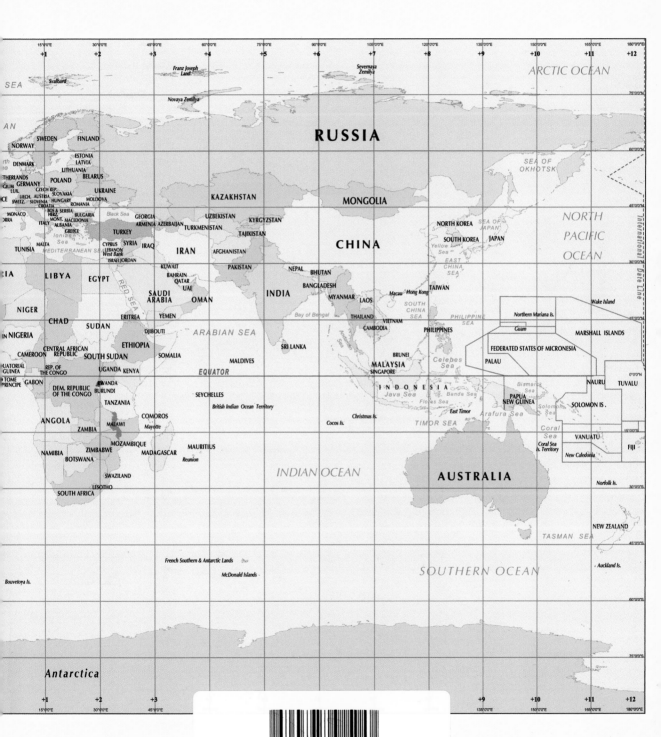

The International Year Book and Statesmen's Who's Who

2014

61st EDITION

INTERNATIONAL AND NATIONAL ORGANISATIONS,
COUNTRIES OF THE WORLD AND OVER 3,000 BIOGRAPHIES
OF LEADING PERSONALITIES IN PUBLIC LIFE

MARTINUS NIJHOFF PUBLISHERS
LEIDEN / BOSTON

Editorial Policy

Below are the criteria we have applied when selecting information for inclusion within *The International Year Book and Statesmen's Who's Who*; anyone who has information concerning the following, or who wishes to be included, is invited to write to the Editorial Manager.

Entry is not a matter for payment nor is it dependent upon purchase of this or any other publication.

International Organisations

The international organisations section covers the United Nations, together with its specialized and affiliated agencies. The European Union and its main bodies are comprehensively covered along with major inter-governmental organisations making significant contributions to political/commercial decision making.

There are additional listings of organisations split into the following categories: agriculture, farming and fisheries; commodities; communications and media; development; economics and finance; education; environment; government and politics; health and medicine; law; religion; science; tourism; trade and industry; transport; and welfare and human rights. For this edition, there is expanded coverage of legal and human rights organisations.

States of the World

Information on every country in the world. This includes information at state level in federal countries such as the USA, Canada, India, and Germany. The profile fields are as follows:

Capital; Constitution and Government including cabinet list; Legal System; Local Government; Area and Population; Employment; Banking and Finance; Manufacturing, Mining and Services; Communications and Transport; Health; Education; Religion; Communications and Media; Environment; and Space Programme.

Biographies

This section contains the biographies of men and women who have had a demonstrable impact upon international affairs or who are of sufficient importance within their own country as to be of interest to anyone wishing to learn more about them. Our definition of 'Statesmen' includes the following:

Politicians: including cabinet ministers, parliamentarians, heads of government and relevant heads of state
Diplomats: for example, ambassadors.
Legal: for example, judges and legal experts
For more extensive biographical coverage, please consult *The International Year Book and Statemen's Who's Who Online*. In addition to further profiles of political leaders and individuals of international and national significance, *The International Year Book and Statesmen's Who's Who Online* also includes biographies from *Who's Who in Public International Law*, a project conceived by Sir Eli Lauterpracht, CBE, QC. Detailed profiles of over 600 experts in the field of international law are published. Those included in the publication have participated in international tribunals, international criminal courts, and human rights courts.

Acknowledgement

We would like to thank the many embassies, government agencies and information sources who have helped us with our research for this 61st edition. We would like to thank http://www.politics1.com, US National Governors Association (http://www.nga.org) and Statistics Canada Website for their permission to use material from their websites. Statistics Canada information is used with the permission of Statistics Canada. Users are forbidden to copy this material and/or redisseminate the data, in an original or modified form, for commercial purposes, without the expressed permission of Statistics Canada. Information on the availability of the wide range of data from Statistics Canada can be obtained from Statistics Canada's Regional Offices, its World Wide Web site at http://www.statcan.ca, and its toll-free access number 1-800-263-1136. ABS data used with permission from the Australian Bureau of Statistics.

Printed and bound in Great Britain by Antony Rowe, Chippenham

INTRODUCTION

Martinus Nijhoff Publishers are pleased to present the 61st edition of *The International Year Book and Statesmen's Who's Who*. More detailed information than ever before has been included. Even more content is available in the **online edition** of *The International Year Book and Statesmen's Who's Who* at http://referenceworks.brillonline.com/browse/international-year-book-and-statesmens-who-s-who. Users of the online edition also have access to the highly-prestigious *Who's Who in Public International Law*. Holders of the print edition now have access to the online edition at no extra charge using the token on the dust jacket of the book. More information on how to gain access is given in the letter sent with this volume. If the letter is missing, please contact sales-us@brill.com (for customers in the Americas) or sales-nl@brill.com for more information.

The Year Book is presented in three main sections. For ease of use these sections are cross-referenced.

International Organisations This section profiles the structure and functions of the world's major international and national organisations from United Nations agencies to economic and trade organisations. The section has been re-organised and now also includes over 500 international organisations ordered by subject matter including business, education, health, human rights and law.

States of the World A current and comprehensive overview of the political, economic and social landscape of the world's countries, arranged alphabetically. Dependencies or state entries are listed after the ruling federal nation.

As well as being a reference book, *The International Year Book and Statesmen's Who's Who* also publishes thousands of central contact addresses. These include ministry addresses, government bodies, banks, top companies, chambers of commerce and many more. Thousands of up-to-date e-mail and internet addresses are also published. As well as providing direct links to ministries and embassies, links are provided to full text constitutions.

The section is complemented by a full-colour plate section of flags. Colour endpapers also show political boundaries and time zones.

Biographies Over 3,000 major international figures are profiled in this section, from heads of state and politicians to diplomats, heads of inter-governmental organisations, senior legal figures and heads of central banks.

Details include: political and professional career summaries, education, professional memberships, publications and recreations. E-mail and internet addresses are also published.

The International Year Book and Statesmen's Who's Who Online also includes biographies from *Who's Who in Public International Law*, a project conceived by Sir Eli Lauterpracht, CBE, QC.

Who's Who in Public International Law aims to present biographies of experts working in the arena of international law including such areas as trade, investment, the environment, humanitarian law, human rights and international criminal law. It is the only directory which focuses on prominent people working in International Law. Those included in the publication have participated in international tribunals, international criminal courts, and human rights courts.

The profiles include details on education, involvement in international law, publications, memberships and areas of special interest.

Further useful information may be found in the preliminary section of *The International Year Book and Statesmen's Who's Who*. For quick and easy reference, there is a matrix detailing country membership of major international organisations.

Every care is taken to check the information supplied for the preparation of the articles in this volume, but the publishers cannot take responsibility for any omissions or inaccuracies. They will be glad to receive any authoritative correction.

THE INTERNATIONAL YEAR BOOK AND STATESMEN'S WHO'S WHO

is researched and compiled by:

Jennifer Dilworth, *Editorial Manager*
Megan Stuart-Jones, *Assistant Editor*

Hans van der Meij, *Publisher*

The International Year Book and Statesmen's Who's Who
Martinus Nijhoff Publishers
(an imprint of Koninklijke Brill NV)
P.O. Box 9000
2300 PA Leiden
The Netherlands
e-mail: iyb@brill.com
URL: http://www.brill.com/
Tel.: +31 (0)71 535 3500 Fax: +31 (0)71 531 7532

ISSN: 0074-9621
ISBN-13: 978-90-04-24374-3
© 2013 by Koninklijke Brill NV, Leiden, The Netherlands

Koninklijke Brill NV incorporates the imprints Brill, Global Oriental, Hotei Publishing, IDC Publishers and Martinus Nijhoff Publishers.

http://www.brill.com

CONTENTS

CONTENTS

OTHER INTERNATIONAL AND NATIONAL ORGANISATIONS

STATES OF THE WORLD

CONTENTS

CONTENTS

CONTENTS

DEPENDENT STATES AND TERRITORIES

CONTENTS

ABBREVIATIONS

A

AAA	American Arbitration Association
AB	Aktiebolaget (Bachelor of Arts)
ADC	Aide-de-Camp
ADE	Anorthotiko Komma Ergazomenou (Progressive Party of the Working People)
ADISOK	Ananestiko Demokratico Socialistiko Kinema (Democratic Socialist Reform Movement)
admin.	administration, administrative, administrator
ADP	Agrarian Democratic Party
AEC	Atomic Energy Commission
AEU	Amalgamated Engineering Union
AFHQ	Allied Forces Headquarters
AG	Aktiengesellschaft (joint stock company)
AGALEV	Anders Gaan Leven (Another Way of Life-Ecologist Party)
AIB	Associate of the Institute of Bankers
AIC	Agrupacion Independiente de Canarias (Independent Association of the Canary Islands)
AICA	Associate Member, Commonwealth Institute of Accountants
AICE	Associate of Institute of Civil Engineers
AID	Agency for International Development (Intermunicipal Association for Purification)
AIL	Associate – Institute of Linguistics
AIME	Associate – Institute of Mining Engineers
AIMM	Associate – Institute of Mining and Metallurgy
A. Inst. CE	Associate of the Institute of Civil Engineers
AIV	Association des Ingénieurs sortis de l'Ecole supérieure des Textiles de Verviers (Association of Engineer Graduates of the Verviers Higher School of Textiles)
AKEL	Anorthotiko Komma Ergazomenou Laou (Progressive Party of the Working People)
ALÖ	Alternative Liste Österreichs (Austrian Alternative List)
AM	Assembly Member
Amb. Ex. & Plen.	Ambassador Extraordinary and Plenipotentiary
AN	Alleanza Nazionale (National Alliance)
ANAP	Anavatan Partisi (Motherland Party)
AOV	Algemeen Ouderen Verbond (General Alliance for the Elderly)
AP	Alianza Popular (Popular Alliance Party)
Apdo.	Apartado (PO Box number)
APEX	Association of Professional, Executive, Clerical and Computer Staff
approx.	approximately
apptd.	appointed
Apr.	April
ARC	Rainbow Group in the European Parliament
ARCVS	Associate of the Royal College of Veterinary Surgeons
AREV	Alternative Rouge et Verte
ARIBA	Associate of the Royal Institute of British Architects
ARIC	Associate of the Royal Institute of Chemistry

ASBL	Association sans but lucratif (Non Profit-Seeking Association)
ASEAN	Association of Southeast Asian Nations
Assn.	Association
Assoc.	Associate
Asst.	Assistant
AUF	Labour Party Youth Organisation (Norwegian)
Aug.	August
AWEPPA	Association of West European Parliamentarians for Action Against Apartheid

B

b.	born (né(e), geboren, nacido)
BA	Bachelor of Arts
B.Agr.	Bachelor of Agriculture
B.Arch.	Bachelor of Architecture
barr.	Barrister (lawyer)
BA.Sc.	Bachelor of Applied Science
BAO	Bachelor of Art of Obstetrics
BBA	Bachelor of Business Administration
BBC	British Broadcasting Corporation
BCE	Bachelor of Civil Engineering
B.Ch.	Bachelor of Surgery
B.Chir.	Bachelor of Surgery
BCL	Bachelor of Civil Law
B.Comm.	Bachelor of Commerce
BD	Bachelor of Divinity
Bd.	Board
BD.Sc.	Bachelor of Dental Science
BE&A	Bachelor of Engineering and Architecture
B.Ed.	Bachelor of Education
BEE	Bachelor of Electrical Engineering
BEF	British Expeditionary Force
BEM	British Empire Medal
BENELUX	Belgium-Netherlands-Luxembourg (Committee)
B. en H.	Bachiller en Humanidades (Bachelor of Humanities)
B. és A.	Bachelor of Arts
B. és L.	Bachelor of Letters
B. és S.	Bachelor of Science
BIM	British Institute of Management
BIS	Bank for International Settlements
BL	Bachelor of Laws
B.Litt.	Bachelor of Letters
blvd.	boulevard
BMA	British Medical Association
B.Phil.	Bachelor of Philosophy
Bros.	Brothers
BS	Bachelor of Surgery
BSA	Bachelor of Science in Agriculture
B.Sc.	Bachelor of Science
BSE	Bovine Spongiform Encephalopathy
B.Soc.Sc.	Bachelor of Social Sciences
BSP	Bulgarska Sotsialisticheska Partiya (Bulgarian Socialist Party)
Bt.	Baronet

ABBREVIATIONS

B.V.Sc.	Bachelor of Veterinary Science
BZNS	Bulgarska i Zemeldeski Naroden Sayuz (Bulgarian Agrarian National Union)

C

CA	Chartered Accountant
Capt.	Captain
CARICOM	Caribbean Community
CB	Companion of the Order of the Bath
CBE	Commander of the Order of the British Empire
CBI	Confederation of British Industry
CBSS	Council of the Baltic Sea States
CC	County Councillor; County Council
CCAMLR	Commission for the Conservation of Antarctic Marine Living Resources
CD	Centrum-Demokraterne (Centre Democratic Party)
CDA	Christen Democratisch Appèl (Christian Democratic Appeal); Obbcanská democratická aliance (Civic Democratic Alliance)
CDP	Obcanská demokratická strana (Civic Democratic Party)
CDPF	Christian Democratic Popular Front
Cdr.	Commander
CDS	Centro Democrático y Social (Centre Democratic and Social Party); Partido do Centro Democrático Social (Centre Democratic Party)
CDU	Christlich Demokratische Union (Christian Democratic Union); Obcanská demokratická unia (Civic Democratic Union)
CE	Civil Engineer
CEA	European Court of Arbitration
CEMAC	Communauté Economique et Monétaire de l'Afrique Centrale
C.Eng.	Chartered Engineer
CERN	Centre Européen de Recherche Nucléaire
CG	Left Unity
CGIA	City and Guilds of London Insignia Award
CGSP	Centrale générale des Services publics (General Public Services Group)
CGT	Confédération Générale du Travail (General Confederation of Labour)
ch.	children
CH	Companies of Honour
Ch.B.	Bachelor of Chemistry
Ch.D.	Doctor of Chemistry
Chllr.	Chancellor
Ch.M.	Master of Surgery
Chmn.	Chairman
CHP	Cumhuriyet Halk Partisi (Republican People's Party)
Chwn.	Chairwoman
Cia.	Compañia (Company)
CIE	Companion of the Order of the Indian Empire
Cie.	Compagnie (Company)
cif	cost, insurance and freight
CIGS	Chief of the Imperial General Staff
C-in-C	Commander-in-Chief
CIO	Congress of Industrial Organisation

CIS	Commonwealth of Independent States
Ciu	Convèrgencia i Unió (Convergence and Union Party)
Cllr.	Councillor
CLRAE	Standing Conference of Local and Regional Authorities of Europe
CM	Master in Surgery
Cmdr.	Commander
Cmdre.	Commodore
CMG	Companion of the Order of St. Michael and St. George
Cmmw.	(The) Commonwealth
Cmn.	Commission
Cmnr.	Commissioner
Cncl.	Council
CND	Campaign for Nuclear Disarmament
CNIP	Centre National des Indépendants et Paysans
CO	Commanding Officer
Co.	Company
Coll.	College
comm.	commission
Cons.	Conservative (and Unionist) Party
Co-op.	Co-operative
Corp.	Corporation
CP	Centerpartiet (Centre Party)
CPCS	Kommunistická strana Ceskoslovenská (Communist Party of Czechoslovakia)
cr.	created
CSDP	Ceská strana sociálne demokratická (Czech Social Democratic Party)
CSI	Companion of the Order of the Star of India
CSP	Centrale des Services Publics (Public Services Group)
C.St.J.	Commander of the Order of St. John of Jerusalem
CSU	Christlich Soziale Union (Christian Social Union)
CTBTO	Preparatory Commission for the Comprehensive Nuclear-Test-Ban Treaty Organization
Cttee(s).	Committee(s)
CVO	Commander of the Royal Victorian Order
CVP	Christelijke Volkspartij (Christian People's Party)

D

d.	daughters (filles, töchter, hijas)
DBA	Doctor of Business Administration
DBE	Dame Commander of the Order of the British Empire
DBERR	Department of Business, Enterprise and Regulatory Reform
DC	Partito della Democrazia Cristiana (Christian Democrats)
D.Com.L.	Doctor of Commercial Law
D.Comm.	Doctor of Commerce
DCS	Doctor of Commercial Sciences
DD	Doctor of Divinity
DDS	Doctor of Dental Surgery
Dec.	December
decd.	deceased
D.Econ.	Doctor of Economics
Deleg.	Delegation

D. en D.	Docteur en Droit
D.Eng.	Doctor of Engineering
D. en L.	Doctor en Leyes (Doctor of Law)
D. en M.	Doctor en Médicine (Doctor of Medicine)
Dep.	Deputy
dept.	department
D. és L.	Doctor of Letters
dev.	development
DFC	Distinguished Flying Cross
Dfld	Department of International Development
DFM	Distinguished Flying Medal
DHL	Doctor of Humane Letters
DIANA	Demokratiki Ananestasi (Democratic Renewal Party)
DIKO	Dimokratiko Komma (Democratic Party)
D. in D.	Dottore in Diretto (Doctor of Law)
Dip.Ing.	Diplom Ingenieur (Diploma of Engineering)
Dip.Law	Diploma in Law
Dir.	Director
Dir-Gen.	Director-General
diss.	dissolved
DISY	Demokratikos Synagemos (Democratic Rally)
Div.	Division
DK	Deutsche Kommunistische Partei (German Communist Party)
DL	Deputy Lieutenant
D.Litt.	Doctor of Literature
DLPL	Democratic Labour Party of Lithuania
DnA	Det norske Arbeiderparti (Norwegian Labour Party)
Dott.Ing.	Dottore in Ingegneria (Doctor of Engineering)
Dott.	Dottore (Doctor)
DP	Demokrat Parti (Democrat Party)
DPS	Dvizhenie za Prava i Svobodi (Movement for Rights and Freedom)
D.Psych.	Doctor of Psychology
Dr.	Doctor(ate)
Dr.Ing.	Doktor Ingenieur (Doctor of Engineering)
Dr. Jur.	Doctor of Jurisprudence (Law)
Dr.rer.pol.	Doctor of Political Science
Dr.rer.nat.	Doctor of Natural Science
Drs.	Doctor Doctor, Doctorates
DS	Demokratická strana (Democratic Party)
DSC	Distinguished Service Cross
D.Sc.(Agric.)	Doctor of (Agricultural) Science
DSM	Distinguished Service Medal
DSO	Distinguished Service Order
DSP	Demokratik Sol Parti (Democratic Left Party)
Dtech	Dr. of Technology
DTI	Department of Trade and Industry
DUP	Democratic Unionist Party
DV.Sc.	Doctor of Veterinary Science
DYP	Dogru Yol Partisi (True Path Party)
D.Zool.	Doctor of Zoology
D66	Democraten 66 (Democrats 66)

E

EA	Eusko Alkartasun (Basque Solidarity)
EBU	European Broadcasting Union
EC	European Community
ECA	Economic Co-operation Administration

ECE	European Central Inland Transport Association
Ecolo.	Ecology Party
econ.	economics
ECO	Economic Co-operation Organization
ECOSOC	Economic and Social Council for the United Nations
ED	European Democratic Group
EDEK	Ethniki Demokratiki Enosi Kyprou (Cyprus National Democratic Union)
EDIK	Enosi Demokratikou Kentrou (Democratic Centre Union)
EE	Euskadiko Ezkerra (Basque Left Party)
EEC	European Economic Community
EFTA	European Free Trade Association
EIB	European Investment Bank
EKD	Evangelische Kirche in Deutschland (Protestant Church in Germany)
ELDR	European Liberal Democratic and Reformist Group
EN	Europe of the Nations Group
EN.Ex. & Min.Plen.	Envoy Extraordinary and Minister Plenipotentiary
ENIP	Estonian National Independence Party
EP	European Parliament
ERA	European Radical Alliance Group
EPEN	Greek National Political Society
ERD	Emergency Reserve Decoration (Army)
ESA	European Space Agency
est	established
e.t.	en titre
etc.	et cetera (and so on)
ETH	Eidgenossische Technische Hochschule
EU	European Union
EUL/NGL	European United Left/Nordic Green Left Group
EURATHOM	European Atomic Energy Community
Exec.	Executive

F

FAO	Food and Agriculture Organization
FBA	Fellow of the British Academy
FBP	Fortschrittliche Bürgerpartei (Progressive Citizens Party)
FCA	Fellow of the Institute of Chartered Accountants
FCIB	Fellow of the Corporation of Insurance Brokers
FCO	Foreign and Commonwealth Office
FCWA	Fellow of the Institute for Cost and Works Accountants
FDF	Front Démocratique des Francophones (French Speaking Democratic Front)
FDP	Freie Demokratische Partei (Free Democratic Party)
Feb.	February
Fed.	Federation, Federal
F. Eng.	Fellowship in Engineering
FICE	Fellow, Institute of Civil Engineers
FIDESZ	Fiatal Demokraták Szövetsége (Federation of Young Democrats)
FK	Faelles Kurs (Common Course)

ABBREVIATIONS

FL	Freie Liste (Free List)		HDZ BiH	Hrvatska Demokratska Zajednica Bosné i Hercegovina (Croatian Democratic Union of Bosnia-Herzegovina)
fmr.	former			
fmrly.	formerly		HE	His Eminence, His Excellency
FN	Front National (National Front)		HKDS	Hrvatska Krscanska Demokratska Stranka (Croatian Christian Democratic Party)
FNRS	Fonds national de la Recherche Scientifique (National Fund for Scientific Research)		HM	His (Her) Majesty
fob	free on board		HNS	Hrvatska Narodna Stranka (Croatian People's Party)
FP	Folkpartiet liberalerna (Liberal Party)			
FPÖ	Freiheitliche Partei Österreichs (Freedom Party of Austria)		Hon.	Honourable, Honorary
			Hon. Consul.	Honorary Consul, Consulate
FRAe.S	Fellow, Royal Aeronautical Society		Hosp.	Hospital
FRHS	Fellow, Royal Historical Society		HQ	Headquarters
FRICS	Fellow, Royal Institute of Chartered Surveyors		HRH	His (Her) Royal Highness
FRS	Fellow, Royal Society		HRP	Hristiyan-Republikanska Partiya (Christian Republican Party)
FRSL	Fellow, Royal Society of Literature			
FSD	Fédération des Socialistes Démocrates (Federation of Social Democrats)		HSH	His (Her) Serene Highness
			HSLS	Hrvatska Socijalno Liberalna Stranka (Croatian Social-Liberal Party)
FSE	Fellow, Society of Engineers		HSP	Hrvatska Stranka Prava (Croatian Party of Right)
FSM	Federal States of Micronesia			
			HSS	Hrvatska Seljacka Stranka (Croatian Peasant Party)

G

GATT	General Agreement on Tariffs and Trade		HZDS	Hnutie za Demokratické Slovensko (Movement for a Democratic Slovakia)
GB	Great Britain			
GBE	Knight (or Dame) Grand Cross of the Order of the British Empire			

I

GCB	Knight Grand Cross of the Order of the Bath		IAEA	International Atomic Energy Agency
GCIE	Knight Grand Commander of the Order of the Indian Empire		IATA	International Air Transport Association
			IBA	Institute of British Architects
GCMG	Knight Grand Cross of the Order of St. Michael and St. George		IBC	International Broadcasting Corporation
			IBRD	International Bank for Reconstruction and Development
GCSI	Knight Grand Commander of the Order of the Star of India		ICA	International Court of Arbitration
GCVO	Knight Grand Cross of the Royal Victorian Order		ICAO	International Civil Aviation Organization
			ICC	International Chamber of Commerce
GDP	Gross Domestic Product		ICE	Institute of Civil Engineers (Catholic Institute of Advanced Business Studies)
GDR	German Democratic Party			
Gebr.	Gebrüder (Bros.; Brothers)		ICRC	International Committee of the Red Cross
GLC	Greater London Council		IDA	International Development Association
GM	George Medal		IFAD	International Fund for Agricultural Development
GMB	General and Municipal Boilermakers Union			
GmbH	Gesellschaft mit beschränkter Haftung (company with limited liabilities)		IGO	Intergovernmental Organisation
			ILO	International Labour Office, International Labour Organisation
GNI	Gross National Income (a term now used instead of GNP in national accounts)		IMCO	Inter-governmental Maritime Consultative Organisation
GNP	Gross National Product			
Govt.	Government		IMF	International Monetary Fund
Gp.	Group		IMO	International Maritime Organization
GPO	General Post Office		INASEP	Intercommunale Namuroise de Services Publics (Namur Intermunicipal Public Services Association)
GPV	Gereformeerd Politiek Verbond (Reformed Political Association)			
Grüne	Die Grünen (The Greens)		INASTI	Institut National d'Assurances Sociales pour Travailleurs Indépendants (National Institute of Social Insurance for Independent Workers)
GUE	Group for the European Unitarian Left			
			Inc.	Incorporated

H

			Ing.	Ingenieur; Ingegnere (Engineer)
H	Hoyre (Conservative)		Inst.	Institute
h.c.	honoris causa		Instn.	Institution
HDS	Hrvatska Demokratska Stranka (Croatian Democratic Party)		Int.	International
			INTERPOL	International Criminal Police Organization
HDUR	Unionea Democrata a Maghiarilor din Romnia (Hungarian Democratic Union of Romania)		IP	Sjálfstaedisflokkurinn (Independence Party)
			IPU	Inter-Parliamentary Union

IRE — Institut National des Radioéléments (National Institute of Radio-elements)

ITU — International Telecommunication Union

J

Jan. — January
JP — Justice of the Peace
Jr. — Junior
JSD — Doctor of the Science of Law
jt. — joint
Jul. — July
Jun. — June

K

KBE — Knight Commander of the Order of the British Empire
KCB — Knight Commander of the Order of the Bath
KCIE — Knight Commander of the Order of the Indian Empire
KCMG — Knight Commander of the Order of St. Michael and St. George
KCSG — Knight Commander of the Order of St. Gregory
KCSI — Knight Commander of the Order of the Star of India
KCVO — Knight Commander of the Royal Victorian Order
KDH — Krestansko-demokratické hnutie (Christian Democratic Movement)
KDNP — Keresztéugdemokrata Néppart (Christian Democratic People's Party)
KdS — Kristdemokratiska Samhällspartiet (Christian Democratic Party)
KDS — Krestanskodemokratická strana (Christian Democratic Party)
KDU-CSL — Krestanská a demokratická unie-Ceskoslovanksá strana lidová (Christian Democratic Union – Czechoslovak People's Party)
KED — Kinema ton Eleftheron Dimokraton (Movement of Free Democrats)
KF — Det Konservative Folkeparti (Conservative People's Party)
KG — Knight of the Order of the Garter
K.GaA. — Kommandit-Gesellschaft auf Aktien (private company partly organised as a joint-stock company)
KKE — Kommunistiko Komma Elladas (Communist Party of Greece)
KLD — Kongres Liberalno - Demokratyczny (Liberal Democratic Congress)
KLJ — Knight, St. Lazarus of Jerusalem
KLM — Koninklijke Luchtvaart Maatschappij NV (Royal Dutch Airlines)
KNP — Konfederacja Polski Niepodleglej (Confederation for an Independent Poland)
KODISO — Democratic Socialist Party of Greece
KOK — Kansallinen Kokoomus (National Coalition Party)
KP — Keskustapuolue (Centre Party)
KPB — Belgian Communist Party
KPN — Konfederacja Polski Niepodleglej (Confederation for an Independent Poland)

KPO — Kommunistische Partei Osterreichs (Communist Party of Austria)
KrF — Kristelig Folkeparti
KSG — Knight of St. Gregory the Great
K.St.J. — Knight of the Order of St. John of Jerusalem
KT — Knight of the Order of the Thistle
Kt. — Knight
KUL — Katholieke Universiteit te Leuven (Catholic University of Louvain)
KVP — Katholieke Volks Partij (Catholic People's Party)

L

Lab. — Labour Party
LBO — Liberal Bosniak Organisation
LCIA — London Court of International Arbitration
LCR — Ligue Communiste Révolutionnaire (Revolutionary Communist League)
LDDP — Lithuanian Democratic Labour Party
L. de Phil. — Licencié de Philosophie (Licentiate in Philosophy)
LDR — Liberal, Democratic and Reformist Group
LDS — Liberalna Demokraticna Stranka (Liberal Democratic Party)
L. em C. — Licenciado em Ciencia
L. em C.E. — Licenciado en Ciencias Economicas
L. em D. — Licenciado em Direito
L. en L. — Licenciado en Leyes
L. en D. — Licencié en Droit; Licenciado en Derecho
L. és L. — Licencié en Lettres
L. és Sc. — Licencié en Sciences
LHB — Bachelor of Humane Letters
LHD — Doctor of Humane Letters
Lib. — Liberal Party
LK — Liberaalinen Kansanpuolue (Liberal People's Party)
Lic. — Econ. Licenciate in Economic Sciences
Lic.iur — Jur.Licenciate in Law
Lic.L. — Licentiate of Law
Lic. Med. — Licentiate in Medicine
LKP — Lithuanian Communist Party
LL.B — Bachelor of Laws
LL.D — Doctor of Laws
LL.L — Licentiate of Laws
LL.M — Master of Laws
LM — Licentiate of Medicine
LNNK — Latvian National Independence Movement
LO — Lutte Ouvière (Workers Struggle)
LRCP — Licentiate of the Royal College of Physicians
LRD — Liberal and Democratic Reformist Group
LSA — Licentiate of the Society of Apothecaries
LSDP — Lithuanian Social Democratic Party
LSDSP — Latvian Social Democratic Workers Party
LSE — London School of Economics
Lt. — Lieutenant
Ltd. — Limited
LTF — Popular Front of Latvia
LZP — Latvian Green Party

ABBREVIATIONS

M

m.	married, marriage (marié(e), verheiratet, casado)
MA	Master of Arts, Member of Assembly
MACGP	Master of Royal College of General Practitioners
Mag.	Magister
Man.Dir.	Managing Director
Mar.	March
marr.	married
May.	Mayor
MB	Bachelor of Medicine
MBA	Master of Business Administration
MBE	Member of the Order of the British Empire
MBO	Muslimanska-Bosnjacka Organizacija (Muslim-Bosnian Organization)
MC	Military Cross
MCC	Marylebone Cricket Club
M.Ch.	Master of Surgery
MCL	Master of Civil Law
MCP	Milliyetci Hareket Partisi (Nationalist Movement Party)
MCS	Master of Commercial Science
MD	Doctor of Medicine
MDF	Magyar Demokrata Forum (Hungarian Democratic Forum)
MDP/CDE	Movimento Democrático Portugês (Portuguese Democratic Movement)
ME	Master of Engineering
M.Ec.	Master of Economics
mem.	member
M.Eng.	Master of Engineering (Dublin)
MEP	Member of European Parliament
MFA	Ministry of Foreign Affairs
MGP	Mouvement Gaulliste Populaire (Popular Gaullist Movement)
Mgr.	Manager
MHA	Member of the House of Assembly
MHR	Member of the House of Representatives
MIGA	Multilateral Investment Guarantee Agency (MIGA)
Mij.	Maatschappij
Min.	Ministry
Min.Plen.	Minister Plenipotentiary
MLA	Member of Legislative Assembly
MLC	Member of Legislative Council
MLP	Malta Labour Party
MM	Military Medal
MMP	Magyar Munkáspárt (Hungarian Workers Party)
MNP	Magyar Néppart (Hungarian People's Party)
MP	Member of Parliament
M.Phil.	Master of Philosophy
MoD	Ministry of Defence
Mr	Meester in de Rechten (Dutch Law Degree)
MRCS	Member of the Royal College of Surgeons
MRG	Mouvement des Radicaux de Gauche (Radical Left Movement)
MRI	Member of the Royal Institution
MRIA	Member of the Royal Irish Academy
MRP	Mouvement Républicain Populaire

MS	Master of Sciences; Master of Surgery; Moderata Samlings partiet (Moderate Party)
M.Sc.	Master of Science
MSF	Union for Manufacturing, Science and Finance
MSI-DN	Movimento Sociale Italiano - Destra Nazionale (Italian Social Movement National Right)
MSP	Magyar Szocialiste Párt (Hungarian Socialist Party)
MSZ	Magyar Szocialiste Munkáspárt (Hungarian Socialist Workers Party)
Mt.	Mount
My.	Maatschappy

N

NACRO	National Association for the Care and Rehabilitation of Offenders
NAFTA	North American Free Trade Agreement
Nat.	National
NATO	North Atlantic Treaty Organization
ND	Nea Demokratia (New Democracy)
NEC	National Executive Committee
NEDC	National Economic Development Council
née	refers to maiden name
NEI	Netherlands East Indies
NGO	Non-Governmental Organisation
NI	Non-attached
NLP	Partidul National Liberal (National Liberal Party)
Nov.	November
NPD	Nationaldemokratische Partei Deutschlands (National Democratic Party of Germany)
NSF	Frontul Salvarii Nationale (National Salvation Front)
NSS	Narodna saborna stranka (People's Assembly Party)
NUM	National Union of Mineworkers
NUT	National Union of Teachers
NV	Naamloze Vennootschap (Limited Company)
NVV	Dutch Association of Trade Unions

O

Oct.	October
ODP	Ozone Depleting Potential
ODS	Obcanská demokratická strana (Civic Democratic Party)
OECD	Organisation for Economic Co-operation and Development
OECS	Organisation of Eastern Caribbean States
OH	Obcanská hnutí (Civic Movement)
OM	Member of the Order of Merit
OPCW	Organisation for the Prohibition of Chemical Weapons
OPEC	Organisation of the Petroleum Exporting Countries
opp.	opposition
OSCE	Organization on Security and Co-operation in Europe
O.St. J	Officer of the Most Venerable Order of the Hospital of St. John of Jerusalem
OUP	Official Unionist Party

ÖVP	Österreichisches Volkspartei (Austrian People's Party)	PPR	Politieke Partij Radikalen (Political Party of Radical Democrats)
Oy.	Osakeyhtio (Limited Company)	PPS	Parliamentary Private Secretary; Polska Partia Socjalistyczma (Polish Socialist Party)

P

		PR	Partito Radicale (Radical Party); Parti Republicain (Republican Party)
PA	Althydubandalag (People's Alliance); Partido Andalucista (Andalucian Party)	PRC	Partito della Rifondazione Comunista (Communist Re-establishment Party)
PAKOP	Pankyprio Komma Prosfygon ke Pligenton (Refugee Party)	PRD	Partido Renovador Democrático (Democratic Renewal Party)
PAR	Partido Argonés Regionalista (Aragon Regional Party)	Pref.	Prefecture
Parly.	Parliamentary	Pres.	President
PASH	Partie Agrare Shqiptare (Albanian Agrarian Party)	PRI	Partito Repubblicano Italiano (Italian Republican Party)
PASOC	Partido de Acción Socialista (Socialist Action Party)	PRL	Parti des Réformes et de la Liberté (Party for Reform and Freedom)
PASOK	Panellinion Socialistikon Kinema (Panhellenic Socialist Movement)	PRO	Public Relations Officer
		Prof.	Professor
PBEC	Pacific Basin Economic Council	PRS	Partia Republikana Shqipërisë (Albanian Republican Party)
PBS	Partia e Blertë Shqiptare (Albanian Green Party)	PS	Parti Socialiste; Partido Socialista (Socialist Party)
PCB	Parti Communiste de Belgique (Belgian Communist Party)	PSC	Parti Social Chrétien (Christian Social Party)
PCE	Partiso Comunista de Espana (Communist Party of Spain)	PSD	Partido Social Democrata (Social Democratic Party); Parti-Social-Démocrate (Social Democratic Party)
PCF	Parti Communiste Français (French Communist Party)	PSDI	Partito Socialista Democratico Italiano (Italian Social Democrat Party)
PCP	Partido Communista Português (Portuguese Communist Party)	PSDS	Partia Socialdemokratike ë Shqipërisë (Social Democratic Party of Albania)
PCS	Parti Chrétien Social (Christian Social Party)	PSI	Partito Socialista Italiano (Italian Socialist Party)
PDA	Stranka Demokratske Akcije (Party of Democratic Action)	PSL	Polskie Stronnictwo Ludowe (Polish Peasant Party)
PDM	Partit Demokratico Malti (Malta Democratic Party)	PSOE	Partido Socialista Obrero Español (Spanish Socialist Workers Party)
PDS	Partia Demokratike Shqipërisë (Albanian Democratic Party); Partei des Demokratischen Socialismus (Party of Democratic Socialism); Partito Democratico della Sinistra (Democratic Party of the Left)	PSP	Pacifistisch Socialistische Partij (Pacifist Socialist Party)
		PSS	Partia Socialist Shqipërisë (Albanian Socialist Party)
PECC	Pacific Economic Cooperation Council	PSU	Parti Socialiste Unifié (Unified Socialist Party)
PEN	Poets, Playwrights, Essayists, Editors and Novelists (Club)	PTB	Parti du Travail de Belgique (Belgian Labour Party)
PES	Partie Ecologie Shqipërisë (Albanian Ecology Party)	Ptnr.	Partner
		PvdA	Partij van de Arbeid (Labour Party)
PGCE	Post Graduate Certificate of Education	PW	Partij voor Vrijheid en Vooruitgang (Party for Reform and Freedom)
Ph.D.	Doctor of Philosophy	PWU	Postal Workers Union
PL	Partido Liberal (Liberal Party); Porozumienie Centrum (Centre Alliance)		

Q

PLC or plc	Public Limited Company	QC	Queen's Counsel
PLI	Partito Liberale Italiano (Italian Liberal Party)		
PLO	Palestine Liberation Organisation		

R

PLP	Parliamentary Labour Party		
PM	Pjóovaki (People's Movement)	RA	Royal Academy, Royal Artillery
PN	Partit Nazzjonalista (National Party)	RAC	Royal Automobile Club
PNV	Partido Nacionalista Vasco (Basque Nationalist Party)	RAF	Royal Air Force
		RC	Roman Catholic
Pol.	Politics	RD	Royal Naval and Marine Forces Reserve Decoration
POSL	Parti Ouvrier Socialiste Luxembourgeois (Socialist Workers Party)		
PP	Partido Popular (Popular Party)	RDE	Group of the European Democratic Alliance
PPE	Group of the European People's Party (Christian-Democratic Group)	RDP	Radikalna Demokraticheska Partiya (Radical Democratic Party)
PPI	Partito Popolare Italiano (Italian Popular Party)	Regt.	Regiment

ABBREVIATIONS

REP	Die Republikaner (Republican Party)
resd.	resigned
retd.	retired
Rev.	Reverend
RFC	Rugby Football Club
RIBA	Royal Institute of British Architects
RIIA	Royal Institute of International Affairs
RMC	Royal Military College
RN	Royal Navy
ROC	Republic of China
RP	Refah Partisi (Welfare Party)
RPF	Rassemblement du Peuple Français (Rally for the French People); Reformaatorishce Pilitieke Federatie (Evangelical Political Federation)
RPR	Rassemblement pour la République (Rally for the Republic)
RSA	Royal Soc. of the Arts
Rt.Hon.	(The) Right Honourable
Rt.Rev.	(The) Right Reverend

S

S	Socialist Group
s.	sons (fils, Söhne, hijos)
SA	Société Anonyme, Sociedad Anonima (Limited Company)
SAARC	South Asian Association for Regional Cooperation
SAR	Special Administrative Region
SARS	Severe Acute Respiratory Syndrome
Sch.	School
Scot.	Scotland
SD	Svobodní demokraté (Free Democrats); Stronnictwo Demokratyczne (Democratic Party)
SDA	Stranka Demokratske Akcije (Party of Democratic Action)
SDAP	Sveriges Socialdemokratiska Arbetare-partiet (Swedish Social Democratic Labour Party)
SDL	Strana demokratickej lavice (Party of the Democratic Left)
SDLP	Social Democratic and Labour Party
SDP	Social Democratic Party; Suomen Sosialidemokraattinen Puolue (Finnish Social Democratic Party); Stranka Demokratskila Promjena (Party of Democratic Reform); Sosyal Demokrat Partisi; Partidul Social Democrat Romn (Romanian Social Democratic Party); Stranka Demokratskih Reformi (Slovenian Party of Democratic Reform)
SDRB	Société de Développement régionale de Bruxelles (Brussels Regional Development Society)
SDS	Srpska Demokratska Stranka (Serbian Democratic Party)
SDSH	Socijaldemokratska Stranka Hrvatske (Croatian Social-Democratic Party)
SDSS	Social demokraticna stranka Slovenije (Social Democratic Party of Slovenia)
SELA	Latin American Economic System
Sec.	Secretary
Sec.-Gen.	Secretary-General
SEP	Svenska Folkpartiet (Swedish People's Party)
Sep.	September
SETCA	Syndicat des Employés, Techniciens et Cadres de Belgique (Union of Belgian Employees, Technicians and Executives)
SF	Socialistisk Folkeparti (Socialist People's Party)
SFP	Svenska Folkpartiet (Swedish People's Party)
SGP	Staakundig Gereformeerde Partij (Political Reformed Party)
SI	Socialisti Italiani (Italian Socialists)
SIAEE	Société Intercommunale d'Aménagement et d'Equipement Economique (Intermunicipal Society of Economic Planning and Development)
SITC	Standard International Trade Classification
SKD	Slovenska Krscanski Demokrati (Slovene Christian Democrats)
SKDL	Suomen Kansen Demokrattinen Liitto (Finnish People's Democratic League)
SKL	Suomen Kristillinen Liittoo (Finnish Christian Union)
SKP	Suomen Kommunistinen Puolue (Communist Party of Finland)
SKZ	Slovenska Kmecka Zveza (Slovene Peasant League)
SLD	Social and Liberal Democrats (now called Liberal Democrats)
SLP	Partidul Socialistal Muncii (Socialist Labour Party)
SLS	Slovenska ljudska stranka (Slovenian People's Party)
SMP	Suomen Masseuden Puolue (Finnish Rural Party)
SNCF	Société Nationale des Chemins de Fer Français (National French Railway Company)
SNL	Société national de logement (National Accommodation Society)
SNP	Scottish National Party
SNS	Slovenska nacionalna stranka (Slovenian National Party); Slovenská narodná strana (Slovak National Party)
Soc.	Society
Soc.Dem.	Social Democrat
SP	Socialistische Partij (Socialist Party); Senterpartiet
SPA	Societa per Azioni (Joint Stock Company)
SPC	Secretariat of the Pacific Community
SPD	Sozialdemokratische Partei Deutschlands (Social Democratic Party of Germany)
SPÖ	Sozialistische Parei Österreichs (Socialist Party of Austria)
SPRL	Société privée à Responsabilité Limitée (Private Society of Limited Responsibility)
SPS	Socijalisticka partija Srbije (Socialist Party of Serbia)
Sr	Senior
SRLW	Société Régionale de logement Wallon (Walloon Regional Accommodation Society)
SRM	Srpski pokret obnove (Serbian Renewal Movement)
SRS	Srpska Radikalna Stranka (Serbian Radical Party)
SSH	Socijalisticka Stranka Hrvatske (Croatian Socialist Party)
SSR	Soviet Socialist Republic

SSS Socialisticna Stranka Slovenije (Socialist Party of Slovenia)
St. Saint, Street
Str. Straße (Street)
Supt. Superintendent
SVP Sosialistik Venstrepartei; Sudtiroler Volkspartei (South Tyrol People's Party)
SZDS Szabad Demoktraták Szövetsége (Alliance of Free Democrats)

T

TCD Trinity College, Dublin
TD Territorial Decoration
TGWU Transport and General Workers' Union
Treas. Treasurer
TUC Trades Union Congress
TV Television

U

UBP Ulusal Birlik Partisi (National Unity Party)
UCL Université Catholique de Louvain (Catholic University of Louvain)
UCR Union Centriste et Radicale (Centrist and Radical Union)
UD Unia Demokratyczna (Democratic Union)
UDF Union pour la Démocratie Française (Union for French Democracy)
UDP Uniao Democratico Popular (People's Democratic Union)
UEMOA Union Economique et Monétaire Ouest Africaine
UEO Union européenne occidentale (Western European Union)
UK United Kingdom
ULB Université Libre de Bruxelles (Free University of Brussels)
UNCHS United Nations Centre for Human Settlements
UNCTAD United Nations Conference on Trade and Development
UND Union Nationale et Démocratique (National and Democratic Union)
UNDP United Nations Development Programme
UNEP United Nations Environment Programme
UNESCO United Nations Educational, Scientific and Cultural Organization
UNHCR United Nations High Commission for Refugees
UNICEF United Nations Children's Fund
UNIDO United Nations Industrial Development Organization
Univ. University
UN(O) United Nations (Organisation)
UNRRA United Nations Relief and Rehabilitation Administration
UPOV International Union for the Protection of New Varieties of Plants
UPU Universal Postal Union
USA United States of America
UUP Ulster Unionist Party

UV Union Valenciana (Valencian Union Party)
UVCB Union des villes et communes de Belgique (Association of Belgian Cities and Municipalities)

V

V The Green Group in the European Parliament
V. Venstre, Danmarks Liberale Parti (Liberal Party)
VC Victoria Cross
VGÖ Vereinte Grune Österreichs (United Green Party of Austria)
Vice-Chmn. Vice-Chairman
Vice-Pres. Vice-President
VLD Vlaamse Liberalen en Demokraten (Flemish Liberals and Democrats: Liberal Party - Flemish speaking)
VP Vänsterpartiet (Left Party)
VU Volksunie (People's Union); Vaterlandische Union (Fatherland Union)
VVD Volkspartij voor Vrijheid en Democratie (People's Party for Freedom and Democracy)

W

WA Samtök um Kvennalista (Women's Alliance)
WCU World Conservation Union
WEU Western European Union
WFTU World Federation of Trade Unions
WHO World Health Organization
WIPO World Intellectual Property Organization
WMO World Meteorological Organization
WTO World Trade Organization

Y

YDP Yeni Dogus Partisi
YMCA Young Men's Christian Association
YWCA Young Women's Christian Association

Z

Zch-N Zjedurczenie Chrzescijansko-Narodowe (Christian National Union)
ZRS Zdruzenie robotníkov Slovenska (Association of Workers of Slovakia)

COUNTRY MEMBERSHIP OF MAJOR ORGANISATIONS

Column groups: **UN** | **UN SPECIALISED AGENCIES** (FAO[2] through WMO, World Tourism Organization) | **UN RELATED ORGANISATIONS** (CTBTO Prep.com, IAEA, OPCW, World Trade Organization[2])

Country	UN	FAO[2]	ICAO	IFAD	ILO	IMF	IMO	ITU	UNESCO	UNIDO	UPU	WHO	WIPO	WMO	World Tourism Organization	CTBTO Prep.com	IAEA	OPCW	World Trade Organization[2]
Afghanistan	★	★	★	★	★	★		★	★	★	★	★	★	★	★	★	★	★	★[7]
Albania	★	★	★	★	★	★	★	★	★	★	★	★	★	★	★	★	★	★	★
Algeria	★	★	★	★	★	★	★	★	★	★	★	★	★	★	★	★	★	★	★[7]
Andorra	★	★	★					★	★			★	★		★	★		★	★[7]
Angola	★	★	★	★	★	★	★	★	★	★	★	★	★	★		★	★		★
Anguilla														★[3]					
Antigua & Barbuda	★	★	★	★	★	★	★	★	★		★	★	★	★		★		★	★
Argentina	★	★	★	★	★	★	★	★	★	★	★	★	★	★	★	★	★	★	★
Armenia	★	★	★	★	★	★		★	★	★	★	★	★	★	★	★	★	★	★
Aruba				★					★[4]		★			★[4]					
Ascension											★								
Australia	★	★	★		★	★	★	★	★		★	★	★	★	★	★	★	★	★
Austria	★	★	★	★	★	★	★	★	★	★	★	★	★	★	★	★	★	★	★
Azerbaijan	★	★	★	★	★	★	★	★	★	★	★	★	★	★	★	★	★	★	★[7]
Bahamas, The	★	★	★	★	★	★	★	★	★	★	★	★	★	★	★	★		★	★[7]
Bahrain	★	★	★		★	★	★	★	★	★	★	★	★	★	★	★	★	★	★
Bangladesh	★	★	★	★	★	★	★	★	★	★	★	★	★	★	★	★	★	★	★
Barbados	★	★	★	★	★	★	★	★	★	★		★	★	★		★		★	★
Belarus	★	★	★		★	★		★	★	★	★	★	★	★	★	★	★	★	★[7]
Belgium	★	★	★	★	★	★	★	★	★	★	★	★	★	★	★[10,4]	★	★	★	★
Belize	★	★	★	★	★	★	★	★	★	★	★	★	★	★		★	★	★	★
Benin	★	★	★	★	★	★	★	★	★	★	★	★	★	★	★	★	★	★	★
Bermuda														★[3]					
Bhutan	★	★	★	★		★		★	★	★	★	★	★	★	★	★		★	★[7]
Bolivia	★	★	★	★	★	★	★	★	★	★	★	★	★	★	★	★	★	★	★
Bosnia & Herzegovina	★	★	★	★	★	★	★	★	★	★	★	★	★	★	★	★	★	★	★[7]
Botswana	★	★	★	★	★	★		★	★	★	★	★	★	★	★	★	★	★	★
Brazil	★	★	★	★	★	★	★	★	★	★	★	★	★	★	★	★	★	★	★
British Virgin Islands									★[4]					★[3]					
Brunei Darussalam	★	★	★		★	★	★	★	★		★	★	★	★	★	★		★	★
Bulgaria	★	★	★		★	★	★	★	★	★	★	★	★	★	★	★	★	★	★
Burkina Faso	★	★	★	★	★	★		★	★	★	★	★	★	★	★	★	★	★	★
Burundi	★	★	★	★	★	★		★	★	★	★	★	★	★	★	★	★	★	★
Cambodia	★	★	★	★	★	★	★	★	★	★	★	★	★	★	★	★	★	★	★
Cameroon	★	★	★	★	★	★	★	★	★	★	★	★	★	★	★	★	★	★	★
Canada	★	★	★	★	★	★	★	★	★		★	★	★	★		★	★	★	★
Cape Verde	★	★	★	★	★	★	★	★	★	★	★	★	★	★	★	★	★[11]	★	★
Cayman Islands									★[4]					★[3]					
Central African Republic	★	★	★	★	★	★		★	★	★	★	★	★	★	★	★	★	★	★
Chad	★	★	★	★	★	★		★	★	★	★	★	★	★	★	★	★	★	★
Chile	★	★	★	★	★	★	★	★	★	★	★	★	★	★	★	★	★	★	★
China	★	★	★	★	★	★	★	★	★	★	★	★	★	★	★	★	★	★	★
Colombia	★	★	★	★	★	★	★	★	★	★	★	★	★	★	★	★	★	★	★
Comoros	★	★	★	★	★	★	★	★	★	★	★	★	★	★		★		★	★[7]
Congo, Democratic Republic of	★	★	★	★	★	★	★	★	★	★	★	★	★	★	★	★	★	★	★
Congo, Republic of	★	★	★	★	★	★	★	★	★	★	★	★	★	★	★	★	★	★	★
Cook Islands		★	★	★			★		★			★		★		★		★	
Costa Rica	★	★	★	★	★	★	★	★	★	★	★	★	★	★	★	★	★	★	★
Côte d'Ivoire	★	★	★	★	★	★	★	★	★	★	★	★	★	★	★	★	★	★	★
Croatia	★	★	★	★	★	★	★	★	★	★	★	★	★	★	★	★	★	★	★
Cuba	★	★	★	★	★		★	★	★	★	★	★	★	★	★	★	★	★	★
Curacao					★				★[4]		★			★					

WORLD BANK GROUP					INTER-GOVERNMENTAL ORGANISATIONS														
IBRD	IFC	IDA	MIGA	ICSID	ADB	ASEAN	CARICOM	Commonwealth	EBRD14	EU	Franc Zone	IADB	INTERPOL	League of Arab States	NATO	OECD	OPEC	OSCE	
★	★	★	★	★	★								★						Afghanistan
★	★	★	★	★					★	★9			★		★			★	Albania
★	★	★	★	★									★	★			★		Algeria
													★					★	Andorra
★	★	★	★										★				★		Angola
							★4												Anguilla
★	★		★				★	★					★						Antigua & Barbuda
★	★	★	★	★								★	★						Argentina
★	★	★	★	★	★				★				★					★	Armenia
													★						Aruba
																			Ascension
★	★	★	★	★	★			★	★				★			★			Australia
★	★	★	★	★	★				★	★		★	★			★		★	Austria
★	★	★	★	★	★				★				★					★	Azerbaijan
★	★	★	★	★			★	★				★	★						Bahamas, The
★	★		★	★									★	★					Bahrain
★	★	★	★	★	★			★					★						Bangladesh
★	★	★	★	★			★	★				★	★						Barbados
★	★		★	★				★					★					★	Belarus
★	★	★	★	★	★			★	★	★		★	★		★	★		★	Belgium
★	★	★	★	★17			★	★				★	★						Belize
★	★	★	★	★							★		★						Benin
							★4												Bermuda
★	★	★			★								★						Bhutan
★	★	★	★									★	★						Bolivia
★	★	★	★	★					★	★9			★					★	Bosnia & Herzegovina
★	★	★	★	★				★					★						Botswana
★	★	★	★									★	★						Brazil
							★4												British Virgin Islands
★				★	★	★		★					★						Brunei Darussalam
★	★		★	★					★	★			★		★			★	Bulgaria
★	★	★	★	★							★		★						Burkina Faso
★	★	★	★	★									★						Burundi
★	★	★	★	★	★	★							★						Cambodia
★	★	★	★	★				★			★		★						Cameroon
★	★	★	★	★17	★			★	★			★	★		★	★		★	Canada
★	★	★	★	★									★						Cape Verde
							★4												Cayman Islands
★	★	★	★	★							★		★						Central African Republic
★	★	★	★	★							★		★						Chad
★	★	★	★	★								★	★			★			Chile
★	★	★	★	★	★							★	★						China
★	★	★	★	★								★	★						Colombia
★	★	★	★	★							★		★	★					Comoros
★	★	★	★	★									★						Congo, Democratic Republic of
★	★	★	★	★							★		★						Congo, Republic of
					★														Cook Islands
★	★	★	★	★								★	★						Costa Rica
★	★	★	★	★							★		★						Côte d'Ivoire
★	★	★	★	★					★	★		★	★		★			★	Croatia
													★						Cuba
													★						Curaçao

COUNTRY MEMBERSHIP OF MAJOR ORGANISATIONS

	UN	FAO	ICAO	IFAD	ILO	IMF	IMO	ITU	UNESCO	UNIDO	UPU	WHO	WIPO	WMO	World Tourism Organization	CTBTO Prep.com	IAEA	OPCW	World Trade Organization
		UN SPECIALISED AGENCIES														UN RELATED ORGANISATIONS			
Cyprus	★	★	★	★	★	★	★	★	★	★	★	★	★	★	★	★	★	★	★
Czech Republic	★	★	★		★	★	★	★	★	★	★	★	★	★	★	★	★	★	★
Denmark	★	★	★	★	★	★	★	★	★	★	★	★	★	★		★	★	★	★
Djibouti	★	★	★	★	★	★	★	★	★	★	★	★	★	★	★		★	★	★
Dominica	★	★		★	★	★	★	★	★	★	★	★	★	★	★			★	★
Dominican Republic	★	★	★	★	★	★	★	★	★	★	★	★	★	★	★	★	★	★	★
Ecuador	★	★	★	★	★	★	★	★	★	★	★	★	★	★	★	★	★	★	★
Egypt	★	★	★	★	★	★	★	★	★	★	★	★	★	★	★	★	★		★
El Salvador	★	★	★	★	★	★	★	★	★	★	★	★	★	★	★	★	★	★	★
Equatorial Guinea	★	★	★	★	★	★	★	★	★	★	★	★	★			★		★	★[7]
Eritrea	★	★	★	★	★	★	★	★	★	★	★	★	★	★	★	★		★	
Estonia	★	★	★		★	★	★	★	★		★	★	★	★		★	★	★	★
Ethiopia	★	★	★	★	★	★	★	★	★	★	★	★	★	★	★	★	★	★	★[7]
Faroe Islands		★[4]					★[4]		★[4]										
Fiji	★	★	★	★	★	★	★	★	★		★	★	★	★		★	★	★	★
Finland	★	★	★	★	★	★	★	★	★	★	★	★	★	★		★	★	★	★
France	★	★	★	★	★	★	★	★	★	★	★	★	★	★	★	★	★	★	★
French Polynesia															★				
Gabon	★	★	★	★	★	★	★	★	★	★	★	★	★	★	★	★	★	★	★
Gambia, The	★	★	★	★	★	★	★	★	★	★	★	★	★	★	★	★		★	★
Georgia	★	★	★	★	★	★	★	★	★	★	★	★	★	★	★	★	★	★	★
Germany	★	★	★	★	★	★	★	★	★	★	★	★	★	★	★	★	★	★	★
Ghana	★	★	★	★	★	★	★	★	★	★	★	★	★	★	★	★	★	★	★
Greece	★	★	★	★	★	★	★	★	★	★	★	★	★	★	★	★	★	★	★
Grenada	★	★	★	★	★	★	★	★	★	★	★	★	★			★		★	★
Guatemala	★	★	★	★	★	★	★	★	★	★	★	★	★	★	★		★	★	★
Guinea	★	★	★	★	★	★	★	★	★	★	★	★	★	★	★	★		★	★
Guinea-Bissau	★	★	★	★	★	★	★	★	★	★	★	★	★	★	★	★		★	★
Guyana	★	★	★	★	★	★	★	★	★	★	★	★	★	★		★		★	★
Haiti	★	★	★	★	★	★	★	★	★	★	★	★	★	★	★	★	★	★	★
Holy See								★			★		★		★[7]	★	★	★	★[8]
Honduras	★	★	★	★	★	★	★	★	★	★	★	★	★	★	★	★	★	★	★
Hong Kong, SAR							★[4]								★	★[4]			★
Hungary	★	★	★	★	★	★	★	★	★	★	★	★	★	★	★	★	★	★	★
Iceland	★	★	★	★	★	★	★	★	★		★	★	★	★		★	★	★	★
India	★	★	★	★	★	★	★	★	★	★	★	★	★	★	★		★	★	★
Indonesia	★	★	★	★	★	★	★	★	★	★	★	★	★	★	★	★	★	★	★
Iran	★	★	★	★	★	★	★	★	★	★	★	★	★	★	★	★	★	★	★[7]
Iraq	★	★	★	★	★	★	★	★	★	★	★	★	★	★	★	★	★	★	★[7]
Ireland	★	★	★	★	★	★	★	★	★	★	★	★	★	★		★	★	★	★
Israel	★	★	★	★	★	★	★	★	★	★	★	★	★	★	★	★	★		★
Italy	★	★	★	★	★	★	★	★	★	★	★	★	★	★	★	★	★	★	★
Jamaica	★	★	★	★	★	★	★	★	★	★	★	★	★	★	★	★	★	★	★
Japan	★	★	★	★	★	★	★	★	★	★	★	★	★	★	★	★	★	★	★
Jordan	★	★	★	★	★	★	★	★	★	★	★	★	★	★	★	★	★	★	★
Kazakhstan	★	★	★	★	★	★	★	★	★	★	★	★	★	★	★	★	★	★	★[7]
Kenya	★	★	★	★	★	★	★	★	★	★	★	★	★	★	★	★	★	★	★
Kiribati	★	★	★	★	★	★	★	★	★		★	★	★	★		★		★	
Korea, DPR (North)	★	★	★	★			★	★	★	★	★	★	★	★	★	★			
Korea, Republic of (South)	★	★	★	★	★	★	★	★	★	★	★	★	★	★	★	★	★	★	★
Kosovo						★													
Kuwait	★	★	★	★	★	★	★	★	★	★	★	★	★	★	★	★	★	★	★
Kyrgyzstan	★	★	★	★	★	★		★	★	★	★	★	★	★	★	★	★	★	★
Lao People's Democratic Republic	★	★	★	★	★	★		★	★	★	★	★	★	★	★	★	★	★	★

Country	WORLD BANK GROUP					INTER-GOVERNMENTAL ORGANISATIONS													
	IBRD	IFC	IDA	MIGA	ICSID	ADB	ASEAN	CARICOM	Commonwealth	EBRD[14]	EU	Franc Zone	IADB	INTERPOL	League of Arab States	NATO	OECD	OPEC	OSCE
Cyprus	★	★	★	★	★				★	★	★			★					★
Czech Republic	★	★	★	★	★					★	★			★		★	★		★
Denmark	★	★	★	★	★	★				★	★		★	★		★	★		★
Djibouti	★	★	★	★										★	★				
Dominica	★	★	★	★				★	★					★					
Dominican Republic	★	★	★	★	★[17]								★	★					
Ecuador	★	★	★	★									★	★				★	
Egypt	★	★	★	★	★						★			★	★				
El Salvador	★	★	★	★	★								★	★					
Equatorial Guinea	★	★	★	★								★		★					
Eritrea	★	★	★	★										★					
Estonia	★	★	★	★	★					★	★			★		★	★		★
Ethiopia	★	★	★	★	★[17]									★					
Faroe Islands																			
Fiji	★	★	★	★	★	★			★[13]					★					
Finland	★	★	★	★	★	★				★	★		★	★			★		★
France	★	★	★	★	★	★				★	★	★	★	★		★	★		★
French Polynesia																			
Gabon	★	★	★	★	★							★		★					
Gambia, The	★	★	★	★	★				★					★					
Georgia	★	★	★	★	★	★				★				★					★
Germany	★	★	★	★	★	★				★	★		★	★		★	★		★
Ghana	★	★	★	★	★				★					★					
Greece	★	★	★	★	★					★	★			★		★	★		★
Grenada	★	★	★	★	★			★	★					★					
Guatemala	★	★	★	★	★								★	★					
Guinea	★	★	★	★	★									★					
Guinea-Bissau	★	★	★	★	★[17]							★		★					
Guyana	★	★	★	★	★			★	★				★	★					
Haiti	★	★	★	★	★			★					★	★					
Holy See														★					★
Honduras	★	★	★	★	★								★	★					
Hong Kong, SAR						★													
Hungary	★	★	★	★	★					★	★			★		★	★		★
Iceland	★	★	★	★	★					★	★[5]			★		★	★		★
India	★	★	★	★		★			★					★					
Indonesia	★	★	★	★	★	★	★							★					
Iran	★	★	★	★										★				★	
Iraq	★	★	★	★										★	★			★	
Ireland	★	★	★	★	★	★				★	★			★			★		★
Israel	★	★	★	★	★					★			★	★			★		
Italy	★	★	★	★	★	★				★	★		★	★		★	★		★
Jamaica	★	★		★	★			★	★				★	★					
Japan	★	★	★	★	★	★				★			★	★			★		
Jordan	★	★	★	★	★					★				★	★				
Kazakhstan	★	★	★	★	★	★				★				★					★
Kenya	★	★	★	★	★				★					★					
Kiribati	★	★	★			★			★										
Korea, DPR (North)																			
Korea, Republic of (South)	★	★	★	★	★	★				★			★	★			★		
Kosovo	★	★	★	★	★					★	★[9]								
Kuwait	★	★	★	★	★									★	★			★	
Kyrgyzstan	★	★	★	★	★[17]	★				★				★					★
Lao People's Democratic Republic	★	★	★	★		★	★							★					

COUNTRY MEMBERSHIP OF MAJOR ORGANISATIONS

	UN	UN SPECIALISED AGENCIES														UN RELATED ORGANISATIONS			
	UN	FAO	ICAO	IFAD	ILO	IMF	IMO	ITU	UNESCO	UNIDO	UPU	WHO	WIPO	WMO	World Tourism Organization	CTBTO Prep.com	IAEA	OPCW	World Trade Organization
Latvia	★	★	★		★	★	★	★	★		★	★	★	★		★	★	★	★
Lebanon	★	★	★	★	★	★	★	★	★	★	★	★	★	★		★	★	★	★[7]
Lesotho	★	★	★	★	★	★		★	★	★	★	★	★	★	★	★	★	★	★
Liberia	★	★	★	★	★	★	★	★	★	★	★	★	★	★	★	★	★	★	★[7]
Libya	★	★	★	★	★	★	★	★	★	★	★	★	★	★	★	★	★	★	★[7]
Liechtenstein	★							★			★		★			★	★		
Lithuania	★	★	★		★	★	★	★	★		★	★	★	★	★	★	★	★	★
Luxembourg	★	★	★	★	★	★	★	★	★	★	★	★	★	★		★	★	★	★
Macao, SAR							★[4]		★[4]					★	★[4]				★
Macedonia, former Yugoslav Republic	★	★	★	★	★	★	★	★	★	★	★	★	★	★	★	★	★	★	★
Madagascar	★	★	★	★	★	★	★	★	★	★	★	★	★	★	★	★	★	★	★
Madeira															★[4]				
Malawi	★	★	★	★	★	★	★	★	★	★	★	★	★	★	★	★	★	★	★
Malaysia	★	★	★	★	★	★	★	★	★	★	★	★	★	★	★	★	★	★	★
Maldives	★	★	★	★	★	★	★	★	★	★	★	★	★	★	★	★		★	★
Mali	★	★	★	★	★	★		★	★	★	★	★	★	★	★	★	★	★	★
Malta	★	★	★	★	★	★	★	★	★	★	★	★	★	★	★	★	★	★	★
Marshall Islands	★	★	★	★	★	★	★	★	★			★				★	★	★	
Mauritania	★	★	★	★	★	★	★	★	★	★	★	★	★	★	★	★	★	★	
Mauritius	★	★	★	★	★	★	★	★	★	★	★	★	★	★	★	★	★	★	★
Mayotte											★								
Mexico	★	★	★	★	★	★	★	★	★	★	★	★	★	★	★	★	★	★	★
Micronesia, Fed. Sts. Of	★	★	★		★			★	★		★			★		★		★	
Moldova	★	★	★	★	★	★	★	★	★	★	★	★	★	★	★	★	★	★	★
Monaco	★	★	★				★	★	★	★	★	★	★	★	★	★	★	★	
Mongolia	★	★	★	★	★	★	★	★	★	★	★	★	★	★	★	★	★	★	★
Montenegro1	★	★	★		★	★	★	★	★	★	★	★	★	★	★	★	★	★	★
Montserrat															★[3]				
Morocco	★	★	★	★	★	★	★	★	★	★	★	★	★	★	★	★	★	★	★
Mozambique	★	★	★	★	★	★	★	★	★	★	★	★	★	★	★	★	★	★	★
Myanmar	★	★	★	★	★	★	★	★	★	★	★	★	★	★	★	★	★		★
Namibia	★	★	★	★	★	★	★	★	★	★	★	★	★	★	★	★	★	★	★
Nauru	★	★	★	★				★	★		★	★				★		★	
Nepal	★	★	★	★	★	★	★	★	★	★	★	★	★	★	★	★	★	★	★
Netherlands	★	★	★	★	★	★	★	★	★	★	★	★	★	★	★	★	★	★	★
New Caledonia															★				
New Zealand	★	★	★	★	★	★	★	★	★		★	★	★	★	★	★	★	★	★
Nicaragua	★	★	★	★	★	★	★	★	★	★	★	★	★	★	★	★	★	★	★
Niger	★	★	★	★	★	★		★	★	★	★	★	★	★	★	★	★	★	★
Nigeria	★	★	★	★	★	★	★	★	★	★	★	★	★	★	★	★	★	★	★
Niue		★		★				★				★		★		★		★	
Norway	★	★	★	★	★	★	★	★	★	★	★	★	★	★	★	★	★	★	★
Occupied Territories									★						★[7]				
Oman	★	★	★	★	★	★	★	★	★	★	★	★	★	★	★	★	★	★	★
Overseas Territories (UK)											★								
Pakistan	★	★	★	★	★	★	★	★	★	★	★	★	★	★	★	★	★	★	★
Palau	★	★	★		★	★		★			★					★	★	★	
Panama	★	★	★	★	★	★	★	★	★	★	★	★	★	★	★	★	★	★	★
Papua New Guinea	★	★	★	★	★	★	★	★	★	★	★	★	★	★	★	★	★	★	★
Paraguay	★	★	★	★	★	★	★	★	★	★	★	★	★	★	★	★	★	★	★
Peru	★	★	★	★	★	★	★	★	★	★	★	★	★	★	★	★	★	★	★
Philippines	★	★	★	★	★	★	★	★	★	★	★	★	★	★	★	★	★	★	★
Poland	★	★	★		★	★	★	★	★	★	★	★	★	★	★	★	★	★	★
Portugal	★	★	★	★	★	★	★	★	★	★	★	★	★	★	★	★	★	★	★
Puerto Rico															★[4]				

COUNTRY MEMBERSHIP OF MAJOR ORGANISATIONS

WORLD BANK GROUP					INTER-GOVERNMENTAL ORGANISATIONS														
IBRD	IFC	IDA	MIGA	ICSID	ADB	ASEAN	CARICOM	Commonwealth	EBRD14	EU	Franc Zone	IADB	INTERPOL	League of Arab States	NATO	OECD	OPEC	OSCE	
★	★	★	★	★					★	★			★		★			★	Latvia
★	★	★	★	★									★	★					Lebanon
★	★	★	★	★				★					★						Lesotho
★	★	★	★	★									★						Liberia
★	★	★	★										★	★18			★		Libya
									★				★					★	Liechtenstein
★	★	★	★	★					★	★			★		★			★	Lithuania
★	★	★	★	★	★				★	★			★		★	★		★	Luxembourg
																			Macao, SAR
★	★	★	★	★					★	★5			★					★	Macedonia, former Yugoslav Republic
★	★	★	★	★									★						Madagascar
																			Madeira
★	★	★	★	★				★					★						Malawi
★	★	★	★	★	★	★		★					★						Malaysia
★	★	★	★		★			★					★						Maldives
★	★	★	★	★							★		★						Mali
★	★		★	★				★	★	★			★					★	Malta
★	★	★			★								★						Marshall Islands
★	★	★	★	★									★	★					Mauritania
★	★	★	★	★				★					★						Mauritius
																			Mayotte
★	★	★	★						★			★	★			★			Mexico
★	★	★	★	★	★														Micronesia, Fed. Sts. Of
★	★	★	★	★					★				★					★	Moldova
													★					★	Monaco
★	★	★	★	★	★				★				★					★	Mongolia
★	★	★	★	★					★	★5			★					★	Montenegro1
							★												Montserrat
★	★	★	★	★					★				★	★					Morocco
★	★	★	★	★				★					★						Mozambique
★	★	★	★16		★	★							★						Myanmar
★	★		★	★17				★					★						Namibia
					★			★					★						Nauru
★	★	★	★	★	★								★						Nepal
★	★	★	★	★	★				★	★		★	★		★	★		★	Netherlands
																			New Caledonia
★	★	★	★	★	★			★					★			★			New Zealand
★	★	★	★	★								★	★						Nicaragua
★	★	★	★	★							★		★						Niger
★	★	★	★	★				★					★				★		Nigeria
																			Niue
★	★	★	★	★	★				★			★	★		★	★		★	Norway
														★					Occupied Territories
★	★	★	★	★									★	★					Oman
																			Overseas Territories (UK)
★	★	★	★	★	★			★					★						Pakistan
★	★	★	★		★														Palau
★	★	★	★	★								★	★						Panama
★	★	★	★	★	★			★					★						Papua New Guinea
★	★	★	★	★								★	★						Paraguay
★	★	★	★	★								★	★						Peru
★	★	★	★	★	★	★							★						Philippines
★	★	★	★						★	★			★		★	★	★		Poland
★	★	★	★	★	★				★	★		★	★		★	★	★		Portugal
																			Puerto Rico

COUNTRY MEMBERSHIP OF MAJOR ORGANISATIONS

	UN	UN SPECIALISED AGENCIES														UN RELATED ORGANISATIONS			
	UN	FAO	ICAO	IFAD	ILO	IMF	IMO	ITU	UNESCO	UNIDO	UPU	WHO	WIPO	WMO	World Tourism Organization	CTBTO Prep.com	IAEA	OPCW	World Trade Organization
Qatar	★	★	★	★	★	★	★	★	★	★	★	★	★	★	★	★	★	★	★
Romania	★	★	★	★	★	★	★	★	★	★	★	★	★	★	★	★	★	★	★
Russian Federation	★	★	★		★	★	★	★	★	★	★	★	★	★	★	★	★	★	★
Rwanda	★	★	★	★	★	★		★	★	★	★	★	★	★	★	★	★[11]	★	★
St. Kitts and Nevis	★	★	★	★	★	★	★	★	★	★	★	★	★			★		★	★
St. Lucia	★	★	★	★	★	★	★	★	★	★	★	★	★	★		★		★	★
St. Vincent & the Grenadines	★	★	★	★	★	★	★	★	★	★	★	★	★			★		★	★
Samoa	★	★	★	★	★	★	★	★	★	★	★	★	★	★		★		★	★
San Marino	★	★			★	★	★	★	★		★	★	★		★	★	★[11]	★	
São Tomé & Príncipe	★	★	★	★	★	★	★	★	★	★	★	★	★	★	★	★		★	★[7]
Saudi Arabia	★	★	★	★	★	★	★	★	★	★	★	★	★	★	★	★	★	★	★
Senegal	★	★	★	★	★	★	★	★	★	★	★	★	★	★	★	★	★	★	★
Serbia	★	★	★		★	★	★	★	★	★	★	★	★	★	★	★	★	★	★[7]
Seychelles	★	★	★	★	★	★	★	★	★	★	★	★	★	★	★	★	★	★	★[7]
Sierra Leone	★	★	★	★	★	★	★	★	★	★	★	★	★	★	★	★	★	★	★
Singapore	★	★	★		★	★	★	★	★		★	★	★	★		★	★	★	★
Sint Maarten					★				★[4]		★			★					
Slovak Republic	★	★	★		★	★	★	★	★	★	★	★	★	★	★	★	★	★	★
Slovenia	★	★	★		★	★	★	★	★	★	★	★	★	★	★	★	★	★	★
Solomon Islands	★	★	★	★	★	★	★	★	★		★	★		★		★		★	★
Somalia	★	★	★	★	★	★	★	★	★	★	★	★		★		★		★	
South Africa	★	★	★	★	★	★	★	★	★	★	★	★	★	★	★	★	★	★	★
South Sudan	★	★	★	★	★			★	★		★	★		★		★			
Spain	★	★	★	★	★	★	★	★	★	★	★	★	★	★	★	★	★	★	★
Sri Lanka	★	★	★	★	★	★	★	★	★	★	★	★	★	★	★	★	★	★	★
Sudan	★	★	★	★	★	★	★	★	★	★	★	★	★	★	★	★	★	★	★[7]
Suriname	★	★	★	★	★	★	★	★	★	★	★	★	★	★		★		★	★
Swaziland	★	★	★	★	★	★		★	★	★	★	★	★	★	★	★	★	★	★
Sweden	★	★	★	★	★	★	★	★	★		★	★	★	★		★	★	★	★
Switzerland	★	★	★	★	★	★	★	★	★	★	★	★	★	★	★	★	★	★	★
Syria	★	★	★	★	★	★	★	★	★	★	★	★	★	★	★	★	★		★[7]
Taiwan																			★
Tajikistan	★	★	★	★	★	★		★	★	★	★	★	★	★	★	★	★	★	★
Tanzania	★	★	★	★	★	★	★	★	★	★	★	★	★	★	★	★	★	★	★
Thailand	★	★	★	★	★	★	★	★	★	★	★	★	★	★	★	★	★	★	★
Timor-Leste	★	★	★	★	★	★	★	★	★	★	★	★				★		★	
Togo	★	★	★	★	★	★	★	★	★	★	★	★	★	★	★	★		★	★
Tokelau		★[4]							★[4]										
Tonga	★	★	★	★		★	★	★	★		★	★	★	★		★	★[11]	★	★
Trinidad & Tobago	★	★	★	★	★	★	★	★	★	★	★	★	★	★		★	★	★	★
Tunisia	★	★	★	★	★	★	★	★	★	★	★	★	★	★	★	★	★	★	★
Turkey	★	★	★	★	★	★	★	★	★	★	★	★	★	★	★	★	★	★	★
Turkmenistan	★	★	★		★	★	★	★	★	★	★	★	★	★	★	★		★	
Turks & Caicos Islands																★[3]			
Tuvalu	★	★		★	★	★	★	★	★	★	★	★		★		★		★	
Uganda	★	★	★	★	★	★	★	★	★	★	★	★	★	★	★	★	★	★	★
Ukraine	★	★	★		★	★	★	★	★	★	★	★	★	★	★	★	★	★	★
United Arab Emirates	★	★	★	★	★	★	★	★	★	★	★	★	★	★	★	★	★	★	★
United Kingdom	★	★	★	★	★	★	★	★	★		★	★	★	★		★	★	★	★
United States of America	★	★	★	★	★	★	★	★	★		★	★	★	★		★	★	★	★
Uruguay	★	★	★	★	★	★	★	★	★	★	★	★	★	★	★	★	★	★	★
Uzbekistan	★	★	★	★	★	★		★	★	★	★	★	★	★	★	★	★	★	★[7]
Vanuatu	★	★	★	★	★	★	★	★	★	★	★	★	★	★	★	★		★	★
Venezuela	★	★	★	★	★	★	★	★	★	★	★	★	★	★	★	★	★	★	★
Vietnam	★	★	★	★	★	★	★	★	★	★	★	★	★	★	★	★	★	★	★

WORLD BANK GROUP					INTER-GOVERNMENTAL ORGANISATIONS														
IBRD	IFC	IDA	MIGA	ICSID	ADB	ASEAN	CARICOM	Commonwealth	EBRD[14]	EU	Franc Zone	IADB	INTERPOL	League of Arab States	NATO	OECD	OPEC	OSCE	
★	★		★	★									★	★			★		Qatar
★	★		★	★					★	★			★		★			★	Romania
★	★	★	★	★[17]					★				★			★[15]		★	Russian Federation
★	★	★	★	★				★					★						Rwanda
★	★	★	★	★			★	★					★						St. Kitts and Nevis
★	★	★	★	★			★	★					★						St. Lucia
★		★	★	★			★	★					★						St. Vincent & the Grenadines
★	★	★	★	★	★			★					★						Samoa
★													★					★	San Marino
★	★	★	★	★									★						São Tomé & Príncipe
★	★	★	★	★									★	★			★		Saudi Arabia
★	★	★	★	★							★		★						Senegal
★	★	★	★	★					★	★[5]			★					★	Serbia
★	★		★	★				★					★						Seychelles
★	★	★	★	★				★					★						Sierra Leone
★	★	★	★	★	★	★		★					★						Singapore
													★						Sint Maarten
★	★	★	★	★					★	★			★		★	★		★	Slovak Republic
★	★	★	★	★					★	★		★	★		★	★		★	Slovenia
★	★	★	★	★	★			★											Solomon Islands
★	★	★		★									★	★					Somalia
★	★	★	★					★					★						South Africa
★	★	★	★	★									★						South Sudan
★	★	★	★	★	★				★	★		★	★		★	★		★	Spain
★	★	★	★	★	★			★					★						Sri Lanka
★	★	★	★	★									★	★					Sudan
★	★		★				★					★	★						Suriname
★	★	★	★	★				★					★						Swaziland
★	★	★	★	★	★				★	★		★	★			★		★	Sweden
★	★	★	★	★	★				★			★	★			★		★	Switzerland
★	★	★	★	★									★	★[18]					Syria
					★														Taiwan
★	★	★	★		★				★				★					★	Tajikistan
★	★	★	★	★				★					★						Tanzania
★	★	★	★	★[17]	★	★							★						Thailand
★	★	★	★	★									★						Timor-Leste
★	★	★	★	★							★		★						Togo
																			Tokelau
★	★	★		★	★			★					★						Tonga
★	★	★	★	★			★	★				★	★						Trinidad & Tobago
★	★	★	★	★				★					★	★					Tunisia
★	★	★	★	★	★				★	★[5]			★		★	★		★	Turkey
★	★		★	★	★				★									★	Turkmenistan
							★[4]												Turks & Caicos Islands
★		★			★			★					★						Tuvalu
★	★	★	★	★				★					★						Uganda
★	★	★	★	★					★				★					★	Ukraine
★	★	★	★	★									★	★			★		United Arab Emirates
★	★	★	★	★	★			★	★	★		★	★		★	★		★	United Kingdom
★	★	★	★	★	★				★			★	★		★	★		★	United States of America
★	★		★	★								★	★						Uruguay
★	★	★	★	★	★				★				★					★	Uzbekistan
★	★	★	★		★			★											Vanuatu
★	★		★									★	★				★		Venezuela
★	★	★	★		★	★							★						Vietnam

COUNTRY MEMBERSHIP OF MAJOR ORGANISATIONS

	UN	UN SPECIALISED AGENCIES														World Tourism Organization	UN RELATED ORGANISATIONS			
	UN	FAO	ICAO	IFAD	ILO	IMF	IMO	ITU	UNESCO	UNIDO	UPU	WHO	WIPO	WMO	World Tourism Organization	CTBTO Prep.com	IAEA	OPCW	World Trade Organization
Yemen	★	★	★	★	★	★	★	★	★	★	★	★	★	★	★	★	★	★	★[7]
Zambia	★	★	★	★	★	★		★	★	★	★	★	★	★	★	★	★	★	★
Zimbabwe	★	★	★	★	★	★[6]	★	★	★	★	★	★	★	★	★	★	★	★	★

Legend

★[1] Following Montenegro's acceptance of the declaration of independence on 3 June 2006, the membership of the State Union of Serbia and Montenegro in the UN including all organisations is continued by the Republic of Serbia.

★[2] EU also a member

★[3] Territory member, British Caribbean Territories

★[4] Associate Member

★[5] Candidate country

★[6] Voting rights suspended

★[7] Observer state

★[8] Observer state, but unlike other WRO observer states, does not have to start accession negotiations within five years of becoming an observer

★[9] Potential candidate country

★[10] Flemish Community of Belgium only

WORLD BANK GROUP					INTER-GOVERNMENTAL ORGANISATIONS														
IBRD	IFC	IDA	MIGA	ICSID	ADB	ASEAN	CARICOM	Commonwealth	EBRD[14]	EU	Franc Zone	IADB	INTERPOL	League of Arab States	NATO	OECD	OPEC	OSCE	
★	★	★	★	★									★	★					Yemen
★	★	★	★	★				★					★						Zambia
★	★	★	★	★									★						Zimbabwe

★[11] Membership approved. Membership will take effect once the necessary legal instruments are deposited.

★[12] Member in arrears

★[13] Suspended from the Councils of the Commonwealth in December 2006 following a military coup

★[14] EC & EIB also members

★[15] Started accession talks

★[16] In the process of fulfilling membership requirements

★[17] Signed but not ratified membership

★[18] Membership suspended

CALENDAR OF FORTHCOMING ELECTIONS

September 2013
7 September	Presidential election scheduled in the **Maldives**.
9 September	Parliamentary elections scheduled in **Norway**.
14 September	Parliamentary elections scheduled in **Australia**.
15 September	Parliamentary elections scheduled in **Macau**.
16 September	Parliamentary elections scheduled in **Rwanda**.
20 September	Legislative elections scheduled in **Swaziland**.
22 September	Parliamentary elections scheduled in **Germany**.
27 September	Parliamentary elections scheduled in **Aruba**.
29 September	Legislative elections scheduled in **Austria**.

October 2013
	Presidential election due in **Ethiopia**.
	Presidential election due in **Georgia**.
	Second round of presidential elections due in **Madagascar**.
16 October	Presidential election scheduled in **Azerbaijan**.
29 October	Legislative elections scheduled in **Argentina**.

November 2013
	Legislative elections due in **Falkland Islands**.
	Legislative elections due in **Nepal**.
	Presidential election due in **Tajikistan**.
5 November	Parliamentary elections scheduled in **Northern Mariana Islands**.
17 November	First round of presidential and legislative elections scheduled in **Chile**.
24 November	Parliamentary elections scheduled in **Guinea-Bissau**.
24 November	Presidential and legislative elections scheduled in **Honduras**.

December 2013
	Second round of presidential elections due in **Georgia**.
15 December	Parliamentary elections scheduled in **Turkmenistan**.

January 2014
	Legislative elections due in **Bangladesh**.

February 2014
2 February	Presidential and parliamentary elections scheduled in **Costa Rica**.
2 February	First round of presidential election scheduled in **El Salvador**.

March 2014
	Legislative elections due in **Antigua and Barbuda**.
	Legislative elections due in **Colombia**.
	Legislative elections due in **Iraq**.
	Presidential election due in **Macedonia**.
	Presidential election due in **Slovakia**.
9 March	Second round of presidential election due in **El Salvador**.

April 2014
	Presidential election due in **Afghanistan**.
	Presidential election due in **Algeria**.
	Parliamentary elections due in **Hungary**.
	Parliamentary elections due in **Indonesia**.
	Presidential election due in **Malta**.
	Parliamentary elections due in **South Africa**.

May 2014
	Presidential election due in **Colombia**.
	Legislative elections due in **Czech Republic**.
	Legislative elections due in **Dominican Republic**.
	Parliamentary elections due in **India**.
	Presidential election due in **Lebanon**.
	Presidential election due in **Lithuania**.
	Parliamentary elections due in **Maldives**.
	Presidential election due in **South Africa**.
	Presidential election due in **Syria**.
4 May	Presidential and legislative elections due in **Panama**.
20 May	Presidential and parliamentary elections due in **Malawi**.
22 May	Parliamentary elections due in the **European Union**.
25 May	Parliamentary elections due in **Belgium**.
25 May	Parliamentary elections due in **Luxembourg**.

July 2014
	First round of presidential elections due in **Indonesia**.
	Presidential election due in **Israel**.
	Presidential election due in **Macau**.
	Presidential election due in **Mauritania**.

August 2014
	Presidential election due in **Turkey**.
	Parliamentary elections due in **São Tomé and Príncipe**.
	Parliamentary elections due in **Solomon Islands**.

September 2014
	Parliamentary election due in **Fiji**.
	Parliamentary elections due in **Sweden**.
	Presidential election due in **Vanuatu**.
	Parliamentary election due in **Tuvalu**.

October 2014
	Parliamentary election due in **Bahrain**.
	Presidential and parliamentary elections due in **Bosnia and Herzegovina**.
	Presidential and parliamentary elections due in **Botswana**.
	Presidential and parliamentary elections due in **Mozambique**.
5 October	Presidential and parliamentary elections due in **Brazil**.
26 October	First round of presidential elections and legislative elections due in **Uruguay**.

November 2014
	Legislative elections due in **Haiti**.
	Parliamentary elections due in **Lebanon**.
	Parliamentary elections due in **Moldova**.
	Presidential & parliamentary elections due in **Namibia**.
	Presidential election due in **Romania**.
4 November	Legislative elections due in **American Samoa**.
4 November	Legislative elections due in **USA**.

December 2014
	Presidential and parliamentary elections due in **Bolivia**.
	Parliamentary elections due in **Comoros**.
	Presidential and parliamentary elections due in **Uzbekistan**.

FLAGS

 AFGHANISTAN

 ÅLAND ISLANDS

 ALBANIA

 ALGERIA

 AMERICAN SAMOA

 ANDORRA

 ANGOLA

 ANGUILLA

 ANTARCTICA

 ANTIGUA & BARBUDA

 ARGENTINA

 ARMENIA

 ARUBA

 AUSTRALIA

 ABORIGINAL FLAG

 AUSTRALIAN CAPITAL TERRITORY

 NEW SOUTH WALES

 NORTHERN TERRITORY

 QUEENSLAND

 SOUTH AUSTRALIA

 TASMANIA

 VICTORIA

 WESTERN AUSTRALIA

 AUSTRIA

 AZERBAIJAN

 BAHAMAS

 BAHRAIN

 BANGLADESH

 BARBADOS

... BELARUS

 BELGIUM

 BELIZE

 BENIN

 BERMUDA

 BHUTAN

 BOLIVIA

 BONAIRE

 BOSNIA-HERZEGOVINA

 BOTSWANA

 BRAZIL

 BRITISH VIRGIN ISLANDS

 BRUNEI

 BULGARIA

 BURKINA FASO

 BURUNDI

 CAMBODIA

 CAMEROON

 CANADA

 ALBERTA

 BRITISH COLOMBIA

 MANITOBA

 NEW BRUNSWICK

 NEWFOUNDLAND AND LABRADOR

 NORTHWEST TERRITORIES

FLAGS

 NOVA SCOTIA

 NUNAVUT

 ONTARIO

 PRINCE EDWARD ISLAND

 QUEBEC

 SASKATCHEWAN

 YUKON

 CANARY ISLANDS

 CAPE VERDE

 CAYMAN ISLANDS

 CENTRAL AFRICAN REPUBLIC

 CHAD

 CHILE

 CHINA

 CHRISTMAS ISLAND

 COCOS ISLANDS

 COLOMBIA

 COMOROS

 DEMOCRATIC REPUBLIC OF CONGO

 REPUBLIC OF CONGO

 COOK ISLANDS

 COSTA RICA

 CÔTE D'IVOIRE

 CROATIA

 CUBA

 CURAÇAO

 CYPRUS

 CZECH REPUBLIC

 DENMARK

 DJIBOUTI

 DOMINICA

 DOMINICAN REPUBLIC

 ECUADOR

 EGYPT

 EL SALVADOR

 ENGLAND

 EQUATORIAL GUINEA

 ERITREA

 ESTONIA

 ETHIOPIA

 FALKLAND ISLANDS

 FAROE ISLANDS

 FIJI

 FINLAND

 FRANCE

 FRENCH POLYNESIA

 FRENCH SOUTHERN & ANTARCTIC TERRITORIES

 GABON

FLAGS

GALAPAGOS ISLANDS

GAMBIA

GEORGIA

GERMANY

BADEN WÜRTTEMBERG

BAVARIA

BERLIN

BRANDENBURG

BREMEN

HAMBURG

HESSE

LOWER SAXONY

MECKLENBURG WESTERN POMERANIA

NORTH-RHINE WESTPHALIA

RHINELAND-PALATINATE

SAARLAND

SAXONY

SAXONY-ANHALT

SCHLESWIG-HOLSTEIN

THURINGIA

GHANA

GIBRALTAR

GREECE

GREENLAND

GRENADA

GUAM

GUATEMALA

GUERNSEY

GUINEA

GUINEA-BISSAU

GUYANA

HAITI

HONDURAS

HONG KONG

HUNGARY

ICELAND

INDIA

INDONESIA

IRAN

IRAQ

IRELAND

ISLE OF MAN

ISRAEL

ITALY

JAMAICA

JAPAN

JERSEY

JORDAN

KAZAKHSTAN

KENYA

KIRIBATI

KOREA (NORTH)

KOREA (SOUTH)

KOSOVO

FLAGS

 KUWAIT

 KYRGYZSTAN

 LAOS

 LATVIA

 LEBANON

 LESOTHO

 LIBERIA

 LIBYA

 LIECHTENSTEIN

 LITHUANIA

 LUXEMBOURG

 MACAO

 MACEDONIA

 MADAGASCAR

 MADEIRA

 MALAWI

 MALAYSIA

 MALDIVES

 MALI

 MALTA

 MARSHALL ISLANDS

 MARTINIQUE

 MAURITANIA

 MAURITIUS

 MAYOTTE

 MEXICO

 MICRONESIA

 MOLDOVA

 MONACO

 MONGOLIA

 MONTENEGRO

 MONTSERRAT

 MOROCCO

 MOZAMBIQUE

 MYANMAR

 NAMIBIA

 NAURU

 NEPAL

 NETHERLANDS

 NEW CALEDONIA AND DEPENDENCIES

 NEW ZEALAND

 NICARAGUA

 NIGER

 NIGERIA

 NIUE

 NORFOLK ISLAND

 NORTHERN CYPRUS

 NORTHERN IRELAND

 NORTHERN MARIANAS

 NORWAY

 OCCUPIED PALESTINIAN TERRITORIES

 OMAN

 PAKISTAN

PALAU

FLAGS

 PANAMA

 PAPUA NEW GUINEA

 PARAGUAY

 PERU

 PHILIPPINES

 PITCAIRN ISLANDS

 POLAND

 PORTUGAL

 PUERTO RICO

 QATAR

 REUNION ISLAND

 ROMANIA

 RUSSIAN FEDERATION

 RWANDA

 SABA

 SAINT KITTS & NEVIS

 SAINT EUSTATIUS

 SAINT HELENA

 SAINT LUCIA

 SAINT MARTIN-SINT MAARTEN

 SAINT VINCENT & GRENADINES

 SAINT PIERRE AND MIQUELON

 SAMI

 SAMOA

 SAN MARINO

 SÃO TOMÉ E PRÍNCIPE

 SARK

 SAUDI ARABIA

 SCOTLAND

 SENEGAL

 SERBIA

 SEYCHELLES

 SIERRA LEONE

 SINGAPORE

 SLOVAK REPUBLIC

 SLOVENIA

 SOLOMON ISLANDS

 SOMALIA

 SOUTH AFRICA

 SOUTH GEORGIA

 SOUTH SUDAN

 SPAIN

 SRI LANKA

 SUDAN

 SURINAME

 SWAZILAND

 SWEDEN

 SWITZERLAND

FLAGS

 SYRIA

 TAIWAN

 TAJIKISTAN

 TANZANIA

 THAILAND

 TIMOR-LESTE

 TOGO

 TOKELAU

 TONGA

 TRINIDAD & TOBAGO

 TUNISIA

 TURKEY

 TURKMENISTAN

 TURKS AND CAICOS

 TUVALU

 UGANDA

 UKRAINE

 UNITED ARAB EMIRATES

 UNITED KINGDOM

 UNITED STATES OF AMERICA

 ALABAMA

 ALASKA

 ARIZONA

 ARKANSAS

 CALIFORNIA

 COLORADO

 CONNECTICUT

 DELAWARE

 DISTRICT OF COLUMBIA

 FLORIDA

 GEORGIA

 HAWAII

 IDAHO

 ILLINOIS

 INDIANA

 IOWA

 KANSAS

 KENTUCKY

 LOUISIANA

 MAINE

 MARYLAND

 MASSACHUSETTS

 MICHIGAN

 MINNESOTA

 MISSISSIPPI

 MISSOURI

 MONTANA

 NEBRASKA

 NEVADA

 NEW HAMPSHIRE

 NEW JERSEY

 NEW MEXICO

 NEW YORK STATE

 NORTH CAROLINA

FLAGS

 NORTH DAKOTA

 OHIO

 OKLAHOMA

 OREGON

 PENNSYLVANIA

 RHODE ISLAND

 SOUTH CAROLINA

 SOUTH DAKOTA

 TENNESSEE

 TEXAS

 UTAH

 VERMONT

 VIRGINIA

 WASHINGTON

 WEST VIRGINIA

 WISCONSIN

 WYOMING

 URUGUAY

 US VIRGIN ISLANDS

 UZBEKISTAN

 VATICAN CITY

 VANUATU

 VENEZUELA

 VIETNAM

 WALES

 WALLIS & FUTUNA

 YEMEN

 ZAMBIA

 ZIMBABWE

 AFRICAN UNION

 ANDEAN COMMUNITY

 ASEAN

 CARICOM

 CIS

 COMMONWEALTH

 EAST AFRICAN COMMUNITY

 EUROPEAN UNION

 IFRC

 ISLAMIC CONFERENCE

 NATO

 NORDIC COUNCIL

 INTERNATIONAL OLYMPIC COMMITTEE

 OPEC

 PACIFIC COMMUNITY

 UN

 UNICEF

UNITED NATIONS

The name 'United Nations' was devised by the late President Roosevelt, and was first used in the Declaration by United Nations on 1 January 1942, when representatives of 26 nations pledged their governments to continue fighting together against the Axis powers. In the aftermath of World War II, the United Nations helped stabilise international relations and give peace a more secure foundation.

The Charter of the United Nations was drawn up by the representatives of 50 countries at the Conference on International Organization (San Francisco, USA; 25 April - 26 June 1945) and was signed on the latter date. The representatives worked on the basis of principles which had been formulated by representatives of the United Kingdom, the USA, the Soviet Union and China at Dumbarton Oaks from August to October 1944.

The states invited to the San Francisco Conference were those which had declared war on the Axis powers and adhered to the Declaration by United Nations of 1 January 1942. In this declaration the 26 nations which were the original signatories and the 21 others which subsequently adhered to it formally subscribed to the purposes and principles of the Atlantic Charter and agreed not to make a separate peace. The invitation to Poland was held over owing to the fact that a Provisional Government of National Unity had not yet been formed. Four other countries were invited by the Conference itself, making a total of 51. These 51 states are the original members of the United Nations.

The United Nations officially came into existence on 24 October 1945, when the United Kingdom, the USA, France, the then USSR and China, and a majority of other signatories, ratified the Charter. All the signatories had ratified it by 31 December 1945, Poland having signed on 15 October.

Functions

The function of the United Nations is set forth in the Preamble to the Charter, which states that the Peoples of the United Nations are determined to prevent war, " ... reaffirm faith in fundamental human rights, in the dignity and worth of the human person, in the equal rights of men and women and of nations large and small ... ", to maintain treaty obligations and the observance of international law; and to " ... promote social progress and better standards of life in larger freedom ... " Although the Charter does not authorise the United Nations to intervene in matters which come essentially within the national province of any state, the Charter states that this principle shall not prejudice the application of enforcement measures under Chapter VII concerning action with respect to threats to the peace, breaches of the peace and acts of aggression.

The UN is not only a peace-keeper and a forum for conflict resolution. Eighty per cent of the work of the UN system is devoted to helping developing countries build the capacity to help themselves. This includes promoting and protecting democracy and human rights; saving children from starvation and disease; providing relief assistance to refugees and disaster victims; countering global crime, drugs and disease; and assisting countries devastated by war and the long-term threat of landmines.

Membership

Membership is open to all nations who are prepared to accept the obligations of the Charter, and is effected on the recommendation of the Security Council by the General Assembly. Following Montenegro's acceptance of independence on 3 June 2006 from Serbia, Montenegro became a member in its own right on 28 June 2006.

The 193 Member States of the United Nations, and the date of their admission to the Organization, are as follows:

Afghanistan	19 November 1946
Albania	14 December 1955
Algeria	8 October 1962
Andorra	28 July 1993
Angola	1 December 1976
Antigua and Barbuda	11 November 1981
Argentina*	24 October 1945
Armenia	2 March 1992
Australia*	1 November 1945
Austria	14 December 1955
Azerbaijan	9 March 1992
Bahamas	18 September 1973
Bahrain	21 September 1971
Bangladesh	17 September 1974
Barbados	9 December 1966
¹Belarus*	24 October 1945
Belgium*	27 December 1945
Belize	25 September 1981
Benin	20 September 1960
Bhutan	21 September 1971
Bolivia*	14 November 1945
²Bosnia and Herzegovina	22 May 1992
Botswana	17 October 1966
Brazil*	24 October 1945
Brunei Darussalam	21 September 1984
Bulgaria	14 December 1955
Burkina Faso	20 September 1960
Burundi	18 September 1962
Cambodia	14 December 1955
Cameroon	20 September 1960
Canada*	9 November 1945
Cape Verde	16 September 1975

- continued

Central African Republic	20 September 1960
Chad	20 September 1960
Chile*	24 October 1945
People's Republic of China*	24 October 1945
Colombia*	5 November 1945
Comoros	12 November 1975
Republic of the Congo	20 September 1960
Democratic Republic of Congo	20 September 1960
Costa Rica*	2 November 1945
Côte d'Ivoire	20 September 1960
³Croatia	22 May 1992
Cuba*	24 October 1945
Cyprus	20 September 1960
⁴Czech Republic	19 January 1993
Denmark*	24 October 1945
Djibouti	20 September 1977
Dominica	18 December 1978
Dominican Republic*	24 October 1945
Ecuador*	21 December 1945
⁵Egypt*	24 October 1945
El Salvador*	24 October 1945
Equatorial Guinea	12 November 1968
Eritrea	28 May 1993
Estonia	17 September 1991
Ethiopia*	13 November 1945
Fiji	13 October 1970
Finland	14 December 1955
France*	24 October 1945
Gabon	20 September 1960
Gambia	21 September 1965
Georgia	31 July 1992
⁶Germany	18 September 1973
Ghana	8 March 1957
Greece*	25 October 1945
Grenada	17 September 1974
Guatemala*	21 November 1945
Guinea	12 December 1958
Guinea-Bissau	17 September 1974
Guyana	20 September 1966
Haiti*	24 October 1945
Honduras*	17 December 1945
Hungary	14 December 1955
Iceland	19 November 1946
India*	30 October 1945
⁷Indonesia	28 September 1950
Iran* (Islamic Republic of)	24 October 1945
Iraq*	21 December 1945
Ireland	14 December 1955
Israel	11 May 1949
Italy	14 December 1955
Jamaica	18 September 1962
Japan	18 December 1956
Jordan	14 December 1955
Kazakhstan	23 January 1992
Kenya	16 December 1963
Kiribati	14 September 1999
Democratic People's Republic of Korea	17 September 1991
Republic of Korea	17 September 1991
Kuwait	14 May 1963
Kyrgyzstan	2 March 1992
Lao People's Democratic Republic	14 December 1955
Latvia	17 September 1991
Lebanon*	24 October 1945
Lesotho	17 October 1966
Liberia*	2 November 1945
Libya	14 December 1955
Liechtenstein	18 September 1990
Lithuania	17 September 1991
Luxembourg*	24 October 1945
⁸The Former Yugoslav Republic of Macedonia	8 April 1993
Madagascar	20 September 1960
Malawi	1 December 1964
⁹Malaysia	17 September 1957
Maldives	21 September 1965
Mali	28 September 1960
Malta	1 December 1964
Marshall Islands	17 September 1991
Mauritania	7 October 1961
Mauritius	24 April 1968
Mexico*	7 November 1945
Micronesia, Federated States of	17 September 1991
Republic of Moldova	2 March 1992
Monaco	28 May 1993
Mongolia	27 October 1961
¹¹Montenegro	28 June 2006

UNITED NATIONS

- continued

Morocco	12 November 1956
Mozambique	16 September 1975
Myanmar	19 April 1948
Namibia	23 April 1990
Nauru	14 September 1999
Nepal	14 December 1955
Netherlands*	10 December 1945
New Zealand*	24 October 1945
Nicaragua	24 October 1945
Niger	20 September 1960
Nigeria	7 October 1960
Norway*	27 November 1945
Oman	7 October 1971
Pakistan	30 September 1947
Palau	15 December 1994
Panama*	13 November 1945
Papua New Guinea	10 October 1975
Paraguay*	24 October 1945
Peru*	31 October 1945
Philippines*	24 October 1945
Poland*	24 October 1945
Portugal	14 December 1955
Qatar	21 September 1971
Romania	14 December 1955
[10]Russian Federation	24 October 1945
Rwanda	18 September 1962
St. Kitts and Nevis	23 September 1983
St. Lucia	18 September 1979
St. Vincent and the Grenadines	16 September 1980
San Marino	2 March 1992
Sao Tome and Principe	16 December 1975
Samoa	15 December 1976
Saudi Arabia*	24 October 1945
Senegal	28 September 1960
[11]Serbia	1 November 2000
Seychelles	21 September 1976
Sierra Leone	27 September 1961
Singapore	21 September 1965
[12]Slovak Republic	19 January 1993
[13]Slovenia	22 May 1992
Solomon Islands	19 September 1978
Somalia	20 September 1960
South Africa*	7 November 1945
[17]South Sudan	14 July 2011
Spain	14 December 1955
Sri Lanka	14 December 1955
Sudan	12 November 1956
Suriname	4 December 1975
Swaziland	24 September 1968
Sweden	19 November 1946
Switzerland	10 September 2002
[14]Syria*	24 October 1945
Tajikistan	2 March 1992
[15]Tanzania	14 December 1961
Thailand	16 December 1946
Timor Leste	27 September 2002
Togo	20 September 1960
Tonga	14 September 1999
Trinidad and Tobago	18 September 1962
Tunisia	12 November 1956
Turkey*	24 October 1945
Turkmenistan	2 March 1992
Tuvalu	5 September 2000
Uganda	25 October 1962
Ukraine*	24 October 1945
United Arab Emirates	9 December 1971
United Kingdom*	24 October 1945
United States of America*	24 October 1945
Uruguay*	18 December 1945
Uzbekistan	2 March 1992
Vanuatu	15 September 1981
Venezuela*	15 November 1945
Vietnam	20 September 1977
[16]Yemen	30 September 1947
Zambia	1 December 1964
Zimbabwe	25 August 1980

* Original member

[1] Byelorussia informed the United Nations on 19 September 1991 that it had changed its name to Belarus.

[2] Bosnia and Herzegovina. The Socialist Federal Republic of Yugoslavia was an original Member of the United Nations, the Charter having been signed on its behalf on 26 June 1945 and ratified 19 October 1945, until its dissolution following the establishment and subsequent admission as new members of Bosnia and Herzegovina, the Republic of Croatia, the Republic of Slovenia, the former Yugoslav Republic of Macedonia and the Federal Republic of Yugoslavia. The Republic of Bosnia and Herzegovina was admitted as a Member of the United Nations by a General Assembly resolution on 22 May 1992.

[3] Croatia. The Socialist Federal Republic of Yugoslavia was an original Member of the United Nations, the Charter having been signed on its behalf on 26 June 1945 and ratified 19 October 1945, until its dissolution following the establishment and subsequent admission as new members of Bosnia and Herzegovina, the Republic of Croatia, the Republic of Slovenia, the former Yugoslav Republic of Macedonia and the Federal Republic of Yugoslavia. The Republic of Croatia was admitted as a Member of the United Nations by a General Assembly resolution on 22 May 1992.

[4] Czechoslovakia was an original member of the United Nations, joining on 24 October 1945. A letter dated 10 December 1992 informed the Secretary-General that as of 31 December 1992 the Czech and Slovak Federal Republic would cease to exist. The Czech Republic and Slovak Republic would as successor states apply for membership. After receiving their applications the Security Council recommended to the General Assembly, that the Czech Republic and Slovak Republic be admitted. They were admitted on 19 January 1993 as member states.

[5] Egypt and Syria were original Members of the United Nations from 24 October 1945. Following a plebiscite on 21 February 1958, the United Arab Republic was established by a union of Egypt and Syria and continued as a single Member. On 13 October 1961, Syria having resumed its status as an independent State, resumed its separate membership of the United Nations. On 2 September 1971, the United Arab Republic changed its name to the Arab Republic of Egypt.

[6] The German Democratic Republic was admitted to membership in the United Nations on 18 September 1973. Through its accession to the Federal Republic of Germany with effect from 3 October 1990, the two German States have united to form one sovereign State.

[7] By letter of 20 January 1965, Indonesia announced its decision to withdraw from the United Nations "at this stage and under the present circumstances". By telegram of 19 September 1966, it announced its decision "to resume full co-operation with the United Nations and to resume participation in its activities". On 28 September 1966, the General Assembly took note of this decision and the President invited the representatives of Indonesia to take seats in the Assembly.

[8] The Socialist Federal Republic of Yugoslavia was an original Member of the United Nations, the Charter having been signed on its behalf on 26 June 1945 and ratified 19 October 1945, until its dissolution following the establishment and subsequent admission as new members of Bosnia and Herzegovina, the Republic of Croatia, the Republic of Slovenia, the former Yugoslav Republic of Macedonia and the Federal Republic of Yugoslavia. On 8 April 1993 The General Assembly decided to admit to United Nations membership the state being provisionally referred to for all purposes within the United Nations as 'The Former Yugoslav Republic of Macedonia' pending settlement of the difference that had arisen over its name.

[9] The Federation of Malaya joined the United Nations on 17 September 1957. On 16 September 1963, its name changed to Malaysia, following the admission to the new federation of Singapore, Sabah (North Borneo) and Sarawak. Singapore became an independent State on 9 August 1965 and a United Nations Member on 21 September 1965.

[10] The Union of Soviet Socialist Republics was an original Member of the United Nations from 24 October 1945. In a letter dated 24 December 1991, Boris Yeltsin, the President of the Russian Federation, informed the Secretary-General that the membership of the Soviet Union in the Security Council and all other United Nations organs was being continued by the Russian Federation with the support of 11 member countries of the Commonwealth of Independent States.

[11] The membership of the State Union Serbia and Montenegro in the United Nations, including all organs and organizations of the United Nations system is continued by the Republic of Serbia on the basis of Article 60 of the Constitutional Charter of Serbia and Montenegro, activated by the Declaration of Independence adopted by the National Assembly of Montenegro on 3 June 2006. The Republic of Monenegro was admitted as a Member of the United Nations by General Assembly resolution 60/264 of 28 June 2006.

[12] Czechoslovakia was an original member of the United Nations, joining on 24 October 1945. A letter dated 10 December 1992 informed the Secretary-General that as of 31 December 1992 the Czech and Slovak Federal Republic would cease to exist. The Czech Republic and Slovak Republic would as successor states apply for membership. After receiving their applications the Security Council recommended to the General Assembly, that the Czech Republic and Slovak Republic be admitted. The Slovak Republic was admitted on 19 January 1993 as a Member State.

[13] Slovenia. The Socialist Federal Republic of Yugoslavia was an original Member of the United Nations, the Charter having been signed on its behalf on 26 June 1945 and ratified 19 October 1945, until its dissolution following the establishment and subsequent admission as new members of Bosnia and Herzegovina, the Republic of Croatia, the Republic of Slovenia, the former Yugoslav Republic of Macedonia and the Federal Republic of Yugoslavia. The Republic of Slovenia was admitted as a Member of the United Nations by a General Assembly resolution on 22 May 1992.

[14] Egypt and Syria were original Members of the United Nations from 24 October 1945. Following a plebiscite on 21 February 1958, the United Arab Republic was established by a union of Egypt and Syria and continued as a single Member. On 13 October 1961, Syria having resumed its status as an independent State, resumed its separate membership of the United Nations.

[15] Tanganyika was a United Nations Member from 14 December 1961 and Zanzibar was a Member from 16 December 1963. Following the ratification on 26 April 1964 of Articles of Union between Tanganyika and Zanzibar, the United Republic of Tanganyika and Zanzibar continued as a single Member, changing its name to United Republic of Tanzania on 1 November 1964.

[16] Yemen was admitted to membership of the United Nations on 30 September 1947 and Democratic Yemen on 14 December 1967. On 22 May 1990, the two countries merged and have since been represented as one Member with the name Yemen.

17 The Republic of South Sudan formally seceded from Sudan on 9 July 2011 as a result of an internationally monitored referendum held in January 2011, and was admitted as a new Member State by the United Nations General Assembly on 14 July 2011.

Principal Organs of the United Nations

The UN has six main organs, all except The International Court of Justice located at the UN HQ in New York. The International Court of Justice is located at The Hague, the Netherlands. The main organs are:

The General Assembly

All UN Member States are represented in the General Assembly - a parliament of nations which meets to consider the world's most pressing problems. Each Member State has one vote. Important matters are decided by two-thirds majority. Others by simple majority. The Assembly holds its annual regular session from September to December.

The Security Council

The UN Charter gives the Security Council primary responsibility for maintaining international peace and security. The Council may convene at any time peace is threatened. There are 15 Council members, five permanent - China, France, the Russian Federation, the United Kingdom and the United States. The other ten are elected for two-year terms by the General Assembly.

The Economic and Social Council

The Economic and Social Council co-ordinates the economic and social work of the UN and the UN family. It fosters international co-operation for development. It has 54 members, elected by the General Assembly for three-year terms. It meets throughout the year. Beginning in 1998, the Economic and Social Council expanded its discussions to include humanitarian themes.

The Secretariat

The Secretariat carries out the substantive and the administrative work of the United Nations as directed by the General Assembly, the Security Council and the other organs. At its head is the Secretary-General.

The International Court of Justice

The International Court of Justice, also known as the World Court, is the main judicial organ of the United Nations. It consists of 15 judges elected by the General Assembly and the Security Council and decides disputes between countries.

The Trusteeship Council

Established to provide international supervision for 11 Trust Territories administered by 7 Member States and to ensure steps were taken to prepare the Territories for self-government or independence. By 1994 all Territories had attained self-government or independence and now the Trusteeship Council will only meet as and when the occasion demands.

The UN System

The International Monetary Fund, the World Bank group and other independent organisations known as "specialized agencies" are linked to the UN through co-operative agreements. These agencies are autonomous bodies created by intergovernmental agreement and have wide-ranging international responsibilities in the economic, social, cultural, educational, health and related fields.

In addition, a number of UN offices, programmes and funds work to improve the economic and social condition of people around the world. These bodies report to the General Assembly or the Economic and Social Council. All these organisations have their own governing bodies, budgets and secretariats. Together with the UN, they are known as the UN family or the UN system. Some 40,000 people work in the UN the Secretariat.

Achievements
Peacekeeping

The UN does not have an army. Member States voluntarily provide troops and equipment, for which they are compensated from a special peace-keeping budget. The United Nations peacekeepers are dispatched by the Security Council and help implement peace agreements, monitor cease-fires, patrol demilitarized zones and create buffer zones between opposing forces. The success of peacekeeping depends, ultimately, on the consent and co-operation of the opposing parties. As of March 2013, there were currently 15 ongoing operations (14 peacekeeping operations and one special political mission in Afghanistan) and some 92,968 uniformed personnel, provided by over 110 countries.

Following the September 2001 terrorist attack on the United States, the Security Council adopted a wide-ranging resolution which obligates States to ensure that any person who participates in financing, planning, preparing, perpetrating or supporting terrorist acts is brought to justice.

During the 1990s, there have been major changes in the patterns of conflict with more than 90 per cent of conflicts taking place within, rather than between, states. The UN has therefore reshaped and enhanced the range of instruments at its command, emphasizing conflict prevention, continually adapting peacekeeping operations, involving regional organisations, and strengthening post-conflict peace-building. The UN played a major role in ending war and fostering reconciliation in El Salvador, Guatemala, Cambodia and Mozambique.

Other conflicts (e.g. Somalia, Rwanda and the former Yugoslavia), often characterised by ethnic violence, have brought new challenges to the UN peacekeeping role.

Continuing crises in the Democratic Republic of the Congo, East Timor, Kosovo, Liberia, Côte d'Ivoire, Haiti, Sudan and Ethiopia-Eritrea led the Council to establish eight new missions in 1999-2006. The UN continues to maintain two peacekeeping forces in the area of Arab/Israeli

conflict - the Golan Heights and Southern Lebanon. The most recent operations were established in the Central African Republic and Chad (2007) and Darfur, Sudan. The UN is also helping to prepare a referendum on the future of Western Sahara. As of March 2013 the missions were: UN Organization Stabilization Mission in the DRC (MONUSCO); African Union-UN Hybrid Operation in Darfur (UNAMID); UN Mission in South Sudan (UNMISS); UN Operation in the Cote d'Ivoire (UNOCI); UN Mission in Liberia (UNMIL); UN Mission for the Referendum in Western Sahara (MINURSCO); UN Stabilization Mission in Haiti (MINUSTAH); UN Military Observer Group in India and Pakistan (UNMOGIP); UN Assistance Mission in Afghanistan (UNAMA); UN Peacekeeping Force in Cyprus (UNFICYP); UN Interim Administration Mission in Kosovo (UNMIK); UN Disengagement Observer Force, Syria Golan Heights (UNDOF); United Nations Interim Force in Lebanon (UNIFIL); UN Truce Supervision Organization, Middle East (UNTSO); UN Security Force for Abyei, Sudan (UNISFA)

Approved resources for peacekeeping operations for the period 1 July 2012 to 30 June 2013 amount to US$7.33 billion. This excludes the costs of special missions covered by the regular budget. Approximately $3.34 billion was outstanding (as of 31 January 2013).

Most peace-keeping troops are supplied by developing countries. The main contributors as of 2013 were Bangladesh (approx. 8,780), Pakistan (8,200), India (7,840), Ethiopia (6,500), Nigeria (5,500), Nepal (4,500), Jordan (3,500).

The UN is increasingly concentrating on peacebuilding, addressing the underlying causes of conflict.

Disarmament

Halting the spread of arms and reducing and eliminating weapons of mass destruction are major goals of the UN. It has provided an ongoing forum for negotiations, making recommendations and initiating studies. Negotiations have produced agreements such as the Nuclear Non-Proliferation Treaty (1968), the Comprehensive Nuclear-Test-Ban Treaty (1996) and the treaties establishing nuclear-free zones. Other treaties prohibit the development, production and stockpiling of chemical weapons (1992) and bacteriological weapons (1972). An international conference in 2001 adopted a range of political undertakings to prevent, combat and eradicate the trade in small arms. By 2009, 156 nations had signed the Ottawa Convention outlawing landmines.

The International Atomic Energy Agency ensures that nuclear materials and equipment intended for peaceful uses are not diverted for military purposes and the Organisation for the Prohibition of Chemical Weapons collects information on chemical facilities worldwide and conducts routine inspections to ensure adherence to the chemical weapons convention.

Promoting Development

At the Millennium Summit of September 2000, world leaders adopted a set of Millennium Development Goals aimed at eradicating extreme poverty, achieving universal primary education, promoting gender equality and empowering women, reducing child mortality, improving maternal health and combating HIV/AIDS, malaria and other diseases. A set of measurable targets is to be achieved by the year 2015. A status report was published in June 2006.

The UN system's annual expenditure on operational activities for development, excluding contributions from the World Bank and the IMF, amount to more than US$4 billion. This is spent mostly on economic and social programmes to help the world's poorest countries. The UN Development Programme has supported more than 5,000 projects - agricultural, industrial, educational and environmental - with a current budget of US$2 billion. It is the largest multilateral source of grant development assistance.

Through the efforts of the UN Industrial Development Organization, the UN has promoted investment in developing countries.

Promoting Human Rights

Since adopting the Universal Declaration of Human Rights in 1948, the United Nations has helped enact comprehensive agreements on political, civil, economic, social and cultural rights. The UN Human Rights Commission has focused world attention on cases of torture, disappearance, and arbitrary detention. Two tribunals have been established to try people accused of war crimes in former Yugoslavia and Rwanda, and an International Criminal Court was set up in 1998.

A long-term objective of the United Nations has been to improve the lives of women and to empower women to have greater control over their lives. The UN Development Fund for Women and the International Research and Training Institute for the Advancement of Women have supported programmes and projects to improve the quality of life for women in over 100 countries.

Protecting the Environment

The UN has played a significant part in creating a global programme to protect the environment. The "Earth Summit," the UN Conference on Environment and Development held in Rio de Janeiro in 1992, resulted in treaties on biodiversity and climate change, and all countries adopted "Agenda 21" - a blueprint for sustainable development whilst protecting natural resources. The UN Environment Programme and the World Meteorological Organization have been instrumental in highlighting the damage caused to the earth's ozone layer. As a result of a treaty, known as the Montreal Protocol, there has been a global effort to reduce chemical emissions of substances that have caused the depletion of the ozone layer. Through three international conferences, the UN spearheaded international effort to promote a comprehensive global agreement - the UN Convention on the Law of the Sea 1994 - for the protection, preservation and peaceful development of the oceans.

Emergency Assistance

In 2005, through the Office for the Co-ordination of Humanitarian Affairs, UN organisations raised nearly US$2 billion for the victims of war and natural disasters. The UN family of organisations, in partnership with intergovernmental and non-governmental organisations, provide food, shelter, medicines and logistical support.

UNITED NATIONS

Finance

The UN runs on assessed contributions from Member States under the terms of its 1945 Charter. It relies on countries to honour their treaty obligations and to pay their membership dues in full, on time and without conditions. Each country's contribution is calculated, according to a formula approved by all Member States, on the basis of its share of the world economy and ability to pay. In December 2011 the General Assembly adopted a budget of $5.15 billion for the biennium 2012-2013.

The top contributors are: the US, Japan, Germany, the UK and France. In 2011, the USA contributed $582 million of the total $2,414.7 million.

Significant arrears in payments to the Regular Budget remain. At the end of 2010, Member States owed the United Nations Regular Budget over $US348 million for current and past assessments. Total unpaid assessed contributions to the peacekeeping budget stood at US$2.6 billion.

Under the UN Charter, if at the beginning of the year a country owes the same or more than its total gross assessments for the previous two years, it automatically loses its right to vote in the General Assembly. As of February 2013, the following Member States were in arrears

and were not able to vote: Dominican Republic, Marshall Islands, Seychelles, Sierra Leone, Vanuatu, Venezuela and Zimbabwe. The following countries were also in arrears but were allowed to vote as they had shown that conditions beyond their control had been a factor: the Central African Republic, The Comoros, Guinea-Bissau, Sao Tome and Principe, and Somalia.

Secretary-General: Ban Ki-moon (page 1383)

United Nations Regional Information Centres, URL: http://unic.un.org/

United Nations Headquarters, New York: First Avenue at 46th Street, New York, NY 10017, USA. Tel: +1 212 963 4475, fax: +1 212963 0071, e-mail: inquiries@un.org, URL: http://www.un.org/

United Nations Headquarters, Geneva: Palais des Nations, 8-14 Avenue de la Paix, 1211 Geneva 10, Switzerland. Tel: +41 (0)22 917 1234, fax: +41 (0)22 917 0123, e-mail: webmaster@unog.ch, URL: http://www.un.org/

GENERAL ASSEMBLY

67th Annual Session, September 2012- September 2013

The General Assembly is the main deliberative organ of the United Nations and the work of the UN derives largely from the decisions of the General Assembly. Whilst these decisions have no legally binding force for Governments, they carry the weight of world opinion on major international issues, as well as the moral authority of the world community.

The General Assembly comprises all 193 United Nations Member States each of which may have not more than five representatives and may decide the way in which to choose its representatives, but has only one vote. It meets regularly once a year, sessions usually take place between September and December, but special sessions can be convened at the request of the Security Council, of a majority of members or of one member supported by a majority of members. Whilst decisions are usually made on the basis of a simple majority, important issues can only be passed by a two-thirds majority.

Function

The General Assembly's functions are:
- To consider and make recommendations on the principles of general co-operation in the maintenance of international peace and security, including the principles governing disarmament and the regulation of armaments;

- To discuss any problem affecting peace and security and make recommendations on it, except where a dispute or situation is currently being discussed by the Security Council (in 1956 the Assembly decided that if the Security Council, because of lack of unanimity of the permanent members, fails to exercise its primary responsibility for the maintenance of international peace and security in any case where there appears to be a threat to the peace, breach of the peace, or act of aggression, the Assembly shall consider the matter immediately with a view to making recommendations to Members for collective measures, including in the case of a breach of the peace or act of aggression, the use of armed force when necessary);

- To discuss and, with the same exception, to make recommendations on any question within the scope of the Charter affecting the powers and functions of any organ of the United Nations;

- To initiate studies and make recommendations to promote international political co-operation, the development of international law and its codification, the realisation of human rights and fundamental freedoms for all, and international collaboration in economic, social, cultural, education and health fields;

- To receive and consider reports from the Security Council and other organs of the United Nations;

- To make recommendations for the peaceful settlement of any situation, regardless of origin, which might impair friendly relations among nations;

- To supervise, through the Trusteeship Council, the execution of the Trusteeship Agreements for non-strategic areas;

- To elect the ten non-permanent members of the Security Council, the 54 members of the Economic and Social Council, those members of the Trusteeship Council which are elected; to take part (with the Security Council) in the election of the judges of the International Court of Justice; and, on the recommendation of the Security Council, to appoint the Secretary-General;

- To consider and approve the budget of the United Nations, apportion the contributions among members, and examine the administrative budgets of specialised agencies.

The General Assembly deals with its work through six main committees on which all members are entitled to be represented:

First Committee (Disarmament and International Security), Chair: Mr Desra Percava (Indonesia)
Second Committee (Economic and Financial), Chair: Mr George Wilfred Talbot (Guyana)

Third Committee (Social, Humanitarian and Cultural), Chair: H.E. Mr Henry Mac-Donald (Suriname)
Fourth Committee (Special Political and Decolonization), Chair: Mr Noel Nelson Messone (Gabon)
Fifth Committee (Administrative and Budgetary), Chair: Mr Miguel Berger (Germany)
Sixth Committee (Legal)

In addition to these main committees, the Assembly may constitute other committees on which all members have the right to be represented.

Proceedural Committees

There are also two procedural committees, the **Credentials Committee** and the **General (or Steering) Committee**.

The **Credentials Committee** is made up of nine members appointed by the Assembly at the beginning of each session. The members as of 2013 (67th Session) were: Angola, China, Peru, Russian Federation, Seychelles, Sweden, Thailand, Trinidad and Tobago, and the United States.

The **General (or Steering Committee)** is composed of 25 members (the President of the Assembly, 21 vice-presidents and the six main committee chairmen). At the beginning of each session the General Committee considers the agenda and makes recommendations to the Assembly. It also makes recommendations as to the closing date of the session. It helps the President and the General Assembly in drawing up the agenda. It does not decide any political questions.

The president of the 67th session of the General Committee is H.E. Vuk Jeremić (Qatar). The 21 vice-presidents as of March 2013, were from: Afghanistan, Algeria, Angola, Bangladesh, China, Congo, France, Ghana, Honduras, Israel, Kenya, Lebanon, Nepal, Netherlands, Palau, Peru, Russian Federation, Sierra Leone, Trinidad and Tobago, United Kingdom, United States.

As a rule, the Assembly refers all questions on its agenda to one of the main Committees, to a joint committee, or to a specially appointed *ad hoc* committee. These committees then submit proposals for approval to a plenary meeting of the Assembly. Voting in committees and sub-committees is by simple majority.

The Assembly may adopt resolutions without reference to any committee. The Assembly is further assisted by two standing committees: the Advisory Committee on Administrative and Budgetary Questions, (nine members), and the Committee on Contributions (10 members).

Subsidiary Organs
The Human Rights Council

The Human Rights Council is an inter-governmental body within the UN system made up of 47 States responsible for strengthening the promotion and protection of human rights around the globe. The Council was created by the UN General Assembly on 15 March 2006 with the main purpose of addressing situations of human rights violations and making recommendations on them.
President (2013): Remigiusz Achilles Henczel (Poland)

Council of the United Nations University

The University comprises UNU Centre in Tokyo and a worldwide network of Research and Training Centres and Programmes assisted by numerous associated and co-operating institutions. These units work in collaboration with each other as well as with a wide network of several designated UNU Associated Institutions and many co-operating institutions, acdemics and researchers worldwide.

There are also two governing councils; the Governing Coucnil of the UN Environment Programme and the Governing Council of the UN Human Settlements Programme.

Budget

The General Assembly approves the regular budget to cover administrative and other expenses of the Secretariat and other principal organs of the United Nations. All member states contribute to the regular budget in accordance with a scale of assessments specified by the

General Assembly. How much a State pays is determined primarily by its total national income in relation to that of other Member States. The General Assembly has fixed a maximum of 25 per cent and a minimum of 0.01 per cent of the budget for any one contributor.

President
The President of the General Assembly is elected by the Assembly and holds office until the close of the session at which he was elected. The election is held by secret ballot and there are no nominations. The President is elected by a simple majority and due regard is given to equitable geographical rotation on the following basis:

(a) African States
(b) Asian States
(c) Eastern European States
(d) Latin American States
(e) Western European and other States

President: Vuk Jeremić (page 1449)(Republic of Serbia)

General Assembly, URL: http://www.un.org/en/ga/

SECURITY COUNCIL

The Security Council has primary responsibility, under the UN Charter, for the maintenance of international peace and security. To achieve this, the Council may undertake mediation, issue cease-fire directives, send UN peace-keeping forces to help reduce tensions in troubled areas and keep opposing forces apart or impose economic sanctions. The Security Council may decide on collective military action where this is appropriate. Under the terms of the UN Charter, member states must comply with the decisions of the Security Council.

Members
There are 15 members of the Security Council, of which five are designated as permanent members by the UN Charter. The ten non-permanent members are elected for two-year terms by the General Assembly. A State may not immediately succeed itself on the expiration of its term. (Terms expire on 31 December of the year indicated in parentheses.)

- **Permanent Members:** China, France, Russian Federation, United Kingdom of Great Britain and Northern Ireland, United States of America

- **Non-permanent Members:** Argentina (2014), Azerbaijan (2013), Australia (2014), Guatemala (2013), Luxembourg (2014), Morocco (2013), Pakistan (2013), Republic of Korea (2014), Rwanda (2014) and Togo (2013).

Every member of the Council is entitled to one vote. Voting on all matters other than questions of procedure, when a decision is made by an affirmative vote of any nine members, requires the vote of nine members including the concurring votes of permanent members; but any member, whether permanent or not, may not vote when it is party to a dispute.

The Council is so organised as to be able to function continuously and a representative of each of its members must always be present at the headquarters of the United Nations. It may meet at places other than at headquarters if considered advisable.

A country which is a member of the United Nations but not of the Council may take part in its discussions when the Council considers that country's interests are particularly affected. Both members and non-members are invited to take part in the Council's discussions when they are parties to disputes under the Council's consideration. In the case of a non-member the Security Council lays down the conditions under which it may participate.

Presidency
Presidency of the Security Council changes monthly on an alphabetical basis (based on English names). The presidency will be held by the following countries for one month during 2013 (in order of rotation): Pakistan, Republic of Korea, Russian Federation, Rwanda, Togo, UK, US, Argentina, Australia, Azerbaijan, China, France.

Function
The Security Council is primarily responsible for maintaining international peace and security. The UN Charter specifically empowers it:
- To maintain international peace and security in accordance with the Purposes and Principles of the United Nations;
- To investigate any dispute or situation which might lead to international friction;
- To recommend methods of adjusting such disputes or terms of settlement;
- To formulate plans for the establishment of a system to regulate armaments;
- To determine the existence of a threat to the peace or act of aggression and to recommend what action should be taken;
- To call on Members to apply economic sanctions and other measures short of war in order to prevent or stop aggression;
- To take military action against an aggressor;
- To recommend the admission of new members and the terms on which non-members of the United Nations may become parties to the Statute of the International Court of Justice;
- To exercise the trusteeship functions of the United Nations in 'strategic areas';
- To submit annual and special reports to the General Assembly;
- To recommend the appointment of the Secretary-General to the General Assembly and, in consultation with the Assembly, to elect International Court Judges.

The Military Staff Committee
The Military Staff Committee, which is composed of the Chiefs of Staff of the five permanent members or their representatives, according to the Charter, advises and assists the Security Council on such questions as the Council's military requirements for the maintenance of peace, the strategic direction of armed forces placed at its disposal, the regulation of armaments, and possible disarmament.

General and complete disarmament is one of the major objectives of the United Nations and over the years some 20 multilateral and bilateral arms regulations and disarmament agreements have been reached, including:
1959 - Antarctic Treaty forbidding military activity in that zone;

1963 - Moscow Treaty banning nuclear tests in the atmosphere, in outer space and under water;
1967 - Outer Space Treaty banning nuclear weapons from outer space;
1968 - Treaty on the Non-Proliferation of Nuclear Weapons;
1972 - Sea-bed Treaty prohibiting emplacement of nuclear and other weapons of mass destruction in that environment;
1975 - Convention banning the development, production and stockpiling of bacteriological weapons and calling for the early destruction of existing stocks;
1976 - Convention on the Prohibition of Military or any other Hostile Use of Environmental Modification Techniques;
1983 - Convention on certain inhumane weapons.

In addition to a Disarmament Commission composed of all Members of the United Nations, there is a Conference on Disarmament open to all nuclear weapon States and to 35 other countries representing all political tendencies and geographical groupings. The major goal of this Committee is to draw up elements of a comprehensive programme for disarmament.

Committees
The Security Council also includes Standing Committees and Ad Hoc Committees.

There are currently three **Standing Committees**, all of which comprise representatives of every Security Council Member State, discuss Rules of Procedure and the Admission of New Members. The current Standing Committees are:
- Security Council Committee of Experts
- Security Council Committee on Admission of New Members
- Security Council Committee on Council meetings away from Headquarters

The **Ad Hoc Committees**, are established as and when necessary, also comprise every Council Member. They meet in closed session. Currently the Ad Hoc Committees are: The United Nations Compensation Commission; The Counter-terrorism Committee; and the 1540 Committee. The **Counter-terrorism Committee** was established in response to the terrorist attack in New York in September 2001. The **1540 Committee** was established in April 2004 to implement resolution 1540 which addresses the issue of the proliferation of nuclear, chemical and biological weapons.

Further subsidiary bodies include:
Peacebuilding Commission: set up on 20 December 2005 (resolution 60/180 and 1645) which advises and proposes integrated strategies for post-conflict recovery;
Sanctions Committees: Under Chapter VII of the Charter, the Security Council can take enforcement measures to maintain or restore international peace and security. Such measures range from economic and/or other sanctions not involving the use of armed force to international military action. The Sanctions Committees report on specific Resolutions relating to Somalia, Eritrea, the Democratic Republic of Congo, Cote d'Ivoire, Sudan, Libya, and Guinea-Bissau. There are also enforcement measures relating to any individual or entity associated with al-Qaida and associated individuals.
Governing Council of the UN Compensation Commission: Created in 1991 to process claims and pay compensation for losses and damage resulting from Iraq's unlawful invasion of Kuwait. The UN received 2.7 million claims totalling US$32.5 billion.
The Security Council Working Group on Documentation and Other Procedural Questions (IWG): established in June 1993 to improve procedures within the Security Council relating to its documentation and other procedural questions. The Working Group meets as agreed by members of the Security Council.
Working Group on Children and Armed Conflict: established in 2005 in response to SC Resolution 1612.

International Tribunals
Two International Tribunals are currently in existence:
- International Tribunal for the Prosecutions of Persons Responsible for Serious Violations of International Humanitarian Law in the Territory of the Former Yugoslavia;
- International Tribunal for the Prosecution of Persons Responsible for Serious Violations of International Humanitarian Law Committed in the Territory of Rwanda and Rwandan Citizens Responsible for such Violations Committed in the Territory of Neighbouring States.

Working Groups
There are currently five Security Council Working Groups: Peacekeeping Operations; Ad Hoc Working Group on Conflict Prevention and Resolution in Africa; Working Group established pursuant to resolution 1566 (2004); Working Group on Children and Armed Conflict; Informal Working Group on Documentation and Other Procedural Questions.

Peace-keeping Operations
Since 1948, there have been 67 United Nations peace-keeping operations.

UNITED NATIONS

The Peacebuilding Fund was launched in October 2006. It is administered by the Peacebuilding Commission which will use resources at the disposal of the international community to advise and propose integrated strategies for post-conflict recovery, focusing attention on reconstruction, institution-building and sustainable development, in countries emerging from conflict.

At March 2013 there were 14 peacekeeping missions and one special political mission* in operation covering Africa, the Middle East, Asia and the Pacific, Europe and the Americas. Tasks range from keeping hostile parties apart to helping them work peacefully together. This means helping to implement peace agreements, monitoring ceasefires, creating buffer zones, and helping in the creation of political institutions.

MINURSO (UN Mission for the Referendum in Western Sahara), April 1991, Approx. approved budget 2012-2013: US$61.3 million;
MINUSTAH (UN Stablization Mission in Haiti), June 2004, Approx. approved budget 2012-2013: US$648.4 million;
MONUSCO (UN Organization Stabilization Mission in the DRC), July 2010- (currently approved until June 2013), Approx. approved budget 2012-2013: US$1,347.5 million
UNAMID (African Union-UN Hybrid Operation in Darfur), July 2007-, Approx. approved budget 2012-2013: US$1,448.6 million;
UNDOF (UN Disengagement Observer Force), June 1974-, Approx. approved budget 2012-2013: US$46 million;
UNFICYP (UN Peacekeeping Force in Cyprus), March 1964, Approx. approved budget 2012-2013: US$56.1 million;
UNIFIL (UN Interim Force in Lebanon), March 1978-, Approx. approved budget 2012-2013: US$524 million;
UNISFA (UN Interim Security Force for Abyei), June 2011, Approx. approved budget 2012-2013: US$257.9 million;
UNMISS (UN Mission in South Sudan), July 2011-, Approx. approved budget 2012-2013: US$839.5 million;
UNOCI (UN Mission to Cote d'Ivoire), April 2004-, Approx. approved budget 2012-2013: US$575 million;
UNMIK (UN Interim Administration Mission in Kosovo), June 1999, Approx. approved budget 2012-2013: US$47 million;
UNMIL (UN Mission in Liberia), September 2003-, Approx. approved budget 2012-2013: US$496.5 million;
UNMOGIP (UN Military Observer Group in India and Pakistan), January 1949-, Approx. appropriation 2012-2013: US$21 million;

UNTSO (UN Truce Supervision Organization), May 1948, Approx. appropriation 2012-2013: US$70 million;

The UN Peacekeeping Operations budget for 2012/13 was approximately US$7.33 billion. Approximate resources as of 2013 were: 81,000 serving troops and military observers, 12,200 police personnel, 5,500 international civilian personnel, 16,800 local civilian staff and 2,000 UN Volunteers. 114 countries contributed military and police personnel. There have been approximately 3,085 fatalities in peacekeeping operations since 1948.

In May 2003 Security Council Resolution number 1483 recognised that Iraq still posed a threat to international peace and security. It expressed the will to encourage the people of Iraq to form a representative government based on equal rights and justice for all, the need for humanitarian relief and set in place a Special Representative to co-ordinate the activities of the UN in the post-conflict process. The UN provided support and technical assistance to enable elections to be held in January 2005 to establish a representative government including the Transitional National Assembly and in June 2006, the UN Security Council welcomed the formation of Iraq's first constitutionally-elected Government. It also agreed upon the continuation of the Multinational Force, certain arrangements for a Development Fund (DFI) and an International Advisory and Monitoring Board.

The International Compact with Iraq, which was launched on 3rd May 2007, is an initiative of the Government of Iraq for a new partnership with the international community. The Compact is a five-year national plan that includes benchmarks and mutual commitments from both Iraq and the international community, all with the aim of helping Iraq on the path towards peace, sound governance and economic reconstruction. The Compact affirms the Iraqi Government's vision that, in five years, Iraq shall be a united, federal and democratic country, at peace with its neighbours and itself, well on its way to sustainable economic self-sufficiency and prosperity, and well integrated in its region and the world.

In 2012, resolutions were passed on the situations in Afghanistan, Bosnia & Herzegovina, Cyprus, DRC, Guinea-Bissau, Côte d'Ivoire, Haiti, the Western Sahara, Somalia, Timor Leste, Liberia, Libya, Mali, the Middle East, Sierra Leone, Sudan, non-proliferation DPRK, the International Tribunal in the Former Yugoslavia and the International Criminal Tribunal for Rwanda.

As of March 2013, resolutions had been passed on the situations in Guinea-Bissau, sanctions in Sudan, Burundi, Cyrpus, Central African Republic, non-proliferation DPRK, UN Peacekeeping Operations.

Security Council, URL: http://www.un.org/sc/

ECONOMIC AND SOCIAL COUNCIL

The Economic and Social Council (ECOSOC) was established by the UN Charter as the principal organ to co-ordinate the economic, social and related work of the UN's specialized agencies, functional commissions and regional commissions. It also receives reports from 11 UN funds and programmes. ECOSOC provides a central point for discussion of international economic and social issues and for formulating policy.

Its responsibilities are:
- to promote higher standards of living, full employment and economic and social progress
- to find solutions to social, health and economic problems
- to encourage international education and cultural co-operation
- to promote universal respect for human rights and freedoms

In 2005, ECOSOC was mandated to hold Annual Ministerial Reviews (AMR) and a biennial Development Co-operation Forum (DCF). The aim of the AMR is to assess progress in achieving internationally agreed development goals. The DCF works to increase the effectiveness of different development partners.

Members
ECOSOC has 54 members elected for three-year terms by the General Assembly. Seats on the General Assembly are allocated by geographical representation. Fourteen are allocated to African states, eleven to Asian states, six to Eastern European states, ten to Latin American and Caribbean states and thirteen to Western European and other states. It meets annually in, alternately, New York and Geneva for a five- to six-week session. This session includes a ministerial discussion of key social and economic issues. Additionally, there is an organisational session held in New York. A one-member-one-vote system is used to carry assembly decisions.

The Council is currently composed of the following 54 States (the term of office for each member expires on 31 December of the year indicated in parentheses):

Albania	(2015)
Austria	(2014)
Belarus	(2014)
Benin	(2015)
Bolivia	(2015)
Brazil	(2014)
Bulgaria	(2013)
Burkina Faso	(2014)
Cameroon	(2013)
Canada	(2015)
China	(2013)
Colombia	(2015)
Croatia	(2015)
Cuba	(2014)

- continued

Denmark	(2013)
Dominican Republic	(2014)
Ecuador	(2013)
El Salvador	(2014)
Ethiopia	(2014)
France	(2014)
Gabon	(2013)
Haiti	(2015)
India	(2014)
Indonesia	(2014)
Ireland	(2014)
Japan	(2014)
Kuwait	(2015)
Kyrgryzstan	(2015)
Latvia	(2013)
Lesotho	(2014)
Libya	(2014)
Malawi	(2013)
Mexico	(2013)
Nepal	(2015)
Netherlands	(2015)
New Zealand	(2013)
Nicaragua	(2013)
Nigeria	(2014)
Pakistan	(2013)
Qatar	(2013)
Republic of Korea	(2013)
Russian Federation	(2013)
San Marino	(2015)
Senegal	(2013)
South Africa	(2015)
Spain	(2014)
Sudan	(2015)
Sweden	(2013)
Tunisia	(2015)
Turkey	(2014)
Turkmenistan	(2015)
United Kingdom of GB and NI	(2013)
United States of America	(2015)

Retiring members are eligible for re-election.

Structure

The Council functions through commissions, sub-commissions and committees.

There are five regional commissions under the Council's authority whose aim is to assist in the economic and social development of their respective regions and to strengthen economic relations of the countries in each region, both among themselves and with other countries of the world:

Economic Commission for Africa (ECA), P O Box 3001, Addis Ababa, Ethiopia. Tel: +251 11 551 7200, fax: +251 11 551 0365, e-mail: ecainfo@uneca.org, URL: http://www.uneca.org/

Economic and Social Commission for Asia and the Pacific (ESCAP), The United Nations Building, Rajadamnern Nok Avenue, Bangkok 10200, Thailand. Tel: +66 (2) 288 1234, fax: +66 (2) 288 1000, URL: http://www.unescap.org

Economic Commission for Europe (ECE), Palais des Nations, Office 256, CH-1211 Geneva 10, Switzerland. Tel: 41 (0)22 917 1234, fax: +41 (0)22 917 0505, e-mail: info.ece@unece.org, URL: http://www.unece.org

Economic Commission for Latin America and the Caribbean (ECLAC), Casilla de Correo 179-D, Santiago de Chile, Chile. Tel: +56 (2) 2000 2085051, fax: +56 (2) 210 2080252, e-mail: prensa@cepal.org, URL: http://www.eclac.cl

Economic and Social Commission for Western Asia (ESCWA), P O Box 11-8575, Riad el-Solh Square, Beirut, Lebanon. Tel: +961 (1) 981301, fax: +961 (1) 981510, URL: http://www.escwa.un.org/

Economic and social matters are also dealt with by the following bodies and programmes, who all report to the Economic and Social Council and/or the General Assembly: the United Nations Children's Fund, the Office of the United Nations High Commissioner for Refugees, the World Food Programme, the United Nations Conference on Trade and Development, the United Nations Development Programme, the United Nations Environment Programme, and the United Nations International Drug Control Programme.

There are also nine United Nations **Functional Commissions** and one UN Forum which come under the auspices of the Economic and Social Council:

- **Statistical Commission** - established in 1946, this Commission assists the Council in promoting the development of national statistics and the improvement of their comparability. It co-ordinates the statistical work of specialised agencies and helps to develop the central statistical services of the Secretariat. It advises the organs of the UN on general questions relating to the collection and analysis of statistical information and assists the developing countries in strengthening their statistical systems.

Statistical Commission, Statistics Division, United Nations, UN Plaza, New York, NY 10017, USA. Fax: +1 212 963 4116, e-mail: statistics@un.org, URL: http://unstats.un.org/unsd/

- **Commission on Population and Development** - initially established in 1946 but renamed in 1994, this Commission assists the Economic and Social Council by arranging for studies and advising the Council on population trends and issues; integrating population and development strategies; population and related development policies and programmes; provision of population assistance to developing countries and giving advice on any other population and development questions. It also monitors, reviews and assesses the implementation of the Programme of Action of the International Conference on Population and Development at national, regional and global levels. Composed of 47 member states.

Commission on Population and Development, 2 UN Plaza, Room DC2-1950, New York, NY 10017, USA. Tel: +1 212 963 3179, fax +1 212 963 2147, URL: http://www.un.org/esa/population/cpd/aboutcom.htm

-**Commission for Social Development**
This commission is the key UN body in charge of implementing the Copenhagen Declaration and Programme of Action. Each year the Commission takes up a key social development issue, the theme for 2009 being social integration. Composed of 46 members.

Commission for Social Development, United Nations, UN Plaza, Room DC2-1320, New York, NY 10017, USA. Tel: +1 212 963 5855, fax: +1 212 963 3062, e-mail: social@un.org, URL: http://www.un.org/esa/socdev/csd/index.html

-**Commission on the Status of Women** - established in 1946, the mandate of this Commission is to prepare recommendations and reports to the Council on promoting women's rights in political, economic, civil, social and educational fields. The objective of the Commission is to promote implementation of the principle that men and women shall have equal rights.

Commission on the Status of Women, 2 UN Plaza, DC2-12 Floor, New York, NY 10017, USA. Fax: +1 212 963 3463, URL: http://www.un.org/womenwatch/

- **Commission on Narcotic Drugs** - this is the central body within the UN system dealing with drug-related matters. It analyses the world drug situation and develops proposals to strengthen the international drug control system to combat the world drug problem. Through the Secretariat of this Commission, the UNDCP manages organisational and administrative matters as well as ensuring a permanent monitoring system for follow-up on resolutions and decisions by the Commission, the Economic and Social Council, and the General Assembly.

Commission on Narcotic Drugs, Vienna International Centre, PO Box 500, A-1400 Vienna, Austria. Tel: +43 (0)1 260600, fax: +43 (0)1 26060 5866, URL: http://www.undcp.org/

- **Commission on Crime Prevention and Criminal Justice** - this replaced the Committee on Crime Prevention and Control in 1992 and its remit is to provide policy guidance to the UN in the field of crime prevention and criminal justice. It also develops, monitors and reviews the implementation of the UN crime prevention and criminal justice programme and helps to co-ordinate the activities of the UN institutes in these fields.

Commission on Crime Prevention and Criminal Justice, Vienna International Centre, PO Box 500, A-1400 Vienna, Austria. Tel: +43 (0)1 260600, fax: +43 (0)1 26060 5866, URL: http://www.unodc.org/

- **Commission on Science and Technology for Development** - this commission was established in 1992 to provide the Council with high-level advice on relevant issues through analysis and appropriate policy recommendations. The Commission acts as a forum for the examination of science and technology questions and their implications for development, the advancement of understanding on science and technology policies and the formulation of recommendations and guidelines on science and technology matters within the UN system.

Commission on Science and Technology for Development, UNCTAD, Palais des Nations, 8 - 14 Av. De la Paix, 1211 Geneva 10, Switzerland. Tel: +41 (0)22 907 1234 fax: +41 (0)22 907 0043, e-mail: stdev@unctad.org, URL: http://www.unctad.info/en/Science-and-Technology-for-Development---StDev/

- **Commission on Sustainable Development** - this Commission was created in December 1992 to ensure effective follow-up on the UN Conference on Environment and Development (UNCED) and to monitor and report on implementation of the Earth Summit agreements at local, national, regional and international levels. The Commission ensures the high visibility of sustainable development issues within the UN system and helps to improve the UN's co-ordination of environment and development activities. The programme of work is organised on two-year cycles focused on selected issues. The 2007 to 2008 cycle will focus on agriculture, rural development, land, drought, desertification, and Africa.

Commission on Sustainable Development, UN Plaza, Room DC2-2220, New York, New York 10017, USA. Tel: +1 212 963 8102, fax: +1 212 963 4260, e-mail: dsd@un.org, URL: http://sustainabledevelopment.un.org/csd.html

- **UN Forum on Forests** - this was established in 2000 to promote the management, conservation and sustainable development of all types of forests, and to strengthen long-term political commitment to this end. It promotes the implementation of internationally agreed actions on forests at national, regional and global levels.

UN Forum on Forests, United Nations, UN Plaza, Room DC - 1245, New York, NY 10017, USA. Tel: +1 212 963 3160/3401, fax: +1 917 367 3186, URL: http://www.un.org/esa/forests/

ECOSOC Standing Committees

There are three standing committees: Committee for Programme and Co-ordination, Committee on Non-Governmental Organizations; Committee on Negotiations with Intergovernmental Agencies.

Over 2,000 non-governmental organisations have consultative status with the Council. These NGOs may send observers to public meetings of the Council and its subsidiary bodies, and may submit written statements relevant to the Council's work. The Council classifies NGOs into three categories: Category I are those NGOs concerned with most of the Council's activities, Category II are those that have special competence in specific areas and the third category are those organisations that can occasionally contribute to the Council and are placed on a roster for ad hoc consultations.

President: H.E. Mr Néstor Osorio (page 1490)

Economic and Social Council, United Nations, UN Plaza, New York, NY 10017, USA, e-mail: ecosocinfo@un.org, URL: http://www.un.org

TRUSTEESHIP COUNCIL

The Trusteeship Council was set up to ensure that Trust Territories were adequately prepared for independence or self-government by those Governments responsible for their administration. With the independence of Palau (1 October 1994), the last remaining United Nations Trust territory, the Trusteeship Council's task was completed and operations were suspended on 1 November 1994. The Council agreed that it would no longer meet on an annual basis, but would convene should circumstances require it.

It comprises the five permanent members of the Security Council: China, France, the Russian Federation, the United Kingdom and the United States.

Functions and Powers
According to its Charter, the Trusteeship Council is empowered to consider Administering Authorities' reports on the advancement - political, economic, social and educational - of those living in Trust Territories. Additionally, the Council can undertake specific missions to Trust Territories.

Trusteeship Council, URL: http://www.un.org/

INTERNATIONAL COURT OF JUSTICE (ICJ)

The International Court of Justice (ICJ), established in 1946, is the principal judicial organ of the United Nations. Its Statute is an integral part of the United Nations Charter. The seat of the Court is at the Peace Palace in The Hague (Netherlands). Of the six principal organs of the United Nations, it is the only one not located in New York. Independent of the United Nations Secretariat, the ICJ is assisted by a Registry, its own international secretariat, whose activities are both judicial and diplomatic, as well as administrative. The official languages of the Court are French and English. Also known as the "World Court", it is the only court of a universal character with general jurisdiction.

Functions
The Court has a twofold role: first, to settle, in accordance with international law, legal disputes submitted to it by States (its judgments have binding force and are without appeal for the parties concerned); and, second, to give advisory opinions on legal questions referred to it by duly authorized United Nations organs and agencies of the system.

Parties
Contentious cases between States: The Court is open to the parties to its Statute, which automatically includes all Member States of the United Nations. A State which is not a Member of the United Nations may become a party to the Statute on conditions determined in each case by the General Assembly upon the recommendation of the Security Council. All countries which are parties to the Statute of the Court can be parties to cases before it. Other States can refer cases to it under conditions laid down by the Security Council. In addition, the Security Council may recommend that a legal dispute be referred to the Court.
Advisory Procedures: The General Assembly and the Security Council can ask the Court for an advisory opinion on any legal question. Other organs of the United Nations and the specialised agencies, when authorised by the General Assembly, can ask for advisory opinions on legal questions within the scope of their activities.

Cases
Between 1946 and 22 March 2013, the Court delivered 112 Judgements on disputes concerning inter alia land frontiers and maritime boundaries, territorial sovereignty, the non-use of force, non-interference in the internal affairs of States, diplomatic relations, hostage-taking, the right of asylum, nationality, guardianship, rights of passage and economic rights. It also has given 27 advisory opinions, concerning inter alia admission to UN membership, reparation for injuries suffered in the service of the United Nations, territorial status of South-West Africa (Namibia) and Western Sahara, judgements rendered by international administrative tribunals, expenses of certain UN operations, and applicability of the UN Headquarters Agreement 1947, the status of human rights rapporteurs, the legality of the threat or use of nuclear weapons and the legal consequences of the construction of a wall in the occupied Palestinian Territory.

Jurisdiction
The jurisdiction of the Court covers all questions which States refer to it, and all matters provided for in the United Nations Charter or in treaties or conventions in force. States may bind themselves in advance to accept the jurisdiction of the Court in special cases, either by signing a treaty or convention which provides for referral to the Court, or by making a special declaration to that effect (as at 22 March 2013, the declarations of 69 States were in force). Such declarations accepting compulsory jurisdiction may exclude certain classes of cases.

In accordance with Article 38 of its Statute, the Court, in deciding disputes submitted to it, applies: international conventions establishing rules recognised by the contesting States; international custom as evidence of a general practice accepted as law; the general principles of law recognised by nations; and judicial decisions and the teachings of the most highly qualified publicists of the various nations, as a subsidiary means for determining the rules of law.

Composition
The Court consists of 15 Judges elected by the General Assembly and the Security Council, voting independently. They are chosen on the basis of their qualifications, not on the basis of nationality, and care is taken to ensure that the principal legal systems of the world are represented in the Court. No two Judges can be nationals of the same State. The Judges serve for a term of nine years and may be re-elected. They cannot engage in any other occupation during their term of office. The Court normally sits in plenary session, but it may further form so-called "ad hoc" chambers if the parties in a case so request. Judgements given by the chambers are considered as rendered by the full Court.

As of 22 March 2013, the composition of the Court was as follows (in order of seniority, with country and year of expiry given in parentheses):
President: Judge Peter Tomka (page 1526) (Slovakia, 2021)
Vice-President: Judge Bernardo Sepúlveda-Amor (page 1512) (Mexico, 2015)

Judges: Hisashi Owada (page 1491) (Japan, 2021), Ronny Abraham (page 1371) (France, 2018), Kenneth Keith (page 1455) (New Zealand, 2015), Mohamed Bennouna (page 1387) (Morocco, 2015), Leonid Skotnikov (page 1516) (Russia, 2015), Antonio A. Cancado Trindade (page 1399) (Brazil, 2018), Abdulqawi Ahmed Yusuf (page 1542) (Somalia, 2018), Christopher Greenwood (page 1433) (United Kingdom and Northern Ireland, 2018), Xue Hanqin (page 1540) (China, 2021), Joan E. Donoghue (page 1416) (USA, 2015), Giorgio Gaja (Italy, 2015) (page 1428), Julia Sebutinde (page 1510) (Uganda, 2021), Dalveer Bhandari (page 1388)(India, 2018).

Registrar: Philippe Couvreur (page 1409) (Belgium, 2014)

International Court of Justice, Peace Palace, 2517 KJ The Hague, Netherlands. Tel: +31 (0)70 302 2337, fax: +31 (0)70 364 9928, URL: http://www.icj-cij.org

SECRETARIAT

The Secretariat carries out the day-to-day work of the United Nations and services the other principal organs of the Organization, administering the programmes and policies laid down by them.

The Secretariat performs duties ranging from the administration of peace-keeping operations to the mediation of international disputes. Additionally, the organisation can examine social and economic trends; study issues such as human rights and sustainable development; arrange international conferences on world issues; monitor in what way UN decisions are effected; translate and interpret documents and speeches into the UN's official languages; and promulgate information about the UN to the world's media.

Staff
At its head is the Secretary-General, the chief administrative officer of the United Nations, who is appointed by the General Assembly on the recommendation of the Security Council, and who serves a five-year renewable term.

The Secretariat shares its Headquarters with the United Nations Headquarters in New York and maintains a significant presence in Addis Ababa, Bangkok, Beirut, Geneva, Nairobi, Santiago and Vienna, as well as having offices all over the world.

The Secretary-General acts as chief administrative officer at all meetings of the General Assembly, the Security Council, the Economic and Social Council and the Trusteeship Council, and performs such other functions as are entrusted to him by these organs. He is required to submit an annual report to the General Assembly on the work of the Organization. One of the special powers of the Secretary-General is the fact that he may bring to the attention of the Security Council any matter which in his opinion may threaten the maintenance of international peace and security.

The Secretary-General and his staff are responsible for their work only to the UN and swear an oath not to take instructions from any outside institution.

Secretary-General: Ban Ki-moon (page 1383)

FOOD AND AGRICULTURE ORGANIZATION OF THE UNITED NATIONS (FAO)

The founding Conference of the Food And Agriculture Organization (FAO) took place in Quebec City in 1945, with the aim of raising levels of nutrition and standards of living, improving agricultural productivity and improving conditions in rural areas. Today, it is one of the largest specialised agencies within the United Nations system with 192 member states plus the EC (Member Organization) and employs more than 3,500 staff. It is a technical agency that also serves as an information centre, an adviser to governments and a neutral forum. Despite halving the proportion of hungry people since the 1960s, more than 1 billion still go hungry in the developing world.

Structure

FAO is governed by the Conference of Member Nations which then elects a Council of 49 member states to act as an interim governing body (those elected serve rotating terms of three years). The Conference also elects a Director-General to head the agency and he serves a six-year term. The Council is advised by five specialist committees - each concerned with either agriculture, world food security, fisheries, forestries or commodities - on management strategies to cope with current trends in their particular fields. The Council then reports back to the Conference, which meets every two years and is responsible for the Budget and Programme of Work to be followed for the next two years. Among the current priority Programmes are the 'Special Programme for Food Security' and the 'Emergency Prevention System for Transboundary Animal and Plant Pests and Diseases'.

FAO is divided into seven departments: Agriculture and Consumer Protection; Economic and Social Development; Fisheries and Aquaculture; Forestry; Corporate Services; Human Resources and Finance; Natural Resources Management and Environment; and Technical Cooperation. Its work is divided into two categories - the Regular Programme which oversees internal matters such as the maintenance of staff providing support for field work, advising governments on planning and policy or servicing various development needs, and the Field Programme which implements development strategies and provides assistance to both governments and rural communities, as well as assisting in the rebuilding of agricultural infrastructures following emergencies.

FAO is currently undergoing a major reform programme aimed at bringing expertise closer to member countries and streamlining administrative, financial and management processes. Measures include opening several more decentralized offices and reorganizing departments at headquarters in order to increase thier efficiency.

FAO has launched special activities and programmes to mobilise governments, international organisations and all sectors of civil society in a coordinated campaign to eradicate hunger.

At the World Food Summit of 1996, 186 countries pledged to reduce the number of hungry from 840 million to half that number by 2015. FAO announced in 2006 that current projections suggest the goal will not be met, and that without increased efforts the number of hungry people will stand at 582 milion by 2015. However, the target remains achievable through a twin approach of direct action, such as nutrition programmes, and a focus on agriculture and rural development.

FAO hosts international conferences to cover areas of particular concern, including the Conference on Nutrition (1991), the World Food Summit (1996), World Forestry Congress (1997), the World Food Summit: Five Years Later (2002), the High-Level Conference on World Food Security and the Challenges of Climate Change and Bioenergy (2008) and the World Summit on Food Security (2009).

The Special Programme for Food Security targets the low-income food-deficit countries that are home to the vast majority of the world's chronically undernourished people and the annual TeleFood campaign, dedicated to helping the hungry help themselves, pays for small sustainable agriculture and livestock projects that help poor families produce more food.

FAO's International Code of Conduct for Responsible Fisheries establishes a framework for sustainable management and conservation of the living resources of the high seas.

Development Assistance

In addition to ensuring adequate food supplies, FAO also aims to benefit overall national development by creating employment and generating income through farming. Its goal is not only to provide immediate relief but also to find long-term sustainable solutions to the fundamental problems of poverty and hunger. FAO attains this goal by giving practical help in the form of various technical assistance projects that are designed with social, economic and environmental factors in mind. A successful way of ensuring a co-operative approach to the development has been to combine people's participation and local expertise with new skills, ideas and technologies.

On average, FAO has approximately 1,800 field projects operating at any one time.

Information and Support Services

The FAO World Agricultural Information Centre (WAICENT) has been set up to give internal and external users easier access to the Organization's statistical data banks in agriculture, fisheries, forestry, nutrition and rural development. Through the WAICENT information services, FAO is able to organise and disseminate its wealth of information resources on agriculture, fisheries and forestry, and to play a key role world-wide in providing vital data for the analysis, review and improvement of agricultural policies on food security. Internet offers a unique and unlimited capacity to disseminate information in a cost-effective manner to millions of users around the world, in Arabic, English, French and Spanish. As part of efforts to expand access to WAICENT, especially in member countries where the Internet is not yet widely available, a set of WAICENT CD-ROMs has been developed, which includes, among others, FAOSTAT, AGRIS and CARIS, Gender and Food Security, and Combating Desertification.

FAO's Global Information and Early Warning System (GIEWS) monitors the world food outlook through satellite data, agricultural statistics and field reports. GIEWS assists countries in improving their national early warning systems as well as data-gathering, and provides other technical support. As a centre of independent information and expertise, FAO is called upon by many member governments to assist in formulating national and regional plans for agricultural development.

FAO operates several specialised databases and information systems, among them: the International Information System for the Agricultural Sciences and Technology (AGRIS), Current Agricultural Research Information System (CARIS), Interlinked Computer Storage and Processing System of Food and Agricultural Commodity Data (ICS), Aquatic Sciences and Fisheries Information System (ASFIS), Fisheries Statistical Data Base (FISHDAB), Forest Resources Information System (FORIS), International Fish Market Indicators (GLOBEFISH) and Fishery Project Information System (FIPIS).

Government Relations

FAO collaborates with governments to promote agricultural and rural development and to encourage international co-operation on matters such as food standards, fair trade, environmental management and conservation of genetic resources. It offers advice on agricultural policy and planning, administrative and legal structures in order to ensure that national strategies are formed concerning rural development and the alleviation of hunger and poverty.

FAO's mediation on an international level has resulted in an number of intergovernmental agreements. These include the International Treaty on Plant Genetic Resouces for Food and Agriculture, an international framework for conservation, sustainable use, and fair and equitable sharing, and the International Plant Protection Convention, which counters the spread of plant pests. Another example is the World Soil Charter, which sets out guidelines for the best use of the world's land resources.

Budget

In 2009, FAO-assisted projects used US$699.1 million from donor agencies and governments for agricultural and rural development projects and emergencies. Some 82.1 per cent of Field Programme finances were taken from national trust funds. During the same year, FAO itself contributed 9.2 per cent (or US$66.4 million), provided by the Regular Programme budget through its Technical Cooperation Programme and its programmes for food security. In 2010-11, programmes and projects were implemented to a value of US$1.7 million. The budget for the 2012-13 biennium is $1,005.6 million, up 1.4 per cent from the previous period. Voluntary contributions were expected to exceed US$1.4 billion in 2012-13.

Publications

Each year FAO publishes about 150 books on agriculture, forestry, fisheries and rural development as well as numerous CD-ROMs, technical papers, newsletters and periodicals. It also publishes authoritative reports on global conditions and trends, including The State of Food Insecurity in the World, The State of Food and Agriculture, The State of the World's Forests, The State of the World's Fisheries and Aquaculture and The World Food Survey.

FAO established the Edouard Saouma Award (1993) in honour of a former Director-General. The US$25,000 prize is presented every two years to a regional institution managing a particularly efficient project funded under FAO's Technical Co-operation Programme.

Membership

There are currently 191 member nations, two associate members and one member organization, the European Union. For details of the membership of FAO please consult the matrix of *Country Membership of Major Organisations* in the preliminary section.

Director General (2012-2015): José Graziano da Silva (page 1433)

Food and Agriculture Organization of the United Nations, Viale delle Terme di Caracalla, 00153 Rome, Italy. Tel: +39 (0) 6 57051, fax: +39 (0) 6 5705 3152, e-mail: FAO-HQ@fao.org, URL: http://www.fao.org

INTERNATIONAL BANK FOR RECONSTRUCTION AND DEVELOPMENT (IBRD)

The World Bank

The International Bank for Reconstruction and Development (IBRD) was established in 1944 as the original institution of the World Bank Group.

As of March 2013, it had 188 member countries. The World Bank's purpose is to help raise the standard of living in its developing member countries by financing high priority development projects, by providing technical assistance and by conducting an economic policy dialogue with borrower governments. Its main aim is to reduce poverty by emphasising investments that directly affect the well-being of people in developing countries by making them more productive and integrating them as active partners in the development process.

The Bank is funded principally through the world's capital markets.

Together with the International Development Association (IDA) the IBRD is known as the World Bank. The International Development Association (IDA), funded partly by government contributions and is intended to lend to the poorest countries at concessional terms. (Please see separate entry for more information on the IDA).

Partnerships

The IBRD has three other affiliates: the International Finance Corporation (IFC), promoting private enterprises in developing countries through equity participation and loans; the Multilateral Investment Guarantee Agency (MIGA), established in 1988, providing insurance against non-commercial risks for investments in developing countries; and the International Centre for Settlement of Investment Disputes (ICSID), providing facilities for the settlement of disputes between foreign investors and host countries. Together these closely associated institutions make up the World Bank Group. Dr Jim Yong Kim is the President of all five institutions. (Please see separate entries for more information on the affiliates).

All members of the Bank must first join the International Monetary Fund, although the two institutions are independent of one another.

Structure

All the powers of the Bank are vested in a Board of Governors composed of one Governor and an alternate appointed by each member country. This Board meets annually, two consecutive years in Washington DC, and the third year in the capital of another member country. Most of its powers have been delegated to the Executive Directors, of whom five are appointed by the five largest shareholders (France, Germany, Japan, the United Kingdom and the United States), and 19 are elected by the remaining members. Once a year the Board of Governors of the IBRD meets with the Board of Governors of the IMF for the Annual Meeting.

Operations of the Bank are carried out by an international staff headed by the President, who is selected by the Executive Directors. The President is *ex officio* Chairman of the Executive Directors and chief of the Bank's operating staff; he is responsible, subject to the direction of the Executive Directors on policy questions, for the conduct of the Bank's business, and for the organisation, appointment, and dismissal of its officers and staff.

The IBRD has five standing committees: the Audit Committee, the Committee on Development Effectiveness, the Budget Committee, the Personnel Committee and the Committee on Executive Directors' Administrative Affairs. An informal advisory group, the executive directors' Steering Committee, also has regular meetings. The Bank has established a Presidential Fellows Programme in order to attract scholars and leaders to the Bank and so increase its effectiveness.

Function

The Bank lends to member governments, governmental agencies or private enterprises. All loans must be for productive purposes, and if the borrower is not a government, the guarantee of the member government concerned is required. Before lending, the Bank studies the economic position of the country concerned and satisfies itself that the country can earn the foreign exchange needed for repayment; it also examines, on the spot, the economic and technical justification for the project and requires regular reports on the project's progress after the loan is made.

Structural and sectoral adjustment loans in support of economic programmes designed to reduce current account deficits and restore the momentum of economic growth have become increasingly important in recent years as part of the World Bank's efforts to assist countries with a heavy external debt burden. The World Bank is integrating environmental concerns more and more into its operations to ensure sustainable development as well as attempting to increase the role of women in development. The Bank continues to foster close co-ordination of external assistance to developing nations through more than 35 co-ordinating groups that it has helped create at the request of the developing countries whose development programmes have attracted sufficient support to justify them.

The Bank works jointly with several UN agencies in order to strengthen the capacity of developing countries to implement and sustain policy reform. Representatives of the International Monetary Fund, the OECD, the United Nations Development Programme and the relevant regional development banks regularly attend meetings of World Bank sponsored co-ordinating groups. The United Nations Development Programme (UNDP)/ World Bank trade expansion programme provides technical and policy advice and the Social Dimension of Adjustment Programme is executed by the Bank in collaboration with the UNDP, the African Development Bank and bilateral donors. A new Business Partnership Center was launched in 1997 to serve as a focal contact point for business groups.

Investments

The IBRD raises almost all of its money in the world's financial markets, around US$18 - 20 billion each year. It issues bonds to raise money, and then passes on the low interest rates to its borrowers.

Projects approved for IBRD assistance in recent years have included:
- helping countries to build education systems that can respond to the poverty and knowledge challenges of the 21st Century. The Bank manages a Catalytic Fund with initial commitments of $250 million, to provide start-up funding to countries implementing good policies but lacking sufficient donor support.

- protecting people from the impoverishing effects of illness, malnutrition and high fertility. In 2006, support to health and other social services programmes totalled more than US$2.2 billion, while support to improve water, sanitation and flood protection exceeded US$1.7 billion.

- the New Voices initiative which was launched in 2004 with the aim of bringing children and youth into the policy dialogue on global development issues.

- In May 2008 support for global efforts to overcome food crisis with a new $1.2 billion to address immediate needs, including $200 million in grants for the vunerable in the poorest countries.

Debt Relief

At the July 2005 G8 Summit in Gleneagles, Scotland, G8 leaders pledged to cancel the debt of the world's most indebted countries, most of which are located in Africa. Debt cancellation will be provided by the International Development Association IDA of the World Bank, the International Monetary Fund and the African Development Fund to countries that have graduated (called reaching the "completion point") from the Enhanced Heavily Indebted Poor Countries (HIPC) Initiative.

Initially, 17 HIPC countries were eligible for 100 per cent debt cancellation. There are now 39 HIPCs. As of March 2013, 35 countries have reached the completion point: Afghanistan, Benin, Bolivia, Burkina Faso, Burundi, Cameroon, Central African Republic, Comoros, Congo, Cote d'Ivoire, DRC, Ethiopia, the Gambia, Ghana, Guinea, Guyana, Guinea-Bissau, Haiti, Honduras, Madagascar, Malawi, Mali, Mauritania, Mozambique, Nicaragua, Niger, the Republic of Congo, Rwanda, Sao Tome and Principe, Senegal, Sierra Leone, Tanzania, Uganda, and Zambia. Chad is an interim country (between decision and completion point). Three countries remain potentially eligible for HIPC debt relief: Eritrea, Somalia, and Sudan. Total Bank debt relief was estimated to total about US$58 billion at the end of 2011.

Financial Crisis

Although the World Bank expects the world economy to grow by 2.5 per cent in 2012 and 3.0 per cent in 2013 and expects the recovery to be higher in developing countries, their growth rates are expected to fall to 5.3 per cent and it expects demand for Bank assistance to continue to be high. Food prices remain high and additionally there is the threat of drought in the Horn of Africa. In total the World Bank has provided over $280 billion of help since the start of the current financial crisis in 2008. IBRD commitments were estimated at $20.6 billion for 2012, down on its record commitments of $44.2 billion in FY10 and $32.9 billion in FY09 when the crisis was at its peak in developing countries.

Membership stands at 188 countries. For details of the membership of the IBRD, please consult the matrix of *Country Membership of Major Organisations* in the preliminary section.

President: Dr Jim Yong Kim (page 1449)

International Bank for Reconstruction and Development (The World Bank), 1818 H Street, NW, Washington, DC 20433, USA. Tel: +1 202 473 1000, fax: +1 202 477 6391, e-mail: pic@worldbank.org, URL: http://www.worldbank.org

INTERNATIONAL CENTRE FOR SETTLEMENT OF INVESTMENT DISPUTES (ICSID)

Established in 1966, the International Centre for Settlement of Investment Disputes (ICSID), is an autonomous international institution. It was established under the Convention on the Settlement of Investment Disputes between States and Nationals of Other States (the ICSID or Washington Convention). ICSID is part of the World Bank Group. The primary purpose of ICSID is to provide facilities for conciliation and arbitration of international investment disputes.

As of March 2013, there were 158 signatory States to the ICSID Convention. Of these, 147 have ratified the convention to become a Contracting State. All of ICSID's members are also members of the World Bank.

Recourse to ICSID's conciliation and arbitration is entirely voluntary. However, once the parties have consented to arbitration under the ICSID Convention, neither can unilaterally withdraw its consent. All member states, whether or not parties to the dispute, are required by the Convention to recognise and enforce ICSID arbitral awards.

Provisions on ICSID arbitration can be found in investment contracts between governments of member countries and investors from other member countries. Advance consents by governments to submit investment disputes to ICSID arbitration can also be found in about thirty investment laws and in over 1,500 bilateral investment treaties.

ICSID arbitration is one of the main mechanisms for the settlement of investment disputes under four recent multilateral trade and investment treaties: (the North American Free Trade Agreement, the Energy Charter Treaty, the Cartagena Free Trade Agreement and the Colonia Investment Protocol of Mercosur).

Since 1978, the Centre has a set of *Additional Facility Rules* which enable the Secretariat to administer certain proceedings which fall outside the scope of the Convention. These include disputes where one of the parties is not a member of ICSID and for cases which do not involve an investment dispute but relates to a transaction which has "features that distinguishes it from an ordinary commercial transaction". ICSID can also be used for fact-finding. ICSID is considered to be the leading arbitration institution involved in investor-State dispute settlement.

Structure
ICSID has an Administrative Council and a Secretariat. The Administrative Council is the governing body of ICSID and is chaired by the World Bank's President and consists of one representative of each member countries. Unless a government makes a contrary designation, its Governor for the World Bank sits *ex-officio* on ICSID's Administrative Council. Annual meetings of the Council are held in conjunction with the joint World Bank / International Monetary Fund annual meetings. Principal functions of the Administrative Council include the election of the Secretary-General and the Deputy Secretary-General, the adoption of regulations and rules for the institution and conduct of ICSID proceedings, the adoption of the ICSID budget, and the approval of the annual report on the operation of ICSID.

Secretariat
The Secretariat consists of a Secretary-General, a Deputy Secretary-General and staff. The Secretary-General is the legal representative of ICSID, the registrar of ICSID proceedings and the principal officer of the Centre.

The Secretariat's administrative costs are financed out of the World Bank's budget; the costs of ICSID proceedings are borne by the disputing parties.

Publications
Investment Laws of the World (looseleaf collection); Investment Treaties (looseleaf collection); ICSID Review-Foreign Investment Law Journal (biannual); ICSID Annual Report

For details of the membership of ICSID please consult the matrix of *Country Membership of Major Organisations* in the preliminary section.

Secretary-General: Meg Kinnear (page 1457)

International Centre for Settlement of Investment Disputes (ICSID), 1818 H Street, N.W, Washington, DC 20433, USA. Tel: +1 202 458 1534, fax: +1 202 522 2615, e-mail: ICSIDsecretariat@worldbank.org, URL: http://www.worldbank.org/icsid

INTERNATIONAL CIVIL AVIATION ORGANIZATION (ICAO)

The Convention on International Civil Aviation was adopted by the representatives of 52 states at the Chicago International Civil Aviation Conference on 7 December 1944. ICAO was formally established on 4 April 1947, 30 days after the convention had been ratified by 26 states. The member states number 191.

Purpose
The aims and objectives of ICAO, as stated in Article 44 of the Convention, are to develop the principles and techniques of international air navigation and to foster the planning and development of international air transport.

The Assembly of the ICAO has endorsed Strategic Objectives for the period 2001-2013 which are intended to provide a framework for the Organisation's adaptation to future issues in international civil aviation.

1) Safety - Enhance global civil aviation safety
2) Security - Enhance global civil aviation security
3) Environmental Protection & Sustainable Development of Air Transport - Foster harmonized and economically viable development of international civil aviation that does not unduly harm the environment

Structure
The ICAO consists of an Assembly, a Council and a Secretariat.

The Assembly, is the sovereign body of the ICAO. It is composed of delegates from member nations, and meets at least once in a three-year period to review the organisation and set policy. It also sets a triennial budget.

The Council, ICAO's executive body, is composed of representatives of 36 states elected by the Assembly for a three-year term. In the election, adequate representation is given to states of chief importance in air transport, states which make the largest contribution to the provision of facilities for civil air navigation and states whose inclusion will ensure that all regions of the world are represented. The Council is assisted by the Air Navigation Commission (technical matters), the Air Transport Committee (economic matters), the Committee on Joint Support of Air Navigation Services and the Finance Committee.

ICAO's Secretariat is divided into five principal sections; the Air Navigation Bureau, the Air Transport Bureau, the Technical Co-operation Bureau, the Bureau of Administration and Services, and the Legal Bureau. For purposes of administration the ICAO recognises nine different geographical regions that must each be treated differently when planning for the provision of air navigation facilities and services. There are seven Regional Offices; Asia and the Pacific; the Middle East; East and South Africa; West and Central Africa; North America, Central America and the Caribbean; South America; Europe and the North Atlantic.

ICAO also works in co-operation with organisations such as the World Meteorological Organization (WMO), the World Trade Organization (WTO), the World Health Organization (WHO), the Universal Postal Union (UPU) and the International Telecommunication Union (ITU).

Function
ICAO has many functions within the technical, economic and legal fields of aviation. It facilitates the adoption of international law instruments and promotes the adoption and amendment of the ICAO International Standards, Recommended Practices (Annexes to the Convention on International Civil Aviation) and Procedures, which are designed to ensure safety, regularity and efficiency in air navigation. Furthermore, ICAO works to improve the reporting of aircraft accident and incident data, the application of computers in meteorological services, the automation of air traffic services, the carriage of dangerous goods by air, all-weather operations, aircraft noise levels and engine emissions.

In tandem with the United Nations Development Programme (UNDP), the ICAO provides technical assistance for the improvement of civil aviation in developing countries, particularly in the development of aerodromes, air traffic control, and communications and meteorological services - ICAO also provides assistance to members who are in the process of improving their aviation security facilities and procedures. The Organization has also created or helped to create several civil aviation training centres throughout the world, at which over 100,000 students have attended to date.

There are currently 191 member contracting states. For details, please consult the *Matrix of Country Membership of Major Organisations* in the preliminary section.

Secretary-General: Raymond Benjamin (Egypt) (page 1386)
President of the Council: Mr Roberto Kobeh González (Mexico) (page 1458)

International Civil Aviation Organization (ICAO), 999 University St, Montreal, Quebec HC3 5H7, Canada. Tel: +1 514 954 8219, fax +1 514 954 6077, e-mail: icaohq@icao.int, URL: http://www.icao.int

INTERNATIONAL DEVELOPMENT ASSOCIATION (IDA)

The International Development Association (IDA), was formally established on 24 September 1960, to provide assistance for the same purposes as the International Bank for Reconstruction and Development (IBRD), but to concentrate primarily on the poorer developing countries, aiming to eliminate poverty by providing long-term loans (credits) and grants at zero interest. Together with the International Bank for Reconstruction and Development it makes up the World Bank.

Function

IDA lends only to countries that have a per capita income, in 2012, of less than US$1,175 or that lack the financial ability to borrow from the IBRD. IDA credits (so-called in order to distinguish them from IBRD loans), are made to governments only; they have grace periods of 10 years, maturities of 20, 35 or 40 years and no interest. A small annual service fee of 0.75 per cent is charged on both disbursed and non-disbursed portions of each credit.

Eighty-one countries, home to 2.5 billion people, are currently eligible to borrow from IDA, 39 of them in Africa. When a member's GNP exceeds IDA's eligibility threshold it is deemed to have 'graduated' from IDA and must then borrow from IBRD at market rates. 'Graduates' from IDA include China, Egypt, Macedonia and the Philippines. In total, 36 countries have developed their economies beyond the IDA eligibility threshold, although some have subsequently become eligible once more. There are certain countries - such as India, Indonesia and Pakistan - who qualify for both IDA credits and IBRD loans, and these are known as 'blend' borrowers.

Budget

Funds used by IDA come mostly in the form of subscriptions, general replenishments from IDA's more industrialised and developed members, special contributions and transfers from the net earnings of the IBRD. Donors replenish IDA funds once every three years. The 15th replenishment was for the period July 2008- June 2011. Total funds for this period were SDR 27.3 billion (US$41.6 billion), of which donor contributions accounted for 60 per cent. 52 countries contributed to the funds. The largest pledges came from the US, the UK, Japan, Germany, France, Canada, Italy and Spain. The 16th replenishment will last for the period July 2011 and June 2014. 51 countries contributed to this fund which totalled US$49.3 billion.

Initial subscriptions of each member country of IDA are proportioned to that member's subscription to the capital stock of the IBRD: wealthier countries pay their subscriptions entirely in convertible form, while less developed countries pay only 10 per cent of their subscriptions in convertible form; the remaining 90 per cent is paid in each member's national currency and cannot be used by IDA for lending to other countries without the member's consent.

The bulk of usable resources available to IDA is usually contributed by the wealthier countries: Canada, France, Germany, Italy, Japan, the Netherlands, the UK, and the USA. Turkey and Korea, once borrowers from IDA, are now donors. Countries currently eligible to borrow from IBRD - Argentina, Brazil, the Czech Republic, Hungary, Mexico, Poland, Russia, the Slovak Republic, South Africa and Venezuela - were also donors to the 14th Replenishment. Other contributors are Australia, Austria, Barbados, The Bahamas, Belgium, Denmark, Finland, Greece, Iceland, Ireland, Israel, Kuwait, Luxembourg, New Zealand, Norway, Portugal, Saudi Arabia, Singapore, Spain, Sweden, and Switzerland. Cumulative contributions since IDA's beginning total US$124 billion equivalent. IDA lending by sector is as follows: Infrastructure 35 per cent; public administration and law 19 per cent; social sector 26 per cent; agriculture 13 per cent; industry 4 per cent and finance 3 per cent.

The top ten borrowers in FY11 were: Bangladesh (US$2,139 million), India (US$2,072 million), Pakistan (US$1,292 million), Vietnam (US$1,280 million), Ethiopia (US$630 million), Ghana (US$605 million), Nigeria (US$535 million), Kenya (US$490 million), Tanzania (US$420 million), and Mozambique (US$413 million).

In Fiscal Year 2012 (ended 30 June 2012), IDA commitments totalled US$14.8 billion, of which 15 per cent was provided on grant terms. New commitments in Fiscal Year 2012 comprised 160 new operations. Since 1960, IDA has lent US$222 billion to 108 countries. Annual lending figures have increased steadily and averaged about US$15 billion over the last three years, approximately 50 per cent of which goes to Africa.

Structure

Each member country is represented by the same governor and Executive Director that represents it in the IBRD. The President of IBRD is *ex officio* President of IDA and Chairman of IDA Executive Directors. The Executive Directors have the same broad powers as they have in IBRD and, although legally and financially distinct, both organisations are served by the same officers and staff. Furthermore, a country must be a member of IBRD before it can join IDA.

Key Programmes

Fighting the spread of HIV/AIDS: IDA has so far committed a total of more than US$1.8 billion globally for HIV/AIDS prevention, care, support and treatment. In 2004, the Bank, in partnership with the Global Fund to Fights AIDS, Tuberculosis and Malaria, UNICEF and the Clinton Foundation, announced agreements that will make it possible for developing countries to purchase high-quality AIDS medicines at the lowest possible prices.

Education: The goal of the World Bank and IDA is to ensure that by 2015, every girl and boy in the developing world has access to and completes a free and compulsory primary education of good quality. Over the past decade, US$8 billion in support has been channeled to 71 countries, with substantial support focused on Africa and South Asia.

Private Sector Development: Private sector development is about promoting growth, reducing poverty and helping people to improve their quality of life. The Doing Business Project aims to speed reform and in some cases progress has been dramatic. For example, Pakistan and Honduras have cut the time required to register a business by 45 per cent or more.

Gender: Limited access to financial services constrains economic participation. IDA supports investment and growth and helps to alleviate poverty by making financial services available to more lower-income persons, including women.

Heavily-Indebted Poor Countries (HIPC) and Multilateral Debt Relief Initiative (MDRI): The MDRI was formed at the G8 Summit at Gleneagles, Scotland in July 2005 and calls for 100 percent cancellation of IDA, AfDF and IMF debt for countries that reach the HIPC completion point. IDA's estimated costs from debt cancellation would be equivalent to about US$37 billion. This will be compensated by additional donor resources from regular replenishments.

There are currently 172 member countries. For membership details, please consult the matrix of *Country Membership of International Organisations* in the preliminary section.

President: Dr Jim Yong Kim (page 1449)

International Development Association (IDA), 1818 H Street, NW, Washington, DC 20433, USA. Tel: +1 202 473 1000, fax +1 202 477 6391, URL: http://www.worldbank.org/ida/

INTERNATIONAL FINANCE CORPORATION (IFC)

The International Finance Corporation (IFC), an affiliate of the World Bank, was established in 1956 to assist less developed member countries by promoting growth in the private sector of their economies. Today IFC is the largest multilateral source of loan and equity financing for private sector projects in the developing world. Its primary goal is to improve lives and raise the living standards of those in developing countries.

The IFC aims to increase support for capital market development and a broad range of financial institutions including commercial banks, leasing companies, venture capital funds and discount houses account for the financing approved from the Corporation's own account. The Corporation has also taken significant steps to strengthen its commitment to supporting only those projects that are environmentally responsible and has intensified its efforts to encourage private investment in the environmental goods and services sector in developing countries.

Its purpose is to create opportunity for people to escape poverty and improve their lives by:
-Promoting open and competitive markets in developing countries
-Providing support to companies and private sector partners
-Helping to generate productive jobs and deliver essential services

IFC offers a full array of financial products and services to companies in its developing member countries. These include: Long-term loans in major and local currencies, at fixed or variable rates; Equity investments; Quasi-equity instruments (such as subordinated loans, preferred stock, income notes, convertible debt); Syndicated loans; Risk management (such as

intermediation of currency and interest rate swaps, provision of hedging facilities; Intermediary finance. The IFC continues to develop new financial tools to help companies manage risk. IFC also mobilises additional financing in the international capital markets and provides advisory services to both businesses and governments on issues related to private investment.

Global Financial Crisis

The World Bank expected the global economy to grow by 3.2 per cent in 2011, with recovery stronger in developing countries. However, the Bank expects 64 million more people will fall into extreme poverty (living on less than US$1.25 per day) because of the financial crisis. Since 2007, the IFC has donated almost US$2 billion to the World Bank's Fund for the poorest countries. The IFC foresees a gradual recovery in 2013.

In response to the global financial crisis the IFC is committed to providing liquidity support and to rebuilding the financial infrastructure. Its activities include an expansion of its global trade finance program from $1 billion to $4 billion. It provides guarantees where commercial banks can not and enables support for an additional $6 billion of trade each year. Its Global Trade Liquidity Program works with major international banks and development banks to support $50 billion of trade per year. IFC has invested an estimated $300 million into its Infrastructure Crisis Facility.

Structure

The Corporation co-ordinates its activities with the other institutions in the World Bank Group - the International Bank for Reconstruction and Development (IBRD, the International Development Association (IDA) and the Multilateral Investment Guarantee Agency (MIGA) - but it is legally and financially independent, with its own Articles of Agreement, shareholders, financial structure, management and staff.

To join IFC, countries must first be a member of the IBRD. Its programmes and activities are guided by its 184 member countries through its Board of Governors and Board of Directors. Each country appoints a governor and an alternate. The five largest shareholders, France, Germany, Japan, the United Kingdom and the United States appoint an executive director, while other member countries are represented by 19 executive directors. IFC's corporate powers are vested in its Board of Governors, which delegates most of these powers to the Board of Directors. The 24 directors meet at World Bank Group headquarters to approve project financing operations.

The President of the World Bank Group, Dr Jim Yong Kim, also serves as the IFC's president. The Executive Vice President, Lars Thunell, is responsible for the overall management of day-to-day operations. He is assisted by the Senior Management Group which consists of regional vice presidents, network vice presidents and other vice presidents.

The IFC is divided into six Regional Departments - Europe and Central Asia; Sub-Saharan Africa; South Asia; the Middle East and North Africa; Latin America and the Caribbean; and East Asia and the Pacific.

Budget and Funding

The Corporation's share capital is provided by its 184 member countries and voting is in proportion to the number of shares held. IFC's authorised capital is US$2.45 billion which is made up of loans, equity, guarantees, swaps and standby arrangements. All IFC's loans are made at market rates of interest and carry maturities of three to 13 years. The percentage of IFC equity investments increases as the Corporation helps to reduce reliance on debt financing by businesses in developing countries. 22 per cent of IFC's financing is approved for projects in the very poorest countries, with per capita incomes of US$400 or less.

Since its founding, IFC has committed more than US$56 billion of its own funds, and arranged US$25 billion in syndications in 140 developing countries. In FY 2011 the IFC's total financing amounted to US$18.7 billion, including a record $6.5 billion in mobilization, more than $180 million in AS project spend and $0/7 billion in AMC commitments. Approximately 48 per cent of investment projects were in IDA countries.

As of March 2013 there were 184 member states. For details of the membership of the IFC please consult the matrix of *Country Membership of Major Organisations* in the preliminary section.

President: Dr Jim Yong Kim (page 1449)
CEO: Jin-Yong Cai

International Finance Corporation, 2121 Pennsylvania Avenue, Washington, DC 20433, USA. Tel: +1 202 473 1000, URL: http://www.ifc.org

INTERNATIONAL FUND FOR AGRICULTURAL DEVELOPMENT (IFAD)

The International Fund for Agricultural Development (IFAD) is an international financial institution and a specialized United Nations agency dedicated to eradicating poverty and hunger in rural areas of developing countries. It was established in 1977.

Through low-interest loans and grants, IFAD develops and finances programmes and projects that fit within national systems and respond to the needs, priorities and constraints identified by poor rural people themselves.

Structure

Membership in IFAD is open to any state that is a member of the United Nations, its specialized agencies or the International Atomic Energy Agency. The Governing Council is IFAD's highest decision-making authority, with 169 Member States (as of May 2013) represented by a Governor and an Alternate Governor. The Council meets annually.

IFAD's second main governing body is its Executive Board, which reports to the Governing Council and is responsible for overseeing general operations and approving funding for IFAD's programmes and projects. The Board, which is composed of 18 elected Members and 18 Alternate Members, meets three times a year.

The President of IFAD is the organization's chief executive officer and chair of its Executive Board. Presidents are elected for a four-year term, and IFAD presidencies are renewable once.

The current President of IFAD is Kanayo F. Nwanze, who was re-elected for a second four-year term in 2013.

Function

IFAD works with partners from around the world to design and finance programmes and projects that ensure poor rural people have access to the assets they need to overcome poverty. Such assets include water, land and other natural resources, agricultural technologies, financial services, markets and opportunities for enterprise.

IFAD also helps local organizations strengthen their capacity to lead the development of their communities over the long term. As a result, poor rural people are able to increase their food production sustainably, raise their incomes, and improve their health, nutrition and education.

IFAD tackles poverty not only as a lender but also as an advocate for poor rural people. Its multilateral base provides a natural global platform to discuss key issues that influence their lives. IFAD plays an important role in promoting pro-poor agricultural research through grants to international agricultural research centres.

The bulk of IFAD's financing for investment programmes and projects is in the form of loans on highly concessional terms. In 2010, the value of highly concessional loans represented 66.3 per cent of the year's financing for programmes and projects. In addition, approximately 20 per cent of financing was provided on grant terms.

IFAD is fully committed to the Heavily Indebted Poor Countries Debt Initiative (HIPC), which aims to reduce the external debt of the world's poorest, most heavily indebted countries to sustainable levels, subject to satisfactory economic performance. Since the HIPC Debt Initiative was set up, many countries have made substantial progress in gaining access to debt relief. Over 90 per cent of eligible countries (35 out of 38) have passed their decision points, qualifying for HIPC Debt Initiative assistance from IFAD. Thirty-one countries have now reached completion point - at which they get full and irrevocable debt reduction - and seven are in the interim period between the decision and completion points.

At its December 2010 session, the IFAD Executive Board approved a decision point document for debt relief for the Comoros. In addition, five countries - the Congo, the Democratic Republic of the Congo, Guinea-Bissau, Liberia and Togo - reached their respective completion points and qualified for irrevocable debt relief. Total commitments amounted to approximately US$715.3 million of debt service relief in nominal terms.

Aims

IFAD's goal is to empower poor rural women and men in developing countries to achieve higher incomes and improved food security. IFAD works with a range of partners to ensure that poor rural people have better access to, and the skills and organization they need to take advantage of:

-natural resources, especially land and water, and improved natural resource management and conservation practices
- improved agricultural technologies and effective production services,
- a broad range of financial services,
- transparent and competitive markets for agricultural inputs and produce,
- opportunities for rural off-farm employment and enterprise development, and
- local and national policy and programming processes

Six principles of engagement guide our work:
- We focus on our strengths in agricultural and rural development, working with partners to meet other needs of poor rural communities.
- We target the poorest and most vulnerable people with the capacity to benefit from the programmes and projects we support.
- We empower poor rural women and men - individually and collectively.
- We encourage innovation and work with partners to scale up successes.
- We work in partnership to multiply the effectiveness of our interventions.
- We design and manage programmes and projects for quality, impact and sustainability.

All of IFAD's decisions - on regional, country and thematic strategies, poverty reduction strategies, policy dialogue and development partners - are made with these principles and objectives in mind. IFAD is committed to achieving the Millennium Development Goals, in particular the target to halve the proportion of hungry and extremely poor people by 2015. Central to IFAD's work is the conviction that, if poverty is to be eradicated, poor rural people must be empowered to lead their own development and to have a say in the decisions and policies that affect their lives.

In the period 1978-2011, IFAD invested US$12.865 billion in 892 projects and programmes that have reached some 400 million poor rural governments. In the same period, grant approvals amounted to 2,398 (US$799.9 million). In the same period, co-financing amounted to US$9,183 million (of which multilateral US$7,203.1 million, bilateral US$1,500.3 million, NGO US$41.4 million, other US$438.2 million). Loan disbursements amounted to US$8,216.9 million and loan repayments US$2,809.8 million.

At the end of 2012, IFAD was financing a total of 256 ongoing programmes and projects in 97 countries. IFAD investments in these activities were worth US$4.2 billion (2010). An estimated 400 million poor rural people were expected to benefit.

IFAD's annual programme of work is growing significantly. In 2010, the programme of work achieved was a record US$852.8 million, an increase of 18.8 per cent compared to 2009. 2010 was the first year of IFAD's Medium-Term Plan 2010-2012 in which a cumulative programme of work of US$3 billion over the three-year timeframe was proposed. The 2011 programme of work was approved at US$1 billion by the Executive Board in December 2010.

In addition to its own programme of work in 2011, an additional US$0.5 billion of commitments entrusted to IFAD Management, but mobilized from non-regular resources, has also been proposed.

IFAD's investments in Asia and the Pacific make up the largest regional portfolio. At the end of 2012, IFAD was providing more than US$1.6 billion in financing for 60 ongoing programmes and projects in 19 countries. IFAD also provides regional and country-specific grants amounting to more US$3 billion.

Selected programmes and projects
In Ghana, IFAD is helping to develop cassava production, processing and marketing. More than 750,000 farmers have planted new varieties developed with IFAD support. The initiative is also helping create new cassava products, such as flour used in bread, snacks and biscuits. The project has helped link 60 farmer groups to markets through processors in their communities, and trained 167 processing groups in product utilization, business development and marketing.

In Rwanda, IFAD is helping small-scale tea growers improve their yields and obtain financial services and secure access to land. In one community, Nshili, profits were low because the processing factory was 50 kilometres away. When the private sector built a factory in Nshili, the project helped a farmers' cooperative gain a 15 per cent stake. The collaboration among farmers is also aiding reconciliation from the genocide of the 1990s.

In the South Pacific, the IFAD-supported MORDI project (Mainstreaming of Rural Development Innovations) has helped dozens of island communities. In the village of Hunga, in Tonga, it helped build a paved road to the wharf to facilitate transporting goods to market. Funds were raised by appealing to overseas families and friends through a social networking site set up by a young person from the community.

In Guatemala, the poor and isolated El Quiché area now has new roads, irrigation systems and processing centres built through a project supported by IFAD. Smallholder farmers are harvesting cash crops such as onions and French beans. Through the Guatemalan Exporters Association, they are selling their produce to some of the biggest retailers in the world. Smallholder farmers' associations have taken in more than US$800,000 in gross revenues.

In Egypt, unemployed college and vocational school graduates are finding new life on farms created from reclaimed land in the desert. The IFAD-supported project offers loans to buy land plus training and other support. The 36,000 farmers helped to date are supplying produce like oranges, peanuts and mozzarella cheese to high-end domestic and international markets. Meanwhile they are creating a community in the desert.

In Bosnia and Herzegovina, women are overcoming traditional attitudes to succeed in non-traditional areas with help from IFAD. One woman, formerly a single mother, used a retail background to start a business, 'Flores', that exports medicinal herbs and mushrooms. After three years of searching for credit, she got a loan of US$25,000 from the project supported by IFAD. Flores now has about 2,000 seasonal workers, most of them women.

President: Kanayo F. Nwanze (page 1488)

International Fund for Agricultural Development, Via Paolo di Dono 44, Rome 00142, Italy. Tel: +39 06 54591, fax: +39 06 504 3463, e-mail: ifad@ifad.org, URL: http://www.ifad.org

INTERNATIONAL LABOUR ORGANIZATION (ILO)

The ILO was created in 1919 as part of the Treaty of Versailles that ended World War I to reflect the belief that universal and lasting peace can be accomplished only if it is based on social justice. In 1946, it became the first specialized agency associated with theUnited Nations (UN), and is unique within the UN system as being its only tripartite organisation, representing workers, employers and governments. In 1969 the Nobel Committee awarded its peace prize to the ILO. The ILO's 2008 Declaration on Social Justice for a Fair Globalization reflects the central role of the Decent Work Agenda in steering a more balanced course for the global economy, as has been widely recognized at national, regional and global levels.

As at May 2013, the number of ILO member countries currently stood at 185. For membership details, please consult the matrix of *Country Membership of Major Organisations* in the preliminary section.

Purpose
The ILO is devoted to advancing opportunities for women and men to obtain decent and productive work in conditions of freedom, equity, security and human dignity. The ILO's four strategic objectives are to promote rights at work, encourage decent employment opportunities, enhance social protection; and strengthen social dialogue in handling work-related issues.

Structure
The International Labour Conference is the supreme deliberative body of the ILO, meeting annually in Geneva. National delegations are composed of two Government delegates, one Employers' delegate and one Workers' delegate. Delegates can speak and vote independently. The Governing Body, elected by the Conference, functions as the Organisation's executive council; it meets three times a year and is composed of 28 Government members, 14 Employers' members and 14 Workers' members.

The International Labour Office is the Organisation's secretariat, operational headquarters, research centre and publishing house, and there are regional, area and branch offices in 40 countries. Multidisciplinary teams, geared to delivering technical guidance on policy issues and development programmes, have been set up in Africa, the Americas, Asia and the Pacific, Central and Eastern States and the Arab States. Most of these teams include specialists in international labour standards and advisors on employers' and workers' activities, so continuing the link between standards and technical co-operation.

Function
The ILO brings issues of employment, social protection, labour standards and rights at work, and social dialogue on to the international agenda through the instruments of standard-setting, technical co-operation activities and research and publishing.

One of the ILO's most important functions is the adoption of the International Labour Conference of Conventions and Recommendations to set international standards of labour. Each Convention is a legal instrument regulating some aspect of labour administration, social welfare or human rights; it is conceived as a model for national legislation. Recommendations, too, are designed to guide governments. Member countries are obliged to report periodically on the implementation of the Conventions they have ratified and also on their position with respect to Conventions they have not ratified and to the Recommendations. The Conventions and Recommendations of the ILO cover a wide range of issues such as labour administration, industrial relations, employment policy, freedom of association, collective organisation and bargaining rights, forced labour, discrimination, general working conditions, social security, occupational health and safety, the employment of women, of children, and of special categories such as migrant workers and seafarers. By May 2013 there had been 189 Conventions and 202 Recommendations.

The ILO has adjusted its programme to take account of the main trends in the world labour markets and so enhance its capacity to respond effectively to increasing requests for assistance, particularly as issues such as respect for freedom of association, child labour and health and safety have become more and more pertinent.

The ILO's technical co-operation programmes also focus on policies for development, alleviation of poverty and the creation of jobs; and enterprise and co-operative development, mainly through assisting in the creation of health and safety departments, social security systems and worker education programmes. The ILO also provides research, analysis and advice to assist national policy makers in their quest for full employment.

The ILO has an International Training Centre in Turin (established in 1965) for government officials, directors of vocational training centres and systems, senior and middle management in the public and private sectors, managers of human development resources and leaders of both workers' and employers' organisations, while its International Institute for Labour Studies promotes the study and discussion of issues relating to the interaction between labour institutions, economic development and society.

Budget
At the 304th Session in March 2009, the governing body of the ILO endorsed the strategic policy framework for 2010-2015. The ILO's proposed regular budget for the 2012/13 biennium was US$861 million, up from US$726 million in 2010-11. The ILO's Programme and budget sharpens the focus of ILO activities by setting out four strategic objectives for the ILO at the turn of the century: to promote and realise fundamental principles and rights at work; to create greater opportunities for women and men to secure decent employment and income; to enhance the coverage and effectiveness of social protection for all; and, to strengthen tripartism and social dialogue.

Under each strategic objective, a number of global programmes (InFocus) concentrate and integrate activities already under way while responding to new needs and demands. Global programmes such as the Programme on Promoting the Declaration on Fundamental Principles and Rights at Work, the International Programme on the Elimination of Child Labour (IPEC), Strategies against Social Exclusion and Poverty (STEP), the Programme on Safety and Health at Work and the Environment (SAFEWORK), the ILO Programme on HIV/AIDS and the World of Work (ILO/AIDS), the Programme on Crisis Response and Reconstruction (ILO/CRISIS), the Social Finance Programme, and the Programme on Boosting Employment through Small Enterprise Development (EMPISEED) are the cornerstones of the ILO's technical co-operation programme.

Director-General: Guy Ryder (UK) (page 1507)

International Labour Organization (ILO), 4 route des Morillons, CH 1211 Geneva 22, Switzerland. Tel: +41 (0)22 799 61 11, fax: +41 (0)22 799 86 85, e-mail: ilo@ilo.org, URL: http://www.ilo.org

INTERNATIONAL MARITIME ORGANIZATION (IMO)

The International Maritime Organization (IMO), a specialised agency of the United Nations, was established by a UN Maritime Conference at Geneva in 1948 although it did not hold its first meeting until 1959. Its headquarters are in London and it currently has 170 Member States and three Associate Members.

Function

The IMO deals with the technical aspects of shipping, with special emphasis on safety of life at sea, maritime security, prevention of pollution of the sea from ships, and on liability and compensation issues. When IMO came into being, its chief concern was to develop international treaties and other legislation concerning safety and marine pollution prevention. By the late 1970s, when most of this work had been completed, the organisation began to place stronger emphasis on improving and implementing legislation. This policy has been so successful that many Conventions now apply to more than 98 per cent of the world merchant shipping tonnage. The international nature of merchant shipping as well as the growth in global trade means that the IMO has an increasingly important role to play in encouraging countries to implement minimum shipping standards. The Organization is in the process of institutionalizing its Member State audit Scheme to make it mandatory.

The International Convention for the Safety of Life at Sea (SOLAS) is the most important treaty covering ship safety and maritime security, while the MARPOL treaty covers accidental and operational oil pollution as well as pollution by chemicals, goods in packaged form, sewage, garbage and air pollution and emissions from ships. Amendmetns adopted in 2011 cover energy efficiency measures, representing the first -ever nabdaatory measures covering emissions of CO_2 from international transport.

IMO has achieved considerable success in its primary goals of safer shipping and cleaner oceans. The rate of serious casualties at sea has fallen considerably since the 1980s and the number of oil spills have decreased significantly since the 1970s.

Structure

The Organization consists of an Assembly, a Council and five main Committees: the Maritime Safety Committee; the Marine Environment Protection Committee; the Legal Committee; the Technical Co-operation Committee and the Facilitation Committee. A number of sub-committees support the work of the main technical committees.

The **Assembly of IMO**, consisting of representatives from all Member States, is the sovereign body of the Organization and normally meets every two years. It is responsible for approving the work programme, voting the budget and determining the financial arrangements of the Organization.

The **40-Member Council** is elected by the Assembly for a term of two years; it meets twice a year and is IMO's governing body between sessions of the Assembly.

The members in 2012-13 are as follows:
Group (a): China, Greece, Italy, Japan, Norway, Panama, Republic of Korea, Russian Federation, United Kingdom, United States
Group (b): Argentina, Bangladesh, Brazil, Canada, France, Germany, India, Netherlands, Spain, Sweden
Group (c): Australia, Bahamas, Belgium, Chile, Cyprus, Denmark, Egypt, Indonesia, Jamaica, Kenya, Liberia, Malaysia, Malta, Mexico, Morocco, Philippines, Singapore, South Africa, Thailand, Turkey.

All committees and subsidiary bodies are open to all Member States to participate equally.

The **Maritime Safety Committee** deals with all aspects of maritime safety and maritime security.
The **Marine Environment Protection Committee** executes and co-ordinates all activities of IMO relating to the prevention and control of pollution from ships.

The MSC and the MEPC are supported by:
Sub-Committee on Dangerous Goods, Solid Cargoes and Containers: deals with regulations for carriage of grain in bulk, the Code of Safe Practice for Bulk Cargoes and the International Maritime Dangerous Goods Code. These are regularly kept up to date.
Sub-Committee on Bulk Liquids and Gases: this body deals with issues concerning the transport of oil, chemicals and gases.
Sub-Committee on Fire Protection: deals with fire protection measures for ships, including tankers.
Sub-Committee on Radiocommunications and Search and Rescue: deals with questions pertaining to, radiocommunications and search and rescue.
Sub-Committee on Safety of Navigation: deals with questions pertaining to safety of navigation, including those relevant to new types of craft.
Sub-Committee on Ship Design and Equipment: deals with all matters relating to ship equipment, including life-saving appliances and arrangements, and has produced codes for the construction and equipment of ships carrying dangerous chemical substances and for ships carrying liquefied gases in bulk; aims to recommend suitable design criteria, construction standards and other safety measures.
Sub-Committee on Standards of Training and Watch-keeping: responsible for matters relating to the International Convention on Standards of Training, Certification and Watchkeeping for Seafarers, and other international standards, as well as human element issues.
Sub-Committee on Stability and Load Lines and on Fishing Vessels Safety: deals with questions of subdivision, stability and load lines and safety aspects of fishing vessels, including operation.
Sub-Committee on Flag State Implementation: acts as a forum for both flag and port States to improve the way in which IMO standards are enforced and has an important role in casualty analysis, in order to develop lessons learned from maritime casualties.
The **Legal Committee** was established by the Council in June 1967 to deal initially with legal problems related to liability adn compensation connected with the loss of the tanker Torrey Canyon. Its mandate was subsequently extended to cover all legal questions within IMO's field of interest.
The Technical Co-operation Committee: performs advisory functions in respect of IMO's programme of technical assistance to developing countries.
The Facilitation Committee: Its task is to standardise and simplify documentation concerning ship arrivals and departures, cargo and passengers and the implementation of the Convention of Facilitation of Maritime Traffic and introduction of measures to that end.

Budget

The total budget for the 2012-13 biennium was £62.2 million. Contributions to the IMO budget are based on a formula that is different from that used in other United Nations agencies: the amount paid by each Member State depends primarily on the tonnage of its merchant fleet.The top ten contributors for 2012 were assessed as follows: Panama, Liberia, Marshall Islands, UK, Bahamas, Singapore, Malta, Greece, China and Japan.

The Secretariat is composed of the Secretary-General and 300 personnel based at the headquarters of the Organization.

For details of the membership of IMO please consult the matrix of *Country Membership of Major Organisations* in the preliminary section.

Secretary-General: Koji Sekimizu (page 1511)

International Maritime Organization (IMO), 4 Albert Embankment, London SE1 7SR, United Kingdom. Tel: +44 (0)20 7735 7611, fax: +44 (0)20 7587 3210, e-mail: info@imo.org, URL: http://www.imo.org, Facebook: https://www.facebook.com/IMOHQ, Twitter: https://twitter.com/imohq

INTERNATIONAL MONETARY FUND (IMF)

The International Monetary Fund was established on 27 December 1945 as an independent international organization and began financial operations on 1 March 1947. An agreement of mutual cooperation with the United Nations came into force on 15 November 1947.

Aims as set out in the IMF's Articles of Agreement: To promote international monetary cooperation, the expansion of international trade and exchange rate stability; to assist in the removal of exchange restrictions and the establishment of a multilateral system of payments; and to alleviate any serious disequilibrium in members' international balance of payments by making the financial resources of the IMF available to them, usually subject to economic policy conditions to ensure the revolving nature of IMF resources.

Amendments to the Articles of Agreement: The first amendment, creating the special drawing right (SDR), the IMF's reserve asset, took effect on 28 July 1969. (The SDR's value changes daily; on 1 July 2011, 1 US$ = 0.6248 SDR). The second amendment took effect on 1 April 1978, and established a new code of conduct for exchange arrangements in the wake of the collapse of the par value system. The third amendment came into force on 11 November 1992; it allows for the suspension of voting and related rights of a member that fails to settle its outstanding obligations to the IMF. The fourth Amendment, which came into force on 10 August 2009, provides for a special one-time allocation of SDRs. The articles were further amended in 2011 to facilitate a move to a more representative, all-elected Executive Board.

IMF activities

Each member of the IMF undertakes a broad obligation to collaborate with the IMF and other members to ensure orderly exchange arrangements and to promote a system of stable exchange rates. In addition, members are subject to certain obligations relating to domestic and external policies that can affect the balance of payments and the exchange rate. The IMF makes its lending resources available, under proper safeguards, to its members to meet short-term or medium-term payment difficulties. It also provides technical assistance to its member countries.

Surveillance

The IMF is mandated to oversee the international monetary system and monitor the economic and financial policies of its 188 member countries. This activity is known as surveillance, and takes place at the global and country levels. The IMF highlights possible risks to domestic and external stability and advises on needed policy adjustments. In this way, it helps the international monetary system serve its essential purpose of facilitating the exchange of goods, services, and capital among countries, thereby sustaining strong and stable economic growth. Financial sector issues are receiving increasing coverage under surveillance, and analytical tools for integrating financial sector and capital markets analysis into macroeconomic assessments are being developed.

Lending

A core responsibility of the IMF is to provide loans to member countries experiencing balance of payments problems. This financial assistance enables countries to rebuild their international reserves, stabilize their currencies, continue paying for imports, and restore conditions for strong economic growth, while undertaking policies to correct underlying problems. Unlike development banks, the IMF does not lend for specific projects.

The IMF has various loan instruments, or "facilities," that are tailored to address the specific circumstances of its diverse membership. Nonconcessional loans are provided mainly through Stand-By Arrangements (SBA) and the Extended Fund Facility (which is useful primarily for longer-term needs). The Flexible Credit Line (FCL) was introduced in 2009, for countries with very strong fundamentals, policies, and track records of policy implementation. Disbursements under the FCL would not be phased or subject to conditionality.

The IMF also offers special financing facilities for low-income countries. A new Poverty Reduction and Growth Trust is expected to become effective in late 2009, with three new lending windows: the Extended Credit Facility, which provides flexible medium-term support; the Standby Credit Facility, which addresses short-term and precautionary needs; and the Rapid Credit Facility, which offers emergency support with limited conditionality. The IMF also provides emergency assistance to support recovery from natural disasters and conflicts, in some cases at concessional interest rates.

A major reform of the IMF's lending facilities took place in March 2009. Conditions linked to IMF loan disbursements are to be better focused and more adequately tailored to the varying strengths of countries' policies and fundamentals. The flexibility of the SBA has been enhanced. In addition, access limits have been doubled, the cost and maturity structure of the Fund's lending has been simplified, and its lending facilities have been streamlined. There were further reforms in 2010 and 2011. Most recently, its lending instruments were improved in order to provide crisis prevention tools. In low-income countries the IMF doubled loan access limits and increased its lending to the world's poorer countries with interest rates set at zero per cent until the end of 2014.

Technical assistance

IMF technical assistance supports the development of the productive resources of member countries by helping them to manage their economic policy and financial affairs more effectively. The IMF provides technical assistance in its areas of core expertise: macroeconomic policy, tax policy and revenue administration, expenditure management, monetary policy, the exchange rate system, financial sector sustainability, and macroeconomic and financial statistics. About 90 per cent of IMF technical assistance goes to low and lower-middle income countries. The IMF operates seven regional technical assistance centres: in the Pacific (Fiji), the Caribbean (Barbados), three in Africa (Gabon, Mali, and Tanzania), the Middle East (Lebanon), and Central America (Guatemala).

How the IMF finances itself

Quotas. Quota subscriptions from member countries are the IMF's main source of financing. A member's quota is largely determined by its economic position relative to other members; it is also linked to their drawing rights on the IMF, their voting power and their share of SDR allocations. Quotas are reviewed at least every five years.

Borrowing. The IMF can supplement its resources through borrowing if it believes that resources might fall short of members' needs. There are a range of options available for temporarily supplementing the Fund's resources, including entering into bilateral loan agreements, issuing notes to the official sector, and enlarging existing borrowing arrangements.

General Arrangements to Borrow (GAB) and New Arrangements to Borrow (NAB). The GAB and NAB are credit arrangements between the IMF and a group of member countries and institutions to provide supplementary resources to the IMF to forestall or cope with an impairment of the international monetary system or to deal with an exceptional situation that poses a threat to the stability of that system. The GAB, established in 1962, enables the IMF to borrow specified amounts of currencies from 11 industrial countries (or their central banks), under certain circumstances, at market-related rates of interest. The potential amount of credit available to the IMF under the GAB totals SDR 17 billion, with an additional SDR 1.5 billion available under an associated arrangement with Saudi Arabia. The NAB, which came into effect in 1998, is a set of credit arrangements between the IMF and 26 member countries and institutions. Importantly, the NAB is the facility of first and principal recourse vis-à-vis the GAB. The maximum amount of resources available to the IMF under the NAB and GAB is SDR 34 billion.
In April 2009, the G-20 agreed to increase the lending resources available to the IMF by up to US$500 billion, thereby tripling the total pre-crisis lending resources. The increase is to be made in two steps: first, through immediate bilateral financing from IMF member countries; and second, by subsequently incorporating this financing into an expanded and more flexible NAB increased by up to $500 billion. This objective was achieved by September 2009.

Bilateral loans. Under such an agreement, the member normally commits to allow the Fund to make drawings up to a specified ceiling during the period for which drawings can be made. During the course of 2009, the IMF signed a number of bilateral loan agreements.

IMF notes. Some official creditors may prefer to invest in paper or notes issued by the IMF. In 2009, the IMF's Executive Board approved a new framework for issuing notes to the official sector. The issuance of notes would enable members to invest in IMF paper, while providing an immediate supplement to IMF resources for financial assistance to members. China is the first country to have signed such a note purchase agreement.

SDR allocations. The IMF may allocate SDRs to members in proportion to their IMF quotas. Such an allocation provides each member with a costless asset. There have been three general SDR allocations, made in response to a long-term global need for reserve assets: (i) SDR 9.3 billion, distributed in 1970-72; (ii) SDR 12.3 billion, distributed in 1979-81; and (iii) SDR 162.1 billion, distributed in August 2009. A special one-time allocation of SDRs amounting to SDR 21.4 billion was implemented on 9 September 2009. This allocation corrected for the fact that countries that joined the Fund after 1981 - more than one fifth of the IMF membership - had never received an SDR allocation.

Figures for 2013

As of March 2013, total quotas amounted to US$360 million with additional pledged or committed resources of US$1 trillion. Committed loans amounted to US$226 billion of which US$166 billion has not been drawn. The biggest borrrowers are Greece, Portugal and Ireland. The biggest precautionary loanns were were for Mexico, Poland and Colombia.

Governance reform

On April 28, 2008, a large-scale quota and voice reform was adopted by the IMF's Board of Governors. It aims to make quotas more responsive to economic realities by increasing the representation of fast-growing economies and at the same time giving low-income countries more say in the IMF's decision making. The reform builds on an initial step agreed by the IMF's membership in September 2006 to have ad hoc quota increases for four countries - China, Korea, Mexico, and Turkey. In October 2009, the IMF membership expressed its support for a shift in quota share to dynamic emerging market and developing countries of at least five percent from over-represented countries to under-represented countries using the current quota formula as the basis to work from. In December 2010 the Governors agreed to double the IMF's quota resources to US$730 billion and to realign the quota shares. In April 2012, member countries announced additional pledges to increase the IMF's resouces by over US$430 billion to help strengthen the global economy and enhance financial stability.

Organization

The highest authority is the Board of Governors, on which each member government is represented. Normally the Governors meet once a year, and may take votes by mail or other means between meetings. The Board of Governors has delegated many of its powers to the 24 executive directors in Washington, who are appointed or elected by individual member countries or groups of countries. The managing director is selected by the executive directors and serves as chairman of the Executive Board, but may not vote except in case of a tie. The term of office is for five years, but may be extended or terminated at the discretion of the executive directors. The managing director is responsible for the ordinary business of the IMF, under the direction of the executive directors, and supervises a staff of about 2,500. There are three deputy managing directors. As of May 2013, the IMF had 188 members. For full details, consult the Matrix of *Country Membership of International Organisations* in the Preliminary Section.

The IMF has eight functional departments that carry out its policy, analytical, and technical work and manage its financial resources. Five area, or regional, departments are responsible for advising member countries on macroeconomic polices and the financial sector, and for putting together, when needed, financial arrangements to support economic reform programs.

The IMF Institute is a specialized department providing training in macroeconomic analysis and policy, and related subjects, for officials of member countries. In addition to training offered in Washington D.C., the IMF also offers training for country officials through a network of seven regional training institutes and programs. These are: the IMF-Singapore Regional Training Institute; the Joint Africa Institute (in Tunisia); the Joint China-IMF Training Program

(in Dalian, China); the Joint IMF-Arab Monetary Fund Regional Training Program (in the United Arab Emirates), the Joint India-IMF Training Program (in Pune, India), the Joint Regional Training Center for Latin America (in Brazil), and the Joint Vienna Institute (in Austria).

Publications
Publications information may be found online at: http://www.imf.org/external/pubind.htm

Managing Director: Christine Lagarde (page 1459)

International Monetary Fund, HQ, 700 19th St. NW, Washington, D.C., 20431, USA. European office in Paris, and regional offices in Tokyo and Warsaw. URL: http://www.imf.org

INTERNATIONAL TELECOMMUNICATION UNION (ITU)

The Union was established on 17 May 1865 (Paris) as the International Telegraph Union with the adoption of the first convention relating to telecommunications and the First Telegraph Regulations. The Union's name was changed to the International Telecommunication Union in 1934 and it became a specialised agency of the United Nations on 15 October 1947. The Union currently has a membership of 193 countries and over 700 private sector entities and academic associations. Please consult the matrix of *Country Membership of Major Organisations* for further details.

Purpose
The ITU exists in order to maintain and extend international co-operation among all Members of the Union for the improvement and rational use of telecommunications of all kinds. Other responsibilities include the orderly recording and registration of frequency assignments and positions of geostationary satellites, promotion of telecommunications development world-wide, organisation of major international telecommunications conferences and exhibitions, and responding to new global challenges including lessening the impact of climate change and increasing cyber security.

Structure
The Plenipotentiary Conferences is the highest policy-making body. It adopts the fundamental policies of the organisation and decides on the organisation and activities of the Union through the International Telecommunication Convention. The Plenipotentiary Conference is composed of delegations representing Members and is convened every four years.

In Geneva, December 1992, the Plenipotentiary Conference decided that a new constitution should be adopted for the ITU. The new constitution now divides the ITU's work into three sectors: Radiocommunications; Telecommunications Standardization; and Telecommunication Development. The ITU's work and the decisions made at the Plenipotentiary Conferences are implemented by a council. The Plenietentary Conference also elects the 12 members of the Radio Regulations Board.

The ITU Council (originally the Administrative Council) was established in 1947. It comprises a maximum of 25 per cent of the total number of the Member States. The Administrative Council meets once a year and is composed of 46 Members of the Union elected by the Plenipotentiary Conference with due regard to the need for equitable distribution of the seats on the Council among all regions of the world. It also performs any duties assigned to it by the Plenipotentiary Conference. It must also consider broad telecommunications environment.

The other legal bodies of the ITU are the General Secretariat, the World and Regional Radiocommunication Conferences, the Radio Communication Assemblies, the Radio Regulations Board, Radio Communication Study Groups and Advisory Group, Radiocommunication Bureau, World Telecommunication Standardization Assemblies, Telecommunication Standardization Study Groups and Advisory Group Telecommunication Standardization Bureau, World and Regional Teleconnmunication Development Conferences, Telecommunication Development Study Groups and Advisory Group, the Telecommunication Development Bureau, and the World Conferences on International Telecommunications.

Sectors
The work of the ITU is organised through three main sectors: Radiocommunications; Standardization; and Development.

Funding
The main source of funding is from contributions from Member States. Income in 2008 was CHF169.1 million, of which 81 per cent came from contributions (69 per cent from Member States and 11 per cent from sector members and 1 per cent from Associates). Expenditure fell to CHF146.4 million in 2008.

Secretary-General: Dr. Hamadoun Touré (Mali) (page 1527)

International Telecommunication Union, Place des Nations, CH 1211 Geneva 20, Switzerland. Tel. +41 (0) 22 730 5111, fax. +41 (0) 22 733 7256, Central ITU e-mail: itumail@itu.int, URL: http://www.itu.int/

MULTILATERAL INVESTMENT GUARANTEE AGENCY (MIGA)

Established in April 1988, the Multilateral Investment Guarantee Agency (MIGA), is an independent, self-supporting member of the World Bank Group. Its aim is to promote private foreign investment in for economic development in developing countries by guaranteeing investments made by foreign investors against political risks and helping to create an attractive climate for private investment in member countries. Its strategy concentrates on specific areas including: infrastructure development; frontier markets; investment in conflict-affected countries;and investments between developing countries.

Function
MIGA is the only global multilateral investment insurer and ranks among the top providers of investment insurance world-wide. The MIGA guarantee offers protection against four types of non-commercial risk: currency inconvertibility and transfer restrictions; war and civil disturbance; expropriation; and breach of contract. Guarantees are available for certain types of investments going into its developing member countries. These include cross-border investments, multi-country projects and capital market and performance bonds. In 2010 substantial changes were approved to its constitution to ensure increased investment and higher development impact. The scope for investment projects has increased: projects must be financially and economically viable, environmentally sound and consistent with the development objectives of the host country. More specifically MIGA is now able to insure project debt even if the agency is not insuring a portion of the equity investment.

Since its inception in 1988, MIGA has issued guarantees worth more than US$24 billion for more than 650 projects in more than 100 developing countries. For the year ending June 30, 2011 MIGA issued $2.1 billion in investment guarantees for 38 projects in developing

countries, a record high and significantly up on $1.5 billion in 2010. This included projects in Iraq, Kosovo, Liberia and the Republic of Congo. For the period FY 2012-14, MIGA expects to issue at least US$2 billion each year.

Structure
MIGA is an agency affiliated with the World Bank. It is owned by its member countries and has a Capital Stock of SDR1 billion. The President of the World Bank is Chairman of the MIGA Board of Directors and President of the Agency. The Agency's Executive Vice-President is its chief operating officer.

Membership is open to all member countries of the World Bank. As at March 2013, 179 nations had completed their membership requirements. For details of the membership of MIGA please consult MIGA's website or the matrix of *Country Membership of Major Organisations* in the preliminary section.

President: Dr Jim Yong Kim (page 1449)
Executive Vice President: Izumi Kobayashi
Vice President and CEO: Michel Wormser

Multilateral Investment Guarantee Agency (MIGA), 1818 H Street, NW, Washington, DC 20433, USA. Tel: +1 202 458 2538, fax: +1 202 522 0316, URL: http://www.miga.org

UNITED NATIONS EDUCATIONAL SCIENTIFIC AND CULTURAL ORGANIZATION (UNESCO)

UNESCO was established on 4 November 1946, when the instruments of acceptance of 20 signatories of its Constitution were deposited with the Government of the United Kingdom. This followed a conference of representatives of 44 countries meeting in London, who laid down the basis of the Organization at the recommendation of the United Nations Conference of San Francisco.

The main objective of UNESCO is to contribute to peace and security in the world by promoting collaboration among nations through education, science, culture, communication and information, and human sciences in order to further universal respect for justice, for the rule of law and for the human rights and fundamental freedoms which are affirmed for the peoples of the world by the Charter of the United Nations. The Organization focuses particularly on two global priorities: Africa and Gender Equality. Overriding aims include: achieving good education for all; sustainable development; addressing emerging social and ethical issues; foster cultural diversity and peace.

UNESCO is actively working towards the UN Millennium Development Goals, specifically:
- to halve the number of people living in extreme poverty in developing countries by 2015
- to achieve universal primary education in all countries by 2015
- to eliminate gender disparity in primary and secondary education
- to help countries realise strategies for sustainable development and to preserve and develop environmental resources

Education
UNESCO's most important activities are in the sphere of education. There has been significant progress in recent years, but as of 2009, 75 million children remained out of primary school and millions leave without obtaining basic literacy and numeracy skills. UNESCO is spearheading objectives of achieving universal primary education for all by 2015. Objectives include the eradication of illiteracy, universal primary education, secondary and higher education reform and the improvement of technical and vocational training, adult, non-formal and permanent education, population education, and the education of women and girls. It also places special emphasis on the attainment of education by people with disabilities. Each year UNESCO sends expert missions to member states on request to advise on all matters concerning education, and provides fellowships and travel grants. In these forms of assistance, priority is given to the rural regions of developing member countries.

Natural Sciences
While the main emphasis in UNESCO's work in science and technology is on harnessing these to development, and above all on fulfilling the needs of developing countries, the Organization is also active in promoting and fostering collaborative international projects among the highly industrialised countries. UNESCO's activities can be divided into three levels: international, regional and sub-regional, and national.

At the international level, UNESCO has established various forms of intergovernmental co-operation concerned with environmental sciences and research on natural resources and in the basic sciences, UNESCO helps promote international and regional co-operation in close collaboration with the world scientific communities, with which it maintains close co-operative links particularly through its support to ICSU and member unions.

Examples of these include the **Man and Biosphere Programme (MAB)** which has undertaken more than 1,000 programmes in 100 countries, involving local people in solving practical problems of environmental resource management in arid lands, humid tropical zones, mountain ecosystems, urban systems, etc.; the **International Geological Correlation Programme (IGCP)**, covering the different fields in earth sciences; the **International Hydrological Programme (IHP)** which deals with the assessment, management and scientific aspects of water resource; and the **World Water Assessment Programme (WWAP)** which seeks to improve the supply and quality of global freshwater resources.UNESCO is also helping countries develop renewable energy programmes.

At the regional and sub-regional level, UNESCO develops co-operative scientific and technological research programmes through organisation and support of scientific meetings and contacts with research institutions, and the establishment or strengthening of co-operative networks. Periodically, regional ministerial conferences are organised on science and technology policy and on the application of science and technology to development. More specialised regional and sub-regional meetings are also organised.

At the national level, UNESCO assists member states in policy-making and planning in the field of science and technology generally, and by organising training and research programmes in basic sciences, engineering sciences and environmental sciences, particularly work relevant to development, such as the use of small-scale energy sources for rural and dispersed populations.

Social and Human Sciences
UNESCO's co-operation with the United Nations Fund for Population Activities (UNFPA) led to a technical assistance programme which benefits developing countries in the areas of population education and communication. Other research activities concern modifications in the spatial distribution of populations (e.g. urbanisation), the ways in which societies react to global climate and environmental change, and changes affecting women and families.

UNESCO gives high priority to young people who are the first victims of unemployment, economic and social inequalities and the widening gap between developing and industrialised countries. It focuses on the educational and cultural dimensions of physical education and sport and their capacity to preserve and improve health. It aims to combat marginalisation and to encourage integration of young people in society. One activity targeted at young people is education for the prevention of AIDS.

UNESCO also focuses on the promotion and protection of human rights and democracy through education, information and documentation, and research, particularly rights related to its fields of competence. It disseminates scientific information aimed at combating racial prejudice, works to improve the status of women and their access to education, and promotes equality between men and women.

UNESCO has been one of the principal promoters of the reflection on ethics of living. In 1993, the International Bioethics Committee of UNESCO (IBC) was formed. It keeps abreast of progress in genetics, whilst taking care to ensure respect for the values of human dignity and freedom in view of the potential risks of irresponsible attitudes in biomedical research. The IBC is an international forum for debate, particularly with regard to the implementation of the Universal Declaration on the Human Genome and Human Rights.

UNESCO has also established the **World Commission on the Ethics of Scientific Knowledge and Technology (COMEST)** as a forum for ethical debate and action with regard to the progress in scientific knowledge and technology. It deals in particular with questions arising from progress in the field of energy production and consumption, the information society, the ethics of outer space and questions over the use of freshwater.

Culture
There are three parts to UNESCO's cultural programme: protecting and conserving cultural property; international safeguarding campaigns to help member states to conserve and restore monuments and sites; and training museum managers and conservationists and the promotion of public awareness of the cultural heritage.

The **World Heritage Programme** aims to protect historic sites and natural landmarks of outstanding universal significance by providing financial aid for restoration, technical assistance, training and management planning. As of March 2013 the 'World Heritage List' comprises over 940 sites including the Great Barrier Reef in Australia, the Galapagos Islands (Ecuador), Chartres Cathedral (France), the Taj Mahal (India), Auschwitz concentration camp (Poland), Machu Picchu (Peru), and the Serengeti National Park (Tanzania). Two sites were added to the World Heritage List in Danger: Río Plátano Biosphere Reserve (Honduras), Tropical Rainforest Heritage of Sumatra (Indonesia). UNESCO added 26 new sites to the World Heritage List in July 2012, including the Gonbad-e Qabus tomb in Iran, the Landscape of Grand Pré, Canada and the Archaeological heritage of the Lennong Valley of Malaysia. Chad, Congo, Palau and Palestine had sites inscribed for the first time.

UNESCO encourages the translation and publication of literary works, publishes albums of art, and produces records, audio-visual programmes and travelling art exhibitions. It supports the development of book publishing and distribution and the training of editors and managers in publishing and is active in preparing and encouraging the enforcement of international legislation on copyright.

Communication and Information
UNESCO's Communication and Information programme was established in 1990 and has three main objectives: to promote the free flow of ideas and universal access to information; to promote the expression of pluralism and diversity in the media and world information networks; and to promote access for all to ICTs.

UNESCO also aims at reinforcing the **International Programme for the Development of Communication (IPDC)** to increase resources for the development of communication. As UNESCO's main operational arm, the IPDC receives project proposals from all regions of the world and can support projects emanating from sources other than the public sector. Funds are pledged by donors once a year at the meetings of its Intergovernmental Council which decides on their allocation.

The **General Information Programme (GIP)** was established in 1976 to provide a focus for UNESCO's activities in the fields of specialised information systems, documentation, libraries and archives for economic and social development, especially in the developing Countries. An Intergovernmental Council of 30 members, elected by the UNESCO General Conference, is responsible for guiding the programme, through pilot projects, preservation and conservation efforts under the Records and Archives Management Programme (RAMP); the training of users of library and information services; the reinforcement of activities relating to the micro version of the CDS/ISIS software package and implementation of activities relating to the establishment of the Bibliotheca Alexandrina.

UNESCO's programme in the field of informatics is through the **Intergovernmental Informatics Programme (IIP)** which was set up to reinforce the promotion of international co-operation in increasing resources for collaborative efforts in informatics, while emphasizing the role of computer science and its applications in extending human knowledge.

Structure
UNESCO is governed by a General Conference composed of representatives of the 195 member states and seven associate member states which meets every two years and decides the policy, programme and budget of the Organization. An Executive Board of 58 members elected by the General Conference supervises the execution of conference decisions.

The International Secretariat, headed by the Director-General, elected for a six year term, carries out the work of the Organization. There are approximately 2,000 staff from 170 countries, of whom over 700 work around the world in one of UNESCO's 50 field offices.

Budget
UNESCO's regular budget for 2012-2013 was US$653 million (a zero nominal growth on 2011-12) which is made up of mandatory contributions from member states and other sources, mainly the UNDP and other UN agencies. Extra-budgetary funding amounted to US$308 million in 2011.

As of March 2013, UNESCO had 195 Member States and seven Associate Members. For details of the membership of UNESCO please consult the matrix of *Country Membership of Major Organisations* in the preliminary section.

Director-General: Irina Bokova (page 1391)

UNESCO, 7 Place de Fontenoy, 75352 Paris 07 SP, France. Tel: +33 (0)1 45 68 10 00, fax: +33 (0)1 45 67 16 90, e-mail: bpi@unesco.org, URL: http://www.unesco.org

UNITED NATIONS INDUSTRIAL DEVELOPMENT ORGANIZATION (UNIDO)

Established in 1966 by the UN General Assembly to act as the central co-ordinating body for industrial activities within the UN system, UNIDO became the sixteenth UN specialised agency in 1985. 174 countries are Member States of the United Nations Industrial Development Organization. It promotes sustainable development by mobilising industry-related knowledge, skills, information and technology to encourage productive employment, competitive economy and a sound environment.

Purpose
The purpose of UNIDO's activities, to enhance productivity and improve the competitiveness of developing countries, is to help these countries alleviate poverty and share the benefits of globalisation.

Structure
UNIDO has two policy-making organs: the General Conference (GC) and the Industrial Development Board (IDB). The Programme and Budget Committee is a subsidiary organ of the IDB.

General Conference - the chief policy-making organ of the Organisation, comprising representatives of all 174 Member States, takes place every two years.

The **Programme and Budget Committee** - consisting of 27 members elected by the General Conference for a two-year term, is a subsidiary organ of the Board, and assists it in preparing work programmes and budgets.

The **Industrial Development Board** - comprising 53 Member States, reviews the implementation of the work programme, the regular and operational budgets and, every four years, recommends a candidate for Director-General to the General Conference for appointment. The Director-General heads the UNIDO Secretariat. The current DG, Kandeh K. Yumkella, was elected in December 2005.

The UNIDO Secretariat carries out programmes and activities approved by its policy-making organs. The Director-General is assisted by three Managing Directors and approximately 600 staff members at Headquarters in Vienna and 100 staff members in the field.

In addition, UNIDO draws on outside experts for over 2,000 short and long-term assignments all over the world. UNIDO has a number of offices worldwide: There are 13 Investment and Technology Promotion Offices (ITPOs), 59 Subcontracting and Partnership Exchanges (SPX), 35 National Cleaner Production Centres (NCPs), established by UNIDO and UNEP and 10 International Technology Centres (ITCs) at various stages of development, that work closely with the ITPOs.

Activities
The broad objectives and priorities of UNIDO are given in the Business Plan on the Future Role and Functions of UNIDO, endorsed by the seventh session of the General Conference in 1997.

This Business Plan grouped the activities of UNIDO into two areas of concentration: (a) strengthening industrial capacities, including programmes in support of the global forum function and policy advice; and (b) cleaner and sustainable industrial development. In addition, while maintaining the universal character and vocation of UNIDO, the Business Plan provided for the Organisation's activities to be focused geographically on least developed countries, in particular in Africa; sectorally on agro-based industries; and thematically on small and medium enterprises (SMEs).

UNIDO achieves these objectives through Integrated Programmes (IPs) or Country Service Frameworks (CSFs), based on combinations of its eight service modules or in stand-alone projects involving only one or two service modules.

UNIDO's eight Service Modules are: Industrial governance and statistics; Investment and technology promotion; Quality and productivity; Small business development; Agro-industries; Industrial energy and Kyoto Protocol; Montreal Protocol; Environment management.

Integration within an IP also has to be achieved at the level of donor mechanisms, national counterparts and other development activities in the country or region.

UNIDO is focusing on three themes, which directly respond to international development priorities: Poverty Reduction through Productive Activities; Energy and Environment; and Trade Capacity Building.

Financial Resources
There are three components to UNIDO's (biennial) budget, these components are designated as the Regular Budget (financed by assessed contributions payable by Member States), the Operational Budget (financed from the reimbursement of support costs received from technical cooperation and other services), and Voluntary Contributions.

The main source of funds for technical cooperation activities are Voluntary Contributions, received via: the Industrial Development Fund (IDF), trust funds received from donor countries and institutions; the Multilateral Fund for the Implementation of the Montreal Protocol; the Global Environment Facility (GEF); the Common Fund for Commodities (CFC).

The estimated total volume of UNIDO's operations for the biennium 2010-2011 was $361 million. The value of UNIDO's ongoing technical cooperation programmes and projects totalled $882 million as of 31 December 2011. The value of technical cooperation programmes in 2011 was $166.7 million.

Publications
Industrial Development Report, UNIDO Annual Report. For more information on publications, see www.unido.org/publications.

UNIDO has also developed a variety of databases such as the Biosafety Information Network Advisory Service (BINAS), the Business Environment Strategic Toolkit (BEST), and Industrial Development Abstracts (IDA) which is the source of information on UNIDO technical co-operation and other industrial activities. UNIDO Comfar software facilitates the financial and economic appraisal of investment projects.

UNIDO-supported centres are: International Centre for Science and High Technology (ICS) in Trieste, Italy; International Centre for Advancement of Manufacturing Technology (ICAMT) in Bangalore, India; International Centre for Application of Solar Energy (CASE) in Perth, Western Australia; International Centre for Medicine Biotechnology (ICMB) in Obolensk, Moscow Oblast of the Russian Federation and International Materials Assessment and Application Centre in Rio de Janeiro, Brazil.

For membership details please consult the matrix of *Country Membership of International Organisations* in the preliminary section.

Director General: Li Yong (page 1464)

United Nations Industrial Development Organization, Wagramerstr.5, PO Box 300, Vienna International Centre, A 1400 Vienna, Austria. Tel: +43 (0)1 260 260, fax: +43 (0)1 269 2669, e-mail: unido@unido.org, URL: http://www.unido.org

UNIVERSAL POSTAL UNION (UPU)

The Universal Postal Union, located in Berne, Switzerland, is a UN agency specialising in international postal relations. It was formed by the 1874 Treaty of Berne to organise and improve international postal services. The Constitution of the Universal Postal Union (UPU) was adopted in 1964 (six additional protocols were adopted at successive Universal Congresses) and the Acts that help govern it came into force on 1 January 2001.

The objectives of the UPU are: to guarantee the provision of a good quality, affordable universal postal service; to improve the quality and raise the level of efficiency of the international postal network so that customers have a secure, reliable and affordable service; increase knowledge of the commnications markets; to reform the postal sector to ensure sustainable development of the postal services; to increase co-operation and interaction among postal industry stakeholders.

In March 2013 the UPU numbered 192 member countries.

Structure
The Universal Postal Congress, the supreme legislative authority of the Union, consists of representatives of all member countries and is convened every four years. Its main function is to study and revise the Acts of the Union, taking as a basis proposals put forward by member countries, the Council of Administration or the Postal Operations Council. However, although its main purpose is to debate legislation, more recently it has focused on broader policy issues. In addition to setting the budget for the next four years, Congress also elects the Director-General and the Deputy Director-General, as well as members of the Council of Administration and Postal Operations Council. The 25th Universal Postal Congress took place in September 2012, in Qatar.

The Council of Administration (CA), composed of 41 member countries, meets each year at UPU headquarters. It ensures the continuity of the Union's work between Congresses, supervises Union activities and examines regulatory, administrative, legislative and legal issues that are of interest to the Union. The CA agrees the Union's annual budget and accounts, in addition to yearly updates of the UPU's Programme and budget. Finally, it has responsibility for the promotion and co-ordination of all aspects of technical assistance among member countries.

The Postal Operations Council (POC), composed of 40 member countries elected by Congress, meets annually at UPU headquarters. It is primarily responsible for technical operations in the sphere of international postal services, specifically assisting postal services to modernise and upgrade their products. Additionally, the POC promotes new postal products by collecting, analysing and publishing the results of tests and research. It also makes recommendations to member countries about standards for technological and operational processes to promote uniformity of practice.

The International Bureau is the UPU's Headquarters and is situated in Berne. It provides support and secretariat facilities for the various bodies of the UPU as well as liaison, information, and consultation among the Union's members. It also acts as a clearing-house in settling accounts between postal administrations and inter-administration charges for the exchange of postal items and international reply coupons. The International Bureau also represents the Union externally, particularly with international organisations.

There are two co-operatives; the Telematics Co-operative and the EMS Co-operative.

Funding
The annual budget amounts to CHF37 million. These expenses are borne jointly by all member countries which, for this purpose, are divided into ten contribution classes, the least-developed countries contributing one half of a unit and major economies contributing a maximum of 50 units.

For details of the membership of the UPU, please consult the matrix of *Country Membership of Major Organisations* in the preliminary section.

Director-General of the International Bureau (2013-17): Bishar Hussein (Kenya) (page 1446)

Universal Postal Union, International Bureau, Case postale 13, CH-3000 Berne 15, Switzerland. Tel: +41 (0)31 350 3111, fax: +41 (0)31 350 3110, email: info@upu.int, URL: http://www.upu.int

WORLD BANK

The World Bank is one of the primary sources of financial and technical assistance to developing countries around the world.

The World Bank was set up in 1944 to manage the global post-war economy. Its first loan of $250 million was to France in 1947 for post-war reconstruction. Reconstruction remains an important focus of the Bank's work but its main aim is now poverty reduction.

It is made up of two development institutions owned by 188 member countries - the International Bank for Reconstruction and Development (IBRD) and the International Development Association (IDA).

The IBRD concentrates on middle income and creditworthy poor countries, while the IDA focuses on the poorest countries. Together they provide low-interest loans, interest-free credits and grants to developing countries for investments in education, health, public administration, infrastructure, financial and private sector development, agriculture, and environmental and natural resource management.

World Bank Group
The World Bank has three affiliates: the International Finance Corporation (IFC); the Multilateral Investment Guarantee Agency (MIGA); the International Centre for Investment Disputes (ICSD). These three affiliates together with the IDA and the IBRD make up the World Bank Group.

Aims
The overall aim of the World Bank is to reduce poverty. The World Bank focuses on achieving the Millennium Development Goals. Its aims are:
- poverty reduction and sustainable growth in the poorest countries
- responding to the challenges of post-conflict countries
- regional and global issues - climate change, trade, disease
- development and financing for middle income countries
- greater development in the Arab World
- pooling of global knowledge to support development

Financial Crisis
Although the World Bank expects the world economy to grow by 2.5 per cent in 2012 and 3.0 per cent in 2013 and expects the recovery to be higher in developing countries, their growth rates are expected to fall to 5.3 per cent and it expects demand for Bank assistance to continue to be high. Food prices remain high and additionally there is the threat of drought in the Horn of Africa. In total the World Bank has provided over $280 billion of help since the start of the current financial crisis in 2008.

The World Bank has focused significantly on food security. Approximately 40 million people have been helped through the Global Food Crisis Response Program (GFRP) which has contributed $1.5 billion. The Bank is also supporting the Global Agriculture and Food Security Program (GAFSP), set up by the World Bank Group in April 2010 at the G20's request, to support country-led agriculture and food security plans and help promote investments in smallholder farmers. As of 2013, pledges totalled over $1 billion. Donors include states and the Gates Foundation.

Organisation
The 188 member states are represented by a Board of Governors, who are the ultimate policy makers. The governors are the ministers of finance or development of the member countries. They meet once a year at the Annual meetings of the Board of Governors of the World Bank Group and the IMF. There are 24 Executive Directors who work on site. The largest shareholders (France, Germany, Japan, the UK and the US) appoint an executive director. The other member states are represented by 19 executive directors. The meetings of the Board of Directors are chaired by the President of the World Bank. The President is elected by the Board of Governors for a five-year renewable term. As the US is the Bank's largest shareholder, the president is traditionally from the US. The president is the president of all the World Bank group bodies.

Dr Jim Yong Kim replaced Robert Zoellick as president of the World Bank group on 1 July 2012.

World Bank Inspection Panel
The World Bank Inspection Panel was set up in 1993 to ensure that the Bank's operations stick to the Bank's policies and procedures.

Funding
The World Bank raises money in several different ways to support the loans and grant activity of the IBRD and the IDA. IBRD's lending is mainly financed by selling AAA-rated bonds in the world's financial markets. The Bank's capital is also lent out. Shareholder support is also important.

For further information on the bodies that make up the World Bank Group, please consult their individual entries.

President: Jim Yong Kim (page 1449)

The World Bank, 1818 H Street, NW, Washington, DC 20433, USA. Tel: +1 202 473 1000, fax: +1 202 477 6391, e-mail: pic@worldbank.org, URL: http://www.worldbank.org

WORLD HEALTH ORGANIZATION (WHO)

The Constitution of the World Health Organization (WHO) was adopted on 22 July 1946 by the International Health Conference (convened by the Economic and Social Council), and came into being on 7 April 1948.

WHO's aim is that all people should attain the highest possible level of health; 'health', as defined in the WHO Constitution, as being not just an absence of disease or infirmity, but also a state of complete physical, mental and social well-being.

Structure
WHO policy is made by its World Health Assembly, which meets on an annual basis, while its Executive Board meets twice a year. The Organization is divided into six regional organisations meeting once a year, each with its own Regional Director, Regional Committee and Regional Office. The Secretariat is headed by the Director - General and the Regional Directors, and consists of administrative and technical staff. There are some 8,000 staff in total.

Function
The WHO acts as the directing and co-ordinating authority on international health work, striving to improve health conditions for all people, but in particular for the poorest. It assists governments by supplying knowledge, evidence based technical assistance and/or emergency aid, and by helping them to strengthen their health services and health policy.

The Organization establishes international standards for foods and biological, pharmaceutical and related products, whilst also proposing conventions, agreements, regulations and recommendations concerning international nomenclature of diseases, causes of death and public health practices.

The Organization promotes and co-ordinates technical co-operation and biomedical and health service research throughout the medical world, and tries to improve standards of teaching and training in the health, medical and related fields.

The WHO works on the prevention and control of epidemic, endemic and other diseases. The Organization (in co-operation with other agencies if necessary) also promotes improving environmental factors that influence health, through the improvement of nutrition, housing and sanitation, recreation, economic/working conditions, and other contributing factors.

Projects
One of the most significant events in WHO's first 50 years was the global eradication of smallpox, which had disfigured and killed millions before its elimination in 1980. Other diseases such as polio and guinea-worm are on the threshold of eradication, and thanks to improved methods of treatment, leprosy is also being overcome. Recently, WHO has turned its focus on diseases that cause or perpetuate poverty, such as malaria, tuberculosis, HIV/AIDS, childhood diseases and maternal mortality. It is working to scale up the global fight against these diseases while also tackling the growing threat of non-communicable diseases in developing countries, in particular the large threat of tobacco-related diseases.

WHO strategy emphasises partnerships with Member States, other international organisations, civil society and the private sector. In addition, almost 1,200 leading health-related institutions from around the World are officially designated as WHO Collaborating Centres.

Budget
The WHO budget is made up of assessed contributions from its 193 Member States and Associate Members, as well as voluntary contributions from Member States and various other sources. The framework for the financial resources and expenditures of WHO is derived from the 11th General Programme of Work, which covers the period 2006-15. From 2008, a medium-term strategic plan will form the framework for WHO's results-based management. The six-year plan (2008-13) covers three biennial budget periods, starting with 2008-2009. Total operating revenue for 2010 was US$2323 million (compared to US$2759 million 2008-09). Operating expenses amounted to US$2,078 million of which $1,945 million related to expenditure for the programme budget. Financial income amounted to US$42 million. The overall recorded surplus carried forward to 2011 was US$287 million. The proposed budget for 2012-13 was revised down to US$3959 million. Assessed contributions remain at their 2010-2011 level, providing approximately 24 per cent of the financing. The remaining 76 per cent will need to be financed through volntary contributions.

For details of the membership of the WHO please consult the matrix of *Country Membership of Major Organisations* in the preliminary section.

Director-General: Dr. Margaret Chan (page 1402)

World Health Organization, 20 Ave Appia, 1211 Geneva 27, Switzerland. Tel: +41 (0)22 791 2111, fax: +41 (0)22 791 3111, e-mail: info@who.int, URL: http://www.who.org

WORLD INTELLECTUAL PROPERTY ORGANIZATION (WIPO)

The World Intellectual Property Organization (WIPO) was established in 1967, with the conclusion of the Convention establishing WIPO which entered into force on 26th April 1970. WIPO became a specialised organisation of the United Nations in 1974. WIPO's mission is to promote the protection of intellectual property (IP) rights worldwide and to extend the benefits of the international IP system to all member states. Intellectual property covers industrial property (patents, trademarks, industrial designs, etc.) and copyright (for works in the literary, musical, artistic, photographic and audio-visual fields).

WIPO administers 25 treaties that deal with different legal and administrative aspects of intellectual property (IP). These include the Paris Convention for the Protection of Industrial Property (174 states are party to this as of May 2013), and the Berne Convention for the Protection of Literary and Artistic Works (166 states are party to this treaty as of May 2013). Full details of all WIPO-administered treaties are available at : http://www.wipo.int/treaties/en.

WIPO's programme of work covers three main areas of activity, namely, development of the international intellectual property legal archituecture, technical assistance and capacity-building in the field of IP and the delivery of services which facilitate the process of obtaining IP rights internationally. Also, the WIPO Arbitration and Mediation Center offers Alternative Dispute Resolution (ADR) options and mediation for the resolution of international commercial disputes between private parties. The Center is also a leading dispute resolution service provider for challenges related to abusive registration and use of Internet domain names, commonly known as 'cybersquatting'.

Structure
WIPO's governing bodies are the WIPO General Assembly, the WIPO Conference and the WIPO Coordination Committee composed of representatives of both WIPO member states and the Unions that WIPO administers (see http://www.wipo.int/treaties/en/convention/). The Secretariat of WIPO has some 1,300 staff from over 100 countries.

As of May 2013, there were 186 member states. For details of the membership of WIPO please consult the matrix of *Country Membership of Major Organisations* in the preliminary section.

Budget
WIPO generates over 90 per cent of its annual budget, financing its activities from revenues acquired through the provision of services to the private sector in the form of international filing of patents and international registration of trademarks and designs as well as its alternative dispute resolution services. The remainder comes from contributions by Member States. WIPO's annual income amounts to over 300 million Swiss francs. WIPO's budget for the 2012-13 biennium is approximately CHF 647 million.

Director-General: Francis Gurry (Australia) (page 1435)

World Intellectual Property Organization, 34, Chemin des Colombettes, 1211 Geneva 20, Switzerland. Tel: +41 (0)22 338 9111, URL: http://www.wipo.int

WORLD METEOROLOGICAL ORGANIZATION (WMO)

The World Meteorological Organization (WMO) is a specialized agency of the United Nations. It is the UN system's authoritative voice on the state and behaviour of the Earth's atmosphere, its interaction with the oceans, the climate it produces and the resulting distribution of water resources. It aims to provide world leadership and expertise thus contributing to the well-being and safety of people worldwide and to the global economy.

WMO has a membership of 191 Member States and Territories (as of March 2013). It originated from the International Meteorological Organization (IMO), which was founded in 1873. Established in 1950, WMO became the specialized agency of the United Nations in 1951 for meteorology (weather and climate), operational hydrology and related geophysical sciences.

Mission
The top-level objectives of WMO are:
- To facilitate co-operation and establish a world-wide network of research stations relating to meteorological, hydrological and geophysical issues
- To produce more accurate, timely and reliable forecasts and warnings of weather, climate, water and related environmental elements;
- To further the application of meteorology to shipping, water, aviation, agriculture and other human activities;
- To improve the delivery of weather, climate, water and related environmental information and services to the public, governments and other users;
- To provide scientific and technical expertise and advice in support of policy- and decision-making and implementation of the agreed international development goals and multilateral agreements
- To encourage further research and training in meterology and related research.

Structure
World Meteorological Congress, the supreme body of the Organization, brings together the delegates of Members once every four years to determine general policies for the fulfilment of the purposes of the Organization, to approve long-term plans, to authorize maximum expenditure for the following financial period, to adopt Technical Regulations relating to international meteorological and operational hydrological practice, to elect the President and Vice-Presidents of the Organization and members of the Executive Council and to appoint the Secretary-General.

The Executive Council, the executive body of the Organization, is responsible to Congress for the coordination of the programmes of the Organization and the utilization of its budgetary resources in accordance with the decision of Congress. Composed of 37 directors of National Meteorological or Hydrometeorological Services, it meets at least once a year to implement the programmes approved by Congress and review the activities of the Organization.

The six regional associations are each composed of Members whose task it is to coordinate meteorological, hydrological and related activities within their respective Regions (Africa; Asia; South America; North America, Central America and the Caribbean; South-West Pacific; and Europe).

The eight technical commissions, composed of experts designated by Members, study matters within their specific areas of competence. The Commissions are currently: Basic Systems (CBS); Instruments and Methods of Observation (CIMO); Hydrology (CHy); Atmospheric Sciences (CAS); Aeronautical Meteorology (CAeM); Agricultural Meteorology (CAgM); Climatology (CCl) and the Joint WMO-IOC Commission for Oceanography and Marine Meteorology (JCOMM).

The Secretariat, headed by the Secretary-General, serves as the administrative, documentation and information centre of the Organization. It prepares, edits, produces and distributes the publications of the Organization, carries out the duties specified in the Convention and other Basic Documents and provides support to the work of the constituent bodies of WMO described above.

The Secretariat hosts Regional Offices for Africa, Asia and the South-West Pacific, the Americas, and Europe. The Regional Offices supervise related WMO offices in the field. There are two liaison offices: one in New York and one in Brussels.

WMO programmes
WMO carries out its work through several major scientific and technical programmes. These are designed to assist all Members to provide, and benefit from, a wide range of meteorological and hydrological services and to address present and emerging problems. The programmes of WMO make possible the provision of meteorological and related services in all countries at costs far below those that would be incurred if each Member acted alone. Programmes include: World Weather Watch (WWW); Global Atmosphere Watch Programme (GAW); World Weather Research Programme (WWR); Hydrology and Water Resources Programme (HWRP); World Climate Research Programme (WCRP); WMO Space Programme; World Climate Programme (WCP); WMP Programme for the least developed countries; Regional Programme (RP); Disaster Risk Reduction Programme (DRR) and Aeronautical Meteorology Programme.

The strategic plan for 2012-15 was approved in Geneva 2011. The plan is centres around three global needs: improved protection of life and property; poverty alleviation, development of sustainable livelihoods and economic growth; and sustainable use of natural resources and improved environmental quality. The plan will be achieved through five key policy themes: improvment of service quality; scientific research and development and implementation of technology; improved capacity; strengthening parternships; increased good governance.

Budget
The results-based budget for the period 2008-2011 was CHF 393,800,000, including regular resources of CHF 269,800,000 and CHF 124,000,000 from extra-budgetary resources.

President: David Grimes (Canada)
Secretary-General: Michel Jarraud (France) (page 1449)

WMO, 7 bis, avenue de la Paix, PO Box 2300, CH 1211 Geneva 2, Switzerland, Tel: +41 (0)22 730 8111, fax: +41 (0)22 730 8181, e-mail: wmo@wmo.int, URL: http://www.wmo.int

WORLD TOURISM ORGANIZATION (UNWTO / OMT)

The World Tourism Organization is the successor to the International Union of Official Tourist Publicity Organisations (est. 1925) and the International Union for Official Tourism Organisations (IUOTO) which was set up following the Second World War. As international tourism grew, national governments became more involved until, in 1974, the IUOTO was renamed the World Tourism Organisation. The WTO Secretariat was installed in Madrid in 1975.

The WTO serves as a global forum for tourism policy issues. It aims to promote the development of responsible, sustainable, accessible tourism, with particular emphasis on the interests of developing countries. It is a strong supporter of the Global Code of Ethical Tourism and is committed to the UN's millennium goals.

Activities
One of the WTO's fundamental tasks is the transfer of tourism knowledge and experience to developing countries. All WTO projects are based on the policy of sustainability, ensuring that the economic benefits of tourism development do not damage the environment or the local cultures. Long term projects in this area have included the Tourism Master Plan in Ghana (1996), the Reconstruction and Development Plan in Lebanon (1997) and the Action Plan for Sustainable Tourism Development in Uzbekistan (1997). Recent short-term projects have included a pilot eco-tourism development in Congo, protection of historic sites in the Philippines, resort marketing in China and resort management in the Maldives.

As global competition in tourism intensifies, WTO's section for Quality of Tourism Development aims to help member destinations become more competitive through trade liberalisation, safety and security measures, and improved technical standards. WTO's activities are guided by a series of policy instruments adopted by members of the organisation: The Tourism Bill of Rights and Tourist Code; Recommended Measures for Safety; Creating Tourism Opportunities for Handicapped People in the Nineties; Health Information and Formalities in International travel; WTO Statement on the Prevention of Organized Sex Tourism. It co-operates with other international organisations working in these fields - Interpol, UNCTAD, the WTO, the WHO, and the World Customs Organisation. WTO's regional representatives carry out direct actions that strengthen and support the efforts of National Tourism Administrations.

Structure
The General Assembly is the supreme organ of the WTO. It meets every two years to approve the programme of work and to debate topics of importance to the tourism sector. The General Assembly is composed of voting delegates representing Full and Associate Members. As of March 2013, there were 155 Member States, six Associate Members, and over 400 Affiliate Members. For membership details please consult the matrix of *Country Membership of International Organisations* in the preliminary section.

The Executive Council is WTO's governing board, responsible for ensuring that the organisation carries out its work and stays within its budget. It is composed of 29 members elected by the General Assembly and meets twice a year. Romania holds the chair for 2013.

WTO has six regional commissions - Africa, the Americas, East Asia and the Pacific, Europe, the Middle East and South Asia - whose activities are designed to help increase the stature of National Tourism Administrations within their own countries at the same time as improving each nation's tourism sector. The commissions meet at least once a year to discuss the organisation's activities and priorities for the future.

Specialised committees of WTO members advise on management and programme content.

A Secretary-General, elected by the General Assembly for a four-year term, heads the Secretariat. There are about 110 full-time staff at the Madrid Headquarters of WTO and there is also a regional support office for Asia-Pacific in Japan. The Secretariat is responsible for implementing WTO's programme of work and serving the needs of the members.

Funding
WTO is mainly financed by members' contributions. Full Members pay an annual quota calculated according to their level of economic development and the importance of tourism in each country. Associate Members pay a fixed annual contribution of US$30,000 and Affiliate Members pay US$2,000 per annum. Membership dues account for about 90 per cent of the budget, the remainder coming from UNDP support costs, investment income and sales of publications and electronic products.

Secretary-General: Taleb Rifai (Jordan)

World Tourism Organization (UNWTO / OMT), Calle Capitan Haya 42, 28020 Madrid, Spain. Tel: +34 (9)1 567 8100, fax: +34 (9)1 571 3733, e-mail: omt@unwto.org, URL: http://www.unwto.org

INTERNATIONAL ATOMIC ENERGY AGENCY (IAEA)

Established on 29 July 1957, the International Atomic Energy Agency (IAEA) is an autonomous member of the United Nations that serves as the world's centre for nuclear co-operation. Operating on an annual budget of approximately €315 million provided by its 159 Member States, the IAEA aims at four primary goals: safeguarding nuclear non-proliferation; enhancing the security of nuclear facilities and radioactive materials; ensuring the safety of nuclear facilities and technologies; and promoting nuclear science to meet basic human needs.

Article II of the IAEA Statute states that "The Agency shall seek to accelerate and enlarge the contribution of atomic energy to peace, health and prosperity throughout the world. It shall ensure, so far as it is able, that assistance provided by it or at its request or under its supervision or control is not used in such a way as to further any military purpose."

Principal Achievements
The IAEA is active in almost every country of the world through its safeguards, safety, security and technical co-operation programmes. Under the Treaty of the Non-Proliferation of Nuclear Weapons (NPT), The IAEA is charged with ensuring that states commit not to use nuclear material for explosive purposes. The Treaty requires that all non-nuclear-weapon States conclude comprehensive IAEA safeguard agreements and submit all nuclear material to IAEA monitoring.

The IAEA safeguards are thus designed to ensure that countries using nuclear technologies are not secretly developing nuclear weapons. Governments sign agreements with the IAEA pledging to disclose their nuclear materials and activities; the IAEA then applies accounting methods and on-site inspections to verify that the declarations continue to be accurate and complete.

IAEA verification is further strengthened through an "Additional Protocol" to a country's comprehensive safeguards agreement. Under such a Protocol, States are required to provide the IAEA with broader information on all aspects of its nuclear fuel cycle-related activities. They must also grant the Agency wider access rights and enable it to use the most advanced verification technologies.

The IAEA accounts for all "source and special fissionable material" in countries under comprehensive safeguards. Safeguards activities focus on materials that are crucial to making nuclear weapons - Plutonium-239, Uranium-233 and -235. Safeguards are applied routinely at over 900 facilities in 71 countries. As of 1 July 2012, 175 states had safeguard agreements in force, involving 2,153 safeguard inspections during the year.

The IAEA has established a vast body of safety standards covering nuclear energy, radiation protection, radioactive waste management and the transport of radioactive materials. These are updated regularly to ensure that state-of-the-art methods for achieving the highest level of safety are provided. More importantly, they are coordinated with the guidance associated with other industrial and technical organisations.

To ensure that its standards are rigorously applied, the IAEA conducts safety reviews for appraising compliance and provides advisory services to users and regulatory authorities. These reviews and services are conducted by experts from throughout the world, under the leadership of the IAEA.

The IAEA has established a system to facilitate emergency assistance to Member States in the event of radiation accidents. The IAEA has prepared three international conventions, namely, the Convention on Early Notification of a Nuclear Accident (entered into force on 27 October 1986), the Convention on Assistance in the Case of a Nuclear Accident or Radiation Emergency (1987) and the International Convention on Nuclear Safety (1996), which were endorsed in the light of the Chernobyl nuclear accident.

Additional international conventions administered by the IAEA are the Vienna Convention on Civil Liability (1977), the Convention on Supplementary Compensation for Nuclear Damage (not yet in force), the Convention of Physical Protection of Nuclear Material (1987) and the Joint Convention on the Safety of Spent Fuel Management and the Safety of Radioactive Waste Management.

The IAEA prepares feasibility and market studies for nuclear power and operates three laboratories. The Agency also assists Member States to strengthen their capabilities to fight terrorism: by providing advisory services and training; by promoting international standards and guidelines and by supplying critical information services and technical support.

The IAEA's technical cooperation programme promotes research, adaptation and the transfer of nuclear science for meeting basic human needs. Working together with bilateral, multilateral and non-governmental aid partners, the IAEA contributes to the social and economic development of its Member States and delivers sizeable human benefits. Nuclear techniques are helping to boost production of tropical plants and to combat insects and diseases. Nuclear tools are improving food safety. Radiotherapy is saving the lives of cancer sufferers throughout the developing world.

Medium Term Strategy 2012-2017
In 1999, a Medium Term Strategy (MTS) was developed to provide a review of issues and developments in the 'nuclear world', in particular: the present situation regarding nuclear power; the advantages of nuclear related techniques in food and agriculture, human health, water resources management and environmental monitoring; the Agency's efforts to create a global nuclear safety culture; the efforts to conclude Additional Protocols to safeguard agreements; outreach to non-traditional partners and gaining a better understanding of the needs of Member States

The MTS is used as a starting point and reference document in the formulation of programme proposals. The latest IAEA Medium Term Stategy covers the period 2012 - 2017. This MTS recognises the world has changed since its first MTS, with increasing globalization meaning greater travel of people and ideas. There are greater threats to international security from nuclear proliferation and nuclear terrorism. Greater technology must also be taken into account. Its six strategic objectives are:
- facilitating access to nuclear power;
- increasing promotion of nuclear science, technology, and applications;
- improving nuclear safety and security;
- providing effective technical co-operation;
- strengthening the Agency's safeguards and verification activities;
- providing efficient and innovative management and strategic planning.

Budget
The IAEA's regular budget for 2012 was €331 million. The target for voluntary contributions to the Technical Co-operation Fund for 2012 was US $88 million.

Structure
Headquartered at the Vienna International Centre, the IAEA is led by a 35-member Governing Board chosen from 154 member states at the Annual General Conference of all Member States. The Agency operates field and liaison offices in New York, Geneva, Canada and Tokyo, laboratories in Austria and Monaco and a research centre in Italy, administered by UNESCO.

The IAEA Secretariat carries out programmes and activities approved by the Agency's policymaking organs. The Secretariat is headed by the Director-General, who is the chief administrative officer and is appointed for a four-year term. Assisting him are six Deputy Director Generals who each head their own separate departments. In 2012, there were over 2,300 professional and support staff within the Secretariat.

There are six major departments: management, nuclear sciences and applications, nuclear energy, nuclear safety and security, technical co-operation, and safeguards and verification.

As of February 2013, the IAEA had 159 members.

For details of the membership of IAEA, please consult the matrix of *Country Membership of Major Organisations* in the preliminary section.

Director-General: Yukiya Amano (page 1377)

International Atomic Energy Agency, Vienna International Centre, Wagramerstrasse 5, PO Box 100, A-1400 Vienna, Austria. Tel: +43 (0)1 26000, fax: +43 (0)1 26007, e-mail: Official.Mail@iaea.org, URL: http://www.iaea.org

INTERNATIONAL CENTRE FOR SCIENCE AND HIGH TECHNOLOGY

The International Centre for Science and High Technology was an initiative of Nobel prize-winner Abdus Salam. In 1988 Salam's intention was to create a centre for science and high technology with goals of technology transfer and promotion of industry in developing countries. This was to complement and extend the theoretical research and transfer of scientific know-how activities of ICTP, the International Centre for Theoretical Physics he directed at Miramare, Trieste, Italy for three decades until 1993. Following an Institutional Agreement between the Italian government and UNIDO, ICS was recognised as an autonomous institution within the legal framework of UNIDO. This agreement came into force in February 1996.

The institutional mandate of ICS was to promote the transfer of knowledge in applied science and high technology to developing countries and countries in economic transition to support local industrial growth for an economically, environmentally and socially sustainable development.

The International Centre for Science and High Technology (ICS-UNIDO) closed in 2012.

INTERNATIONAL CRIMINAL COURT

The ICC is the first ever permanent, treaty based, international criminal court established to promote the rule of law and ensure that the gravest international crimes do not go unpunished. The ICC complements national criminal jurisdictions and will only act if states are unwilling or unable to prosecute. The ICC can exercise jurisdiction with respect to the crimes of genocide, crimes against humanity and war crimes committed on or after 1 July 2002 by a national of a state party or in the territory of a state party. Definitions of these crimes are provided by the Statute and further elaborated by the Elements of Crimes. In the main, the court's procedures come from a mix of the civil and adversarial systems.

History
The UN first recognised the need for an international criminal court in 1948 and on 9 December 1948 the General Assembly of the United Nations adopted the Convention on the Prevention and Punishment of the Crime of Genocide. In the same resolution, the General Assembly invited the International Law Commission "to study the desirability and possibility of establishing an international judicial organ for the trial of persons charged with genocide." Between 1949 and 1954, the International Law Commission prepared several draft statutes for an ICC but differences of opinion forestalled further developments.

In 1989, in response to a request by Trinidad and Tobago, the United Nations General Assembly requested the International Law Commission (ILC) to resume work on an international criminal court with jurisdiction to include drug trafficking.

In 1993, The International Criminal Tribunal for the former Yugoslavia (ICTY) was established by Security Council resolution 827. The Tribunals authority is to prosecute and try four clusters of offences: grave breaches of the 1949 Geneva Conventions; violations of the laws or customs of war; genocide; and crimes against humanity committed on the territory of the former Yugoslavia since 1991.

In 1994, the United Nations Security Council established the International Criminal Tribunal for Rwanda (ICTR) by resolution 955 of 8 November 1994. This enabled the prosecution of persons responsible for genocide and other serious violations of international humanitarian law committed in the territory of Rwanda between 1 January 1994 and 31 December 1994 and Rwandan citizens responsible for the same violations in the territory of neighbouring States.

The International Criminal Court (ICC) was established by the Rome Statute of the International Criminal Court on 17 July 1998, when 120 States participating in the "United Nations Diplomatic Conference of Plenipotentiaries on the Establishment of an International Criminal Court" adopted the Statute. The Statute sets out the Court's jurisdiction, structure and functions. On 11 April 2002 the requisite number of nations ratified the Rome statute of 1998. The statute came into force on 1 July 2002. Anyone who commits any of the crimes under the Statute after this date will be liable for prosecution by the Court.

In November 2011, the ICC issued a warrant for the arrest of the former president of the Côte d'Ivoire, Laurent Gbagbo, on charges of crimes against humanity. He will be the first former head of state to be tried by the ICC. The ICC has issued only two other warrants for serving or former heads of state: President Omar al-Bashir of Sudan, who is still at large, and the late former Libyan leader Col. Muammar Gaddafi.

In March 2012, the ICC found the Congolese warlord, Thomas Lubanga, guilty of recruiting and using child soldiers between 2002 and 2003. It is the Court's first verdict. He was sentenced to 14 years.

As of 2013, 18 cases in 8 situations (Uganda, DRC, Darfur, CAR, Kenya, Libya, Cote d'Ivoire, Mali) have been brought before the ICC. The Office of the Prosecutor is currently conducting preliminary examinations including Afghanistan, Georgia, Guinea, Colombia, Honduras, Korea and Nigeria.

Structure
The Court is an independent institution. It is not part of the UN but has a co-operative relationship. The Court is composed of four organs: the Presidency; the Judicial Divisions; Office of the Prosecutor; and the Registry.

The Presidency is responsible for the overall administration of the Court. It is composed of three judges of the Court, elected by their fellow judges, for three years. The Judicial Divisions consist of 18 judges organised into the Pre-Trial Division, the Trial Division and the Appeals

Dividsion. The judges of each division sit in chambers whcih are responsible for conducting the proceeds of the court of different stages. The Office of the Prosecutor is responsible for receiving referrals on crimes within the jurisdiction of the Court, and for conducting investigations and prosecutions before the Court. The Office is headed by the Prosecutor, Luis Moreno Ocampo (Argentina). The Prosecutor is elected by the States Parties for a time of nine years. The Registry is responsible for the non-judicial aspects of the administration of the court. The Registry is headed by the Registrar who is the principal administrative office of the Court. The current registrar is Ms Silvania Arbia.

Member States
As of March 2013, 121 countries were State Parties to the Rome Statute. Only seven nations voted against the treaty in 1998: USA, China, Iraq, Libya, Yemen, Qatar and Israel. Although the USA did sign the treaty under President Clinton in 2000, President Bush was opposed to the treaty.

As of March 2013 the states that had ratified the treaty were: Afghanistan, Albania, Andorra, Antigua & Barbuda, Argentina, Australia, Austria, Bangladesh, Barbados, Belgium, Belize, Benin, Bolivia, Bosnia & Herzegovina, Botswana, Brazil, Bulgaria, Burkina Faso, Burundi, Cambodia, Canada, Cape Verde, Central African Republic, Chad, Chile, Colombia, Comoros, Congo, Cook Islands, Costa Rica, Croatia, Cyprus, Czech Republic, Dem. Rep. of the Congo, Denmark, Djibouti, Dominica, Dominican Republic, Ecuador, Estonia, Fiji, Finland, France, Gabon, Gambia, Georgia, Germany, Ghana, Greece, Grenada, Guatemala, Guinea, Guyana, Honduras, Hungary, Iceland, Ireland, Italy, Japan, Jordan, Kenya, Latvia, Lesotho, Liberia, Liechtenstein, Lithuania, Luxembourg, Madagascar, Malawi, Maldives, Mali, Malta, Marshall Islands, Mauritius, Mexico, Mongolia, Montenegro, Namibia, Nauru, Netherlands, New Zealand, Niger, Nigeria, Norway, Panama, Paraguay, Peru, Philippines, Poland, Portugal, Republic of Korea, Republic of Moldova, Romania, Samoa, San Marino, Senegal, Serbia, Seychelles, Sierra Leone, Slovakia, Slovenia, South Africa, Spain, St. Kitts and St. Nevis, St. Lucia, St.Vincent and the Grenadines, Suriname, Sweden, Switzerland, Tajikistan, the former Yugoslav Republic of Macedonia, Timor-Leste, Trinidad and Tobago, Tunisia, Uganda, United Kingdom of Great Britain and Northern Ireland, United Republic of Tanzania, Uruguay, Vanuatu, Venezuela and Zambia.

Funding
The International Criminal Court is funded by contributions made by States Parties, voluntary contributions from Governments, international organisations, individuals, corporations and other entities. The court is separate from the UN, however, in special circumstances, the UN could provide funds.

President: Judge Sang-Hyun Song (Republic of Korea) (page 1518)
First Vice-President: Sanji Mmasenono Monageng (Botswana)
Second Vice-President: Judge Cuno Tarfusser (Italy)

Judges of the Court
The judges of the Court are: Sang-Hyun Song (Republic of Korea), Sanji Mmasenono Monageng (Botswana), Cuno Tarfusser (Italy), Hans-Peter Kaul (Germany), Akua Kuenyehia (Ghana), Erkki Kourula (Finland), Anita Ušacka (Latvia), Ekaterina Trendafilova (Bulgaria), Joyce Aluoch (Kenya), Christine van den Wyngaert (Belgium), Silvia Alejandra Fernandez de Gurmendi (Argentina), Kuniko Ozaki (Japan), Miriam Defensor-Santiago (Philippines), Howard Morrison (United Kingdom), Anthony T. Carmona (Trinida and Tobago, Olaga Herrera Carbuccia (Dominican Republic), Robert Fremr (Czech Republic) and Chile Eboe-Osuji (Nigeria). The following judges are continuing in office to complete their trials: Judge Elizabeth Odio Benito (Costa Rica), Judge René Blattmann (Bolivia), Judge Fatoumata Dembele Diarra (Mali), Judge Sir Adrian Fulford (UK), Judge Svlvia Steiner (Brazil) and Judge Bruno Cotte (France).

Office of the Prosecutor
The Office of the Prosecutor is responsible for receiving referrals and any substantiated information on crimes within the Court's jurisdiction, examining them and for conducting investigations and prosecutions before the Court. The office is headed by the Prosecutor who is elected by the states parties for a term of nine years.
Prosecutor: Mrs Fatou Bensouda (The Gambia)

International Criminal Court, Maanweg - 174, 2516 AB The Hague, The Netherlands. Postal address: PO Box 19519, 2500 CM, Den Haag, The Netherlands. Tel: +31 (0)70 515 8515, fax: +31 (0)70 515 8555, URL: http://www.un.org/law/icc

INTERNATIONAL CRIMINAL TRIBUNAL FOR RWANDA

The Security Council created the International Criminal Tribunal for Rwanda (ICTR) by resolution 955 of 8 November 1994. The International Criminal Tribunal for Rwanda was established to prosecute persons responsible for genocide and other serious violations of international humanitarian law committed in Rwanda between 1 January 1994 and 31 December 1994. It may also deal with the prosecution of Rwandan citizens responsible for genocide and other such violations of international law committed in the territory of neighbouring States during the same period.

Its aim is to help the process of reconciliation and help maintain peace in the region. It hopes that through its work there will never be a repeat of genocide in Africa. Its work should ensure that all, even those in positions of high power, become accountable for their actions. The Tribunal's work is providing important precedents for the International Criminal Court and various national jurisdictions.

ICTR Law
The ICTR is governed by its Statute, which is annexed to Security Council Resolution 955. The Tribunal consists of three organs: the Chambers and the Appeals Chamber; the Office of the Prosecutor, in charge of investigations and prosecutions; and the Registry, responsible for providing overall judicial and administrative support to the Chambers and the Prosecutor. Some 77 nationalities are represented at the Tribunal (Arusha, Kigali, the Hague and New York).

Resources
For biennium 2010-2011, the General Assembly approved initial appropriations for ICTR of $245,295,800 gross and authorized 693 posts for 2010 and 628 posts for 2011. Expenditure in 2012-13 was forecast to be $188 million and income $175 million.

President: Khalida Rachid Khan (page 1456)

International Criminal Tribunal for Rwanda, Arusha International Criminal Conference Centre, PO Box 6016, Arusha, Tanzania. Tel: +255 27 250 27 4207-4211 / +1 212 963 2850, fax: +255 27 250 4000 / +1 212 963 2848, URL: http://www.ictr.org

INTERNATIONAL CRIMINAL TRIBUNAL FOR THE FORMER YUGOSLAVIA

Established in 1993, the International Criminal Tribunal for the former Yugoslavia (ICTY) is a United Nations court of law dealing with war crimes that took place during the conflicts in the Balkans in the 1990s. The ICTY was the first war crimes court created by the UN and the first international war crimes tribunal since the Nuremberg and Tokyo tribunals. It was established by the Security Council in accordance with Chapter VII of the UN Charter.

In its precedent-setting decisions on genocide, war crimes and crimes against humanity, the Tribunal has shown that an individual's senior position can no longer protect them from prosecution. Through its work, it has shown that those suspected of the greatest responsibility for atrocities committed can be called to account as individuals. By bringing perpetrators to trial, the ICTY aims to deter future crimes and bring justice to thousands of victims and their families. The final indictments were issued at the end of 2004. In 2011, the last remaining fugitives, Ratko Mladić and Goran Hadžić, were arrested and transferred to The Hague. None of the 161 individuals indicted by the Tribunal remain at large. At at March 2013, the Tribunal has concluded proceedings against 136 of the 161 individdals indicted by the Tribunal. Currently one indivdual is preparing for trial, 25 individuals have ongoing proceedings. Of the 126 proceedings that have concluded, 18 have been acquitted, 68 have been sentenced, 13 refered to a national jurisdiction, 20 have had their indictments withdrawn, and 16 are deceased.

The Tribunal remains impartial. It takes no side in the conflict and trials are determined on the basis of evidence presented.

The Tribunal will close when its work is completed. It is expected that four trials will conclude during 2013. The case of Radovan Karadzic is currently expected to finish in 2014 and the trials of Hadzic and Mladic in 2015 and 2016 respectively. There is also ongoing appellate work: judgements in the Perisic , Dordevic and Sainovic et al appeals cases will be delivered in 2013. The Popovic et al appeals case is expected to be completed by July 2014.

Structure
The ICTY is made up of three main branches: the Chambers, the Registry and the Office of the Prosecutor. The Chambers is made up of three Trial chambers and an Appeals Chamber. Each Trial Chamber is composed of three permanent judges and a maximum of six ad litem judges. Three judges are assigned to hear each case, and at least one judge per case must be a permanent judge. The Appeals Chamber consists of seven permanent Judges, five of whom are permanent judges of the ICTY and two of whom are permanent judges of the International Criminal Tribunal for Rwanda (ICTR). These seven judges also constitute the Appeals Chamber of the ICTR. Each appeal is heard and decided by a bench of five judges of the Appeals Chamber. The Tribunal's President and Vice-President are elected from among the ICTY judges.

The ICTY employs approximately 1,000 staff members representing some 80 nationalities.

President: Judge Theodor Meron (USA) (page 1476)
Vice-President: Judge Carmel Agius (Malta) (page 1372)
Prosecutor: Serge Brammertz (page 1393)

International Criminal Tribunal Yugoslavia, PO Box 13888, 2501 EW The Hague, The Netherlands. Tel: +31 (0)70 5128752, fax: +31 (0)70 512 5355, URL: http://www.icty.org/

INTERNATIONAL INSTITUTE ON AGEING

The Vienna International Plan of Action on Ageing, adopted by the World Assembly on Ageing in 1982 and endorsed by the United Nations General Assembly in its resolution 37/51, recommended, inter alia, the establishment of training institutes for the promotion of training and research, as well as the exchange of information and knowledge, to provide an international basis for social policies and action, especially in developing countries. Following its long-standing interest in international co-operation within the field of ageing, and in harmony with the spirit and objectives of the Vienna Plan of Action, the Maltese Government proposed that a United Nations International Institute on Ageing should be established in Malta to help developing countries prepare for the inevitable consequences of a dramatic increase in their elderly populations. As a result, the International Institute on Ageing (INIA) was established by resolution 1987/41 by the United Nations Economic and Social Council. On the 9th October, 1987, the United Nations signed an official agreement with the Government of Malta to establish the International Institute as an autonomous body under the auspices of the United Nations. The Institute was inaugurated on 15 April 1988 by the United Nations Secretary-General, His Excellency Mr Javier Pérez de Cuéllar.

Mandate
Its mandate is to empower less developed countries to cope with mass longevity and enable and train their own personnel to formulate and realise appropriate policies; to establish regional training centres in less developed countries; to provide continuing support to sustain both individual personnel and the centres by modern information technology; and to promote interactive networks and parternships to sustain these initiatives.

Objectives
The Institute's main objective is to fulfil the training needs of developing countries and to facilitate the implementation of the Vienna International Plan of Action on Ageing.

The Institute provides multi-disciplinary education and training in the following areas: Social Gerontology, Health and Longevity; Economic and Financial Aspects of Ageing, Medical Gerontology and the Demographic Aspects of Population Ageing. These programmes are oriented towards persons who hold positions as policy-makers, planners, programme executives, educators and professionals who work, or intend to work, in the field of Ageing or with older persons.

The training programmes are reinforced by the Institute's other activities, these being: data collection, documentation, information exchange and technical co-operation, as well as research and publications.

International Activities
The Collaborating Network of International Organisations is an initiative undertaken by INIA in 1989 to facilitate the exchange of information on the issue of Ageing and thus fulfil its role as a bridge between and among developed and developing countries.
Collaborating Agreements: in accordance with the Agreement signed between the United Nations and the Government of Malta, INIA has developed arrangements for active and close co-operation with UN specialised agencies and other organisations and institutions.

Research
A study to assess the prevalence of Dementia across different countries and cultures was carried out on the initiative of the Research programme on Ageing of WHO based in Maryland, USA. Malta was one of the countries engaged in the study, with the particular advantage that its sample was representative of the entire elderly Malta population. Other countries involved were Canada, Chile, Nigeria, Spain and USA. The INIA conducted the Malta study.

Finance
The Institute's major source of funding derives from the Malta Government and the United Nations Population Fund (UNFPA). INIA has also received grants from the Merck Institute of Ageing and Health, Washington. These funds support the educational activities of Fellows from developing countries attending the short-term programmes as well as students participating in the nine-month Postgraduate Diploma Course in Gerontology and Geriatrics at the University of Malta.

Structure
The Institute is an independent organisation under the auspices of the United Nations. Its activities are guided by an international Board of Governors, currently composed of ten members: a chairperson and seven members (with due regard to the principle of equitable geographical distribution) appointed by the Secretary-General of the United Nations, and two members appointed by the Government of Malta. The Director is appointed by the Government of Malta after consultation with the UN Secretary-General.

Publications
Journal BOLD (4 issues per year in English); Proceedings of Expert Group Meetings on: Long-Term Training in Gerontology and Geriatrics; Short-term training in Social Gerontology; Short-term Training in Income Security for the Elderly in Developing Countries and Short-term Training in Geriatrics and An Ageing World; Short-term training in Demographic Aspects of Ageing; Short-term training in Physical and Occupational Therapy for Older Persons. Proceedings of conferences and other meetings organised by the Institute. In a joint project with CICRED (France), INIA has published 20 country monographs on population ageing. INIA's Documentation Centre is a depository of documents, publications and audio-visual material related to ageing.

Director: Professor Joseph Troisi
Chair, International Board: Mr Sha Zukang, Under Sec.-Gen., Department of Economic & Social Afffairs, UN

International Institute on Ageing (United Nations - Malta), 117 St. Paul Street, Valletta, VLT07, Malta. Tel: +356 21 243044/5/6, fax: +356 21 230248, e-mail: info@inia.org.mt, URL: http://www.inia.org.mt

INTERNATIONAL SEABED AUTHORITY

The International Seabed Authority ("the Authority") formally came into existence on 16 November 1994 upon the entry into force of the 1982 United Nations Convention on the Law of the Sea ("the Convention") and became fully operational in 1996. It is an autonomous international organisation. The Authority is the organisation through which its members, that are the parties to the Convention, organize and control activities in the Area, particularly with a view to administering the mineral resources of the Area. The Area means the seabed and ocean floor and subsoil thereof, beyond the limits of national jurisdiction.

Structure
The supreme organ is the Assembly which has the power to establish policies and is made up of all ISA members. Members are all parties to the Law of the Sea Convention. As of January 2013 there were 165 members. The Assembly also elects the members of the the

Authority's Council and other bodies, also the Secretary-General. It sets the two-year budgets and approves any rules, regulations and procedures. Other organs of the Authority are the Legal and Technical Commission, the Finance Committee and the Secretariat.

The office of the Secretary-General (OSG) co-ordinates and supervises the work of the Secretariat. It also keeps a list of Permanent Representatives and persons accredited to the Authority.

Secretary General: Nii A. Odunton (Ghana) (page 1488)

International Seabed Authority, 14-20 Port Royal Street, Kingston, Jamaica. Tel: +1 876 922 9105, fax: +1 876 922 0195, URL: http://www.isa.org.jm

INTERNATIONAL TRADE CENTRE (ITC)

The International Trade Centre (ITC) is the joint agency of the World Trade Organization and the United Nations. ITC enables small and medium enterprises in developing countries to become more competitive in global markets, leading to inclusive, sustainable economic development and contributing to the achievement of the Millennium Development Goals.

Set up in 1964, ITC's strategic objectives are to strengthen the international competitiveness of private sector enterprises, develop the capacity of trade service providers to support businesses, and support policymakers in integrating the business sector into the global economy.

ITC is headed by an Executive Director who reports to the Secretary General of the United Nations Conference on Trade and Development and to the Director General of the WTO. The Senior Managment Committee is made up of the two executive officers and the heads of I TCs' four divisions (Market Development; Country Programmes; Programme Support; Business and Institutional Support)

Executive Director: Patricia Francis (page 1426)

International Trade Centre (ITC), Palais des Nations, 1211 Geneva 10, Switzerland. Tel: +41 (0)22 730 0111, fax: +41 (0)22 733 4439, URL: http://www.intracen.org/

INTERNATIONAL UNION FOR THE PROTECTION OF NEW VARIETIES OF PLANTS (UPOV)

Established in 1961, the International Union for the Protection of New Varieties of Plants (UPOV) is an intergovernmental organisation whose object is to provide an internationally harmonized system of intellectual property rights of plant breeders. The mission of UPOV is to provide and promote an effective system of plant variety protection, with the aim of encouraging the development of new varieties of plants, for the benefit of society.

Activities
On the basis of the International Convention for the Protection of New Varieties of Plants, exclusive property rights may be granted to breeders of new varieties of plants. To be eligible for this protection, varieties have to be: distinct from existing, commonly known varieties; sufficiently uniform; stable; and new in the sense that they must not have been commercialised prior to certain dates.

UPOV promotes international harmonisation and co-operation between members on legal and technical aspects of the protection of new varieties of plants, and assists countries and certain intergovernmental organisations in the introduction of plant variety protection legislation.

The Union maintains close contacts with a number of IGOs and NGOs with interests in the field of plant variety protection and related areas.

Membership
As of March 2013 there were 71 members: Albania, Argentina, Australia, Austria, Azerbaijan, Belarus, Belgium, Bolivia, Brazil, Bulgaria, Canada, Chile, China, Colombia, Costa Rica, Croatia, Czech Republic, Denmark, Dominican Republic, Ecuador, Estonia, European Union, Finland, France, Georgia, Germany, Hungary, Iceland, Ireland, Israel, Italy, Japan, Jordan, Kenya, Kyrgyzstan, Latvia, Lithuania, Mexico, Morocco, Netherlands, New Zealand, Nicaragua, Norway, Oman, Panama, Paraguay, Peru, Poland, Portugal, Republic of Korea, Republic of Moldova, Romania, Russian Federation, Serbia, Singapore, Slovakia, Slovenia, South Africa, Spain, Sweden, Switzerland, The former Yugoslav Republic of Macedonia, Trinidad and Tobago, Tunisia, Turkey, Ukraine, United Kingdom, United States of America, Uruguay, Uzbekistan and Vietnam.

Secretary General: Francis Gurry (page 1435)

International Union for the Protection of New Varieties of Plants (UPOV), 34 Chemin des Colombettes, CH-1211 Geneva 20, Switzerland. Tel: +41 (0)22 338 9111, fax: +41 (0)22 733 0336, e-mail: upov.mail@upov.int, URL: http://www.upov.int

IUCN (INTERNATIONAL UNION FOR CONSERVATION OF NATURE)

Founded in 1948 at an international conference sponsored by UNESCO and the French Government at Fontainebleau, France, IUCN is an independent union of sovereign states, government agencies and non-governmental organisations. Its mission is to influence, encourage and assist societies throughout the world to conserve the integrity and diversity of nature and to ensure that any use of natural resources is equitable and ecologically sustainable.

The IUCN was originally known as the International Union for the Protection of Nature (IUPN). It changed its name in1956 to the International Union for Conservation of Nature and Natural Resources in 1956. The use of the name 'World Conservation Union', in conjunction with IUCN, began in 1990. From March 2008 this name is no longer commonly used.

Aims
To monitor the state of the planet's living resources - the plants, animals and ecosystems on which the survival and wellbeing of humanity depend; to determine scientific priorities for conservation action; to mobilise scientific and professional resources to investigate the most serious conservation problems and recommend solutions to them; to develop, within a coherent global strategy, programmes of action to protect, sustain and use rationally the most important and threatened species and ecosystems; to assist governments and other bodies to devise, initiate and carry out projects for the conservation of wild living resources.

Membership
IUCN currently has over 1,200 member organizations in 140 countries, including more than 200 government and 900 non-government organizations. There are approximately 11,000 voluntary scientists and experts, grouped into six Commissions.

The 92 state members of the IUCN are:
Algeria, Angola, Argentina, Australia, Bangladesh, Belgium, Benin, Bhutan, Botswana, Burkina Faso, Cameroon, Canada, Central African Republic, China, Democratic Republic of Congo, Republic of Congo, Costa Rica, Côte d'Ivoire, Cyprus, Czech Republic, Denmark, Ecuador, Egypt, El Salvador, Equatorial Guinea, Estonia, Fiji, Finland, France, Georgia, Germany, Greece, Guinea, Guinea-Bissau, Iceland, India, Iran, Iraq, Ireland, Italy, Japan, Jordan, Kenya, Korea (RK), Kuwait, Lao People's Democratic Republic, Lesotho, Liberia, Liechtenstein, Luxembourg, Madagascar, Malaysia, Mali, Mauritania, Mauritius, Mexico, Monaco, Morocco, Nauru, Nepal, Netherlands, New Zealand, Niger, Nigeria, Norway, Oman, Pakistan, Panama, Peru, Portugal, Russia, Rwanda, Samoa, Saudi Arabia, Senegal, Seychelles, Solomon Islands, South Africa, Spain, Sri Lanka, Swaziland, Sweden, Switzerland, Thailand, Tonga, Tunisia, Turkey, Uganda, United Kingdom, United States of America, Vanuatu, Vietnam, Zambia.

Function
The members, commissions, scientists and associated professionals provide the authoritative information and advice on which IUCN bases its programmes. IUCN monitors the status of threatened species, protected areas and areas in need of protection, major actual or impending ecological changes and their causes and consequences, and major issues regarding the management of natural resources. Essential information is published in key source documents, notably the IUCN Red List of Threatened Species (describing all threatened species of mammals, amphibians and reptiles, fish, plants, and invertebrates) and the United Nations List of National Parks and Protected Areas. No other organisation monitors the status of species and ecosystems on a global basis, and the IUCN Red List of Threatened Species and the UN List of National Parks and Protected Areas are the only authoritative sources of comprehensive information on the status of threatened species and protected ecosystems throughout the world.

IUCN Global Programme 2013-16
The Global Programme with developed and approved by IUCN member organizations every four years. The programme for 2013-16 has three priority areas of work: Valuing and Conserving Nature; Effective and Equitable Governance of Nature's Use; Deploying Nature-based Solutions to Global Challenges in Climate, Food and Development.

Partnerships
IUCN has formal working relations with a wide range of intergovernmental and international organisations and works especially closely with UNEP, FAO, and UNESCO. Many of IUCN's activities aim to improve the effectiveness of international environmental Conventions, including the Convention on Biological Diversity, the Ramsar Convention on Wetlands of International Importance, and the United Nations Framework Convention on Climate Change.

IUCN has special relationships with the Council of Europe, the Organization of African Unity, and the Organization of American States, and with the following non-governmental organisations: International Association on Water Pollution Research, International Council for Bird Preservation, International Council of Scientific Unions, International Geographical Union, International Union of Forestry Research Organizations, International Youth Federation for Environmental Studies and Conservation, World Society for the Protection of Animals, and World Wildlife Fund.

It has official Observer Status at the UN General Assembly.

Expenditures and Financial Support
Total income was projected to be CHF121 million in 2012, compared to CHF 142 million in 2008. The total financial plan for the 2013-16 Programme is projected to be CHF 512 million (i.e an average of CHF 128 million per year, with annual increases in the range of 3-4 per cent. Of this, CHF 47 million is expected to come from membership dues, CHF 359 million from governments and mulitaterals; and CHF 16 million from non-goverment organizations. Breakdown by IUCN Progamme Area is: valuing and conserving nature CHF 120 million; effective and equitable governance of nature's use CHF 90 million; and deploying nature-based solutions to global challenges CHF 185 million.

Structure
IUCN consists of: (a) the President; (b) the World Conservation Congress; (c) the Council; (d) the IUCN member committees; (e) the Commissions and (f) the Secretariat.

World Conservation Congress
The World Conservation Congress is the world's largest and most diverse conservation event. Held every four years, the Congress aims to improve how we manage our natural environment for human, social and economic development.

Bureau
Consist of the President as Chair, the Treasurer, one Commission Chair, four other Councillors each from different Regions and the Chairs of the Programme and Policy Committee and the Finance and Audit Committee.

Council
Members of the Union elect the Council every four years at the World Conservation Congress. The 2012-16 Council is made up of: a President, four vice-presidents (elected by Council) a Treasurer, the Chairs of the six Commissions, three Regional Councillors from each of the eight Statutory Regions, and a councillor from the State in which IUCN has its seat (Switzerland). The Council functions in a similar way to a Board of Directors, meeting once or twice a year to direct Union policy, approve finances and decide on strategy. The Council may appoint up to six additional Councillors.

IUCN Council President: Zhang Xinsheng (China)

Member Committees
Member organisations participate in national and regional committees. These committees coordinate conservation action and policy at the national or regional level and play an important role in the development of the global IUCN Programme, as well as its governance through the World Conservation Congress.

Commissions
IUCN maintains a global network of more than 10,000 scientists and professionals organised into six commissions:

Education and Communication Commission (CEC): champions the strategic use of communication and education to empower and educate stakeholders for the sustainable use of natural resources. Members: 600. Chair: Juliane Ziedler (Germany) http://www.iucn.org/cec/

Environmental Law Commission (CEL): advances environmental law by developing new legal concepts and instruments, and by building the capacity of societies to employ environmental law for conservation and sustainable development. Members: 500.Chair: Antonio Herman Benjamin (Brazil)http://www.iucn.org/about/union/commissions/cel/ **Commission on Environmental, Economic and Social Policy (CEESP):** provides expertise and policy advice on economic and social factors for the conservation and sustainable use of biological diversity. Members: 500. Chair: Aroha Te Pareake Mead (New Zealand)http://www.iucn.org/about/union/commissions/ceesp/

World Commission on Protected Areas (WCPA): promotes the establishment and effective management of a worldwide representative network of terrestrial and marine protected areas. Members: 1,300. Chair: Ernesto Hoeflich (Mexico)http://www.iucn.org/about/union/commissions/wcpa/

Species Survival Commission (SSC): advises the Union on the technical aspects of species conservation and mobilizes action for those species that are threatened with extinction. Members: 7,500. Chair: Dr Simon Stuart (UK) http://www.iucn.org/

Commission on Ecosystem Management (CEM): provides expert guidance on integrated ecosystem approaches to the management of natural and modified ecosystems. Members: 400. Chair: Piet Wit (Netherlands) http://www.iucn.org/about/union/commissions/cem/

Director General: Julia Marton-Lefèvre (page 1472)

IUCN (International Union for Conservation of Nature), Rue de Mauverney 28, 1196 Gland, Switzerland. Tel: +41 (0)22 999 0000, fax: +41 (0)22 999 0002, URL: http://www.iucn.org

IUCN Environmental Law Centre, Godesbergeralle 108-112, 53175 Bonn, Germany. Tel: +49 (0)228 269 2231, fax: +49 (0)228 269 2250, e-mail: ELCSecretariat@iucn.org

OFFICE OF THE UNITED NATIONS HIGH COMMISSIONER FOR HUMAN RIGHTS (OHCHR)

The Office of the United Nations High Commissioner for Human Rights (OHCHR) has a unique mandate to promote and protect all human rights. At the World Conference on Human Rights in 1993, the international community decided, as stated in the Vienna Declaration and Programme of Action, to establish a robust human rights mandate with stronger institutional support. Accordingly, the General Assembly (Resolution 48/141) in December 1993 established the position of the High Commissioner for Human Rights to spearhead the United Nations' human rights efforts. OHCHR offers leadership, works objectively, educates and takes action to empower individuals and assist States in upholding human rights. OHCHR, a part of the United Nations Secretariat, is headquartered in Geneva.

Through its unique access, OHCHR works with Governments to help promote and implement human rights worldwide. It also assists other entities with responsibility to protect human rights to fulfil their obligations, and speaks out objectively in the face of human rights violations. OHCHR is tasked with injecting a human rights perspective into all United Nations programmes in order to ensure that peace and security, development, and human rights - the three pillars of the United Nations system - are interlinked and mutually reinforcing. This human rights mainstreaming task is essential at a time when the United Nations is undergoing its most far-reaching reform as a follow up to the World Summit of September 2005.

In carrying out its mission, OHCHR:
- Gives priority to addressing the most pressing human rights violations, both acute and chronic, particularly those that put life in imminent peril;
- Focuses attention on those who are at risk and vulnerable on multiple fronts;
- Pays equal attention to the realization of civil, cultural, economic, political, and social rights, including the right to development; and
- Measures the impact of its work through the substantive benefit that is accrued, through it, to individuals around the world.

OHCHR Plan of Action and its Strategic Management Plan 2012-2013
OHCHR is committed to becoming a results-based organization. In accordance with this, OHCHR has translated its mandate into eleven identifiable changes. The Global Expected Accomplishjments relate to three types of changes: changes in national human rights protection systems; changes in the international human rights protection systems; and changes in the involvement of other actors in human rights work.

Structure
The High Commissioner is appointed by the Secretary General with the approval of the General Assembly, for a fixed term of four years with the possibility of renewal for a further term of four years. The High Commissioner heads the Office of the High Commissioner for Human Rights and is assisted by a Deputy High Commissioner.

OHCHR has its headquarters in Geneva, an office at the United Nations in New York and field presences in over 40 countries and regions. In addition to the Executive Office of the High Commissioner and a number of units that report to the Deputy High Commissioner,

OHCHR has four substantive divisions: the Human Rights Council and Treaties Division, the Special Procedures Division, the Field Operations and Technical Cooperation Division, and the Research and Right to Development Division.

In addition to their other functions, the four divisions provide substantive, secretariat, and research support to: the Human Rights Council, which has replaced the 60-year-old United Nations Commission on Human Rights since June 2006 as the key United Nations intergovernmental body responsible for human rights; its independent experts on different thematic or country mandates (special rapporteurs); various working groups; four human rights voluntary trust funds; and the expert treaty bodies.

The treaty bodies refer to the current eight expert committees mandated to monitor implementation of the core international human rights treaties. They include: Human Rights Committee (HRC); Committee on Economic, Social and Cultural Rights (CESCR); Committee on the Elimination of Racial Discrimination (CERD); Committee on the Elimination of Discrimination against Women (CEDAW); Committee against Torture (CAT); Committee on the Rights of the Child (CRC); Committee on Migrant Workers (CMW); and the Committee on the Rights of Persons with Disabilities (CRPD).

OHCHR's method of work focuses on three major dimensions: standard-setting, monitoring, and implementation. In recent years, OHCHR has strengthened its efforts in ensuring the implementation of international human rights standards on the ground through greater country engagement and its field presences. OHCHR has also increased its presence in the field, reaching out to the people who need it the most. OHCHR field offices and presences play an essential role in identifying, highlighting, and developing responses to human rights challenges, in close collaboration with governments, the United Nations system, non-governmental organizations, and members of civil society.

Staffing and Funding
To implement its comprehensive mandate, OHCHR employs some 990 staff, based in New York, 12 country offices and 12 regional offices around the world. Two new country offices were established in 2010 in Guinea and Mauritania, and mandates were extended in Bolivia, Columbia and Nepal. More than 400 staff are based at Geneva Headquarters. OHCHR is funded from the United Nations regular budget and from voluntary contributions. Regular budget funding amounted to US$141.4 million in 2010-2011. Additional funding comes from voluntary donors. In 2010 voluntary contributions fell to US$109 million, down from US$118 million in 2009. The top three voluntary contributors in this period were the US, Norway and the Netherlands.

UN High Commissioner: Ms Navanethem Pillay (page 1495)

Office of the United Nations High Commissioner for Human Rights (OHCHR), 1211 Geneva 10, Switzerland. Tel: +41 (0)22 917 9000, fax: +41 (0)22 917 9008, e-mail: InfoDesk@ohchr.org, URL: http://www.ohchr.org

ORGANISATION FOR THE PROHIBITION OF CHEMICAL WEAPONS (OPCW)

The mission of the Organisation for the Prohibition of Chemical Weapons (OPCW) is to implement the provisions of the Chemical Weapons Convention in order to achieve a world free of chemical weapons and, in so doing, contribute to international security and stability, complete disarmament and economic development and promote the peaceful uses of chemistry.

The Chemical Weapons Convention (CWC) was opened for signature in Paris on 13 January 1993. As at March 2013, it has been ratified or acceded to by 188 States that have deposited their instruments of ratification or accession with the United Nations Secretary-General. It is the first disarmament agreement negotiated within a multilateral framework that provides for the elimination of an entire category of weapons of mass destruction under a stringent verification regime. It also recognises the prohibition of the use of herbicides as a method of warfare.

The CWC succeeds the Geneva Protocol of 1925 (a reaction to the 91,000 chemical weapon fatalities of the First World War) which prohibited the use of chemical and biological weapons in war and the Biological Weapons Convention of 1972 which outlawed biological and toxin weapons and required their destruction.

The basic obligations under the Chemical Weapons Convention are contained in Article I of the Convention and are, in brief:
1. Each State Party undertakes never to: develop, produce, stockpile or retain chemical weapons, or transfer chemical weapons to anyone; use chemical weapons; engage in any military preparations to use chemical weapons.
2. Each State Party undertakes to destroy chemical weapons it owns or that are located within its jurisdiction.
3. Each State Party undertakes to destroy all chemical weapons it abandoned on the territory of another State Party.
4. Each States Party undertakes to destroy any chemical weapons production facilities it owns or that are located under its jurisdiction.
5. Each State Party undertakes not to use riot control agents as a method or warfare.

Function
The principal functions of the OPCW in implementing the Convention are:

- to ensure a credible regime to verify the destruction of chemical weapons and prevent their re-emergence, whilst protecting legitimate national security and proprietary interests;
- to provide protection and assistance against the threat or use of chemical weapons;
- to encourage international co-operation in the peaceful uses of chemistry.

Two fundamental principles underline the approach of the OPCW: the centrality of the Convention's multilateral character and the non-discriminatory and equal application of the provisions of the Convention to all States Parties.

Structure
The OPCW is an independent, autonomous international organisation with a working relationship with the UN.

The **Conference of the States Parties** is the principal organ of the Organisation. Composed of all Member States of the OPCW, it meets in regular annual sessions, though special sessions can also be convened including Review Conferences, which are held every five years.

The **Executive Council** is the executive organ of the organisation and is composed of 41 representatives elected for two-year terms from among the Member States. Allocation of seats is based on geographical quotas to ensure equitable geographical distribution, as follows:
Africa - 9 seats, Asia - 9 seats, Eastern Europe - 5, Latin America and the Caribbean - 7 seats, Western European and other States - 10. In addition 1 seat is designated consecutively by the regions of Asia and Latin America and the Caribbean.

Due regard is also paid to the importance of the chemical industry and to political and security interests of the regions.

The **Technical Secretariat** has the primary responsibility for carrying out the activities mandated by the Convention. These include carrying out verification activities, providing assistance if chemical weapons are used, supporting the Conference and the Executive Council and communicating on behalf of the OPCW. The Director-General is the head and chief administrative officer of the Technical Secretariat. The post is for a term of four years and renewable only once.

The **Scientific Advisory Board** provides specialised advice in the areas of science and technology. It consists of independent experts.

OPCW Inspectors play a very significant role in the implementation of the verification regime of the Convention. The routine monitoring regime involves submission by States Parties of initial and annual declarations to the OPCW, initial visits and systematic inspections of declared chemical weapons storage, production and destruction facilities. Routine verification also applies to chemical industry facilities that produce, process or consume chemicals listed in the three Schedules of the Convention. The regime of challenge inspections allows each State Party to have an inspection conducted at any facility or location without right of refusal, at short notice, in order to clarify and resolve questions of possible non-compliance.

Every Member State must implement the provisions under the Chemical Weapons Convention at the national level. Each Member State is obliged to provide other Member States with its fullest cooperation to expedite prosecution.

The budget in 2013 was €69.8 million.

For membership details, please consult the matrix of *Country Membership of International Organisations* in the preliminary section. As of March 2013, there were 188 member states.

Director-General: Ahmet Üzümcü (Turkey)

Organization for the Prohibition of Chemical Weapons, Johan de Wittlaan 32, 2517 JR, The Hague, Netherlands. Tel: +31 (0)70 416 3300, fax: +31 (0)70 306 3535, e-mail: media@opcw.org, inquiries@opcw.org, URL: http://www.opcw.org

PREPARATORY COMMISSION FOR THE COMPREHENSIVE NUCLEAR-TEST-BAN TREATY ORGANIZATION (CTBTO)

The Preparatory Commission for the Comprehensive Nuclear-Test-Ban Treaty Organization (CTBTO) is an international organisation established by the States Signatories to the Treaty on 19 November 1996. It carries out the necessary preparations for the effective implementation of the Comprehensive Nuclear-Test-Ban Treaty, and prepares for the first session of the Conference of the States Parties to the Treaty.

The Commission's main task is the establishment of the International Monitoring System and the International Data Centre as well as the development of operational manuals.

The Treaty
The Comprehensive Nuclear-Test-Ban Treaty (CTBT) is an important part of the international regime for the non-proliferation of nuclear weapons and an essential foundation for the pursuit of nuclear disarmament. Its total ban of any nuclear weapon test explosion in any environment will constrain the development and improvement of existing nuclear weapons and halt the development of advanced new types of these weapons.

Following in the path of the Partial Test Ban Treaty (1963) and the Non-proliferation Treaty (1968), the CTBT was adopted by the United Nations General Assembly, and opened for signature in September 1996. 183 countries have signed the Treaty, of which 159 have also ratified it (as of April 2013), including three of the nuclear weapon States: France, the Russian

Federation and the United Kingdom. The latest state to ratify was Chad on 8 February 20132. However 44 specific nuclear technology holder countries must sign and ratify before the CTBT can enter into force. Of these, eight are missing: China, Egypt, India, Iran, Israel, North Korea, Pakistan and the USA. India, North Korea and Pakistan have yet to sign the CTBT.

Membership
There are currently 183 Member States (159 ratifications). Six international organisations are accredited to the Preparatory Commission: UN, IAEA (International Atomic Energy Agency), ITU (International Telecommunications Union), OPCW (Organization for the Prohibition of Chemical Weapons), WHO (World Health Organization) and WMO (World Meteorological Organization). Member States oversee the work of the Preparatory Commission and fund its activities.

Organisation Structure
There are two main organs, the plenary body and the Provisional Technical Secretariat.

The plenary body, also known as the Preparatory Commission, is composed of all the States Signatories and has three subsidiary groups: Working Group A deals with budgetary and administrative matters including legal issues; Working Group B examines verification issues and the Advisory Group advises on financial and associated administration matters. This group is composed of experts from the States Signatories with recognised standing and experience in international financial matters. Working Groups A and B make proposals and recommendations for consideration and adoption by the Preparatory Commission.

With a staff of approximately 260 drawn from State Signatories, the Provisional Technical Secretariat (PTS) assists the Commission to carry out such functions as the Commission determines, including the verification activities listed in the Treaty.

The annual budget is around US120,000,000 (€82,000,000).

For membership details, please consult the matrix of *Country Membership of International Organisations* in the preliminary section.

Executive Secretary of the Preparatory Commission and Head Administrative Officer of PTS: Mr Tibor Toth (Hungary) (page 1527)

CTBTO Preparatory Commission, Vienna International Centre, PO Box 1200, A-1400 Vienna, Austria. Tel: +43 (0)1 26030 6200, fax: +43 (0)1 26030 5823, e-mail: info@ctbto.org, URL: http://www.ctbto.org

SECRETARIAT FOR THE CONVENTION ON THE RIGHTS OF PERSONS WITH DISABILITIES (SCRPD)

SCRPD (United Nations Enable) works to advance the rights of persons with disabilities in society and development through various human rights and development instruments including: World Programme of Action concerning Disabled Persons (1982), the Standard Rules on Equalization of Opportunities for Persons with Disabilities (1994) and the Convention on the Rights of Persons with Disabilities (2006).

Within the UN it focuses its work on: supporting inter-governmental bodies such as the General Assembly; servicing the Conference of States Parties to the Convention on the Rights of Persons with Disabilities; implementing international norms; technical co-operation and supporting the Millennium Development goals.

As of April 2013, there were 130 ratifications/accessions to the Convention and 155 signatures. Most recently, Singapore signed the Convention on 30 November 2012. Iraq ratified the Convention on 20 March 2013, Barbados on 27 February 2013 and Albania on 11 February 2013.

During the 67th Session of the General Assembly, the UN adopted three resolutions on disability:

-Status of the Convention on the Rights of Persons with Disabilities and the Optional Protocol thereto
-Realizing the Millennium Development Goals and other internationally agreed development goals for persons with disabilities towards 2015 and beyond
-Addressing Socio-Economic Needs of Individuals, Families and Societies affected by Autism Spectrum Disorders (ASD), Developmental Disorders (DD) and associated disabilities

SCRPD promotes and supports partnerships among governments, UN organisations, academic institutions and other organziations of persons with disabilities in particular.

The UN has designated 3 December as the International Day of Persons with Disabilities. The theme for 2012 is: Removing barriers to create an inclusive and accesible society for all.

United Nations Enable, Secretariat for the Convention on the Rights of Persons with Disabilities, Department of Economic and Social Affairs, United Nations, S-2906, New York, NY 10017, USA. Fax: +1 212 367 5102, e-mail: enable@un.org, URL: http//www.un.org/disabilities

UNAIDS

Established in 1994 by a resolution of the UN Economic and Social Council and launched in January 1996, UNAIDS' mission is to lead and inspire the world in achieving universal access to HIV prevention, treatment, care and support. Its goal is a world with no new HIV infections, no discrimination and no AIDS-related deaths.

UNAIDS has five goals:
- Leadership and advocacy for effective action on the epidemic
- Providing strategic information and policies to guide effortsin the AIDS response worldwide
-Tracking, monitoring and evaluation of the epidemic & to become the world's leading resource for AIDS-related data and analysis
- Development of strategic partnerships
- Mobilize resources to support an effective response.

In 2006 a Political Declaration on HIV/AIDS was adopted unanimously by UN Member States at the close of the United Nations General Assembly 2006 High Level Meeting on AIDS. It provides a strong mandate to help move the AIDS response forward and reaffirmed the 2001 Declaration of Commitment and the Millennium Development Goals, in particular the goal to halt and begin to reverse the spread of AIDS by 2015.

A new Political Declaration was issued in 2011. Its targets and elimination commitments are: to achieve universal access to HIV prevention, treatment, care and support by 2015; to reduce sexual transmission; prevent HIV among drug users; to eliminate new HIV infections

among children; to avoid TB deaths; to close the resource gap; to eliminate gender inequalities; to eliminate stigma and discrimination; to eliminate travel restrictions; to strengthen HIV integration.

In 2010, UNAIDS estimated that more than 34 million people were living with HIV, including more than 2.5 million children aged under 15 years. An estimated 2.6 million people were newly infected with HIV/AIDS in 2009, down from 3.1 million in 1999. In 2011, there were 1.7 million AIDS-related deaths, lower than the 2.3 million in 2005.

UNAIDS Co-Sponsors
UNAIDS co-sponsors are: UNHCR, UNICEF, WFP, UNDP, UNFPA, UNODC, ILO, UNESCO, WHO and the World Bank. The co-sponsors and the UNAIDS Secretariat make up the Committee of Cosponsoring Organisations which meets annually. UNAIDS is supported by voluntary contributions from governments, foundations, corporations, private groups and individuals.

Executive Director: Michel Sidibe, Under-Secretary General of the UN (page 1514)

UNAIDS Secretariat, 20 Avenue Appia, CH-1211 Geneva 27, Switzerland. Tel: +41 (0) 22 791 3666, fax: +41 (0)22 791 4187, URL: http://www.unaids.org

UNITED NATIONS CAPITAL DEVELOPMENT FUND (UNCDF)

UNCDF is the UN's capital investment agency for the world's least developed countries. It increases access to investment capital and finance and aims to promote sustainable growth for all.

Mandate
Its mandate from the UN General Assembly (1966) is to 'assist developing countries in the development of their economies by supplementing existing sources of capital assistance by means of grants and loans'. The mandate was amended in 1974 to focus on the least developed among the developing countries.

To fulfill its mandate UNCDF uses both public and private financing mechanisms. Within the public sector it supports decentralization and strong financial management within the systems, with the aim of more effective allocation of public resources, more responsive governments

and better public investment to improve quality of life and sustainable economic growth. Within the private sector it works to ensure that financial services reach both small businesses and the poor.

Structure
UNCDF is an autonomous voluntarily funded UN organization, affiliated with UNDP. The executive Board of UNDP serve as UNCDF's executive board. The board meets three time a year and is made up of 36 member states from regional groupings. The executive board is under the authority of the Economic and Social Council, and ultimately the General Assembly of the UN. The UNDP administrator also acts as UNCDF's managing director. Management of UNCDF is mostly delegated to an executive director.

It is based in New York, with three regional offices and over 35 country programme offices, most of which are co-located with UNDP.

Funding
Funding comes from UN member states, foundations and the private secor. UNCDF raises its own funding and income is approximately $60 million per year.

Executive Secretary: Marc Biechler

UN Capital Development Fund (UNCDF), 2 UN Plaza, New York, NY 10017, USA. Tel: +1 212 906 6565, fax: +1 212 906 6479, e-mail: info@uncdf.org, URL: http://www.uncdf.org

UNITED NATIONS CHILDREN'S FUND (UNICEF)

UNICEF is the leading organization in the world focusing on children and the rights of children. It works with local communities, partners and governments in more than 190 countries across to world to ensure that the rights of children are upheld.

The United Nations Children's Fund was created by a resolution of the United Nations General Assembly (Resolution 57(1), 11 December 1946) as a temporary agency to aid the children of war-devastated Europe. In 1950 the General Assembly changed UNICEF's mandate in order to respond to the needs of children throughout the world. UNICEF became a permanent branch of the UN system in 1953, receiving the Nobel Peace Prize in 1965.

UNICEF's ultimate goal is for all children to enjoy the basic rights set out in the Convention on the Rights of the Child (concerning children's rights to survival, development, protection and participation regardless of race, sex, creed or social standing) which was adopted unanimously by the UN General Assembly on 20 November 1989. Less than 10 months after its adoption, the Convention entered into force as the required 20 states had ratified it and incorporated it into their national legislation. The Convention has now been ratified by nearly every country in the world.

Focus Areas
The priority areas are:
Child Development and Survival: UNICEF believes every child has the right to survive and it works to end preventable child deaths. Although child mortality has fallen by 35 per cent across the globe over the last 20 years, in 2010, over 7.5 million children died before reaching the age of five.

Basic Education and Gender Equality: Every child regardless of gender, ethnicity or social situation, has the right to free, compulsory, quality education. UNICEF supports programmes targeted at the world's most vulnerable children including girls, the poor, victims of conflict, the disabled and those affected by HIV/AIDs.

HIV/AIDS and children: UNICEF focuses on prevention of mother-to-child transmissions; providing treatment and care; preventing infection among young people; protecting and supporting children affected by HIV and AIDS.

Child Protection: All children have the right to be protected from violence, abuse and exploitation. UNICEF works to improve the protection of children in various ways including the improvement of child protection systems, and promotion of positive social norms.

Policy Advocacy and Partnerships: UNICEF focuses on child poverty, inequalities, social protection, migration and social budgeting. UNICEF works to ensure that the rights of children are included in public policies.

Structure
UNICEF is a semi-autonomous member of the United Nations system. UNICEF has its own governing body, the Executive Board, which meets once a year. The Executive Board is responsible for providing inter-governmental support to and supervision of the activities of UNICEF, in accordance with the overall policy guidance of the General Assembly and the Economic and Social Council. The Board consists of 36 members, elected on the basis of annual rotation for three-year terms by the Economic and Social Council with the following regional allocation of seats: 8 African States, 7 Asian States, 4 Central and Eastern European States, 5 Latin American and Caribbean States and 12 Western European and Other States (including Japan).

The Executive Board Members for 2013 are:
Africa: Central African Republic, DRC, Djibouti, Egypt, Gambia, Ghana, Kenya, Namibia.
Asia: China, India, Indonesia, Iran, Pakistan, Republic of Korea, Thailand.
Eastern Europe: Albania, Bulgaria, Estonia, Russian Federation
Latin America and the Caribbean: Antigua and Barbuda, Colombia, Cuba, Guyana, Haiti.
Western Europe and others: Belgium, Canada, Denmark, Finland, France, Greece, Ireland, Israel, Norway, Portugal, Sweden, Switzerland, USA.

The officers of the Board, constituting the Bureau, are elected by the Board from among Board members, at the first session of the calendar year. There are five officers - the President and four Vice-Presidents. They are elected for a one-year term.

The Office of the Secretary of the Executive Board (OSEB) is responsible for maintaining strong relations between the Board and the UNICEF secretariat; organising Board sessions and Bureau meetings, and providing editorial and technical services for documentation relating to Board meetings. The Executive Director, who is responsible for the administration of UNICEF, is appointed, in consultation with the Board, by the United Nations Secretary-General.

UNICEF carries out work in 190 countries through national programmes and National Committees. There are eight regional offices and 126 country offices worldwide. Of the 7,200 workforce, some 6,500 positions are in the fieldwork. UNICEF's secretariat is headquartered in New York and there are offices in Geneva, Brussels, Tokyo and Copenhagen as well as a research centre in Florence.

The National Committees for UNICEF, predominantly organised in industrialised countries, play a crucial role in generating a better understanding of the needs of children in developing countries and of the work of UNICEF. There are 37 National Committees providing fundraising and advocacy support to UNICEF.

The 10-member Committee on the Rights of the Child, consisting of independent experts from all parts of the world, monitors the implementation of the Convention. The Committee also works with UNICEF, other United Nations agencies and non-governmental organisations to promote the effective implementation of the provisions contained in the Convention's 54 Articles.

Relations With Non-Governmental Organisations
UNICEF has always worked closely with the voluntary sector. Many international non-government organisations (NGOs) concerned with the situation of children have become working partners with UNICEF - providing channels for targeted advocacy, raising funds and collaborating directly in programmes. NGOs are often leaders in providing services to children in the developing countries and so can provide UNICEF with information and advice on the basis of their experience and some have collaborated in projects of mutual interest.

Relations Within The United Nations System
UNICEF is part of the pattern of co-operative relationships that links the various development organisations of the United Nations system, bilateral aid agencies and non-governmental organisations. Collaboration within the United Nations system ranges from sharing of expertise to systematic exchanges on policies and relevant experience.

UNICEF does not duplicate services available from the specialised agencies of the United Nations but benefits from their technical advice, particularly from the World Health Organization (WHO), but also from the Food and Agriculture Organization (FAO), the United Nations Educational, Scientific and Cultural Organization (UNESCO) and the International Labour Organisation (ILO). These exchanges occur through the machinery of the Administrative Committee on Co-ordination (ACC), as well as through periodic inter-secretariat consultations, e.g. the joint UNICEF/WHO Committee on Health Policy which meets biannually to advice on policies of co-operation in health programmes and undertakes periodic reviews.

UNICEF co-operates in country programmes with other funding agencies of the United Nations system, such as the World Bank, the United Nations Fund for Population Activities (UNFPA), and the World Food Programme (WFP). In the case of emergencies UNICEF works with the Office of the United Nations Disaster Relief Co-ordinator (UNDRO), WFP, the United Nations Development Programme (UNDP), the United Nations High Commissioner for Refugees (UNHCR), and other agencies of the United Nations system, as well as with the International Committee of the Red Cross and National Red Cross, Red Crescent Societies or their international body, the League of Red Cross and Red Crescent Societies.

Budget
All UNICEF income comes from voluntary contributions - from governments, inter-governmental agencies, non-governmental organisations and individuals. Almost all countries, industrialised and developing, make annual contributions which account for 63 per cent of UNICEF income. As UNICEF is not a 'membership' organisation with an 'assessed' budget, individuals and organisations around the world are an important source of funding. Material support from the public comes through the buying of greeting cards, individual contributions, the proceeds from benefit events, grants, and collections by school children. Such fund-raising efforts are often sponsored by the National Committees.

Income totalled US$3,711 million in 2011, up 1 per cent on the previous year. Overall income was ahead of planned programme expenditure. In 2009, US$1,955 million came from governments and US$916 million from private sources. Inter-organization arrangements contributed $296 million and other income amounted to $89 million. Expenditure for 2009 totalled US$3,298 million, up 6 per cent on the previous year. Over 50 per cent of the expenditure was directed at programmes for children's survival and development needs. Over 55 per cent of the budget went to Africa and 30 per cent to Asia. In 2011, the top government contributor was the US ($345.4 million) followed by the UK ($290.7 million).

Executive Director: Anthony Lake (page 1459)

United Nations Children's Fund, UNICEF House, 3 United Nations Plaza, New York, NY 10017, USA. Tel: +1 212 326 7000, fax: +1 212 887 7465, URL: http://www.unicef.org

United Nations Children's Fund, European Headquarters, Palais des Nations, 1211 Geneva 10, Switzerland. Tel: +41 (0)22 909 5111, fax: +41 (0)22 909 5900, e-mail: askgeneva@unicef.org

UNITED NATIONS CONFERENCE ON TRADE AND DEVELOPMENT (UNCTAD)

The United Nations Conference on Trade and Development (UNCTAD) is the principal organ of the UN General Assembly in the fields of trade, investment and development. It was established as a permanent intergovernmental body in 1964 in Geneva with a view to accelerating trade and economic development, particularly in developing countries. UNCTAD discharges its mandate through policy analysis, intergovernmental deliberations, consensus-building and negotiation, implementation of actions and follow-up, and technical co-operation.

Structure

UNCTAD is composed of 194 member states and a number of governmental and non-governmental organisations with observer status. Its Secretariat forms part of the United Nations Secretariat. It has a staff of some 400, mainly in Geneva, and is headed by a Secretary-General. The Conference meets every four years at ministerial level to formulate major policy guidelines and set work programmes. The executive body, the Trade and Development Board, holds its regular session in the autumn and can convene up to three executive sessions a year. It reports to the General Assembly through the Economic and Social Council.

Two Commissions of the Board formulate policy for their particular field of work. These are: the Trade and Development Commission and the Investment, Enterprise and Development Commission. These two Commissions meet once a year for five days, and in order to receive the best level of technical expertise possible, they may convene up to 10 meetings of experts a year.

UNCTAD has also been assigned the responsibility of servicing the Commission on Science and Technology for Development (CSTD), a body of the Economic and Social Council (ECOSOC).

There are six divisions: Division on Gloablization and Development Strategies; Division on Investment and Enterprise; Division on International Trade in Goods and Services, and Commodities; Division on Technology and Logistics; Division for Africa, Least Developed Countries and Special Programmes; Division of Managment.

Functions

The main focus of UNCTAD's work is outlined as follows:

- **Trade and Commodities:** Promotes commodity diversification and development; assists in competition and consumer policies; trade negotiations and commercial diplomacy; trade analysis and information system; trade and environment.

- **Investment and enterprise development:** investment policy reviews; investment guides and capacity building; promotes entrepreneurship; international investment and technology arrangements.

- **Macroeconomic policies, debt and development financing:** Policy analysis and research, technical and advisory support to the G24 group of developing countries; management of external debt.

- **Technology and Logistics:** includes an integrated customs system (ASYCUDA); cargo tracking system (ACIS); e-tourism initiative; technology reveiws and development; training networks.

- **Africa, least developed countries, landlocked developing coutries and small island developing States:** increasing understanding of African development efforts, supporting NEPAD; providing analytical work and technical assistance to developing states.

UNCTAD is also responsible for administering the Generalized System of Preferences (GSP), established in 1971, allowing preferential tariffs for certain manufactured exports from developing countries. It lends particular support to the world's least developed countries (LDCs) and assists developing countries in their trade negotiations and in matters of debt management.

UNCTAD established the Common Fund for Commodities (to facilitate the financing of commodity agreements and support research for individual commodities) in 1989; the only universally applicable Set of Principles and Rules on competition policy in 1980; the Agreement on the Global System of Trade Preferences in 1989; and has also introduced many conventions in maritime transport particularly in liner shipping conferences (1974), multimodal transport of goods (1980), ship registration (1986) and the Convention of Maritime Liens and Mortgages (1993).

Relationships with other Organisations

Within the United Nations, UNCTAD works closely with the World Trade Organization, the International Trade Centre, UN Regional Commissions, UNDP and the IMF. Over 110 other intergovernmental bodies have gained accrediation as observers to UNCTAD's Trade and Development Board.

Budget

The Secretariat's annual regular budget is approximately US$68 million, drawn from the United Nations regular budget. Technical co-operation activities, financed from extrabudgetary resources provided by donor and beneficiary countries, amount to approximately US$38 million a year. There are three main funding sources for technical co-operation activities: trust funds, UNDP, UN programe budget. The proposed UNCTAD 2012-2013 programme budget amounted to US$135.5 million.

Membership

Afghanistan, Albania, Algeria, Andorra, Angola, Antigua and Barbuda, Argentina, Armenia, Australia, Austria, Azerbaijan, Bahamas, Bahrain, Bangladesh, Barbados, Belarus, Belgium, Belize, Benin, Bhutan, Bolivia, Bosnia and Herzegovina, Botswana, Brazil, Brunei Darussalam, Bulgaria, Burkina Faso, Burundi, Cambodia, Cameroon, Canada, Cape Verde, CAR, Chad, Chile, China, Colombia, Comoros, Congo, Costa Rica, Côte d'Ivoire, Croatia, Cuba, Cyprus, Czech Republic, DPR of Korea, DRC, Denmark, Djibouti, Dominica, Dominican Republic, Ecuador, Egypt, El Salvador, Equatorial Guinea, Eritrea, Estonia, Ethiopia, Fiji, Finland, France, Gabon, Gambia, Georgia, Germany, Ghana, Greece, Grenada, Guatemala, Guinea, Guinea-Bissau, Guyana, Haiti, Holy See, Honduras, Hungary, Iceland, India, Indonesia, Iran, Iraq, Ireland, Israel, Italy, Jamaica, Japan, Jordan, Kazakhstan, Kenya, Kiribati, Kuwait, Kyrgyzstan, Laos, Latvia, Lebanon, Lesotho, Liberia, Libya, Liechtenstein, Lithuania, Luxembourg, Madagascar, Malawi, Malaysia, Maldives, Mali, Malta, Marshall Islands, Mauritania, Mauritius, Mexico, Micronesia, Moldova, Monaco, Mongolia, Montenegro, Morocco, Mozambique, Myanmar, Namibia, Nauru, Nepal, Netherlands, New Zealand, Nicaragua, Niger, Nigeria, Norway, Oman, Pakistan, Palau, Panama, Papua New Guinea, Paraguay, Peru, Philippines, Poland, Portugal, Qatar, Republic of Korea, Romania, Russian Federation, Rwanda, Saint Kitts and Nevis, Saint Lucia, Saint Vincent and the Grenadines, Samoa, San Marino, Sao Tome and Principe, Saudi Arabia, Senegal, Serbia, Seychelles, Sierra Leone, Singapore, Slovakia, Slovenia, Solomon Islands, Somalia, South Africa, South Sudan, Spain, Sri Lanka, Sudan, Suriname, Swaziland, Sweden, Switzerland, Syria Arab Republic, Tajikistan, Thailand, The former Yugoslav Republic of Macedonia, Timor-Leste, Togo, Tonga, Trinidad and Tobago, Tunisia, Turkey, Turkmenistan, Tuvalu, Uganda, Ukraine, United Arab Emirates, United Kingdom, United Republic of Tanzania, USA, Uruguay, Uzbekistan, Vanuatu, Venezuela, Vietnam, Yemen, Zambia, Zimbabwe.

Secretary General: Dr. Supachai Panitchpakdi (page 1492)

United Nations Conference on Trade and Development (UNCTAD), Palais des Nations, 8-14 Avenue de la Paix, CH-1211 Geneva 10, Switzerland. Tel: +41 (0)22 917 1234, fax: +41 (0)22 917 0057, e-mail: info@unctad.org, URL: http://www.unctad.org

UNITED NATIONS CONVENTION TO COMBAT DESERTIFICATION (UNCCD)

The 1992 Rio Earth Summit identified desertification, along with climate change and the loss of biodiversity, as some of the greatest challenges to sustainable development. The United Nations Convention to Combat Desertification (UNCCD) was established in 1994 and is only legally binding international agreement linking environment and development to sustainable land management.

The UNCCD established a ten-year strategy (2008-18) with the specified aim: "to forge a global partnership to reverse and prevent desertification / land degradation and to mitigate the effects of drought in affected areas in order to support poverty reduction and environmental sustainability".

As of March 2013, 195 states have signed the Convention. The UNCCD works closely with the other two Rio Conventions; the Convention on Biological Diversity (CBD) and the UN Framework Convention on Climate Change (UNFCCC).

The supreme body of the Convention is the Conference of the Parties (COP) and it is made up of all parties belonging to the Convention. As of 2001, sessions are held biannually. It has two subsidiary bodies: the Committee on Science and Technology (CST) and the Committee for the Review of the Implementation of the Convention (CRIC).

The Secretariat of the Convention was established in Article 23 of the UNCCD. Its key function is to service the sessions of the COP and its subsidiary bodies. Under its 2012-2015 workplan it is focused on increasing political momentum, moving towards global target-setting and improving conditions for national implementation. It is focused on building and strengthening partnerships with relevant programmes and institutions.

Executive Secretary: Luc Gnacadja

United Nations Convention to Combat Desertification, PO Box 260129, D-53153 Bonn, Germany. Tel: +49 228 815 2800, fax: +49 228 815 2898 / 99, e-mail: secretariat@unccd.int, URL: http://www.unccd.int

UNITED NATIONS DEMOCRACY FUND (UNDEF)

UNDEF was established in 2005 as a United Nations General Trust Fund to support democracy worldwide. UNDEF supports projects that promote human rights, and encourage the participation of all groups in democratic processes. Most UNDEF funds go to local civil society organizations.

UNDEF funding is based entirely on voluntary contributions from governments; in 2010, it received more than $110 million dollars in contributions from 39 donor countries, including many middle- and low-income States in Africa, Asia and Latin America. UNDEF has supported a total of more than 330 projects in more than 110 countries in the following main areas: Community development; Rule of law and human rights; Tools for democratization; Women; Youth; Media. Approximately 60-70 projects receive funding each year. In 2012, UNDEF received 2,014 project proposals from 133 countries for funding. Approximately 26 per cent were for community development projects, 25 per cent for rule of law and human rights and 20 per cent for women.

The Democracy Fund has its own Executive Head and staff. The Executive Head reports directly to the Advisory Board on substantive matters and reports to the Executive Director of UN Office for Partnerships for administrative purposes. Administrative support is provided by the UN Office for Partnerships.

Executive Head: Roland Rich (page 1502)

United Nations Democracy Fund (UNDEF), 1 United Nations Plaza, Room DC1-1300, New York, NY 10017, USA. Tel: +1 212 963 3399, fax: +1 212 963 1486, e-mail: democracyfund@un.org, URL: http://www.un.org/democracyfund/

UNITED NATIONS DEVELOPMENT PROGRAMME (UNDP)

The United Nations Development Programme (UNDP) was established in 1965 through the merger of two predecessor programmes for UN technical co-operation. The UNDP is the UN's principal provider of development advice, advocacy and grant support. It helps countries build their capacities for development whilst protecting the environment.

Function
The UNDP focuses on five main areas; Poverty Reduction, Democratic Governance, Crisis Prevention and Recovery, Energy and the Environment and HIV/AIDS. It also focuses on the empowerment of women.

In September 2000, at the United Nations Millennium Summit, world leaders pledged to cut poverty in half by 2015. The UNDP is involved in making this happen through providing developing countries with knowledge-based consulting services and by building national, regional and global coalitions for change.

In 1990, UNDP published its first Human Development Report, an annual book that ranks countries on a Human Development Index combining measurements of life expectancy, literacy, per-capita income and respect for women's rights. Since then, the UNDP has helped 135 countries to produce their own National Human Development Reports, which provide a basis for informed local debate about priorities and policies.

In addition to UNDP's main programme, the organisation's Administrator has responsibility for several associated Funds, each responding to a specific development need. These include: The United Nations Capital Development Fund (UNCDF), United Nations Development Fund for Women (UNIFEM), the United Nations Volunteers (UNV), the United Nations Revolving Fund for Natural Resources Exploration (UNRFNRE), United Nations Sudano-Sahelian Office (UNSO), United Nations Fund for Science and Technology for Development (UNFSTD), and the Global Environment Facility (GEF).

As of 2013 UNP was working in 177 countries. As of 2012, 128 countries were receiving support from UNDP for democratic governance and 60 countries were receiving elections support.

Structure
The UNDP is headed by an Administrator, who is responsible to an Executive Board based in New York, and composed of 36 representatives of both donor and programme countries. The Executive Board decides policy and programming and reports to the UN General Assembly through the Economic and Social Council. The Programme operates through 135 country offices throughout the world, each one headed by a Resident Representative who is, in most cases, also the Resident Co-ordinator of relief efforts following emergencies or disasters and the co-ordinator of any UN-related assistance for development in the country or countries served.

The Membership of the Executive Board in 2013 is as follows (membership expires on the last day of the year indicated):

Membership of Executive Board

State	End of term
AFRICAN STATES	
Angola	2015
Congo, Republic of	2015
Djibouti	2013
Ethiopia	2015
Lesotho	2015
Liberia	2014
Morocco	2014
Niger	2015
ASIAN AND PACIFIC STATES	
Bangladesh	2013
China	2013
Fiji	2015
Indonesia	2014
Iran	2015
Pakistan	2015
Republic of Korea	2014
LATIN AMERICAN AND CARIBBEAN STATES	
Argentina	2013
Brazil	2014

- continued
El Salvador 2013
Guatemalaa 2015
Nicaragua 2014
EASTERN EUROPEAN AND OTHER STATES
Belarus 2013
Bulgaria 2015
Czech Republic 2013
Russian Federation 2014
*WESTERN EUROPEAN AND OTHER STATES
France
Germany
Ireland
Japan
Netherlands
New Zealand
Norway
Portugal
Spain
Sweden
United Kingdom
United States
*WEOG has had its own rotation scheme since April 2006

Funding

Ninety per cent of UNDP's unrestricted programme resources go to 66 low-income countries that are home to ninety per cent of the world's people in absolute poverty. Funds are mostly directed to the provision of national/international experts, sub-contracts for technical services, fellowships for people in programme countries and equipment. Region by region, the largest share of allocated funds goes to Sub-Saharan Africa, then the Asia/Pacific region, followed by Latin America and the Caribbean, the Arab States, Eastern Europe and the Commonwealth of Independent States.

Total resources for 2012-13 amounted to $12.89, including and openeing balance of $3.16 billion, contributions of $9.60 billion and other income of $0.13 billion. Projected use of resource was estimated to be $11.73 billion, of which development activities of $10.33 billion.

President of the Bureau 2013: H.E. Mr Roble Olhaye (Djibouti)
Vice-Presidents of the Bureau 2013: Mr Andy Rachmianto (Indonesia), H.E. Eduardo Poretti (Argentina), Boyan Belev (Bulgaria), Ms Merete Dyrud (Norway)

Administrator: Helen Clark (page 1405)

United Nations Development Programme (UNDP), 1 United Nations Plaza, New York, NY 10017, USA. Tel: +1 212 906 5000, fax: +1 212 906 5364, e-mail: hq@undp.org, URL: http://www.undp.org

UNITED NATIONS ENTITY FOR GENDER EQUALITY AND THE EMPOWERMENT OF WOMEN (UN-WOMEN)

In July 2010, the United Nations General Assembly created UN Women, the United Nations Entity for Gender Equality and the Empowerment of Women. UN Women develops the work of four previously distinct parts of the UN system: Division for the Advancement of Women (DAW); International Research and Training Institute for the Advancement of Women (INSTRAW); Office of the Special Adviser on Gender Issues and Advancement of Women (OSAGI); United Nations Development Fund for Women (UNIFEM).

Over many decades, the UN has made significant progress in advancing gender equality but many gender inequalities remain deeply embedded throughout the world. Women may still face occupational segregation and gender wage gaps, or be prevented from obtaining employment. Females are still denied access to basic education and health care and remain under-represented in political and economic decision-making processes.UN Women was created to address the challenges the UN has faced in tackling gender inequality, including inadequate funding. Its aims include:
- elimination of discrimination against women and girls;
- empowerment of women; and
- achievement of equality between women and men as partners and beneficiaries of development, human rights, humanitarian action and peace and security

The main roles of UN Women are:
- To support inter-governmental bodies, such as the Commission on the Status of Women, in their formulation of policies, global standards and norms.
- To help Member States to implement these standards, providing technical and financial support to those countries when appropriate, and developing effective partnerships with civil society.
- To ensure the UN system meets its own commitments on gender equality.

UN Women is funded by both the voluntary contributions and the regular UN budget. Its minimum annual budget is US$500 million.

Under Secretary-General and Executive Director: Michelle Bachelet (page 1381)

UN Women, 304 East 45th Street, 15th Floor, New York, NY 10017 ,USA. Tel: +1 212 906 6400, fax: +1 212 906 6705, URL: http://www.unwomen.org

UNITED NATIONS ENVIRONMENT PROGRAMME (UNEP)

UNEP was founded on 15 December 1972 by the UN General Assembly. It was established as a result of the UN Conference on the Human Environment in Stockholm, June 1972.

Objectives
To provide leadership and encourage partnership in caring for the environment by inspiring, informing and enabling nations and peoples to improve their quality of life without compromising that of future generations.

Structure
UNEP has the following main components: the **Governing Council**, composed of 58 member States elected for four years, which reports to the UN General Assembly through ECOSOC. The Council assesses the state of the world environment, establishes UNEP's programme priorities, and approves the budget. The membership of the Governing Council is made up on the following geographical basis: Africa (16), Asia (13), Latin America and the Caribbean (10), Eastern Europe (6), Western Europe, North America, and other (13).

A **High-Level Committee of Ministers and Officials (HLCOMO)** was established by a decision of the Governing Council in April 1997 as a subsidiary body of the Council. It has the mandate to consider the international environmental agenda and to make reform and policy recommendations to the Governing Council. It also provides guidance and advice to UNEP's Executive Director on emerging environmental issues; enhances the collaboration and co-operation of UNEP with other relevant multilateral bodies as well as with the environmental conventions and their secretariats; and supports the Executive Director in mobilizing adequate and predictable financial resources for UNEP's implementation of the global environmental agenda approved by the Council. The Committee consists of 36 members elected from among members of the UN and its specialized agencies. Members serve for two years, taking into account the principle of equitable regional representation as reflected in the composition of the Council.

The **Committee of Permanent Representatives**, the other subsidiary organ of the Governing Council, whose membership is open to Permanent Representatives accredited to UNEP from among members of the UN and its specialized agencies, has the mandate to: review, monitor, and assess the implementation of decisions of the Council; review reports on the effectiveness, efficiency, and transparency of the functions and work of the secretariat and make recommendations thereon to the Council; and prepare draft decisions for consideration by the Council.

The Secretariat, headed by the Executive Director, supports the Governing Council, co-ordinates environmental programmes within the UN system, and administers the Environment Fund. There are six regional offices (Nairobi, Kenya; Bangkok, Thailand; Geneva, Switzerland; Mexico City, Mexico; Washington DC, USA; Manama, Bahrain).

Activities
UNEP's most important function is to serve as a forum for addressing existing and emerging environmental issues at the global and regional levels. UNEP assesses global, regional and national environmental conditions; it develops international environmental agreements; helps develop institutions manage the environment; integrates economic development and environmental protection; facilitates technology and knowledge transfers to aid sustainable development; encourages new partnerships.

UNEP has developed a medium term strategy (2010-2013) with six cross-cutting thematic priorities. These are: climate change disasters and conflicts; ecosystem management; environmental governance; harmful substances and hazardous waste; resource efficiency - sustainable consumption and production.

UNEP's programme is implemented through eight divisions:

AFFILIATED AGENCIES OF THE UNITED NATIONS

Division of Early Warning and Assessment (DEWA)

DEWA performs the function of bringing better information into the decision-making process in order to link analysis with decisions and to obtain the best available description of the implications of policy choices. The Global Environment Outlook (GEO) process and report series relies on a network of collaborating centres, advisory groups, scientists and policy makers, and linkages with other UN bodies. The main output of the process is the GEO report series, which aims to reflect the best information and perspectives available on the global environment.

In February 2001 DEWA launched the UNEP.Net to ensure better public access to environmental information, while supporting environmental assessment for well-informed decision making. It also provides a platform for UN national focal points, UNEP partners, and collaborating institutions and centres to share among themselves and with the public the environmental information they possess. UNEP.Net is the result of a partnership with two institutions from the private sector in the field of environment information, the Environment Systems Research Institute (ESRI) and the National Geographic.

DEWA also incorporates the UNEP World Conservation Monitoring Centre (UNEP-WCMC), which was established in June 2000 as the key biodiversity assessment centre of UNEP.

Division of Communications & Public Information (DCPI)

DCPI works to raise UNEP's profile and influence attitudes, behaviour and decisions related to the local and global environment. It disseminates the environmental message through the media, the Internet and audiovisual and printed products, and through a wide variety of events, awards and partnerships.

Division of Environmental Policy Implementation (DEPI)

There are four branches to this Division:
- Capacity-building - DEPI provides technical and advisory services to partners around the globe. It develops and implements pilot projects and participates in the identification and dissemination of best practices.
- Global Programme of Action for the protection of the Marine Environment from Land-based Activities (GPA).
- Disaster management. The DEPI spearheads UNEP's response to environmental emergencies and promotes the enforcement of, and compliance with, multilateral environmental agreements (MEAs)
- Implementation of environmental law. A priority task of DEPI has been to develop draft framework guidelines on compliance and enforcement of environmental agreements and prevention of environmental crime. The guidelines will not be legally binding, but they will provide general guidance to countries in their efforts to improve on their compliance with and the enforcement of environmental agreements and to prevent and combat environmental crime.

Division of Technology, Industry, and Economics (DTIE)

DTIE works as a catalyst and encourages decision-makers in government, industry, and business to develop and adopt environmentally sound policies, strategies, practices, and technologies. This involves raising awareness, building international consensus, codes of practice, and economic instruments, strengthening capabilities, exchanging information, and initiating demonstration projects.

Division of Regional Co-operation (DRC)

DRC is focused on harmonization of regional environmental actions by strengthening intergovernmental policy dialogue through ministerial forums and increased regional and sub-regional co-operation. These developments are underpinned by enhanced information exchange within regions and the building of public environmental awareness on environmental issues.

Division of Environmental Conventions

DEC leads the following functions of UNEP: To promote the progressive development and implementation of environmental law to respond to environmental challenges, in particular by supporting States and the international community in strengthening their capacity to develop and implement legal frameworks; and To support the implementation of Multilateral Environmental Agreements (MEAs) by parties, and facilitate interlinkages and synergies, while respecting the legal autonomy of MEAs and the decisions taken by their respective governing bodies.

Division of Global Environment Facility Coordination (DGEF)

DGEF promotes international co-operation and fosters action to protect the global environment. It was established in 1991 and restructured in 1994 with a capital of US$2 billion. The DGEF was established on the basis of collaboration and partnership between UNEP, the UN Development Programme (UNDP) and the World Bank. It has been designated as a financial mechanism providing new and additional financial resources to eligible countries, to meet the agreed incremental costs of measures aimed at achieving global environmental benefits in the areas of biological diversity, climate change, international waters, and the protection of the ozone layer. In addition, activities related to land degradation, in particular desertification and deforestation, are eligible as they relate to one of the four focal areas. UNEP has a key role in the DGEF. It provides scientific and technical analysis, advances environmental management in DGEF-financed activities, and provides guidance on environmental assessments and policy frameworks.

UNEP provides the secretariat of the Scientific and Technical Advisory Panel (STAP) of the DGEF, comprising 12 world-renowned experts in the fields relevant to the DGEF activities and designated by the Executive Director of UNEP.

There is also a **Regional Co-operation Division.**

Conventions

Main conventions on the environment under the auspices of UNEP:
- Convention on International Trade in Endangered Species of Wild Fauna and Flora (CITES), Washington, DC, 1973;
- Convention on the Conservation of Migratory Species of Wild Animals (CMS), Bonn, 1979;
- Vienna Convention for the Protection of the Ozone Layer, Vienna, 1985, including the Montreal Protocol on Substances that Deplete the Ozone Layer, Montreal, 1987;
- Convention on the Control of Transboundary Movements of Hazardous Wastes and their Disposal (Basel Convention), Basel, 1989;
- Convention on Biological Diversity (CBD), adopted in Nairobi and opened for signature in Rio de Janeiro, 1992;
- Lusaka Agreement on Co-operative Enforcement Operations Directed at Illegal Trade in Wild Fauna and Flora, Lusaka, 1994;
- Convention on the Prior Informed Consent Procedure for Certain Hazardous Chemicals and Pesticides in International Trade (Rotterdam Convention on PIC), Rotterdam, 1998 (see Agreements). Operated jointly with the Food and Agriculture Organization (FAO);
- Stockholm Convention on Persistent Organic Pollution (Stockholm Convention on POPs), Stockholm, 2001.

Finance

UNEP is financed through the regular budget of the UN, the Environment Fund, Trust Funds, and counterpart contributions. The contribution from the UN Regular Budget is less than 4 per cent of the total budget and UNEP depends mainly on voluntary support. The Enivronment Fund is the main source of funding. The total budget for UNEP for the years 2012 and 2013 was approved at $474 million.

Special funds

The Environment Fund is a voluntary fund used to finance the costs of the implementation of UNEP's programme of work. Some programmes are financed totally by the Environment Fund, but most are funded from more than one source, including the Trust Funds and counterpart contributions. Contributions in 2011 reached US$80,053,859. The top donor in 2012 was the Netherlands (approx US$10 million) followed by Germany (approx US$9.9 million).

Membership of Governing Council, 2012-15

Albania, Antigua and Barbuda*, Argentina*, Australia*, Bangladesh, Belgium*, Brazil*, Canada*, Central African Republic*, Chile, China*, Colombia, Congo, Cuba, Czech Republic*, Ecuador, Egypt, France*, Fiji, Gabon*, Georgia, Germany*, India, Indonesia*, Iran, Israel, Italy, Japan*, Kenya*, Lesotho*, Liberia, Malaysia*, Mauritania*, Mauritius, Mexico, Mozambique*, Netherlands, Nigeria, Pakistan*, Poland, Republic of Korea*, Romania*, Russian Federation*, Saudi Arabia, Senegal, Spain, Sudan, Switzerland*, Thailand, Togo, Trinidad and Tobago*, UK, United Republic of Tanzania*, USA*, Uruguay* and Zambia*.
* Term ends in 2013.

Executive Director: Achim Steiner (page 1520)

UN Environment Programme (UNEP), Secretariat, United Nations Avenue, Gigiri, PO Box 30552 00100, Nairobi, Kenya. Tel: +254 2 762 1234, fax: +254 2 762 3927, e-mail: unepinfo@unep.org, URL: http://www.unep.org

UNITED NATIONS HIGH COMMISSIONER FOR REFUGEES (UNHCR)

The United Nations High Commissioner for Refugees began work on 1 January 1951 as a subsidiary body of the General Assembly of the United Nations. It replaced the International Refugee Organisation (1946-49), originally intended as a temporary specialised agency of the UN charged primarily with resettling 1.2 million European refugees left homeless in the aftermath of World War II. However, it was decided that the scale of the international refugee problem called for further action and today more than 34 million people in 110 countries fall under UNHCR's concern. Initially set up for a period of three years, its mandate was extended every five years as refugee crises mushroomed around the world. In December 2003, the UN General Assembly decided to remove the time limitation on UNHCR's mandate until the refugee problem is solved.

Under its Statute, UNHCR concerns itself with any person who, owing to a well-founded fear of being persecuted for reasons of race, religion, nationality, membership of a particular social group, or political opinion, is outside the country of his/her nationality, and is unable to or, owing to such fear, is unwilling to avail himself/herself of the protection of that country. Refugees meeting this criteria are entitled to the protection of the Office of the United Nations High Commissioner for Refugees irrespective of their geographical location. UNHCR has participated in more than 30 operations to help internally displaced people (IDPs) since the 1970s, including Timor, Kosovo, Colombia, Afghanistan and more recently the Sudanese region of Darfur. In late 2005, UN and other specialized agencies agreed to a more coordinated and cohesive approach to tackle the problem of internally displaced civilians. Under this new 'collaborative approach', UNHCR will in future take a lead role in overseeing the protection and shelter needs of IDPs as well as in the coordination and management of any camps which are established. Globally there are an estimated 23.7 million IDPs who have fled their homes, usually as a result of civil war, of whom UNHCR helps some 6 million.

Function

UNHCR's most important responsibility, known as 'international protection', is to ensure respect for the basic human rights of these refugees, including their ability to seek asylum and to ensure that no one is returned involuntarily to a country where he or she has reason to fear persecution. The organisation promotes international refugee agreements and monitors government compliance with international law. UNHCR also seeks durable solutions for refugees in three main areas: voluntary repatriation to their original homes, local integration in countries where they first sought asylum, or resettlement to a third country. Material assistance is provided in co-operation with other inter-governmental and non-governmental agencies. UNHCR's actions include measures to prevent refugee problems, such as institution-building and training initiatives in countries likely to produce refugees and in countries needing to offer asylum.

Structure

The High Commissioner is elected by the UN General Assembly on the nomination of the Secretary-General and submits a written report annually to the UN General Assembly. The High Commissioner's programmes are approved and supervised by UNHCR's Executive Committee, currently composed of the following 87 member countries (October 2012-October 2013): Algeria, Argentina, Australia, Austria, Azerbaijan, Bangladesh, Belgium, Benin, Brazil, Bulgaria, Cameroon, Canada, Chile, China, Colombia, Congo, Costa Rica, Côte d'Ivoire, Croatia, Cyprus, Denmark, Djibouti, DRC, Ecuador, Egypt, Estonia, Ethiopia, Finland, France, Germany, Ghana, Greece, Guinea, the Holy See, Hungary, India, the Islamic Republic of Iran, Ireland, Israel, Italy, Japan, Jordan, Kenya, Lebanon, Lesotho, Luxembourg, Madagascar, Mexico, Montenegro, Morocco, Mozambique, Namibia, Netherlands, New Zealand, Nicaragua, Nigeria, Norway, Pakistan, the Philippines, Poland, Portugal, Republic of Korea, Republic of Moldova, Romania, the Russian Federation, Rwanda, Serbia, Slovenia, Somalia, South Africa, Spain, Sudan, Sweden, Switzerland, Thailand, the former Yugoslav Republic of Macedonia, Togo, Tunisia, Turkey, Turkmenistan, Uganda, United Kingdom, United Republic of Tanzania, USA, Venezuela, Yemen and Zambia.

Partnerships

UNHCR works with a variety of UN bodies, inter-governmental (IGOs) and non-governmental organisations (NGOs). Major UN partners include the World Food Programme (WFP), which supplies food and basic commodities to refugees; the UN Children's Fund (UNICEF), the World Health Organization (WHO), UN Development Programme (UNDP), the Office for the Coordination of Humanitarian Affairs (OCHA), and the UN High Commissioner for Human Rights. Other partners include the International Committee of the Red Cross (ICRC), the International Federation of Red Cross and Red Crescent Societies (IFRC), the International Organization for Migration (IOM) and more than 570 non-governmental organisations.

In recent years, as refugee problems have become more complex, UNHCR has expanded its links with non-traditional organisations which themselves have become more involved in crises. They include the UN peacekeepers who played a vital role in the former Yugoslavia, Kosovo and East Timor; and financial institutions such as the World Bank.

Recent Statistics

In 2011 the UNHCR was helping 10.5 million refugees, slightly down on 2010. A further 4.7 million reigstered refugees are looked after in approximately 60 camps in the Middle East by UNRWA, set up to look after displaced Palestinians. More than half the refugees of concern to UNHCR are in Asia and 22 per cent in Africa. In the same year there were some 826,00 asylum-seekers of concern to UNHCR. UNHCR lobbies governments to treat asylum seekers fairly, recognising the difficulties of documenting persecution. There were approximately 26 million internally displaced people (IDP) around the world in 2008, of whom the UNHCR was caring for around 14.4 million. The most significant new displacement in 2008 came in the Philippines, where 600,000 people fled fighting between the government and armed groups in the south. Other large-scale displacements of 200,000 people occured in the following countries: Sudan, Kenya, Democratic Republic of the Congo, Iraq, Pakistan, Somalia, Colombia, Sri Lanka and India. In 2012, UNHCR expressed concern over the deteriorating situation in Mali.

Budget

UNHCR is funded entirely by voluntary contributions, principally from governments, but also from inter-governmental organisations, corporations and individuals. As the number of persons of concern to UNHCR jumped to a high of 27 million in 1994, its budget rose accordingly, from $564 million in 1990 to more than $1 billion annually for most of the 1990s. The 2012 annual budget was a record US$3.59 billion. The top five donors in 2009 were the United States (US$640.7 million, 37 per cent), the European Commission (7 per cent), Japan (6 per cent), Sweden (6 per cent) and the Netherlands (5 per cent).

In addition to voluntary contributions, UNHCR receives a limited subsidy - less than 4 per cent of the total - from the regular budget of the United Nations, which covers a fraction of its administrative costs.

Contributions "in kind" which include such things as tents, medicines, trucks, air transportation and specialised personnel, complement UNHCR's resources, especially in rapidly developing major emergencies.

The agency has a national and international staff of approximately 7,700 working in approximately 126 countries.

High Commissioner: Antonio Guterres (Portugal) (page 1435)

Office of the United Nations High Commissioner for Refugees, Case postale 2500, CH 1211 Geneva 2, Switzerland. Tel: +41 (0)22 739 8111, fax: +41 (0)22 739 7315, URL: http://www.unhcr.org

UNITED NATIONS HUMAN SETTLEMENTS PROGRAMME - UN-HABITAT

The United Nations Commission on Human Settlements (Habitat) was established in 1978, two years after the United Nations Conference on Human Settlements, held in Vancouver, Canada. Based in Nairobi, Kenya, the organisation's main functions are to act as the agency for the human settlements development activities of the United Nations and as the centre for the global exchange of information about human settlements, regarding living conditions and trends. In January 2002, the Centre was elevated to the status of a full UN Programme, and its name was changed accordingly to the United Nations Human Settlements Programme or UN-HABITAT for short.

The Programme focuses on promoting housing for all, improving urban governance, reducing urban poverty, improving the living environment and managing disaster mitigation and post-conflict rehabilitation.

Its mandate comes from the following documents: the Vancouver Declaration on Human Settlements; Habitat Agenda; Istanbul Declaration on Human Settlements; the Declaration on Cities and other Human Settlements; and Resolution 56/206.

Activities and Programmes
UN-HABITAT currently operates in over 70 countries, concentrating in the areas of capacity-building, human settlements management and development, basic services and infrastructure, and housing. To improve in-country programme preparation and management, UN-Habitat has three regional offices in Rio de Janeiro, Brazil; Fukuoka, Japan; and Nairobi, Kenya. UN-Habitat works with a number of other UN organisations such as the United Nations Development Programme (UNDP), the United Nations Children's Fund (UNICEF), and the World Health Organisation (WHO), to promote its aims throughout the World. Habitat also works closely with bilateral and external assistance agencies, international and national non-governmental organisations (NGOs), associations of local authorities, parliamentary associations, women and youth organisations and private sector bodies.

UN-Habitat's priorities ahead of the Habitat III summit in 2016 are: Urban legislation, land and governance; Urban planning and design; Urban economy; Urban basic services; Housing and slum upgrading; Risk reduction and rehabilitation; Urban research and capacity development.

UN Millennium Goals
One of the UN Millennium Goals is to improve the lives of at least 100 million slum dwellers by 2020, and this task was mandated to UN-HABITAT. UN-HABITAT believes that this 100 million population represents only 10 per cent of the present worldwide slum population,

and if unchecked the slum population could reach 3 billion by 2050. In many cities, especially in developing countries, more than 50 per cent of the population have little or no access to shelter, water and sanitation.

Budget
The budget comes from four main sources: contributions from unilateral and bilateral partners for technical cooperations; governments and other partners; and around 5 per cent from the regular UN budget.

World Habitat Day
The UN has designated the first Monday of each year as World Habitat Day. It is intended to remind the world of its collective resonsibility for human habitat and represent a chance to reflect on the basic right of adequate shelter for all.

Governing Council (2013)
African States (16): Algeria, (2014), Benin (2016), Burkina Faso (2015), Central African Republic (2014), Congo (2015), Gabon (2014), Lesotho (2015), Lesotho (2015), Madagascar (2016), Mali (2014), Morocco (2016), Mozambique (2014), Nigeria (2014), Somalia (2016), South Africa (2015), Uganda (2016), United Republic of Tanzania (2015).

Latin American and Caribbean States (10): Antigua and Barbuda (2016), Argentina (2014), Brazil (2015), Chile (2014), Colombia (2016), El Salvador (2016), Grenada (2014), Haiti (2015), Mexico (2015), Venezuela (2014).

Eastern European States (6): Albania (2014), Russian Federation (2014). Four vacant seats.

Western European and Other States (13): Finland (2014), France (2016), Germany (2015), Israel (2015), Norway (2016), Spain (2016), Sweden (2014), Turkey (2014), United States of America (2014). Three vacant seats.

Asia-Pacific States (13): Bahrain (2015), Bangladesh (2016), China (2016), India (2015), Indonesia (2014), Iran, Islamic Republic of (2014), Japan (2014), Jordan (2015), Pakistan (2014), Republic of Korea (2016), Saudi Arabia (2015), Sri Lanka (2016), Thailand (2015).

Executive Director: Dr Joan Clos (Spain) (page 1406)

UN-HABITAT, POB 30030, Nairobi, Kenya. Tel: +254 20 762 3210, fax: +254 20 762 3477, e-mail: infohabitat@unhabitat.org, URL: http://www.unhabitat.org

UNITED NATIONS INSTITUTE FOR DISARMAMENT RESEARCH (UNIDIR)

UNIDIR is an autonomous institute within the UN. It undertakes research on security and disarmament with the aim of helping countries worldwide in their disarmament policies and programmes. Its work covers small arms to tactical nuclear weapons. Its statute was approved at the 39th session of the UN General Assembly, 17 December 1984 and came into effect on 1 January 1985.

Its mandate is based on the Final Document of the First Special Session of the UN General Assembly devoted to disarmament. It also takes into account recommendations of the General Assembly. Its work programme is reviewed annually and must be approved by the UN Secretary-General's Advisory Board on Disarmament Matters. UNIDIR works with researchers, diplomats, government officials, NGOs and other institutions. UNIDIR provides a communications link between the research sector and the United Nations Member States.

UNIDIR's activities are grouped into three main areas: global security and disarmament; regional security and disarmament; and human security and disarmament.Global security and disarmament covers international arms control agreements and their implementation as well as international security, missiles and weapons of mass destruction. Regional security and disarmament works on issues concentrated in specific areas. Human security and disarmament looks at disarmament, human rights and development, for example

anti-personnel mines, small arms and peace-building. UNIDIR carries out its programme of work through four different types of activities: research projects, meetings and conferences, a fellowship programme and the Geneva Forum.

UNIDIR is funded by voluntary donations from governments and private funders. It also receives some money from the UN's regular budget to cover some of its administrative costs.

In 2012, funding came from the following governments: Finland, France, Germany, Hungary, India, Indonesia, Ireland, Israel, Japan, Luxembourg, Malaysia, Mexico, Netherlands, Norway, Pakistan, People's Republic of China, Russia, Switzerland, Turkey, and the USA. Public donations were received from the EC, the Foundation for International Relations and Development Studies, the Organisation internationale de la Francophonie (OIF), the Secure World Foundation and the Simons Foundation.

Director: Theresa Hitchens (page 1442)

UNIDIR, Palais des Nations, 1211 Geneva 10, Switzerland. Tel: +41 (0)22 917 3186, fax: +41 (0)22 917 0176, e-mail: unidir@unog.ch, URL: http://www.unidir.org

UNITED NATIONS INSTITUTE FOR TRAINING AND RESEARCH (UNITAR)

The United Nations Institute for Training and Research (UNITAR) was established in 1965 as an autonomous body within the United Nations system with the purpose of enhancing the effectiveness of the UN through appropriate training and research.

Aims

UNITAR's mission is to deliver innovative training and conduct research on knowledge systems to develop the capacity of beneficiaries. Our goal is to be a centre of excellence recognized within and outside the United Nations system for standard-setting methodologies, high-quality training, and research capacity on knowledge systems.

UNITAR's mandate is to:
- carry out a wide range of training programmes in the field of peace and security as well as social, environment and economic development.
- carry out result-oriented research, in particular, research on and for training and to develop pedagogical materials including distance learning training packages, work books, as well as softwares and video training packs.
- establish and strengthen cooperation with other inter-governmental organizations, faculties and academic institutions, in particular for the development of research and training activities.
- conduct training programmes in multilateral diplomacy and international cooperation for diplomats accredited to the United Nations and national officials involved in work related to United Nations activities.

UNITAR's vision of training and capacity-building is based on the conviction that training should be linked to international, national and local efforts to initiate change, and should result in a measurable impact. Taking action for training is a sustainable development guarantee for future generations.

Numerous contacts and exchanges exist among the training and research institutes; at the same time, they all have institutional relationships with other UN partners that represent important strategic and operational alliances for their ongoing work programmes. There is

active collaboration across the United Nations system and a fair degree of awareness of what other organizations do. This allows for the development of partnerships that create synergies in the delivery of services, particularly in the field of training.

Research

UNITAR's research activities are focusing on knowledge systems and their practical applications. Taking into consideration capacity development requirements such activities allow the Institute to develop methodologies that are particularly relevant for lifelong learning. Research supports the Institute's training activities through the provision of learning environments adapted to respond to the needs of adult learners, thus facilitating the increase, efficiency and outreach of the Institute's capacity development activities.

UNOSAT

UN Operational Satellite Applications Programme is a UNITAR programme which benefits from infrastructure support provided by the European Organisation of Nuclear Research (CERN). By delivering integrated satellite-based solutions for human security, peace and socio-economic development, its goal is to make satellite solutions and geographic information easily accessible to the UN family and through training and capacity development projects. Since 2003, UNOSAT has established a rapid mapping service for the international humanitarian community and UN Member States.

Funding

The Institute is supported by voluntary contributions from governments, intergovernmental organizations, foundations, and develops working relationships with other UN entities, the private sector and renowned academic institutions. Becoming one of our partners contributes to our goal and enables the exchange of knowledge through collaboration.

UN Assistant Secretary-General and Director ad-interim: Sally Fegan-Wyles

UNITAR, Palais des Nations, 1211 Geneva 10, Switzerland. Tel: +41 (0)22 917 8400, fax: +41 (0)22 917 8047, e-mail: info@unitar.org, URL: http://www.unitar.org

UNITED NATIONS INTERNATIONAL COMPUTING CENTRE

The United Nations International Computing Centre (ICC) was established in 1971 as an inter-agency facility providing electronic data processing services.

ICC focuses on the provision of ICT services to UN and other not-for-profit organizations and thus has extensive experience in the implementation and support of ICT solutions specific to its clients. ICC understands the complex operational model of UN organizations and offers them the security of keeping their data and applications within the UN family. ICC applies industry best practices.

Reform initiatives of the United Nations give Common Services a prominent position. ICC consolidates IT services and delivers economies of scale through sharing of infrastructure, technology skills and management expertise. By using ICC services, partners realise savings which are generally greater than those they might achieve individually, or by outsourcing to commercial providers.

More than 25 organizations, funds and programmes of the United Nations System use ICC's services and participate in its governance, as Partner Organizations. In addition, governmental and inter-governmental entities, NGOs as well as other not-for-profit institutions use ICC's services.

ICC has offices in Geneva, New York, Rome and Brindisi.

Structure

ICC is governed by a Management Committee, comprised of one senior manager from each Partner Organization. The Management Committee provides broad policy guidelines and reviews ICC's work programme and associated budgets. The ICC Secretariat is the operating organ and is headed by the Director of ICC, who is its Chief Executive Officer.

Finance

ICC is self-funding and operates on the basis of recovering the cost of service provision.

United Nations International Computing Centre, Palais des Nations, 1211 Geneva 10, Switzerland. Tel: +41 (0)22 929 1411, e-mail: callcentre@unicc.org, URL: http://www.unicc.org

UNITED NATIONS INTERREGIONAL CRIME AND JUSTICE RESEARCH INSTITUTE (UNICRI)

The United Nations Interregional Crime and Justice Research Institute (UNICRI), formerly called the United Nations Social Defence Research Institute (UNSDRI) was established in 1968. Its aims are to contribute through applied research, training, technical co-operation, field activities and the collection, exchange and dissemination of information to the formulation and implementation of improved policies in the field of crime prevention and criminal justice.

Aims

The Institute's specific goals are to: advance understanding of crime-related problems; foster just and efficient criminal justice systems; support respect for international instruments and other standards, facilitate international law enforcement cooperation and judicial assistance, promote the exchange of information by, inter alia, maintaining an international documentation centre on criminology and related disciplines. UNICRI's principal areas of

focus are: security governance, international criminal law, judicial reform, juvenile justice, corruption, victim protection, organized crime, counterfeiting and drugs. The Documentation Centre supports the Institute's research, training and field activities and enables the Institute to serve the needs of international organizations, national institutions, NGOs, experts and professionals.

Funding

UNICRI is funded by voluntary contributions from States, international organizations and public or private institutions.

AFFILIATED AGENCIES OF THE UNITED NATIONS

Structure

UNICRI is governed by a Board of Trustees composed of eminent experts from different countries. Seven of these are selected by the Commission on Crime Prevention and Criminal Justice on the principle of equitable geographical distribution. They are nominated by the Secretary-General and endorsed by ECOSOC. Representatives of the host country, the Secretary-General, the Administrator of UNDP and the Director of the Institute serve as ex-officio members of the Board.

Director: Dr Jonathan Lucas (page 1467)

UNICRI, Viale Maestri del Lavoro, 10, 10127 - Turin, Italy. Tel: +39 (0)11 653 7111, fax: +39 (0)11 631 3368, e-mail: information@unicri.it, URL: http://www.unicri.it

UNITED NATIONS OFFICE FOR PARTNERSHIPS

The United Nations Office for Partnerships serves as a portal for partnership opportunities with the UN. It promotes new collaborations and partnerships in support and fulfillment of the Millennium Development Goals (MDGs) and provides support to new initiatives of the Secretary-General.

UNOP manages the United Nations Fund for International Partnerships (UNFIP), established by the Secretary-General in March 1998 to serve as the liaison in the partnership between the UN system and the UN Foundation, and the United Nations Democracy Fund (UNDEF), established by the Secretary-General in July 2005 to support democratization throughout the world. UNOP also provides advisory services to other bodies.

The UN Foundation was set up as the charity responsible for administering the $1 billion contribution of Ted Turner in support of UN causes. Through UNFIP, funds mobilised by the UN Foundation are channelled to the UN system, for implementation of projects focused on

Children's Health, Women and Population, Environment, and Peace, Security and Human Rights. To date over US$1 billion has been programmed for over 500 projects implemented by 33 United Nations entities in over 120 countries.

The Office, headed by Mr. Roland Rich, Officer-in-Charge, reports to the Secretary-General, Ban Ki-moon.

Officer-in-charge, UNOP & Executive Head, UNDEF: Roland Rich

United Nations Office for Partnerships, 1 United Nations Plaza, Room DC1-1330, New York, NY 10017, USA. Tel: +1 212 963-1000, fax: +1 212 963-1486, e-mail: partner@un.org, URL: http://www.un.org/partnerships/index.html

UNITED NATIONS OFFICE OF LEGAL AFFAIRS

The UN Office of Legal Affairs (OLA) provides a central legal service for the UN Secretariat as well as for the principal and other organs of the UN. It also contributes to the development and codification of international public and trade law, and aims to strengthen and effectively implement the international law of the seas and oceans through consistent application of the 1982 United Nations Convention on the Law of the Sea.

OLA is headed by an Under-Secretary-General who is assisted by some 160 staff members. Its biennial budget is currently around US$36 million.

Under-Secretary-General: Ms. Patricia O'Brien

United Nations Office of Legal Affairs, United Nations Headquarters, New York, NY 10017, USA. Fax: +1 212 963 6430, URL: http://untreaty.un.org/ola/Default.aspx

UNITED NATIONS OFFICE ON DRUGS AND CRIME (UNODC)

The United Nations Office on Drugs and Crime (UNODC), established in 1997, is a global leader in the struggle against illicit drugs and international crime, and the lead United Nations entity for delivering legal and technical assistance to prevent terrorism. Headquartered in Vienna, UNODC operates 54 field offices around the world, covering more than 150 countries.

UNODC is governed by two functional Commissions of the Economic and Social Council: the Commission on Narcotic Drugs and the Commission on Crime Prevention and Criminal Justice. Their decisions and resolutions provide policy guidance and oversight to UNODC in their respective areas, and they also approve UNODC's budget and workplan. (The United Nations regular budget component, which accounts for approximately 8.6 percent of the total UNODC budget, is approved by the General Assembly.)

The Commission on Narcotic Drugs is the central policymaking body within the United Nations system dealing with drug-related matters. It monitors the world drug situation, develops strategies on international drug control and recommends measures to combat the world drug problem, including through reducing demand for drugs, promoting alternative development initiatives and adopting supply reduction measures.

The Commission on Crime Prevention and Criminal Justice is the central body within the United Nations system providing policy guidance on crime prevention and criminal justice. It formulates international policies and recommendations on criminal justice issues, including trafficking in persons, transnational crime and aspects of terrorism prevention. It monitors the use and application of relevant United Nations standards and norms and it guides policy development in response to new issues.

Both Commissions provide Member States with a venue to exchange expertise, experiences and information on relevant matters and to develop a coordinated response.

Crime, drugs and terrorism are high-priority issues for the United Nations. At a time when these problems without borders are becoming widely recognized as threats to individuals and nations alike, requests for coordinated UNODC initiatives at the national, regional and transnational levels continue to grow. UNODC's efforts enhance security and improve the everyday lives of people across the globe.

Mandates

UNODC is guided by international mandates based on the rule of law. Within these mandates, UNODC gathers and analyses evidence that identifies trends and serves as a platform for action. This foundation of research, which undergirds all of UNODC's work, enables it to identify needs on the basis of facts. Because UNODC provides relevant stakeholders with unbiased data, it can serve as an honest broker in defining policy on key issues.

Crime-related Treaties

The United Nations Convention against Transnational Organized Crime is the main international instrument to counter organized crime and a critical force to spur coordinated international cooperation to fight organized crime. Also known as the Palermo Convention, it is supplemented by three protocols that target trafficking in persons, especially women and children; smuggling of migrants; and illicit manufacturing and trafficking of firearms.

The United Nations Convention against Corruption is the first legally binding global anti-corruption instrument. It obliges the States that have ratified it to prevent and criminalize corruption, promote international cooperation, recover stolen assets and improve technical assistance and information exchange. The Convention applies to both the public and private sectors, and it provides all national, regional and multinational anti-corruption efforts with a single set of agreed-upon anti-corruption obligations and guidelines.

Drug-related Treaties
- Single Convention on Narcotic Drugs and its Protocol
- Convention on Psychotropic Substances
- United Nations Convention against Illicit Traffic in Narcotic Drugs and Psychotropic Substances

The three major international drug control treaties are mutually supportive and complementary. An important purpose of the first two treaties is to codify internationally applicable control measures to ensure the availability of narcotic drugs and psychotropic substances for medical and scientific purposes, and to prevent their diversion into illicit channels. They also include general provisions on trafficking and drug abuse.

Terrorism-related Treaties

The 16 universal legal instruments against terrorism are a major element of the global regime against terrorism and form an important framework for international cooperation in countering terrorism. Most of these instruments are punitive, requiring State Parties to penalize various types of terrorist violence in their domestic law and to provide no safe haven for terrorists.

Key Programmes

The UNODC strategy for confronting crime, drugs and terrorism integrates both thematic and regional approaches to ensure that its initiatives are proactive, focused and effective. Its work falls into five interrelated thematic areas:

- Organized crime and trafficking
- Corruption
- Crime prevention and criminal justice reform
- Health and livelihoods
- Terrorism prevention

UNODC country and regional programmes support and complement these themes and translate them into action. To consolidate its presence where the threat from crime, drugs and terrorism is particularly severe or rapidly growing, UNODC has established a series of regional programmes with the goal of creating localized hubs of action and expertise. It has begun its work in the following regions, with others to follow:

- East Asia and the Pacific
- South Eastern Europe
- East Africa
- Central America and the Caribbean

Working directly with Governments, international organizations, other United Nations entities and civil society groups, UNODC acts as a catalyst for action by developing and implementing programmes that are tailored to the needs of the countries and regions it assists and fully coordinated with its key areas of focus.

Tools and Services

UNODC offers countries in-depth expertise and a broad array of innovative services, tools and resources to counteract the destructive impact of organized crime, illicit drugs and terrorism. UNODC provides accurate and reliable evidence-based research and threat analysis to inform and support policy and operational decisions; a wide range of technical assistance to enhance the capacity of States to build and sustain safe and stable societies; norms and standards that establish and promote best practices and encourage compliance with international obligations; international networks that encourage exchange of information and experience; and advocacy services to raise public awareness about key issues and mobilize all sectors of society to help bring about change.

Central to every kind of assistance UNODC provides is a commitment to building local capacity. UNODC helps countries develop and strengthen their own institutions so that they are better able to confront and disrupt criminal organizations and terrorist networks and put a stop to trafficking and other illicit activities. Because the problems UNODC addresses do not respect borders, many of its efforts involve international cooperation, whether at the regional, transnational or global level.

Publications

UNODC publishes a number of authoritative research reports on global, regional and national trends and threats in drugs and crime. Its premier publication, the annual World Drug Report, provides comprehensive, balanced information on drug trends and an analysis of drug markets at the global, regional and national levels.

UNODC threat assessment reports on particular regions or on issues such as transnational organized crime, the transnational trade in Afghan heroin or the impact of drug trafficking on security provide evidence of, and raise awareness about, the links between drug trafficking, organized crime, development and security issues.

UNODC also produces survey reports on illicit crop cultivation, drug use, crime victimization and corruption. Illicit crop monitoring reports include an annual Afghanistan opium poppy survey report and regular updates on coca cultivation in the Plurinational State of Bolivia, Colombia and Peru, opium poppy cultivation in the Lao People's Democratic Republic and Myanmar, and cannabis plant cultivation in Morocco.

UNODC also tracks crime statistics and produces specialized reports on crime, such as the 2009 Global Report on Trafficking in Persons. Gathering and analysing data on crime is particularly challenging and UNODC is working to develop and refine measurements and standards to improve the ability of Governments and international institutions to perform this work.

UNODC also produces a wide variety of resource publications for practitioners, including legislators, policymakers, law enforcement and criminal justice officials, health-care providers, NGOs and others who work in areas covered by the UNODC mandate. These include handbooks, manuals, model laws, case studies, assessment instruments, training modules and other resources and reference tools.

Many UNODC publications, including its in-depth research reports and crop surveys, can be accessed on the UNODC website. Many are available in more than one language.

Funding

For the years 2010-2011, the UNODC budget was approved at a level of US$463 million. Approximately US$42 million of that amount was provided from the United Nations regular budget, with the remaining US$426 million expected to be raised through voluntary donor contributions.

UNODC Executive Director: Yury Fedotov (page 1423)

United Nations Office on Drugs and Crime, Vienna International Centre, P.O. Box 500, A-1400 Vienna, Austria. Tel: +43 1 260 60-0, fax: +43 1 260 605 866, email: unodc@unodc.org, URL: http://www.unodc.org

UNITED NATIONS PEACEBUILDING COMMISSION

The Peacebuilding Commission (PBC) was created in 2005 by both the General Assembly and the Security Council in their respective resolutions A/60/180 and SC 1645 (2005). It is an intergovernmental advisory that supports peace efforts in countries emerging from conflict.

Its mandate is to "marshal resources and to advise on and propose integrated strategies for post-conflict peacebuilding and recovery." The PBC supports reconstruction, institution-building and sustainable development, in countries emerging from conflict.

It is specifically mandated to:

- Propose integrated strategies for post-conflict peacebuilding and recovery;
- Help to ensure financing for both in immediate short term and longer term of conflicts and their aftermath
- Focal global attention on post-conflict recovery;
- Develop best practices for its political, security, humanitarian and development support partners.

Structure

The PBC's Organizational Committee is made up of 31 countries: Seven from the Security Council (including the five permanent members); Seven from the Economic and Social Council (ECOSOC), Five from the top 10 financial contributors to the UN budgets, including voluntary contributions to UN agencies and programs and the Peacebuilding Fund; Five from the top 10 providers of military personnel and civilian police to UN missions; and Seven additional

members, to ensure geographical balance and include countries with post-conflict experience. These are be elected by the General Assembly. A Peacebuilding Support Office (PBSO) was established in the United Nations Secretariat to support the Peacebuilding Commission in all its deliberations. The PBSO is headed by an Assistant Secretary-General.

The Peacebuilding Commission is being reviewed to assess its progress so far and determine its future direction.

Peacebuilding Fund

The Peacebuilding Fund (PBF) was set up so that immediate funding needs may be available for countries in need when other funding mechanisms are not available. As of 2013, it was supporting more than 220 projects in 22 countries. In 2010, the PBF immediate response facility allocated over US$25 million to fund projects in Burundi, Central African Republic, Côte d'Ivoire, Guinea, Haiti, Liberia, Kenya, Sierra Leone, Somalia, Sri Lanka, Sudan and Timor Leste. The Peacebuilding and Recovery Facility allocated US$196 million to fund projects in Burundi, CAR, Comoros, Côte d'Ivoire, Democratic Republic of Congo, Guinea, Guinea Bissau, Liberia, Nepal, and Sierra Leone.

Chair, Peacebuilding Commission: Ambassador Ranko Vilović (Republic of Croatia) (page 1532)

UN Peacebuilding Commission, First Avenue at 46th Street, New York, NY 10017, USA. Tel: +1 212 963 4475, fax: +1 212 963 0071, URL: http://www.un.org/en/peacebuilding/

UNITED NATIONS POPULATION FUND (UNFPA)

UNFPA, the United Nations Population Fund, a subsidiary organ of the United Nations General Assembly, is the largest internationally funded source of population assistance. It promotes the right of all individuals to develop to their fullest potential. It is supported entirely by voluntary contributions. Since it began operations in 1969 as the United Nations Fund for Population Activities, the UNFPA has provided nearly $6 billion in assistance to 155 developing countries. A quarter of the world's population assistance from donor nations to developing countries is channelled through UNFPA.

Mission

UNFPA's mission statement summaries its aim: UNFPA "supports countries in using population data for policies and programmes to reduce poverty and to ensure that every pregnancy is wanted, every birth is safe, every young person is free of HIV/AIDS and every girl and woman is treated with dignity and respect."

AFFILIATED AGENCIES OF THE UNITED NATIONS

Purpose

At present, UNFPA's work is guided by the Programme of Action adopted at the International Conference on Population and Development in 1994 and the Millennium Development Goals adopted in 2000. From ICPD, the following goals were agreed:
- universal access to reproductive health services by 2015
- universal primary education and closing the gender gap in education by 2015
- reduction of maternal mortality by 75 per cent by 2015
- reduction in infant mortality
- increase in life expectancy.

These goals were amplified in 1999, one of the most important additions being:
- HIV infection rates in persons aged 15-24 should be reduced by 25 per cent in the most affected countries by 2005, and by 25 per cent globally by 2010.

Subsequent international agreements at ICPD+5, the Millennium Summit (2000) and the World Summit (2005) have linked UNFPA's mandate to specific goals and place greater stress on the Fund's role in HIV prevention and poverty reduction.

In 2007, a plan for 2008-2011 a new strategic plan was introduced entitled 'Accelerating Progress and National Ownership of the IPCD Programme of Action'. A major re-organisation is also underway including a decentralisation of resources from headquarters to the country and regional levels. Following a review of UNFPA's recent work, a revised Strategic Plan was introduced for 2011-2013. The plan centres on the promoting the right to sexual and reproductive health. Priority will be given to two areas; reducing maternal deaths and achieving universal access to reproductive health, including family planning.

Policies

UNFPA is a grant-providing agency and its programmes provide equipment, expertise and training designed to meet each country's needs. The projects themselves are generally executed by governments, United Nations agencies, and non-governmental organisations. UNFPA provides assistance only upon the request of governments and supports only non-coercive population policies. The Fund has been guided by two major principles in providing assistance for population activities. First, that every nation has the sovereign right to determine its own population policies and programmes. Second, that all couples and individuals have the basic right to decide freely and responsibly the number and spacing of their children. In accordance with the recommendations of the 1984 International Conference on Population, abortion is not regarded by UNFPA as a means of family planning. UNFPA does not provide support for abortion. Rather, it maintains that effective contraception reduces the demand for abortion. UNFPA supports family planning activities as a human right; for the improvements in family health that they bring; for demographic change; and as an adjunct to socio-economic development.

Since 2007, UNFPA has decentralized its operations in order to become more field-centred and efficient. It established five regional and six sub-regional offices in the field that help co-ordinate work in about 150 countries, areas and territories through a network of 129 country offices.

Programme

In keeping with directives issued by the Governing Council of the United Nations Development Programme, which also functions as UNFPA's Governing Council, the Fund concentrates its efforts in the following programme areas, in descending order of priority:
- family planning programmes, which may be oriented towards the individual or the family. These are often integrated with maternal and child health services in the primary health care context, and may also be integrated with other programmes as appropriate to social and cultural conditions;
- information, education and communication activities including population education, motivation and social mobilisation. The information disseminated deals primarily with family planning, and addresses a broad range of population-related issues such as environmental concerns;
- basic data collection and analysis through, for example, national population and housing censuses, sample surveys, and vital registration systems;

- population dynamics, comprising mainly research on demographic and socio-economic interrelationships; population policy, which involves assisting governments, at their request, in formulating, implementing, and evaluating population policies.

UNFPA allocates about 50 per cent of its resources to reproductive health, including maternal and child health care and family planning. A further 20 per cent goes towards related population information, education and communication. The balance is allocated to such areas as population data collection and analysis, research on demographic and socio-economic relationships, and the formation and evaluation of population policy.

Special programmes cover the following areas: women, population and development; youth; ageing; AIDS; and population and environment. Programmes on women, population and development seek to enhance women's integration into the development process through increased and improved participation in education and employment, as well as a broad range of social, economic, and political activities. UNFPA addresses AIDS-related problems mainly through public information activities and education. AIDS-related activities are integrated into UNFPA-supported maternal and child health and family planning programmes. UNFPA supports research into the interrelationships between population and the environment, and assists countries and organisations, at their request, in examining these interrelationships.

Funding

UNFPA is wholly funded by voluntary contributions, the main donors being governments and intergovernment organisations, as well as private sector groups and individuals. Total revenue for 2011 was US$934 million including US$450.7 million in voluntary contributions from governments and private donors.

The Fund is a subsidiary organ of the UN General Assembly. It reports to the UNDP/UNFPA Executive Board of 36 UN Member States on administrative and financial matters. It receives overall policy guidance from ECOSOC.

Priority countries

UNFPA uses a set of criteria to decide which developing countries are most in need of population assistance. Priority country status is given to those countries with a per capita gross national product of US$750 or less and which meet any two of the following criteria: annual population increment of 100,000 or more; gross reproduction rate of 2 or more; infant mortality rate of 120 per 1,000 live births or more; female literacy rate of 40 per cent or less; and rural population density of 2 or more people per hectare.

Monitoring and Evaluation

UNFPA uses the Programme Review and Strategy Development (PRSD) exercise to assist countries in formulating, monitoring, and updating their population policies and programmes. Undertaken jointly with national governments, the PRSD serves as a means to analyse a country's current population situation and trends. It helps to determine the country's population goals and targets, the role of national institutions in achieving these goals, the assistance requirements from UNFPA and other donors, and the role to be played by international and local non-governmental organisations. All UNFPA-funded projects are monitored through annual progress reports; tripartite project reviews which involve the government, UNFPA, and the executing agency; and mid-cycle reviews conducted half-way through a programme period. In addition, UNFPA uses outside experts to conduct independent, in-depth evaluations. Results of evaluations are regularly published by UNFPA and disseminated to governments, project staff, and others interested in the Fund's activities.

To see the membership of the Governing Council, please consult the entry for UNDP.

Executive Director: Dr Babatunde Osotimehin (page 1490)

United Nations Population Fund (UNFPA), 220 East 42nd Street, New York, NY 10017, USA. Tel: +1 212 297 5000, fax: +1 212 370 0201, e-mail: hq@unfpa.org, URL: http://www.unfpa.org

UNITED NATIONS RELIEF AND WORKS AGENCY FOR PALESTINE REFUGEES IN THE NEAR EAST (UNRWA)

The United Nations Relief and Works Agency for Palestine Refugees in the Near East (UNRWA) was created by resolution 302 (IV) of the UN General Assembly on 8 December 1949 and began operations on 1 May 1950. In the absence of a solution to the Palestine Refugee problem, the General Assembly has renewed UNRWA's mandate every three years (most recently extending it until 30 June 2014) and is expected to renew until settlement of the refugee problem is reached.

Envisaged initially as a temporary organisation, UNRWA originally provided, in co-operation with host governments, emergency relief to some three quarters of a million people, mostly Palestinian Arabs, who had lost their homes and livelihood as a result of the 1948 Arab-Israeli conflict and fled to neighbouring Arab countries, especially the present Lebanon, Syria, Jordan and the West Bank and Gaza Strip. Today UNRWA is the main provider of essential services - health, education, relief and social services - to 5 million registered Palestine refugees in the Middle East.

Programmes

UNRWA's main programmes are:
Relief and Social Services: Provides a minimum standard of nutrition and shelter. It also facilitates longer-term social and economic development for refugees and their communities.

Education: It has been the main provider of basic education to Palestinian refugees for 60 years. Education is UNRWA's largest activity accounting for nearly 50 per cent of its budget and 70 per cent of its staff. In 2011/12 its programme included: nearly 700 schools, approximately 19,200 educational staff, approximately 486,75 pupils, 10 vocational training centres, over 6,600 training places, 890 teachers in training and 1,700 student teachers.
Health: More than 3,600 health workers provide health care to Palestinian refugees in over 130 centres. In 2011, UNRWA staff performed 10.7 million medical and dental consultations.
Micro Finance: Aims to promote economic development and to alleviate poverty among Palestine refugees and other poor and marginalised groups. It has helped finance over 150,000 enterprises.
Infrastructure and Camp Improvement: Created in response to the Geneva Conference on UNRWA (2004) to tackle the deteriorating living conditions of Palestine refugees in camps. Of the 4.7 million Palestine refugees registered wtih UNRWA, approximately 1.3 million live in its 58 recognised refugee camps. The department is not funded by UNRWA's regular budget and is dependent on specific grants from donors.

General Programmes

Gaza: Approximately 1.1 million Palestine refugees live in the tiny Gaza Strip, living in eight camps.
Jordan: More than 2 million registered refugees live in Jordan. There are ten official and three unofficial camps. Most Palestinian refugees have full Jordanian citizenship.

Lebanon: Around 425,000 refugees are registered with UNRWA in 12 refugee camps. Palestinian refugees account for some 10 per cent of Lebanon's total population.

Syria: UNRWA is mandated to provide health, education, and relief and social services to more than 467,000 Palestine refugees living in nine official and three unofficial camps. The current political situation in Syria has adversely affected the economy. Factors including the decrease in value of the Syrian pound, rising cost of basic commodieis and decreased employment have impacted both Syrians and the Palestinian refugee community. UNRWA is working to help refugees' ability to cope and to achieve sustainable livelihoods.

West Bank: Approximately 780,000 registered refugees. Approximately 25 per cent live in 19 refugee camps.

Emergency Programmes

Lebanon

Conflict between the militant group Fatah al-Islam and the Lebanese army and the Nahr el-Bared refugee camp destroyed the entire camp and the neighbouring UNRWA compound which included schools and health clinics. At least 27,000 refguuees had to abandon their homes. Most moved to the Beddawi refugee camp which struggled to cope with the influx. UNRWA's initial emergency response is now a sustained relief programme. The Agency continues to provide most of the displaced refugees with their most fundamental daily needs: shelter, food, water and sanitation. Reconstruction began in 2009 with rebuild costs for 2009-11 estimated to be almost $330 million.

West Bank

722,302 registered refugees lived in the West Bank in 19 camps. UNRWA has provided expanded medical aid and relief and has worked to improve living conditions by repairing and reconstructing refugees' shelters and promoting major improvements in environmental health. It also seeks to protect human rights. It has also been able to create jobs.

Gaza

Approximately 1.1 million Palestine refugees lived in the tiny Gaza Strip, living in eight camps. As in the West Bank, economic depression, high unemployment and reduced job opportunities have contributed to an increase in poverty. Approximately 50,000 refugees live in the eight refugee camps.

Present Emergency

The Intifadah which broke out in September 2000 obliged the Agency to launch an appeal for emergency funds to cover special operations in the West Bank and Gaza Strip. A further appeal for funds was launched in January 2002 following Israeli military incursions into occupied Palestinian territories in Israel which resulted in large-scale destruction of shelters, water and electricity supplies and the basic services required for the minimum standards of life.

Since the beginning of current emergency, UNRWA has worked to alleviate the impact of violence, curfews and closures on the refugee population in the West Bank and Gaza Strip. The effect of closures on the Palestinian economy has resulted in an estimated 50 per cent unemployment, putting 60 per cent of the population under the poverty line. As part of its emergency relief activities UNRWA has increased its provision of food aid, and now targets almost 220,000 families in the West Bank and Gaza. The Agency also provides temporary jobs, which indirectly support 160,000 women and children in Gaza alone. It assists over 5,000 refugees whose homes have been damaged during military operations.

The UNRWA's health programme has responded to increased demands due to injuries and psychological trauma caused by the conflict, and their medical teams attempt to bring healthcare to communities isolated by closures for long periods. The education of refugee children has been severely disrupted, as teachers and pupils are often unable to reach their schools, which have themselves come under fire and been used as military outposts.

Financing

UNRWA is funded almost entirely by voluntary contributions mostly from governments and the European Commission, which account for 98 per cent of all income. Most contributions are received as financial assistance, although 5 per cent of income is received in kind - mainly as donations of food commodities. The largest contributor in 2009 was the USA (US$268 million), followed by the European Commission (US$232.7 million).However, the funding target for 2009 was not reached. In 2009, UNRWA's total budget for its core programmes, emergency activities and special projects was US$1.2 billion, for which the Agency received US$948 million. UNRWA's biennium regular budget for 2010 and 2011 was US$1.23 billion

Organisation

The Commissioner-General, appointed by the UN General Assembly, is the head of all UNRWA operations assisted by an Advisory Commission. UNRWA's five fields of operation in Lebanon, Syria, Jordan, West Bank and Gaza are supervised and supported by a Headquarters in Vienna (Austria) and Amman (Jordan) and Gaza City (Gaza). There are field offices in the Gaza Strip, Jordan, Lebanon, Syria, and the West Bank and Liaison Offices in Egypt and the USA.

UNRWA employs over 27,000 local staff, most of whom are locally recruited Palestinians. The UN employs 110 international staff posts and there are senior secondments from UNESCO and WHO.

Commissioner-General: Filippo Grandi

United Nations Relief and Works Agency for Palestine Refugees in the Near East (UNRWA) Headquarters, HQ Gaza, PO Box 140157, Amman 11814, Jordan. Tel: +972 8 677 7333, fax: +972 8 677 7555, URL: http://www.unrwa.org

UNRWA HQ Amman, Bayader Wadi Seer, PO Box 140157, Amman 11814, Jordan. Tel: +962 6 580 8100, fax: +962 6 580 8335

UNITED NATIONS RESEARCH INSTITUTE FOR SOCIAL DEVELOPMENT

The United Nations Research Institute for Social Development (UNRISD) is an autonomous UN agency established in 1963. UNRISD is concerned with reseach into the effects on social development as economies grow and contract.

UNRISD hosts international, regional meetings and global conferences through which it aims to build working relationships with researchers and experts as well as inspire new research programmes and review ongoing projects. It also exists to bridge the gap between academic and professional researchers and the policy makers who can use and implement the information.

UNRISD Board

The UNRISD Board of Advisors, which has included academics, activists, ambassadors and individuals from the private sector, puts forth ideas for further elaboration

Funding

When UNRISD was established in 1963 the Netherlands granted a US$1 million start up fund. UNRISD does not receive funding from the general budget of the UN but receives contributions from governments, non-governmental organizations, foundations, and United Nations agencies usually given as grants for specific projects. The Institute has an annual operating budget of approximately US$4 million. Total expenditure in 2011 was US$3.9 million. Core funding in 2011 was provided by Denmark, Finland, Mexico, South Africa, Sweden and the UK.

Director: Sarah Cook (page 1408)

United Nations Research Institute for Social Development (UNRISD), Palais des Nations, 1211 Geneva 10, Switzerland. Tel: + 41 (0)(0)22 917 3020, fax: +41 (0)22 917 0650, e-mail: info@unrisd.org, URL: http://www.unrisd.org

UNITED NATIONS VOLUNTEERS (UNV)

The United Nations Volunteers (UNV) programme is the UN organization that aims to contributes to peace and development through voluntary work worldwide. UNV seeks to harness the benefits to both society and the individual that volunteerism can bring including socially and economically.

The progamme works to foster recognition of volunteers. It works with partners to integrate volunteerism into development programming, and helps to mobilize an increasing number of volunteers throughout the world.

UNV helps countries to foster and develop volunteerism as a force for sustainable development. It provides strategic advice on the role and contribution of volunteerism and options for community involvement in development programmes. UNV has partnerships with governments and with the UN, non-profit and private sector organizations in order to support development programmes.

More than 7,500 UN Volunteers are active each year. Approximately 80 per cent coming from developing countries, and more than 30 per cent volunteering within their own countries. Volunteers mobilized by UNV have helped to organize and run local and national elections and have supported numerous peacekeeping and humanitarian projects. Approximately 33 per cent of international civilians working in UN peacekeeping operations are UN Volunteers. The UNV Online Volunteering service acts as a portal for advice and service providers.

UNV is represented worldwide through the offices of the United Nations Development Programme (UNDP) and reports to the UNDP Executive Board. It is active in approximately 130 countries.

Executive Coordinator: Richard Dictus (Netherlands)

United Nations Volunteers, POB 260 111, D-53153 Bonn, Germany. Tel: +49 228 815 2000, fax: +49 228 815 2001, e-mail: information@unvolunteers.org, URL: http://www.unv.org/

WORLD FOOD PROGRAMME

Established in 1963, the World Food Programme (WFP) is the United Nations frontline agency in the fight against global hunger. Hunger affects one out of every seven people on earth, and some 24,000 people die every day from hunger and related causes. WFP envisages a world in which everyone has access at all times to the nourishment they require to lead a full life. Since its inception, the organisation has invested over US$27.8 billion to combat hunger, promote economic and social development and provide relief assistance in emergencies throughout the world.

Function
WFP's strategic plan for the period 2008-2013 reflects the beginning of its transition from a food agency to a food assistance agency. Broadly, its aims are:

- To save lives and protect livelihoods in emergencies
- To prevent hunger and prepare for disaster and disaster mitigation
- To rebuild livelihoods post-disaster or post-conflict
- To reduce chronic hunger and undernutrition
- To assist countries to reduce hunger through handover strategies and local purcahses

The WFP has three main areas of activity:

Emergencies and Rehabilitation: in emergencies, WFP provides fast, efficient, life-sustaining relief to millions of people who are the victims of natural or man-made disasters. This includes refugees and internally displaced people. Today, 80 per cent of WFP resources are used for relief activities.

Development: these projects target the most vulnerable people - babies, school children, pregnant and breast-feeding women and the elderly. WFP uses food aid as a preventive medicine. The WFP school feeding projects use food aid to encourage millions of hungry children to come to school. In countries such as Haiti, Pakistan, Morocco and Mozambique, the WFP food also draws mothers into health clinics as well as literacy and nutrition classes.

Food for Work: where people are chronically hungry, WFP promotes self-reliance through food-for-work projects. Workers are paid with food aid to allow communities to devote more time to development. Examples of this work are roads and ports built in Ghana and Lesotho, repaired dykes in Bangladesh and terraced hillsides in China and Guatemala.

During the year 2010, 109.2 million people in 75 countries benefited directly from the food aid supplied through the WFP. Those helped in 2010 included: 89 million women and children, 15.4 million internally displaced persons, 2.1 million refugees, and 2.5 million people affected by HIV/AIDS. Some 21.1 million children received school meals aid. Some 4.6 million metric tons of food were delivered. In 2011, WFP aimed to reach more than 90 million people in more than 70 countries. In 2011, over 2.4 million metric tons of food valued at US$1.2 billion from 87 nations were delivered. In 2011, WFP raised more than US$43.8 billion from voluntary donations.

Structure
The Executive Board consists of 36 members, of which 18 are elected by the Economic and Social Council of the UN (ECOSOC) and 18 by the Council of Food and Agriculture. Each member serves a three-year term and is eligible for re-election.

WFP's Executive Board Member States for the year 2013 are:
Expiring 31 December 2013: Australia, Cameroon, Canada, Cuba, Germany, Haiti, Morocco, Norway, Republic of Korea, Saudi Arabia, South Africa, Sudan.
Expiring 31 December 2014: Belgium, Brazil, China, Czech Republic, Ghana, Guatemala, Japan, Slovak Republic, Sweden, Tunisia, United Kingdom, Zambia.
Expiring 31 December 2015: Afghanistan, India, Iraq, Italy, Mexico, Netherlands, Philippines, Russian Federation, Sierra Leone, Switzerland, Uganda, USA.

The Executive Board oversees WFP's humanitarian and development food aid activities; helps to evolve and co-ordinate short and long term food aid policies; reviews, modifies and approves programmes, projects and activities as well as their budgets and reports annually to the substantive session of ECOSOC and the Council of FAO.

At the First Session of each year, the Executive Board elects, from among its members, a Bureau comprising a President, Vice President and three other members. Their function is to facilitate the functioning of the Board, in particular strategic planning, the preparation and organisation of Board meetings and the promotion of dialogue.

The Executive Director, who heads the Secretariat based in Rome, is elected by the UN Secretary General and the Director General of the FAO, for five years.

Funding
WFP relies entirely on voluntary contributions to finance its humanitarian and development projects. Donations are made either as cash, food such as flour, beans, oil, salt and sugar, or the basic items necessary to grow, store and cook food - kitchen utensils, agricultural tools, warehouses.

The principal source of funding is the 70 plus governments who voluntarily finance WFP projects. In the year 2011, the grand total of funding was US$3,714.6 million. The main donor was the USA (US$1,276.01 million).

Executive Director: Ertharin Cousin (page 1409)

World Food Programme, Via C.G. Viola 68, Parco dei Medici, 00148 Rome, Italy. Tel: +39 (0)6 65131, fax: +39 (0)6 6513 2840, e-mail: wfpinfo@wfp.org, URL: http://www.wfp.org

WORLD TRADE ORGANIZATION (WTO)

The World Trade Organization (WTO) was established on 1 January 1995, as a successor to the General Agreement on Tariffs and Trade (GATT).

GATT
GATT was established on a provisional basis on 1 January 1948 and was the only multilateral treaty on the rules of conduct for world trade. The General Agreement arose from an intention to provide a framework for international trade relations and a forum in which countries could negotiate and discuss factors such as employment, commodity agreements, restrictive practices, international investment and services and the reduction of trade barriers. This was done through 'trade rounds' - multilateral trade negotiations - of which GATT held 8 between the years 1947-93. Most of the early trade rounds were concerned solely with the reduction

of tariffs, but the so-called 'Kennedy Round' (1964-67) included a GATT Anti-Dumping Agreement and there were attempts from the 1970s onwards to address a wider range of factors such as intellectual property rights, dispute settlements, and issues in services, agriculture and the textiles and clothing trades. By the 1980s GATT was less effective, in that its own success in reducing tariffs (to just 4.7 per cent as opposed to the 40 per cent in existence when GATT started) had caused countries to seek to protect their trade sectors from overseas competition through bilateral agreements and subsidies. This undermined GATT's credibility as a multilateral agreement. Furthermore, GATT did not cover the increasingly important trade in services; there were several heavily exploited loopholes in the agreements covering agriculture, textiles and clothing; the dispute settlement system was too slow; and world trade was in general more complex than it had been in the 1940s.

Purpose

The WTO is the result of the decision by GATT members to create a permanent institution that would deal with the rules of global trade. Its primary aim is to ensure the best possible flow of trade between nations. It aims to improve the welfare of its member states.

The Multilateral Trading System

GATT and the WTO have helped create a strong trading system. The system was developed through a series of trade negotiation held under GATT. Most rounds dealt with tariff reductions. The 1986-94 Uruguay Round led to the creation of the WTO. Further negotiations have taken place. In 1997 agreements were reached on telecommunications, IT and financial services.

In 2000, new negotiations began on agriculture and services. These have been incorporated into the broader Doha Development Agenda (DDA), launched in 1991. The agenda also includes work on non-agricultural tariffs, trade and environment and various other issues raised by developing countries.

The WTO agreements form the basis of the Multilateral Trading System. The agreements are negotiated by a majority of member states, signed and ratified by their parliaments. The agreements form the basic rules of international trade. They guarantee important trade rights and ensure that governments keep their trade policies within agreed limits for everyone's benefit.

WTO Agreements

The current set of agreements are the outcome of the 1986-84 Uruguay Round which include a substantial revision of the original GATT. GATT remains the agreement for trade in goods. The Uruguay Round created more rules for trading in services, intellectual property, dispute settlements and trade policy reviews. There are some 30 agreements in total with separate commitments for specific areas.

-Goods

The revised GATT is the umbrella agreement for trade in goods. It has annexes dealing with specific sectors such as agriculture, or issues including state trading, subsidies and anti-dumping measures,

-Services

The General Agreement on Trade in Services (GATS) ensures that the services industry, including banks, insurance firms, telecommunications companies, tourism firms, also now has the same principles of freer and fairer trade.

-Intellectual Property

The WTO Intellectual Property means that the WTO now provides rules for trade and investment ideas, how to copyright and protect designs etc.

-Dispute Settlement

The system encourages member states to settle trade disputes through consultation. Countries may bring disputes to the WTO if they think their rights have been infringed. More than 300 cases have been dealt with in the last 10 years.

-Trade Policy Review

The purpose of the review is to improve transparency and create a better understanding of the policies of individual member states, and the potential impact these policies may have.

Developing Countries

All the agreements contain special provisions for developing of least developing countries (which form approximately 70 per cent of the WTO membership). The 2001 Ministerial Conference in Doha held many negotiations on the rights of developing countries. A WTO Committee on Trade and Development, supported by a sub-Committee on Least Developed Countries, studies the special needs of developing countries.

The WTO also organizes technical assistance and training through technical co-operation missions and reference centres.

Structure

The governing body is the Ministerial Conference (representatives of all members of WTO) which meets every two years to decide on the direction of WTO's programme. The General Council, also composed of all members, reports to the Conference and acts as the Dispute Settlement Body and the Trade Policy Review Body. The General Council delegates responsibility to the Council for Trade in Goods, the Council for Trade in Services and the Council for Trade Related Aspects of Intellectual Property Rights, and all three may establish their own subsidiary bodies when necessary.

Five other bodies report to the General Council: the Committee on Trade and Development, the Committee on Trade and Environment, the Committee on Balance of Payments; the Committee on Budget, Finance and Administration and the Committee on Regional Trade Agreement. In addition, there is a separate management body reporting to the General Council for WTO's plurilateral agreements - the Committee on Trade in Civil Aircraft and the Committee on Government Procurement.

The Trade Negotiations Committee for the Doha Development Agenda also reports to the General Council.

As at March 2013, WTO had 159 member states. As a result of increasing economic integration certain members have common trade interests and are able, under Article XXIV, to act together as a single entity within WTO. The European Commission, the Association of South East Asian Nations (ASEAN); the Cairns Group (developed and developing agricultural exporting nations); and to a lesser extent the Latin American Economic System (SELA) and the African, Caribbean and Pacific Group (ACP) often present united fronts.

The WTO makes decisions through the consensus of its members, although if consensus is not possible, the WTO Agreement provides for four voting situations: a three-quarters majority may vote for an interpretation of a proposed agreement; the same majority may vote to have an obligation imposed on a particular member waived; any part of a multilateral agreement may be amended through either a two-thirds or full majority (this depends on the nature of the amendment in question and in any case is effective only on those members who accept the amendment): a two-thirds majority of members can vote for the admittance of a new member.

The WTO Secretariat comprises approximately 640 staff and is based in Geneva, Switzerland. The WTO 2012 budget was 196 million Swiss Francs, consisting of contributions (calculated on the basis of trade share volume) from member states and miscellaneous income.

For details of the membership of the WTO please consult the matrix of *Country Membership of Major Organisations* in the preliminary section.

Outgoing Director General: Pascal Lamy
Incoming Director General (September 2013): Roberto Azevedo

World Trade Organization (WTO), Centre William Rappard, 154 rue de Lausanne, CH 1211 Geneva 21, Switzerland. Tel: +41 (0)22 739 5007, fax: +41 (0)22 731 4206, e-mail: enquiries@wto.org, URL: http://www.wto.org

EUROPEAN UNION

The object of the European Community, as set out in the 1957 Treaty of Rome, is 'to lay the foundation of an ever-closer union among the peoples of Europe'. The EU adopted its present form with the ratification of the Maastricht Treaty in 1993. The European Union is a political and economic alliance which currently consists of 28 Member States representing a population of 497 million people.

Origins of the Community

The need to restore the shattered economies of Western Europe following World War II gave political impetus to the creation of structures that would unite past enemies. The first of these structures, the Organization for European Economic Co-operation (established in 1947) and the Council of Europe (created in 1949) did not satisfy those Europeans who wanted a more federal structure for Western Europe.

One step towards this end was the *Schuman Plan*, aimed at pooling the coal and steel resources of Western Europe under a single authority and creating a single market. At that time coal and steel were seen not only as basic to economic revival, but also major elements in the development of national military power. The Plan was adopted under the Treaty of Paris in 1951 by Belgium, the Netherlands, Luxembourg, France, West Germany and Italy, establishing the European Coal and Steel Community (ECSC). The institutions of the ECSC included a High Authority advised by a Consultative Committee, a Council of Ministers, a Common Assembly and a Court of Justice. Its objectives were the economic expansion and rationalisation of the two industries, the abolition of duties and the elimination of restrictive practices.

The success of the ECSC encouraged the six members to plan further economic integration. In 1955 a report on a complete merger of the six economies and a common organisation for the development of nuclear energy was commissioned. Britain was invited to participate but declined. On the 25 March 1957, the Treaty of Rome was signed by the Six member countries, and this established the European Economic Community (EEC) and the European Atomic Energy Community (EAEC, commonly known as Euratom), as from 1 January 1958. Since both the EEC and Euratom had parallel institutions to those of the ECSC; under the Merger Treaty of 1965, the three Communities were merged in 1967 into the European Communities (EC), with common institutions vested in the European Commission, the Council of Ministers, the European Assembly or Parliament, and the European Court of Justice. The Treaty also established a single Economic and Social Committee.

Enlargement

The economic success of the EEC led successive British governments to apply for membership, first in July 1961 and again in May 1967 when Denmark and Ireland applied to join. Norway applied later. Three of the applicants for membership (excluding Ireland) were members of the European Free Trade Association (EFTA) which had been created in 1960 in an attempt to counter the economic influence of the EEC. The applications were rejected, possibly due to the influence of President General de Gaulle; when he left office in 1969, the Six members agreed in principle to an enlargement of the Community.

On 22 January 1972, Accession Treaties to the Community were signed. Referenda in Ireland (10 May 1972) and Denmark (2 October 1972) approved membership, but in Norway membership was rejected on a referendum on 26 September. In the UK the European Communities Act received the Royal Assent on 17 October 1972. On 1 January 1973 Denmark, Ireland and the UK became members of the enlarged Community of the Nine.

When the governments of Greece, Portugal and Spain became democratic in the mid-1970s, those countries became eligible for membership of the EEC. Greece, which had had an Association Agreement with the Community since 1962 (frozen from 1967-1974 under the Colonels' regime) became the 10th member country on 1 January 1981. Portugal and Spain started accession negotiations in October 1978 and February 1979 respectively, and both countries joined the Community on 1 January 1986. However, in Greenland (a part of Denmark with home rule) a referendum showed a majority in favour of withdrawing from the EC, and Greenland left the community on 1 January 1985, subject to agreement on fishing. Applications to join the European Community were tabled by Turkey in 1987, Austria in 1989, from Cyprus and Malta in 1990, Sweden in 1991 and Finland in 1992. Finland, Sweden and Austria became members from January 1995.

In December 2002, the EU reached agreement with 10 candidate countries that they could join the EU on 1 May 2004. Cyprus, the Czech Republic, Estonia, Hungary, Latvia, Lithuania, Malta, Poland, Slovakia and Slovenia became members on 1 May 2004. The European Council agreed in 1993 that Bulgaria and Romania could join the EU on 1st January 2007. Croatia joined the EU on 1 July 2013 as the 28th member.

In December 2004, accession talks with Turkey began. The Former Yugoslav Republic of Macedonia, Iceland, Montenegro, and Serbia are also candidate countries. Potential candidate countries are Albania, Bosnia and Herzegovina, and Kosovo under UN Security Council Resolution 1244.

Current Membership (28)

Member State	Year of Entry
Belgium	Founder member
France	Founder member
Germany	Founder member
Italy	Founder member
Luxembourg	Founder member
The Netherlands	Founder member
Ireland	1973
Denmark	1973
United Kingdom	1973
Greece	1981

- continued

Portugal	1986
Spain	1986
Austria	1995
Finland	1995
Sweden	1995
Cyprus	2004
Czech Republic	2004
Estonia	2004
Hungary	2004
Latvia	2004
Lithuania	2004
Malta	2004
Poland	2004
Slovakia	2004
Slovenia	2004
Bulgaria	2007
Romania	2007
Croatia	2013

Main Treaties

The Single European Act (SEA)

The Community has political as well as economic aspirations. The Single European Act (SEA) for the creation of a single Community market came into force on 1 July 1987. It amended the 1957 Treaty of Rome with a modest range of reforms, including amended voting procedures, powers of the European Parliament, a treaty on European Political Co-operation and bringing the European Monetary System (EMS) into the scope of the Treaty of Rome.

Merger Treaty

The Merger Treaty, signed in Brussels on 8 April 1965 and in force since 1 July 1967, which provided for a Single Commission and a Single Council of the then three European Communities.

Treaty of Rome

The Treaty of Rome established the European Economic Community (EEC). It was signed in Rome on 25 March 1957 and entered into force on 1 January 1958. The Treaty establishing the European Atomic Energy Community (Euratom) was signed at the same time and the two are jointly known as the Treaties of Rome.

Treaty on European Union (Maastricht Treaty)

In December 1991, the Treaty on European Union (aka the Maastricht Treaty) was signed by the heads of government of the then twelve members. This treaty extended the Community's objective of ever closer union among the peoples of Europe by, *inter alia*: setting a timetable for economic and monetary Union; introducing the 'principle of subsidiarity' into the domain of Community intervention at national level; widening the power of the European Parliament, and introducing the Committee of the Regions. It also brought new areas such as foreign policy and defence, immigration and asylum policies under the EC umbrella and introduced the concept of European citizenship. With the ratification of the Maastricht Treaty, the European Community became known as the European Union.

Treaty of Nice

This treaty was agreed in order to reform the EU institutions so that they could function efficiently following the Union's enlargement to 25 member states. The Treaty of Nice entered into force on 1 February 2003.

Treaty of Amsterdam

The Treaty of Amsterdam, signed on 2 October 1997, entered into force on 1 May 1999. It amended and renumbered the EU and EC Treaties.

European Convention

On 20 June 2003 a draft constitution, the European Convention, was submitted to the EU Summit at Thessaloniki. The proposed Convention included changes to the presidency and parliamentary powers and voting. It required the approval of all 27 governments. A "Treaty establishing a constitution for Europe" was adopted by the Heads of State and Government at the Brussels European Council in June 2004 and signed in Rome on 29 October 2004, but it was never fully ratified; although nine members had ratified it by the end of April 2005, at the end of May, France and the Netherlands rejected the treaty by referendum. The remaining member states were therefore no longer required to continue the ratification process, and the European Convention did not proceed.

The Treaty of Lisbon

The main objectives of this treaty are to make the EU more democratic, fulfilling the Europeans citizens' expectations for high standards of openness, accountability, transparency and participation. It is hoped that the Treaty will make the EU more efficient and empowered to tackle global challenges such as climate change, security and sustainable development. The treaty is similar to the failed draft constitution but rather than replacing all earlier EU treaties, the Lisbon treaty amends the Treaty on the European Union and the Treaty Establishing the European Community. The Lisbon Treaty was signed on 13 December 2007, and will have to be ratified by all 27 Member States before it could enter into force. It was hoped that this would happen before the next European Parliament elections in June 2009.

By June 2009, 25 countries had ratified the treaty; Irish voters rejected it in the only referendum to be held on the treaty, in 2008. The president of the Czech Republic also rejected it. The future of the treaty was therefore unclear, but in October 2009 Ireland held a second referendum and voted in favour of the treaty and the Czech Republic ratified it in November 2009. The Lisbon Treaty came into force on December 1 2009.

EU Presidency
Under the terms of the Lisbon treaty the post of President and High Representative for Foreign Affairs were created. In November voting began to elect the first President and Belgian prime minister Herman van Rompuy (page 1530) was unanimously elected to the post with Baroness Catherine Ashton (page 1380) of the United Kingdom being elected High Representative for Foreign Affairs.

Convention
Convention for the Protection of Human Rights and Fundamental Freedoms
Entered into force on 3 September 1953. The "European Convention on Human Rights" details a number of fundamental rights and freedoms (right to life, prohibition of torture, prohibition of slavery and forced labour, right to liberty and security, right to a fair trial, no punishment without law, right to respect for private and family life, freedom of thought, conscience and religion, freedom of expression, freedom of assembly and association, right to marry, right to an effective remedy, prohibition of discrimination). Parties undertake to secure these rights and freedoms to everyone within their jurisdiction. The Convention also establishes an international enforcement machinery. All alleged violations of human rights are referred directly to the Court

COMMUNITY LAW
Community Law has its origin in the Rome and Paris Treaties which laid down certain obligatory commitments, such as the Customs Union, the Common Agricultural Policy, and the 'approximation' or harmonisation of national laws. Article 235 of the EEC Treaty allows for the development of other activities (e.g. establishment of the Regional Fund). Community legislation is binding on member countries, but implementation of the law varies according to whether it takes the form of a Regulation, Directive, Decision, Recommendation or Opinion and on national customs and institutions. Enforcement is usually left to national governments, but the Commission is empowered to take direct action against governments or firms that breach rules against restrictive practices, or to refer infringements of Community law to the European Court of Justice. The Court ruling is expected to be obeyed by governments or other bodies concerned. Implementation of Community law operates at different levels within member countries and may be devolved by governments to regional or local authorities.

FINANCIAL ORGANS
The Budget
Originally the Community was financed by direct contributions from each member country on an agreed basis, but it was always intended that this system should be replaced by financing from Community taxes or 'own resources'. The Six decided to introduce own resources in 1970, but the system did not become fully operational until January 1980. Budget revenues are raised from four resources: customs duties levied at the EU's external borders; agricultural levies on products imported from third countries; a proportion of VAT on goods and services across the EU; and a proportion of each Member State's GNP. The first Delors package, agreed in February 1988, set the pattern for Community income and expenditure for the five years until 1992. It was then agreed that the Community's income (its 'own resources') should not be higher than 1.24 per cent of GNP by the end of the period. This figure has now been revised to 1.27 per cent.

The overall EU budget for 2012 was $129.1 billion in payments (an increase of over 1.8 per cent) and €147.2 billion for commitments, an increase of 3.8 per cent on the 2011 budget. For commitments, $67.5 billion was allocated to sustainable growth (45.9 per cent of total budget), €60.0 billion for preservation and management of natural resources (40.8 per cent of total budget); €2.1 billion for citizenship, freedom, security and justice (1.4 per cent of total budget); €9.4 billion on EU as a global player (6.4 per cent of total budget); €8.3 billion on administration (of which the Commission €3.3 billion). The budget for 2012 forecasts €129.1 in payments, up 1.8 per cent on 2011: $55.3 billion was allocated to sustainable growth, €57.0 billion for preservation and management of natural resources; €1.5 billion for citizenship, freedom, security and justice, €6.9 billion on EU as a global player; €8.3 billion on administration (of which the Commission €3.3 billion).The key objective of the 2012 Budget was to support the European economy and EU citizens.

A multi-year budget for 2014-2020 was agreed in February 2013. The Multi-Annual Financial Framework (MFF) amounts to €960 billion (£812 billion, US$1.3 trillion), representing a 3.3 per cent cut on the previous seven-year-budget. The MFF is approximately 1 per cent of total GDP across the EU countries. Agricultural subsidies are expected to be cut under the new budget. Actual budget spending is forecast to be lower than the budget (€908 billion). The proposed budget breaks down thus: Cohesion €325 billion; Competitiveness and growth €125.6 billion; Common Agricultural Policy €278 billion; Rural development and fisheries €95 billion; Security and Citizenship €15.7 billion; EU as a global player €59 billion; Administration €62 billion. Outside of the budget, a further €37 billion is proposed for the period 2014-2020, mainly overseas aid. The budget must be passed by the European Parliament.

The budget is adopted through a series of European Parliament readings. A preliminary draft proposal by the Commission at the end of April of each year is the basis for the Council's first reading. Following consultations with a delegation from the European Parliament, the Council amends the preliminary draft and adopts the draft budget. This is then analysed by Parliament's Committee on Budgets, specialised committees, individual members and political groups. Any amendments or modifications appearing at this stage are considered in the Committee on Budgets and then in plenary in Parliament's first reading, usually in October. The amended draft budget is then referred back to the Council for its second reading, which usually takes place in November. Finally, Parliament's second reading establishes both policy priorities and funding levels, and ultimately adopts the final budget. This takes place in December.

As well as the budget, the Community uses the following organs to make loans and grants:

The European Investment Bank (EIB)
This is the European Union's financing institution. It was established under Article 129 of the EEC Rome Treaty, with an annual lending volume of ECU 33 billion. The bank offers or guarantees loans for projects in the less developed regions of the Community, for industrial modernisation programmes, and for projects of common interest to several member countries that cannot be financed by national means. Its annual lending volume reached €79 billion in 2009. It has since been aiming to reduce it and in 2012, the annual lending volume was €52 billion.

European Development Fund (EDF)
assists development programmes of countries that have acceded to the Lomé Convention. Financial aid, in the form of loans or grants, is also available for various industrial, research and educational projects.

Structural Funds
The European Union has Structural Funds which address structural economic and social problems to overcome inequalities between different regions and social groups.

The European Social Fund (ESF)
Established in 1960, the ESF is the main instrument of Community social policy. During the period 2007-13 its intervention will focus on four key areas: increasing adaptability of workers and enterprises; enhancing access to employment and participation in the labour market; reinforcing social inclusion; and promoting partnership for reform in the fields of employment and inclusion.

European Regional Development Fund (ERDF)
This was established in 1975 to help correct regional imbalances within the European Union. Grants from the ERDF help finance development initiatives in both private and public sectors in government-designated Assisted Areas. Financial assistance from the ERDF is mainly targeted at: supporting small and medium-sized enterprises; promoting productive investment; improving infrastructure; furthering local development. The ERDF is the largest of the EU's Structural Funds, representing almost half of the total budget for the Structural Funds.

The **Cohesion Fund** provides additional structural assistance to those EU countries where the per capita GDP is lower then 90 per cent of the EU average. Grants are awarded to projects concerning the environment or transport infrastructure.

COMMUNITY INSTITUTIONS
The major Community Institutions are the European Parliament, the Council of Ministers, the European Commission, the European Court of Justice and the European Council (created 2009). Since 1974, summit meetings of Heads of State and Governments have been institutionalised as the European Council, which now meets at least twice a year. Other institutions are: The European Court of Auditors, The European Investment Bank, the Economic and Social Committee, the Committee of the Regions, the European Ombudsman and the European Central Bank. A short description of each institution follows; please refer to individual entries for further information.

European Parliament
This is largest multinational Parliament in the world. It represents the 493 million citizens of the Union and its primary objectives are the same as other parliaments - to pass good laws and to monitor and control the use of executive power. The Single Act of 1987 and the Treaty of European Union of 1993 have widened its responsibilities and increased its powers.

Since 1979, the Members of the European Parliament (MEPs) have been directly elected by the citizens of the Member States. Elections are held every five years. The most recent election was held in June 2009.

Since December 2011, the Parliament has had 754 seats allocated as follows: Austria 19 seats; Belgium 22; Bulgaria 18; Cyprus 6; Czech Republic 22; Denmark 13; Estonia 6; Finland 13; France 74; Germany 99; Greece 22; Hungary 22; Ireland 12; Italy 73; Latvia 9; Lithuania 12; Luxembourg 6; Malta 6; Netherlands 26; Poland 51; Portugal 22; Romania 33; Republic of Slovenia 8; Slovak Republic 13; Spain 54; Sweden 20 and UK 73. During the present parliamentary term, the number of MEPs was increased to the maximum provided for in the Treaty of Lisbon. For the 2014 election, according to the Lisbon Treaty, the number of seats will vary from six for Cyprus, Estonia, Malta and Luxembourg to 96 for Germany. Croatia will be able to elect 12 MEPs who will serve one year until the 2014 elections.

There are currently 7 political groups in the European Parliament; Group of the European People's Party (Christian Democrats); Group of the Progressive Alliance of Socialists and Democrats in the European Parliament; Group of the Alliance of Liberals and Democrats for Europe; Group of the Greens/European Free Alliance; European Conservatives and Reformists Group; Confederal Group of the European United Left - Nordic Green Left; Europe of Freedom and Democracy Group.

The European Parliament has three main locations: Brussels, Luxembourg and Strasbourg. The administrative offices (the General Secretariat) is in Luxembourg, and meetings of the whole Parliament (plenary sessions) normally take place in Strasbourg. MEPs sit according to political grouping rather than nationality.

The Parliament's main work is done in 20 standing committees, two subcommittees, 1 special committee on organised crime, corruption and money laundering (set up in March 2012) and 41 delegations. The Committees present reports to plenary sessions of the Parliament which may approve Commission proposals or suggest amendments, which are embodied in a Resolution or Opinion to the Council and Commission. Neither is obliged to heed them, but they increasingly do.

Members of the European Parliament (MEPs) can question both the Council and the Commission about any aspect of the Community's business, particularly where the interests of those they represent are likely to be directly affected. The Commission must submit an Annual Report to the Parliament. The European Parliament shares, with the Council, equal responsibility for adopting the EU budget. The Parliament can reject a proposed budget, and it has done so on several occasions. When this happens, the entire budget procedure has to be re-started. The European Commission proposes the draft budget, which is then debated by the Council and the European Parliament.

EUROPEAN UNION

The European Parliament exercises democratic supervision over the Union, and has the power to dismiss the Commission by adopting a motion of censure. This requires a two-thirds majority. It also supervises the day-to-day management of EU policies by putting oral and written questions to the Commission and the Council.

The Parliament is run by a Bureau, normally comprising the President and 14 Vice-Presidents who are elected by secret ballot to serve for two-and-a-half years. Additionally, five quaestors are responsible, in a purely consultative capacity, for financial and administrative affairs which affect Members. All business is conducted in the 28 official languages of the Community and all documents are published in these languages.

European Parliament, URL: http://www.europarl.europa.eu/portal/

Council of the European Union (also known as the Council of Ministers)
The Council is the Community's supreme legislative authority; apart from limited exceptions, it has to approve all Commission legislative proposals before these can become law. Furthermore, the Council co-ordinates the national policies of Member States and resolves differences between them and other institutions.

Each member country has its own representative Minister on the Council depending on the issues under discussion, e.g. Foreign Ministers on foreign and general affairs, Agricultural Ministers on Agriculture, and so on. Important Councils usually meet at least once a month.

The Presidency of the Council is held for a six-month term by each member country, from January until June, and from July until December. The Presidency must arrange and preside over all meetings; elaborate acceptable compromises and find pragmatic solutions; and secure consistency in decision making. The current and forthcoming presidencies are: 2013, Jan.-June: Ireland, July-Dec.: Lithuania; 2014: Jan.-June: Greece, July-Dec.: Italy; 2015: Jan.-June: Latvia, July-Dec.: Luxembourg.

Some Council decisions previously taken unanimously in accordance with the Luxembourg Agreement of 28 January 1966 can now be adopted by majority votes under the Single European Act. Those policy areas still requiring unanimity include taxation, industry, culture, regional and social funds, the framework programme for research and technology development, Common Foreign and Security Policy, Justice and Home Affairs. While the general principle of a new policy requires unanimous approval, implementation of that principle through regulations or directives can be carried out by qualified majority voting. A minimum of 225 votes out of 345 is required to reach a qualified majority.

On 3 May 2011 the United Nations General Assembly adopted a resolution upgrading the status of the European Union's participation in the United Nations 192-member body. The resolution was adopted by 180 UN Member States. Syria and Zimbabwe abstained and 10 countries did not vote. It will allow senior EU representatives to present the common positions of the Union to the Assembly.

The Council has its own Secretariat, consisting of about 2,500 officials, mostly in Brussels.

Council of the European Union, URL: http://www.consilium.europa.eu/homepage

The Commission
The Commission has four main roles: it proposes legislation to Parliament and the Council; it enforces Community law (jointly with the Court of Justice); it administers and implements Community policies and it acts as a mouthpiece for the European Union, negotiating international trade and co-operation agreements.

The Commission also manages the Union's annual budget and runs the Structural Funds, which attempt to even out disparities between the richer and poorer parts of the Union.

The Commission is headed by a college of 27 Commissioners (as at May 2013). One Commissioner is nominated by the national government of each Member State. Commissioners are appointed for a five-year renewable term, and pledge themselves to act independently in the Community interest. The President of the Commission is appointed on a two-year renewable term. The President is chosen by the EU Heads of State or Government meeting in the European Council. The President for the 2009-14 term is José Manuel Barroso. (page 1384)

In addition to its initiatory and executive function the Commission has certain delegated decision making powers under the Treaties in connection with the Common Agricultural Policy (CAP) and Community competition policy.

The Commission employs about 15,000 people (out of a total of some 23,500 in all Community Institutions), including translators and interpreters. It works through 40 Directorates-General (DGs) and specialised services, each responsible to a Commissioner. There are Representation Offices in the capitals of the member states, and external delegations in nearly 60 countries.

European Commission, URL: http://ec.europa.eu/index_en.htm

European Council
Since 1974 summit meetings of Heads of State and Governments have become institutionalised as the European Council or European Summit, which meets now at least twice a year. The European Council sets priorities, gives political direction, provides impetus for the development of the Union and resolves issues the Council of Ministers is unable to. After each meeting the European Council submits a report to the European Parliament as well as an annual report on the Union's progress. With the entry into force of the Lisbon Treaty on 1 December 2009, the European Council became an institution in its own right.

European Council, URL: http://www.european-council.europa.eu/

Court of Justice
The Court of Justice provides the legal framework for the decisions and regulations made by the Council and the Commission. The Court consists of 27 judges and 8 advocates-general. One judge is chosen from each member country, and is appointed for a six year renewable term. The President is elected from among the judges for a three year term. The Registrar, appointed by the Court of Justice to hold office for a term of six years, also acts as secretary-general of the institution.

The Court's judgement is final and cannot be referred to any other Court. It arbitrates on disputes between member countries solely on Community matters and on infringements of Community law brought to its attention by the Commission; it acts as a tribunal on complaints by individuals or bodies directly affected by Community legislation, and in cases between the Community and its employees. National courts can refer to the Court for an interpretation of Community law, thus ensuring its uniform application throughout the Community.

Court of Justice, URL: http://curia.europa.eu/

European Court of Auditors
This consists of 27 members originating from the Member States, appointed for a term of six years. It has some 550 staff, 250 of whom are auditors. Its responsibility is the monitoring of Community finance - checking that the European Union spends its money according to its budgetary rules and regulations and for the purposes for which it is intended.

The Court of Auditors publishes an annual report concerning the implementation of the EU budget for each financial year and a statement of assurance on the reliability of the accounts for each financial year.

The Court of Auditors has no judicial power but passes irregular cases to the responsible community bodies for them to take appropriate action.

The current President of the Court of Auditors is Vitor Caldeira. (page 1398)

URL: http://eca.europa.eu/

Economic and Social Committee (ESC)
The ESC consists of 344 members drawn from European economic and social interest groups. The primary task of the ESC is to provide advice on matters referred to it by the Commission and the Council, and act as a forum for the single market, hosting events designed to make the EU more accessible to people.

Members are nominated by governments and appointed by the Council of the European Union for a four-year term of office (renewable). Membership is divided between the Member States in the following way (2010-15): Germany, France, Italy and the United Kingdom have 24 members each, Spain and Poland have 21, Romania has 15, Belgium, Bulgaria, Greece, the Netherlands, Portugal, Austria, Sweden, Czech Republic and Hungary have 12, Denmark, Ireland, Finland, Lithuania and Slovakia have nine, Estonia, Latvia and Slovenia have seven, Luxembourg and Cyprus have six and Malta has five.

Every two year and a half years the ESC elects a bureau of 37 members, a president and two vice-presidents to organise and coordinate the work of its various bodies. The Committee meets in plenary session ten times a year. It is served by a secretariat-general which is led by a secretary-general reporting to the president. The current president (2013) is Henri Malosse (Belgium) (page 1470).

URL: http://www.eesc.europa.eu/

Committee of the Regions
The Committee was created as a consultative body by the Treaty on European Union and holding its first session in March 1994. There is now a legal obligation to consult the representatives of local and regional authorities on a variety of matters that affect them directly and to involve them more actively in the development and implementation of EU policies. Subsidiarity is a key principle in the Treaty on European Union.

As regional presidents, mayors of cities or chairmen of city and county councils, up to 350 members are elected to the Committee as officials from the levels of government closest to the citizen. As of May 2013 there were 344 members.

The Committee is made up of six standing commissions. The Bureau, elected for a two-year term, organises the work of the Committee of the Regions. the current president (May 2013) is Ramon Luis Valcarcel Siso (page 1530).

URL: http://cor.europa.eu/

European Ombudsman
All European citizens have the right to apply to the European Ombudsman if they think they have suffered due to "maladministration" by any of the EU institutions or bodies. The Ombudsman has wide ranging powers of inquiry. He can also act as a conciliator between citizens and the EU administration. The Ombudsman can make recommendations to EU institutions and can refer cases to the European Parliament. Currently the position is held by Mr. P. Nikiforas Diamandouros. He is due to retire in October 2013. His successor has been named as Emily O'Reilly.

URL: http://www.ombudsman.europa.eu/start.faces

European Investment Bank (EIB)
This is the European Union's financing institution. It was established under Article 129 of the EEC Rome Treaty, with an annual lending volume of ECU 33 billion. The bank offers or guarantees loans for projects in the less developed regions of the Community, for industrial modernisation programmes, and for projects of common interest to several member countries that cannot be financed by national means.

European Investment Bank, URL: http://www.eib.org/

European Central Bank
The main objective of the European Central Bank is to maintain price stability. It defines and implements the monetary policy of the European Union; conducts foreign exchange operations; holds and manages the official foreign reserves of the participating Member States; promotes the smooth operation of payments systems; contributes to the smooth conduct of policies pursued by the component authorities relating to the prudential supervision of credit institutions and the stability of the financial system.

European Central Bank, URL: http://www.ecb.int/

European External Action Service
The High Representative is assisted by the European External Action Service (EEAS). The European External Action Service (EEAS) was established following the ratification of the Lisbon Treaty and came into operation on December 1 2010. The EEAS operates as a diplomatic corps representing the EU and comes under the jurisdiction of the High Representative for Foreign Affairs and Security Policy. Abroad, the Union is represented by a network of 136 EU Delegations, which have a similar function to those of an embassy. EEAS staff come from the European Commission, the General Secretariat of the Council and the Diplomatic Services of EU Member States. The initial budget was €9.5 million. EEAS is based in Brussels.
High Representative: Baroness Catherine Ashton (page 1380)
Executive Secretary-General: Pierre Vimont (page 1532)
URL: http://eeas.europa.eu

ECONOMIC INTEGRATION
The Single Common Market
The aim of the EEC Rome Treaty was to establish a common market and the progressive harmonisation of the economic policies of the member countries. This required the establishment of a Customs Union and Common External Tariff (CET) and the abolition of internal trade barriers within the Union.

Customs Union
The Customs Union was achieved by the six founder members in 1968, and extended to all new member countries. Competition policy in the Community is governed by Articles 85/86 of the Rome treaty, which prohibit agreements among enterprises which adversely affect trade between member countries. Article 100 requires that governments should seek to harmonise national laws or administrative laws that affect the proper functioning of the Market.

In 1988, the Single Administrative Document replaced separate documents previously used by the customs administrations in all the different Member States, greatly simplifying customs procedures. The single market entered into force in 1993, ensuring free circulation of goods, persons, services and capital in a frontier-free internal market. A framework for the Community's import and export procedures was set up in 1994 and customs legislation was consolidated into the customs code.

The Customs Union, through Member State customs services, carries out import controls concerning: health risks in foodstuffs imported from third countries; radioactive material; the environment (control of imported waste and dangerous goods, control of ozone endangering products); and surveillance/prevention of international trade in endangered species. Under national legislation controls are also used to prevent illicit trade in narcotics, firearms and ammunition, and pornographic material.

In 1996, the Parliament and the Council adopted a Commission proposal for a programme, which has since been updated as Customs 2002; its main aim is to avoid operational customs differences at national level through monitoring practice among Member States customs procedures; exchanges between customs officials and training programmes; and the computerisation of customs procedures at Union level.

Common Customs Tariff
The Common Customs Tariff (CCT) applies to the import of goods across the external borders of the Customs Union. It is common to all members of the Union, but the rates of duty vary according to goods and provenance. The CCT ensures that EU producers can compete fairly and equally on the Community market with manufacturers from other countries.

The Community has been able to cut tariffs in world trade using the CCT as a steering instrument (under the General Agreement of Tariffs and Trade - GATT). The European Union is at present the biggest trading bloc in the world, accounting for about a sixth of total global trade in goods. It is a significant player in the World Trade Organisation (WTO). The EU has also arranged "preferential" agreements with individual countries or groups of countries by means of free trade agreements and customs.

Free Trade Agreements
European Economic Area
The EU and most of the members of the Free Trade Association (EFTA) - Iceland, Norway and Liechtenstein - together established the European Economic Area (EEA), which came into being on the 1st January 1993. There is a separate free trade agreement with Switzerland (the EFTA member that did not join the EEA).

The European Union has Custom Union agreements with Turkey, San Marino and Andorra. The organisation also assists developing countries by providing "preferential" access (reduced rates of customs duty). This is the case with the Lomé Convention (ACP), a co-operative agreement with countries in Africa, the Caribbean and the Pacific. The EU has Mediterranean Agreements with Morocco, Algeria, Tunisia, Egypt, Israel, the Palestine Liberation Organisation, Syria, Lebanon, Malta and Cyprus. Finally, there is a general system of preferences (GSP) for developing countries; this allows industrial member countries to independently grant trade concessions to countries such as those in Asia and Latin America.

The European Monetary System (EMS)
The EMS came into effect on 13 March 1979, and sought to create a zone of monetary stability in Europe, involving co-operation among participating member countries in keeping the fluctuation of their exchange rates against each other within narrow limits. It also offered medium term loans for economic assistance to the less prosperous member states in the EMS. It was the forerunner of Economic and Monetary Union which lead to the Euro.

Economic and Monetary Union (EMU)
The decision to form an Economic and Monetary Union (EMU) was taken by the European Council in Maastricht in 1991 and was later formalized in the Treaty on European Union (the Maastricht Treaty). All EU member states take part in the economic union, some also adopt the euro. EMU should lead to greater economic stability, higher growth and higher employment through internal efficiency and the benefits of greater size.

The key points of EMU are: coordination of economic polices; co-ordination of fiscal policies including limits on government debt and deficit; an independent monetary policy run by the ECB; the single currency and the euro area. Responsibility for economic policy is split between Member States and EU institutions. The process of economic integration generally develops along the following lines: preferential trading area; free trade area; customs union; single market; economic and monetary union; and finally complete economic integration.

Single European Currency ECU / Euro
Initially the Union used units of account (u.a.) for its financial activities. The unit was independent of national currencies, but linked to them by conversion rates; this enabled single common prices to be established for the whole of the Union. The unit, known as the European Currency Unit (ECU), was defined in terms of a 'basket' of the currencies of the member countries. The value of the ECU varied from day to day in any one national currency according to movements in all the exchange rates involved. The ECU was never legal tender and nor was it represented by official banknotes and coins. It did become a store of value because volumes of public and private debt were denominated in ECU and it was used as a means of payment between companies and in foreign trade. It was never a fully-fledged currency.

The ECU became the euro on a 1:1 basis on midnight 31 December 1998 - 1 January 1999.

The euro is the currency of the European Monetary Union. The name "euro" was adopted by the European Heads of State or Government at the European Council meeting in Madrid in December 1995. (The official abbreviation for the euro is 'EUR'). It is a true currency in its own right, and is issued by the European Central Bank. It was adopted by 11 States from January 1 1999: Belgium, Germany, Spain, France, Ireland, Italy, Luxembourg, the Netherlands, Austria, Portugal and Finland. Local currency ceased to be valid for everyday use in those countries after 1 July 2002.

Greece adopted the euro in January 2001. Slovenia was the first of the countries from the 2004 enlargement to meet the criteria and adopted the euro on 1 January 2007. Cyprus and Malta adopted the Euro from 1 January 2008. Slovakia adopted the Euro in 2009 and Estonia in 2011.

The adoption of the euro as the single currency of the European Community eliminates transaction costs; it allows true economies of scale, and removes the differentials in interest rates between long-term capital markets; it allows the European Union to compete in external trade, with the euro granted the status of a major international currency to rank with the dollar and the yen.

All EMU members are eligible to adopt the euro but Denmark and the United Kingdom have opted to remain outside the euro for the time being. The following countries have not adoped the euro. Bulgaria, the Czech Republic, Hungary, Poland, Romania and Sweden. Lithuania and Lativa are members of the exchange rate mechanism. Lativa, which initially wanted to join in 2014, has said it will only join once the eurozone debt crisis has calmed.

OTHER POLICIES
Common Agricultural Policy
The aim of the Common Agricultural Policy (CAP) as set out in the EEC Rome Treaty, was to create a single common market in the majority of agricultural products, to ensure stability of prices and a fair standard of living for those who work in the industry.

When the CAP was set up, there were deficits of most products. Mechanisms of intervention were devised to support prices and incomes. However, this stimulated agricultural output at a rate far higher than the capacity of the market; production grew by two per cent per year between 1973 and 1988 while consumption grew only 0.5 per cent per year. The result was a build-up of surpluses or 'mountains' and 'lakes' of agricultural products.

The Inter-institutional Agreement of 29 June 1988 set in place reform mechanisms. which succeeded in some areas, but the surpluses of beef, sheep meat, butter, skimmed milk powder, tobacco and wine continued to grow. In the early 1990s, a new approach was adopted; prices for key products were lowered, and the impact of these cuts on producer incomes was offset by direct payments.

Further reform became necessary in the late 1990s, due to growing world demand for food, greater consumer interest in food safety and animal welfare, and the requirement laid down in the Treaty of Amsterdam that environmental concerns should be integrated into all EU legislation. The Agenda 2000 CAP reform aimed to simplify by decentralising, streamlining and simplifying programme procedures and regulations; in the wine sector, for example, there is now one regulation where previously there were 23.

Yet more reforms were introduced in 2004 and 2005, including the single farm payment (SFP) for EU farmers independent of production and payments linked to environmental, food safety, animal and plant health and welfare standards. A major review was conducted in

EUROPEAN UNION

2008 including reducing SFPs to large farms. Further proposals including subsiding farmers who grow crops for biofuels and abolishing the set aside scheme. Since 2009, receipients of SFPs are in the public domaine. The CAP is due to be reviewed in 2013.

The CAP is funded by the EAGGF and accounted for approximately 34.9 per cent of the Community budget during the 2007-13 period.

Charter of Fundamental Social Rights for Workers
At the meeting of the European Council in Strasbourg on 8 and 9 December 1989, the heads of State or Government of the European Community Member States, with the exception of the United Kingdom, adopted the Charter of Fundamental Social Rights for Workers. The Charter is both a solemn statement of progress already made in the social field and a preparation for new advances - so that the same importance may be given to the social dimension of the Community as to its economic aspects.

In the preamble to the Charter, the Heads of State or Government underline the priority which they attach to job creation, the importance of the social consensus as a factor in economic development and their rejection of all forms of discrimination or exclusion.

Developing Countries
EU/ACP Partnership
The community has maintained close economic links with former European colonies, first through the Yaounde Agreements and, following British accession to the EC in 1973, through the Lomé Conventions I, II, III and IV of 1975, 1980, 1985 and 1990.

Signatories to Lomé III included 66 countries from Africa, the Caribbean and the Pacific, known as the ACP States. Emphasis was put on food security, rural development and measures to halt soil erosion and the advance of the desert. Investment aid to ACP countries (1985-1990) totalled 8,500m ECU.

Five years later, cash shortages had become the biggest worry for many ACP States. The text of Lomé IV (effective from 1990-95) contained measures to help arrest the economic crisis, such as enterprise development, a greater role for the private sector, and investment protection to attract more foreign investors. There was new emphasis on the protection of the environment. The European Development Fund (EDF) aid increased to 12,000m ECU, most in the form of grants.

The EDF budget for 1995-2000 was 12.9 billion ECU (the first time the EDF had not increased in real terms). The expiry of the Lomé IV in the new millennium heralded a time of change;statistics indicated that, despite generous trade preferences, ACP countries were not experiencing satisfactory economic development. In sub-Saharan Africa, and in most of the Caribbean and Pacific islands, almost half the people were still living in conditions of absolute poverty, forced to survive on less than US$1 a day, as a result of serious economic problems and political instability.

On June 23 2000, the European Union signed a twenty-year partnership agreement with 77 ACP Group states (representing a total of more than 650 million people). The Cotonou Agreement replaced the Lomé Convention. It focuses on poverty reduction through political dialogue, development aid and closer economic and trade co-operation. It is based on respect for human rights and establishes consultation procedures and appropriate sanctions for dealing with human rights violations and serious corruption. It also encourages greater participation by civil society, the private sector and trade unions.

A €13.5 billion European Development Fund covered the Agreement's first five years. The system of trade preferences will be replaced gradually by a series of new economic partnerships based on the progressive and reciprocal removal of trade barriers. The Agreement came into force on 1 April 2003, and will be open to revision every five years.

The 10th EDF (2008-2013) is governed by the ACP-EC partnership agreement (signed in 2000 and revised in 2005) and the amended Overseas Association Decision. The 10th EDF has a budget of €22 682 million, comprising: €21 966 million to the ACP countries (97 per cent of the total),€286 million to the OCTs (1 per cent); €430 million to the Commission as support expenditure for programming and implementation of the EDF (2 per cent). The amount for the ACP countries breaksdown thus: €17 766 million to the national and regional indicative programmes (81 per cent of the total), €2 700 million to intra-ACP and intra-regional cooperation (12 per cent), €1 500 million to Investment Facilities (7 per cent).

External Assistance
The Community now provides over 10 per cent of total official development aid in the world. Originally concentrated on the ACP countries, Community aid now has a global reach and covers new areas such as reconstruction, institution-building, macro-economic support, electoral observation and human rights. External aid programmes constitute over 60 per cent of all the European Commission's accounts.

To meet the challenge of growth in external assistance, the European Commission announced reform of assistance programmes from May 2000. This included: an overhaul of programming; integration of the project cycle from identification through to implementation; creation of a single body in charge of project implementation; extensive devolution of project management to the Commission's external delegations and authorities in third countries; urgent measures to eliminate old and dormant commitments.

In May 2005, as a part of the review of the UN's Millennium Development Goals in September 2005, the European Commission agreed to a new collective target of an additional €20 billion of aid by 2010.

The European Union is the largest donor of humanitarian aid in the world. The European Commission has approved humanitarian and food aid, including emergency assistance to relieve famine or provide help after earthquakes, worth a total of €800 million annually in the current funding cycle. The aid is managed by the European Community Humanitarian Office (ECHO).

European Research Area Committee (ERAC)
ERAC (fomerly CREST) is a strategic policy advisory body to support research and technological development. ERAC (fomerly CREST) was set up in the 1970s. It was given a revised mandate in 2010. It was renamed as the European Research Area Committee to reflect its new role. Its main mission is to provide strategic input to the Council , the Commission and the Member states on R&D issues relevant to the development of European research, seen as vital for Europe's economic development and competitiveness.

European Union: URL: http://www.europa.eu

EUROPEAN PARLIAMENT

One of the major institutions of the European Union and the largest multinational parliament in the world, the European Parliament represents the 500 million citizens of the EU. All European citizens have the right, whether in groups or individually, to petition the Parliament.

The Treaty of Rome (1957) provided for a European assembly, initially nominated from national parliaments, but later directly elected. In 1962 the European Assembly was re-named the European Parliament; the first direct elections were held on 7-10 June 1979. The responsibilities and powers of the European Parliament were increased through the Single Act of 1987, the Treaty of European Union of 1993 and the Treaty of Amsterdam of 1997.

European Convention
In 2003 Valéry Giscard d'Estaing, head of the drafting convention, presented official copies of the draft European Convention to the EU Thessaloniki Summit.

Key proposals included:
- A person, not a country, to hold the presidency. The term of office to increase from 6 months to 30 months.
- The position of External Affairs Commissioner and Foreign Policy Representative to be combined into one post of Foreign Minister.
- Each of the 27 countries to have an EU Commissioner, though only 15 at any one time to have voting rights.
- Europe to adopt one foreign policy and eventually one defence policy.
- Some power of legislation veto to be lost, although not on foreign policy, tax or defence.
- The Charter of Fundamental Human Rights to be included in the constitution.

On 29 October 2004, the Heads of State or Government of the 25 Member States and the three candidate countries signed the Treaty establishing a Constitution for Europe. This Treaty could only enter into force when it has been adopted by each of the signatory countries in accordance with its own constitutional procedures. By the end of April 2005, nine members had ratified the constitutional treaty. However, at the end of May 2005, France and the Netherlands rejected the Treaty by referendum. A period of reflection, explanation and discussion by all Member States followed, and a draft for a revised treaty, the Lisbon Treaty, was drawn up in 2007.

Lisbon Treaty
A final draft of the revised treaty was agreed in October 2007, and in December 2007 the member states signed the so-called Lisbon Treaty. The treaty is similar to the rejected European Constitution draft, but rather than replacing all earlier EU treaties, the Lisbon treaty amends the Treaty on the European Union and the Treaty Establishing the European Community. By mid 2009, 25 countries had ratified the treaty, but Irish voters rejected the treaty in the only referendum held on the treaty, and the Czech President Vaclav Klaus,was opposed to ratification making its future unclear as all 27 countries had to ratify the treaty before it could come into effect. Ireland held a second referendum and on 2 October 2009 Ireland voted in favour of the Treaty. The Czech Republic ratified the Treaty on 3 November 2009. The treaty became law on 1 December 2009.

Powers
The powers of the European Parliament fall into three categories: legislative, budgetary, and supervisory of the executive.

Legislative Power
Initially, the Parliament was only consultative; the Commission proposed and the Council of Ministers decided legislation. However, later treaties have increased the Parliament's powers so that Parliament and the Council of Ministers now share the power of decision in a wide range of areas. Most Commission proposals have to be referred to the Parliament and its views are increasingly taken into account by the Commission and the Council of Ministers before adoption of legislation. In most areas, Parliament can improve proposed legislation by amendment. After two readings, members can review and amend the Commission's proposal and the Council's preliminary position on it. A conciliation committee - made up of equal numbers of Members of Parliament and of the Council, with the Commission present - can seek a compromise on a document that the Council and Parliament can both endorse. Parliament can reject the proposal if an agreement is not reached.

The Parliament has the absolute power to dismiss the Commission as a whole (which it has never done) and Parliament's assent is required for important international agreements, for example the accession of new Member States, association agreements with third countries and the powers of the European Central Bank.

Budgetary Power
The European Parliament approves the Union's annual budget. Modifications and amendments to the Commission's initial proposals may be made and to the Council's position. The Parliament has the absolute power to reject the budget (which has happened in exceptional circumstances). The President of the Parliament signs the budget into law. Parliament also makes an assessment each year of the Commission's management of the budget before approving the accounts.

Supervision of the Executive
Executive power in the European Union is shared between the Commission and the Council of Ministers. Parliament exercises overall political supervision of these institutions. Parliament appoints the President and members of the Commission every five years. It scrutinises monthly and annual reports submitted by the Commission. Parliament can pass a motion of censure on the Commission and force it to resign.

The President of the Council presents a programme at the beginning of their term of office and accounts for it to Parliament at the end of that time. The President of the Council also reports to the Parliament on the results of each European Council and on the development of foreign and security policy. At the start of all European Council meetings, the President of Parliament presents Parliament's positions on the subjects on the agenda of the Heads of State or Government.

It is open to Members of the European Parliament (MEPs) to question both the Council and the Commission about any aspect of the Community's business, particularly where the interests of those they represent are likely to be directly affected.

The Parliament also appoints the Ombudsman, who can investigate allegations of misadministration brought against the European Union by its citizens.

Organisation
There are currently 754 members. The members are elected once every five years by voters across the Member States (27 at time of last election, Croatia became the 28th state when it joined the EU in 2013). Once elected, members organise along political lines. Currently there are seven groups. Parliamentary documents are published in all the official languages of the EU.

Since December 2011, the Parliament has had 754 seats allocated as follows: Austria 19 seats; Belgium 22; Bulgaria 18; Cyprus 6; Czech Republic 22; Denmark 13; Estonia 6; Finland 13; France 74; Germany 99; Greece 22; Hungary 22; Ireland 12; Italy 73; Latvia 9; Lithuania 12; Luxembourg 6; Malta 6; Netherlands 26; Poland 51; Portugal 22; Romania 33; Republic of Slovenia 8; Slovak Republic 13; Spain 54; Sweden 20 and UK 73.

During the present parliamentary term, the number of MEPs was increased to the maximum provided for in the Treaty of Lisbon. For the 2014 election, according to the Lisbon Treaty, the number of seats will vary from six for Cyprus, Estonia, Malta and Luxembourg to 96 for Germany. Croatia will have the right to elect 12 MEPs. They will serve for one year ahead of the 2014 elections.

The current political groupings are: Group of the European People's Party (Christian Democrats); Group of the Progressive Alliance of Socialists and Democrats in the EU: Alliance of Liberals and Democrats for Europe; European Conservatives and Reformists Group; Group of the Greens/European Free Alliance; European United Left - Nordic Green Left; Europe of Freedom and Democracy Group.

For the main part of their work, Parliament and the MEPs meet in Brussels where its specialist committees scrutinise proposals for new EU laws. The current standing committees: Foreign Affairs, Human Rights, Security and Defence; Development; International Trade; Budgets; Budgetary Control; Economic and Monetary Affairs; Employment and Social Affairs; Environment, Public Health and Food Safety; Industry, Research and Energy; Internal Market and Consumer Protection; Transport and Tourism; Regional Development; Agriculture and Rural Development; Fisheries; Culture and Education; Legal Affairs; Civil Liberties, Justice and Home Affairs; Constitutional Affairs; Women's Rights and Gender Equality; Petitions. There are two Special committees: organisted crime, corruption and money laundering. In addition, the European Parliament can set up subcommittees, temporary committees or committees of enquiry, examples of which have been the committee on foot and mouth disease; committee of inquiry into BSE and the committee on human genetics and other new technologies of modern medicine.

The Parliament meets in Strasbourg for plenary sessions for one week a month and MEPs sit according to political grouping rather than nationality. Elections take place every five years. Results of the 2009 elections gave the centre-right European People's Party (EPP/Christian Democrats) the majority, with 265 seats; the Progressive Alliance of Socialists and Democrats in Europe has 184 seats and the Alliance of Liberals and Democrats for Europe is the third largest party with 84 seats. The Green/European Free Alliance won 55 seats while the European Conservatives and Reformists Group won 54 seats. The European United Left-Nordic Green Left has 35 seats, the Europe of Freedom and Democracy (Eurosceptic) has 32 seats, and 27 MEPs are non-attached.

Within the UK, the Conservatives hold 25 seats, Labour 13 seats, Liberal Democrats 11 seats, UK Independence Party 13 seats, Scottish National Party 2 seats, Green Party 2 seats, Plaid Cymru 1 seat, and the BNP 2 seats. In Northern Ireland, the Democratic Unionists, Sinn Fein and the Ulster Unionists all have a seat each. The 25 British Conservative Party MEPs left the European People's Party to form the European Conservatives and Reformists Group (ECR).

The Parliament is run by a Bureau, normally comprising the President and 14 Vice-Presidents who are elected by secret ballot to serve for two-and-a-half years. Additionally, five quaestors are responsible, in a purely consultative capacity, for financial and administrative affairs that affect Members. The Conference of Presidents (the chairmen of the political groups and the President of the Parliament) organises the Parliament's work and draws up the sessions' agenda.

The General Secretariat of the European Parliament is based in Luxembourg, committees meet in Brussels and plenary sessions take place in Strasbourg.

The Parliament employs 3,500 people, a third of whom work in the linguistic services. All business is now conducted in the 27 official languages of the Union and all documents are published in these languages. The long term budget for the European Parliament for 2007 - 2013 is EUR 866.4 billion.

President: Martin Schulz (page 1510)

European Parliament, Allée du Printemps, B.P. 1024, F-67070 Strasbourg Cedex. Tel: +33 (0)3 88 17 40 01, fax: +33 (0)3 88 17 48 60, URL: http://www.europarl.europa.eu/

General Secretariat of the European Parliament, Plateau du Kirchberg, B.P. 1601, L-2929, Luxembourg. Tel: +352 43001, fax: +352 43 002 4842, URL: http://www.europarl.europa.eu/

European Parliament, Brussels, Rue Wiertz, B-1047 Brussels, Belgium. Tel: +32 (0)2 284 2111, URL: http://www.europarl.europa.eu/

European Parliament Information Office, United Kingdom, 2 Queen Anne's Gate, London SW1H 9AA, UK. Tel: +44 (0)20 7227 4300, fax: +44 (0)20 7227 4302, e-mail: eplondon@europarl.eu.int, URL: http://www.europarl.org.uk

COUNCIL OF THE EUROPEAN UNION (COUNCIL OF MINISTERS)

Functions

The Council of the European Union (officially the Council and commonly referred to as the Council of Ministers) is the EU's main decision-making body. It is also called the Consilium as a Latin-language compromises. It exercises legislative power, in many cases legislating jointly with the European Parliament. In addition, it coordinates the general economic policies of the member states and defines and implements the Common Foreign and Security Policy, on the basis of general guidelines identified by the European Council. It concludes, on behalf of the Community and the Union, international agreements between the EU and one or more states or international organisations, and co-ordinates the action of member states, and takes measures, relating to police and judicial co-operation in criminal matters. The Council, together with the European Parliament, forms the budgetary authority which adopts the Community's budget.

Composition of the Council

The Council brings together the ministers of the member states. It meets in nine different configurations, depending on the subject being discussed (foreign affairs, financial affairs, social affairs, transport, agriculture, etc.). For example, the General Affairs and External Relations configuration brings together Foreign Affairs ministers.

The Council proceedings are prepared and coordinated by the Permanent Representatives Committee (COREPER), which is composed of the permanent representatives of the member states in Brussels and their deputies. The work of this Committee is itself prepared by more than 150 committees and working parties consisting of delegates from the member states.

Decision-making:

In principle, the Council legislates on the basis of proposals drafted by the European Commission. On a broad range of issues, Community legislation is adopted jointly by the Parliament and the Council under what is known as the co-decision procedure.

The Treaties define the cases in which the Council acts by a simple majority (mainly used for procedural decisions), qualified majority or unanimously. The most common voting procedure is qualified majority, whereby the member states' votes are weighted as follows: France, Germany, Italy and the UK have 29 votes each; Spain and Poland have 27 votes each; Romania has 14 votes; the Netherlands has 13 votes; Belgium, the Czech Republic, Greece, Hungary and Portugal have 12 votes each; Austria, Bulgaria and Sweden have 10 votes each; Finland, Denmark, Ireland, Lithuania and Slovakia have 7 votes each; Luxembourg, Cyprus, Estonia, Latvia and Slovenia have 4 votes each and Malta has 3 votes (Total: 345 votes). Until Croatia becomes a full member of the EU on 1 July 2013 it will participate as an active observer.

Qualified majority is reached if a majority of member states (in some cases a two-thirds majority) are in favour of the proposal and at least 255 votes are cast in favour, out of the total of 345 votes. In addition, a member state may ask for confirmation that the votes in favour represent at least 62 per cent of the total population of the Union. If this is found not to be the case, the decision is not taken.

Unanimity is required in particularly sensitive areas such as taxation, social security, energy, culture, common foreign and security policy, and in many areas of justice and home affairs.

General Secretariat of the Council of the EU

The Council's General Secretariat, under the direction of its Secretary-General, ensures every support that the Institution and its preparatory bodies need to do their work. With about 3,300 staff working mainly in Brussels, the General Secretariat advises the Presidency, ensures the continuity of proceedings and prepares and follows up meetings. Legal advice is provided by the Council's Legal Service.

The Deputy Secretary-General is responsible for the running of the General Secretariat. He is appointed by the Council.

Presidency of the Council of the EU

The Presidency of the Council is held by each member state in turn, for a period of six months (from January to June, and from July to December), in accordance with a pre-established rota. The Presidency plays an essential role in organising the Council's work, particularly in taking the legislative and political decision-making process forward. It is responsible for organising and chairing all meetings (European Council, COREPER, working parties and committees) and brokering compromises. Lithuania holds the Presidency for the period July-December 2013, followed by Greece (January-June 2014) and Italy (July-December 2014).

Budget

The Council of the European Council and Council (EC/C) have one common budget structure. The EC/C budget for 2013 was €535,5 million, an increase of 0.3 per cent on the previous year.

European Council / Council of Europe

The Council of the European Union should not be confused with the European Council or the Council of Europe.

The European Council brings together the heads of state or government of the European Union and the president of the Commission. It defines the general political guidelines of the European Union. The decisions taken at the European Council meetings are a major impetus in defining the general political guidelines of the European Union.

The Council of Europe is not part of the European Union but an international organisation in its own right. Its headquarters are in Strasbourg and its main role is to strengthen democracy, human rights, and the rule of law throughout its member states. Although the 27 member states of the European Union are all members of the Council of Europe, both organisations are quite distinct.

Please see separate entries for further details.

President: rotating.

Secretary-General: Uwe Corsepius (page 1409)

Council of the European Union/Council of Ministers, Rue de la Loi/Wetstraat 175, B-1048 Brussels, Belgium. Tel: +32 (0)2 281 6111, fax: +32 (0)2 281 6999, URL: http://www.consilium.europa.eu

EUROPEAN COMMISSION

Established under the Merger Treaty of 1965, which brought into being the European Communities (EC), the European Commission is one of the European Union's major institutions, and is at the centre of all EU policy-making.

Purpose

The Commission works alongside the other European institutions and with the governments of the Member States. Its main concern is to defend the interests of the Union and Europe's citizens and companies in general, rather than on behalf of sectoral interests or individual countries.

Function

The Commission has four main roles: it proposes legislation to Parliament and the Council; it enforces Community law (jointly with the Court of Justice); it administers and implements Community policies and it acts as a mouthpiece for the European Union, negotiating international trade and co-operation agreements.

Proposals for Legislation

The Commission's proposals relate to areas defined by the Treaties, in particular transport, industry, social policies, agriculture, the environment, energy, regional development, trade relations and development co-operation. Legislation is only initiated in areas where the EU can take action more effectively than individual Member States.

The first stage of the legislative process is extensive research and discussion with representatives of governments, industry, trade unions, and experts in the area in question. Often there are conflicting interests which the Commission must take into account when it prepares its proposals. The proposal is then submitted to the Council of Ministers and the European Parliament. In agreement with the Commission, the Council can amend a proposal. The European Parliament shares co-decision with the Council in most areas and has to be consulted in others. The Commission is required to take Parliament's amendments into consideration when revising its proposals.

Whilst the Commission has the right of initiative, the Council of Ministers and the European Parliament take the main decisions on European Policy.

Community Law
The Commission ensures that EU legislation is applied correctly in the Member States in order to maintain a climate of mutual confidences between the States, economic operators and private individuals. If necessary, it can take action against public or private sector organisations who breech European Law and bring them before the European Court of Justice. The Commission is also responsible for the vetting of EU subsidies and can impose fines on authorities or companies that infringe the law.

If a situation cannot be settled through the infringement procedure, the Commission refers the matter to the Court of Justice, which ultimately ensures that the law is observed.

Community Policies
The Commission acts as the executive body for the European Union both implementing and managing policy. It manages the Union's annual budget (€133.8 billion in payments in 2009) under the supervision of the Court of Auditors and runs the Structural Funds, which attempt to even out disparities between the richer and poorer parts of the Union.

In addition to its initiatory and executive function the Commission has certain delegated decision making powers under the Treaties in connection with trade policy, the Common Agricultural Policy (CAP) and Community competition policy.

Mouthpiece for the EU
The Commission is an important representative of the European Union on the international stage, negotiating international agreements. The creation of the World Trade Organisation (WTO) was negotiated by the Commission on the Union's behalf, as was the Uruguay Round Trade Liberalisation Accord and the Lomé Convention which associates the EU with developing countries in Africa, the Caribbean and the Pacific is another example.

Structure
A Commission with too many members would be unworkable. Until 1 May 2004 there were 20 commissioners - two from each of the most heavily populated member states and one from each of the other EU countries. When ten more countries joined the EU on 1 May 2004, the number of commissioners rose to 30. From November 2004, when the 2004-09 Commission took office, the number of commissioners was reduced to 25 - one per country. This number increased to 27 when Bulgaria and Romania joined the EU on 1st January 2007. Croatia became the 28th member of the European Union on 1 July 2013.

The President of the Commission is appointed on a two-year renewable term by the EU Heads of State or Government. This choice has to be approved by the European Parliament, as does the choice of the other Commissioners.

The Commission employs about 15,000 people (out of a total of some 23,500 in all Community Institutions), including translators and interpreters. The Union has 23 official languages. It works through 40 Directorates-General (DGs) and specialised services, each responsible to a Commissioner.

The Commission also has Representation Offices in the capitals of the member states, and external delegations in nearly 60 countries.

The adoption of the White Paper on Reform on 1 March 2000 started the process of internal modernisation of the Commission. The reform strategy centres on balancing tasks with resources; a thorough overhaul of management and human resources policies; and improved financial management, efficiency and accountability.

Other Responsibilities
The Commission works closely with the Committee of Permanent Representatives (COREPER) composed of member country ambassadors to the Community, which tries to reconcile national differences in considering Community legislative proposals referred to it from the Council of Ministers.

The Commission has responsibilities for aid and development in third countries. It manages the PHARE and TACIS programmes of financial and technical assistance to the countries of Central and Eastern Europe and to the Republics of the former Soviet Union.

European Convention
Under the terms of the draft constitution submitted at the June 2003 Thessaloniki EU Summit there would be several changes to the workings of the European Commission. Each country will have a commissioner but only 15 would have voting rights at any one time. The presidency would be held by a person not a country for a proposed term of 30 months. At the end of May 2005, France and the Netherlands rejected the constitutional treaty by referendum. There was a period of reflection and discussion, and in October 2007 the member states signed the Treaty of Lisbon; however, this treaty was still to be ratified by two countries - Ireland and the Czech Republic. Ireland and the Czech Republic ratified the treaty in October and November respectively and the treaty came into force on December 1 2009. For more details see the entry of the European Union.

Members of the European Commssion, 2010-2014

President: José Manuel Durão Barroso (page 1384)
High Representative of the Union for Foreign Affairs and Security and Vice President of the Commission: Baroness Catherine Ashton (page 1380)
Vice President Justice, Fundamental Rights and Citizenship: Viviane Reding (page 1501)
Vice President, Competition: Joaquin Almunia (page 1376)
Vice President, Transport: Siim Kallas (page 1453)
Vice President, Digital Agenda: Neelie Kroes (page 1458)
Vice President, Industry and Entrepreneurship: Antonio Tajani (page 1523)
Vice President, Inter-Institutional Relations and Administration: Maroš Šefčovič (page 1511)
Vice President, Economic and Monetary Affairs: Olli Rehn (page 1501)
Commissioner, Environment: Janez Potočnik (page 1497)
Commissioner, Development: Andris Piebalgs (page 1495)
Commissioner, Internal Market and Services: Michel Barnier (page 1383)
Commissioner, Education, Culture, Multilingualism and Youth: Androulla Vassiliou (page 1531)
Commissioner, Taxation and Customs Union, Audit and Anti-Fraud: Algirdas Šemeta (page 1511)
Commissioner, Trade: Karel De Gucht (page 1414)
Commissioner, Research and Innovation: Maire Geoghegan-Quinn (page 1429)
Commissioner, Financial Programming and Budget: Janusz Lewandowski (page 1463)
Commissioner, Maritime Affairs and Fisheries: Maria Damanaki (page 1411)
Commissioner, International Cooperation, Humanitarian Aid and Crisis Response: Kristalina Georgieva (page 1430)
Commissioner, Energy: Günter Oettinger (page 1488)
Commissioner, Regional Policy: Johannes Hahn (page 1436)
Commissioner, Climate Action: Connie Hedegaard (page 1440)
Commissioner, Enlargement and European Neighbourhood Policy: Štefan Füle (page 1427)
Commissioner, Employment, Social Affairs and Inclusion: László Andor (page 1378)
Commissioner, Home Affairs: Cecilia Malmström
Commissioner, Agriculture and Rural Development: Dacian Ciolos (page 1405)
Commissioner, Health and Consumer Policy: Tonio Borg (page 1392)
Commissioner, Consumer Policy: Nevan Mimica (page 1478)

Nevan Mimica became Croatia's first EC Commissioner on 1 July 2013.

European Commission, rue de la Loi 200, B-1049 Brussels, Belgium. Tel: +32 (0)2 299 1111, fax: +32 (0)2 299 1970, URL: http://www.europa.eu

EUROPEAN COUNCIL

The European Council defines the general political direction and priorities of the European Union. With the entry into force of the Treaty of Lisbon on 1 December 2009, it became an institution.

Lisbon Treaty
The Treaty of Lisbon entered into force on 1 December 2009. In summary the main changes are: On 1 December 2009 the European Community was replaced by the European Union which succeeded it and took over all its rights and obligations. The Treaty on European Union kept the same name and the Treaty establishing the European Community became the Treaty on the functioning of the European Union. For the first time, the role of full-time president of the European Council was created. The President's main tasks are to ensure the preparation and continuity of the the work of the European Council - which becomes an institution in its own right - and to faciliate concessions. The role is for a term of two and a half years, renewable once. A High Representative of the Union for Foreign Affairs and Security Policy was created. The High Representative acts as both the Council's representative for Common Foreign and Security Council, the President of the Foreign Affairs Council and a Vice-President of the Commission. The High Representative is responsible for setting foreign policy and common defence policy. The term is five years.

Functions
The European Council provides the Union with the necessary impetus for its development and defines the general political directions and priorities thereof. It does not exercise legislative functions. The European Council consists of the Heads of State or Government of the Member States, together with its President and the President of the Commission. The High

Representative of the Union for Foreign Affairs and Security Policy takes part in its work. When the agenda so requires, the members of the European Council may decide each to be assisted by a minister and, in the case of the President of the Commission, by a member of the Commission. The European Council meets twice every six months, convened by its President. When the situation so requires, the President will convene a special meeting of the European Council. Except where the Treaties provide otherwise, decisions of the European Council are taken by consensus. In some cases, it adopts decisions by unanimity or by qualified majority, depending on what the Treaty provides for. The European Council elects its President by qualified majority. The President's term of office is two and a half years, renewable once. The European Council usually meets in Brussels, in the Justus Lipsius building. It is assisted by the General Secretariat of the Council.

History
The European Council was created in 1974 with the intention of establishing an informal forum for discussion between Heads of State or Government. It rapidly developed into the body which fixed goals for the Union and set the course for achieving them, in all fields of EU activity. It acquired a formal status in the 1992 Treaty of Maastricht, which defined its function as providing the impetus and general political guidelines for the Union's development. On 1 December 2009, with the entry into force of the Treaty of Lisbon, it became one of the seven institutions of the Union.

Council of the European Union / Council of Europe
The European Council should not be confused with the Council of the European Union or the Council of Europe.

EUROPEAN UNION

The **Council of the European Union** is the Union's legislative body; for a wide range of Community issues, it exercises that legislative power in co-decision with the European Parliament. The Council is composed of one representative at ministerial level from each Member State. Council members are politically accountable to their national parliaments.

The **Council of Europe** is not part of the European Union but an international organisation in its own right. Its headquarters are in Strasbourg and its main role is to strengthen democracy, human rights, and the rule of law throughout its member states. Although the 27 member states of the European Union are all members of the Council of Europe, both organisations are quite distinct.

Please see individual entries for further information.

President of the European Council: Herman Van Rompuy (page 1530)
High Representative of the Union for Foreign Affairs and Security Policy: Baroness Catharine Ashton (page 1380)

European Council, Rue de la Loi 175, B-1048 Brussels, Belgium. Tel: +32 (0)2 281 6111, fax: +32 (0)2 281 6934, URL: http://www.european-council.europa.eu/

COURT OF JUSTICE OF THE EUROPEAN UNION

Since the establishment of the Court of Justice of the European Union in 1952, its mission has been to ensure that "the law is observed" "in the interpretation and application" of the Treaties.

The Court thus constitutes the judicial authority of the European Union and, in cooperation with the courts and tribunals of the Member States; it ensures the uniform application and interpretation of European Union law.

The Court of Justice of the European Union consists of three courts: the Court of Justice, the General Court (created in 1988) and the Civil Service Tribunal (created in 2004).

In 2013, the budget was €354,88 million.

Function
The Court of Justice, like the General Court, has the duty to ensure that the law is observed in the interpretation and application of the founding Treaties of the European Union and of the provisions adopted by the competent institutions.

The Court of Justice, which can also be consulted for an opinion by the Member States and the institutions, has a broad jurisdiction. It has jurisdiction in particular to give preliminary rulings, at the request of the national courts or tribunals, on the interpretation of the Treaties and on the validity and interpretation of acts of the institutions, bodies, offices or agencies of the Union; to rule, at the request of the Commission or a Member State, on the failure of a Member State to fulfil an obligation under the Treaties; to hear and determine actions for annulment and actions for failure to act brought by a Member State against the Parliament and/or the Council (apart from certain Council measures) or brought by one institution against another; to rule on appeals against decisions of the General Court.

Structure
The Court of Justice is composed of 28 Judges (one Judge from each Member State) (as of July 2013) and is assisted by eight Advocates General. The Judges and the Advocates General are appointed by common accord of the governments of the Member States after consultation of a panel responsible for giving an opinion on candidates' suitability. They are appointed for a term of office of six years, which is renewable. The Registrar is appointed by the Court of Justice to hold office for a term of six years. The Registrar also acts as secretary-general of the institution.

The Court of Justice may sit in plenary session, in Grand Chamber of 13 judges or in chambers of three or five judges.

Approximately 17,200 judgements and orders have been delivered since 1952. In 2012, 631 cases were introduced and 595 cases closed.

Order of Precedence of the Court of Justice as at 01 April 2013
President: Vassilios Skouris (page 1516)
Vice-President: K. Lenaerts (page 1462)
President of the First Chamber: Antonio Tizzano (page 1526)
President of the Second Chamber: Rosario Silva de Lapuerta (page 1514)
President of the Third Chamber: Marko Ilesic (page 1446)
President of the Fourth Chamber: L. Bay Larsen (page 1385)
President of the Fifth Chamber: T. von Danwitz (page 1532)
First Advocate General: N. Jääskinen (page 1448)
President of the Tenth Chamber: A. Rosas
President of the Seventh Chamber: G. Arestis (page 1379)
President of the Ninth Chamber: J. Malenovský (page 1469)
President of the Sixth Chamber: Maria Berger (page 1387)
President of the Eighth Chamber: E. Jarašiunas (page 1449)
Advocate General: Juliane Kokott
Judge: Endre Juhasz
Judge: George Arestis
Judge: Anthony Borg Barthet
Judge: U. Lõhmus (page 1466)
Judge: Eglis Levits
Judge: Aindrias O Caoimh
Advocate General: Eleanor Sharpston
Advocate General: Paolo Mengozzi
Advocate General: Yves Bot (page 1392)
Judge: J.-C. Bonichot
Judge: A. Arabadjijev (page 1379)
Judge: Camelia Toader
Judge: J.-J. Kasel (page 1454)
Judge: M. Safjan
Judge: D. Šváby (page 1522)

Advocate General: P. Cruz Villalón
Judge: A. Prechal
Judge: C.G. Fernlund
Judge: J.L. da Cruz Vilaça
Advocate General: M. Wathelet
Judge: C. Vajda
Advocate General: N. Wahl
Registrar: A. Calot Escobar

Composition of the Chambers of the Court of Justice as at 1 April 2013
First Chamber: *President of Chamber:* A. Tizzano (page 1526); *Judges:* M. Berger, A. Borg Barthet, E. Levits, J.-J. Kasel
Second Chamber: *President of Chamber:* R. Silva de Lapuerta (page 1514); *Judges:* G. Arestis, J.C. Bonichot, A. Arabadjiev, J.L. da Cruz Vilaça
Third Chamber: *President of Chamber:* M. Ilesic (page 1446); *Judges:* E. Karasiunas, A.Ó Caoimh, C. Toader, C.G. Fernlund
Fourth Chamber: *President of Chamber:* L. Bay Larsen (page 1385); *Judges:* J. Malenovský, U. Lõhmus, M. Safjan, A. Prechal
Fifth Chamber: *President of Chamber:* T. von Danwitz (page 1532); *Judges:* A. Rosas, E. Juhász, D. Šváby, C. Vajda
Sixth Chamber: *President of Chamber:* M. Berger (page 1387); *Judges:* A. Borg Barthet, E. Levits, J.-J. Kasel
Seventh Chamber: *President of Chamber:* G. Arestis (page 1379); *Judges:* J.C. Bonichot, A. Arabadjiev, J.L. da Cruz Vilaça
Eighth Chamber: *President of Chamber:* E. Jarasiunas (page 1449); *Judges:* A.Ó Caoimh, C. Toader, C.G. Fernlund
Ninth Chamber: *President of Chamber:* J. Malenovský (page 1469); *Judges:* U. Lõhmus, M. Safjan, A. Prechal
Tenth Chamber: *President of Chamber:* A. Rosas: *Judges:* E. Juhász, D. Šváby, C. Vajda

The General Court
As the number of cases brought before the Court of Justice has rapidly increased since its establishment in 1952, it has set up a new judicial body to deal with cases more quickly. The General Court was created in 1989 and introduced a second tier of judicial authority, which concentrates on strengthening the judicial safeguards available to individuals, while the Court of Justice focuses on the uniform interpretation of EU Law.

The General Court is made up of at least one Judge from each Member State (28 as of June 2013). The Judges are appointed by common accord of the governments of the Member States after consultation of a panel responsible for giving an opinion on candidates' suitability. They are appointed for a term of office of six years, which is renewable. They appoint their President, for a period of three years, from amongst themselves. They appoint a Registrar for a term of office of six years.

It has no permanent advocates. It usually sits in chambers of three or five judges but can also sit in Grand Chamber of 13 judges in particularly important cases.

Approximately 8,700 judgements and orders have been delivered since 1989. In 2012, 617 cases were introduced and 688 cases closed.

Order of Precedence of the General Court at 1 April 2013
President of the General Court: Marc Jaeger
President of Chamber: J. Azizi
President of Chamber: N. J. Forwood
President of Chamber: O. Czúcz
President of Chamber: I. Pelikánová
President of Chamber: S. Papasavvas
President of Chamber: A. Dittrich
President of Chamber: L. Truchot
President of Chamber: H. Kanninen
Judges: M.E. Martins Ribeiro; F. Dehousse; I. Wizniewska-Bialecka; V. Vadapalas; K. Jürimäe; I. Labucka; M. Prek; S. Soldevila Fragoso; S. Frimodt Nielsen; K.O'Higgins; J.Schwarcz; M. van der Woude; D. Gratsias; A. Popescu, M. Kancheva, G. Berardis, E. Buttigieg, C. Wetter
Registrar: E. Coulon

The General Court Extended Composition of the Chambers as of 8 April 2013
First Chamber: *President of Chamber:* J. Azizi; *Judges:* I. Labucka, S. Frimodt Nielsen, D. Gratsias, M. Kancheva, E. Buttigieg
Second Chamber: *President of Chamber:* N. J. Forwood; *Judges:* F. Dehousse, I. Wiszniewska-Bialecka, M. Prek, J. Schwarcz

Third Chamber: *President of Chamber:* O. Czúcz; *Judges:* I. Labucka, S. Frimodt Nielsen, D. Gratsias, M. Kancheva, E. Buttigieg
Fourth Chamber: *President of Chamber:* I. Pelikanova; *Judges:* V. Vadapalas, K. Jurimae, K. O'Higgins, M. van der Woude
Fifth Chamber: *President of Chamber:* S. Papasavvas; *Judges:* V. Vadapalas, K. Jurimae, K. O'Higgins, M. van der Woude
Sixth Chamber: *President of Chamber:* H. Kanninen; *Judges:* M.E. Martins Ribeiro, S. Soldevila Fragoso, A. Popescu, G. Berardis, C. Wetter
Seventh Chamber: *President of Chamber:* A. Dittrich; *Judges:* F. Dehousse, I. Wiszniewska-Bialecka, M. Prek, J. Schwarcz
Eighth Chamber: *President of Chamber:* L. Truchot; *Judges:* M.E. Martins Ribeiro, S. Soldevila Fragoso, A. Popescu, G. Berardis, C. Wetter

The Civil Service Tribunal
The European Union Civil Service Tribunal is composed of seven Judges appointed by the Council for a period of six years which may be renewed. The Judges of the Tribunal elect their President from among their number for a term of three years which may be renewed.

The Tribunal sits in Chambers of three Judges. However, whenever the difficulty or importance of the questions of law raised justifies it, a case may be referred to the full court. Furthermore, in cases determined by its Rules of Procedure, it may sit in a Chamber of five Judges or as a single Judge.

The Judges appoint a Registrar for a term of six years.

The Civil Service Tribunal whose special field is disputes involving the European Union civil service, this jurisdiction having previously been exercised by the Court of Justice and then, following its creation in 1989, by the Court of First Instance.

Approximately 900 judgements and orders have been delivered since 2005. In 2012, 178 cases were introduced and 121 cases closed.

Order of Precedence of the Civil Service Tribunal (07.10.2011-30.09.2014)
President of the Civil Service Tribunal: S. Van Raepensbusch (page 1530)
President of Chamber: H. Kreppel
President of Chamber: M.I. Rofes i Pujol
Judges: I. Boruta, E. Perillo, R. Barents, K. Bradley
Registrar: W. Hakenberg

First Chamber: *President of Chamber:* H. Kreppel; *Judges:* E. Perillo, R. Barents
Second Chamber: *President of Chamber:* M.I. Rofes i Pujol ; *Judges:* I. Boruta, K. Bradley
Third Chamber: *President of Chamber:* S. Van Raepenbusch; *Judges:* a) I. Boruta, E. Perillo
b) R. Barents, K. Bradley

For further information contact the Press and Information Division.

Court of Justice of the European Union, Rue du Fort Niedergrünewald, L-2925 Luxembourg, Tel.: (352) 4303-1, Fax: (352) 43 37 66, http://www.curia.europa.eu

EUROPEAN INVESTMENT BANK (EIB)

The European Investment Bank (EIB) was established in 1958 as part of the decision to create a European Economic Community. Its aims are to contribute to the steady and balanced development of the European Union by providing loans for capital investment projects furthering Union policy objectives, in particular: the strengthening of economic and social cohesion; the promotion of business activity to foster the economic advancement of the less favoured regions; the improvement of infrastructure and services in the health and education sectors; the development of transport, telecommunications and energy transfer infrastructure networks with a Community dimension; the preservation of the natural and urban environment; the securing of the energy supply base; assistance in the development of SMEs and, under the "Innovation 2000 Initiative (i2i)", support for investments which promote the information society, research and development, innovation and competitiveness as well as human capital.

While most of its lending is for projects located within the EU, the EIB also participates in the implementation of the Union's development policy in countries outside the European Union; in Accession countries, in countries of the Euro-Mediterranean Partnership, in African Caribbean and Pacific (ACP) states, in South Africa, Latin America and Asia (ALA) and in the Balkans.

The EIB operates under three-year rolling plans. The plan for 2011-13 aims to work towards the gradual return to pre-crisis lending figures and the Bank's focus for operations and regions where its added value is most significant. Its ultimate aim is to have a positive impact on the growth potential of the European economy. It also aims to contribute to the Europe 2020 strategy of smart and sustainable growth as well as support for Climate Action.

European Investment Fund
The European Investment Fund is part of the EIB group. It has several shareholders: EIB 61 per cent, EC 30 per cent, other European Financing Institutions 9 per cent. Both the EIB and the EIF support SMEs. The EIB provides long term loans to large capital investment projects. The EIF concentrates on investment in innovative SIMS in the EU and the Enlargement area through venture capital funds.

Structure
The Board of Governors consists of the ministers designated by each of the Member States, usually the Finance Ministers. It lays down general directives on credit policy, approves the balance sheet and annual report, commits the Bank with respect to financing operations outside the Union and decides on capital increases.

The Board of Directors consists of 28 Directors and 18 Alternates appointed by the Board of Governors. The Board meets ten times a year and ensures that the Bank is managed within European Treaties, the EIB's statute and the directives, it approves the granting of loans, authorises conclusion of guarantees and borrowings and recommends changes in the Bank's credit policy. It is chaired by the President of the Bank. The Management Committee, the executive body, controls all current operations, recommends decisions to Directors and is responsible for carrying them out. The Audit Committee verifies the operations of the Bank have been conducted and that books are kept in a proper manner.

Key Figures
The EIB had subscribed capital as of 31.12.2011 of €232,393 million. In 2011, projects to the cost of €53,467 million were approved, €46,201 million in the EU and €7,266 million in partner countries. Subscribed capital in the European Investment Fund as of 31.12.2011 was €3,000 million.

Annual lending was approximately €45 billion in the mid-2000s before increasing to €79 billion in 2009 in response to the global economic crisis. In 2012, lending was approximately €52 billion.

Croatia became an EIB shareholder upon joining the Union on 1 July 2013.

President of the EIB: Werner Hoyer (Germany) (page 1444)

European Investment Bank, 100 boulevard Konrad Adenauer, L- 2950 Luxembourg. Tel: +352 4379 1, fax: +352 437704, URL: http://www.eib.org

EUROPEAN CENTRAL BANK

The European Central Bank was founded in June 1998. Together with the EU national central banks (NCBs) which have adopted the euro, it makes up the European System of Central Banks (ESCB). The NCBs of the Member States which have not adopted the euro are members of the ESCB with a special status. They do not take part in decision- making regarding the single monetary policy.

Objectives
The main objective of the European Central Bank is to maintain price stability. It should always act in accordance with the principle of an open market economy with free competition, favouring an efficient allocation of resources. The basic tasks of the bank are as follows:

- the definition and implementation of the monetary policy of the euro area
- the conduct of foreign exchange operations
- the holding and management of the official foreign reserves of the euro area countries (portfolio management)
- the promotion of the smooth operation of payment systems

Structure
The process of decision-making in the Eurosystem is centralised through the Governing Council and the Executive Board of the ECB. As long as there are Member States that have not adopted the euro, a third decision-making body, the General Council, shall also exist.

The **Governing Council** comprises all the members of the Executive Board and the governors of the NCBs of the Member States of those counties which have adopted the euro. The main responsibilities of the Governing Council are to adopt the guidelines and take the decisions necessary to ensure the performance of the tasks entrusted to the Eurosystem; to formulate the monetary policy of the euro area including, as appropriate, decisions relating to monetary objectives, key interest rates, the supply of reserves in the Eurosystem and to establish the necessary guidelines for their implementation.

The **Executive Board** comprises the President, the Vice-President and four other members chosen from among persons of professional experience in monetary or banking matters. The main responsibilities of the Board are to implement monetary policies, to execute those powers assigned to it by the Governing Council and to prepare Governing Council meetings.

EUROPEAN UNION

The **General Council** comprises the President, the Vice-President and the governors of the NCBs of all 27 Member States. It performs the tasks which the ECB took over from the EMI and which, owing to the derogation of one or more Member States, still have to be performed in Stage Three of Economic and Monetary Union (EMU). The General Council also contributes to the ECB's advisory functions, the collection of statistical information, the preparation of the ECB's annual reports, the establishment of rules for standardising accounting and reporting of operations undertaken by the NCBs and the necessary preparations for irrevocably fixing the exchange rates of the currencies of the Member States with a derogation against the euro.

Finances

With effect from 29 December 2010, the ECB increased its subscribed capital by €5 billion, from €5.76 billion to €10.76 billion. The euro area NCBs paid their first instalment of their additional capital contributions on 29 December 2010 and the remaining two instalments were paid at the end of 2011 and 2012, respectively.

The paid-up capital of euro area NCBs amounts to €5,196,932,289.36 breaks down as follows:

Euro area NCBs (as of 1 April 2013)

National Central Bank	Capital key %	Paid up capital €
Euro Area		
Nationale Bank van Belgie Banque Nationale de Belgique	2.4256	261,010384.68
Deutsche Bundesbank	18.9373	2,037,777,027.43
Eesti Bank	0.1790	19,261,567.80
Central Bank of Ireland	1.1107	119,518,566.24
Bank of Greece	1.9649	211,436,059.06
Banco de España	8.3040	893,564,575.51
Banque de France	14.2212	1,530,293,899.48
Banca d'Italia	12.4966	1,344,715,688.14
Central Bank of Cyprus	0.1369	14,731,333.14
Banque centrale du Luxembourg	0.1747	18,798,859.75
Central Bank of Malta	0.0632	6,800,732.32
De Nederlandsche Bank	3.9882	429,156,339.12
Oesterreichische Nationalbank	1.9417	208,939,587.70
Banco de Portugal	1.7504	188,354,459.65
Banka Slovenije	0.3288	35,381,025.10
Narodna Banka Slovenska	0.6934	74,4614,363.76
Suomen Pankki - Finlands Bank	1.2539	134,927,820.48
Total	**69.7905**	**7,529,282,289.35**

Source: http://www.ecb.europa.eu

The EU's 10 non-euro area NCBs are required to contribute to the operational costs incurred by the ECB in relation to their participation in the European System of Central Banks (ESCB) by paying up a minimal percentage of their subscribed capital. Since 29 December 2010 these contributions represent 3.75 per cent of their subscribed capital, amounting to a total of €121,176,379.25 as follows:

Non-euro area NCBs (as of 1 April 2013)

NCB	Capital Key %	Paid Up Capital (€)
Bulgarian National Bank	0.8686	3,505,013.50
Ceska narodni banka	1.4472	5,839,806.06
Danmarks Nationalbank	1.4835	5,986,285.44
Latvijas Banka	0.2837	1,144,798.91
Lieutuvos bankas	0.4256	1,717,400.12
Magyar Nemzeti Bank	1.3856	5,591,234.99
Narodowy Bank Polski	4.8954	19,754,136.66
Banca Nationala a Romaniei	2.4645	9,944,860.44
Sveiges Riksbank	2.2582	9,112,389.47
Bank of England	14.5172	58,580,453.65
Total	**30.0295**	**121,176,379.25**

Source: http://www.ecb.europa.eu

The non-euro area NCBs are not entitled to receive any share of the distributable profits of the ECB, nor are they liable to fund any losses of the ECB.

Latvia, which joined the European Union in 2004, is expected to become the 18th member of the eurozone in January 2014.

Financial Crisis

The ECB's main focus during the crisis has been price stability in the euro area which is defined as keeping euro area HIPC inflation below, but close to 2 per cent over the medium term.

President: Mario Draghi (page 1417)
Vice-President: Vitor Constâncio

European Central Bank, Kaiserstrasse 29, D-60311 Frankfurt am Main, Germany. Tel: +49 (0) 69 13440, fax: +49 (0) 69 13446000, e-mail: info@ecb.europa.eu, URL: http://www.ecb.europa.eu

AFRICAN DEVELOPMENT BANK GROUP

The African Development Bank Group comprises the African Development Bank established in 1964; the African Development Fund, established in November 1972 to provide development finance on concessionary terms to African Member countries; and the Nigeria Trust Fund established in February 1976 to assist in the development effort of the poorer African Development Bank members.

The AfDB is one of the five multilateral development banks in the world. The others are the European Bank for Reconstruction and Development (EBRD), the Asian Development Bank (AsDB) and the Inter-American Development Bank (IAfDB). The AfDB and the World Bank have a close relationship, especially with regard to partnership and financing but the AfDB is totally independent of the World Bank.

Its mission is to help reduce poverty, improve living conditions for Africans and mobilize resources for Africa's economic and social development. The Bank Group finances economic and social development projects and programmes in African countries through loans, equity investments and technical assistance.

Structure
The African Development Bank Group's highest policy-making body is its Board of Governors, which consists of one governor for each member country and which issues general directives concerning the operational policies of the Bank. The approval of the Bank's Governors is required for amendments to the Bank's Agreement, the admittance of new members and capital increases. With the exception of certain powers specifically reserved to it under the Agreement, the Board of Governors has delegated its powers to a Board of Directors made up of 18 Executive Directors (12 from the regional members and 6 from the non-regional members) for a period of three years. The Board of Directors is responsible for the conduct of the general operations of the Bank including the approval of its budget and general operations. The President is elected by the Board of Governors upon the recommendation of the Board of Directors for a term of five years. The three Vice-Presidents, who assist the President in the day to day management of the Bank, are appointed by the Board of Directors on the recommendation of the President.

Budget
The financial resources of the Bank consist of ordinary capital resources, comprising subscribed capital, reserves, funds raised through borrowings, and accumulated net income. The Bank's capital is subscribed such that the Regional Member Countries hold 60 per cent of total subscribed capital, and non-regional members hold 40 per cent.

The Bank lends at variable rates calculated on the basis of the cost of borrowings. The rate is adjusted twice a year. The other terms include a commitment charge of 1 per cent and maturities of up to 20 years, including a five-year grace period. In 2011 ADB's authorised

capital was UA 66.05 billion. Its subscribed capital amounted to UA 37.32 billion and its paid up capital UA3.29 billion. Between 1967 and 2011 it had funded 3,661 operations totalling a commitment of UA$60.06 billion. In 2011, 184 operations totalled UA5.72 billion.

Activities
The Bank's operations cover the major sectors, with particular emphasis on agriculture, public utilities, transport, industry, the social sectors of health and education, and concerns cutting across sectors - such as poverty reduction, environmental management, gender main-streaming, and population activities. Most Bank financing is designed to support specific projects. However, the Bank also provides programme, sector, and policy-based loans to enhance national economic management. The Bank also finances non-publicly guaranteed private sector operations. The Bank actively pursues co-financing activities with bilateral and multilateral institutions.

Membership
The African Development Bank Group has a total of 78 member countries, comprising 53 independent African countries (regional) and 25 non-African countries (non-regional).

The 53 regional member countries are: Algeria, Angola, Benin, Botswana, Burkina-Faso, Burundi, Cameroon, Cape Verde, Central African Republic, Chad, Comoros, Congo, Democratic Republic of Congo, Côte d'Ivoire, Djibouti, Egypt, Equatorial Guinea, Eritrea, Ethiopia, Gabon, The Gambia, Ghana, Guinea, Guinea-Bissau, Kenya, Lesotho, Liberia, Libyan Arab Jamahiriya, Madagascar, Malawi, Mali, Mauritania, Mauritius, Morocco, Mozambique, Namibia, Niger, Nigeria, Rwanda, Sao Tomé and Principe, Senegal, Seychelles, Sierra Leone, Somalia, South Africa, Sudan, Swaziland, Tanzania, Togo, Tunisia, Uganda, Zambia and Zimbabwe.

The 24 non-regional member countries are: Argentina, Austria, Belgium, Brazil, Canada, China, Denmark, Finland, France, Germany, India, Italy, Japan, Korea, Kuwait, Netherlands, Norway, Portugal, Saudi Arabia, Spain, Sweden, Switzerland, United Kingdom, United States of America and the United Arab Emirates.

President: Donald Kaberuka (page 1452)

African Development Bank Group, Rue Joseph Anoma, 01 BP 1387 Abidjan 01, Côte d'Ivoire. E-mail: afdb@afdb.org, URL: http://www.afdb.org

The AFDB is temporarily based in Tunisia. **African Development Bank Group**, 15 Avenue du Ghana, PO Box 323-1002, Tunis-Belvedere, Tunisia. Tel: +216 71 103900, fax: +216 71 351933, e-mail: afdb@afdb.org, URL: http://www.afdb.org

AFRICAN UNION (AU)

The Organisation of African Unity was founded in 1963 when its aim was to promote unity among African countries, improve the general living standards on the continent, defend the territorial integrity and independence of its states and promote international co-operation. Membership comprised 53 of the 54 African states, the only exclusion being Morocco.

At an Extraordinary Summit in Sirte on 9.9.99, the African Leaders decided to establish an African Union to be a successor to the OAU. All 53 OAU members have now ratified the Constitutive Act of African Union, and the Durban Summit in July 2002 constituted the Inaugural Summit for the African Union.

The objectives of the African Union are:
- to provide the appropriate framework within which the necessary partnership between Governments, peoples' representatives, economic operators and civil society can be strengthened in order to promote the economic and social development of the Continent;
- to promote the democratic aspirations of the African peoples;
The Constitutive Act of the African Union contains new provisions on the observance of human rights, the rule of law and gender issue;
- to promote peace and security and thereby encourage socio-economic progress.

Structure
The organs of the union are:
Assembly of the Union: Composed of Heads of State and Government or their representatives. The Assembly is the supreme organ of the AU.
TheExecutive Council: The Composed of Ministers of the members states. The Council is responsible to the Assembly.
The Commission: Made up of the Chair, the Deputy Chair, eight Commissioners (each with a portfolio) and staff members.
The Permanent Representatives Committee: Made up of Permanent Representatives of Member States accredited to the Union.
The Peace and Security Council (PSC): The decision to create the PSC was made in 2001 in Lusaka. The Protocol is still in the process of being ratified.
The Pan-African Parliament: The protocol relating to the composition, powers, functions and organization of the Pan-African Parliament has been signed by Member States and is in the process of ratification.
ECOSOCC (Economic Social and Cultural Council): An advisory organ, made up of different professional and social groups from the member states. The statutes on its functions, composition and powers are to be submitted at the Maputo Summit.

Court of Justice: To be established. The statutes will be submitted to the Assembly in Maputo.
The Specialized Technical Committees: Rural Economy and Agricultural Matters; Monetary and Financial Affairs; Trade, Customs and Immigration Matters; Industry, Science and Technology, Energy, Natural Resources and Environment; Transport, Communications and Tourism; Health, Labour and Social Affairs; and Education, Culture and Human Resources. Represented at ministerial level.
The Financial Institutions: The African Monetary Fund, the African Investment Bank and the African Central Bank. These will constitute the economic foundation of the African Union, geared towards economic development and the eradication of poverty on the Continent.

The AU Commission
The AU is the principal organ and plays a central role in the management of the AU. Its responsibilities include: to represent the Union and defend its interests; to elaborate common positions of the Union; to prepare strategic plans and studies for the consideration of the Executive Council; to elaborate, promote, coordinate and harmonize the programmes and policies of the Union with those of the RECs; and to ensure gender is addressed in the activities of the Union.

Members
Algeria, Angola, Benin, Botswana, Burkina Faso, Burundi, Cameroon, Cape Verde, Central African Republic, Chad, Comoros, Republic of the Congo, Cote d'Ivoire, Democratic Republic of the Congo, Djibouti, Egypt, Equatorial Guinea, Eritrea, Ethiopia, Gabon, Gambia, Ghana, Guinea, Guinea-Bissau, Kenya, Lesotho, Liberia, Libya, Madagascar, Malawi, Mali, Mauritania, Mauritius, Mozambique, Namibia, Niger, Nigeria, Rwanda, Democratic Republic Arab of the Sahara, Sao Tome and Principe, Senegal, Seychelles, Sierra Leone, Somalia, South Africa, Sudan, South Sudan, Swaziland, United Republic of Tanzania, Togo, Tunisia, Uganda, Zambia, Zimbabwe.

Chair, African Union: Hailemariam Desalegn (Ethiopia)
Chair, African Union Commission: H.E. Dr Nkoazana C. Dlamini Zuma

African Union, PO Box 3243, Addis Ababa, Ethiopia. Tel: +251 11 551 7700, fax: +251 11 551 7844, URL: http://www.au.int/

AGENCY FOR THE PROHIBITION OF NUCLEAR WEAPONS IN LATIN AMERICA AND THE CARIBBEAN (OPANAL)

Organismo para la Proscripción de las Armas Nucleares en la América Latina y el Caribe

The Agency for the Prohibition of Nuclear Weapons in Latin America and the Caribbean (OPANAL) is an inter-governmental agency created to ensure that the obligations of the Treaty of Tlatelolco are met. This Treaty was signed on 14 February 1967 and has been in force since April 1969. It is also known as the Treaty for the Prohibition of Nuclear Weapons in Latin America and the Caribbean, and sets out to:

- Ensure the absence of nuclear weapons within an agreed zone (the entire Latin American and Caribbean region and some areas of the Pacific and Atlantic Oceans)
- To promote general and complete disarmament
- Contribute to nuclear non-proliferation
- Use nuclear materials and facilities only for peaceful purposes
- Prohibit testing, production, acquisition and storage of nuclear weapons.

Structure
The three main bodies are the General Conference, the Council and the Secretariat General.

The highest authority is the **General Conference**. It rules on all issues, establishes procedures, elects members of its council, elects the secretary-general, reviews the organisation's special reports, establishes agreements with governments and international organisations, approves the budget, approves rules of procedure and establishes such subsidiary organisations as are necessary.

The **Council** consists of five members elected for a four-year term. The current members (2013) are Argentina, Bolivia, Brazil, Chile and Mexico. The Council oversees the work of the organisation and produces reports.

The **SecretaryGeneral** is the highest administrative official of the Agency. The Secretary-General is elected by his peers and serves a four-year term, renewable once. The post cannot be occupied by a national of the host country.

There are two subsidiary bodies, the **Committee on Contributions, Administrative and Budgetary Matters** and the **Good Offices Committee**. The current (2013) members of the Committee on Contributions, Administrative and Budgetary Matters are Belize, Brazil, Cuba, Guatemala and Nicarugua.

Membership
The following countries have all signed the treaty and are full parties to the treaty: Antigua & Barbuda, Argentina, Bahamas, Barbados, Belize, Bolivia, Brazil, Chile, Colombia, Costa Rica, Cuba, Dominica, Dominican Republic, Ecuador, El Salvador, Grenada, Guatemala, Guyana, Haiti, Honduras, Jamaica, Mexico, Nicaragua, Panama, Paraguay, Peru, St. Kitts & Nevis, St. Lucia, St. Vincent & the Grenadines, St; Lucia, Suriname, Trinidad & Tobago, Uruguay and Venezuela.

Additional Protocols
Protocol I, for States that have territories under their responsibility in implementing the Treaty Area. This Protocol has been signed and ratified by the United Kingdom, the Netherlands, France and the United States of America.
Protocol II, led to the nuclear powers recognized by the international community, has been signed and ratified by China, the United States of America, France, Britain and the USSR (now Russia).

Secretary-General: H.E. Mme Gioconda Úbeda Rivera (2010-December 2013)

Agency for the Prohibition of Nuclear Weapons in Latin America and the Caribbean (OPANAL), Schiller 326 - 5 piso, Col. Chapultepec Morales, Mexico DF, 11570 Mexico. Tel: +52 55 5255 2914, fax: +52 55 5255 3748, e-mail: info@opanal.org, URL: http://www.opanal.org

ANDEAN COMMUNITY

The Andean Community is a sub-regional organisation with international status. It is made up of Bolivia, Columbia, Ecuador and Peru, and the bodies and institutions comprising the Andean Integration System. Located in South America, the four Andean countries group together over 100 million persons living in an area of 4,700 square kilometres whose Gross Domestic Product was US$340 billion in 2008. Its aim is to form the Union of South American Nations (Unasur).

History
The Andean Community dates back to 1969, when five South American countries (Bolivia, Chile, Columbia, Ecuador and Peru) signed the Cartagena Agreement in order to jointly improve their peoples' standard of living through integration and economic and social co-operation. On October 30, 1976, Chile withdrew from it. Venezuela was a member from February 13, 1973, until April 22, 2006.

Almost all the Andean bodies and institutions were created during the first ten years of the integration process, except for the Andean Council of Presidents, which was set up in 1990. The policy or model that predominated in the 1970s was the 'import substitution' or 'closed model' that protected national industry by imposing high duties on products brought into the country. This model entered a stage of crisis, making the 1980s a lost decade for both the Andean countries and Andean integration. None of the countries in the region, from Mexico to Argentina, emerged unscathed from the debt crisis, which was reflected in the stagnation of the integration process.

It was decided at a meeting held in Galapagos (Ecuador) in 1989, to replace the model of closed development with one of open development. Trade and the market became the driving forces and this was reflected in the adoption of Strategic Design and a Working Plan in which trade occupied the leading position. The Andean countries eliminated tariffs on their trade with each other and in 1993 formed a free trade area. This gave a strong boost to trade within the Community, which increased heavily, creating thousands of new jobs. Trade in services was also liberalized, particularly the different modes of transportation. In 1997, the member countries decided, through the Trujillo Protocol, to introduce reforms to the Cartagena Agreement in order to bring it into line with the changes that have taken place on the international scene. These reforms put the leadership of the process in the hands of the Presidents and made the Andean Councils of Presidents and of Foreign Ministers a part of the institutional structure. The Andean Community was created to replace the Andean Pact.

Since 2003, the integration process was given a social content as well. An Integral Plan for Social Development was established by Presidential mandate. The Secretariat's Working Plan for 2008, which provides for action in the areas of the Social and Political Area, Environment, External Relations and Economic and Trade Area. The Working Program for 2009 provided

for the development of items in different political, social, cultural, environmental, trade and other spheres that will, icontribute to national efforts to fight poverty, inequality and social exclusion, as well as recover the harmony and balance between man and nature.

At a Special Meeting of the Andean Council of Presidents in 2011 the presidents of the member states reiterated their commitment to strengthen the AC and to work together with Mercosur and Unasur with a view towards a possible future convergence of the three.

Areas of Action
Social and Policial: To contribute to national efforts to overcome poverty, exclusion, inequality and asymmetries by promoting civil society participation and boosting actions to deepen political co-operation. Its programs are: Social Development, Food Security and Regional Development, Migration and Labor, Civil Society, Communication and Political Affairs.

Environment: An Andean Environmental Agenda comprising subregional actions to promote sustainable development is being implemented as a way of responding effectively to global threats to the environment. Programs: Climate Change, Biodiversity, Water and Disasters.

External Relations: The CAN's joint external projection within the framework of its Common Foreign Policy (CFP) reinforces the Member Countries' negotiating capacity and is conducive to their playing a more important role within the dynamic international context. Its programs are: Latin America and the Caribbean, European Union and Other Countries and Organizations.

Economic and Trade Area: The aim is to consolidate the enlarged market in order to guarantee the unhampered flow of goods and services within the subregion and to contribute to job creation. Programs: Goods, Macroeconomics, SMEs, Services, Investment and IP.

Institutional Area: Aim is to achieve an efficient management of the integration process by means of progress that address the General Secretariat's other work areas. Its programs are: Legal Counseling, Andean Integration System, Statistics, Technical Cooperation, Administration, IT, Institutional Services.

Structure
The Andean Integration System (SAI) is a set of bodies and institutions forming part of the Andean Community, designed to allow for an effective co-ordination between them in order to maximize sub-regional Andean integration, promote their external projection and strengthen the actions relted to the integration process.

The SAI comprises the following bodies and institutions: Andean Presidential Council; Andean Council of Foreign Affairs Ministers; the Andean Community Commission; Andean Community General Secretariat; Andean Community Court of Justice (URL: http://www.tribunalandino.org.ec/); Andean Parliament (URL: http://www.parlamentoandino.org/); Andean Development Corporation (URL: http://www.caf.com); Latin American Reserve Fund (URL: http://www.flar.net); Andean Business Advisory Council; Andean Labor Advisory Council (URL: http://www.ccla.org.pe); Símón Rodriguez Agreement; Andean Health Organization - Hipólito Unanue Agreement (URL: http://www.orasconhu.org/); Símón Bólivar Andean University (URL: http://www.uasb.edu.bo/web/); and Consultative Council of Indigenous Peoples.

Members
Bolivia, Columbia, Ecuador, Peru
Associate members: Argentina, Brazil, Chile, Paraguay, Uruguay

Secretary-General: Adalid Contreras Baspineiro

Andean Community General Secretariat, Paseo de la Republica 3895, San Isidro, Lima 27, Peru. Tel: +51 (0)1 710 6400, fax: +51 (0)1 221 33 29, URL: http://www.comunidadandina.org/endex.htm

ARAB MAGHREB UNION

The Arab Maghreb Union (AMU) was born of the idea of a unified northern Africa, initially thought of by nationalists in the 1920s and later gaining widespread support following the turbulence of World War II and the independence movements of the 1950s and 1960s. Territorial disputes and political differences meant that it was not until the late 1980s that momentum was regained and the treaty of the 'Greater Arab Maghreb' was signed on 17 February 1989 in Marrakech.

There are five member states: Algeria, Libya, Mauritania, Morocco and Tunisia.

The AMU aims to safeguard the region's economic interests, foster and promote economic and cultural co-operation and increase mutual commercial exchanges. It is intended that this will lead to integration and the creation of a North African Common Market (Maghreb Economic Space). The AMU Treaty also includes key aspects of common defence issues and undertakings not to interfere in the domestic affairs of the partners.

Secretary-General: Habib Ben Yahia (page 1540)

Arab Maghreb Union, 14 rue Tensift, Agdal Rabat, Morocco. Tel: +212 537 6813, fax +212 537 681377, e-mail: sg.uma@maghrebarabe.org, URL: http://www.maghrebarabe.org

ARAB MONETARY FUND

The Arab Monetary Fund was founded in 1976. Its objectives are:
- to correct imbalances in the balances of payments of member states;
- to remove restrictions on current payments between member states;
- to establish policies and structures for Arab monetary co-operation;
- to advise on policies related to the investment of the financial resources of member states in foreign markets;
- to promote the development of Arab financial markets;
- to facilitate the creation of a unified Arab currency; and
- to promote trade among member states.

Activities
To achieve its aims, the Fund provides credit facilities to member states, promotes trade and encourages capital movements between member states. It manages funds placed in its charge by member states, conducts the research required to achieve the Fund's goals and holds periodic consultations with members on their economic conditions and the policies they pursue. It also provides technical assistance to banking and monetary institutions.

The managment of the AMF consists of the Board of Governors (General Assembly) and the board of executive directors chaired by the Director General Chairman of the board. The AMF is composed of:
Offices: the Internal Audit Office and the Director's General Office;
Departments: Economic and Technical; Economic Policy Institute; Treasury and Investment Administration; Finance and Computer; Legal; and
Committees: Loans Committee; Investment Committee; and the Administration Committee.

Membership
There are currently 22 member countries of the AMF: Algeria, Bahrain, Comoros, Djibouti, Egypt, Iraq, Jordan, Kuwait, Lebanon, Libya, Mauritania, Morocco, Oman, Palestinian Authority, Qatar, Saudi Arabia, Somalia, Sudan, Syria, Tunisia, United Arab Emirates and Yemen.

Director General and Chairman of the Board: Dr. Jassim Al Mannai (page 1376)

Arab Monetary Fund, P.O. Box 2818, Abu Dhabi, United Arab Emirates. Tel: +971 2 617 1400, fax: +971 2 632 6454, e-mail: centralmail@amfad.org.ae, URL: http://www.amf.org.ae

ARCTIC COUNCIL

The Ottawa Declaration of 1996 formally established the Arctic Council to address the common concerns and challenges faced by the Arctic governments and their people. The Arctic covers one sixth of the earth's landmass; more than 30 million km^2 and twenty-four time zones. It has a population of some four million, including over thirty different indigenous peoples and many languages. The Arctic is a region of vast natural resources and a very clean environment compared with most areas of the world. The main activities of the Council focus on the protection of the Arctic environment and sustainable development as a means of improving the economic, social and cultural well-being of the north.

Activities
The work of the Council is undertaken by the Arctic Council Working Groups, of which there are six:
- Arctic Contaminants Action Programme (ACAP)
- Arctic Monitoring and Assessment Program (AMAP)
- Conservation of Arctic Flora and Fauna (CAFF)
- Emergency Prevention, Preparedness and Response (EPPR)
- Protection of the Arctic Marine Environment (PAME)
- Sustainable Development Working Group (SDWG)

Current action plans are the Arctic Climate Impact Assessment programme, the Arctic Council Action Plan to Eliminate Pollution and the Regional Programme for Action for the protection of the Arctic Marine Environment from Land-Based Activities.

The Tromso Declaration on protecting and preserving the Arctic's environment was signed on the 29th of April 2009 in Tromso, Norway.

Structure
The Council meets at ministerial level twice a year. Senior Arctic officials also meet twice a year. The Chair and Secretariat of the Council rotates among the Arctic States. The Chairman is the Minister of Foreign Affairs of the relevant country. Canada holds the chair in the period May 2013-2015. It will then pass to Canada, followed by the USA.

Members
Current members of the Council are: Canada, Denmark (including Greenland & the Faroe Islands), Finland, Iceland, Norway, the Russian Federation, Sweden and the United States of America.

Permanent Participants in the Council are: the Russian Association of Indigenous Peoples of the North, the Inuit Circumpolar Conference, the Saami Council, the Aleut International Association, the Arctic Athabaskan Council and the Gwich'in Council International.

The 8th Arctic Council Ministerial Meeting took place on 15 May 2013.

Chairman, 2013-15: Leona Aglukkaq (Canada) (page 1372)

Arctic Council Secretariat, Polarmiljøsenteret, 9296 Tromsø, Norway. Tel: +47 7775 0140, fax: +47 7775 0501, e-mail: ac-chair@arctic-council.org, URL: http://www.arctic-council.org

ASIAN DEVELOPMENT BANK

The Asian Development Bank was established in 1966 to facilitate economic and social development in the Asia-Pacific region. Its aims are:
- to promote investment of public and private capital for development;
- to use the resources at its disposal as loans for the development of its developing members;
- to meet the requests of its developing members for assistance in co-ordinating their economic development plans and policies;
- to provide technical assistance to help prepare, finance and carry out development projects and programmes and advisory services.

A long-term strategic framework was adopted in 2008. Under Strategy 2020, the ADB will have three main agendas: inclusive growth, environmentally sustainable growth, and regional integration.

Structure
This consists of a Board of Governors, a Board of Directors, a President, three Vice-Presidents (Operations 1, Operations 2, Finance and Administration) and support staff. The Bank has a staff of over 2,000 drawn from 50 countries, working in 24 offices and its Headquarters in Manila.

The Board of Governors is the organisation's highest policy-making body. Each member country nominates one Governor and one Alternate Governor. This governor exercises that country's voting rights. The Board of Governors delegates its authority to the Board of Directors.

The Board of Directors consists of 12 members, 8 of whom are elected by regional members and 4 by non-regional members. Directors hold office for two years and may be re-elected. Each director appoints an alternate director. Directors are responsible for the Bank's general operations, approve the budget and submit accounts to the Board of Governors. The Board of Directors normally meets once a week.

The President is elected by the Board of Governors and is the Chairperson of the Board of Directors. The term of office is five years but the incumbent is eligible for re-election. The Vice-Presidents are appointed by the Board of Directors on the recommendation of the President. Currently, there are four Vice-Presidents. They are responsible, respectively, for the Operations 1 (South Asia, Mekong and Private Sector Operations), Operations 2 (East & Central Asia, Southeast Asia, Pacific and Central Operation Services), Knowledge, Management and Sustainable Development and Finance and Administration.

Finance
The financial resources of the bank consist of ordinary capital resources, comprising subscribed capital, reserves and funds raised through borrowings; and special funds comprising contributions made by member countries, past loan repayments, and amounts previously set aside from the paid-in capital. The bank also receives co-financing funds from official aid agencies, export credit agencies and market institutions.

In 2010, ADB approved $16.5 billion in financing operations, among these were 118 loans of around $11.5 billion, 40 grants amounting to $982 million, five guarantees of $982 million and eight equity investments maounting to $175 million. Technical assistance amounted to $175.5 million for 243 projects. The Trade Program also supported amost $2.8 billion in trade through guarantees and bank loans. In 2011, there were 558 ongoing projects.

The Japanese Fund for Poverty Reduction (JFPR) was established in 2000 through a special $90 million contribution by the Government of Japan. It provides additional assistance in ADB's fight against poverty. At October 2002, approved JFPR projects amounted to US$68.73 million.

Technical Assistance
The bank's main objective is to assist development as effectively as possible, not only through the amount of finance loaned but also through technical assistance. Funding in 2011 amounted to US$21.7 billion. Loans in 2011 included: US$250 million for a metro rail system in Bangalore, US$500 million to improve services in Georgia and US$650 million to help rebuild Pakistan's flood damaged infrastructure.

Membership
The Bank has 67 members, 48 of which are from the Asian and Pacific region and 19 of which are from outside.

Regional Members: Afghanistan, Armenia, Australia, Azerbaijan, Bangladesh, Bhutan, Brunei Darussalam, Cambodia, China, Cook Islands, Fiji, Georgia, Hong Kong SAR, India, Indonesia, Japan, Kazakhstan, Kiribati, Republic of Korea, Kyrgyzstan, Laos, Malaysia, Maldives, Marshall Islands, Micronesia, Mongolia, Myanmar, Nauru, Nepal, New Zealand, Pakistan, Palau, Papua New Guinea, Philippines, Singapore, Samoa, Solomon Islands, Sri Lanka, Tajikistan, Taipei, Thailand, Timor-Leste, Tonga, Turkmenistan, Tuvalu, Uzbekistan, Vanuatu, Vietnam

Non-Regional Members: Austria, Belgium, Canada, Denmark, Finland, France, Germany, Ireland, Italy, Luxembourg, Netherlands, Norway, Portugal, Spain, Sweden, Switzerland, Turkey, United Kingdom, USA

Its main partners are governments, the private sector , non-government organizations, development agencies, community-based organizations and foundations.

President: Takehiko Nahao (page 1483)

Asian Development Bank, 6 ADB Avenue, Mandaluyong City 1550, Manila, Philippines. Tel: +63 2 632 4444, fax: +63 2 636 2444, URL: http://www.adb.org

ASIA-PACIFIC ECONOMIC CO-OPERATION (APEC)

Asia-Pacific Economic Co-operation (APEC) was formed in 1989 as a result of the growing interdependence among Asia-Pacific economies. Originally intended as an informal dialogue group with limited participation and scope, APEC has become the most important regional vehicle for promoting trade and economic co-operation. It operates as a co-operative economic and trade forum. The organisation's main aim is to advance Asia-Pacific economic growth and sense of community. APEC has 21 members which account for approximately 40 per cent of the world's population, approximately 54 per cent of world GDP and approximately 44 per cent of world trade.

Objectives
APEC works in three areas to meet its objectives of free and open trade and investment in the Asia-Pacific by 2010 for developed economies and 2020 for developing economies:
- Trade and Investment Liberalisation - reducing and eliminating tariff and non-tariff barriers to trade and investment, and opening markets.
- Business Facilitation - reducing the costs of business transactions, improving access to trade information and bringing into line policy and business strategies to facilitate growth, and free and open trade.
- Economic and Technical Co-operation (ECOTECH) - assisting member economies build the necessary capacities to take advantage of global trade and the New Economy.

Another area of co-operation among APEC members is the environment, with Asia-Pacific economies pledging to protect the quality of air, water and green spaces, whilst managing energy sources and renewable resources to ensure sustainable growth and provide a more secure future in the Asia-Pacific area.

In 2011, the APEC Leaders issued the Honolulu Declaration in which they committed to the further development of the regional economy; support of green growth objectives; and increased regulatory co-operation and convergence. Specifically APEC aims for reduced tariff rates on environmental goods by 2015; reduction of aggregate energy intensity by 45 per cent by 2035; and better regulatory practices by 2013.

Structure

Ministerial and Senior Officials Meetings
The APEC Chair, which rotates annually among members, is responsible for hosting the annual ministerial meeting of foreign and economic ministers. Senior Officials Meetings (SOM) are held regularly prior to every ministerial meeting. Senior officials make recommendations to the Minister and carry out their decisions. They oversee and co-ordinate the budgets and work programmes of the APEC fora.

APEC Business Advisory Council (ABAC)
In 1995 the APEC Business Advisory Council (ABAC) was established as a permanent council composed of up to three senior business people from each member economy to provide advice on the implementation of APEC action plans and on other specific business sector priorities. Chairmanship of the ABAC rotates each year according to which economy chairs APEC.

APEC Fora
At each Ministerial Meeting, members define and fund work programmes for APEC's four committees, eleven working groups and other APEC fora.

The APEC Secretariat was established in Singapore in 1993 to serve as the core support mechanism for the APEC processes. It comprises 23 officials seconded from member economies and a similar number of local support staff.

Each member economy provides small annual funding contributions. From 2009 these will total US$5 million. Funding is used to fund the Secretariat and various projects. Japan has provided additional funds since 1997.

Membership
There are currently 21 members: Australia, Brunei Darussalam, Canada, Chile, People's Republic of China, Hong Kong SAR, Indonesia, Japan, Republic of Korea, Malaysia, Mexico, New Zealand, Papua New Guinea, Peru, the Philippines, the Russian Federation, Singapore, Chinese Taipei, Thailand, United States of America, Vietnam.

Publications
APEC publishes many titles. A cyber bookstore has been set up at http://www.ecomz.com/apec.

Executive Director: Dr Alan Bollard

APEC Secretariat, 35 Heng Mui Keng Terrace, Singapore 119616. Tel: +65 68 919 600, fax: +65 68 919 690, e-mail: info@apec.org, URL: http://www.apec.org

ASSOCIATION OF CARIBBEAN STATES

The Association of Caribbean States is an organisation for consultation, co-operation and action among the countries of the Greater Caribbean. Its main objectives are to strengthen the integration process, to preserve the environmental integrity of the Caribbean Sea and to promote sustainable development in the Greater Caribbean region.

Membership
The following are currently member states: Antigua and Barbuda, Bahamas, Barbados, Belize, Colombia, Costa Rica, Cuba, Dominica, Dominican Republic, El Salvador, Grenada, Guatemala, Guyana, Haiti, Honduras, Jamaica, Mexico, Nicaragua, Panama, St. Kitts and Nevis, St. Lucia, St. Vincent and the Grenadines, Suriname, Trinidad and Tobago and Venezuela.

Activities
The current focus of the Association is on co-operation in four areas: trade, transport, sustainable tourism and natural disasters.

Trade: The Association fosters co-operation and integration by uniting the efforts of ACS member countries to build and consolidate an enhanced economic space for trade and investment in the Greater Caribbean. It also promotes understanding and convergence of positions in areas of mutual interest within the major negotiation processes, such as the FTAA and the WTO, particularly with respect to the treatment of small economies. It holds business forums and meetings of trade promotion organisations annually.

Transport: The main goal of the Association is the signing of the Air Transport Agreement, which will grant regional airlines of signatory countries increased access to the other members' skies. The ACS is also building a Port and Maritime Information Database which will include factors such as freight costs and services available in ACS territories. The Association has signed co-operation agreements with other agencies to deal with security training, thus promoting the safety of travellers and helping to stem the illegal drug trade.

Sustainable Tourism: A primary objective of the Association is the establishment of the Sustainable Tourism Zone of the Caribbean (STZC). The Convention establishing the STZC guides destinations in the sustainable development of the tourism industry.

Natural Disasters: The Association encourages co-operation between the bodies responsible for disaster planning and response in the region. It provides tools to strengthen national organisations in prevention and mitigation of natural disasters and backs projects in development that will lead to early warning systems in the region and an improvement in the information systems of the national and regional bodies.

Organisation Structure
The Ministerial Council, comprising the Foreign Affairs Ministers of member states, is the principal policy-making body of the Association, and the Secretariat is the executive arm of the organisation. There are five Special Committees: Trade Development and External Economic Relations; Sustainable Tourism; Transport; Natural Disasters; and Budget and Administration. There is also a Council of National Representatives for the Special Fund, responsible for overseeing resource mobilisation and project development. The Special Committees meet twice a year.

Secretary General: Dr Alfonsos Minera Cavadio

Association of Caribbean States, 5-7 Sweet Briar Road, St. Clair, P.O. Box 660, Port of Spain, Trinidad and Tobago. Tel: +868 622 9575, fax: +868 622 1653, e-mail: mail@acs-aec.org, URL: http://www.acs-aec.org

ASSOCIATION OF SOUTHEAST ASIAN NATIONS (ASEAN)

The Association of Southeast Asian Nations or ASEAN was established on 8 August 1967 in Bangkok, Thailand, with the signing of the Bangkok Declaration by the five original ASEAN Member States, namely, Indonesia, Malaysia, Philippines, Singapore and Thailand. At present, the ten Member States comprise Brunei Darussalam, Cambodia, Indonesia, Lao PDR, Malaysia, Myanmar, Philippines, Singapore, Thailand and Vietnam.

As set out in the Bangkok Declaration, the aims and purposes of ASEAN are:
1. To accelerate the economic growth, social progress and cultural development in the region through joint endeavours in the spirit of equality and partnership in order to strengthen the foundation for a prosperous and peaceful community of Southeast Asian Nations;
2. To promote regional peace and stability through abiding respect for justice and the rule of law in the relationship among countries of the region and adherence to the principles of the United Nations Charter;
3. To promote active collaboration and mutual assistance on matters of common interest in the economic, social, cultural, technical, scientific and administrative fields;
4. To provide assistance to each other in the form of training and research facilities in the educational, professional, technical and administrative spheres;
5. To collaborate more effectively for the greater utilisation of their agriculture and industries, the expansion of their trade, including the study of the problems of international commodity trade, the improvement of their transportation and communications facilities and the raising of the living standards of their peoples;
6. To promote Southeast Asian studies; and
7. To maintain close and beneficial cooperation with existing international and regional organisations with similar aims and purposes, and explore all avenues for even closer cooperation among themselves.

As of 2009, the ASEAN region has a population of about 580 million, a total area of 4.5 million square kilometres, a combined gross domestic product of almost US$1,500 billion.

ASEAN Secretariat
In 1976, the ASEAN Member States decided to establish the ASEAN Secretariat as the central administrative organ. The basic mandate of the ASEAN Secretariat is 'to provide for greater efficiency in the coordination of ASEAN organs and for more effective implementation of ASEAN projects and activities'. The operational budget of the ASEAN Secretariat is prepared annually and funded through equal contribution of all ASEAN Member States. The ASEAN Secretariat is located in Jakarta, Indonesia and is headed by the Secretary-General. The Secretary-General is appointed on merit and accorded ministerial status for a five-year term. He is mandated to initiate, advise, coordinate, and implement ASEAN activities. The ASEAN Secretariat has an approximate total of 200 staff.

ASEAN Community
The ASEAN Vision 2020, adopted by the ASEAN Leaders on the 30th Anniversary of ASEAN, agreed on a shared vision of ASEAN as a concert of Southeast Asian nations, outward looking, living in peace, stability and prosperity, bonded together in partnership in dynamic development and in a community of caring societies. At the 12th ASEAN Summit in January 2007, the Leaders affirmed their strong commitment to accelerate the establishment of an ASEAN Community by 2015 and signed the Cebu Declaration on the Acceleration of the Establishment of an ASEAN Community by 2015.

ASEAN Security Community
To build on what has been constructed over the years in the field of political and security cooperation, the ASEAN Leaders have agreed to establish the ASEAN Security Community (ASC). The APSC shall aim to ensure that countries in the region live at peace with one another and with the world in a just, democratic and harmonious environment. It will be built on the strong foundation of ASEAN processes, principles, agreements, and structures, which evolved over the years and are contained in the following major political agreements:

-Bangkok Declaration, Bangkok, 8 August 1967
-Zone of Peace, Freedom and Neutrality Declaration, Kuala Lumpur, 27 November 1971
-Declaration of ASEAN Concord, Bali, 24 February 1976
-Treaty of Amity and Co-operation in Southeast Asia, Bali, 24 February 1976
-ASEAN Declaration on the South China Sea, Manila, 22 July 1992
-Treaty on the Southeast Asian Nuclear Weapon-Free Zone, Bangkok, 15 December 1995
-ASEAN Vision 2020, Kuala Lumpur, 15 December 1997
-ASEAN Declaration on Joint Action to Counter Terrorism, Bandar Seri Begawan, 5 November 2001

In recognition of security interdependence in the Asia-Pacific region, ASEAN established the ASEAN Regional Forum (ARF) in 1994. The ARF discusses major regional security issues in the region, including the relationship amongst the major powers, non-proliferation, counter-terrorism and transnational crime, among others. Its approach includes preventative diplomacy and conflict resolution.

ASEAN Economic Community
The ASEAN Economic Community (AEC) shall be the goal of regional economic integration by 2015. ASEAN Leaders adopted the ASEAN Economic Blueprint in November 2007. Its aims are a highly competitive economic region, equitable economic development and regional integration into the global economy.

INTER-GOVERNMENTAL ORGANISATIONS

The ASEAN Socio-Cultural Community

Among the aims of the ASEAN Socio-Cultural Community (ASCC),are raising the standard of living of disadvantaged groups and the rural population; involving all sectors of society, in particular women, youth, and local communities; employment generation; alleviating poverty and socio-economic disparities; and ensuring economic growth with equity; working together.

External Relations

ASEAN has eleven Dialogue Partners, namely, Australia, Canada, China, the European Union, India, Japan, the Republic of Korea, New Zealand, the Russian Federation, the United States of America, and the United Nations Development Programme (UNDP). ASEAN also promotes cooperation with Pakistan in some areas of mutual interest. To support the conduct of ASEAN's external relations, ASEAN has also established Committees in Third Countries, composed of heads of diplomatic missions, in the following capitals: Ankara, Beijing, Berlin, Brussels, Canberra, Geneva, Islamabad, London, Moscow, New Delhi, New York, Ottawa, Paris, Riyadh, Seoul, Tokyo, Vienna, Washington D.C. and Wellington. Consistent with its resolve to enhance cooperation with other developing regions, ASEAN maintains contact with other inter-governmental organisations, namely, the Economic Cooperation Organisation, the South Asian Association for Regional Cooperation, the Shanghai Cooperation Organisation, the South Africa Development Cooperation, the Arab League and the United Nations, MERCOSUR, the Gulf Cooperation Council, the Rio Group, the South Pacific Forum, and the Asian-African Sub-Regional Organisations Conference.

Structure and Mechanisms

The highest decision-making body in ASEAN is the annual meeting of the ASEAN Heads of State and Government, called the ASEAN Summit. The ASEAN Standing Committee, under the Chairmanship of the Foreign Minister of the country-in-chair, is mandated to coordinate the work of ASEAN in between the annual ASEAN Ministerial Meeting (AMM), where the Foreign Ministers of ASEAN meet. ASEAN Chair is elected based on English alphabetical rotation of all ASEAN Member States. Ministerial meetings are held regularly. Committees of senior officials, technical working groups and task forces support the ministerial bodies. ASEAN has several specialised bodies and arrangements promoting intergovernmental cooperation in various fields such as ASEAN Centre for Energy, ASEAN Foundation, and ASEAN Centre for Biodiversity. In addition, ASEAN promotes dialogue and consultations with professional and business organisation with related aims and purposes, such as the ASEAN-Chambers of Commerce and Industry, ASEAN Business Forum, and ASEAN Intellectual Property Association. Furthermore, there are 58 Civil Society Organisations (CSOs), which have formal affiliations with ASEAN.

ASEAN Charter

The ASEAN Charter is a constitution for ASEAN, which will serve as a legal and institutional framework of ASEAN to support the realisation of its goals and objectives. It will confer a legal personality to ASEAN and determine the functions, develop areas of competence of key ASEAN bodies and their relationship with one another in the overall ASEAN structure. The Charter was signed on 20 November 2007 by the Leaders of the ten ASEAN Member States at the 13th ASEAN Summit in Singapore. It will come into force on the 30th day after the deposit of the tenth instrument of ratification (or instrument of acceptance) with the Secretary-General of ASEAN. The charter came into force on 15 December 2008. The ASEAN Charter will bring about institutional changes. Essentially, the improved structure will enable ASEAN to improve coordination, ensure prompt implementation of decisions and agreements, and speedy response to new opportunities and challenges. Important changes include:

-Convening ASEAN Summit twice a year, instead of once a year
-ASEAN Foreign Ministers to serve as the ASEAN Coordinating Council
-Single Chairmanship for key high-level ASEAN bodies
-Appointment of Member States' Permanent Representatives to ASEAN to form a Committee of Permanent Representatives in Jakarta
-Establishment of an ASEAN human rights body
-Establishment of the ASEAN Community Councils, under which purview the relevant ASEAN Sectoral Ministerial Bodies
-Enhance role and mandate of the Secretary-General of ASEAN

At the 12th ASEAN Summit in January 2007, the Leaders signed the Cebu Declaration on the Acceleration of the Establishment of an ASEAN Community by 2015. The ASEAN Community is comprised of three entities: the ASEAN Political-Security Community, ASEAN Economic Community and ASEAN Socio-Cultural Community. Each has its own plan of action, and, together with the Initiative for ASEAN Integration (IAI) Strategic Framework and IAI Work Plan Phase II (2009-2015) they form the Roadmap for and ASEAN Community 2009-2015.

In 2009 a Free Trade Agreement was signed between ASEAN and New Zealand and Australia. It is hoped that the agreement will boost the aggregate GDP by more than US$48 billion in the period up to 2020.

Secretary-General (2013-17): H.E. Le Luong Minh (Vietnam) (page 1462)

ASEAN Secretariat, 70A Jalan Sisingamangaraja, Jakarta 12110, Indonesia, Tel: +62 21 7262991, fax: +62 21 7398234, e-mail: public@asean.org, URL: http://www.asean.org

BEAC (BANQUE DES ETATS DE L'AFRIQUE CENTRALE)

Bank of Central African States

The Central Africa Central Bank (Banque des Etats de l'Afrique Centrale, BEAC) was established in November 1972. It is a multinational African organisation which operates under the rules of the Convention of the Central African Monetary Union (UMAC), and the Convention of Monetary Co-operation agreed between France and UMAC signatories.

The members of BEAC are: Cameroon, Central African Republic, Chad, Republic of Congo, Gabon and Equatorial Guinea.

The Bank's purpose is to define and promote monetary policy in the member countries, conduct currency exchanges, protect and maintain the monetary reserves and support the effective functioning of payment systems.

The monetary unit is the Franc of Financial Co-operation in Central Africa (F CFA). Parity with the French franc is fixed.

The Bank is administered by a governor and an Administrative Council. The Administrative Council is made up of 14 people nominated by the governments of the member states including the governor of the bank who has the position of President of the Council. There are four representatives for Cameroon, one for the Central African Republic, one for Chad, one for Congo, two for Gabon, one for Equatorial Guinea and three for France.

Other institutions include the Ministerial Committee of the Monetary Union of Central Africa, comprised of two ministers from each member state; and the Financial Policy Committee, in addition to the President, this committee has 14 members (two per member state) and two from France. The Bank's leadership comprises six members: a governor, vice-governor, a secretary general and three other directors.

Governor: Lucas Abaga Nchama
Vice-Governor: Tahir Hamid Nguilin
Secretary General: Daniel Ngassiki

Banque des Etats d'Afrique Centrale, 736 Avenue Monseigneur Vogt, B.P. 1917, Yaoundé, Cameroon. Tel: +237 223 4030, fax: +237 223 3329, e-mail: beac@beac.int, URL: http://www.beac.int

BENELUX UNION

Benelux was formed in 1944, when the governments of Belgium, the Netherlands and Luxembourg signed a customs agreement creating a single economic region free of internal border controls. This became known as the 'Benelux-agreement'. Liberalisation of trade during the late forties and early fifties proved largely successful and in 1954 the national trade policies of the three countries were replaced by a common Benelux policy. One significant result of the creation of the Benelux 'formula' was the proposal by the Benelux foreign ministers of a blueprint for European economic co-operation, to their partners in the ECSC. A conference was convened in Messina, where most of the Benelux proposals were adopted. This conference led to the establishment of the European Economic Community in 1957.

The Benelux countries safeguarded their mutual co-operation within the EEC through Article 233 of the Treaty of Rome and drew up their own Economic Union Treaty in 1958 which enabled the free movement of capital, services and personnel within the three countries. Financial (including monetary), economic, and social policy co-ordination was a central

objective. In this realm the common visa policy deserves special mention. It was the precursor of the so-called Schengen-co-operation. National laws regarding the protection of trade marks, designs and models, were replaced by common Benelux legislation.

Gradually, the original objectives have been attained and new ones added. Benelux is considered as the laboratory of European integration. It played a key-role in the establishment and support of the Schengen-co-operation (1985-1999), which aimed at freedom of movement throughout Europe. The Schengen-co-operation was transferred to the European Union on 1 May 1999.

June 2008 Treaty

A new Benelux treaty was signed on 17 June 2008 by the prime ministers and ministers of foreign affairs of Belgium, the Netherlands and Luxembourg, as will as the minister-presidents of Flanders, the Walloon government, the French community and the German community of

Belgium and the minister-chairman of Brussels Capital Region. The two main objectives of the new Treaty are to continue with Benelux co-operation as a laboratory for Europe and to enlarge cross-border co-operation.

The co-operation focuses on the three main areas of internal market and economic union; durability; and justice and home affairs. There is a four-year common work programme executed by annual plans.

The structure of the Union has also been simplified. Five institutions remain: the Benelux Committee of Ministers; the Benelux Council; the Benelux Parliament; the Benelux Court of Justice; and the Benelux Secretariat General. The Benelux Organisation for Intellectual Property is also mentioned in the Treaty.

The official name of the Benelux also changed from Benelux Economic Union to Benelux Union

Secretary General: Dr. J P R M van Laarhoven (page 1530)
Deputy Secretary General - Belgium: Mr L. Willems
Deputy Secretary General - Luxembourg: A. de Muyser

Benelux Union, 39 Rue de la Régence, 1000 Brussels, Belgium. Tel: +32 (0)2 519 3811, fax: +32 (0)2 513 4206, e-mail: info@benelux.int, URL: http://www.benelux.int

BLACK SEA ECONOMIC COOPERATION ORGANIZATION

In June 1992 the Heads of State and Government of eleven countries (Albania, Armenia, Azerbaijan, Bulgaria, Georgia, Greece, Moldova, Romania, Russia, Turkey and Ukraine) attended a summit in Istanbul which resulted in the signing of the Summit Declaration on Black Sea Economic Co-operation. Serbia and Montenegro joined in 2002. The membership is now held by Serbia. The aim is to promote interaction and accord among the participating states resulting in increased prosperity and security across the region and in Europe.

The Council of Ministers of the BSEC meets twice a year in April and October and is the highest decision-making body. The meetings are held in the member states on a rotational basis. The Minister of Foreign Affairs who hosts the meeting is the chairperson until the next meeting. The Committee of Senior Officials meets before the Council of Ministers and if necessary undertakes groundwork for decisions. The Permanent International Secretariat is responsible for maintaining communication between the member states and co-ordinates the activities of the working groups. Armenia holds the chairmanship from 1 July to 31 December 2013.

The BSEC related bodies and affiliated centres are: BSEC Parliamentary Assembly (PABSEC), BSEC Business Council (BSEC BC), Black Sea Trade and Development Bank (BSTDB), International Centre for Black Sea Studies (ICBSS), BSEC Coordination Center for the Exchange of Statistical Data and Economic Information.

Secretary General: Dr Victor Tvircun

Black Sea Economic Cooperation Organization, Sakip Sabanci Caddesi, Mucir Fuad Paca Yalisi, Eski Tersane, 34460 Istanbul, Turkey. Tel: +90 212 229 633035, fax: +90 212 229 6336, e-mail: info@bsec-organization.org, URL: http://www.bsec-organization.org

CABI

Established in 1910, CABI (formerly CAB International) is a not-for-profit inter-governmental organisation that improves people's lives by providing information and applying scientific expertise to solve problems in agriculture and the environment. Its mission and direction is influenced by its 48 member countries who help guide the activities undertaken. CABI's activities contribute directly to achieving global development objectives, particularly those concerned with poverty reduction, environmental sustainability and partnership for development.

Publishing
CABI produces key scientific publications, including the CAB Abstracts database as well as multi-media compendia, books, e-books and internet resources.

Development projects and research
CABI staff research, and find solutions to, agricultural and environmental problems using science, information and communication tools. CABI alleviates poverty and increases food security by improving crop yields, and safeguards the environment by combating invasive plants, diseases and insects and finding natural alternatives to pesticides.

Microbial services
CABI manages one of the world's largest genetic resource collections, the UK's National Collection of Fungus Cultures. CABI holds over 28,000 live and 400,000 dried organisms including Sir Alexander Fleming's penicillin producing culture.

Chief Executive Officer: Dr Trevor Nicholls

CABI, Nosworthy Way, Wallingford, OX10 8DE, UK. Tel: +44 (0)1491 832111, fax: +44 (0)1491 833508, e-mail: enquiries@cabi.org, URL: http://www.cabi.org

CARIBBEAN COMMUNITY (CARICOM)

The CARICOM Single Market and Economy (CSME) was established in order to achieve sustained economic development based on international competitiveness, co-ordinated economic and foreign policies, functional co-operation and enhanced trade and economic relations with third States and enhanced effectiveness of the decision-making and implementation processes of the Caribbean Community.

The Treaty establishing the Caribbean Community including the Caribbean Common Market, and the Agreement establishing the Common External Tariff for the Caribbean Common Market, were first signed by the Prime Ministers of Barbados, Guyana, Jamaica and Trinidad and Tobago at Chaguaramas, Trinidad on 4 July 1973, and entered into force on 1 August 1973. The Revised Treaty of Chaguaramas establishing the Caribbean Community including the CARICOM Single Market and Economy (CSME) was signed by the Heads of Government of the Caribbean Community on July 5th 2001 at their 22nd Meeting of the Conference in Nassau, The Bahamas.

CARICOM now comprises 15 Member Countries: Antigua and Barbuda, The Bahamas (not a member of the Caribbean Common Market), Barbados, Belize, Dominica, Grenada, Guyana, Haiti, Jamaica, Montserrat, Saint Kitts and Nevis, Saint Lucia, St. Vincent and the Grenadines, Suriname, and Trinidad and Tobago. British Virgin Islands and the Turks and Caicos Islands were given Associate membership of the Caribbean Community in July 1991, Anguilla in July 1998, Cayman Islands in May 2002 and Bermuda in July 2003.

The aims of the Caribbean Community are as follows:
- improved standards of living and work
- full employment

- accelerated, co-ordinated and sustained economic development and convergence
- expansion of trade and economic relations with third States
- enhanced levels of international competitiveness
- organisation for increased production and productivity
- a greater measure of economic leverage and effectiveness of Member States in dealing with third States
- enhanced co-ordination of Member States' foreign and (foreign) economic policies and
- improved co-operation with regard to the common services and activities of the peoples of the Member States, with greater understanding among the people and the advancement of social, cultural and technological development as well as improvements in such areas as health, education, transport and telecommunications.

Structure
The **Conference of Heads of Government** is the principal organ of the Community, and its primary responsibility is to determine the policy of the Community. It is the final authority of the Community for the conclusion of treaties and for entering into relationships between the Community and international organisations and States. It is responsible for financial arrangements for meeting the expenses of the Community but has delegated this function to the Community Council. Decisions of the Conference are generally taken unanimously.

INTER-GOVERNMENTAL ORGANISATIONS

The **Bureau of the Conference of Heads of Government** comprises a Chairman, who is the Chairman of the Conference, the incoming and outgoing Chairmen, and a Chief Executive Officer in the person of the Secretary-General. The Bureau is responsible for initiating proposals, updating consensus, mobilising action and securing the implementation of CARICOM decisions.

The **Caribbean Community Council**, which replaced the Common Market Council in 1992, is the second highest body of the Community, and consists of a Minister of Government designated by each member State. It is responsible for the development of Community strategic planning and co-ordination in the areas of economic integration, functional co-operation and external relations.

The **Caribbean Community (CARICOM) Secretariat**, successor to the Commonwealth Caribbean Regional Secretariat, is the principal administrative organ of the Community. It services meetings of the Organs and Bodies of the Community, organises and conducts studies on various issues and provides, on request, services to Member States on matters relating to the achievement of Community objectives. The Secretary-General shall be appointed by the Conference on the recommendation of the Council for a term not exceeding five years and may be reappointed. The Secretary-General shall act in that capacity in all meetings of the Conference, the Bureau, the Council, and of the institutions of the Community.

Secretariat Programmes, Sub-Programmes and Projects
Executive Management; Internal Oversight; Strategic Planning, Monitoring and Evaluation; Human Resource Management; Corporate Services; Finance; Statistics; Development and Operation of the Single Market and Economy; Coordination of Economic Policy and Sectoral Programmes; Sustainable Development; External Economic and Trade Relations; Foreign Policy and Community Relations; Mobilisation of Resources From External Agencies and Caribbean Community Technical Assistance Services; Human Resource Development; Health Sector Development; Culture and Community Development; Legal and Institutional Framework; Crime and Security; Economic Development Policy, Tax Administration and Research (EDPR); Energy; PAN Caribbean Partnership Against HIV/AIDS (PANCAP); CARIFORUM; Information and Communication Technology for Development; Trade Negotiations.

The Principal Organs of the Community are assisted in the performance of their functions by the following four Ministerial Councils:

- **The Council for Trade and Economic Development (COTED)** which promotes trade and economic development of the Community and oversees the operations of the CARICOM Single Market & Economy (CSME).
- **The Council for Foreign and Community Relations (COFCOR)** which determines relations with international organisations and third states.
- **The Council for Human and Social Development (COHSOD)** which promotes human and social development.
- **The Council for Finance and Planning (COFAP)** which co-ordinates economic policy and financial and monetary integration of Member States.

Secretary-General: H.E. Amb. Irwin LaRocque (Dominica)
Chairman: H.E. Michel Joseph Martelly (President of Haiti) (page 1471)

Caribbean Community Secretariat, PO Box 10827, Georgetown, Guyana, South America. Tel: +592 222 0075 fax: +592 222 0171, e-mail: doccentre@caricom.org, URL: http://www.caricom.org

CARIBBEAN DEVELOPMENT BANK

The Caribbean Development Bank (CDB) was established in January 1970, its purpose being to contribute to the economic growth and development of the member countries in the Caribbean and to promote economic co-operation and integration among them, with special regard to the needs of the less developed members of the region.

The Bank's Mission Statement states that the "CDB intends to be the leading catalyst for development resources into the region, working in an efficient, responsive and collaborative manner with our Borrowing Members and other development partners, towards the systematic reduction of poverty in their countries, through social and economic development".

Membership
There are now 26 members - 18 regional (Anguilla, Antigua and Barbuda, the Bahamas, Barbados, Belize, British Virgin Islands, Cayman Islands, Dominica, Grenada, Guyana, Haiti, Jamaica, Montserrat, St. Kitts and Nevis, St. Lucia, St. Vincent and the Grenadines, Trinidad and Tobago, Turks and Caicos Islands) three other regional members (Colombia, Mexico, Venezuela), and five non-regional members (Canada, China, Germany, Italy, United Kingdom and Venezuela).

Functions
- to assist regional members in the co-ordination of their development programmes with a view to achieving better utilisation of their resources; making their economies more complementary and promoting the orderly expansion of their international trade, in particular intra-regional trade;
- to mobilise within and outside the region additional financial resources;
- to finance projects and programmes contributing to the development of the region;
- to provide appropriate technical assistance to its regional members, particularly by undertaking or commissioning pre-investment surveys and by assisting in the identification and preparation of project proposals;
- to promote public and private investment in development projects;
- to co-operate and assist in other regional efforts designed to promote regional and locally controlled financial institutions and a regional market for credit and savings;

- to stimulate and encourage the development of capital markets within the region;
- and to undertake or promote such other activities as may advance its purpose.

Structure
The Board of Governors is the highest policy-making body of the CDB. Each Member Country nominates one governor and one Alternate Governor. Voting power is roughly proportional to shares subscribed, with slight weighting in favour of the smaller Member Territories. The Board of Governors meets annually, but may be summoned as required.

The Board of Directors is responsible for the general policy and direction of the operations of the CDB. It comprises 17 Directors, 12 representing the Regional Members of CDB and 5 from the non-Regional Members. The President of the CDB is also the Chairman of the Board of Directors and serves a five-year term, though he may be re-elected.

Finance
The Bank's Board of Governors approved an increase in the Bank's ordinary capital by USD1 billion, the largest expansion of resources in the Bank's history. The new funds will enable the Bank to increase its financial assistance to its Borrowing Member Countries (BMCs) to deal with the impact of the global financial and economic crisis as well as to execute their medium-term programmes for poverty reduction and economic and social development. It will also ensure that the Bank can implement the programmes of assistance from its Strategic Plan 2010-2014.

Chairman of the Board of Directors and President of CDB: Hon. W. McKeeva Bush OBE

Caribbean Development Bank, PO Box 408, Wildey, St. Michael, BB 11000, Barbados. Tel: +246 431 1600, fax: +246 426 7269, e-mail: info@caribank.org, URL: http://www.caribank.org

CENTRAL AMERICAN BANK FOR ECONOMIC INTEGRATION (CABEI)

Founded in 1960, the Central American Bank for Economic Integration (CABEI) is a multilateral development bank established to promote the integration of the isthmus and to encourage balanced economic and social growth in the Central American countries. It aims to achieve its goals through its support of public and private programmes and projects that generate employment and contribute to improvements in productivity and competitiveness. It is now the largest financial institution in Central America.

Objectives
Its strategic objectives are: the fight against poverty; regional integration and competing in the global economy.

Activities
The Central American Bank for Economic Integration specialises in the capturing and channelling of foreign resources. It is also expert in fostering investment and trade relations. The Bank studies and promotes investment opportunities in strategic sectors. It grants short, medium and long-term loans and issues liabilities in international financial markets. It obtains loans and guarantees from other governments and financial institutions and acts as a fiduciary for resources entrusted to it by countries and regions in order to further specific objectives.

CABEI provides financial resources in the following fields: electricity generation; irrigation; drainage and soil conservation; expansion of infrastructure; development of non-traditional exports; development and promotion of tourism; industrial reactivation and modernisation; agriculture; infrastructure of the municipalities; sustainable development; encouragement of micro, small and medium-sized businesses and the facilitation of international trade. It also provided financial assistance in the aftermath of Hurricane Mitch.

Its institutional strategy for the period 2010-14 focuses on: social development; regional integration and competitiveness; environmental sustainability; and gender equality.

Membership
The five founding Member States of CABEI are: Costa Rica, El Salvador, Guatemala, Honduras and Nicaragua. They have been joined by the following regional members: Panama and the Dominican Republic. The following are non-regional members: Mexico, Taiwan, Argentina, Colombia, and Spain, Panama and the Dominican Republic. Belize is a beneficiary member. To date, Panama, the Dominican Republic, Argentina and Colombia have the dual role of member and beneficiary country.

President: Nick Rischbieth Glöe

Central American Bank for Economic Integration, Edificio Sede BCIE, Boulevard Suyapa, Tegucigalpa, Honduras. Tel: +504 240 2243, fax: +504 240 2185, URL: http://www.bcie.org

CENTRAL AMERICAN INTEGRATION SYSTEM (SICA)
Sistema de la Integración Centroamericana

The Central American Integration System (SICA) was constituted on 13th December 1991, under the auspices of the Organisation of Central American States (ODECA). SICA is supported by the United Nations, and its fundamental aim is the unification of Central America and the creation of a Region of Peace, Freedom, Democracy and Development, based on respect and the promotion of human rights.

The ODECA, formed in 1951 in El Salvador, contributed to the integration of transport systems, education programmes and customs processes within the region. It was involved in drawing up the General Treaty of Central American Economic Integration, 1960, a precursor to the creation of the Central American Bank of Economic Integration. The Protocol of Tegucigalpa was signed in December 1991 at the XI Summit Meeting of Central American Presidents, and this led to the creation of the Central American Integration System, a new legal-political framework within which all aspects of integration (economic, social, cultural, political and environmental) could be addressed.

Structure
The Protocol of Tegucigalpa established a pro-tempore President, who is appointed to the six month post on hosting the Presidents' Meeting. The governing bodies of the Central American Integration System are the Meeting of the Presidents and the Board of Foreign Ministers who outline policy and pass this to the Executive Committee for implementation. The General Secretariat (SG-SICA), based in El Salvador, coordinates and executes the policies of the governing bodies with recourse to the Consultative Committee, specialized institutions and regional bodies.

The organisation works within partnerships on social and economic projects, and singly when working on projects to improve tourism in the region.

The SICA initiative is supported by the UN General Assembly and SICA's regional bodies and institutions may interact with the United Nations system.

Membership
The members of SICA are Belize, Costa Rica, El Salvador, Guatemala, Honduras, Nicaragua and Panama. The Dominican Republic is an associate member. Mexico, Argentina, Chile, Brazil, Peru and the USA are regional observers. Taiwan, Spain, Italy, Japan, Australia, South Korea, France and the Holy See are extraregional observers. Colombia, Ecuador, Haiti and Uruguay are in the process of joining SICA as Regional Observers. The UK is in the process of joining as an Extra Regional Observer. Their participation was approved in December 2012.

Purpose
The aims of the Central American Integration System are as follows:
- to consolidate democracy and strengthen institutions based on Governments elected by universal, free and secret suffrage, and on respect for Human Rights,
- to consolidate a new model of regional security based on a reasonable balance of forces, the strengthening of civil power, the eradication of extreme poverty, the encouragement of sustainable development, the protection of the environment and the eradication of violence, corruption, terrorism, drug trafficking and arms dealing
- to promote freedom within government, ensuring that the individual and society reach their full and harmonious potential
- to achieve regional wellbeing and social and economic justice for the Central American people
- to achieve economic union and the strengthen the Central American financial system
- to strengthen the region as an economic block which can compete successfully within the international economy
- to reaffirm and strengthen the self-determinism of Central America vis-a-vis external relations through a strategy of increasing the region as a whole's participation in the international sphere
- to encourage the sustained economic, social, cultural and political development of the member states as well as the region as a whole
- to establish actions for the preservation of the environment, through respect for nature, ensuring the balanced development and careful exploitation of the natural resources in the area, with the possible establishment of an New Ecological Order in the region
- to reach an shared institutional and legal framework founded on mutual respect between the member states.

Budget
The Central Amercian Integration System is financed through annual subscriptions from the member states.

Secretary General: Juan Daniel Alemán Gurdián

Central American Integration System, Boulevard Orden de Malta, 470, Urb. Santa Elena, Antiguo Cuscatlán, El Salvador. Tel: +503 2248 8800, fax: +503 2248 8899, URL: http://www.sica.int

CENTRAL EUROPEAN INITIATIVE

Founded in 1989 as Quadrangular Cooperation, the Central European Initiative is the oldest and largest of sub-regional co-operation initiatives that emerged in Central and Eastern Europe in the wake of the collapse of communism. It was established as an inter-governmental forum for economic, political and cultural co-operation among its member states.

Membership

From the four founding members (Austria, Italy, Hungary and Yugoslavia) membership has expanded to 18 Member States: Albania, Austria, Belarus, Bosnia and Herzegovina, Bulgaria, Croatia, the Czech Republic, Hungary, Italy, Macedonia, Moldova, Montenegro, Poland, Romania, Serbia, Slovakia, Slovenia and Ukraine. The territory covers over 2.4 million sq. kilometres and has a population of nearly 260 million.

Functions

Its main objectives are to bring the countries of Central, Eastern and South-Eastern Europe closer together and assist them in their transition to stable democracies and market economies as well as in their preparation process for EU membership. During the last years, the CEI has undergone a transformation from being predominantly oriented towards policy dialogue to an organisation emphasizing economic growth and human development as main priorities. Regions for main concern of CEI assistance are the countries of the Western Balkans and those part of the EU's neighbourhood policy, namely Belarus, Moldova and the Ukraine. The CEI co-operates with European organisations and institutions, in particular with the European Union, the Council of Europe, the OECD, the OSCE and other regional co-operation initiatives in areas of mutual interest. CEI co-operation activities are also carried out with the UN.

Structure

The CEI operates through various structures, such as the annual Summit of the Heads of Government, and the annual Meeting of the Ministers of Foreign Affairs, held in the country holding the rotating CEI presidency (Hungary, 2013), other ministerial or special events at expert level and meetings of the Committee of National Co-ordinators. The Ministers of Economic sectors meet at the annual CEI Summit Economic Forum.

Thought its networks of Focal Points, designated by the respective governmental bodies of its Member States, the CEI is active in the following priority areas: Climate, Environment and Sustainable Energy, Enterprise Development including Tourism, Human Resource Development; Information Society and Media; Intercultural Cooperation including Minorities; Multimodal Transport; Science and Technology; Sustainable Agriculture.

The CEI working bodies are supported by the CEI Executive Secretariat (CEI-ES), based in Trieste with the legal status of an International Organisation, and the CEI Project Secretariat, operative at the EBRD in London with offices both in Trieste and London. The CEI-ES, headed by a Secretary General, provides administrative support to both the decision-making and operational bodies of the CEI. The main areas of support are:
- information and documentation
- organisation, preparation and follow-up of meetings
- participation in CEI meetings and other CEI-related events
- CEI programmes and projects

Finances

The CEI Co-operation Fund, covered by annual contributions of Member States, finances the implementation of multilateral activities, such as seminars, workshops and training courses taking place in the CEI region. The CEI Trust Fund at the EBRD, contributed by Italy, provides "seed money" for the identification, promotion and appraisal of technical cooperation linked to EBRD investment projects as well as for co-funding the Summit Economic Forum and the Know-How Exchange Programme. The Solidarity Fund, based on voluntary contributions from Member States, is used to assist participation of representatives and experts at the CEI events.

Secretary General: Ambassador Giovanni Caracciolo di Vietri

CEI, Executive Secretariat, Via Genova, 9 - 34121 Trieste, Italy. Tel: +39 (0)40 778 6777, fax: +39 (0)40 360640, e-mail: cei@cei.int, URL: http://www.ceinet.int

COLOMBO PLAN FOR CO-OPERATIVE ECONOMIC AND SOCIAL DEVELOPMENT

(Asia and the Pacific)

Founded by seven Commonwealth countries in 1950, (as the Colombo Plan for Co-operative Economic Development in South and Southeast Asia), the Colombo Plan was subsequently joined by more countries in Asia and the Pacific as well as the USA and Japan. The Plan's life has been extended from time to time at five-year intervals and from 1980 was extended indefinitely.

There are now 27 permanent member countries: Islamic State of Afghanistan, Australia, Bangladesh, Bhutan, Brunei Darussalam, Fiji, India, Indonesia, Islamic Republic of Iran, Japan, Korea, Laos, Malaysia, Maldives, Mongolia, Myanmar, Nepal, New Zealand, Pakistan, Papua New Guinea, Philippines, Saudi Arabia, Singapore, Sri Lanka, Thailand, United States of America and the Socialist Republic of Vietnam.

Function

The Plan embodies the concept of a collective inter-governmental effort toward the economic and social development of member countries in the Asia-Pacific region. It provides a forum for discussion of development needs of member countries and through consensus implements programmes in response to their identified needs. One specific long-term objective has been to encourage developing member countries to become donors themselves of capital and technical co-operation assistance to other member countries. The primary focus of all Colombo Plan Activities is human resources development in the Asia-Pacific region.

The administrative costs of the Council and the Secretariat are borne equally by all member governments. The programmes are voluntarily funded by donors. However from 1996, the revised Constitution of the Colombo Plan stipulates that programmes could also be funded through non-member governments, international/regional aid agencies, public and private sector foundations/enterprises and other entities.

Programmes

Important programmes conducted by the Colombo Plan are:
- the Programme for Public Administration which was established in 1995 and undertook the task of imparting training and thereby enhancing the capability of senior administrators of developing member countries;
- the Programme for Private Sector Development which focuses on small and medium enterprises and entrepreneurship development;
- the Drug Advisory Programme (DAP) established in 1973 addresses the issue of drug abuse prevention and aspects of treatment, rehabilitation, training and gender related matters. In 1999, the DAP implemented training programmes in treatment and rehabilitation in prison/correctional settings in Bangladesh, India and the Maldives. Training programmes in relapse prevention, after-care and re-integration are being conducted in Indonesia and the Philippines. Greater attention will be paid to gender issues that relate to drug abuse prevention and control and also the special problems that face vulnerable groups such as women, children and slum dwellers.

- the Programme on Environment which focuses on the area of environment and related issues.
- the Long Term Fellowship Programme, which was approved by the Council at its 249th session, and re-established in 2005 offers scholarships leading to master degrees / graduate diplomas in a wide variety of subjects. Thailand, Malaysia Korea and Singapore have commenced the implementation of this programme by offering courses of excellence in their respective countries.

Besides its regular programmes, the Colombo Plan also undertakes training formulated on a project-by-project basis that addresses the development needs of developing member countries. The Colombo Plan Staff College for Technician Education is based in Manila, the Philippines. Its primary goal is to enhance the growth and development of technician education systems in developing member countries.

Structure

The **Consultative Committee** is the principal policy-making, review and deliberative body of the Colombo Plan. It consists of all member countries. It meets every two years. The Committee reviews the economic and social progress of members, exchanges views on technical co-operation programmes and, generally, reviews the activities of the Colombo Plan.

The **Colombo Plan Council** meets several times a year in Colombo, Sri Lanka and consists of all members. The heads of member countries' diplomatic missions resident in Colombo represent their countries at Council sessions. The Council's major functions include identification of important development issues in the region; recommendation of necessary measures to be taken by the Colombo Plan for consideration by the Consultative Committee; and ensuring implementation of the Consultative Committee's directives.

The **Colombo Plan Secretariat** participates, in an advisory capacity, at Consultative Committee Meetings and assists the Council in the discharge of its functions. It also services committees of the Council and provides administrative support to the programmes of the Colombo Plan. The Secretary-General of the Colombo Plan Secretariat gives guidance to the programmes and is in overall charge of all financial and administrative matters on which he/she reports to the Council.

Secretary-General (FY 2012-13): H.E. Ashok K. Kantha

Colombo Plan, No.31, Wijerama Road, Colombo 7, Sri Lanka. Tel: +94 11 2684 188, Colombo, fax: +94 11 2684 386, e-mail: info@colombo-plan.org, URL: http://www.colombo-plan.org

COMMON MARKET FOR EASTERN & SOUTHERN AFRICA (COMESA)

Established in 1994, COMESA replaced the Preferential Trade Area for Eastern and Southern Africa (PTA). The current 19 member countries are Burundi, Comoros, Democratic Republic of Congo, Djibouti, Egypt, Eritrea, Ethiopia, Kenya, Libya, Madagascar, Malawi, Mauritius, Rwanda, Seychelles, Sudan, Swaziland, Uganda, Zambia and Zimbabwe. Overall they cover a population of over 389 million people and have an import bill of approximately US$32 billion and an export bill of approximately US$82 billion.

Structure
The Heads of States of the member countries are at the top of the decision-making structure. A Council of Ministers is responsible for making policy. There are also 12 technical committees and several advisory bodies. The Secretariat is based in Lusaka, Zambia.

Purpose
COMESA's aim is to deepen and broaden the integration process among member States through more comprehensive trade liberation measures such as the complete elimination of tariff and non-tariff barriers to trade and the elimination of customs duties. It encourages the free movement of capital, labour and goods and works towards standardised technical specifications and quality control.

Free Trade
The COMESA Free Trade Area (FTA) was launched on 31 October 2000 with nine participating countries: Djibouti, Egypt, Kenya, Madagascar, Malawi, Mauritius, Sudan, Zambia and Zimbabwe. Burundi and Rwanda joined the FTA on 1 January 2004.

Institutions
Several institutions have been created to help promote sub-regional co-operation and development. These include: The Eastern and Southern African Trade and Development Bank (PTA), Nairobi, Kenya; FEMCOM (Federation of National aSsociatios of Women in Business in COMESA; The COMESA Clearing House; The PTA Re-Insurance Company, Nairobi, Kenya and the COMESA Court of Justice.

Court of Justice
Created under the COMESA Treaty, it became operational in 1998. In 2003 it was decided that the seat of the Court should be in Khartoum, Sudan. The Court took over the functions of the (Preferential Trade Area for Eastern & Southern African States (PTA) Tribunal, the PTA Administrative Appeals Board and the PTA Centre for Commercial Arbitration. The aim of the Court of Justice is to act as a strong and unified judicial body.

Secretary-General: Sindiso Ngwenya

Common Market for Eastern & Southern Africa, Comesa Centre, Ben Bella Road, PO Box 30051, Lusaka, Zambia. Tel: +260 211 229725, fax: +260 211 225107, URL: http://www.comesa.int

COMMONWEALTH

The Commonwealth is an association of independent countries consulting and co-operating in the common interests of their peoples and in the promotion of international understanding and world peace. The association has no constitution or charter, but members commit themselves to a number of principles and values. The basis of these is the Declaration of Commonwealth Principles, agreed at Singapore in 1971, and reaffirmed in the Harare Commonwealth Declaration of 1991. The fundamental political values underpinning the Commonwealth are outlined in The Mission Statement of the Commonwealth Secretariat as follows: "We work as a trusted partner for all Commonwealth people as a force for democracy and good governance, a platform for global consensus building and a source of practical help for sustainable development".

The Commonwealth's membership of 54 countries, with a total population of 2 billion people, represents 30 per cent of the membership of the United Nations and of the world's population. The Commonwealth, which comes second only to the UN in size as an international association, is a powerful voice in international forums. The fact that it is a 'family' of nations sharing a common heritage in many fields, including a common language, enables member states to work together in an atmosphere of co-operation and understanding.

On 26 April 2009 the sixtieth anniversary of the London Declaration was celebrated. In April 1949, Commonwealth prime ministers met in London issued a Declaration which changed membership from one which was based on common allegiance to the British Crown to one in which members recognised the British monarch as the Heath of the Commonweath. Thus the British Commonwealth ended and the modern Commonwealth began.

Members
The member countries of the Commonwealth are: Antigua and Barbuda, Australia, The Bahamas, Bangladesh, Barbados, Belize, Botswana, Brunei Darussalam, Cameroon, Canada, Cyprus, Dominica, Fiji Islands, The Gambia, Ghana, Grenada, Guyana, India, Jamaica, Kenya, Kiribati, Lesotho, Malawi, Malaysia, Maldives, Malta, Mauritius, Mozambique, Namibia, Nauru, New Zealand, Nigeria, Pakistan, Papua New Guinea, Rwanda, St Kitts and Nevis, St Lucia, St Vincent and the Grenadines, Samoa, Seychelles, Sierra Leone, Singapore, Solomon Islands, South Africa, Sri Lanka, Swaziland, the United Republic of Tanzania, Tonga, Trinidad and Tobago, Tuvalu, Uganda, United Kingdom, Vanuatu and Zambia.

Pakistan was suspended from the councils of the Commonwealth following a military coup in October 1999, in which the democratically elected government of Prime Minister Nawaz Sharif was ousted in a coup led by General Pervez Musharraf. It was readmitted in May 2004.

The 2003, Commonwealth Heads of Government Meeting (CHOGM) established a committee to examine the issue of Zimbabwe and wished to facilitate the early return of Zimbabwe to the Councils of the Commonwealth. In 2003 however Zimbabwe's suspension was extended to December 2003. Zimbabwe then left the Commonwealth.

The Fiji Islands were suspended from the Commonwealth on 1 September 2009. Nauru is a Member in Arrears.

Of the Commonwealth's member countries, 32 are classified as small states either because they have small populations (less than 1.5 million) or because they face many of the same circumstances and challenges as other small states. The Commonwealth pays particular attention to the needs and concerns of its small states.

The Commonwealth also includes self-governing states associated with member countries, as well as dependent territories. These are eligible for Commonwealth technical assistance and take part in a variety of Commonwealth activities. With a combined total population estimated at about 6 million, they include: the external territories of Australia, namely Norfolk Island, Coral Sea Islands Territory, Australian Antarctic Territory, Heard Island and McDonald Islands, Cocos (Keeling) Islands, Christmas Island, Territory of Ashmore and Cartier Islands; the New Zealand territories of Tokelau and the Ross Dependency (Antarctic); Cook Islands and Niue, which are self governing countries in free association with New Zealand; and the UK overseas territories of Anguilla, Bermuda, British Antarctic Territory, British Indian Ocean Territory, British Virgin Islands, Cayman Islands, Falkland Islands, Gibraltar, Montserrat, Pitcairn, Henderson, Ducie and Oeno Islands, St Helena and St Helena Dependencies (Ascension and Tristan da Cunha), South Georgia and the South Sandwich Islands, and Turks and Caicos Islands.

All of the member states, with the exception of Mozambique and Rwanda, have had a constitutional or administrative link with the United Kingdom or another Commonwealth country. The modern Commonwealth emerged on 27 April 1949 when its leaders issued the London Declaration which dropped the expression "common allegiance to the Crown" as the basis of membership and accepted India's request to retain its membership even though it was to become a republic.

All nations of the Commonwealth accept HM Queen Elizabeth II as the symbol of their free association and thus Head of the Commonwealth. The position of Head implies no executive or constitutional power and is independent of any other status the Queen may have under any member's constitution.

Structure
The Commonwealth has three intergovernmental organisations: the Commonwealth Secretariat, the Commonwealth Foundation and the Commonwealth of Learning.

The Commonwealth Secretariat
The Commonwealth Secretariat, established in 1965, is the main intergovernmental agency of the association, its civil service. The Secretariat is based at Marlborough House in central London and is headed by the Commonwealth Secretary-General, assisted by three Deputies. The Secretariat employs approx. 260 staff drawn from over 30 countries.

The Secretariat is responsible to Commonwealth governments collectively, is the main agency for multilateral communication between them, and provides the central organisation for joint consultation and co-operation in many fields. The Secretariat's functions are shared among 12 divisions responsible for: administration, economic affairs, economic and legal advisory services, export and industrial development, gender and youth affairs, general technical assistance services, human resource development, information and public affairs, legal and constitutional affairs, management and training services, political affairs, and science and technology. Within the office of the Secretary-General, there is also a Strategic Planning and Evaluation Unit and an NGO Desk.

Meetings of Heads of Government
Every two years, Commonwealth Heads of Government - for the most part, Presidents and Prime Ministers - meet for a few days of intensive discussion. These summits provide a unique forum for consultation at the highest level of government.

INTER-GOVERNMENTAL ORGANISATIONS

To encourage frank exchanges of views, every effort is made to promote an informal atmosphere. After a public opening session, discussions are held in camera, the number of advisers restricted and written speeches discouraged. Each meeting includes a 'Retreat' when Commonwealth leaders, unaccompanied by other ministers or officials, have complete privacy. Many important initiatives have emerged from these Retreats.

The most recent CHOGM was held in Perth, Australia in October 2011.

In addition to the biennial CHOGMs, there are also regular ministerial and officials' meetings which enable member countries to share ideas on common issues, and task forces are set up to resolve crises when the need arises. Ministers of Finance meet annually, and Ministers of Education, Health, Law, Women's Affairs and Youth hold full consultations every three years. There are also ministerial-level consultations on the environment and on small states.

Commonwealth Programmes
The work of the Secretariat is funded by several budgets and funds. All member governments contribute to the Secretariat's budget on an agreed scale, based on income and population size. In advancing the Commonwealth's fundamental political values, the Secretariat organises workshops on deepening democracy, deploys the good offices of the Secretary-General to defuse situations of potential conflict at the request of member governments, and sends missions to observe elections in member countries.

The Secretariat also organises the meetings of the **Commonwealth Ministerial Action Group**, which was set up in 1995 to address serious or persistent violations of Commonwealth principles as outlined in the Harare Declaration. It was reconstituted by Heads of Government at Durban in November 1999, and now comprises Ministers from Australia, Bangladesh, Barbados, Botswana, Canada, Malaysia, Nigeria and the United Kingdom.

To advance the Commonwealth's fundamental values, the Secretariat organises various forms of co-operation in legal and constitutional matters. This has included the development of a framework for promoting good governance and combating corruption, human rights workshops, and mutual assistance in combating such international crime as money laundering, drug-trafficking, and computer-related crime.

As well as organising the annual Commonwealth Finance Ministers Meetings, the Secretariat promotes the economic development of member countries in a variety of ways. Regional investment funds have been launched in all four main regions of the developing Commonwealth, to boost private investment in member countries. The Commonwealth has also participated actively in efforts to relieve the debt burden of heavily indebted poor countries (HIPCs). The Secretariat has hosted meetings and developed proposals to refine the HIPC initiative framework and the linkage between debt relief, aid and poverty reduction.

Other significant groups include: the Commonwealth Consultative Group on Environment, The Commonwealth Science Council (CSC), The Commonwealth Youth Programme (CYP), The Commonwealth Fund for Technical Co-operation (CFTC).

Other Intergovernmental Organisations
The **Commonwealth Foundation**, in London, provides support for the non-governmental organisations (NGOs) of the association. Established in 1966, it runs programmes to promote and strengthen NGO co-operation and capacity-building and also supports cultural exchanges. One of its major activities is the sponsorship of the annual Commonwealth Writers Prize.

The **Commonwealth of Learning (COL)**, based in Vancouver, Canada, helps extend, improve and link distance education in member countries. Its ultimate aim is to enable anyone in the Commonwealth who desires educational self-improvement to have access to that knowledge wherever it is available in the Commonwealth. Heads of Government decided to establish COL at the 1987 summit in Vancouver and it was set up the following year.

The People's Commonwealth
The Commonwealth provides excellent opportunities for networking and information-sharing among member countries, not only at the government level, but also among professional associations and NGOs.

The Secretariat works closely with the Commonwealth Business Council (CBC), set up by Commonwealth Heads of Government in 1997 as an association of companies and corporations to promote international trade and investment. Through its annual Commonwealth Business Forum, the CBC promotes public-private sector partnerships and enables input from the private sector to be incorporated into the Commonwealth's consultative mechanisms and policy debates.

It also works with such professional associations as the Commonwealth Association for Public Administration, the Commonwealth Association for Corporate Governance, the Commonwealth Local Government Forum, the Commonwealth Magistrates' and Judges Association, the Commonwealth Lawyers' Association, the Commonwealth Parliamentary Association and the Commonwealth Network in Information Technology (COMNET-IT), a computer network linking institutions and professionals for the exchange of knowledge and information on economic development and management.

The Secretariat collaborates with international and local NGOs working on the ground in developing countries, in such areas as human rights, export and enterprise development, renewable resource development, science and technology, and environmental conservation.

Commonwealth Day and Week
The second Monday in March every year is Commonwealth Day, focusing on schools. A special theme is chosen every year. The Head of the Commonwealth, Her Majesty The Queen, attends a multi-faith observance held in Westminster Abbey in London, and the Commonwealth Secretary-General reads out her message which is broadcast in member countries. The first Commonwealth Week was held in 2008.

Secretary-General: Mr Kamalesh Sharma (page 1513)

Commonwealth Secretariat, Marlborough House, Pall Mall, London SW1Y 5HX, United Kingdom, Tel: +44 (0)20 7747 6500, fax: +44 (0)20 7930 0827, e-mail: info@commonwealth.int, URL: http://www.thecommonwealth.org, http://www.youngcommonwealth.org

Commonwealth Foundation, Marlborough House, Pall Mall, London SW1Y 5HY, United Kingdom, Tel: +44 (0)20 7930 3783, fax: +44 (0)20 7839 8157, e-mail: foundation@commonwealth.int, URL: http://www.commonwealthfoundation.com

Commonwealth of Learning, 1055 West Hastings Street, Suite 1200, Vancouver, British Columbia, V6E 2E9, Canada, Tel: +1 604 775 8200, fax: +1 604 775 8210, e-mail: info@col.org, URL: http://www.col.org

COMMONWEALTH FOUNDATION

The Commonwealth Foundation is a development organisation resourced by and reporting to Commonwealth governments. Founded in 1965, its mandate was to strengthen civil society and thereby enhance development and democracy in the Commonwealth. It worked on behalf of the Commonwealth of Nations, spanning 54 countries and almost a third of the world's population. It relaunched in November 2012 with a revised mandate. It develops the capacity of civil cosociety to act together and learn from each other.

Aims
The vision of the Commonwealth Foundation is for a world where: every person is able to participate in and contribute to the sustainable development of an equal and peaceful society. Its mission is: to 'develop the capacity of Civil Society to act together and learn from each other to engage with the institutions that shape people's lives'.

Its core values are: diversity; collaboration; integrity; and ingenuity.

Its strategic plan for 2012-16 is based on the following programmes: Capacity Development; Knowledge Management: Building a CUlture of Learning and Performance; Mainstreaming Cross-Cutting Outcome Areas; Promoting Synergy and Co-ordination.

All 54 Commonwealth governments may apply for membership of the CF. Membership as of 2013 was 47 countries. Associated states or overseas territories may apply for associate member status and Gibraltar is currently an associate member.

Director: Vijay Krishnarayan

Commonwealth Foundation, Marlborough House, Pall Mall, London SW1Y 5HY, UK. Tel: +44 (0)20 7930 3783, fax: +44 (0)20 7839 8157, e-mail: foundation@commonwealth.int, URL: http://www.commonwealthfoundation.com/

COMMONWEALTH OF INDEPENDENT STATES (CIS)

The Commonwealth of Independent States (CIS) was founded in Minsk on 8 December 1991 by the leaders of the Republic of Belarus, the Russian Federation and the Ukraine. In the Commonwealth Agreement they state: "We, the Republic of Belarus, the Russian Federation (RF) and the Ukraine, the states which founded the Union of Soviet Socialist Republics and signed the 1922 Union Treaty, hereinafter referred to as the High Contracting Parties, declare that the USSR no longer exists as a subject of international law and geo-political reality."

The Articles of the Agreement state:
1. The High Contracting Parties form a Commonwealth of Independent States.

2. The High Contracting Parties shall guarantee their citizens equal rights and freedoms regardless of their nationality and other distinctions.
3. Wishing to encourage the expression ... and identity of the ethnic minorities ... on their territories, the High Contracting Parties shall undertake to protect them.
4. The High Contracting Parties shall promote ... beneficial co-operation between their peoples and states.

COMMONWEALTH OF INDEPENDENT STATES (CIS)

5. The High Contracting Parties shall recognise and respect the territorial integrity of one another and the inviolability of existing borders within the Commonwealth. They ... guarantee the openness of the borders, freedom of movement of citizens and the flow of information within the Commonwealth.

6. The Commonwealth States shall co-operate in safeguarding international peace and security ... The Parties shall respect their mutual wish to achieve the status of a non-nuclear zone and neutral state. The Commonwealth States shall preserve and maintain under joint command their common military-strategic space, including single control over nuclear weapons. They shall also jointly guarantee the requisite conditions for the deployment, functioning and financial and social maintenance of the strategic armed forces.

7. The High Contracting Parties have agreed ... through joint co-ordinating institutions of the Commonwealth on:
- joint foreign policy activities;
- the creation and development of a common economic space and common European and Eurasian markets;
- the development of transport and communications systems;
- environmental protection.

8. The Parties recognise the global implications of the Chernobyl nuclear ... disaster and pledge to pool and co-ordinate their efforts to minimise and eliminate its aftermath.

9. Each of the High Contracting Parties shall preserve the right to suspend this Agreement or any clause thereof at a year's notice.

10. The use of any laws of other states, including the former USSR, shall be prohibited on the territory of the states that have signed this Agreement from the moment of its signing.

11. The High Contracting Parties shall guarantee the fulfilment of international obligations arising for them from the treaties and agreements of the former USSR.

In a separate declaration it was stated that the Community is open to all member states of the USSR and to other countries sharing the aims and principles of the Commonwealth.

At a meeting in Alma-Ata on 21 December 1991, eight further Republics from the former USSR joined, and in December 1993 Georgia also joined the Commonwealth.

Membership of the Commonwealth of Independent States
Armenia, Azerbaijan, Belarus, Georgia, Kazakhstan, Kyrgyzstan, Moldova, Russian Federation, Tajikistan, Turkmenistan, Uzbekistan and Ukraine.

Institutions
Council of Heads of State
One of the supreme organs of the Commonwealth, the Heads of State convene at least twice a year. Meetings are presided over by the Heads of State alternately in Russian alphabetical order of names of Commonwealth states. Their main function is to deal with questions of co-ordinating the activities of the Commonwealth states in the spheres of common interest, including the abolition of institutions of the former USSR.

Council of Heads of Government
The Council of Heads of Government convenes at least once in three months and is also a supreme policy-making institution.

The Executive Committee
Based in Minsk, Belarus, the Executive Committee is the legal successor to the CIS Executive Secretariat. On April 2 1999, the Council of the Heads of State adopted the Decision on reorganisation of the Secretariat into the CIS Executive Committee. At the same time they also elected Yuri Yarov as the Chairman of the Executive Committee-Executive Secretary of the Commonwealth. The leading positions at the Executive Committee are occupied by the representatives of the member states of the Commonwealth, while the staff is mainly Belarusian nationals.

The Executive Committee services the Council of the Heads of State and the Council of Heads of Government. It also co-ordinates the activities of member states, statutory and sectoral organs of the Commonwealth; working closely with the Economic Council, Council of Foreign Ministers, Council of Defence Ministers, Council of Border Troops Commanders, Secretariat of the Interparliamentary Assembly, the Interstate Committee for Statistics, the Council of Railway Transport Ministers and other organs.

One of the major activities of the Executive Committee is ensuring the development of partnerships between the CIS and other international organisations. The CIS now works with UNCTAD, ILO, WHO, UNHCR, OSCE and the European Union. The CIS works alongside the European Commission and has established an exchange of legal and economic information through the EU TACIS programme.

On March 24 1994, the CIS was granted observer status in the UN General Assembly.

Development of the Commonwealth
After the establishment of the CIS, the initial meetings of the Councils of the Heads of State and Heads of Government focused primarily on collective security and military issues:
Strategic Forces: Under the Agreement of 31.12.1991 the members of the Commonwealth "recognise the necessity of establishing a Joint Command of the Strategic Forces and maintaining a single command of nuclear and other mass destruction weapons of the former USSR." By 1992, agreements had been signed on the principles of the CIS United Armed Forces (UAF) formation and service; on the Chief Commander of the UAF; and the powers of the CIS supreme Councils on defence issues.

Nuclear Weapons: Of the former Republics of the USSR, Belarus, Kazakhstan, the Russian Federation and the Ukraine have nuclear weapons on their territory. An agreement, signed 23 December 1991 reaffirms the non-proliferation of atomic weapons, their elimination from the territories of Belarus and the Ukraine and their eventual destruction.

Space Exploration: Space exploration and the use of outer space are to be carried out jointly on the basis of inter-state programmes by the joint strategic forces and financed by the participating states.

Border Troops: While the members of the Commonwealth retain the right to create their own armed forces, guarding the external borders will remain a common task. Agreements were also signed on the groups of military observers and collective peace-keeping forces in the CIS.

Financial and economic matters then took precedence. September 1993 saw the Heads of States signing the Treaty on establishment of the Economic Union. The Treaty covers the principles of free movement of goods, services, workers, capital; elaboration of money and credit, tax, price, customs and foreign economic policies; rapprochement of the methods of management of economic activities, and creation of favourable conditions for development of direct production links. Documents were also adopted on the foundation of the Interstate Bank and the regulation of the interstate securities market. On 15 April 1994 all the CIS states signed the Agreement on Establishment of the Free Trade Zone.

More recent priorities have been the struggle against organised crime; the presence of collective CIS peace-keeping forces in the conflict zones of Abkhazia, Georgia and Tajikistan; a united system for air defence; and the on-going process of integration development of the CIS.

Chairman of the Council of Heads of State, 2013: A. Lukashenko (page 1467) (President of Belarus)

CIS Executive Secretariat, 17 Kirov St., Minsk 22050, Belarus. Tel: +375 17 229 3434 / 229 3517, fax: +375 17 272339, e-mail: postmaster@cis.minsk.by, URL: http://www.cis.minsk.by

COMMUNAUTÉ ECONOMIQUE ET MONÉTAIRE DE L'AFRIQUE CENTRALE (CEMAC)

The Central African Economic and Monetary Community was founded in 1994, succeeding the Central African Economic and Customs Union of 1964. Its purpose is to promote regional economic and monetary integration. An economic regional programme was launched in 2010 with the aim of creating an integrated, secure and sustainable economic zone by 2025.

The members of CEMAC are Cameroon, Central African Republic, Chad, Congo, Equatorial Guinea and Gabon. As of 2010, the region covered an estimated population of 36.7 million. The average GDP growth rate for the region 4.08 per cent with average inflation of 2.33 per cent.

The main organs of CEMAC are the Conference of the Heads of State, the Council of Ministers of the UEAC (Economic Union of Central Africa), the Ministerial Committee of UMAC (Monetary Union of Central Africa), and the Executive Secretariat. A Court of Justice and a

parliament have also been established. The Court of Justice has 13 judges, from whom they elect the first president. The Council of Ministers is made up of three members from each member state. The Ministerial Committee is made up of two members from each member state. The inaugural meeting of the Parliament took place on 15 April 2010 at its seat in Malabo. The parliament has 30 members, five from each member state.

The presidency of CEMAC rotates.

President of Commission: Pierre Moussa (Congo)

Central African Economic and Monetary Community, Immeuble CEMAC, Avenue des martyrs, BP 969, Bangui, Central African Republic. Tel: + 236 21 61 47 81, fax: +236 70 14 15 66, URL: http://www.cemac.int/

COMMUNITY OF LATIN AMERICAN AND CARIBBEAN STATES (CELAC)

CELAC is a regional bloc of Latin American and Caribbean nations created on 23 February 2010 at the Rio Group-Caribbean Community Summit held in Mexico. It is made up of the 33 sovereign countries in the Americas and covers an estimated 600 million people. Its aims include to increase Latin American integration, promote trade and development and to end American imperialism. It is seen as a successor to the Rio Group and the Latin American and Caribbean Summit (CALC) and as an alternative to the Organization of American States (OAS). The US and Canada are not included.

In July 2010 CELAC appointed President Hugo Chavez of Venezuela and President Sebastian Pinera of Chile as co-chairs of the forum to draft the statutes of the organisation. The group was formally established in July 2011 at a summit in Caracas. The inaugural summit was held in December 2011 and focused on the global economic crisis and its effect on the region. The 2012 summit took place in Chile.

Membership
Antigua & Barbuda, Argentina, Bahamas, Barbados, Belize, Bolivia, Brazil, Chile, Columbia, Costa Rica, Cuba, Dominica, Dominican Republic, Ecuador, El Salvador, Grenada, Guatemala, Guyana, Haiti, Honduras, Jamaica, Mexico, Nicaragua, Panama, Paraguay, Peru, Saint Lucia, Saint Kitts & Nevis, Saint Vincent and the Grenadines, Suriname, Trinidad and Tobago, Uruguay, Venezuela.

CELAC, URL: http://www.celac.gob.ve

CONGRESS OF LOCAL AND REGIONAL AUTHORITIES OF THE COUNCIL OF EUROPE

Congress of Local and Regional Authorities of the Council of Europe, Congrès des Pouvoirs Locaux et Régionaux du Conseil de l'Europe, Kongress der Gemeinden und Regionen des Europarates. The Standing Conference of Local and Regional Authorities of Europe (the European Conference of Local and Regional Authorities betwwen 1957 and 1975) was established in 1957 and was replaced in 1994 by the Congress of Local and Regional Authorities. It has two Chambers: the Chamber of Local Authorities and the Chamber of Regions. The two-Chamber assembly comprises 318 elected members and 318 substitutes representing over 200,000 regional and local authorities in the Council's 47 member states. The Congress meets twice a year in Strasbourg and welcomes delegations from approved European organisations and some non-member states as guests or observers.

The Congress is the voice of Europe's regions and municipalities. It provides a forum where delegates can discuss problems, pool experience and express their views to governments. It advises the Committee of Ministers and the Parliamentary Assembly of the Council of Europe on all aspects of local and regional policy and co-operates closely with national and international organisations representing local government. Dialogue is not confined to institutions; the Congress also organises hearings and conferences locally and regionally, reaching the wider public whose involvement is essential to a working democracy.

Aims
These include:
- monitoring the application of the European Charter of Local Self-Government;
- promoting effective local and regional government structures in all Council of Europe member states;
- examining the state of local and regional democracy in member states;
- developing initiatives to enable citizens to participate effectively in local and regional democracy;
-representing the interests of local and regional government in the shaping of European policy;
- encouraging regional and cross-border co-operation for peace, tolerance and sustainable development in order to safeguard our regions for future generations;
- encouraging the setting up of Euro-regions;
- observing local and regional elections.

Structure
The Standing Committee, drawn from all national delegations, meets between plenary sessions. Four Statutory Committees (Institutional Committee, Committee on Sustainable Development, Culture and Education Committee, Committee on Social Cohesion) deal with specific issues. The Bureau establishes the programmes and timetable of the Congress and is composed of the President and 16 Vice-Presidents.

Achievements
The European Charter of Local Self-Government (adopted in 1985); the European Outline Convention on Transfrontier Co-operation between Territorial Communities or Authorities (adopted in 1980); the European Convention on the Participation of Foreigners in Public Life at Local Level (adopted in 1992); the European Charter for Regional or Minority Languages (adopted in 1992); the European Urban Charter (adopted in 1992); the Charter on the Participation of Young People in Municipal and Regional Life (adopted in 1992 and revised in 2003); the European Network of Training Organizations for Local and Regional Authorities (ENTO); the Local Democracy Agencies (LDA); the network of National Associations of Local Authorities of South East Europe (NALAS); the Adriatic Euroregion (est. 2006); New Congress Charter (2007); the Black Sea Euroregion (est. 2008). In 2011, the Committee of Ministers of the Council of Europe adopted the new Congress Charter.

Members
Albania, Andorra, Armenia, Austria, Azerbaijan, Belgium, Bosnia and Herzegovina, Bulgaria, Croatia, Cyprus, Czech Republic, Denmark, Estonia, Finland, France, Georgia, Germany, Greece, Hungary, Iceland, Ireland, Italy, Latvia, Liechtenstein, Lithuania, Luxembourg, Malta, Moldova, Monaco, Montenegro, Netherlands, Norway, Poland, Portugal, Romania, Russian Federation, San Marino, Serbia, Slovak Republic, Slovenia, Spain, Sweden, Switzerland, the Former Yugoslav Republic of Macedonia, Turkey, Ukraine, United Kingdom

Observers: Major international associations of local and regional authorities

Secretary General, 2012-14: Herwig van Staa (Austria, EPP/CD)

Congrès des Pouvoirs Locaux et Régionaux du Conseil de l'Europe, Secretariat, c/o Conseil de l'Europe, F-67075 Strasbourg Cedex, France. Tel: +33 (0)3 88 41 21 10, fax: +33 (0)3 88 41 27 51, e-mail: congress.web@coe.int, URL: http://www.coe.int/congress

CO-OPERATION COUNCIL FOR THE ARAB STATES OF THE GULF

Also known as the Gulf Co-operation Council, the GCC formally came into being on May 25, 1981.

The objectives of the GCC are to achieve unity between Member States and strengthen relations between them; to formulate similar regulations in various fields such as economic and financial affairs, commerce, customs and communications, education and culture, social and health affairs, information and tourism, and legislative and administrative affairs; to stimulate scientific and technological progress in the fields of industry, mining, agriculture, water and animal resources, and establish scientific research; and to encourage co-operation by the private sector for the good of their people.

On January 1st 2008 a GCC common market was launched.

There are currently six member countries: Bahrain, Kuwait, Oman, Qatar, Saudi Arabia, United Arab Emirates. Yemen is in negotiation for membership and hopes to join by 2016.

Structure
The Supreme Council is the GCC's highest authority and is composed of the heads of Member States. Presidency is rotated annually on the basis of the alphabetical order of Member States. The Supreme Council gives policy direction, reviews reports and recommendations, appoints the Secretary-General and approves the budget of the Secretariat-General. It meets twice yearly though Extraordinary sessions can be convened.

The Commission for the Settlement of Disputes is attached to the Supreme Council and is formed on an 'ad-hoc' basis according to each particular case and the nature of the dispute. The Commission submits recommendations to the Supreme Council.

The Consultative Commission for the Supreme Council has 30 members. Seats are equally distributed among the six member countries. Established in 1998, it provides advice on subjects referred to it by the Supreme Council.

The Ministerial Council is composed of Foreign Ministers or other ministers that the member states choose to delegate. Its Chairman is rotated annually. It proposes policies and prepares recommendations and studies. It meets every three months.

The Secretariat-General is headed by the Secretary-General, who is appointed by the Supreme Council for a three-year term, renewable only

In 2012, it was announced that the Council would move from a regional bloc to a confederation.

Secretary-General: Abdul Latif Bin Rashid Al Zayani (Bahrain)

Co-operation Council for the Arab States of the Gulf, PO Box 7153, Riyadh, 11462, Saudi Arabia. Tel: +996 482 7777, fax: +996 482 9089, URL: http://www.gcc-sg.org/

COUNCIL OF ARAB ECONOMIC UNITY

CAEU was created in 1964 to implement the Arab Economic Unity Agreeemnt (AEUA) among the member states of the Arab League. The Agreement was ratified by 12 states: Egypt, Iraq, Jordan, Kuwait, Libya, Mauritania, Palestine, Somalia, Sudan, Syria and the two Yemen states. The Council's goal is to create economic unity among its members. Objectives include the creation of a unified Arab custom area, co-ordination of foreign trade policies, achievement of monetary unity and co-ordination of tax and duties legislation.

There are currently 12 member states: Egypt, Iraq, Jordan, Kuwait, Libya, Mauritania, Occupied Palestinian Territories, Somalia, Syria, Sudan, United Arab Emirates and Yemen.

The Council is the legislative instrument of the CAEU. Each member is state is represented on a ministerial level. The Permanent Committee carries out research for the Council to aid its decision making and the General Secretariat is responsible for the implementation of any decisions.It also represents the Council at other bodies. The Council is chaired by a representative from each country for one year.

Council of Arab Economic Unity, 1113 Corniche el Nil, Cairo, Egypt. Tel: +20 2 575 5321, fax: +20 2 575 4090, e-mail: caeu@idsc.net.org, URL: http://www.caeu.org.eg/

COUNCIL OF EUROPE

The Statute bringing into existence the Council of Europe was signed at St. James's Palace, London, on 5 May 1949 (one year after The Hague Congress had called for its creation). The requisite seven ratifications were obtained shortly afterwards and in August 1949 the principal organs of the Council - the intergovernmental Committee of Ministers and the Parliamentary Consultative Assembly opened their first meetings in Strasbourg, where the Secretariat had already been installed.

Statute of the Council of Europe
The Statute is the Constitution of the Council of Europe. It defines its aims and governs the conditions of entry of new Members; it also provides for the organs of the Council and determines their competence.

Aims of the Council
Article I of the Statute states that the aim of the Council of Europe is to achieve a greater unity between its Members for the purpose of safeguarding and realising the ideals and principles which are their common heritage and facilitating their economic and social progress. The Statute goes on to state that this aim shall be pursued through the organs of the Council by discussion of questions of common concern and by agreements and common action in economic, social, cultural, scientific, legal and administrative matters and in the maintenance and further realisation of human rights and fundamental freedoms. This reference to human rights is taken up again in Articles III and IV, in which acceptance of the principles of the rule of law is made a condition of membership of the Council. The functions of the Council are thus general and extend to all fields of European co-operation, with the sole exception of questions of national defence excluded by Article I (d).

Member States
As of May 2013, there were 47 member states. The 10 Governments that originally signed the Statute were Belgium, Denmark, France, Ireland, Italy, Luxembourg, the Netherlands, Norway, Sweden and the United Kingdom. During the first Session held in August 1949, the Committee of Ministers invited Greece, Turkey and Iceland to join the Council; Turkey and Greece in fact sent representatives to the first Session of the Consultative Assembly, while Iceland became a member in March 1950. Countries that have joined subsequently are the Federal Republic of Germany (Associate Member 1950, full Member 1951), Austria (1956), Cyprus (1961), Switzerland (1963), Malta (1965), Portugal (1976), Spain (1977), Liechtenstein (1978), San Marino (1988), Finland (1989), Hungary (1990), Poland (1991), Bulgaria (1992), Estonia, Lithuania, Slovenia, the Slovak Republic, the Czech Republic and Romania (1993).

The Saar, admitted as an Associate Member in 1950, ceased to have separate representatives in the Council at the end of 1956, following its political integration into the Federal Republic of Germany. Greece withdrew from the Council in December 1969, but was re-admitted in November 1974. Countries that have recently joined are Andorra (1994), Albania, Latvia, Moldova, the former Yugoslav Republic of Macedonia, Ukraine (1995), Croatia and the Russian Federation (1996), Georgia (1999), Armenia and Azerbaijan (2001), Bosnia and Herzegovina (2002), Serbia (2003), Monaco (2004), Montenegro, Azerbaijan (2007). Croatia became a fully fledged member on 1 July 2013.

Any European State which is deemed to be able and willing to fulfil the provisions of Article III (regarding the respect of human rights and fundamental freedoms) may be invited to become a member of the Council of Europe by the Committee of Ministers. By statutory resolution the Ministers have agreed that such invitations shall be launched only after consultation of the Assembly. The Ministers have also stated their willingness to admit non-member countries to certain activities of the Council: an example is the participation (on an equal footing) of the Holy See in the elaboration and execution of the Council's cultural, educational and sport programmes. A number of Central and Eastern European countries were granted Special Guest Status by the Council's Parliamentary Assembly in 1989 and subsequently became member states.

Belarus is an applicant country. Its special guest status has been suspended due to its lack of respect for human rights and democracy.

The Holy See, the US, Canada, Japan and Mexico are observer countries.

Budget
The Council of Europe is financed by the governments of the member states in proportion to their population and respective wealth. For the period 2012-13, the Council of Europe's budget amounted to €240 million.

Structure
Committee of Ministers
The Committee of Ministers is the decision-making body of the Council of Europe. It alone can accept the text of conventions or agreements and take the decision to open them to signature; it makes recommendations to Governments and may require them to inform it of what action they have taken in regard to such recommendations; it adopts the budget; and

INTER-GOVERNMENTAL ORGANISATIONS

it takes binding decisions on all matters relating to the internal organisation and arrangements of the Council of Europe. It also provides a permanent forum for the member States to discuss a wide range of political issues with a view to taking a common position. The Committee of Ministers takes the decisions on political action to be undertaken by the Organisation, though it does not take decisions on defence issues. Over 200 Conventions have been drawn up, mainly concerning human democratic, social and cultural cohesion.

The Committee consists of the Foreign Ministers of the 47 Member States, who usually meet twice a year; decisions are taken on their behalf by a body of high-ranking national officials known as the Ministers' Deputies who hold meetings once a week.

Members undertake to accept the principles of the rule of law and their people's prerogative to basic human rights and fundamental freedoms. They also undertake to collaborate to achieve greater unity and to facilitate economic and social progress. In the event of a serious violation by a member state under the Statute, the Committee of Ministers can suspend that State's representation, invite it to withdraw or decide that it has ceased to be a member of the Council.

The Committee of Ministers has strengthened its dialogue with Europe's elected representatives at national and local levels and extended its political discussions to non-member countries, including a number of non-European states with observer status (the United States, Holy See, Canada, Japan and Mexico). It has intensified its co-operation with other European organisations, particularly the European Union and the Organisation for Security and Co-operation in Europe (OSCE).

The Chairmanship of the Committee rotates on a six-monthly basis on alphabetical order (English). Andorra held it for the period November 2012-May 2013 followed by Armenia (May-November 2013).

Parliamentary Assembly (PACE)

The Assembly consists of 318 representatives from the 47 member countries. The size of delegations varies from 18 (United Kingdom, Germany, Italy, France and Russia) to two (Liechtenstein, San Marino, Monaco and Andorra), according to the population of the member state concerned. Representatives are elected or appointed by national parliaments from among their members, and, although they speak and vote in all freedom, according to their conscience and convictions as individuals, their party affiliations are taken into account so as to mirror the strength of the democratic parties in their particular national assemblies.

The Assembly has five political groups: the Socialist Group (SOC), Group of the European People's Party (EPP/CD), the European Democratic Group (EDG), the Alliance of Liberals and Democrats for Europe (ALDE) and the Group of the Unified European Left (UEL). Some members of the Assembly choose not to belong to any political group. Each of the groups has a chair, who may initiate discussions or appoint spokespersons in Assembly debates. Representatives must be Members of Parliament. Each representative is entitled to a substitute who may speak and vote in his or her stead. A proposal in its final form may be either a recommendation or a resolution. The former is, after adoption, communicated by the Assembly to the Committee of Ministers for their consideration. A resolution may be adopted by a simple majority only and it gives formal expression to the opinion of the Assembly on a particular point.

The Assembly holds regular debates on European and world events and, more generally, matters where action at European level is needed. The Assembly's debates and adopted texts provide important pointers for the activities of the Committee of Ministers. Its political debates have frequently been based on the findings of on-the-spot visits and ongoing dialogue with the states concerned.

In 1989, the Parliamentary Assembly created special guest status, allowing parliamentary delegations from central and eastern Europe to attend the Assembly's plenary sessions and committee meetings. The contacts and exchanges established facilitated their accession to the Council of Europe.

Close relations are developed with the European Union (particularly since the creation, in 1974, of a Council of Europe Brussels Office), the OECD, the European Bank for Reconstruction and Development (EBRD), the UN and other international organisations in Geneva. The majority of European (and some world) intergovernmental organisations submit regular reports for debate by the Parliamentary Assembly, which has long been recognised as the 'Forum of Europe'. Democratic European and non-European non-member states of the Council of Europe also participate in some parliamentary debates (e.g. on development issues and OSCE).

The Assembly elects its President, traditionally for three consecutive one-year terms. The current president is Jean-Claude Mignon.

Joint Committee

The task of co-ordinating the work of the two main statutory bodies of the Council of Europe devolves mainly to the Joint Committee. This is a joint consultative committee, without power to take executive decisions. It is composed of members of the Assembly and of the Committee of Ministers.

The Congress of Local and Regional Authorities of Europe

The Congress of Local and Regional Authorities of Europe, like the Parliamentary Assembly, has 636 members (316 representatives and 316 substitutes). It is composed of two chambers, one representing local authorities and the other, regions. Its function is to strengthen democratic institutions at the local level, and in particular to strengthen transfrontier and inter-regional co-operation in Greater Europe.

Co-operation with non-governmental organisations (NGOs)

Over 395 NGOs have participatory status with the Council of Europe. Various consultation arrangements (including discussions and colloquies) enable NGOs to participate in a number of interparliamentary and intergovernmental activities.

Secretariat

The Secretariat, comprising about 1,800 permanent officials drawn from member states, is governed partly by the Statute, partly by internal Administrative Regulations. The Statute provides that the Secretary-General, the Deputy Secretary-General and the Secretary General of the Parliamentary Assembly are appointed by the Parliamentary Assembly on the recommendation of the Committee of Ministers.

Survey of Achievements

The Committee of Ministers' decisions are sent to governments as recommendations or embodied in European conventions and agreements, which are legally binding on states that ratify them. The European Convention on Human Rights was the Council of Europe's first treaty and is its greatest achievement.

European Court of Human Rights (ECHR)

The European Convention for the Protection of Human Rights and Fundamental Freedoms was drawn up within the Council of Europe, was opened for signature in Rome on 4 November 1950 and entered into force on 3 September 1953. The authors' aim was to take the first steps for the collective enforcement of certain of the rights stated in the United Nations Universal Declaration of Human Rights of 1948. In addition to laying down a catalogue of civil and political rights and freedoms, the Convention set up a system to enforce the obligations entered into by Contracting States. Three institutions were entrusted with this responsibility: the European Commission of Human Rights (set up in 1954), the European Court of Human Rights (set up in 1959) and the Committee of Ministers of the Council of Europe.

Since the Convention's entry into force, 14 protocols have been adopted, some adding further rights to those already guaranteed. From the 1980s onwards, the steady growth in the number of cases brought before the Convention institutions made it increasingly difficult to keep the length of proceedings within acceptable limits.

Reform of the procedure was necessitated by the increasing number of applications, their growing complexity and the widening of the Council of Europe" membership from 23 in 1989 to 40 in 1996. To this end, a new protocol to the European Convention on Human rights, Protocol No. 11, entered into force on 1 November 1998, setting up a single permanent European Court of Human Rights in place of the Convention's two existing institutions.

A single Court of Human Rights

The European Court of Human Rights is now directly accessible to the individual and its jurisdiction is compulsory for all contracting states. It sits on a permanent basis and deals with all the preliminary stages of a case, as well as giving judgement on the merits.

The Court consists of a number of judges equal to the number of contracting states to the Convention. Judges are elected by the Parliamentary Assembly of the Council of Europe. Although candidates are initially put forward by each government, judges enjoy complete independence in the performance of their duties, and do not represent the states which proposed them.

Any cases that are clearly unfounded are sifted out of the system at an early stage by a unanimous decision of the Court, sitting as a three-judge committee. In the large majority of cases, the Court sits as a seven-judge Chamber. If applications are then judged admissible, the Chamber may attempt to reach a friendly settlement with the parties. If this is impossible, the Chamber delivers its judgement.

Monitoring the Court's judgements in which a violation is found is the task of the Committee of Ministers, which ensure that states take any general measures needed to prevent further violations.

Conventions

The Council of Europe has drawn up a number of conventions to meet growing new challenges and needs:

The European Social Charter: The 1961 European Social Charter, its Additional Protocol (1998) and the Revised Charter (1996) guarantee a series of fundamental social rights. States which have ratified the Charter or the Revised Charter must regularly submit reports on how they have put it into practice. These are examined by the European Committee of Social rights (ECSR), made up of independent experts, who assess whether the Charter is being complied with.

The Convention for the Prevention of Torture: The Convention supplements the protection under the ECHR by establishing a European Committee for the Prevention of Torture (CPT), made up of independent and impartial experts with the power to make unannounced visits to places of detention throughout Europe.

The **Framework Convention for the Protection of National Minorities** is the first legally-binding multilateral instrument to protect national minorities in general. It sets out the principles to be respected by states that ratify it. These include equality before the law, measures to preserve and develop culture and safeguard identity, religion languages and traditions, to ensure access to the media, to establish free and peaceful contact across borders with people legally resident in other states, and to protect the use of minority languages for hoardings and inscriptions.

The **Criminal Law Convention on Corruption** and the **Civil Law Convention on Corruption** were adopted as part of the Council's action programme against corruption. A major convention to combat cyberspace crime entered into force on 1st July 2004.

The **Convention on Human Rights and Biomedicine** is the first internationally binding legal text for protecting human beings against the possible misuse of new biological and medical techniques. Its basic aim is to safeguard fundamental rights and freedoms and the dignity and identity of individuals. Its Additional Protocol, signed in January 1998, prohibits the cloning of human beings.

The **European Cultural Convention** is a vast framework convention which was adopted in 1954. Some of the important sectors which it covers are education, higher education and research, culture, heritage, sport and youth policy. It serves as a basis for close dialogue and extensive co-operation between 48 countries, including the 46 Council of Europe member states.

The **European Charter of Local Self-Government** is considered the constitutional text for local self-government in Europe. The Charter serves as a model in new democracies and some states have already incorporated its principles into constitutions.

The **Outline Convention on Transfrontier Co-operation** provides a legal framework to facilitate co-operation between territorial communities or authorities in border regions.

A **Charter for Regional or Minority Languages** aims to halt the decline of non-official languages traditionally used within a state by its own nationals and to promote their spoken and written use in public life.

The **Convention on the Conservation of European Wildlife and Natural Habitats** is the basic legal instrument guiding Council of Europe action in the field of environmental protection in Europe.

The **Convention on the Prevention of Terrorism** increases the effectiveness of existing international texts on the fight against terrorism. It aims to strengthen member states' efforts to prevent terrorism.

The **Convention on Action Against Trafficking in Human Beings** is a comprehensive treaty mainly focused on the protection of victims of trafficking and the safeguard of their rights. It also aims at preventing trafficking as well as prosecuting traffickers.

Institutional Structures
The Council of Europe has created diverse institutional structures to take a whole range of action in a number of key areas:

A Commissioner for Human Rights: A new post of Commissioner for Human Rights was created in 1999. The Commissioner is responsible for promoting education, awareness and respect for human rights in member states and ensuring full and effective respect of Council of Europe texts. The Commissioner plays a supporting and essentially preventive role, performing different functions from those of the European Court of Human Rights.

Democratic Stability programmes: Increase in membership has been accompanied by a growing emphasis on co-operation and assistance programmes to strengthen democratic stability. The Council of Europe has been involved in a variety of ways: from short-term expert missions to fully-fledged Council of Europe's offices on the ground (eg. Tirana, Sarajevo, Podgorica, Chisinau, Tbilisi, Pristina, Yerevan, Baku, Skopje and Belgrade) as well as human rights experts in Chechnya.

The **European Commission against Racism and Intolerance (ECRI)** was set up in 1993 to fight all forms of racism, xenophobia and anti-Semitism. It evaluates the efficiency of all existing national and international measures against racism.

Programmes of education for Democratic Citizenship: The Council runs several programmes on education in human rights and democratic citizenship, history and language teaching, teacher training, secondary education with a European dimension, access to higher education, student mobility and recognition of qualifications. For example, the European Year of Citizenship through Education, 2005.

Youth Centres: There are practical programmes to promote youth mobility and exchanges throughout Europe. The European Youth Foundation, based in Strasbourg, provides financial support for international activities.

Social Cohesion: This was created in 1998 to encourage efforts being made in this area. It also launched a programme promoting a child-friendly society where children are protected and parents are provided with the means to carry out their child-raising tasks. Promotion, participation and protection are its keywords.

Partial Agreements: Since 1956, the Council of Europe has concluded a number of Partial Agreements which allow a number of states to carry out a specific activity of common interest with the consent of other members:

The **Commission for Democracy through Law (Venice Commission)** based in Italy provides legal advice on the development and functioning of democratic institutions and constitutional law.

The **Council of Europe Development Bank** aims to provide funds for social projects such as aid to refugees and victims of natural disasters, housing, job creation in run-down areas and social infrastructure.

The **Pompidou Group** is the main European forum to take a multi-disciplinary approach to the problems caused by drug abuse and trafficking.

The **European Centre for Global Interdependence and Solidarity (North-South Centre)** was established in 1990 to encourage co-operation between Europe and the South. It works to develop links with governments, local authorities, NGOs, in other parts of the world to promote human rights, democracy and education.

The **European Pharmacopoeia** sets out common and compulsory standards to guarantee the quality of medicines in all member states.

Eurimages is the European fund for co-production and distribution of feature films and documentaries. Its objectives are primarily cultural in that it endeavours to support works which reflect the multiple facets of a European Society.

The **European Audiovisual Observatory** sends out Europe-wide statistics and data on audiovisual matters to 36 European states.

The **European Centre for Modern Languages** in Graz trains teacher-trainers, the authors of language textbooks and experts in language curricula.

The partial agreement in the social and public health field includes the protection of public health and the rehabilitation and integration of people with disabilities.

EUR-OPA Major Hazards Agreement is an intergovernmental platform for cooperation in the field of major natural and technological disasters using prevention through knowledge, risk management, post-crisis analysis and rehabilitation.

GRECO, Group of States Against Corruption, evaluates through a dynamic process of peer pressure, the compliance with undertakings contained in the legal instruments of the Council of Europe in order to fight against corruption.

Awareness Campaigns
The Council of Europe has organised 'years' or 'campaigns' including most recently: Combat Violence Against Women (2006); Dosta! Roma and Travellers (2007); and One in Five (Stopping sexual abuse against children) (2010). The No Hate Speech Movement was launched in March 2013.

Secretary-General, Council of Europe: Thorbjørn Jagland (page 1448)

Council of Europe, 67075 Strasbourg Cedex, France. Tel: +33 (0)3 88 41 20 33, fax: +33 (0)3 88 41 27 45, e-mail: infopoint@coe.int, URL: http://www.coe.int

COUNCIL OF THE BALTIC SEA STATES

The Council of the Baltic Sea States (CBSS) was established in March 1992 with the signing of the Copenhagen declaration. The Council serves as an overall regional forum focusing on the need for greater co-operation among the Baltic Sea States in order to achieve democratic development in the region, closer unity between member countries and favourable economic development.

Membership
There are eleven member states of the Council of the Baltic Sea States plus the European Union: Denmark, Estonia, Finland, Germany, Iceland, Latvia, Lithuania, Norway, Poland, Russia, Sweden. France, Italy, Slovak Republic, The Netherlands, Ukraine, the United Kingdom and the United States of America all enjoy Observer status in the CBSS.

Organisation Structure
The **Council** is the principal decision and policy-making body of the Organisation and consists of the Ministers for Foreign Affairs of each Member State and a member of the European Commission. Chairmanship rotates on an annual basis. Russia held it for the June 2012-June 2013 period with specific attention to: modernisation and innovation, energy co-operation, and prevention of the spread of extremism. The Foreign Minister of the presiding country is responsible for co-ordinating the Council's ongoing activities between Ministerial Sessions and is assisted in this by a Committee of Senior Officials. The Council

meets at the level of Ministers for Foreign Affairs every other year. During those years that Council meetings are not held, Heads of Government convene for the Baltic Sea States Summits in the country holding the CBSS presidency.

The **CBSS Secretariat**, inaugurated in October 1998, is the permanent international Secretariat of the Council of the Baltic Sea States. It provides technical and organisational support to the Chairman of the CBSS, the working bodies and the structures of the Council. The long term priorities for the Baltic Sea Cooperation are: environment, economic development, energy, education & culture and civil security & human dimension. The budget of the Secretariat is raised through contributions paid by the governments of the 11 CBSS Member States.

The **Committee of Senior Officials (CSO)** consists of high-ranking representatives of the Ministries for Foreign Affairs of the Member States and of the European Commission. The CSO can designate specific tasks to three Working Groups and a special Task Force.
- Working Group on Democratic Institutions (WGDI)
- Working Group on Economic Co-operation (WGEC)
- Working Group on Nuclear Safety and Radiation Protection (WGNRS)
- Task Force against Trafficking in Human Beings (TF-THB) which liaises with government offices, IGOs, NGO, and public institutions working in the area of trafficking in human beings with a focus on adults and working with WGCC.

INTER-GOVERNMENTAL ORGANISATIONS

The Baltic Sea Region Energy Cooperation (BASREC) was established in October 1999 to support the development of an effective, efficient and environmentally sound energy market for the Baltic Sea Region. The cooperation runs with the Presidency, while the operative function is no longer situated in the Secretariat.

The Baltic 21 Network consists of CBSS countries, the European Union, intergovernmental organisations, international financial institutions and non-governmental organisation and network. Emphasis is on seven economic sectors of importance for the development in the region: Agriculture, Energy, Fisheries, Forests, Industry, Tourism and Transport, and Spatial Planning. Education has been added to the Baltic 21 process. The **Agenda 21 for the Baltic Sea Region** comprises the agreed goals and an Action Programme for Sustainable Development, including timeframes, actors and proposals for financing. Four applications submitted under the first call of the Baltic Sea Programme 2007-2013 have been accepted and the projects will be entitled Eco Region, SPIN - sustainable production through innovation in small and medium enterprises, The Baltic Sea Bioenergy Promotion Programme and UrbanRural - New Bridges.

The **Working Group on Children at Risk (WGCC)** was established in 2001 and is tasked to identify, support and implement cooperation on children at risk with the states and partner organisations in the region.

Ars Baltica Organising Committee is a forum for multilateral cultural cooperation with an emphasis on common projects within the Baltic Sea Region. It gives priority to art, culture and cultural history.

The **EuroFaculty** was established in 1994 to assist in reforming higher education in Law, Economics, Public Administration and Business Administration in the three Baltic countries of Estonia, Latvia and Lithuania. In addition, the project was successfully implemented also in Kaliningrad, the Russian Federation. A new stage of the project is to commence in Pskov, the Russian Federation.

Other working bodies include the Working Group on Youth Affairs , the Business Advisory Council, Ars Baltica and the Baltic Sea Monitoring Group on Heritage Cooperation which was established in 1998 and its work is organised in four sub-groups: Building preservation and Maintenance in practise, Underwater Heritage, Coastal Culture and Maritime Heritage and Sustainable historic towns.

The Russian presidency for the period 2012-13 began on 1 July 2012.

Director General: Jan Lundin

CBSS Secretariat, P O Box 2010, 10311 Stockholm, Slussplan 9, Sweden. Tel: +46 (0)8 440 1920, fax: +46 (0)8 440 1944, e-mail: cbss@cbss.org, URL: http://www.cbss.org

DANUBE COMMISSION

The Danube Commission has been in operation since 1954. Its function is to act according to the 18 August 1948 Convention on the Navigation of the Danube, a treaty that aims to guarantee free navigation of the Danube. The treaty was originally signed by Bulgaria, Hungary, Romania, Czechoslovakia, Ukraine, the Soviet Union and Yugoslavia, and now has 11 country members: Austria, Bulgaria, Croatia, Germany, Hungary, Moldova, Romania, Russia, Slovak Republic, Ukraine and Serbia. France and Turkey have expressed interest in membership. Each country has one representative on the Commission. The Commission elects a president, vice-president and secretary who each serve for three years.

The official languages of the Commission are French, German and Russian.

President: Ambassador Mrs Biserka Benisheva (Bulgaria) (page 1386)
Vice-President: Ambassador Alexandru Codreanu (Moldova)

Danube Commission, Benczúr Utca 25, H-1068 Budapest, Hungary. Tel: +36 1 461 8010, fax: +36 1 352 1839, e-mail: secretariat@danubecom-intern.org, URL: http://www.danubecommission.org/

EASTERN CARIBBEAN CENTRAL BANK (ECCB)

The Eastern Caribbean Central Bank was established in October 1983. Its purpose is to maintain the stability of the Eastern Caribbean dollar, maintain the banking system and support the growth and development of member states.

There are eight member states: Anguilla, Antigua & Barbuda, Dominica, Grenada, Montserrat, St Kitts and Nevis, St Lucia, and St Vincent and the Grenadines.

The governing bodies of the ECCB are the Monetary Council and the Board of Directors. The Monetary Council is the highest decision making authority. It is made up of one minister appointed by each member-state government. It provides directives on monetary and credit policy to the Bank. The Board of Directors is made up of one director appointed by each member state and a Governor and Deputy Governor.

Governor: Sir K. Dwight Venner (page 1531)

Eastern Caribbean Central Bank, PO Box 89, Basseterre, St. Kitts and Nevis. Tel: +1 869 465 2537, fax: +1 869 465 9562, e-mail: info@eccb-centralbank.org, URL: http://www.eccb-centralbank.org

ECONOMIC COMMUNITY OF WEST AFRICAN STATES (ECOWAS)

First founded in 1975, the Economic Community of West African States (ECOWAS) is a regional group of fifteen countries. It aims to promote economic integration in all aspects of economic activity, concentrating primarily on industry, transport, telecommunications, energy, agriculture, natural resources, commerce, monetary and financial questions and social and cultural matters.

The 15 member states are: Benin, Burkina Faso, Cape Verde, Côte d'Ivoire, Gambia, Ghana, Guinea, Guinea Bissau, Liberia, Mali, Niger, Nigeria, Senegal, Sierra Leone and Togo.

Structure

ECOWAS institutions are: The Commission (formerly the Authority of Heads of State and Government); The Community Parliament; The Community Court of Justice; The ECOWAS Bank for Investment and Development (EBID). The two main institutions are the Commission and EDIB (more often called the Fund). They implement policies, and carry out development projects. On-going projects include agricultural, energy and water resources development and road construction and telecommunications.

Commission

The newly created Commission was formed to increase the effectiveness of ECOWAS. It is headed by a president, and supported by a vice-president and seven commissioners, each with a clearly defined sector. The Commission should consolidate the community spirits, enhance its powers, and develop supra-nationality. A new legal regime will be adopted. The current president of the Commission is Kadré Désiré Ouedraogo. (page 1491)

Community Parliament

The protocol authorising the parliament was signed in 1994 and came into force in 2002. It is the Assembly for the peoples of the Community. the Parliament is composed of 115 seats and each member state has a minimum of five seats, the rest are allocated according to population. Distribution is thus: Nigeria 35 seats, Ghana 8, Cote d'Ivoire 7, Burkina Faso 6, Guinea 6, Mali 6, Niger 6, Senegal 6. Benin, Cape Verde, Gambia, Guinea Bissau, Liberia, Sierra Leone and Togo each have 5 seats. The Parliament is headed by a president, currently Sen. Ike Ekweremadu.

EBID

Its main objective is to contribute towards the economic development of West Africa through the financing of ECOWAS and NEPAD (New Partnership for Africa 's Development) projects and programmes, notable among which are programmes relating to transport, energy, telecommunications, industry, poverty alleviation, the environment and natural resources. The initial authorised capital of the EBID is UA (Units of Account) 603,000,000 or approximately US$ 750,000,000. Regional members control 67 per cent of the capital and 33 per cent is offered for subscription by non-regional members. Its decision-making bodies are the board of Governors, the Board of Directors and the President. The president is currently Mr Bashir Ifo.

Community Court of Justice

ECOWAS decided in 1999 to establish a Court of Justice as a permanent institution. The Court addresses complaints from member states and institutions of ECOWAS as well as issues relating to defaulting nations. The court has a president, chief registrar and seven judges. Justice Nana Awa Daboye of Togo was elected president of the court in 2009 and Justice Benfeito Mosso Ramos of Cape Verde was elected vice president.

Chairman, ECOWAS: Alassane Dramane Ouattara (Côte d'Ivoire) (page 1491)

Economic Community of West African States (ECOWAS), ECOWAS Commission, 101 Yakubu Gowon Crescent, Asokoro District P.M.B. 401 Abuja, Nigeria, Tel: +234 (9) 314 7647-9, fax: +234 (9) 314 3005, e-mail: info@ecowas.info, URL: http://www.ecowas.int

ECONOMIC CO-OPERATION ORGANIZATION (ECO)

Established in 1985, the Economic Co-operation Organization (ECO) succeeded the Regional Co-operation for Development (1964-1979) and is an intergovernmental regional organisation whose principal purpose is to promote economic, technical and cultural co-operation among its Member States.

The original organisation numbered just the three states of Iran, Pakistan and Turkey, but these were later joined by a further seven member states in 1992, following the break-up of the former Soviet Union.

The Treaty of Izmir, signed in 1977 as the legal framework for the RCD, was adopted as the basic Charter of ECO and amended in 1996 following the expansion of the organisation.

Membership

There are currently 10 member states: Islamic Republic of Afghanistan, Republic of Azerbaijan, Islamic Republic of Iran, Republic of Kazakhstan, Kyrgyz Republic, Islamic Republic of Pakistan, Republic of Tajikistan, Republic of Turkey, Turkmenistan and Republic of Uzbekistan.

Objectives

ECO has seven principal aims:
(1) Sustainable economic development of its Member States, to be achieved through the progressive removal of trade barriers and the promotion of interregional trade. A greater role of the ECO region in the growth of world trade and gradual integration of the Member States economies with the world economy.
(2) Development of transport and communications infrastructure linking the Member States with each other and the outside world.
(3) Economic liberalisation and privatisation.
(4) Mobilisation and utilisation of ECO region's material resources.
(5) Effective use of the agricultural and industrial potential of the region.
(6) Regional cooperation for drug abuse control, ecological and environmental protection and strengthening of historical and cultural ties among the peoples of the ECO region, and
(7) Mutually beneficial co-operation with regional and international organisations.

Organisational Structure

The Council of Ministers (COM) is the highest policy and decision-making body and is composed of Ministers of Foreign Affairs or such other representatives of Ministerial rank as may be designated by the member government. The Council of Ministers meets at least once a year by rotation among the Member States.

The Council of Permanent Representatives (CPR) consists of the Permanent Representatives or Ambassadors of the Member States to the Islamic Republic of Iran and to the ECO, and the Director General for ECO Affairs at the Iranian Ministry of Foreign Affairs.

The Regional Planning Council (RPC) is composed of the Head of the Planning Organization of the Member States or such other representatives of corresponding authorities.

The General Secretariat consists of seven Directorates under the supervision of the Secretary General and his two Deputies. The Directorates evolve projects and programmes in the fields of trade and investment; transport and telecommunications; energy, minerals and environment; industry and agriculture; project and economic research and statistics. There are approximately 60 members of staff.

Secretary General: H.E. Ambassador Shamil Aleskerov

Secretariat of Economic Co-operation Organization, No. 1, Golobu Alley, Kamranieh, PO Box 14155-6176, Tehran, Iran. Tel: +98 21 2283 1733-4 / 2229 2066, fax: +98 21 2283 1732, e-mail: Registry@ECOsecretariat.org, URL: http://www.ecosecretariat.org

EUROPEAN BANK FOR RECONSTRUCTION AND DEVELOPMENT (EBRD)

The European Bank, with its headquarters in London, was established in May 1990 and inaugurated in April 1991. It was the first international institution of the post Cold War period. Its purpose was to foster the transition towards open market oriented economies and promote private and entrepreneurial initiative in the countries of Central and Eastern Europe and the Commonwealth of Independent States (CIS) committed to multiparty democracy, pluralism and market economics. Today, the EBRD helps build market economies and democracies in countries from central Europe to central Asia. The EBRD is the single largest investor in the region.

There are currently 64 state members, plus the European Community and the European Investment Bank. Membership is open to European countries as well as non-European countries that are members of the International Monetary Fund. For full details of membership, please consult the matrix of membership of major organisations in the preliminary section. Tunisia and Jordan joined in 2011 and Kosovo in 2012.

The EBRD endeavours to help the economies of these countries integrate into the international economy, with particular concern for strengthening democratic institutions, respect for human rights and for environmentally sound policies.

As the Bank has developed, it has become a centre for the accumulation and exchange of knowledge on specific problems of the countries of the region and on the transition to a market economy. The EBRD helps its members to implement structural and sectoral economic reforms, including demonopolization, decentralization and privatisation. It merges the principles of private or privatisable enterprises in the competitive sector through sound banking principles, which includes the full range of private sector financing skills and experience.

It carries out its funding of physical and financial infrastructure projects through Development Banking, which includes the full range of development bank financing and economic, country and sectoral expertise. The kinds of finance the Bank offers include loans, guarantees, underwriting and equity investment. Advisory services and technical assistance are a major feature of the Bank's activities. The terms of the Bank's funding are designed to enable it to co-operate both with international financial institutions and public and private financial institutions through co-financing arrangements.

Structure

The powers of the European Bank are vested in a Board of Governors. Each member appoints one Governor and one Alternate to be presented on the Board of Governors. The Board of Governors has delegated powers to a Board of Directors comprising 24 members, who hold office for a term of three years. The Board of Directors is responsible for the general direction of the European Bank, including the approval if its budget and of its general operations. The President is elected by the Board of Governors for a term of four years. Vice Presidents are appointed by the Board of Directors on the recommendation of the President.

The EBRD has the following departments: Banking, Finance, Evaluation, Secretary-General, Chief Economist, General Counsel, Political Department, Communications, Risk Management, Human Resources, Internal Audit, Chief Compliance Officer, President's Office.

Funding

EBRD is owned by its 64 member/shareholder countries, the European Community and the European Investment Bank. The Bank Share Capital (totalling €21 billion) is provided by the Members.

Countries of Operations

The EBRD invests and operates in the following 30 countries (as of 2013): Albania, Armenia, Azerbaijan, Belarus, Bosnia and Herzegovina, Bulgaria, Croatia, Estonia, FYR Macedonia, Georgia, Hungary, Kazakhstan, Kosovo, Kyrgyz Republic, Latvia, Lithuania, Moldova, Mongolia, Montenegro, Poland, Romania, Russia, Serbia, Slovak Republic, Slovenia, Tajikistan, Turkey, Turkmenistan, Ukraine and Uzbekistan. The EBRD ceased making new investments in the Czech Republic in 2007, but still manages a portfolio.

Global Financial Crisis

The EBRD has developed crisis response packages and to date projects worth US$800 million have been aproved or are under consideration to help stimulate businesses affected by the crisis. In 2011, EBRD's portfolio grew to €35 billion with a record level of investment of €9.1 billion in 380 projects. In total, since 3,644 projects have been invested in with a total project value €235.2 billion.

President (2012-16): Sir Suma Chakrabati (page 1402)
Secretary General: Enzo Quattrociocche

European Bank for Reconstruction and Development, 1 Exchange Square, London, EC2A 2JN, UK. Tel: +(0)20 7338 6000/ 7496 6000, fax: +(0)20 7338 6100 / 7496 6100, URL: http://www.ebrd.com

EUROPEAN COURT OF HUMAN RIGHTS

The European Court of Human Rights is an international court set up in 1959. It rules on individual or State applications alleging violations of the civil and political rights set out in the European Convention on Human Rights. Since 1998 it has sat as a full-time court and individuals can apply to it directly. It has delivered more than 10,000 judgments. In 2011, it delivered 1,157 judgments concerning 1,511 applicants. On 1 June 2010 Protocol no 14 came into force, which has the aim of guaranteeing the long-term efficiency of the Court. The Court is based in Strasbourg. It looks after the human rights of the 800 million European citizens of its 47 member States.

European Convention on Human Rights

The European Convention on Human Rights is an international treaty under which the member States of the Council of Europe promise to secure fundamental civil and political rights, not only to their own citizens but also to everyone within their jurisdiction. The Convention was signed on 4 November 1950 in Rome and entered into force in 1953.

The Convention guarantees: the right to life; the right to a fair hearing, the right to respect for private and family life, freedom of expression, freedom of thought, conscience and religion, and the protection of property. It prohibits torture and inhuman treatment, slavery and forced labour, the death penalty, arbitrary and unlawful dentention.

Composition of the Court
(in order of precedence as at 02.01.2013)
Dean Peilmann, President, Luxembourg
Josep Casadevall, Vice-President, Andorra
Guido Raimondi, Vice-President, Italy
Ineta Ziemele, Section President, Latvia
Iabelle Berro-Lefèvre, Section President, Monaco
Corneliu Bîrsan, Romania
Peer Lorenzen, Denmark
Boštjan Zupančič, Slovenia
Elisabeth Steiner, Austria
Alvina Gyulumyan, Armenia
Khanlar Hajiyev, Azerbaijan
Davíd Thór Björgvinsson, Iceland
Danutė Jočienė, Lithuania
Ján Šikuta, Slovak Republic
Dragoljub Popović, Serbia
Päivi Hirvelä, Finland
George Nicolaou, Cyprus
Luis López Guerra, Spain
András Sajó, Hungary
Mirjana Lazarova Trajkovska, The former Yugoslav Republic of Macedonia
Ledi Bianku, Albania
Nona Tsotsoria, Georgia
Ann Power-Forde, Ireland
Zdravka Kalaydjieva, Bulgaria
Işıl Karakaş, Turkey
Nebojša Vučinić, Montenegro
Kristina Pardalos, San Marino
Ganna Yudkivska, Ukraine
Vincent A. De Gaetano, Malta
Angelika Nußberger, Germany
Julia Laffranque, Estonia
Paulo Pinto de Albuquerque, Portugal
Linos-Alexandre Sicilianos, Greece
Erik Møse, Norway
Helen Keller, Switzerland
André Potocki, France
Paul Lemmens, Belgium
Helean Jäderblom, Sweden
Paul Mahoney, United Kingdom
Aleš Pejchal, Czech Republic
Johannes Silvis, Netherlands
Krysztof Wojtyczek, Poland
Valeriu Gritco, Republic of Moldova
Faris Vehabović, Bosnia & Herzegovina
Ksenija Turković, Croatia
Dmitry Dedov, Russian Federation

President: Dean Spielmann (page 1519)

European Court of Human Rights, Council of Europe, 67075 Strasbourg Cedex, France. Tel: +33 (0)3 88 41 20 18, fax: +33 (0)3 88 41 27 30, URL: http://www.echr.coe.int

EUROPEAN ECONOMIC AREA (EEA)

The Agreement on the European Economic Area (EEA) is an agreement between the European Community (EC) and its 27 Member States on the one side and the three out of four EFTA States: Norway, Iceland and Liechtenstein. Switzerland is an EFTA country but not part of the EEA Agreement, which entered into force on 1 January 1994.

EEA has the following objectives and principles:
- free movement of goods
- free movement of persons, services and capital
- free competition
- co-operation in a number of economic and educational areas.

Structure
EEA Council
The EEA Council is composed of EEA-EFTA foreign ministers and the EU. The EU is represented by foreign ministers, the European Commissioner for External Relations and the High Representative for the EU's Common Foreign and Security Policy. The EEA Council meets twice a year. The presidency of the EEA Council will be held alternately for a period of six months, by a member of the EU and a member of the Government of an EFTA-EEA State. The EA Council provides support for the development of the agreement and guidelines for the EEA Joint Committee. It also takes into consideration resolutions adopted by the EEA Joint Parliamentary Committee and the EEA Consultative Committee.

The EEA Joint Committee
The EEA Joint Committee consists of representatives of the Contracting Parties and ensures the effective implementation and operation of the EEA agreement. To this end, it carries out exchanges of views and information and takes decisions by agreement. The EEA Joint Committee meets, in principle, at least once a month. The presidency rotates in the same way as that of the EEA Council.

The EEA Joint Parliamentary Committee
The EEA Joint Parliamentary Committee is composed of equal numbers of members of the European Parliament and members of Parliaments of the EFTA-EEA States. It holds sessions alternately in the EC and in an EFTA State. It shall contribute, through dialogue and debate, to a better understanding between the EC and the EFTA States in the areas covered by the EEA.

The EEA Consultative Committee
The EEA Consultative Committee is composed of equal numbers of members of the Economic and Social Committee of the EC and members of the EFTA Consultative Committee representing the social partners from the EEA countries. It may express its views in the form of reports and resolutions.

European Economic Area, c/o EFTA Secretariat, Rue Joseph II, 12-16, 1000 Brussels, Belgium. Tel: +32 (0)2 286 1711, fax: +32 (0)2 286 1750, e-mail: mail.bxl@efta.int, URL: http://www.efta.int

EUROPEAN FREE TRADE ASSOCIATION (EFTA)

The European Free Trade Association (EFTA) was founded in 1960 by the Stockholm Convention. It is an intergovernmental organisation set up for the promotion of free trade and economic integration to the benefit of its four Member States: Iceland, Liechtenstein, Norway and Switzerland.

History
EFTA was founded on the premise of free trade as a means as achieving growth and prosperity amongst its Member States as well as promoting closer economic co-operation between the Western European Countries. The EFTA Convention was agreed in Stockholm in November 1959 and entered into force on 3 May 1960. The seven founding members were: Austria, Denmark, Norway, Portugal, Sweden, Switzerland, and the United Kingdom. The agreement was updated in 2001 with the Vaduz Convention. There have been several changes in membership. Finland became an Associate Member in 1961 and a full member in 1986. Iceland joined in 1970 and Liechtenstein in 1991. Denmark and the UK left to become members of the EC in 1973. Portugal joined the EC in 1986 as did Austria, Sweden and Finland in 1995. EFTA celebrated its 50th anniversary in 2010.

Purpose
The Association has responsibility for the management of :
- The EFTA Convention;
- The European Economic Area (EEA) Agreement; and
- EFTA's worldwide network of free trade and partnership agreements.

The EFTA Convention
The Convention regulates the free trade relations between the four EFTA Members States and provides the legal framework for EFTA as an organisation. It covers trade in goods and services and includes areas such as investment and the free movement of persons. The updated EFTA Convention, the Vaduz Convention, was signed in Vaduz, Liechtenstein, on 21 June 2001. It came into force on 1 June 2002 with the following main changes:

Expanded Scope: to include new areas such as trade in services and investment, mutual recognition of conformity assessments, free movement of persons, social security and mutual recognition of diplomas, land and air transport, public procurement and intellectual property rights.

Broader Functions: The functions of the EFTA Council were broadened to reflect the historical changes in EFTA's mission, in particular with repsect to EFTA's free trade regime with partner countries.

The European Economic Area
The Agreement of the EEA brings together the 27 EU members and the 3 EFTA states (Iceland, Liechtenstein and Norway) in a single market. The agreement provides for the inclusion of EU legislation on the free movement of goods, services, capital and persons into the legal systems of the three EFTA EEA states, and covers co-operation in key areas such as R&D, education, social policy, the environment, consumer protection and culture.

The EFTA Free Trade Network
Cross-border trade and investment are central to the growth of the EFTA countries. Approximately 80 per cent of EFTA's total merchandise trade is covered by preferential arrangements. As of March 2012, the EFTA states have 24 free trade agreements covering 33 countries.

Structure
The operation of the EFTA Convention is the responsibility of the EFTA Council which meets regularly at the level of ministers or ambassadors. The Council is assisted by a Secretariat and a number of standing committees. Each EFTA country holds the chairmanship of the Council for six months.

Secretariat
The Secretariat has its headquarters in Geneva, with other offices in Brussels and Luxembourg. Its annual budget is approximately 25 million Swiss francs. There are approximately 100 staff members.

EFTA Court
The EFTA Court, based in Luxembourg, corresponds to the Court of Justice of the European Union in matters relating to the EEA EFTA States. The Court deals with infringement actions brought by the EFTA Surveillance Authority against an EFTA State with regard to the implementation, application or interpretation of an EEA rule. The Court also handles the settlement of disputes between two or more EFTA States. It also hears appeals against decisions taken by the EFTA Surveillance Authority and gives advisory opinions to courts in the EFTA States on the interpretation of EEA rules.

The EFTA Court consists of three Judges who serve for a period of three years. The Judges elect their president for a term of three years.
PJudges (2013): Carl Baudenbacher (page 1385) (President) (Liechtenstein); Pall Hreinsson (Iceland); Per Christiansen (Norway).

Secretary-General: Kristinn Arnason (Iceland) (page 1379)
Deputy Secretary-General (Brussels): Helge Skaara
Deputy Secretary-General (Geneva): Ivo Kaufmann

European Free Trade Association, 9-11 rue de Varembé, CH-1211 Geneva 20 Switzerland. Tel: +41 (0)22 332 2600, fax: +41 (0)22 332 2677, e-mail: mail.gva@efta.int, URL: http://www.efta.int

EFTA Brussels Office, 12-16 Rue Joseph II, B 1000, Brussels, Belgium. Tel: +32 (0)2 286 1711, fax: +32 (0)2 286 1750, e-mail: mail.bxl@efta.int

EFTA Statistical Office, Batiment Joseph Bech, 5 rue Alphonse Weicker, L-2721 Luxembourg. Tel: +352 430 133894, fax: +352 430 132145, e-mail: efta.lux@ec.europa.eu

EFTA Court, URL: http://www.eftacourt.int

EUROPEAN SPACE AGENCY (ESA)

The idea for an independent European space power emerged in the early 1960s, although ESA did not gain legal status until 1980 when eleven countries ratified the Convention. The European Space Agency (ESA) was established in order to provide and promote collaboration among European States in space research and technology while ensuring that this research and technology was applied only for peaceful purposes.

Function
ESA shapes the development of Europe's space capability, implementing a European Space Programme. ESA provides technical facilities to each of the scientific agencies of its member states and is responsible for projects such as the European telecommunications and meteorology satellite programmes, 'Spacelab' and the Ariane rockets. ESA comprises the ESTEC European Space Research and Technology Centre (Netherlands), the ESOC European Space Operations Centre (Germany), the ESRIN European Space Research Institute (Italy), the EAC European Astronaut Centre (Germany) and the European Space Astronomy Centre (Spain), and Guiana Space Centre (CSG), French Guiana. A new ESA site has also opened in Harewell, Oxfordshire. There are also liaison offices in Belgium, US and Russia.

Achievements
Ariane rockets developed by ESA now command the commercial market in space launches, especially for communications satellites, despite intense competition from the USA, Russia, China and Japan.

Global standards for the present generation of telecommunications satellites are based on techniques demonstrated by ESA, and over 50 telecom satellites have been built by European aerospace companies.

ESA leads the world in monitoring the ozone hole, ice sheets, ocean winds and currents, and other health checks for our planet. Meteosat, which gives the familiar daily movies of the weather in Europe and Africa, was also developed by ESA. Scientific spacecraft built by ESA have achieved a leading role in the study of the Sun and its effects on the Earth, in investigating comets, in mapping the stars from space, and in unveiling the Universe by infrared light and X-rays.

ESA's own astronauts have flown in space in US Shuttle missions and spent several sojourns on the Russian space station Mir. They fly to the International Space Station, to which ESA contributes as a full partner.

Europe's astronomers benefit from guaranteed use of Hubble Space Telescope, the famous visible-light space telescope thanks to ESA's partnership with NASA and practical contributions to this ESA/NASA collaboration project.

Members
There are 20 member states: Austria, Belgium, Zech Republic, Denmark, Finland, France, Germany, Greece, Ireland, Italy, Luxembourg, Netherlands, Norway, Poland, Portugal, Romania Spain, Sweden, Switzerland, and the United Kingdom. Canada takes part in some projects under a Cooperation agreement. Romania signed its Accession Agreement with ESA on 20 January 2011 became the 19th Member State on 22 December 2011. Poland exchanged enhanced Acession Agreements with ESA in September 2012. Hungary, Estonia and Slovenia are 'European Cooperating States'. Other countries have signed cooperation agreements with ESA.

Organisation
The policies of the ESA are agreed by a Council made up of Representatives from the member states. Each member state has one vote. Council meetings are held every three months at delegate level and every two to three years at ministerial level. Specific programmes are overseen by specialised Programme Boards and the running of the Agency is divided between a Science Programme Committee, an Administrative and Finance Committee, an Industrial Policy Committee and an International Relations Committee.

Budget
The budget for 2012 was an estimated €4,020 million, rising to €4,282.1 million in 2013. Of this, approximately 23 per cent is allocated to earth observation, 17 per cent to navigation, 16 per cent to launchers, 12 per cent to scientific programmes, 9.3 per cent to human spaceflights, and 7.3 per cent to telecom & integrated applications.

Director-General: Jean-Jaques Dordain (page 1417)

European Space Agency (ESA), 8-10 rue Mario Nikis, 75738 Paris Cedex 15, France. Tel: +33 (0)1 53 69 76 54, URL: http://www.esa.int

FRANC ZONE

The Franc Zone was founded in 1945 to create a monetary union with those African nations which once formed part of the French Colonial empire and whose own currencies were linked to the Franc. After accession to independence, the majority of the new states chose to remain in a common monetary system with a renewed institutional framework. The currencies are now linked to the euro.

As the financial instrument of the Franc Zone, the central Bank of France co-operates with the African Member states to ensure the smooth running of the common institutions of the Franc Zone.

Member States
Fourteen states from sub-Saharan Africa: Benin, Burkina Faso, Cameroon, Central African Republic, Chad, Republic of Congo, Côte d'Ivoire, Equatorial Guinea, Gabon, Guinea-Bissau, Mali, Niger, Senegal, Togo; Comoros and France.

Franc Zone, Direction Générale des Etudes et des Relations Internationales (Service de la Zone Franc), Banque de France, 31 rue Croix-des-Petits-Champs, Paris Cédex 01, France. Tel: +33 (0)1 42 92 42 92, URL: http://www.banque-france.fr

INDIAN OCEAN COMMISSION

The Indian Ocean Commission (IOC) was established in 1982. The Foreign Affairs Ministers of Madagascar, Mauritius and Seychelles met in Port Louis, Mauritius to discuss ways and means to establish closer links among themselves and co-operate in a number of ways. By 1986 two other countries of the South-West Indian Ocean Region, Comoros and France (on behalf of its DOM Reunion) had joined the organisation.

Purpose
The basic aims of IOC are: diplomatic, political and security co-operation; economic and trade co-operation; co-operation in the fields of agriculture and fisheries; preservation of the environment; cultural, scientific, technical and legal co-operation.

Structure
The highest organ is the Summit of Heads of State or Government. The IOC's governing body is the Council of Ministers where each country is represented either by its Minister of External Affairs or Planning or a Minister to whom the co-operation portfolio has been entrusted. A

meeting takes place annually. Co-ordination of the various activities at the national level is carried out by a Permanent Liaison Officer (OPL) in each country. These OPLs report directly to the Council of Ministers. A number of technical committees have also been set up to advise and deal with specific technical projects and programmes.

The activities of the IOC are co-ordinated by a General Secretariat. The Secretariat is located in Mauritius and is headed by a Secretary General and a small staff. Since its inception the IOC has launched a number of projects in such fields as tuna research, aromatic and medicinal plants, meteorology, trade exchanges, tourism development and environment.

Secretary-General: Jean-Claude de l'Estrac

IOC General Secretariat, Blue Tower, 3rd Floor, Rue de l'institut, Ebène, Mauritius. Tel: +230 402 6100, fax: +230 465 6798, email: secretariat@icoi-ioc.org, URL: http://www.coi-ioc.org/

INTER-AMERICAN DEVELOPMENT BANK

Created in 1959 with 19 member countries the Inter-American Development Bank was designed to combat poverty and to help and promote economic and social growth among countries in Latin America and the Caribbean. Today there are 48 member countries of which 26 are borrowing members in Latin America and the Caribbean. It works with governments, companies and civil society organizations. The client base varies from small businesses to municipal authorities to central governments. The IDB is the main source of multilateral financing and expertise for sustainable economic, social and institutional development in Latin America and the Caribbean.

The financial resources of the Bank consist of the ordinary capital account comprised of subscribed capital, reserves and funds raised through borrowing; and Funds in Administration which are contributions made by member countries. The Bank also has a Fund for Special Operations for lending on concessional terms for projects in countries classified as economically less developed.

The Bank uses the resources of its Ordinary Capital, which currently totals US$101 billion, for most of its lending operations. On average the IADB lends US$10 billion per annum, mainly financing projects in key sectors such as infrastructure, energy, water, education and health. In 2012, an estimated US$11.4 billion was loaned. In 2009, total subscribed capital amounted to US$104.9 bn. Total assets were US$84.0 bn and loans amounted to US$58.0 bn. Total equity to loans ratio was 34.2 per cent. In 2008, the assets of the Fund for Special Operations totalled US$6.3 billion. In 2010, it was propopsed that the Bank's Ordinary Capital be increased by $70 billion in response to the global financial crisis. There was also a proposal to increase, by $479 million, the Fund for Special Operations which provides assistance to the region's poorest nations. These proposals have been improved and should be implemented in 2015. The Inter-American Investment Corporation provides an average US$400 million in loans and guarantees to SMEs in the region. The Multilateral Investment Fund provides US$100 million in grants per annum. There are approximately 2,000 employees.

As well as the Bank, the IDB Group consists of the **Inter-American Investment Corporation (ICC)** and the **Multilateral Investment Fund (MIF)**. The IIC is an autonomous affiliate of the Bank and was established to finance small and medium-scale private enterprises and promote economic development within the region. The MIF was created in 1992 to promote investment reforms and to stimulate private-sector development. The IADB was realigned in 2007 to meet the new demands of Latin America and the Caribbean. It connects with more new clients and has more personnel in country offices. It aims to achieve sustainable economic growth, increase competitiveness, modernize public sector institutions and encourage free trade and regional integration.

Structure
The Board of Governors is the Bank's highest authority, on which each member country is represented, usually by the Ministers of Finance, Presidents of Central Banks or officers of comparable rank. The Board of Governors has delegated many of its operational powers to the Board of Executive Directors.

The Bank has Country Offices in each of its borrowing member countries and in Paris and Tokyo.

President: Luis Alberto Moreno (page 1480)

Inter-American Development Bank, 1300 New York Avenue, NW, Washington, DC 20577, United States of America. Tel: +1 202 623 1000, fax: +1 202 623 3096, URL: http://www.iadb.org

INTERGOVERNMENTAL AUTHORITY ON DEVELOPMENT

The Intergovernmental Authority on Development (IGAD) was formed in 1996 to supersede the Intergovernmental Authority on Drought and Development (IGADD) which was created in 1986. IGADD was formed after individual countries realised that individual efforts could not combat the magnitude of problems (famine, ecological degradation, economic hardship) that the region faced. In 1986 Djibouti, Ethiopia, Kenya, Somalia, Sudan and Uganda took action through the UN to set up an intergovernmental body for development and drought control. The Heads of State met in Djibouti in January 1986 to sign the agreement. Eritrea became the seventh member in 1993. South Sudan officially split from Sudan in 2011 and became a member that same year.

On 21 March 1996 the Heads of State and Government of the member countries signed a 'Letter of Instrument to Amend the IGADD Charter/Agreement' which revitalised the body and gave it its new name. The new body has expanded areas of regional co-operation and a new organisational structure.

Aims
The IGAD strategy was drawn up in 2003 and adopted by the 10th Summit of heads of State and Government. Its three main priority sectors are: agriculture and environment; political and humanitarian affairs; and economic co-operation. The aims of IGADD are to help the region achieve peace and prosperity including food security and environmental protection; promotion and maintenance of peace and security, and humanitarian affairs; and economic co-operation and integration.

Objectives
Objectives include:
-promotion of joint development strategies, co-ordination of economic policies;
-harmonization of various policies including trade, customs, transport, agriculture, promotion of free trade;
-create an environment for foreign, cross-border and domestic trade and investment;
-initiative and develop programmes and projects to achieve food security;
-create mechanisms to promote peace and stability, management and prevention of intra-regional conflicts through dialogue
-promote the objectives of the Common Market for Eastern and Southern Africa (COMESA)

Structure
The supreme policy making organ is the Assembly of Heads of State and Government. It determines the objectives, guidelines and programmes and meets annually. A chairman is elected from among the member states in rotation. The Council of Ministers is composed of the ministers of foreign affairs and one other minister designated by each member state. The Council formulates policy, approves the work programme and the budget. The Committee of Ambassadors is made up of ambassadors or plenipotentiaries from the members states accredited to the country of IGAD headquarters. It convenes as required to advise the Executive Secretary. The Secretariat is headed by an Executive Secretary appointed by the Assembly of Heads of State and Government for a term of four-years renewable once. The Secretariat assists member states in formulating regional projects. The Executive Secretary is assisted by four directors.

The IGAD Inter-Parliamentary Union (IPU-IGAD) came into force on 28 November 2007 after it was ratified by four states (Ethiopia, Djibouti, Sudan, and Somalia). The first meeting of the Conference of the Speakers of Parliament of IGAD member states, the highest organ of the Union , took place on 28 November 2008. The first meeting of the IPU Executive Council, the second highest organ of the Parliamentary Union took place on 25-26 May 2008.

In order to establish formal relationships with partners who work closely with the Secretariat, the IGAD Partners Forum (IPF) was created in 1997. In addition to states, partners also include the European Commission, the International Organization for Migration, the UNDP, and the World Bank. The first Joint Ministerial Meeting of IPF was held in Rome in 1998.

In 2009 the member states agreed on a draft Convention on Extradition and a Convention on Mutual Legal Assistance.

Executive Secretary: Amb. (Eng.) Mahboub M. Maalim

Intergovernmental Authority on Development, IGAD Secretariat, PO Box 2653, Djibouti. Tel: +253 354050, fax: +253 356994, e-mail: igad@igad.org, URL: http://www.igad.org

INTERNATIONAL CRIMINAL POLICE ORGANISATION (INTERPOL)

Interpol is an international intergovernmental organisation founded in 1923 and reconstituted in 1946. Its main purpose is to ensure and promote the widest possible mutual assistance between all criminal police authorities within the limits of their own laws and the spirit of the Universal Declaration of Human Rights. It also aims to establish and develop institutions likely to contribute effectively to the prevention and suppression of ordinary law crimes. It is the largest international police organisation with 190 member countries.

In pursuance of these aims, Interpol acts as a point of reference for international enquiries, a conduit for international police communication, a source of information on crimes and criminals, an international police liaison service and also offers assistance with policy for international police co-operation.

Interpol therefore provides a secure worldwide police communication system, global databases and data services for police and international operational support services for police in key crime areas.

These services are provided through a co-ordination centre (known as the General Secretariat) for its 190 member countries. Priority areas of activity include drugs and organised crime, public safety and terrorism, financial and high tech crime, trafficking in human beings and tracking fugitives.

Governance Structure
The General Assembly is the organisation's governing body. It is composed of delegates appointed by the member countries of the organisation. Each country has one vote and all votes carry equal weight.

Interpol's Executive Committee is composed of the president of the organisation, three vice-presidents and nine delegates. It meets three times a year and supervises the execution of the decisions of the General Assembly, and oversees the work of the Secretary General who is the organisation's chief executive.

The General Secretariat in Lyon, France is the centre for co-ordinating the fight against international crime. Its activities, undertaken in response to requests from the police services and judicial authorities in its member countries, focus on crime prevention and law enforcement.

There are approximately 670 staff members at the General Secretariat and the regional offices. There are seven regional offices in Argentina, Cameroon, Cote d'Ivoire, El Salvador, Kenya, Thailand and Zimbabwe. Interpol also has a special representative at the UN in New York, and at the EU in Brussels. A Global Complex for Innovation, a research and development facility, is scheduled to open in 2014.

Finance: The annual budget for 2010 was €48.6 million which was mainly funded from annual dues paid by member countries. For the financial year 2011, the operating income amounted to €60 million of which over 80 per cent was contributed by member countries. Operating expenditure amounted to €58 million.

For a full list of members, please consult the Matrix of Country Memberships of Major Organisations in the preliminary section.

President: Mrs Mireille Ballestrazzi
Secretary General: Ronald K. Noble

International Criminal Police Organization - Interpol, 200 quai Charles de Gaulle, 69006 Lyon, France. Tel: + 33 (0)4 72 44 70 00, fax: + 33 (0)4 72 44 71 63, e-mail: cp@interpol.int; URL: http://www.interpol.int
Mailing Address: BP 6041, 69411 LYON CEDEX 06, France

INTERNATIONAL ORGANIZATION FOR MIGRATION

Established initially as the Intergovernmental Committee for European Migration (ICEM) to help solve the post-war problems of migrants, refugees and displaced persons in Europe and to assist in their orderly migration, IOM's focus has since expanded and now includes a wide variety of migration management activities.

IOM believes that international migration is an opportunity for co-operation and development, and acts with its partners in the international community to: encourage social and economic development through migration; uphold the dignity and well-being of migrants; assist in meeting the operational challenges of migration and advance understanding of migration issues.

Since 1951, IOM has assisted over 11 million refugees and migrants to settle in other counties. Membership numbered 149 member states in March 2013 and 13 observer states.

With operations on every continent, IOM helps migrants, governments and civil society through a large variety of field-based operations and programmes. It defines its outlook on migration issues through six service areas, which form the backbone of the Organization's expertise:

Movements: Resettlement, repatriation and transportation assistance for migrants constitutes the core of IOM's activities. Aspiring to provide the most efficient and humane movement service for migrants, governments and other partners, IOM organises safe and reliable transfer of migrants for resettlement, work, studies or any other purpose of orderly migration. Regular movement services include selection, processing, language training, orientation activities, medical examinations and various activities to facilitate integration. One of the most prominent movement programmes implemented by IOM since the early 1950s is the US Refugee Programme (USRP).

Assisted Returns: Most migrants wish to return to their country of origin. Others may be subject to return from a country of intended residence after being denied the permission to stay. IOM believes that migrants should be able to return in safety and dignity. IOM's assisted return activities comprise both voluntary return programmes for individuals and migration diplomacy, with IOM acting as an independent and neutral broker and facilitator.

Migration Health and Medical Services: IOM has, over time, gathered considerable experience from the medical screening of millions of migrants and, based on this experience, the Organization provides appropriate treatment and preventive health services to migrants. It also promotes and assists in the standardisation of immigration, travel and international health legislation/guidelines and the IOM Medical Services offer support to training and education of staff involved in migration health care. The link between migration and HIV/AIDS is of particular concern and IOM is working closely with UNAIDS on research and programme development.

Technical Co-operation and Capacity Building: IOM's technical co-operation on migration helps governments facilitate co-operation amongst themselves and to develop the necessary legislation, administrative structures, knowledge and the human resources to better manage migration. IOM is especially active in the CIS countries and in South Eastern Europe where capacity building programmes are implemented. In early 2001, IOM presented the "Migration for Development in Africa" programme that aims to mobilise Africa's human resources in the diaspora and to associate them to the development of their home countries, to counter the negative effects of the brain drain.

Counter-trafficking: An increasing number of migrants are trafficked world-wide every year, generating large amounts of money for organised criminal networks. These networks misinform would-be migrants by exploiting their ignorance and often expose them to physical harm and danger, economic despair, forced labour and vulnerability in destination countries. IOM contributes to the prevention of trafficking by providing factual information on the dangers of irregular migration. IOM also provides assistance to victims by offering protection, counselling and voluntary return and reintegration. IOM's work in the fight against trafficking also involves research, compilation of data, dissemination of information and experience and assistance to governments to enhance their capacity to combat this phenomenon.

Migration Information: Migrants as well as governments need to make decisions on the basis of accurate, reliable and timely information. Based on thorough research, IOM develops efficient public information campaigns targeted and adapted to specific audiences.

Recent Activities
In Indonesia, following the tsunami of December 2004, the IOM is building thousands of transitional housing units and 55 Satellite Health Clinics (SHC). These SHCs will serve as the primary centres for basic health care for the tsunami-affected population in Aceh.

Following the South Asia earthquake in October 2005, the IOM is providing return assistance to families currently living in more than 150 planned camps and transportation to those living with relatives or in small, unplanned camps.

Since February 2007, more than 26,000 IDPs have been helped to return to South Kordofan and South Sudan.

In mid 2000, IOM was designated to be a partner organisation of the Federal Foundation handling claims and paying compensation to former forced slave labourers under the Nazi regime. IOM is in charge of claims from non-Jewish victims living anywhere in the world except in nine countries in Central and Eastern Europe, which are covered by other partner organisations. As of December 2001, the expiration of the filing deadline, 308,000 claims for slave labour, personal injury and death of a child had been received, and 48,000 claims for property loss had been submitted. In December 2000, IOM was also designated as an implementing organisation of the Holocaust Victims Assets Programme, a claims programme designed to compensate victims of Nazi persecution arising out of litigation against Swiss banks. By December 2001, the expiration of the filing deadline, 22,000 claims had been received.

Field locations have increased from 119 in 1998 to more than 470 in 2013. Active projects have increased from 686 in 1998 to more than 2,300 in 2013. Operational staff have increased from approximately 1,100 in 1998 to approximately 7,800 in 2013, almost entirely in the field.

Manila and Panama Administrative Centres
In order to manage growth and achieve efficiencies, IOM has set on an exercise to tranfer some functions from Headquarters and high cost locations to lower costs. The Manila Administrative Centre currently offers global support in the following areas - finance, information technology, human resources, staff security, project tracking, and health claims processing.

Partnerships
The IOM co-ordinates its refugee activities with the UN High Commissioner for Refugees and with governmental and non-governmental organisations. It is represented at the UN General Assembly as an observer. In 1993 the UN General Assembly granted IOM the right to draw on the resources available in the Central Emergency Revolving Fund (CERF). In 1996 a Co-operation Agreement was signed with the UN. Other agreements exist with individual UN agencies, such as UNDP, UNAIDS, UNFPA, UNHCR and WHO.

Budget
Total expenditure has increased from US$242.2 million in 1998 to over US$1.3 billion in 2011. In 2011 more than 97 per cent of IOM's funding was in the form of voluntary contributions for projects.

Director General: William Lacey Spring

International Organization for Migration, 17, Route des Morillons, POB 71, CH 1211 Geneva 19, Switzerland. Tel: +41 (0)22 717 9111, fax: +41 (0)22 798 6150, e-mail: hq@iom.int, URL: http//www.iom.int

INTERNATIONAL RED CROSS AND RED CRESCENT MOVEMENT

The International Red Cross and Red Crescent Movement is the world's largest humanitarian organization. It is dedicated to protecting human life and dignity world-wide, thereby promoting lasting peace. The millions of people in the Movement help those hurt by armed conflict, natural disasters and other tragedies, regardless of political, racial, religious or ideological differences.

Structure of the Movement
The Movement is comprised of:
- The International Committee of the Red Cross (ICRC)
- The International Federation of Red Cross and Red Crescent Societies
- National Red Cross and Red Crescent Societies

The ICRC, the Federation and the National Societies are independent bodies.

International Committee of the Red Cross
The International Committee of the Red Cross (ICRC) is an impartial, neutral and independent organisation whose exclusively humanitarian mission is to protect the lives and dignity of victims of war and internal violence and to provide them with assistance. It directs and co-ordinates the international relief activities conducted by the Movement in situations of conflict. It also endeavours to prevent suffering by promoting and strengthening humanitarian law and universal humanitarian principles. Established in 1863, the ICRC is at the origin of the International Red Cross and Red Crescent Movement.

The primary role of the ICRC is to protect victims of international and internal armed conflicts as defined in the four Geneva Conventions of 1949 and their Additional Protocols of 1977. The Committee, which promoted these international treaties, works for their development and world-wide dissemination.

To date more than 190 states have signed the Geneva Conventions of 1949. In fulfilling its mandate, the ICRC may take on any or all of the following roles: protecting, visiting and helping noncombatants (namely the wounded, prisoners of war, and civilian inhabitants of occupied territories); searching for people missing as a result of armed conflicts; exchanging messages to and from members of separated families; facilitating the establishment of hospital and security zones; organising and co-ordinating international aid programmes and medical assistance in aid of refugees, displaced people, and other civilians who are victims of armed conflicts.

In addition, the ICRC works for the development and the dissemination of international humanitarian law applicable in armed conflicts. As a neutral and independent institution, it may take any humanitarian initiative, such as visiting political detainees. The ICRC is a private, non-political, independent institution. The Committee itself is composed of a maximum of 25 Swiss citizens. The permanent ICRC headquarters is in Geneva, Switzerland. There are approximately 12,000 staff working in 80 countries world-wide. Approximately 30 per cent of its activities are carried out in co-operation with National Societies. The ICRC has an annual budget of approximately 1 billion Swiss francs. In 2013, the ICRC asked for 1.17 billion Swiss francs to cover its operations.

In 2013, key countries of operation include: Afghanistan, Central African Republic, Iraq, Somalia & Syria.

International Federation
The International Federation was founded in 1919. The Movement comprises the International Federation, the consisting of 187 member Red Cross and Red Crescent societies, a secretariat, and more than 60 delegations around the world. Worldwide there are 13 million volunteers working for the Movement, helping the Movement reach 150 million people.

The International Federation's work concentrates on four main areas: promoting humanitarian values; disaster response; disaster preparedness; and health and community care.

It has member National Societies, the National Societies in their own right and the International Committee of the Red Cross (ICRC). Its network of National Societies covers almost all countries in the world. Its day-to-day work is performed by millions of members and volunteers who sustain Red Cross and Red Crescent programmes world-wide.

Each Red Cross and Red Crescent unit has its own governing boards. The highest decision-making body of the Movement is the International Conference of the Red Cross and Red Crescent which meets every four years. Participating are the ICRC, the Federation, internationally recognised National Societies and governments signatories of the Geneva Conventions.

ICRC Finance
The ICRC is funded through voluntary contributions from Governments and National Societies. In 2010, the IFRC received 500 million Swiss francs in voluntary contributions . Total income was 556 million Swiss francs. Total restricted expenditure for 2010 amounted to 472 million Swiss francs. The operating expenditure of the Secretariat amounted to 63 million Swiss francs.

The International Federation of Red Cross and Red Crescent Societies
The Federation helps co-ordinate relief efforts for victims of natural disasters and promotes the humanitarian activities of National Red Cross and Red Crescent Societies. It was founded in 1919 in Paris, as the League of Red Cross Societies in the aftermath of the First World War. Since 1939 its secretariat has been in Geneva, Switzerland.

The role of the Federation is to represent National Societies internationally; to organise and co-ordinate international disaster relief operations and preparedness planning; develop and support health and care in the community, especially around AIDS and infectious diseases; and promote the Red Cross and Red Crescent Principles and Values.

The Federation's General Assembly in 1999 adopted Strategy 2010, the culmination of two years of consultation with the National Societies. This Strategy guides the Federation's actions, defining three directions for the Federation and its member National Societies to follow in order to achieve their common mission to improve the lives of vulnerable people by mobilizing the power of humanity. The three directions are:

- National Society programmes focused on the areas where they can add greatest value: promotion of humanitarian values and principles, disaster response, disaster preparedness, health and care in the community.
- well functioning National Societies that can mobilize support and carry out their humanitarian mission, contributing to the building of civil society.
- working together effectively through programme co-operation, long-term partnerships and funding, as well as more active advocacy.

The International Federation supports some 250 million people per year through its programmes.

International Federation Finance
The Federation's primary source of funds comes from voluntary contributions for relief operations and development. The remainder is provided by voluntary contributions to the Strategic Work Plan, investment income and statutory contributions paid by National Societies. Income for 2006 was CHF 62 million and operational expenditure was CHF 43 million.

Structure of the Federation
The General Assembly of all member National Societies meets every two years and is the supreme body of the Federation. It is responsible for appointing the Secretary General, who directs the Secretariat and its delegations. The Governing Board meets twice yearly. The Board comprises the Federation's President and Vice Presidents, representatives from elected member Societies and the chairman of the Finance Commission. The Federation has a Secretariat staff of over 230 employees of 50 nationalities in Geneva and maintains some 200 delegates in the field.

National Societies
There are currently 187 National Red Cross and Red Crescent Societies around the world. National Societies embody the work and the principles of the International Red Cross and Red Crescent Movement. They provide relief and development activities tailored to each country's specific needs and act as auxiliaries to their country's public authorities by providing a range of services - from disaster relief to social assistance to first aid courses. In order to gain Federation membership, each National Society is required to adhere to a 10 point Code of Conduct.

INTER-GOVERNMENTAL ORGANISATIONS

Emblems

The International Red Cross and Red Crescent Movement currently have three emblems in use: the red cross, the red crescent and the red crystal. National societies must use one of the emblems. The Red Cross and Red Crescent have been used as universally recognized symbols of assistance for victims of natural disasters and armed conflicts for decades. In 2005 a third symbol, the red crystal, was added for those National Societies that do not wish to use either the red cross or the red crescent. All the emblems have the same international status and offer the same level of protection under international humanitarian law.

Strategy 2020

Strategy 2020 is the 10-year plan for the International Federation of Red Cross and Red Crescent Societies (IFRC). It was adopted in 2009 after extensive consulation within the International Movement and its external partners. It has three strategic aims and three enabling actions for the IFRC and its member National Societies in order to achieve a common vision of preventing and alleviating human suffering through humanitarian actions, thus promoting human dignity and world peace.

The strategic aims are:
1. Save lives, protect livelihoods, and strengthen recovery from disasters and crises
2. Enable healthy and safe living

3. Promote social inclusion and a culture of non-violence and peace

These aims will be delivered by building and maintaining strong National Red Cross and Red Crescent Societies, use of humanitarian diplomacy, and effective functioning of the International Federation.

President, International Federation of Red Cross and Red Crescent Societies: Tadateru Konoé
Secretary-General, International Federation of Red Cross and Red Crescent Societies: Mr Bekele Gelata
President, International Committee of the Red Cross: Peter Maurer

International Federation of Red Cross and Red Crescent Societies, Box 372, 17, Chemin des Crêts, CH 1211 Geneva 19, Switzerland. Tel: +41 (0)22 730 4222, fax: +41 (0)22 733 0395, e-mail: secretariat@ifrc.org, URL: http://www.ifrc.org

International Committee of the Red Cross, 19 avenue de la Paix, CH 1202 Geneva, Switzerland. Tel: +41 (0)22 734 60 01, fax: +41 (0)22 733 2057, URL: http://www.icrc.org, http://www.redcross.int

INTER-PARLIAMENTARY UNION

The Inter-Parliamentary Union is an international organisation that brings together the parliaments of sovereign States. As such it is the sole organisation representing the legislative branch of government on a global scale. There are currently 155 members and nine associate members.

The mission of the IPU, as defined in Article 1 of its Statutes, is to strive for peace and co-operation among peoples and for the firm establishment of representative institutions. Within this mandate, the organisation works to strengthen parliamentary democracy throughout the world.

The IPU holds two assemblies each year. These are large conferences bringing together hundreds of MPs to discuss the most salient issues on the international agenda. The assemblies form the backdrop for parliamentary diplomacy.

Part of the IPU's work is to invigorate and defend representative institutions. Its Committee on the Human Rights of Parliamentarians takes up cases of breaches of individual MPs' rights, from unlawful revocation of parliamentary privilege to murder. The IPU also helps fledgling parliaments with technical assistance.

The Meeting of Women Parliamentarians was established in 1978 and brings together nearly 150 women parliamentarians from around 100 countries, who discuss topics relating to the status of women. Women MPs are in a small minority, and the IPU runs a programme of seminars designed to advance the interests of women politicians throughout the world.

The United Nations granted observer status to the organisation in 2002. Co-operation agreements have been signed between IPU and FAO, UNDP, UNESCO and ILO.

The IPU strategy for 2012-2017 is titled 'Better parliaments, stronger democracy'.

Structure

The organs of the IPU are the plenary Assembly (with its three Standing Committees on international peace and security; sustainable development, financing and trade; and democracy and human rights), the Governing Council (governing body), Executive Committee (12 members), Study Committees, The Meeting of Women Parliamentarians and the permanent Secretariat under a Secretary General. The President of the IPU is elected for a term of three years; he is also ex-officio member and President of the Executive Committee.

Budget

The IPU is financed by its members out of public funds. The budget for 2013 is based on a gross-operating expenditure of CHF 13.6 million. Existing member contributions were frozen at the 2012 level. New member contributions are expected to amount to CHF 50,000 in 2013 and 2014. Voluntary contributions and grants was expected to amount to CHF 1.5 million.

President of the Inter-Parliamentary Union: Dr Abdelwahad Radi
Secretary General: Anders B. Johnsson (page 1450)

Inter-Parliamentary Union, 5 Chemin du Pommier, Case postale 330, CH-1218 Le Grand-Saconnex, Geneva, Switzerland. Tel: +41 (0) 22 919 4150, fax: +41 (0) 22 919 4160, e-mail: postbox@mail.ipu.org, URL: http://www.ipu.org

ISLAMIC DEVELOPMENT BANK

Established in 1973 and formally opened in 1975, the Islamic Development Bank fosters the development and social progress of its member countries and Muslim communities in accordance with the principles of Shari'ah (Islamic Law).

Function

- To participate in equity capital and grant loans for productive projects and enterprises;
- to provide financial assistance to member countries; to establish and operate special funds for specific purposes - including a fund for assistance to Muslim communities in non-member countries;
- to assist in the promotion of foreign trade, especially in capital goods;
- to provide technical assistance to member countries and extend training facilities for personnel engaged in development activities in Muslim countries.

Present membership consists of 56 countries and is limited to members of the Organisation of the Islamic Conference.

The headquarters are in Jeddah, with regional offices in Morocco, Malaysia, Kazakhstan and Senegal.

President: H.E. Dr. Ahmad Mohamed Ali Al Madani (page 1374)

Islamic Development Bank, P.O. Box 5925, Jeddah 21432, Saudi Arabia. Tel: +966 2 636 1400, fax: +966 2 636 6871, URL: http://www.isdb.org

LATIN AMERICAN AND CARIBBEAN ECONOMIC SYSTEM (SELA)

Established on 17 October 1975, the Latin American and Caribbean Economic System is a regional intergovernmental organisation whose main aims are to achieve common strategies for the Latin American and Caribbean region on economic issues when dealing with the international community and to foster co-operation and integration among the countries of the region.

Membership
There are currently 28 member states: Argentina, Bahamas, Barbados, Belize, Bolivia, Brazil, Colombia, Costa Rica, Cuba, Chile, Dominican Republic, Ecuador, El Salvador Grenada, Guatemala, Guyana, Haiti, Honduras, Jamaica, Mexico, Nicaragua, Panama, Paraguay, Peru, Suriname, Trinidad & Tobago, Uruguay and Venezuela.

Activities
In the area of regional and international co-operation, SELA promotes the exchange of information about the implementation of public policies and projects that may lead to optimum use of official financial aid for development as well as improved technical co-operation among developing countries (TCDC). With the support of bilateral and multilateral agencies, SELA promotes the implementation of programmes aimed at strengthening of regional and sub-regional integration, particularly in Central America and the Caribbean.

SELA carries out studies of intra-regional trade and investments, and analyses co-operation programmes among Latin American and Caribbean countries. The organisation follows the progress of other regional integration organisations such as MERCOSUR, the Andean Community, CARICOM, and the Association of Caribbean States.

In the international arena, SELA aims to raise mutual awareness, take advantage of business and investment opportunities and increase international co-operation with countries outside the Latin American and Caribbean region. It studies the trends and negotiations in multilateral trade.

Structure
The Latin American Council is the principal decision-making body of SELA. Each member state sends one representative to the Council, which meets annually and is responsible for establishing the general policies and work programme of the organisation.

The Permanent Secretariat is the administrative body of SELA and is headed by a permanent secretary who is elected by the Council every four years.

The Action Committees are set up when two or more countries are interested in promoting joint programmes in specific areas. These Committees are either dissolved upon accomplishing their objectives or they become Permanent Bodies of SELA.

Permanent Secretary (2013-17): Roberto Guarnieri (page 1434)

Permanent Secretariat Latin American and Caribbean Economic System, Torre Europa, Fourth floor, Campo Alegre, av Francisco de Miranda, Caracas 1060- Venezuela. Tel: +58 212 955 7111, fax: +58 212 951 5292, e-mail: diffusion@sela.org, URL: http://www.sela.org

LATIN AMERICAN INTEGRATION ASSOCIATION (ALADI)

ALADI unites 12 countries covering 20 million sq. km. and more than 510 million people. It was established in 1980 with the Montevideo Treaty which provides its global legal framework. It follows the general principles of pluralism, convergence, flexibility, differential treatment and multiplicity.

Its aim is to create a Latin-American common market including the creation of an area of economic preferences in the region, through three mechanisms:
- regional tariff preference granted to products originating in the member countries
- regional scope agreement, among member countries
- partial scope agreements, between two or more countries
Agreements may cover tariff relief, trade promotion, agricultural trade, customs, finance, health co-operation; environmental protection, tourism, and many other fields.

Membership is open to all Latin-American countries. It currently has 13 members. The founding members were: Argentina, Bolivia, Brazil, Chile, Colombia, Cuba, Ecuador, Mexico, Paraguay, Peru, Uruguay and Venezuela. Panama joined in 2012.

Secretary-General: Carlos Alberto Alvarez (Argentina)

Latin American Integration Association (ALADI), Cebollati 1461, CP 11200, Montevideo, Uruguay. Tel: +598 2 410 1121, fax: +598 2 419 0649, e-mail: sgaladi@aladi.org, URL: http://www.aladi.org

LEAGUE OF ARAB STATES

The Pact establishing the League of Arab States was signed at Cairo on March 22, 1945.

The movement towards Arab unity existed long before World War I. However the peace settlement of 1919, placing a great part of the Arab world - Syria, Lebanon, Palestine, Transjordan and Iraq - temporarily under British and French control, thwarted the ambitions of Arab nationalists. In the aftermath of World War II, these mandated territories, excluding Palestine, attained independence. While the war was still in progress, a conference of Arab states met in Alexandria, Egypt. Representatives of the governments of Egypt, Syria, Lebanon, Transjordan, Iraq, Saudi Arabia and Yemen took part in the conference. A delegation representing the Palestinians also attended. The conference resulted in the birth of the protocols that formed the basis of the Pact of the Arab League.

The following year the Pact which established the Arab League's framework was signed by representatives of Egypt, Lebanon, Syria, Transjordan, Iraq, Saudi Arabia and Yemen. It laid down the principle of joint Arab action while maintaining the individual sovereignty of its member states. The purpose of the League is to bring about a closer union among the various Arab states and to foster political and economic co-operation. In the spirit of this union an agreement for collective defence and economic co-operation was signed in Cairo in 1950.

The constitution of the Arab League stipulates that other Arab countries may join on attaining independence. Hence, the League is currently comprised of 21 members - Algeria, Bahrain, Comoros, Djibouti, Egypt, Iraq, Jordan, Kuwait, Lebanon, Libya, Mauritania, Morocco, Oman, Palestine, Qatar, Saudi Arabia, Somalia, Sudan, Tunisia, the United Arab Emirates and Yemen. Syria's membership was suspended following the recent uprising and government response. In 2003, Eritrea joined the League as an observer. Brazil, India and Venezuela are also observer states.

In January 2011 the Arab League warned regional leaders to take note of the political upheaval in Tunisia, saying its issues were common to all Arab states. In Febuary, it banned Libya from attending meetings after several hundred citizens were killed in an anti-government uprising. Syria was suspended as a member in November 2011 after it refused to allow Arab League monitors into the country to monitor the situation.

Structure
The Council of the League is the highest executive body representing all the member states. Its task is to adopt resolutions within the context of joint Arab action and to oversee that they are implemented. It meets in ordinary session twice a year in March and in September and in extraordinary session whenever it is deemed necessary.

The Treaty for Joint Defence and Economic Co-operation provided for the establishment of a Defence Council, formed of the foreign and defence ministers of member states. The same treaty also provided for the establishment of an Economic Council, which developed into an Economic and Social Council.

Specialised ministerial councils hold regular meetings and draw up common policies for the regulation and advancement of co-operation in various fields.

The General Secretariat is in charge of implementing the Council's resolutions. It is headed by the Secretary General who is appointed by the General Council for a five-year term of office, subject to renewal. He is helped by Assistant Secretaries General (recommended by the Secretary General and approved by the Arab League Council).

The Secretariat divides its work among many departments which include: Arab Affairs, Economic Affairs, International Affairs, Palestine Affairs, Legal Affairs, Social and Cultural Affairs, Information and Administrative and Financial Affairs. The General Secretariat has

INTER-GOVERNMENTAL ORGANISATIONS

representative offices abroad, in Washington, Bonn, London, Paris, Rome, Ottawa, Madrid, Buenos Aires, Brasilia, New Delhi, Tokyo, Dakar and Lagos. It also has permanent delegations attached to the UN in both New York and Geneva.

Affiliated to the Arab League are various specialised agencies such as: the Arab Organisation for Mineral Resources, the Arab Monetary Fund, the Arab Satellite Communications Organisation, the Arab Academy of Maritime Transport, the Arab Bank for Economic Development in Africa, the Arab League Educational Cultural & Scientific Organisation and the Council of Arab Economic Unity.

Secretary General: Dr Nabil El Araby (page 1420)

League of Arab States, P.O. Box 11642, Maidane Al-Tahrir, Cairo, Egypt. Tel: +20 2 575 2966 / 575 0511, fax: +20 2 574 0331/ 577 9546, URL: http://www.lasportal.org

MERCOSUR

Mercosur is an economic integration project whose participants are Argentina, Brazil, Paraguay and Uruguay. Bolivia, Chile, Colombia, Ecuador and Peru currently have associate member status, and Venezuela is awaiting ratification of full membership; this was turned down in 2009. The bloc currently represents some 263 million people. Mercosur was initiated in 1991, by the Treaty of Asunción. This was later amended and updated in 1994, with the Treaty of Ouro Preto.

Its main objectives are the integration of member states through the movement of goods and services, the establishment of common external taxes as well as a common trade policy, the coordination of macroeconomic policy, and legal harmonisation where relevant.

Since its inception, Mercosur has become a stabilising factor in the region; political links have grown through the network of trade relations, and tendencies towards regional fragmentation have been minimized. The member states recognise that strength of democratic institutions is essential for integration to progress, and that regional peace is also an essential element in Mercosur's development. The member governments have agreed to further cooperate on security and defence issues, and to consolidate international agreements on nuclear disarmament and the non-proliferation of nuclear weapons.

Structure
The Council of the Common Market is the highest policy making body of the organisation. It seeks to fulfil the objectives established in the Treaty of Asuncion and the final implementation of the Common Market. Longer term plans include a free-trade bank for the region and the creation of a Mercosur development bank.

The Common Market Group is the executive body of Mercosur. Together with the Trade Commission, it is charged with overseeing the implementation of the common commercial policy. The Joint Parliamentary Commission is the representative body of the parliaments of the member states, and the Social and Economic Advisory Forum represents the economic and social sectors. The Administrative Secretariat of Mercosur gives operational support to the organisation and is headquartered in Montevideo, Uruguay.

The founding of the Mercosur Parliament was agreed at the December 2004 presidential summit. It began meeting in 2007 in Uruguay.

The presidency of Mercosur rotates on a six-monthly-basis between the group members.

Secretariat of Mercosur, Dr. Luis Piera 1992, Edif. Mercosur, C.P. 11.200, Montevideo, Uruguay. Tel: +598 2 412 9024, fax: +598 2 410 0958, e-mail: secretariat@mercosur.org.uy, URL: http://www.mercosur.int/

NEW PARTNERSHIP FOR AFRICA'S DEVELOPMENT (NEPAD)

NEPAD was created to address the current challenges of Africa including increasing poverty, Africa's undevelopment and its marginalization. The Organisation of African Unity (now the African Union) gave a mandate to the five initiating Heads of State (Algeria, Egypt, Nigeria, Senegal and South Africa). The 37th Summit of the OAU in July 2001 formally adopted the resulting strategic framework document.

In February 2010, the 14th AU Assembly established the NEPAD Planning and Coordinating Agency (NEPAD Agency) as a technical body of the AU to replace the NEPAD Secretariat. The NEPAD Agency is a key outcome of the integration of NEPAD into the AU

Purpose
The primary objectives of NEPAD are:
- To eradicate poverty;
- Sustained growth and development for African countries;
- Stop any marginalisation of Africa and ensure it is fully integrated into the global economy;
- To speed up the empowerment of women;
- To integrate Africa into the global economy.

There are six main programme areas: agriculture and food security; climate change and national resource management; regional integration and infrastructure; human development; economic and corporate governance; and cross-cutting issues including gender, capacity building and ICT.

Structure
NEPAD is a programme of the African Union. The NEPAD governance structures are: The Assembly of the African Union; The NEPAD Heads of State & Government Orientation Committee (HSGOC); and the NEPAD Steering Committee (SC).

The NEPAD Heads of State and Government Implementation Committee (HSGIC) was established through the Declaration of the 2001 OAU Summit in Lusaka, Zambia. In February 2010 it became the NEPAD Heads of State and Government Orientation Committee (HSGOC). The HSGOC provides leadership, sets policies and prioirties. Current membership stands at 20: Algeria, Benin, Cameroon, Congo, DRC, Egypt, Ethiopia, Gabon, Lesotho, Libya, Madagascar, Malawi, Mali, Namibia, Nigeria, Rwanda, Senegal, South Africa, Sudan, Tunisia.

The NEPAD Agency is overseen by the NEPAD HSGOC Chairperson, currently H.E. Dr Jean Ping, Chair of the African Union Commission.

NEPAD HSGOC Chairperson: H.E. Dr Jean Ping (page 1496), Chair of the African Union Commission.

NEPAD, NPCA, P.O. Box 1234, Halfway House, Midrand 1685, South Africa. Tel: +27 11 256 3600, fax: +27 11 313 3684, URL: http://www.nepad.org

NORDIC COUNCIL AND NORDIC COUNCIL OF MINISTERS

The Nordic Council is a forum for co-operation between the Parliaments and Governments of the Nordic countries. The Council was set up in 1952. Co-operation between the countries is based on the 1962 Helsinki Treaty, in which the Nordic states undertook to preserve and further develop co-operation in legal, cultural, social, economic and communications spheres. 1971 saw the establishment of The Nordic Council of Ministers in which the Governments of the Nordic countries work together.

The Nordic region consists of Denmark, Finland, Iceland, Norway and Sweden with the autonomous territories of the Faeroes, Greenland and the Åland Islands. Its population totals about 24 million.

The Nordic countries constitute a free labour market. Laws and regulations have been introduced to facilitate co-operation in areas such as labour market, trade and communications, and resources are also co-ordinated in such sectors as energy and industry.

In addition, the Nordic countries work together on legislative issues, culture, research and education, and assume a shared responsibility for the environment. Decisions concerning foreign and security policy cannot be taken by joint Nordic bodies. However, to promote co-operation in specific areas, special agreements have been signed.

Nordic Council

The Nordic Council's functions are to take initiatives and press for action, follow up and give advice on matters involving co-operation between the Nordic countries. It has two types of members: those nominated by national Parliaments and those appointed from among members of Governments or the executive bodies of the autonomous territories. In all, 87 members are chosen by the Parliaments, as follows: Denmark (Folketing) 16, Faeroes (Lagting) 2, Greenland (Landsting) 2, Finland (Eduskunta/Riksdag) 18, Åland Islands (Landsting) 2, Iceland (Althing) 7, Norway (Storting) 20, Sweden (Riksdag) 20.

Political Organs of the Nordic Council

The Nordic Council's political organs are the Plenary Assembly, the Presidium and the standing committees.

Plenary Assembly

The Plenary Assembly consists of the 87 parliamentary members of the Council and some 80 Government representatives, and normally holds one session a year. It is the highest decision-making body of the Nordic Council. Among other things, it adopts recommendations and statements of opinion, determines the Nordic Council's Rules of Procedure, elects the Council's Presidium, decides on the number of standing committees and their spheres of responsibility, and fixes the place and date of the next session of the Council.

Presidium

The Nordic Council's Presidium consists of eleven MPs, and a president and vice-president. All countries and party group should be represented. The term is for one year and president and vice-president come from the host country. The Presidium looks after the day-to-day business of the Council during and between sessions. It makes decisions on consultation procedures and adopts the Council's budget.

Standing Committees

The Nordic Council has five specialist committees, a Control Committee and a Voting Committee. The committees are empowered to set up temporary sub-committees or working parties. The members, chairperson and deputy chairperson of the various committees are elected at the annual session of the Nordic Council and serve for the following calendar year. The committees are: Culture, Education and Training; Citizens' and Consumer Rights; Environment and Natural Resources Committee; Welfare Committee; Business & Industry Committee.

Nordic Council of Ministers

The Council of Ministers consists of one minister from each of the five countries. The executive bodies of the Faeroes, Greenland and the Åland Islands also send their representatives. Which ministers attend depend on the issues being discussed, e.g. the Ministers of Social Affairs for social matters. Each country appoints one of its ministers as Minister for Nordic Co-operation, whose primary responsibility is the activities of the Nordic Council of Ministers. The Council of Ministers leads the Nordic co-operation, submits proposals to the Nordic Council for its session and follows up the Council's recommendations, which lead to agreements, conventions and other joint measures. Unanimous decisions by the Nordic Council of Ministers are binding for the governments of the individual countries.

A thorough revision of Nordic co-operation and its institutional framework has been undertaken. The Council of Ministers wishes to promote Nordic co-operation within the financial scope available. The focus of this activity is related to the Nordic region and Europe, and in particular the Baltic republics and Eastern Europe. The Nordic region may play a special role in relation to co-operation with the countries around the Baltic sea, not least as regards the environment, resources and infrastructure.

Budget

The annual budget of the Council of Ministers is 900 million Danish Kroner and 30 million Danish Kroner for the Nordic Council. Denmark contributes 21.6 per cent, Finland 17.4 per cent, Iceland 1.2 per cent, Norway 28.1 per cent and Sweden 31.7 per cent. Approximately 25 institutions are funded by Nordic budget appropriations.

Information/Publications

The Information Department of the Nordic Council of Ministers is responsible for presenting the results of ongoing political co-operation within the framework of the two councils. A weekly newsletter is issued every Monday, and an international newsletter, Top of Europe, is issued monthly covering the Nordic co-operation. A substantial number of publications, studies, reports and statistics are published annually, most of which are available to the public through the internet (http://www.norden.org), and through National Commissioners.

Sweden holds the presidency of the Nordic Council for 2013.

Secretary General of Nordic Council of Ministers: Dagfinn Høybråten (page 1444) (Norway)

Nordic Council, Ved Stranden 18, 1061 Copenhagen K, Denmark. Tel: +45 3396 0400, e-mail: nordisk-rad@norden.org, URL: http://www.norden.org

Nordic Council of Ministers, Ved Stranden 18, 1061 Copenhagen K, Denmark. Tel: +45 3396 0200, e-mail: nmr@norden.org, URL: http://www.norden.org

NORTH AMERICAN FREE TRADE AGREEMENT (NAFTA)

The North American Free Trade Agreement (NAFTA) was signed on December 17 1992. The signatories are the United States, Mexico and Canada. Formal negotiations on the agreement were begun in June 1991. Legislation to implement the agreement was passed by Congress in 1993. The agreement came into operation on January 1 1994. NAFTA is the largest market in the world; a combined US, Mexican and Canadian economy of $17 trillion and more than 450 million people.

The aim of the agreement is to facilitate trade between the three countries. It sets rules for most services, including finance, accountancy, architecture, land transport, publishing, consulting, commercial services, education, environmental services, enhanced telecommunications, advertising, broadcasting, construction, tourism, engineering, health care, management and legal services. It excludes aviation, maritime and basic telecommunications.

The countries agreed to end tariffs on goods that qualified as North American items. This was carried out in a series of stages from immediate elimination to 15-year phaseout. The sectors covered include automobiles, textiles, agriculture, energy, finance, intellectual property and telecommunications. All duties and restrictions were finally eliminated, as scheduled, in 2008.

The agreement also affects other areas of the economy including:

Investment: The principles of national treatment and most-favoured nation treatment would apply to investments by enterprises in a NAFTA country, but country-specific exceptions would be made.

Cross-Border Trade in Services: the countries are prohibited from discriminating against service providers from another NAFTA country, but they are allowed to list exceptions to this rule to permit selective discrimination.

Land Transportation: Over a period of 10 years the participating countries opened their markets to cross-border bus and truck service and to investment in domestic bus and truck companies.

Emergency Action (Safeguards): If the Agreement were to cause a surge of imports that damaged a domestic industry the importing country could suspend its tariff elimination for a temporary period 3-4 years.

Secretariat

The NAFTA Secretariat is composed of a Canadian Section (Ottawa); Mexican Section (Mexico City) and the US Section (Washington DC). The Secretariat administers the NAFTA procedures to resolve trade disputes between national industries and governments in an impartial and timely manner. The Secretariat is accountable to the NAFTA Free Trade Commission which comprises the minister responsible for international trade in the three NAFTA partner countries.

NAFTA Secretariat, Room 2061, 14th St. & Constitution Ave, N.W., Washington, DC 20230, USA. Tel +1 202 482 5438, fax: +1 202 482 0148, e-mail: usa@nafta-sec-alena.org, URL: http://www.nafta-sec-alena.org

NORTH ATLANTIC TREATY ORGANIZATION (NATO)

The North Atlantic Alliance was established on the basis of the 1949 North Atlantic Treaty as a defensive political and military alliance of independent countries in accordance with the terms of the United Nations Charter. It provides common security for its members through cooperation and consultation in political, military and economic as well as scientific and other non-military fields. NATO is the organisation that enables the goals of the Alliance to be implemented.

Membership

There are 28 member states of NATO: Albania, Belgium, Bulgaria, Canada, Croatia, Czech Republic, Estonia, Denmark, France, Germany, Greece, Hungary, Iceland, Italy, Lativa, Lithuania, Luxembourg, the Netherlands, Norway, Poland, Portugal, Romania, Slovakia, Slovenia, Spain, Turkey, the United Kingdom, and the United States.

NATO's Membership Action Plan (MAP) is designed to assist aspiring countries meet NATO's standards and prepare for possible future membership. The former Yugoslav Republic of Macedonia has been participating since 1999. Montenegro was invited to join in 2009. Bosnia & Herzegovina was invited to join MAP in April 2010 subject to the country's government meeting defence requirements. NATO continues to maintain an open door policy.

Partnerships

The **North Atlantic Co-operation Council (NACC)** was established in December 1991 as the institutional framework for the Alliance's new partnership with the countries of Central and Eastern Europe and the states on the territory of the former Soviet Union. In 1997 the NACC was replaced by the Euro-Atlantic Partnership Council (EAPC). There are currently 50 EAPC member states: the 28 members of the Alliance, as well as Armenia, Austria, Azerbaijan, Belarus, Bosnia and Herzegovina, Finland, Georgia, Ireland, Kazakhstan, Kyrgyzstan, the former Yugoslav Republic of Macedonia, Malta, Moldova, Montenegro, Russia, Serbia, Sweden, Switzerland, Tajikistan, Turkmenistan, Ukraine and Uzbekistan. The role of the EAPC is to facilitate cooperation on security and related issues between the participating countries at all levels, to oversee the process of developing closer institutional ties as well as informal links between them and to act as the multilateral political framework for the Partnership for Peace (PfP) programme, established in 1994.

Consultations and cooperation with EAPC partners focus on such issues as: peacekeeping; defence planning; democratic concepts of civilian-military relations and democratic control of armed forces; civil/military co-ordination of air traffic management; and economic issues such as defence industry conversion. EAPC countries also participate in NATO's scientific, environmental and information programmes. EAPC activities are based on a two-year action plan.

The **Partnership for Peace (PfP)** promotes cooperation among the NATO allies and individual partner countries on a bilateral basis, through many security-related activities. There are currently 22 countries in the partnership. Bosnia & Herzegovina, Montenegro and Serbia have joined the Partnership, a first step towards their membership of NATO.

In 1997, in addition to Russian participation in the EAPC and the Partnership for Peace, a new basis for bilateral NATO-Russia cooperation was established with the signature of the NATO-Russia Founding Act and the creation of a NATO-Russia Permanent Joint Council. The Founding Act remains the basis for NATO-Russia relations, but in 2002 a new **NATO-Russia Council** replaced the former Permanent Joint Council, bringing the members of NATO and Russia together on the basis of the equality of all the participating countries.

A programme of special cooperation is also being pursued, in the context of **NATO's Mediterranean Dialogue**, with seven non-NATO Mediterranean countries (Algeria, Egypt, Israel, Jordan, Mauritania, Morocco and Tunisia). The Dialogue is based on the recognition of the importance of security in the Mediterranean area to the wider security of the Euro-Atlantic area. Its aim is to enhance security and stability and to contribute to a better understanding in the region of NATO goals and policies.

To date, four countries from the Gulf Co-operation Council have joined the **Istanbul Cooperation Initiative (IC)**: Bahrain, Qatar, Kuwait and the UAE.

NATO also provides a forum for active cooperation among its member states and partner countries in areas such as civil emergency planning and disaster relief. For example, the EADRCC also played a key role in coordinating humanitarian aid from NATO and partner countries to Kosovar refugees and assist neighbouring countries during the Kosovo conflict in 1999 and has been used on other occasions to coordinate support for EAPC member countries struck by earthquakes, major flooding, fires and other disasters.NATO is currently cooperating with Afghanistan, Australia, Iraq, Japan, Pakistan, REpublic of Korea, New Zealand and Mongolia.

NATO also co-operates with various international organizations including the UN, the EU and the OSCE.

Activities

With the demise of the Warsaw Pact and the end of the Cold War, the Atlantic Alliance began a process of fundamental transformation of its structures and policies, following the London (July 1990) and Rome (November 1991) Summits, to meet the new security challenges in Europe. These changes and innovations included a new Strategic Concept; a reduced and more flexible force structure; increased coordination and cooperation with other international institutions; active involvement, and in some cases a leadership role, in international peacekeeping operations; and intensive cooperation and consultation with the countries of Central and Eastern Europe and the former Soviet Union.

The Strategic Concept adopted at the 1991 Rome Summit outlined a broad approach to security based on dialogue and cooperation, as well as the maintenance of a collective defence capability; it brought together political and military elements of NATO's security policy, establishing cooperation with new partners in Central and Eastern Europe and the former Soviet Union as an integral part of the Alliance's strategy. The Concept, which was updated in 1999, provided for reduced dependence on nuclear weapons and introduced major changes in NATO's integrated military forces, including substantial reductions in their size and readiness, improvements in their mobility, flexibility and adaptability to different contingencies, greater use of multinational formations and the creation of a multinational Rapid Reaction Corps. Measures were also taken to streamline NATO's military command structure and to adapt the Alliance's defence planning arrangements and procedures. While the Alliance's primary role of providing for the collective security of its member nations remained unchanged, it also took on expanded tasks in the field of peace-keeping and peace-support operations. A further updating of the strategic concepts wasadelivered at the Lisbon Summit 2010 following consultation of a group of experts and members led by former US Secretary of State, Madeleine Albright.

These tasks include promoting security and stability throughout Europe, and playing a major role in response to UN requirements for support for crisis management and peacekeeping initiatives. To this end from 1992, NATO provided concrete support for UN peacekeeping efforts in the Balkans, drawing on its unique assets and capabilities, including its experience of political and military cooperation and training, its integrated military structure and its command and control facilities.

A NATO-led Implementation force (IFOR), including forces from many partner countries including Russia, was deployed to Bosnia-Herzegovina at the end of December 1995, to implement the military aspects of the Dayton Peace Agreement signed earlier that month. In December 1996, IFOR was replaced by a similar but smaller NATO-led Stabilisation Force (SFOR). SFOR concluded its work at the end of 2004 when responsibility for this operation was taken over by the European Union with NATO support, in accordance with detailed arrangements worked out between the two organisations for such eventualities under the Berlin Plus agreement of March 2003.

The North Atlantic Council authorised NATO air strikes on 23 March 1999, against strategic targets in the Federal Republic of Yugoslavia, with the aim of ending the repression of Kosovo Albanians by the Yugoslav government. The air strikes ended on 10 June 1999 following the agreement of the Yugoslav security forces to withdraw. On 12 June a NATO-led peacekeeping force (KFOR) was established in accordance with a UN mandate to lay the basis for future stability and reconstruction.

Russia suspended cooperation with NATO following the beginning of the air campaign initiated by the Alliance. However, when the air campaign ended, Russia agreed to contribute significant forces to the NATO-led Kosovo Force (KFOR). Regular ministerial meetings of the Permanent Joint Council between Russia and NATO were resumed.

Marking NATO's 50th anniversary, the Washington Summit in April 1999 consolidated the changes that have taken place in NATO in the 1990s. These include: the enlargement process; the reshaping of the Alliance's military structures to enable it to handle new roles in the field of crisis management, peace-keeping and peace-support; and the strengthening of the European role in security matters.

On 12 September 2001, following the attacks on Washington and New York, NATO invoked Article 5 of the North Atlantic Treaty for the first time, declaring that the attack against the United States was considered an attack against all members of the Alliance.

These events, and the universal threat they represented, acted as a catalyst for the opening of a new chapter in NATO's relations with Russia. Since May 2002, NATO countries and Russia have worked together in the framework of a new NATO-Russia Council, which serves as a forum in which they seek to identify and pursue opportunities for joint action, in areas of common concern, as equal partners. The relationship has had further difficulties: Russia has expressed concern over the NATO expansion of 2004 which mean that NATO's reach extended to its borders. Relations deterioriated after the Rusian-Georgian war of August 2008 but in March 2009 NATO announced that it was to resume high level contact with Russia.

Further major actions were taken in 2003 and 2004 to transform and strengthen the civilian and military structures of the Alliance in line with today's much-changed security environment. In particular, NATO partner countries have undertaken major steps to improve and adapt their military capabilities in order to address new challenges including the fight against terrorism and the proliferation of weapons of mass destruction.

The Alliance has also taken on new operational tasks including, in August 2003, the leadership of the International Security Assistance Force (ISAF) in Afghanistan, previously led by individual nations, and now the NATO's largest ever force in operation; and in July 2004, the establishment of a NATO Training Mission to assist the interim Iraqi government in the training and equipment of national security forces. At the NATO Istanbul Summit Meeting in June 2004, other initiatives were also taken including the expansion of the role of ISAF in order to assist the government in extending its authority beyond Kabul to the regions of Afghanistan outside the capital; the enhancement of the Alliance's existing Mediterranean Dialogue and the launching of a Istanbul Cooperation Initiativein 2004 inviting contacts and cooperation with interested countries in the broader Middle East region. To date, Bahrain, Qatar, Kuwait and the UAE have joined the ICI. On 5 October 2006, in an important step for NATO; the command of the international military forces in eastern Afghanistan was taken by NATO-ISAF from the US-led Coalition.

Libya

On March 27, NATO Allies decided to take on the whole military operation in Libya under United Nations Security Council Resolution 1973. The purpose of Operation Unified Protector was to protect civilians and civilian-populated areas under threat of attack. NATO implemented all military aspects of the UN Resolution. OUP ended successfully on 31 October 2011.

Active NATO operations as of April 2013

Operation Active Endeavour: This maritime operation, launched in October 2001 amid the aftermath of 9/11, aims to detect and deter terrorist activity in the Mediterranean. Initially targeted at the eastern Mediterranean region, the operation was extended to the whole of the Mediterranean in March 2004.

Kosovo Force

KFOR is a NATO-led multinational peacekeeping force established under the auspices of the UN, in accordance with UN Security Council Resolution 1244 of 10 June 1999. Following the declaration of independence on 17 February 2008, it was agreed that KFOR shall remain in Kosovo unless the Security Council decides otherwise. KFOR will continue to co-operate closely with the population of Kosovo, the UN, the EU and other international actors wherever appropriate. There are currently some 5,500 troops from KSFOR deployed in Kosovo.

African Union (AU) Assistance

At the request of the AU, NATO has provided support to the AU Mission in Sudan. It is also providing assistance to the AU Mission in Somalia and capacity-building support to the AU's long-term peace-keeping capabilities, in particular the African Standby Force.

International Security Assistance Force

This is a UN-mandated international force created to assist the Afghan authorities in establishing a secure and stable environment in Afghanistan. NATO has been leading ISAF since August 2003. The ISAF force is NATO's largest military operation. The number of ISAF troops grew from the initial 5,000 to more than 130,000 troops from many countries, including all 28 NATO member nations. As of April 2013, there were approximately 102,00 troops from 50 different countries. The ISAF mission is due to end in 2014.

NATO's objective in Afghanistan is to provide security in the country, preventing it from being a safe haven for terrorists. The NATO-led International Security Assistance Force (ISAF) undertake security operations and train the Afghan National Security Forces. The aim is for the Afghan Security Forces to have full responsibility for security by 2014. NATO's commitment to Afghanistan will remain beyond transition.

Operation Ocean Shield

Focuses on at-sea counter-piracy operations off the Horn of Africa. Approved on 17 August 2009 by the North Atlantic Council, this operation is contributing to international efforts to combat piracy in the area. It is also offering, to regional states that request it, assistance in developing their own capacity to combat piracy activities.

Members of the North Atlantic Council

Secretary General of NATO: Anders Fogh Rasmussen (page 1500)
Deputy Secretary General: Sergio Balanzino

The Military Committee

Chairman: Gen. Knud Bartels

The NATO Strategic Commanders

Supreme Allied Commander Europe (SACEUR): Admiral James G. Stavridis (US)
Supreme Allied Commander Transformation (SACT): General Jean-Paul Paloméros (France)

North Atlantic Treaty Organization, Blvd. Leopold III, B 1110 Brussels, Belgium. Tel: +32 (0)2 707 4111, fax: +32 (0)2 707 4117, e-mail: natodoc@hq.nato.int, URL: http://www.nato.int

ORGANISATION FOR ECONOMIC CO-OPERATION AND DEVELOPMENT (OECD)

The Organisation for Economic Co-operation and Development is principally a forum for discussion, development and refinement of social and economic policies. Its 34 member states produce over 75 per cent of world trade, and donate over 96 per cent of all development assistance.

The OECD was formed on 30 September 1961, after ratification of a convention signed on 14 December 1960. The Organisation succeeded the OEEC (Organisation for European Economic Co-operation), which was limited to European countries and founded in 1948 to administer American aid offered under the Marshall Plan and to undertake a joint effort for European economic recovery from the effects of WWII.

As a result of the reconstitution of the Organisation, Canada and the United States, formerly Associated countries, became full members, while the Organisation's objectives were enlarged, notably by including action in favour of the developing world. Japan, Finland, Australia and New Zealand joined in 1964, 1969, 1971, and 1973 respectively. Mexico joined in 1994, the Czech Republic in 1995, Hungary, Korea and Poland in 1996, the Slovak Republic in 2000 and Chile, Slovenia, Israel and Estonia in 2010. The OECD's Members are now: Australia, Austria, Belgium, Canada, Chile, Czech Republic, Denmark, Estonia, Finland, France, Germany, Greece, Hungary, Iceland, Ireland, Israel, Italy, Japan, Korea, Luxembourg, Mexico, Netherlands, New Zealand, Norway, Poland, Portugal, Slovak Republic, Slovenia, Spain, Sweden, Switzerland, Turkey, United Kingdom, and the United States. The Commission of the European Communities generally takes part in the work of the Organisation.

The aims of the Organisation are:
(1) to promote economic and social welfare throughout the OECD area by assisting its Member Governments in the formulation of policies designed to this end and by co-ordinating these policies;
(2) to contribute to the sound and harmonious development of the world economy and improve the lot of the developing countries, particularly the poorest.

Recent Developments

In May 2007, OECD countries agreed to invite Chile, Estonia, Israel, Russia and Slovenia to open discussions for membership of the Organisation and offered enhanced engagement, with a view to possible membership, to Brazil, China, India, Indonesia and South Africa. At the G8 Summit held in Heiligendamm in June 2007, the G8 Heads of State and Government decided to embark on an active dialogue with the emerging economies (Brazil, China, India, Mexico and South Africa). In December 2008, the approval of so-called road maps marked the start of accession talks with Chile, Estonia, Israel, Russia and Slovenia. Chile joined in May 2010, Slovenia in July 2010, Israel in September 2010 and Estonia in December 2010.

OECD is in the process of reforming its management and is looking at making OECD a more effective instrument of international co-operation. Its Paris headquarters have been renovated and a new conference centre has been built.

Structure

The supreme body of OECD is the Council on which each of the 31 Member countries is represented by a Permanent Representative having the rank of an ambassador. It meets regularly at Official level under the chairmanship of the Secretary-General to develop general directives on the work to be undertaken and once a year, at Ministerial level, when the Ministers of Foreign Affairs, Economics, Finance and Trade address the most prominent problems and set work priorities for the following year. The Council is responsible for all matters of general policy and may establish subsidiary bodies as required to achieve the objectives of the Organisation. Normally the Organisation works through informal consensus. The Council may, however, take formal 'Decisions' requiring unanimity which are binding for all Member Governments. The Council is assisted by the Executive Committee (open to all member countries), whose general task is to prepare the work of the Council. Apart from its regular meetings, the Executive Committee meets several times a year in 'Special Sessions' attended by very senior government officials.

The major part of the OECD's work is prepared and carried out in numerous specialised bodies, called either Committees or Working Parties, of which there are approximately two hundred. All Members are represented by these bodies. Committees normally reach decisions by consensus and each country's position is given equal weight. Some of the Committees meet occasionally at Ministerial level.

The OECD also has a Secretariat, a group of 700 eminent specialists whose function is to research and gather facts which they compare and analyse in order to be able to forecast changes in an extensive range of spheres. The Secretariat is headed by the Secretary-General who has four deputies.

Special bodies have been set up within the framework of the Organisation, namely: Africa Partnership Forum; Financial Action Task Force; Heiligendamm Dialogue Process Support unit; the International Energy Agency; the Nuclear Energy Agency; the Development Centre; Partnership of Democratic Governance Advisory unit; Sahel and West Africa Club and the International Transport Forum.

The various Committees and bodies are, as a rule, composed of civil servants coming either from capitals or from Permanent Delegations to the OECD which are established as normal diplomatic missions and are headed by ambassadors. They are assisted by an international Secretariat, independent of any national government and headed by the Secretary-General. Approximately 40,000 senior officials come to OECD committee meetings from national administrations each year to request, review and contribute to work undertaken by the OECD secretariat.

Mission

OECD brings together the governments of countries committed to democracy and the market economy from around the world to:
- Support sustainable economic growth
- Increase employment
- Raise living standards
- Maintain financial stability
- Assist other countries' economic development
- Contribute to growth in world trade

Activities

OECD uses its wealth of information on a broad range of topics to help governments foster prosperity and fight poverty through economic growth and financial stability. It makes sure that environmental implications of economic and social development are taken into account.

INTER-GOVERNMENTAL ORGANISATIONS

The main organ for the consideration and direction of economic policy among the Member countries is the Economic Department. OECD's work is based on monitoring of events in member countries as well as outside the OECD area, and includes regular forecasts of short and medium-term economic developments. The OECD Secretariat collects and analyses data, after which committees discuss policy regarding this information, the Council makes decisions and recommendations to governments.

Relations with other international Organisations
Under a Protocol signed at the same time as the OECD Convention, the European Commission generally takes part in the work of the Organisation. EFTA may also send representatives to OECD meetings. Formal Relations exist with a number of other international organisations, including the ILO, FAO, IMF, IBRD, UNCTAD, IAEA and the Council of Europe. A few non-governmental organisations have been granted consultative status, notably the Business and Advisory Committee to the OECD (BIAC) and the Trade Union Advisory Committee to the OECD (TUAC). The OECD also maintains close relationships with parlimentatians in member countries, mainly through its close and long-standing links with the Council of Europe and its parliamentary Assembly.

Budget
It is OECD's 34 member countries who finance the work of the Secretariat. The OECD does not dispense money. The Council decides on the size of the budget and the amount that each member country contributes towards it, which is calculated according to the weight of its economy, the United States being the biggest contributor (22 per cent). Countries may also make additional voluntary donations for particular programmes or projects. The OECD's budget for 2013 is €347 million. Unlike the World Bank or the International Monetary Fund, OECD does not dispense grants or make loans.

Publications
OECD provides a considerable number of publications on a wide variety of subjects in the form of printed publications, microfiches, and electronic publications. The list of publications may also be accessed at http://www.oecd.org/publications. Some 250 titles are published each year.

Secretary-General: Angel Gurría (page 1435)
Deputy Secretaries-General: Richard Boucher (page 1392), Pier Carlo Padoan, Rintaro Tamaki, Yves Leterme (page 1463)

Organisation for Economic Co-operation and Development, 2 rue André-Pascal, 75775 Paris Cédex 16, France. Tel: +33 (0)1 45 24 82 00, fax: +33 (0)1 45 24 85 00, URL: http://www.oecd.org

ORGANISATION OF EASTERN CARIBBEAN STATES (OECS)

The Organisation of Eastern Caribbean States (OECS) was established on June 18, 1981 when seven Eastern Caribbean countries signed the Treaty of Basseterre, agreeing to promote unity and solidarity among members.

The principal objectives of the OECS are to promote co-operation among the Member States and to defend their sovereignty, territorial integrity and independence; to assist the Member States in the realisation of their obligations and responsibilities to the international community; to establish and maintain whatever possible arrangements for joint overseas representation and common services; to promote economic integration among Member States and to pursue these aims through discussion of questions of common concern and by agreement on common action.

Activities
OECS is currently running several projects:
- Caribbean Culture and Internet: this project seeks to establish an online network involving over 50 cultural organisations.
- Health Sector Reform Project: established with the help of the French Government to strengthen the Ministries of Health, re-organise health systems, improve quality and facilitate regional sharing of health services.
- Judiciary and Legal Reform Project: to strengthen the role of the legal and judicial system in providing a sustainable and enabling environment for social and economic development.
- Telecommunications Reform Project (TELECOMS): this is to address the need for competition in the telecommunications sector which is recognised as being a critical element for economic diversification.
- Trade Policy Assistance Project: this project is funded by the Canadian International Development Agency (CIDA). It seeks to strengthen the capacity of the OECS to participate fully and compete in the global economy.

A new treaty, the Treaty of Basseterre, to establish the OECS Economic Union was ratified on 18 June 2010. The organisation's aim is to assist its members to respond to today's fast-changing economic environment.

Organisation Structure
The OECS is administered by a Central Secretariat located on Morne Fortune, Castries, Saint Lucia. The Secretariat is headed by the Director General who is responsible to the Authority. Over the years several subsidiary and autonomous institutions have been created.

The Islands share a single currency, the Eastern Caribbean Dollar ($2.70 ECD = 1 USD). The operation of the currency is overseen by the Eastern Caribbean Central Bank, the monetary authority for the seven OECS governments and the government of Anguilla (The British Virgin Islands uses the US Dollar as their de facto currency).

The Islands also share a common Supreme Court: The Eastern Caribbean Supreme Court, with its two divisions, the High Court and the Court of Appeal. The Supreme Court is headed by the Chief Justice. High Court judges are based in each Member State, but the judges of the Court of Appeal are resident in Saint Lucia and travel to each territory to hear appeals from the High Court. Final appeals go to the Privy Council in the UK.

The functions of the Organisation are co-ordinated by the Secretariat, under the direction and management of the Director General. The Director is responsible to the Authority, which is the highest organ of the organisation. The Authority comprises the Heads of Government (Prime Ministers of the independent countries as well as the Chief Ministers and Premier of the non-independent countries) whose policy decisions direct the work of the Organisation as required. The chairmanship of the Authority changes every year, rotating alphabetically by country. The OECS Authority meets twice yearly, and from time to time in Special Session as and when required. There are four main divisions in the Secretariat: Division of the Office of the Director General, Social and Sustainable Development Division, Corporate Services Division and Economic Affairs Division. These four Divisions oversee the strategic direction of the Organisation, as well as the work of a number of specialised institutions, work units or projects located in six countries - Commonwealth of Dominica, Saint Lucia, Belgium, Switzerland, Canada, and the USA. In carrying out its mission, the OECS works along with a number of sub-regional and regional agencies and institutions. These include the Eastern Caribbean Telecommunications Authority (ECTEL), Eastern Caribbean Civil Aviation Authority, Eastern Caribbean Central Bank (ECCB), and the Eastern Caribbean Supreme Court.

Membership
The members of the OECS are: Anguilla, Antigua and Barbuda, British Virgin Islands, Dominica, Grenada, Montserrat, St. Kitts and Nevis, Saint Lucia, St. Vincent and the Grenadines. In 2008 Venezuela expressed interest in membership.

Director General: Dr Len Ishmael

Organisation of Eastern Caribbean States, Morne Fortune, P.O. Box 179, Castries, Saint Lucia. Tel: +758 452 2537, fax: +758 453 1628, e-mail: oesec@oecs.org, URL: http://www.oecs.org

ORGANISATION OF ISLAMIC COOPERATION (OIC)

Originally founded in 1969, the Organisation of Islamic Cooperation (formerly the Organisation of the Islamic Conference) has 57 member states and five observer states. The present Charter of the Organization was adopted by the Eleventh Islamic Summit held in Dakar on 13-14 March 2008. The Organization aims, inter alia, to enhance and consolidate the bonds of fraternity and solidarity among the Member States; to respect, safeguard and defend the national sovereignty, independence and territorial integrity of all Member States and to promote cooperation in political, economic, trade, science and technology, social, cultural and information fields.

Structure
Its main bodies are (i) Islamic Summit, (ii) Council of Foreign Ministers, and (iii) the General Secretariat.

The Islamic Summit is composed of Kings and Heads of State and Government of Member States and is the supreme authority of the Organization. It takes policy decisions and provides guidance on all issues pertaining to the realization of the objectives as provided for in the Charter and consider other issues of concern to the Member States and Ummah, and is held triennially.

The Council of Foreign Ministers considers the means for the implementation of the general policy of the Organization and is convened once a year.

The General Secretariat, headed by the Secretary-General who is the Chief Administrative Officer of the Organization, follows up the implementation of decisions, resolutions and recommendations of the Islamic Summits and the Council of Foreign Ministers. The Secretary-General is elected by the Council of Foreign Ministers for a period of five years, renewable once only.

In order to advance issues of critical importance to the Organization and its Member States, the Organization has formed the following Standing Committees: (i) Al Quds Committee, (ii) Standing Committee for Information and Cultural Affairs (COMIAC) (iii) Standing Committee for Economic and Commercial Cooperation (COMCEC), (iv) Standing Committee for Scientific and Technological Cooperation (COMSTECH). The Standing Committees are chaired by Kings and Heads of State and Government.

The following have been established as subsidiary organs: Statistical, Economic, Social Research & Training Center for Islamic Countries (SESRIC); Research Center for Islamic History, Art & Culture (IRCICA); Islamic University of Technology (IUT); Islamic Center for the Development of Trade (ICDT); International Islamic Fiqh Academy (IIFA); and the Islamic Solidarity Fund and its Waqf.

Four specialised institutions and organs have been established with the OIC framework. Their budgets are independent of the budget of the General Secretariat. The organs are: the Islamic Development Bank (IBD); Islamic Educational, Scientific and Cultural Organization; Islamic Broadcasting Union (IBU); International Islamic News Agency (IINA); and the Islamic Committee of the International Crescent (ICIC).

Member States

Afghanistan, Albania, Algeria, Azerbaijan, Bahrain, Bangladesh, Benin, Brunei-Darussalam, Burkina-Faso, Cameroon, Chad, Comoros, Côte d'Ivoire, Djibouti, Egypt, Gabon, Gambia, Guinea, Guinea-Bissau, Guyana, Indonesia, Iran, Iraq, Jordan, Kazakhstan, Kuwait, Kyrgyz Republic, Lebanon, Libya, Malaysia, Maldives, Mali, Mauritania, Morocco, Mozambique, Niger, Nigeria, Oman, Pakistan, Palestine, Qatar, Saudi Arabia, Senegal, Sierra Leone, Somalia, Sudan, Suriname, Syria, Tajikistan, Togo, Tunisia, Turkey, Turkmenistan, Uganda, United Arab Emirates, Uzbekistan, Yemen.

Observer States

Bosnia-Herzegovina, Central African Republic, Thailand, the Russian Federation and Turkish Cypriot State.

Other Observers

Moro National Liberation Front, Parliamentary Union of the OIC Member States, United Nations, Non-Aligned Movement, League of Arab States, African Union, Economic Co-operation Organization.

Activities:

- *The Palestine Question:* the OIC calls for an end to the Israeli occupation, the establishment of a fully independent and sovereign Palestinian state on all Palestinian territories occupied by Israel in 1967, with East Jerusalem as its capital, and the right of Palestinian refugees to return to their homes according to UN resolution 194. The OIC supports the Middle East Peace Road Map, adopted by the UN Security Council. OIC member states are major financial donors to the Palestinians.

- *Iraq:* OIC is engaged in the national reconciliation process. It brought together high ranking representatives of Sunni and Shiite authorities in Makkah, 2006, resulting in the signing of the Makkah Declaration, aimed at ensuring the sanctity of human life and at ending the bloodshed in Iraq. The OIC opened an office in Baghdad in 2008.
- *Somalia:* the OIC endeavours to restore durable peace and stability to the country. It has participated in two round of UN coordinated peace talks, which resulted in an historic peace agreement between the Transitional Government and the opposition Alliance for the Re-Liberation of Somalia, as well as a ceasefire agreement in October 2008.
- *Terrorism:* the OIC Convention on combating international terrorism was adopted in 1999, and remains a comprehensive instrument in the fight against international terrorism. It safeguards the right of people who fight against occupation, aggression, colonialism and hegemony.
- *Muslim Minorities:* the OIC cooperates with international organisations and governments of states with resident Muslim minorities, to resolve the problems of the Muslim communities whilst respecting the sovereignty and laws of the states.
- *Humanitarian Affairs:* the OIC has established a department dedicated to humanitarian assistance and emergency relief. Humanitarian missions have been deployed in Gaza, Somalia and Somali refugee camps in Kenya. Appeals were made following natural disasters in Algeria, Balgldesh, Indonesia, Kyrgyzstan, Mozambique, Pakistan, Turkmenistan and the Yemen. The department also administers development and reconstruction funds in Afghanistan, Bosnia, Indonesia and Sierra Leone.
- *Economic Dimension:* the OIC Ten-Year Plan of Action (2005) emphasizes the need to make best use of the human, natural and economic resources of the Muslim world to promote economic cooperation and establish a Free Trade Area among member states.
- *Science and Technology:* The third extraordinary Islamic Summit called on member states to take steps to achieve scientific and technological development, especially self-sufficiency in the peaceful use of nuclear technology within the framework of the International Atomic Energy Agency (IAEA), with a view to supporting sustainable development in member states.
- *Higher Education:* the OIC calls for the improvement and reform of educational institutions and curricula, and the facilitating of academic interaction and exchange of knowledge among the academic institutions of the member states.
- *Environment and Health:* the OIC develops ways to address health and environment issues, and aims to increase cooperation among the member states in combating epidemic diseases such as AIDS, Malaria, Tuberculosis and Polio.

Other areas of discussion at the OIC Islamic Summits have included the combating of intolerance and discrimination against Muslims, and women and their role in the development of Islamic Societies.

The third extraordinary session of the Islamic Summit held in 2005 laid down the blue print called the Ten-Year Program of Action. The plan includes: promotion of tolerance and moderation, modernization, refeorms, good governance and promotion of human rights.

Funding

The budget of the General Secretariat and subsidiary organs are borne by member states, proportional to their national incomes.

Secretary General: Prof. Dr., Dr.h.c. mult. Ekmeleddin Ihsanoglu

Organisation of Islamic Cooperation Kilo 6, Mecca Road, PO Box 178, Jeddah 21411, Saudi Arabia. Tel: +966(2) 690 0001, fax: +966 (2) 275 1953, e-mail: cabinet@oic-oci.org, URL: http://www.oic-oci.org

ORGANIZATION FOR SECURITY AND CO-OPERATION IN EUROPE (OSCE)

The Organization for Security and Co-operation in Europe (OSCE) is the world's largest regional security organization, involving 57 participating States from Europe, Central Asia, and North America. Under chapter VIII of the Charter of the United Nations, the OSCE is recognised as a primary instrument for resolving conflict, from early warning and conflict prevention to crisis management and post-conflict rehabilitation. The Conference on Security and Co-operation in Europe (CSCE) was a series of multilateral conferences for dialogue and negotiation started in the early 1970s. Following the Budapest Summit in 1994, the OSCE changed its name from the CSCE and acquired permanent institutions and operational capabilities, taking up its new role in response to the new challenges of the post-Cold War period.

Guided by the 10 Principles of the Helsinki Final Act (1975) governing the behaviour of States, and the Charter of Paris for a New Europe (1990), the Organization deals with three dimensions of security - the politico-military, the economic and environmental, and the human dimension. A wide range of security concerns addressed in this context include arms control, confidence- and security-building measures, human rights, ethnic minorities situation, media freedom, policing strategies, counter-terrorism, trafficking in human beings, and economic and environmental activities. All 56 participating States have equal status; decisions are taken by consensus and are politically binding.

The OSCE maintains special relations with 11 countries which are known as Partners of Co-operation. These are as follows: Mediterranean: Algeria, Egypt, Israel, Jordan, Morocco, Tunisia: Asian: Japan, South Korea, Thailand, Afghanistan. In 2009, Australia was granted the status of Partner for Co-operation and invited to particiapte in the meetings.

Structures & Institutions

The main decision-making bodies of the OSCE are the Summit, which consists of the Heads of State and Government and meets periodically, the Ministerial Council, which is an annual meeting of the Foreign Ministers of the OSCE members (except when there is a Summit) and the Permanent Council, a regular body for political consultation and decision-making which meets weekly in Vienna.

The Forum for Security Co-operation meets weekly to discuss the politico-military dimension of security.

Responsibility for executive action is the province of the Chairman-in-Office (CiO). The Chairmanship changes annually, and the post is held by the Foreign Minister of a participating State. The Chairman works alongside the previous and future Chairmen, known collectively as the Troika.

The Secretary General is the representative of the Chairman-in-Office, providing support in the achievement of OSCE's aims and objectives. Based in Vienna, the Secretary General also manages OSCE's structures and operations. The post has a three-year term.

A number of institutions make up the OSCE. The Secretariat, based in Vienna, supports the Organization's operations and the Prague Office provides assistance, particularly with information, research and documentation.

The **Office for Democratic Institutions and Human Rights (ODIHR),** based in Warsaw, monitors elections, promotes human and electoral rights, as well as the development of NGOs and civil society, trains journalists, OSCE human rights and election monitors, and forms the contact point for Roma and Sinti issues.

The **High Commissioner on National Minorities** provides an early warning and conflict prevention service. Based in The Hague, the Commissioner assesses and tries to defuse situations involving national minority issues through quiet diplomacy.

The **Parliamentary Assembly** consists of 320 parliamentarians from all OSCE states. In its annual July session it debates matters and passes resolutions which are relevant to the OSCE's work. It also plays an important role in election monitoring. The Assembly's Secretariat is based in Copenhagen.

The **OSCE Representative on Freedom of the Media,** based in Vienna, provides a rapid response to serious cases of non-compliance with OSCE principles and commitments relating to freedom of expression and of the media.

A **High-Level Planning Group is** responsible for preparing an OSCE peacekeeping force for Nagorno-Karabakh. There is also the **OSCE Assistance in Implementation of Bilateral Agreements,** comprising the OSCE representative to the Russian-Latvian Joint Commission on Military Pensioners.

There are three OSCE-related bodies. A **Joint Consultative Group** promotes the implementation of the CFE Treaty. The group meets in Vienna. The **Open Skies Consultative Commission** promotes the implementation of the Open Skies Treaty. The Commission also meets in Vienna. Finally, the **Court of Conciliation and Arbitration** in Geneva settles disputes relating to participating States who are signatories to the Convention on Conciliation and Arbitration. The Court was established in 1995 by the Convention on Conciliation and Arbitration. Thirty-three States are currently (2013) Parties to the Convention. The Court is composed of experts in the field of international law who are appointed by the States Parties to the Convention. The conciliators and arbitrators are headed by a Bureau.

Structure & Functions of the Secretariat

The **Conflict Prevention Centre** is responsible for supporting OSCE work in relation to early warning, conflict prevention and crisis management.
The **Office of the Co-ordinator of OSCE Economic and Environmental Activities** seeks to identify and address economic and environmental threats to security.
The **Action Against Terrorism Unit** in the OSCE's Secretariat, coordinates assistance to OSCE participating States in implementing international conventions related to the fight against terrorism.
The **Office of the Special Representative and Co-ordinator for Combating Trafficking in Human Beings** supports participating States in their initiatives to prevent trafficking in human beings, to prosecute traffickers and to protect victims.
The **Strategic Police Matters Unit** helps to build up police capacity in the OSCE participating States.

Budget

The Secretariat's activities are financed by the contributions of the participating States, with the exception of the salaries of the diplomatic personnel which remain the responsibility of the seconding administrations. The OSCE's 2013 budget was €144.8 million. The Secretariat and OSCE Institutions employ around 550 staff. Field operations employ approximately 2,300 people.

Key Programmes

There are 16 missions or field operations in South-Eastern Europe (Presence in Albania, Mission to Bosnia and Herzegovina, Mission to Montenegro, Mission to Serbia, Mission in Kosovo, Mission to Skopje), Eastern Europe (Mission to Moldova, Project Co-ordinator in Ukraine), the Caucasus (Office in Baku, Office in Yerevan, Personal Representative of the Chairman-in-Office on the Conflict Dealt with by the OSCE Minsk Conference) and Central Asia (Center in Ashgabad, Center in Astana, Centre in Bishkek, Office in Tajikistan, Project Co-ordinator in Uzbekistan).

Field missions and operations conduct projects on surplus small arms and light weapons, toxic rocket fuel components and offer assistance with their destruction, monitor elections, rule of law, human rights, ethnic minorities, media freedom and freedom of expression, train police, legal experts and journalists, educate young people on environmental protection, business and democracy, offer expertise on border management, fight against human trafficking, and terrorism.

For details of the membership of OSCE please consult the matrix of *Country Membership of Major Organisations* in the preliminary section.

Secretary General: Ambassador Lamberto Zannier (page 1542)

OSCE Secretariat, Wallnerstrasse 6, A-1010 Vienna, Austria. Tel: +43 (0)1 5143 66000, fax: +43 (0)1 5143 66996, e-mail: info@osce.org, URL: http://www.osce.org

ORGANIZATION OF AMERICAN STATES (OAS)

The Organization of American States (OAS) is the world's oldest international regional organisation created by governments to preserve the peace, ensure freedom and security, and promote the welfare of the peoples of its member states. It is also a forum for dialogue.

On April 14, 1890, in Washington, DC, the First International Conference of American States founded the international Union of American Republics. Its members at that time were: Argentina, Bolivia, Chile, Brazil, Colombia, Costa Rica, Ecuador, El Salvador, Guatemala, Haiti, Honduras, Mexico, Nicaragua, Paraguay, Peru, United States of America, Uruguay and Venezuela. In 1910, the International Union became the Union of American Republics and in 1948 a Charter was signed in Bogota, transforming the Union of American Republics into the Organization of American States. The OAS Charter has been amended three times in 1967, 1970 and 1985. The most recent reform to the Charter occurred in 1997, through the ratification of the Protocol of Washington. The OAS now has the right to suspend a member state whose democratically elected government is overthrown by force.

The OAS member states have intensified their co-operation since the end of the Cold War, taking on new and important challenges. In 1994 the region's 34 democratically elected presidents and prime ministers met in Miami for the First Summit of the Americas, where they established broad political, economic and social development goals. They have continued to meet periodically since then to examine common interests and priorities. Through the ongoing Summits of the Americas process, the region's leaders have entrusted the OAS with a growing number of responsibilities to help advance the countries' shared vision.

Membership
Today, the OAS membership includes all 35 independent states of the Americas and constitutes the main political, juridical, and social governmental forum of the Americas. In addition, it has granted permanent observer status to 67 states, as well as to the European Union (EU). State membership is as follows: Antigua and Barbuda, Argentina, Bahamas, Barbados, Belize, Bolivia, Brazil, Canada, Chile, Colombia, Costa Rica, Cuba, Dominica, Dominican Republic, Ecuador, El Salvador, Grenada, Guatemala, Guyana, Haiti, Honduras, Jamaica, Mexico, Nicaragua, Panama, Paraguay, Peru, Saint Kitts and Nevis, Saint Lucia, Saint Vincent and the Grenadines, Suriname, Trinidad and Tobago, USA, Uruguay and Venezuela. On June 3, 2009, OAS revoked Cuba's suspension.

Permanent Observers to the OAS
As of April 2013 there were 68 permanent observers: Albania, Algeria, Angola, Armenia, Austria, Azerbaijan, Belgium, Benin, Bosnia and Herzegovina, Bulgaria, China, Croatia, Cyprus, Czech Republic, Denmark, Egypt, Equatorial Guinea, Estonia, European Union, Finland, Former Yugoslav Republic of Macedonia, France, Georgia, Germany, Ghana, Greece, Holy See, Hungary, Iceland, India, Ireland, Israel, Italy, Japan, Kazakhstan, Republic of Korea, Latvia, Lebanon, Lithuania, Luxembourg, Malta, Monaco, Morocco, Netherlands, Nigeria, Norway, Pakistan, Philippines, Poland, Portugal, Qatar, Romania, Russian Federation, Saudi Arabia, Serbia, Slovakia, Slovenia, Spain, Sri Lanka, Sweden, Switzerland, Thailand, Tunisia, Turkey, Ukraine, United Kingdom of Great Britain and Northern Ireland, Vanuatu, and Yemen.

Purposes
The OAS proclaims the following essential purposes:
a) To strengthen the peace and security of the continent
b) To promote and consolidate representative democracy with due respect for the principle of nonintervention.
c) To prevent possible causes of difficulties and to ensure the pacific settlement of disputes that may arise among the Member States.
d) To provide for common action on the part of those States in the event of aggression.
e) To seek the solution of political, judicial and economic problems that may arise among them.
f) To promote, by co-operative action, their economic, social, and cultural development and address the complex problems caused by poverty, drugs and corruption.
g) To achieve an effective limitation of conventional weapons that will make it possible to devote the largest amount of resources to the economic and social development of the member States.

Structure
The main organs are as follows:

The General Assembly
The General Assembly, the supreme organ of the Organization, convenes annually in regular session. Special sessions may also be convoked. All member States have the right to be represented in the General Assembly. Each State has the right to one vote. The General Assembly decides the general action and policy of the Organization, determines the structure and functions of its organs, and considers any matter relating to friendly relations among the American States.

The Meeting of Consultation of Ministers of Foreign Affairs
Held in order to discuss either urgent matters of issues of common interest. Any state may request a meeting. The Permanent Council votes on whether such a meeting should take place.

The Councils
- Permanent Council
The Permanent Council is composed of one representative of each member State, especially appointed by the respective Government with the rank of ambassador. It meets regularly at OAS headquarters in Washington to guide ongoing policies and actions. The chairmanship of the Permanent Council rotates every three months, in alphabetical order of countries. Each member state has an equal voice, and most decisions are forged through consensus.
-Inter-American Council for Integral Development
Composed of all Member States. The body is directly answerable to the General Assembly and its purpose is to promote co-operation among is Member states with regard to integral development and in particular to try to eliminate extreme poverty.

Inter-American Judicial Committee
An advisory body to the Organization on juridical matters, promotes the development and codification of international law.

Inter-American Commission on Human Rights
Formally established in 1960. Its Rules of Procedure were first adopted in 1980, and have been amended several times, most recently in 2006. Its seven members are elected by the General Assembly for four-year terms. They may be re-elected only once. Its mission is to promote and protect human rights.

General Secretariat
The central and permanent organ of the OAS.

Specialized Conferences
Inter-governmental meetings for special technical matters of for specific policy issues.

Specialized Organizations
Established by multilateral agreements. They are autonomous but take into account recommendations of the General Assembly and the Councils. The organizations include: the Pan American Health Organizations (PAHO), the Inter-American Children's Institute (IIN), the Inter-American Commission of Women (CIM), the Pan American Institute of Geography and History (PAIGH), the Inter-American Indian Institute (III), the Inter-American Institute for Co-operation on Agriculture).

Secretary General: José Miguel Insulza (page 1447)

Organization of American States, 17th Street & Constitution Avenue, NW, Washington, DC 20006, USA. Tel. +1 202 458 3000, URL: http://www.oas.org

ORGANIZATION OF ARAB PETROLEUM EXPORTING COUNTRIES (OAPEC)

The Organization of Arab Petroleum Exporting Countries (OAPEC) was established on 9 January 1968 by the governments of Saudi Arabia, Kuwait and Libya. Its aims are to co-ordinate efforts and encourage co-operation between member countries in the various forms of economic activity in the petroleum industry.

Activities
The promotion and co-ordination of activities leading to the development of petroleum industry infrastructure in Arab countries; the establishment of joint ventures in the Arab oil industry and the dissemination of information on energy and economics through a library, a database and publications. The OAPEC convenes the Arab Energy Conference, specialised symposia and co-operation seminars with non-Arab countries. The ninth Arab Energy Conference took place in Doha in May 2010 with a theme of 'Energy and Arab Co-operation'. The tenth will take place in 2014.

Joint Undertakings: Arab Maritime Petroleum Transport Company (AMPTC), Arab Petroleum Services Company (APSC), Arab Petroleum Investments Corporation (APICORP), Arab Petroleum Training Institute (APTI), Arab Shipbuilding and Repair Yard Services Company (ASRY).

Members: Algeria, Bahrain, Egypt, Iraq, Kuwait, Libya, Qatar, Saudi Arabia, Syria and the United Arab Emirates. Tunisia withdrew its membership in 1986.

Budget: Member countries contribute to the organisation's budget in equal shares.

Structure
Council of Ministers: The supreme authority of OAPEC, it is responsible for drawing up its general policy, governing and directing its activities. Comprising oil ministers or comparable officials from each member country. Convenes twice a year, chairmanship rotates annually in alphabetical order of countries.

INTER-GOVERNMENTAL ORGANISATIONS

Executive Bureau: The Executive Bureau assists the Ministerial Council in supervising OAPEC's affairs. The Bureau comprises senior officials from each member country, chairmanship by rotation. It convenes prior to meetings of the Ministerial Council.

General Secretariat: The General Secretariat administers and realises the organization's activities. It is headed by the Secretary-General, who is accountable to the Council. The Secretary General is the official spokesperson. Within the General Secretariat are the Arab Center for Energy Studies, the Technical Affairs Department, the Economics Department, the Information and Library Department, and the Finance Administration Department.

Judicial Tribunal: The Judicial Tribunal was established by a special Protocol signed in Kuwait on 9 May 1978. The judges of the Tribunal were first elected on 6 May 1981. The number of judges varies between seven and eleven. The Tribunal hears cases between members countries; member countries and petroleum companies operating within that country; and member countries and the national oil company of another member state.

Secretary General: H.E. Dr Abdul Hussain bin Alli Mirza

OAPEC Head Office, PO Box 20501 Safat, 13066 Kuwait. Tel: +965 495 9000, fax: +965 495 9755, e-mail: oapec@oapecorg.org, URL: http://www.oapecorg.org

ORGANIZATION OF THE PETROLEUM EXPORTING COUNTRIES (OPEC)

The Organization of the Petroleum Exporting Countries (OPEC) was established in September 1960. The principal aims of the Organization are to co-ordinate and unify the petroleum policies of Member Countries and determine the best means for safeguarding their interests, individually and collectively; to devise ways and means of ensuring the stabilization of prices in international oil markets with a view to eliminating harmful and unnecessary fluctuations; and to secure a steady income for the producing countries, an efficient, economic and regular supply of petroleum to consuming nations, and a fair return on their capital to those investing in the petroleum industry.

OPEC Sovereigns and Heads of State also made a 'Solemn Declaration' in 1975 to assist other developing countries in their efforts to establish a new international economic order.

The 12 Member Countries are: Algeria, Angola, Ecuador, Islamic Republic of Iran, Iraq, Kuwait, Socialist People's Libyan Arab Jamahiriya, Nigeria, Qatar, Saudi Arabia, United Arab Emirates and Venezuela. Membership is open to any other country having substantial net exports of crude petroleum, which has fundamentally similar interests to those of Member Countries. Gabon was a member from 1975-1994. Indonesia suspended its membership in January 2009.

The Member Countries currently supply more than 40 per cent of the world's oil and they possess about 78 per cent of the world's total proven crude oil reserves.

Structure
The Conference is the supreme authority of the organisation and generally meets twice a year. It is responsible for the formulation and implementation of policy.

The OPEC secretariat is a permanent inter-governmental body. The Secretariat, which has been based in Vienna since 1965, provides research and administrative support to the Member Countries and also disseminates news and information.

Summits
Heads of State and Government of member countries held the first OPEC summit in Algiers in 1975 and a second summit in Caracas, Venezuela in 2000. The Third Summit was held in Riyadh, Saudi Arabia in November 2007. The recent summits had three key themes of stable energy markets, sustainable development and the environment. A comprehensive long-term strategy was adopted in 2005. As part of global efforts to address the economic crisis, OPEC has supported the oil industry following soaring prices in 2004 and the collapse of oil prices in 2008. An international seminar took place in Vienna in June 2012.

Secretary-General: Abdalla Salem El-Badri (Libya) (page 1420)

Organization of the Petroleum Exporting Countries, 93 Obere Donaustrasse, A-1020 Vienna, Austria. Tel: +43 (0)1 211120, fax: +43 (0)1 216 4320, e-mail: prid@opec.org, URL: http://www.opec.org

PACIFIC ECONOMIC COOPERATION COUNCIL (PECC)

The Pacific Economic Cooperation Council was formed in September 1980 when the Pacific Community Seminar called for the establishment of an independent, regional mechanism to advance economic co-operation and market-driven integration. PECC is a tripartite partnership of leaders in the fields of business and industry, government and intellectual circles. It aims to be policy-oriented, pragmatic and anticipatory in the areas of trade, investment, finance and all major industrial sectors.

Membership
PECC has 26 Member Committees, including associate and institutional member from economies in the Pacific region: Australia, Brunei Darussalam, Canada, Chile, China, Colombia, Ecuador, Hong Kong, Indonesia, Japan, Korea, Malaysia, Mexico, Mongolia, New Zealand, Peru, the Philippines, Singapore, Pacific Islands Forum, Chinese Taipei, Thailand, the United States and Vietnam. France (Pacific Territories) is an Associate Member. Institutional Members are Pacific Trade and Development Conference (PAFTAD) and Pacific Basin Economic Council (PBEC).

Each Member Committee comprises of senior representatives from business, government and academic circles.

Structure
The Standing Committee is the Pacific Economic Co-operation Council's governing body. It meets once a year and is composed of representatives from all of the full Member Committees, the two institutional members and associate Member Committees. The Co-chairs are elected for 3-year terms, Dr Charles E. Morrison, President of the East West Center and Mr Jusuf Wanandi, Senior Fellow and Vice-Chair of the Board of Trustees of the Centre for Strategic and International Studies are the current co-chairs. The Executive Committee is a subset of the Standing Committee. It is composed of 11 members and the Secretary General. The Executive Committee oversees the day-to-day work of the PECC.

Task Forces carry out the PECC work program. Each group is composed of representatives from the member committees as well as other invited institutions and individuals. As official observers to the APEC process, PECC provides assistance and support to APEC.

The chair is elected for a three-year term.

PECC Co-Chairs: Dr Charles E. Morrison, President of the East West Center and Mr Jusuf Wanandi, Senior Fellow and Vice-Chair of the Board of Trustees of the Centre for Strategic and International Studies

PECC International Secretariat, 29 Heng Mui Keng Terrace, Singapore 119620. Tel: +65 6737 9822, fax: +65 6737 9824, e-mail: info@pecc.org, URL: http://www.pecc.org

PACIFIC ISLANDS FORUM

Established in 1971, the Pacific Islands Forum is a regional inter-governmental organisation whose aim is to enhance economic and political co-operation, improve living standards, protect the environment and ensure sustainable development throughout the region.

The Forum meets once a year at Head of Government level. This meeting is immediately followed by a post-Forum dialogue which is conducted at Ministerial level with the Forum's dialogue partners. The Forum works to a corporate plan, the 2013 plan is under discussion.

Membership
The 16 member countries of the Forum are: Australia, Cook Islands, Federated States of Micronesia, Fiji, Kiribati, Nauru, New Zealand, Niue, Palau, Papua New Guinea, Republic of the Marshall Islands, Samoa, Solomon Islands, Tonga, Tuvalu and Vanuatu. New Caledonia and French Polynesia, previously Forum Observers, became Associate Members in 2006. There are five Forum Observers: Tokelau, Wallis and Futuna, the Commonwealth, the Asia Development Bank and the World Bank (2010). Timor Leste is a Special Observer. The Forum's 14 dialogue partners are: Canada, China, European Union, France, India, Indonesia, Italy, Japan, Korea, Malaysia, Philippines, Thailand, United Kingdom and the USA.

Organisation Structure

The administrative arm of the Pacific Islands Forum is the Secretariat, originally established in 1972 as a Trade Bureau. It undertakes the programmes and activities under guidelines decided by the Forum leaders and is funded by contributions from member governments and donors. The Secretariat employs about 80 staff in Suva, Fiji and has responsibilities for the Pacific Islands Trade and Investment Commissions in Auckland and Sydney; Pacific Islands Forum Trade Office in Beijing and Pacific Islands Centre in Tokyo.

The Secretariat is headed by a Secretary General and two Deputies. The work programme is determined by a governing body comprising senior officials from all Forum member governments, known as the Forum Officials Committee, and is focused on the four Forum goals of economic growth, sustainability, good governance and security. The Secretariat budget was FJ$36 million.

The Forum Secretary General also chairs the Council of Regional Organisations in the Pacific (CROP), which brings together eleven main regional organisations in the Pacific region.

Secretary General: Tuiloma Neroni Slade (Samoa)

Pacific Islands Forum Secretariat, Private Mail Bag, Suva, Fiji. Tel: +679 331 2600, fax: +679 330 5573, e-mail: info@forumsec.org.fj, URL: http://www.forumsec.org

RIO GROUP
Grupo de Rio

The Grupo de Rio was established in December 1986, following a meeting of Heads of Government in Rio de Janeiro, as a forum for the discussion of issues of common interest to the countries of Latin America and the Caribbean.

Its membership comprised 23 states: Argentina, Belize, Bolivia, Brazil, Chile, Colombia, Costa Rica, the Dominican Republic, Ecuador, El Salvador, Guatemala, Guyana, Haiti, Honduras, Jamaica, Mexico, Nicaragua, Panama, Paraguay, Peru, Uruguay and Venezuela.

It has now been superceded by CELAC (Community of Latin American and Caribbean States).

SECRETARIAT OF THE PACIFIC COMMUNITY (SPC)

The South Pacific Commission, as SPC was formerly called, was founded in Australia in 1947 under the Canberra Agreement by the six 'participating governments' that then administered territories in the Pacific: Australia, France, New Zealand, the Netherlands, the United Kingdom and the United States of America. They established the organisation to restore post-war stability to the region, to assist in administering their dependent territories and to benefit the people of the Pacific.

On 6 February 1998, the South Pacific Commission (SPC) became the 'Pacific Community'. The title 'Pacific Community' defines the consortium of states and territories within the organisation called 'The Secretariat of the Pacific Community' (SPC).

The Secretariat of the Pacific Community is a technical assistance, training and research agency with 26 members serving its 22 Pacific Island members (countries and territories), with:
a) Enhanced technical, professional, management and research capability in Pacific Island countries and territories.
b) Enhancement of 'informed' decision making, through increased availability of technical and research information to member countries and territories on a timely basis.
c) Enhanced awareness in member countries and territories concerning the intricate relationship between resource management (including human, land, marine) and sustainable development.
d) Established partnerships and improved co-operation and collaboration with member and donor governments, funding agencies, non-governmental organisations, international organisations and other regional organisations.
e) Gender focused, culturally sensitive, efficient, effective and transparent regional organisation with a commitment to service.

Members

American Samoa, Australia, Cook Islands, Federated States of Micronesia, Fiji Islands, France, French Polynesia, Guam, Kiribati, Marshall Islands, Nauru, New Caledonia, New Zealand, Niue, Northern Mariana Islands, Palau, Papua New Guinea, Pitcairn, Samoa, Solomon Islands, Tokelau, Tonga, Tuvalu, United States of America, Vanuatu, Wallis and Futuna.
The United Kingdom withdrew at the beginning of 1996 from SPC, rejoined in 1998 and withdrew again in January 2005. The Netherlands withdrew in 1962.

Structure

The governing body of the Pacific Community is the 'Conference of the Pacific Community', replacing the South Pacific Conference. The Conference meets every two years. The Pacific Community is serviced by its Secretariat (SPC). The Conference's committee of the whole, the Committee of Representatives of Governments and Administration (CRGA), meets annually. The SPC is led by a Director-General, who is the Chief Executive Officer of the Secretariat. The Director General is appointed directly by the representatives of the 26 member countries and territories at the Conference of the Pacific Community. Over 350 staff members work for the SPC, most of whom are based at the headquarters in Noumea and at the Suva office.

Programme Officers travel extensively in the region and staff are also based in various countries to conduct short-term training programmes. The official working languages are English and French.

SPC Programmes

The SPC has an integrated work programme in land, marine and social resources that encompasses a diverse range of issues identified as priority areas by the Pacific Island countries and territories themselves.

Land Resources: Amongst issues concerning agriculture, special attention is given to general agriculture, plant protection, animal health and production, crop improvement, resource economics, forestry and the availability of agricultural information.
Marine Resources: A Coastal Fisheries Programme addresses the long-term social and economic value of small-scale fisheries and aquatic resources in Pacific Island waters. An Oceanic Fisheries Programme provides member countries with the scientific information and advice necessary to manage fisheries exploiting the region's resources of tuna, billfish and related species. A regional maritime programme offers legal and training advisory services to ensure that island countries adopt international, regional and national policies that will result in safer ships and cleaner seas.
Social Resources: The Community Health Programme aims to strengthen the establishment of public health surveillance and communicable disease control, minimise the transmission of STDs and HIV/AIDS, prevent non-communicable diseases, strengthen health management capacity, prevent and control tuberculosis, improve planning, delivery and management of health promotion activities, and prevent and control vector-borne diseases, including malaria, dengue and filariasis. The Socio-economic programme offers technical advice and assistance, as well as training, in areas such as youth and women's issues, cultural affairs, demography and population, statistics, rural energy development, community education, media, reproductive health and population advocacy. There is also an Information and Communication Programme.

In 2011, the Pacific Islands Applied Geoscience Commission transferred its core functions to SPC.

Finances

The Secretariat of the SPC draws its regular budget from the contributions of all of its 26 member countries, each of which is assessed on an agreed formula. The largest contributors are the governments of Australia, France, New Zealand, the USA and the EU. Voluntary contributions (extra budgetary) are also provided by some member countries, other governments, various aid agencies and international organisations, and other external sources. The annual 2007 budget was CFP 43 million (US$48 million).

Director-General: Dr. Jimmie Rodgers

Secretariat of the Pacific Community (SPC), BP D5, 95 Promenade Roger, Laroque, Anse Vata, 98848 Noumea Cedex, New Caledonia. Tel: +687 262000, fax: +687 263818, email: spc@spc.int, URL: http://www.spc.int

SOUTH ASIAN ASSOCIATION FOR REGIONAL COOPERATION (SAARC)

The South Asian Association for Regional Cooperation (SAARC) was established in 1985 when its charter was formally adopted by the Heads of State or Government of Bangladesh, Bhutan, India, Maldives, Nepal, Pakistan and Sri Lanka. Afghanistan became a fully-fledged member of SAARC during the 14th SAARC Summit.

As at 2013, Australia, China, the European Union, Iran, Japan, Republic of Korea, Mauritius, Myanmar and the USA are the observers of SAARC.

The primary objective of the Association is the acceleration of the process of economic and social development in member states, through collective action in agreed areas of cooperation. These include Agriculture and Rural Development; Biotechnology; Culture; Economic; Energy; Environment; Funding mechanisms; Human Resource Development; Information, Communication and Media; People-to-People Contacts; Poverty Alleviation; Science and Technology; Security; Tourism.

A SAARC Preferential Trading Arrangement (SAPTA) designed to reduce tariffs on trade between SAARC member states was signed in April 1993 and entered into force in December 1995. With the objectives of moving towards higher levels of trade and economic co-operation in the region by removing barriers to cross-border flow of goods, a Committee of Experts was established to draft a comprehensive treaty regime for creating a free trade area. The agreement on the South Asian Free Trade Area (SAFTA) entered into force with effect from 1 January 2006.

Structure
The highest authority rests with the Heads of State or Government of each member country. The Council of Ministers, which meets twice a year is made up of the Foreign Ministers of each state and formulates policies and considers new projects. The Standing Committee comprising of Foreign Secretaries monitors and coordinates the Association's cooperative programmes and meets twice a year. Technical Committees are responsible for individual areas of SAARC's activities. The Secretariat coordinates, monitors, facilitates and promotes SAARC's activities and serves as a channel of communication between the Association and other regional and inter-governmental institutions. The Secretariat is composed of the Secretary General, seven Directors and the General Services Staff.

Regional Centres
There are nine regional centres: SAARC Agricultural Information Centre (SAIC), Dhaka, Bangladesh; SAARC Tuberculosis Centre (STC), Kathmandu, Nepal; SAARC Documentation Centre (SDC), New Delhi, India; SAARC Meteorological Research Centre (SMRC), Dhaka, Bangladesh; SAARC Human Resource Development Centre (SHRDC), Islamabad, Pakistan; SAARC Coastal Zone Management Centre, Male', Maldives; SAARC Information Centre, Kathmandu, Nepal, SAARC Forestry Centre, Thimphu, Bhutan, SAARC Disaster Management Centre (SDMC), New Delhi, India, SAARC Energy Centre (SEC), Islamabad, Pakistan, SAARC Cultural Centre, Kandy, Sri Lanka and the SAARC Forestry Centre, Bhutan.

Finances
The activities of the Secretariat and the Regional Centres of SAARC are funded through assessed subscriptions of the Member States though the host country finances part of the office expenses. It has a current fund of about $6.6 million.

Secretary-General: H.E. Ahmed Saleem

South Asian Association for Regional Cooperation, P.O. Box 4222, Tridevi Marg, Kathmandu, Nepal. Tel: +977 1 422 1794 / 1785 / 6350, fax: +977 1 422 7033 / 3991, e-mail: saarc@saarc-sec.org, URL: http://www.saarc-sec.org

SOUTHERN AFRICAN DEVELOPMENT COMMUNITY (SADC)

The Southern African Development Community (SADC), formerly the Southern African Development Co-ordination Conference (SADCC), was formed in Lusaka, Zambia, on 1 April 1980, following the adoption of the Lusaka Declaration: "Southern Africa Towards Economic Liberation" by the nine founding Member States.

There are now 15 member states: Angola, Botswana, Democratic Republic of Congo (DRC), Lesotho, Madagascar, Malawi, Mauritius, Mozambique, Namibia, Seychelles, South Africa, Swaziland, United Republic of Tanzania, Zambia and Zimbabwe.

Objectives
The objectives of SADC are to:
- achieve development and economic growth, alleviate poverty, enhance the standard and quality of life of the peoples of Southern Africa and support the socially disadvantaged through regional integration;
- evolve common political values, systems and institutions;
- promote and defend peace and security;
- promote self-sustaining development on the basis of collective self-reliance, and the inter-dependence of member states;
- achieve complementarity between national and regional strategies and programmes;
- promote and maximise productive employment and utilisation of the resources of the region;
- achieve sustainable utilisation of natural resources and effective protection of the environment;
- and strengthen and consolidate the long-standing historical, social and cultural affinities and links among the peoples of the region.

SADC Member States emphasise the need to ensure that poverty alleviation is addressed in all SADC activities and programmes so that solutions are found to liberate the peoples of the SADC region from abject poverty. HIV/AIDS is seen as a major threat to the attainment of the objectives of SADC and, as such, is accorded priority in the health programme and other relevant sectors.

Milestones
SADC launched its Free Trade Area in August 2008 during the 28th Summit of SADC Heads of State and government. Further milestones are to achieve Customs Union by 2010, the Common Market by 2015, the Monetary Union by 2016, and the Single Currency by 2018. However, in August 2010 SADC announced it would have to postpone the launch of the Customs Union. A taskforce is to review the situation and report to SADC.

Common Agenda
SADC's Common Agenda includes the following: the promotion of sustainable and equitable economic growth and socio-economic development that will ensure poverty alleviation and ultimately its eradication; the promotion of common political values, systems and other shared values which are transmitted through democratic, legitimate and effective institutions; and the consolidation and maintenance of democracy, peace and security.

Budget
The SADC budget for operational costs of running the Secretariat and Commissions is funded from contributions by member states in equal amounts agreed by the SADC Council of Ministers.

Structure
SADC comprises the following institutions; the Summit of Heads of State & Government, Summit Troika of the Organ, the SADC Tribunal, Council of Ministers, Sectoral/Cluster Ministerial Committees, Standing Committee of Senior Officials, SADC Secretariat, SADC National Committees and the SADC Parlimentarium Forum.

The Summit
The Summit comprises the Heads of State and/or Government of the Member States and is the supreme policy-making institution of SADC. It is responsible for the overall policy direction and control of the Community functions. The Summit meets at least twice a year and elects a Chairperson and Deputy at this meeting.

SADC Tribunal
The SADC Tribunal was established in 1992 as the judicial institution of SADC. The inauguration of the Tribunal and the swearing in of the Members took place on 18th November 2005 in Windhoek, Namibia. The Tribunal consists of ten members including the President of the Tribunal appointed from SADC Member States. Under international law the Tribunal is considered an international court just like the European Court of Justice or the East African Court of Justice. The day to day functions of the Tribunal are headed by the Registrar , who is the Chief Executive of the Tribunal, supported by a Librarian, Finance and Administration Officer. The first dispute was lodged in August 2007.

Council of Ministers
The Council consists of ministers from each member State, usually from the Ministries of Foreign Affairs or Economic Planning or Finance. The Council is responsible for overseeing the functioning and development of SADC and ensuring that policies are properly implemented. The Council meets four times a year.

Organ on Politics, Defence and Security
This organ is managed on a Troika basis and is responsible for promoting peace and security. This body reports to the Chairperson of SADC. Its structure, operations and functions are regulated by the Protocol on Politics, Defence and Security Co-operation, signed by the Summit in August 2001. The Chairperson of the Organ is assisted by a Deputy and the Chairperson of the previous year. All three are Heads of Member States. The SADC Secretariat services the organ on Politics, Defence and Security.

Integrated Committee of Ministers
The object of this new institution is to ensure proper policy guidance, co-ordination and harmonisation of cross-sectoral activities. It oversees the activities of the four core areas of integration: Trade, Industry, Finance and Investment; Infrastructure and Services; Food,

Agriculture and Natural Resources and Social and Human Development and Special Programmes, including the implementation of the Regional Indicative Strategic Development Plan.

SADC National Committees
Composed of key people from government, the private sector and civil society in Member States, these Committees help in the formulation of regional policies and strategies as well as co-ordinating and overseeing the implementation of programmes at a national level.

SADC Parliamentarian Forum
It is an inter-parliamentary institution. It shares all rights and privilegs of the other institutions of the SADC. it was launched in 1996 and official approved in 1997. It has five programme areas: democracy and governance; parliamentary capacity development; regional development and integration programme, HIV/AIDS and Public Health Programme, and Gender Equality & Empowerment Programme.

Secretariat
The Secretariat is the principal executive institution of the SADC and is responsible for the strategic planning, coordination and management of programmes. It is based in Gaborone, Botswana and is headed by an Executive Secretary.

Secretary General: Mr Tomaz Augusto Salomao

Southern African Development Community, SADC Secretariat Building, Private Bag 0095, Gaborone, Botswana. Tel: +267 395 1863, fax: +267 397 2848, e-mail: registry@sadc.int, URL: http://www.sadc.int

UNION ECONOMIQUE ET MONÉTAIRE OUEST AFRICAINE (UEMOA)
Economic and Monetary Union of West Africa

UEMOA was created on 10 January 1994 when the Heads of State and Government of seven West African countries signed the Treaty of Dakar. The seven countries share a single currency and monetary policy and are Benin, Burkina Faso, Côte d'Ivoire, Mali, Niger, Senegal and Togo. They were joined by Guinea-Bissau in May 1997.

The aims of the Union are:
- to strengthen the competitiveness of the financial and economic programmes of the member states within the framework of an open market;
- to ensure the compatibility of the members' economic policies through the institution of a multilateral inspection procedure;
- to create a common market based on the free circulation of people, goods, services and capital. As of January 2000, intra-UEMOA tariffs were lifted and a common external tariff was applied to all other imports;
- to structure policy co-operation in national sectors through implementing shared projects and eventually common policies, especially in the fields of human resources, land management, agriculture, energy, industry, mines, transport, infrastructure and telecommunications;

- to harmonise the laws of the Member States, especially fiscal laws.

Structure
The management structure of UEMOA is composed of the Conference of the Heads of State, the Council of Ministers, and the UEMOA Commission. The control organs are the Court of Justice, the Revenue Court, and the Interparliamentary Committee. The Central Bank of West African States (BCEAO) and the West African Development Bank (Banque Ouest-Africaine de Dévelopment) act as autonomous specialised institutions.

President of the Commission: M. Sheikh Hadjibou Soumare (Senegal)

Commission de l'UEMOA, 380, Pr Joseph Ki-Zerbo Avenue, 01 BP 543 Ouagadougou 01, Burkina Faso. Tel: +226 31 8873, fax: +226 31 8872, e-mail: Commission@uemoa.int, URL: http://www.uemoa.int / http://www.izf.net

UNION OF SOUTH AMERICAN NATIONS (UNASUR)
Unión de Naciones Suramericanas

The aims of the Union of South American Nations, which replaces the South American Community of Nations (CSN), are to boost economic and political intergration in the region, and to unite the existing intergovernmental bodies of Mercosur and the Andean Community.

At the Third South American Summit on 8 December 2004 representatives from 12 South American nations signed the Cuzco Declaration which announced the aim of founding a South American Community, modelled after the European Union including a parliament, currency and passport.

The UNASUR Constitutive Treaty was signed in Brasilia on 23 May 2008.

Structure
At the First South American Community of Nations Heads of State Summit held in Brazil in September 2005 it was agreed that the community would use the exisiting institutions belonging to previous trade blocs. There will be annual meetings between the presidents of each member nation, and six monthly meetings between the foreign ministers of each member nation. Representatives from Mercosur and the Andean Community will also attend. The organisation is to be headed by a secretary general and a permanent secretariat established in Quito, Ecuador. The presidency of the organisation will be held for a year and rotate anually

among the members. The South American Parliament will be situated in Cochabamba, Boliva. The Bank of the South will be located in Bogota, Colombia and should become operational in 2013.

UNASUR's Constitutive Treaty entered into force on 11 March 2011.

There are nine Ministerial Councils of the UNASUR: Social Development; Fight Against Drug Traffic; Health; Education, Culture, Science & Technology; Defense; Energy; Economy & Finances; Infrastructure & Planning; Electoral Council.

Members
Members are Argentina, Bolivia, Brazil, Chile, Colombia, Ecuador, Guyana, Paraguay, Peru, Suriname, Uruguay and Venezeula.

The organisation will affect some 376 million people.

President: Ollanta Humala
Seecretary General: Ali Rodriguez Araque

UNASUR, URL: http://www.uniondenacionessuramericanas.com / http://www.comunidadandina.org

Agriculture, Farming and Fisheries

ARAB AUTHORITY FOR AGRICULTURAL INVESTMENT AND DEVELOPMENT

The 20 member states of AAAID aim to develop the agricultural resources of its member states, produce the maximum possible amounts of food products and increase the exchange of agricultural products between Arab countries.

President: Ali Bin Saeed Al-Sharhan

Arab Authority for Agricultural Investment and Development, P.O. Box 2102, Khartoum, Sudan. Tel: +249 187 096100, e-mail: info@aaaid.org, URL: http://www.aaaid.org

ARAB ORGANISATION FOR AGRICULTURAL DEVELOPMENT

The Arab Organisation for Agricultural Development was founded in 1970 to create and develop links between Arab states in all agricultural activities.

Arab Organisation for Agricultural Development, 7 Amarat Street, P.O.Box 474, Khartoum 11111, Sudan. Tel: +249 18 347 2176, fax: +249 18 347 1402, e-mail: info@aoad.org, URL: http://ww.aoad.org

AVRDC - WORLD VEGETABLE CENTER

AVRDC- The World Vegetable Center (formerly the Asian Vegetable Research and Development Center) focuses on vegetable research and development. It aims to reduce poverty and malnutrition in developing countries by improved production and consumption of vegetables.

Director General: Dr Junne-Jih Chen

AVRDC - World Vegetable Center, P.O. Box 42, Shanhua, Tainan 74199, Taiwan ROC. Tel: +886 6583 7801, fax: +886 6583 0009, e-mail: avrdcbox@avrdc.org, URL: http://www.avrdc.org

COLLABORATIVE INTERNATIONAL PESTICIDES ANALYTICAL COUNCIL (CIPAC)

CIPAC aims to promote the international agreement on methods of analysis of pesticides used in crop protection.

Chairman: Dr Ralf Hanel (Germany)

Collaborative International Pesticides Analytical Council (CIPAC), Abteilung 2, Pflanzenschutzmittel, Referat 206, Messenweg 11/12, D-38104 Braunsenweig, Germany. Tel: +49 (0)531 299 5306, fax: +49 (0)531 299 3002, e-mail: cipac@acw.admin.ch, URL: http://www.cipac.org

EUROPEAN AND MEDITERRANEAN PLANT PROTECTION ORGANIZATION (EPPO)

EPPO is an intergovernmental organisation responsible for European cooperation in plant health. Its objectives are to protect plants, to develop international strategies against the introduction and spread of dangerous pests and to promote safe and effective control methods. EPPO's membership has grown from 15 member states to 50.

Director-General: Mr R. Arnitis

European and Mediterranean Plant Protection Organization (EPPO) (Organisation Européenne et Méditerranéenne pour la Protection des Plantes), 21 boulevard Richard Lenoir, 75011 Paris, France. Tel: +33 (0)1 45 20 77 94, fax: +33 (0)1 70 76 65 47, e-mail: hq@eppo.fr, URL: http://www.eppo.org

EUROPEAN ASSOCIATION FOR ANIMAL PRODUCTION (EAAP)

Aims to improve the condition of animal production and meet consumer demand.

Secretary General: Andrea Rosati

European Association for Animal Production (EAAP), Via G. Tomassetti 3, 1/A, 00161 Rome, Italy. Tel: +39 06 4420 2639, fax: +39 06 8632 9263, e-mail: eaap@eaap.org, URL: http://www.eaap.org

EUROPEAN GRASSLAND FEDERATION (EGF)

EGF is a forum for research workers, advisors, teachers, farmers and policy makers with active interest in all aspects of grasslands in Europe. These aspects include management of all types of grasslands for production, utilization, amenities and conservation purposes.

General Secretary: Dr. Willy Kessler

European Grassland Federation (EGF), Reckenholzstrasse 191, CH- 8046 Zürich, Switzerland. Tel: +41 (0)44 377 7276, fax: +41 (0)44 377 7201, e-mail: fedsecretary@europeangrassland.org, URL: http://www.europeangrassland.org

EUROPEAN LIVESTOCK AND MEAT TRADING UNION (UECBV)

Aims to serve and defend the legitimate interests of the livestock and meat trade with particular regard to: common agricultural policy; veterinary issues (public health, animal health, animal welfare); international trade; and competition. UECBV represents approximately 20,000 firms and 230,000 jobs.

Secretary General: Jean-Luc Mériaux

European Livestock and Meat Trading Union (UECBV), P.O. Box 9, 81A Rue de la Loi, 1040 Brussels, Belgium. Tel: +32 (0)2 230 4603, fax: +32 (0)2 230 9400, e-mail: info@uecbv.eu, URL: http://www.uecbv.eu

INTER-AMERICAN INSTITUTE FOR COOPERATION ON AGRICULTURE

Founded in 1942, the IICA became the specialized agency for agriculture of the OAS. It has a leading role in agricultural development, modernization and integration.

Director General: Dr Victor Villalobos

Inter-American Institute for Cooperation on Agriculture, 600 m Norte del Cruce Ipis-Coronado, Apartado 55-2000, San Isidro de Coronado, San José, Costa Rica. Tel: +506 2216 0222, fax: +506 2216 0222, e-mail: iicahq@icca.ac.cr, URL: http://www.iica.int

INTER-AMERICAN TROPICAL TUNA COMMISSION (IATTC)

IATTC is responsible for the conservation and management of fisheries for tunas and other species taken by tuna-fishing vessels in the eastern Pacific Ocean. It also has significant responsibilities for the implementation of the International Dolphin Conservation Program (IDCP).

Director: Guillermo A. Compean

Inter-American Tropical Tuna Commission (IATTC), 8604 La Jolla Shores Drive, La Jolla CA 92037-1508, California, USA. Tel: +1 858 546 7100, fax: +1 858 546 7133, e-mail: info@iattc.org, URL: http://www.iattc.org

INTERNATIONAL ASSOCIATION FOR CEREAL SCIENCE AND TECHNOLOGY (ICC)

ICC is: an independent, internationally recognised organisation of experts; a neutral forum for all cereal scientists and technologists; publisher of international standard methods and an organiser of national and international events.

Secretary General: Dr. Roland E. Poms

International Association for Cereal Science and Technology (ICC), Marxergasse 2, A-1030 Vienna, Austria. Tel: +43 (0)1 7077 2020, fax: +43 (0)1 7077 2040, e-mail office@icc.or.at, URL: http://www.icc.or.at

INTERNATIONAL ASSOCIATION FOR VEGETATION SCIENCE (IAVS)

IAVS is an international association for all individuals interested in vegetation science. Its aims are to promote research and education in vegetation science; to facilitate scientific and personal contacts among vegetation scientists of all countries and; to promote applications of vegetation science.

President: Martin Diekmann

International Association for Vegetation Science (IAVS), URL: http://www.iavs.org

INTERNATIONAL ASSOCIATION OF AGRICULTURAL ECONOMISTS (IAEE)

A worldwide confederation of agricultural economists and others concerned with agricultural economic problems, including problems related to the use of renewable resources and the environment.

President: Keijiro Otsuka, Japan
President Elect: Johan Swinner, Belgium

International Association of Agricultural Economists (IAEE), 555 East Wells Street, Suite 1100, Milwaukee, WI 53202, USA. Tel: +1 414 918 3199, fax: +1 414 276 3349, e-mail: iaae@execinc.com, URL: http://www.iaae-agecon.org

INTERNATIONAL ASSOCIATION OF HORTICULTURAL PRODUCERS (IAHP)

A coordinating body representing horticultural producers' organisations all over the world. It aims to stimulate international marketing of flowers, plants and landscaping services.

President: Doeke Faber

International Association of Horticultural Producers (IAHP), Oude Herenweg 10, 2215 RZ Voorhout, The Netherlands. E-mail: sg@aiph.org, URL: http://www.aiph.org

INTERNATIONAL BEE RESEARCH ASSOCIATION (IBRA)

A charity working to increase awareness of the vital role of bees in the environment and to encourage the use of bees as wealth creators.

President: Prof. Octaaf Van Laere

International Bee Research Association (IBRA), 16 North Road, Cardiff CF10 3DY, UK. Tel: +44 (0)29 2037 2409, fax: +44 (0)5601 135640, e-mail: mail@ibra.org.uk, URL: http://www.ibra.org.uk

INTERNATIONAL COMMISSION FOR THE CONSERVATION OF ATLANTIC TUNAS (ICCAT)

An inter-governmental fishery organisation responsible for the conservation of tunas and tuna-like species in the Atlantic Ocean and its adjacent seas.

Executive Secretary: Mr Driss Meski

International Commission for the Conservation of Atlantic Tunas (ICCAT), 8 Calle Corazón de María, Sixth Floor, 28002 Madrid, Spain. Tel: +34 91 416 5600, fax: +34 91 415 2612, e-mail: info@iccat.int, URL: http://www.iccat.int

INTERNATIONAL DAIRY FEDERATION (IDF)

An organisation created by the dairy sector worldwide where dairy specialists of all kinds meet to resolve common issues and exchange ideas and experience. IDF work is strategically focused on providing science-based information on which governments and legislators can develop policy and regulations.

Director General: Christian Robert

International Dairy Federation (IDF), 70/B, Boulevard Auguste Reyers, 1030 Brussels, Belgium. Tel: +32 (0)2 733 9888, fax: +32 (0)2 733 0413, e-mail: info@fil-idf.org, URL: http://www.fil-idf.org

INTERNATIONAL FEDERATION OF BEEKEEPERS' ASSOCIATIONS (APIMONDIA)

Promotes scientific, ecological, social and economic apicultural development in all countries and the cooperation of beekeepers' associations, scientific bodies and of individuals involved in apiculture worldwide.

President: Gilles Ratia

International Federation of Beekeepers' Associations (APIMONDIA), Corso Vittorio Emanuele II, I-00186 Rome, Italy. Tel.: +39 06 685 2286, fax: +39 06 685 2287, e-mail: Apimondia@mclink.it, URL: http://www.apimondia.org

INTERNATIONAL INSTITUTE OF TROPICAL AGRICULTURE (IITA)

IITA's mission is to enhance food security and improve livelihoods in Africa through research for development.

Director General: Mr Hartmann

International Institute of Tropical Agriculture (IITA), Oyo Road, PMB 5320, Ibadan, Oyo State, Nigeria. Tel: +234 803 403 5281-3, fax: +234 2 2412221, e-mail: hartmann@cgiar.org, URL: http://www.iita.org

INTERNATIONAL LIVESTOCK RESEARCH INSTITUTE (ILRI)

Focussed on livestock and poverty, bringing high-quality science and capacity-building to bear on poverty reduction and sustainable development. ILRI works in Africa, Asia and Latin America, with offices in East and West Africa, South and Southeast Asia, China and Central America.

Director General: Jimmy Smith

International Livestock Research Institute (ILRI), P.O. Box 30709, Nairobi 00100, Kenya. Tel: +254 20 422 3000, fax: +254 20 422 3001, e-mail: ILRI-Kenya@cgiar.org, URL: http://www.ilri.org

INTERNATIONAL ORGANISATION FOR BIOLOGICAL AND INTEGRATED CONTROL OF NOXIOUS ANIMALS AND PLANTS (IOBC)

IOBC promotes environmentally safe methods of pest and disease control. It is a voluntary organisation of biological-control workers. Membership in IOBC gives individuals and organizations the opportunity to participate in biological control activities beyond their specific jobs and workplaces, to step outside their bureaucracies, and to contribute to the promotion of biological control worldwide.

President: Prof. Dr. Barbara Barratt

International Organisation for Biological and Integrated Control of Noxious Animals and Plants (IOBC), University of Hawaii at Manoa, Kauai Agricultural Research Center, 7370 Kuamoo Road, Kapaa, Hawaii, USA 96746. Tel: +1 8088 2249 8431, e-mail: messing@hawaii.edu, URL: http://www.iobc-global.org

INTERNATIONAL RICE COMMISSION

Promotes national and international action in respect of production, conservation, distribution and consumption of rice.

Executive Secretary: Peter Kenmore

International Rice Commission, Agriculture Department, Food and Agriculture Organization of the United Nations (FAO), Via delle Terme di Caracalla, 00100 Rome, Italy. Tel: +39 (0)6 5705 6265, fax: +39 (0)6 5705 6347, e-mail: nguu.nguyen@fao.org, URL: http://www.fao.org

INTERNATIONAL RICE RESEARCH INSTITUTE (IRRI)

IRRI is a nonprofit research and training organization. It develops new rice varieties and rice crop managment techniques in order to improved the qyuality and yield of rice in an environmentally sustainable way. It mission includes reduction of poverty and hunger.

Director General: Robert S. Zeigler

International Rice Research Institute (IRRI), P.O Box 7777, Manila, Philippines. Tel: +63 2 580 5600, fax: +63 2 580 5699, e-mail: irri@cgiar.org, URL: http://www.irri.org

INTERNATIONAL SEED TESTING ASSOCIATION (ISTA)

ISTA members work together to achieve the vision of Uniformity in seed quality evaluation worldwide. The Association produces internationally agreed rules for seed sampling and testing, accredits laboratories, promotes research, provides international seed analysis certificates and training, and disseminates knowledge in seed science and technology. This facilitates seed trading nationally and internationally, and also contributes to food security.

Secretary General: Dr. Michael Muschick

International Seed Testing Association (ISTA), Zürichstrasse 50, 8303 Bassersdorf, Switzerland. Tel: +41 (0)44 838 6000, fax: +41 (0)44 838 6001, e-mail ista.office@ista.ch, URL: http://www.seedtest.org

INTERNATIONAL SOCIETY FOR HORTICULTURAL SCIENCE (ISHS)

Aims to promote and to encourage research in all branches of horticulture and to facilitate cooperation of scientific activities and knowledge transfer on a global scale by means of its publications, events and scientific structure. It has more than 700 members in 150 countries.

Executive Director: Jozef Van Assche

International Society for Horticultural Science (ISHS), P.O Box 500, 3001 Leuven 1, Belgium. Tel: +32 (0)1 622 9427, fax: +32 (0)1 622 9450, e-mail: info@ishs.org, URL: http://www.ishs.org

NATIONAL FARMERS' FEDERATION OF AUSTRALIA

The National Farmers' Federation was established in 1979 and is the national voice for Australian farmers. It is a federation of Australian farm organisations representing Australian farmers through its member organisations. Its principal goals focus on three core policy areas: - Reducing farmers' costs (through industrial relations, tax policy, fuel, interest rates etc.); Increasing the size of markets (through our trade efforts and addressing market dominance in the domestic market); and Improving the sustainability of agriculture (through ensuring water and land resource security and ensuring policies encourage farmers to manage their resources sustainably).

President: Jock Laurie

National Farmers' Federation of Australia, NFF House, 14-16 Brisbane Avenue, Barton, ACT 2600, Australia. Tel: +61 (0)2 6273 3855, fax: +61 (0)2 6273 2331, e mail: nff@nff.org.au, URL: http://www.nff.org. au

OTHER INTERNATIONAL AND NATIONAL ORGANISATIONS

NATIONAL INSTITUTE OF AGRICULTURAL BOTANY (NIAB)

An independent charitable company that provides technical services to governments, supra-governmental agencies, agribusiness, the food industry and farmers.

Chief Executive Officer: Dr. Tina Barsby

National Institute of Agricultural Botany (NIAB), Huntingdon Road, Cambridge CB3 0LE, UK. Tel: +44 (0)1223 342200, fax: +44 (0)1223 277602, e-mail: info@niab.com, URL: http://www.niab.com

NORTHWEST ATLANTIC FISHERIES ORGANIZATION

The 12 member countries (Canada, Cuba, Denmark (in respect of Faroe Islands and Greenland), European Union, France (in respect of Saint Pierre and Miquelon), Iceland, Japan, Republic of Korea, Norway, Russian Federation, Ukraine and USA) aim to contribute to the optimum use, rational management and conservation of the fish resources of the Convention Area.

General Council Chairman and President: Veronika Veits (EU)

Northwest Atlantic Fisheries Organization, 2 Morris Drive, Suite 100, P.O.Box 638, Dartmouth, Nova Scotia, Canada B2Y 3Y9. Tel: +1 902 468 5590, fax: +1 902 468 5538, e-mail: info@nafo.int, URL: http://www.nafo.int

SOIL ASSOCIATION

A worldwide charity, founded in 1946, to promote a fuller understanding of the vital relationship between soil, plant, animal and man. It encourages an ecological approach and offers organic husbandry as a viable alternative to modern intensive methods.

Royal Patron: HRH The Prince of Wales (page 1403)
Director: Helen Browning

Soil Association, South Plaza, Marlborough Street, Bristol, BS1 3NX, UK. Tel: +44 (0)117 314 5000, fax: +44 (0)117 314 5001, e-mail: info@soilassociation.org, URL: http://www.soilassociation.org

WORLD ORGANISATION FOR ANIMAL HEALTH (OIE)

The World Organisation for Animal Health (OIE) is an intergovernmental organisation with a mandate from its 178 Members to improve world animal health. The OIE is responsible for ensuring transparency of the world animal disease situation, including diseases transmissible to humans, as well as for the sanitary safety of international trade of animals and animal products. The organisation elaborates international standards recognized by the World Trade Organization in all fields relevant to its mandate, which include animal welfare. The OIE maintains permanent relations with 45 other international and regional organisations and has Regional and sub-regional Offices on every continent.

Director General: Dr Bernard Vallat

World Organisation for Animal Health, 12 rue de Prony 75017 Paris, France. Tel: +33 (0)1 44 15 18 88, fax: +33 (0)1 42 67 09 87, e-mail: oie@oie.int, URL: http://www.oie.int

WORLD'S POULTRY SCIENCE ASSOCIATION (WPSA)

Strives to advance knowledge and understanding of all aspects of poultry science and the poultry industry. Its major role is to encourage liaison among research scientists and educators, and between those in research and education and those working in the many diverse sectors of the industry.

President: Dr. R.A.E. Pym
Secretary: Dr. R.W.A.W. Mulder

World's Poultry Science Association (WPSA), P.O Box 31, 7360 AA Beekbergen, The Netherlands. Tel: +31 (0)55 506 3250, fax: +31 (0)55 506 4858, e-mail: wpsa@xs4all.nl, URL: http://www.wpsa.com

Commodities

AFRICA RICE CENTER

Africa Rice Center (formerly WARDA) is the premier research centre for rice development in sub-Saharan Africa. It also serves as a hub for rice-related research and development networks in the region.

Director General: Dr Papa Abdoulaye Seck

Africa Rice Center, 01 B.P 2551, Bouaké 01, Côte d'Ivoire. Tel: +225 3165 9300, fax: +225 3165 9311, URL: http://www.africarice.org/

ASIAN AND PACIFIC COCONUT COMMUNITY (APCC)

An inter-governmental organisation which promotes and co-ordinates production, processing, marketing and research of coconut products in 17 major coconut producing countries.

Executive Director: Romulu N. Arancon, Jnr

Asian and Pacific Coconut Community, 3rd Floor, Lina Building, Jl. H.R. Rasuna Said Kav.B7, Kuningan, Jakarta 12920, Indonesia. P.O Box 1343, Jakarta 10013, Indonesia. Tel: +62 (21) 522 1712, fax: +62 (21) 522 1714, e-mail: apcc@indo.net.id, URL: http://www.apccsec.org

ASSOCIATION OF THE EUROPEAN SUGAR INDUSTRY (CEFS)

CEFS represents and defends the interests of all European sugar manufacturers and refiners among the European Institutions and among different international organisations and provides its members with all relevant information on the development of European legislation. It promotes dialogue and exchanges of information, participates in scientific research, carries out economic studies and arranges for the adoption of common positions whenever necessary.

Director-General: Marie-Christine Ribera

Association of the European Sugar Industry (CEFS) (Comité Européen des Fabricants de Sucre), Avenue de Tervuren 182, 1150 Brussels, Belgium. Tel: +32 (0)2 762 0760, fax: +32 (0)2 771 0026, e-mail: cefs@cefs.org, URL: http://www.cefs.org

COCOA PRODUCERS' ALLIANCE (COPAL)

Consists of 10 cocoa producing countries which account for 75 per cent of the world's coca production. COPAL aims to exchange technical and scientific information, discuss problems of mutual interest and to advance social and economic relations between producers.

Coca Producing Alliance (COPAL), National Assembly Complex, Tafawa Balewa Square, P.O.Box 1178, Lagos, Nigeria. Tel: +234 1 263 5574, fax: +234 1 263 5684, e-mail: info@copal-cpa.org, URL: http://www.copal-cpa.org

EUROPEAN ALUMINUM ASSOCIATION (EAA)

The overall objective of the EAA is to secure sustainable growth of aluminium in its markets and to maintain and improve the image of the aluminium industry towards target audiences.

Secretary General: Patrick de Schrynmakers

European Aluminum Association (EAA), Avenue de Broqueville 12, B-1150 Brussels, Belgium. Tel: +32 (0)2 755 6363, fax: +32 (0)2 779 0531, e-mail: eaa@aluminium.org, URL: http://www.eaa.net

EUROPEAN ASSOCIATION FOR THE TRADE IN JUTE AND RELATED PRODUCTS

Maintains contacts between national associations, carries out scientific research and encourages the exchange of information.

Secretary General: L. van der Ziel

European Association for the Trade in Jute and Related Products (EUROJUTE), P.O. Box 93002, 2509 AA, The Hague, The Netherlands. Tel: +31 (0)70 3349 0750, fax: +31 (0)70 349 0775, e-mail: info@eurojute.com, URL: http://www.eurojute.com

INTERNATIONAL GRAINS COUNCIL (IGC)

Administers the two conventions contained in the International Grains Agreement 1995 concerning grain trade and food aid. The Grains Trade Convention (GTC) applies to trade in wheat, maize, barley, sorghum and other grains, and their products. Under the Food Aid Convention (FAC) donors pledge to provide annually specified minimum amounts or values of food aid to developing countries in the form of grains and other eligible products. Current memberships is 25 states and the European Union.

International Grains Council: 1 Canada Square, Canary Wharf, London E14 5AE, United Kingdom. Tel : +44 (0)20 7513 1122, fax: +44 (0)20 7513 0630, e-mail: igc@igc.org.uk, URL: http://www.igc.int

INTERNATIONAL ORGANISATION OF VINE AND WINE (OIV)

Promotes and guides scientific and technical research and experimentation; draws up recommendations and monitors the implementation of such recommendations in liaison with its members, especially in the following areas: conditions for grape production, oenological practices, definition and/or description of products, labelling and marketing conditions, methods for analysing and assessing vine products.

President: Mr. Yves Bénard

International Organisation of Vine and Wine (OIV), 18 Rue d'Aguesseau. 75008 Paris, France. Tel: +33 (0)1 44 94 80 80, fax: +33 (0)1 42 66 90 63, e-mail: contact@oiv.int, URL: http://www.oiv.int

INTERNATIONAL PEPPER COMMUNITY (IPC)

Co-ordinates and stimulates research on technical and economic aspects of production, including research on diseases affecting the pepper plant and research on development of disease-resistant and high-yielding varieties; facilitates the exchange of information on programmes and policies and on any other aspects relating to production; and develops programmes for increasing consumption in traditional and new markets, including programmes of co-operation in promotion activities.

Executive Director: S. Kannan

International Pepper Community (IPC), 4th Floor LINA Building, Jln. H.R. Rasuna Said Kav. B7, Kuningan, Jakarta 12920, Indonesia. Tel: +62 21 522 4902, fax: +62 21 522 4905, e-mail: mail@ipcnet.org and ipc@indo.net.id, URL: http://www.ipcnet.org

INTERNATIONAL PLATINUM GROUP METALS ASSOCIATION (IPA)

A non-profit association that represents the worldwide leading mining, production and fabrication companies in the global platinum group metals (PGMs) industry, comprising platinum, palladium, iridium, rhodium, osmium and ruthenium. Its major activities cover areas of emission control legislation, environment, health & safety, sustainable development, and communication.

President: Alexander Wood

International Platinum Group Metals Association (IPA), Schiess-Staett-Strasse 30, Munich D-80339, Germany. Tel: +49 (0)89 5199 6770, fax: +49 (0)89 5199 6719, e-mail: info@platinuminfo.net, URL: http://www.ipa-news.com

INTERNATIONAL TOBACCO GROWERS' ASSOCIATION (ITGA)

A non-profit organisation founded in 1984 with the objective of presenting the cause of millions of tobacco farmers to the world. It develops contact between tobacco growers around the world, shares non-competitive information about the crop with its members and forms strategies to stabilise supply and prices.

Chief Executive: Mr Antonio Abrunhosa

International Tobacco Growers' Association, Av. Gen. Humberto Delgado 30, 6000-081 Castelo Branco, Portugal. Tel.: + 351 272 325 901, fax: + 351 272 325 906, e-mail: itga@tobaccoleaf.org, URL: http://www.tobaccoleaf.org

INTERNATIONAL TROPICAL TIMBER ASSOCIATION

A commodity organisation which brings together countries which produce and consume tropical timber, to exchange information and develop policies on all aspects of the world tropical timber economy.

Executive Director: Dr. Emmanuel Z. Meka

International Tropical Timber Association, International Organizations Center, 5th Floor, Pacifico-Yokohama 1-1-1, Minator-Mirai, Nishi-Ku, Yokohama, 220-0012, Japan. Tel: +81 45 223 1110, fax: +81 45 223 1111, e-mail: itto@itto.or.jp, URL: http://www.itto.or.jp

INTERNATIONAL TUNGSTEN INDUSTRY ASSOCIATION (ITIA)

Promotes the use of tungsten and tungsten products; monitors global regulations on health, safety and the environment; collects scientific data on tungsten; and organises regular meetings for the tungsten industry worldwide.

International Tungsten Industry Association (ITIA), 4 Heathfield Terrace, London, W4 4JE, United Kingdom. Tel: +44 (0)20 8996 2221, fax: +44 (0)20 8994 8728, e-mail: info@itia.info, URL: http://www.itia.info

REGIONAL ASSOCIATION OF OIL AND NATURAL GAS COMPANIES IN LATIN AMERICA AND THE CARIBBEAN (ARPEL)

ARPEL works together with its members on issues that contribute to sustainable development in the Region: regional energy integration, refining fuels, climate change, atmospheric emissions, oil spill contingency plans and best practices in environment and occupational health and safety management, corporate social responsibility, relations with indigenous peoples, gender analysis and transparency.

Regional Association of Oil and Natural Gas Companies in Latin America and the Caribbean (ARPEL), Javier de Viana 1018, 11200 Montevideo, Uruguay. Tel: +598 2 410 6993, fax: +598 2 410 9207, URL: http://www.arpel.org

WORLD ASSOCIATION OF BEET AND CANE GROWERS (WABCG)

The only international organisation that brings together national-level organisations of beet and cane growers on a worldwide basis to provide a forum to discuss common interests, problems and solutions.

President: Alf Cristaudo (Australia)

World Association of Beet and Cane Growers (WABCG), 60 rue Saint-Lazare, 75009 Paris, France. Tel: +33 (0)1 45 26 05 53, fax: +33 (0)1 48 74 72 12, e-mail: wabcg@ifap.org, URL: http://www.wabcg.org

WORLD FEDERATION OF DIAMOND BOURSES (WFDB)

Aims to provide bourses trading in rough and polished diamonds and precious stones with a common set of trading practises and to promote understanding and closer co-operation between peoples all over the world who earn their livelihood in the diamond and precious stones trade.

Secretary General: Mr Michael H. Vaughan

World Federation of Diamond Bourses (WFDB), Pelikaanstraat 62, B-2018 Antwerpen, Belgium. Tel: +32 (0)3 234 9121, fax: +32 (0)3 226 4073, e-mail: info@worldfed.com, URL: http://www.worldfed.com / http://www.wfdbmark.com

WORLD GOLD COUNCIL

An organisation formed and funded by the world's leading gold mining companies with the aim of stimulating and maximising the demand for, and holding of, gold by consumers, investors, industry, and the official sector.

Chief Executive Officer: Aran Shishmanian

World Gold Council, 10 Old Bailey, London EC2M 7NG, UK. Tel. +44 (0)20 7826 4700, fax: +44(0)20 7826 4799, e-mail: info@gold.org, URL: http://www.gold.org

WORLD SUGAR RESEARCH ORGANISATION (WSRO)

An international scientific research organisation supported by the sugar industry globally. WSRO's objective is to monitor and communicate research on the role of sugar, and other carbohydrates, in nutrition and health.

Director-General: Dr Richard Cottrell

World Sugar Research Organisation (WSRO), 70 Collingwood House, Dolphin Square, London SW1V 3LX, UK. Tel: +44 (0)20 7821 6800, fax: +44 (0)20 7834 4137, e-mail: wsro@wsro.org, URL: http://www.wsro.org

Communications & Media

ASSOCIATION OF EUROPEAN JOURNALISTS (AEJ)

AEJ brings together individual journalists through their membership of the national sections. It was formed to defend the freedom of information and freedom of the press in Europe and to promote European harmony.

Secretary-General: N. Peter Kramer

Association of European Journalists (AEJ), 145 Avenue Baron Albert d'Huart, B 150 Kraainem, Belgium. E-mail: npkramer@skynet.be, URL: http://www.aej.org

COMMONWEALTH TELECOMMUNICATIONS ORGANISATION

The Commonwealth Telecommunications Organisation is an inter-governmental development partnership between Commonwealth and non-Commonwealth governments, telecommunications businesses, international organisations and civil society organisations which is dedicated to promoting social and economic development in the Commonwealth and beyond by helping to bridge the digital divide.

Chairman: Anusha Palpita

Commonwealth Telecommunications Organisation, 64-66 Glenthorne Road, London W6 0LR, UK. Tel: +44 (0)208 600 3800, e-mail: info@cto.int, URL: http://www.cto.int

DISTRIPRESS

Distripress is the association for the promotion of international press distribution. Links distributors, publishers and their suppliers on an international level and supports the promotion of the international distribution of newspapers, magazines and pocket books. Distripress promotes business contacts, supports a fair and efficient trade and intervenes in favour of press freedom.

President: Tony Jashanmal

Distripress, Beethovenstrasse 20, CH-8002 Zürich, Switzerland. Tel: +41 (0)44 202 4121, fax: +41 (0)44 202 1025, e-mail: info@distripress.net, URL: http://www.distripress.net

OTHER INTERNATIONAL AND NATIONAL ORGANISATIONS

ENGLISH-SPEAKING UNION

The English-Speaking Union (ESU) is committed to creating international understanding through English at a time when English has become the working language of the global village. At the heart of ESU's response is the role of public speaking, discussion and debate.

Patron: HM Queen Elizabeth II (page 1420)
President: HRH The Prince Philip Duke of Edinburgh KG KT (page 1419)
Chairman: The Rt. Hon. The Lord Hunt of Wirral MBE PC (page 1445)
Director-General: Michael Lake CBE

English-Speaking Union, Dartmouth House, 37 Charles Street, London W1J 5ED, UK. Tel: +44 (0)20 7529 1550, fax: +44 (0)20 7495 6108, e-mail: esu@esu.org, URL: http://www.esu.org

EUROPEAN BROADCASTING UNION (EBU)

The EBU serves 85 national media organizations in 56 countries in and around Europe. It represents its members and promotes the values and distinctiveness of public service media in Europe and around the world. The Eurovision and Euroradio networks deliver news, sports, events and music to EBU members and other media organizations. Services to members range from legal advice, technical standardization and development to co-production and exchange of quality European content.

President: Jean-Paul Philippot (RTBF, Belgium)
Secretary General: Ingrid Deltenre

European Broadcasting Union, Ancienne Route 17A, CH 1218 Grand-Saconnex (GE), Switzerland. Tel: +42 (0)22 717 2111, fax: +41 (0)22 747 4999, e-mail: ebu@ebu.ch, URL: http://www.ebu.ch

INTER-AMERICAN PRESS ASSOCIATION (IAPA)

IAPA is a non-profit organization committed to defending freedom of speech and freedom of the press in the Americas.

Executive Director: Milton Coleman (USA)

Inter-American Press Association (IAPA), Jules Dubois Building, 1801 S.W. 3rd Avenue, Miami, Florida 33129, USA. Tel: +1 305 634 2465, fax: +1 305 635 2272, URL: http://www.sipiapa.org

INTERNATIONAL ASSOCIATION FOR MARINE ELECTRONICS COMPANIES (CIRM)

CIRM is the principal international association for marine electronics. Members include major manufacturers, suppliers, system operators and service providers, covering the whole field of marine navigation, communications and information systems.

Secretary General: Michael Rambaut

International Association for Marine Electronics Companies (CIRM), Southbank House, Black Prince Road, London SE1 7SJ, Tel: +44 (0)20 7587 1245, fax: +44 (0)20 7587 1436, e-mail: SECGEN@CIRM.ORG, URL: http://www.cirm.org

INTERNATIONAL COUNCIL OF FRENCH-SPEAKING RADIO AND TELEVISION ORGANIZATIONS (CIRTEF)

Aims to: establish, throughout the world, a permanent dialogue between broadcasting organizations which use the French language entirely or partially in their national or regional programs and promote the role of radio and television in the development of the community.

Secretary General: Guila Thiam

International Council of French-speaking Radio and Television Organizations (CIRTEF), 52 Boulevard Auguste-Reyers, 1044 Brussels, Belgium. Tel: +32 (0)2 732 4585, fax: +32 (0)2 732 6240, e-mail: cirtef@rtbf.be, URL: http://www.cirtef.org

INTERNATIONAL FEDERATION OF THE PERIODICAL PRESS (FIPP)

Works for the benefit of magazine publishers around the world; promoting the common editorial, cultural and economic interests of consumer and business-to-business publishers, both in print and electronic media.

President: David Hill

International Federation of the Periodical Press (FIPP), Queens House, 55-56 Lincoln's Inn Fields, London WC2A 3LJ, UK. E-mail: info@fipp.com, URL: http://www.fipp.com

INTERNATIONAL PEN

International PEN is the world association of writers. Its aim is to engage with, and empower, societies and communities across cultures and languages, through reading and writing. It does this through the promotion of literature; international campaigning on issues such as translation and freedom of expression; and improving access to literature at regional, national and international levels.

International President: John Ralston Saul

International Secretary: Tori Takeaki

International PEN Headquaters, Brownlow House, 50/51 High Holborn, London WC1V 6ER, UK. Tel: +44 (0)20 7405 0338, fax: +44 (0)20 7405 0339, e-mail: executivedirector@internationalpen.org.uk, URL: http://www.internationalpen.org.uk

INTERNATIONAL PRESS INSTITUTE (IPI)

A global network of editors, media executives and leading journalists, dedicated to the furtherance and safeguarding of press freedom, the protection of freedom of opinion and expression, the promotion of the free flow of news and information, and the improvement of the practices of journalism.

Director: Alison Bethel McKenzie

International Press Institute (IPI), Spiegelgasse 2, A-1010 Vienna, Austria. Tel: +43 (0)1 512 9011, fax: +43 (0)1 512 9014, e-mail: ipi@freemedia.at, URL: http://www.freemedia.at

INTERNATIONAL PRESS TELECOMMUNICATIONS COUNCIL (IPTC)

A consortium of the world's major news agencies, news publishers and news industry vendors. It develops and maintains technical standards for improved news exchange that are used by major news organization throughout the world.

Managing Director: Michael Steidl

International Press Telecommunications Council (IPTC), Royal Albert House, Sheet Street, Windsor, Berkshire SL4 1BE, UK. Tel: +44 (0)1753 705051, fax: +44 (0)1753 831541, e-mail: office@iptc.org, URL: http://www.iptc.org

INTERNET CORPORATION FOR ASSIGNED NAMES AND NUMBERS (ICANN)

ICANN is responsible for the global coordination of the Internet's system of unique identifiers. These include domain names as well as the addresses used in a variety of Internet protocols.

President: Rod Beckstrom

Internet Corporation for Assigned Names and Numbers (ICANN), 4676 Admiralty Way, Suite 330, Marina del Rey, California 90292-6601, USA. Tel: +1 310 823 9358, fax: +1 310 823 8649, e-mail: icann@icann.org, URL: http://www.icann.org

WORLD ASSOCIATION OF NEWSPAPERS AND NEWS PUBLISHERS (WAN-IFRA)

WAN-IFRA was formed in 2009 with the merger of the World Association of Newspapers and IFRA. The global organisation of the world's press, WAN-IFRA defends and promotes press freedom, strong journalism and the development of press business. It represents more than 18,000 publications, 15,000 online sites and over 3,000 companies in over 120 countries.

President: Jacob Mathew

World Association of Newspapers and News Publishers (WAN-IFRA), Washingtonplatz 1, 64287 Darmstadt, Germany. Tel: +49 6151 733 6, fax: +49 6151 733 800, e-mail: info@wan-ifra.org, URL: http://www.wan-ifra.org/

Development

ACTIONAID

Actionaid works in partnership with the poorest and most vulnerable people to eradicate poverty by overcoming the injustice and inequality that cause it.

Chief Executive: Joanna Kerr

Actionaid UK, 33-39 Bowling Green Lane, London, EC1R 0BJ, UK. Tel: +44 (0)20 3122 0734, fax: +44 (0)20 7278 5667, URL: http://www.actionaid.org

AFRICAN CAPACITY BUILDING FOUNDATION (ACBF)

Aims to build and strengthen sustainable human and institutional capacity in the core public sector, in the sector's interface areas with the private sector and civil society, in training and research institutions as well as within regional organizations in order to spur economic growth, poverty reduction, good governance and effective participation by Africa in the global economy.

Executive Secretary: Dr. Frannie Léautier

African Capacity Building Foundation (ACBF), Z B Life Towers 7th, 14th & 15th Floors, Cnr Sam Nujoma St. & Jason Moyo Avenue, P.O. Box 1562, Harare, Zimbabwe. Tel: +263 4 790398, fax: +263 4 702915, e-mail: root@acbf-pact.org, URL: http://www.acbf-pact.org

AFRICAN TRAINING AND RESEARCH CENTRE IN ADMINISTRATION FOR DEVELOPMENT (CAFRAD)

The African Training and Research Centre in Administration for Development (CAFRAD) is a Pan African intergovernmental organization, established in 1964 by African governments, with the support of UNESCO; making it the first uniquely Pan-African training and research center in the continent for the improvement of public administration and governance systems in Africa. Its headquarters is located in Tangier (Morocco). Membership is open to all African countries: at present, CAFRAD has a membership of 36 States.

Director General: Dr. Simon Mamosi Lelo

African Training and Research Centre in Administration for Development (CAFRAD), P.O. Box 310, Tangier 90001, Morocco. Tel: +212 39 322707, fax: +212 39 325785, e-mail: cafrad@cafrad.org, URL: http://www.cafrad.org

ATD FOURTH WORLD

ATD Fourth World is an anti-poverty organisation that engages with individuals and institutions to find solutions to eradicate extreme poverty.

Chairperson: Rev. Nick Edwards

ATD Fourth World (UK), 48 Addingon Square, London, UK. Tel: +44 (0)20 7703 3231, fax: +44 (0)20 7252 4276, e-mail: atd@atd-uk.org, URL: http://www.atd-uk.org

CARITAS INTERNATIONALIS

Caritas provides aid to tens of millions of women, men and children in times of hardship and contributes to the development of social justice in times of peace. Caritas' mandate includes integral development, emergency relief, advocacy, peace building, respect for human rights and support for proper stewardship of the planet's environment and resources.

Secretary General: Lesley-Anne Knight

Caritas Internationalis, Palazzo San Calisto, 00120 Vatican City, Italy. Tel: +39 6 698 79799, fax: +39 6 698 87237, e-mail: caritas.internationalis@caritas.va, URL: http://www.caritas.org

DEVELOPING EIGHT (D-8)

The objectives of D-8 are to improve developing countries' positions in the world economy, diversify and create new opportunities in trade relations, enhance participation in decision-making at the international level, and provide better standards of living.

Secretary General: H.E. Widi Pratikto

Developing Eight (D-8), Maya Akar Center, Buyukdere Cad. 100 - 102, Kat:22, D:87, Esentepe 34390, Istanbul, Turkey. Tel: +90 212 356 1823, fax: +90 212 356 1829, e-mail: secretariat@developing8.org, URL: http://www.developing8.org

ENTERPRISEWORKS / VITA (EWV)

EWV works to combat poverty by helping small producers and other entrepreneurs build sustainable businesses that create jobs and increase productivity, market opportunities and incomes. EWV achieves this by expanding access to appropriate technologies, technical assistance, knowledge and finance. In 2009, Enterprise Works/VITA merged with Relief International.

Chairman: Simon Goodall

EnterpriseWorks / VITA, 1100 H Street NW, Suite 1200, Washington DC 2005, USA. Tel: +1 202 639 8660, fax: +1 202 639 8664, e-mail: info@enterpriseworks.org, URL: http://www.enterpriseworks.org

INTERNATIONAL CO-OPERATION FOR DEVELOPMENT AND SOLIDARITY (CIDSE)

A network of Catholic development organisations in Europe and North America promoting solidarity and justice.

Secretary General: Bernd Nilles

International Co-operation for Development and Solidarity (CIDSE), Street Stévin 16, B-1000 Brussels, Belgium. Tel: +32 (0)2 230 7722, fax: +32 (0)2 230 7082, e-mail: postmaster@cidse.org, URL: http://www.cidse.org

LATIN AMERICAN ASSOCIATION OF DEVELOPMENT FINANCING INSTITUTIONS (ALIDE)

Aims to strengthen the action and participation of the financial institutions in the economic and social process of Latin America and the Caribbean and develop the cooperation between its members. It has more than 70 members in 22 countries.

Secretary General: Roberto Smith

Latin American Association of Development Financing Institutions (ALIDE), Paseo de la República 3211, San Isidro, Lima 27, Peru. Tel: +51 1 442 2400, fax: +51 1 442 8105, e-mail: sg@alide.org.pe, URL: http://www.alide.org.pe

MEKONG RIVER COMMISSION (MRC)

An agreement between the governments of Cambodia, Lao PDR, Thailand and Viet Nam on the joint management of their shared water resources and the development of the economic potential of the river.

Mekong River Commission (MRC), P.O.Box 6101, Vientiane, Laos. Tel: +856 21 263263, fax: +856 21 263264, e-mail: mrcs@mrcmekong.org, URL: http://www.mrcmekong.org

NILE BASIN INITIATIVE

Cooperative venture between nations who share the waters of the Nile river to achieve water security and avert conflicts over water resources. Members include Burundi, Democratic Republic of Congo, Egypt, Ethiopia, Kenya, Rwanda, Sudan, Tanzania and Uganda. Eritrea is as an observer.

Executive Director: Dr Wael Khairy

Nile Basin Initiative, P.O. Box 192, Entebbe, Uganda. Tel: +256 41 321424, fax: +256 41 320971, e-mail: nbisec@nilebasin.org, URL: http://www.nilebasin.org

NORDIC DEVELOPMENT FUND

A multilateral financing organisation. Its aims is to address the mitigation of climate change and support the adaptation to climate change, providing grants to climate change related interventions in low income developing countries. NDF is the joint development finance institution of the Nordic countries (Denmark, Finland, Iceland, Norway and Sweden). NDF finances projects in cooperation with other development institutions. It has financed 190 development assistance credits valued at €1 billion.

Managing Director: Helge Semb

Nordic Development Fund, P.O. Box 185, FIN-00171 Helsinki, Finland. Tel: +358 1 061 8002, fax: +358 9 622 1491, e-mail: info.ndf@ndf.fi, URL: http://www.ndf.fi

PARTNERS IN POPULATION AND DEVELOPMENT (PPD)

Dedicated to the promotion of South-South partnerships to facilitate the improvement of technical and managerial capacities of individuals and institutions in developing countries in order to strengthen their respective reproductive health programmes.

Executive Director: Dr. Harry S. Jooseery

Partners in Population and Development (PPD), IPH Building (2nd Floor), Mohakhali, Dhaka-1212, Bangladesh. Tel: +880 2 988 1882, fax: +880 2 882 9387, e-mail: partners@ppdsec.org, URL: http://www.partners-popdev.org

POPULATION COUNCIL

An international, non-profit, non-governmental organisation, which seeks to improve the well-being and reproductive health of current and future generations around the world and to help achieve a humane, equitable, and sustainable balance between people and resources.

President: Peter J. Donaldson

Population Council, One Dag Hammarskjold Plaza, New York 10017, USA. Tel: +1 212 339 0500, fax: +1 212 755 6052, e-mail: pubinfo@popcouncil.org, URL: http://www.popcouncil.org

VIENNA INSTITUTE FOR DEVELOPMENT AND COOPERATION (VIDC)

Arranges cultural exchanges between Austria and countries from Africa, Asia and Latin America in order to encourage anti-racist and integrative measures in sport, in particular football.

President: Barbara Prammer

Vienna Institute for Development and Cooperation (VIDC), Möllwaldplatz 5/3, 1040 Vienna, Austria. Tel: +43 (0)1 713 3594, fax: +43 (0)1 713 3594, e-mail: office@vidc.org, URL: http://www.vidc.org

WOMANKIND WORLDWIDE

The purpose of the charity is to enhance the lives of women in developing countries. Through partnerships with 37 local organisations in 15 countries, Womankind Worldwide aims to improve the standards of health care and education and to combat poverty, illiteracy and violence against women.

Executive Director: Sue Turrell

Womankind Worldwide, 2nd Floor, Development House, 56 - 64 Leonard Street, EC2A 4LT, UK. Tel: +44 (0)20 7549 0360, fax: +44 (0)20 7549 0361, e-mail: info@womankind.org.uk, URL: http://www.womankind.org.uk

Economics and Finance

AMERICAN BANKERS ASSOCIATION

Organised in 1875, the American Bankers Association is the national organisation of banking. Its membership consists of commercial banks, multi-bank holding companies and the equivalent of US commercial banks in foreign countries.

Chairman: Albert Kelly, Jr

American Bankers Association, 1120 Connecticut Avenue, NW, Washington DC 20036, USA. Tel: +1 202 663 5000, fax: +1 202 663 7543, URL: http://www.aba.com

ARAB FUND FOR ECONOMIC AND SOCIAL DEVELOPMENT

The Arab Fund for Economic and Social Development is an autonomous regional Pan-Arab development finance organisation. Its membership consists of all states who are members of the League of Arab States.

Director General/Chairman of the Board of Directors: Abdlatif Yousef al-Hamad

Arab Fund for Economic & Social Development, PO Box 21923 Safat, 13080 Kuwait. Tel: +965 2495 5000, fax: +965 248 15750 / 60 / 70, e-mail: hq@arabfund.org, URL: http://www.arabfund.org

ASIAN CLEARING UNION (ACU)

A simple form of payment arrangement whereby the members settle payments for intra-regional transactions among the participating central banks on a multilateral basis. This facilitates payments among member countries for eligible transactions, thereby economising on the use of foreign exchange reserves and transfer costs, as well as promoting trade among the participating countries.

Secretary General: Mrs. Lida Borhan-Azad

Asian Clearing Union (ACU), 193 Pasdaran Avenue, P.O. Box 15875/7177, Tehran, Iran. Tel: +98 21 2284 2076, fax: +98 21 2284 7677, e-mail: acusecret@cbi.ir, URL: http://www.asianclearingunion.org

ASIAN REINSURANCE CORPORATION (ARC)

An intergovernmental organisation established under the auspices of UN-ESCAP operating as a professional reinsurer and a development organization providing technical assistance to countries in the Asia-Pacific region.

Chairman: Dr. Abdolnaser Hemmati

Asian Reinsurance Corporation (ARC), 17th Floor, Tower B Chamnan Phenjati Business Center, 65 Rama 9 Road, Huaykwang, Bangkok 10320, Thailand. Tel: +66 2 245 2169, fax: +66 2 248 8011, e-mail: asianre@asianrecorp.com, URL: http://www.asianrecorp.com

ASSOCIATION OF CHARTERED CERTIFIED ACCOUNTANTS

Founded in 1904, the Association of Chartered Certified Accountants is the second largest of the four bodies of professional accountants which are recognised by statute in the United Kingdom and Irish Republic. It supports 147,000 members and 424,00 students through a network of 83 offices.

Chief Executive: Mark Gold

Association of Chartered Certified Accountants, 29 Lincoln's Inn Fields, London WC2A 3EE, Tel: +44 (0)20 7059 5000, fax: +44 (0)20 7059 5050, e-mail: info@accaglobal.com, URL: http://www.accaglobal.com

CENTRE FOR LATIN AMERICAN MONETARY STUDIES (CEMLA)

The regional association of Latin American and Caribbean central banks. Its main objective since 1952 is cooperation amongst its members in order to promote a better knowledge of monetary and financial topics in the region.

Director General: Lic. Javier Guzmán Calafell

Centre for Latin American Monetary Studies (CEMLA), Durango 54, Col. Roma, Del. Cuauhtémoc, Mexico D.F., Mexico. Tel: +52 55 5061 6641, fax: +52 55 5061 6695, e-mail: cemla@cemla.org, URL: http://www.cemla.org

ECONOMETRIC SOCIETY

An international society for the advancement of economic theory in its relation to statistics and mathematics. The main activities of the Society are: publication of the journal Econometrica; publication of a research Monograph Series and; organisation of scientific meetings in six regions of the world.

General Manager: Claire Sashi

Econometric Society, Department of Economics, New York University, 19 West Fourth Street, 6th Floor, New York, NY 10012, USA. Tel: +1 212 998 3820, fax: +1 212 995 4487, e-mail: sashi@econometricsociety.org, URL: http://www.econometricsociety.org

EUROPEAN FEDERATION OF FINANCE HOUSE ASSOCIATIONS (EUROFINAS)

Studies the development of instalment credit financing in Europe, collates and publishes instalment credit statistics, and promotes research into instalment credit practice. It is estimated that Eurofinas members financed over €320 billion worth of new loans in 2009.

Director General: Tanguy van de Werve

European Federation of Finance House Associations (EUROFINAS), Boulevard Louis Schmidt 87 b.3, 1040 Etterbeek, Brussels, Belgium. URL: http://www.eurofinas.org

EUROPEAN FINANCIAL MANAGEMENT & MARKETING ASSOCIATION (EFMA)

EFMA promotes innovation in retail finance by fostering debate and discussion among peers supported by an array of information services and numerous opportunities for direct encounters.

Chairman: Roberto Nicastro

European Financial Management & Marketing Association (EFMA), 8 rue Bayen, 75017 Paris, France. Tel : +33 (0)1 47 42 52 72, fax: +33 (0)1 47 42 56 76, e-mail: info@efma.com, URL: http://www.efma.com

EUROPEAN PRIVATE EQUITY AND VENTURE CAPITAL ASSOCIATION (EVCA)

EVCA represents the European private equity sector and promotes the asset class both within Europe and throughout the world.

Secretary General: Dörte Höppner

European Private Equity and Venture Capital Association (EVCA), Place du Champ de Mars 5, B-1050 Brussels, Belgium. Tel.: +32 (0)2 715 0020, fax: +32 (0)2 725 0704, e-mail: info@evca.com, URL: http://www.evca.com

FINANCIAL ACTION TASK FORCE (FATF)

An inter-governmental body whose purpose is the development and promotion of national and international policies to combat money laundering and terrorist financing. There are currently 36 members of the FATF; 34 jurisdictions and 2 regional organisations (the Gulf Cooperation Council and the European Commission).

President: Giancarlo Del Bufalo

Financial Action Task Force (FATF), 2 rue André Pascal, 75775 Paris Cedex 16, France. Tel: +33 (0)1 45 24 90 90, fax: +33 (0)1 44 30 61 37, e-mail: Contact@fatf-gafi.org, URL: http://www.fatf-gafi.org

INTERNATIONAL ASSOCIATION FOR RESEARCH IN INCOME AND WEALTH

The Association's aims are to further research on national, economic and social accounting, including the concepts and definitions for the measurement and analysis of income and wealth.

Executive Director: Andrew Sharpe

International Association for Research in Income and Wealth, 151 Slater Street, Suite 710, Ottawa, Ontario K1P 5H3, Canada. Tel: +1 613 233 8891, fax: +1 613 233 8250, e-mail: info@iariw.org, URL: http://www.iariw.org

INTERNATIONAL BUREAU OF FISCAL DOCUMENTATION (IBFD)

Offers expertise on cross-border taxation. The IBFD produces independent tax research, international tax information and education with the aim to enable customers to do their work more quickly and efficiently.

Chairman of the Executive Board: Sam Van der Feltz

International Bureau of Fiscal Documentation (IBFD), P.O. Box 20237, 1000 HE Amsterdam, (Visiting address: HJE Wenckebachweg 210, 1096AS Amsterdam), The Netherlands. Tel.: +31 (0)20 554 0100, fax: +31 (0)20 622 8658, e-mail: info@ibfd.org, URL: http://www.ibfd.org

INTERNATIONAL FISCAL ASSOCIATION (IFA)

Its objects are the study and advancement of international and comparative law in regard to public finance, specifically international and comparative fiscal law and the financial and economic aspects of taxation. Membership of IFA now stands at more than 12,000 from 106 countries.

President: M.E. Tron (Mexico)

International Fiscal Association (IFA), World Trade Center, Beursplein 37, P.O. Box 30215, 3001 DE Rotterdam, The Netherlands. Tel: +31 10 405 2990, fax: +31 10 405 5031, e-mail: a.gensecr@ifa.nl, URL: http://www.ifa.nl

INTERNATIONAL UNION FOR HOUSING FINANCE (IUHF)

Established in 1914, the International Union for Housing Finance (IUHF) is a worldwide networking organisation that enables its members to keep up-to-date with the latest developments in housing finance from around the world and to learn from each other's experiences.

Secretary General: Mrs Annik Lambert

International Union for Housing Finance (IUHF), Avenue de Cortenbergh 71, 8th Floor, B-1000 Brussels, Belgium. E-mail: info@housingfinance.org, URL: http://www.housingfinance.org

NORDIC INVESTMENT BANK

An international financial institution which aims to promote sustainable growth in the economies of its member countries through the long-term financing of projects in the private and public sectors. Its members are: Denmark, Finland, Iceland, Norway, Sweden, Estonia, Latvia and Lithuania.

President and CEO: Johnny Åkerholm

Nordic Investment Bank, Fabianinkatu 34, PO Box 249, FI-00171 Helsinki, Finland. Tel: +358 1 061 8001, fax: +358 1 06180 725, e-mail: info@nib.int, URL: http://www.nib.int/

WORLD COUNCIL OF CREDIT UNIONS (WOCCU)

As a worldwide representative organization, WOCCU is the world's leading advocate, platform for knowledge exchange, and development agency for credit unions. Membership includes 188 million members and 53,000 credit unions from 100 countries.

President: Brian Branch

World Council of Credit Unions (WOCCU), 5710 Mineral Point Rd., P.O. Box 2982, Madison, WI 53705-4493, USA. Tel: +1 608 395 2000, fax: +1 608 395 2001, e-mail: mail@woccu.org, URL: http://www.woccu.org

WORLD SAVINGS BANKS INSTITUTE (WSBI)

WSBI is the global voice of savings and retail banking. WSBI represents the interests of savings and retail banks at an international level and fosters members' cooperation.

President and Chairman of the Board: José Antonio Olavarrieta Arcos

World Savings Banks Institute (WSBI), Rue Marie-Thérèse 11, B-1000 Brussels, Belgium. Tel: +32 (0)2 211 1111, fax: +32 (0)2 211 1199, e-mail: info@savings-banks.com, URL: http://www.savings-banks.com

Education

ASSOCIATION FOR CHILDHOOD EDUCATION INTERNATIONAL

Aims to promote and support worldwide the education and development of children, from birth through early adolescence, and to influence the professional growth of all those who are committed to the needs of children in a changing society.

President: Debora Wisneki

Association for Childhood Education International, 17904 Georgia Ave, Suite 215, Olney, Maryland 20832, USA. Tel: +1 301 570 2111, fax: +1 301 570 2212, e-mail: headquarters@acei.org, URL: http://www.acei.org

ASSOCIATION MONTESSORI INTERNATIONALE (AMI)

Founded in 1929 by Dr. Maria Montessori to maintain the integrity of her life's work, and to ensure that it would be perpetuated after her death. AMI's activities include: providing guidance for AMI training courses; co-ordinating a Training of Trainers programme; guiding the manufacturers recognised by AMI in the production of approved Montessori materials; and overseeing the publication of Dr. Montessori's books.

President: André Roberfroid

Association Montessori Internationale, Koninginneweg 161, 1075 CN Amsterdam, The Netherlands. Tel: + 31 20 679 8932, fax: + 31 20 676 7341, e-mail: info@montessori-ami.org, URL: http://www.montessori-ami.org

ASSOCIATION OF ARAB UNIVERSITIES

Aims to enhance co-operation between institutions and co-ordinate their activities in order to raise university and higher education.

Secretary General: Prof. Dr. Saleh Hashem

Association of Arab Universities, P. O. Box 401, Jubeiha 11941, Hashemite, Kingdom of Jordan. Tel: +962 6 506 2048, fax: +962 6 506 2051, e-mail: secgen@aaru.edu.jo, URL: http://www.aaru.edu.jo

ASSOCIATION OF COMMONWEALTH UNIVERSITIES

The Association of Commonwealth Universities is a voluntary body whose aim is to promote contact and co-operation between its member universities in all the regions and countries of the Commonwealth.

Secretary General: Professor E. Nigel Harris (University of the West Indies, Jamaica)

Association of Commonwealth Universities, Woburn House, 20-24 Tavistock Square, London, WC1H 9HF, UK. Tel: +44 (0)20 7380 6700, fax: +44 (0)20 7387 2655, e-mail: info@acu.ac.uk, URL: http://www.acu.ac.uk

ASSOCIATION OF EUROPEAN RESEARCH LIBRARIES (LIBER)

The aim of LIBER is to assist research libraries in Europe to become a functional network across national boundaries in order to ensure the preservation of the European cultural heritage, to improve access to collections in European research libraries, and to provide more efficient information services in Europe.

Executive Director: Wouter Schallier

Lique des Bibliotheques Europeennes de Recherche / Association of European Research Libraries (LIBER), Koninklijke Bibliotheek, National Library of the Netherlands, PO Box 90407, 2509 The Hague, The Netherlands. Fax: +31 (0)70 314 0197, e-mail: liber@kb.nl, RL: http://www.libereurope.eu

BRITISH ACADEMY

The British Academy, established by Royal Charter in 1902, is the national academy for the humanities and the social sciences. It aims to provide leadership in representing the interests of research and learning nationally and internationally and to give recognition to academic excellence and achievement.

Chief Executive and Secretary: Dr. R Jackson

British Academy, 10 Carlton House Terrace, SW1Y 5AH, London, UK. Tel: +44 (0)20 7969 5200, fax: +44 (0)20 7969 5300, e-mail: chiefexec@britac.ac.uk, URL: http://www.britac.ac.uk

BRITISH COMPUTER SOCIETY

The mission of BCS is to enable the information society. It promotes wider social and economic progress through the advancement of IT science and practice. BCS brings together industry, academics, practitioners and government to share knowledge, promote new thinking, inform the design of new curricula, shape public policy and inform the public.

Chief Executive: David Clarke

British Computer Society, 1st Floor, Block D, North Star House, North Star Avenue, Swindon SN2 1FA, Wiltshire, UK. Tel: +44 (0)1793 417417, fax: +44 (0)1793 417444, e-mail: bcshq@hq.bcs.org.uk, URL: http://www.bcs.org

CARIBBEAN EXAMINATIONS COUNCIL (CXC)

A regional examining body that provides examinations for secondary and post-secondary candidates in Caribbean countries. Also provides technical assistance and consultancy services to both the public and private sectors across the region.

Caribbean Examinations Council (CXC), The Garrison, St Michael, Jamaica. Tel: +1 246 227 1700, fax: +1 246 429 5421, e- mail: cxcwzo@cxc.org, URL: http://www.cxc.org

CARNEGIE TRUST FOR THE UNIVERSITIES OF SCOTLAND

The Trust assists Scottish universities with development and research and gives support towards tuition fees to Scottish students.

Chairman of the Trustees: The Rt Hon Sir David Edward KCMG QC LLD Drhc FRSE

Carnegie Trust for the Universities of Scotland, Andrew Carnegie House, Pittencrieff Street, Dunfermlaine, Fife, KY12 8AW Scotland, UK. Tel: +44 (0)1383 724990, fax: +44 (0)1383 749799, e-mail: jgray@carnegie-trust.org, URL: http://www.carnegie-trust.org

CATHOLIC INTERNATIONAL FEDERATION OF PHYSICAL AND SPORTING EDUCATION (FICEP)

Promotes the development of sportsmen and women in the Christian spirit, while warning against the dangers, such as doping, in the field of the sport.

OTHER INTERNATIONAL AND NATIONAL ORGANISATIONS

President: Elke Haider

Catholic International Federation of Physical and Sporting Education (FICEP), 22 rue Oberkampf, Paris 75011, France. Tel: +33 (0)1 43 38 50 57, e-mail: info@ficep.org, URL: http://www.ficep.org

ENGINEERING AND PHYSICAL SCIENCE RESEARCH COUNCIL (EPSRC)

EPSRC is the UK's main agency for funding research in engineering and the physical sciences. EPSRC invests in high-quality basic, strategic and applied research and related postgraduate training to help the nation exploit the next generation of technological change. The areas covered range from information technology to structural engineering, and mathematics to materials science.

EPSRC works alongside sister Research Councils with responsibility for other areas of research in the UK.

Chair: John Armitt CBE
CEO: Professor David Delpy

Engineering and Physical Science Research Council, Polaris House, North Star Avenue, Swindon SN2 1ET, UK. Tel:+44 (0)1793 444000, URL: http://www.epsrc.ac.uk

EUROPEAN ASSOCIATION FOR THE EDUCATION OF ADULTS (EAEA)

EAEA is a European NGO with 127 member organisations in 43 countries. Its main roles are: policy advocacy for lifelong learning at a European level; development of practice through projects, publications and training; provision of information and services for our members; international co-operation.

President: Sue Waddington

European Association for the Education of Adults (EAEA), Rue de l'Arlon 40, B-1000 Brussels, Belgium. Tel: +32 (0)2 234 3763, fax: +32 (0)2 235 0539, e-mail: eaea-office@eaea.org, URL: http://www.eaea.org

EUROPEAN FOUNDATION FOR MANAGEMENT DEVELOPMENT (EFMD)

EFMD provides a forum for information, research, networking and debate on innovation and best practice in management development.

Director General & CEO: Eric Cornuel

European Foundation for Management Development (EFMD), Rue Gachard 88 - box 3, 1050 Brussels, Belgium. Tel: +32 (0)2 629 0810, fax: +32 (0)2 629 0811, URL: http://www.efmd.org

EUROPEAN UNIVERSITY ASSOCIATION (EUA)

Represents and supports higher education institutions in 46 countries, providing them with a forum to co-operate and keep abreast of the latest trends in higher education and research policies. Members of the Association are European universities involved in teaching and research, national associations of rectors and other organisations active in higher education and research.

President: Prof. Jean-Marc Rapp

European University Association, Rue d'Egmont 13, 1000 - Brussels, Belgium. Tel.: +32 (0)2 230 5544, fax: +32 (0)2 230 5751, e-mail: info@eua.be, URL: http://www.eua.be

INSTITUTE OF COMMONWEALTH STUDIES

The only postgraduate academic institution in the UK devoted to the study of the Commonwealth. It is the national and international centre of excellence for policy-relevant research and teaching on Commonwealth studies, focusing on North-South relations, global peace and security, development, good governance, human rights and the politics of society.

University of London Institute of Commonwealth Studies, 2nd Floor, South Block, Senate House, Malet Street, London WC1E 7HU, UK. Tel: +44 (0)20 7862 8844, fax: +44 (0)20 7862 8813, e-mail: ics@sas.ac.uk, URL: http://www.commonwealth.sas.ac.uk

INSTITUTE OF FINANCIAL SERVICES

The IFS School of Finance is a registered charity incorporated by Royal Charter. We provide financial education to financial services professionals the world over, and to consumers in the UK.

Chairman: Dr Paul Fisher

Institute of Financial Services, IFS House, 4-9 Burgate Lane, Canterbury, Kent CT1 2XJ, UK. Tel: +44 (0)1227 818609, fax: +44 (0)1227 784331, e-mail: customerservices@ifslearning.com, URL: http://www.ifslearning.com

INSTITUTION OF MECHANICAL ENGINEERS

IMechE promotes the education, training and professsional development of engineers and acts as an international centre for technology transfer in mechanical engineering.

President: John Wood FIMechE
Chief Executive: Stephen Tetlow MBE

Institution of Mechanical Engineers, 1 Birdcage Walk, Westminster, London SW1H 9JJ, UK. Tel: +44 (0)20 7222 7899, fax: +44 (0)20 7222 4557, URL: http://www.imeche.org

INTERNATIONAL ASSOCIATION FOR EDUCATIONAL AND VOCATIONAL GUIDANCE (IAEVG)

Advocates that all citizens who need and want educational and vocational guidance and counselling should receive this counselling from a competent and recognized professional; recommends the basic nature and quality of service that should typify the service provided to students and adults and recommends the essential training and other qualifications that all counsellors in educational and vocational guidance should have.

Secretary General: Ms. Linda Taylor

International Association for Educational and Vocational Guidance (IAEVG), 119 Ross ave, Suite 202, Ottawa ON K1Y 0N6, Canada. Tel: +1 613 729 6164, fax: +1 613 729 3515, URL: http://www.iaevg.org

INTERNATIONAL BACCALAUREATE ORGANIZATION

A non-profit educational foundation founded in 1968 which works with schools, governments and international organizations to develop challenging programmes of international education and rigorous assessment. These programmes encourage students across the world to become active, compassionate and lifelong learners who understand that other people, with their differences, can also be right.

Director General: Mr Jeff Beard

International Baccalaureate Organization, Route des Morillons 15, Grand-Saconnex, Genève CH-1218, Switzerland. Tel: +41 (0)22 791 7740, fax: +41 (0)22 791 0277, e-mail: ibhq@ibo.org, URL: http://www.ibo.org

INTERNATIONAL COUNCIL FOR OPEN AND DISTANCE LEARNING (ICDE)

Aims to promote intercultural co-operation and understanding through flexible learning and teaching throughout the world; to contribute to the development of new methodologies and technologies in order to improve lifelong learning; to foster international collaboration in flexible learning and teaching; and to support and develop networks for flexible learning and teaching at national, regional and global levels.

Secretary General: Gard Titlestad

International Council for Open and Distance Learning (ICDE), Lilleakerveien 23, 0283 Oslo, Norway. Tel: +47 22 06 2630, fax: +47 22 06 2631, e-mail: icde@icde.org, URL: http://www.icde.org

INTERNATIONAL FEDERATION OF CATHOLIC UNIVERSITIES (IFCU)

Aims to ensure a strong bond of mutual assistance among all Catholic universities; to help solve problems of growth and development and; to co-operate with other international organizations.

Secretary General: Pr. Mgr Guy-Réal Thivierge

International Federation of Catholic Universities (IFCU), 21 Rue d'Assas, 75270 Paris, France. Tel: +33 (0)1 44 39 52 26, fax: +33 (0)1 44 39 52 28, e-mail: sgfiuc@bureau.fiuc.org, URL: http://www.fiuc.org

INTERNATIONAL FEDERATION OF LIBRARY ASSOCIATIONS AND INSTITUTIONS (IFLA)

IFLA is an independent, international, non-governmental, not-for-profit organization. It aims to: promote high standards of provision and delivery of library and information services; encourage widespread understanding of the value of good library and information services and; represent the interests of its members throughout the world.

President: Ms Ellen Tise

International Federation of Library Associations and Institutions (IFLA), P.O. Box 95312, 2509 CH The Hague, The Netherlands. Tel: +31 (0)70 314 0884, fax: +31 (0)70 383 4827, e-mail: IFLA@ifla.org, URL: http://www.ifla.org

INTERNATIONAL FEDERATION OF UNIVERSITY WOMEN (IFUW)

An international, non-profit organisation of women graduates working to promote lifelong education, to improve the status of women and girls, and to enable women to effect positive change for a peaceful, sustainable future.

President: Marianne Haslegrave, Great Britain

International Federation of University Women (IFUW), 10 rue du Lac, CH-1207 Geneva, Switzerland. E-mail: info@ifuw.org, URL: http://www.ifuw.org

INTERNATIONAL FEDERATION OF WORKERS' EDUCATION ASSOCIATIONS (IFWEA)

An international organisation responsible for the development of workers' education. It brings together national and international trade unions, workers' education associations, NGOs and social-democratic foundations engaged in the provision of adult education opportunities for workers and the communities in which they live throughout the world.

General Secretary: Sahra Ryklief

International Federation of Workers' Education Associations (IFWEA), c/o Labour Research Service, PO Box 376, Woodstock 7915, Cape Town, South Africa. Tel: +27 21 447 1677, fax: +27 21 447 9244, E-mail: ifweasecretariat@lrs.org.za, URL: www.ifwea.org

INTERNATIONAL READING ASSOCIATION (IRA)

Promotes professional development for reading educators at all levels; supports research, practice, and policy that improve instruction for the benefit of all teachers and learners; and encourages research that informs decision making by educators, policymakers, and the public.

Acting Executive Director: Mark Mullen

International Reading Association (IRA), 800 Barksdale Road, P.O. Box 8139, Newark, DE 19714-8139, USA. Tel: +1 302 731 1600, fax: +1 302 731 1057, URL: http://www.reading.org

INTERNATIONAL SCHOOLS ASSOCIATION (ISA)

Aims to further world peace and international understanding through education; encourage the creation of new international schools; encourage co-operation among international or internationally-minded schools through consultation on teaching and administrative questions; nurture interest in national schools of international matters as a means of improving international understanding.

Chair: Luis Martinez Zorzo
Executive Administrator: Lisa Venegas

International Schools Association (ISA), US Office, Boca Prep International School, 10333 Diego Drive South, Boca Raton, FL 33428, USA. Tel: +1 561 883 3854, fax: +1 561 483 2004, URL: http://www.isaschools.org

INTERNATIONAL SOCIETY FOR MUSIC EDUCATION (ISME)

ISME believes that lived experiences of music, in all their many aspects, are a vital part of the life of all people. ISME's mission is to enhance those experiences by: building and maintaining a worldwide community of music educators characterized by mutual respect and support; fostering global intercultural understanding and cooperation among the world's music educators; and promoting music education for people of all ages in all relevant situations throughout the world.

International Society for Music Education (ISME), P.O. Box 909, Nedlands WA 6909, Australia. Tel: +61 8 9386 2654, fax: +61 8 9386 2658, e-mail: isme@isme.org, URL: http://www.isme.org

PAN-AMERICAN INSTITUTE OF GEOGRAPHY AND HISTORY

Encourages,co-ordinates and promotes the study of cartography, geophysics, geography, history, anthropology and archaeology as well as other related scientific studies of interest to the Americas.

Secretary General: Dr Santiago Borrero Mutis M.Sc (Colombia)

Pan-American Institute of Geography and History, Ex-Arzobispado 29, Col. Observatorio, 11860 Mexico City DF, Mexico. Tel: +52 55 5277 5888, fax: +52 55 5271 6172, e-mail: secretariageneral@ipgh.org, URL: http://www.ipgh.org

PRINCE'S TRUST

A leading UK youth charity for 14-30 year olds. Its programmes are targeted at people who are unemployed or facing barriers in life. It gives opportunities to develop confidence, learn new skills, move into work, education and training.

President: HRH The Prince of Wales (page 1403)
Chairman: Charles Dunstone
Chief Executive: Martina Milburn

Prince's Trust, 18 Park Square East, London NW1 4LH, UK. Tel: +44 (0)20 7543 1234, fax: +44 (0)20 7543 1200, e-mail: info@princes-trust.org.uk, URL: http://www.princes-trust.org.uk

RHODES TRUST

Administers the estate of the late Cecil Rhodes, and in particular the Scholarships (tenable at Oxford University) established under his will in 1902. The scholarships are available to citizens of certain countries of the Commonwealth, the USA and Germany.

Chief Executive of the Rhodes Trust / Warden of Rhodes House: Dr Donald Markwell

Rhodes Trust, Rhodes House, Oxford OX1 3RG, UK. Tel: +44 (0)1865 270902, fax: +44 (0)1865 270914, e-mail: admin@rhodeshouse.ox.ac.uk, URL: http://www.rhodeshouse.ox.ac.uk

SOUTHEAST ASIAN MINISTERS OF EDUCATION ORGANIZATION (SEAMEO)

The Southeast Asian Ministers of Education Organization (SEAMEO) was established in 1965, to promote cooperation in education, science and culture in Southeast Asia, through the establishment of networks and partnerships, provision of intellectual fora for policy makers and experts, and promotion of sustainable human resource development. SEAMEO develops the capacities of teachers and school managers in Southeast Asia through its network of 19 specialed training institutions and research programmes in various fields of education, science and culture.

Member Countries: Brunei Darussalam; Cambodia; Indonesia; Lao PDR; Malaysia; Myanmar; Philippines; Singapore; Thailand; Timor-Leste; Socialist Republic of Vietnam.

Publications: SEAMEO Education Agenda, semi-annual

President: H E Dr Mona D Valisno, Philippines
Director: Dato' Dr Ahamad bin Sipon,

Southeast Asian Ministers of Education Organization (SEAMEO), Mom Luang Pin Malakul Centenary Building, 920 Sukhumvit Road, Bangkok 10110, Thailand. Tel: +662 391 0144, fax: +662 381 2587, e-mail: secretariat@seameo.org, URL: http://www.seameo.org

UNION OF UNIVERSITIES OF LATIN AMERICA AND THE CARIBBEAN (UDUAL)

Aims to promote the academic interchange of professors and students, contribute to the development of a free, peaceful and democratic society and to obtain the cultural integration of Latin America.

Secretary General: Dr Roberto Escalante Semerena

Union of Universities of Latin America and the Caribbean (UDUAL), General Secretariat, Northwest Circuit Olympic Stadium, University City, Coyoacán 04510 Mexico. Tel: +52 55 5616 2383, e-mail: contacto@udual.org, URL: http://www.udual.org/Ingles/IndiceIngles.htm

UNITED NATIONS UNIVERSITY

The academic arm of the UN system, UNU is a global research and teaching organization with 15 institutes and programmes in 13 countries world wide. It has close relationships with other UN system organizations.

Rector: Dr David M. Malone (Canada)

United Nations University, 5-53-70 Jingumae, Shibuya-ku, Tokyo, 150-8925, Japan. Tel: +81 3 5467 1212, fax: +81 3 3499 2828, URL: http://unu.edu/

UNIVERSAL ESPERANTO ASSOCIATION

With members in 118 countries, UEA works not only to promote Esperanto, but to stimulate discussion of the world language problem and to call attention to the necessity of equality among languages.

Universal Esperanto Association, Nieuwe Binnenweg 176, 3015 BJ Rotterdam, The Netherlands. Tel: +31 10 436 1044, fax: +31 10 436 1751, e-mail: info@co.uea.org, URL: http://www.uea.org

US-UK FULBRIGHT COMMISSION

The purpose of the commission is to promote Anglo-American understanding through educational exchange. It achieves this goal through its Fulbright Awards programme.

Honorary Chairman: Ambassador Louis B Susman
Executive Director: Penny Egan

Fulbright Commission, Battersea Power Station, Gate 2, 188 Kirtling Street, London SW8 5BN, UK. Tel: +44 (0)20 7498 4010, fax: +44 (0)20 7498 4023, e-mail: programmes@fulbright.co.uk, URL: http://www.fulbright.co.uk

WORLD FEDERATION OF MODERN LANGUAGE ASSOCIATIONS (FIPLV)

Aims to: promote the teaching and learning of living languages in order to facilitate and improve communication, understanding, cooperation and friendly relations between all peoples of the world and; develop, support and promote policies designed to diversify the languages taught, to improve the quality of language teaching and make this teaching available to all.

President: Terry Lamb

World Federation of Modern Language Associations (FIPLV), P.O. Box 216, Belgrave 3160, Australia. e-mail: fiplv@telia.com, URL: http://www.fiplv.org

WORLD UNIVERSITY SERVICE (WUSC)

WUSC is a network of individuals and postsecondary institutions who believe that all peoples are entitled to the knowledge and skills necessary to contribute to a more equitable world. Its mission is to foster human development and global understanding through education and training.

World University Service (WUSC), 1404 Scott Street, Ottawa K1Y 4M8, Canada. Tel: +1 613 798 7477, fax: +1 613 798 0990, e-mail: wusc@wusc.ca, URL: http://www.wusc.ca

Environment

BIRDLIFE INTERNATIONAL

A global partnership of conservation organisations that strives to conserve birds, their habitats and global biodiversity, working with people towards sustainability in the use of natural resources.

Chairman: Dr. Peter John Schei
Director: Dr. Marco Lambertini

BirdLife International, Wellbrook Court, Girton Road, Cambridge CB3 0NA, UK. Tel: +44 (0)1223 277318, fax: +44 (0)1223 277200, e-mail: birdlife@birdlife.org, URL: http://www.birdlife.org

CENTRE FOR ALTERNATIVE TECHNOLOGY

A leading eco centre in Europe, CAT was established over 30 years ago as a visitor education centre demonstrating environmental building, renewable energy, energy efficiency, organic growing and water and sewage treatment.

Centre for Alternative Technology, Machynlleth, Powys, SY20 9AZ, UK. Tel: +44 (0)1654 705950, fax: +44 (0)1654 702782, e-mail: info@cat.org.uk, URL: http://www.cat.org.uk

COMMISSION FOR THE CONSERVATION OF ANTARCTIC MARINE LIVING RESOURCES (CCAMLR)

CCAMLR was established under the Convention on the Conservation of Antarctic Marine Living Resources (negotiated under the auspices of the Antarctic Treaty) which came into force on 7 April 1982. It is responsible for implementing the Convention and for the conservation of marine living resources in waters south of about 40 degrees South (the 'Convention Area'). The aims of the Commission are based on an 'ecosystem approach' which is designed both to ensure the conservation of harvested populations and species and to take into account ecological interactions between key species in the Antarctic marine ecosystem. The CCAMLR conservation programme regulates all existing, new and exploratory fisheries, including fishing for research purposes. Over the last 30 years, the CCAMLR has established a comprehensive code of responsibility for its 25 Member States through the adoption and implementation of over 200 conservation measures.

As of 2013, the Commission had 25 members. A further 11 countries had acceded to the Convention.

Commission for the Conservation of Antarctic Marine Living Resources, P.O. Box 213 North Hobart 7002, Tasmania, Australia. Tel: +61 3 6210 1111, fax: +61 3 6224 8744, e-mail: ccamlr@ccamlr.org, URL: http://www.ccamlr.org

EUROPEAN ORGANISATION FOR THE EXPLOITATION OF METEOROLOGICAL SATELLITES (EUMETSAT)

Aims to establish, maintain and exploit European systems of operational meteorological satellites; contribute to the operational monitoring of the climate and the detection of global climatic changes and assist in environmental monitoring.

Director-General: Dr. Lars Prahm
Chairman of Council: Prof. Petteri Taleas

European Organisation for the Exploitation of Meteorological Satellites (EUMETSAT), Eumetsatallee 1, D-64295 Darmstadt, Germany. Tel: +49 6151 807345, fax +49 6151 807555, e-mail press@eumetsat.int, URL: http://www.eumetsat.int

FRIENDS OF THE EARTH INTERNATIONAL

The world's largest grassroots environmental network which unites 76 diverse national member groups and some 5,000 local activist groups on every continent with approximately 2 million members and supporters around the world. Campaigns on today's most urgent environmental and social issues, challenges the current model of economic and corporate globalization and promotes solutions that will help to create environmentally sustainable and socially just societies.

Chair: Nnimmo Bassey

Friends of the Earth International, P.O. Box 19199, 1000 GD Amsterdam, The Netherlands. Tel: +31 (0)20 622 1369, fax: +31 (0)20 639 2181, e-mail: foei@foei.org, URL: http://www.foei.org

GREEN CROSS INTERNATIONAL

Aims to help ensure a just, sustainable and secure future for all by fostering a value shift and cultivating a new sense of global interdependence and shared responsibility in humanity's relationship with nature.

Founding Chairman: Mikhail Gorbachev
Chairman: Jan Kulczyk

Green Cross International, 9-11 rue de Varembé, 1202 Geneva, Switzerland. Tel: +41 (0)22 789 1662, fax : +41 (0)22 789 1695, e-mail: gcinternational@gci.ch, URL: http://www.greencrossinternational.net

GREENPEACE INTERNATIONAL

Greenpeace is an independent campaigning organisation that aims to expose global environment problems and to force solutions which it believes are essential to ensure the ability of the earth to nurture life in all its diversity. It uses non-violent direct confrontation to achieve these objectives.

International Executive Director: Kumi Naidoo (South Africa)

Greenpeace International, Ottho Heldingstraat 5, 1066 AZ Amsterdam, The Netherlands. Tel: +31 (0)20 718 2000, fax: +31 (0)20 514 8151, e-mail: supporter.services@int.greenpeace.org, URL: http://www.greenpeace.org

INTERNATIONAL EMISSIONS TRADING ASSOCIATION

Works for the development of an active, global greenhouse gas market, consistent across national boundaries and involving all flexibility mechanisms. Promotes an integrated view of the emissions trading system as a solution to climate change, participates in the design and implementation of national and international rules and guidelines and aims to provide the most up-to-date and credible source of information on emissions trading and greenhouse gas market activity.

Chief Executive Officer: Henry Derwent

International Emissions Trading Association, 24, rue Merle d'Aubigné, CH-1207 Genève, Switzerland. Tel: +41 (0)22 737 0500, fax: +41 (0)22 737 0508, e-mail: secretariat@ieta.org, URL: http://www.ieta.org

INTERNATIONAL WHALING COMMISSION

88 member nations meet at least once a year largely to keep under review and revise as necessary the measures laid down in the Schedule to the Convention governing the conduct of whaling.

Vice Chairman: Ambassador Anthony Liverpool (Antigua & Barbuda)

International Whaling Commission, The Red House, 135 Station Road, Impington, Cambridge, CB4 9NP, UK. Tel: +44 (0)1223 233971, fax: +44 (0)1223 232876, e-mail: secretariat@iwcoffice.org, URL: http://www.iwcoffice.org

JOINT NATURE CONSERVATION COMMITTEE

The forum through which the four country nature conservation agencies - the Countryside Council for Wales, Natural England, Scottish Natural Heritage and the Council for Nature Conservation and the Countryside (CNCC) - deliver their statutory responsibilities for the United Kingdom as a whole and internationally. The Joint Nature Conservation Committee (JNCC) is the statutory adviser to the UK Government and devolved administrations on UK and international nature conservation. Its work contributes to maintaining and enriching biological diversity, conserving geological features and sustaining natural systems.

Chairman: Peter Bridgewater
Managing Director: Marcus Yeo

Joint Nature Conservation Committee, Monkstone House, City Road, Peterborough PE1 1JY, UK. Tel: +44 (0)1733 562626, fax: +44 (0)1733 555948, e-mail: communications@jncc.gov.uk, URL: http://www.jncc.gov.uk

NATIONAL TRUST FOR PLACES OF HISTORIC INTEREST OR NATURAL BEAUTY

Exists to preserve the best of the UK countryside and the finest buildings for the enjoyment of future generations. It is a charity, independent of the State, financed by gifts, legacies and members' subscriptions and the income from its property.

President: HRH Prince Charles (page 1403)
Director-General: Dame Fiona Reynolds DBE

National Trust, 32 Queen Anne's Gate, London, SW1H 9AB, United Kingdom. Tel: +44 (0)1793 817400, URL: http://www.nationaltrust.org.uk

SIERRA CLUB

The oldest and largest environmental organisation in the world; it has over 1 million members, 65 chapters and 409 local groups. It promotes conservation of the natural environment by influencing public policy decisions, whether legislative, administrative, legal or electoral.

President: RobinMann

Sierra Club, 2nd Floor, 85 2nd Street, San Fransisco, CA 94105, USA. Tel: +1 415 977 5500, fax: +1 415 977 5799, e-mail: information@sierraclub.org, URL: http://www.sierraclub.org

WETLANDS INTERNATIONAL

A global NGO dedicated to the conservation and wise use of wetlands. Works globally, regionally and nationally to achieve the conservation and wise use of wetlands, to benefit biodiversity and human well-being.

Chief Executive Officer: Jane Madgwick

Wetlands International, PO Box 471, 6700 AL Wageningen, The Netherlands. Tel: +31 (0)318 660910, fax +31(0) 318 660950, URL: http://www.wetlands.org

WORLD SOCIETY FOR THE PROTECTION OF ANIMALS

Its aims are to promote effective means for the protection and conservation of animals and the relief of suffering of animals throughout the world; to maintain effective liaison between, and seek co-operation with, localised organisations having similar objectives; to provide facilities for membership of approved animal welfare societies and individuals interested in animal welfare; to seek recognition and representation on suitable bodies; to study international and national legislation relating to animal welfare and to promote international efforts for the protection of animals. WSPA has consultative arrangements with the United Nations, the Council of Europe, and the European Community, and maintains a fully trained field staff.

Director General: Michael Baker

World Society for the Protection of Animals, 5th Floor, 222 Grays Inn Road, London, WC1X 8HB, UK. URL: http://www.wspa.org.uk

WORLD WATER COUNCIL

Provides a platform to encourage debates and exchanges of experience and aims to reach a common strategic vision on water resources and water services management amongst all stakeholders in the water community.

Director General: Loïc Fauchon

World Water Council, URL: http://www.worldwatercouncil.org

WORLD WIDE FUND FOR NATURE (WWF)

One of the world's largest private international conservation organisations. Its mission is to stop the degradation of the planet's natural environment and to build a future in which humans live in harmony with nature.

President: Yolanda Kakabadse (page 1453)
Director-General: James P. Leape

World Wide Fund for Nature, Avenue du Mont-Blanc, CH 1196 Gland, Switzerland. Tel: +41 (0)22 364 9111, fax: +41 (0)22 364 8836, URL: http://www.wwf.org/

Government & Politics

AFRICAN ASSOCIATION FOR PUBLIC ADMINISTRATION AND MANAGEMENT (AAPAM)

An international professional association for African public administrators and managers. Provides a forum for the articulation and dissemination of ideas on human capacity building and development issues in the African region and a link between the many parties involved in development policy management.

President: Tlohang Sekhamane

African Association for Public Administration and Management (AAPAM), Britak Centre, Ragati & Mara Roads, P.O.Box 48677, 00100 GPO, Nairobi, Kenya. Tel. +254 20 273 0505, e-mail: aapam@aapam.org, URL: http://www.aapam.org

ARAB TOWNS ORGANIZATION (ATO)

Aims to reinforce Arab local authorities and encourage decentralization, raise the level of municipal services and utilities in Arab cities and foster cooperation and exchange of expertise between Arab cities.

Arab Towns Organization (ATO), P.O. Box 68160 Kaifan, 71962 Kuwait. Tel : +965 484 9705, fax: +965 484 9319, e-mail: ato@ato.net, URL: http://www.ato.net

ASIA-EUROPE MEETING (ASEM)

Aims to facilitate dialogue and co-operation on an informal basis between the EU Member States, the European Commission, 16 Asian countries and the ASEAN Secretariat. Areas covered by ASEM include political, economic and cultural issues. The idea behind ASEM is to strengthen understanding and mutual respect between the two regions.

Asia-Europe Meeting (ASEM), c/o Asia-Europe Foundation, 31 Heng Mui Keng Terrace, Singapore 119595. Tel: +65)6874 9718, fax: +65 6872 1206, e-mail: admin@aseminfoboard.org, URL: http://www.aseminfoboard.org/

ASSOCIATION OF SECRETARIES GENERAL OF PARLIAMENTS (ASGP)

Seeks to facilitate personal contacts between holders of the office of Secretary General in different parliamentary assemblies. Studies the law, procedure, practice and working methods of different parliaments and proposes measures for improving those methods and for securing co-operation between the services of different parliaments.

Association of Secretaries General of Parliaments (ASGP), URL: http://www.asgp.info

BROOKINGS INSTITUTION

The Brookings Institution is a private, non-profit organisation devoted to non-partisan research, education, and publication in economics, government, foreign policy, and the social sciences. It was founded in 1916 and named after Robert Brookings who was instrumental in its development. The organisation aims to influence public policy issues through through the work of its scholars and publications. Its Centre for Public Policy Education organises conferences and serves as a forum for informed debate.

The Board of Trustees supervises the Institution, approving its fields of investigation and safeguarding its independence. The President is the chief administrative officer, responsible for formulating and co-ordinating policies, recommending projects, approving publications, and selecting staff.

President: Strobe Talbott

Brookings Institution, 1775 Massachusetts Avenue, NW Washington DC 20036-2188. Tel.: +1 202 7976000, fax: +1 202 797 6195, URL: http://www.brookings.edu

BUSINESSEUROPE

Known as the Union of Industrial and Employers' Confederations of Europe (UNICE) until January 2007, BUSINESSEUROPE provides a framework within which industry and employers examine European policies and proposed legislation in order to prepare joint positions, promote their policies and positions at Community and national level, and persuade European legislators to take them into account.

President: Jurgen Thumann
Secretary-General: Philippe de Buck

BusinessEurope, Avenue de Cortenbergh 168, 1000 Brussels, Belgium. Tel: +32 (0)2 237 6511, fax: +32 (0)2 231 1445, URL: http://www.businesseurope.eu

COMMONWEALTH PARLIAMENTARY ASSOCIATION

The Commonwealth Parliamentary Association provides the means for regular consultation between Commonwealth parliamentarians and encourages understanding and co-operation among them, promoting the study of and respect for parliamentary institutions and the advancement of good democratic practices.

Secretary-General: Dr. William F. Shija

Commonwealth Parliamentary Association, Westminster House Suite 700, 7 Millbank, Westminster, London SW1P 3JA, UK. Tel: +44 (0)20 7799 1460, fax: +44 (0)20 7222 6073, e-mail: pirc@cpahq.org, URL: http://www.cpahq.org

COMMONWEALTH WAR GRAVES COMMISSION

The Commission is responsible for the permanent marking and care of the graves of members of the forces of the Commonwealth who lost their lives in the 1914-18 and 1939-45 wars, and the commemoration by name of those who have no known grave.

President: HRH The Duke of Kent KG GCMG GCVO ADC
Chairman (ex officio UK Secretary of State for Defence): Rt. Hon. Dr Liam Fox (page 1426)

Commonwealth War Graves Commission, 2 Marlow Road, Maidenhead, Berkshire SL6 7DX, UK. Tel: +44 (0)1628 634221, fax: +44 (0)1628 771208, e-mail: Casualty & Cemetery Enquiries: casualty.enq@cwgc.org, URL: http://www.cwgc.org

EAST AFRICAN COMMUNITY (EAC)

EAC aims at widening and deepening co-operation among the partner states in, among others, political, economic and social fields for their mutual benefit. Formed in 1999 by Kenya, Uganda and Tanzania and enlarged in 2007 by Rwanda and Burundi.

Secretary General: Ambassador Juma Volter Mwapachu

OTHER INTERNATIONAL AND NATIONAL ORGANISATIONS

East African Community (EAC), Arusha International Conference Centre (AICC) Building, Kilimanjaro Wing, 5th Floor, P.O. Box 1096, Arusha, Tanzania. Tel: +255 27 250 4253, fax: +255 27 250 4255, e-mail: eac@eachq.org, URL: http://www.eac.int/

EUROPEAN MOVEMENT (UK)

The European Movement was founded in 1948. It played a major role in the creation of the Council of Europe and the European Communities. Today the European Movement UK has branches and members throughout Britain and campaigns for a European Economic Union based on an enlarged European community with effective and democratic institutions.

Chairman: Peter Luff (page 1467)
Vice Chairmen: Veronica Stiastny, Richard Corbett
President: Rt. Hon. Charles Kennedy, MP (page 1455)
Vice-Presidents: Rt. Hon Kenneth Clarke QC MP (page 1405), Rt. Hon. Baroness Joyce Quin

European Movement (UK), 203 Southbank House, Black Prince Road, London SE17SJ, UK. Tel: +44 (0)20 3176 0543, e-mail: emoffice@euromove.org.uk, URL: http://www.euromove.org.uk

FEDERAL TRUST FOR EDUCATION AND RESEARCH

The Federal Trust for Education and Research aims to contribute to the achievement of a more just, harmonious and peaceful world by studying the application of federalist principles to the organisation of society, states and international relations.

Director: Brendan Donnelly

Federal Trust for Education and Research, 31 Jewry Street, London EC3N 2EY, UK. Tel: +44 (0)20 7320 3045, e-mail: info@fedtrust.co.uk, URL: http://www.fedtrust.co.uk

HANSARD SOCIETY

The Hansard Society is the UK's leading independent, non-profit political research and education charity.

President: John Bercow (page 1387), Speaker of the House of Commons
Chairman: Peter Riddell

Hansard Society for Parliamentary Democracy, 40 -43 Chancery Lane, London WC2A 1JA, UK. Tel: +44 (0)20 7438 1222, fax: +44 (0)20 7438 1229, e-mail: hansard@hansard.lse.ac.uk, URL: http://www.hansardsociety.org.uk

INTERNATIONAL ALLIANCE OF WOMEN (IAW)

The International Alliance of Women was founded originally in 1904 to get the votes for Women. Affiliated and associated societies from all parts of the world belong to the Alliance, and also many hundreds of individual members all working towards greater equality, education and health needs for women worldwide. Affirms that full and equal enjoyment of human rights is due to all women and girls. The IAW maintains that a prerequisite to securing these rights is the universal ratification and implementation without reservation of the Convention on the Elimination of All Forms of Discrimination against Women (CEDAW).

President & Chief Representative to the UN: Lyda Verstegen

International Alliance of Women (IAW), P.O. Box 380, Nambucca Heads, 2448 NSW, Australia. Tel: +61 2 6568 6239, e-mail: iawsec@womenalliance.org, URL: http://www.womenalliance.org

INTERNATIONAL BUREAU FOR PUBLICATION OF CUSTOMS TARIFFS

Translates and publishes in English, French, German, Italian and Spanish the customs tariffs of all countries, together with such modifications as may be introduced from time to time.

International Bureau for Publication of Customs Tariffs, 38 Rue de l'Association, B-1000 Brussels, Belgium. Tel: +32 (0)2 501 8774, fax: +32 (0)2 218 3025, e-mail: dir@bitd.org, URL: http://www.bitd.org

INTERNATIONAL COMMISSION FOR THE HISTORY OF REPRESENTATIVE AND PARLIAMENTARY INSTITUTIONS

Aims to promote research into the origin, growth and development of representative and parliamentary institutions throughout the world in all periods. It facilitates the international exchange of bibliographical information and is concerned with the political theory and institutional practice of representation as well as with the internal organization and the social and political background to parliaments and assemblies of estates.

President: Maria Sofia Corciulo (Italy)
Secretary-General: Estevao do Rezende Martins (Brazil)

International Commission for the History of Representative and Parliamentary Institutions (ICHRPI), Department of History, Carleton University, 400 Peterson Hall, 1125 Colonel By Drive, Ottawa, Ontario, Canada KIS 5B6. URL: http://www.ichrpi.org/default.html

INTERNATIONAL DEMOCRAT UNION (IDU)

Aims to advance the social and political values on which democratic societies are founded, including basic personal freedoms and human rights, as defined in the Universal Declaration of Human Rights.

Executive Secretary: Eirik Moen

International Democrat Union (IDU), P.O. Box 1536 Vika, N-0117 Oslo, Norway. Tel: +47 2282 9000, fax: +47 2282 9080, e-mail: secretariat@idu.org, URL: http://www.idu.org

INTERNATIONAL LESBIAN AND GAY ASSOCIATION

A world-wide network of national and local groups dedicated to achieving equal rights for lesbian, gay, bisexual and transgendered (LGBT) people everywhere.

Co-Secretaries General: Gloria Careaga (Mexico) and Renator Sabbadini (Italy)

International Lesbian and Gay Association, 17 Rue de la Charité, 1210 Brussels, Belgium. Tel: +32 (0)2 502 2471, fax: +32 (0)2 609 5419, e-mail:ilga@ilga.org, URL: http://www.ilga.org

INTERNATIONAL UNION OF SOCIALIST YOUTH (IUSY)

The aim of IUSY is to put into practice and defend the ideals of democratic socialism; freedom and human rights, equality, democracy, universal solidarity and political solutions to problems.

Secretary General: Viviana Piñeiro (JSU, Uruguay)

International Union of Socialist Youth (IUSY), Amtshausgasse 4, A-1050 Vienna, Austria. Tel: +43 (0)1 523 1267, fax: +43 (0)1 5231 2679, e-mail: iusy@iusy.org, URL: http://www.iusy.org

NETHERLANDS INSTITUTE OF INTERNATIONAL RELATIONS CLINGENDAEL

The Netherlands Institute of International Relations Clingendael works to identify and analyze developing political and social situations for the benefit of governments and the public. It operates as a think tank and an diplomatic academy.

To achieve its aims, Clingendael carries out research and organises courses and training programmes as well as publishing its studies and findings. It hosts conferences and seminars to which international political leaders, diplomats and journalists are invited.

Director: Prof. Ko Colijn

Netherlands Institute of International Relations Clingendael, Clingendael 7, 2597 VH The Hague, The Netherlands. Tel: +31 (0)70 324 53 84, e-mail: info@clingendael.nl, URL: http://www.clingendael.nl

NUCLEAR CONTROL INSTITUTE

An independent policy research centre which monitors nuclear programmes in the United States and other countries. It develops and pursues strategies to halt the spread and reverse the growth of nuclear arms.

Vice-President: Sharon Tanzer

Nuclear Control Institute, Suite 400, 1000 Connecticut Avenue NW, Washington DC 20036, USA. Tel: +1 202 822 8444, fax: +1 202 452 0892, e-mail: mail@nci.org, URL: http://www.nci.org

POLICY STUDIES INSTITUTE

An independent, non-party political and non-profit making institute that aims to contribute to better planning and policy making, particularly in government and industry and in the relations between them.

Director: Malcolm Rigg

Policy Studies Institute, 50 Hanson Street, London W1W 6UP, UK. Tel: +44 (0)20 7911 7500, fax: +44 (0)20 7911 7501, e-mail: website@psi.org.uk, URL: http://www.psi.org.uk

SOCIALIST INTERNATIONAL

The worldwide organisation of social democratic, socialist and labour parties. It brings together over 170 political parties and organisations from all continents. As a non-governmental organisation, the Socialist International has consultative status (Category 1) with the United Nations and works internationally with a large number of other organisations.

President: George A. Papandreou (President of the Panhellic Socialist Movement, PASOK, Greece)
Secretary General: Luis Ayala

Socialist International, Maritime House, Old Town, Clapham, London SW4 0JW, UK. Tel: +44 (0)20 7627 4449, fax: +44 (0)20 7720 4448//7498 1293, e-mail: secretariat@socialistinternational.org, URL: http://www.socialistinternational.org

SOCIALIST INTERNATIONAL WOMEN

Aims to; strengthen relations between its member organisations; promote action programmes to overcome any discrimination in society and promote knowledge and understanding amongst women of the aims and tasks of democratic socialism. There are currently 145 member organizations.

President: Pia Locatelli, Italian Socialist Party, PSI

Socialist International Women, Maritime House, Old Town, London SW4 0JW, UK. Tel: +44 (0)20 7720 0568, fax: +44 (0)20 7498 1293, URL: http://www.socintwomen.org

SOCIETY FOR INTERNATIONAL DEVELOPMENT

An international network of individuals and organisations founded in 1957 to promote social justice and democratic participation. There are 65 local chapters, 45 institutional members and 3,000 individual members in 80 countries.

Managing Director: Stefano Prato

Society for International Development, Via Panisperna 207, 00184 Rome, Italy. Tel: + 39 06 487 2172, fax: +39 06 487 2170, e-mail: sid@aed.org, URL: http://www.sidint.org

STOCKHOLM INTERNATIONAL PEACE RESEARCH INSTITUTE (SIPRI)

Conducts research on questions of conflict and cooperation of importance for international peace and security, with the aim of contributing to an understanding of the conditions for peaceful solutions of international conflicts and for a stable peace.

Director: Bates Gill

Stockholm International Peace Research Institute (SIPRI), Signalistgatan 9, SE-169 70 Solna, Sweden. Tel: +46 8 655 9700, fax: +46 8 655 9733, e-mail: sipri@sipri.org, URL: http://www.sipri.org

TRANSPARENCY INTERNATIONAL

Transparency International (TI), the global civil society organisation leading the fight against corruption, brings people together in a powerful worldwide coalition to end the devastating impact of corruption on men, women and children around the world. TI's mission is to create change towards a world free of corruption.

TI challenges the inevitability of corruption, and offers hope to its victims. Since its founding in 1993, TI has played a lead role in improving the lives of millions around the world by building momentum for the anti-corruption movement. TI raises awareness and diminishes apathy and tolerance of corruption, and devises and implements practical actions to address it.

Chairman: Dr. Huguette Labelle

Transparency International, Alt-Moabit 96, 10559 Berlin, Germany. Tel: +49 (0)30 343 8200, fax: +49 (0)30 3470 3912, e-mail: ti@transparency.org, URL: http://www.transparency.org

TRILATERAL COMMISSION

Formed by private citizens of Pacific Asia, Europe (European Union countries), and North America (United States, Mexico and Canada) to foster closer co-operation among these core democratic industrialized areas of the world with shared leadership responsibilities in the wider international system.

Executive Committee Chairman: Edmond Alphandéry

Trilateral Commission, 1156 Fifteenth Street NW, Washington, DC 20005, USA. Tel: +1 202 467 5410, fax: +1 202 467 5415, e-mail: contactus@trilateral.org, URL: http://www.trilateral.org

UNITED CITIES AND LOCAL GOVERNMENTS

A global organisation of local governments and their national associations. It gives a voice to every type of local government - large and small, rural and urban - representing and defending their interests at global level and addressing key issues for the future of cities and their citizens. It has members in 136 of the 192 UN member states, representing over half of the world's population.

Presidency: Kadir Topbas, Mayor of Istanbul (Turkey)

United Cities and Local Governments, Carrer Avinyo 15, 08002 Barcelona, Spain. Tel: +34 (0)93 342 8750, fax: +34 (0)93 342 8760, e-mail: info@cities-localgovernments.org, URL: http://www.cities-localgovernments.org

UNITING FOR PEACE

Uniting for Peace was formed when the World Disarmament Campaign combined with Action for UN Renewal. It campaigns for worldwide disarmament, both nuclear and non-nuclear, for military expenditure to be diverted to sustainable development, the eradication of poverty through the UN, and for the reform and strengthening of the United Nations for enhanced global security.

Chair: Vijay Melton

Uniting for Peace, 97 Commercial Road, London, El 1RD, UK. Tel: +44 (0)207 377 2111, e-mail: vijay@vmpeace.org, URL: http://www.world-disarm.org.uk

UNREPRESENTED NATIONS AND PEOPLES ORGANISATION

Founded in 1991 to represent nations and peoples who are not represented in today's main international organisations such as the United Nations. It aims to provide a legitimate forum for and effective channels to communicate with the international community, including governments, NGOs, IGOs and the media to empower more effectively all sectors of society to participate in determining the destiny of their nations and peoples.

General Secretary: Marino Busdachin

Unrepresented Nations and Peoples Organisation, P.O. Box 85878, 2508 CN, The Netherlands. Tel: +31 (0)70 364 6504, fax: +31 (0)70 364 6608, e-mail: unpo@unpo.org, URL: http://www.unpo.org

WOMEN'S INTERNATIONAL DEMOCRATIC FEDERATION (WIDF)

Develops solidarity and encourages women to show resistance towards conflicts, occupations, blockades and fundamentalism. The Federation encourages women to work for peace, liberty, political parity, democracy and social development.

Women's International Democratic Federation (WIDF), Guimarães Passos street, 422, Vila Mariana, São Paulo SP 04107-031, Brazil. Tel: +55 11 5082 44 18, e-mail: fdim.sec@terra.com.br, URL: http://www.fdim-widf.com.br/indexingles.htm

WORLD ECONOMIC FORUM

An independent non-governmental organisation that integrates leaders from business, government, academia, the media and civil society in a partnership committed to improving the state of the world. The Forum seeks to create opportunities for leaders around the world to address key economic, social and political issues on the global and regional agendas.

Founder and Executive Chairman: Klaus Schwab (page 1510)

World Economic Forum, 91 - 93 route de la Capite, CH-1223 Cologny / Geneva, Switzerland. Tel: +41 (0)22 869 1212, fax: +41 (0)22 786 2744, e-mail: contact@weforum.org, URL: http://www.weforum.org

WORLD FEDERALIST MOVEMENT (WFM) Mouvement Fédéraliste Mondial (MFM)

A network of organisations, national and international, working to achieve a just world order through a strengthened United Nations. The WFM has over 28 member and associated organisations as well as 25,000 individual members in 80 countries.

President: Dr Lloyd Axworthy
Executive Director: William R. Pace

World Federalist Movement, 708 Third Avenue, 24th Floor, New York, NY 10017, USA. Tel: +1 212 599 1320, fax: +1 212 599 1332, e-mail: info@wfm.org, URL: http://www.wfm.org

WORLD PEACE COUNCIL (WPC)

WPC is a broad coalition of movements and organizations which, on the international level, choose to combine their diverse activities for the achievement of a common goal: the creation and strengthening of a secure and just peace for all the peoples of the world.

General Secretary: Athanossios Pafilis

World Peace Council (WPC), 10 OthonosSt., Athens 10557, Greece. Tel: +30 210 331 6326, fax: +30 210 322 4302, e-mail: info@wpc-in.org, URL: http://www.wpc-in.org

WORLD WIDE PEACE

The charity was founded in 1984 based. The aims of WWP are international conflict mediation, environmental co-operation and international cultural understanding. It transcends all existing political, ethnical, cultural and religious barriers and values the implications of the Helsinki accord. It is registered in over 100 countries.

President: Prof. Manuel Dittmers BA MEd MSc FRSA FInstD

World Wide Peace, P.O. Box 551042, D-22570 Hamburg, Germany. Tel: +49 (0)40 865995, e-mail: info@worldwidepeace.com, URL: http://www.world-wide-peace.com

YOUTH OF THE EUROPEAN PEOPLE'S PARTY (YEPP)

Aims: to develop contacts and exchanges between the youth movements of different states and regions of Europe, by allowing them to meet and compare their experiences and; to participate in any initiative taken by the European Union or the Council of Europe, likely to contribute to a better knowledge of the process of co-operation and integration in Europe.

President: Laurent Schouteten

Secretary General: Carlo de Romanis

Youth of the European People's Party (YEPP), Rue du Commerce 10, 1000 Brussels, Belgium. Tel: +32 (0)2 285 4163, fax: +32 (0)2 285 4165, e-mail: yepp@epp.eu, URL: http://www.yepp-eu.org

Health & Medicine

AEROSPACE MEDICAL ASSOCIATION (ASMA)

An umbrella group providing a forum for many different disciplines to come together and share their expertise. The Association has provided its expertise to a multitude of federal and international agencies on a broad range of issues including aviation and space medical standards, the ageing pilot, and physiological stresses of flight.

Executive Director: Jeffrey Sventek

Aerospace Medical Association, 320 South Henry Street, Alexandria, VA 22314-3579, USA. Tel:+1 703 739 2240, fax: +1 703 739 9652, e-mail: rrayman@asma.org, URL: http://www.asma.org

ASSOCIATION OF NATIONAL EUROPEAN AND MEDITERRANEAN SOCIETIES OF GASTROENTEROLOGY (ASNEMGE)

Contributes to the study and progress of gastroenterology in Europe and the Mediterranean area and encourages and supports co-operative research.

President: M. Hull

Association of National European and Mediterranean Societies of Gastroenterology (ASNEMGE), URL: http://www.asnemge.org

CYSTIC FIBROSIS WORLDWIDE

Works to promote access to appropriate care and education to those people living with the disease in developing countries and to improve the knowledge of CF among medical professionals and governments worldwide.

President: Mr. Mitch Messer

Cystic Fibrosis Worldwide, 210 Park Avenue #267, Worcester, MA 01609, USA. Tel.: +1 508 762 4232, e-mail: information@cf-europe.info, URL: http://www.cfww.org

EUROPEAN ASSOCIATION FOR CANCER RESEARCH (EACR)

The largest member organisation for cancer research in Europe, established in 1968, with a membership of over 7,500. It supports cancer research and facilitates communication through a variety of Fellowship Programmes, meetings and workshops.

President Elect: Moshe Oren
Secretary General: Richard Marais

European Association for Cancer Research (EACR), School of Pharmacy, University of Nottingham, Nottingham NG7 2RD,United Kingdom. Tel: +44 (0)115 951 5114, fax: +44 (0)115 951 5115, e-mail: eacr@nottingham.ac.uk, URL: http://www.eacr.org

EUROPEAN ASSOCIATION FOR THE STUDY OF DIABETES

Based on individual membership and embraces scientists, physicians, laboratory workers, nurses and students from all over the world who are interested in diabetes and related subjects. Annually holds an EASD Scientists Training Course and a Robert Turner Clinical Research Course to attract new talent to diabetes research in different centres throughout the world.

President: A. Boulton

European Association for the Study of Diabetes, Rheindorfer Weg 3, Dusseldorf D-40591, Germany. Tel: +49 (0)211 758 4690, fax: +49 (0)211 7584 6929, e-mail: secretariat@easd.org, URL: http://www.easd.org

EUROPEAN BRAIN AND BEHAVIOUR SOCIETY (EBSS)

Its purpose is the exchange of information between European scientists interested in the relationship of brain mechanisms and behaviour. To this avail the Society organises a General Meeting every year.

President: Carmen Sandi

European Brain and Behaviour Society, Einsteinweg 55, Leiden, 2333 CC, The Netherlands. Tel: +31 (0)71 527 6289, fax: +31 (0)71 527 4277, URL: http://www.ebbs-science.org

EUROPEAN FEDERATION OF INTERNAL MEDICINE (EFIM)

Brings together the National Societies of Internal Medicine of different countries across Europe, and currently has 33 member societies. Its purpose is to re-emphasize the importance of Internal Medicine in patient care in a world of increasing specialisation.

Secretary-General: Dr J.W.F. Elte

European Federation of Internal Medicine, 287 Avenue Louise, 4th Floor, 1050 Brussels, Belgium. Tel: +32 (0)2 6433 2040, fax: +32 (0)2 645 2671,e-mail: info@efim.org, URL: http://www.efim.org

EUROPEAN HEALTH MANAGEMENT ASSOCIATION (EHMA)

Focuses on managerial issues and on management development in the health sector. Fosters activities between health service organisations and institutions in the field of healthcare management education and training. There are 160 members in more than 30 countries in the European area.

President: Prof. Aad de Roo

European Health Management Association, Rue Belliard 15-17, 6th Floor, 1040 Brussels, Belgium. Tel: +32 (0)2 502 6525, fax: +32 (0)2 503 1007, URL: http://www.ehma.org

EUROPEAN LEAGUE AGAINST RHEUMATISM (EULAR)

Represents the patient, health professional and scientific societies of rheumatology of all the European nations. EULAR endeavors to stimulate, promote, and support the research, prevention, treatment and rehabilitation of rheumatic diseases.

President-elect: Prof. Maurizio Cutolo

European League Against Rheumatism (EULAR), Seestrasse 240, CH-8802 Kilchberg, Zurich, Switzerland. Tel +41 (0)44 716 3030, fax +41 (0)44 716 3039, e-mail: eular@eular.org, URL: http://www.eular.org

EUROTRANSPLANT INTERNATIONAL FOUNDATION

Responsible for the mediation and allocation of organ donation procedures in Austria, Belgium, Germany, Luxemburg, the Netherlands, Slovenia and Croatia. In this international collaborative framework, the participants include all transplant hospitals, tissue-typing laboratories and hospitals where organ donations take place.

President: Dr. Priv.-Doz. B. Meiser
General Director: Dr. A. Oosterlee
Medical Director: Dr. A. Rahmel

Eurotransplant International Foundation, P.O. Box 2304, 2301 CH Leiden, The Netherlands. Tel: +31 (0)71 579 5795, fax: +31 (0)71 579 0057, URL: http://www.eurotransplant.nl

FDI WORLD DENTAL FEDERATION

Aims to develop and disseminate policies, standards and information related to all aspects of oral health care around the world. It does this through the publication of FDI Policy Statements; declarations that lay out the current thinking on various issues related to oral health, oral health policies and the dental profession.

President: Orlando Monteiro da Silva

FDI World Dental Federation, Tour de Cointrin, Avenue Louis Casai 84, Case Postale 3, 1216 Cointrin, Geneva, Switzerland. URL: http://www.fdiworldental.org

INSTITUTE OF NUTRITION OF CENTRAL AMERICA AND PANAMA (INCAP)

An international scientific organisation which aims to study food and nutrition problems and to assist member countries in their solution.

Institute of Nutrition of Central America and Panama (INCAP), Calzada Roosevelt, Zona 11, Apartado Postal 1188, 01901 Guatemala City, Guatemala, Central America. Tel: +502 2472 3762, fax: +502 473 6529, URL: http://www.incap.org.gt

INTERNATIONAL ACADEMY OF AVIATION AND SPACE MEDICINE

An international, organisation with membership from 46 countries worldwide. Its object is the promotion and search for new knowledge in aerospace medicine, and the contribution to international co-operation among those devoted to education and research in this particular field.

President: Tony Batchelor (UK)
Secretary General: Dr Claude Thibeault (Canada)

International Academy of Aviation and Space Medicine, URL: http://www.iaasm.org

INTERNATIONAL ACADEMY OF CYTOLOGY

An international, scientific, nonprofit organization of cytologists and professional persons concerned with research in clinical cytology. It aims to encourage co-operation among those persons who are actively engaged in the practice of clinical cytology; to foster and facilitate the international exchange of knowledge and information on specialized problems of clinical cytology; and to standardize terminology.

President: Dr Diane Solomon
Secretary General: Dr Fernando Schmitt

International Academy of Cytology, Burgunderstrasse 1, 79104 Freiburg, Germany. Tel: +49 (0)761 292 3802, fax: +49 (0)761 292 3802, e-mail: centraloffice@cytology-iac.org, URL: http://www.cytology-iac.org

INTERNATIONAL AGENCY FOR THE PREVENTION OF BLINDNESS (IAPB)

Established as a coordinating umbrella organization to lead an international effort in mobilizing resources for blindness prevention activities. IAPB aspires to link professional bodies, NGOs, educational institutions and interested individuals with national programs for the prevention of blindness. It currently has a global initiative: VISION 2020: The right to sight.

Chairman, Board of Trustees: Christian Garms
CEO: Peter Ackland

International Agency for the Prevention of Blindness (IAPB), London School of Hygiene and Tropical Medicine, Keppel Street, London WC1E 7HT, United Kingdom. Tel: +44 (0)207 927 2973, URL: http://www.iapb.org

INTERNATIONAL ASSOCIATION FOR DENTAL RESEARCH (IADR)

Aims to advance research and increase knowledge for the improvement of oral health worldwide and to facilitate the communication and application of research findings.

Executive Director: Christopher H. Fox

International Association for Dental Research (IADR), 1619 Duke Street, Alexandria, VA 22314-3406, Tel: +1 703 548 0066, fax: +1 703 548 1883, e-mail: research@iadr.org, URL: http://www.iadr.org

INTERNATIONAL ASSOCIATION FOR THE STUDY OF OBESITY

Aims to improve global health by promoting the understanding of obesity and weight-related diseases through scientific research and dialogue, whilst encouraging the development of effective policies for their prevention and management.

President: Prof. Philip Jones
President-Elect: Prof. Walmir Coutinho

International Association for the Study of Obesity, Charles Darwin House, 12 Roger Street, London WC1N 2JU, UK. Tel: +44 (0)20 7685 2580, fax: +44 (0)20 7685 2581, e-mail: enquiries@iaso.org, URL: http://www.iaso.org

INTERNATIONAL ASSOCIATION OF AGRICULTURAL MEDICINE AND RURAL HEALTH (IAAMRH)

An independent association for agricultural and rural health professionals which aims to: help member organizations adopt a scientific approach in the field of agricultural medicine and rural health and assist in its practical application; establish effective collaboration with other branches of medicine, health, agricultural, environmental and other related sciences and to study the effects of social , physical and environmental conditions on human health.

President: Dr. Ashok Patil
President-Elect: Prof. Hans-Joachim Hannich
Secretary General: Dr. Syusuke Natsukawa

International Association of Agricultural Medicine and Rural Health (IAAMRH), Saku Central Hospital, 197 Usuda Saku City, Nagano Pref., 384-0301, Japan. Tel: +81 267 82 3131, fax: +81 267 82 7533, URL: http://www.iaamrh.org

INTERNATIONAL ASSOCIATION OF APPLIED PSYCHOLOGY (IAAP)

The mission of the IAAP is to bring applied psychologists in world-wide contact with each other. To this end, every four years IAAP organizes a world congress of applied psychology which serves as a review of advances in applied psychology and unites several thousand psychologists from all over the world.

President-Elect: José M. Peiro
Secretary-General: Janel Gauthier

International Association of Applied Psychology (IAAP), Colegio Oficial de Psicólogos, Cuesta de San Vicente 4, 28008 Madrid, Spain. Tel: 34 91 394 3236, fax: +34 91 351 0091, e-mail: iaap@psi.ucm.es, URL: http://www.iaapsy.org

INTERNATIONAL ASSOCIATION OF BIOETHICS

Studies the ethical, social, legal, philosophical and other related issues arising in health care and in the biological sciences and aims to be truly international, linking all those working in bioethics and related fields, facilitating mutual contact, and encouraging the discussion of cross-cultural aspects in bioethics.

President: Professor Nikola Biller-Andorno

International Association of Bioethics, PO Box 280, University of the Philippines, Diliman, Quezon City 1101, Philippines. Tel: +63 2 436 8873, fax: +63 2 426 9590, e-mail: bioethics-international@kssp.upd.edu.ph, URL: http://www.bioethics-international.org

INTERNATIONAL ASSOCIATION OF GERONTOLOGY AND GERIATRICS

Aims to promote the highest quality of life and well being of all people as they experience ageing at individual and societal levels. Promotes the highest levels of achievement of gerontological research and training worldwide, and interacts with other international, inter-governmental, and non-governmental organizations in the promotion of gerontological interests globally.

President: Bruno Vellas

International Association of Gerontology and Geriatrics, Hopital de la Citadelle, Bld. du XIIème de Ligne, B400 Liège, Belgium. URL: http://www.iagg.info

INTERNATIONAL BRAIN RESEARCH ORGANIZATION (IBRO)

An independent, non-governmental organization founded in 1960 in response to the growing demand from scientists in many countries and different disciplines for the creation of a central organization for the better mobilization and utilization of the world's scientific resources for research on the brain.

Executive Director: Stephanie de La Rochefoucauld

International Brain Research Organization (IBRO), 255 rue Saint-Honoré, 75001 Paris, France. Tel: +33 (0)1 46 47 92 92, fax: +33 (0)1 46 47 42 50, e-mail: admin@ibro.info, URL: http://www.ibro.org

INTERNATIONAL BUREAU FOR EPILEPSY (IBE)

Established in 1961 as an organisation of laypersons and professionals interested in the medical and non-medical aspects of epilepsy. The IBE addresses such social problems as education, employment, insurance, driving licence restrictions and public awareness.

President: Mike Glynn

International Bureau for Epilepsy, 11 Priory Hall, Stillorgan, Dublin 18, Ireland. Tel: +353 1 210 8850, fax: +353 1 210 8450, e-mail: ibedublin@eircom.net, URL: http://www.ibe-epilepsy.org

INTERNATIONAL CHIROPRACTORS' ASSOCIATION

Encourages the highest professional, technical, and ethical standards for chiropractors and maintains and promotes chiropractic's unique identity as a non-therapeutic, drugless and surgical-free health science.

President: Gary Walesemann, DC

International Chiropractors' Association, 6400 Arlington Boulevard, Ste. 800, Falls Church, VA 22042 USA. Tel: +1 800 423 4690, URL: http://www.chiropractic.org

INTERNATIONAL COLLEGE OF SURGEONS (ICS)

A global organization dedicated to bringing together surgeons and surgical specialists of all nations, races, and creeds to promote surgical excellence for the benefit of all of mankind and to foster fellowship worldwide.

Executive Director: Max C. Downham

International College of Surgeons (ICS), 1516 N. Lakeshore Drive, Chicago, IL 60610, USA. Tel +1 312 642 3555, fax +1 312 787 1624, e-mail: info@icsglobal.org, URL: http://www.icsglobal.org

INTERNATIONAL COMMISSION ON OCCUPATIONAL HEALTH (ICOH)

An international non-governmental professional society whose aims are to foster the scientific progress, knowledge and development of occupational health and safety in all its aspects. It has a membership of 2,000 professionals from 93 countries.

President: Dr. Kazutaka Kogi
Secretary General: Dr. Sergio Iavicoli INAIL

OTHER INTERNATIONAL AND NATIONAL ORGANISATIONS

International Commission on Occupational Health (ICOH), Via Fontana Candida 1, I-00040 Monteporzio Catone (Rome), Italy. Tel: +39 06 9418 1506, fax: +39 06 9418 1556, e-mail: icoh@inail.it, URL: http://www.icohweb.org

INTERNATIONAL COMMISSION ON RADIOLOGICAL PROTECTION (ICRP)

ICRP provides recommendations and guidance on all aspects of protection against ionising radiation to regulatory and advisory agencies and offers advice intended to be of help to management and professional staff with responsibilities for radiological protection.

Scientific Secretary: Christopher Clement

International Commission on Radiological Protection, 280 Slater Street, Ottawa, Ontario, K1P 5SP, Canada. URL: http://www.icrp.org

INTERNATIONAL DIABETES FEDERATION (IDF)

A worldwide alliance of 200 diabetes associations in 160 countries, who have come together to enhance the lives of people with diabetes everywhere. The Federation is committed to raising global awareness of diabetes, promoting appropriate diabetes care and prevention, and encouraging activities towards finding a cure for the different types of diabetes.

President: Sir Michael Hurst

International Diabetes Federation (IDF), 166 Chaussée de la Hulpe, B-1070 Brussels, Belgium. Tel: +32 (0)2 5385 511 l, fax: +32 (0)2 538 5114, e-mail: info@idf.org, URL: http://www.idf.org

INTERNATIONAL FEDERATION OF GYNECOLOGY AND OBSTETRICS (FIGO)

Brings together professional societies of obstetricians and gynecologists on a global basis with member societies in 113 countries or territories. It aims to promote the well-being of women and their children and to raise the standard of practice in obstetrics and gynecology around the world.

President: Prof. Gamal Serour (Egypt)
President-Elect: Sir Sabaratnam Arulkumaran (UK)

International Federation of Gynecology and Obstetrics, FIGO House, Suite 3 - Waterloo Court, 10 Theed Street, London SE1 8ST. UK. Tel: +44 (0)20 7928 1166, fax: +44 (0)20 7928 7099, e-mail: figo@figo.org, URL: http://www.figo.org

INTERNATIONAL FEDERATION OF SURGICAL COLLEGES

Brings together all the principal established colleges and associations of surgeons throughout the world in a unified federation in order to improve and maintain standards of surgery throughout the world.

Secretary-General: Professor S.W.A. Gunn, Geneva, Switzerland

International Federation of Surgical Colleges, c/o Royal College of Surgeons in Ireland, 123 St. Stephen's Green, Dublin 2, Ireland. Tel.: +35 31 4022707, e-mail: ifsc@rcsi.ie, URL: http://www.ifsc-net.org

INTERNATIONAL LEAGUE AGAINST EPILEPSY (ILAE)

An association of physicians and other health professionals working towards a world where no persons' life is limited by epilepsy. Its mission is to provide the highest quality of care and well-being for those afflicted with the condition and other related seizure disorders.

President: Solomon Bosche

International League Against Epilepsy (ILAE), 342 North Main Street, West Hartford, CT 06117-2507, USA. Tel: +1 860 586 7547, fax: +1 860 586 7550, URL: http://www.ilae-epilepsy.org

INTERNATIONAL NARCOTICS CONTROL BOARD (INCB)

An independent and quasi-judicial monitoring body for the implementation of the United Nations international drug control conventions.

President: Hamid Ghodse

International Narcotics Control Board, P.O. Box 500, A-1400 Vienna, Austria. Tel: +43 (0)1 260 604277, fax: +43 (0)1 260 605867, e-mail: secretariat@incb.org, URL: http://www.incb.org

INTERNATIONAL ORGANIZATION FOR MEDICAL PHYSICS (IOMP)

Represents over 16,500 medical physicists worldwide, 6 regional organisations and 80 adhering national member organisations. Its mission is to advance medical physics practice worldwide by disseminating scientific and technical information, fostering the educational and professional development of medical physicists and promoting the highest quality medical services for patients.

President: Prof. Fridtjof Nüsslin
Secretary General: Dr. Madan Rehani

International Organization for Medical Physics (IOMP), Fairmount House, 230 Tadcaster Road, York YO24 1ES, UK. URL: http://www.iomp.org

INTERNATIONAL PHARMACEUTICAL FEDERATION (FIP)

The FIP is the global federation of national associations of pharmacists and pharmaceutical scientists. It has 124 Member Organisations and represents and serves more than two million practitioners and scientists around the world.

General Secretary: Mr Ton Hoek

International Pharmaceutical Federation (FIP), PO Box 84200, 2508 AE The Hague, The Netherlands. Tel.: +31 (0)70 302 1970, fax: +31 (0)70 302 1999, e-mail: fip@fip.org, URL: http://www.fip.org

INTERNATIONAL PLANNED PARENTHOOD FEDERATION

Bases its work on the belief that access to sexual and reproductive health and rights information is a basic human right. It has consultative status with the United Nations and its major specialised agencies. Approximately 300 people are employed within the global headquarters and six regional offices. IPPF works in over 170 countries and in 2010 there were approximately 33 million clients.

Director-General: Tewodros Melesse

International Planned Parenthood Federation, 4 Newhams Row, London SE1 3UZ, UK. Tel: +44 (0)20 7939 8200, fax: +44 (0)20 7939 8300, e-mail: info@ippf.org, URL: http://www.ippf.org

INTERNATIONAL PSYCHOANALYTICAL ASSOCIATION (IPA)

The IPA is the world's primary accrediting and regulatory body for psychoanalysis. Its mission is to assure the continued vigour and development of psychoanalysis for the benefit of psychoanalytic patients and to stimulate debate and research in the field.

Director General: H. Gunther Perdigão

International Psychoanalytical Association, Broomhills, Woodside Lane, London N12 8UD, UK. Tel: +44 (0)20 8446 8324, fax: +44 20 8445 4729, e-mail: ipa@ipa.org.uk, URL: http://www.ipa.org.uk

INTERNATIONAL SOCIETY OF AUDIOLOGY

Concerned with advancement of the interests of all those working in audiology or related fields, the interests of the hearing impaired and deaf community and the development of measures to prevent deafness and hearing impairment.

President: Dr Jose Juan Barajas de Prat
Secretary-General: Dr George Mencher

International Society of Audiology, URL: http://www.isa-audiology.org

INTERNATIONAL SOCIETY OF SURGERY (ISS)

Aims to act as an umbrella organization for all those interested in problems of general interest to all surgical specialties such as intensive care, wound treatment, shock, multiple trauma, antibiotic policy, suture matncerial and deontological problems. The ISS is also interested in upkeeping general surgery as an important training base for surgery.

President: Professor Kenneth O. Boffard

International Society of Surgery, Seltisbergerstrasse 16, CH-4419 Lupsingen, Switzerland. Tel: +41 (0)61 815 9666, fax: +41 (0)61 811 4775, e-mail: surgery@iss-sic.ch, URL: http://www.iss-sic.ch

INTERNATIONAL SPINAL CORD SOCIETY

An international impartial, non-political and non-profit making association whose purpose is to study all problems relating to traumatic and non-traumatic lesions of the spinal cord. This includes causes, prevention, basic and clinical research, medical and surgical management, clinical practice, education, rehabilitation and social reintegration.

President: Prof. F. Biering-Sorensen (Denmark)
Executive Administrator: Mrs Marianne Bint (UK)

International Spinal Cord Society, National Spinal Injuries Centre, Stoke Mandeville Hospital, Aylesbury, Bucks HP21 8AL, UK. Tel: +44 (0)1296 315866, fax: +44 (0)1296 315870, e-mail: admin@iscos.org.uk, URL: http://www.iscos.org.uk

INTERNATIONAL UNION AGAINST CANCER (UICC)

Founded in 1933, the UICC, an international NGO, is the largest cancer-fighting organisation of its kind in the world, with more than 360 member organisations across 115 countries. UICC's mission is to eliminate cancer as a life threatening disease for future generations. UICC is non-profit, non-political and non-sectarian. It works closely with its member organizations and partners to implement its strategies. UICC is supported by membership dues and donations from foundations, corporations and individuals.

President: Prof. David Hill (Australia)
CEO: Cary Adams (UK)

International Union Against Cancer (UICC), 62 route de Frontenex, 1207 Geneva, Switzerland. Tel: +41 (0)22 809 1811, fax: +41 (0)22 809 1810, e-mail: info@uicc.org, URL: http://www.uicc.org

INTERNATIONAL UNION AGAINST TUBERCULOSIS AND LUNG DISEASE (THE UNION)

The mission of the International Union Against Tuberculosis and Lung Disease (The Union) is to bring innovation, expertise, solutions and support to address health challenges in low-and middle-income populations. Its scientific departments focus on tuberculosis, HIV, lung health and non-communicable diseases, tobacco control and research. http://www.theunion.org

President: Dr S. Bertel Squire (UK)
Secretary General: Dr Camilo Roa Jr (Philippines)

International Union Against Tuberculosis and Lung Disease, 68 boulevard Saint Michel, 75006 Paris, France. Tel : +33 (0)1 44 32 03 60, fax : +33 (0)1 43 29 90 87, e-mail: union@theunion.org, URL: http://www.theunion.org

INTERNATIONAL UNION FOR HEALTH PROMOTION AND EDUCATION (IUHPE)

Promotes global health and contributes to the achievement of equity in health between and within countries of the world. IUHPE fulfils its mission by building and operating an independent, global, professional network of people and institutions to encourage the free exchange of ideas, knowledge, know-how, experiences, and the development of relevant collaborative projects, both at global and regional levels.

President: Michael Sparks (Australia)

International Union for Health Promotion and Education, 42 Boulevard de la Liberation, 93202 Saint-Denis Cedex, France. Tel: +33 (0)1 48 13 71 20, fax: +33 (0)1 48 09 17 67, e-mail: iuhpe@iuhpe.org, URL: http://www.iuhpe.org

MEDICAL RESEARCH COUNCIL

Aims to promote the balanced development of medical aid and related biological research and to advance knowledge that will lead to the maintaining and improvement of human health.

Chairman: Sir John Chisholm
Chief Executive: Sir John Savill

Medical Research Council, 14th Floor, One Kemble Street, London Wc2B 4AN / 2nd Floor David Phillips Building, Polaris House, North Star Avenue, Swindon, SN2 1FL, United Kingdom. Tel: +44 (0)1793 416200, URL: http://www.mrc.ac.uk

MEDICAL WOMEN'S INTERNATIONAL ASSOCIATION

Aims to promote the cooperation of medical women throughout the world and to develop friendship and understanding between them; actively work against gender related inequalities in the medical profession including career opportunities and economical aspects; and offer medical women the opportunity to meet to discuss questions concerning the health and well-being of humanity.

Secretary-General: Shelly Ross MD

Medical Women's International Association, 7555 Morley Drive, Burnaby, B.C., Canada, V5E 3Y2. Tel.: +1 604 439 899, fax: +1 604 439 8994, URL: http://www.mwia.net

MERLIN

Merlin specialises in health, saving lives in times of crisis and helping to rebuild shattered health services. Merlin works with existing health systems to realise everyone's right to accessible, affordable health care. Merlin works in up to 20 countries at anytime and helps more than 20 million people.

Chair: Lord Jay of Ewelme
Chief Executive: Carolyn Miller

Merlin, 12th Floor, 207 Old Street, London EC1V 9NR, UK. Tel: +44 (0)20 7014 1600, fax: +44 (0)20 7014 1601, e-mail: hq@merlin.org.uk, URL: http://www.merlin.org.uk

MULTIPLE SCLEROSIS INTERNATIONAL FEDERATION (MSIF)

Established in 1967 as an international body linking the activities of national MS societies around the world, MSIF aims to lead the global MS movement by stimulating research into the understanding and treatment of MS and by improving the quality of life of people affected by MS.

Chief Executive Officer: Peer Baneke

Multiple Sclerosis International Federation, 3rd Floor Skyline House, 200 Union Street, London SE1 0LX, UK. Tel: +44 (0)20 7620 1911, fax: +44 (0)20 7620 1922, e-mail: info@msif.org, URL: http://www.msif.org

PAN AMERICAN HEALTH ORGANIZATION

An international public health agency whose purpose is to improve health and living standards with the Americas. It promotes primary health care strategies and targets the most vulnerable groups such as the poor, the displaced, the elderly and children.

Director: Dr Carissa Etienne

Pan American Health Organization, 525 23rd Street, NW, Washington DC 20337, USA. Tel: +1 202 974 3000, fax: +1 202 974 3663, URL: http://www.paho.org

REHABILITATION INTERNATIONAL (RI)

RI is a global and diverse network of persons with disabilities, NGOs, government agencies, service providers and advocates who work together to advance the rights and inclusion of people with disabilities worldwide.

Secretary General: Ms Venus Ilagan

Rehabilitation International (RI), 25 East 21 Street, 4th floor, New York, NY 10010, USA. Tel.: +1 212 420 1500, fax: +1 212 505 0871, e-mail: ri@riglobal.org, URL: http://www.riglobal.org

ROYAL SOCIETY FOR THE PROMOTION OF HEALTH

Promotes the continuous improvement in human health world-wide though education, communication and the encouragement of scientific research.

Chief Executive: Professor Richard Parish

Royal Society for the Promotion of Health, 38A St George's Drive, London SW1V 4BH, UK. Tel: +44 (0)20 7630 0121, fax: +44 (0)20 7976 6847, e-mail: rsh@rsh.org, URL: http://www.rsh.org

WELLCOME TRUST

An independent research-funding charity which seeks to raise awareness of the medical, ethical and social implications of research and to promote dialogue between scientists, the public and policy makers. The trust's vision is to achieve extraordinary improvements in human and animal health. In pursuit of this, it supports the brightest minds in biomedical research and the medical humanities.

Director: Sir Mark Walport
Chairman: Sir William Castell

Wellcome Trust, Gibbs Building, 215 Euston Road, London NW1 2BE, UK. tel: +44 (0)20 7611 8888, fax: +44 (0)20 7611 8545, e-mail: contact@wellcome.ac.uk, URL: http://www.wellcome.ac.uk

WORLD ALLERGY ORGANIZATION (WAO)

An international umbrella organisation whose members consist of 89 regional and national allergology and clinical immunology societies from around the world. By collaborating with member societies, WAO provides direct educational outreach programs, symposia and lectureships to members in 100 countries.

President: Dr Richard Lockey

World Allergy Organization (WAO), 555 East Wells Street, Suite 1100, Milwaukee, WI 53202-3823, USA. Tel: +1 414 276 1791, fax: +1 414 276 3349, e-mail: info@worldallergy.org, URL: http://www.worldallergy.org

WORLD CONFEDERATION FOR PHYSICAL THERAPY (WCPT)

An international non-profit professional organisation which works to improve global health by representing the physical therapy profession internationally; encouraging high standards of physical therapy research, education and practice; supporting communication and exchange of information; and collaborating with international and national organisations.

President: Marilyn Moffat
Secretary General: Brenda Myers

OTHER INTERNATIONAL AND NATIONAL ORGANISATIONS

World Confederation for Physical Therapy, Victoria Charity Centre, 11 Pelgrove Road, London, SW1V 1RB, UK. Tel: +44 (0)20 7471 6765, fax: +44 (0)20 7471 6766, e-mail: info@wcpt.org, URL: http://www.wcpt.org

WORLD FEDERATION FOR MENTAL HEALTH

Aims to: heighten public awareness about the importance of mental health and to gain understanding and improve attitudes about mental disorders; promote mental health and prevent mental disorders and; improve the care, treatment and recovery of people with mental disorders.

World Federation for Mental Health, PO Box 807, Occoquan, VA 22125, USA. URL: http://www.wfmh.org

WORLD FEDERATION OF NEUROLOGY

Aims to improve human health worldwide by promoting prevention and the care of persons with disorders of the entire nervous system. It does this by: fostering the best standards of neurological practice; educating, in collaboration with neuroscience and other international public and private organisations; and facilitating research through its Research Groups and other means.

President: Dr Vladimir Hachinski

World Federation of Neurology, Hill House, Heron Square, Richmond, TW9 1EP, UK. Tel: +44 (0)20 8439 9556, fax: +44 (0)20 8439 9499, e-mail: info@wfneurology.org, URL: http://www.wfneurology.org

WORLD FEDERATION OF OCCUPATIONAL THERAPISTS

The key international representative for occupational therapists and occupational therapy around the world and the official international organisation for the promotion of occupational therapy.

President: E. Sharon Brintnell

World Federation of Occupational Therapists, PO Box 30, Forrestfield, Western Australia, Australia 6058. Fax: + 61 8 9453 9746, e-mail: admin@wfot.org.au, URL: http://www.wfot.org

WORLD FEDERATION OF PUBLIC HEALTH ASSOCIATIONS

An international, non-governmental organisation bringing health workers throughout the world together for professional exchange, collaboration, and action.

President: Dr. Ulrich Laaser
Secretary General: vacant
Vice President/President Elect: James Chauvin

World Federation of Public Health Associations, Office of the Secretariat, c /o Institute for Social and Preventive Medicine, University of Geneva, CMU, 1, rue Michel Servet CH-1211 Genève 4, Switzerland. Tel: +41 22 379 04 53, fax: +41 22 379 04 52, URL: http://www.wfpha.org

WORLD HEART FEDERATION

Helps people achieve a longer and better life through prevention and control of heart disease and stroke, with a focus on low and middle income countries. A non-governmental organization committed to helping the global population achieve a longer and better life through prevention and control of heart disease and stroke, with a focus on low and middle income countries. Comprised of medical societies and heart foundations from over 100 countries, the World Heart Federation is recognised by WHO as its leading non-governmental partner in the prevention and control of cardiovascular disease.

President: Akira Matsumori (Japan)
Chief Executive Officer: Johanna Ralston (Switzerland)

World Heart Federation, 7 rue des Battoirs, 1211 Geneva, Switzerland. Tel: +41 22 807 0320, fax: +41 22 807 0339, URL: http://www.worldheart.org

WORLD MEDICAL ASSOCIATION (WMA)

Aims to achieve the highest international standards in all aspects of medical education and practice and to encourage closer co-operation between doctors and national medical associations in order to address problems confronting the medical profession.

President: Dr José Luiz Gomes Do
Secretary General: Dr Otmar Kloiber

World Medical Association, 13, ch. du Levant, CIB - Bâtiment A, 01210 Ferney-Voltaire, France. Tel: +33 (0)4 50 40 75 75, fax: +33 (0)4 50 40 59 37, e-mail: wma@wma.net, URL: http://www.wma.net

Law

AMERICAN ARBITRATION ASSOCIATION (AAA)

Founded in 1926, the American Arbitration Association (AAA) is a non-profit organisation whose aims are to implement arbitration as an out-of-court solution to resolving disputes. The AAA provides administrative services to those engaged in dispute resolution through its International Centre for Dispute Resolution (ICDR). The organisation helps in the appointment of mediators and arbitrators, and gives users information on resolution options. The AAA aims to move cases through arbitration or mediation in an impartial manner. Through its worldwide offices, the organisation develops alternative dispute resolution systems for corporations, unions, government agencies, law firms, and the courts, as well as providing education, training, and publications on the subject of alternative dispute resolution.

American Arbitration Association, 1633 Broadway, 10th Floor, New York, New York 10019, USA. Tel: +1 212 716 5800, fax: +1 212 716 5905, URL: http://www.adr.org/

AMERICAN SOCIETY OF INTERNATIONAL LAW (ASIL)

The American Society of International Law is a non-profit, non-partisan educational organisation. Founded in 1906, its mission is to foster the study of international law and to promote the establishment and maintenance of international relations on the basis of law and justice. ASIL's programmes are delivered through meetings, publications, information services and outreach programmes. The organisation holds consultative status to the UN Economic and Social Council. There are currently around 4,000 members from almost 100 countries. They include lawyers, academics, corporate counsel, judges, government representatives and international civil servants.

President-Elect: Donald Donovan, ASIL

American Society of International Law (ASIL), 2223 Massachusetts Avenue, NW, Washington DC 20008, USA. Tel: +1 202 939 6000, URL: http://www.asil.org

AMSTERDAM LAW SCHOOL

The Amsterdam Law School and the Amsterdam Graduate School of Law are the educational institutes of the Amsterdam Law School (ALS). The Amsterdam Graduate School of Law is responsible for the Faculty's English-taught LLM programmes, including the degree programmes in European Private Law and International and European Law. The Amsterdam Law School also manages the Amsterdam Exchange Programme. The ALS has won several European Commission contract competitions for training national civil servants and European Community officials. The Faculty of Law has an estimated 3,500 students and 350 staff members.

In September 2008 the Amsterdam Law School joined with the Columbia School of Law to offer the Masters in International Criminal Law course. This is the first course which recognises international criminal law as a distinct field of study.

Dean: Prof. dr. C.E. Du Perron

University Amsterdam - Faculty of Law, International Office, Amsterdam Law School, Oudemanhuispoort 4-6, 1012 CN Amsterdam, The Netherlands. Or: PO Box 1030, 1000 BA Amsterdam, The Netherlands. Tel: +31 (0)20 525 3359, e-mail: als-fdr@uva.nl, URL: http://www.studeren.uva.nl/law-programmes

ASIAN HUMAN RIGHTS COMMISSION

The Asian Human Rights Commission (AHRC) was founded in 1986. It is an independent, non-governmental body, and seeks to bring a greater awareness of human rights issues to the forefront in the Asian region by promoting international public awareness of issues of the area. AHRC promotes civil and political rights, as well as economic, social and cultural rights and seeking redress for victims of human right abuses.

Listed among its objectives are the need to: Protect and promote human rights by monitoring, investigation, advocacy, and taking solidarity actions; Work towards social equality, with particular emphasis on social groups who have suffered discrimination in the past, such as women and children and minorities, including Dalits; Develop cultural and religious programmes for the promotion of human rights; Encourage ratification of UN instruments and development of local legislation, law enforcement and judicial practices in keeping with such instruments, and assist the formation and functioning of national human rights commissions.

Chair of the Board of Directors: John Joseph Clancey (Hong Kong)

Asian Human Rights Commission, Unit 701A, Westley Square, 48 Hoi Yuen Road, Kwun Tong, Hong Kong, China. Tel: +852 2698 6339, fax: +852 2698 6367, e.mail: ahrc@ahrc.asia, URL: http://www.humanrights.asia

ASSOCIATION INTERNATIONALE DE DROIT DES ASSURANCES (AIDA)

Formed in 1960, AIDA is a non-profit making international association. Its members are nationally organised insurance law associations, which are grouped regionally. Its aims are to promote the study and knowledge of international and national insurance law and related matters. AIDA proposes measures with a view to the insurance industry adopting them at a national and international level, leading to harmonisation of insurance law or means for resolution of insurance disputes. The organisation holds a World Congress every four years and publishes the resultant papers. AIDA also issues periodicals and a quarterly electronic newsletter.

President: Mr Michael Gill, DLA Phillips Fox Lawyers, Sydney, Australia

Association Internationale de Droit des Assurances. E-mail: aidaworld@btinternet.com, URL: http://www.aida.org.uk/about.asp

ASSOCIATION INTERNATIONALE DU DROIT DE LA MER (ASSIDMER)
International Association of Maritime Law

The Association Internationale du Droit de la Mer (AssIDMer) is an international non-profit making organisation whose objectives are to promote cooperation and research in the field of maritime law, and to develop greater understanding and equal application of such law. The organisation holds conferences and forums on relevant subjects, encourages research, prepares reports and articles for publication, and maintains links with other judicial and scientific groups concerned with maritime law. The international membership of AssIDMer is composed of academics, judges, diplomats, lawyers, businessmen and lawyers.

The founder and honorary president Daniel Vignes died in 2011.

President: Giuseppe Cataldi

Association Internaitonale du Droit de la Mer, Via Partenope 10/A con accesso alla Via Chiatamone 61/61, 80121 Naples, Italy. URL: http://www.assidmer.org

ASYLUMLAW.ORG

Asylumlaw.org was founded in 1999. Its aim is to use the internet in helping lawyers and other accredited representatives around the world to prepare the best asylum cases they can. Around 10,000 lawyers now use the site who have collectively represented an estimated 100,000 asylum seekers.

CEO: David Berton

Asylumlaw.org, 1638 N. Wolcott Avenue, Chicago, Illinois 60622, USA. URL: http://www.asylumlaw.org

AUCKLAND UNIVERSITY, FACULTY OF LAW

Auckland University's law faculty currently consists of around 40 full-time staff and approximately 1,800 students. Located close to New Zealand's busiest High Court, it is in the heart of the New Zealand's commercial district. The Faculty staff includes leaders in all subjects from commercial and public law to human rights and environmental law. The School offers a broad-based legal education; as well as teaching the core law subjects, it offers the largest range of optional courses in New Zealand. Around 10 per cent of Auckland's final-year students spend one or two terms at law schools abroad.

Dean: Dr Andew Stockley

Faculty of Law Office, University of Auckland, Private Bag 92019, Auckland Mail Centre, Auckland 1142, New Zealand. Tel: +64 9 373 7599, URL: http://www.law.auckland.ac.nz/uoa/

AUSTRALIAN AND NEW ZEALAND SOCIETY OF INTERNATIONAL LAW (ANZIL)

ANZSIL was established in 1992 in order to develop, promote and support the teaching of international law. Through its annual conference, it provides a forum for discussion for academics, government lawyers, NGOs and students, and aims to increase public awareness and understanding of international law. ANZSIL is organised through the Australian National University's Centre for International and Public Law and the Victorian University of Wellington's New Zealand Centre for Public Law.

President of the Executive Council: Andrew Byrnes

Australian and New Zealand Society of International Law, Centre for International and Public Law, Australian National University, Canberra ACT 0200, Australia. Tel: +61 2 6125 0454, e-mail: anzsil@law.anu.edu.au, URL: http://law.anu.edu.au/anzsil/index.html

AVOCATS SANS FRONTIÈRES (ASF)

Founded in 1992 in Belgium, Avocats Sans Frontières (ASF- Lawyers without Borders) is an international non-governmental organisation of lawyers, solicitors and magistrates whose aim is to contribute to the establishment of a just and united society through the promotion and protection of the political, economic, social and cultural rights of the most vulnerable people. To this end, ASF distributes legal aid, and organises access to justice, as well as supporting local law practitioners and informing populations about their rights. ASF is based in Brussels, Belgium. There are also permanent offices iin Burundi, Democratic Republic of Congo, Rwanda, Uganda and Nepal.

President: Hafida Talhaoui

Avocats Sans Frontières, Rue de Namur 72, 1000 Brussels, Belgium. Tel: +32 2 223 36 54, e-mail: info@asf.be, URL: http://www.asf.be/

BRITISH INSTITUTE OF INTERNATIONAL AND COMPARATIVE LAW (BIICL)

Formed in 1895, the British Institute of International and Comparative Law (BIICL) is an independent legal research institute with charitable status. It aims to develop the understanding of international and comparative law, and to promote the rule of law in international affairs.The organisation seeks to achieve these aims through research, publications and events. It currently has around 800 members, comprising barristers, solicitors, judges, government and NGO counsels, academics and students.

President and Chairman: Dame Rosalyn Higgins DBE QC (page 1441)

British Institute of International and Comparative Law, Charles Clore House, 17 Russell Square, London, WC1B 5JP, United Kingdom. Tel: +44 020 7862 5151, fax: +44 020 7862 5152, URL: http://www.biicl.org

CENTRE FOR ISLAMIC AND MIDDLE EASTERN LAW

The Centre for Islamic & Middle Eastern Law (CIMEL) forms part of the School of Oriental and African Studies (SOAS) at the University of London. It aims to promote the study and understanding of Islamic law and modern Middle Eastern legal systems, through lectures, publications, conferences and academic exchanges. In 1990, the Centre established the Middle East Legal Practitioners' Forum (MELPF) in order to foster the links with lawyers in London and in the Middle East. CIMEL encourages research projects on Islamic law, and fosters links between those involved in this specialised field, such as legal practitioners, members of the business community, and government officials.

Chair, CIMEL Advisory Council: Professor His Honour Judge Eugene Cotran

Centre for Islamic & Middle Eastern Law, School of Oriental and African Studies, University of London, Thornhaugh Street, Russell Square, London WC1H 0XG. Tel: +44 020 7637 2388, URL: http://www.soas.ac.uk/cimel/

CHARTERED INSTITUTE OF ARBITRATORS

The Chartered Institute of Arbitrators (CIArb) is a non-profit charity with over 30 branches and.around 12,000 members around the world. It aims to promote, facilitate and develop all forms of private dispute resolution, and offers the only globally recognised professional qualifications in the field. The Institute provides training for arbitrators, mediators and adjudicators, and acts as a centre for policy makers, academics and those in business concerned with the cost-effective and early settlement of disputes.

President: Jeffrey Elkinson FCIArb (Bermuda)

Chartered Institute of Arbitrators, 12 Bloomsbury Square, London WC1A 2LP, UK. Tel: +44 (0)20 7421 7444, fax: +44 (0)20 7404 4023, e-mail: info@ciarb.org, URL: http://www.ciarb.org/

CHINA-EU SCHOOL OF LAW (CESL)

Forming part of the China University of Political Science and Law (CUPL), the China-EU School of Law (CESL) is a joint project of the Government of the P.R. China and the European Union. The school aims to cultivate a generation of legal professionals who are proficient in both Chinese and international law. CESL offers a programme of Chinese Juris Master and LL.M of EU Law, as well as a Professional Training Program for lawyers, judges and prosecutors. There is also a Research and Consultancy Program, leading to a Ph.D qualification. Lectures on European and international law are given by visiting professors from European universities. The School is administered by two Co-Deans (one of Chinese nationality, one of a nationality other than Chinese).

Co-Deans: Prof. Fang Liufang and Prof. Thomas Bruha

China-EU School of Law (CESL), University of Political Science and Law, No. 27, Fuxue Road, Changping District, Beijing 102249, China. URL: http://www.cesl.edu.cn

CHINESE UNIVERSITY OF HONG KONG (CUHK), FACULTY OF LAW

The CUHK Faculty of Law (formerly the School of Law) admitted its first students in 2006. It offers LLB degrees and graduate JD, LLM, MPhil and PhDs. The LLB degree offers students a general law grounding, and some can choose a double degree option towards the end of their first year. The double degree options are Law and Business, Law and Translation, and Law and Sociology.

The post-graduate JD, LL.M. and PCLL classes are held in the central business district of Hong Kong, close to Hong Kong High Court, the Legislative Council Building , and law firms.

Dean: Professor Christopher Gane

Faculty of Law, 6/F, Lee Shau Kee Building, The Chinese University of Hong Kong, Shatin, New Territories, Hong Kong. Tel: +852 3163 4399, e-mail: law@cuhk.edu.hk, URL: http://www.law.cuhk.edu.hk/
Graduate Law Centre, 2/F, Bank of America Tower, 12 Harcourt Road, Central, Hong Kong. Tel: +852 3529 5900, e-mail: law@cuhk.edu.hk

OTHER INTERNATIONAL AND NATIONAL ORGANISATIONS

COALITION FOR THE INTERNATIONAL CRIMINAL COURT (CICC)

The Coalition for the International Criminal Court (commonly known as CICC) is an international non-governmental organisation which advocates a fair, effective and independent International Criminal Court (ICC). Its members aim to strengthen international cooperation with the ICC; to ensure that the court is fair, effective and independent; to make justice both visible and universal, and to promote stronger national laws which ensure justice for victims of war crimes, crimes against humanity and genocide. The CICC national coalitions and regional networks comprise a range of civil society groups, including NGOs, academics, lawyers and bar associations. Funding is provided by the EU, various governments and other foundations. As of April 2012, 139 countries had signed the ICC Treaty and 121 had ratified it.

Convenor: William Pace

Coalition for the International Criminal Court, 708 3rd Avenue, New York, NY 10017-4210, USA. Tel: +1 212 687 2176, URL: http://www.iccnow.org/

COLUMBIA LAW SCHOOL

Columbia Law School is a leading center of legal scholarship. There are around 1,200 JD students enrolled at any one time. Columbia has expanded its programs in international and comparative law over the past decade, increasing the availability and choice of joint degree programmes and encouraging study abroad programmes. The number of international internships has also grown. The Law School collaborates with foreign educational institutes, governments and NGOs all over the world.

There are centers for Chinese, Japanese, Korean and European legal studies, and the Law School organises conferences and research programmes in many other regions of the world in collaboration with such entities as the Center for Global Legal Problems, the Human Rights Institute and the Parker School for Foreign and Comparative Law.

Dean: David M. Schizer

Columbia Law School, 435 West 116th Street, Mail Code 4004, New York, NY 10027-7297, USA. Tel: +1 212 854-2640, URL: http://www.law.columbia.edu/

COMMONWEALTH LAWYERS ASSOCIATION

The CLA promotes and maintains the rule of law throughout the Commonwealth.

The stated aims of the CLA as laid down in its constitution are as follows: Ensuring that a common bond of Commonwealth is preserved and fostered; Strengthening professional links between members of the legal profession; Maintaining the honour and integrity of the profession; Promoting uniformity in the standards of professional ethics; Encouraging improved standards of education; Promote the administration of justice and protection of human rights in accordance with the principles enshrined in the Harare Declaration of 1991, Milbrooke Action Programme of 1995 and the Latimer House Guidelines of the Commonwealth of 1998 (now referred to as the Commonwealth (Latimer House) Principles on the accountability of and relationship between the three branches of Government).

President, Council, 2011-2013: Boma Ozobia (Nigeria)
Vice-President: Mark Stephens (England and Wales)

Executive Committee Chair: Laurie Watt

Commonwealth Lawyers Association, 17 Russell Square, London, WC1B 5DR, UK. Tel: +44 (0)207 862 8824, fax: +44 (0)207 862 8816, email: cla@sas.ac.uk, URL: http://www.commonwealthlawyers.com

COMMONWEALTH MAGISTRATES AND JUDGES ASSOCIATION

Founded in 1970, the Commonwealth Magistrates and Judges Association (CMJA) is a charitable organisation whose aims are threefold: to advance the administration of the law by promoting judicial independence; to support legal education, as well as the administration of justice, the treatment of offenders and the prevention of crime within the Commonwealth; and to disseminate information and literature on all matters of interest concerning the legal process within Commonwealth countries.

Secretary General: Dr Karen Brewer

Commonwealth Magistrates and Judges Association, CMJA, Uganda House, 58-59 Trafalgar Square, London, WC2N 5DX. Tel: +44 (0)20 7976 1007, fax: +44 (0)20 7976 2394, e-mail: info@cmja.org, URL: http://www.cmja.org/

CORNELL LAW SCHOOL

Founded in 1887 in Ithaca, NY, Cornell Law School is one of the five Ivy League law schools. It currently has around 603 enrolled J.D. students and is the third smallest law school in the USA.

Cornell has specialised in international law since 1948, and initiated the Cornell International Law Journal in 1968. It has a partnership with the University of Paris I law faculty, as well as a summer law institute in Suzhou, China. The Clarke Program in East Asian Law and Culture was established in 2002. Cornell Law is home to the Legal Information Institute (LII), an online provider of public legal information. It offers all opinions of the US Supreme Court handed down since 1990.

Dean: Stewart J. Schwab

Cornell Law School, Myron Taylor Hall, Ithaca, NY 14853-4901, USA. URL: http://www.lawschool.cornell.edu/

COUNCIL OF BARS AND LAW SOCIETIES OF EUROPE

The CCBE is the official representative organisation for the legal profession in the EU and the EEA. It represents the bar associations and law societies of the member states, and the lawyers who belong to them before the European institutions. It has consultative status with the Council of Europe.

President (2012): Marcella Prunbauer-Glaser

Council of Bars and Law Societies of Europe, 1-5 ave. de la joyeuse entrée, 1040 Brussels, Belgium. Tel: +32 (0)2 234 6510, fax: +32 (0)2 234 6511, email: ccbe@ccbe.eu, URL: http://www.ccbe.eu

COURT OF ARBITRATION FOR SPORT (CAS)

Created in 1984, the Court of Arbitration for Sport (CAS) is an independent organisation which facilitates the settlement of sports-related disputes through arbitration or mediation adapted to the specific requirements of the sports world. It functions under the administrative and financial authority of the International Council of Arbitration for Sport (ICAS). The CAS registers approximately 300 cases each year, and calls on almost 300 arbitrators from 87 countries, chosen for their specialist knowledge of arbitration and sports law. The CAS also gives advisory opinions concerning legal questions related to sport, and sets up non-permanent tribunals for major events such as the Olympic Games.

Secretary General: Matthieu Reeb

Court of Arbitration for Sport, Château de Béthusy, Avenue de Beaumont 2, CH-1012 Lausanne, Switzerland. Tel: +41 21 613 50 00, fax: +41 21 613 50 01, e-mail: info@tas-cas.org, URL: http://www.tas-cas.org/

COURT OF CONCILIATION AND ARBITRATION

The Court of Conciliation and Arbitration provides a mechanism for the peaceful settlement of disputes between States. The Court was established in 1995 by the Convention on Conciliation and Arbitration. Thirty-three States are currently (as of July 2013) Parties to the Convention. The Court's mandate is to settle, by means of conciliation or arbitration, the disputes between States submitted to it. The conciliation commissions and arbitral tribunals are created by the Court on an ad hoc basis and the Court therefore is not a permanent body. It is composed of recognized experts in the field of international law who are appointed by the States Parties to the Convention. The conciliators and arbitrators are headed by a Bureau, currently chaired by Robert Badinter, former Minister of Justice of France and President of the Court. His term is due to end in 2013.

President of the Court: Robert Badinter

OSCE Court of Conciliation and Arbitration, 9-11 rue de Varembé, CH-1202 Geneva, Switzerland. Tel: +41 (0)22 758 0025, fax: +41 (0)22 758 2510, e-mail: cca.osce@bluewin.ch, URL: http://www.osce.org/cca

COURT OF JUSTICE OF THE EUROPEAN UNION

See entry in European Union section.

DURHAM LAW SCHOOL

Based at Durham University, the Law School is one of the leading centres of legal research in the UK. In was ranked 4th in the RAE 2008. The School has over 30 full-time academic staff, whose research interests include topics as diverse as bioethics and medical law, commercial law, human rights, gender studies, European law, legal history and criminal law and criminology.

Durham Law School , 50 North Bailey, Durham DH1 3ET, UK. Tel: +44 191 334 2800, fax: +44 191 334 2801, URL: http://www.dur.ac.uk/law/

EUROPEAN SOCIETY OF INTERNATIONAL LAW (ESIL)

Founded in 2004 in response to growing globalisation, the European Society of International Law aims to contribute to the rule of law in international relations and to promote the study of public international law. The society encourages research and the exchange of ideas on matters of common interest to international lawyers in Europe and elsewhere, providing a forum for European-wide discussions. It promotes the involvement of students, and fosters greater awareness and understanding of international law within the general public. Membership is open to all those with an interest in international law.

President: Anne Peters

European Society of International Law, Academy of European Law, Villa Schifanoia, Via Boccaccio 121, 50133 Florence, Italy. Tel: +39 055 468 5512, e-mail: esil.secretariat@eui.eu, URL: http://www.esil-sedi.eu/

EUROPEAN UNIVERSITY INSTITUTE
The EUI was set up in 1972 by the founding members of the European communities to provide high level legal academic traiinng to doctoral researchers and to promote research at the highest level. The Department of Law has a well-established reputation for European law, international law, comparative private and public law and social and cognitive theories of law.

President: Joseph Borrell Fontelles

European University Institute, Department of Law, Badia Fiesolana, Via dei Roccettina 9, 50016 San Domenico di Fiesole, Italy. URL: http://www.eui.eu/About/Index.aspx

FAIR TRIALS INTERNATIONAL
Fair Trials International (FTI) is an organisation which works to promote fair trials according to international standards of justice and also defends the rights of people facing charges in a country other than their own.

FTI 's stated mission is to provide individual legal assistance through its expert casework practice. It also addresses the root causes of injustice through broader research and campaigning and builds local legal capacity through targeted training, mentoring and network activities.

Chief Executive: Jago Russell

Fair Trials International, 3/7 Temple Chambers, Temple Avenue, London EC4Y 0HP, United Kingdom. Tel: +44 (0)207 822 2370, fax: +44(0)207 822 2371, URL: http://www.fairtrials.net

FEDERATION OF EUROPEAN EMPLOYERS (FEDEE)
Initially established with EU funding in 1989, but now an independent organisation, FedEE provides practical resources for companies operating across Europe, with a focus on employment law, pay and labour relations. The organisation provides legal support through the use of international employment lawyers who provide information covering subjects such as employment contracts, employee participation, working time, equal opportunities and employee dismissal.

Founder & Secretary General: Robin Chater

Federation of European Employers, Adam House, 7-10 Adam Street, The Strand, London, WC2N 6AA, UK. Tel: +44 0207 520 9264, fax: +44 0207 520 9265, URL: http://www.fedee.com/

FREIE UNIVERSITAT (FU) BERLIN (FREE UNIVERSITY OF BERLIN)
FU Berlin is the largest university in Berlin and one of the largest in Germany. It holds the nations's largest law library and several significant law institutes. Prominent alumni include the former German president Roman Herzog and the former president of the German Supreme Court, Jutta Limbach.

Freie Universität (FU) Berlin, Fachbereich Rechtswissenschaft, Van't-Hoff-Str. 8, 14195 Berlin, Germany. URL: http://www.jura.fu-berlin.de/studium/vorschriften/llm/

GENEVA UNIVERSITY LAW SCHOOL
The Geneva University Law School is home to several research centres including the Centre for Banking and Financial Law, the Centre for European Legal Studies and the Art Law Centre, and has a strong focus on international and comparative law. It attracts students from around the world and the language of instruction is English. One of the school's most renowned courses is the Master of Advanced Studies in International Dispute Settlement which covers such fields as international commercial and investment arbitration, WTO dispute resolution and proceedings before the International Court of Justice.

Geneva Law School and Graduate Institute of International and Development Studies, P.O. Box 136, 1211 Geneva 21, Switzerland. Tel: +41 22 9089 4487, fax: +41 22 908 4499, e-mail: info@mids.ch, URL: http://mids.ch

GEORGETOWN UNIVERSITY LAW CENTER
Established in 1870, Georgetown University Law Center (Georgetown Law) is the second largest law school in the USA with a full-time enrollment of approximately 1,600 students. It receives over 10,000 applications each year, more than any other law school in the U.S. This is partly due to its location in the Capitol Hill area of Washington D.C., and its close proximity to federal agencies and the US Supreme Court.

J.D. students choose between a traditional law curriculum (which includes contracts, constitutional law, torts, property, criminal procedure, civil procedure, and legal research), and a more interdisciplinary, theoretical approach to legal study (contracts and torts, constitutional law and criminal procedure, administrative law, jurisprudence, legal research, civil procedure, and property).

Dean: William Treanor BA, JD, Yale; Ph.D, Harvard

Georgetown University Law Center, 600 New Jersey Avenue, N.W. Washington D.C. 20001, USA. Tel: +1 202 662 9000, URL: http://www.law.georgetown.edu/

GHENT UNIVERSITY LAW SCHOOL
The Law School offers an LL.M programme in European Law including EU law, international law and member state law. The Law School is a European Jean Monnet Centre of Excellence, recognised for its expertise and resources in European Union Law. The programme is directed by Prof.dr. Marc de Vos.

Dean: Prof. dr. Dr. Piet Taelman

Ghent University Law School, Universiteitstraat 4, 9000 Ghent, Belgium. URL: http://www.law.ugent.be/

GOETHE UNIVERSITAT FRANKFURT AM MAIN
The university was founded in 1914 through private funding. and is one of the major institutions of higher education in Germany. In total there are over 41,000 students from more than 129 nations. The Institute for International and European Law and Comparative Law is headed by Prof. Dr. Peter von Wilmowsky. It also well known for its study of International Business Law.

Faculty of Law, Dean: Prof. Dr. Cornelius Prittwitz

Goethe Universität Frankfurt am Main, Department of Law, Grüneburgplatz 1, 60323 Frankfurt am Main, Germany. Tel: +49 (0)69 798 34206, URL: http://www.jura.uni-frankfurt.de/index.html

HAGUE ACADEMY OF INTERNATIONAL LAW
The Hague Academy of International Law was established in 1923 with funding received from the Carnegie Foundation in Washington. It has since become a centre for research and teaching in both public and private international law.

As the Academy is a stand alone institution and not part of a university it does not have a permanent teaching staff and so the Curatorium can call upon academics, lawyers, diplomats or anyone it feels qualified to deliver lectures. Courses are made up of a series of lectures given in English and French which are published in the Collected Courses of the Academy of International Law.

Curatorium President: Boutros Boutros-Ghali

Hague Academy of International Law, Peace Palace, Carnegieplein 2, 2517 KJ The Hague, The Netherlands. Tel: +31 (0)70 302 4242, URL: http://www.hagueacademy.nl

HARVARD LAW SCHOOL
Harvard Law School prepares students for careers in law practice, business, public service and teaching. There are more than 100 full-time professors and over 150 visiting professors and lecturers. Approximately 1,900 students attend HLS each year (1,680 JD students, 160 LL.M students and 50 SJD candidates). The student body is drawn from every state in the U.S. and more than 80 countries around the world.

The curriculum features more than 260 courses and seminars that cover a broad range of traditional and emerging legal fields. The Law School also runs research programmes and publishes books, periodicals and newsletters. Over half the Harvard Law faculty incorporates international and comparative perspectives in its teaching, and Harvard's research centers host hundreds of workshops, and conferences with an international focus. There are specialised courses in international law, a student-edited international law journal, and an international law library.

Dean: Martha Minow

Harvard Law School, 1563 Massachusetts Avenue, Cambridge, MA 02138, USA. Tel: +1 617 495 3100, URL: http://www.law.harvard.edu/

IE LAW SCHOOL
The IE Law School was founded in 1973. The main course offered is the Master of Laws (LL.M.) in International Legal Practice. The IE also works in partnership with the Northwestern University School of Law to offer an Executive LL.M. programme. The languages of instruction are Spanish and English.

Dean: José M. De Areilza S.J.D

IE Law School, María de Molina, 11, 28006 Madrid, Spain. E-mail: law@ie.edu, URL: http://www.ie.edu/IE/site/php/en/school_law.php

INSTITUT DU DROIT INTERNATIONAL
Institute of International Law
The Institute of International Law was founded in 1873 in response to the apparent flouting of the Convention for the Amelioration of the Condition of the Wounded in Armies in the Field (1864) during the Franco-Prussian War of 1870-71. The aims of the Institute are to contribute to the development of international law and to ensure its implementation. The Institute establishes scientific commissions to study relevant themes, and the resultant Resolutions may be brought to the attention of government authorities. The Institute of International Law received the Nobel Peace Prize in 1904.

Secretary-General: M. Joe Verhoeven

Institut du Droit International, 24, rue de Morsaint, B-1390 Grez-Boiceau, Belgium. Tel: +32 10 84 53 96, URL: http://www.idi-iil.org

OTHER INTERNATIONAL AND NATIONAL ORGANISATIONS

INTER-AMERICAN COMMERCIAL ARBITRATION COMMISSION (IACAC)

The Inter-American Commercial Arbitration Commission was established in 1934 under the Organisation of American States. It has established, maintains and administers a system for settlement of international commercial disputes by arbitration or conciliation. The system includes National Sections or Representatives in almost all countries in the Western Hemisphere. The Commission coordinates the activities of National Sections (representing the business and legal communities of their respective countries), as well as providing administrative services and appointing arbitrators. The Commission promotes educational activities designed to foster a knowledge and use of international commercial arbitration, and supports conciliation in misunderstandings and trade disputes.

President: Dr. Julio Gonzalez Soria

Inter-American Commercial Arbitration Commission (IACAC). E-mail: sice@sice.oas.org, URL: http://www.sice.oas.org/dispute/comarb/iacac/iacac1e.asp

INTERNATIONAL ASSOCIATION FOR REFUGEE LAW JUDGES

Amongst the stated aims of the organisation in its constitution are that it seeks to foster recognition that protection on account of race, religion, nationality, membership in a particular social group, or political opinion is an individual right established under international law, and that the determination of refugee status and its cessation should be subject to the rule of law.

The organisation commits itself to: Promote within the judiciary and quasijudicial decision makers world-wide a common understanding of refugee law principles and to encourage the use of fair practices and procedures to determine refugee law issues; To foster judicial independence and to facilitate the development within national legal systems of independent institutions applying judicial principles to refugee law issues; To encourage the sharing of information and databases relating to conditions in countries of origin and countries of transit of asylum seekers; To encourage the development of norms of access by asylum seekers to judicial systems that are compatible with international law standards; To promote or undertake research initiatives, publications and projects that further the attainment of the objects of the Association; While keeping in mind the independence of the members of the Association in their judicial functions, to co-operate with the United Nations High Commissioner for Refugees and other agencies, both international and national, that are concerned with the promotion of an understanding of refugee law issues.

President: Sebastiaan de Groot

International Association of Refugee Law Judges, P.O. Box 1621, 2003 BR Haarlem, The Netherlands. Tel: +31 23 888 3956, fax: +31 23 888 3979, URL: http://www.iarlj.org/general/

INTERNATIONAL ASSOCIATION OF PENAL LAW

The International Association of Penal Law (AIDP), (L'Association Internationale de Droit Penal) was founded in Paris in 1924. It grew out of the organisation the International Union of Penal Law (UIDP), which had been founded in Vienna in 1889. The AIDP is the oldest global organisation which brings together specialists on the criminal law. The organisation is open to anyone anywhere in the world who is concerned with the study and implementation of criminal law and who wishes to promote the development of legislation and institutions and who has a view towards providing a more humane and efficient system for its administration.

The main areas of interest to the organisation are Criminal policy and the codification of penal law; Comparative criminal law; Human rights in the administration of criminal justice; and International criminal law; International criminal justice.

President: José Luis de la Cuesta

International Association of Penal Law (AIDP), POB 60118, 33008 Bordeaux CEDEX, France. TEl: +33 (0)5 56 06 66 73, fax: +33 (0)1 44 04 92 89, e-mail: secretariat@penal.org, URL: http://www.penal.org

INTERNATIONAL ASSOCIATION OF WOMEN JUDGES

Founded in 1991, the International Association of Women Judges (IAWJ) is a non-profit, organisation which aims to unite women judges from different legal systems who share a commitment to justice and the rule of law. Currently, it has over 4,000 members, drawn from over 100 countries. The IAWJ is committed to protect and empower women, and works to advance human rights, and to eliminate discrimination on the basis of gender, through judicial education programmes.

President: Lady Brenda Hale, Supreme Court of the United Kingdom
President-Elect: Hon. Eusebia Nicholas Munuo

International Association of Women Judges, 1850 M Street NW Suite 350 Washington DC 20036 USA. Tel: +1 202 223 4450, +1 202 223 4480, URL: http://www.iawj.org

INTERNATIONAL BAR ASSOCIATION

The world's largest international organisation of Law Societies, Bar Associations and individual lawyers engaged in international practice. The IBA has consultative status with the UN and Council of Europe. It has a membership of more than 45,000 individual lawyers and over 200 bar associations and law societies.

President: Akira Kawamura
Secretary General: David W. Rivkin

International Bar Association, 4th Floor, 10 St Bride Street, London EC4A 4AD, UK. Tel: +44 (0)20 7842 0090, fax: +44 (0)20 7842 0091, URL: http://www.ibanet.org

INTERNATIONAL CENTRE FOR CRIMINAL LAW REFORM AND CRIMINAL JUSTICE POLICY

The International Centre for Criminal Law Reform and Criminal Justice Policy (ICCLR) is an independent, international institute based in Vancouver, Canada. Founded in 1991, ICCLR is a joint initiative of the Government of Canada, the University of British Columbia, Simon Fraser University, the International Society for the Reform of Criminal Law, and the Province of British Columbia. It is officially affiliated with the United Nations pursuant to a formal agreement in 1995 between the Government of Canada and the UN. The Centre contributes to the priorities of Canada and the United Nations in the field of criminal law and criminal justice.

The mandate of the Centre is to promote the rule of law, democracy, human rights, and good governance in criminal law and the administration of criminal justice, domestically, regionally and globally.

To fulfill its mandate, the Centre cooperates closely with a network of local, national and international experts including representatives from Federal and Provincial governments, the legal and academic communities, as well as other members of the United Nations Programme Network of Institutes. The Centre undertakes the development and delivery of technical assistance programs, develops tools including handbooks and manuals, and conducts research and policy analysis. Further, the Centre provides public information, consultation and education relating to crime, protecting victims, developing more effective and fair justice systems and supporting international cooperation to fight against serious crimes.

President: Daniel C. Préfontaine QC

International Centre for Criminal Law Reform and Criminal Justice Policy, 1822 East Mall, Vancouver, BC V6T 1Z1, Canada. Tel: +1 604 822 9875, e-mail: icclr@law.ubc.ca. URL: http://www.icclr.law.ubc.ca

INTERNATIONAL CENTRE FOR THE SETTLEMENT OF INVESTMENT DISPUTES (ICSID)

The International Centre for the Settlement of Investment Disputes (ICSID) is an autonomous institution established under the 1965 Convention on the Settlement of Investment Disputes, a multilateral treaty formulated by the World Bank. Its main function is to provide facilities for conciliation and arbitration of international investment disputes. It currently has a membership of over 140 States. The President of the World Bank is ex officio Chairman of the ICSID Administrative Council but has no vote. ICSID is considered to be the leading international arbitration institution devoted to investor-State dispute settlement.

For further details, please consult its main entry under 'Affiliated Agencies of the United Nations'.

Secretary-General: Meg Kinnear

ICSID, 1818 H Street, N.W., Washington, D.C. 20433, U.S.A. Tel: +1 202 458 1534, fax: +1 202 522 2615, URL: http://icsid.worldbank.org/ICSID/

INTERNATIONAL COUNCIL FOR COMMERCIAL ARBITRATION (ICCA)

The International Council for Commercial Arbitration (ICCA) is a worldwide organisation devoted to promoting the use and improving the processes of arbitration, conciliation and other forms of resolving international commercial disputes. Its activities include convening conferences, sponsoring dispute resolution publications, and promoting the harmonisation of arbitration and conciliation rules, laws, procedures and standards. The 37 members and 20 advisory members are drawn from 32 developed and developing nations, and are recognized specialists in the field of dispute resolution.

Secretary General: Kap-You (Kevin) Kim

International Council for Commercial Arbitration, URL: http://www.arbitration-icca.org/about.html

INTERNATIONAL CRIMINAL COURT

See entry in Affiliated Agencies of the United Nations section

INTERNATIONAL CRIMINAL LAW NETWORK

The International Criminal Law Network (ICLN), was founded in 2002 by Science Alliance with the support of the Dutch Ministries of Defence and Foreign Affairs and the Municipality of The Hague.

The organisation's stated mission to organise professional and social interaction on a worldwide level between academics, policymakers and legal professionals in the area of international criminal law. In order to realise this goal, ICLN organises successful activities on a wide scale, such as an Annual Conference, several lectures per year, the ICC Trial Competition and regional training workshops.

President: Prof. Michael P. Scharf

International Criminal Law Network, Koninginnegracht 27, The Hague 2514 AB, The Netherlands. Tel: +31 70 362 6579, fax:+ 31 70 362 9768, URL: http://www.icln.net/cms/

INTERNATIONAL CRIMINAL POLICE ORGANISATION (INTERPOL)

See entry in Inter-Governmental Organisations section.

INTERNATIONAL CRIMINAL TRIBUNAL FOR RWANDA

See entry in Affiliated Agencies of the United Nations section.

INTERNATIONAL CRIMINAL TRIBUNAL FOR THE FORMER YUGOSLAVIA

See entry under Affiliated Agencies of the United Nations.

INTERNATIONAL INSTITUTE FOR THE UNIFICATION OF PRIVATE LAW (UNIDROIT)

Originally established in 1926 in association with the League of Nations, the International Institute for the Unification of Private Law is an independent intergovernmental organisation whose purpose is to study needs and methods for modernising, harmonising and co-ordinating private and in particular commercial law between States and groups of States. Unidroit's 63 member States, drawn from the five continents, represent a variety of different legal, economic and political systems as well as different cultural backgrounds.

International Institute for the Unification of Private Law, 28 Via Panisperna, 00184 Rome, Italy. Tel.: +39 06 696211, fax: +39 06 699 41394, e-mail: info@unidroit.org, URL: http://www.unidroit.org/

INTERNATIONAL INSTITUTE OF SPACE LAW

The International Institute of Space Law (IISL) was founded in 1960. Its aim is to foster the development of space law with the cooperation of the appropriate international organisations and national entities. The Institute also researches the legal and social aspects of the exploration and use of outer space, and organises meetings, colloquia and competitions on these aspects of space activities. The proceedings of the colloquia are published by the American Institute of Aeronautics and Astronautics. Membership of the IISL is by election only, members being distinguished for their contributions to space law development.

President: Mrs Tanja L. Masson-Zwaan (Netherlands)

International Institute of Space Law, 94bis, Avenue de Suffren, 75015 Paris, France. E-mail: cmj@advancingspace.com, URL: http://www.iislweb.org/

INTERNATIONAL LAW ASSOCIATION

A private membership organisation whose objectives include the study, elucidation and advancement of international law, the study of comparative law, the making of proposals for the solution of conflicts of law and for the unification of law.

President: Professor Nicolaas Schrijver
Secretary General: David Wyld

International Law Association, Charles Clore House, 17 Russell Square, London WC1B 5DR, UK. Tel: +44 (0)20 7323 2978, fax: +44 (0)20 7323 3580, e-mail: info@ila-hq.org, URL: http://www.ila-hq.org

INTERNATIONAL LAW COMMISSION

The International Law Commission held the first of its annual sessions in 1949. Its stated aim is the promotion of the progressive development of international law and its codification. The Commission concerns itself primarily with public international law, and has worked principally in the area of international criminal law.

The Secretary-General of the United Nations provides the staff and facilities of Commission. It currently has 34 members, drawn from the international legal community, academia, the diplomatic corps, government ministries and international organisations.

International Law Commission, Room M-13065, 405 E 42nd Street, New York, N.Y. 10017, USA. URL: http://www.un.org/law/ilc

INTERNATIONAL LAW INSTITUTE

The International Law Institute is an independent, non-profit educational institution. Its aim is to raise levels of professional competence in legal, economic and financial fields so that professionals can achieve practical solutions to common problems in ways that best suit

their nations' particular requirements. Over the years, the ILI has expanded its activities from pure research to practical training and education, advice to governments and NGOs, and publishing. It has trained approximately 28,000 officials from 185 countries.

Chairman: Professor Don Wallace

International Law Institute, 1055 Thomas Jefferson St., Suite M-100, N.W., Washington, D.C. 20007, USA. Tel: +1 202 247 6006, fax: +1 202 247 6010, URL: http://www.ili.org

INTERNATIONAL MARITIME COMMITTEE (COMITE MARITIME INTERNATIONAL)

Aims to contribute to the unification of maritime law in all its aspects.

President: Karl-Johan Gombrii
Secretary General: Nigel Frawley

International Maritime Committee (Comite Maritime International), Everdijstraat 43, B-2000 Antwerp, Belgium. Tel: +32 (0)3 227 3526, fax: +32 (0)3 227 3528, e-mail: admini@cmi-imc.org, URL: http://www.comitemaritime.org

INTERNATIONAL PEACE INSTITUTE

Until 2008 the International Peace Institute was known as the International Peace Academy. It was founded by a group of people from both inside and outside of the UN in 1970 who felt a completely independent institution, free from official constraints, would be able to make a unique contribution to multilateral efforts to prevent and settle armed conflicts around the world. Today, the Institute is an independent, international not-for-profit think tank staffed by people of around 20 nationalities.

Honorary Chair: H.E. Ban Ki-moon (page 1383)
President: Terje Rød-Larsen

International Peace Institute, 777 United Nations Plaza, New York, NY 10017-3521, USA. Tel: +1 212 687 4300, e-mail: ipi@ipinst.org, URL: http://www.ipinst.org

INTERNATIONAL SOCIETY FOR THE REFORM OF CRIMINAL LAW

The International Society for the Reform of Criminal Law (ISRCL) was founded in 1988 following a conference in London of legal experts from around the world who met to discuss the reform of criminal law and the criminal justice system.

The organisation's stated purpose is to encourage members to develop their individual interests and, in turn, provide a network to enable others to support their interests. The Society encourages joint research and policy development among individuals and government bodies from different jurisdictions.

President: The Hon. Chief Justice Lance S. G. Finch

International Society for the Reform of Criminal Law, (ISRCL), Suite 1000, 840 Howe Street, Vancouver, V6Z 2M1, British Columbia, Canada. Tel: +1 604 643 1252, fax: +1 604 643 1200, e-mail: secretariat@isrcl.org, URL: http://www.isrcl.org

INTER-PACIFIC BAR ASSOCIATION

An international association of business and commercial lawyers with a focus on the Asia-Pacific region. It has approximately 1,600 members from 67 different national jurisdictions. Its aims include the development of the legal profession within the Asia-Pacific Region.

President: Lalit Bhasin (India)
President-Elect: Young-Moo Shin (Republic of Korea)

Inter-Pacific Bar Association, Roppongi Hills North Tower 7F, 6-2-31 Roppongi, Minato-ku, Tokyo 106-0032 Japan. Tel.: +81 3 5786 6796, fax: +81 3 5786 6778, e-mail: ipba@ipba.org, URL: http://www.ipba.org

KING'S COLLEGE SCHOOL OF LAW

Founded over 175 years ago, the King's College School of Law benefits from its location close to government departments, the Royal Courts of Justice, the Inns of Court and the offices of all major City law firms. The School currently has around 60 full-time academic staff members. The School is particularly well regarded in the areas of commercial, competition, financial and European law.

Research centres based at the College include the Centre of European Law, the Centre of Medical Law and Ethics; and the Centre for Technology, Law, Ethics and Society. The King's Law Journal publishes scholarly articles and comments on legal issues.

Head of School: Professor Timothy Macklem

King's College London School of Law, Strand, London, WC2R 2LS, United Kingdom. Tel: +44 (0)20 7836 5454, URL: http://www.kcl.ac.uk/

OTHER INTERNATIONAL AND NATIONAL ORGANISATIONS

LEIDEN UNIVERSITY - LEIDEN LAW SCHOOL

Leiden Law School is the oldest in the Netherlands and has a permanent teaching staff of around 300. Courses are taught in either Dutch or English and the school enjoys an excellent international reputation. The Leiden Law School also has a centre in The Hague, the Grotius Centre for International Legal Studies.

The Masters curriculum offers several courses including Public International Law and European Law.

Leiden Law School publishes several journals including the Common Market Law Review and the Leiden Journal of International Law.

Dean: Professor Rick Lawson

Leiden Law School, PO Box 9520, 2300 RA Leiden, The Netherlands. URL: http://law.leiden.edu/

LONDON COURT OF INTERNATIONAL ARBITRATION

Dating back to the 1880s, the London Court of International Arbitration (LCIA) is one of the oldest international institutions for commercial dispute resolution. The Court appoints tribunals, sets out the challenges to the arbitrators and controls costs. It comprises 35 members, drawn from leading practitioners in commercial arbitration. The subject matter of contracts in dispute includes all aspects of international commerce, including telecommunications, insurance, oil and gas exploration, construction, shipping, aviation, pharmaceuticals, shareholders agreements, IT, finance and banking. The current rules of the LCIA were promulgated in 1998 and are currently under review.

President: William W. Park, USA

London Court of International Arbitration, 70 Fleet Street, London EC4Y 1EU, UK. Tel: +44 (0)20 7936 7007, fax: +44 (0)20 7936 7008, e-mail: lcia@lcia.org, URL: http://www.lcia.org/

LONDON SCHOOL OF ECONOMICS, FACULTY OF LAW

Founded over a century ago, the LSE law faculty teaches the foundations of legal knowledge, as well as offering optional subjects and teaching students to develop analytical and research skills. It also runs LL.M and Ph.D programmes. The LSE International Humanitarian Law Project promotes the study of international humanitarian law, aiming to engage the interest of governments, organisations and academic institutions concerned with humanitarian issues. The Transnational Law Project promotes research and the teaching of transnational regulation and dispute resolution.

Law Department, London School of Economics, Houghton Street, London, WC2A 2AE, UK. Tel: +44 (0)207 955 7688, fax: +44 (0)207 955 7366, e-mail: lawdepartment@lse.ac.uk, URL: http://www.lse.ac.uk/collections/law/index.htm

MAX PLANCK INSTITUTE FOR COMPARATIVE PUBLIC LAW AND INTERNATIONAL LAW

The Max Planck Society consists of nearly 80 research institutes which operate independently from but in close co-operation with universities across Europe. The Institute for Comparative Public Law and International Law is one of the most important research institutes in the German speaking world in the fields of international law, European law, comparative public law and transnational law. The Institute performs advisory functions for parliament and administrative organs and courts and has provided expert testimony and counsel for the German Federal Constitutional Court, the Parliament and government. It is directly involved in the creation of legal institutions in several countries including Sudan. Its vast library contains over 610,000 volumes. Its regular publications include the Max Planck Yearbook of United Nations Law.

Director: Prof. Dr. Armin von Bogdandy

Max Planck Institute for Comparative Public Law and International Law, Im Neuenheimer Feld 535, D-69120, Heidelberg, Germany. Tel: +49 (6221 482 1, URL: http://www.mpil.de/ww/en/pub/news.cfm

MCGILL UNIVERSITY FACULTY OF LAW

Established in 1848, in Montreal, Quebec, the McGill Faculty of Law is the oldest law school in Canada. It currently enrols around 170 undergraduate students per year. Its graduates obtain both a Bachelor of Laws (LL.B.) and Bachelor of Civil Law (B.C.L.), allowing them to practice in the Canadian, US and UK common law system as well as Quebec's civil law system. The Faculty also offers the degrees of D.C.L. (Doctor of Civil Law) and LL.M. (Master of Laws). McGill Law has a tradition of supporting international human rights; Prof. John Peters Humphrey drafted the UN Declaration of Human Rights in 1948.

Dean: Professor Daniel Jutras

McGill University Faculty of Law, Day, Chancellor, Hall, 3644 Peel Street, Montreal, Quebec H3A 1W9, Canada. Tel.: +1 514 398 6666, URL: http://www.mcgill.ca/law/

NATIONAL LAW SCHOOL OF INDIA UNIVERSITY NLSIU

Founded in 1987, the National Law School of India University (NLSIU) is based in Bangalore. Students are selected on the basis of an all-India entrance exam. There are currently approximately 400 undergraduate students, and around one hundred postgraduate students. The NLSIU law degree takes five years, with courses in the liberal arts included in the first two years. The Law School has exchange programmes with Georgetown University in the USA, the National University of Singapore, Canada's Osgoode Hall Law School and Germany's Hamburg University and University of Munich.

Chancellor: Chief Justice of India
Vice-Chancellor & Professor of Law: Prof. (Dr) R. Venkata Rao

National Law School of India, PO Bag 7201, Nagarbhavi, Bangalore 560 072, India. Tel: +91 80 2321 3160, fax: +91 80 23160534, URL: http://www.nls.ac.in/

NATIONAL UNIVERSITY OF SINGAPORE FACULTY OF LAW

First established in 1956, the National University of Singapore Faculty of Law is one of the two law schools in Singapore.

Students take compulsory modules in the first two years, and then specialise in options such as Asian legal studies, banking and finance, biomedical law, commercial law, comparative law, corporate law, criminal law, intellectual property, international law, jurisprudence, legal process and skills, public law, and transportation law. The law school has an extensive exchange programme with dozens of law schools all over the world, including Columbia University, University of Toronto, UCL, McGill University, National University School of India, University of Sydney, University College Dublin, and Beijing University. From 2011, the International Court of Justice and the World Bank is offering three fellowships.

Dean: Prof. Simon Chesterman

National University of Singapore, Faculty of Law, Eu Tong Sen Building, 469G Bukit Timah Road, Singapore 259776. Tel: +65 6516 1305, URL: http://law.nus.edu.sg

NETHERLANDS INSTITUTE OF HUMAN RIGHTS (SIM)

The Netherlands Institute of Human Rights has several databases housing its document collection. The public may search these databases through the Institute's internet site. Its Case Law databases provide access to the databases containing the case law of international supervisory organs. These contain jurisprudence of the Human Rights Committee ('CCPR'), the Committee Against Torture ('CAT'), the Committee on the Elimination of Racial Discrimination ('CERD') and the Committee on the Elimination of Discrimination against Women ('CEDAW'). There is a database containing information on judgements of the European Court of Human Rights ('ECHR') and concluding observations of the United Nations treaty bodies and case law from the International Criminal Tribunals.

Netherlands Institute of Human Rights, Drift 15, 3512 BR Utrecht, The Netherlands. Tel: +31 30 2538033, fax: +31 30 2537168, email: sim.documentation@uu.nl, URL: http://sim.law.uu.nl/SIM/Dochome.nsf?Open

NEW YORK UNIVERSITY LAW SCHOOL

Founded in 1835, New York University School of Law currently has an enrollment of around 1,700 students. It was one of the first law schools to admit women. At its campus in Greenwich Village, it offers programmes in Business, Clinical, Constitutional, Criminal, Environmental, Innovation, Interdisciplinary, International, Procedure, Public Interest and Tax Law. The Law School's international law program aims to prepare students for the challenges and opportunities of globalisation. The faculty involves students in work on issues such as international commercial law, climate change, transitional justice, World Trade Organization disputes, global antitrust litigation, Security Council powers, and antiterrorism.

Dean: Richard Revesz

New York University School of Law, 40 Washington Square South, NY, NY 10012, USA. Tel: +1 212 998 6060, URL: http://www.law.nyu.edu/index.htm

NORTHWESTERN UNIVERSITY SCHOOL OF LAW

The Northwestern University School of Law (Northwestern Law) was founded in 1859 in Chicago as a private law school. There are approximately 780 students enrolled. The faculty has a particularly strong reputation for academic strength in tax, international law, trial advocacy, alternative dispute resolution, and legal writing. Northwestern was one of the first law schools to offer a Supreme Court Clinic, allowing students the opportunity to work on cases pending before the US Supreme Court.

The law school sponsors six student-run legal journals, amongst which is the Northwestern University Law Review and the Journal of Criminal Law and Criminology.

Dean: Daniel B. Rodriguez

Northwestern University School of Law, 375 East Chicago Avenue, Chicago, Illinois 60611-3069, USA. Tel: +1 312 503 3100, URL: http://www.law.northwestern.edu/

OSGOODE LAW SCHOOL, YORK UNIVERSITY

Established in 1889, Osgoode Law School now has a faculty of around 140 full-time academic staff and there are around 194 undergraduate and post-graduate students enrolled. Its degree in law is accepted for bar admission in every province except Quebec, as well as in Massachusetts and New York. The School runs Canada's largest graduate law programme. It also offers a US JD degree in conjunction with New York University School of Law. Osgoode Hall Law School replaced the Bachelor of Laws designation with a Juris Doctor degree. The School leads in the areas of constitutional law, the Charter and human rights, and international law.

Dean: Lorne Sossin

Osgoode Law School, York University, Ignat Kaneff Building, 4700 Keele Street Toronto, Canada, M3J 1P3. Tel: +1 416 736 5030, URL: http://www.osgoode.yorku.ca/

PEKING UNIVERSITY LAW SCHOOL

Whilst officially inaugurated in 1999, Peking University (PKU) Law School was originally known as the Law Department of Peking University, founded in 1904, and is therefore the oldest law school in China. PKU Law School currently has 40 full-time faculty professors, and 33 associate professors. There are some 700 undergraduate students, and 1,128 postgraduate students. A further 217 students are studying for a Ph.D. There are over 100 foreign students at the Law School. The four core subjects are Legal Theory Studies, Constitution and Administrative Law Studies, Economic Law Studies, and Criminal Law Studies.

PKU Law School has exchange relationships with Japan, Singapore, Canada, the US, the UK, Taiwan and Hong Kong, as well as with international organisations such as the World Trade Organization, and the UN International Criminal Tribunal.

Dean: Zhang Shouwen

Peking University Law School, No.5 Yiheyuan Road Haidian District, Beijing, P.R.China 100871. URL: http://english.pku.edu.cn/

PERMANENT COURT OF ARBITRATION

The Permanent Court of Arbitration (PCA) is an international organisation, which offers a wide range of arbitration services to resolve disputes between States, as well as disputes between private parties and those involving inter-governmental organisations. In certain circumstances private cases may be brought to the PCA for support and assistance.

Established after the adoption of the Convention for the Pacific Settlement of International Disputes (1899), the PCA was one of the most important results of the First International Peace Conference, held in The Hague in 1899. In 1907, the American philanthropist Andrew Carnegie donated US$1.5m for the construction, on land made available by the Netherland's government, of a "temple of peace". Today it is known as the Peace Palace, and also houses the International Court of Justice and the Hague Academy of International Law.

Acting Secretary-General: Brooks W. Daly

International Bureau, Permanent Court of Arbitration, The Peace Palace, Carnegieplein 2, 2517 KJ, The Hague, Netherlands. Tel: +31 (0)70 302 4165, fax: +31 (0)70 302 4167, e-mail: bureau@pca-cpa.org, URL: http://www.pca-cpa.org

PUBLIC INTERNATIONAL LAW & POLICY GROUP

Operating as a non-profit global law firm, the Public International Law & Policy Group (PILPG) provides free legal assistance to developing states and organisations involved in conflicts. PILPG advises on the legal aspects of peace negotiations and constitution-drafting, as well as providing policy formulation advice and training on matters related to conflict resolution. There are four main areas of activity: Peacebuilding, International Justice, Post-Conflict Political Development, and Public International Law. PILPG relies on volunteer assistance from former international lawyers, diplomats, and pro bono assistance from international law firms. In 2005, PILPG was nominated for the Nobel Peace Prize.

Co-founder & President: Dr Paul R. Williams

Public International Law & Policy Group (PILPG), e-mail: info@pilpg.org, URL: http://www.publicinternationallaw.org/

RAOUL WALLENBERG INSTITUTE OF HUMAN RIGHTS AND HUMANITARIAN LAW

RWI is an independent academic institute for research, education, and training regarding all aspects of international human rights law. Its mission is to develop knowledge and understanding of international human rights law and to promote human rights.

Director: Marie Tuma

Raoul Wallenberg Institute (RWI), Stora Gråbrödersg. 17 B, PO Box 1155, SE-221 05 Lund, Sweden. Tel: + 46 46 222 1200, fax: +46 46 222 1222, URL: http://www.rwi.lu.se

SOUTHAMPTON UNIVERSITY SCHOOL OF LAW

One of the leading law schools in the UK, Southampton University School of Law currently has a full-time academic staff of 35. As well as offering the traditional LLB course, Southampton Law School offers an LLB (Hons) European Legal Studies Programme, enabling students to study law in a European country for one year, and an International Legal Studies LLB programme allowing students to study law in an English-speaking jurisdiction outside the EU (currently Canada, Chile, Hong Kong and Singapore) for one academic year. Southampton Law School has specialised in Maritime Law for many years, and has strong connections with the Institute of Maritime Law and London's Baltic Exchange.

Head of School: Professor Nathalie Lee

University of Southampton Law School, University Road, Southampton, SO17 1BJ, UK. Tel +44 023 8059 2420, fax +44 023 8059 3131, URL: http://www.soton.ac.uk/law/

STANFORD LAW SCHOOL

Dating back to 1893, Stanford is one of the top US law schools, offering over 200 courses. Its basic mission is to achieve the highest standards of excellence in legal scholarship. In pursuit of its belief that lawyers should be educated more broadly, the School is committed to interdisciplinary education, working with other schools within the university to develop joint degree programmes in fields such as economics and public policy. Stanford's International Human Rights Clinic (IHRC) explores international human rights, represents clients in humanitarian matters, and helps implement the rule of law in developing countries. The Environmental Law Clinic is involved in efforts to effect changes in law and public policy around global warming. The Immigrants' Rights Clinic (IRC) is committed to protecting the human rights of all non-citizens regardless of immigration status.

Dean: Larry Kramer

Stanford Law School, Crown Quadrangle, 559 Nathan Abbott Way, Stanford, CA 94305-8610, USA. Tel: +1 650 723 2465, fax: +1 650 725 0253, URL: http://www.law.stanford.edu/

SYDNEY LAW SCHOOL

One of Australia's first law schools, established in 1855, Sydney Law School remains one of the most prestigious law schools of Australia. It has over 70 full time academic staff. It is particularly reknown in the areas of international and comparative law as well as taxation, corporate and criminal law. The School also offers specialist courses environmental and health law and introduced a Juris Doctor degree in 2011. Sydney Law School partners Harvard Law School, as well as other Ivy League and Russell Group law schools.

Dean: Professor Gillian Triggs

Sydney Law School, Eastern Avenue, Camperdown Campus, University of Sydney NSW 2006, Australia. Tel: +61 2 9351 2222, URL: http://sydney.edu.au/law/

TRINITY COLLEGE DUBLIN, SCHOOL OF LAW

Situated close to the courts and Irish parliament buildings, the School of Law, Trinity College Dublin is Ireland's oldest Law School. It is committed to the service of society through education, research and public service activities. The School currently has a student population of approximately 510 undergraduates and 170 postgraduates. Faculty members are involved in writing and editing textbooks, casebooks and commentaries on conflict of laws, constitutional law, European Union law, environmental law, human rights law, international law, sports law and trade union law, amongst other subjects.

Students publish the Dublin University Law Journal, and the Trinity College Law Review.

Head of School: Professor Hilary Biehler

Trinity College Dublin School of Law, House 39, New Square, Trinity College Dublin 2, Ireland. Tel: +353 1 896 1000, URL: http://www.tcd.ie/Law/

UK ASSOCIATION OF EUROPEAN LAW

The Association was founded in 1974 to promote the study of the laws and institutions of the EU and to disseminate such knowledge, as well as to understand the relationship between EU laws and those of its national member states. It achieves these objectives through holding meetings, conferences and study groups, promoting and carrying out research, and enabling the publication of relevant materials. Its membership is drawn principally from members of the judiciary in the UK and teachers of law.

UK Association of European Law, Law School, King's College, London, WC2R 2LS. Tel: +44 (0) 20 7848 1768, fax: +44 (0) 20 7848 2443, e-mail: ukael@kcl.ac.uk, URL: http://www.ukael.org/index.html

UNION INTERNATIONALE DES AVOCATS

Membership of the UIA is open to lawyers worldwide. More than 200 bar associations, organisations or federations (representing nearly two million lawyers) as well as several thousand individual members from over 110 countries are included. Its aims include the defence of the legal profession, development of legal knowledge at an international level and the establishment of an international legal order based on justice and defence of human rights.

President, 2012: Mr Driss Chater

Union Internationale des Avocats, 25 rue du Jour, 7001 Paris, France. Tel: +33 (0)1 44 88 55 66, fax: +33 (0)1 44 88 55 77, email: uiacentre@uianet.org, URL: http://www.uianet.org/index.jsp

OTHER INTERNATIONAL AND NATIONAL ORGANISATIONS

UNITED NATIONS INTERREGIONAL CRIME AND JUSTICE RESEARCH INSTITUTE (UNICRI)

Together with the Faculty of Law at the University of Turin, UNICI holds an LL.M in International Crime and Justice. The program focuses on the following topics: International Criminal Law and International Humanitarian Law; International Criminal Jurisdictions and International Criminal Proceedings; Relationships between International Criminal Law and National Legislation; Interstate Co-operation on Criminal Matters; Transnational Organized Crime (Trafficking in Persons, Corruption and Terrorism); Activities and Organizations of the United Nations System.

For further details on UNICRI see its entry under Affiliated Agencies of the United Nations.

UNICRI, Viale Maestri del Lavoro, 10, 10127 - Turin, Italy. Tel: +39 (0)11 653 7111, fax: +39 (0)11 631 3368, e-mail: information@unicri.it, URL: http://www.unicri.it

UNIVERSITAT BONN

The University of Bonn is one of Germany's foremost research universities. Law has been taught at the university since 1819 and there are now several law institutes including an Institute for International and Comparative Law, Institute of German, European and International Family Law, an Institute for International Law and an Institute for German and International Civil Procedure and Conflict Management.

Managing Director: Prof. Dr. Matthias Herdegen

Universität Bonn, Adenauerallee 24-42, 53113 Bonn, Germany. Tel: +49 (0)228 73-3932, fax: +49 (0)228 73-9171, URL: http://jura.uni-bonn.de/index.php?id=883

UNIVERSITAT DES SAARLANDES, EUROPA INSTITUT

The university was founded in 1948 under the aegis of the French government and the University of Nancy. The Europa-Institute was founded in 1951 and is the second eldest institution of its kind in Europe. Today the Institute focuses on European Law and international law. Its specializations include European Economic Law and European Protection of Human Rights. The current directors of the Institute are Prof. Dr. Werner Meng and Prof. em. Dr. iur. Dr. rer. pol. Dr. hc mult. Georg Ress

Universität des Sarlandes, Europa Institut, Sektion Rechtswissenschaft, Postbox 15 11 50, D-66041 Saarbrücken, Germany. URL: http://www.europainstitut.de/

UNIVERSITAT WIEN (UNIVERSITY OF VIENNA)

The University of Vienna (Universität Wien) opened in 1365. Today over 63,000 students are enrolled. The LL.M in International Legal Studies and the Law School are aimed at expanding understanding of fundamental structures and key issues in international law. There are four modules: Fundamental Issues of International Law, International Economic Law, International Organizations and International Dispute Settlement. Classes are taught in English. The faculty includes top scholars and practitioners of international alaw, including arbitrators and experts in international investment, dispute settlement, expert advisors to foreign ministries and international organizations and other legal experts to various UN bodies.

Faculty of Law, Dean: Heinz Mayer

University of Vienna (Universität Wien), International Legal Studies, Department of European, International & Comparative Law, Schottenbastei 10-16, 1-1010 Vienna, Austria. URL: http://www.juridicum.at/index.php?id=182

UNIVERSITÉ DE LAUSANNE (UNIL)

Law has been taught at the University of Lausanne since 1537. Today the law school is known as the Faculty of Law and Criminal Sciences of the University of Lausanne. The LL.M. course offers specialisations in International Economic Law and International and European Business Law. The languages of instruction are French and English. The Faculty of Law and Criminal Sciences has become recognised as Switzerland's most important centre for the teaching of International Economic, International Commercial and European Union law within the Center for Comparative, European and International Law. Partner institutions include the Europa Institute in Saarbrucken and the University Adolfo Ibanez, Chile.

Université de Lausanne (UNIL), BFSH 1, 1015 Lausanne, Switzerland. Tel: +41 21 692 27 90, URL: http://www.unil.ch/llm

UNIVERSITÉ DE LIÈGE, INSTITUTE FOR EUROPEAN LEGAL STUDIES

The Institute IEJE (Institut d'Etudes Juridiques Européenes) is an international research centre dedicated to European law. Many EU law specialists including: F. Dehousse, P. Demaret, R. Joliet, P. Pescatore, S. Van Raepenbusch and M. Wathelet have been associated with the Institute. Several of its former professors and members have been appointed Judges of the European Court of Justice.

Université de Liège, Institute for European Legal Studies, Law Faculty, Blvd. du rectorat 3, bâtiment B 33, Liège B-4000, Belgium.URL: http://www.ieje.net/

UNIVERSITÉ PARIS 1 PANTHÉON-SORBONNE

The Université Paris 1 is one of the largest French universities. It aims to become one of the major centres for research and knowledge in 21st century Europe. It contains the Sorbonne Law School, one of the most prestigious law faculties in the world. There are 15 research institutes within the Law School including the Centre for Study and Research into International Law (CERDIN). The School has links with other universities including Kings College London, the University of Cologne, Columbia University and Cornell University.

Université Paris 1 Panthéon-Sorbonne Sorbonne Law School, Bureau 311 B 12 place du Panthéon, 75005 Paris, France. E-mail: ecole-droit-sorbonne@univ-paris1.f URL: http://www.univ-paris1.fr/

UNIVERSITY COLLEGE DUBLIN SCHOOL OF LAW

Established almost a century ago, University College Dublin's School of Law is the larges law school in Ireland. It offers a range of undergraduate law degree programmes, both as single subject and in combination with other disciplines. The Law School also offers graduate degrees, specialising in European law, commercial law and employment law as well as in arbitration and criminology and criminal justice. There is also a doctoral programme. Through UCD's participation in the ERASMUS/Socrates European Exchange Programme, students can choose to study abroad for part of their course.

Dean: Professor Colin Scott

UCD School of Law, Roebuck Castle, University College Dublin, Belfield, Dublin 4, Ireland URL: http://www.ucd.ie/law/

UNIVERSITY COLLEGE LONDON, FACULTY OF LAWS

Since 1826, the Faculty of Laws at University College London (UCL) has thrived on the grea traditions of legal education. It is now one of the world's leading law schools.

UCL Laws has a student body comprising over 550 undergraduate, 480 taught graduate students and 50 research students. The faculty has some 65 academic staff, many visiting professors, and distinguished judicial and other visiting academic staff. It provides some o the finest, research-led Laws learning in the world.

UCL Laws is particularly well-regarded for its teaching of Commercial and Competition Law Criminal Justice; Family and Social Welfare; EU Law; Environmental Law and Policy; Human Rights Law; Intellectual Property Law; Litigation and Dispute Resolution; Jurisprudence and Legal Theory.

Dean: Dame Hazel Genn DBE, QC

Faculty of Laws, University College London, Bentham House, Endsleigh Gardens, London WC1H 0EG. Tel: +44 (0)20 7679 2000, URL: http://www.ucl.ac.uk/laws/

UNIVERSITY OF ABERDEEN, SCHOOL OF LAW

Established over 500 years ago, the Law faculty of Aberdeen University currently has some 800 undergraduates enrolled. There are over 100 students studying for LLM programmes, and around 60 for the research LLM and the PhD. There are about 40 full-time equivalent members of the academic staff, engaged in both teaching and in research. The School has a long tradition of legal research, and, as well as teaching the traditional courses, it offers courses in dispute resolution and environmental law. Furthermore it offers degrees of Law with French, German, Gaelic and Spanish, which include a year spent in a European law school. There are also LLB degrees with options in Economics, Accounting, or Management Studies.

Acting Head of the Law School: John Paterson

University of Aberdeen, School of Law, Taylor Building, Aberdeen AB24 3UB, UK. Tel: +44 (0)1224 274260, fax: +44 (0)1224 272442, URL: http://www.abdn.ac.uk/law/

UNIVERSITY OF CALIFORNIA, BERKELEY SCHOOL OF LAW

The University of California, Berkeley School of Law, commonly referred to as Berkeley Law and Boalt Hall, is one of the top ten law schools in the USA. It is a public Law School, and currently has 850 enrolled J.D. students, 160 LL.M/J.S.D. students, and 40 MA/Ph.D students. The School runs specialised programmes in Business, Law and Economics, Comparative Legal Studies, Environmental Law, International Legal Studies, Law and Technology, and Social Justice. Berkeley School of Law was the first U.S. law school to offer M.A. and Ph.D. degrees in Jurisprudence and Social Policy.

The faculty runs research progammes to find solutions to wide-ranging challenges, such as the development of business strategies to combat global warming, and how to protect intellectual property within the global economy.

Dean: Christopher Edley, Jr.

University of California, Berkeley School of Law, 2850 Telegraph Avenue, Suite 500, Berkeley, CA 94705-7220, USA. Tel: +1 510 642 1741, URL: http://www.law.berkeley.edu

UNIVERSITY OF CAMBRIDGE, LAW FACULTY

Law has been studied at Cambridge University since the thirteenth century. The Faculty currently has over 70 teaching staff, around 700 undergraduate students, 180 LL.M. students and 100 graduate research students. Five degrees are available in Law, the B.A., LL.M., M.Litt, Ph.D. and LL.D. There is also a MPhil in Criminology, and a Diploma in International Law.

University of Cambridge, Faculty of Law, 10 West Road, Cambridge CB3 9DZ, United Kingdom. Tel: +44 (0)1223 330033, fax: +44 (0)1223 330055, URL: http://www.law.cam.ac.uk/

UNIVERSITY OF CHICAGO LAW SCHOOL

The University of Chicago Law School was founded in 1902 and currently has approximately 590 enrolled students. It is noted for its influence on the economic analysis of law. The School is committed to the teaching of abroad and basic knowledge of law, an understanding of the functioning of the legal system, and the development of analytic abilities. The Law school's research mission is broad, encompassing the range of thought from the empirical to the theoretical; from pure legal topics to interdisciplinary inquiry; and from the state and federal laws of the USA to international and comparative law.

Dean: Michael Schill, Harry N. Wyatt Professor of Law

University of Chicago Law School, 1111 East 60th Street, Chicago, Illinois 60637, USA. Tel: +1 773 702 9494, URL: http://www.law.uchicago.edu/

UNIVERSITY OF DUNDEE, SCHOOL OF LAW

Originally part of the University of St. Andrews, the University of Dundee's School of Law dates back to 1410. Dundee is the only British law school to offer undergraduate degrees in both Scots law and English law and thus allowing them to undertake professional training in any part of the United Kingdom. There are over 60 students in the LLM programme, drawn from around the world. The school has partnerships with the University of Cergy-Pontoise for the teaching of international commercial law and the University of Toulouse for the teaching of comparative and European private international law. The School runs a distance learning LLM in International Dispute Resolution, allowing legal professionals to specialise in one of the fastest growing areas of legal practice. It also offers a distance learning programme in healthcare law and ethics which is designed for healthcare professionals.

Dean of School: Professor Alan C. Page

University of Dundee, School of Law, Nethergate, Dundee, DD1 4HN, Scotland, UK. Tel: +44 (0)1382 384461, URL: http://www.dundee.ac.uk/law

UNIVERSITY OF FRIBOURG

The law school at the University of Fribourg is home to the Federalism Institute, the European Law Institute, the International Institute of Construction Law and the Economic Law Institute. Since 2008 the law school has hosted a new Centre for Advanced Studies in Transnational, International and European Business Law which offers the Master of Laws in Cross-Cultural Business Practice Program and a interdisciplinary Doctoral Program in European Studies. The Faculty of Law has 1,700 students and offers instruction in French and German as well as English.

University of Fribourg, Center of Advanced Studies, School of Law, Av. de Beauregard 11, Office # 5.608, 1700 Fribourg, Switzerland. URL: http://www.unifr.ch/mlcbp

UNIVERSITY OF LEICESTER SCHOOL OF LAW

The University of Leicester School of Law is one of the top law schools in the UK. Around 250 students are enrolled each year on the LLB course, which provides a grounding in English law, teaches the skills of legal research and practice and allows for specialisation. The School is one of the most international in the UK, which is reflected in the research activities of its staff. European Law is taught to all students, and there are options to study law at a European or International law school for one year. The post-graduate programme also includes options in international and European specialisations.

Head of Law School: Prof. Mark Bell

University of Leicester School of Law, University Road, Leicester, LE1 7RH, UK. Tel: +44 (0)116 252 2363, e-mail: law@leicester.ac.uk, URL: http://www.le.ac.uk/la/

UNIVERSITY OF MELBOURNE, MELBOURNE LAW SCHOOL

Established in 1857, the School of Law at the University of Melbourne is one of Australia's oldest and most highly regarded law schools. It currently has around 3,500 students, and in recent years has placed increasing emphasis on its designation as a graduate law school; from 2008 the Melbourne JD is the only degree offered by the School that leads to admission to legal practice. The JD is taught at the masters level and designed for students with an undergraduate degree in a discipline other than law or a degree in law from a different legal system. The Faculty of Law is home to some key research institutes and centres, including the Asian Law Centre, the Centre for Resources Energy and Environmental Law and the Institute for International Law and the Humanities.

Dean: Prof. Carolyn Evans

Melbourne Law School, 185 Pelham Street, Carlton, University of Melbourne, Victoria 3010 Australia. Tel: +61 3 8344 4475, URL: http://www.law.unimelb.edu.au

UNIVERSITY OF MICHIGAN LAW SCHOOL

Founded as a public law school in 1859, the University of Michigan Law School (Michigan Law) currently has an enrollment of around 1,200 students, and offers J.D., L.L.M and S.J.D. qualifications. The Law School has over 70 full-time faculty members.

Michigan Law offers a broad range of scholarship, and encourages an interdisciplinary approach. There are clinical programmes following completion of the first year, and the School has partnerships with many universities and institutes in Europe and the Far East which encourage exchange programmes. Michigan Law School students publish six well-regarded law journals including the Michigan Law Review.

Dean: Evan Caminker

University of Michigan Law School, 625 South State Street, Ann Arbor, Michigan 48109-1215, USA. Tel: +1734 764 1358, URL: http://www.law.umich.edu/

UNIVERSITY OF NOTTINGHAM SCHOOL OF LAW

Consistently ranking among the top Law Schools in the UK, Nottingham University Law School currently has around 40 full-time academic staff and approximately 900 enrolled students. The undergraduate programme establishes a knowledge and understanding of legal principles and of the operation of law in society, whilst the postgraduate courses offer a diverse range of more specialised learning. There are opportunities for research in most areas of the law. Members of the Faculty serve on over 40 different journals and book series, some in groundbreaking areas of law. The School is home to the Human Rights Law Review, as well as to the Public Procurement Research Group and the Human Rights Law Centre.

Head of School: Stephen Bailey

University of Nottingham School of Law, Law and Social Sciences Building, University Park, Nottingham NG7 2RD, UK. Tel: +44 (0) 115 951 5700, fax: +44 (0) 115 951 5696, URL: http://www.nottingham.ac.uk/law/index.aspx

UNIVERSITY OF OSLO, DEPARTMENT OF PUBLIC AND INTERNATIONAL LAW

The Department of Public and International Law at the University of Oslo offers courses covering Environmental Protection, Refugees, International Crimes, Women's law, Globalization, Democracy, Human Rights and Use of Force as well as research opportunities in the more modern areas of Environmental Law and eCommerce. The faculty is also home to the Department of Criminology and Sociology of Law and a Centre for Human Rights.

University of Oslo, Department of Public and International Law, Postbox 6706, St. Olavs plass, N-0130 Oslo, Norway. Tel: +47 228 59500, e-mail: postmottak@jus.uio.no, URL: http://www.jus.uio.no/english

UNIVERSITY OF OTTAWA, FACULTY OF LAW

Founded in 1953, the University of Ottawa has the largest law faculty in Canada with a current enrollment of around 1,380 students. It is located close to the Supreme Court of Canada, and federal government agencies. The faculty is renowned for its international law, law and technology, social justice and environmental law components.

Studies are divided into civil law and common law sections; the civil law section is instructed entirely in French, the common law section in both English and French. A new Programme de droit canadien now allows students to earn both a common law and civil law degree (LL.B. and LL.L.) in three years. The faculty also offers a joint LL.B.- M.B.A. degree; a unique LL.B.-J.D. program in partnership with two American law schools; and a joint LL.B.-M.A. program in International Relations.

Dean (Common Law): Bruce Feldthusen

University of Ottawa, Faculty of Law, Fauteux Hall, 57 Louis Pasteur St., Ottawa, Ontario K1N 6N5, Canada. Tel: +1 613 562 5794, URL: http://www.commonlaw.uottawa.ca/ or http://www.droitcivil.uottawa.ca/

UNIVERSITY OF OXFORD, FACULTY OF LAW

The study of law at Oxford dates back some 800 years. Today Oxford University's Law faculty is the largest in the UK, joining the 30 individual college law schools. The student-to-faculty ratio is approximately 7:1. Approximately half the Faculty has studied abroad; around 15 per cent of undergraduate students and 85 percent of post-graduate students are from overseas. Oxford has the largest doctoral progamme in Law in the English-speaking world.

Dean of the Faculty: Timothy Endicott

Faculty of Law, University of Oxford, St Cross Building, St Cross Road, Oxford OX1 3UL, UK. Tel: T: +44 (0)1865 271491, fax: +44 (0)1865 271493, e-mail: lawfac@law.ox.ac.uk, URL: http://www.law.ox.ac.uk/

UNIVERSITY OF TORONTO FACULTY OF LAW

Established in 1887, the University of Toronto Faculty of Law currently has 60 full-time faculty members, and 600 undergraduate and graduate students. It is particularly well known for its teaching of corporate law, international law, law and economics, and legal theory. The Faculty offers Canada's most extensive program in pro bono work and international human rights law. Toronto Faculty of Law was the first law school in Canada to offer the Juris Doctor (J.D.) rather than the Bachelor of Laws (LL.B).

Dean: Prof. Mayo Moran

University of Toronto Faculty of Law, 84 Queen's Park, Toronto, ON, M5S 2C5, Canada. Tel: +1 416 978 0210, URL: http://www.law.utoronto.ca/

OTHER INTERNATIONAL AND NATIONAL ORGANISATIONS

UNIVERSITY OF TURIN, FACULTY OF LAW (UNITO)

Law has been studied at the University of Turin since its founding in 1404. It is one of the leading law schools in Euope especially in the fields of comparative law and private law. The faculty offers an LL.M in international criminal law in conjunction with the United Nations Interregional Crime and Justice Research Institute (UNICRI). The program is designed to provide a deeper knowledge of international criminal law.

UNITO, Via Verdi 8, 10124 Turin, Italy. Tel: +39 (0)11 670 6111, URL: http://www.giurisprudenza.unito.it/do/home.pl

UTRECHT UNIVERSITY SCHOOL OF LAW

Utrecht University School of Law is one of the oldest law schools in the Netherlands. The school has a staff of approximately 280 professors and associate professors teaching 80 Ph.D and 740 LL.M students and 2,350 bachelor's students and 150 international exchange bachelor's students. The school is also home to the Netherlands Institute of Human Rights, Willem Pompe Institute of Criminal Law and Criminology, Centre for Intellectual Property Law, and the Centre for Environmental Law and Policy.

The language of instruction is English.

Utrecht University School of Law, Janskerkhof 3, Utrecht 3512 BK, The Netherlands. URL: http://www.law.uu.nl/

VRIJE UNIVERSITEIT BRUSSEL (VUB)
Institute of European Studies

The LL.M programme at the University was created in 1971 and is still known as the Program on International Legal Cooperation (PILC). The focus has gradually moved from international and comparative law to international and European Law. The degree has now changed to the LL.M in International and European Law. The faculty includes full time academics, lawyers and EU officials. In 2001, PILC was incorporated into the Institute for European Studies (IES) at the VUB. The Master Program still retains its links to the Law Faculty.

Vrije Universiteit Brussel (VUB), Institute for European Studies, Pleinlaan 2, 1050 Brussels, URL: http://www.ies.be/pilc/

WORLD JURIST ASSOCIATION

A free and open forum for legal professionals to support the institutions that govern and enforce the administration of international law.

President: Alexander Belohlavek (Czech Republic)

World Jurist Association, 7910 Woodruff Avenue, Suite # 1440, Bethesda MD 20814, USA. E-mail: wja@worldjurist.org, URL: http://www.worldjurist.org

YALE LAW SCHOOL

With approximately 690 students from 48 states and 32 countries, and a student/faculty ratio of 7.7 to one, Yale Law School is relatively small. The faculty runs over 180 courses each year, and encourages independent research. Yale Law School has a tradition of emphasising public as well as private law, and around 60 per cent of students participate in public interest activities, through clinics or voluntary student groups.

The Law School has an international tradition and many legal issues are approached from a global perspective. Courses are run in international and foreign law, and students who hold foreign law degrees come to Yale Law School for a graduate law education.

Dean: Robert Post

Yale Law School, P.O. Box 208215, New Haven, CT 06520-8215, USA. Tel: +1 203 432 4995, URL: http://www.law.yale.edu/

Religion

ALLIANCE ISRAÉLITE UNIVERSELLE (AIU)

Aims to promote a type of Judaism that is simultaneously faithful to tradition while being tolerant and open to the modern world. Furthermore, the Alliance strives to promote French language and culture abroad. The largest Judaica library in Europe: more than 130,000 volumes; over a million archive documents.

Director: Jo Toledano

Alliance Israélite Universelle (AIU), 45 rue de la Bruyère, 75428 Paris Cedex 09, France. Tel: +33 (0)1 53 32 88 55, fax: +33 (0)1 48 74 51 33, e-mail: info@aiu.org, URL: http://www.aiu.org

ANGLICAN COMMUNION

The Anglican Communion comprises all the Anglican or Episcopalian Churches and dioceses throughout the world. All are in full communion with the see of Canterbury.

President: The Archbishop of Canterbury (page 1537)

Anglican Communion Office, St. Andrew's House, 16 Tavistock Crescent, London W11 1AP, UK. Tel: +44 (0)20 7313 3900, fax: +44 (0)20 7313 3999, e-mail: aco@anglicancommunion.org, URL: http://www.anglicancommunion.org

BAPTIST WORLD ALLIANCE

The Baprist World Alliance (BWA) is a fellowship of 214 Baptist conventions and unions comprising a membership of 37 million baptized believers and a community of 105 million. The BWA began in London, England in 1905 at the first Baptist World Congress.

General Secretary: Neville Callum

Baptist World Alliance, 405 North Washington Street, Falls Church, Virginia 22046 USA. Phone: +1 703 790 8980, fax: +1 703 893 5160, e-mail: bwa@bwanet.org, URL: http://www.bwanet.org

CARIBBEAN CONFERENCE OF CHURCHES

The recognized Regional Ecumenical Organization (REO) of the Caribbean and one of the major development agencies at work in the Caribbean today. It was founded in 1973 and is currently comprised of 33 member churches in 34 territories across the Dutch, English, French and Spanish speaking territories of the region.

General Secretary: Gerard Grenado

Caribbean Conference of Churches, P.O. Box 876, Port of Spain, Trinidad and Tobago. Tel.: +1 868 662 3064, fax.: +1 868 662 1303, e-mail: trinidad-headoffice@ccc-caribe.org URL: http://www.ccc-caribe.org

CHRISTIAN CONFERENCE OF ASIA

A regional ecumenical organisation representing 17 National Councils and over 100 churches and denominations in 21 countries.

General Secretary: Dr. Henriette Hutabarat Lebang

Christian Conference of Asia, c/o Payap University, Muang, Chiang Mai 50000 Thailand. Tel: +66 53 243906/7, fax: +66 53 247303, e-mail: cca@cca.org.hk, URL http://www.cca.org.hk

CONFERENCE OF EUROPEAN CHURCHES (CEC)

A fellowship of 120 Orthodox, Protestant, Anglican and Old Catholic Churches along with 40 associated organisations from all countries on the European continent. CEC was founded in 1959 and has offices in Geneva, Brussels and Strasbourg.

Interim General Secretary: Revd. Prof. Dr. Viorel Ionita

Conference of European Churches (CEC), P.O. Box 2100, 150 route de Ferney, CH-1211 Geneva 2, Switzerland. Tel: +41 22 791 6228, fax: +41 22 791 6227, e-mail: cec@cec-kek.org, URL: http://www.ceceurope.org

EUROPEAN BAPTIST FEDERATION

The EBF was founded in 1949 to unite European Baptists as Europe emerged from the devastation of World War Two. During the Cold War the EBF maintained contact with believers behind the Iron Curtain who were suffering for their faith. It aims to strengthen and draw together Baptists in Europe and the Middle East on the basis of their Christian beliefs.

General Secretary: Anthony Peck

European Baptist Federation, Nad Habrovkou 3, Jeneralka, CZ-164 00 Praha 6, Czech Republic. Tel: +420 296 392250, fax: +420 296 392254, e-mail: office@ebf.org, URL http://www.ebf.org

FEDERATION OF JEWISH COMMUNITIES

Aims to restore Jewish life, culture and religion throughout the lands of the former Soviet Union by providing professional assistance, educational support and funding to member communities.

Executive Director: Rabbi Avraham Berkowitz

Federation of Jewish Communities, 5A 2nd Vysheslavtzev Pereulok, Moscow 127055 Russia. Tel: +7 495 737 8275, fax: +7 495 783 8471, e-mail: info@fjc.ru, URL http://www.fjc.ru

FRIENDS (QUAKERS) WORLD COMMITTEE FOR CONSULTATION

A non-governmental organisation with consultative status at the United Nations. It aims to encourage and strengthen the spiritual life within the Society of Friends and to promote understanding between Friends everywhere and members of other branches of the Christian Church and also other religious faiths.

General Secretary: Nancy Irving

Friends (Quakers) World Committee for Consultation, Friends' House, 173 Euston Road, London NW1 2AX, UK. Tel: +44 (0)20 7663 1199, URL: http://www.fwccworld.org

INTERNATIONAL ASSOCIATION FOR RELIGIOUS FREEDOM

Aims to work for freedom of religion and belief at a global level by encouraging interfaith dialogue and tolerance. There are over 90 affiliated member groups in approximately 25 countries, from a wide range of faith traditions including among others Buddhism, Christianity, Hinduism, Islam, Shintoism and Sikhism.

President: Most. Rev. Mitsuo Miyake (Japan)

International Association for Religious Freedom, Secretariat, c/o Konko Church of Izuo, 3-8-21 Sangenya-Nishi, Taisho-ku, Osaka 551-0001, Japan. Tel: +91 (0) 675 035 02, e-mail: hq@iarf.net, URL: http://www.iarf.net

INTERNATIONAL COUNCIL OF CHRISTIANS AND JEWS

Promotes understanding and cooperation between Christians and Jews based on respect for each other's identity and integrity; addresses issues of human rights and human dignity deeply enshrined in the traditions of Judaism and Christianity and counters all forms of prejudice, intolerance, discrimination, racism and the misuse of religion for national and political ends.

President: Dr. Deborah Weissman

International Council of Christians and Jews, Martin Buber House, P.O. Box 11 29, D - 64629 Heppenheim, Germany. Tel: +49 62 526 896810, fax: +49 62 526 8331, e-mail: info@iccj.de, URL: http://www.iccj.org

INTERNATIONAL FELLOWSHIP OF RECONCILIATION

Has a vision of a world where conflicts are resolved through nonviolent means, where systems that foster fear and hatred are dismantled, and where justice is sought as a basis for peace. While coming from diverse religious backgrounds, members share a common belief in the transforming power of nonviolence and reconciliation.

International Fellowship of Reconciliation (IFOR), Spoorstraat 38, Alkmaar, 1815 BK, The Netherlands. Tel + 31 72 512 3014, fax: + 31 72 515 1102, e-mail: coordinator@ifor.org, URL: http://www.ifor.org

INTERNATIONAL HUMANIST AND ETHICAL UNION

The world union of Humanist, rationalist, secular, ethical culture, atheist and freethought organizations. Aims to represent and support the global Humanist movement and achieve a Humanist world in which human rights are respected and all can live a life of dignity.

President: Sonja Eggerickx

International Humanist and Ethical Union, 1 Gower Street, London WC1E 6HD, UK. Tel: + 44 (0)870 288 7631, fax +44 (0)870 288 7631, e-mail: office-iheu@iheu.org, URL: http://www.iheu.org

LUTHERAN WORLD FEDERATION

A global communion of Christian churches in the Lutheran tradition. Founded in 1947 in Lund, Sweden, the LWF now has 145 member churches in 79 countries all over the world representing over 70 million Christians.

General Secretary: Rev. Martin Junge

Lutheran World Federation, 150 route de Ferney, P.O. Box 2100, CH-1211 Geneva 2, Switzerland. Tel: +41 (0)22 791 6111, fax: +41 (0)22 791 6630, e-mail: info@lutheranworld.org, URL: http://www.lutheranworld.org

OPUS DEI

Aims to help people turn their work and daily activities into occasions for growing closer to God, for serving others, and for improving society. Opus Dei complements the work of local churches by offering lessons, talks, retreats and Catholic pastoral care that help people develop their personal spiritual life and apostolate.

Prelate: Bishop Javier Echevarría

Opus Dei, Viale Bruno Buozzi 73, 00197 Rome, Italy. Tel: +39 06 808961, email: newyork@opusdei.org, URL: http://www.opusdei.org

ROMAN CATHOLIC CHURCH

The supreme government of the Church is vested in the Pope, with the advice and assistance of the College of Cardinals and the Synod of Bishops.

The Visible Head of the Catholic Church on Earth: His Holiness Pope Benedict XVI (page 1386)
The Apostolic Nuncio (Great Britain): Archbishop Faustino Sainz Muñoz

The Apostolic Nunciature, 54 Parkside, London SW19 5NE UK. Tel: +44 (0)20 8944 7189, fax: (0)20 8947 2494, URL: http://www.vatican.va/
The Vatican, Piazza Pio XII, 4-00120 Vatican City. Tel: +39 (0)6 6982, URL: http://www.vatican.va

SALVATION ARMY

The primary function has always been to act as a mission to the unconverted. The Salvation Army now operates in 124 countries, preaching the Christian gospel in more than 175 languages. It is believed also to be the biggest voluntary social work agency in the world.

Worldwide Head: General Linda Bond
Territorial Commander (UK): Commissioner John Matear

Salvation Army (UK Headquarters), 101 Newington Causeway, London SE1 6BN, UK. Tel: +44 (0)20 7367 4700, fax: +44 (0)20 7367 4728, URL: http://www.salvationarmy.org.uk

UNITED BIBLE SOCIETIES

Aims to achieve the widest possible effective distribution of the Bible in a language which can be easily understood and is faithful to the original texts, without sectarian doctrinal note or comment and at a price which people can afford.

United Bible Societies, URL: http://www.biblesociety.org

WORLD COMMUNION OF REFORMED CHURCHES

A fellowship of 80 million Reformed Christians in 230 churches in 108 countries. Its member churches are Congregational, Presbyterian, Reformed and United churches with roots in the 16th-century Reformation led by John Calvin, John Knox and others.

General Secretary: Rev. Dr. Setri Nyomi

World Communion of Reformed Churches, 150 route de Ferney, PO Box 2100, 1211 Geneva 2, Switzerland. Tel: +41 (0)22 791 6240, fax: +41 (0)22 791 6505, e-mail: wcrc@wcrc.ch, URL: http://www.wcrc.ch

WORLD CONFERENCE OF RELIGIONS FOR PEACE

A international coalition of representatives from the world's religions dedicated to promoting peace. Brings together hundreds of key religious leaders every five years to discuss the great issues of our time, meeting most recently in 2011.

Secretary General: Dr.William F. Vendley

World Conference of Religions for Peace, 777 United Nations Plaza, New York NY 10017, USA. Tel: +1 212 687 2163, fax: +1 212 983 0566, e-mail: info@wcrp.org, URL: http://www.wcrp.org

WORLD CONGRESS OF FAITHS

Arranges a variety of conferences, meetings, retreats, visits and group travel. These provide occasions to learn what others believe, what they think about life today and how they pray, meditate and worship with the aim of encouraging good community relations, moral and spiritual renewal and world peace.

President: The Reverend Marcus Braybrooke

World Congress of Faiths, London Inter Faith Centre, 125 Salusbury Rd, London NW6 6RG, UK. Tel: +44 (0)20 8959 3129, fax: +44 (0)20 7604 3052, e-mail: enquiries@worldfaiths.org, URL: http://www.worldfaiths.org

WORLD COUNCIL OF CHURCHES

The Council comprises 349 members churches in over 110 countries and represents about 560 million Christians. Its purpose is to call one another to visible unity in one faith and in one eucharistic fellowship.

General Secretary: Rev. Dr. Olva Tykse Tveit (Norway)

World Council of Churches, 150 route de Ferney, P.O. Box 2100, 1211 Geneva 2, Switzerland. Tel: +41 (0)22 791 6111, fax: +41 (0)22 791 0361, URL: http://www.oikoumene.org/

WORLD EVANGELICAL ALLIANCE

Seeks to strengthen local churches through national alliances, supporting and coordinating grassroots leadership. Seeks practical ways of showing the unity of the body of Christ and joins together to give a worldwide identity, voice and platform to Christians worldwide.

International Director: Dr. Geoff Tunnicliffe

World Evangelical Alliance, 74 Trinity Place, Suite 1400, New York, NY 10006-2122, USA. Tel: +1 212 233 3046, fax: +1 646 957 9218, e-mail: info@worldevangelical.org, URL: http://www.worldevangelical.org

WORLD FELLOWSHIP OF BUDDHISTS

Aims to promote among the members strict observance and practice of the teachings of the Buddha; to secure unity, solidarity, and brotherhood amongst Buddhists; and to propagate the sublime doctrine of the Buddha.

President: Mr. Phan Wannamethee

OTHER INTERNATIONAL AND NATIONAL ORGANISATIONS

World Fellowship of Buddhists, 616 Benjasiri Park, Soi Medhinivet, Sukhumvit 24, Bankok 10110, Thailand. Tel. +66 (0)2 661 1284, fax.+66 (0)2 661 0555, URL: http://www.wfb-hq.org

WORLD METHODIST COUNCIL

An association of the Churches in the Methodist/Wesleyan tradition throughout the world that promotes unity and seeks to deepen fellowship, foster Methodist participation in the ecumenical movement and advance unity of theological and moral standards.

General Secretary: Dr. George H. Freeman

World Methodist Council, P.O. Box 518, 545 North Lakeshore Road, Lake Junaluska, North Carolina 28745, USA. Tel: +1 828 456 9432, fax: +1 828 456 9433, e-mail: georgefreeman@charter.net, URL: http://www.worldmethodistcouncil.org

WORLD UNION FOR PROGRESSIVE JUDAISM

Strengthens Jewish life in Israel and worldwide by establishing and supporting modern, pluralistic congregations and institutions, developing Jewish communal and youth leadership and advancing social justice.

Chairman: Michael Grabiner

World Union for Progressive Judaism, 13 King David Street, Jerusalem 94101, Israel. Tel: +972 2 620 3447, fax: +972 2 620 3525, e-mail: wupjis@wupj.org.il, URL: http://www.wupj.org

WORLD UNION OF CATHOLIC WOMEN'S ORGANIZATIONS

Aims to promote the presence, participation and co-responsibility of Catholic women in society and Church, in order to enable them to fulfil their mission of evangelisation and to work for human development.

Secretary General: Gillian Badcock

World Union of Catholic Women's Organizations, 37 rue Notre-Dames-des-Champ, 75006 Paris, France. Tel: +33 (0)1 45 44 27 65, fax: +33 (0)1 42 84 04 80, e-mail: wucwoparis@wanadoo.fr, URL: http://www.wucwo.org

Science

CERN - EUROPEAN ORGANIZATION FOR NUCLEAR RESEARCH (ORGANISATION EUROPÉENNE POUR LA RECHERCHE NUCLÉAIRE)

The world's largest particle physics centre where scientists unite to study the building blocks of matter and the forces that hold them together. CERN exists primarily to provide them with the necessary tools i.e. accelerators, which accelerate particles to almost the speed of light and detectors to make the particles visible.

Director General: Dr Rolf-Dieter Heuer

CERN - European Organization for Nuclear Research, CH-1211 Genève 23, Switzerland. Tel: +41 (0)22 767 6111, fax: +41 (0)22 767 6555, e-mail: press.office@cern.ch, URL: http://www.cern.ch

EUROPEAN ASSOCIATION OF GEOSCIENTISTS AND ENGINEERS

A European based organisation with a worldwide membership providing a global network of commercial and academic professionals to all members. The association is multi-disciplinary and international in form and pursuits.

President: John Underhill

European Association of Geoscientists & Engineers, PO Box 59, 3990 DB Houten, The Netherlands. Tel: +31 (0)30 635 4055, fax: +31 (0)30 634 3524, e-mail: eage@eage.org, URL: http://www.eage.org

EUROPEAN ATOMIC FORUM (FORATOM)

Promotes the use of nuclear energy in Europe and acts as the voice of the industry in energy policy discussions involving the EU institutions. Provides a bridge between the industry and the institutions (Members of the European Parliament and key policy-makers in the European Commission). As of October 2011, there were 102 members.

President: Dr Ralf Gudner

European Atomic Forum (FORATOM), Rue Belliard 65, 1040 Brussels, Belgium. Tel.: +32 (0)2 502 4595, fax: +32 (0)2 502 3902, e-mail: foratom@foratom.org, URL: http://www.foratom.org

EUROPEAN MEDITERRANEAN SEISMOLOGICAL CENTRE (EMSC)

Aims to establish and operate a system for rapid determination of the European an Mediterranean earthquake epicentres (location of major earthquakes within a delay c approximately one hour). The EMSC, acting as the central authority, is responsible fo transmitting these results immediately to the appropriate international authorities and t the members in order to meet the needs of protection of society, scientific progress an general information.

Secretary General: Rémy Bossu

European Mediterranean Seismological Centre (EMSC), c/o LDG, BP12, 9168 Bruyères-le-Châtel, France. Tel: +33 (0)1 69 26 78 14, fax: +33 (0)1 69 26 70 00, e-mai csem@csem-csem.org, URL: http://www.emsc-csem.org

EUROPEAN MOLECULAR BIOLOGY ORGANIZATION (EMBO)

Promotes excellence in molecular life sciences through targeted programmes and activities fosters talented scientists at all stages of the scientific career path through courses,workshops conferences and fellowships and promotes international scientific co-operation.

Director: Professor Maria Leptin

European Molecular Biology Organization (EMBO), Postfach 1022.40, D-6901 Heidelberg, Germany. Tel: +49 (0)6 2218 8910, fax: +49 (0)6 2218 891 200, e-mai embo@embo.org, URL: http:// www.embo.org

FEDERATION OF EUROPEAN BIOCHEMICAL SOCIETIES

FEBS seeks to promote, encourage and support biochemistry, molecular cell biology an molecular biophysics throughout Europe in a variety of different ways. It has nearly 40,000 members from 43 countries.

Federation of European Biochemical Societies, National Medical Center, Diosze, u. 64, 1113 Budapest, Hungary. Tel. +36 1 372 4316, fax. +36 1 372 4353, e-mail secretariat@febs.org, URL: http://www.febs.org

HIGH ALTITUDE RESEARCH STATIONS JUNGFRAUJOCH AND GORNERGRAT

Dedicated to providing the infrastructure and support for scientific research of internationa significance that must be carried out at an altitude of 3,000-3,500 meters above sea leve or for which a high alpine climate and environment are necessary. The Research Station an Sphinx Laboratory at Jungfraujoch, together with the two astronomical observatories Gornergrat South and Gornergrat North, are run for this purpose.

President: Professor Dr. Erwin O. Fluckiger

High Altitude Research Stations Jungfraujoch and Gornergrat Internationa Foundation, Sidlerstrasse 5, CH-3012 Bern, Switzerland. Tel: +41 (0)31 631 4052, fax +41 (0)31 631 4405, e-mail: louise.wilson@space.unibe.ch, URL: http://www.ifjungo.ch

INSTITUTE OF GENERAL SEMANTICS

A not-for-profit corporation established in 1938 by Alfred Korzybski, located in Fort Worth Texas with members and subscribers in over 30 countries. Conducts educational seminars workshops and programmes around the country.

President: Martin H. Levinson

Institute of General Semantics, 72-11 Austin Street 233, Forest Hills, NY 11375, USA Tel: +1 212 729 7973, URL: http://www.generalsemantics.org

INTERNATIONAL ASSOCIATION FOR EARTHQUAKE ENGINEERING (IAEE)

Aims to promote international cooperation among scientists, engineers and other professional in the broad field of earthquake engineering through interchange of knowledge, ideas, result of research and practical experience.

President: Dr Polat Gulkan

International Association for Earthquake Engineering (IAEE), Ken chiku-kaika Bldg., 3rd Floor, Minatoku Shiba 5-Chome 26-20, Tokyo 108-0014, Japan. E-mai secretary@iaee.or.jp, URL: http://www.iaee.or.jp

INTERNATIONAL ASSOCIATION FOR MATHEMATICAL GEOLOGY

The mission of the IAMG is to promote, worldwide, the advancement of mathematics, statistic and informatics in the geosciences.

President: Vera Pawlowsky-Glahn (Spain)
Secretary General: Dan Tetzlaff (USA)

International Association for Mathematical Geology, 5868 Westheimer Rd, 537, Houston TX 77057, Canada. Tel: +1 832 380 8833, URL: http://www.iamg.org

INTERNATIONAL ASSOCIATION FOR PLANT TAXONOMY

IAPT is dedicated to organismal biodiversity: the extent, recognition, organisation, evolution, and naming of plants and fungi, both living and fossil. It carries out projects of interest and concern to systematic biologists, especially those which require or profit from international cooperation.

Managing Secretary: Eva Senkova

International Association for Plant Taxonomy, Institute of Botany, Slovak Academy of Sciences, Dubravska cesta 9, SK-845-23 Bratislava, Slovakia. Tel.: +421 2 5942 6150 , fax: +421 2 5942 6151, URL: http://www.iapt-taxon.org

INTERNATIONAL ASSOCIATION FOR THE PHYSICAL SCIENCES OF THE OCEANS

IAPSO has the prime goal of promoting the study of scientific problems relating to the oceans and the interactions taking places at the sea floor, coastal, and atmospheric boundaries insofar as such research is conducted by the use of mathematics, physics, and chemistry.

Secretary General: Professor Johan Rodhe

International Association for the Physical Sciences of the Oceans, Dept. of Earth Science, U?niv. of Gothenburg, Box 460, Gothenburg, SE 40530, Sweden. Tel: +46 317 862876, URL: http://iapso.iugg.org/

INTERNATIONAL ASSOCIATION OF METEOROLOGY AND ATMOSPHERIC SCIENCES

Provides the scientific community with platforms to present, discuss and promote the newest achievements in meteorology, atmospheric science and related fields. It also facilitates and coordinates research which requires international cooperation.

President: Athéna Coustenis (France) (2011-15)
Secretary General: Hans Volkert (Germany) (2007-15)

International Association of Meteorology and Atmospheric Sciences, General Secretariat, Deutsches Zentrum fuer Luft und Raumfahrt e.V., Institut fuer Physik der Atmosphaere, Muencher Strasse 20, D-82234 Oberpfaffenhofen, Germany. Email: Hans.Volkert@DLR.de, URL: http://www.iamas.org

INTERNATIONAL ASSOCIATION OF SEDIMENTOLOGISTS (IAS)

Founded in 1952 with the goal to promote the study of sedimentology and the interchange of research, particularly where international cooperation is desirable.

President: Poppe De Boer (Netherlands)
General Secretary: Vincenzo Pascucci (Italy)

International Association of Sedimentologists (IAS), Department of Geology and Soil Science, Ghent University, Krijgslaan 281/S8, 900 Ghent, Belgium, URL: http://www.iasnet.org

INTERNATIONAL ASSOCIATION OF THEORETICAL AND APPLIED LIMNOLOGY

Promotes and communicates new and emerging knowledge among limnologists to advance the understanding of inland aquatic ecosystems and their management.

President: Prof. Dr. Brian Moss (UK)

International Association of Theoretical and Applied Limnology, URL: http://www.limnology.org

INTERNATIONAL ASTRONAUTICAL FEDERATION (IAF)

Encourages the advancement of knowledge about space and the development and application of space assets for the benefit of humanity. Disseminates information and provides a significant worldwide network of experts in the development and utilisation of space.

President: Berndt Feuerbacher
Executive Director: Philippe Willekens

International Astronautical Federation (IAF), 94bis Avenue de Suffren, 75015 Paris, France. Tel : +33 (0)1 45 67 42 60, fax : +33 (0)1 42 73 21 20, e-mail: info@iafastro.org, URL: http://www.iafastro.org

INTERNATIONAL ASTRONOMICAL UNION (IAU)

Promotes and safeguards the science of astronomy in all its aspects through international cooperation. The key activity of the IAU is the organization of scientific meetings.

General Secretary: Dr. Ian F. Corbett

International Astronomical Union (IAU), 98bis Bd Arago, 75014 Paris, France. Tel: +33 (0)1 43 25 83 58, fax +33 (0)1 43 25 26 16, e-mail iau@iap.fr, URL: http://www.iau.org

INTERNATIONAL BUREAU OF WEIGHTS AND MEASURES (BIPM)

The task of the BIPM is to ensure world-wide uniformity of measurements and their traceability to the International System of Units (SI). It does this with the authority of the Convention of the Metre, a treaty between fifty-five nations.

Director: Dr Martin J.T. Milton
Head of Secretariat: Mrs C. Fellag-Ariouet

International Bureau of Weights and Measures (BIPM), Pavillon de Breteuil, F-92312 Sèvres Cedex, France. Tel.: +33 (0)1 45 07 70 70, fax: +33 (0)1 45 34 20 21, e-mail: cfellag@bipm.org, URL: http://www.bipm.org

INTERNATIONAL CARTOGRAPHIC ASSOCIATION

ICA is the world authoritative body for cartography; the discipline dealing with the conception, production, dissemination and study of maps. Its mission is to promote the discipline and profession of cartography in an international context.

President: William Cartwright
Secretary-General: David Fairbairn

International Cartographic Association, School of Civil Engineering and Geosciences, Newcastle University, Newcastle upon Tyne, NE1 7RU United Kingdom. Tel: +44(0)191 222 6353, fax: +44(0)191 222 6902, email: dave.fairbairn@ncl.ac.uk, URL: http://www.icaci.org

INTERNATIONAL COMMISSION FOR OPTICS (ICO)

Its objective is to contribute, on an international basis, to the progress and diffusion of knowledge in the field of optics. In addition to its Congresses, ICO initiates international topical meetings, and acts as a co-sponsor for a number of international scientific meetings organised by other bodies.

President: Maria L. Calvo (Spain)

International Commission for Optics (ICO), URL: http://www.ico-optics.org

INTERNATIONAL COMMISSION ON RADIATION UNITS AND MEASUREMENTS (ICRU)

Aims to develop internationally acceptable recommendations regarding; quantities and units of radiation and radioactivity; procedures suitable for the measurement and application of these quantities in diagnostic radiology, radiation therapy, radiation biology, and industrial operations; and physical data needed in the application of these procedures, the use of which tends to assure uniformity in reporting.

Chairman: Hans Georg Menzel (Switzerland)

International Commission on Radiation Units and Measurements (ICRU), 7910 Woodmont Avenue, Suite 400, Bethesda, MD 20814-3095, USA. Tel: +1 301 657 2652, fax: +1 301 907 8768, e-mail: icru@icru.org, URL: http://www.icru.org

INTERNATIONAL COMMISSION ON ZOOLOGICAL NOMENCLATURE

ICZN was founded in 1895 in order to create, publish and, periodically, to revise the International Code of Zoological Nomenclature. The Commission also considers and rules on specific cases of nomenclatural uncertainty. These rulings are published as 'Opinions' in the Bulletin of Zoological Nomenclature.

President: Jan van Tol (Netherlands)

International Commission on Zoological Nomenclature, Natural History Museum, Cromwell Road, London SW7 5BD, UK. Tel.: +44 (0)20 7942 5653, e-mail: iczn@nhm.ac.uk, URL: http://www.iczn.org

INTERNATIONAL COUNCIL FOR SCIENCE (ICSU)

Aims to promote international scientific activity in the different branches of science and their applications for the benefit of humanity.

President: Catherine Bréchignac
Executive Director: Deliang Chen

International Council for Science (ICSU), 5 Rue Auguste Vacquerie, 75016 Paris, France. Tel: +33 (0)1 45 25 03 29, fax: +33 (0)1 42 88 94 31, e-mail: secretariat@icsu.org, URL: http://www.icsu.org

OTHER INTERNATIONAL AND NATIONAL ORGANISATIONS

INTERNATIONAL COUNCIL FOR SCIENTIFIC AND TECHNICAL INFORMATION

Offers a unique forum for interaction between organizations that create, disseminate and use scientific and technical information. ICSTI's mission cuts across scientific and technical disciplines, as well as international borders, to give member organisations the benefit of a truly global community.

President: Roberta Shaffer (USA)

International Council for Scientific and Technical Information (ICSTI), 5 rue Ambroise Thomas, 75009 Paris, France. Tel: +33 (0)6 14 65 16 57, URL: http://www.icsti.org

INTERNATIONAL COUNCIL FOR THE EXPLORATION OF THE SEA

An inter-governmental marine science organisation whose aims are the promotion, co-ordination and dissemination of research on the physical, chemical and biological systems in the North Atlantic.

General Secretary: Gerd Hubold

International Council for the Exploration of the Sea, H.C. Andersens Boulevard 44 - 46, DK 1553 Copenhagen V, Denmark. Tel: +45 3338 6700, fax: +45 3393 4215, e-mail: info@ices.dk, URL: http://www.ices.dk

INTERNATIONAL COUNCIL OF PSYCHOLOGISTS

The purpose of ICP is to advance psychology and the application of its scientific findings throughout the world. To this end, ICP seeks to strengthen international bonds between psychologists and to widen, deepen, and clarify channels of communication between individual psychologists.

President: Dr Ludwig Lowenstein

International Council of Psychologists, URL: http://www.icpweb.org

INTERNATIONAL FEDERATION OF SOCIETIES FOR MICROSCOPY

IFSM's aim is to contribute to the advancement of microscopy in all its aspects. It comprises microscopy societies from all around the world.

General Secretary: Professor C. Barry Carter

International Federation of Societies for Microscopy, URL: http://www.ifsm.uconn.edu

INTERNATIONAL FOOD INFORMATION SERVICE (IFIS)

A not-for-profit organisation established in 1968 to serve the international food science, food technology and human nutrition community, by: providing information products and services, including the FSTA - Food, Science and Technology Abstracts database. IFIS's mission is to communicate and promote knowledge of the sciences related to food in order to stimulate global education, research and vocational training for the future benefit of humanity.

Managing Director: Richard Hollingsworth

International Food Information Service (IFIS), Lane End House, Shinfield Road, Shinfield, Reading RG2 9BB, UK. Tel: +44 (0)118 988 3895, fax: +44 (0)118 988 5065, e-mail: ifis@ifis.org, URL: http://www.foodsciencecentral.com

INTERNATIONAL GEOGRAPHICAL UNION

Aims to promote the study of geographical problems; initiate and co-ordinate geographical research requiring international co-operation and to promote its scientific discussion and publication; and provide for the participation of geographers in the work of relevant international organizations.

Secretary-General and Treasurer: Michael Meadows

International Geographical Union, Department of Environmental & Geographical Science, South Lane, University of Cape Town, Rondebosch, 7701, Cape Town, South Africa, URL: http://www.igu-net.org

INTERNATIONAL GLACIOLOGICAL SOCIETY (IGS)

Founded in 1936 to provide a focus for individuals interested in practical and scientific aspects of snow and ice. It aims to stimulate interest in and encourage research into the scientific and technical problems of snow and ice in all countries and to facilitate and increase the flow of glaciological ideas and information. The Society publishes scientific journals in the field of glaciology and cryospherics and organizes symposia and workshops worldwide in furtherance of its goals.

Secretary General: Magnús Már Magnússon

International Glaciological Society, Scott Polar Research Institute, Lensfield Road, Cambridge CB2 1ER, UK. Tel: +44 (0)1223 355974, fax: +44 (0)1223 354931, e-mail: igsoc@igsoc.org, URL: http://www.igsoc.org

INTERNATIONAL HYDROGRAPHIC ORGANIZATION

The International Hydrographic Organization is a competent international organization, a referred to in the United Nations Convention on the Law of the Sea, which coordinates on a worldwide basis the setting of standards for the production of hydrographic data and the provision of hydrographic services and which facilitates capacity building of nationa hydrographic services.

Directing Committee: Vice Admiral Maratos (Greece), Captain Hugo Gorziglia (Chile) Captain Robert Ward (Australia)

International Hydrographic Organization, 4 Quai Antoine 1er, B.P. 445, MC 9801 Monaco Cedex, Principality of Monaco. Tel: +377 93 108100, fax: +377 93 108140, e-mai info@ihb.mc, URL: http://www.iho.int

INTERNATIONAL INSTITUTE OF REFRIGERATION (IIR)

A scientific and technical intergovernmental organization enabling pooling of scientific an industrial know-how in all refrigeration fields on a worldwide scale.

Director: Didier Coulomb

International Institute of Refrigeration (IIR), 177, boulevard Malesherbes, 7501 Paris, France. Tel: +33 (0)1 42 27 32 35, fax: +33 (0)1 47 63 17 98, URL: http://www.iifiir.org

INTERNATIONAL INSTITUTE OF WELDING

Aims to encourage the development of welding and to provide for the exchange of scientifi and technical information relating to research and education.

President: Prof. Dr.-Ing. Ulrich Dilthey

International Institute of Welding, 90 rue des Vanesses, 93420 Villepinte, France Tel: +33 (0)1 49 90 36 08, fax: +33 (0)1 49 90 36 80, e-mail: iiw@iiwelding.org, URL http://www.iiwelding.org

INTERNATIONAL ORGANIZATION OF LEGAL METROLOGY (OIML)

Established in 1955 in order to promote the global harmonization of legal metrolog procedures. OIML has developed a worldwide technical structure that provides its member with metrological guidelines for the elaboration of national and regional requirement concerning the manufacture and use of measuring instruments for legal metrolog applications.

Director: Stephen Patoray

International Organization of Legal Metrology (OIML), 11 rue Turgot, F-7500 Paris, France. Tel: +33 (0)1 48 78 12 82, fax: +33 (0)1 42 82 17 27, URL: http://www.oiml.org

INTERNATIONAL PEAT SOCIETY (IPS)

An international, non-governmental and non-profit organisation with approximately 1,45 members from 36 countries. It is dedicated to fostering the advancement, exchange an communication of scientific, technical and social knowledge and understanding for the wis use of peatlands and peat.

President: Mr Donal Clarke (Ireland)

International Peat Society, Vapaudenkatu 12, 40100 Jyväskylä, Finland. Tel: +35 (0)14 338 5440, fax: +358 (0)14 338 5410, e-mail: ips@peatsociety.org, URL http://www.peatsociety.org

INTERNATIONAL PHONETIC ASSOCIATION (IPA)

The aim of the IPA is to promote the scientific study of phonetics and the various practica applications of that science. In furtherance of this aim, the IPA provides the academi community world-wide with a notational standard for the phonetic representation of al languages - the International Phonetic Alphabet (also IPA). The latest version of the IPA Alphabet was published in 2005.

Vice President: Prof. Daniel Recasens

International Phonetic Association (IPA), Aristotle University of Thessaloniki, Schoo of English, Department of Theoretical and Applied Linguistics, Thessaloniki, 54124, Greece Tel: +30 2310 997429; fax: +30 2310 997432, e-mail: knicol@enl.auth.gr, URL http://www.langsci.ucl.ac.uk/ipa

INTERNATIONAL RADIATION PROTECTION ASSOCIATION (IRPA)

Aims to provide a medium whereby those engaged in radiation protection activities in al countries may communicate more readily with each other and through this process advanc radiation protection in many parts of the world. This includes those involved in science medicine, engineering, technology and law.

President: Ken Kase
Executive Officer: Jacques Lochard

International Radiation Protection Association (IRPA), c/o CEPN, 28 rue de la Redoute, Fontenay-aux-Roses 92260, France. Tel: +33 (0)1 55 52 19 47, fax: +33 (0)1 55 52 19 21, e-mail: irpa.exof@irpa.net, URL: http://www.irpa.net

INTERNATIONAL SOCIETY FOR ROCK MECHANICS

Aims to encourage international collaboration and exchange of ideas and information between Rock Mechanics practitioners; encourage teaching, research, and advancement of knowledge in Rock Mechanics; and promote high standards of professional practice among rock engineers so that civil, mining and petroleum engineering works might be safer, more economic and less disruptive to the environment.

President: Professor Xia-Ting Feng

International Society for Rock Mechanics, Av. Brasil, 101, 1700-066 Lisbon, Portugal. Tel.: +351 21 844 3419, fax: +351 21 844 3021, e-mail: secretariat.isrm@lnec.pt, URL: http://www.isrm.net

INTERNATIONAL SOCIETY FOR STEREOLOGY (ISS)

Includes members from the fields of mathematics, statistics, biology and materials science. The official journals of the Society are the Journal of Microscopy and Image Analysis & Stereology. The International Congress for Stereology is held every four years, and the European Congress for Stereology is also held every four years. ISS also supports courses and workshops on stereology.

President: Professor Jens R. Nyengaard

International Society for Stereology, URL: http://www.stereologysociety.org

INTERNATIONAL SOCIETY OF BIOMETEOROLOGY (ISB)

Aims to provide an international forum for the promotion of interdisciplinary collaboration between meteorologists, health professionals, biologists, climatologists, ecologists and other scientists and to develop research agendas in the field of biometeorology.

President: Paul Beggs (Australia)
Secretary: Prof. Mark D. Schwartz

International Society of Biometeorology (ISB), Department of Geography, University of Wisconsin-Milwaukee, Milwaukee, WI 53201, USA. Tel: +1 414 229 3740, e-mail: mds@uwm.edu, URL: http://www.biometeorology.org

INTERNATIONAL STATISTICAL INSTITUTE

An autonomous society devoted to the development and improvement of statistical methods and their application throughout the world.

Director-Secretary/Treasurer: Mrs Ada Van Krimpen

International Statistical Institute, c/o Netherlands Statistics, Leidschenveen, The Hague, The Netherlands. URL: http://www.isi-web.org/

INTERNATIONAL UNION FOR PURE AND APPLIED BIOPHYSICS

Its function is to support research and teaching in biophysics. Its principal regular activity is the triennial International Congresses and General Assemblies. Its members come from 50 countries.

President Elect: Professor Gordon Roberts
Secretary General: Professor Cris G. dos Remedios

International Union for Pure and Applied Biophysics, URL: http://www.iupab.org

INTERNATIONAL UNION OF BASIC AND CLINICAL PHARMACOLOGY (IUPHAR)

The main objectives of IUPHAR are to foster international cooperation in pharmacology by promoting cooperation between societies that represent pharmacology and related disciplines throughout the world and sponsoring international and regional congresses and meetings.

Secretary-General: Dr. S.J. Enna

International Union of Basic and Clinical Pharmacology (IUPHAR), University of Kansas Medical Center, 3901 Rainbow Boulevard, Mail Stop 4016, Kansas City, Kansas 66160, USA. Tel: +1 913 588 7533, fax: +1 913 588 7373, e-mail: IUPHAR@kumc.edu, URL: http://www.iuphar.org

INTERNATIONAL UNION OF BIOCHEMISTRY AND MOLECULAR BIOLOGY

Unites biochemists and molecular biologists in 77 countries. Devoted to promoting research and education in biochemistry and molecular biology throughout the world and gives particular attention to areas where the subject is still in its early development.

General Secretary: Professor Michael P. Walsh

International Union of Biochemistry and Molecular Biology, Department of Biochemistry & Molecular Biology, Faculty of Medicine, university of Calgary, 3330 Hospital Drive NW, Calgary, Alberta, T2N 4N1, Canada. Tel: +1 403 220 3021, fax: +1 403 270 2211, URL: http://www.iubmb.org/

INTERNATIONAL UNION OF BIOLOGICAL SCIENCES (IUBS)

A non-governmental, non-profit organisation, established in 1919. Its objectives are: to promote the study of biological sciences; to initiate, facilitate and coordinate research and other scientific activities necessitating international, interdisciplinary cooperation; to ensure the discussion and dissemination of the results of cooperative research, particularly in connection with IUBS scientific programmes; and to support the organisation of international conferences and assist in the publication of their reports.

President: Giorgio Bernardi (Italu)

International Union of Biological Sciences (IUBS), Batiment 442, Université de Paris Sud XI, 91405 Orsay Cedex, France. Tel: +33 (0)1 69 15 50 27, URL: http://www.iubs.org

INTERNATIONAL UNION OF CRYSTALLOGRAPHY

Its objectives are; to promote international co-operation in crystallography and to contribute to all aspects of crystallography; to promote international publication of crystallographic research; to facilitate standardization of methods, units, nomenclatures and symbols; and to form a focus for the relations of crystallography to other sciences.

President: Prof. Gautam Desiraju

International Union of Crystallography, 2 Abbey Square, Chester CH1 2HU, UK. Tel: + 44 (0)1244 345431, fax: + 44 (0)1244 344843, e-mail: execsec@iucr.org, URL: http//www.iucr.org

INTERNATIONAL UNION OF FOOD SCIENCE & TECHNOLOGY (IUFOST)

Promotes international co-operation and exchange of scientific and technical information among scientists, food technologists and specialists of member nations, supports international progress in both theoretical and applied areas of food science and aims to advance technology in the processing, manufacturing, preservation, storage and distribution of food products.

Chairman and President: Prof. Geoffrey Campbell-Platt (UK)
Secretary-General and Treasurer: Ms. Judith Meech (Canada)

International Union of Food Science & Technology (IUFoST), PO Box 61021, Number 19, 511 Maple Grove Road, Oakville, Ontario, Canada, L6J 6X0. Tel: +1 905 815 1926, fax: +1 905 815 1574, e-mail: secretariat@iufost.org, URL: http://www.iufost.org

INTERNATIONAL UNION OF GEODESY AND GEOPHYSICS (IUGG)

An international organization dedicated to advancing, promoting, and communicating knowledge of the Earth system, its space environment, and the dynamical processes causing change.

President (2011-15): Harsh Gupta (India)

International Union of Geodesy and Geophysics (IUGG), Karlsruhe Institute of Technology, Geophysical Institute, Hertzstr. 16, 76187 Karlsruhe, Germany. URL: http://www.iugg.org

INTERNATIONAL UNION OF IMMUNOLOGICAL SOCIETIES

An umbrella organisation for many of the regional and national societies of immunology throughout the world. It aims to organize international co-operation in immunology and to promote communication between the various branches of immunology and allied subjects.

President: Stefan H.E. Kaufmann

International Union of Immunological Societies, c/o Vienna Academy of Postgraduate Medical Education and Research, Alser Strasse 4, A - 1090 Vienna, Austria. Tel: +43 (0)1 405 138313, fax: +43 (0)1 405 138323, e-mail: iuis-central-office@medacad.org, URL: http://www.iuisonline.org

INTERNATIONAL UNION OF MICROBIOLOGICAL SOCIETIES (IUMS)

IUMS is one of the 29 Scientific Unions of the International Council of Scientific Unions. Aims to promote the study of microbiological sciences internationally; initiate, facilitate and coordinate research and other scientific activities which involve international cooperation; and ensure the discussion and dissemination of the results of international conferences.

President Elect: Geoffrey L. Smith (UK)
Secretary General: Robert Samson (Netherlands)

International Union of Microbiological Societies (IUMS), PO Box 85167, 3508 AD Utrecht, The Netherlands. Tel: +31 (0)30 212 2600, fax: +31 (0)30 251 2097, e-mail: r.samson@cbs.knaw.nl, URL: http://www.iums.org

OTHER INTERNATIONAL AND NATIONAL ORGANISATIONS

INTERNATIONAL UNION OF NUTRITIONAL SCIENCES (IUNS)

Aims to promote advancement in nutrition science, research and development through international cooperation at the global level. Encourages communication and collaboration among nutrition scientists and disseminates information in nutritional sciences.

Secretary General: Prof. Rekia Belahsen

International Union of Nutritional Sciences (IUNS), IUNS Secretariat, Gonzalo de Bilbao, 23, Planta 2 - Módulos 9 y 10
41003 Seville, Spain. Tel: +34 954 22 40 95, fax: +34 954 21 02 15, URL: http://www.iuns.org

INTERNATIONAL UNION OF PHYSIOLOGICAL SCIENCES (IUPS)

The unifying objective of physiologists is to increase mankind's understanding of the functions of cells, tissues, organs and organ systems of animals and humans. The objectives of the IUPS are to encourage the advancement of the physiological sciences, facilitate the dissemination of knowledge in the field of physiological sciences and to promote the International Congresses of Physiological Sciences.

Secretary General: Walter Boron

International Union of Physiological Sciences (IUPS), URL: http://www.iups.org

INTERNATIONAL UNION OF RADIO SCIENCE

A non-governmental and non-profit organisation responsible for stimulating and co-ordinating, on an international basis, studies, research, applications, scientific exchange and communication in the fields of radio science.

President: Prof. Phil Wilkinson (Australia)
Secretary-General: Professor Paul Lagasse (Belgium)

International Union of Radio Science, c/o INTEC, Ghent University, Sint-Pietersnieuwstraat 41, B-9000 Ghent, Belgium. Tel: +32 (0)9 264 3320, fax: +32 (0)9 264 4288, e-mail info@ursi.org, URL: http://www.ursi.org

INTERNATIONAL UNION OF TOXICOLOGY (IUTOX)

Fosters international scientific cooperation among toxicologists and promotes global acquisition, dissemination, and utilization of knowledge in the world of science of toxicology and ensures continued training and development of toxicologists worldwide.

President: Dr. Kai Savolainen

International Union of Toxicology (IUTOX), 1821 Michael Faraday Drive, Suite 300, Reston, VA 20190, USA. Tel: +1 703 438 3103, fax: +1 703 438 3113, e-mail: iutoxhq@iutox.org, URL: http://www.iutox.org

INTERNATIONAL WATER ASSOCIATION (IWA)

Connects water professionals worldwide to lead the development of effective and sustainable approaches to water management.

Executive Director: Paul Reiter

International Water Association (IWA), Alliance House, 12 Caxton Street, London SW1H 0QS, UK. Tel: +44 (0)207 654 5500, fax: +44 (0)207 654 5555, e-mail: water@iwahq.org.uk, URL: http://www.iwahq.org/1nb/home.html

MEDITERRANEAN SCIENCE COMMISSION

Aims to better understand, monitor and protect a fast-changing, highly impacted Mediterranean Sea. CIESM runs expert workshops, collaborative programs and regular congresses, delivering authoritative, independent advice to national and international agencies.

Director General: Prof. Frédéric Briand

Mediterranean Science Commission (CIESM), 16 bd de Suisse, MC 98000 Monaco. Tel: +377 9330 3879, e-mail: contacts@ciesm.org, URL: http://www.ciesm.org

PUGWASH CONFERENCES ON SCIENCE AND WORLD AFFAIRS

Brings together, in private as individuals, influential scholars and public figures from around the world who are concerned with reducing the danger of armed conflict and seeking cooperative solutions for global problems. In 1995, Pugwash and Prof. Joseph Rotblat jointly received the Nobel Peace Prize.

President: Jayantha Dhanapala

Pugwash Conferences on Science and World Affairs, via dei Riari 86, 1-00165 Rome, Italy. Tel: +39 06 687 8376, e-mail: pugwash@iol.it, URL: http://www.pugwash.org

ROYAL SOCIETY

A learned society for the promotion of natural and applied sciences such as engineering and medicine, as well as mathematics. It encourages both national and international activities in a similar way to national academies overseas.

President: Prof. Martin Rees, Lord Rees of Ludlow Kt PRS
Executive Secretary: Stephen Cox CVO

Royal Society, 6 - 9 Carlton House Terrace, London SW1Y 5AG, UK. Tel: +44 (0)20 7451 2500, fax: +44 (0)20 7930 2170, e-mail: webmanager@royalsociety.org, URL http://www.royalsociety.org

WORLD ORGANISATION OF SYSTEMS AND CYBERNETICS (WOSC)

Aims for the recognition of cybernetics as a fundamental science. Organizes and sponsors tri-annual international congresses with exhibitions of automation and computer equipment.

Director-General: Dr Alex Andrew

World Organisation of Systems and Cybernetics (WOSC), 95 Finch Road, Earley, Reading RG6 7JX, UK. Tel: +44 (0)118 926 9328, e-mail: alexandrew@tiscali.co.uk, URL: http://www.cybsoc.org/wosc

Tourism

CARIBBEAN TOURISM ORGANIZATION (CTO)

CTO is a trade organization whose main objective is the development of sustainable tourism for the economic and social benefit of Caribbean people. Comprised of government and private sector operatives in the tourism industry across the Caribbean, CTO collects and disseminates research and data on the development of the regional industry.

Secretary General: Hugh Riley

Caribbean Tourism Organization (CTO), 1 Financial Place, Collymore Rock, St. Michael, Barbados. Tel: +1 246 427 5242, fax: +1 246 429 3065, e-mail: ctobar@caribsurf.com, URL: http://www.onecaribbean.org

INTERNATIONAL ASSOCIATION OF SCIENTIFIC EXPERTS IN TOURISM (AIEST)

Supports the activity of scientific institutes of tourism, or other centres of research and education specialising in tourism, and develops relations between them. Organises and co-operates in congresses and other meetings and courses on tourism of a scientific nature.

Secretary General: Prof. Dr. Christian Laesser

International Association of Scientific Experts in Tourism (AIEST), Dufourstrasse 40a, CH-9000 St. Gallen, Switzerland. Tel: +41 (0)71 224 2530, fax: +41 (0)71 224 2536, e-mail: aiest@unisg.ch, URL: http://www.aiest.org

INTERNATIONAL CONGRESS & CONVENTION ASSOCIATION (ICCA)

Aims to evaluate practical ways to get the travel industry involved in the rapidly expanding market of international meetings and to exchange information related to their operations in this market. ICCA is made up of over 950 member companies and organisations in 87 countries.

CEO: Martin Sirk

International Congress & Convention Association (ICCA), Toren A, De Entree 57, 1101 BH Amsterdam, The Netherlands. Tel: +31 (0)20 398 1919, fax: +31 (0)20 699 0781, e-mail: icca@icca.nl, URL: http://www.iccaworld.org

INTERNATIONAL HOTEL & RESTAURANT ASSOCIATION (IH&RA)

Monitors issues that are raised by major international organisations involved in tourism, represents the collective industry interests before policy makers and lobbies for better recognition of the hospitality industry worldwide.

President: Dr. Ghassan Aïdi

International Hotel and Restaurant Association (IH&RA), 42 Avenue General Guisan , Lausanne, 1009 Pully, Switzerland. Tel: +41 (0)21 711 4283, e-mail: info@ih-ra.com, URL: http://www.ih-ra.com

SOUTH PACIFIC TOURISM ORGANISATION

Aims to facilitate the sustainable development of the tourism sector in the South Pacific, strengthen capacity within the region, and sustainably plan, market and manage development of the tourism sector.

South Pacific Tourism Organisation, PO Box 13119, Suva, Fiji Islands. Tel: +679 330 1177, fax: +679 330 1995, URL: http://www.spto.org

UNITED FEDERATION OF TRAVEL AGENTS ASSOCIATIONS (UFTAA)

JFTAA's mission is to be an international forum where matters affecting the world travel industry are addressed, representing and defending the interests of incoming and outgoing tour operators, travel and tourism agencies before the governmental bodies, suppliers and other entities of international scope.

Chairman: Mr Prasad Challagalla

United Federation of Travel Agents Associations (UFTAA), 19 avenue des Castelans, MC98000 Monaco. Tel: +377 92 052829, fax: +377 92 052987, e-mail: uftaa@uftaa.org, URL: http://www.uftaa.org

Trade & Industry

AFRICAN ORGANISATION FOR STANDARDISATION (ARSO)

Founded by the Organisation of African Unity (now the African Union) and the UN Economic Commission for Africa in 1977. Aims to improve and promote market access and consumer protection in order to enhance inter-African and global trade.

President: Dr Eng. Kioko Mang'eli

African Regional Organisation for Standardisation (ARSO), International House 3rd Floor. P.O. Box 57363 -00200 City Square, Nairobi, Kenya. Tel: +254 020 224561, fax: +254 020 218792, e-mail: info@arso-oran.org, URL: http://www.arso-oran.org

ARAB-BRITISH CHAMBER OF COMMERCE

Founded in 1975, the Arab-British Chamber of Commerce exists to encourage trade and economic co-operation between the United Kingdom and the 21 members of the League of Arab States.

Secretary-General and Chief Executive: Dr Afnan Al Shuaiby

Arab-British Chamber of Commerce, 43 Upper Grosvenor Street, London, W1K 2NJ, UK. Tel +44 (0)20 7235 4363, fax: +44 (0)20 7245 6688, e-mail: info@abcc.org.uk, URL: http://www.abcc.org.uk

ASIAN PRODUCTIVITY ORGANIZATION (APO)

A regional intergovernmental organisation. Its mission is to contribute to the socio-economic development of Asia and the Pacific through enhancing productivity. The APO is non-political, non-profit, and non-discriminancy.

Secretary-General: Ryuichiro Yamazaki (Japan)

Asian Productivity Organization (APO), Hirakawa-cho Dai-ichi Seimei Bldg. 2F, 1-2-10 Hirakawa-cho, Chiyoda-ku, Tokyo 102-0093, Japan. Tel: +81 (0)3 5226 3920, fax: +81 (0)3 5226 3950, e-mail: apo@apo-tokyo.org, URL: http://www.apo-tokyo.org

BRITISH CHAMBERS OF COMMERCE

Formed in 1860, the British Chambers of Commerce (BCC) is the largest business representative body in the UK representing all sizes of businesses in all sectors of the economy.

President: Martyn Pellew

British Chambers of Commerce, 65 Petty France, London SW1H 9EU, UK. Tel: +44 (0)20 7654 5800, fax: +44(0)20 7654 5819, e-mail: info@british.chambers.org.uk, URL: http://www.britishchambers.org.uk

CHARTERED INSTITUTE OF PUBLIC RELATIONS

The Chartered Institute of Public Relations is a professional organisation for individual practitioners. The institute defines public relations as the planned and sustained effort to establish and maintain goodwill and mutual understanding between an organisation and its public.

President-Elect: Sally Sykes

Chartered Institute of Public Relations, CIPR Public Relations Centre, 52-53 Russel Square, London WC1B 4HP, UK. Tel: +44 (0)20 7631 6900, e-mail: info@cipr.co.uk, URL: http://www.cipr.co.uk

CHEMICALS INDUSTRY ASSOCIATION

The Chemicals Industry Association aims to assist its members to secure sustainable profitability and to improve recognition of their contribution to society by working with them to influence relevant people and policies.

Chief Executive: Steve Elliott

Chemicals Industry Association, Kings Buildings, Smith Square, London SW1P 3JJ, UK. Tel: +44 (0)20 7834 3399, fax: +44 (0)20 7834 4469, e-mail: enquiries@cia.org.uk, URL: http://www.cia.org.uk

CONSUMERS INTERNATIONAL (CI)

An independent global campaigning voice for consumers. CI aims to promote a fairer society through defending the rights of all consumers, especially the poor, marginalised and disadvantaged, by: supporting and strengthening member organisations and the consumer movement in general and campaigning at international level for policies which respect consumer concerns.

President (2011-15): Jim Guest (USA)

Consumers International (CI), 24 Highbury Crescent, London N5 1RX, UK. Tel: +44 (0)20 7226 6663, fax: +44 (0)20 7354 0607, e-mail: consint@consint.org, URL: http://www.consumersinternational.org

EUROCHAMBRES
European Association of Chambers of Commerce and Industry

EUROCHAMBRES is the Association of European Chambers of Commerce and Industry. It is the sole European body that serves the interests of every sector and every size of European business. It forms one of the key pillars of business representation to the European institutions.

President: Alessandro Barberis
Secretary General: Arnaldo Abruzzini

Eurochambres (European Association of Chambers of Commerce and Industry), The Chamber House, Avenue des Arts 19A/D, 1000 Brussels, Belgium. Tel: +32 (0)2 282 0850, fax; +32 (0)2 230 0038, e-mail: eurochambres@eurochambres.be, URL: http://www.eurochambres.be

EUROPEAN ASSOCIATION OF COMMUNICATIONS AGENCIES (EACA)

EACA aims to promote honest, effective advertising, high professional standards, and awareness of the contribution of advertising in a free market economy and to encourage close co-operation between agencies, advertisers and media in European advertising bodies.

President: Mory MacLennan

European Association of Communications Agencies (EACA), 152 Blvd. Brand Whitlock, B-1200 Brussels, Belgium. Tel: +32 (0)2 740 0710, fax: +32 (0)2 740 0717, URL: http://www.eaca.be

EUROPEAN CHEMICAL INDUSTRY COUNCIL (CEFIC)

Aims to maintain and develop a prosperous chemical industry in Europe by promoting the best possible economic, social and environmental conditions to bring benefits to society with a commitment to the continuous improvement of all its activities including the safety, health and environmental performance.

Director General: Hubert Mandery

European Chemical Industry Council (Cefic), Avenue E. van Nieuwenhuyse, 4 box 1, B-1160 Brussels, Belgium. Tel: + 32 (0)2 676 7211, fax: + 32 (0)2 676 7300, e-mail: mail@cefic.be, URL: http://www.cefic.org

EUROPEAN COMMITTEE FOR STANDARDIZATION (CEN)

Contributes to the objectives of the European Union and European Economic Area with voluntary technical standards which promote free trade, the safety of workers and consumers, interoperability of networks, environmental protection, exploitation of research and development programmes, and public procurement.

President Elect: Dipl. Ing. Friedrich Smaxwil (Germany)

European Committee for Standardization (CEN), Avenue Marnix 17, B - 1000 Brussels, Belgium. Tel: + 32 (0)2 550 0811, fax: + 32 (0)2 550 0819, URL: http://www.cen.eu

EUROPEAN CONFEDERATION OF IRON AND STEEL INDUSTRIES (EUROFER)

Encourages co-operation amongst the national federations and companies in all matters that contribute to the development of the European steel industry, and represents the common interests of its members vis-à-vis third parties, notably the European institutions and other international organisations.

Director General: Gordon Moffat

OTHER INTERNATIONAL AND NATIONAL ORGANISATIONS

European Confederation of Iron and Steel Industries (EUROFER), 5 Avenue Ariane, Building "Integrale" E3 (3rd floor), B-1200 Brussels, Belgium. Tel: +32 (0)2 738 7920, fax: +32 (0)2 736 3001, e-mail: mail@eurofer.eu, URL: http://www.eurofer.eu

EUROPEAN PATENT OFFICE (EPO)

An intergovernmental organisation that was set up on 7 October 1977 on the basis of the European Patent Convention (EPC) signed in Munich in 1973. It has two bodies, the European Patent Office and the Administrative Council, which supervises the Office's activities.

President: Benoit Battistelli

European Patent Office (EPO), Isar building, Erhardtstr. 27, 80469 Munich, Germany. Tel: +49 (0)89 2399 1101, fax: +49 (0)89 2399 2891, URL: http://www.epo.org

EUROPEAN TRADE UNION CONFEDERATION (ETUC)

ETUC was created in 1973 to promote the interests of working people at European level and to represent them in the EU institutions. At present, the ETUC has in membership 83 National Trade Union Confederations from 36 European countries, as well as 12 European industry federations, making a total of 60 million members, plus observer organisations in Macedonia and Serbia.

General Secretary: Bernadette Ségol

European Trade Union Confederation, International Trade Union House, 5 Boulevard Roi Albert II, B-1210 Brussels, Belgium. Tel: +32 (0)2 224 0411, fax: +32 (0)2 224 0454, e-mail: etuc@etuc.org, URL: http://www.etuc.org

EUROPEAN TRAVEL COMMISSION (ETC)

Its main objectives are to promote Europe as an attractive tourist destination particularly in overseas markets; assist member National Tourist Offices to exchange knowledge and work collaboratively; provide industry partners and other interested parties with easy access to material and statistics regarding inbound tourism to Europe.

Executive Director: Raf De Bruyn

European Travel Commission, Head Office, Avenue Marnix 19A/25, 1000 Brussels, Belgium. Tel: +32 (0)2 548 9000, fax: +32 (0)2 514 1843, e-mail: info@visiteurope.com URL: http://www.etc-corporate.com / http://www.visiteurope.com

EXPORT CREDITS GUARANTEE DEPARTMENT

ECGD, the Exports Credits Guarantee Department, is the UK's official export credit agency. It works with exporters, project sponsors, banks and buyers to help UK exporters of capital equipment and project-related goods and services, by providing insurance against non-payment risks to UK exporters and guarantees for bank loans to facilitate the arranging of finance to buyers of UK goods. It also provides insurance against political risks to UK investors in overseas markets.

Chief Executive: Patrick Crawford

Export Credits Guarantee Department, 2 Exchange Tower, Harbour Exchange Square, London E14 9GS, UK. Tel: +44 (0)20 7512 7000, fax: +44 (0)20 7512 7649, e-mail: help@ecgd.qsi.gov.uk, URL: http://www.ecgd.gov.uk

FAIRTRADE INTERNATIONAL (FLO)

Fairtrade International (FLO) is a non-profit multi-stakeholder organization. FLO is responsible for the strategic direction of Fairtrade, the Fairtrade Standards and producer support. The Fairtrade Certification Mark is a registered trademark of FLO which shows that a product meets international Fairtrade standards.

Chair of the FLO Board: Jean Louis Homé

Fairtrade International (FLO), Bonner Talweg 177, 53129 Bonn, Germany. Tel +49 (0)228 949230, fax: +49 (0)228 242 1713, e-mail: info@ fairtrade.net, URL: http://www.fairtrade.net

GULF ORGANIZATION FOR INDUSTRIAL CONSULTING (GOIC)

GOIC, founded in 1976, by GCC Member States (UAE, Bahrain, Saudi Arabia, Oman, Qatar and Kuwait) targets developing industries throughout the GCC by means of providing both the industrial and economic sectors with distinctive knowledge, consultancy and technical services.

Secretary General: H.E. Mr Abdulaziz bin Hamad Al-Ageel

Gulf Organization for Industrial Consulting (GOIC), P.O. Box 5114, Corniche Road, West Bay Area, Doha, Qatar. Tel: +974 485 8888, fax: +974 483 1465, e-mail: goic@goic.org.qa, URL: http://www.goic.org.qa

INSTITUTE OF CHARTERED SECRETARIES AND ADMINISTRATORS

In addition to being the professional qualifying body for company secretaries, the Institute identifies and promulgates best practice; contributes to the drawing up of relevant legislation regulation and codes of practice; and provides members with assistance in carrying out their roles.

Chief Executive: David Wilson FCIS FSA

Institute of Chartered Secretaries and Administrators, 16 Park Crescent, London W1B 1AH, UK. Tel: +44 (0)20 7580 4741, fax: +44 (0)20 7323 1132, e-mail: info@icsa.co.uk, URL: http://icsa.org.uk

INSTITUTE OF DIRECTORS

An international organisation committed to high standards of corporate governance. The UK Institute actively represents the interests of members to both UK Government and to the European Community Institutions.

Director General: Miles Templeman

Institute of Directors, 116 Pall Mall, London SW1Y 5ED, UK. Tel: +44 (0)20 7839 1233, fax: +44 (0)20 7930 1949, e-mail: enquiries@iod.com, URL: http://www.iod.com

INTERNATIONAL ADVERTISING ASSOCIATION (IAA)

The IAA champions advertising as a force for growth in all free market societies. It provides its members with an international, multi-industry forum for the global exchange of knowledge, best practices, professional development, intelligence, experience and ideas.

Chairman and World President: Joseph Ghossoub

International Advertising Association (IAA), IAA World Service Center, 521 Fifth Avenue, Suite 1807, New York NY 10175, USA. Tel: +1 212 557 1133, fax: +1 212 983 0455, e-mail: membership@iaaglobal.org, URL: http://www.iaaglobal.org

INTERNATIONAL ASSOCIATION FOR SOAPS, DETERGENTS AND MAINTENANCE PRODUCTS (AISE)

The industry develops and markets products that are essential to society such as detergents and maintenance products for either household or industrial and institutional use.

President: Hans Bender

International Association for Soaps, Detergents and Maintenance Products (AISE), Third Floor, Avenue Herrmann Debroux 15A, 1160 Brussels, Belgium. Tel: + 32 (0)2 679 6260, fax: +32 (0)2 679 6279, e-mail: aise.main@aise.eu, URL: http://www.aise.eu

INTERNATIONAL BOOKSELLERS FEDERATION (IBF)

IBF offers a variety of services to its Members, which range from worldwide networking, information and professional expertise to the promotion of the bookshop as the place to buy books. IBF also provides its Members with help and support when they need to lobby their governments on issues affecting the book trade.

President: Inara Belinkaja (Latvia)

International Booksellers Federation (IBF), Rue de la Science 10, 1000 Brussels, Belgium. Tel: +32(0)2 223 4940, fax:+32(0)2 223 4938, e-mail: ibf.booksellers@skynet.be URL: http://www.ibf-booksellers.org

INTERNATIONAL CHAMBER OF SHIPPING

Promotes the interests of its members internationally on matters of general policy including navigation, marine safety, ship construction and design, marine law and marine insurance questions, pollution control and trade documentation.

Secretary-General: Peter Hinchcliffe

International Chamber of Shipping, 12 Carthusian Street, London EC1M 6EZ, UK. Tel: +44 (0)20 7417 8844, fax: +44 (0)20 7417 8877, e-mail: ics@marisec.org, URL: http://www.marisec.org

INTERNATIONAL COCOA ORGANIZATION

To complement its mandate of working towards a sustainable world cocoa economy, ICCO also funtions as a centre to address matters of importance in world cocoa, in conjunction with governments and the private sector.

Executive Director: Dr. Jean-Marc Anga

International Cocoa Organization, Commonwealth House, 1 - 19 New Oxford Street, London WC1A 1NU, UK. Tel: +44 (0)20 7400 5050, fax: +44 (0)20 7421 5500, e-mail: info@icco.org, URL: http://www.icco.org

INTERNATIONAL COFFEE ORGANIZATION

Aims to achieve a reasonable balance between world supply and demand on a basis which will assure adequate supplies of coffee at fair prices to consumers and markets for coffee at remunerative prices to producers, and which will be conducive to long-term equilibrium between production and consumption.

Council Chairman: Henry Ngabirano (Uganda)
Executive Director: Robério Oliveira Silva (Brazil)

International Coffee Organization, 22 Berners Street, London W1T 3DD, UK. Tel: +44 (0)20 7612 0600, fax: +44 (0)20 7612 0630, e-mail: info@ico.org, URL: http://www.ico.org

INTERNATIONAL CO-OPERATIVE ALLIANCE (ICA)

An independent, non-governmental organisation which unites, represents and serves co-operatives worldwide. It is the largest non-religious, non-governmental organisation in the world. The International Co-operative Alliance was established by co-operatives around the world in 1895 to advance the co-operative enterprise model. It has members in 90 countries representing a billion members of co-operatives. Individual members own and democratically control their co-operative and share in net proceeds.

The ICA works with global bodies to create a legislative environment that allows co-operatives to form and grow. It informs the media and public about the importance of the values-based business model of the co-operative for economic and social policy, and also helps co-operatives around the world support one another, one of seven key principles that the co-operative movement has established as defining what it means to be co-operative.

The ICA has four regional offices: Brussels, Belgium; Nairobi, Kenya; New Delhi, India; San Jose, Costa Rica.

Director-General: Charles Gould

International Co-operative Alliance (ICA), 15 route des Morillons, 1218 Grand-Saconnex, Geneva, Switzerland. Tel: +41 (0)22 929 8838, fax: +41 (0)22 798 4122, e-mail: ica@ica.coop, URL: http://www.ica.coop

INTERNATIONAL COTTON ADVISORY COMMITTEE

An inter-governmental organisation which observes and keeps in close touch with developments affecting the world cotton situation; it disseminates statistics, and it suggests to the governments represented measures considered suitable for the furtherance of international collaboration in order to maintain and develop a sound world cotton economy.

Chair: Patrick Packnett

International Cotton Advisory Committee, Suite 702, 1629 K Street, NW, Washington DC 20006-1636, USA. Tel: +1 202 463 6660, fax: +1 202 463 6950, e-mail: secretariat@icac.org, URL: http://www.icac.org

INTERNATIONAL COUNCIL OF SOCIETIES OF INDUSTRIAL DESIGN (ICSID)

A global not-for-profit organisation that promotes better design around the world. Today, ICSID has over 150 members in more than 50 countries, representing an estimated 150,000 designers.

President Elect: Prof. Soon-In Lee (South Korea)

International Council of Societies of Industrial Design (ICSID), 455 St-Antoine W. Suite SS10, Montréal, Quebec H2Z 1J1, Canada. Tel: +1 514 448 4949, fax: +1 514 448 4948, e-mail: office@icsid.org, URL: http://www.icsid.org

INTERNATIONAL FAIR TRADE ASSOCIATION (IFAT)

A global network of over 270 fair trade organisations in more than 60 countries, which works to improve the livelihoods and well-being of disadvantaged people in developing countries and to change the unfair structures of international trade.

Executive Director: Carol Wills

International Federation of Alternative Trade (IFAT), 30 Murdock Road, Bicester, Oxon OX6 7RF. United Kingdom. Tel: +44 (0)1869 249819, fax: +44 (0)1869 246381, e-mail: info@ifat.org.uk, URL: http://www.catgen.com/ifat

INTERNATIONAL FEDERATION OF PHARMACEUTICAL MANUFACTURERS AND ASSOCIATIONS (IFPMA)

Encourages a global policy environment that is conducive to innovation in medicine, both therapeutic and preventative, for the benefit of patients around the world.

Director General: Mr. Eduardo Pisani

International Federation of Pharmaceutical Manufacturers and Associations (IFPMA), 15 Ch. Louis-Dunant, PO Box 195, 1211 Geneva 20, Switzerland. Tel: +41 (0)22 338 3200, fax: +41 (0)22 338 3299, e-mail: info@ifpma.org, URL: http://www.ifpma.org

INTERNATIONAL FERTILIZER INDUSTRY ASSOCIATION (IFA)

Promotes efficient and responsible production and use of plant nutrients to maintain and increase agricultural production worldwide in a sustainable manner and improves the operating environment of the fertilizer industry in the spirit of free enterprise and fair trade.

President: William J. Doyle (Canada)

International Fertilizer Industry Association (IFA), 28 rue Marbeuf, 75008 Paris, France. Tel: +33 (0)1 53 93 05 00, fax: +33 (0)1 53 93 05 45, e-mail: ifa@fertilizer.org, URL: http://www.fertilizer.org

INTERNATIONAL FRAGRANCE ASSOCIATION (IFRA)

The mission of IFRA is to serve and advance the collective interests of the fragrance industry worldwide through the imposition of a consistent system of standards for the good manufacture and safe use of fragrances, which is based on broadly recognised scientific principles and aims to protect the consumer and the environment.

International Fragrance Association (IFRA), Avenue des Arts 6, 1210 Brussels, Belgium. Tel: +32 (0)2 214 2060, fax: +32 (0)2 214 2069, e-mail: secretariat@ifraorg.org, URL: http://www.ifraorg.org

INTERNATIONAL FUR TRADE FEDERATION (IFTF)

Through its work, and the activities of members, IFTF seeks to protect fur trade interests and promote innovation, high standards and a positive factual image of fur and the fur industry worldwide. It includes 42 member organisations in 25 countries.

International Fur Trade Federation (IFTF), PO Box 495, Weybridge KT13 8WD, Surrey, UK. e-mail: pressoffice@iftf.com, URL: http://www.iftf.com

INTERNATIONAL LEAD AND ZINC STUDY GROUP

An autonomous intergovernmental organisation which provides opportunities for regular intergovernmental consultations on international trade in lead and zinc.

Secretary General: Donald Smale

International Lead and Zinc Study Group, Rua Almirante Barroso 38, 5th Floor, Lisbon 1000-013, Portugal. Tel: +351 21 359 2420, fax: +351 21 359 2429, e-mail: root@ilzsg.org, URL: http://www.ilzsg.org

INTERNATIONAL OLIVE COUNCIL

Provides a forum for debate and decision-making and co-ordinates national production and marketing policies for olive oils and table olives.

Executive Director: Jean-Louis Barjol

International Olive Council, Principe de Vergara 154, 28002 Madrid, Spain. Tel: +34 91 590 3638, fax: +34 91 563 1263, e-mail: iooc@internationaloliveoil.org, URL: http://www.internationaloliveoil.org

INTERNATIONAL ORGANIZATION FOR STANDARDIZATION

ISO links the national standards institutes of 162 countries. Aims to promote the development of standardisation and related activities in the world with a view to facilitating international exchange of goods and services and to developing co-operation in the sphere of intellectual, scientific, technological and economic activity.

President: Dr Boris Aleshin (Russia)
Secretary-General: Rob Steele

International Organization for Standardization, 1 ch. de la Voie-Creuse, Case Postale 56, CH-1211 Geneva 20, Switzerland. Tel: +42 (0)22 749 0111, fax: +41 (0)22 733 3430, e-mail: central@iso.org, URL: http://www.iso.org

INTERNATIONAL ORGANIZATION OF MOTOR VEHICLE MANUFACTURERS (OICA)

The general purposes of the organization are to defend the interests of the vehicle manufacturers, assemblers and importers grouped within their national federation and, in particular to link the national automobile associations and study issues of mutual interest relating to the development and future of the automobile industry.

President: Patrick Blain (CCFA - France)

International Organization of Motor Vehicle Manufacturers (OICA), 4 rue de Berri, F 75008 Paris, France. Tel: +33 (0)1 43 59 00 13, fax: +33 (0)1 45 63 84 41, e-mail: oica@oica.net, URL: http://www.oica.net

OTHER INTERNATIONAL AND NATIONAL ORGANISATIONS

INTERNATIONAL PUBLISHERS ASSOCIATION (IPA)

IPA is the global non-governmental organisation representing all aspects of book and journal publishing worldwide. Established in 1896, IPA's mission is to promote and protect publishing and to raise awareness for publishing as a force for cultural and political advancement worldwide.

President: Youngsuk Chi

Secretary General: Jens Bammel

International Publishers Association (IPA), 3 avenue de Miremont, 1206 Geneva, Switzerland. Tel : +41 (0)22 704 1820, fax : +41 (0)22 704 1821, e-mail : secretariat@internationalpublishers.org, URL: http://www.internationalpublishers.org

INTERNATIONAL RUBBER STUDY GROUP

A forum for the discussion of matters affecting the supply and demand for synthetic and natural rubber. The group covers all aspects of the world rubber industry, including marketing, shipping, distribution, trade in raw materials and the manufacture and sale of rubber products.

Secretary-General: Dr. Stephen V. Evans

International Rubber Study Group, 111 North Bridge Road, 23-06 Peninsula Plaza, Singapore 179098, Singapore. Tel: +65 6837 2411, fax: +65 6339 4369, e-mail: irsg@rubberstudy.com, URL: http://www.rubberstudy.com

INTERNATIONAL SUGAR ORGANIZATION

Provides a forum for intergovernmental consultations on sugar and on ways to improve the world sugar economy and facilitates trade by collecting and providing information on the world sugar market and other sweeteners.

Executive Director: Dr. Peter Baron (page 1383)

International Sugar Organization, 1 Canada Square, Canary Wharf, London E14 5AA, UK. Tel: +44 (0)20 7513 1144, fax: +44 (0)20 7513 1146, e-mail: exdir@isosugar.org, URL: http://www.isosugar.org

INTERNATIONAL TEA COMMITTEE

A statistical and information centre partly funded by several producing and consuming tea board associations.

Chairman: M. J. Bunston

International Tea Committee, 1 Carlton House Terrace, London SW1Y 5DB, UK. Tel: +44 (0)20 7839 5090, e-mail: info@inttea.com, URL: http://www.inttea.com

INTERNATIONAL TEXTILE MANUFACTURERS FEDERATION (ITMF)

A global forum for discussion of matters within the common interest and concern of textile companies.

President: Bashir H. Ali Mohammad (Pakistan)
Vice Presidents: Josué C. Gomes da Silva (Brazil), Wang Tian Eai (China)
Treasurer: Bassem Sultan (Egypt)
Director General: Christian Schindler

International Textile Manufacturers Federation (ITMF), Wiedingstrasse 9, CH-8055 Zurich, Switzerland. Tel: +41 283 6380, fax: +41 283 6389, e-mail: secretariat@itmf.org, URL: http://www.itmf.org

INTERNATIONAL WOOL TEXTILE ORGANIZATION

Aims to maintain a permanent connection between the organisations in the wool textile industry and to represent the production, commerce and industry of wool textiles in all branches of international economic activity.

President: Peter Ackroyd

International Wool Textile Association, Rue de l'Industrie 4, 1000 Brussels, Belgium, Tel: +32 (0)2 505 4010, fax: +32 (0)2 503 4785, e-mail: info@iwto.org, URL: http://www.iwto.org

INVOLVEMENT AND PARTICIPATION ASSOCIATION (IPA)

An independent not-for-profit organisation, concerned specifically with the development of all forms of employee involvement, consultation and partnership at work.

President: Lord John Monks
Director: Nita Clarke

Involvement and Participation Association (IPA), 17-18 Britton Street, London, EC1M 5TP, UK. Tel: +44 (0)20 7880 6220, URL: http://www.ipa-involve.com

LONDON CHAMBER OF COMMERCE AND INDUSTRY

Provides support to the development of international and domestic trade. Established over 100 years ago, it is the largest membership organisation of its kind in the world.

President: Willie Walsh
Chief Executive: Colin Stanbridge

London Chamber of Commerce and Industry, 33 Queen Street, London EC4R 1AP, UK. Tel: +44 (0)20 7248 4444, fax: +44 (0)20 7489 0391, e-mail: lc@londonchamber.co.uk, URL: http://www.londonchamber.co.uk

PACIFIC BASIN ECONOMIC COUNCIL

Founded in 1967, the Pacific Basin Economic Council is an association of business leaders dedicated to expanding trade and investment in the region, supporting open markets to lower trade barriers and addressing emerging issues that are likely to shape the regional and global economies. The Pacific Basin Economic Council represents about 1,000 major corporations in 20 economies in the region, including China, Japan and the United States. Its member corporations account for more than US$4 trillion in global sales and they employ more than 10 million people.

Interim Chairman: Warren Luke

PBEC International Secretariat, Room 1304, Wing On Centre, 111 Connaught Road Central, Hong Kong. Tel: +852 2815 6550, fax: +852 2545 0499, e-mail: info@pbec.org, URL: http://www.pbec.org

TEXTILE INSTITUTE

An international non-profit making association which aims to facilitate learning, recognise achievement, reward excellence and disseminate information within the texile and related industries. It has corporate and individual members in up to 80 countries.

World President: Andreas Weber CText FTI

Textile Institute, 1st Floor, St. James' Building, Oxford Street, Manchester, M1 6QF, Uk. Tel: +44 (0)161 237 1188, fax: +44 (0)161 236 1991, e-mail: tihq@textileinst.org.uk, URL: http://www.textileinstitute.org

US CHAMBER OF COMMERCE

The US Chamber is a non-profit membership organization representing the unified interests of US business before Congress, government agencies, and the courts. It represents over 3 million businesses of varying sizes, and many state and local chambers of commerce, business associations and American Chambers of Commerce abroad.

President and CEO: Thomas J. Donohue

US Chamber of Commerce, 1615 H Street NW, Washington DC 20062 - 2000, USA. Tel: +1 202 659 6000, fax: +1 202 463 5686, URL: http://www.uschamber.com

WORK FOUNDATION

A non-profit making organisation, offering new thinking, research and solutions to the challenge of making workplaces more effective, successful and fulfilling. Its 12,000 corporate members include industrial and commercial companies, central and local government departments, nationalized industries, trade unions and employers' associations. Lancaster University acquired the Work Foundation in 2010.

Executive Vice-Chair: Will Hutton

Work Foundation, 21 Palmer Street, London SW1H 0AD, UK. Tel: +44 (0)20 7976 3565, e-mail: contactcentre@theworkfoundation.com, URL: http://www.theworkfoundation.com

WORLD ASSOCIATION OF OPINION AND MARKETING RESEARCH PROFESSIONALS (ESOMAR)

ESOMAR's aim is to promote the value of market and opinion research in illuminating real issues and bringing about effective decision-making. ESOMAR creates and manages a programme of industry-specific and thematic conferences, publications and communications as well as advocating self-regulation and the worldwide code of practice.

President: Dieter Korczak

World Association of Opinion and Marketing Research Professionals (ESOMAR), Euroenter 2, 11th floor, Barbara Strozzilaan 384, 1083 HN Amsterdam, The Netherlands. Tel: +31 20 664 2141, fax: +31 20 664 2922, URL: http://www.esomar.org

WORLD ASSOCIATION OF TRAVEL AGENCIES (WATA)

A worldwide organisation of selected travel agencies dedicated to the enhancement of the professionalism and profitability of member agents through mutual cooperation and global networking. Its members are committed to the highest standards of business ethics and quality of service to clients.

President: Adel Zaki (Egypt)

World Association of Travel Agencies (WATA), Tranchepied 25, 1278 La Rippe, Switzerland. Tel: +41 (0)79 239 7279, fax: +41 (0)22 362 0753, e-mail: wata@wata.net, URL: http://www.wata.net

WORLD CUSTOMS ORGANIZATION

An independent intergovernmental body which aims to enhance the effectiveness and efficiency of customs administrations and assist them to contribute to national development goals, particularly in the areas of trade facilitation, revenue collection, community protection and supply chain security. It represents 177 customs administrations around the world that cover approximately 98 per cent of world trade.

Secretary General: Kunio Mikuriya (Japan)

World Customs Organization, 30 rue du Marché, B-1210 Brussels, Belgium. Tel: +32 (0)2 209 9211, fax: +32 (0)2 209 9292, URL: http://www.wcoomd.org

WORLD TRADE CENTERS ASSOCIATION (WTCA)

WTCA is a not-for-profit, non-political association dedicated to the establishment and effective operation of World Trade Centers as instruments for trade expansion.

Chairman: Ghazi Abu Nahl

World Trade Centers Association (WTCA), 420 Lexington Avenue, Suite 518, New York NY 10170, USA. Tel: +1 212 432 2604, e-mail: wtca@wtca.org, URL: http://www.wtca.org

Transport

AFRICAN AIRLINES ASSOCIATION (AFRAA)

Aims to promote the development of safe, reliable, economical and efficient air transport services to, from, within and through Africa and to study problems connected therein and fosters closer commercial and technical co-operation among African air transport enterprises.

Secretary General: Dr Elijah Chingosho

African Airlines Association (AFRAA), P.O. Box 20116, Nairobi 00200, Kenya. Tel: +254 20 232 0144, fax: +254 20 232 0148, e-mail: afraa@afraa.org, URL: http://www.afraa.org

AIRPORTS COUNCIL INTERNATIONAL (ACI)

ACI advances the interests of the world's airports and promotes professional excellence in airport management and operations.

Director General: Angela Gittens

Airports Council International (ACI), PO Box 16, 1215 Geneva 15, Switzerland. Tel: +41 (0)22 717 8585, fax: +41 (0)22 717 8888, e-mail: aci@aci.aero, URL: http://www.aci.aero

ARAB AIR CARRIERS ORGANIZATION (AACO)

Aims to promote the highest safety standards, provide a framework for a better economic environment for airline operations and promote high standards of consumer driven services.

Secretary General: Mr Abdul Wahab Teffaha

Arab Air Carriers Organization (AACO), P.O. Box 13-5468, Beirut, Lebanon. Tel: +961 1 861297, fax: +961 1 863168, e-mail: info@aaco.org, URL: http://www.aaco.org

ASSOCIATION OF ASIA PACIFIC AIRLINES (AAPA)

The primary purpose of AAPA is to serve as a trade association for international airlines based in the Asia Pacific region. The Association addresses a wide range of policy issues relating to commercial air transport.

Director General: Andrew Herdman

Association of Asia Pacific Airlines (AAPA), 9/F Kompleks Antarabangsa, Jalan Sultan Ismail, 50250 Kuala Lumpur, Malaysia. Tel: +603 2145 5600, fax: +603 2145 2500, e-mail: info@aapa.org.my, URL: http://www.aapairlines.org

BIMCO

BIMCO, the Baltic and International Maritime Council, aims to ensure that new initiatives for legislation are practical and justified and reflect the true state of shipping today. It advocates international rather than regional or national regulations, implemented on an equal basis in all states.

President: Yudhishthir Khatau

BIMCO, Bagsværdvej 161, 2880 Bagsværd, Denmark. Tel: +45 44 366800, fax: +45 44 366868, e-mail: mailbox@bimco.org, URL: http://www.bimco.org

EUROPEAN CIVIL AVIATION CONFERENCE (ECAC)

Aims to promote the continued development of a safe, efficient and sustainable European air transport system. In so doing, ECAC seeks to harmonise civil aviation policies and practices amongst its 44 Member States and promote understanding on policy matters between its Member States and other parts of the world.

Executive Secretary: Salvatore Sciacchitano

European Civil Aviation Conference (ECAC), 3 bis Villa Emile Bergerat, 92522 Neuilly sur Seine Cedex, France. Tel : +33 (0)1 46 41 85 44, fax : +33 (0)1 46 24 18 18, e-mail: info@ecac-ceac.org, URL: http://www.ecac.ceac.org

EUROPEAN CONFERENCE OF MINISTERS OF TRANSPORT (ECMT)

International Transport Forum, formerly the European Conference of Ministers of Transport (ECMT), is an inter-governmental organisation with 52 member countries. Its aim is to help shape the transport policy agenda world wide and to act as as a think tank for transport policy.

Secretary General: Carole Coune

International Transport Forum, 2 rue André Pascal, F-75775 Paris Cedex 16, France. Tel: +33 (0)1 45 24 97 10, fax: +33 (0)1 45 24 97 42, e-mail: itf.contact@oecd.org, URL: http://www.internationaltransportforum.org/

EUROPEAN ORGANISATION FOR THE SAFETY OF AIR NAVIGATION (EUROCONTROL)

Develops, coordinates and plans for implementation of short-, medium- and long-term pan-European air traffic management strategies and their associated action plans in a collective effort involving national authorities, air navigation service providers, civil and military airspace users, airports, industry, professional organisations and relevant European institutions. There are 39 member states.

Director General: David McMillan

European Organisation for the Safety of Air Navigation (EUROCONTROL), 96 Rue de la Fusée, B-1130 Brussels, Belgium. Tel: +32 (0)2 729 3501, fax: +32 (0)2 729 9100, URL: http://www.eurocontrol.int

INTERGOVERNMENTAL ORGANISATION FOR INTERNATIONAL CARRIAGE BY RAIL (OTIF)

Aims to establish and develop uniform system of law in the following areas: contracts of carriage for the international carriage of passengers and goods (CIV and CIM), carriage of dangerous goods (RID), contracts of use of vehicles (CUV), contract on the use of railway infrastructure (CUI), validation of technical standards and adoption of uniform technical prescriptions for railway material (APTU), procedure for the technical admission of railway vehicles and other railway material used in international traffic (ATMF).

Secretary General: Stefan Schimming

Intergovernmental Organisation for International Carriage by Rail (OTIF), Gryphenhübeliweg 30, CH - 3006 Berne, Switzerland. Tel: + 41 (0)31 359 1010, fax: + 41 (0)31 359 1011, e-mail: info@otif.org, URL: http://www.otif.org

INTERNATIONAL AIR TRANSPORT ASSOCIATION (IATA)

IATA's mission is to lead, represent and serve the air transport industry. IATA seeks to improve understanding of the industry among decision makers and increase awareness of the benefits that aviation brings to national and global economies. IATA also works to improve the safety, security and efficiency of this critical industry.

Director General: vacant

International Air Transport Association (IATA), 33 Route de l'Aeroport, PO Box 416, Geneva - 15 Airport, Switzerland. Tel: +41 (0)22 770 2525, fax: +41 (0)22 798 3553, e-mail: corpcomms@iata.org, URL: http://www.iata.org

INTERNATIONAL ASSOCIATION OF PORTS AND HARBOURS (IAPH)

Its principal objective is to develop and foster good relations and cooperation among all ports and harbors in the world by proving a forum to exchange opinions and share experiences on the latest trends of port management and operations.

Secretary General: Susumu Naruse

International Association of Ports and Harbours (IAPH), 7th Floor, South Tower New Pier Takeshiba, 1-16-1 Kaigan, Minato-ku, Tokyo 105-0022, Japan. Tel: +81 3 5403 2770, fax: +81 3 5403 7651, e-mail: info@iaphworldports.org, URL: http://www.iaphworldports.org

OTHER INTERNATIONAL AND NATIONAL ORGANISATIONS

INTERNATIONAL ASSOCIATION OF PUBLIC TRANSPORT (UITP)

UITP works to mobilise political will with its sound evidence, and to create a favourable climate for the sector and to defend the interests of public transport. UITP represents the entire mobility market.

Secretary General: Hans Rat

International Association of Public Transport (UITP), Rue Sainte-Marie 6 (Quai de Charbonnages), B-1080 Brussels, Belgium. Tel: +32 (0)2 673 6100, fax: +32 (0)2 660 1072, e-mail: hans.rat@uitp.org, URL: http://www.uitp.org

INTERNATIONAL CONTAINER BUREAU

The BIC is the international organization elected by the International Organization for Standardization (ISO) and the World Customs Organization (WCO) as the official registrar office for the attribution and the protection of the owner codes used to identify containers in the International Trade.

Secretary General: Bertrand Geoffray

International Container Bureau, 38 rue des Blancs Manteaux, 75004 Paris, France. Tel: +33 (0)1 47 66 03 90, fax: +33 (0)1 47 66 08 91, e-mail: bic@bic-code.org, URL: http://www.bic-code.org

INTERNATIONAL FEDERATION OF FREIGHT FORWARDERS ASSOCIATIONS (FIATA)

Aims to unite the freight forwarding industry worldwide; represent, promote and protect the interests of the industry by participating as advisors or experts in meetings of international bodies dealing with transportation and; familiarise trade and industry and the public at large with the services rendered by freight forwarders.

Director General: Marco Sangaletti

International Federation of Freight Forwarders Associations (FIATA), Schaffhauserstr. 104, P.O. Box 364, CH-8152 Glattbrugg, Switzerland. Tel: +41 43 211 6500, fax: +41 43 211 6565, e-mail: info@fiata.com, URL: http://www.fiata.com

INTERNATIONAL RAILWAY TRANSPORT COMMITTEE (CIT)

A federation of railway and shipping companies. CIT forms the interface of the railways between transport law and practical application.

President: Jean-Luc Dufournaud

International Railway Transport Committee (CIT), Weltpoststrasse 20, CH-3015 Bern, Switzerland. Tel: +41 (0)31 350 0190, fax: +41 (0)31 350 0199, e-mail: info@cit-rail.org, URL: http://www.cit-rail.org

INTERNATIONAL ROAD FEDERATION

An international, non-profit making organisation whose objective is to encourage better road and transportation systems worldwide and to help apply technology and management practices to attain maximum economic and social returns from national road investments.

International Road Federation, 2 chemin de Blandonnet, 1214 Vernier, Geneva, Switzerland. Tel: +41 (0) 22 306 0260, fax: +41 (0) 22 306 0270, e-mail: info@irfnet.org, URL: http://www.irfnet.org

INTERNATIONAL ROAD SAFETY ORGANISATION (PRI)

PRI devotes itself to place and to keep road safety high on the political and public agenda and to encourage safe behaviour. The key tasks of PRI are raising awareness for road safety, lobbying decision makers, transferring knowledge from its members on education and communication and mobilizing public support. There are more than 55 members in 45 countries.

President: Joop Goos (Netherlands)

International Road Safety Organisation (PRI) (La Prevention Routière Internationale), Rietgors 1, 3755 GA Eemnes, The Netherlands. Tel: +216 98 90 87 58, fax: +216 71 35 45 78, e-mail: contact@lapri.org, URL: http://www.lapri.org

INTERNATIONAL ROAD TRANSPORT UNION (IRU)

The IRU, through its national associations, represents the entire road transport industry world-wide. It speaks for the operators of coaches, taxis and trucks, from large transport fleets to driver-owners. In all international bodies that make decisions affecting road transport, the IRU acts as the industry's advocate.

President: Janusz Lacny
Secretary General: Martin Marmy

International Road Transport Union (IRU), 3 rue de Varembé, BP 44, 1211 Geneva 20, Switzerland. Tel: +41 (0)22 918 2700, fax: +41 (0)22 918 2741, e-mail: iru@iru.org, URL: http://www.iru.org

INTERNATIONAL UNION OF RAILWAYS (UIC)

A world-wide organisation for international cooperation among railways and the promotion of rail transport which aims to meet the challenges of mobility and sustainability. The organisation includes 200 members across five continents.

Chairman: Yoshio Ishida
Director-General: Jean-Pierre Loubinoux

International Union of Railways (UIC), 16 rue Jean Rey, 75105 Paris, France. Tel +33 (0)1 44 49 20 20, fax: +33 (0)1 44 49 20 29, e-mail: (surname)@uic.org, URL http://www.uic.org

NORDISK DEFENCE CLUB

A mutual freight, demurrage and defence club whose membership is comprised of international shipowners and charterers worldwide.

Chairman: Nils Dyvik

Nordisk Defence Club, Kristinelundveien 22, P.O. Box 3033 Elisenberg, 0207 Oslo, Norway. Tel: +47 22 135600, fax: +47 22 430035, e-mail: post@nordisk.no, URL: http://www.nordisk.no

UNIFE (THE ASSOCIATION OF THE EUROPEAN RAIL INDUSTRY)

UNIFE's mission is to enhance the competitiveness of the railway industry and promote the development of rail as the preferred mode of transportation in Europe and beyond.

Director General: Philippe Citroën

UNIFE (The Association of the European Rail Industry), 221 Avenue Louise (Bte 11), B-1050 Brussels, Belgium. Tel: +32 (0)2 626 1260, fax: +32 (0)2 626 1261, e-mail: unife@unife.org, URL: http://www.unife.org

WORLD AIRLINES CLUBS ASSOCIATION (WACA)

Aims to unite, coordinate, advise and arbitrate the activities of the airlines/interlines clubs throughout the world; publicise, encourage, promote and extend the Airlines/Interlines clubs movement; and unite the members of the Airlines/Interline Clubs in friendship, good fellowship and mutual understanding.

President: Maga Ramasamy

World Airlines Clubs Association (WACA), 800 Place Victoria, PO Box 113, Montreal, Quebec H4Z 1M1, Canada. Tel: +1 514 874 0202 (ext 3243), fax: +1 514 874 1753, e-mail: info@waca.org, URL: http://www.waca.org

Welfare & Human Rights

AMNESTY INTERNATIONAL

A worldwide movement of more than 3 million supporters, members and activists who campaign for internationally recognised human rights as enshrined in the Universal Declaration of Human Rights. The organisations stated mission is to conduct research and generate action to prevent and end grave abuses of human rights and to demand justice for those whose rights have been violated.

Secretary-General: Salil Shetty (page 1514)

Amnesty International Secretariat, Peter Benenson House, 1 Easton Street, London, WC1X 0DW, UK. Tel: +44 (0)20 7413 5500, fax: +44 (0)20 7956 1157, e-mail: amnestyis@amnesty.org, URL: http://www.amnesty.org

ANTI-SLAVERY INTERNATIONAL

Works at local, national and international levels to eliminate the system of slavery around the world by: urging governments of countries with slavery to develop and implement measures to end it; lobbying governments and intergovernmental agencies to make slavery a priority issue; and educating the public about the realities of slavery and campaigning for its end.

Director: Aidan McQuade

Anti-Slavery International, Thomas Clarkson House, The Stableyard, Broomgrove Road, London SW9 9TL, UK. Tel: +44 (0)20 7501 8920, fax: +44 (0)20 7738 4110, e-mail: info@antislavery.org, URL: http://www.antislavery.org

ASSOCIATION FOR WOMEN'S RIGHTS IN DEVELOPMENT

The Association for Women's Rights in Development (AWID) is an international organisation. It is committed to achieving gender equality, sustainable development and women's human rights through support of women's rights advocates, organizations and movements internationally which exist to advance the rights of women.

President: Lina Abou-Habib

Association for Women's Rights in Development, 215 Spadina Ave, Suite 150, Toronto, Ontario, M5T 2C7, Canada. Tel: +1 416 594 3773, fax: +1 416 594 0330, e-mail: contact@awid.org, URL: http://www.awid.org

ASSOCIATION FRANÇOIS-XAVIER BAGNOUD

Association François-Xavier Bagnoud (FXB International) is an international organization that aims to provide support to children affected by theAIDS pandemic and poverty. Children in extreme poverty and those who have been left orphaned and vulnerable by AIDS are best supported FXB in sustainable communities.

One of the main projects of FXB are the FXB villages which are home to around 500 people, mainly children. The villages exist to support individuals and teach them skills which ultimately mean they will become physically, financially and socially independent.

FXB has projects running in China, India, Myanmar, Thailand, Burundi, Rwanda, South Africa, Uganda, Brazil, Colombia, Uruguay and Switzerland.

Interim CEO: Lydia Clemmons

Association François-Xavier Bagnoud, 44, rue de Lausanne, 1201 Geneva, Switzerland. Tel.: +41 (0)22 741 0030, fax: +41 (0)22 731 1757, e-mail: info@fxb.org, URL: http://www.fxb.org

ASSOCIATION INTERNATIONALE DE LA MUTUALITÉ (AIM)

A grouping of autonomous health insurance and social protection bodies acting as the member's link to governments, non-governmental organisations and stakeholders in the field of social and health services and as the spokesman of the health and social mutual societies.

President: Mr Willi Budde

Association Internationale de la Mutualité (AIM), 50 rue d'Arlon, B-1000 Brussels, Belgium. Tel + 32 (0)2 234 5700, fax + 32 (0)2 234 5708, e-mail: aim.secretariat@aim-mutual.org, URL: http://www.aim-mutual.org

BRITISH HELSINKI HUMAN RIGHTS GROUP

The British Helsinki Human Rights Group is a non-governmental organization which monitors human rights in the 56 participating States of the Organization for Security and Co-operation in Europe (OSCE). It is not affiliated to the Helsinki Committee for Human Rights. Amongs its activities are the Monitoring the conduct of elections in OSCE member states; Examining issues relating to press freedom and freedom of speech; Reporting on conditions in prisons and psychiatric institutions; Covering asylum and immigration issues.

The British Helsinki Human Rights Group, URL: http://www.bhhrg.org

BUSINESS AND HUMAN RIGHTS RESOURCE CENTRE

The Business and Human Rights Resource Centre is an independent non profit resource covering business and human rights. Balance is sought through dialogue which is encouraged with companies over allegations of misconduct. The website covers 180 countries and topics discussed include discrimination, environment, poverty and development, labour, access to medicines, health and safety, security, and trade.

Director: Christopher Avery

Business and Human Rights Resource Centre, 1-3 Charlotte Street, 3rd floor, London W1T 1RD, United Kingdom. Tel: +44 (020) 7636-7774, fax: +44 (020) 7636-7775, URL: http://www.business-humanrights.org

CARTER CENTER

The Carter Center, was founded by former US president Jimmy Carter in 1982. It is in partnership with Emory University, and aims to advance human rights, alleviate unnecessary human suffering and improve the quality of life for people in more than 70 countries. It also aims to prevent and resolve conflicts, enhance freedom and democracy, and improve health.

The Center is a non-partisan organisation and acts as a neutral in dispute resolution activities.

Founder and Trustee: Jimmy Carter
President and CEO: John Hardman, MD

The Carter Center, One Copenhill, 453 Freedom Parkway, Atlanta, GA 30307, USA. E-mail: carterweb@emory.edu. URL: http://www.cartercenter.org

CENTER FOR ECONOMIC AND SOCIAL RIGHTS (CESR)

The Center for Economic and Social Rights (CESR) aims to promote social justice through human rights guaranteeing the right to education, health, food, water, housing, work, and other economic, social and cultural rights essential to human dignity.

Executive Director: Ignacio Saiz

Center for Economic and Social Rights, Fuencarral, 158-1ºA, 28010 Madrid, Spain. Tel: +34 91 448 3971, fax: +34 91 448 3980, E-mail: rights@cesr.org URL: http://www.cesr.org

CENTER FOR GENDER AND REFUGEE STUDIES

The Center for Gender and Refugee Studies (CGRS) was set up to protect the basic human rights of refugee women and girls by advancing gender-sensitive asylum laws, as well as helping and raising awareness of women in need of protection

CGRS is actively involved in scholarly research, policy work, and impact litigation, as well as carrying out research and advocacy initiatives around human rights violations in specific countries.

Director: Karen Musalo

Center for Gender & Refugee Studies, University of California, Hastings College of the Law, 200 McAllister Street, San Francisco, CA 94102, USA. Tel: +1 415 565 4877, URL: http://cgrs.uchastings.edu

CENTER FOR HUMAN RIGHTS AND GLOBAL JUSTICE

The Center for Human Rights and Global Justice was established at the New York University School of Law to bring together teaching, research, clinical, internship, and publishing activities undertaken within the Law School on issues relating to international human rights law. Amongst its stated aims are: Generate substantive, cutting-edge and sophisticated contributions to human rights research and legal scholarship on the part of faculty, staff, students, fellows and visitors; and actively engage in public affairs and make original and constructive contributions to on-going policy debates relating to human rights.

Faculty Directors and Co-Chairs: Philip Alston, Ryan Goodman

Center for Human Rights and Global Justice, New York University School of Law, 110 West Third Street, Room 204, New York, NY 10012, USA. Tel: +1 212 998 6714, fax: +1 212 995 4646, e-mail: law.chrgj@nyu.edu, URL: http://www.chrgj.org

CENTER FOR HUMAN RIGHTS AND HUMANITARIAN LAW

The Center for Human Rights and Humanitarian Law was established in 1990 by Washington College of Law to work with students, faculty and the international legal community to provide scholarship and support for human rights initiatives around the world.

The Center is committed to creating opportunities for students in the field human rights through training, complementary education, workshops and conferences as well as research and publications. Current programs include the Academy for Human Rights and Humanitarian Law, the War Crimes Research Office, the Inter-American Human Rights Moot Court Competition, and the Human Rights Brief.

Executive Director: Hadar Harris

The Center for Human Rights and Humanitarian Law, 4801 Massachusetts Ave, NW, Washington, DC 20016-8187, USA. Tel: +1 202 274 4180, fax; +1 202 274 0783, e-mail: humlaw@wcl.american.edu. URL: http://www.wcl.american.edu/humright/center/

CENTER FOR HUMAN RIGHTS AND THE ENVIRONMENT (CEDHA)

The Center for Human Rights and Environment (CEDHA) was established in 1999 and is a non-profit organization. CEDHA seeks to find a better relationship between the environment and people. It works to guarantee human rights for victims of environmental degradation, or due to non-sustainable management of natural resources, and to prevent future violations. CEDHA is working towards the creation of inclusive public policy that promotes inclusive socially and environmentally sustainable development, this can be achieved through community participation and public interest litigation.

Honourary President: Romina Picolotti

Center for Human Rights and the Environment (CEDHA), General Paz, 186 - 7mo. Piso, "A", X5000JLO Córdoba, Argentina. Tel: + 54 351 425 6278. E-mail: cedha@cedha.org.ar. URL: http://www.cedha.org.ar

CENTER FOR MIGRATION STUDIES

The Center for Migration Studies of New York (CMS) was founded in 1964 and is a non-profit organization. It exists to provide research and a forum for debate on international migration.

Executive Director: Mr René Manenti

Center for Migration Studies, 27 Carmine Street, New York, NY 10014-4423, USA. Tel: +1 212 675 3993. Fax: +1 212 255 1771. E-mail: cms@cmsny.org. URL: http://cmsny.org

CENTER FOR VICTIMS OF TORTURE

The Center for Victims of Torture (CVT) is a private, nonprofit, organisation that was founded in 1985. Its headquarters are in Minneapolis, Minnesota. The organisation also has a base in Washington, D.C., and operates centres in Jordan, Sierra Leone and the Democratic Republic of Congo.

OTHER INTERNATIONAL AND NATIONAL ORGANISATIONS

CVT's stated mission is to heal the wounds of torture on individuals, their families and their communities and to stop torture worldwide.

Executive Director: Douglas A. Johnson, MPPM

Center for Victims of Torture, 717 E. River Parkway, Minneapolis, MN 55455, USA. Tel: +1 612 436 4800, e-mail: cvt@cvt.org, URL: http://www.cvt.org

CENTRE ON HOUSING RIGHTS AND EVICTIONS

The Centre on Housing Rights and Evictions (COHRE) is a non-governmental, not-for-profit human rights organisation which was established in 1994 in the Netherlands. Its focus is on the human right to housing and on forced evictions at the international level. COHRE works with partner organisations and community activists around the world.

COHRE's stated objectives are: Promoting the full enjoyment of the human right to adequate housing for everyone, everywhere; Preventing forced evictions and securing restitution or compensation where evictions cannot be prevented; Protecting the housing rights of vulnerable, disadvantaged and threatened groups and communities throughout the world; Fostering tolerance, social justice, equality and mutual respect for all; Strengthening popular education and awareness of international housing rights standards and the role these can and should play at the local and international levels.

Chairperson: John Packer

COHRE, 83, rue de Montbrillant, 1202 Geneva, Switzerland. E-mail: cohre@cohre.org. URL: http://www.cohre.org

CHILD RIGHTS INFORMATION NETWORK

The organisation works towards ensuring that each child can enjoy all of the human rights promised by the United Nations, regional organisations, and national governments. CRIN provides information services and publications to child rights professionals and children.

Director: Veronica Yates

Child Rights Information Network (CRIN), East Studio, 2, Pontypool Place, London, SE1 8QF, United Kingdom. Tel: +44 20 7401 2257, e-mail: info@crin.org, URL: http://www.crin.org/contact/contact.asp

CHILD SOLDIERS INTERNATIONAL

Works to prevent the recruitment and use of children as soldiers, to secure their demobilization and to ensure their rehabilitation and reintegration into society. Its main activities are research and monitoring, advocacy and capacity building.

Chair, Board of Trustees: Demelza Hauser

Child Soldiers International, 9, Marshalsea Road, London SE1 1EP, UK. Tel: +44 (0) 207 367 4110 fax: +44 (0) 207 367 4129, email: info@child-soldiers.org, URL: http://www.child-soldiers.org

CHILDREN IN CRISIS

Children in Crisis was established in 1993 in the UK to give children in some of the world's poorest countries the education they need to transform their lives. In its overseas programmes Children in Crisis works in partnership with local organisations to provide educational opportunities for vulnerable children.

Founder and Life President: The Duchess of York (page 1424)
President: Olivier de Givenchy

Children in Crisis, 206-208 Stewart's Road, London SW8 4UB, UK. Tel: +44 (0)20 7627 1040, fax +44 (0)20 7627 1050, e-mail: info@childrenincrisis.org, URL: http://www.childrenincrisis.org

CHILDWATCH INTERNATIONAL

The Childwatch International Research Network, founded in 1993, is a global, non-profit, non-governmental network of institutions that work together to promote children's rights and to improve child well being.

Childwatch International's states aims are: Promoting Child Rights through Child Research; Raise the profile of Child Research; Improve resources for child research; Building the Capacity of Child Research Institutions, through promoting: Collaborative research; Research relevant to local contexts.

President: Robbie Gilligan, Children's Research Centre, Trinity College, Dublin, Ireland

Childwatch International, P.O. Box 1132 Blindern, N-0317 OSLO, Norway. Tel: +47 22 85 43 50, fax: +47 22 85 50 28, e-mail: childwatch@uio.no, URL: http://www.childwatch.uio.no

CHRISTIAN AID

Christian Aid began its work in response to the needs of refugees in Europe during the Second World War. Today it is the official relief and development agency of 41 British and Irish Churches. Its vision is an end to poverty.

Director: Loretta Minghella OBE

Christian Aid, Inter-Church House, 35 Lower Marsh, London, SE1 7RL, UK. Tel: +44 (0)20 7620 4444, fax: +44 (0)20 7620 0719, e-mail: info@ christianaid.org, URL: http://www.christianaid.org.uk

CITIZENS FOR GLOBAL SOLUTIONS

Citizens for Global Solutions is an American based organisation that wants to educate regarding global inter-dependence and informing concerns of a global nature to relevant public figures.

The aims are to envision a future in which nations work together to abolish war, protect our rights and freedoms, and solve the problems facing humanity that no nation can solve alone. This vision requires effective democratic global institutions that will apply the rule of law while respecting the diversity and autonomy of national and local communities.

Chief Executive Officer: Don Kraus

Citizens for Global Solutions, 418 7th Street SE, Washington, DC 20003-2796, USA. Tel: +1 202 546 3950, fax: +1 202 546 3749. URL: http://www.globalsolutions.org

COMMONWEALTH HUMAN RIGHTS INITIATIVE

The Initiative was originally set up in London and is a non-partisan independent international non-governmental organisation.

Its stated mandate is to promote awareness of and adherence to the Harare Principles, the Universal Declaration of Human Rights and other internationally recognised human rights instruments and declarations made by the Commonwealth Heads of Governments as well as domestic instruments supporting human rights in the Commonwealth.

CHRI believes that the promotion and protection of human rights is the responsibility of governments but that the active participation of civil society acting in concert is vital to ensuring rule of law and the realisation of human rights.

Director: Maja Daruwala

Commonwealth Human Rights Initiative (CHRI), B-117, Second Floor, Sarvodaya Enclave,v New Delhi - 110 017, India. Tel: +91 11 2685 0523, fax: +91 11 2686 4688, e-mail: info@humanrightsinitiative.org, URL: http://www.humanrightsinitiative.org/

DECEMBER 18

December 18 is a non-profit organization working for the promotion and protection of the rights of migrants worldwide. The organisation gets its name from the day when the General Assembly of the United Nations adopted the "International Convention on the Rights of All Migrant Workers and Members of their Families". The18th of December is also now known as International Migrants Day.

December 18 stated aims are to: advocate for a world where migrants are not discriminated against because of their sex, race, colour, language, religion or conviction, political or other opinion, national, ethnic or social origin, nationality, age, economic position, property, marital status, birth or any other status. A world that understands and accepts migration as normal and takes place within a framework that applies universal human rights norms and standards to all migrants and members of their families.

The mission of December 18 is to promote the protection of the rights of migrants worldwide. Our goal is to ensure that the human rights of all migrants are known, recognized and protected effectively, and that an environment is created for migrants to be full participants in any society. We promote an approach to migration policies that is based on existing international and regional human rights instruments and mechanisms.

Director: René Plaetevoet

December 18, 323 Rue du Progrès, 1030 Brussels, Belgium. Tel: +32 (0)2 274 1435, fax: +32 (0)2 274 1438. E-mail: info@december18.net. URL: http://www.december18.net

DEFENCE FOR CHILDREN INTERNATIONAL

Defence for Children International (DCI) was founded in 1979 , the International Year of the Child, and is an independent non-governmental organisation that aims to promote and protect children's rights on a global, regional, national and local level.

Defence for Children International, Rue de Varembé 1, Case Postale 88, Geneva 20, CH-1211, Switzerland. Tel: +41 22 734 0558, fax: +41 22 740 1145, e-mail: info@dci-is.org. URL: http://www.defenceforchildren.org

DISABLED PEOPLES' INTERNATIONAL

The Disabled Peoples' International (DPI) is a network of national organizations and assemblies of disabled people. The organisation was established to promote human rights of disabled people through full participation, equal opportunities and development.

The stated goals of the DPI are to promote the human rights of disabled persons; promote economic and social integration of disabled persons; develop and support organizations of disabled persons.

The network currently covers Africa, Asia/Pacific, Caribbean, Europe & Latin America. Within 2012 it will expand to cover ten countries within the Arab region.

DPI Chairperson: Wilfred Guzman Jara

Disabled Peoples' International, 874 Topsail Road, Mount Pearl, Newfoundland, A1N 3J9, Canada. Tel: +1 709 747 7600, fax: 709 747 7603, e-mail: info@dpi.org, URL: http://v1.dpi.org

EARTHRIGHTS INTERNATIONAL

EarthRights International (ERI) is a non-governmental, non-profit organisation which seeks to combine the power of law and the power of people in defence of earth rights. Its stated aims are: fact-finding, legal actions against perpetrators of earth rights abuses, training grassroots and community leaders, and advocacy campaigns. Through these strategies, ERI seeks to end earth rights abuses, to provide real solutions for real people, and to promote and protect human rights and the environment in the communities where ERI works.

Co-Founder and Executive Director: Ka Hsaw Wa

Earthrights International, Washington Office, 1612 K Street, NW, Suite 40, Washington, DC 20006, USA. Tel:. +1 202 466 5188, e-mail: infousa@earthrights.org, URL: http://www.earthrights.org

EQUALITY NOW

Equality Now was founded in 1992 and works to promote and protect the human rights of women everywhere. Its stated aims are to take action to protest these violations against women and bring to public attention human rights violations against women. The Women's Action Network is committed to voicing a worldwide call for justice and equality for women. Issues of urgent concern to Equality Now include rape, domestic violence, reproductive rights, trafficking of women, female genital mutilation, and the denial of equal access to economic opportunity and political participation.

Executive Director: Taina Bien-Aimé

Equality Now, PO Box 20646, Columbus Circle Station, New York, NY 10023, USA. E-mail: info@equalitynow.org, URL: http://www.equalitynow.org.
Equality Now Africa Regional Office, PO Box 2018, 00202 Nairobi, Kenya, Tel: +254 20 271 9913/9832, e-mail: equalitynownairobi@equalitynow.org

EUROPEAN COURT OF HUMAN RIGHTS

See entry for European Court of Human Rights and also entry for Council of Europe in the Inter-Governmental Organisations section.

FOUNDATION FOR INTERNATIONAL ENVIRONMENTAL LAW AND DEVELOPMENT (FIELD)

Created in 1989, the Foundation for International Environmental Law and Development is a non-profit charity consisting of a group of international lawyers who assist communities in their negotiations for fairer international environmental laws. Working with local partners, NGOs and institutions, the organisation aims to protect the environment and promote sustainable development, through campaigns, research and legal intervention.

Director: Joy Hyvarinen

Foundation for International Environmental Law and Development, 3 Endsleigh Street, London WC1H 0DD, United Kingdom. Tel: +44 020 7872 7200, fax: +44 (0)20 7388 2826, URL: http://www.field.org.uk/

GENOCIDE WATCH

Genocide Watch is the co-ordinator of the International Alliance to End Genocide. The stated mission of the organisation is to predict, prevent, stop and punish genocide and other forms of mass murder. It seeks to raise awareness and influence public policy concerning potential and actual genocide. The purpose is to build an international movement to prevent and stop genocide.

President: Dr. Gregory H Stanton

Genocide Watch, P.O. Box 809, Washington, D.C. 20044 USA. Tel: +1703 448 0222, e-mail: genocidewatch@aol.com, URL: http://www.genocidewatch.org

GLOBAL RIGHTS

Global Rights: Partners for Justice, works to assist foreign advocates and groups with their domestic human rights abuses. Its stated mission is that the organisation is a human rights advocacy group that partners with local activists to challenge injustice and amplify new voices within the global discourse. It has offices in countries around the world, that help local activists create just societies through proven strategies for effecting change. It seek justice for victims of human rights abuses. It works to promote racial and gender equality and help people and communities feel empowered to change their societies. It works on the ground, over extended periods of time, partnering with local human rights advocates to strengthen their effectiveness in combating abuses in their countries. It focuses on developing the skills of local activists that are essential to addressing human rights concerns and promoting justice such as: documenting and exposing abuses, conducting community education and mobilization, advocating legal and policy reform in countries and internationally, and using the courts to increase access to justice for disadvantaged populations. It helps local activists to engage with the international community, including the United Nations, to further their human rights objectives at home.

Interim Executive Director: Susan Farnsworth

Global Rights, 1200 18th Street NW, Suite 602, Washington, DC 20036, USA. Tel: +1 202 822 4600. URL: http://www.globalrights.org

HUMAN RIGHTS FIRST

Human Rights First is an independent non-profit, non-partisan international human rights organisation. The organisation works to build respect for human rights as well as the rule of law to promote dignity to which everyone is entitled.

Among the projects it is engaged in are: Crimes Against Humanity; Fighting Discrimination: Human Rights Defenders; Refugee Protection; Law and Society.

President and CEO: Elisa Massimino

Human Rights First, 333 Seventh Avenue, 13th Floor, New York, NY 10001-5108, USA: Tel: +1 212 845 5200, fax: +1 212 845 5299. URL: http://www.humanrightsfirst.org

HUMAN RIGHTS WATCH

An organisation which aims to prevent discrimination, uphold political freedom, protect people from inhumane conduct in wartime and bring offenders to justice.

Executive Director: Kenneth Roth

Human Rights Watch, 350 Fifth Avenue, 34th Floor, New York, NY 10118-3299, USA. Tel: +1 212 290 4700, fax: +1 212 736 1300, e-mail: hrwny@hrw.org, URL: http://www.hrw.org

ICARE

ICare was founded in 1999 to provide a portal for anti-racism on the internet. ICare's stated purpose is to provide a virtual network to support and to be used by those who are committed to improving universal human rights standards and particularly non-discrimination principles. ICARE is the information-disseminator for the European NGO-community working in the fields of anti-discrimination, human rights, anti-semitism, diversity and migration, with a focus on anti-racism. ICARE is a NGO community networking system, an environment where large and small organizations can work on local, national, regional and international issues. The purpose of ICARE is the empowerment of democratic, non-violent Human Rights and antiracism work by offering information and reporting on events taking place, by facilitating communication, advocacy, campaigns and actions and by stimulating intersectional and international co-operation of NGOs. ICARE is a Magenta Foundation project.

ICare: Internet Centre Anti Racism Europe: E-mail: info@icare.to, URL: http://www.icare.to

INCLUSION EUROPE

A non-profit organisation that campaigns for the rights and interests of people with intellectual disabilities and their families throughout Europe. Respect, solidarity and inclusion are the fundamental values of the movement.

Secretary General: Ivo Vykydal

Inclusion Europe, Galeries de la Toison d'Or, 29 Chaussée d'Ixelles, B-1050 Brussels, Belgium. Tel.: +32 (0)2 502 2815, fax: +32 (0)2 502 8010, e-mail : secretariat@inclusion-europe.org, URL: http://www.inclusion-europe.org

INSTITUTE FOR DEMOCRACY AND HUMAN RIGHTS

The Institute for Democracy and Human Rights (IDHR) is an independent non-governmental organizsation founded in 1999.

The stated mission of the IDHR is to contribute to the development of democratic statehood based on the principles of human rights and social justice. It believes that this is the prerequisite for Armenians, as individuals and as a collective, to develop free, dignified, and prosperous lives full of opportunity for human development.

President, Head of Operations: Arpineh Galfayan

Institute for Democracy and Human Rights, Aygedzor Str. 4/1, Yerevan 0019, Armenia. Tel:(+374 1026 4712. E-mail: info@idhr.am. URL: http://www.idhr.am

INSTITUTE OF RACE RELATIONS

The Institute of Race Relations (IRR) was established as an independent educational charity in 1958 to carry out research, publish and collect resources on race relations throughout the world. Today, the IRR leads research and analysis of the struggle for racial justice in Britain, Europe and internationally.

Institute of Race Relations, 2-6 Leeke Street, London WC1X 9HS, United Kingdom. Tel: +44 (0)20 7837 0041, fax: +44 (0)20 7278 0623, e-mail: info@irr.org.uk, URL: http://www.irr.org.uk

INTER-AMERICAN CHILDREN'S INSTITUTE (IIN)

The IIN is a specialized agency of the OAS working to help children and adolescents and to promote their rights and a better quality of life.

Director General: Maria de los Dolores Aguilar Marmolejo

OTHER INTERNATIONAL AND NATIONAL ORGANISATIONS

Inter-American Children's Institute (Instituto Interamericano del Nino, la Nina y Adolescentes) (IIN), Av. de Octobre 2904, Casilla de Correo 16212, Montevideo 11600, Uruguay. Tel: +598 2487 2150, fax: +598 2487 3242, e-mail: iin@iinoea.org, URL: http://www.iin.oea.org

INTER-AMERICAN COMMISSION OF WOMEN (CIM)

Established in 1928, the CIM was the first inter-governmental agency established to promote women's rights and gender equality. It is a specialized agency of the Organization of American States. Each of the OAS member states designates a delegate. They meet every three years during the Assembly of Delegates.

Executive Secretary: Carmen Moreno Toscano (page 1480)

Inter-American Commission of Women, 1889 F. Street, N.W. Washington, DC 20006, USA. URL: http://www.oas.org/en/cim/

INTERNATIONAL ASSOCIATION FOR SUICIDE PREVENTION (IASP)

IASP provides a forum for national and local suicide prevention organizations, researchers, volunteers, clinicians and professionals to share knowledge provide support and collaborate in suicide prevention around the world.

President: Lanny Berman, Ph.D.
General Secretary: Dr Tony Davis

International Association for Suicide Prevention (IASP), Canterbury Suicide Project, University of Otago, Christchurch, P.O Box 4345, Christchurch, New Zealand. Tel: +61 (3) 3720 408, fax: +61 (3) 3720 407 e-mail: znnette.beautrais@chmeds.ac.nz URL: http://www.iasp.info

INTERNATIONAL ASSOCIATION OF CHILDREN'S INTERNATIONAL SUMMER VILLAGES (CISV)

A global community of volunteers creating opportunities for all ages to experience the excitement and enrichment of cultural diversity through educational programmes. Founded on the belief that peace is possible through friendship - and that the real difference can be made by starting with children.

International Association of Children's International Summer Villages (CISV), MEA House, Ellison Place, Newcastle upon Tyne NE1 8XS, UK. Tel: +44-(0)191 232 4998, fax: +44 (0)191 261 4710, e-mail: international@cisv.org, URL: http://www.cisv.org

INTERNATIONAL ASSOCIATION OF SCHOOLS OF SOCIAL WORK (IASSW)

IASSW promotes the development of social work education throughout the world, develops standards to enhance quality of social work education, encourages international exchange, provides forums for sharing social work research and scholarship, and promotes human rights and social development through policy and advocacy activities.

President: Angelina Yuen Tsang

International Association of Schools of Social Work (IASSW), c/o Graduate School of Social Work, Addis Ababa University, PO Box 1176, Ethiopia. Tel: +251 11 123 1084, fax: +251 11 123 9768, e-mail: abyetas@aau.edu.et, URL: http://www.iassw-aiets.org

INTERNATIONAL ASSOCIATION OF SOCIAL EDUCATORS (AIEJI)

Aims to: unite social educators from all countries and promote quality practice that seeks to ensure the best for people served by the profession and; encourage the richness of diversity by promoting the working together of people of different backgrounds and cultures through the international membership of AIEJI.

General Secretary: Lars Steinov

International Association of Social Educators (AIEJI), 22 rue Halévy, 59000 Lille, France. URL: http://www.aieji.net

INTERNATIONAL CIVIL DEFENCE ORGANISATION (ICDO)

Aims to develop partnerships between potential donors of civil defence equipment and design and implement training programmes for civil protection in all matters concerning population protection and the safeguard of property and the environment in case of disaster.

Secretary General: Nawaf B. Al Sleibi

International Civil Defence Organisation, ch. de Surville 10-12, 1213 Petit-Lancy, Geneva, Switzerland. Tel.: +41 (0)22 879 6969, fax: +41 (0)22 879 6979, e-mail: icdo@icdo.org, URL: http://www.icdo.org

INTERNATIONAL COMMISSION OF JURISTS

The International Commission of Jurists (ICJ) is made up of up to sixty lawyers who work to ensure respect for international human rights standards through the law. The commissioners are respected in their fields and known for their experience, knowledge and fundamental commitment to human rights. The composition of the Commission aims to reflect the geographical diversity of the world and its many legal systems. The ICJ has an impartial and objective appraoch to the protection and promotion of human rights through the rule of law.

President: Pedro Nikken

International Commission of Jurists, P.O. Box 91, 33 rue des Bains, 1211 Geneva 8, Switzerland. Tel: +41 22 979 3800, e-mail: info@icj.org, URL: http://www.icj.org

INTERNATIONAL COUNCIL OF HUMAN RIGHTS POLICY

The International Council of Human Rights (ICHRP), was established in 1994 by Philip Alston, Thomas Hammarberg and Margo Picken. They wished to create a forum where human rights policy dilemmas and difficult implementation problems that arise could be discussed. The organisation now provides a forum for applied research on matters of international human rights policy.

Chair: Hina Jilani

International Council of Human Rights Policy, Rue Ferdinand-Hodler 17, CH-1207 Geneva, Switzerland. Tel: +41 (0)22 775 3300, e-mail: ichrp@ichrp.org, URL: http://www.ichrp.org

INTERNATIONAL COUNCIL OF WOMEN (ICW - CIF)

An international, non-political, non-governmental organisation which represents millions of women in its affiliated councils in all continents. Aims to: help women help themselves; promote equal rights and responsibilities for both men and women; promote recognition and respect for human rights; bring together women from all continents in unity within diversity; and encourage the integration of women in development.

President: Cosima Schenk

International Council of Women (ICW - CIF), 13 rue Caumartin, 75009 Paris, France. Tel: +33 (0)1 47 42 19 40, fax: +33 (0)1 42 66 26 23, e-mail: info@icw-cif.com, URL: http://www.icw-cif.org

INTERNATIONAL FEDERATION FOR HUMAN RIGHTS LEAGUES (FIDH)

The aim of the FIDH is to obtain effective improvements in the protection of victims, the prevention of human rights abuse and the prosecution of those responsible.

President: Souhayr Belhassen

International Federation for Human Rights Leagues (FIDH), 17 passage de la main d'or, 75011 Paris, France. Tel: +33 (0)1 43 55 25 11, fax: +33 (0)1 43 55 18 80, e-mail: fidh@fidh.org, URL: http://www.fidh.org

INTERNATIONAL FEDERATION OF PERSONS WITH PHYSICAL DISABILITY (FIMITIC)

FIMITIC promotes the equalisation of opportunities for disabled persons and fights against their discrimination.

President: Miguel Angel García Oca

International Federation of Persons with Physical Disability (FIMITIC), Plittersdorfer Strasse 103, D-53173 Bonn, Germany. Tel: +49 (0)228 935 9191, fax: +49 (0)228 935 9192, e-mail: fimitic@t-online.de, URL: http://www.fimitic.org

INTERNATIONAL FEDERATION OF SOCIAL WORKERS (IFSW)

A global organisation striving for social justice, human rights and social development through the development of social work, best practices and international cooperation between social workers and their professional organisations.

President: Gary Bailey

International Federation of Social Workers, PO Box 6875, Schwarztorstrasse 22, CH-3001 Berne, Switzerland. Tel: +41 (0)31 382 6015, fax: +41 (0)31 382 1125, URL: http://www.ifsw.org

INTERNATIONAL HUMAN RIGHTS LAW INSTITUTE

The International Human Rights Law Institute (IHRLI) was founded in 1990. The organisation is concerned with research and preparing its students for work in the field of Human Rights. It is involved in international projects including post-conflict justice; human rights documentation and analysis; capacity building for legal professionals; gender rights and human trafficking.

Executive Director: Charles E. Tucker, Jr., B.A., J.D.

International Human Rights Law Institute, DePaul University College of Law, 25 East Jackson Boulevard, Chicago, IL 60604, USA. +1 312 362 5919. E-mail: ihrli@depaul.edu. URL: http://www.law.depaul.edu/centers_institutes/ihrli

INTERNATIONAL LEAGUE FOR HUMAN RIGHTS

This governmental non-profit organisation has special consultative status at the United Nations, the Council of Europe and the International Labor Organization. The organisation is based in New York and Geneva and works to keep human rights at the forefront of international affairs its stated mission is to defend individual human rights advocates who have risked their lives to promote the ideals of a just and civil society in their homelands.

President: Robert Arsenault

International League of Human Rights (ILHR), 352 Seventh Avenue, Suite 1234, New York, NY 10001, USA. Tel: +1 212 661 0480, fax: +1 212 661 0416, e-mail: info@ilhr.org, URL: http://www.ilhr.org

INTERNATIONAL ORGANISATION OF THE FRANCOPHONIE

Fosters and develops links and relations between French-speaking nations. The organisation also promotes peace and human rights. There are currently 53 member states, two associated members and 13 observer states.

Secretary General: Abdou Diouf (page 1415)

International Organisation of the Francophonie, 28 rue de Bourgogne, 75007 Paris, France. Tel: +33 (0)1 44 11 12 50, fax: +33 (0)1 44 11 12 76, e-mail: oif@francophonie.org, URL: http://www.francophonie.org/

INTERNATIONAL RED CROSS AND RED CRESCENT MOVEMENT

See entry in Inter-Governmental Organisations section.

INTERNATIONAL SOCIAL SECURITY ASSOCIATION (ISSA)

The constitutional mandate of the ISSA is "to co-operate, at the international level, in the promotion and development of social security throughout the world (...) in order to advance the social and economic conditions of the population on the basis of social justice."

The ISSA is guided by a strategic vision to promote dynamic social security as the social dimension in a globalizing world through supporting excellence in social security administration. The ISSA believes that in order to face the evolving needs of the world's population, social security must dynamically adapt and innovate to foster integrated, pro-active and forward-looking social security policies with the aim of better ensuring universal access to social security.

Secretary General: Hans-Horst Konkolewsky

International Social Security Association (ISSA), 4 route des Morillons, Case postale 1, CH-1211 Geneva 22, Switzerland. Tel: +41 (0)22 799 6617, fax: +41 (0)22 799 8509, e-mail: issa@ilo.org, URL: http://www.issa.int

INTERNATIONAL SOCIAL SERVICE (ISS)

ISS is an international non-governmental organisation dedicated to helping individuals and families with personal or social problems resulting from migration and international movement.

Secretary General: Jean Ayoub

International Social Service (ISS), 32 quai du Seujet, 1201 Geneva, Switzerland. Tel.: +41 (0)22 906 7700, fax: +41 (0)22 906 7701, e-mail: info@iss-ssi.org, URL: http://www.iss-ssi.org

INTERNATIONAL WOMEN'S RIGHTS ACTION WATCH

The International Women's Rights Action Watch (IWRAW) was founded in 1985 at the Third World Conference on Women in Nairobi, Kenya. It aims to to promote recognition of women's human rights as accorded by the United Nation's Convention on the Elimination of All Forms of Discrimination against Women (CEDAW). The stated premise of IWRAW is that the human rights of women and girls are essential to development and that equality between women and men will only be achieved through use of international human rights principles and processes. Since its inception, IWRAW's program has expanded to encompass advocacy for women's human rights under all the international human rights treaties.

Director: Dr Marsha Freeman

International Women's Rights Action Watch (IWRAW), University of Minnesota, 229-19th Avenue South, Minneapolis, MN 55455, USA. Tel: +1 612 625 4985, e-mail: mfreeman@umn.edu. URL: http://www1.umn.edu/humanrts/iwraw/index.html

LIBERTY

Liberty is also known as the National Council for Civil Liberties. Founded in 1934, it is a cross-party, non-party membership organisation at the heart of the movement for fundamental rights and freedoms in England and Wales. It promotes the values of individual human dignity, equal treatment and fairness as the foundations of a democratic society.

Director: Shami Chakrabarti

Liberty, 21 Tabard Street, London, SE1 4LA, UK. URL: http://www.liberty-human-rights.org.uk/

MÉDECINS SANS FRONTIÈRES

A private, non profit-making, international organisation whose objective is to provide medical aid to populations in crisis without discrimination and to raise awareness of the plight of those populations. Over 3,000 volunteers, of 445 different nationalities, are currently working in more than 60 countries alongside locally recruited personnel.

President, MSF International: Dr Unni Karunakara
UK Executive Director: Marc DuBois

Médecins Sans Frontières UK, 67 - 74 Saffron Hill, London, EC1N 8QX, UK. Tel: +44 (0)20 7404 6600, fax: +44 (0)20 7404 4466, e-mail: office-ldn@london.msf.org, URL: http://www.uk.msf.org

MONTREAL INSTITUTE OF GENOCIDE AND HUMAN RIGHTS

The Institute's aims are to discover the underlying reasons for genocide and other crimes against humanity and to find recommendations to resolve conflicts in their early stages.

Founding Co-Directors: Professor Frank Chalk, Professor Kurt Jonassohn

Montreal Institute for Genocide and Human Rights Studies, Concordia University, 1455 De Maisonneuve Blvd. West, Montreal, Quebec, H3G 1M8, Canada. Tel: +1 514 848 2424, URL: http://migs.concordia.ca/

NORDIC COMMITTEE FOR HUMAN RIGHTS (NCHR)

The Committee is an international non-governmental organisation working for the protection of rights of individuals and families in the Nordic countries. Its actions ensure that civil servants who abuse their power are brought to justice and works to bring about changes in current policies that mean unnnecessary interference in the private lives of citizens of the Nordic countries.

President: Ruby Harrold-Claesson, Lawyer, Sweden

Nordic Commitee for Human Rights, Ströms Väg 37, S-424 71 Olofstorp, Sweden. Tel: +46 31 70 20 385, URL: http://www.nkmr.org/

NUFFIELD FOUNDATION

Awards grants to UK organisations for research and innovative work in the following areas: the family justice system; child protection; access to justice and education, in particular, science education. Also funds its own initiatives.

Director: Anthony Tomei

Nuffield Foundation, 28 Bedford Square, London WC1B 3JS, UK. Tel: +44 (0)20 7631 0566, fax: +44 (0)20 7323 4877, e-mail: info@nuffieldfoundation.org, URL: http://www.nuffieldfoundation.org

OFFICE OF THE UNITED NATIONS HIGH COMMISSIONER FOR HUMAN RIGHTS (OHCHR)

See entry in Affiliated Agencies of the United Nations Section

OXFAM

Aims to bring relief and humanitarian help to people, irrespective of religious or political boundaries. Oxfam works in over 80 countries, often where conflict makes life almost unsupportable for innocent victims.

Chair, International Secretariat: Keith Johnston
Chairman, UK: John Gaventa

Oxfam, Oxfam House, John Smith Drive, Cowley, Oxford OX4 2JY. Tel: +44 (0)1865 473727, e-mail: oxfam@oxfam.org.uk, URL: http://www.oxfam.org.uk

PAN PACIFIC AND SOUTH EAST ASIA WOMEN'S ASSOCIATION (PPSEAWA)

PPSEAWA's objectives are to strengthen the bonds of peace by fostering a friendship and better understanding among women in all areas of the Pacific and Southeast Asia and to promote cooperation among women of these regions for the study and improvement of social, economic, and cultural conditions.

President: Teresa Hintzke

OTHER INTERNATIONAL AND NATIONAL ORGANISATIONS

Pan Pacific and South East Asia Women's Association (PPSEAWA), P.O. Box 119 Nuku'alofa, Tonga. Tel: +676 41 403, fax: +676 41 404, e-mail: info@ppseawa.org, URL: http://www.ppseawa.org

REDRESS

Founded in 1992 by Keith Carmichael, a torture survivor, the mission of Redress is to help torture survivors obtain justice and reparation; and to hold governments and perpetrators accountable.

Director (on leave): Carla Ferstman

Redress, 87 Vauxhall Walk, London, SE11 5HJ, United Kingdom. Tel: +44 (0)20 7793 1777, fax: +44 (0)20 7793 1719, e-mail: info@redress.org, URL: http://www.redress.org

REPORTERS WITHOUT BORDERS

Reporters Without Borders has fought for press freedom since 1985. It defends journalists and media assistants who are imprisoned and exposes any mistreatment and torture, fights against censorship, works to improve the saftety of journalists and gives financial aid to journalists in difficulties, as well as to the families of imprisoned journalists.

Reporters Without Borders, International HQ, 47 rue Vivienne, 75002 Paris, France. Tel: +33 (0)1 44 83 84 84, fax: +33 (0)1 45 23 11 51, e-mail: rsf@rsf.org, URL: http://www.rsf.org

ROCKEFELLER FOUNDATION

Founded in 1913 by John D. Rockefeller to "promote the well-being of mankind throughout the world". The Foundation's programmes are currently concentrated in the following areas: health equity, food security, working communitites, creativity and culture and global inclusion.

President: Judith Rodin

Rockefeller Foundation, 420 Fifth Avenue, New York, NY 10018-2702, USA. Tel: +1 212 869 8500, fax: +1 212 764 3468, URL: http://www.rockfound.org

ROKPA INTERNATIONAL

ROKPA International is a distinctive relief organisation that was founded in 1980. The headquarters of the organisation are in Zurich, Switzerland; however, the organisation has branches in 20 countries worldwide. ROKPA's goal is to improve the lives of people in need, wherever necessary, independent of religion and culture. Priority countries are Tibet and Nepal, Zimbabwe and South Africa. ROKPA is Tibetan and means 'to help' or 'to serve'. To date, ROKPA has supported over 200 projects initiated by the local population - always under the motto 'helping others to help themselves'. ROKPA projects are invariably initiated through requests for assistance from the local population. This mechanism ensures that the sort of assistance provided is exactly that which is required and welcome.

President: Dr. Akong Tulku Rinpoche
Vice-President: Lea Wyler

ROKPA International: Bökimstrasse 27, CH-8032 Zurich, Switzerland. Tel: +41 (0)44 262 6888, fax: +41 (0)44 262 6889, e-mail: info@rokpa.ch, URL: http://www.rokpa.org

ROTARY INTERNATIONAL

An organisation of business and professional leaders who participate in and administer a wide range of humanitarian and educational programmes and activities designed to improve the human condition and advance the organisation's ultimate goal of world understanding and peace.

President: Ray Klinginsmith

Rotary International, 1 Rotary Center, 1560 Sherman Avenue, Evanston, IL 60201, USA. Tel: +1 847 866 3000, fax: +1 847 328 8554, e-mail: forename.surname@rotary.org, URL: http://www.rotary.org

SAVE THE CHILDREN FUND

The UK's leading international children's charity, working to create a better future for children. The organisation champions the right of all children to a healthy and secure childhood and aims to build a better world for present and future generations.

President: HRH The Princess Royal GCVO (page 1378)
Chief Executive: Justin Forsyth

Save the Children, 1 St. John's Lane, London, EC1M 4AR, UK. Tel: +44 (0)20 7012 6400, fax: +44 (0)20 7012 6963, URL: http://www.savethechildren.org.uk

SERVICE CIVIL INTERNATIONAL (SCI)

A peace organisation that co-ordinates international voluntary projects for people of all ages, cultures, religious and economic backgrounds, based on the belief that all people are capable of living together and co-operating with mutual respect and without recourse to violence to solve conflict. The organisation has over 40 branches and groups worldwide and many partner organisations.

International Coordinator: Margherita Serafini

Service Civil International (SCI), St-Jacobsmarkt 82, B-2000 Antwerp, Belgium. Tel: +32 (0)3 226 5727, fax: +32 (0)3 232 0344, e-mail: info@sciint.org, URL: http://www.sciint.org

SIMON WIESENTHAL CENTER

The Center is an international Jewish human rights organisation dedicated to confronting anti-semitism, terrorism and promoting human rights and dignity, defending the safety of Jews and promoting knowledge of the Holocaust so that it may never be forgotten. It as accredited as an NGO at several international organisations including the UN, UNESCO and the Council of Europe.

The Simon Wiesenthal Center, International HQ, 1399 South Roxbury Drive, Los Angeles, California 90035, USA. Tel: +1 303 553 9036, fax: +1 310 533 4521, e-mail: information@wiesenthal.net, URL: http://www.wiesenthal.com/

SOCIETY OF SAINT-VINCENT DE PAUL

A charitable organisation which works among the poor and the marginalized and contributes to the advancement of suffering people through training, education and development projects.

Secretary General: Bruno Menard

Society of Saint-Vincent de Paul, 6, rue de Londres, 75009 Paris, France. Tel: +33 (0)1 53 45 87 53, fax: +33 (0)1 42 61 72 56, e-mail: cgi.information@ozanet.org, URL: http://www.ozanet.org

SOLIDAR

SOLIDAR is a European network of 52 NGOs active in over 90 countries helping to advance social justice in Europe and worldwide. SOLIDAR voices the concerns of its member organisations to the EU and international institutions across the policy sectors social affairs, international co-operation and life long learning.

Secretary General: Conny Reuter

SOLIDAR, 22 rue du Commerce, B1000, Brussels, Belgium. Tel: +32 (0)2 500 1020, fax: +32 (0)2 500 1030, e-mail: solidar@solidar.org, URL: http://www.solidar.org

SOROPTIMIST INTERNATIONAL

A worldwide organization for women in management and professions, working through service projects to advance human rights and the status of women.

International President: Hanne Jensbo

Soroptimist International, 87 Glisson Road, Cambridge, CB1 2HG, UK. Email: hq@soroptimistinternational.org, URL: http://www.soroptimistinternational.org

UNITED NATIONS HIGH COMMISSIONER FOR REFUGEES (UNHCR)

See entry in Affiliated Agencies of the United Nations section.

VITAL VOICES GLOBAL PARTNERSHIP

Vital Voices Global Partnership is an NGO whose mission is to identify, train and empower emerging female leaders and social leaders, enabling them to transform lives and communities and improve the economic, political and social status of women worldwide. More than 8,000 emerging women leaders from 127 countries have been trained and mentored. In turn, these women have trained over 500,000 women and girls in their own countries. The organisation also works to combat human trafficking and other forms of violence against females.

Founder: The Hon. Hillary Rodham Clinton (page 1406)
Honorary Chairs: The Hon. Nancy Kassebaum Baker, The Hon. Kay Bailey Hutchinson

Vital Voices Global Partnership, 1625 Massachusetts Avenue, NW, Suite 850, Washington, DC 20036, USA. Tel: +1 202 861 2625, fax: +1 292 296 4142, URL: http://vitalvoices.org/

WITNESS

Witness is an international human rights organisation that supports local groups to use film/video footage in their human rights advocacy campaigns. In addition to providing equipment, the organisation also helps to expose the issues world wide.

Executive Director: Yvette Alberdingk Thijm

Witness, 80 Hanson Place, 5th Floor, Brooklyn, NY 112117, USA. Tel: +1 718 783 2000, fax: + 1 718 783 1593, URL: http://www.witness.org/

WOMEN'S INITIATIVES FOR GENDER JUSTICE

The organisation works for gender-inclusive justice and is working towards an independent ICC. The organisation does advocacy for inclusion of gender-based crimes in the investigations of the International Criminal Court and promotes the rights of women through the justice process.

Executive Director: Brigid Inder

Women's Initiatives for Gender Justice, e-mail: info@iccwomen.org, URL: http://www.iccwomen.org/index.php

WOMEN'S INTERNATIONAL LEAGUE FOR PEACE AND FREEDOM

WILPF works for peace, disarmament and gender equality. Founded in 1915, the organisation has consultative status with ECOSOC, UNESCO, UNCTAD, and has special relations with several including the ILO, the FAO, and UNICEF.

Co-Presidents: Annelise Ebbe and Kerstin Greback

WILPF, 1 rue de Varembé, Case Postale 28, 1211 Geneva 20, Switzerland. Tel: +41 (0)22 919 7080, fax: +41 (0)22 919 7080, URL: http://www.wilpfinternational.org/

WOMEN'S REFUGEE COMMISSION

Campaigns for policies, laws and programmes to improve the lives and protect the human rights of refugee and displaced women, young people and children. The Commission works to empower the displaced.

Executive Director: Sarah Costa

Women's Refugee Commission, 122 East 42nd Street, New York, NY 10168, USA. Tel: + 212 551 3115, URL: http://womensrefugeecommission.org/

WORLD BLIND UNION (WBU)

Speaks on behalf of blind and partially sighted persons of the world, representing 168 million blind and visually impaired persons from about 600 different organisations in 190 countries. WBU is a non-political, non-religious, non-governmental and non-profit-making organisation.

President: Maryanne Diamond

World Blind Union (WBU), c/o Almansa 66, 28039 Madrid, Spain. Tel: +34 91 436 5366, fax: +34 91 589 4749, e-mail: umc@once.es, URL: http://www.worldblindunion.org/en/

WORLD FEDERATION OF THE DEAF (WFD)

An international non-governmental organisation representing approximately 70 million deaf people worldwide. Ensures that deaf people in every country have the right to preserve their own sign languages, organisations, and cultural and other activities.

President: Mr Markku Jokinen

World Federation of the Deaf (WFD), P.O. Box 65, 00401 Helsinki, Finland. Fax: +358 (0)9 580 3572, e-mail: Info@wfdeaf.org, URL: http://www.wfdeaf.org

WORLD ORGANISATION AGAINST TORTURE (OMCT)

A coalition of international non-governmental organisations fighting against torture and other inhuman treatments. It works to protect and promote human rights world wide and provides medical, legal and social assistance to torture victims. OMCT has consultative status with many institutions including ECOSOC, the ILO, the African Commission on Human and Peoples' Rights and the Council of Europe.

World Organisation Against Torture (OMCT), PO Box 21, 8 rue du Vieux-Billard, CH-1211 Geneva 8, Switzerland. Tel: +41 (0)22 809 4939, fax: +41 (0)22 809 4929, e-mail: omct@omct.org, URL: http://www.omct.org/

WORLD VETERANS FEDERATION

An international non-governmental organisation whose main objective since its inception in 1950 has been to bring together all those who have fought and experienced the suffering of wars, to work together to contribute towards the building of a peaceful, just and free world within the principles of the United Nations Charter and the Universal Declaration of Human rights. Among its stated aims are The aims of the WVF are: To defend the spiritual and material interests of veterans and victims of war and their families by all available legal means; To maintain international peace and security by the application to the letter and in spirit of the Charter of the United Nations and by respecting the human rights and fundamental freedoms set forth in the International Bill of Human Rights and other international instruments; To promote the full integration of veterans and victims of war in their respective communities by providing appropriate rehabilitation and other relevant legislation and actions to overcome the physical and psycho-social consequences of armed conflict; To further friendly relations among national as well as international organizations of veterans and victims of war.

Secretary General: Mr Mohammed Benjelloun

World Veterans Federation, 17 rue Nicolo, 75116 Paris, France. Tel: +33 (0)1 40 72 61 00, fax: +33 (0)1 40 72 80 58, e-mail: wvf@wvf-fmac.org, URL: http://www.wvf-fmac.org

WORLD YWCA

The World Young Women's Christian Association (World YWCA) is a global network of women leading social and economic change in 125 countries worldwide. It advocates for peace, justice, health, human dignity, freedom and care of the environment, and has been at the forefront of raising the status of women since it was founded in 1894. The World YWCA develops women's leadership to find local solutions to the global inequalities women face. Each year, it reaches more than 25 million women and girls through work in 22,000 communities. This grassroots development experience shapes the organisation's global advocacy agenda. YWCA work is inspired by Christian principles and a commitment to women's full and equal participation in Society. It is a volunteer membership movement, inclusive of women from many faiths, backgrounds and cultures.

Aims: A fully inclusive world where justice, peace, health, human dignity, freedom and care for the environment are promoted and sustained through women's leadership.

Purpose: The purpose of the World YWCA is to develop the leadership and collective power of women and girls around the world to achieve justice, peace, health, human dignity, freedom and a sustainable environment for all people.

President: Susan Brennan

World YWCA, 16 Ancienne Route, 1218 Grand Saconnex, Geneva, Switzerland. Tel: +41 (0)22 929 6040, fax: +41 (0)22 929 6044, e-mail: worldoffice@worldywca.org, URL: http://www.worldywca.org

Y CARE INTERNATIONAL

The overseas development agency of the YMCAs in Great Britain and Ireland. It works in the poorest areas of over 30 countries in the developing world providing financial support to long term development projects.

President: Terry Waite CBE (page 1533)
Chief Executive: Chris Roles

Y Care International, Kemp House, 152 - 160 City Road, London EC1V 2NP, UK. Tel: +44 (0)20 7549 3150, fax: +44 (0)20 7549 3151, e-mail: enq@ycareinternational.org, URL: http://www.ycare.org.uk, http://www.ycareinternational.org

STATES
OF THE WORLD

AFGHANISTAN
The Islamic State of Afghanistan
Jomhuri-ye Eslami-ye Afghanestan

Capital: Kabul (Population estimate, 2011: 3.9 million)

Head of State: Hamid Karzai (President) (page 1454)

Vice President: Mohammad Qasim Fahim

Vice President: Abdul Karim Khalili

National Flag: Three equal horizontal stripes of black, red and green with the national arms in the centre

CONSTITUTION AND GOVERNMENT

Constitution

Under the 1964 constitution Afghanistan became a parliamentary democracy in which legislative authority rested with a National Assembly of two houses. The legislative, executive and judicial branches of government were separated. Certain powers, such as the appointment of the Prime Minister and judges of the Supreme Court, rested with the King, who was a constitutional monarch. The monarchy was overthrown in a military coup d'état in July 1973.

The country was ruled by Presidential Decree until February 1977 when a new constitution was approved by a *Loya Jirga* (Grand Assembly). The 1977 constitution was annulled shortly after the 1978 coup and the former 'Republic of Afghanistan' became the 'Democratic Republic of Afghanistan'. The People's Democratic Party of Afghanistan (PDPA) was the only political party. The supreme state body was the Revolutionary Council, the president of which was de facto head of state.

In 1987 the *Loya Jirga* approved a new constitution which provided for a Senate and a National Assembly, though without executive powers. The Revolutionary Council was abolished and political parties other than the PDPA permitted. The word 'Democratic' was dropped from the country's name, which became the Islamic State of Afghanistan.

After the withdrawal of Soviet troops in February 1989, efforts were resumed to agree an end to the civil war; the leaders of ten Mujahidin groups agreed on the formation of an Interim Council. Its 50 members consisted of 30 Mujahidin commanders, 10 religious leaders, and ten other members nominated by the guerrillas. It was shortly replaced by a more broadly based Interim Government, known as the Islamic Council of the Islamic State of Afghanistan.

On 27 September 1996, President Burhanuddin Rabbani's Government was displaced by the Islamic Taliban movement who re-named the country the Islamic Emirate of Afghanistan and formed a new Interim Council, subsequently known as the Supreme Council, led by Mullah Mohammad Omar. Most foreign countries refused to officially recognise the new government.

Following its failure to hand over Osama bin Laden, suspected of masterminding the terrorist attacks on New York and Washington on 11 September 2001, Afghanistan's Taliban regime became the target of air strikes by the US and the UK. By the end of 2001 the Taliban had been displaced by the military action.

Agreement was reached on 29 November 2001 on the structure of an interim government: a total of 42 seats split equally between the Northern Alliance and supporters of former King Zahir Shah. In June 2002 the Loya Jirga elected Hamid Karzai as interim head of state, and the new cabinet was sworn in on 24 June 2002. In November 2003 Afghanistan's 35-member Constitutional Committee unveiled the new draft constitution; the country was renamed the Islamic Republic of Afghanistan and the constitution based on Islamic principles. Under the constitution all Afghans have equal rights; there is now programme of education for women, a right denied them under the Taliban regime. The constitution was adopted on 16 January 2004.

To consult the full constitution, please visit: http://www.moj.gov.af/pdf/constitution2004.pdf.

International Relations

There were tensions between Afghanistan and some of her neighbours during the Taliban regime: Russia was angered by Taliban support for Chechen rebels, and gave support to the Northern Alliance; Pakistan initially recognised the Taliban regime, but altered its position following the terrorist attacks of September 11 2001 and the Taliban's harsh treatment of Afghanistan's Shi'a minority led to Iranian support of the Northern Alliance.

Since the end of the Taliban regime in 2001, Afghanistan has become an active member of the international community. In December 2002, Afghanistan's six neighbours signed a 'Good Neighbor' Declaration, pledging to respect Afghanistan's independence and territorial integrity. Since then Afghanistan and its neighbours have also signed Declarations on trade, transit and investment, designed to develop economic links and to strengthen relations. The international community supports Afghanistan and assists in her reconstruction efforts. Many UN agencies working in the country have been consolidated under one organisation, the UN Mission in Afghanistan (UNAMA).

Recent Events

On 19 December 2005 the first parliament for more than 30 years held its inaugural session. President Karzai described the event as a 'step toward democracy'. However, fighting and violence have risen steadily. The authorities have little control beyond Kabul.

The first half of 2006 saw a sharp increase in the number of attacks by the Taliban and their allies, as well as growing anti-US feeling. In October 2006, NATO took over from the US-led coalition forces. In February 2007, the British government announced that a further 7,700 UK troops were to be deployed in Afghanistan, mainly in Helmand Province, to counter an expected Spring offensive by the Taliban.

In June 2007, the annual World Drug Report revealed that, despite a ban on poppy crops, over 90 per cent of the world's illegal opium now originates from Afghanistan, and over 50 per cent comes from Helmand province alone. The report stated that Afghanistan is unlikely to regain real security until the production of illegal drugs is tackled; the state of lawlessness is fuelled by the opium trade.

The former King of Afghanistan, Zahir Shah (92), died on 23rd July 2007. He had been a symbol of national unity; deposed in 1973, he had returned from exile after the fall of the Taliban in 2002.

On the 13th June, Taliban militants from across the border in Pakistan attacked a jail in Kandahar. Around 1,000 prisoners escaped, of whom 350 were Taliban. President Hamid Karzai responded by threatening to send troops over the border into Pakistan to confront militants. Pakistan warned it would not tolerate outside interference in its affairs.

In June 2008, the UN Office on Drugs and Crime estimated that the Taliban had made around $100 million in 2007 from the opium trade; the money was raised through a ten per cent tax on farmers in Taliban-controlled areas, and it is thought that the Taliban raise further funds through other activities related to the opium trade, such as offering protection at laboratories and during transport of the drugs.

On the 16th September 2008, the UN reported that there had been 1,445 civilian deaths between January and August - a rise of 39 per cent on the same period in 2007- and that August 2008 had the highest number of deaths (330) since the overthrow of the Taliban in 2001. Fifty-five percent of the 2008 civilian deaths were attributed to the Taliban; pro-government forces were responsible for 577 of the civilian deaths. In October, NATO gave the go ahead for its troops to attack opium factories and distribution networks for the first time. Up until then, International Security and Assistance Force (Isaf) and US-led troops had concentrated on eradicating poppy crops, whilst Afghan forces had been leading the fight against the drugs industry, to little effect.

Fighting continued into 2009. In February 2009, US President Barack Obama authorised up to 17,000 more US troops; the 8,000 marines, 4,000 army soldiers, and 5,000 support staff will serve in the south.

In March, the Supreme Court ruled President Hamid Karzai could stay in office until elections in August 2009. The constitution stipulates that his term should have expired on 21 May, but elections were postponed for security reasons. In April, Nato agreed to boost troop numbers to cover the election; US President Obama said his alliance partners would deploy about 5,000 troops, and the US would commit an additional 21,000 troops.

Insurgent attacks on security forces increased in the run-up to the presidential election on 20th August 2009. There were 30 candidates, including the incumbent, Hamid Karzai, former Foreign Minister Abdullah Abdullah and former Finance Minister Ashraf Ghani. On the day there were sporadic incidents of violence across the country. Even once the polls had closed and the counting was underway, the attacks continued. Hamid Karzai was declared the winner despite widespread allegations of fraud.

Also in February 2010, Operation Moshtarak was launched by Nato. The operation was a major offensive operation to secure control of the province of Helmand. February 2010 also saw the capture of leading Afghan Taliban military commander Mullah Abdul Ghani Baradar in Pakistan.

In June 2010 US General Stanley McChrystal was sacked as commander of the forces in Afghanistan after openly criticising political leaders in the USA and Afghanistan. US General David Petraeus was appointed to take command of the 130,000 international forces.

In November 2010 at a Nato summit in Lisbon a plan was agreed to hand control of security to Afghan forces by end of 2014.

In January 2011, President Karzai made an official state visit to Russia, the first time an Afghan leader had made such a visit since the end of the Soviet invasion in 1989.

Fighting continues in Afghanistan but the coalition has begun to put dates on its withdrawal. President Barack Obama has announced the withdrawal of 10,000 US troops in 2011 and another 23,000 by the end of 2012. At least 68,000 US troops will remain but are scheduled to withdraw by 2013 provided that Afghan forces are ready to take over security. Britain has said it will withdraw its forces by 2015 if circumstances permit. The Afghan security army continues to grow and is expected to reach 171,500 by October 2011. National Police officers

AFGHANISTAN

should reach 134,000 by October 2011. May 2011 was the worst month for coalition casualties since 2010. The number of Afghan civilians killed is also reported to be rising. Taliban tactics have changed to include the use of snipers and more remotely detonated devices.

In September 2011, the Taliban launched an attack on Kabul which took almost a day to quell. They attacked the US embassy, the NATO-led Interregional Security Assistance Force and other diplomatic buildings. At least 27 people were confirmed dead. The High Peace Council chief Burhanuddin Rabbani, tasked with negotiating with the Taliban, was killed by a suicide bomber on 20 September, while meeting with Taliban representatives.

In October 2011, Assadullah Khalid, the minister of border and tribal affairs, survived a suicide bomb attack in Kandahar. Two bystanders died in the attack. In the same month in one of the worst ground attacks on foreign troops since 2001, a suicide bomber attacked a bus carrying members of the International Security Assistance Force in the capital Kabul, killing 17 people.

An estimated 59 people were killed in by two bomb attacks on Shia worshippers on 6 December raising fears of a return to sectarian violence. At least 19 civilians were killed by a roadside bomb in southern Helmand province in the same week.

In March 2012 an American soldier from a base in Kandahar province is alleged to have gone into two Afghan homes and shot the occupants, 16 in all including children. The Taliban said there would be reprisals for the attack.

In April the Taliban attacked the diplomatic quarter of Kabul. In May 2012 Arsala Rahmani a member of the High Peace Council and former Taliban Minister was shot dead in Kabul, the Taliban denied it was involved in his death.

In August 2012, almost 50 people were killed and more than 130 others injured in a series of bombings in the south-west and north of Afghanistan. Most of the victims were civilians. The bombings followed a series of attacks by infiltrators of the Afghan security forces.

In September 2012, violent protests took place in several countries following the release of an amateur anti-Islam video made in the USA. Protesters attacked Nato's Camp Bastion, killing two marines.

In June 2013, the Afghan army took command of all military and security operations from Nato forces.

Also that month, planned peace talks in Qatar with the Taliban were put into jeopardy when President Hamid Karzai said that he would stay away unless foreign powers allowed the process to be run by the Afghans, the US had said that they would hold direct talks with the Taliban. The Taliban opened a political office in Qatar in June, on the same day that Nato handed over security for the whole of Afghanistan to the Afghan government.

In July 2013 a suicide bomber attacked a police station in Uruzgan, 12 people were killed and several injured. The Taliban has consistently targeted the police.

Legislature

Afghanistan had no legislature since the abolition of the bicameral National Assembly (*Meli Shura*) in 1992. A Loya Jirga was convened on 11 June 2002, consisting of 1,051 delegates (160 seats reserved for women and six for religious leaders). A new Constitution was drafted in 2003 and adopted early in 2004. Under the terms of the 2004 Constitution, the legislature (Jirga), first elected in September 2005, is bicameral.

The upper house, the House of Elders (Meshrano Jirga) has 102 members, of whom 34 are indirectly elected by provincial councils for three-year terms and a further 34 are indirectly elected by district councils for four-year terms. The remaining 34 are appointed by the president for five-year terms, and must include 17 women, two representatives for the disabled and two for the Kuchi people.

The lower chamber, the House of the People (Wolesi Jirga), has 249 members; 10 seats are reserved for the Kuchi ethnic group (at least three of them for women) and a further 65 seats at least must be held by women. All members are directly elected for a five-year term.

Cabinet (as at June 2013)

Minister of Foreign Affairs: Dr Zalmai Rasul (page 1500)
Minister of Defence: Gen. Ghulam Mushtaba Patang
Minister of the Interior: Gen. Besmillah Mohammadi
Minister of Finance: Dr Omar Zakhailwal (page 1542)
Minister of Education: Dr. Gholam Faruq Wardaq
Minister of Borders & Tribal Affairs: vacant
Minister of Commerce and Industry: Dr Anwar-ul-Hag Ahadi
Minister of Mines: Wahidollah Shahrani
Minister of Economy: Abdul Hardi Arghandiwal
Minister of Women's Affairs: Prof. Dr Husn Banu Ghazanfar (acting)
Minister of Public Health: Dr Suraya Dalil (acting)
Minister of Agriculture and Irrigation: Mohammad Asef Rahimi
Minister of Justice: Habibullah Ghaleb
Minister of Communications and Information Technology: Amir Zai Sangeen (acting)
Minister of Information and Culture: Dr Sayed Makhdum Rahin
Minister of Refugee and Repatriation: Jamahir Anwari
Minister of Haj and Religious Affairs: Dr Mohammad Yousuf Niazi
Minister of Energy and Water: Gen. Mohammad Ismarl Khan (acting)
Minister of Labour, Martyrs, Disabled and Social Affairs: Amina Afzali
Minister of Higher Education: Gholam Sarwar Danesh (acting)
Minister of Transport and Aviation: Dr Daud Ali Najafi (acting)
Minister of Development and Rural Affairs: Jarullah Mansoori
Minister of Counter-Narcotics: Zarar Ahmad Moqbel
Minister of Public Works: Abdul Qudus Hameedi

Minister of Urban Development: Dr Sultan Hussain Hissary (acting)
Minister of Parliamentary Affairs: Dr Hamyoon Azizi

Ministries

Office of the President, Kabul, Afghanistan. Tel: +93 20 25889, e-mai hussain.rahimi@gmail.com, URL: http://www.president.gov.af
Ministry of Finance, Pashtunistan Watt, Kabul, Afghanistan. Tel: +93 20 210 2099 e-mail: hasan@mof.gov.af, URL: http://www.mof.gov.af
Ministry of Foreign Affairs, Malak Azghar Road, Kabul, Afghanistan. Tel: +93 20 21 0366, fax: +93 20 890 9988, e-mail: contact@mfa.gov.af, URL: http://mfa.gov.af
Ministry of Agriculture, Irrigation and Livestock, Jamal Mina, Kart-I-Sakhi, Kabul Afghanistan. Tel: +93 20 250 0315, , URL: http://www.mail.gov.af
Ministry of Border and Tribal Affairs, Kabul Airport Road, 3rd Makrorayan, Kabul Afghanistan. Tel: +93 20 21793
Ministry of Commerce and Industry, Darulaman Watt, Kabul, Afghanistan. Tel: +9 20 250 0356, fax: +93 20 250 0356, e-mail: info@commerce.gov.af, URL http://www.commerce.gov.af
Ministry of Communications and Information Technology, Mohammad Ja Khan Watt, Kabul, Afghanistan Tel: +93 20 210 2655, fax: +93 20 290022, e-mail:
Ministry of Counter-Narcotics, Jalalabad Road, 3rd Makrorayan, Kabul. Afghanistan Tel: +93 20 242837, e-mail: info@mcn.gov.af, URL: http://www.mcn.gov.af
Ministry of Culture and Youth Affairs, Mohammad Jan Khan Watt, Kabul Afghanistan. Tel: +93 20 210 1301, fax: +93 20 229 0088, e-mail aziza_ahmadyar@hotmail.com
Ministry of Defence, Darulaman Watt, Kabul, Afghanistan. Tel: +93 20 41232, URL http://www.mod.gov.af
Ministry of Development and Rural Affairs, Shah Mohammad Ghazi Watt, Kabul Afghanistan. Tel: +93 70 281750, e-mail: ehsan.zia@mrrd.org, URL: http://www.mrrd.gov.a
Ministry of the Economy, Pashtoonistan Watt, Kabul, Afghanistan. Tel: +93 20 210271.
Ministry of Education, Mohammad Jan Khan Wat, Kabul, Afghanistan. Tel: +93 20 210 0483, e-mail: attaullah.wahidyar@moe.gov.af, URL: http://www.moe.gov.af
Ministry of Energy and Water, Darul Aman Road, Kabul, Afghanistan. Tel: +93 20 25109
Ministry of Haj and Religious Affairs, Sher Pur Shahri Naw, Kabul, Afghanistan.
Ministry of Higher Education, Karte Char, Kabul, Afghanistan. Tel: +93 20 250 0324 e-mail: khelwaty@yahoo.co.uk, URL: http://www.mohe.gov.af
Ministry of Housing and Town Planning, Shar-i-Nau, Kabul, Afghanistan. Tel: +93 20 21273
Ministry of Information and Cultural Tourism, Puli Baghi Umumi, Kabul Afghanistan. Tel: +93 20 210 1312
Ministry of the Interior, Shar-i-Nau, Kabul, Afghanistan. Tel: +93 22 11342, URL http://www.moi.gov.af
Ministry of Justice, Shar Rahi Pashtunistan, Kabul, Afghanistan. Tel: +93 20 23404 e-mail: info@moj.gov.af, URL: http://www.moj.gov.af
Ministry of Labour, Martyrs, Disabled and Social Affairs, Micro-Rayon 1, Kabul Afghanistan.
Ministry of Mines and Industries, Pashtunistan Watt, Kabul, Afghanistan. Tel: +93 20 25841
Ministry of Public Health, Masoud Intersection, Airport Road, Kabul, Afghanistan. Tel +93 20 40851, URL: http://www.moph.gov.af
Ministry of Public Welfare, First Micro-rayon, 1st, 2nd, and 3rd Blocks, Kabul Afghanistan. Tel: +93 20 230 1363
Ministry of Public Works, Micro-Rayon 1, Kabul, Afghanistan. Tel: +93 20 230 1363 fax: +93 20 230 1362, e-mail: omaratefi@yahoo.com
Ministry of Refugees and Repatriation, Jungaluk, off Darlaman Road, Kabul Afghanistan. e-mail: afgmorr@afgmorr.com
Ministry of Transport and Aviation, Ansari Wat, Kabul, Afghanistan. e-mail najafiafg@yahoo.com, URL: http://www.motca.gov.af
Ministry of Women's Affairs, Shahri Naw, Kabul, Afghanistan. Tel: +93 20 220 1378 e-mail: info@mowa.gov.af, URL: http://www.mowa.gov.af

Political Parties

Hezb-e Islami, (Islamic Party)
Hezbi Jumhori Afghanistan, (Republic Party of Afghanistan)
Jamiat-e Islami, (Islamic Society)
Harakat-e Islami-yi, (Islamic Movement of Afghanistan)
Afghan Mellat, (Afghan Social Democratic Party)
Hezb-e Wahdat-e Islami Afghanistan, (Islamic United Party of Afghanistan)
Ittehad-I Islami Bara-yi Azadi Afghanistan, (Islamic Dawah Organisation of Afghanistan)
Hezb jabha nijat mili, (National Rescue Front)

Elections

Presidential elections took place on 9 October 2004 when Hamid Karzai, head of the previous provisional administration, was elected with 55.4 per cent of the vote, beating Yonous Qanooni, of Hezb-e-Nuhzhat-e-Mili, who received 16.3 per cent. In December 2004 he was sworn in.

Parliamentary and provincial elections, postponed from April 2005, took place on 18 September 2005. 53 per cent of the 12.5 million registered voters cast their vote. There are no formal political parties, and members were elected to the Jirga as individuals. The appointment of the new government was announced in March 2006. Parliamentary elections are due in 2010.

The Election Commission scheduled the next presidential election for 20 August 2009. Mr. Karzai's term ended in May, but elections were postponed to allow more time to organise the ballot. The elections took place amidst protests and violence, early results showed that President Hamid Karzai has gained more votes than his nearest rival, Abdullah Abdullah. Mr. Abdullah said he would contest the result as there had been many allegations of vote fraud as well as threats and attacks by the Taliban against voters. As of 8 September, with over 90 per cent of the vote counted, Mr. Karzai was reported to have won over 54 per cent of the vote with his nearest rival Abdullah Abdullah on 28.3 per cent. However the Electoral Complaints Commission ordered several recounts and reported there had been clear incidents of electoral fraud. A second round of elections was to be held but in Mr. Abdullah pulled out of the race stating that not enough had been done to prevent further electoral fraud. In November 2009 Hamid Karzai was sworn in for a second presidential term. In January 2010 President Karzai put forward his cabinet nominees, parliament rejected 17 of them, a further list of 17 nominees was submitted and 10 of those were rejected.

In a move that angered diplomats, in February President Karzai issued a decree which gave him total control of the UN-backed Electoral Complaints Commission, the commission had helped expose massive fraud in the October presidential election. He subsequently announced that foreign observers had been responsible for the fraud in the disputed polls and accused the UN and EU officials of involvement in a plot to put a puppet government in power.

Legislative elections took place on September 18 2010

In June 2010, President Obama sacked his top commander Stanley McChrystal and replaced him with Gen. David Petraeus.

Diplomatic Representation
Embassy of the Islamic State of Afghanistan, 31 Princes Gate, Exhibition Road, London, SW7 1QQ, United Kingdom. Tel: +44 (0)20 7589 8891, fax: +44 (0)20 7581 3452, e-mail: contacts@afghanistanembassy.org.uk, URL: http://afghanistanembassy.org.uk
Ambassador: Mohammad Daud Yaar, Ph.D.
Embassy of the Islamic State of Afghanistan, 2341 Wyoming Avenue, NW, Washington, DC 20008, USA. Tel: +1 202 483 6414, fax: +1 202 483 9523, URL: http://www.embassyofafghanistan.org/
Ambassador: Eklil Ahmad Hakimi
British Embassy, 15th Street, Roundabout Wazir Akbar Khan, PO Box 334, Kabul, Afghanistan. Tel: +93 70 102000, fax: +93 70 102250, e-mail: britishembassy.kabul@fco.gov.uk, URL: http://ukinafghanistan.fco.gov.uk/en
Ambassador: Sir Richard Stagg (page 1519)
US Embassy, The Great Masoud Road, Kabul, Afghanistan. Tel: +93 230 0436, fax: +93 230 1364, e-mail: kabulwebmaster@state.gov, URL: http://kabul.usembassy.gov
Ambassador: James B Cunningham (page 1411)
Afghanistan Mission to the UN, 360 Lexington Avenue, 11th Floor, New York, NY 10017, USA. Tel: +1 212 972 1212, fax: +1 212 972 1216
Permanent Representative: Zahir Tanin

LEGAL SYSTEM

Following the US intervention in Afghanistan, a judicial commission was set up to rebuild Afghanistan's justice system in accordance with Islamic principles. The Afghan Supreme Court (Dadgah Hali) is now the court of last resort, and is made up of nine justices who are appointed for 10 year terms by the President, with the approval of the Wolesi Jirga. The President selects the Chief Justice from the nine justices. Judges can be trained in either civil or Islamic law. Matters of law with no provision in the constitution or other standing laws are judged by Hanafi jurisprudence. Shia law is applicable in cases dealing with personal matters of those who are of the Shia sect.

Initially, the Court was dominated by conservative religious figures and some of its rulings disappointed reform-minded Afghanis, but in 2006 President Karzai appointed several more moderate justices, and replaced the ultra conservative Chief Justice Faisal Ahmad Shinwari with the moderate Abdul Salam Azimi.

Following the Supreme Court are the Appeals courts and the Primary Courts.

Over 2008, the Afghan government increased its power in provincial centres, but the Taliban continued to control some areas. Apart from the extrajudicial killings in these war-torn areas, human rights violations included poor prison conditions and prolonged pretrial detention; restrictions on the freedom of the press; restrictions on religious conversions; abuse of worker rights; and child labor. Afghanistan retains the death penalty for apostasy and murder. Executions have been rare since the fall of the Taliban but at least eight people were executed in 2012.

Supreme Court of Afghanistan: URL: http://www.supremecourt.gov.af/
Supreme Court Chief Justice: Professor Abdul Salam Azimi

Attorney General's Office, URL: http://ago.gov.af/ps
Attorney General: Muhammad Ishaq Aloko

Afghanistan Independent Human Rights Commission, Pul-e-Surkh, Karti 3, Kabul, Afghanistan. Tel: +93 ()20 250 0676, fax: +93 (0)20 250 0677, e-mail: aihrc@aihrc.org.af, URL: http://www.aihrc.org.af/

LOCAL GOVERNMENT

There are 34 provinces, or *velayat*, each administered by a governor who is appointed by the president. The provinces are: Badakhshan, Badghis, Baghlan, Balkh, Bamian, Daykundi, Farah, Faryab, Ghazni, Ghor, Helmand, Herat, Jowzjan, Kabul, Kandahar, Kapisa, Khost, Kunar, Kunduz, Laghman, Lowgar, Nangarhar, Nimruz, Nurestan, Oruzgan, Paktia, Paktika, Panjshir, Parvan, Samangan, Sar-e Pol, Takhar, Vardak, and Zabul. Each of the provinces is divided into districts, altogeher there are around 365 districts. In March, 2010, the Sub National Governance Policy was approved by the Afghan cabinet. If the policy is fully implemented it will strengthen the role of governors and councils and introduce budgets and will increase public accountability of the councils and governors.

Each province is represented in the House of Elders by two representatives.

To view a map of the regions, please consult:
http://www.un.org/Depts/Cartographic/map/profile/afghanis-reg.pdf

AREA AND POPULATION

Area
Afghanistan is an inland country bounded in the north by Tajikistan, Uzbekistan and Turkmenistan, in the east and south by Pakistan, in the north east by China, and in the west by Iran. It has an area of 652,225 sq. km (250,000 sq. mi). The climate ranges from arid to semi-arid, with cold winters and hot summers. Afghanistan's terrain is largely mountainous, almost half the country lying over 2,000 metres above sea level. In the east is the area known as the Hindu Kush where peaks reach around 7,000 metres above sea level.

To view a map, consult: http://www.un.org/Depts/Cartographic/map/profile/afghanis.pdf

Population
According to WHO statistics, the population of Afghanistan in 2010 was 31.412 million, with an estimated annual growth rate of 3.2 per cent in the period 2000-10. Population density is around 38 people per sq. km. Over five million Afghan refugees returned home from Pakistan and Iran during the early 2000s, but, at the end of 2007, there were still almost 3.1 million Afghan refugees (27 per cent of the global refugee population) in more than 70 different asylum countries. 96 per cent were in Pakistan and Iran.

About 23 per cent of the population lived in urban areas in 2010. The largest town is the capital Kabul, with a population of around four million. The last official figures for the smaller towns were: Kandahar, 191,000; Herat, 151,000; Mazar-i Sharif, 111,000; Jalalabad, 58,000; Kunduz, 51,000; and Ghazni, 32,000.

The majority of the population (53 per cent) are aged between 15 and 64 years, with 46 per cent aged up to 14 years, and approximately 4 per cent aged 65 and over. The median age was estimated to be 17.0 years in 2010.

Pashtuns account for up to 45 per cent of the population, with Tajiks making up a quarter (in the north), Hazara between 10 and 19 per cent, and Uzbeks some 6-8 per cent. The official languages are Pashto and Dari (a dialect of Persian). Persian, Uzbek and Turkmen are also spoken. There are over 70 other languages and dialects.

Births, Marriages, Deaths
According to 2010 estimates, the birth rate is 43.6 births per 1,000 people, while the death rate is 15.9 per 1,000 people (2009). Infant mortality is estimated at 103 deaths per 1,000 live births and the child mortality rate is estimated at 149 per 1,000 live births. The fertility rate is 6.3 children born per woman. Life expectancy at birth was estimated at 48 years in 2009 (47 years for men and 50 years for women). Healthy life expectancy was estimated to be 36 years. (Source: http://www.who.int, World Health Statistics 2012)

Public Holidays 2014
14 January: Birth of the Prophet Muhammad*
18 April: Liberation Day
27 April: Revolution Day
1 May: Labour Day
19 August: Independence Day
29 June: Beginning of Ramadan*
29 July: Eid al-Fitr* (end of Ramadan)
5 October: Eid al-Adha (Feast of the Sacrifice)*
25 October: Al Hijira (Islamic New Year)*
3 November: Ashura*
*Islamic holidays: precise date depends on appearance of the moon

EMPLOYMENT

According to Asian Development Bank statistics, Afghanistan's total labour force was estimated at 7.85 million in 2004, up by 1.9 per cent on the previous year. Of these, 7.59 million were employed; 5.2 million in agriculture, 369,000 in industry and 1.9 million in the service sector. The unemployment rate in 2004 was 3.4 per cent, affecting some 265,000 people.

As part of the reconstruction of post-war Afghanistan, the UN Development Programme has trained over 10,000 people in basic computer skills. Those receiving training include the civil service, local government staff and academics, as well as the general public.

BANKING AND FINANCE

The economy was badly damaged by years of war but is recovering following the fall of the Taliban in 2001. Afghanistan is traditionally a rural country with a large nomadic population, estimated at about 15 per cent of the total population. Economic progress is hampered by poor communications, poor infrastructure, corruption, political instability and security problems. The country is landlocked with much of its land consisting of high plateaux and mountains. In April 2007 Afghanistan became a member of the South Asia Association for Regional Co-operation (SAARC). The government is trying to increase regional trade.

Currency
In September 2002, in a move designed to give credibility to a highly devalued currency, 'Old Afghani' notes were exchanged for 'New Afghani' notes, at a ratio of 100-to-1. US dollars are still used for many transactions in Afghanistan. The exchange rate at the end of 2011 was 48.28 New Afghanis per US dollar.

One Afghani (Af, AFA) = 100 puls

AFGHANISTAN

GDP/GNP, Inflation, National Debt

Afghanistan's Gross Domestic Product fell over the period 1980-2000, due to a loss of labour and capital, as well as problems with transport and trade, caused by two decades of war and continuing political turmoil. Since the fall of the Taliban in 2001 there have been signs of economic growth. According to statistics from the Asian Development Bank, GDP (at current market prices) rose from US$4,390 million in 2002 to US$4,769 million in 2003 and then to US$5,733 million in 2004 (12.6 per cent growth), and US$6,852 million in 2005 (10.3 per cent growth). In 2006, it reached US$7,459 million, equivalent to a growth rate of 6.5 per cent. By 2008, it had reached US$10,662 million. The growth rate was 16.4 per cent in 2007, but was expected to fall in 2008. Per capita GDP was US$424. Estimated figures for 2009 put GDP at US$23.35 billion giving a per capita figure of US$800. In 2010, GDP was estimated to have grown to US$27.36 billion, with a growth rate of 82 per cent. GDP per capita was estimated to have grown to US$900.

According to 2009 Asian Development Bank figures, agriculture contributes 32.5 per cent of Afghanistan's GDP (down from 57.0 per cent in 2000 and 93.3 per cent in 1994), with services contributing 45.4 per cent (up from 19.5 per cent in 2000) and industry 22.1 per cent (down from 23.2 in 2000). However, unofficially it is thought that the opium trade accounts for up to 60 per cent of GDP.

GDP by industrial origin is shown on the following table:

GDP by industry (Million Afghanis, current market prices

Industry	2007	2008	2009
Agriculture	184,134	150,133	196,990
Mining, Manufacturing and Utilities	1,783	2,481	2,921
Manufacturing	77,553	91,879	80,435
Utilities	645	527	629
Construction	42,568	43,741	49,955
Trade	51,974	48,097	49,812
Transport and communications	44,778	91,481	111,784
Finance	9,772	9,222	11,745
Public administration	39,976	57,137	67,170
Others	38,179	32,084	34,171
Indirect taxes less subsidies	14,267	14,330	21,782
TOTAL GDP	505,630	541,112	627,395

Source: Asian Development Bank

The national Consumer Price Index (March 2004=100) rose from 113 in 2005 to 121 in 2006 and to 135 in 2007. In Kabul, CPI rose to 136.4, an increase of 8.6 per cent, in 2007. The cost of food went up by 12.2 per cent over 2007. As at the end of 2006, external debt was US$1,771 million, 99.4 per cent of which was long-term debt. External debt stood at 23.7 per cent of GDP. (Source: Asian Development Bank)

Foreign Investment

Pledges of assistance totalled almost $15 billion in 2006. In March 2004, President Karzai urged foreign donors at a conference in Berlin to renew their commitments to Afghanistan, while presenting the donors with a $28 billion, seven year economic development program. Overseas aid and assistance is administered by United Nations High Commissioner for Refugees (UNHCR) and Oxfam. In 2011, the IMF approved a new credit facility worth US$133 million designed to help the country move towards a more stable and sustainable economy.

Balance of Payments / Imports and Exports

Afghanistan is a member of many international trade organisations including the Asian Development Bank, the Colombo Plan, the International Bank for Reconstruction and Development and the Islamic Development Bank.

Trade is supervised by the government through the Ministries of Commerce and Finance and the Afghanistan Bank. The government monopoly controls the import of petrol and oil, sugar, cigarettes and tobacco, motor vehicles and consignment goods from bilateral trading countries.

Export revenue, import costs and trade balance are shown on the following table:

External Trade

External Trade (US$ million)	2006	2007	2008	2009
Exports	416	454	545	403
Imports	2,744	3,022	3,020	3,336
Trade balance	-2,328	-2,568	-2,475	-2,933
Annual change, %				
Exports	8.3	9.1	20.0	-26.1
Imports	11.1	10.1	-0.1	10.5

Source: Asian Development Bank

The following tables show external trade for according to international trading partner:

Exports by destination country, (US$m)

Country	2008	2009	2010
India	118.7	109.7	116.2
Pakistan	84.7	108.5	111.5
United States	79.0	113.0	79.3
Tajikistan	61.0	40.2	41.3
Russian Federation	13.5	13.1	13.5
Total exports	**475.2**	**448.3**	**469.6**

Source: ADB

Imports by country of origin, (US$m)

Country	2008	2009	2010
Pakistan	2,051.5	1,493.3	1,534.5
United States	529.9	1,662.7	2,367.6
India	398.5	516.1	521.8
Germany	428.5	340.7	341.2
Russia	189.8	285.7	293.6
Total	**5,653.4**	**6,689.4**	**7,437.3**

Source: Asian Development Bank

Afghanistan is the largest opium poppy producing country in the world, producing 93 per cent of total global supply in 2007. The opium trade is thought to represent between 40 and 60 per cent of the country's GDP. It is thought that opium is grown in 28 of the 34 provinces, over some 61,000 hectares. The southern provinces, close to the border with Pakistan and under the control of the Taliban, are the most productive regions. It is generally believed that the opium trade funds the Taliban militants. Despite efforts by the government and international forces, the production of opium continues to grow; farmers argue that no alternative has been offered to them. Total opium cultivation increased by almost 60 per cent in 2006 and production by almost 50 per cent. (Source: Energy Information Administration, EIA)

Central Bank

Da Afghanistan Bank (Bank of Afghanistan), Ibni Sina Wat, Kabul, Afghanistan. Tel: +93 24075 (5 lines), URL: http://www.centralbank.gov.af
Governor: Noorullah Delawari

MANUFACTURING, MINING AND SERVICES

Primary and Extractive Industries

Afghanistan has mineral resources in the form of natural gas, petroleum, coal, copper, chromite, barites, talc, lead, sulfur, iron ore, zinc, salt and semi and semi-precious stones.

Afghanistan's proven natural gas reserves were estimated by the former Soviet Union at 3,530 billion cubic feet in 2005. In the mid-1970s natural gas production had reached 275 million cubic feet per day. However, output declined to some 220 million cubic feet by the beginning of the 1980s, largely as a result of falling reserves. By 2000 gas production had fallen to just 22 million cubic feet, all of which was put to domestic use. EIA figures put natural gas production and consumption at five billion cubic feet in 2010.

Proven oil and condensate reserves were estimated by the former Soviet Union at 95 million barrels in 1978. All oil exploration and development, including plans for a 10,000 barrels per day refinery, were halted following the Soviet invasion in 1979. At present, Afghanistan still imports all of its oil requirements. In 2006, according to EIA statistics, Afghanistan imported and consumed 5,030 barrels per day. A small amount of crude oil (300 barrels per day) is produced by the Angot field in the northern Sar-i-Pol province. Figures for 2011 show that no oil production took place.

Coal reserves are thought to be of a significant quantity, estimated at 73 million tons, according to recent figures. Annual coal production fell from over 100,000 short tons in the early 1990s to a low of 5,000 short tons in 1995. Production has begun to pick up from 2002, and 99,000 short tons was mined in 2005 but had fallen in 2010 to 39,000 short tons.. Most of Afghanistan's coal is found in the north of the country, between Herat and Badashkan. Afghanistan uses all of the coal produced.

Energy

Afghanistan's power grid has been severely damaged by years of war. Until the end of 1999, Afghanistan imported much of its electricity requirements from Uzbekistan; however, supplies were cut due to arrears in payments. More recently, Turkmenistan supplied power to the north-west of Afghanistan. A power transmission line connects the power plant in the east of Turkmenistan to the west of Afghanistan. Hydro-electricity is generated at the 66 MW Mahipar plant, although sporadic droughts limit production. At present, less than 10 per cent of Afghans have access to electricity supplies, and Kabul suffers power shortages.

Electricity capacity was 0.49 gigawatts (GWe) in 2010. Power generation stood at 0.99 billion kWh in 2010 and consumption was 2.49 kWh, according to EIA statistics.

Manufacturing

Industries include cement, coal-mining, cotton textiles, small vehicle assembly plants, fruit canning, carpet making, leather tanning, footwear manufacture, sugar manufacture, cotton seed oil, furniture, prefabricated buildings, glass, bicycles, mechanical spares, fertilisers, preparation of hides and skins and building. Most of these are relatively small and, with the exception of hides and skins, carpets and fruits, do not meet domestic requirements. Manufacturing relies on the agricultural sector for most of its raw materials. Foreign aid has been allocated for the building of a cement factory and a new oil refinery is planned in Jowzjan.

Service Industries

Tourism was formerly an important contributor to Afghanistan's foreign currency reserves but owing to internal political instability there has been negligible tourism since 1979.

Agriculture

Although the greater part of Afghanistan is more or less mountainous with land too dry and rocky for successful cultivation, many fertile plains and valleys also exist where, with the aid of irrigation from small rivers or wells, crops of fruit, vegetables and cereals are possible. It is estimated that there are 14 million hectares of cultivable land in the country of which less than six per cent is currently cultivated.

Principal crops are wheat, fruit and vegetables, maize, rice, barley, cotton, sugar-beet, sugar-cane and oil seeds. Livestock raised include sheep, cattle, goats and poultry with donkeys, horses, camels, mules and buffaloes kept as draught animals. Most forest exploitation is for fuel wood.

Fruit and bread are staple foods for many people throughout the year. The staple meat is the fat-tailed sheep, whose tail provides grease as a butter substitute. Wool and skins provide material for warm clothing and are also one of the more important export commodities of the country, along with Persian lambskins (Karakuls). Preserved fruit is also exported in large quantities.

Opium has developed into a major source of income, following the Soviet withdrawal; in 2008, the World Drug Report stated that 93 per cent of illegal opium now originates in Afghanistan (up dramatically from 30 per cent in the 1980s), despite the presence of over 30,000 international troops. In 2008, Afghanistan produced 7,700 tons of opium, with an export value estimated at £2.7 billion. It is estimated that Helmand province alone cultivates almost half the world's illegal opium. Afghanistan began implementing counter-narcotics programmes late in 2005; they included the promotion of alternative livelihoods, public information campaigns and targeted eradication policies. By August 2007, it was estimated that the government had eradicated around 19,000 hectares of opium poppy, under 10 per cent of the area under poppy cultivation.

Over 80 per cent of the labour force is employed in farming. Food output is currently below the level required to feed the existing population; traditional crops of grain, rice, fruit, nuts and vegetables were severely affected by drought in recent years. The end of civil war produced the largest wheat harvest in 25 years in 2003, with production increasing by 58 per cent on the previous year. However, millions of Afghans remained dependent on food aid.

The following table shows recent estimated agricultural production:

Agricultural Production in 2010

Produce	Int. $'000	Tonnes
Wheat	665,682	4,532,000
Cow milk, whole	437,198	1,401,000
Indigenous cattle meat	353,670	130,922
Grapes	349,441	611,320
Indigenous sheep meat	293,627	107,840
Rice, paddy	181,174	672,000
Almonds, with shell	165,254	56,000
Vegetables fresh nes	124,371	660,000
Indigenous goat meat	105,907	44,200
Sheep milk, whole, fresh	78,272	201,000
Anise, badian, fennel, corian	56,378	10,200
Berries nes	51,223	29,400

Source: http://faostat.fao.org/site/339/default.aspx Food and Agriculture Organization of the United Nations, Food and Agricultural commodities production

COMMUNICATIONS AND TRANSPORT

Travel Requirements
All visitors to Afghanistan must possess a valid passport and an Afghan visa. The basic tourist visa entitles a traveller to 30 days stay in Afghanistan. Visas for six months or one year are available, depending on the purpose of the visit. It is recommended that visas be obtained prior to travelling to Afghanistan. A return ticket is also required.

National Airlines
The national airline is Ariana and operates regular services to Dubai, Istanbul, Tehran, Frankfurt, Islamabad, New Delhi, Tashkent and Baku. URL: http://www.flyariana.com.

International Airports
There are 53 airports in Afghanistan, 19 of which have paved runways, and four of which has a runway over 3,049 metres long. The main international airport, Kwaja Rawash, is located 16 kilometres from Kabul and has been expanded with Russian assistance. New runways at Kabul and Kandahar airports have also been completed. Provincial all-weather airports have been constructed at Herat, Qunduz, Jalalabad and Mazar-i Sharif and internal air services operate between them. Local services are provided by Kam Air, URL: http//www.flykamair.com. nternational flights are provided by the national airline, Ariana as well as Pakistan International Airlines (PIA), Iran Air and Air India. In May 2012 was announced an international airport was to be built in the northern province of Balkh. The Mazar-e Sharif airport will receive $60 million investment from the EU and the UAE and will be the country's biggest airport.

There are also 11 heliports in the country.

Railways
There are no railways in the country but the Oxus bridge, opened in 1982, brought the Soviet railway into Afghanistan. The bridge was reconstructed, and reopened in 2007, opening vital trade routes. A 200 km line of 1.520 mm gauge was authorised from Termez to Pul-i Khumri.

Roads
All roads are in a poor state of repair as a result of the war. The most reliable recent statistics listed the following roads:
Internal: Kabul-Kandahar (310 miles); Kandahar-Herat (350 miles); Mazar-I-Sharif-Kabul (380 miles). Also Kabul-Khanabad-Faizabad (450 miles); Kabul-Gardez (80 miles); Herat-Maimana-Mazar-I-Sharif (500 miles) and Kabul-Bamiyan (140 miles are unsurfaced roads suitable only for vehicles with four wheel drive. They are usually impassable in winter.) Roads to the frontiers: Kabul-Khyber (175 miles); Kandahar-Chaman (70 miles) and roads from Herat to the former Soviet and Persian borders.

In December 2003, the Salang Tunnel linking northern and southern Afghanistan was reopened, and the main highway between Kabul and Kandahar was restored, cutting travel time between the two cities from two days to just five hours. Other roads forming the national "ring-road" system, are due to be repaired, with foreign assistance.

Buses run regularly from Jalalabad to Peshawar in Pakistan and between Herat and Mashad in Iran.Vehicles are driven on the right.

Ports and Harbours
A port has been built at Qizil Qala on the Oxus river where barge traffic is increasing. Three river ports on the Amu Darya have been built at Sherkhan Bandar, Tashquzar and Hairatan, and are linked by road to Kabul.

Afghanistan signed a trilateral trade agreement with Iran and India in 2003. The agreement designates the Iranian port of Chabahar as a major port for Afghan industry. Afghans will pay reduced rates for port fees and warehousing, and they will be able to transport goods through Iran, a major development in view of Afghanistan's landlocked location.

HEALTH

Since the fall of the Taliban in 2001, the international community has assisted the Afghan government in rebuilding the primary health-care system through a variety of development projects. There are now over 900 clinics and approximately 40 per cent of the population have access to healthcare. However, most inhabitants lack access to safe drinking water and sanitary facilities. Disease and malnutrition are widespread and around 6.5 million people depend on food aid.

In 2005-10, there were 7,248 doctors (2.1 per 10,000 people), 17,257 nurses and midwives (5 per 10,000 people), and around 1,035 dentists. In 2009, the government spent the equivalent of 7.6 per cent of GDP on health; per capita total expenditure on health amounted to US$34 (US$4 government expenditure) in the same year. External resources for health accounted for 34.3 per cent of the total expenditure on health. There are approximately 4 hospital beds per 10,000 population.

Life expectancy averages 48 years in Afghanistan (males 47 years, females 50 years). The infant mortality rate fell to 103 deaths per 1,000 live births in 2010 compared to 140 per 1,000 live births in 1990. The under-five mortality rate is 149 per 1,000 live births, compared to 209 in 1990. The most common causes of child (under 5 years) mortality in 2010 were pneumonia (25 per cent) and diarrhoea (16 per cent). In the years 2000-10 approximately 59.3 per cent of children aged less than 5 years were stunted for their age and 32.9 per cent were underweight. The Ministry of Health has established a Child and Adolescent Health Department and a Department of Women and Reproductive Health to tackle high infant and maternal mortality rates.

Major diseases are tuberculosis and malaria. The Afghan Government has been assisted by the WHO in delivering treatments and preventative measures for both these diseases. In March 2006, a Ministry of Public Health, UNICEF and World Bank nationwide campaign was launched to immunise seven million children, in all of Afghanistan's 34 provinces, against polio. Since 2002 UN agencies have administered 16 million vaccinations against measles. Immunization rates have increased dramatically: 62 per cent of one year olds were immunized against measles in 2010 compared to 27 per cent in 2000. Approximately 66 per cent received the DTP3, Hib3 and HepB3 vaccinations in 2010. Cholera and diarrhoeal diseases are being tackled through health education, water chlorination and the construction of wells throughout the country. In 2008, an estimated 78 per cent of the urban population and 39 per cent of the rural population had access to improved drinking water. An estimated 60 per cent of the urban population and 30 per cent of the rural population had access to improved sanitation. (Source: http://www.who.int, Global Health Statistics, 2012)

EDUCATION

Elementary and Secondary
Both elementary and secondary education is free. In 2007 there were a total of 9,476 schools. General Education has 9,062 schools: 5,024 Primary, 2,506 Lower Secondary and 1,532 Higher Secondary schools. There were also 336 Islamic Schools, 34 Teacher Training Centres and 44 Technical Vocational schools.

The government's goals for 2010 are for net enrollment in primary school for girls and boys to be at least 60 per cent and 75 per cent respectively; for the number of women teachers to increase by 50 per cent over the figure for 2005, and for 70 per cent of teachers to be fully qualified.

In 2007, according to President Karzai, around 300,000 children in the south of the country had to stay at home due to the Taliban insurgency. Pupils and teachers have been attacked on their way to school. Many other children are deprived of an education because their families would rather girls worked in the household or boys herded livestock.

However, in more stable areas of the country, the intake figures are more encouraging, with a million new admissions in 2007-08. About 5.9 million students enrolled in primary and secondary education, and teacher training programmes. A further 280,000 students enrolled in literacy courses across the country in nearly 5,000 classes. Overall, the student population in 2007 was approximately two-thirds male to one third female, and this ratio was the same in teacher training programmes. However, by grade 12 of secondary education, the ratio was 75 male to 25 female. This may change as the present and future school populations go through the new system.

In 2007, there were 149,417 teachers, of whom 142,508 were employed in General Education. 27.69 per cent of General Education teachers were female. Within the Islamic Education system, employing 3,474 teachers, just 1.91 per cent were female.

Higher Education
Kabul University was founded in 1932 and has nine faculties (medicine, science, agriculture, engineering, law and political science, literature, economics, theology and pharmacology). There are four other universities and a polytechnic.

The adult literacy rate (over 15s), according to 2004 estimates, is 28.1 per cent. This reflects an improvement on the figures for 1999 (31 per cent literacy: 47 per cent for men and 15 per cent for women), though the figures for rural areas are likely to be lower. Among the 15-24 year old age group, the literacy rate was estimated to be 34.3 per cent.

RELIGION

Afghanistan is an Islamic country where more than 99 per cent of the population is Muslim. Most Afghans are of the Sunni sect (80 per cent). Shia Muslims make up most of the remainder, though a small percentage of the population is Hindu.

Children and teenagers undergo religious training in the family, mosque and in school. Religious training is carried out in Darul Hefazes, schools where the holy Qur'an is memorised. These schools are funded by the government. The Theology Faculty of the Kabul University is the highest centre for acquiring religious instruction.

Afghanistan has a religious liberty rating of 2 on a scale of 1 to 10 (10 is most freedom). (Source: World Religion Database)

COMMUNICATIONS AND MEDIA

Media laws prohibit material that is seen as anti Islamic.

Newspapers
There are currently at least 100 press titles under varied ownership. Titles include:
The Daily Afghanistan (http://www.dailyafghanistan.com/), **Anis** (in Dari and Pashtu); **Haywad** (in Dari and Pashtu); **Mojahid** (in Dari and Pashtu), **Weesa** (Trust) (http://www.weesa.net). There are a number of weekly and monthly magazines such as: **Kabul Weekly** (URL: http://www.kw/af/english/index.php), **Heydayat Weekly.**

Bakhtar News Agency (URL: http://www.bakhtarnews.com.af/) is Afghanistan's national news agency.

Broadcasting
The local media were severely restricted under Taliban rule. Radio Afghanistan was renamed Radio Voice of Shariah and reflected Islamic fundamentalist values, whilst TV was viewed as a source of corruption and banned. The state-run Radio Afghanistan was on the air again by the end of 2001. Kabul Radio and a number of provincial stations broadcast in Pashtu and Persian. Taliban radio re-emerged in April 2005; the operators were said to be using a mobile transmitter.

Since the end of the Taliban era, the number of private television stations has increased and there are now numerous radio and TV stations. The press has also flourished. Ownership ranges from the state, provincial powers and private owners to foreign sponsors.

The national broadcaster is National Radio and Television Afghanistan (URL: http://rta.org.af/). The main private network is Tolo Tv (URL: http://www.tolo.tv/). This was initally supported by US aid. The first private radio station was Arman FM (URL: http://www.arman.fm/).

Telecommunications
The telephone system is centred on Kabul but has not been well developed throughout the country. There are telegraphic communication facilities between all the larger towns and with other parts of the world. According to 2008 estimates, there were 450,000 mainline telephones.

There are now multiple mobile phone service providers. According to figures from Afghan Wireless, owners of the first network to go live in Afghanistan, more mobile phone calls are made in Kabul than in downtown Manhattan. In 2008, it was estimated that there were over 8.4 million mobile phones in use.

The UN Development Programme is currently training the civil service, local government staff, academics and the general public in computer skills, including MS Office and the internet. For many Afghans, the availability of cheap PCs, and the limited broadcasts on the local television network, mean that those that can afford television receivers are buying computers instead.

In 2008, there were approximately 500,000 internet users.

ENVIRONMENT

Afghanistan suffers from natural hazards such as flooding and earthquakes in the Hindu Kush mountain region. Current environmental problems include desertification, deforestation, overgrazing, and soil degradation. Afghanistan is a party to the following environmental agreements: Biodiversity, Climate Change, Desertification, Endangered Species, Environmental Modification, Marine Dumping, Ozone Layer Protection. Afghanistan has signed, but not ratified: Hazardous Wastes, Law of the Sea, Marine Life Conservation.

In 2006 Afghanistan's emissions from the consumption and flaring of fossil fuels totalled 0.80 million metric tons of carbon dioxide. EIA figures for 2010 show that carbon dioxide emissions from consumption of fossil fuels was 0.79 million metric tons.

In 2012, Afghanistan's first national park was opened, it is situated in Bamiyan and is part of an environmental protection project.

ALBANIA
Republic of Albania
Republika e Shqipërisë

Capital: Tirana (Population estimate: 400,000)

Head of State: Bujar Nishani (President) (page 1487)

National Flag: Red, bearing at the centre a double-headed eagle black, with wings displayed

CONSTITUTION AND GOVERNMENT

Constitution
The 1928 constitution established a monarchy; however, the former Kingdom of Albania's royal family fled from the country in 1939 after an invasion by Italian troops. The monarch at that time, King Zog, died abroad in 1961, and his son, King Leka, claims that the constitution is still valid. King Leka returned to Albania in April 1997, and held a referendum in June 1997 on whether to return Albania to a constitutional monarchy. The results indicated that 66.7 per cent wished to retain a republic, whilst 33.3 per cent wanted to restore the monarchy. However, the pro-monarchist Legality Movement Party disputed the results and accused the electoral commission of malpractice.

Albania existed as a single party Communist state until President Alia Ramiz responded to extensive protests throughout the autumn of 1990 and promised greater freedom and democracy and the introduction of a multi-party system. Free elections were promised for 10 February, but were postponed to 31 March after the opposition parties declared that this would not give them sufficient time to make preparations. Renewed protests and strikes resulted in President Alia taking over all power on 19 February 1991, appointing a Presidential Council consisting of eight members and reshuffling the existing cabinet.

An effort to stem the continuing economic decline, as well as pressure on the government, led to the appointment of the first non-communist prime minister in June 1991. But neither this move nor the promise of early elections restored order. New elections were held in March 1992, after which the former opposition Democratic Party gained 68 per cent of the vote, while the Socialists (the former Communist Party) only polled 22 per cent.

In April 1992 Ramiz Alia resigned as president. He was replaced by Sali Berisha, the Democratic Party leader. A draft Constitution was approved by referendum on 22 November 1998. Under its terms, Albania's head of state is the president, indirectly elected by the People's Assembly for a maximum of two successive five-year terms. The president appoints the head of government, the prime minister, whose appointment must also be approved by the People's Assembly. The Council of Ministers is also appointed by the People's Assembly.

To consult the full constitution, please visit:
http://www.president.al/english/pub/kushtetuta.asp

International Relations
Albania is actively pursuing membership of the EU; formal negotiations to join were opened in 2003 and made a formal application for membership in 2009, it is forecast that Albania will become a member of the EU in 2015. Albania also formally applied to join NATO, and became a member in 2009.

Recent Events
January 1997 saw large anti government protests following the collapse of pyramid financial schemes; state armories were looted and more than 13,000 refugees fled to Italy. The government resigned and a Socialist led coalition government came to power led by the prime minister, Fatos Nano.

In 1998-99 continuing unrest in neighbouring Kosovo and the Nato air strikes against Yugoslav military targets saw thousands of Kosovan refugees arriving in Albania.

In June 2006 a stabilisation and association agreement was signed with the EU in recognition of the economic and political reform that Albania had achieved. The majority of the population wants Albania to join the EU. In April 2008 Albania was invited to join Nato. Membership is expected in 2009.

A general election took place in June 2009. It was narrowly won by the centre-right Democratic Party led by Sali Berisha. Amidst allegations of vote-rigging the opposition Socialist party staged a series of demonstrations. Opposition to the result continued and in May 2010 Edi Rama, the leader of the Socialists, called for the government to order a partial recount or face a long campaign of civil disobedience.

In November 2010 the EU rejected Albania's request for EU candidate status, but it agreed to ease visa requirements for Albanians.

In February 2011, former economy minister Dritan Prifti was stripped of his immunity so that he could be charged with corruption, former prime minister Ilan Meta was also being investigated over a deal to build a power station.

Legislature
Albania's unicameral legislature consists of the People's Assembly (*Kuvendi Popullor*). The People's Assembly comprises 140 deputies elected for four-year terms, of whom 100 are directly elected, with the balance elected by proportional representation.

People's Assembly, Bul "Deshmoret e Kombit" Nr.4, Tirana, Albania. Tel: +355 (0)4 362003, fax: +355 (0)4 227949, e-mail: marlind@yahoo.com, URL: http://www.parlament.al
Speaker: Jozefina Çoba Topalli

Cabinet (as at June 2013)
Prime Minister: Sali Berisha (page 1387)
Deputy Prime Minister, Minister of Education and Sciences: Dr Mygyrem Tafaj
Minister of Foreign Affairs: Aldo Bumci
Minister of Health: Dr Halim Kosova
Minister of the Interior: Flamur Noka
Minister of Justice: Eduard Halimi
Minister of Defence: Arben Imami (page 1446)
Minister of European Integration: Dr Majlinda Bregu (page 1394)
Minister of Finance: Ridvan Bode (page 1390)
Minister of Public Works and Transport: Sokol Olldashi
Minister of Labour, Social Affairs and Equal Opportunities: Spiro Ksera
Minister of Agriculture, Food and Consumer Protection: Dr Genc Ruli
Minister of Tourism, Culture, Youth and Sports: Visar Zhiti
Minister of the Environment: Fatmir Mediu
Minister of Innovation and Information and Communication Technology: Genc Pollo

---

Ministries
Council of Ministers, Këshilli i Ministrave, Tirana, Albania. Tel: +355 (0)4 228210, fax: +355 (0)42 27888
Office of the President, Bulevardi Dëshmorët e Kombit, Tirana, Albania. Tel: +355 (0)4 228313, fax: +355 (0)4 233761, e-mail: presec@presec.tirana.al, URL: http://www.president.al
Office of the Prime Minister, Bulevardi Dëshmorët e Kombit, Tirana, Albania. Tel: +355 4 225 0474, fax: +355 4 223 7501, e-mail: kryeministri@km.gov.al, URL: http://www.km.gov.al
Ministry of Foreign Affairs, Bulevardi Gjergj Fishta 6, Tirana, Albania. Tel: +355 4 236 4090, fax: +355 4 236 2084, e-mail: info@mfa.gov.al, URL: http://www.mfa.gov.al
Ministry of European Integration, Bulevardi Dëshmorët e Kombit, Tirana, Albania. Tel: +355 4 222 8645, fax: +355 4 222 8645, e-mail: majlinda.bregu@mie.gov.al, URL: http://www.mie.gov.al
Ministry of Defence, Bulevardi Dëshmorët e Kombit, PO Box 203/1, Tirana, Albania. Tel: +355 4 222 6601, fax: +355 4 222 8325, e-mail: kontakt@mod.gov.al, URL; http://www.mod.gov.al
Ministry of Public Order, Sheshi "Skënderbej", Nr.3, Tirana, Albania. Tel: +355 (0)4 2228167, e-mail: mrp@mpo.gov.al, URL: http://www.mpo.gov.al
Ministry of Agriculture and Food, Sheshi Skenderbej Nr. 2, Tirana, Albania. Tel: +355 (0)4 228379, e-mail: ibrov@icc-al.org, URL: http://www.mbu.gov.al
Ministry of Finance, Bulevardi Dëshmorët e Kombit 4, Tirana, Albania. Tel: +355 (0)4 267654, fax: +355 (0)4 226111, e-mail: secretary.minister@minfin.gov.al, URL: http://www.minfin.gov.al
Ministry of the Economy, Trade and Energy, Bulevardi Zhan d'Ark, Tirana, Albania. Tel: +355 4 236 4633, fax: +355 4 236 4639, e-mail: gruli@mete.gov.al, URL: http://www.minek.gov.al
Ministry of Transport and Telecommunications, Rruga Abdi Toptani 5, Tirana, Albania. Tel: +355 (0)4 234674, fax: +355 (0)4 232389, e-mail: spmt@albmail.com, URL: http://www.mtt.gov.al
Ministry of Public Works and Planning,Rruga Abdi Toptani 4, Tirana, Albania. Tel: +355 (0)4 233503, fax: +355 (0)4 233503, e-mail: mpptt@mpptt.gov.al, URL: http://www.mpp.gov.al
Ministry of Justice, Bulevardi Dëshmorët e Kombit, Tirana, Albania. Tel: +355 (0)4 224041, fax: +355 4 228359, e-mail: ministidre@albaniaonline.net, URL: http://www.justice.gov.al
Ministry of Industry and Energy, Bulevardi Dëshmorët e Kombit, Tirana, Albania. Tel: +355 (0)4 227617, fax: +355 (0)4 234052, e-mail: dpzh@abissnet.com.al, URL: http://www.mepp.gov.al
Ministry of Health and Environment, Rruga Durrësit 27, Tirana, Albania. Tel: +355 (0)4 270630, fax: +355 (0)4 270624, URL: http://www.moe.gov.al
Ministry of Education and Science, Rruga Durrësit 23, Tirana, Albania. Tel: +355 (0)4 226307, fax: +355 (0)4 232002, e-mail: rspahia@mash.gov.al, URL: http://www.mash.gov.al
Ministry of Tourism, Cultural Affairs, Youth and Sports, Bulevardi Dëshmorët e Kombit, Tirana, Albania. Tel: +355 4 222 3474, fax: +355 4 223 2488, e-mail: ypango@mktrs.gov.al, URL: http://www.mktrs.gov.al

Ministry of Internal Affairs, Sheshi Skënderbej 3, Tirana, Albania. Tel: +355 4 224 7155, fax: +355 4 222 7520, e-mail: bnishani@moi.gov.al, URL: http://www.moi.gov.al

Political Parties
Christian Democratic Party, Rruga Dëshmorët e 4 Shkurtit, Tirana, Albania. Tel: +355 42 30042, fax: +355 (0)4 234024, URL: http://www.pdkdiaspora.com/
Democratic Alliance Party, 260 Qemal Stafa Street, Tirana, Albania. Tel: +355 (0)4 230468
Democratic Party, Punetoret e Lirise Street, Tirana, Albania. Tel: +355 (0)4 233737, URL: http://www.pd.al
Leader: Sali Berisha
Environmentalist Agrarian Party, 6 Budi Rruga, Tirana, Albania. Tel: +355 (0)4 227481, fax: +355 (0)4 227481
Union for Human Rights Party, Durresi Street, Tirana, Albania. Tel:+355 (0)4 24965, URL: http://www.pbdnj.com
Leader: Vangjel Dule
Republican Party, Sami Frasheri Street, near Petro Nini High School, Tirana, Albania. Tel: +355 (0)4 223090
Leader: Fatmir Mediu
Socialist Party of Albania (SPA), Blvd. Deshmoret e Kombit, Tirana, Albania. Tel:+355 (0)4 227409, fax: +355 (0)4 227417, URL: http://www.ps.al
Leader: Edi Rama
Social-Democratic Party, 26 Asim Voshki Street, Tirana, Albania. Tel: +355 (0)4 226540, fax: +355 (0)4 227485, URL: http://www.psd-al.org/
Socialist Movement for Integration, URL: http://www.lsi.ai
Leader: Ilir Meta
Party for Justice, Integration and Unity, URL: http://www.pdiu.al
Leader: Shpëtim Idrizi

Elections
In July 2007, following four rounds of elections, Bamir Topi, of the ruling Democratic Party, was elected President of Albania. The next presidential election is due in July 2012.

The most recent general election was held on 28 June 2009. The Democratic Party led by former president Sali Berisha won the largest share of the vote as part of the Alliance for Change. The Alliance for Change partners, the Republic Party (PR) and the Party for Justice and Integration (PDI), both won one seat. Overall the coalition was one seat short of an overall majority. The PD then formed a new coalition with the Socialist Movement for Integration. A Cabinet was approved on 16 September. The PDI did not receive a seat. There has been widespread opposition to the result.

The most recent presidential election was held in June 2012, Bujar Nishani a member of the ruling coalition won, the Socialist Party which is the main opposition boycotted the election.

The age of suffrage is 18. Voting is compulsory.

Diplomatic Representation
British Embassy, Rruga Skenderbej N.12, Tirana, Albania. Tel: +355 (0)4 234973/4/5, fax: +355 (0)4 247697, URL: http://ukinalbania.fco.gov.uk/en
Ambassador: Nicholas Cannon OBE (page 1400)
Embassy of the United States, Rruga Elbasanit 103, Tirana, Albania. Tel: +355 (0)4 247285, fax: +355 (0)4 232222, URL: http://tirana.usembassy.gov
Ambassador: Alexander A. Arvizu (page 1379)
Embassy of the Republic of Albania, 2nd Floor, 24 Buckingham Gate, London SW1E 6LB, United Kingdom. Tel: +44 (0)20 7828 8897, fax: +44 (0)20 7828 8869, e-mail: amblonder@hotmail.com, URL: http://www.albanianembassy.co.uk
Ambassador: Mal Bershira
Embassy of the Republic of Albania, 2100 S. Street, NW, Washington, DC 20008, USA. Tel: +1 202 223 4942, fax: +1 202 628 7342, e-mail: albaniaemb@aol.com, URL: http://embassyofalbania.org
Ambassador: Gilbert Galanxhi
Permanent Mission to the United Nations, 320 East 79th Street, New York, NY 10021, USA. Tel: +1 212 249 2059, fax: +1 212 535 2917, e-mail: albania@un.int
Ambassador: Agim Nesho

LEGAL SYSTEM

Justice is administered by a Supreme Court, the Constitutional Court, Court of Cassation, district courts and appeal courts. Justices of the Supreme Court are elected by the People's Assembly for a term of four years. The Constitutional Court deals with all matters and disputes concerning the constitution, whilst the Court of Cassation is the highest appeal court. The High Council of Justice, responsible to the President, nominates officials of the district and appeal courts.

In general, the government respects the rights of its citizens. However, there are cases of police corruption and impunity, and security forces have been known to abuse prisoners and detainees. Prison conditions remain poor. The death penalty was abolished in 2007.

Supreme Court of Albania: http://www.gjykataelarte.gov.al/
Chief Justice: Shpresa Becaj

People's Advocate of Albania, URL: http://www.avokatipopullit.gov.al/

LOCAL GOVERNMENT

Administratively, Albania is divided into 12 prefectures (Qarku i Beratit, Qarku i Dibres, Qarku i Durresit, Qarku i Elbasanit, Qarku i Fierit, Qarku i Gjirokastres, Qarku i Korces, Qarku i Kukesit, Qarku i Lezhes, Qarku i Shkodres, Qarku i Tiranes, Qarku i Vlores). The prefectures

ALBANIA

are divided into 36 *rreths*, or districts, and one municipality. These are further sub-divided into 384 local government units or communes which are headed by a Mayor, and 2,900 villages. Each district administers its affairs through multi-party executive committees. Each region has a Prefect appointed by the Council of Ministers as its representative.

The most recent local government elections took place in May 2011. There was some controversy over some of the voting but Lulzim Basha of the Democratic Party was sworn in as the new mayor of Tirania in July.

AREA AND POPULATION

Area
Albania is situated on the Adriatic Sea, bounded in the north by Montenegro, in the east by Macedonia, in the north east by Serbia/Kosovo and in the south and south east by Greece. The area of the country is approximately 28,750 sq. km (10,629 sq. miles). The land consists mainly of mountains and plains. Low ground turns quickly to swampland in the winter. The climate on the south coast is Mediterranean.

To view a map, consult: http://www.un.org/Depts/Cartographic/map/profile/albania.pdf

Population
The estimated population in 2010 was 3.412 million, with an estimated annual growth rate of 0.4 per cent over the period 2000-10. Population density in 2000 was 127.7 inhabitants per sq. km. Approximately 23 per cent of the population is aged less than 15 years and 13 per cent over 60 years. Some 52 per cent of the population live in urban areas, the majority of the population live near the coast. The major cities are Tirana, Durres, with an estimated population of 200,000, Elbasan, Shkoder and Vlore. Albanians are the principal ethnic group with a small Greek minority. Albanian is the official language although Greek is also spoken. Tosk is the official dialect.

Births, Marriages, Deaths
In 2010, the fertility rate was 1.5 for women. Infant mortality in 2009 was 13.0 per 1,000 live births. In 2008 the maternal mortality rate was 31 per 100,000 live births. In 2010 the crude birth rate was 12.8 per 1,000 population and the crude death rate was 8.8 per 1,000 population. Figures for 2001 show that 25,717 marriages and 2,462 divorces took place. According to the WHO, life expectancy at birth in 2009 was 72 years for males and 75 years of females. Healthy life expectancy was 64 years. The median age is 30. (Source: http://www.who.int, World Health Statistics 2012)

Public Holidays 2014
1 January: New Year's Day
18 April: Good Friday
21 April: Easter Monday
5 May: May Day
29 July: Lesser Bairam (End of Ramadan)*
5 October: Greater Bairam (Feast of the Sacrifice)*
28 November: Independence and Liberation Day
25 December: Christmas Day
* Islamic holidays depend on the sighting of the moon, therefore dates can vary.

EMPLOYMENT

According to recent estimates Albania had a total labour force of 1,102,900 in 2008 of which half are employed in agriculture, and half are employed in industry and services. Official unemployment figures for 2006 put the number unemployed as 150,000, estimated figures for September 2010 put unemployment at 13.5 per cent.

The following table shows how the working population were employed in recent years:

Sector	2005	2006
Agriculture, forestry & fishing	545,000	542,000
Mining & quarrying	6,000	5,000
Manufacturing	56,000	58,000
Electricity, gas & water supply	12,000	10,000
Construction	52,000	53,000
Trade	64,000	68,000
Hotels & restaurants	15,000	16,000
Transport, storage & communications	19,000	19,000
Education	47,000	48,000
Health & social work	24,000	25,000
Other	90,000	90,000
Total	932,000	935,000

Source: Copyright © International Labour Organization (ILO Dept. of Statistics, http://laborsta.ilo.org/)

BANKING AND FINANCE

Currency
The unit of currency is the lek (Lk) of 100 qindarka.

GDP/GNP, Inflation, National Debt
A reform programme has been in operation since the early 1990s. The policies included privatisation, financial sector reform, restructuring and financial liberalisation. Farmers' incomes were greatly improved following the privatisation of agricultural land in 1992. Albania's GDP fell in 1997 following the collapse of financial pyramid schemes in which large numbers of the population had invested. Corruption remains a problem; the European Commission published a report in July 2009 which criticised the government's failure in the

fight against corruption and organised crime. EU funding of over 500 million was suspended as of September 2009. Albania remains one of the poorest countries in Europe; in 2005 the World Bank estimated 18 per cent of the population were living below the poverty line.

The following table shows the main macroeconomic indicators at current prices in recent years.

Description	2005	2006	2007*
GDP (current prices) in million Leks	814,797	882,209	971,222
Annual growth rate of GDP at constant prices	5.7%	5.4%	6.0%
GDP per capita in Leks	259,000	280,000	307,000
GDP per capita in €	2,088	2,275	2,491

Source: Institute of Statistics

GDP was estimated at $23.5 billion in 2009, rising to €24.5 billion in 2010 and $25.2 billion in 2011. The real growth rate was estimated at 2 per cent in 2011. Per capita GDP was $7,700 in 2011.

The following table shows GDP by economic activity in recent years:

GDP by economic activities, million leks

Activity	2005	2006	2007(e)
Agriculture, hunting and forestry	151,640	154,648	164,924
Industry	78,319	88,207	81,100
- Mining	5,576	5,894	8,141
- Manufacturing	72,743	82,313	72,959
Construction	101,759	113,724	127,224
Services	405,917	438,606	498,388
-Trade, hotels & restaurants	159,029	166,125	185,038
-Transport	40,986	43,350	47,500
-Post & Communication	28,257	31,614	37,167
-Other services	177,645	197,517	228,677
FISIM (-)	-23,508	-30,446	-34,125
Gross value added at basic prices	**714,128**	**764,739**	**837,512**
Taxes on products	104,158	121,188	136,789
Subsidies on products(-)	3,489	3,718	3,079
GDP at market prices	**814,797**	**882,209**	**971,222**

Source: Institute of Statistics

Albania's inflation rate has fallen considerably over the past decade. The average annual inflation rate for 1990-96 was 67.9 per cent, reaching a peak in 1991 of 250 per cent. The rate decreased to almost 20 per cent in 1996 but then increased again to 50 per cent in 1998. It has stabilised over the last 10 years. Estimates for 2003 put inflation at 4.5 per cent, 2.9 per cent in 2004, 2.4 per cent in 2006, 1.5 per cent in 2009, rising to over 2 per cent in 2010. Inflation was estimated to be 3 per cent in 2012.

Total external debt rose from an estimated US$820 million in 1999 to an estimated US$2.3 billion in 2006.

The Albanian economy was put under severe strain following the NATO bombing in 1999 of Yugoslavia when an estimated 500,000 Albanian refugees from Kosovo entered Albania. Albania relies heavily on remittances sent home by Albanians working abroad. Remittances have declined since the Eurozone crisis in 2008 and as of 2010 accounted for approximately 8 per cent of GDP.

Foreign Investment
In the past, Albania received economic assistance from Russia and the People's Republic of China. More recently, Albania has developed trade links with the European Community. The US is also a large investor. Albania is actively working towards attracting more foreign direct investment.

Balance of Payments / Imports and Exports
Italy is Albania's main export partner, followed by Greece, Germany, Austria, and Turkey. Main import partners are Italy, Greece, Turkey, and Germany. Approximately 85 per cent of exports go to the EU, although only around 10 per cent of Albania's GDP is made up from exports.

Direction of exports (min leke)

	2007	2008
Europe	92,485	108,739
-Italy	66,147	69,593
-Greece	8,092	9,904
Africa	33	62
Americas	629	451
-USA	623	425
Asia	3,504	3,200
Australia-Oceania	4	1
Others	155	188

Source: Institute of Statistics

Imports by origin (min leke)

	2007	2008
Europe	321,821	369,395

- continued

-Italy	100,743	116,462
-Greece	55,040	64,353
-Germany	20,744	26,724
-Turkey	27,454	26,245
Africa	**3,026**	**3,313**
Americas	**11,901**	**15,662**
-Brazil	5,008	6,122
-USA	4,433	5,607
Asia	**38,234**	**50,175**
Australia-Oceania	**268**	**307**
-Australia	184	213
Others	**945**	**1,041**

Source: Institute of Statistics

The trade balance in 2008 was -372,322 min leke.

The following tables show the value of exports and imports by SITC groupings in recent years:

Exports (fob) in Million Leks

Commodity	2006	2007	2008
Food, beverages and tobacco	6,143	7,079	7,215
Minerals, fuels, electricity	5,809	14,987	20,339
Chemical and plastic products	563	786	1,177
Leather and leather manuf.	1,486	2,022	1,738
Wood manufactures and paper	2,504	3,031	3,619
Textile and footwear	42,419	47,069	48,813
Construction materials and metals	13,203	15,386	22,492
Machineries, equipments & spare parts	2,979	3,925	4,578
Others	2,300	2,889	2,600
Total	299,1470	376,194	439,894

Source: Institute of Statistics

Imports in Million Leks

Commodity	2006	2007	2008
Food, beverages and tobacco	53,464	60,895	73,160
Minerals, fuels, electricity	41,472	62,932	78,705
Chemical and plastic products	33,086	39,526	45,465
Leather and leather manuf.	6,528	7,825	6,924
Wood manufactures and paper	10,887	13,323	15,016
Textile and footwear	35,111	39,310	39,582
Construction materials and metals	47,836	59,560	67,827
Machineries, equipments & spare parts	60,369	78,773	97,059
Others	10,393	14,049	16,156
Total	299,147	376,194	439,894

Source: Institute of Statistics

Albania joined the World Trade Organization in July 2000. As a prerequisite to entry, Albania had to liberalise its markets and ensure that legislation conformed to international trade rules. Albania has also negotiated Free Trade Agreements with Macedonia, Croatia, Bulgaria, Bosnia and Herzegovina, Romania, and Moldova.

Central Bank

Bank of Albania, (Banka e Shqiperise), Sheshi 'Skenderbej' 1, Tirana, Albania. Tel: +355 (0)4 235568 / (0)4 222152 / (0)4 222752, fax: +355 (0)4 223558, e-mail: public@bankofalbania.org, URL: http://www.bankofalbania.org
Governor: Ardian Fullani (page 1427)

MANUFACTURING, MINING AND SERVICES

Primary and Extractive Industries

Albania no longer produces a great deal of oil (nearly 15,600 barrels per day in 2011). It consumed 44,000 barrels per day that year, all imported. It has an estimated 200 million barrels of oil reserves. (Source: EIA)

In 2004, Albania, Macedonia and Bulgaria agreed to go ahead with the construction of a US$1.2bn pipeline. It will run from Burgas, Bulgaria on the Caspian Sea to Vlore, Albania on the Adriatic coast. It should be able to transport 750,000 barrels of oil per day. Construction was expected to begin in 2006 and be completed by 2011, but in 2011 work on the project had still not begun.

Production and consumption of primary energy in ktoe*

Total Production	2006	2007
Lignite	0.05	0.04
Crude oil	1.59	1.78
Natural gas	0.03	0.05
Electric power	1.50	0.82
Firewood	0.72	0.68
Others	0.03	0.04
Total production	3.92	3.41
Total consumption		
Lignite	0.05	0.05

- continued

Crude oil	4.03	3.96
Natural gas	0.00	0.00
Electric power	0.94	0.99
Firewood	0.73	0.63
Others	0.01	0.02
Total consumption	5.76	5.70

*ktoe = kilo tonnes of oil of equivalent
Source: Statistics Albania

Energy

Albania has a total electricity generating capacity of 1.62 gigawatts (GWe), according to 2012 figures, mainly hydroelectric. Total electricity generation was 7.48 billion kWh. Electricity consumption in 2012 was 4.67 billion kWh.

Tourism

Tourism is an increasingly important sector with touris arrival increasing from 748,000 in 2005 to 937,000 in 2006 and 1,126,000 in 2007.

Manufacturing

Albania's industrial sector contributed around 12 per cent of GDP in 2003 and, employed over 55,000. Industrial production grew at an estimated rate of 9 per cent in 2000. Agricultural processing is one of the country's main industries, along with mineral and oil extraction, cement manufacture and textiles. Some of these products, particularly minerals such as chrome, ferrochrome, iron, nickel and copper, are present in considerable quantities and the oil and gas reserves are destined for export only if sizeable foreign investment can be attracted.

Agriculture

The agricultural sector contributes about 21 per cent of Albania's annual GDP and employs half of the labour force. The main crops are wheat, corn, potatoes, maize, fruit, vegetables and sugar beet. Eighty per cent of agriculture production is destined for domestic use. Agricultural exports include vegetables, fruits and tobacco. The following table shows estimated crop production in 2010.

Crop	Production (Int$ $'000)	Metric Tonnes
Cow milk. whole, fresh	261,005	930,000
Grapes	105,692	184,900
Indigenous Cattle Meat	95,394	35,313
Tomatoes	73,648	199,283
Olives	56,049	70,000
Wheat	40,061	294,900
Indigenous Sheep Meat	37,801	13,883
Chillies and Peppers, green	30,823	65,475
Sheep milk, whole, fresh	29,385	77,000
Hen eggs, in shell	25,960	31,300
Apples	23,093	54,604
Goat milk, whole, fresh	20,719	63,000

Source: http://faostat.fao.org/site/339/default.aspx Food and Agriculture Organiztion of the United Nations, Food and Agricultural commodities production

COMMUNICATIONS AND TRANSPORT

Visa Requirements

Citizens of the US, Canada, Australia and the EU do not require a visa to enter the country. However, they do need a return travel ticket. An entry stamp valid for a stay of up to 90 days, will be issued at the point. Travellers are sometimes charged an entry fee of €1 (not nationals of the European Union), and the same amount is charged for leaving the country. All travellers entering or exiting Albania must have six months or more validity on their passport. Citizens of other countries are advised to contact the Albanian consulate in their country to check visa requirements.

National Airlines

The Italian airline, Alitalia, runs regular weekly flights between Rome and Tirana, subsidised by the Italian government. There are also regular air services connecting Tirana with Belgrade, Berlin and Budapest.
Ada-Air, URL: http://www.adaair.com
Albanian Airlines, URL: http://www.albanianairlines.com

Airports

Tirana International Airport, Mother Teresa, URL: http://www.tirana-airport.com
Aviation is regulated by the following bodies:
Ministry of Industry, Transport and Trade, 42 Myslym Shryi, Tirana, Albania. Tel: +355 (0)4 228428
General Directorate of Civil Aviation, Albtransport, 202 Rruga Kongresi i Permentit, Tirana, Albania. Tel: +355 (0)4 223026

Railways

In 2010 there was about 895 km of railway track. Trains run from Tirana to Shkodra, Vlora, Fier, Ballsh and Pogradec. Future plans for the railway system include a link between Pogradic and Kicevo in FYR Macedonia and also Florina in Greece.

Roads

The road network in 2002 amounted to about 18,000 km, which included 3,225 km of main roads and 4,300 km of secondary roads. Some 190,004 cars, 25,066 buses and coaches, and 46,809 lorries and vans used Albania road system in 2004. The most widely used public

ALGERIA

transport system in the bus system run by private companies, the main routes run from Shkodra, Korça, Saranda, Gjirokastra, Peshkopia and Durres to Tirana. A daily bus services operates between Ulcinj in Montenegro and Shkoder. Vehicles are driven on the right.

Ports and Harbours
Albania has the following ports: Shëngjin (San Giovanni di Medua), Durrës (Durazzo), Vlora (Valona) and Saranda (Porto Edda). There are 43 km of waterways. Ferry runs between Durrës and Bari and Ancona , Brindisi to Vlore and Corfu to Saranda.

HEALTH

In 2009, general government expenditure on health as a percentage of total government expenditure was 8.4 per cent. Total expenditure was equivalent to 6.9 per cent of GDP. Private expenditure accounts for 58.8 per cent of total expenditure. Total per capita expenditure was equivalent to US$260.

In 2005-10 there were an estimated 3,685 doctors (11.5 per 10,000 population), 12,455 nurses and midwives (39 per 10,000 population). There were a reported 1,035 dentists and 1,237 pharmaceutical personnel. In the period 2005-11 there were an estimated 28 hospital beds and 2.1 psychiatric beds per 10,000 population.

An estimated 94 per cent of the total population have access to improved sanitation and 95 per cent to improved drinking water-sources.

In 2010, the infant mortality rate (likelihood of dying aged less than1 year old) was estimated to be 16 per 1,000 live births and the child (under-five) mortality rate was estimated to be 18 per 1,000 live births. The most common causes of infant mortality (2010) were congenital anomalies 24 per cent, prematurity 19 per cent and pneumonia 11 per cent. Immunization rates for common diseases are high (99 per cent). (Source: http://www.who.int, Global Health Statistics, 2012)

EDUCATION

Primary/Secondary Education
Primary and secondary education is compulsory and free of charge, and lasts between the ages of 6 and 14. Primary school enrolment is put at 96 per cent for males and 94 per cent for females. Secondary education is split into two levels, the second lasting for five years and allowing students to move into higher education. Students must pasta a school certificate to pass from primary into secondary education. In recent years some private schools have opened.

Higher Education
Recent figures indicate that there are nine universities and two institutes of higher education in Albania. The State University of Tirana was inaugurated on 16 September 1957.

Literacy was estimated at 99.0 per cent in 2007.

RELIGION

Albania's ban on religious worship was ended in 1990 with the fall of the USSR. Currently, the country is predominantly Muslim, with about 71 per cent of the population of the Sunni or Bektashi orders. The Eastern Orthodox Church is also represented (20 per cent), as well as the Roman Catholic Church (7 per cent).

Albania has a religious liberty rating of 9 on a scale of 1 to 10 (10 is most freedom). (Source: World Religion Database)

COMMUNICATIONS AND MEDIA

The constitution guarantees freedom of the media but there are reporst of political and business pressure on journalists.

Newspapers
Over 20 dailies are published and over 150 titles in total.
Albania Daily News, URL: http://www.albanianews.com
Koha Jone, URL: http://www.kohajone.com
Rilinja Demokratike, http://www.rilindjademokratike.com/
Skekulli, URL: http://www.skekulli.com
Gazeta Shqiptare, URL: http://www.balkanweb.com/gazetav5/

Broadcasting
On completion of the TV centre in Tirana, regular television transmissions began in 1971 for an initial duration of four hours daily. Now, the state-run Albanian Radio and Television, operates two networks. Private competition has flourished since the 1990s. An estimated 90 per cent of Albanian households have a television. Political parties are not allowed to own private broadcast stations although they may publish newspapers. Regulation has improved. Cable is available as are several international broadcasters.
Albanian Radio & Television (RTsh), URL: http://www.rtsh.al/
Top Channel, URL: http://www.top-channel.tv/ (private)
Arberia TV, URL: http://www.telearberia.tv/ (private)
Top Albania Radio, URL: http://www.topalbaniaradio.com/
National Council of Radio and Television, URL: http://www.kkrt.gov.al

The main news agency is the **Albanian Telegraphic Agency (ATA)**, URL: http://www.ata.gov.al/.

Telecommunications
Although recently there has been investment in the land lines system, the system still does not meet demand and subscriber rates remain low. Mobile phone coverage is much more extensive. As of 2008 it was estimated that there were 315,000 land lines in operation and three million mobile phones.

In 2009, an estimated 750,000 of the population were internet users.

ENVIRONMENT

Major environmental problems in Albania include soil erosion, deforestation, and water pollution from industry and untreated wastewater. In recent years, increased car ownership has resulted in an increase of air pollution in the larger cities particularly Tirana.

Albania is a party to the following environmental agreements: Air Pollution, Biodiversity, Climate Change, Climate Change-Kyoto Protocol, Desertification, Endangered Species, Hazardous Wastes, Law of the Sea, Ozone Layer Protection, and Wetlands.

In 2010 Albania produced 4.89 million metric tons of carbon dioxide from the consumption of fossil fuels.

ALGERIA
The People's Democratic Republic of Algeria
Al Jumhuriyah al Jaza'iriyah ad Dimuqratiyah ash Sha'biyah

Capital: Algiers (Population estimate: 3.2 million)

Head of State: Abdelaziz Bouteflika (President) (page 1392)

National Flag: A crescent and red star on a vertically divided half white and green background

CONSTITUTION AND GOVERNMENT

Constitution
Formerly a French colony, Algeria became independent on 3 July 1962. The country was ruled by the National Liberation Front (FLN) from 1962 until 1988. A referendum in 1989 approved a new constitution that proposed a multi-party democracy and market economy. At the same time religious fundamentalists set up the Islamic Salvation Front (FIS). In the first multi-party elections in 1991, on the expectation that the FIS would win a majority of seats, the electoral process was halted and the Higher Committee of State (HCS) took control. This signalled the start of years of violent unrest. The FIS was banned in 1992. Mohamed Boudiaf was declared head of the five-man HCS in March 1992 but was assassinated three months later. The HCS was disbanded in 1994 and Brigadier-General Liamine Zeroual was appointed President. He was officially elected to the post in 1995 to serve a five-year term but resigned in 1998. Abdelaziz Bouteflika was elected President on 15 April 1999 for a five-year term, and was re-elected in 2004. Under the terms of the Constitution the president is elected by universal adult suffrage for a five-year term. The president appoints the prime minister, who appoints the Council of Ministers. In November 2008 the parliament approved constitutional changes which allow the president to run for three terms.

To consult the full constitution, please visit:
http://www.algeria-un.org/default.asp?doc=-const

Recent History
The Berbers make up around 30 per cent of the population and in 2001 following some unrest, the government agreed to recognise the Berber language of Tamazight. Investment in the predominantly Berber area of Kabylie was promised in the spring of 2005, together with increased recognition of people's culture.

In March 2005, a government report found that the security forces had been responsible for the disappearance of some 6,000 people during the civil conflicts of the 1990s. A 'reconciliation' referendum was held in September, in which voters backed the Government in its plans to amnesty many of those involved in the killings. The first of the Islamist militants were freed from jail in March 2006. In September, Rabah Kebir, leader of the banned Islamic Salvation Front (FIS), returned from self-imposed exile and urged those rebels who were still fighting to disarm.

In January 2007, 10 Islamist militants and five members of Algerian security forces were killed when the militants carried out a rocket attack on an army post in the eastern region of Batna. Earlier in the month, the Salafist Group of Preaching and Combat (GSPC) announced that it had changed its name to al-Qaeda Organisation in the Islamic Maghreb, and the attack is thought to have been carried out by this group. In April 2007, two bomb blasts killed 23 people and injured around 160 in Algiers. It was also possibly the work of the al-Qaeda Organisation in the Islamic Maghreb. The attacks were a blow for the Algerian authorities which have for years fought Islamist militancy.

In May 2007, 18 soldiers and 22 Islamist guerrillas were killed in ambushes and bomb attacks in the east of the country. The armed forces had stepped up operations against the armed groups ahead of the parliamentary elections due on 17th May. Abou Moussab Abdelaouadoud, leader of the al-Qaeda Organisation in the Islamic Maghreb, described the election as a comedy and said that anyone taking part in them would be committing a sin.

On 11 December, two bomb attacks were carried out in Algiers, killing between 26 and 60 people (including 11 UN personnel) and injuring a further 177. The targets were the Constitutional Council and offices of the UN. Al-Qaeda in the Land of the Islamic Maghreb claimed responsibility; they referred to the UN buildings as an 'international infidels' den'.

On the 6th June 2008, a bomb attack by suspected Islamist militants killed six soldiers east of the capital, Algiers. Security forces blamed the al-Qaeda in the Islamic Maghreb movement. In August, the movement claimed responsibility for a series of bombings in towns to the east of Algiers, in which around 60 people were killed.

President Bouteflika won a third term of office in April 2009.

In July 2009, Algeria, Nigeria and Niger signed an agreement to build a US$13 billion pipeline which will carry Nigerian gas across the Sahara to the Mediterranean.

In April 2010, a joint command was set between Algeria, Mauritania, Mali and Niger to tackle threat of terrorism.

As unrest in Arab countries in the Middle East and North Africa at the beginning of 2011 began to spread, Algeria was also affected. From January 2011 President Abdelaziz Bouteflika came under pressure to made constitutional changes including a limit to presidential terms. Strikes and protests continued and were broken up by police when protesters attempted to march through the capital. In February President Bouteflika met a major demand of the protestors and lifted the state of emergency that had been in place for 19 years. As well as demanding political changes protests were also directed at the rising cost of food and rising unemployment. On April 16 President Bouteflika announced he would amend the constitution and a constitutional commission would be set up. The original protests seem to have been triggered by rising food prices and the government is now trying to respond with a large programme of public spending using money from Algeria's oil and gas export wealth.

In September 2012, President Bouteflika appointed the former minister of water, Abdelmalek Sellal to the post of prime minister, ending post-election uncertainty. Elections had taken place in May.

In January 2013 Islamic militants siezed control of a gas complex in the desert close to the Libyan border, they said they were attacking in retaliation for French military operations against Islamists in Mali. Many foreign nationals were taken hostage in the seige. Algerian special forces brought the siege to an end but several hostages had already been killed by the militants.

Legislature
Algeria's bicameral legislature - the Parliament (Barlaman) - comprises the lower house, or National People's Assembly, and the upper house, or National Council.

Upper House
The 144-seat National Council, or Council of the Nation, *Majilis al-Oumma*, is made up of 96 members elected by electoral colleges (formed by local councils), with two members representing each electoral district, and 48 members appointed by the President. Members serve a six-year term, with half replaced every three years.
Council of the Nation, 7 blvd Zirout Youcef, Algiers, Algeria. URL: http://www.majliselouma.dz

Lower House
The National People's Assembly, *Majilis al-Chaabi al-Watani*, has 389 members representing 48 Wilayas. Members are directly elected for a five-year term.
National People's Assembly, 18 blvd Zirout Youcef, Algiers, Algeria. URL: http://www.apn.dx.org

Cabinet (as at March 2013)
Prime Minister: Abdelmalek Sellal (page 1511)
Deputy Prime Minister: Abdelmalek Guenaizia (page 1435)
Minister of Foreign Affairs: Mourad Medelci (page 1476)
Minister of Justice and Keeper of the Seals: Mohamed Charfi (page 1403)
Minister of Finance: Karim Djoudi (page 1416)
Minister of Trade: Mostafa Benbada
Minister of Transport: Amar Tou
Minister of Water Resources: Hocine Necib
Minister of Energy and Mines: Dr Youcef Yousfi
Minister of National Education: Abdelatif Baba Ahmed
Minister of Higher Education and Scientific Research: Dr Rachid Harraoubia
Minister of Public Works: Amar Ghoul
Minister for Communications: Mohand Oussaid Belaid
Minister of Vocational Training and Professional Education: Mohamed Mebarki
Minister of Religious Affairs and Endowments: Pr. Bouabdellah Ghalamallah (page 1430)
Minister of Industry and Promotion of Investments: Cherif Rahmani

Minister of Mujahedin: Mohamed Cherif Abbas (page 1371)
Minister of Labour, Employment and Social Security: Tayeb Louh
Minister of National Solidarity and Family: Souad Bendjaballah
Minister of Housing and Town Planning: Abdelmadjid Teboune
Minister of Fisheries and Marine Resources: Sid Ahmed Ferroukhi
Minister of Culture: Mme Khalida Toumi
Minister of Health, Population and Hospital Reform: Abdelaziz Ziari
Minister for Youth and Sports: Mohamed Tahmi
Minister of Agriculture and Rural Development: Rachid Benaissa
Minister of Town Planning and the Environment: Amara Brnyounes
Minister of Tourism and Handicrafts: Mohamed Benmeradi
Minister for Relations with Parliament: Mahmoud Khoudri
Minister of Postal Services, Information Technology and Telecommunications: Moussa Benhamadi
Minister for the Interior and Local Authorities: Dahou Ould Kablia
Minister of Maghreb and African Affairs: Abdelkader Messahel

Ministries
Office of the President, Présidence de la République, El Mouradia, Algiers, Algeria. Tel: +213 (0)21 691515, fax: +213 (0)21 691595, URL: http://www.el-mouradia.dz
Office of the Prime Minister, rue Docteur Sâadane, Algiers, Algeria. Tel: +213 (0)21 731200, fax: +213 (0)21 717929, URL: http://www.cg.gov.dz/
Ministry of Justice, 8 Place Bir Hakem, El Biar, Algiers, Algeria. Tel: +213 (0)21 921608, fax: +213 (0)21 922956, URL: http://www.mjustice.dz/
Ministry of Interior and Local Communities, 18 rue Docteur Sâadane, Algiers, Algeria. Tel: +213 (0)21 732340, fax: +213 (0)21 605210
Ministry of Foreign Affairs, 1 Rue Ibn Batrane, El-Mouradia, Algiers, Algeria. Tel: +213 (0)21 504545, fax: +213 (0)21 504141, URL: http://www.mae.dz
Ministry of Public Works, Tel: +213 (0)21 914938, fax: +277 (0)21 91 35 85
Ministry of Finance, Place du Pérou, Immeuble Maurétania, Algiers, Algeria. Tel: +213 (0)21 595151, URL: http://www.finance-algeria.org
Ministry of Small and Medium Sized Companies, Immeuble le Colisée, 4 rue Ahmed Bey, Algiers, Algeria. Tel: +213 (0)21 697273, fax: +213 (0)21 230094, URL: http://www.pmeart-dz.org/
Ministry of Energy and Mines, 80 avenue Ahmed Ghermoul, Algiers, Algeria. Tel: +213 (0)21 488526, fax: +213 (0)21 488557, e-mail: info@mem-algeria.org, URL: http://www.mem-algeria.org
Ministry of National Education, 8 Rue de Pékin, Algiers, Algeria. Tel: +213 (0)21 605560, fax: +213(0)21 606702, e-mail: men@men.dz, URL: http://www.meducation.edu.dz
Ministry of Culture, Palais de la Culture "Moufdi Zakaria", Plateau des Annassers, BP 100, Algiers, Algeria. Tel: +213 (0)21 291010, fax: +213 (0)21 292089, e-mail: info@mcc.gov.dz, URL: http://www.mcc.gov.dz
Ministry of Higher Education & Scientific Research, 11 rue Doudou Mokhtar, Algiers, Algeria. Tel: +213 (0)21 912323, fax: +213 (0)21 911722, URL: http://www.mesrs.dz
Ministry of Professional Training, URL: http://www.mfp.gov.dz/
Ministry of Youth and Sports, 3 rue Mohamed Belouizdad, Place du 1er mai, Algiers, Algeria. Tel: +213 (0)21 655555, fax: +213 (0)21 657174, e-mail: mjs@mjs.dz, URL: http://www.mjs.dz
Ministry of Trade, rue Docteur Saâdana, Algiers, Algeria. Tel: +213 (0)21 732340/ 737417, fax: +213 (0)21 692201, URL: http://www.mincommerce.gov.dz/
Ministry for the Posts and Telecommunications, 4 bis boulevard Krim Belkacem, Algiers, Algeria. Tel: +213 (0)21 711200, fax: +213 (0)21 730047, URL: http://www.mptic.dz/
Ministry of Religious Affairs, 4 rue de Timgad, Hydra, Algiers, Algeria. Tel: +213 (0)21 608555, fax: +213 (0)21 600936, URL: http://www.m-moudjahidine.dz/
Ministry of Housing and Urban Affairs, 135 rue de Didouche Mourad, Algiers, Algeria. Tel: +213 (0)21 740722, fax: +213 (0)21 745383, e-mail: mhabitat@wissal.dz, URL: http://www.mhu.gov.dz/
Ministry of Industry and Investment, Immeuble le Colisée, 2 rue Ahmed Bey, Algiers, Algeria. Tel: +213 (0)239043, fax: +213 (0)21 283837, URL: http://www.mipi.dz/index_fr.php
Ministry of Work, Employment and Social Services, 14 boulevard Mohamed Belouizdad, Algiers, Algeria. Tel: +213 (0)21 659999, fax: +213 (0)21 663519, URL: http://www.mtss.gov.dz/
Ministry for National Solidarity, rue Docteur Saâdane, Algiers, Algeria. Fax: +213 (0(21 600936, URL: http://www.msolidarite.gov.dz/
Ministry of War Veterans, 2 avenue de Lieutenant Med Benarfa, El Biar, Algiers, Algeria. Tel: +213 (0)21 922355/922359, fax: +213 (0)21 923516
Ministry of Water Resources, URL: http://www.mre.gov.dz/
Ministry of Health, Population and Hospitals Reform, 125 rue Abderaahmane Laâla, El Madania,16075 Algiers, Algeria. Tel: +213 (0)21 279900 , fax: +213 (0)21 279641, e-mail: webmaster@ands.dz, URL: http://www.ands.dz/
Ministry of National and Regional Development and the Environment, Grand Séminaire, Kouba, Algiers, Algeria. Tel: +213 (0)21 586550, fax: +213 (0)21 585038
Ministry of Agriculture and Rural Development, 4 route des Quatre Canons, Algiers, Algeria. Tel: +213 (0)21 711712, fax: +213 (0)21 745129, URL: http://www.minagri-algeria.org
Ministry of Fishing, URL: http://www.mpeche.gov.dz/
Ministry of Territory, Environment, Tourism and Handicraft, Route Nationale N° 36 El Biar, Algiers, Algeria. Tel: +213 (0)21 432844, fax: +213 (0)21 432861, URL: http://www.matet.dz/
Ministry of Transport, 119 rue de Didouche Mourad, Algiers, Algeria. Tel: +213 (0)21 711366, fax: +213 (0)21 736450
Ministry of Relations with Parliament, URL: http://www.mcrp.gov.dz/Ministere_Arabe/
National Assembly, 18 Boulevard zirout youcef, 16000 Algiers, Algeria. Tel: +213 (0)21 7386 00/10, e-mail: info@apn-dz.org, URL: http://www.apn-dz.org

Elections
The most recent presidential election was held in April 2009 and Abdelaziz Bouteflika, President since 1999, was re-elected in a second landslide victory, winning over 90 per cent of the vote. Mr. Bouteflika had changed the Constitution in order to be able to run for a third

ALGERIA

term in office. Around 74 per cent of those eligible voted, amid a boycott by some opposition parties and charges of election fraud. Mr Bouteflika's nearest rival was Louisa Hanoune of the Trotskyist Workers' Party who won just 4.22 per cent of the vote.

The most recent elections for the National Assembly were held in May 2012. The government coalition led by the National Liberation Front (FLN) was re-elected to power winning 220 seats. Indirect elections for the National Council were most recently held on 12 January 2010.

Political Parties

Rassemblement National Démocratique (National Democratic Rally, RND), 10, les Asphodèles Ben Aknoun, Algeria. Tel: +021 91 64 10 / 29 77, Fax: +021 91 47 40 / 47 74, e-mail: cn@rnd-dz.com, URL: http://www.rnd-dz.com/index.php
Leader: Ahmed Ouyahia
Nationale Libération Front (National Liberation Front, FLN), 7 rue du Stade, Hydra, Algiers, Algeria. Tel: +213 (0)21 592149, URL: http://www.pfln.org.dz
Leader: Abdelaziz Belkhadem
Mouvement de la Société pour la Paix (Movement for a Peaceful Society, MSP), 163 Hassiba Ben Bouali, Algiers, Algeria. URL: http://www.mssalgeria.net
Leader: Bouguerra Soltani
el-Isiah, Movement for National Reform (Isiah); Parti des Travailleurs, Workers Party, PT; Front des Forces Socialistes (FFS); Rassemblement pour la Culture et la Democratie (RCD)
Algerian National Front (Front Nationale Algerien) (FNA), URL: http://www.fna.dz

Diplomatic Representation

British Embassy, 12 Rue Slimane Amirat (Ex Lucien Reynaud), Hydra, Algiers, Algeria. Tel: + 213 (0)21 230068, fax: +213 (0)21 230067, URL: http://ukinalgeria.fco.gov.uk/en/about-us/our-embassy/our-ambassador
Ambassador: Martyn Roper
US Embassy, 4 Chemin Cheikh Bachir El-Ibrahimi, BP 408 (Alger-Gare) 16000, Algiers, Algeria. Tel: +213 (0)21 691255 / 691425, fax: +213 (0)21 693979, URL: http://algiers.usembassy.gov
Ambassador: Henry S. Ensher
Algerian Embassy, 54 Holland Park, London W11 3RS, United Kingdom. Tel: +44 (0)20 7221 7800, fax: +44 (0)20 7221 0488, URL: http://www.algerianembassy.org.uk/
Ambassador: H.E. Amar Abba
Algerian Embassy, 2118 Kalorama Road, NW Washington DC 20008, USA. Tel: +1 202 265 2800, fax: +1 202 667 2174, e-mail: embalgus@cais.com, URL: http://www.algeria-us.org/
Ambassador: Abdallah Baali (page 1381)
Permanent Mission of Algeria to the United Nations, 326 East 48th Street, New York, NY 10017, USA. Tel: +1 212 750 1960, fax: +1 212 759 5274, e-mail: mission@algeria-un.org, URL: http://www.algeria-un.org/
Ambassador: H. E. Mourad Benmehidi

LEGAL SYSTEM

Algeria's legal codes are based on the laws of Islam and of other Northern African and Socialist states, as well as on French law. In civilian courts, Shari'a (Islamic law) is applied to social issues. Military courts have jurisdiction in cases involving military personnel, and also hear some cases in which civilians are charged with security-related and terrorism offenses. The Constitutional Council reviews the constitutionality of treaties and laws, and has the power to nullify unconstitutional laws.

Algeria's judicial system is three-tiered; Daira tribunals are courts of first instance for civil and certain criminal matters; 48 Wilaya Courts in each province hear all cases, and have appellate jurisdiction over lower court decisions in civil suits, and the Supreme Court is the highest court. It comprises a Private Law chamber for civil and commercial cases, a Social Division for social security and labor cases, a Criminal Court, and an Administrative Division. Judges are appointed by the executive branch of government, for a term of ten years.

There are various failures of the Algerian government with regard to human rights issues. These include restrictions on freedom of speech, press and assembly; limitations on religious freedoms; and cases of corruption, official impunity and lack of government transparency. Algeria retains the death penalty for ordinary crimes such as murder, but there have been no executions for over a decade.

National Human Rights Commission of Algeria, Palais du Peuple, Avenue Franklin Roosevelt, 16000 Algiers, Algeria. +213 2123 0311, fax: +213 2123 9037

LOCAL GOVERNMENT

The country is divided into 48 Wilayate (or Provinces) which are led by governors (walis) who report to the Minister of the Interior. The provinces are: Adrar, Chlef, Laghouat, Oum El Bouaghi, Batna, Bejaia, Biskra, Bechar, Blida, Bouira, Tamanrasset, Tebessa, Tlemcen, Tiaret, Tizi Ouzou, Algiers, Djelfa, Jijel, Setif, Saïda, Skikda, Sidi Bel Abbes, Annaba, Guelma, Constantine, Medea, Mostaganem, Msila, Mascara, Ouargla, Oran, El Bayadh, Illizi, Bordj Bou Arreridj, Boumerdes, El Tarf, Tinouf, Tissemsilt, El Oued, Khenchela, Souk Ahras, Tipaza, Mila, Aïn Defla, Naama, Aïn Temouchent, Ghardaia, Relizane.

Each wilaya is further divided into daïras, which in turn are divided in communes. The wilayas and communes are each governed by an elected assembly. The most recent local elections for 1,541 municipal councils and 48 local departments took place in November 2007. Local elections should take place in 2012.

AREA AND POPULATION

Area

Algeria is a country in north-west Africa bounded by Morocco to the west, the Democratic Arab Republic of the Sahara and Mauritania to the south-west, Tunisia and Libya to the east, Mali and Niger to the south and the Mediterranean Sea to the north. With an area of 2,381,741 sq. km. Algeria has 1,200 km of Mediterranean coastline. The country can be divided into two main relief areas: to the north, the Tell and Steppe Atlases (381,000 sq. km) and to the south, the Saharan areas (over 2 million sq. km). The north of the country enjoys a Mediterranean climate, whilst the interior is dry with cold winters and hot summers on the high plateau. The hot, dust/sand-laden sirocco wind is common in summer. The Tell is fairly well watered compared with the drier Sahara.

To view a map, please consult http://www.lib.utexas.edu/maps/cia08/algeria_sm_2008.gif

Population

The population of Algeria was estimated at 35.468 million in 2010 (up from 33.3 million in 2007); the annual growth rate is estimated to be 1.5 per cent. Population density averages 13.3 per square km, though over 90 per cent of the population lives on the coast, constituting just 12 per cent of the land. Approximately 66 per cent of the population lives in urban areas, and around 1.5 million nomads and semi-settled Bedouin still live in the Saharan area of Algeria.

Algeria is made up largely of Arabs; some 30 per cent of whom are Berbers, the original inhabitants until the 7th century. At the beginning of 2001 the Berber population began pressing the Algerian government for political and cultural recognition, and in March 2002 President Bouteflika announced that Tamazight would be recognised within the Algerian constitution as a national language. Algeria's main languages are Arabic, French, and Berber dialects.

Births, Marriages and Deaths

In 2010, the birth rate was estimated at 20.2 births per 1,000 inhabitants, whilst the death rate was put at 5.0 per 1,000 people. According to the latest WHO figures, average life expectancy at birth in 2009 was 71 years for males and 74 years for females. Healthy life expectancy was 62 years. The median age was 26 years. Approximately 27 per cent of the population is aged under 15 years and 7 per cent over 60. The total fertility rate was estimated to be 2.3 per cent.

Public Holidays 2014

1 January: New Year's Day
4 January: Birth of the Prophet*
5 May: Labour Day
5 July: Independence Day.
29 June: Beginning of Ramadan *
29 July: Eid al-Fitr (End of Ramadan) *
5 October: Eid al-Adha (Feast of the Sacrifice)*
1 November: Anniversary of the Revolution
25 October: Al-Hijira (Islamic New Year)*
*These holidays are dependent on the sighting of the moon and dates vary from year to year.

EMPLOYMENT

Figures for 2008 indicate that the total number of people in the labour force that year was 9,465,000. Estimates figures for February 2011 put the unemployment rate at 10 per cent.

Employment by industrial sector (figures in 000s)

Sector	2003	2004
Agriculture, hunting and forestry	1,404.6	1,585.2
Fishing	7.2	31.0
Mining and quarrying	82.9	135.1
Manufacturing	615.7	846.7
Electricity, Gas and Water Supply	104.6	79.1
Construction	799.9	967.6
Wholesale and Retail trade, Repair of Motor Vehicles, Motorcycles and Household Goods	880.9	1,174.4
Hotels and Restaurants	102.5	164.8
Transport, Storage and Communications	405.4	435.9
Financial Services	67.6	68.8
Real Estate, Renting and Business Activities	68.0	72.4
Public Administration and Defence; Compulsory Social Security	1,071.2	1,104.1
Education	627.7	634.0
Health and Social Work	245.0	235.5
Other Community, Social and Personal Services	183.4	208.9
Employees in private households	12.2	34.9
Extra-territorial organisations and bodies	2.9	3.9
Unclassified	1.4	16.2
Total	6,684.1	7,798.4

Source: Copyright © International Labour Organization (ILO Dept. of Statistics, http://laborsta.ilo.org)

BANKING AND FINANCE

Currency

One Algerian Dinar (AD) = 100 centimes

GDP/GNP, Inflation, National Debt

Algeria's economy is dominated by the state and by hydrocarbons. Algeria's economy has grown in recent years, largely due the oil and natural gas sector which accounts for nearly 30 per cent of GDP and over 95 per cent of export revenues. In response to declining oil revenues and high debt repayments, the Algerian government implemented a macro-economic plan and also rescheduled its US$7.5 billion Paris Club debt. The government reforms successfully managed to reduce inflation. It has made limited attempts to diversify the economy. In response to unrest in 2011, the government offered several billion dollars worth of grants and benefit increases. The limited growth there is in the economy is driven by public spending.

GDP rose from US$82 billion in 2004 to an estimated US$92.22 billion in 2006. By 2008, it was estimated to have reached US$150 billion. GDP was estimated to be US$162 billion in 2010 with a growth rate of 3.5 per cent. The economy grew by 2.6 per cent in 2011. ~Growth is forecast to continue: at 3.1 per cent in 2012 and over 4 per cent in 2013. Per capita GDP in 2010 was estimated to be US$4,500 per annum.

Industry accounted for around 62 per cent of GDP in 2010. The service sector contributed 31 per cent and the agricultural sector accounted for around 7 per cent.

Inflation, based on consumer prices, rose from 1.6 per cent in 2005 to 2.5 per cent in 2007. Inflation rose further to 3.8 per cent in 2008 and by 2010 it was estimated to be 5.7 per cent. It was estimated to be 3.9 per cent in 2011.

Algeria's total external debt has been greatly reduced in recent years. It reached a high of US$31,296.50 million in 1995. In the following years it fell gradually. It was US$20,374.12 million in 2004, US$15,457.35 million in 2005, and then fell dramatically to US3,737.97 million in 2006. (Source: AFDB). Latest figures put it at under US$500 million, some 3.5 per cent of GDP.

Balance of Payments / Imports and Exports

Algeria's major export partners in 2010 were the US (22.7 per cent), Italy (14 per cent), Spain (10.8 per cent) and France (9 per cent). The main products were petroleum, natural gas and their products which accounted for 97.5 per cent of total exports. Main import products are food, consumer goods and capital goods. In 2010, the main suppliers were France (16.5 per cent), China (12 per cent), Italy (9 per cent), Spain (5.9 per cent) and the US (5.9 per cent).

In 2010, exports were estimated to be worth US$56.5 billion and imports US$40.2 billion.

Foreign Investment

The UK is Algeria's largest foreign investor. Most foreign investment is in the oil sector. Government control or involvement in other sectors has hindered further foreign investment. Some privatisation programmes are ongoing.

Central Bank

Banque d'Algérie, Immeuble Joly, 38 Avenue Franklin Roosevelt, 16000 Algiers, Algeria. Tel: +213 21 230023, fax: +213 21 66499/66437, e-mail: ba@bank-of-algeria.dz, URL: http://www.bank-of-algeria.dz
Governor: Mohammed Laksaci

Chambers of Commerce and Trade Addresses

Chambre Algérienne de Commerce et d'Industrie (CACI), URL: http://www.caci.dz/

MANUFACTURING, MINING AND SERVICES

Primary and Extractive Industries

According to the Energy Information Administration (EIA), Algeria's hydrocarbon industry contributes around 97 per cent of export revenue and 36 per cent of GDP. Proven oil reserves at the beginning of January 2012 were an estimated 12.2 billion barrels. Experts in the field consider Algeria to be underexplored, and Algeria's National Council of Energy believes that the country still contains vast hydrocarbon potential. Over the last few years, there have been significant new oil and gas discoveries.

Oil production in 2011 was estimated to be 1.27 million barrels per day. Algeria is a member of OPEC and therefore its production in constrained by agreed OPEC quotas. In 2011 Algeria also produced 270,000 million barrels a day of condensate and 340,000 million barrels per day of natural gas liquids. These products do not form part of the OPEC quota. Algeria consumes an estimated 402,000 barrels per day of oil and exports 1.48 million barrels per day. Approximately 37 per cent of Algeria's crude oil exports went to European OECD countries in 2006, and 35 per cent of exports went to the USA. France, Italy, Spain and Germany were the main European importers. Algeria has four refineries, with a combined capacity of 450,000 bbl/d. This fulfills most of the country's refined oil product needs. Algeria uses seven coastal terminals to export crude oil, refined products, liquefied petroleum gas (LPG) and natural gas liquids (NGL). There are facilities located at Arzew, Skikda, Algiers, Annaba, Oran, Bejaia, and La Skhirra in Tunisia.

Sonatrach is the state-owned oil company which dominates the sector. However, the country has sought foreign investment in its oil industry, and the share of production controlled by foreign companies has increased to 44 per cent over the past few years. Sonatrach is in partnership with all foreign companies operating in Algeria, and usually holds majority ownership in production-sharing agreements. In March 2005, the Algerian parliament adopted the hydrocarbon reform bill which encouraged international oil company investment in the industry. However, 2006 amendments to the hydrocarbon bill created a windfall tax on profits whenever oil prices exceed $30 per barrel; this tax can reach up to 50 per cent on some contracts, deflating some investment enthusiasm.

With over 159 billion cubic feet of proven reserves in January 2012, Algeria's natural gas industry is ranked ninth largest in the world. Natural gas production in 2010 was estimated at 2,988 billion cubic feet, whilst consumption was an estimated 1,018 billion cubic feet.

Natural gas represented 62 per cent of the country's total energy consumption in 2004. Algeria exports most of its gas to Europe, where the largest importers in 2005 were Italy (969 billion cubic feet), Spain (506 billion cf) and France (265 billion cf). The USA imported 97 billion cubic feet in the same year.

Algeria is the fourth largest exporter of Liquified Natural Gas (LNG) in the world (behind Indonesia, Malaysia and Qatar), exporting around 13 per cent of the world's total. The main importer is Europe, principal purchasers being France and Spain. During 2005, the United States imported some 15 per cent of its total LNG imports from Algeria.

Sonatrach dominates natural gas production and wholesale distribution, whilst Sonelgaz (also state-controlled) runs retail distribution. The country is increasingly open to foreign investment in the sector. In July 2009, Algeria, Nigeria and Niger signed an agreement to build a US$13 billion pipeline to transport Nigerian gas across the Sahara to the Mediterranean.

The mineral industry produces mercury, iron ore, phosphates, zinc, silver, gypsum and barite.

Energy

Total energy consumption reached an estimated 1.8 quadrillion Btus in 2004, equivalent to 38.6 million Btus per capita. Natural gas accounted for 62 per cent of the energy mix, oil - 36 per cent and coal - one per cent.

Electricity generating capacity stood at around 33.12 billion kilowatthours in 2009. 99.8 per cent of electricity generation was from thermal sources (mainly natural gas), and 0.2 per cent came from hydroelectric sources. Domestic consumption was around 33.68 Bkwh in 2010; the excess was exported to Morocco and Tunisia. Demand has grown sharply in recent years.

New Energy Algeria (NEAL), a joint venture formed in 2002 by Sonatrach and Sonelgaz, is looking at the development of alternative electricity sources, including solar, wind, and biomass.

Manufacturing

The manufacturing industry contributes 14 per cent to GDP. The main areas are electrical, petrochemical, food processing, chemicals, leather, pharmaceuticals, cement and water desalination.

Service Industries

Recent figures indicate that this sector contributed some 32.5 per cent toward GDP in 2006. Algeria has never really developed a tourist industry. Political violence and the socialist government's antipathy towards the west have militated against any tourist development.

Agriculture

The agricultural sector contributed 12 per cent of GDP in 2011 and employed around 14 per cent of the workforce.

Cereals include wheat, barley, oats, maize, sorghum and vegetables such as beans, lentils, potatoes, peas, cucumbers, tomatoes, onions, carrots, melons, artichokes, sunflowers, sugar beets and tobacco. Grapes and a variety of citrus fruits are also grown including oranges, mandarins, lemons, grapefruit and clementines. Exports include olives, figs, dates, wine and tobacco.

Algerian livestock remains greatly dependent on imports of fodder and industrial cattle food. The Algerian fishing industries total catch in 2010 was 95,366 tonnes (Source FAO)

Agricultural Production in 2010

Produce	Int. $'000	Tonnes
Cow milk, whole. fresh	565,267	1,811,400
Potatoes	531,812	3,290,000
Indigenous sheep meat	490,648	180,200
Olives	444,550	555,200
Wheat	433,380	3,100,000
Dates	362,600	710,000
Indigenous chicken meat	358,438	351,640
Indigenous cattle meat	387,877	125,076
Grapes	268,660	470,000
Onions, dry	233,389	1,111,200
Tomatoes	213,867	578,700
Hen eggs in shell	156,755	189,000

Source: http://faostat.fao.org/site/339/default.aspx Food and Agriculture Organization of the United Nations, Food and Agricultural commodities production

COMMUNICATIONS AND TRANSPORT

Travel Requirements

Citizens of the US, Canada, Australia and the EU must have a passport valid for six months, and either a 30 day tourist visa or a 90 day business visa. If a transit stop exceeds 24 hours, a transit permit for up to 48 hours must be obtained from the airport authorities.

Citizens of other countries are advised to contact the Algerian consulate in their country to check visa requirements prior to travelling.

ALGERIA

National Airlines
Air Algerie has been government owned since 1972. It runs domestic services and international services world-wide. It flies to the main business centres of Annaba, Constantine and Oran as well as smaller locations and oil towns including Ghardaia, Ouargla, In Amenas and Hassi Messaoud. Air travel is often the most convenient way to travel because of distance and sand storms.
Air Algerie, URL: http://www.airalgerie.dz/info/index_e.htm

International Airports
Aeroport D'Alger, Houari, Boumediene, Algiers, Algeria. Tel: +213 (0)21 250 9191
Airlines landing at Aeroport D'Alger include Lufthansa, Air Berlin, British Airways, Air France, Iberia, Alitalia, TAP Portugal and Turkish Airlines.

Railways
Société Nationale des Transports Ferroviaires (SNTF) is the railway company of Algeria, URL: http://www.sntf.dz. A daily service operates between Algiers and Oran, Béjaia, Skikda, Annaba and Constantine in the north. In the south services run between Annaba to Tebessa via Souk Ahras, Constantine to Touggourt via Biskra, and Mohammadia to Bechar, some services only run once a day.

An underground system for Algiers was finally completed in 2011 after 28 years of planning and construction. Work halted in 1992 because of the civil war. The 10-stop 6.5 km (4 mile) line cost an estimated 90bn dinar ($1.2 bn). The line connects central Algiers to the suburb of Kouba.

Roads
Vehicles drive on the right in Algeria and anyone driving along desert roads must take supplies of water and fuel. A bus and tram system operates in Algiers and along the coast; a coach system operates for longer distances.

Ports and Harbours
Algeria's main ports include Algiers, Annaba, Skikda, Jijel, Djendjene, Bejaia, Oran and Mostaganem. A government run ferry system operates from the main ports and ferry services connect Algeria with Spain, France and Italy.

HEALTH

Life expectancy in Algeria is 71 years for men and 74 years for women (2009). Child mortality (based on the probability of dying under five years) was estimated at 36 per 1,000 live births in 2010 and infant mortality at 31 per 1,000 live births. The most common causes of death for children aged less than five were prematurity (24 per cent), measles (11 per cent), diarrhoea (7 per cent) pneumonia (12 per cent), birth asphyxia (11 per cent) and congenital abnomalities (13 per cent). An estimated 15.9 per cent of children aged under five years were stunted for their age in the period 2005-11. In 2010, some 95 per cent of children were vaccinated against measles, diptheria and hepatitis B. Major health problems in the country are malnutrition and trachoma and epidemics of malaria and tuberculosis. In 2010 there were 5 reported cases of malaria, 22,326 of tuberculosis, 212 of rubella and 103 of measles.

In 2010, 83 per cent of the population had access to improved drinking water and an estimated 95 per cent of the population had access to improved sanitation.

According to 2011 statistics in the period 2000-10, Algeria had 40,857 doctors (12 per 10,000 people), 11,001 dentists (3 per 10,000 people) and 65,919 nurses and midwives (19 per 10,000 people). There were also 8,232 pharmaceutical personnel and 2,429 environment and public health workers.

Total expenditure on health in 2009 was equivalent to 4.6 per cent of GDP. Government expenditure accounted for 79.3 per cent of total expenditure. Per capita total expenditure was US$181. (Source: http://www.who.int, Global Health Statistics, 2012)

EDUCATION

Primary/Secondary Education
Education in Algeria is free and officially compulsory to the age of 16. Teacher shortages and terrorist attacks on schools during the years of civil conflict have had a detrimental effect on the education system. Since a review in 2000, the government has initiated a series of reforms - specifically the Operational Plan for the Reform of the Algerian Educational System.

In 2007, some 30 per cent of young children attended a nursery school (compared to a regional average of 18 per cent). In the same year, 96 per cent of boys and 95 per cent of girls attended primary school. In 2005, 76 per cent went on to study at secondary level. The pupil/teacher ratio at primary level was 24:1.

Teaching in primary schools is carried out almost entirely in Arabic. After three years French is introduced as a second language. In some secondary schools teaching is totally in Arabic, and in other secondary schools teaching is bilingual in Arabic and French.

In 2006, it was estimated that 74.6 per cent of the population were literate (over 15 years old and able to read and write). In the younger 15-24 year old age group, the literacy rate increases to 92 per cent. Adult male literacy continues to be higher than female, though the gap is narrowing; in 2006, among the 15-24 age group, 94 per cent of males were literate and 89.8 per cent of women were literate, whereas in the overall adult population the relative percentages were 83.7 and 65.3.

Higher Education
There are ten universities in Algeria and 22 per cent of students were enrolled in tertiary education in 2006, in line with the regional average. (Source: UNESCO, UIS, September 2008)

RELIGION

Islam is Algeria's official religion, nearly 98 per cent of the population are Muslim and the vast majority of Algerians are Sunni Muslims. Since the departure of the French, Christianity is a peripheral religion (0.17 per cent of the population).

Algeria has a religious tolerance rating of 3 on a scale of 1 to 10 (10 is most freedom). (Source: World Religion Database)

COMMUNICATIONS AND MEDIA

Television and radio is state-controlled but private newspapers exist and criticism of the authorities is published. There is no direct censorship.

In July 2006 in a significant step towards democracy, President Bouteflika pardoned all journalists convicted of defaming or insulting state institutions. The pardon effectively dismissed the charges against 67 people. However, according to the criminal code, insulting the president, government or judges is still punishable by prison sentence. Nevertheless, the pardon was widely seen as a significant step toward democracy. In September 2011, President Bouteflika announced plans to allow independent radio and television stations for the first time since independence in 1962.

There is some danger to journalists; there have been several murders of journalists thought to be carried out by armed Islamist groups.

Newspapers
El Chaab, URL: http://www.ech-chaab.com/
El Khabar, URL: http://www.elkhabar.com
La Tribune, URL: http://www.latribune-online.com
El Moujahid, URL: http://www.elmujahid.com
Ech Chourouk, URL: http://www.echoroukonline.com/ara/
Le Quotidien d'Oran, URL: http://www.lequotidien-oran.com/

Algeria has more than 45 daily newspapers published in French and Arabic, with a total circulation of more than 1.5 million copies. Algerian newspapers are widely seen to be the freest in the region.

Broadcasting
The state has a monopoly over broadcasting. Satellite television is widespread with access to European and Arab satellite stations. Approximately 40 regional radio stations also operate.
National Television (ENTV), URL: http://www.entv.dz/
BRTV, URL: http://www.brtv.fr/, Berber television, transmitted from France via satellite.
Algerian Radio, URL: http://www.algerian-radio.dz/

The state-run news agency is the Algerian Press Service, URL: http://www.aps.dz/fr/welcome.asp

Telecommunications
In 2005, a consortium led by Egypt's Orascom Telecom won a 15-year license to build and operate a fixed-line network in Algeria. There are fewer than ten main-line telephones per 100 persons, but this is partially offset by the sharp increase in mobile subscribership; in 2007, there were 31 million mobile phones in use. As of 2009, there were an estimated 4 million internet users.

ENVIRONMENT

Algeria's main environmental problems are soil erosion, desertification, the dumping of raw sewage and petroleum refining wastes in rivers and coastal waters, and insufficient supplies of potable water.

Algeria is a party to the following environmental agreements: Biodiversity, Climate Change, Climate Change-Kyoto Protocol, Desertification, Endangered Species, Environmental Modification, Hazardous Wastes, Law of the Sea, Ozone Layer Protection, Ship Pollution, and Wetlands.

According to figures from the EIA, in 2009, Algeria produced 112.19 million metric tons of carbon dioxide emissions from the consumption of fossil fuels. This figure fell to 110.90 million metric tons in 2010. In 2007, Algeria produced 200.0 ODP tons of Ozone depleting CFCs.

SPACE PROGRAMME

The Algerian Space Agency (URL: http://www.asal.dz/) was established in 2002. Algeria launched its first satellite, ALSAT-1 in 2002. It was followed by ALSAT-2A in 2010 which was launched from India. It will be used for observational purposes. It will be followed by ALSAT-2B which will be built in Algeria. A series of telecommunications satellites are also planned.

ANDORRA
Principality of Andorra
Principat d'Andorra

Capital: Andorra-la-Vella (Population estimate: 22,000)

Episcopal Co-Prince: Joan Enric Vives Sicilia (Bishop of Urgell)

French Co-Prince: François Hollande (President of France) (page 1443)

National Flag: A tricolour pole-wise, blue, yellow, red, with the national coat of arms centred in the yellow band

CONSTITUTION AND GOVERNMENT

Constitution
The principality of Andorra is the oldest state in Europe. A number of its institutions date back to the Middle Ages. The heads of state are, in name, the two Co-Princes: the President of France and the Bishop of Urgell, Spain. The role of the two Co-Princes is now largely ceremonial. They appoint one representative each to the Constitutional Tribunal and the Superior Council of Justice. Each Co-Prince appoints a personal representative in Andorra to keep them informed about issues in the principality.

A new constitution was approved by the Andorran people on 14 March 1993 under which Andorra became a sovereign state, with the government having legislative and judicial authority. The constitution was agreed with a majority of 74.2 per cent of all votes, representing 75.7 per cent of the 9,123 registered voters.

The head of government is the President of the General Council-appointed Executive Council.

To consult the full constitution (in French), please visit:
http://www.coprince-fr.ad/index.php?option=com_content&view=article&id=4&Itemid=5&lang=ca

International Relations
Andorra has close relations with Spain and France. The country is not a member of the EU, but is a member of its Customs Union and has a Cooperation Agreement with the organisation. Andorra has no armed forces. The state joined the United Nations in 1993.

Legislature
The unicameral General Council of the Valleys (*Consell General del Valles*) exercises legislative power. It consists of 28 councillors elected for a period of four years. Half the councillors are elected in local elections, with two representatives from each parish, and half in general elections. The General Council elects the Head of Government.

Consell General, Casa de la Vall, Andorra la Vella. Tel: +376 821234, fax: +376 861234, e-mail: conseil.general@andorra.ad, URL: http://www.consellgeneral.ad/
Chairman: Joan Gabriel i Estany

Cabinet (as at June 2013)
President of the Executive Council, Minister for Culture: Antoni Marti (page 1471)
Minister of Foreign Affairs and Co-operation: Gilbert Saboya
Ministry of Economy and Territory: Jordi Alcobé
Minister of Finance and Civil Service: Jordi Cinca
Minister of Health and Welfare: Cristina Rodriguez
Minister of Tourism and the Environment: Francesc Camp
Minister of Education, Youth and Sport: Roser Suñé
Minister of Justice and Minister of the Interior: Marc Vila

Ministries
Government portal: URL: http://www.andorra.ad
Ministry of Health and Welfare, Avda. Príncep Benlloch, 30 Edifici Clara Rabassa - 4th, Andorra la Vella, Andorra. Tel: +376 861933, fax: +376 829347, URL: http://www.salutibenestar.ad
Ministry of Education, Youth & Sports, Avinguda Méritxell 80, Edif. Crédit Centre, Andorra la Vella. Tel: +376 861229, fax: +376 868308
Ministry of Tourism and Culture, Prat de la Creu 62, Andorra la Vella, Andorra. Tel: +376 875702, fax: +376 860184, e-mail: turisme@andorra.ad, URL: http://www.andorra.ad
All other Ministries, Edifici Administratiu, Carrer Prat de la Creu 62-64, Andorra la Vella, Andorra. Tel: +376 875700, fax: +376 875698
Additional contact details:
Ministry of Internal Affairs and Finance URL: http://www.finances.ad
Ministry of Agriculture and Environment, Department of Environment, C. Dr. Vilanova, 13 Edf. Davi, esc. C, 3r, Andorra la Vella, Andorra. Tel: +376 875707, fax: +376 869 833, e-mail: mediaambient@andorra.ad, URL: http://www.mediambient.ad

Elections
The last parliamentary election took place on 26 April 2009 when the Social Democratic Party (PS) won 14 of the 28 seats in the legislature. PS leader Jaume Bartumeu was elected president of the Executive Council.

Political Parties
Democrats for Andorra Party, URL: http://www.democrates.ad
Leader: Antoni Marti (page 1471)
The Social Democrats, URL: http://www.psa.ad

Leader: Jaume Bartumeu
Andorra for Change, URL: http://www.andorrapelcanvi.com
Leader: Eusebi Nomen
Greens for Andorra, http://www.verds.ad
Leader: Isabel Lozano Muñoz
Democratic Renewal, URL: http://www.renovaciodemocratica.ad
Leader: Ricard de Haro

Diplomatic Representation
Embassy of the Principality of Andorra (London Office), 63 Westover Road, London SW18 2RF, United Kingdom. Tel: +44 (0)20 8874 4806, fax: +44 (0)20 8874 4806
British Consulate, Avinguda Sant Antoni 23, Cal Sastre Vell, AD400, La Massana, Principat d'Andorra. Tel: +376 839840, e-mail: britconsul@andorra.ad, URL: http://ukinspain.fco.gov.uk/en/about-us/
Ambassador: Giles Paxman (page 1493) (resident in Madrid)
Embassy of Andorra to Spain, Switzerland, the UK, and Finland, C/Alcalà 73, 28001 Madrid, Spain. +34 91 431 7453, fax: +34 91 577 6341, e-mail: ambaixada@emb-principado-andorra.es
Mission of Andorra to the United Nations, 2 United Nations Plaza, 25th Floor, New York, NY 10017, USA. Tel: +1 212 750 8064, fax: +1 212 750 6630, e-mail: andorra@un.int
Permanent Representative to the UN: Amb. Narcis Casal Fonsdeviela (also Amb. to the USA)

LEGAL SYSTEM

The judicial system is independent. Civil cases are first heard by the batllia court (Courts of the First Instance). Appeals are heard in the Court of Appeals. Final appeals in civil cases are heard by the Supreme Court of Andorra at Perpignan, France, or the Ecclesiastical Court of the Bishop of Seu d'Urgell, Spain. Criminal cases are heard in Andorra la Vella by the Tribunal des Cortes. Sentenced criminals are detained in French and Spanish jails.

A Superior Council of Justice oversees and administers the judicial system. It has five members, each separately appointed by the two co-princes; the head of government; the president of the General Council, and members of the lower courts. Members of the judiciary are appointed for 6-year terms.

There is also a Constitutional Court, consisting of four magistrates who have an eight year term of office; two are appointed by the co-princes and two by the General Council. The Constitutional Court protects the constitution.

The government generally respects the rights of its citizens. The death penalty was abolished in 1990.

Superior Council of Justice, URL: http://www.justicia.ad/en/coneix.html
Constitutional Court, URL: http://www.tribunalconstitucional.ad/

LOCAL GOVERNMENT

The territory of Andorra is divided into seven Parròquies (parishes): Canillo, Encamp, Ordino, La Massana, Andorra la Vella, Sant Julià de Lòria and Escaldes-Engordany. The parishes are represented and administered by *comuns*. The comuns receive capital transfers from the State General Budget.
Comun de Canillo, URL: http://www.canillo.ad/
Comun d'Encamp, URL: http://www.encamp.ad
Comun d'Ordino, URL: http://www.comuordino.ad/
Comun de la Massana, URL: http://www.lamassana.ad/
Comun d'Andorra la Vella, URL: http://www.comuandorra.ad
Comun de Sant Julià de Lòria, URL: http://www.santjulia.ad/
Comun d'Escalades Engordany, URL: http://www.e-e.ad/portal/

Local elections were last held in December 2011.

AREA AND POPULATION

Area
Andorra is a landlocked and mountainous country in the Central Pyrenees, bordered by France and Spain. It has an area of 467.67 sq. km. The climate is temperate.

To view a map, please http://www.lib.utexas.edu/maps/cia08/andorra_sm_2008.gif

Population
The population in 2010 was estimated to be 85,000, of whom some 35 per cent were native Andorrans. The annual population growth rate was estimated at 2.7 per cent in the period 2000-10. Approximately 15 per cent of the population is aged under 15 years and 22 per cent is aged over 60 years. The average age is 41.1 years. The majority of residents are Spanish (over 37 per cent), Portuguese (approx. 13 per cent) and French (6 per cent). An estimated 88 per cent of the population live in urban areas, mainly the Andorra la Vella parish and the Escaldes-Engordany parish.

ANDORRA

Catalan is the official language but French and Spanish are also spoken. English is becoming widely used as the language for commerce.

Births, Marriages, Deaths

In 2009, average life expectancy at birth was estimated at 82 years (79.0 years for men and 85.0 years for women). Healthy life expectancy was 72 years for males and 76 years for females. The infant mortality rate was 3 deaths per 1,000 live births in 2010 and the child mortality rate was 4 deaths per 1,000 live births. The total fertility rate for women was 1.3 in 2010. The crude birth rate was 10 per 1,000 population and the crude death rate in 2009 was 8.0 per 1,000 population. (Source: http://www.who.int, World Health Statistics 2012)

Public Holidays 2014

1 January: New Year's Day
6 January: Epiphany (Twelfth Night)
14 March: Constitution Day
17 April: Holy Thursday
18 April: Good Friday
21 April: Easter Monday
5 May: Labour Day
29 May: Ascension
8 June: Whit Sunday
9 June: Whit Monday
15 August: Assumption
8 September: National Holiday (Mare de Deu de Meritxell)
1 November: All Saints' Day
4 November: St. Charles' Day
8 December: Immaculate Conception
25 December: Christmas
26 December: St. Stephen's Day

EMPLOYMENT

Andorra had an estimated 2007 labour force of 42,230 people. 79.0 per cent of the workforce is employed in the services sector, 20.8 per cent in industry, and 0.3 per cent in agriculture.

BANKING AND FINANCE

Currency

The country has no official currency and adopted the Spanish peseta and French franc until 1 January 2002 when the euro was introduced. There are no exchange restrictions.

GDP/GNP, Inflation, National Debt

Andorra's economy is largely based on tourism which has been hit by the economic crisis in the eurozone. Tourism currently contributes around 50 per cent of GDP, significantly down on earlier years, and employs approximately 78 per cent of the labour force. The banking sector contributes a significant proportion of the economy; Andorra's 'tax haven' status attracts foreign investment, and banking accounts for around 95 per cent of the financial system. Other major economic activities include tobacco production, livestock and furniture making. The weak economic situation throughout the Eurozone is expected to hinder Andorra's growth.

Gross Domestic Product reached an estimated €2.8 billion in 2011, compared to €2.7 billion in 2010, and €2.8 billion in 2009. The growth rate in 2011 was an estimated 0.2 per cent. Growth was forecast to continue in 2012, but at less than 1 per cent. Per capita GDP was estimated at $48,000 in 2011. The inflation rate averaged 1.6 per cent over 2010.

Historically a tax-free haven, an agreement reached with the EU in 1991 set duty-free quotas and placed limits on certain goods, such as tobacco, alcohol and milk. However, Andorra is permitted to maintain price differences from other EU countries. In 2004 the Andorran government signed a series of accords with the Union in the fields of economic, social, and cultural cooperation.

General government debt was estimated to amount to over 40 per cent of GDP in 2011.

Balance of Payments / Imports and Exports

Andorra's main import trading partners are Spain (around 50 per cent of trade), France, and the US. Main import products are consumer goods, electricity, and food. The main export partners are Spain (70 per cent) and France (15 per cent). Major export products include tobacco products and furniture. Exports were estimated to be worth US$69 million in 2009. Imports amounted to US$1,450 million.

A trade agreement was signed on 28 June 1990 with the European Union, which created a customs union for industrial products and terms for agricultural products. The agreement was enlarged in 1995 with the Common Exterior Tariff (CET). Andorra is also a member of the United Nations Conference for Commerce and Development (UNCCD), the World Tourism Organisation, and the Customs Cooperation Council (CCC).

Business Addresses

Duana Andorrana (Customs), URL: http://www.duana.ad
Chamber of Commerce, Industry and Services,
URL: http://www.andorra.ad/ccis/index.html
Association of Andorran Banks - ABA,
URL: http://www.andorraonline.ad/

MANUFACTURING, MINING AND SERVICES

Primary and Extractive Industries

Andorra's natural resources include mineral water, iron ore, timber, lead and mineral water.

Energy

Andorra generates quantities of hydroelectric power from a 26.5 MW plant at Les Escaldes which provides 40 per cent of electricity requirements. Spain provides the balance.

Manufacturing

Andorra's manufacturing industries are handicrafts, cigars, cigarettes, and furniture. Trade in consumer goods, including imported merchandise, is strong, due to the special tax status of the country which allows Andorra to sell goods at reduced prices.

Service Industries

Tourism, particularly skiing, is Andorra's main source of business. Over 9 million people visit the country each year, a large percentage travelling from France and Spain. The country benefits from low taxation on shopping for visitors. The tourist trade employs a significant proportion of the labour force. Tourism has been hard hit by the economic crisis in the Eurozone, particularly Spain.

Sindicat d'Iniciative Oficina de Turisme, Carrer Dr Vilanova, Andorra la Vella, Andorra
Tel: +376 820214, fax: +376 825823, URL: http://www.andorra.ad/ca-ES/Pagines/default.asp

Agriculture

Agriculture was Andorra's main economic activity until the development of the tourist industry. Just 2 per cent of the land is arable. The main crops produced include tobacco, wheat, rye, barley, oats, and vegetables. Sheep are the main livestock to be reared. Most of Andorra's food is imported. Less than one per cent of the population are employed full time in the agricultural sector.

COMMUNICATIONS AND TRANSPORT

Travel Requirements

US, Canadian, Australian, British and other EU citizens do not require a visa to visit Andorra for a period of up to three months. Andorra is not part of the Schengen area, and people entering Europe on a Schengen visa should therefore make sure that their visa entitles them to repeated visits to prevent them from being refused entry to Spain or France following a stay in Andorra.

Nationals of other countries should contact the Sindicat d'Iniciativa Oficina de Turisme (URL: http://www.andorra.ad) to find out their visa requirements.

International Airports

The nearest large airports are at Toulouse in France and Barcelona in Spain.

Roads

There is a good road connecting Andorra with the French and Spanish frontiers at Pas de la Casa and Farga de Moles respectively. There is also a secondary road network which connects the villages of the country. A bus system connects the villages and traffic is driven on the right.

HEALTH

Total expenditure on health was equivalent to 7.6 per cent of GDP in 2009. Government expenditure on health represented 21.3 per cent of its total expenditure. Government expenditure accounted for 70.1 per cent of total expenditure on health. Per capita total spend was US$3,364.

According to the latest WHO figures, in 2005-10 there were 266 physicians (39.1 per 10,000 people), 311 nurses and midwives (45.7 per 10,000 inhabitants), 51 dentists (7.5 per 10,000) and 78 pharmaceutical personnel. There were 26 hospital beds per 10,000 people.

The infant mortality rate (probability of dying by age 1) was 3 per 1,000 live births and rate for children aged less than 5 years was 4 per 1,000 live births. The most common causes were congenital anomalies (34 per cent) and prematurity (20 per cent). The immunization rate for measles was 99 per cent in 2010.

It is estimated that 100 per cent of the population have access to improved sanitation and drinking water supply. (Source: http://www.who.int, World Health Statistics, 2012)

EDUCATION

The education system consists of Andorran, Spanish and French state schools, and private English schools. There is also a church-controlled system. Attendance is free and compulsory in the state sector, up to 16 years. Whilst the state schools are built and maintained by the Andorran authorities, teachers are paid by France or Spain. Approximately 35 per cent of children attend French schools; 29 per cent Andorran and 35 per cent Spanish schools. Andorran and Spanish schools follow the Spanish curriculum. There are three languages of instruction, Catalan, French and Spanish.

The University of Andorra was established in 1997. Due to its small size, it works in conjunction with Spanish and French universities.

Recent figures put literacy rates at 100 per cent. Figures for 2007 show that the equivalent of 2.6 per cent of GDP was spend on education.

RELIGION

Most people follow Christianity, and about 94 per cent are Roman Catholics.

COMMUNICATIONS AND MEDIA

The constitution provides for freedom of speech and the press.

Newspapers
Diari d'Andorra, URL: http://www.diariandorra.ad
El Periódic d'Andorra, URL: http://www.and.ad
Broadcasting
The main radio stations are:
Radio i Televisio Nacional d'Andorra, URL: http://www.rtvasa.ad/index.asp
Radio Valira, http://www.radiovalira.com/

Andorra 1, URL: http://www.andorra1.ad/
A television station, TVA, is run by Radio i Telev ision d'Andorra.

Telecommunications
The use of mobile telephones has surpassed that of mainline phones; in 2008 there were an estimated 37,400 mainline phones in use, and 64,600 mobile phones being used. Figures for 2008 indicate that Andorra has 23,000 hosts and an estimated 59,000 internet users.

ENVIRONMENT

Areas of environmental concern include deforestation, air pollution, and overgrazing leading to soil erosion.

Andorra is party to the following environmental agreements: Biodiversity, Desertification, Hazardous Wastes and Ozone Layer Protection.

ANGOLA
Republic of Angola
República de Angola

Capital: Luanda (Population estimate: 5 million)

Head of State: José Eduardo dos Santos (President) (page 1417)

Vice-President: Manuel Domingos Vicente

National Flag: A yellow cog-wheel, machete and star set on an upper band of red and a lower band of black

CONSTITUTION AND GOVERNMENT

Constitution
A former Portuguese colony, Angola became independent on 11 November 1975, shortly after the outbreak of civil war. The war between the Movement for the Liberation of Angola (MPLA) and the National Union for the Total Independence of Angola (UNITA) lasted 27 years, ending in 2002.

In 1991, the Government amended the Constitution with a view to adopting a multiparty system, where previously the MPLA had been the only legal party. In addition, other legislation was introduced ensuring guarantees for foreign investment, strengthened human rights, freedom of the press and other reforms. Under the terms of the 1975 Constitution, the head of state is the president, elected by universal adult suffrage for a term of five years. However, elections have not taken place since 1992. The president appoints the Council of Ministers. In 1998, a Constitutional Commission was set up to draft a new constitution. The position of prime minister was temporarily suspended during the civil war (from January 1999 to January 2003); during this period the President held both positions.

The draft constitution was approved in January 2010. Under the new constitution, the post of prime minister was abolished and the position of deputy president was created.

To consult the constitution, please visit:
http://www.comissaoconstitucional.ao/pdfs/constituicao-da-republica-de-angola-versao-ingles.pdf.

International Relations
During the civil war Angola's relations with her neighbours suffered but in recent years relations have improved. Through foreign investment in the oil industry Angola now enjoys working relationships with the US. Angola belongs to several organisations for Portuguese speaking nations.

Recent Events
In February 2002 Unita leader Jonas Savimbi was killed in a gunfight with government forces and in April of that year Unita rebels signed a formal ceasefire with the Angolan army. By June of that year many refugees had returned home.

In August 2006 the government signed a ceasefire agreement with FLEC (Front of Liberation of the State of Cabinda). Cabinda is an enclave north of Angola and the oil wells that provide over half of Angola's oil are located off its coast. Cabinda fought for independence from the Portuguese and continued to fight for self determination after the Portuguese left. The ceasefire agreement was not supported by all the opposition factions.

The first parliamentary elections in 16 years took place in September 2008, and the governing MPLA government won a landslide victory. Their main rivals UNITA demanded a re-run of the Luanda poll, which had been mismanaged. Presidential elections are scheduled for September 2009 but were again postponed.

On 21st March 2009, hundreds of thousands of Angolans gathered to hear Pope Benedict XVI celebrate an open-air Mass near Luanda. Catholics account for some 55 per cent of the population.

In January 2010 Angola played host to the football tournament the African Nations Cup. A bus carrying the Togo football team was attacked by Cabinda separatists.

Also that month parliament approved a new constitution abolishing direct elections for the president. From 2012 the post of president will be filled by the top-ranking candidate of the party that wins the parliamentary election.

Legislature
The highest governmental body is the People's Assembly. Its jurisdiction includes making changes to constitutional law, approving legislation and drafting the state budget. Its 223 deputies are elected by popular vote for a four-year period.

The Council of Ministers is the government's highest administrative body and is the executive body of the People's Assembly. It is made up of the President of the Republic, the ministers and the state secretaries.
National Assembly, CP 1204, Luanda, Angola. Tel: +244 (0)2 334021, fax: +244 (0)2 331118, e-mail: assembleianacionale@parlamento.ebonet.net, URL: http://www.parlamento.ao

Cabinet (as at March 2013)
Minister of Finance: Dr Carlos Alberto Lopes (page 1466)
Minister of Foreign Affairs: Georges Rebelo Pinto Chicoty (page 1404)
Minister of the Interior: Angelo de Barros Veiga Tavares
Minister of Defence: Candido Pereira dos Santos Van Dunem
Minister of Agriculture and Rural Development: Afonso Canga
Minister of Assistance and Reintegration: Joao Baptista Kussumua
Minister of Commerce: Rosa Escorcio Pacavira De Matos
Minister of Hotels and Tourism: Pedro Mutinde
Minister of Culture: Rosa Maria Martins da Cruz e Silva
Minister of Education: Mpinda Simao
Minister of Oil: Jose Botelho de Vasconcelos
Minister of Health: Jose Vieira Dias Van Dunem
Minister of Geology, Mines and Industry: Francisco Manuel Monteiro De Queiroz
Minister of Social Communication: José Luis De Matos
Minister of Justice and Human Rights: Rui Jorge Carneiro Mangueira
Minister of Energy and Water Resources: Joao Baptista Borge
Minister of Planning: Job Graca
Minister of Telecommunications and IT: Jose Carvalho da Rocha
Minister of Public Administration, Employment and Social Welfare: Dr. António Domingos Pitra Costa Neto (page 1485)
Minister of Higher Education: Adao Gaspar Ferreira do Nascimento
Minister of Science and Technology: Maria de Candid Pereira Teixeira
Minister of Territorial Administration: Dr Bornito De Sousa Baltazar Diogo
Minister of Transport: Augusto da Silva Tomás
Minister for Veterans and Ex-Servicemen's Affairs: Kundi Paihama
Minister of Women and Family Affairs: Maria Filomena de Fatima Lobao Telo Delgado
Minister of the Environment: Maria de Fatima Monteiro Jardim
Minister of Youth and Sports: Goncalves Manuel Muandumba
Minister of Urban Affairs and Housing: Jose Antonio da Conceicao E Silva
Minister of the Economy: Abraao Pio dos Santos Gourgel
Minister for Parliamentary Affairs: Rosa Luis de Sousa Micolo
Secretary of the Council of Ministers: Frederico Manuel dos Santos e Silva Cardoso
Minister of Fisheries: Victoria Francisco Lopes Cristovao de Barros Neto
Minister of Industry: Bernarda Goncalves Martins Henriques Da Silva
Minister of State, Civilian Chief of Staff: Edeltrudes Mauricio Fernandes Gaspar Da Costa
Minister of State, Military Chief of Staff: Gen. Manuel Helder Viera Dias Jr

Ministries
Office of the President, Protocolo de Estado, Rua 17 de Setembro, Luanda, Angola. Tel: +244 22 237 0150, fax: +244 22 233 9855, URL: http://www.angola.org
Office of the Vice President, Cidade Alta, Luanda, Angola. Tel: +244 22 239 7448, fax: +244 22 239 7071, URL: http://www.governo.gov.ao
Ministry of the Economy, Largo da Mutamba, Luanda, Angola. e-mail: geral@minec.gov.ao, URL: http://www.minec.gov.ao
Ministry of Finance, Largo da Mutamba, Luanda, Angola. Tel: +244 22 233 6095, fax: +244 22 233 3016, e-mail: geral@minfin.gov.ao, URL: http://www.minfin.gov.ao

ANGOLA

Ministry of Foreign Affairs, Rua Major Kanhangulo, Luanda, Angola. Tel: +244 22 239 4827, fax: +244 22 239 3246, e-mail: geral@mirex.gov.ao, URL: http://www.mirex.gov.ao
Ministry of Industry, Rua Sequeira Lukoki 25, Luanda, Angola. Tel: +244 22 233 2971, fax: +244 22 239 2400, e-mail: geral@mind.gov.ao, URL: http://www.mind.gov.ao
Ministry of Agriculture and Rural Development, Avenida Comandante Gika 20, Luanda, Angola. Tel: +244 22 232 2694, fax: +244 22 232 3217, e-mail: gabminander@netangola.com, URL: http://www.minagri.gov.ao
Ministry of Commerce, Largo 4 de Fevereiro 3, Palácio de Vidro, Luanda, Angola. Tel: +244 22 231 1191, fax: +244 22 237 0804, e-mail: geral@minco.gov.ao, URL: http://www.minco.gov.ao
Ministry of Culture, Largo António jacinto, Avenida Comandante Gika, Luanda, Angola. Tel: +244 22 232 2070, fax: +244 22 232 3979, e-mail: geral@mincult.gv.ao, URL: http://www.mincult.gov.ao
Ministry of Defence, Rua 17 de Setembro, Luanda, Angola. Tel: +244 22 233 0354, fax: +244 22 233 4276, e-mail: geral@minden.gov.ao, URL: http://www.minden.gov.ao
Ministry of Education, Largo António Jacinto, Luanda, Angola. Tel: +244 22 232 1236, fax: +244 22 232 1592, e-mail: geral@med.gov.ao, URL: http://www.med.gov.ao
Ministry of Energy and Water Resources, Avenida 4 de Fevereiro 105, Luanda, Angola. Tel: +244 22 239 3687, fax: +244 22 239 3687, e-mail: geral@minen.gov.ao, URL: http://www.minen.gov.ao
Ministry of the Environment, Avenida 4 de Fevereiro, Luanda, Angola. e-mail: geral@minam.gov.ao, URL: http://www.minam.gov.ao
Ministry of the Family and Women's Advancement, Largo 4 de Fevereiro, Palácio de Vidro 2 andar, Luanda, Angola. Tel: +244 22 231 0057, fax: +244 22 231 0057, e-mail: geral@minfamu.gov.ao, URL: http://www.minfamu.gov.ao
Ministry of Fisheries, Avenida 4 de Fevereiro 30, Edificio Atlântico, Luanda, Angola. Tel: +244 22 231 0479, fax: +244 22 233 3814, e-mail: geral@minpescas.gov.ao, URL: http://www.minpescas.gov.ao
Ministry of Geology and Mines, Largo António Jacinto, Luanda, Angola. Tel: +244 22 232 2905, fax: +244 22 232 1655, e-mail: geral@mgm.gov.ao, URL: http://www.mgm.gov.ao
Ministry of Health, Rua 17 de Setembro, C.P. 1201, Luanda, Angola. Tel: +244 22 239 1641, fax: +244 22 233 8052, e-mail: geral@minsa.gov.ao, URL: http://www.minsa.gov.ao
Ministry of the Hotel Industry and Tourism, Largo 4 de Fevereiro, Palácio de Vidro, Luanda, Angola. Tel: +244 22 231 1448, fax: +244 22 231 0629, e-mail: geral@minhotur.gov.ao, URL: http://www.minhotur.gov.ao
Ministry of the Interior, Largo do Palácio de Vidro, Rua 25 de Abril 1 R/C, Luanda, Angola. Tel: +244 22 233 5976, fax: +244 22 239 5133, e-mail: geral@minint.gov.ao, URL: http://www.minint.gov.ao
Ministry of Justice, Rua 17 de Setembro, Luanda, Angola. Tel: +244 22 233 6045, fax: +244 22 233 9914, e-mail: geral@minjus.gov.ao, URL: http://www.minjus.gov.ao
Ministry of Oil, Avenida 4 de Fevereiro 105, Luanda, Angola. Tel: +244 22 233 7448, fax: +244 22 238 5847, e-mail: geral@minpet.gov.ao, URL: http://www.minpet.gov.ao
Ministry of Planning, Largo do Palacio, Rua 17 de Setembro, Luanda, Angola. Tel: +244 22 239 0188, fax: +244 22 233 9586, e-mail: geral@minplan.gov.ao, URL: http://www.minplan.gov.ao
Ministry of Public Administration, Employment and Social Welfare, Rua 17 de Setembro 32, CP 1986, Luanda, Angola. Tel: +244 22 233 9656, fax: +244 22 233 9507, e-mail: mapess@ebonet.net, URL: http://www.mapess.gv.ao
Ministry of Public Works, Rua Friedrich Engels 92, Luanda, Angola. Tel: +244 22 233 4429, fax: +244 22 239 2539, e-mail: geral@minop.gov.ao, URL: http://www.minop.gov.ao
Ministry of Science and Technology, Avenida Lenine 106/108, Maianga, Luanda, Angola. Tel: +244 22 230 9794, fax: +244 22 230 9794, e-mail: geral@mct.gov.ao, URL: http://www.mct.gov.ao
Ministry of Social Assistance and Reintegration, Avenida Hoji Ya Henda 117, Luanda, Angola. Tel: +244 22 233 0218, fax: +244 22 233 8210, e-mail: geral@minars.gov.ao, URL: http://www.minars.gov.ao
Ministry of Social Communication (Information), Avenida Comandante Valódia 206, 1 e 2 andares, Luanda, Angola. Tel: +244 22 244 3495, fax: +244 22 244 3495, e-mail: geral@mcs.gov.ao, URL: http://www.mcs.gov.ao
Ministry of Telecommunications and Information Technology, Rua Major Kanhangulo, Luanda, Angola. Tel: +244 22 231 1004, fax: +244 22 233 0776, e-mail: geral@mtti.gov.ao, URL: http://www.mtti.gov.ao
Ministry of Territorial Administration, Avenida Comandante Gika 8, Luanda, Angola. Tel: +244 22 232 1729, fax: +244 22 232 3272, e-mail: geral@mat.gov.ao, URL: http://www.mat.gov.ao
Ministry of Transport, Avenida 4 de Fevereiro 42, Luanda, Angola. Tel: +244 22 231 1800, fax: +244 22 231 1582, e-mail: geral@mintrans.gov.ao, URL: http://www.mintrans.gov.ao
Ministry of Urbanization and Construction, Avenida 4 de Fevereiro 25, Edificio Atlântico 1 andar, Luanda, Angola. Tel: +244 22 231 1073, fax: +244 22 231 0517, e-mail: geral@minuh.gov.ao, URL: http://www.minuh.gov.ao
Ministry of Veterans Affairs, Avenida Comandante Gika 2, Rua Francisco Xavier, CP 3828, Luanda, Angola. Tel: +244 22 232 1648, fax: +244 22 232 0876, e-mail: geral@macvg.gov.ao, URL: http://www.macvg.gov.ao
Ministry of Youth and Sports, Avenida Comandante Valódia 299, 4° andar, Luanda, Angola. Tel: +244 22 244 3521, fax: +244 22 232 1118, e-mail: geral@minjud.gov.ao, URL: http://www.minjud.gov.ao/

Main Political Parties

The Popular Movement for the Liberation of Angola (MPLA), Luanda, Angola. URL: http://www.mpla.org/
Chairman: José Eduardo Dos Santos (page 1417)
National Union for the Total Independence of Angola (UNITA), Rua Comandante Bula, 71-73 S. Paulo, Luanda, Angola.
President: Isaias Samakuva
National Front for the Liberation of Angola, (FNLA), Luanda, Angola. URL: http://www.fnla.net
Leader: Ngola Kabangu,

Elections

UN supervised general elections were held on 29 and 30 September 1992. Twenty-three political parties contended and there were 13 candidates in the simultaneous presidential election. The MPLA polled 57.9 per cent of the votes and UNITA, 31.4 per cent. José Eduardo dos Santos, the MPLA candidate, won 50 per cent and Jonas Savimbi of UNITA 40 per cent. Under electoral law, if no presidential candidate wins over 50 per cent of the vote, a second round is held. There was no second round of voting in the poll but Mr Dos Santos is recognised internationally as Angola's president.

Despite the fact that the UN and other international observers declared the elections to have been free and fair, UNITA alleged widespread fraud, withdrew its generals from the unified armed forces and began moving its troops across the country. The Government offered UNITA further posts, and the UNITA leader, Jonas Savimbi, was subsequently offered one of two vice-presidencies. However, in January 1999, a Parliamentary resolution was passed declaring Jonas Savimbi a war criminal.

A presidential election was due again in 1997 but was postponed indefinitely. The Assembly extended its own mandate for the second time on 17 October 2000. On 24 August 2004 the government announced a timetable for voter enrolment with elections due in September 2006. However, the president said repairs to roads and railways needed to be completed before the vote could take place, citing the inaccessibility of many towns and villages as an obstacle to fair elections. Presidential elections were due to be held in September 2009 but were again postponed.

Parliamentary elections eventually took place on the 5/6 September 2008. Angola's ruling MPLA party won a landslide victory in the country's first parliamentary elections in 16 years. With around half of the votes counted, the MPLA had received 81 per cent of the vote, whilst the main opposition party, Unita, had polled 10 per cent. Unita demanded a re-run in Luanda voting in the capital was chaotic. An EU observer said there was widespread vote-rigging with the governing party offering bribes, and soldiers and MPLA officials appearing to intimidate voters. However, observers from the Southern African Development Community (SADC) said the vote had been "transparent and credible".

The most recent elections took place on August 31 2012, they were declared to have been free, fair, transparent and credible by observers although UNITA wanted a delay due to lack of transparency. The MPLA won a comfortable victory. African Union observers said the elections had been free and fair.

Diplomatic Representation

Embassy of the Republic of Angola, 2100-2108 16th Street, NW, Washington, DC 20009, USA. Tel: +1 202 785 1156, fax: +1 202 785 1258, e-mail: angola@angola.org, URL: http://www.angola.org/
Ambassador: Alberto do Carmo Bento Ribeiro
Embassy of the United States, Rua Houari Boumedienne 32, CP 6468, Luanda, Angola. Tel: +244 (0)2 447028 / 445481, fax: +244 (0)2 446924, e-mail: amembassyluanda@netangola.com, URL: http://angola.usembassy.gov
Ambassador: Christopher J. McMullen, Ph.D.
Embassy of the Republic of Angola, 22 Dorset Street, London W1U 6QY, United Kingdom. Tel: +44 (0)20 77299 9850, fax: +44 (0)20 7486 9397, e-mail: embassyofangola@cwcom.net
Ambassador: H.E. Miguel Gaspar Fernandes Neto
Britsh Embassy, Rua Diogo Cao 4, CP 1244, Luanda, Angola. Tel: +244 (0)2 392991 / +244 (0)2 334582, fax: +244 (0)2 333331, e-mail: Postmaster.Luanda@fco.gov.uk, URL: http://ukinangola.fco.gov.uk/en
Ambassador: Richard Wildash, LVO (page 1537)
Permanent Mission of the Republic of Angola to the United Nations, 125 East 73rd Street, New York, NY 10021, USA. Tel: +1 212 861 5656, fax: +1 212 861 9295, e-mail: themission@angolaun.org, URL: http://www.angolaun.org/
Permanent Representative to the UN: Ismael A. Gaspar Martins

LEGAL SYSTEM

The legal system is based on Portuguese civil law system and traditional law. In 1991, the constitution was amended to guarantee an independent judiciary; however, the president appoints the 16 Supreme Court judges for life, as well as appointing the attorney general.

The court system comprises of the Supreme Court, the Court of Appeals, the people's revolutionary courts and a system of people's courts. The Supreme Court and the Court of Appeals hear cases involving national officials and appeals from lower courts. The system lacks resources and is perceived to be ineffective. A Constitutional Court, was authorised in 1992 but has not yet been established.

The government's human rights record is poor; there have been recent unlawful killings and torture by police, military, and private security forces. There is official corruption, and police carry out arbitrary arrests. The judicial system lacks independence and its inefficiency leads to lengthy pretrial detentions. In recent years, there have been forced evictions without compensation. Angola abolished the death penalty in 1992.

Provedor di Justiça di direitos, Rua 1° Congresso do MPLA, Bairro Mutamba, Luanda, Angola. +244 923 531843, fax: +244 222 359488, URL: http://www.provedor-jus.co.ao/oprovedor.php

Chief Justice: Cristiano André

LOCAL GOVERNMENT

Angola is divided into 18 provinces and 161 districts. Districts are further divided into communes, villages and neighbourhoods. Administration at each level is the responsibility of a commissioner. Provincial People's Assemblies represent the people at local level with 55-85 deputies. The 18 provincial commissioners are ex-officio members of the executive branch of the national government. The provinces are Bengo, Benguela, Bie, Cabinda, Cuando Cubango, Cuanza Norte, Cuanza Sul, Cunene, Huambo, Huila, Luanda, Lunda Norte, Lunda Sul, Malanje, Moxico, Namibe, Uige and Zaire.

In August 2007 a resolution was passed by central government to extend the control of local budgets to some municipalities, this was then extended to cover all municipalities in 2008. Local government elections are scheduled to take place after national elections in late 2012.

AREA AND POPULATION

Area
Angola is on the west coast of Africa below the equator. It extends southward from the mouth of the Congo river for over 1,000 miles. It includes the territory of Cabinda, which is separated from Angola by a strip of land along the north bank of the Congo. Angola shares its borders to the north and east with the Democratic Republic of Congo, to the east with Zambia and to the south with Namibia. The Atlantic Ocean borders the east side. Angola covers an area of 1,246,700 sq. km.

The climate is semi-arid in the south and along the coast. The north is more tropical and humid.

To view a map, consult: http://www.un.org/Depts/Cartographic/map/profile/angola.pdf

The country is divided into 18 provinces as detailed in the following table:

Angolan Provinces

Province	Capital	Area	Population
Bengo	Caxito	33,016	310,000
Benguela	Benguela	31,780	670,000
Bié	Kuito	70,314	1,200,000
Cabinda	Cabinda	7,270	100,000
Cunene	Ondijiva	87,342	200,000
Huambo	Huambo	34,270	1,000,000
Huila	Lubango	75,002	800,000
Kuando-Kubango	Menongue	199,042	150,000
Kwanza Norte	N'Dalantando	24,110	420,000
Kwanza Sul	Sumbe	55,660	610,000
Luanda	Luanda	2,257	3,000,000
Luanda Norte	Lucapa	103,000	250,000
Luanda Sul	Saurimo	77,637	120,000
Malange	Malange	97,602	700,000
Moxico	Luena	223,023	240,000
Namibe	Namibe	58,137	85,000
Uige	Uige	58,698	500,000
Zaire	M'Banza Kongo	40,130	50,000

Source: http://www.angola.org

The official language is Portuguese. There are also five native main languages, Ovimbundu, Kimbundu, Kikongo, Kichokwe and Ovambo.

Population
The population of Angola was estimated to be 19.082 million in 2010 (up from 18.1 million in 2008). The average annual growth rate for the period 2000-10 was 3.1 per cent. The population is very young, with a median age of 17 years. Approximately 47 per cent of the population is under 15 years old. Just 4 per cent is aged over 60 years. Approximately 59 per cent of the population lives in urban areas.

The population is made up as follows: Ovimbundu (37 per cent), Kimbundu (25 per cent), Bakongo (13 per cent), mestico (mixed native African and European, 2 per cent), European (1 percent) and others (2 per cent).

Births, Marriages, Deaths
According to 2010 estimates, the current crude birth rate is 41.6 births per 1,000 people, whilst the death rate is 13.2 deaths per 1,000 people. In 2010 infant mortality was estimated at 98 deaths per 1,000 live births, and life expectancy at birth was 52 years (51 years for men and 53 years for women). Healthy life expectancy was 45 years. The total fertility rate was 5.4 children per woman of child-bearing age. (Source: http://www.who.int, World Health Statistics 2012)

Public Holidays 2014
1 January: New Year
4 January: Martyrs of Colonial Repression Day
4 February: Commencement of Armed Struggle Day (Inicio de Luta Armada)
8 March: International Women's Day
27 March: Victory Day*
4 April: Peace and Reconciliation Day
14 April: Youth Day*
18 April: Good Friday
21 April: Easter Monday
1 May: Workers' Day
2 June: International Children's Day
1 August: Armed Forces Day*

17 September: National Hero's Day (Anniversary of the birth of President Neto)
1 November: All Soul's Day
11 November: Independence Day
1 December: Pioneers' Day*
25 December: Family Day (Christmas Day)
*popular holidays, not officially recognised

EMPLOYMENT

Angola's labour force was estimated at 7.9 million in 2010. An estimated 80 per cent of the labour force work in agriculture (mainly subsistence farming), followed by industry, trade and services employing 20 per cent. Unofficial figures in 2006 estimated unemployment to be 26 per cent.

BANKING AND FINANCE

Currency
One Kwanza Reajustados (KZR) = 100 Lwei

GDP/GNP, Inflation, National Debt
Oil is the mainstay of the Angolan economy, accounting for over 50 per cent of GDP and virtually 100 per cent of exports. Subsistence agriculture still accounts for 85 per cent of employment. The recent economic downturn has lead to a drop in demand and the economy is consequently expected to see lower growth rates in 2009. The economy has been long hindered by corruption, mismanagement and civil war. Since 2000, the government has made some economic reforms. Foreign investment is hard to secure.

GDP was estimated to be US$100 billion in 2011. Industry is the largest contributor (an estimated 65 per cent in 2008 and the oil industry is the largest contributor to this sector), followed by services (25 per cent) and agriculture (9 per cent). The growth rate of GDP slowed temporarily to an estimated 4.9 per cent during 2003, but grew by an estimated 12.2 per cent in 2004, 14.4 per cent in 2005 and 14.6 per cent in 2006. GDP growth reached an estimated 18 per cent in 2008 but slowed dramatically in 2009 due to the global economic downturn and significantly lower oil prices. In 2010 it was estimated to be 2 per cent and 3 per cent in 2011.

Following IMF-agreed economic reforms, inflation has dropped from a high of 268.4 per cent in 2001 to 116.1 per cent in 2001, 106.8 per cent in 2002, 76.7 per cent in 2003, then 31.0 per cent in 2004. The downward trend has continued, falling to 18.5 per cent in 2005, to 12.2 per cent in 2006 and 11.8 per cent in 2007. Figures for 2010 estimated inflation to be running at 14.5 per cent.

Angola's external debt at the end of 2006 was around US$9.5 billion. In November 2009, the IMF approved a 27-month Stand-by Arrangement with Angola for the amount of around US$1.4 billion, the loan was to help Angola cope with the effects of the global economic crisis. In return Angola would work towards making oil revenues more transparent.

Foreign Investment
The World Bank agreed a Second Social Action Fund Credit of US$33 million in July 2000 to finance Angola's poverty aid programmes and in 2003 pledged a US$100 million support package. In 2002, the IMF initiated a Staff Monitored Program to carry through economic reform. As part of this program, an analysis of the oil industry was undertaken, and it was discovered that revenues often did not reach the national bank, and were therefore 'unaccounted'. Angola has signed up to transparency initiatives to assist in securing oil-backed loans, in particular from the IMF.

Foreign direct investment in the oil industry was expected to reach $23 billion between 2003 and 2008. In 2003, the USA made Angola eligible for tariff preference under the African Growth and Opportunity Act, reflecting the importance to the US of Angolan oil imports.

Balance of Payments / Imports and Exports
Total exports were estimated to be US$65 billion in 2011. Angola's largest trading partner is Portugal followed by China which has become Angola's major trade partner. Major export partners include China (35 per cent), USA (20 per cent), India (9 per cent) and Portugal. Total imports were estimated to be US$19 billion in 20110. Approximately 20 per cent of imports come from Portugal, 18 per cent from China, the USA 9.5 per cent and Brazil 7 per cent.

Crude oil was the main export commodity in 2006, accounting for an estimated 90 per cent of all exports. Diamonds made up 8.4 per cent of exports. Other exports included petroleum products, gas, coffee, fish, timber and cotton. The main imports were machinery, vehicles, medicines, food, textiles and military goods.

Central Bank
Banco Nacional de Angola, PO Box 1243/1298, 151 Avenida 4 de Fevereiro, Luanda, Angola. Tel: +244 (0)2 332633, fax: +244 (0)2 395885, e-mail: sec.gvb@bna.ao, URL: http://www.bna.ao
Governor: José de Lima Massano

Chambers of Commerce and Trade Organisations
Angolan Chamber of Commerce and Industry (Camara de Comercio e Industria de Angola), URL: http://www.ccia.ebonet.net/
US-Angola Chamber of Commerce, URL: http://www.us-angola.org

STATES OF THE WORLD

ANGOLA

MANUFACTURING, MINING AND SERVICES

Primary and Extractive Industries

Angola is the second largest producer of crude oil in sub-Saharan Africa (Nigeria is the first) and the ninth largest supplier of crude oil to the United States. The oil sector plays a crucial role in the economy, currently accounting for 95 per cent of total export revenues. Production is worth US$3.5 billion annually. In January 2007, Angola became a member of the Organization of Petroleum Exporting Countries (OPEC) and currently has an oil production quota of between 1.52 and 1.66 million barrels per day.

As at the beginning of January 2012 Angola had proven oil reserves of 9.5 billion barrels. Oil production was estimated at 1.7 million barrels per day in 2011 (up from 742,000 barrels per day in 2001). Angola consumed an estimated 88,000 barrels per day and exported 1.7 million barrels per day in 2011. Refining capacity at the beginning of January 2012 was 39,000 barrels per day, and is set to rise when the long awaited refinery at Lobito comes onstream. Oil exports from Angola to China make up around 15 per cent of China's oil needs.

Angola's national oil company, Sonangol, works with foreign companies through joint ventures and production sharing agreements. Funding is through oil-backed loans. Foreign oil companies operating in Angola include ChevronTexaco, BP, ENI-Agip, ExxonMobil, Shell, and TotalFinaElf.

Several offshore discoveries have led to the creation of the Zone d'Interet Commun (ZIC) with the Republic of Congo in 2003, each country receiving half of all revenues from the exploitation block. Chevron have indicated that they will make a sizeable investment in Angola, following their discovery of a site which could yield over 10,000 barrels of oil per day.

Natural gas reserves were estimated at 11.0 billion cubic feet in January 2012. Production was estimated at 26 billion cubic feet in 2011 the same as natural gas consumption that year.

Angola has substantial deposits of diamonds, iron ore, phosphates, manganese, copper, lead and zinc as well as strategic base metals, chromium, beryl, kaolin, quartz, gypsum, marble and black granite. Before 1975 Angola was the world's fourth largest producer of diamonds but dropped to seventh place during the war as official production was prey to theft, smuggling and transportation problems. Angola recently announced changes to its production program, which outlines its goal to double its present capacity of 6 million carats of diamonds annually. If achieved, this would make Angola the third largest producer in Africa, behind Botswana and the Democratic Republic of Congo.

Diamond mining accounts for 8.4 per cent of Angola's total exports. In an effort to boost government revenues, the Government took steps in 2000 to end the illegal mining of diamonds, which at that time equaled the value of government mining revenues. In 2004 tens of thousands of illegal foreign diamond miners were expelled in a crackdown on illegal mining and trafficking. An estimated 300,000 foreign diamond dealers were also expelled. Figures for 2002 show that the estimated value of diamond production was US$1 billion.

Energy

Total energy consumption was 0.20 quadrillion Btu. in 2009 up from 0.19 Btu. in 2008. Recent figures show that 80 per cent of the population does not have access to electricity.

Angola's electric generation capacity was 5.1 billion kilowatts in 2010. Hydroelectric facilities provide approximately two-thirds of power, using the Matala, Cambambe and Mabubas dams. Two further dams are under construction and rehabilitation of hydropower stations damaged during the war is planned. Angola's state-owned electricity utility is the Empresa Nacional de Electricidade (ENE).

Angola is responsible for coordinating energy policy for the Southern African Development Coordination Conference (SADCC) and SADCC's energy secretariat is based in Luanda. (Source: EIA)

Manufacturing

Industry is Angola's largest economic sector, contributing some 65 per cent of GDP. The war and the subsequent destruction of economic and social facilities were the main causes of the decline in production that Angola has faced since independence. The Peace Accord signed by the Government and UNITA on 31 May 1991 opened up new prospects for Angola to improve production levels.

Angola currently produces beer, soft drinks, sugar, wheatflour, pasta, cooking oil, molasses, salt, textiles, shoes, matches, soap, paint, plastic bottles and glues. Heavy industry makes up 15 per cent of Angola's industrial output including production of cement, oil, tyres, steel and cars.

Agriculture

Agriculture employs 85 per cent of Angola's labour force and contributes about 10 per cent of GDP. Angola was self-sufficient in most food crops and a major exporter of coffee at independence. Prior to the war Angola was the world's fourth largest coffee producer with output totalling 200,000 tons each year. In 1995-96 it more than doubled this amount. Following the war, growth in the agricultural sector has been hampered by landmines, bad transport infrastructure and loss of farming skills.

It is estimated that the country has between 5 and 8 million hectares of prime agricultural land as well as land suitable for grazing. The country's different climate zones enable farmers to grow a variety of different crops including potatoes, cassava, beans, yams, sugar cane, maize, manioc, bananas, sunflowers, cotton, palm oil, citrus and numerous vegetables.

Agricultural Production in 2010

Produce	Int. $'000	Tonne
Cassava	1,447,721	13,858,70
Indigenous cattle meat	284,690	105,38
Maize	142,844	1,072,74
Beans, dry	137,358	250,11
Potatoes	124,338	841,27
Bananas	121,862	432,70
Sweet potatoes	74,513	986,56
Honey, natural	57,466	22,90
Cow milk, whole, fresh	57,357	183,80
Indigenous pigmeat	49,960	32,50
Groundnuts, with shell	47,933	115,16
Vegetables fresh nes	45,716	242,60

Source: http://faostat.fao.org/site/339/default.aspx Food and Agriculture Organization of the United Nations, Food and Agricultural commodities production

Angola has 1,600 km of coastline with excellent fishery resources. The annual catch average 360,000 tons a year, which is much lower than the pre-war total of over 600,000 tons. Ha the boats returned to Portugal post independence, and fish-processing facilities have falle into disrepair.

COMMUNICATIONS AND TRANSPORT

Travel Requirements

Citizens of the USA, Canada, Australia and the EU require a passport valid for six month and a visa, obtained before travelling to Angola. Other nationals are advised to contact the Angolan embassy for entry requirements.

An International Certificate of Vaccination is also required. Travellers whose immunizatior cards do not show inoculations against yellow fever within the past ten years may be subjec to exclusion, on-the-spot vaccination, and/or heavy fines.

National Airlines

The country's main airline is:

TAAG-Angola Airways (Linhas Aereas de Angola), URL: taagangola.pages.web.com TAAG services are scheduled, charter, international, regional, domestic, passenger, and cargo. The airline has a fleet of 13 planes and employs approximately 5,770 people.

Transafrik International, Luanda International Airport, Luanda, Angola. Tel: +244 (0)2 352141, fax: +244 (0)2 354183

Transafrik operates chartered, regional, and cargo services.

Angola Air Charter, CP 3010, Luanda, Angola. Tel: +244 (0)2 330994, fax: +244 (0)2 392229

International Airports

There is an international airport at Luanda in addition to 143 airports 57 of which have pavec runways. Angola has two heliports.

Railways

Three lines with a total of 3,970 km of track run from coast to hinterland, trains run from Luanda to Malanje, Lobito to Dilolo (the Benguela Railway) and Namibe to Menongue. There is also a branch line between Dondo and Golungo Alto. Reconstruction of the railways is underway and both passenger and freight operations have resumed on the Benguela Railway. Railways are operated by PCFT and CFB.

Roads

It is estimated that Angola's 108,000 km of roads almost 60 per cent were in need of repair during the late 1980s. Vehicles drive on the right. A bus system operates in Luanda.

Ports and Harbours

The main shipping ports are Luanda, Lobito and Namibe.

HEALTH

The health situation in Angola deteriorated drastically during the civil war and has yet to recover. It has a poor health infrastructure with limited personnel and resources. Angola is among the worst affected country in terms of landmines, which have left thousands of people disabled.

According to 2009 figures, total expenditure on health was equivalent to 4.9 per cent of GDP. Government spending on health was estimated to be 10.1 per cent of total government expenditure. Private expenditure was estimated to be 10.1 per cent of total health expenditure, all out-of-pocket. Total per capita expenditure on health was US$201 in 2009, compared to US$16 in 2000.

According to WHO statistics, in 2000-10 there were 1,165 doctors (1 per 10,000 population), and 19,485 nurses and midwives (14 per 10,000 population) and 22 dentists. There are an estimated 8 hospital beds per 10,000 population.

Life expectancy rates have risen in the period 1990-2009, from 42 years to 52 years. Angola's major health problems are malaria, AIDS, and tuberculosis. In 2003, nearly 4 per cent of the population (15 to 49 year olds) were infected with HIV/AIDS, the majority of whom were women. Lack of education regarding the spread of the AIDS virus is a problem for Angola. There have been around 21,000 reported deaths. Malaria continues to be prevalent in Angola, as is tuberculosis. In 2010 there were 1.68 million reported cases of malaria and 44,655 of TB. Following four years of no cases, there were eight reported cases of polio in 2007 and 29 in 2009 and 5 in 2011. There were 1,484 reported cases of cholera.

In 2010, the infant mortality rate (probability of dying aged less than 1 year old) was 98 per 1,000 live births and 161 per 1,000 live births for children aged under 5 years old compared to 144 years and 243 years respectively in 1990. The main causes of death (2010) in children aged five or less were diarrhoea 15 per cent, pneumonia 17 per cent, prematurity 13 per cent and malaria 10 per cent. HIV/AIDS accounted for 2 per cent of deaths of children aged less than five. Childhood immunization rates have improved in recent years and currently stand at over 90 per cent for the major diseases compared to approximately 40 per cent for measles in 2000. Only 18 per cent of children are estimated to sleep under insecticide-treated nets and only 29 per cent received treatment for malaria.

In 2008, an estimated 60 per cent of the urban population and 38 per cent of the rural population had access to improved drinking-water source. An estimated 86 per cent of the urban population had access to improved sanitation and 18 per cent in rural areas had access to improved sanitation. (Source: http://www.who.int, Global Health Statistics, 2012)

EDUCATION

Eight years of education is compulsory and free for children from the ages of seven to 15. Primary education lasts for four years and secondary education lasts for up to six years and is divided into two courses (one of four years and the other of two years). There is one university, Agostinho Neto University, located in Luanda.
In 2001, the overall literacy rate was estimated at 42 per cent. Only 29 per cent of women over the age of 15 are considered literate compared to 56 per cent of men. Figures for 2006 show that the equivalent of 2.6 per cent of GDP was spent on education.

RELIGION

A large proportion of the population belongs to the Christian faith, with Roman Catholics accounting for 68 per cent, Protestants 20 per cent and traditional beliefs, 12 per cent. Angola has a small Muslim community (0.58 per cent). Angola has a religious tolerance rating of 8 on a scale of 1 to 10 (10 is most freedom). (Source: World Religion Database)

In March 2009, the Pope Benedict XVI visited Angola. Two people were killed in a stampede when over 50,000 people gathered at a football stadium for an address by the Pope. The following day, hundreds of thousands of people gathered to hear an open-air mass near Luanda.

COMMUNICATIONS AND MEDIA

The constitution provides for freedom of expression but this principle is not always adhered to. The state controls all of the national media. There are some private newspapers and radio stations which do sometimes criticise the government. Television and the internet are very limited outside the capital and radio is the most important medium outside of the capital.

The constitution provides for freedom of expression but this principle is not always adhered to. The state controls all of the national media. There are some private newspapers and radio stations which do sometimes criticise the government. Television and the internet are very limited outside the capital and radio is the most important medium outside of the capital.

Newspapers
Journal De Angola, URL: http://www.jornaldeangola.com (only daily newspaper)
Angola Agency Press (ANGOP), URL: http://www.portalangop.co.ao/

Broadcasting
Television stations exist in Luanda, Bengue and Dalatando. TPA is the only terrestrial broadcasting company and is state owned. TV subscription services are available. Radio is the most important medium for most Angolans. Each of the Angolan provinces operates its own radio station.
Televisao Popular de Angola (TPA), URL: http://www.tpa.ao
Radio National de Angola, URL: http://www.nra.ao/

Telecommunications
The land line system remains very limited despite an increase in providers. There are currently five land line providers including Angola Telecom which is also a mobile phone service provider. There are currently over 110,000 phone lines in use in Angola. Recent figures show an estimated 6.7 million mobile phones were in use in 2008. It is estimated that as of 2008 there were 550,000 internet users.

ENVIRONMENT

Significant environmental problems include pasture overuse and resultant soil erosion, desertification, deforestation of tropical rain forest, water pollution, and insufficient supplies of potable water.

Angola is a party to the following environmental agreements: Biodiversity, Climate Change, Climate Change-Kyoto Protocol, Desertification, Law of the Sea, Marine Dumping, Ozone Layer Protection, and Ship Pollution.

According to figures from the EIA, in 2010, Angola's emissions from the consumption and flaring of fossil fuels totalled 24.2 million metric tons of carbon dioxide. The industrial sector contributes the greatest proportion of carbon emissions, followed by the transport, commercial and residential sectors.

SPACE PROGRAMME

Angola and Russia signed an agreement in 2009 for the building, launch and operation of an Angolan telecommunications satellite (AngoSat). Russia will provide ongoing technical support for the satellite programme. The satellite is due to be launched in 2012 and will have a lifespan of 15 years. It will support the telecommunications infrastructure and digital terrestial television.

ANTIGUA AND BARBUDA

Capital: St John's (Population estimate: 30,000)

Head of State: H.M. Queen Elizabeth II (Sovereign) (page 1420)

Governor-General: Dame Louise Lake-Tack GCMG

National Flag: Inverted triangle centred on a red ground, divided horizontally into three bands of black, blue and white, with the black stripe bearing a symbol of the rising sun in gold

CONSTITUTION AND GOVERNMENT

Constitution
Barbuda became an Associated State of Antigua in 1967 and under the title Antigua and Barbuda the state became an independent member of the Commonwealth on 1 November 1981. Under the terms of the 1981 Constitution, the Queen is Head of State and is represented by the Governor-General. The Government is headed by the Prime Minister, the House of Representatives' leader of the majority, who is appointed by the Governor-General. Members of the Cabinet are also appointed by the Governor-General with the advice of the Prime Minister.

To consult the full constitution, please visit:
http://www.ab.gov.ag/gov_v4/pdf/ab_constitution.pdf

International Relations
Antigua and Barbuda is a member of the Commonwealth where it is strong on advancing the needs of small states.

Recent Events
Antigua and Barbuda's economy has suffered since the downturn in tourism following the September 11 tragedy and the slowdown in the global economy. National debt began to rise. As part of its plan to reduce debt levels, the government sworn pledged to reduce the public sector workforce; the cabinet took a salary cut and income tax was reintroduced in 2005 for people earning more than EC$3,000 a month.

The chief finance regulator was fired in June 2009, accused of alleged corruption in the case of the disgraced financier, Sir Allen Stanford.

In January 2013, Antigua went to the World Trade Organization for permission to run a website selling music, films and software outside copyright law. The US objected to the plan as it felt it amounted to official piracy" of intellectual property.

Legislature
Antigua and Barbuda's bicameral parliament consists of the Senate and the House of Representatives.

Upper House
The 17-member Senate, appointed by the Governor-General, comprises one member nominated at the Governor-General's own discretion, 11 recommended by the Prime Minister, four recommended by the Leader of the Opposition, and one recommended by the Barbuda Council. All members serve for the life of the parliament.
Senate, Parliament Building, Queen Elizabeth Highway, St John's, Antigua. Tel: +1 268 462 4822, fax: +1 268 462 6724
House of Representatives, Parliament Building, Queen Elizabeth Highway, St John's, Antigua. Tel: +1 268 462 4822, fax: +1 268 462 6724, e-mail: parliament@candw.ag

Lower House
The 17 members of the House of Representatives are elected by universal suffrage for a term of five years. In addition, the Speaker and an ex-officio member also sit in the House.
House of Representatives, Parliament Building, Queen Elizabeth Highway, St John's, Antigua. Tel: +1 268 462 4822, fax: +1 268 462 6724, e-mail: parliament@candw.ag

---

Cabinet (as at June 2013)
Prime Minister, Minister of Foreign Affairs: Hon. Winston Baldwin Spencer (page 1518)
Minister of Finance, the Economy and Public Administration: Hon. Harold Lovell (page 1467)
Attorney General, Minister of Legal Affairs: Hon. Justin Simon
Minister of Health, Social Transformation and Consumer Affairs: Hon. Wilmoth Daniel
Minister of National Security & Employment: Hon. Dr. Leon Errol Cort
Minister of Agriculture, Lands, Housing and the Environment: Hon. Hilson Baptiste

ANTIGUA AND BARBUDA

Minister of Education, Sports, Youth and Gender Affairs: Hon. Dr. Jacqui Quinn-Leandro (BPM)
Minister of Tourism, Civil Aviation and Culture: Hon. John Herbert Maginley
Minister of Works and Transport: Hon. Trevor Myke Walker

Ministers of State
Minister of State attached to the Ministry of Agriculture, Lands, Housing and the Environment: Hon. Chanlah Codrington
Minister of State attached to the Ministry of Tourism, Civil Aviation and Culture: Hon. Eleston Montgomery Adams
Minister of State attached to the Office of the Prime Minister: Senator the Hon. Dr. Edmond Mansoor
Minister of State attached to the Ministry of Education, Sports and Youth Affairs: Hon. Winston V. Williams
Minister of State attached to the Ministry of Legal Affairs: Senator the Hon. Joanne Maureen Massiah
Minister of State attached to the Ministry of Works and Transport: Senator the Hon Elmore Charles
Minister of State attached to the Ministry of National Security: Colin Derrick

Ministries
Government portal: URL: http://www.ab.gov.ag/gov_v2/index.php
Office of the Prime Minister, Queen Elizabeth Highway, St. John's, Antigua. Tel: +1268 462 4956, fax: +1268 462 3225
Office of the Attorney-General and Ministry of Justice and Legal Affairs, Nevis Street, St. John's, Antigua. Tel: +1268 462 8867, fax: +1268 462 2465
Ministry for Foreign Affairs, Queen Elizabeth Highway, St. John's, Antigua. Tel: +1 268 462 1052, fax: +1 268 462 2482, e-mail:foreignaffairs@ab.gov.ag, URL: http://www.foreignaffairs.gov.ag
Ministry for Public Utilities, Housing, Transport and Aviation, St. John's Street, St. John's, Antigua. Tel: +1268 462 3851, fax: +1268 462 2516
Ministry of Home Affairs, Urban Development and Renewal and Social Improvement, Queen Elizabeth Highway, St. John's, Antigua. Tel: +1268 462 5933, fax: +1268 462 3225
Ministry of Economic Development, Trade, Industry and Commerce, Redcliffe Street, St. John's, Antigua. Tel: +1268 462 4302, fax: +1268 462 1622
Ministry of Education, Culture and Technology, Church Street, St. John's, Antigua. Tel: +1268 462 4959, fax: +1268 462 4970
Ministry of Health and Social Improvement, Cross Street, St. John's, Antigua. Tel: +1268 4610 9425, fax: +1268 462 5003
Ministry of Tourism and Environment, Administration Building, Queen Elizabeth Highway, St. John's, Antigua. Tel: +1268 432 0787, fax: +1268 432 2836
Ministry of Labour, Cooperatives and Public Safety, State Insurance Building, Redcliffe Street, St. John's, Antigua. Tel: +1268 462 0567, fax: +1268 462 1595
Ministry of Agriculture, Lands and Fisheries, Nevis and Temple Streets, St. John's, Antigua. Tel: +1268 462 1543, fax: +1268 462 6104
Ministry of Planning, Implementation and Public Service Affairs, Church Street, St, John's, Antigua. Tel: +1268 462 5935, fax: +1268 462 6104
Ministry of Information, Broadcasting, Sports and Carnival, Cassada Gardens, St. John's, Antigua. Tel: +1268 562 1675, fax: +1268 562 1681
Ministry of Finance, High & Long Streets, St. John's, Antigua. Tel: +1268 462 4302, fax: +1268 462 4622
Ministry of Public Works, Communication and Insurance, Queen Elizabeth Highway, High Street (Finance), St. John's, Antigua. Tel: +1268 462 5933, fax: +1268 426 3225

Political Parties
Antigua Labour Party (ALP), St. Mary's Street, St. John's, Antigua. Tel: +1 268 462 1059, URL: http://www.votealp.com/home.jsp
Leader: Hon. Lester Bryant Bird
United Progressive Party (UPP), Nevis Street, St John's, Antigua. Tel: +1 268 462 1818, URL: http://www.uppantigua.ag/
Leader: Hon. Baldwin Spencer (page 1518)
Barbuda People's Movement (BPM), Codrington, Barbuda.
National Movement for Change; Organisation for National Development ; Barbudans for a Better Barbuda; Democratic People's Party; National Reform Movement

Elections
The last parliamentary election took place on 12 March 2009 when the ruling United Progressive Party (UPP) was returned to power with a very narrow majority. Winston Spencer subsequently announced a smaller cabinet which includes one member of the Barbuda People's Movment. Elections take place every five years. The voting age is 18.

Diplomatic Representation
High Commission for Antigua and Barbuda, 2nd Floor, 45 Crawford Place, London W1H 4LP, United Kingdom. Tel: +44 (0)20 7258 0070, fax: +44 (0)20 7258 7486, e-mail: antiguabarbudaUK@hotmail.com, URL: http://www.antigua-barbuda.com
High Commissioner: Carl Roberts (page 1503)
Embassy of Antigua and Barbuda, 3216 New Mexico Avenue, NW, Washington, DC 20016, USA. Tel: +1 202 362 5122, fax: +1 202 362 5225, e-mail: embantbar@aol.com
Ambassador: Deborah Mae Lovell
British High Commission, Price Waterhouse Centre, 11 Old Parham Road, P.O. Box 483, St. John's, Antigua. Tel: +1 268 462 0008, fax: +1 268 562 2124, e-mail: britishc@candw.ag, URL: http://ukinbarbados.fco.gov.uk/en/
High Commissioner: Duncan Taylor
The USA does not have an embassy in Antigua and Barbuda but the embassy in Barbados is accredited.

Permanent Mission of Antigua and Barbuda to the United Nations, 305 E 47th Street, New York, NY 10017, USA. Tel: +1 212 541 4117, fax: +1 212 757 1607, emai antigua@un.int, URL: http://www.antiguabarbudamission.org/index.htm
Ambassador: Dr. John W. Ashe

LEGAL SYSTEM

Justice in Antigua and Barbuda is based on UK common law. Antigua and Barbuda is member of the Eastern Caribbean court system, based in St. Lucia and interprets the law based on UK common law. Decisions by local Magistrates Courts and High Courts can be appealed to the Court of Appeal, which travels to each Member State at specified dates to hear appeals in both civil and criminal matters.

The government generally respects the human rights of its citizens. However, the state retain the death penalty.

Eastern Caribbean Court System: URL: http://www.eccourts.org/
Chief Justice: Hon. Janice Mesadis Pereira

Office of the Ombudsman, Deanery Place & Dickenson Bay Street, St John's, Antigua and Barbuda. Tel: +1 268 462 9364, fax: +1 268 462 9355, URL http://www.ombudsman.gov.ag

LOCAL GOVERNMENT

Administratively, Antigua and Barbuda is divided into six parishes (Saint George, Saint John Saint Mary, Saint Paul, Saint Peter, and Saint Philip) and two dependencies Barbuda, and the uninhabited island of Redonda. The Barbuda Council is responsible for the administration of local government and comprises nine directly-elected members and two ex-officio members Partial elections are held every two years. The next election is due in 2013.

AREA AND POPULATION

Area
The three islands of Antigua, Barbuda and the uninhabited Redonda form part of the Leeward Islands in the Eastern Caribbean. Their total area is 440 sq. km. Antigua is 281 sq. km (108 sq. miles), Barbuda is 161 sq. km (62 sq. miles), and Redonda is 1.6 sq. km. The climate is tropical and the area is also subject to hurricanes.

To view a map, please consult http://www.lib.utexas.edu/maps/americas/antiguabarbuda.jpg

Population
The population in 2010 was put at 89,000. The population of Barbuda was put at 1,400 most of whom live in or near the capital of Codrington. The annual population growth rate was estimated at 1.3 per cent over the period 2000-10. The capital, St. John's, has an estimated population of 30,000. The majority of the population (66 per cent) is aged between 15 and 64, with 24 per cent aged up to 14 years. The islands' population is predominantly of African origin, with a minority of Portuguese, British and Levantine Arabs. Since the devastating volcano in Montserrat around 1,200 Montserratians live on the islands. The official language is English.

Births, Marriages, Deaths
The crude birth rate in 2010 was estimated at 16 births per 1,000 of the population, whilst the death rate was an estimated 6.6 deaths per 1,000 of the population. Infant mortality in 2010 was estimated at 7 deaths per 1,000 live births. Average life expectancy at birth in 2009 was 74 years (73 years for men and 76 years for women). (Source: http://www.who.int, World Health Statistics 2012)

Public Holidays 2014
1 January: New Year's Day
18 April: Good Friday
21 April: Easter Monday
1 May: Labour Day
7 June: Queen's Birthday
9 June: Whit Monday
6 July: Caricom Day
5-6 August: Carnival
1 November: Independence Day
9 December: National Heros Day
25-26 December: Christmas

EMPLOYMENT

Recent estimates put the total labour force at 30,000. The major employment sector is the restaurant and hotel industry, which employs 31.9 per cent of the labour force. Other important employment areas are services (24 per cent), construction (11.6 per cent) and transport and communications (9 per cent). Estimated figures for 2011 put the unemployment rate at 11 per cent.

Total Employment by Economic Activity

Occupation	2001
Agriculture, hunting & forestry	691
Fishing	255
Mining & quarrying	106
Manufacturing	1,541
Electricity, gas & water supply	513

continued

Construction	3,122
Wholesale & retail trade, repairs	4,846
Hotels & restaurants	5,081
Transport, storage & communications	2,808
Financial intermediation	1,049
Real estate, renting & business activities	1,460
Public admin. & defence; compulsory social security	4,376
Education	1,711
Health & social work	1,716
Other community, social & personal service activities	2,686
Households with employed persons	1,304
Extra-territorial organisations & bodies	503
Other	2,467

Source: Copyright © International Labour Organization (ILO Dept. of Statistics, http://laborsta.ilo.org)

Antigua and Barbuda has one of the lowest unemployment in the Caribbean. Ninety per cent of the labour force is in employment. However, the 2005 budget included measures to cut the public service salary bill by 20 per cent by cutting approximately 2,600 jobs of the 13,000 public sector workforce.

BANKING AND FINANCE

Currency
The unit of currency is the Eastern Caribbean Dollar, which has a fixed exchange rate with the US dollar. EC$2.70 = US$1.00.

Antigua is a member of the Eastern Caribbean Currency Union (ECCU), whose members share a common currency issued by the Eastern Caribbean Central Bank (ECCB), and is also a member of CARICOM and the Organization of Eastern Caribbean States.

GDP/GNP, Inflation, National Debt
The islands' economy is primarily based on tourism and services sector. Tourism accounts for over half of GDP, although hurricanes since 1995 have caused damage to the tourism infrastructure and reduced the number of tourists visiting the islands. Antigua was also adversely affected by the events of September 11 2001, as tourists decided not to travel. In 2008 over 200,000 tourists visited the islands, up from 190,000 in 2007.

To try to counterbalance its dependency on tourism, Antigua has sought to develop other industries such as financial services, communications, transport and more recently, internet gambling. Industry contributes just over 22 per cent to GDP, whilst agriculture contributes 4 per cent.

GDP was estimated at US1,164 million in 2007 (compared to US$818 million in 2004), with an annual growth rate of 6.1 per cent. Per capita GDP in 2007 was estimated to be US$13,600. Figures for 2009 put GDP at US$1.1 billion, a per capita figure of US$18,000. In keeping with the world economic downturn, GDP growth in 2009 was recorded at -6.4 per cent. Estimates for 2010 put GDP at US$1.433 billion with a growth rate of -4 per cent. Growth was estimated at -0.5 per cent in 2011 with a total GDP of US$1.6 billion.

Inflation (consumer prices) in 2000 was 2.5 per cent and 2.0 per cent in 2004, falling to 1.0 per cent in 2005 and averaged 1.0 per cent in 2009. In 2010, it was estimated to be 2.8 per cent, rising to 3 per cent in 2011.

Recent figures put external debt at 125 per cent of GDP.

Balance of Payments / Imports and Exports
The economy is small and open, and consequently the country is affected by changes in the economic conditions of countries from which it imports goods and services. To some extent the effect of imported prices on the economy is moderated by the fixed exchange rate with the US dollar. Estimated figures for 2011 put the cost of imports at US$420 million and the value of merchandise exports at US$43.5 million. Major imports are food and live animals, machinery and transport equipment, chemicals and oil. Major exports are petroleum products, manufactured goods, food and live animals, and machinery and transport equipment. Top trading partners in 2005 were the EU, the US, Barbados, the Netherlands Antilles, St. Kitts and Nevis, and Trinidad and Tobago.

Antigua and Barbuda has significant trade links with the US, and benefits from the US Caribbean Basin Initiative. The country also belongs to the Caribbean Community and Common Market (CARICOM).

Trade or Currency Restrictions
Antigua and Barbuda practices a very liberal trade regime with no restrictions on imports and no non-tariff barriers.

Chambers of Commerce and Trade Organisations
Antigua and Barbuda Chamber of Commerce and Industry, P.O. Box, Redcliffe Street, St. John's, Antigua. Tel: +1 268 462 0743, fax: +1 268 462 4575

MANUFACTURING, MINING AND SERVICES

Primary and Extractive Industries
Antigua and Barbuda does not produce its own oil but relies on imports for consumption needs. Imports of oil were 6.00 thousand barrels a day in 2011, mainly jet fuel, distillate, and gasoline. It exports a small quantity (0.16 thousand barrels a day) of petroleum products, largely gasoline and distillate. Oil consumption in the same year totalled 6.00 thousand barrels a day, most of which was jet fuel, distillate and gasoline.

Energy
Antigua and Barbuda consumed 0.010 quadrillion Btu of energy in 2009. All of the country's energy is produced by petroleum. Installed electricity capacity was 0.03 million kW in 2010. Net generation in the same year was estimated at 0.12 billion kWh.

Manufacturing
Industry is the second largest contributor to GDP: 22 per cent according to recent estimates. The industry sector employs around 7 per cent of the labour force. Primary manufacturing industries include assembly for export, bedding, handicrafts, and electronic components.

Service Industries
The services industry is a major part of the economy, contributing nearly 75 per cent towards GDP in 2002. Commerce and services employs over 80 per cent of the labour force. Antigua and Barbuda is an active offshore financial sector. Tourism is a key sector, accounting for half of GDP. Over one third of tourist arrivals are from the US. Tourist arrivals have since been affected by hurricane damage to the infrastructure and the global downturn in travel following the terrorist attacks of September 11. Figures for 2002 show that visitors were beginning to return and tourism receipts for that year totalled US$240 million. In 2004, the islands had 245,456 visitors who stayed on the islands and over 500,000 cruise ship visitors. The Cricket World Cup was held in the Caribbean in 2007. As a result of this the tourist sector benefited from an increase in tourists as well as the building of new hotels. Figures for 2008 show that 203,741 visitors arrived in the first nine months of the year.

Antigua & Barbuda Department of Tourism, URL: http://www.antigua-barbuda.com

Agriculture
Agricultural revenue represented 3.8 per cent of GDP in 2011, whilst the sector employed just over seven per cent of the workforce. While sugar was the main agricultural crop for many years, its importance has diminished and among the main products are now fruit and vegetables, particularly mangoes, guava and melons. Cotton and meat are also produced. Livestock production includes cattle, pigs, goats and sheep. The agriculture sector is mainly geared towards the domestic market.

Agricultural Production in 2010

Produce	Int. $'000*	Tonnes
Fruit, tropical fresh nes	2,616	6,400
Cow milk, whole, fresh	1,779	5,700
Indigenous cattle meat	1,513	560
Mangoes, mangosteens, guavas	779	1,300
Indigenous pigmeat	323	210
Indigenous chicken meat	308	216
Indigenous goat meat	300	125
Hen eggs, in shell	228	275
Indigenous sheep meat	190	70
Other melons (inc. cantaloupes)	153	830
Tomatoes	133	360
Lemons & limes	131	330

* unofficial figures

Source: http://faostat.fao.org/site/339/default.aspx Food and Agriculture Organization of the United Nations, Food and Agricultural commodities production

COMMUNICATIONS AND TRANSPORT

Travel Requirements
British citizens do not require a visa to enter Antigua and Barbuda on holiday or business; however, for visits of over one month, an extension of stay must be obtained through the Antigua and Barbuda Immigration Department. Citizens of the USA, Canada, Australia and most of the EU do not require a visa; people from Cyprus, Czech Republic, Latvia, Lithuania and Slovak Republic do need a visa.

Immigration officials require exact information about where visitors are staying, and may request to see a return ticket or ticket for onward travel, as well as proof of sufficient funds to cover the cost of the visitor's intended stay. There is a departure tax payable when departing the country.

Nationals of countries other than those mentioned above should contact the Antigua and Barbuda High Commission for any further information on visa and entry requirements.

International Airports
VC Bird International Airport, 6 km north-east of St. John's, is large enough to accommodate international aircraft. It is used for regular direct flights from Britain and Germany as well as the USA, and connections to other Caribbean Islands. The main airlines serving the country are Air Canada, American Airlines, British Airways, British West Indies Airways, Condor and the Leeward Islands Air Transport (LIAT).

Carib Aviation operates flights between Antigua and Barbuda.

Roads
The country has a combined road network of about 1,165 km, of which 384 km is paved. A major road resurfacing project was due to be completed in 1999. Vehicles are driven on the left.

Shipping
St. John's has two ports served by international lines. Ferries operate from St. Johns to Barbuda, journey time is around 90 minutes.

STATES OF THE WORLD

ARGENTINA

Ports and Harbours
The main regional and international port for cargo and passengers is St. John's Deep Water Harbour, which provides a sea link from Canada, the USA, Europe and the Far East.

HEALTH

The country is presently served by a general hospital, with 220 beds, a private clinic, seven health centres and 17 clinics. A new EC$80 million hospital complex in St. John's provides a further 187 beds. According to the latest WHO figures, there are 12 doctors and 233 nurses and midwives.

Total expenditure on health in 2009 represented 4.9 per cent of GDP. Government expenditure makes up 67.1 per cent of the total health expenditure and represents 8 per cent of its total expenditure. Per capita total expenditure on health is US$601.

In 2010, the infant mortality rate (likelihood of dying before first birthday) was 7 per 1,000 live births and the child mortality rate was 8 per 1,000 live births.(Source: http://www.who.int, Global Health Statistics, 2012)

EDUCATION

Education is compulsory between the ages of five and 16. Primary education lasts from the age of five to the age of 10, whilst secondary education lasts from 11 to 16. There are currently 65 primary schools, 11 secondary schools, Antigua State College, The University of West Indies Extra Mural Centre and the Antigua and Barbuda International Institute of Technology. Recent figures put adult literacy rates at 89 per cent and that the equivalent of 3.9 per cent of GDP is spent annually on education.

RELIGION

Christianity is the main religion in the country with nearly 98 per cent of the population, the main denomination being Anglican. Other denominations include Roman Catholic, Methodist, Lutheran, Moravian, Pentecostalist, Baptist, and Seventh Day Adventist. Antigua has a religious liberty rating of 9 on a scale of 1 to 10 (10 is most freedom). (Source: World Religion Database)

COMMUNICATIONS AND MEDIA

Most of the broadcast stations are controlled by the Antigua Labour Party. Newspapers can criticism of the government.

Newspapers
The main newspapers are:
The Daily Observer, URL: http://www.antiguaobserver.com/
The Antigua Sun, URL: http://www.antiguasun.com/

Broadcasting
The Antigua and Barbuda Broadcasting Service (ABS) provides the country's radio and television services. In addition there are a number of commercial radio stations and a 13-channel cable system, CTV Entertainment Systems. Estimates put the number of television receivers at 35,000 and the number of radio sets at 50,000.

Telecommunications
There is a good domestic automatic service. In 2008, it was estimated there were 130,000 mobile phones in use compared to 38,000 landlines. Figures for 2008 show that Antigua has 7,000 internet service providers and around 65,000 internet users.

ENVIRONMENT

There is much concern over the shipment of nuclear waste through the Caribbean Sea. Any accident could cause severe long term, ecological, economic and health problems, including cancer and the contamination of food supplies, agricultural production and seafood. In addition, there are problems with limited fresh water resources as a result of tree clearing.

In 2010, Antigua and Barbuda's emissions from the consumption of fossil fuels totalled 0.72 million metric tons of carbon dioxide. (Source: EIA)

Antigua and Barbuda is a party to the following international environmental agreements: Biodiversity, Climate Change, Climate Change-Kyoto Protocol, Desertification, Endangered Species, Environmental Modification, Hazardous Wastes, Law of the Sea, Marine Dumping, Ozone Layer Protection, Ship Pollution, Wetlands, and Whaling.

ARGENTINA

Argentine Republic

República Argentina

Capital: Buenos Aires (Population estimate: 3.4 million; greater Buenos Aires metropolitan area: 12 million)

Head of State: Cristina Fernandez de Kirchner (page 1424)

Vice President: Amado Boudou (page 1392)

National Flag: A dual colour fesswise, light blue, white, light blue; the centre stripe charged with a gold sun in splendour with 32 rays and a human face

CONSTITUTION AND GOVERNMENT

Constitution
The Republic of Argentina gained its independence from Spain on 9 July 1816. According to the current Constitution (24 August 1994) executive power is exercised by the President of the Republic with the advice and assistance of the Ministers of State, who are appointed by, and responsible to, the President. The President is head of government and Commander-in-Chief of the armed forces, and serves a maximum of two four-year terms.

To consult the full constitution, please visit:
http://www.argentina.gov.ar/argentina/portal/documentos/constitucion_ingles.pdf

International Relations
Argentina is a member of the regional common market bloc Mercosur, the world's fourth largest integrated market with a combined population of about 200 million people. Trade between Argentina and the other members has increased significantly over the last five years. Argentina is also a member of the Rio Group. The dispute over two pulp mills in Uruguay has marred the relationship between the two countries recently.

Argentina plays an active role in international affairs; it was a non-permanent member of the UN Security Council until the end of 2006, and Argentine troops have been deployed on UN peacekeeping operations in Cyprus, Kosovo, the Middle East and Haiti. It has a police contingent in Darfur. Argentina was elected to the Human Rights Council in May 2008.

Argentina has strong historic links with the UK. Following the Falklands conflict, diplomatic relations were restored in 1990 and issues relating to the South Atlantic are discussed jointly by Argentina and the UK. The British government maintains that no negotiations over sovereignty will take place unless and until that is the wish of the Islanders.

Recent Events
On 20 December 2001 President Fernando de la Rua resigned from office after widespread protests at austerity measures imposed by the government. On 23 December 2001 Adolfo Rodriguez Saa was sworn in as President, only to resign on 30 December. Eduardo Duhalde became Argentina's third president in two weeks on 1 January 2002. The financial crisis also claimed the minister of economy, Domingo Cavallo, who resigned in December 2001. In April 2002 the minister of economy Jorge Remes Lenicov resigned following the delaying of a vote on his package to prevent the collapse of the banking system. Dr. Roberto Lavagna was appointed the new economic minister. Early elections were held in May 2003 and the Presidency was won by Nestor Kirchner, of the PJ (Peronist) party.

By 2003, economic recovery was beginning to be felt and the IMF agreed to a new loan in March 2004. However talks were suspended in August 2004 ending the restructuring of the country's debt, the biggest sovereign default in modern history, amounting to around US$100 billion. 76 per cent of the creditors of Argentina's massive debt agreed to a restructured repayment plan in February 2005. For every defaulted bond with a face value of $1, a new bond, with a market value of 35 cents, was issued. In January 2006, Argentina repaid its debt to the IMF.

In June 2005, the Supreme Court abolished the amnesty law protecting former military officers suspected of human rights abuses during the years 1976 to 1983. Between 10,000 and 30,000 people were killed or disappeared before Argentina returned to civilian rule. The victims became known as 'Los Desaparecidos'.

Argentina's relationship with neighbouring Uruguay was put under strain in May 2006, when Argentina filed a complaint against the construction of two pulp mills on the bordering Uruguay River, citing environmental concerns. In July, the International Court of Justice in The Hague ruled that whilst construction of the mills could continue, the court would investigate the environmental aspect. In September 2007, hundreds of Argentinians protested outside the paper pulp mill.

In February 2008, Argentina and Brazil agreed to build a joint nuclear reactor to counter looming energy shortages. The agreement came as part of a plan by South America's two biggest economies to extend defence and energy projects. Each country currently has two operating nuclear plants, and both have signed the Nuclear Non-Proliferation Treaty.

In March 2008, Argentine farmers held nationwide protests after the government refused to back down on tax rises of up to 45 per cent on some agricultural exports. The government uses taxes on grain and commodity exports to boost state revenues. Trade at Argentina's largest grain and cattle markets ground to a halt, while many shops reported shortages of supplies. Thousands of Argentines protested in support of the farmers.

In April 2008, fires on grassland outside Buenos Aires caused health fears in the city, as people complained of sore throats and eyes. The health ministry said the smoke was not toxic although it contained high levels of carbon monoxide. The air was so thick that airports and highways had to be closed. Farmers clearing land to graze cattle were blamed for the fires.

In June 2008, the Argentine Senate narrowly rejected the controversial tax increases on agricultural exports. The vote was a blow to President Cristina Fernandez who had intended to use the tax to fund the building of schools, roads and hospitals. The strikes by farmers had led to food shortages in some parts of the country. The president cancelled the controversial taxes in July, and the Agriculture Secretary resigned, along with the Cabinet Chief.

In November, former President of Argentina, Carlos Menem, was formally charged with involvement in arms-trafficking. He was accused of authorising the sale of weapons, to Croatia and Ecuador at a time when Croatia was under a UN arms embargo because of its involvement in the violent break-up of the former Yugoslavia and when Ecuador was involved in a month-long conflict with neighbouring Peru. Mr. Menem maintained that the shipments were destined for Panama and Venezuela.

Towards the end of December 2008, it was announced that former President, (and husband of the present President), Nestor Kirchner would be investigated over corruption allegations, and links with the Venezuelan President, Hugo Chavez. The investigation was requested by opposition leader Elisa Carrio who alleged that Mr. Kirchner distributed big construction contracts and government-owned licences to drill for oil in return for financial rewards. Under the terms of an agreement with President Chavez, Argentina was to buy Venezuelan fuel and Venezuela would purchase Argentine manufactured goods. It is alleged that $90m in Argentine government funds used to complete to deal disappeared.

The government declared a national state of emergency in January 2009 after Argentina suffered its worst drought for decades.

In April 2009, Argentina handed over documents to the UN which formally laid claim to an ocean area which extended to the Antarctic and includes the Falkland Islands and in February 2010 it imposed controls on ships passing through its water to the Falkland Islands, this was in response to British plans to drill for oil near the Falkland Islands.

In July 2010, Argentina became the first Latin American country to legalise same-sex marriage.

A former naval officer, Alfredo Astiz, was jailed in October 2011 for crimes against humanity during military rule in 1976-83. Fifteen other former military and police officers were also sentenced. All worked at the Naval Mechanical School in Buenos Aires (ESMA) which was a secret torture centre. Of the approximately 5,000 prisoners taken to Esma it is alleged that only 10 per cent survived.

Towards the end of 2011 as the 30th aniversary of the Falklands Conflict with the UK approached, tensions between Argentina and the UK increased. Argentina persuaded members of Mercosur to close their ports to ships flying the flag of the Falkland Islands. In February 2012, Argentina made an official complaint to the UN that Britain was 'militarising' the area around the Falkland Islands. The UK dismssed the claims. In March 2013, the Falkland Islanders held a referendum and voted overwheimngly in favour of remaining a British territory. Argentina dismissed the referendum as meaningless.

Legislature
Legislative power is vested in the Federal Congress (*Congreso de la Nacion*) which consists of two houses, the Senate (*Senado*) and the Chamber of Deputies (*Camara de Diputados*).

Upper House
The Senate is composed of 72 members, directly elected for six years, three from each province. One third of the Senate becomes renewable every three years. The current voting system replaces that operating until October 2001 when Senators were indirectly elected by the provinces for nine years.
Senate (Senado de la Nacion), Hipólito Yrigoyen 1849 1er. Piso, Buenos Aires, Argentina. Tel: +54 (0)11 4010 3000, e-mail: losada@senado.gov.ar, URL: http://www.senado.gov.ar
President: Julio C. Cleto Cobos

Lower House
Seats in the Chamber of Deputies are distributed among the different political parties according to their share of the popular vote. The Chamber of Deputies has 257 members who are elected for a four year term, one half being renewed every two years.
Chamber of Deputies (Camera de Diputados), Av. Rivadavia 1864, 1033 Buenos Aires, Argentina. Tel: +54 (0)11 4370 7100, URL: http://www.diputados.gov.ar
President, Chamber of Deputies: Dr. Eduardo Alfredo Fellner

Cabinet (as at June 2013)
Cabinet Chief: Dr Juan Manuel Abal Medina
Minister of Interior: Florencio Randazzo
Minister of Foreign Affairs, International Trade and Religion: Hector Marcos Timerman (page 1525)
Minister of Defence: Aguatin Rossi
Minister of the Economy and Public Finance: Hernan Lorenzino
Minister of Justice and Human Rights: Julio Alak
Minister of Education: Alberto Sileoni

Minister of Labour, Employment and Human Resources: Carlos Tomado (page 1526)
Minister of Health: Juan Luis Manzur
Minister of Science and Technology: Dr. Lino Baranao
Minister of Industry: Debora Giorgi
Minister of Agriculture, Livestock and Fisheries: Norberto Yahuar
Minister of Social Development and Environment: Alicia Kirchner
Minister of Tourism, Carlos Enrique Meyer
Minister of Federal Planning and Public Investment: Julio de Vido (page 1415)

Ministries
Office of the President, Balcarce 50, 1064 Buenos Aires, Argentina. Tel: +54 (0)11 4344 3600, fax: +54 (0)11 4344 3700 / 3800, e-mail: webmaster@presidencia.gov.ar, URL: http://www.presidencia.gov.ar
Office of the Vice President, Balcarce 50, 1064 Buenos Aires, Argentina. Tel: +54 (0)11 4379 5858, fax: +54 (0)11 4954 4707, e-mail: webmaster@presidencia.gov.ar, URL: http://www.presidencia.gov.ar
Office of the Cabinet, URL: http://www.jgm.gov.ar/
Ministry of the Interior, 25 de Mayo 101/145, C1002ABC Buenos Aires, Argentina. Tel: +54 (0)11 4339 0800, fax: +54 (0)11 4343 0880, e-mail: info@mininterior.gov.ar, URL: http://www.mininterior.gov.ar/
Ministry of Foreign Affairs, International Trade and Religion, Esmeralda 1212, 1007 Buenos Aires, Argentina. Tel: +54 (0)11 4819 7000, fax: +54 (0)11 4819 7501, e-mail: web@cancilleria.gov.ar, URL: http://www.mrecic.gov.ar/
Ministry of Defence, Azopardo 250, Pisos 10, 11 y 13, 1328 Buenos Aires, Argentina. Tel: +54 (0)11 4346 8800, fax: +54 (0)11 4346 8800, URL: http://www.mindef.gov.ar
Ministry of Economy and Production, Hipólito Yrigoyen 250, 1310 Buenos Aires, Argentina. Tel: +54 (0)11 4349 5000, fax: +54 (0)11 4349 8815, e-mail: Webmaster@mecon.gov.ar, URL: http://www.mecon.gov.ar
Ministry of Planning, Public Investment and Services, Hipólito Yrigoyen 250, 1310 Buenos Aires, Argentina. Tel: +54 (0)11 4349 5000 / 5010, fax: +54 (0)11 4318 9432; http://www.minplan.gov.ar
Ministry of Justice, Security and Human Rights, Sarmiento 329, 1041 Buenos Aires, Argentina. Tel: +54 (0)11 4328 3015, URL: http://www.jus.gov.ar
Ministry of Education, Science and Technology, Pizzurno 935, 1020 Buenos Aires, Argentina. Tel: +54 (0)11 4129 1000, fax: +54 (0)11 4812 6493, e-mail: webmaster@prensa.me.gov.ar, URL: http://www.me.gov.ar
Ministry of Labour, Employment and Social Security, Avenue Leandro N. Alem 650, 1001 Buenos Aires, Argentina. Tel: +54 (0)11 4310 6000, fax: +54 (0)11 4310 6424, e-mail: consultas@trabajo.gov.ar, URL: http://www.trabajo.gov.ar
Ministry of Health, Avenue 9 de Julio 1925, 1001 Buenos Aires, Argentina. Tel: +54 (0)11 4379 9000, e-mail: consultas@msal.gov.ar, URL: http://www.msal.gov.ar
Ministry of Social Development, Av. 9 de Julio 1925, 1332 Buenos Aires, Argentina. Tel: +54 (0)11 4379 3600, URL: http://www.desarrollosocial.gov.ar

Political Parties
Partido Justicialista (PJ) (Peronist party), Matheu 130, (1082) Buenos Aires, Argentina. Tel: +54 (0)11 4952 4555, fax: +54 (0)11 4954 2421, URL: http://www.pj.org.ar/
President: Daniel Scioli
Frente para la Victoria. (an offshoot of PJ). URL: http://www.frenteparalavictoria.org
President: Nestor Kirchner
Unión Civica Radical (UCR, Radical Civic Union), Alsina 1786, (1088) Federal Capital, Argentina. URL: http://www.ucr.org.ar/
President: Ángel Rozas
Socialist Party (PS), URL: http://www.partidosocialista.com.ar
Leader: Rubén Giustiniani
Republican Proposal (PRO), URL: http://www.pro.com.ar
Leader: Mauricio Macri
Civic Coalition ARI, URL: http://www.coalicioncivica.org.ar
Leader: Elisa Carrió

Elections
Presidential elections took place on 24 October 1999 and saw the Peronist Carlos Menem replaced by the Radical Party's Fernando de la Rua, who gained 48 per cent of the vote. President de la Rua resigned on 21 December 2001 following violent protests against austerity measures imposed by the government and was replaced by Ramon Puerta on 20 December 2001, Adolfo Rodriguez Saa on 23 December 2001, and Eduardo Duhalde on 1 January 2002.

Presidential elections were held in May 2003 and were won by Nestor Kirchner, of the Front for Victory party. He won 22 per cent of the vote, ahead of Carlos Menem with 19.4 per cent. In October 2007, Cristina Fernandez de Kirchner (wife of the incumbent President) won the presidential elections with 44.92 per cent of the vote, to become Argentina's first elected female president. The most recent presidential election took place in October 2011 when Cristina Fernandez de Kirchner was re-elected with 54 per cent of the vote.

Elections were also held in October 2007 for 130 of the 257 members of the Argentine Chamber of Deputies and for 24 of the 72 members of the Argentine Senate. In the Chamber of Deputies, the Front for Victory now has 153 MPs (up 13), the Civic Coalition Confederation has 27 MPs (up 13), and the Radical Civic Union has 30 (down 7). In the Senate, the Front for Victory and the Civic Coalition Confederation both gained seats, whilst the Radical Civic Union again lost seats. Further elections took place in June 2009 for half of the Chamber and one third of the Senate. Half of the Chamber was elected in 2011.

Voting in Argentine elections is compulsory.

Diplomatic Representation
Embassy of the United States of America, Avenue Colombia 4300, 1425 Buenos Aires, Argentina. Tel: +54 ((11) 5777 4533, fax: +54 (11) 5777 4240, URL: http://buenosaires.usembassy.gov
Ambassador: Vilma Martinez

ARGENTINA

British Embassy, Dr Luis Agote 2412, C1425EOF, 1425 Buenos Aires, Argentina. Tel: +54 (11) 4808 2200, fax: +54 (11) 4808 2274, e-mail: askconsular.baires@fco.gov.uk, URL: http://ukinargentina.fco.gov.uk
Ambassador: Shan Morgan
Embassy of Argentina, 1600 New Hampshire Avenue, NW, Washington, DC 20009, USA. Tel: +1 202 238 6400, fax: +1 202 332 3171, URL: http://www.embassyofargentina.us
Ambassador: Alfredo Vicente Chiaradia
Embassy of Argentina, 65 Brook Street, London W1Y 1YE, United Kingdom. Tel: +44 (0)20 7318 1300, fax: +44 (0)20 7318 1301, URL: http://www.argentine-embassy-uk.org/index_eng.shtml
Ambassador: Alicia Castro (page 1401)
Brazilian Embassy, Cerrito 1350, 1010 Buenos Aires, Argentina. Tel: +54 (11) 4515 2400, fax: +54 (11) 4515 2400, e-mail: webmaster@embrasil.org.ar, URL: http://www.brasil.org.ar
Permanent Mission to the United Nations, One United Nations Plaza, 25th Floor, New York, NY 10017, USA. Tel: +1 212 688 6300, fax: +1 212 980 8395, e-mail: argentina@un.int, URL: http://www.un.int/argentina
Ambassador and Permanent Representative: S.E. Sr. Jorge Martín Arturo Argüello

LEGAL SYSTEM

The legal system of Argentina is a mix of both common law and civil law, the civil law element being based on the 1853 Constitution of Argentina and the 1871 Civil Code.

The National Judicial Power, through the nine-member Supreme Court of Justice, has jurisdiction over the entire country, and used to have jurisdiction over the Federal Capital. However, when the Constitution of the Autonomous Government of the City of Buenos Aires was established in 1994, the capital acquired a judicial system similar to that of the other provinces. Each autonomous province has a Supreme Court, Appeal Courts, Courts of First Instance and minor courts. Federal Appeal Courts sit in all the major cities of the interior - La Plata, Paraná, Córdoba, Rosario, Bahia Blanca, Mendoza, Resistencia and Tucumán.

Judges on the Supreme Court of Justice are appointed by the Argentinian president, with the approval of the Senate. Judges of lower courts are proposed to the Senate by the Council of Judges which consists of members of Congress, the Supreme Court, and professional organisations.

Whilst in general the government respects the human rights of its citizens, Argentinian prisons are overcrowded, and prisoners suffer prolonged pretrial detention due to a slow judicial system. Conditions in the prisons are substandard. In 2008 there were reports of the use of excessive force by police and security forces, and some cases of official corruption. In 2008, the government convicted several perpetrators of human rights abuses committed during the 1976-83 military dictatorship, and brought back to trial some people who had been pardoned of human rights abuses during that era.

In 1984, Argentina abolished the death penalty for ordinary crimes (exceptional crimes were those committed under military law or in exceptional circumstances), and in 2008, it was abolished for all crimes.

Supreme Court of Justice
Corte Suprema, URL: http://www.csjn.gov.ar
Members of the Supreme Court of Justice:
President: Dr. Ricardo Luis Lorenzetti (page 1466)
Vice President: Dra. Elena Highton de Nolasco
Justices: Dr. Enrique Santiago Petracchi, Dr. Juan Carlos Maqueda, Dra. Carmen Maria Argibay, Dr Eugenio Raul Zaffaroni

Defensoria del Pueblo de la Nacion Argentina (Office of the Ombudsman), URL: http://www.dpn.gob.ar

LOCAL GOVERNMENT

Argentina is a republic consisting of one autonomous district (Federal Capital) and 23 provinces: Buenos Aires, Catamarca, Chaco, Chubut, Cordoba, Corrientes, Entre Rios, Formosa, Jujuy, La Pampa, La Rioja, Mendoza, Misiones, Neuquen, Rio Negro, Salta, San Juan, San Luis, Santa Cruz, Santa Fe, Santiago del Estero, Tierra del Fuego - Antartica e Islas del Atlantico Sur, Tucuman.

Each of the provinces has its own constitution, laws, authorities, form of government, etc., though these must comply with the national constitution and laws. Some provinces have two legislative houses, others only one, but all are elected by popular vote. The Governor of each Province is also elected. All provinces except Buenos Aires are divided into districts called departments (departamentos), which are in turn divided into municipalities (cities, towns and villages). The Federal Capital, Buenos Aires, was declared an autonomous city in the 1994 constitutional reform. Its mayor is elected by the people, and carries the title of Jefe de Gobierno. The most recent local elections took place in 2011.

AREA AND POPULATION

Area
Argentina is the eighth largest country in the world with a land area of 1,073,393 sq. miles. The coastline to the east stretches for 1,600 miles along the Atlantic Ocean. To the west, the frontier with Chile runs along the Andean mountains, to the north are Bolivia and Paraguay, and to the north-east Brazil. Argentina also shares and eastern border with Uruguay. Argentina has five major geographical regions: the rain forest areas of the far-northeast along its border with Brazil; the flat, swampy Chaco plain; the fertile grasslands of the central Pampas, one of the largest fertile plains in the world covering nearly a third of the Argentina's land area; the Patagonian plateau stretching down to Tierra del Fuego, and the Andes

Mountains along its western border with Chile. To the south, the Argentine Andes have advancing glaciers, as well as the continent's highest mountain, the Cerro Aconcagua, at 22,835 ft. Major rivers include the Colorado, Negro, Paraguay, Parana, Salado and Uruguay, along which are found some 250 waterfalls, including the Iguazu Falls. Argentina has the world's southernmost city - Ushuaia.

As Argentina extends from the Tropic of Capricorn to the South Pole its climate ranges from subtropical in the north to sub arctic in far south. The higher slopes of the Andes are very cold, with frequent snow in the southern peaks. Eleven per cent of the land is cultivated (31 million ha), approximately 33 per cent is grassland, and 16 per cent is forest.

To view a map, consult http://www.lib.utexas.edu/maps/cia08/argentina_sm_2008.gif

Population
Estimates by the Instituto Nacional de Estadística y Censos indicate that the population grew to 39.745 million people in 2008, assuming growth of 0.97 per cent per annum. The WHO estimated the population to be 40.4 million in 2010 with a annual growth rate of 0.9 per cent over the period 2000-10. Buenos Aires has the greatest number of inhabitants at over 13 million, followed by Córdoba province (3.05 million) and Santa Fe province (2.97 million). Current population density is 13 inhabitants per sq. km. Over 90 per cent of the population live in urban areas, with over a third of the population in the Federal Capital, Buenos Aires. Other major cities are Cordoba, La Plata, Mendoza, Rosario and Santa Fé.

Most Argentines are of European origin, especially Spanish and Italian. Many came from France, Poland, Russia and Germany. The Jewish community is the seventh largest in the world outside Israel. There are also more than a million people of Arab descent. Only one per cent of the population is indigenous, living mainly in the north and west.

The official language is Spanish. The Inca language of Quechua is still spoken in some parts of Jujuy, Salta, Catamarca, Tucumán and Santiago del Estero. English, German and Italian are also widely spoken or understood.

Births, Marriages, Deaths
According to 2010 estimates, the birth rate is 17.2 per 1,000 population, whilst the death rate is 7.9 per 1,000. Average life expectancy at birth in 2010 was 75 years (72 years for men and 79 years for women). The median age was 30 years in 2010. Approximately 25 per cent of the population is aged under 15 years and 15 per cent over 60 years. The infant mortality rate is 12 deaths per 1,000 live births and the fertility rate is 2.2 children born per woman. (Source: http://www.who.int, World Health Statistics 2012)

Public Holidays 2014
1 January: New Year's Day
24 March: Truth and Justice Day
2 April: Veterans' Day / Malvinas Day
17 April: Maundy Thursday
18 April: Good Friday
21 April: Easter Monday
1 May: Labour Day
25 May: Revolution (1810) Day
14 June: Flag Day
9 July: Independence (1816) Day
17 August: Death of General J. de San Martin
11 October: Race Recognition Day
8 December: Immaculate Conception
25 December: Christmas Day

EMPLOYMENT

The total urban work force aged 15 and above in 2006 numbered 11,051,500, and represented 61.5 per cent of the total population. 10,040,500 people aged over 10 years were employed in the second half of the year in urban areas.

The unemployment rate reached a peak of 20 per cent in 2002, before falling to around 10.6 per cent of the workforce in 2005 and 9.5 per cent in 2006. Estimated figures for 2008 put the
labour force at 16.2 million with one per cent employed in agriculture, 24 per cent in industry and 75 per cent in the service sector, unemployment that year was estimated at 7.9 per cent. Figures for 2009 show that 72 per cent of the workforce was employed in the service sector, 23 per cent in the industry and commerce and five per cent in agriculture. Unemployment figures from the International Labour Organisation put the unemployment rate at 8.5 per cent in 2007, 7.8 per cent in 2008 and 8.6 per cent in 2009.

Employment according to industry, 2006

Industry	Number employed
Agriculture, hunting and forestry	72,900
Fishing and associated activities	9,000
Mines and quarries	39,800
Manufacturing industries	1,410,700
Electricity, gas and water	44,100
Construction	884,700
Wholesale and retail trade	2,018,600
Restaurants and hotels	380,800
Transport, storage and communication	644,000
Financial services	189,400
Real Estate	809,800
Public administration, defence and social security	768,700
Education	809,800
Health and social work	590,200

- continued

Community, social and personal services	546,700
Domestic services	797,000
Services to overseas companies	2,200
Miscellaneous	25,000
Total	**10,040,500**

Source: International Labour Organisation

BANKING AND FINANCE

Currency
One Peso = 100 centavos
On 7 January 2002, Argentina's minister of economy, Jorge Remes Lenicov, announced the devaluation of the peso. Pegged to the dollar for the past ten years on a 1 to 1 basis, the peso eventually lost about 70 per cent of its value.

GDP/GNP, Inflation, National Debt
Argentina entered a recession in 1998 which culminated in a collapse at the end of that year. Strict controls on bank withdrawals were imposed amid widespread public protests and in early January 2002, Argentina officially defaulted on its external debt of around US$100 billion. The 2002 budget was reduced by one-fifth, pension payments were cut, and bank accounts frozen. Over 2002 the economy shrank by 10.9 per cent. The social impact was enormous; 50 per cent of the population was living below the poverty line. By 2003, there were signs of economic recovery. The International Monetary Fund agreed a new loan and the country's record-breaking debt was restructured in February 2005.

Argentina's economic recovery was initially impressive. Since 2003, growth has averaged nearly 9 per cent per annum. In January 2006, Argentina paid its $9.8 billion International Monetary Fund (IMF) debt out of the country's international reserves. However, by 2007, the economy had begun to overheat, inflation was rising and tax revenues had decreased with a decline in export prices. In 2008, the economy cooled down to around 5 per cent with a further reduction anticipated for 2009. In order to address some of the economic prices, the government is following a programme of unpopular taxation increases. There were protests in 2012 over rising inflation. Argentina is facing censure and possible sanctions from the IMF for lack of transparency.

Figures for 2009 showed that GDP was US$306.7 billion, giving a per capita figure of around US$7,472. GDP was estimated to be US$380 billion with growth of over 9 per cent. The government has predicted that growth will be over 3 per cent is 2012 and over 4 per cent in 2013. Growth is being sustained by high demand from Brazil and a bumper soybean crop.

In 2009 the services sector accounted for around 61 per cent of GDP; industry contributed around 32 per cent of GDP, and the agriculture sector accounted for 7 per cent.

GDP Sector (million pesos at 1993 market prices)	2006	2007*
Agriculture, livestock, hunting and forestry	17,265	19,037
Fishing	497	465
Mining and quarrying	5,219	5,195
Manufacturing	54,975	59,153
Utilities	9,023	9,541
Construction	20,751	22,806
Wholesale and retail trade	41,587	46,219
Hotels and restaurants	8,079	8,745
Transport, storage and communications	33,049	37,568
Financial intermediation	14,573	17,280
Real estate, business services and rentals	43,959	46,018
Civil service and defense	15,561	16,134
Education, social services and health	25,749	26,996
Other community, social and personal services	18,854	20,054
Total GDP at Market Prices	**330,565**	**359,170**

*Preliminary figures
Source: Direccion Nacional de Cuentas Nacionales, INE, October 2008

Although there are price controls on key goods and utilities, inflation remains in double figures and is a matter of consumer concern. Food prices increased by 30 per cent over 2007, and by more in the first half of 2008. Official inflation was put at 12 per cent in 2012 but is thought to be higher.

Balance of Payments / Imports and Exports
The production of grains, cattle, and other agricultural goods continues to be the backbone of Argentina's export economy. Energy products, high technology goods, and services are emerging as significant export sectors. Annual export revenue rose from US$34.5 billion in 2004 to an estimated US$46.6 billion in 2006, and to US$55.4 billion in 2007. Foreign trade is becoming increasingly important to the Argentine economy and by 2010, exports were estimated to be US$68 billion. Main export partners are Brazil (19 per cent), the EU (18 per cent), China (9 per cent) and the US (6 per cent).

Import costs have risen from US$13.27 billion in 2003 to an estimated US$34.2 billion in 2006, and to an estimated US$56 billion in 2010. Most imports came from Brazil (30 per cent), USA (13 per cent) and China (10 per cent). Main imports are machinery, vehicle and transport products and petroleum and natural gas.

Central Bank
Banco Central de la Republica Argentina, Reconquista 266, 1003 Buenos Aires, Argentina. Tel: +54 (0)11 4348 3500, fax: +54 (0)11 4348 3955/6, e-mail: sistema@bcra.gov.ar, URL: http://www.bcra.gov.ar
Governor: Mercedes Marco del Pont

Chambers of Commerce
Cámara Argentina de Comercio, URL: http://www.cac.com.ar
Cámara de Comercio Industria y Producción de la Republica Argentina, URL: http://www.cacipra.org.ar/
Cámara de Comercio Exterior de Rosario, URL: http://www.commerce.com.ar
Secretaria de Relaciones Economicas Internacionales, URL: http://www.mrecic.gov.ar
Asociacion de Importadores y Exporadores de la Republica Argentina, URL: http://www.aiera.org/

MANUFACTURING, MINING AND SERVICES

Primary and Extractive Industries
Argentina's high level of economic growth in recent years led to a corresponding increase in the demand for energy; however, domestic production of oil and natural gas have stagnated and exports have declined, and this imbalance has led to sporadic shortages of electricity and natural gas, such as in June 2007, when the country experienced unusually cold weather.

Proven oil reserves were estimated at 2.5 billion barrels at the beginning of January 2012 (up from 2.3 billion in 2006). Production in 2011 was put at 747.74,470 barrels per day, and oil consumption was an estimated 685,000 barrels per day. Net oil exports were 62.74 barrels per day in 2011. EIA figures from that year show that 40 per cent of exported crude oil went to the USA, 34 per cent to Chile, 19 per cent to China and seven per cent to Brazil. At present, Argentina's oil industry has a crude oil refining capacity estimated at 631,000 barrels per day

Energía Argentina Sociedad Anónima (ENARSA), is the state energy company. The largest petroleum company was Repsol-YPF, formed by a merger of the former state company Yacimientos Petroliferos Fiscales (YPF) and the Spanish oil company Repsol however in 2012 legislation was passed confirming expropriation. The expropriation only concerned Repsol's 51 per cent share of the company. The government felt that Repsol and been under investing leading to lower than possible production. Many foreign firms such as Shell, Exxon, Pan American Energy, Astra and Bridas have local subsidiaries trading in the petroleum industry in Argentina. The Bridas Corporation is a 50-50 joint venture with China National Offshore Oil Corporation. Chevron, Petrobras and and Sinopec Group also have operations in Argentina.

After Venezuela and Mexico, Argentina has the largest proven reserves of natural gas in Latin America. At the beginning of January 2010 natural gas reserves totalled 14 trillion cubic feet. Estimated production in 2010 was 1,416 billion cubic feet and estimated consumption in the same year was 1,529 billion cubic feet.

Net natural gas imports were 113 billion cubic feet in 2010. Argentina had been an exporter of gas but as consumption outstripped production this has changed. Chile had been Argentina's largest customer for natural gas. . In October 2006, the Argentina and Bolivia signed a deal for Argentina to import natural gas for 20 years; under the terms of the deal, Argentina will eventually import close to one billion cubic feet per day (Bcf/d), a fourfold increase from current levels, and the price will eventually become linked to market rates. Concerns have recently been voiced over rising gas prices following Bolivia's announced plans to renationalise its gas industry.

The largest natural gas reserves are located in the Neuquen, Austral, and Noroeste basins, with the Neuquen basin producing more than 60 per cent of Argentine natural gas.

Argentina has limited coal resources. According to 2006 estimates, coal reserves were 467 million short tons, all of which is lignite and sub-bituminous. Coal production in 2010 reached 0.090 million short tons, and the country's consumption reached 1.829 million short tons.

Metals and minerals found in Argentina include zinc, lead, tin, copper, silver, uranium, salt, manganese, argil, gypsum, bentonite and borate. The law regarding mining was changed in 1993 to encourage foreign investment. (Source: Energy Information Administration, EIA)

Energy
In 2004, Argentina suffered an energy crisis; state controls, imposed to keep prices low, led to a sharp increase in demand that outstripped supply. The government broke its natural gas export contract with Chile, and imported natural gas from Bolivia. It also introduced energy rationing. To avoid a recurrence of the crisis, the government introduced reforms: a new, state-owned energy company (Enarsa) was set up; incentives for greater investment in downstream infrastructure were initiated, and there are plans to eventually liberalize energy prices.

Argentina's total energy consumption in 2009 was estimated at 3.3 quadrillion Btu, according to latest EIA statistics. Natural gas provided 51 per cent of all power in 2005, whilst oil contributed 33 per cent of the mix, hydroelectricity 12 per cent, nuclear 3 per cent and coal 1 per cent.

In 2010, electricity generation capacity reached an estimated at 32 gigawatts. Production was 119 billion kilowatthours, 111 billion kWhs of which were consumed by the domestic market. Argentina is the third-largest energy consumer in South America. (Source: EIA)

Manufacturing
Industry accounts for just over 31 per cent of GDP. Exports of industrial non-agricultural products earned US$14,825,921,000 in 2006, whilst agricultural/fishing industrial products earned US$15,244,205,000 in exports. Principal industries are meat refrigeration and packing, flour milling, sugar refining, wine making, oil extraction, textiles, tobacco, chemicals, petrochemicals, rubber, glass and ceramics, vehicles and machinery, and leather. Argentina has an expanding motor-car industry, mostly developed with foreign capital.

STATES OF THE WORLD

ARGENTINA

Tourism

Tourism has boomed in the last few years, reaching a record high in 2006 with 4.1 million foreign tourists, up from 3.3 million visitors in 2003. Tourism generated a revenue of US$2 billion in 2003 rising to US$3.0 billion in 2006. Most visitors came from the neighbouring countries of Chile, Brazil, Paraguay and Uruguay. The main tourism areas are: the Iguazú Falls area, the glaciers and lakes of the southwest, the Lago Argentino, the Perito Moreno glacier and the Andean Mountains with their pre-Columbian ruins.
Secretaría de Turismo de la Nación, URL: http://www.turismo.gov.ar

Agriculture

Argentina is one of the world's largest producers and exporters of agricultural and pastoral products. Of a total land area of approximately 700 million acres, farms occupy about 425 million acres. About 60 per cent of the farmland is used as pasture, 10 per cent in annual crops, 5 per cent in permanent crops and the remaining 25 per cent in forest and wasteland. A large proportion of the land is still held in large estates devoted to cattle raising but the number of small farms is increasing.

The agriculture sector accounts for around nine per cent of GDP and half of all exports in terms of value (including agribusiness). The principal crops are wheat, maize, oats, barley, rye, linseed, sunflower-seed, alfalfa, sugar and cotton. Argentina is pre-eminent in the production of beef, mutton and wool, self-sufficient in basic foodstuffs and conducts a large export trade in many others.

Considerable progress has been made to expand the production of plantation crops such as rice, tea, sugar, tobacco, cotton, groundnuts and fruit and there are now exportable surpluses in some instances. The vine is cultivated in the provinces of Mendoza, San Juan and Rio Negro and there is a large and growing wine industry centred in Mendoza. Argentina is now the world's fifth largest producer of wine. Olives, citrus and deciduous fruits are cultivated on a large scale. The products of stock-raising account for about 50 per cent of total exports; they include chilled, frozen and canned meat, wool and hides.

Agricultural Production in 2010

Produce	Int. $'000	Tonnes
Soybeans	14,171,833	52,675,500
Indigenous cattle meat	7,095,056	2,626,460
Cow milk, whole, fresh	3,277,233	10,501,900
Maize	2,768,066	22,676,900
Indigenous chicken meat	2,275,291	1,597,360
Wheat	2,270,404	14,914,500
Grapes	1,495,699	2,616,610
Sugar cane	820,925	25,000,000
Sunflower seed	611,303	2,232,030
Apples	444,060	1,050,000
Lemons and limes	441,434	1,113,380
Indigenous pigmeat	431,965	281,000

Source: http://faostat.fao.org/site/339/default.aspx Food and Agriculture Organization of the United Nations, Food and Agricultural commodities production

Argentina is naturally endowed with one of the most extensive ocean submarine platforms in the world, covering more than a million sq. km. Production by Argentine fisheries was estimated at 811,750 tonnes in 2010

COMMUNICATIONS AND TRANSPORT

Travel Information

Passport holders of the EU, the United States, Canada and Australia do not require a visa for Argentina, for stays of up to 90 days. Other passport holders should contact the Argentine embassy, or refer to
http://www.argentine-embassy-uk.org/version%20ingles/information/visaslistapaises.html. A return ticket is required.

National Airlines

Aerolineas Argentinas, URL:http://www.aerolineas.com.ar
In July 2008, the Argentine government renationalised Aerolineas Argentinas, nearly 20 years after it was privatised. Aerolineas was in debt by nearly $900m and was losing around $1m per day.

International Airports

The international airports are Ezeiza, Jorge Newbery, Córdoba, Jujuy, Resistencia, Rosario, Rio Gallegos, San Carlos de Bariloche, Corrientes, Salta and Ushuaia. Ezeiza is the largest airport, and is used for jets, cargo and international passenger traffic.

There are 1,140 airfields 156 of which have paved runways, four of which have runways of over 3,047 metres. 30 airfields has runways of over 2,438 metres. There was two heliports in Argentina in 2010.

Aerolíneas Argentinas; Austral; Aerochaco; Andes Líneas Aéreas; LADE; LAER; LAN Argentina and Sol Líneas Aéreas all operate domestic flights.

Railways

Argentina's 31,900 km of railway were privatised in 1992. The railway system is now divided into six freight units and three passenger companies. Per year some 17 million tonnes of freight is transported. The railway system is currently being updated and there are plans for a high speed rail link between Buenos Aires and Rosario. Buenos Aires has an underground system known as the Subte, the city is also served by an urban railway system linking the city and suburbs. The city of Rosario has its own urban train and tram system. A rail connection linking Chile and Argentina is currently under construction.

Roads

There are now 231,144 km of roads of which some 734 km are highways and 69,400 km are paved. The road network carries the bulk of freight traffic but many roads now need renewing. The government has awarded concessions to private operators to operate some toll roads. All cities and towns have bus services. Vehicles are driven on the right.

Shipping

International shippers using Argentine ports include Columbus Line CSAV, NYK Line, Nanta Line, Global Lines, and Pan-American Independent Line of Uruguay.

Regular hydrofoil ferries link Buenos Aires with Montevideo and Colonia in Uruguay.

Ports and Harbours

The main ports are Buenos Aires, La Plata, Bahía Blanca, Concepcion del Uruguay, Necochea Rio Gallegos, Rosario, Santa Fe, Ushuaia, Mar del Plata and Comodoro Rivadavia. Almost 90 per cent of Argentina's foreign trade is transported by water; the country has 3,500 km of navigable waterways.

Administración General de Puertos, Avda Ing. Huergo 431, Buenos Aires, Argentina Tel: +54 (0)11 342 6826, fax: +54 (0)11 342 8710

HEALTH

According to the latest WHO figures, in 2009 total expenditure on health represented 9.5 per cent of GDP. Government expenditure accounted for 66.4 per cent of total expenditure on health. Health spending accounts for 22.2 per cent of total government expenditure. Per capita total expenditure was US$734 in 2009. Out-of-pocket expenditure accounts for 59.2 per cent of private expenditure on health.

Figures for 2003 indicate that there are around 8,000 hospitals and clinics in Argentina, with approximately 77 beds. Around 2,000 of the health facilities are in Buenos Aires. In 2000-07, there were 108,800 doctors (30 per 10,000 population), 29,000 nurses and midwives (8 per 10,000 population) and 28,900 dentists (8 per 10,000 population). 98 per cent of births were attended by a skilled midwife or nurse.

The prevalence of HIV/AIDs in 2005 was thought to be around 0.45 per cent of adult Argentines. In 2010, the infant mortality rate was 12 per 1,000 live births in 20109 and the under-five mortality rate was 14 per 1,000 live births. The most common causes of childhood mortality are prematurity (24 per cent) and congenital anomalies (25 per cent).

In 2008, an estimated 98 per cent of the urban population and 80 per cent of the rural population had access to an improved drinking water. In the same year, 91 per cent of the urban population and 77 per cent of the rural population had access to improved sanitation. (Source: http://www.who.int, Global Health Statistics, 2012)

EDUCATION

Primary/Secondary Education

Education is free at all levels and compulsory between 6 and 14. 97.5 per cent of children aged 6-12 attended school. According to recent statistics, pre-school institutions currently have 1,145,919 students, whilst primary schools have 5,123,256, middle schools have 2,463,608 and higher (non university level) schools have 356,585. 81 per cent of children attend secondary schools.

There are 14,549 pre-schools, 21,495 primary schools, 5,914 middle schools and 1,452 higher (non-university level) schools.

The number of teachers working in Argentina's primary and secondary schools are as follows: 309,081 in primary schools; 2,842,926 in middle schools; and 409,511 in higher, non university level, schools. (Source: Instituto Nacional de Estadistica y Censos)

The adult literacy rate in 2010 was 99.0 per cent, rising to 99.1 per cent among the 15-24 age group. In 2006, 16.0 per cent of government expenditure went on education (Source: UNESCO)

Higher Education

There are 29 state and 23 private universities. The national University of Córdoba, founded in 1613, is the oldest; the largest is the University of Buenos Aires founded in 1821. Recent figures show that there are 812,308 students at public universities and 124,524 students at private universities.

The most popular university courses are economics, medicine and law.

Approximately 2,000 Argentine students are studying in the USA at graduate and undergraduate levels.

RELIGION

The Roman Catholic Church is recognised in the Constitution of the Republic and more than 90 per cent of the country is Roman Catholic. The rest of the population is Protestant (two per cent), Jewish (1.2 per cent). Muslim, (2.0 per cent).

COMMUNICATIONS AND MEDIA

The constitution guarantees media freedom but there are reports of attacks on media freedom. Argentina is a leading media market with a strong newspaper market, hundreds of commerical radio stations, numerous TV stations and and high subscription rates to cable TV.

Newspapers

There are some 150 daily newspapers in circulation. Approximately 60 per cent of newspapers are sold in the capital. Newspapers with significant circulation include:

Clarin, URL: http://www.clairn.com.ar
Crónica (Argentina), URL: http://www.cronica.com.ar/
La Nación (Argentina), URL: http://www.lanacion.com.ar
La Prensa, URL: http://www.laprensa.com.ar/
El Cronista Comercial, URL: http://www.cronista.com.ar

Press Association

Asociación de Entidades Periodísticas Argentinas (ADEPA), URL: http://www.adepa.org.ar/

Broadcasting

There are 42 TV broadcasters and 444 repeater stations. The main state-run channel is Canal 7 (URL: http://www.tvpublica.com.ar/tvpublica/). The private sector operates the main television stations and hundreds of commercial radio stations. Grupo Clarin operates television and radio channels. Radio Nacional (URL: http://www.radionacional.com.ar/) is the state-run channel. Satellite and cable TV is very popular.

The state-run news agency is Telam (URL: http://www.radionacional.com.ar/).

Telecommunications

Many improvements have been made in recent years aided by thliberalization of the market in 1998. Competiton and foreign investment have enabled infrastructure improvements. Fibre optic cable trunk lines have been installed between major cities and the major networks are fully digitalised. In 2010, there were 10 million mainline telephones in use, and 57 million mobile phones. Argentina has over 16 million internet users.

ENVIRONMENT

The central government environmental agency, the Secretaría de Recursos Naturales y Ambiente Humano (Secretariat of Natural Resources and Human Environment), is responsible for working with provincial governments in establishing environmental policies with limited success. Most provinces have their own legislation which further hampers an effective policy.

The country's major environmental problems are air pollution, soil erosion and degradation, desertification, and urban area water pollution. Buenos Aires suffers particularly badly from air pollution. Attempts have been made to reduce car emissions and encourage the use of public transport in the city.

Recently the number of beavers on the island of Tierra del Fuego (jointly owned by Chile and Argentina), has increased to the level where they are officially considered a plague. It is estimated that there are now up to 250,000 beavers on the island, and they are breeding at a rate of around 20 per cent per annum. Imported from Canada with the idea of creating a fur industry in the 1940s, they now have no natural predators. The environmental impact has been to kill off many of the trees in the region.

According to figures from the EIA, Argentina's emissions from the consumption of fossil fuels totalled 169.82 million metric tons of carbon dioxide in 2010.

Argentina is a party to the following international environmental agreements: Antarctic-Environmental Protocol, Antarctic-Marine Living Resources, Antarctic Seals, Antarctic Treaty, Biodiversity, Climate Change, Climate Change-Kyoto Protocol, Desertification, Endangered Species, Environmental Modification, Hazardous Wastes, Law of the Sea, Marine Dumping, Ozone Layer Protection, Ship Pollution, Wetlands, and Whaling. Argentina has signed, but not ratified the agreement on Marine Life Conservation Argentina has played a leading world role in setting voluntary environmental targets.

SPACE PROGRAMME

The National Space Activities Commission is responsible for the national space programme. It was set up as a civilian agency in 1991. It has signed agreeements with NASA and ESA and developed a number of earth observation satellites including SAC-C in 2000. The most recent launch was SAC-D in 2011 as part of a research mission. A new rocket, Tronador II, is under development, and is currently scheduled to start test flights in 2012. Defence missile and rocket development has been restarted under President Kirchner.

National Commission for Space Activity (Comision Nacional de Activadedes Espaciales), URL: http://www.conae.gov.ar/

ARMENIA

Republic of Armenia

Hayastani Hanrapetoutiun

Capital: Yerevan (Population estimate: 1.2 million)

Head of State: Serge Sargsyan (President) (page 1508)

National Flag: Consists of three horizontal stripes: red, dark blue and orange.

CONSTITUTION AND GOVERNMENT

Constitution

The Sovereign state of the Republic of Armenia declared itself independent of the Soviet Union on 23 September 1991 and in December became a member of the Commonwealth of Independent States. It joined the United Nations in March 1992.

Armenia introduced a new Constitution in 1995 to replace the Soviet Constitution of 1978. Under this Constitution the President appoints the Prime Minister, and the Cabinet based on the recommendation of the Prime Minister. The President himself is elected by the people for a term of five years and can serve no more than two consecutive terms. Executive power rests in the hands of the Prime Minister and the Cabinet.

A nine-member Constitutional Court was created on 6 December 1995, its function being to assess the constitutionality of Government resolutions, Presidential decrees and Armenian law. Amendments to the Constitution were approved by referendum in November 2005.

To consult the full constitution, please visit:
http://www.president.am/library/constitution/eng/

International Relations

Armenia's closest relations are with Russia, although it is also looking to integrate more with Europe. Its relations with Turkey are more troubled and their border has been closed since 1992. Turkey and Armenia have prepared a draft agreement on establishing diplomatic relations, but it is not expected that the Turks will sign it until the Nagorno-Karabakh conflict is resolved. Despite the troubled relationship, the Turks and Armenians work together in the Black Sea Economic Co-operation Organisation. Relations with Georgia are generally good, particularly in economic terms.

Armenia is a member of the United Nations, the Council of Europe, the Organization for Security and Cooperation in Europe (OSCE), the Commonwealth of Independent States, NATO's Partnership for Peace, the Collective Security Treaty Organization (CSTO), the Organization of the Black Sea Economic Cooperation organization (BSEC), the Euro-Atlantic Partnership Council, the International Monetary Fund, the International Bank for Reconstruction and Development, and the World Trade Organization. Albania made a formal application for membership of the European Union in 2009.

Nagorno-Karabakh

Armenia has a longstanding dispute with Azerbaijan over the Nagorno-Karabakh region. Mainly populated by Armenians, the region was assigned by Moscow to Azerbaijan in the 1920s but is currently held by Armenian forces. Nagorno-Karabkh declared itself unilaterally as an independent republic in 1991. A cease-fire was agreed between both countries in May 1994 and still holds, though there have been sporadic clashes. It is estimated that over 15,000 people have been killed with at least 900,000 Azeris and 300,000 Armenians displaced. In 1998 President Ter-Petrossian resigned following opposition to his plans for a compromise with Azerbaijan. Talks were held over the future of the region in 2001, but nothing came of them. In 2006, an overwhelming majority of Nagorno-Karabakh residents - mostly ethnic Armenians - voted in favour of declaring a sovereign state, but this was not recognised internationally. At the beginning of November 2008, Armenia and Azerbaijan signed a joint agreement aimed at resolving the dispute.

Recent Events

In 1999 gunmen entered the parliament and shot the prime minister, speaker and six other officials in a protest against the government's economic policies. In 2003 those involved in the shootings were sentenced to life imprisonment.

A referendum on constitutional amendments took place in November 2005. The proposals strengthened the role of parliament while restricting presidential powers. The result was a yes vote but there were allegations of vote-rigging.

In February 2007, Parliament adopted a bill allowing dual citizenship; this eases the naturalisation process for Armenia's foreign diaspora which is currently estimated at around 8 million people. In March 2007, the PM, Andranik Markaryan, died of a heart attack and was replaced by Serge Sargsyan. Parliamentary elections were held on 12 May 2007. The Republican Party of Armenia won 33.9 per cent of the votes (64 seats), whilst their closest rivals Prosperous Armenia, won 15.1 per cent (18 seats). In February 2008, presidential elections were held; the incumbent Prime Minister, Serge Sargsyan of the Republican Party of Armenia, ran against the former President, Levon Ter-Petrossian. Mr. Sargsyan won, but there were allegations of election rigging by the opposition. In March, a three-week state of emergency was declared in the capital following eleven days of protests. International observers judged the poll to be generally democratic. Demonstrations also occurred on the anniversary of the elections.

ARMENIA

In recent years, efforts have been made to improve relations with Turkey. In September 2008, in a landmark event, the president of Turkey, Abudllah Gul visited Armenia, the first Turkish president so to do. The following October the two governments agreed to normalise relations, establish diplomatic links and re-open the border between the two countries. However, the opposition accused the government of failing to tackle the genocide question. In April 2010, parliament suspended ratification of the accord, accusing Turkey of imposing conditions, particularly that Armenia should resolve its dispute with Azerbaijan. In October 2010, in a deal brokered by Russia, Armenia and Azerbaijan agreed to an exchange of prisoners captured during the Nagorno-Karabakh conflict.

In June 2011, Prime Minister Serge Sarkisian announced that Armenia was ready to establish diplomatic relations with Turkey.

Legislature

Legislative power rests with the single-chamber National Assembly (*Azagayin Joghov*). The chairman of the National Assembly is elected by its Deputies, whilst its Deputies are elected by both proportional and single member district representation. With effect from the 2000 parliamentary elections the National Assembly was reduced from 190 to 131 Deputies elected for a four-year term.

National Assembly, 19 Marshall Bagramyan Avenue, Yerevan, 375095, Armenia. Tel: +374 1 58 82 25, fax: +374 1 52 98 26, e-mail: miba@parliament.am, URL: http://www.parliament.am

> **Cabinet (as at June 2013)**
> *Prime Minister:* Tigran Sargsian (page 1508)
> *Deputy Prime Minister and Minister of Territorial Administration:* Armen Gevorgian
> *Minister of Sport and Youth Affairs:* Yuri Vardanyan
> *Minister of Healthcare:* Derenik Dumanyan
> *Minister of Economy:* Vahram Avanesyan
> *Minister of Justice:* Hrair Tovmasian
> *Minister of Foreign Affairs:* Edward Nalbandian (page 1483)
> *Minister of Conservation:* Aram Harutyunya
> *Minister of Agriculture:* Sergo Karapetyan
> *Minister of Labour and Social Security:* Artem Asatryan
> *Minister of Energy and Natural Resources:* Armen Movsissyan (page 1481)
> *Minister of Education and Science:* Armen Ashotyan
> *Minister of Culture:* Hasmik Poghosyan
> *Minister of Defence:* Seyran Ohanyan
> *Minister of Transport and Communication:* Gagik Beglaryan
> *Minister of Urban Development:* Samvel Tadevosyan
> *Minister of Finance:* David Sargsyan
> *Minister of Emergency Situations:* Armen Yeritzyan
> *Minister of Diaspora Affairs:* Hranush Hacobyan

Ministries

Office of the President, Baghramian Avenue 26, 375077 Yerevan, Armenia. Tel: +374 1054 4052, fax: +374 1052 1551, e-mail: press@president.am, URL: http://www.president.am
Office of the Prime Minister, Republic Square, Government House 1, Yerevan, Armenia. Tel: +374 1052 8712, fax: +374 10 528712, e-mail: press@arminco.com, URL: http://www.gov.am/en/
Ministry of Agriculture, Ministry of Agriculture, Government House 3, Republic Square, 375010 Yerevan, Armenia. Tel: +374 10 524641, fax: +374 10 151583, e-mail: naxartex@yahoo.com, URL: http://www.minagro.am
Ministry of Urban Development, Government House 3, Republic Square, Yerevan 375010, Armenia. Tel: +374 10 589080, fax: +374 10 524367
Ministry of Culture, Government House 3, Republic Square, 375010 Yerevan, Armenia. Tel: +374 10 529349, fax: +374 10 523922, e-mail: mincult@xter.net, URL: http://www.mincult.am
Ministry of Defence, Gevork Chaush Street 60, Yerevan 357088, Armenia. Tel: +374 10 523332, fax: +374 10 287203, URL: http://www.mil.am
Ministry of Education and Science, Governmet House 3, Yerevan 375010, Armenia. Tel: +374 10 566602, fax: +374 10 151651, URL: http://www.edu.am/
Ministry of Energy & Natural Resources, Republic Square, Government House 2, Yerevan 375010, Armenia. Tel: +374 10 521964, fax: +374 10 151687, URL: http://www.minenergy.am/
Ministry of Finance and Economy, Republic Square, Government House 1, Yerevan 375010, Armenia. Tel: +374 2 527342, fax: +374 2 151069, URL: http://www.mfe.am/mfeengweb/indexeng.htm
Ministry of Foreign Affairs, Republic Square, Government House 2, Yerevan, Armenia. Tel: +374 10 506167, fax: +374 10 562543, URL: http://www.armeniaforeignministry.am/
Ministry of Health, Republic Square, Government House 3, Yerevan 375010, Armenia. Tel: +374 10 582413, fax: +374 10 151097, URL: http://www.arminhealth.am/
Ministry of Trade and Economic Development, M Mkrtchyan Street 5, Yerevan 375008, Armenia. Tel: +374 10 526134, fax: +374 10 151675, URL: http://www.minted.am
Ministry of Justice, Vasgen Sarkissian Street 3, Yerevan 375010, Armenia. Tel: +374 10 582157, fax: +374 10 582442, URL: http://www.justice.am
Ministry of Natural and Environmental Protection, Government House 3, Yerevan 375010, Armenia. Tel: +374 10 521099, URL: http://www.mnpiac.am
Ministry of Labour and Social Security, Government House 3, Yerevan 375010, Armenia. Tel: +374 10 526831, URL: http://www.mss.am/
Ministry of Transport & Communications, Nalybandian Street 28, Yerevan 375010, Armenia. Tel: +374 10 563391, URL: http://www.mtc.am/
Ministry of Youth and Sport, Government House 3, Republic Square, 375010 Yerevan, Armenia. Tel: +374 10 529349, fax: +374 10 523922

Political Parties

Armenian Revolutionary Federation (ARF), 2 Myasnyak Avenue, 375025 Yerevan, Armenia. URL: http://www.arfd.am/
Chairman: Hrant Markarian

Republican Party of Armenia (HHK), 23 Tumanian Street, Yerevan, Armenia. Tel +374 10 581882, fax: +374 10 566034, URL: http://www.hhk.am
Leader: Serge Sargsyan (page 1508)
Prosperous Armenia (BHK), URL: http://www.bhk.am
Leader: Gagik Tsarukian
Rule of Law (OEK), URL: http://www.oek.am
Leader: Artur Baghdasarian
Heritage, URL: http://www.heritage.am
Chairman: Raffi Hovannisian

Elections

The minimum voting age in Armenia is 18. Both parliamentary and presidential elections are held every five years.

In March 2007, Prime Minister Andranik Markaryan died of a heart attack. The Minister of Defence, Serge Sargsyan, replaced him, and in May 2007, the Prime Minister's Armenian Republican Party won over 33 per cent of votes cast in the parliamentary elections. The new coalition government included the RPA, the Armenian Revolutionary Federation - Dashnaktsutyun (ARF-D), the United Labour Party (ULP) and the Prosperous Armenia Party.

The most recent parliamentary election took place in May 2012, the governing Republican Party won a majority.

Prime Minister Robert Kocharyan won the presidential election on 30 March 1998, and was re-elected in 2003 with 67.5 per cent of the vote. He was not eligible to stand for a third term. The presidential elections of February 2008 were contested by the standing Prime Minister, Serge Sargsyan of the Republican Party of Armenia, and the former President, Levon Ter-Petrossian. Mr Sargsyan won 52.9 per cent of the vote, whilst Mr. Ter-Petrosian trailed on 21.5 per cent. Supporters of Mr Ter-Petrosian claimed the vote had been rigged and staged a rally in the capital Yerevan. The Organisation for Security and Co-operation in Europe said the poll broadly met democratic standards. The most recent presidential election took place in February 2013 and President Serge Sarkisian was re-elected with nearly 59 per cent of the vote.

Diplomatic Representation

Embassy of the United States of America, 1 American Avenue, Yerevan, Armenia. Tel: +374 10 464700; fax: +374 10 464742, URL: http://armenia.usembassy.gov
Ambassador: John A. Heffern
British Embassy, 34 Baghramyan Avenue, Yerevan, Armenia. Tel: +374 10 264301, fax: +374 10 264318, URL: http://ukinarmenia.fco.gov.uk/en
Ambassadors: Mr Jonathan Aves and Ms Katherine Leach
Embassy of the Republic of Armenia, 2225 R Street, NW, Washington DC 20008, USA. Tel: +1 202 319 1976, fax: +1 202 319 2982, e-mail: amembusadm@msn.com, URL: http://usa.mfa.am/en
Ambassador: Tatoul Markarian
Embassy of the Republic of Armenia, 25A Cheniston Gardens, London, W8 6TG, United Kingdom. Tel: +44 (0)20 7938 5435, fax: +44 (0)20 7938 2595, e-mail: armemb@armenianembassyuk.com, URL: http://www.armenianembassy.org.uk/
Ambassador: Gagik Kirakosian
Permanent Mission of the Republic of Armenia to the United Nations, 119 East 36th Street, New York, NY 10016, USA. Tel: +1 212 686 9079, fax: +1 212 686 3934, e-mail: armenia@un.int, URL: http://www.un.int/armenia
Ambassador and Permanent Representative: Garen Nazarian

LEGAL SYSTEM

The judiciary is independent, and consists of district courts of the first instance, an Appeals Court and a Court of Cassation. Judges have to be approved by the President, and serve for life, unless removed for malfeasance. The Constitutional Court was created in 1995. It consists of nine members, of which five are appointed by Parliament and four by the President. The Court judges the constitutionality of laws, Presidential decrees, government resolutions and international agreements. It also resolves disputes regarding the results of elections.There is a Council of Justice, which is led by the President and includes the Attorney General, the Minister of Justice and fourteen further member appointed by the President. The Council appoints judges. There is also a Council of Court Chairs consisting of 21 judges, which is responsible for financial and budgetary cases. Review of the judiciary is ongoing.

In July 2003 the President of Armenia, Robert Kocharyan, commuted all outstanding death sentences and in September Armenia abolished capital punishment in peacetime by ratifying Protocol No 6 to the European Convention on Human Rights.

Armenia held a seriously flawed presidential election in February 2008; large crowds of demonstrators protested the conduct and results, and clashes between protesters and security forces resulted in the deaths of 10 persons. The government imposed a 20-day state of emergency; citizens were subject to arrest, detention, and imprisonment. Prison conditions are unhealthy. The authorities impose restrictions on freedom of assembly and the press, as well as on religious freedom.

Constitutional Court, URL: http://www.concourt.am/english/index.htm
President: Harutyunyan Gagik

Human Rights Defender of Armenia, URL: http://www.ombuds.am/main/en/

LOCAL GOVERNMENT

As a result of restructuring, Armenia's 38 administrative districts were amalgamated into one city and 10 provinces or regions (*marz*), each with its own provincial Governor. These provinces are the City of Yerevan, Aragatsotn, Ararat, Armavir, Gegharkunik, Kotaik, Lori, Shirak, Siunik, Tavush and Vayots Dzor. The provinces are further divided into communities (*hamaynk*).

A reform of Yerevan's status, to that of a community as required by the 2005 constitutional referendum, is currently underway. Once the parliament enacts legislation to change the capital's status, the mayor will no longer be appointed by the president but instead be chosen by city councillors. The most recent local elections took place in 2008.

AREA AND POPULATION

Area

Armenia is situated on the southern edge of the Caucasian Mountains and 90 per cent of its 29,800 sq. km (11,500 sq. miles) area is over 1,000 m above sea level. The Republic is landlocked, and bordered by the Republic of Georgia to the north, the Republic of Azerbaijan to the east and south west (Azerbaijan - Naxcivan enclave), Iran to the South and Turkey to the west. Armenia's terrain is largely mountainous with high plateaux. The area is prone to earthquakes.

The climate is continental with hot summers and cold winters.

To view a map, consult: http://www.un.org/Depts/Cartographic/map/profile/armenia.pdf

Population

Armenia had an estimated population in 2010 of 3.092 million, with an annual growth rate of 0.1 per cent over the period 2000-10. The population density was 109 people per km sq. Some 64 per cent of the population lives in urban areas, and 35 per cent live in the capital, Yerevan. An estimated 65 per cent of Armenians are aged between 15 and 60 years, with 20 per cent aged under 15. The median age is 32 years. In recent years the number of families emigrating from Armenia has begun to cause concern, with some estimates showing that 25 per cent of the population has left; young families seek what they hope will be a better life abroad.

The official language is Armenian, with Russian, French and English also spoken. Almost 95 per cent of the population is Armenian, with the remaining 5 per cent made up largely of Azeris, Greeks, Jews, Kurds, Malakans, Russians and Yezidis although figures suggest that by the end of 1993 nearly all Azeris had left.

Births, Marriages, Deaths

The estimated birth rate in 2010 was 15.3 per 1,000 inhabitants, whilst the estimated death rate was 14.0 per 1,000 people in the same year.

In 2009, average life expectancy at birth was 66 years for men and 74 years for women. Healthy life expectancy was put at 59 and 63 years respectively. Infant mortality in 2010 was 18 deaths per 1,000 live births. Neonatal mortality was 11 per 1,000 live births in 2010. The maternal mortality rate was estimated to be 29 per 100,000 population. The total fertility rate was estimated to be 1.7 births per female. (Source: http://www.who.int, World Health Statistics 2012)

Public Holidays 2014

1-2 January: New Year
6 January: Armenian Orthodox Christmas
8 March: Women's Day
18 April: Good Friday
21 April: Easter Monday
24 April: Genocide Memorial Day
1 May: Labour Day
9 May: Victory Day (World War II)
28 May: First Republic Day
5 July: Constitution Day
21 September: Independence Day
31 December: New Year's Eve

EMPLOYMENT

Armenia's workforce was estimated at 1.168 million in 2007, 1.085 million of whom were employed. The official unemployment rate was 7.1 per cent, affecting 82.700 people. (Source: Asian Development Bank) Figures from the International Labour Organisation show that the number of people employed in 2008 was 1,117,600 of whom 44,200 were employed in the agricultural sector, 188,000 in industry, and 435,900 in the service sector.

The agricultural sector continued to be the largest employer in 2007, with around 502,700 workers. 140,000 people worked in the manufacturing industry whilst 442,600 worked in the services sector.

Total Employment by Economic Activity

Occupation	2007
Agriculture, hunting & forestry	433,800
Fishing	400
Mining & quarrying	17,100
Manufacturing	81,500
Electricity, gas & water supply	35,400
Construction	91,400

- continued

Wholesale & retail trade, repairs	116,300
Hotels & restaurants	11,000
Transport, storage & communications	72,200
Financial intermediation	14,000
Real estate, renting & business activities	17,300
Public admin. & defence; compulsory social security	70,500
Education	110,600
Health & social work	57,100
Other community, social & personal service activities	52,000
Households with employed persons	4,300
Extra-territorial organisations & bodies	3,600

Source: Copyright © International Labour Organization (ILO Dept. of Statistics, http://laborsta.ilo.org)

BANKING AND FINANCE

Currency

1 Dram (ADM) = 100 Iouma
The Dram replaced the Russian Rouble in 1993.

GDP/GNP, Inflation, National Debt

Armenia's economy suffered following the breakup of the Soviet Union in 1991, and a further blow came with the shutting of the borders with Azerbaijan and Turkey in 1994 due to the disputed Nagorno Karabakh border. GDP fell and the country suffered hyper inflation. The government began carrying out economic reforms which reduced inflation and resulted in steady economic growth. Armenia has adopted new industries such as precious stone processing (particularly diamonds) and jewellery making, as well as communications and technology. The country has completed a six-year programme of economic reforms, which included an overhaul of the infrastructure, the refurbishment of power stations, and a shifting towards a more market-driven economy. Armenia joined the WTO in 2003. The economy into recession in 2009. There have been Armenia receives aid from Russia, the IMF and other organisations. Armenia is dependent on Russia; most of its gas is imported from Russia and Russia either owns or manages much of the country's energy infrastructure.

According to the National Statistical Service of Armenia, nominal GDP was US$6,386.7 million in 2006 and real GDP growth was 13.3 per cent in the same year. This was the fifth consecutive year of double-digit growth, boosted by good agricultural results and a construction boom. In the first eight months of 2006 growth was recorded at 9.8 per cent. GDP reached 3,650.0 billion drams in 2008 at an annual growth rate of 6.8 per cent. Estimated figures for 2009 put GDP growth at -14.1 per cent, rising to 2.1 per cent in 2010. Per capita GDP was 1,075 million drams in 2010. (Source: ADB)

GDP by industrial origin at current market prices, billion Drams

	2008	2009	2010
Total GDP	3,568.2	3,141.7	3,501.6
-Agriculture	581.9	531.3	609.4
-Mining, Manufacturing and utilities	474.3	421.4	519.0
-Construction	903.0	584.4	600.3
-Trade	428.1	419.8	480.5
-Transport and communications	242.3	226.0	237.4
-Finance, Public administration, Others	588.4	676.8	719.1
-Less: Financial intermediation services indirectly measured	55.0	50.6	53.1
-Taxes less subsidies on products	405.2	332.6	389.0
Net factor income from abroad	144.2	60.3	..
GNI	3,712.4	3,202.0	..

Source: ADB

GDP was estimated at US$10 billion in 2011.

Recent figures show that Albania's GDP was comprised of the service sector, 21 per cent; transport 5.4 per cent; communications 4.6 per cent; agriculture, 19 per cent; construction, 13 per cent; industry, 28 per cent; and remittances, nine per cent.

Inflation was estimated at 3.2 per cent in 2012.

Foreign debt amounted to US$1,872.9 million in 2004. It fell to US$1,860.7 in 2005 before climbing to US$2,072.8 million in 2006.

Foreign Investment

In 2003 Armenia joined the World Trade Organization. In 2010, foreign direct investment in Armenia totalled US$560 million. Most foreign investment is within the mining and telecommunications sectors. As of 2012, Canada was the largest investor in Armenia.

Balance of Payments / Imports and Exports

Total export revenue has risen steadily over the past few years, from US$685 million in 2003 to US$$1,057 million f.o.b. in 2008. They fell in 2009 to US$710.5 million before rising to US$1,011.2 million in 2010. Armenia's main export trading partners are Russia ($160.8 million in 2010), Germany (US$132.6 million) and the Netherlands ($98.6 million). Major exports include diamonds, pig iron, energy, scrap metal, machinery and equipment, copper ore, foodstuffs and brandy.

ARMENIA

Main import trading partners are China ($505.8 million, 2008), Germany ($213.7 million) and Italy (US$122.6 million). Main imported products include petroleum, natural gas, food, and tobacco. Total import costs were US$1,279 million in 2003, rising to US$4,426.1 million in 2008. They fell to US$3,321.1 million in 2009 before rising to US$3,782.9 million in 2010.

The trade deficit stood at US$2,771.7 million in 2010. (Source: ADB)

Trade Restrictions
As of 2013, there is currently an arms embargo in force on Armenia, imposed by the UN. The borders with Turkey are closed.

Central Bank
Central Bank of the Republic of Armenia, V Sargsyan Str 6, 375010 Yerevan City, Yerevan, Armenia. Tel: +374 10 583841, fax: +374 10 151107, e-mail: mcba@cba.am, URL: http://www.cba.am
Chairman: Arthur Javadyan

MANUFACTURING, MINING AND SERVICES

Primary and Extractive Industries
Armenia has no reserves of fossil fuels and no crude oil refining capacity. The country therefore has to import all of its fuel requirements, which, since the Azerbaijani fuel embargo of 1991, come from Turkmenistan (gas) and Georgia (petroleum products). In the absence of oil pipelines into Armenia, imported oil is transported by railway or road. Oil consumption was 55,000 bbld in 2011.

Natural gas consumption in 2010 was an estimated 61 billion cubic feet, all imported. Natural gas accounts for 50 per cent of Armenia's total energy consumption. Gas distribution is the responsibility of Armrosgazprom, owned by the government (45 per cent), Russia's Gazprom (45 per cent), and Itera (10 per cent). Since the Nagorno-Karabakh conflict, Armenia no longer receives shipments of natural gas from Azerbaijan through the pipeline between the two countries. As a result, imports must come through the Georgian-Russian pipeline to the north of the country. Construction was completed in 2008 of the 35 billion cubic feet Armenia-Iran gas pipeline, although supplies have not yet begun. In April 2006 it was announced that Russia was to take control of Armenian pipelines and a power station in return for setting gas prices at US$110 per 1,000 cubic metres until 2009; this almost doubled the pre-existing price, but kept it well below European costs.

Coal consumption was 66,000 short tons in 2010.

Armenia has large deposits of iron ore, especially at Abovian and Hrazdan where there are estimated to be 400 million and 150 million tons, respectively. There are also large deposits of copper molybdenum ore, which is mined at the Kadjaran factory. The Alaverdi copper works is being restored and a new modern plant is being constructed at Kapan. Lead and zinc ores are found in Armenia, and amongst these ores are gold and other rare elements. There are also gold deposits in Zod, Meghradzor and Terterasar. Building materials found in Armenia include marble, granite, travertine, limestone and gypsum. Mineral water is produced from about 700 springs or wells.

Energy
Armenia's total energy consumption was an estimated 0.208 quadrillion Btu in 2009 and consumption was 0.208 quadrillion Btu. The industrial sector uses almost 50 per cent of total energy.

Armenia generates electricity primarily by thermal power (42 per cent), as well as nuclear power (32 per cent), and hydropower (26 per cent). Armenia has privatised much of its electricity industry, and much of the country's distribution network is either owned or operated by foreign investors. The Russian electricity monopoly, Unified Energy Systems (UES), has effectively taken control of the Caucasus electricity industry; in Armenia, UES offered to cancel out the debt for nuclear fuel with the acquisition of Armenia's electricity infrastructure. In addition, UES gained a license to operate Armenia's only nuclear power plant, Metsmamor, as well as other thermal and hydroelectric facilities.

A US$300 million programme is currently underway to build 38 small and three large hydroelectric power plants with a total capacity of 296 MW. The programme will be part financed by the World Bank and the EBRD.

The Metsamor nuclear plant at Yerevan has a total capacity of 815 MW. The plant was closed in 1989 due to safety fears but was re-opened in 1995 because of a lack of alternative generating plants. Armenia has been under pressure to close the plant but as of 2012 it remained open. Plans have been put forward to build a new 1,000 MWe unit at Metsamor, if the project goes ahead it would be commissioned in 2019. There are three thermal power plants in the country.

Electricity generation capacity was 3.17 billion kilowatthours in 2010, with electricity generation at 6.25 billion kWh. Electricity consumption was 4.71 billion kWh. Armenia and Iran have linked their electricity grids and both countries take advantage of seasonal differences in demand. During the summer Armenia exports its electricity to Iran, and in the winter imports it back.

Manufacturing
Armenia's heavy industry specialises in the manufacture of machines and machine tools, presses, foundry equipment and chemicals. As the country is so high in mineral deposits one of the most significant arms of its industrial production is non-ferrous metallurgy. Light industry is of particular importance to Armenia, accounting for a quarter of its total output. Armenia is a net exporter in this field. The bulk of this output comes from the production of processed and canned food, consumer durables (such as radios, bikes and washing machines), and knitwear, clothes and footwear (although it has to import cotton, wool and silk in order to do this). The country is an important producer of goods such as computers and calculators

that use semiconductor electronics. Jewelry is an important export sector. There are diamond polishing plants using diamonds from Russia and European Union countries. The diamond processing industry, which was one of the leading export sectors in 2000-2004 and also a major recipient of foreign investment, has since suffered a dramatic drop in output due to raw material supply problems with Russia and a general decline in international diamond markets. Other industrial sectors driving industrial growth include energy, metallurgy, and food processing. Jewelry is produced by private and state-run companies from diamonds, gold, silver and semi-precious stones.

The manufacturing sector in Armenia employs around 15 per cent of the workforce and contributes 45 per cent of GDP. The industrial production growth rate was an estimated 12 per cent in 2007.

Services
Armenia has much potential as a tourist destination and recent figures indicate that some success is being achieved in attracting visitors. Almost 40 per cent of the workforce is employed in this sector, and it generates approximately 40 per cent of GDP. Figures for 2006 show that Armenia had 381,000 visitors generationg tourist receipts of US$193 million.

Agriculture
Agriculture accounts for 19 per cent of GDP, and employs almost 45 per cent of the workforce. Armenia was the first former Soviet Republic to introduce a land privatisation programme (1991) and now 95 per cent of agricultural output comes from private farms. 46 per cent of Armenia's land is used for farmland, and 36 per cent is mountainous and so used for raising cattle and sheep. The principal crops are potatoes, wheat, pulses, tomatoes, sugar beets, vegetables and fruit (especially grapes and citrus fruits). Although Armenia has to import 65 per cent of its food it is a net exporter of fruits. Tobacco is grown and plants are cultivated for their oil, which is distilled in order to make perfume. Each year the country produces 20 to 21 tons of geranium oil distillate, one of the more valuable goods on world markets. The country also produces wine and brandy. Armenia has 286,000 ha of watered fertile land. Two separate state bodies are responsible for maintaining the water supply and irrigation systems.

Agricultural Production in 2010

Produce	Int. $'000	Tonnes
Cow milk, whole, fresh	161,742	557,293
Indigenous cattle meat	129,579	47,968
Grapes	127,416	222,905
Tomatoes	93,099	251,916
Potatoes	58,931	481,956
Vegetables fresh nes	37,786	200,517
Hen eggs, in shell	32,031	38,620
Apples	21,835	56,487
Indigenous sheep meat	19,895	7,307
Berries nes	17,569	10,084
Cabbages and other brassicas	16,802	114,279
Wheat	16,788	183,500

Source: http://faostat.fao.org/site/339/default.aspx Food and Agriculture Organization of the United Nations, Food and Agricultural commodities production

COMMUNICATIONS AND TRANSPORT

Travel Requirements
All visitors to Armenia require a visa. It is possible to get one on arrival at the airport or the main land border crossings of Bagratashen and Meghri, or by applying for an e-visa via the website: http://www.armeniaforeignministry.am.

National Airlines
Armenian Airlines (AAL), (state-owned) Zvartnots Airport, Yerevan 375042, Armenia. Tel +374 10 773313, URL: http://www.armenianairlines.com/
The governing body of Armenian aviation is the Main Administration of Civil Aviation - Armenia.
Main Administration of Civil Aviation - Armenia, Zvartnots Airport, Yerevan 375042, Armenia. Tel: +374 10 282066 / 772030, fax: +374 10 772211 / 282641 / 284142 / 281597

International Airports
Armenia has 13 airports, 11 with paved runways.
Shirak Airport, 377500 Giumri. Tel: +374 8856 922158
Yerebuni Airport, Arshakuniantsa Prospect 135, Yerevan. Tel: +374 10 484272
Zvartnots Airport (Yerevan), 375042, Yerevan. Tel +374 10 773097, International and domestic flights

Railways
850 km of track (not including industrial track). The capital Yerevan has a small underground network and a tram system. Armenia has a rail link which runs once a day to Tbilisi, Georgia.

Roads
There are 11,300 km of roads. Most towns and cities operate a minibus service, coaches are used for longer distances.

HEALTH

In 2009, total expenditure on health as a percentage of GDP was 4.6 per cent. General government expenditure accounts for 43.5 per cent of total health expenditure. Per capita total expenditure on health was US$129 in 2009. External resources account for 8.4 per cent of total health expenditure. In 2005-10, there were an estimated 11,234 physicians (3.76

per 1,000 inhabitants), 14,386 nurses and midwives (4.82 per 1,000), 1,943 dentists (0.65 per 1,000 inhabitants) and 204 pharmacists (0.07 per 1,000 residents). In 2005-11, there were 37 hospital beds per 10,000 population and 4.8 psychiatric beds per 10,000 population.

It was estimated in 2005 that 0.1 per cent of adults had HIV/AIDs.

In 2010 the infant mortality rate (probability of dying aged less than 1 year old) was 18 per 1,000 live births and the rate for children aged less than five years old was 20 per 1,000 live births. In 2009, some 25 per cent of the deaths were caused by prematurity, 22 per cent by congenital anomalies and 11 per cent by pneumonia. Immunization rates (2010) for children aged less than 1 year were as follows: measles 97 per cent, DTP3 94 per cent, HepB3 94 per cent and Hib3 48 per cent.

In 2010, 98 per cent of the population had sustainable access to an improved water source. In the same period, 90 per cent of the population had sustainable access to improved sanitation. (Source: http://www.who.int, Global Health Statistics, 2012)

EDUCATION

In 2006, some 36 per cent of pre-primary children attended a nursery school.

Education is compulsory from the age of six to 16. At primary level 82 per cent of the relevant age-group enrolled in primary school in 2006, and 91 per cent of children completed the full primary course, leaving 9 per cent out of school. The pupil/teacher ratio was 21:1. An estimated 86 per cent of relevant-aged pupils went on to secondary education in the same year.

32 per cent of students went on to study at tertiary education level. This was well above the regional average of 25. There are 25 public institutions of higher education, including seven colleges, with 26,000 students.

Some 99.5 per cent of the population are literate. This figure increases to 99.8 per cent among the 15-24 year old age group. Figures for 2006 show that 14.0 per cent of government spending went on education. (Source: UNESCO)

RELIGION

Armenia adopted Christianity as its state religion in 301 AD, the first country to do so. The Armenian Apostolic Church is the leading denomination, an Orthodox church with its centre at Echmiadsin. The head of the Church - the Catholicos of All Armenians - is Karekin II. There are also Orthodox, Yazidi and Islamic communities, the latter primarily comprised of Muslim Azerbaijanis. More than 90 per cent of the population is nominally affiliated with the Armenian Apostolic Church, which is considered to be the national church of Armenia. Just 2.2 per cent of the population is Muslim.

Armenia has a religious tolerance rating of 4 on a scale of 1 to 10 (10 is most freedom). (Source: World Religion Database)

COMMUNICATIONS AND MEDIA

Censorship is prohibited by law but defamation is punishable by prison terms. A state of emergency was briefly imposed in 2008 which meant that the news had to be sanctioned by the government. Television is the most popular medium.

Newspapers
Newspapers are not the primary source of information. Most publications are either owned by individuals or politiacl parties. Main newspapers are: Hayastani Hanrapetutyun (URL: http://www.hhpress.am/); Aykakan Ahanamak (URL: http://www.hzh.am/), owned by the opposition Democratic Homeland party; Respublika Armenia (URL: http://www.ra.am/, government); Azg (URL http://www.azg.am/); Aravot (URL: http://www.aravot.am/); Yerkir (URL: http://www.yerkir.am/); Golos Armenii (URL: http://www.golos.am/), Iravunk Weekly (URL: http://www.iravunk.com/).

Broadcasting
The state broadcaster is Armenian State Television (AST) (URL: (http://www.armtv.com/). There are approximately 40 private broadcasters including Armenian TV (URL: http://www.armeniatv.am/)and Prometheus TV which are both national, commercial broadcasters. There are two main independent cable channels - Mayr Hayrenik and Shant - as well as several smaller channels.

The state radio station is the Public Radio of Armenia (URL: http://www.armradio.am/). There are several private radio stations including Hit FM, Radio Alfa and Radio Van (URL: http://www.radiovan.am).

The state-run news agency is Armenpress,
URL: http://www.armenpress.am/eng/news/news.htm.

Telecommunications
Armenia had 650,000 land-line telephones and over 2 million cellular phones in 2008. In 2010, Armenia had some 208,000 internet users.

ENVIRONMENT

Major environmental problems include the chemical pollution of soil, the pollution of the Hrazdan and Aras rivers, deforestation due to the energy blockade of Azerbaijan, the draining of Lake Sevan for hydropower, and the re-use of the Metsamor nuclear power station which closed in 1989 because of safety fears; despite pressure from the international community, the government is reluctance to decommission this power plant unless there is a reliable alternative source of energy. Armenia has agreed to conduct a preliminary Environmental Impact Assessment (EIA) and Feasibility Study for a new nuclear power generation unit.

According to figures from the EIA, in 2010, Armenia's emissions from the consumption of fossil fuels totalled 11.56 million metric tons of carbon dioxide.

Armenia is a party to the following environmental agreements: Air Pollution, Biodiversity, Climate Change, Climate Change-Kyoto Protocol, Desertification, Environmental Modification, Hazardous Wastes, Law of the Sea, Ozone Layer Protection, and Wetlands. Armenia has signed, but not ratified the agreement on Air Pollution-Persistent Organic Pollutants.

Armenia has set up a Ministry of Nature Protection and has introduced a pollution fee system by which taxes are levied on air and water emissions and solid waste disposal, with the resulting revenues used for environmental protection activities.

SPACE PROGRAMME

Armenia signed a memorandum of understanding with Russia in July 2012, ordering a commercial communications satellite. The satellite, Armenia's first, is expected to carry 15 transponders. The satellite is to be made by the Russian satellite maker Reshetnev Information Satellite Systems.

AUSTRALIA
Commonwealth of Australia

Capital: Canberra (Population estimate, 2012: 367,000)

Head of State: Her Majesty Queen Elizabeth II (Sovereign) (page 1420)

Governor-General: Quentin Bryce (page 1396)

National Flag: On a blue background the British blue ensign appears in the upper hoist-side quadrant; below the ensign is the Commonwealth Star in white, and on the fly half of the flag appears the Southern Cross, also in white.

CONSTITUTION AND GOVERNMENT

Constitution
The six former British colonies of Australia became an independent federation in 1901. Under the terms of the 1901 Federal Constitution, executive power is vested in the Queen. Queen Elizabeth II is currently Queen of Australia and is represented in the country by the Governor-General, who exercises executive power on her behalf. The Governor-General is appointed by the Queen on the advice of the Prime Minister, and usually serves a term of five years, although this can be extended.

The head of government is the Prime Minister, appointed by the Governor-General and responsible to Parliament. The Prime Minister chooses the Cabinet, which is appointed by the Governor-General.

To consult the full constitution, please visit:
http://www.aph.gov.au/senate/general/constitution/

International Relations
Australia is an outward-looking nation actively involved in international affairs. The country has close links with Europe and North America, and engages actively with Asian and Pacific states. Australia has mediated between warring groups in Papua New Guinea and the Solomon Islands, and deployed thousands of peacekeepers in newly-independent East Timor. In 2008, PM Kevin Rudd proposed the creation of a new Asia-Pacific bloc which would co-operate in economic, security and political matters, and would have a broader remit than such bodies as Apec, Asean and the East Asia Summit.

The USA is one of Australia's top merchandise trading partners, its largest services trading partner and the leading source of foreign investment. The Australia-US Free Trade Agreement entered into force on 1 January 2005. The USA is also a close security ally; The ANZUS Treaty of 1951 binds the two counties in cooperation on military and security issues. Australia invoked the Treaty for the first time following the terrorist attacks of 11 September 2001, and deployed forces to Afghanistan.

China's increasing economic, political and strategic weight in the Asia-Pacific region and the global economy has led to increased bilateral cooperation. In 2006, China became Australia's second largest trading partner and one of its fastest growing export markets.

AUSTRALIA

Australia has close ties with many countries in Europe. Australia and the UK in particular have strong trade and investment links. The UK is Australia's second-largest foreign investor and the second-largest destination for Australian foreign investment.

Australia has begun seeking election as a non-permanent member of the UN Security Council from 2013.

Recent Events
Organisers estimated that around 150,000 people across Australia took part in Walk Against Warming rallies on 11 November 2007. Campaigners want greenhouse gas emissions to be cut by 30 per cent by 2020. With per capita carbon dioxide emissions of 20.24 metric tons in 2005, Australia is one of the worst polluters in the world. On being sworn into office in December 2007, Prime Minister Rudd's first act was to sign documents ratifying the Kyoto Protocol on climate change, reversing the previous administration's policy. Australia's new stance on Kyoto isolated the US as the only developed nation not to have ratified the treaty.

In February 2008, the last asylum seekers left a detention camp on Nauru; Prime Minister Kevin Rudd had pledged to end the 'Pacific Solution' immigration policy which meant that people seeking asylum in Australia were sent to detention on small Pacific islands. On the 13th February, the government made a formal apology for the wrongs that successive governments had committed against the Aboriginal population. The motion was passed unanimously by the Australian parliament. Prime Minister Rudd made specific mention of the 'Stolen Generation', children forcibly removed from their families to be brought up as white.

At a government-led summit on the future of Australia in April 2008, there were renewed calls for a republic and the end of the British monarch as the head of state. PM Rudd is a longstanding republican but the government does not consider the establishment of a republic a priority, giving it a target of 12 years. Aboriginal issues and climate change were also on the Australia 2020 agenda.

In September 2008, Quentin Bryce was sworn in as the new governor-general; she is the first woman to hold the post.

In southern Australia, bushfires caused the deaths of some 210 people in early February 2009. Wildfires are an annual event, but a drought, dry bush and one of the most powerful heat waves in memory made them particularly intense. The state of Victoria was the worst hit, but South Australia and New South Wales were also affected. At the same time, northern Queensland was suffering heavy flooding, with some areas cut off for three weeks. In May, torrential rains and strong winds lashed the east coast; up to 20,000 people were cut off by the floodwaters in NSW and Queensland, and large areas were declared disaster zones. The flooding is the most extensive in the two states for 30 years.

In April 2010 a Chinese bulk carrier, the Shen Neng 1, ran aground off Queensland and caused widespread damage to the Great Barrier Reef. The Australian government has not ruled out a prosecution, as the ship ran aground in a no-go zone.

In June 2010 Prime Minister Kevin Rudd faced a leadership challenge. He did not stand in the leadership vote as he knew he would lose. Deputy prime minister Julia Gillard won the vote and became Australia's first female prime minister. A general election was then held in August. No party won a working majority and so coalition talks began. On September 7 it was announced that Julia Gillard had won the backing of the independent MPs and so was able to form a government.

Severe flooding occurred again in Queensland in December 2010-January 2011 killing 35 people and making hundreds homeless. Queensland was then hit by Cyclone Yasi.

In February 2012, the foreign minister Kevin Rudd resigned his post in order to mount an ultimately unsuccessful challenge to Prime Minister Gillard's leadership.

In April 2012 Senator Bob Brown, leader of the Green Party, resigned his post.

In July 2012, a controversial carbon tax was proposed, the tax would penalise large polluters, Prime Minister Gillard fells it is needed to meet Australia's climate change obligations, however, opponents of the tax say it will cost jobs and raise prices.

In September 2012, an independent panel recommended the setting up holding centres in Nauru and Papua New Guinea to cope with increasing numbers of asylum seekers.

Also in September, Australia signed an agreement with Papua New Guinea to conduct offshore processing on Manus Island.

In March 2013, Prime Minister Gillard survived another leadership challenge, afterwards she announced a major cabinet reshuffle in order to oust supporters of the challenge. In June 2013, Kevin Rudd mounted another challenge and ousted Julia Gillard as leader of the Labor Party and prime minister in a Parliamentary vote. At the end of June, Kevin Rudd was sworn in as prime minister and announced a new cabinet.

Legislature
Commonwealth legislative power is vested in the Commonwealth Parliament, comprising the House of Representatives and the Senate, which are directly elected by the people of Australia. Government is by the Westminster system of government and Ministers of State must be members of either the Upper or Lower House. Apart from the constitutional requirement that all financial legislation must originate in the House of Representatives and that the Senate cannot amend such legislation, the two houses have similar powers. The fact that the Senate can reject financial legislation makes it potentially one of the most powerful upper houses in the world.

Upper House
In the 76-seat Senate, each of the six States, regardless of population size, has equal representation with 12 seats. In addition, the two Territories - the Australian Capital Territory and the Northern Territory - both elect two Senators each. Under the Commonwealth Electoral Act, senators who represent the Territories are elected every three years, whilst those who represent the States are elected every six years. Under section 57 of the Constitution, the Governor-General may dissolve both Houses of the Parliament, leading to a general election for all divisions in both Houses.

The electoral system is quota-based proportional representation, and an absolute majority is not required. The candidate needs to receive a quota of the vote based on a calculation of votes cast within the relevant state by the number of vacancies, plus one. In a half Senate election, which generally takes place at the same time as a General Election, and where six seats are being contested, the candidate needs to obtain one seventh of the total formal vote, plus one.

Department of the Senate, Parliament House, Canberra, ACT 2600, Australia. Tel: +61 (0)2 6277 7111, fax: +61 (0)2 6277 3199 (Clerk), e-mail: infoservices.sen@aph.gov.au, URL: http://www.aph.gov.au/Senate/
President of the Senate: Hon. John Joseph Hogg (page 1442)

Lower House
The House of Representatives is composed of 150 members, one member per electoral division, who serve three-year terms. The boundaries of electoral divisions do not cross State or Territory borders. The apportionment of House of Representatives seats to state/territory is as follows: New South Wales, 50; Victoria, 37; Queensland, 27; Western Australia, 15; South Australia, 12; Tasmania, 5; Australian Capital Territory, 2; Northern Territory, 2.

The voting system used is a full preferential voting system, i.e. the voter must mark their preference against all the candidates for the vote to be counted. Each Member of the House is elected for a Division under an absolute majority system, where a candidate must receive 50 per cent plus one of the votes in a Division for election. First preferences are counted first; if, after this, a candidate does not have an absolute majority then later preferences are taken into account.

To be entitled to be nominated as a candidate to the Federal Parliament, candidates must be Australian citizens, be over the age of 18, an elector or eligible to become an elector. Members of State or Territory legislatures may not be nominated for election to the Federal Parliament unless they resign their state positions.

Department of the House of Representatives, Parliament House, Canberra 2600, Australia. Tel: +61 (0)2 6277 7111, fax: +61 (0)2 6277 2006 (Clerk), URL: http://www.aph.gov.au/house/
Speaker of the House of Representatives: Hon. Anna Burke (page 1397)

Cabinet (as at July 2013)
Prime Minister: Kevin Rudd (page 1506)
Deputy Prime Minister, Minister of Infrastructure and Transport, Broadband, Communications and the Digital Economy, Leader of the House: Anthony Albanese (page 1373)
Minister for Foreign Affairs: Bob Carr (page 1401)
Minister for Climate Change, Environment, Heritage and Water: Mark Butler
Attorney-General, Minister of Emergency Management, Special Minister of State and Minister for the Public Service and Integrity: Mark Dreyfus QC
Minister for Industry and Innovation, Science and Research, Minister of Higher Education: Kim Carr (page 1401)
Minister of Defence: Stephen Smith (page 1517)
Minister of Trade: Richard Marles
Minister for Health and Medical Research: Tanya Plibersek (page 1496)
Minister of Finance and Deregulation, Leader of the Government in the Senate: Penny Wong (page 1539)
Minister of Agriculture, Fisheries and Forestry: Joel Fitzgibbon (page 1425)
Minister of Resources and Energy, Small Businesses and Tourism: Gary Gray
Minister of Family, Housing, Community Services and Indigenous Affairs, Minister of Disability Reform: Jenny Macklin (page 1468)
Minister for Immigration, Multicultural Affairs and Citizenship: Tony Burke (page 1397)
Minister for Education, Minister for Workplace Relations: Bill Shorten
Minister of Employment, Skills and Training: Brendan O'Connor (page 1488)
Minister of Mental Health and Ageing: Jacinta Collins (page 1407)
Minister for Regional Australia, Minister of Local Government and Territories: Catherine King
Minister for Community Services, Housing and Homelessness, Minister for Indigenous Employment and Economic Development: Julie Collins
Treasurer: Chris Bowen (page 1392)

Outer Ministry (as at July 2013)
Minister of Home Affairs, Minister of Justice: Jason Clare
Minister for Veterans Affairs, Defence Science and Personnel, Indigenous Health, Centenary of ANZAC: Warren Snowdon (page 1517)
Minister for Employment Participation and Childcare, Minister for the Status of Women: Kate Ellis (page 1420)
Minister of Assistant Treasurer, Assisting for Deregulation, Assisting for Finance and Superannuation: David Bradbury
Minister for Human Services: Jan McLucas (page 1475)
Minister of Multicultural Affairs, Assisting for Industry and Innovation: Kate Lundy (page 1467)
Minister of Sport, Minister assisting on Tourism: Don Farrell
Minister for Regional Development, Regional Communities, and as Minister for Road Safety: Sharon Bird

AUSTRALIA

Minister of Human Services: Jan McLucas (page 1475)
Minister of International Development: Melissa Parke

Ministries

Office of the Prime Minister, 3-5 National Circuit, Barton, ACT 2600, Australia. Tel: +61 2 6271 5111, fax: +61 2 6271 5414, URL: http://www.pm.gov.au

Department of Agriculture, Fisheries and Forestry, Edmund Barton Building, Kings Avenue, Barton, ACT 2600 (GPO Box 858, Canberra ACT 2601), Australia. Tel: +61 2 6272 3933, fax: +61 2 6272 3008, URL: http://www.affa.gov.au/index.cfm

Attorney-General's Department, Central Office, Robert Garran Offices, National Circuit, Barton ACT 2600, Australia. Tel: +61 2 6250 6666, fax: +61 2 6250 5900, URL: http://law.gov.au, http://www.ag.gov.au/

Department of Broadband, Communications and the Digital Economy, GPO Box 2154, Canberra ACT 2601, Australia. Tel: +61 2 6271 1000, fax: +61 2 6271 1901, URL: http://www.dbcde.gov.au/

Department of Defence, Russell Offices, Canberra, ACT 2600, Australia. Tel: +61 2 6265 9111, fax: +61 2 6273 4118, URL: http://www.defence.gov.au

Department of Education, Employment and Workplace Relations, GPO Box 9879, Canberra, ACT 2601, Australia. Tel: +61 2 6121 6000, fax: +61 2 6121 7542, URL: http://www.deewr.gov.au/

Department of Environment, Water, Heritage and the Arts, John Gorton Building, King Edward Terrace, Parkes, ACT 2600 (PO Box 787, Canberra, ACT 2601), Australia. Tel: +61 2 6274 1111, fax: +61 2 6274 1123, URL: http://www.environment.gov.au/

Department of Innovation, Industry, Science and Research, GPO Box 9839, Canberra, ACT 2601, Australia. Tel: +61 2 6213 6000, fax: +61 2 6213 7000, URL: http://www.industry.gov.au

Department of Family, Community Services and Indigenous Affairs, (GPO Box 7788, Canberra Mail Centre, ACT 2610) Tuggeranong Office Park, Athllon Drive, Greenway ACT 2905, Australia. Tel: +61 2 6244 7788, fax: +61 2 6244 7988, e-mail: facs.internet@facs.gov.au, URL: http://www.facsia.gov.au/

Department of Finance and Deregulation, Parkes Place, Parkes, ACT, Australia. (Postal address: John Gorton Building, King Edward Terrace, Parkes, ACT 2600, Australia.) Tel: +61 2 6215 2222, URL: http://www.finance.gov.au/

Department of Foreign Affairs and Trade, R.G. Casey Building, John McEwen Crescent, Barton, ACT, 0221 Australia. Tel: +61 2 6261 1111, fax: +61 2 6261 1038, URL: http://www.dfat.gov.au

Department of Health and Ageing, (GPO Box 9848, Canberra City ACT 2601) Furzer Street and Bowers Street, Woden Town Centre, Canberra, Australia. Tel: + 61 2 6289 1555, fax: +61 2 6281 6946, URL: http://www.health.gov.au

Department of Human Services, PO Box 3959, Manuka, ACT 2603, Australia. Tel: +61 2 6223 4000, fax: +61 2 6223 4499, URL: http://www.humanservices.gov.au

Department of Immigration and Citizenship, PO Box 25, Belconnen ACT 2616, Australia. Tel: +61 2 6264 1111, fax: +61 2 6225 6970, URL: http://www.immi.gov.au

Department of Resources, Energy and Tourism, GPO Box 9839, Canberra, ACT 2601, Australia. Tel: +61 2 6213 6000, fax: +61 2 6213 7000, URL: http://www.industry.gov.au

Department of Infrastructure, Transport, Regional Development and Local Government, GPO Box 594, Canberra, ACT 2601, Australia. Tel: +61 2 6274 7111, fax: +61 2 6257 2505, URL: http://www.infrastructure.gov.au/

Department of the Treasury, Langton Crescent, Parkes, ACT 2600, Australia. Tel: +61 2 6263 2111, fax: +61 2 6273 2614, e-mail: department@treasury.gov.au, URL: http://www.treasury.gov.au/

Department of Veterans' Affairs, PO Box 21, Woden, ACT 2606, Australia. Tel: +61 2 6289 6736, fax: +61 2 6289 6257, URL: http://www.dva.gov.au

Political Parties

Australian Greens, GPO Box 1108, Canberra ACT 2601, Australia. Tel: +61 (0)2 6162 0036, fax: +61 (0)2 6277 6455, e-mail: frontdesk@greens.org.au, URL: http://www.greens.org.au/
Leader: Christine Milne

Australian Labor Party, Centenary House, 19 National Circuit, Barton, ACT 2600, (PO Box E1, Kingston ACT 2604) Australia. Tel: +61 (0)2 6120 0800, fax: +61 (0)2 6120 0801, e-mail: info@cbr.alp.org.au, http://www.alp.org.au
Leader: Julia Gillard

Communist Party of Australia, 65 Campbell Street, Surry Hills, NSW 2010, Australia. Tel: +61 2 9212 6855, fax: +61 2 9281 5795, e-mail: cpa@cpa.org.au, URL: http://www.cpa.org.au

Country Liberal Party, PO Box 40945, Casuarina, NT 0811, Australia. Tel: +61 (0)8 8927 8233, fax: +1 (0)8 8927 8233, email: secretariat@clp.org.au, URL: http://www.clp.org.au/
Leader: Terry Mills

Liberal Party of Australia, Federal Secretariat, Corner of Blackall and Macquarie Streets, Barton, ACT 2600, Australia. (Postal address: PO Box 6004, Kingston, ACT 2604, Australia.) Tel: +61 (0)2 6273 2564, fax: +61 (0)2 6273 1534, e-mail: admin2@liberal.org.au, URL: http://www.liberal.org.au/
Leader: Tony Abbott

National Party of Australia, 7 National Circuit, John McEwen House, Barton ACT 2600, Australia. (Postal address: PO Box 6190, Kingston, ACT 2604, Australia) Tel: +61 (0)2 6273 3822, fax: +61 (0)2 6273 1745, URL: http://www.nationals.org.au
Leader: Warren Truss

Australian Democrats, National Office, Unit 9, Level 1, 16 National Circuit, Barton, ACT 2600, Australia. (Mailing address: PO Box 5089, Kingston ACT 2604, Australia) Tel: +61 (0)2 6273 1059, fax: +61 (0)2 6273 1251, e-mail: inquiries@democrats.org.au, URL: http://www.democrats.org.au
National President: Darren Churchill

Elections

All citizens of Australia over the age of 18 must be enrolled on the Commonwealth Electoral Roll and must vote in federal elections and referenda to change the Constitution. Failure to vote or register to vote is punishable by a fine. Only those non-resident citizens who were voters before 25 January 1984 are required to vote and entitled to nominate for election.

Parliamentary elections took place on 24th November 2007. The opposition centre-left Australian Labor Party, led by Kevin Rudd, won the election against the incumbent centre-right coalition government which had been in power since 1996. Following his loss at the election, PM Howard announced his immediate retirement. He was replaced as leader of the Liberal Party by Dr. Brendan Nelson.

The most recent parliamentary election took place in August 2010, Labor Prime Minister Kevin Rudd faced a leadership challenge and did not stand in a vote for leader as he knew he would lose, deputy prime minister Julia Gillard won the vote and became Australia's first female prime minister. Following the August election no party won an overall majority and after several weeks of negotiations it was announced on September 7 that Julia Gillard had won the backing of the independent MPs and so was able to form a government. The next election will be held in September 2013.

On 6 November 1999 a referendum was held to decide whether Australia should become a republic. Specifically, two proposals were put to the people of the Commonwealth of Australia:
1) To alter the Constitution to establish the Commonwealth of Australia as a republic with the Queen and Governor-General being replaced by a President elected by a two-thirds majority of the members of the Commonwealth Parliament.
2) To alter the Constitution to insert a preamble.

A total of 11,785,000 votes were cast by 95.13 per cent of the electorate. In response to the first proposal, 54.87 per cent voted 'no', and 45.13 per cent voted 'yes'. In response to the second proposal, 60.66 per cent voted 'no', whilst 39.34 per cent voted 'yes'. Consequently, neither question was carried, either by a majority of voters in Australia as a whole or by a majority of voters in a majority of the States.

Diplomatic Representation

British High Commission, Commonwealth Avenue, Yarralumla, Canberra, ACT 2600, Australia. Tel: +61 (0)2 6270 6666, fax: +61 (0)2 6273 3236, e-mail: bhc.canberra@uk.emb.gov.au, URL: http://ukinaustralia.fco.gov.uk
High Commissioner: Paul Madden (page 1469)
Embassy of the United States of America, Moonah Place, Yarralumla, Canberra, ACT 2600, Australia. Tel: +61 (0)2 6214 5600, fax: +61 (0)2 6214 5970, e-mail: info@usembassy-australia.state.gov, URL: http://canberra.usembassy.gov
Ambassador: Jeffrey L. Bleich
Australian High Commission, Australia House, Strand, London, WC2B 4LA, United Kingdom. Tel: +44 (0)20 7379 4334, fax: +44 (0)20 7240 5333, URL: http://www.uk.embassy.gov.au/lhlh/aboutus.html
High Commissioner: Hon. Mike Rann (page 1500)
Australian Embassy, 1601 Massachusetts Avenue, NW, Washington, DC 20036-2273, USA. Tel: +1 202 797 3000, fax: +1 202 797 3168, e-mail: library.washington@dfat.gov.au, URL: http://www.usa.embassy.gov.au
Ambassador: Mr Kim Beazley, AC (page 1385)
Australian Mission to the United Nations, 150 East 42nd Street, 33rd Floor, New York, NY 10017-5612, USA. Tel: +1 212 351 6600, fax: +1 212 351 6610, e-mail: australia@un.int, URL: http://www.unny.mission.gov.au/unny/home.html
Ambassador: Gary Quinlan (page 1499)

LEGAL SYSTEM

The judicial power of the Commonwealth is vested in the High Court of Australia, in the federal courts created by Parliament, and in the State courts invested by Parliament with federal jurisdiction. The nature and extent of the judicial power of the Commonwealth is prescribed in the Australian Constitution.

The High Court has original jurisdiction in matters as conferred on it under the Constitution or by Parliament, and jurisdiction to hear and determine appeals arising from determinations of any Justice or Justices exercising the original jurisdiction of the High Court, any other federal court or court exercising federal jurisdiction, and, in certain matters, from determination of State or Territory Supreme Courts. The High Court consists of a Chief Justice and six other Justices, and has its principal seat in Canberra. The High Court may sit in other cities as required.

Parliament has created four other Federal courts: the Federal Court of Australia, the Federal Court of Bankruptcy, the Australian Industrial Court and the Family Court of Australia. From February 1977 the jurisdiction formerly held by the Australian Industrial Court and by the Federal Court of Bankruptcy respectively, except in the case of proceedings commenced and part heard in these Courts before that date, is now exercised by the Federal Court of Australia.

The judicial power of the States and Territories is vested in the Supreme Court and other courts of the respective States and Territories. Each State and Territory Supreme Court consists of a Chief Justice and a varying number of other Judges. The denominations and functions of intermediate and lower courts vary from State to State and Territory to Territory. All State courts of general State jurisdiction have also been vested with Federal jurisdiction.

The government generally respects the human rights of its citizens. There were some instances of discrimination against Aboriginal people by the general public in 2008. The death penalty was abolished in 1985 (Queensland, 1922; Tasmania, 1968; The Northern Territory; Australian Capital Territory and the Commonwealth, 1973; Victoria, 1975; South Australia, 1976; Western Australia, 1984; and New South Wales, 1985).

High Court of Australia, Parkes Place, Parkes, Canberra, ACT 2600, Australia. (Postal address: PO Box 6309, Kingston, Canberra, Australian Capital Territory, 2604, Australia.) Tel: +61 (0)2 6270 6811, fax: +61 (0)2 6273 3025, e-mail: enquiries@hcourt.gov.au, URL: http://www.hcourt.gov.au/
Chief Justice: Robert Shenton French (page 1427)

AUSTRALIA

Federal Court of Australia Law Courts Building, Queens Square, Sydney NSW 2000, Australia. Tel: +61 (0)2 9230 8281, fax: +61 (0)2 9230 8535, URL: http://www.fedcourt.gov.au/index.html
Chief Justice: The Hon. Patrick Keane

Family Court of Australia Corner Childers Street and University Avenue, Canberra, Australia. (Postal address: GPO Box 9991 Canberra, ACT 2601) (DX Box: DX 5652 Canberra) Tel: +61 (0)2 6267 0511, fax: +61 (0)2 6257 1586, URL: http://www.familycourt.gov.au/

Human Rights and Equal Opportunity Commission, URL: http://www.humanrights.gov.au

LOCAL GOVERNMENT

At the head of each State is a Governor representing the Sovereign and a Cabinet headed by the Premier. The various state legislatures consist of upper and lower houses, except in the case of Queensland where the upper house was abolished in 1922. The functions discharged by the State Governors vary according to local conditions. General education, health, police, the operation of railways, transport and undertakings and public utilities are, generally, administered by the State Governments.

The Northern Territory and Norfolk Island both have an administrator, appointed by the Governor-General. The Australian Capital Territory has a Chief Minister.

The following are the State Governors of Australia and Administrators of the Northern Territory and the Island Territories:

Australian Capital Territory: Katy Gallagher
New South Wales: Her Excellency Prof. Marie Bashir, AO (page 1384)
Victoria: The Hon. Alex Chernov, AO, QC
Queensland: Her Excellency Penelope Wensley, AO (page 1535)
Western Australia: His Excellency Malcolm McCusker AO, QC
South Australia: His Excellency Rear Admiral Kevin Scarce, AO, CSC, RANR (page 1509)
Tasmania: His Excellency the Hon. Peter Underwood AO (page 1529)
Northern Territory: Her Honour the Hon. Sally Thomas AM
Christmas Island: Hon. Brian Lacy (Administrator)
Cocos (Keeling) Islands: Hon. Brian Lacy (Administrator)
Norfolk Island: Owen Walsh (Acting Administrator)

Assembly elections were held in 2010 in South Australia, Tasmania and Victoria. New South Wales had a lower house general election in 2011. Assembly elections are due in 2012 for the ACT, the Northern Territory and Queensland. Western Australia should have an election either late 2012 or early 2013.

The Australian Local Government Association is the national voice of local government, representing 560 councils across the country. The Association is a federation of state and territory local government associations. Since 2001, membership has included the Government of the Australian Capital Territory which combines both state and local government functions. (URL: http://www.alga.asn.au/about/)

AREA AND POPULATION

Area
The total area of Australia, including Tasmania, is 7,692,030 sq. km., making it the sixth largest country in area. Its coastline is 36,735 kilometres. The interior of the country (known as the Outback) is sparsely populated semi-desert and tropical wetlands. Nearly a third of the continent lies in the tropics and the rest is in the temperate zone. The coldest areas are in the south east where the only regular snowfall occurs.

Most of the population live in the South Eastern cities of Sydney, Melbourne, Brisbane and Adelaide, as well as the west coast city of Perth; the overall population density in Australia is 2.9 persons per sq. km although there are wide regional variations. Among the states and territories, the Australian Capital Territory had the highest population density at 152.5 people per sq km, followed by Victoria with 24.4, New South Wales with 9.0 and Tasmania with 7.5. The remaining states and territories all had population densities below the Australian average, with the Northern Territory having the lowest at just 0.2 people per sq km. Only 15 per cent live in rural areas.

To view a map, consult http://www.lib.utexas.edu/maps/cia08/australia_sm_2008.gif

The following table shows the estimated areas of the States/Territories (sq. km):

State/Territory	Area (sq. km)	Total area (%)
New South Wales	800,640	10.41
Victoria	227,420	2.96
Queensland	1,730,650	22.50
South Australia	983,480	12.79
Western Australia	2,529,880	32.89
Tasmania	68,400	0.89
Northern Territory	1,349,130	17.54
Australian Capital Territory	2,360	0.3
Jervis Bay Territory	70	---
Australia	7,692,030	100.0

Source: Australian Bureau of Statistics

Population
Australia's total population was estimated at 22.9 million as of March 2013, with an annual population increase of around 1.6 per cent. Natural increase over the year 2012 made up an estimated 42 per cent of the overall population increase, whilst net overseas migration accounted for around 58 per cent of the increase.

All states and territories experienced positive population growth over the year; Western Australia recorded the largest percentage gain (3.3 per cent), and Tasmania recorded the smallest (0.2 per cent).

The following table gives a breakdown of the population by state:

Estimated Resident Population - June 2012 (E)

Area	Population	12 month change (%)
New South Wales	7,290,300	1.1
Victoria	5,623,500	1.6
Queensland	4,560,100	1.9
South Australia	1,654,800	1.0
Western Australia	2,430,300	3.3
Tasmania	512,000	0.2
Northern Territory	234,800	1.5
Australian Capital Territory	374,700	1.9
Australia	**22,686,600**	1.6

(Source: ABS, 3101.0 Australian Demographic Statistics, 2013)

(All figures sourced from the ABS are quoted with the permission of the Australian Bureau of Statistics)

By 2008, the Indigenous population of Australia had reached an estimated 520,350 (2.5 per cent of the total Australian population). Some 90 per cent of the Indigenous people identify themselves as Aboriginal, whilst 6 per cent are Torres Strait Islanders, and the remaining 4 per cent count themselves as being of both Aboriginal and Torres Strait Islander origin. In 2008, just over two-thirds of Indigenous people lived outside the major cities, with 44 per cent living in regional areas and 24 per cent living in remote (or very remote) areas. More than half of the Indigenous population lived in either New South Wales (30 per cent) or Queensland (28 per cent). Approximately 13 per cent lived in Western Australia and 12 per cent in the Northern Territory.

Immigration has doubled the population of Australia since 1945, and between 1995 and 2000 a total of 1.4 million people arrived in Australia with the intention of staying for 12 months or longer. In 2006-07, net overseas migration added an estimated 177,620 people to the Australian population, the highest ever recorded. In the year ended 30 June 2007, all states and territories experienced growth in net overseas migration; New South Wales recorded the highest gain (54,890 people), followed by Victoria (47,150) and Queensland (33,540). Overall, 59 per cent of overseas immigrants were aged between 15 and 34 years. Figures for 2009-10 showed that net overseas migration was 215,600 persons, down by 11 per cent on the previous year. People arriving from the United Kingdom remain the largest group accounting for 5.3 per cent of the resident population as at 30 June 2010, with 2.4 per cent of the population having born in New Zealand, 1.7 per cent born in China and 1.0 per cent born in Italy. (ABS data used with permission from the Australian Bureau of Statistics)

Over the twelve months to 30 June 2007, 23,000 people born in China settled in Australia. 22,840 UK-born people, 21,420 New Zealand-born people and 17,420 Indians migrated to Australia. Over the decade to 2006, people born in Sudan recorded the largest average increase, at 27 per cent per year, followed by those born in Afghanistan (13 per cent) and Iraq (10 per cent). The number of immigrants from Southern and Central Asia, and Sub-Saharan Africa, increased by 6 per cent per year over the same period.

Over 2006-07, net migration of Australians to other countries totalled 22,700 people.

Births, Marriages, Deaths
There were 297,900 births registered in Australia in 2010, an increase of approximately 2,200 on the previous year. Figures for 2007 show that Australia's total fertility rate in 2007 was 1.93 babies per woman, the highest since 1981 (1.94). Among indigenous women, the rate was higher, at 2.4 children. The increase in fertility rate was largely due to births to women aged 25 to 34 years, though the fertility of women in all age groups increased.

All states and territories recorded a higher number of births in 2007 than in 2006: Queensland and Victoria recorded the largest increase in number of births, and the largest percentage increases, at 16.3 per cent (though this is due to changes in processing birth registrations) and 7.8 per cent respectively. South Australia also had a high percentage increase of 7.7 per cent. The median age of all mothers who gave birth in Australia in 2006 was 30.7 years.

The number of deaths registered in 2010 was 143,500. With increased population growth, and continued population ageing, the number of deaths is projected to rise. However, the overall crude death rate has declined from 7.2 deaths per 1,000 population in 1986 to six deaths per 1,000 population in 2007. The highest death rate in 2007 was in Northern Territory (8.9 per 1,000 people), whilst the lowest was in the Australian Capital Territory (5.6 per 1,000 inhabitants). Figures for 2008 showed there were 143,900 deaths registered, around 6,100, 4.4 per cent than the number registered in 2007. The number of indigenous deaths registered in 2006 was 2,300. The indigenous population has age-standardised death rates twice that of the total population.

The 2010 infant mortality rate was 4.1 infant deaths per 1,000 children who survive their first year, down on the 2006 rate of 4.7 deaths per 1,000 survivors. The indigenous infant mortality rate is higher than that of the rest of the Australian population.

Life expectancy at birth continued to increase in 2007, when it stood at 79 years for males and 83.7 years for females. The Australian Capital Territory recorded the highest life expectancy at birth for both males (80.3 years) and females (84 years) in 2007, while the Northern Territory recorded the lowest life expectancy at birth for both males (72.4 years) and females (78.4 years).

The Aboriginal and Torres Strait Islander population is relatively young. In 2008, almost half (49 per cent) of the Indigenous population was aged under 20 years and a further 16 per cent were aged between 20 and 30 years. Just 3 per cent of the Indigenous population were aged 65 years and over in 2008. It is estimated that indigenous men have a life expectancy of 59 years, and indigenous women 64 years.

Marriages numbered 120,100 in 2009, indicating an increase on figures for the previous decade. The preliminary crude marriage rate was 5.5 marriages per 1,000 inhabitants, up on 2003 but down on the 1998 rate of 5.9 per 1,000. The median age of a first marriage was 31.5 years for men and 29.2 years for women. 62.9 per cent of marriages were performed by civil celebrants, and 76.8 per cent of couples who married had lived together prior to marriage.

Divorces numbered 52,400 in 2005, continuing a downward trend that began in 2000. The crude divorce rate was 2.3 per 1,000 population in 2009. (Source: ABS Cat. nos. 3301.0; 3302.0; and 3412, 2008)

Public Holidays 2014
1 January: New Year's Day
26 January: Australia Day
18 April: Good Friday
21 April: Easter Monday
25 April: Anzac Day
9 June: Queen's Official Birthday (except Western Australia) (second Monday in June)
25 December: Christmas Day
26 December: Boxing Day

For holidays specific to individual states please refer to the individual state entries.

EMPLOYMENT

According to ABS seasonally adjusted employment statistics, the number of people employed numbered 11,541,600 in January 2013, and the number of unemployed people was 657,800. (Source: ABS, 6202.0)

The overall employment participation rate in January 2013 was 65.0 per cent. Employment participation rates in the states, in January 2012, were as follows: New South Wales, 63.4 per cent; Victoria, 65.0 per cent; Queensland, 67.4 per cent; South Australia, 63.3 per cent; Western Australia, 68.9 per cent; Tasmania, 60.5 per cent; Northern Territory, 74.7 per cent; Australian Capital Territory, 72.3 per cent. (ABS Labour Force, 6202.0, Mar. 2012)

Unemployment amongst the States in January 2012 was as follows: NSW, 5.3 per cent; Victoria, 5.2 per cent; Queensland, 5.4 per cent; South Australia, 5.2 per cent; Western Australia, 4.2 per cent; Tasmania, 6.6 per cent; Northern Territory, 4.2 per cent; Australian Capital Territory, 3.7 per cent. (ABS Labour Force, 6202.0, Mar. 2012)

Employed Persons by Industry 2008

Industry	No. employed
Agriculture, Forestry and Hunting	343,500
Fishing	11,200
Mining and Quarrying	133,000
Manufacturing	1,102,100
Electricity, Gas and Water Supply	98,500
Construction	987,000
Wholesale and Retail Trade; Repairs	1,847,100
Hotels and Restaurants	708,300
Transport, Storage and Communications	695,600
Financial intermediation	401,500
Real estate, renting & business activities	1,326,300
Public admin. and defence; compulsory social security	644,500
Education	807,500
Health and social work	1,129,600
Other community, social and personal services	502,500
Private Household employees	2,100
Total No. of Employed people	**10,740,500**

Source: Copyright © International Labour Organization (ILO Dept. of Statistics, http://laborsta.ilo.org)

BANKING AND FINANCE

Currency
One Australian Dollar (A$) = 100 cents

GDP/GNP, Inflation, National Debt
The Australian economy had enjoyed 19 years of uninterrupted growth. This slowed a little in 2006 due to the effects of a long drought and global oil price hikes. However, a boom in resource and minerals exports led to an increased growth rate for 2007. The growing prosperity of East Asia has been a major factor in Australia's economic growth; China's industrial development requires Australian minerals and fuels, while the rise of the region's middle class has expanded markets for Australia's foods businesses. There is concern that the size and skills of the workforce may limit export potential in the future.

Australia's resources-based economy began to struggle since the global financial turmoil began in the middle of 2008. Mining firms reduced capital spending and cut staffing levels. In February 2009, the government announced a A$42 billion stimulus plan; A$28.8bn will be invested in schools, housing and roads and another A$12.7bn will provide cash support for lower-income families as from March. The country's central bank cut interest rates to 3.25 per cent - the lowest level in 45 years. The government halved its economic growth forecast for 2008/09 to one per cent. Latest figures show that the economy grew by 0.4 per cent in the first quarter of 2009 and 0.6 per cent in Q2. Australia recorded a quarter of negative growth at the end of 2009 but didn't enter into recession. In Q2 2010 the Australian economy grew by its fastest pace in three years, with growth stimulated by demand for iron ore and other commodities (mainly from China). GDP expanded 1.2 per cent in Q2 up from 0.7 per cent in 2010. The beginnings of global economic recovery have stimulated Australia's exports and figures for 2011 showed a growth in foreign trade. As a result economic growth has strengthened and GDP was forecast to grow by 3.4 per cent in the years 2011-12 and 2012-13.

GDP and other selected aggregates. Chain volume measures A$million

Aggregate	2008-09	2009-10	2010-11
GDP	1,263,934	1,293,380	1,318,554
Real gross domestic income	1,275,871	1,293,380	1,371,035
Real net nat. disposable income	1,033,645	1,034,942	1,100,781
Domestic final demand	1,272,240	1,301,913	1,343,991
Non-farm GDP	1,238,764	1,268,590	1,291,429
Gross nat. expenditure	1,267,681	1,298,000	1,348,168

Source: ABS (13500D0001_201203)

Forecast figures for 2012 put GDP at current prices at US$1,542.1 billion up from US$1,487.4 billion inn 2011, this gives a year on year growth figure of 2.3 per cent in 2011 and 3.3 per cent in 2012.

Gross State Product at annual chain volume measure in A$m

State/Territory	June 2008	June 2009
New South Wales	381,720	382,314
Victoria	281,504	283,784
Queensland	223,450	224,187
South Australia	76,905	77,991
Western Australia	155,449	156,603
Tasmania	22,261	22,564
Northern Territory	15,879	16,297
Australian Capital Territory	24,582	24,916
Australia (GDP)	1,181,750	1,194,496

Source: Australian Bureau of Statistics

GDP per capita (current prices) averaged A$67,983 in 2012 up from US$67,983 in 2011. Every state had positive growth in GSP per capita.

Australia's market economy is dominated by the services sector which contributes some 71 per cent of GDP. However, it is agriculture and mining (jointly accounting for just eight per cent of GDP) that contribute over 50 per cent of Australia's goods and services exports; whilst rich in natural resources, Australia has a small domestic market of just 20 million inhabitants. The manufacturing sector has been in decline for several decades, and now accounts for around 10 per cent of GDP. The sector is unable to compete with foreign imports and is handicapped by a relatively high Australian Dollar.

Over the year 2009-10 the main contributing industries to gross value added growth were mining, manufacturing, construction, and financial and insurance services.

Industry Gross Value Added - chain volume measures at basic prices A$million

Industry	2009-10	2010-11
Agriculture, forestry, fishing	28,764	31,443
Mining	96,105	95,548
Manufacturing	107,707	107,634
Electricity, gas, water & waste services	28,623	28,892
Construction	95,804	101,481
Wholesale trade	55,128	54,803
Retail trade	58,258	58,598
Accommodation and food services	29,474	29,941
Transport, postal and storage	65,392	67,732
Information, media and telecommunications	41,823	42,434
Finance and insurance services	125,399	127,334
Rental, hiring and real estate services	27,260	26,661
Professional, scientific and technical services	81,043	86,471
Administrative and support services	30,246	32,008
Public administration and safety	64,117	65,266
Education and training	57,546	58,821
Health care and social assistance	72,627	76,347
Arts and recreation services	10,911	11,124
Other services	23,548	22,685
Ownership of dwellings	103,271	106,003
Gross value added at basic prices	1,203,046	1,231,227
Taxes less subsidies on products	90,334	90,986
TOTAL	**1,293,380**	**1,318,554**

Source: ABS http://www.ausstats.abs.gov.au 13500DO001-201203

AUSTRALIA

The Consumer Price Index (CPI) for the weighted average of eight capital cities (all groups) rose by 3.7 per cent over the year to December 2008. The main factors contributing to the increase were rises in financial services (seven per cent), housing (6.5 per cent), Alcohol and tobacco (5.8 per cent) and food (5.6 per cent). A fall of 1.2 per cent was recorded for transportation costs.

Net foreign debt was A$657,961 million at the end of 2008, an increase of $55,254 million on the figure for the end of 2007. Net debt was expected to reach 8.8% of GDP in 2011-12.

Foreign Investment
Foreign investment in Australia reached $1,728,215 million at the end of 2008. Portfolio investment accounted for $982,178 million of total foreign investment, whilst direct investment contributed $382,332 million, financial derivatives, $96,196 million and other investments $267,509 million. The leading investor countries are the USA, the UK and Japan.

Australian investment abroad reached $995,211 million at the end of 2008. Direct investment abroad accounted for $292,756 million, portfolio investment, $413,384 million, financial derivatives, $98,881 million, and other investments, A$177,582 million. The countries in which Australia has most investments are the USA, the UK, New Zealand and Japan. (Source: ABS, 5302.0, 2008). Australia's net International Investment Position rose A$12.4 billion to a net liability position of $768.6 billion in December 2009.

Balance of Payments / Imports and Exports
The following table shows total merchandise exports and imports in recent years:

Year	Exports (A$m)	Imports (A$m)	Balance (A$m)
2008-09	230,829	219,485	11,344
2009-10	200,720	203,590	-2,870
2010-11	245,724	214,080	31,644

Source: ABS 13500DO002_201203

The trend estimate of the balance on goods and services was a surplus of $1,729m in March 2011, a decrease of $65m on the revised surplus in February 2011. In seasonally adjusted terms, the balance on goods and services was a surplus of $1,740m in March 2011. In seasonally adjusted terms, goods and services exports rose 9 per cent to $24,991m from February to March 2011. Non-rural goods rose 11 per cent and non-monetary gold rose 59 per cent. Rural goods fell 2 per cent and net exports of goods under merchanting remained steady at $26m. Services credits rose one per cent. In March 2011, in seasonally adjusted terms, goods and services imports rose to $23,251m.

The top international export trading partners are shown on the following table:

Top International Export Trading Partners, 2006-07

Country	A$ million	Share of total exports %
Japan	32,627	19.4
China	22,845	13.6
Korea, Rep. of	13,071	7.8
India	10,099	6.0
USA	9,453	5.8
New Zealand	9,160	5.6
Taiwan	6,192	3.7
United Kingdom	6,160	3.7
Singapore	4,625	2.7
Thailand	4,260	2.5

Source: Year Book Australia 2008 (1301.0, 31.9 Merchandise Exports by country)

Top Ten International Import Trading Partners, 2006-07

Country	A$ million	Share of total imports %
China	27,138	15.0
USA	24,927	13.8
Japan	17,409	9.6
Singapore	10,135	5.6
Germany	9,274	5.1
United Kingdom	7,402	4.1
Thailand	7,210	4.0
Malaysia	6,625	3.7
Korea, South	6,010	3.3
New Zealand	5,605	3.1

Source: Year Book Australia 2008 (1301, 31.10 Merchandise Imports by country

Merchandise Imports and Exports by Industry of Origin, April 2007 (A$m)

Industry	Imports	Exports
Agriculture, forestry, fishing and hunting		
Agriculture	76	605
Services to agriculture & hunting	1	29
Forestry and logging	1	5
Commercial fishing	10	46
Total Agriculture	88	685
Mining		
Coal mining	1	1,817
Oil and gas extraction	1,167	1,071
Metal ore mining	79	2,221
Other mining	8	22
Total mining	1,255	5,130
Manufacturing		

- continued

Food, beverage, tobacco	658	1,413
Textile, clothing, footwear and leather	658	141
Wood and paper products	338	200
Printing, publishing and recorded media	153	41
Petroleum, coal, chemical and associated products	2,716	866
Non-metallic mineral products	143	22
Metal products	1,374	3,049
Machinery and equipment	6,734	1,340
Other manufacturing	412	93
Total manufacturing	13,186	12,295
Other	50	877
Total	14,579	13,859

Source: ABS (5368.0 -Merchandise Exports and Imports by industry, tables 32 & 35)

Australia is an important participant in the following regional economic cooperations: APEC (Asia Pacific Economic Cooperation), the Australian ASEAN Forum and the South Pacific Regional Trade and Economic Cooperation Agreement (SPARTECA).

Trade or Currency Restrictions
There is no limit to the amount of Australian or foreign currency that it is possible to bring into the country although amounts greater than $A5,000 must be reported on arrival. All goods arriving in Australia unaccompanied by a person must be cleared by Customs. To clear commercial samples a series of applications forms (Carnet A) should be filled in.

Central Bank
Reserve Bank of Australia, 65 Martin Place, Sydney, NSW 2000, Australia. Tel: +61 2 9551 8111, fax: +61 2 9551 8000, e-mail: rbainfo@rba.gov.au, URL: http://www.rba.gov.au Governor: Glenn Stevens (page 1520)

Chambers of Commerce and Trade Organisations
Australian Chamber of Commerce and Industry, URL: http://www.acci.asn.au/
Chamber of Commerce and Industry of Western Australia (CCIWA), URL: http://www.cciwa.asn.au
Queensland Chamber of Commerce and Industry, URL: http://www.qcci.com.au
New South Wales Business Chamber, URL: http://www.nswbusinesschamber.com.au/
Tasmanian Chamber of Commerce and Industry, URL: http://www.tcci.com.au/tcci/
Victorian Employers' Chamber of Commerce and Industry, URL: http://www.vecci.org.au
Australian Trade Commission , URL: http://www.austrade.gov.au

MANUFACTURING, MINING AND SERVICES

Primary and Extractive Industries
Australia is a natural resource-rich country with significant petroleum, natural gas and coal reserves.

The world's largest exporter and fourth largest producer of coal, Australia has estimated recoverable reserves of 86,600 billion short tons, almost all of it on the eastern seaboard. The continent exports around 60 per cent of its annual production, and accounts for 29 per cent of global coal exports, (and over 50 per cent of global coking coal). In 2010 coal production was an estimated 463 million short tons, most of which was bituminous hard coal. Consumption was an estimated 1545.156 million metric short tons.

Substantial oil and gas discoveries have been made in Australia in the last three decades. Proven oil reserves were estimated at 1.4 billion barrels at the beginning of January 2012. Crude refining capacity was an estimated 409,000 barrels per day in 2011, down from 755,000 barrels per day in 2005. Crude oil and concentrates are produced from 10 basins, the largest is the Gippsland basin off the coast of Victoria which produces 58 per cent of the country's total production. A further 30 per cent comes from the Bonaparte basin off the north-west coast and the Carnarvon basin off the central west coast. Australian demand for petroleum products is satisfied mainly by domestic refining capacity, using both domestic and imported crudes. Oil production in 2011 was estimated at 517,000 barrels per day. However, consumption in the same year was an estimated 1,023,000 barrels per day and net imports were 505,000 bbld. It is predicted that Australia's oil demand will increase over the next decade, and that the continent will depend on imports for some 78 per cent of its requirements. At present, the main suppliers are the UAE, Malaysia, Vietnam and Papua New Guinea.

Woodside Petroleum and Santos are the largest Australian companies operating in the oil industry, international companies working in Australia include, ExxonMobil, Shell, Chevron, ConocoPhillips, Japex, Total, BHP Billiton, and Apache.

Australia's natural gas reserves, estimated at 110 billion cubic feet in January 2011, are amongst the largest in the Asia pacific region. The most concentrated reserves are located offshore of the north-western coast in the Carnarvon Basin, or Northwest Shelf. At present, natural gas is not a major source of energy in the Australian fuel mix (around 17 per cent), but consumption is predicted to rise rapidly, reaching 24 per cent of total energy consumption by 2020. In 2011, the country produced an estimated 1.489 billion cubic feet of natural gas, and consumed an estimated 973 billion cubic feet. (Source: EIA)

Around half of the gas that Australia produces is converted into LNG which can then be exported. Figures from the EIA show that in 2010, 70 per cent of Australia's LNG was exported to Japan, 21 per cent to China, five per cent to South Korea and four per cent of Taiwan.

Australia has proven resources of more than 15,000 million tonnes of high grade iron ore and is the world's fourth-largest producer of this commodity. Western Australia produces most of Australia's iron ore. The continent is also the world's largest producer of both bauxite and alumina, and the fourth-largest producer of aluminium. Australia exports three-quarters of its alumina, accounting for about half the world's alumina trade. Australia is also a world leader in the export of lead and zinc, which are mined mainly in NSW, Queensland, Tasmania and Western Australia.

Several major deposits of copper were discovered in the 1980s. More than half the country's output of refined copper, about 250,000 tonnes, is exported. Australia ranks third in world nickel production, and exports nearly all of it. Australia is the leading producer of retile, zircon, monazite and alluvial ilmenite - all minerals with high-technology applications.

There has been a significant upsurge in gold exploration since the early 1980s, placing Australia third among the developed nations producers; gold ranks third among Australia's export-income earners. Advances in gold mining and processing technology have meant that the industry has grown dramatically. There are substantial proven resources, mainly in Western Australia and Queensland.

Australia's reasonably assured uranium resources represent nearly a third of the western world's uranium resources. The major deposits are in the Northern Territory, South Australia and Western Australia. Uranium mining and export are permitted from only the Ranger mine in the Northern Territory and the Olympic Dam mine in South Australia and are subject to stringent safeguard requirements. Nabarlek ceased production in 1988. Annual production is approximately 8,000 tons a year.

The Australian Nuclear Science and Technology Organisation (ANSTO), a statutory body, helped develop Australia's uranium resources and its use of various forms of nuclear energy. ANSTO's research establishment, the major centre for peaceful nuclear research in Australia, is part of the Lucas Heights Research Laboratories, about 30km south-west of Sydney, NSW. It operates Australia's two nuclear reactors, used only for research.

Mineral production is shown on the following table:

Mineral, Oil & Gas Production, 2008-09

Mineral	Value AUS$ million
Bauxite	855
Copper (metal content)	5,775
Gold (metal content)	8,260
Iron ore & concentrate	34,217
Lead (metal content)	1,112
Nickel (metal content)	3,210
Silver (metal content)	1,073
Uranium oxide	1,007
Zinc (metal content)	2,377
Black coal (saleable)	61,392
Brown coal	na
Crude oil	11,971
Condensate	4,156
Natural gas	3,646
Liquefied natural gas	10,830
Diamonds	432
Salt	412
Ilmenite	97
Phosphate rock	147
Synthetic rutile	414
Leucoxene	19
Manganese ore	1,880

Source: Australian Bureau of Statistics 8415.0

Australia produces opals, sapphires and diamonds (22,791,833 ct in 2004-05). (All figures sourced from the ABS are quoted with the permission of the Australian Bureau of Statistics)

Energy

Australia's total energy consumption was estimated at 5.590 quadrillion Btu in 2009. Per capita energy consumption in 2005 was an estimated 264 million Btu. (Source: EIA)

In 2010 Australia had an electricity generating capacity of 59.1 gigawatts. In the same year electricity generation was 228.17 billion kilowatthours (Bkwh) of electricity (up from 215.8 billion kWh in 2003), whilst electricity consumption was 213.54 billion kWh. Approximately 75 per cent of electricity was produced from coal with around 55 per cent being black coal. In June 2004, the Australian government forecast that energy demands would grow 50 per cent by 2020. The Government 'White Paper' on energy endorsed the increased use of coal, which was controversial with environmental groups and the public.

As of 2004, Australia generated 2.5 BkWh of electricity from renewable sources. Australia's Mandatory Renewable Energy Target (MRET) is set at 9.5 BkWh of total electricity generation. There are many investments currently being made in the renewable energy sector across Australia.

The Australian Energy Regulator (AER) was formed in 2005. As of 2007, this body assumed responsibility for electricity transmission and wholesale energy prices, natural gas transmission and prices and the enforcement of market rules. (Source: EIA)

Manufacturing

The manufacturing sector produced AU$105.2b of IVA in 2008-09. The food product manufacturing subdivision contributed U$16.5 billion, followed by primary metal and metal product manufacturing ($14.05 bn) and machinery and equipment manufacturing with $11.8 bn. The manufacturing industry produced $420.9 billion sales and service income and paid out $53.2 bn wages and salaries. Employment in manufacturing amounted to 1,007,800 in 2008-09.

The manufacturing sector continues to dominate Australia's merchandise exports, accounting for 50.7 per cent of total export in 2006-07. Over the five years to 2006-07, the value of exports of manufactured goods has risen from A$69,111 million to A$85,343 million. Japan, New Zealand and the USA imported A$8.5 billion, A$7.7 billion and A$7.4 billion respectively in 2006-07.

Principal manufactured items are food, beverage and tobacco products, with production centred mainly in Queensland; machinery and equipment, based mainly in South Australia; metal products and the printing, publishing and recorded media industries are largely based in New South Wales. Manufacture of goods in the textile, clothing, footwear and leather industries takes place mainly in Victoria. (Source: Australian Bureau of Statistics)

Manufacturing Industry, 2010-11

Industry subdivision	Wages & salaries $m	Industry Value Added $m	Employment end of June
Food product manufacturing	9,619	17,754	206,658
Beverage and tobacco product manufacturing	1,968	6,561	30,827
Textile, leather, clothing and footware	1,531	2,807	44,218
Wood product	2,137	4,105	44,319
Pulp, paper and converted paper products	1,520	2,966	20,789
Printing	2,347	4,075	45,150
Petroleum and coal products	586	1,797	6,003
Basic chemical and chemical products	3,709	8,766	44,646
Polymer product and rubber product	2,753	4,881	45,573
Non-metallic mineral product	2,712	5,437	41,689
Primary metal and metal product	4,669	9,528	56,652
Fabricated metal product	6,221	10,683	118,887
Transport equipment	5,137	8,745	83,245
Machinery and equipment	6,739	10,696	107,805
Furniture and other manufacturing	1,470	2,632	39,456
TOTAL	53,117	101,4349	935,987

Source: Australian Bureau of Statistics. 81550DO001_201011

Service Industries

Australia's service industries account for an estimated 70 per cent of the country's economy.

The following table shows service industry sectors according to GVA:

Industry Value Added and No. of employees, 2005-06

Service	A$m	Average annual growth 2001-06 %
Wholesale trade	44,886	4.0
Retail trade	53,242	3.8
Accommodation, cafes and restaurants	20,204	4.2
Transport and storage	42,037	4.7
Communication services	25,331	5.8
Finance and insurance services	65,883	3.6
Property and business services	108,434	3.0
Government administration and defence	35,195	1.6
Education (private)	38,556	1.5
Health and community services (private)	55,455	4.2
Cultural and recreational services	13,506	4.5
Personal and other services	17,686	2.6

Source: ABS, 1301.0 Year Book Australia, 2008

Average annual total employment in the service industries over 2006-07 was 7,724,600 people, and represented three quarters of all employment. Most people were employed in the retail sector (1.4 million people). Real estate and business services employed around 1.2 million, Health and community services employed just over one million, and the Education sector employed around 718,000 people.

Tourism

Tourism accounted for A$37.6 billion of total GDP in 2005-06 (3.9 per cent), an increase of 5.5 per cent over the previous year. Domestic visitors generated 75.8 per cent of tourism industry GDP whilst international visitors generated 24.2 per cent.

There were almost 5.5 million international visitor arrivals to Australia during 2005-06, which represented an increase of 1.4 per cent on the previous year. Growth over the preceding two years was stronger, at 6.9 per cent and 8.6 per cent. Most international visitors came from New Zealand, the UK, Japan and the USA.

Tourism continues to contribute significantly to employment and Australia's exports. The tourism industry share of total employment fell slightly in 2005-06 to 4.6 per cent. The sector contributed 11 per cent of total exports of goods and services ($20 billion) in the same year.

Tourism Australia, URL: www.tourism.australia.com, http://www.australia.com

AUSTRALIA

Agriculture

Agriculture, hunting and forestry employed 515,000 people in 2009-09. Gross value of agricultural production rose from A$28,764 million in 2009-10 to A$31,443 million in 2010-11. In 2005-06, the value of Australian agricultural production was A$37 billion; the value of crop production rose to A$19.6 billion, benefiting from good seasonal conditions and increased prices, whilst the value of livestock products rose to A$5.8 billion as a result of the increased value of milk and eggs offsetting a fall in wool prices. The value of slaughterings and other disposals (such as exports) fell to A$12 billion:

There are about 127,500 properties in Australia that have an estimated value of agricultural operations of A$20,000 or more. These cover about 470 hectares, or 61 per cent of the total land area. The agricultural sector accounts for approximately 20 per cent of Australia's total export income.

Australia is the world's largest wool producing country, producing around a quarter of total world production. However, worldwide production has been declining over the past decade due to competition from cheaper synthetic fibres; since 1990, Australian wool production has almost halved, to around 475,000 tonnes in 2005. Most of Australia's wool is exported, mainly to China, Italy, Taiwan and India. In 2006, the gross value of wool was estimated at just over A$2 billion. Meat is another key sector and the country's beef products are the highest earning rural export commodity.

Until 1994-95 Australia supplied about 14 per cent of the world wheat market and average exports were 15 million tonnes. The drought of 1994-95 reduced the annual crop to under 9 million tonnes. The yield rose to over 10 million tonnes in 2002-03, contributing to a total cereals for grain value of A$7,604.8 million in 2006. Total production in 2008-09 was put at 21.8 million tonnes. Sugar is another major crop and Australia is one of the word's top sugar exporters. 37,822,000 tonnes were produced in 2005, yielding an income of A$997.7 million. Sugar production in 2009-10 was put at 31 million tonnes. It is exported mainly to Canada and the far East. Queensland produces about 95 per cent of Australia's total output.

There had been a reduction in rice production, down to 339,000 tonnes in 2005 from 1,643,000 in 2001; the area cultivated for the crop was reduced from 159,000 ha in 2001 to 51,000 ha in 2002. However, in recent years rice production had begun to increase again and figures for 2009-10 show that production was at 197,000 tonnes. Cotton production has also declined, from 698,000 tonnes in 2000 to 563,000 tonnes in 2005; again, the amount of land used to grow this crop has been reduced (from 435,000 ha to 304,000 ha.). Figures for 2009-10 show that the land used for cotton production had begun to increase after years of decline and was up to 196,000 ha with 352,000 tonnes being produced.

The Australian wine and grape industry experienced a second consecutive record harvest in 2004-05 with increased wine production levels. 1,925,490 tonnes of grapes were crushed in 2004-05; beverage wine production was a record 1,422.8 million litres, an increase of 1.3 per cent on 2003-04. Exports of Australian produced wine increased by 14.6 per cent, reaching 669.7 million litres and the value of these exports increased by 8.9 per cent, to A$2.7 billion. There was a drop of 0.6 per cent in beverage wine production in 2005-06; however, exports grew by 7.8 per cent to 722.2 million litres. The main markets are the UK, US, Canada, Sweden, New Zealand and Japan. The main grape-growing areas are in South Australia, Victoria, NSW and Western Australia.

Gross Value of Commodities Produced, 2011

Commodity	$m
Crops	
Cereals for grain	9,845
Cotton (inc. value of cotton lint and cotton seed)	1,902
Legumes for grain	953
Grapes	1,013
Nursery production	1,263
Oilseeds	1,328
Sugar cane cut for crushing	950
Vegetables	3,338
Total crops	25,048
Livestock slaughterings & other disposals	
Apples	264,401
Bananas	302,173
Mangoes	44,342
Selected Vegetables	
Cattle & calves	7,824
Sheep & lambs	2,862
Pigs	919
Poultry	2,077
Other livestock	12
Total livestock slaughterings & other disposals	13,795
Livestock Products	
Wool (inc. dead wool & wool on skins)	2,673
Whole milk	3,932
Eggs	572
Total livestock products	7,177
Total agriculture	46,020

Source: Australian Bureau of Statistics 7106.0

The period 2001-07 was marked by below average rainfall, leading to the worst drought in over a century. Conditions were so bad, particularly in rural areas, that a significant number of farmers in South Australia, Victoria and NSW abandoned their crops. In May 2007, heavy rains fell in the South Eastern regions, giving Australians hope that an agricultural watering ban could be avoided, and in January 2008, heavy rains flooded parts of NSW and Queensland, but analysts thought it too early to judge the drought over.

Forestry

The extensive forests in the higher rainfall zones of eastern and south-west Australia are highly productive. With plantations of exotic and native species, many of these forests are the resource base for major industries. Native forests cover nearly 163 million hectares, 127 million of which are dominated by eucalyptus. Plantations for timber production total about 1.8 million hectares.

The value of exports of forest products in 2005-06 totalled A$2.1 billion, of which 40 per cent were woodchips and 28 per cent paper and paperboard products. The value of imports of forest products over the same year was A$4.0 billion, indicating a trade deficit in forest products of A$1.9 billion over the year. (Source: 1301 Year Book Australia, 2008)

Fishing

Many varieties of fish are caught commercially, the main catch being tuna, prawns, rock lobster, abalone, scallops and oysters. In 2005-06, some 240,980 tonnes were caught, with a total value of A$2.133 million. In quantity terms, production declined by 13 per cent during 2005-06, with finfish (other than tuna), prawns and rock lobster the major contributors to the total; however, the gross value of the catch increased by one per cent, the first rise in five years. Main importers of Australian fish are Japan, Hong Kong and the USA. (Source: 3101 Year Book Australia, 2008)

COMMUNICATIONS AND TRANSPORT

Visa Information

With the exception of citizens from New Zealand who are automatically issued visas at the passport control point, all travellers must obtain a visa or an Electronic Travel Authority. The ETA is an electronically stored authority for travel to Australia for tourism, short-term business or elective study purposes. It allows multiple entries for stays of up to three months for people from the USA, Canada, and the EU (except Bulgaria, Cyprus, Czech Republic, Estonia, Hungary, Latvia, Lithuania, Poland, Romania, Slovak Republic and Slovenia). The ETA is valid for 12 months from date of issue, or for the life of the passport if it is less than 12 months. Visitors not eligible for an ETA, or requiring a longer stay, should apply for Tourist (Non ETA) and Business Short-stay (Non ETA) visas. There are also student visas, employers' visas for overseas workers and sponsored family visitor visas available. Further information is available at the Australian High Commission.

Customs Restrictions

There are strict laws prohibiting or restricting the entry of drugs, steroids, firearms and weapons and certain articles subject to quarantine in Australia. The following items should also be declared: animals, foodstuffs, plants and plant products, animal products, wildlife and wildlife products, cordless telephones, facsimile and CB radios, prescription medicines, motor vehicles, caravans and trailers, yachts and leisure craft. Business samples should also be declared. National heritage items and fauna and flora should not be taken out of the country without a permit.

Most goods imported into Australia are exempt from import restrictions, although many (with the exception of textiles, clothing, footwear, cars and agricultural machinery) are subject to a customs duty of up to 5 per cent. Most customs duties have been abolished on trade between Australia and New Zealand, with all import licensing and tariff quotas removed. The Australian consulate or relevant customs board should be contacted for further details.

Transport

Because of the great distances involved and the distribution of most of the population around the State capitals, the transport network is extensive, and includes nearly 840,000 km of roads, 240,000 km of unduplicated air routes and 40,000 km of government railways.

The State governments deal mainly with roads, ports, intrastate shipping and railways. The Federal Government deals with shipping and air transport between States and Territories and the Australian National Railways network. In addition, the Federal Government maintains an interest in all transport matters and financially assists State railway and road construction projects.

National Airlines

In 1992 the Government introduced measures to deregulate air services, including allowing Qantas to operate on domestic routes and working towards the development of a single aviation market for Australia and New Zealand. The government sold its stake in Qantas and sold Australian Airlines to Qantas. (URL: http://www.quantas.com.au)

International Airports

The main international airports in Australia are: Perth, Adelaide, Melbourne, Sydney, Brisbane, Cairns and Darwin.

Railways

Australia's railways are owned and operated mainly by government. New South Wales, Victoria, Queensland and Western Australia have their own railway systems. The National Rail Corporation, established in 1991, is a commercial organisation, separate from government involvement. The metropolitan railways in Adelaide are owned and operated by the South Australian Government. The Federal Government railways are run by the Australian National Railways Commission trading as Australian National.

Privately-owned railways operate in each State serving mining, agricultural and industrial areas. The largest private railway operations serve iron-ore mining in the north-west of Western Australia. Queensland has an extensive tramway network to serve mills in sugar-producing areas.

All state capitals have a suburban railway system. Melbourne and Adelaide have a tram system.

National Rail Corporation, URL: http://www.nationalrail.com.au/

Rail Australia, URL: http://www.railaustralia.com.au

Roads

Australian roads are funded approximately equally by all three tiers of government. The 16,000 km National Highway System, which links all capitals, is a federal responsibility. Federal road programs have been funded since the early 1980s from the excise levied on petrol and diesel fuel. More recently, additional funds have been allocated to the states and territories for public transport, road safety research and rail systems. Traffic drives on the left.

Shipping

Australia trades with about 200 countries and territories and annually exports almost 260 million tonnes of freight by sea. Imports by sea total almost 24 million tonnes. Australia is served mainly by foreign-flag vessels in its overseas trade. The Australian flag share of tonnage is about 4.2 per cent. The government has recently restructured the shipping industry, cutting manning on Australian ships.

Ports and Harbours

Australian ports are the responsibility of State government authorities and departments or private operators. Australia has about 70 ports of commercial significance. The main ports serve the State capitals and industrial and mining centres. These include: Sydney; Melbourne; Geelong; Fremantle; Adelaide; Brisbane.

HEALTH

The central government determines policy but the states and territories are primarily responsible for delivering public health services. Funding comes from both Commonwealth and state/territory level. The aim of Australia's national health service is to give universal access to health care while allowing choice for individuals through private sector involvement in delivery and financing. In 1984 the Government introduced Medicare, a health insurance system. Medicare is funded by a range of taxes including income tax and a levy of 1.5 per cent on taxable incomes above a certain rate. The Government also provides a number of welfare benefits including pensions, unemployment, sickness, and family allowance. Private health insurance provides some 11 per cent of total national health care funding.

According to World Health Organization statistics, total expenditure on healthcare in 2009 amounted to 8.7 per cent of GDP, equivalent to some US$3,945 per capita. Most of the financing was through Government resources (66.0 per cent). Some 33.6 per cent was from private sources, over 59 per cent in the form of out-of-pocket expenditure.

In the period 2005-10 there were estimated to be 62,800 physicians (29.9 per 10,000 population), 201,300 nurses and midwives (95.9 per 10,000 population), 14,500 dentists (6.9 per 10,000 population), 21,800 pharmaceutical personnel (10.4 per 10,000 population), and 1,012 community and health workers. There were an estimated 38 hospital beds and 3.9 psychiatric beds per 10,000 population.

The infant mortality rate (likelihood of dying before first birthday) was 4 per 1,000 live births and the under-fives mortality rate was 5 per 1,000 live births in 2010. The most common causes of childhood deaths are prematurity (20 per cent) and congenital anomalies (24 per cent). In 2010, the immunization coverage rates were: measles 94 per cent, diptheria & hepatitis 92 per cent. (Source: http://www.who.int, Global Health Statistics, 2012)

EDUCATION

School attendance is compulsory throughout Australia between the ages of six and 15, except in Tasmania where the leaving age is 16. In all States, tuition at government primary and secondary school is free. The Federal Government is responsible for education services in Australia's external territories. The States and Territories are responsible for providing education services although the Federal Government provides grants. Most Australian children begin school before the compulsory school age and many attend pre-school centres within the school system that provide sessions for children from the age of four. In 2008, an estimated 82 per cent of pre-school children attended pre-primary schools.

Primary/Secondary Education

Secondary schooling begins in year seven or year eight and continues to year 12. The most common type of secondary school is the co-educational comprehensive or multi-purpose high school, offering a wide range of subjects and activities. Schools of the Air uses two-way radio to provide 'classroom' experience for children in the remote parts of Australia.

In 2010, there were 9,468 schools in Australia, 6,743 of which were government schools and 2,725 were non-government schools (1,708 Catholic, 1017 Independent). This breaks down to: 6,357 primary schools, 1,409 secondary schools, 1,286 combined primary/secondary schools and 416 special schools. In the same year, there were 3,510,875 full-time school students; 66 per cent of these attended a government-run school.

There were an estimated 162,831 indigenous full-time school students were enrolled in Australian schools in 2010, reflecting a 4 per cent increase on the previous year. The Northern Territory had the highest proportion of students identified as indigenous (41 per cent) whereas Queensland and NSW had the highest numbers (50,000).

In 2010, non-government teaching staff numbers increased by 32 per cent from 77,490 to 102,410 while government teaching staff numbers increased by 10 per cent from 166,507 to 183,725. The full-time equivalent student to teaching staff ratio in Australia is estimated at 15.7: 1 for primary schools (down from 17.3: 1) and in secondary schools it stands at 12.0: 1 (down from 12.6 : 1). (Source: ABS, Australia, 2010, 4221.0)

Higher Education

There are 36 publicly funded universities, four colleges and two private universities. In 2006, 984,100 students were enrolled on higher education courses. This represented a 3 per cent increase on the number in 2005. 55 per cent of the students were women, and around 66 per cent of the total were full time. The most popular subjects were those in the field of management and commerce. In 2004, just 0.9 per cent of students were indigenous (8,895), down 1 per cent on the previous year.

Vocational Training

The Australian National Training Authority co-ordinates the vocational and educational training system. There are over 4,400 registered training organisations in Australia, most of them private; however, most vocational students study under publicly-funded training providers. These are predominately government-administered TAFE colleges or institutes. During 2006, there were 1.7 million students enrolled in a publicly-funded VET course. Enrolments by males aged 19 years or younger increased by 11 per cent, and females by 12 per cent, between 2005 and 2006.

RELIGION

About three-quarters of Australians profess Christianity. Of these about 26 per cent are Catholics and 18 per cent Anglican and 16 per cent Protestant. Many non-Christian faiths are followed, including Judaism (0.45 per cent), Buddhism (2.10 per cent), Hinduism (0.75 per cent) and Islam (1.7 per cent).

Australia's first woman bishop, Kay Goldsworthy, was consecrated in Perth, in May 2008. A minority of Australian Anglicans warned that the appointment would split the church. Opponents of the ordination of women include the head of the Sydney diocese, Archbishop Peter Jensen.

National Council of Churches in Australia, URL: http://www.ncca.org.au
President: The Revd. Michael Putney
National Office of the Anglican Church, URL: http://www.anglican.org.au/
Primate: Most Rev., Dr. Phillip Aspinall
Australian Catholic Bishops' Conference, URL: http://www.catholic.org.au
President: Most Rev Philip Wilson, Archbishop of Adelaide

COMMUNICATIONS AND MEDIA

In 2007, the government changed the rules on cross-media ownership. Greater cross-ownership of press and TV is now permitted. Higher levels of foreign ownership are also permitted. News Limited and John Fairfax Holdings are the largest newspaper publishers in metropolitan areas, with the Fairfax subsidiary Rural Press is one of the most important in regional areas.

Newspapers
Newspapers include:
The Age, URL: http://www.theage.com.au
The Courier-Mail, URL: http://www.news.com.au/couriermail
The Australian, URL: http://www.theaustralian.news.com.au/
The Sydney Morning Herald, URL: http://www.smh.com.au
The West Australian, URL: http://www.thewest.com.au

Broadcasting
Radio and television broadcasting services are provided by national, commercial, multicultural and public organisations. National (non-commercial) services are provided by the Australian Broadcasting Corporation (ABC), URL: http://www.thewest.com.au. The ABC comprises two national television services; three national radio networks; a local radio network; a 24-hour news and parliamentary broadcast radio service; Radio Australia, an external broadcasting service to the Asia-Pacific; and Australia Network, an international television service to the Asia-Pacific.

The Special Broadcasting Service (SBS) provides multilingual radio and multicultural television services and financial and programme support to public broadcasters presenting multilingual programs. T. SBS television broadcasts programming in over 60 languages while the national radio service broadcasts 650 hours of programming each week in 68 languages - more than any other radio network in the world.

There are currently three main retail pay television service providers in Australia. The largest operator is Foxtel, which provides more than 100 channels to its 1.44 million subscribers. Foxtel's service is 100 per cent digital.

There are 274 commercial radio licences over more than 100 licence areas in Australia. Major commercial radio network owners include DMG Radio Australia, Macquarie Regional Radioworks, Fairfax Media, the Australian Radio Network, Austereo Pty Ltd, and Broadcast Operations Group.

The Australian Communications and Media Authority is responsible for the regulation of broadcasting, radio communications, telecommunications and online content.

The National Transmission Agency operates Australia's transmission stations. Radio Australia is the international shortwave service of the ABC. It broadcasts in English 24 hours a day and for varying periods in Indonesian, Mandarin, Cantonese, French, Japanese, Neo-Melanesia (Pidgin), Thai and Vietnamese.

Commercial radio and television stations operate under licenses from the Australian Broadcasting Tribunal. The tribunal has powers to hold public inquiries into the granting, renewal and transfer of commercial and public broadcasting licenses as well as into such matters as setting standards of broadcasting practice. There are more than 170 commercial

AUSTRALIA

radio stations, most broadcasting on the AM band and a growing proportion (approximately 20 per cent) on the FM band. Australia's public broadcasting stations are non-commercial, and cater for education, community or special interests.

Australian Broadcasting Corporation (ABC), URL: http://www.abc.net.au/

The major news agencies are Australia Associated Press (http://aap.com.au/) and ABC (http://www.abc.net.au/news/default.htm).

Post and Telecommunications
The major post operator is Australia Post. In 2011, there were an estimated 10.5 million mainline telephones in use, and over 24 million mobile cellular phones. Around 15.8 million Australians regularly use the internet and there are over 15 million hosts. The National Broadbank Network (NBN) was launched in New South Wales in May 2011.

ENVIRONMENT

Nearly seven million square kilometres, or 91 per cent of Australia, is covered by native vegetation. There are 17 Australian properties on the World Heritage List: The Great Barrier Reef, the Tasmanian Wilderness, the Wet Tropics of Queensland and Shark Bay, Kakadu National Park, Uluru-Kata Tjuta National Park, Purnululu National Park, Willandra Lakes region and the Tasmanian Wilderness, the Australian Fossil Mammal Sites (Naracoorte/Riversleigh), Lord Howe Island Group, Central Eastern Rainforest Reserves (Australia), Fraser Island, Macquarie Island, Heard Island and McDonald Islands and the Greater Blue Mountains Area. Approximately 10.5 per cent of mainland Australia's natural environment is protected by national environmental legislation.

Australia is one of the most biologically diverse countries on the planet. It is home to more than one million species of plants and animals, many of which are found nowhere else in the world. It is estimated that as many as 85 per cent of marine species found in southern Australian waters occur nowhere else. About 85 per cent of flowering plants, 84 per cent of mammals, more than 45 per cent of birds, and 89 per cent of inshore, freshwater fish are unique to Australia.

Australia's major environmental problems include soil erosion and salinity, desertification, and limited fresh water supplies. Australia's soils and seas are among the most nutrient poor and unproductive in the world. Australia is the driest inhabited continent on earth, with the

least amount of water in rivers, the lowest run-off and the smallest area of permanent wetlands of all the continents. Pollution is one of Australia's most serious problems and the vast majority of marine pollution is caused by land based activities. Approximately 7 per cent of Australia's marine territory is identified as marine protected areas.

Energy related carbon emissions were estimated at 437 million metric tons in 2008, of which coal 55 per cent and oil 31 per cent. Per capita carbon emissions in 2008 were an estimated 20.8 metric tons. Australia's energy consumption is dominated by coal, and the fuel share of carbon emissions is similarly dominated by coal. Figures for 2010 put carbon dioxide emissions from the consumption of fossil fuels at 405.34 million metric tons, down from 411.60 million metric tons the previous year. (Source: EIA)

Australia is a party to the following international environmental agreements: Antarctic-Environmental Protocol, Antarctic-Marine Living Resources, Antarctic Seals, Antarctic Treaty, Biodiversity, Climate Change, Climate Change-Kyoto Protocol, Desertification, Endangered Species, Environmental Modification, Hazardous Wastes, Law of the Sea, Marine Dumping, Marine Life Conservation, Ozone Layer Protection, Ship Pollution, Tropical Timber 83, Tropical Timber 94, Wetlands, and Whaling.

On being sworn into office in December 2007, Prime Minister Rudd's first act was to sign documents ratifying the Kyoto Protocol on climate change, reversing the previous administration's policy. Australia's new stance on Kyoto isolates the US as the only developed nation not to have ratified the treaty. However, Mr Rudd subsequently adopted conservative greenhouse emissions target cuts of between 5 and 15 per cent by 2020. Under his successor, Julia Gillard, the Australian Senate backed a controversial law on pollution. The Clean Energy Act will force the country's 500 worst-polluting companies to pay a tax on their carbon emissions from 1 July 2012.

SPACE PROGRAMME

Australia first launched a satellite in the 1960s. It provided launch facilities until 1970 when launch activities moved to French Guiana. Its space-related activities are limited and are administered through various government agencies including the Department of Industry, Innovation, Science, Research and Tertiary Education. Its current priorities are protecting national security; developing domestic space industry; support research; ensuring access to space services (including communications, global positioning and earth observation).
Australian Space Programme, URL: http://www.space.gov.au/Pages/default.aspx

AUSTRALIAN CAPITAL TERRITORY

Capital: Canberra (Population estimate: 375,000)

Chief Minister: Katy Gallagher

State Flag: At the centre of the gold fly is the coat of arms of the City of Canberra. The Southern Cross is set on a blue bar at the hoist. The flag uses the blue and gold of Canberra's city colours.

CONSTITUTION AND GOVERNMENT

Constitution
An area of 2,359 sq. km was transferred to the Commonwealth of Australia by the State of New South Wales in 1911, to become the Australian Capital Territory (ACT). A further 73 sq. km was transferred in 1915 to serve as a port. On 11 May 1989 self-government was proclaimed. Australia's capital, Canberra, is located in the north of the ACT.

Two Federal Senators and two Members of the Federal House of Representatives represent the Australian Capital Territory in the Australian Parliament.

Legislature
The Territory has an elected Legislative Assembly with 17 members (or MLAs) who serve a four year term. The Legislative Assembly is unique in having responsibilities and power to make law at both state and local level. All members vote to elect a Chief Minister, who in turn selects a maximum of four ministers to form a cabinet. The Chief Minister occupies the roles of State Premier and Mayor, and allocates ministerial responsibilities to each minister. Currently, the Assembly is divided in the following way: Australian Labor Party, 7 seats; Liberal Party, 6 seats; ACT Greens, 4 seats.

Legislative Assembly for the Australian Capital Territory, Civic Square, London Circuit, GPO Box 1020, Canberra ACT 2601. Tel: +61 (0)2 6205 0439, fax: +61 (0)2 6205 3109, e-mail: secretariat@parliament.act.gov.au, URL: http://www.parliament.act.gov.au
Speaker: Vicki Dunne

Cabinet (as at May 2013)
Chief Minister, Treasurer, Minister for Health, Minister for Industrial Relations: Hon. Katy Gallagher
Deputy Chief Minister, Treasurer, Minister for Economic Development, Minister for Tourism, Sport and Recreation: Hon. Andrew Barr
Attorney General, Minister for Police and Emergency Services, Minister for Environment & Sustainable Development: Hon. Simon Corbell (page 1408)
Minister for Education and Training, Minister for Disability, Children and Young People, Minister for the Arts, Minister for Women, Minister for Multicultural Affairs Minister for Racing and Gaming: Hon. Joy Burch

---

Minister for Minister for Territory and Municipal Services, Minister for Corrections, Minister for Housing, Minister for Aboriginal and Torres Strait Islander Affairs Minister for Ageing: Shane Rattenbury

Ministries
Office of the Premier, ACT Legislative Assembly, Civic Square, London Circuit, GPO Box 1020, Canberra ACT 2601, Australia. Tel: +61 2 6205 0439, fax: +61 2 6205 3109, e-mail: secretariat@act.gov.au, URL: http://www.legassembly.act.gov.au/
Chief Minister's Department, (GPO Box 158, Canberra ACT 2601) Canberra Nara Centre, Cnr Constitution Ave & London Circuit, Canberra City, Australia. Tel: +61 2 6207 5111, fax: +61 2 6207 0167, e-mail: cmdwebmaster@act.gov.au, URL: http://www.cmd.act.gov.au/
ACT Department of Education, Youth and Family Services, (PO Box 1584 Tuggeranong, ACT 2901) Manning Clark Offices, 186 Reed Street, Greenway, ACT 2900, Australia. Tel: +61 2 6207 5111, fax: +61 2 6205 9333, e-mail: decs.webmaster@act.gov.au, URL: http://www.decs.act.gov.au/
ACT Department of Justice and Community Safety, (GPO Box 158 Canberra ACT 2601) Level 3 GIO House, 250 City Walk, Canberra ACT 2601, Australia. Tel: +61 2 6207 0500, fax: +61 2 6207 0499, e-mail: jcs.webadmin@act.gov.au, URL: http://www.jcs.act.gov.au/main.html
ACT Department of Urban Services, (P.O. Box 158, Canberra City, ACT 2601) Macarthur House, 12 Wattle Street, Lyneham, ACT 2602, Australia. Tel: +61 2 6207 5111, e-mail: urbanservices@act.gov.au, URL: http://www.urbanservices.act.gov.au
ACT Department of Health, (GPO Box 825, Canberra ACT 2601) Level 2, North Building, London Circuit, Canberra City, ACT 2601, Australia. Tel: +61 2 6205 5111, fax: +61 2 6207 5775, e-mail: HealthACT@act.gov.au, URL: http://www.health.act.gov.au/
ACT Department of Treasury and Infrastructure, (GPO Box 158, Canberra City ACT 2601) Canberra Nara Centre, Cnr Constitution Ave & London Circuit, Canberra City, Australia. Tel: +61 2 6207 5111, fax: +61 2 6207 0167, e-mail: dtwebmaster@act.gov.au, URL: http://www.treasury.act.gov.au/
ACT Department of Disability, Housing and Community Services, GPO Box 158 Canberra ACT 2601, Australia. Tel: +61 2 62075111, e-mail: dhcs@act.gov.au, URL: http://www.dhcs.act.gov.au

Elections
Elections for the ACT Legislative Assembly take place every four years. The last Legislative Assembly election was held on 20 October 2012. The current Legislative Assembly is divided as follows: Australian Labour Party, 8 seats (up one seat); Liberal Party, 8 seats (up one seat); ACT Greens, one seat (down three seats).

LEGAL SYSTEM

The ACT Supreme Court consists of the Chief Justice and three Justices. It is known as the Court of Appeal when exercising its appellate jurisdiction. The Court of Appeal sits in February, May, August and November, usually for two weeks in each sitting.
Supreme Court, Knowles Place, Canberra City, ACT 2601, Australia. Tel: +61 6267 2707, fax: +61 6257 3668, URL: http://www.courts.act.gov.au/supreme
Chief Justice: Terence John Higgins

LOCAL GOVERNMENT

As well as the National Capital of Australia, Canberra is a self-governing city-state with more than 300,000 inhabitants.

AREA AND POPULATION

Area
The Australian Capital Territory (ACT) is the smallest of the Australian States and Territories, and is the only State/Territory without a sea border. The total area of the ACT is just over 2,400 sq. km. Temperatures in the ACT range from about 37°C degrees to -6°C. Average annual rainfall is about 630 mm, with just over 100 days of rain per year. There is an average of 7.5 hours per day of sunshine.

Population
The population in 2010 was an estimated 358,571, with an approximate annual growth rate of 1.5 per cent. Population density was estimated at 152.5 people per km^2. The majority of people live and work in the capital Canberra (population of over 300,000). Major statistical subdivisions of the city include Tuggeranong, 89,800; Belconnen, 85,600; and North Canberra, 40,800. In 2009, the median age of the ACT population was 33.7 years; the national median age of Australia's population was 36.6 years. The population is projected to reach 400,000 by 2018. It is also an ageing population. As of 2009, those aged 65 and over accounted for 10.2 per cent of the total population. This is set to increase to 21.9 per cent by 2059.

Births, Marriages, Deaths
There were 4,858 births registered in 2009 up from 4,804 in 2008. The fertility rate in the same year was 1.8 births per woman up from 1.7 in 2008. The number of deaths recorded in 2009 was 1,648 (a death rate of 5.6 per 1,000 people). There were 5.3 marriages per 1,000 residents in 2004. (Source: 1307.8 - Australian Capital Territory in Focus)

Regional Holidays 2014
10 March: Canberra Day

EMPLOYMENT

Labour Force (Trend)

	Unit	Jan. 2012	Jan. 2013
Civilian population 15 years and over	'000	296.0	302.6
Employed persons	'000	206.2	209.7
Unemployed persons	'000	7.6	9.9
Unemployment rate	%	3.6	4.5
Participation rate	%	72.2	72.7

Source: Labour Force, Australia, March 2013 (cat. no. 6202.0).

The following table shows employment by industry at the end of February 2006:

Employment by industry, February 2006

Sector	No. of employed
Agriculture, forestry, fishing	1,400
Mining	-
Manufacturing	4,500
Electricity, gas and water	1,200
Construction	11,100
Wholesale trade	4,300
Retail trade	20,700
Accommodation, cafes, restaurants	6,600
Transport and storage	4,200
Communication services	2,800
Finance and insurance	4,000
Property and business services	26,700
Government administration	46,100
Education	16,100
Health and community service	15,800
Cultural and recreational services	6,000
Personal and other services	7,700

Source: ABS 1307.8 - Australian Capital Territory in Focus, 2006

BANKING AND FINANCE

GDP/GNP, Inflation, National Debt
Gross State Product (at current prices) rose from A$19,994 million in 2005-06 to A$21,586 million in 2006-07, indicating growth of 8 per cent. The ACT Gross State Product in 2005-06 accounted for just 2.1 per cent of Australia's total Gross Domestic Product (the third lowest in Australia). GSP per capita in the same year was A$64,591 the third highest in Australia.

AUSTRALIAN CAPITAL TERRITORY

GSP grew by 0.9 per cent in the period 2009-10 in real terms compared to the national rate of 2.3 per cent. GSP amounted to A$27,773 million. The most significant contributors to GSP are Public administration and construction.

Gross State Product, Chain volume measures

Year	A$m	% change from previous year
2007-08	27,483	301
2008-09	28,618	4.1
2009-10	29,509	3.1
2010-11	30,455	3.2
2011-12	31,511	3.5

Source: Australian Bureau of Statistics 5220.0

The Consumer Price Index for Canberra (all items) rose by 2.5 per cent from 2001-02, by 3.3 per cent over 2002-03 and by 2.6 per cent over the year 2003-04 (slightly above the weighted average of eight capital cities in Australia of 2.4 per cent). The biggest rises in 2003-04 were in health (8 per cent) and housing (7 per cent). There were falls in the price of clothing and footwear (1 per cent) and recreation (2 per cent). (Source: Australian Bureau of Statistics)

Balance of Payments / Imports and Exports
ACT merchandise exports amounted to A$9 million in 2009, including arms & ammunition A$2.4 million and artwork and antiques A$2 million. Services were exported to the value of $1 billion and account for 99 per cent of the Territory's exports.

Chambers of Commerce and Trade Organisations
ACT and Region Chamber of Commerce and Industry, URL: http://www.actchamber.com.au

MANUFACTURING, MINING AND SERVICES

Manufacturing
While a major part of the Territory's economy centres around the Government sector, the manufacturing sector is also important. The manufacturing sector employed 5.1 per cent of the state's workforce in 2004-05 and contributed A$965 million in sales and service income. Printing, publishing and recorded media created the most revenue (A$291 million), followed by machinery and equipment manufacture (A$148 million in sales and service income).

Tourism
Tourism is a growth industry, with over 1.25 million visitors a year. The accommodation industry employed over 2,500 people in 2004, and the sector generated A$34.3 million over the year.

The following table shows tourist accommodation in 2006 and 2007:

Hotels, motels and guest houses	2006	2007
Establishments	59	57
Guest rooms	5,055	5,023
Bed spaces	14,145	14,885
Room occupancy rates %	69.3	69.3
Takings from accommodation A$'000	41,324.3	45,747.9

Source: Australian Bureau of Statistics (2007 Australian Capital Territory at a Glance, 1314.8)

Agriculture
Agricultural establishments numbered 88 in 2004 (down from 96 in 2002). The total area of agricultural land was 50,000 hectares in the same year (down from 52,000 in 2002). Livestock numbers in 2006 were: cattle and calves, 17,000; poultry, 376,600, and sheep and lambs, 111,000.

Agricultural production in 2006 produced an income of A$19.2 million, of which A$5.5 million was from crops, A$8.9 million from livestock products, and A$4.8 million from livestock slaughterings.

COMMUNICATIONS AND TRANSPORT

International Airports
Canberra International Airport, URL: http://www.canberraairport.com.au

HEALTH

In 2004, there were 1,945 medical practitioners in Australian Capital Territory, as well as 3,902 nurses and 250 dentists.

In the same year 52 per cent of the population was covered by private medical insurance; the national average rate of cover is 43 per cent.

EDUCATION

Primary/Secondary Education
In 2006 there were 95 government schools, and 44 non-government schools. Government primary and secondary students numbered 35,076 (continuing a downward trend since 1991), whilst non-government primary and secondary students numbered 24,460, an increase on previous years. The Apparent Retention Rate from Year 10 to Year 12 was 88.9 per cent (well above the national average of 76.1 per cent).

In 2006, there were 1,127 indigenous students in the Territory's schools. In the same year, there were 4,785 teachers.

Higher Education
There were four higher education institutions in 2004 with 26,031 students. Most attended the Australian National University (13,278) or the University of Canberra (10,248). The Australian Catholic University had 596 students enrolled, whilst the Australian Defense Force Academy had 1,909 students. 0.8 per cent (199) of students were indigenous.

Vocational Education and Training
In 2003 there were three vocational education and training institutions, with a total of 18,500 students.

COMMUNICATIONS AND MEDIA

Newspapers
The Canberra Times, URL: http://www.canberratimes.com.au

Telecommunications
In 2003, 80 per cent of households had access to a home computer, and 66 per cent of households had internet access. Both figures were well above the national average.

NEW SOUTH WALES

Capital: Sydney (Population estimate: 4.2 million)

Governor: Prof. Marie Bashir AC (page 1384)

State Flag: A British Blue Ensign on which is superimposed the state badge: the cross of St. George in red on a white disc; at the end of each arm of the cross is a gold, eight pointed star, and in the centre of the cross is a golden lion

CONSTITUTION AND GOVERNMENT

Constitution
The Governor is the Queen's representative and has all of Her Majesty's powers in the State with the exclusion of the power to appoint and terminate the appointment of the Governor. Advice on such appointments is tendered to Her Majesty by the Premier of the State. The Governor's most important duties include appointing the Executive Council and presiding at its meetings, appointing the Premier and other ministers from among the members of the executive Council, and summoning and dissolving the legislature.

Recent Events
At the end of February 2012, New South Wales was hit by devastating floods, 70 per cent of the state was either flooded or under threat.

Legislature
The Parliament of New South Wales consists of two Chambers: the Legislative Council and the Legislative Assembly.
Parliament of New South Wales, Parliament House, Macquarie Street, Sydney NSW 2000, Australia. Tel: +61 (0)2 9230 2111, URL: http://www.parliament.nsw.gov.au/

Upper House
The Legislative Council consists of 42 members, elected by the people of the State as a single electorate. Members serve for a term of office equivalent to two terms of the Legislative Assembly; that is, eight years. Half of the members retire or stand for re-election at every general election.
Legislative Council, Macquarie Street, Sydney, NSW 2000, Australia. Tel: +61 (0)29230 2319, fax: +61 (0)2 9230 2876, e-mail: council@parliament.nsw.gov.au: URL: http://www.parliament.nsw.gov.au/
President: Hon. Don Harwin MLC

Lower House
The Legislative Assembly consists of 93 members who serve a maximum period of four years.
Legislative Assembly, Macquarie Street, Sydney, NSW 2000, Australia. Tel: +61 (0)2 9230 2616, fax: +61 (0)2 9230 2828, e-mail: assembly@parliament.nsw.gov.au, URL: http://www.parliament.nsw.gov.au/
Speaker of the Legislative Assembly: Hon Shelley Hancock

Cabinet (as at June 2013)
Premier: Barry O'Farrell (page 1488)
Deputy Premier, Minister for Trade & Investment, Minister for Regional Infrastructure & Services: Andrew Stoner
Minister for Health, Minister for Medical Research: Jillian Skinner
Minister for Education: Adrian Piccoli
Minister for Police and Emergency Services, Minister for the Hunter, Vice President of the Executive Council: Michael Gallacher
Minister for Roads and Ports: Duncan Gay
Minister for Planning and Infrastructure: Brad Hazzard
Minister for Resources and Energy, Special Minister of State, Minister for the Central Coast: Chris Hartcher
Minister for Transport: Gladys Berejiklian
Minister for Tourism, Minister for the Arts: George Souris
Treasurer: Mike Baird
Minister for Finance and Services, Minister for the Illawarra: Greg Pearce
Minister for Primary Industries, Minister for Small Business: Katrina Hodgkinson
Minister for Ageing, Minister for Disability Services: Andrew Constance
Attorney General, Minister for Justice: Greg Smith
Minister for Local Government, Minister for the North Coast: Don Page
Minister for Family and Communities, Minister for Women: Pru Goward
Minister for Fair Trade: Anthony Roberts
Minister for Mental Health, Minister for Healthy Lifestyles, Minister for Western NSW: Kevin Humphries
Minister for the Environment, Minister for Heritage: Robyn Parker

---

Minister for Citizenship and Communities, Minister for Aboriginal Affairs: Victor Dominello
Minister for Sport and Recreation: Graham Annesley

Ministries
Premier's Department, Level 39, Governor Macquarie Tower, 1 Farrer Place, Sydney, NSW, Australia 2000 (GPO Box 5341, Sydney, Australia 2001). Tel: +61 2 9228 5555, fax: +61 2 9228 3522, e-mail: info@premiers.nsw.gov.au, URL: http://www.premiers.nsw.gov.au/
Department of Aboriginal Affairs, Level 13, Tower B, Centennial Plaza, 280 Elizabeth St, Sydney NSW 2000, Australia. Tel: +61 2 9219 0700, fax: +61 2 9219 0790, e-mail: enquiries@daa.nsw.gov.au, URL: http://www.daa.nsw.gov.au/
Department of Ageing, Disability and Home Care, Level 13, 83 Clarence Street, Sydney NSW 2000, Australia. Tel: +61 2 8270 2000, fax: +61 2 9689 2879, e-mail: service@dadhc.nsw.gov.au, URL: http://www.dadhc.nsw.gov.au/
Department of Community Services, Level 25, 9 Castlereagh Street, Sydney NSW 1044, Australia. Tel: +61 2 9228 5360, fax: +61 2 9228 5366, e-mail: carmel.tebbutt@juvjus.minister.nsw.gov.au, URL: http://www.community.nsw.gov.au/
Department of Education and Training, Level 2, 35 Bridge Street, Sydney, NSW 2000, (GPO Box 33, Sydney, NSW 2001) Australia. Tel: +61 2 9561 8000, fax: +61 2 9561 8185, e-mail: webteam@det.nsw.edu.au, URL: http://www.det.nsw.edu.au
Department of Fair Trading, 1 Fitzwilliam Street, Parramatta, NSW 2150, Australia. Tel: +61 2 9895 0111, fax: +61 2 9895 0222, e-mail: enquiry@fairtrading.nsw.gov.au, URL: http://www.dft.nsw.gov.au/
Department of Housing, 2223-239 Liverpool Road, Ashfield NSW Australia 2131, Australia (Locked Bag 4001, Ashfield BC NSW Australia 1800). Tel: +61 2 8753 8000, fax: 8753 8888, e-mail: feedback@housing.nsw.gov.au, URL: http://www.housing.nsw.gov.au
Department of Commerce - Office of Industrial Relations, 1 Oxford Street, Darlinghurst, NSW 2010 (PO Box 847, Darlinghurst, NSW 1300), Australia. Tel: +61 2 131 628, fax: +61 2 9020 4700, e-mail: info@lspc.nsw.gov.au, URL: http://www.dir.nsw.gov.au
Department of Juvenile Justice, Levels 5, 8, 10, Roden Cutler House, 24 Campbell Street, Haymarket 2000 (PO Box K399, Haymarket 1240), Australia. Tel: +61 02 9289 3333, fax: +61 2 9289 3399, e-mail: djj@djj.nsw.gov.au, URL: http://www.djj.nsw.gov.au/
Department of Infrastructure, Planning and Natural Resources, 20 Lee St Sydney 2000, (GPO Box 3927, Sydney 2001), Australia. Tel: +61 2 9762 8000, fax +61 2 9762 8701, e-mail: information@planning.nsw.gov.au, URL: http://www.dipnr.nsw.gov.au
Department of Local Government, 5 O'Keefe Avenue, Nowra, NSW, (Locked Bag 3015, Nowra, NSW 2541), Australia. Tel: +61 2 4428 4100, fax: 61 2 4428 4199, e-mail: dlg@dlg.nsw.gov.au, URL: http://www.dlg.nsw.gov.au
Department of Mineral Resources, Minerals and Energy House, 29-57 Christie Street, St Leonards, NSW 2065 (PO Box 536, St Leonards, NSW 1590), Australia. Tel: +61 2 9901 8888, fax: +61 2 9901 8777, e-mail: webcoord@minerals.nsw.gov.au, URL: http://www.minerals.nsw.gov.au
Department of Public Works and Services, McKell Building, 2-24 Rawson Place, Sydney, NSW 2000, Australia. Tel: +61 2 9372 8877, fax: +61 2 9372 8640, e-mail: feedback@dpws.nsw.gov.au, URL: http://www.dpws.nsw.gov.au/Home.htm
Department of State and Regional Development, Level 35, Governor Macquarie Tower, 1 Farrer Place, PO Box N818, Sydney NSW 1220, Australia. Tel: +61 2 9228 3111, fax: +61 2 9228 3626, e-mail: invest@nswg.co.uk, URL: http://www.business.nsw.gov.au/
Department of Transport, Level 17, 227 Elizabeth Street, Sydney NSW 2000 (GPO Box 1620, Sydney NSW 2001), Australia. Tel: +61 2 9268 2800, fax: +61 2 9268 2900, e-mail: mail@transport.nsw.gov.au, URL: http://www.transport.nsw.gov.au/
Department of Lands, Level 3, 1 Prince Albert Road, Queen's Square, Sydney NSW 2000, (GPO Box 15, Sydney NSW 2001), Australia. Tel: +61 2 9228 6666, fax: + 61 2 9236 7632, URL: http://www.lands.nsw.gov.au

Elections
Both Houses of Parliament of New South Wales are directly elected by all the citizens of New South Wales aged 18 and over. Elections take place every four years. Elections for the 55th Legislature were held on 26 March 2011. The whole of the Legislative Assembly and half of the Legislative Council was up for election. The incumbent Australian Labor Party which had been in power for sixteen years was defeated by the Liberal-National coalition led by Barry O'Farrell.

The Legislative Assembly is made up of the following political parties: Liberal/National Coalition Party, 69 seats (Liberal 51 seats, National 18); Labour, 20 seats; Greens, 1 seat, Independents 3 seats.

The Legislative Council currently consists of: Australian Labour Party, 14 seats; Liberal/National Coalition, 19 seats; The Greens, 5 seats; Christian Democratic Party, 2 seats; Shooters Party, 2 seats.

LEGAL SYSTEM

The New South Wales court system consists of the Supreme Court, Compensation Court, Coroner's Court, District Court, Drug Court, Land and Environment Court, and local courts. The Supreme Court comprises the Chief Justice, the President of the Court of Appeal, 10 Judges of Appeal, one Chief Judge at Common Law, one Chief Judge in Equity, 33 Judges, eight Acting Judges, and four Masters.

Supreme Court of New South Wales, Law Courts Building, Queens Square, 184 Phillip Street, Sydney, NSW 2000 (GPO Box 3, Sydney, NSW 2001), Australia. Tel: +61 28 9230 8111, fax: +61 28 9230 8628, e-mail: Supreme_Court@agd.nsw.gov.au, URL: http://www.lawlink.nsw.gov.au/sc
Chief Justice: Hon. Tom. Bathurst QC
Attorney General: Hon. Gregory Smith

LOCAL GOVERNMENT

New South Wales is divided into 14 regions: Central West, Far West, Hunter, Illawara, Murrumbidgee, Murray, Mid-North Coast, Northern, North Western, Richmond-Tweed, South Eastern, Sydney Inner, Sydney Outer, and Sydney Surrounds. There are Shire Councils, Municipal Councils, and City Councils.

New South Wales Department of Local Government, URL: http://www.dlg.nsw.gov.au/dlg/dlghome/dlg_home.asp

AREA AND POPULATION

Area
The area of New South Wales is 800,628 sq. km, equivalent to 10.4 per cent of the total area of Australia. Lord Howe Island, situated off the South Pacific coastline 702 km northeast of Sydney, is officially part of New South Wales and is included in its administration. The state is defined by four regions: the coast, the tableland, the western slopes of the Great Dividing Range, and the western plains.

The climate of NSW is temperate; however, very high temperatures can occur in the north-west, and it can turn very cold in the south.

In June 2007, gale-force winds and flood waters forced the evacuation of thousands of people in New South Wales. At least nine people were killed by the heavy storms.

Population
Although it accounts for only 10 per cent of the total area of Australia, New South Wales is home to 33.1 per cent of the country's total population. The population is the highest of all the Australian states and territories; at the end of June 2011, there were 7.3 million inhabitants, an increase of 1.1 per cent) on the previous year. Net overseas migration is the largest contributor to the population increase. Around 62.9 per cent of the total NSW population lives in the Sydney Statistical Division. The population is expected to reach 8.6 million by 2036.

Most of the population (67.1 per cent in June 2009) is aged between 15 and 64 years, with 18.9 per cent aged under 14 years and 13.9 per cent aged 65 years or over. The median age in 2009 was 37.1 years.

Births, Marriages, Deaths
There were around 97,900 live births registered in New South Wales in 2009, up from 92,300 in 2008. There were 48,800 deaths in 2009 In 2008 state lost 24,000 people through interstate migration in 2006, but 42,200 people moved to NSW from overseas over the year.

The fertility rate in 2008 was 2.23 children per woman, and life expectancy was 78 years for men and 83 years for women. Infant mortality was 4.6 deaths per 1,000 children surviving their first year. Marriages numbered 36,900 in 2003 (5.5 per 1,000 population), while divorces numbered 16,300 (2.4 per 1,000 population). (Source: Australian Bureau of Statistics)

Regional Holiday 2014
4 August: Bank Holiday

EMPLOYMENT

Labour Force (seasonally adjusted)

	Unit	Jan. 2012	Jan. 2013
Civilian population 15 years and over	'000	5,966.5	6,044.2
Employed persons	'000	3,580.8	3,635.0
Unemployed persons	'000	195.5	194.4
Unemployment rate	%	5.2	5.1
Participation rate	%	63.3	63.4

Source: Labour Force, Australia, March 2013 (cat. no. 6202.0)

Employees per Industry

Sector	2010
Agriculture, forestry and fishing	97,500
Mining	33,600
Manufacturing	306,100
Electricity, gas, water & waste services	40,400
Construction	292,600

- continued

Wholesale trade	138,700
Retail trade	365,200
Accommodation and restaurants	248,800
Transport, Postal and warehousing	184,800
Information media & telecommunications	82,800
Financial & insurance services	168,900
Rental, hiring & real estate services	58,100
Professional, scientific & technical services	288,900
Administrative & support services	115,200
Public administration & safety	203,800
Education & training	249,800
Health care & social assistance	385,000
Arts & recreation services	56,900
Other services	144,800
Total	3,461,900

Source: ABS 13381.3 NSW Regional Statistics

BANKING AND FINANCE

GDP/GNP, Inflation, National Debt
New South Wales's Gross State Product (GSP) accounts for some 32 per cent of Australia's total Gross Domestic Product, the highest proportion of all the states and territories. GSP (current prices) rose from A$300,636 million over 2004-05 to A$315,709 million in 2005-06, an increase of 5 per cent. In 2007-08 GSP was estimated to be $345.3 billion, as measured by the chain volume estimates of Gross State Product (GSP), representing 2.8 per cent growth, lower than the national growth rate of 3.7 per cent for the same period. Per capita GSP rose 4.1 per cent, from A$44,619 to A$46,431, over 2005-06.

Gross State Product, Chain volume measures

Year	A$m	% change from previous year
2007-08	412,244	2.9
2008-09	416,293	1.0
2009-10	424,547	2.0
2010-11	435,547	2.6
2011-12	446,169	2.4

Source: Australian Bureau of Statistics 5220.0

The annual change for the Consumer Price Index (all groups) for Sydney, 2005-06 was three per cent. The main rises were seen in education, transport and food costs. The House Price Index for established houses fell by 2.9 per cent, but rose by 2.3 per cent with regard to project homes. (Source: ABS 1338.1 NSW in Focus 2007, Consumer Price Index)

Balance of Payments / Imports and Exports
New South Wales is Australia's largest overseas trading state, contributing 17.6 per cent of national export revenues and 38.7 per cent of import costs in the year 2005-06.

In 2007-08, total export revenues reached $30,000 million (17 per cent of Australia's export total). The most important trading partners was Japan ($7.9 billion). Main exports are mineral fuels, manufactured goods and crude materials. Major export commodities are coal and coke, aluminium, meat, wool, and cereals.

Over the year 2007-08, import costs rose to over $76 billion, representing 38 per cent of Australian total. The main sources of origin were China ($15.1 billion), USA ($9.6 billion) and Japan ($6.4 billion). Main imports are machinery and transport equipment, computers and computer parts, and manufactured articles.

Top import and export commodities are shown on the following tables:

Top Export Commodities by Revenue, 2005-06

Export Commodity	A$m
Mineral fuels, oils and products of their distillation; bituminous subs.; mineral waxes	6,324
Aluminium and articles thereof	2,107
Ores, slag and ash	1,857
Pharmaceutical products	1,422
Meat and edible meat offal	1,146

Source: ABS 1338.1 NSW in Focus 2007

Top Import Commodities by Revenue, 2005-06

Commodity	A$m
Boilers, machinery; mechanical appliances & nuclear reactors; parts thereof	11,811
Electrical machinery & equip. and parts thereof	9,692
Vehicles (not rail or tramway rolling stock) and accessories thereof	5,944
Mineral fuels, oils and products of their distillation; bituminous subs.; mineral waxes	5,509
Pharmaceutical products	5,230

Source: ABS 1338.1 NSW in Focus 2007

From 2006-07 to 2007-08, the value of the NSW international trade deficit increased by 9.9 per cent ($4.1 billion) to $45.9 billion. The increase was the result of imports growth ($6.1 billion) exceeding exports growth ($2.0 billion). (Source: ABS, 1388.1)

AUSTRALIA

Chambers of Commerce
State Chamber of Commerce (NSW), URL: http://www.thechamber.com.au

MANUFACTURING, MINING AND SERVICES

Primary and Extractive Industries

A huge basin of black coal lies under the central coast and Blue Mountains area and is mined extensively in the Hunter River Valley, around Lithgow and on the Illawarra coast.

The following table shows key indicators for mining in NSW and Australian Capital Territory:

Selected NSW mining industries

	Unit	2005-06
Summary of operations		
Sales and service income	A$m	12,376
Wages and salaries	A$m	1,460
Industry value added	A$m	6,138
Mineral Production		
Metallic mineral	A$m	2,759
Coal, oil and gas	A$m	8,531
Construction materials	A$m	369
Other non-metallic minerals	A$m	124

Source: ABS 1338.1 NSW in Focus, Mining

Energy

Australia's deregulated gas market is administered by the individual states. New South Wales's gas requirements are almost entirely supplied by the Cooper Basin fields, owned and operated by Santos.

The Illawarra region of New South Wales is a major coal-producing area, and supplies coking and thermal coal mined by BHP Billiton, the second largest mining company in the world.

New South Wales and Victoria have combined their electricity industries to become a two-state regional market. Australia's largest electricity producer is the New South Wales-owned Macquarie Generation.

Manufacturing

Measured by sales and service income, NSW manufacturing industry dominates the national industry; this is particularly evident in the printing, publishing and recorded media subdivision, where the state contributes 45 per cent of national sales and service income, 40 per cent of Industry Value Added and 38 per cent of national employment.

Manufacturing Industry, 2009-10

Industry subdivision	Wages & salaries $m	Sales & service income $m	Employment end of June
Food product manufacturing	2,905	23,489	65,787
Beverage and tobacco product manufacturing	593	5,787	8,063
Textile, leather, clothing and footware	492	2,959	13,455
Wood product	626	3,835	14,042
Pulp, paper and converted paper products	402	2,915	5,930
Printing	897	3,714	18,717
Petroleum and coal products	206	10,366	1,908
Basic chemical and chemical products	1,268	10,335	16,130
Polymer product and rubber product	834	4,396	14,435
Non-metallic mineral product	835	4,563	12,355
Primary metal and metal product	1,247	12,908	16,796
Fabricated metal product	1,519	7,822	31,402
Transport equipment	1,445	6,155	17,772
Machinery and equipment	2,317	12,430	38,689
Furniture and other manufacturing	439	2,449	12,153
TOTAL	16,025	114,123	287,633

Source: Australian Bureau of Statistics. 8159.0

Tourism

The most visited parts of NSW are Sydney, the North Coast, Explorer Country and The Murray.

The number of hotels and motels in 2005-06 was 1,418, up from 1,396 in 2004-05. The rate of room occupancy was 61.9 per cent, whilst accommodation takings increased to A$2,119,684,000. The industry employed around 33,754 people. (Source: Australian Bureau of Statistics)

Agriculture

The period 2001-06 was marked by below average rainfall, leading to the worst drought in over a century. Conditions had become so bad in 2006-07 that a significant number of farmers in South Australia, Victoria and NSW abandoned their crops. In 2003-04, there were 40,827 farms in the state.

Gross Value of Selected Agricultural Production 2010

	A$ million
Cereals for grain	1,681.4
Cotton	452.8
Fruit & nuts	474.3
Grapes	173.8
Nursery production	299.8
Vegetables	375.2
Cattle & calves	1,487.6
Sheep and lamb	584.3
Wool	641.1
Total Agricultural production	8,359.2

Source: ABS 7123.1.55.001 - Agricultural State Profile, New South Wales

COMMUNICATIONS AND TRANSPORT

International Airports

Sydney Airport's facilities were improved for the 2000 Olympic Games.

Railways

All railways are administered by the state except for a few short lines maintained by industrial undertakings. A state-of-the-art rail link was constructed to transport passengers between Sydney Airport and the Olympic Stadium in Sydney Olympic Park.

Ports and Harbours

The NSW Maritime Authority is connected with a maritime history that can be traced back to 1811 when the first harbour master was appointed to control the port of Sydney.

The main ports are Sydney, Newcastle, Port Kembla, Port Botany and Kurnell. Major port and harbour facilities are under government control through the Maritime Services Board. Sydney Ports Corporation consists of Port Botany, Sydney Harbour, Darling Harbour, White Bay, and Glebe Island.

HEALTH

In 2008 there were 20,006 hospital beds in the public sector, and 6,792 in the private sector.

In the same year, 53.8 per cent of the New South Wales population was covered by private health insurance, and in 2007 some A$30.8 billion was spent on health care.

22.6 per cent of adults aged 18 or over were smokers in 2005, 13 per cent have high risk alcohol consumption and 70.6 per cent have a low exercise level. 47.1 per cent of those aged 15 years or over were overweight or obese. (Source: 1338.1 - New South Wales in Focus)

EDUCATION

Primary/Secondary Education

Schools numbered 3,097 in 2009 (2,181 government and 916 non-government). There were 2,133 primary schools and 525 secondary schools, as well as 439 combined and special schools. Pupils (full time and part time) numbered 1,110,900 in the same year; 618,700 full time pupils attended primary school and 492,200 were in secondary.

There were 84,627 teachers in 2006. The teacher/pupil ratio was one to 16.4 in primary schools and one to 12.1 in secondary schools. The participation rate for full-time students from Year 10 to Year 12 in 2006 was 73 per cent.

Higher Education

The participation rate in higher education, for those aged 20-24 years, was 38 per cent. (Source: Australian Bureau of Statistics)

COMMUNICATIONS AND MEDIA

Newspapers

New South Wales's newspapers include the Australian Financial Review (URL: http://afr.com/) and the Sydney Morning Herald (URL: http://www.smh.com.au/).

NORTHERN TERRITORY

Capital: Darwin (Population estimate, 2010: 77,290)

Administrator: Her Honour the Hon. Sally Thomas AM

State Flag: Superimposed on an ochre field in the centre of the fly is a stylised Sturt's Desert Rose with seven petals, whilst at the hoist is a white Southern Cross on a black panel.

CONSTITUTION AND GOVERNMENT

Constitution

The Northern Territory was established in 1978 and given authority to carry out specific political functions within its borders. In accordance with the provisions of the Northern Territory (Self Government) Act 1978 the Administrator of the Northern Territory is appointed by the Governor-General by Commission under the Seal of Australia. The Administrator's role is similar to that of the State Governor and the position has a maximum term of two years.

Legislature

The Northern Territory has a unicameral legislature, the Legislative Assembly, which has 25 members elected by popular franchise for four years. It is led by the Chief Minister and eight Ministers. The current structure of the Legislative Assembly is as follows: Australian Labour Party, 19 seats; Country Liberal Party, 4 seats; Independents, 2 seats.

The Legislative Assembly of the Northern Territory, GPO Box 3721, Darwin, NT 0801, Australia. Tel: +61 (0)8 8946 1521 (Clerk), fax: +61 (0)8 8941 2437 (Clerk), e-mail: tableoffice.la@nt.gov.au, URL: http://www.nt.gov.au/lant/
Speaker: Kezia Purick

Cabinet (as at July 2013)

Chief Minister, Minister for Police, Fire and Emergency Services, Minister for Transport, Minister for Infrastructure, Minister for Trade, Minister for Local Government: Hon. Adam Graham Giles
Minister for Justice and Attorney-General, Minister for Corporate and Information Services, Minister for Correctional Services : Hon. John Wessel Elferink
Minister for Lands, Planning and the Environment, Minister for Housing, Minister for Education: Hon. Peter Glen Chandler
Minister for Health, Minister for Alcohol Rehabilitation and Policy, Minister for Business, Minister for Employment and Training: Hon. Robyn Lambley
Minister for Tourism and Major Events, Minister for Parks and Wildlife, Minister for Arts and Museums, Minister for Central Australia: Hon. Matt Escott Conland
Minister for Primary Industry and Fisheries, Minister for Mines and Energy, Minister for Land Resource Management, Minister for Public Employment,
Minister for Essential Services: Hon. Willem Westra van Holthe
Minister for Regional Development, Minister for Indigenous Advancement, Minister for Children and Families, Minister for Women's Policy: Hon. Alison Anderson
Minister for Sport and Recreation, Minister for Racing, Minister for Statehood, Minister for Young Territorians, Minister for Senior Territorians: Hon. Peter Styles

Ministries

Office of the Chief Minister, (GPO Box 3146) Parliament House, Darwin, Northern Territory 0800. Tel: +61 8 8901 4000, fax: +61 8 8901 4099, e-mail: chiefminister.nt@nt.gov.au, URL: http://www.dcm.nt.gov.au
Department of Justice, GPO Box 1722 Darwin NT 0801, Australia. Tel: +61 8 8999 5047, fax: +61 8 8999 7095, e-mail: dojwebmanager.doj@nt.gov.au, URL: http://www.nt.gov.au/justice
NT Treasury, 38 Cavenagh Street, Darwin, Northern Territory (GPO Box 1974, Darwin, NT 0801), Australia. Tel: +61 8 8999 7406, fax: +61 8 8999 6150, e-mail: nt.treasury@treasury.nt.gov.au, URL: http://www.nt.gov.au/ntt/
Department of Employment, Education and Training, GPO Box 4821, Darwin, NT 0801, Australia. Tel: +61 8 8924 4452, fax: +61 8 8924 4450, e-mail: infocentre.deet@nt.gov.au, URL: http://www.ntde.nt.gov.au
NT Department of Business, Industry and Resource Development, (GPO Box 3000, Darwin NT 0801), Development House, 76 The Esplanade, Darwin NT 0800, Australia. Tel: +61 8 8982 1700, fax: +61 8 8982 1725, e-mail: info.dbird@nt.gov.au, URL: http://www.dbird.nt.gov.au
NT Department of Business, Industry and Resource Development - Office for Primary Industry and Fisheries, (GPO Box 3000, Darwin NT 0801) Berrimah Farm, Makagon Road Berrimah NT 0828, Australia. Tel: +61 (8) 8999 2210, fax: +61 (8) 8999 2023, e-mail: web.dpif@nt.gov.au, URL: http://www.nt.gov.au/dbird/dpif
NT Department of Corporate and Information Services, GPO Box 2391, Darwin NT 0801, Australia. Tel: +61 8 8999 5511, fax: +61 8 8999 1710, e-mail: dcis.webmanager@nt.gov.au, URL: http://www.nt.gov.au/dcis/
Department of Community Development, Sport & Cultural Affairs, RCG Building, Corner Smith and Briggs Street, Darwin NT 0800, (GPO Box 4621, Darwin NT 0801), Australia. Tel: +61 8 8901 4700, fax: +61 8 8999 8488, e-mail: webadmin.dcdsca@nt.gov.au, URL: http://www.dcdsca.nt.gov.au/
Department of Health and Community Services, Health House, 87 Mitchell St, Darwin, (PO Box 40596, Casuarina NT 0811), Australia. Tel: +61 8 8999 2400, fax: +61 8 8999 2700, e-mail: sitemaster.ths@nt.gov.au, URL: http://www.health.nt.gov.au/
Department of Infrastructure, Planning and Environment, PO Box 2520, Darwin, NT 0871, Australia. Tel: +61 8 892 47024, fax: +61 8 892 47079, e-mail: infoact.DIPE@nt.gov.au, URL: http://www.ipe.nt.gov.au/

Elections

The most recent legislative election was held in August 2012. The Country Liberal Party won 16 seats and the Australian Labor Party won 8 seats and there was one independent.

LEGAL SYSTEM

The Northern Territory's court system comprises the Supreme Court and Magistrates Courts. The Supreme Court consists of the Chief Justice, five judges, two additional judges, and one acting judge.
Supreme Court, Supreme Court Building, State Square, Darwin NT 0800, (GPO Box 3946, Darwin NT 0801) Australia. Fax: +61 (0)8 8999 5446, URL: http://www.nt.gov.au/ntsc/
Chief Justice: Hon. Trevor Riley

LOCAL GOVERNMENT

The Northern Territory is divided into Municipalities, Community Government, Special Purpose Towns, and Incorporated Associations.

Office of Local Government and Regional Development, URL: http://www.dcdsca.nt.gov.au/

AREA AND POPULATION

Area

The total area of the Northern Territory is 1,351,961.8 sq. km, approximately one sixth of the Australian landmass. The Northern Territory is the third largest of the states and territories after Western Australia and Queensland. The capital city, Darwin, is as close to Singapore and Manila as it is to Sydney and Melbourne. The northern region has two seasons; the wet season of humidity and heavy rainfall lasts from October to April while the dry season runs from May to September. The southern region has cool winters and hot dry summers.

Population

Total population at June 2010 was estimated at 234,800, indicating an increase on the previous year's figure of 229,711.

According to figures from June 2010 the indigenous population numbered 64,005, 31,514 male and 32,491 female). The Northern Territory has the lowest population of the Australian states and territories.

Major towns and cities, together with their populations (2010), are as follows: Darwin City (77,290); Alice Springs (27,957); Palmerston (30,140); Litchfield (19,414); and Katherine (10,104). (Source: Australian Bureau of Statistics)

Births, Marriages, Deaths

According to Australian Bureau of Statistics figures for 2009, there were 3,819 births in NT, equating to a crude birth rate of 18.1 births per 1,000 population. The fertility rate was 2.18 per 1,000 inhabitants, though it averaged 2.12 among the indigenous population. The Northern Territory has the highest teenage fertility rate of 48 per 1,000 population. In an estimated 17 per cent of births, paternity is not acknowledged. Deaths numbered 953 of which 431 were from the indigenous population. The crude death rate was 4.7 per 1,000 population. Life expectancy is 72.1 years for men, and 78.1 years for women. The median age in 2009 was 31 years. In 2005 marriages numbered 774 (3.8 per 1,000 population), whilst divorces numbered 470 (2.3 per 1,000 population). (Source: ABS, 33030, 2009)

EMPLOYMENT

Labour Force (seasonally adjusted)

	Unit	Jan. 2012	Jan. 2013
Civilian population 15 years and over	'000	173.0	176.3
Employed persons	'000	124.2	125.2
Unemployed persons	'000	5.4	5.1
Unemployment rate	%	4.2	3.9
Participation rate	%	74.9	74.0

Source: Labour Force, Australia, March 2013 (cat. no. 6202.0)

Employment by Industry, February 2011

Industry	No. of employed
Agriculture, forestry, fishing	2,100
Mining	4,300
Manufacturing	4,400
Electricity, gas, water & waste services	2,200
Construction	12,800
Wholesale & retail trade	16,900
Accommodation, cafes, restaurants	9,500
Transport and storage	4,900
Communication services	1,800
Finance and insurance	1,100
Property services	2,400
Professional, scientific & technical services	6,100

AUSTRALIA

- continued

Admin. and support services	3,900
Public admin. & safety	18,100
Education & training	9,300
Health and community services	14,300
Arts and recreation services	2,800
Other services	6,000
TOTAL	122,900

Source: ABS (Northern Territory at a Glance, 2011)

BANKING AND FINANCE

GDP/GNP, Inflation, National Debt

Mining, tourism and defence are major contributors to the Northern Territory economy.

Gross State Product rose from $12 693 million in 2005-06 to $13 405 million in 2006-07, an increase of 6 per cent. The Northern Territory's GSP per capita was estimated to be A$63 548), 33 per cent higher than GDP per capita for Australia ($47 954); the Territory has the highest per capita GSP in Australia.

Gross State Product, Chain volume measures

Year	A$m	% change from previous year
2007-08	16,135	3.1
2008-09	16,917	4.1
2009-10	17,118	3.1
2010-11	17,322	3.2
2011-12	18,086	3.5

Source: Australian Bureau of Statistics 5220.0

The Consumer Price Index (CPI) in Darwin rose by 3.2 per cent over the year to September 2007. The weighted average CPI of eight capital cities went up by 1.9 per cent over the same period. The higher result for Darwin was due to larger increases in housing (7 per cent compared to 4.2 per cent elsewhere) and recreation, and a smaller reduction in transportation costs than the other cities.

Balance of Payments / Imports and Exports

The Northern Territory is a net exporter, due to its mineral and energy resources which account for a large proportion of all exports. Revenues are volatile due to fluctuation in production levels and in world oil prices.

The total value of exports increased from A$5,222 million in 2009 to A$5,407 million in 2010. The territory's main export commodities are petroleum products, minerals (uranium, bauxite, manganese, alumina), food and live animals, and crude materials. Major export trading partners in 2009 included: Japan (A$1,952 million), China (A$1,225 million) and the USA (A$446 million).

Import costs fell from S$5,222 million in 2009 to A$5,407 million in 2010. Imports include machinery and transport, manufactured goods, unclassified commodities, and mineral fuels. Major import trading partners in 2009 included: Singapore (A$550m), Kuwait (A$331m), Japan (A$169m) and the US (A$131m). (Source: DFAT)

Chambers of Commerce and Trade Organisations

Department of Industries and Business, Territory Business Centre, URL: http://www.nt.gov.au/business/

MANUFACTURING, MINING AND SERVICES

Primary and Extractive Industries

The Northern Territory has extensive deposits of uranium, manganese, gold, bauxite, and alumina, as well as oil and gas. Diamonds are also mined in the state. In 2005-06 the mining industry continued to be a major contributor to the state economy, with a total value of A$1.93 billion. Metallic mineral production yield revenues of A$1677.4 million; non metallic mineral production had a value of A$17.8 million; and energy minerals earned A$233.8 million. Figures from February 2009 show that 4.0 per cent of the working population were employed in the mining sector.

Mining industry statistics

Mineral Commodities	2007-08	2008-09
Total fuel minerals, $m	3,695	4,401
-Crude oil ,$m	720	511
-Liquefied natural gas, $m	1,274	2,306
Total metallic minerals, $m	1,547	1,455
-Gold, $m	430	320
-Uranium oxide, $m	461	557
Total industrial minerals, $m	1,040	1,448
-Manganese ore, $m	1,025	1,446
Total mineral commodities, $m	6,293	7,316

Source: ABS, Northern Territory at a Glance, 2011

The costs of exploration have risen in all mining sectors, apart from gold. The largest increase in expenditure has been in the petroleum subdivision, where exploration costs soared from A$99.2 million over the year 2004-05 to A$299.2 million over the following year.

Manufacturing

In 2004-05, manufacturing contributed around 5.9 per cent of state Total Factor Income a 4,700 people were employed in the sector at the end of February 2009. The Sales and servi income totalled A$1,507 million, most income coming from the machinery and equipme and the food, beverage and tobacco sectors. (Source: Australian Bureau of Statistics)

Tourism

Tourism is one of the fastest growing industries in the Northern Territory, with around 1 million visitors per year. Around 75 per cent are domestic visitors.

Tourist accommodation

Hotels, motels, guest houses etc.	Unit	Sept.Qtr. 2010	Dec.Qtr. 201
Establishments	No.	96	9
Employees	No.	3,217	3,10
Takings from accommodation	A$ million	93.2	58
Room occupancy rate	%	79.8	60.

Source: ABS Northern Territory at a Glance, 2009

Agriculture

The agricultural, forestry and fishing sector employed 2.3 per cent of the labour force i February 2009 and contributed 5.1 per cent to the Territory's total exports in 2006.

Total agricultural land covers nearly 135 million ha., though most of this is used for livestoc rearing. Just 7,000 ha. is used for crop growing.

Processing industries have now been established and they are increasingly contributing t the territory's earnings. Live cattle exports to European, American, Asian and Pacifi destinations are the main source of exports revenue in this sector.

Main Agricultural and Fishing Exports A$'000

	2009	201
Live cattle	200,165	183,60
Meat	1,484.9	1,093.
Fish	132.9	9.
Hides & skins of saltwater crocodiles	8,730.4	8,622.
Fruit & nuts	2,056.2	1,605.8
Vegetables	121.2	4.

Source: ABS, Northern Territory at a Glance, 2011

Over the year 2004-05, revenue from livestock slaughterings and products reached A$25 million, and crops and horticulture earnings reached A$65.4 million. The value of the fishin catch over the same period was A$119.4 million, of which the prawn catch was worth A$63. million.

COMMUNICATIONS AND TRANSPORT

International Airports

Darwin is a first port of call for many international flights from Asia.

Ports and Harbours

Darwin has the foremost deep water port in the north of Australia. Two further ports in the Northern Territory are managed by mining companies, Milner Bay and Grove.

HEALTH

In 2005-06 the Territory had five public hospitals with 569 hospital beds. A total of 6,118 day surgeries were carried out in 2005-06, up from 5,699 the previous year.

EDUCATION

School is compulsory between six and 15. In some areas Indigenous students are also taught in their native language.
Education participation rates for the Northern Territory's 15 to 19 year olds are the lowest in Australia at just under 40 per cent for boys and around 43 per cent for girls.
In 2006, the Government of Northern Territory was responsible for 151 schools, and there were 35 independent schools, 15 of which were catholic. There were 186 schools in total; of these, 99 were primary schools, 17 were secondary and 65 were combined primary/secondary schools.
There were 37,580 full time students in 2006, and 1,176 part-time students. 25,194 full time pupils were in primary school, and 12,386 were in secondary. Indigenous students number 14,630. School participation rates fell from 80 per cent among the 15 year olds to 71.5 per cent at 16 years, 47.7 per cent at 17 years and 10 per cent at 18 years. 3.1 per cent of 19 year olds continue in education.
There were 3,205 teachers in 2006. The ratio of students to teacher in primary schools was 14:1 and in secondary schools, it was 11:1.
The University's Institute of Technical and Further Education provides a wide range of trade and technical courses, as well as programs designed to develop managerial and supervisory skills.

COMMUNICATIONS AND MEDIA

Around 35,000 households now have internet access, equivalent to 60 per cent.

QUEENSLAND

Capital: Brisbane (Population estimate: 1.8 million)

Governor General: Her Excellency Penelope Wensley, AO (page 1535)

State Flag: The Blue Ensign imposed with a Royal Crown superimposed on a Maltese cross.

CONSTITUTION AND GOVERNMENT

Constitution

Following the Westminster system of government, Queensland has three separate arms of government: legislature, executive (which includes the Governor, the Cabinet and the public service), and judiciary. The Governor is the Sovereign's representative and has the power to summon and dissolve Parliament, grant Royal Assent to Legislative Assembly Bills and issue State Election 'writs'. The Government, led by the Premier, is responsible to Parliament. The Cabinet comprises 19 ministers.

Recent Events

In January 2011, Queensland was hit by devastating floods. More than 20 towns were either flooded or cut off completely and over 200,000 people were affected. Nearly all the states mines were shut down. In January 2013 Queensland was hit again by devastating floods.

Legislature

Queensland is the only Australian State to have a single Chamber Parliament. The upper house or Legislative Council was abolished in 1922. There is now only one chamber, the Legislative Assembly or Lower House, comprising 89 members or MLAs, one for each of Queensland's electorates. Members are elected for a period of three years by the eligible Queensland electorate.

Queensland Legislative Assembly, Parliament House, Cnr. George and Alice Streets, Brisbane QLD 4000 CDE M29, Australia. Tel: +61 7 3406 7111, fax: +61 7 3221 7475, URL: http://www.parliament.qld.gov.au
Speaker: Hon. R. John Mickel

Cabinet (as at June 2013)

Premier of Queensland: Campbell Newman (page 1485)
Deputy Premier, Minister of State for Development, Infrastructure and Planning: Jeff Seeney
Treasurer and Minister of Trade: Tim Nicholls
Minister for Health: Lawrence Springborg
Minister for Education, Training and Employment: John-Paul Langbroek
Minister for Police and Community Safety: Jack Dempsey
Attorney-General and Minister for Justice: Jarrod Bleijie
Minister for Transport and Main Roads: Scott Emerson
Minister for Housing and Public Works: Tim Mander
Minister for Agriculture, Fisheries and Forestry: John McVeigh
Minister for Environment and Heritage Protection: Andrew Powell
Minister for Natural Resources and Mines: Andrew Cripps
Minister for Energy and Water Supply: Mark McArdle
Minister for Local Government, Community Recovery and Resilience: David Crisafulli
Minister for Communities, Child Safety and Disability: Tracy Davis
Minister for Science, Information Technology, Innovation and the Arts: Ian Walker
Minister for National Parks, Recreation, Sport and Racing: Steven Dickson
Minister for Tourism, Major Events, Small Business and the Commonwealth Games: Jann Stuckey
Minister for Aboriginal and Torres Strait Islander and Multicultural Affairs and Minister Assisting the Premier: Glen Elmes

---

Ministries

Office of the Premier, PO Box 185, Brisbane Albert Street Qld 4002, QLD 4000, Australia. Tel: +61 7 3224 4500, fax: +61 7 3221 3631, e-mail: Premiers@ministerial.qld.gov.au, URL: ThePremier@premiers.qld.gov.au, http://www.thepremier.qld.gov.au/
Office of the Deputy Premier, Treasurer and Minister State Development, 9th Floor, Executive Building, 100 George Street, Brisbane QLD 4000 (GPO Box 611, Brisbane QLD 4001 CDE M49), Australia. Tel: +61 7 3224 6900, fax: +61 7 3229 0642, e-mail: Treasurer@ministerial.qld.gov.au, URL: http://www.treasury.qld.gov.au
Office of the Minister for Police and Corrective Services, PO Box 195, Brisbane Albert Street QLD 4002, Australia. Tel: +61 7 3239 0199, fax: +61 7 3221 9985, e-mail: Information@dcs.qld.gov.au, Police@ministerial.qld.gov.au, URL: http://www.correctiveservices.qld.gov.au
Office of the Minister for Families, and the Minister for Aboriginal and Torres Strait Islander Policy, Minister for Disability Services, Level 7, 111 George Street, Brisbane QLD 4000, Australia. Tel: +61 7 3224 7477, fax: +61 7 3210 2190, e-mail: askus@datsip.qld.gov.au, families@ministerial.qld.gov.au, mailbox@disability.qld.gov.au, URL: http://www.indigenous.qld.gov.au/, http://www.families.qld.gov.au/index.html, http://www.disability.qld.gov.au/
Office of the Minister for Employment, Training and Youth, and Minister for the Arts, 17th Floor, Mineral and Energy Centre, 61 Mary Street, Brisbane QLD 4000 (GPO Box 69, Brisbane QLD 4001 CDE M20), Australia. Tel: +61 7 3224 2170, fax: +61 7 3229 9346, e-mail: Employment@ministerial.qld.gov.au, URL: http://www.det.qld.gov.au, www.arts.qld.gov.au
Office of the Minister for Transport and Main Roads, Level 13, Capital Hill Building, 85 George Street, Brisbane QLD 4000, (GPO Box 1549 Brisbane QLD 4001), Australia. Tel: +61 7 3237 1949, fax: +61 7 3224 4242, e-mail: Transport@ministerial.qld.gov.au, URL: http://www.transport.qld.gov.au

Office of the Minister for Health, Level 19, State Health Building, 147-163 Charlotte Street, Brisbane QLD 4000, (GPO Box 48, Brisbane QLD 4001), Australia. Tel: +61 7 3234 1191, fax: +61 7 3229 4731, e-mail: Health@ministerial.qld.gov.au, URL: http://www.health.qld.gov.au
Office of the Attorney-General and Minister for Justice, Level 18, State Law Building, 50 Ann Street, Brisbane QLD 4000, (GPO Box 149, Brisbane QLD 4001), Australia. Tel: +61 7 3239 3478, fax: +61 7 3220 2475, e-mail: Attorney@ministerial.qld.gov.au, URL: http://www.justice.qld.gov.au
Office of the Minister for Innovation and Information Economy, Level 13, 111 George Street, Brisbane QLD 4000 (PO Box 187, Brisbane Albert Street QLD 4002), Australia. Tel: +61 7 3225 4280, fax: +61 7 3210 2186, e-mail: iie@ministerial.qld.gov.au, URL: http://www.iie.qld.gov.au
Office of the Minister for Natural Resources and the Minister for Mines, 13th Floor, Mineral House, 41-59 George Street, Brisbane, QLD 4000 (PO Box 456, Brisbane Albert Street QLD 4002), Australia. Tel: +61 7 3896 3688, fax: +61 7 3210 6214, e-mail: NR&Mines@ministerial.qld.gov.au, URL: http://www.nrm.qld.gov.au
Office of the Minister for Primary Industries and Rural Communities, Level 8, Primary Industries Building, 80 Ann Street, Brisbane QLD 4000 (GPO Box 46, Brisbane QLD 4001), Australia. Tel: +61 7 3239 3000, fax: +61 7 3229 8541, e-mail: DPI@ministerial.qld.gov.au, URL: http://www.dpi.qld.gov.au
Office of the Minister for Emergency Services, Queensland Emergency Services Complex, Cnr Park Road and Kedron Park Road, Kedron QLD 4031, (GPO Box 1377, Brisbane QLD 4001), Australia. Tel: +61 7 3247 8190, fax: +61 7 3247 8195, e-mail: emergency@ministerial.qld.gov.au, URL: http://www.emergency.qld.gov.au
Office of the Minister for Tourism and Racing and Minister of Fair Trading, Level 26, 111 George Street, Brisbane QLD 4000 (GPO Box 1141, Brisbane QLD 4001), Australia. Tel: +61 7 3224 2004, fax: +61 7 3229 0434, e-mail: tourism@ministerial.qld.gov.au, URL: http://www.dtrft.qld.gov.au
Office of the Minister for Public Works and Housing, Level 7 (Parliament House End), 80 George Street, Brisbane QLD 4000, (GPO Box 2457, Brisbane QLD 4001), Australia. Tel: +61 7 3237 1832, fax: +61 7 3210 2189, e-mail: Works&Housing@ministerial.qld.gov.au, URL: http://www.publicworks.qld.gov.au, http://www.housing.qld.gov.au
Office of the Minister for Environment, Level 17, 160 Ann Street, Brisbane QLD 4000, (PO Box 155, Brisbane Albert Street QLD 4002), Australia. Tel: +61 7 3225 1800, fax: +61 7 3229 6920, e-mail: environment@ministerial.qld.gov.au, URL: http://www.epa.qld.gov.au
Office of the Minister for Education, Level 22, Education House, 30 Mary Street, Brisbane QLD 4000, (PO Box 33, Brisbane Albert Street QLD 4002), Australia. Tel: +61 7 3237 1000, fax: +61 7 3229 5335, e-mail: education@ministerial.qld.gov.au, URL: http://education.qld.gov.au
Office of the Minister for State Development, Level 12, Executive Building, 100 George Street, Brisbane QLD 4000, (PO Box 168, Brisbane Albert Street QLD 4002), Australia. Tel: +61 7 3224 4600, fax: +61 7 3224 4781, e-mail: statedevelopment@ministerial.qld.gov.au, URL: http://www.sd.qld.gov.au
Office of the Minister for Local Government and Planning, Level 18, Mineral House, 41-59 George Street, Brisbane QLD 4000, (PO Box 31, Brisbane Albert Street QLD 4002), Australia. Tel: +61 7 3227 8819, fax: +61 7 3221 9964, e-mail: localgovernment&planning@ministerial.qld.gov.au, URL: http://www.dlgp.qld.gov.au/
Office of the Minister for Industrial Relations, Level 6, Block B, Neville Bonner Building, 75 William Street, Brisbane QLD 4000, (GPO Box 69, Brisbane QLD 4001), Australia. Tel: +61 7 3225 2210, fax: +61 7 3221 4802, e-mail: industrialrelations@ministerial.qld.gov.au, URL: http://www.dir.qld.gov.au/

Elections

The most recent election took place on 24th March 2012 when the Liberal National Party won, beating the Labor Party who had been in power for five consecutive terms. The Liberals won 78 of the 89 seats and the Labor Party, seven seats.

Peter Beattie resigned in September 2007, and was replaced as Premier by Anna Bligh, the first woman Premier of Queensland. Premier Bligh was later elected Premier in 2009, and became the first elected woman Premier in Australia.

Political Parties

Australian Labor Party, URL: http://www.qld.alp.org
Liberal Party, URL: http://www.qld.liberal.org.au
National Party, URL: http://www.qld.nationals.org.au/

LEGAL SYSTEM

Supreme Court, 304 George Street, Brisbane (PO Box 167, Brisbane Albert Street, Qld, 4002), Australia. Tel: +61 73 247 4313, fax: +61 73 247 5316, URL: http://www.courts.qld.gov.au/
Chief Justice: Hon. Paul de Jersey A.C.
President of Court of Appeal: Hon. Justice Margaret A. McMurdo (page 1475)

LOCAL GOVERNMENT

For administrative purposes Queensland is divided into 125 councils. Local government personnel are numbered as follows: Councillors, 1,037; Mayors, 125; CEOs, 125; and Senior Officers, 655. Local government elections are held every four years when more than 1,100 councillors were elected for four-year terms.

AUSTRALIA

AREA AND POPULATION

Area
The area of Queensland is 1,734,190 sq. km, with 22.5 per cent of the area of the Australian continent, making it the second largest of Australia's states/territories. The climate ranges from the tropical north to the subtropical south, from the wet coastal plains to the drier inland. Average annual rainfall ranges from 4,000 mm in the north-eastern coast to just 150 mm in the south-western desert.

Population
The estimated population is at June 2011 was 4,47 million and comprises approximately 20 per cent of the total Australian population. Queensland was the fastest growing state in Australia over the twelve months to March 2007. The total population is projected to reach 9 million by 2036. The two most populous cities in Queensland are Brisbane and Gold Coast. Queensland's population mainly resides in the south-eastern corner of the state, with the Statistical Divisions of Brisbane, the Gold Coast, the Sunshine Coast and Moreton having 66 per cent of the population.

The majority of the population is aged between 25 and 64 years (53 per cent), with 20 per cent aged up to 14 years, 12 per cent aged 65 years and over, and 14 per cent aged between 15 and 24 years. The median age is 36 years. (Source: Australian Bureau of Statistics, 2009)

Births, Marriages, Deaths
In 2010 there were 64,467 births and 27,289 deaths. There were 26,530 marriages and 11,418 divorces that year. (Source: Australian Bureau of Statistics)

EMPLOYMENT

Labour Force (seasonally adjusted)

	Unit	Jan. 2012	Jan. 2013
Civilian population 15 years and over	'000	3,693.4	3,767.3
Employed persons	'000	2,352.2	2,354.6
Unemployed persons	'000	135.8	137.8
Unemployment rate	%	5.5	5.5
Participation rate	%	67.4	66.2

Source: Labour Force, Australia, March 2013 (cat. no. 6202.0)

Recent figures show that most people worked in the retail industry (324,700), property and business services (257,400) and the construction industry (225,100).

BANKING AND FINANCE

GDP/GNP, Inflation, National Debt
The volume measure of gross state product (GSP) grew by 4.9 per cent in the year 2005-06, to $187,339 million. Queensland's annual GSP was the third highest of the Australian states and territories (after New South Wales and Victoria). However, GSP per capita, at A$45,369 in 2005-06, was the third lowest in the country. (Source: Australian Bureau of Statistics) Despite the worldwide economic crisis, the economy in Queensland continued to grow, by 1.1 per cent in 2008-09 and by 2.3 per cent in 2009-10. A demand for coal from China helped strengthen exports.

Gross State Product, Chain volume measures

Year	A$m	% change from previous year
2007-08	260,796	4.8
2008-09	263,465	1.0
2009-10	267,221	1.4
2010-11	269,880	1.0
2011-12	280,622	4.0

Source: Australian Bureau of Statistics 5220.0

There was growth of 9.8 per cent in Queensland's Total Factor Income; compensation of employees grew by 11.6 per cent, and gross operating surplus also experienced strong growth.

The following table shows industry gross value added at chain volume measures, figures are in A$ million.

Industry	2009-10	2010-11
Agriculture, forestry and fishing	6,807	7,475
Mining	22,937	18,887
Manufacturing	20,034	19,407
Electricity, gas and water supply	5,776	5,785
Construction	20,681	23,154
Wholesale trade	12,395	12,353
Retail trade	12,883	13,079
Accommodation and restaurants	6,146	5,988
Transport and storage	15,663	16,258
Communication services	5,103	5,309
Financial & insurance services	16,738	17,223
Property services	5,488	5,375
Professional, scientific & technical services	14,355	13,950
Admin. & support services	4,456	4,827
Public admin. and safety	12,973	13,312
Education & training	10,027	10,332

- continued

Health care and social assistance	14,803	15,12*
Arts & recreation services	1,538	1,58*
Other services	4,534	4,15*
Ownership of dwellings	21,336	21,92*
Gross value added at basic prices	234,645	235,51*

ABS 5220.0 Australian National Accounts: State Accounts

The Consumer Price Index for Brisbane (all groups) rose by 2.6 per cent in the year to 2006 This is higher than the 2.1 per cent average increase of the eight Australian capital cities of (1989-90 = 100.0). (Source: Australian Bureau of Statistics)

Balance of Payments / Imports and Exports
Foreign and interstate trade was as follows:

External merchandise trade ($million)

Exports	2009-10	2010-11
- Foreign	43,266	49,368
- Interstate	20,969	18,849
- Total	64,235	68,217
Imports		
- Foreign	31,035	33,088
- Interstate	36,305	35,490
- Total	67,340	68,578

Source: Queensland at a Glance

Exports rose 4.5 per cent in 2009-10. Japan is Queensland's top export trading partner, contributing around 23 per cent of total export revenue in 2009-10. Other top export trading partners are the China (16 per cent), India (12.1 per cent) and South Korea (10.9 per cent). Total overseas exports amounted to A$43,275 million in 2009.

Japan is also the source of around 17 per cent of Queensland's imports. Other major import trading partners are the US, Papua New Guinea, China, New Zealand, Malaysia, Germany, Indonesia, Thailand, Vietnam, South Korea and the UK.

Top commodity exports are mineral fuels and lubricants, food and live animals, crude materials, and manufactured goods. Top commodity imports include machinery and transport equipment, mineral fuels and lubricants, and manufactured goods.

Major Banks
Bank of Queensland Limited, URL: http://www.boq.com.au

Chambers of Commerce and Trade Organisations
Queensland Chamber of Commerce and Industry, http://www.qcci.com.au

MANUFACTURING, MINING AND SERVICES

Primary and Extractive Industries
The following table provides statistics about Queensland's mining industry:

	Unit	2008-09	2009-10
Value of mineral commodities produced	A$m	49,430	29,661
Black coal (saleable)	'000 tonnes	190,895	205,719
Bauxite	'000 tonnes	17,415	17,890
Copper (metal content)	'000 tonnes	355	215
Lead (metal content)	'000 tonnes	411	427
Zinc	'000 tonnes	880	832
Gold (metal content)	kilograms	18,110	13,191
Silver (metal content)	tonnes	1,560	1,695

Source: Australian Bureau of Statistics, Queensland at a Glance

Manufacturing
Manufacturing industry according to sector is shown on the following table:

Manufacturing Industry, 2009-10

Industry subdivision	Wages & salaries $m	Sales & service income $m	Employment end of June
Food product manufacturing	1,921	14,759	46,116
Beverage and tobacco product manufacturing	136	1,589	2,330
Textile, leather, clothing and footware	202	1,169	6,382
Wood product	511	2,885	11,178
Pulp, paper and converted paper products	130	1,065	2,082
Printing	250	393	6,747
Petroleum and coal products	121	6,494	1,171
Basic chemical and chemical products	536	3,994	6,680
Polymer product and rubber product	398	2,924	7,530
Non-metallic mineral product	526	4,095	9,030
Primary metal and metal product	1,067	10,019	14,643
Fabricated metal product	1,291	6,115	26,554

continued

Transport equipment	747	4,445	14,340
Machinery and equipment	1,033	5,961	19,156
Furniture and other manufacturing	233	1,148	7,076
TOTAL	9,102	67,603	181,014

Source: Australian Bureau of Statistics. 8159.0

Tourism

Accommodation revenues in 2007-08 were: A$2,076 million. Occupancy rates averaged 65.9 per cent over all types of accommodation. There were 1,116 establishments with 60,422 rooms in the year 2007-08. (ABS, Queensland at a Glance, 2009)

Agriculture

Agricultural establishments numbered 27,656 in 2006-07 (down from 27,900 farms in 2001-02) with a total area for farming of 143,871,000 (down from 144,288,000 in 2003-04). Crop farming used 2,215,000 ha (down from 2,745,000 ha in 2003-04).

Gross Value of Selected Agricultural Production 2010

	A$ million
Cereals for grain	524.5
Cotton	301.1
Fruit & nuts	1,009.7
Nursery production	327.8
Grapes	35.7
Sugar cane for crushing	1,316.2
Vegetables	868.8
Cattle & calves	3,228.7
Sheep and lamb	45.1
Wool	87.2
Total Agricultural production	9,137.1

Source: ABS 7503.0

Queensland produces some 93 per cent of Australia's total sugar cane output, and 44 per cent of the nation's cotton crop. In 2006-07, the state raised 11,495,000 meat cattle and 189,000 dairy cattle, as well as 4,378,000 head of sheep and lamb, and 695,000 pigs. (Source: ABS, Queensland at a Glance 2009)

COMMUNICATIONS AND TRANSPORT

Railways

Queensland Rail saw increases in both passenger journeys (up to 54,100,000) and freight tonnage (183,460,000) in 2005-06. Earnings rose to A$2,574.3 million.

HEALTH

Queensland is divided into healthcare districts, each of which is serviced by one or more hospitals (178 in all), supported by some 277 nursing homes, community health centres and outpatient clinics. The state also has 55 private hospitals and 46 private day hospitals. The health service employs around 44,000 people.

The northern part of Queensland lies in the tropics and suffers a greater incidence of tropical diseases such as Dengue Fever and Ross River Fever.

Aboriginal and Torres Strait Islander communities have a lower life expectancy that the rest of the Queensland inhabitants, particularly those living in remote areas. These communities have higher rates of diabetes, kidney disease and drug and alcohol abuse compared to the rest of the state. Queensland's indigenous people die 18 to 19 years earlier than non-Indigenous Queenslanders.

EDUCATION

In 2010, Queensland had 1,235 government schools and 467 non-government run schools, of which 288 were run by the catholic church. In the same year, there were 731,617 students enrolled 492,114 attending government schools and 239,503 non-government schools.

In 2006, there were 54,578 teachers in the schools. The ratio of pupils to teacher in primary schools was 15.5:1 and, in secondary schools it was 13:1.

78.5 per cent of students remained in full-time education to year 12, above the national average of 74.7 per cent.

COMMUNICATIONS AND MEDIA

Newspapers
Courier Mail, URL: http://www.news.com.au/couriermail/queensland
Daily Mercury, URL: http://www.dailymercury.com.au/

ENVIRONMENT

In March 2009, a Hong Kong-registered ship damaged by Cyclone Hamish leaked 230 tonnes of oil along the coast of Queensland. The toxic sludge threatened wildlife and dozens of beaches along the Sunshine Coast were declared disaster zones. The ship's owner, Swire Shipping, faced fines of up to A$1.5m if found guilty of environmental breaches, as well as clean-up costs of A$100,000 a day. Hundreds of people worked to clean the beaches and save affected wildlife. Moreton Bay, a marine sanctuary worst hit by the oil spill, is home to a range of sea birds as well as turtles, dolphins and pelicans.

SOUTH AUSTRALIA

Capital: Adelaide (Population estimate: 1.1 million)

Governor: Rear Admiral Kevin Scarce AO CSC RANR (page 1509)

Lieutenant Governor: Hieu Van Le (page 1530)

State Flag: The State flag comprises the Blue Ensign with the State Badge in the fly. The State Badge consists of an Australian Piping Shrike standing on the staff of a gum tree.

CONSTITUTION AND GOVERNMENT

The Governor is the Queen's representative in South Australia. The Governor summons and prorogues Parliament at the beginning and end of each session. The Lieutenant Governor is appointed by the Queen on the advice of the Premier. The Lieutenant Governor's role is largely to deputise in the absence or incapacity of the Governor.

The government of South Australia is based on a Cabinet Government. The Cabinet is headed by the Premier and comprises 13 Ministers who may be members of the House of Assembly or Legislative Council. The Cabinet advises the Governor. Every Cabinet member is also a member of the Executive Council - the executive arm of government presided over by the Governor.

Recent Events
In November 2012, South Australia was hit by bushfires which scorched 2,000 hectares of land near Port Lincoln and destroyed several homes.

Legislature
South Australia's bicameral legislature comprises the Legislative Council and House of Assembly. A system of preferential voting is in operation and voting is compulsory for Australian citizens over the age of 18.
Parliament of South Australia, Parliament House, Adelaide, SA, 5000, Australia. URL: http://www.parliament.sa.gov.au/

Upper House
The Legislative Council is composed of 22 members presided over by the President. Every alternate election 11 Legislative Council members are elected by a proportional representation system of voting for terms of at least six years.

Legislative Council, Parliament House, Adelaide, SA, 5000, Australia. Tel: +61 (0)8 8237 9100, fax: +61 (0)8 8212 5792, URL: http://www.parliament.sa.gov.au/LegislativeCouncil/

Lower House
The House of Assembly consists of 47 members, each representing a separate electorate, elected by secret ballot for a minimum term of three years and a maximum term of four. A candidate must receive a majority of votes (over 50 per cent) to be elected.
House of Assembly, GPO Box 572, Adelaide SA 5001, Australia. Tel: +61 (0)8 8237 9467, fax: +61 (0)8 8237 9482, assembly@parliament.sa.gov.au, URL: http://www.parliament.sa.gov.au/house
Speaker of the House of Assembly: Lynette Breuer

> **Cabinet (as at June 2013)**
> *Premier, Minister, Treasurer, Minister for State Development, for the Public Sector, and for the Arts:* Jay Wilson Weatherill
> *Minister for Industrial Relations:* John Rau
> *Minister for State / Local Government Relations:* Gail Gago
> *Minister for Finance:* Michael O'Brien
> *Minister Assisting the Minister for the Arts:* Chloe Fox
> *Minister for Aboriginal Affairs and Reconciliation:* Ian Hunter

Ministries
Office of the Premier, (GPO Box 2343, Adelaide, South Australia 5001) State Administration Centre, 200 Victoria Square, Adelaide, South Australia, 5000. Tel: +61 8 8463 3166, fax: +61 8 8463 3168, e-mail: premier@saugov.sa.gov.au, URL: http://www.premier.sa.gov.au/, http://www.premcab.sa.gov.au/
Attorney General's Department, (GPO Box 464, Adelaide, SA 5001) 10th Floor, Mercantile Mutual Centre, 45 Pirie Street, Adelaide SA 5000, Australia. Tel: +61 8 8207 1555, fax: +61 8 8207 2520, e-mail: agd@agd.sa.gov.au, justice@justice.sa.gov.au, URL: http://www.justice.sa.gov.au
Department for Primary Industries and Resources, 17th Floor, Grenfell Centre, 25 Grenfell Street, Adelaide, South Australia 5000. Tel: +61 8 8226 0322, fax: +61 8 8226 0316, e-mail: ministers.office@pi.sa.gov.au, URL: http://www.pir.sa.gov.au/
Department of Justice, 11th Floor, 45 Pirie Street, Adelaide, South Australia 5000. Tel: +61 8 8207 1723, fax: +61 8 8207 1736, e-mail: justice@justice.sa.gov.au, URL: http://www.justice.sa.gov.au/

AUSTRALIA

Department of Industry & Trade, Level 10, Terrace Towers, 178 North Terrace, Adelaide, DX 452 Adelaide, GPO Box 2832 Adelaide, South Australia 5001. Tel: +61 8 8303 2500, fax: +61 8 8303 2410, URL: http://www.dit.sa.gov.au

Department of Treasury and Finance, (GPO Box 1045, Adelaide South Australia 5001) State Administration Centre, 200 Victoria Square, Adelaide South Australia 5000. Tel: +61 8 8226 9500, fax: + 61 8 8226 3819, e-mail: treasuryweb@saugov.sa.gov.au, URL: http://www.treasury.sa.gov.au/

Department for Correctional Services, (GPO Box 1747 Adelaide SA 5001) 25 Franklin Street Adelaide SA 5000, Australia. Tel: +61 8 8226 9000, fax: +61 8 8226 9226, e-mail: DCS.Central@saugov.sa.gov.au, URL: http://www.corrections.sa.gov.au/

Department of Human Services, Citicentre Building, 11 Hindmarsh Square, Adelaide SA 5000, (PO Box 287, Rundle Mall, Adelaide SA 5000), Australia. Tel: +61 8 8226 8800, fax: +61 8 8226 0725, e-mail: webmaster@dhs.sa.gov.au, URL: http://www.dhs.sa.gov.au

Department for Transport, Urban Planning, (PO Box 8245, Hindley Street, Adelaide SA 5000) Level 9, Roma Mitchell House, 136 North Terrace, Adelaide, 5000, South Australia. Tel: +61 8 8204 8200, fax: +61 8204 8216, URL: http://www.dtup.sa.gov.au/

Office for the Status of Women, Roma Mitchell House, 136 North Terrace, Adelaide 5000, (PO Box 8020, Station Arcade, Adelaide, SA 5000) South Australia. Tel: +61 8 8303 0961, fax: +61 8 8303 0963, e-mail: SocialJustice@saugov.sa.gov.au, URL: http://www.osw.sa.gov.au/

Department for Environment and Heritage, GPO Box 1047, Adelaide SA 5001, Australia. Tel: +61 8 8204 9000, fax: +61 8 8204 1919, e-mail: environmentshop@saugov.sa.gov.au, URL: http://www.environment.sa.gov.au/

Department of State Aboriginal Affairs and Reconciliation, Division of Department of Environment, Heritage and Aboriginal Affairs, Level 1, Centrepoint Building, 22 Pulteney Street, Adelaide SA 5000, Australia. Tel: +61 8 8226 8900, fax: +61 8 8226 8999, URL: http://www.dosaa.sa.gov.au/intro-main.html

Department of Education and Children's Services, 31 Flinders Street Adelaide SA 5000, (GPO Box 1152, Adelaide, SA 5001), Australia. Tel: +61 8 8226 1527, e-mail: decscustomers@saugov.sa.gov.au, URL: http://www.decs.sa.gov.au/

Department for Administrative and Information Services, Government ICS, DAIS Level 4, Wakefield House, 30 Wakefield Street, Adelaide South Australia 5000, (GPO Box 1484, Adelaide, South Australia 5001), Australia. Tel: 61 8 8226 3558, fax: 61 8 8226 3666, URL: http://www.government.ics.sa.gov.au/

Elections

In the March 2006 elections, in the House of Assembly, the Australian Labor Party, in government since 2002 under Premier Mike Rann, won six Liberal-held seats to bring their total number of seats to 28, and hence the first Labor majority government since the 1985. The Liberal Party were left with 15 seats, Independents won three seats, and there was one National Party seat. The Labor Party under Premier Mike Rann was re-elected for a third term in the March 2010 elections

In the Legislative Council, the Australian Labor Party and the Liberal party both won eight seats each. The No Pokies independent, Nick Xenophon, won an unprecedented 20.5 per cent of the poll. Family First won two seats, the Democrats were left with just one seat, and the Greens won a seat for the first time.

LEGAL SYSTEM

The judicial system includes a Supreme Court (composed of a Chief Justice, 12 judges and three masters), District Courts, Local Courts, Magistrates Courts, Youth Court, Coroner's Court, Environment Resources and Development Court, Industrial Relations Court.

Supreme Court of South Australia, Registrar's Office, 1 Gouger Street, Adelaide, South Australia, 5000, Australia. Tel: +61 (0)8 8204 0471, fax: +61 (0)8 8212 7154, URL: http://www.courts.sa.gov.au/
Chief Justice: The Hon Justice Kourakis

LOCAL GOVERNMENT

Under the Local Government Acts in South Australia there are 68 Councils. In addition there are six Local Governing Authorities located in remote areas of South Australia: Anangu Pitjantjatjara; Maralinga Tjarutja; Yalata Community Inc.; Nepabunna Community Council; Gerard Reserve Inc.; and The Outback Areas Community Development Trust.

Office of Local Government, URL: http://www.localgovt.sa.gov.au/

AREA AND POPULATION

Area

The area of South Australia is 984,377 sq. km, representing 12.8 per cent of the total area of Australia. It has a coastline of 1,700 km. The mean summer temperature is 22.3°C and the mean winter temperature 11.8°C. South Australia is the driest of all the states and territories; in 2006, the second driest year since records began in 1839, total rainfall in Adelaide reached just 288 mm (average annual rainfall being 558 mm in Adelaide). In January 2009, the state suffered a heatwave when temperatures exceeded 43°C (46 °C in urban areas).

Population

The estimated population for South Australia was 1,650,400 at the end of 2010, an increase of 15,600 persons (1.0 per cent) over the year.

South Australians comprise just 7.5 per cent of the total population of Australia. Around 73 per cent of the population of South Australia lives in the Adelaide Statistical Division. According to 2007 figures, life expectancy is 78.8 years for men and 83.9 years for women.

In 2008, the median age was 39 years, compared to 36.9 for Australia as a whole. Approximately 18.1 per cent of the population is aged 14 or under, 66.6 per cent were aged 15-64 years, and 15.3 per cent were aged over 65 years.

The indigenous population (those of Aboriginal and Torres Strait Islander origin) numbered an estimated 28,100 in 2006. (Source: South Australia at a Glance, 2007)

Births, Marriages, Deaths

There were 20,200 births in 2007-08 and 12,400 deaths. The infant mortality rate stood at 5.1 deaths per 1,000 inhabitants.

The marriage rate rose from 4.9 per 1,000 in 2005 to 5.1 per cent in 2007, whilst the divorce rate fell from 2.4 per 1,000 inhabitants in 2005, to 2.2 per 1,000 in 2007. The fertility rate was 1.79 per woman in 2005. (Source: South Australia at a Glance, 2009)

EMPLOYMENT

Labour Force (seasonally adjusted) Unit Jan. 2012 Jan. 2013 Civilian population 15 years and over'0001,367.01,381.5Employed persons'000820.2817.2Unemployed persons'00043.853.0Unemployment rate%5.16.1Participation rate%63.263.0Source: Labour Force, Australia, March 2013 (cat. no. 6202.0)

BANKING AND FINANCE

GDP/GNP, Inflation, National Debt

South Australia's Gross State Product (GSP) (current prices) rose from $65,177 million in June 2006 to A$69,540 million in June 2007, indicating an increase of 6.7 per cent over the year. South Australia's GSP comprises 6.6 per cent of the total national GSP. South Australia's GSP per capita rose by 5.6 per cent in the year to June 2007, reaching A$44,281. This is second lowest national rate. (Source: 5220.0 - Australian National Accounts: State Accounts, 2006-07). GSP grew by 1.5 per cent in 2009-10, to A$80.4 billion.

Gross State Product, Chain volume measures

Year	A$m	% change from previous year
2007-08	84,855	5.8
2008-09	86,450	1.9
2009-10	87,346	1.0
2010-11	89,322	2.3
2011-12	91,217	2.1

Source: Australian Bureau of Statistics 5220.0

Although agriculture accounts for 4.9 per cent of Australia's GSP, it is an important sector and includes over 42 per cent of Australia's total vineyard area and nearly one third of the barley area, South Australia's economy is primarily based on agricultural and horticultural products (including wine). Other major economic sectors are machinery, minerals, and aquaculture. The services sector contributes 60.4 per cent of GDP, manufacturing 11.6 per cent, mining 3.8 per cent and other 19.5 per cent.

The Consumer Price Index (all groups) for the capital, Adelaide, rose by three per cent over the year to December 2006. Preliminary figures for the house price index for established housing indicate a rise of 6.4 per cent over the year to September 2006. (Source: ABS, South Australia at a Glance, 2007)

Balance of Payments / Imports and Exports

The value of South Australia's merchandise exports in 2007-08 were A$10,338 million. The value of merchandise imports rose to A$732.4 million in 2007-08 compared to A$511 million in July 2007.

Main exported commodities are shown below:

Main export revenues, in A$ million

Export Group	2003-04
Metals and metal manufactures	799
Fish and crustaceans	400
Road vehicles, parts etc.	1,277
Meat and meat preparations	299
Wine	1,398
Wheat	693

Source: Australian Bureau of Statistics: 2005 South Australia at a Glance

South Australia's top trading partners are listed in the table below:

Main trading partners, 2003-04

Exports to:	A$ million
- United States of America	1,390
- Japan	695
- New Zealand	557
Total Exports	7,608
Imports from:	
- European Union	1,038
- Japan	891
- Middle East	669
- United States of America	652

continued

otal Imports	5,163

ustralian Bureau of Statistics: South Australia at a Glance

hambers of Commerce and Trade Organisations
nternational Trade Association South Australia, URL:
ttp://www.exportsouthaustralia.com/
outh Australian Chamber of Mines & Energy, URL: http://www.resourcessa.org.au/

MANUFACTURING, MINING AND SERVICES

rimary and Extractive Industries
outh Australian mineral production largely concentrates on copper, uranium oxide, opal, atural gas, crude oil, and liquid petroleum gas (LPG). The industry has around 17 mining stablishments and employed 4,000 in 2002-03 (up from 2,200 people in 2001-02). Various stablishments have closed and new ones opened. By the end of 2010 there are expected o be 16 operational sites. The state's second significant gold mine was opened at White Dam in June 2010. Production is scheduled to be 50,000 ounces per annum.

he following table shows the value of mineral production in recent years:

Value of Mineral Production, 2001-03 (A$m)

Mineral	2001-02	2002-03
Copper	476.6	514.6
Uranium oxide	153.4	131.3
Opal (estimate)	35.9	33.0
Natural gas	353.1	336.1
Crude oil	144.9	192.5
LPG	115.9	67.2
Other condensates	88.1	47.8
Construction materials	99.7	95.7
Industrial materials	52.4	46.1
Total mineral value	1,692.4	1,655.2

Source: Australian Bureau of Statistics: 2005 South Australia at a Glance

Manufacturing
Manufacturing forms an important part of South Australia's economy. A total of 97,100 people were employed in the sector in 2004-05 and revenue from the sector reached A$27.2 million. Machinery and equipment manufacturing is the largest subsector, accounting for 35 per cent of sales and service income and 32 per cent of South Australia's manufacturing employment. The State leads the country in wine and brandy production and is a significant supplier of meat, wood, printing, cement and concrete products, iron and steel, and appliances and electrical equipment.

Manufacturing Industry, 2009-10

Industry subdivision	Wages & salaries $m	Sales & service income $m	Employment end of June
Food product manufacturing	656	5,494	16,675
Beverage and tobacco product manufacturing	493	3,087	8,966
Textile, leather, clothing and footwear	84	460	2,515
Wood product	199	1,161	4,075
Pulp, paper and converted paper products	169	632	2,229
Printing	107	402	2,791
Petroleum and coal products	4	196	53
Basic chemical and chemical products	170	1,337	2,347
Polymer product and rubber product	213	1,185	3,757
Non-metallic mineral product	200	1,544	3,181
Primary metal and metal product	306	3,039	4,016
Fabricated metal product	424	2,170	8,832
Transport equipment	692	3,816	8,887
Machinery and equipment	589	3,107	11,224
Furniture and other manufacturing	93	491	2,830
TOTAL	4,398	28,121	82,377

Source: Australian Bureau of Statistics. 8159.0

Tourism
Tourist accommodation in 2003 and 2004 is shown on the following table:

Accommodation Hotels, motels, guest houses and serviced apartments	June qtr.2003	June qtr. 2004

- continued

	249	247
Number at 30th June	249	247
Guest rooms	11,764	11,910
Guest arrivals ('000s)	456.4	453
Takings from accommodation (A$'000)	56,754	60,907

Source: Australian Bureau of Statistics (South Australia at a Glance)

In the September qtr., 2006,there were 251 hotels and motels, and there were 556,000 guest arrivals.

Agriculture
In 2005, the number of agricultural establishments in South Australia had fallen to 14,111 (from 15,435 in 2001). As at the 30th June of 2005, 54,107,000 ha of land were used for agriculture; of this, 4,397,000 were used for crop-growing. Principal primary agricultural production includes wheat for grain and other cereals, fruit, vegetables and wool.

South Australia has about 42.3 per cent of Australia's vineyards. There were approximately 67,000 hectares of bearing vines in South Australia in 2005, with a further 4,400 hectares planted but not yet bearing fruit. The main varieties of wine produced are Cabernet Sauvignon, Shiraz, Chardonnay and Merlot.

The period 2001-07 has been marked by below average rainfall, leading to the worst drought in over a century. Conditions become so bad in 2006-07, that a significant number of farmers in South Australia, Victoria and NSW abandoned their crops. Total agricultural income slumped from A$1,233 million in 2005-06, to A$596 million in 2006-07, which is marginally greater than 25 per cent of the income derived from this sector in 2001-02 of A$2,311 million.

Gross Value of Selected Agricultural Production 2010

	A$ million
Cereals for grain	1,182.5
Fruit & nuts	287.0
Nursery production	63.2
Grapes	385.4
Vegetables	480.0
Cattle & calves	308.2
Sheep and lamb	448.4
Wool	284.0
Total Agricultural production	4,578.9

Source: ABS 7503.0

COMMUNICATIONS AND TRANSPORT

South Australia has more than 95,000 km of roads; more than 2,400 km are classified as national highways.

Railways are operated by the Federal and State governments.

HEALTH

South Australia has 80 public hospitals, 55 private hospitals as well as approximately 160 nursing homes. Approximately 6,550 beds are available (excl. day surgery beds) and the mean length of stay was 3.5 days.

EDUCATION

Primary/Secondary Education
In 2006, there were 604 government-run schools in South Australia and 201 non-government schools, of which 106 were Catholic. In total, South Australia had 546 primary schools, 94 secondary schools, and 142 combined primary and secondary schools.

There were 156,861 pupils enrolled in primary school in 2006, and 93,065 pupils registered in secondary school. Teachers numbered 19,854. In primary school, the ratio of pupils to teacher was 15.9:1 and in secondary schools, the ratio was 12.2:1. An estimated 7,986 indigenous people attended South Australian schools in 2006.

COMMUNICATIONS AND MEDIA

Newspapers
South Australia's newspapers include the Adelaide Advertiser (URL: http://www.adelaidenow.com.au/), the Murray Pioneer (URL: http//www.murray-pioneer.com.au/), the Sunday Mail (URL: http://www.couriermail.com.au/news/sunday-mail), and the Yorke Peninsula Country Times (URL: http://www.ypct.com.au/). Also published is the Sunday Mail/Advertiser (URL: http://www.theadvertiser.news.com.au/)

Telecommunications
The number of South Australia's internet subscribers rose from 453,000 in 2006 to 4496,000 in 2007-08. Approximately 62 per cent of households have an internet connection.

TASMANIA

Capital: Hobart (Population estimate: 200,000)

Governor: His Excellency the Hon. Peter Underwood, AO (page 1529)

State Flag: A British Blue Ensign on which is superimposed the state badge: a red lion on a white disc.

CONSTITUTION AND GOVERNMENT

Constitution
Van Diemen's Land was established in September 1803 by Lieutenant John Bowen. Australia's second oldest settlement, it took over its own administration on 3 December 1825 before its name was changed to Tasmania in 1856. In the same year the bicameral parliament met for the first time. The structure of the constitution has remained the same since then.

According to the Constitution the head of state is the Governor who is appointed by the Queen on the advice of the Premier. The Governor's responsibilities include the appointment of the Premier and, on the advice of the Premier, the appointment of Ministers.

Legislature
The Tasmanian Parliament is made up of three parts houses: the Crown, the Legislative Council and the House of Assembly. All three set Tasmania's state laws. All people aged 18 years and over vote to elect both houses.

Upper House
The Legislative Council consists of 15 members, one member for each constituency, and all elected for six years. There are no General Elections for the Legislative Council; rather, there are elections held for two or three electorates per year. Three members retire each year, except in every sixth year when four retire. The Legislative Council is currently composed of 12 Independent seats, and 3 Australian Labor Party (ALP) seats.
Tasmanian Legislative Council, Parliament House, Hobart 7000, Tasmania, Australia. Tel: +61 (0)3 6233 2300, fax: +61 (0)3 6231 1849, e-mail: council@parliament.tas.gov.au, URL: http://www.parliament.tas.gov.au/lc/council.htm

Lower House
The House of Assembly consists of 25 members. There are five House of Assembly divisions, corresponding to the Commonwealth electoral divisions, each returning five members elected under a system of proportional representation. The term of the House of Assembly is four years. The House meets annually, with sessions from March to May and then from August to December. The House is currently composed of 10 ALP seats, 10 Liberal seats, and 5 Tasmanian Green seats.
House of Assembly, Parliament House, Hobart, Tasmania 7000, Australia. Tel: +61 (0)3 6233 2200, fax: +61 (0)3 6223 6266, e-mail: assembly@parliament.tas.gov.au, URL: http://www.parliament.tas.gov.au/ha/house.htm

Cabinet (as at June 2013)
Premier, Treasurer, Minister for the Arts: Lara Giddings (page 1430)
Deputy Premier, Minister for Primary Industries & Water, Minister for Energy and Resources, Minister for Local Government, Minister for Planning, Minister for Racing: Bryan Green
Minister for Health, for Children, and for Sport and Recreation: Michelle O'Byrne
Minister for Infrastructure, for Workplace Relations, for Economic Development, Science, Innovation and Technology, and Minister for the Police & Emergency Management: David O'Byrne
Attorney General, Minister for Justice, Minister of Environment, Parks and Heritage: Brian Wightman
Minister for Education and Skills, for Corrections and Consumer Protection, for Sustainable Development: Nick McKim
Minister for Human Services, Minister for Community Development, for Climate Change, and for Aboriginal Matters: Cassy O'Connor
Minister for Tourism, Minister for Finance, Minister for Hospitality, and Minister for Veterans' Affairs and Skills: Scott Bacon

Ministries
Office of the Premier, (GPO Box 123B Hobart, Tasmania 7001) 11th Floor, 15 Murray Street, Hobart, Tasmania 7000. Tel: +61 (0)3 6233 3464, fax: +61 (0)3 6234 1572, e-mail: Premier@dpac.tas.gov.au, URL: http://www.premier.tas.gov.au/
Office of the Attorney-General and Ministry for Justice and Industrial Relations, 1st Floor, Public Building, 53 St John Street, Launceston, Tasmania 7250. Tel: +61 (0)3 6336 3400, fax: +61 (0)3 6331 3705, e-mail: Records@justice.tas.gov.au, URL: http://www.justice.tas.gov.au/
Department of Treasury and Finance, The Treasury Building, 21 Murray Street, Hobart, Tasmania 7000, (GPO Box 147, Hobart Tasmania 7001). Tel: +61 (0)3 6233 3100, fax: 61 (0)3 6223 2755, e-mail: reception@treasury.tas.gov.au, URL: http://www.tres.tas.gov.au
Department of Primary Industries, Water and Environment, Marine Board Building, 1 Franklin Wharf, Hobart, TAS 7001 (GPO Box 44, Hobart, Tasmania 7001). Tel: +61 (0)3 6233 8001, fax: +61 (0)3 6234 1335, e-mail: FAF.Enquiries@dpiwe.tas.gov.au, URL: http://www.dpiwe.tas.gov.au/
Department of Education, 116 Bathurst Street, Hobart 7000 (GPO Box 169, Hobart 7001), Tasmania. Tel: +61 (0)3 6233 7055, fax: +61 (0)3 6231 1576, e-mail: web.support@education.tas.gov.au, URL: http://www.education.tas.gov.au/
Department of Health and Human Services, 34 Davey Street, Hobart (GPO Box 125B, Hobart, Tasmania 7001), Tasmania. Tel: +61 (0)3 6233 3185, fax: +61 (0)3 6233 4580, e-mail: internetco-ordinator@dhhs.tas.gov.au, URL: http://www.dhhs.tas.gov.au/

Ministry for Infrastructure, Energy and Resources, 10 Murray Street, Hobart 7000 (GPO Box 936, Hobart, Tasmania 7001) Tasmania. Tel: +61 (0)3 6233 2001, e-mail info@dier.tas.gov.au, URL: http://www.dier.tas.gov.au/
Department of Economic Development, (GPO Box 646 Hobart) 22 Elizabeth Street, Hobart, Tasmania, Australia 7000. Tel: +61 (0)3 62 335888, fax: +61 (0)3 62 335800, e-mail. info@development.tas.gov.au, URL: http://www.development.tas.gov.au/
Department of Tourism, Parks, Heritage and the Arts, GPO Box 771, Hobart Tasmania 7001. Tel: +61 (0)3 6233 5732, fax: +61 (0)3 6233 5555, e-mail info@dtpha.tas.gov.au, URL: http://www.dtpha.tas.gov.au/
Department of Police and Public Safety, 43 Liverpool St, Hobart 7000, Tasmania (GPO Box 308C, Hobart, Tasmania 7001). Tel: +61 (0)3 6230 2375, e-mail tasmania.police@police.tas.gov.au, URL: http://www.police.tas.gov.au/

Political Parties
Australian Labor Party (ALP), URL: http://www.tas.alp.org.au/
Tasmanian Greens, URL: http://www.tas.greens.org.au/

Elections
In the legislative elections for the House of Assembly, held 18 March 2006, the ALP won a third successive term in office, with 49.3 per cent of the vote (14 seats). The Liberal party won 31.9 per cent (7 seats) and the Greens won 16.6 per cent (4 seats). In the most recent elections held in March 2010, both the ALP and the Liberal Party won 10 seats and the Greens won 5 seats, their best ever result.

Because the Legislative Council can never be dissolved for a general election, a limited number of seats go to election annually, usually in May.

LEGAL SYSTEM

Tasmania's court system comprises the Supreme Court, Magistrates Court (Criminal and General, Small Claims, Civil, and Coronial Divisions), and Coroner's Court. The Supreme Court consists of the Chief Justice and five Judges.
Supreme Court of Tasmania, Salamanca Place, Hobart, Tasmania 7000 or GPO Box 167B, Hobart, Tasmania 7001. Tel: +61 3 6233 3427 (Registry), fax: +61 3 6233 7816 (Registry), URL: http://www.supremecourt.tas.gov.au/home
Chief Justice: Hon Ewan Crawford

LOCAL GOVERNMENT

Tasmania is divided into 30 municipalities, the largest of which is Launceston with 62,830 inhabitants.

AREA AND POPULATION

Area
Tasmania is an island that lies off the south-east coast of Australia. It is surrounded by smaller islands, the most important of these being Flinders, King and Bruny. The smallest of Australia's six states, Tasmania has an area of 68,102 sq. km (including the lesser islands), equivalent to about 0.9 per cent of the total area of Australia. The state is separated from the Australian mainland by Bass Strait, and the remaining coastline is bounded by the Southern Ocean on the south and west and the Tasman Sea on the east.

Hobart, Tasmania's capital city, is in the south of the state.

Population
The estimated resident population of Tasmania was an estimated 507,626 in 2010, and comprised around 2.4 per cent of the total population of Australia. The population growth rate over the year to March 2007 was 0.6 per cent. Natural growth increased the population by 758 people, overseas migration added 330 but interstate migration lost 22 people, giving a net increase of 1,066 people. Population density increased slightly in 2004 to 7.1 persons per sq. km.

Births, Marriages, Deaths
In 2006, the number of registered births in Tasmania was recorded as 6,316 and the number of registered deaths was 3,938. There were 24 infant deaths in 2006. Tasmania's fertility rate in 2008-09 was 2.2 babies per woman, the highest since 1975. Life expectancy in 2006-08 was 77.7 for males and 82.3 years for females. The median age of the population was 39.6 years.

Marriages in 2005 took place at the rate of 5.4 per 1,000 inhabitants, and divorces occurred at the rate of 2.8 per 1,000 people. (Source: Australian Bureau of Statistics)

Regional Public Holidays 2014
8 January: Devonport Cup (Municipal area of Devonport only)
10 February: Royal Hobart Regatta (Hobart and south of Hobart only)
26 February: Launceston Cup
10 March: Eight Hours Day
2 May: AGFEST (Circular Head only)

EMPLOYMENT

Labour Force (seasonally adjusted)

	Unit	Jan. 2012	Jan. 2013
Civilian population 15 years and over	'000	413.5	415.9
Employed persons	'000	232.5	230.4
Unemployed persons	'000	17.2	19.4
Unemployment rate	%	6.9	7.8
Participation rate	%	60.4	60.1

Source: Labour Force, Australia, March 2013 (cat. no. 6202.0)

Employment according to Industry, November Quarter

Industry	2005	2010
Agriculture, forestry and fishing	15.2	14.8
Mining	2.7	3.6
Manufacturing	23.0	19.2
Electricity, gas, water and waste services	2.7	3.8
Construction	15.1	18.5
Wholesale trade	7.8	7.3
Retail trade	25.6	27.5
Accommodation, cafes, restaurants	16.2	16.8
Transport, postal and warehousing	9.5	11.9
Communication services	5.3	3.8
Finance and insurance	6.0	4.0
Rental, hiring & real estate services	3.4	3.1
Professional, scientific & technical services	9.8	13.7
Administrative & support services	7.2	6.5
Public admin. & safety	16.8	15.5
Education & training	16.5	20.5
Health care & social assistance	26.0	31.1
Arts & recreation services	5.5	4.8
Other services	8.2	9.4
Total	222.5	235.8

Source: ABS (Tasmania at a Glance, 2011)

BANKING AND FINANCE

GDP/GNP, Inflation, National Debt

Over the year 2006-07, Tasmania's Gross State Product (chain volume measures) rose by 2.1 per cent to A$21,088 million (current prices). This was slightly below the average annual rise over the decade to 2007, of 2.7 per cent. In 2005-06, the main contributors to GSP were the business services sector (13 per cent) and manufacturing industry, though the percentage contribution of this sector has fallen from 15 per cent in 2000 to 11 per cent in 2006.

Gross State Product, Chain volume measures

Year	A$m	% change from previous year
2007-08	23,592	2.9
2008-09	24,154	2.4
2009-10	24,168	0.1
2010-11	24,218	0.2
2011-12	24,345	0.5

Source: Australian Bureau of Statistics 5220.0

The Consumer Price Index (CPI) (all items) rose from 148 in March 2005 to 155.4 in March 2007. There was an increase of 2.1 per cent over the year to March 2007. The established House Price Index indicated a rise of 10.5 per cent over the year to March 2007.

Balance of Payments / Imports and Exports

Tasmania is rich in mineral resources, and it produces more primary produce than its small population requires.

Tasmanian merchandise export revenue rose to A$3,706 million at the year end June 2007, up from A$2,895 million by June 2006. Merchandise import costs rose to A$615 million over the twelve months to June 2007, up from A$515 million by June 2006. Export of services earned A$385 million over the year to June 2007 and the import of services cost A$198 million over the same year. Figures for 2009-10 showed that total imports (customs value) was A$714.9 million and total exports (f.o.b.) that year were valued at A$3,004.2 million.

Tasmania's international exports have historically been mainly composed of raw materials and their products.

Main Exported Commodities, 2005-06, A$000s

Zinc	589,622
Aluminium	487,711
Wood in chips or wood waste	336,958
Copper ores and concentrates	214,485
Fish, crustaceans and molluscs	145,062
Meat and meat preparations	134,225
Dairy produce and eggs	98,696
Iron ore and concentrates	82,568
Cork and wood manufactures (excl. furniture)	51,651

Source: 1384.6 Statistics-Tasmania, 2006

The following tables show monthly export revenue and import costs according to top international trading partners:

Tasmania's Major Export Markets (A$'000)

Trading Partner	2004-05	2005-06
Japan	711,518	555,207
Hong Kong	241,502	439,021
Rep. of Korea	263,332	324,180
China	201,872	250,419
USA	222,053	181,577
ASEAN - Total	263,662	294,375
- Indonesia	70,239	94,854
- Singapore	78,691	34,460
- Thailand	30,161	70,409
- Malaysia	44,917	57,992
- Philippines	27,024	24,796
European Union Total	97,923	126,756

Source: Australian Bureau of Statistics (1384.6 - Statistics - Tasmania, 2006)

The most valuable import category in 2005-06 was pulp and waste paper, which accounted for 11.6 per cent of the total. Cocoa was second, accounting for 8.9 per cent of imports. Other major imports included general industrial machinery and equipment and machine parts; power generating machinery and equipment, and petroleum, petroleum products and related materials.

Chambers of Commerce and Trade Organisations

Derwent Valley Chamber of Commerce and Industry, URL: http://www.tased.edu.au/tasonline/dvcc/contents.htm

Tasmanian Chamber of Commerce and Industry Ltd., URL: http://www.tcci.com.au/

MANUFACTURING, MINING AND SERVICES

Primary and Extractive Industries

Tasmanian mining is concentrated in the north and west of the State. Both metallic minerals and non-metallic minerals, including fuel minerals, are produced. Tasmania's most significant known resources are: copper, lead, zinc, nickel, tin, gold and iron ore. There are also operations for mining clay and limestone, as well as coal. Around 3,600 people are employed in the mining sector.

Energy

Lacking abundant supplies of coal and oil, Tasmania has promoted the development of hydroelectricity for industrial and general use. The total installed generating capacity, in 2004 is 2,502 MW. Production in 2002 amounted to 10,195 GWh, of which 10,133 GWh was provided by the hydroelectric network and 62 was provided through thermal means.

Tasmania is in the path of prevailing westerly winds, the Roaring Forties, which ensure ideal conditions for producing electricity through wind power. Research has indicated that wind turbines could create enough energy to supply electricity in Tasmania and to mainland Australia. In May 2003, there are four wind farm sites or potential sites in Tasmania: Woolnorth, King Island's Huxley Hill, Heemskirk and Musselroe.

Hydro Tasmania, URL: http://www.hydro.com.au/

Manufacturing

Cheap bulk electricity for industrial use has attracted a number of major industries to Tasmania, principally associated with metal refining (zinc, aluminium, iron ore pelletizing, and ferro-alloy production) and paper and newsprint production. In 2009-10 manufacturing sales and service income amounted to A$8,263 million The industry employs around 19,000 people.

Manufacturing Industry, 2009-10

Industry subdivision	Wages & salaries $m	Sales & service income $m	Employment end of June
Food product manufacturing	324	1,877	6,648
Beverage and tobacco product manufacturing	18	121	427
Textile, leather, clothing and footware	28	113	629
Wood product	71	399	1,739
Pulp, paper and converted paper products	113	273	441
Printing	22	67	548
Petroleum and coal products	4	19	61
Basic chemical and chemical products	41	358	547
Polymer product and rubber product	34	166	679
Non-metallic mineral product	38	334	714
Primary metal and metal product	138	1,311	1,893
Fabricated metal product	75	308	1,712
Transport equipment	57	217	962
Machinery and equipment	79	564	1,449
Furniture and other manufacturing	16	82	590

AUSTRALIA

- continued

TOTAL	1,059	6,208	19,038

Source: Australian Bureau of Statistics. 8159.0

Tourism

Total adult visitors to Tasmania rose from 748,500 in 2004 to 904,000 in 2010. Visitors' expenditure rose from A$1,093,0000 to A$1,526,000 over the same period. Most visitors came from Australia, and 124,1000 were visiting relatives or friends. 385,500 people visited Tasmania for a holiday. (Source: Australian Bureau of Statistics)

Agriculture

Tasmania had a total agricultural land area of 6.84 million hectares in 2003, of which 74,000 hectares was used for crops. The total number of agricultural establishments with an estimated value of A$5,000 or more was 4,286 in 2004 (down from 4,286 in 2001). In 2004-05, gross farm product was $661 million, the equivalent to 4.1 per cent of GSP. In 2006, 14,100 people were employed in this sector.

Main Farm Products, 2009-10

Product	Quantity
Livestock numbers	
Milk cattle	192
Meat cattle	446
Sheep & lambs	1,991
Pigs	11
Production	
Red meat (carcass weight) tonnes	62,885
Milk, million litres	674
Wool, tonnes	10,275
Barley for grain, tonnes	28,800
Apples, tonnes	31,229
Gross value of agricultural commodities produce, A$m	1,087.8

Source: Tasmania at a Glance

Fishing

The fishing industry employs approximately 1,500 people and produces over A$300 million in revenue.

COMMUNICATIONS AND TRANSPORT

National Airlines

Regular jet flights operate between Hobart and Melbourne, the journey taking about an hour, and there are regular interstate and intrastate services to other main centres. Direct flights to and from New Zealand are also run.

International Airports

Hobart International Airport(URL: http://www.hobartairpt.com.au/) is located at Llanherne, Hobart.

Railways

The Tasmanian railway system consists of 867 km of primarily freight track. The only passenger services are for small tourist networks.

Roads

Tasmania has about 24,000 km of roads, with a further 6,000 km of four-wheel drive track private roads and fire trails. The State Road Network is managed by the Department of Infrastructure, Energy and Resources. The National Highway consists of the Midland Highway and the Bass Highway West, and joins the four major population centres.

Shipping

Several roll-on roll-off type vessels provide regular shipping services for freight and passenger between Tasmania and the mainland states.

Ports and Harbours

Hobart Ports Corporation, URL: http://www.hpc.com.au
Burnie Port Corporation, e-mail: info@burnieport.com.au

HEALTH

Tasmania has three major hospitals for acute conditions, located in Hobart, Launceston and Burnie. There are 20 smaller district hospitals and health centres which provide local care and there are around 10 privately funded hospitals.

Average male life expectancy is 76.6 years and female 81.4 years.

The most frequent causes of early death in Tasmanian men are ischaemic heart disease, lung cancer, and stroke. In women, the most frequent causes are ischaemic heart disease, stroke and breast cancer. 25 per cent of Tasmanian men, and 23.7 per cent of women, were regular smokers in 2001.

EDUCATION

There was a total of 80,841 full time students in 2010. The number of students in government schools fell from 61,976 in 2002 to 57,331in 2010. Conversely, the number of students in non-government schools rose from 20,821 in 2001 to 226,783 in 2010.

Government schools numbered 202 in 2010, whilst non-government schools numbered 66.

Total university enrolment numbered 26,783 in 2010.

COMMUNICATIONS AND MEDIA

Newspapers

Tasmania's newspapers include The Advocate (URL: http://nwtasmania.yourguide.com.au), the Launceston Examiner (URL: http://northerntasmania.yourguide.com.au), The Mercury (URL: http://www.themercury.com.au/), and The Sunday Tasmanian.

Telecommunications

The number of homes with internet access reached 99,000 in 2006, equivalent to 49 per cent of total households.

ENVIRONMENT

In May 2009, the Tasmanian devil, the world's largest surviving marsupial carnivore, was given an 'endangered' status; the population is thought to have fallen by 70 per cent since the 1990s. The Tasmanian devils are suffering an incurable facial tumor disease, which is highly contagious and is spread through biting.

VICTORIA

Capital: Melbourne (Population estimate, 2012: 4,077,035)

Governor: Alex Chernov AC QC (page 1403)

State Flag: A British Blue Ensign on which is superimposed the state badge: the Southern Cross surmounted by the St Edwards Crown.

CONSTITUTION AND GOVERNMENT

Constitution

From 1836 to 1842 Victoria was a district of New South Wales, governed from Sydney. In 1851 it became a self-governing colony when the Legislative Council of Victoria was formed. The constitution was drafted by the Legislative Council in 1853-54 and came into effect on 23 November 1855. The constitution required the Parliament of Victoria to include the Crown, a Legislative Council and a Legislative Assembly. Elections for the lower house first took place in 1856, and on 25 November the Parliament of Victoria was sworn in. On 1 January 1901 Victoria became a State in the federation of Australia.

Following the Australia Acts of 1986, the Governor exercises the powers and functions of the Crown for Victoria, other than the Governor's appointment or dismissal which is the responsibility of the Queen. As the Queen's representative, the Governor has the power to summon or dissolve Parliament, appoint or dismiss ministers, and act as Governor in Council.

The Lieutenant-Governor is appointed or dismissed by the Queen on the advice of the Premier, and exercises the powers and functions of the Governor in his or her absence. In the absence of the Lieutenant-Governor, the Administrator - who is the Chief Justice or next most senior judge of the Supreme Court - is empowered to act.

Recent Events

Bushfires caused the deaths of over 130 people in southern Australia in early February 2009. Victoria was the worst affected state. The wildfires were exacerbated by drought, dry bush and one of the most powerful heat waves in memory. Temperatures in parts of Melbourne reached 118 degrees Fahrenheit (48 degrees Celsius), and dozens of heat-related deaths were reported. One massive bushfire tore through several towns, destroying everything in its path. Many people died in cars whilst trying to flee and others were killed in their homes. Some escaped by jumping in swimming pools or farm reservoirs. More than 750 houses were destroyed and some 78 people were admitted to hospital with serious burns and injuries. It was thought that some of the fires were deliberately lit and the authorities declared one devastated town a crime scene. In February and March 2012 bush fires again struck large areas of Victoria.

Legislature

There are currently two legislative chambers: the Legislative Council and the Legislative Assembly.
Parliament of Victoria, Parliament House, Melbourne, Victoria 3002, Australia. Tel: +61 3 9651 8911, fax: +61 3 9654 5284, e-mail: info@parliament.vic.gov.au, URL: http://www.parliament.vic.gov.au/

Upper House
In November 2006, the Victorian Legislative Council elections were held under a new multi-proportional representation system. The State of Victoria is now divided into eight electorates, each of which is represented by five representatives elected by Single Transferable Vote proportional representation. The total number of members was reduced from 44 to 40 and their term of office is now four years. Elections for the Victorian Parliament are now fixed and occur in November every four years.
Legislative Council, Parliament House, Melbourne, Victoria 3002, Australia. Tel: +61 (0)3 9651 8673, fax: +61 (0)3 9650 5253, e-mail: council@parliament.gov.vic.au, URL: http://www.parliament.vic.gov.au/council/default.htm
President of the Legislative Council: Bruce Atkinson MLC

Lower House
The Legislative Assembly consists of 88 members, elected for the duration of Parliament, which is limited to a minimum of three and a maximum of four years. Each member is elected for a single electoral district.
Legislative Assembly, Parliament House, Spring Street, Melbourne 3002, Australia. Tel: +61 (0)3 9651 8564, fax: +61 (0)3 9654 7245, e-mail: assembly@parliament.vic.gov.au, URL: http://www.parliament.vic.gov.au/assembly
Speaker of the Legislative Assembly: Ken Smith

Cabinet (as at June 2013)
Premier, Minister for Regional Cities; Minister for Racing: Denis Napthine (page 1484)
Deputy Premier, Minister for Regional and Rural Development, Minister for State Development: Peter Ryan
Minister for Innovation, Services and Small Business, Minister for Tourism and Major Events, Minister for Employment: Louise Asher
Attorney General, Minister for Finance, Minister for Industrial Relations: Robert Clark
Minister for Health, Minister for Ageing: David Davis
Minister for Sport and Recreation, Minister for Veterans' Affairs: Hugh Delahunty
Minister for Education: Martin Dixon
Minister for Planning: Matthew Guy
Minister for Higher Education and Skills: Peter Hall
Minister for Ports, Minister for Major Projects; Minister for Manufacturing: David Hodgett
Minister for Multicultural Affairs and Citizenship; Minister for Energy and Resources: Nicholas Kotsiras
Minister for Housing, Minister for Children and Early Childhood Development: Wendy Lovell
Minister for Public Transport, Minister for Roads: Terry Mulder
Treasurer: Michael O'Brien
Minister for Corrections, Minister for Liquor and Gaming Regulation, Minister for Crime Prevention: Edward O'Donohue
Minister for Local Government, Minister for Aboriginal Affairs: Jeanette Powell
Assistant Treasurer, Minister for Technology: Gordon Rich-Phillips
Minister for Environment and Climate Change, Minister for Youth Affairs: Ryan Smith
Minister for the Arts, Minister for Women's Affairs; Minister for Consumer Affairs: Heidi Victoria
Minister for Agriculture and Food Security, Minister for Water: Peter Walsh
Minister for Police and Emergency Services; Minister for Bushfire Response: Kim Wells
Minister for Mental Health; Minister for Community Services; Minister for Disability Services and Reform: Mary Wooldridge

Ministries
Office of the Premier, 1 Treasury Place, Melbourne, Australia 3000. Tel: +61 3 9651 5000, fax: +61 3 9651 5054, e-mail: premier@dpc.vic.gov.au, URL: http://www.premier.vic.gov.au/
Department of Infrastructure, Nauru House, 80 Collins Street, Melbourne 3000, (GPO Box 2797Y, Melbourne 3001), Australia. Tel: +61 3 9655 6666, fax: +61 3 9655 6752, e-mail: infrastructure@doi.vic.gov.au, URL: http://www.doi.vic.gov.au
Department of Treasury and Finance, 1 Treasury Place, Melbourne, Victoria 3002. Tel: +61 3 9651 5111, fax: +61 3 9654 7215, e-mail: information@dtf.vic.gov.au, URL: http://www.dtf.vic.gov.au/
Department of Education and Training, 2 Treasury Place, East Melbourne (GPO Box 4367, Melbourne, VIC 3001), Victoria 3002. Tel: +61 3 9637 2000, fax: +61 3 9637 3260, e-mail: edline@edumail.vic.gov.au, URL: http://www.det.vic.gov.au/det/
Department of Human Services, Enterprise House, 555 Collins Street, Melbourne 3000, (GPO Box 4057, Melbourne Vic 3001), Victoria. Tel: +61 3 9616 7777, fax: +61 3 9616 8329, URL: http://www.dhs.vic.gov.au/
Local Government and Regional Services Division, Department of Infrastructure,
Level 19, 80 Collins Street, Melbourne 3000, (GPO Box 2797Y, Melbourne 3001), Australia. Tel: +61 3 9655 6666, fax: +61 3 9655 6752, e-mail: infrastructure@doi.vic.gov.au, URL: http://www.doi.vic.gov.au/doi/internet/localgov.nsf
Department of Innovation, Industry and Regional Development, 55 Collins Street, Melbourne Victoria 3000 (GPO Box 4509 RR, Melbourne, Victoria 3001) Australia. Tel: +61 3 9651 9999, fax: +61 3 9651 9770, e-mail: enquiries@iird.vic.gov.au, URL: http://www.iird.vic.gov.au/
Department of Justice, 55 St Andrews Place, Melbourne 3002, (GPO Box 4356 QQ, Melbourne 3001), Australia. Tel: +61 3 9651 0333, fax: +61 3 9651 0555, e-mail: penny.armitage@justice.vic.gov.au, URL: http://www.justice.vic.gov.au/
Department of Sustainability and Environment, 8 Nicholson Street, East Melbourne VIC 3002, (PO Box 500, East Melbourne 3002), Australia. Tel: +61 3 9637 8000, fax: +61 3 9637 8100, e-mail: customer.service@dse.vic.gov.au, URL: http://www.dse.vic.gov.au
Department of Primary Industries, 8 Nicholson Street, East Melbourne 3002, (PO Box 500, East Melbourne 3002), Australia. Tel: +61 3 9637 8000, fax: +61 3 9637 8100, e-mail: customer.service@dpi.vic.gov.au, URL: http://www.dpi.vic.gov.au/

Department of Planning (Department of Infrastructure), Level 20, Nauru House, 80 Collins Street, Melbourne, Vic 3000 (GPO Box 2797Y, Melbourne Vic 3001), Australia. Tel: +61 03 9655 6666, fax: +61 03 9655 6752, URL: http://www.doi.vic.gov.au/doi/internet/planning.nsf
Department for Victorian Communities, Level 48, 80 Collins Street, Melbourne 3000, (GPO Box 2392V, Melbourne 3001), Australia. Tel: +61 3 9666 4200, fax: +61 3 9666 4394, e-mail: dvc@dvc.vic.gov.au, URL: http://www.dvc.vic.gov.au/

Elections
The most recent state legislative elections took place on 27 November 2010. All seats in both houses of parliament were up for election. In the Legislative Assembly the incumbent Australian Labor Party won most seats but did not gain an overall majority. The Labor Party won 43 seats (down 12 on the previous election), the Liberal Party 35 (up 12) and the National Party 10 seats. The new Liberal/National coalition government was sworn in on 2 December 2010. Daniel Andrews became the new Labor leader.

In the Legislative Council the Liberal/National Coalition won 21 of the 40 seats, the Australian Labor Party 16 and the Australian Greens three.

LEGAL SYSTEM

Victoria's court system consists of the Supreme Court, Court of Appeal, County Courts, and Magistrates Courts.

Supreme Court of Victoria, 210 William Street, Melbourne, Victoria 3000, Australia. Tel: +61 (0)3 9603 6111, fax: +61 (0)3 9603 6352, e-mail: webmaster@supremecourt.vic.gov.au
URL: http://www.supremecourt.vic.gov.au

LOCAL GOVERNMENT

Victoria is divided into a total of 79 local governments consisting of metropolitan and rural councils. Metropolitan councils are headed by a Chief Executive Officer and a Mayor. Rural councils are headed by a Chief Executive Officer and a Mayor or Shire President. Local government elections usually take place every three years on the third Saturday in March.

Department for Victorian Communities, URL: http://www.dvc.vic.gov.au

AREA AND POPULATION

Area
The area of the State of Victoria is 227,600 sq. km, 2.96 per cent of the Australian total or sixth in terms of geographic size. Victoria generally has a temperate climate though the coastal areas can get cold fronts with Southern Ocean winds. The Alpine areas have the most extreme weather conditions. The capital, Melbourne, enjoys average temperatures ranging from 25°C in summer to 7°C in winter. Average annual rainfall is 641 mm.

In January 2009, the state suffered a heatwave, with temperatures reaching 43°C (46°C in urban areas). Wildfires in the west of the state destroyed 2,000 hectares of forest and grassland, and forced residents to flee their homes.

Population
Victoria's total population at the end of June 2011 was 5,624,100, an increase of 84,200 or 1.5 per cent on the previous year's figure. Victoria has about 25 per cent of Australia's total population and is Australia's second most populous state after New South Wales. There are around 21.6 people per sq. km. Over 73 per cent of the population lives in the capital city; Melbourne, which had a population of 4.0 million in Jan. 2012. For year ended 30 September 2009, Victoria's preliminary net overseas migration estimate was 82,060 persons, this accounted for over 66 per cent of the state's population increase.

Births, Marriages, Deaths
In 2009, the number of births was estimated to be 70,920. The crude birth rate in 2006 was 12.7 births per 1,000 inhabitants. The fertility rate for 2009 was 1.8 children per woman. The standardised death rate for Victoria is approximately 6.3 deaths per 1,000 inhabitants. The marriage rate in the same year was 5.2 per 1,000 people, whilst the divorce rate was 2.5 per 1,000 people. (Source: Australian Bureau of Statistics)

EMPLOYMENT

Labour Force (seasonally adjusted)

	Unit	Jan. 2012	Jan. 2013
Civilian population 15 years and over	'000	4,630.4	4,706.4
Employed persons	'000	2,857.7	2,859.1
Unemployed persons	'000	155.4	186.8
Unemployment rate	%	5.2	6.1
Participation rate	%	65.1	64.7

Source: Labour Force, Australia, March 2013 (cat. no. 6202.0)

Employees per industry, Nov. 2010

Industry	'000 employees
Agriculture, Fishing and Foresty	49.9
Mining	9.4
Manufacturing	264.9
Electricity, Gas and Water	31.3

AUSTRALIA

- continued

Construction	218.4
Wholesale trade	96.7
Retail trade	166.9
Accommodation and Restaurants	77.0
Transport and storage	116.9
Communications	46.9
Finance and Insurance	101.3
Rental, hiring and real estate services	35.1
Professional, scientific & technical services	170.3
Admin. & support services	39.2
Public admin. & safety	61.5
Education & training	49.6
Health care & social assistance	52.6
Arts & recreation services	22.8
Other services	52.8
Total	1,298.3

Australian Bureau of Statistics

BANKING AND FINANCE

GDP/GNP, Inflation, National Debt
Gross State Product, Chain volume measures

Year	A$m	% change from previous year
2007-08	298,320	3.5
2008-09	301,548	1.1
2009-10	307,193	1.9
2010-11	315,571	2.7
2011-12	322,833	2.3

Source: Australian Bureau of Statistics 5220.0

The following table shows the industry gross value added in chain volume measures in recent years, figure are in A$ million.

Industry	2009-10	2010-11
Agriculture, forestry and fishing	7,471	7,767
Mining	7,243	7,101
Manufacturing	28,714	27,970
Electricity, gas and water supply	5,821	5,985
Construction	19,065	20,021
Wholesale trade	14,408	13,814
Retail trade	14,596	15,123
Accommodation and restaurants	6,582	6,881
Transport and storage	13,964	14,295
Communication services	11,554	11,532
Financial & insurance services	33,570	34,620
Property and business services	6,059	6,067
Professional, scientific & technical services	21,111	24,136
Admin. & support services	7,951	8,386
Public admin. and safety	10,611	10,898
Education & training	15,976	16,265
Health care and social assistance	17,446	17,955
Arts & recreation services	3,121	3,284
Other services	5,152	5,161
Ownership of dwellings	23,317	23,929
Gross value added at basic prices	273,732	281,191

ABS 5220.0 Australian National Accounts: State Accounts

The Consumer Price Index (CPI) stood at 156.9 (Base index: 1989-90 = 100.0) in Melbourne as at September 2007. This indicated an increase of 0.8 per cent over the quarter, and an increase of 2.1 per cent over the year. For the year ending September 2007, the inflation rate for Melbourne was higher than the average for the eight capital cities which stood at 1.9 per cent.

Balance of Payments / Imports and Exports
Balance of International Merchandise Trade in A$m

Year	Exports	Imports	Balance
2007-08	20,539	56,058	-35,520
2008-09	20,375	56,457	-36,082
2009-10	18,427	53,118	-34,691

Source: ABS 13672DO019_201012 State and Regional Indicators, Victoria, Dec 2010

Goods exported, (figures in A$m)

Selected Goods	2008-09	2009-10
Beverages & tobacco	295	279
Crude materials, inedible, except fuels	1,691	2,002
Mineral fuels, lubricants & related materials	1,044	785
Animal & vegetable oils, fats & waxes	123	110
Chemicals & related products, n.e.c.	2,445	2,380
Manufactured goods classified chiefly by material	2,741	2,162
Machinery & transport equipment	4,014	3,603
Miscellaneous manufactured articles	1,014	950
Commodities & transactions merchandise trade , n.e.c. gold, non-monetary (excl gold ores & concentrates	16	24
Combines confidential items of trade	881	694
Total	20,375	18,427

ABS, 13672DO020_201012 State and Regional Indicators, Victoria, Dec 2010

Goods imported, (figures in A$m)

Selected Goods	2008-09	2009-10
Beverages & tobacco	471	422
Crude materials, inedible, except fuels	815	655
Mineral fuels, lubricants & related materials	5,506	5,361
Animal & vegetable oils, fats & waxes	294	256
Chemicals & related products, n.e.c.	1,415	5,216
Manufactured goods classified chiefly by material	6,530	6,049
Machinery & transport equipment	21,673	21,124
Miscellaneous manufactured articles	9,931	8,835
Commodities & transactions merchandise trade , n.e.c. gold, non-monetary (excl gold ores & concentrates	23	12
Combines confidential items of trade	2,506	2,067
Total	56,457	53,118

ABS, 13672DO020_201012 State and Regional Indicators, Victoria, Dec 2010

Main trading partners in the year 2009-10 were as follows:

Foreign Trade	A$ million
Export partners:	
- China	2,380
- New Zealand	1,989
- Japan	1,561
- United States of America	1,513
- Saudi Arabia	1,069
Import partners:	
- China	10,476
- United States of America	6,024
- Japan	5,108
- Germany	3,655
- Thailand	2,727
- Singapore	2,519

Source: ABS 13672DO021_201012 State and Regional Indicators, Victoria

Chambers of Commerce and Trade Organisations
Victorian Employers' Chamber of Commerce and Industry, URL: http://www.vecci.org.au/

MANUFACTURING, MINING AND SERVICES

Manufacturing

Victoria is second to New South Wales in Australian manufacturing industry. The dominant subdivision is machinery and equipment manufacturing, which makes up 35 per cent of national total sales and service income. This is followed by food, beverage and tobacco manufacturing, and petroleum, coal, chemical and associated products. Victoria produces 44 per cent of the national sales and service income in the textiles, clothing, footwear and leather sector.

Manufacturing industry according to sector is shown on the following table:

Manufacturing Industry, 2009-10

Industry subdivision	Wages & salaries $m	Sales & service income $m	Employment end of June
Food product manufacturing	2,762	23,776	58,650
Beverage and tobacco product manufacturing	553	6,112	7,891
Textile, leather, clothing and footware	681	3,769	17,933
Wood product	586	2,887	12,609
Pulp, paper and converted paper products	590	4,400	8,833
Printing	785	3,354	16,893
Petroleum and coal products	199	3,548	1,947
Basic chemical and chemical products	1,186	9,242	14,194
Polymer product and rubber product	1,059	5,962	17,415
Non-metallic mineral product	690	4,034	11,379
Primary metal and metal product	672	5,479	9,260
Fabricated metal product	1,411	6,993	28,839
Transport equipment	1,980	13,936	30,635
Machinery and equipment	1,545	7,526	28,753
Furniture and other manufacturing	473	2,312	12,593
TOTAL	15,173	103,330	277,823

Source: Australian Bureau of Statistics. 8159.0

Tourism
In the June Quarter 2005, 1,554,300 people visited Victoria, with an average stay lasting 2.1 days. Revenue from the industry, over the quarter, amounted to A$249,554,000. The XVIII Commonwealth Games took place in Melbourne between 15-26 March 2006.

Agriculture
Victoria is an agricultural state producing wheat, oats and barley as well as fruit and wine. Victoria has around 22 million hectares of agricultural land, 3.3 million ha. of which is used to grow crops. At the turn of the century, there were about 37,000 farms producing a total revenue of A$6,310 million. Figures for 2002 indicate 33,500 farms.

Main agricultural commodities in 2010 are shown below:

Agricultural produce	$m (E)
Total Crops	**4,452.3**
-Barley	337.0
-Wheat	644.2
-Apples	202.8
-Grapes	372.9
-Other fruit and nuts	529.7
-Hay	813.5
-Nursery production	433.8
-Vegetables	666.5
Total livestock and other disposals	**3,002.1**
-Cattle & calves	1,276.3
-Sheep & lambs	1,045.6
-Pigs	166.7
-Poultry	487.1
Total livestock products	**2,491.8**
Wool	435.1
Milk	1,961.9
Eggs	94.8
Total livestock products	**9,946.3**

Austats: Agricultural State Profile

The period 2001-07 has been marked by below average rainfall, leading to the worst drought in over a century. Conditions have become so bad in 2006-07, that a significant number of farmers in South Australia, Victoria and NSW were forced to abandon their crops.

There were 1.7 million tonnes of grapes crushed in the 2008-09 financial year, down 5.4 per cent decrease on the previous financial year. There were 1.2 billion litres of beverage wine produced in 2008-09, a 5.9 per cent decrease on 2007-08. However, 2008-09 exports of Australian produced wine rose 5.2 per cent (to 752 million litres) compared to the previous financial year, while domestic sales of Australian wine also increased slightly to 430 million litres. (Source: ABS)

COMMUNICATIONS AND TRANSPORT

Roads
There are 151,681 km of roads in Victoria.

Ports and Harbours
Victoria's main ports are Melbourne, Geelong, Portland, and Hastings.
Melbourne Port Corporation, URL: http://www.melbport.com.au/

HEALTH

There are 144 public hospitals in Victoria, as well as several government-funded primary health care services. There are 81 private hospitals and 61 day procedure centres. Life expectancy is metropolitan areas is higher than the national average (for males, 78.5 years and for females, 83.3 years). Ischaemic heart disease is the leading cause of death for both men and women. There are an estimated 2.3 hospital beds per 1,000 population and 306 doctors per 100,000 population.

EDUCATION

Primary/Secondary Education
In 2006, there were 1,605 government-run schools in Victoria (down from 1,625 in 2001), and 694 independent schools (down from 696 in 2001). 1,642 schools were primary, 368 were secondary and 194 were primary and secondary combined. Victoria had 453,739 full-time pupils in primary education in 2006, and 376,096 full-time students enrolled in secondary education. 4,121 students were indigenous.

97 per cent of people aged 15 are enrolled in school; this figure drops to 91.4 per cent among 16 year olds, to 78.9 per cent among 17 year olds, and to 22.7 per cent among 18 year olds.

There were 68,697 teachers employed in 2006. The ratio of students to teacher in primary schools is 15.9:1, and in secondary schools the ratio is 11.9:1.

COMMUNICATIONS AND MEDIA

Newspapers
Victorian newspapers include The Age (http://www.theage.com.au/), Benalla Ensign (http://www.ensign.benalla.net.au/), Cobram Courier, The Courier (http://www.courier.cobram.net.au/), Cranbourne Independent (http://www.starnewsgroup.com.au/news/cranbourne/), Frankston & Hastings Independent (http://www.frankstonweekly.com.au/), Geelong Advertiser (http://www.geelongadvertiser.com.au), Herald Sun (http://www.heraldsun.com.au/), Herald-Sun Sunday, Kilmore Free Press, The Warrandyte Diary, and the Warrnambool Standard.

WESTERN AUSTRALIA

Capital: Perth (Population estimate: 1.45 million)

Governor: Malcolm McCusker AO QC (page 1474)

State Flag: A British Blue Ensign on which is superimposed the state badge: a native Black Swan on a yellow disc, the swan facing the hoist.

CONSTITUTION AND GOVERNMENT

Constitution
When Western Australia was colonised in 1829 it inherited the English system of government and law. The 1889 Constitution makes the Governor the representative of the Queen and established a bicameral legislature based on the Westminster model of government.

Legislature
The first legislative body, the Legislative Council, convened for the first time on 7 February 1832 and was composed of the Governor of Western Australia and four nominated members. In 1890 the Legislative Assembly was formed, which at the time consisted of 30 elected members. Western Australia has retained its bicameral Parliament which still consists of the Legislative Council and the Legislative Assembly. Both Chambers are now elected.

Western Australia is the only Australian state to use a zonal electoral system for both its houses of parliament, which effectively means that, in general, rural voters have twice the voting influence of city voters.

Upper House
There are 34 members of the Legislative Council, two of the six electoral regions returning seven members, the remaining four returning five each. The member elected holds office for a fixed term of four years, beginning on 22 May of each four year period. Currently, the Legislative Council is composed of the following political parties: Australian Labour Party (11 members), Liberal Party of Australia (16), Greens (4) and National Party of Australia (5). **Legislative Council**, Parliament House, Perth, WA 6000, Australia. Tel: +61 8 9222 7214 (Clerk), fax: +61 8 9222 7809 (Clerk), URL: http://www.parliament.wa.gov.au/index.htm

Lower House
The Legislative Assembly is composed of 57 members who are elected from single member electoral districts (34 metropolitan and 23 county) for a term of four years. A system of preferential voting is in operation. Current members of the Legislative Assembly were elected in September 2008. Currently, the Legislative Assembly is composed of the following political parties: Australian Labour Party (28 members), Liberal Party (24), National Party of Australia 45), Others (3). **Legislative Assembly**, Parliament House, Perth, WA 6000, Australia. Tel: +61 8 9222 7215 (Clerk), fax:+61 8 9222 7818 (Clerk), URL: http://www.parliament.wa.gov.au/index.htm

---

Cabinet (as at June 2013)
Premier, Minister for State Development; Science: Hon. Colin Barnett (page 1383)
Deputy Premier; Minister for Health; Tourism: Hon. Dr. Kim Hames
Minister for Regional Development and Lands: Hon. Brendon Grylls
Minister for Education; Aboriginal Affairs; Electoral Affairs: Hon. Peter Collier
Treasurer; Minister for Transport; Fisheries: Hon. Troy R. Buswell
Minister for Planning, Culture and the Arts; Science and Innovation: Hon. John Day
Minister for Police; Road Safety; Small Business; Women: Hon. Liza Harvey
Minister for Training & Workforce: Hon. Terry Redman
Minister for Mental Health; Disability Services: Hon. Helen Morton
Attorney General; Minister for Commerce: Hon. Michael Mischin
Minister for Mines and Petroleum; Housing: Hon. W.R. Marmion
Minister for Sport, Recreation, Racing and Gaming: Hon. Terry Waldron
Minister for Agriculture and Food: Hon. Ken Baston
Minister for Energy; Finance; Citizenship and Multiculturalism: Dr Mike Nahan
Minister for Local Government, Community Services; Seniors & Volunteers; Youth: Hon. A.J. Simpson
Minister for the Environment; Heritage: Hon. Albert P. Jacob
Minister for Emergency Services; Corrective Services; and Veterans: Hon. Joe Francis

---

Ministries
The Office of the Premier, 24th Floor, 197 St. George's Terrace, Perth, Western Australia 6000. Tel: +61 8 9222 9888, fax: +61 8 9322 1213, e-mail: wa-government@dpc.wa.gov.au, URL: http://www.premier.wa.gov.au/
Aboriginal Affairs Department, (PO Box 7770, Cloister's Square, Perth, Western Australia, 6850) Level 1, 197 St Georges Terrace, Perth, Western Australia. Tel: +61 8 9235 8000, fax: +61 8 9235 8088, e-mail: info@aad.wa.gov.au, URL: http://www.aad.wa.gov.au/

AUSTRALIA

Department of Conservation and Land Management, Hackett Drive, Crawley 6009, Western Australia. Tel: +61 8 9442 0300, fax: +61 8 9386 1578, e-mail: info@calm.wa.gov.au, URL: http://www.calm.wa.gov.au/

Department of Education and Training, 151 Royal Street, East Perth WA 6004. Tel: +61 8 9264 4111, fax: +61 8 9264 5005, e-mail: websupport@det.wa.edu.au, URL: http://www.eddept.wa.edu.au/

Department of Environmental Protection, Level 8 Westralia Square Building, 141 St Georges Terrace, Perth, Western Australia 6000, (PO Box K822, Perth WA 6842). Tel: +61 8 9222 7000, fax: +61 8 9222 7099, e-mail: info@environ.wa.gov.au, URL: http://www.environ.wa.gov.au

Department of Health, 189 Royal Street, East Perth WA 6004 (PO Box 8172, Perth Business Centre, Perth WA 6849), Australia. Tel: +61 8 9222 4222, fax: +61 8 9222 4046, e-mail: PRContact@health.wa.gov.au, URL: http://www.health.wa.gov.au/

Department of Housing and Works, 99 Plain St, East Perth, 6004 Western Australia. Tel: +61 8 9222 4666, fax: +61 8 9211 1388, e-mail: askdhw@dhw.wa.gov.au, URL: http://www.dhw.wa.gov.au/

Department of Justice, 141 St Georges Terrace, Perth 6000, Western Australia. Tel: +61 8 9264 1711, URL: http://www.justice.wa.gov.au/home.asp

Department of Local Government and Regional Development, Level 1 Dumas House, 2 Havelock St, West Perth 6005, (PO Box R1250, Perth WA 6844), Australia. Tel: +61 8 9217 1500, fax: +61 8 9217 1555, e-mail: info@dlg.wa.gov.au, URL: http://www.dlgrd.wa.gov.au/

Department of Industry and Resources, Mineral House, 100 Plain Street, East Perth, WA 6004, Australia. Tel: +61 8 9222 3333, fax: +61 8 9222 3862, e-mail: webmaster@doir.wa.gov.au/, URL: http://www.doir.wa.gov.au/

Department for Community Development, 189 Royal Street, East Perth WA 6004, Australia. Tel: +61 8 9222 2614, URL: http://www.communitydevelopment.wa.gov.au/

Department of Culture and the Arts, Level 7, 573 Hay Street, Perth WA 6000, (PO Box 8349, Perth Business Centre, WA 6849), Australia. Tel: +61 8 9224 7300, fax: +61 8 9224 7301, e-mail: info@dca.wa.gov.au, URL: http://www.cultureandarts.wa.gov.au/

Industrial Relations Commission, Level 16, 111 St George's Terrace, Perth WA 6000, Australia. Tel: +61 8 9420 4444, fax: +61 8 9420 4511, email: webmaster@wairc.wa.gov.au, URL: http://www.wairc.wa.gov.au

Department of Industry and Technology, Dumas House, 2 Havelock Street, West Perth, Western Australia 6005, Australia. Tel: +61 8 9222 5555, fax: +61 8 9222 5055, e-mail: arie.valkhoff@doir.wa.gov.au, URL: http://www.indtech.wa.gov.au/

Department of Land Information, (P.O. Box 2222, Midland 6936, Western Australia), 1 Midland Square, Morrison Road, Midland, Western Australia, 6936. Tel: +61 8 9273 7373, fax: +61 8 9273 7666, e-mail: mailroom@dli.wa.gov.au, URL: http://www.dola.wa.gov.au/corporate.nsf

Department of Productivity and Labour Relations, 2 Havelock Street, West Perth, Western Australia 6005. Tel: +61 8 9222 7700, fax: +61 8 9222 7777, e-mail: labourrelations@docep.wa.gov.au, URL: http://www.docep.wa.gov.au/

Department of Consumer and Employment Protection, 219 St. Georges Terrace, Perth Western Australia 6000, (Locked Bag 14, Cloisters Square, Western Australia 6850). Tel: +61 8 9282 0777, fax: +61 8 9282 0850, e-mail: consumer@docep.wa.gov.au, URL: http://www.docep.wa.gov.au/

Elections

The most recent legislative election was held in March 2013. In the Legislative Assembly, the Australian Labour Party won 28 seats (the same as the previous election), the Liberal Party of Australia won 24 seats (also the same as the previous election), the National Party of Australia won 4 seats down one) and there were three other party seats.

LEGAL SYSTEM

Western Australia's court system consists of the Supreme Court, Probate Registry, District Court, Family Court, Liquor Licensing Court, Magistrates' Courts, Court of Petty Sessions, Local Court, and the Children's Court.

The Supreme Court comprises the Chief Justice, 16 Judges, and two Masters.

Supreme Court of Western Australia, Stirling Gardens, Barrack Street, Perth 6000, Australia. Tel: +61 (0)8 9421 5333, fax: +61 (0)8 9221 4436, e-mail: supreme.court.reception@justice.wa.gov.au, URL: http://www.supremecourt.wa.gov.au

LOCAL GOVERNMENT

Western Australia is divided into 142 local government councils. Local governments are separate, semi-autonomous, legal entities bound by the Local Government Act and other laws. Local government councillors are elected.

AREA AND POPULATION

Area

The area of Western Australia is 2,532,400 sq. km, equivalent to 32.9 per cent of the total area of Australia, making it the largest of Australia's states and territories. It has a total coastline of 12,500 km, equivalent to 34.0 per cent of Australia's coastline. In Perth, the capital of Western Australia, temperatures range from 17.9C° to 29.7C° in January, and 9.0C° to 17.4C° in July. Mean annual rainfall in Perth is 72.4 mm.

Population

Despite its large land area, Western Australia has less than 10 per cent of Australia's population. The estimated resident population in mid-2010 was 2,296,400 in 2010, up from 2,163,200 in 2008, representing an annual increase of 2.2 per cent, the fastest growth rates of all the states. For the year ending 30 June 2010, net overseas migration contributed almost 60 per cent of the estimated resident population growth.

The population of Perth Statistical Division was estimated at 1,507,900 in 2006, over 70 per cent of the total population of Western Australia. Within the statistical division, the population of the capital city itself is estimated to be 1,270,500. The majority of Western Australians are aged between 20 and 59 years (1,368,200 in 2008), with 426,500 aged under 15 years, 368.600 aged 65 and over, and 152,200 aged between 15 and 19 years.

Births, Marriages, Deaths

According to ABS statistics for the year 2010, there were 30,878 live births representing a crude birth rate of 13.7 per 1,000 population. In 2007 there were 12,283 deaths. Life expectancy at birth in 2009 was 79.5 years for males and 84.1 years for females. In 2009, the infant mortality rate was 3.0 deaths per 1,000 inhabitants (2.7 non-indigenous rate, indigenous rate 7.7). In 2007, there were 12,290 registered marriages and 4,932 divorces. (Source: Australian Statistics Bureau)

EMPLOYMENT

Labour Force (seasonally adjusted)

	Unit	Jan. 2012	Jan. 2013
Civilian population 15 years and over	'000	1,927.2	1,990.6
Employed persons	'000	1,275.7	1,315.7
Unemployed persons	'000	54.8	55.5
Unemployment rate	%	4.1	4.0
Participation rate	%	69.0	68.9

Source: Labour Force, Australia, March 2013 (cat. no. 6202.0)

Number of Employees by Industry

Industry	Nov. 2009	Nov. 2010
Agriculture, forestry, fishing	38,100	47,100
Mining	65,000	86,900
Manufacturing	97,400	84,900
Electricity, gas, water	12,200	16,500
Construction	127,400	137,500
Wholesale trade	41,600	40,900
Retail trade	128,200	120,400
Accommodation, cafes, restaurants	73,400	69,500
Transport, storage	58,300	52,000
Communication Services	18,100	15,600
Finance and insurance services	27,300	30,900
Rental, hiring and real estate services	19,200	22,000
Professional, scientific and technical services	85,200	93,400
Administrative & support services	39.4	44.1
Public admin. and safety	64.2	68.5
Education & training	98.4	97.6
Health and community services	115.1	120.7
Arts & recreation services	20.0	18.6
Other services	49,300	58,600
Total	1,177,400	1,225,800

Source: ABS, 1367.5 Western Australia at a Glance

BANKING AND FINANCE

GDP/GNP, Inflation, National Debt
Gross State Product, Chain volume measures

Year	A$m	% change from previous year
2007-08	195,973	3.9
2008-09	204,354	4.3
2009-10	213,354	4.3
2010-11	221,574	4.0
2011-12	236,338	6.7

Source: Australian Bureau of Statistics 5220.0

Mining is the state's highest earning industries, with Gross Value Added (GVA) at A$36,498 million in 2006-07 (up 12.6 per cent over the year). Property and business services was the second highest earning sector, with GVA of A$11,569 million. The agricultural sector GVA saw a loss of 35.2 per cent over the year. (Source: ABS, 5220.0 National Accounts, State Accounts, 2005-06)

The CPI rose by 2.8 per cent over the year to September 2003, and by 2.1 per cent from September 2003 to September 2004. The greatest increases were seen in health care and housing costs, whilst small decreases were recorded in clothing and recreation costs. (Source: Australian Bureau of Statistics)

Balance of Payments / Imports and Exports

In the period 2009-10 the main export destinations were China (A$30,800 million, 37 per cent), Japan (A$14,245 million, 17 per cent) and India (A$8,584 million, 10 per cent). The main import destinations were Thailand (A$4,528 million, 16 per cent), US (A$2,822 million, 10 per cent), and China (A$2,820 million, 10 per cent).

Major export commodities include iron ore & concentrates, gold and crude petroleum. Main import commodities are gold, crude petroleum oils, motor vehicles, computer equipment, aircraft, specialised machinery, civil engineering plants, and fertilizers.

Chambers of Commerce and Trade Organisations
Chamber of Commerce & Industry of Western Australia, URL:
http://www.cciwa.com/

MANUFACTURING, MINING AND SERVICES

Primary and Extractive Industries
With more than 270 operating mines, Western Australia is a leading supplier of many commodities including alumina, diamonds, iron ore and mineral sands. The State also produces 70 per cent of Australia's gold and significant exports of salt, nickel, and numerous other metals.

Production from the mining industry is shown below:

Mining

Production	Unit	Sept. 2009	Sept. 2010
Iron Ore	'000 tonnes	103,517	106,146
Diamonds	'000 carats	2,333	2,471
Bauxite	'000 bauxite	10,642	10,801

Source: ABS, Western Australia at a Glance

Energy
Western Australia is a major oil, gas and coal producing region. It has extensive natural gas reserves and the State supplies liquefied natural gas (LNG) to Japan, and is developing markets in Taiwan and Korea.

Manufacturing
Manufacturing Industry, 2009-10

Industry subdivision	Wages & salaries $m	Sales & service income $m	Employment end of June
Food product manufacturing	575	4,489	14,435
Beverage and tobacco product manufacturing	138	1,048	3,132
Textile, leather, clothing and footware	98	632	3,151
Wood product	204	1,368	4,214
Pulp, paper and converted paper products	47	315	842
Printing	133	508	3,460
Petroleum and coal products	94	4,961	1,104
Basic chemical and chemical products	412	5,108	4,841
Polymer product and rubber product	215	1,380	3,946
Non-metallic mineral product	374	2,355	5,631
Primary metal and metal product	1,080	25,481	10,985
Fabricated metal product	1,001	4,757	18,321
Transport equipment	394	1,703	6,239
Machinery and equipment	646	3,777	11,637

- continued			
Furniture and other manufacturing	178	749	4,873
TOTAL	5,590	58,632	96,840

Source: Australian Bureau of Statistics. 8159.0

Tourism
There are around 320 hotels and other accommodation facilities in Western Australia. Residents departing short term in 2005-06 numbered 562,290, whilst short-term visitors arriving numbered 498,622. Of those arriving by air, around 26 per cent came from the United Kingdom and Ireland, 16.5 per cent were from Singapore, and almost 12 per cent came from Japan. Over 8.8 per cent came from Malaysia.
Western Australian Tourism Commission, URL: http://www.westernaustralia.com/

Agriculture
Total area of agricultural land in Western Australia is around 104,646 ha. In 2004-05, there were 11,745 farms.

Gross Value of Selected Agricultural Production 2010

	A$ million
Cereals for grain	2,345.9
Fruit & nuts	217.1
Nursery production	144.2
Grapes	112.5
Vegetables	316.1
Cattle & calves	537.1
Sheep and lamb	460.9
Wool	415.4
Total Agricultural production	5,752.8

Source: ABS 7503.0

EDUCATION

According to the Australian Bureau of Statistics, in 2010, there were 768 government-run schools in Western Australia, and 297 non-government schools.

In 2010, there were 233,839 government school students and 124,530 non government students enrolled.

RELIGION

According to 2004 ABS statistics, 24.4 per cent of Western Australians are Catholic, 22.4 per cent are Anglican, 33.7 per cent have other religious affiliations, while 19.5 per cent have no religion.

COMMUNICATIONS AND MEDIA

Newspapers
Western Australia's newspapers include the Augusta Margaret River Mail (http://www.margaretrivermail.com.au/), the Hutt River Guardian, the Kimberley Echo, Post Newspapers, The Sunday Times, and The West Australian (http://www.thewest.com.au).

TERRITORIES OF AUSTRALIA

CONSTITUTION AND GOVERNMENT

Constitution
The Commonwealth Government administers the Territories of Jervis Bay, the Cocos (Keeling) Islands, Christmas Island, Norfolk Island, the Coral Sea Islands, Ashmore and Cartier Islands, Heard and McDonald Islands and the Australian Antarctic Territory.

The Commonwealth Government conferred self-government on the Northern Territory on 1 July 1978 and on the Australian Capital Territory on 11 May 1989. The Australian Antarctic Territory, with an estimated area of 6,199,846 sq. kilometres out of an approximate total of 13,991,340 sq. km. for the entire Antarctic Continent, was established by an Order in Council, dated 7 February 1933, which placed under the control of the Commonwealth that part of the Territory in the Antarctic Seas which comprises all the islands and territories, other than Adelie Land, situated south of the 60th parallel of south latitude, and lying between the 160th and 45th meridians of east longitude.

ASHMORE AND CARTIER ISLANDS

Capital: Administered from Canberra, Australia

CONSTITUTION AND GOVERNMENT

Constitution
The Ashmore and Cartier Islands were placed under the authority of the Commonwealth of Australia in 1931, the Ashmore Islands having been annexed by Great Britain in 1878 and the Cartier Islands in 1909. The Islands were accepted by Australia through the Ashmore and Cartier Islands Acceptance Act 1933 under the name of the Territory of Ashmore and Cartier Islands. The Territory was subsequently annexed to, and deemed to form part of, the Northern Territory. With the granting of self government to the Northern Territory on 1 July 1978, the administration of the Islands became a direct responsibility of the Commonwealth government administered by the Australian Ministry for the Environment, Sport, and Territories.

LEGAL SYSTEM

The Islands' laws are those of the Northern Territory and the Commonwealth.

AREA AND POPULATION

Area
Ashmore Islands (known as Middle, East and West Islands) and Cartier Island are situated in the Indian Ocean some 850-790 km west of Darwin. The islands lie at the outer edge of the continental shelf. They are small and low and are composed of coral and sand. Vegetation consists mainly of grass. The total land area is about 5 sq. km, with 74.1 km of coastline.

To view a map, please consult:
http://www.lib.utexas.edu/maps/cia08/ashmore_cartier_sm_2008.gif

Population
The islands have no permanent inhabitants.

Indonesian fishermen are allowed access to the lagoon and fresh water at Ashmore Reef's West Island, under the provisions of a Memorandum of Understanding signed by the Australian and Indonesian governments; this permits the fishermen to fish areas of the sea which they have accessed traditionally for centuries, although there are now restrictions placed on all fishing and access by the general public within the Nature Reserve. These are aimed at the protection and preservation of the wide range of wildlife resident on the reef.

Cartier Island and its surrounding areas (within a radius of 10 kilometres) is a Defence Practice Area and has been used as an air weapons range by the Department of Defence since World War II. There is a risk of unexploded ordnance, and visitor access is prohibited. The Australian Nature Conservation Agency (ANCA) has designated the area as a possible National Nature Reserve.

Due to its proximity to Indonesia, the Ashmore Reef was a destination for smugglers transporting asylum seekers to Australia; asylum seekers could claim to have entered Australian territory once they reached Ashmore. The Australian government took the stance that it was not responsible for the so-called boat people, and discouraged the practise.

MANUFACTURING, MINING AND SERVICES

Primary and Extractive Industries
The Jabiru and Challis oil fields are located within the adjacent area of the territory. The extraction of petroleum in the area adjacent to the Northern Territory is the administrative responsibility of the Northern Territory Department of Mines and Energy.

COMMUNICATIONS AND TRANSPORT

Ports and Harbours
The islands have no ports or harbours; the only available anchorage is offshore.

ENVIRONMENT

On 16 August 1983, a national nature reserve was declared over the 583 sq. km. Ashmore Reef and that area is now known as Ashmore Reef National Nature Reserve. Although the Islands are uninhabited, Indonesian fishing boats, which have traditionally plied the area to fish within the Territory under an agreement between the governments of Australia and Indonesia. To provide a sovereignty presence and to prevent any abuse of landing rights or destruction of protected wildlife, the Australian Government has established an Australian presence in the Territory during the period from March to November each year.

Periodic visits are made to the Islands by ships of the Royal Australian Navy, and aircraft of the Royal Australian Air Force and the Civil Coastal Surveillance Service make aerial surveys of the Islands and neighbouring waters. Bird life is plentiful on the islands of Ashmore Reef and access to the main breeding sites at East and Middle Islands is by permit only. Turtles are plentiful at certain times of the year and beche-de-mer are abundant. Regular visits are made to the Reef by officers of the Australian Nature Conservation Agency.

CHRISTMAS ISLAND

Capital: The Settlement

Head of State: Hon. Brian Lacy (Administrator)

CONSTITUTION AND GOVERNMENT

Constitution
Following annexation by the United Kingdom in 1888, Christmas Island was incorporated for administrative purposes with the Straits Settlements (now Singapore and part of Malaysia) in 1900. Japanese forces occupied the Island from March 1942 until the end of the WWII. In 1946 Christmas Island became a dependency of Singapore.

In 1948 the mining industry was taken over by a partnership of the Australian and New Zealand Governments, and managed by British Phosphate Commissioners. The first permanent population of the Island took place over the period 1949 to 1958 when a massive expansion program led to the recruitment of labour from Cocos, Malaya and Singapore.

In 1957 the Australian government acquired Christmas Island from the Singapore Government for a sum of just under £3 million. Administration was then transferred to the United Kingdom on 1 January 1958, pending a final transfer to Australia. The transfer took place on 1 October 1958 - a date celebrated on Christmas Island as Territory Day. The Christmas Island Act 1958 provides the basis for the administrative, legislative and judicial systems. The head of Government is the Administrator, appointed by the Governor-General of Australia, on the recommendation of the Federal Cabinet. Christmas Island comes under the administration of the Australian Department of Transport and Regional Services, but has a local Shire Council to provide local government services; this consists of nine members who each serve a four year term. Christmas Island residents who are Australian citizens also vote in federal elections.

The next parliamentary election is due in October 2013.

Administration Headquarters, URL: http://www.christmas.shire.gov.cx

LEGAL SYSTEM

Courts and judicial officers of Western Australia exercise jurisdiction in the territory.

The Christmas Island Police service is operated by the Australian Federal Police. As well as usual police duties they are responsible for customs and immigration, search and rescue and registration of vehicles on the island.

LOCAL GOVERNMENT

With the introduction of new state-like laws, the Christmas Island Services Corporation and the Christmas Island Assembly was replaced in 1992 by the Christmas Island Shire Council, established under the Local Government Act (WA) (CI). The Christmas Island Shire Council has normal local government responsibilities in most parts of the Territory.

Shire of Christmas Island, URL: http://www.christmas.shire.gov.cx

AREA AND POPULATION

Area
Christmas Island is an isolated, oceanic island 360 km south of Java Head (Indonesia) in the Indian Ocean. The nearest point on the Australian coast is North West Cape, 1,408 km to the southeast. The area is 135 sq. km (52 sq. miles), mainly tropical rainforest; 65 per cent of the island is a national park. The climate is tropical, with heat and humidity moderated by trade winds.

There is a narrow reef surrounding the island. Christmas Island's isolation has created a unique set of ecological relationships characterised by the evolution of new species and sub-species restricted to Christmas Island, and by profound changes in the biology of immigrant species establishing their niche on the island. The island is also a focal point for sea birds of various species.

To view a map of the island, please consult
http://www.lib.utexas.edu/maps/cia08/christmas_island_sm_2008.gif

Population
In 2010, the population was estimated to be 1,400. The island's ethnic groups are approximately 70 per cent Chinese, 10 per cent Malay and 20 per cent European.

Whilst English is the official language of Christmas Island, other languages spoken include Malay, Indonesian and four Chinese dialects: Hakka, Hainese, Hokkien and Teochew.

Public Holidays 2014
As Australia plus:
31 January: Chinese New Year
1 May: Labour Day
29 July: Hari Raya Puasa (Eid al Fitr)
August: Month of the Hungry Ghost
August: Mooncake Festival
1 October: Territory Day
5 October: Hari Raya Haji (Eid al Adha)
23 October: Divali

BANKING AND FINANCE

Phosphate mining has been the only significant economic activity on Christmas Island. In December 1987 the Australian Government closed the phosphate mine, but it was reopened in 1991 by a consortium which included former mine workers. The authorities have tried to diversify the economy; in 1993 a casino was opened in 1993, but was then closed five years later. In 2001, plans for a commercial spaceport were launched, but no progress has been made. Tourism is a sector of potential expansion; the Island is rich in flora and fauna, and is ringed by a reef. The Australian Government built a temporary immigration detention centre on the island in 2001. It was subsequently replaced with a larger, modern facility located at North West Point.

Currency
Australian currency is used.

Balance of Payments / Imports and Exports
Phosphate is exported mainly to South East Asian markets (Malaysia, Indonesia, Japan and Taiwan). According to recent statistics, exports of natural phosphates reach 270,000 tonnes annually. However, supplies are very depleted.

Chambers of Commerce and Trade Organisations
Christmas Island Chamber of Commerce, Christmas Island (Indian Ocean), via Perth Mail Exchange WA 6798. Tel: +61 (0)8 9164 8249

MANUFACTURING, MINING AND SERVICES

Primary and Extractive Industries
A phosphate mine is operated by Christmas Island Phosphates and continues to supply the South East Asian market with low-grade phosphate. In February 1998 the Commonwealth signed a 21 year lease with Phosphate Resources Ltd for the supply phosphate and limestone subject to appropriate environmental standards. The Commonwealth receives royalties according to the tonnage of mined material shipped, from which a conservation levy is taken. This levy is contributes to the rehabilitation of rainforest and is overseen by Parks Australia.

Energy
The island electricity (Consumer voltage 240V, 50 cycles) is generated by diesel plants in the power station located on the island.

Water is pumped from several springs and underground streams. The water is treated and supplied in accordance with Western Australian standards and is tested periodically by hospital staff.

Tourism
Tourism is a growing industry. Christmas Island offers birdwatching, snorkelling and diving, and fishing holidays as well as beach and relaxation holidays. Ecotourism is particularly popular; the Christmas Island National Park currently protects 85 square kilometres, including the reef. The park preserves the ecological systems of the rainforests, the ocean shores and the reefs.

There are twelve hotels on the islands, and the Port of Christmas Island welcomes yachts at Flying Fish Cove; new deep water moorings have been installed.

Christmas Island Tourism Association, URL: http://www.christmas.net.au

COMMUNICATIONS AND TRANSPORT

Visa Information
No passport or visa is required when visiting Christmas Island from the Australian mainland. Travel to the island via Singapore or Indonesia, however, is regarded as international travel and is subject to passport requirements.

National Airlines
National Jet Systems (NJS) operates a weekly return service between Christmas Island, Cocos (Keeling) Islands and Perth.
National Jet Systems, e-mail: lenn@natjet.com.au,
URL: http://www.nationaljet.com.au/

International Airports
Christmas Island Airport is a 24-hour, international airport.

Roads
There are good roads in the developed areas and four wheel drive tracks through many parts of the National Park.

Shipping
Cargo vessels from Perth deliver supplies to the island every 6 - 8 weeks. The phosphate mining company exports phosphate rock and bagged dust to South East Asia via small (11,000 tonnes) ore ships. There are about 20-30 journeys per annum. Island bound cargo capacity on these ships is limited.

HEALTH

Christmas Island has one hospital with eight inpatient beds and an Accident and Emergency department, services are supplied by the Indian Ocean Territories Health Service. Patients who require specialist treatment are evacuated to Perth.

EDUCATION

Pre-school Education
Silver City Kindergarten and Playgroup Association, a privately operated organisation provides kindergarten sessions for children over three years of age. A weekly Playgroup also meets on the premises. An Early Childhood Centre is run by the Christmas Island Women's Association and operates from the Tom Paterson School, catering for children from 2-4 years. A childcare centre run by the Christmas Island Shire Council offers occasional and full time care.

Primary/Secondary Education
Education is free and compulsory from age 6 to 15. The Christmas Island District High School provides education from pre-school level through to Year 10 secondary level. The school is staffed by teachers from the Education Department of Western Australia and follows the state curriculum. A number of senior secondary students attend years 11-12 in WA schools. These students may be eligible for assistance under government schemes for assistance to isolated students.

RELIGION

It is estimated that 12 per cent of residents are Buddhist, 19 per cent Muslim, and 24 per cent Christian. There are many other adherents of various Chinese deities. Within the Christian churches, Christmas Island lies in the jurisdiction of both the Anglican and Roman Catholic Archdioceses of Perth in Western Australia.

Christmas Island has a religious liberty rating of 10 on a scale of 1 to 10 (10 is most freedom). (Source: World Religion Database)

COMMUNICATIONS AND MEDIA

Newspapers
The Islander is a fortnightly newsletter published by the Shire of Christmas Island.

Broadcasting
Christmas Island does not have its own television station. A commercial TV network broadcasts from Western Australia, as do ABC and SBS. Many residents have also had their own small satellite dish installed to receive other stations.

Radio VLU2 is the local radio station, staffed by volunteer announcers, and transmits on 1422 kHz and 102.2 FM in English, Malay and Chinese. Christmas Island also receives ABC Classical Radio and WAFM, a commercial station based in Western Australia.

Telecommunications
There is STD telephone and fax access to and from the Australian mainland, as well as Telstra services. GSM mobile telephone service replaced older analog system in February 2005. Christmas Island telephone numbers are listed in the Great Northern WA phone book.

At present there are over 1,800 internet hosts.

ENVIRONMENT

Over 60 per cent of the Island is designated a National Park. The Park also extends to 50 meters of the low water mark. The Island supports a wide range of species. It contains the last remaining nesting habitat in the world of the endangered Abbott's booby and supports the world's largest remaining robber crab population.

SPACE PROGRAMME

Construction on a satellite launch facility, the Asia Pacific Space Centre (APSC), began in 2001. The centre comprises a technical complex, a launch complex and amission control. It is expected to have a life space on 15-20 years. The first launch took place in 2003 for the National Space Development Agency of Japan. The Australian government cancelled an upgrade to its satellite communications on the Island in 2012. The upgrade will be delayed until at least 2015.

COCOS (KEELING) ISLANDS

Head of State: Hon. Brian Lacy (Administrator)

CONSTITUTION AND GOVERNMENT

Constitution

The territory was administered as part of the colony of Singapore until the UK transferred sovereignty over the Cocos (Keeling) Islands to Australia in 1955. In 1886 Queen Victoria granted in perpetuity all land in the islands to George Clunies-Ross, reserving the right to resume any of the lands and prohibiting its alienation without prior approval of the crown. The Australian Government purchased most of the Clunies-Ross family property in 1978. This land, except for Crown land on West Island retained for administrative purposes, was vested in the Cocos (Keeling) Islands Council in Trust for the benefit and advancement of the Cocos Islander population. The remaining 12 acres on Home Island, including the family home, was purchased by the Australian Government in 1993.

On 1 July 1992 the Territories Law Reform Act 1992 was introduced which applied the bulk of Commonwealth legislation to the territory and replaced the old colonial based Singapore laws with a body of state law modelled on that of Western Australia. In accordance with the Cocos (Keeling) Islands Act 1955, an Administrator, appointed by the Governor General, administers the territory on behalf of the Commonwealth. Subject to the direction of a Parliamentary Secretary appointed by the Minister responsible for territories, the Administrator is responsible for law, order and good government. For the purposes of enrolment and voting in elections for the Federal Parliament, the Cocos (Keeling) Islands are part of the Electoral District of the Commonwealth Division of the Northern Territory. There is a unicameral Cocos (Keeling) Islands Shire Council that consists of seven seats, members are elected for four years.

Cocos (Keeling) Islands Administration, Cocos (Keeling) Islands (Indian Ocean), PO Box 1094 Indian Ocean WA 6799. Tel: +61 8 9162 6769, fax: +61 8 9162 6697

LEGAL SYSTEM

The islands' legal system is based on Australian law as well as local laws. Courts and judicial officers of Western Australia exercise jurisdiction in the territory.

LOCAL GOVERNMENT

With the introduction of new state-like laws, the Cocos (Keeling) Islands Council was replaced in 1992 by the Cocos (Keeling) Islands Shire Council, established under the Local Government Act 1960. The Cocos (Keeling) Islands Shire Council has normal local government responsibilities in most parts of the territory. Council elections take place every two years in October, with three or four of the seven Councilors being up for re-election. The next election is due in 2011. The President is elected every two years from within the elected Councilors, and represents the combined electorate.

Shire of the Cocos (Keeling) Islands, URL: http://www.shire.cc

AREA AND POPULATION

Area

Located in the Indian Ocean approximately 2,950 km northwest of Perth, the Cocos (Keeling) Islands are one of Australia's most distant and isolated territories. The islands form two low-lying coral atolls consisting of 27 separate islands, having a land area around 14 sq. km. The main group of islands is roughly circular in shape with North Keeling Island, a separate atoll, some 24 km to the north. The highest point of the islands is 5 metres. The islands are covered in thick vegetation.

To view a map, please consult http://www.lib.utexas.edu/maps/cia08/cocos_sm_2008.gif

The climate is equable and generally under the influence of southeast trade winds, but cyclonic conditions can and do occur. Temperatures vary from 19-31°C (69-88°F) with average rainfall of 2,000 mm per annum.

Population was an estimated 596 in 2010, down from 635 in 2000. It consists mostly of Cocos Islanders resident on Home Island. The majority are Malay and speak Cocos Malay, a variant of Malay. Most are followers of Islam. West Island, 12 km across the lagoon, is the administrative centre with a population of 130, principally government employees and their families on short term postings.

EMPLOYMENT

Unemployment on the islands is currently in the region of 60 per cent of the total workforce. The islands' main employers are the Shire Council and the Co-operative. Despite some Co-operative enterprises related to tourism and minor private business ventures, few opportunities for new employment exist.

BANKING AND FINANCE

In 1827, the Cocos (Keeling) Islands were occupied by John Clunies-Ross, who brought labourers with him to establish and develop coconut plantations at a time when the copra trade was flourishing. The Malay community can trace its ancestors to East Africa, China, Java, Borneo and Malacca. In 1980, the copra industry ceased operation on the Islands, and the economy now relies on fishing. There is also a small tourist industry.

Currency
Australian currency is used.

GDP/GNP
The largest private sector is provision of services to the community. Tourism is a small industry, limited by the inaccessibility of the islands.

MANUFACTURING, MINING AND SERVICES

Service Industries
Tourism represents a growing source of economic activity in the territory. There are a few small enterprises providing services associated with the tourism industry and a number of part time retail agencies operating on the islands. Cocos Islands Cooperative Society Limited conducts the business enterprises of the Cocos Islanders. Activities include tourist accommodation and building construction and maintenance.

North Keeling Island, an atoll approximately 75km north of the southern atoll, is protected as a World Heritage Reserve under the control of Parks Australia Cocos (Keeling) Islands.

Cocos Island Tourism Commission, URL: http://www.cocos-tourism.cc/

Agriculture
Agricultural products include vegetables, bananas and pawpaws. Very small quantities of fruit and vegetables are produced for local consumption but most food requirements come from Australia. Coconut is the only cash crop grown. Fishing contributes to the local food supply.

COMMUNICATIONS AND TRANSPORT

Visa Information
There are no passport or visa requirements when visiting the Cocos Islands from the Australian mainland. Visitors from outside Australia, however, are subject to the usual immigration rules.

National Airlines
The only passenger transport connection with the rest of the world are a twice a week airflights to Christmas Island and Perth.

Shipping
Cargo vessels from Perth deliver supplies to the island every 6-8 weeks.

Ports and Harbours
There are no ports or harbours in the Cocos (Keeling) Islands. Lagoon anchorage only is provided.

HEALTH

The Indian Ocean Territories Health Service (IOTHS) operates a clinic on both Home Island and West Island. A doctor, nurses, health workers, a community services officer and a dental assistant reside on the Cocos (Keeling) Islands. Specialist services are not usually available on Cocos.

EDUCATION

Education is free and compulsory from ages six to 15. The islands has one primary school and one secondary school.

RELIGION

The majority of Home Island residents are Sunni Muslims (representing over 65 per cent of the total islands' population, according to recent statistics) and on West Island most are Christian (just over 27 per cent). The Cocos (Keeling) Islands lie within both the Anglican and Roman Catholic archdiocese of Perth in Western Australia.

The islands have a religious liberty rating of 10 on a scale of 1 to 10 (10 is most freedom). (Source: World Religion Database)

COMMUNICATIONS AND MEDIA

Broadcasting
Radio VKW Cocos (URL: //http://onlineradio2.com/listen/Voice_of_the_Cocos_960) provides a daily, non commercial domestic broadcasting service. Radio stations outside the islands include ABC Radio National and the Western Australian commercial FM station WAFM. The Australian Broadcasting Corporation Overseas Television Service, and several other radio and television stations are received via satellite.

ENVIRONMENT

Current environmental problems include limited fresh water, usually found only in natural underground reservoirs.

CORAL SEA ISLANDS

CONSTITUTION AND GOVERNMENT

Constitution
In 1968, the British Government formally recognized the control which Australia had exercised over the islands for a number of years. The Australian Government then declared the islands an Australian Territory by the Coral Sea Islands Act of 1969. In 1997 the Coral Sea Islands Act was amended to include 1,880 sq. km of seabed around the Elizabeth and Middleton Reefs located 160 km north of Lord Howe Island.

Most of the islands have been surveyed and are visited regularly by Royal Australian Navy vessels. The government has control over the activities of visitors to the Territory.

The laws of the Australian Capital Territory apply in the Coral Sea Islands Territory. The Ministry for the Environment and Water Resources is responsible for matters affecting the Territories.

Recent Events
On 14th June 2004, a group of gay activists from Queensland established The Gay and Lesbian Kingdom of the Coral Sea, as a protest at the Australian government's refusal to recognise same-sex marriages. The kingdom has a high court, chief justice and an absolute ruler, His Majesty Emperor Dale. The kingdom's claims are not recognised by any state, and as no permanent settlement has been established, the Coral Sea Islands remain uninhabited.

LEGAL SYSTEM

The laws of the Australian Capital Territory apply to the Coral Sea Islands. The Supreme Court of Norfolk Island (consisting of Federal Court Judges) has legal jurisdiction in the Territory. Where additional legislation for the territory is necessary (for the purposes of peace, order and good government), responsibility falls to the Governor-General to create Coral Sea Islands Territory Ordinances.

AREA AND POPULATION

Area
The Coral Sea Islands Territory is situated east of Queensland between the Great Barrier reef and longitude 156°06. The territory comprises all the sea islands in a sea area of approximately 780,000 sq. km. The islands are formed largely of coral and sand. Some have a cover of grassy or scrub-type vegetation. The better known among them are Cato Island, Chilcott Islet in the Coringa Group, and those of the Willis Group. Apart from Willis Island, the islands are uninhabited due to their small size and the absence of permanent fresh water.

In the 19th Century many ships were wrecked in the area, and the reefs and islands are often named after the ships which foundered there. Navigational aids exist on several of the reefs and islands. There have been a number of scientific expeditions to the region since 1859 and many specimens of flora and fauna are now housed in Australian herbariums and museums. As there are occasional tropical cyclones in the area, meteorological data is relayed to the mainland from a number of automatic weather stations.

To view a map, please consult
http://www.lib.utexas.edu/maps/cia08/coral_sea_islands_sm_2008.gif

Population
A meteorological station, staffed by four people, has been on Willis Island since 1921. The remaining islands are uninhabited.

MANUFACTURING, MINING AND SERVICES

Agriculture
The Australian Fisheries Management Authority is responsible for granting permission for commercial fishing in the area of the Coral Sea Islands.
Australian Fisheries Management Authority, URL: http://www.afma.gov.au

COMMUNICATIONS AND TRANSPORT

There are no ports or harbours on the Coral Sea Islands, only offshore anchorage.

ENVIRONMENT

The Coral Sea Islands Territory is also an area of world natural and ecological importance. A number of the reefs and islands within the Territory have been identified as important nesting sites for seabirds and marine turtles. The Lihou Reef and Coringa-Herald National Nature Reserves were declared under the National Parks and Wildlife Conservation Act 1975 in August 1982 in order to provide protection for the wide variety of wildlife in these areas. Six species of sea turtle nest in the Coral Sea Islands Territory, including the largest species in the world, Dermochelys Coriacea which is regarded as one of the most endangered of the world's sea turtles. There are at least 24 bird species in the territory; a number of these species are protected under Australia-Japan and Australia-China agreements on endangered and migratory birds.

A number of Australian agencies are responsible for environmental concerns in the Coral Sea Islands, including the Australian Nature Conservation Agency (ANCA). The Royal Australian Navy and Coastwatch (Australian Customs) are responsible for aerial and sea surveillance.

JERVIS BAY

CONSTITUTION AND GOVERNMENT

Constitution
Although the Jervis Bay Territory is a territory in its own right, the laws of the Australian Capital Territory (so far as they are applicable) apply under the Jervis Bay Territory Acceptance Act 1915. The Commonwealth Minister for Regional Services Territories is responsible for the provision and maintenance of municipal and territory services, the management of the Jervis Bay Nature Reserve in sympathy with the rest of the territory and the surrounding region, matters relating to leases, and the management of other lands and waters in the territory. A Regional Director supervises four staff in providing a range of services.

Residents of the territory vote in the Federal electorate of Fraser for representation in the House of Representatives and the Senate but are excluded from representation in the Australian Capital Territory (ACT) Legislative Assembly. A local residents' forum, the Jervis Bay Residents' Group, was established in 1989. Representatives from each of the four communities of the territory (HMAS Creswell, Jervis Bay Village, Wreck Bay and the private leases) play an active role in representing the views of residents. Additionally, the Wreck Bay Aboriginal Community Council has been granted limited powers to create by-laws. In 1986 the Aboriginal Land Grant (Jervis Bay Territory) Act was passed to assist the grant of land at the Wreck Bay Village to the Aboriginal Community.

LEGAL SYSTEM

Courts and judicial officers of the Australian Capital Territory (ACT) exercise jurisdiction in the territory. The Wreck Bay Aboriginal Community Council was granted limited powers to make by-laws in 1995; however, to date, that power has not been exercised.

Following a Royal Commission enquiry into aboriginal deaths in custody, the Aboriginal Justice Advisory Committee was set up.

AREA AND POPULATION

Area
The Jervis Bay Territory comprises 73 sq. km (7,400 hectares) on the southern shore of Jervis Bay, about 195 km south of Sydney. The mainland area is about 6,500 hectares, marine waters within the territory cover about 800 hectares, and, in addition, the territory includes the 51 hectare Bowen Island. About 90 per cent of the territory is Aboriginal Land, most of which is the Booderee National Park, which is leased back to the Director of National Parks. The remainder of the land is used for Department of Defence purposes, Aboriginal land (Wreck Bay), a few private leases and other Commonwealth land. The former Australian National Parks and Wildlife Service (now known as Australian Nature Conservation Agency) assumed management responsibility for the Jervis Bay National Park on 1 July 1992.

AUSTRALIA

Population

The population of the Territory is gradually decreasing; total permanent population is now about 611 (down from 750 in 2003), comprising 331 at HMAS Creswell, 180 at Wreck Bay Village, 82 in the Jervis Bay Village and the balance on private leases. The population fluctuates according to intake numbers on HMAS Creswell, which can rise to 1,000.

Jervis Bay is populated by Aboriginal people whose ancestors first inhabited the area 20,000 years ago, and is regarded as being the birthplace of the 13 tribes of the south coast. The Aboriginal people living in the area were granted land rights of over 400 hectares in 1986.

BANKING AND FINANCE

Currency
Australian currency is used.

GDP/GNP, Inflation, National Debt
Tourism is the most significant economic activity in the Jervis Bay Territory. Approximately 750 000 tourists visit the Booderee National Park each year.

Government services are funded administratively through Territories Office appropriations and are generally based on service standards in the surrounding region. Most government services have been privatised in line with Government policy.

MANUFACTURING, MINING AND SERVICES

Service Industries
Tourism is the major industry in Jervis Bay. Some 750,000 tourists visit the area annually.

EDUCATION

The Jervis Bay School is situated on the HMAS Creswell, Navy Base. Figures for 2008 show that the school had 64 students.

ENVIRONMENT

The Jervis Bay region lies between the northern and southern climatic zones, and its habitats include oceanic waters, bay waters of varying depths, intertidal rock platforms and beaches, estuarine waters, recent and ancient dune systems, coastal cliffs, heaths, forests, swamps and lakes.

In 1992 the Jervis Bay Nature Reserve was made the responsibility of the Australian Nature Conservation Agency and renamed Jervis Bay National Park. In 1995 Jervis Bay National Park and Jervis Bay Botanic Gardens Annex were given to Wreck Bay Aboriginal Community Council and leased back to the Commonwealth. The Jervis Bay National Park was renamed the Booderee National Park in 1998. The Booderee National Park is home to over 200 species of birds, 27 species of mammals, 23 species of reptiles, 15 species of amphibians, and 180 species of fish.
Booderee National Park, URL: http://www.environment.gov.au/parks/booderee/

NORFOLK ISLAND

Capital: Kingston (administrative centre); Burnt Pine (commercial centre)

Head of State : Neil Pope (Administrator) (page 1497)

Territory Flag: Three vertical stripes - green, white, green - with a width ratio of 7:9:7, on the middle panel of which is superimposed a green image of the Norfolk Island pine tree

CONSTITUTION AND GOVERNMENT

Constitution
In 1914 the island became a territory under the authority of the Commonwealth of Australia. From 1914-79 the island was administered directly by Australia through a resident Administrator advised by a group of local residents.

The Norfolk Island Act 1979 provides the island with a large measure of internal self-government consistent with its constitutional status as a non-dependent Australian Territory. Under the Act, the Norfolk Island community gained its own legislature and executive government responsible for a range of matters.

The Administrator is the senior Commonwealth representative in the territory. He is appointed by the Governor-General and is responsible to the Australian Federal government. In exercising his powers the Administrator acts on the advice of the Executive Council in relation to those matters within the responsibility of the Norfolk Island Government. In all other matters the Administrator acts on instructions from the Australian government.

Recent Events
On 20 February 2006, the Minister for Local Government, Territories and Roads announced the Australian Government's decision to review governance arrangements on Norfolk Island; the Australian Government were concerned that the governance and financial arrangements on Norfolk Island were unsustainable and that alternative arrangements should be canvassed. In December 2006, the decision was reached not to proceed with changes to the governance. In making its decision, the Australian Government took into account the assurances made by the Norfolk Island Government to increase revenue and promote tourism growth on the Island. However, the global economic crisis has had dire consequences for the Norfolk economy and in 2011, the federal government took back some powers in return for financial aid.

In 2010, Norfolk Island was made a World Heritage site.

Legislature
Wide powers are exercised by an elected nine-member Legislative Assembly and by an Executive Council, comprising the Executive Members of the Legislative Assembly, who have ministerial-type responsibilities. Australian citizens on Norfolk Island have the right of optional enrolment for voting in Federal elections. Eligible Norfolk Islanders who can establish a relevant connection with a State subdivision are permitted to enroll in that subdivision. Voters who cannot establish a connection are entitled to vote in the Division of Canberra.

The Legislative Assembly is elected for a period of three years by the residents of Norfolk Island. The Legislative Assembly consists of nine members, whilst the Executive Council is composed of four of the nine members of the Legislative Assembly. Each member holds the position of minister for one or more portfolios. The Executive Council advises the administrator. **Legislative Assembly**, Old Military Barracks, Quality Row, Kingston, Norfolk Island, South Pacific. Tel: +672 322003, fax: + 672 322624, e-mail: executives@assembly.gov.nf, URL: http://www.norfolkislandgovernment.com/members.html

Executive Council (as at June 2013)
Chief Minister: Hon. David E. Buffet (page 1396)
Minister for Finance and the Attorney General: vacant
Minister for Tourism, Industry and Development: André N. Nobbs
Minister for Community Services: Timothy Sheridan

Ministries
Office of Ministries, Old Military Barracks, Kingston, Norfolk Island 2899, URL: www.norfolkislandgovernment.com/
Office of the Administrator, Norfolk Island, South Pacific 2899. Tel: +672 322152, fax: +672 322681, URL: http://www.norfolk.gov.nf/

Elections
The Thirteenth Legislative Assembly was elected on 17 March 2010 and sworn in on 24 March 2010.

LEGAL SYSTEM

The judicial system consists of a Supreme Court, situated at Kingston, and a Court of Petty Sessions. The Supreme Court may sit in Norfolk Island, New South Wales, Victoria or the Australian Capital Territory in determining a non-criminal matter. The court has original jurisdiction in serious criminal matters and in matters of a civil nature where damages sought amount to more than $10,000. Criminal matters may be heard by a jury of Norfolk Islanders. The court consists of the Chief Justice, appointed by the Governor-General of Australia, and such other judges as the Governor-General sees fit to appoint.

The Court of Petty Sessions hears criminal matters punishable by fine or summary conviction and may hear minor civil matters. Three magistrates sit on the bench during a hearing, and are appointed from the Australian Capital Territory. A Coroner's Court and an Employment Tribunal may also hear matters of a specific nature.

As Norfolk Island is a part of the Commonwealth of Australia, appeals to the Australia Federal court system are possible. Norfolk Island's courts also have jurisdiction in the Coral Sea Territory.

Supreme Court of Norfolk Island, Norfolk Island, South Pacific 2899. Tel: +672 3 23691, fax: +672 3 23403

AREA AND POPULATION

Area
Norfolk Island is an Australian Territory off the eastern coast of Australia in the Pacific Ocean, about 1,400 km east of Brisbane, 750 km to the south of New Caledonia and 640 km north of New Zealand. The territory also comprises the uninhabited Nepean and Phillip Islands, 1 km and 7 km south of the main island, respectively. The territory covers a total area of 34.6 sq. km (13.3 sq. miles).

Norfolk Island's geography is largely rolling plains with some volcanic mountains. Average temperatures range from 20°C to 25°C in February to 13°C to 18°C in July. Annual average rainfall is about 1,400mm.

Population
Norfolk Island had a recorded population of 2,037 at the last census in 2001; the figure was estimated to be 2,160 in 2011. The average life expectancy is 78 years.

Of the permanent population, nearly half are descendants of the Pitcairn Islanders, who originally settled in 1856.

Under the Citizenship Act 1948 a person born on Norfolk Island is an Australian by birth as long as one parent is an Australian citizen or a permanent Australian resident. 82 per cent are Australian citizens and 14 per cent are New Zealanders.

English is the official language although a local Polynesian dialect is spoken by some residents.

Public Holidays 2014
6 March: Foundation Day
8 June: Bounty Day: Pitcairners Arrival Day (1856)
26 November: Thanksgiving Day

EMPLOYMENT

Around 10 per cent of the labour force is engaged in agriculture and 90 per cent in industry and services.

BANKING AND FINANCE

Currency
Australian currency is used.

GDP/GNP, Inflation, National Debt
Tourism is the main economic activity and had increased steadily over recent years. Revenues from tourism helped the agricultural sector become self sufficient. Philatelic sales (stamps and postcards) were also a source of income. However, a severe decline in the tourism industry in 2011 has caused a major economic collapse. In 2012 it was revealed that more than US$37 million had been provided in emergency funding by the Department of Regional Australia (more than US$20,000 per permanent resident). However, the economic situation remains dire and the federal government has warned that the tax system will need to be reformed and government-owned enterprises will have to be sold.

Australian income tax does not have to be paid for income earned within the Territory. Although other Federal taxes do not apply to the Territory either, local and indirect taxes are levied by the NIG.

Balance of Payments / Imports and Exports
The main export commodities are postage stamps, seeds of the Norfolk pine and Kentia palm, and small quantities of avocado. Main export partners are Australia, other Pacific islands and New Zealand.

Chambers of Commerce and Trade Organisations
Norfolk Island Chamber of Commerce, POB 370, Norfolk Island 2899. Tel: +672 3 22018, fax: +672 3 23106

MANUFACTURING, MINING AND SERVICES

Service Industries
Tourism is Norfolk Island's main source of revenue. Up to 40,000 tourists visit each year, 80 per cent of them from the Australian mainland. The sector employs around 90 per cent of the workforce.

Tourism almost totally funds the Island's needs. Additional monies are contributed by the Commonwealth of Australia towards the management of the National Park, the salary and operations expenses of the Administrator's Office, a local meteorological office and towards a percentage of the costs of maintaining the Kingston and Arthur's Vale Historical Area which contains many of the remains of the British Penal Colony buildings

Agriculture
The key agricultural crops are Norfolk Island pine seed, Kentia palm seed, cereals, vegetables, and fruit. In order to preserve the growing environment, importation of fresh fruit and vegetables is prohibited. There are also cattle and poultry industries. Twenty five per cent of the land is under permanent pasture.

In order to preserve fishing stocks a major natural resource for the islanders. The Australian Government controls territorial sea claims to three nautical miles from the island.

COMMUNICATIONS AND TRANSPORT

National Airlines
Flight West and Norfolk Jet Express link Norfolk Island with Brisbane, whilst Air New Zealand links the island with New Zealand. There are also charter flights from Lord Howe Island and, with Air Caledonie, New Caledonia.

Roads
There are about 80 km of roads, 50 km of which are paved and 30 km are unpaved.

Shipping
Norfolk Island is serviced by shipping lines. Small tankers deliver petroleum products and liquid propane gas to the island.

Ports and Harbours
Norfolk Island has no ports or harbours; however, loading jetties exist at Cascade and Kingston.

HEALTH

Norfolk Island has a 28-bed hospital, four doctors, and a range of dental services. Emergency services are provided on a 24-hour basis and if necessary patients may be evacuated by the RAAF.

A compulsory Healthcare Scheme is run by the Norfolk Island Government for residents over the age of 18.

EDUCATION

Infant, primary and secondary education is compulsory and is provided free of charge by the Norfolk Island government. The education system is based on that in New South Wales with an extension to include Years 11 and 12. The Island receives teachers, assistance and services from the New South Wales Department of Education. The Norfolk Island Central School, takes pupils from kindergarten through to Higher School Certificate level in year 12.

Bursaries and scholarships are available for vocational training outside of the island.

RELIGION

The population is divided as follows: Anglican (39 per cent), Roman Catholic (11.7 per cent), Uniting Church in Australia (16.4 per cent), Seventh-Day Adventist (4.4 per cent), none (9.2 per cent), unknown (16.9 per cent), other (2.4 per cent).

Norfolk Island has a religious liberty rating of 10 on a scale of 1 to 10 (10 is most freedom). (Source: World Religion Database)

COMMUNICATIONS AND MEDIA

Newspapers
There are two weekly newspapers, Norfolk Island Government Gazette and Norfolk Islander.
Norfolk Island Government Gazette, Kingston, Norfolk Island 2899. Tel: +672 3 22001, fax: +672 3 23177
Norfolk Islander, Greenways Press, POB 150, Norfolk Island 2899. Tel: +672 3 22159, fax: +672 3 22948

Broadcasting
Three FM radio broadcast stations operate on the island. Norfolk Island Broadcasting Service is government-owned and non-commercial. Australian Broadcasting Service programmes are relayed by satellite. By 2005, there was one local television station and 2 repeater stations that broadcast Australian programmes.

Telecommunications
There are approximately 2,550 mainline telephones in use. Mobile phones have been operational on the island since 2007. Wireless internet and ADSL broadband is available throughout the island.

AUSTRIA
Republic of Austria
Republik Österreich

Capital: Vienna (Population estimate: 1.68 million)

Head of State: Heinz Fischer (President) (page 1425)

National Flag: Three stripes fesswise, red, white, red.

CONSTITUTION AND GOVERNMENT

Constitution
The Republic of Austria was proclaimed on 12 November 1918, following the break-up of the Austro-Hungarian Empire. Austria's present constitution goes back to the constitution of 1929 which came back into force on 19 December 1945 after the German occupation during World War II. Austria's 1955 State Treaty made the country 'permanently neutral'.

The supreme head of the republic is the Federal President, directly elected by universal adult suffrage for a maximum of two consecutive six-year terms. The Federal President appoints the Chancellor and, on his proposal, other members of the Federal Government.

For further information on the constitution, please consult:
www.bmeia.gv.at/en/foreign-ministry/austria/government-and-politics/parliamentary-democracy.html

International Relations
Following the second World War Austria was occupied by the USSR, US, UK and France, gaining her independence in May 1955. Since then Austria has followed a line of neutrality and as a result is home to several UN organisations. Austria joined the European Union in 1995 and is a member of the UN but with regard to its neutrality is not a member of NATO.

Recent Events
The inclusion of the right wing Freedom Party in the government, following the 1999 General Election, led to protests within Austria and around the world; the Freedom Party (FPÖ) and the Austrian People's Party (ÖVP) won 52 seats each, and formed a coalition. The EU announced a freezing of bilateral contacts and Israel recalled their Ambassador. The party leaders, Jörg Haider and Wolfgang Schüssel, signed an agreement which stated that the federal government stands for respect, tolerance and understanding for all human beings irrespective of their origin, religion or philosophy, and that the federal government works for an Austria in which xenophobia, anti-Semitism and racism have no place.

In February 2000 Jörg Haider resigned as leader of the FPÖ, his place being taken by Vice-Chancellor Susanne Riess-Passer. In-fighting within the FPÖ led to several cabinet resignations in August and September 2002. Chancellor Schüssel announced an early general election for November 2002 in an attempt to prevent hardliners from the FPÖ gaining cabinet positions. Susanne Reiss-Passer resigned as leader of the FPÖ and was succeeded by Mathias Reichold, who in turn resigned in October 2002. Herbert Haupt subsequently became leader. The FPÖ won just 18 seats in the November elections; the OVP won 79 seats. Unable to form a coalition with either the SDP or the Greens, Wolfgang Schüssel announced a coalition with the FPÖ. In April 2005 Jörg Haider announced that he was forming a new party called the Alliance for Austria's Future. In October 2008 Jörg Haider was killed in a car crash.

In May 2005 Austria ratified the EU Constitution but as France and The Netherlands had rejected it, it was no longer viable in its existing form and the debate continued.

In July 2008 the Conservative People's Party withdrew from the grand coalition with the Social Democrats resulting in a snap general election which was held at the end of September. The Social Democrats won the most votes but far-right parties made large gains. The new leader of the Social Democrat Party, Werner Faymann, formed a new coalition with the Austrian People's Party and the new government was sworn in on 2 December.

Austria served as a non-permanent member of the UN Security Council in the period 2009/10.

Legislature
The legislative branch of government is the bicameral Federal Assembly (*Bundesversammlung*), which comprises the Federal Council (*Bundesrat*) and the National Council (*Nationalrat*).
Parliament: http://www.parlinkom.gv.at

Upper House
The *Bundesrat* has 62 members although this number varies from time to time. Representation is by province and seats are allocated according to the population of each province. All legislation presented to the lower house must also be passed by the upper house.
Bundesrat (Federal Council), Ballhausplatz 2, 1014 Vienna, Austria. Tel: +43 (0)1 53115, fax: +43 (0)1 535 0338, URL: http://www.austria.gv.at/ http://www.parlinkom.gv.at

Lower House
The *Nationalrat* has 183 members. It approves federal legislation and any new government. Members are elected for a period of four years. Voting is by secret ballot and by a system of proportional representation.
Nationalrat (National Council), Dr. Karl Renner-Ring 3, A-1017 Vienna, Austria. Tel: +43 (0)1 401100, fax: +43 (0)1 40110/2345, URL: http://www.parlinkom.gv.at

President: Barbara Prammer (page 1497)

Cabinet (as of July 2013)
Federal Chancellor: Werner Faymann (page 1423)
Vice Chancellor, Federal Minister for European and International Affairs: Michael Spindelegger (page 1519)
Federal Minister for Economic Affairs Family and Youth: Reinhold Mitterlehner (page 1478)
Federal Minister for Education, Art and Culture: Claudia Schmied (page 1509)
Federal Minister of Finance: Maria Fekter (page 1424)
Federal Minister for Transport, Innovation and Technology: Doris Bures (page 1397)
Federal Minister for Defence and Sports: Gerald Klug
Federal Minister for Agriculture, Forestry, Environment and Water Management: Nikolaus Berlakovich (page 1387)
Federal Minister for Health: Alois Stöger (page 1520)
Federal Minister for Women and Civil Service: Gabriele Heinisch-Hosek
Federal Minister of Justice: Beatrix Karl
Federal Minister for Interior: Johanna Mikl-Leitner
Federal Minister for Social Affairs, Labour, and Consumer Protection: Rudolf Hundstorfer
Federal Minister of Science and Research: Karlheinz Tochterle

Ministries
Office of the Federal President, Hofburg, Leopoldinischer Trakt, 1014 Vienna, Austria. Tel: +43 (0)1 534 22, URL: http://www.hofburg.at/
Federal Chancellery, Ballhausplatz 2, 1014 Vienna, Austria. Tel: +43 (0)1 531150, fax: +43 (0)1 535 0338, e-mail: praesidium@bka.gv.at, URL: http://www.austria.gv.at/
Federal Ministry for Health, Family and Youth, Radetzkystr. 2, 1030 Vienna, Austria. Tel: +43 (0)1 711000, fax: +43 (0)1 711 00 1430 e-mail: buergerservice@bmgf.gv.at, URL: http://www.bmgf.gv.at
Federal Ministry for Foreign Affairs, Minoritenplatz 8, 1014 Vienna, Austria. Tel: +43 (0)1 501150, fax: +43 (0)1 535 4530, URL: http://www.bmaa.gv.at
Federal Ministry of the Interior, Herrengasse 7, 1010 Vienna, Austria. Tel: +43 (0)1 531260, fax: +43 (0)1 53126 2569, e-mail: ministerbuero@bmi.gv.at, URL: http://www.bmi.gv.at
Federal Ministry of Finance, Himmelpfortgasse 8, 1015 Vienna, Austria. Tel: +43 (0)1 514330, fax: +43 (0)1 512 7869, e-mail: post@bmf.gv.at, URL: http://www.bmf.gv.at
Federal Ministry for Economic Affairs and Labour, Stubenring 1, 1010 Vienna, Austria. Tel: +43 (0)1 711000, fax: +43 (0)1 713 7995, e-mail: service@bmwa.gv.at URL http://www.bmwa.gv.at
Federal Ministry for Social Affairs and Consumer Protection, Stubenring 1 1010 Vienna, Austria. Tel: +43 (0)1 71100, fax: +43 (0)1 715 8258, e-mail einlaufstelle@bmsg.gv.at, URL: http://www.bmsg.gv.at
Federal Ministry for Agriculture and Forestry, the Environment and Water Management, Stubenring 1, 1010 Vienna, Austria. Tel: +43 (0)1 711000, fax: +43 (0)1 71100-2127, URL: http://www.lebensministerium.at
Federal Ministry for Education, Arts and Culture, Minoritenplatz 5, 1014 Vienna Austria. Tel: +43 (0)1 531200, fax: +43 (0)1 53120-7797 / -3099, e-mail ministerium@bmbwk.gv.at, URL: http://www.bmbwk.gv.at
Federal Ministry of Justice, Museumstrasse 7, 1070 Vienna, Austria. Tel: +43 (0)1 521520, fax: +43 (0)1 52152 2727, e-mail: post@bmj.gv.at, URL: http://www.bmj.gv.at
Federal Ministry for Transport, Innovation and Technology, Radetzkystrasse 2, 1030 Vienna, Austria. Tel: +43 (0)1 711620, fax: +43 (0)1 71162 8199, URL http://www.bmvit.gv.at
Federal Ministry of Defence and Sports, Rossauer Laende 1, 1090 Vienna, Austria Tel: +43 (0)1 52000, fax: +43 (0)1 5200-17041, e-mail: buergservice@bmlv.gv.at, URL http://www.bmlv.gv.at
Federal Ministry of Science and Research, Minoritenplatz 5, 1014 Vienna, Austria Tel: +43 (0)1 53120-0, URL: http://www.bmwf.gv.at
Federal Ministry for Women and Public Administration, Ballhausplatz 2, 1014 Vienna, Austria. Tel: +43 (0)1 531150, fax: +43 (0)1 535 0338, URL http://www.frauen.bka.gv.at/

Political Parties
Österreichische Volkspartei (ÖVP, People's Party), Lichtenfelsgasse 7, A-1010 Vienna Austria. Tel: +43 (0)1 401260, fax: +43 (0)1 402 7889, e-mail: email@oevp.at, URL http://www.oevp.at
Chairman: Josef Pröll
Sozialdemokratische Partei Österreichs (SPÖ, Social Democratic Party) Löwelstr. 18, A-1014 Vienna, Austria. Tel: +43 (0)1 534270, fax: +43 (0)1 535 9683/5342 extn.282, URL: http://www.spoe.at
Chairman: Werner Faymann (page 1423)
Freiheitliche Partei Österreichs (FPÖ, Austrian Freedom Party), Esslinggasse 14-16, A-1010 Vienna, Austria. Tel: +43 (0)1 512 35350, fax: +43 (0)1 512 35359, e-mail bqst@fpoe.at, URL: http://www.fpoe.at
Leader: Heinz-Christian Strache
Die Grünen-die Grüne Alternative (Grüne, The Greens-The Green Alternative), Lindengasse 40, A-1071 Vienna, Austria. Tel: +43 (0)1 521250, fax: +43 (0)1 526 9110, e-mail: dialogbuero@gruene.at, URL: http://www.gruene.at
Leader: Eva Glawischnig

Bündnis Zukunft Österreich (BZO The Alliance for Austria's Future), (formed in April 2005) Kärntner Ring 11-13/7/4, A-1010 Vienna, Austria. URL: http://www.bzoe.at
Leader: Joseph Bucher

Liberales Forum (LIF, Liberal Forum), Dürergasse 6/10, A-1060 Vienna, Austria. URL: http://www.liberale.at
Leader: Angelika Mlinar

Bürgerforum Österreich (FRITZ, Citizens' Forum Austria), URL: http://www.listefritz.at/
Leader: Fritz Dinkhauser

Liste Hans-Peter Martin (HPM Hans-Peter Martin's List), URL: http://www.weisse.at/
Leader: Hans-Peter Martin

Elections

All men and women aged 18 years and over are entitled to vote. New legislation for national elections was introduced in 1993. This aimed to avoid party political fragmentation and reduce the size of regional constituencies. There are presently nine major constituencies.

The most recent presidential election took place in April 2010 when Heinz Fischer was re-elected to the post.

Elections held in October 2006 resulted in the Social Democratic Party (FPÖ) led by Alfred Gusenbauer winning 35.3 per cent of the vote, the People's Party (ÖVP) 34.3 per cent, the Greens, 11.05 per cent and Jörg Haider's Alliance for the Future of Austria 4.1 per cent. Alfred Gusenbauer was invited to form a coalition government as leader of the largest party and talks began with the People's Party. The talks soon broke down but eventually an agreement between the two parties was settled and in January 2007 the new government was sworn in. In July 2008 the Conservative People's Party withdrew from the grand coalition with the Social Democrats resulting in a snap general election which was held at the end of September. Although the Social Democrats won most votes, far right parties did very well. The Freedom Party won 18.1 per cent of the vote and the Alliance for the Future of Austria won 10.9 per cent. A coalition government was formed by the Social Democrats and the People's Party. For the first time in a general election in an EU country 16 and 17 year olds were able to vote.

Diplomatic Representation

Austrian Embassy, 18 Belgrave Mews West, London, SW1X 8HU. Tel: +44 (0)20 7235 3731, fax: +44 (0)20 7344 0292, e-mail: embassy@austria.org.uk, URL: http://www.bmeia.gv.at/botschaft/london.html
Ambassador: Dr. Emil Brix (page 1394)

Austrian Embassy, 3524 International Court NW, Washington, DC 20008-3035, USA. Tel: +1 202 895 6700, fax: +1 202 895 6750, URL: http://www.austria.org
Ambassador: Dr. Hans Peter Manz (page 1470)

US Embassy, Boltzmanngasse 16, A-1090 Vienna, Austria. Tel: +43 (0)1 31339, fax: +43 (0)1 310 06820, e-mail: embassy@usembassy.at, URL: http://vienna.usembassy.gov
Ambassador: William C. Eacho, III (page 1419)

British Embassy, Jauresgasse 12, 1030 Vienna, Austria. Tel: +43 (0)1 716130, fax: +43 (0)1 7161 32999, e-mail: info@britishembassy.at, URL: http://www.britishembassy.at
Ambassador: Susan le Jeune d'Allegeershecque (page 1462)

Austrian Mission to the United Nations, 823 United Nations Plaza, 8th Floor, New York, NY 10017, USA. Tel: +1 212 949 1840, fax: +1 212 953 1302, e-mail: austria@un.int, URL: http://www.bmeia.gv.at/en/austrian-mission/austrian-mission-new-york.html
Ambassador: Martin Sajdik

LEGAL SYSTEM

The Austrian legal system is divided between courts concerned with public law matters, and those of ordinary jurisdiction.

The Courts of public law jurisdiction are the Constitutional Court (Verfassungsgerichtshof) and the Administrative Courts. The Constitutional Court protects the civil rights of the people, and ensures that legislation conforms with the Constitution. It also adjudicates disputes between the federation and the federal provinces. The various Administrative tribunals and Court review the actions and decisions of the administrative authorities. Proceedings before the tribunals (which are not strictly courts) fulfill the fair trial requirement of the European Convention of Human Rights (ECHR). The only administrative court in Austria is the Verwaltungsgerichtshof which reviews the decisions and the exercise of power of the entire public administration.

The Courts of ordinary Jurisdiction deal with matters of private and criminal law. There are two kinds of Courts of First Instance - District Courts and Regional Courts. The severity of the a crime in a criminal case, or the amount claimed in a civil case, determines which court will hear the case. Decisions are taken by a single judge in District Courts, and also in civil cases before Regional Courts. The composition of the Regional Court in criminal matters differs according to the nature of the case.

Regional Courts can act as a Court of second instance where a civil case was originally brought before a District Court. Where a Regional Court already decided in the first instance, appeals go before a Province Court (Oberlandesgericht). In criminal matters, the Province Courts are always the second instance courts.

The Supreme Court (Oberster Gerichtshof) is the highest court in civil and criminal cases. It has 6 Senates for criminal cases, 10 for civil cases and 2 additional for labour cases and social cases. The Supreme Court hears cases only on appeal.

The government respects the rights of its citizens.

The death penalty was abolished in 1968 by Constitution.

Supreme Constitutional Court (Verfassungsgerichtshof): URL: http://www.vfgh.gv.at
President: Gerhart Holzinger

Supreme Administrative Court (Verwaltungsgerichtshof): URL: http://www.vwgh.gv.at
President: Prof. Dr. Clemens Jabloner (page 1448)

Supreme Judicial Court (Oberster Gerichtshof): URL: http://www.justiz.gv.at

Austrian Ombudsman Board, Singerstrasse 17, PO Box 20, A-1015 Vienna, Austria. Tel: +43 1 515 05-0, URL: http://www.volksanw.gv.at/i_english.htm

LOCAL GOVERNMENT

Austria is divided into nine provinces (Länder), each having its own Provincial Government with a Provincial Governor (Landeshauptmann) at its head, elected by the Provincial Diet (Landtag). Elections take place every five or six years.

Provincial Governors (Landeshauptmänner)

Vienna (Vienna): Dr Michael Häupl (SPO), URL: http://www.wien.gv.at/
Burgenland (Eisenstadt): Hans Niessl (SPO), URL: http://www.burgenland.at
Carinthia (Klagenfurt): Gerhard Dörfler (FPK), URL: http://www.ktn.gv.at
Lower Austria (Sankt Pölten): Dr Erwin Pröll (OVP), URL: http://www.noe.gv.at
Upper Austria (Linz): Dr Josef Pühringer (OVP), URL: http://www.land-oberoesterreich.gv.at/cps/rde/xchg/ooe
Salzburg (Salzburg): Gabi Burgstaller (SPO), URL: http://www.salzburg.gv.at
Styria (Graz): Franz Voves (SPO), URL: http://www.steiermark.at
Tyrol (Innsbruck): Günther Platter (OVP), URL: http://www.tirol.gv.at
Vorarlberg (Bregenz): Dr Herbert Sausgruber (OVP), URL: http://www.voralberg.at

The following table shows the population of each Länder on January 1 2010:

Länder	Population
Burgenland	283,965
Carinthia	559,315
Lower Austria	1,607,976
Upper Austria	1,411,238
Salzburg	529,861
Styria	1,208,372
Tyrol	706,873
Vorarlberg	368,868
Vienna	1,698,822

Source: Statistik Austria

AREA AND POPULATION

Area

Austria is a land-locked country in central Europe bounded in the north by Germany and the Czech Republic, in the east by the Slovak Republic and Hungary, in the south by Slovenia and Italy and in the west by Liechtenstein and Switzerland. It has a total area of 83,859 sq. km (32,369 sq. miles). The climate ranges from cool temperate to mountain conditions according to the region. Winters are cold with considerable snowfall, whilst summers are warm. The wettest months are from May to August. The river Danube flows through Austria for 350 km (220 miles). The highest mountain is the Grossglockner at (3,797 metres (12,530 feet).

To view a map, consult http://www.lib.utexas.edu/maps/cia08/austria_sm_2008.gif

Population

Figures for the beginning of 2012 put the population at approximately 8,443,018, up from 8,233,000 in 2005. The main towns 2012) are Vienna (1.7 million), Graz (265,000), Linz (191,000), Saltzburg (149,000) and Innsbruck (121,000). (Source: Statistik Austria).

The official language is German but the rights of Slovenian, Croatian and Hungarian speaking minorities are protected. Ninety-two per cent of the population speak German, with linguistic minorities of Slovenes (29,000), Croats (60,000), Hungarians (33,000) and Czechs (19,000).

Births, Marriages, Deaths

In 2011 there were 78,109 births (down from 78,742 the previous year) and 76,479 deaths (down from 77,199 the previous year). That year there were 36,426 marriages and in 2011, and 17,295 divorces. Figures for 2010 show that 114,398 people immigrants arrived in Austria and 86,703 people emigrated to other countries. Life expectancy is 77.62 years for men and 82.97 years for women. In 2008, of a total population of 8,336,549, approximately 1,269,556 people were under 15 years old, 5,198,511 were aged between 15 and 59 years, and 1,880,482 were aged 60 years or over. (Source: Statistik Austria)

Public Holidays 2014

1 January: New Year's Day
6 January: Epiphany
18 April: Good Friday
21 April: Easter Monday
1 May: Labour Day
29 May: Ascension Day
9 June: Whit Monday
19 June: Corpus Christi
15 August: Assumption Day
26 October: National Day
1 November: All Saints Day
8 December: Immaculate Conception

AUSTRIA

25 December: Christmas Day
26 December: St Stephen's Day

EMPLOYMENT

Figures for 2011 put the total workforce at 4,322,900 of which 4,143,900 were employed and 179,000 were unemployed. Figures for 2010 put the total workforce at 4,285,000 of which 4,096,000 were employed and 188,000 were unemployed. Unemployment has been amongst the lowest in Europe although unemployment figures rose between 2002 and 2005 reaching 5.2 per cent. Since then unemployment rates have fallen from 4.7 per cent in 2006 to 4.4 per cent in 2007, 3.8 per cent in 2008, 4.8 per cent in 2009, 4.4 per cent in 2010 and 4.2 per cent in 2011

Employment figures for 2011

Economic Sector	No. of employed,'000
Agriculture, forestry & fishing	29,000
Mining & quarrying	11,000
Manufacturing	624,000
Electricity, gas, steam & air conditioning supply	31,000
Water supply, sewerage, waste management	17,000
Construction	329,000
Wholesale & retail trade, repairs	561,000
Transportation & storage	193,000
Accommodation & food service	207,000
Information & communication	84,000
Financial & insurance activities	141,000
Real estate activities	32,000
Professional. scientific, technical activities	157,000
Admin. & support service activities	128,000
Public admin. & defence, compulsory social security	278,000
Education	248,000
Human health & social work activities	352,000
Arts, entertainment & recreation	52,000
Other service activities	89,000
Activities of households as employers	8,000
Activities of extraterritorial organisations & bodies	6,000
Unemployment rate	4.8 %

Source: Statistik Austria

Trade Unions in Austria

GPA - Gewerkschaft der Privatangestellten - Private Sector Employee's Union, URL: http://www.gpa.at
Österreichischer Gewerkschaftsbund (ÖGB) (Austrian Trade Union Fed.), URL: http://www.oegb.at
Gewerkschaft Kunst, Medien, Sport, freie Berufe (Trade Union Arts, Media, Sports, Freelancer), URL: http://www.kmsfb.at

BANKING AND FINANCE

Currency
One euro = 100 cents
€ = 13.7603 schillings (European Central Bank irrevocable conversion rate)
On 1 January 1999 the euro was launched as an electronic currency across the 12 member states of the EU. On 1 January 2002 the euro became legal tender in Austria. Austria's old currency, the schilling, ceased to be legal tender from 28 February 2002. Euro banknotes come in denominations of 5, 10, 20, 50, 100, 200, and 500. Euro coins come in denominations of 2 and 1 euros, 50, 20, 10, 5, 2, and 1 cents.

GDP/GNP, Inflation, National Debt
Since the early 1990s Austria has embarked on a programme of economic reforms including the telecommunications and energy sectors as well as banks and some industries, liberalization of markets and tax cuts.

Austria's economy has grown steadily since joining the European Union on 1 January 1995 and since 2003 has grown faster than the average for Eurozone countries; growth in 2006 was put at 3.3 per cent compared to the Eurozone average of 2.7 per cent. Economic growth has been driven in recent years by strong export growth and rising investments. In 2007 growth was put at 3.4 per cent but by the end of the year growth began to decline slightly as globally financial markets failed and many countries began to fear a recession. Given that in the changing economic market export driven economies were hit, and growth for 2008 was put at 2.1 per cent, Austria's recession lasted until the third quarter of 2009. Austria has an austerity package in place which aims to balance the budget by 2016. GDP in 2009 contracted by 3.8 per cent before recovering in 2010 with a growth rate of 1.3 per cent followed by growth of 1.4 per cent in 2011. Forecast figures for 2012 predict that growth will fall.

The following table shows the value of GDP in recent years:

Year	GDP, current prices in bil. €	% change on previous year
2000	210.4	5.2
2005	244.4	3.9
2006	257.2	4.7
2007	270.8	3.1
2008	281.9	4.1
2009	274.8	-2.8

- continued

2010	286.2	4.1
2011	301.3	5.3

Source: Statistik Austria

Make up of GDP in euro billion at current prices

Sector	2010 € bn	2010 % change	2011	2011
Agriculture, forestry & fishing	3.8	11.5	4.2	9.5
Mining & quarrying, Manufacturing	46.6	5.8	52.5	12.8
Utilities	8.8	3.7	9.9	12.9
Construction	17.7	-1.1	18.6	5.0
Wholesale & retail trade & repairs	35.1	8.5	36.1	2.6
Transport & storage	12.1	1.1	12.3	1.6
Accommodation & food service activities	12.6	2.6	13.1	3.5
Information & communication	8.1	-1.0	7.9	-2.5
Financial & insurance activities	12.8	7.6	13.4	5.0
Real estate services	24.5	3.0	25.4	3.7
Professional, scientific, technical activities	23.3	5.8	24.3	4.4
Public administration & defence compulsory social insurance	15.3	1.6	15.4	0.8
Education, human health, social work activities	30.6	2.8	31.3	2.4
Other service activities	7.4	2.8	7.6	2.9
Gross value added at basic prices, total	258.6	4.2	272.0	5.1
Taxes on products	32.8	2.6	34.0	3.7
Subsidies on products	5.3	-3.5	4.7	-10.8
GDP at market prices	286.2	4.1	301.3	5.3

Source: Statistics Austria

Per capita GDP was put at €33,850 in 2009, 3.2 per cent higher than the previous year.

Inflation was recorded at 2.3 per cent in 2004, 2.1 per cent in 2005, 1.7 per cent in 2006 and 2.2 per cent in 2007. In June 2008, inflation reached 3.9 per cent, its highest rate for 15 years, due mainly to increased prices in energy and food. By October 2008 it had fallen to 3.1 per cent and fell again in 2009 to an average of 0.5 per cent. Figures for 2010 put inflation in 2010 at 1.7 per cent, rising to 3.6 per cent in 2011. Figures for 2010 put debt at 71.9 per cent of GDP, rising to 72.2 per cent of GDP in 2011.

Foreign Investment
Foreign direct investments in Austria in 2007 amounted to approximately €108 billion.

Balance of Payments / Imports and Exports
Foreign trade is the mainstay of the Austrian economy. The following tables show foreign trade by category of goods in 2010. Figures are in € billion:

Foreign Trade by Selected Goods

Goods	Import	Export	Balance
Total	113.7	109.4	-4.3
Food & live animals	6.7	5.7	-1.0
Beverages & tobacco	0.9	1.6	0.7
Crude materials	5.8	3.7	-2.1
Mineral fuels, lubricants & related materials	12.1	3.5	-8.7
Animal & vegetable oils, fats & waxes	0.4	0.2	-0.2
Chemicals & related products	14.4	14.2	-0.3
Manufactured goods	18.1	25.2	7.1
Machinery & transport equipment	37.0	41.4	4.4
Miscellaneous manufactured article	16.5	12.9	-3.6
Commodities n.e.s.	1.8	1.1	-0.7

Source: Statistik Austria

In 2010 the total cost of imports was €113.7 billion. Export earnings were recorded at €109.4 billion. In 2011, the figures were €130.8 billion and €122.2 billion respectively.

The following table shows Austria's international trading partners:

Imports and exports according to country groups 2010

Country Groups	Imports	Annual Change %	Exports	Annual Change %
In total	113.7	16.54	109.4	16.7
Europe	94.3	15.6	89.8	16.0
Africa	2.0	71.2	1.4	3.8
America	4.9	26.1	7.7	25.8
Asia	12.4	14.3	9.7	19.3
Australia and Oceania	0.1	1.3	0.7	0.6
EU27	82.3	15.5	77.1	16.0
Third countries	31.3	19.1	32.2	18.4

- continued

Euro-area	68.3	14.1	59.2	16.1
Neighbouring countries	69.9	14.7	60.7	17.3
EFTA	6.7	5.9	6.1	15.5

Source: Statistics Austria

More than 40.6 per cent of all imported goods (€48.5 billion) came from Germany and almost a third of all products exported from Austria (€35 billion) were sent to Germany. Other major EU-trading partners are Italy, Czech Republic and France.

Central Bank

Österreichische Nationalbank, PO Box 61, Otto-Wagner Platz 3, A-1090 Vienna, Austria. Tel: +43 (0)1 40420, fax: +43 (0)1 40420 2398, e-mail: oenb.info@oenb.co.at, URL: http://www.oenb.at
Governor: Ewald Nowotny (page 1487)

Oesterreichische Kontrollbank AG, URL: http://www.oekb.co.at

Chambers of Commerce and Trade Organisations

Wirtschaftskammer Österreich (Austrian Economic Chamber), URL: http://www.wko.at
Austrian Trade Commission, URL: http://www.austriantrade.org/uk
Verband Österreichischer Banken und Bankiers (Assn. of Austrian Banks and Bankers), URL: http://www.voebb.at
Verband der Versicherungsunternehmen Österreichs (Assn. of Austrian Insurance Companies), URL: http://www.vvo.at

MANUFACTURING, MINING AND SERVICES

Primary and Extractive Industries

Extensive mineral resources are mined. Mined products include, dolomite, iron ore and mica, basalt, limestone and marble, quartz and brown coal. Figures for 2007 show that 8,800 were employed in the mining and quarrying sectors.

Oil

Oil production in 2011 was 30,000 barrels per day, approximately 50 per cent of which was crude oil. A total of 209 thousand barrels per day were refined in 2012, most of which was crude oil. Refinery capacity is 209 thousand bbl/d. Consumption of oil in 2011 was 262.9 thousand barrels per day. OMV, Austria's biggest petroleum and chemical group, presently drills for oil in the eastern and central oil fields and supplies approximately 70 per cent of domestic needs. OMV also handles the oil imported along the Adriatic-Vienna pipeline from the port of Trieste. Chief suppliers are Russia, Kazakhstan and Saudi Arabia. There are 777 km of pipelines.

Gas

Natural gas gross production in 2011 was 63 billion cubic feet, whilst consumption was 318 billion cubic feet. The majority of natural gas requirements are met by imports primarily from the Russia and Norway.

Coal

There was no coal produced in 2009 or 2010. In 2005 the coal mines in Styria were closed and as a result Austria now imports all its coal requirements. In 2010, coal consumption was 5.094 million short tons, all imported.

Energy

Austria's main natural source of energy is hydropower, with 1,300 power stations in operation. The largest of these is Altenworth which has an average annual output of 1,950 million kWh. Total electricity capacity was 21.11 Gwe in 2010. Net generation was 64.82 billion kWh in 2010. Net consumption was 63.80 billion kWh in 2010. (Source: EIA)

Austria has refrained from using nuclear power for the purposes of electricity generation.

Manufacturing

The country relies largely on food production, iron and steel, textiles, chemicals and production of motor vehicles to sustain its industry. Manufacturing and industry are distributed throughout Austria in the following way: Upper Austria - steel, iron, mechanical engineering and the chemical industry; Salzburg - electrical and paper industry and tourism; Vorarlberg - textiles and clothing; Carinthia - wood and paper industry, and tourism; Styria - iron and steel, and processing industries; Tirol - tourism and glass.

As in common with many large economies Austria suffered from the global economic downturn in 2008 and 2009. In 2009 domestic production decreased by 9.3 per cent compared to 2008 figures. Manufacture of machinery and equipment fell and production of motor vehicles in particular fell in in 2009 by 25 per cent of 2008 figures.

The following table shows preliminary results for industry in 2008.

Industry and Construction

Sector	No. of enterprises	Personnel	Turnover in Thsd €
Total	58,097	964,083	231,930,687
Mining and quarrying	332	6,378	2,270,177
Manufacturing	26,128	637,985	162,640,820
- machinery and equipment	1,466	76,189	19,866,828
- food products	3,558	68,470	13,629,937
- wood and wood products	2,921	36,571	7,180,303
- paper and paper products	155	18,367	6,213,995

- continued

- chemicals and chemical products	337	17,666	7,771,716
- rubber and plastic products	596	29,381	6,171,423
- basic metals	169	35,776	14,881,183
- fabricated metal products (except machinery & equipment)	3,971	75,185	14,230,487
- electrical equipment	478	45,446	11,120,860
- motor vehicles, trailers and semi-trailers	294	33,215	13,157,030
Electricity, Gas, Steam and Air Conditioning Supply	1,428	27,945	26,482,485
Water Supply, Sewerage, Waste Management	1,301	15,230	3,496,811
Construction	28,908	276,545	37,040,394

Source: Statistics Austria

Service Industries

The service industry accounts for approximately 60 per cent of GDP. The well established financial services sector consists of over 1,000 banking institutions. Turnover in the services sector fell by 4.7 per cent in 2009 compared to 2008.

Tourism

In the calendar year 2011 there were a reported 126.0 million overnight stays reported, up 0.9 per cent from 2010. Domestic overnight stays rose by 1.7 per cent compared. Tyrol traditionally has the most tourist visitors and the country's 88 lakes and mountainous areas are a chief attraction. The majority of visitors come from Germany, the Netherlands and Britain. In 2008, the direct value added created by the tourism industry was around €15.05 billion. This declined in 2010.

Agriculture

Approximately 46 per cent of land is covered by forest and woodland, with pastures and arable land covering the greater part of the remaining area. Timber plays an important role as a raw material in the economy.

Only 1 per cent of land use is devoted to permanent crops. The main agricultural production areas are to the north of the Alps and along both banks of the Danube. Agriculture accounts for approximately 3 per cent of GDP and the principal crops are fruit, potatoes and grain, with livestock including poultry, cattle and pigs. In 2007 the total number of farms and forestry operations was 187,000 (compared to 217,500 in 1999). Farms are almost exclusively family run and some are run on a part-time basis.

In 2009, total bovine livestock of approximately 2,026,000 cattle, 3,137,000 swine, 345,000 sheep and 68,200 goats. In 2008, meat production (animals slaughtered) was as follows: 5,557,000 pigs, 610,000 cattle, 80,700 calves, 319,000 sheep, 45,000 goats, and 903 horse and foals. In 2008, 527,000 dairy cows were kept in Austria, with an average annual yield of of 6,059 kg. Some 8,000 tonnes of raw sheep milk and 17,200 tonnes of raw goat milk were also produced.

In 2009, the cereal production (including grain and maize) came to 4.8 million tons, higher than the average for the decade but down on the record harvest of 2008 by 11 per cent. Approximately 1.9 million tons of grain maize were produced. Oilseeds and leguminous plants brought 364,100 tons and root crops with 3.8 million tons. Despite unfavourable weather conditions the fruit harvest was above the decade average in 2009. Approximately 264,200 tons of dessert fruits were produced (up 10 per cent compared to 2008). Apricots achieved a record production of 6,000 tons (up 32 per cent from 2008) and strawberries 15,200 tons. Vegetable production came to 594,600 tons in 2009 although wet weather adversely affected leafy and stalked vegetables.

Aquaculture production for 2008 totalled 2,889 tons, down 14.,4 per cent less than in 2007. Rainbow trout production decreased by 26.2 per cent to 1,205 tons.

Production from forestry products has increased in recent years from €1.01 billion in 2001 to €1.13 billion in 2002 and to €1.23 billion in 2003.

COMMUNICATIONS AND TRANSPORT

Travel Requirements

A valid passport is required. EU citizens can travel to Austria without a visa up to the expiry date of their passports. Other citizens need at least three months' validity on their passport. Austria is a signatory to the 1995 Schengen Agreement; citizens of the USA, Australia and Canada can stay without a visa for tourist/business for up to 90 days in each six-month period. That 90-day period begins when you enter any of the Schengen countries. An entry permit, valid for up to six months, is required for a period of up to six months. See http://www.eurovisa.info/SchengenCountries.htm for details.

Nationals of countries other than those listed above should contact the Austrian embassy to check visa requirements.

National Airlines

Österreichische Luftverkehrs AG (Austrian Airlines), URL: http://www.aua.com
Austrian Air Transport (Austrian Air Cargo), URL: http://www.austriancargo.com
Tiroler Luftfahrt (Tyrolean Airways), URL: http://www.aua.com

International Airports

There are international airports in Vienna, Linz, Salzburg, Graz, Klagenfurt and Innsbruck.
Graz Airport, URL: http://www.flughafen-graz.at
Innsbruck Airport, URL: http://www.innsbruck-airport.com

AUSTRIA

Klagenfurt, Wörthersee Airport, URL: http://www.klagenfurt-airport.at
Linz Airport, URL: http://www.flughafen-linz.at
Salzburg Airport, URL: http://www.salzburg-airport.com
Vienna Airport, URL: http://www.viennaairport.com
Total passengers in 2009: 22.5 million (arrivals and departures)
Total cargo in 2009: 190,800 tonnes
Total aircraft movements in 2009: 318,000 (incl. take-offs and landings)

Railways

Austrian Railways are almost completely nationalised under the Federal Railways (ÖBB). The total length of the track is 5,643 km of which 61 per cent is electrified. 191.3 million passengers travelled by rail in 2005 and 93.1 million tons of freight in 2009.
Österreichische Bundesbahnen (ÖBB) (Austrian Federal Railways), URL: http://www.oebb.at
General-Dir: Rüdiger vorm Walde

Vienna has an underground system as well as a light railway and tram system.

Roads

There are 110,000 km of roads of which 35,000 km are paved and 1,634 km are motorways. Speed limits are 100 km per hour on highways, 130 km per hour on freeways and 50 km per hour in residential areas. In 2010 there were 4.4 million private cars registered. Vehicles are driven on the right.

Shipping

Austria has no sea frontier, but cargo is carried on the Danube. The main Austrian shipping company is the DDSG (Danube Steamship Company). There are 350 km of navigable waterway. Figures for 2009 show that 9.3 million tons of freight was carried on the Danube.

HEALTH

Austria has a system of social insurance which covers almost the whole population. It provides earnings related benefits in the event of injuries at work, maternity, invalidity, death, sickness and old age.

Figures from the WHO show that in 2005-10 there were 40,026 physicians (48.5 per 10,000 population) 64,910 nurses and midwives (78.8 per 10,000 population), 4,685 dentists (5.7 per 10,000 population) and 5,579 pharmaceutical personnel (6.8 per 10,000 population) and 1,653 psychiatrists (2.0 per 10,000 population). In the period 2005-11 there were 77 hospital beds and 4.0 psychiatric beds per 10,000 population.

In 2009, 16.2 per cent of total government expenditure was allocated to health, equivalent to 11.0 per cent of GDP. Government expenditure accounts for 77.7 per cent of total health spend, with the rest being private expenditure. Pre-paid plans account for 19.6 per cent of private expenditure. Per capita total expenditure on health was US$5,035.

In 2010, the infant mortality rate (probability of dying by the age of 1 year) was 4 per 1,000 live births and the rate for children aged less than 5 years was 4 per 1,000 live births. The main causes of death among children aged less than five years were (2010) prematurity (25 per cent), congenital anomalies (32 per cent), birth asphyxia (6 per cent) and pneumonia (2 per cent). In 2005-10 immunization coverage among 1-year-olds was: measles 76 per cent, DTP3 83 per cent, HepB3 83 per cent, and Hib3 83 per cent. (Source: http://www.who.int, Global Health Statistics, 2012)

EDUCATION

Elementary education is free and compulsory. It normally begins in that school year which follows the day of the 6th birthday, and lasts nine years. In addition to the state-run education system about 10 per cent of schools are private and the majority of these are run by the Roman Catholic Church.

In the academic year 2010/11 there were 327,700 pupils in elementary schools, 226,900 in lower secondary schools, 200,700 in secondary academic schools, 355,300 in secondary technical and vocational schools. There were approximately 265,000 university level students in 2010/11. (Source: Statistics Austria)

University education was free until 2001, since then students are subject to fees. Austrian universities include: University Vienna; University Graz; University Innsbruck; University Salzburg; Technical University Vienna; Technical University Graz; Mining University Leoben; University of Agriculture in Vienna; University of Veterinary Medicine in Vienna; University of Economics and Business Administration in Vienna; University for Social and Economic Sciences in Linz; University of Educational Sciences, Klagenfurt; Academy of Fine Arts; College of Applied Arts, Vienna; College of Music and Dramatic Arts, Vienna; College of Music and Dramatic Arts 'Mozarteum', Salzburg; College of Music and Dramatic Arts, Graz; College of Art and Industrial Design, Linz.

Literacy in Austria is estimated at 98 per cent.

RELIGION

Freedom of legally recognised churches is guaranteed within the constitution. Religious education is given in schools and covers all faiths.

79 per cent of the population are Christian, with 74 per cent following the Roman Catholic faith. There are two Roman Catholic Archbishoprics: one in Vienna, with bishoprics at St. Pölten, Linz and Eisenstadt; and the other in Salzburg, with bishoprics at Graz-Seckau, Gurk-Klagenfurt, Innsbruck and Feldkirch.

A further 5 per cent profess to be Protestant, and 4.8 per cent are Muslim, 0.10 per cent are Jewish and 0.9 per cent Hindu.

Austria has a religious liberty rating of 7 on a scale of 1 to 10 (10 is most freedom). (Source: World Religion Database)

Ökumenischer Rat der Kirchen in Österreich (Ecumenical Council of Churches in Austria), URL: http://www.kirchen.at
Österreichische Bischofskonferenz (Bishops' Conference), URL: http://www.bischofskonferenz.at
Archbishop of Vienna, Wollzeile 2, 1010 Vienna, Austria. Tel: +43 (0)1 515520, fax: +43 (0)1 51552760
Most Reverend Dr. Christoph Schönborn (page 1510)
Bund der Baptistengemeinden in Österreich (Federation of Baptist Communities), URL: http://www.evangelikale.at
Israelitische Kultusgemeinde (Jewish Community), URL: http://www.ikg-wien.at

COMMUNICATIONS AND MEDIA

Newspapers
The newspaper industry remains strong in Austria. Main newspapers include:
Der Standard, URL: http://www.derstandard.at
Kronen-Zeitung, URL: http://www.krone.at
Der Kurier, URL: www.kurier.at/zeitung
Kleine Zeitung, URL: http://www.kleinezeitung.at
Die Presse, URL: http://www.diepresse.at
Wirtschaftsblatt, URL: http://www/wirtschaftsblatt.at
Wiener Zeitung, URL: http://www.wienerzeitung.at

Austrian Newspaper Association, URL: http://en.voez.at/b1m1

Broadcasting
Broadcasting is dominated by the public broadcaster, Osterreichischer Eundfunk (ORF). Private broadcasting is a relatively recent development. The commercial station ATV commenced broadcasting in 2000.

Austrian Broadcasting Corporation - ORF Radio, URL: http://www.orf.at
Austrian Broadcasting Corporation - ORF Television, URL: http://www.orf.at
ATV, URL: http://atv.at/

Telecommunications
There were over 3.3 million telephone connections and over 13 million mobile phones in use as of 2011. Figures for 2009 show that Austria had 6.1 million regular internet users. Approximately 70 per cent of households had access to the internet, and in 2009 some 58 per cent used broadband to connect. Approximately 40 per cent of the population use the internet for online purchases.

ENVIRONMENT

The principal threats to the environment in Austria are forest degradation caused by air pollution from industrial plants, and soil pollution from chemicals such as pesticides.

88.0 million tons of carbon dioxide equivalent of greenhouse gases were emitted in 2007, 3.9 per cent down on 2006 figures. The Kyoto target for 2008-10 is for 68.8 million tons per year. Per capita emissions of greenhouse gases were put at 11.0 tons in 2006, compared to the EU 27 average of 10.4 tons.

In 2006, €9.4 billion was spent on environmental protection. Eco-taxes raised €7.2 billion in 2007. (Source: Statistics Austria)

Austria is a party to the following international agreements: Air Pollution, Air Pollution-Nitrogen Oxides, Air Pollution-Persistent Organic Pollutants, Air Pollution-Sulfur 85, Air Pollution-Sulphur 94, Air Pollution-Volatile Organic Compounds, Antarctic Treaty, Biodiversity, Climate Change, Climate Change-Kyoto Protocol, Desertification, Endangered Species, Environmental Modification, Hazardous Wastes, Law of the Sea, Ozone Layer Protection, Ship Pollution, Tropical Timber 83, Tropical Timber 94, Wetlands, and Whaling.

SPACE PROGRAMME

Austria joined the European Space Agency (ESA) in 1987 and has participated in the following programmes: science; telecommunications; navigation satellite programme Galileo; earth observations; Ariane-5; Aurora exploration; various technology programmes. Its space programme is administered by the Osterreichische Forschungsforderungsgesellschaft (FFG), Austrian Research Promotion Agency. FFG was founded in 2004 and aims to develop Austria as one of the world's leading research centres. The Austrian space budget is mainly financed by the Ministry for Transport, Innovation and Technology. In 2009 the budget was an estimated €60 million.

Austria is a member on the UN Committee on the Peaceful Uses of Outer Space (COPUOS).

Austrian Research Promotion Agency, URL: http://www.ffg.at

AZERBAIJAN
Republic of Azerbaijan
Azarbaijchan Respublikasy

Capital: Baku (Population estimate: 1.9 million)

Head of State: Ilham Aliyev (President) (page 1375)

National Flag: Blue, red and green horizontal bands; a white crescent and an eight-pointed star in the red band

CONSTITUTION AND GOVERNMENT

Constitution
The Azerbaijan SSR was formed on 28 April 1920 and formed part of the Transcaucasian Soviet Republic from 1922-36. It became a Union Republic on 5 December 1936. The former republic's Communist party left the Communist Party of the then Soviet Union on 29 August 1991 and declared independence from the USSR on 30 August 1991. The Azeri Popular Front protested against the leadership's support of the coup against President Gorbachev on 19 August, and direct presidential elections on 8 September were boycotted by the opposition. Azerbaijan joined the Commonwealth of Independent States on 24 September 1993.

The Constitution of Azerbaijan was adopted by universal referendum on 12 November 1995, making it a democratic republic. The most recent changes to the Constitution were ratified by referendum on 24 August 2002. Under the terms of the constitution executive power is given to the President who, as Head of State, is elected by the people for a term of five years. In 2009, voters backed the removal of the two-term presidential limit. The President appoints the Prime Minister as head of government, and the Cabinet of Ministers, Azerbaijan's highest executive body.

To consult the full constitution, please visit:
http://www.azerbaijan.az/portal/General/Constitution/constitution_01_e.html

International Relations
The major domestic and international issue affecting Azerbaijan is the dispute over Nagorno-Karabakh, a predominantly ethnic Armenian region in south-western Azerbaijan. When Azerbaijan gained independence from Russia, relations were quite cool but in recent years there have been several meetings between the presidents of both countries and talks of increased trade and security. Mainly populated by Armenians, the region was assigned by Moscow to Azerbaijan in the 1920s but is currently held by Armenian forces. Nagorno-Karabkh declared itself unilaterally as an independent republic in 1991. A cease-fire was agreed between both countries in May 1994 and still holds, though there have been sporadic clashes. It is estimated that over 15,000 people have been killed with at least 900,000 Azeris and 300,000 Armenians displaced. In 2006, an overwhelming majority of Nagorno-Karabakh residents - mostly ethnic Armenians - voted in favour of declaring a sovereign state, but this was not recognised internationally. At the beginning of November 2008, Armenia and Azerbaijan signed a joint agreement aimed at resolving the dispute.

Recent Events
Azerbaijan joined the United Nations on 2 March 1992, the Organization of Security and Cooperation in Europe (OSCE) on 30 January 1992, and became a full member of the Council of Europe on 17 January 2001.

The ethnic Armenian-populated enclave of Nagorno Karabakh was at war with the surrounding Azeri population between1988 and 1994. The region unilaterally declared itself an independent state in 1991. Some 30,000 people were killed and more than a million fled their homes. A ceasefire was negotiated in 1994, but peace talks stalled and refugees remain stranded. Violence continues to flare up sporadically in the region. Azerbaijan declared illegitimate a referendum held in the region in December 2006. The vote approved a new constitution and referred to Karabakh as a sovereign state.

In May 2006, the opening ceremony for the Baku-Tblisi-Ceyhan pipeline was disrupted by an opposition rally, quelled violently by police. The pipeline, running from Baku, through Georgia, to the Turkish coast, is the means to export the anticipated wealth of energy resources from landlocked Azerbaijan. Objections are based on the political and seismic instabilities of the regions through which the pipeline passes. In 2007 the Azerbaijani state oil company stopped pumping oil to Russia in a dispute over oil prices.

In March 2008 fighting erupted in Nagorno-Karabakh and several soldiers on both sides were killed. Armenia and Azerbaijan accused each other of instigating the violence.

In November 2008, Armenia and Azerbaijan signed a joint agreement aimed at resolving their dispute over Nagorno-Karabakh.

In September 2010 BP announced plans to build a gas pipeline from Azerbaijan to Europe, which would by-pass Russia.

In September 2012, tensions flared between Azerbaijan and Armenia when Azerbaijan pardoned an army officer who had been jailed in Hungary for killing an Armenian colleague, the previous June there had been clashes on the Aberbaijan-Armenian border which resulted in military fatalities on both sides.

Legislature
Legislative power is given to the unicameral National Assembly (Milli Majlis), consisting of 125 deputies, 100 of whom are directly elected, the remaining 25 being elected by proportional representation. Both the President and the National Assembly are elected for five years.
National Assembly, (Milli Majlis), 1 Parliamentary Avenue, 1152 Baku, Azerbaijan. Tel: +994 12 439 97 50, e-mail: azmm@meclis.gov.az, URL: http://meclis.gov.az
Speaker: Oktay Asadov

Cabinet (as at June 2013)
Prime Minister: Artur Rasizade (page 1500)
First Deputy Prime Minister: Yaqub Abdulla Eyyubov (page 1422)
Deputy Prime Ministers: Elchin Efendiyev (page 1419) , Abid Sharifov (page 1513) , Ali Hasanov (page 1439)
Minister of Finance: Samir Sharifov
Minister of Labour and Social Security: Fuzuli Alekbarov
Minister of Foreign Affairs: Elmar Mammadyarov
Minister of Defence: Col.-Gen. Safar Abiyev
Minister of Internal Affairs: Ramil Usubov
Minister of National Security: Eldar Mahmudov
Minister of Agriculture: Ismat Abbasov
Minister of Ecology and Natural Resources: Huseyn Bagirov
Minister of Health: Oqtay Shiraliyev
Minister of Culture and Tourism: Abulfaz Garayev (page 1428)
Minister of Education: Mikail Jabbarov
Minister of Justice: Fikret Farrukh Mamedov
Minister of Communications and Information: Ali Mamad oglu Abbasov
Minister of Economic Development: Shahin Mustafyev
Minister of Taxation: Fazil Mamedov (page 1470)
Minister of Transport: Ziya Mammadov
Minister of Industry and Energy: Natiq Aliyev
Minister of Emergencies: Kyamaleddin Heydarov
Minister of Defence Industry: Yavar Camalov
Minister of Youth and Sport: Azad Rahimov

Ministries
Office of the President, Istiklal küç. 19, 1066 Baku, Azerbaijan. Tel: +994 12 492 7906, fax: +994 12 498 0822, e-mail: office@apparat.gov.az, URL: http://www.president.az
Office of the Prime Minister, Lermontov küç. 63, 1001 Baku, Azerbaijan. Tel: +994 12 495 7528, fax: +994 12 498 9786
Ministry of Finance, Samed Vurghun küç. 83, 1022 Baku, Azerbaijan. Tel: +994 12 493 8103, fax: +994 12 493 0562, e-mail: office@maliyye.gov.az, URL: http://www.maliyye.gov.az
Ministry of Foreign Affairs, Shikhali Gurbanov küç. 4, 1009 Baku, Azerbaijan. Tel: +994 12 492 9692, fax: +994 12 498 8480, e-mail: secretariat@mfa.gov.az, URL: http://www.mfa.gov.az
Ministry of Internal Affairs, Gusi Hajiyev küç. 7, 1001 Baku, Azerbaijan. Tel: +994 12 492 6623, fax: +994 12 492 4590, URL: http://www.mia.gov.az
Ministry of Justice, Inshaatchilar prospekti 1, 1073 Baku, Azerbaijan. Tel: +994 12 430 0977, fax: +994 12 430 0981, e-mail: mincus@azdata.net, URL: http://www.justice.gov.az
Ministry of Agriculture, 3rd floor Government House, U. Hajibayov 40, 1000 Baku, Azerbaijan. Tel: +994 12 493 0884, fax: +994 12 493 3745, e-mail: agry@azerin.com, URL: http://www.agro.gov.az
Ministry of Communication and Information Technologies, Azerbaijan Avenue 33, 1000 Baku, Azerbaijan. Tel: +994 12 498 5838, fax: +994 12 498 7912, e-mail: mincom@mincom.gov.az, URL: http://www.mincom.gov.az
Ministry of Culture and Tourism, Government House, Azadlyg Ave 1, 1000 Baku, Azerbaijan. Tel: +994 12 493 4398, fax: +994 12 493 5605, e-mail: mugam@culture.gov.az, URL: http://www.mct.gov.az
Ministry of Ecology and Natural Resources, B. Agayev 100-A, 1073 Baku, Azerbaijan. Tel: +994 12 438 0481, fax: +994 12 492 5907, URL: http://www.eco.gov.az
Ministry of Economic Development, Niyazi küç. 23, 1066 Baku, Azerbaijan. Tel: +994 12 492 4110, fax: +994 12 492 5895, e-mail: office@economy.gov.az, URL: ttp://economy.gov.az
Ministry of Education, Kh‬ t‬küç. 49, 1008 Baku, Azerbaijan. Tel: +994 12 496 0647, fax: +994 12 496 3483, e-mail: office@edu.gov.az, URL: http://edu.gov.az
Ministry of Health, Kiçik D‬ n‬küç. 4, 1014 Baku, Azerbaijan. Tel: +994 12 493 2977, fax: +994 12 498 8559, e-mail: mednet@mednet.az, URL: http://www.mednet.az
Ministry of Industry and Energy, Gasanbek Zardabi küç. 88, 1012 Baku, Azerbaijan. Tel: +994 12 447 0584, fax: +994 12 431 9005, e-mail: mfe@azdata.net, URL: http://www.mia.gov.az
Ministry of Labour and Social Protection of Population, Government House, U. Hajibayov Street 40, 1000 Baku, Azerbaijan. Tel: +994 12 493 9310, fax: +994 12 493 9472, e-mail: mlspp@mlspp.gov.az, URL: http://www.mlspp.gov.az
Ministry of National Security, Parliament Avenue 2, 1152 Baku, Azerbaijan. Tel: +994 12 493 7622, fax: +994 12 493 7622, e-mail: cpr@mns.gov.az, URL: http://www.mns.gov.az
Ministry of Taxes, Landau küç. 16, 1073 Baku, Azerbaijan. Tel: +994 12 438 8681, fax: +994 12 438 5587, e-mail: office@taxes.gov.az, URL: http://www.taxes.gov.az
Ministry of Transport, Tbilisi Avenue 1054, 1122 Baku, Azerbaijan. Tel: +994 12 433 9941, fax: +994 12 433 9942, URL: http://www.mot.gov.az
Ministry of Youth and Sport, Olympiya küç. 4, 1072 Baku, Azerbaijan. Tel: +994 12 465 6442, fax: +994 12 465 6438, e-mail: myst@myst.gov.az, URL: http://www.myst.gov.az

AZERBAIJAN

Political Parties
There are currently 31 political parties in Azerbaijan, the main ones being:
The New Azerbaijan Party, URL: http://www.yap.org.az
The Azerbaijan Democratic Party
Azerbaijani Popular Front Party (APFP)
The Musavat Party, URL: http://www.musavat.com
The Motherland Party, URL: http://avp.az
Civic Solidarity Party, URL: http://vhp.az

Elections
Presidential elections took place in October 1998 when the New Azerbaijan Party's Heydar Aliyev won 78 per cent of the vote. His son Ilham Aliyev won the October 2003 presidential election. Some independent observers criticised the campaign. The most recent presidential election took place in October 2008. Ilham Aliyev was re-elected although several opposition parties boycotted the election.

Parliamentary elections were held on 6th November 2005, and were won by the ruling New Azerbaijan Party. There were allegations of election fraud, and independent observers said that the elections did not meet democratic standards, citing intimidation, stuffing of ballot boxes and violations in the counting procedure. Protesters demanded a rerun when the ruling New Azerbaijan Party won by a large majority. The most recent parliamentary elections were held in November 2010, the New Azerbaijan Party retained power although several opposition parties said that some candidates had been prevented from registering and observers said the election had been overly restrictive.

Diplomatic Representation
British Embassy, 45 Khagani Street, AZ1010 Baku, Azerbaijan. Tel: +994 (0)12 4975190, fax: +994 (0)12 4972739, e-mail: generalenquiries.baku@fco.gov.uk, URL: http://ukinazerbaijan.fco.gov.uk/en
Ambassador: Peter Bateman (page 1384)
Embassy of Azerbaijan, 4 Kensington Court, London W8 5DL, United Kingdom. Tel: +44 (0)20 7938 3412 / 5482, fax: +44 (0)20 7937 1783, URL: http://www.azembassy.org.uk/
Ambassador: H.E. Mr Fakhraddin Gurbanov
Embassy of Azerbaijan, 2741 34th Street, NW Washington DC 20008, USA. Tel: +1 202 337 3500, fax: +1 202 337 5911, e-mail: azerbaijan@azembassy.com, consul@azembassy.com, URL: http://www.azembassy.com/
Ambassador: H.E. Elin Suleymanov (page 1522)
US Embassy, Azadliq Prospekt 83, AZ1007 Baku, Azerbaijan. Tel: +994 (0)12 4980335, fax: +994 (0)12 4656-671, e-mail: consularbaku@state.gov, URL: http://azerbaijan.usembassy.gov/
Ambassador: Richard L. Morningstar
Permanent Representative of the Republic of Azerbaijan to the United Nations, 866 United Nations Plaza, Suite 560, New York, NY 10017, USA. Tel: +1 212 371 2559 / 2832 / 2721, fax: +1 212 371 2784 / 2672, e-mail: azerbaijan@un.int, URL: http://www.un.int/azerbaijan/
Ambassador and Permanent Representative: H.E. Mr. Agshin Mehdiyev

LEGAL SYSTEM

The sources of law in the Azerbaijani legal system are the Constitution, acts adopted through referendum, Azerbaijani legislation, resolutions of Cabinet Ministers and international treaties.

The Constitutional Court is made up of a Chairman and eight judges nominated by the President and confirmed in office by the National Assembly (Milli Majlis). The Supreme Court is the highest judicial body in civil, criminal, administrative and other cases that are referred to it by the general courts. It exercises control over the activity of the general courts. Judges of the Supreme Court of the Azerbaijan Republic are nominated by the President and approved by the Milli Mejlis. The Supreme Court serves as a court of appeals; below it are the district and municipal courts, which serve as trial courts. The Economic Court of the Republic of Azerbaijan is the highest legal body deciding economic disputes.

The government's human rights record remains poor. There are arbitrary arrests and detentions, and law enforcement officials act with impunity. Prison conditions are harsh and pretrial detention can be long. The government continued to imprison persons for politically motivated reasons. There is pervasive corruption. Restrictions on freedom of assembly continues, particularly in terms of political organizing. The UN Human Rights Council undertook a Universal Periodic Review in 2012.

In 1998, the death penalty was abolished.

Constitutional Court, URL: http://www.constcourt.gov.az/en
Supreme Court, URL: http://www.supremecourt.gov.az/
Human Rights Commissioner of Azerbaijan, URL: http://ombudsman.gov.az/

LOCAL GOVERNMENT

For administrative purposes, Azerbaijan is divided into 59 districts (*rayons*), 11 cities and one autonomous republic, Naxcivan Muxtar Respublikasi (Nakhchevan). The cities are Ali Bayramli Sahari, Baki Sahari, Ganca Sahari, Lankaran Sahari, Mingacevir Sahari, Naftalan Sahari, Saki Sahari, Sumqayit Sahari, Susa Sahari, Xankandi Sahari and Yevlax Sahari. The President of Azerbaijan appoints the governors of these units, while the government of Nakhchivan is elected and approved by the parliament of Nakhchivan Autonomous Republic.

AREA AND POPULATION

Area
The Republic of Azerbaijan occupies the eastern part of Transcaucasia and includes the area of Nakhchvan and Nagorno Karabakh. It is bounded in the south by Iran and Turkey, and by Russia to the north. The Caspian Sea forms its eastern border, and Georgia and Armenia are to the west. The country covers an area of 86,600 sq. km.

Azerbaijan extends 400 km from north to south, and 500 km from west to east. There are three mountain ranges, which combined cover around 40 per cent of the land area: the Greater Caucasus, the Lesser Caucasus, and the Talysh Mountains. Almost half of all the mud volcanoes on Earth can be found in Azerbaijan. 8,350 rivers drain into the Caspian Sea in the east of the country. The largest lake is Sarısu (67 km²) and the longest river is the Kura (1,515 km).

The climate is dry, with hot summers and mild winters. The Greater Caucasus shelters Azerbaijan from the cold northern winds, leading to a largely subtropical climate.

To view a map, consult http://www.un.org/Depts/Cartographic/map/profile/azerbaij.pdf

Population
In 2010, the WHO reported a population of 9.188 million and annual population growth of 1.2 per cent over the period 2000-10. Azerbaijan has a relatively high migration rate, estimated in 2006 at 4.38 emigrants per 1,000 inhabitants. The population density is around 99 people per sq. km, some 52 per cent of the Azeris live in urban areas. Of Azerbaijan's 60 towns those with populations over 200,000 include Baku, Kirovobad, and Sumgait. Baku has a population of about 2,100,000.

Azerbaijanis comprise 90 per cent of the total population, the remainder being Russian (2.5 per cent), Armenian (2 per cent) and others including Lezghians, Avars, Kurds, Udi, Georgians and Turks. The separatist Nagorno-Karabakh region is populated almost entirely by ethnic Armenians.

The official language of Azeri, spoken by over 90 per cent of the population, was adopted in 2001. Russian and Armenian are also spoken.

Births, Marriages, Deaths
Latest estimates (2010) put the birth rate at 19.8 births per 1,000 population and the crude death rate was 9.1 per 1,000 population. According to the latest WHO statistics, the infant mortality rate was 39 deaths per 1,000 live births in 2010, with the fertility rate at 2.2 children born per woman. Average life expectancy at birth in 2009 was estimated at 68 years (66 years for men and 70 years for women). The median age was 30 years. In 2009 the adult mortality rate (probability of dying between 15 and 60 years) was estimated at 177 per 1,000 population. (Source: http://www.who.int, World Health Statistics 2012)

Public Holidays 2014
1 January: New Year's Day
20 January: Day of the Martyrs*
8 March: Women's Day
20-21 March: Novruz Bayramy (Persian New Year)*
18 April: Good Friday
21 April: Easter Monday
9 May: Victory Day
28 May: Republic Day
15 June: National Salvation Day
26 June: Army and Navy Day
29 July: End of Ramadan*
18 October: National Independence Day
5 October: Feast of Sacrifice*
12 November: Constitution Day
17 November: Day of National Revival
31 December: Day of Solidarity of Azerbaijanis throughout the World
* Variable

EMPLOYMENT

Azerbaijan's workforce numbered 4,295,000 in 2007, with a participation rate of 74.4 per cent. 4,014,000 people were employed and 261,000 were unemployed (6.5 per cent of the population). The main employment sectors were services (2,210,000), agriculture and forestry (1,560,000), and manufacturing (198,000). 45,000 people were employed in the mining sector. Figures for 2009 show that 4,071,595 people were employed 1,573,020 of whom were employed in agriculture, 524,441 in industry and 1,974,134 in the services sector. Unemployment that year was recorded as 6.0 per cent. (International Labour Organization, ILO Dept. of Statistics, http://laborsta.ilo.org)

Total Employment by Economic Activity

Occupation	2008
Agriculture, hunting & forestry	1,601,400
Fishing	4,500
Mining & quarrying	45,300
Manufacturing	195,500
Electricity, gas & water supply	44,600
Construction	206,600
Wholesale & retail trade, repairs	657,400
Hotels & restaurants	23,400
Transport, storage & communications	167,000
Financial intermediation	35,000
Real estate, renting & business activities	194,800

- continued

Public admin. & defence; compulsory social security	249,500
Education	311,300
Health & social work	180,500
Other community, social & personal service activities	136,600
Households with employed persons	-
Extra-territorial organisations & bodies	500

Source: Copyright © International Labour Organization (ILO Dept. of Statistics, http://laborsta.ilo.org)

BANKING AND FINANCE

Currency

The unit of currency is the manat. The rouble was withdrawn from circulation on 1 January 1994.

GDP/GNP, Inflation, National Debt

Following the collapse of the Soviet Union and the fall of real GDP by nearly 60 per cent, a formal programme of economic reform was adopted in 1995. The following five years saw privatisations and foreign investment in Azerbaijan's oil and gas industries. A major overhaul of the financial sector was also implemented in line with International Monetary Fund (IMF) and World Bank advice and resources.

Azerbaijan's hope for sustained economic growth rests in large part with its sizeable hydrocarbon resources in the Caspian Sea region, through effective management of the resulting revenue, and non-oil sector diversification. In 1999, a State Oil Fund was set up to manage the revenues, and to use money obtained from oil-related foreign investment for education, poverty reduction, and raising rural living standards. Assets in the Fund have grown from US$816 million in 2003 to US$3.09 billion in 2007, and it was anticipated that the Fund would increase to $36 billion by 2010. (EIA)

Real GDP grew steadily at around 10 per cent per annum between 1997-2004, then rose sharply by an estimated 26.4 per cent in 2005. It rose by 34.5 per cent in 2006 and by 25.1 per cent in 2007 to reach an estimated US$28.94 billion. In 2008, growth fell to 10.8 per cent. Total GDP was 38,005.7 million new manats. Per capita GDP in 2010 was 4,593.9 New Manats. GDP growth in 2008 was estimated at 10.8 per cent, at 9.3 per cent in 2009 and at 5.0 per cent in 2010. (Source: Asian Development Bank) GDP was estimated at US$60 billion in 2011. Growth was estimated at 2.2. per cent in 2012.

GDP at current market prices, per economic sector (figures in Million New Manats)

Sector	2008	2009	2010
GDP at current market prices	4,013.2	35,601.5	41,574.7
-Agriculture	2,236.0	2,179.5	2,221.1
-Mining	21,164.5	15,090.4	19,131.6
-Manufacturing	1,888.6	1,967.3	2,255.9
-Electricity, Gas and Water	443.8	418.1	465.0
-Construction	2,800.3	2,554.3	3,134.3
-Trade	2,534.3	2,729.6	3,182.8
-Transport and Communications	2,693.8	3,117.2	3,281.6
-Finance	709.3	760.4	785.3
-Public Administration	599.2	764.9	783.5
-Others	2,959.4	3,778.7	3,823.4
-Less: Financial intermediation services indirectly measured	580.7	568.9	456.8
-Taxes less subsidies on products	2,688.6	2,810.0	2,967.0
Net factor income from abroad	-4,124.7	-2,628.0	..
GNI	26,012.5	32,973.5	..

Source: Asian Development Bank

The industrial sector contributed 64 per cent of GDP in 2010, followed by services (30.4 per cent) and agriculture (5.7 per cent). Oil sector revenue as a share of GDP grew from 9.8 per cent in 2005 to 19.7 per cent in 2007.

Inflation was estimated at 8 per cent in 2011. External debt rose from an estimated US$1,300 million in 2002 to US$1,600 million in 2003 and to an estimated US$1,873 million in 2005.

Foreign Investment

Since Azerbaijan's lucrative oil and gas sector opened up to foreign investment in 1992, the country has received around US$65 billion in foreign investment (as at 2011). Most investment has been targetted towards Azerbaijan's oil industry.

Balance of Payments / Imports and Exports

Estimated merchandise export revenues rose 25.5 per cent in 2010 from US$21,096.8 million in 2009 to US$26,476 million in 2010. Major export goods are mineral products, transport equipment, base metals and articles thereof, cotton and foodstuffs. Azerbaijan's main export trading partners in 2010 were Italy (US$5,899.6 million), USA (US$1,855.7 million) and France (US$1488.4 million).

Estimated merchandise import costs rose from an estimated US$6125.57 million in 2009 to US$9460.76 million in 2010. Major import goods include machinery and electrical equipment, base metals, oil products, foodstuffs and chemicals. Major import trading partners in 2010 were Germany (US$958.1 million), China (US$928.9 million), Belarus (US$166.0 million) and France (US$150.4 million).

The trade balance stood at US$346.2 million in 2007.

Central Bank

National Bank of Azerbaijan, 32 R. Behbudov Str, Baku AZ 1014, Azerbaijan. Tel: +994 (0)12 4931122, fax: +994 (0)12 4935541, URL: http://www.cbar.az
Chairman of the Board: Elman S Rustamov

Chambers of Commerce and Trade Organisations
US-Azerbaijan Chamber of Commerce, URL: http://www.usacc.org/

MANUFACTURING, MINING AND SERVICES

Primary and Extractive Industries

Azerbaijan has large resources of mineral oil, natural gas, and iron ore. It is one of the oldest oil-producing areas in the world. Crude oil and oil products account for around 90 per cent of total exports and almost 53 per cent of GDP.

The country had proven oil reserves of 7,000 million barrels in January 2012. Oil refining capacity was 399,000 barrels per day and production was estimated at 989.28 thousand barrels per day, 99 per cent of which was crude oil. Domestic consumption was 168,000 barrels per day in 2011. Net oil exports that year were 821,000 barrels per day, most of which went to Russia, Italy, Turkey, and Germany.

Most of the country's oil is produced in the Caspian Sea. Oil and gas are also extracted in the Apsheron Peninsula, the Kura-Arak lowland and in the open sea (Neftyznye Kamni deposit). Major oil refineries include the 242,000 barrels per day plant at Baku and the 200,000 barrels per day plant at Heydar Aliev. The Azeri government has signed a number of major deals with a variety of consortia for the exploration and development of various offshore fields. The State Oil Company of the Azerbaijan Republic (SOCAR), retains a partial share in all of them.

Almost all of Azerbaijan's oil exports are transported via the BTC pipeline system, which bypasses Russia. The pipeline runs 1,040 miles from the capital city of Baku, via Georgia, to the Turkish port of Ceyhan, and has a capacity of one million barrels per day. It took six months for the line to be filled. Headed by BP, it was a controversial project. Critics are concerned that the area through which the pipeline runs is politically volatile, and that it has been built in a seismic zone. The Baku-Novorossiysk pipeline transports oil from the Azeri, Chirag and Guneshli fields. Construction and repair works on the Baku-Supsa pipeline continue.

Proven total natural gas reserves at the beginning of January 2010 were around 30 trillion cubic feet. Azerbaijan produced an estimated 589 billion cubic feet in 2010 and consumed the same amount. Until then the country was producing less than it consumed and imported gas from Turkmenistan and Iran. Over the next 10 years, SOCAR plans to invest $224 million to expand natural gas production by drilling 23 gas wells, expanding existing platforms, and building underwater gas pipelines.

Azerbaijan's major natural gas production increases are expected to come from the development of the Shah Deniz offshore field, which is thought to be one of the largest discoveries in 20 years. It contains between 15 and 35 trillion cubic feet of natural gas. The Shah Deniz consortium members began producing natural gas for export during 2007. The main pipeline for exports is the South Caucasus Pipeline (SCP - also known as "Baku-T'bilisi-Erzurum") which runs parallel to the BTC pipeline for most of its route. (Source: Energy Information Administration, EIA)

Energy

Azerbaijan's total energy consumption was an estimated 0.699 quadrillion Btu in 2006 , up from 0.605 in 2003. Per capita energy consumption was 82.8 million Btu in the same year, below the regional average of 160.4 million Btu.

Azerbaijan has an electricity generation capacity of 5.5 gigawatts and generates an estimated 20.4 billion kilowatthours (kWh) per annum. There are eight state-owned thermal electric power stations (accounting for about 80 per cent of Azerbaijan's generating capacity) and six hydroelectric plants. Electricity consumption has remained at around 20.4 billion kWh for several years; a sharper increase is anticipated with the economic growth resulting from the BTC and SCP pipelines becoming operational. Azerbaijan imports the shortfall in electricity from Russia, Turkey, Iran, and Georgia. Azerenerjy is the state power generation company. (Source: EIA). In 2007 Azerbaijan produced 21,847 million kWh of electricity, 19,051 from thermoelectric stations, 2,364 million kWh from hydroelectric stations and 432 million kWh from mobile generators. (Azerbaijan Statistical Yearbook)

Manufacturing

Oil equipment and machine-building are Azerbaijan's most promising manufacturing sectors. In addition, ferrous and non-ferrous metallurgy, mechanical engineering and a building materials industry are being developed, as are the production of cotton, silk and woollen fabrics. Flour grinding, wine-making, fishing and tobacco processing are among the well-established industries that have been considerably expanded. Other sectors are light industry and electrical equipment. Figures from the Azerbaijan Statistical Yearbook show that earnings from manufacturing in 2007 were 22,441 million manet and people employed numbered 195,5 million.

Industrial Production in 2007

Product	'000 Tonnes
Crude petroleum	42,598
Natural gas, million cubic metres	16,560
Iron ore, iron content	17
Salt	7
Cement	1,691

AZERBAIJAN

- continued

Wheat flour	1,422
Crude steel	468
Suphuric acid	25
Caustic soda	20

Source: Asian Development Bank

Agriculture

Over recent years, the contribution of the agricultural sector to national GDP has fallen from 29.3 per cent in 1990 to 5.5 per cent in 2010, due largely to growth in the oil sector. In financial terms, the sector has grown steadily, and earned New Manats 1,564.6 million in 2007 (up from NM.1,329.3 million the previous year). A wide range of fruits and vegetables are grown and exported, mostly to Russia. Buffalo account for a significant share of cattle. Silkworm breeding is well developed.

Agricultural Production in 2010

Produce	Int. $'000	Tonnes
Cow milk, whole, fresh	414,347	1,507,430
Indigenous cattle meat	308,546	114,218
Indigenous sheep meat	200,861	73,770
Tomatoes	160,404	434,036
Potatoes	126,808	953,710
Wheat	111,282	1,272,340
Apples	89,516	211,665
Indigenous chicken meat	89,421	62,768
Grapes	74,045	129,536
Fruit fresh nes	66,282	189,900
Hen eggs, in shell	58,878	70,990
Hazelnuts, with shell	47,212	29,454

Source: http://faostat.fao.org/site/339/default.aspx Food and Agriculture Organization of the United Nations, Food and Agricultural commodities production

The Caspian fishing industry is concentrated on dwindling stocks of sturgeon and beluga. Th etotal catch in 2010 was estimated to be 1,080 tonnes, down from 10,890 tonnes in 2001.

COMMUNICATIONS AND TRANSPORT

Visa Requirements
US, Canadian, Australian and EU citizens require a visa, valid for at least six months, to visit Azerbaijan. Some nationals may be eligible for a visa on arrival. Foreign nationals intending to remain in Azerbaijan for more than 30 days must register with local police within three days of their arrival and apply for an ID card. Citizens of countries not mentioned above are advised to contact the embassy to check visa requirements.

National Airlines
The state-owned airline, Azerbaijan Airlines (AZAL), was part of the Soviet Union national airline Aeroflot prior to the split in 1991. Comprising some 20 aircraft, it flies passengers and cargo to destinations in Europe, Asia and the Middle East. It also operates a cargo service and a helicopter service.
Azerbaijan Airlines, URL: http://icd_azal.com

International Airports
State Concern Azerbaijan Hava Yollari, Baku, Azerbaijan. Tel: +994 (0)12 934434
Baku-Heydar Aliyev International Airport, Baku, Azerbaijan. Tel: +994 12 972732, URL: http://www.airport.az
Lenkaran Airport, Azerbaijan. Tel: +994 (0)12 491 3840
There are also airports at Gyandzha and Nakhichevan City. Figures for2010 show that Azerbaijan had a total of 35 airports, 27 of which had paved runways. There was also one heliport.

Railways
The total length of the railway in 2010 was 2,918 km. Azerbaijan is connected to Tiblisi in Georgia, and Makhachkala in the Russian Federation, as well as Moscow. A new rail link between Azerbaijan and Turkey via Georgia is currently under construction and was expected to be completed in 2012.

Roads
The road network is currently some 59,140 km, much of which is in poor condition. Road freight by lorry totals 447.2 m tonnes annually. There are daily bus services from Georgia, Turkey, Iran and Russia. Vehicles are driven on the right.

HEALTH

Azerbaijan has its own social security system, including provision for free health care. Benefits include sick and maternity leave, temporary disability, and burial. Funding comes by way of the Social Protection Fund, the Employment Fund, and the Disabled Persons' Fund. In 2002, it was estimated that 49 per cent of the population were living below the poverty line (Source: Azerbaijani Embassy).

In 2009, total expenditure on health was equivalent to 5.8 per cent of GDP. Government expenditure accounts for 23.1 per cent of the total expenditure on health. Per capita total expenditure on health was estimated at US$283. In 2005-10, there were 32,798 doctors (37.8 per 10,000 population), 72,356 nurses and midwives (83.4 per 10,000 population) and 2,457 dentists (2.8 per 10,000 people), 1,652 pharmaceutical personnel (1.9 per 10,000 people). In 2005-11 there were 75 hospital beds and 4.3 psychiatric beds per 10,000 population.

In 2008, life expectancy at birth was 68 years. In 2010, the infant mortality rate (death of children aged less than one year) was 39 per 1,000 live births, the child mortality rate (deaths of children of five years and under) was 46 per 1,000, whilst the adult mortality rate (people aged 15-59) stood at 221 per 1,000 for males and 134 per 1,000 for females. The most common causes of death for young children were (2010) prematurity (22 per cent), pneumonia (17.0) and diarrhoea (8 per cent). The immunization coverage among 1-year-olds were: measles 67 per cent, DTP3 72 per cent and HepB3 49 per cent.

In 2010, an estimated 80 per cent of the population had access to improved drinking-water sources and 82 per cent of the population had access to improved sanitation. Approximately 26.8 per cent of the children aged less than five years old were considered to be stunted. (Source: http://www.who.int, Global Health Statistics, 2012)

EDUCATION

In 2007, 30 per cent of small children attended a pre-primary school (up from 24 per cent in 2004). In the same year, 95 per cent of the relevant age-group attended primary school, and 83 per cent of the concerned age-group were enrolled in secondary education. 15 per cent of older students were enrolled in tertiary education. The figures are all below the average for the region.

The pupil:teacher ratio in primary schools in 2007 was 12:1. In the same year, 12.6 per cent of total government expenditure went on education. The adult literacy rate was estimated to be 99.5 per cent (100 per cent among 15-24 year olds) (Source: UNESCO, UIS, August 2009)

RELIGION

Most people (over 88 per cent) are Muslim and most of those are Shi'a Muslims. There are also Russian Orthodox (2.5 per cent), Armenian Orthodox (2.3 per cent) and others (1.8 per cent), including Jewish communities.

Azerbaijan has a religious liberty rating of 3 on a scale of 1 to 10 (10 is most freedom) (Source: World Religion Database)

COMMUNICATIONS AND MEDIA

The constitution guarantees freedom of speech but there are reports that opponents of the regime face sanctions. The public-broadcaster is supposed to be free of government control.

Newspapers
There are currently more than 600 newspapers and information agencies officially registered in Azerbaijan. The country's official information agency is AzerTaj, based in the capital, Baku. Newspapers are published in Azerbaijani, Russian and English. the Azarbaycan is a government produced daily newspaper. Some 95 journals are published including 55 in Azerbaijani. Total press circulation is more than 3,730,000, of which 3,265,000 publications are in Azerbaijani
Azadliq, URL: http://www.azadliq.az/
Ekho, URL: http://www.echo-az.com/index.shtml
Eksoress, URL: http://www.express.com.az/
Baku Sun, URL: http://www.bakusun.az/ (English and Azeri)

Broadcasting
Azerbaijan National Television and Radio broadcasts in Azerbaijani and Russian and is state run, URL: http://www.aztv.az. There are four commercial national stations and several regional stations. There is limited availability of cable television. Radio Baku broadcasts in Azerbaijani, Arabic, English and Turkish. English-language news services include the Azartac news agency (URL: http://www.azertag.com/index_en.html).

Telecommunications
Fixed-lines and other telecom services are controlled by a state telecommunications monopoly and growth has been stagnant; more competition exists in the mobile-cellular market with four providers in 2009. There were an estimated 1.3 million main line telephones and around 6.5 million mobile phones in 2008. In 2008 there were 1.5 million internet users.

ENVIRONMENT

Azerbaijan's main environmental problems include severe pollution to the Caspian Sea, from which much of the country's oil industry operates; soil in the region was contaminated by DDT and toxic defoliants used in cotton production during the Soviet era. Local scientists believe that the Absheron Peninsula and the Caspian Sea are the most ecologically devastated areas in the world due to air, water and soil pollution.

Over-fishing threatens the survival of Caspian sturgeon stocks, the source of most of the world's supply of caviar. The Convention on International Trade in Endangered Species (CITES) imposed a ban on most Caspian caviar in January 2006, but lifted it in January 2007.

In 2010, Azerbaijan's emissions from the consumption of fossil fuels totalled 35.12 million metric tons of carbon dioxide. The oil industry produces the greatest proportion of carbon emissions, followed by the natural gas industry. (Source: EIA)

Azerbaijan is a party to the following environmental agreements: Air Pollution, Biodiversity, Climate Change, Climate Change-Kyoto Protocol, Desertification, Endangered Species, Hazardous Wastes, Marine Dumping, Ozone Layer Protection, Ship Pollution, and Wetlands.

SPACE PROGRAMME

The Scientific and Industrial Association for Space Research was established in Baku in 1975 as part of the Soviet Union's vast space programme. Azerbaijan is due to launch its first communications satellite through Arianespace at the Guiana space station by the end of 2012.

BAHAMAS
Commonwealth of The Bahamas

Capital: Nassau (Population estimate: 233,000)

Head of State: HM Queen Elizabeth II (Head of the Commonwealth) (page 1420)

Governor General: Sir Arthur Foulkes (page 1426)

National Flag: A black equilateral triangle against the mast superimposed on a horizontal background made up of two colours on three equal stripes: aquamarine, gold and aquamarine

CONSTITUTION AND GOVERNMENT

Constitution
The Bahamas became a parliamentary democracy in July 1973 when it became a sovereign independent state. The Government consists of the Governor-General, the representative of the Monarch, and a bicameral parliament consisting of a Senate and a House of Assembly. The constitution of the Bahamas provides for separation of powers under the Governor General, who represents the Queen as Head of State. Power held by the Governor General is titular. Governance effectively rests with Parliament, the Executive and the Judiciary.

The executive branch of government consists of a Cabinet of at least nine members, including the Prime Minister and the Attorney General. All cabinet ministers must be members of Parliament and the Prime Minister and Minister of Finance must be members of the House of Assembly. Up to three ministers can be appointed from among senators.

In 2003 the Government appointed a bi-partisan Constitutional Commission to provide a review of the constitution. The Commission presented its preliminary report to the prime minister in March 2006. It proposed that The Bahamas should become a democratic parliamentary republic and that a President be elected or appointed by the two houses of Parliament as Head of State of The Bahamas. There is to be a period of public consultation.

To consult the full constitution, please visit: http://www.bahamas.gov.bs/

International Relations
The Bahamas enjoys a close trading relationship with her Caribbean neighbours and is a member of the Caribbean Community (CARICOM), the African Caribbean and Pacific (ACP) Group of States, CARIFORUM (CARICOM plus the Dominican Republic and Cuba), the Association of Caribbean States (ACS), the Caribbean Export Development Agency (CEDA), and the Caribbean Tourism Organisation (CTO). The Bahamas has applied for membership of the World Trade Organisation and is involved in on-going negotiations with the United States and Canada over a Free Trade Area for the Americas.

Upper House
The Senate has 16 members, nine appointed by the Governor-General on the advice of the Prime Minister, four on the advice of the Leader of the Opposition and three on the advice of the Prime Minister after consultation with the Leader of the Opposition. This arrangement provides for the Opposition to have not less than four members in the Senate and to claim up to three more based on its numerical strength in the House of Assembly. Members are appointed following a general election for the lower house and members serve the same term as their Assembly colleagues.
Senate, PO Box N 7147, Nassau, Bahamas. Tel: +1 242 322 2427, fax: +1 242 328 8294

Lower House
The House of Assembly must have at least 38 members, (and usually has 40) elected at least every five years by universal adult suffrage. This number may be increased on the recommendation of the Constituencies Commission which is charged with reviewing electoral boundaries at least every five years. The present membership was reduced from 49 to 40 in March 1997.
House of Assembly, PO Box N 3003, Nassau, Bahamas. Tel: +1 242 322 2041, fax: +1 242 322 1118, URL: http://www.bahamas.gov.bs

Cabinet (as at June 2013)
Prime Minister, Minister of Finance: Hon. Perry Christie (page 1405)
Deputy Prime Minister; Minister of Works and Urban Development: Hon. Philip B. Davies
Minister of Foreign Affairs and Immigration: Hon. Frederick Mitchell (page 1478)
Minister of Agriculture, Marine Resources and Local Government: Alfred Gray
Minister of Labour and National Insurance: Hon. Shane Gibson
Minister of Transport and Aviation: Hon. Glenys Hannah Martin
Minister of Social Services: Hon. Melanie Griffin
Minister for Grand Bahama: Hon. Dr Michael Darville
Minister of Health: Hon. Dr Perry Gomez
Minister of the Environment and Housing: Hon. Kendred Dorsett
Minister of Youth, Sports and Culture: Hon. Daniel Johnson
Minister of State in the Office of the Prime Minister, in charge of Investments: Hon. Khaalis Rolle

Minister of National Security; Government Leader in the House of Assembly: Hon. Dr Bernard Nottage
Minister of Tourism: Hon. Obediah Wilchombe
Minister of Education, Science and Technology: Hon. Jerome Fitzgerald
Minister of Financial Services: Hon. Ryan Pinder
Attorney General; Legal Affairs: Hon. Sen. Allyson Maynard
Minister of State for Transport and Aviation: Hon. Hope Strachan
Minister of State for Legal Affairs: Hon. Damian Gomez
Minister of State for Finance: Hon. Michael Halkitis
Minister of State for National Security: Hon. Sen. Keith Bell

Ministries
Government portal: URL: http//www.bahamas.gov.bs
Office of the Governor General, Government House, Government Hill, PO Box N-8301, Nassau, The Bahamas. Tel: +1 242 322 1875, fax: +1 242 322 4659, URL: http://www.bahamas.gov.bs/bahamasweb/home.nsf
Office of the Prime Minister and Cabinet Office, PO Box CB-10980, Nassau, The Bahamas. Tel: +1242 327 5826, fax: +1242 327 5806, e-mail: info@opm.gov.bs, URL: http://www.opm.gov.bs
Ministry of National Security, East Hill Street, PO Box N-3217, Nassau, The Bahamas. Tel: +1 242 322 6792, fax: +1 242 328 8212, URL: http://www.bahamas.gov.bs
Ministry of Foreign Affairs, Goodmans Bay Corporate Center, West Bay St, PO Box N-3746, Nassau, The Bahamas. Tel: +1 242 322 7624, fax: +1 242 328 8212, e-mail: mfabahamas@batelnet.bs, URL: http://www.mfabahamas.org
Ministry of Social Development and Housing, PO Box N-275/N-3206, Nassau, The Bahamas. Tel: +1 242356 0765/323 3333, fax: +1242 323 3883/323 3737
Ministry of Health, Poinciana Building, Meeting Street, PO Box N-3729, Nassau, The Bahamas. Tel: +1 242 502 4700, fax: +1 242 325 5421, URL: http://www.bahamas.gov.bs/health
Ministry of Transport, Aviation and Local Government, PO Box N-3008, Nassau, The Bahamas. Tel: +1242 394 5095, fax: +1242 394 5023
Ministry of Finance, Cecil Wallace-Whitfield Centre, Cable Beach, PO Box N-3017, Nassau, The Bahamas. Tel: +1 242 327 1530, fax: +1 242 327 1618, e-mail: mofgeneral@bahamas.gov.bs, URL: http://www.bahamas.gov.bs/finance
Ministry of Tourism, Bolam House, George Street, PO Box N-3701, Nassau, The Bahamas. Tel: +1 242 322 7500, fax: +1 242 356 3967, e-mail: tourism@batelnet.bs, URL: http://www.bahamas.com
Ministry of Agriculture and Fisheries, PO Box N-3028, Nassau, The Bahamas. Tel: +1242 325 7502, fax: +1242 322 1767, URL: http://www.bahamas.gov.bs
Ministry of Education, Youth and Sports, PO Box N-3913, Nassau, The Bahamas. Tel: +1242 322 8140, fax: +1242 322 8491, URL: http://www.bahamaseducation.com
Ministry of Labour and Immigration, 2nd Floor Post Office Building, East Hill Street, PO Box N-3008, Nassau, The Bahamas. Tel: +1 242 323 7814, fax: +1 242 325 1920, URL: http://www.investbahamas.org
Ministry of Public Works, John F. Kennedy Drive, PO Box N-8156, Nassau, The Bahamas. Tel: +1 242 322 4830, fax: +1 242 326 6629, e-mail: admin@mowt.bs, URL: http://www.bahamas.gov.bs/publicworks
Office of the Attorney General, 7th Floor Post Office Building, East Hill Street, PO Box N-3007, Nassau, The Bahamas. Tel: +1 242 502 0400, fax: +1 242 322 2255, URL: http://www.bahamas.gov.bs
Ministry of Youth, Sports and Culture, Thompson Boulevard, P O Box N-4891, Nassau, The Bahamas. Tel: +1 242 502 0600, fax: +1 242 326 0085, e-mail: desmondbannister@bahamas.gov.bs, URL: http://www.bahamas.gov.bs/culture
Ministry of Lands and Local Government, Manx Building, West Bay Street, PO Box N-3040, Nassau, The Bahamas. Tel: +1 242 328 2700, fax: +1 242 328 1324, URL: http://www.bahamassupremecourt.gov.bs/
Ministry of Housing, Claughton House, Frederick Street, PO N-4849, Nassau, The Bahamas. Tel: +1 242 322 6027, fax: +1 242 322 6005, URL: http://www.bahamas.gov.bs

Elections
General elections take place every five years and are held under universal adult suffrage. Local government elections take place every three years. The most recent parliamentary elections took place in May 2012. The opposition Progressive Liberal Party won the election, beating the incumbent Free National Movement.

Political Parties
Free National Movement (FNM), URL: http://www.freenationalmovement.org
Progressive Liberal Party (PLP), URL: http://www.myplp.com
Coalition for Democratic Reform (CDR); Bahamian Freedom Alliance (BFA)

Diplomatic Representation
The Embassy of the Commonwealth of the Bahamas, 2220 Massachusetts Avenue, NW, Washington, DC 20008, USA. Tel: +1 202 319 2660, fax: +1 202 319 2668
Ambassador: vacant
The High Commission for the Commonwealth of the Bahamas, 10 Chesterfield Street, London, W1X 8AH, United Kingdom. Tel: +44 (0)20 7408 4488, fax: +44 (0)20 7499 4937, URL: http://www.bahamashclondon.net/

STATES OF THE WORLD

BAHAMAS

Ambassador: Eldred E. Bethel (page 1388)
British High Commission, (There is no resident British diplomatic mission in the Bahamas. Contact BHC in Jamaica). PO Box 575, 28 Trafalgar Road, Kingston 10, Jamaica, URL: http://ukinjamaica.fco.gov.uk/en/
High Commissioner: Howard Drake
US Embassy, PO Box N-8197, Nassau, The Bahamas. Tel: +1 242 322 1181, fax: +1 242 356 0222, URL: http://nassau.usembassy.gov
Ambassador: vacant
The Permanent Mission of the Commonwealth of the Bahamas to the United Nations, 231 46th Street, New York, NY 10017, USA. Tel: +1 212 421 6925, fax: +1 212 759 2135, URL: http://www.un.int/bahamas/
Ambassador: Paulette Bethel

LEGAL SYSTEM

The Constitution provides for an independent judiciary including a Court of Appeal, a Supreme Court and Magistrate Courts. Final appeal is to the Privy Council in London, England. The Constitution also provides for a Public Service Commission, a Public Service Board of Appeal, a Judicial and Legal Service Commission and a Police Service Commission.

The Court of Appeal is the highest resident tribunal in the country. Juridicially and administratively, it is separate and apart from the Supreme Court and functions as an independent institution. It consists of five judges: the president, two resident judges and two non-resident judges - all appointed by the Governor-General. Appeals from the Court of Appeal go before the Privy Council. The Supreme Court comprises the Chief Justice and eight justices, also appointed by the Governor-General.

The government generally respects the human rights of its citizens, thought there have been cases of discrimination against persons of Haitian descent. There has also been criticism of the inefficient and slow judicial system, and of substandard conditions in prisons. The Bahamas retain the death penalty.

Supreme Court of the Bahamas: http://www.bahamassupremecourt.gov.bs/
Chief Justice: The Hon. Michael L. Barnett

LOCAL GOVERNMENT

The islands are divided into 31 districts for administrative purposes: Acklins Islands, Berry Islands, Bimini, Black Point, Cat Island, Central Abaco, Central Andros, Central Eleuthera, City of Freeport, Crooked Island and Long Cay, East Grand Bahama, Exuma, Grand Cay, Harbour Island, Hope Town, Inagua, Long Island, Mangrove Cay, Mayaguana, Moore's Island, North Abaco, North Andros, North Eleuthera, Ragged Island, Rum Cay, San Salvador, South Abaco, South Andros, South Eleuthera, Spanish Wells, West Grand Bahama.

Local elections took place in June 2011. Councillors serve three-year terms.

AREA AND POPULATION

Area
The Bahamas comprises 700 islands, approximately 37 of which are inhabited, lying about 50 miles off the coast of Florida, stretching south-easterly along the coast of Cuba to within 60 miles of Haiti. The land area of the Bahamas is 5,383 sq. miles (13,880 sq. km). The land is low and flat and the climate is semi-tropical.

To view a map, consult http://www.lib.utexas.edu/maps/cia08/bahamas_sm_2008.gif

Population
Figures for 2010 estimated the population to be 343,000 up from the 2008 estimated figure of 338,000. The annual growth rate was estimated to be 1.4 per cent over the period 2000-10. In 2010 the median age was estimated to be 31 years. An estimated 23 per cent of the population was aged under 15 years and 10 per cent over 60 years. Approximately 85 per cent are of African descent, 12 per cent of European descent, the remainder being of Hispanic and Asian origin. The official language is English. Creole is also spoken, mainly by immigrants from Haiti. It is estimated that the Bahamas is home to an estimated 60,000 illegal immigrants from Haiti who have fled unrest. Approximately 84 per cent of the population lives in urban areas.

Births, Marriages, Deaths
Live births per 1,000 of the population in 2010 were estimated at 15.5. The number of deaths per 1,000 of the population in 2009 was estimated at 5.3. The infant mortality, according to 2010 statistics, was 14.0 per 1,000 live births. Maternal mortality was estimated at 49 per 100,000 live births. In 2009 average life expectancy was 76 years (72 for males, 78 for females). Healthy life expectancy was 63 and 68 years respectively. The total fertility rate per woman was 1.9 children. (Source: http://www.who.int, World Health Statistics 2012)

Public Holidays 2014
1 January: New Year's Day
18 April: Good Friday
21 April: Easter Monday
1 May: Labour Day
9 June: Whit Monday
10 July: Independence Day
7 August: Emancipation Day
12 October: Discovery Day
25 December: Christmas Day
26 December: Boxing Day

EMPLOYMENT

The following table shows employment according to industry in 2008:

Industry	No. of employed
Agriculture, hunting, forestry and fishing	5,120
Mining, quarrying, & utilities	2,690
Manufacturing	6,250
Construction	19,370
Wholesale and retail trade, repairs	24,480
Hotels and restaurants	27,230
Transport, storage & communication	14,100
Real estate, renting and business activities	20,120
Public Administration and Defence; Compulsory Social Security, Education, Health and Social Work, Other Community,Social and Personal Service Activities	54,800
Unclassified	780
Total	174.920

Source: Copyright © International Labour Organization (ILO Dept. of Statistics, http://laborsta.ilo.org)

Figures for 2005 put the unemployment rate at 10.2 per cent this had fallen to 7.9 per cent in 2007, it rose to 8.7 per cent in 2008 and 14.2 per cent in 2009.

On average the majority of female workers earned three quarters of their male counterparts wage. In the service sector women earned only 57.4 per cent of the male wage, and in the elementary occupations they earned 85.3 per cent. Women employed in financial services, manufacturing industries and in the wholesale and retail trades earned just over half of what their male colleagues earned. Women employed in the construction, transportation and utilities industries earned just over 80 per cent of what their male colleagues earned.

BANKING AND FINANCE

Currency
1 Bahamian dollar = 100 cents

GDP/GNP, Inflation, National Debt
The Bahamian economy is dominated by tourism and financial services. Tourism and related industries are thought to provide over 60 per cent of GDP and employ some 50 per cent of the workforce. The economy is heavily dependent on trade with the US and as such has been adversely affected by the US economic situation. Tourism has decreased in the last year. Several projects relating to tourism are planned to help develop the economy. Many of the projects involve foreign investment and the government is increasingly turning to new partners including China to help finance developments. China is financing a new sports stadium and some road construction. A slight recovery was forecast for 2011, aided by investment in construction and an upturn in tourism.

GDP was estimated at B$7,234 million in 2007, indicating a growth rate of 5.2 per cent on the 2006 figure of B$6,876 million. It was estimated at $7.564 billion (current price) in 2008, with a growth rate of 0.8 per cent. GDP growth in 2009 was put at just under one per cent. It was estimated to be $7.7 billion in 2010 with a growth rate of -0.5 per cent. Growth was estimated at 2 per cent for the first two quarters of 2012. GDP is made up mainly by the service sector (90 per cent). Financial services make up 11.5 per cent of GDP, business services and real estate 18 per cent, construction 11 per cent. Agriculture contributed 1.5 per cent and industry 8 per cent. Per capita GDP was estimated to be $28,500 in 2010. GNI was estimated to be B$5,498 million in 2007, up from B$5,276 million in 2006.

Figures for 2010 put inflation at 1.3 per cent, rising to over 2 per cent in 2011, due largely to rising fuel costs. Inflation was estimated to be 2.5 per cent in 2012.

The total national debt was estimated to be almost $5 billion in 2012.

Balance of Payments / Imports and Exports
Imports to the Bahamas include foodstuffs, manufactured goods, mineral fuels, petroleum and petroleum products, chemicals and machinery and transportation equipment. Total imports in 2009 cost an estimated US$2.6 billion. The USA provided over 25 per cent of imports in 2008, followed by South Korea and Japan. Exports from the Bahamas include pharmaceuticals, chemicals, cement, rum, crawfish, fruit and vegetables, salt and aragonite and exports in 2009 earned US$330 million. The EU is the greatest export partner (55 per cent). Approximately 22 per cent of exports go to the USA.

Foreign Investment
Foreign investment is encouraged by incentives through the Industries Encouragement Act, The Agriculture Manufacture Act, The Hotels Encouragement Act and The Spirits and Beer Manufacturing Act. These acts offer customs duty relief. Foreign investment has also benefited through the setting up for two duty free zones, one at Freeport on Grand Bahama Island, the other on the island of New Providence.

Bahamas Investment Authority, URL: http://www.bahamas.gov.bs/

Central Bank
Central Bank of the Bahamas, PO Box N-4868, Frederick Street, Nassau, Bahamas. Tel: +1 242 322 2193, fax: +1 242 322 4321, e-mail: cbob@batelnet.bs, URL: http://www.centralbankbahamas.com
Governor: Mrs Wendy Craigg

Chambers of Commerce and Trade Organisations
Bahamas Chamber of Commerce, URL: http://www.thebahamaschamber.com/

MANUFACTURING, MINING AND SERVICES

Energy

The Bahamas consumed a total of 0.074 quadrillion Btu in 2009. In 2010 the Bahamas generated 1.93 billion kWh of electricity and consumed 1.79 billion kWh.

The Bahamas imports all the oil it uses, 41,000 barrels per day in 2011.

Manufacturing

Industrial output accounts for 10 per cent of GDP, about 50 per cent of industrial employment and about 4 per cent of employment. There are various tax incentives to encourage manufacturers. Main industrial firms include PFC Bahamas, a pharmaceutical firm, BORCO oil facility, the Commonwealth Brewery and Bacardi Corporation. Main products include cement, salt, rum, pharmaceuticals, steel pipes and the processing of agricultural products.

Service Industries

Tourism, which annually attracts more than four million visitors to the Bahamas, continues to be the major sector in the Bahamian economy. It accounts for more than 70 per cent of the country's foreign exchange earnings from the export of goods and services, and 65 per cent of employment and contributes 48 per cent of GDP. In 1997 there were 3,361,331 foreign arrivals in the Bahamas. Of these 1,617,595 were stop-over visitors (that is, they stayed 24 hours or more), 1,743,736 were cruise visitors. This represents a decrease of nearly 1.6 per cent over the 1996 figure of 3,414,944. Total visitor spending (October 1998) was estimated at B$2,906,801. The two main tourist centres are New Providence and Grand Bahama. Over 80 per cent of tourists are from America.

The banking and finance sector is the second largest earner in the Bahamian economy, contributing around 15 per cent of GDP and employing over 4,500 people. More than 300 banks and trust companies are represented in the Bahamas.

Agriculture

This new but fast growing sector employs about 5.0 per cent of the population and contributes about 2 per cent of GDP. However, it only provides 20 per cent of the food requirement for the country. The remaining 80 per cent must be imported. Winter vegetables, citrus and avocados are among the crops exported and they are mainly grown on the islands of Abaco and Andros. 95 per cent of export crops go to the USA.

Approximately 32 per cent of the total land area of the Bahamas is covered with natural pine forests. These are found on the northern islands of Grand Bahama, Abaco, Andros and New Providence. The total pine forest cover was estimated to be some 500,000 acres (204,000 ha) of which 90 per cent is state owned and 10 per cent privately owned forest. At present there are no forest based industries.

The government wants to encourage foreign investment in the agriculture sector particularly beef and pork production, dairy and winter vegetable production and shrimp farming.

Agricultural Production in 2010

Produce	Int. $'000	Tonnes
Indigenous chicken meat	8,884	6,237
Grapefruit (inc. pomelos)	4,294	19,100
Lemons and limes	4,044	10,200
Vegetables Fresh nes	3,373	17,900
Sugar cane	1,888	57,500
Tomatoes	1,404	3,800
Fruit, tropical fresh nes	1,390	3,400
Bananas	1,211	4,300
Hen eggs, in shell	1,078	1,300
Goat milk, whole, fresh	604	1,800
Indigenous pigmeat	484	315
Goat milk, whole, fresh	316	1,050
Indigenous pigmeat	484	315

Source: http://faostat.fao.org/site/339/default.aspx Food and Agriculture Organization of the United Nations, Food and Agricultural commodities production

Fishing

It is estimated that the fishing sector provides employment for about 2,500 people and contributes about 5 per cent of GDP. Currently, fisheries development is expanding at a rapid rate. The fishing industry currently earns more than B$50 million per year, mainly from lobster exports. All commercial fishing boats must be solely Bahamian owned.

COMMUNICATIONS AND TRANSPORT

Visa Information

USA, Canadian, Australian and most EU nationals do not require a visa to stay in the Bahamas for up to eight months. Visits longer than eight months need approval for extension of stay. Nationals of Bulgaria, the Czech Republic, Estonia, Hungary, Latvia, Lithuania, Poland, Romania, the Slovak Republic and Slovenia do need a visa, and citizens of Austria, Cyprus, Finland, France, Germany, Ireland, Malta, Portugal, Spain and Sweden need a visa for visits of over three months. Nationals of Belgium, Denmark, Greece, Italy, Luxembourg, The Netherlands and the UK require a visa for stays of over eight months.

Please contact a Bahamanian Embassy for further information.

Customs Restrictions

Most consumable goods brought into the Bahamas attract customs duties which are levied on an *ad valorem* basis on entry. Tariff value depends on the item being imported but can vary between 0 per cent and 260 per cent. Usually luxury items attract higher tariffs, whilst breadbasket items and printed material are almost duty free. However, such goods attract a 7 per cent stamp tax. Food also carries a stamp tax of 2 per cent.

National Airlines

Bahamasair, URL: http://www.bahamasair.com
Provides services from Atlanta and points in Florida to Nassau and Freeport in addition to its inter-island schedule service.

International Airports

The Bahamas is accessible by air from all major cities in western Europe, North America, South America and the Caribbean. An estimated 3.1 million passengers passed through its main airport in 2011. The airport is currently undergoing expansion and should be able to handle 5 million passengers per year by 2015.
Lynden Pindling International Airport (formerly Nassau International Airport), URL: http://www.vantageairportgroup.com
There are also 39 smaller airports and airfields and one heliports.

Roads

There are 240 miles of paved roads in New Providence, and 426 miles in Grand Bahama. The major islands together have 400 miles of driveable roads, vehicles are driven on the left. There are no railways.

Ports and Harbours

There are regular freight services to Nassau, operated by companies from the Caribbean, UK, US, Canada and the Far East.
Grand Bahama Port Authority, URL: http://www.gbpa.com/

HEALTH

There are four hospitals in Nassau: The Princess Margaret Hospital, Doctors Hospital, Sandilands Rehabilitation Centre, and the Lyford Cay Hospital / Bahamas Heart Institute. In Freeport, Grand Bahama, there is one general hospital, Rand Memorial Hospital, and two specialist medical centres, The Sunrise Medical Centre and Lucayan Medical Centre.

In 2000-07, there were 32 hospital beds per 10,000 population. The number of health practitioners, per 100,000 of the population, as of 2004 were: 105.5 physicians (312 in total), 45 registered nurses and midwives (1,323), and 7.2 dentists (21).

Child (aged five or less) mortality rates were put at 16 per 1,000 live births in 2009 and infant mortality rates at 14 per 1,000 live births. Most common causes of death (2010) were prematurity (9 per cent), congenital anomalies (12 per cent) and pneumonia (27 per cent). Approximately 1 per cent of child deaths were due to HIV/AIDS.

In 2009, total expenditure on health was 8.3 per cent of GDP. Government expenditure on health accounted for 46.8 per cent of total expenditure on health. Spending on health accounted for 15.2 per cent of the government's total spending. Total per capita expenditure on health was US$1,741 in 2009.

An estimated 98 per cent of the population have access to improved water sources and 100 per cent to improved sanitation. (Source: http://www.who.int, Global Health Statistics, 2012)

EDUCATION

Bahamian education is under the jurisdiction of the Ministry of Education. Schools in the Bahamas are categorised as primary (ages 5 - 11) and secondary schools (ages 11 - 16). Education between the ages of 5 and 16 is compulsory. There are 226 schools in the Commonwealth of the Bahamas. Of these, 185 (81.9 per cent) are fully maintained by Government, and 41 (18.1 per cent) are independent schools. There are 35 government-owned schools in New Providence and 150 on the Family Islands. 26 independent schools are located in New Providence and 15 on the Family Islands.

There are also central secondary schools in the Family Islands. Special education schools (all ages) cater for students with severe learning disabilities. Free education is available in Ministry schools in New Providence and the Family Islands. Courses lead to the Bahamas Junior Certificate (BJC) usually after 9 - 10 years; and the Bahamas General Certificate of Secondary Education (BGCSE), which replaces the traditional General Certificate of Education (GCE), after 11 - 12 years. Independent schools provide education at primary and secondary levels. The term 'college' in their names does not mean a university-type school. Recent figures show 37,438 students in primary education, and 24,594 in secondary education.

Several private schools of continuing education offer secretarial and academic courses. The government-operated Princess Margaret Hospital offers a Nursing Course through the school of nursing. Four institutions in the Bahamas offer higher education: the government-sponsored college of the Bahamas, established in 1974; the University of the West Indies (regional), affiliated with the Bahamas since 1960; the Bahamas Hotel Training College, sponsored by the Ministry of Education and the Hotel Industry; and the Industrial Training Programme established to provide the basic trade skills. Tertiary education is offered through the University of Miami, Nova University, University College, St John's University, Bahamas Campus.

In 2007, 91 per cent of the relevant age-group attended primary school, and 86 per cent of the concerned age-group were enrolled in secondary education.

BAHRAIN

The pupil:teacher ratio in primary schools in 2007 was 14:1. In the same year, 19.7 per cent of total government expenditure went on education. The adult literacy rate was estimated to be 91.0 per cent (97 per cent among 15-24 year olds). (Source: UNESCO, UIS, August 2009)

RELIGION

The population is predominantly Christian, with the major denomination being Baptist (32 per cent). Other denominations include Anglican (20 per cent), Roman Catholic (19 per cent), Protestant (12 per cent), Methodist and Church of God (6 per cent). Other faiths represented include Judaism, Islam, and Bahai.

The Bahamas have a religious tolerance rating of 9 on a scale of 1 to 10 (10 is most freedom). (Source: World Religion Database)

COMMUNICATIONS AND MEDIA

Newspapers
Newspapers are allowed to carry criticise the government. The main newspapers are:
The Nassau Guardian, URL: http://www.thenassauguardian.com
The Tribune (Bahamas), URL: http://access.tribune242.com/
Freeport News, URL: http://www.freeport.nassauguardian.net
Bahama Journal, URL: http://www.jonesbahamas.com

Broadcasting
The government operates a radio network and the only TV station. There are also priva radio stations and cable television is widely available.
ZNS Television, URL: http://www.znsbahamas.com
Cable Bahamas, URL: http://www.cablebahamas.com

Telecommunications
The systems is modern. A submarine networks links 14 of the islands. In 2008 there wer estimated to be 133,000 land lines in operation and 355,000 mobiles.

In 2008 there were around 106,000 internet users.

ENVIRONMENT

The main environmental concerns for the islands is the decay of surrounding coral reefs ar the disposal of solid waste.

In 2010, the Bahamas' emissions from the consumption of fossil fuels totalled 5.57 millic metric tons of carbon dioxide. (Source: EIA)

The Bahamas is a party to the following international agreements: Biodiversity, Climat Change, Climate Change-Kyoto Protocol, Desertification, Endangered Species, Hazardou Wastes, Law of the Sea, Ozone Layer Protection, Ship Pollution, and Wetlands.

BAHRAIN
Kingdom of Bahrain
Mamlakat Al-Bahrayn

Capital: Manama (Population estimate: 160,000)

Head of State: King Hamad Bin Isa Al Khalifa (page 1375)

Crown Prince, Chair of the National Economic Development Council: Shaikh Salman bin Hamad al-Khalifa

National Flag: Red; a white stripe pale-wise at the hoist, with a serration of eight teeth towards the fly

CONSTITUTION AND GOVERNMENT

Constitution
Bahrain gained full independence from British protection in 1971, and a Constitution was finalised in 1973. The Constitution was approved by a Constituent assembly consisting of both elected and nominated members, together with representatives of the Council of Ministers.

Bahrain became a member of the United Nations and the Arab League in 1971. In 1981 it joined its five neighbours - Saudi Arabia, Oman, Kuwait, the United Arab Emirates and Qatar - to form the strategic alliance called the Gulf Co-operation Council (GCC).

Shaikh Isa Bin Sulman Al Khalifa, former ruler of Bahrain, died in March 1999 and was succeeded by his eldest son, Shaikh Hamad Bin Isa Al Khalifa, the crown prince and heir apparent since 1964.

In December 2000 a national charter was drafted which allowed for a constitutional monarchy, an independent judiciary and a partially elected parliament. Under the old system the Emir was the authority, whilst the ruling family held most of the cabinet posts. The charter was voted for by the people in a referendum in February 2001, with 98.4 per cent voting for the changes. On 14 February 2002 Bahrain became a constitutional monarchy, the Emir became King and the country became known as the Kingdom of Bahrain.

To consult the full constitution, please visit: http://www.e.gov.bh

International Relations
Bahrain is a member of the Gulf Co-operation Council. In March 2001, the International Court of Justice (ICJ) awarded sovereignty over the Hawar Islands and Qit'at Jaradah to Bahrain and sovereignty over Zubarah, which forms part of the Qatar peninsula, Janan Island and Fasht ad Dibal to Qatar, and redrew the international maritime border. There has subsequently been renewed co-operation between the two countries. Bahrain maintains strong relations with its largest financial backers, Saudi Arabia, Kuwait and the U.A.E. Bahrain-Iran relations have remained strained since an Iran-sponsored coup plot in Bahrain was discovered.

Bahrain became a member of the United Nations and the Arab League in 1971. Bahrain has a strategic partnership with the US; the two countries signed a Defense Cooperation Agreement in October 1991, which granted U.S. forces access to Bahraini facilities and the right to pre-position material for future crises. Bahrain is the headquarters of the U.S. Navy's Fifth Fleet. Bahrain provided basing and overflight clearances for many US aircraft during both Iraq wars. Bahrain has delivered humanitarian support and technical training to assist in the reconstruction of Iraq.

Recent Events
In February 2001, Shaikh Hamad pardoned all political prisoners and detainees, includin those who had been imprisoned, exiled or detained on security charges. He also abolishe the State Security Law and the State Security Court, which had permitted the governmer to detain individuals without trial for up to 3 years. On February 14 2002, Shaikh Hama pronounced Bahrain a constitutional monarchy and changed his status from Amir to King.

Municipal elections were held on 9 May 2002. Women were allowed to vote and stand fo office for the first time. The first General Election was held in October 2002, and there wer 177 candidates, eight of whom were women. In April 2004, Nada Haffadh became the firs woman to hold a ministerial position, that of Health Minister. In March of 2005, protest took place in favour of a fully-elected parliament.

In 2006, US President George Bush signed a bill to enact the 2004 US-Bahrain free-trad agreement.

In November 2006, the Shia opposition won 40 per cent of the vote in the general election and a Shia Muslim, Jawad bin Salem al-Oraied, was appointed deputy prime minister.

Houda Nonoo, a Jewish woman, was appointed Bahrain's ambassador to the USA in May 2008. She is believed to be the Arab world's first Jewish ambassador.

In April 2009, the King pardoned more than 170 prisoners charged with endangering nationa security.

In January 2011 popular demonstrations broke out in the Arab world. Following successfu demonstrations in Egypt and Tunisia, protestors took to the streets of Manama. The demonstrators faced the security forces and seven anti-government protesters were killed As a conciliatory gesture the king released some political prisoners and the prominent Shia opposition figure Hassan Mushaima returned from exile after charges against him were dropped. The cabinet was also reshuffled but, contrary to the demands of the protesters, the prime minister kept his position. The protesters are predominantly Shia Muslims, and they have been demonstrating against economic hardship, the lack of political freedom and the discrimination in jobs in favour of the governing Sunni Muslim minority. By March the protests had grown and troops arrived from neighbouring Gulf states including Saudi Arabia and the United Arab Emirates ostensibly to guard key installations. The protesters occupied the centre of the capital and on March 16 King Hamad cleared the protesters camp in a show of force which the UN said was 'shocking'. Despite this, protests continued and in April the Government moved to ban two main political parties representing the Shia majority. By June the state of emergency was lifted but security on the streets remained heavy. It has beer estimated that around 30 people have been killed during the protests. It has also been claimed that around 400 activists including human rights activists and opposition supporters have been detained by the authorities.

Following an inquiry into the crackdown on protestors earlier in 2011, the head of the security agency was replaced. The enquiry found that excessive force had been used; at least 40 people died during the protests. Sheikh Khalifa bin Abdullah was moved to another security role, the secretary general of the Supreme Defence Council. Abel bin Khalifa Hamad al-Fadhel was named as acting security chief.

In April 2012 protests were still continuing and focused on the agreement between Formula 1 racing and Bahrain as the country agreed to host the Grand Prix. The race went ahead despite the death of an activist.

Legislature

Prior to 2002, there was no elected legislature. The 2002 Constitution allows for a directly elected lower house, the Council of Representatives, which has 40 members. Thirty-two of the Council's 40 members represent Sunni and Shia Islamist societies. The upper house, the Shura, is appointed by the king and also has 40 members. Both houses have legislative powers and serve a four year term.

Council of Representatives (Majlis al-Nuwab), PO Box 54040, Manama, Bahrain, URL: http://www.nuwab.gov.bh/
Consultative Council (Majlis al-Shura), PO Box 10105, Manama, Bahrain. URL: http://www.shura.gov.bh

Cabinet (as at July 2013)

Prime Minister: H.H. Shaikh Khalifa Bin Salman Al-Khalifa (page 1375)
Deputy Prime Minister: H.E. Shaikh Ali Bin Khalifa Al-Khalifa (page 1375)
Deputy Prime Minister: H.E. Shaikh Mohammed Bin Mubarak Al-Khalifa (page 1375)
Deputy Prime Minister: Jawad al Arrayed Al-Oraied
Deputy Prime Minister, Minister in the Prime Minister's Office: Shaikh Khalid bin Abdulla al Kahlifa
Minister of the Interior: Lt. Gen. Shaikh Rashid bin Abdulla bin Amhed al-Khalifa
Minister of Foreign Affairs: H.E. Shaikh Khalid bin Ahmed bin Mohammed al Khalifa (page 1375)
Minister of Justice and Islamic Affairs: Shaikh Khalid bin Ali al Khalifa
Minister of Energy, Oil, Electricity and Water Authority: H.E. Abdulhussein bin Ali Mirza (page 1446)
Minister of Industry and Commerce: H.E. Dr Hassan bin Abdulla Fakhro
Minister of Finance: H.E. Shaikh Ahmed bin Mohammed Al Khalifa (page 1375)
Minister of Works: Issam bin Abdallah Khalaf
Minister of Culture: Sheikh May Bint Mohammed Al Khalifa
Minister of Municipalities and Town Planning: Dr Juma Ahmed Al-Kaabi
Minister of Education: H.E. Dr Majed bin Ali Al Nuaimi (page 1376)
Minister of Labour: Jameel Hmaidan
Minister of Health: Sadiq bin Abdul Karim Al-Shehabi
Minister for Human Rights and Social Development: Dr Fatimah Al-Bulushi
Minister of Transport and Communications: Kamal bin Ahmed Mohadded
Minister of State for Shura Council and Parliament Affairs: Abdulaziz al Fadhel
Minister of State for Defence: Dr Sheikh Mohammad bin Abdullah al-Khalifa
Minister of Housing: Dr Bassem bin Yacoub Al-Hamer
Minister of State for Follow-up Affairs: Dr Shaikh Mohammed Al Mutawa
Minister of State for Foreign Affairs: Dr Ganem Al-Buainain
Minister of State for Information Affairs: Sameera Rajab
Minister of State for Human Rights Affairs: Salah Ali
Minister of State for Interior Affairs: Major Gen. Adel bin Khalifa Al-Fadhel

Ministries

Office of the Prime Minister, PO Box 1000, Rifa'a, Bahrain. Tel: +973 17 200000, fax: +973 229022, URL: http://www.e.gov.bh
Ministry of Defence, PO Box 245, West Rifa'a, Bahrain. Tel: +973 17 665599, fax: +973 17 663923
Ministry of Finance and National Economy, PO Box 333, Manama, Bahrain. Tel: +973 17 530800, fax: +973 17 532713, e-mail: mfmoahs@mofne.gov.bh, URL: http://www.mofne.gov.bh
Ministry of Cabinet Affairs and Information, PO Box 100, Rifa'a, Bahrain. Tel: +973 17 223366, fax: +973 17 225202, URL: http://www.bna.bh/
Ministry of Industry, PO Box 10908, Manama, Bahrain. Tel: +973 17 291511, fax: +973 17 290157, e-mail: industry@industry.gov.bh, URL: http://www.industry.gov.bh/
Ministry of Housing, Municipalities and Environment, PO Box 5802, Manama, Bahrain. Tel: +973 17 533000, fax: +973 17 534115, URL: http://www.mohme.gov.bh/
Ministry of Works and Agriculture, PO Box 5, Manama, Bahrain. Tel: +973 17 535222, fax: +973 17 533095
Ministry of Electricity and Water, PO Box 2, Manama, Bahrain. Tel: +973 17 533133, fax: +973 17 533035
Ministry of Commerce, PO Box 5479, Diplomatic Area, Manama, Bahrain. Tel: +973 17 531531, fax: +973 17 530455, e-mail: drmansoor@commerce.gov.bh, URL: http://www.commerce.gov.bh/
Ministry of Foreign Affairs, PO Box 547, Manama, Bahrain. Tel: +973 17 227555, fax: +973 17 212603
Ministry of the Interior, PO Box 13, Manama, Bahrain. Tel: +973 17 272111, fax: +973 262169
Ministry of Transportation, PO Box 10325, Manama, Bahrain. Tel: +973 17 534534, fax: +973 17 537537
Ministry of Education, PO Box 43, Manama, Bahrain. Tel: +973 17 258400, fax: +973 17 687866, e-mail: webmaster@education.gov.bh, URL: http://www.education.gov.bh/
Ministry of Health, PO Box 12, Manama, Bahrain. Tel: +973 17 255555, fax: +973 17 252569, e-mail: webmaster@health.gov.bh, URL: http://www.moh.gov.bh/
Ministry of Labour and Social Affairs, PO Box 32333, Isa Town, Manama, Bahrain. Tel: +973 17 687800, fax: +973 17 686954, e-mail: jamalq@bah-molsa.com, URL: http://www.bah-molsa.com/
Ministry of Justice and Islamic Affairs, PO Box 450, Manama, Bahrain. Tel: +973 17 531333, fax: +973 17 536343, e-mail: info@undernit.com, URL: http://www.moia.gov.bh/
Ministry of State for Legal Affairs, PO Box 790, Manama, Bahrain. Tel: +973 17 259990, fax: +973 17 270303

Political Parties

Political parties are not permitted. However, there are four political societies: al Wifag, al Asala, al Minbar, al Mustaqbil

Elections

Elections to the 40-seat Chamber of Deputies took place on 25 November 2006. The election was the first in which the Shiite-led opposition made a strong run in parliament, after boycotting the elections in 2002; the Shia Al-Wefaq National Islamic Society won 18 seats,

whilst the pro-government Sunnis won 22 seats. A large number of women candidates stood for election, and one, Lateefa Al Gaood, won by default before polling began when her two opponents withdrew from the race. She is the first woman to serve in an elected parliament in the Gulf. Critics accused the government of engineering her victory since it was unlikely that a woman would have been elected.

The most recent parliamentary election took place in October 2010. The Shia Al-Wefaq National Islamic Society again won 18 of the 40 seats, pro-government Sunnis retained power.

Diplomatic Representation

British Embassy, 21 Government Avenue, PO Box 114, Manama 306, Bahrain. Tel: +973 17 574100, fax: +973 17 574161, e-mail: britemb@batelco.com.bh, URL: http://ukinbahrain.fco.gov.uk/
Ambassador: H.E. Iain Lindsay
Embassy of the Kingdom of Bahrain, 30 Belgrave Square, London SW1X 8QB. Tel: +44 (0)20 7201 9170, fax: +44 (0)20 7201 9183, e-mail: info@bahrainembassy.co.uk, URL: http://www.bahrainembassy.co.uk/
Ambassador: H.E. Ms. Alice Thomas Samaan
US Embassy, Bldg 979, Road 3119, Block 331, Zinj (PO Box 26431, Manama), Bahrain. Tel: +973 17 273300, fax: +973 17 272594, URL: http://bahrain.usembassy.gov
Ambassador: H.E. Thomas C. Krajeski (page 1458)
Embassy of Bahrain, 3502 International Drive NW, Washington DC 20008, USA. Tel: +1 202 342 1111, fax: +1 202 362 2192, e-mail: information@bahrainembassy.org, URL: http://www.bahrainembassy.org/
Ambassador: H.E. Ezra Nonoo (page 1487)
Permanent Mission of the Kingdom of Bahrain to the United Nations, 866 Second Avenue, 14th & 15th Floors, New York, NY 10017, USA. Tel: +1 212 223 6200, fax: +1 212 319 0687, e-mail: Bahrain@un.int, URL: http://bahrain.un.int
Ambassador: Jamal Faris al-Ruwayi

LEGAL SYSTEM

In theory, the judiciary is an independent and separate branch of government. However, the amir retains the power of pardon. Bahrain has a dual court system, with both civil and Sharia courts.

The civil court system consists of summary courts and a Supreme court. Summary courts of first instance are located in all communities and include separate civil and criminal sections. The Supreme Court of Appeal is the highest appellate court in the country, and also rules on the constitutionality of laws and regulations.

The Sharia courts mainly deal with personal matters, such as marriage, divorce, and inheritance. Sharia courts of first instance are located in all communities, and a Sharia Court of Appeal sits at Manama. Appeals beyond the jurisdiction of the Sharia Court of Appeal are taken to the Supreme Court of Appeal.

Citizens do not have the right to change their government. The government restricts civil liberties such as the freedom of press, speech, assembly, association, and some religious practices. There is discrimination on the basis of gender, religion, nationality, and sect, and restrictions on the rights of expatriate workers remain a problems, though the government passed comprehensive antitrafficking legislation in 2008, and successfully prosecuted its first case under this law in December 2008.

Bahrain retains the death penalty. One person was reported to have been executed in 2010. As of 2012, five people were believed to be on death row.

LOCAL GOVERNMENT

For administrative purposes Bahrain is divided into five governorates which are overseen by an appointed governor. The country is further divided into 12 *manatiq*, or municipalities, all of which are administered from the capital Manama. They are Al Hadd, Al Manamah, Al Mintaqah al Gharbiyah, Al Mintaqah al Wusta, Al Mintaqah ash Shamaliyah, Al Muharraq, Ar Rifa' wa al Mintaqah al Janubiyah, Jidd Hafs, Madinat Hamad, Madinat 'Isa, Juzur Hawar and Sitrah.

AREA AND POPULATION

Area

Bahrain, a group of 36 islands with a total area of 717.5 sq. km, is situated in the Arabian Gulf, off the east coast of Saudi Arabia. The state takes its name from the largest island, Bahrain, which has an area of 586.5 sq. km. The four main islands are joined by causeways, and make up about 95 per cent of the total land area. The principal towns are Manama, Muharrag, Isa Town, Rifaa and Awali. Following an International Court of Justice ruling in March 2001, the Hawar Islands now belong to Bahrain. The ownership of the islands had been the subject of a dispute with Qatar.

The climate is hot and humid with very little rain.

To consult a map, visit: http://www.un.org/Depts/Cartographic/map/profile/bahrain.pdf

Population

Bahrain's total population was estimated to be 1.262 million in 2010 (compared with 776,000, including about 235,100 non-nationals, in 2008). It is one of the most densely populated countries in the world; just under 90 per cent of the population live in the two principal cities of Manama and Al Muharrak. Annual population growth over 2000-2010 was approximately 6.8 per cent. An estimated 63 per cent of the population are Bahraini Arabs, whilst 19 per

BAHRAIN

cent are from Asia, 10 per cent from other Arab states and 8 per cent are Iranian. An estimated 77 per cent of the population (2010) is aged between 15 and 60 years old, with 20 per cent aged 14 or less. The median age is 30 years.

In 2002, the King decreed that citizens of the Gulf Cooperation Council (GCC) could take up dual Bahraini nationality; opposition groups believe that the government is granting citizenship to foreign nationals who have served in the Bahraini armed forces and security services in order to alter the demographic balance of the country, which is primarily Shi'a. About 40,000 individuals have been naturalised over the past 50 years, amounting to around 10 per cent of the total population.

The official language is Arabic, although English is widely used for business purposes. Urdu and Farsi are also spoken.

Births, Marriages, Deaths
Recent figures suggest that the birth rate for the year 2010 stood at 19.5 per 1,000 people, whilst the death rate was 2.9 per 1,000 population. Life expectancy in 2009 was 73 years for men and 76 years for women. Healthy life expectancy was 66 years. The infant mortality rate was 9.0 per 1,000 live births in 2009. In 2009, the neonatal mortality rate was 4 per 1,000 live births and the maternal mortality rate was estimated at 19 per 100,000 population. The fertility rate among Bahraini women was 2.5 children per woman. (Source: http://www.who.int, World Health Statistics 2012)

Public Holidays 2014
1 January: New Year
14 January: Birth of the Prophet* (Milad al-Nabi)
29 June: Ramadan begins*
29 July: Eid Al Fitr* (End of Ramadan)
5 October: Festival of the Sacrifice (Eid Al Adha)*
25 October: Al-Hijira (Islamic New Year)*
16 December: National Day
*Islamic holidays are dependent on the sighting of the moon and so precise dates may change

EMPLOYMENT

Estimates for the year 2006 suggest a total workforce of 359,500, a large proportion of which (44 per cent) is foreign. 6,805 people were registered as unemployed, of whom 5,280 were women. The unemployment rate in 2005 was estimated at 15 per cent.

Paid employment by economic activity

Sector	2006
Agriculture, hunting, forestry and fishing	3,737
Mining and quarrying	8
Manufacturing	61,942
Electricity, gas and water	1,313
Construction	89,407
Wholesale and retail trade, restaurants, hotels	72,795
Transport, storage and communication	13,009
Financing, insurance, real estate and business	14,298
Community, social and personnel services	40,298

Source: Copyright © International Labour Organization (ILO Dept. of Statistics, http://laborsta.ilo.org)

In June 2006, Bahrain passed laws legalizing the existence of multiple trade federations and codifying several protections for workers engaged in union activity. As part of the government's labor reform program, it has formed a Labor Market Regulatory Authority and established a fund to support the training of Bahraini workers.

BANKING AND FINANCE

Currency
One Bahrain dinar (BD) = 1,000 fils

GDP/GNP, Inflation, National Debt
Bahrain is rich in oil, natural gas, aluminium, fish and pearls. Although rich in oil, the economy is fairly diversified and has a developed financial and banking sector. Bahrain has been relatively unaffected by the global economic crisis. There has been some decline in the demand for petrocarbons, but this is expected to reverse. The construction market has also been hit. Stockmarkets have also suffered losses. The economy is primarily dependent upon the services industry, which contributed an estimated 65 per cent of annual GDP in 2009. Industry accounted for 33 per cent of GDP in the same year, with agriculture contributing less than 1 per cent.

Petroleum production and refining continues to play a major role in the economy; revenues from the sector currently account for 10 per cent of GDP and provide about 76 per cent of government income. However, reserves are expected to run out within 10 to 15 years.

Bahrain has become a major financial center and the sector is currently the largest contributor to GDP (30 per cent). Some 370 offshore banking units and representative offices are located in Bahrain, as well as 65 American firms. Bahrain is home to the largest concentration of Islamic financial institutions in the Middle East. Currently over 30 Islamic commercial, investment and leasing banks are located in the islands, as well as Islamic insurance (takaful) companies. Bahrain is also developing other service industries such as information technology, healthcare and education.

Recent increases in oil prices have helped Bahrain's economic growth. Real GDP rose from US$11.6 billion in 2005 and to US$12.07 billion in 2006. In 2007, GDP was an estimated US$18.4 billion with a growth rate of 6.7 per cent. In 2009, it was estimated to be US$20.5 billion. GDP was estimated to be 9,710 million BD in 2011. Annual GDP growth was estimated to be 5.4 per cent in 2009, rising to 2.2 per cent in 2011. Growth in 2012 was forecast to be over 4 per cent. Transport and communications showed the biggest growth. GDP was estimated at US$38,000.

Inflation was estimated at 2 per cent over the period 2008-11. It rose over 2012 reaching 3.7 per cent in September 2012. Public debt amounted to 3170 million BD in 2011 (32.5 per cent of GDP).

In 2002, Bahrain set up the International Islamic Financial Market. The market deals only in products that comply with Sharia law.

Balance of Payments / Imports and Exports
Oil accounts for some 60 per cent of the country's export earnings, much of it in the form of refined oil, originally from Saudi Arabia. Industrial diversification has created a range of business opportunities. Strategically located as a 'gateway to the Middle East', Bahrain promotes capital and energy intensive industries, with strong emphasis on exports.

Export revenue was US$12.5 billion in 2009. The main products exported were petroleum and petroleum products, aluminium and textiles. Bahrain exports mainly to the USA, Saudi Arabia, India and Japan.

Principal import products are crude oil, machinery, and chemicals. Import costs were US$10.4 billion in 2009. Main import trading partners are: Saudi Arabia (27 per cent), Japan, USA and China.

In January 2006, the US President George W Bush signed a bill to enact the US-Bahrain free-trade agreement, following its approval by the US Congress. It has since generated increased US commercial interest in Bahrain.

Central Bank
Central Bank of Bahrain, PO Box 27, Manama, Bahrain. URL: http://www.cbb.gov.bh
Governor: H.E. Mr Rasheed Mohammed Al Maraj

Chambers of Commerce and Trade Organisations
Bahrain Chamber of Commerce and Industry,
URL: http://www.bahrainchamber.org.bh/
Bahrain Stock Exchange, URL: http://www.bahrainstock.com

MANUFACTURING, MINING AND SERVICES

Primary and Extractive Industries
Bahrain produces a limited amount of oil, all of which comes from the Awali field. Proven oil reserves at the beginning of January 2012 were 120 million barrels. Production in 2011 was an estimated 47,430 barrels per day (of which 35,000 barrels of crude). Bahrain had an estimated 2012 refining capacity of 254 thousand barrels per day. Estimated consumption was 45,000 barrels a day in 2011. Because domestic production is much lower than the country's refining capacity, Bahrain imports about 225,000 bbl/d of Arab Light crude oil from Saudi Arabia via a pipeline linking the two countries; Bahrain Petroleum Company refines this oil and exports much of it via tanker, mostly to India and other Asian markets.

Bahrain was the first country in the Southern Gulf region to have an oil-based economy. The island's first refinery opened in 1935; however, the Government realised from the outset that the country's oil reserves were limited, so a deliberate policy of diversification into hydrocarbon linked industries and use of all oil associated products was adopted. It is anticipated that reserves will be exhausted in ten to fifteen years time. Gas and oil production together now only contribute 11 per cent of Bahrain's GDP but still provide around 60 per cent of government income.

The Awali site is Bahrain's only oilfield. The Abu Safa field was jointly controlled by Saudi Aramco but in 1997 all proceeds from the field were given to Bahrain by Saudi Arabia. This contributes about US$115 million per year to government revenue. In 2001 an ongoing dispute about sovereignty of the Hawar Islands with Qatar was resolved in Bahrain's favour. The islands lie just off Qatar's main offshore oil field and this has generated interest in exploration in this area.

It is estimated that Bahrain has natural gas reserves of 3.0 trillion cubic feet. Natural gas production in 2010 was estimated at 451 billion cubic feet, all of which was consumed domestically. (Source: Energy Information Agency, EIA)

Energy
Bahrain's total (estimated) energy consumption in 2009 was 0.557 quadrillion Btu, equivalent to about 0.1 per cent of world energy consumption. Domestic production was 0.554 quadrillion Btu in the same year.

Bahrain has three main power plants: Rifa'a, Manama and Sitra. The government is building a new power and water-desalination plant at Hidd. In November, 2007 the Ministry of Electricity and Water announced plans for a $1 billion electric power and desalination project. The new power station will be located at Al Dour should be fully operational by 2013.

Electric generation capacity in 2010 was 3.17 gigawatts. Production of electricity in the same year was an estimated 12.4 billion kWh., whilst consumption reached 11.6 billion kWh. (Source: EIA)

Manufacturing

Second to oil, aluminium is Bahrain's oldest and most established industry. The introduction of a smelter to the state was the first step towards diversifying the economy in an attempt to reduce exclusive dependence on oil, while at the same time providing employment opportunities and increasing industrial development. Aluminium Bahrain (Alba) has grown to become one of the Gulf's largest non-oil industrial undertakings, and production capacity is 500,000 tonnes per year. It employs over 2,300 people and supports secondary manufacturers including a rolling mill.

The Arab Shipbuilding and Repair Yard has a capacity of 500,000 dead-weight tonnes and a second dock is planned. Traditional industries such as pearling, boat building, and weaving have declined as the government's policy of industrial diversification has developed.

Manufacturing industry contributed some 12.4 per cent of GDP in 2006.

Services

As part of the diversification process, Bahrain has developed as a major financial centre in the region, and this sector is now the second largest contributor to GDP (around 30 per cent in 2008). Over a hundred foreign banks and representative offices are located on the island, and it plays host to the largest concentration of Islamic financial institutions. Other growing service industries include information technology, education and healthcare. Tourism is becoming a significant source of income; the government favours large-scale tourism projects. It opened the only Formula One race track in the Middle East in 2004, and has awarded tenders for several tourist complexes. Oil revenues have been used to build an advanced infrastructure in transportation and telecommunications, which accounted for almost 9 per cent of GDP in 2006. Real estate contributed 9.2 per cent and government services accounted for 14.8 per cent.

Agriculture

Only eight per cent of Bahrain's total area is suitable for agricultural purposes. This is due to housing and industrial development that has encroached upon agricultural land; the soil which is nutrient deficient and the hostile climate, which is part desert, part maritime. The sector contributed less than 1 per cent to GDP in 2011. The Government introduced measures to increase agricultural production to meet 15 per cent of local requirements but most food continues to be imported. Bahrain's main agricultural products are fruit, vegetables, poultry, dairy products, shrimp and fish. Estimated figures for production are shown in the following table.

Agricultural Production in 2010

Produce	Int. $'000	Tonnes
Dates	7,150	14,000
Cow milk. whole, fresh	2,902	9,300
Hen eggs, in shell	2,488	3,000
Indigenous cattle meat	2,419	895
Fruit fresh nes	2,094	6,000
Tomatoes	1,404	3,800
Indigenous chicken meat	1,133	796
Vegetables fresh nes	905	4,800
Nuts, nes	843	460
Indigenous sheep meat	420	154
Lemons and limes	416	1,050
Lettuce and chicory	327	700

Source: http://faostat.fao.org/site/339/default.aspx FAOSTAT, Statistics Division, Food and Agriculture Organization of the UN

The fishing industry suffered from lack of manpower and steps have been taken to improve fishing methods, train the workforce and restore the marine life which has suffered due to land reclamation and pollution. The total catch for 2010 was estimated at 13,490 tonnes.

COMMUNICATIONS AND TRANSPORT

Travel Requirements

Citizens of the USA, Australia, Canada and the EU require a visa to enter Bahrain. Nationals of EU countries (except nationals of Bulgaria, Cyprus, the Czech Republic, Estonia, Hungary, Latvia, Lithuania, Malta, Poland, Romania, the Slovak Republic and Slovenia), Australia, Canada and USA may obtain visas on arrival at Bahrain International Airport or King Fahad Causeway if holding valid passports and return/onward tickets for tourist or business stays of up to two weeks.

Nationals not referred to above are advised to contact the embassy to check requirements.

International Airports

Bahrain International Airport is situated in Muharraq 6.5 km from Manama. It handles over 3.4 million passengers a year, has a fully automatic landing system, and a large automated air cargo terminal. It is a scheduled stop for numerous airlines, including Gulf Air, British Airways, Cathay Pacific, Saudia, Lufthansa, KLM, Air India and UTA. The passenger terminal can handle up to 10 million passengers a year. Gulf Air has its headquarters in Bahrain, and offers a service to most Middle East destinations, European cities, and many other international destinations.

Gulf Air, URL: http://www.gulfairco.com

Roads

Bahrain's road network has expanded to 3,850 km, of which 3,121 km is surfaced, 440 km is main highways, and 450 km is secondary roads. The 25 km link to Saudi Arabia, the King Fahad Causeway, puts Bahrain within one hour of the major population centres of the Eastern Province of Saudi Arabia and about four hours of driving to Kuwait and Riyadh. There are also causeways to Muharraq Island and Sitrah. Vehicles drive on the right and most road signs are in Arabic and English.

Ports and Harbours

The major sea port, Mina Sulman, was established in 1954 and can accommodate vessels up to 65,000 tonnes. It has a large covered storage area and comprehensive marine engineering and repair facilities. A new port is currently being constructed at Hidd. It will cover 640 hectares and will have two 300 metre container berths. There are also ports at Mina' Salman and Sitrah.

HEALTH

Total expenditure on health in 2009 was equivalent to 4.7 per cent of GDP, equating to around US$771 per capita. Government expenditure accounts for 70.1 per cent of the total expenditure. This represented 11.4 per cent of total government expenditure.

In 2005-10, there were 1,103 physicians (14.4 per 10,000 population), 2,856 nurses and midwives (37.3 per 10,000 population), 273 dentists (3.6 per 10,000 population). In 2008 there were an estimated 186 pharmacists (2.4 per 1,000 population) and 294 public and environmental health workers (0.40 per 1,000 population). In the period 2005-11, there were 18 hospital beds and 2.8 psychiatric beds per 10,000 population.

The infant mortality rate (probability of dying aged less than 1 year old) in 2010 stood at 9 per 1,000 live births and the under-five mortality rate was 10 per 1,000 live births. The most common causes of death for children aged under five years old were congenital abnormalities (32 per cent), prematurity (19 per cent), birth asphyxia (9 per cent), injuries (6 per cent) and pneumonia (2 per cent).

An estimated 100 per cent of the population have access to improved-drinking water sources and sanitation. (Source: http://www.who.int, World Health Statistics, 2012)

EDUCATION

The government pays for all schooling costs, including for non-nationals and higher education. Whilst education is not compulsory in Bahrain, attendance levels are high at the state and private schools. There are commercial schools as well as schools offering education in English, Japanese, French, Indian and other Asian languages.

In 2006, 52 per cent of small children were enrolled in pre-primary school, well above the regional average of 18 per cent. Around 98 per cent of the relevant age-group registered for primary education, and 96 per cent of girls and 91 per cent of boys enrolled in secondary school.(Source: UNESCO, UIC, October 2008)

Higher education is available at the Bahrain University, Arabian Gulf University and specialised institutes including the College of Health Sciences, which trains doctors, nurses, pharmacists, and paramedics. The Bahrain Training Institute provides training in manufacturing, construction, commercial and service industries, and the Bahrain Institute for Banking & Finance offers courses in banking, finance and insurance. The government has identified providing educational services to the Gulf Cooperation Council as a potential economic growth area, and is actively working to establish Bahrain as a regional center for higher education. In 2006, 32 per cent of the population of tertiary age enrolled in higher education.

According to latest UNESCO figures, in 2006 the literacy rates for males aged 15+ was 90 per cent and for females it was 85.5 per cent. For the age group 15-24 years it was 99.6 for males and 99.7 for females.

The pupil:teacher ratio in primary schools in 2002 was 16:1.

RELIGION

Islam is the state religion. Around 98 per cent of the population are Muslim. Although around 70 per cent of the indigenous population is Shi'a Muslim, the ruling family and the majority of government, military, and corporate leaders are Sunni Muslims, which make up around 28 per cent. There are small Christian, Jewish, Buddist, Baha'is and Hindu communities.

Bahrain has a religious tolerance rating of 4 on a scale of 1 to 10 (10 is most freedom). (Source: World Religion Database)

COMMUNICATIONS AND MEDIA

A press law allows for independence for journalists, but self censorship is practised. Insulting the king may be punished by jail terms.

Newspapers
Akhbar Al-Khaleej, URL: http://www.akhbar-alkhaleej.com/
Al Ayam, URL: http://www.alayam.com/
Gulf Daily News, URL: http://www.gulf-daily-news.com/
Alwasat Newspaper, URL: http://www.alwasatnews.com/

Broadcasting
The Bahrain Radio and Television Corporation (URL: http://www.bahraintv.com/testbars/) is the state run corporation and operates five terrestrial channels. Bahrain has Arabic and English-language television channels, broadcasting a mixture of news, international programmes, films and other material. Additionally, English channels can be received from Saudi Arabia, Qatar, Kuwait, Dubai and Abu Dhabi. Most homes have satellite television subscriptions.

BANGLADESH

The main news agency is the Bahrain News Agency (BNA), URL: http://english.bna.bh/

Telecommunications

Bahrain was the first country in the Middle East to install a satellite communication system and its telecommunication system is among the most advanced in the region with over 90 per cent of its network equipped with digital transmission. The system was run exclusively by the state-owned Batelco until 2003, when its monopoly was broken.

In 2008 there were 220,000 mainline telephones and 1.4 million mobile phones in use. According to 2008 estimates there are around 400,000 internet users in Bahrain.

ENVIRONMENT

Energy related carbon dioxide emissions were estimated at 23.5 million metric tons in 2002, equivalent to about 0.1 per cent of world carbon emissions. Per capita carbon emissions were 9.0 metric tons in the same year (compared with 5.5 metric tons in the US). The natural gas industry produces the greatest proportion of carbon emissions (76.9 per cent in 2002), followed by the oil industry (23.1 per cent).

Main environmental concerns for Bahrain include the effects of industrialisation, rising sea levels, limited natural fresh water resources, droughts and the threat of damage to coastline from oil spills in the Gulf. Lack of freshwater resources.

In 2010, Bahrain's emissions from the consumption and flaring of fossil fuels totalled 30.6 million metric tons of carbon dioxide, this was down slightly on the 2009 figure of 30.81 million metric tons. (Source: EIA)

Bahrain is a party to the following international agreements: Biodiversity, Climate Change, Climate Change-Kyoto Protocol, Desertification, Hazardous Wastes, Law of the Sea, Ozone Layer Protection, Ship Pollution and Wetlands.

BANGLADESH

People's Republic of Bangladesh

Prajatantri Bangladesh

Capital: Dhaka (Population estimate, 2005: 11 million)

Head of State: Abdul Hamid (President) (page 1437)

National Flag: Green with a central red disc

CONSTITUTION AND GOVERNMENT

Constitution

Bangladesh was under Muslim rule for five and a half centuries and passed into British hands in 1757. During British rule it was part of the British Indian province of Bengal and Assam. In August 1947 it gained independence along with the rest of India and formed part of Pakistan. It was known as East Pakistan until 26 March 1971 when it emerged as an independent country.

The Constitution of Bangladesh provides for a parliamentary system (effective from September 1991) and government where the President is the Head of State, and where the Prime Minister is the Head of Government. The Constitution is based on the principle of absolute trust and faith in the Almighty Allah, nationalism, democracy and socialism, the latter meaning economic and social justice.

The Constitution was amended in 1996 to make provision for a caretaker government to govern the country in between the dissolution of Parliament and the formation of a new government. During this period the President's role would become more significant.

To consult the full constitution, please visit: http://www.banglaembassy.com.bh/Constitution.html

International Relations

Geographically and culturally Bangladesh has a close relationship with India although there have been some difficulties over the issues of shared water supplies and India accuses some Indian separatists of taking refuge in Bangladesh, something which Bangladesh has denied. There has been some discussion regarding the setting up of a Free Trade Zone between the two countries. Bangladesh is a member of Bangladesh is a member of the Commonwealth, the UN, South Asian Association for Regional Cooperation, (SAARC) and the Organisation of Islamic Conference (OIC).

Recent Events

On 21 June 2002 President Chowdhury resigned following a dispute over protocol. In September, when Iajuddin Ahmed was elected to the presidency, the main opposition party, the Awami League, did not field a candidate. In 2003 the Awami party began to boycott parliamentary sessions, claiming that it was not allowed to criticise the government. In June 2004 it resumed its place in parliament as the main opposition party.

Sham A M S Kibria, a leading politician of the Awani party, was killed in a grenade attack in January 2005. The party called for a general strike in protest. In February 2006 the party ended its year-long parliamentary boycott.

Economist Muhammad Yunus and his Grameen Bank won the 2006 Nobel Peace Prize for his anti-poverty work

The mandate of PM Khaleda Zia ended on 27 October 2006 and she handed power to a caretaker authority pending elections in 2007. Violent protests followed the government's choice of interim administration and President Ahmed assumed the role of prime minister until the January 2007 elections. The interim government promised to clean up corruption ahead of elections. It tried to exclude two leading women politicians, arguing that the presence of the two party leaders was stopping it from carrying out constitutional reforms. However, violence between supporters of the two women led to the cancellation of the 2007 general election and the imposition of a state of emergency. Dr Fakhruddin Ahmed became head of the caretaker government in January, and elections were re-scheduled for December 2008.

In April 2007, former PM Sheikh Hasina was charged with murder and former PM Begum Khaleda Zia was placed under virtual house arrest. Other politicians were arrested in an anti-corruption drive.

In November 2007, a devastating cyclone hit Bangladesh. At least 2,500 people were killed and hundreds of thousands left homeless.

Postponed elections finally took place in December 2008. The Awani League Alliance led by the former prime minister Sheikh Hasina won a landslide victory.

Border guards protesting against their pay and conditions led a mutiny in February 2009. An estimated 74 people, mainly army officers, were killed at the guards' Dhaka compound headquarters. Over 1,000 border guards were later charged in connection with the mutiny.

In September 2011, hundreds of Jamaat-e-Islami supporters were arrested on charges of inciting violence during nation-wide protests. The opposition Bangladesh Nationalist Party announced it would be holding a country-wide strike to protest against price rises and the alleged repression of opposition parties.

In April 2013, Prime Minister Sheikh Hasina rejected demands by Islamists to change blasphemy laws. Protesters wanted a new anti-blasphemy law to punish anyone defaming Islam and the Prophet Muhammed. The Prime Minister felt the present laws were sufficient.

In April 2013, an eight storey factory building situated near the capital Dhaka collapsed. It was the country's worst industrial disaster with more than 700 people killed and 2,500 injured. The factory housed garment workers and had reportedly been built illegally. Following the disaster, many European retailers agreed to sign an accord to improve safety conditions in factories and after workers protested, the government pledged to raise the minimum wage and make it easier for workers to form unions. In July 2013, 70 retailers agreed a plan which would allow for inspections to take place of garment factories. Several large retailers have signed up to the agreement including Sweden's H & M, which is the largest buyer of Bangladeshi-made clothes.

Legislature

The Constitution provides for a single Chamber of Parliament (called 'Bangladesh Jatiya Sangsad'), consisting of 330 members. Of these, 300 members are elected directly by the people and 30 women members are elected by the Members of Parliament. In May 2004 the constitution was amended to reserve 45 seats in parliament for female MPs. As a result the total number of MPs is now 345. The term of each Parliament lasts five years.

Parliament, Jatiya Sangsad, Parliament House, Shere-e-Banghla Nagar, Dhaka 1207, Bangladesh. Tel: +880 2 811 1600, fax: +880 2 881 2267, URL: http://www.parliamentofbangladesh.org

---

Cabinet (as at June 2013)

Prime Minister, Minister for Power, Energy and Mineral Resources; Establishment; Housing and Public Works; Women and Children's Affairs; Defence: Sheikh Hasina Wajed (page 1533)
Minister of Law, Justice and Parliamentary Affairs: Shafiq Ahmed
Minister of Foreign Affairs: Dipu Moni (page 1479)
Minister of Finance: Abul Maal Abdul Muhith (page 1481)
Minister of Agriculture: Motia Chowdhury
Minister of Home Affairs: Dr Mohiuddin Khan Alamgir
Minister of Industry: Dilip Barua
Minister of Commerce: Ghulam .M. Quader
Minister of Planning: Air Vice Marshal (Ret'd.) A. K. Khandoker

---

Minister of Water Resources: Ramesh Chandra Sen
Minister of Fisheries and Livestock: Abdul Latif Biswas
Minister of Land: Mohammed Rezaul Karim Hira
Minister of Information: Hasanul Haq Inu
Minister of Cultural Affairs: Abul Kalam Azad
Minister of Civil Aviation and Tourism: Lt. Col. (Ret'd) Faruq Khan
Minister of Jute and Textiles: Abdul Latid Siddiqui
Minister of Local Government, Rural Development and Co-operatives: Syed Ashraful Islam
Minister of Education: Nurul Islam Nahid
Minister of Expatriates' Welfare and Overseas Employment: Khandaker Mosharraf Hossain
Minister of Labour and Employment: Rajiuddin Ahmed Raju
Minister of Health and Family Welfare: Dr A. F. M. Ruhul Haque
Minister of Social Welfare: Enamul Huq Mustafa Shahid
Minister of Shipping: Shahkahan Khan
Minister of Posts and Telecommunications: Shahara Khatun
Minister of Communications: Obaidul Quader
Minister of Railways: Mujibul Hoque
Minister of Food: Dr Mohammed Abdur Razzaque
Minister of Primary and Mass Education: Dr Mohammad Afsaryl Ameen
Minister of Information and Communication Technology: Mostafa Faruque Mohammad
Minister of Disaster Management and Relief: Abul Hasan Mohmud Ali
Minister of State for the Environment and Forests: Dr Hasan Mahmud
Minister of Communications, Roads and Bridges: Obdaidul Quader
Minister without Portfolio: Suranjit Sen Gupta

Ministries

Government portal: URL: http://www.pmo.gov.bd
Office of the Prime Minister, Old Sangshad Bhaban, Tejgaon, Dhaka - 1000, Bangladesh. Tel: +880 2 811 5100, fax: +880 (0)2 811 3244, e-mail: pm@pmobd.org, URL: http://www.pmo.gov.bd
Ministry of Finance, Bangladesh Secretariat, Bldg 7 (3rd Flr), Dhaka 1000, Bangladesh. Tel: +880 2 861 5950, fax: +880 2 861 5581, URL: http://www.mof.gov.bd/
Ministry of Foreign Affairs, Topkhana Road, Dhaka, Bangladesh. Tel: +880 (0)2 236020, fax: +880 (0)2 411281, e-mail: pspmo@bangla.net, URL: http://www.mofabd.org
Ministry of Agriculture, Bangladesh Secretariat, Bhaban 4, 2nd Storey, Dhaka, Bangladesh. URL: http://www.bangladesh.gov.bd/moa
Ministry of Commerce, Bhaban No. 3, 3rd Floor, Secretariat, Dhaka-1000, Bangladesh. Tel: +880 (0)2 862826, fax: +880 (0)2 865741,
Ministry of Communications, Bhaban No. 7, 8th Floor, Secretariat, Dhaka 1000, Tel: +880 (0)2 862866, fax: +880 (0)2 866636, URL: http://www.moc.gov.bd
Ministry of Defence, Old High Court Building, Dhaka, Bangladesh. Tel: +880 (0)2 259082
Ministry of Education, Bangladesh Secretariat, Bhaban 7, 2nd 9 Storey Building, 6th Floor, Dhaka, Bangladesh. Tel: +880 (0)2 861 1395, fax: +880 (0)2 861 7577
Ministry of Energy and Mineral Resources, Bhaban No. 6, 1st Floor, Secretariat, Dhaka 1000, Bangladesh. Tel: +880 (0)2 866188, fax: +880 (0)2 861110
Ministry of Food, Bangladesh Secretariat, Bhaban 4, 2nd 9 Storey Building, 3rd Floor, Dhaka, Bangladesh. Tel: +880 (0)2 861 6262, fax: +880 (0)2 861 9623, URL: http://www.mofdm.gov.bd
Ministry of Health and Family Welfare, Bangladesh Secretariat, Main Building, 3rd Floor, Dhaka, Bangladesh. Tel: +880 (0)2 861 5515, fax: +880 (0)2 861 9077
Ministry of Home Affairs, School Building, 2nd & 3rd Floor, Bangladesh Secretariat, Dhaka, Bangladesh. Tel: +880 (0)2 861 1155, fax: +880 (0)2 861 9667
Ministry of Industries, 91 Motijheel, Dhaka1 000, Bangladesh. Tel: +880 (0)2 956 7024, fax: +880 (0)2 860588, Telex: 672830
Ministry of Information, Bangladesh Secretariat, 2nd 9 Storey Building, 8th Floor, Dhaka, Bangladesh. Tel: +880 (0)2 235111, URL: http://www.moi-gob.org
Ministry of Labour and Manpower, Bangladesh Secretariat, 1st 9 Storey Building, 4th Floor, Dhaka, Bangladesh. Tel: +880 (0)2 861 8845, fax: +880 (0)2 861 8660
Ministry of Land, Bangladesh Secretariat, Bhaban 4, 2nd 9 Storey Building, 3rd Floor, Dhaka, Bangladesh. Tel: +880 (0)2 861 9644, fax: +880 (0)2 861 2989
Ministry of Local Government, Rural Development and Co-operatives, Bangladesh Secretariat, Bhaban 7, 1st 9 Storey Building, 6th Floor, Dhaka, Bangladesh. Tel: +880 (0)2 861 9176, fax: +880 (0)2 861 4374
Ministry of Liberation and War Affairs: URL: http://www.mlwa.gov.bd
Ministry of Public Works, Bangladesh Secretariat, Main Extension Building, 2nd Floor, Dhaka, Bangladesh.
Ministry of Shipping, Bhaban No. 6, 8th Floor, Secretariat, Dhaka1000, Bangladesh. Tel: +880 (0)2 868033, fax: +880 (0)2 868122
Ministry of Social Welfare and Women's Affairs, Bangladesh Secretariat, Bhaban 5, New Building, Dhaka, Bangladesh.
Ministry of Planning, Block No. 7, Room 7, Sher-e-Banglanager, Dhaka 1000, Bangladesh. Tel: +880 (0)2 686033, fax: +880 (0)2 868122
Ministry of Posts & Telecommunications, Bhaban No. 7, 6th Floor, Secretariat, Dhaka 1000, Bangladesh. Tel: +880 (0)2 832160, fax: +880 (0)2 865755
Ministry of Textiles, Bhaban No. 6, 11th Floor, Secretariat, Dhaka 1000, Bangladesh. Tel: +880 (0)2 867266, fax: +880 (0)2 860600
Ministry of Civil Aviation & Tourism, Bhaban No. 6, 19th Floor, Secretariat, Dhaka 1000, Bangladesh. Tel: +880 (0)2 867244, fax: +880 (0)2 869206
Ministry of Science and Technology, Bangladesh Secretariat, Building 6, 9th Floor, Dhaka 1000, Bangladesh. URL: http://www.most-bd.org
Ministry of Law, Justice and Parliamentary Affairs, Bangladesh Secretariat, Bldg 4 (7th Flr), Dhaka 1000, Bangladesh. Tel: +880 2 861 0577, fax: +880 2 861 8557, URL: http://www.minlaw.gov.bd
Ministry of Liberation War Affairs, Ellenbari, Tejgaon, Dhaka 1215, Bangladesh. Tel: +880 2 913 6420, fax: +880 2 815 3468, e-mail: secmolwa @ bttb.net.bd, URL: http://www.mlwa.gov.bd
Ministry of Planning, Sher-e-Banglanagar, Dhaka 1207, Bangladesh. Tel: +880 2 811 5175, fax: +880 2 811 7581, URL: http://www.bangladesh.gov.bd

Ministry of Post and Telecommunications, Bangladesh Secretariat, Bldg 8 (4th Flr), Dhaka 1000, Bangladesh. Tel: +880 2 861 1155, fax: +880 2 861 9667, URL: http://www.mopt.gov.bd
Ministry of Power, Energy and Mineral Resources, Bangladesh Secretariat, Bldg 6 (1st and 2nd Flrs), Dhaka 1000, Bangladesh. Tel: +880 2 861 9199, fax: +880 2 861 5097, URL: http://www.emrd.gov.bd
Ministry of Religious Affairs, Bangladesh Secretariat, Bldg 8 (2nd Flr), Dhaka 1000, Bangladesh. Tel: +880 2 861 0682, fax: +880 2 861 5040, URL: http://www.mora.gov.bd
Ministry of Science and Technology, Bangladesh Secretariat, Bldg 6 (9th Flr), Dhaka 1000, Bangladesh. Tel: +880 2 861 6484, fax: +880 2 861 9606, e-mail: most@bangla.net, URL: http://www.mosict.gov.bd
Ministry of Shipping, Bangladesh Secretariat, Bldg 6 (8th Flr), Dhaka 1000, Bangladesh. Tel: +880 2 861 8155, fax: +880 2 861 8122, URL: http://www.bangladesh.gov.bd
Ministry of Social Welfare, Bangladesh Secretariat, Dhaka 1000, Bangladesh. URL: http://www.msw.gov.bd
Ministry of Textiles and Jute, Bangladesh Secretariat, Bldg 6 (7th Flr), Dhaka 1000, Bangladesh. Tel: +880 2 861 1643, fax: +880 2 861 8766, URL: http://www.motj.gov.bd
Ministry of Water Resources, Bangladesh Secretariat, Bldg 6 (4th Flr), Dhaka 1000, Bangladesh. Tel: +880 2 861 6500, fax: +880 2 861 2400, URL: http://www.mowr.gov.bd
Ministry of Women's and Children's Affairs, Bangladesh Secretariat, Bldg 6 (2nd and 3rd Flrs), Dhaka 1000, Bangladesh. Tel: +880 2 861 0568, fax: +880 2 861 7550, URL: http://www.mowca.gov.bd
Ministry of Youth, Sports and Cultural Affairs, Bangladesh Secretariat, Bldg 7 (5th Flr), Dhaka 1000, Bangladesh. Tel: +880 2 861 0683, fax: +880 2 861 2344, URL: http://www.moysports.gov.bd

Political Parties
Awami League (AL), 23 Bangabandhu Avenue, Dhaka, Bangladesh. URL: http://www.albd.org/
28 member central executive committee, 15 member central advisory committee and a 13 member presidium. President: Sheikh Hasina (page 1533)
Bangladesh Jatiyatabadi Dal (Bangladesh Nationalist Party-BNP). URL: http://www.bnpbd.com/
Chairman: Khaleda Zia
National Party (NP, allied to the Awami League).

Elections
Parliamentary elections were due in January 2007, but threats of a boycott by the Awami League, who questioned the fairness of the elections, led to violence, a state of emergency and the postponement of elections until late December 2008. The election was won by Sheikh Hasina's Awami League with a landslide victory. The alliance won 250 of the 300 seats in parliament. The Bangladesh Nationalist Party (BNP) headed by Khaleda Zia accepted the result after initially alleging electoral fraud. Outside observers judged the election to be generally fair.

Presidential elections were held in October 2001. Iajuddin Ahmed became president in 2002, having been the only candidate to register. The last presidential elections took place in January 2009; the sole candidate for the presidency was Zillur Rahman, who took office in February 2009.

Diplomatic Representation
British High Commission, United Nations Road, Baridhara, Dhaka, Bangladesh. Tel: +880 (0)2 882 2705, fax: +880 (0)2 882 6181, URL: http://ukinbangladesh.fco.gov.uk/en
High Commissioner: H.E. Robert Winnington Gibson CMG (page 1430)
US Embassy, Consulate Section, GPO Box 323, Dhaka, Bangladesh. Tel: +880 (0)2 884700-722, fax: +880 (0)2 883744, URL: http://dhaka.usembassy.gov
Ambassador: Dan W. Mozena
Embassy of Bangladesh, 2201 Wisconsin Avenue, N.W., Suite 300-325, Washington, DC 20007, USA. Tel: +1 202 342 8372-8376, fax: +1 202 333 4971, e-mail: banglaemb@aol.com, URL: http://www.bdembassyusa.org
Ambassador: Akramul Qader
Bangladesh High Commission, 28 Queen's Gate, London, SW7 5JA, United Kingdom. Tel: +44 (0)20 7584 0081, fax: +44 (0)20 7581 7477, email: bdesh.lon@dial.pipex.com, URL: http://www.bhclondon.org.uk
High Commissioner: Mohamed Mijarul Quayes
Bangladesh High Commission, 56 Ring Road, Lajpat Nagar-III, New Delhi 110024, India. Tel: +91 11 683 4668, fax: +91 11 683 9237, e-mail: Bdoot.del@smy.Sprintrpg.ems.vsnl,net.in
Permanent Mission to the United Nations, 821 United Nations Plaza, 8th Floor, New York, NY 10017, USA. Tel: +1 212 867 3434-37, fax: +1 212 972 4038, e-mail: bgdun@undp.org
Ambassador & Permanent Representative of Bangladesh to the United Nations: Abdulkalam Abdul Momen

LEGAL SYSTEM

The legal system is based in part on English common law and in part on Islamic family law. The judiciary is organised at two levels; a Supreme Court with Appellate and High Court Divisions, and subordinate courts.

The government's human rights record remains poor. During the state of emergency of 2007-08; many fundamental rights, including freedom of expression and freedom of association, were curtailed, and the government banned political activities. Whilst the number of extrajudicial killings by security forces went down, the police and army abused their power, with arbitrary arrests and detentions, and the harassment of journalists. Bangladesh retains the death penalty. At least nine people were executed in 2010 and five in 2011.

Supreme Court: URL: http://www.supremecourt.gov.bd/
Chief Justice: Md. Muzammel Hossain

BANGLADESH

LOCAL GOVERNMENT

The country is divided into seven administrative divisions: Barisal, Dhaka, Chittagong, Rajshahi, Khulna, Sylhet and Rangpur. Each is headed by a Divisional Commissioner. A division has a number of districts, administered by a Deputy Commissioner. There are 64 districts in total. Each district is divided into several *thanas*. A *thana* consists of several *unions*, *mouzas* and *villages*. In each *union* there is a *Union Parishad* responsible and accountable to the local people who acts as the local government at the lowest tier. The Village Council and District Council Bill passed by parliament states that for every three local government wards, one seat is reserved for a woman and women have the right to contest general seats. Local elections were held in 2009.

AREA AND POPULATION

Area

Bangladesh is situated in southern Asia and is bordered by India in the east, north and west, the Bay of Bengal in the south and Myanmar. It covers an area of approximately 147,570 sq. km (56,977 sq. miles), and has more than 355 rivers flowing through it making it very fertile. Bangladesh is generally low lying, flat alluvial plain. The country is more hilly in the south east. Bangladesh is situated on the delta of the rivers Ganges, Meghna and Brahmaputra and is therefore prone to flooding especially in the monsoon season. July 2004 saw the start of some of the worst floods to hit Bangladesh. Around 1,000 people died and more than 30 million people lost their homes or were stranded. The climate is generally tropical with mild winters and hot humid summers. The monsoon season is from June to October.

To view a map, consult http://www.un.org/Depts/Cartographic/map/profile/banglade.pdf

Population

Estimates for 2010 put the country's population at 148.69 million, 72 per cent of which lives in rural areas. The density of 1,198 inhabitants per sq. km is one of the world's highest. The approximate populations of the largest cities are: Dhaka, 11,000,000; Chittagong, 2,800,000; Khulna, 1,800,000; Rajshahi, 1,000,000. Population growth is currently estimated at an average of 1.4 per cent per year over the period 2000-10.

The official language of Bangladesh is Bangla (Bengali) although English is widely spoken.

Births, Marriages and Deaths

Life expectancy at birth was estimated to be 64 years for males and 66 years for females in 2009. Healthy life expectancy was estimated at 56 years for males and 55 for females. The median age was estimated to be 24 years. Approximately 31 per cent of the population is under 15 years old and 7 per cent is over 60 years. (Source: http://www.who.int, World Health Statistics 2012)

Public Holidays 2014

1 January: New Year
21 February: International Mother Language Day
14 January: Birth of the Prophet*
26 March: Independence Day
15 April: Bangla New Year
18 April: Good Friday
21 April: Easter Monday
1 May: Labour Day
17 May: Buddha Purnima
29 July: End of Ramadan*
15 August: National Mourning Day
5 October: Feast of the Sacrifice*
20 October: Evening of Destiny
25 October: Islamic New Year*
7 November: National Revolution Day
16 December: Victory Day
25 December: Christmas Day
26 December: Boxing Day
* Islamic holidays are dependent on the sighting of the moon and therefore can vary.

EMPLOYMENT

Figures for 2003 show that Bangladesh has a workforce of more than 46 million, 22.9 million of whom were employed in the agricultural sector, 4.30 million in the manufacturing sector, 100,000 in mining, and 17.0 million in other areas. Estimated figures for 2007 put the unemployment rate at 2.5 per cent.

In 1995 Bangladesh signed an agreement to outlaw child labour in the garment industry. Due to the size of the Bangladesh population around 2 million people join the workforce every year. A large number of the workforce are employed abroad, particularly in Saudi Arabia, Kuwait, UAE, Oman, Qatar, Malaysia, and Singapore.

In 2005 the government floated the idea of reducing the working week to five days down from six, in an effort to make savings especially on transport and fuel costs.

Figures for 2009 put the unemployment rate at 5.0 per cent.

Employed Persons by Economic Activity in 2005

Occupation	Employed ('000s)
Agriculture, hunting & forestry	21,672
Fishing	1,095
Mining & quarrying	51
Manufacturing	5,224

- continued

Electricity, gas & water supply	7
Construction	1,52
Wholesale & retail trade, repairs	7,10
Hotels & restaurants	71
Transport, storage & communications	3,97
Financial intermediation	50
Real estate, renting & business activities	23
Public admin. & defence	88
Education	1,30
Health & social work	36
Other community social & personal services	2,62
Households with employed persons	47,35
Unemployed	2,10

Source: Copyright © International Labour Organization (ILO Dept. of Statistics, http://laborsta.ilo.org)

BANKING AND FINANCE

Currency

One Taka (Tk) =100 Paisas

GDP/GNP, Inflation, National Debt

Bangladesh is one of the world's poorest and most populated countries. The economy i primarily agriculture-based but there can be adverse climatic conditions with periodic floodin and droughts. However, there are believed to be substantial reserves of gas. The infrastructur needs development. Aid has been provided with the aim of supporting the government economic reforms. However there are still concerns over the level of corruption in the countr and the speed of reforms.

GDP growth has been adversely affected in recent years by floods. Growth of 5.5 per cen was achieved in 2000 and an estimated 5.9 per cent in 2001. Predictions of a 6.0 per cen rise for 2005 had to be revised down to 4.8 per cent, following devastating floods in Ju and August 2004. The agricultural sector and infrastructure were particularly badly hit. GD growth was estimated at 6 per cent in 2008, 5.7 per cent in 2009 and 6 per cent in 2010 GDP was estimated at US$103 billion in 2010 and US$110 billion in 2011. GDP is forecas to grow at 5.8 per cent in 2013.

15 years ago agriculture made up half of the GDP. Now it represents about 19 per cent, wit industry contributing 29 per cent, and commercial services making up the remainder. As th agriculture sector declines many Bangladeshis having been seeking work abroad not alway legally. In an effort to diversify the economy, industrial development has become a governmen priority. It is also hoped that recent discoveries of oil and gas off shore will boost the econom although whether the reserves will be used for domestic use or used for export is still unde discussion.

The following table shows the make up of GDP at current market prices (figures in billio Taka):

Industry	2008	2009	2010
Agriculture	999.9	1,112.3	120.
Mining	61.5	70.9	82.
Manufacturing	939.0	1,064.5	1,192.
Utilities	60.7	65.4	71.
Construction	438.5	501.3	563.
Trade	782.2	882.8	988.
Transport & communications	569.1	642.8	713.
Finance	89.5	102.5	116.
Public admin.	144.3	163.6	190.
Others	1,175.0	1,333.3	1,512.
Net factor income from abroad	483.9	559.0	657.
GDP by industrial origin	5,458.2	6,147.9	6,923.
GNI at current market prices	5,942.1	6,706.9	7,571.

Source: Asian Development Bank

Inflation was estimated at 8 per cent in 2010.

Total external debt was estimated at US$23.5 billion in 2008.

Foreign Investment

The government has tried to implement several policy reforms designed to create a more favourable conditions for foreign and doemstic investment. Ithas liberalized its trade regime and reformed tariffs. Its privatisation programme has also opened up opportunities for foreign investment. The UK is Bangladesh's largest aid donor (£1 billion in the period 2011-15).

Bangladesh also receives aid from the IMF and World Bank. In November 1998 the Worl Bank made a US$200 million credit available to aid flood recovery, and the Asian Developmen Bank also made a loan of over US$100 million. Bad flooding was again recorded in Augus 2000. In June 2003 the International Monetary Fund approved the granting of a Povert Reduction and Growth Facility worth US$490 million. To secure this loan facility Banglades had to change from an exchange rate pegged to the US dollar to a managed floatin exchange, and this came into effect in May 2003. The IMF also agreed a US$987 million loa in 2012 under its Extended Credit Facility.

Balance of Payments / Imports and Exports

The following tables show the Bangladesh trade balance and the cost of selected imports and exports (figures in billion Taka):

External Trade	2008	2009	2010
Exports, fob	968.0	1071.9	1123.5
Imports, cif	1,483.7	1558.7	1642.4
Trade balance	-515.7	-486.8	-518.9

Exports by HSC	2005	2006	2007
Animals & animal products	26.5	30.4	38.6
Textile & textile products	371.4	455.7	583.6
Hides & skin	13.6	16.6	18.5
Vegetable products	3.0	5.1	5.0
Prepared foodstuffs	1.8	2.2	2.6
Mineral products	2.0	3.6	4.4
Footwear, headgear	4.9	6.0	7.3
Base metals & articles thereof	3.4	3.4	6.8

Imports by HSC	2005	2006	2007
Textile & textile articles	166.2	204.6	236.9
Machinery & mechanical	133.2	150.9	199.1
Appliances			
Transportation equipment	44.0	46.7	60.5
Mineral products	77.2	127.3	95.8
Vegetable products	66.7	62.4	82.2
Chemical products	62.4	74.9	83.3
Animal & animal products	6.3	6.1	7.3
Base metals & articles thereof	41.9	65.9	68.0
Wood pulp products	15.0	19.0	21.4

Source: Asian Development Bank

The main destinations for Bangladesh's exports are the USA (US$3,945.8 million in 2010), Germany (US$2,143 million), the UK (US$1,375 million), France, Italy and the Netherlands. Imported goods come mainly from China (US$6,133 million in 2010), India US$3,253 million), Singapore (US$1,796 million), Japan, Hong Kong and South Korea.

Central Bank
Bangladesh Bank, PO Box 325, Motijheel Commercial Area, Dhaka, Bangladesh. Tel:+880 (0)2 955 5000-19, fax: +880 (0)2 956 6212 , e-mail: BanglaBank@Bangla.Net, URL: http://www.bangladesh-bank.org
Governor: Dr. Atiur Rahman

Trade Organisations
Federation of Bangladesh Chambers of Commerce and Industry, URL: http://www.fbcci-bd.org

MANUFACTURING, MINING AND SERVICES

Primary and Extractive Industries
Petrobangla, the state-owned holding corporation, is the sponsoring agency for oil, gas and mining activities in the country. In recent years foreign oil companies such as Shell, Texaco and Holland Sea Search have been working with Petrobangla in exploration work. As of 1 January 2011 Bangladesh had proven oil reserves of 30.0 million barrels, and produced 5,720 barrels per day, of which 5,000 barrels per day was crude oil. Consumption was 110,000 barrels per day.

About 1.5 million tons of crude oil is imported by Bangladesh Petroleum Corporation (BPC), which is refined in the refinery at Chittagong. Bangladesh has a refining capacity of 33,000 billion barrels per day.

Proved reserves of natural gas were 7 trillion cubic feet in 2011, although recent exploration has led estimates to be revised up to 80 trillion cubic feet. Natural gas production is in 2010 was 703 billion cubic feet the same as consumption..

Mining of limestone and china clay is carried out in Bangladesh, 31,000 tonnes of limestone was produced in 2007 and 19,000 tonnes of china clay.

There are thought to be 3.3 billion tonnes of coal reserves and the country is researching the construction of coal-firing power plants.

Energy
Most of Bangladesh's power supplies come from old gas-fired plants. There are daily shortages and the poor energy infrastructure is being blamed for hindering growth. Roughly 50 per cent of rural domestic energy in the country comes from wood. Hydroelectricity is generated locally, and at present about 500 million cubic feet per day of gas is being used through an approximately 1,000 km long gas transmission system. Figures for 2010 show that 39.7 billion kWh of electricity was produced, mainly from natural gas, with the remainder coming from oil or hydro sources. 38.8 billion kWh was consumed. Total energy consumption was estimated to be 0.9 quadrillion Btu. in 2009.

In November 2011 Bangladesh announced it had signed a deal with Russia to build two nuclear power plants each with a capacity of 1000 MW. Construction is scheduled to start in 2013 and should be completed by 2018. Russia is to supply technical support, funding and fuel. The power stations are being constructed to address Bangladesh's energy shortfalls; the country currently has a daily electricuty shortfall of about 2,000 MW. The cost was estimated to be around US$2 billion, and is scheduled to begin operating by 2018.

Manufacturing
The main industrial activities involve jute products such as sacking, textiles, paper and carpet backing; Bangladesh produces one quarter of the world's jute. Other industries include the manufacture of leather goods, chemicals, textiles, including ready made garments and sugar. In order to attract foreign investment in manufacturing industries the government has set up export processing zones and tax concessions for industries particularly suited to export. The government is also preparing to privatise some state owned businesses. Industrial production showed a growth of 7.2 per cent in 2003. The following table shows manufacturing production in recent years. Figures are in thousand metric tonnes:

Product	2005	2006	2007
Fertilizer compound	2,102	1,927	1,982
Cement	2,943	3,211	3,439
Sugar	107	133	162
Jute goods	275	255	263
Soyabean oil	53	63	67
Cotton yarn	104	121	156
Paper	24	26	23

Source: Asian Development Bank

Tourism
Recent figures show that around 200,000 people visit Bangladesh per year, generating around US$80 million.
Bangladesh Parjatan Corporation (National Tourism Organisation), URL: http://www.parjatan.org

Agriculture
The economy of Bangladesh is still predominantly agricultural, and accounts for around 18 per cent of GDP. Rural development has been assigned priority in the framework of the overall economic development programme, including development of agriculture through irrigation, drainage facilities and small flood control measures.

20.16 million acres of land are cultivated, of which 9.69 million hectares is arable and permanently cropped land, and 600,000 hectares is permanent pasture.

Jute and tea are the main cash crops although rice production is increasing and is the staple food of Bangladesh. Non-traditional crops such as wheat, potato and pulses have been successful. Sugar cane, tobacco, pulses, spices and cotton are also grown, although repeated natural disasters, such as the severe floods in 1998 and 2004, have necessitated emergency food imports. Bangladesh is prone to floods but after each flood a deposit of nutrient-rich silt is left behind which can boost agricultural production. Livestock and the exports of hides, skins and related products also form a large part of the agricultural economy.

The agricultural sector was severely hit by the devastating floods in 2004, when more than a million hectares of crops were destroyed as well as large scale loss of livestock.

Agricultural Production in 2010

Produce	Int. $'000	Tonnes
Rice, paddy	12,926,461	50,061,200
Potatoes	1,265,014	7,930,000
Goat milk, whole fresh	837,608	2,496,000
Mangoes, mangosteens, guavas	627,837	1,047,850
Indigenous cattle meat	510,657	189,036
Indigenous goat meat	457,892	191,100
Fruit, tropical fresh nes	447,292	1,094,500
Jute	340,018	1,200,600
Cow milk, whole, fresh	258,886	829,600
Vegetables fresh nes	243,089	1,290,000
Bananas	230,446	818,254
Indigenous chicken meat	228,092	160,131

Source: http://faostat.fao.org/site/339/default.aspx Food and Agriculture Organization of the United Nations, Food and Agricultural commodities production

Fishing
The fisheries sub-sector contributes about 3.5 percent to the GDP and about 12 per cent to the national export earning. About 1.2 million people are directly engaged in activities related to the fisheries, with about 10 million people indirectly related. The inland fisheries of the country cover some 4.5 million hectares. Estimated figures for 2010 put the total catch for Bangladesh at 1.726,585 tonnes.

COMMUNICATIONS AND TRANSPORT

Travel Requirements
A passport valid for three months after departure is required by citizens of the USA, Canada, Australia and the EU, as is a visa. Citizens of countries where there is a Bangladesh Mission must obtain a visa before going to Bangladesh. Some tourist and business travellers who do not have a mission for Bangladesh in their country of origin can obtain 30-day visas (for business and investment purposes) on arrival, provided they hold a letter of invitation from a company based in Bangladesh. All travellers to Bangladesh are advised to contact the embassy to check exact requirements.

National Airlines
Biman Bangladesh Airlines, URL: http://www.bangladeshonline.com/biman/

International Airports
Dhaka-Zia International Airport (URL: http://www.dhakaairport.com/index.html), Dhaka, Chittagong and Sylhet. There are eight other airports at Barisal, Comilla, Cox's Bazar, Ishurdi, Jessore, Rajshahi, Syedpur and Thakurgaon. Several companies provide domestic flights including, Aero Bengal Airlines, Air Parabat, Bengal Airlift LTD, Biman Bangladesh Airlines (BG) and GMG Airlines.

BANGLADESH

Railways
Bangladesh has about 2,750 km of railroad, with 502 stations. Express trains run between the main cities. In 2008 the rail link between Bangladesh and India was re-opened and trains run twice a week between Dhaka and Kolkata.
Bangladesh Railway, Rail Bhaban, Abdul Ghani Road, Dhaka 1000, Bangladesh. Tel: +880 (0)2 956 1200, fax: +880 (0)2 864370

Roads
There are over 200,000 km of road and it is estimated that around 70 per cent of passenger travel and transportation of cargo is by road. Vehicles are driven on the left. In 1998 the Bangabandhu Bridge was opened over the Jamuna River, connecting east and west Bangladesh. It is 4.8 km long, and carries road and rail transport, as well as electricity, a natural gas pipeline and telecommunication links. Bus links connect Bangladesh to India, Dhaka to Kolkata, Dhaka to Siliguri and Dhaka to Agartala.

Shipping
Bangladesh Shipping Corp, BSC Bhaban, Saltgola Road, P.O. Box 641, Chittagong 4100, Bangladesh. Tel: +880 (0)31 505062, +880 (0)31 710506, Telex: 66277; 24 vessels.
Bangladesh Inland Water Transport Corp 5 Dilkusha Commercial Area, Dhaka 1000, Bangladesh. Tel: +880 (0)2 257092; 273 vessels.
During the monsoon season there are about 8,372 km of navigable waterways. This goes down to about 5,200 in the dry season.

Ports and Harbours
The two seaports of Bangladesh are Chittagong and Mongla. There are eight river ports and six terminals including Dhaka, Narayanganj, Chandpur, Barisal and Khulna. There are roughly 8,433 km of perennial and seasonal waterways. Ferry services run between ports on the south coast and the Ganges River delta, there is also a regular ferry between Dhaka and Khulna.
Chittagong Port Authority, P.O. Box 2013, Chittagong 4100, Bangladesh. Tel: +880 (0)31 505041, Telex: 66264

HEALTH

Health care is provided through union and Thana health clinics, district hospitals and medical college hospitals. In 2005-10 there were 43,315 physicians (3 per 10,000 population), 39,992 nurses and midwives (2.7 per 10,000 population), 2,742 dentists, an estimated 9,411 pharmacists (0.06 per 1,000 population), and 6,091 public and environmental health workers (0.04 per 1,000 population). In 2005-11 there were 3 hospital beds and 0.1 per psychiatric beds per 10,000 population. In 2009, total expenditure on health as a percentage of GDP was 3.4 per cent, equating to a per capita total expenditure of US$21. Government expenditure makes up 33.0 per cent of total expenditure on health. Almost all private expenditure on health is out-of-pocket.

In 2008, 85 per cent of the urban population and 78 per cent of the rural population had access to an improved water source. An estimated 56 per cent of the population had sustainable access to improved sanitation in 2010.

Contraceptive prevalence rate is now at 50.9 per cent, reducing population growth rate to below 2 per cent. The infant mortality rate was 38 per 1,000 live births in 2010 and the child mortality rate was 48 per 1,000 live births. The maternal mortality rate is estimated at 340 per 100,000 population. The most common causes of death for children aged less than 5 years according to 2010 figures, were prematurity (29 per cent), birth asphyxia (14 per cent), diarrhoea (6.0 per cent), pneumonia (14 per cent), measles (1 per cent) and injuries (6 per cent). The immunization rates for common diseases such as measles is now approximately 95 per cent. Approximately 43.2 per cent of children aged five or less were considered stunted in the period 2005-11.

In 2010, there were 91,227 reported cases of malaria, 3,848 of leprosy, 788 of measles and 710 of tetanus. (Source: http://www.who.int, World Health Statistics, 2012)

EDUCATION

Primary education (for ages five to nine) is free whilst most secondary schools (ages 10-14) and higher secondary schools (ages 15-24) are private, although they are often government subsidised. Approximately 84 per cent of relevant age groups are enrolled in primary education. Ninety-five per cent go onto secondary education.

Children can attend one year of pre-primary education at age five. Primary school starts at age six and lasts for five years. The pupil: teacher ratio was put at 45:1 in 2007. Secondary school starts at age 11 and lasts for seven years.

There are 11 government and 18 non-government universities in the country. There are 13 government and five non-government medical colleges, four engineering colleges, 2,845 colleges, 20 polytechnic institutes, 12,553 secondary schools, and 78,595 primary schools.

There is also a parallel system known as Madrasah that offers Islamic education up to post-graduate level.

The adult literacy rate for 15 years plus is 58.7 per cent for males and 48.0 per cent for females (2007). In the age group 15 to 24 years it was 71.1 per cent and 73.2 per cent respectively. (Source: UNESCO)

RELIGION

About 89 per cent of the population is Muslim. Three other major religions are Hinduism (9 per cent), Buddhism (0.65 per cent) and Christianity (0.52 per cent).

Bangladesh has a religious tolerance rating of 2 on a scale of 1 to 10 (10 is most freedom). (Source: World Religion Database)

COMMUNICATIONS AND MEDIA

Press freedom is guaranteed in principle by the constitution but some harassment of journalists has been reported. The main broadcasters are state-owned and there is little coverage of the political opposition.

Newspapers
There are more than 1,000 newspapers and periodicals including 286 daily papers in the country. Total circulation of newspapers exceeds 2 million. Both Bangla and English language dailies are widely read. The government closed down state-owned newspapers in 1997 in line with the privatisation policy.
Bangladesh Sangbad Sangstha (National News Agencies), URL: http://www.bssnews.net/
Bangladesh Observer, URL: http://www.bangladeshobserveronline.com
Dainik Ittefaq, URL: http://www.ittefaq.com
Daily Star, URL: http://www.thedailystar.net
The New Nation, URL: http://nation.ittefaq.com

Broadcasting
Radio Bangladesh and Bangladesh Television (BTV) are state-owned. Television is the most popular medium, especially in urban areas. BTV is the only terrestial TV Channel. State-run radio covers most of the country. Bangladesh Betar (Radio) now has ten regional stations and reaches 60 million listeners. Its external service broadcasts in seven languages.
Betar Bangladesh, URL: http://www.betar.org.bd/
Bangladesh Television (BTV), URL: http://www.btv.com.bd/

The official news agency is Bangladesh Sangbad Sangstha, URL: http://www.bssnews.net/

Telecommunications
There are an estimated 1.4 million landlines, approximately 1 per 100 people. As of 2009, it was estimated that Bangladesh currently has 45 million mobile phone users. There were an estimated 500,000 internet users as of 2008. This represents 0.3 per cent of the population.

ENVIRONMENT

Deforestation, destruction of wetlands and depletion of soil nutrients result in environmental problems in Bangladesh. These problems are exacerbated by over population and a lack of environmental awareness. Bangladesh has also been beset with natural disasters like floods, cyclones and tidal bores which lead to severe socio-economic and environmental damage. In July 2004, Bangladesh was hit by the worst flooding for several years resulting in the deaths of 300 people and affecting hundreds of thousands of others and in November 2007, Cyclone Sidr hit, killing thousands of people.

Environment Courts have been set up recently to take action against environmental pollution. The Environment Conservation Rules 1997 was also passed as a means of controlling pollution. According to the EIA, in 2010, Bangladesh's emissions from the consumption of fossil fuels totalled 56.74 million metric tons of carbon dioxide.

Bangladesh is party to the following conventions: Climate Change, Climate Change-Kyoto Protocol, Desertification, Endangered Species, Environmental Modification, Hazardous Wastes, Law of the Sea, Ozone Layer Protection, Ship Pollution, and Wetlands.

SPACE PROGRAMME

The Bangladesh Space Research and Remote Sensing Organization (SPARRSO) was founded in 1980 as an autonomous R&D organization of the government. It acts as the centre of excellence for the peaceful application of space science, remote sensing and GIS. It collaborates with other national, regional and international organizations and advised the government on space technology.
SPARRSO, URL: http://www.sparrso.gov.bd/intro.html

BARBADOS

Capital: Bridgetown (Population estimate: 140,000)

Head of State: H.M. Queen Elizabeth II (page 1420)

Governor General: H.E. Elliot Belgrave (page 1386)

National Flag: Three equal stripes of blue, gold and blue. A black trident is superimposed onto the gold band

CONSTITUTION AND GOVERNMENT

Constitution
A new constitution came into being in November 1966 when Barbados became an independent sovereign state. The legislature consists of the Governor-General (representing the British monarch), a Senate and a House of Assembly. The Governor-General appoints the Prime Minister, and, on his advice, appoints other ministers to become members of the Cabinet. In May 1995 the government formed a ten-member commission to advise on future reform of the constitution and political institutions. Whilst the Queen is presently head of state, a referendum, to be held in the future, is expected to establish Barbados as a republic headed by a ceremonial president.

To consult the full constitution, please visit: http://www.gov.bb

International Relations
Barbados is an active member of CARICOM and has good relations with all its CARICOM neighbours. There was a dispute between Barbados and Trinidad and Tobago about the location of a sea border. The dispute went to arbitration and, in April 2006, the ruling went mainly in Barbados' favour. As a result Barbados began oil exploration.

Recent Events
In March 2009 PM David Thompson survived a no-confidence vote over his handling of the country's financial crisis. Prime Minister David Thompson died in office on 23 October 2010, he had reshuffled his cabinet in September reducing his responsibilities due to illness. Deputy prime minister Freundel Stuart was sworn in as prime minister on the same day.

Lower House
The House of Assembly consists of 30 members elected every five years by adult suffrage. In 1963 the voting age was reduced to 18. The cabinet consists of the Prime Minister and not less than five other ministers appointed by the Governor-General on the advice of the Prime Minister.
House of Assembly, Parliament Buildings, Bridgetown, Barbados. Tel: +1 246 436 3712, fax: +1 246 436 4143, URL: http://www.parliamentbarbados.gov.bb

Upper House
The Senate is comprised of 21 members. Of these, 14 are appointed on the advice of the Prime Minister, two on the advice of the Leader of the Opposition, and the other seven by the Governor-General alone. Senators serve a five year term.
Senate, Parliament Buildings, Bridgetown, Barbados. Tel: +1 246 426 5331, fax: +1 246 436 4143, URL: http://www.barbadosparliament.com/the_senate.php

Cabinet (as at July 2013)
Prime Minister: Freundel Stuart (page 1521)
Minister of Home Affairs and Attorney General: Adriel Brathwaite
Minister of Foreign Affairs and Foreign Trade: Maxine McClean
Minister of Social Care, Constituency Empowerment, & Community Development: Steven Blackett
Minister of Housing, Lands and Rural Development: Denis Kellman
Minister of Tourism and International Transport: Richard Sealy
Minister of Education, and Human Resource Development: Ronald Jones
Minister of Finance and Economic Affairs: Christopher Sinckler
Minister of Transport and Works: Michael Lashley
Minister of Agriculture, Food, Fisheries, Industry and Small Business Development: David Eastwick
Minister of Culture, Youth Affairs and Sports: Stephen Lashley
Minister of Health: John Boyce
Minister of Environment, Water Resources and Drainage: Denis Lowe
Minister of Industry, International Business, Commerce and Small Business Development: Donville Inniss
Minister of Labour: Esther Byer-Suckoo
Minister in the Office of the Prime Minister: Darcy Boyce
Minister of State in the Office of the Prime Minister: Patrick Todd
Parliamentary Secretary in the Ministry of Tourism and International Transport: Mrs Irene Sandiford-Garner
Parliamentary Secretary in the Ministry of Finance and Economic Affairs: Jepter Ince
Parliamentary Secretary in the Ministry of Education, Science, Technology and Innovation: Harry Husbands

Ministries
Office of the Prime Minister, Government Headquarters, Bay St, St Michael, Barbados. Tel: +1 246 436 3179, fax: +1 246 436 9280, URL: http://www.primeminister.gov.bb/
Ministry of Finance and Economic Affairs, Government Headquarters, Bay St, St Michael, Barbados. Tel: +1 246 426 2814, fax: +1 809429 4032, URL: http://www.barbadosbusiness.gov.bb/
Ministry of Tourism, Sherbourne Conference Centre, 2 Mile Hill, St. Michael, Barbados. Tel: +1 246 430 7500, URL: http://www.barmot.gov.bb/

Ministry of International Transport, Port Authority Building, University Row, St. Michael, Bridgetown, Barbados. Tel: +1 246 427 5163
Ministry of Foreign Affairs, Foreign Trade and International Business, 1 Culloden Rd., St Michael, Barbados. Tel: +1 246 429 7108, fax: +1 246 429 6652, URL: http://www.foreign.gov.bb/
Ministry of Home Affairs, Level 5, General Post Office Building, Cheapside, Bridgetown, St. Michael, Barbados. Tel: +1 246 228 8950, fax: +1 246 437 3794
Office of the Attorney General, Sir Frank Walcott Building, Culloden Road, St. Michael, Barbados. Tel +1 246 431 7750
Ministry of Agriculture and Rural Development, Graeme Hall, Christ Church, Barbados. Tel: +1 246 428 4061, fax: +1 246 420 8444, URL: http://www.barbados.gov.bb/bgis.htm
Ministry of Environment and Energy, Sir Frank Walcott Building, Culloden Road, St. Michael, Barbados. +1 246 426 5080 , URL: http://environment.gov.bb/
Ministry of Education, Youth Affairs and Culture, Dame Elsie Payne Complex, Constitution Road, St. Michael, Barbados. Tel: +1 246 426 5416, fax: +1 246 436 2411, URL: http://www.mes.gov.bb/pageselect.cfm?page=101/
Ministry of Health, Jemmotts Lane, St. Michael, Barbados. Tel: +1 246 426 4669, fax: +1 246 426 5570, URL: http://www.mha.gov.bb/
Ministry of Labour, Sports, and Public Sector Reform, National Insurance Building, Fairchild Street, Bridgetown, St. Michael, Barbados. Tel: +1 246 427 2326, fax: +1 246 426 8959, URL: http://labour.gov.bb/blmis2/default.asp
Ministry of Public Works, and Transport, The Pine, St. Michael, Barbados. Tel: +1 246 429 3495, fax: +1 246 437 8133, URL: http://www.publicworks.gov.bb
Ministry of Commerce, Consumer Affairs and Business Development, Reef Road, Fontabelle, St. Michael, Barbados. Tel: +1 246 426 4452, fax: +1 431 0056, URL: http://www.commerce.gov.bb/
Ministry of Housing and Lands, Sir Frank Walcott Building, Culloden Road, St. Michael, Barbados. Tel: +1 246 431 7600, URL: http://housing.gov.bb/

Elections
Elections held in January 2008 was won by the opposition Democratic Labour Party led by David Thomson. The DLP took 20 seats in parliament and the BLP 10. The most recent elections took place in February 2013, the DLP retained power.

Political Parties
Barbados Labour Party, Grantley Adams House, 111 Roebuck Street, Bridgetown, Barbados. Tel: +1 246 429 1990, URL: http://blp.org.bb
Leader: Rt. Hon.Owen Arthur
Democratic Labour Party, George Street, Belleville, St Michael, Barbados. Tel: +1 246 429 3104, fax: +1 246 429 3104, URL: http://www.dlpbarbados.org/cms
Leader: Freundel Stuart (page 1521)

Diplomatic Representation
British High Commission, Lower Collymore Rock, PO Box 676, Bridgetown, Barbados. Tel: +1 246 430 7800 fax: +1 246 430 7851, URL: http://ukinbarbados.fco.gov.uk/en/
High Commissioner: Paul Brummell (page 1396)
US Embassy, Canadian Imperial Bank of Commerce Building, Broad Street, Bridgetown, PO Box 302, Barbados. Tel: +1 246 436 4950, fax: +1 246 429 5246, URL: http://barbados.usembassy.gov
Ambassador: Larry L. Palmer (page 1492)
High Commission of Barbados, 1 Great Russell Street, London, WC1B 3JY, United Kingdom. Tel: +44 171 631 4975, fax: +44 171 323 6872, e-mail: london@foreign.gov.bb
High Commissioner: Hugh Arthur
Embassy of Barbados, 2144 Wyoming Avenue, NW Washington DC 20008, USA. Tel: +1 202 939 9200, fax: +1 202 332 7467
Ambassador: John E. Beale
Permanent Mission to the United Nations, 820 Second Avenue, 9th Floor New York, N.Y. 10017, USA. Tel: +1 212 551 4300
Perm. Representative: Joseph Goddard

LEGAL SYSTEM

The legal system comprises the Magistrates Court, a High Court and a Court of Appeal. Magistrates Courts deal with lesser offences. The High Court and the Court of Appeal comprise the Supreme Court of Judicature. Each appeal court consists of four judges. Judges of the Supreme Court are appointed by the governor acting on recommendations of the prime minister. The leader of the opposition is also consulted. The final court of appeal was Her Majesty's Privy Council in London, but this was replaced by the Caribbean Court of Justice in 2005.

In general, the government of Barbados respects the human rights of its citizens. Barbados retains the death penalty.

Supreme Court, URL: http://www.lawcourts.gov.bb/Supreme.html
Chief Justice: The Hon. Mr Justice Marston Gibson

Office of the Ombudsman, Trident House, Lower Broad Street, Bridgetown, Barbados. Tel: +1 246 436 8179, fax: +1 246 426 4444

BARBADOS

LOCAL GOVERNMENT

The former locally elected government bodies were abolished in 1967 and replaced by eleven parishes and the city of Bridgetown, each under the control of central government. The parishes are: Christ Church, Saint Andrew, Saint George, Saint James, Saint John, Saint Joseph, Saint Lucy, Saint Michael, Saint Peter, Saint Philip, and Saint Thomas.

AREA AND POPULATION

Area
Barbados is the most easterly of the Caribbean islands. It is nearly 21 miles long, 14 miles wide and covers an area of about 430 sq. km. The land is mainly flat with low hills in the interior. In the north-east the hills are higher, up to 340 metres. The island is surrounded by coral reefs. The climate is tropical with a rainy season from June to October.

To view a map, consult http://www.lib.utexas.edu/maps/cia08/barbados_sm_2008.gif

Population
The population in 2010 was estimated to be 273,000, with a density of 625 inhabitants per sq. km. The annual population growth rate is estimated at 0.2 per cent. An estimated 44 per cent of the population live in urban areas. Over 80 per cent of the population are of African descent and around 4 per cent are of European descent. The median age is 37 years. Approximately 17 per cent of the population is aged less than 15 years and 16 per cent over 60 years. The official language is English. A local Bajan dialect is also spoken.

Births, Marriages, Deaths
According to recent estimates, the birth rate has gone down to 10.9 per 1,000 population in 2010 from 13.6 per 1,000 population in 2001, whilst the crude death rate has stayed relatively stable at 8.8 per 1,000 inhabitants. The total fertility rate was estimated to be 1.6 births per female in 2008. The adolescent fertility rate is estimated at 51 per cent. The infant mortality rate is 17 per 1,000 inhabitants.

According to 2009 estimates, life expectancy at birth is estimated at 76 years (73 for males and 80 years for females). Healthy life expectancy is estimated at 67 years (65 years for males and 69 years for females). (Source: http://www.who.int, World Health Statistics 2012)

Public Holidays 2014
1 January: New Year's Day
21 January: Errol Barrow Day
18 April: Good Friday
21 April: Easter Monday
28 April: National Heroes' Day
1 May: Labour Day
9 June: Whit Monday
1 August: Emancipation Day
2 August: Kadooment Day
30 November: Independence Day
25 December: Christmas Day
26 December: Boxing Day

EMPLOYMENT

Figures for 2004 put the work force at 146,300. The majority are employed in the community, social and personal services sector. The sugar industry, once the largest industry, is now in decline and employs around 800. Figures for 2008 put the workforce at 143,800 with an unemployment rate at 8.1 per cent (11,600 people), compared to 9.8 per cent in 2004 and 10.6 in 2003.

Workforce employed by Sector, 2004

Sector	Workforce
Agriculture	4,400
Manufacturing	7,600
Electricity, gas & water	1,800
Construction	13,400
Wholesale & retail, restaurants & hotels	19,600
Transport, storage & communications	5,200
Finance, insurance & personnel services	56,400
Other	12,200

Source: International Labour Organization

BANKING AND FINANCE

Currency
1 Barbados Dollar = 100 cents

GDP/GNP, Inflation, National Debt
The economy used to be dominated on sugar cultivation but it has diversified into tourism and light industry. A deep recession in the 1980s was marked by the decline of the tourist industry. The economy recovered in the 1990s and was further boosted by government economic programmes. In 2001 the Prime Minister did away with the traditional budget speech and instead presented the Economic Programme. The key points included a new telecommunications regime to end the monopoly of Cable and Wireless & legislation to provide regulations of e-commerce and internet access. Following a sustained period of growth in the 1990s, the economy, especially the tourism sector, slowed following the events

of September 11 2001. Subsequent investment in construction and the development of top-end tourism stimulated growth. However, the global economic crisis caused a decline in the luxury tourism market.

In 2010, GDP (market prices) was estimated to be $8,500 million, down from $8,800 million in 2009. GDP per capita was estimated to be US$13,500 in 2009.

The service sector contributes 76 per cent of GDP from the tourist, banking and data processing industries. The agriculture sector has declined recently and contributes 4 per cent of GDP, of which 2.5 per cent comes from sugar. Manufacturing and construction contribute 17 per cent, mainly from food and beverages, textiles, paper and chemicals.

Figures for 2010 show that national debt was estimated to be $7,900 million, over 95 per cent of GDP.

Inflation was estimated at 5.5 per cent in 2007.

Balance of Payments / Imports and Exports
Estimated figures for 2010 show that exports earned US$470 million, up from U$440 million in 2009, and the cost of merchandise imports rose to approximately US$2,400 million, down from US$2,700 million in 2009. The main exports markets and import suppliers are the US, other CARICOM countries, UK and Canada.

Central Bank
Central Bank of Barbados, Spry Street, Bridgetown, Barbados. Tel: +1 246 436 6870, fax: +1 246 427 9559, e-mail:hrinfo@centralbank.org.bb, URL: http://www.centralbank.org.bb Governor: Dr DeLisle Worrall

Chambers of Commerce and Trade Organisations
Barbados Chamber of Commerce & Industry, URL: http://bdscham.com
Barbados Investment & Development Corporation, URL: http://www.bidc.com

MANUFACTURING, MINING AND SERVICES

Primary and Extractive Industries
Mining and quarrying account for only one per cent of the GDP. Consequently, minimal mining of natural resources has been undertaken. Sand is extracted for use in building construction and road industries, it is mined for the construction industry from the St. Andrew area, and restrictions are in place to limit ecological damage. Limestone, found over about 370 sq. km of Barbados, is used for cement manufacturing. Production of slaked lime is used for the iron, steel and chemical industries.

Energy
Some crude oil and natural gas is produced. Barbados has crude oil reserves of around 2.5 million barrels and five billion cubic feet of natural gas. Production of oil in 2011 was an estimated 1,000 barrels per day. Barbados does not have its own refinery so its oil is exported to Trinidad for refining and then imported for consumption, Barbados consumes around 9,000 barrels per day of which some 8,000 bb/d are imported. Barbados produces enough natural gas to satisfy local demand but as demand increases, gas will have to be imported to meet needs. The National Petroleum Company distributes the country's natural gas. In 2010 production was estimated at 1.0 billion cubic metres, all of which was consumed domestically. Gas reserves were estimated at 135.8 million cubic metres in 2006.

Large amounts of solar energy are available and have provided a viable substitute for water heating since 1974. Barbados receives one of the highest levels of solar radiation in the world, representing about 5.8 kWh per sq. metre per day, and has made such natural energy commercially available. In comparison, the Barbados Light and Power Company provides 152,000 kW from two generating stations.

Manufacturing
The manufacturing industry, which showed a decline in the 1980s, began to show signs of improvement in the 1990s. Main manufactured goods include food and beverages, textiles, electronic components, paper and chemicals and component assembly for export.

Service Industries
Tourism has taken over from sugar as the main contributor to GDP and has become the main foreign exchange earner. The services sector as a whole accounts for two thirds of the country's economy. Figures for 2000 show that there were 556,000 visitors to Barbados generating receipts of US$745 million. Long stay arrivals were up by 5 per cent and cruise passenger figures were up by 22 per cent. The tourism industry was hit by a downturn in visitors following the September 11 2001 attacks. A government led initiative on marketing the island to the UK and US markets saw visitor numbers begin to rise and by 2006 tourist figures had begun to rise particularly the numbers of cruise ship passengers. In 2006 a new direct flight between Florida in the US and Barbados was established.

Agriculture
Agriculture is well developed. Sugar cane is the main crop, dominating over 7,000 hectares of land and providing about 535,000 metric tons of produce. It is an industry in decline following the fall in the EU offset price which was exacerbated by the strong Euro, further cuts in 2009 and 2010 wer expected. Sugar now only contributes around one per cent of GDP. However, recent years have seen attempts at crop diversification (for example, cotton and cut flowers) and sugar is no longer the primary foreign exchange earner. Root crops now cover over 2,000 hectares of land and include yams, sweet potatoes, pumpkins and carrots. Fruits grown commercially include bananas, guavas, grapefruit, avocados, cherries and limes. Apart from sugar refining the other main agro-industry is rum making. The banana sector also faces cuts in the EU tariff and quota system which is currently being challenged by Ecuador, Colombia and the USA in the World Trade Organisation.

Agricultural Production in 2010

Produce	Int. $'000	Tonnes
Indigenous chicken meat	20,879	14,658
Sugar cane	8,498	258,800
Indigenous pigmeat	4,235	2,755
Cow milk, whole, fresh	2,091	6,701
Hen eggs, in shell	1,850	2,231
String beans	1,049	1,100
Vegetables fresh nes	792	4,200
Fruit, tropical fresh nes	654	1,600
Pulses, nes	544	1,000
Indigenous cattle meat	446	165
Avocados	437	630
Indigenous turkey meat	355	272

Source: http://faostat.fao.org/site/339/default.aspx Food and Agriculture Organization of the United Nations, Food and Agricultural commodities production

Fishing

A gradual increase in the tonnage of fish caught in recent years has led to improved fishing techniques and equipment. In 2004 a disagreement regarding sea borders flared between Barbados and Trinidad and Tobago. Barbados took the dispute to a UN backed tribunal. Estimated figures for 2010 put the total catch for Barbados at 3,269 tonnes.

COMMUNICATIONS AND TRANSPORT

Travel Requirements

British citizens do not require a visa to enter Antigua and Barbuda for visits of up to six months; for longer visits, visa extensions and work permits must be applied for at the Immigration Department, Careenage House, The Wharf, Bridgetown. Citizens of the USA, Canada, Australia and most of the EU do not require a visa for visits of up to six months; people from the Czech Republic, Estonia, Hungary, Lithuania, Poland, Portugal, Slovak Republic and Slovenia require a visa for stays of 28 days and over. Citizens of Latvia require a visa on entry.

Immigration officials may request to see a return ticket or ticket for onward travel. There is a departure tax payable when leaving the country. Nationals of countries other than those mentioned above should contact the High Commission for any further information on visa and entry requirements.

International Airports

Grantley Adams International Airport is owned and operated by the Government of Barbados. Services are provided by many international airlines to European cities, the United States and Caribbean.

National Airlines

Caribbean Airlines, the national airline, ceased operating in 1987.

Roads

The total length of road open for traffic is 1,600 km, of which 1,570 km have an asphalt surface. Vehicles drive on the right. Recent figures show that there are 42,900 private cars on the roads, and over 1,500 hire cars and nearly 1,000 taxis. Buses and passenger carrying mini-vans operate throughout the island.

Shipping

A number of steamship companies operate from Bridgetown Harbour, including Royal Cruise Line, Cunard Lines, Princess Cruises and Royal Caribbean Cruise Lines.
Barbados Shipping & Trading Company Ltd., URL: http://www.bsandtco.com

Ports and Harbours

The deep water Bridgetown Harbour (opened in 1961) has recently been modernised. It now provides berths for 8 ships between 500 and 600 feet in length, and with draughts up to 9.6 metres, including one specially built for bulk-loading sugar. Facilities include a Container Park, able to accommodate up to 3,000 containers, seven straddle carriers and one gantry crane with a 40-ton lifting capacity. The recently refurbished Passenger Terminal offers about 20 duty-free shops.
The Barbados Port Authority, University Row, Princess Alice Highway, Barbados. URL: http://www.barbadosport.com/

HEALTH

In 2009, total expenditure on health was the equivalent of 5.9 per cent of GDP on health care, equating to a per capita expenditure of US$843. Government expenditure represented 58.6 per cent of the expenditure. The remainder was mainly out-of-pocket private expenditure.

According to the latest WHO figures, in the period 2005-10 there are an estimated 489 doctors (18.1 per 10,000 population), 94 dentists (3.5 per 10,000 population) and 1,311 nurses and midwives (48.6 per 10,000 population). In 2000-08 there were 32 hospital beds per 10,000 population. In the period 2005-11 there were 18 hospital beds and 2.8 psychiatric beds per 10,000 population.

In 2010 the infant mortality rate was 17 per 1,000 live births and the child (under 5 years) mortality rate was 20 per 1,000 live births. The main causes of death were congenital abnormalities (31 per cent), prematurity (21 per cent), birth asphyxia (12 per cent) and pneumonia (7 per cent). (Source: http://www.who.int, World Health Statistics 2012)

EDUCATION

Education in Barbados is provided free of charge and is compulsory for pupils aged between 5 and 16. UNESCO figures for 2007 show that 91 per cent of pre-school age children were enrolled at nursery or kindergarten. 97 per cent of girls and 96 per cent of boys of primary school age were enrolled at primary school and 93 per cent of girls and 88 per cent of boys of secondary school age were enrolled at secondary school. In primary school the pupil: teacher ratio was 15:1.

Pupils are prepared for Caribbean Examination Council (CXC) examinations. Erdiston Training College for teachers provides courses for teachers on the island. Further education is provided by the Samual Jackman Prescod Polytechnic, Barbados Community College and The University of the West Indies. In addition, the Barbados Institute of Management and Productivity (BIMAP), offers management and business training. The government's Skills Training Programme, established in 1979, provides locally based vocational training.

In 2007 the government spent an estimated 6.4 per cent of GDP on education.

Literacy is estimated at over 99 per cent. (Source: UNESCO)

RELIGION

The population is mainly Christian (95 per cent) the majority are Protestant and a small percentage are Catholic. Other religions followed include Baha'i (1.4 per cent), Islam (0.89 per cent) and Hinduism (0.38 per cent). An estimated 2 per cent are not religious.

Barbados has a religious tolerance rating of 9 on a scale of 1 to 10 (10 is most freedom). (Source: World Religion Database)

COMMUNICATIONS AND MEDIA

There is freedom of expression. The media is free of censorship and state control.

Newspapers

Newspapers are privately owned.
The Nation, URL: http://www.nationnews.com
Barbados Advocate, URL: http://www.barbadosadvocate.com/

Broadcasting

The government-owned Caribbean Broadcasting Corporation (CBC) founded in 1963, provides programmes for radio and television via CBC Radio and CBC TV. A subscription television service (Multi Choice TV) also provides an additional thirty channels including Cable News Network (CNN). There are several other well established commercial radio channels.
CBC, URL: http://www.cbc.bb/
Caribbean News Agency, URL: http://www.cananews.net/

Telecommunications

Approximately 150,000 main telephone lines were in use (approximately 50 per 100 population) according to 2008 estimates. Recent figures show around 400,000 mobile phones are in use and there are around 190,000 internet users.

ENVIRONMENT

One of the main environmental concerns for Barbados is the pollution of its waters by ships. Soil erosion is another major problem.

In 2010, Barbados' emissions from the consumption of fossil fuels totalled 1.57 million metric tons of carbon dioxide. (Source: EIA)

Barbados is party to the following international agreements: Biodiversity, Climate Change, Climate Change-Kyoto Protocol, Desertification, Endangered Species, Hazardous Wastes, Law of the Sea, Marine Dumping, Ozone Layer Protection, Ship Pollution, and Wetlands.

BELARUS

Republic of Belarus

Respublika Belarus

Capital: Minsk (Population estimate, 2011: 1,864,500)

Head of State: Alexander G. Lukashenko (President) (page 1467)

National Flag: Red with a green strip along the lower edge, and in the hoist a vertical red and white ornamental pattern

CONSTITUTION AND GOVERNMENT

Constitution

Constitutionally, state power is divided into executive, legislative, and judicial branches of government. The supreme standing representative body and the only legislative body is the Supreme Soviet of the Republic of Belarus. The President of Belarus is the head of both the state and the executive power.

In 1922 Belarus became part of the USSR under the name 'Belorussian Soviet Socialist Republic'. The Supreme Soviet declared the republic sovereign in July 1990. At the end of June 1991 the Belorussian Supreme Soviet voted to create the post of directly elected president. The Chairman of the Supreme Soviet, Nikolai Dementei, who had expressed support for the coup of 19 August against the Soviet President Gorbachev, resigned later that month and the Supreme Soviet voted on independence. At the same time the Communist Party of Belorussia resigned from the Communist Party of the Soviet Union, and its property was nationalised. Eventually the Communist Party was suspended.

On 19 September 1991 Belorussia was renamed the 'Republic of Belarus', and Stanislav Shushkevich was elected to the post of Chairman of the Supreme Soviet. In March 1994 a new constitution was introduced. This stipulated that the president had to be elected. In July 1994 Alexander Lukashenko was elected the first President of the Republic of Belarus.

A national referendum held on 24 November 1996 introduced amendments to the 1994 constitution. 84.14 per cent of the total number of the country's electors appeared at the vote. 70.45 per cent of the electors noted in the voters' list (7,346,397 people) endorsed the proposals of the President on amendments and additions to the Constitution, 9.39 per cent endorsed the proposals of the Supreme Soviet. President Lukashenko's first term as President was extended by two years (to 2001) in the referendum, and further extended to 2002 in June 1997. The opposition contested the legitimacy of these extensions and attempted to hold presidential elections in May 1999, when Lukashenko's five-year term should have been coming up for renewal. The EU also indicated in July 1999 that it might not continue to recognise Lukashenko as head of state. Elections were eventually held in September 2001.

Under the current 1994 constitution the head of state is the president, directly elected by universal adult suffrage. The president appoints the chair of the Council of Ministers who is the head of government. The Council of Ministers is accountable to the president, and responsible to the National Assembly.

To consult the full constitution, please visit: http://www.president.gov.by/en/press10669.html

International Relations

The Republic of Belarus was the original signatory to the Commonwealth of Independent States Agreement on 9 December 1991, together with the Russian Federation and the Ukraine, and later signed the Alma Ata Declaration of 21 December 1991. In April 1997 Belarus and Russia signed a joint supreme council to co-ordinate social, economic and military policy. It is chaired in turn by the presidents of each country, both of them holding a veto. In December 1999 Belarus and Russia signed a number of documents which make provisions for a still closer social, economic and financial union between the two countries. The treaty will create a joint supranational body, establishing a joint council of officials to co-ordinate policy. It proposes that Belarus adopt the Russian rouble as legal tender as a single currency in 2005, and harmonise legislation on tax, customs and defence by 2008. The new body is supposed to have limited powers to issue decrees and directives. The leaders of Russia and Belarus will take turns in government.

Since gaining its independence following the collapse of the Soviet Union, Belarus has kept close ties with Russia a policy that President Lukashenko has pursued with talk of a union between the two countries but so far this has come to nothing.

Since 1997 the European Union suspended ministerial and high level contacts with Belarus over concerns on constitution and human rights issues. The EU has expressed its wish to form closer ties with Belarus if democratic and economic reforms are undertaken. In May 2007 Belarus failed to win a seat on the United Nations Human Rights Council. Belarus is a member of the IMF and the World Bank.

Recent Events

After negotiations during which Moscow threatened to cut supplies, a new gas deal was signed with Russia in December 2006, which more than doubled the price of gas and phased in further increases over four years. In January 2007, Russia cut the supply along an oil export pipeline to Europe amid a row with Belarus over taxation and allegations of siphoning. The dispute ended after Russia agreed to cut the oil tax on Belarus. In August 2007 Russian again

said it would reduce gas supplies because of unpaid debts, prompting President Lukashenko in October to announce that Belarus would have to build a nuclear power station to meet the energy needs of the country.

In March 2007, thousands of opposition supporters held a rally in Minsk, calling for an end to President Lukashenko's rule. Tensions arose with the US in 2008. Belarus withdrew its ambassador to the US over disputed sanctions and later asked the US Ambassador, Karen Stewart, to leave amidst allegations of US spy activities. Belarus expelled a further 11 US diplomats in a row over Belarus's human rights record. Relations with the West appeared to start improving in August 2008 when Belarus freed three dissidents including the former opposition presidential candidate Alexander Kozulin. The EU also lifted its travel ban on President Lukashenko in October 2008.

General elections took place in September 2008 when government candidates won all the seats. Opposition parties alleged irregularities & EU observers said that the election did not meet international standards. There have since been several resignations and reshuffles.

The EU lifted its travel ban on President Lukashenko in October 2009.

In January 2010, tensions arose with Russia over energy supplies and Belarus threatened to cut electricity supplies to Russia. An agreement was eventually reached over the amount of duty free oil that Russia would supply to Belarus. The following June President Lukashenko ordered the transit route of gas from Russia to Europe to be shut down after supplies to Belarus were cut because of arguements over debt. Supplies returned to normal after Belarus paid the outstanding debt. In July despite ongoing disputes about Russian duty on oil and gas, Belarus signed a customs union with Russia and Kazakhstan.

In April 2011 a bomb left at a station on the Minsk metro exploded killing 12.

Parliamentary elections were held on September 23 2012, President Lukashenko's supporters won the election which opposition parties claimed were neither free nor fair.

Legislature

The Belarusian Parliament, the National Assembly (*Natsionalnoye Sobranie*), consists of two houses: the House of Representatives (*Palata Predstaviteley*) and the Council of the Republic (*Soviet Respubliki*). Members of both houses serve a four year term.

Upper House

The Council of the Republic consists of 64 members, 56 elected at sittings of the Deputies of the local Soviets of Deputies of the basic level (eight from each of the six regions of the Republic and of the city of Minsk), and eight appointed by the president, all members serve a four year term. The Council of the Republic is the house of territorial representation.
Council of the Republic, ul Krasnoarmeiskaya 4, 220 016 Minsk, Belarus. Tel: +375 172 891181, fax: +375 172 272318, e-mail: cr@sovrep.gov.by, URL: http://www.sovrep.gov.by

Lower House

The House of Representatives comprises 110 deputies and the Supreme House. The deputies are elected to the House of Representatives directly by the voters for a maximum of four years.
House of Representatives, Natsionalnoye Sobranie, Sovetskaya St. 11, 220 010 Minsk, Belarus. Tel: +375 172 273784, fax: +375 172 223178, e-mail: gertsik@house.gov.by, URL: http://www.house.gov.by

---

Cabinet (as at July 2013)
Prime Minister: Mikhail Myasnikovich (page 1483)
First Deputy Prime Minister: Vladimir I. Semashko (page 1511)
Deputy Prime Minister: Valeriy Ivanov
Deputy Prime Minister: Anatoly Kalinin
Deputy Prime Minister: Sergey Rumas
Deputy Prime Minister: Anatoly Tozik
Minister of Economy: Nikolai Snopkov
Minister of Architecture and Construction: Anatoli Nichkasov
Minister of Internal Affairs: Ihar Shunevich
Minister of Health: Vasily Zharko
Minister of Foreign Affairs: Vladimir Makei
Minister of Culture: Boris Svetlov
Minister of Defence: Yuri Zhadobin
Minister of Education: Sergey Maskevich
Minister of Emergencies: Vladimir Vashchenko
Minister of Natural Resources and Environmental Protection: Vladimir Tsalko
Minister of Industry: Aleksandr Radzkevich
Minister of Information: Oleg V. Proleskovsky
Minister of Agriculture and Food: Leonid Zaitsev
Minister of Labour and Social Security: Marianna Shchetkina
Minister of Sports and Tourism: Alexander Shamko
Minister of Trade: Valentin S. Chekanov
Minister of Transport and Communications: Ivan Shcherba
Minister of Finance: Andrey Kharkavets (page 1456)
Minister of Justice: Oleg Slizhevskiy
Minister of Communications and Information Technology: Nikilai Pantelei

---

Minister of Energy: Vladimir Potupchik
Minister of Housing and Communal Services: Vladimir M. Belokhvostov
Minister of Forestry: Mikhail Amelyanovich
Chair of State Committee on Science and Technology: Igor Voitov
Chair of the International Statistical Committee: Vladimir I Zinovsky
Minister of Revenues: Vladimir of Revenues

Ministries

Office of the President, Dom Urada, vul. Karl Marksa 38, 220016 Minsk, Belarus. Tel: +375 17 222 3217, fax: +375 17 226 0610, e-mail: contact@president.gov.by, URL: http://www.president.gov.by

Office of the Prime Minister, House of Government, Independence Square, 220010 Minsk, Belarus. Tel: +375 17 222 6905, fax: +375 17 222 6665, e-mail: contact@government.by, URL: http://www.government.by

Ministry of Agriculture and Food, 15 Kirov Street, 220050 Minsk, Belarus. Tel: +375 17 227 3751, fax: +375 17 227 4388, e-mail: kanc@mshp.minsk.by, URL: http://mshp.minsk.by

Ministry of Architecture and Construction, 39 Myasnikov Street, 220079 Minsk, Belarus. Tel: +375 17 227 2642, fax: +375 17 220 7424, URL: http://www.mas.by

Ministry of Communications and Information Technology, 10 F Skoriny Avenue, 220050 Minsk, Belarus. Tel: +375 17 227 2157, fax: +375 17 226 0848, URL: http://www.mpt.gov.by

Ministry of Culture, 11 Pobeditelei Avenue, 220004 Minsk, Belarus. Tel: +375 17 203 7574, fax: +375 17 223 5825, URL: http://www.kultura.by

Ministry of Defence, 1 Kommunisticheskaya Street, 220001 Minsk, Belarus. Tel: +375 17 239 2379, fax: +375 17 227 3564, URL: http://www.mod.mil.by

Ministry of the Economy, 14 Bersona Street, 220050 Minsk, Belarus. Tel: +375 17 222 6048, fax: +375 17 222 6335, URL: http://www.economy.gov.by

Ministry of Education, 9 Sovetskaya Street, 220010 Minsk, Belarus. Tel: +375 17 227 4736, fax: +375 17 220 8057, e-mail: root@minedu.unibel.by, URL: http://www.minedu.unibel.by

Ministry of Emergencies, 5 Revolutsionnaya Street, 220004 65-50 Minsk, Belarus. Tel: +375 17 203 6550, fax: +375 17 229 3439, e-mail: mcs@infonet.by, URL: http://www.rescue01.gov.by

Ministry of Energy, 14 K Marksa Street, 220050 Minsk, Belarus. Tel: +375 17 229 8359, fax: +375 17 229 8468, URL: http://www.minenergo.gov.by

Ministry of Finance, 7 Sovetskaya Street, 220010 Minsk, Belarus. Tel: +375 17 222 6137, fax: +375 17 222 4593, e-mail: web_mf@open.by, URL: http://www.ncpi.gov.by/minfin

Ministry of Foreign Affairs, 19 Lenina Street, 220030 Minsk, Belarus. Tel: +375 17 227 2922, fax: +375 17 227 4521, e-mail: mail@mfabelar.gov.by, URL: http://www.mfa.gov.by

Ministry of Forestry, 6 Chkalova Street, 220039 Minsk, Belarus. Tel: +375 17 224 4705, URL: http://www.mlh.by

Ministry of Housing and Communal Services, 16 Bersona Street, 220050 Minsk, Belarus. Tel: +375 17 200 1545, fax: +375 17 220 3894, URL: http://www.mjkx.gov.by

Ministry of Industry, 2/4 Partizansky Avenue, 220033 Minsk, Belarus. Tel: +375 17 224 9595, fax: +375 17 224 8784, e-mail: minprom1@ntc.niievm.minsk.by, http://www.minprom.gov.by

Ministry of Information, 11 Pobeditelei Avenue, 220004 Minsk, Belarus. Tel: +375 17 203 9231, fax: +375 17 223 3435, URL: http://www.mininform.by

Ministry of Internal Affairs, 4 Gorodskoy Val, 220050 Minsk, Belarus. Tel: +375 17 218 7808, fax: +375 17 223 9918, URL: http://www.mvd.gov.by

Ministry of Justice, 10 Kollektornaya Street, 220084 Minsk, Belarus. Tel: +375 17 206 3728, fax: +375 17 220 9684, URL: http://www.minjust.by

Ministry of Labour and Social Protection, 23/2 Pobeditelei Avenue, 220004 Minsk, Belarus. Tel: +375 17 206 3884, fax: +375 17 223 4521, URL: http://www.mintrud.gov.by

National Statistical Committee, 12 Partizansky Avenue, 220033 Minsk, Belarus. Tel: +375 17 249 5200, fax: +375 17 249 2204, e-mail: minstat@mail.belpak.by, URL: http://www.belstat.gov.by

Ministry of Natural Resources and Environmental Protection, 10 Kollektornaya Street, 220048 Minsk, Belarus. Tel: +375 17 200 6691, fax: +375 17 220 5583, e-mail: minproos@mail.belpak.by, URL: http://www.minpriroda.by

Ministry of Public Health, 39 Myasnikova Street, 220096 Minsk, Belarus. Tel: +375 17 222 6033, fax: +375 17 222 6297, URL: http://www.minzdrav.by

Ministry of Revenues, 9 Sovetskaya Street, 220010 Minsk, Belarus. Tel: +375 17 222 6450, fax: +375 17 222 6450, URL: http://www.nalog.by

Ministry of Sports and Tourism, 8/2 Kirova Street, 220600 Minsk, Belarus. Tel: +375 17 227 7237, fax: +375 17 227 7622, e-mail: inter.sport@solo.by, URL: http://www.mst.by

Ministry of Trade, 8/1 Kirova Street, 220050 Minsk, Belarus. Tel: +375 17 227 6121, fax: +375 17 227 2480, URL: http://www.mintorg.gov.by

Ministry of Transport and Communications, 21 Chicherina Street, 220000 Minsk, Belarus. Tel: +375 17 234 1152, fax: +375 17 220 7424, URL: http://www.mintrans.by

State Committee on Science and Technology, 1 Akademicheskaya Street, 220072 Minsk, Belarus. Tel: +375 17 284 0760, URL: http://www.gknt.org.by

Elections

Parliamentary elections for the House of Representatives took place in October 2004. The Communist party of Belarus remained the largest party in the parliament. At the same time a referendum was held on whether to lift a constitutional ban on the president running for a third term; it was claimed that there was a 90 per cent turnout, with over 70 per cent of voters agreeing to lifting the ban. However, observers were very critical of the result and the way the vote was conducted. The most recent parliamentary elections took place on 28 September 2008. Opposition candidates did not win any seats and complained that the elections were neither free or fair.

Presidential elections were held in September 2001 when Alexander Lukashenko was re-elected with 75 per cent of the vote. This election was also criticised by outside observers. The most recent presidential election took place in December 2010 when Lukashenko was again re-elected, outside observers criticised the election for being flawed.

The most recent parliamentary election took place on September 23 2012. Supporters of President Lukashenko won the election, the main opposition parties boycotted the elections which meant that in some constituencies there was only one candidate. The opposition parties claimed the elections were neither free not fair.

Political Parties

Belaruskaya Syalanskaya Partya (Belarusian Peasant Party), 220108 Minsk, vul. Gaya 38, POB 333, Belarus. Tel: +375 172 771905, fax: +375 (8)172 779651

Belaruskyaya Satsiyaldemokratychnaya Hramada (Belarusian Social Democratic Assembly), 220026 Minsk, pr. Partizanski 83, room 53, Belarus. Tel: +375 172 464691, fax: +375 (8)172 457852, URL: http://www.bsdp.org/?q=en

Partya Kamunista Belarusi (Communist Party of Belarus), 220071 Minsk, vul. Lunacharskaga 5, Belarus. Tel: +375 172 337757, fax: +375 172 323123, URL: http://www.comparty.by
Leader: Tatsyana Holubeva

Natsyianal-Demokratychnaya Partya Belarusi (National Democratic Party of Belarus), 220116 Minsk, vul. Timashenki 24, Belarus. Tel: +375 172 570823, fax: +375 172 369972

Belarusian Popular Front; the United Civic Party; the Social Democratic Party ; Women's Party 'Nadzeya'; Belarusian Independence Bloc.

Diplomatic Representation

British Embassy, 37 Karl Marx Street, Minsk 220030, Belarus. Tel: +375 (8)172 105920, fax: +375 17 2292306, e-mail: britinfo@nsys.by, URL: http://ukinbelarus.fco.co.uk
Ambassador: Rosemary Thomas

US Embassy, 46 Starovilenskaya Street, Minsk 220002, Belarus. Tel: +375 (8)172 101283 , fax: +375 17 2347853, URL: http://minsk.usembassy.gov
Chargé d'Affaires: Michael Scanlan

Embassy of Belarus, 6 Kensington Court, London, W8 5DL, United Kingdom. Tel: +44 (0)20 7937 3288, fax: +44 (0)20 7361 0005, e-mail: uk@belembassy.org, URL: http://belarus.embassyhomepage.com
Ambassador: Aleksandr Mikhnevich

Embassy of Belarus, 1619 New Hampshire Avenue NW, Washington, DC 20009, USA. Tel: +1 202 986 1604, fax: +1 202 986 1805, e-mail: usa@belarusembassy.org, URL: http://usa.mfa.gov.by
Ambassador: vacant

Permanent Mission of the Republic of Belarus to the United Nations, 136 East 67 Street, New York, N.Y. 10021. Tel: +1 212 535 3420, fax: +1 212 734 4810, URL: http://www.un.int/belarus
Ambassador Extraordinary & Plenipotentiary: Andrey Dapkyunas

LEGAL SYSTEM

The Constitutional Court exists to ensure the conformity of laws, decrees and edicts of the President, international agreements, all courts and the laws of the parliament to the constitution. The Constitutional Court is formed on the parity base: six judges appointed by the President and six judges elected by the Council of the Republic (the Upper House of Parliament). The Chairman of the Constitutional Court is appointed among the judges by the President with the consent of the Council of the Republic. Currently there are 11 judges in court, each with a term of 11 years.

The court system is split into three main groups - the Constitutional Court, the general courts and the economic courts. An appeal against a District Court decision can go before a Regional Court, and ultimately before the Supreme Court. There are also specialist courts, such as the Court of Minsk City, and military courts.

At present, power is concentrated in the presidency. Since his election in 1994 as president, Alexander Lukashenka has consolidated his power over all institutions and undermined the rule of law through authoritarian means. The 28th September 2008 parliamentary election failed to meet international standards. Prison conditions remain poor, and there are reports of abuse of prisoners and of arbitrary arrests and imprisonment of citizens for political reasons.

Belarus is the only country in Europe to retain the death penalty. Capital punishment is currently permissable for various acts including: terrorism; genocide; crimes against the security of humanity; certain cases of murder; treason that results in loss of life; conspiracy to seize power; sabotage; murder of a police officer; and use of weapons of mass destruction. Two people were reported to have been executed in 2010, two in 2011 and two in 2012.

Constitutional Court of Belarus: URL: http://www.kc.gov.by/en/main.aspx
Chairman: Petr P. Miklashevich
National Center of Legal Information, URL: http://notes.ncpi.gov.by/work/EnglSite.nsf

LOCAL GOVERNMENT

Belarus consists of six regions (oblasts) - Brest, Gomel, Grodna, Minsk, Mogilev, and Vitebsk - and one municipality (Minsk City). The municipalities are in turn divided into districts (rayons).

Self-government is exercised through local Councils of Deputies, executive and management bodies, bodies of territorial public self-management, local referenda and meetings. The Councils are voted in for a term of four years and they have jurisdiction over programs of economic and social development, local budgets and local taxes.

Regional Population Figures (000s)

Region	2005	2011
Brest	1,439.4	1,394.8
Vitebsk	1,289.5	1,221.8

BELARUS

Gomel	1,484.2	1,435.0
Grodno	1,122.1	1,065.9
Minsk	1,470.5	1,411.5
Mogilev	1,147.3	1,088.1
Minsk City	1,744.6	1,864.1

Source: Ministry of Statistics & Analysis

AREA AND POPULATION

Area

The Republic of Belarus is a landlocked country and is bounded in the west by Poland, in the north by Latvia and Lithuania, in the east by Russia, and in the south by the Ukraine. The total land area is 207,600 sq. km. The rivers, Dniepper, Prypyats and Nyoman run through Belarus. The terrain is generally flat with many marshes.

The climate is continental with cold winters and more maritime, cool summers.

To view a map, consult: http://www.un.org/Depts/Cartographic/map/profile/belarus.pdf

Population

The population in 2010 was estimated to be 9,595,000 (compared to 9,724,723 in 2007). Population numbers have been falling since 1993. The majority of the population (67 per cent) are aged between 15 and 60 years, with 15 per cent aged up to 14 years, and 18 per cent aged 60 and over. The majority of the population (75 per cent in 2010) lives in urban areas. Those *voblastsi* with populations over 200,000 are Minsk, Homel, Vitsebsk, Mahilev and Brest. Minsk has a population of approximately 1.8 million, about one fifth of the total population of Belarus.

Population size and decrease

Indicator	1999	2003	2005	2006
Total population ('000s)	10,019	9,849	9,751	9,714
- Males ('000s)	4,703	4,610	4,556	4,535
- Females ('000s)	5,316	5,239	5,195	5,179
- Urban (% of total)	69.7	71.5	72.4	72.8
- Rural (% of total)	30.3	28.5	27.6	27.2
- Under working age ('000s)	2,065	1,757	1,620	1,574
- Of working age* ('000s)	5,809	6,010	6,061	6,066
- Over working age ('000s)	2,145	2,082	2,070	2,074
Natural increase of population ('000s)	-49.0	-54.7	-51.4	-41.7

*males 16-59 years old, females 16-54 years
Source: Ministry of Statistics and Analysis

According to recent figures, the population is composed of 81.2 per cent Belarusians, 11.4 per cent Russians, the other 7.0 per cent are made up of Poles, Ukrainians, Jews with Tatars, Gypsies and Lithuanians accounting for 0.1 per cent of the population each.

Belarusian and Russian are the official state languages, with English and German spoken in business.

Births, Marriages, Deaths

Estimates for 2010 put the birth rate at 11.1 births per 1,000 population, and the death rate at 14.1 deaths per 1,000 population. Life expectancy at birth in 2009 was 70 years (64 years for men and 76 years for women). Healthy life expectancy was respectively 58 and 66 years. The infant mortality rate is 4 deaths per 1,000 live births, whilst the fertility rate is 1.3 children born per woman. (Source: http://www.who.int, World Health Statistics 2012)

Public Holidays 2014

1 January: New Year's Day
3 July: Liberation from German Occupation
7 January: Orthodox Christmas
15 March: Constitution Day
18 April: Orthodox Good Friday
20 April: Orthodox Easter Sunday
28 April: Memorial Day
5 May: Labour Day
9 May: Victory Day
8 June: Orthodox Pentecost
2 November: Commemoration Day
25 December: Christmas Day (Catholic)

EMPLOYMENT

In 2006, the economically active population was 4,466,100, of which 2,099,700 were male and 2,366,400 were female. The workforce was up in number from 4,428,200 in 2004. The number of unemployed fell from 83,000 in 2004 to 67,900 in 2005 and 52,000 in 2006. The registered unemployment rate fell from 1.9 per cent in 2004 to 1.5 per cent in 2005 and 1.2 per cent in 2006. (Source: Ministry of Statistics and Analysis) Figures for 2008 put the economically active at 4,638,100, 2,188,700 were male and 2,449,400 were female.

Percentage employed by sector

Sector	1995	2005
Industry	27.6	26.8
Agriculture	19.1	10.7
Construction	6.9	7.7

Transport & Communications	7.0	7
Trade & Public Catering	10.7	13.
Health Care	6.5	7.
Education	9.5	10.
Other	12.7	15

Source: Ministry of Statistics and Analysis

BANKING AND FINANCE

Currency

The unit of currency is the rouble which is divided into 100 copeks. As of 1 January 2000 the devaluation of the Belarusian rouble took place (a thousandfold decrease in the face value of money unit). In November 2001 it was announced that Belarus was to undertake obligations set down by the IMF so that the Belarusian rouble would become convertible.

GDP/GNP, Inflation, National Debt

Since President Lukashenko's election in 1994 Belarus has moved the economy away from the Western open-market model to a form of market socialism. Closer relations with Russia have isolated Belarus from the West and have influenced Belarusian economic policy accordingly. There is little foreign investment. The economy has been dependent on oil deals with Russia. The economic situation worsened in 2011. It has been boosted by multi-million dollar loans from Russia, the EU, and the sale of Beltrangaz to Russia. Belarus had to deal with hyper-inflation in 2011. The government has said its priority for 2013 will be to ease inflation and to rebuild its gold and foreign currency reserves.

Gross Domestic Product (GDP) (ppp) was estimated to be US$125 billion in 2009, rising to US$135 billion in 2010 and $140 million in 2011. The growth rate was estimated to be over 7 per cent in 2010 and 5 per cent in 2011. Per capita GDP was estimated at US$15,000 in 2011.

Industry makes up 44 per cent of GDP, agriculture 9.5 per cent, and services 46 per cent.

Inflation was estimated at 7 per cent in 2010. A currency crisis in 2011 meant that it spiralled into hyperinflation to over 100 per cent before falling back in 2012 to an estimated 50 per cent inn August 2012. The government hopes that the rate will fall to 15 per cent in 2013.

National debt was estimated to be US$18 million in 2010.

Foreign Investment

Since 1995, when President Lukashenko began the policy of 'market socialism', the state has had the right to intervene in the management of private businesses.

Balance of Payments / Imports and Exports

Belarus does most of its foreign trade with other Commonwealth of Independent State Countries (CIS). By 2009, exports were estimated to be worth US$25 billion and imports cost US$30 billion.

Central Bank

National Bank of the Republic of Belarus, 20, Nezavisimosty Avenue, 220008 Minsk, Belarus. Tel: +375 (8)172 192303, fax: +375 (8)172 274879, e-mail: Email@nbrb.by, URL: http://www.nbrb.by
Chairman: Nadezhda Ermakova

Chambers of Commerce and Trade Organisations

Belarusian Chamber of Commerce and Industry, URL: http://www.cci.by/

MANUFACTURING, MINING AND SERVICES

Primary and Extractive Industries

Belarus has reserves of various mineral deposits, including potassium, rock salt, clay, sand, cement, concrete ingredients, iron ore, cobalt, phosphate, silver and gold in varying quantities.

Belarus has a small oil industry, with the largest reserves and production capacity in the Baltic Sea region. Oil reserves are about 1200 million barrels (2012) but oil production is only about 31,000 barrels per day (2011). The crude oil refining capacity was 493,000 barrels per day in 2012. Two refineries operate in Belarus: the Naftan refinery in Navapolatsk Vitsebsk Region, and the Mzyr refinery in the Homel Region. Oil consumption had fallen by half in the past decade, from 375,000 barrels per day in 1992 to 138,000 barrels per day in 2001, but figures for 2011 showed that consumption was 194,000 barrels per day. Belarus must import about 75 per cent of its oil from Russia (162,000 barrels per day, in 2010). Belarusnafta, the state-owned oil production monopoly, estimates that active oil deposits will last for a further 17 years at an oil-extraction rate of 40,000 barrels per day.

Belarus produced just 8.0 billion cubic feet of natural gas in 2010 and is therefore heavily reliant on imports from Russia. Natural gas consumption rose from 692 billion cubic feet in 2000 to 771 billion cubic feet in 2010. Baltransgaz is Belarus's state-run natural gas distributor and operates 4,100 miles of natural gas pipelines, eight compressor stations, 250 distribution stations, and two storage reservoirs. A 350-mile stretch of the 2,500-mile, trans-continental Yamal-Europe natural gas pipeline runs through Belarus, carrying Russian natural gas exports to European consumers. Belarus relies heavily on imported gas from Russia; the Russian gas company Gazprom has announced that all customers will have to pay full prices in the future. Belarus was paying around a fifth of the market price for gas from Russia but in 2006 Russia raised the price and said it would phase in further increases over the next four years. In January 2007 Russia introduced an export duty of $52.7 per ton of oil.

Belarus has no coal reserves. In 2010, consumption was 0.084 million short tons.

Energy
Total energy consumption in 2009 was 1.04 quadrillion Btu, the highest in the Baltic Sea region. Natural gas production consumes the greatest proportion of energy (66.6 per cent in 2000), followed by the petroleum (28.7 per cent), coal (1.9 per cent), and hydroelectric (0.02 per cent) industries.

Belarus has a power-generating capacity of 8.03 gigawatts. Almost all of the country's power generation is made up of oil and natural gas-fired power plants, with hydroelectric generation accounting for just 0.1 per cent. Belarus remains a net importer of electricity for about 20 per cent of its annual power demand, due mainly to a decaying power infrastructure and a lack of investment in the industry. Consequently, consumption outstrips generation. Electricity imports come mainly from Russia (over 5 billion kWh from Russia and 0.9 billion kWh from Lithuania in 2001). In 2007 President Lukashenko said that Belarus would have to build a nuclear power station in order for the country to meet its energy needs and in July 2012, Belarus and Russia signed an agreement that Russian would help finance and build a nuclear power plant. The plant will be situated in Belarus' western Grodno region.

Manufacturing
Belarus has an important automotive and chemical industry. The country builds heavy-duty lorries, heavy tippers and multi-use tractors. The country is rich in peat and manufactures machinery for the peat industry. Production of peat by Belarus has dropped since the disaster at the Chernobyl nuclear plant, as peat became contaminated. The engineering industry produces river boats, metal cutting machines and farm machinery. Instrument making, radio and electronic engineering, potassium production, glass, timber and woodworking industries feature prominently. Textiles are a leading branch of the light industry, while meat and milk production predominate in the food processing industry. Industrial output (current prices) rose from 48,530 billion roubles in 2004 to 62,545 billion roubles in 2005. Figures for 2005 show that 1,062,000 are employed in the industry sector. (Source: Ministry of Statistics and Analysis)

Sectors of Industrial Production (%), 2005

Sector	%
Electric power	6.2
Fuel	21.7
Chemical and petro-chemical	11.3
Machinery and metalworking	22.4
Logging, wood-working	4.5
Building materials	4.2
Light industry	4.7
Food	16.2
Other	8.5

Source: Ministry of Statistics and Analysis

Output of major industrial products

Product	2004	2005
Electric power, bln. kWh	32.2	31.0
Primary oil refining, thsd. tons	18,451	19,802
Mineral fertilizers, thsd. tons	5,403	5,669
Synthetic resins & plastics, thsd. tons	433	457
Chemical fibres & filaments	203.4	210.8
Tyres, thsd. units	3,198	3,052
Metal-cutting machines, thsd units	5.4	3.7
Tractors, thsd. units	34.0	41.5
Trucks, thsd. units	21.5	22.3
Buses, thsd. units	610	1,263
Trolleybuses, units	118	147
Excavators, units	383	512
Sawn wood, thsd. cubic metres	2,727	2,667
Cement, thsd. units	2,731	3,131

Source: Ministry of Statistics and Analysis

Tourism
In 1999 there were 355,000 visitors to Belarus, an increase on the figure for 1997 of 250,000. Figures for 2004 showed that visitors to Belarus had fallen to 67,000.

Agriculture
About 45 per cent of the land is used for agricultural purposes, although much of this is poor as the climate is harsh. Belarus is an important producer of flax, potatoes, rye, wheat, buckwheat, barley and oats. Hemp and sugar beet are also grown. There is a fairly large timber industry. Agriculture contributes over nine per cent to GDP.

Agricultural Production in 2010

Produce	Int. $'000*	Tonnes
Cow milk, whole, fresh	1,736,654	6,594,500
Indigenous cattle meat	832,137	308,042
Indigenous pigmeat	618,471	402,325
Indigenous chicken meat	346,396	243,186
Potatoes	342,813	7,831,110
Hen eggs, in shell	162,560	196,000
Sugar beet	139,274	3,773,390
Tomatoes	114,624	310,159
Apples	97,507	525,552
Vegetables fresh nes	75,889	522,720
Rapeseed	74,494	374,522
Strawberries	59,720	44,000

- continued
* unofficial figures
Source: http://faostat.fao.org/site/339/default.aspx FAOSTAT, Statistics Division, Food and Agriculture Organization of the UN

COMMUNICATIONS AND TRANSPORT

Travel Requirements
A passport valid for 90 days after departure is required by citizens of the USA, Canada, Australia and the EU. All foreign nationals must register their passports at the local police station within three days of their arrival. If staying at a hotel, reception will do this automatically. A visa is also required by US, Canadian, Australian and EU citizens. Transit visas are required even for travelers transiting on direct overnight trains with no stops or transfers on Belarussian territory. Transit visas should be obtained prior to any journey that requires travel through Belarus . All foreign nationals (except British) must hold medical insurance. Foreign citizens visiting and transiting Belarus also should be prepared to demonstrate sufficient financial means to support their stay. Most CIS nationals do not require a visa.

Customs Restrictions
The basis of the customs legislation of the country is formed by the Customs Code of the Republic of Belarus and the Law of the Republic of Belarus 'on Customs Tariff'. After signing the Customs Union Agreement between Belarus, Russian Federation, Kazakhstan and Kyrgyzstan, the territory of the Republic became the part of the common customs space. Within the Union of the Republic of Belarus and Russia, all customs duties and quantitative restrictions concerning mutual trade have been cancelled.

The following goods are duty-free: printed advertising materials, goods meant for demonstration with the purpose of concluding a foreign trade deal, or for using at exhibitions to design expositions, and humanitarian aid goods (food stuffs, clothes, footwear, children's toys, articles for medical purposes etc).

National Airlines
Belavia, URL: http://www.belavia.by
Belair, Korotkeivicha Str 5, 222039 Minsk, Belarus. Tel: +375 (8)172 250702, fax: +375 (8)172 227509

International Airports
Airports are stationed in Minsk, Brest, Grodno, Vitebsk, Mobilev and Gomel and use of airspace is controlled by the following state bodies:
Belaeronavigatsyia Committee on Aerospace Use and Air Traffic Control, 220147 Minsk, Zhodinskaya str. 21, Belarus. Tel: +375 (8)172 636185/647872
Byelorussian Centre of Air Traffic Organisation, 220039 Minsk, Belarus. Tel: +375 (8)172 768672
State Committee on Aviation of the Republic of Belarus, 22050 Minsk, Aerodromnaya str. 4, Belarus. Tel: +375 (8)172 225592
Ministry of Transport-Belarus, 220745 Minsk, Lenina str. 17, Belarus. Tel: +375 (8)172 964463, fax: +375 (8)172 964364
Minsk-2 Airport, Tel: +375 (8)172 971838, fax: +375 (8)172 791629
Minskavia-Minsk-1-Airport, 220039 Minsk, Korotkeivicha str., 7, Belarus. Tel: +375 (8)172 253464/250444
Vitebsk Airport, 210039 Vitebsk, Belarus. Tel: +375 (8)212 254045

Railways
The total length of railway track is 5,590 km. Most towns and cities are connected by the rail netwerk, trains also run to Warsaw, Poland and Moscow, Russia. The capital Minsk has a subway system which is currently being expanded as well as a tram system.
Belarus Railways, URL: http://www.rw.by

Roads
The total length of roads is 92,200 km, of which 60,900 km is hard surfaced. Vehicles are driven on the right.

Shipping
Belarus has no coast but has 2 navigable rivers, the Dnepr and the Pripyat. The Dnepr takes barges of up to 1,000 tonnes as far north as Zhlobin. The Pripyat carries barges from Ukraine to Brest on the Polish border. There is also a canal system in use.

Freight Turnover by Types of General Purpose Transport (mln ton-km)

Transport Type	1995	2005
Railway	25,510	43,559
Motor road inc. transport of Organisations	9,539	15,055
Air	60	59
Inland waterway	133	90

Source: Ministry of Statistics & Analysis

Passenger Turnover by Types of General Purpose Transport (mln passenger-km)

Transport type	1995	2005
Railway	12,505	10,351
Motor road inc. buses	9,308	9,231
Air	1,228	684
Inland waterway	2	2

Source: Ministry of Statistics & Analysis

BELGIUM

HEALTH

Belarus has a special Chernobyl tax which funds health care and pensions for victims of the disaster at the Chernobyl nuclear plant in 1986. Total government expenditure in 2009 on health was equivalent to 6.1 per cent of GDP, which accounts for a per capita expenditure of US$311. General government expenditure on health accounts for 8.4 per cent of total government expenditure. Government expenditure accounts for 64.0 per cent of the total expenditure on health. Private expenditure accounts for 36 per cent of total expenditure on health, of which approximately 74.8 per cent is out-of-pocket expenditure.

Latest figures from the WHO (2005-10), show that Belarus has 49,380 physicians (51.8 per 10,000 population), 125,032 midwives and nurses (131.1 per 10,000 population), 5,182 dentists (5.4 per 10,000 population), 3,053 pharmaceutical personnel (3.2 per 10,000 population). There are approximately 111 hospital beds and 6.3 psychiatric beds per 10,000 population).

The infant mortality rate in 2010 (probability of dying before one year old) was 4 per 1,000 live births. The under-five mortality rate was 6 per 1,000 live births. The most common causes of death in the under-fives was congenital abnormalities (34 per cent), 19 per cent prematurity, 8 per cent birth asphyxia, and pneumonia 9 per cent.

In 2010, an estimated 100 per cent of the population have access to improved drinking-water sources and 93 per cent of the population had access to improved sanitation.(Source: http://www.who.int, World Health Statistics 2012)

EDUCATION

Belarus is a country of total literacy with a wide network of higher, secondary and specialised secondary education establishments as well as scientific and research institutions. According to the 1989 census, 899 of every 1,000 people employed in the national economy have completed higher or secondary education. Despite economic difficulties, the number of pupils and students has changed very little in recent years.

Schooling is compulsory and free; primary education starts for children aged six and lasts for four years. Secondary level education starts at age ten and lasts for seven years, five in lower and two in upper. In the academic year 2005-06 there were 1,240,900 pupils enrolled in secondary education. In the academic year 2005-06 there were 4,187 general secondary schools and 204 specialised schools. There were 55 institutions providing higher education with a total enrollment of 383,000.

Literacy is estimated at 99.8 per cent. In recent years annual expenditure on education was the equivalent of 5.2 per cent of GDP.

RELIGION

The major faith is Christianity (74 per cent), with the Orthodox Church the largest denomination. The Catholic, Protestant, Jewish (0.27 per cent) and Muslim (0.28 per cent), faiths are also represented.

Belarus has a religious liberty rating of 4 on a scale of 1 to 10 (10 is most freedom). (Source: World Religion Database)

COMMUNICATIONS AND MEDIA

Lack of media freedom is a serious concern. The government has been accused of supressing freedom of speech and blocking the independent and opposition press. Restrictive media laws have recently been passed. There is government control of telecommunications technology. There is more freedom on the internet and this is widely used by the opposition.

Newspapers
There are several newspapers, both state-run and private. However, government publications benefit from subsidies whilst the opposition press has faced increasing charges and obstacles. The main newspapers are:
Narodnaya Hazeta (People's Newspaper), URL: http://www.ng.by/ (opposition)
Sovetskaya Belorossiya, URL: http://www.sb.by/ (Russian language, main government daily)
Zvyazda, URL: http://www.zvyazda.minsk.by/
Narodnaya Volya, URL: http://www.http://www.nv-online.info/ (private, printed in Russia)

Broadcasting
At present there are four state run television channels and a radio station. The national state-owned TV and Radio Broadcasting Company of Belarus (URL: http://www.tvr.by/eng/) is a member of the European Broadcasting Union. The non-governmental air and cable TV networks have been developing since 1991, and there are now more than 170 registered local cable TV networks. Recent figures show that there are over 2.5 million televisions in use.

Telecommunications
According to recent estimates there are over 3.7 million telephone mainlines in use and 8.6 million mobile telephones (2008). The state-owned Beltelcom is the sole provider of the fixed line service. Modernisation of the system is ongoing. Internet users number an estimated 3.7 million. The opposition uses the internet most successfully to spread its message as its not controlled by the government to the same extent.

ENVIRONMENT

Main environmental issues include contamination in the south of the country by fallout from the disaster at Ukraine's Chernobyl nuclear reactor in 1986, and pollution of soil from pesticides.

In 2010, Belarus's emissions from the consumption of fossil fuels totalled 68.24 million metric tons of carbon dioxide, the highest in the Baltic Sea region.

Belarus is a party to the following international environmental agreements: Air Pollution, Air Pollution-Nitrogen Oxides, Air Pollution-Sulfur 85, Biodiversity, Climate Change, Climate Change-Kyoto Protocol, Desertification, Endangered Species, Environmental Modification, Hazardous Wastes, Law of the Sea, Marine Dumping, Ozone Layer Protection, Ship Pollution, and Wetlands.

SPACE PROGRAMME

The national space program for 2013- 2017 includes development of remote sensing and space communications. Belarus also hopes to launch a satellite in 2012 for independent space data collection.
National Academy of Sciences, URL: http://www.nasb.gov.by

BELGIUM

Kingdom of Belgium

Royaume de Belgique / Koninkrijk België

Capital: Brussels (Population estimate, 2008: 1,048,491)

Head of State: King Philippe (page 1495), in July 2013 the reigning King Albert II (page 1373)announced that he would abdicate in favour of his son Prince Phillippe.

National Flag: A pale-wise tricolour of black, yellow and red.

CONSTITUTION AND GOVERNMENT

Constitution
Following independence from the Netherlands, the government and administrative structure of Belgium were laid down by the constitution promulgated in 1831. Belgium has a hereditary constitutional monarchy. The monarchy is hereditary by order of progeniture, and has no powers other than those provided under the constitution. According to the constitution, the King has immunity and his ministers are liable for him. He is the guardian of the country's unity and independence and receives a civil list. Women have been eligible to accede to the throne since 1991.

Since 1831 successive institutional reforms made in 1970, 1980, 1988 and 1993 have devolved power to the various communities in the country. The article of the Belgian Constitution states 'Belgium is a federal state which consists of communities and regions'. The divisions are as follows: the national government with responsibility for foreign and defence policy, internal security, monetary affairs and the budget and social security; the three 'Language Communities' (Flemish, French and German speaking) which deal with cultural matters, education, health policy, language use and protection of the youth; the three 'Regions' (Flanders, Wallonia and Brussels) which have authority over socio-economic matters such as urban planning, housing, economic development, employment, energy, public works and transport.

There are ten 'Provinces': Antwerp, Flemish Brabant, Hainaut, Liege, Limburg, Luxembourg, Namur, Oost-Vlaanderen, West-Vlaanderen, and Walloon Brabant, as well as 589 'Communes' which operate at an administrative local government level.

Under the terms of the 1831 constitution the prime minister is the head of government, appointed by the monarch, and is responsible to the Chamber of Representatives. The monarch appoints the cabinet on the advice of the prime minister.

The most recent reforms made in 1993 provided for the following major amendments: reduction in the number of members of the Chamber of Representatives and the Senate; the Chamber to become the main legislative body; the Senate to be essentially a revising chamber; parliaments for Flanders and Wallonia to be directly elected; the bilingual province of Brabant to be divided into independent French and Dutch-speaking halves; powers over foreign trade, agriculture, scientific policy and some aspects of international relations to be transferred to the regions.

To consult the full constitution (in French), please visit: http://www.senate.be/doc/const_fr.html

International Relations
Belgium is an active member of the EU, the UN and NATO as well as other organisations. Belgium is currently a non-permanent member of the UN Security Council (2007-09). Both NATO and the EU are headquartered in Brussels, and Belgium is in favour of further strengthening economic and political integration within the EU.

The Kingdom maintains close links to its former colonies in Central Africa, especially the Democratic Republic of Congo, Rwanda and Burundi. In 1948, Belgium formed the Benelux customs grouping, with the Netherlands and Luxembourg, and later became one of the six founding members of the EU.

Recent Events
In January 2003 Belgium pledged to invest more in renewable energy sources and natural gas legislation was passed to shut down all seven of her nuclear reactors by 2025 and ban the building of any new reactors.

On 15th December 2007, thousands of trade union members protested in Brussels against rising food and fuel prices, and the failure of Belgium's politicians to form a government over the six months since the general election. Dutch and French-speaking political parties remained split over autonomy plans, and policies could be enacted due to the political paralysis. On the 18th December, the king asked the caretaker prime minister, Mr. Verhofstadt, to form an interim government to start negotiations leading to institutional reform. Mr. Verhofstadt's party, the Flemish Liberals, had been beaten in the June 2007 elections. In March 2008, some nine months after the election, the new government was sworn in, with Yves Leterme as prime minister.

In December 2008, Yves Leterme offered his government's resignation amid a growing row over the break-up and sale of the Fortis bank.

In January 2009, Christian Democrat Herman Van Rompuy was confirmed as prime minister, heading a coalition that was largely unchanged from that of his predecessor. In November Prime Minister Van Rompuy was elected as the first president of the European Union, Yves Leterme took over as prime minister.

The Belgian home affairs parliamentary committee voted unanimously in March 2010 to ban face-covering Islamic veils from being worn in public. This vote could pave the way for approval by parliament in which case the ban would become law and would be the first such law in Europe.

In April 2010 the government collapsed when a key coalition partner pulled out in a row over francophone rights in Dutch-speaking areas near Brussels. Prime Minister Leterme handed in his resignation and an early election was then held in June. On 6 May the Chamber of Representatives voted to dissolve itself, ahead of the elections held on 13 June. The separatist New Flemish Alliance became the largest single group after the election, although the French and Flemish Socialists together had more seats overall. Prime Minister Leterme agreed to stay on in the role of Prime Minister heading a caretaker cabinet until coalition talks were finished and a new cabinet was announced. As of May 2011 a government was still not in place and on 16 May King Albert asked the Francophone socialist leader Elio Di Rupo to form a new federal government.

In September 2011, the caretaker prime minister, Yves Leterme, said he was to retire from politics to take a job at the OECD. Talks to form a coalition government continued.

In November 2011, the rating's agency Standard & Poor's cut Belgium's credit rating from AA+ to AA amidst concerns over funding and market pressures.

On 1 December 2011 it was reported that a new government was to be formed. Six parties agreed on a new government headed by the French-speaking Socialist Elio Di Rupo.

In mid-December a gunman went on the rampage in the town of Liege; he threw hand grenades and shot at panicing Christmas shoppers before killing himself. Five people died in the attack and 125 were injured.

In October 2012, the Flemish Nationalist Party (NVA) made major gains at local elections, this made it the largest political force in Flanders. Leader Bart De Wever became mayor of Antwerp.

In July 2013, King Albert announced that he was abdicating in favour of his son Crown Prince Philippe. The official abdication was to take place on July 21, Belgium's National Day.

Legislature
Belgium's bicameral legislature, the Federal Chambers (*Chambres Législatives Fédérales/Federal Wetgevende Kamers*), consists of the Senate (*Sénat/Senaat*) and the Chamber of Representatives (*Chambre des Représentants/Kamer van Volksvertegenwoordigers*).

Upper House
The Senaat/Sénat (Senate) has 71 members, of which 40 are directly elected, 21 are assigned by the Community Councils, and 10 are co-opted. Of the 40 directly elected Senators 25 are elected by the Flemish electoral college and 15 by the French electoral college. All are elected for a period of four years. Of the 21 assigned senators, the Flemish Council and the French Community Council each designate 10 of their members, whilst the German Community Council designates one of its members. Of the 10 co-opted senators, the Dutch speaking senators of the two previous groups assign six members, whilst the French speaking senators of the two previous groups assign four members.

Two linguistic groups make up the Senate: the Dutch and the French. The Dutch linguistic group is composed of 41 senators: 25 directly elected by the Dutch speaking electoral college, 10 assigned by the Flemish Council, and six co-opted by both of the above groups. The French linguistic group is composed of 29 senators: 15 directly elected by the French speaking electoral college, 10 assigned by the French community Council, and four co-opted by the above groups. Senators are elected for four-year terms.

In addition to the Senate's 71 members, two members of the royal family are appointed by right: His Royal Highness Prince Philippe and Her Royal Highness Princess Astrid. Under the terms of the constitution those senators appointed by right are the children of the King over 18 years of age or, in the absence of children, Belgian descendants of the branch of the royal family called upon to reign.

Senate, Rue de la Loi 8, 1009 Brussels, Belgium. Tel: +32 (0)2 501 7070 / 7658, fax: +32 (0)2 514 0685 / 7587, e-mail: info@senate.be, URL: http://www.senate.be
President: Sabine de Bethune

Lower House
The Kamer van Volksvertegenwoordigers/Chambre des Représentants (Chamber of Representatives) has 150 members, directly elected by proportional representation, who serve a four year term. The deputies are divided into a French language and a Dutch language group. There are currently 88 Dutch-speakers and 62 French-speakers in the Chamber. Some laws require a majority within each language group. The composition of the senate is as follows: CD&V 17 seats, cdH 9 seats, Ecolo-Groen! 13 seats; Independent 1, LDD 1 seats; MR 18 seats, N-VAN-VA 27 seats, Open Vld 13 seats, PS 26 seats, sp.a 13 seats, VB 12 seats.

Chamber of Representatives, Rue de Louvain 13, 1000 Brussels, Belgium. Tel: +32 (0)2 549 8111 / 8136, fax: +32 (0)2 549 8302, URL: http://www.lachambre.be
President: André Flauhert

Cabinet (as at July 2013)
Prime Minister: Elio Di Rupo (PS) (page 1415)
Deputy Prime Minister, Minister for Finance and Sustainable Development, Minister responsible for the Civil Service: Koen Geens (CD&V) (page 1429)
Deputy Prime Minister and Minister of Social Affairs and Public Health: Laurette Onkelinx (PS) (page 1490)
Deputy Prime Minister, Minister for Pensions: Alexander De Croo (Open VLD)
Deputy Prime Minister, Minister for Foreign Affairs, Foreign Trade and European Affairs: Didier Reynders (MR) (page 1502)
Deputy Prime Minister, Minister for the Interior: Joelle Milquet (cdH) (page 1478)
Deputy Prime Minister, Minister for Economy, Consumers and the North Sea: Johan Vande Lanotte (MR) (page 1530)
Minister for SMEs, Independents, Agriculture and Middle Classes: Sabine Lauruelle (MR) (page 1461)
Minister of Justice: Annemie Turtelboom (page 1528) (Open VLD)
Minister for Defence: Pieter de Crem (CD&V) (page 1413)
Minister of Public Enterprises, Science Policy and Development Co-operation, Minister for Urban Affairs: Paul Magnette (PS) (page 1469)
Minister for Employment: Monica de Coninck (SP.A)
Minister of Budget and Administrative Simplification: Oliver Chastel

Ministries
Office of the Prime Minister, 16 Rue de la Loi, B-1000 Brussels, Belgium. Tel: +32 (0)2 501 0211, fax: +32 (0)2 512 6953, URL: http://www.premier.fgov.be
Ministry of Defence, 8 rue Lambermont, 1000 Brussels, Belgium. Tel: +32 (0)2 701 3111 2811, fax: +32 (0)2 550 2919, URL: http://mod.fgov.be
Ministry of Economic Affairs, 23 Square de Meeus, 1040 Brussels, Belgium. Tel: +32 (0)2 506 5111, fax: +32 (0)2 230 1824, URL: http://mineco.fgov.be
Ministry of Employment and Labour, 51-53 rue Belliard, 1040 Brussels, Belgium. Tel: +32 (0)2 233 4111, fax: +32 (0)2 233 4257, e-mail: info@meta.fgov.be, URL: http://meta.fgov.be
Ministry of Finance, 12 rue de la Loi, 1000 Brussels, Belgium. Tel: +32 (0)2 233 8111, fax: +32 (0)2 233 8003, URL: http://www.minfin.fgov.be/
Ministry of Foreign Affairs, Foreign Trade and International Cooperation, 15 rue de Petit Carmes, 1000 Brussels, Belgium. Tel: +32 (0)2 501 8111, fax: +32 (0)2 514 3067, e-mail: info@diplobel.org, URL: http://diplobel.fgov.be
Ministry of the Interior, 66 rue Royale, 1000 Brussels, Belgium. Tel: +32 (0)2 500 2048, fax: +32 (0)2 500 2039, e-mail: info@ibz.fgov.be, URL: http://www.ibz.fgov.be/
Ministry of Justice, 115 boulevard de Waterloo, 1000 Brussels, Belgium. Tel: +32 (0)2 542 6604, fax: +32 (0)2 538 7039, e-mail: info@just.fgov.be, URL: http://just.fgov.be
Ministry of Civil Service, Résidence Palace, 51 rue de la Loi, 1040 Brussels, Belgium. Tel: +32 (0)2 287 5800, fax: +32 (0)2 233 0590, URL: http://www.mazfp.fgov.be
Ministry of Social Affairs, Health and Environment, 66 rue de la Loi, 1040 Brussels, Belgium. Tel: +32 (0)2 210 4511, fax: +32 (0)2 230 3895, URL: http://minsoc.fgov.be
Ministry of Communications and Infrastructure, Rue d'Arlon 104, 1040 Brussels, Belgium. Tel: +32 (0)2 233 1211, fax: +32 (0)2 230 1824, e-mail: info@mobilit.fgov.be, URL: http://vici.fgov.be

Political Parties
Groen! (formerly Anders Gaan Leven -Agalev-, Green Party), Sergeant de Bruynestraat 78-82, 1070 Anderlecht, Belgium. Tel: +32 (0)2 219 1919, fax: +32 (0)2 223 1090, e-mail: info@groen.be, URL: http://www.groen.be
Leader: Wouter Van Besien
Christen-Democratisch en Vlams (CD&V), Wetstraat 89, 1040 Brussels, Belgium. Tel: +32 (0)2 238 3866, fax: +32 (0)2 238 3871, e-mail: inform@cdenv.be, URL: http://www.cdenv.be
Leader: Wouter Beke
Ecolo (Ecologist Party, French Speaking), Espace Kegeljan, Av. de la Marlagne, 52, B-5000 Namur, Belgium. Tel.: +32 (0)81 227871, fax: +32 (0)81 230603, e-mail: info@ecolo.be, URL: http://www.web4.ecolo.be

BELGIUM

Co-presidents: Jean-Michel Javaux, Sarah Turine
Front Démocratique des Francophones (FDF, French Speaking Democratic Front), 127 chaussée de Charleroi, 1060 Brussels, Belgium. Tel: +32 (0)2 538 8320, fax: +32 (0)2 539 3650, e-mail: fdf@fdf.be, URL: http://www.fdf.be
President: Olivier Maingain
Front National (FN), Clos du Parnasse 12/8, 1050 Ixelles, Belgium. Tel: +32 (0)81 74 2572, e-mail: fn@frontnational.be, URL: http://www.frontnational.be
President: Patrick Cocriamont
Nieuw-Vlaamse Alliantie (NVA), (VU & ID21 split into N-VA and SPIRIT) Barrikadenplein 12, 1000 Brussels, Belgium. Tel: +32 (0)2 219 4930, fax: +32 (0)2 217 3510, e-mail: info@n-va.be, URL: http://www.n-va.be/
President: Bart de Wever
Mouvement Réformateur (MR), rue de Naples 39, 1050 Brussels, Belgium. Tel: +32 (0)2 500 3543, fax: +32 (0)2 500 3542, e-mail: mr@mr.be, URL: http://www.mouvementreformateur.be/
President: Charles Michel
Parti Socialiste (PS, French Wing), 13 Boulevard de l'Empereur, 1000 Brussels, Belgium. Tel: +32 (0)2 548 3211, fax: +32 (0)2 548 3380, e-mail: info@ps.be, URL: http://www.ps.be
President: Elio Di Rupo (page 1415)
Centre Démocrate Humaniste (CDH), (formerly the Parti Social Chrétien) rue des Deux Eglises 41, 1000 Brussels, Belgium. Tel: +32 (0)2 238 0111, fax: +32 (0)2 238 0129, e-mail: info@lecdh.be, URL: http://www.lecdh.be/
Leader: Benoît Lutgen
Socialistische Partij Anders (SP, Flemish Wing), Agoragalerij, Grasmarkt 105/37, B-1000 Brussels, Belgium. Tel: +32 (0)2 552 0200 / 0328, fax: +32 (0)2 552 0255 / 0329, e-mail: info@s-p-a.be, URL: http://www.sp.be
Vlaams Belang, (Flemish Interest) previously Vlaams Blok, Madouplein 8/9 - 1210 Brussels, Belgium. Tel: +32 (0)2 219 60 09, e-mail: info@vlaamsbelang.org, URL: http://www.vlaamsbelang.org/
President: Bruno Valkeniers
Vlaamse Liberalen en Demokraten (VLD, Flemish Liberals and Democrats: Liberal Party - Flemish Wing), 34 rue Melsens, 1000 Brussels, Belgium. Tel: +32 2 549 0020, fax: +32 (0)2 512 6025, e-mail: vld@vld.be, URL: http://www.vld.be
Leader: Alexander De Croo

Elections

Voting is compulsory, and suffrage is universal from 18 years. General elections are held every four years.

Elections to the Chamber of Representatives and the Senate last took place on 10 June 2007. The liberal fraction (MR, VLD) with 41 seats became the largest group in parliament, followed by the Christian Democrats (CD&V, Cdh) and N-VA with 40 seats. The Flemish alliance CD&V and N-VA became the biggest party (25 seats for CD&V and 5 for N-VA), and led coalition talks for a new government.

On June 13, 2007, King Albert II appointed MR leader Didier Reynders informateur. He assessed the possibilities for government coalitions and presented his report to the King on July 4, 2007. Mr. Leterme was asked to form a government on 15 July, but, after several weeks of failed negotiations, he resigned his mandate. The king then commissioned the Chamber of Representatives Speaker Herman Van Rompuy (Flemish Christian Democrat) to negotiate a way out of the political crisis; he too failed, and Leterme took over the negotiations again. On 1st December 2007, Yves Leterme, abandoned efforts to form a coalition government, having failed to find a compromise between Dutch- and French-speaking politicians, and again resigned as coalition negotiator. French-speaking politicians in Wallonia had rejected his demands for greater autonomy for the country's regions. On the 18th December, the king asked the caretaker PM, Guy Verhofstadt, to form an interim government and begin negotiations leading to institutional reform. The political crisis prompted speculation of a possible end to Belgium's 177-year existence, and a separation into French and Flemish speaking states. Leterme was eventually sworn into office with a reshuffled government on 20 March 2008. On 19 December Leterme offered his government's resignation, and on the 22 December Van Rompuy was asked to form a new government. His cabinet, comprising the same coalition parties and only four new ministers (including Van Rompuy himself), was sworn in on 30 December.

Elections were held on 13 June 2010. The NVA remained the largest party. Breakdown of seats was as follows: NVA 27 seats; PS 26 seats; MR 18 seats; CD&V 17 seats; SP.A 13 seats; Open VLD 13 seats; VB 12 seats; CDH 9 seats; others 15 seats. In the Senate, results were as follows: NVA 14 seats; PS 13 seats; MR 8 seats; CD&V 7 seats; SP.A 7 seats; Open VLD 6 seats; others 16 seats. A government was finally formed in December 2011.

Diplomatic Representation

Embassy of Belgium, 17 Grosvenor Crescent, London SW1X, United Kingdom. Tel: +44 (0)20 7470 3700, fax: +44 (0)20 7470 3795 / 3710, e-mail: uk@diplobel.org, URL: http://www.diplomatie.be/london
Ambassador: H.E. Johan Verbeke (page 1531)
Embassy of Belgium, 3330 Garfield Street, NW Washington DC 20008, USA. Tel: +1 202 333 6900, fax: +1 202 333 5457, e-mail: Washington@diplobel.org, URL: http://www.diplobel.us
Ambassador: H.E. Jan Matthysen (page 1472)
British Embassy, Avenue d'Auderghem 10, 1040 Brussels, Belgium. Tel: +32 (0)2 287 6211, fax: +32 (0)2 287 6355 (Political) / 6360 (Press and Public Affairs), e-mail: info@britain.be, URL: http://ukinbelgium.fco.gov.uk/en/
Ambassador: Jonathan Brenton (page 1394)
US Embassy, 27 boulevard de Régent, 1000 Brussels, Belgium. Tel: +32 (0)2 508 2111, fax: +32 (0)2 333 3079, URL: http://brussels.usembassy.gov/
Ambassador: Howard Gutman
Permanent Mission to the United Nations, 823 United Nations Plaza, 345 East 46th Street, 4th Floor, New York, NY 10017. Tel: +1 212 378 6300, fax: +1 212 681 7618, e-mail: belgium@un.int, URL: http://www.un.int/belgium
Ambassador & Permanent Representative: Jan K.F. Grauls

Reigning Royal Family

The present King, Albert II, took oath on 9th August 1993 following the death of his brother King Baudouin. He has been married to Paola Ruffo di Calabria since 2 July 1959. Their children are as follows: Crown Prince Philippe (page 1495); Prince Laurent; Princess Astrid. In December 1999, Crown Prince Philippe married Mathilde d'Udekem d'Acoz. Their daughter Princess Elisabeth was born in October 2001, their son Prince Gabriel was born on 20 August 2003, and Prince Emmanuel was born on 4 October 2005. Their youngest daughter, Princess Eléonore, was born in 2008.

LEGAL SYSTEM

Belgian law is modeled on the French legal system. The judiciary is independent. Belgium's court system consists of the Supreme Court, five courts of appeal, eleven assize courts for the trial of political and criminal cases, and district courts of first instance.

Minor offenses are dealt with by justices of the peace and police tribunals. More serious offenses and civil lawsuits are brought before district courts of first instance, which include commercial and labor tribunals. Verdicts may be appealed before five regional courts of appeal or five regional labour courts in Antwerp, Brussels, Ghent, Mons, and Liège. All offenses punishable by prison sentences of more than five years are dealt with by the eleven courts of assize (one for each province and the city of Brussels), the only jury courts in Belgium.

The supreme Court of Cassation's function is to verify that the law has been properly applied and interpreted. The court comprises three chambers with 16 judges. Each chamber has a Dutch and a French division. Each chamber has a chief judge, called the President, and two heads of division, one for each language group. The entire court is headed by a chief judge - the First President.

The Council of State is the Supreme Administrative Court of Belgium. Its functions include assisting the executive with legal advice and being the supreme court for administrative justice.

The Court of Arbitration was created in 1984 following the development of Belgium from a unitary state into a federal state. Its function is to supervise the observance of the constitutional division of powers between the federal state, the communities and the regions. In May 2007, the court was renamed Constitutional Court. The Court is composed of 12 judges (2 linguistic groups of which 6 Dutch and 6 French speakers) appointed for their lifetime by the King.

A system of military tribunals handle offenses involving military personnel. These consist of four officers and a civilian judge.

Whilst the government respects the rights of its citizens, the prisons are overcrowded and pretrial detention can be lengthy. The detention conditions for failed asylum applicants were poor. The death penalty was abolished for all crimes in Belgium in 1996.

Supreme Court of Appeal (Cour de Cassation): URL: http://www.just.fgov.be

LOCAL GOVERNMENT

Belgium is divided into 10 provinces: Antwerp, East Flanders, Hainaut, Limberg, Liège, Luxembourg, Namur, Flemish Brabant, Walloon Brabant and West Flanders. Each province is ruled by a governor and a provincial council. There are 589 communes, each of which is headed by a mayor (*Bourgmestre*) and a town council. Both provinces and communes enjoy a large measure of local autonomy. Voting in communal elections is by proportional representation.

The most significant long-term factor in Belgian politics is the gradual devolution of power to the autonomous regional governments. There is currently no hierarchy between the levels of state, regions and language communities and none can interfere in matters under the jurisdiction of the others. In total there are five levels of power: federal, community, regional, provincial and communal.

The Communities have authority for people-related issues including education (with some exceptions), cultural matters, family policies.

The Regions have authority for territory-related matters including regional development, agriculture, housing, water, regional energy, regional economy, regional transport and environment. The regions took on responsibility for agriculture and communal and provincial legislation in 2002. Development co-operation is currently a federal responsibility but this may move to a regional responsibility.

The Provinces may intervene in all areas which are of interest to them but must respect the authority of the Communes and all other higher authorities. The Communes may act in a similar way.

The most recent regional elections took place on 7 June 2009. Elections are next due in 2014.

Autonomous Regional Governments
The Walloon Government (as at April 2013)
Minister-President: Rudy Demotte (page 1414)
Vice-President and Minister for Sustainable Development, the Public Office, Energy, Housing and Research: Jean-Marc Nollet
Vice-President and Minister for Budget, Finances, Employment, Formation, Sports and the Airport Policy André Antoine
Vice-President and Minister for Economy, External Trade and New Technologies: Jean-Claude Marcourt
Minister for Local Responsibilities, Towns and Tourism: Paul Furlan

244

Minister for Health, Equality and Social Action: Eliane Tillieux
Minister for Environment, Land Management and Mobility: Philippe Henry
Minister for Public Works, Agriculture, Rural Affairs, Nature and Forests: Benoit Lutgen

Parliament
Walloon Parliament, URL: http://parlement.wallonie.be/content
President: P. Dupriez

Ministries
Office of the Minister-President of the Walloon Region, 25-27 rue Mazy, 5100 Jambes, Belgium. Tel: +32 (0)81 333160, fax: +81 (0)81 333166, e-mail: dircom@mrw.wallonie.be, URL: http://mrw.wallonie.be
General Secretariat, Place de la Wallonie 1, 5100 Namur, Belgium. Tel: + 32 (0)81 333111, +32 (0)81 333777, URL: http://mrw.wallonie.be/sg/sec
Chancellery, Place de la Wallonie 1, 5100 Namur, Belgium. Tel: +32 (0)81 333030, fax: +32 (0)81 333033, e-mail: a.paulet@mrw.wallonie.be
Ministry of Transport and Equipment, blvd. du nord 8, B-5000 Namur, Belgium. e-mail: interent@met.wallonie.be, URL: http://met.wallonie.be/opencms/opencms/fr/
Ministry of the Walloon Region, Place de la Wallonie, 1 (5ème étage), 5100 Jambes, Belgium. URL: http://mrw1.wallonie.be/
General Directorate for Agriculture, Chaussée de Louvain, 14-5000 Namur, Belgium. URL: http://agriculture.wallonie.be/apps/spip_wolwin/
General Directorate for Economy, URL: http://economie.wallonie.be/
General Directorate for the Environment, Avenue Prince de Liège 15, Namur B-5100, Belgium. URL: http://environnement.wallonie.be/
General Directorate for Land Management, Housing and Heritage, URL: http://mrw.wallonie.be/dgatlp/dgatlp/default.asp

The Flemish Government (as at April 2013)
Minister-President and Minister of Economy, Foreign Policy, Agriculture and Rural Policy: Kris Peeters (CD&V)
Vice-Minister-President and Minister for Innovation, Public Investment, Media and Poverty Reduction: Ingrid Lieten (sp.a)
Vice-Minister-President and Minister for Administrative Affairs, Local and Provincial Government, Civic Integration, Tourism and the Vlaamse Rand: Geert Bourgeoius (N&VA)
Minister for Welfare, Public Health and Family: Jo Vandeurzen (CD&V)
Minister for Mobility and Public Works: Hilde Crevits (CD&V)
Minister for Energy, Housing, Cities and Social Economy: Freya Van den Bossche (sp.a)
Minister for Finance, Budget, Work, Town and Country Planning and Sport: Philippe Muyters (N-VA)
Minister for Environment, Nature and Culture: Joke Schauvliege (CD&V)
Minister for Education, Youth, Equal Opportunities and Brussels Affairs: Pascal Smet (sp.a)

Parliament
Flemish Parliament, Sint-Gillislaan 45, 92000 Dendermonde, Belgium. Tel: +32 (0) 52 218 856, fax: +32 (0)52 380 771, e-mail: norbert.debatselier@vlaamsparlement.be, URL: http://www.vlaamsparlement.be/vp/index.html

Departments
Coordination Department (Foreign Affairs and Communications), Boudewijngebouw, Boudewijnlaan 30, 1000 Brussels, Belgium. Tel: +32 (0)2 553 5968, fax +32 (0)2 553 5863, e-mail: info@coo.vlaanderen.be
General Affairs and Finance Department, Boudewijngebouw, Boudewijnlaan 30, 1000 Brussels, Belgium. Tel: +32 (0)2 553 5171, fax: +32 (0)2 553 5021, e-mail: info@azf.vlaanderen.be
Department of Science, Innovation and Media, Koning Albert II-laan 7, 1210 Brussels, Belgium. Tel: +32 (0)2 553 4535, fax: +32 (0)2 553 4537, e-mail: info@wim.vlaanderen.be
Department of Education, Hendrik Consciencegebouw, Koning Albert II-laan 15, 1210 Brussels, Belgium. Tel: +32 (0)2 553 8611, fax: +32 (0)2 553 9655, URL: http://www.ond.vlaanderen.be/infolijn
Department of Welfare, Public Health and Culture, Markiesgebouw, Markiesstraat 1, 1000 Brussels, Belgium. Tel: +32 (0)2 553 3110, fax: +32 (0)2 553 3140, e-mail: info@wvc.vlaanderen.be, URL: http://www.wvg.vlaanderen.be/welzijnengezondheid/
Department of Economics, Employment, Home Affairs and Agriculture, Markiesgebouw, Markiesstraat 1, 1000 Brussels, Belgium. Tel: +32 (0)2 553 3902, fax: +32 (0)2 553 4067, e-mail: info@ewbl.vlaanderen.be
Department of Environment and Infrastructure, Graaf de Ferrarisgebouw, Koning Albert II-laan 20 bus2, 1210 Brussels, Belgium. Tel: +32 (0)2 553 7102, fax: +32 (0)2 553 7105, e-mail: leefmilieu.infrastructuur@lin.vlaanderen.be, URL: http://www.lin.vlaanderen.be/

The Brussels-Capital Government (as at April 2013)
Minister-President, responsible for Local Administration, Land Management, Monuments and Sites, Co-operation and Development and Regional Statistics: Charles Picqué
Minister responsible for Finance, Budget, & Foreign Relations: Guy Vanhengel
Minister responsible for Environment, Energy, Water Policy and Urban Renovation: Evelyne Huytebroeck
Minister responsible for Public Works, Transport, IT and Brussels Port: Brigitte Grouwels
Minister responsible for Employment, Economy, Foreign Trade and Scientific Research: Celine Fremault
Secretary of State with responsibility for Town Planning and Public Hygiene: Rachid Madrane
Secretary of State with responsibility for Mobility & Equal Opportunities: Bruno de Lille

Secretary of State with responsibility for Housing, Fire Prevention and Emergency Medical Aid: Christos Doulkeridis

Parliament
Brussels Regional Parliament, URL: http://www.parlbruparl.irisnet.be/
President: Eric Tomas

Administrations
General Secretariat Services, Boulevard du Jardin Botanique, 1035 Brussels, Belgium. Tel: +32 (0)2 204 2111, fax: +32 (0)2 518 1739, URL: http://www.brussels.irisnet.be
Local Authorities Administration, Boulevard du Jardin Botanique, 1035 Brussels, Belgium. Tel: +32 (0)2 204 2111
Finance & Budget Administration, Centre des Communications du Nord, Rue du Progres 80, 1030 Brussels, Belgium. Tel: +32 (0)2 204 2111, fax: +32 (0)2 204 1517
Equipment and Transport Administration, Centre des Communications du Nord, Rue du Progres 80, 1030 Brussels, Belgium. Tel: +32 (0)2 204 2111, fax: +32 (0)2 204 1512
Housing and Spatial Development Administration, Centre des Communications du Nord, Rue du Progres 80, 1030 Brussels, Belgium. Tel: +32 (0)2 204 2111, fax: +32 (0)2 204 0135
The Economy and Employment Administration, Boulevard du Jardin Botanique, 1035 Brussels, Belgium. Tel: +32 (0)2204 2111, e-mail: expan.eco@mrbc.irisnet.be

Government of the French Community (as at April 2012)
Minister-President: Rudy Demotte (page 1414)
Vice-President, and Minister for Children, Research and Civil Service: Jean-Marc Nollet
Vice-President, and Minister for the Budget, Finance, and Sport: André Antoine
Vice-President and Minister of Higher Education: Jean-Claude Marcourt
Minister of Culture, Health and Equal Opportunities: Fadila Laanan
Minister of Compulsory Education: Marie-Dominique Simonet
Minister of Youth: Evelyne Huytebroeck

Parliament
Parliament of the French Community, Rue de la Loi 6, 1012 Brussels, Belgium. Tel: +32 (0)2 506 3811, fax: +32 (0)2 506 3978, URL: http://www.pcf.be

Ministries
Ministry of the French Community, Boulevard Leopold II, 44, 1080 Brussels, Belgium. Tel: +32 (0)2 413 2311, fax: +32 (0)2 413 3443, URL: http://www.cfwb.be

Government of the German Community (as at April 2013)
Minister-President, Minister for Local Authorities: Karl-Heinz Lambertz (SP) (page 1460)
Minister for Education, Employment and Training: Oliver Paasch
Minister for Family, Health and Social Affairs: Harald Mollers
Minister for Culture, Media and Tourism: Isabelle Weykmans (PFF)

Parliament
Council of the German-speaking Community (Rat der Deutschsprachigen Gemeinschaft Belgiens), Kaperberg 8, B-4700 Eupen, Belgium. Tel. + 32 (0)87 590720, fax + 32 (0)87 590730, e-mail: verwaltung@rdg.be, URL: http://www.dgparlament.be/

Ministries
Government of the German-speaking Community (Regierung der Deutschsprachigen Gemeinschaft Belgiens), Klötzerbahn 32, B-4700 Eupen, Belgium. Tel: + 32 (0)87 596400, fax: +32 (0)87 740258, e-mail: regierung@dgov.be, URL: http://www.dgov.be, http://www.dglive.be
Ministry of the German-speaking Community, Postanschrift Gospert 1-5, 4700 Eupen, Belgium. Tel: +32 (0)87 596300, fax: +32 (0)87 552891, e-mail: ministerium@dgov.be

AREA AND POPULATION

Area
Belgium is located in western Europe, north of France, south of the Netherlands and east of Germany and Luxembourg. The north-west of the country borders the north sea. The total area of Belgium is 32,545 sq. km. The terrain is generally flat, but is hilly and forested in the southeast (Ardennes) region.

The Walloon region covers 55.2 per cent of the total area of Belgium, slightly more than the Flemish area of 44.3 per cent.

The climate is temperate, with moderate temperatures and frequent rain.

To view a map, consult http://www.lib.utexas.edu/maps/cia08/belgium_sm_2008.gif

Population
The population on 1 January 2011 was estimated at 10,951,266. This was the largest increase since 1965, and was mainly due to the rise in net migration to Belgium. Figures from January 1 2011 show that residents of Belgium with a foreign nationality numbered 1,119,256, many coming from other countries of the EU. The main countries of origin are Italy, France, the Netherlands, Spain, Germany, Portugal, Poland, Turkey and Romania. The population was estimated to be 10,807,396 in 2010 and forecast to rise to 11.5 million by 2020.

As at 1st January 2011, the population was structured in the following way: 0-17 years, 2,231,033; 18-64 years, 6,837,428; 65 years and above, 1,882,805. By 2050 the population aged 65 and over is expected to exceed 2,860,000. In 2005 the density of the population per sq. km. was 342.2; the most densely populated area is the Brussels-Capital region with 6,238.3 inhabitants per sq. km.

BELGIUM

The number of those reaching 100 years old has increased from 546 in 1990 to 1,381 in 2008; 10.4 per cent of Belgian men reached their centenary (a reduction of almost ten per cent on 1990), whilst 89.6 per cent of women attained 100 years, (an increase of 9.6 per cent on 1990). In 2009, life expectancy at birth was 79.84 (77.15 males, 82.43 females). Life expectancy in the Brussels-Capital region was 79.65 years, in the Flemish speaking region 80.66 years, and in Walloon 78.40 years.

Various languages are dominant in specific regions. These include Flemish-speaking regions (57 per cent of the population), French-speaking (32 per cent) and German-speaking (0.7 per cent). A further 10 per cent in Brussels are bilingual.

Approximately 57.8 per cent of the population lives in the Flemish region, 32.4 per cent in the Walloon region and 9.8 per cent the Brussels capital region. The following table shows population figures amongst the different regions and provinces:

Regional population, 1st January 2010

Area	Inhabitants
REGION	
Brussels capital region	1,089,538
Flemish region	6,251,983
Walloon region	3,498,384
PROVINCE	
Antwerp	1,744,862
Vlaams Brabant	1,076,924
Hainaut (2005)	1,286,275
Limburg	838,505
Liège	1,067,685
Luxembourg	269,023
Namur	472,281
Oost Vlaanderen	1,432,326
Walloon Brabant	379,515
West Flanders	1,159,366

Source: National Institute of Statistics

Births, Marriages, Deaths

In 2009, there were an estimated 127,297 births down from 128,049 births in 2008. In 2009 there were 104,509 deaths. In 2008 there were 45,613 marriages (approximately 4.13 per 1,000 inhabitants) and 35,366 divorces (approximately 3 per 1,000 inhabitants). In 2008 there were an estimated 2,183 same sex marriages and 161 same sex divorces. In 2007 there were 49,189 cohabitation contracts.(Source: INS)

Public Holidays 2014

1 January: New Year's Day
18 April: Easter Monday
1 May: Labour Day
29 May: Ascension Day
9 June: Whit Monday
21 July: Independence Day
15 August: Assumption Day
1 November: All Saints' Day
11 November: Armistice Day
25 December: Christmas Day

Community Public Holidays

8 May: Brussels Capital Region
11 July: Flemish Community
15 September: Walloon Community
27 September: French Community
15 November: German-speaking Community

EMPLOYMENT

Figures for 2008 show that 62.4 per cent of the labour force was employed which fell to 61.6 per cent in 2009 before climbing again to 62 per cent in 2010. The unemployment rate in 2008 was 7.0 per cent, rising to 7.9 per cent in 2009, to 8.3 per cent in 2010, falling to 7.2 per cent in 2011. (Source: URL: http://www.statbel.fgov.be)

The following table shows a breakdown of employment by activity:

Employment according to industry, 2008

Sector	No. of Employees
Source: Copyright © International Labour Organization (ILO Dept. of Statistics, http://laborsta.ilo.org)	
Agriculture, hunting, and forestry	79,400
Fishing	1,000
Mining and quarrying	6,200
Manufacturing	727,500
Utilities	40,400
Construction	321,800
Wholesale and retail, repairs,	571,000
Hotel and restaurants	141,900
Transport, storage and communications	331,800
Financial services	175,700
Real Estate, renting and business activities	417,900
Public admin. and defence; compulsory social services	436,900
Education	375,600
Health and social work	564,100

- continued	
Other community, personal services	181,800
Household servants	42,100
Extra territorial organisations and bodies	30,700
Total	4,445,900

Over 50 per cent of private and public sector employees belong to a union. The main unions are the Belgian Socialist Confederation of Labour, the Confederation of Catholic Labour Unions, and the Confederation of Liberal Labour Unions.

Average household incomes are higher in Flanders than in Brussels or Wallonie, but there is a larger concentration of wealthy households in Brussels. In Flanders, 11 per cent of the population live below the poverty threshold, whilst in Wallonie, this figure reaches 17 per cent. In 2006, an estimated 14.7 per cent of the population were classified as poor. (Source: http://www.statbel.fgov.be)

In recent years the number of people working part time has risen. The number of part time employees rose to over 1,020,000 in 2011, of which 819,000 were women.

BANKING AND FINANCE

Currency

On 1 January 2002 the euro became legal tender. Prior to that the currency was the Belgian Franc of 100 centimes
€= 40.3399 Belgian francs (European Central Bank irrevocable conversion rate)
1 euro (€) = 100 cents
Bank notes are in denominations of 5, 10, 20, 50, 100, 200 and 500 euro. Coins are in denominations of 1, 2, 5, 10, 20 and 50 cents and 1 and 2 euro.

GDP/GNP, Inflation, National Debt

Over recent years, the economic priority has been the reduction of a large public debt, which fell below 100 per cent of GDP in 2003 for the first time in nearly 30 years, and continued to fall, reaching 88.2 per cent of GDP in 2006. However, faced with the global economic crisis (2009/10), progress in debt reduction will no longer be at the forefront of economic policy, and public debt grew to over 92 per cent of GDP by 2010.

The downturn has had a severe impact on Belgium; in February 2009, 789 businesses closed down, bringing the total of failing businesses over the quarter to 2,423 (up 25.7 per cent over the same period in 2008). Industry saw an increase of 44.2 per cent in businesses closing, the trade sector saw an increase of 17.2 per cent and the transport and other services sector saw an increase of 25.1 per cent of closed businesses. The Belgian state-owned Fortis Bank recorded an estimated net loss of up to €19bn over 2008 due to the financial crisis and the break-up of the banking and insurance group that owned it. The bank was one of the first European financial firms to seek a government bail-out. However, the Belgian economy has proved more resiliant that that of its neighbours, largely due to relatively low levels of debt in households and businesses.

The economy grew by 2.7 per cent over 2007, slightly lower than in 2006 when growth peaked at 2.9 per cent. Growth slowed to 1.1 per cent over 2008, contracting to -3.0 per cent over 2009 (compared to -4.1 per cent in the eurozone), before growing by an estimated 2.2 per cent in 2010, and was forecast to grow by 2.4 per cent in 2011 and 2.2 per cent in 2012. GDP at market prices in 2008 was €346,385.0 million, €340,788.0 million in 2009, €354,688.0 million in 2010 and 368,304.0 in 2011.

The services sector accounts for approximately for 68 per cent of GDP, followed by industry (15 per cent), construction (five per cent) and agriculture, forestry and fishing (less than one per cent). Other components accounted for 10 per cent. The following table shows estimated Gross Value Added according to branch of activity:

GVA according to branch of activity (current prices), (€ million)

Sector	2010	2011	2011-10 +/- %
Source: National Institute of Statistics, Key Figures 2012			
Agriculture, forestry, fisheries	2,319	2,015	-13.1
Industry	52,491	56,242	7.1
Construction	17,999	18,967	5.4
Services	243,369	251,567	3.4
Trade, transport and communications	77,170	80,125	3.8
Financial and business activities, estate agencies and renting	89,533	91,528	2.2
Government and education	46,210	48,066	4.0
Other services	30,456	31,848	4.6
Other components	38,510	39,513	2.6
Total GDP	354,688	368,304	3.8

Private and public consumption increased over 2007 (by 2.5 per cent and 2.1 per cent respectively). Public and business investment increased both increased by over five per cent. Both consumption and investment are likely to be affected by the global downturn, due to public lack of confidence.

Inflation averaged 1.8 per cent over 2007, and 4.5 per cent over 2008. Inflation was 0.9 per cent in 2009 rising to an average of 2.19 per cent in 2010, and 3.5 per cent in 2011.

Belgium's public debt reached a peak in 1993 when public debt represented almost 135 per cent of GDP. The public debt ratio has been reduced since, but climbed to nearly 90 per cent of GDP in 2008, due in part to government bank bailouts. It is expected to remain high for several years. In 2009 it was 96.7 per cent of GDP. Estimated figures for the end of 2011 put total public debt at about 96.8 per cent of GDP.

Foreign Investment
The largest foreign investors in Belgium are France, the Netherlands, Germany and the United States. Foreign direct investment totaled over US$705 billion in 2009. US and other foreign countries employ about 11 per cent of the workforce.

Foreign businesses are treated the same as Belgian companies. There are no restrictions on repatriation of capital and profits, and no requirement that a Belgian national own part of the company's equity. Special corporate tax rules exist for foreign companies intending to set up distribution and service centres in Belgium.

Balance of Payments / Imports and Exports
Belgium is one of the largest trading nations in the world. Belgium chiefly imports part produced goods, finishes them and re-exports them. Around 76 per cent of Belgium's trade is with other EU countries.

Provisional figures for the value of traded commodities in December 2008 are listed below:

Trade in Commodities, December 2008 (€ million - provisional)

Commodity	Exports	Imports
Food and Animal products	1,797.7	1,528.3
Beverages and Tobacco	160.9	266.4
Raw materials, except fuels	400.7	716.5
Minerals, lubricants and fuels	1,527.6	2,928.8
Oils and fats of animal or vegetable origin	78.7	135.1
Chemicals and related products	3,657.6	3,019.3
Manufactured articles classified by primary material	2,946.2	2,526.5
Machines and transport equipment	4,149.7	4,970.9
Other manufactured articles	1,644.2	1,979.0
Articles and transactions not included above	43.5	67.1

Source: National Institute of Statistics

The following table shows provisional trade figures by major destination for the year 2010:

Imports and Exports by major destination, 2010

Country	€000 (provisional)
Source: Banque Nationale de Belgique	
Exports	
Total	**310,068,435.93**
China	5,417,976.27
Germany	57,987,904.71
Spain	9,286,178.34
France	51,576,632.68
United Kingdom	21,545,233.44
India	6,823,977.84
Italy	14,254,861.55
Luxembourg	5,452,587.88
Netherlands	36,891,377.07
Poland	5,014,988.06
US	17,696,785.58
Imports	
Total	**294,318,387.25**
China	12,009,547.64
Germany	47,915,987.82
France	33,181,951.64
UK	15,701,780.91
Ireland	15,514,919.7
Italy	9,073,205.69
Japan	6,606,955.55
Netherlands	55,812,586.44
Russia	6,224,269.46
United States	16,418,573.05

Central Bank
Banque Nationale de Belgique SA (Nationale Bank van Belgie NV), Boulevard de Berlaimont 14, B 1000 Brussels, Belgium. Tel: +32 2 2212111, fax: +32 2 2213101, e-mail: secretariat@nbb.be, URL: http://www.nbb.be
Governor: Luc Coerne (page 1407)

Chambers of Commerce and Trade and Investment Organisations
Belgian National Federation of Chambers of Commerce and Industry, URL: http://www.cci.be
Flanders Foreign Investment Office, URL: http://www.ffio.com
Chambre de Commerce et d'Industrie de Bruxelles, URL: http://www.ccib.be
Féderation des Entreprises de Belgique (Belgian Business Federation), URL: http://www.vbo-feb.be
Brussels Stock Exchange, URL: http://www.euronext.com

MANUFACTURING, MINING AND SERVICES

Primary and Extractive Industries
Belgium has few natural resources. Although it has no oil reserves, according to EIA estimates, the country had a refinery capacity of 740 thousand barrels per day in 2012. Oil consumption reached 644.44 thousand barrels per day in 2011. Natural gas consumption was 475 billion cubic feet in 2011, all of it imported, and coal consumption fell to 3.287 million short tons in 2010. (Source: EIA)

In 2005, oil products continued to dominate the energy market (39.5 per cent), though its share was slightly down on 2000. Nuclear energy also increased its share to 22.1 per cent. Renewable sources of energy increased from 1.6 per cent to 2.5 per cent of the market. There has been a drop in solid fuels percentage share of the market, from 14.1 per cent in 2000 to 9.7 per cent in 2005. There has also been a drop in the consumption of natural gas 700 billion cubic feet in 2010 and 475 billion cubic feet in 2011.

Energy
Electricity generation in 2010 reached 88.41 billion KWh, approximately 50 per cent of which was nuclear and some 40 per cent GWh thermal. Installed capacity was 17.49 GWe. Total electricity consumption in 2010 was 84.68 billion kWh. Total primary energy production was 0.527 quadrillion Btu in 2009 and consumption was 2.605 quadrillion Btu. Energy intensity (Btu per 2005 US$) was 7.465. (Source: EIA)

Nuclear power is dominant in the production of electricity, supplying 55.4 per cent of total requirements in 2004. The first nuclear power station went on line in 1974 at Doel, on the left bank of the Scheldt below Antwerp; a second has been in operation since 1975 at Tihange along the Meuse, 30 km upstream from Liège. These two sites were later expanded, and today Belgium has seven nuclear power stations. In 1988 the government announced that nuclear power was to be gradually phased out starting in 2015. (Source: FPS Economy, DG Statistics)

Manufacturing
The main industrial centres are Antwerp, Brussels and Ghent. Belgium has around 500 industrial parks covering 40,000 hectares. The manufacturing sector employed a total of 727,500 in 2008, and the construction industry employed almost 321,800 in the same year. Manufacturing contributed 17 per cent of Belgium's GDP in 2006, and €53,500 million towards the national Gross value added. The construction industry accounted for five per cent of GDP in the same year, and earned some €14,256 million.

Production of Manufactured Goods in € Million

Sector	2004
Food products not inc. meat & dairy	19.425
Processed meat	1.523
Processed fruit & vegetables	371
Fruit & vegetable based products	2.106
Beverages	1.457
Fabric & textiles	1.095
Paper and paperboard	3.818
Chemicals	29.518
Pharmaceuticals	4.555
Toiletries, & perfumes	1.318
Rubber & plastic	4.891
Glass & glass materials	1.680
Machinery and equipment	7.295
Office machinery	279,71
Machinery, electrical apparatus	4.075
Radio, Television & communication equipment	2.345
Motor vehicles	11.515
Furniture	1.965

Source: BelgoStat

Service Industries
The service industry is Belgium's largest employer; around 3,124,000 people worked in the sector in 2006. The trade sector employed 559,000; financial, real estate, renting and business activities 559,000; Health and social work, 529,000, and public administration, defence and social services 422,000. Services contributed €208,627 million to the Belgian Gross Value Added in 2006, up from €198,638 million in 2005.

Belgium is home to many international organisations including the European Commission and NATO.

Of the 6,747 foreigners day visitors to Belgium in 2005, most were Dutch, French or British. A further 15,553 foreigners had overnight stays; these were mainly from the Netherlands (4,925), the UK (2,199) and Germany (1,952).
Belgium Tourist Reservations, URL: http://www.trabel.com/

Agriculture
Belgium had 17,352 sq. km of farmland in 2007 (down from 17,653 in 2000), which was used as follows: arable land, 8,387 sq. km.; permanent crops, 235 sq. km; pasture, 5,073 sq. km and other agricultural use, 3,658 sq. km. A further 6,059 sq. km. is forested or woodland.

Whilst the number of farms has decreased over the years, (to 39,528 in 2011), the total area used for farming has been reduced only slightly, indicating an increase in the size of the average farming establishment. The number of full-time farm workers is shrinking; in 2011, 74,399 people employed in agriculture down from 83,865 in 2009. Despite an increase in the number of organic farms, (from 135 in 1991 to 712 according to recent figures), organic farming remains marginal, representing just one per cent of farming establishments. (Source: Stabel)

BELGIUM

The agriculture, forestry and fisheries industry contributed €2,831 million towards Belgium's GDP in 2006, down from €2,925 million in 2005. The sector now represents under 1 per cent of total GDP.

Belgium is almost self-supporting in meat production and has a surplus for export as well as some milk products, sugar, and horticultural and agricultural products. Horticulture supplies most of the country's needs. Production of fruits, vegetables and flowers is large enough to allow quantities to be exported.

Agricultural Production (ha)	2010	2011
Cereals	339,102	327,679
Winter wheat	206,282	182,709
Winter barley	40,512	39,641
Grain Maize	62,531	72,025
Industrial crop	92,491	94,162
Sugar Beet	59,303	62,199
Flax	11,048	11,296
Rapeseed	11,279	12,016
Potatoes	81,760	82,341
Fodder crops	267,409	269,405
Silage maize	176,313	173,540
Outdoor vegetables	40,941	40,038
Fallow land	95,920	7,307
Cultivation of perennial plants	21,674	21,671
Permanent pastures	499,687	488,924
Greenhouse crops	2,140	1,819

Source: http://statbel.fgov.be

In 2010 there were an estimated 2,593,000 cattle of which milk cows were 521,000. There were 6,430,000 pigs and an estimated 34 million poultry. An estimated 812,541 head of cattle were slaughtered in 2008 (430,234,441 kg) and 11,157,415 pigs (1,320,211,586 kg). An estimated 614 million litres of milk were produced, 133.8 million litres of cream, 175.6 tonnes of butter, and 62.8 tonnes of cheese.

In 2008, 17.064 tonnes of fish were caught (down from 18.680 tonnes in 2006), with a value of €66.5 million, down from €79.4 million the previous year. Plaice and sole are the largest catches, at 4.264 tonnes and 3.58 tonnes respectively. (Source: http://statbel.fgov.be)

COMMUNICATIONS AND TRANSPORT

Travel Requirements
Citizens of most EU member states do not require a passport if they have a National Identity card. Nationals of the USA, Canada, Australia, Denmark, Sweden and the UK require a passport valid for at least three months beyond length of stay. USA, Canadian, Australian and EU citizens do not require a visa for stays of up to three months.

Belgium is a signatory to the 1995 Schengen Agreement.
See http://www.eurovisa.info/SchengenCountries.htm for details.

Customs Restrictions
Belgium applies the common external tariff to goods imported from non-EU countries. For goods imported from an EU country there are no customs duties.
Administration of Customs and Excise, URL: http://www.fiscus.fgov.be

National Airlines
SN Brussels Airlines, (formed from Sabena and Delta Air Transport), URL: http://www.brussels-airlines.com
Virgin Express, URL: http://www.brusselsairlines.com/

International Airports
Civil aviation is administered by the Minister of Communications. Air transport and general policy matters are dealt with by the Administrator General. The main airports are operated by a government agency, the 'Régie des Voies Aériennes'. The main international airports are Brussels National, which carries around 95 per cent of passenger traffic and 85 per cent of freight traffic, Antwerp, Ostend, Charleroi (Gosselies) and Liège (Bierset). Air services link Brussels with most of the capitals of Europe and the Middle East, Africa, the USA, Canada and Mexico and the Far East. Belgium has a total of 42 airports.
Belgian Airport Company (formerly the Belgian Airways and Airport Agency), URL: http://www.brusselsairport.be/
Antwerp, Deurne Airport, URL: http://www.antwerp-airport.be/
Passengers, 2007: 175,000; Aircraft movement: 51,200
Brussels, National Airport, URL: http://www.brusselsairport.be
Passengers, 2006: 146,355; Aircraft movement: 26,850
Charleroi, Gosselies Airport, URL: http://www.charleroi-airport.com/
Passengers, 2007: 2.458 million; Aircraft movments, 2007: 70,725
Liège, Bierset Airport, URL: http://www.liegeairport.com/
Passengers, 2007: 332,848
Ostend Airport, URL: http://www.ost.aero/
Passengers, 2007: 180,063

Railways
The total railway network covers 3,380 km (2,507 km electrified; 2,163 km are fitted for 120 km/h; and 71 km are fitted for 300 km/h). Belgium is also part of the Thalys network which is a joint venture between Belgian, French, Dutch and German railways. Eurostar connects Brussels with London by rail. Both Brussels and Antwerp have a Metro system as well as trams. Tram systems operate in the towns of Charleroi, Ghent and Ostend. In 2009, the percentage of total freight transport by land in tonnes-kilometres was 15 per cent.

Roads
The number of vehicles on the roads continues to increase; by mid 2011, there were over 6.8 million vehicles, of which approximately 5.4 million were passenger cars, almost one car per inhabitant. Whilst the number of accidents on the roads remains stable at around 50,000, the number of fatalities has gone down by 20 per cent over four years. However, there are still over a thousand deaths per year. In 2006, 348.5 million tonnes of goods were transported by road. Vehicles drive on the right. In 2009, the percentage of total freight transport by land in tonnes-kilometres was 69 per cent.

Waterways
Belgium has a large inland waterway system, incorporating the rivers Muese and Scheldt, the Albert Canal, the Sambre Canal and the Antwerp-Brussels-Charleroi Canal (ABC), the Canal du Centre, the Nimy-Blaton-Péronnes Canal and the Scheldt. The network is around 1,530 km long. In 2009, the percentage of total freight transport by waterways in tonnes-kilometres was 16 per cent. Within Europe, only the Netherlands has a higher percentage. Total traffic was approximately 130,350 million tonnes in 2008. (Source: Statbel)

Shipping
Main ports and harbours are Antwerp, Brugge, Gent, Hasselt, Liege, Mons, Namur Oostende and Zeebrugge. In 2006 there were 58,829 dockings and departures. In 2006 there were also 375,000 passenger arrivals and 374,000 departures. Transported tonnage was 93.6 million tonnes loaded and 125.6 million tonnes unloaded.

The merchant marine totals 25 ships (1,000 GRT or above), 2 bulk ships, 7 cargo ships, 5 chemical tankers, 1 liquefied gas tanker, and 10 oil tankers.

HEALTH

Health care is paid for by a welfare system made up of employer and employee contributions. In 2005-10 there were 31,578 doctors (30.1 per 10,000 population), 12,109 pharmacists, 7,655 dentists (7.3 per 10,000 population), 5,637 nurses and midwives (5.4 per 10,000 population), and 12,450 pharmaceutical personnel (11.9 per 10,000 population). There were 65 hospital beds per 10,000 population in the period 2005-11.

In 2009, the government spent approximately 15.1 per cent of its total budget on healthcare (up from 12.3 per cent in 2000), accounting for 75.1 per cent of all healthcare spending. Social security expenditure on health accounted for 84.9 per cent of government health expenditure. Private expenditure accounted for 24.9 per cent; pre-paid plans account for 19.1 per cent of health expenditure. Total expenditure on healthcare equated to 10.8 per cent of the country's GDP. Per capita expenditure on health was approximately US$4,749, compared with US$1,844 in 2000.

The infant mortality rate in 2010 was 4 per 1,000 live births. The child mortality rate (under 5 years) was down to 4 per 1,000 live births. The main causes of childhood mortality are (2010): congenital anomalies (27 per cent), prematurity (14 per cent), birth asphyxia (8 per cent), diarrhoea (1 per cent), pneumonia (1 per cent), neonatal sepsis (3 per cent) and injuries (8 per cent). In 2012, there were 40 reported cases of measles, 31 of mumps, and 814 of TB. (Source: http://www.who.int, World Health Statistics 2012)

Over the decade to 2006, cigarette sales increased by 8 per cent, whilst cigar sales went down by 5 per cent. However, cigarette sales fell by 7 per cent over 2007. Approximately 17 per cent of Belgians are obese and 22 per cent of those over 15 years old are regular smokers; more men than women smoke, and there is a greater smoking prevalence among French-speakers than amongst the Flemish community.

HIV/AIDs prevalence was estimated at 162 cases per 100,000 people.

EDUCATION

The complex organisation of the education system in Belgium reflects its linguistic and religious diversity; the two education ministries cover the French (plus the German minority) and the Dutch speaking areas, respectively. Federal legislation only covers such things as the age of compulsory education and funding of the communities, otherwise education is the province of the communities (French, Dutch or German speaking). Education is free and compulsory for both sexes, with excellent facilities are available for primary, secondary and higher education. Literacy is estimated at 99 per cent (99.7 per cent for those aged 15-24 years).

Compulsory schooling lasts from 6 to 18, and schools are organised by three education networks: community schools, subsidised schools (predominantly Catholic), and subsidised official schools which are organised by communes and provinces. Most children also attend both pre- and post-compulsory education. Primary school education is for six years. Secondary education has altered from selective to comprehensive, and also lasts for six years. Students an choose different types of secondary education, General Secondary Education; Technical Secondary Education; Vocational Secondary Education; Art Secondary Education. Secondary education is divided into three grades, each grade covering two years. During the first year of each grade pupils study the same education programme; during the second year of each grade pupils may choose from a range of options. In addition, provisions exist for special education and adult education. There are universities at Brussels, Leuven, Louvain-La-Neuve, Antwerp, Mons, Ghent and Liège. Leuven is the oldest, having been founded in 1426. Belgium also has a system of non-university institutions that provide higher education and training in areas such as technical and teacher training.

Figures for the school year 2006-07 show that there were a total of 2,300,217 students: 418,268 at nursery school, 736,802 at primary school, 830,258 at secondary school and 321,472 students in higher education, including university. In 2006, 8.1 per cent of the total population had obtained a university degree, and a further 16.3 per cent had received qualifications from other Higher Education establishments. (Source: FPS Economy, DG

Statistics) The pupil/teacher ratio in primary education was estimated at 11:1. An estimated 99 per cent of pupils move onto secondary education from primary education. Public expenditure on education was estimated to be 6 per cent of GDP in 2007, representing 12.4 per cent of total government expenditure. Of this, 43 per cent is allocated to secondary education. Approximately 63 per cent of pupils went on to tertiary education in 2008. (Source: UNESCO)

RELIGION

The majority of the inhabitants (75 per cent) of Belgium are Roman Catholic. There is full religious freedom and the State does not interfere in the internal affairs of the churches, paying part of the income of ministers of the denominations specified by the law out of the national treasury. Belgium has over 390,000 Muslims, 27,900 Jews, 25,800 Buddhists and 3,200 Hindus.

Belgium has a religious tolerance rating of 7 on a scale of 1 to 10 (10 is most freedom). (Source: World Religion Database)

Bishops' Conference, URL: http://www.catho.be/
Consistoire Central Israélite de Belgique (Central Council of the Jewish Communities of Belgium), URL: http://www.jewishcom.be

COMMUNICATIONS AND MEDIA

Newspapers
Het Laaste Nieuws, URL: http://www.hln.be
La Meuse, URL: http://www.lameuse.be
La Libre Belgique, URL: http://www.lalibre.be/index.php
Het Nieuwsblad, URL: http://www.nieuwsblad.be
Le Soir (Belgium), URL: http://www.lesoir.be
De Standaard, URL: http://www.standaard.be
Het Volk, URL: http://www.hetvolk.be
De Morgen, URL: http://www.demorgen.be
De Tijd, URL: http://www.tijd.be

Business Journals
De Financieel Ekonomische Tijd, URL: http://www.tijd.be
Trends, URL: http://www.trends.be
L'Echo, URL: http://www.lecho.be
The Bulletin, URL: http://www.thebulletin.be

Broadcasting
There are two public bodies that operate Belgian radio and television: the Radiodiffusion Télévision Belge de la Communauté Française (RTBF) for French transmissions and Vlaamse Radio en Televisie-omroep (formerly BRT - Belgische Radio en Televisieomroep) for Dutch transmissions. RTBF operates RTBF1, RTBF 2 and an international satellite channel. Over 95 per cent of Belgians have access to cable television. The switchover to digital television was completed in 2011.
Radio-Télévision Belge de la Communauté Française (RTBF), URL: http://www.rtbf.be
Vlaamse Radio en Televisieomroep, URL: http://www.tvl.be
Commercial stations include:

Canal Plus Belgique, URL: http://www.canalplus.be
Vlaamse Televisie Maatschappij (VTM), URL: http://www.vtm.be
VT4, URL: http://www.vt4.be/home.php
Radio Télévision Luxembourg (RTL), URL: http://www.rtlinfo.be/index.php
Belgischer Rundfunk (BRF), URL: http://www.brf.be/brf

National Press Agency (BELGA), URL: http://www.belga.be

Telecommunications
Recent figures show that over 4.2 million telephone lines and an estimated 12.4 million mobile phones are in use. The government auctioned off a fourth mobile phone license in January 2010.

The number of internet users has soared to around 8.1 million in 2009. Over 73 per cent of all households gave internet access and over 80 per cent of households with children have an internet connection. Approximately 28.3 per cent of the population had broadband connections in 2008. The majority of internet users use the internet daily. It is increasingly used for online banking; an estimated 66 per cent of the population used it for this in 2010. In 2009, there were an estimated 174,524 new registrations of '.be' domains, amounting to a total of 977,998.

ENVIRONMENT

Flooding is an issue for the areas of reclaimed coastal land; these are currently protected from the sea by concrete dikes. Other current issues include urbanization, industrial air pollution, and water pollution, specifically the Meuse River which is a major source of drinking water and is polluted by steel production wastes.

Belgium is party to the following international agreements: Air Pollution, Air Pollution-Nitrogen Oxides, Air Pollution-Persistent Organic Pollutants, Air Pollution-Sulfur 85, Air Pollution-Sulfur 94, Air Pollution-Volatile Organic Compounds, Antarctic-Environmental Protocol, Antarctic-Marine Living Resources, Antarctic Seals, Antarctic Treaty, Biodiversity, Climate Change, Climate Change-Kyoto Protocol, Desertification, Endangered Species, Environmental Modification, Hazardous Wastes, Law of the Sea, Marine Dumping, Marine Life Conservation, Ozone Layer Protection, Ship Pollution, Tropical Timber 83, Tropical Timber 94, Wetlands, and Whaling.

Total carbon dioxide emissions from the consumption of fossil fuels in 2009 amounted to 130.88 million metric tons; this fell to 127.19 million metric tons in 2010. (Source: EIA)

Belgium produces lower than average waste for a European country: 493 kg / inhabitant compared to the European average of 524 kg / inhabitant. In 2008, 35 per cent of waste was recycled, 25 per cent was composted and 35 per cent was incinerated with energy recovery in almost all cases. Approximately 5 per cent was landfill. (Source: Stabel)

SPACE PROGRAMME

Belgium has been involved in European space policy since the 1960s and was one of the founding member states of the European Space Agency. Its international bilateral co-operation programmes include working with France in the Earth observation programme SPOT and with Russia on the MIRAS programme.

BELIZE

Capital: Belmopan (Population estimate: 20,000)

Head of State: Her Majesty Queen Elizabeth II (Sovereign) (page 1420)

Governor-General: Sir. Colville Young GCMG, MBE (page 1541)

National Flag: A rectangular dark blue background with narrow red stripes at the top and bottom and with the country's coat of arms on a white circle in the centre

CONSTITUTION AND GOVERNMENT

Constitution
Belize was formally declared a British Colony in 1871 when the Crown Colony system of Government was introduced and the Legislative Assembly was replaced by a nominated Legislative Council. This constitution, with minor changes, continued until 1935. Further constitutional advances came in 1954 with the introduction of universal adult suffrage and an elected majority in the Legislature; the ministerial system was adopted in 1961. In 1970 the capital Belize City was replaced by Belmopan. The country's name was changed on 1 June 1973 from British Honduras to Belize. Belize achieved full independence on 21 September 1981.

The Government of Belize is operated on the principles of parliamentary democracy based on the Westminster system. The country is a sovereign, democratic state. A Prime Minister and Cabinet make up the executive branch, while a 29-member elected House of Representatives and 8-member appointed Senate form a bicameral legislature. Her Majesty Queen Elizabeth II is the titular Head of State. She is represented in Belize by a Governor-General who must be a Belizean. The Cabinet consists of a Prime Minister, other Ministers and Ministers of State who are appointed by the Governor-General on the advice of the Prime Minister.

To consult the full text of the constitution, please visit: http://www.belizelaw.org/e_library/constitution.html.

International Relations
An area covering over half of Belize has always been claimed by Guatemala, the reason for the British Army presence in the country. Whilst Guatemala recognised Belize's independence in 1991, it never formally relinquished its claim, and in 2000 the claim was renewed. Talks were held in Washington to try to resolve the situation and, in 2002, the two nations agreed a draft settlement. This was due to be the subject of referenda in both countries, but in 2003 Guatemalan officials notified the OAS (Organization of American States who were acting as facilitators) that they could not accept the recommendations for constitutional reasons. In 2007 the OAS recommended that the dispute be referred to the International Court of Justice.

Belize is a member of the Commonwealth, UN and OAS. It has strong ties with Caribbean states through its membership of CARICOM and is strengthening ties with its Central American neighbours through membership of SICA.

Recent Events
A strike involving both public and private sector workers took place in January 2005, the areas of dispute being tax increases and demands for salary increases. In April of the same year, there were anti-government protests. In April 2006, Belize began commercial exploitation of its oil reserves.

In September 2011, the USA added Belize to its blacklist of countries whoe are considered to be major producers or transit routes for illegal drugs.

Legislature
A 29-member elected House of Representatives and eight-member appointed Senate form a bicameral legislature. Five senators are appointed by the Governor-General on the advice of the Prime Minister, two on the advice of the Leader of the Opposition, and one on the

BELIZE

advice of the Belize Advisory Council. The Speaker of the House of Representatives and the President of the Senate are elected either from among the members of these Houses (providing they are not ministers) or from among persons who are not members of either house. Members of the House of Representatives are directly elected for a five-year term.

House of Representatives, National Assembly Building, PO Box 139, Cayo District, Belmopan, Belize. Tel: +501 (0)822 2141, fax: +501 (0)822 3889, e-mail: nationalassembly@belize.gov.bz

---

Cabinet (as at June 2013)

Prime Minister, Minister of Finance: Dean Barrow (page 1384)

Deputy Prime Minister, Minister of Natural Resources and Agriculture: Gaspar Vega (page 1531)

Minister of Foreign Affairs and Foreign Trade; Attorney General: Wilfred Elrington (page 1420)

Minister of Tourism amd Culture: Maneul Heredia

Minister of Human Development and Social Transformation: Anthony Martinez

Minister of Housing and Urban Development: Michael Finnegan

Minister of Trade, Investment, Private Sector Development and Consumer Protection: Erwin Contreras

Minister of Health: Pablo Marin

Minister of Education, Youth and Sports: Patrick Faber

Minister of Labour, Local Government and Rural Development: Godwin Hulse

Minister of Public Service, Elections and Boundaries: Charles Gibson

Minister of Works and Transport: Rene Montero

Minister of National Security, Police and Belize Defense Force: John Saldivar

Minister of Foresty, Fisheries, Sustainable Development and Indigenous People: Senator Liselle Alamilla

Minister of Energy, Science and Technology and Public Utilities: Senator Joy Grant

Minister with Special Emphasis on the Conscious Youth Development Programme and the Gang Truce Programme: Mark King

---

Ministries

Office of the Governor-General, Belize House, Belmopan, Belize. Tel: +501 822 2521, fax: +501 822 2050, URL: http://www.belize.gov.bz

Office of the Prime Minister, 2nd Floor, Sir Edney Cain Building, Belmopan, Belize. Tel: +501 822 2345, fax: +501 822 0898, e-mail: primeminister@belize.gov.bz, URL: http://www.belize.gov.bz/pm/welcome.shtml

Ministry of Finance, 2nd Floor Sir Edney Cain Building, Belmopan, Belize. Tel: +501 822 2345, fax: +501 822 0898, e-mail: finsec@btl.net, URL: http://www.mof.gov.bz

Ministry of Foreign Affairs, 2nd Floor Nemo Building, Belmopan, Belize. Tel: +501 822 3789, fax: +501 822 2854, e-mail: belizemfa@btl.net, URL: http://www.mfa.gov.bz

Ministry of Foreign Trade, 1st Floor Sir Edney Cain Building, Belmopan, Belize. Tel: +501 822 2832, fax: +501 822 2837, URL: http://www.foreigntrade.gov.bz

Ministry of Agriculture and Fisheries, 1st Floor, West Block Building, Belize. Tel: +501 822 2241, fax: +501 822 2409, e-mail: info@agriculture.gov.bz, URL: http://www.agriculture.gov.bz

Office of the Attorney General, Ground Floor, East Block Building, Belmopan, Belize. Tel: +501 822 2504, fax: +501 822 3390, e-mail: access@btl.net, URL: http://www.belizelaw.org

Ministry of Economic Development, Commerce, Industry and Consumer Protection, Ground Floor, Sir Edney Cain Building, Belmopan, Belize. Tel: +501 822 2526, fax: +501 822 3673, e-mail: econdev@btl.net, URL: http://www.belizeinvest.org.bz

Ministry of Education, 2nd Floor West Block Building, Belmopan, Belize. Tel: +501 822 3380, fax: +501 822 3389, e-mail: moeducation.moes@gmail.com, URL: http://www.moes.gov.bz

Ministry of Health, 2nd Floor East Block Building, Belmopan, Belize. Tel: +501 822 2497, fax: +501 822 2942, e-mail: dhsmoh@yahoo.com, URL: http://www.health.gov.bz

Ministry of Housing and Urban Development, 1st Floor Sir Edney Cain Building, Belmopan, Belize. Tel: +501 822 1039, fax: +501 822 3337, e-mail: info@housing.gov.bz, URL: http://www.belize.gov.bz

Ministry of Human Development and Social Transformation, Ground Floor, West Block Building, Belmopan, Belize. Tel: +501 822 2161, fax: +501 822 3175, e-mail: mhd@btl.net, URL: http://www.mohd.gov.bz

Ministry of Labour, Local Government and Rural Development, 6/8 Trinity Boulevard, Belmopan, Belize. Tel: +501 822 2297, fax: +501 822 0156, e-mail: secretary@labour.gov.bz, URL: http://www.belize.gov.bz

Ministry of Natural Resources and Environment, Market Square, Belmopan, Belize. Tel: +501 822 2226, fax: +501 822 2333, e-mail: info@mnrei.gov.bz, URL: http://www.mnrei.gov.bz

Ministry of Police and Public Security, Curl Osmond Thompson Building, Belmopan, Belize. Tel: +501 822 2231, fax: +501 822 2195, e-mail: minofnatsec@mns.gov.bz, URL: http://www.belizedefenceforce.net

Ministry of Public Service, Governance Improvement and Elections and Boundaries Department, Ground Floor, Sir Edney Cain Building, Belmopan, Belize. Tel: +501 822 2204, fax: +501 822 2206, e-mail: ceo@mps.gov.bz, URL: http://www.elections.gov.bz

Ministry of Public Utilities, Transport, Communications and National Emergency Management, Nemo Building, Belmopan, Belize. Tel: +501 822 2692, fax: +501 822 3317, e-mail: belizetransport@yahoo.com, URL: http://www.belize.gov.bz

Ministry of Tourism, Civil Aviation and Culture, Constitution Drive, Belmopan, Belize. Tel: +501 822 2801, fax: +501 822 2810, e-mail: tourismdpt@btl.net, URL: http://www.belizetourism.org

Ministry of Works, Power Lane, Belmopan, Belize. Tel: +501 822 2136, fax: +501 822 3282, e-mail: works@btl.net, URL: http://www.belize.gov.bz

Ministry of Youth, Sports, Information and Broadcasting, 1st Floor East Block Building, Belmopan, Belize. Tel: +501 822 3336, fax: +501 822 0433, e-mail: youthbelize@gmail.com, URL: http://www.belize.gov.bz

Political Parties

People's United Party (PUP), Independence Hall, 3 Queen Street, Belize City, Belize. URL: http://www.pup.org.bz
Leader: John Briceño
United Democratic Party (UDP), Belize City, Belize. URL: http://www.udp.org.bz
Leader: Dean Barrow (page 1384)

Elections

General elections are held at intervals of not longer than five years. The voting age is 18 and above. The Prime Minister has the right to advise the Governor-General to dissolve the National Assembly and so determine the date of the general elections.

The most recent election was held in February 2008. The United Democratic Party (UDP) won, unseating the People's United Party which had been in power for 10 years. Dean Barrow became the new prime minister.

Diplomatic Representation

Embassy of Belize, 2535 Massachusetts Avenue NW, Washington, DC 20008, USA. Tel: +1 202 332 9636, fax: +1 202 332 6888, e-mail: belize@aos.org, URL: http://www.embassyofbelize.org
Ambassador: H.E. Nestor Mendez
American Embassy, Gabourel Lane and Hutson Street, Belize City, Belize. Tel: +501 2 77161, fax: +501 2 30802, URL: http://belize.usembassy.gov
Ambassador: Vinai Thummalapally
Belize High Commission, Third Floor, 45 Crawford Place, London, W1H 4LP, UK. Tel: +44 (0)20 7723 3603, fax: +44 (0)20 7723 9637, e-mail: bzhc-lon@btconnect.com, URL: http://www.belizehighcommission.com
High Commissioner: H.E. Ms Kamela Palma
British High Commission PO Box 91, Belmopan, Belize. Tel:+501 822 2146/7, fax: +501 822 2761, e-mail: brithicom@btl.net , URL: http://ukinbelize.fco.gov.uk/en
High Commissioner: Peter Hughes OBE
Permanent Mission of Belize to the United Nations, 675 Third Ave. Suite 1911, New York, NY 10017, USA. Tel: +1 212 593 0999, fax: +1 212 593 0932, e-mail: blzun@belizemission.com, URL: http://www.un.int/belize/staff.htm
Permanent Representative: Janine Elizabet Coye-Felson

LEGAL SYSTEM

The legal system is based on English law. The Chief Justice has overall responsibility for the administration of justice in Belize, and is appointed by the Governor General after being advised by the Prime Minister.

There are three Supreme Court Judges - the Chief Justice and two other judges, known as Puisne Judges. Belize has six judicial districts each of which has a court which is presided over by a Magistrate. Appeals go to the Supreme Court and are heard by a jury. If a second appeal is heard this goes to the Court of Appeal, which sits 3-4 times a year, with four justices. In 2010, the Caribbean Court of Justice replaced the Judicial Committee of the Privy Council as the final Court of Appeal in civil and criminal matters.

The government generally respects the human rights of its citizens. However, lengthy pretrial detention remains a problem, as do discrimination against women and child labour. Belize retains the death penalty.

Supreme Court of Belize, URL: http://www.belizelaw.org/supreme_court/
Office of the Ombudsman, URL: http://www.ombudsman.gov.bz
Caribbean Court of Justice, URL: http://www.caribbeancourtofjustice.org/

LOCAL GOVERNMENT

There are six districts: Belize, Cayo, Corozal, Orange Walk, Stann Creek and Toledo. Its system of local government comprises two city councils (Belize and Belmopan), seven town councils and a network of 192 village and community councils. Belmopan, now the capital of Belize, has its own city council. Direct election of mayors was introduced in 2000. Belize City is administered by an 10-member elected City Council.

AREA AND POPULATION

Area

Belize is situated on the east coast of Central America with Mexico to the north and Guatemala to the west and south. The area of the country is 8,866 sq. miles. The major towns in Belize are Corozal Town, Orange Walk Town, Belize City, San Pedro Town, San Ignacio, Benque Viejo del Carmen, Belmopan, Dangriga and Punta Gorda.

Much of the land is forested. There are many lagoons near to the coast. It also has the world's fifth longest barrier reef and a coral stretching 184 miles along the offshore islands.

The climate is tropical with pronounced dry and wet seasons, with some regional variations. Temperatures vary according to elevation and tend to be higher inland.

To view a map of Belize, please consult:
http://www.lib.utexas.edu/maps/americas/belize_pol_03.pdf

Population

The population in 2010 was approximately 312,000. Approximately 67 per cent of the population live in urban areas. Belmopan, the capital, has a population of around 20,000, but the most inhabited urban area continues to be Belize City with 63,670 inhabitants. The average annual growth rate is 1.8 per cent.

The main ethnic groups are Creole, of African or Caribbean descent, 25 per cent, Mestizo (Spanish-Mayan) 53 per cent, Mayan 10 per cent and Garifuna six per cent (African Descent). Ethnic groups are heavily intermixed. There are a number of people of Spanish and East Indian descent as well as a small Mennonite community of European origin. The multi-racial make-up of the Belizean society also includes Chinese and Arabs.

The official language of Belize is English, which is used for instruction. Spanish is now very widely spoken. Mayan and Creole are also used.

Births, Marriages, Deaths
The population of Belize is young, with a median age of 22 years. An estimated 36 per cent of the population is 14 years and younger and just 7 per cent is aged over 60 years. In 2010 the birth rate was estimated to be 26.5 births per 1,000 population and the death rate was 6.5 deaths per 1,000 population. The infant mortality rate was 14 per 1,000 live births in 2010. The total fertility rate was 2.8 per female. The average life expectancy was 71 years for men and 76 years for women in 2009. Healthy life expectancy was 57 years for males and 63 years for females. (Source: http://www.who.int, World Health Statistics 2012)

Public Holidays 2014
1 January: New Year's Day
17 March: Commonwealth Day
18 April: Good Friday
22 April: Easter Monday
10 September: National Day
21 September: Independence Day
14 October: Columbus Day
25 December: Christmas Day
26 December: Boxing Day

EMPLOYMENT

The labour force in Belize consisted of 112,807 people in 2006. Of these, 102,223 were employed (67,000 men and 34,000 women). The unemployment rate in the same year stood at 9.4 per cent and affected 10,573 people. (Source: Statistical Institute of Belize). Figures for 2008 showed that the labour force numbered 124,600 with an unemployment of 8.2 per cent.

Figures for 2006 indicate that the service sector is the largest employer, employing around 60 per cent of the working population. This is to be expected with tourism becoming an important part of the economy. The agriculture sector employs around 22 per cent and industry and commerce, 18 per cent.

Total Employment by Economic Activity

Occupation	2005
Agriculture, hunting & forestry	17,548
Fishing	1,792
Mining & quarrying	211
Manufacturing	9,575
Electricity, gas & water supply	934
Construction	6,884
Wholesale & retail trade, repairs	16,928
Hotels & restaurants	8,740
Transport, storage & communications	6,365
Financial intermediation	1,594
Real estate, renting & business activities	2,114
Public admin. & defence; compulsory social security	6,771
Education	6,170
Health & social work	2,682
Other community, social & personal service activities	3,853
Households with employed persons	5,818
Extra-territorial organisations & bodies	554
Other	146

Source: Copyright © International Labour Organization (ILO Dept. of Statistics, http://laborsta.ilo.org)

BANKING AND FINANCE

Currency
The currency unit is the Belizean dollar (BZ$) of 100 cents. The Belize dollar is tied to the US dollar.

GDP/GNP, Inflation, National Debt
The Belize economy is based largely on tourism, forestry, fishing and agriculture, and agro-industry such as fruit processing and sugar refining. Tourism is now the largest foreign currency earner, having overtaken agriculture, but the industry has been affected by the global economic downturn. Sugar, the chief crop, accounts for nearly half of exports, while the banana industry is the country's largest employer. New technology has made oil extraction in Belize viable, and an oil field has recently been found in Central Belize. The economy is hindered by a poor infrastructure.

GDP was estimated at US$1.38 billion in 2008, and US$1.4 billion in 2009 reflecting a growth rate of 0.8 per cent. It was estimated to be US$1.43 billion in 2010. Growth rates for the years 2004 and 2005 were estimated to be 9.2 per cent and 5.1 respectively, slowing to an estimated 4 per cent in 2006. The growth rate fell to 1.2 per cent in 2007 but was expected to rise slighly to 2.0 per cent in 2008. Per capita income was estimated at US$4,150 in 2010.

According to the Statistical Institute of Belize, the services sector continued to be the greatest contributor to GDP in 2006, accounting for some 60.9 per cent, largely due to the growing importance of tourism in Belize. Agriculture, forestry, fishing and mining together accounted for 12.5 per cent of the country's GDP and the manufacturing sector contributed 17.8 per cent.

Over recent years, the cost of living has gradually increased; the inflation rate has risen from 0.6 per cent in 2000, to 4.3 per cent in 2006. In 2006, the highest increases were in transport and communications (6.9 per cent) and food, beverages and tobacco (4.3 per cent). (Source: Statistical Institute of Belize) Inflation was estimated at 6.4 per cent in 2008 and had fallen into negative figures for 2009 of -1.1 per cent.

Belize has an external debt of almost US$1 billion. The Government announced in July 2006 that they would not be able to meet external debt payments and sought to reschedule the debt.

Foreign Investment
Capital expenditure is financed through economic cooperation programmes with the UK, Canada and the USA and loans received from the Caribbean Development Bank. Belize has received BZ$20.0 million under the US Caribbean Basin Initiative to assist in private and public sector projects.

Balance of Payments / Imports and Exports
Figures for the year 2010 indicate that revenue from merchandise exports amounted to US$325 million. Cane sugar and citrus products, together with bananas, fish, lobster, farmed shrimp and clothing, were the main export products. The main markets were the USA (49 per cent), the EU and Caribbean Community countries.

Import costs reached an estimated US$709 million in 2010, the main products being food, consumer goods, building materials, vehicles and machinery. Most goods were imported from the USA (45 per cent), China and Mexico.

Central Bank
Central Bank of Belize, PO Box 852, Gabourel Lane, Belize City, Belize. Tel: +501 (0)223 6194, fax: +501 (0)223 6219, e-mail: cenbank@btl.net, URL: http://www.centralbank.org.bz Governor: Glenford Ysaguirre

Chambers of Commerce and Trade Organisations
The Belize Chamber of Commerce and Industry, URL: http://www.belize.org
Commercial Free Zone Management Office, URL: http://www.belizefreezones.com

MANUFACTURING, MINING AND SERVICES

Primary and Extractive Industries
Following 50 years of exploration for oil in Belize, technology has recently made its extraction viable. An oil field of around 10 million barrels was found in Central Belize in 2005, and oil production in 2008 was 3,500 barrels per day, though the field could potentially supply considerably more. Oil production in 2010 was put at 4,000 barrels per day all of which was crude. That year Belize consumed 7,000 barrels per day. Belize has no refineries, so exports the oil for processing before it is sold on the international market, mostly to the US. In the first half of 2007, Belize consumed 7,400 barrels of oil per day; Venezuela supplies oil to Belize at preferential terms under the PetroCaribe initiative.

Belize Natural Energy's (BNE) is the state's oil company.

Belize neither produces nor consumes natural gas.

Energy
Belize imports around 50 per cent of the electricity it needs from Mexico. The remainder is supplied by the hydroelectric facility at Mollejon and through heating plants fuelled by diesel. The Chalillo dam is currently under construction on the Upper Macal River. The dam is designed to increase Belize's own electricity production making the country less dependent on exports from Mexico.

In 2005, Belize completed construction of the 5.3-MW Chalillo hydropower project, the cause of much controversy with environmental groups who tried to block the construction. Figures for 2010 put net generation of electricity at 0.52 billion kilowatthours and consumption at 0.63 billion kilowatthours.

Manufacturing
Belize has a small manufacturing base, the main industries being garment production and food processing, particularly sugar, citrus fruits and bananas. In the garment industry typically cloth was imported from the US made up into garments then re-exported. The manufacturing sector accounted for 17.6 per cent of GDP in 2008 and employed 18 per cent of the workforce.

Service Industries
Belize is pursuing eco-tourism, promoting the longest barrier reef in the Western Hemisphere, fishing, wildlife reserves, Mayan ruins and beaches. In 2006, the number of tourists reached 900,000, 90 per cent of whom were from the USA. The number of hotels has quadrupled in the last twenty years to over 400. In order to accommodate the growing tourist trade, Belize has built a Tourism Village in Belize City, which includes a new passenger terminal building and docking facilities.
Belize Tourist Board, URL: http://www.travelbelize.org/

Agriculture
Agriculture in 2011 provided an estimated 10.0 per cent of the country's GDP, and employed approximately 11 per cent of the total labour force, both figures showing a contraction of the section since 2003. Although about 1,998,230 acres or 38 per cent of the total land area

BELIZE

is considered potentially suitable for agricultural use, only 10 to 15 per cent is in use in any one year; furthermore, about half of this is under pasture. The remainder is used for a variety of permanent and annual crops.

The agricultural sector is dominated by the sugar industry, which is concentrated in the Corozal and Orange Walk Districts. Sugar contributes over 33 per cent of agricultural export earnings. Annual production of sugar is around 80,000 tons from 60,000 acres of sugar cane. A statutory Sugar Board controls and regulates the sugar industry and the production of cane. The citrus industry, centred in the Stann Creek District, is the second major contributor to export earnings. The bulk of output from 57,000 acres of orange and grapefruit groves is processed into concentrates, oil and squash for export means. The Citrus Control Board is responsible for regulating the industry.

Bananas are the third largest export crop and are mainly grown in the Stann Creek District. Despite damage caused by hurricanes and drought in the 1970s, more than 5,000 acres are now established. Funds from the Caribbean Development Corporation have enabled the expansion of the industry.

Cacao is becoming increasingly important as an export crop. Hershey Food Corporation of the United States has established a commercial plantation in the Cayo District. Mangoes are also grown commercially, but production fluctuates, mainly due to climatic conditions. The Government is always looking for ways to diversify in the agricultural sector and recently invested in the production, processing and marketing of soybeans. Other agricultural products include honey, maize beans, rice, poultry and eggs.

Agricultural Production in 2010

Produce	Int. $'000*	Tonnes
Oranges	45,841	237,200
Sugar cane	30,135	917,728
Bananas	19,742	70,100
Indigenous chicken meat	18,336	12,873
Grapefruit (inc. pomelos)	8,094	36,000
Papayas	7,124	25,100
Rice, paddy	5,169	18,900
Indigenous cattle meat	4,291	1,589
Maize	2,951	54,300
Beans, dry	2,562	4,500
Indigenous pigmeat	1,847	1,201
Hen eggs, in shell	1,742	2,100

* unofficial figures

Source: http://faostat.fao.org/site/339/default.aspx Food and Agriculture Organization of the United Nations, Food and Agricultural commodities production

Forestry
There has been a resurgence in forestry. Reforestation and natural regeneration in the pine forest as well as artificial regeneration of fast-growing tropical hardwood species are in progress. Of the total land area, 4.4 per cent is considered to be suitable for forest production.

Fishing
Belize has a viable fishing industry. Export markets for scale fish are mainly in the United States, Mexico and Jamaica. Farmed shrimp and lobster are important products within the fishing industry.

COMMUNICATIONS AND TRANSPORT

Travel Requirements
US, Canadian, Australian and EU citizens require a passport valid for six months and evidence of sufficient funds (minimum £50 per day) and proof of return or onward ticket at the point of entry. A visa is not required for periods of up to 30 days, apart from nationals of Bulgaria and Romania. Visitors for purposes other than tourism, or who wish to stay longer than 30 days, must obtain visas from the government of Belize. Nationals not referred to above are advised to contact the embassy/high commission to check visa requirements.

National Airlines
The number of domestic flights between 1994 and 1998 decreased by 20 per cent, due, it is believed, to an increase in the use of passenger boats by tourists.

International Airports
There are 43 airports in Belize, five with paved runways. The main airport, Philip S.W. Goldson International Airport, is situated 10 miles from Belize City, and is owned and operated by the Government. Regular international services are maintained by six airlines to and from the United States of America, Central America and Mexico.

Roads
There are 2,872 km or roads in Belize of which around 480 are paved. Some roads are impassable during the rainy season. Buses from Guatemala City and Belmopan run to Flores in Guatemala, and to Chetumal in Mexico. Vehicles are driven on the right.

Shipping
Nine major shipping lines move cargo to and from Belize to Central and North America, Europe and Japan. Passenger boats are becoming an increasingly popular form of transport, especially amongst tourists; there are 825 km of navigable waterways in Belize.

Ports and Harbours
The main port is Belize City, now equipped with a modern deep water port able to handle containerized shipping. The second largest port, Commerce Bight, just south of Dangriga, can accommodate the medium sized vessels required to handle increased exports of bananas and citrus products. There are also ports at Big Creek, Corozol and Punta Gorda.

HEALTH

Total expenditure on health in Belize represented 5.5 per cent of GDP in 2009, which equated to a total per capita spend of US$242. Government expenditure accounts for 63.8 per cent of the total expenditure on health (11.8 per cent of its total expenditure). Private expenditure accounts for 36.2 per cent of expenditure of which 74 per cent is out-of-pocket.

There are government hospitals in Belmopan and in Belize City, as well as hospitals in three regions and three community hospitals The government runs a system of dental care and nutritional education. Medical services in rural areas are provided by rural health care centres, and mobile clinics operate in remote areas. According to the latest WHO figures, in 2005-10, there were 241 doctors (8.3 per 10,000 population), 570 nurses and midwives (19.6 per 10,000 population, 112 pharmaceutical personnel and 12 dentists. There were 12 hospital beds per 10,000 population.

Major causes of death include heart disease, diabetes and road traffic accidents. Belize has one of the highest rates of HIV/AIDs in the region. In 2010, the infant mortality rate (probabilty of dying by age 1) was 14 per 1,000 live births and the under-five mortality rate was 17 per 1,000 live births. In the period 2005-10, 22.2 per cent of the under-fives were classified as stunted. The major causes of childhood mortality were: diarrhoea (10 per cent), pneumonia (7 per cent), birth asphyxia (48 per cent), congenital abnormalities (7 per cent), and injuries (12 per cent).

In 2010, 98 per cent of the population were using improved drinking-water sources and 90 per cent were using improved sanitation. (Source: http://www.who.int, World Health Statistics 2012)

EDUCATION

Primary education is compulsory throughout the country for children between the ages of six and 14. Primary and secondary education is free although uniforms and books have to be provided by parents, attendance is estimated at 60 per cent and parents can be fined if their children do not attend regularly. The schools are almost all denominational. The Government maintains one special school for mentally disabled children and another for children with physical disabilities.

Recent figures put the adult literacy rate at 76.5 per cent. Annual expenditure on education has been put at 5.4 per cent of GDP.

Vocational Training
Specialised training is available at other institutions: the Belize Technical College offers craft and technical courses, whilst the Belize Teachers College runs a two-year diploma course leading to trained teacher's status. The Belize Vocational Training Centre in Belize City provides courses for primary school-leavers, while the Belize Youth Development Centre and the Belize College of Agriculture offer training for those interested in entering the field of agro-industry. Advanced training is provided to Belizeans in the professional and technical fields at Belize's first university, the University College of Belize.

RELIGION

The Constitution provides for freedom of religion. About 62 per cent of the population are Roman Catholics and the remainder Protestants. This includes Anglicans, Methodists, Seventh Day Adventists, Mennonites, Nazarenes, Jehovah's Witnesses and others. There are small number of Baha'is (7,700), (Muslims (1,600), Buddhists (15,000), and Hindus (6,200).

Belize has a religious liberty rating of 10 on a scale of 1 to 10 (10 is most freedom). (Source: World Religion Database)

COMMUNICATIONS AND MEDIA

The constitution guarantees media freedom. There are exceptions for national security.

Newspapers
Among the leading newspapers are: The Amandala (URL: http://www.amandala.com.bz/), The Belize Times (People's United Party) (URL: http://www.belizetimes.bz/), The Reporter and The Guardian (URL: http://www.guardian.bz/), all of which are published weekly. There are no daily newspapers.

Broadcasting
There are currently 8 privately-owned TV stations. Multi-channel cabel TV is also available. State-run radio was privatised in 1998. Some 35 radio stations operate. Wave Radio is affiliated to the United Democratic Party.

Telecommunications
The trunk network largely uses microwave radio relay. Landline telephone subscribers numbered approximately 31,000 in 2008, and there were around 160,000 mobile telephone users in the same year. Figures for 2008 show that Belize has around 34,000 internet users.

ENVIRONMENT

Concerns regarding the effects of pesticides on the ecosystem were raised in 1996, and led to the implementation of the National Pesticide Certification Program, training farmers on the classification, safe handling and rational use of pesticides. The Pesticide Control Board controls all aspects of pesticides.

Of concern to environmentalists was the construction of the Chalillo dam, which was given the go-ahead in 2004. It was thought that the dam would destroy the habitat of macaws, tapirs and other species. There is also a threat to the environment posed by increased tourism. Other environmental concerns are deforestation and water pollution from sewage, industrial effluents, agricultural runoff; as well as solid and sewage waste disposal.

In order to preserve Belize's natural heritage 55 protected areas covering 43.2 per cent of the total land area have been set aside for scientific, educational and recreational use. Belize has the longest (184 miles) coral reef in the Western Hemisphere and the fifth longest barrier reef in the world.

In 2010, carbon dioxide emissions from the comsumption of fossil fuels was 0.98 million metric tons. (Source: EIA)

Belize is a party to the following international agreements: Biodiversity, Climate Change, Climate Change-Kyoto Protocol, Desertification, Endangered Species, Hazardous Wastes, Law of the Sea, Ozone Layer Protection, Ship Pollution, Wetlands, and Whaling.

BENIN
Republic of Benin
République du Bénin

Capital: Porto Novo (Population estimate: 295,000)

Seat of Government: Cotonou (Population estimate: 2 million)

Head of State: Dr Thomas Yayi Boni (page 1391)

National Flag: Green vertical stripe, at the hoist two horizontal stripes yellow and red.

CONSTITUTION AND GOVERNMENT

Constitution
Benin is the former French colony of Dahomey, the core of which was the traditional kingdom of Danhomé. It became independent as the Republic of Dahomey in August 1960. Its name was changed to Benin in December 1975. The present constitution dates from 1990.

Major-General Mathieu Kérékou came to power in 1972. He took a nationalist, anti-French stance and in November 1974 Marxism-Leninism was declared to be the national ideology. A reorganisation of the French-style administrative system began and various mainly French-owned companies were nationalised. Relations with France were seriously affected; in particular co-operation and aid agreements were curtailed. After three years of economic uncertainty and a further 12 months of transition, the prime minister, Nicéphore Soglo, was elected president on 24 March 1991. He was succeeded by Major-General Mathieu Kérékou in March 1996, who was re-elected in March 2001. The current President took office in 2006.

Executive power is held by the president, who is elected by universal adult suffrage for a five-year term, renewable once. The 83-member Assemblée Nationale holds legislative power and is elected in the same way for a term of four years. The president chooses the Council of Ministers, subject to approval by parliament.

To consult the full constitution (in French), please visit: http://www.gouv.bj/spip.php?article2

Recent Events
The cabinet was reshuffled in October 2008, the third reshuffle by Yayi Boni since he came to power in 2006.

Benin announced in 2009 it had discovered significant quantities of oil offshore near Seme, near the border with Nigeria.

In April 2009 the EU banned all of Benin's air carriers from flying to the EU due to safety concerns.

In August 2010, fifty MPs demanded that President Yayi be charged concerning an alleged swindle which resulted in thousands of people losing their life savings.

In October 2010, Benin was hit by severe flooding; thousands of people were left homeless.

In August 2011, the London marine insurance market put Benin on its list of areas deemed high risk due to an escalation of pirate attacks in the area.

Also in August 2011, the Benin parliament abolished the death penalty.

In October 2012, President Boni's neice, doctor and an ex-minister were arrested over an alleged plot to poison him. In March 2013, police announced they had foiled a coup against the president, those arrested incuded a cabinet member and someone who was linked to the previous poisoning attempt.

International Relations
Benin maintains strong links with Nigeria, and has good relations with its Francophone neighbours. France and China are also important allies. Benin's democracy, stability, and positive role in international peacekeeping ensure the country's international standing. A long-term border dispute with Niger was settled in 2005 when the ICJ ruled on disputed islands on the Niger River, awarding 16 islands to Niger and nine to Benin. Both countries accepted the ruling.

National Assembly, (Assemblée Nationale), PO Box 371, Porto-Novo, Benin. E-mail: guedegbe@assembleebenin.org, URL: http://www.assembleebenin.org
President: Mathurin Nago

Cabinet (as at June 2013)
Prime Minister: Pascal Irénée Koupaki (page 1458)
Minister of State for Presidential Affairs: Issifou Kogui N'Douro
Minister of Heath: Akoko Kinde Gazard
Minister of Justice and Keeper of the Seals, Minister for Legislation and Human Rights: Marie Elise Gbedo
Minister Delegate of Micro-Finance and Youth and Women's Employment: Reckiat Madougou
Minister Delegate of Transport and Public Works: Lambert Koty
Minister of Industry, and Small and Medium Sized Enterprises: Madina Sephou
Minister of Secondary Education, Vocational Education and Technical Training: Djimba Soumanou
Minister of Economy and Finance: Jonas Aliou Gbian
Minister of Foreign Affairs, African Integration and Co-operation, Francophonie and Beninese Expatriates: Nassirou Arifari Bako
Minister of the Environment and Conservation, Housing and Urban Affairs: Blaise Ahanhanzo-Glele
Minister of Work and Civil Service: Maimouna Kora Zaki
Minister of Agriculture, Livestock and Fishery: Katé Sadai
Minister of the Interior and National Security: Benoit Assouan Degla
Minister of Culture, Literacy Handicrafts and Tourism: Jean-Michel Abimbola
Minister of Youth, Sports and Leisure: Didier Aplogan
Minister of Communications and Information Technology: Max Aweke
Minister Delegate with responsibility for relations with Political and Religious Institutions: Safiatou Bassabi
Minister of Nursery and Primary Education: Eric N'Dah
Minister of the Family, Social Affairs, National Solidarity, the Handicapped and the Elderly: Fatouma Amadou Djibril
Minister of Local Government, Land Management and Decentralisation: Raphael Edou
Minister of Higher Education and Scientific Research: Francois Abiola
Minister of Administration and Institutional Reform: Martial Sounton
Minister of Economic Analysis, Development and Planning: Marcel De Souza
Minister of Energy, Oil and Mining Research, Water and Development of Renewable Energy: Sophiat Onifade
Minister Delegate to the President of the Republic, responsible for Maritime Economy and Harbour Infrastructure, Government Spokesman: Valentin Djenontin-Agossou

Ministries
Office of the President, BP 1288, Place de l'Independence, Cotonou, Benin. Tel: +229 21 30 02 28, fax: +229 21 30 06 36, URL: http://www.gouv.bj
Ministry of Foreign Affairs and African Integration, 06 BP 318, Cotonou, Benin. Tel: +229 21 30 04 00, fax: +229 21 30 19 64, e-mail: sg@etranger.gouv.bj, URL: http://www.etranger.gouv.bj
Ministry of the Economy and Finance, BP 302, Cotonou, Benin. Tel: +229 21 30 12 47, fax: +229 21 30 18 51, e-mail: sg@finance.gouv.bj, URL: http://www.finance.gouv.bj
Ministry of Agriculture, Livestock and Fishery, 01 BP 2900, Cotonou, Benin. Tel: +229 21 30 04 10, fax: +229 21 30 03 26, e-mail: sgm@agriculture.gouv.bj, URL:ttp://www.agriculture.gouv.bj
Ministry of Commerce, Industry and Small and Medium-sized Enterprises, 01 BP 363, Cotonou, Benin. Tel: +229 21 30 76 45, fax: +229 21 30 30 24, e-mail: sg@commerce.gouv.bj, URL: http://www.commerce.gouv.bj
Ministry of Communications and Information Technology, 01 BP 120, Cotonou, Benin. Tel: +229 21 31 43 34, fax: +229 21 31 59 31, e-mail: sg@communication.gouv.bj, URL: http://www.communication.gouv.bj
Ministry of Culture, Literacy, Handicrafts and Tourism, 01 BP 2037, Guincomey, Cotonou, Benin. Tel: +229 21 30 70 10, fax: +229 21 30 70 31, e-mail: sg@tourisme.gouv.bj, **URL: http://www.tourisme.gouv.bj**
Ministry of Decentralization, Local Government and Regional Planning, Cotonou, Benin. URL: http://www.gouv.bj
Ministry of the Environment and Protection of Nature, 01 BP 3621, Cotonou, Benin. Tel: +229 21 31 50 58, fax: +229 21 31 50 81, e-mail: sg@environnement.gouv.bj, URL: http://www.environnement.gouv.bj
Ministry of Family and National Solidarity, 01 BP 2802, Cotonou, Benin. Tel: +229 21 31 67 07, fax: +229 21 31 64 62, e-mail: sg@famille.gouv.bj, URL: http://www.famille.gouv.bj

BENIN

Ministry of Higher Education and Scientific Research, 01 BP 348, Cotonou, Benin. Tel: +229 21 30 19 91, fax: +229 21 30 57 95, e-mail: sg@recherche.gouv.bj, URL: http://www.recherche.gouv.bj

Ministry of the Interior and Public Security, BP 925, Cotonou, Benin. Tel: +229 21 30 11 06, fax: +229 21 30 01 59, e-mail: sg@securite.gouv.bj, URL: http://www.securite.gouv.bj

Ministry of Justice, BP 2493, Cotonou, Benin. Tel: +229 21 30 05 36, fax: +229 21 30 18 21, e-mail: sg@justice.gouv.bj, URL: http://www.justice.gouv.bj

Ministry of Labour and Civil Service, BP 907, Cotonou, Benin. Tel: +229 21 31 26 18, fax: +229 21 31 06 29, e-mail: sgm@travail.gouv.bj, URL: http://www.travail.gouv.bj

Ministry of Mines, Energy and Water Resources, 04 BP 1412, Cotonou, Benin. Tel: +229 21 31 29 07, fax: +229 21 31 35 46, e-mail: sg@energie.gouv.bj, URL: http://www.energie.gouv.bj

Ministry of National Defence, 01 BP 2493, Cotonou, Benin. Tel: +229 21 30 05 36, fax: +229 21 30 18 21, e-mail: sg@defense.gouv.bj, URL: http://www.defense.gouv.bj

Ministry of Planning and Development, BP 342, Cotonou, Benin. Tel: +229 21 30 00 30, fax: +229 21 30 16 10, e-mail: sg@planben.gouv.bj, URL: http://www.gouv.bj

Ministry of Primary Education and National Languages, 01 BP 10, Porto Novo, Cotonou, Benin. Tel: +229 20 21 33 27, fax: +229 20 21 50 11, e-mail: sg@enseignement.gouv.bj, URL: http://www.enseignement.gouv.bj

Ministry of Public Health, 01 BP 882, Cotonou, Benin. Tel: +229 21 33 21 41, fax: +229 21 33 04 62, e-mail: sg@sante.gouv.bj, URL: http://www.sante.gouv.bj

Ministry of Public Works and Transport, BP 351, Cotonou, Benin. Tel: +229 21 31 46 33, fax: +229 21 31 06 17, e-mail: sg@transport.gouv.bj, URL: http://www.transport.gouv.bj

Ministry for Relations with Institutions, 01 BP 406, Cotonou, Benin. Tel: +229 21 30 60 93, fax: +229 21 30 78 94, e-mail: sg@exterieur.gouv.bj, URL: http://www.exterieur.gouv.bj

Ministry of Urban Affairs, Housing, Land Reform and the Fight against Coastal Erosion, Cotonou, Benin. URL: http://www.gouv.bj

Ministry of Youth, Sport and Leisure, 03 BP 2103, Cotonou, Benin. Tel: +229 21 30 36 14, fax: +229 21 38 21 26, e-mail: sg@jeunesse.gouv.bj, URL: http://www.jeunesse.gouv.bj

Political Parties
There are over a hundred registered parties; the major parties in government at present include:

Cauri Forces for an Emerging Benin (FCBE)
Leader: Yayi Boni
Parti du Renouveau Democratique (PRD), Immeuble Babo Oganla, Porto Novo, Benin.
Leader: Adrien Houngbedji
Alliance Etoile (AE)
Social-Democrat Party (PSD)
Mouvement Africain pour La Democratie et le Progès (MADEP), Leader: Séfou Fagbohoun
Key Force (FC),
Front for Action for Renewal, Democracy and Development (FARD-ALAFIA),
National Solidarity Party (PNE)
Union for Progress and Democracy (UPD-GAMESU)
Union for Democracy and National Solidarity (UDS)
Ladder for Democracy and Development (EDD)

Elections
The most recent parliamentary elections were held in April 2011. The Cauri Forces for an Emerging Benin (FCBE) again became the largest party in the National Assembly with 41 seats The Union Makes the Nation opposition alliance won 31 seats.

The most recent presidential election was held in March 2011. Thomas Yayi Boni was re-elected with 53.2 per cent of the vote.

Local elections were held in 2008.

Diplomatic Representation
US Embassy, rue Caporal Bernard Anani, BP 2012, Cotonou, Benin. Tel: +229 300650 / 300513 / 301792, fax: +229 301439 / 301974, e-mail: amemb.coo@intnet.bj, URL: http://cotonou.usembassy.gov/about.html
Ambassador: Michael Raynor
Benin Embassy, 2124 Kalorama Road, NW, Washington DC 20008, USA. Tel: +1 202 232 6656, fax: +1 202 200 1996, URL: http://www.beninembassy.us/
Ambassador: Cyrille S. Oguin
UK Embassy, based at High Commission in Nigeria. URL: http://ukinnigeria.fco.gov.uk/en/
British High Commissioner: Dr Andrew Pocock (page 1496)
Benin Embassy to UK, 87 avenue Victor-Hugo, 75116 Paris, France. (Millenium Business Centre, Humber Road, London NW2 6DW UK.) Tel: +33 (0)1 45 00 98 82 (+44 (0)20 8954 8800), fax: +33 (0)1 45 01 82 02 (+44 (0)20 8954 8844), e-mail: ambassade-benin@gofornet.com, URL: http://beninconsulate.co.uk
Ambassador: H.E. A. Agossou
Permanent Mission of Benin to the UN, 125 East 38th Street, New York, NY 10016, USA. Tel: +1 212 684 1339, URL: http://www.un.int/benin/
Permananet Representative: Jean-Francis R. Zinsou

LEGAL SYSTEM

Benin's judicial system comprises the Constitutional Court, the Supreme Court, and the High Court of Justice. The Constitutional Court is the regulatory body of public power. The Supreme Court has the highest level of jurisdiction in legal matters. It is designed as a check on the executive, and also acts in a consultative role. The High Court of Justice, which cannot include the President, is made up of members of the Constitutional Court, Parliament and the president of the Supreme Court. It alone can judge the President.

In general, the government respects the human rights of its citizens. However, there are reports that police occasionally use excessive force. Corruption continues to be a problem, and arbitrary arrest can lead to lengthy pre-trial detention in harsh prison conditions. Benin retained the death penalty for ordinary crimes such as murder and armed robbery, until parliament voted to end capital punishment in August 2011. It was formally abolished in 2012.

Supreme Court, BP 330, Cotonou, Benin. Tel: +229 313105 / 315047, fax: 315492, URL: http://supremecourt1.tripod.com/courtact2.htm
Chief Justice: Hon. Justice Idris Legbo Kutigi

Benin Human Rights Commission, 04 BP 607, Cadjoun, Cotonou, Benin. Tel: +229 933672, fax: +229 305271

LOCAL GOVERNMENT

For administrative purposes Benin is divided into 12 departments, each of which falls under the authority of a civilian prefect. The departments are Alibori, Atakoro, Atlantique, Borgou, Collines, Couffo, Donga, Littoral, Mono, Oueme, Plareau and Zou.

Local elections took place in April 2008. Parties linked to President Yayi won a majority of local council seats, but the opposition did well in the south.

AREA AND POPULATION

Area
The People's Republic of Benin is situated on the west coast of Africa. It is bordered by Togo to the west and Nigeria to the east, and by Burkina Faso and Niger to the north. It has a coastline of about 100 km on the Gulf of Guinea. Its area is 112,622 sq. km. In 2005, the International Court of Justice awarded most of the river islands along the disputed Benin-Niger border to Niger. The land is generally flat with some hills and low mountains. The highest point is Mount Sokbaro at 658 m.

To view a regional map, please consult:
http://www.un.org/Depts/Cartographic/map/profile/westafrica.pdf

The south of Benin has an equatorial climate, varying from hot and dry from January to April and during August, to rainy from May to July and September to December. The north has more extreme temperatures, hot and dry between November and June, cooler and very wet between July and October.

Population
The population in 2010 was estimated at around 8.850 million assuming an annual growth rate of 3.1 per cent over 2000-10. The main ethnic groups are the Fon and other Adja-speakers 60 per cent, the Bariba 10 per cent and the Yoruba and Mahi 9 per cent.

The chief cities are Cotonou, the chief port, business centre and seat of government, and Porto Novo, the capital and administrative centre. Cotonou has approximately 800,000 inhabitants, whilst Port Novo has an estimated 250,000 and Parakou has 150,000. Forty-two per cent of the population lives in urban areas.

The official language is French, although Bariba and Fulani are spoken in the north and Fon and Yoruba in the south. There are over 20 dialects spoken in Benin. English is also spoken in some areas.

Births, Marriages, Deaths
In 2010, the estimated birth rate was 39.6 births per 1,000 people, and there were approximately 10.9 deaths per 1,000 people. The fertility rate was 5.3 in 2009. The infant mortality rate was 73 per 1,000 live births. In 2009, life expectancy at birth was 54 years for males and 60 years for females. The median age was 18 years. Some 44 per cent of the population is aged under 15 years and 5 per cent aged over 60 years. (Source: http://www.who.int, World Health Statistics 2012)

Public Holidays 2014
1 January: New Year's Day
10 January: Vodoun (Traditional Day)
14 January: Prophet's Birthday*
21 April: Easter Monday
1 May: Workers' Day
29 May: Ascension Day
9 June: Whit Monday
29 July: End of Ramadan (Eid al-Fitr)*
1 August: Independence Day
15 August: Assumption
5 October: Feast of the Sacrifice (Eid al-Adha)*
26 October: Armed Forces Day
1 November: All Saints' Day
30 November: National Day
25 December: Christmas Day
* Muslim holidays are based on sightings of the moon and therefore vary from year to year.

EMPLOYMENT

According to estimates, the labour force numbered 5.38 million in 2007. There is a heavy reliance on informal employment, family helpers, and the use of apprentices. Agriculture (including hunting, forestry and fishing) is Benin's largest employment sector. Other major employment sectors are trade, restaurants and hotels, employing 432,500; community, social and personal services, employing 164,500; and manufacturing, employing 160,500.

BANKING AND FINANCE

Currency
The unit of currency is the Communauté Financière Africaine (CFA) franc comprising of 100 centimes. Notes are in denominations of 10,000, 5,000, 2,500, 1,000 and 500 and coins in 250, 100, 50, 25, 10, 5 and 1. Benin is part of the French Monetary Area. The financial centre is Cotonou.

GDP/GNP, Inflation, National Debt
Despite its growth since its transition to a democratic government in 1990, the economy of Benin remains underdeveloped and dependent on subsistence agriculture, cotton production, and regional trade. Benin's major export is cotton, the value of which fluctuates with volatile world prices. The cotton industry also faces competition from subsidised cotton growers in the USA and elsewhere. Other main products include palm and cocoa. Re-export trade is another significant contributor to the economy although much is unrecorded. In 2006, the African Development Bank and the World Bank approved debt relief for several countries including Benin. Benin relies on outside aid. France is a major donor. In 2005 Benin was ranked 162 out of 177 countries on the UNDP Human Development index.

Exploration for oil has started but exploitable reserves are not yet known.

GDP

	2005	2006	2007
GDP (current market prices), US$ million	4,468.04	4,721.45	5,637.91
GDP growth rate (%)	2.9	3.8	4.2
GNI per inhabitant	510	640	..

Source: African Development Bank

Estimated figures for 2009 put GDP at US$6.2 billion with a growth rate that year of 3.2 per cent. GDP growth was estimated to be 3.0 per cent in 2010 and 3.3 per cent in 2011. GDP was estimated to be US$7.3 billion in 2011. Agriculture contributed around 33 per cent of GDP, whilst the growing services sector accounted for an estimated 52.3 per cent. Industry contributed around 14.5 per cent.

Inflation was 0.9 per cent in 2004, 5.4 per cent in 2005, 3.8 per cent in 2006 and 1.5 per cent in 2007. Inflation was estimated to be 4 per cent in 2009, falling to 2.7 per cent in 2011.

Total external debt was put at US$7,62.44 million in 2005, falling to US$782,10 million in 2006. (Source: AFDB)

Balance of Payments / Imports and Exports
Benin's major exports are cotton, crude petroleum, manufactured articles, cotton yarn and fabrics. Major imports are food products, beverages and tobacco, refined petroleum products, machinery and transport equipment, miscellaneous manufactured articles. Main trading partners are Nigeria, Côte d'Ivoire, France, China, Brazil, Italy, Libya and the UK. China is now the main supplier of imports. Most exports and re-exports go to Nigeria. It is estimated that 70 per cent of imports into the port of Cotonou are then exported to Nigeria. The government relies on customs receipts for about half of its income. Nigerian trade policy is therefore critical to the health of the economy.

External Trade, US$ million

	2005	2006	2007
Trade balance	-406.79	-508.23	-592.97
Exports	324.56	251.05	302.03
Imports	731.34	759.28	895.00

Source: African Development Bank

Central Bank
Banque Centrale des Etats de l'Afrique de l'Ouest, BP 3108, Avenue Abdoulaye Fadiga, Dakar, Senegal. Tel: +221 33 839 05 00, fax: +221 33 823 83 35, e-mail: webmaster@bceao.int, URL: http://www.bceao.int/
Governor: Tiémoko Meyliet Kone

Chambers of Commerce and Trade Organisations
Chamber of Commerce and Industry Benin, e-mail: ccib@bow.intnet.bj, URL: http://www.lamaisondelafrique.com/cci_benin.html

MANUFACTURING, MINING AND SERVICES

Primary and Extractive Industries
There are deposits of phosphates, chrome and iron in the north of Benin. In the past oil has been drilled from the Sémé offshore fields, although government revenue from this declined by the mid-1980s and reserves had dwindled to 0.008 billion barrels by 2006. However, exploration of new sites is ongoing. In February 2009 Benin announced that significant quantities of oil had been found off-shore near Seme, near the Nigeria-Benin border. In 2011 no oil was being produced. Benin consumed 28,000 barrels per day, all of which was imported.

Energy
In 2010, the total net electricity generated was 0.14 billion kWh and consumption was 0.87 billion kWh. All home produced electricity is generated from fossil fuels. Benin's national gas company, Société Beninoise de Gaz, is part of a consortium with Ghana and Togo which has studied the feasibility of a West Africa Gas Pipeline. Ghana currently accounts for a significant proportion of the country's imports. Benin is trying to attract foreign capital to build electricity generation facilities within the country, in order to break this dependency. In 2006 Benin and Togo announced plans to build a hydro-electric dam on the Mona River, the dam is currently under construction.

Manufacturing
The manufacturing sector is confined to light industry, mainly involved in processing primary products and the production of consumer goods. Palm oil is produced in the south of the country and used to produce margarine and soap. Locally grown cotton is used in the textile industry.

Tourism
Benin's tourism is focused around its game reserves and national parks. The country has around 180,000 visitors each year.

Agriculture
Agriculture accounted for an estimated 36 per cent of GDP in 2011. Benin's economy is still dominated by cash-crop exports and the production of food crops. The latter have usually been produced in sufficient quantities to satisfy local demand and allow largely unrecorded exports to Nigeria. The cash-crop exports have become more diversified in recent years, although this has been accompanied by export instability. Principal crops are cassava (manioc), palm oil, yams, beans rice, peanuts, maize and cotton. In recent years encouragement has been given to farmers to diversify into cash crops such as coffee, cocoa, ground nuts (peanuts), and kerite (shea nuts).

Agricultural Production in 2010

Produce	Int. $'000	Tonnes
Yams	419,729	2,389,900
Cassava	375,649	3,596,000
Cotton lint	109,048	76,300
Maize	101,352	1,132,700
Beans, dry	93,938	160,000
Indigenous cattle meat	70,452	26,080
Tomatoes	67,372	182,300
Pineapples	62,938	220,800
Cashew nuts, with shell	61,009	69,700
Groundnuts, with shell	48,805	117,000
Rice paddy	46,092	167,000
Fruit fresh nes	45,933	131,600

Source: http://faostat.fao.org/site/339/default.aspx Food and Agriculture Organization of the United Nations, Food and Agricultural commodities production

Principal livestock are cattle, goats and sheep. In 2004, there were an estimated 1.75 million head of cattle and buffaloes and 2 million head of sheep.

In 2004 Benin removed 332,000 cubic metres of industrial roundwood, an estimated 162,000 cubic metres of wood fuel, 205,000 cubic metres of wood charcoal and 31,000 cubic metres of sawn wood.

Principal fish catches are tilapias, freshwater fish, and marine fish. Total fish catch in 2004 was approximately 34,000 tonnes. Locally caught shrimp are exported to Europe.

COMMUNICATIONS AND TRANSPORT

Travel Requirements
US, Canadian, Australian and EU nationals require a visa obtained before travelling to Benin. Visitors to Benin should also have the WHO Yellow Card ("Carte Jaune") indicating that they have been vaccinated for yellow fever. Nationals of other countries are advised to contact the Benin embassy to check entry requirements.

International Airports
As well as the international airport at Cotonou (Cotonou-Cadjehoun), there are airports at Parakou, Natitingou, Kandi, Abomey, Savè and Porga. The Benin government has a share in Air Afrique. Government run air services operate between Cotonou, Parakou, Natitingou, Djougou and Kandi.

In 2009 the EU banned air carriers from Benin from flying to the EU over safety fears.

Railways
Railways connect Cotonou with Parakou, a journey time of 12-14 hours (northwards for 438 km), with a branch line running westwards to Ouidah and Segboroué (34 km). A third line runs eastwards to Porto Novo and then north-eastwards to Pobé (107 km). A rail line from Parakou (via Gaya) to Niamey in Niger is currently under construction; this will provide the first rail link with Niger. In total Benin has approximately 750 km of rail track.
Organisation Commune Bénin-Niger des Chemins de Fer et des Transports (OCBN), Cotonou, Benin.

Roads
There are about 16,000 km of roads. In the region of 2,700 km of Benin's roads are paved, including many of those from Cotonou to Dassa, and Parakou to Malanville. Two main roads connect Cotonou with Niamey in Niger, and the other connects Lagos with Porto Novo. Tracks are passable during the dry season. Vehicles travel on the right.
Compagnie de Transit et de Consignation du Bénin (TCB), Cotonou, Benin.

BHUTAN

Ports and Harbours

Benin's main port is at Cotonou. It handled about 5.2 million tonnes of cargo in 2005 (4.6 million tonnes imports, 600,000 tonnes exports). Regular cargo services are run by several shipping lines from Marseille. Local shipping from Lagos arrives in Porto Novo.

Port Autonome de Cotonou, Cotonou, Benin. URL: http://www.portdecotonou.com/

HEALTH

Benin's healthcare service was funded in 1995 by the International Development Association, which contributed US$27.8 million to a US$33.4 million project. Total 2009 expenditure on health was approximately 4.3 per cent of GDP. Government expenditure accounts for 53.8 per cent of the total expenditure. Private expenditure accounted for 46.2 per cent of expenditure on health, almost all of which is out-of-pocket. Per capita expenditure in 2009 was US$34. Medical facilities outside major towns are limited. In 2005-10 there were estimated to be 542 doctors (0.6 doctors per 10,000 population), 7,129 nurses and midwives (7.7 per 10,000 population), 20 pharmacists, 37 dentists and 217 environment and public health workers. There are currently 5 hospital beds per 10,000 population.

A programme of immunization has been undertaken. Reported cases of major diseases such as measles, polio and tetanus have fallen. Immunization coverage among 1-year-olds in 2010 were 69 per cent for measles, DTP3 83 per cent, HepB3 83 per cent and Hib3 83 per cent. In 2010 there were 983 reported cases of cholera, 227 of leprosy, 392 of measles (compared to 18,635 in 1980), 3,756 of TB and 233 of meningitis. In 2007, HIV prevalence among adults was estimated at 1.2 per cent. There were no reported cases of polio (compared to 21 in 2008).

In 2005-11 an estimated 44.7 per cent of children aged 5 or under were stunted and an estimated 20.2 per cent were underweight. In 2010 the infant mortality rate (probability of dying before age one) was 73 per 1,000 live births. The mortality rate for under-fives was 115 per 1,000 live births. In 2008, the most common causes of death for children under 5 were malaria (23 per cent), prematurity (12 per cent), diarrhoeal diseases (10 per cent), pneumonia (17 per cent), and birth asphyxia (9 per cent). HIV/AIDs accounted for approximately 1 per cent of deaths of children aged under 5. Approximately 20 per cent of children sleep under treated insect nets.

In 2010, an estimated 75 per cent of the population had sustainable access to improved water sources and 13 per cent of the population had sustainable access to improved sanitation compared to an estimated 59 per cent of the urban population and 11 per cent of the rural population in 2006.(Source: http://www.who.int, World Health Statistics 2012)

EDUCATION

Education is free for primary aged children and education in Benin has since 1975 been under state control. Primary education lasts from the age of six until the age of 11 with an enrolment figure of 76 per cent. The pupil teacher ration is 44:1. Secondary education begins at 12 and lasts for a maximum of seven years. Recent statistics show that there are 3,100 primary schools, 13,900 teachers and 722,100 pupils. Secondary schools number 193, with 118,100 students. Higher education currently has 9,047 enrolled students. Fifty-one per cent of primary pupils go onto secondary school. Twenty-three per cent of pupils repeat primary education. In 2006, the government spent 3.9 per cent of GDP on education.

In 2007 the literacy rate was estimated to be 35.6 per cent (47.9 per cent for males, 23.3 per cent for females). (Source: UNESCO)

RELIGION

Approximately 54 per cent of the population is Christian the majority of whom are Catholic, and 22 per cent is Muslim; however, many nominal Muslims and Christians continue to practice animistic traditions. Voodoo originated in Benin and was introduced to Brazil and the Caribbean Islands by African slaves taken from this part of the Slave Coast.

Benin has a religious liberty rating of 10 on a scale of 1 to 10 (10 is most freedom). (Source: World Religion Database)

COMMUNICATIONS AND MEDIA

The constitution guarantees freedom of the media. However, libel laws are occasionally used against journalists and the government sometmes interevenes. Radio is the main source of information particularly in rural areas.

Newspapers

There are six daily newspapers published in Benin: *La Nation*, the official newspaper, (URL: http://www.gouv.bj/presse/lanation); *Le Matinal*, (URL: http://www.lematinalonline.com), Fraternité, Le Republicain, L'Aurore and L'Evenement du Jour. The *Journal Officiel de la République du Bénin* is issued fortnightly by the government information bureau.

Broadcasting

The state-owned radio and television broadcasting network is the Office de Radiodiffusion et de Télévision du Bénin based in Cotonou. It operates a television station with multiple channels. Satellite television is available. The government body responsible for the media is: **Haute Autorité de l'Audio Visuel et de la Communication**, Cotonou, Benin. Tel: +229 315429.

There are also several commercial television channels and over 30 state, commercial and local radio stations. Further expansion of private and commercial channels and stations is expected. Commercial television channels include LC2 (URL: http://www.lc2international.tv/) and Golfe TV. Golfe FM is one of the commercial radio stations. It is estimated that over 620,000 radio sets are in use and more than 60,000 televisions.

Telecommunications

In 2008 there were an estimated 159,000 main lines and 3.6 million mobile telephones in use. In 2008 an estimated 500,000 people were internet users.

ENVIRONMENT

Main environmental concerns in Benin are deforestation and desertification. Wildlife is threatened by poaching. There is also a lack of potable water.

According to figures from the EIA, in 2010 Benin's emissions from the consumption of fossil fuels totalled 3.65 million metric tons of carbon dioxide.

Benin is party to the following international agreements: Biodiversity, Climate Change, Climate Change-Kyoto Protocol, Desertification, Endangered Species, Environmental Modification, Hazardous Wastes, Law of the Sea, Ozone Layer Protection, Ship Pollution, Wetlands, and Whaling.

BHUTAN

Kingdom of Bhutan

Druk-Yul

Capital: Thimphu (Population estimate: 80,000)

Head of State: King Jigme Khesar Namgyal Wangchuk (page 1484)

National Flag: Divided diagonally, fly to hoist yellow over orange with a dragon centred white, clasping jewels in the claws

CONSTITUTION AND GOVERNMENT

Constitution

Bhutan gained its independence from India on 8 August 1949. It became a constitutional monarchy with a Royal Advisory Council and a Council of Ministers (cabinet) responsible to the National Assembly or Tsogdu. Despite the absence of a formal constitution, in 1998 King Jigme Singye Wangchuck gave the legislature the right to remove him from power (with a two-thirds vote) and appoint the Council of Ministers. The Council of Ministers served five-year terms.

In March 2005, a new constitution was proposed, in which Bhutan would become a parliamentary democracy in 2008. In December 2005, King Jigme Singye Wangchuk announced his intention to abdicate at the time of the 2008 democratic elections, but in the event he abdicated on 15 December 2006, in favour of his son Crown Prince Jigme Kesar Kamgyal.

Under the 2008 Constitution the legislature is bicameral. The lower chamber, the National Assembly (Dzongkhag Tshogdu), has up to 55 members who serve a maximum five-year term. There are currently 47 members. Members are directly elected from two parties chosen in primary elections. The upper chamber, the National Council (Gewog Tshogde) has 25 members, 20 directly elected (one from each province) and five appointed by the monarch. All are appointed for a five-year term.

The head of the government is the prime minister, the leader of the larger party in the National Assembly. The prime minister is formally appointed by the king. The prime minister can serve a maximum of two terms. Ministers must be members of the National Assembly.

To consult the constitution, please visit: http://www.constitution.bt/

Recent Events

King Jigme Khesar Namgyel Wangchuck, 28, was crowned on 6 November, 2008, the most auspicious date for the occasion according to three of the country's astrologers. The Oxford-educated King became the fifth hereditary king of Bhutan, and the world's youngest monarch. Both the new government and the opposition took the opportunity to reiterate their commitment to the royal philosophy of Gross National Happiness - or GNH - which aims to strike a better balance between the spiritual and the material.

Bhutan became a constitutional monarchy, and held its first democratic elections for a new parliament and prime minister in March 2008.

Legislature

Bhutan's unicameral legislature, the National Assembly (or Tsogdu), was established in 1953 and consists of 154 members, 105 of whom are indirectly elected by villages, 12 reserved for ecclesiastical bodies, and 37 officials appointed by the monarch (ministers, their deputies and members of the Royal Advisory Council). The Tsogdu has a three year term and meets twice a year, enacting laws, advising on constitutional and political matters, and debating issues.

Under Bhutan's first written constitution, there will be two legislatures, the National Assembly (Tsogdu) with 47 directly elected members, and the National Council (Gewog Tshogde), with 20 directly elected members and five members appointed by the king. Both houses will have a five year term. Elections took place on 24 March 2008. Several members of the Council of Ministers resigned in 2007 in order to prepare for the general elections.

National Assembly (Tsogdu), PO Box 139, Gyelyong Tshogduthimpu, Thimphu, Bhutan. Tel: +975 2 32729, fax: +975 2 34210

```
Council of Ministers (as at June 2013)
Prime Minister:  Jigme Thinley (page 1525)
Minister of Agriculture: Pemo Gyamtsho
Minister of Finance:  Wangdi Norbu
Minister of Foreign Affairs: Ugyen Tshering
Minister of Economic Affairs:  Khandu Wangchuk (page 1534)
Minister of Health:  Zangley Dukpa
Minister of Information and Communications: Nandalal Rai
Minister of Education: Thakur Singh Powdyel
Minister of Labour and Human Resources: Dorji Wangdi
Minister of Home and Cultural Affairs: Minjur Dorji
Minister of Works and Human Settlements: Yeshey Zimba
Chief Justice:  Sonam Tobgye
```

Ministries

Office of the King, Royal Palace, Tashichhodzong, Thimpu, Bhutan. Tel: +975 2 322521, fax: +975 2 322079

Ministry of Economic Affairs, Tashichhodzong, Thimphu, Bhutan. Tel: +975 2 322211, fax: +975 2 323617, e-mail: khandu_wangchuk@hotmail.com, URL: http://www.mti.gov.bt

Ministry of Finance, Tashichhodzong, PO Box 117, Thimphu, Bhutan. Tel: +975 2 324867, fax: +975 2 333976, e-mail: wnorbu@mof.gov.bt, URL: http://www.mof.gov.bt

Ministry of Foreign Affairs and Trade, PO Box 103, Gyalyong Tshokhang, Thimphu, Bhutan. Tel: +975 2 322359, fax: +975 2 331465, e-mail: ugyen@mfa.gov.bt, URL: http://www.mfa.gov.bt

Ministry of Agriculture, PO Box 252, Thimphu, Bhutan. Tel: +975 2 322129, fax: +975 2 323153, e-mail: pgyamtsho@moa.gov.bt, URL: http://www.moa.gov.bt

Ministry of Education, PO Box 112, Thimphu, Bhutan. Tel: +975 2 323825, fax: +975 2 326424, e-mail: powdyel@gmail.com, URL: http://www.education.gov.bt

Ministry of Health, PO Box 726, Kawajangsa, Thimphu, Bhutan. Tel: +975 2 323973, fax: +975 2 323973, e-mail: zangleydrukpa@health.gov.bt, URL: http://www.health.gov.bt

Ministry of Home and Cultural Affairs, Tashichhodzong, PO Box 133, Thimpu, Bhutan. Tel: +975 2 322643, fax: +975 2 32214, e-mail: lmd@mohca.gov.bt, URL: http://www.mohca.gov.bt

Ministry of Information and Communications, PO Box 278, Thimphu, Bhutan. Tel: +975 2 327932, fax: +975 2 328154, e-mail: nanday@moic.gov.bt, URL: http://www.moic.gov.bt

Ministry of Labour and Human Resources, Thonsel Lam, Lower Motithang, PO Box 1036, Thimphu, Bhutan. Tel: +975 2 327127, fax: +975 2 327126, e-mail: horseme@molhr.gov.bt, URL: http://www.molhr.gov.bt

Royal Court of Justice, Thimpu, Bhutan. Tel: +975 2 322613, fax: +975 2 322921, e-mail: judiciary@druknet.bt, URL: http://www.judiciary.gov.bt

Ministry of Trade and Industry, Tashichhodzong, PO Box 141, Thimphu, Bhutan. Tel: +975 2 322211, fax: +975 2 323617, e-mail: mtinet@druknet.bt, URL: http://www.mti.gov.bt

Ministry of Works and Human Settlements, Tashichhodzong, PO Box 791, Thimphu, Bhutan. Tel: +975 2 322218, fax: +975 2 323144, e-mail: secretary@mowhs.gov.bt, URL: http://www.mowhs.gov.bt

Political Parties

Bhutan Peace and Prosperity Party (DPT), (Druk Phuensum Tshogpa), URL: http://www.dpt.bt
Leader: Jigme Thinley

People's Democratic Party (PDP), URL: http://www.pdp.bt
Leader: Tshering Tobgay

Elections

Elections for members of the National Assembly were not held on any one date but took place on the expiry of each member's term. Following the proposed changes to the constitution, elections for the new National Council took place in December 2007 and January 2008. Elections for the new National Assembly took place on 24 March 2008; the Bhutan Harmony Party won most votes. The most recent elections were held in June 2013, a second round was scheduled for in July.

Diplomatic Representation

Permanent Representative of the Kingdom of Bhutan to the United Nations, Two UN Plaza, 27th Floor, New York NY 10017, USA. Tel: +1 212 826 1919, fax: +1 212 826 2998, URL: http://www.un.int/wcm/content/site/bhutan
Permanent Representative: Amb. Lhatu Wangchuk

LEGAL SYSTEM

The legal system is based on English common law and Indian law. There is no written constitution, although a draft for one was submitted in December 2002. The monarch is the final court of appeal. Bhutan's court system consists of the Royal High Court, the Dzongkhag Courts (District), the Dungkhag Courts (Sub-District), and other special courts that may be convened by the King on the recommendation of the National Judicial Commission. Judges are appointed for life by the king. Minor offenses are adjudicated by village headmen. In 2000, a Department of Legal Affairs was created to investigate and prosecute criminal and civil cases against civil servants.

Transition to a parliamentary democracy has improved the human rights situation; however, there are difficulties with the regulation of religion, and there is some discrimination against the ethnic Nepalese minority. Bhutan does not accept International Court of Justice jurisdiction.

The death penalty was abolished in 2004.

Chief Justice: Sonam Tobgye
Royal High Court of Bhutan: URL: http://www.judiciary.gov.bt/

LOCAL GOVERNMENT

For administrative purposes Bhutan is divided into 20 districts or *dzongkhag*. Bumthang, Chhukha, Chirang, Daga, Gasa, Geylegphug, Ha, Lhuntshi, Mongar, Paro, Pemagatsel, Punakha, Samchi, Samdrup Jongkhar, Shemgang, Tashigang, Tashi Yangtse, Thimphu, Tongsa and Wangdi Phodrang.

Local elections took place in 2011.

AREA AND POPULATION

Area

The total area of Bhutan is 18,147 sq. miles (47,000 sq. km). It is bordered by China to the north and India to the south, west and east.

There are three regions in Bhutan: the Duar plain in the south, 300 to 2,000 metres above sea level with a tropical climate; the central Middle Himalayan area, up to 3,000 metres above sea level with a temperate climate; and the Great Himalayan area in the north, up to 8,000 metres above sea level with snow all year round.

To view a map, consult http://www.lib.utexas.edu/maps/cia08/bhutan_sm_2008.gif

Population

The estimated population in 2009 was 697,000, with an estimated annual population growth rate of 2.5 per cent. The population density in 2004 was 20 inhabitants per sq. km. Approximately 36 per cent of the population live in urban areas; the capital, Thimphu, has an estimated population of 35,000. The median age is 24 years. Approximately 31 per cent of the population is under 15 years old and an estimated 7 per cent over 60 years old. The majority of people are Butias and Tibetans, with a further 25 per cent Nepalese and a minority of Lepchas (native people) and Santals (descendants of Indian immigrants).

The official language is Dzongkha, although Nepalese, Tibetan, and other dialects are also spoken. English is the working language of the administrative system.

Births, Marriages, Deaths

According to 2004 estimates the birth rate was 34.4 births per 1,000 population, whilst the death rate was 13.2 deaths per 1,000 population. Average life expectancy at birth is 63 years (62 years for males and 65 years for females). Healthy life expectancy is 54 and 56 years respectively. The estimated fertility rate is 2.6 children born per woman. (Source: WHO)

Public Holidays

17 December: National Day

EMPLOYMENT

Approximately 93 per cent of people are employed in agriculture, 5 per cent in services and 2 per cent in industry and commerce. There is a severe shortage of skills among the people. Figures from the International Labour Organisation put the workforce in 2009 at 325,700 with 12,900 (4.0 per cent) unemployed.

Total Employment by Economic Activity

Occupation	2005
Agriculture, hunting & forestry	108,030
Fishing	-
Mining & quarrying	2,839
Manufacturing	4,882
Electricity, gas & water supply	4,116
Construction	30,887
Wholesale & retail trade, repairs	6,747
Hotels & restaurants	4,017
Transport, storage & communications	8,057
Financial intermediation	2,287
Public admin. & defence; compulsory social security	17,494
Education	7,832

STATES OF THE WORLD

BHUTAN

- continued
Health & social work 2,521
Other community, social & personal service activities; 48,734
Extra-territorial organisations & bodies; Other
Source: Copyright © International Labour Organization (ILO Dept. of Statistics, http://laborsta.ilo.org)

BANKING AND FINANCE

Currency
One Ngultrum (Nu) = 100 chetrums. Indian currency is also legal tender.

GDP/GNP, Inflation, National Debt
The Government of Bhutan operates five-year plans to develop its economy, the tenth of which runs from 2008 to 2013. The country has applied for membership of the World Trade Organisation, and is a member of several regional trading associations. Bhutan has seen major development in the hydroelectricity field, and the current five-year economic plan envisages expansion in the areas of tourism and information and communications technology. However, Bhutan's economy is at present reliant on agriculture. The economy has strong monetary and trade links with India.

GDP at current market prices in 2003, according to the Asian Development Bank, was Ngultrum 28,542 million. GDP growth has been strong in recent years. According to the ADB it was estimated at 6.3 per cent in 2006, rising to over 20 per cent in 2007. Per capita GDP was an estimated Ngultrum 89,586 in 2009, at current market prices. Estimated figures for 2009 put GDP at Nu 54,149.7 million reflecting a growth rate of 5.0 per cent.

GDP by Industry 2007-09 (at Current Prices), Million Ngultrum

Sector	2007	2008	2009
	49,456.6	54,713.0	61,223.5
Agriculture	9,234.1	10,078.3	11,158.7
Mining	890.5	1,252.0	1,392.0
Manufacturing	4,033.2	4,593.4	5,017.2
Electricity, gas and water	10,082.0	11,520.9	11,816.4
Construction	6,781.0	6,251.0	7,469.7
Trade	2,865.3	3,263.8	3,472.9
Transport and Communications	4,468.8	5,365.8	5,989.9
Finance	4,105.4	4,576.5	4,962.1
Public Administration	5,311.8	5,930.4	7,963.3
Other	241.9	267.7	276.4

Source: Asian Development Bank

GDP was estimated at US$1.65 billion in 2011.

Services contributes about 35 per cent of GDP whilst industry and commerce contribute approximately 15 per cent and agriculture 19 per cent.

Inflation in 2011 was an estimated 9.5 per cent, up from 2.9 per cent in 2009. The rise has been driven by higher food prices.

Total external debt was just under US$815 million in 2010.

Foreign Investment
Bhutan receives multilateral assistance from various international agencies such as the United Nations Development Programme, United Nations Children's Fund, World Food Programme and United Nations Fund for Population Activities. In addition, bilateral financial and technical assistance is provided by Australia, New Zealand, Japan, United Kingdom, Singapore, United States of America, Switzerland and Austria. It has an annual subsidy from the Government of India of Rs500,000 through a treaty amended in 1949. Direct foreign investment amounted to US$16 million in 2011.

Balance of Payments / Imports and Exports
Major export commodities are electricity, calcium carbide, recorded media, palm oil and copper wire. Cardamom is a major agricultural export commodity, as is timber. Imports include fuel and lubricants, grain, machinery and parts, consumer goods, cereals and textiles.

External Trade in Million Ngultrum

Year	Exports, fob	Imports, cif	Trade Balance
2008	22,590.6	23,495.1	-904.5
2009	23,973.9	25,522.9	-1,549.0
2010	24,897.1	38,588.4	-13,661.3

Source: Asian Development Bank

Bhutan's major trading partners in 2010

Exports to:	Million US Dollars
India	156.4
Hong Kong	0.4
Bangladesh	12.1
Japan	3.1
Italy	0.5
Imports from:	
India	121.3
Japan	20.4
Korea	6.7

- continued
Germany 6.
Source: Asian Development Bank

Central Bank
Royal Monetary Authority of Bhutan, P.O. Box 154, Thimphu, Bhutan. Tel: +975 322540 / 2 323110 / 2, fax: +975 2 322847, e-mail: rma-rsd@druknet.net.bt, URL http://www.rma.org.bt
Chairman: H.E. Yeshey Zimba

MANUFACTURING, MINING AND SERVICES

Primary and Extractive Industries
Bhutan has no reserves of natural gas or oil. Imports of oil account for 100 per cent of consumption which, in 2011, were estimated at 1,000 barrels per day (mainly distillate kerosene and gasoline). Bhutan has coal reserves of 1.3 million short tons, and produced an estimated 108,000 tons in 2009 (all bituminous). Coal production has increased in recent years and whereas Bhutan used to import coal to meet demands in 2010 it exported 18,000 million short tons.

Energy
Bhutan's total energy consumption in 2009 was estimated at 0.52 quadrillion Btu, less than 0.1 per cent of world energy consumption. In terms of energy consumption in the commercial sector, hydroelectric power consumes the most energy (80 per cent in 2002), followed by petroleum (13 per cent) and coal (7 per cent).

Almost all of Bhutan's energy consumption is from biomass, largely firewood. Commercially, energy consumption comes mainly from oil, imported coal and hydroelectricity. Hydroelectric projects are located in Chukha, Thimphu, Paro, Wangdiphodrang, Tashigang, Gidakom and Mongar. Currently, Bhutan's electricity generating industry does not provide power to the whole of the country, and many areas also suffer shortages and power cuts. In 1999, the Asian Development Bank (ADB) agreed a US$10 million loan for a Sustainable Rural Electrification Project which will provide over 6,000 people in remote areas of the country with access to electricity.

Total electricity generation capacity in 2010 was around 7.23 billion kilowatthours (kWh), net consumption that year was 1.68 (kWh). Bhutan is a net exporter of hydroelectricity.

Manufacturing
A cement plant with a production capacity of 1,000 tons a day operates in Pugli in southern Bhutan. There is a chemical plant and a timber factory and Bhutan also produces processed foods. Most manufacturing is centered near the Indian border.

Tourism
The Kingdom of Bhutan has a cautious approach to tourism, wishing to avoid the negative impact of tourism on the country's culture and environment. All tourists must travel on a pre-planned, pre-paid, guided package tour through a registered tour operator in Bhutan or their counterparts abroad. However, tourism is an area that the Government of Bhutan wishes to expand, taking advantage of its location and ecosystem. The tourism industry in Bhutan is founded on the principle of sustainability; it must be environmentally and ecologically friendly, socially and culturally acceptable and economically viable. The number of tourists visiting Bhutan is also regulated to a manageable level because of the lack of infrastructure. In 1999, the sector earned the country US$8.88 million, and there were just over 7,000 visitors.
Bhutan Tourism Corporation Limited (BTCL), URL http://www.kingdomofbhutan.com/

Agriculture
Around 44 per cent of the Bhutan workforce is engaged in agricultural activity and animal husbandry. Main crops are barley, wheat, maize and rice, with some production of fruit and vegetables including chillies, citrus fruits, potatoes, peaches and nectarines. A virus wiped out much of the orange crop in 2009. Oranges are a significant export for Bhutan. Because of strict environmental controls, Bhutan's forests have increased in area since the 1960s to over 70 per cent of the country's area.

Agricultural Production in 2010

Produce	Int. $'000*	Tonnes
Rice, paddy	18,855	71,637
Indigenous cattle meat	13,777	5,100
Arecanuts	12,720	7,280
Cow milk, whole, fresh	12,110	38,807
Chillies and peppers, dry	11,283	10,300
Oranges	10,169	52,621
Maize	7,819	57,663
Apples	7,332	17,337
Potatoes	6,796	44,014
Citrus fruit, nes	6,464	14,300
Roots and tubers, nes	4,275	25,000
Chillies and peppers, green	3,152	6,696

* unofficial figures
Source: http://faostat.fao.org/site/339/default.aspx Food and Agriculture Organization of the United Nations, Food and Agricultural commodities production

COMMUNICATIONS AND TRANSPORT

Visa Information
All visitors to Bhutan require a visa, approved and issued prior to entry. Visas take at least ten days to process, and, since airline tickets cannot be purchased without visa clearance, they should be applied for at least two months before travelling. Visas are initially granted for stays of up to 15 days, but the Bhutan Tourism Corporation Limited (BTCL) can apply for an extension of tourist visas. The government may refuse entry to those wishing to visit for mountaineering, publicity and research activities.

National Airlines
The national airline is Druk Air, which is the only airline serving Bhutan. (URL: http://www.drukair.com.bt)

International Airports
There is an international airport at Paro.

Railways
At present Bhutan has nor railways system but a linl to Phuentsholing from India is under construction.

Roads
Bhutan has more than 4,000 km of roads, but over 3,980 of them are not paved. Vehicles are driven on the left.

HEALTH

There are 28 general hospitals, 44 dispensaries, 65 basic health units, two indigenous dispensaries, one mobile hospital, three leprosy hospitals, one health school and 15 malaria eradication centres. There are 18 hospital beds per 10,000 population. In the period 2015-10, there were 52 doctors (0.2 per 10,000 population), 545 nurses and midwives, 65 dentists and 165 community health workers. In 2009, total expenditure on health was equivalent to 5.1 per cent of GDP. Government expenditure makes up 86.5 per cent of this. External resources amounted to 8.1 per cent of total expenditure. Total per capita expenditure on health was US$91.00.

According to latest figures, the infant mortality rate stood at 44 per 1,000 live births in 2010 and the child mortality rate per 56 per 1,000 live births (compared to 109 in 2000). The main causes of child mortality are prematurity (23 per cent), diarrhoea (7 per cent), pneumonia (20 per cent), measles (1 per cent), and HIV/AIDS (1 per cent). The measles immunization rate was 95 per cent in 2010. In the period 2005-11, 33.5 per cent of children aged less than five years old were classified as stunted.

In 2010, 96 per cent of the population had access to improved drinking water and an estimated 44 per cent of the rural population had access to improved sanitation. (Source: http://www.who.int, World Health Statistics 2012)

EDUCATION

Recent figures suggest that Bhutan has 145 primary schools, 22 junior high schools, six central schools, two teacher training institutes, two technical schools, two schools for Buddhist studies and one junior college. There are a certain number of private and Government aided schools. In the year 2000, almost 115,000 pupils enrolled in schools, and a further 1,800 enrolled in other educational institutions. The ratio of pupils to teachers was 39 to one. English and the national language of Dzongkha are taught in schools.

Approximately 60 per cent of males and 35 per cent of females are literate. Recent figures show that 17.0 per cent of government spending went on education.

RELIGION

Three quarters of Bhutan's population are Lamaistic Buddhist (66 per cent), whilst a quarter (mainly Nepalese) are Hindu. There are also very small numbers of Christians and Muslims.

Bhutan has a religious tolerance rating of 4 on a scale of 1 to 10 (10 is most freedom). (Source: World Religion Database)

COMMUNICATIONS AND MEDIA

Media freedom is restricted.

Newspapers
Kuensel, URL: http://www.kuenselonline.com/ (weekly). The first daily newspaper (Bhutan Today) was launched in 2008.

Broadcasting
Television broadcasting was only introduced in 1999 as part of the King's Jubilee celebrations. Radio and television programmes are broadcast by the state owned Bhutan Broadcasting Service (URL: http://www.bbs.com.bt/). Cable television is also available.

Telecommunications
The towns and district headquarters have telecommunications systems. The rural service is poor. A total of 27,000 telephone mainlines were estimated to be in use in 2008, and there were some 252,000 mobile phones. An international telephone service is provided between Thimphu, Phuntsholing and other countries. Internet users numbered 40,000 in 2008.

ENVIRONMENT

Bhutan has strict environmental conservation policies, including limits on the number of visiting tourists, bans on the export of raw timber, and controls on industrial and infrastructure projects. Current environmental problems include restricted potable water and soil erosion.

In 2010, Bhutan's emissions from the consumption of fossil fuels totalled 0.28 million metric tons of carbon dioxide, the lowest in the South Asia region. (Source: EIA)

Bhutan is a party to the following international agreements: Biodiversity, Climate Change, Climate Change-Kyoto Protocol, Desertification, Endangered Species, Hazardous Wastes, and Ozone Layer Protection.

BOLIVIA

Republic of Bolivia

República de Bolivia

Capital: Sucre (Population estimate, 2010: 225,000)

Administrative Capital: La Paz (Population estimate, 2009: 831,000)

Head of State: Evo Morales (President) (page 1480)

Vice-President: Alvaro M. Garcia Linera (page 1428)

National Flag: Three horizontal bands of red, yellow and green with the coat of arms centered on the yellow band

CONSTITUTION AND GOVERNMENT

Constitution
The first Bolivian constitution was framed in 1826 after the country won its independence from Spain the year before. The current constitution was promulgated in 1947 but implementation was interrupted by the 1952 revolution.

Although Sucre is the legal capital of Bolivia, its administrative capital and seat of government is La Paz.

The executive branch of Bolivia's political system is made up of the President who is elected with the Vice President every five years. The Constitution was reformed in 1995. Under this Constitution an incumbent President cannot seek immediate re-election. The President appoints a cabinet of 14 members.

A constituent assembly was established in the summer of 2006 with a mandate to draft a new constitution, giving more rights to the indigenous majority. Since the outset, the assembly faced political deadlock over the constituent assembly's voting rules. In August, the legality of a vote to exclude the location of the capital was contested by the opposition; agreement could not be reached, and the opposition delegates walked out of the assembly. The MAS approved a constitution without the opposition vote in November 2007. In January 2009 the new constitution was approved by more than 60 per cent of voters in a referendum.

To consult the constitution, please visit: http://www.presidencia.gob.bo/download/constitucion.pdf

International Relations
Bolivia has maintained normal diplomatic relations with all its neighbours except Chile. Relations with Chile have been strained since the War of the Pacific (1879-83) when Bolivia lost its only coastal province, Atacama. Relations were most recently severed in 1978, over the inability of the two countries to reach an agreement that might have granted Bolivia access to the sea.

BOLIVIA

Under President Morales, relations between Bolivia and Cuba have improved, as have relations with Venezuela, which now provides financial assistance to Bolivian municipalities, armed forces and police. The government recently announced it would pursue formal relations with Iran and Libya.

Traditionally, the USA and Bolivia have enjoyed a cooperative relationship, but this has come under recent pressure as President Morales has been publicly critical of US policies. The control of illegal narcotics is a major issue in the bilateral relationship. In 1988, a new law, Law 1008, recognized only 12,000 hectares in the Yungas as sufficient to meet the legal demand of coca and the law called for the eradication of all "excess" coca. Successive Bolivian governments instituted programs offering cash compensation to coca farmers who eradicated voluntarily. Beginning in 1997, the government launched a policy of physically uprooting the illegal coca plants, and Bolivia's illegal coca production fell over the next four years by up to 90 per cent. The Morales government has embarked on a policy of voluntary eradication and social control, and plans to expand legal coca production to 20,000 hectares.

Bolivia has recently become more active in the regional economic groups such as the Organization of American States (OAS), the Rio Group, the Latin American Integration Association (ALADI), and Amazon Pact. It is an associate member of Mercosur. It is also a member of the UN, the Non-Aligned Movement and the World Trade Organization among others.

Recent History
Victor Paz Estenssoro returned from exile to become president in 1952 following a revolution led by peasants and miners. He introduced social and economic reforms. In 1964 Vice-President Rene Barrientos staged a successful military coup and remained in power (despite an attempted coup by 'Che' Guevaro in 1967) until 1969, when he was killed in a plane crash. His successor, President Salinas was removed by the army in the same year. In 1971 Col. Hugo Banzer came to power after staging a military coup and in 1980 General Luis Garcia staged a successful coup in 1980 following disputed elections. He was later replaced by General Torrelio Villa who resigned in 1982. The country was then headed by Siles Zuazo who resigned in 1985 following an attempted coup and strike action. In 1989 Jaime Paz Zamora became president and entered a power-sharing pact with the former dictator, Hugo Banzer, who was elected president in 1997. He was replaced in 2001 by Vice-President Jorge Quiroga. In 2002 Gonzales Sanchez de Lozada won the presidential elections. However civil unrest continued with violent protests against income tax proposals, and government plans to export natural gas. President Lozada resigned and was replaced by Carlos Mesa. In 2004 there were protests calling for Sr. Mesa's resignation after he signed a natural gas export deal. He was eventually forced to resign in June 2005, and was replaced by a caretaker president.

In December 2005, Socialist leader Evo Morales won the presidential election and became the first indigenous Bolivian to become President. He pledged to bring the benefits of the nation's resources to the people, through increasing state control over the natural gas industry. Although he stated that he would not expropriate the property of energy firms, in May 2006 he placed the energy sector under state control. In June 2006, the President began a programme of land reform, giving 30,000 square km. of land to indigenous peasant communities. A land reform bill, calling for the redistribution of 'under-used' land to rural communities, was passed by congress early in November 2006.

In October 2007, as part of a dispute that has set Bolivia's richest regions against the central government, President Morales sent troops into the airport of the province of Santa Cruz; local officials were demanding landing fee payments to be paid directly to the local authorities, rather than to federal government. Some 7,000 protesters rallied at the airport and the troops pulled back to avoid clashes. Santa Cruz leaders want autonomy and a larger share of natural gas revenues; they also oppose attempts by President Morales to nationalise key industries and redistribute land.

One day strikes against the draft constitution were held in six of Bolivia's nine provinces on 29th November 2007. Opposition leaders claimed the constitution will concentrate too much power in the hands of the government, and objected to the way reforms were being introduced by an assembly with no opposition delegates. In December, the provinces of Santa Cruz, Beni, Pando and Tarija (Bolivia's richest regions) declared autonomy in protest against constitutional reforms which include greater state control of the economy. President Morales said the moves were "illegal".

Bolivian opposition members announced a referendum on 4 May 2008 to demand autonomy for the eastern province of Santa Cruz. The Santa Cruz autonomy referendum took place on 5th May, and 80 per cent of voters backed plans to give their region more powers. A vote of confidence referendum was held in August 2008; President Morales won 60 per cent of the vote, but four opposition governors also remained in power. Protests continued, and on the 10th September, anti-government protesters stormed public buildings in eastern Bolivia; hundreds of people raided the state-run telecommunications company, the tax agency, the local state TV network and the land reform institute in the city of Santa Cruz. On the 11th September, Bolivia expelled the US Ambassador, claiming that he had incited the riots, and the following day, the USA expelled the Bolivian Ambassador to Washington. The following day, President Evo Morales declared a state of emergency in the northern province of Pando, where 30 people had been killed in riots. President Morales accused the region's governor of hiring foreign hitmen to attack his peasant supporters; the governor rejected the claim. On the 14th September, government officials met the governor of Tarija region to try to ease tension in energy-rich eastern areas held by the opposition.

In October 2008, the date was set for a referendum on the new constitution: 25 January 2009. President Morales agreed to seek only one more five-year term. The new constitution includes a bill of rights, including a chapter dedicated to Bolivia's 36 indigenous peoples. It increases state control over the economy, limits the size of big land holdings and redistributes revenues from the important gas fields in the eastern lowlands to poorer parts of the nation. Indigenous people would be granted autonomy over their traditional lands and a "priority"

share of the revenue from natural resources; however, many of the areas where natural resources are found are governed by the opposition and would also be granted greater autonomy.

On the 2nd November, President Morales announced an indefinite suspension of US Drug Enforcement Administration operations in Bolivia, accusing the agency of having encouraged anti-government protests. President Morales once served as the leader of the country's union of coca-growers. Bolivia is a major producer of cocaine, but millions of the country's people also chew coca leaves as part of their daily routine, believing the leaf has health benefits. In October 2010 the government scrapped a new law which would have cut cocaine production the law was abandoned in response to anger from coca growers.

On the 25th January, President Morales claimed victory in a referendum on the new constitution; exit polls estimated that 60 per cent of voters had voted in favour of it. Many mixed-race people in the fertile eastern lowlands rejected the charter and four of Bolivia's nine provinces had a majority no vote. Support for Mr Morales was highest in the western highlands where Indians are a majority. In April 2009, President Morales went on hunger strike for five days, to encourage the senate to pass a new electoral bill. The bill allows Mr Morales to run for a second term in office in elections in December, as well as giving greater political power to Bolivia's indigenous majority. In January 2012, Bolivia temporarily left the UN Conventions on Narcotics as a protest against classification of coca as an illegal drug, Bolivia later signed an agreement with the US and Brazil to help reduce the production of illegal cocaine

In February 2011, there were demonstrations following steep rises in the price of basic foodstuffs.

In August and September 2011 protests were held against plans to build a major road through a rainforest reserve, the government says the road is essential for future development. In April 2012, President Morales rescinded the contract awarded to OAS of Brazil to build the road.

In May 2012 the president nationalised the Spanish-owned electric power company REE on the grounds that it had not invested enough in Bolivia.

In June 2012, police protests over pay and conditions turned violent as the police seized control of several stations. The government accused them of plotting a coup; a claim the police denied. An agreement over pay was signed in eight regions.

In May 2013, a law was passed by parliament allowing President Morales to stand for a third time.

Legislature
Legislative power resides with the National Congress which is divided into two chambers: the Senate and the Chamber of Deputies.
URL: http://www.congreso.gov.bo/indice.asp

Upper House
The Senate is made up of 27 directly elected senators, three for each department, who hold office for five years.
URL: http://www.senado.bo

Lower House
The Chamber of Deputies consists of 130 members who also hold office for five years. Under the 1995 Constitution 50 per cent of the deputies are elected under party lists, whilst the other half run for representation of a particular district.
URL: http://www.diputados.bo/

Cabinet (as at June 2013)
Minister of Finance: Luis Alberto Arce Catacora (page 1379)
Minister of Foreign Affairs: David Choquehuanca Céspedes (page 1404)
Minister of National Defence: Ruben Saavedra Soto
Minister of Productive Development and Plural Economy: Ana Teresa Morales Olivere
Minister of the Presidency: Oscar Coca Antezana
Minister of Education: Roberto Aguilar Gomez
Minister of Public Services, Public Works and Housing: Walter Juvenal Delgadillo Terceros
Minister of Health and Sports: Nila Heredia Miranda
Minister of Labour, Employment and Social Security: Carmen Trujillo Cardenas
Minister of Rural Development and Lands: Nemesia Achacollo Tola
Minister of Mines and Metallurgy: Jose Pimentel Castillo
Minister of Culture: Zulma Yugar Parraga
Minister of Autonomy: Carlos Romero Bonifaz
Minister of the Environment and Water: Julieta Monje
Minister of Planning and Development: Elba Viviana Caro Hinojosa
Minister of State Legal Affairs: Elizasbeth Arismendi Chumacero
Minister of the Interior: Wilfredo Chavez
Minister of Hydrocarbons and Energy: Jose Luis Gutierrez
Minister of Justice: Nilda Copa Condori
Minister of Transparency of Institutions and the Fight against Corruption: Nardi Suxo Iturri

---

Ministries
Seat of Government, Palacio de Gobierno, Plaza Murillo, La Paz, Bolivia. Tel: +591 2 371302 / 359736, fax: +591 2 367421
Presidential Office, URL: http://www.presidencia.gob.bo/
Legislative Seat of Government, Palacio Legislativo, Plaza Murillo, La Paz, Bolivia. Tel: +591 2 311117 / 310458 / 391680, fax: +591 2 392606
Foreign Office, Calle Ingavi esq. Junin, Le Paz, Bolivia. Tel: +591 2 371150, fax: +591 2 392134 / 365590, URL: http://www.rree.gov.bo/

Ministry of the Interior, Av Arce esq. Belisario Salínas No. 2409, La Paz, Bolivia. Tel: +591 2 370460 / 431851 / 431708, URL: http://www.mingobierno.gov.bo/

Ministry of Finance, Palacio de Communicaciones (piso 19), Avenida Mariscal Santa Cruz, La Paz, Bolivia. Tel: +591 2 392540 / 392779 / 392220, fax: +591 2 359955, URL: http://www.hacienda.gov.bo/

Ministry of Economic Development, Palacio de Communicaciones, Avenida Mariscal, Santa Cruz, La Paz, Bolivia. Tel: +591 2 369674 / 356741 / 375000, fax: +591 2 375000 / 360534, URL: http://www.desarollo.gov.bo

Ministry of Sustainable Development and Environment, Avenida Arce 2147, Le Paz, Bolivia. Tel: +591 2 363331 / 372378 / 372063, fax: +591 2 392892

Ministry of Health and Social Security, Plaza del Estudiante, La Paz, Bolivia. Tel: +591 2 371373-9, fax: +591 2 371376 / 375462, URL: http://www.sns.gov.bo/

Ministry of Defence, Plaza Abaroa esq. 20 de Octubre, La Paz, Bolivia. Tel: +591 2 430130, fax: +591 2 433159, URL: http://www.mindef.gov.bo/

Ministry of Labour, Yanacocha esq. Mercado, Le Paz, Bolivia. Tel: +591 2 364164 / 391449 / 359036, fax: +591 2 371387

Ministry of Justice, PO Box 6966, La Paz, Bolivia. Tel: +591 2 373620 / 361037, fax: +591 2 391570

Ministry of Education, PO Box 6500, La Paz, Bolivia. Tel: +591 2 372060 / 372145, fax: +591 2 371376, URL: http://www.veips.gov.bo/

Ministry of Housing, Avenida Saavedra 2273, La Paz, Bolivia. Tel: +591 2 360469 / 372241, fax: +591 2 371335

Ministry of International Trade and Investment, Palacio de Communicaciones, Avenida Mariscal, Santa Cruz, La Paz, Bolivia. Tel: +591 2 36652, fax: 591 2 377451, URL: http://www.mcei.gov.bo/

Ministry of Agriculture, Avenida Camacho No. 1471, La Paz, Bolivia. Tel: +591 2 367936, fax: +591 2 359480, URL: http://www.maca.gov.bo/

Ministry of External Relations and Worship, URL: http://www.rree.gov.bo/

Ministry of Gas and Oil, URL: http://www.veips.gov.bo/

Ministry of Mining, URL: http://www.rree.gov.bo/

Major Political Parties

Movement towards Socialism (MAS)
Leader: Evo Morales
Social and Democratic Power (PODEMOS) -until 2002, known as Nationalist Democratic Action (ADN)
Leader: Jorge Quiroga
National Unity (UN)
Nationalist Revolutionary Movement (MNR)
Progress Plan for Bolivia - National Convergence (PPB-CN)
Social Alliance (AS)

Elections

Presidential elections took place in June 2002 but, since there was no clear winner, Congress chose between the two top candidates: former president Gonzalo Sanchez de Lozada and leader of the coca growers, Evo Morales. Gonzalo Sanchez de Lozada was inaugurated in August 2002, but resigned in October 2003, following protests over tax and gas exports. He was succeeded by Carlos Mesa, who in turn resigned and was replaced by a caretaker president, Sr. Rodriguez Veltze who called an election for December 2005. Evo Morales won a landslide victory, with the support of the majority indigenous people.

The last parliamentary elections took place in December 2005. The Movement towards Socialism party won 53.7 per cent of the vote, and now hold 72 of the 130 Chamber of Deputies seats and 12 of the 27 Senate seats.

A vote of confidence referendum was held on 10 August 2008, on whether President, Evo Morales, his vice-president and eight governors should stay in office. The Senate has repeatedly challenged the government; Sr. Morales reforms have brought him up against rebellious regional governors. President Morales won 60 per cent of the referendum vote of confidence. However, the vote did little to ease Bolivia's deep divisions, as four of the opposition governors also won the right to remain in their positions.

The next presidential and legislative elections were due in December 2010 but were called early on 6 December 2009. All citizens over 18 are entitled, and required by law, to vote. President Morales was elected for a second term as president.

Diplomatic Representation

US Embassy, Avenida Arce 2780, PO Box 426, La Paz, Bolivia APO AA 34032. Tel: +591 (0)2 2430251, fax: +591 (0)2 2433900, URL: http://bolivia.usembassy.gov
Chargé d'Affairs: Larry L. Memmott
British Embassy, Avenida Arce 2732, Casilla 697, La Paz, Bolivia. Tel: +591 (0)2 2433424, fax: +591 (0)2 2431073, URL: http://ukinbolivia.fco.gov.uk/en
Ambassador: Ross Denny (page 1415)
Embassy of Bolivia, 106 Eaton Square, London, SW1W 9AD, United Kingdom. Tel: +44 (0)20 7235 4248 / 2257, fax: +44 (0)20 7235 1286, e-mail: info@embassyofbolivia.co.uk, URL: http://www.embassyofbolivia.co.uk
Ambassador: H.E. Mrs Maria Beatriz Souviron (page 1518)
Embassy of Bolivia, 3014 Massachusetts Avenue, NW, Washington DC 20008, USA. Tel: + 1 202 483 4410, fax: +1 202 3283712, URL: http://www.bolivia-usa.org/
Charge d:Affaires: Freddy Bersatti
Permanent Representative of Bolivia to the United Nations, 211 East 43rd Street, 8th Floor (Room 802), New York, N.Y. 10017, USA. Tel: +1 212 682 8132, fax: +1 212 687 4642, e-mail: bolnu@aol.com
Charge d:Affaires: Rafael Archondo Quiroga

LEGAL SYSTEM

The judiciary is formed by the Supreme Court, the district courts and other tribunals and judgeships.

The Supreme Court consists of a president and eleven justices who are appointed for 10 years by the Chamber of Deputies. It has its seat in Sucre. It is divided into three chambers, dealing with civil cases, criminal cases, and social and administrative cases. Each chamber has three judges. The President of the Supreme Court presides over all sections. The Supreme Court also has the power to determine the constitutionality of laws, decrees, and resolutions approved by the government, and it can try public officers, including the president, for crimes committed while in office.

There are nine superior district courts which hear appeals in both civil and criminal matters from decisions rendered by trial courts in each department. There are civil and criminal trial courts in departmental towns and cities throughout Bolivia. The criminal sections have investigating judges who prepare criminal cases for trial by sectional judges. Commercial and civil matters on personal and property actions are heard by the civil sections of the trial courts.

In 2012, President Evo Morales replaced existing judges with elected officials and 56 judges elected by national ballot were sworn in and will serve in the country's four highest courts. The move has been denounced by some as a politicization of the judicial system.

In general, the government respects the human rights of its citizens. However, prison conditions are harsh, and there are arbitrary arrests. There have been recent attacks on the judiciary by the executive branch, as well as threats to civil liberties, including legal rights and press freedom. There is corruption and a lack of transparency in government. Bolivia retains the death penalty, but only for exceptional crimes such as those committed under military law or in exceptional circumstances.

The Supreme Court ruled on 2,206 cases in 2011. Approximately 29,000 cases were pending as of January 2012.

Supreme Court: URL: http://suprema.poderjudicial.gob.bo/
President, Supreme Court: Dr. Eddy Walter Fernández Gutiérrez

Defence of the People, Calle Colombia 440, San Pedro, La Paz, Bolivia. URL: http://www.defensor.gov.bo/

LOCAL GOVERNMENT

Bolivia is divided into nine administrative departments: La Paz, Chuquisaca, Oruro, Beni, Santa Cruz, Potosí, Tarija, Cochabamba and Pando.

Each elects three senators for Congress, and each has its own municipal council which controls revenue and expenditure. A prefect holds political, military and administrative authority within each department. Bolivians chose their departmental prefects by popular vote for the first time on December 18, 2005. Departments are further divided into provinces (of which there are 112) and municipalities (of which there are 312), and are each administered by a sub-prefect. The provinces and municipalities are sub-divided into cantons (of which there are 1,384).

In a July 2006 referendum, Bolivia's four eastern departments voted in favor of increasing regional autonomy, and the other five provinces opposed the measure. The autonomy movement rallied around Sucre's August 2007 demand that the constituent assembly consider moving all branches of government to the traditional capital. In December 2007, the provinces of Santa Cruz, Beni, Pando and Tarija declared themselves autonomous, in protest at proposed reforms under the new constitution. The four lowland provinces hold the country's gas reserves and are home to important agribusinesses. Their political leaders argue that the new constitution is illegal since it was drawn up during an opposition boycott of parliament. Santa Cruz held a popular referendum on its autonomy statute on May 4, 2008, in which the majority of voters voted for autonomy. The Bolivian Government considered this referendum to be illegal and did not recognise its results.

Bolivian cities and towns are governed by directly elected mayors and councils. Municipal elections were last held in April 2010, with councils elected to 5-year terms. Some government-aligned parliamentarians have advocated popular elections for the civic committees, which they claim disproportionately represent elite and opposition interests.

AREA AND POPULATION

Area

Bolivia is a landlocked republic in the centre of South America. It is bounded in the north and east by Brazil, in the south by Paraguay and Argentina, in the south-west by Chile, and in the west by Peru. It has a total area of 1,098,581 sq. km. or approximately 424,164 sq. miles.

The Andes run through Bolivia, but as well as mountainous terrain with its high plateaux, the country has semi-tropical lowlands. Bolivia and Peru share Lake Titicaca, the world's highest navigable lake (at 3,805 metres above sea level) and the administrative capital, La Paz, is the highest capital city in the world, at 3,640 metres.

The climate varies according to altitude, from tropical to cold.

To view a map, consult: http://www.un.org/Depts/Cartographic/map/profile/bolivia.pdf

Population

The population of Bolivia, estimated at approximately 9.93 million in 2010 (compared to 9.1 million in July 2007), is largely (55 per cent) indigenous. Population growth is around 1.8 per cent per year. Ethnic groups include the Quechua (30 per cent), the Aymara (25 per cent). The Mestizo, those of mixed European and Indian descent make up around 30 per cent and Europeans make up the remaining 15 per cent. Population density ranges from less than one

BOLIVIA

person per square kilometer in the southeastern plains to about ten per square kilometer in the central highlands. Approximately 67 per cent of the population lives in urban areas. The population of La Paz, the administrative capital, was recently put at 831,000, with Sucre, the official capital, 225,000. Other major cities include Santa Cruz, with a population of 1,486,115; Cochabamba, 587,220; and El Alto, (13,800 ft. above sea level), 858,716.

Almost two-thirds of the people live in poverty. The official languages of Bolivia are Spanish, Quechua and Aymara, although Spanish is spoken by only 50 per cent of the population.

Births, Marriages, Deaths

In 2010, the birth rate was estimated at 26.5 per 1,000 population and the death rate was around 6.5 per 1,000 population. Average life expectancy was 66 years for men and 70 for women. The median age was 22 years. Approximately 35 per cent of the population is aged under 15 years and 7 per cent over 60 years. The fertility rate is currently around 3.3 children per woman. (Source: http://www.who.int, World Health Statistics 2012)

Public Holidays 2014

1 January: New Year
February: Fiesta (Oruru only)*
April: Fiesta (Tarija only)*
18 April: Good Friday
21 April: Easter Monday
1 May: Labour Day
19 June: Corpus Christi
May: Fiesta (Sucre only)*
July: Fiesta (La Paz only)*
6 August: Independence Day
September: Fiesta (Cochabamba only)*
September: Fiesta (Santa Cruz and Pando only)*
14 October: Columbus Day
1 November: All Saints' Day
November: Fiesta (Potosi only)*
November: Fiesta (Beni only)*
25 December: Christmas
*variable

EMPLOYMENT

Figures for 2008 indicate that Bolivia had a workforce of 4.4 million, of which 2.48 million were in non-agricultural sectors, 42 per cent were engaged in services including government departments and 58 per cent were engaged in industry and commerce.

Industry	No. of employed
Agriculture, hunting and forestry	1,673,000
Fishing	13,500
Mining & utilities	72,400
Manufacturing	514,900
Utilities	15,500
Construction	316,300
Wholesale and retail trade, repairs	673,800
Hotels and restaurants	159,300
Transport, storage & communication	272,300
Financial intermediation	28,100
Real estate, renting and business activities	136,900
Public Administration and Defence; Compulsory Social Security	152,100
Education	223,100
Health & social work	109,500
Other community, social & personal service activities	148,900
Households with employed persons	160,800
Extra-Territorial organisations & bodies	2,000
Total	4,672,400

Source: Copyright © International Labour Organization (ILO Dept. of Statistics, http://laborsta.ilo.org)

BANKING AND FINANCE

Currency

The monetary unit has been the Boliviano (Bs, BOB) since July 1992.
1 Boliviano = 100 centavos

GDP/GNP, Inflation, National Debt

Although rich in mineral resources and in agricultural potential, Bolivia is counted among the poorest and least developed countries in South America. Approximately two thirds of the population live in poverty. Recommendations by the IMF have not been carried out due to previous governments' fear of social protests. The country has rich reserves of minerals and natural gas and these represent Bolivia's main exports. The economy has been boosted in recent years because of high commodity prices, however global prices have fallen in the global economic downturn and Bolivia's economy has consequently suffered. Its infrastructure needs to develop to maximise its extraction and export industries.

Estimated figures for 2010 put GDP at US$19.8 billion, a per capita figure of US$1,850, up from US$17.4 billion in 2009 giving a per capita figure of US$1,765. The annual growth rate was 4.1 per cent in 2010 rising to over 5 per cent in 2011. GDP in 2011 was estimated to be US$24.5 billion. Inflation in 2006 was around 4.3 per cent but this rose to 11.7 per cent in 2007. It has remained high and in 2011 was estimated to be just under 10 per cent. The

agricultural sector accounts for approximately 10.5 per cent of GDP, while manufacturing contributes 36 per cent and the services sector (including government) accounts for 51 per cent of GDP.

Foreign Investment

New financial laws were introduced in the 1990s to promote investment. Exchange controls were removed and bank interest rates allowed to float freely. The privatisation of state-owned companies and trade liberalisation encouraged foreign investors during the decade; they were accorded national treatment, and foreign ownership of companies was virtually unrestricted. Many of these reforms are currently under review, and an increased role for the state in the economy has become a primary goal of the Morales administration.

Currently there is a degree of investor uncertainty; in 2000, government plans to privatise the water utility in Cochabamba led to national protests and the plans were cancelled. Investors were only compensated in 2006. Foreign investment fell over the years 2004 and 2005, and the new Hydrocarbons Law, together with the nationalisation of hydrocarbons announced in May 2006, increased investor caution. Foreign direct investment inflows have decreased, as has long-term investment across most industrial sectors.

Balance of Payments / Imports and Exports

Bolivia has several regional trade agreements. It is a member of the Andean Community (CAN) and an associate member of MERCOSUR (Southern Cone Common Market). The Andean Trade Promotion and Drug Eradication Act, which expired in 2006, allowed many exports to the USA to travel duty-free.

In 2008, there was an overall merchandise trade surplus of US$1.9 million; exports of goods earned an estimated US$6.8 billion, and imports cost the country $4.9 billion. Estimated figures for 2009 put exports at US$5.2 billion and imports at US$4.3 billion. Exports were estimated to be US$8 billion in 2011 and imports US$7.1 billion.

Principal exports were gas, soybeans, coffee, zinc, tin, silver, gold, jewelry, wood and petroleum products. Brazil was the main purchaser in 2011, buying over 40 per cent of all exports. The USA (12 per cent), South Korea, Peru, Argentina and Japan were also significant markets.

Between them Chile and Brazil supply almost half of imports. Other major suppliers include Argentina, the US, Peru and China. Vehicles, machinery, consumer products, construction and mining equipment were the principal commodities imported.

International Trade Agreements

Bilateral trade agreements have been signed with Argentina, Belgium, Canada, China, Germany, France, Italy, Mexico, The Netherlands, Peru, Spain, Sweden, Switzerland, United Kingdom, United States.

Bolivia is a chartered member of the United Nations (UN) and of the Organization of American States (OAS). It is also a member of the World Trade Organization (WTO), the Multilateral Investment Guarantee Agreement (MIGA), as well as the Overseas Private Investment Corporation (OPIC). In a move which potentially threatenes thousands of jobs, the US government recently withdrew some freed trade benefits in response to some of President Morales' policies. Bolivia withdrew from ICSID and threatened to renegotiate its bilateral investment treaties.

Bolivia is a member of the Latin American Integration Association (ALADI) and is an associate member of the South American organisation Mercosur.

Central Bank

Banco Central de Bolivia, PO Box 3118, Calle Mercado esq Ayacucho, La Paz, Bolivia. Tel: +591 2 374151, fax: +591 2 239 2998, e-mail: bancocentraldebolivia@bcb.gov.bo, URL: http://www.bcb.gob.bo/
President: Marcelo Zabalaga Estrada

MANUFACTURING, MINING AND SERVICES

Primary and Extractive Industries

Bolivia has a diverse mineral production. Mining of silver has now overtaken that of tin and there has been a considerable increase in zinc and gold production. Future ventures include mining of lithium and iron. Bolivia's top mining company is Comsur.

Figures for 2011 show that Bolivia had proven oil reserives of 209 million barrels of oil and produced 49,000 barrels per day but consumed 62,000 barrels.Oil production in primarily concentrated in two fields, Sabalo which produces around 37 per cent of Bolivia's oil and San Alberto which produces around 21 per cent. The state-owned YPFB Transporte controls the majority of Bolivia's petroleum transportation network, whcih covers 1,553 miles (2,500 km.) of pipelines.

Bolivia has the second-largest proven natural gas reserves in South America, behind Venezuela, and gas exports provide an important source of revenue. Bolivia currently exports gas to Brazil and Argentina; plans to export liquefied natural gas (LNG) to Mexico and the USA, have been delayed by political debate.

At the beginning of 2010 proven natural gas reserves stood at 27 trillion cubic feet. Over the same year, production rose to 507 billion cubic feet and consumption rose to around 96 billion cubic feet. Over 85 per cent of the country's total reserves are in Tarija, and Santa Cruz department holds over 10 per cent.

In July 2004 there was a referendum on the gas industry and the people backed returning reserves to the ownership and control of the state, high royalties on production and export through Peru rather than through Chile. President Mesa, author of the bill, resigned in June 2005, amid political turmoil regarding energy policy. In May 2005, the Hydrocarbons Law as passed, as a result of which an extra 32 per cent tax on oil and gas production was vied (on top of the pre-existing 18 per cent royalty) and existing contracts had to be nverted to the terms of the new law.

May 2006, President Evo Morales announced the re-nationalizing of the entire natural as sector: foreign companies could no longer own natural gas reserves and the state-run acimientos Petroliferos Fiscales Bolivianos now holds the majority stake in all natural gas rojects. Private companies have to operate under service agreements, producing natural as on behalf of YPFB for a fee. The privatisation policy will have a profound impact on rther development of the energy sector.

olivia meets its needs from domestic oil production; figures for 2008 indicate that onsumption was an estimated 60,000 barrels per day and production reached around 39,000 arrels per day. Proven oil reserves stood at an estimated 0.4 billion barrels at the beginning * 2008. In May 2007, YPFB re-acquired the country's two refineries from Petrobras. These eet domestic demand for gasoline and jet fuel, but the country still imports other refined etroleum products due to a lack of suitable domestic refining capacity. (Source: Energy formation Administration)

nergy
ectricity generation capacity is in the region of 1.6 gigawatts, and Bolivia's electricity roduction of 5.8 billion kWh supplies more than the country requires. Bolivia has plans to xport to Brazil. 75 per cent of electricity is thermoelectric and 25 per cent hydroelectric. In lay 2010 President Morales ordered the nationalisation of four Bolivian electricity firms, his would mean that the government controlled 80 per cent of the country's power eneration.

gures from the EIA for 2011 show that 45 per cent of Bolivia's total energy consumption ame from petroleum, 34 per cent from natural gas, 14 from biomass, six per cent from ydroelectric power and one per cent from other renewable sources.

Manufacturing
ndustry contributed some 36 per cent of Gross Domestic Product in 2006. The main subsectors were mineral and hydrocarbon extraction, manufacturing, textiles, food processing, chemicals, lastics, mineral smelting, and petroleum refining. Goods produced on a smaller scale include wood products and furniture, printing and publishing, plastic, glass, rubber products, industrial hemicals and pharmaceuticals.

ervices
he services sector, including government, accounted for over 51 per cent of GDP in 2006. ourism is growing and visitors in 2006 numbered 515,000 up from 284,000 in 1995.

Agriculture
Agriculture is an important growth industry in Bolivia. Half a million hectares of soybeans, orghum, wheat, corn, sunflowers, rice, sugar and cotton are being farmed commercially in he east where excellent soil conditions and favourable climates allow double-cropping, reating high productivity. There are two large areas of tropical forest where forestry is lanned, although dependent upon improvements in transport facilities.

Bolivia is the world's third largest grower of coca (after Colombia and Peru). It was originally grown to be used in indigenous rituals and for chewing, but cultivation increased in response o the growth of the illegal drug trade in the 1970s. In 1988, Law 1008, effectively illegalised he cultivation of coca in all but 12,000 hectares in the Yungas area. Successive governments ried to replace coca crops with crops such as tropical fruits, offering the farmers financial ncentives to change over. In 1997, the government of the day started a policy of physically uprooting the plants, and production fell by up to 90 per cent over the next four years. However, in 2001 farmers rejected a government offer of US$900 each in exchange for the eradication of the coca crop. In 2003, an estimated 28,000 hectares were being used for coca cultivation, an increase of around 23 per cent on the previous year. The current government is following a policy of voluntary eradication and has increased the area allowed for legal coca cultivation to 20,000 hectares.

Agricultural Production in 2010

Produce	Int. $'000	Tonnes
Indigenous chicken meat	604,902	424,669
Indigenous cattle meat	546,351	202,249
Soybeans	396,577	1,917,150
Sugar cane	191,316	5,826,230
Indigenous pigmeat	128,848	83,818
Potatoes	125,137	975,418
Rice, paddy	120,237	449,482
Cow milk, whole, fresh	115,986	371,676
Sunflower seed	85,548	310,841
Plantains	65,071	338,901
Indigenous sheep meat	57,858	21,250
Hen eggs, in shell	56,813	68,500

* unofficial figures
Source: http://faostat.fao.org/site/339/default.aspx Food and Agriculture Organization of the United Nations, Food and Agricultural commodities production

Forestry
In response for calls to save the rain forest and provide ecologically sustainable wood products Bolivia has introduced Community Forestry. Indigenous communities own the land and use sustainable forestry practices to ensure an income for their communities and the survival of the forest.

COMMUNICATIONS AND TRANSPORT

Travel Requirements
Citizens of the US, Canada, Australia and the EU must have a passport valid for six months. Most EU, Australian and Canadian citizens can travel as tourists to Bolivia for up to three months without a visa, but nationals of Bulgaria, Cyprus, Malta, Romania and the USA do need a tourist visa; on 1 January 2007, the Bolivian president decreed that all US citizens wishing to enter Boliva, for any purpose, would require a visa. US nationals wishing to enter Bolivia are advised to contact the nearest Bolivian consulate for further information.

All nationals travelling on business require a Specific Purpose visa. Citizens of countries not listed above are advised to contact the Bolivian consulate in their country to check visa requirements prior to travelling.

International Airports
El Alto airport, La Paz, is Bolivia's main airport. There is a second international airport, Viru-Viru, at Santa Cruz.

Railways
The railway network extends for 3,700 miles. Bolivia currently has two unconnected rail networks, the Eastern network and Western network. To connect them would involve a 480 km track at an estimated cost of US$1.5 billion.

Roads
In 2002, there were about 60,000 km of roadways in service, nearly 4,000 km of which are paved. The Pan-American highway links Argentina with Peru, whilst a 560 km highway connects Santa Cruz with Cochabamba. Bus services link Bolivia with Argentina and Peru. Vehicles are driven on the right.

By 2010 it is hoped that as many as 11 major international highways will be completed. Bus services link Bolivia with Argentina and Peru.

Waterways
Bolivia shares control of Lake Titicaca, the world's highest navigable lake, with Peru. It has free port privileges in Argentine, Chilean, Brazilian and Paraguayan maritime ports. Ferry services operate on Lake Titicaca.

HEALTH

In 2009, total expenditure on health equated to 5.1 per cent of GDP, representing a per capita spend of US$90. The Bolivian government spent 64.6 per cent of total expenditure on the health sector in 2009. Out of pocket expenditure accounts for 96.3 per cent of private expenditure on health. Government benefits are paid in the event of accident, sickness, old age or death. Pension reform is being undertaken in Bolivia. In 2000-10, there were 10,329 doctors (12 per 10,000 population) and 18,091 nurses and midwives (21 per 10,000 population).

Approximately two thirds of the population lives in poverty in Bolivia. Approximately 96 per cent of the urban population and 67 per cent of the rural population had access to improved drinking-water sources in 2008. In the same year 34 per cent of the urban population and 9 per cent of the rural population had access to improved sanitation. In 2010, 88 per cent of the population had access to improved drinking water and 27 per cent to improved sanitation.

Infant mortality (probability of dying before age one) stands (2010) at 42 deaths per 1,000 live births and child mortality (under-fives) at 54 deaths per 1,000 live births. Major causes of childhood deaths are prematurity (21 per cent), diarrhoea (9 per cent) and pneumonia (15 per cent). The immunization rate for diseases such as measles, diptheria and hepatitis B stands at over 81 per cent. The prevalence of HIV among adults aged 15-49 was 0.2 per cent in 2007. (Source: http://www.who.int, World Health Statistics 2012)

EDUCATION

Elementary education is free and compulsory for all children between the ages of six and 14. Schools are maintained by the municipalities and the State. Recent figures show there were about 2,300 pre-primary schools and 12,600 primary schools. In 2007, 49 per cent of children were enrolled in pre-school education, 94 per cent of girls and 93 per cent of were enrolled in primary school and 70 per cent of girls and 70 per cent of boys were enrolled in secondary school.

There are universities at La Paz, Sucre, Cochabamba, Oruro, Potosi, Santa Cruz and Tarija.

UNESCO figures for 2007 estimated that the government spent just over 18 per cent of its total budget on education. In the same year, the adult literacy rate was 90.7 per cent. The rate rose to over 99 per cent among the 15-24 year old age-group.

In December 2008, President Morales declared the country to be 'illiteracy free', following a 30-month campaign to teach thousands of poor Bolivians to read and write. The campaign was designed by Cuba and financed by Venezuela. Under Unesco standards, a country can be declared free of illiteracy if 96 per cent of its population over the age of 15 can read and write. Political opponents of President Morales dismissed the announcement as political propaganda.

RELIGION

In 1961 the church was separated from the State. There is now complete freedom of worship. The established religion, however, is Roman Catholic, accounting for about 80 per cent of the population. The main authority of the Catholic Church is the Conferencia Episcopal Boliviana. Other denominations include Anglican and Protestant (13 per cent). Other faiths include Judaism and the Bahá'ís.

In May 2010 President Morales met with the Pope and urged him to consider allowing priests to marry.

Bolivia has a religious tolerance rating of 10 on a scale of 1 to 10 (10 is most freedom). (Source: World Religion Database)

COMMUNICATIONS AND MEDIA

Bolivia enjoys relative press freedom. Much of the press is in private hands.

Newspapers
Major newspapers include:
La Razon, La Paz, Bolivia. URL: http://www.la-razon.com/
El Diario, La Paz, Bolivia.URL: http://www.eldiario.net/
Los Tiempos, Cochabamba, Bolivia. URL: http://www.lostiempos.com/
El Deber, Santa Cruz, Bolivia. URL: http://www.lostiempos.com/
High illiteracy levels limit readership of the newspapers.

Broadcasting
There are 208 radio stations in the country. Radio is the most significant medium especially in rural areas. There is a national official television channel and a national independent channel in addition to a number of private TV channels in each department.

Empresa Nacional de Televisión Boliviana-Canal 7, La Paz, Bolivia. UR http://www.televisionboliviana.tv.bo/
Asociación Boliviana de Radiodifusoras (ASBORA), La Paz, Bolivia.

Telecommunications
The state telephone company is Entel, providing direct dialling between most cities and lor distance and overseas services. In 2008 there were over 690,000 mainline telephones in us and some 4.8 million mobile phone users. By 2008, there were over one million interne users.
Empresa Nacional de Telecomunicaciones (ENTEL), La Paz, Bolivia.

ENVIRONMENT

Bolivia's main environmental problems are caused by deforestation as a result of internation tropical timber demand and agricultural land clearing; soil erosion, desertification, industri water pollution; and loss of biodiversity. The slash and burn technique for cultivation is als causing concern.

In 2010, Bolivia's emissions from the consumption of fossil fuels totalled 12.29 million metr tons of carbon dioxide. (Source: EIA)

Bolivia is a party to the following international agreements: Biodiversity, Climate Chang Climate Change-Kyoto Protocol, Desertification, Endangered Species, Hazardous Waste Law of the Sea, Marine Dumping, Ozone Layer Protection, Ship Pollution, Tropical Timbe 83, Tropical Timber 94, and Wetlands.

SPACE PROGRAMME

The Bolivian Space Agency was created in 2010. A communications satellite, which will b built and launched with Chinese help, is due to be launched in 2013.

BOSNIA AND HERZEGOVINA
Bosna i Hercegovina

Capital: Sarajevo (Population estimate: 388,000)

Head of State, Presidency of Bosnia and Herzegovina
Rotating Chairs of Presidency: Nejobsa Radmanovic (page 1499) (Serb), Bakir Izetbegović (page 1447)(Bosniac), Zelijko Komsic (page 1458) (Croat)

National Flag: Medium blue band on the fly side; a yellow isosceles triangle abuts the blue band and the top of the flag; the remainder of the flag is medium blue, with seven full five-pointed stars and two half stars along the hypotenuse of the triangle

CONSTITUTION AND GOVERNMENT

Constitution
At the end of the Second World War, Bosnia Herzegovina came under Communist rule as part of the Socialist Federal Republic of Yugoslavia. The constitution of the former Yugoslavia provided for a collective presidency. Forty years later, a civil war between 1992 and 1995 marked the break up of the former federation of Yugoslavia into independent states. In 1991, Bosnia-Herzegovina declared independence and in May 1992 it was recognised internationally as an independent country. In March 1994 the State of Bosnia and Herzegovina was created in which the governmental office of Prime Minister was to be rotated annually between Muslim and Croat ethnic groups. The Chair of the Council of Ministers is nominated by the Presidency and approved by the House of Representatives. The Chair of the Council of Ministers (Prime Minister) is then responsible for appointing a Foreign Minister, Minister of Foreign Trade and others as appropriate.

The General Framework Agreement for Peace in Bosnia and Herzegovina (often known as the Dayton Peace Treaty) signed in December 1995 agreed to preserve Bosnia and Herzegovina as a state with a 51:49 division of territory between the Muslim/Croat Federation and the Serb-led Republika Srpska. The agreement provided for democratic elections and a three-member presidency, comprising one Muslim, one Croat and one Serb. The presidency governs at republican level, with governments existing within the two constituent parts simultaneously: the Bosniac-Croat Federation of Bosnia and Herzegovina and the Republika Srpska (RS). The agreement provided for the creation of a republican bicameral assembly (comprising a House of Peoples and a House of Representatives). Current constitutions were amended to conform with the peace agreement. The Bosnian-Serb Republic passed a law in 2010 to make it easier to hold referendums on national issues. This could pave the way to a referendum on independence.

To consult the full constitution, please visit:
http://www.ccbh.ba/eng/article.php?pid=825&kat=518&pkat=500

Recent Events
Bosnia and Herzegovina has now begun the process of becoming a member of the European Union. In 2005 EU foreign ministers gave the go-ahead for talks on Stabilisation and Association Agreement to start.

In February 2005 the genocide case brought by Bosnia-Herzegovina against Serbia an Montenegro opened at the International Court of Justice at the Hague. In the same year th Srebrenica Massacre trial opened at the UN war crimes tribunal at the Hague. In 2007 it wa ruled that the massacre did constitute genocide but Serbia was cleared of direct involvement

In January 2007 Nikola Spiric, a Bosnian-Serb, formed a government after the party leader agreed on a coalition. He resigned in November of the same year in protest at EU-backe reforms.

Various individuals wanted on charges of war criminals have been arrested in recent years Zdravko Tolimir, was arrested in May 2007 on charges relating to the Srebrenica massacre The former Bosnian Serb police chief Stojan Zupljanin was arrested in 2008 on charges o war crimes, and the former Bosnian Serb leader Radovan Karadzic was arrested in Belgrad in July 2008 after 13 years on the run. He was charged with 11 counts of war crimes. M Karadzic does not recognise the legitimacy of the court but pleas of not-guilty have bee entered on his behalf. His trial began in October 2009.

In March 2010 the former Bosnian Muslim leader Ejup Ganic was arrested in Britain fo alleged war crimes under an extradition warrant issued by Serbia.

In May 2011, the former Bosnian Serb military chief Ratko Mladic was arrested. His trial fo alleged war crimes began in The Hague in May 2012.

In December 2011, Bosnia's Muslim, Croat and Serb political leaders reached an agreemen on formation of new central government. As a result of this Croat Vjekoslav Bevanda wa elected to the post of prime minister.

In December 2012, Bosnian Serb former general Zdravko Tolimir, was sentenced to lif imprisonment by the Hague UN war crimes tribunal for his part in the genocide of the Srebrenica massacre.

In February 2013, prime minister of the Republika Srpska Aleksandar Dzombic resigned Former minister of economic relations Zeljka Cvijanovic was nominated for and assumed the role. Her new cabinet was sworn in the following month.

State of Bosnia and Herzegovina:
The head of state is a three-member presidency, one member representing each of the three ethnic groups: Bosnian, Croat, and Serb. The chair of the presidency rotates among its members every eight months. Since December 2002 the post of prime minister has a four-year term instead of rotating every eight months from Bosniac to Croat to Serb representatives.

Upper House
The House of Peoples (Dom Naroda) comprises 15 delegates, two-thirds of whom come from the Federation (five Croats and five Bosniacs) and one-third from the RS (five Serbs). Nine members of the House of Peoples constitutes a quorum, provided that at least three delegates from each group are present. Members of the House of Peoples serve for a two-year term.
House of Peoples, Parliamentary Assembly, Trg BIH 1, 71000 Sarajevo, Bosnia & Herzegovina. Tel: +387 3366 6585
Chairman, House of Peoples: Velimir Jukic

Lower House

The House of Representatives (Predstavnicki Dom) is composed of 42 members, two-thirds to be elected from the territory of the Federation and one third from the Serb Republic. Representatives serve a two-year term.

House of Representatives, Trg BIH 1, 71000 Sarajevo, Bosnia & Herzegovina. Tel: +387 366 6585

Chairman, House of Representatives: Sefik Dzaferovic

Presidency of Federation of Bosnia and Herzegovina (as at June 2013)
Federation President: Zivko Budimir (Croat)
Federation Vice President: Mirsad Kebo (Bosniac) (page 1454)
Federation Vice Presidency: Svotozar Pudaric (Serb)

Council of Ministers of Bosnia and Herzegovina (as at June 2013)
Prime Minister, Chair of the Council of Ministers, Minister of European Integration: Vjekoslav Bevanda (page 1388)
Minister of Security: Fahrudin Radoncic
Minister of the Treasury and Finance: Nikola Spiric (page 1519)
Minister of Foreign Affairs: Zlatko Lagumdzija
Minister of Defence: Zerkerijah Osmic
Minister of Human Rights and Refugees: Damir Ljubic
Minister of Civil Affairs: Sredoje Novic
Minister of Transport and Communications: Damir Hadzic
Minister of Justice: Barisa Colak
Minister of Foreign Trade and Economic Relations: Mirko Sarovic

Ministries
Office of the President, Musala 5, 71000 Sarajevo, Bosnia and Herzegovina. Tel: +387 366 4941, fax: +387 3347 2791, e-mail: mar.jovan@bih.net.ba, URL: http://www.predsjednistvobih.ba
Office of the Chair of the Council of Ministers, Vojvode Putnika 3, 71000 Sarajevo, Bosnia and Herzegovina. Tel: +387 3366 4941, fax: +387 3344 3446, e-mail: kabprem@fbihvlada.gov.ba, URL: http://www.fbihvlada.gov.ba
The Treasury and Finance, Trg Bosne i Hercegovine 1, 71000 Sarajevo, Bosnia and Herzegovina. Tel: +387 3320 5345, fax: +387 3347 1822, URL: http://www.vijeceministara.gov.ba
Ministry of Foreign Affairs, Musala 2, 71000 Sarajevo, Bosnia and Herzegovina. Tel: +387 3328 1100, fax: +387 3347 2188, e-mail: info@mvp.gov.ba, URL: http://www.mvp.gov.ba
Ministry of Foreign Trade and Economic Relations, Musala 9, 71000 Sarajevo, Bosnia and Herzegovina. Tel: +387 3320 6142, fax: +387 3368 8060, e-mail: info@vet.gov.ba, URL: http://www.vet.gov.ba
Ministry of Civil Affairs, Vojvode Putnika 3, 71000 Sarajevo, Bosnia and Herzegovina. Tel: +387 3378 6822, fax: +387 3378 6944, URL: http://www.fbihvlada.gov.ba
Ministry of Defence, Trg Bosne i Hercegovine 1, 71000 Sarajevo, Bosnia and Herzegovina. Tel: +387 3326 3180, fax: +387 3320 6094, URL: http://www.vijeceministara.gov.ba
Ministry of Human Rights and Refugees, Trg Bosne i Hercegovine 1, 71000 Sarajevo, Bosnia and Herzegovina. Tel: +387 3320 6273, URL: http://www.mhrr.gov.ba
Ministry of Justice, Trg Bosne i Hercegovine 1, 71000 Sarajevo, Bosnia and Herzegovina. Tel: +387 3322 3501, fax: +387 3322 3504, e-mail: kontakt@mpr.gov.ba, URL: http://www.mpr.gov.ba
Ministry of Security, Trg Bosne i Hercegovine broj 1, 71000 Sarajevo, Bosnia and Herzegovina. Tel: +387 3321 3623, fax: +387 3321 3628, e-mail: bdautbasic@smartnet.ba, URL: http://www.vijeceministara.gov.ba
Ministry of Transport and Communications, Alipasina 41, 71000 Sarajevo, Bosnia and Herzegovina. Tel: +387 3366 8907, fax: +387 3366 7866, URL: http://www.fmpik.gov.ba

---

Federation of Bosnia and Herzegovina (Federacija Bosne i Hercegovine):
The Bosniac-Croat Federation has its own directly elected president.

Legislature
The Bosniac-Croat Federation parliament is bicameral, consisting of the House of Peoples and the House of Representatives.
Parlament Federacije Bosne i Hercegovine, Hamdije Kresevljakovica 3, Sarajevo, Bosnia and Herzegovina. Tel: +387 (0)33 219190, fax: +387 (0)33 445390, URL: http://www.parlamentfbih.gov.ba/

Upper House
The House of Peoples consists of 74 members, made up of 30 Bosniacs, 30 Croats, and 14 members indirectly elected by the cantonal assemblies. Members serve two-year terms.

Lower House
The House of Representatives comprises 140 members who also serve a term of two years.

Cabinet of the Bosniac-Croat Federation (as at June 2013)
Prime Minister: Nermin Niksic (page 1487)
Deputy Prime Minister, Minister of Agriculture, Water Management and Forestry: Jerko Ivankovic-Lijanovic
Deputy Prime Minister, Minister of Physical Planning: Desnica Radivojevic
Minister of Interior: Predrag Kurtes
Minister of Finance: Ante Krajina
Minister of Justice: Zoran Mikulic
Minister of Education and Science: Damir Masic
Minister of Energy, Mining and Industry: Erdal Turhulj
Minister of Transport and Communications: Enver Bijedic
Minister of Labour and Social Affairs: Vjekoslav Camber
Minister for Refugees and Displaced Persons: Adil Osmanovic
Minister of Health: Rusmir Mesihovic
Minister of Trade: Milorad Bahilj
Minister of Tourism and Environment: Branka Duric

Minister of Development and Entrepreneurship: Sanjin Halimic
Minister of Veterans' Issues: Zukan Helez
Minister of Sport and Culture: Salmir Kaplan

Ministries
Office of the President, Marsala Tita 16, 71000 Sarajevo, Zmaja od Bosne 3. Tel: +387 (0)33 206656 / 657 / 658
Office of the Vice President, Marsala Tita 16, 71000 Sarajevo, Zmaja od Bosne 3. Tel: +387 (0)33 472618
Office of the Prime Minister, Marsala Tita 16, 71000 Sarajevo, Zmaja od Bosne 3. Tel: +387 (0)33 650457 / 656963, fax: +387 (0)33 664816
Ministry of Defence, Hamdije Kreševljakovica 98, Sarajevo. Tel: +387 (0)33 650677, URL: http://www.fbihvlada.gov.ba/engleski/index.html
Ministry of Energy, Mining and Industry, Adema Buce 34, Mostar. Tel: +387 (0)36 580020, fax. +387 (0)36 580015, e-mail: fmeri-mo@bih.net.ba, URL: http://www.fbihvlada.gov.ba/engleski/index.html
Ministry of Finance, Mehmeda Spahe 5, Sarajevo. Tel: +387 (0)33 203147, fax: +387 (0)33 203152, e-mail: info@fmf.gov.ba, URL: http://www.fmf.gov.ba
Ministry of Foreign Affairs, 71000 Sarajevo, Zmaja od Bosne 3. Tel: +387 (0)33 213777, fax: +387 (0)33 653592
Ministry of Health, Titova 9, Sarajevo. Tel: +387 (0)33 664245, fax: +387 (0)33 664245, URL: http://www.fbihvlada.gov.ba/engleski/index.html
Ministry of Interior, Mehmeda Spahe 7, Sarajevo. Tel: +387 (0)33 664904 / 472593, URL: http://www.fmup.ba
Ministry of Justice, Valtera Perica 15, Sarajevo. Tel: +387 (0)33 213151, fax: +387 (0)33 213155, URL: http://www.fbihvlada.gov.ba/engleski/index.html
Ministry of Transport and Communications, Ivana Krndelja bb, Mostar. Tel: +387 (0)36 550025, fax: +387 (0)36 550024, URL: http://www.fmpik.gov.ba

Serb Republic Government:
The Republika Srpska has its own directly elected president. As well as being the supreme commander of the armed forces, the Serb Republic president also nominates the prime minister to the National Assembly.

Legislature
The Serb Republic legislature consists of the unicameral National Assembly. Its 83 Deputies serve two-year terms and are elected by proportional representation.
Speaker of the Serb Assembly: Dragan Kalinic

Cabinet of the Serb Republic Government (as June 2013)
President: Milorad Dodik (Serb) (page 1416)
Vice President: Emil Vlajki (Croat)
Vice President: Enes Suljkanovic (Bosniac)
Prime Minister: Zeljka Cvijanovic (page 1411)
Deputy Prime Minister, Minister of Education and Culture: Goran Mutabdzija
Minister of Trade and Tourism: Maida Ibrisaqic Hrstic
Minister of Justice: Gorana Zlatkovic
Minister of Finance: Dr Zoran Tegeltija
Minister of Economic Affairs and Regional Co-ordination: Igor Vidovic
Minister of Administration and Local Government: Lejla Resic
Minister of Transport and Communications: Nedeljko Cubrilovic
Minister of Industry, Energy and Development: Dr Zeljko Kovacevic
Minister of Urban Planning, Construction and Ecology: Srebrenka Golic
Minister of Labour and Veterans: Peter Djokic
Minister of Refugees and Displaced Persons: Davor Cordas
Minister of Technology and Science: Dr Jasmin Komic
Minister of Health and Social Welfare: Dr Slobodan Stnic
Minister of Agriculture, Water Management and Forestry: Stevo Mirjanic
Minister of Internal Affairs: Radislav Jovicic
Minister of Family, Youth and Sports: Nada Tesanovic

Ministries
Prime Minister's Office, Banja Luka. Tel: +387 (0)51 331322, e-mail: kabinet@vladars.net
Ministry of Finance, Vuka Karadzica 4, 51000 Banja Luka, Bosnia and Herzegovina. Tel: +387 (0)51 331350, fax: +387 (0)51 331351, e-mail: mf@mf.vladars.net
Ministry of Interior, Jug Bogdana 108, 78000 Banja Luka, Bosnia and Herzegovina. Tel: +387 (0)51 331100, e-mail: mup@mup.vladars.net, URL: http://www.mup.vladars.net
Ministry of Defence, Bana Lazarevica 15, 51000 Banja Luka, Bosnia and Herzegovina. Tel: +387 (0)51 218823, fax: +387 (0)51 300243, e-mail: mo@mo.vladars.net
Ministry of Justice, Vuka Karadzica 4, 51000 Banja Luka. Bosnia and Herzegovina. Tel: +387 (0)51 331582, fax: +387 (0)51 331593, e-mail: mpr@mpr.vladars.net
Ministry of Administration and Local Government, Vuka Karadzica 4, 51000 Banja Luka, Bosnia and Herzegovina. Tel: +387 (0)51 331680, Fax: +387 (0)51 331681, e-mail: muls@muls.vladars.net
Ministry of Economy, Energy and Development, Vuka Karadzica 4, 51000 Banja Luka, Bosnia and Herzegovina. Tel: +387 (0)51 331710, fax: +387 (0)51 331702, e-mail: mer@mer.vladars.net
Ministry of Economic Affairs and Coordination, Vuka Karadzica 4, 51000 Banja Luka, Bosnia and Herzegovina. Tel: +387 (0)51 331430, fax: +387 (0)51 331436, e-mail: meoi@meoi.vladars.net
Ministry for Veterans and Labour, Vuka Karadzica 4, 51000 Banja Luka, Bosnia and Herzegovina. Tel: +387 (0)51 331651, fax: +387 (0)51 331652, e-mail: mpb@mpb.vladars.net
Ministry of Trade and Tourism, Vuka Karadzica 4, 51000 Banja Luka, Bosnia and Herzegovina. Tel: +387 (0)51 331523, fax: +387 (0)51 331499, e-mail: mtt@mtt.vladars.net
Ministry of Transport and Communications, Vuka Karadzica 4, 51000 Banja Luka, Bosnia and Herzegovina. Tel: +387 (0)51 331611, fax: +387 (0)51 331612, e-mail: msv@msv.vladars.net
Ministry of Agriculture, Forestry and Water Management, Vuka Karadzica 4, 51000 Banja Luka, Bosnia and Herzegovina. Tel: +387 (0)51 331634, fax: +387 (0)51 331 631, e-mail: mps@mps.vladars.net

BOSNIA AND HERZEGOVINA

Ministry of Urbanism, Civil Engineering and Ecology, Trg srpskih junaka 4, 51000 Banja Luka, Bosnia and Herzegovina. Tel: +387 (0)51 215511, fax: +387 (0)51 215548, e-mail: migrs@migrs.vladars.net

Ministry of Education and Culture, Vuka Karadzica 4, 51000 Banja Luka, Bosnia and Herzegovina. Tel: +387 (0)51 331422, fax: +387 (0)51 331423, e-mail: mp@mp.vladars.net

Ministry for Refugees and Displaced Persons, Vuka Karadzica 4, 51000 Banja Luka, Bosnia and Herzegovina. Tel: +387 (0)51 331470, fax: +387 (0)51 331471, e-mail: mirl@mirl.vladars.net

Ministry of Health and Social Walfare, Zdrave Korde 8, 51000 Banja Luka, Bosnia and Herzegovina. Tel: +387 (0)51 216600, fax: +387 (0)51 331601, e-mail: mszs@mszs.vladars.net

Ministry of Science and Technology, Vuka Karadzica 4, 51000 Banja Luka, Bosnia and Herzegovina. Tel: +387 (0)51 331542, fax: +387 (0)51 331 548, e-mail: mnk@mnk.vladars.net

Political Parties

Hrvatska Demokratska Zajednica Bosne i Hercegovine - HDZ BIH (CDU - BH, Croatian Democratic Union of Bosnia and Herzegovina), 71000 Sarajevo. URL: http://www.hdzbih.org
Leader: Dragan Čović

Hrvatska stranka prava (HSP BiH The Croatian Party of Rights), Zagreb, Croatia. URL: http://hsp.hr
Leader: Daniel Srb

Stranka Demokratske Akcije (SDA, Party of Democratic Action), 71000 Sarajevo. URL: http://www.sda.ba
Leader: Sulejman Tihić

Stranka za Bosnu i Hercegovinu, (Party for Bosnia-Herzegovina, SBiH), URL: http://www.zabih.ba
Leader: Haris Silajdžić

Partija demokratskog progresa, (Party of Democratic Progress PDP), URL: http://www.pdpinfo.net
Leader: Mladen Ivanić

Social Demokratska Partija (SDP BiH Socialist Democrat Party), 71000 Sarajevo, Dure Dakovica 41. Tel: +387 (0)33 216644, fax: +387 (0)33 218168,URL: http://www.sdp.ba
Leader:: Zlatko Lagumdžija

Socijalisticka partija Srbije za Republiku Srpsku (SPS, Socialist Party of Serbia for the Bosnian Serb Republic)

Savez nezavisnih socijaldemokrata, (Alliance of Independent Social Democrats, SNSD); URL: www.snsd.org
Leader: Milorad Dodik

Union for a Better Future of Bosnia & Herzegovina (Savez za bolju budućnost BiH, SBB BiH), URL: http://www.sbbbh.ba
Leader: Fahrudin Radončić

Other Parties

Stranka za Bosnu i Hercegovinu (SBiH, Party for BiH)
Stranka Nezavisnih Socijaldemokrata (SNSD, Party of Independent Social Democrats)
Koalicija (Coalition)
- Hrvatska Demokratska Zajednica (Croatian Democratic Community)
- Demokrscani (Christian-Democrats)
Partija demokratskog progresa RS (PDP RS, Party for Democratic Progress)
Socialisticka Partija Republike Srpske (SPRS, Socialist Party RS)
Bosanska Stranka (BOSS, Bosnian Party)
Stranka Penzionera Umirovljenika BiH (SPU)
Demokratski Narodni Savez (DNS, Democratic People's League)
Demokratska Narodna Zajednica (DNZ, Democratic People's Community)
Nova Hrvatska Inicijativa (NHI, New Croatian Initiative)
Ekonomski Blok HDU - Za Boljitak (EB)

Elections

The most recent elections for the House of Representatives of Bosnia and Herzegovina were held in October 2010.

House of Representatives, 1 October 2010

Party	No. of seats
SDP BiH	8
SNSD	8
SDA	7
SDS	4
SBB BiH	4
HDZ BiH	3
Others	8

Members of the Federation House of Representatives were also elected in October 2010. The following table shows the results of the vote:

Federation House of Representatives, October 2010

Party	Seats
SDP BiH	28
SDA	23
SBB BiH	13
HDZ BiH	12
SBiH	9
Others	13

Elections for the Serb People's Assembly were held on 3 October 2010. The SNSD retained its majority.

The most recent elections for the Presidency of the Federation were held in March 2011.

Diplomatic Representation

British Embassy, 8 Tina Ujevica, 71000 Sarajevo, Bosnia and Herzegovina. Tel: +38 (0)33 444429, fax: +387 (0)33 666131, e-mail: britemba@bih.net.ba, URL http://ukinbih.fco.gov.uk/en
Ambassador: Michael Tatham

British Embassy, 8 Simeuna Dzaka, Banja Luka, Serb Republic of Bosnia and Herzegovina Tel: +387 (0)51 212395, fax: +387 (0)51 216842, e-mail sarajevoBLOffice.sarajevo@fco.gov.uk

US Embassy, Alipasina 43, 71000 Sarajevo, Bosnia and Herzegovina. Tel: +387 (0)7 445700 fax: +387 (0)71 659722 , URL: http://sarajevo.usembassy.gov
Ambassador: Patrick Moon

Embassy of Bosnia and Herzegovina, 5-7 Lexham Gardens, London, W8 5JJ, United Kingdom. Tel:+44 (0)20 7373 0867, fax: +44 (0)20 7373 0871, URL: http://bhembassy.co.uk/e
Ambassador: NJ.E. Mustafa Mujezinović

Embassy of Bosnia and Herzegovina, 2109 E Street, NW, Washington, DC 20037 USA. Tel: +1 202 337 1500, fax: +1 202 337 1502, email: info@bhembassy.org, URL http://www.bhembassy.org/
Ambassador: Jadranka Negodic

Permanent Representative of the Republic of Bosnia and Herzegovina to the United Nations, 866 United Nations Plaza, Suite 580, New York, NY 10017, USA Tel: +1 212 751 9015, fax: +1 212 751 9019, e-mail: bosnia@un.int, URL http://www.un.int/bosnia/
Ambassador: H.E. Ms. Mirsada Čolaković

LEGAL SYSTEM

The legal system is based on civil law. It is organised on three levels with minor courts, higher courts and supreme courts, as well as the Office of the Public Attorney - all supervised by the Ministry of Justice. Separate judicial systems exist in the Bosnian Federation and the Serb Republic.

The Constitutional Court of Bosnia and Herzegovina is the supreme, final arbiter in legal matters. It is composed of nine members; four members are selected by the House of Representatives of the Federation, two by the Assembly of the RS and three by the President of the European Court of Human Rights after consultation with the Presidency. Terms of initial appointees are five years, unless they resign or are removed for cause by consensus of the other judges. Once appointed, judges are not eligible for reappointment. Judges subsequently appointed will serve until the age of 70.

The legal system of the Serb Republic consists of the Constitutional Court, the Supreme Court, District and Basic Courts. The Constitutional Court is solely responsible for all matters of constitutional law as well as the annulment of any administrative acts. The Supreme Court is the Serb Republic's highest appellate court.

The government's human rights record is poor. There have been recent reports of police abuses, harsh prison conditions, intimidation of journalists and members of civil society, and discrimination against ethnic and religious minorities.

The former Bosnian-Serb leader Ratko Mladic is currently on trial at The Hague for genocide and other war crimes.

The death penalty was abolished in 1998.

Constitutional Court, URL: http://www.ccbh.ba
Ombudsman of Bosnia and Herzegovina, URL: http://www.ombudsmen.gov.ba/IndexEn.aspx

LOCAL GOVERNMENT

For administrative purposes Bosnia and Herzegovina is divided into the Federation of Bosnia and Herzegovina, the Republic of Srpska and the district of Brcko. The Federation of Bosnia and Herzegovina is divided into 10 Cantons: Una - Sana Canton; Posavina Canton; Tuzla Canton; Zenica - Doboj Canton; Bosnian Podrinje Canton; Central Bosnia Canton; Herzegovina - Neretva Canton; West Herzegovina Canton; Sarajevo Canton; and West Bosnia Canton. These cantons are then divided into 79 municipalities. The Republic of Srpska is divided into 62 municipalities. The district of Brcko is a self-governing administrative unit under the sovereignty of Bosnia and Herzegovina. The District is still under international supervision.

Local elections took place in October 2008. Nationalist parties did well. The next local elections should take place in 2012.

AREA AND POPULATION

Area

The state of Bosnia and Herzegovina is situated in the southeast of Europe. It has boundaries with Croatia to the north and west, Serbia to the east and Montenegro to the southeast. There is a short strip of coastline on the Adriatic at Neum. Bosnia and Herzegovina covers an area of 51,129 sq. km, with 23.5 km of coastline. The capital of Bosnia and Herzegovina is Sarajevo.

To view a map, consult: http://www.un.org/Depts/Cartographic/map/profile/bosnia.pdf

The Republic of Srpska is located in the central Balkan Peninsula and covers an area of 25,053 sq. km. Its two main regions are the north-west - consisting of the regions of Banja Luka Krajina and Posavina - and the east - consisting of the regions of Semberija, Majevica, Drina, Sarajevo and Romanija, and Herzegovina. The Republic of Srpska's capital is Banja Luka, which is the Republic's seat of government, administrative and business centre.

The terrain is quite mountainous with a high point of 2,386 metres (Maglic). Winters are generally cold and summers hot. There are some variations depending on elevation. Higher areas have shorter, cooler summers with long, harsh winters. Along the coast, the winter is milder with increased precipitation.

The main languages of Bosnia and Herzegovina are Bosnian, Serbian and Croatian. The Muslims (Bosniaks and Croats) use the Roman alphabet whilst the Cyrillic script is used by the Serbs.

Population
The estimated population in 2010 was 3.77 million with an average annual population growth rate of 0.2 per cent over the period 2000-10, and population density of 85.2 per sq. km. The majority of the population (66 per cent) is aged between 15 and 60 years, with 15 per cent aged under 15 years, and 19 per cent aged 60 and over. Approximately 49 per cent of the population lives in urban areas. The population of the capital, Sarajevo, is approximately 388,000.

The population comprises the following ethnic groups: Bosniak, 48 per cent; Serb, 34 per cent; Croat, 15 per cent.

Births, Marriages, Deaths
Estimates for 2010 put the birth rate at 8.5 per 1,000 population and the death rate at 9.8 per 1,000. Average life expectancy at birth in 2009 was 75 years (73 years for men and 78 years for women). Healthy life expectancy was respectively 65 and 68 years. The infant mortality rate is 8.0 deaths per 1,000 live births. The total fertility rate was 1.2 children born per woman. (Source: http://www.who.int, World Health Statistics 2012)

Public Holidays 2014
1-2 January: New Year
1 March: Independence Day (Sarajevo and Mostar)
1April: Easter Monday (Banja Luka)
18 April: Good Friday (Banja Luka)
21 May: Labour Day
15 August: Assumption
21 November: National Statehood Day
25 November: National Day
25 December: Christmas Day

EMPLOYMENT

The total work force was estimated to be 1,863,000 people in 2007, of whom 48 per cent worked in the services sector, 32 per cent in industry and mining and 20 per cent in agriculture. Figures for 2010 put the workforce at1,478,000 of whom 315,000 were unemployed.

BANKING AND FINANCE

After the Dayton Peace Treaty of 1995, the official reconstruction of the economy began. The fragmentation of the country's infrastructure and the shortage of foreign exchange were the principal obstacles to overcome. As a member of the World Bank from 1 April 1996, loans of US$269 million were immediately secured for emergency projects.

Currency
The konvertible marka (KM, BAM) was introduced in the summer of 1998 and is pegged to the euro.
1 konvertibilna marka = 100 pfeninga

GDP/GNP, Inflation, National Debt
Despite strong growth in GDP and massive increase of exports since the end of the war in 1995, an estimated 20 per cent of the population lives in poverty. Three has been some structural reform and the banking sector is privatised and modernised. However other sectors have been less successful in their reform processes. Bosnia needs to attract more foreign investment to grow the economy but foreign investors have been put of by various factors including excessive bureaucracy and corruption.

Although economic output recovered in 1996-99, following the civil war, output growth slowed in 2000-02, and the current GDP remains far below its 1990 level. Total GDP was estimated at US$7,300 billion in 2002. Per capita GDP in the same year was US$1,900. The GDP growth rate fell by a third in 1999, from 18.0 per cent in 1998 to 12.0 per cent the following year, and was estimated in 2000 at 8 per cent, falling to 2.3 per cent in 2001. Growth in 2002 was put at 3.9 per cent with a projected growth of 5.0 per cent in 2004. Figures for 2005 put GDP at US$9.4 billion with a per capita figure of US$2,405. GDP was estimated to have grown to US$15.14 billion in 2007 with a growth rate of 5.5 per cent. Estimated figures for 2009 put GDP at US$17.1 billion, giving a per capita figure of US$4,700. The growth rate was estimated to be -3.2 per cent. In 2011, two ratings agencies lowered its sovereign credit rating of the country because of its negative outlook. However, in 2011 the economy returned to growth and GDP was estimated to be $17.8 billion in 2011, with a growth rate of 1.7 per cent.

According to 2008 estimates, Bosnia and Herzegovina's services sector makes the greatest contribution to GDP (62 per cent), followed by industry (29 per cent), and agriculture (9 per cent).

Figures for 2008 show that around 20 per cent of the population are living below the poverty line with another 30 per cent living on incomes only just above it. Public expenditures are very high and collection of revenues is difficult; with this in mind, VAT was introduced on 1 January 2006.

Inflation fell from an estimated 5.0 per cent in 1998 to an estimated 3.0 per cent in 1999. It rose to around 3.5 per cent in 2002 before falling to 1.1 per cent in 2004. As a result of Bosnia's strict currency board regime, inflation has remained relatively low throughout the Federation and Republic of Srpska. Inflation was estimated to be 0.6 per cent in 2009 rising to over 2 per cent in 2010 and to over 3 per cent in 2011.

Total public debt was estimated to be approximately 40 per cent of GDP in 2011.

According to World Bank estimates, GDP growth was 62 per cent in the Muslim/Croat Federation and 25 per cent in Republika Srpska (RS) in 1996. In 1997 it was 35 per cent in the Federation and flat in the RS. Growth continued in the Federation in 1998. Growth in the RS should see dramatic increases following recent upsurges in donor investment. Support for Eastern European Democracy (SEED) assistance accounts for 20-25 per cent of economic growth in Bosnia.

Foreign Investment
In the first three years since the Dayton Accords were signed, over US$5.1 billion in foreign aid was been received in Bosnia, about US$800 million came from SEED funds. This support has been key to the growth and revitalisation of the economy and infrastructure in the Republic. The country received economic aid of about US$1,000 million in 1999.

Balance of Payments / Imports and Exports
Exports were estimated to be worth US$4.4 billion in 2010. Main export commodities are clothing, metals, and wood products. Major export trading partners are Germany (17 per cent), Italy, Switzerland, and Croatia.

Merchandise imports were an estimated US$8 billion in 2010. Main import commodities include chemicals, machinery and equipment, food, and fuels. Major import trading partners are Croatia (17 per cent), Italy, Slovenia, Germany.

Central Bank
A central bank based in Sarajevo was created under the provisions of the Dayton Peace Agreement to be the sole authority for monetary policy and the issuing of domestic currency. The IMF appointed the bank's governor.
Centralna banka Bosne i Hercegovine, Marsala Tita Street 25, 71000 Sarajevo, Bosnia-Herzegovina. Tel: +387 (0)33 278 100, fax: +387 (0)33 278 299, email: contact@cbbh.gov.ba, URL: http://www.cbbh.ba
Governor: Kemal Kozaric

Chambers of Commerce and Trade Organisations
Chamber of Commerce and Foreign Trade of Bosnia and Herzegovina, URL: http://www.komorabih.com
Chamber of Economy of Federation BH, URL: http://www.kfbih.com
Chamber of Commerce of Republika Serbia, URL: http://www.pkrs.inecco.net

MANUFACTURING, MINING AND SERVICES

Primary and Extractive Industries
Bosnia and Herzegovina has rich deposits of a number of minerals, including coal, iron ore, bauxite, manganese, copper, chromium, lead, zinc, rock salt, barite and various types of clay. Resources of coal have been estimated at 3.1 billion tonnes and those of iron ore at 750 billion tonnes.

The country has no oil resources of its own and is entirely reliant on imports. In 2011 an estimated 35,000 barrels per day of oil was imported for domestic consumption most of which was distillate, gasoline, and residual.

Similarly, supplies of natural gas are imported for domestic consumption; a total of 8,000 million cubic feet in 2008 (up from 7,060 million cubic feet in 1998).

Coal production was 12.146 million short tons in 2010, nearly 60 per cent of which was lignite and nearly 40 per cent bituminous hard coal. All was used for domestic consumption.

Energy
In 2010, installed capacity was 4.30 GWe. Bosnia and Herzogovina produced 16.50 billion kilowatthours of electicity and consumed 11.07 billion kilowatthours.

Manufacturing and Industry
The economy of Bosnia and Herzegovina is predominantly industry-based, with primary and raw material sectors particularly production of steel, iron ore, lead, zinc, manganese and bauxite. Industrial production is highly developed, especially in the fields of micro-electronics and equipment for the nuclear power industry. Other areas of production include vehicle assembly, textiles, tobacco products, wooden furniture, tank and aircraft assembly, domestic appliances and oil refining. Industry accounted for an estimated 23 per cent of GDP in 2006.

Bosnia and Herzegovina was one of the least developed of the members of the former Yugoslavian Federation. Severely affected by the war, industrial production grew by 87 per cent in 1996 in the Federation and 38 per cent in the Serb Republic. Overall, industrial production grew at an estimated rate of 11.5 per cent in 2008.

Service Industries
The service industry is the country's greatest contributor to GDP, accounting for 66 per cent according to 2006 estimates. An estimated 256,000 visitors went to Bosnia and Herzegovina that year generating tourist expenditure of $643 millions.

BOSNIA AND HERZEGOVINA

Agriculture

Because of geographical features, Bosnia's agriculture does not play an important role, but cattle breeding is well developed and agricultural crops, produced on 2.5 million hectares, include wheat, maize, fruit, vegetables, wine and tobacco. The 2.8 million hectares of woodland are one of the country's main resources. The wood and timber industries are well developed. Agriculture contributed about 8.0 per cent of GDP in 2011.

Agricultural Production in 2010

Produce	Int. $'000	Tonnes
Cow milk, whole, fresh	185,864	715,600
Plums and sloes	94,028	157,562
Vegetables fresh nes	86,363	458,300
Maize	78,438	853,376
Indigenous chicken meat	51,957	36,476
Potatoes	48,430	378,707
Indigenous cattle meat	46,128	17,076
Apples	30,306	71,659
Chillies and peppers, dry	28,043	25,600
Chillies and peppers, green	18,076	38,397
Hen eggs, in shell	17,251	20,800
Raspberries	15,358	7,937

*unofficial figures

Source: http://faostat.fao.org/site/339/default.aspx Food and Agriculture Organization of the United Nations, Food and Agricultural commodities production

COMMUNICATIONS AND TRANSPORT

Travel Requirements

A passport is required by citizens of the USA, Canada, Australia and most of the EU (except holders of valid national identity cards issued to nationals of Austria, Belgium, Finland, France, Germany, Greece, Italy, Luxembourg, The Netherlands, Norway, Portugal, Spain and Sweden). A visa is not required by nationals referred to above for stays of up to three months. Citizens of countries not mentioned above are advised to check visa requirements with the embassy. Citizens of Croatia and Serbia can enter Bosnia and Herzegovina with ID only.

International Airports

In addition to the international airport at Sarajevo there are three further civil airports. The resumption of commercial flights to Bosnia's airports following the civil war has been tentative. Sarajevo airport was reopened in August 1996.

National Airlines

BH Airlines, URL: http://www.bhairlines.ba

Railways

The railway system includes 1,040 km of track, of which 75 km is electrified. The state railway company was split into three regional state owned companies after hostilities broke out, namely the Bosnia and Herzegovina Railway Company (Sarajevo based); Herzeg-Bosnia Railway Company (Croat); and the Serb Republic Railway and Transport Company (Banja Luka).

Roads

Over a third of the country's 21,677 km. of roads and bridges were damaged or disrupted during the civil war. The Dayton Agreement set down the establishment of the Transport Corporation to take control of and run the road, port and railway systems. There are 450,298 passenger cars in the country, vehicles are driven on the right.

HEALTH

The entire population is covered by a state-operated health service. This was greatly disrupted during the civil war when only international relief organisations could provide basic healthcare. According to the latest WHO figures, total expenditure on health equated to approximately 10.9 per cent of GDP in 2009. Total per capita expenditure on health in 2009 was US$495. Government expenditure accounts for 61.3 per cent of this. Private expenditure is virtually all out-of-pocket. Health expenditure represented 15.1 per cent of total government expenditure in 2009.

In 2005-10, according to World Health Organisation statistics, there were 6,443 doctors (16.4 per 10,000 inhabitants). In the same year, there were 19,825 nurses and midwives (50.4 per 10,000 people), 685 dentists (1.7 per 10,000 inhabitants) and 364 pharmaceutical personnel. In 2005-11, there were 34 hospital beds and 2.4 psychiatric beds per 10,000 population.

In 2008, there were 1,321 reported cases of TB, 45 cases of measles, 209 of mumps, and 2,784 rubella. The infant mortality rate (probability of dying before age one) stood at 8 per 1,000 live births in 2010 and the under-fives mortality rate at 8 per 1,000 live births. The most common causes of death in the under-fives were prematurity 23 per cent, congenital abnormalities 31 per cent, pneumonia 9 per cent and injuries 5 per cent. Approximately 11.8 per cent of the population aged five or under were classified as stunted in the period 2005-11.

In 2010, an estimated 98 per cent of the population and 79 per cent of the population had access to improved sanitation. (Source: http://www.who.int, World Health Statistics 2012)

EDUCATION

Elementary education lasts for eight years and is free and compulsory.

At the secondary level there are a number of vocational, apprentice schools, art schools and teacher training institutions. There are 250,000 students in 407 primary schools and 80,000 students in 171 secondary schools. Higher education is covered by seven universities in Sarajevo, Banja Luka, Mostar, Bihac, Foca and Tuzla. In addition, Bosnia and Herzegovina has its own Academy of Arts and Sciences.

The literacy rates are estimated at 99 per cent for males and 94.4 per cent for females (2001). For the age group 15-24 years the literacy rate is 99 per cent. (Source:UNESCO).

RELIGION

Approximately half the population are divided between the Greek Orthodox (21 per cent) and the Roman Catholic (13 per cent) church. The main religion, however, is Islam (58 per cent) and its followers are primarily Bosniaks or ethnic-Muslims who converted to Islam under the Ottomans. The minority are ethnic Albanian and Turkish Muslims, though all are followers of the Sunni sect. Protestants make up less than 1 per cent and others 8 per cent.

Bosnia and Herzegovina has a religious liberty rating of 5 on a scale of 1 to 10 (10 is most freedom). (Source: World Religion Database)

COMMUNICATIONS AND MEDIA

The media is highly politicised. A new national public broadcasting service is being developed under the supervision of the Office of the High Representattive. The media is free but is subject to political pressure.

Newspapers

Oslobodjenje (Liberation), URL: http://www.slobodjna-bosna.ba/
Dnevni Avaz, Sarajevo, URL: http://www.avaz.ba
Nezavisne Novine, Banja Luka, URL: http://www.nezavisne.com
Glas Srpske, Banja Luka, URL: http://www.glassrpske.com
Dnevni List, Mostar, URL: http://www.dnevni-list.ba

Broadcasting

The Sarajevo radio and television station is the central broadcasting station for the Republic. In addition, private radio and television companies are now permitted to operate.
Public Broadcasting Service of Bosnia-Hercegovina, is a public broadcaster, operates BHTV1 channel, URL: http://www.bhrt.ba/lat/
Federation TV (FTV), public TV service, Bosnian Muslim-Croat, URL: http://www.rtvfbih.ba/
Serb Republic Radio-TV (RTRS), TV service, Bosnian Serb, URL: http://www.rtrs.tv/
Commercial stations include
Mzera Plus, URL: http://www.mrezaplus.ba/
Open Broadcast Network, URL: http://www.obn.ba/

Radio stations include:
Radio and TV of Bosnia, the state-wide public broadcaster, URL: URL: http://www.bhrt.ba/lat/
Radio FBiH, public, Bosnian-Croat, URL: http://www.rtvfbih.ba/
Serb Republic Radio, URL: http://www.rtrs.tv/

Telecommunications

Recent 2008 estimates put the number of telephone main lines in use at approximately 1,000,000, and the number of mobile phones at 3.7 million.

Approximately 1.3 million of the population were internet users in 2008.

ENVIRONMENT

Bosnia and Herzegovina is a party to the following international environmental agreements: Air Pollution, Biodiversity, Climate Change, Climate Change-Kyoto Protocol, Desertification, Hazardous Wastes, Law of the Sea, Marine Life Conservation, Ozone Layer Protection, and Wetlands.

Current environmental problems include water shortage and destruction of infrastructure as a result of the 1992 civil war; air pollution; and limited sites for the disposal of urban waste.

Carbon dioxide emissions from the consumption of fossil fuels was 20.14 million metric tons in 2010. (Source: EIA)

BOTSWANA
Republic of Botswana

Capital: Gaborone (Population estimate, 2011: 250,000)

Head of State: Lt. Gen. Seretse Khama Ian Khama (page 1456)

Vice-President: Dr Ponatshego Kedikilwe (page 1455)

National Flag: Light-blue flag split by horizontal black stripe with white border.

CONSTITUTION AND GOVERNMENT

Botswana (formerly Bechuanaland) became a republic within the British Commonwealth on 30 September 1966.

The Head of State is the President who is elected for a period of five years by the National Assembly. He is also the executive Head of Government and presides over a cabinet consisting of the Vice-President, 14 other ministers and 2 assistant ministers.

The legislative power of the Republic is vested in the Parliament of Botswana, which consists of the President and the National Assembly. The National Assembly consists of 57 members (of whom four are specially elected) and an Attorney-General who can speak but not vote in the Assembly.

Under the Constitution there is also a House of Chiefs with advisory functions. It consists of the chiefs of the eight principal tribes of Botswana as permanent *ex-officio* members, four other members elected from among the sub-chiefs in the Chobe, Francistown, Ghanzi and Kgalagadi Districts, and three specially elected members. The House of Chiefs is available to advise the Government in the exercise of its responsibilities. The National Assembly is prohibited from proceeding with any bill which particularly affects a defined range of subjects relating to matters of tribal concern, unless a draft of it has been referred to the House of Chiefs.

In 2003 following a commissioned report it was announced that the number of seats available in parliament was to be increased by 17 ready for the 2004 election.

To consult the constitution, please visit: http://www.parliament.gov.bw/docs/documents/constitution.pdf.

International Relations
Botswana is host to refugees from Namibia and an increasing number from Zimbabwe.

Recent Events
In April 2008 Seretse Khama Ian Khama became president of Botswana. He succeeded Festus Mogae and is the son of Botswana's first president, Sir Seretse Khama. Earlier in 2008 there had been calls for the post of president to be elected by the people but this was rejected by parliament.

The former president Festus Mogae won a US$5 million prize for good governance in Africa.

In November 2009 the economy of Botswana recorded a large recovery after diamond production was increased, this overturned a decision made in earlier that year to halve production in the face of falling demand.

In November 2010, Survival International, a human rights group called for a boycott of Botswanan diamonds, it accused the government of trying to force Basarwa bushmen away from their ancestral lands. In January 2011 an appeal court overturned a decision from the previous July which had deprived the indigenous Basarwa bushmen of the right to drill for water on their land.

Legislature
Botswana has a unicameral legislature with 57 directly elected members who serve a five-year term.
National Assembly, PO Box 240, Gaborone, Botswana. Tel: +2 391 3103, fax: +2 397 3200, e-mail: parliament@gov.bw, URL: http://www.gov.bw/home.html

Cabinet (as at June 2013)
Minister of Presidential Affairs and Public Administration: Mokgweetsi Masisi
Minister of Infrastrucutre, Science and Technology: Johnnie Swartz
Minister of Finance and Development Planning: Kenneth Matambo
Minister of Foreign Affairs: Phandu Skelemani (page 1515)
Minister of Agriculture: Christian de Graaf
Minister of Defence, Justice and Security: Dikgakgamatso Seretse
Minister of Environment, Wildlife & Tourism: Kitso Mokaila
Minister of Education and Skills Development: Pelonomi Venson-Moitoi
Minister of Labour and Home Affairs: Edwin Batshu
Minister of Local Government: Peter Siele
Vice President, Minister of Minerals, Energy and Water Affairs: Ponatshego Kedikilwe (page 1455)
Minister of Trade and Industry: Dorcas Makgatho-Malesu
Minister of Transport and Communications: Nonofo Molefhi
Minister of Youth, Sports and Culture: Shaw Kgathi
Minister of Health: John Seakgosing
Minister of Lands and Housing: Lebonaamang Mokalake

Ministries
Government portal, URL: http://www.gov.bw
Office of the President, Private Bag 001, Gaborone, Botswana. Tel: +267 395 0800, fax: +267 395 0888, e-mail: op.registry@gov.bw, URL: http://www.gov.bw/
Office of the Vice President, Private Bag 006, Gaborone, Botswana. URL: http://www.gov.bw/government/ministry_of_state_president.html
Ministry of Foreign Affairs and International Cooperation, Private Bag 00368, Gaborone, Botswana. Tel: +267 3600 700, fax: +267 313366, mofaic@registry.gov.bw, URL: http://www.gov.bw/government/ministry_of_foreign_affairs.html
Ministry of Education, Private Bag 005, Gaborone, Botswana. Tel: +267 356 5400, fax: +267 356 5458, e-mail: moe.webmaster@gov.bw, URL: http://www.gov.bw/moe/index.html
Ministry of Labour and Home Affairs, Private Bag 002, Gaborone, Botswana. Tel: +267 361 1100, fax: +267 313-584, e-mail: msetimela@gov.bw, URL: http://www.gov.bw/government/ministry_of_labour_and_home_affairs.html
Ministry of Local Government, Private Bag 006, Gaborone, Botswana. Tel: +267 3548400, e-mail: bsentle@gov.bw, URL: http://www.gov.bw/government/ministry_of_local_government.html
Ministry of Health, Private Bag 0038, Gaborone, Botswana. Tel: +267 397 4104, fax: +267 3902 584, e-mail: mchakalisa@gov.bw, URL: http://www.gov.bw/government/ministry_of_health.html
Ministry of Agriculture, Private Bag 003, Gaborone, Botswana. Tel: +267 3950 602, fax: +267 3975 805, URL: http://www.gov.bw/government/ministry_of_agriculture.html
Ministry of Finance and Development Planning, Private Bag 008, Gaborone, Botswana. Tel: +267 350100, fax: +267 300325, e-mail: gmapitse@gov.bw, URL: http://www.gov.bw/government/ministry_of_finance_and_development_planning.html
Ministry of Minerals, Energy and Water Affairs, Private Bag 0018, Gaborone, Botswana. Tel: +267 365 6600, fax: +267 372738, URL: http://www.gov.bw/government/ministry_of_minerals_energy_and_water_affairs.html
Ministry of Works and Transport, Private bag 007, Gaborone, Botswana. Tel: +267 3958 500, fax: +267 3913 303, URL: http://www.gov.bw/government/ministry_of_works_and_transport.html
Ministry of Trade and Industry, Private Bag 0014, Gaborone, Botswana. Tel: +267 395 7406, fax: +267 397 2910, e-mail: dia.hq@gov.bw, URL: http://www.mti.gov.bw/
Ministry of Lands Housing and Environment, Private bag BO66, Gaborone, Botswana. Tel: +267 301 402 URL: http://www.gov.bw/government/ministry_of_lands_and_housing.html
Attorney General Chambers, Private Bag 009, Gaborone, Botswana. Tel: +267 354700, fax: +267 357089, URL: http://www.gov.bw/government/attorney_generals_chambers.html

Political Parties
Botswana Congress Party, URL: http://www.bcp.org.bw
Leader: Dumelang Saleshando
Botswana Alliance Movement
Leader: Ephraim Lepetu Setshwaelo
Botswana Democratic Party (BDP)
Leader: Ian Khama
Botswana National Front (BNF)
Leader: Duma Boko

Elections
The most recent parliamentary elections were held on 16 October 2009. The ruling Botswana Democratic Party (BDP) retained its majority in the National Assembly. President Ian Khama also retained the presidency in the presidential elections which took place on 18 October 2009. He named his cabinet on 22 October.

Diplomatic Representation
High Commission of the Republic of Botswana, 6 Stratford Place, London, W1C 1AY, United Kingdom. Tel: +44 (0)20 7499 0031, fax: +44 (0)20 7495 8595
Ambassador: Roy Blackbeard (page 1390)
British High Commission, Private Bag 0023, Gaborone, Botswana. Tel: +267 395 2841, fax: +267 395 6105, e-mail: bhc@botsnet.bw, URL: http://ukinbotswana.fco.gov.uk/en
High Commissioner: Nick Pyle
Embassy of the Republic of Botswana, 1531-33 New Hampshire Avenue, NW, Washington DC 20036, USA. Tel: +1 202 244 4990, fax: +1 202 244 4164, URL: http://www.botswanaembassy.org
Ambassador: Ms. Tebelelo Seretse (page 1512)
US Embassy, PO Box 90, Gaborone, Botswana. Tel:+267 353982, fax: +267 395 6947, e-mail: usembgab@mega.bw, URL: http://botswana.usembassy.gov
Ambassador: Michelle Gavin (page 1429)
Permanent Mission of the Republic of Botswana to the United Nations, 866 Second Avenue, New York, USA. Tel: +1 212 244 2164, fax: +1 212 725 5061, URL: http://www.botswanaun.org
Ambassador: Charles Thembani Ntwaagae

LEGAL SYSTEM

The legal system of Botswana is based on a mix of Roman-Dutch law and local custom law. The constitution provides for a high court, a court of appeal, and subordinate courts. Traditional, tribal courts, presided over by chiefs, handle minor offenses, marital matters and property disputes. The judiciary is independent of the executive and the legislative branches.

BOTSWANA

The High Court for Botswana has initial jurisdiction in all criminal and civil proceedings. The Court consists of the Chief Justice and such number, if any, of puisne judges as may be prescribed from time to time. The Botswana Court of Appeal has jurisdiction for criminal and civil appeals emanating from the High Court of Botswana. In certain circumstances, further appeal can be made to the Judicial Committee of the Privy Council. There are subordinate courts, and courts with limited jurisdiction, in each of the 12 administrative districts of the country. Each district has a Magistrate's Court.

In general, the government respects the human rights of its citizens. There are, however, poor prison conditions and lengthy delays in the judicial process. There is some restriction on press freedom, as well as a restriction of the right to strike. Botswana retains the death penalty for various crimes including treason, murder and mutiny. One person was reported to have been executed in 2010 and one in 2012.

In 2006, the High Court ruled that the Botswana government's eviction of the Kalahari Bushmen was 'unlawful and unconstitutional', and that they had the right to live on their ancestral land inside the Central Kalahari Game Reserve, and to hunt and gather there. However, the judges also said that the government was not obliged to provide services to Bushmen in the reserve. Since the ruling, the government has arrested more than 50 Bushmen for hunting, and banned the Bushmen from using their water borehole. Hundreds of bushmen are still in resettlement camps, unable to return home. In 2013, the Bushmen took their case to court again.

LOCAL GOVERNMENT

The system of local government is based upon nine district councils, Central, Ghanzi, Kgalagadi, Kgatleng, Kweneng, North East, North West, South East and Southern, each one represented by a district commissioner, and five town councils, Gaborone, Lobatse, Silebi-Pikwe, Jwaneng and Francistown. Revenue comes mainly from a local government tax on income, levied on people resident in a council area.

Local elections take place every five years, most recently in 2009. The Botswana Democratic Party retained its large majority winning 333 of the 490 seats.

AREA AND POPULATION

Botswana is bounded on the south and east by the Republic of South Africa, on the northeast by Zimbabwe, on the north by the Zambesi and Chobe Rivers, and on the west by the territory of Namibia. The country's area is estimated at 581,730 sq. km. The Kalahari Desert makes up a large proportion of the land.

The climate is semi-arid with hot summers and warm winters.

To view a map, consult: http://www.lib.utexas.edu/maps/cia08/botswana_sm_2008.gif

Population
Estimates for 2010 put the population at 2.007 million (compared to 1.84 million in 2007). The population figures are beginning to rise following a fall to an estimated 1,562,000 in 2004 which was due to the fact that Botswana had the second highest levels of HIV infection in Africa; an estimated 40 per cent of the adult population were infected. The median age in 2010 was 23 years. Approximately 33 per cent of the population are aged under 15 years old and just 6 per cent over 60 years.

The population density is three people per sq km. Around 90 per cent of the population are ethnically Tswana and the rest of the population is made up of Herero, Mbukushu, Yei and Mazezuru. The Bushmen are Basarwa or San. They traditionally lead a hunter gatherer existence in the Kalahari desert, but in recent years the government has tried to encourage them to move to towns. In 2006, a group of Bushmen won a four-year legal battle to hold onto their ancestral lands.

Population figures for 2010 show that 61 per cent of the population live in urban areas. The capital and seat of government, Gaborone, has a population of about 250,000. Other towns include: Francistown (83,023), Selebi-Pikwe (49,849), Molepolole (54,561), Kanye (40,628), Serowe (42,444), Mahalapye (39,719), Lobatse (29,689), Maun (43,776), Mochudi (36,962). Setswana is the national language, but English is the official language. Tribal languages are also spoken.

Births, Marriages, Deaths
The estimated birth rate in 2010 was 23.6 births per 1,000 population and the infant mortality rate was 70 per 1,000 live births. Estimated figures for the death rate in 2010 were 9.1 deaths per thousand population, resulting in a population growth of -0.90 per cent. In 1997 life expectancy from birth was 47 years but by 2000 life expectancy was down to 39 years because of the spread of the HIV/AIDS virus. It had fallen further to 30 years in 2004. According to WHO estimates it had risen to 61 years by 2009. The total fertility rate was estimated to be 2.8 per cent. (Source: http://www.who.int, World Health Statistics 2012)

Public Holidays 2014
1 January: New Year
18 April: Good Friday
21 April: Easter Monday
1 May: Labour Day
29 May: Ascension Day
1 July: Sir Seretse Khama Day
15 July: President's Day
30 September: Independence Day
25-26 December: Christmas

EMPLOYMENT

Total Employment by Economic Sector in 2003

Sector	Thousands
Agriculture, forestry & fishing	98,102
Mining & quarrying	13,764
Manufacturing	44,557
Electricity, gas & water supply	4,412
Construction	41,917
Wholesale & retail trade, repairs	61,658
Hotels & restaurants	14,744
Transport, storage & communications	12,599
Financial intermediation	4,930
Real estate, renting & business activities	14,340
Public admin. & defence, compulsory social security	67,232
Education	38,703
Health & social work	13,964
Other community, social & personal services	9,556
Private households with employed persons	21,621
Extra-territorial orgs. & bodies	223
Other	43
Total	462,366

Source: International Labour Organization

Agriculture (mainly subsistence and cattle raising) provides a living for over 80 per cent of the population but only contributes three per cent of the GDP. Although diamonds contribute 38 per cent of the GDP, mining only employs 3.6 per cent of the population.

Recent figures put the unemployment rate officially at 7.5 per cent. Figures for 2010 put the workforce at 1,036,000.

BANKING AND FINANCE

Currency
The unit of currency is the Pula divided into 100 thebe. The financial centre is Gaborone.

GDP/GNP, Inflation, National Debt
Botswana's economy has developed strongly over the last 30 years although it has slowed because of the current global economic crisis. It is judged to be the least corrupt economy in Africa and the economy has been well managed. Diamonds account for 30 per cent of GDP, and the future diversification of the economy is an economic challenge that Botswana has to face although safari-based tourism is already proving successful.

Estimated figures for 2009 put nominal GDP at US$12 billion giving a per capital figure of US$6,200. In 2010, GDP was estimated to be US$14.8 billion, rising to US$17.4 billion in 2011. Over the period 1967-2006, the growth rate was an average of 9 per cent. It slowed during 2007 and 2008 to 3 per cent, before falling into negative figures in 2009. In 2010, growth was estimated to be 7.5 per cent falling to 5 per cent in 2011. The service sector is the largest contributor to GDP, making up 52 per cent, 45 per cent comes from industry and just 2 per cent from agriculture. Tourism is a growth industry. Diamonds are the most significant commodity accounting for 30 per cent of GDP. Demand for diamonds fell in 2009 but began to recover in 2011. It is forecast to recover to pre-global crisis levels in 2013.

Following the introduction of VAT, inflation in 2001 and 2002 rose to nearly 10 per cent, but in 2003 had fallen, as was expected, to 6.4 per cent. Figures for 2007 put the average inflation rate at 7.1 per cent. In 2012, the medium term target was 3-6 per cent.

Total external debt was put at US$1.9 billion in 2011.

Balance of Payments / Imports and Exports
Botswana's main trading partners are the members of the African Customs Union (SACU), the United Kingdom and other European countries and the USA. In 2011, Botswana's imports cost an estimated US$6.3 billion. Its exports were worth US$6.5 billion.

The main export of Botswana is diamonds. It also exports nickel, copper, meat products, textiles, hides, skins, and soda ash. Main imports include foodstuffs, petroleum products, machinery, transport equipment, manufactured goods, and chemicals.

Central Bank
Bank of Botswana, Private Bag 154, Khama Crescent, Government Enclave, Gaborone, Botswana. Tel: +267 360 6000, fax: +267 3913890, URL: http://www.bankofbotswana.bw
Governor: Linah K. Mohohlo

In 2012, foreign exchange reserves were estimated to be US$7,834 million.

Chambers of Commerce and Trade Organisations
Botswana Chamber of Commerce and Industry, Gaborone, Botswana. Tel: +267 395 3721 / 3433

MANUFACTURING, MINING AND SERVICES

Primary and Extractive Industries
Botswana is one of the largest producers of uncut diamonds in the world, with an output of about 28 million carats per annum. There are three diamond mines, Jwaneng, Orapa and Letlhakane, which are jointly owned by the De Beers Mining Company and the Botswana Government under the company name of Debswana. In 2000 the production of Opapa mine was doubled. In 2004 the carat value of diamonds produced by Debswana was a record 31

million. Diamond sales in 1999 reached 10 billion Pula, an increase of 67 per cent on 1998. Earnings from diamonds account for around 30 per cent of GDP and over 50 per cent of foreign exchange earnings. In 2008 De Beers opened the Diamond Trading Centre moving operations of shift sorting, cutting, polishing, aggregating, and marketing from London to Gaborone. However, in 2009, the government announced that it was to cut dramatically diamond production because of falling demand.

The country also has major deposits of copper, nickel, coal, gold, and a variety of other metals and minerals and recently coal bed methane gas has been discovered in the northeast.

Energy

Botswana has no oil resources of its own and imports around 15,000 barrels per day.

Electricity is supplied by the Botswana Power Corporation, and comes from fossil fuels. A programme of rural electrification has been ongoing. The company Eltel completed a US$90,000,000 project in 2010 which linked 100 villages to the national grid. Figures for 2010 show that Botswana had a generating capacity of 0.13 billion Kwh. Botswana produced 0.43 billion KWh of electricity in 2010 and consumed 3.46 billion KWh.

Manufacturing

This has not yet been developed to any significant degree. However, Botswana's light industrial sector has a good potential for growth and the government strongly supports expansion in this area. Textiles, footwear, construction materials, furniture and health and beauty aids are among the promising sectors. Cement, food, and beer are also produced.

Service Industries

Tourism is one of the fastest growing sectors of the economy. Over 17 per cent of Botswana is national park or game reserve. Botswana is one of the most popular African tourist destinations and the Department of Tourism has a mandate to preserve rather than exploit, and to pursue a policy of high income and low-volume tourism. Revenues from tourism are around US$539 million per year. Figures for 1999 show that Botswana had 740,000 visitors; this rose to 975,000 in 2003 and 1,675,000 in 2006. Tourism now accounts for around 12 per cent of GDP.

Agriculture

The role of agriculture in Botswana's overall economy has declined in recent years, partly as a result of six years of drought combined with a decline in traditional farming, and partly because of the growing importance of other sectors. Main agricultural products are maize, sorghum, pulses, fruit and vegetables. Cattle still account for the largest part of livestock farming, and beef exports remain important particularly to the EC.

In 2000 a National Master Plan for Agricultural Development (NAMPAD) was drawn up. Among its suggestions were a move away from subsistence farming to commercial farming and diversification into such fields as game farming, forestry, bee keeping and horticultural production.

Traditionally cattle raising has played a large part both socially and economically in the life of Botswana. Beef exports are still important and there are between two and three million cattle in the country.

Agricultural Production in 2010

Produce	Int. $'000*	Tonnes
Indigenous cattle meat	98,593	36,497
Game meat	50,480	23,200
Cow milk, whole, fresh	35,628	114,170
Roots and tubers, nes	16,999	99,400
Indigenous goat meat	13,194	5,507
Indigenous chicken meat	6,976	4,898
Sorghum	6,138	41,000
Vegetables fresh nes	5,163	27,400
Indigenous sheep meat	4,881	1,793
Sunflower seed	4,390	16,000
Hen eggs, in shell	3,732	4,500
Fruit fresh nes	1,885	5,400

* unofficial figures
Source: http://faostat.fao.org/site/339/default.aspx Food and Agriculture Organization of the United Nations, Food and Agricultural commodities production

COMMUNICATIONS AND TRANSPORT

Travel Requirements

US, Canadian, Australian and most EU nationals require a passport with six months validity, but do not require a visa for visits of up to 90 days. Citizens of Bulgaria, Czech Republic, Estonia, Hungary, Latvia, Lithuania, Poland, Romania, Slovak Republic and Slovenia do need a visa. Nationals of other countries are advised to contact the Botswana embassy to check entry requirements.

National Airlines

Air Botswana, Sir Seretse Khama Airport, P.O. Box 92 The Mall, Gaborone, Botswana. Tel: +267 352812, fax: +267 375408. Has scheduled flights to Francistown, Gaborone, Harare, Johannesburg, Kasane, Maun, Victoria Falls.

Several airlines cater for people travelling to Botswana for Safaris, Delta Air, URL: http://www.okavango.bw/air.html; Mack Air, Moremi Air Services, URL: http://www.moremiair.com; Northern Air, URL: http://www.sefofane.com.

International Airports

There are five international airports, the largest being Sir Seretse Khama Airport at Gabarone, the capital. According to recent figures there are 27 government-owned airports.

Railways

Botswana's railway system consists of 880 km of main line linking South Africa (Mafeking) with Zimbabwe (Bulawayo), and 250 km of branch lines to mines. A journey from Johannesburg to Gaborone takes about 12 hours. The main stations are Lobatse, Ramotswa, Gaborone, Pilane, Mahalapye, Palapye, Serule, Selebi Phikwe and Francistown. In 1998 Botswana Railways (BR) made a profit of P10 million, nearly 90 per cent of its earnings come from freight. Working in conjunction with the National Railways of Zimbabwe and Spoornet (RSA), Botswana Railways can provide links to Namibia, Swaziland, Zambia, the Democratic Republic of Congo, Angola, Malawi, Tanzania and Mozambique.

Roads

Botswana has approximately 20,000 kilometres of roads, out of which 10,000 km are hard-surfaced, including the 595 km Trans-Kgalagadi Highway which links Gaborone with Windhoek, Namibia. The road network links all communities of over 100 people, approximately 90 per cent of the population. In 1995 a total of 107,675 vehicles were registered. Vehicles are driven on the left.

In 2006 an agreement was reached to build a bridge at Kazungula, on the Zambezi river, the bridge will cost an estimated US$70 million to build and will link Botswana, Zambia and Zimbabwe. Bus services connect Botswana with Johannesburg, South Africa, Windhoek, Namibia and Victoria Falls, Zimbabwe.

HEALTH

Figures from the World Health Organisation show that in 2009, total expenditure on health equated to 10.0 per cent of GDP, representing US$581 per capita. Government expenditure represents 76 per cent of total health expenditure. External resources accounted for 19.5 per cent of total expenditure on health. Private expenditure accounted for 24 per cent of expenditure of which 29.5 per cent was out-of-pocket.. In 2005-10 Botswana had 591 physicians (3.4 per 10,000 population), 5,006 nurses and midwives (28.4 per 10,000 population), 38 dentists, 333 pharmacists and 172 public and environmental health workers. There were an estimated 18 hospital beds per 10,000 population.

Children under the age of 12 receive free medical care. Botswana has a comprehensive system of immunisation with the majority of babies being immunised against diptheria, tetanus, measles and tuberculosis before their first birthday. The infant mortality rate was put at 36 per 1,000 live births in 2010 and the child mortality rate was 48 per 1,000 live births. The major causes of death are prematurity (19 per cent), HIV/AIDS (15 per cent, compared to 48 per cent in 2000), pneumonia (13 per cent), birth asphyxia (10 per cent) and diarrhoea (6 per cent). Approximately 31.4 per cent of the under-fives were classified as stunted in the period 2005-10.

In 2010, 96 per cent of the population had access to improved drinking water. An estimated 74 per cent of the urban population and 39 per cent of the rural population had access to improved sanitation in 2008. (Source: http://www.who.int, World Health Statistics 2012)

By the mid-1990s AIDS, (Acquired Immune Deficiency Syndrome) had reached epidemic proportions. Life expectancy in Botswana fell from 47 years in 1997 to 39 years in 2000 and further still to 30 in 2004. UN figures show that by 2003 Botswana had the world's highest known rate for HIV/Aids infection with one in three adults being infected. Botswana now has one of the most advanced treatment programmes for the disease in Africa; anyone infected with the HIV virus can now get government-provided free anti-retroviral drugs. In 2004 following his re-election, President Mogae pledged to continue the fight against the spread of AIDS and his aim for Botswana to be free of the disease by 2016. According to WHO figures, by 2007 the prevalence of HIV among adults aged 15-49 years was 23.9 per cent.

EDUCATION

Figures from UNESCO for 2004 show that 64 per cent of girls and 58 per cent of boys of secondary school age were enrolled. The University of Botswana was founded in 1982 and has over 8,000 students. Higher education also covers teacher training as well as engineering courses at the Botswana Polytechnic. Primary education is provided free of charge but secondary school fees have been charged since 2006.

According to the latest UNESCO figures (2007), the literacy figure for males aged 15 years and older was 82.8 per cent and for females 82.9 per cent. For those aged 15-24 the rates rise to approximately 92.9 per cent and 95.3 per cent respectively.

The pupil: teacher ratio in primary schools in 2004 was 24:1. In the same year, 21.0 per cent of total government expenditure went on education. (Source: UNESCO, UIS, August 2009)

RELIGION

Approximately 50 per cent of the population hold indigenous or animist beliefs, and 27 per cent Christian beliefs.

COMMUNICATIONS AND MEDIA

Freedom of expression is provided for by the constituion and although some opposition groups have alleged intereference this is generally respected.

BRAZIL

Newspapers

Newspapers include the state-owned *The Botswana Daily News* (URL: http://www.gov.bw/cgi-bin/news.cgi), *The Botswana Guardian* (URL: http://www.botswanaguardian.co.bw/) and several weekly papers: *Mmegi*, (The Reporter), URL: http://www.mmegi.bw, *Botswana Gazette* (URL: http://www.gazette.bw) and *The Midweek Sun* (URL: http://www.midweeksun.co.bw/) and *The Voice* (URL: http://www.thevoicebw.com/). Newspaper circulation is mainly limited to urban areas.

Broadcasting

Radio is the most important broadcasting medium in rural areas. Radio Botswana, a government-funded station located in Gabarone, broadcasts for 119 hours per week in Setswana and English, and there are plans to expand the network. There are two privately owned radio stations Ya Rona FM and GABZ FM.

Botswana TV (URL: http://www.btv.gov.bw/) is government owned and has been broadcasting since 2000. Satellite television is available.

Telecommunications

The telecommunications system has developed in recent years and a fully digital system is being developed. Landlines are in decline and as of 2008 there were estimated to be 142,000 in use. By comparison, mobile phone usage has dramatically increased and there are now estimated to be 1,486 million in use. In 2009 there were an estimated 120,000 internet users.

ENVIRONMENT

Environmental issues of concern include overgrazing and desertification. Nearly 40 per cent of the land is set aside as conservation areas, 17 per cent is national parks and game reserves and just over 20 per cent is given over to wildlife management. No permanent structures can be built on conservation land, and so game lodges and other buildings are built on land leased from the government for 15 years at a time.

At the end of 2012 the Botswana government announced plans to stop commercial hunting from January 2014, the ban was introduced due to growing concerns about the falling numbers of wildlife.

In 2010, Botswana's emissions from the consumption of fossil fuels totalled 3.84 million metric tons of carbon dioxide. (Source: EIA)

Botswana is a party to the following international agreements: Biodiversity, Climate Change, Climate Change-Kyoto Protocol, Desertification, Endangered Species, Hazardous Wastes, Law of the Sea, Ozone Layer Protection, and Wetlands

BRAZIL
Federative Republic of Brazil
República Federativa do Brasil

Capital: Brasília (Population estimate, 2011: 2,500,000)

Head of State: Dilma Rousseff (President) (page 1506)

Vice President: Michel Temer (page 1524)

National Flag: Green, bearing at the centre a diamond yellow charged with a blue celestial globe; on it one star for each of the twenty-six states and the federal district. It is inscribed in green on white round the equator with 'Ordem e Progresso'

CONSTITUTION AND GOVERNMENT

Constitution
Brazil gained independent from Portugal on 7 September 1822.

The Constitution provides for three independent powers: the Executive, the Legislative and the Republic. This system has been in place since the first constitution in 1891, after the abolition of the monarchy, and has remained fundamental over six subsequent republican constitutions. The most recent constitution, promulgated in 1988, included more powers for the legislature in its dealing with the executive, and concepts for environmental protection. Legislative power is exercised by the National Congress, which is composed of the Chamber of Deputies and the Federal Senate.

To consult the full constitution (in Portuguese), please visit: http://legis.senado.gov.br/con1988/CON1988_19.12.2006/CON1988.htm

International Relations
Brazil has traditionally played an important role in the inter-American community and leads in efforts to deepen Latin American integration, through its membership of Mercosul, the Organization of American States (OAS), the Rio Group, ALADI and other regional groupings. Under the present government, Brazil has increasingly engaged with other emerging powers, such as India, South Africa, China and Russia. As a leader within Latin America, Brazil encourages closer co-operation between the region and the Middle East.

Brazil is a member of the UN and has contributed troops to UN peacekeeping efforts in the Middle East, the Congo, Angola and East Timor, amongst others. The state is currently leading the UN peacekeeping force in Haiti. Brazil is lobbying for a permanent position on the enlarged UN Security Council.

Recent Events
In March 2005, at least 30 people on the outskirts of Rio de Janeiro were killed in the city's worst massacre for over a decade. Rogue police were said to be responsible. In October 2005, Brazil held a referendum on the question of whether the country should prohibit the sale of firearms. 63.94 per cent of voters were against the prohibition. Brazil has the world's second largest number of fatal shootings, after Venezuela; around 39,000 people die of shot wounds each year.

Presidential and legislative elections were held in October 2006. The incumbent President Lula was re-elected to office.

In July 2007, the government's anti-slavery team freed over a thousand labourers who were working on a sugar cane plantation in the Amazon. Farmers in debt are forced to work almost for free, to repay their debt; it is believed that up to 40,000 people could be working in conditions akin to slavery.

In August 2007, the government announced that environmental policies had slowed the destruction of the Amazon rainforest. Over the year to July 2006, deforestation in the Amazon fell by 25 per cent, to the lowest rate since 2000. In February 2008, Argentina and Brazil agreed to build a joint nuclear reactor to counter looming energy shortages. The agreement came as part of a plan by South America's two biggest economies to extend defence and energy projects. Each country currently has two operating nuclear plants, and both have signed the Nuclear Non-Proliferation Treaty.

Towards the end of November 2008, flooding and landslides in the southern state of Santa Catarina caused the deaths of 97 people. A further 19 people went missing, and almost 80,000 had to move from their homes. Many towns and cities were declared disaster zones, and the government pledged over $1bn to Santa Catarina and other affected states.

In December 2008, eight of the Supreme Court's 11 judges voted to keep a reservation in the Amazonian state of Roraima as a single territory. The large area of land in the far north of Brazil, known as Raposa Serra do Sol, is home to 19,000 Amazonian Indians and was approved as an official reservation in 2005. There are more than 100 similar cases before the Supreme Court and the ruling establishes an important legal precedent.

On October 31 2010 Dilma Rousseff was elected to the post of president, she became Brazil's first female leader. She was sworn in on January 1 2011.

There have been several resignations over corruption allegations. The chief minister, Antonio Palocci, resigned in June 2011 over corruption allegations. The minister of transport, Alfredo Nascimento, resigned in July 2011 after reports of corruption within his ministry. In October 2011 the sports minister, Mr Orlando Silva, also resigned after corruption allegations.

In May 2012 the government announced some more tax cuts to try and stimulate the economy in response to the global economic crisis. Measures included a temporary tax reduction on some car sales. The automotive sector accounts for approximately 20 per cent of the country's industrial GDP.

In June 2013, hundreds of thousands of people took to the streets to protest against rising transport costs, which they believe are a result of the cost of hosting the World Cup in 2014 and the Olympic Games in 2016. The main cities involved in the demonstrations were Rio de Janeiro, Belo Horizonte, Salvador, Fortaleza and the capital, Brasilia.

Legislature
Executive power is exercised by the President of the Republic. The President is assisted by a Cabinet composed of a number of Ministers of State.

The Chamber of Deputies is elected for a four-year term by proportional representation from the 26 States and the Federal District. There are 513 seats.

The Federal Senate of 81 seats is elected by the majority principle on the basis of three Senators for each state. The Senatorial mandate is eight years, and the representation of each state is renewed every four years, alternately, by one-third and two-thirds.

The president and vice-president are elected for four-year terms.

Câmara dos Deputados (Chamber of Deputies): Palácio do Congresso Nacional, Praça dos Três Poderes, Brasília - DF. Tel: +55 (0)61 3216 0000, URL: http://www2.camara.gov.br
Senado Federal (Federal Senate): Palácio do Congresso Nacional, Praça dos Três Poderes - Brasília DF - CEP 70165-900. Tel: +55 (0)61 3311 4141, URL: http://www.senado.gov.br/sf/

Cabinet (as at June 2013)

Chief of Staff of the Presidency: Gleisi Hoffmann
Minister of Finance: Guido Mantega (page 1470)
Minister of Foreign Relations: Antonio Patriota (page 1493)
Minister of Defence and Civil Aviation: Celso Amorim (page 1377)
Minister of Agriculture, Livestock and Supply: Antonio Andrade
Minister of State for Institutional Security in the Office of the President: Jose Elito Carvalho Siqueira
Minister of Fisheries and Aquaculture: Marcelo Crivella
Minister of Science and Technology: Marco Antonio Raupp
Minister of Culture: Marta Suplicy
Minister of Development, Industry and Foreign Trade: Fernando Pimentel
Minister of Education: Aloizio Mercadante
Minister of Sport: Aldo Rebelo
Minister for National Integration: Fernando Bezerra Coelho
Minister of Justice: Jose Eduardo Cardozo
Minister of Environment: Izabella Teixeira
Minister of Mining and Energy: Edison Lobao
Minister of Planning, Budget and Management: Miriam Belchior
Minister of Tourism: Gastro Vieira
Minister of Communications: Paulo Bernardo Silva
Minister of Health: Alexandre Padilha
Minister of Labour and Employment: Manoel Dias
Minister of Social Security: Garibaldi Alves Filho
Minister of Transport: Cesar Borges
Minister of Social Development and Hunger Alleviation: Tereza Campelo
Attorney General: Luis Inacio Lucena Adams (page 1372)
Comptroller General of the Union: Jorge Hage Sobrinho
Minister of Agrarian Development: Jose 'Pepe' Vargas
Governor of the Central Bank of Brazil: Alexandre Tombini

Ministries

Office of the President, Palacio do Planalto, 30 Andar, 70150-900 Brasilia DF, Brazil. Tel: +55 (0)61 411 1202, fax: +55 (0)61 411 2222, URL: http://www.planalto.gov.br
Office of the Vice President, Palacio do Planalto, Anexo I I, Terrreo, 70150-900 Brasilia DF, Brazil. Tel: +55 (0)61 411 2230, fax: +55 (0)61 226 9871
Ministry of Justice, Esplanada dos Ministerios, Bl. T, 4th Floor, 70064-900 Brasilia DF, Brazil. Tel: +55 (0)61 429 3000, fax: +55 (0)61 322 6817, URL: http://www.mj.gov.br
Ministry of Defense, Qg/Ex. Bloco A, 40 Pavimento - Smu, 70630-901 Brasilia DF, Brazil. Tel: +55 (0)61 415 5200, fax: +55 (0)61 415 4379, URL: http://www.defesa.gov.br
Ministry of External Relations, Esplanada Ministerios, Pal. Itamaraty, 70170-900 Brasilia DF, Brazil. Tel: +55 (0)61 224 3129, fax: +55 (0)61 226 1762, e-mail: webmaster@mre.gov.br, URL: http://www.mre.gov.br
Ministry of Finance, Esplanada dos Ministerios, Bloco P, 70048-900 Brasilia DF, Brazil. Tel: +55 (0)61 412 2000 / 3000, fax: +55 (0)61 226 9084, e-mail: se.df@fazenda.gov.br, URL: http://www.fazenda.gov.br
Ministry of Transport, Esplanada dos Ministerios, Bl. R, 6th Floor, 70044-900 Brasilia DF, Brazil. Tel: +55 (0)61 224 0185, fax: +55 (0)61 226 4864, URL: http://www.transportes.gov.br
Ministry of Agriculture, Esplanada dos Ministerios, Bloco D, 8th Floor, 70043-900 Brasilia DF, Brazil. Tel: +55 (0)61 226 321 5498, fax: +55 (0)61 225 9046, e-mail: cenagri@agricultura.gov.br, URL: http://www.agricultura.gov.br
Ministry of Education, Esplanada dos Ministerios, Bloco L, 8th Floor- Gab, 70047-900 Brasilia DF, Brazil. Tel: +55 (0)61 410 8484, fax: +55 (0)61 410 9198, URL: http://www.mec.gov.br/
Ministry of Culture, Esplanada dos Ministerios, Bloco B, 3th Floor, Room 301, 70068-900 Brasilia DF, Brazil. Tel: +55 (0)61 316 2170, fax: +55 (0)61 225 9162, e-mail: info@minc.gov.br, URL: http://www.cultura.gov.br/
Ministry of Labour, Esplanada dos Ministerios, Bloco F, 5th Floor 70059-900 Brasilia DF, Brazil. Tel: +55 (0)61 317 6000, fax: +55 (0)61 224 5844, URL: http://www.mte.gov.br
Ministry of Social Security and Assistance, Esplanada dos Ministerios, Bloco F, 8th Floor, 70059-900 Brasilia DF, Brazil. Tel: +55 (0)61 224 5831, fax: +55 (0)61 317 5407, URL: http://www.mpas.gov.br
Ministry of Health, Esplanada dos Ministerios, Bloco G, 5th Floor, 70058-900 Brasilia DF, Brazil. Tel: +55 (0)61 315 2425, fax: +55 (0)61 315 2879, e-mail: imprensa@saude.gov.br, URL: http://www.saude.gov.br
Ministry of Industry and Foreign Trade, Esplanada dos Ministerios, Bloco J, 6th Floor, Room 600, 70053-900 Brasilia DF, Brazil. Tel: +55 (0)61 325 2001, fax: +55 (0)61 325 2230, e-mail: webmaster@desenvolvimento.gov.br, URL: http://www.mdic.gov.br
Ministry of Communications, Espalanda dos Ministerios, Bloco R, 8th Floor, 70046-900 Brasilia DF, Brazil. Tel: +55 (0)61 225 9381, fax: +55 (0)61 226 3980, URL: http://www.mc.gov.br
Ministry of Administration and Planning, Esplanada dos Ministerios, Bloco K, 7th Floor, 70040-906 Brasilia DF, Brazil. Tel: +55 (0)61 429 4343, fax: +55 (0)61 225 7287, URL: http://www.planejamento.gov.br
Ministry of Science and Technology, Esplanada dos Ministerios, Bloco E, 4th Floor, 70067-900 Brasilia DF, Brazil. Tel: +55 (0)61 224 4364, fax: +55 (0)61 225 7496, e-mail: webgab@mct.gov.br, URL: http://www.mct.gov.br
Ministry of the Environment, Esplanada dos Ministerios, Bloco B, 5-9th Floor, 70068-900 Brasilia DF, Brazil. Tel: +55 (0)61 322 8239, fax: +55 (0)61 226 7101, URL: http://www.mma.gov.br
Ministry of Sport, Esplanada dos Ministerios, Bloco A, 7th Floor, 70054-906 Brasilia DF, Brazil. Tel: +55 (0)61 217 1800, fax: +55 (0)61 217 1707, URL: http://www.met.gov.br
Ministry for Rural Development, Esplanada dos Ministerios, Bloco A, 8th Floor, 70068-900 Brasilia DF, Brazil. Tel: +55 (0)61 223 8076, fax +55 (0)61 223 1630, e-mail: communicacaosocial@mda.gov.br, URL: http://www.mda.gov.br
Ministry of National Integration, Esplanada dos Ministérios, Bloco E, 8th Floor, 70067-901 Brasilia DF, Brazil. Tel: +61 414 5972, URL: http://www.integracao.gov.br/

Political Parties

Partido do Movimento Democrático Brasileiro (PMDB, Brazilian Democratic Movement Party), URL: http://www.pmdb.org.br
President: Michel Temer
Partido da Social Democracia Brasileira (PSDB, Brazilian Social Democracy Party), URL: http://www.psdb.org.br
Leader: Sérgio Guerra
Partido da Frente Liberal (PFL, Liberal Front Party), URL: http://www.pfl.org.br
President: Jorge Bornhausen
Partido dos Trabalhadores (PT, Worker's Party), URL: http://www.pt.org.br/portalpt/index.php
Presidente: Ricardo Berzoini
Partido Progressista do Brasil (PPB, Progressive Party), URL: http://www.pp.org.br/
President: Francisco Dornelles
Partido Democrático Trabalhista (PDT, Worker's Democratic Party), URL: http://www.pdt.org.br
President: Carlos Roberto Lupi
Partido Socialista Brasileiro (PSB, Brazilian Socialist Party), URL: http://www.psbnacional.org.br/
President: Eduardo Campos
Partido Liberal (PL, Liberal Party), URL: http://www.pl.org.br
President: Professor Sergio Tamer
Partido Comunista do Brasil (PC do B, Brazilian Communist Party), URL: http://www.vermelho.org.br/pcdob/
Leader: Renato Rebelo
Partido Verde (PV), URL: http://www.pv.org.br
Leader: Jose Luiz de Franca Penna

Elections

President, Luiz Inacio Lula da Silva (Lula) of the Worker's Party, stood down in October 2010 when presidential and parliamentary elections most recently took place. Dilma Rousseff, also of the Worker's Party, won the second round of the presidential election with 56 per cent of the vote. President Rouseff is Brazil's first female leader.

Thirteen parties won seats in the Federal Senate in 2006, the four parties with the most being the PFL (18), the PMDB (15), the PSDB (15) and the PT (11). In the Chamber of Deputies, twenty-nine parties are represented, the four largest being the PMDB (89), the PT (83), the PFL (65) and the PSDB (65). President Lula's PT party failed to win a majority in either house and had to form a coalition.

Diplomatic Representation

Embassy of Brazil, 3006 Massachusetts Avenue, NW, Washington, DC 20008, USA. Tel: +1 202 238 2700, fax: +1 202 238 2827, e-mail: webmaster@brasilemb.org, URL: http://www.brasilemb.org
Ambassador: Mauro Luiz Iecker Viera (page 1531)
Embassy of Brazil, 32 Green Street, London, W1K 4AT, United Kingdom. Tel: +44 (0)20 7499 0877, fax: +44 (0)20 7399 9100, URL: http://www.brazil.org.uk
Ambassador: Roberto Jaguaribe
British Embassy, Setor de Embaixadas Sul, Quadra 801, Conjunto K, Brasilia DF 70408-900, Brazil. Tel: +55 (61) 3329 2300, fax: +55 (61) 3329 2369, e-mail: britemb@terra.com.br, URL: http://www.reinounido.org.br
Ambassador: Alan Charlton (page 1403)
US Embassy, SES, Avenue das Nações, Quadra 801, Lote 3, 70403-900 Brasília DF, Brazil. Tel: +55 (61) 3312 7000, fax: +55 (61) 3312 7241, URL: http://www.embaixada-americana.org.br
Ambassador: Thomas A. Shannon, Jr.
Permanent Mission of Brazil to the United Nations, 747 Thrid Avenue, 9th Floor, New York, NY 10017, USA. Tel: +212 372 2600, fax: +212 371 5716, e-mail: delbrasonu@delbrasonu.org, URL: http://www.un.int/brazil
Permanent Representative: H. E. Ambassador Maria Luiza Ribeiro Viotti

LEGAL SYSTEM

The Brazilian legal system is based on Civil Law. The Judiciary is organized into federal and state branches.

The Federal Supreme Court sits in Brasília and is composed of 11 judges appointed by the President of the Republic following approval by the Federal Senate. The Supreme Court is is the guardian of the Constitution. The Superior Court of Justice, which has both primary and appellate jurisdiction, is composed of 33 judges appointed by the President of the Republic, again subject to the approval of the Federal Senate. There are also military, electoral and labour courts, each with their own judges.

State-level justice in Brazil consists of state courts and judges. The states of Brazil organize their own judicial systems, with court jurisdiction defined in each state constitution.

The federal government generally respects the human rights of its citizens, but the record of several state governments is poor. In recent years, there have been cases of unlawful killings and the use of excessive force by police and prison security forces. Prison conditions are harsh and there are long delays in the judicial system. There is widespread forced labor; and child labor in the informal sector. Human rights violators often enjoy impunity. Brazil retains the death penalty but only for exceptional crimes such as those committed under military law or in exceptional circumstances.

In October 2011, the Senate voted to set up a truth commission to investigate human rights abuses including those committed during military rule from 1964-1985. The Commission was inaugurated in 2012.

Supreme Federal Tribunal: URL: http://www.stf.jus.br/portal/principal/principal.asp

STATES OF THE WORLD

273

BRAZIL

President: Joaquim Barbosa

LOCAL GOVERNMENT

Brazil is divided into 26 States and one Federal District (Brasilia). The states have considerable autonomy, being responsible for such issues as security and education. They have separate legislatures, administrations and judiciaries. Furthermore, they have their own constitutions and may make their own laws, provided that these accord with the constitutional principles of the federal government.

The members of the legislature for each state are elected by popular vote, as are the state governors. The most recent municipal elections took place in 2008 with voting taking place in over 5,500 municipalities for mayors and city councillors. The next elections are due to take place in 2012.

The 26 states are Acre, Alagoas, Amapa, Amazonas, Bahia, Ceara, Espirito Santo, Goias, Maranhao, Mato Grosso, Mato Grosso do Sul, Minas Gerais, Para, Paraiba, Parana, Pernambuco, Piaui, Rio de Janeiro, Rio Grande do Norte, Rio Grande do Sul, Rondonia, Roraima, Santa Catarina, Sao Paulo, Sergipe and Tocantins.

AREA AND POPULATION

Area

Brazil is bounded in the north by Colombia, Venezuela, the Guianas and Suriname, in the north and east by the Atlantic Ocean, in the south by Uruguay and in the west by Argentina, Bolivia, Paraguay and Peru. It covers an area of 8,511,970 sq. km and is the fifth largest country in the world. Two of the largest rivers in the world flow through Brazil, the Amazon system in the north and the Parana to the south.

In 2007, researchers claimed to have established as a scientific fact that the Amazon is the longest river in the world; whilst the Amazon has been recognised as the largest river by volume, it has generally been regarded as second in length to the River Nile. The research established the source of the Amazon as being an ice-covered mountain in southern Peru called Mismi. This is further south than had previously been thought, giving the Amazon a total length of 6,800 km compared to the Nile's 6,695 km.

Brazil is divided into five major regions. The Amazon Basin (covering 60 per cent of the country) in the north consists of lowlands covered by rain forest and rivers and is the largest virgin land area in South America. The north-eastern 'sertao' is an area of rocky plateaux and scrub vegetation where the main activity is cattle raising and the climate is semi-arid. The coastal strip, known as the 'zona de mata', is more humid: sugar cane and cocoa are produced here. The Carajás mountain range is home to one of the world's largest mineral reserves, rich in manganese, bauxite, copper, nickel and iron. The south, where Rio de Janeiro and São Paulo are to be found, is an area of vast plateaux where industry and economic activity are concentrated.

Brazil has a variety of climatic zones, from the warm Amazon region to the hot dry Northeast with temperatures of over 40°C and to the Uruguayan border, where the average temperature is around 18°C.

To view a map, consult: http://www.lib.utexas.edu/maps/cia08/brazil_sm_2008.gif

Population

Brazil is the fifth most populous country in the world with a population of around 194.946 million in 2010. The annual growth rate averages 1.1 per cent. Some 87 per cent of the population now lives in urban areas, where poverty and violence are rife. The major cities are São Paulo (over 11 million inhabitants (2012) with a density of 7,247 people per sq. km, this is the fourth most populated city in the world), Brasilia, Rio de Janeiro (6,136,652 people), Salvador, Curitiba, Recife, Porto Alegre and Belo Horizonte.

There are six main population groups within Brazil: Portuguese, African, other Europeans, Middle Eastern peoples, Asians and indigenous peoples. There are around 350,000 indigenous people still living in Brazil, though their livelihoods are threatened by deforestation, disease and mining.

The official language of Brazil is Portuguese, although Spanish, English and French are spoken.

Births, Marriages and Deaths

Life expectancy in 2009 was 73 years (70 for men and 77 for women). Healthy life expectancy was estimated to be 64 years. The median age is 29 years. Approximately 25 per cent of the population is under 15 years old and 10 per cent over 60 years old. The total fertility rate was put at 1.8 births per female. (Source: http://www.who.int, World Health Statistics 2012)

Public Holidays 2014

1 January: New Year's Day
20 January: Founding of Rio de Janeiro (Rio only)
25 January: Founding of São Paulo (São Paulo only)
28 February - 4 March: Carnival
18 April: Good Friday
21 April: Easter Monday
21 April: Tiradentes
1 May: Labour Day
19 May: Corpus Christi
7 September: Independence Day
12 October: Our Lady of Aparecida (Patron Saint of Brazil)
1 November: All Saints Day
15 November: Proclamation of the Republic
25 December: Christmas Day

EMPLOYMENT

The labour force (over the age of fifteen) in 2006 was estimated to be 95,620,000, representing almost 69 per cent of the total population. 89.3 million people (over the age of ten) were employed in September 2006, and 8.2 per cent of the workforce (10+) were unemployed. In 2007, around 1.6 million new jobs were created - the highest ever increase. Since 2004, there has been a 50 per cent increase in the minimum wage. Estimated figures for 2009 put the workforce at 101.7 million.

Employment by economic activity, 2007

Sector	No. of employees
Agriculture, hunting and forestry	16,207,200
Fishing	371,700
Mining and quarrying	378,700
Manufacturing	13,105,100
Electricity, gas and water supply	362,700
Construction	6,107,000
Wholesale and retail trade; Repair of motor vehicles and personal and household goods	16,308,900
Hotels and restaurants	3,350,900
Transport, storage and communications	4,374,000
Financial services	1,181,400
Real estate, renting and business activities	5,499,300
Public administration and defence; Compulsory social security	4,504,200
Education	5,052,300
Health and Social work	3,327,100
Other community, social and personal service activities	3,311,300
Private household with employed persons	6,731,700
Extra-territorial organisations and bodies	3,400
Not classifiable by economic activity	209,000

Source: Copyright © International Labour Organization (ILO Dept. of Statistics, http://laborsta.ilo.org)

Critics have accused producers of exploiting workers in the sugar cane and ethanol industry. It is estimated that between 25,000 and 40,000 people have fallen into debt slavery in Brazil, by paying for transportation to work far from where they live and by buying overpriced tools and food. In July 2007, over a thousand labourers were freed by the government's anti-slavery team from inhumane conditions on a sugar cane plantation in the Amazon. An ethanol-producing company which owns the plantation denied allegations of abusing the workers and claimed that the workers were paid good wages by Brazilian standards.

BANKING AND FINANCE

Currency

One Real (R$) = 100 centavos
Before the introduction of the Real Plan the currency was the Cruzeiro.

GDP/GNP, Inflation, National Debt

Brazil has enjoyed over ten years of financial stability, steady growth and a fall in unemployment, and is currently experiencing a period of economic optimism. At a time of rising global demand for food and energy, Brazil is in a strong position. The country is one of the world's most important agricultural producers, and is close to becoming an important oil exporter. On his election in 2002, President Lula da Silva pledged to close the gap between rich and poor in Brazil, and the impact of orthodox economic policies such as a floating exchange rate, inflation targeting and fiscal restraint initiated under former President Cardoso (1995-2002) and expanded under the da Silva administration, began to be felt; as incomes rose and a quarter of Brazil's population entered the consumer market for the first time. With its consequent expanding domestic markets, Brazil is now attracting huge amounts of foreign direct investment. The government also started several programs to improve Brazil's infrastructure including transport and energy supply, which should further improve its economy.

GDP grew for a third consecutive year in 2007, to an estimated US$1.838 trillion (purchasing power parity), an increase of 4.5 per cent on the previous year. GDP growth reached an estimated 8 per cent in 2008 with GDP (ppp) at US$1.977 trillion. Estimated figures for 2009 show GDP (ppp) rose to US$2.022 trillion, giving a per capita figure of US$10,600. GDP was estimated to be US$2.3 trillion in 2011. The services sector accounts for 67 per cent of GDP, industry contributes 28 per cent and agriculture, 6 per cent.

However, since the beginnings of the global financial downturn, Brazil's economy has been affected by sharp falls in world commodity prices, and the country's currency and stock markets have suffered as foreign investors sell off assets to cover domestic losses. The economy as a whole remains strong, with a growing export market, moderate inflation and a fall in unemployment. However, despite initial strong growth in 2008 Brazil entered into recession in 2009 after two quarters of negative growth. Growth soon returned: official figures put growth in Q2 2009 at 1.9 per cent and the economy boomed in 2010, growing by 7.5 per cent. In 2011, the central bank cut the growth forecast to 3.5 per cent, citing the gloomy international outlook and also spending cuts including the removal of stimulus packages. Growth was zero per cent in 3Q 2011, and growth was estimated to be 2.7 per cent for the whole of 2011. The government announced tax cuts in mid-2012 in an attempt to stimulate the economy. Its target growth rate for the year is 4.5 per cent but this is expected to be revised downwards.

Brazil is now a net creditor nation. It repaid its IMF debt of US$15.5 billion in 2005, two years ahead of schedule. However, local currency government debt remains high. In 2009, Brazil offered US$10 billion to the IMF to help developing nations gain credit.

Inflation ran at 3.14 per cent in 2006, down from 5.7 per cent in 2005, 7.6 per cent in 2004 and 9.5 per cent in 2003. It averaged 5.9 per cent in 2009. In 2011, the government was to implement US$30 billion of spending cuts to help curb inflation. Inflation was estimated at 5.5 per cent in that year.

Brazil attracted an estimated $66 billion of foreign direct investment in 2011.

Balance of Payments / Imports and Exports
Estimated figures for 2011 put the trade surplus at US20 billion; exports earned US$202 billion and imports cost US$182 billion.

Brazil's main exports are manufactured products, coffee and iron ore. Main imports are raw materials for industry, capital goods and petroleum, and other fuels and consumer goods. Major trade partners include China and the USA.

Brazil is a founder member of Mercosul, along with Argentina, Paraguay and Uruguay. Bolivia, Chile, Peru, Venezuela and Mexico are associate members, and Free Trade Agreements have been signed with Colombia and Ecuador. Mercosul is the world's fourth biggest integrated market and the second largest in the Americas after the North American Free Trade Area (NAFTA) with a combined population of over 220 million people. Mercosul is negotiating an Association Agreement with the European Union, and Free Trade Agreements with India and South Africa.

Central Bank
Banco Central do Brasil, Setor Bancario Sul, Quadra 3, Bloco B, 70074-900, Brasilia (DF), Brazil. Tel: +55 (0)61 414 1000 / 61 414 2000, fax: +55 (0)61 223 1033 / 61 223 2716, URL: http://www.bcb.gov.br
Governor: Alexandre Tombini

Banking Association
Federação Brasileira das Associações de Bancos: URL: http://www.febraban.com.br

Chambers of Commerce and Trade Organisations
Confederação Nacional do Comércio, URL: http://www.cnc.com.br/
Câmara de Comércio e Indústria do Rio de Janeiro, URL: http://www.caerj.org.br/

MANUFACTURING, MINING AND SERVICES

Primary and Extractive Industries
Mining operations are largely concentrated in the State of Minas Gerais where deposits of iron ore, mica, beryl, nickel, marble, manganese and limestone are found. Many other minerals are extracted including potash, nickel, lead, zinc, quartz, crystal, gem stones, industrial graphite, chromium, molybdenum, niobium, tungsten, uranium and gold. 90 per cent of the world's aquamarines, topazes, tourmalines and amethysts are supplied from mines in Minas Gerais. Brazil's gold reserves, found mainly in Para and Bahia, are estimated at 33,000 tons. Niobium deposits were discovered in 1990.

In the early 1980s, Brazil was a large net oil importer (importing approximately 70 per cent of its needs), but production has now nearly caught up with consumption and the country aims to become a net oil exporter in the near future. In January 2012 Brazil had proven oil reserves of 14 billion barrels, following the discoveries in the Campos Basin and the Santos Basin. Estimated oil production rose to 2.7 million barrels per day in 2011, whilst consumption climbed to 2.7 million barrels per day. Imports come from Africa and the Middle East. Brazil has 1.9 million bbl/d of crude oil refining capacity spread amongst 13 refineries. The state controlled Petrobras remains dominant in the oil sector although it no longer holds a monopoly. Petrobras aims to increase refining capacity to more than 3 million by 2020 to meet rising demand.

Brazil is one of the world's largest producers of ethanol and is the largest exporter of the fuel. In 2010, Brazil produced 486,000 billion barrels per day of ethanol. Most new cars sold in Brazil are flex-fuel vehicle, which means that they can run on pure ethanol, or an ethanol-petrol mix. Furthermore, all petrol in Brazil contains ethanol, with blending levels varying from 20-25 per cent. Brazilian ethanol comes from sugar cane, which is grown in the country's tropical climate. A poor sugar cane harvest and underinvestment in the industry led to a fall in production in 2011 to an estimated 390,000 bbl/d.

Brazil has estimated natural gas reserves of 14.7 trillion cubic feet (as at January 2012). The country produced 590 billion cubic feet of gas in 2011 and consumed 943 billion cubic feet, importing the balance from Bolivia and Argentina. A lack of natural gas transportation infrastructure in the interior regions of the country has hindered the consumption, production and exploration of natural gas.

Petrobras operates the domestic natural gas transport sytem which extends over 4,000 miles. In 2010, the Southeast Northeast Incoonnection Gas Piplein linked the system sin the north and south of the country for the first time. In 2009, construction of the Urucu pipline inking Urucu to Manaus, in the Amazonas state was completed.

Recent estimates put the country's recoverable coal reserves at 11.1 billion short tons. Production was 6.2 million short tons in 2010, whilst consumption for the same year was 25.3 million short tons. (Source: EIA)

Energy
Brazil is the third largest producer and consumer of electricity in the Western Hemisphere, and the tenth largest consumer in the world. Total energy production was 8.455 quadrillion Btu in 2008 and consumption was 10.6 quadrillion Btu. EIA figures for 2010 showed that 39 per cent of Brazil's primary energy consumption came from oil and other liquids, 29 per cent from hydroelectricity, 21 per cent from the other renewables, seven per cent from natural gas, three per cent from coal, and one per cent from nuclear.

The country has an installed generating capacity of 106 gigawatts. Net electricity generation was approximately 458 billion kWh in 2009, whilst consumption for the same year was 417 billion kWh.

Hydroelectric power is the source of 83 per cent of Brazil's installed generating capacity. In partnership with Paraguay, Brazil operates the Itaipu power plant on the river Parana, the largest hydroelectric plant in the world, with a 12.6 gigawatt capacity. Thermal (oil, natural gas and coal) generation accounts for around 7 per cent of capacity, with renewable sources and nuclear generating 4 per cent and 3 per cent respectively. Brazil has two nuclear power plants, with a third currently under construction.

In 2007, following two years of consultation, the government gave the go-ahead for the construction of two hydro-electric dams to be built on the longest tributary of the Amazon River, the Madeira River. Once built, the two dams could supply around up to 10 per cent of the national demand for electricity. Environmentalists fear it will cause damage to the Amazon and the surrounding areas of the projected dams. The river is said to have one of the most diverse fish stocks in the world. (Source: EIA)

Manufacturing
Brazil has one of the most advanced industrial sectors in Latin America. Manufacturing accounts for around 28 per cent of GDP. Vehicle production is now an important industry in the country; most manufacturers have a production plant in Brazil. Brazil's aerospace industry has also grown rapidly and is now the sixth largest aircraft industry in the world. Other major industries include steel, iron ore, timber, textiles, cement, tin and petrochemicals, computers and consumer durables.

Service Industries
At the end of 2005, some 7.58 million people worked in the services sector, most in the business and transport sub-sectors. There were 948,420 companies operating, 299,000 involved in services to families and 224,000 in the business sector. (Source: Brasil em Sintese, Instituto Brasileiro de Geografia e Estatística, IBGE)

Telecommunications and post are financially the most important industries in this sector, followed by banking and commerce, energy and computing. Tourism has been targeted as an area of growth; in 2002, there were 3.8 million visitors to Brazil, generating revenue of over US$3 billion. Figures for 2006 show visitors numbered 4.0 million generating revenue of US$4.5 billion. Vistors were estimated to number over 5 million in 2010.

Agriculture
Agriculture still accounts for a major part of economic activity, contributing around 5 per cent of GDP (25 per cent when including agribusiness), employing almost one quarter of the working population and contributing 36 per cent of export revenue. Brazil is the world's largest producer of coffee and sugarcane, tropical fruits and concentrated orange juice. The country is a leading producer of cocoa, tobacco and cotton.

Soyabean production has increased enormously in response to Chinese demand and a decline in US production of the crop. The acreage dedicated to this crop has increased dramatically, causing concern to environmentalists: there has been large-scale deforestation due to land clearance for soyabean crop production.

Beef, poultry and pork production have risen over the years, as have exports in these sectors, particularly to Europe. Brazil's has the world's largest commercial cattle herd; at 170 million head, it is 50 per cent larger than that of the USA.

Agricultural Production in 2010

Produce	Int. $'000*	Tonnes
Indigenous cattle meat	25,192,925	9,325,960
Sugar cane	23,362,278	717,462,000
Soybeans	16,799,930	68,756,300
Indigenous chicken meat	15,288,160	10,733,000
Cow milk, whole, fresh	9,489,244	30,715,500
Indigenous pigmeat	3,498,298	3,078,840
Oranges	3,498,298	1,810,700
Coffee, green	3,122,434	2,906,320
Rice, paddy	3,072,187	11,236,000
Maize	2,961,862	55,394,800
Bananas	1,960,938	6,962,790
Beans, dry	1,811,816	3,158,910

*unofficial figures
Source: http://faostat.fao.org/site/339/default.aspx Food and Agriculture Organization of the United Nations, Food and Agricultural commodities production

Brazil's timber reserves are the third largest in the world. Three-quarters of the timber is found in the Amazon region where 400 marketable varieties of hardwood grow. Hardwoods also predominate in the Atlantic coastal zone and only the southern States of Paraná, Santa Catarina and Rio Grande do Sul produce the soft wood known as Paraná pine, used in the construction and pulp and paper industries. In recent years the government has implemented plans, including an Environmental Crimes Law, to stop illegal burning of rainforest for clearing.

Fishing has always been important, particularly in the northeast where there are plenty of fish and shellfish of high commercial value. At the mouth of the river Amazon the world's largest shrimp bank is found and there is tuna along the Brazilian coastline. Figures for 2010 put the total catch for Brazil was 785,370 tonnes.

BRAZIL

COMMUNICATIONS AND TRANSPORT

Travel Requirements
All travellers must have a passport valid for at least six months from date of entry and must have onward or return tickets and sufficient funds to cover their stay. Nationals of most EU countries do not require a visa for tourist and business stays of up to 90 days; the exceptions are citizens of Cyprus, Estonia, Latvia, Lithuania and Malta who do require a visa. The nationals of the USA, Canada and Australia do require a visa. Citizens from Argentina, Bolivia, Chile, Colombia, Ecuador, Paraguay, Peru, Uruguay and Zambia may enter the country with a valid ID card. Citizens of other countries should contact the Brazilian consulate to find out about visa requirements.

National Airlines
Varig (Viação Aérea Rio-Grandense), URL: http://www.varig.com.br
Vasp, URL: http://www.vasp.com.br
TransBrasil, URL: http://www.transbrasil.com.br

International Airports
The most important airfields are Brasilia International and Congonhas arirport serving Sao Paulo). Due to the size of the country air travel is often the cheapest and easiest way to travel long distances, figures from 2010 show that Brazil had 4,072 airports. In preparation for the 2014 football world cup and the 2016 Olympics, Brazil is improving its transport infrastructure. A new terminal is planned for the international airport, however construction was halted in 2011 due to concerns over the bidding process. The terminal should double the passenger capacity to 52.7 million.
Empresa Brasileira de Infra-Estrutura Aeroportuária (INFRAERO), URL: http://www.infraero.com.br

Due to the size of the country, air travel is ususally the quickest and most convenient form of travel. All cities are linked by air routes. Shuttle services exist between São Paulo and Rio de Janeiro; São Paulo and Brasilia; Brasilia and Belo Horizonte, (Beagá).

Railways
The total length of track is over 29,412 km (18,330 miles), including urban rail. A high speed link is planned between São Paulo and Rio de Janeiro.

Roads
The total length of roads is 1,724,929 km, of which almost 95 km is tarmacked. Vehicles are driven on the right.
All the state capitals are linked by paved roads and major cities like Sao Paolo and Rio de Janeiro have motorways. Long distance bus services connect Brazil with neighbouring countries, services run to Buenos Aires, Asunción, Montevideo, Santiago de Chile, and Lima.
Departamento Nacional de Estradas de Rodagem (DNER)(National Roads Development), URL: http://www.dner.gov.br

Ports and Harbours
Brazil's largest ports are Santos, Rio de Janeiro, Paranagua, Recife and Vitoria. The two largest, Rio and Santos, handle about half the cargo loaded and discharged through the 36 main deep-water ports in Brazil. New ports such as Tubarao, from where the bulk of Brazil's iron ore is shipped abroad, and Icomi, from where manganese is transported, are playing an increasing role.

There are also ports at Belem, Fortaleza, Ilheus, Imbituba, Manaus, Porto Alegre, Rio Grande and Salvador. Ferries operate from most ports.

HEALTH

According to World Health Organization statistics, in 2009 total expenditure on health equates to 8.8 per cent of GDP, equating to US$734 per capita. Government spending represents 43.6 per cent of health expenditure. Private expenditure accounted for the rest, of which some 56.4 per cent was out-of-pocket expenditure and approximately 41.0 per cent came from pre-paid plans. In the period 2005-10, there were 341,849 doctors (17.6 per 10,000 population), 1,243,804 nurses and midwives (64.2 per 10,000 population), 227,141 dentists (11.7 per 10,000 population) and 104,098 pharmaceutical personnel (5.4 per 10,000 population). There were approximately 24 hospital beds and 1.9 psychiatric beds per 10,000 population.

In 2010, an estimated 98 per cent of the population had sustained access to improved drinking water. In the same year, an estimated 79 per cent of the population were using improved sanitation. In 2008, an estimated 87 per cent of the urban population and 37 per cent of the rural population had sustained access to improved sanitation.

In 2009, the infant mortality rate (probability of dying by age one) was 17 per 1,000 live births. The rate of under-fives mortality for year 2009 was 19 deaths in every 1,000 live births. The main causes of child deaths are prematurity (22 per cent), congenital anomalies (19 per cent), diarrhoea (3 per cent), and pneumonia (7 per cent). Diabetes affects some 4.5 million Brazilians, the second highest rate in the Americas (following the USA). Abortion is currently the subject of intense debate; some Brazilians are pushing for the legalisation of terminations which the Catholic Church vehemently opposes. Abortion is only permitted in the cases of rape or danger to the mother. The World Health Organisation estimates that illegal abortions numbered more than a million in Brazil in 2006.

AIDS/HIV affected an estimated 560 000 people in 2003, rising to an estimated 620,000 in 2005. An estimated 14,000 people died of the illness in 2005. Brazil's Aids programme has succeeded in stabilising the rate of HIV infection and reducing the number of Aids-related deaths. The country has used generic copycat Aids medicines in order to achieve this. In 2007 the prevalence of HIV/AIDS in adults aged 15-49 years was 0.6 per cent.

In the first seven months of 2007, more than 438,000 cases of dengue fever were reported in Brazil, with 98 deaths. At the beginning of 2008, there was another outbreak, and hospitals in Rio de Janeiro province reported over 2,000 new cases per day. Around 48 people died in the state within the first three months of the year, most within the city, where stagnant waters are an attractive breeding ground for mosquitoes. In January 2008, there was an outbreak of yellow fever, with 12 suspected cases, three of which were fatal. More than 560,000 people were vaccinated against the disease. Yellow fever is transmitted by infected mosquitoes and is generally confined to rural or jungle areas of Brazil. In 2010, there were 32 reported cases of diptheria, 34,894 of leprosy, 334,618 of malaria, 68 of measles, 477 of pertussis, 308 of tetanus, 74,395 of TB. (Source: http://www.who.int, World Health Statistics 2012)

EDUCATION

The Brazilian education system includes both public and private institutions. Education is free at all levels and compulsory between the ages of 7 and 15. Secondary education takes place from 15 to 18 or 19 years.

In 2004, 34,012,000 students aged between 7 and 14 years olds were registered at a school, representing approximately 98 per cent of the school-aged population.

In 2007, 16.2 per cent of total government expenditure went on education. An estimated 7 per cent of public expenditure went on pre-primary education, 32 per cent on primary, 44 per cent on secondary and 16 per cent on tertiary. (Source: UNESCO)

Universities and Higher Education
The Ministry of Education controls higher education. The Federal Government maintains at least one Federal university in each state. Upon completion of a full academic course of study, university students may obtain the Bachelor Degree (Bacharelado) and may also have an additional year's teacher training (Licenciatura). In 2009, 36 per cent of students went on to study at tertiary level.

The adult literacy rate is estimated to be 90.3 per cent among those over 15 years old. This figure goes up to 97.2 per cent among the age group 15-24. (Source, UNESCO)

RELIGION

Brazil is the world's most populous Catholic nation with around 125 million followers in 2000; 74 per cent of the population is Roman Catholic. Connection between Church and State was abolished in 1889, restored in 1934 and again abolished under the 1946 constitution.

There are many protestant churches (15 per cent of the population are protestant) including Episcopal, Methodist, Lutheran and Baptist as well as some Jews, Muslims and Buddhists.

In May 2007, during a visit to Brazil, Pope Benedict XVI canonised the first native-born saint, Friar Galvao, an 18th Century monk. The Church attributed two miracles to Friar Galvao and credited him with 5,000 miracle cures.

Conselho Nacional de Igrejas Cristâs do Brazil (CONIC) (National Council of Christian Churches in Brazil), URL: http://www.conic.org.br
Exec. Secretary: Revd. Luiz Alberto Barbosa
Bishops' Conference, Conferência Nacional dos Bispos do Brasil, URL: http://www.cnbb.org.br

COMMUNICATIONS AND MEDIA

Freedom of the press is guaranteed by the constitution.

Newspapers
O Dia, URL: http://odia.terra.com.br/
Correio Braziliense, URL: http://www.correioweb.com.br
O'Estado de Sao Paulo, URL: http://www.estado.com.br
Folha de Sao Paulo, URL: http://www.folha.com.br
Gazeta Mercantil (Financial Newspaper), URL: http://www.gazeta.com.br
O'Globo, URL: http://www.globo.com.br
Jornal do Brasil, URL: http://www.jbonline.terra.com.br

Broadcasting
Brazil has thousands of radio stations and hundreds of TV channels. Globo, Brazil's most-successful broadcaster, dominates the market and runs TV and radio networks, newspapers and pay-TV operations. Brazil is developing digital TV services and aims to switch off analogue transmissions from 2016.
Associação Brasileira de Emissoras de Rádio e Televisâo (ABERT), URL: http://www.abert.org.br
TV Band, commercial network, URL: http://www.band.com.br/
Rede Globe, commercial network, URL: http://redeglobo.globo.com/
SBT, URL: http://www.sbt.com.br/home/
Radiobraz, state-run, URL: http://www.ebc.com.br/

Telecommunications
Figures for 2010 indicate that there were 42 million mainline phones and 200 million mobile phone lines in use. By 2010 there were an estimated 74 million internet users.

ENVIRONMENT

Brazil has one of the highest levels of biodiversity in the world, encompassing Amazon rainforest, coastal and marine waters, savannah lands, wetlands and Atlantic forest.

Due to developmental and economic pressures, the rainforest in Brazil has suffered extensive damage from deforestation over the years. In the year to August 2004, 26,000 sq. km. of forest was chopped down, much of the clearance occurring in the Mato Grosso area, in order to grow soyabean crops. In 2005, the government reported that one fifth of the Amazon forests had been cleared.

Measures have been taken by successive Brazilian governments to reduce the impact of development on the environment: in 1998 the President signed decrees to protect two areas in the Atlantic forest and two in the Amazon region from development in perpetuity and in 1999 the President signed an environmental crime bill, which meant that pollution and deforestation became crimes punishable by a fine or jail sentence. In August 2007, the government announced that these policies were having a positive effect; the rate of deforestation fell by 25 per cent in the year to July 2006, preventing the release of 410 million tonnes of greenhouse gases and halting the destruction of 600,000 trees. However, over the months to January 2008, there was a sharp increase in forest clearance; 3,235 sq km were lost. In November 2008, officials said that the destruction of the Amazon rainforest had accelerated for the first time in four years; 11,968 sq km of land was cleared in the year to July, nearly 4 per cent higher than the year before. Demand for land to raise cattle and grow soya increased as commodity prices rose. The government said that the deforestation would have been considerably worse if it had not taken action against illegal logging. In the period 2010-11 an estimated 6,250 km² was felled. In total an estimated 20 per cent of the Amazon has been cleared. Controversial environmental laws were discussed in 2012 which some fear will lead to increased deforestation. In May 2012, President Rousseff vetoed parts of a controversial bill which regulated how much land farmers had to preserve as forest. Among the articles she vetoed were an amnesty for illegal loggers and farming close to river banks.

In November 2009, Brazil and France agreed a common aim on fighting global warming, and announced that their goal was to reduce industrialised nations' emissions to 50 per cent below 1990 levels by 2050.

In 2007, following two years of consultation, the government gave the go-ahead for the construction of two hydro-electric dams to be built on the Madeira River, the longest tributary of the Amazon River which is thought to have one of the most diverse fish stocks in the world. Environmentalists fear the dams will damage the ecosystem of the Amazon and put pressure on resources in the area. The government has attached 33 conditions on the construction of the dams, in an effort to minimise the environmental impact.

There are fears amongst environmentalists that Brazil, one of the world's largest emitters of CO_2 gas, will soon become a net polluter, as the absorbing properties of the rainforest are reduced and more felled trees are burned. In 2005, Brazil emitted 360.57 million metric tonnes of CO_2 gases into the atmosphere, equivalent to 1.94 metric tonnes per capita. In 2006, Brazil's emissions from the consumption and flaring of fossil fuels totalled 377.24 million metric tons of carbon dioxide. By 2010 emissions had risen to 453.87 million metric tons. (Source: EIA)

Brazil is party to the following treaties: Antarctic-Environmental Protocol, Antarctic-Marine Living Resources, Antarctic Seals, Antarctic Treaty, Biodiversity, Climate Change, Climate Change-Kyoto Protocol, Desertification, Endangered Species, Environmental Modification, Hazardous Wastes, Law of the Sea, Marine Dumping, Ozone Layer Protection, Ship Pollution, Tropical Timber 83, Tropical Timber 94, Wetlands, and Whaling.

SPACE PROGRAMME

Brazil's National Policy on the Development of Space Activities focuses on the development of space-related systems - such as the ECCO communications satellites - that can be used for commercial reasons. The Brazilian Congress approved the creation, as a civil agency, of the Brazilian Space Agency in February 1994. The Brazilian Space Agency currently co-ordinates the Alcantara Launch Center (CLA) and the Barreira do Inferno Launch Center. It also manages the Aeronautics and Space Institute. Brazil launched its first space rocket in October 2004.
Brazilian Space Agency, URL: http://www.aeb.gov.br/

BRUNEI DARUSSALAM

State of Brunei Darussalam

Negara Brunei Darussalam

Capital: Bandar Seri Begawan (Population estimate: 64,000)

Head of State: His Majesty Sir Hassanal Bolkiah (Sovereign) (page 1532)

Crown Prince: His Majesty Prince Al-Muhtadee Billah

National Flag: Yellow, with two diagonal stripes, white and black, extending from the upper hoist to the lower fly; in the centre the State crest of flag, Royal Umbrella, wing of feathers, a crescent above a scroll and is flanked by two upraised hands

CONSTITUTION AND GOVERNMENT

Constitution

Brunei assumed its full international responsibility as a Sovereign and Independent State in January 1984, having been a British protected state since the late nineteenth century.

The constitution, set up in 1959, provided for a Privy Council, a Council of Ministers, a Legislative Council, a Religious Council and a Council of Succession. Parliament consisted of 33 members, 16 of whom were directly-elected. However, the elected body was disbanded in 1962 by the present Sultan's father after voters backed the left-wing Brunei People's Party. He declared a state of emergency that is still in place. Subsequent demands for greater democracy and the abolition of the monarchy were rejected and the armed revolt that followed was crushed with British military help.

The seat of Government is in Bandar Seri Begawan. The supreme executive authority of the State is vested in the Sultan; the underpinning political philosophy is that of a 'Malay Muslim Monarchy'. The Sultan is also Prime Minister and Minister of Defence. In September 2004, a Parliament of 21 appointed MPs was re-opened after twenty years of suspension and the Sultan signed a constitutional amendment allowing for the election of 15 members of the next parliament. Elections have not yet been called.

To consult the constitution, please visit:
http://www.agc.gov.bn/agc1/images/LOB/cons_doc/constitution_i.pdf.

Recent Events

In 2005, the Sultan took steps towards reform when he reshuffled the cabinet, introducing younger members with more private sector experience. He also removed the conservative Education Minister, who wanted to expand the religious curriculum. In August 2005, the National Development Party was registered as a political party.

In February 2007, Brunei, Indonesia and Malaysia, signed the Rainforest Declaration; the agreement promised to conserve a large area of Borneo which is home to some rare species.

The former finance minister and Sultan's brother, Prince Jefri Bolkiah, lost an appeal at Brunei's highest court in November, and was ordered to return property, cash and luxury goods allegedly acquired through misappropriated state funds, and in June 2008, a UK judge issued a warrant for his arrest when he failed to attend a court hearing regarding the return of the missing funds.

In December 2007, Amnesty international criticised Brunei's corporal punishment laws, reporting that 68 foreigners had been flogged over the year for immigration offences.

In December 2010 Brunei and Malaysia agreed to develop two oil areas off Borneo together, this brought about the end of a border dispute that had been going on for seven years.

Legislature
The legislature consists of the Council of Cabinet Ministers, the Religious Council, and the Privy Council.

> **Cabinet (as at June 2013)**
>
> *Sultan, Prime Minister, Minister of Defence and Minister of Finance:* HM Sultan Haji Hassanal Bolkiah Mu'izzaddin Waddulah Ibni Al-Marhum Sultan Haji Dmar 'Ali Saifuddien Sa'adul Khairi Waddien (page 1532)
> *Minister of Foreign Affairs:* HRH Prince Mohamed Bolkiah, Duli Yang Teramat Mulia Paduka Seri Pengiran Perdana Waziz Sahibul Himmah Wal-Waqar Pengiran Muda
> *Minister of Home Affairs:* Pehin Ustaz Badaruddin bin Pengarah Othman
> *Minister of Education:* Pehin Dato Abu Bakar bin Haji Apong
> *Minister of Industry and Primary Resources:* Pehin Dato Yahya bin Begawan Mudim Bakar
> *Minister of Religious Affairs:* Pehin Dato Mohammad bin Abd Rahman
> *Minister of Development:* Pehin Dato Suyoi bin Osman
> *Minister of Culture, Youth and Sports:* Pehin Dato Hazair bin Abdullah
> *Minister of Communications:* Pehin Dato Abdullah bin Begawan Bakar
> *Minister of Health:* Pehin Dato Adanan Yussof
> *Minister of Energy:* Pehin Dato Mohammad Yasmin bin Umar
> *Second Minister of Finance:* Pehin Dato Haji Awang Abd. Rahman bin Haji Ibrahim
> *Second Minister of Foreign Affairs:* Pehin Dato Lim Jock Seng

Ministries
Prime Minister's Office, Istana Nurul Iman, BA1000, Bandar Seri Begawan, Brunei Darussalam. Tel: +673 222 9988, fax: +673 224 1717, e-mail: PRO@jpm.gov.bn, URL: http://www.pmo.gov.bn/
Ministry of Communications, Old Airport, Berakas, 1150 Bandar Seri Begawan, Brunei Darussalam. Tel: +673 238 3838, fax: +673 238 0127, URL: http://www.mincom.gov.bn
Ministry of Culture, Youth and Sports, Jalan Residency, 1200 Bandar Seri Begawan, Brunei Darussalam. Tel: +673 224 0585, fax: +673 224 1620, URL: http://www.kkbs.gov.bn

BRUNEI DARUSSALAM

Ministry of Defence, Bolkiah Garrison, 1100, Bandar Seri Begawan, Brunei Darussalam. Tel: +673 223 0130, fax: +673 223 0110, URL: http://www.mindef.gov.bn

Ministry of Development, Old Airport, Berakas, 1190, Bandar Seri Begawan, Brunei Darussalam. Tel: +673 224 1911, URL: http://www.mod.gov.bn

Ministry of Education, Old Airport, Berakas, 1170 Bandar Seri Begawan, Brunei Darussalam. Tel: +673 224 4233, fax: +673 224 0980, URL: http://www.moe.gov.bn/

Ministry of Finance, 1130 Bandar Seri Begawan, Brunei Darussalam. Tel: +673 224 2405, fax: +673 224 1829, URL: http://www.finance.gov.bn

Ministry of Foreign Affairs, Jalan Subok, 1120 Bandar Seri Begawan, Brunei Darussalam. Tel: +673 224 1177, fax: +673 222 4709, URL: http://www.mfa.gov.bn

Ministry of Health, Old Airport, Berakas, 1210 Bandar Seri Begawan, Brunei Darussalam. Tel: +673 222 6640, fax: +673 224 0980, URL: http://www.moh.gov.bn

Ministry of Home Affairs, 1140, Bandar Seri Begawan, Brunei Darussalam. Tel: +673 222 3225, fax: +673 224 1247, URL: http://www.home-affairs.gov.bn/

Ministry of Industry and Primary Resources, Old Airport, Berakas 1220, Bandar Seri Begawan, Brunei Darussalam. Tel: +673 238 2822, fax: +673 238 3811, URL: http://www.industry.gov.bn/

Ministry of Law, Bandar Seri Begawan 1160, Brunei Darussalam. Tel: +673 222 4872, URL: http://www.judicial.gov.bn/

Ministry of Religious Affairs, 1180, Bandar Seri Begawan, Brunei Darussalam. Tel: +673 224 2565, fax: +673 238 2330, URL: http://www.religious-affairs.gov.bn/

Political Parties
There are three parties, but they play little role in the day to-day life of the country and are not elected.
Brunei National Solidarity Party (BNSP)
National Development Party
Brunei People's Awareness Party

Diplomatic Representation
Embassy of Brunei Darussalam, 3520 International Court, NW, Washington DC 20008, USA. Tel: +1 202 237 1838, fax: +1 202 885 0560, e-mail: info@bruneiembassy.org, URL: http://www.bruneiembassy.org/
Ambassador: H.E. Dato Yusoff Abdul Hamid
High Commission of Brunei Darussalam, 19-20 Belgrave Square, London, SW1X 8PG, UK. Tel +44 (0)20 7581 0521, fax: +44 (0)20 7235 9717, e-mail: bruhighcomlondon@hotmail.com, URL: http://bdhcl.ashtron.com/en
High Commissioner: H.E. Mohd. Aziyan bin Abdullah
British High Commission, 2.01, 2nd Floor, Block D, Kompleks Yayasan Sultan Haji Hassanal Bolkiah, Bandar Seri Begawan BS 8711, Brunei Darussalam. (Postal address: PO Box 2197, Bandar Seri Begawan 8674, Brunei Darussalam.) Tel: +673 (0)2 222231, fax: +673 (0)2 234315, e-mail: brithc@brunet.bn, URL: http://ukinbrunei.fco.gov.uk/en
High Commissioner: Robert Fenn (page 1424)
Embassy of the United States of America, 3rd Floor, Teck Guan Plaza, Jalan Sultan, Bandar Seri Begawan 2085, Brunei Darussalam. Tel: +673 (0)2 3339670, fax: +673 (0)2 2225293, e-mail: amembassy_bsb@state.gov, URL: http://brunei.usembassy.gov
Ambassador: Daniel Shields
Permanent Representative of Brunei Darussalam to the United Nations, 771 First Avenue, New York, NY 10017, USA. Telephone: +1 212 697 3465, fax: +1 212 697 9889, e-mail: info@bruneimission-ny.org., URL: http://www.un.int/wcm/content/site/brunei
Permanent Representative: Emran Bahar

LEGAL SYSTEM

Brunei's legal system is based on the Indian penal code and English Common Law, with an independent judiciary, a corpus of written common law judgements and statutes and legislation enacted by the Sultan. The judicial system consists of three courts: the Supreme Court, the Intermediate Court, and the Subordinate Courts (Magistrates Courts). Decisions of the High Court can be taken to the Court of Appeal, presided over by the president and two commissioners appointed by the Sultan. The Supreme Court consists of the High Court and the Court of Appeal.Appeals in civil cases can still be made to the Judicial Committee of the English Privy Council and the final Court for Brunei. Matters relating to Islamic Law are dealt with by the Islamic Courts.

The sultan maintains control over the security forces. There are limits on freedom of speech, press and assembly, as well as restrictions on religious freedom. Citizens of Brunei cannot change their government. Brunei Darussalam retains the death penalty for ordinary crimes such as murder, but no executions have been carried out since before 1999.

Supreme Court of Brunei Darussalam, URL: http://www.judicial.gov.bn:81/
Chief Justice of the Supreme Court: Dato Seri Paduka Mohammed Saied

LOCAL GOVERNMENT

For administrative purposes Brunei Darussalam is divided into four regions: Brunei/Muara, Belait, Tutong, and Temburong. All districts are represented by District Officers, who are responsible to the Prime Minister and Home Minister. Bandar Seri Begawan is the capital of Brunei Darussalam with an area of about 16 sq. km.

AREA AND POPULATION

Area
Brunei is situated on the north-west coast of Borneo and borders Sarawa, a Malaysian state. The country has an area of 5,769 sq. km. The western part of Brunei Darussalam is characterised by hilly lowlands of below 91 metres rising to 300 metres in the hinterland.

The eastern part of the state consists of rugged mountain terrain, rising 1,850 metres above sea level. Brunei Darussalam has an equatorial climate, with high temperatures, high humidity and heavy rainfall.

To view a map of Brunei Darussalam, please consult:
http://www.lib.utexas.edu/maps/cia08/brunei_sm_2008.gif

Population
The population in 2010 was estimated at 399,000 (compared to 390,000 in July 2007), with an annual growth rate of 2.0 per cent. Population density is around 68 people per sq. km, though 76 per cent of the people live in urban areas. The Brunei/Muara District has the largest share of the population (247,200 inhabitants in 2003), followed by Belait (59,600) and Tutong (41,600). Temburong has the smallest population (9,400 inhabitants).

Around 68 per cent of the population is aged between 15 and 64 years, with 26 per cent aged up to 15 years, and 6 per cent aged 60 years and over. The population is made up mainly of Malays (approximately 73 per cent), as well as Chinese (15 per cent) and other races (12 per cent).

The official language is Malay, but English is widely spoken and used in education.

Births, Marriages, Deaths
The birth rate per 1,000 of the population has fallen in recent years, from 24 in 1997 to 19.2 in 2010. The death rate per 1,000 of the population has risen from 3.0 in 1997 to 3.5 in 2010. Average life expectancy at birth in 2009 was 76.5 years (76 years for males and 77 years for females). Healthy life expectancy was estimated to be 66 years. The infant mortality rate in the same year was 6 deaths per 1,000 live births. The total fertility rate was estimated to be 2.0 children per female. (Source: http://www.who.int, World Health Statistics 2012)

Public Holidays 2014
1 January: New Year's Day
14 January: Birth of the Prophet*
31 January: Chinese New Year**
23 February: National Day
31 May: Anniversary of Royal Brunei Regiment
29 June: Ramadan begins*
15 July: Sultan's Birthday
29 July: Eid Al Fitr, Ramadan ends*
25 December: Christmas Day
* Islamic holidays: may vary from the dates given
** First moon of the lunar calendar

EMPLOYMENT

Brunei's total labour force was estimated to be around 180,000 in 2006, with an unemployment rate of four per cent. Foreign workers make up a significant proportion of Brunei's labour force, numbering up to 100,000 people, despite the fact that work permits are issued for short periods and have to be regularly renewed. Estimated figures for 2008 put the workforce at 188,800, with unemployment running at 3.7 per cent.

Over half of Brunei Darussalam's labour force are civil servants; around 40 per cent work in construction and the oil and gas production industry, and 10 per cent in agriculture, forestry and fishing.

Employment by economic activity in 2001

Sector	No. of employees
Agriculture, hunting and forestry	1,518
Fishing	476
Mining and quarrying	3,954
Manufacturing	12,455
Electricity, gas and water supply	2,639
Construction	12,301
Wholesale and retail trade; Repair of motor vehicles and personal and household goods	12,931
Hotels and restaurants	7,107
Transport, storage and communications	4,803
Financial services, real estate, renting & business activities	819
Public administration and defence; compulsory social security, education, social work, other	79,880

Source: Copyright © International Labour Organization (ILO Dept. of Statistics, http://laborsta.ilo.org)

BANKING AND FINANCE

Currency
Brunei dollar (B$) = 100 cents.

GDP/GNP, Inflation, National Debt
Brunei is the third largest oil producer in south east Asia and its economy is largely based on exports of crude oil and natural gas, which together account for around 50 per cent of GDP, 90 per cent of exports, and 80 per cent of government revenues.

Brunei is attempting to diversify the economy away from its heavy dependence on the oil and gas sectors. The Brunei Economic Development Board was set up in 2002 to identify suitable industrial projects such as petrochemicals, oil refining, and aluminum smelting, and the country is marketing its eco-tourism, as well as attracting the luxury tourist market. Other non-petroleum industries include agriculture, forestry, fishing, aquaculture, and banking. A the planning stage are a power plant in the Sungai Liang region to power a proposed aluminum smelting plant and a giant container hub at the Muara Port facilities. The government has announced plans for Brunei to become an international offshore financial centre and a centre for Islamic banking, and is looking into the possibility of establishing a 'cyber park' to develop an information technology industry.

GDP by industrial origin at current market prices (Million Brunei Dollars)

	2008	2009	2010
	20,398	15,611	16,867
Agriculture	130	142	128
Mining	11,672	7,390	8,572
Manufacturing	2,796	2,181	2,036
Electricity, gas and water	115	122	132
Construction	534	518	524
Trade	558	591	623
Transport and communications	534	556	576
Finance	593	574	583
Public Administration	2,152	2,190	2,313
Others	1,314	1,348	1,381

Source: Asian Development Bank

Foreign Investment
The government of Brunei actively encourages foreign investment, with plans to diversify the economy into areas such as communications technology, financial services, and oil refining. Taking advantage of the country's location, there are plans to make the country a major shipping hub. New business enterprises that fulfill certain criteria are relieved of income tax on profits for up to five years. Personal income tax and capital gains tax are not levied. FDI was estimated to be US$3235 million in 2009.

Balance of Payments / Imports and Exports
Merchandise export revenue in 2010 was estimated at US$9,340 million, whilst import costs were US$2,456 million. The merchandise trade balance in 2010 was an estimated US$6884 million.

Export commodities are mainly crude oil, natural gas and refined products. Main export partners are Japan (US$3,732 million), Indonesia, Korea, Australia and India. Main suppliers include Singapore, Malaysia, China and Japan. (Source: Asian Development Bank, ABD)

Chambers of Commerce
National Chamber of Commerce and Industry of Brunei Darussalam, URL: http://www.nccibd.com/

MANUFACTURING, MINING AND SERVICES

Primary and Extractive Industries
Brunei has extensive reserves of oil and natural gas. Commercial oil production began in 1929, with offshore production of oil and gas following in 1963. Brunei Darussalam is the third largest oil producer in Southeast Asia and the fourth largest producer of liquefied natural gas in the world. Revenues from the sector account for around 50 per cent of gross domestic product (GDP), around 90 per cent of merchandise exports, and 80 per cent of government revenues. The main oil export destinations are the ASEAN nations, Japan, South Korea, Taiwan, and the United States.

Brunei had proven oil reserves of 1.1 billion barrels at the beginning of January 2011. In order to prolong hydrocarbon reserves, the government controls oil production levels. Deep-sea exploration in 2004 and 2005 by Brunei Shell Petroleum has yielded new oil finds of an 100 million barrels of recoverable reserves. Estimated oil production was 150,100 barrels per day in 2011, 123,900 barrels per day of which was crude oil. Brunei has just one refinery, with a capacity of 9,000 barrels per day. This meets 50 per cent of Brunei's domestic petroleum product requirements, and the country imports small amounts of petroleum products from neighboring countries to meet domestic demand. Oil consumption in 2011 was an estimated 17,000 barrels per day, and the remaining crude oil was exported to other countries in the region.

Brunei Shell Petroleum, a joint venture in which the Brunei government and Royal Dutch/Shell both have a 50 per cent share, is responsible for the production and processing of oil, gas and petrochemical products. Brunei has an outstanding territorial dispute with neighbouring Malaysia over the deep-sea acreage that includes blocks J and K off the coast of Borneo. In 2003, Murphy Oil (U.S.) and Petronas (Malaysia) discovered a large oil field which may extend into Block J. Brunei is counting on Blocks J and K to maintain the country's oil and gas output another decade or more. Malaysian officials have offered to devise a joint-development zone with Brunei, but this would necessitate Brunei redrawing its contracts with Shell, Conoco, and Mitsubishi. In March 2004 Shell Malaysia announced a new oil discovery at Gumusut, near the disputed territory. The status of oil development in these disputed areas remains unresolved, despite talks between the heads of state in 2006.

Proven natural gas reserves were estimated at 14 trillion cubic feet at the beginning of January 2011. Production of natural gas was 417 billion cubic feet in 2011, with consumption at 105 billion cubic feet. Brunei exported 357 Bcf of Liquified Natural Gas in 2004; Japan imported around 88 per cent and South Korea bought the remaining 12 per cent. (Source: EIA)

Energy
Total energy consumption in 2009 was estimated at 0.126 quadrillion Btus. Fuel share of energy consumption in 2004 was as follows: natural gas, 73.9 per cent; oil, 26.1 per cent.

Electric generation capacity was 0.7 gigawatts in 2010, and production in the same year was 3.6 billion kilowatthours. Brunei's power demand is growing at a rapid rate of 7 to10 per cent annually; consumption reached 3.2 billion kilowatthours in 2010.

Manufacturing
Brunei's industry sector contributes about 45 per cent of GDP, according to 2001 estimates. Industries include petroleum production and refining, liquified natural gas, and construction. The government is encouraging foreign investment in manufacturing industry, in order to diversify the economy. It is targetting areas such as communications technology, petrochemicals and oil refining. A 500-megawatt power plant, a new jetty and a container port in the Sungai Liang area are planned, to help establish new industries. Manufacturing that currently exists include food and beverage processing, cement, and garments. Future projects include furniture manufacture, ceramic tiles, chemicals and glass.

Service Industries
The services sector accounts for half of Brunei's GDP and the civil service employs around 50 per cent of the labour force. The government is hoping to diversify into areas such as tourism and financial services, as well as taking advantage of Brunei's important location (linking the Indian and Pacific oceans) to become a major shipping centre.

Agriculture
Just 2 per cent of the land in Brunei is used for arable farming, and 1 per cent for pasture. Most of the arable land is not irrigated. Brunei's agriculture is primarily based on small units, cultivating rice, vegetables, tropical fruits and field crops. In 2004 there were 6,000 head of cattle and buffalo, and around 5,000 head of goats and sheep (Source: FAO Statistical Year Book 2005-2006)

The government assists farmers with re-stocking and veterinary services. Despite these measures, Brunei needs to import about 80 per cent of its food requirements. The government owns a ranch in Australia, which assists in meeting the country's beef requirements. Poultry and eggs are reared locally, but most food requirements are met through imports.

Agricultural Production 2010

Produce	Int $'000*	Tonnes
Indigenous chicken meat	20,044	14,072
Hen eggs, in shell	5,818	7,015
Fruit fresh nes	1,815	5,200
Vegetables fresh nes	773	4,100
Leguminous vegetables, nes	481	1,400
Indigenous cattle meat	462	171
Indigenous duck meat	445	270
Cucumbers and gherkins	397	2,000
Indigenous buffalo meat	388	144
Pineapples	285	1,000
Cassava	282	2,700
Rice, paddy	265	1,072

*unofficial figures
Source: http://faostat.fao.org/site/339/default.aspx Food and Agriculture Organization of the United Nations, Food and Agricultural commodities production

More than two thirds of Brunei is covered by tropical forests with fruit yielding plants. Logging is controlled by the Forestry Department, as are exports of wood. Efforts are now underway to promote value added activities such as furniture production.

Fishing
Although fishing was a traditional form of livelihood for a long time, the industry declined dramatically since the increase in oil prices in the 1970s. A Fisheries Department was created to revitalise the industry but in 1995 the industry contributed only 0.2 per cent of national GDP. More recently, the government has begun to promote the industry, as part of the strategy to diversify the economy and a 200-nautical mile fisheries limit is now in existence. FAO figures for 2010 put the total catch at 2,272 tonnes.

COMMUNICATIONS AND TRANSPORT

Travel Requirements
US, Canadian, Australian and EU citizens require a passport valid for at least six months from date of departure and a return ticket in the case of visa-free trips. Visitors must show sufficient funds to support themselves whilst in the country. British passport holders and EU citizens do not require a visa for visits of up to 30 days. Australians are advised to get a visa before arrival; Canadians can stay up to 14 days without a visa, whilst US citizens can stay for up to 90 days. Israelis may not be granted entry to Brunei. Nationals not referred to above are advised to contact the embassy to check visa requirements.

As of June 12, 2004, immigration offenses are punishable by caning. Workers who overstay their visas can face jail sentences and three strokes of the cane. Those associated with violators, such as contractors or employers, are subject to the same penalties if found guilty.

National Airlines
Royal Brunei Airlines, PO Box 737, Bandar Seri Begawan 1907, Negara, Darussalam, Brunei. Tel: +673 (0)2 240 500, fax: +673 (0)2 244737

International Airports
Brunei International Airport handles 1.5 million passengers per year.

Roads
There are some 3,650 km of roads in Brunei, 2,819 km paved with a permanent road surface. Vehicles are driven on the left.

BULGARIA

Shipping
The Brunei, Belait and Tutong rivers play an important role in maintaining communications with inland areas. Regular freight services are operated to Singapore, Malaysia, Hong Kong, Thailand, Taiwan, the Philippines and Indonesia from the country's two main ports at Muara and Kuala Belait. Water taxis are also available.

Ports and Harbours
The ports of Muara, Bandar Seri Begawan, and Kuala Belait provide shipping facilities for the entire region.

HEALTH

Oil revenues have allowed Brunei to build up one of the most comprehensive welfare systems in the world. The government provides for all medical services and subsidizes food and housing. The health service is free for citizens of Brunei, with a nominal charge for permanent residents, foreign citizens and their dependants. Health care consists of a three-tier system, with health clinics providing primary care, health centres secondary care, and district hospitals tertiary and specialised care. Total expenditure on health in 2009 was 3.0 per cent of GDP, equating to US$833 per capita. Government expenditure makes up 85.2 per cent of the total expenditure on health and represents 7.5 per cent of its total expenditure.

In 2005-10, there were 564 doctors (14.2 per 10,000 population), 1,941 nurses and midwives (48.8 per 10,000 population), and 65 dentists (2 per 10,000 population). There are an estimated 30 hospital beds per 10,000 population.

Malaria has been eradicated in the country, and cholera has almost disappeared. There were no reported cases of either disease in 2010.

In 2010, the infant mortality rate (probability of dying by age one) was 6 deaths per 1,000 live births. The under-fives mortality rate was 7 per 1,000 population. The main causes of death were 29 per cent congenital abnormalities, 25 per cent prematurity and 4 per cent birth asphyxia. (Source: http://www.who.int, World Health Statistics 2012)

EDUCATION

Overall responsibility for primary and secondary education, adult education, teacher training and higher education lies with the Ministry of Education.

Education is free from the age of five for children who are citizens and lasts nine years. There are 122 kindergarten and primary schools and 50 secondary schools. Higher education is provided by the University of Brunei Darussalam. Whilst most of Brunei's college students go abroad to finish their education, over 3,000 attend the University of Brunei. Other institutions at tertiary level include eight technical and vocational colleges, three institutes and a teacher training college.

Religious education in schools is compulsory for every Muslim child.

Some 50 per cent of children were enrolled in nursery schools in 2007. Figures from the same year show that 93 per cent of girls and 93 per cent of boys were enrolled in primary school. For students of secondary school age the enrolment figures were 91 per cent of girls and 87 per cent of boys. An estimated 15 per cent of students of the relevant age studied at tertiary

level within Brunei in 2005, though others went abroad to study for a degree. In primary education, the pupil/teacher ratio was 13:1, and 100 per cent of pupils continued to grade 5. Ninety per cent of pupils went from primary to secondary school.

In 2005, 9.1 per cent of total government spending went on education. The adult literacy rate was estimated to be 92.7 per cent in 2001, rising to 98.9 per cent among the youth. These figures are above the regional average in 2005 of 91.7 (Source: UNESCO, UIS, October 2007)

RELIGION

Islam is the official religion of Brunei Darussalam with around 58 per cent of the population being followers and the Sultan is the head of the Islamic faith in the country. Other faiths practiced include Christianity (14 per cent) and Buddhism (9 per cent).

Brunei has a religious liberty rating of 3 on a scale of 1 to 10 (10 is most freedom). (Source: World Religion Database)

COMMUNICATIONS AND MEDIA

Freedom of expression does not exist in Brunei. The royal family owns or controls much of the media. Political and religious self-censorship is also prevalent.

Newspapers
Main newspapers are:
The Borneo Bulletin (daily) also covering Sabah and Sarawak, in English. URL: http://www.brunei-online.com/bb/
Media Permata (daily), issued in Malay.

Broadcasting
Radio Television Brunei (URL: http://www.rtb.gov.bn/) is state controlled. Foreign TV is available via cable.

Telecommunications
Brunei has a sophisticated telephone network which includes the use of two satellite stations. Direct telephone links to remote areas are available through microwave and solar-powered telephones. According to 2008 estimates there are some 76,000 telephone main lines, with 375,000 mobile phones. Internet users numbered an estimated 320,600 in 2010.

ENVIRONMENT

In 2010 Brunei's emissions from the consumption of fossil fuels totalled 8.27 million metric tons of carbon dioxide. The industrial sector generates the greatest proportion of carbon emissions, followed by the commercial, transport and residential sectors. (Source: EIA)

Brunei is affected by seasonal smoke emanating from forest fires in Indonesia. In 2007, Brunei, signed a "Rainforest Declaration", with Indonesia and Malaysia, agreeing to conserve a large area of Borneo that is home to rare species.

Brunei is a party to the following environmental agreements: Biodiversity, Climate Change, Desertification, Endangered Species, Hazardous Wastes, Law of the Sea, Ozone Layer Protection, and Ship Pollution. Brunei is not a signatory to the Kyoto Protocol.

BULGARIA
Republic of Bulgaria
Republika Bulgaria

Capital: Sofia (Population estimate: 1.2 million)

Head of State: Rosen Plevneliev (President) (page 1496)

Vice President: Margarita Popova (page 1497)

National Flag: A tricolour fesswise, white, green and red

CONSTITUTION AND GOVERNMENT

Constitution
Germany invaded Bulgaria during World War II and Soviet troops invaded in 1944. In 1946 a referendum abolished the monarchy. The Communists assumed power in Bulgaria after the Second World War and were ousted in 1989. Within a few months the pre-war parties were reinstituted and new ones set up. In the elections for a Grand National Assembly held in June 1990 the Bulgarian Socialist Party (formerly the Communist Party) won 53 per cent of the seats against 36 per cent for the UDF. The Republic of Bulgaria now has a parliamentary system of government. The people exercise their power directly through political parties and through bodies established by the constitution, passed in July 1991.

This constitution is the supreme law of the Republic of Bulgaria and its provisions apply directly. The power of the state is clearly divided between the three branches - legislative, executive and judicial. The Head of State is the president. He is elected directly by the people

for five years and is eligible for re-election only once. The president is the supreme commander-in-chief of the armed forces. He schedules the elections, promulgates laws, appoints and dismisses ambassadors and permanent representatives to international organisations. The president, after consulting parliamentary groups, appoints the prime minister from the party holding the majority in Parliament. In international affairs the president personifies the state, concludes treaties, and has the power to declare war and make peace.

To consult the full constitution, please visit: http://www.parliament.bg/?page=const&lng=en

International Relations
Bulgaria became a member of NATO in March 2004 and has since sent troops to Afghanistan and Iraq. In October 2004 the European Community said that Bulgaria would be able to join the EU on 1 January 2007, but made it clear that it still had some concerns in the areas of human rights, justice, agriculture and aviation safety. Bulgaria is a member of the World Trade Organisation.

Recent Events
In June 2001, the last king of Bulgaria, former King Simeon Saxe-Coburg-Gotha who had reigned from 1943-46, was elected to the post of prime minister when his party, National Movement Simeon II, won parliamentary elections. His party lost the next election in 2001 as the people felt the reforms he had promised were not happening fast enough.

In April 2004, Bulgaria signed the EU accession treaty.

In December 2006, five Bulgarian medics were found guilty in Libya of deliberately infecting children with the HIV, and given death sentences. Bulgarian officials condemned the sentences by a Libyan court. The medics were returned to Bulgaria in the summer of 2007, and pardoned by their government.

In January 2007, Bulgaria joined the European Union and held its first European parliament elections in May.

In July 2008 the European Commission suspends EU aid worth hundreds of millions of euros following criticism of the Bulgarian government over its failure to tackle corruption and organised crime. In September the Commission permanently took away half of the aid frozen in July.

In January 2009 Bulgaria suffered a severe gas shortage as the energy dispute between Russian and Ukraine resulted in supplies being cut.

In September 2010 the EU called on Bulgaria to take action on tackling crime and corruption. In December both France and Germany blocked Bulgaria from joining the Schengen passport-free zone as they felt the country still had to work on the fight against corruption and organised crime.

In February 2013, 14 people were injured during clashes with police at anti austerity protests leading to the resignation of Prime Minister Borisov.

Legislature

Bulgaria has a unicameral legislature, The National Assembly is the supreme legislative authority. Its 240 members are elected for four years. General elections by secret ballot are held within two months from the expiry of the preceding Parliament. The Council of Ministers is in charge of implementing the state's domestic and foreign policy. The functions of the cabinet also include managing the budget and state's assets, the determination of economic policy, and coordination of ministries, departments and other offices of state. The Council of Ministers is free to ask for the National Assembly's vote of confidence and resigns if it fails to receive it. In 2009 some changes were made to how the National Assembly is elected. 31 of the MPs are elected by majority vote and 209 by proportionate vote, the electorate select candidates from party or coalition lists in each of the twenty-eight administrative divisions. A party or coalition must receive at least four per cent of the national vote to enter parliament.

Narodno Sobraniye (National Assembly), Narodno Sobranie Square, 1169 Sofia, Bulgaria. Tel: +359 2 93939, URL: http://www.parliament.bg
Chairman: Tsetska Tsacheva Dangovska

Cabinet (as at June 2013)

Prime Minister: Pamen Oresharski (page 1490)
Deputy Prime Minister, Minister in charage of EU funds, Minister of Justice: Zinaida Zlatanova (page 1543)
Minister of the Interior: Prof. Tsvetlin Yovchev
Minister of Foreign Affairs: Kristian Vigenin (page 1531)
Minister of Labour and Social Affairs: Hassan Ademov
Minister of Economy and Energy: Dragomir Stoynev
Minister of Agriculture and Food: Dimitar Grekov
Minister of Education and Science: Aneliya Klisarova
Minister of Health: Tanya Lyubomirova-Raynova
Minister of the Environment and Water: Iskra Mihaylova-Koparova
Minister of Defence: Angel Naydenov
Minister of Transport, Information Technology and Communications: Daniel Papazoff
Minister of Regional Development: Desislava Terzieva
Minister of Culture: Dr Petar Stojanovic
Minister of Youth and Sport: Mariana Georgieva

Ministries

Office of the President, 2 Boulevard Knjaz Dondukov, 1123 Sofia, Bulgaria. Tel: +359 (0)2 83839, fax: +359 (0)2 980 4484, e-mail: press@president.bg, URL: http://www.president.bg/

Office of the Prime Minister, 1 Boulevard Knjaz Dondukov, 1194 Sofia, Bulgaria. Tel: +359 (0)2 8501, fax: +359 (0)2 981 8170, e-mail: primeminister@gov.bg, URL: http://www.government.bg

Ministry of State Administration, Boulevard Knjaz Dondukov, 1194 Sofia, Bulgaria.

Ministry of Regional Development and Public Works, 17-19 Sts. Kiril and Metodii St., 1202 Sofia, Bulgaria. Tel: +359 (0)2 94059, fax: +359 (0)2 987 5856, e-mail: press@mrrb.government.bg, URL: http://www.mrrb.government.bg/

Ministry of Education and Science, 2A Boulevard Knjaz Dondukov, 1000 Sofia, Bulgaria. Tel: +359 (0)2 988 2693, fax: +359 (0)2 988 3693, e-mail: press_mon@minedu.government.bg, URL: http://www.minedu.government.bg/

Ministry of Foreign Affairs, 2 Aleksander Zhendov St., 1113 Sofia, Bulgaria. Tel: +359 (0)2 737987, fax: +359 (0)2 703041, e-mail: iprd@mfa.government.bg, URL: http://www.mfa.government.bg/

Ministry of Finance, 102 G.S. Rakovski St., 1000 Sofia, Bulgaria. Tel: +359 (0)2 9859 2024, fax: +359 (0)2 980 6863, e-mail: feedback@minfin.government.bg, URL: http://www.minfin.bg

Ministry of the Interior, 29 Shesti Septemvri St., PO Box 192, 1000 Sofia, Bulgaria. Tel: +359 (0)2 987 7511, fax: +359 (0)2 824047, e-mail: office@mvr.bg, URL: http://www.mvr.bg/

Ministry of Defence, 1 Aksakov St., 1000 Sofia, Bulgaria. Tel: +359 (0)2 9220 922, fax: +359 (0)2 873228, e-mail: reforma_BA@md.government.bg, URL: http://www.md.government.bg/

Ministry of Justice, 1 Slavjaska St., 1000 Sofia, Bulgaria. Tel: +359 (0)2 867 3274, fax: +359 (0)2 981 9157, e-mail: pr@mjeli.government.bg, URL: http://www.mjeli.government.bg/

Ministry of Transport and Communications, 9 Diakon Ignatiy St, 1000 Sofia, Bulgaria. Tel: +359 (0)2 9409 500 / 764, fax: +359 (0)2 987 18 05, e-mail: press@mtc.government.bg, URL: http://www.mtc.government.bg

Ministry of Agriculture and Forestry, 55 Hristo Botev Boulevard, 1040 Sofia, Bulgaria. Tel: +359 (0)2 985 11255, fax: +359 (0)2 980 6256, e-mail: press@mzgar.government.bg, URL: http://www.mzgar.government.bg/

Ministry of Labour and Social Policy, 2 Triaditza St., 1051 Sofia, Bulgaria. Tel: +359 (0)2 91408, fax: +359 (0)2 988 4405 / 986 1318, e-mail: mlsp@mlsp.government.bg, URL: http://www.mlsp.government.bg/

Ministry of Health, 5 Sveta Nedelj St., 1000 Sofia, Bulgaria. Tel: +359 (0)2 981 1830, fax: +359 (0)2 981 2639, URL: http://www.mh.government.bg/

Ministry of the Environment and Water, 67 William Gladstone St., 1000 Sofia, Bulgaria. Tel: +359 (0)2 940 6222, fax: +359 (0)2 986 25 33, e-mail: feedback@moew.government.bg, URL: http://www.moew.government.bg/

Ministry of Culture, 17 Alexander Stamboliiski Boulevard, 1000 Sofia, Bulgaria. Tel: +359 (0)2 980 6191, fax: +359 (0)2 981 8559, e-mail: press.culture@bta.bg

Ministry of Economy, 8 Slavianska St., 1000 Sofia, Bulgaria. Tel: +359 (0)2 940 7638, fax: +359 (0)2 988 5532, e-mail: public@mi.government.bg, URL: http://www.mi.government.bg/

Ministry of Energy and Energy Resources, 8 Triaditza str., 1040 Sofia, Bulgaria. Tel: +359 (0)2 987 8425 / 549 0325, fax: +359 (0)2 986 5703 / 987 84 25, e-mail: pressall@doe.bg, URL: http://www.doe.bg/cgi-bin/i.pl

Political Parties

Bulgarska Sotsialisticheska Partija (BSP, Bulgarian Socialist Party), 20 Positano St., POB 382, 1000 Sofia, Bulgaria. Tel: +359 (0)2 881951, fax: +359 (0)2 871292, URL: http://www.bsp.bg
Chairman: Sergei Stanishev

Natsionalen sayuz Ataka (National Union Attack), URL: http://www.ataka.bg
Leader: Volen Siderov

Grazhdani za Evropeysko Razvitie na Balgariya (Citizens for European Development of Bulgaria), URL: http://www.gerb.bg
Leader: Boyko Borisov

Demokrati za silna Bulgaria (Democrats for a Strong Bulgaria), URL: http://www.dsb.bg
Leader: Ivan Kostov

Dvizhenie za Prava i Svobodi (Movement for Rights and Freedoms), URL: http://www.dps.bg
Leader: Ahmed Dogan

Red, Zakonnost, Spravedlivost, (Order, Law and Justice), URL: http://www.rzs.bg
Leader: Yane Yanev

Sayuz na Demokratichnite Sili (Union of Democratic Forces), URL: http://www.sds.bg
Leader: Martin Dimitrov

Elections

The penultimate general election took place in June 2005. The Coalition for Bulgaria led by the Bulgaria's Socialist Party (BSP) won 31 per cent of the vote and its leader Sergei Stanishev tried to form a coalition with the liberal Turkish Movement for Rights and Freedoms, (MRF) but this was defeated by parliament. President Parvanov approached the NMS to try to form a government, but this too ended in failure. In August Sergey Stanishev finally became prime minister after agreeing a coalition government of his BSP party, the NMSII and the ethnic Turkish Movement for Rights and Freedoms party, (MRF).

Parliamentary elections last took place on the 5th July 2009. The centre-right opposition party, the Citizens for European Development of Bulgaria (Gerb) won by a wide margin with 116 seats, but it was five seats short of a majority. The party, led by Boiko Borisov, the mayor of Sofia, promised to end corruption and tackle the economic crisis. Mr Borisov formed a coalition with small right-wing parties.

The most recent parliamentary elections took place in May 2013. Although the ruling Citizens for European Development of Bulgaria (CEDB) remained the largest party with 98 seats it did not win a majority; the Bulgarian Socialist Party (BSP), won 86 seats, the Movement for Rights and Freedoms (MRF), won 33 seats and Attack won 23 seats. The CEDB failed to form a coalition government and so the BSP was passed the mandate and a coalition was formed between the BSP and the MRF.

The most recent presidential election was held in November 2011, Rosen Plevneliev was elected to the post.

Diplomatic Representation

Bulgarian Embassy, 1621 22nd Street, NW, Washington DC 20008, USA. Tel: +1 202 387 0174, fax: +1 202 234 7973, e-mail: office@bulgaria-embassy.org, URL: http://www.bulgaria-embassy.org
Ambassador: Elena Poptodorova

Bulgarian Embassy, 186-188 Queen's Gate, London SW7 5HL, United Kingdom. Tel: +44 (0)20 7584 9400, fax: +44 (0)20 7584 4948, URL: http://www.bulgarianembassy-london.org
Ambassador: Konstantin Stefanov Dimitrov

British Embassy, 9 Moskovska Street, Sofia, Bulgaria. Tel: +359 (0)2 933 9222, fax: +359 (0)2 933 9219, e-mail: britembinf@mail.orbitel.bg, URL: http://ukinbulgaria.fco.gov.uk/en
Ambassador: Jonathan Allen

US Embassy, 16 Kozyak Street, 1407 Sofia, Bulgaria. Tel: +359 (0)2 980 5241, fax: +359 (0)2 981 8977, e-mail: irc@usembassy.bg, URL: http://bulgaria.usembassy.gov
Ambassador:

Permanent Mission to the UN in New York: URL: http://www.mfa.bg/new-york-un
Ambassador: Rayko Raytchev

BULGARIA

LEGAL SYSTEM

The Bulgarian legal system became independent from the government following the 1991 reform of the Constitution. There were further reforms in 1994 and 2003. The judicial system consists of regional, district and appeal courts. The Supreme Court of Cassation and the Supreme Administrative Court are the highest courts of appeals. There is a military court system for military matters.

The Supreme Judicial Council is the administrative body of the Judiciary. It is composed of 25 members, 11 of whom are elected within the Judiciary, 11 by the National Assembly, and three are the presidents of SCC, of SAC and the Chief Prosecutor. The Constitutional Court determines if laws and international agreements are in compliance with the Constitution. It consists of 12 judges.

Jurors are elected at local government elections. The Prosecutor General and judges are elected by the Supreme Judicial Council, established in 1992.

The government generally respects the human rights of its citizens. However, there are harsh conditions in prisons, and there have been cases of arbitrary arrest and detention, and of police abuse of pretrial detainees and prison inmates. There is widespread corruption in the executive, legislative, and judicial branches of government. There is discrimination against minority groups. Capital punishment was abolished in 1999.

Supreme Administrative Council: http://www.sac.government.bg/
Constitutional Court, URL: http://www.constcourt.bg/
Ombudsman of the Republic of Bulgaria, URL: http://www.anticorruption.bg/ombudsman/

LOCAL GOVERNMENT

Bulgaria is divided into 28 regions and 264 municipalities. The regions are administrative units used to implement government regional policy and are managed by a governor appointed by the Council of Ministers. Municipalities are run by mayors and have independent budgets.

The 28 regions are Sofia (capital), Sofia region, Burgas, Varna, Plovdiv, Russe, Haskovo, Lovetch, Montana, Sliven, Yambol, Dobritch, Silistra, Shumen, Gabrovo, Pleven, Vidin, Vratza, Veliko Tarnovo, Pazardjik, Smolian, Razgrad, Targovishte, Blagoevgrad, Pernik, Kardjali, Kjustendil and Stara Zagora.

The most recent local elections were held in October 2011.

AREA AND POPULATION

Area
Bulgaria is situated in the south-east of Europe and is bordered by Romania, Serbia, Greece, the former Yugoslav republic of Macedonia, Turkey and the Black Sea. The country's total area is 110,993.6 sq. km. Bulgaria is a mountainous country with lowlands in the north and south east. It has three main rivers the Danube, Maritsa, and Strouma.

The climate is temperate with cold, damp winters and hot, dry summers.

To view a map, please http://www.lib.utexas.edu/maps/cia08/bulgaria_sm_2008.gif

Population
Its population was estimated in 2010 to be 7,494,000 with an annual population growth rate of -0.7 over the period of 2000-10. Around 71 per cent of the population lived in urban areas. 85.6 per cent of the population are Bulgarian and 9.5 per cent are Turkish with minority races including Gypsy, Armenian, Jewish, Wallach, Tartar, Greek and Russian. The largest city is Sofia, with a population of 1,200,000. This is followed by Plovdir, with 368,500, and Varna with 350,000. The official language is Bulgarian, written in the Cyrillic script.

Births, Marriages, Deaths
The population growth for Bulgaria is in the negative as indicated by the following birth and death rates. Between the years 1991-95 the birth rate averaged 9.9 per cent compared to an average death rate of 13.02 per cent. During the years 1996-2000 the average birth rate was 8.4 per cent and the average death rate was 14.14 per cent. In order for the population to remain stable Bulgaria would need a birth rate of 2.2 but in 2009 it was 1.4. The fall in population growth is exacerbated by the amount of people particularly the younger generation leaving to find work abroad and this migration of workers was expected to get bigger after Bulgaria joined the EU in 2007. In 2010, the crude birth rate was put at 10.1 per 1000 population and the crude death rate was 14.4 per 1,000 population.

In 2010, the median age was 42 years. An estimated 24 per cent of the population were aged over 60 years and 14 per cent aged less than 15 years.

The average life expectancy is 70 years for men and 77 years for women. Healthy life expectancy is 63 years for males and 69 years for females. (Source: http://www.who.int, World Health Statistics 2012)

Public Holidays 2014
1 January: New Year's Day
7 January: Orthodox Christmas
3 March: National Day
18 April: Orthodox Good Friday
21 April: Easter Monday
1 May: Labour Day
6 May: Army Day
24 May: St Cyril and Methodius Day/Education Day/Culture Day

6 September: Reunification of Bulgaria
22 September: Independence Day
1 November: Leaders of Bulgarian National Revival Day
24-26 December: Christmas Holiday

EMPLOYMENT

Employees by economic activity groupings, 2008

Activity	Employees
Agriculture, hunting, forestry & fishing	268,600
Mining & quarrying	36,100
Manufacturing	798,700
Electricity, gas & water supply	43,000
Construction	355,900
Wholesale & retail trade and repairs	546,700
Accomodation & food service activities	178,100
Transport, storage & communications	193,800
Financial & insurance activities	58,000
Real estate, renting & business activities	141,600
Information & communications	73,500
Professional, scientific & technical activities	85,000
Public admin. & defence, compulsory social security	243,000
Health & social work	161,800
Admin, & support service activities	81,000
Education	211,000
Arts, entertainment & recreation	44,900
Other service activities	44,700
Activities of households as employers	7,600
Activities of extraterritorial organisations & bodies	1,100
Other	67,000

Source: Copyright © International Labour Organization (ILO Dept. of Statistics, http://laborsta.ilo.org)

Figures for 2006 put unemployment at 9.0 per cent down from 10.1 per cent in 2005. It fell to an estimated 6 per cent in 2008. Estimated figures for 2010 put the workforce at 2,499,000, with an unemployment rate of 9.5 per cent. Figures for 2011 estimated the workforce to be 2,530,000 with an unemployment rate of 8.8 per cent. An estimated 6 per cent of the population exist on less than US$2 a day.

BANKING AND FINANCE

GDP/GNP, Inflation, National Debt
One lev = 100 stotinki.
In July 1999 a new lev was introduced. The new lev has the value of 1,000 old lev. Currently the lev is pegged to the Euro at a rate of €1 = BGN1.955

GDP/GNP, Inflation, National Debt
Bulgaria's transition to a market economy after communism has not been straightforward, not helped by periods of political instability. Following an economic crisis in 1996 where the country suffered from hyperinflation and economy collapsed, the government stabilized the economy with the help of a programme initiated by the World Bank and the IMF in March 1997. In 1998 GDP was US$11.6 billion, rising to US$13.8 billion in 1999 and growth was approximately 5 per cent in 2000. In August 2001 the new government under King Simeon II announced plans to reform the economy. The reforms included raising the minimum wage and a system of interest free loans to stimulate private enterprise. Bulgaria signed an EU accession treaty in 2005 and joined in 2007. In 2008, the EU said it was suspending aid worth thousands of euros after it found that the Bulgarian government had failed to tackle corruption. Some of the aid was later permanently withdrawn. Bulgaria has pledged to tackle the problem.

Bulgaria has enjoyed an extended period of growth in recent years, driven by exports and Foreign Direct Investment as well as an increase in domestic spending but foreign investments have fallen with the global economic crisis and domestic spending has also weakened. An estimated 60 per cent of Bulgaria's exports go to the eurozone and this market has been adversely affected by the global economic crisis. By 2010, GDP was estimated at €47 billion with a growth rate of 0.2 per cent. GDP grew by an estimated 1 per cent in 2011 and was estimated to be US$52 billion in 2011. Per capita GDP was estimated to €6,522. Due to the economic crisis, growth is expected to fall to 0.5 per cent in 2012 before rising in 2013.

In 2011 services contributed 64 per cent to GDP, industry 31 per cent and agriculture 5.0 per cent.

Inflation fell from 22.3 per cent in 1998 to 11.4 per cent in 1999, and was forecast between 5 and 7 per cent for 2001. From 2003 onwards there has been an upward trend to inflation. In 2007 it reached an estimated 11.5 per cent, 2008, 7.1 per cent before falling to 1.5 per cent in 2009. Inflation was estimated at 4.4 per cent in 2010.

Public debt was estimated to be 16.5 per cent of GDP in 2011.

Foreign Investment
Six Duty-Free Zones have been established since 1987, each located at points strategic to international markets; the ports of Vidin and Rouse on the Danube, Dragoman near the Serbian border, Svilengrad near the Turkish border, Plovdir (the second largest city in the country) and Bourgas, adjacent to the largest Bulgarian port on the Black Sea. These zones have attracted such foreign companies as Plexus, Hyundai and Groupe Schneider.

igures for 2004 show an increase in direct foreign investment to US$2.4 billion since when nvestment has remained high and has become one of the driving forces behind the growing conomy; figures for 2006 put foreign direct investment at €4.1 billion, the highest in Central nd Eastern Europe.

oreign reserves were estimated to be US$17 billion in 2011.

Balance of Payments / Imports and Exports

here has been a change in Bulgaria's trading patterns in recent years; markets in the former oviet Union have collapsed and imports from countries from the former COMECON bloc ave had to be paid for with hard currency rather than by a process of barter. More than 50 er cent of Bulgaria's exports now go to European Community countries. The main market or Bulgarian exports is Turkey (11.5 per cent), followed by Germany, Italy, Greece, Belgium nd Romania. The main country for imports is Russia (12.5 per cent), followed by Germany, taly, Ukraine, Turkey, Greece, Romania and Austria. Main exported goods are raw materials, netals, clothing and footwear, and consumer goods. Estimated figures for 2010 show that xports earned €15.5 billion and imports cost €18.7 billion.

Central Bank

Bulgarska Narodna Banka (Bulgarian National Bank), 1 Alexander Battenberg q, 1000 Sofia, Bulgaria. Tel: +359 (0)2 91459, fax: +359 (0)2 980 2425 / (0)2 980 6493, -mail: press_office@bnbank.org, URL: http://www.bnb.bg
Governor: Ivan Iskrov

Chambers of Commerce and Trade Organisations

Bulgarian Chamber of Commerce and Industry (BCCI), URL: http://www.bcci.bg
American Chamber of Commerce in Bulgaria, URL: http://amcham.bg/

MANUFACTURING, MINING AND SERVICES

Primary and Extractive Industries

errous metallurgy has been developing in recent decades, mostly on imported ores because roduction of home-mined ferrous ore is insignificant. Arasel-Medet Inc. of Pirdup, in south entral Bulgaria, is the country's biggest non-ferrous metallurgical reserve. Arasel-Medet as an annual capacity of 7.5 million tonnes of copper ore. The transition to a market economy nd ecological issues were among the reasons for a fundamental re-consideration of the ountry's metallurgical sector from 1990 onwards. Recent figures show that ferrous metallurgy ccounted for 6.2 per cent of industrial output, while non-ferrous metallurgy accounted for .8 per cent of industrial output.

igures for 2011 show that Bulgaria had proven reserves of 20 million barrels of oil, and roduced 1,000 barrels per day while consuming 134,000 barrels per day. Since 1994 foreign ompanies have been granted permission to perform research into the availability of oil and as in the Black Sea continental shelf, although these are estimated to be limited. In 2010, ulgaria consumed 90 billion cubic feet of natural gas, all of which was imported. It has stimated gas reserves of 210 billion cubic feet. In 2012 Bulgaria banned exploratory drilling or shale gas using the extracation method called 'fracking', a system which used induced ydraulic fracturing to extract hydrocarbons.

ecent figures estimate that Bulgaria has coal reserves of approximately 2,400 million short ons. In 2010, Bulgaria produced 32.3 million short tons and consumed 35.6 million short ons, mainly anthracite for use in her power stations. Net coal imports were 102.6 trillion tu.

nergy

ne adverse effects of the Gulf crisis on Bulgaria's energy sector as well as repeated droughts nd mismanagement, contributed to a severe energy crisis in the winter of 1990-91 which esulted in drastic cuts in electricity supply and heating.

here have been a number of ventures and donations involving foreign companies and overnments in recent years. Under an agreement with the IMF the state electricity company NEK was split into separate units to deal with power generation, transmission and distribution. he electricity sector is being opened up to private investors and joint ventures are being set p to refurbish generating plants with foreign companies. Many plants operate at a loss and he plan is to increase prices to cover costs. In 1999 the US power plant developer AES nnounced plans to build a US$750 million plant which will supply 10 per cent of Bulgaria's lectricity. In 2011 the partnership announced they were to build a second wind power park o be situated in the northeast of the country.

ecent figures show that just over 40 per cent of Bulgaria's electricity is generated from uclear power. There were six reactors at the Kozloduy nuclear power installation on the anube near the border with Romania. As part of its accession agreements to join the EU, ulgaria agreed to close four of the six reactors by 2006 and in return received EU funding o upgrade the remaining two and compensation for the loss of electricity exports from the lant. The plant was of a similar design to that at Chernobyl in the Ukraine. In January 2005 ulgaria announced plans to open a new nuclear power plant at Belene but this plan was crapped and instead a thermal powerplant was built on the site instead.

otal primary energy production in 2009 was 0.396 quadrillion Btu and consumption was .746 quadrillion Btu.

Manufacturing

ndustry accounts for around 31 per cent of GDP and the growth rate of industrial production was put at 1.5 per cent in 2008. The chemical sector remains Bulgaria's largest industrial ector, producing plastics, paints, detergents, perfumes and pharmaceuticals. It accounts for 1.6 per cent of industrial output and 19.4 per cent of export revenue. The food processing, everages and tobacco industry is second in the manufacturing sector and accounts for 18.4 er cent of output and 16.1 per cent of exports. The main areas are meat processing, dairy,

canning, sugar, vegetable oils, wine, brewing, fish, milling and tobacco. The next largest sector is mechanical engineering which provides 13.8 per cent of output in a number of areas including machine-tools, forklifts, tractors, harvesters, buses, ship-building and cars.

Service Industries

Figures for 2000 show that there were 2,354,000 tourists visiting Bulgaria - this figure had risen to 5,158,000 in 2006, generating tourism receipts of US$3.3 million.

Agriculture

Bulgaria possesses very fertile soil and a favourable climate. However agriculture in Bulgaria has been until recently neglected and often mismanaged; previously existing cooperative farms were amalgamated to form largely ineffective agro-industrial complexes. Investments in industry were given priority over agriculture, although this sector is now considered to be a priority target. Foreign investors are being encouraged to buy land and the government is investing in the dairy sector to create modern dairy farms. The government also wants producers and processors to improve their standards to EU requirements.

Agricultural Production in 2010

Produce	Int. $'000*	Tonnes
Wheat	492,136	3,994,900
Sunflower seed	353,960	1,506,120
Cow milk, whole, fresh	294,930	1,124,360
Maize	199,257	2,044,100
Anise, badian, fennel, corian	193,453	35,000
Indigenous chicken meat	158,081	110,980
Rapeseed	151,685	544,800
Grapes	131,585	230,198
Indigenous pigmeat	106,400	69,215
Hen eggs, in shell	74,035	89,264
Barley	71,763	833,300
Indigenous cattle meat	67,507	24,990

*unofficial figures
Source: http://faostat.fao.org/site/339/default.aspx Food and Agriculture Organization of the United Nations, Food and Agricultural commodities production

COMMUNICATIONS AND TRANSPORT

Travel Requirements

Citizens of the USA, Canada, Australia and the EU (apart from those with a National Identity Card) require a passport valid for at least three months. EU members do not require a visa for stays of up to 90 days. Bulgaria is a member of the Schengen Agreement but has not yet fully implemented it. US, Canadian and Australian citizens do need a visa. Possession of a return ticket and sufficient funds for the length of the visit are required. Nationals not referred to above are advised to contact the embassy to visa requirements.

International Airports

Bulgaria has four international airports at Sofia, Varna, Bourgas, Plovdiv and Gorna Oryahovitsa Airport in Northern Bulgaria.

National Airlines

Bulgaria Air is the main air carrier serving Bulgaria. The foreign lines from Sofia include those to Athens, Istanbul, Damascus, Beirut, Baghdad, Cairo, Khartoum, Amsterdam, Bengazi, Berlin, Brussels, Vienna, Copenhagen, London, Moscow, Paris, Rome, and Luanda.

Bulgaria Air, Sofia Airport, Sofia 1540, Bulgaria. Tel: +359 (0)2 881800 / 652997, fax: +359 (0)2 791206 / 652997, URL: http://www.air.bg

Railways

The principal railways are: Dragoman - Svilengrad (part of the international railway Munich - Istanbul); Sofia - Varna; Rousse - Podkova; Sofia - Kulata (Sofia - Aegean line); Voluyak - Gyueshevo; Mezdra - Vidin; Plovdiv - Bourgas; Rousse - Kaspitchan. BDZ, the Bulgarian State Railways Company has been restructured. A rail link is due to start construction in 2013 between Bulgaria and Macedonia. International rail links exist to many cities Kiev, Istanbul and Vienna. The total distance of rail track in Bulgaria is around 4,150 km. with 245 km of narrow gauge. Sofia has a small city centre based subway system that was expanded in 2012 and now covers 20.5 km servicing 16 stations.
Bulgarian State Railways, URL: http://www.bdz.bg

Roads

There is a programme of improvements to the national road network, the Trans-European Motorway (TEM) and a ring road around the Black Sea coast. Total distance covered by the road system is around 40,230 km. used by 1.8 million cars. Vehicles are driven on the right. Sofia has a tram system.

Ports and Harbours

The main seaports are Varna and Bourgas and the main ports on the river Danube are Rousse and Lom.

HEALTH

Health care is provided by the state and is free of charge. Private health care also exists. Total expenditure on health was 7.2 per cent of GDP in 2009. Per capita total expenditure on health was US$463. Government expenditure on health accounts for 55.4 per cent of total expenditure on health. Expenditure on health accounts for 9.8 per cent of government expenditure.

BURKINA FASO

In 2005-10 there were an estimated 27,988 doctors (37.3 per 10,000 population), 35,250 nurses and midwives (47 per 10,000 population) and 6,493 dentists (8.7 per 10,000 population). In 2005-11 there were an estimated 66 hospital beds per 10,000 population.

In 2010 there were 22,004 reported cases of measles, 317 of mumps, and 2,412 of TB. In 2010, the infant mortality rate (probability of dying by age 1) was 11 per live births. The under-fives mortality rate was 13 per 1,000 cases. The main causes of death were pneumonia 24 per cent, prematurity 21 per cent, congenital abnormalities 19 per cent, and birth asphyxsia 11 per cent. Approximately 1 per cent of deaths were caused by diarrhoea. (Source: http://www.who.int, World Health Statistics 2012)

EDUCATION

Education at all levels is entirely free and run by the state. It is compulsory for children from 7 to 16. The first private schools were opened in 1991. Higher education is provided at the Universities of Sofia, Plovdiv, Veliko Turnovo and Varna, and at 14 regionally distributed colleges. An American University was also opened in the town of Blagoevgrad. Recent figures show that there are 3,889 schools, 110,541 teachers and a total of 1,403,892 students.

In 2007 an estimated 81 per cent of children are enrolled in pre-primary school and 94 per cent of girls and 95 per cent of boys were enrolled. Approximately 2 per cent of children have to repeat a year. The pupil to teacher ratio is estimated at 16:1. The transition to secondary school is approximately 96 per cent. Enrolment in secondary school for 2007 was estimated at 87 per cent of girls and 89 per cent of boys. An estimated 46 per cent of the population of tertiary age are in tertiary education.

In 2006 11.6 per cent of government spending was allocated to education, of which 16 per cent on tertiary education, 46 per cent was on secondary education, 20 per cent on primary education and 8 per cent on pre-primary education.

The literacy rate for adults is estimated at 98.3 per cent. The youth literacy rate is 97.6 per cent. (Source: UNESCO)

RELIGION

The majority of the believers in the country belong to the Eastern Orthodox Church (83 per cent). Of the smaller religious communities the largest is the Muslim community (12 per cent). There are also Roman Catholics, Protestants, Jews and Armenian Gregorians.

Bulgaria has a religious liberty rating of 4 on a scale of 1 to 10 (10 is most freedom). (Source: World Religion Database)

COMMUNICATIONS AND MEDIA

Newspapers
Freedom of the press is guaranteed under the constitution although there are allegations of threats from both organised crime and political circles. There are more than a hundred different newspapers and magazines at present in the country. Some of the larger ones are

24 Chasa, Daily, URL: http://www.24chasa.bg
Trud, Daily, URL: http://www.trud.bg/
Dnevnik, Daily, URL: http://news.dnevnik.bg
Telegraf, Daily, URL: http://telegraf.bg
Standart, Daily, URL: http://www.standartnews.com

Broadcasting
The public broadcaster is Bulgarian National Television (URL: http://www.bnt.bg). The first national commercial channel was bTV (URL: http://www.btv.bg) and in 2003 a second national commercial TV licence was awarded to Nova TV (URL: http://ntv.bg). The public radio broadcaster is Bulgarian National Radio (URL: http://www.bnr.bg). Darik Radio is a private national broadcaster. Both BNT and BNG have been granted independence from the state. Global media conglomerates have bought into the Bulgarian media market.

Telecommunications
The antiquated telecommunications system which dated from the Soviet times is being improved with a modern digital trunk line now connecting most regions. There were an estimated 2.3 million landlines in use in 2010. The number of mobile phones exceeds that of landlines: as of 2010 there were an estimated 10.6 million mobile phones in use. By 2008 over 3.3 million people were regular internet users.

ENVIRONMENT

Main environmental concerns are river pollution, particularly from heavy metals and detergents, air pollution from industry, and soil contamination, again from heavy metals. Forests are also being damaged by acid rain.

In 2010, Bulgaria's emissions from the consumption of fossil fuels totalled 42.17 million metric tons of carbon dioxide. (Source: EIA)

Bulgaria is a party to the following international agreements: Air Pollution, Air Pollution-Nitrogen Oxides, Air Pollution-Persistent Organic Pollutants, Air Pollution-Sulfur 85, Air Pollution-Sulfur 94, Air Pollution-Volatile Organic Compounds, Antarctic-Environmental Protocol, Antarctic-Marine Living Resources, Antarctic Treaty, Biodiversity, Climate Change, Climate Change-Kyoto Protocol, Desertification, Endangered Species, Environmental Modification, Hazardous Wastes, Law of the Sea, Marine Dumping, Ozone Layer Protection, Ship Pollution, and Wetlands.

SPACE PROGRAMME

Bulgaria has observer status at the European Space Agency.

BURKINA FASO

République Démocratique du Burkina Faso

Capital: Ouagadougou (Population estimate: 1,000,000)

Head of State: Captain Blaise Compaoré (President) (page 1408)

National Flag: Equal stripes of red and olive green, with red at top. Five pointed star in centre.

CONSTITUTION AND GOVERNMENT

Constitution
The former French colony of Upper Volta (a territory of Afrique Occidentale Française) became independent in August 1960 as the Republic of Upper Volta. Its name was changed to Burkina Faso in August 1984. Since independence the country has had a number of military governments.

In 1991 a referendum adopted a new constitution by which an elected president holds executive power with an elected government. In 1997 the constitution was amended to allow the president to hold power for more than two terms. In April 2000 parliament voted to fix the presidential mandate to five years, with a maximum of two terms.

To consult the constitution (in French), please visit:
http://www.legiburkina.bf/codes/constitution_du_burkina_faso.htm

International Relations
Relations with Cote d'Ivoire have been problematic since 2000 when there were claims that President Compaore supported the rebels. However mediation headed by President Comapore led to the Ouagadougou Accords. Since 2002, many of the 2 million Burkinabe nationals who worked in Cote d'Ivoire have returned home, adding to unemployment. Burkina Faso has strong links with Libya. France is its main western ally and trading partner.

Recent Events
In September 2009 Burkina Faso was hit by the worst floods for nearly 100 years, the area around the capital Ouagadougou was the worst hit with 150,000 people made homeless. An estimated 30cm of rain fell in 10 hours washing away homes, roads, bridges and an electrical plant.

In January 2011 a new government was announced which included a minister for political reforms, it was expected that this new ministry would look into lifting the limit on the terms the president can serve.

In April 2011, thousands of people took to the streets to protest over rising food prices, also that month soldiers and presidential guards mutinied over unpaid allowances. In response the president sacked the prime minister, reshuffled the cabinet and appointed new governors to its 13 states. In July, it detained the alleged ringleaders of several recent mutinies and dismissed some soldiers. The National Assembly also dissolved the National Electoral Commission so that a new chairman could be appointed in preparation for the legislative and municipal elections.

In November 2012, President Compaore acted as a regional mediator to try to resolve the crisis in Mali.

The ruling party won December's legislative elections.

Legislature
The legislature has two chambers. The lower chamber, the Assemblée Nationale (National Assembly), has 111 members, directly elected for a five-year term. The upper chamber, the Chambre des Représentants (House of Representatives), has 178 members who serve a three-year term. The members may be directly or indirectly elected by provincial councils or interest groups. It is a consultative body. The judiciary is independent.

Assemblée Nationale, 554 blvd de l'Independance, 01 B.P. 6482 Ouagadougou 01, Burkina Faso. Tel: +226 50 31 44 49, fax: +226) 50 31 45 90, e-mail: an@assembly.gov.bf, URL: http://www.an.bf
President: Roch Marc Christian Kabore

Ministries

Presidency, BP 7030, Ouagadougou, Burkina Faso. URL: http://www.presidence.bf
Office of the Prime Minister, BP 7027, Ouagadougou, Burkina Faso. Tel: +226 5032 7889, fax: +226 5031 4761, URL: http://www.primature.gov.bf/republic/fgouvernement.htm
Ministry of Agriculture and Water Resources, 03 B.P. 705, Ouagadougou 03, Burkina Faso. Tel: +226 324114, URL: http://www.agriculture.gov.bf
Ministry of Animal Resources, URL: http://www.mra.gov.bf
Ministry of Basic Education and Literacy, 03 B.P. 732, Ouagadougou 03, Burkina Faso. Tel: +226 306600, URL: http://www.meba.gov.bf
Ministry of Civil Service and Institutional Development, 03 B.P. 7006, Ouagadougou 03, Burkina Faso. Tel: +226 308285, URL: http://www.fonction-publique.gov.bf/
Ministry of Commerce, Industry and Handicrafts, 01 B.P 514, Ouagadougou 01, Burkina Faso. Tel: +226 314493, URL: http://www.commerce.gov.bf
Ministry of Culture, Arts and Tourism, 03 B.P. 7007, Ouagadougou 03, Burkina Faso. Tel: +226 330963, fax: +226 330964, e-mail: webmestre-culture@liptinfor.bf, URL: http://www.culture.gov.bt
Ministry of Defence, B.P. 496, Ouagadougou 01, Burkina Faso. Tel +226 307214 fax: +226 313610, URL: http://www.defense.gov.bf/
Ministry of Economy and Development, 01 B.P. 3924, Ouagadougou 01, Burkina Faso. Tel +226 324190, fax +226 310086, URL: http://www.medev.gov.bf/
Ministry of Employment, Works and Youth, 0 B.P. 7016, Ouagadougou 01, Burkina Faso. Tel: +226 308568, e-mail: zephirin.kiendrebeog@delgi.gov.bf, URL: http://www.emploi.gov.bf
Ministry of Energy and Mines, 01 BP 604, Ouagadougou 01, Burkina Faso. Tel: +226 318429, URL: http://www.mines.gov.bf
Ministry of the Environment and Quality of Life, B.P. 7044, Ouagadougou, Burkina Faso. Tel +226 324094, URL: http://www.environnement.gov.bf
Ministry of Finance and Budget, URL: http://www.finances.gov.bf/
Ministry of Foreign Affairs & Regional Co-operation, Rue N. 988, Boulevard du Faso, 03 B.P. 7038, Ouagadougou 03, Burkina Faso. Tel: +226 324736, fax: +226 308792, URL: http://www.mae.gov.bf/
Ministry of Health, 03 BP 7009, Ouagadougou, Burkina Faso. +226 324159, URL: http://www.sante.gov.bf
Ministry for Human Rights, URL: http://www.mpdh.gov.bf
Ministry of Information, 03 B.P. 7045, Ouagadougou 03, Burkina Faso. Tel: +226 314572, URL: http://www.information.gov.bf
Ministry of Infrastructure, Transport and Housing, 03 BP 7011, Ouagadougou 03, Burkina Faso. Tel: +226 324905, URL: http://www.mith.gov.bf
Ministry of Justice and Keeper of the Seals, 01 B.P. 526, Ouagadougou 01, Burkina Faso. Tel: +226 324833, e-mail: sepdh.cabinet@justice.gov.bf, URL: http://www.justice.gov.bf
Ministry of Parliament Relations, 03 B.P. 2097, Ouagadougou 03, Burkina Faso. Tel: +226 324070, URL: http://www.mrp.gov.bf
Ministry of Posts and Telecommunication, 03 B.P. 7045, Ouagadougou 03, Burkina Faso. Tel: 226 324833, URL: http://www.mpt.bf
Ministry of Promotion of Women, URL: http://www.mpf.gov.bf
Ministry of Secondary and Higher Education and Scientific Research, 03 B.P. 7130, Ouagadougou 03, Burkina Faso. Tel: +226 324868 / 324552, URL: http://www.messrs.gov.bf

Ministry of Social Action and National Solidarity, 01 B.P. 515, Ouagadougou 01, Burkina Faso. Tel: +226 306875, e-mail: webmaster@delgi.gov.bf, URL: http://www.action-sociale.gov.bf
Ministry of Sport and Leisure, 03 B.P. 7035, Ouagadougou 03, Burkina Faso. Tel: +226 324795, URL: http://www.sports.gov.bf
Ministry of Territorial Administration and Decentralisation, 03 B.P. 7034, Ouagadougou 03, Burkina Faso. Tel: +226 324778, URL: http://www.matd.gov.bf/

Elections

Presidential elections were held in November 2005. Thirteen candidates took part. The incumbent, Blaise Compaoré, won a third term with over 80 per cent of the vote. His closest rival was Bénéwené Sankara who took 4.88 per cent of the vote. In the previous elections in 1988 the opposition boycotted the election. The most recent presidential election took place in November 2010. President Compaore won another term in office.

In April 2009 parliament passed a law which states that henceforth at least 30 per cent of candidates put forward for election must be women. The most recent parliamentary elections were held on 2 December 2012. The ruling Congress for Democracy and Progress won most seats. Provisional results suggested the party had taken at least 70 of the 127 seats. The opposition has alleged fraud.

Political Parties

The main political parties are:
Alliance for Democracy and Federation - African Democratic Rally (ADF-RDA); Congress for Democracy and Progress (CDP); Union for the Republic (UPR).

Diplomatic Representation

Embassy of the USA, 602 Avenue Raoul Follerau, 01 BP 35, Ouagadougou, Burkina Faso. Tel: +226 306723, fax: +226 303890, e-mail: amembouaga@state.gov, URL: http://ouagadougou.usembassy.gov
Ambassador: Thomas Dougherty
British Embassy (all staff reside at Accra), Ambassador: Peter Jones (page 1451)
French Embassy, 33 rue Yalgado Ouedraogo, BP 504, Ouagadougou 01, Burkina Faso. E-mail: ambassade@ambafrance-bf.org, URL: http://www.ambafrance-bf.org
Embassy of Burkina Faso, 2340 Massachusetts Avenue NW, Washington DC 20008, USA. Tel: +1 202 332 5577, fax: +1 202 667 1882, e-mail: ambawdc@verizon.net, URL: http://burkina-usa.org
Ambassador: Seydou Bouda
Embassy of the Republic of Burkina Faso to UK, 16 Place Guy d'Arezzo, 1180 Brussels, Belgium, Tel: +32 345 99 12, fax: +32 345 06 12, e-mail: ambassade.burkina@skynet.be, URL: http://www.ambassadeduburkina.be/
Ambassador: Frederic Assomption Korsaga

LEGAL SYSTEM

Civilian courts replaced revolutionary tribunals in 1993. The legal system is based on French civil law system and customary law. The judicial and administrative jurisdictions are as follows: The Supreme Court of Appeals (Cour de cassation) is the highest court in judicial terms; the Council of State (Conseil d'Etat) is the highest jurisdiction on administrative matters; the Court of Accounts (la Cour des comptes) is the highest jurisdiction when it comes to controlling public finances. There are also tribunals for children and labour tribunals.

There is also a Constitutional Court, whose president is nominated by the state president.

There have been recent reports of security forces using of excessive force against civilians. Arbitrary arrest and detention are widespread, and prison conditions are harsh. The judiciary is regarded as inefficient and lacking in independence, and there is official corruption. Burkina Faso retains the death penalty for ordinary crimes such as murder but no-one is reported to have been executed since before 1999. Three people were reported to have been sentenced to death in 2012.

Conseil Constitutionel (Constitutional Court): URL: http://www.conseil-constitutionnel.gov.bf
La Cour de Cassation (Court of Appeal), URL: http://www.cour-cassation.gov.bf
Le Conseil d'Etat (Council of State), URL: http://www.conseil-etat.gov.bf
La Cour des Comptes (Government Audit Office), URL: http://www.cour-comptes.gov.bf

LOCAL GOVERNMENT

For local administration Burkina Faso is divided into 13 regions and 45 provinces with a High Commissioner for each one.

The provinces are: Bale, Bam, Banwa, Bazega, Bougouriba, Boulgou, Boulkiemde, Comoe, Ganzourgou, Gnagna, Gourma, Houet, Ioba, Kadiogo, Kenedougou, Komondjari, Kompienga, Kossi, Koulpelogo, Kouritenga, Kourweogo, Leraba, Loroum, Mouhoum, Namentenga, Nahouri, Nayaa, Noumbiel, Oubritenga, Oudalan, Passore, Oni, Sanguie, Sanmatenga, Seno, Sissili, Soum, Sourou, Tapoa, Tuy, Yagha, Yatenga, Ziro, Zondonma, Zoundweogo.

351 communes or departments come under prefect administration, arrondissements and communes have mayors, and the 8,228 villages and sectors have delegates. The most recent local government elections took place in 2006. The CDP party won almost two-thirds of the seats. Local elections are due in May 2012.

BURKINA FASO

AREA AND POPULATION

Area
Burkina Faso is a landlocked west African state to the north of the Côte d'Ivoire, Ghana, Togo and Benin, and bordered on the north by Mali and Niger. The area is 274,200 sq. km. Most of the country is arid with poor soil. The land is generally flat, leading to undulating plains and hills in the southeast and west. The climate ranges from dry Sahel in the north to tropical savannah in the south.

To view a map, consult: http://www.un.org/Depts/Cartographic/map/profile/burkina.pdf

Population
In 2010 the population estimate was 16,469 million (compared to 14.74 million in 2007) with a density of 49 inhabitants per sq. km. The annual population growth rate was 2.9 per cent over the period 2000-10. Approximately 74 per cent of the population live in rural areas, although migration to urban areas is put at 8 per cent. The working population is 4.6 million. The principal cities are the capital, Ouagadougou (population: 1 million), Bobo-Dioulasso (450,000), Koudougou (90,000) and Ouahigouya. The official language is French but local languages are also spoken including Moré, Fulfuldé and Dioula.

The main ethnic groups are the Mossi (48.6 per cent), the Peul (7.8 per cent), the Gourmantche (7 per cent), the Bobo (6.8 per cent), the Bisa-Samo (6.5 per cent), the Gurunsi (6 per cent), the Dagari-Lobi (4.3 per cent), the Bwa (3 per cent), the Senufo-Marka-Dioula (2.2 per cent) and others making up 7.8 per cent.

Births, Marriages and Deaths
The birth rate is 43.2 per 1,000, and the death rate 13.1 per 1,000 population. Infant and maternal mortality are both high. On average one child in nine will die before his or her first birthday. Infant mortality was 91 per 1,000 live births in 2006. The neonatal mortality rate was 38 per 1,000 live births. 2009 figures for maternal mortality show that for every 100,000 live births, 560 women died (compared to 1,000 in 2004). The total fertility rate was 5.9 live births per female.

Average life expectancy in 2009 was 49 years for males and 56 years for females. Healthy life expectancy in 2008 was 43 years. The median age is 17 years. An estimated 4 per cent of the population is over 60 years old and 45 per cent under 15 years. (Source: http://www.who.int, World Health Statistics)

Public Holidays 2014
1 January: New Year's Day
14 January: Eid-Milad Nnabi*
21 April: Easter Monday
8 May: Victory Day
1 May: Labour Day
29 May: Ascension Day
29 July: End of Ramadan*
4 August: National Day
15 October: Anniversary of the Coup d'état
5 October: Eid-ul-Adha*
25 October: El am Hejir (New Year)*
1 November: All Saints Day
11 December: Constitution Day
25 December: Christmas Day
* Islamic holidays are dependent on the sighting of the moon and can vary

EMPLOYMENT

Over 90 per cent of the population makes its living from agriculture, and over 80 per cent of the population relies on subsistence farming. 44.5 per cent of the population is below the poverty line (less than F41,099 CFA per year), and 27.8 per cent below the extreme poverty line (less than 3F1,790 CFA per year). The development of agriculture is hindered by the country's climatic conditions, including poor soil, and a poor infrastructure.

Revenue is also generated by selling cash crops such as ground nut, and from fishing and crafts. Large numbers of the working population migrate to neighbouring Côte d'Ivoire and Ghana for harvest employment.

2.1 per cent of the population works in industry and 5.5 per cent works in commerce, services or government. Recent figures show that the workforce was around 6.6 million. Estimated unemployment in 2004 was put as high as 77 per cent.

BANKING AND FINANCE

Currency
The unit of currency is the Communauté Financière Africaine (CFA) franc.
The financial centre is Ouagoudougou.

GDP/GNP, Inflation, National Debt
The economy is primarily based on agriculture and is therefore dependent on world prices and climatic variations. Poverty is severe and widespread. Problems include poor soil, climatic conditions, weak infrastructure and a low literacy rate. Conflict in Cote d'Ivoire has also adversely affected the economy as new trade routes have had to be found. Following economic reforms, the IMF has provided sustained support. There are mineral resources in the country and exploration is ongoing. This diversification should help the economy and gold has now overtaken agriculture as the main source of export revenue.

In 2009 agriculture contributed 34 per cent to GDP, industry (including mining) 26 per cent building. Service industries contributed approximately 40 per cent. In 2009 GDP was US$ billion with an annual growth rate of 3.1 per cent. Per capita GDP was estimated to be US$580 in 2009. GDP was estimated to have risen to US£10.1 billion in 2011, with per capita GDP rising to an estimated US$1,400. Despite the difficult international economic situation growth is expected to continue in the short-term with projections of 5.3 per cent in 2012 and 5.5 per cent in 2013.

Inflation was 6.5 per cent in 2005, compared to -0.2 per cent in 2000. In 2006 it was estimated to be 2.3 per cent, rising to an estimated 4 per cent in 2007. In 2008 it was estimated to be 7.3 per cent and 2.6 per cent in 2009. It is forecast to rise to 4 per cent over 2012.

In 2005 Burkina Faso was ranked 175 out of 177 for the UNDP Human Development Index. In 2002 the World Bank ranked Burkina Faso as the 13th poorest country in the world. Some socio-economic improvements have been made but severe poverty is still widespread. Following economic reforms in the 1990s the IMF has supported several programmes in the country. A three-year IMF-sponsored Poverty Reduction and Growth Facility was successfully completed in 2006. A further IMF PRGF was signed in September 2007. France is the state's largest bilateral donor. In April 2002 Burkina Faso qualified for HIPC status under the IMF-World Bank heavily indebted initiative and received US$930 million debt relief.

Balance of Payments/Imports and Exports
A slow programme of privatisation has been under way since 1998 and the government revised its investment rules in 2004 to try and attract foreign investment. Changes in legislation benefit the mining industry and by 2010, gold had overtaken agriculture as the main export. Gold mining production increased dramatically between 2009 and 2010, and further mining ventures were launched in 2011. Main imported goods included food products, petroleum and machinery and came from Côte d'Ivoire, Togo, Senegal, France and Nigeria. Estimated figures for 2010 put export earnings at US$1.5 billion and the cost of imports at US$1.7 billion.

Central Bank
Banque Centrale des Etats de l'Afrique de l'Ouest, PO Box 3108, Avenue Abdoulaye Fadiga, Dakar, Senegal. Tel: +221 8 390500, fax: +221 8 239335, e-mail: webmaster@bceao.int, URL: http://www.bceao.int
Governor: Tiémoko Meyliet Kone

Chambers of Commerce and Trade Organisations
Chamber of Commerce, Industry and Handicraft, Chambre de Commerce d'Industrie et d'Artisanat du Burkina, 01 BP 502, Ouagadougou 01, Burkina Faso. Tel: +226 3061 14 / 15, fax +226 306116, e-mail: ccia-bf@ccia.bf, URL: http://www.ccia.bf/

MANUFACTURING, MINING AND SERVICES

Primary and Extractive Industries
Burkina Faso has a limited number of mineral resources, including gold, manganese, marble, copper, nickel and limestone. In order to encourage production in this sector the government introduced in October 1997 a number of tax and customs breaks. This resulted in a rise in the number of exploration permits issued.

The gold industry is under-development and is expected to contribute significantly to export earnings in coming years. The most important gold mine is currently at Poura. Reserves are estimated at 1,600,000 tonnes. Other significant mines are Guiro and Bayildiaga. The short-term production forecast is 5-6 tonnes per year. As a result of falling gold prices the government was forced in 1999 to close down the state owned mining company Soremib. In 2006 the government awarded exploration permits to a Canadian company (Goldrush Resources). Gold production continues to increase and it is expected to become the country's second export earner (after cotton).

There are magnesium reserves at Tamboa (discovered in 1959) where mining is hampered by location. Reserves are estimated at more than 19 million tonnes with a content of 55 per cent Mn.

Energy
Burkina Faso has to import most of its energy as it has no mineral resources or refining capacity. However, a number of hydro-electric schemes are being instituted to reduce costs including schemes at Kompiega, Bagré, Comoé and Diébougou, and irrigation partnerships with the Côte d'Ivoire and Ghana. In 2009 total energy consumption was 0.20 quadrillion btu, and production was 0.001 quadrillion btu. In 2011 estimated consumption of petroleum was 9,000 thousand barrels per day, all of which was imported. In 2010, 0.67 billion kWh of electricty was generated.

Manufacturing
Manufacturing is limited and is concentrated on transformation of local materials. The sector employs two per cent of the population (13,000 employees), and contributes 27 per cent to PIB. Only one per cent is exported. Most manufacturing is concentrated in the major towns. The main manufacturing industries are textile production, mainly cotton and leather, and food processing, particularly sugar.

Agriculture
Agriculture is the main industry in Burkina Faso and makes up over 30 per cent of GDP. Over 90 per cent of the population are employed in agriculture, which makes up approximately 50 per cent of exports.

Production is dependent on the climate, and varies significantly. Droughts in recent years have had a devastating effect on the country and damaged Burkina Faso's aim to be self-sufficient in food supplies. Approximately 1 per cent of arable land is irrigated. In 1998 the government adopted a new strategy for sustained growth in the agriculture and livestock market up to 2010. The plan includes the development of markets in rural areas, modernisation, promoting private initiatives in rural areas and improving the economic situation of women in rural areas.

Production of rice is a fast growing area but Burkina Faso only produces 20 per cent of the amount it needs. National per capita crop consumption is 185.5 kg. In order to increase the country's self sufficiency irrigation programmes are being developed, both to increase quantity and variety of crops grown. The most significant crops for the non-domestic market are cotton, shea, and ground nuts and sesame. Cotton represents 70 per cent of Burkina Faso's exports, and 35-40 per cent of GDP. It is affected by falling world prices. On average at least 60,000 tonnes of cotton are exported each year. The main markets are south-east Asia (Taiwan, Indonesia, Thailand, Japan, South Korea and the Philippines) who buy 70 per cent of the produce. Other destinations are China, Brazil and Nigeria.

Cattle breeding is the country's second largest income source after cotton. Estimates for 2003 show there were 7.6 million cattle and buffaloes, 17.2 million sheep and goats and nearly 19 million poultry. Livestock makes up 10 per cent of GDP and 18 per cent of exports. In 1997 a new ministry was created to develop this sector. As part of the new government strategy the government plans to divide the country into three specialised zones: the Northern Zone will specialise in raising young animals for market; the Central Zone will specialise in raising and fattening livestock; and the Southern Zone will specialise in intensive farming.

Agricultural Production in 2010

Produce	Int. $'000*	Tonnes
Indigenous cattle meat	371,093	137,372
Sorghum	300,615	1,990,230
Cotton lint	271,549	190,000
Millet	204,576	1,147,890
Cow peas. dry	230,528	626,113
Maize	158,555	1,133,450
Groundnuts, with shell	153,464	340,166
Indigenous goat meat	81,737	34,113
Cottonseed	79,454	250,000
Rice, paddy	73,558	270,658
Cow milk, whole, fresh	68,466	219,400
Sesame seed	61,363	90,649

*unofficial figures
Source: http://faostat.fao.org/site/339/default.aspx Food and Agriculture Organization of the United Nations, Food and Agricultural commodities production

The Ministry of Environment and Water has trained over 2,000 people in fishing related activities, and the creation of reservoirs has led to increased fish production. Over 14,000 tonnes of freshwater fish were caught in 2010.

COMMUNICATIONS AND TRANSPORT

Travel Requirements
A valid passport, visa, and evidence of yellow-fever vaccination are required for entry into the country.

International Airports
There are two international airports at Ouagadougou and Bobo Dioulasso. There are a further 31 other airports with unpaved runways.
Air Burkina, URL: http:// www.air-burkina.com

Railways
The rail line north from the coast at Abidjan in Côte d'Ivoire to Ouagadougou (1,173 km) via Bobo Dioulasso covers 517 km inside Burkina Faso, and trains run daily.

Roads
Burkina Faso's road network is about 17,000 km, about one quarter of which is all-weather but only 8 per cent of which is tarred. Vehicles are driven on the right. Bus services connect Burkina Faso with Ghana, Mali, and Benin.

HEALTH

In 2009, total expenditure on health as a percentage of GDP was 6.6 per cent. Government expenditure accounts for 49.7 per cent of total expenditure. Private expenditure accounts for 50.3 per cent of total expenditure. External resources account for 26 per cent of expenditure on health. Some 73.8 per cent of private expenditure is out-of-pocket expenditure. Per capita total expenditure on health was US$39. According to WHO figures, in 2005-10 there were an estimated 921 doctors (1 per 10,000 population), 10,539 nurses and midwives (7 per 10,000 population), 28 dentists, 347 pharmacists, 36 public and environmental health workers and 1,238 community health workers.

In 2010, child (one-year-olds) immunization against measles was an estimated 94 per cent (compared to 59 per cent in 2000). In 2000-09 over 26 per cent of children were underweight and 35.1 per cent were stunted. In 2010, the major causes of death for children under 5 were malaria (24 per cent), diarrhoeal diseases (12 per cent) and pneumonia (18 per cent). Only 10 per cent of children sleep under treated insect nets. One per cent of deaths of children under 5 were attributed to HIV/AIDs. In 2003 the official percentage for people (aged 15-24) living with HIV/AIDS was 4.2 per cent. In 2010, there were 804,539 reported cases of malaria, 320 of leprosy, 2,511 of measles, 3,604 of meningitus, and 4,800 of TB.

According to the WHO an estimated 79 per cent of the population had sustainable access to an improved water source in 2008. An estimated 17 per cent of the population had sustainable access to improved sanitation.(Source: http://www.who.int, World Health Indicators 2012)

EDUCATION

Education is free and in theory compulsory, however many families are unable to attend school for financial reasons (both cost of school supplies and many children also work). Primary education is for ages 7-13, and secondary education for ages 13-19. In 2007, approximately 52 per cent of primary-aged children (47 per cent of girls and 57 per cent of boys) were in school. The primary pupil: teacher ratio was 48:1 in 2007. An estimated 31 per cent of primary school children complete the grades. The transition rate to secondary education was 45 per cent in 2006. According to 2007 figures, 12 per cent of secondary-aged children attended school, (10 per cent of girls and 14 per cent of boys).

Burkina Faso schools teach a national curriculum including agricultural production, the school week runs Monday to Saturday with Thursday and Sunday off, many rural schools have a long afternoon break to allow children to return home to work on the land.

There are three universities: Ouagadougou, Bobo-Dioulasso Polytechnic University and Koudougou Ecole Normale Supérieure. The enrolment rate for tertiary education was estimated at 3 per cent.

In 2006, government expenditure on education as a percentage of GDP was 4.5 per cent. (15.4 per cent of total government expenditure). Approximately 66 per cent of this was allocated to primary education.

Adult literacy was approximately 28.7 per cent in 2007 (36.7 per cent for males, 21.6 per cent for females). There are also wide regional variations. For the age group 15-24 years old, the literacy rate is 39.3 per cent (40.4 for males and 27.7 for females). (Source: UNESCO)

RELIGION

The main religions followed are Islam (52 per cent), indigenous beliefs (27 per cent) and Christianity (21 per cent).

Burkina Faso has a religious tolerance rating of 9 on a scale of 1 to 10 (10 is most freedom). (Source: World Religion Database)

COMMUNICATIONS AND MEDIA

The Ministry of Communication and Culture regulates the media. Much of the media practises some self-censorship. There are allegations of threats or arrests against journalists.

Newspapers
Sidwaya (official daily), URL: http://www.sidwaya.bf
L'Observateur Paalga (private), URL: http://www.lobservateur.bf
Le Pays, (private daily) URL: http://www.lepays.bf
L'Indépendant, URL: http://www.independant.bf

Broadcasting
The most popular media is radio. State, private and community stations exist. It is estimated that there are around 370,000 radios in use, with 20 radio stations broadcasting. The state-run station is Radio Burkina. Burkina Faso has one television station (state-run) , and approximately 100,000 televisions are in use.
Radio Burkina, URL: http://www.radio.bf/
Télévision Nationale du Burkina, URL: http://www.tnb.bf
Canal 3, URL: http://www.tvcanal3.com/

Telecommunications
Telephones and internet service providers are relatively reliable. The telephone network is managed by ONATEL (Office National des Télécommunications). In 2006 the government sold a 51 per cent stake in the national companay. In 2008 there were an estimated 144,000 landlines in operation and 2.5 million mobile phones. Less than 1 per cent of the population had access to the internet in 2003. By 2008 there were an estimated 140,000 users.
ONATEL, URL: http://www.onatel.bf
Authorité Nationale de Régulation des Télécommmunications (National Regulatory Telecoms Authority), URL: http://www.artel.bf

ENVIRONMENT

Environmental issues include droughts and desertification, overgrazing, soil degradation and deforestation. In the period 1990-95 the annual rate of deforestation was estimated at 1 per cent. In 2001, total renewable water resources were estimated at 17.5 cu km.

In 2010, Burkina Faso's emissions from the consumption of fossil fuels totalled 1.44 million metric tons of carbon dioxide. (Source: EIA)

Burkina Faso is party to international agreements on: Biodiversity, Climate Change, Climate Change-Kyoto Protocol, Desertification, Endangered Species, Hazardous Wastes, Law of the Sea, Marine Life Conservation, Ozone Layer Protection, and Wetlands.

BURUNDI
Republic of Burundi
Republika y'u Burundi

Capital: Bujumbura (Population estimate: 800,000)

Head of State: Pierre Nkurunziza (CNDD-FDD) (page 1487)

First Vice President: Therence Sinunguruza (Political Affairs) (Uprona)
Second Vice President: Gabriel Rufyikiri (Social And Economic Affairs) (CNDD-FDD)

National Flag: On a field quartered wedge-wise crimson and green, a white saltire; at the centre, a white disc charged with three red stars.

CONSTITUTION AND GOVERNMENT

Constitution
On 1 July 1962 independence from Belgian control was proclaimed and the country became a constitutional monarchy. In November 1966 the monarchy was overthrown and a Republic was founded. Ten years later the Second Republic came into being. Finally on 3 September 1987 Major Pierre Buyoya overthrew the president, Col. Bagaza, and proclaimed the Third Republic. Major Buyoya dissolved opposition parties and suspended the constitution.

The current constitution dates from 2005. It came into force on an interim basis on 1 November 2004 and was endorsed in a referendum on 28 February 2005. Under the terms of this constitution the president is directly elected. The term of office for the president is five years, renewable only once. Two vice-presidents are appointed by the president but must be approved by the National Assembly and the Senate. The first vice-president must be from a different ethnic group and political party from the president.

The parliament is bi-cameral. The lower chamber has 100 directly elected members. Up to 21 members may be co-opted so that there is a split of 40 per cent Tutsi members and 60 per cent Hutu. Three members of the Twa group are also co-opted. There should also be 30 per cent women. The Senate has 49 members, 34 of whom are elected (one Hutu and Tutsi from each province and three co-opted members from the TWA. Former presidents also have a seat in the Senate. Women should make up 30 per cent of the total. All members serve a five-year term.

To consult the constitution, please visit: http://www.burundi-gov.bi/.

Recent Events
Burundi has two main tribes, the Hutu and the Tutsi, and tensions between them became apparent soon after independence. These accelerated into open conflict and massacres. At least 80,000 mainly Hutu civilians were killed in 1972 alone, and hundreds of thousands of people were displaced. President Buyoya eventually set up a Committee for National Unity, which produced a draft charter recommending regulations for equality between the tribes and equal opportunities. The constitution was accepted by referendum (90.2 per cent) and promulgated on 13 March 1992.

In June 1993 Melchior Ndadaye was elected president after winning Burundi's first multi-party elections, but was killed during an attempted coup in October 1993. Hundreds of thousands of Burundians fled to neighbouring countries in the ensuing civil war and over 350,000 people are believed to have been killed. In early 1994 Cyprien Ntaryamira was elected president. Later that year a Convention of Government was agreed between the major political parties. President Ntaryamira died in an aeroplane crash in April 1994.

In July 1996 President Sylvestre Ntibantunganya was deposed by the army, parliament was dissolved and political parties were temporarily prohibited. Major Pierre Buyoya was re-installed as president. The terms of the Constitution and the Convention of Government were suspended for a short time in 1996. Political parties were later re-installed.

From 1995 attempts were made to broker a peace deal between Burundi's Hutu and Tutsi population; they culminated in the 2000 Arusha Accords which provide for a government in which power is shared between Hutu and Tutsi, as well as equal representation in the armed forces. Although four Tutsi parties refused to sign the agreement, it was ratified. As part of the brokered agreement, a peace-keeping force was to be established in Burundi, and President Pierre Buyoya (a Tutsi) was to remain as president until April 2003 when he and his ethnic Hutu vice president would exchange roles. The transitional constitution was adopted on 18 October 2001. However, the Forces for the Defence of Democracy (CNDD-FDD-Ndayikengurikye), a Hutu-dominated armed-opposition group, which had not been party to the negotiations, continued to fight and rejected a ceasefire offer in April in 2002. Further negotiations in September 2002 resulted in a ceasefire agreement which was not respected.

President Buyoya handed over the presidency to his Hutu vice-president, Domitien Ndayizeye, on 30 April 2003. Negotiations continued between the government and the CNDD-FDD (Nkurunziza) and other armed groups. In July 2003, there was a major rebel assault on Bujumbura led by the FNL (Rwasa). In October 2003 the main Hutu-dominated rebel group, the CNDD-FDD Nkurunziza, joined the government and its institutions under a power-sharing agreement.

In November 2003 President Ndayizeye and Pierre Nkurunziza, leader of the CNDD-FDD (Nkurunziza), signed an agreement to end the civil war at a summit of African leaders in Tanzania. Members of the FDD, NFL and FNL were given ministerial positions. However members of the NFL (Forces for National Liberation) continued to fight. A ceasefire agreement in April 2004 was not respected, and conflict continued.

In May 2004, the CNDD-FDD (Nkurunziza) withdrew from the unity government because of what they saw as inadequate representation. The UN Security Council voted to send a peacekeeping force to Burundi. A referendum on the constitution was held on 28 February 2005 and was endorsed by the majority. In April 2005 the parliament extended the mandate of President Ndayizeye until August 2005 when elections were due to take place. In April 2005 the CNDD-FDD (Nkurunziza) withdrew from the governing coalition after the president rejected its choice for interior minister. In March 2006, Frodebu announced its withdrawal from the government, but its three ministers refused to resign, and were expelled from the party.

The last rebel group, the FNL-Rwasa, signed a new ceasefire agreement in September 2006. In January 2007, the UN closed its peacekeeping mission and began focussing on reconstruction operations. The DRC, Rwanda and Burundi relaunched the Great Lakes Countries Economic Community (CEPGL) in April 2007.

There was sporadic fighting in September 2007 with rebel raids in the north of the country and fighting between rival FNL factions in Bujumbura. There have been several recent cabinet reshuffles.

In April 2008 Hussein Radjabu, the former head of the ruling party, was sentenced to prison for 13 years for allegedly plotting an armed rebellion. Some outbreaks of fighting between government troops and rebel forces obliged the UN to postpone an assessment of the peace agreement. The UN is working with the government to disarm rebels and to form a new army. In October 2008 an opposition leader, Alexis Sinduhje of the Movement for Security and Democracy, was imprisoned for allegedly insulting the president.

The last rebel group, the Forces for National Liberation (FNL), ended its armed struggle and changed into a political party. The process was overseen by the African Union.

In March 2009, the Paris club of creditor nations cancelled the total $134.3 million debt Burundi owed to its members.

In January 2010, 13 soldiers were arrested for allegedly plotting a coup to overthrow President Nkurunziza.

In June 2013, a controversial media law was approved by President Nkurunziza. The new law forbids reporting on matters that could undermine national security, public order or the economy. Critics say it will undermine freedom of speech.

Legislature
Burundi has a bicameral legislature. Members of both houses serve a five year term. The executive branch is made up of the president who appoints and presides over the Council of Ministers. The 2004 constitution also specifies the ethnic balance of the cabinet and the number of women it should include.

Upper House
Burundi has a 49-member senate. Within the senate three seats are reserved for former presidents, three for the ethnic Twa minority, 34 elected members (one Hutu and one Tutsi for each province), and eight women are currently co-opted to bring the number of women to 30 per cent. The Senate was first elected in 2005. Members serve a five-year term.
Senate, (Sénat) PO Box 814, Bujumbura, Burundi.

Lower House
The National Assembly has 100 directly elected members. A further 21 members may be co-opted to archive an ethnic balance. Currently 15 members are co-opted Three members of the Ethnic Twa group are also co-opted. Members serve a five-year-term. The Assembly was elected for the first time in 2004.
National Assembly, (Assemblée Nationale), Palais des Congrès de Kigobe, PO Box 120, Bujumbura, Burundi.

Cabinet (as at June 2013)
Head of State: Pierre Nkurunziza (page 1487)
Minister of Agriculture and Livestock: **Odette Kaytesi**
Minister of Civil Service, Labour and Social Security: **Annonciate Sendazirasa**
Minister in the Office of the President, in charge of Good Governance and Privatisation: **Issa Ngendakumana**
Minister of East African Community Affairs: **Hafsa Mossi**
Minister of Communications, Information, Relations with Parliament and Government Spokesman: **Leocadie Nihazi**
Minister of Defence and War Veterans: **Maj.-Gen. Pontien Gaciyubwenge**
Minister of Transport, Public Works and Equipment: **Deogratis Rurimunzu**
Minister of Primary and Secondary Education, Vocational and Professional Training: **Dr Rose Gahiru**
Minister of Energy and Mines: **Ir Come Manirakiza**

Minister for External Relations and Co-operation: Laurent Kavakure
Minister of Finance and Economic Planning: Tabu Abdallah Manirakiza
Minister of the Interior: Edouard Nduwimana
Minister of Justice and Keeper of Seals: Pascal Barandagiye
Minister of Health and the Fight against AIDS: Dr Sabine Ntakarutimana
Minister for Trade, Industry and Tourism: Mme Victoire Ndikumana
Minister of Public Security: Gabriel Nizigama
Minister of Youth and Sports: Adolphe Rukenkanya
Minister for National Solidarity, Repatriment, Reconstruction, Human and Gender ghts: Clotilde Niragira
Minister of Higher Education and Scientific Research: Dr Joseph Butore
Minister of Communal Development: Jean-Claude Ndihokubwayo
Minister of Water, Environment and Land Development: Ir Jean-Claude Nduwayo

Ministries

Government portal: URL: http://www.burundi.gov.bi

Office of the President, Boulevard de l'Uprona, Rohero I, BP 1870, Bujumbura, Burundi. Tel: +257 2222 6063, fax: +257 2222 7490, e-mail: sindamuk@cbinf.com, URL: http://www.burundi-gov.bi

Office of the Vice-President, BP 2800 Bujumbura, Burundi. Tel: +257 3363, fax: +257 26424

Ministry of Finance, BP 1830, Bujumbura, Burundi. Tel: +257 2222 3988, fax: +257 222 3827, URL: http://www.burundi-gov.bi/

Ministry of External Relations and Co-operation, Bdg Grand Bureau, Bvd de la Liberté, BP 1840, Bujumbura, Burundi. Tel: +257 2221 7595, fax: +257 2222 6313, URL: http://www.burundi-gov.bi

Ministry for Interior, 5e étage, Bdg Grand Bureau, BP 1990, Bujumbura, Burundi. Tel: 257 2222 4242, fax: +257 2222 5351, e-mail: mininter@cbinf.com, URL: http://www.burundi-gov.bi

Ministry for Human Rights, Institutional Reforms and Relations, BP 6802 Bujumbura, Burundi. Tel: +257 213682 / 215228 / 213848, fax: +257 243880

Ministry of Justice, Chaussée Prince Rwagasore, Bujumbura, Burundi. Tel: +257 2222 243, fax: +257 2222 2148, URL: http://www.burundi-gov.bi/

Ministry for the Peace Process, BP 6242, Bujumbura, Burundi. Tel: +257 219460, fax: 257 219459, e-mail:peaceproc@cbin.com

Ministry for Labour and Social Security, Chaussée Prince Louis Rwagasore, 2830 Bujumbura, Burundi. Tel: +257 244563 / 244561, fax: +257 245363 / 244561, e-mail: minitrav@cbinf.com

Ministry of Defence, BP 1870 Bujumbura, Burundi. Tel: +257 224611, fax: +257 225686 217505 / 244709

Ministry of Education, Boulevard de l'Uprona, 1990 Bujumbura, Burundi. Tel: +257 222 9450, fax: +257 2222 8477, e-mail: minedu@cbinf.com, URL: http://www.burundi-gov.bi

Ministry of Agriculture and Livestock, Bujumbura, Burundi. Tel: +257 2222 2087, fax: +257 2222 2873, URL: http://www.burundi-gov.bi

Ministry of Youth, Sports and Culture, Bujumbura, Burundi. Tel: +257 2222 2135, fax: +257 2222 6231, URL: http://www.burundi-gov.bi

Ministry of Development and Reconstruction, Avenue de l'Industrie, Bujumbura, Burundi. Tel: +257 225394, fax: +257 224193

Ministry of Commerce and Industry, Bujumbura, Burundi. Tel: +257 2222 5019, fax: +257 2222 5595, URL: http://www.commerceetindustrie.gov.bi/

Ministry of Public Works and Equipment, Bujumbura, Burundi. Tel: +257 226841, fax: +257 226840

Ministry of Transport, Post and Telecommunications, 2000 Bujumbura, Burundi. Tel: +257 223100, fax: +257 226900, e-mail: mtpt@cbinf.com

Ministry of Communication, Chaussée Prince Rwagasore, 2ème Bâtiment de l'INSS, 1080 Bujumbura, Burundi. Tel: +257 224666 / 221766, fax: +257 216318, e-mail: minicom@cbinf.com

Ministry of Energy and Mines, BP 745, Bujumbura, Burundi. Tel: +257 2222 5909, fax: +257 2222 3337, URL: http://www.burundi-gov.bi

Ministry for Reintegration and Resettlement of Displaced and Repatriated People, BP 2645 Bujumbura, Burundi. Tel: +257 216303, fax: +257 218201, e-mail: minicom@cbinf.com

Ministry of Public Health and the Fight against AIDS, BP 1820, Bujumbura, Burundi. Tel: +257 2222 3945, fax: +257 2222 9196, e-mail: minisante_cabinet@usan.net, URL: http://www.burundi-gov.bi

Ministry for Social Action and Women's Promotion, BP 2690 Bujumbura, Burundi. Tel: +257 222431, fax: +257 216102

Ministry of Communal Development, BP 1910 Bujumbura, Burundi. Tel: +257 225267, fax: +257 224678, e-mail: minicom@cbinf.com

Ministry of Handicraft Industry, Training and Adult Literacy, Chaussée du P.L.R 2ème Bâtiment de l'INSS (Institut Nationale de la Sécurité Sociale), Bujumbura, Burundi. Tel: +257 244662 / 241409, fax: +257 244664

Minister of Good Governance and Privatisation, Chaussée Prince Louis RWAGASORE, Bâtiment INSS, 3ième, BP 3539, Bujumbura, Burundi. Tel: +257 243366 / 244832, fax: +257 244835, e-mail: minigouv@cbinf.com

Ministry of Civil Service, Labour and Social Security, 2e Bdg de l'INSS, Chaussée Prince Rwagasore, BP 2830, Bujumbura, Burundi. Tel: +257 2222 5058, fax: +257 2222 4079, e-mail: minitrav@cbinf.com, URL: http://www.burundi-gov.bi

Ministry of Telecommunications, Information, Communications and Relations with Parliament, 2e Bdg de l'INSS, Chaussée Prince Rwagasore, BP 1080, Bujumbura, Burundi. Tel: +257 2222 4666, fax: +257 2221 6318, e-mail: minicom@cbinf.com, URL: http://www.burundi-gov.bi

President of the National Assembly, Bujumbura, Burundi. Fax: +257 233685

Elections

All adults may vote. Presidential elections took place on 1 June 1993 and parliamentary elections on 29 June 2003. Under the peace agreement, legislative and presidential elections were supposed to take place by the autumn of 2004. Both were postponed. President Ndayizeye's term was extended until August 2005, when the assembly and senate elected Pierre Nkurunziza, leader of the CNDD-FDD, to the office.

Parliamentary elections took place on 4 July 2005. The CNDD-FDD (Nkurunziza) won 58 per cent of the vote (59 seats). The mainly Hutu Frodebu party won 22 per cent of the vote and 24 seats. The mainly Tutsi Uprona party won seven per cent of the vote and 10 seats. Other parties won seven seats. Under the terms of the peace process, the 100 MPs will take their seats in an assembly, where 40 per cent of seats are reserved for the Tutsi minority and 60 per cent for Hutus.

The most recent parliamentary elections took place in July 2010. President Nkurunziza was re-elected president in June 2010 although the election was boycotted by the opposition.

Political Parties

There are numerous political parties within Burundi. Many have known or alleged links to the 1993-94 violence. Several of the parties have different factions. The following are represented in parliament:

National Council for the Defense of Democracy (Conseil National Pour la Défense de la Démocratie, CNDD), Leader: Pierre Nkurunziza

FRODEBU (Front pour la Démocratie au Burundi, Front for Democracy in Burundi)

Leader: Jean Minani (Founded 1980s, officially recognised 1992)

UPRONA (Union pour le Progrès National, Union for National Progress), POB 1810, Bujumbura, Burundi. Tel: +257 225028

Leader: Jean-Baptiste Manwangari

CNDD (Conseil National pour la Défense de la Démocratie, National Council for the Defence for Democracy)

Founded 1994 with an armed wing, the Forces pour la Défense de la Démocratie, FDD (Forces for the Defence of Democracy). In 1988 the CNDD and the FDD split and Jean-Bosco Ndayikengurukiye set up a new faction (CNDD-FDD). The CNDD also retained a small armed wing. Jean-Bosco Ndayikengurukiye was ousted in October 2001 and replaced by Pierre Nkurunziza. Jean-Bosco Ndaiukengurikiye claimed leadership over a minority wing of the CNDD-FDD.

MRC (Mouvement pour la Réhabilitation du Citoyen - Rurenzangemero, Movement for the Rehabilitation of Citizens),

Leader: Epitace Bayaganakandia

PARENA (Parti pour le redressement national, Party for National Recovery)

Founder: Jean-Baptise Bagaza (1994)

Diplomatic Representation

Embassy of Burundi, c/o Suite 212, 2233 Wisconsin Avenue, NW, Washington, DC 20007, USA. Tel: +1 202 342 2574, fax: +202 342 2578, URL: http://www.burundiembassydc-usa.org/
Ambassador: Angele Niyuhire

Embassy of the USA, avenue des Etats-Unis, PO Box 1720, Bujumbura, Burundi. Tel: +257 223454, fax: +257 222926, URL: http://burundi.usembassy.gov
Ambassador: Dawn M. Liberi

British Embassy, All staff resident in Kigali, Rwanda. Tel: +250 84098. British Embassy Liaison Office, Bujumbura: Tel: +257 827602, e-mail: belo@cni.cbinf.com
Ambassador: Benedict Llewellyn-Jones OBE

Embassy of Burundi, Square Marie-Louise 46, 1000 Brussels LE, Belgium. Tel: +322 230 535 / 4548, fax: +322 230 7883, email: ambassade.burundi@skynet.be, URL: http://www.ambassade-burundi.be
Ambassador: Laurent Kavakure

Embassy of France, 60 avenue de l'UPRONA, PO Box 1740, Bujumbura, Burundi. Tel: +257 226767, fax: +257 227443
Ambassador: Jean-Pierre Lajaunie

Permanent Representative to the UN, New York: URL: http://www.un.int/wcm/content/site/rwanda
Ambassador: Eugène-Richard Gasana

LEGAL SYSTEM

The Burundi judicial system is based on German and Belgium civil codes and customary law. It comprises a Supreme Court (whose nine justices are appointed by the President), three Courts of Appeal, Tribunals of First Instance, Tribunals of Trade, Tribunals of Labour, and Administrative Courts. The tribunals are used as judicial courts in the provinces. There is also a Constitutional Court. The High Court of Burundi judiciary constitutes the Supreme Court and the Constitutional Court; it is responsible for sentencing the Prime Minister or the President of Burundi for any crime during their tenure.

The human rights record of the government is poor; army, police and National Intelligence Service personnel were responsible for killings, torture, and beatings of civilians and detainees in 2008, though the number of reported cases was down on previous years. Prison conditions are life-threatening, whilst arbitrary arrests and long pre-trial detention continue to be a problem. There is widespread judicial inefficiency and corruption. The government continues to detain political prisoners, and restricts freedom of assembly and association. Burundi abolished the death penalty in 2009.

Supreme Court, PO Box 1460, Bujumbura, Burundi. Tel: +257 222571, fax: +257 222148

LOCAL GOVERNMENT

There are 16 administrative provinces, which are governed by civilians, plus the city of Bujumbura which is divided into two administrative units. Each province is divided into districts, and each district subdivided into communes (129 as of 2011). In 2005 collines (hills) councils were established. The provinces are Bubanza, Bujumbura Mairie, Bujumbura Rural, Bururi, Cankuzo, Cibitoke, Gitega, Karuzi, Kayanza, Kirundo, Makamba, Muramvya, Muyinga, Mwaro, Ngozi, Rutana and Ruyigi.

BURUNDI

Local elections took place on 3 June 2005. The mainly Hutu Forces for the Defence of Democracy won over 50 per cent of the local councils. These were the first national elections to be held in the country since civil war broke out in 1993. The most recent local elections took place in June 2010 and the ruling CNDD-FDD party won over 60 per cent of the vote.

AREA AND POPULATION

Area

The area of Burundi is about 27,834 sq. km. The country has borders with Rwanda in the north, Tanzania in the east and the south, and the Democratic Republic of Congo in the west.

The terrain extends over a number of levels, from about 770 metres above sea level in the west up to about 2,000 metres, and this accounts for various climates, from tropical in the west, to cooler areas along the border with the Democratic Republic of Congo. There are two rainy seasons (March to May; October to December).

To consult a map, visit: http://www.un.org/Depts/Cartographic/map/profile/burundi.pdf

Population

In 2010 the population was estimated at 8.383 million, with an annual population growth rate of 2.7 per cent. Population growth is more rapid in urban areas. Population density is approximately 206 persons per sq. km. The vast majority of the population (89 per cent) lives in rural areas. As of 2004 there were believed to be 490,000 Burundian refugees still living in Tanzania following the 1998-2003 war. Over 150,000 are believed to have returned since 2002.

There are three main ethnic groups: Hutu, 85 per cent of the population; Tutsi, 14 per cent; and the Twa (pygmoids), 1 per cent.

The languages are Kiruandi (the national language), French (the administrative language), and Kiswahili (another spoken language).

Births, Marriages, Deaths

In 2010 the estimated birth rate was 34 births per 1,000 population and the death rate 14 per 1,000 population. In 2009 average life expectancy was estimated to be 49 years for men and 51 years for women, compared to 42 and 47 respectively in 2004. Healthy life expectancy was 42 years for males, 43 for females. In 2009 maternal mortality was estimated at 970 per 100,000 live births. In 2010 an estimated 38 per cent of the population was under 15 years old and 5 per cent was over 60. The median age was 20 years. In 2003 the dependency ratio was 96 per 100. In 2010 the fertility rate per woman was 4.3 children. (Source: http://www.who.int, World Health Statistics 2012)

Public Holidays 2014

1 January: New Year's Day
5 February: Unity Day
21 April: Easter Monday
1 May: Labour Day
29 May: Ascension Day
1 July: Independence Day
15 August: Assumption
18 September: Victory of Uprona Day
13 October: Rwagasore Day
21 October: Ndadaye Day
1 November: All Saints Day
25 December: Christmas Day

EMPLOYMENT

Over 90 per cent of the population, including 97 per cent of women, work in agriculture, mainly subsistence and just over 2.0 per cent work in industry. Estimated figures for 2007 put the labour force at 4.2 million. Per capita gross income was estimated at US$90 in 2004. It is estimated that over 80 per cent of the population is below the poverty line. The World Development Bank estimates that only 15 per cent of women are paid.

Burundi qualified for debt relief under the Highly Indebted Poor Country initiative and received a 66 per cent debt reduction in March 2004. A Poverty Reduction Strategy Paper was leased in conjunction with the IMF and World Bank in 2007.

BANKING AND FINANCE

Currency

One Burundi Franc = 100 centimes.

GDP/GNP, Inflation, National Debt

The instability in the country in the period 1993-96 greatly affected the economy, particularly when neighbouring countries imposed sanctions (now lifted) after the coup in June 1996. During the civil war the infrastructure was also damaged. This led to a period of very low growth and high inflation. Development of the economy is made more difficult by Burundi's distance from the sea and high transport costs. An estimated 65 per cent of the population is below the poverty line. There has been some progress in structural reforms in public finance. The economy is also being helped by the development of the energy sector and the liberalisation of the coffee sector. The crisis in the international economy has had some negative impacts and Burundi also faces uncertainty over how much foreign aid it will receive during the crisis.

GDP

	2005	2006	200
GDP US$ million	795.97	911.74	946.4
GDP growth rate (%)	0.9	5.1	3
GNI per inhabitant	100	100	

Source: African Development Bank

GDP was estimated to be US$1.3 billion in 2010 with a growth rate of 3.4 per cent. Per capi GDP was US$151.

In 2007 the main contributors to GDP were: agriculture, 49 per cent; industry, 19 per cer services, 33 per cent.

Inflation has also improved - from 31.1 per cent in 1997 to 12.5 per cent in 1998. It ros again to a high of 24.3 per cent in 2000. In 2002 it reached a low of -1.3 per cent but ros to 10.7 per cent in 2003. It fell to 8.4 per cent in 2004. It rose to 13.0 per cent in 2005 befor falling to 2.8 per cent in 2006. In 2010, it was 6.4 per cent and by 2011 had risen to 9.7 pe cent. Rising food and transport costs have contributed to rising inflation in 2012; in Q3 was estimated to be over 15 per cent.

Burundi is heavily dependent on foreign aid. In 2003 it received US$105 million. In 2006 external debt was US$1,290.79 million. In 2009, a group of creditor nations cancelled US$13 million of debt.

Balance of Payments / Imports and Exports

Coffee is the main export crop and currently represents over 50 per cent of total exports. I 1995 coffee to the value of US$112.5m was exported (80 per cent of total exports). Howeve the 1996 embargo resulted in a major decline in this market with only US$40.1 million c coffee being exported. The economy was further hit by a poor harvest in 2003. Other expo goods are tea, sugar, cotton, and animal hides. The major export markets are Germany (2 per cent), Switzerland (11 per cent), Belgium (7 per cent) and Rwanda (6.8 per cent).

Principal imports are food, tobacco, chemicals, vehicles, and petroleum. Burundi's mai trading partners are Kenya, UK, Switzerland, France, Germany, Saudi Arabia and Japan.

External Trade, US$ million

	2005	2006	2007
Trade balance	-147.80	-181.11	-252.1
Exports	57.18	58.64	44.5
Imports	204.78	239.75	296.6

Source: African Development Bank

Estimated figures for 2009 put export earnings at US$63.8 million and import costs a US$402.2 million.

Central Bank

Banque de la Republique du Burundi (BRB) Av. du Gouvernement, PO Box 705 Bujumbura, Burundi. Tel: +257 225142, fax: +257 223128, e-mail: brb@cbinf.com, URL http://www.brb.bi/
Governor: Gaspard Sindayigaya

Chambers of Commerce and Trade Organisations

Chambre de Commerce et de l'Industrie du Burundi, URL: http://www.cfcib.org

MANUFACTURING, MINING AND SERVICES

Industrial development has been hindered by the security situation, the geographical locatior of the country (distance to sea), and high transport costs. There have been some attempts at privatisation, notably in the coffee sector. Most industry relates to the processing of coffee

Mining and Extractive Industries

Burundi has several mineral deposts columbium (niobium)-tantalum ore, gold, china clay, tin, and tungsten ore have been mined for export. Limestone, peat, sand, and gravel are alsc produced. There are also deposits of feldspar, kaolin, nickel, phosphate, platinum-group metals, quartzite and vanadium.

Energy

Most of Burundi's energy is generated by hydropower. An estimated 34 million kWh were imported from the Democratic Republic of Congo. In 2010 Burundi's net electricity generation was 0.15 billion kWh and consumption was 0.22 billion kWh. In 2011 Burundi consumed 3,000 barrels of oil per day (all imported). Per capita energy consumption is low: 190 KgPE (petroleum equivalent) compared to the African average of 338 KgPE.

Manufacturing

The manufacturing sector of Burundi is small and underfunded. Main products are beverages, particularly beer and soft drinks, cigarettes, soap, glass, textiles, insecticides, cosmetics, cement, and some food processing.

Service Industries

There is some wildlife tourism but the industry is hampered by the occasional outbreaks of violence. Figures for 2006 show that an estimated 201,000 people visited Burundi spending around $2.0 million.
Office National du Tourisme (ONT), URL: http://www.burunditourisme.com

Agriculture

More than 90 per cent of the population depends upon agriculture for a living. An estimated 650,000 hectares (50 per cent) of the land is arable and some 2 per cent of this is irrigated. Most farming is subsistence. Agriculture is the main source of foreign currency for the country providing more than 50 per cent of GDP and more than 90 per cent of total exports. Prior to the recent civil war, Burundi was virtually self-sufficient in food production. It should be able to produce all it needs but soil erosion, over-cultivation, war and the number of internally displaced people who cannot produce their own food, means that Burundi has to import food. Food accounts for 90 per cent of agricultural imports and 13 per cent of all imports.

Agricultural Production in 2010

Produce	Int. $'000*	Tonnes
Bananas	538,664	1,912,660
Beans, dry	113,841	201,551
Vegetables fresh nes	75,942	403,000
Sweet potatoes	72,986	966,343
Cassava	62,512	598,409
Indigenous cattle meat	42,182	15,615
Fruit fresh nes	35,567	101,900
Rice, paddy	22,829	83,019
Indigenous pigmeat	18,410	11,976
Maize	17,165	126,412
Indigenous goat meat	15,364	6,412
Sorghum	12,572	83,023

* unofficial figures
Source: http://faostat.fao.org/site/339/default.aspx Food and Agriculture Organization of the United Nations, Food and Agricultural commodities production

Coffee is one of the main crops but production fell in 2003 because of floods and insect infestations. There has been some privatisation of the coffee sector.

Tea was introduced into Burundi on an experimental basis at the beginning of the 1930s, although the first treatment plant was not constructed until the 1960s. At present there are four factories operating at Rwegura, Teza, Ijenda and Tora treating the production of some 2,350 acres of tea plants, 4,199 acres being industrial blocks and some 7,904 acres being small village strips cultivated by 25,000 smallholders. The Burundi Tea Bureau (OTB) directs and coordinates the activities of all the factories and industrial blocks. Although production lags far behind coffee, tea is the second largest foreign currency earner for the country. The FAO estimated production to be 8,025 metric tonnes in 2010.

Livestock farming is decreasing in Burundi due to diminishing pastures, and the total figure for livestock has decreased dramatically in recent years. In 200, according to the FAO, there were approximately 325,000 cattle and buffaloes and 980,000 goats and sheep. Latest figures put the number of poultry at 800,000. 950,000 hectares are currently used for pasture.

Fishing

The fishing industry is small. The main fishing areas are the Burundian part of Lake Tanganyika, Cohoha and Rweru lakes, and the Ruvubu, Kagera and Maragarazi rivers. In 2010 fishing was estimated at 17,700 tonnes (compared to 25,000 in 1997). It remains a significant sector in terms of employment.

Forestry

Deforestation is a major problem. Forest covered declined by an estimated 9 per cent to 90,000 ha. Forests have been cultivated to try to counteract the deforestation but are ill-managed. In 2004 an estimated 333,000 tonnes of industrial roundwood were produced and 83,000 tonnes of sawn wood. An estimated 8.4 million tonnes of fuel wood were produced. In 2004 forestry product exports stood at US$1 million.

COMMUNICATIONS AND TRANSPORT

Travel Requirements

Citizens of the USA, Canada, Australia and the EU require a passport valid for six months (with at least one blank page), a visa and evidence of immunization against yellow fever. Travelers with an expired visa are not permitted to leave the country without acquiring an exit visa prior to departure. Travelers to the Democratic Republic of Congo will not be allowed to enter if their passport contains a visa or an entry/exit stamp from Burundi. Nationals from countries other than those listed above should contact the Burundi embassy to check entry requirements.

Roads

There are 14,480 km of roads in Burundi of which 1,950 km are national highways. 1,027 km are surfaced. Vehicles drive on the right.

International Airports

Bujumbura has an international airport and there are services to Europe and other African countries. There are a further six airports with unpaved airways.

In 2007 there were 89,500 passenger arrivals (up 20 per cent from 2006) and 63,000 passenger departures. In 2007, 490 tons of bagage and 2,250 tons of freight were transported into the country, and 400 tons of bagage and 280 tons of freight were transported out of the country.
Air Burundi, 40 avenue du Commerce, PO Box 2460, Bujumbura, Burundi. Tel: +257 223452, fax: +257 223452. The airline ceased operating for a while in 2007 and 2010.

Waterways

Burundi is a landlocked country, linked by lakes to Tanzania and Zambia. Lake Tanganyika is an important trading point and waterway with a major port at Bujumbura. In 2007, 123,000 (down 20 per cent from 2006) tons of goods were brought in, and 12,500 tons (down 10 per cent from 2006) were taken out.

HEALTH

According to WHO figures in the period 2000-10, there were an estimated 200 doctors (0.3 per 10,000 population), 1,348 nurses and midwives (1.9 per 10,000 population), 14 dentists, and 76 pharmaceutical personnel. In 2009, total expenditure on health was 11.4 per cent of GDP, representing a per capita spend of US$19. Government expenditure on health accounts for 36 per cent of the total expenditure on health. External sources account for 45.4 per cent of expenditure on health. Health expenditure accounts for 8.1 per cent of total government expenditure.

Main causes of death are malaria, respiratory diseases, and stomach diseases. In the years 2005-11, 57.5 cent of children under-five were stunted and 35.2 per cent were underweight. In 2009 the infant mortality rate (probability of dying before age 1) was 88 per 1,000 births. The mortality rate for under-fives was 142 per 1,000 live births. The main causes of death were diarrhoea 15 per cent, pneumonia 19 per cent, malaria 4 per cent and prematurity 13 per cent. Approximately 6 per cent of deaths were attributed to HIV/AIDS. AIDS is also a major problem: 80 per cent of long-term hospital patients in Bujumbura have AIDS-related illnesses. According to 2003 figures between 4.1 per cent and 8.8 per cent of adults (aged 15-49) (170,000-350,000) were living with HIV/AIDS. In 2003, there were 25,000 recorded deaths due to HIV/AIDS.

In 2010, 72 per cent of the population (83 per cent urban, 71 per cent rural) had access to improved water supply and 46 per cent to improved sanitation. (Source: http://www.who.int, World Health Statistics 2012)

EDUCATION

One of the country's principal aims is universal education provided free of charge. It had aimed to achieve this by 2000, but the target was revised to 2010. In 2005, the new president, Pierre Nkurunziza, abolished fees (1,500 Burundi Francs / $1.5 per year) for primary education. Many families had been unable to pay. The education system struggled to cope with the massive influx of pupils, with class sizes reaching 150 pupils. In 2007, the average pupil: teacher ratio in primary schools was estimated at 52:1. In 2006, 75 per cent of children aged seven attended primary school. An estimated 36 per cent of children complete primary education. An estimated 29 per cent of children repeat some primary education.

Great efforts are being made to set up more secondary schools, especially technical and vocational establishments. An estimated 25 per cent of children go onto secondary school. Burundi has one university, in Bujumbura, and, according to recent figures, an estimated 2 per cent of students go onto higher education.

In 2004, the average literacy rate was 159.8 per cent overall (67.3 per cent for males, 52.2 per cent for females). For the population aged 15-24 literacy is much higher at 76.8 per cent for males and 70.4 for females. In 2005, 5.2 per cent of GDP was spent on education. (Source: UNESCO)

RELIGION

Ninety three per cent of the population is Christian (Roman Catholic 74 per cent, Protestant 20 per cent). Many of the population also hold indigenous beliefs (mainly the Imana Cult) and 2 per cent are Muslim. Most of the Muslim population live on the Imbo Plain.

Burundi has a religious tolerance rating of 9 on a scale of 1 to 10 (10 is most freedom). (Source: World Religion Database)

COMMUNICATIONS AND MEDIA

There is occasional government censorship. The media also practises some self censorship.

Newspapers

The newspaper industry is hindered by low literacy levels. Burundi's main newspapers are:
La Renouveau du Burundi, PO Box 2870, Bujumbura, Burundi. (government newspaper)
Ubumwe, PO Box 1400, Bujumbura, Burundi. Tel: +257 223929 (government-owned)
Ndongozi, founded by Catholic Church
Arc-en-ciel (Rainbow), private, weekly, French language

Agence burundaise de Presse (ABP), 6 avenue de la Poste, PO Box 2870, Bujumbura, Burundi. Tel: +257 225417

Broadcasting

Radio is the main source of information for most. In 2001 there were estimated to be 440,000 radios. In 2004 an estimated 14 per cent of households had television.
The state radio and television broadcasting company is:
Voix de la Révolution/La Radiodiffusion et Télévision Nationale du Burundi (RTNB), PO Box 1900, Bujumbura, Burundi. Tel: +257 223742, fax: +257 226547
Various other stations have been set up including:
Bonesha FM, funded by international organisations and set up to promote reconciliation.
Radio Publique Afrique, private, has some UN funding.
Radio Isangiro, private, URL: http://www.web-africa.org/isanganiro/

Telecommunications

In 2008 there were an estimated 30,400 telephone lines in use and 450,000 mobile cellular phones. In 2000 there was one Internet Service Provider. According to 2008 figures, 65,500 people have regular access to the internet.

Office nationale des télécommunications (ONATEL), PO Box 60, Bujumbura, Burundi. Tel: +257 223196, fax: +257 226917

ENVIRONMENT

Major environmental concerns are deforestation, over-grazing, soil erosion, and declining bio-diversity. Burundi suffers from both flooding and drought. Wood is the only combustible energy source available to most of the population and has been used without being replanted.

A National Council for the Environment has been set up. Two national parks (Kibira Nation Park in the northwest and Rurubu National Park in the northeast) have been set up in a attempt to protect the wildlife.

In 2010 Burundi's emissions from the consumption of fossil fuels totalled 0.53 million met tons of carbon dioxide.

Burundi is party to the following treaties: Biodiversity, Climate Change, Climate Change-Kyo Protocol, Desertification, Endangered Species, Hazardous Wastes, Ozone Layer Protectio and Wetlands. Burundi has signed but not ratified the Law of the Sea agreement.

CAMBODIA

Kingdom of Cambodia

Preah Reach Ana Pak Kampuchea

Capital: Phnom Penh (Population estimate: 1,000,000)

Head of State: King Norodom Sihamoni (Sovereign) (page 1514)

President of the National Assembly: Heng Samrin

National Flag: Horizontal stripes in blue, red, blue, the red stripe being double the width of the blue, a white three-towered temple is pictured in the centre of the red stripe

CONSTITUTION AND GOVERNMENT

Constitution

A French Protectorate from 1863 until 1953, Cambodia was independent until the *coup d'etat* by General Lon Nol in the 1970s. The resulting civil war between his forces and those of the Khmer Rouge lasted until 1975, when the Pol Pot-led Khmer Rouge overthrew the Lon Nol regime. The year was termed 'Year One' by the Khmers, and ushered in four years of genocide and destruction, during which an estimated two million Cambodians were killed by their government.

Vietnam entered the country at the end of 1978 in order to overthrow Pol Pot. The Paris Peace Agreement was signed by Cambodia's political parties and 19 countries on the 23 October 1991, bringing an end to the conflict. After hiding in Cambodia's jungle for many years, Pol Pot was captured in early 1998 and put on trial. He died soon afterwards.

Following the UN-supervised elections of 1993, a National Assembly was established (originally consisting of 120 elected members), and the Royal Government of Cambodia was formed. The constitution was changed to recognise the private sector of the economy as well as the state-run, co-operative and family sectors. The country is now a constitutional monarchy.

Under the current 1993 Constitution, the head of state is the King. King Norodom Sihanouk was elected by the seven-member Throne Council in September 1993 but abdicated in October 2004 and was succeeded by his son Norodom Sihamoni. The head of government is the Prime Minister, appointed by the King, who appoints the Royal Government of Cambodia.

To consult the full constitution, please visit:
http://www.embassy.org/cambodia/cambodia/constitu.htm

International Relations

Cambodia has good relations with most of its regional neighbours. At the beginning of 2003, relations with Thailand suffered when anti-Thai riots erupted in Phnom Penh, leading to the burning down of the Thai Embassy and the premises of a number of Thai businesses. There are occasional problems with Thailand over the question of the Preah Vehear temple site; the 900-year-old Hindu temple was judged to be on the Cambodian side of the border in 1962 by the International Court of Justice, a decision that continues to irk Thailand. The temple is on the top of a cliff, and only easily accessible from the Thai side of the border.

China, Japan, the US and the EU have invested heavily in the reconstruction of Cambodia. In 2007, international donors contributed assistance amounting to approximately 50 per cent of the national budget. Cambodia is a member of the UN, the Association of Southeast Asian Nations (ASEAN), the Group of 77 at the UN and the Non Aligned Movement (NAM). The government has occasional disagreements with the UN on human rights issues.

Recent Events

Sam Rainsy, the leader of one of the opposition parties, returned to Cambodia in 2006, having fled to France a year earlier following the Government's decision to strip him of his parliamentary immunity. In December 2005, in his absence, he was sentenced to 18 months in jail for defaming both Hun Sen and the then National Assembly President, Prince Norodom Ranariddh. However, he received a royal pardon from the King.

Prince Norodom Ranariddh, was ousted as leader of FUNCINPEC in October 2006 and went abroad after being found guilty in March 2007 of "breaching the trust of the party" and sentenced to 18 months in prison.

In 2007 court tribunals began questioning suspects about the Khmer Rouge alleged genocide In September, Nuon Chea, the most senior surviving member of the Khmer Rouge was charge with crimes against humanity, and in November, a genocide tribunal heard a bail plea fror a former prison chief, Khang Khek Ieu, which was eventually refused in March 2008.

In July 2008, relations with neighbouring Thailand became tense when 40 Thai soldier crossed the frontier into Cambodia following the arrest of three Thai protestors near th Preah Vihear temple. Ownership of the temple has long been a sensitive issue between th two countries; in 1962, the International Court of Justice awarded it to Cambodia. Tensio increased when Cambodia applied for World Heritage status for the temple, which wa approved by Unesco early in July. By mid-July, over 500 Thai and 1,000 Cambodian soldier were stationed on opposite sides of disputed land near Preah Vihear temple. Officials from both sides held talks to resolve the stand-off , but in October, two Cambodian soldiers wer killed in an exchange of fire, several soldiers were wounded on both sides, and 10 Tha soldiers reportedly taken prisoner.

In February 2009 the former Khmer Rouge leader Duch went on trial in Phnom Penh, charge with presiding over the murder and torture of thousands of people when he was head of th Tuol Sleng prison camp.

In July 2010, the former Khmer Rouge prison chief Comrade Duch was found guilty of crime against humanity and sentenced to 35 years in prison.

In September 2010, the exiled opposition leader Sam Rainsy was sentenced in absentia te 10 years in prison having been found guilty of manipulating a map to suggest Cambodi was losing land to Vietnam.

In January 2011, Thai-Cambodian tensions rose when Cambodia brought espionage charge against two Thai citizens who had been arrested after crossing the countries' disputed borde in December. The following month Thai and Cambodian forces exchanged fire across th disputed area near the Preah Vihear temple. The Prime Minister, Hen Sen asked the UN tc send peacekeepers to the area. In December 2011 both Cambodia and Thailand agreed tc withdraw their troops from the area.

In April 2012, environmental activist Chut Wutty was shot during a confrontation with police while travelling in a forested area which was under threat..

In May 2012 the Government suspended the granting of land for development by private companies in an effort to curb evictions and illegal logging.

In October 2012, the former king, Norodom Sihanouk, died of a heart attack aged 89.

In November 2012, the Government approved a plan to build a controversial hydroelectric dam called the Lower Sesan 2 on a tributary of the Mekong.

Legislature

The current legislature is the bicameral Parliament, consisting of the Senate and the National Assembly.

Upper House

The Senate was first approved by the National Assembly in March 1999, and consists of 61 members, 57 of whom are elected by universal adult suffrage, two nominated by the King, and two elected by the National Assembly. All serve for a five-year term.

Senate, Preah Norodom Blvd., Chamkarmon State Building, Phnom Penh, Kingdom of Cambodia. Tel: +855 (0)23 211441 / 42 / 43, fax: +855 (0)23 211446, e-mail: oum_sarith@camnet.com.kh, URL: http://www.khmersenate.org/

Lower House

The National Assembly comprises 122 members directly elected for a term of five years.
The National Assembly, Samdech Sotheatos Blvd., Phnom Penh, Cambodia. Tel: +855 (0)23 214136, fax: +855 (0)23 217769, e-mail: kimhenglong@cambodian-parliament.org, URL: http://www.cambodian-parliament.org

Cabinet (as at March 2013)
Prime Minister: Samdech Hun Sen (page 1445)

Deputy Prime Minister, Minister of Foreign Affairs and International Cooperation: or Namhong
Deputy Prime Minister, Minister of the Interior: Sar Kheng
Deputy Prime Minister, Minister of the Council of Ministers: Sok An
Deputy Prime Minister, Minister of National Defence: Gen. Tea Banh
Deputy Prime Minister, Economy and Finance: Keat Chhon (page 1403)
Deputy Prime Minister: Ke Kim Yan
Deputy Prime Minister: Yim Chai Lyl
Deputy Prime Minister: Gen. Nhoek Bunchhai
Deputy Prime Minister, Minister of National Assembly and Senate Relations and Inspection: Men Sam-on
Deputy Prime Minister: Bin Chhin
Senior Minister, Minister of the Environment: Mok Maret (page 1479)
Senior Minister, Minister of Planning: Chhay Than (page 1524)
Senior Minister, Minister of Commerce: Cham Prasidh (page 1498)
Senior Minister, Land Management, Urbanism and Construction: Im Chhunlim
Senior Minister, Minister for Special Envoys: Serei Kosal
Minister of Rural Development: Chea Sophara
Minister of Education, Youth and Sports: Im Sethy
Minister of Justice: Ang Vong-vattana
Minister of Tourism: Thong Khon
Minister of Industry, Mines and Energy: Suy Sem
Minister of Health: Mam Bunheng
Minister of Rural Development: Chea Sopahara
Minister of Agriculture, Forestry and Fishery: Chan Sarun (page 1402)
Minister of Culture and Fine Arts: Him Chhem
Minister of Social Affairs, Veterans and Youth Rehabilitation: Ith Samheng (page 507)
Minister of Posts and Telecommunications: So Khun
Minister of Women's Affairs: Ing Kantha Phavy
Minister of Public Works and Transport: Tram Iv-tek
Minister of Water Resources: Lim Kean Hao
Minister of Vocational Training and Labour: Vong Soth
Minister of Information and Press: Khieu Kanharith
Minister of Religious Matters: Min Khin
Minister of Health: Mam Bunheng
Minister attached to the Office of the Prime Minister: Chheang Yanara

Ministries

Ministry of Agriculture, Forestry and Fishing, 200 blvd. Norodom, Phnom Penh, Cambodia. Tel: +855 23 211351, fax: +855 23 217320, e-mail: icomaff@camnet.com.kh, URL: http://www.maff.gov.kh

Ministry of Commerce, 20 a-b blvd. Norodom, Phnom Penh, Cambodia. Tel: +855 23 426024, fax: +855 23 426024, e-mail: kunkoet@moc.gov.kh, URL: http://www.moc.gov.kh

Ministry of Religious Affairs, quai Sisowath, cnr rue 240, Phnom Penh, Cambodia. Tel: +855 23 725099, fax: +855 23 725699, e-mail: morac@cambodia.gov.kh, URL: http://www.morac.gov.kh/

Ministry of Culture and Fine Arts, 227 blvd. Norodom, Phnom Penh, Cambodia. Tel: +855 23 217645, fax: +855 23 725749, e-mail: mcfa@cambodia.gov.kn, URL: http://www.mcfa.gov.kh

Ministry of Economy and Finance, 60 rue 92, Phnom Penh, Cambodia. Tel: +855 23 428960, fax: +855 23 447798, e-mail: mefcg@hotmail.com, URL: http://www.mef.gov.kh

Ministry of Education, Youth and Sports, 80 blvd.Norodom, Phnom Penh. Tel: +855 23 360233, fax: +855 23 212512, URL: http://www.moeys.gov.kh/

Ministry of Environment, 48 blvd. Sihanouk, Phnom Penh, Cambodia. Tel: +855 23 427894, fax: +855 23 427844, e-mail: moe-cabinet@camnet.com.kh, URL: http://www.moe.gov.kh

Ministry of Foreign Affairs and International Cooperation, Sisowath Quay, cnr rue 240, Phnom Penh, Cambodia. Tel: +855 23 214441, fax: +855 23 216144, e-mail: mfaicasean@bigpond.com.kh, URL: http://www.mfaic.gov.kh

Ministry of Health, 151 blvd. Kampuchea Krom, Phnom Penh, Cambodia. Tel: +855 23 722873, fax: +855 23 426841, e-mail: procure.pcu@bigpond.com.kh, URL: http://www.moh.gov.kh

Ministry of Interior, 275 blvd. Norodom, Phnom Penh, Cambodia. Tel: +855 23 212707, fax: +855 23 426585, e-mail: moi@interior.gov.kh, URL: http://www.interior.gov.kh

Ministry of Industry, Mines and Energy, 45 blvd. Norodom, Phnom Penh, Cambodia. Tel: +855 23 723077, fax: +855 23 428263, e-mail: mine@cambodia.gov.kh, URL: http://www.mine.gov.kh

Ministry of Information, 62 blvd. Monivong, Phnom Penh, Cambodia. Tel: +855 23 724159, fax: +855 23 427475, e-mail: information@cambodia.gov.kh, URL: http://www.information.gov.kh

Ministry of Justice, 240 blvd. Sothearos, Phnom Penh, Cambodia. Tel: +855 23 360421, fax: +855 23 364119, e-mail: moj@cambodia.gov.kh, URL: http://www.moj.gov.kh

Ministry of Land Management, Urbanism and Construction, 771-773 blvd. Monivong, Phnom Penh, Cambodia. Tel: +855 23 215660, fax: +855 23 217035, e-mail: gdlmup-mlmupc@camnet.com.kh, URL: http://www.mlmupc.gov.kh

Ministry of National Assembly and Senate Relations and Inspection, Jawaharlal Nehru, Phnom Penh, Cambodia. Tel: +855 23 884261, fax: +855 23 884264, e-mail: mnasrl@cambodia.gov.kh, URL: http://www.mnasrl.gov.kh

Ministry of National Defence, Confederation de la Russie, cnr rue 175, Phnom Penh, Cambodia. Tel: +855 23 883184, fax: +855 23 366169, e-mail: info@mond.com.kh, URL: http://www.mond.gov.kh

Ministry of Planning, 386 Blvd Monivong, Phnom Penh, Cambodia. Tel: +855 23 212049, fax: +855 23 210698, e-mail: mop@cambodia.gov.kh, URL: http://www.mop.gov.kh

Ministry of Posts and Telecommunications, Corner of Street 13 & 102, Phnom Penh. Tel: +855 (0)23 426510 / 724809, fax: 855 (0)23 426011, URL: http://www.mptc.gov.kh

Ministry of Public Works, 106 blvd. Norodom, Phnom Penh, Cambodia. Tel: +855 23 427845, fax: +855 23 427852, e-mail: mpwt@mpwt.gov.kh, URL: http://www.mpwt.gov.kh

Ministry of Rural Development, Pochentong Blvd, Phnom Penh, Cambodia. Tel: +855 (0)23 722425, fax: +855 (0)23 426814, URL: http://www.mrd.gov.kh/

Ministry of Social Welfare, Labour and Veterans, 68 Norodom Blvd, Phnom Penh. Tel: +855 (0)23 725191, fax: +855 (0)23 427322, URL: http://www.mosalvy.gov.kh/

Ministry of Tourism, 3 Monivong Blvd, Phnom Penh. Tel: +855 (0)23 426107, fax: +855 (0)23 426364, also represented in Europe by: A.D.T.K., 4 rue Adolphe Yvon, 75016 Paris. Tel: +33 (0)1 60 06 35 96, URL: http://www.mot.gov.kh/default.php

Ministry of Water Resources, 47 blvd. Norodom, Phnom Penh, Cambodia. Tel: +855 23 724289, fax: +855 23 426345, e-mail: mowram@cambodia.gov.kh, URL http://www.mowram.gov.kh

Ministry of Women's Affairs, 3 blvd. Norodom, Phnom Penh, Cambodia. Tel: +855 23 428965, fax: +855 23 428965, e-mail: mwva.cabinet@online.com.kh, URL: http://www.mwva.gov.kh/

Political Parties

The main political parties are

The Cambodian People's Party (CPP, Kanakpak Pracheachon Kâmpuchéa), URL: http://www.thecpp.org
Chair: Chea Sim

The Sam Rainsy Party (PSR, Pak Sam Rainsy), URL: http://www.samrainsyparty.org
Chair, Sam Rainsy

The United National Front for an Independent, Neutral, Peaceful and Cooperative Cambodia (Funcinpec), URL: http://www.funcinpec.info
Chair, Keo Puth Rasmey

The Human Rights Party (HRP), URL: http://www.hrpcambodia.com
Leader: Kem Sokha

Norodom Ranariddh Party (NRP), URL: http://nrparty.org
Leader: Chhim Siek Leng

Elections

According to the Constitution, adults above the age of 18 are eligible to vote.

The most recent elections to the National Assembly were held in July 2008 when the CPP won 72 seats, and the PSR won 27 seats. Funcinpec won just six seats. The CPP retained its coalition with the severely diminished party, but ordered its leaders to stand down and let army general Nek Bhun Chhay take over as the first non-royal party leader. Election observers criticised the disenfranchisement of a large number of voters, but praised the improvement over the 2003 elections. The election fell short of international standards.

The most recent election for the Senate was held in January 2006. The Cambodian People's Party won 43 of the seats, Funcinpec won 12 and Sam Rainsy Party won two seats. The election was criticised by local monitors as being undemocratic.

Diplomatic Representation

British Embassy: 27-29 Street 75, Phnom Penh, Cambodia. Tel: +855 (0)23 427124, fax: +855 (0)23 427125, e-mail: BRITEMB@online.com.kh, URL: http://ukincambodia.fco.co.uk/en/
Ambassador: Mark Gooding

Royal Embassy of Cambodia, 64 Brondesbury Park, Willesden Green, London NW6 7AT, United Kingdom. Tel: +44 (0)20 8451 7850, fax: +44 (0)20 8451 7594, e-mail: cambodianembassy@btconnect.com, URL: http://www.cambodianembassy.org.uk
Ambassador: Hor Nambora

Royal Embassy of Cambodia, 4530 16th Street, NW, Washington, DC 20011, USA. Tel: +1 202 726 7742, fax: +1 202 726 8381, e-mail: cambodia@embassy.org, URL: http://www.embassyofcambodia.org
Ambassador: Hem Heng

Embassy of the United States of America, 16 Street 228 (between streets 51 and 63), Phnom Penh, Cambodia. Tel: +855 (0)23 216436, fax: +855 (0)23 216437, URL: http://cambodia.usembassy.gov/
Ambassador: William Todd

Permanent Representative of the Kingdom of Cambodia to the United Nations, 866 United Nations Plaza, Room 420, New York, NY 10017, USA. Tel: +1 212 223 0676 / 0435 / 0530, fax: +1 212 223 0425, e-mail: cambodia@un.int, URL: http://www.un.int/cambodia/
Ambassador: Kosal Sea

LEGAL SYSTEM

The Cambodian judiciary has three levels: the lower courts, the Appeal Court and the Supreme Court. There is also a military court system. The 1993 constitution provides for a Constitutional Council, and a Supreme Council of Magistrates, which appoints and disciplines judges.

In 2003 the government signed an Agreement with the UN on the formation of an international criminal tribunal to bring to justice those senior individuals most responsible for the deaths of around 1.7 million people during the Khmer Rouge era in Cambodia (1975-1979). A legislative amendment was passed by the Cambodia parliament to allow the formation of the Khmer Rouge Tribunal (aka. the Extraordinary Chambers in the Courts of Cambodia - ECCC). The staff comprises both Cambodian and international judges and personnel, who are nominated by the UN Secretary-General. The international elements (and the costs of the defence teams, witness protection etc) are funded through voluntary contributions by international states, whilst the Cambodian government funds the domestic elements.

In 2007 the Cambodian authorities arrested five former Khmer Rouge leaders: Kaing Guek Eav (known as Duch), Nuon Chea (Brother No2), Ieng Sary and his wife, Ieng Thirith and Khieu Samphan (ex-Head of State). The first trial, that of Kaing Guek Eav (Duch), finally opened in February 2009. He was sentenced in 2010 to 30 years. On appeal, it was increased to life imprisonment. Ieng Sary, a co-founder of the Khmer Rouge (Brother No. 3), died whilst on trial in 2013. In March 2013, Nuon Chea (Brother No. Two) was deemed fit to stand trial.

CAMBODIA

The government's human rights record is poor. With low revenues and high crime rates, the justice system is over-burdened. Many serious crimes, notably political killings, go unsolved. Police corruption and abusive imprisonment conditions remain endemic. The government restricts freedom of speech and the press. The death penalty was abolished in 1989.

Extraordinary Chambers in the Courts of Cambodia, http://www.eccc.gov.kh/en

LOCAL GOVERNMENT

For administrative purposes Cambodia is divided into one capital municipality, 23 provinces, 185districts, over 1,600 communes, and over 13,400 villages. The provinces are Banteay Mean Cheay, Batdambang, Kampong Cham, Kampong Chhnang, Kampong Spoe, Kampong Thum, Kampot, Kandal, Kaoh Kong, Keb, Krachen, Mondol Kiri, Otdar Mean Cheay, Pailin, Pouthisat, Preah Seihanu (Sihanoukville), Preah Vihear, Prey Veng, Rotanah Kiri, Siem Reab, Stoeng Treng, Svay Rieng, and Takev. Local elections took place in 2007.

AREA AND POPULATION

Area
Cambodia is situated in southern Asia with Thailand and Laos to the north, Thailand to the west, south Vietnam to the east, and the Gulf of Thailand to the south-west. The total area of Cambodia is 181,035 sq. km.. Apart from the Cardamom Mountains in the south-west and uplands in the north-east, the country is predominantly flat. In the centre is the largest lake in South East Asia, the Tonle Sap. Phnom Penh, is located at the confluence of the Mekong, Tonle Sap and Bassac rivers. 20 per cent of the land is used for agriculture and approximately 61 per cent is forested.

The climate is tropical monsoon with rainy season lasting from June to October.

To view a map, consult: http://www.un.org/Depts/Cartographic/map/profile/cambodia.pdf

Population
The total population of Cambodia in 2010 was estimated at 14.138 million. The annual growth rate is approximately 1.3 per cent and an estimated 32 per cent of the population is under fifteen years old. Average population density in Cambodia is 81 people per sq. km. though only 20 per cent of people live in urban areas. Around 90 per cent of Cambodians live in the central lowlands where population density rises to 100 people per sq. km. Some 1 million Cambodians live in the capital Phnom Penh; other populous cities are Sihanoukville with 155,700 inhabitants and Battambang, 140,000 inhabitants. The majority of Cambodians (90 per cent) are Khmer, with 5 per cent Vietnamese, and 1 per cent Chinese. The rest of the population includes Cham Muslims and tribal peoples.

Over a third of the people live below the poverty line. In 1999 the government set up various plans to tackle the problem including investment in irrigation, public health, and agriculture. Landmines constitute an obstacle to further rural development, though clearing has reduced the number of injuries over recent years.

The official language of Cambodia is Khmer.

Births, Marriages, Deaths
According to 2010 estimates, the current birth rate is 22.5 births per 1,000 people, whilst the death rate is 8.6 deaths per 1,000 people. Average life expectancy at birth in 2009 was 61 years. Healthy life expectancy is 53 years. The infant mortality rate is 43 deaths per 1,000 live births, whilst the total fertility rate is 2.6 children born per woman. (Source: http://www.who.int, World Health Statistics 2012)

Public Holidays 2014
1 January: New Year's Day
7 January: Victory Day
14 February: Meak Bochea Day
8 March: International Women's Day
13 April: Cambodian New Year
1 May: Labour Day
9 May: Royal Ploughing Ceremony
13 May: King Sihamoni's birthday
14 May: Birth of Buddha
1 June: International Children's Day
24 September: Constitution Day
14 October: Phchum Ben's Day
23 October: Paris Peace Agreement
29 October: King Sihamoni Coronation Day
31 October: Former King Shinaouk's Birthday
9 November: Independence Day
27 November: Water Festival
10 December: Human Rights Day

EMPLOYMENT

Cambodia had a labour force of about 7,496,000 in 2004 (growing at 2.8 per cent per annum). Figures for 2008 show that 8,144,800 people were employed. Around 4,813,100 people were employed in the agriculture sector, 694,700 in manufacturing industry, 16,400 in the mining sector and 2,620,600 in other sectors. (Source ADB).

Total Employment by Economic Activity

Occupation	2004
Agriculture, hunting & forestry	2,577,622

- continued

Fishing	31,47
Mining & quarrying	3,94
Manufacturing	218,31
Electricity, gas & water supply	23
Construction	8,90
Wholesale & retail trade, repairs	404,83.
Hotels & restaurants	25,10
Transport, storage & communications	5,16
Financial intermediation	3,03
Real estate, renting & business activities	4,76
Public admin. & defence; compulsory social security	17,46
Education	33,13
Health & social work	11,88
Other community, social & personal service activities	42,73
Households with employed persons	14,52
Extra-territorial organisations & bodies	2,97

Source: Copyright © International Labour Organization (ILO Dept. of Statistics, http://laborsta.ilo.org)

BANKING AND FINANCE

Currency
One Riel (KHR) = 100 sen
The Cambodian economy continues to suffer the legacy of decades of war and internal strife. The country's infrastructure remains inadequate (although road networks are improving) and most rural households depend on agriculture and its related subsectors. The country remains heavily reliant on foreign assistance; about half of the central government budget depends on donor assistance. In 2006, US$601 million was given, according to the Cambodia Aid Effectiveness Report, and pledges of US$698.2 million have been made for 2007. The main donors are the Asian Development Bank (ADB), UN Development Program (UNDP), World Bank, International Monetary Fund, and various countries including China, the EU, and the U.S.

However, since 2004, the Cambodian economy has expanded by over 10 per cent per annum, largely driven by the garment and tourism sectors. In 2007, GDP grew by 10.2 per cent. In 2008, growth dropped to 6.7 per cent and was predicted to fall as low as 1.0 per cent in 2009. Agriculture, previously the main contributor towards Cambodia's GDP (and employing about 75 per cent of the workforce), contributed 32.5 per cent to GDP (at current market prices) in 2008. The services sector accounted for just over 45.1 per cent and industry contributed around 22.4 per cent of GDP. The services sector experienced the strongest growth (9 per cent). The economy slowed in 2009 but rose in 2010 on the strength of strong exports. The outlook remains uncertain. GDP was estimated at US$12.75 billion in 2011 and US$15 million in 2012.

GDP by industrial origin at current market prices, billion Riels

	2008	2009	2010
GDP at current market prices	41,968.4	43,065.8	45,942.7
-Agriculture	13,745.1	14,420.0	15,547.0
-Mining	164.6	195.9	284.0
-Manufacturing	6,441.1	6,207.6	6,848.1
-Electricity, gas and water	211.9	229.7	251.6
-Construction	2,571.5	2,693.7	2,518.6
-Trade	5,618.8	5,811.6	6,358.0
-Transport and communication	3,102.0	3,223.6	3,433.1
-Finance	549.5	594.1	670.1
-Public administration	767.8	768.5	806.9
-Others	6,263.0	6,303.9	6,426.3
-Less: imputed bank services charges	420.9	471.9	529.1
-Taxes less subsidies on products	2,953.9	3,089.3	3,328.2
-Net factor income from abroad	-406.9	-382.9	-415.6
GNI at current market prices	41,561.5	42,682.9	45,527.1

Source: ADB

Inflation has remained low over the first few years of the decade, standing at 1.2 per cent in 2003 before rising to 3.8 per cent in 2004, 5.8 per cent in 2005, 4.7 per cent in 2006, 5.9 per cent in 2007 and 4.4 per cent in 2009. Inflation was estimated to be 3.5 per cent in 2012.

External debt was an estimated US$3.6 billion in 2012.

As a member of Asean, Cambodia participates in the Association's economic initiatives, including Asean Free Trade Areas (AFTA), Asean Industry Co-operation (AICO) and Asean Investment Areas (AIA). Cambodia is also a member of MIGA.

Foreign Investment
Foreign direct investment (FDI) has increased 12-fold since 2004 as sound economic policies, political stability, regional economic growth, and government openness attract growing numbers of investors. The main commercial investors in Cambodia are: Malaysia, Taiwan, People's Republic of China, Hong Kong, Thailand, United States of America, and Korea. The main sectors for investment in Cambodia are in agriculture, tourism and infrastructure, particularly hydropower.

The Cambodian Investment Law (1994) offers a variety of incentives to foreign investors, such as nine per cent corporate income tax and tax holidays of up to eight years. There is also free repatriation of profits. The Council for Development of Cambodia (CDC) was established in 1994 as a 'one-stop' centre to ease the way for foreign concerns wishing to invest in the country.

Foreign investment was estimated at US$2.6 billion in 2006. China is the country's largest investor, contributing an estimated US$8.8 million over the last twenty years.

Balance of Payments / Imports and Exports
Exports, fob, rose to US$5,068 million in 2010 and imports rose to US$6,782 million. The trade deficit for 2010 was -US$1,714 million.

The main export products were rubber, timber, Soya beans, maize and sesame and Cambodia's main market was the United States. The table below shows selected export partners in recent years (Figures shown in US$ million)

Destination of Exports	2008	2009	2010
Total	5,127.6	4,984.3	4,567.1
United States	1,970.9	1,552.8	2,183.6
Hong Kong	839.9	1,646.3	20.4
Canada	292.0	195.8	346.6
Germany	138.1	108.8	294.6
UK	155.7	179.7	315.0

Source: ADB

Principal import commodities in 2007 were fuels, cigarettes, vehicles, consumer goods and machinery. The main suppliers are listed below: (Figures shown in US$ million)

Source of Imports	2008	2009	2010
Total	4,419.8	3,896.3	9,487.2
Thailand	696.9	464.8	2,574.4
China	934.9	881.3	1,482.0
Singapore	303.8	209.0	2,436.1
Hong Kong	589.6	484.2	645.4
Vietnam	471.0	493.5	507.2

Source: ADB

Central Bank
National Bank of Cambodia, PO Box 25, 22-24 Preah Norodom Blvd, Phnom Penh, Cambodia. Tel: +855 (0)23 428105 / (0)23 722563, fax: +855 (0)23 426117, e-mail: nbc2@bigpond.com.kh, URL: http://www.nbc.org.kh/index.asp
Governor: Chanto Chea

Chambers of Commerce and Trade Organisations
Council for Development of Cambodia (CDC), URL: http://www.cdc-crdb.gov.kh/

MANUFACTURING, MINING AND SERVICES

Primary and Extractive Industries
Cambodia has valuable deposits of gemstones. Sapphires and rubies are mined in Battambang province. There are also deposits of iron and manganese, and contracts have been issued for the offshore exploration of oil and gas. Cambodia produces none of its oil requirements. Figures from 2007 show that around 16,200 people were employed in the mining sector.

Energy
All energy for commercial use is currently imported, although there are estimates that offshore Cambodia may contain a fair amount of oil and nearly 5 trillion cubic feet of gas. Oil imports were 4,000 barrels per day in 2011, mainly gasoline, kerosene, distillate and residual.

Electricity of Cambodia produces and supplies electricity to Phnom Penh, and now the regional towns of Siem Reap, Kandal, Kampong Chain, and Sihanoukville. There are plans to increase the production of hydroelectricity, though this would require substantial damming of the Mekong and feasibility studies regarding the ecological and social implications would need to be carried out.

In 2010 electricity capacity was 0.36 million kilowatts (over 70 per cent of which was thermal, with the balance hydroelectric). Electricity generation in 2010, 0.94 billion kilowatthours (kWh). Electricity consumption was 2.01 billion kWh in the same year.

Manufacturing
Manufacturing contributed an estimated 28 per cent of total GDP in 2007. Industrial manufacturing is increasing after years of being hampered by limited resources and poor infrastructure, and is now a major foreign currency earner. Main sectors include garments and textiles, tools, cigarettes, pharmaceuticals and household goods. The garments and textiles sector employs around 350,000 people, and dominates Cambodia's exports. There were forecasts that the sector would contract following the expiration of the Multifiber Arrangement in 2005, but it has actually expanded by nearly 20 per cent, to an estimated $2.6 billion in 2007. Construction is also a growth industry as the country rebuilds and expands its infrastructure.

Services and Tourism
Services accounted for 43 per cent of GDP in 2007, the main areas being tourism, telecommunications, transportation, and construction.

Tourism is a re-emerging industry; in the 1950s and 60s, Cambodia was a popular destination. Following thirty years of civil war, the country is now developing the industry. The number of tourists coming to Cambodia is currently increasing by 20 to 25 per cent per year, with 1.7 million visitors in 2006 and with two million visitors expected to visit Cambodia in 2008.

The government has established bilateral co-operation with several countries including Thailand, Indonesia, Vietnam, and Japan. Direct flights are now possible from both Ho Chi Minh city, Vietnam and Bangkok.

Agriculture, Livestock and Fishing
Cambodia's annual production of rice continues to grow, most households are involved in production, and rice is a basic of Cambodian diet. The country is now a net exporter of rice.

Agricultural Production in 2010

Produce	Int. $'000	Tonnes
Rice, paddy	2,204,942	8,245,320
Cassava	443,698	4,247,420
Indigenous cattle meat	169,863	62,880
Indigenous pigmeat	150,591	97,962
Maize	103,127	773,269
Vegetables fresh nes	90,508	480,300
Bananas	44,779	159,000
Natural rubber	42,894	37,500
Soybeans	41,835	156,589
Beans, dry	41,501	71,220
Mangoes, mangosteens, guavas	33,553	56,000
Indigenous chicken meat	27,716	19,458
Bananas		

*Unofficial figures
Source: http://faostat.fao.org/site/339/default.aspx Food and Agriculture Organization of the United Nations, Food and Agricultural commodities production

Pulses, pepper, fruit, castor oil, cotton, jute, coffee and tobacco are also grown. The Cambodian government hopes to increase agricultural industry, such as food processing, palm oil refineries and rubber-processing factories.

In 2010, 490,094 tonnes of fish were caught, up from 326,000 tons in 2004 and 2,699,000 metric tons in 2006. Cultivation of prawns and crocodiles has seen a decline over recent years. There is concern that inland fish stocks are in decline due to environmental degradation, over-fishing and the conversion of inundation forests into rice fields.

Forestry
Forest covers about 60 per cent of Cambodia, including a great variety of tropical hardwoods such as teak and rosewood. Industries arising from this include timber, lumber and charcoal. The rubber plantations are second only to the timber industry in providing export earnings. The forestry sector is subject to over-exploitation and illegal logging.

COMMUNICATIONS AND TRANSPORT

Travel Requirements
Visitors from the USA, Canada, Australia and the EU require a passport valid for at least six months after date of return, and a visa. A 30 day visa can be obtained on arrival in Cambodia. Nationals of countries not referred to above are advised to contact the embassy to check visa requirements.

International Airport
Cambodia has two international airports at Phnom Penh and Siem Reap.

Airlines
Siem Reap Airways International, URL: http://www.siemreapairways.com; PMT Air, URL: http://www.pmtair.com

Railways
There are 602 km of track in Cambodia. There are two services running from Phnom Penh to Sihanoukville and Phnom Penh to Battambang.

Roads
Cambodia has around 13,300 km of roads, approx. 2,600 of which are paved. Foreign aid (US/Japanese) has recently been invested in road building and bridge construction. Vehicles are driven on the right. There are bus services linking Cambodia with Thailand, Vietnam and Laos although the latter is not a regular service.

Shipping
Cambodia's rivers are important communication routes and there are over 2,000 km of navigable waterways. The river port of Phnom Penh can be reached by ocean going vessels with a draft of less than 3.3 miles. There is also a river port at Kompong Chang on the Tonle Sap River. There is a seaport at Sihanoukville but most goods are still shipped up the Mekong to Phnom Penh. There is a system of government run ferries including routes linking Phnom Penh to Siem Reap, Siem Reap to Battambang, and Sihanoukville to Koh Kong.

A total of 1,825 vessels are harboured at Phnom Penh and Sihanoukville. A total 1.5m tons of transit goods and 1.3m tons of loaded goods are shipped annually.

HEALTH

Cambodian health is among the poorest in the region. Life expectancy is 61 years and the rate of maternal mortality in childbirth is 540 deaths per 100,000 births. Malaria and dengue fever continue to be widespread. Progress is being made however; the expansion of HIV/AIDS prevention, treatment and care programmes has resulted in a reduction in the prevalence among adults - from 2.6 per cent in 1996 to 0.9 per cent in 2006. There has also been a reduction in the cases of malnutrition; between 2000 and 2009, the percentage of underweight children under 5 years dropped from 42.6 to 29. Infant mortality (probability of dying by

CAMEROON

age1) has declined by some 30 per cent, but the rate is still high at 69 per 1,000 live births. The most common causes of death for children aged under 5 are pneumonia 28 per cent, prematurity 11 per cent and diarrhoea 7 per cent.

As of 2008, an estimated 81 per cent of the urban population and 56 per cent of the rural population had access to improved drinking water. In the same year, 67 per cent of the urban population and 18 per cent of the rural population had access to improved sanitation.

In 2008, total expenditure on health accounted for 5.7 per cent of GDP on health care. General government expenditure represented 23 per cent of total expenditure on health. Over 76 per cent of expenditure on health is private, almost all of which is out-of-pocket. Per capita expenditure on health was US$43. World Health Organization figures for 2000-10 estimated the number of health personnel at: 3,393 doctors (2.3 per 10,000 population), 11,736 nurses and midwives (7.9 per 10,000 population), 258 dentists, and 569 pharmacists. (Source: WHO, 2011) According to the National Institute of Statisics of Cambodia there were 1,185 health establishments and 10,900 beds.

EDUCATION

Schools were re-opened after the war in 1979. During the 1980s the Government concentrated on primary education with the emphasis on practical training for work. There are now over 40,000 primary school teachers.

In 2007, 89 per cent of the relevant age-group were enrolled in primary school, (87 per cent of girls and 91 per cent of boys). 34 per cent of the relevant age-group were registered at a secondary school (32 per cent of girls and 36 per cent of boys. Five per cent went on to tertiary education. The pupil/teacher ratio in 2007 was 51:1.

The literacy rate is estimated to be around 75.6 per cent (85 per cent among men and 66 among women). (Source: UNESCO, UIS)

RELIGION

The population is almost entirely Buddhist (97 per cent). In 1989, Buddhism was again recognised as the state religion having been previously suppressed by the Khmer Rouge. There are 3,685 pagodas, 50,081 monks, 582 Buddhist schools, and 1 Buddhist university. Additionally there are 202 mosques, 190 Surva temples, 150 Muslim schools with 1.6 per cent of the population followers, and 376 churches with 41,026 followers. There are 85 Christian schools.

Cambodia has a religious liberty rating of 9 on a scale of 1 to 10 (10 is most freedom). (Source: World Religion Database)

COMMUNICATIONS AND MEDIA

The press is not entirely free with reports of criminal charges against some journalists. Spreading 'false information' is punishable by a custodial sentence. Many newspapers and broadcasters depend on political support.

Newspapers
Kaoh Santepheap, pro-government daily, URL: http://kohsantepheapdaily.com.kh/
Sapordamean Kampuchea (SPK), Cambodian news agency. Bulletins in Khmer, French and English.
The Cambodia Daily, URL: http://www.cambodiadaily.com/
Phnom Penh Post, URL: http://www.phnompenhpost.com/

Broadcasting
National Television of Cambodia is the state-run broadcaster. Private and commercial broadcasters exist. Satellite television also exists.
National Television of Cambodia, URL: http://www.tvk.gov.kh
TV3, URL: http://www.tv3.com.kh/ (commercial)
TV5, URL: http://www.ch5cambodia.com.(private)
CTN, URL: http://www.ctncambodia.com (private)

Telecommunications
In 2008 there were an estimated 45,500 mainline telephones in use (less than one per 100 people) and 4.2 million mobile phones. Mobile-phone systems are widely used in urban areas to bypass deficiencies in the fixed-line network.

In 2009, it was estimated that there were 74,000 regular internet users, mainly in urban areas. Internet access in rural areas is limited.

ENVIRONMENT

Cambodia remains one of the most heavily forested countries in the region, although deforestation continues at an alarming rate. Mangrove swamps are particularly under threat.

In 2010, Cambodia's emissions from the consumption of fossil fuels totaled 3.59 million metric tons of carbon dioxide. (Source: EIA)

The country is a party to the following international environmental agreements: Biodiversity, Climate Change, Climate Change-Kyoto Protocol, Desertification, Endangered Species, Hazardous Wastes, Marine Life Conservation, Ozone Layer Protection, Ship Pollution, Tropical Timber 94, Wetlands, and Whaling. It has signed, but not ratified the Law of the Sea.

CAMEROON

Republic of Cameroon

République du Cameroun

Capital: Yaoundé (Population estimate: 1.5 million)

Head of State: Paul Biya (President) (page 1389)

National Flag: Three vertical stripes of green, red, and yellow of equal width, stamped with one gold star in a vertical red stripe

CONSTITUTION AND GOVERNMENT

Constitution
Cameroon was colonised by Germany in 1884, and after World War 1 was mandated by the League of Nations to the French and British Governments. Full independence was achieved on 1 October 1961 with the Federal Republic of Cameroon as the new name.

As a result of a national referendum in 1972 a unitary state of 'The United Republic of Cameroon' was approved and a new constitution came into force. In December 1995 the constitution was amended to increase the presidential term from five to seven years with a maximum tenure of two terms. In April 2008, Parliament amended the constitution to allow the President to run for a third term in 2011, despite opposition to the amendment.

The President is Head of State and Commander-in-Chief of the Armed Forces, and is empowered to appoint the Prime Minister and members of the Cabinet. The Prime Minister is head of government, appointed from the majority party.

To consult the constitution (in French), please visit: http://www.prc.cm/instit/consti.htm.

International Relations
Cameroon is a member of the African Development Bank, African Union, Central African Economic and Monetary Community, the Commonwealth, International Organisation of the Francophonie, Economic Community of Central African States, the International Monetary Fund and the United Nations.

Cameroon has had a long standing border dispute with Nigeria over the potentially oil rich area of Bakassi peninsula. In 2002, the UN ruled that the area belonged to Cameroon. Nigeria withdrew its troops from the area in June 2006 and in August 2008 it ended the dispute and handed over the disputed peninsula to Cameroon.

Recent Events
At a meeting of the Paris Club (a group of leading lending countries) in 2006, nearly of all of Cameroon's debt of US$3.5 billion was cancelled.

By the end of 2006 the UNHCR estimated that 30,000 refugees fleeing conflicts in Chad and the Central African Republic had arrived in Cameroon in the preceeding 18 months.

In August 2008, Nigeria handed over the Bakassi peninsula to Cameroon, bringing an end to a long-standing dispute over the territory. The majority of the local population considers itself Nigerian, but an international court ruled in favour of Cameroon in 2002. Around 90 per cent of the area's population, estimated at up to 300,000, is made up of Nigerian fishermen, who were moved to an area with no access to the sea; campaigners say the handover has destroyed their way of life. The offshore waters of the Bakassi peninsula are thought to contain substantial oil fields which Nigeria and Cameroon will now work together to explore.

In January 2011, Cameroon negotiated a loan from China to build a deep sea port at Kribi.

In February 2012 hundreds of elephants were slaughtered for their ivory in the Bouba Ndjida national park. Poachers from Sudan and Chad were blamed.

Legislature
Legislative power is shared by the President, through decrees and ordinances, and the unicameral National Assembly (*Assemblée Nationale*) through laws voted by its members and ratified by the President. The National Assembly has 180 members who are elected for five-year terms.
National Assembly, Tel: +237 222 80 71, fax: +237 222 09 79, e-mail: ancm@assemblee-nationale.cm, URL: http://www.assembleenationale.cm

Cabinet (as at June 2013)

Prime Minister: Philemon Yang (page 1540)
Deputy-Prime Minister with responsibility for Relations with the Assemblies: Amadou Ali (page 1374)
Minister for Agriculture and Rural Development: Menye Lazare Essimi
Minister of Justice and Keeper of the Seals: Laurant Esso
Minister for Culture: Ama Tutu Muna
Minister for Transport: Robert Nkili
Minister of Territorial Administration and Decentralisation: Rene Emmanuel Sadi
Minister for Posts and Telecommunications: Jean-Pierre Biyiti Bi Essam
Minister for Economy, Planning, Development Programming and Regional Development: Emmanuel Nganou Djoumessi
Minister for Foreign Affairs: Pierre Moukoko Mbonjo
Minister of Town Planning and Housing: Jean Claude Mbwentchou
Minister of Finance: Ousmane Mey Alamine
Minister of Industry, Mines and Technological Development: Emmanuel Bonde
Minister of National Education: Alim Youssouf
Minister of Labour and Social Security: Gregroire Owona
Minister of Employment and Vocational Training: Zacharie Perevet
Minister of Livestock, Fisheries and Animal Industries: Dr Taiga
Minister of Youth and Civic Education: Kpatt Ismael Bidoung
Minister of Sports and Physical Education: Adoum Garoua
Minister of Public Health: Andre Mama Fouda
Minister of Secondary Education: Louis Bapes Bapes
Minister of Environment and Protection of Nature: Pierre Hele
Minister of Public Works: Patrice Amba Salla
Minister of Tourism and Leisure: Bello Bouba Maigari
Minister of Forestry and Wildlife: Philip Ngwese Ngole
Minister of Land Tenure: Jacqueline Koung A Bissike
Minister of Higher Education: Jacques Fame Ndongo (page 1485)
Minister of Social Affairs: Catherine Bakang Mbock
Minister of Civil Service and Administrative Reform: Emmanuel Bonde
Minister of Communication: Issa Tchiroma Bakary
Minister of Trade: Luc Magloire Mbarga Atangara
Minister of Advancement of Women and the Family: Marie Theresa Abena Ondoa
Minister of Water and Energy: Basile Atangana Kouna
Minister of Science, Research and Innovation: Madeleine Tchuente
Minister of SMEs and Handicrafts: Laurent Etoundi Ngoa

Ministries

Office of the Prime Minister, Immeuble Etoile, 1000 Yaoundé, Republic of Cameroon. +237 223 5750, fax: +237 235765, e-mail: spm@camnet.cm, URL: http://www.spm.gov.cm/
Ministry of Economy and Finance, BP 18, Yaoundé, Cameroon. Tel: +237 2223 4040, fax: +237 2223 2150, http://www.camnet.cm/investir/minfi/
Ministry of Commercial and Industrial Development, Yaoundé, Republic of Cameroon. Tel: +237 232388, fax: +237 222704, e-mail: mindic@camnet.cm, URL: http://www.camnet.cm/investir/mindic
Ministry of Justice, c/o the Central Post Office, Yaoundé, Cameroon. Tel: +237 2222 0197, fax: +237 2223 5961
Ministry of Territorial Administration and Decentralization, c/o the Central Post Office, Yaoundé, Cameroon. Tel: +237 2223 4090, fax: +237 2222 3735
Ministry for Forests and Wildlife, c/o the Central Post Office, Yaoundé, Cameroon. Tel: +237 2221 1454, fax: +237 2222 9489, e-mail: onadef@camnet.cm, URL: http://www.camnet.cm/investir/envforet/index.htm
Ministry of Communication, 1000 Yaoundé, Republic of Cameroon. Tel: +237 223155, fax: +237 223 3022
Ministry of Youth and Sports, 1000 Yaoundé, Republic of Cameroon. Tel: +237 233257 / 223 1201, fax: +237 223 2610, URL: http://www.camnet.cm/minjes3
Ministry of Public Health, c/o the Central Post Office, Yaoundé, Cameroon. Tel: +237 2222 2901, fax: +237 2222 5785, URL: http://www.camnet.cm/investir/hgy/index.htm
Ministry of Agriculture, 1000 Yaoundé, Republic of Cameroon. Tel: +237 234085
Ministry of Tourism, 1000 Yaoundé, Republic of Cameroon. Tel: +237 224411, fax: +237 221295, e-mail: mintour@camnet.cm, URL: http://www.camnet.cm/mintour/tourisme
Ministry of the Public Service and Administrative Reform, 1000 Yaoundé, Republic of Cameroon. Tel: +237 222 0356, fax: +237 222 0800
Ministry of Social Affairs, 1000 Yaoundé, Republic of Cameroon. Tel: +237 224148, URL: http://www.camnet.cm/investir/afsoc
Ministry of Posts and Telecommunications, c/o the Central Post Office, Yaoundé, Cameroon. Tel: +237 2223 0615, fax: +237 2223 3159, URL: http://www.camnet.cm/investir/minposte/minpost.htm
Ministry of Public Works, 1000 Yaoundé, Republic of Cameroon. Tel: +237 220156
Ministry of Employment, Labour and Social Welfare, 1000 Yaoundé, Republic of Cameroon. Tel: +237 223 3617
Ministry of Fisheries and Livestock, 1000 Yaoundé, Republic of Cameroon. Tel: +237 222 1370 / fax: +237 222 1405
Ministry of Mines, Water and Energy, 1000 Yaoundé, Republic of Cameroon. Tel: +237 233404, fax: +237 223400, e-mail: minmee@camnet.cm, URL: http://www.camnet.cm/investir/minmee
Ministry of Transport, Yaoundé, Republic of Cameroon. Tel: +237 228709, e-mail: mintrans@camnet.cm, URL: http://www.camnet.cm/investir/transport
Ministry of Industry, Mines and Technological Development, c/o the Central Post Office, Yaoundé, Cameroon. Tel: +237 2223 4040, fax: +237 2222 2704, e-mail: mindic@camnet.cm
Ministry of Land Tenure and State Property, c/o the Central Post Office, Yaoundé, Cameroon. Fax: +237 2222 1509, URL: http://www.minpat.gov.com
Ministry of Tourism, BP 266, Yaoundé, Cameroon. Tel: +237 2222 4411, fax: +237 2222 1295, e-mail: mintour@camnet.cm; URL: http://www.camnet.cm/mintour/tourisme
Ministry of Youth and Sports, c/o the Central Post Office, Yaoundé, Cameroon. Tel: +237 2223 3257, fax: +237 2223 2610, URL: http://www.camnet.cm/minjes3/accueil.htm

Political Parties

There are approximately 47 political parties in Cameroon the main ones being: Cameroon People's Democratic Movement (RDPC); National Union for Democracy and Progress (UNDP); Social Democratic Front (SDF).

Elections

The last legislature election was held on 22nd July 2007; the Cameroon People's Democratic Movement (RDPC), led by President Biya, retained its overall majority of seats in the National Assembly. The most recent presidential election was held in October 2011, President Biya was re-elected with 78 per cent of the vote, his apponents alleged fraud.

The most recent parliamentary election was scheduled for 8 July 2012 but was postponed until July 2013. The result was not known at the time of going to press.

Diplomatic Representation

High Commission for the Republic of Cameroon, 84 Holland Park, London, W11 3SB. Tel: +44 (0)20 7727 0771, fax: +44 (0)20 7792 9353, e-mail: info@cameroonhighcommission.co.uk, URL: http://www.cameroonhighcommission.co.uk
High Commissioner: Janet Ekaney
Embassy of the Republic of Cameroon, 2349 Massachusetts Avenue, NW, Washington, DC 20008, USA. Tel: +1 202 265 8790, fax: +1 202 387 3826, URL: http://www.ambacam-usa.org/
Ambassador: Joseph Foe-Atangana
British High Commission, Avenue Winston Churchill, BP 547, Yaoundé, Cameroon. Tel: +237 220545 / 220796, fax: +237 220148, e-mail: BHC.yaounde@fco.gov.uk, URL: http://ukincameroon.fco.gov.uk/en
High Commissioner: Bharat Joshi (page 1452)
US Embassy, Avenue Rosa Parks, P.O. Box 817, Yaounde, Cameroon. Tel: +237 220 1500, fax: +237 220 1500x4531, URL: http://yaounde.usembassy.gov
Ambassador: Robert P Jackson
Permanent Representative of the Republic of Cameroon to the United Nations, 22 East 73rd Street, New York, NY 10021, USA. Tel: +1 212 794 2295, fax: +1 212 249 0533, e-mail: cameroon@un.int, URL: http://www.cameroonmission.org
Ambassador: Michel Tommo Monthe

LEGAL SYSTEM

The Republic of Cameroon is rare in that it administers both civil and common law, legacies of both the French and English legal systems. The North West and South West provinces are attached to the common law, while the rest of the country adheres to the civil law. The policy of the legislature has been to merge the two systems, which to some extent (particularly with criminal legislation and some aspects of the civil law like labour legislation) has been a success.

The judiciary is independent. A higher judicial council, of which the head is the President, acts as a disciplinary organ and studies proposals of nomination of magistrates in the state. The Supreme Court comprises a president and nine judges, and gives the final decision on both civil and criminal matters, as well as the final interpretation on constitutional matters. The High Court of Justice consists of nine judges and six substitute judges, all of whom are elected by the National Assembly.

Traditional Law is applied mainly in rural areas, and only in very limited cases. The judges who preside over Traditional Law Courts are usually appointed by the Minister of Justice from persons knowledgeable in the customs and traditions of the area.

The government's human rights record is poor; security forces have committed unlawful killings, and have tortured prisoners. Prison conditions are life threatening, and there have been incidents of prolonged pretrial detention. The government restricts freedoms of speech and assembly, and official corruption is endemic. Cameroon retains the death penalty for crimes including secession, esponiage and incitement to war. The last reported execution was in 1997. There were estimated to be over 75 people on death row in 2012. One death sentence was reported to be handed down in 2010 and another in 2011.

National Commission on Human Rights, SGBC Building, 2nd Floor, BP 20317 Yaounde, Cameroon. Tel: +237 2 2226117, fax: +237 2 226082

LOCAL GOVERNMENT

The Republic of Cameroon is divided into 10 administrative provinces: Adamaoua, Centre, Est, Extreme-Nord, Littoral, Nord, Nord-Ouest, Ouest, Sud, and Sud-Ouest. Each has a governor who has been appointed by the President and who is resident at the provincial headquarters. The provinces are further divided into 58 departments or divisions, and 349 subprefectures or subdivisions.

Local elections took place most recently in 2007 and are due to take place again in 2012.

AREA AND POPULATION

Area

Cameroon is situated in on the Gulf of Guinea which makes up its western border, it is bordered on the north by the Republic of Chad, the west by Nigeria, the east by the Central African Republic, and on the south by the Republic of Congo, Gabon and Equatorial Guinea. It has an area of 475,000 sq. km, the north of the country is made up of desert plains, the central area is mountainous, the highest altitude being 4,070 metres (Mount Cameroon), and the south and east of the country has rain forests. The main rivers of Cameroon include the Sanaga and Nyong rivers which flow west to the Atlantic Ocean, the Mbéré and Logone rivers flow north into Lake Chad.

CAMEROON

The climate is very varied. The coastal area is very hot and humid, with high precipitation and a short dry season. The South Cameroon Plateau rises from the coastal plan. It is less humid than the coast with wet and dry seasons. Cameroon's mountain chain has a mild climate with high rainfall. The northern lowland is an arid region with high temperatures and low rainfall.

To view a map of Cameroon, please consult:
http://www.un.org/Depts/Cartographic/map/profile/cameroon.pdf

Population

The population in 2010 was estimated at 19.599 million, with an annual population growth rate of 2.2 per cent over the period 2000-10 and a population density of 27.9 people per sq. km. The major ethnic groups are Hausa, Fulbe, Bamileke, Tiker, Bamoun, Fang, Ewondo, Boulou, Eton, Bassa, Bakoko and Douala.

Approximately 58 per cent of the population lives in urban areas. The capital Yaoundé has a population of around 1.5 million. Other major cities are Douala with a population of around 1.7 million, Garoua, 424,000, Maroua, 409,000, Bafoussam, 319,500 and Bamenda, 321,500.

Official languages are English and French. In addition some 100-200 Congo-Kordofanian and Afro-Asiatic languages are also spoken.

Births, Marriages, Deaths

The birth rate in 2010 was estimated at 36.2 births per 1,000 of the population, while the death rate was estimated at 14.4 deaths per 1,000 of the population. Infant mortality was 94 deaths per 1,000 live births. Average life expectancy in 2009 was an estimated 51 years. Healthy life expectancy was 45 years. Approximately 41 per cent of the population is aged under 15 years and 5 per cent over 60 years. The median age is 19. The fertility rate is 4.5 children born per woman. (Source: http://www.who.int, World Health Statistics 2012)

Public Holidays 2014

1 January: New Year's Day and Independence Day
14 January: Birth of the Prophet*
11 February: Youth Day
1 April: Easter Monday
18 April: Good Friday
1 May: Labour Day
29 May: Ascension Day
20 May: Proclamation of the Republic
29 July: Eid Al Fitr (Ramadan ends)*
15 August: Assumption Day
1 October: Reunification
5 October: Eid al-Adha (Festival of Sacrifice)*
25 December: Christmas
*Islamic holiday - precise date depends on sighting of the moon

EMPLOYMENT

Estimates put the total labour force at 7.84 million in 2010. Agriculture provides employment for 70 per cent of the active working population, with industry and commerce employing 13 per cent. The unemployment rate in 2001 was estimated at 30 per cent.

BANKING AND FINANCE

Currency: CFA franc

The CFA franc is pegged to the euro at 655.957.

GDP/GNP, Inflation, National Debt

Cameroon is rich in natural resources which has helped it become the region's best economic performer. Despite its relatively strong export market, the economy has been hindered by corruption and economic mismanagement. Recent structural reforms include liberalising agriculture and industry and the privatisation of the water and electricity utilities and the national oil company. Foreign investment remainled relatively low. Cameroon is unlikely to meet its Millennium goals due to lower than anticipated growth. In response to the global rise in commodity prices the government was forced to reduce food import tariffs to counter social unrest.

Cameroon's economy was historically based on agriculture, fishing and forestry. However, since the mid-1990s, the economy has begun to diversify, particularly in the area of oil production, with the services sector contributing 40 per cent of GDP, industry 31 per cent, and agriculture just 29 per cent. Since then Cameroon's economy has demonstrated reasonable growth, some of which can be attributed to diversification away from agriculture. By 2009 the service sector made up 50 per cent of GDP, industry made up 30 per cent and agriculture just 20 per cent. Other contributors towards Cameroon's stronger economy include improvements in fiscal spending, efforts to reduce the high external debt, and, in particular, a multi-million debt-relief package by the World Bank. However, Cameroon has also been affected adversely by the world economic crisis. In 2010, Cameroon issued its first sovereign bond raising an estimated US$400 million for special projects. Foreign investment in new diamond mining projects have also helped the economy.

In 2010, GDP was estimated to be US$22.5 billion with an annual growth rate of over 3 per cent. Per capita GDP was US$1,100. The estimated inflation rate was 5.1 per cent in 2008 and 5.3 per cent in 2009. In 2010 it was estimated to be 1.3 per cent, the low rate aided by government subsidies on fuel and food. GDP was estimated to be US$25 billion in 2011 with a growth rate of 4 per cent. Growth is expected to continue to be over 4 per cent in 2012 and 2013 due to a recovery in the oil sector.

A US$144 million credit to Cameroon was agreed in 2001 with the IMF following satisfactory economic reforms. In 2006 the Paris Club, a group of leading lending countries reached an agreement whereby nearly of all of Cameroon's debt of US$3.5 billion was cancelled. Further the IFC are providing financial support for small and medium investment projects. In 2009 the IMF approved US$144 million of loans.

Balance of Payments / Imports and Exports

Cameroon's exports in 2011 generated an estimated US$5 billion, whilst imports cost an estimated US$6 billion. Principal export commodities are crude oil and petroleum products, lumber, cocoa beans, wood, aluminium, cotton, and coffee. Principal import products are machinery and electrical equipment, transport equipment, food, and fuel. The EU is the main trading partner accounting for over 50 per cent of exports and 40 per cent of imports. France and China are the main trading countries.

Central Bank

Banque des États de l'Afrique Centrale (BEAC), PO Box 1917, Rue du Docteur Jamot, Yaounde, Cameroun. Tel: +237 234030 / 234060, fax: +237 233329, URL: http://www.beac.int
Governor: Lucas Abaga Nchama

MANUFACTURING, MINING AND SERVICES

Primary and Extractive Industries

Exploration for petroleum began in the 1950s and is controlled by the national oil company, Société Nationale de Hydrocarbures (SNH), formed in 1980. Major international oil companies involved in Cameroon's oil industry include Chevron, TotalFinaElf, Exxon Mobil, Petronas, Royal Dutch/Shell (Pecten), and Texaco. Today, Cameroon's oil industry concentrates on refining and sales rather than production. The sale of petroleum products contributes a third of government and export revenues, whilst accounting for less than 5 per cent of GDP.

Cameroon is the sixth largest oil producer in sub-Saharan Africa, becoming a net oil exporter in 1995. Proven oil reserves at the beginning of January 2012 were estimated at 200 million barrels. Oil production increased in 1996 with the development of the Kribi area and discovery of the Ebome field, and in 1999 crude oil production reached 84,800 barrels per day. However, with the exhausting of existing fields, and the absence of newly-discovered ones, production is declining in the long term. Oil production was 61,990 barrels per day in 2011 with 27,000 barrels per day being used domestically the rest going for export. The crude oil refining capacity in at the beginning of January 2012 was 37,000 barrels per day.

Cameroon was in dispute with Nigeria over oil rights in the oil-rich Bakassi Peninsula. The International Court of Justice (ICJ) ruled in October 2002 in favour of Cameroon; however, Nigeria rejected the ruling. In 2005, President Paul Biya and Nigerian president, Olusegun Obasanjo, met UN Secretary General Kofi Annan to discuss the situation and in June 2006 Nigeria's troops withdrew from the area. In August 2008 Nigeria agreed to hand over the Bakassi peninsula to Cameroon.

Cameroon had natural gas reserves of 5.0 trillion cubic feet at the beginning of January 2012; production began in 2006 with one billion cubic feet produced all of which was consumed. Reserves have been discovered in the Rio Del Rey, Douala and Kribi-Campo basins but they have not been developed. Figures for 2011 put production at 7.0 billion cubic feet and consumption at 5.0 billion cubic feet.

Coal production was 1,000 short tons in 2001, all of which was bituminous. In recent years no coal has been produced. The Golf of Mamfe holds deposits of lead, zinc, sapphire and salt. Salt is exploited in Mbankang and Manakang villages.

Analysis of iron ore deposits show a hematite content of 40 per cent to 50 per cent and magnetite content of 35 per cent to 70 per cent. As part of the South West research project rare earths have been discovered in the basin close to Mont des Éléphants. Bauxite deposits are known to exist in Cameroon at two locations. Nickel deposits exist in the Lomie region.

Energy

Cameroon's total energy consumption in 2006 was 0.088 quadrillion Btu.

Cameroon has 110 possible hydroelectric sites with a combined potential capacity of 500,000 megawatts, making it the country with the greatest power potential in Africa (alongside the Democratic Republic of Congo). Cameroon has an electric generation capacity of 819,000 kilowatts, 88 per cent of which is obtained from hydro-electric generation and 12 per cent of which is thermal. Generation in 2001 was 3.90 billion kilowatthours (kWh). Consumption in the same year was 332 billion kWh.

Cameroon's major hydro power stations, Edea and Song-Loulou, are located on the Sananga River. Approximately 30 diesel power stations are available as a back-up system to assist when water levels at the hydro dams are insufficient. Feasibility studies have also been carried out by Hydro-Quebec regarding the construction of a new power station. Further, an agreement has been signed for the development of a gas turbine power station near the port town of Kribi. The main production site for oil and petroleum products is the Limbe based SONARA plant. The state-owned utility Société Nationale d'Electricité de Cameroun (SONEL) is responsible for generation and distribution of electricity, and is part-owned by AES-SONEL.

Other sources of energy include charcoal, bio-gas and solar. There is a prototype installation for the electrification of the Mefomo rural dispensary, 20 km from Yaoundé, and 10 stations for measuring sun rays are already operational.

Manufacturing

The annual growth rate in this sector is approximately 6 per cent, and accounts for some 25 per cent of exports. Main products are enamel utensils and sheet iron products, beer, shoes, soap, oil, liquid air, meat products, bread, fruit juices, powdered milk, chocolate, corn and palm oil, mineral water, batteries, vegetable oils, textile goods, chemical products, cement and tobacco products.

Service Industries

The government's influence in economic activities is particularly felt in companies such as Cameroon Airlines, Cameroon Shipping Lines and the Railway Company, as well as public utility industries like water (SNEC) and electricity (SONEL). Private enterprise is concentrated on small- and medium-sized industries.

Figures for 2006 showed that there were 176,000 visitors to Cameroon generating earnings of $212 million.

Agriculture

Cameroon's economy is essentially agricultural. Agriculture, forestry and fishing contributes about 44 per cent of GDP, employs about 80 per cent of the working population, and creates over 50 per cent of total export earnings. The country's geographical position enables it to offer a wide and varied range of products for export and home consumption. Agricultural products are divided into two groups, cash crops and food crops.

Cash crops are basically intended for export and include: coffee, cocoa, rubber, tea, cotton, tobacco, banana, oil palm and pineapples.

Food crops are mainly for home consumption and can be divided into four sections: (1) Cereals: maize, millet and sorgum, rice; (2) Tubers and Plantains: cocoyams-taro, cassava yams, sweet potato, Irish potato; (3) Leguminous plants: groundnuts, soya beans, beans, peas, egusi, sesame; (4) Fruits: mangos, pears, pineapples, bananas, oranges, guavas.

Agricultural Production in 2008

Produce	Int. $'000	Tonnes
Plantains	310,534	1,400,000
Indigenous cattle meat	179,867	86,964
Cassava	162,135	2,500,000
Cocoa beans	144,433	187,532
Maize	125,658	1,200,000
Bananas	116,858	820,000
Beans, dry	101,595	250,000
Game meat	101,528	62,000
Tomatoes	99,510	420,000
Taro (cocoyam)	98,899	1,200,000
Vegetables fresh nes	90,072	480,000
Sorghum	70,754	600,000

Source: http://faostat.fao.org/site/339/default.aspx FAOSTAT, Statistics Division, Food and Agriculture Organization of the UN

The Cameroonian forest covers a total area of 20 million hectares. The average area of forest exploited annually is 423,700 hectares.

The main forestry products are timber, lumber and firewood. The exploitation of firewood, which is the people's main source of heat energy, is still haphazard. Annual consumption is estimated at 7.6 million cubic metres. Other forest products are mainly medicinal plants.

COMMUNICATIONS AND TRANSPORT

Travel Requirements

US, Canadian, Australian and EU subjects require a passport valid for a minimum of six months and a visa to enter Cameroon. Evidence of yellow-fever vaccination, and current immunization records may also be required; travellers should obtain the latest information and details from the Embassy.

Nationals not referred to above are advised to contact the embassy to check visa requirements.

National Airlines

Cameroon's national airline is:
Cameroon Airlines, BP 4092, 3 avenue General de Gaulle, Douala, Littoral, Cameroon. Tel: +237 4 22525, fax: +237 4 33543

International Airports

Cameroon has over 36 airports of various categories. The principal ones are Douala, Yaounde and Garoua, which are all of international standard. Douala airport is used by such international carriers as Alitalia, UTA, Swiss, Iberian Airways, Air France and Cameroon Airlines.

Railways

The oldest railroad in the country links Yaoundé and Douala to Nkongsamba (172 km). In the South-West province, the Cameroon Development Corporation operates a 150 km network of railroad of narrow gauge through its plantations. The longest railroad is the Trans-Cameroon that links Douala to Ngaoundere (628 km). This is to be extended to the Central African Republic and Chad.

Roads

Cameroon has a classified road network of 28,681 km, of which 2,500 km is tarred. In all, there are about 65,000 km of highways but many are unsuitable for vehicles, especially in the rainy season. Cameroon's vehicle stock is estimated at 70,000, with a rate of 83.3 people per motor vehicle. Vehicles drive on the right.

Shipping

In the North province the river Benue, a tributary of the Niger, passes through Garoua. During the months of July, August and September the water level is high enough to ship goods on barges.

Ports and Harbours

Cameroon has four principal ports, Douala-Bonaberi being the most important, followed by the Bota and Tiko ports in the south-west and the Kribi port in the Southern Province.

HEALTH

There are three central hospitals situated in Garoua, Yaoundé and Douala, approximately 75 general hospitals, 680 health centres and 45 centres for mother and child care.

In 2009, the government spent approximately 7.3 per cent of its total budget on healthcare, accounting for 25.9 per cent of all healthcare spending. Total expenditure on healthcare equated to 4.9 per cent of the country's GDP. Per capita expenditure on health was approximately US$41. Figures from the WHO for the period 2000-10 estimated that there were 3,124 physicians (2 per 10,000 population), 26,042 nurses and midwives (16 per 10,000 population) and 147 dentists. There are an estimated 15 hospital beds per 10,000 population. (Source: World Health Organisation, NB Statistics based on scarce data)

According to the latest WHO figures, in 2010 approximately 77 per cent of the population had access to improved drinking water. In the same year, 49 per cent of the population had access to improved sanitation.

The infant mortality rate in 2009 was 84 per 1,000 live births. The child mortality rate (under 5 years) was 136 per 1,000 live births. The main causes of childhood mortality are: prematurity (11 per cent), diarrhoea (13 per cent), pneumonia (15 per cent), malaria (16 per cent) and HIV/AIDs (5 per cent). An estimated 13 per cent of children sleep under insecticide-treated nets. Immunization rates have risen: approximately 79 per cent of children now receive the measles vaccination and over 80 per cent received DTP3, HepB3 and Hib3 vaccinations. (Source: http://www.who.int, World Health Statistics 2012)

Recent figures show that around 550,000 people are living with the HIV/AIDS virus.

EDUCATION

Education is free of charge and lasts for six years. Primary education lasts from the age of six until 12 and is compulsory and there is a pupil: teacher 44:1. Secondary education lasts from 12 to 18 (four at lower level and three at upper level). Attendance is usually based on whether the parents can afford the fees. The primary school age population is 2.14 million, with the gross enrolment ratio down from 101 per cent in 1990 to 88 per cent in 1996. The secondary school-age population is 2.05 million, with the gross enrolment ratio down from 28 per cent in 1990 to 27 per cent in 1996. Public current expenditure on education as a percentage of GDP was 3.9 per cent in 2007.

Cameroon has seven universities. Seven per cent of tertiary age students were in further education in 2007.

The adult literacy rate in 2007 was put at 71 per cent for men and 51 per cent for women, one of the highest in Africa.

RELIGION

Cameroon is a secular state practising freedom of religion. Approximately 57 per cent of the population is Christian, whilst 19 per cent is Muslim and 22 per cent holds traditional beliefs.

Cameroon has a religious tolerance rating of 7 on a scale of 1 to 10 (10 is most freedom). (Source: World Religion Database)

COMMUNICATIONS AND MEDIA

There are strict government controls on the media and there are severe libel laws. State broadcasting held a monopoly until 2007 when two licences to private broadcasters were issued. There are several unlicensed private broadcasters in operation. Foreign news broadcasters must partner with the government-owned national broadcaster.

Newspapers

Main newspapers include: the state-owned Cameroon Tribune (state-owned, French & English daily), URL: http://www.cameroon-tribune.net/; The Post (private, English), URL: http://www.postnewsline.com; Le Messager (daily), URL: http://www.lemessager.net/; La Nouvelle Expression, (French), URL: http://www.lanouvelleexpression.net

Broadcasting

The Cameroon Radio and Television Corporation (CRTV) (URL: http://www.crtv.cm/) operates at least one provincial radio station for each province and a national station based in the capital Yaoundé. At present the only television station is situated in Yaoundé. However, Government policy is to open more television stations in the provinces.

Telecommunications

The telephone system is old and unreliable in many parts of the country. Subscriptions for landlines are low at less than 200,000 whilst mobile phone subscriptions have risen sharply to over 6 million in 2008. There were approximately 725,000 regular internet users.

CANADA

ENVIRONMENT

Cameroon's main environmental issues are water-borne diseases, deforestation, overgrazing, desertification, poaching and over fishing.

Carbon dioxide emissions were estimated at 6.81 million metric tons in 2005, equivalent to 0.39 metric tons per capita. Figures for 2010 put carbon dioxide emissions at 7.36 metric tons.

On an international level the Republic of Cameroon is a party to conventions on: Biodiversity, Climate Change, Climate Change-Kyoto Protocol, Desertification, Endangered Species, Hazardous Wastes, Law of the Sea, Ozone Layer Protection, Tropical Timber 83, Tropical Timber 94, Wetlands, and Whaling.

In July 1998, 90 national and international human rights and environmental non-governmental organisations petitioned the World Bank to axe plans to run an oil pipeline from Chad to Cameroon, through areas of jungle inhabited by the Bagyeli, or Pygmies. As a result, the consortium re-routed the pipeline.

CANADA

Capital: Ottawa (Population estimate, 2012) 1,200,000

Head of State: HM Queen Elizabeth II (Sovereign) (page 1420)

Governor-General: Hon. David Johnston (page 1451)

National Flag: A single maple leaf with eleven points on a white square, flanked by vertical red bars one half the width of the square

CONSTITUTION AND GOVERNMENT

Constitution
The Government of Canada was established under the provisions of the British North America Act 1867, with amendments from the Constitution Act 1982. This statute forms the written basis of the Constitution of Canada. The Canadian Constitution combined the British Cabinet system of responsible government with a Canadian adaptation of the United States principle of federation.

The provinces united under this Act were Upper and Lower Canada (now Ontario and Quebec), Nova Scotia and New Brunswick. Provision was made for the later admission of British Columbia, Prince Edward Island, the Northwest Territories and Newfoundland. The province of Manitoba, formed out of the Northwest Territories, was admitted on 15 July 1870, British Columbia on 20 July 1871 and Prince Edward Island on 1 July 1873, having previously refused to join. The Yukon Territory joined in 1898. The new provinces of Alberta and Saskatchewan were admitted on 1 September 1905. Newfoundland, who had with Prince Edward Island originally refused to join, entered the Dominion on 31 March 1949 as the result of a plebiscite held in July 1948.

In 1993 two pieces of legislation were passed in order to pave the way for the creation of a new territory, Nunavut, in response to Inuit land claims: the Nunavut Land Claims Agreement Act which ratified the land claim, and the Nunavut Act which divided the Northwest Territories in order to create the new territory. The territory officially came into being on 1 April 1999 when elections were held for the first Nunavut Government.

The Queen is represented in Canada by a Governor-General, who holds the same position in relation to the administration of public affairs in Canada as the Queen holds in Britain. The Canadian Parliament comprises the Queen (represented by the Governor-General), the Senate and the House of Commons. The Governor-General is appointed by the Queen, on the advice of the Prime Minister of Canada, usually for a term of five years. Canada's system of government is based on that of the British by which a Cabinet (composed of members of the House of Commons or the Senate) is responsible to Parliament. The Cabinet is actually a committee of the Queen's Privy Council for Canada. Members of the Cabinet are chosen by the prime minister; each generally assumes charge of one of the various Departments of Government.

The national Parliament has power "to make laws for the peace, order and good government of Canada," except for "subjects assigned exclusively to the legislatures of the provinces". The provincial legislatures have power over direct taxation in the province for provincial purposes, natural resources, prisons (except penitentiaries), charitable institutions, hospitals (except marine hospitals), municipal institutions, licenses for provincial and municipal revenue purposes, local works and undertakings (with certain exceptions), incorporation of provincial companies, solemenenisation of marriage, property and civil rights in the province, the creation of courts and the administration of justice, fines and penalties for breaking provincial laws, matters of a merely local or private nature in the province, and education (subject to certain rights of the Protestant and Roman Catholic minorities in any province, and of particular denominations in Newfoundland)

To consult the full constitution, please visit: http://laws.justice.gc.ca/en/const/index.html

International Relations
Canada historically has close ties with the United Kingdom and is a member of the Commonwealth. Geographically Canada has close ties with USA with which it does a large volume of trade. Canada is a member of the North America Free Trade Association, North Atlantic Treaty Organisation (NATO); Organisation of American States (OAS); G8; World Trade Organisation (WTO); La Francophonie. Canada had up to 2009 around 600 troops in Afghanistan. Although Canada didn't send troops to fight in the US-led war in Iraq, it has spent Can$300 million on reconstruction and humanitarian projects in that country since 2003.

In recent years Canada has been asserting its sovereignty in the Arctic involving dialogue with the USA and Denmark. The Arctic is believed to have large reserves of oil and gas.

Canada was a key member of the 2011 NATO mission in Libya. Also that year Canadian Forces began a training mission in Afghanistan.

Recent Events
In December 2003, the leader of the Liberal Party Jean Chretien retired as Prime Minister following 10 years in office. Paul Martin was sworn in as prime minister. The following February, the party became embroiled in a scandal concerning the misuse of money intended for advertising and sponsorship; accusations were made of kickbacks being paid to ensure government contracts. The Liberal Party won the general election held in June 2004, but lost its majority. The financial scandal continued to cause problems for the party and in May 2005 the government survived a vote of no-confidence by just one vote. In November, the commission set up to look into the scandal delivered its report; Prime Minister Paul Martin was exonerated but the former prime minister, Jean Chretien was criticised. That month the government failed to win a second no-confidence vote and elections were scheduled for January 2006. The election was won by Stephen Harper's Conservative party, ending a 12 year run of Liberal Governments.

In November 2006, the Canadian parliament agreed a proposal put forward by Prime Minister Harper that the Quebecois should be considered a 'nation' within Canada. The proposal was put to a vote and was approved by 266 votes to 16.

In December 2008, opposition parties united to bring down the minority Conservative government in response to the global economic crisis. A vote of no confidence was avoided by Prime Minister Harper when he asked the Governor General to suspend parliament until January 2009. In February a stimulus package was agreed by parliament negating the need for the vote. The package was worth Can$40 billion. Although Canada has escaped some of the dramatic losses experienced by many countries the stock marked fell sharply in 2008 and Canada has experienced the knock on effect of the crisis in the USA as it is Canada's main trading partner.

In February 2010 Canada hosted the Winter Olympics.

At the November 2011 UN Climate Summit, Canada announced it would not make further cuts in its greenhouse emissions under the Kyoto Protocol and may begin formally withdrawing. Canada has not met its existing commitment (a reduction of 6 per cent compared to 1990). In fact, emissions have risen by over 30 per cent since 1990. In December Canada formally withdrew from the protocol.

In September 2012, Canada broke off diplomatic relations with Iran in an effort to strengthen sanctions against Tehran over its nuclear programme and support for the Assad government in Syria.

In February 2013, the Canadian penny was withdrawn from circulation as production costs exceeded its monetary value.

In July 2013, a runaway freight train carrying crude oil derailed and blew up in the Quebec town of Lac-Megantic. Five people were initially reported as having been killed but more than 40 were still missing and 30 buildings in the town had been completely destroyed in the ensuing fires.

Upper House
The Upper House of the Canadian Parliament, the Senate, consists of 105 Senators appointed by the Governor General on the advice of the Prime Minister. The Senate has all of the powers of the House of Commons except that of initiating financial legislation. Each province and territory is represented by Senators according to its population. Senators serve until the age of 75 and are appointed by the Governor General following recommendation by the Prime Minister. The following table shows the make up of the Senate as of February 2013.

Province/Territory	Senators
Alberta	6
British Columbia	5
Manitoba	6
New Brunswick	10
Newfoundland & Labrador	6
Nova Scotia	10
Northwest Territories	1
Nunavut	1
Ontario	24
Prince Edward Island	4
Quebec	24
Saskatchewan	6
Yukon	1
Party	
Liberal Party	36

- continued

Conservative Party	65
Progressive Conservative	1
Independent	2

Senate, Senate Building, Wellington Street, Ottawa, Ontario K1A 0A4, Canada. Tel: +1 613 992 2493, fax: +1 613 992 7959, URL: http://www.parl.gc.ca

Lower House

Canada's Lower House is the House of Commons. Made up of 302 Members, this is the elected part of the Parliament of Canada and elections take place every five years. Although the Cabinet has the sole power to prepare and introduce bills providing for the expenditure of public money or imposing taxes, these bills must be introduced first in the House of Commons. The House cannot initiate them, or increase either the tax or the expenditure without a royal recommendation in the form of a message from the Governor General. The Senate cannot increase either a tax or an expenditure. However, any Member of either House can move a motion to decrease a tax or an expenditure, and the House concerned can pass it, though this hardly ever happens. The representation of provinces in the house is adjusted after each census in accordance with the wishes of Parliament. For electoral purposes, each province is divided into districts, returning a member on a plurality of votes taken by ballot.
House of Commons, Parliament Buildings, Wellington Street, Ottawa K1A 0A6, Ontario, Canada. Tel: +1 613 943 5959, fax: +1 613 992 3674, URL: http://www.parl.gc.ca
Speaker: Hon. Andrew Scheer (page 1509)

Cabinet (as at May 2013)
Prime Minister: The Rt. Hon. Stephen Harper (page 1438)
Leader of the Government in the House of Commons: Peter Van Loan (page 1530)
Federal Minister of International Trade, Minister of Asia Pacific Gateway: Edward Fast
Federal Minister of Labour: Lisa Raitt (page 1499)
Federal Minister of National Revenue: Gail Shea (page 1513)
Federal Minister of Fisheries and Oceans; Minister of the Atlantic Gateway: Keith Ashfield (page 1379)
Federal Minister of Veterans Affairs: Steven Blaney
Leader of the Government in the Senate: Marjory LeBreton (page 1461)
Federal Minister of Agriculture and Agri-Food and Minister of the Canadian Wheat Board: Gerry Ritz (page 1503)
Federal Minister of Natural Resources: Joe Oliver
Federal Minister of Foreign Affairs: John Baird (page 1381)
Federal Minister of Public Safety: Vic Toews (page 1526)
Federal Minister of Justice and Attorney General of Canada: Robert Nicholson
Federal Minister of the Environment: Peter Kent (page 1455)
Federal Minister of National Defence: Peter MacKay (page 1468)
Federal Minister of Canadian Heritage and Official Languages: James Moore (page 1479)
President of the Treasury Board, Minister for the Federal Economic Development Initiative for Northern Ontario: Tony Clement (page 1406)
Federal Minister of Industry; Minister of State for Agriculture: Christian Paradis (page 1492)
Federal Minister of Transport, Infrastructure and Communities; Canada Economic Development Agency for the Regions of Quebec; President of the Queen's Privy Council for Canada, Minister of Intergovernmental Affairs: Denis Lebel (page 1461)
Federal Minister of Health; Minister of the Canadian Northern Economic Development Agency: Leona Aglukkaq (page 1372)
Federal Minister of Finance: James Flaherty (page 1425)
Federal Minister of International Co-operation: Julian Fantino
Federal Minister of Aboriginal Affairs and Northern Development: Bernard Valcourt (page 1530)
Minister of Public Works and Government Services, Minister for the Status of Women: Rona Ambrose (page 1377)
Minister of Human Resources and Skills Development: Diane Finley (page 1424)
Minister of Citizenship and Immigration: Jason Kenney (page 1455)
Minister of State and Chief Whip: Gordon O'Connor (page 1488)
Minister of State for Small Business and Tourism: Maxime Bernier
Associate Minister of National Defence: Kerry-Lynne Findlay
Federal Minister of State for Western Economic Diversification: Lynne Yelich (page 1541)
Federal Minister of State for Transport: Steven John Fletcher (page 1425)
Federal Minister of State for Science and Technology: Gary Goodyear (page 1432)
Federal Minister of State for Finance: Ted Menzies (page 1476)
Federal Ministerof State for Democratic Reform: Tim Uppal
Federal Minister of State for Senior: Alice Wong
Federal Minister of State for Sport: Bal Gosal
Minister of State for Foreign Affairs (Americas): Diane Ablonczy (page 1371)

Parliamentary Secretaries Office of the Prime Minister
Parliamentary Secretary: Dean Del Mastro
Ministry of Indian Affairs and Northern Development
Parliamentary Secretary: Greg Rickford
Ministry of Agriculture
Parliamentary Secretaries: Pierre Lemieux
Ministry of Foreign Affairs
Parliamentary Secretary: Deepak Obhrai, (page 1488) Bob Dechert
Ministry of International Co-operation
Parliamentary Secretary: Lois Brown
Ministry of Industry
Parliamentary Secretary: Mike Lake
Ministry of Public Safety
Parliamentary Secretary: Candice Bergen

Ministry of the Status of Women
Parliamentary Secretaries: Susan Truppe
Ministry of Official Languages
Parliamentary Secretary: Jacques Gourde (page 1432)
Ministry of Canadian Heritage
Parliamentary Secretary: Paul Calandra
Ministry of Human Resources and Social Development
Parliamentary Secretary: Dr. Kellie Leitch
Ministry of Veterans Affairs
Parliamentary Secretary: Eve Adams
Ministry of National Defence
Parliamentary Secretary: Chris Alexander
Minister of Health
Parliamentary Secretary: Dr. Colin Carrie
Ministry of Citizenship and Immigration
Parliamentary Secretary: Richard Dykstra
Ministry of Justice
Parliamentary Secretaries: Robert Goguen
Ministry of Finance
Parliamentary Secretary: Shelly Glover
Ministry of Fisheries and Oceans and the Asia-Pacific Gateway
Parliamentary Secretary: Randy Kamp (page 1453)
Ministry of International Trade
Parliamentary Secretary: Gerald Keddy (page 1455)
Ministry of Multiculturalism
Parliamentary Secretary: Chungsen Leung
Ministry of National Revenue
Parliamentary Secretary: Cathy McLeod
Office of the Leader in the House of Commons
Parliamentary Secretary: Tom Lukiwski (page 1467)
Ministry of the Environment
Parliamentary Secretary: Michelle Rempel
Office of the President of the Treasury Board
Parliamentary Secretary: Andrew Saxton
Ministry of Transport, Infrastructure and Communities
Parliamentary Secretaries: Pierre Poilievre (page 1496)

Ministries
Office of the Prime Minister, 80 Wellington Street, Ottawa, ON K1A 0A2, Canada. Tel: +1 613 992 4211, fax: +1 613 941 6900, e-mail: pm@pm.gc.ca, URL: http://pm.gc.ca
Agriculture and Agri-Food Canada, Sir John Carling Building, 930 Carling Avenue, Ottawa, ON K1A 0C5, Canada. Tel: +1 613 759 1000, fax: +1 613 759 7977, URL: http://www.agr.gc.ca
Canadian Heritage, 15 Eddy Street, Gatineau, Quebec, K1A 0M5, Canada. Tel: +1 819 997 0055, fax: +1 819 953 5382, URL: http://www.canadianheritage.gc.ca
Citizenship and Immigration Canada, Jean Edmonds South Tower, 365 Avenue Laurier Ouest, Ottawa, ON K1A 1L1, Canada. Tel: +1 613 954 9019, fax: +1 613 954 2221, URL: http://www.cic.gc.ca
Environment Canada, 70 Crémazie Street, Gatineau, Quebec, K1A 0H3, Canada. Tel: +1 819 997 2800, fax: +1 819 994 1412, URL: http://www.ec.gc.ca
Finance Canada, l'Esplanade Laurier, 140 O'Connor Street, Ottawa, ON K1A 0G5, Canada. Tel: +1 613 996 7861, fax: +1 613 995 5176, URL: http://www.fin.gc.ca
Fisheries and Oceans Canada, 200 Kent Street, Ottawa, ON K1A 0E6, Canada. Tel: +1 613 993 0999, fax: +1 613 990 1866, URL: http://www.dfo-mpo.gc.ca
Foreign Affairs and International Trade Canada, Lester B. Pearson Building, 125 Sussex Drive, Ottawa, ON K1A 0G2, Canada. Tel: +1 613 944 4000, fax: +1 613 996 9709, URL: http://www.international.gc.ca
Health Canada, Brooke Claxton Building, Tunney's Pasture, Ottawa, ON K1A 0J9, Canada. Tel: +1 613 957 2991, fax: +1 613 952 1154, URL: http://www.hc-sc.gc.ca
Human Resources Development Canada, Place du Portage, Phase IV, Gatineau, K1A 0J9, Canada. Tel: +1 819 994 6313, fax: +1 819 953 3981, URL: http://www.hrsdc.gc.ca
Indian and Northern Affairs Canada, Les Terrasses de la Chaudière, Ottawa, ON K1A 0H4, Canada. Tel: +1 819 953 1160, fax: +1 819 953 5491, email: reference@inac.gc.ca, URL: http://www.ainc-inac.gc.ca
Industry Canada, C.D. Howe Building, 235 Queen Street, Ottawa, ON K1A 0H5, Canada. Tel: +1 613 954 5031, fax: +1 613 954 1894, URL: http://www.ic.gc.ca
Justice Canada, 284 Wellington Street, Ottawa, ON K1A 0H8, Canada. Tel: +1 613 957 4222, fax: +1 613 954 0811, URL: http://www.justice.gc.ca
National Defence Canada, National Defence Headquarters, Major-General George R. Pearkes Building, 101 Colonel By Drive, Ottawa, ON K1A 0K2, Canada. Tel: +1 613 995 2534, fax: +1 613 992 4739, URL: http://www.forces.gc.ca
Labour and the Economic Development Agency, Place du Portage, Phase II, 11th Floor 165 Hôtel de Ville Street, Gatineau, Quebec, K1A 0J2. Tel: +1 819 953 5646; fax: +1 819 994 5168
Natural Resources Canada, 580 Booth Street, Ottawa, ON K1A 0E4, Canada. Tel: +1 613 995 0947, fax: +1 613 992 7211, URL: http://www.nrcan-rncan.gc.ca
Public Works and Government Services Canada, Place du Portage, rue Laurier, Gatineau, QC, K1A 0S5, Canada. Tel: +1 819 997 5421, fax: +1 819 956 8382, URL: http://www.pwgsc.gc.ca
Transport Canada, 330 Sparks Street, Ottawa, ON K1A 0N5, Canada. Tel: +1 613 990 2309, fax: +1 613 954 4731, URL: http://www.tc.gc.ca
Treasury Board, West Tower, l'Esplanade Laurier, 300 Laurier Ave. West, Ottawa, ON K1A 0R5, Canada. Tel: +1 613 957 2400, fax: +1 613 998 9071; URL: http://www.tbs-sct.gc.ca
Veterans Affairs Canada, 66 Slater Street, Ottawa ON K1A 0P4, Canada. Tel: +1 613 996 4649, fax: +1 613 954 1055; URL: http://www.vac-acc.gc.ca
Western Economic Diversification Canada, Canada Place, 9700 Jasper Avenue, Suite 1500, Edmonton, AB T5J 4H7, Canada. Tel: +1 403 495 4164, fax: +1 403 495 6876; URL: http://www.wd.gc.ca

CANADA

Political Parties

Liberal Party, 81 Metcalfe, Suite 400, 4th floor, Ottawa, ON K1P 6M8. Tel: +1 613 237 0740, fax: +1 613 235 7208, URL: http://www.liberal.ca
Interim Leader: Bob Rae

Bloc Québécois, 3750 Crémazie Blvd. East, Suite 307, Montréal, QC H2A 1B6, Canada. Tel: +1 514 526 3000, fax: +1 514 526 2868, URL: http://www.blocquebecois.org
Leader: Daniel Paillé

In October 2003 The Progressive Conservative Party and the Canadian Alliance agreed to merge and form a united party to be called The Conservative Party of Canada.

The Conservative Party of Canada, 1720 - 130 Albert Street, Ottawa, Ontario, K1P 5G4, Canada. URL: http://www.conservative.ca
Leader: Stephen Harper (page 1438)

New Democratic Party, 1001-75 Albert Street, Suite 802, Ottawa, ON K1P 5E7, Canada. Tel: +1 613 236 3613, fax: +1 613 230 9950, URL: http://www.ndp.ca
Leader: Tom Mulcair

Green Party of Canada, 244 Gerrard Street East, Toronto, ON M5A 2G2, Canada. Tel.: +1 416 929 2397, fax: +1 416 929 7709, e-mail: webadmin@green.ca, URL: http://green.ca
Leader: Elizabeth May

Canadian Action Party, 99 Atlantic Avenue, Suite 302, Toronto, ON M6K 3J8, Canada. Tel: +1 416 535 4144, fax: +1 416 535 6325, e-mail: info@canadianactionparty.ca, URL: http://www.canadianactionparty.ca
Interim Leader: Christopher Porter

Elections

In early 1993 Brian Mulroney resigned as Prime Minister. His successor, Kim Campbell, lost the federal election in October 1993. The following government was led by Jean Chrétien of the Liberal Party. Elections took place on 2 June 1997 and the Liberal Party was returned to power with 38 per cent of the vote. Mr Chrétien called an early election for November 2000, only three years into the term because he felt he could win a third term based on the strength of the Canadian economy. His Liberal party won 41 per cent of the popular vote. In August 2002 Chrétien announced he would step down in December 2003. Elections held within the Liberal party resulted in former finance minister Paul Martin becoming prime minister. The next election was due in 2005 but was called early and held in June 2004. Although Paul Martin was returned as Prime Minister, the Liberal Party lost its majority. In May 2005 allegations were made about the Liberal Party being involved in a financial scandal, and the Liberal Party narrowly survived a vote of no-confidence. A further vote of no-confidence was held in November 2005 following the release of a report into the scandal; the government lost the vote and elections were scheduled for January 2006. Stephen Harper's, Conservative party won the election, ending a 12 year run of Liberal Governments. However, although the Conservatives had won the 2006 election they did not have a majority and so relied on opposition support to pass new bills. Prime Minister Harper called the situation 'deadlocked and dysfunctional' and accordingly called an early election in October 2008. Although the Conservatives increased the number of their seats they were still 11 short of a majority.

The most recent election was held in May 2011; the Conservatives won a third consecutive term and a parliamentary majority.

Seats won in recent elections

Party	2004	2006	2008	2011
Liberal Party	135	103	76	34
Conservative Party	99	124	143	167
Bloc Québécois	54	51	50	4
New Democratic Party	19	29	37	102
Non Partisan	1	1	2	1

Diplomatic Representation

British Embassy, 80 Elgin Street, Ottawa, ON, K1P 5K7, Canada. Tel: +1 613 237 1530, fax: +1 613 237 7980, e-mail: BHC@fco.gov.uk, URL: http://ukincanada.fco.gov.uk/en
Acting High Commissioner: Corin Robertson

American Embassy, 490 Sussex Drive, Ottawa, ON, K1N 1G8, Canada. Tel: +1 613 238 5335, URL: http://canada.usembassy.gov
Ambassador: David Jacobson (page 1448)

Canadian High Commission, MacDonald House, 1 Grosvenor Square, London, W1X 0AB, United Kingdom. Tel: +44 (0)20 7258 6600, fax: +44 (0)20 7258 6474, URL: http://www.london.gc.ca
High Commissioner: Gordon Campbell (page 1399)

Canadian Embassy, 501 Pennsylvania Avenue, Washington, DC 20001, USA. Tel: +1 202 682 1740, fax: +1 202 682 7726, URL: http://www.canadianembassy.org
Ambassador: Gary Doer (page 1416)
Permanent Representative to the UN, New York: John A. McNee

LEGAL SYSTEM

The administration of justice in Canada follows the English system.

The Supreme Court of Canada, first established in 1875 by the Supreme and Exchequer Court Act, is now governed by the Supreme Court Act. The Supreme Court sits at Ottawa and exercises general appellate jurisdiction throughout Canada in civil and criminal cases. The judgement of the Court is final and conclusive.

The Court is also required to advise on questions referred to it by the Governor in Council. Under section 55 of the Supreme Court Act important questions concerning the interpretation of the Constitution Act, the constitutionality or interpretation of any federal or provincial law, the powers of Parliament or of the provincial legislatures or of both levels of government, among other matters, may be referred by the Government to the Supreme Court for consideration.

In civil cases, appeals may be brought from any final judgment of the highest court of last resort in a province. The Supreme Court will grant permission to appeal if it is of the opinion that a question of public importance is involved, one that transcends the immediate concerns of the parties to the litigation. In criminal cases, the Court will hear appeals concerning indictable offences where an acquittal has been set aside or where there has been a dissenting judgement on a point of law in a provincial court of appeal. The Supreme Court may, in addition, hear appeals on questions of law concerning both summary convictions and indictable offences.

There are normally three sessions of the Court each year, beginning on the fourth Tuesday in January, the fourth Tuesday in April and the first Tuesday in October. The Court consists of a Chief Justice and eight puisne judges. They are appointed by the Governor in Council but are removable by the Governor General on address of the Senate and the House of Commons. They cease to hold office on attaining the age of 75 years. The Court is responsible for its own administration and budgeting. The Registrar has the rank of Deputy Head and, subject to the direction of the Chief Justice, is responsible for the Registry, the Library, the Supreme Court Reports as well as personnel.

Supreme Court of Canada, URL: http://www.scc-csc.gc.ca
Chief Justice: The Rt. Hon. Beverley McLachlin (page 1475)

Judges:
The Hon. Mr. Justice Louis LeBel
The Hon. Mr. Justice Morris J. Fish
The Hon. Madam Justice Rosalie Silberman Abella
The Hon. Mr. Justice Marshall Rothstein
The Hon. Mr. Justice Thomas Albert Cromwell
The Hon. Mr. Justice Michael J. Moldaver
The Hon. Mr. Justice Andromache Karakatsanis
The Hon. Mr. Justice Richard Wagner

The Federal Court of Appeal has jurisdiction on appeals from the Trial Division, appeals from Federal Tribunals, review of decisions of Federal Boards and Commissions, appeals from Tribunals and reviews under section 28 of the Federal Court Act, and references by Federal Boards and Commissions. The Trial Division of the Federal Court of Canada has jurisdiction in claims against the Crown, claims by the Crown, miscellaneous cases involving the Crown, claims against or concerning Crown Officers and Servants, relief against Federal Boards, Commissions and other Tribunals, Inter-Provincial and Federal-Provincial disputes, industrial, industrial property matters, admiralty, income tax and estate tax appeals, citizenship appeals, aeronautics, Inter-Provincial works and undertakings, residuary jurisdiction for relief if there is no other Canadian court that has such jurisdiction and jurisdiction in specific matters conferred by Federal Statutes.

The Federal Court consists of a Chief Justice and 32 other judges. At present, there are also seven deputy judges, and six prothonotaries whose authority includes mediation, case management, practice motions and trials of actions in which up to $50,000 is claimed.

Federal Court and Federal Court of Appeal, URL: http://www.fct-cf.gc.ca
Chief Justice: The Hon. Paul S. Crampton

Provincial Courts

Each of the Canadian provinces has its own judicial system: each province has a two-tier court system, the provincial courts, which deal with criminal matters and smaller civil cases and superior courts, which usually have a trial level and an appeal level.

Human Rights

The Canadian government respects the rights of its citizens. The death penalty was abolished in 1976 and the last executions took place in 1962.

Canadian Human Rights Commission, 344 Slater Street, 8th Floor, Ottawa, Ontario K1A 1E1, Canada. Tel: +1 613 995 1151, fax: +1 613 996 9661, URL: http://www.chrc-ccdp.ca/

LOCAL GOVERNMENT

Canada is divided into 10 provinces and three territories. Each has a unicameral legislative assembly which functions in a way very similar to the House of Commons. All bills put forward must go through three readings and receive Royal Assent by the Lieutenant-Governor. The Lieutenant-Governor of each province is appointed by the Governor-General in Council, and governs with the advice and assistance of the Ministry or Executive Council, which is responsible to the Legislature and resigns when it ceases to enjoy the confidence of that body.

Members of the legislature are elected from constituencies established by the legislature roughly in proportion to population, and whichever candidate gets the largest number of votes is elected, even if their vote is less than half the total.

Municipal governments - cities, towns, villages, counties, districts, metropolitan regions - are set up by the provincial legislatures, and have such powers as the legislatures see fit to give them. Mayors, reeves and councillors are elected on a basis that the provincial legislature prescribes. There are now close to 5,000 municipal governments in the country.

Population of the Provinces and Territories as at July 1 2012

Province	Population
Newfoundland and Labrador	512,700
Prince Edward Island	146,100
Nova Scotia	948,700
New Brunswick	756,000
Quebec	8,054,800

- continued

Ontario	13,505,900
Manitoba	1,267,000
Saskatchewan	1,080,000
Alberta	3,873,700
British Columbia	4,622,600
Territories	
Yukon Territory	36,100
Northwest Territories	43,300
Nunavut	33,700

Source: Statistics Canada, CANSIM table 051-0001 Feb. 2013

AREA AND POPULATION

Area

Canada, the second largest country in the world in terms of land area, stretches from the Atlantic Ocean in the east to the Pacific in the west. The area covered is some 3,845,000 sq. miles, (9,984,670 sq. km of which 891,163 sq km is fresh water). Canada covers some six time zones. It borders the US along its southern border (8,893 km) and the US state of Alaska (2,477 km), to the north west. Canada is home to around two million lakes including the great lakes, Huron, Superior, Erie and Ontario, and the inland sea, the Hudson Bay. It is estimated that 891,163 sq km. (344,080.0 sq miles) of Canada's total area is covered by freshwater, roughly nine per cent.

Geographically, Canada is divided into seven distinct regions. The Pacific Coast provides the warmest climate in Canada. The Cordillera, which stretches from British Columbia to Alberta and is known for its mountains including the Rocky Mountains and the St. Elias Mountains. The Prairies of Alberta, Saskatchewan and Manitoba provide some of the most fertile soil in Canada. The Canadian Shield is home to the Hudson Bay. The Great Lakes and St Lawrence Lowlands in Southern Quebec and Ontario is home to over 50 per cent of Canadians and 70 per cent of manufactured goods are produced there. New Brunswick, Nova Scotia, Prince Edward Island and Newfoundland form the Atlantic Provinces or the Appalachian Region and finally there is the Arctic region.

The climate varies from sub-arctic and arctic in the north to temperate in the south.

To view a map, please consult:
http://atlas.nrcan.gc.ca/site/english/maps/reference/can_political_e (With permission of Natural Resources Canada 2008, courtesy of the Atlas of Canada)

Population

In mid-2012 the total population of Canada was estimated to be 34,880,500. According to figures for 2011, the most densely metropolitan areas were Toronto (5,838,800), Montreal (3,908,700), Vancouver (2,419,700) and Ottawa (1,258,900). Nearly 80 per cent of the population lives in urban centres, with over 30 per cent of the population being based in Toronto, Montreal and Vancouver. Around 85 per cent of the population lives in a 300 km wide corridor with the US border.

English and French are the official languages with figures for 2006 showing that English was spoken by 17.8 million people, and French was spoken by 6.8 million.

Births, Marriages and Deaths
Population Growth July 2011-June 2012

	Total
Births	381,598
Deaths	252,242
Immigration	259,969
Emigration	51,350
Returning emigrants	33,199
Net temporary emigrants	29,133
Net interprovincial migration	0
Net non-permanent residents	54,475

Source: Statistics Canada, CANSIM Table 051-0004 Feb. 2013

Statistics Canada information is used with the permission of Statistics Canada. Users are forbidden to copy this material and/or redisseminate the data, in an original or modified form, for commercial purposes, without the expressed permission of Statistics Canada. Information on the availability of the wide range of data from Statistics Canada can be obtained from Statistics Canada's Regional Offices, its World Wide Web site at http://www.statcan.ca, and its toll-free access number 1-800-263-1136.

Public Holidays 2014

1 January: New Year's Day
2 January: New Year (Quebec only)
17 February: Family Day (Alberta, Saskatchewan and Ontario only)
19 March: St. Patrick's Day (Newfoundland only)
18 April: Good Friday
21 April: Easter Monday
23 April: St. George's Day (Newfoundland only)
19 May: Victoria Day
23 June: Discovery Day (Newfoundland only)
24 June: St. Jean Baptiste Day (Quebec only)
1 July: Canada Day
1 July: Memorial Day (Newfoundland only)
9 July: Orangemen's Day (Newfoundland only)
4 August: Civic Holiday (except Quebec and Yukon)
18 August: Discovery Day (Yukon only)
1 September: Labour Day

13 October: Thanksgiving
11 November: Remembrance Day
25 December: Christmas Day
26 December: Boxing Day

If Canada Day falls on a Sunday, the following Monday is observed as a holiday. Holidays in Newfoundland are observed on the nearest Monday.

EMPLOYMENT

The Canadian labour force in December 2012 numbered 19,026,000 people, of whom 17,667,600 were employed and 1,358,400 unemployed, giving an unemployment rate of 7.1 per cent, down from 8.0 per cent in 2010.

Employment by Sector

Sector	Dec. 2011	Dec. 2012
Agriculture	55,800	56,400
Forestry, fishing, mining, oil & gas	37,500	35,300
Utilities	27,500	25,300
Construction	228,600	250,300
Manufacturing	477,400	506,800
Trade	636,200	629,800
Transportation & warehousing	179,700	164,500
Finance, insurance, real estate & leasing	218,300	231,100
Professional, scientific & technical services	300,100	296,600
Business, building & other support services	139,600	153,100
Educational services	281,000	303,200
Health care & social assistance	490,900	571,200
Information, culture & recreation	157,400	186,700
Accommodation & food services	257,500	228,800
Other services	183,600	179,500
Public administration	238,000	226,700

Source: Statistics Canada, CANSIM Table 282-0088 Feb. 2013

The following table shows the unemployment rate by province for 2012.

Province	Unemployment rate %
Newfoundland & Labrador	12.5
Prince Edward Island	11.3
Nova Scotia	9.0
New Brunswick	10.2
Quebec	7.8
Ontario	7.8
Manitoba	5.3
Saskatchewan	4.7
Alberta	4.6
British Columbia	6.7

Source: Statistics Canada CANSIM, table 282-0002 Feb. 2013

BANKING AND FINANCE

Currency

One Canadian Dollar (Can$) = 100 cents

GDP/GNP, Inflation, National Debt

Canada is one of the world's richest and most developed countries, with generally low inflation and steady growth. It is services-dominated but has a strong manufacturing base. Its relationship with America is key and the two countries share the world's largest trade relationship. Since the signing of the NAFTA agreement, two-way trade has increased by approximately 265 per cent. In 2007, trade between the two countries reached US$650 billion. However, as so much trade is linked to the US, the Canadian economy is linked to the state of the US economy, and as such, has suffered in the current economic crisis. Canada does not, however, have the same sub-prime mortgage problem. Canada was hit hard hit by the global economic slowdown, with both its exports and imports falling. The government responded by cutting interest rates and creating various stimulus plans. In February 2009, the parliament passed a Can$40 billion economic stimulus package. The economy shrank by 5.4 per cent in Q1 of 2009. In December 2009, Prime Minister Stephen Harper announced that he was proroguing parliament for two months, because the government needed more time to adjust its budget. He prorogued parliament for a second time in January 2010. In recent years trading with the Asian market, particularly China, has become increasingly important to Canada's economy.

The following table shows expenditure based GDP in recent years.

Year	Can$ millions
2000	1,076,577
2001	1,108,048
2002	1,152,905
2003	1,213,178
2004	1,290,906
2005	1,373,845
2006	1,450,405
2007	1,566,015
2008	1,645,875
2009	1,564,790
2010	1,664,762
2011	1,762,432

Source: Statistics Canada, CANSIM, table 384-0038 Feb. 2013

STATES OF THE WORLD

CANADA

By mid-2001, the growth of the Canadian economy began to slow in response to the economic downturn of the US economy with which it is closely linked. It is estimated that trade between Canada and the US is the equivalent to US$1.4 billion a day in goods, services and investments.

The weak US dollar again contributed to slow growth in 2003, along with the strengthening Canadian dollar, the outbreak of the SARS virus in Toronto and lower beef exports due to the incidence of BSE. The US has since re-opened its market to imports of Canadian beef products but only for certain cuts of meat. Since then, the Canadian economy grew due to the economic recovery of the US economy coupled with the rising prices of oil and gas, which make up a substantial part of Canada's exports.

Economic growth was forecast to remain steady from 2007 at around 2.8 per cent, but revised figures put growth to be 1.4 per cent in 2008 and 2.3 per cent in 2009. This is mainly due to the slowing down of the US economy. Canada in common with the rest of the world has been hit by the global economic downturn and credit crisis particularly as its economy is so closely linked to the fortunes of the US economy. In December 2008, Prime Minister Harper's Government was threatened by a vote of no confidence over its handling of the economic crisis. A stimulus package worth Can$40 billion was agreed, with the aim of encouraging consumer spending. In March 2009 the Bank of Canada reduced its interest rate to 0.5 per cent. By the end of 2009 it became apparent that Canada has survived the global recession better than some other major economies. Forecast figures for 2009 had put GDP growth for that year at -2.4 per cent. However, figures for the fourth quarter of 2009 growth showed positive growth of 1.2 per cent, the largest quarterly growth since 2000.

GDP was estimated to be 3.5 per cent in 3Q 2011, higher than expected. The growth was driven by stronger exports and housing purchases. It represented the biggest quarterly growth since 2004.

Economic growth in 2011 was put at 2.4 per cent, higher that the 2.1 per cent originally predicted. Forecast figures for 2012 put economic growth down to 2.0 per cent, the fall in part due to the crisis in the Eurozone and its impact on other economies. Predicted figures for 2013 put economic growth at 2.8 per cent.

Average inflation was put at 1.8 per cent in 2004, 2.2 per cent in 2005 and 2.0 per cent in 2006. Inflation was put at 3.1 per cent in 2008 and 0.2 per cent in 2009. Average inflation in 2011 was put at 2.9 per cent.

The following table shows the make up of GDP in recent years; figures are in Can$ millions of chained dollars (2007):

Industry	2010	2011
Agriculture, forestry, fishing & hunting	23,965	24,566
Mining & oil & gas extraction	117,317	124,158
Manufacturing	162,056	166,131
Construction industries	103,005	106,066
Utilities	36,642	38,084
Transportation & warehousing	61,326	63,759
Information & cultural industries	49,891	50,671
Wholesale trade	78,676	81,682
Retail trade	80,798	82,361
Finance and insurance	97,746	99,675
Real estate & rental & leasing	181,609	187,130
Professional, scientific & technical services	77,636	79,468
Management of companies & enterprises	11,842	11,955
Admin. & support, waste management & remediation services	38,977	39,407
Educational services	81,231	82,046
Health care & social assistance	105,059	107,230
Arts, entertainment & recreation	11,710	11,572
Accommodation & food services	31,168	31,902
Other services (except public admin.)	30,733	31,478
Public admin.	105,943	107,230

Source: Statistics Canada, CANSIM, table 379-0031, Feb. 2013

In 2006, gross federal debt was put at Can$619,701 million, falling to Can$618,765 million in 2007 and Can$594,390 million in 2008.

Foreign Investment

The United States, United Kingdom, Japan and Germany are the major sources of foreign investment in Canada. In 1993, stock of direct foreign investment amounted to Can$145.9 billion compared to Can$114.9 billion in 1988 (the period which preceded the Canada-United States Free Trade Agreement). Canada has a low corporate tax rate that encourages investment. The following tables show direct foreign investment in and out of Canada in recent years.

Canadian Direct Investments Abroad

Year	Can$ millions
2006	518,839
2007	513,140
2008	642,026
2009	621,181
2010	616,689
2011	684,500

Source: Component of Statistics Canada catalogue no,. 11-001-X

Foreign Direct Investments in Canada

Year	Can$ millions
2006	437,171
2007	510,139
2008	542,732
2009	547,578
2010	561,616
2011	607,500

Source: Component of Statistics Canada catalogue no,. 11-001-X

Balance of Payments / Imports and Exports

Canada in common with the rest of the world has been hit by the global economic downturn and credit crisis particularly as its economy is so closely linked to the fortunes of the US economy. Canada's economy has been particularly hit by the fall in foreign trade, leading in 2009 to the recording of a negative trade balance. The following table shows recent figures for imports and exports on a balance of payments basis:

Imports/Exports of Goods (Can$ Million)

Year	Exports	Imports	Trade Balance
2000	429,372.2	326,336.7	67,035.5
2001	420,730.4	350,071.2	70,659.2
2002	414,038.5	356,727.1	57,311.4
2003	399,122.1	342,709.5	56,412.6
2004	429,005.8	363,157.8	65,848.0
2005	450,210.0	387,837.8	62,372.2
2006	451,971.5	404,510.1	47,461.4
2007	461,385.2	415,790.7	45,594.5
2008	487,261.6	443,592.0	43,669.6
2009	367,429.9	373,984.4	-6,554.5
2010	403,071.3	413,847.6	-10,776.3
2011	456,518.0	455,606,1	911.9

Source: Statistics Canada, CANSIM, table 228-0058 Feb. 2013

The following table show values of imports and exports for selected sectors:

Exports/Imports 2011 (Can$ Million)

Sector	Exports	Imports
Farm, fishing & intermediate food products	24,136.4	12,110.1
Energy products	103,459.4	46,222.5
Metal ores and non-metallic minerals	19,937.6	10,559.7
Metal & non-metallic mineral products	59,008.0	44,053.5
Basic & industrial chemical, plastic & rubber products	35,767.5	35,824.2
Forestry products & building & packaging materials	30,460.5	18,571.1
Industrial machinery, equipment & parts	25,397.8	42,269.0
Electronic & electrical equipment & parts	23,397.8	55,060.7
Motor vehicles & parts	59,590.0	74,148.1
Aircraft & other transportation equipment & parts	16,248.7	12,773.1
Consumer goods	49,846.3	89,414.9
Special transactions trade	2,390.5	5,173.7
Other balance of payments adjustments	7,052.1	9,425.8
Total	456,518.0	455,606.1

Source: Statistics Canada, CANSIM, table 228-0059 Feb. 2013

Foreign Trade on a balance-of-payments basis in 2010 and 2011 (figures in Can$ million)

Country/Grouping	Exports	Imports	Balance
2010			
USA*	296,672.0	259,952.7	36,719.3
Japan	9,716.6	10,067.2	-350.6
United Kingdom	16,985.8	9,560.6	7,452.2
Other EEC Countries	19,475.8	30,788.3	-11,312.5
Other OECD**	17,908.3	29,012.9	-11,104.6
Other Countries***	44,075.7	74,451.1	-30,375.4
Total	404,834.2	413,832.8	-8,998.6
2011			
USA*	331,226.4	281,226.1	50,000.3
Japan	11,348.2	9,368.4	1,979.8
United Kingdom	19,431.4	10,581.2	8,850.2
Other EEC Countries	22,978.2	35,280.8	-12,302.6
Other OECD**	20,524.5	32,687.0	-12,162.5
Other Countries***	52,682.6	86,730.1	-34,047.5
Total	458,191.3	455,873.5	2,317.8

* Inc. Puerto Rico & Virgin Islands
**OECD excluding. USA, Japan, UK & EEC
***Countries not included in EEC or OECD
Source: Statistics Canada, CANSIM table 228,0003 Feb. 2013

Figures for 2006 show that nearly 80 per cent of Canada's exports went to the USA, the main products being motor vehicles and spare parts, crude petroleum and natural gas, forest products, agricultural products, metals, industrial machinery, and aircraft.

Trade or Currency Restrictions

Canada signed the Final Act of GATT (General Agreement on Tariffs and Trade) in 1994. The North American Free Trade Agreement (NAFTA) with the United States and Mexico came into force on 1 January 1994. Tariffs between Canada and the US are being phased out and there is a 10 year programme of reduction of most tariffs with Mexico.

In April 2001, the Summit of the Americas took place in Quebec; leaders of 34 countries from North, Central and South America and the Caribbean met to set up a free trade zone, expanding the North American Free Trade Agreement.

Financial Centres: Toronto, Montreal, Vancouver

Central Bank

Bank of Canada, 234 Wellington Street, Ottawa, Ontario K1A 0G9, Canada. Tel: +1 613 782 8111, fax: +1 613 782 8655, e-mail: paffairs@bankofcanada.ca
URL: http://www.bank-banque-canada.ca
Governor and Chairman of the Board of Directors: Stephen S. Poloz (page 1496)

Development Bank

Business Development Bank of Canada, URL: http://www.bdc.ca

Chambers of Commerce and Trade Organisations

Canadian Chamber of Commerce, URL: http://www.chamber.ca
Canadian Venture Exchange (TSX Venture Exchange), URL: http://www.tsx.com
Bourse de Montréal, URL: http://www.m-x.ca/accueil_fr.php
Toronto Stock Exchange, , URL: http://www.tsx.com
Canadian Association of Importers and Exporters (CAIE), URL: http://www.caie.ca
Canadian International Trade Tribunal, URL: http://www.citt.gc.ca
Export Development Corporation, URL: http://www.edc.ca
Alliance of Manufacturers and Exporters, Canada, URL: http://www.cme-mec.ca

MANUFACTURING, MINING AND SERVICES

Primary and Extractive Industries

Canada has large resources of potash, uranium, nickel, zinc, asbestos, lead, copper gold, cobalt, iron ore and gypsum. Diamonds and quartz are also mined.

The Canadian oil industry is based mainly in western Canada, particularly Alberta, which holds more than 80 per cent of the country's reserves of conventional crude oil, over 90 per cent of its natural gas and all of its bitumen and oil-sands reserves.

There have been recent developments in Eastern Canada including the massive Hibernia field (located on the Grand Banks of Newfoundland and containing three billion barrels of low-sulphur oil) which was developed by a consortium of oil companies with federal assistance, and came on-line in November 1997 producing around 150,000 barrels per day. Currently in development, and also on the Grand Banks, are the Terra Nova field (with an estimated 300-400 million barrels of recoverable oil reserves) and the Whiterose field (with an estimated 250 million barrels of recoverable oil reserves). These both came into production in 2002. It is believed that the far northern reaches of Canada also contain oil reserves. Exploration is currently under way in the Jeanne d'Arc Basin off the coast of Newfoundland. The White Rose started producing in 2004.

Canada had proven oil reserves of some 174 billion barrels as at January 2012, 95 per cent of which was oil sands. Estimated figures for 2011 show that oil production levels were at 3.5 million barrels per day, of which 2.9 million barrels per day were crude. Oil from oil sands are becoming a larger part of production. The domestic market consumed approximately 2.3 million barrels per day of the total.

Oil exports to the US were on average 2.4 million barrels per day during 2007. Canada has an extensive system of pipelines to transport oil; the Enbridge Pipeline covers 8,700 miles transporting oil from Edmonton, Alberta to Eastern Canada, the US, Montreal and Quebec, and the Trans Mountain Pipe Line which transports from Alberta to refineries in Vancouver and to Puget Sound. There is a 30 year old ban against exploration in the Pacific Ocean. This plan is to be reviewed as it is thought that the area near Queen Charlotte Island holds large oil and natural gas deposits. Recent figures show that 99 per cent of Canada's exports oil goes to the US.

As of 1 January 2011 Canada had natural gas reserves of approximately 62 trillion cubic feet, over 80 per cent of which is located in Alberta; an additional 50 trillion cubic feet is thought to lie off the coast between Nova Scotia and Newfoundland. Major gas discoveries have also been made in the frontier and offshore regions. Production in 2011 was around 5.2 trillion cubic feet, of which the domestic market used around 3.1 trillion cubic feet.

Canada has coal reserves of approximately 7.2 billion short tons. In 2011 an estimated 74 million short tons were produced, of which the domestic market used 47 million short tons. Despite a fall in coal prices, due to the reduction of steel-making in Japan and world oversupply, the industry has been boosted by an all-time high steel demand in Canada itself, and the fact that Ontario Hydro was forced to close seven nuclear-power plants and replace their energy generation with coal. Around 80 per cent of coal exports go to Japan. (All figures provided by the US EIA.)

Canadian Association of Petroleum Producers, URL: http://www.capp.ca
Canadian Gas Association, URL: http://www.cga.ca
Mining Association of Canada, URL: http://www.mining.ca

Energy

Energy is Canada's second-most important export (after automobiles) and accounts for approximately ten per cent of the nation's exports and four per cent of world energy production. Among OECD countries, only the United States ranks higher. Canada's major

energy export, by value, is heavy crude oil, most of which is sold to the United States. About half of all Western Canadian coal production is exported to power the Japanese steel industry. Canada is the fifth largest energy producer in the world.

Electricity is one of Canada's fastest growing energy sources. Canada ranks fifth in the world in total electrical generating capacity and electric power production. The largest source of electrical energy is hydroelectric power. Canadian rivers generate 15 per cent of the world's hydroelectric power, and about 59 per cent of the nation's electricity supply. Other main sources include nuclear power, coal, oil and natural gas. Recent figures show that Canada produced over 690 billion kWh of electricity, 57 per cent of which was generation from hydroelectric sources, 27 per cent from conventional thermal sources and 12 per cent from nuclear sources. Two per cent comes from other renewable sources. In the first 11 months of 2004, Canada exported nearly 30 billion kWh of electricity to the US.

Canada is an international leader in nuclear power technology, and generated 84.1 billion kWh of electricity by this method in 1997; production has remained around this level since. In total, there are 18 operating reactors, and a further two currently undergoing refurbishment. All of Canada's reactors are of the CANDU (Canadian Deuterium Uranium) type, and the CANDU station at Pickering, Ontario, is the largest producer of commercial nuclear power in the world. Canada has approximately 30 per cent of the world's uranium resources and exports approximately three quarters of it production, mainly to the US. Other key markets for Canadian uranium are Japan and Western Europe. In 2004 the Canadian government introduced the idea of building a new nuclear power plant; it would be located in Ontario and would be the first new plant for 20 years, helping Canada fulfill her Kyoto agreement obligations. No decision has yet been reached. In March 2011, approximately 73,000 litres of contaminated water spilled into Lake Ontario.

Energy Production in 2009

Energy	Terajoules
Crude oil	5,447,476
Natural gas	6,23.6,021
Natural gas liquids	635,164
Coal	1,361,322
Primary electricity, hydro & nuclear	1,645,665
Refined petroleum products	4,419,867

Source: Canadian Statistics CANSIM 128-0009 Feb. 2013

Canadian Electricity Association, 1 Place Westmount, Bureau 1600, Montreal, PQ H3Z 2P9, Canada. Fax: +1 514 937 6498

Manufacturing Industries

Figures for 2000 show that 557,000 were employed in construction, 255,500 in the production of transport equipment, 211,100 in the production of food, 191,500 in the production of metal goods, 262,500 in paper, printing, publishing and related industries, 139,700 in the production of electrical and electronic goods and 95,700 in the production of chemicals and chemical products.

The following tables shows manufacturing sales in Can$ million in recent years:

Manufacturing Sales by Subsector $ million

Industry	2010	2011
Food	80,493.1	83,721.9
Beverage & tobacco products	10,686.0	10,622.8
Textile mills	1,538.9	1,606.7
Textile product mills	1,687.0	1,600.4
Leather & allied products	395.6	403.3
Clothing	2,294.6	2,247.3
Paper	26,470.1	26,206.0
Printing & related support activities	8,749.0	8,436.1
Petroleum & coal products	68,083.1	79,673.9
Chemicals	43,883.3	47,086.1
Plastics & rubber products	20,906.4	22,477.5
Wood products	18,850.9	18,491.3
Non-metallic mineral products	12,990.3	13,165.2
Primary metals	41,963.2	48,522.5
Fabricated metal products	30,645.0	33,447.1
Machinery	28,888.7	34,588.5
Computer & electronic products	15,491.6	15,815.7
Electrical equipment, appliances & components	9,640.9	10,147.5
Transportation equipment	85,293.4	90,996.2
Furniture & related products	10,713.8	10,591.7
Miscellaneous manufacturing	10,182.1	11,381.7
All manufacturing industries	529,847.0	571,229.4

Source: Statistics Canada CANSIM Table 304-0014 Feb. 2013

Canadian Manufacturers and Exporters, URL: http://www.cme-mec.ca/national/index-en.asp

Service Industries

Figures from Statistics Canada show that, in 2011, Canada's finance and insurance industries, real estate business and business services contributed over Can$286.8 millions to the country's GDP. Figures for 2007 show that Canada had over 30 million visitors, over 25 million of whom were from the USA. In 2007 over 175 million trips were made by Canadians within Canada. The Winter Olympics were held in Whistler, British Columbia in February 2010 providing a boost for the tourism industry. Figures for 2010 show that 24,669,000 visitors arrived in Canada.

Canadian Tourism Commission: URL: http://www.canada.travel/splash.en-gb.html

CANADA

Agriculture

The agricultural sector employs almost 500,000 farmers, which represents about 3.5 per cent of the work force. Another 1.8 million people are employed in the food services and related industries.

There are four main types of farm in Canada: livestock farms, grain farms, mixed grain and livestock farms, and special crop farms. Geographically they can be divided into the following regions: the Atlantic Region, where mixed farming is most common; the Central Region, where, because of favourable climate and soil conditions, varied farming takes place; the Prairie Region, where grain farming and livestock farming takes place; the Pacific Region, mainly livestock and dairy farming and the Northern Region, where there is some grazing but crops are restricted by the harsh climate. Figures from 2011 show that there were 205,730 farms in Canada covering a total area of 64,812,723 hectares.

Canada's most important crop is wheat. The annual crop is over 25 million tonnes, of which some 80 per cent is exported. Total farm cash receipts for all crops and livestock in 2011 was over Can$49 billion. The Canadian livestock population is large: the beef cattle population is over 12 million; dairy cows, 1.8 million; and swine, over 10 million, of which over one million are for breeding. Farm receipts for livestock in 2002 were over Can$18.2 billion. Fur production is also a major industry, with approximately 2.5 million pelts produced in 1997, valued at over Can$69 million. According to Statistics Canada, over half this number is trapped in the wild. The following tables show cash receipts from selected crops and livestock in recent years:

Cash receipts in tonnes, selected crops

Crop	2011	2012
Barley	7,891,500	8,012,300
Canary seed	128,600	124,900
Canola	14,608,100	13,309,500
Chick peas	85,600	157,500
Corn for grain	11,358,700	13,060,100
Lentils	1,523,300	1,472,800
Mustard seed	130,000	118,600
Oats	3,157,600	2,683,900
Soybeans	4,297,700	4,929,600
Sunflower seed	19,800	86,900
Wheat, all	25,288,000	27,205,200
Wheat, durum	4,172,100	4,626,600
Wheat, spring	18,018,600	18,845,400
Wheat, winter remaining	3,097,300	3,733,200

Source: Statistics Canada, CANSIM Table 001-0010 JFeb. 23013

Cash receipts in Can$ thousands

Livestock & products	2009	2010
Cattle & calves	5,863,981	6,132,090
Pigs	2,912,410	3,363,820
Poultry & eggs	3,136,726	3,056,240
Sheep & lambs	133,484	141,750
Milk & cream	5,449,917	5,523,912
Other livestock products	610,073	700,168
Total livestock farm cash receipts	18,106,591	18,917,980

Source: Statistics Canada, www40.statcan.ca/l01/cst01/AGRI03A-eng.htm Jan. 2012

The agri-food processing and manufacturing sector is one of the top economic sectors in terms of employment and shipment. It purchases some Can$25 billion in crops, livestock and fish each year. This, combined with Can$5 billion of raw imports such as cane sugar, is converted into Can$55 billion of processed food and vegetables. Can$12 billion of this is exported. There are over 3,100 food processing establishments in Canada, mainly in Ontario and Quebec.

Forestry

The forested areas of Canada are about 3,417,000 km sq. (49 per cent of the country's total land area), and are mainly coniferous. A little less than two per cent of forest land is reserved for parks and other areas where harvesting is not allowed. The total stand of timber of merchantable size is estimated to be 17,229 million miles sq. There are more than 150 native tree species. Spruce, of which there are five species, is the most important softwood. It is particularly valuable for pulp, owing to its light colour, freedom from resins and the characteristics of its fibres. Other significant woods are Balsam and Douglas fir, pine, cedar, hemlock and larch. Only ten per cent of the nation's deciduous trees or "hardwoods" have commercial significance. Poplar is the most important hardwood. Birch and maple are used for veneers and plywood as well as, for example, furniture and cabinetwork. Recent figures show that logging and forestry employs 114,200 people. In 2002 relations between Canada and the US were put under pressure when the US announced the imposition of a 29 per cent tariff on imported softwood timber from Canada. Currently US imports of Canadian timber amount to US$6 billion per year.

Fishing

With the largest coastline in the world and thousands of rivers and lakes, Canada has for centuries benefited from prosperous fisheries. Canada is the second largest exporter of fish products (in terms of value) in the world and exports three-quarters of its product. The United States accounts for the largest share of exports, followed by Japan and European Economic Community. The most popular export items are cod, herring, crab, and scallop from the Atlantic Coast, and halibut and salmon from the Pacific Coast.

The following table shows aquaculture, production and value in 2010.

Aquaculture, Production and Value in 2010

Fish	Tonnes	Can$ 00
Salmon	101,385	690,91
Trout	6,883	32,62
Other finfish	993	12,26
Clams	1,938	8,29
Oysters	10,862	20,30
Mussels	24,484	36,20
Scallops	702	2,91
Other shellfish	777	5,64
Total aquaculture	160,924	919,46

Source: www.statcan.gc.ca/pub/23-222-x/2010000/t013-eng.pdf Jan/ 2012

Canadian Federation of Agriculture, URL: http://www.cfa-fca.ca/pages/home.php
Canadian Dairy Information Centre, URL: http://www.dairyinfo.gc.ca/index_e.php
Fisheries Council of Canada, URL: http://www.fisheriescouncil.ca

COMMUNICATIONS AND TRANSPORT

Travel Requirements

To enter Canada, EU and Australian citizens require a passport valid for at least one day beyond the intended departure date from Canada. US citizens with proof of citizenship (eg US birth certificate or US naturalisation papers) do not require a passport. Persons entering from St Pierre & Miquelon or the USA who are legal permanent residents of the USA and hold a US alien registration card (Green Card) do not require a passport to enter Canada nor do citizens of France who are residents of and entering from St Pierre & Miquelon.

Visas are not generally required by US, Australian and EU citizens for stays of up to six months. Bulgarian and Romanian citizens do require a visa, as do those visiting Canada who also visit the USA or St Pierre & Miquelon and return directly to Canada as visitors within the period authorised on their initial entry.

Visitors to Canada must satisfy an examining officer at the Port of Entry that they are in good health, with no criminal convictions, and have sufficient funds to maintain themselves during their stay, as well as evidence of confirmed onward reservations out of Canada.

Nationals not referred to above are advised to contact the High Commission to check visa requirements.

Industry Figures

Recent figures from Statistics Canada show that Canada's transportation and warehousing industries contributed over Can$63.0 million to its GDP in 2011, of which the truck transport industries contributed approximately Can$16.9 billion, the air transport industries contributed over Can$6.1 billion, the railway transport industries contributed roughly Can$5.5 billion and water transportation contributed Can$992 million.

National Airlines

Civil aviation comes under the jurisdiction of the Federal Government; it is administered under the authority of the Aeronautics Act and the National Transportation Act. The Aeronautics Act has been divided into three parts. Part I deals with registration of aircraft, licensing of airmen, airports and facilities for air navigation, air traffic control, accident investigation and safe operation of aircraft. Part II is concerned with the economics of commercial air services and Part III deals with internal administration and the implementation of enactments. On international routes scheduled services are offered by the two national flag carriers Air Canada and CP Air. Charter flights for groups of people are also offered by these airlines but there are many charter flights operated by the Regional carriers and by other Canadian airlines as well.

Air Canada, URL: http://www.aircanada.ca
Air Transat, URL: http://www.airtransat.com
First Air, URL: http://www.firstair.com

Railways

Today, the Canadian National and Canadian Pacific Railways are the two main systems in Canada. The rail network includes almost 90,000 km of track. Together Canadian National and Canadian Pacific own over 90 per cent of the track, 86 per cent mainline, 97.2 per cent of branch lines and 90.5 per cent of yards, industrial track and sidings. These two railways also accounted for 78.4 per cent of lines jointly owned or operated under lease, contract or trackage rights, 64 per cent of mainline, 92.7 per cent of branch lines and 83.4 per cent of yards, industrial track and sidings. Recent figures show that 4.3 million passengers travel by rail each year and total non-intermodal traffic loaded was 313,769,000 metric tonnes in 2010.

Montreal and Toronto both have subway systems. Vancouver has an urban railway known as the Skytrain. Calgary and Edmonton both have light rail transit systems.

BC Rail, URL: http://www.bcrail.com
CN Rail, 9URL: http://www.cn.ca
Ontario Northland Transportation Commission, URL: http://www.ontc.on.ca
VIA Rail Canada Inc, URL: http://www.viarail.ca

Roads

There are over 300,000 km of surfaced roads in Canada and 53,000 km of unpaved roads. Vehicles drive on the right. The Trans-Canadian highway is the world's longest national highway and is 7,775 km long. Canada is very auto-dependant and has one of the world's highest automobile to person ratios: there is at least one car for every two Canadians. A lot of freight travels by road, and approximately 50 per cent of road freight comes from the trucking industry. There are more than 1,000 bus operators offering passenger services.

Canadian Institute of Traffic and Transportation, URL: http://www.citt.ca/

Shipping

The shipping industry is in decline in Canada, particularly freight traffic. The drop in international tonnage has resulted primarily from the reduction in tonnage of American cargo unloaded at Canadian ports. Domestic tonnage has also decreased over the last decade. Historically, the international sector (overseas plus United States) has dominated shipping activity in Canada, contributing approximately two-thirds of the total tonnage handled.

Shipping
St. Lawrence Seaway Management Corporation, URL: http://www.seaway.ca
British Columbia Ferry Services Inc, URL: http://www.bcferries.bc.ca
Fednav Ltd, URL: http://www.fednav.com
Groupe Desgagnés Inc, URL: http://www.groupedesgagnes.com
Marine Atlantic Inc, URL: http://www.marine-atlantic.ca

Ports and Harbours
The federal ports system consists of 14 ports operated under the Ports Canada system, nine mainly autonomous harbour commissions and approximately 300 public ports which are administered by the Canadian Coast Guard. There are also a few municipal ports and some 500 private ports.

Recent figures show that over 400 million tonnes of traffic passes through the ports of the Canada Ports Corporation every year. Revenues have recently risen to around $228.3 million. Approximately 185 million tonnes of cargo is transported of which 113 million is dry bulk, 45 million tonnes is liquid bulk, 15 million tonnes containerised and 11 million tonnes non-containerised. Of the total, over 80 per cent is handled by the seven local port corporations and some 20 per cent is handled through the divisional ports administered through the Canada Ports Corporation.

HEALTH

Funding for health care comes from a federal insurance scheme.

Total expenditure on health equates to 11.4 per cent of GDP. General government expenditure accounts for 70.6 per cent of total expenditure on health; the remainder is private expenditure of which 49.6 per cent is out-of-pocket expenditure and 43.2 per cent is from pre-paid plans. Per capita expenditure on health amounts to US$4,519.

Recent figures estimated medical personnel to be as follows: physicians 65,440 (19.8 per 10,000 population), 348,499 nurses and midwives (104.3 per 10,000 population), 41,798 dentistry personnel (12.6 per 10,000 population), 30,553 pharmaceutical personnel (9.2 per 10,000 population) and 1,245 environment and public health workers. In 2005-11 there were estimated to be 32 hospital beds per 10,000 population.

In 2010, the infant mortality rate (probability of dying by first birthday) was an estimated 5 per 1,000 live births and the child mortality rate (dying before age 5) was 6 per 1,000 live births. Immunization coverage is high: 93 per cent of one-year-olds have had a vaccination to prevent measles, 80 per cent DTP, 17 HepB3 and 80 per cent Hib3. (Source: http://www.who.int, World Health Statistics 2012)

EDUCATION

Education is free and compulsory in all provinces for ages seven to 16, apart from Ontario and New Brunswick, where the compulsory education goes up to the age of 18. Literacy is estimated at 99 per cent.

Education is a provincial responsibility except for certain special areas reserved for the Federal Government, such as schools for the indigenous population (which is overseen by the Department of Indian and Northern Affairs Canada), inmates of penitentiaries, and the armed services. The Federal Government also contributes to vocational education and higher education. Education at the elementary and secondary levels is provincially administered, although the local school districts administer the schools under the School Law. The costs of public elementary and secondary education are met through local tax levies on real estate, and grants from the provincial governments.

Despite certain differences there is a basic pattern to the various provincial systems. Each province has established a Department of Education operating under the direction of a cabinet minister and has enacted a School Law or Laws governing the establishment of public schools, conditions of attendance, qualifications of teachers and other requirements. Quebec differs from the other provinces in that it operates a dual system: the Roman Catholic, which has developed in the French tradition; and the Protestant, which is similar to the systems in force in the other provinces. In Newfoundland the schools are denominational, but operate under uniform regulations regarding attendance, curricula, teacher qualifications, and so forth. Schools of technology, open to high school graduates, provide advanced training of a practical nature designed to fit people for skilled occupations just below the professional level.

Recent figures show that Canada spends the equivalent of 7 per cent of GDP annually on education.

RELIGION

Canada has complete freedom of worship and about 30 Christian denominations are represented. Recent figures show that: 37.3 per cent of the population is Catholic, 17.4 per cent Protestant, Jewish 1.2 per cent, Muslim, 1.7 per cent, Buddhist 1.24 per cent, Hindu 1.1 per cent, Sikh 1.15 per cent and Chinese folk religionists, 1.9 per cent. Over 30 per cent said they had no religious affiliation.

Canada has a religious tolerance rating of 9 on a scale of 1 to 10 (10 is most freedom). (Source: World Religion Database)

Canadian Council of Churches, URL: http://www.ccc-cce.ca
General Synod of the Anglican Church of Canada, URL: http://www.anglican.ca/gs2007
Canadian Conference of Catholic Bishops, URL: http://www.cccb.ca

COMMUNICATIONS AND MEDIA

Newspapers
The Toronto Star, URL: http://www.thestar.ca
Le Journal de Montréal, URL: http://www.journalmtl.com
Toronto Sun, URL: http://www.cyberpresse.ca
The Vancouver Sun, URL: http://www.vancouversun.com
The Glose and Mail, URL: http://www.theglobeandmail.com
La Presse, URL: http://www.cyberpresse.ca
National Post, URL: http://www.canada.com/nationalpost/index.html

Broadcasting
Broadcasting is regulated in Canada by the Canadian-Radio-Television and Telecommunications Commission. It is an independent agency and reports to Parliament through the Minister of Canadian Heritage. It also has responsibility for regulating telecommunications carriers. Over recent years broadcast facilities and output have increased steadily. There are over 115 television stations, approximately 700 radio stations and over 2,000 cable television systems broadcasting in Canada. At least 99 per cent of Canadians have direct access to CBC television and radio services. There is also a high level of accessibility to cable services.

A ruling by the broadcasting regulator states that between 30 and 35 per cent of material broadcast on television and radio must be Canadian material.

Canadian Association of Broadcasters, URL: http://www.cab-acr.ca
Canadian Broadcasting Corporation/Société Radio Canada, URL: http://www.cbc.ca
Canadian Radio-Television and Telecommunications Commission (CRTC), URL: http://www.crtc.gc.ca
Canadian Satellite Communications Inc. (Cancom), URL: http://www.cancom.ca
CTV Television Network, URL: http://www.ctv.ca
Telesat Canada, URL: http://www.telesat.ca
Societe Radio-Canada: URL: http://www.radio-canada.ca
TVA: URL: http://tva.canoe.ca

Post and Telecommunications
Recent figures show that the communications industry contributed over Can$24.3 billion to Canada's GDP, of which telecommunication carriers contributed over Can$16.8 billion, telecommunication broadcasters contributed over Can$3.7 billion and postal and courier services contributed over Can$3.6 billion.

Canada has a very developed telecommunications network: there are two coast-to-coast fibre optic networks. There are over 20 million telephone landlines in use and more than 27 million cellular phones. All major telephone companies operating in the provinces and territories are regulated by the CRTC.

Recent figures show that Canada has over 27 million regular internet users.

ENVIRONMENT

The federal and provincial governments share responsibility for Canada's environment. The federal government is responsible for international or interprovincial issues but natural resources are the responsibility of the provinces and territories. Canada has nearly nine per cent of the earth's water and to counteract the stresses that industrial development and urbanisation have put on these resources, it has developed a national water policy. There are drinking water treatment plants for nearly 80 per cent of Canadians. A National Air Pollution Monitoring Network was set up in 1989 to monitor air quality in Canadian cities.

Sustainable practices have been introduced to manage natural resources better. There is a Sustainable Agriculture Initiative, which provides research and development assistance and education to increase sustainability in the agri-food industry. To prevent the decline in ground fish stocks, Canada introduced a moratorium on fishing for northern cod in 1992 and on certain other ground stocks in 1993. Canada is trying to increase measures to control high-seas fishing to prevent over-fishing.

In the year 2000, Canada's federal, provincial and territorial governments were committed to completing a network of protected areas and to accelerate protection of marine regions and certain wildlife habitats. This should result in at least 12 per cent of the country being designated protected space. An Arctic Environmental Strategy focuses on contaminants, water, waste and environment-economic integration to protect this region.

Canada supported the Earth Summit held in Rio de Janeiro in 1992 and has signed major international conventions to protect the global environment. The North American Commission for Environmental Cooperation established under the North American Agreement on Environmental Co-operation (signed by USA, Canada and Mexico) is based in Montreal.

CANADA

The US EIA put Canada's total energy-related carbon dioxide emissions at 631.26 million metric tons in 2005, up from 586.45 million metric tons in 2002. Per capita emissions were estimated to be 19.24 metric tons in the same year, above the North American regional average of 16.07 metric tons, and just short of the US per capita emissions of 20.14 metric tons.

Canada is a party to the following agreements: Air Pollution, Air Pollution-Nitrogen Oxides, Air Pollution-Persistent Organic Pollutants, Air Pollution-Sulfur 85, Air Pollution-Sulfur 94, Antarctic-Environmental Protocol, Antarctic-Marine Living Resources, Antarctic Seals, Antarctic Treaty, Biodiversity, Climate Change, Climate Change-Kyoto Protocol, Desertification, Endangered Species, Environmental Modification, Hazardous Wastes, Law of the Sea, Marine Dumping, Ozone Layer Protection, Ship Pollution, Tropical Timber 83, Tropical Timber 94, and Wetlands. Canada has signed but not ratified agreements on Air Pollution-Volatile Organic Compounds, and Marine Life Conservation.

In February 2007 politicians in Canada's cabinet voted in favour of a motion that would force the government to meet its Kyoto targets. However, at the November 2011 UN Climate Summit, Canada announced it would not make further cuts in its greenhouse emissions under the Kyoto Protocol and may begin formally withdrawing. Canada has not met its existing emissions commitment (a reduction of 6 per cent compared to 1990 levels). In fact, emissions have risen by over 30 per cent since 1990.

SPACE PROGRAMME

Canada's first venture into space was in 1962 with the launch of research satellite Alouet 1. It became the first country to have its own commercial geostationary communicatio satellite network with the launch of Anik A1, and in 1976 the Hermes communicatio satellite was launched through a co-operative effort between Canada and the US.

In December 1989 the Canadian Space Agency (CSA) was established by an act of parliament This organisation coordinates Canada's space programme including work on the Internation Space Station along with the US, the European Space Agency (ESA) and Japan. Canada involved in the design and production of the Mobile Servicing System (MSS). In 1995 th CSA launched RADARSAT an earth observation satellite to help Canada monitor i environment, and which was used to monitor the Manitoba floods in 1997.

The Canadian space agency's mandate is to promote the peaceful use and development space, to advance the knowledge of space through science and to ensure that space scienc and technology provide social and economic benefits for Canadians.

Canadian Space Agency, URL: http://www.asc-csa.gc.ca/

ALBERTA

Capital: Edmonton (Population estimate. 731,000)

Lieutenant-Governor: Col. (Ret'd.) The Hon Donald S. Ethell OC OMM AOE MSC CD (page 1422)

Provincial Flag: Blue with the coat of arms in the centre

CONSTITUTION AND GOVERNMENT

Constitution
Alberta became a province of Canada on 1 September 1905.

Upper House
Although the province has no upper house it is represented in the Canadian Senate by six senators; Douglas Black, Bert Brown, Elaine McCoy, Grant Mitchell, Claudette Tardif and Betty E. Unger.

Lower House
Legislative authority is granted to the Legislative Assembly which has 83 elected members who serve a five year term.
Legislative Assembly, Legislature Building, 10800 - 97 Avenue, Edmonton T5K 2B6, Canada. URL: http://www.assembly.ab.ca

---

Cabinet (as at June 2013)
Premier, President of Executive Council: Alison Redford QC (page 1501)
Deputy Premier, Thomas Lukaszuk
President of Treasury Board and Enterprise, Minister Responsible for Corporate Human Resources Minister of Finance: Doug Horner (page 1443)
Minister of Human Services, Government House Leader: Dave Hancock (page 1437)
Minister of International and Intergovernmental Relations: Cal Dallas
Minister of Energy: Ken Hughes
Minister of Transportation: Ric McIver
Minister of Justice and Attorney General, Deputy Government House Leader: Jonathan Denis
Minister of Human Services, Government House Leader: Dave Hancock
Minister of Aboriginal Relations, Deputy House Leader: Robin Campbell
Minister of Environment and Minister of Sustainable Resource Development: Diana McQueen
Minister of Health and Wellness: Fred Horne
Minister of Infrastructure: Wayne Drysdale
Minister of Culture and Community Spirit: Heather Kilmchuk
Minister for Service Alberta: Manmeet Bhullar
Minister of Tourism, Parks and Recreation: Richard Starke
Minister of Municipal Affairs: Doug Griffiths
Minister of Education: Jeff Johnson
Minister of Agriculture and Rural Development: Verlyn Olson
Minister of Municipal Affairs: Doug Griffiths
Minister of Transportation, Deputy House Leader: Ric McIver

Ministries
Office of the Premier, Legislative Building, Room 307, 10800 - 97 Avenue, Edmonton, Alberta, T5K 2B6, Canada. Tel: +1 780 427 2251, fax: +1 780 427 1349, email: Premier@gov.ab.ca, URL: http://www.gov.ab.ca/premier
Ministry of Municipal Affairs and Housing,18th floor, Commerce Place, Edmonton, AB T5J 4L4, Alberta, T5K 2B6, Canada. Tel: +1 780 427 2732, fax: +1 780 422 1419, URL: http://www.municipalaffairs.gov.ab.ca
Ministry of International, Intergovernmental and Aboriginal Relations, 12th floor, Commerce Place Building, 10155-102 Street, Edmonton, Alberta, T5J 4G8, Canada. Tel: +1 780 422-1510, fax: +1 780 423 6654, URL: http://www.international.gov.ab.ca
Ministry of Justice, 3rd floor, Bowker Building 9833 - 109 Street, Edmonton, Alberta, T5K 2E8, Canada. URL: http://www.justice.gov.ab.ca

Ministry of Health, Room 228, 10800 - 97 Avenue, Edmonton, Alberta, T5K 2B6, Canad. Tel: +1 780 427 3665, fax: +1 780 422 6621, URL: http://www.health.gov.ab.ca
Ministry of Environment, Petroleum Plaza South Tower, 9915-108 Street, Edmonto AB T5K 2G8, Canada. Tel: +1 780 427 2700, fax: +1 780 422 4086, UR http://www3.gov.ab.ca/env
Ministry of Sustainable Resource Development, Room 420, Legislative Buildin 10800-97 Avenue, Edmonton, Alberta, T5K 2B6, Canada. Tel: +1 780 415 4815, fax: +1 78 415 4818, URL: http://www.srd.alberta.ca
Ministry of Infrastructure and Transportation, Twin Atria Building, 4999-98 Avenu Edmonton, Alberta T6B 2X3, Canada. Tel: +1 780 427 2731, fax: +1 780 466 3166, UR http://www.infratrans.ca
Ministry of Employment, Immigration and Industry, 10th Floor, Labour Buildin 10808 - 99 Avenue, Edmonton AB T5K 0G5, Canada. Tel: +1 780 427 8305, fax: +1 780 42 9205URL: http://www.employment.alberta.ca
Ministry of Agriculture and Food, J. G. O'Donoghue Building, 203, 7000 - 113 St Edmonton, AB T6H 5T6, Canada. Tel: +1 403 742 7901, fax: +1 780 422 603 URL:http://www.agric.gov.ab.ca
Ministry of Children's Services, Communications, 12th Floor, Sterling Place, 9940-1C Street, Edmonton, Alberta T5K 2N2, Canada. URL: http://www.child.gov.ab.ca
Ministry of Education, Room 204, 0800 - 97 Avenue, Edmonton, Alberta, T5K 2B Canada. Tel: +1 427 2025, fax: +1 427 5582, email: learning.minister@gov.ab.ca, UR http://www.education.gov.ab.ca
Ministry of Advanced Education and Technology, UR http://www.advancededandtech.gov.ab.ca
Ministry of Finance, Room 224, 10800 - 97 Avenue, Edmonton, Alberta T5K 2B6, Canad. Tel: +1 780 427 8809, fax: +1 780 428 1341, www.finance.gov.ab.ca
T5K 2B6, Canada. Tel: +1 780 415-9390, fax: +1 780 415-9412, UR http://www.trans.gov.ab.ca
Ministry of Energy, Room 404, 10800 - 97 Avenue, Edmonton, Alberta T5K 2B6, Canad. Tel: +1 780 427 3740, fax: +1 780 422 0195, URL: http:// www.energy.gov.ab.ca
Ministry of Seniors and Community Supports, PO Box 3100, Edmonton, Albert T5J 4W3, Canada. Tel: +1 780 415 9550, fax: +1 780 415 9411, UR http://www.seniors.gov.ab.ca
Service Alberta, URL: http://www.servicealberta.gov.ab.ca
Ministry of Tourism, Parks, Recreation and Culture, 299 Legislature Building 10800 - 97 Avenue, Edmonton, Alberta T5K 2B6, Canada. Tel: +1 780 427 4928, UR http://www.tprc.alberta.ca
Treasury Board, 204 Legislature Building, 10800 - 97 Avenue, Edmonton AB T5K 2B Canada. Tel: +1 780 415 4855, fax: +1 780 422 4853, URL http://www.treasuryboard.gov.ab.ca

Elections
The most recent elections were held on 23 April 2012 when the Progressive Conservative retained power, winning 61 seats.

LEGAL SYSTEM

There are three courts in Alberta: The Court of Appeal of Alberta; The Court of Queen's Benc of Alberta; The Provincial Court of Alberta. Appeals from these courts can be referred to Th Supreme Court of Canada. The Provincial Court of Alberta has a family division, a civil divisior a criminal division and a youth division.

LOCAL GOVERNMENT

For the purposes of local government, Alberta is divided into municipalities each with a elected council which oversees services such as road maintenance, water and sewer service and rubbish collection.

AREA AND POPULATION

Area

Alberta covers an area of 661,185 sq. km, including 16,796 sq. km of freshwater, and is the fourth largest province in Canada. The land area is comprised of prairies, parkland (mixed forests and plains), forests and mountain region.

To view a map of Alberta, please consult
http://atlas.nrcan.gc.ca/site/english/maps/reference/provincesterritories. (With permission of Natural Resources Canada 2008, courtesy of the Atlas of Canada)

Population

Alberta's population in 2012 was 3,873,700. It has increased 50 per cent over the past 30 years and is culturally diverse, consisting of various peoples who have settled in Alberta in the last two decades. About 80 per cent of the population live in urban areas, concentrated in the two major centres of Edmonton (recent population 817,500), and Calgary (1,096,830). Ten per cent of the Canadian population live in Alberta.

Births, Marriages and Deaths

In the period July 2011-June 2012 there were 52,145 births, up from 51,175 the previous year. The same year saw 22,730 deaths. During the year July 2006-June 2007, 131,441 immigrants arrived from other Canadian provinces and 80,272 Albertans left Alberta for other Canadian provinces, 20,116 foreign immigrants arrived and 5,082 Albertans left for foreign countries.

In addition to the standard days celebrated in Canada, Alberta also celebrates the following:

Public Holidays 2014

17 February: Family Day
19 May: Victoria Day
4 August: Heritage Day
13 October: Thanksgiving Day
11 November: Remembrance Day

EMPLOYMENT

Figures for 2012 show that the workforce of Alberta was 2,478,900. An estimated 2,312,500 were employed and 166,400 were unemployed giving an unemployment rate of 6.7 per cent. Alberta's employment figures have been hit by the global economic downturn and credit crisis and there have been large losses in jobs in construction and manufacturing. The following table shows how the working population was recently employed:

Industry	Dec. 2011	Dec. 2012
Agriculture	55,500	61,800
Forestry, fishing, mining, oil & gas	166,600	164,900
Utilities	14,600	22,800
Construction	218,400	220,500
Manufacturing	136,400	150,000
Trade	335,400	325,300
Transportation & warehousing	109,100	126,400
Finance, insurance, real estate & leasing	100,100	108,500
Professional, scientific & technical services	164,200	158,600
Business, building & other support services	72,600	72,200
Educational services	124,600	126,600
Health care & social assistance	233,200	230,700
Information, culture & recreation	78,500	72,000
Accommodation & food services	125,700	132,200
Other services	110,100	101,900
Public administration	85,900	90,700

Source: Statistics Canada, CANSIM table 282-0088 Feb. 2013

BANKING AND FINANCE

GDP/GNP, Inflation, National Debt

Expenditure based GDP in Alberta is set out below.

Year	Can$ millions
2004	189,743
2005	219,810
2006	238,886
2007	258,850
2008	294,716
2009	244,827
2010	271,012
2011	295,276

Source: Statistics Canada CANSIM, table 384-0038 Feb. 2013

The economy of Alberta has traditionally been based upon agriculture, including forestry, oil and gas and tourism. More recent growing economic sectors include telecommunications, chemical and petrochemical production, aerospace, software and industrial machinery and equipment.

Alberta's economy has benefited from good economic policy and much from the oil and gas industry particularly the new extractions of oils sands. As a result the province has been able to clear all its debt. In 2006, its budget surplus enabled the province to give every taxpayer a rebate of Can$400.

Balance of Payments / Imports and Exports

Estimated figures for 2003 show that the value of domestic exports was Can$57.4 billion. Over 90 per cent of Alberta's exports went to the USA, Japan, South Korea, Mexico and China. Main exported goods were natural gas, crude petroleum oil, wood pulp, beef, transmission equipment, wheat and lumber. Alberta's main exports include, gas and gas liquids; crude petroleum; petrochemicals; processed food and beverages; metals and machinery; electronic and electrical produces, forest products; livestock; crops; refined petroleum products.

MANUFACTURING, MINING AND SERVICES

Primary and Extractive Industries

Alberta has 80 per cent of Canada's reserves of crude oil and accounts for around 65 per cent of Canada's oil production and 77 per cent of Canada's natural gas production. With gradually falling reserves of oil Alberta may benefit from exploration for heavy crude and utilising its large reserves of oil sands. Estimates from 2005 put the potential reserves of oil from Alberta's oil sands at 175 billion barrels, second only to Saudi Arabia. The extraction of oil from oil sands had previously been too expensive to be economically viable, but with the price of oil continuing to rise it now becomes a worthwhile project. The oil is close to the surface but is mixed with heavy sand. Huge amounts of energy and water are needed to release the oil by pumping in steam which separates the oil and pumps it upward for collection. Fort McMurray is the centre of the growing oil sands business. Production figures for 2004 show that 1.1 million barrels of crude oil were produced daily from oil sands. In January 2011 there was an explosion and fire at the Horizon Oil Sands facility, which injured four workers and operations were suspended for a while. Figures from the plant for 2010 showed that it produced around 90,000 barrels of synthetic crude oil per day.

Alberta has a network of pipelines to export its oil to Eastern Canada and the USA. It has 90 per cent of the country's reserves of natural gas and accounts for 80 per cent of output. The United States is the largest customer of Alberta's natural gas, receiving 51 per cent of its current production. Alberta now supplies an increased 11.6 per cent of the US natural gas market. Coal is another natural Albertan energy source which, at home, creates 90 per cent of the province's electricity, and abroad is currently exported to 12 countries. Alberta contributes half of all Canada's coal. Alberta's oil and gas production is responsible for a quarter of Alberta's GDP and around 70 per cent of exports

The following table shows selected mineral and fuel production by value in 2007.

Mineral and Fuel Production

Product	Can$ million
Gold	1.3
Sand & gravel	405.8
Crude petroleum	36,438.2
Natural gas	42,356.7

Source: Statistics Canada: CANSIM Catalogue no. 26-202-X Jan. 2012

Energy

Around two thirds of energy produced in Canada comes from Alberta. Electricity on the whole comes under the jurisdiction of each province. Alberta was the first province to introduce legislation to privatise its electricity industry, and as of January 2001 customers could choose who supplied their electricity. In 2010, Alberta generated 20.3 per cent of Canada electricity which translated at 805,700 kilowatts.

Manufacturing

Food and beverage processing is the major industry but other important sectors include petrochemicals which alone produces around Can$9 billion annually, plastics, machinery, and aerospace equipment.

The following tables show the value of manufacturing sales in recent years:

Manufacturing sales

Year	Can$ million
2000	44,429,8
2001	45,479.6
2002	45,407.2
2003	48,076.0
2004	53,299.2
2005	60,435.0
2006	65,090.7
2007	65,730.6
2008	70,146.2
2009	53,950.7
2010	60,073.7
2011	70,874.2

Source: Statistics Canada, CANSIM, tables 304-0014 and 304-0015 Feb. 2013

Manufacturing Sales by Subsector, figures in Can$ million

Industry	2010	2011
Food	10,739.7	11,272.5
Beverage & tobacco products	744.4	880.4
Wood products	2,079.2	2,182.1
Paper	1,934.2	1,776.8
Printing & related support activities	827.1	834.7
Petroleum & coal products	14,701.4	18,833.5
Chemicals	10,504.1	12,837.0
Plastics & rubber products	1,422.9	1,498.2

CANADA

- continued

Non-metallic mineral products	1,957.4	2,031.5
Fabricated metal products	4,426.7	5,422.4
Machinery	6,178.5	8,208.3
Computer & electronic products	460.4	486.9
Electrical equipment, appliances & components	402.0	473.6
Furniture & related products	819.5	789.4
Miscellaneous manufacturing	631.2	707.2

Source: Statistics Canada CANSIM, table 304-0015 Feb. 2013

Service Industries
The service sector accounts for more than 60 per cent of the province's GDP. Tourism is the largest of the service industries, employing an estimated 100,000 Albertans on a full- and part-time basis and contributing nearly Can$3 billion to the economy. In 1988 Calgary, Alberta hosted the Winter Olympics and in 2002 a G8 summit took place just outside Calgary. Other important service industries are finance, oil and gas services, transportation and communication, retail, health, education, community and cultural services.

Agriculture
Over 210,292 sq km of land is designated for agricultural use and there are 57,000 farms and ranches. Over 11 million hectares of cultivated land are used to grow grains, oilseeds, forages, forage seeds and special crops. A further 8.4 million hectares of uncultivated land are used as pasture and forage for livestock. Crop production recently totalled 20 million tonnes. Wheat is the major crop. The production of new varieties of existing crops continues to expand and Alberta remains the only province to produce sugar from sugar beet. Figures for 2005 show that Alberta produced over a third of Canada's wheat, barley, oats, canola and dry peas. Alberta has the largest livestock population in Canada. Recent figures show that the province produced 54 per cent of all slaughter cattle (2.4 million head in 2003) in Canada and accounted for 16 per cent of the country's slaughter hog production. It also accounted for 32 per cent of all lamb and mutton and 8 per cent of cornish, broiler and roaster chicken and turkey production.

Alberta's secondary agricultural processing currently represents 12.6 per cent of the entire Canadian food and beverage industry.

The following table shows the value of Alberta's major agricultural products in recent years, figures are in tonnes:

Product	2010	2011
Barley	4,688,000	4,563,300
Canola	5,347,900	4,898,800
Chick peas	10,400	16,200
Corn for grain	35,600	35,600
Mustard seed	26,800	35,900
Oats	738,700	518,200
Wheat, all	8,839,600	8,368,800
Wheat, duram	620,500	732,100
Wheat, spring	7,957,800	7,429,900
Wheat, winter remaining	261,300	206,800

Source: Statistics Canada CANSIM table 001-0017 Feb. 2013

Forestry
Recent figures show that 682,000 sq. km. of land was forested with 257,000 sq. km. under production. Alberta's forest product shipments earned in the region of Can$ 3.8 billion. annually and industry employs around 48,000 people.

Agricultural Financial Services Corporation (AFSC), URL: http://www.afsc.ca

Alberta Grain Commission,
URL: http://www1.agric.gov.ab.ca/$department/deptdocs.nsf/all/agc2620
Farmers' Advocate of Alberta,
URL: http://www1.agric.gov.ab.ca/$department/deptdocs.nsf/all/ofa2621

COMMUNICATIONS AND TRANSPORT

International Airports
There are international airports at Edmonton and Calgary as well as several other smalle airports including Lethbridge, Grande Prairie, Fort McMurray and Peace River.

Railways
The two main railway systems, Canadian Pacific Railway and Canadian National Railwa have a total track of 10,234 km. Alberta is also home to the third largest railway, Railinl Edmonton and Calgary also have light rail networks. Bulk commodities moved include whea and other grains, coal, sulphur, petrochemicals and timber products.

Roads
There are 155,325 km of roads, of which 23,562 are paved, 110,555 are gravelled and 21,20 are either graded or oil-treated. Figures for 2008 show that a total of 4,071,831 vehicle were registered in Alberta.

HEALTH

Alberta is divided into 17 regional health authorities and has more than 300 hospital auxiliary facilities and nursing homes. There are major medical centres at the University Alberta Hospital in Edmonton and the Foothills Hospital Centre in Calgary. Recent figure indicate that per 1,000 population, there are 16.2 beds in health-care institutions. Spendin on health in 2009 totalled Can$8.64 billion.

EDUCATION

Education from kindergarten to pre-university stage is free. There are nominal tuition fee for advanced education programs at Alberta's colleges, universities and technical institute

The post-secondary institutions include four universities, 15 public colleges, fou degree-granting private colleges, two technical institutes and the Banff Centre for Continuin Education.

Figures for recent years show a rise in the number of students enrolled in general educatio 567,979 in the 2009-10 school year. Expenditure per student in public general education i 2008-09 was Can$12,765. (Statistics Canada)

ENVIRONMENT

Alberta Environmental Protection is responsible for safeguarding the region's air, land an water; specifically its forests, parks, wildlife, and fish. Current legislation includes: the Fores Act; the Provincial Parks Act; the Water Resources Act; the Wildlife Act; and the Wildernes Areas, Ecological Reserves and Natural Areas Act. Such legislation can, for example, requir proposed industrial projects to seek approval, apply standards for the conservation of natura resources, and control waste products for the protection of the environment. Standards ar maintained by means of codes of practice, approvals and guidelines, and specifically affec water quality, surface water quality, industrial effluent, waste water, air quality, and a emissions.

BRITISH COLUMBIA

Capital: Victoria (Population estimate: 320,000)

Lieutenant Governor: Steven L. Point, OBE (page 1496)

Provincial Flag: Top half is the Union Jack with a crown in the centre, and the bottom half has seven wavy stripes, alternating blue and white, with a yellow sun rising from the base.

CONSTITUTION AND GOVERNMENT

Constitution
British Columbia became a province on 20 July 1871. Some 36 elected British Columbian members of parliament sit on Canada's 301-seat House of Commons, whilst up to six senators sit on the 104-seat Canadian Senate. The current senators are, Larry Campbell, Mobina Jaffer, Yonah Martin, Richard Neufeld, Nancy Greene Raine and Gerry St. Germain.

To consult the constitution, please visit:
http://www.bclaws.ca/EPLibraries/bclaws_new/document/ID/freeside/00_96066_01

Upper House
Although the province has no upper house, it is represented on the Canadian Senate and the House of Commons. The members of the House of Commons are elected while the members of the Senate are appointed. The representatives in the Senate are: Larry Casmpbell, Mobina Jaffer, Yonah Martin, Richard Neufeld and Nancy Greene Raine.

Lower House
The Legislative Assembly consists of the Lieutenant Governor and 75 members and is electe for five years.
Parliament Buildings, Victoria, BC V8V 1X4, Canada. URL: http://www.legis.gov.bc.ca

Cabinet (as at June 2013)
Premier: Hon Christy Clark (page 1405)
Deputy Premier, Minister of Natural Gas Development and Minister Responsibl for Housing: Rich Coleman
Minister of Education: Peter Fassbender
Minister of Finance and Government House Leader: Michael de Jong
Minister of Agriculture: Pat Pimm
Minister of Justice abd Attorney General: Suzanne Anton
Minister of Children and Family Development: Stephanie Cadieuxl
Minister of Community, Sport and Cultural Development: Coralee Oakes
Minister of Mines and Energy: Bill Bennett
Minister of Forests, Lands and Natural Resources: Steve Thomson
Minister of Health Services: Terry Lake
Minister of Labour, Citizens' Services and Open Government: Margaret MacDiarmi
Minister of Advanced Education: Anrik Virk
Minister of Environment: Mary Polak
Minister of Aboriginal Relations and Reconciliation: John Rustad
Minister of Jobs, Tourism and Skills Training: Shirley Bond
Minister of Multiculturalism: John Yap
Minister for Transportation and Infrastructure, Deputy House Leader: Todd Stone
Minister for Tourism and Small Businesses: Naomi Yamamoto

Minister of Social Development and Social Innovation: Don McRae
Minister of Technology, Innovation adn Citizens Services: ANdrew Wilkinson
Minister of International Trade, Minister Respnsible for Asia Pacific Strategy and Multiculturalism: Teresa Wat

Ministries

Ministry of Agriculture and Lands, PO Box 9120, Stn Prov Govt, Victoria, BC, V8W 9B4. Tel: +1 250 387 6121, URL: http://www.agf.gov.bc.ca

Ministry of Aboriginal Affairs, PO Box 9100, Stn Prov Govt, Victoria, BC, V8W 9B1. Tel: +1 250 356 8281, fax: +1 250 387 1785, URL: http://www.gov.bc.ca/arr/index.html

Ministry of Children and Families, PO Box 9770 Stn Prov Govt, Victoria, BC V8W 9S5, URL: http://www.gov.bc.ca/mcf/index.html

Ministry of Education, 3rd Floor, 835 Humboldt St., Victoria, BC, V8W 9H8. Tel: +1 250 387 2026, fax: +1 250 356 2011, URL: http://www.gov.bc.ca/bced/index.html

Ministry of Advanced Education, Training and Technology, 3rd Floor, 835 Humboldt St., Victoria, B.C., V8W9T6. Tel: +1 250 356 5170, fax: +1 250 356 5468, URL: http://www.gov.bc.ca/aved/index.html

Ministry of Energy and Mines, PO Box 9324, Stn Prov Govt, Victoria, B.C., V8W 9N3. Tel: +1 250 952 0525, fax: +1 250 952 0626 / 0627, URL: http://www.gov.bc.ca/empr/index.html

Ministry of Finance and Corporate Relations, Parliament Buildings, Victoria, BC, V8V 1X4. Tel: +1 250 387 3347, URL: http://www.gov.bc.ca/fin/index.html

Ministry of Forests, Room 128, Parliament Buildings, Victoria, BC, V8V 1X4. Tel: +1 250 387 6240, fax: +1 250 387 1040, URL: http://www.gov.bc.ca/for/index.html

Ministry of Health and Ministry Responsible for Seniors, Room 133 Parliament Buildings, Victoria, BC, V8V 1X4. Tel: +1 250 952 1742, URL: http://www.gov.bc.ca/health/index.html

Ministry of Human Resources, PO Box 9058, Stn Prov Govt, Victoria, BC, V8W 9E2. Tel: +1 250 387 6485, fax: +1 250 356 7801

Ministry of Transportation and Highways, 5B 940 Blanshard Street, Victoria, BC, V8W 3E6. Tel: +1 250 387 7788, fax: +1 250 356 7706, http://www.gov.bc.ca/tran/index.html

Elections

The most recent elections were held in May 2013. The BC Liberal Party led by Christy Clark were re-elected to power for a fourth term.

LEGAL SYSTEM

The British Columbian judicial system comprises the Court of Appeal, the supreme Court and the Provincial Court (of which the Small Claims Court and Family Court are part). The Court of Appeal of British Columbia consists of a Chief Justice and 15 Justices of Appeal. The supreme Court of British Columbia comprises a chief justice and 34 puisne justices. The chief justice is also responsible for general supervision of 47 county court judges in the province. The Provincial Court of British Columbia consists of a chief judge, and approximately 118 provincially appointed judges.

LOCAL GOVERNMENT

British Columbia is divided administratively into 152 incorporated municipalities (cities, districts, towns and villages), regional districts, school districts, regional hospital districts and special purpose improvement districts. Incorporated municipalities are responsible for the provision of roads, sewers and waterworks. Regional districts are responsible for those services shared by a larger area. Funding for both municipal and regional services is generated by property tax and provincial government grants. Local government elections are held every three years.

AREA AND POPULATION

Area

British Columbia is Canada's westernmost province and lies on Canada's Pacific coast it has an area of 947,800 sq. km. including Vancouver Island on which the capital is situated. It is Canada's third largest province, occupying almost 10 per cent of the country's land surface. British Columbia borders Alberta in the east, Northwest and Yukon territories to the North and the US States of Washington, Idaho and Montana to the South and Alaska to the northwest. The terrain is very diverse, from an island studded coastline to the Rocky Mountains, and including rain forests, steppes, fertile river valleys and prairies.

To view a map of British Columbia, please consult http://atlas.nrcan.gc.ca/site/english/maps/reference/provincesterritories. (With permission of Natural Resources Canada 2008, courtesy of the Atlas of Canada)

Population

Thirteen per cent of Canada's population live in British Columbia. Some 320,000 people live in the capital, Victoria. The ten main languages spoken are English, Chinese, Punjabi, German, French, Dutch, Italian, Tagalog, Spanish and Japanese. The province also has many aboriginal people known as First Nations. Among the 197 bands are Gitsan, Haida, Nisga'a and Squamish. (Source: Government of BC and statcan). Figures from Statcan put the population in 2012 at 4,622,600.

Births, Marriages, Deaths

The birth rate had been dropping since 1995 when for the period July 1995-June 1996 there were 46,853 births. For the same period in 2005-2006, there were 40,465 births, up from the July 2003-June 2004 of 40,039. Figures for the year 2008-09 showed that the number of births had risen again to 44,554 and then fell again in 2009-10, to 44,497 in 2010-11 to 43,745 and in 2011-12 to 43,677. The death rate has been increasing from 26,970 in the period July 1995-June 1996 when there were 26,970 deaths compared with the same period for 2002-2003 when there were 28,757 deaths. An estimated 30,001 deaths were recorded

between July 2004-2005, 31,214 in the year 2008-09 and 31,174 in 2009-10, 2010-11, 31,519 and in 2011-12, 32,056. Immigration figures for the year 2011-12 show that 67,334 immigrants arrived from other Canadian provinces and 56,688 people left British Colombia for other Canadian provinces. In 2011-12, 36,222 immigrants arrived in British Columbia and 8,847 people emigrated from the province. Provisional figures for 2008 show that there were 20,632 marriages. (Source: Statistics Canada website, www.statcan.ca.)

In addition to the standard days celebrated in Canada, British Columbia also celebrates the following:

Public Holidays 2014
19 May: Victoria Day
4 August: British Columbia Day
13 October: Thanksgiving Day
11 November: Remembrance Day

EMPLOYMENT

The workforce in British Columbia has increased from 1.9 million in 1996 to 2.4 million in 2012 of which 2,312,500 were employed and 166,400 unemployed giving an unemployment rate of 6.7 per cent. The following table shows how the population were employed recently, figures are seasonally adjusted:

Employment Sector	Dec. 2011	Dec. 2012
Agriculture	26,700	27,900
Forestry, fishing, mining, oil and gas	43,500	48,700
Utilities	10,500	16,600
Construction	207,100	206,300
Manufacturing	168,800	164,700
Trade	357,900	362,000
Transportation & warehousing	127,500	119,000
Finance, insurance, real estate and leasing	132,800	135,600
Professional, scientific & technical services	194,000	174,400
Business building & other support services	82,300	94,600
Educational services	162,300	186,800
Health care & social assistance	278,800	265,100
Information, culture & recreation	113,700	121,500
Accommodation & food services	178,700	176,000
Other services	104,300	105,400
Public admin.	105,100	108,800

Source: Statistics Canada, CANSIM Table 282-0088 Jan 2013

BANKING AND FINANCE

GDP/GNP, Inflation, National Debt
The following table shows expenditure based GDP in recent years:

Year	Can$ millions
2004	157,675
2005	169,664
2006	182,251
2007	196,996
2008	203,820
2009	195,670
2010	208,295
2011	217,749

Source: Statistics Canada, CANSIM, table 384-0038 Jan. 2013

Traditionally the economy has been based on forestry, mining, fishing and agriculture but new areas are becoming increasingly important, including eco-tourism, agri-tourism, film and television production and technology based industries.

Manufacturing Sales

Year	Can$ Millions
2005	42,882.6
2006	44,479.9
2007	42,418.5
2008	39,434.6
2009	32,797.8
2010	35,542.0
2011	37,859.4

Source: Statistics Canada: CANSIM, tables 304-0014 and 304-0015 Jan. 2013

Balance of Payments / Imports and Exports
The main exported good of British Columbia are wood products, paper and food. British Columbia's largest foreign markets both for imports and exports are the USA, Japan, China and South Korea.

MANUFACTURING, MINING AND SERVICES

Primary and Extractive Industries
British Columbia's rich natural resources are due to a geological formation in which it lies: the Western Cordillera. The major products mined are coal, natural gas, copper, zinc, lead, silver and gold. Total metals production in 2007 generated Can$2,9 billion and Can$2,6 billion in 2008, copper was the largest earner. British Columbia accounts for around 30 per cent of Canada's coal production and in 2007 generated Can$1.9 billion.

CANADA

The following table shows the value of mineral production in 2007.

Value in Million Can$

Mineral	2007
Copper	1,980.3
Gold	287.2
Silver	119.4
Zinc	108.4
Sand & gravel	198.8
Coal	1,964.6
Crude petroleum	757.8
Natural gas	6,815.9

Source: Manufacturing and Energy Division, 2008, Canada's Mineral Production, Preliminary Estimates, 2007, Catalogue no. 26-202-X

Energy

British Columbia is self-sufficient in all sources of energy with the exception of oil, most of which is imported from Alberta. The province is the second largest producer of natural gas in Canada and contains one third of Canada's fresh water supply and, in 2003, hydro-electric plants generated 56,689 gigawatts of electricity.

Manufacturing

Manufacturing is largely resource-based with a major emphasis on forest products, food, refined petroleum products and primary metals. Major manufacturing centres are Greater Vancouver and Vancouver Island. The key manufacturing export destination is the United States. The value of manufacturing shipments in 2008 was Can$40 billion and the sector employed around 187,000 persons.

Electronics, telecommunications equipment and pharmaceuticals, known collectively as the high technology sector, increased its real domestic product by seven per cent to Can$1.9 billion. This represents 2.8 per cent of the province's economy. Like manufacturing, the major high technology export market is the United States, although domestic demand has now reduced exports from 48 per cent, in 1995, to 40 per cent.

The British Columbian retail trade generated Can$56 billion in 2008. Metropolitan Vancouver is the province's main trading location, contributing more than one half of provincial retail sales. The major retail trade sector is automotive sales. Food stores and general merchandise stores are the next highest generators of retail trade revenue and contributed over Can$11,400 million in the same year.

Manufacturing Sales by Subsector, figures in Can$ million

Industry	2010	2011
Food	5,997.5	6,301.2
Beverage & tobacco products	1,174.6	1,153.1
Leather & allied products	9.4	14.9
Wood products	5,695.1	5,944.2
Paper	5.026.2	5,198.8
Printing & related support activities	617.0	619.9
Plastics & rubber goods	1.053.7	1,170.9
Non-metallic mineral products	1,327.4	1,310.6
Primary metals	2,234.6	2,697.2
Machinery	1.726.4	2,085.2
Computer & electronic products	1,095.6	1,055.6
Transportation equipment	1,097.9	1,360.4
Furniture & related products	847.6	831.9
Miscellaneous manufacturing	1,170.1	1,184.5

Source: Statistics Canada, CANSIM, table 304-0015 Jan. 2011

Tourism

In 2003, nearly 22 million people visited British Columbia and spent Can$8.9 billion. The majority of visitors were from Canada, whilst North American tourists were the province's second largest sources of revenue. Overseas visitors made up just under 8 per cent of the province's tourists. Generally, they visited British Columbia's national, provincial, regional and local parks, its ecological reserves and its marine parks. Tourism peaked in February 2010 with British Columbia hosting the Winter Olympics in Whistler.

Agriculture

Agriculture in British Columbia is very diverse. Activities include dairy farming, cattle ranching, poultry-raising, and the growing of tree fruits, vegetables, berries, grapes, greenhouse vegetables, mushrooms, bulbs, ornamental flowers and shrubs. The land available for arable cultivation is just three per cent of the total area of the province. Farm size varies by type of activity. In 2011 there were 19,759 farms covering 6.4 million acres. Total farm receipts amounted to Can$2.3 billion in 2006. The following table shows the value of major commodities of farm income:

Production in Metric Tonnes

Crop	2011	2012
Barley	64,200	55,800
Canola	56,000	82,800
Oats	86,400	48,600
Wheat, all	121,600	96,000
Wheat, spring	121,600	96,000

Source: Statistics Canada, CANSIM table 001-0010

Forestry

British Columbia's commercial forests cover 46 per cent of the province's land area. Som 49.9 million hectares of provincial forest land support more than 8 billion cubic metres o mature timber, about 96 per cent of which are coniferous (softwood). British Columbia' topography and climate divides the province into two distinct forest regions: the coast, where hemlock species dominates, and the interior, where the main species are spruce and lodgepol pine. Other valuable commercial species are Douglas fir, balsam and western red cedar. 200. saw British Columbia experience one of the driest summers on record, as a result of this th province suffered from large forest fires in August of that year resulting in the loss of 430,00 hectares of forest.

The following tables show manufacturing shipment by industry (Can$ million) and the timbe harvest:

Industry	Value
Wood	7,284
Paper Products and allied products	3.88
Food	3,04
Refined petroleum and coal	1,81
Fabricated Metal Products	1,32
Primary Metals	798
Printing and Publishing	95
Chemicals and Chemical Equipment	653
Transportation Equipment	657
Non-metallic Minerals	765
Machinery (except electrical)	57
Beverages	77
Electrical and Electronic Products	466
Plastics	443
Furniture and Fixtures	210
Clothing	21
Textile Products	108
Other	32
Total	24,322

Species	Volume ('000 cubic metres)	Percent
Lodgepole pine	19,298	26.2
Spruce	14,244	19.3
Hemlock	12,510	17.
Balsam	10,175	13.8
Douglas fir	7,296	9.9
Cedar	7,220	9.8
Other species	2,932	4.
Total	73,676	100.

The fishing industry in British Columbia is cyclical with landings dependent on fluctuation in stocks of individual species. Salmon is the most important catch, followed by shellfish groundfish and herring. The majority of exported fish goes to the US, followed by Japan.

COMMUNICATIONS AND TRANSPORT

National Airlines

Air BC, Parent company: Air Canada, URL: http://www.aircanada.ca/
Kelowna Flightcraft Air Charter, URL: http://www.flightcraft.ca/

International Airports

Vancouver International Airport (URL: http://www.yvr.ca/) is Canada's second busiest airport

Railways

British Columbia has approximately 6,800 km of railway track. There are a number o operators, including British Columbia Rail, CN Rail and CP Rail.

Roads

There are 22,053 km of paved roads and 21,584 km of unpaved roads. The network of road covers most of the province.

Ports and Harbours

Local port corporations:
Prince Rupert Port Authority, URL: http://www.rupertport.com
Vancouver Port Corporation, URL: http://www.portmetrovancouver.com
Total port traffic at the Prince Rupert port is some 11.5 million tonnes, a reduction of 17 pe cent from traffic levels three years ago. This decline is mainly due to reduced handling of dry goods such as coal and grain. Traffic increased at the Vancouver port, rising by 6 per cen to over 71 million tonnes. This was due mainly to strong exports from west Canada of product such as coal, sulphur and containerised goods.

Waterways

Major rivers in British Columbia are the Columbia, Fraser, Peace and Skeena rivers.

HEALTH

Recent figures show that there are currently 14.3 beds in approved health care institution per 1,000 population. This breaks down to 6.0 per 1,000 in hospitals and 8.3 per 1,000 i residential care facilities. The provincial government's 2009 healthcare expenditure wa Can$10.1 billion.

EDUCATION

The school system is free from kindergarten to grade 12. There are 1,713 public schools in the province, including 1,341 elementary schools, 337 secondary schools and 35 continuing education colleges. Figures for recent years show a fall in the number of students enrolled in general education: 571,415 in the 2007-08 school year falling to 562,902 in the 2009-10 school year. Expenditure per student in public general education in 2009-10 was Can$11,820. (Statistics Canada)

There are five publicly funded universities in British Columbia which enroll 44 per cent of the province's student population: the University of British Columbia, the Simon Fraser University, in Vancouver; the University of Victoria and the Royal Roads University in Victoria; and the University of Northern British Columbia in Prince George. The University of Northern British Columbia accepted its first students in 1992 and opened its main campus in 1994. Post-secondary facilities also exist, including schemes for academic, technical, vocational, career and adult basic education.

COMMUNICATIONS AND MEDIA

Newspapers
Newspapers published in British Columbia include The Vancouver Sun (URL: http://www.vancouversun.com), The Province (URL: http://www.theprovince.com), Times Colonist (URL: http://www.timescolonist.com), Daily News, Daily Courier and Daily Townsman.

Broadcasting
British Columbia's broadcasting, cable and telecommunications industries fall within the federal jurisdiction and are regulated by the Canadian Radio-Television and Telecommunications Commission (CRTC).

Post and Telecommunications
BC Telecom currently provides in the region of 2.5 million access lines, whilst cellular communications companies have more than 500,000 subscribers.

ENVIRONMENT

In order to protect British Columbia's extensive wildlife and wilderness areas, the province has in place a Protected Areas System. Areas under protection account for 11.8 per cent of the province and include the Tatshenshini-Alsek region. The Khutzeymateen Valley is under permanent protection as a grizzly bear habitat. The Great Bear Rainforest covers and area of 64,000 sq. km. and is the world's largest temperate rainforest. In 2006, the federal government announced that it would allocate Can$30 million which would be matched by the provincial government to protect the area.

MANITOBA

Capital: Winnipeg (Population estimate: 630,000)

Lieutenant Governor: Hon. Philip S. Lee, C.M., O.M. (page 1462)

Provincial Flag: Red Ensign with a Union Jack in the top left hand corner and the provincial coat of arms is centred in the right hand half of the flag.

CONSTITUTION AND GOVERNMENT

Constitution
Manitoba became a province of Canada on 15 July 1870.

Upper House
Although the province has no upper house, it is represented on the Canadian Senate by six Senators: JoAnne L. Buth, Maria Chaput , Janis Johnson (page 1450) , Donald Neil Plett, Terry Stratton , Rod Zimmer.

Lower House
The Legislative Assembly consists of the Lieutenant Governor and 60 elected members.
Legislative Assembly, 450 Broadway, Winnipeg, MB R3C 0V8, Canada. URL: http://www.gov.mb.ca/legislature/homepage.html
Speaker: Hon. Daryl Reid

Cabinet (as at June 2013)
Premier, President of the Executive Council, Minister of Federal-Provincial Relations, Minister Responsible for Francophone Affairs: Hon. Gregory Selinger (page 1511)
Minister of Infrastructure and Transportation: Hon. Steve Ashton
Minister of Innovation, Energy and Mines: Hon. David Walter Chomiak (page 1404)
Minister of Conservation and Water Stewardship: Hon. Gord Mackintosh (page 1468)
Minister of Aboriginal Affairs and Northern Affairs: Hon. Eric Robinson (page 1504)
Minister of Finance: Hon. Stan Struthers (page 1521)
Minister of Education: Hon. Nancy Allan
Minister of Healthy Living, Seniors & Consumer Affairs: Jim Rondeau (page 1505)
Minister of Entrepreneurship, Training and Trade: Hon. Peter Bjornson
Minister of Immigration and Multiculturalism: Hon. Christine Melnick
Minister of Health: Hon. Theresa Oswald
Minister of Housing and Community Development: Hon. Kerri Irvin-Ross
Minister of Justice and Attorney General: Hon. Andrew Swan
Minister of Labour and Family Service: Hon. Jennifer Howard
Minister of Advanced Education and Literacy: Erin Selby
Minister of Culture, Heritage and Tourism: Flor Marcelino
Minister of Children and Youth Opportunities: Hon. Kevin Chief
Minister of Agriculture, Food and Rural Initiatives: Hon. Ron Kostyshyn

Ministries
Office of the Premier, President of the Executive Council, Minister of Federal-Provincial Relations, 204 Legislative Building, 450 Broadway, Winnipeg, Manitoba, R3C 0V8, Canada. Tel: +1 204 945 3714, fax: +1 204 949 1484, e-mail: premier@leg.gov.mb.ca, URL: http://www.gov.mb.ca/minister/premier/
Ministry of Agriculture and Food, 165 Legislative Building, 450 Broadway, Winnipeg, Manitoba, R3C 0V8, Canada. Tel: +1 204 945 3722, fax: +1 204 945 3470, e-mail: minagr@leg.gov.mb.ca, URL: http://www.gov.mb.ca/agriculture
Ministry of Family Services and Consumer Affairs, 314 Legislative Building, 450 Broadway Avenue, Winnipeg, Manitoba, R3C 0V8, Canada. Tel: +1 204 945 4256, fax: +1 204 945 4009, e-mail: mincca@leg.gov.mb.ca, URL: http://www.gov.mb.ca/cca/
Ministry of Culture, Heritage and Tourism, 118 Legislative Building, 450 Broadway Avenue, Winnipeg, Manitoba, R3C 0V8, Canada. Tel: +1 204 945 3729, fax: +1 204 945 5223, e-mail: mincht@leg.gov.mb.ca, URL: http://www.gov.mb.ca/chc

Ministry of Education and Training, 168 Legislative Building, 450 Broadway Avenue, Winnipeg, Manitoba, R3C 0V8, Canada. Tel: +1 204 945 3720, fax: +1 204 945 1291, e-mail: minna@leg.gov.mb.ca, URL: http://www.edu.gov.mb.ca/edu
Ministry of Aboriginal and Northern Affairs, 344 Legislative Building, 450 Broadway Avenue, Winnipeg, Manitoba, Canada, R3C 0V8. Tel: +1 204 945 3719, fax: +1 204 945 8374, e-mail: minem@leg.gov.mb.ca, URL: http://www.gov.mb.ca/ana
Ministry of Conservation, 333 Legislative Building, 450 Broadway Avenue, Winnipeg, Manitoba, R3C 0V8, Canada. Tel: +1 204 945 3522, fax: +1 204 945 3586, e-mail: mincon@leg.gov.mb.ca, URL: http://www.gov.mb.ca/conservation
Ministry of Entrepreneurship, Training and Trade, URL: http://www.gov.mb.ca/ctt
Ministry of Finance, 103 Legislative Building, 450 Broadway Avenue, Winnipeg, Manitoba, R3C 0V8, Canada. Tel: +1 204 945 3952, fax: +1 204 945 6057, e-mail: minfin@leg.gov.mb.ca, URL: http://www.gov.mb.ca/finance/index.html
Ministry of Health, 302 Legislative Building, 450 Broadway Avenue, Winnipeg, Manitoba, R3C 0V8, Canada. Tel: +1 204 945 3731, fax: +1 204 945 0441, e-mail: minhlt@leg.gov, URL: http://www.gov.mb.ca/health
Ministry of Healthy Living, Youth, and Seniors, URL: http://www.gov.mb.ca/healthyliving
Ministry of Housing and Community Development, URL: http://www.gov.mb.ca/housing/index.html
Ministry of Transportation and Infrastructure, 203 Legislative Building, 450 Broadway Avenue, Winnipeg, Manitoba, R3C 0V8, Canada. Tel: +1 204 945 3723, fax: +1 204 945 7610, URL: http://www.gov.mb.ca/mit/
Ministry of Energy and Mines, URL: http://www.gov.mb.ca/stem
Ministry of Local Government, 301 Legislative Building, 450 Broadway Avenue, Winnipeg, Manitoba, R3C 0V8, Canada. Tel: +1 204 945 3788, fax: +1 204 945 1383, email: minia@leg.gov.mb.ca, URL: http://www.gov.mb.ca/ia
Ministry of Justice and Office of the Attorney-General, 104 Legislative Building, 450 Broadway Avenue, Winnipeg, Manitoba, R3C 0V8, Canada. Tel: +1 204 945 3728, fax: +1 204 945 2517, e-mail: minjus@leg.gov.mb.ca, URL: http://www.gov.mb.ca/justice/index.html
Ministry of Labour & Immigration, 317 156 Legislative Building, 450 Broadway Avenue, Winnipeg, Manitoba, R3C 0V8, Canada. Tel: +1 204 945 4079, fax: +1 204 945 3266, e-mail: minlab@leg.gov.mb.ca, URL: http://www.gov.mb.ca/labour
Ministry of Water Stewardship: URL: http://www.gov.mb.ca/waterstewardship

Elections
The most recent election was held in October 2011 when the New Democrats Party was re-elected with 37 seats. The Progressive Conservative Party of Manitoba won 19 seats and the Manitoba Liberal Party won one seat.

LEGAL SYSTEM

Manitoba has three levels of Courts. The Provincial Court is the primary court of criminal jurisdiction. The Manitoba Court of Queen's Bench is the highest trial court and can hear civil and criminal cases. The Manitoba Court of Appeal is the senior level court, and hears appeals from the Provincial and Queen's Bench Courts.

LOCAL GOVERNMENT

Manitoba is divided into municipalities each with its own government, autonomous within its own municipality.

CANADA

AREA AND POPULATION

Area
Manitoba covers an area of 650,000 sq. km. It is in the centre of Canada and borders Saskatchewan to the west, Nunavut to the North, Hudson Bay in the North East, Ontario in the west and the USA (North Dakota and Minnesota) to the South. The province has around 100,000 lakes. The north of the province is glaciated and is dominated by forests of pine, hemlock and birch.

To view a map of Manitoba, please consult http://atlas.nrcan.gc.ca/site/english/maps/reference/provincesterritories. (With permission of Natural Resources Canada 2008, courtesy of the Atlas of Canada)

Population
The population in 2012 was 1,267,000, half of which live in the capital, Winnipeg. The chief cities are: City of Winnipeg, with a population in 2001 of 625,500; Brandon, 38,567; Flin Flon, 7,119; Portage la Prairie, 13,186; Thompson, 14,977. In 2012, 237,700 of the population is aged 0-14, 849,200 are aged 15 to 64 years and 180,100 were over 65 years of age.

Births, Marriages, Deaths
Figures for July 2011-June 2012 put the number of births at 16,250 and the number of deaths at 10,459. In the year July 2006-June 2007, 17,325 immigrants arrived from other provinces and 23,177 Manitobans left for other provinces, 10,789 foreign immigrants arrived and 1,767 Manitobans left for other countries. In 2008 there were an estimated 5,804 marriages and in 2005 2,429 divorces. The current life expectancy at birth is 75 years for males and 80.8 years for females. (Source: Statistics Canada)

In addition to the standard days celebrated in Canada, Manitoba also celebrates the following:

Public Holidays 2014
17 February: Louis Riel Day
19 May: Victoria Day
4 August: Civic Holiday
13 October: Thanksgiving Day
11 November: Remembrance Day

EMPLOYMENT

Latest statistics show that in 2012 out of a total labour force of 665,400, 35,300 were out of work. This gave an unemployment rate of 5.3 per cent, down from 5.4 per cent in 2010. In 1998, 1999, 2002 and 2003 Manitoba had the lowest average provincial unemployment rate.

The following table shows how the working population were employed in recent years:

Sector	Dec. 2011	Dec. 2012
Agriculture	22,200	23,900
Forestry, fishing, mining, oil & gas	6,500	7,500
Utilities	8,200	8,000
Construction	43,000	48,700
Manufacturing	61,500	60,900
Trade	93,700	92,600
Transportation & warehousing	36,200	36,400
Finance, insurance, real estate & leasing	36,700	35,100
Prof. scientific & technical services	26,000	29,400
Business building & other support services	18,300	20,500
Educational services	46,800	50,300
Health care & social assistance	95,700	94,300
Information, culture & recreation	23,400	25,600
Accommodation & food services	44,300	41,000
Other services	26,100	28,400
Public administration	38,800	35,900

Source: Statistics Canada, CANSIM table 282-0088

BANKING AND FINANCE

GDP/GNP, Inflation, National Debt
The following table shows expenditure based GDP in recent years:

Year	Can$ millions
2004	39,748
2005	41,681
2006	45,173
2007	49,263
2008	51,899
2009	50,828
2010	53,266
2011	55,894

Source: Statistics Canada,CANSIM, table 384-0038 Jan. 2012

In 2005, the Manitoban economy grew by 2.9 per cent, an estimated 3.2 per cent in 2006, 3.1 per cent in 2007 and by 2.3 per cent in 2008.

Balance of Payments / Imports and Exports
Manitoba Exports by Industry in 2005

Industry	Can$ millions
Agriculture	1,907

- continued

Mining	592
Electrical power	596
Other	381
Manufacturing	6,411
Total	9,886

Source: Government of Manitoba

Manitoba's Export Destinations in 2005

Country	Can$ millions
United States	7,534.7
Japan	524.5
China	243.9
Mexico	199.6
Hong Kong	129.7
Korea, South	100.3
Belgium	92.8
United Kingdom	86.1
Australia	64.1
Taiwan	60.5
Other Countries	850.4

Source: Government of Manitoba

Manitoba Top Import Commodities, 2005

Commodity	Can$ millions
Bulldozers, etc.	407
Cars	402
Tractors	369
Harvesting equipment	294
Vehicle parts	285
Taps, cocks, valves	227
Printed publications	219
Insecticides	215
Turbo-jet & gas turbines	204
Trucks	200
Other	8,852
Total imports	11,675

Source: Government of Manitoba

Manitoba Imports by Country, 2005

Country	Can$ millions
United States	9,561
China	375
Mexico	235
Germany	233
Japan	184
Italy	108
United Kingdom	107
Taiwan	105
Denmark	69
France	68
Other Countries	729

Source: Government of Manitoba

Chambers of Commerce and Trade Organisations
Canada Business Service Centre, URL: http://www.cbsc.org
Manitoba Chamber of Commerce, URL: http://www.mbchamber.mb.ca/

MANUFACTURING, MINING AND SERVICES

Primary and Extractive Industries
Metals mined in Manitoba include nickel, zinc, copper, silver and gold. Minerals mined include gravel, dolomite, ceseum, lithium, tantalum, peat, lime and gypsum. The value of mineral production is around Can$1 million per annum.

The following table shows selected mineral and fuel production by value in 2007.

Mineral and Fuel Production

Product	Can$ million
Copper	436.0
Gold	88.7
Nickel	1,357.9
Silver	18.4
Zinc	377.1
Sand & gravel	50.7
Crude petroleum	618.7

Source: Statistics Canada: www40.statcan.gc.ca/l01/cst01/envi38b-eng.htm Jan. 2012

Energy
At 9.7 billion kWh, Manitoba generates more power than its present needs. A total of 14 hydro-electric power stations contribute to Manitoba's generating capacity of 4,974 MW: six on the Winnipeg River (560 MW); one on the Saskatchewan River (472 MW); five on the Nelson River (3,932 MW); and two on the Laurie River (10 MW). Manitoba has in the region

of 5,060 MW of potential hydro-electric power at 10 sites in the province. In 2002 an agreement was signed to provide Minnesota, USA with 500 MW of electricity, starting in 2005.

Manufacturing

Manufacturing contributes around 13 per cent of the province's GDP. In 2005 manufacturing sales earned Can$13.6 million up slightly from the 2004 figure of Can$13.2 million. This rose to Can$14.8 million in 2006 and Can$16.1 million in 2007. Due to the agricultural base of the province, primary forest products contribute the most to this sector. Currently, it generates Can$1.1 billion in sales and Can$500 million in export shipments. The primary wood products sector, including market pulp, newspaper, paperboard, lumber and plywood, employs 2,000 people and generates some Can$440 million. Converted wood products, including kitchen cabinets, windows and doors, employs about 3,600 people and generates Can$320 million in shipments. The furniture industry has doubled its revenues over the past five years and presently has factory shipments valued at Can$290 million, employing more than 2,800 people. The food and beverage group of industries is another key manufacturing industry and is valued at Can$1,367 million, whilst transportation equipment generates Can$797 million. Manitoba is the largest manufacturer of buses in North America. Manitoban manufacturing sales in 2006 were worth Can$14,972.4 million and Can$16,167.6 million in 2007.

Manufacturing Shipments by Subsector, figures in Can$ millions

Industry	2010	2011
Food	3,675.6	3,560.1
Wood products	433.0	424.5
Paper	347.3	359.7
Printing & related support activities	400.9	353.2
Chemicals	913.5	1,223.4
Plastics & rubber products	607.2	601.3
Non-metallic mineral products	245.9	261.9
Primary metals	2,103.7	2,372.8
Fabricated metal products	801.7	846.0
Machinery	1,366.9	1,697.4
Electrical equipment, appliances & components	257.6	213.8
Transportation equipment	1,859.0	1,975.3
Total	14,421.9	15,316.0

Source: Statistics Canada, CANSIM, table 304-0015 Jan. 2013

Service Industries

Over 1.7 million people work in the tourism sector, contributing Can$1,166 million to the economy.

Recent figures show that the commercial services sector (transportation, communications, finance, retail etc) contributes 52 per cent of the GDP and accounts for nearly half of all jobs, making it the fastest growing area of the economy.

Agriculture

Approximately 5 per cent of Manitoba's GDP comes from agriculture. The sector employs 9 per cent of the working population and earns around 20 per cent of exports. In 2007 total farm income was Can$4.3 billion rising to Can$5.0 billion in 2010. Crops and livestock contributed almost equally: Can$1.4 billion from crop receipts and Can$1.3 billion from livestock receipts. Figures for 2011 showed that Manitoba had a total of 11,330 farms, down from 21,071 in 2001.

In 2004, there were 1.45 million head of cattle and calves, 2.852 million pigs, 82,000 sheep and lambs, 27.546 million chickens. In the same year, 78.744 million dozen eggs were produced. (Source: Statistics Canada www.statcan.ca March 2004)

Production of principal field crops in tonnes is set out in the following table:

Crop	2012
Barley	618,300
- continued	
Canola	2,100,100
Corn for grain	815,400
Oats	569,100
Soybeans	759,300
Sunflower seed	86,900
Wheat, all	3,923,000

Source: Statistics Canada, CANSIM table 001-0010

Forestry

Just over 50 per cent of Manitoba is covered in productive forestland with around 2.15 million cubic metres of wood harvested per year.

COMMUNICATIONS AND TRANSPORT

National Airlines

Air Manitoba, Hangar T67, 620 Ferry Road, Winnipeg International Airport, Winnipeg, Manitoba, R3H 0T7, Canada.

Main International Airports

Winnipeg International Airport is one of the few North American terminals to open 24 hours a day. It is a major centre for cargo transport.

Railways

There are 3,415 miles of railways in Manitoba. The two major railroads are Canadian Pacific with 1,222 miles of railway and Canadian National with 2,193 miles.

Roads

Highways and provincial roads total some 18,000 km.

Ports and Harbours

The main ports and harbours in Manitoba are located in Churchill and Gimli.

HEALTH

There are 69 hospitals in rural and northern Manitoba; nine are in Winnipeg. The most recent figures show that the total number of approved beds per 1,000 population is 17.5 (5.8 in hospitals and 11.6 within residential care facilities). Figures for 2009 show that total expenditure on health was Can$3.3 billion.

EDUCATION

Education is compulsory for all children ages 6 - 16. Education is controlled through locally elected school divisions. Figures for recent years show a fall in the number of students enrolled in general education: 179,320 in the 2007-08 school year falling to 177,962 in the 2008-09 school year. Expenditure per student in public general education in 2008-09 was Can$12,277. (Statistics Canada)

Recent figures show that education expenditure in the Manitoba province totalled Can$2,164.41 million, compared with Canada's overall educational expenditure of Can$58,621.83 million. Elementary and secondary schools drew Can$1,467.41 million of funding, whilst universities drew Can$455.92 million. The major sources of funding were provincial governments, municipal governments and the federal government.

COMMUNICATIONS AND MEDIA

Newspapers

There are 115 Manitoba community newspapers including ethnic media publications five business journals.

NEW BRUNSWICK

Capital: Fredericton (Population estimate: 49,000)

Lieutenant-Governor: Hon. Graydon Nicholas (page 1486)

Provincial Flag: Yellow with black ship with white sail and three red flags sailing on wavy blue and white lines, golden lion in red in chief.

CONSTITUTION AND GOVERNMENT

New Brunswick was one of the original four provinces. It entered the confederation in 1867, and is Canada's only officially bilingual Province having passed into law an Official Languages Act which recognises both the English language and the French language.

Recent Events

In 2006 the government launched its Five in Five initiative, a series of goals to make New Brunswick known as: The Smart Province, with the highest increase in workers with post-secondary education in Canada; The Investment Province, with a lower tax rate and the largest decrease in the unemployment rate in Canada; The Wellness Province, which hopes to see the largest increase in participation in physical activities of any province; The Clean Province, with the greatest reduction in air and water pollution in Canada; The Inclusive Province, aims to achieve the largest poverty-rate reduction in Canada.

Upper House

Although the province has no upper house, it is represented on the Canadian Senate and the House of Commons. The members of the House of Commons are elected while the members of the Senate are appointed. The representatives in the Senate are: Joseph Day, Noel Kinsella, Sandra Lovelace-Nicholas, Paul McIntyre, Percy Mockler, Rose-May Poirier, Pierrette Ringuette, John D. Wallace, Carolyn Stewart Olsen and Fernand Robichaud.

Lower House

New Brunswick's legislature is unicameral, although in all other respects is based on the British Parliamentary System where each of the members of the Legislative Assembly is elected to represent a constituency or district. The Legislative Assembly has 55 seats, meeting once, and occasionally twice, a year.
Legislative Assembly of New Brunswick, PO Box 6000, 706 Queen Street, Fredericton, NB E3B 5H1, Canada. Tel +1 506 453 2506, fax: +1 506 453 7154, e-mail: www.leg@gov.nb.ca, URL: http://www.gnb.ca/legis/index.asp
Speaker of the Legislative Assembly: Hon. Dale Graham

CANADA

Cabinet (as at June 2013)

Premier, President of the Executive Council, Minister Responsible for the Premier's Council on the Status of Disabled Persons, for Citizens' Engagement, for the Office of Government Review: David Alward (page 1377)
Minister for Economic Development, Minister Responsible for Regional Development Corp., Invest NB, Northern New Brunswick Initiative, Francophonie: Paul Robichaud
Attorney General, Minister of Justice, Minister responsible for Women's Equality: Marie-Claude Blais
Minister of Public Safety and Solicitor General: Robert Trevors
Minister of Finance, Minister responsible for NB Liquor Corp, for NB Investment Management: Blaine Higgs
Minister for Transportation & Infrastructure: Claude Williams
Minister for Healthy Communities: Dorothy Shephard
Minister for Natural Resources: Bruce Northrup
Minister for Energy & Mines: Craig Leonard
Minister for Human Resources: Troy Lifford
Minister for Agriculture, Aquaculture & Fisheries: Michael Olscamp
Minister for Health: Hugh Flemming
Minister for Tourism, Heritage & Culture: Trevor Holder
Minister for Government Serivces, responsible for Service New Brunswick, New Brunswick Internal Services: Sue Stultz
Minister for Post-Secondary Education, Training and Labour: Danny Soucy
Minister for Education and Early Childhood Development: Jody Carr
Minister of Environment and Local Government, responsible for Efficiency New Brunswick: Bruce Fitch

Ministries

Office of the Premier and President of the Executive Council, Room 212, Centennial Building, Fredericton, NB, Canada. Tel: +1 506 453 2144, fax: +1 506 453 7407, URL: http://www2.gnb.ca/content/gnb/en/departments/premier.html

Department of Justice, Office of the Attorney-General, Office of Government House Leader, Room 412, Centennial Building, Fredericton, NB, Canada. Tel: +1 506 453 2583, fax: +1 506 453 3651, URL: http://www.gnb.ca/0227/index-e.asp

Department of Public Safety, PO Box 6000, Fredericton, NB, Canada. Tel: +1 506 453 2662, fax: +1 506 444 502, URL: http://www.gnb.ca/0276/index-e.asp

Department of Finance, Room 371, Centennial Building, Fredericton, NB, Canada. Tel: +1 506 444 2627, fax: +1 506 457 4989, URL: http://www.gnb.ca/0024/index-e.asp

Department of Supply and Services, Marysville Place, 4th Floor, 20 McGloin Street, Fredericton, NB, Canada. Tel: +1 506 453 2591, fax: +1 506 462 5049, URL: http://www.gnb.ca/0099/index-e.asp

Department of Transportation, Kings Place, 2nd Floor, 440 King Street, Fredericton, NB, Canada. Tel: +1 506 453 2559, fax: +1 506 453 2900, URL: http://www.gnb.ca/0113/index-e.asp

Department of Natural Resources and Energy, Hugh John Flemming Forestry Complex, 13/50 Suite 310, Regent Street Extension, Fredericton, NB, Canada. Tel: +1 506 453 2510, fax: +1 506 453 2930, URL: http://www.gnb.ca/0078/index-e.asp

Department of Agriculture, Fisheries and Aquaculture, 850 Lincoln Road, Research Station, Lincoln, NB, Canada. Tel: +1 506 453 2662, fax: +1 506 453 3402, URL: http://www.gnb.ca/0027/index-e.asp

Department of Family and Community Services, 5th Floor, 520 King Street, Carelton Place, Fredericton, NB, Canada. Tel: +1 506 453 2001, fax: +1 506 453 2164, URL: http://www.gnb.ca/0017/index-e.asp

Department of Training and Employment Development, Chestnut Complex, 3rd Floor, 470 York Street, Fredericton, NB, Canada. Tel: +1 506 453 2342, fax: +1 506 453 3038, URL: http://www.gnb.ca/0105/index-e.asp

Department of Education, 250 King Street, Fredericton, NB, Canada. Tel: +1 506 453 2523, fax: +1 506 457 4960, URL: http://www.gnb.ca/0000/index-e.asp

Ministry of Environment and Local Government, 20 McGloin Street, 3rd Floor, Marysville Place, Fredericton, NB, E3A 5T8Canada. Tel: +1 506 453 2558, fax: +1 506 453 3377, http://www.gnb.ca/0009/index-e.asp

Department of Health and Wellness, P.O. Box 5100, Fredericton, NB E3B 5G8 Canada. Tel.: +1 506 453- 536, fax: +1 506 444 4697 URL: http://www.gnb.ca/0051/index-e.asp

Department of Business New Brunswick, PO Box 6000, Fifth Floor, Centennial Building, Fredericton, NB, Canada. Tel: +1 506 453 3984, fax: +1 506 444 4586, URL: http://www.gnb.ca/0398/index-e.asp

Solicitor General's Office, 4th Floor, Barker House, 570 Queen Street, Fredericton, NB, Canada. Tel +1 506 457 7886, fax: +1 506 453 3870

Department for Aboriginal Affairs, URL: http://www.gnb.ca/0227/index-e.asp

Political Parties

Progressive Conservative Party (PC), East Block, PO Box 6000, Legislative Assembly, Parliament Square, Fredericton, NB, E3B 5H1, Canada. Tel: +1 506 453 7494, fax: +1 506 453 3461, URL: http://www.pcnb.org

Liberal Party (L), Office of the Official Opposition, East Block, PO Box 6000, Legislative Assembly, Parliament Square, Fredericton, NB, E3B 5H1, Canada. Tel: +1 506 453 2548, fax: +1 506 453 3956, URL: http://www.nblib.nb.ca

New Democratic Party, East Block, PO Box 6000, Legislative Assembly, Parliament Square, Fredericton, NB, E3B 5H1, Canada. Tel: +1 506 453 3305, fax: +1 506 453 3688, URL http://www.ndp-npd.nb.ca

New Brunswick Green Party, URL: www.greenpartynb.ca

Elections

The present Legislative Assembly was elected on 27 September 2010 and has 55 members. Party representation is as follows: Liberal Party (13 seats); Progressive Conservative (42).

LEGAL SYSTEM

New Brunswick has a number of courts. Besides county or district courts there are also family courts, juvenile courts, probate courts, magistrates courts and small claims courts dealing in matters less than Can$6,000. Within these courts most matters are settled.

Chief Justice of New Brunswick: Hon. J. Ernest Drapeau

LOCAL GOVERNMENT

New Brunswick has eight cities, 28 towns and 68 villages. These are administered by local governments which look after services including sewers, street lighting and recreation. There are large areas which have a sparse population and these are divided into 272 local service districts.

AREA AND POPULATION

Area

New Brunswick is located in the east of Canada and borders Nova Scotia, Quebec and the US State of Maine, its eastern border is coastal with the Gulf of St Lawrence and Northumberland Strait. Prince Edward Island is off its coast. It has an area of 73,444 sq. km. New Brunswick is joined to Nova Scotia by the 15-mile wide Isthmus of Chignecto, and connects to Prince Edward Island by the Confederation Bridge.

To view a map, please consult http://atlas.nrcan.gc.ca/site/english/maps/reference/provincesterritories. (With permission of Natural Resources Canada 2008, courtesy of the Atlas of Canada)

Population

In 2012, the population of New Brunswick was 756,000. Recent figures show the populations of the main cities as follows: Fredericton, 46,507; Saint John, 72,494; Moncton, 59,313 and Bathurst, 13,815. New Brunswick is the only province which is officially bilingual and around 33 per cent of the population speak French.

Births, Marriages, Deaths

Provisional figures for the period July 2011-June 2012 show that there were 7,313 births and 6,743 deaths. During the year July 2006-June 2007 14,722 immigrants arrived from other Canadian provinces and 15,866 people left New Brunswick for other Canadian provinces, 1,630 foreign immigrants arrived and 464 people emigrated from New Brunswick to foreign countries. Provisional figures for 2008 show that 3,451 marriages took place. The most recent figures available for the number of divorces in the province show that 1,444 divorces were granted in 2005.

In addition to the standard days celebrated in Canada, New Brunswick also celebrates:

National Day 2014
4 August: New Brunswick Day

EMPLOYMENT

Figures for 2012 show that New Brunswick had a labour force of 391,400, of whom 351,400 were employed and 40,000 were unemployed. The unemployment was 10.2 per cent. The following table shows the number of people employed by industry:

Industry	Dec. 2011	Dec. 2012
Agriculture	3,800	5,000
Forestry, fishing, mining, oil & gas	10,100	12,800
Utilities	4,600	3,800
Construction	28,100	23,100
Manufacturing	30,400	28,300
Trade	56,600	56,000
Transportation & warehousing	15,800	16,400
Finance, insurance, real estate and leasing	16,400	17,100
Professional, scientific & technical services	15,600	14,600
Business building & other support	16,100	17,500
Educational services	26,400	26,800
Health care & social assistance	51,600	54,900
Information, culture & recreation	12,800	13,000
Accommodation & food services	23,800	21,900
Other services	14,900	14,900
Public administration	27,600	21,900

Source: Statistics Canada, CANSIM table 282-0088, Jan. 2013

BANKING AND FINANCE

GDP/GNP, Inflation, National Debt

Expenditure based GDP in recent years is set out below.

Year	Can$ millions
2000	20,085
2001	20,684
2002	21,169
2003	22,366
2004	23,672
2005	24,716
2006	25,847

- continued

2007	27,966
2008	28,533
2009	29,026
2010	30,941
2011	32,180

Source: Statistics Canada, CANSIM, table 384-0038 Jan. 2013

Growth in the economy has been due mainly due to major construction projects in energy and transportation (such as the natural gas pipeline through the southern part of New Brunswick), as well as improved performance in the trade, communications, manufacturing, tourism, business services and information technology sectors. (Source: The New Brunswick Economy)

The following table shows GDP by industry. Figures are in Can$ million (Chained 2002 Dollars)

Industry	2006	2007
Agriculture, forestry, fishing & hunting	868.9	819.6
Mining, oil & gas	213.8	204.4
Utilities	727.3	755.5
Construction	1,414.4	1,535.1
Manufacturing	2,724.5	2,692.0
Wholesale trade	1,200.8	1,183.8
Retail trade	1,392.9	1,456.4
Transportation & warehousing	1,069.9	1,081.5
Information & cultural Industries	766.9	772.0
Financial services	3,708.5	3,812.9
Professional, scientific & technical services	6002.5	617.6
Admin. & support	497.1	502.6
Educational services	1,104.8	1,121.7
Health care & social assistance	1,615.2	1,645.9
Arts, entertainment & recreation	134.2	136.7
Accommodation & food services	465.2	472.4
Other services	15,097.0	15,387.2
Public administration	1,998.5	2,033.8

Source: Government of New Brunswick

Balance of Payments / Imports and Exports

Major export destinations are the United States, Japan, UK and Brazil. The following table shows domestic exports by commodity in Can$ millions in recent years.

Commodity	2007	2008
Live animals	3.4	8.2
Fish & fish preparations	652.6	742.3
Fruit & vegetables & preparations	204.8	239.6
Meat & meat preparations	1.2	0.5
Petroleum oils, other than crude	6,289.3	7,930.6
Electrical energy	131.5	88.6
Lumber	305.6	195.3
Woodpulp	478.4	497.4
Paper & paperboard	755.1	467.2
Fertilizers	184.3	351.8
Ores	276.4	269.4
Inorganic chemicals	62.2	76.7
Organic chemicals	2.8	0.02
Machinery & equipment	471.1	335.1
Automotive products	39.9	21.0
Consumer goods	80.7	113.9
Special transactions	113.9	122.5
Total	11,182.5	12,766.4

Source: Government of New Brunswick

Chambers of Commerce and Trade Organisations

Fredericton Chamber of Commerce, URL: http://www.frederictonchamber.ca

MANUFACTURING, MINING AND SERVICES

Primary and Extractive Industries

New Brunswick possesses a great variety of mineral resources, metals, industrial minerals, fuels and structural materials, including antimony, bismuth, cadmium, copper, gold, lead, silver and zinc, marl, peat moss, potash, silica, salt and sulphur, oil, natural gas and coal. Structural materials include lime, sand and gravel, stone. New Brunswick ranks first in Canada in the production of bismuth, zinc and lead, second in antimony and silver and fifth in the production of copper. The New Brunswick mining industry has been adversely affected by the drop in international prices as a result of a reduction in industrial demand and an international over-production of particular metals. Noranda Inc. is investing Can$5 million to upgrade its Brunswick smelter in an effort to become independent and to offset the life expectancy of Brunswick mining which is estimated to be less than ten years.

In response to falling production, the New Brunswick Exploration Assistance Program has, in recent years, created Can$6.7 million of employment for 200 people.

The following table shows the value of mineral production in 2007.

Value in Million Can$

Mineral	2007
Copper	69.9
Zinc	872.2

- continued

Silver	87.4
Gold	5.5
Sand and gravel	13.0

Source: Statcan http://www40.statcan.gc.ca/l01/cst01/envi38a-eng.htm

Energy

New Brunswick is one of Canada's main oil refining provinces, with a capacity of 237,500 billion barrels a day. The main refinery, owned by Irving Oil Ltd and located at Saint John.

The province also contributes to the nuclear industry with a power reactor owned and operated by the New Brunswick Power Corporation at Point Lepreau, Saint John. New Brunswick generates 4000 MW of electricity from its nuclear power plant, hydro plants, thermal and combustion turbines.

Manufacturing

Forest products such as pulp, paper and timber form the major manufacturing group, followed by foods, oil refining, shipbuilding and general manufacturing, including electronics, cooking and heating equipment, chemicals and fertilizers and diversified other products.

Figures for 2000 show that over 1,300 manufacturing firms employed over 51,000 people. Saint John is the principal manufacturing centre. Manufacturing sales for 2006 were put at Can$14,730.4 millions, rising to Can$15,575.6 millions in 2007 and Can$17,766.1 millions in 2008.

Manufacturing Sales by Subsector, figures in Can$ millions

Industry	2010	2011
Food	2,083.8	2,091.7
Clothing	4.7	5.1
Wood products	912.7	866.8
Printing & related support activities	33.4	28.2
Plastics & rubber products	200.4	186.5
Non-metallic mineral products	219.5	205.9
Fabricated metal products	391.3	398.4

Source: Statistics Canada, CANSIM, table 304-0015 Jan. 2013

Service Industries

Figures for 2009 show that total tourist expenditures amounted to Can$932 million down from the 2008 figure of Can$989, million.

Agriculture

Recent figures show that there are in the region of 3,252 farms in the province, with a total farm land area of 375,631 hectares. The average farm size is about 116 hectares, with an average improved farm land area of 46 hectares. Total farm cash receipts from the sale of agricultural products in the province were Can$533,283 million in 201 Crops are New Brunswick's main farming product, with potatoes the major crop, representing 54.3 per cent of the province's total. New Brunswick's main livestock include poultry, cattle, calves, and hogs. Dairy products represent 18.9 per cent of total cash receipts. The following table shows the value of major commodities of farm income:

Production in Metric Tonnes

Crop	2011	2012
Barley	18,700	26,700
Canola	na	7,800
Corn for grain	20,600	33,400
Oats	15,900	21,200
Soybeans	8,400	9,300
Wheat, all	4,800	6,300
Wheat, spring	4,000	4,900
Wheat, winter remaining	800	1,400

Source: Statistics Canada, CANSIM table 001-0010

Total Receipts from Livestock and Livestock Products in Can$000

Commodity	2011
Cattle	21,302
Calves	2,306
Hogs	13,636
Lambs	653
Dairy products	98,951
Eggs	20,788
Honey	885
Furs	4,166
Total receipts from direct payments	24,891

Source: Statistics Canada, CANSIM 002-0001 Jan. 2013

Fishing

Major fish harvests are snow crab, lobster, herring, salmon, oysters, mussels, arctic char, trout, eel, halibut, haddock, winter flounder, giant sea scallops, bar clams, quahogs and the soft-shell clam. Exports go mainly to the US and Japan. Recent figures show that the industry supports 7,233 fishermen and over 2,700 boats.

COMMUNICATIONS AND TRANSPORT

Airports

New Brunswick has national airports located at Fredericton, Moncton and Saint John. There are regional airports at Bathurst, Charlo, Miramichi and St. Leonard.

CANADA

Railways

New Brunswick is served by a number of railways including the Canadian National Railway, which connects Montreal and Halifax with a branch line to St John, the Springfield Terminal Railway, which connects New Brunswick with Maine, US, the Canadian Atlantic Railway (a division of the Canadian Pacific Railway), the New Brunswick Southern Railway and the New Brunswick East Coast Railway.

Roads

The main highway system, including the Trans-Canada Highway, links the province with the principal roads in Quebec, Nova Scotia, Prince Edward Island, as well as the Inter-state Highway System in the eastern seaboard states of the USA. A road link which is one of the busiest border crossings in Canada exists between St. Stephen, New Brunswick and Calais, Maine. The total road system in New Brunswick runs for 21,301 km.

Ports and Harbours

Ocean vessels are accommodated at various ports in New Brunswick, three of which are ice-free ports. The others are accessible by icebreakers. The largest ice-free port in New Brunswick is Port New Brunswick (formerly Port of Saint John) located in Saint John. At Port Belledune the traffic increased due to a rise in coal imports. There are also ports at Dalhousie, Bayside, (St. Stephen) and Miramichi which is a river port.

Port New Brunswick, URL: http://www.sjport.com
Port Belledune, URL: http://www.portofbelledune.ca/

HEALTH

Recent figures indicate that there are an average of 17.3 approved beds per 1,000 people, 6.3 in hospitals and 11.1 in residential care facilities. Over 47,000 people are employed in the health sector.

EDUCATION

Public education is free and non-sectarian, and is offered in both official languages but unlike the rest of Canada compulsory education goes up to the age of 18 not 16. There are currently more than 129,131 students (including kindergarten) and 7,695 full-time equivalent professional educational staff in the province's 355 schools.

The following table shows recent educational expenditure (in Can$ million) according to level.

Level	New Brunswick	Canada
Elementary and secondary	819.39	36,424.71
Community college	58.51	4,531.82
University	302.72	11,801.98
Vocational training	182.49	6,185.20
Total expenditure	**1,363.10**	**58,943.71**

Source: Statistics Canada

Higher Education

There are 10 colleges administered by the New Brunswick Department of Education with campuses in Moncton, Saint John, St. Andrews, Bathurst, Campbellton, Edmundston, Woodstock, Dieppe, Miramichi and Grand-Sault. There is also a College of Craft and Design.

There are four universities, the University of New Brunswick, is located in Fredericton and with a branch campus in Saint John; St. Thomas University (formerly of Chatham) is located on the Fredericton campus of the University of New Brunswick; Mount Allison University, is at Sackville; and L'Université de Moncton, is the major French speaking degree granting institution.

COMMUNICATIONS AND MEDIA

Newspapers

There are five daily newspapers, (one in French) and 18 weekly papers.

Broadcasting

A Can$4.5 million digital television service, the first in New Brunswick, has been launched by Fundy Communications: MAX TV. The New Brunswick network, TVNB, was taken over in 2000 and is now Rogers Television.

ENVIRONMENT

New Brunswick's Department of the Environment regulates the environment through legislation that includes seven statues: the Clean Water Act, the Clean Air Act, the Clean Environment Act, the Pesticides Control Act, Beverage Containers Act, Environmental Trust Fund Act and the Unsightly Premises Act. All acts set out a number of Regulations some of which are: the Regional Solid Waste Commissions Regulation, the Water Quality Regulation, the Portable Water Regulation, the Water Well Regulation, the Protected Area Exemption Regulation, the Ozone Depleting Substances Regulation and the Environmental Impact Assessment Regulation.

NEWFOUNDLAND AND LABRADOR

Capital: St. John's (Population estimate: 100,000)

Lieutenant-Governor: Hon. John C. Crosbie (page 1410)

Provincial Flag: White background divided by a while saltire cross. The left side is divided into two dark blue triangles intersected by the saltire. The right side shows two red triangles separated by a gold arrow or sword.

CONSTITUTION AND GOVERNMENT

Newfoundland and Labrador was admitted into the Confederation of Canada in 1949.

Upper House

Although the province has no upper house, it is represented on the Canadian Senate. The following members of the Newfoundland and Labrador political parties are also Canadian Senators: George Baker (page 1382), Norman Doyle, (page 1417) George Furey (page 1427), Fabian Manning (page 1470), Elizabeth Marshall, (page 1471) David Wells

Lower House

Newfoundland and Labrador's legislature is unicameral. It has a Lower House which is known as the House of Assembly and currently has 48 seats. The maximum duration of the Assembly is five years. The House of Assembly Speaker is currently Hon. Ross Wiseman

House of Assembly, Confederation Building, PO Box 8700, St. John's NL A1B 4J6, Canada. URL: http://www.gov.nf.ca/hoa

---

Cabinet (as at June 2013)
Premier: Hon. Kathy Dunderdale (page 1418)
Minister of Intergovernmental Affairs and Aboriginal Affairs: Felix Collins
Minister of Fisheries and Aquaculture: Derrick Dalley
Minister of Transportation and Works, and responsible for Newfoundland Labrador: Paul Davis
Minister of Tourism, Culture and Recreation: Hon. Terry French
Minister of Environment and Conservation, Minister responsible for the Multi Materials Stewardship Board, and for the Office of Climate Change, Energy Efficiency and Emissions Tranding: Hon. Thomas J. Hedderson (page 1440)
Minister of Innovation, Trade and Rural Development and Minister responsible for the Rural Secretariat; the R&D Corp.; & Office of Public Engagement: Keith Hutchings
Minister of Education: Hon. Clyde Jackman
Minister of Child, Youth and Family Services, Minister responsible for the Status of Women: Charlene Johnson

---

Minister for Finance; President of the Treasury Board; Minister responsible for the HR Secretariat; for the Public Service Commission; for the Newfoundland & Labrador Liquor Corporation: Jerome Kennedy, QC
Minister of Justice, Government House Leader; Minister responsible for the Labour Relations Agency: Darin King
Minister of Natural Resources, Attorney General, and Minister responsible for the Forestry and Agrifoods Agency: Thomas Marshall QC
Minister of Service NL, Minister Responsible for Labrador Affairs, for the Government Purchasing Agency; for the Office of the CIO, for Workplace Health, Safety and Compensation Commission: Nick McGrath
Minister of Municipal Affairs, Minister responsible for Fire & Emergency Services, and Labrador Registrar General: Kevin O'Brien
Minister of Advanced Education & Skills, Minister responsible for the Status of Persons with Disabilities and for Youth Engagement: Hon. Joan Shea (page 1513)
Minister of Health and Community Services, Minister responsible for Aging and Seniors, and Francophony: Susan Sullivan

Ministries

Office of the Premier, St. John's, NF, Canada. Tel: +1 709 729 3570, e-mail: premier@gov.nf.ca, URL: http://www.premier.gov.nl.ca/premier
Ministry of Environment and Labour, PO Box 8700, Confederation Building, St. John's, NF, A1B 4J6, Canada. Tel: +1 709 729 2574, fax: +1 709 729 0112, e-mail: minister@env.gov.nf.ca, URL: http://www.gov.nl.ca/env
Ministry of Education, PO Box 8700, Confederation Building, St. John's, NF, A1B 4J6, Canada. Tel: +1 709 729 5040, fax: +1 709 729 0414, URL: http://www.ed.gov.nl.ca/edu
Ministry of Finance, PO Box 8700, Confederation Building, St. John's, NF, A1B 4J6, Canada. Tel: +1 709 729 2858, fax: +1 709 729 2232, URL: http://www.fin.gov.nl.ca/fin
Ministry of Fisheries and Aquaculture, PO Box 8700, Confederation Building, St. John's, NF, A1B 4J6, Canada. Tel: +1 709 729 3705, fax: +1 709 729 6082, e-mail: minister@fish.gov.nf.ca, URL: http://www.gov.nl.ca/fishaq
Ministry of Government Services and Lands, PO Box 8700, Confederation Building, St. John's, NF, A1B 4J6, Canada. Tel: +1 709 729 4712, fax: +1 709 729 4754, e-mail: minister@mapa.gov.nf.ca, URL: http://www.gov.nl.ca/gs
Ministry of Health and Community Services, PO Box 8700, Confederation Building, St. John's, NF, A1B 4J6, Canada. Tel: +1 709 729 3124, fax: +1 709 729 0121, e-mail: minister@health.gov.nf.ca, URL: http://www.health.gov.nl.ca/health
Ministry of Human Resources and Employment, PO Box 8700, Confederation Building, St. John's, NF, A1B 4J6, Canada. Tel: +1 709 729 3580, fax: +1 709 729 6996, e-mail: minister@hre.gov.nf.ca, URL: http://www.hrle.gov.nl.ca/hrle

Ministry of Innovation, Trade and Rural Development, PO Box 8700, Confederation Building, St. John's, NF, A1B 4J6, Canada. Tel: +1 709 729 7000, fax: +1 709 729 0654, e-mail: ITRDinfo@gov.nl.ca, URL: http://www.intrd.gov.nl.ca/intrd
Ministry of Labrador and Aboriginal Affairs, PO Box 8700, Confederation Building, St. John's, NF, A1B 4J6, Canada. Tel: +1 709 729 4776, fax: +1 709 729 4900, e-mail: laa@gov.nl.ca, URL: http://www.laa.gov.nl.ca/laa
Ministry of Natural Resources, Natural Resources Building, 50 Elizabeth Ave., P.O. Box 8700, St. John's, NL A1B 4J6, Canada. Tel: +1 709 729 4715, fax: +1 709 729 2076, URL: http://www.nr.gov.nl.ca/nr
Ministry of Municipal and Provincial Affairs, PO Box 8700, Confederation Building, St. John's, NF, A1B 4J6, Canada. Tel: +1 709 729 3048, fax: +1 709 729 0943, e-mail: MAPAinfo@gov.nl.ca, URL: http://www.mpa.gov.nl.ca/mpa
Ministry of Tourism, Culture and Recreation, PO Box 8700, Confederation Building, St. John's, NF, A1B 4J6, Canada. Tel: +1 709 729 0657, fax: +1 709 729 0662, e-mail: tcrinfo@mail.gov.nl.ca, URL: http://www.tcr.gov.nl.ca/tcr
Ministry of Works, Services and Transportation, PO Box 8700, Confederation Building, St. John's, NF, A1B 4J6, Canada. Tel: +1 709 729 3678, fax: +1 709 729 4285, e-mail: WSTMinister@gov.nl.ca, URL: http://www.wst.gov.nl.ca/wst
Ministry of Justice, Department of Justice, 4th Flr., East Block, Confederation Building, Box 8700, St. John's, NL A1B 4J6, Canada. Tel: +1 709 729 5942, fax: +1 709 729 2129, e-mail: justice@gov.nl.ca, URL: http://www.justice.gov.nl.ca/just

Elections

The last general election was held on October 11 2011, when the Progressive Conservatives won 37 seats, the Liberal Party won 6 seats and the New Democratic Party won 5 seats. Elections are held every five years.

LEGAL SYSTEM

The highest court in Newfoundland and Labrador is the Supreme Court of Newfoundland. It is a court of appeal and can hear appeals in criminal and civil matters.
Supreme Court of Newfoundland (Court of Appeal), 287 Duckworth Street, St. John's, NF A1C 5M3, Canada. Tel: +1 709 729 0066, fax: +1 709 729 0074.

The Supreme Court of Newfoundland (Trial Division) hears criminal, civil and family cases as well as appeals from the provincial court.
Supreme Court of Newfoundland (Trial Division), Court House, Duckworth Street, St. John's, NF A1C 5M3, Canada. Tel: +1 709 7291099, fax: +1 709 729 6174.

The Provincial Court of Newfoundland hears criminal, civil actions (for an action not exceeding Can$3,000), family and youth cases.
Provincial Court of Newfoundland, 4th floor, Atlantic Place, St. John's, NF A1C 5M3, Canada. Tel: +1 709 729 0106, fax: +1 709 729 2161

LOCAL GOVERNMENT

Newfoundland and Labrador is divided into 175 local service districts and 287 towns.

AREA AND POPULATION

Area
Newfoundland and Labrador is situated in the north-east of Canada. Its total area is 405,720 sq. km. Newfoundland covers 111,390 sq. km. and is situated in the Gulf of St. Lawrence. Labrador is just above Newfoundland and is located on the mainland of Canada bordering Quebec. It has an area of 294,330 sq. km.

To view a map, please consult
http://atlas.nrcan.gc.ca/site/english/maps/reference/provincesterritories. (With permission of Natural Resources Canada 2008, courtesy of the Atlas of Canada)

Population
The population in 2012 was 510,700.

Births, Marriages, Deaths
In the period 1 July 2011 - 30 June 2012 the number of births fell to 4,823 from 4,875 the previous year. The number of deaths rose to 4,675 up from 4,561 the previous year. In the period 1 July 2007 - 30 June 2008 598 people immigrated to the province and 287 people emigrated from the province. Provisional figures for 2008 show that 2,650 marriages took place and in 2005 789 divorces were granted. (Source: Statistics Canada)

In addition to the standard days celebrated in Canada, Newfoundland and Labrador also celebrates the following:

Public Holidays 2014
18 March: St. Patrick's Day
23 April: St. George's Day
23 June: Discovery Day
1 July: Memorial Day
12 July: Orangemen's Day

Holidays are usually observed on the closest Monday

EMPLOYMENT

Figures for 2012 show that Newfoundland and Labrador had a labour force of 263,300. During that period the number unemployed was 32,800, giving an unemployment rate of 12.5 per cent. In 2010 Newfoundland and Labrador recorded record growth in employment;

the labour force numbered 326,300 of whom 219,400 were employed, giving an unemployment rate of 14.4 per cent. The following table shows how the active population was employed in December 2011 and 2012.

Sector	Dec. 2011	Dec. 2012
Agriculture	1,200	1,900
Forestry, fishing, mining, oil & gas	15,000	14,600
Utilities	2,500	3,300
Construction	20,300	20,000
Manufacturing	12,000	10,300
Trade	37,400	33,100
Transportation & warehousing	10,100	12,600
Finance, insurance, real estate & leasing	9,200	10,100
Professional, scientific & technical services	9,200	9,000
Business building & other support	6,000	6,900
Educational services	17,600	19,600
Health care & social assistance	34,300	37,700
Information, culture & recreation	7,200	7,400
Accommodation & food services	13,200	14,900
Other services	12,300	14,900
Public administration	19,700	19,400

Source: Statistics Canada, CANSIM Table 282-0088 Jan. 2013

BANKING AND FINANCE

GDP/GNP, Inflation, National Debt
The following table shows the province's expenditure GDP in recent years.

Year	Can$ millions
2004	19,407
2005	21,960
2006	26,064
2007	29,735
2008	31,447
2009	24,989
2010	28,621
2011	33,624

Source: Statistics Canada, CANSIM, table 384-0038 Jan. 2013

Manufacturing Sales

Year	Can$ Millions
2006	4,292.9
2007	5,113.6
2008	6,574.3
2009	4,377.0
2010	5,167.3
2011	5,517.1

Source: Statistics Canada CANSIM, tables 304-0014 and 304-0015 Jan. 2013

Balance of Payments / Imports and Exports
Figures for 2004 show that exports earned Can$4.56 billion down from Can$4.79 billion in 2003. Over 50 per cent of exported goods go to the USA. Main exports include offshore oil, fish products, minerals particularly iron ore, newsprint and electricity.

In 2004, foreign imports cost the province Can$2.55 billion, down slightly from Can$ 2.56 billion in 2003. 55 per cent of total imports come from other Canadian provinces mainly Ontario and Quebec. Main imports include refined petroleum, food stuffs, consumer products and transportation services.

Chambers of Commerce and Trade Organisations
Alliance of Manufacturers and Exporters Canada - Newfoundland, URL: http://www.cme-mec.ca/
St. John's Board of Trade, URL: http://www.bot.nf.ca/

MANUFACTURING, MINING AND SERVICES

Primary and Extractive Industries
The value of mineral products for 2008 were estimated at Can$1.9 billion. This reflected a rise following a period of stagnation due to fluctuations in global market prices. Iron ore is the main product and accounts for 90 per cent of mineral earnings. The steel industry is the main destination for iron ore, traditionally Newfoundland and Labrador has supplied the EU and US but increasingly China is becoming a larger market. Other minerals include gold, silver, asbestos, limestone, slate, dolomite and gravel. The province had one gold mine on the Baie Verte Peninsula which ceased production due to depletion, however two small mines were proposed in the area in 2010 which would start production subject to further exploration, approval and permits being issued..

Recent discoveries of nickel, cobalt and copper in the Voisey's Bay area means that mineral production and employment is set to rise. Full production started in 2006 for the open-pit mine. Underground mining is expected to start in 2018.

Energy
The province is a major eastern Canadian supplier of oil and figures for 2008 put production at 134.4 million barrels per day falling slightly to 125.2 million barrels in 2009. This comes mostly from the province's main oil developments, the Hibernia and Terra Nova fields, both owned by Mobil's subsidiary, Mobil Canada. The Can$5.8 billion Hibernia field, on the Grand Banks of Newfoundland, began production in 1997 and presently contains some 3 billion

CANADA

barrels of light, low sulphur oil, of which 750 million to 1 billion barrels is regarded as recoverable. It is being developed by six companies: Mobil Oil Canada, Chevron Canada Resources, Petro-Canada, Canada Hibernia Holding Corporation, Murphy Atlantic Offshore Oil Co., and Norsk Hydro, as well as the Canadian government itself.

The Terra Nova field, some 22 miles east of Hibernia, contains an estimated 300-400 million barrels of recoverable oil, 100,000 billion barrels a day of low sulphur, crude oil and (from 2001) 75 million cubic feet per day of gas.

About ten miles east of Terra Nova is the Whiterose oil and gas development. This contains an estimated 250 billion barrels of oil, with production predicted to reach 75,000 to 80,000 billion barrels a day. Production started in 2005. Production in this field was expected to push total production up to 150 million barrels.

Whilst Alberta has most of Canada's gas reserves, some 50 trillion cubic feet of potential reserves is located between Newfoundland and Nova Scotia. Oil production in January to November 2010 totalled 92.7 million barrels, up nearly 4.0 million barrels on the same period in 2009.

In addition to the 5,400 MW hydro-electric plant on the Churchill Falls, proposals have recently been unveiled by the Canadian Hydropower Association for a Can$7 billion, 3,000 MW dam on the river, which lies along the boundaries of Newfoundland and Quebec. Current electricity production totals around 40 billion kWh per year. Most of the electricity produced at Churchill Falls is exported to Quebec.

Newfoundland Power, URL: http://www.nfpower.nf.ca

Manufacturing
Fish and paper products are the main areas but there is manufacture of items such as boats, lumber, chemical and oil-based products and food and clothing products. Around 12 local companies are engaged in secondary fish processing (the manufacture of consumer-ready fish products). It is a sector which produces around Can$60 million. Most of the Province's manufactured goods are destined for the US.

Manufacturing Sales by Subsector in 2011

Year	Can$ Millions
Food	1,632.5
Wood products	55.1
Chemicals	14.0
Electrical equipment, appliances & components	12.8
Transportation equipment	65.0

Source: Statistics Canada CANSIM, Table 304-0015 Jan. 2013

Service Industries
This sector accounts for over two thirds of the province's GDP and tourism attracts around 300,000 visitors per year. This figure rose to 480,000 in 2008. Recent years have seen an increase in visitors arriving on cruise ships.

Agriculture
Figures for 2010 show that sales of agricultural products was worth Can$132.3 million up from Can$122.0 million in 2009.

The following chart sets out the number of farms whose total gross receipts exceed Can$2,500 according to product.

Product	Newfoundland	Canada
Census farms	**573**	**252,839**
Cattle (beef)	28	67,531
Grain and oilseed (except wheat)	-	51,577
Wheat	-	29,526
Miscellaneous specialty	139	28,715
Dairy	63	24,411
Field crop (except grain and oilseed)	39	16,245

- continued		
Hog	13	8,063
Fruit	36	7,107
Livestock combination	15	6,217
Other combination	60	5,007
Poultry and egg	54	4,833
Vegetable	126	3,607

Source: Statistics Canada

An area for growth in the province's agriculture sector is the greenhouse sector, with floriculture and nursery products now accounting for around 10 per cent of total farm receipts. Dairy farming is also becoming increasingly important. Figures for 2011 show that Newfoundland and Labrador had 510 farms, down from the 2006 figure of 558 farms. Figures for July 2011 show that the province had 11,100 head of cattle including 5,900 dairy cows.

Fishing
During 2003 northern and gulf cod fisheries were closed in order to help preserve cod stocks. As a result for that year Newfoundland and Labrador fisherman landed more clam, shrimp, mackerel, flatfish and turbot.

COMMUNICATIONS AND TRANSPORT

National Airlines
Air Labrador, URL: http://www.airlabrador.com

International Airports
The province's two international airports are at St. John and Gander. Other mainland airports are located in Happy Valley-Goose Bay, Churchill Falls, Wabush, whilst those on the islands are in Stephenville, Deer Lake and St. Anthony.

Ports and Harbours
The main port is St. John's. Recent figures suggest that total traffic has decreased by 6 per cent to 866,000 tonnes.
St. John's Port Authority, URL: http://www.sjpa.com

HEALTH

Recent figures indicate that there are 12.8 approved beds per 1,000 population in Newfoundland for all health care institutions. This breaks down to 5.3 per 1,000 for hospitals and 7.5 for residential care facilities. Recent figures show that the provincial budget for health care is around Can$1.3 billion.

EDUCATION

Figures for 2004 show that Newfoundland and Labrador had 303 public schools, seven private schools, five French first-language schools, two native schools, one youth centre, and the Newfoundland School for the Deaf. Over 65 per cent of the schools were based in rural areas.

Figures for recent years show a decline in the number of students enrolled in general education: 69,665 in the 2009-10 school year down from 72,109 in 2007-08. Expenditure per student in public general education in 2009-10 was Can$12,946.

COMMUNICATIONS AND MEDIA

Newspapers
The Telegram, URL: http://www.thetelegram.com

Broadcasting
The province's main television broadcasting networks are NTV and CBC - Newfoundland Links. Its radio stations include VOCM and OZ-FM.
NTV (Newfoundland Broadcasting Company), URL: http://www.ntv.ca

NORTHWEST TERRITORIES

Capital: Yellowknife (Population estimate: 18,500)

Commissioner: George Tuccaro (page 1528)

Provincial Flag: Vertically, blue, white, blue with the white of double width and bearing the shield of the territory.

CONSTITUTION AND GOVERNMENT

Constitution
The Northwest Territories is governed by a Government Leader, with a seven member cabinet and a Legislative Assembly. A Commissioner of the Northwest Territories acts as a lieutenant governor and is the federal government's senior representative in the Territorial government. The government is run on the consensus system rather than a party political system. Once Members of the Legislative Assembly have been elected in their constituencies, a territorial leadership meeting is held where the Speaker, Premier and Ministers are elected by secret ballot after each MLA has given a presentation. The seat of government was transferred from Ottawa to Yellowknife when it was named Territorial capital on 18 January 1967.

Recent Events
On 1 April 1999 the Northwest Territories were divided into two territories, east and west. Whilst the western territory will retain the name Northwest Territories for the time being, the eastern territory is now called Nunavut, or "Our Land", and comprises the regions of Kitikmeot, Keewatin and Baffin. Its capital is Iqaluit. The area of 1.9 million sq. km contains a population of 24,000, of which 85 per cent are Inuit.

Legislature
Legislative powers are exercised by the Executive Council on such matters as taxation within the Territories in order to raise revenue, maintenance of justice, licences, solemnisation of marriages, education, public health, property, civil rights and generally all matters of a local nature. The Legislative Assembly has 19 elected members and operates under a consensus system.

The Northwest Territories is represented in the federal government by one MP and one Senator, Nick Sibbeston.
Legislative Assembly of the NWT, Legislative Assembly Building, Yellowknife, NT, X1A 2L9, Canada. URL: http://www.assembly.gov.nt.ca/index.html

Cabinet (as at June 2013)

Premier, Minister of Aboriginal Affairs and Intergovernmental Relations, Minister of the Executive, Minister responsible for New Energy Initiatives, for the Status of Women: Hon. Bob McLeod (page 1475)

Deputy Premier, Minister of Education, Culture and Employment, Minister responsible for the Worker's Safety and Compensation Commission: Hon. Jackson Lafferty

Minister of Finance, Chairman of the Financial Management Board, Minister of Environment and Natural Resources, Minister Responsible for the Northwest Territories Power Corporation, Government House Leader: J. Michael Miltenberger (page 1478)

Minister Responsible for the Northwest Territories Housing Corporation, Minister of Municipal and Community Affairs, Minister Responsible for Homelessness, Minister Responsible for Youth: Hon. Robert McLeod

Minister of Health and Social Services, Minister Responsible for Seniors, Minister Responsible for Persons with Disabilities: Tom Beaulieu

Minister of Industry, Tourism and Investment, Minister of Transportation: Hon. David Ramsay

Minister of Justice, Minister of Human Resources, Minister of Public Works and Services, Minister Responsible for the Public Utilities Board: Glen Abernethy

Ministries
Office of The Premier, Aboriginal Affairs, The Executive Council and Ministry of Intergovernmental Affairs, PO Box 466, Fort Simpson, NWT X0E 0N0. Tel: +1 867 669 2311, fax: +1 867 873 0169, URL: http://www.premier.gov.nt.ca
Ministries of Transportation, Public Works and Services, and of Municipal and Community Affairs, PO Box 55, Tuktoyaktuk, NWT X0E 1C0. Tel: +1 867 669 2377, fax: +1 867 977 2181, URL: http://www.dot.gov.nt.ca/_live/pages/wpPages/home.aspx
Ministries of Education, Culture and Employment, of Youth, and Offices of the Workers Compensation Board, and the Public Utilities Board, 102 Wilderness Drive, Fort Smith, NWT X0E 0P0. Tel: +1 867 669 2344, fax: +1 872 669 5642, URL: http://www.ece.gov.nt.ca
Ministries of Resources, Wildlife and Economic Development, of Justice, and of National Constitutional Affairs, PO Box 1320, Yellowknife, NWT X1A 2L9. Tel: +1 867 669 2366, fax: +1 867 873 0169, URL: http://www.iti.gov.nt.ca
Ministries of Finance, Offices of the Financial Management Board, the NWT Power Corporation, and the Woman's Directorate, PO Box 1320, Yellowknife, NWT X1A 2L9. Tel: +1 867 669 2355, fax: +1 867 669 0169, URL: http://www.fin.gov.nt.ca
Office of the Deputy Premier, Ministries of Health and Social Services, and of Seniors, and the Office of the NWT Housing Corporation, PO Box 1998, Inuvik, NWT X0E 0T0. Tel: +1 867 669 2333, fax: +1 867 873 0169, URL: http://www.hlthss.gov.nt.ca

Elections
The most recent election was held on October 2011 and Bob McLeod was subsequently elected as premier.

LOCAL GOVERNMENT

The Northwest Territories is divided into one city, four towns, one village, 11 hamlets, two settlements, four charter communities and 10 designated authorities.

AREA AND POPULATION

Area
The Northwest Territories comprises the Inuvik and Fort Smith Regions, all of Canada north of the 60th parallel except the portions within the Yukon Territory and the provinces of Quebec, Newfoundland and the newly created territory of Nunavut in the east. Major towns are: Inuvik (north of the Arctic Circle), Norman Wells, Fort Simpson, Yellowknife (the capital), Hay River and Fort Smith. The Northwest Territories covers an area of 1.171,918 sq. km. The Northwest Territories is home to the Great Bear lake the largest lake entirely within Canada, other large lakes include the Keller and Great Salve Lakes, the highest point is Mount Nirvana near the border with Yukon.

To view a map, please consult
http://atlas.nrcan.gc.ca/site/english/maps/reference/provincesterritories. (With permission of Natural Resources Canada 2008, courtesy of the Atlas of Canada)

Population
According to 2011 estimated population figures, 43,300 people lived in the Northwest Territories, down from the 2010 figure of 44,200. Before becoming two territories, the region consisted of three ethnic groups: the Inuit or Eskimo (37 per cent), Dene (17 per cent), and Metis (7 per cent).

The Northwest Territories has a broad spectrum of languages and cultures, including English, French, Euro-Canadian, Chipewyan, Metis, Dogrib, Inuvialuit, Slavey and Gwich'in.

Births, Marriages, Deaths
Figures for the period July 2011-June 2012 show that there were 706 births and 199 deaths. Over the period July 2006-June 2007, 2,808 people from other Canadian provinces immigrated to the Northwest Territories and 3,154 from the Northwest Territories migrated to other Canadian provinces. 98 foreign immigrants arrived and 14 people emigrated to other countries. Provisional figures for 2008 show that 130 marriages took place and in 2005, 65 divorces were granted. (Source: Statistics Canada website)

Public Holidays 2014
19 May: Victoria Day
23 June Aboriginal Day
4 August: Civic Holiday
13 October: Thanksgiving Day
11 November: Remembrance Day

EMPLOYMENT

The following table shows employment by selected characteristics in recent years.

	2005	2006	2007
Population age 15+	31,400	31,100	30,700
Labour force	23,900	24,100	23,900
Employed	22,700	22,800	22,600
Unemployed	1,300	1,300	1,300
Not in Labour force	7,500	7,000	6,800
Participation rate	76.1	77.5	77.9
Unemployment rate	5.4	5.4	5.4
Employment rate	72.3	43.3	73.6

Source: Government of Northwest Territories

The following table shows how the experienced labour force (15 years and over) was employed in 2006:

Occupation	Employees
Management	2,855
Business, finance & admin.	4,185
Natural & applied sciences & related	1,695
Health	1,005
Social science, education, gov. service, religion	2,585
Art, culture, recreation & sport	705
Sales & service	5,300
Trades, transport & equipment operators & related occupations	4,265
Occupations unique to primary industry	635
Occupations unique to processing, manufacturing & utilities	210

Source: Statistics Canada, February 2010

BANKING AND FINANCE

GDP/GNP, Inflation, National Debt
GDP, expenditure based in recent years is as follows:

Year	Can$ million
2005	4,267
2006	4,282
2007	4,598
2008	5,005
2009	4,055
2010	4,633
2011	4,791

Source: Statistics Canada, CANSIM, table 384-0038

The mining, oil and gas extraction sector is the largest contributor to GDP.

Balance of Payments / Imports and Exports
The value of manufacturing shipments in 2001 was Can$39.2 million, Can$56.6 million in 2002, Can$78.3 million in 2003, Can$80.5 million in 2004 and Can$86.6 million in 2005. Retail trade in 2000 was worth Can$394 million growing to Can$679.1 million in 2007 and rising to Can$693.0 million in 2009. The value of the wholesale merchant sales was put at Can$159 million in 2000 rising to Can$657.4 million in 2007 before falling to Can$638.6 million in 2008 and Can$552.1 million in 2009.

Chambers of Commerce and Trade Organisations
Fort Simpson Chamber of Commerce, URL: http://www.fschamber.com

MANUFACTURING, MINING AND SERVICES

Primary and Extractive Industries
The management of oil and gas production in the Northwest Territories is the responsibility of the Northern Oil and Gas Directorate of the Federal Department of Indian Affairs and Northern Development in Ottawa.

Mineral Shipments in 2007

Product	Can$ '000	Volume
Crude oil	497,409	1,110 ('000m³)
Natural gas	54,459	235 (million m³)
Diamonds	1,744,988	16,638 ('000 carats)
Tungsten	71,875	2,700 (tonnes)

Source: Government of Northwest Territories

Northern Oil and Gas Directorate, URL: http://www.ainc-inac.gc.ca/oil/index_e.html

Crude oil is produced at Norman Wells and transported via pipeline to Alberta. The field produces between 11 and 12 million barrels a year with an annual value of between Can$250 million and Can$300 million (1997 prices). Natural gas is also produced at Norman Wells

CANADA

and Pointed Mountain. The Pointed Mountain field, which began production in 1972, is expected to have used its reserves in the next few years. New discoveries in the Fort Liard area came online in 2000.

Active mines in the Northwest Territories are the Ekati Diamond Mine, the Diavik mine came on line in 2003, the Polaris Mine, the Nanasivik Mine and the Royal Oak Giant Mine. The Polaris and Nanasivik mines both produce lead and zinc. The territory's gold mines are all located in the Slave Geological Province. The Northwest Territories' mines produce 16.5 per cent of Canada's zinc, 15 per cent of its lead, 8 per cent of its gold and 1.5 per cent of its silver.

The Northwest Territories' primary mineral commodities are zinc and gold, and it is Canada's third largest producer of zinc and fourth largest producer of gold. Figures for 2004 show that the Northwest Territories produced 511 kg of gold (Can$8,752,000) and 1 tonne of silver (Can$27,000).

The Northwest Territories has recently made discoveries of more diamond deposits. There are mines in operation at Ekati, Diavik, and Snap Lake. Annual production is approximately eight million carats. There are also three diamond polishing factories.

Northwest Territories Chamber of Mines, URL: http://www.miningnorth.com

Manufacturing
Value of Manufacturing Sales in Recent Years

Year	Can$ Million
2003	78.3
2004	80.8
2005	90.7
2006	64.2
2007	45.8
2008	39.6
2009	16.1
2010	9.2
2011	9.3

Source: Statistics Canada, CANSIM, tables 304-0014 and 304-0015

Agriculture
In the NWT there are 1.3 million caribou, 130,000 musk oxen and 1,500 wood bison. Around 50,000 caribou are harvested annually at a value of Can$30m. There are 12,700 polar bears with a harvest quota of 500 worth Can$4m per year.

Forest land area in the NWT consists of 61.4m ha which is about 18 per cent of the land area. The principal trees are white and black spruce, jack-pine, tamarack, balsam poplar, aspen and birch. Recently, 56,000 cu. metres of timber valued at Can$1.83m was produced.

Commercial inshore fisheries, principally on Great Slave Lake and around Baffin Island, produce approximately 1.2m kg of fish and fish products worth Can$2.4m. Principal species include whitefish, char and turbot.

Figures for 2009 show that the value of fur pelts produced was Can$830.9.

COMMUNICATIONS AND TRANSPORT

National Airlines
First Air (includes the former Northwest Territorial Airways), URL: http://www.firstair.ca/

Air Nunavut, URL:http://www.airnunavut.ca/
Aklak Air, URL: http://www.aklakair.ca

Figures for 2007 show that take off and landings numbered 108,461.

Railways
There is one railway in the Northwest Territories which runs from Hay River, on the sou[t] shore of Great Slave Lake, 700 km to Grimshaw, Alberta where it connects with the Canadia[n] National Railways.

Roads
The Northwest Territories has 2,200 km of all weather road and 1,300 km of winter-ice road[s] These roads connect South Mackenzie communities to Alberta and Beaufort Delta communitie[s] to the Yukon through the Dempster Highway system. The winter and ice roads interconnec[t] Mackenzie and Beaufort communities to the major community centres. Figures for 200[ ] show that over 37,635 vehicles were registered.

HEALTH

Recent figures show that there are currently 7.3 beds in approved health care institution[s] per 1,000 population. This breaks down to 2.0 in hospitals and 5.3 in residential care facilitie[s] Figures for 2007 show that government expenditure in the Northwest Territories on healt[h] amounted to Can$230 million. Figures from Statcan for 2009 show that Can$238,907,00[ ] was spent on health.

EDUCATION

Figures for recent years show a decline in the number of students enrolled in genera[l] education: 9,048 in the 2007-08 school year falling to 8,762 in the 2008-09 school yea[r] Expenditure per student in public general education in 2008-09 was Can$22,278.

ENVIRONMENT

Recent figures show that the territorial government spent Can$715,000 on pollutio[n] abatement and control measures.

The Department of Resources, Wildlife and Economic Development, as well as bein[g] responsible for the quality and condition of the environment also encourages economi[c] self-sufficiency through the development and management of natural resources.

The Department of Resources, Wildlife and Economic Development is a major contributor t[o] The West Kitikmeot/Slave Study Society (WKSS), which brings together a number of aborigina[l] and environmental organisations, as well as government and industry, in the study of th[e] effects of development on the environment and people of the West Kitikmeot and Slave area Current WKSS-funded projects include the study of water quality, habitat/vegetatio[n] classification, community health, wolverine ecology, the state of Caribou habitat and grizzl[y] bear population.

Other ecological organisations include the Canadian Arctic Resources Committee, Ecolog[y] North, the World Wildlife Fund, the Canadian Nature Federation and the Norther[n] Environmental Coalition.

NOVA SCOTIA

Capital: Halifax (Population estimate: 119,000)

Lieutenant-Governor: John James Grant (page 1432)

Provincial Flag: A blue cross of St. Andrew is set over a white background in the centre of which is an orange shield bearing a red lion.

CONSTITUTION AND GOVERNMENT

Constitution
Nova Scotia was one of the four original provinces, entering the confederation in 1867. The government of the province consists of a 52-member elected House of Assembly and a Lieutenant-Governor who is the Queen's representative in the province. The Lieutenant-Governor is appointed by the Governor General on the advice of the Prime Minister and the federal cabinet. The age of suffrage is 18.

Lower House
Members of the Executive Council (Cabinet) are selected by the Premier from the elected representatives of the majority party. These ministers are answerable to the leader of the cabinet. The speaker of the house presides over the legislature. The assembly is elected for a statutory term of five years but may be dissolved at any time within that period by the Lieutenant Governor or on the advice of the Premier. The legislature's maximum term is five years. At least fifteen members of the House including the Speaker must be present in order for the House to meet and exercise its powers.

House of Assembly, Province House, 1726 Hollis Street, Halifax, Nova Scotia, B3J 2Y3, Canada. Tel: +1 902 424 4661, fax: +1 902 424 0574, URL: http://www.gov.ns.ca/legislature

Eleven members of parliament represent Nova Scotia in the federal government. A Nova Scotia MP is usually selected by the Prime Minister to represent the province at the Cabinet Table. In the Upper House the province is allocated ten seats. Members of Nova Scotia's political parties who are also representatives on the Canadian Senate currently number 10 and are: Gerard Comeau, Jane Cordy, James Cowan, Stephen Greene, Michael MacDonald, Thomas McInnis, Terry Mercer, Wilfred P. Moore, Kelvin K. Ogilvie and Donald H. Oliver.

Cabinet (as of June 2013)
Premier, President of the Executive Council, Minister of Policy and Priorities, Minister of Intergovernmental Affairs, Minister of Aboriginal Affairs: Hon. Darrell Dexter (page 1415)
Deputy Premier, Deputy President of the Executive Council, Chair of Treasury Board; Minister of Labour & Advanced Education; Minister of Immigration: Frank Corbett
Minister of Finance; Minister of African Nova Scotian Affairs: Maureen MacDonald
Minister of Agriculture, Minister of Service Nova Scotia and Municipal Relations: John MacDonell
Minister of Transportation and Infrastructure Renewal, Minister of Gaelic Affairs: Maurice Smith
Minister of the Public Service Commission; Minister of Communication: Marilyn More
Minister of Fisheries and Aquaculture, Minister of Environment: Sterling Belliveau

Minister of Economic & Rural Development &Tourism, Minister responsible for Nova Scotia Business Inc.: Graham Steele
Minister of Community Services, Minister of Seniors: Denise Peterson-Rafuse
Minister of Education and Early Childhood: Ramona Jennex
Attorney General and Minister of Justice: Ross Landry
Minister of Natural Resources, Minister of Energy: Charlie Parker
Minister of Health and Wellness, Minister of Acadian Affairs: David Wilson
Minister of Communities, Culture and Heritage: Leonard Preyra

Ministries
Office of the Premier, Halifax, Nova Scotia, Canada. E-mail: premier@gov.ns.ca, URL: http://www.gov.ns.ca/premier
Attorney-General's Office, Ministry of Justice, 5151 Terminal Road, PO Box 7, Halifax, Nova Scotia B3J 2L6, Canada. Tel: +1 902 424 4044, fax: +1 902 424 0510, e-mail: justweb@gov.ns.ca
Department of Agriculture, PO Box 12223, Halifax, Nova Scotia, B3J 3C4, Canada. Tel: +1 902 424 6734, fax: +1 902 424 3948, URL: http://www.gov.ns.ca/agri
Department of Community Services, PO Box 2561, Halifax, Nova Scotia, BJ3 3N5, Canada. Tel: +1 902 424 4150, fax: +1 902 424 0578, URL: http://www.gov.ns.ca/coms
Department of Economic Development, World Trade Centre, floors 5, 6 and 7, PO Box 519, 1800 Argyle Street, Halifax, Nova Scotia, Canada B3J 2R7. Tel: +1 902 424 8920, e-mail: econ.edt@gov.ns.ca, URL: http://www.gov.ns.ca/econ
Department of Education, PO Box 578, 2021 Brunswick Street, Suite 402, Halifax, Nova Scotia, B3J 2S9, Canada. Tel: +1 902 424 5168, fax: +1 902 424 0511, e-mail: Webmaster@EDnet.ns.ca, URL: http://www.ednet.ns.ca
Department of the Environment and Labour, 5151 Terminal Road, 5th floor, PO Box 697, Halifax, NS, B3J 2T8, Canada. Tel: +1 902 424 5300, fax: +1 902 424 0503, URL: http://www.gov.ns.ca/enla
Department of Finance, Provincial Building, 1723 Hollis Street, Box 187, Halifax, Nova Scotia, B3J 2N3, Canada. Tel: +1 902 424 5554, fax: +1 902 429 0257, URL: http://www.gov.ns.ca/finance/en/home/default.aspx
Ministry of Health, PO Box 488, Halifax, Nova Scotia, B3J 2R8, Canada. URL: http://www.gov.ns.ca/health
Ministry of Service Nova Scotia and Municipal Relations, Summit Place, 4th Floor, 1601 Lower Water Street, Halifax, Nova Scotia, B3J 1S2, Canada. Tel: +1 902 424 4141, fax: +1 902 424 0531, URL: http://www.gov.ns.ca/snsmr
Ministry of Human Resources, One Government Place, 1700 Granville Street, PO Box 943, Halifax, Nova Scotia, B3J 2V9, Canada. Tel: +1 902 424 7660, fax: +1 902 424 0611, e-mail: webmaster@gov.ns.ca
Ministry of Natural Resources, 1701 Hollis Street, PO Box 698, Founders Square, Halifax, NS, B3J 2T9, Canada. Tel: +1 902 424 5935, fax: +1 902 424 7735, URL: http://www.gov.ns.ca/natr
Ministry of Transportation and Public Works, Purdy's Wharf, Tower II, 4th Floor, 1969 Upper Water Street, PO Box 186, Halifax, NS, B3J 2N2, Canada. Tel: +1 902 424 2297, fax: +1 902 424 0171, e-mail: russelro@gov.ns.ca, URL: http://www.gov.ns.ca/tran
Ministry of Labour and Workforce Development, PO Box 697, 5151 Terminal Road, Halifax, Nova Scotia B3J 2T8. Tel: +1 902 424 5301, fax: +1 902 424 0503, URL: http://www.gov.ns.ca/lwd

Elections
An election was held in June 2006 with the Progressive Conservative Party winning 23 of the seats, the New Democratic Party won 20 seats and Liberal Party won 9 seats. The Nova Scotia House of Assembly was dissolved on 5 May 2009 following a government defeat in the House. Elections were held on 9 June and the government defeated. New Democrats took 31 seats, Liberals 11, Progressive Conservatives 10, Independent one.

LEGAL SYSTEM
Nova Scotia's highest court is the Court of Appeal. The Supreme Court is the highest trial court and also acts as appeal court for cases from the Provincial Court. Nova Scotia also has Family, Small Claims, Bankruptcy and Probate Courts.

LOCAL GOVERNMENT
The province is made up of municipal units that have local governments. These have the power to enact by-laws governing affairs such as planning. The municipalities are: Annapolis; Antigonish; Cape Breton; Colchester; Cumberland; Digby; Guysborough; Halifax; Hants; Inverness; Kings; Lunenburg; Pictou; Queens; Richmond; Shelburne; Victoria; Yarmouth.

AREA AND POPULATION
Area
The province of Nova Scotia covers an area of over 53,000 sq km. The Atlantic coastline stretches for 7,400 km. The overall length of the province is 575 km. with an average width of 130 km., the area of Nova Scotia includes Cape Breton Island, which is joined to the mainland by the Canso Causeway. Nova Scotia has a border with New Brunswick and neighbours Prince Edward Island.

To view a map, please consult http://atlas.nrcan.gc.ca/site/english/maps/reference/provincesterritories. (With permission of Natural Resources Canada 2008, courtesy of the Atlas of Canada)

Population
The population in mid-2012 was 948,700. Figures for 2012 show that 137,400 of the population were aged 14 or below, 648,400 were aged between 15 and 64, and 162,900 were over 65.

Births, Marriages, Deaths
In the period July 2011-June 2012 there were 8,848 births. In the same period 8,706 deaths were recorded. During the year July 2006-June 2007, 19,598 immigrants arrived from other Canadian Provinces and 21,999 Nova Scotians left for other Canadian provinces, 2,715 foreign immigrants arrived and 825 Nova Scotians left for foreign countries. Provisional figures for 2009 show that 4,459 marriages took place. (Source: Statistics Canada, www.statcan.ca)

In addition to the standard days celebrated in Canada, Nova Scotia also celebrates the following:

Public Holidays 2014
4 August: Natal Day
11 November: Remembrance Day

EMPLOYMENT
Figures for December 2012 show that the province had a workforce numbering 495,800, and had an unemployment rate of 9.3 per cent. The following table shows how the working population were employed in December 2011 and 2012:

Employment sector	Dec. 2011	Dec. 2012
Agriculture	4,900	6,100
Forestry, fishing, mining, oil & gas	11,600	10,700
Utilities	3,300	4,400
Construction	31,600	29,300
Manufacturing	33,200	30,700
Trade	76,600	69,700
Transportation & warehousing	22,300	20,400
Finance, insurance, real estate & leasing	23,200	22,200
Professional. scientific & technical services	24,200	28,700
Business building & other support services	19,800	21,400
Educational services	38,600	36,600
Health care & social assistance	68,500	67,700
Information, culture & recreation	20,600	18,600
Accommodation & food services	28,000	34,600
Other services	20,900	20,200
Public administration	31,000	58,500

Source: Statistics Canada CANSIM table 282-0088

BANKING AND FINANCE
GDP/GNP, Inflation, National Debt
Expenditure based GDP in recent years is shown in the following table:

Year	Can$ millions
2004	29,853
2005	31,199
2006	31,644
2007	33,852
2008	35,394
2009	34,921
2010	36,350
2011	37,015

Source: Statistics Canada CANSIM, table 384-0038

GDP by Industry (Can$ millions chained 1997)

Industry	2000	2005
Goods producing	4,980	5,406
Other Primary	608	649
Mining & oil & gas extraction	581	442
Utilities	500	548
Manufacturing	2,130	2,379
Construction	1,161	1,388
Service producing	15,803	17,966
Transportation & warehousing	960	1,036
Trade	2,395	2,772
Finance, insurance, real estate, & renting & leasing	4,366	5,051
Community, business & personal services	5,338	5,086
Public administration	2,244	2,398
Other service	501	559
Total	20,860	23,255

Figures may not add due to rounding
Source: Government of Nova Scotia

Balance of Payments / Imports and Exports
The value of Nova Scotia's manufacturing shipments of own goods in 2005 was Can$9,994.7 million, falling to Can$9,558.5 million in 2006 before rising to Can$9,838.2 million in 2007, Can$10,638.0 million in 2008 and falling to Can$8,955.8 million in2009. (Source: Statistics Canada, www.statcan.ca, February 2011).

Nova Scotia's main exported goods include fish, paper and paperboard, transportation equipment, non-metallic minerals, lumber and wood pulp.

CANADA

Exports by Major Commodity Groups (Can$ Millions)

Commodity	2000	2005
Fish & fish preparations	1,098	1,027
Paper & paperboard	540	588
Transportation equipment	328	174
Wood pulp & similar pulp	247	175
Non metallic minerals, mineral fuels	940	1,577
Lumber	242	214
Other commodity groups	1,824	2,074
Total	5,219	5,829

Source: Government of Nova Scotia

MANUFACTURING, MINING AND SERVICES

Primary and Extractive Industries
Principal minerals mined in Nova Scotia are gypsum, salt, coal, dolomite, clay and limestone. Over 3.2 million tonnes of thermal and metallurgical coal are mined annually.

More than 120 offshore wells have been drilled over the last 30 years. Substantial reserves of oil are concentrated in the Sable Island area. Since 1992 two small oil fields have been brought into production. They produce some 6,300 cubic metres of oil per day.

Nova Scotia has estimated potential reserves of natural gas in the region of 53 trillion cubic feet. Its main gas production fields are located at Sable Island and are developed by a consortium including Mobil Canada, Shell Canada and Nova Scotia Resources and currently produce around 500 million cubic feet of natural gas per day. This consortium has expanded into the Alma field, which is 40 miles from Sable. Presently, gas fields with a potential production capacity of 3 trillion cubic feet are being developed, with markets in Atlantic Canada and the northeast of the United States. Environmental concerns have limited the number of fields to be developed to 6 out of a total of 24. Shell Canada and Nova Scotia power will oversee production, which is estimated to be in the region of 60 million cubic feet of natural gas a day for the next 10 years. Forthcoming gas pipeline proposals include a Can$1.3 billion link between Sable Island and the northeast of the US. Currently Nova Scotia exports around 70 per cent of its natural gas to the New England area of the USA. Figures for 2007 show that Crude petroleum production was worth Can$347.7 million and natural gas was worth Can$1,094.9 million.

Energy
A tidal power plant at the Bay of Fundy is in operation.

Manufacturing
Oil refining, fish processing, primary steel operations, pulp and paper manufacturing, type manufacturing, saw-milling and a variety of food processing operations are the province's principal manufacturing industries.

Manufacturing Sales

Year	Can$ million
2003	9,138.0
2004	9,596.2
2005	9,994.7
2006	9,558.5
2007	9,761.9
2008	10,643.1
2009	8,818.9
2010	9,798.9
2011	10,813.4

Source: Statistics Canada CANSIM, tables 304-0014 and 304-0015

Manufacturing Shipments by Industry Group (Can$ Million)

Industry	2009	2010
Food	1,964.6	1,983.5
Wood product	450.0	529.6
Plastics & rubber products	1,006.2	1,220.5
Non-metallic mineral products	198.4	199.9
Computer & electronic products	191.1	195.1
Transportation equipment	696.7	759.1
Total all industries	8,818.9	9,798.9

Source: Statistics Canada http://www40.statcan.ca/l01/cst01/manuf28-eng.htm Jan. 2012

Service Industries
Total annual tourism receipts were recently reported to be Can$1,100,000,000. The industry also generates over 33,000 jobs. Around 100 cruise ships arrive annually at the port of Halifax. Sport fishing is also a growing industry and currently generates almost Can$70 million each year.

Agriculture
Approximately 7.7 per cent of the total land area of Nova Scotia of 397,031 hectares was classified as farm land in a recent census. The major agricultural economic contributor is the dairy sector. The following table shows farm cash receipts for selected products.

Farm Cash Receipts

Product	2010	2011
Cattle	21,286	20,082
Calves	2,699	2,246

- continued

	2010	2011
Dairy products	120,595	124,53
Hens & chickens	70,423	r
Total eggs	29,609	32,27
Wheat excl. durum	1,492	2,06
Corn	3,369	5,45
Potatoes	6,232	5,50
Total livestock & livestock products receipts	357,059	373,71
Total crops receipts	130,108	136,74
Total farm cash receipts	499,912	526,59

Source: Statistics Canada CANSIM Table 002-0001

Total value of agricultural production in 2008 was Can$551,102,000, up from the 2007 figure of Can$543,531,000 but down from Can$553,869,000 in 2006.

Forestry
There are about 4.1 million hectares of forested lands in Nova Scotia or about 74 per cent of the total land area. Roughly 31 per cent is held by the Crown (28 per cent provincial and 3 per cent federal); 69 per cent in private ownerships. Primary forest products include sawlogs, pulpwood, pit props, poles and piling, veneer logs and Christmas trees. Secondary activities include sawmilling, pulp and paper manufacturing, other wood-using industries (for example planning mills, box and barrel factories). The total value of exported primary wood, paper and allied industries is approximately Can$700 million each year.

Fishing
Nova Scotia is one of the leading Canadian fishing provinces. In recent years groundstock fishing quotas have been reduced to protect stock so the industry is trying to diversify through other species such as skate and shark. The industry is also able to expand through aquaculture which enables it to produce fish such as scallops, salmon and oysters. Nova Scotia is the world's largest exporter of lobster.

COMMUNICATIONS AND TRANSPORT

International Airports
There are major airports at Yarmouth, Sydney and Halifax. Airlines serving national and international points from major airports include Air Canada, Canadian Airlines International, Air Nova and Inter-Canadian.

National Airlines
Air Canada Regional (Air Nova), URL: http://www.airnova.com

Railways
The railway network covers some 7,000 km, owned mainly by the Canadian National Railways. The Windsor and Hansport Railway serves part of the Annapolis Valley, connecting Windsor and New Minas, while the Cape Breton and Central Nova Scotia railway operates the line between Sydney and Truro. A transcontinental passenger service is operated by VIA Rail connecting Halifax and Montreal.

Roads
Nova Scotia has a network of 26,800 km. of roads. Of this total over 13,000 km. are paved. Over 585,000 people have vehicle operator licences.

Shipping
A consortium of firms and public sector offices called Ediport Atlantic is responsible for shipping through the Port of Halifax. It has recently developed an electronic management and tracking system for cargo.

Ferry services operate all year round and connect Nova Scotia with Maine USA, Newfoundland, Prince Edward Island and New Brunswick.

Ports and Harbours
The Port of Halifax is Nova Scotia's largest port.
Halifax Port Authority, URL: http://www.portofhalifax.ca

HEALTH

Recent health figures indicate that there are 16.2 approved beds per 1,000 population in healthcare institutions in Nova Scotia. The ratio within hospitals was 6.1 per 1,000 population and in residential care facilities, 10.1. There are 36 hospitals with 3,233 beds in Nova Scotia including one psychiatric hospital and one specialising in maternity and paediatric care. There are also 70 long-term care facilities with 5,874 beds. Recent figures show that there were 2,030 physicians employed in Nova Scotia, along with 9,279 registered nurses, 485 dentists and 1,016 pharmacists. Figures for 2009 show that total expenditure on health was Can$1,9 billion.

EDUCATION

Elementary and high school education is compulsory and free. Figures for recent years show a decline in the number of students enrolled in general education: 135,303 in the 2007-08 school year falling to 133,134 in the 2008-09 school year. Expenditure per student in public general education in 2008-09 was Can$10,761.

At the post-secondary level, there are 12 universities and 10 non-university institutions within Nova Scotia.

COMMUNICATIONS AND MEDIA

Newspapers
Nova Scotia currently has seven daily newspapers and over 40 periodicals.

Broadcasting
There are currently five network televisions stations operating in Nova Scotia: CBHT-TV Halifax (CBC affiliated), CJCH-TV Halifax (CTV owned), CIHF-TV Halifax (owned by Global Communications Ltd), CBIT-TV Sydney (CBC owned), CJCB-TV Sydney (owned by CTV). There are also more than 16 cable television stations operating.

CBHT-TV Halifax, URL: http://www.halifax.cbc.ca
CJCH-TV Halifax, URL: http://www.ctv.ca/
Newcap Broadcasting Limited (Radio), URL: http://www.ncc.ca

Post and Telecommunications
Total revenue from this sector recently exceeded Can$750 million. There is a very high ratio per capita of use of the internet. Latest figures indicate that there are nearly 371,000 residential telephone lines and more than 181,200 business lines.

NUNAVUT

Capital: Iqaluit (Population estimate: 6,000)

Head of State: Edna Elias (Commissioner) (page 1420)

Provincial Flag: Divided in two vertically, left hand side gold, right hand side white, in the centre is a drawing of a stone monument (inuksuk) in red, the top right hand corner has a northern star in blue.

CONSTITUTION AND GOVERNMENT

Constitution
In 1993 two pieces of legislation were passed in order to pave the way for the creation of a new territory, Nunavut, in response to Inuit land claims: the Nunavut Land Claims Agreement Act which ratified the land claim, and the Nunavut Act which divided the Northwest Territories in order to create this new territory. The territory officially came into being on 1 April 1999 and elections were held for the first Nunavut Government on 15 February 1999. The official language of the government is Inuktitut. Inuinnaqtun, English and French is also used.

The Nunavut Legislative Assembly consists of 19 members who serve five-year terms. The cabinet members are appointed by the members of the legislative assembly from among themselves.
Legislative Assembly, Iqaluit, NU X0A 0H0, Canada. URL: http://www.gov.nu.ca
Speaker: Hunter Tootoo

Nunavut is represented in the Canadian Senate by senator Dennis Patterson.

Cabinet (as at June 2013)
Premier, Minister of Executive and Intergovernmental Affairs, Minister Responsible for Immigration, Minister of Aboriginal Affairs, Minister of Education: Eva Aariak (page 1371)
Deputy Premier, Minister of Economic Development and Transportation, Minister Responsible for Nunavut Business Credit Corporation; Nunavut Development Corporation; Mines; Energy; and Nunavut Housing Corporation: Peter Taptuna
Government House Leader, Minister of Community & Government Services, Minister responsible for the Workers' Safety and Compensation Commission: Lorne Kusugak
Minister of Finance, Minister of Health, Minister responsible for Public Agencies Council: Keith Peterson
Minister of Justice, Minister Responsible for Nunavut Arctic College, for Labour Standards Board, for Liquor Licensing Board: Daniel Shewchuk
Minister of Culture & Heritage; Languages; Environment; Minister Responsible for the Utility Rates Review Council: James Arreak
Minister of Family Services, Minister Responsible for Homelessness; Qulliq Energy Corp.; Status of Women: Monica Ell

Ministries
Government portal: URL: http://www.gov.nu.ca/
Office of the Premier, Grinnell Place, PO Box 800, Iqaluit, NT X0A 0H0, Canada. Tel: +1 867 979 5822, fax: +1 867 979 5833
Ministry of Community Government, Housing and Transportation, Brown Building, PO Box 800, Iqaluit, NT X0A 0H0, Canada. Tel: +1 867 975 5300, fax: +1 867 975 5305
Ministry of Culture, Language, Elders and Youth, PO Box 333, Igloolik, NT X0A 0L0, Canada. Tel: +1 867 934 8335, fax: +1 867 934 8685
Ministry of Education, PO Box 800, Iqaluit, NT X0A 0H0, Canada. Tel: +1 867 975 5600, fax: +1 867 975 5605
Ministry of Executive and Intergovernmental Affairs, Grinnell Place, PO Box 800, Iqaluit, NT X0A 0H0, Canada. Tel: +1 867 979 4802, fax: +1 867 979 4774
Ministry of Finance and Administration, Building 1079, Bag 800, Iqaluit, NT X0A 0H0, Canada. Tel: +1 867 975 5800, fax: +1 867 975 5844
Ministry of Health and Social Services, Brown Building, First Floor, Box 800, Iqaluit, NT X0A 0H0, Canada. Tel: +1 867 979 6020, fax: +1 867 975 5705
Ministry of Human Resources, Building 1091, Box 800, Iqaluit, NT X0A 0H0, Canada. Tel: +1 867 975 6200, fax: +1 867 975 6220
Ministry of Justice, Court House, Bag 800, Iqaluit, NT X0A 0H0, Canada. Tel: +1 867 979 6000, fax: +1 867 979 5977
Ministry of Public Works, Telecommunications and Technical Services, Brown Building, Bag 1000, Iqaluit, NT X0A 0H0, Canada. Tel: +1 867 975 5400, fax: +1 867 975 4748
Ministry of Sustainable Development, Brown Building, Third Floor, PO Box 1340, Iqaluit, NT X0A 0H0, Canada. Tel: +1 867 979 5134, fax: +1 867 979 5920
Office of the Commissioner, URL: http://www.commissioner.gov.nu.ca/

Elections
The first Nunavut Legislative Assembly was elected on 15 April 1999 when 88 per cent of the 12,210 eligible voters cast their ballots. The most recent elections were held in October 2008. The next election is scheduled to take place on 28 October 2013.

LEGAL SYSTEM

The justice system is a Single-Level Trial Court system, which is unique in Canada. It is a combination of the Supreme and Territorial courts.

LOCAL GOVERNMENT

Nunavut is divided into 26 communities: Arctic Bay, Arviat, Baker Lake, Bathurst Inlet, Cambridge Bay, Cape Dorset, Chesterfield Inlet, Clyde River, Gjoa Haven, Grise Fiord, Hall Beach, Iglulik, Iqaluit, Kimmirut, Kugluktuk, Nanisivik, Pangnirtung, Pelly Bay, Pond Inlet, Qikiqtarjuaq, Rankin Inlet, Repulse Bay, Resolute, Sanikiluaq, Taloyoak, and Whale Cove. The communities range in population from 25 to 6,000, and all but one are situated on the coast.

AREA AND POPULATION

Area
Nunavut occupies a total area of 1.9 million sq. km., nearly one third of the area of Canada.

To view a map, please consult http://atlas.nrcan.gc.ca/site/english/maps/reference/provincesterritories. (With permission of Natural Resources Canada 2008, courtesy of the Atlas of Canada)

Population
On July 2012 the population was 33,700 up from 30,800 in 2006. 85 per cent of the population are Inuit. Population per sq. km. is 0.01, compared with 2.9 in Canada as a whole. The largest community in Nunavut is the capital, Iqaluit, which has a population of around 6,000. Estimated figures show half of the population is located in the Baffin region. Around 60 per cent of the population is under 25 (the youngest population in Canada). The main languages spoken are Inuktitut, Inuinnaqtun, and English. The following figures show a breakdown of the population: population aged under 15 years, 10,700; population aged 15 to 64, 21,900; population aged 65 years and over, 1,100.

Births, Marriages, Deaths
During the year July 1, 2011 - June 30, 2012 there were 835 births and 176 deaths. In the year 2008-09, 32 immigrants arrived and 20 people emigrated from Nunavut. (Source: Statistics Canada).

Public Holidays
In addition to the standard days celebrated in Canada, Nunavut also celebrates the following:
1 April: Nunavut Day

EMPLOYMENT

Figures for the end of 2009 show that the labour force numbered 11,100 and the unemployment rate was 12.7 per cent. The following table shows how the labour force was employed in 2006:

Occupation	Employees
Management	1,275
Business, finance & admin.	1,880
Natural & applied sciences & related	420
Health	310
Social science, education, gov. service, religion	1,985
Art, culture, recreation & sport	645
Sales & service	3,170
Trades, transport & equipment operators & related occupations	2,040
Occupations unique to primary industry	215
Occupations unique to processing, manufacturing & utilities	140

Source: Statistics Canada, February 2010

CANADA

BANKING AND FINANCE

GDP/GNP, Inflation, National Debt
The average income per household in Nunavut is just under Can$31,500, compared with Can$45,250 in Canada as a whole. Expenditure based GDP in recent years is shown in the following table.

Year	GDP, Can$ millions
2004	1,074
2005	1,137
2006	1,226
2007	1,343
2008	1,592
2009	1,545
2010	1,863
2011	1,964

Source: Statistics Canada CANSIM, table 384-0038 last modified: 2012-11-19

Average annual growth of the economy has been put at 2.4 per cent. Sustainable development is to be the cornerstone of Nunavut's economy. Recent figures show that real GDP (chained 1997) growth was 6.4 per cent in 2002, falling to -4.8 per cent in 2004 and rising to 0.5 per cent in 2004. The fall in 2003 was mainly due to the closure of a gold mine, a lead mine and a zinc mine resulting in a drop in international export figures. GDP growth was put at 8 per cent in 2008. Inflation was 2.3 per cent.

Balance of Payments / Imports and Exports
Government figures for 2008 show that imports cost Can$522 million and exports generated Can$46 million. The major export markets are the US (10.4 per cent), China (9.7 per cent and the UK (8.4 per cent).

Chambers of Commerce and Trade Organisations
Baffin Regional Chamber of Commerce, URL: http://www.baffinchamber.ca/

MANUFACTURING, MINING AND SERVICES

Primary and Extractive Industries
Under the Nunavut Land Claims Agreement, control was given to nearly 38,000 sq km of land which included title to subsurface (mineral) rights.

In the High Arctic region there are two lead and zinc mines. There is also a gold mine at Luin in the Western Arctic. A diamond mine located in the Kitikmeot area came into production in 2006. Mining revenues amounted to approximately Can$6 million in 2008. More mines are expected to open in the coming years.

Recent estimates show that 5 per cent of Canada's oil reserves are located in Nunavut along with 15 per cent of her natural gas reserves. More reserves are expected to be found in the coming years. Gas extraction revenues amounted to over Can$6 million in 2008.

Manufacturing
The manufacturing sector is currently very small and is centred around food processing and arts and crafts.

Manufacturing Sales

Year	Can$ millions
2005	6.3
2006	7.0
2007	6.5

- continued

2008	5.
2009	4.
2010	5.
2011	3.

Source: http://www40.statcan.gc.ca/l01/cst01/manuf28-eng.htm Dec. 2011

Fishing
According to recent government figures, the value of the catch for the Atlantic fisherie amounted to over Can$80 million. A turbot fishery was recently established in the Baffi region. The region has four fish processing plants.

Service Industries
Tourism is seen as a growth area with many visitors to Auyuittuq National Park. Variou types of tourism are being developed including adventure holidays and eco-tourism. Cruis ships currently stop at Pond Inlet, Cape Dorset, Kimmirut and Pangnirtung.

COMMUNICATIONS AND TRANSPORT

National Airlines
Air Inuit, URL: http://www.airinuit.com
Air Nunavut, PO Box 1239, Iqaluit NT, XOA OHO, Canada. Tel: +1 867 979 2400, fax: +1 867 979 4318

International Airports
Iqaluit Airport is based in the Qikiqtaaluk (Baffin) region of Nunavut and receives flights from Greenland, Montreal and Ottawa.

Roads
Nunavut has only about 20 km. of highways, mainly between Arctic Bay and Nanisivik Consequently, there are virtually no roads linking communities in Nunavut.

HEALTH

Nunavut has one hospital, the Baffin Regional Hospital which is situated in Iqaluit, as well as 26 health centres (one in each community), with nursing services for community care.

EDUCATION

Figures for recent years show a rise in the number of students enrolled in general education 9,023 in the 2007-08 school year rising to 9,280 in the 2008-09 school year. Expenditure per student in public general education in 2008-09 was Can$15,875.

Higher Education
Nunavut Arctic College, Iqaluit, offers post-secondary courses at its Nunatta campus.

COMMUNICATIONS AND MEDIA

Broadcasting
The Inuit Broadcasting Corporation (IBC), (URL: http://www.inuitbroadcasting.ca/) broadcasts programmes several hours a week.

Telecommunications
The Inuit language, Inukititut, is a syllabic language and computer programming now makes the language available for use on the internet, so aiding communications between communities.

ONTARIO

Capital: Toronto (Population estimate: 5.1 million)

Lieutenant-Governor: Hon. David C. Onley (page 1490)

Provincial Flag: The Canadian Red Ensign bears the Union Jack in the top left hand corner and the Ontario shield of arms on the right hand side in the centre.

CONSTITUTION AND GOVERNMENT

Constitution
Ontario was one of the four original provinces, entering the Confederation in 1867.

Upper House
Although the province has no upper house, it is represented in the Canadian Senate. The following members of the Ontario political parties are also Canadian Senators: Salma Ataullahjan, Lynn Beyak, David Braley, Marie-P. Charette-Poulin, Anne C. Cools, Nicole Eaton, Art Eggleton, Tobia C. Enverga Jr., Doug Finley, Linda Frum, Irving Gerstein, Mac Harb, Colin Kenny, Marjory LeBreton, Don Meredith, Jim Munson, Ruth Nancy, Rhanh Hai Ngo, Robert Runciman, Hugh Segal. Asha Seth, David Smith and Vernon White.

Lower House
The Lower House is known as the Legislative Assembly and has 107 seats.

Legislative Assembly, Legislative Building, Queen's Park, Toronto, Ontario, M7A 1A2, Canada. URL: http://www.ontla.on.ca

Cabinet (as at June 2013)
Premier, Minister of Agriculture: Kathleen Wynne (page 1540)
Minister of Finance: Charles Sousa
Minister of Energy: Bob Chiarelli
Minister of Intergovernmental Affairs, Minister Responsible for Women's Issues: Laurel C. Broten
Minister of the Environment: Jim Bradley
Minister of Training, Colleges and Universities: Brad Duguid
Minister of Labour: Yasir Naqvi
Minister of Natural Resources: David Orazietti
Minister of Citizenship and Immigration: Michel Coteau
Attorney General: John Gerretsen
Minister of Community Safety and Correctional Services, Minister Responsible for Francophone Affairs: Madeleine Meilleur
Minister of Labour: Yasir Naqvi
Minister of Northern Development and Mines: Michael Gravelle
Minister of Municipal Affairs and Housing: Linda Jeffrey
Minister of Rural Affairs: Jeff Leal
Minister of Economic Development and Innovation: Dr Eric Hoskins
Minister of Culture, Sport and Tourism, Minister Responsible for the 2015 Pan and Parapan American Games: Michael Chan

Minister of Health and Long Term Care: Deb Matthews
Minister of Consumer Services: Tracy MacCharles
Minister of Community and Social Services:
Minister of Research and Innovation: Reza Moridi
Minister of Government Services: John Milloy
Minister of Transportation, Minister of Infrastructure: Glen R. Murray
Minister of Children and Youth Services: Teresa Piruzza
Minister of Education: Liz Sandals
Minister of Aboriginal Affairs: David Zimmer
Minister Responsible for Seniors: Mario Sergio

Ministries
Office of the Premier and Cabinet Office, Room 281, Legislative Building, Queen's Park, Toronto M7A 1A1, Canada. Tel: +1 416 325 1941, fax: +1 416 325 7578, URL: http://www.premier.gov.on.ca
Ministry of Finance, Frost Bldg. S., & Queen's Park Crescent, Toronto, ON M7A IY7, Canada. Tel: +1 416 325 0400, Fax: +1 416 325 0374, URL: http://www.gov.on.ca/FIN/english/enghome.htm
Ministry of Agriculture and Food, 1 Stone Road West, 2nd Floor, Guelph, ON N1G 4Y2, Canada. Tel: +1 519 826 3100, URL: http://www.gov.on.ca/OMAFRA/english/index.html
Minister of the Environment and Energy, 135 St Clair Ave W., Toronto ON M4V 1P5, Canada. Tel: +1 416 325 4000, fax: +1 416 325 3159, URL: http://www.ene.gov.on.ca/index.htm
Office of the Attorney-General, 720 Bay Street, Toronto ON M5G 2K1, Canada. Tel: +1 416 326 2220, fax: +1 416 326 4007, -mail: jusig.mag.webmaster@jus.gov.on.ca, URL: http://www.attorneygeneral.jus.gov.on.ca
Ministry of Education and Training, Colleges and Universities, Mowat Block, 2nd Floor, 900 Bay Street, Toronto ON M7A 1L2, Canada. Tel: +1 416 325 2929, fax: +1 416 325 6348, URL: http://www.edu.gov.on.ca/eng/welcome.html
Ministry of Energy, Science & Technology, Hearst Block, 4th Floor, 900 Bay Street, Toronto ON M7A 2E1, Canada. Tel: +1 416 327 6758, fax: +1 416 327 0033, URL: http://www.energy.gov.on.ca/
Ministry of Health, Hepburn Block, 10th Floor, 80 Grosvenor Street, Toronto ON M7A 1C4, Canada. Tel: +1 416 327 4327, URL: http://www.health.gov.on.ca
Ministry of Intergovernmental Affairs, Mowat Block, 5th Floor, 900 Bay Street, Toronto ON M7A 1C2, Canada. Tel: +1 416 325 4800, URL: http://www.mia.gov.on.ca/mia-main.htm
Ministry of Consumer and Commercial Relations, 250 Yonge Street, Toronto ON M5B 2N5, Canada. Tel: +1 416 326 8555, URL: http://www.cbs.gov.on.ca/mcbs/english/welcome.htm
Ministry of Economic Development & Trade, 8th Floor, Hearst Block, 900 Bay Street, Toronto ON M7A 2E1, Canada. Tel: +1 416 325 6666, fax: +1 416 325 6688, URL: http://www.ontariocanada.com/ontcan/en/home.jsp
Ministry of Municipal Affairs and Housing, 17th Floor, 777 Bay Street, Toronto ON M5G 2E5, Canada. Tel: +1 416 585 7041, fax: +1 416 585 6227, URL: http://www.mah.gov.on.ca/scripts/index_.asp
Ministry of Community and Social Services, Hepburn Block, 7th Floor, 80 Grosvenor Street, Toronto ON M7A 1E9, Canada. Tel: +1 416 325 5666, fax: +1 416 314 8721, URL: http://www.cfcs.gov.on.ca/cfcs/en/default.htm
Ministry of Citizenship, 6th floor, 77 Bloor St. West, Toronto, Ontario, M7A 2R9, Canada. Tel: +1 416 327 2422, fax: +1 416 314 4965, URL: http://www.gov.on.ca/citizenship/index.html
Ministry of Tourism and Recreation, 900 Bay Street, 9th Floor, Hearst Block, Toronto, Ontario, Canada. Tel: +1 416 326 9326, fax: +1 416 326 9338, URL: http://www.tourism.gov.on.ca/english
Ministry of Transportation, 301 St Paul Street, St Catharines ON L2R 7R4, Canada. Tel: +1 905 704 2000, fax: +1 416 327 9185, URL: http://www.mto.gov.on.ca/english/index.html
Ministry of Labour, 400 University Avenue, Toronto ON M7A 1T7, Canada. Tel: +1 416 326 7160, fax: +1 416 326 6546, URL: http://www.gov.on.ca/LAB/english
Ministry of Women's Issues, Mowat Block, 6th Floor, 900 Bay Street, Toronto ON M7A 1L2, Canada. Tel: +1 416 326 1600, fax: +1 416 326 1656, URL: http://www.gov.on.ca/citizenship/owd/index.html

Elections
The most recent elections were held in October 2011 when the Liberal Party won 53 seats, the Progressive Conservative Party won 37 and the New Democratic Party won 17.

LEGAL SYSTEM

Court administration is the responsibility of the Attorney General. Provincial judges are appointed by the Attorney General, on the recommendations of the Judicial Advisory Committee. Courts in the province are managed by the Courts Services Division through a regional structure. Each region is the responsibility of a senior justice and a regional senior judge, both in the Ontario Court. Regional courts are divided into three levels: the Court of Appeal, the Ontario Court (General Division and General Division Small Claims Court) and the Ontario Court (Provincial Division).

LOCAL GOVERNMENT

Ontario is divided for administrative purposes into Municipalities. Each has an elected Council. The responsibilities of the councils include provision of public utilities, road building and maintenance, planning, health care and social services, libraries and police and fire department cover.

AREA AND POPULATION

Area
The area of Ontario is 412,580 sq. miles (1,068,580 sq. km), of which some 344,100 sq. miles (891,190 sq. km) are land area and some 68,480 sq. miles (177,390 sq. km) are lakes, including the Great Lakes and fresh water rivers. The province extends 1,050 miles (1,690 km) from east to west and 1,075 miles (1,730 km) from north to south. It is bounded on the north by Hudson Bay and James Bay, on the east by Quebec, on the west by Manitoba, and on the south by the Great Lakes and the USA. Ottawa, the capital city of Canada is located in Ontario but the provincial capital is Toronto.

To view a map, please consult http://atlas.nrcan.gc.ca/site/english/maps/reference/provincesterritories. (With permission of Natural Resources Canada 2008, courtesy of the Atlas of Canada)

Population
The province's population in 2012 was 13,3505,900 (approximately one third of the total population of Canada), and represents an increase of nearly 139,000 on the previous year. The majority of people, 7.9 million, have English as their first language, whilst over 480,000 speak French primarily. The majority of the French-speaking population live in eastern and northern Ontario. Immigration has made Ontario a multicultural province with many languages now spoken there, including German, Italian, Chinese, Portuguese, Greek, Indo-Iranian, Spanish, Polish, Dutch, Ukrainian, Arabic and Punjabi. Major aboriginal languages spoken are Algonquian and Ojibway. Discussions are presently underway between the Ontario government and First Nations over land rights and self-government with a view to giving Aboriginal governments more political autonomy.

The majority of the population live in urban areas. In 2006, Toronto had an estimated population of 5.1 million.

Births, Marriages and Deaths
In the year July 2011-June 2012 the number of births was 141,799, up from 140,267 the previous year. The number of deaths in the province rose to 96,201 from 93,141 the previous year. During the period July 2006-June 2007, 71,394 people from other Canadian provinces emigrated to Ontario and 107,590 people left Ontario for other Canadian provinces. An estimated 115,497 foreign immigrants arrived in Ontario and 19,523 people emigrated from Ontario to foreign countries. Provisional figures for 2008 saw 63,962 marriages take place and 28,805 divorces were granted in 2005. (Source: Statistics Canada, www.stancan.ca)

In addition to the standard days celebrated in Canada, Ontario also celebrates the following:

Public Holidays 2014
19 May: Victoria Day
4 August: Civic Holiday
13 October: Thanksgiving Day
26 December: Boxing Day

EMPLOYMENT

In 2012 Ontario had a labour force of 7,357,200, of whom 6,783,700 were employed and 573,500 were unemployed. The unemployment rate was 7.8 per cent. The following table shows employment by sector.

Industry	Dec. 2011	Dec. 2012
Agriculture	93,500	85,100
Forestry, fishing, mining, oil & gas	37,100	34,200
Utilities	56,400	55,400
Construction	445,900	429,400
Manufacturing	783,600	802,100
Trade	974,600	1,034,900
Transportation & warehousing	312,200	329,200
Finance, insurance, real estate & leasing	480,800	524,800
Professional, scientific & technical services	595,200	546,800
Business building & other support services	292,700	293,700
Educational services	480,100	523,600
Health care & social assistance	768,300	769,500
Information, culture & recreation	343,400	326,700
Accommodation & food services	406,000	428,400
Other services	284,300	286,400
Public administration	397,300	384,100

Source: Statistics Canada, CANSIM table 282-0088 Feb. 2013

BANKING AND FINANCE

GDP/GNP, Inflation, National Debt
Traditionally the economy of Ontario has been based on timber, fur trading and mineral extraction. Growing economic sectors now include tourism, financial and business services. The GDP of Ontario has shown a consistent growth in recent years. Expenditure based GDP in millions in recent years is shown in the following table:

Year	Can$ millions
2004	516,106
2005	537,383
2006	560,576
2007	587,912
2008	604,164
2009	593,916
2010	625,045

CANADA

- continued
2011   654,561
Source: Statistics Canada, CANSIM, table 384-0038 Feb. 2013

Balance of Payments / Imports and Exports
In 2010 manufacturing sales earned Can$243,306.52 million, up from Can$218,810.2 million in 2009 but still down on the 2008 figures of Can$269,383.7 million. Main exported goods are cars and car parts, food, plastics and electrical goods. Ontario's largest trading partner is the US.

Chambers of Commerce and Trade Organisations
Ontario Chamber of Commerce, URL: http://www.occ.on.ca

MANUFACTURING, MINING AND SERVICES

Primary and Extractive Industries
Ontario has reserves of gold, silver, platinum, zinc, nickel and copper. Ontario also mines limestone, gypsum, talc and salt.

Almost two-thirds of Canada's crude oil refining capacity of 1.85 million billion barrels a day is located in three provinces: Ontario, Quebec and Alberta. Ontario generates some 54,500 billion barrels a day from its refineries.

Ontario and Quebec generate more than half of Canada's electricity. More than half of Ontario's electric power is generated by nuclear plants, whilst 29 per cent comes from its hydroelectric facilities and 14 per cent from coal-fired plants. Major electricity export destinations are New England and New York.

There are currently 12 nuclear power reactors in Ontario, all owned by Ontario Hydro: four at Darlington, east of Pickering; and eight at the Bruce site on the shore of Lake Huron (although four are not presently generating). (Source: US Energy Information Administration)

The following table shows selected mineral and fuel production by value in 2007.

Mineral and Fuel Production

Product	Can$ million
Copper	1,403.1
Gold	1,258.6
Nickel	4,605.9
Silver	61.1
Zinc	300.0
Sand & gravel	490.4
Crude petroleum	51.5
Natural gas	61.1

Source: Statistics Canada: www40.statcan.gc.ca/l01/cst01/envi38b-eng.htm Jan. 2012

Manufacturing
Around 60 per cent of all Canada's manufactured goods come from Ontario. Recent figures show that 94 per cent of Ontario's goods exports are from the manufacturing sector and 90 per cent of manufacturing exports go to the US. Principal manufacturing industries include cars, car, truck and vehicle parts, wood products including pulp and paper, the aerospace industry, food processing, computer, electrical and electronic goods, fabricated metal products, plastics and textiles.

Manufacturing Sales by Subsector, in Can$ millions

Industry	2010	2011
Food	32,015.9	32,981.5
Beverage & tobacco products	4,282.4	4,038.0
Textile mills	616.2	635.1
Textile product mills	799.5	718.2
Clothing	544.7	517.1
Leather & allied products	112.9	145.1
Wood products	3,355.3	3,191.9
Paper	7,305.5	7,426.9
Printing & related support activities	4,095.0	3,929.7
Petroleum & coal products	18,187.0	20,516.3
Chemicals	19,664.3	20,460.5
Plastics & rubber products	10,756.8	11,593.9
Non-metallic mineral products	5,472.1	5,481.3
Primary metals	15,012.6	17,717.1
Fabricated metal products	15,201.0	16,150.6
Machinery	12,669.1	14,815.0
Computer & electronic products	10,371.8	10,405.1
Electrical equipment, appliances & components	4,606.9	5,111.4
Transportation equipment	68,032.1	70,803.9
Furniture & related products	5,024.9	5,031.7
Miscellaneous manufacturing	5,180.5	6,338.7

Source: Statistics Canada
www.statcan.gc.ca/tables-tableaux/sum-som/l01/cst01/manuf33g-eng.htm Feb. 2013

Service Industries
The service sector includes business and financial services, scientific technical, arts and culture services and a large media sector.

Agriculture
Over 56,168 sq km of Ontario's land is classified as farmland. Ontario's main farm produc are cattle (beef), grain and oilseed, fruit and vegetables, dairy, corn, wheat, barley, pigs, fru and general livestock. The major fishing industry product is trout, 4,250 tonnes of whic were caught in 1997, generating Can$23.1 million. (Source: Statistics Canada)

The following table shows selected crop production in recent years:

Crop Production in Tonnes

Crop	2011	201
Barley	161,100	165,50
Canola	73,700	49,90
Corn for grain	7,722,000	8,598,30
Oats	64,400	54,70
Soybeans	3,020,900	3,274,00
Wheat, all	2,407,900	1,883,40
Wheat, spring	162,600	133,40
Wheat, winter remaining	2,245,300	1,750,00

Source: Statistics Canada, CANSIM 001-0010 Feb. 2013

Figures from January 2008 for farm animals are set out in the following table.

Animals	'000 hea
Milk cows	325.
Beef cows	370.
Dairy heifers	174.
Beef heifers	183.
Calves	556.
Pigs	3,69
Sheep & lambs	23

Source: Statistics Canada, adapted from www.statcan.ca March 2008

Forestry
The forestry sector employs around 90,000 people and sales are valued at an average c Can$15 billion a year.

COMMUNICATIONS AND TRANSPORT

Regional Airlines
First Air, URL: http://www.firstair.ca
Air Jazz, URL: http://www.flyjazz.ca
Bearskin Airlines, URL: http://www.bearskinairlines.com

International Airports
The Lester B. Pearson International Airport, operated by the Greater Toronto Airports Authority (GTAA), comprises four main runways, 30 taxiways, 79 aircraft gates and serves 56 carriers Some 40 per cent of the country's cargo is handled by the airport's air cargo operations and the airport has generated more than Can$11 billion for local businesses.
Lester B. Pearson International Airport, URL: http://www.gtaa.com

Roads
Ontario has more than 16,000 km of provincial highways. One of the busiest roads in the world is situated here linking Windsor to the Quebec border.

Railways
Operated by the Ontario Northland Transportation Commission , more commonly Ontario Northland, URL: http://www.ontarionorthland.ca/).

Waterways
Ontario has a well developed system of waterways and canals including the Welland and Rideau canals and the St. Lawrence Seaway which enables ships to travel between Thunder Bay through the great lakes on to the Atlantic.

HEALTH

The most recent figures available show that the approved bed within a health care institution ratio to 1,000 population is 14.9. The ratio within hospitals is 5.2 and within residential care facilities, 9.8.

EDUCATION

Like the rest of Canada education in Ontario is free and compulsory but unlike the rest of Canada it is compulsory up to the age of 18 not 16. Figures for recent years show a decline in the number of students enrolled in general education: 2,087,588 in the 2007-08 school year falling to 2,061,390 in the 2009-10 school year. Expenditure per student in public general education in 2008-09 was Can$11,480.

Ontario has 18 universities, those with the highest enrolments are: The University of Toronto; York University; University of Western Ontario; Université d'Ottawa; and Ryperson Polytechnic University.

COMMUNICATIONS AND MEDIA

Broadcasting
Ontario's public television network is run by TVOntario.
TVOntario, URL: http://www.tvo.org

CJBN-TV, URL: http://www.gokenora.com/cjbn/
CHEX-TV, URL: http://www.chextv.com/

CITY-TV Toronto, URL: http://www.citytv.com
CBC - English Network Radio, http://www.cbc.ca

PRINCE EDWARD ISLAND

Capital: Charlottetown (Population estimate: 32,000)

Lieutenant-Governor: Hon. H. Frank Lewis (page 1463)

Provincial Flag: A banner of the arms, i.e. a white field bearing three small trees and a large tree on a compartment, all green, and at the top a red band with a golden lion, on three sides a border of red and white rectangles.

CONSTITUTION AND GOVERNMENT

Constitution
Prince Edward Island entered the Confederation of Canada in 1873. The Provincial government is administered by the Executive Council (Cabinet) which makes decisions on government direction and policy. On the advice of the First Minister, ministers on the Executive Council are appointed by the Lieutenant-Governor and advise him.

Upper House
Although the province has no upper house, it is represented on the Canadian Senate. The following are Canadian Senators representing Prince Edward Island: Catherine Callbeck, Michael Duffy, Percy Downe and Elizabeth Hubley.

Lower House
The province's parliament is unicameral. The Legislative Assembly has 27 members who are elected for a statutory five years.
Legislative Assembly, Province House, Richmond Street, PO Box 2000, Charlottetown, PEI, C1A 7N8, Canada. Tel: +1 902 368 5970, fax: +1 902 368 5175, URL: http://www.gov.pe.ca

Executive Council (as at June 2013)
Premier and President of Executive Council, Minister responsible for Intergovernmental Affairs, for Acadian and Francophone Affairs, and for Aboriginal Affairs: Hon. Robert W.J. Ghiz (page 1430)
Deputy Premier and Minister of Agriculture & Forestry: Hon. George Webster
Minister of Fisheries, Aquaculture and Rural Development: Hon. Ronald MacKinley
Minister of Health & Wellness: Hon. Doug W. Currie
Minister of Finance, Energy and Municipal Affairs: Hon. Wesley Sheridan
Minister of Community Services & Seniors, Minister responsible for the status of Women: Hon. Valerie Docherty
Minister of Environment, Labour and Justice: Hon. Janice Sherry
Minister of Transportation and Infrastructure Renewal: Hon. Robert Vessey
Minister of Tourism and Culture: Hon. Robert Henderson
Minister of Education and Early Childhood Development: Hon. J. Alan McIsaac
Minister of Innovation and Advanced Learning: Hon. Allen F. Roach

Ministries
Office of the Premier, Fifth Floor, Shaw Building, 95 Rochford Street, P.O. Box 2000, Charlottetown, PE, C1A 7N8, Canada. Tel. +1 902 368 4400, fax: +1 902 368 4416, URL: http://www.gov.pe.ca/premier/
Department of Agriculture and Forestry, Fifth Floor, Jones Building, 11 Kent Street, PO Box 2000, Charlottetown, PEI, C1A 7N8, Canada. Tel: +1 902 368 4880, fax: +1 902 368 4857, URL: http://www.gov.pe.ca/af/index.php3
Office of the Attorney General, Fourth Floor, Shaw Building, 95 Rochford Street, PO Box 2000, Charlottetown, PEI, C1A 7N8, Canada. Tel: +1 902 368 4550, fax: +1 902 368 4910, URL: http://www.gov.pe.ca/oag/index.php3
Department of Tourism, PO Box 2000, Charlottetown, PE, C1A 7N8, Canada. Tel: +1 902 368 5540, fax: +1 902 368 4438, URL: http://www.gov.pe.ca/tourism/index.php3
Department of Education, Second Floor, Sullivan Building, 16 Fitzroy Street, PO Box 2000, Charlottetown, PEI, C1A 7N8, Canada. Tel: +1 902 368 4610, fax: +1 902 368 4699, URL: http://www.gov.pe.ca/education/index.php3
Department of Community and Cultural Affairs, PO Box 2000, Charlottetown, PEI, CIA 7N8, Canada. Tel: +1 902 368 5250, fax: +1 902 368 4121, URL: http://www.gov.pe.ca/commcul/index.php3
Department of Fisheries, Aquaculture and Environment, Fourth Floor, Jones Building, 11 Kent Street, PO Box 2000, Charlottetown, PEI, C1A 7N8, Canada. Tel: +1 902 368 5000, fax: +1 902 368 5830, URL: http://www.gov.pe.ca/fa/index.php3
Department of Health and Social Services, Second Floor, Jones Building, 11 Kent Street, PO Box 2000, Charlottetown, PE, C1A 7N8, Canada. Tel: +1 902 368 4900, fax: +1 902 368 4969, URL: http://www.gov.pe.ca/health/index.php3
Department of Transportation and Public Works, Second and Third Floors, Jones Building, 11 Kent Street, PO Box 2000, Charlottetown, PEI, C1A 7N8, Canada. Tel: +1 902 368 5120, fax: +1 902 368 5385, URL: http://www.gov.pe.ca/tpw/index.php3
Department of Innovation and Advanced Learning, Shaw Building, 5th Floor, 105 Rochford Street, PO Box 2000, Charlottetown, PEI, C1A 7N8, Canada. Tel: +1 902 368 4240, fax: +1 902 368 4242, URL: http://www.gov.pe.ca/ial/index.php3
Provincial Treasury, Second Floor South, Shaw Building, 95 Rochford Street, PO Box 2000, Charlottetown, PEI, C1A 7N8, Canada. Tel: +1 902 368 4050, fax: +1 902 368 6575, URL: http://www.gov.pe.ca/pt/index.php3

Elections
The last provincial general election took place in 2011 when the Liberals won 22 seats and the Progressive Conservative party won 5 seats.

LEGAL SYSTEM
The Supreme Court of Prince Edward Island consists of an Appeal Division and a Trial Division.

The Supreme Court Appeal Division comprises a Chief Justice, The Hon.Chief Justice David H. Jenkins, and two Justices.

The Supreme Court Trial Division comprises a Chief Justice, Jacqueline R. Matheson, four Justices, three Deputy Registrars (Estates, Family and Small Claims), and four Court Clerks. In addition, the Supreme Court is represented in Summerside.

There are also Provincial Courts in Charlottetown, Summerside, Alberton, Souris and Georgetown.

LOCAL GOVERNMENT
The City of Charlottetown has a mayor-council form of municipal government, as does the City of Summerside. The city councillors are elected by residents of voting age within local districts called wards. Everyone of voting age elects the Mayor.

Towns in Prince Edward Island elect a mayor and six councillors every three years, villages have elected village commissioners who are also elected for three years. Prince Edward Island has 75 incorporated municipalities.

AREA AND POPULATION

Area
The province has an area of 5,684 sq. km and is situated in the Gulf of St. Lawrence on the east coast of Canada between New Brunswick and Nova Scotia. It is the smallest province in Canada.

To view a map, please consult http://atlas.nrcan.gc.ca/site/english/maps/reference/provincesterritories. (With permission of Natural Resources Canada 2008, courtesy of the Atlas of Canada)

Population
Figures for mid-2012 put the population of Prince Edward Island at 146,100. Prince Edward Island is divided into three counties: Kings, had a population in 2006 of 18,608; Queens, a population of 72,744; and Prince, a population of 44,499. The chief municipalities with their 2006 populations are Charlottetown, 32,174 and Summerside,14,500. (Source: www.gov.pe.ca)

Births, Marriages, Deaths
In the period 1 July 2011 - 30 June 2012 there were 1,420 births and 1,344 deaths. During the year 1 July 2006 - 30 June 2007 approximately 33,575 immigrated to Prince Edward Island from other Canadian provinces and 3,841 people left Prince Edward Island for other Canadian provinces, 732 foreign immigrants arrived and 27 people emigrated to foreign countries. Provisional figures for 2008 show that there were 831 marriages and in 2005 there were 283 divorces. (Source: Statistics Canada)

Public Holidays 2014
In addition to the standard days celebrated in Canada, Prince Edward Island also celebrates the following:
4 August: Natal Day

EMPLOYMENT
Figures for 2012 show that Prince Edward Island had a total work force of 82,000 of whom 72,800 were employed. During that period the average unemployment rate was 11.3 per cent. The following table shows how the working population were employed in recent years:

Sector	Dec. 2011	Dec. 2012
Agriculture	4,000	4,400
Forestry, fishing, mining, oil & gas	3,500	2,400
Utilities	400	300
Construction	5,300	5,300
Manufacturing	5,300	5,000
Trade	9,300	10,500
Transportation & warehousing	2,400	2,400
Finance, insurance, real estate & leasing	2,700	2,800
Professional, scientific & technical services	3,000	3,200
Business, building & other support services	2,400	2,200
Educational services	5,600	6,900
Health care & social assistance	10,100	9,600
Information, culture & recreation	2,800	3,000
Accommodation & food services	5,800	5,900
Other services	2,700	3,200

CANADA

Public administration   8,200   7,800

Source: Statistics Canada, CANSIM table 282-0088

BANKING AND FINANCE

GDP/GNP, Inflation, National Debt
Expenditure Based GDP

Year	Can$ millions
2004	3,983
2005	4,096
2006	4,315
2007	4,543
2008	4,764
2009	4,909
2010	5,161
2011	5,353

Source: Statistics Canada, CANSIM, table 384-0038

A slowdown in growth in 2001 was recorded and was mainly due to a dry season resulting in a 40 per cent reduction in potato production. Although other sectors of agricultural production grew this was cancelled out by such a large decline. Figures for 2002 show that potato production recovered and a stronger GDP growth was recorded. Figures for 2006 and 2007 put GDP growth at an average of 2.4 per cent and 0.9 per cent in 2008. Figures for 2009 showed that GDP growth contracted by 0.1 per cent and was forecast to grow by 1.9 per cent in 2010. Estimated figures for 2011 show that the economy of Prince Edward Island grew by 1.1 per cent.

Balance of Payments / Imports and Exports
Manufacturing Sales

Year	Can$ millions
2005	1,275.8
2006	1,332.6
2007	1,429.4
2008	1,335.6
2009	1,316.1
2010	1,206.9
2011	1,210.6

Source: Statistics Canada, CANSIM, tables 304-0014 and 304-0015

Food products make up the largest export commodity, which include frozen seafood products, and potato and vegetables. Aerospace products and parts also form an important export commodity.

Chambers of Commerce and Trade Organisations
Canada/Prince Edward Island Business Service Centre, URL: http://www.canadabusiness.ca/
Greater Charlottetown Area Chamber of Commerce, URL: http://www.charlottetownchamber.com/

MANUFACTURING, MINING AND SERVICES

Energy
Prince Edward Island is supplied with electricity from other provinces via an undersea cable that links the island with New Brunswick. Generation on the island itself is in the region of 785 MWh.

Manufacturing
Some two thirds of Prince Edward Island's manufacturing industry is represented by the food industry, mainly potato processing plants. Bakeries, dairies, the feed industry and fish processing are all large sectors in the province. Other growth areas are chemicals, transportation equipment, fabricated metal products and wood. The manufacturing sector contributes about 10 per cent of GDP. The following table shows the value of manufacturing sales in recent years. Figures are in Can$ million:

Industry	2010	2011
Food	659.5	710.7
Wood products	13.9	10.2
Printing & related activities	12.4	12.3
Chemicals	106.9	110.7

Source: Statistics Canada, CANSIM, table 304-0015

Service Industries
Since the opening of the Confederation Bridge between Borden-Carleton, Prince Edward Island and Cape Jourimain, New Brunswick in May 1997 visitor figures have risen dramatically. The bridge has two lanes of traffic and is open continually. It takes approximately 10 minutes to cross.

Agriculture
The total area of farmland in the province occupies approximately 2,830.2 sq km. The following table shows farm cash receipts in Can$ thousands of the main agricultural products.

Product	2009	2010	2011
Potatoes	215,837	199,913	251,966
Cattle & calves	19,104	22,522	21,803
Hogs	10,744	14,706	14,720

Dairy	71,243	71,267	73,94

Source: Statistics Canada CANSIM: Farm Cash Receipts: Table 002-0001

Crop Production in 2011

Crop	Tonne
Wheat	29,80
Oats	10,50
Barley	65,60
Mixed grains	6,50
Soy beans	49,00
Tame hay	249,50
Fodder corn	88,90

Source: Statistics Canada, CANSIM 001-0010 Jan. 2012

The largest cash crop grown in Prince Edward Island is potatoes. In 2001 the crop suffered from a dry season which meant production was down by 40 per cent. Recent figures show that 109,000 acres are given over to potato production. Figures for 2010 show that that the farm cash receipts fell as a result of a fall in potato prices.

Forestry
Forests cover some 280,000 hectares of Prince Edward Island.

Fishing
Main fish harvested include lobster, mussels, salmon, trout and oysters.

COMMUNICATIONS AND TRANSPORT

International Airports
The province's international airport is situated in Charlottetown. Airlines using Charlottetown are Air Canada/Air Nova and Prince Edward Air. Total passenger traffic for 2000 was 166,849.
Charlottetown Airport, URL: http://www.flypei.com/
Summerside Airport, URL: http://www.summersidepei.ca/

Railways
There are bus connections to Prince Edward Island from Moncton, New Brunswick connecting to rail services to Montreal and Halifax.

Roads
There are some 5,300 km of roads of which 3,806 km are paved. Access to Prince Edward Island by road is possible via the 12.9 km Confederation Bridge which links Borden-Carleton, Prince Edward Island, with Cape Jourimain, New Brunswick. The longest bridge in the world over ice, the toll-bridge is open 24 hours a day and takes about ten minutes to cross.

Shipping
Northumberland Ferries links the Island to Caribou, Nova Scotia. The journey, to the Wood Islands port, takes 75 minutes. The ferry runs from May to December, ice permitting. A ferry link also exists between Prince Edward Island and the Magdalen Islands.
Northumberland Ferries Ltd., URL: http://www.nfl-bay.com

HEALTH

The approved health care bed ratio is 22.3 per 1,000 population. There are nine hospitals in the province, two of which are in Charlottetown, and 17 clinics, five of which are in Charlottetown.

EDUCATION

Figures for recent years show a decline in the number of students enrolled in general education: 20,813 in the 2007-08 school year falling to 19,955 in the 2009-10 school year. Expenditure per student in public general education in 2008-09 was Can$10,210.

There is one university, University of Prince Edward Island, in Charlottetown. The post-secondary sector also includes a veterinary college and a Master of Science programme, all in Charlottetown. Holland College provides training for employment in business, applied arts and technology, with approximately 13 campuses province-wide offering professional and vocational career programmes.

COMMUNICATIONS AND MEDIA

Newspapers
Newspapers and magazines published in the province include, Coffee News PEI, Pomeroy's, The Buzz, Voice for Island Seniors, Island Edition, Island Web Classifieds, The Arc Quarterly and Write Me (Young Writers of PEI). Other newspapers include The PEI Times, Atlantic Fish Farming, Atlantic Gig, Eastern Graphic, Island Farmer, West Prince Graphic, The Beacon and La Voix Acadienne (http://journaux.apf.ca/lavoixacadienne/). The Guardian (http://www.theguardian.pe.ca/) and the Journal Pioneer (http://www.journalpioneer.com/) are published daily.

Broadcasting
Television networks operate in Charlottetown: ATV/ASN, CBC Prince Edward Island. In Summerside one community channel operates: Eastlink Community Television.
ATV/ASN, URL: http://www.ctvnews.com
CBC Prince Edward Island, URL: http://www.charlottetown.cbc.ca

A total of six radio broadcast stations operate in the province, five of them on the capital and one in Summerside.

Telecommunications

Telecommunications companies operate from Charlottetown: IslandTelecom and IslandTelMobility. There are five internet service providers in the province: AT&T Canada, Island Services Network, Island Telecom, Auracom and Eastlink.

QUEBEC

Capital: Quebec (Population estimate: 490,000)

Lieutenant-Governor: Hon. Pierre Duchesne (page 1418)

Provincial Flag: Four fleur-de-lis on a blue background with a white cross.

CONSTITUTION AND GOVERNMENT

Constitution

Quebec was one of the original four provinces, and entered the confederation in 1867. Since this time Quebec has questioned its membership in the Canadian confederation and over the last two decades the question of sovereignty has been much debated.

The Quebec charter of Human Rights and Freedoms guarantees every citizen, regardless of race, gender or religion, the right to equal recognition and equal exercise of democratic rights. The charter also recognizes freedom of speech and peaceful assembly. Various commissions and acts have been created to protect these rights.

Quebec's parliamentary system is based on the British model. The National Assembly (parliament) is made up of 125 members elected by universal suffrage, each representing an electoral division. Executive power is exercised by the Prime Minister and cabinet who administer legislation and regulate matters. The assembly is elected for five years. Members are elected under a single-member constituency plurality system. All citizens 18 years of age and over are entitled to vote.

Recent Events

Quebec is a predominantly French speaking province and in 1995 a referendum was held on independence for the province. This resulted in a narrow victory of only 1 per cent for the 'No' vote.

In November 2006, the federal parliament of Canada agreed a proposal put forward by Prime Minister Harper that the Quebecois should be considered a 'nation' within a United Canada. The proposal was put to a vote and was approved by 266 votes to 16.

In December 2007, an agreement was signed between the governments of Canada and Quebec and representatives of the Inuit region of Quebec. The agreement will give the Inuit semi-autonomous status with a regional assembly responsible for areas such as education and health. The agreement was expected to come into force in 2009 but outstanding land claims were only resolved in 2011. A referendum on a regional government for the Inuit region of Nunavik was rejected in 2011 and negotiations are expected to continue.

Legislature

National Assembly, Reception and Information Service, Parliament Building, Office 0.190, Québec, G1A 1A4, Canada. Tel: +1 418 643 7239, fax: +418 646 4271, email: accueil@assnat.qc.ca, URL: http://www.assnat.qc.ca/eng

Although the province has no upper house, it is represented on the Canadian Senate. The following members of the Quebec political parties are also Canadian Senators: Diane Nellemare, Patrick Brazeau, Pierre-Hugues Boisvenu, Claude Carignan, Andrée Champagne, Jean-Guy Dagenais, Roméo Dallaire, Dennis Dawson, Pierre De Bané, Jacques Demers, Suzanne Fortin-Duplessis, Joan Fraser, Céline Hervieux-Payette, Leo Housakos, Serge Joyal, Ghislain Maltais, Paul Massicotte, Pierre Claude Nolin, Michel Rivard, Jean-Claude Rivest, Judith Seidman, Larry Smith, Josee Verner, and Charlie Watt.

Cabinet (as at June 2013)

Premier: Pauline Marois (page 1471)
Deputy Premier, Minister of Agriculture, Fisheris and Food: François Gendron
Minister responsible for Government Affairs; responsible for Saguenay-Lac-Saint-Jean: Stéphane Bédard
Minister for Finance & Economy; responsible for Solidarity; for the Capital Nation region and the Chaudière-Appalaches region: Agnès Maltais
Minister of International Relations, Francophonie and Exterior Trade, responsible for Montreal: Jean-François Lisée
Minister for the Family; Minister responsible for the Laval region: Nicole Léger
Minister for Education, Leisure, Sport: Marie Malavoy
Minister responsible for Democratic Institutions & Civic Participation: Bernard Drainville
Minister for Transport; Municpal Affairs; Regions; and Land Management: Sylvain Gaudreault
Minister of Culture & Communications: Maka Kotto
Minister of Justice: Bertramd St-Arnaud
Minister of Health & Social Services; responsible for the Elderly and for the Estrie Region: Réjean Hébert
Deputy Minister, Intergovernmental Canadian Affairs, Francophone Canadian Matters and Canadian Sovereignty: Alexandre Cloutier
Minister of Natural Resources: Martine Ouellet
Minister of Higher Education, Research, Science & Technology: Pierre Duchesne
Minister of Immigration and Cultural Communities: Diane de Courcey
Minister of Sustainable Development, Envionrment, Fauna and Parks: Yves-François Blanchet

Minister of Public Security, responsible for the Outaouis region: Stéphane Bergeron
Deputy Minister, Social Services & Youth Protection: Véronique Hivon
Deputy Minister, Tourism; responsible for the Bas-Saint-Laurent Region: Pascal Bérubé
Deputy Minister, Economic Development Bank of Quebec: Elaine Zakaib
Deputy Minister, Regions; responsbile for the Gaspésie-Iles-de-la-Madeleine: Gaétan Lelièvre
Also attend cabinet:
Chief Government Whip: Marjolain Dufour
Chair of Government Caucus: Sylvain Pagé

Ministries

Office of the Lieutenant-Governor, URL: http://www.lieutenant-gouverneur.qc.ca/index.html
Office of the Premier, URL: http://www.premier-ministre.gouv.qc.ca/
Ministry of Agriculture, Fisheries and Food, 200-A, chemin Sainte-Foy, 12e étage, Québec, G1R 4X6, Canada. Tel: +1 418 380 2100, fax: +1 418 643 8422, email: info@agr.gou.qc.ca, URL: http://www.agr.gouv.qc.ca
Ministry for Canadian Intergovernmental Affairs, 875, Grande Allée Est, Bureau 2.600, Québec, G1R 4Y8, Canada. Tel: +1 418 646 5950, fax: +1 418 643 8730, URL: http://www.pco-bcp.gc.ca/aia/index.asp?lang=eng
Ministry of Child and Family Welfare, 600 rue Fullum, Montréal, QC, H2K 457, Canada. Tel: +1 514 873 2322, URL: http://www.mfe.gouv.qc.ca
Ministry of Culture and Communications, 225, Grande Allée Est, Québec, G1R 5G5, Canada. Tel: +1 418 380 2300, fax: +1 418 380 2364, URL: http://www.mcc.gouv.qc.cq
Ministry of Education and Youth, 1035, rue de la Chevrotière, Édifice Marie-Guyart, 16e étage, Québec, G1R 5A5, Canada. Tel: +1 418 643 7095, fax: +1 418 646 6561, email: cim.rens@meq.gouv,qc.ca, URL: http://www.meq.gouv.qc.ca
Ministry of the Environment, Édifice Marie-Guyart, 675, boulevard René-Lévesque Est, Québec, G1R 5V7, Canada. Tel: +1 418 643 8259, fax: +1 418 646 5974, email: info@menv.gouv.qc.ca, URL: http://www.menv.gouv.qc.ca
Ministry of Finance, 12, rue Saint-Louis, 1er étage, Québec, G1R 5L3, Canada. Tel: +1 418 691 2233, fax: +1 418 646 1631, URL: http://www.finances.gouv.qc.ca
Ministry of Public Works and Government Services, Édifice "H", 875, Grande Allée Est, Bureau 1.64, Québec (Québec), G1R 5R8, Canada. Tel: +1 418 646 3018, fax: +1 418 646 3730, URL: http://www.tpsgc-pwgsc.gc.ca/comm/index-eng.html
Ministry of Health and Social Services, 1075, chemin Sainte-Foy, 15e étage, Édifice Catherine-de-Longpré, Québec, G1S 2M1, Canada. Tel: +1 418 646 7343, fax: +1 418 644 4534, URL: http://www.msss.gouv.qc.ca
Ministry of Industry and Trade, 710, Place d'Youville, 6e étage, Québec, G1R 4Y4, Canada. Tel: +1 418 691 5650, fax: +1 418 644 0118, email: info@mic.gouv.qc.ca. URL: http://www.mic.gouv.qc.ca
Ministry of International Relations, 525, boul. René-Lévesque Est, 4e étage, Québec, G1R 5R9, Canada. Tel: +1 418 649 2319, fax: +1 418 643 4804, URL: http://www.mri.gouv.qc.ca
Ministry of Justice, Edifice Louis-Phillippe-Pigeon, 1200, route de l'Église, 6e étage, Sainte-Foy, G1V 4M1, Canada. Tel: +1 418 643 5140, fax: +1 418 646 4449, email: communications.justice@justice.gouv.qc.ca, URL: http://www.justice.gouv.qc.cq
Ministry of Labour and Social Security, 425 rue Saint-Amable, Québec, G1R 5Si, Canada. Tel: +1 418 643 4721, fax: +1 418 643 4855, email: DBRP@mess.gouv.qc.ca, URL: http://www.mess.gouv.qc.ca
Ministry of Municipal Affairs and Greater Montréal, Édifice Cook-Chauveau, 20, rue Pierre-Olivier-Chauveau, 3e étage, Secteur B, Québec, G1R 4J3, Canada. Tel: +1 418 691 2050, fax: +1 418 643 1795
Ministry of Natural Resources, 5700, 4e Avenue Ouest, Bureau A-308, Charlesbourg, G1H 6R1, Canada. Tel: +1 418 637 8600, fax: +1 418 643 0720, email: service.citoyens@mrn.gouv.qc.ca, URL: http://www.mrn.gouv.qc.ca
Ministry of Public Security, 2525, boulevard Laurier, Tour des Laurentides, 5e étage, Sainte-Foy (Québec), G1V 2L2, Canada. Tel: +1 418 643 2112, fax: +1 418 646 6168, URL: http://www.msp.gouv.qc.ca
Ministry of Regions, 900 place d'Youville, 5e étage, Edifice André-Laurendeau, Québec, G1R 3P7, Canada. Tel: +1 418 643 0060, fax: +1 418 644 5610, URL: http://www.mreg.gouv.qc.ca
Ministry of Cultural Communities and Immigration, Edifice Gérald-Godin, 360 rue McGill, Montréal, Québec, G1R 5E6, Canada. Tel: +1 514 873 8624, URL: http://www.mrci.gouv.qc.ca
Ministry of Research, Science and Technology, Edifice Gérard-D. Levesque, 12 rue Saint-Louis, 1er étage, Québec, GR 5L3, Canada. URL: http://www.mrst.gouv.qc.ca
Ministry of Transport, 700, boul. René-Lévesque Est, Place Haute-Ville, 27e étage, Québec, G1R 5H1, Canada. Tel: +1 418 643 6864, fax: +1 418 643 1269, email: communications@mtq.gouv.qc.ca, URL: http://www.mtq.gouv.qc.ca

Political Parties

Parti libéral du Québec (Quebec Liberal Party), URL: http://www.plq.org
Action démocratique du Québec, URL: http://www.adq.qc.ca
Parti Québécois, URL: http://www.pq.qc.ca
Parti vert du Québec (Green Party of Quebec), URL: http://ww.pvq.qc.ca
Québec solidaire, URL: http://www.quebecsolidaire.net
Parti démocratie chrétienne du Québec, URL: http://www.partidcq.qc.ca
Coalition Avenir Québec party, URL: http://www.coalitionavenirquebec.org

CANADA

Elections
The most recent general election took place on 4 September 2012. Parti Québécois were elected to a minority government with 54 seats and leader Pauline Marois became the first female Premier of Quebec. The Quebec Liberal Party came second with 50 seats and the newly formed Coalition Avenir Québec party came third with 19 seats. The Québec Solidaire party won two seats.

Diplomatic Representation
Quebec Delegation, 59 Pall Mall, London, SW1Y 5JH, United Kingdom. Tel: +44 (0)20 7766 5900, URL: http://www.quebec.org.uk
Bureau du Quebec, 1101 17th Street, North West, Suite 1006, Washington, DC 20036, USA. Tel: +1 202 659 8991, URL: http://www.quebec-washington.org

LEGAL SYSTEM

The court system comprises Legal Courts (the Québec Court of Appeal, the Québec Superior Court, and the Court of Québec); Municipal Courts; Administrative tribunals; and Specialized Courts.

The Courts of Justice Act stipulates that the Québec Superior Court is made up of 143 judges appointed by the federal government. It has two regional divisions one for western Québec and the other for eastern Québec. A chief justice, an associate justice and an assistant justice preside over the Superior Court.

The Québec Court of Appeal is the general appeal court in Québec. It is made up of 20 judges appointed by the federal government. It sits in Montréal and Québec City. A chief justice, also the chief justice of the Court of Appeal, presides over the Court of Appeal.

The Court of Quebec is the court of original jurisdiction and has three divisions: Civil, Penal and Youth.

LOCAL GOVERNMENT

Québec has 17 administrative regions: Bas-Saint-Laurent; Saguenay-Lac-Saint-Jean; Capitale-Naitonale; Mauricie; Estrie; Montréal; Outaouais; Abitibi-Témiscamingue; Côte-Nord; Nord du Québec; Gaspésie-Iles de la Madeleine; Chaudière-Appalaches; Laval; Lanaudière; Laurentides; Montérégie; Centre-du-Québec.

For municipal management, land management and development Quebec is divided into approximately 1,398 municipalities, 96 regional council municipalities, three urban communities, and one regional government.

Local municipalities are administered by a mayor and councillors who are elected. They exercise power in finance, environment, sanitation, health, recreation, urban planning, transport, and territorial development.

Municipalities within regions form regional council municipalities (RCM) which are headed by a council composed of mayors of the member municipalities. RCMs are responsible for regional plans, urban development and intermunicipal infrastructures.

Three urban communities have been set up by special legislation in Montreal, Quebec and the Outaouais region. These urban communities cover 50 municipalities and work in collaboration with the member municipalities.

The Kativik Regional Government (KRG) has been set up to administer the territory north of the 55th parallel. This encompasses 14 northern villages, one Naskapi village and a non-organised territory. The KRG has special powers which include responsibility for local administration, police services, transportation, communications, training and homes construction.

AREA AND POPULATION

Area
The area of Quebec is 1,667,926 sq. km with a varied terrain and climate. It is bordered by Ontario to the west, Newfoundland and Labrador to the east, New Brunswick to the south east and by the United States of America in the south. It is almost completely surrounded by water, by Hudson Strait to the north, James Bay and Hudson Bay to the west and the St. Lawrence River and Gulf to the south.

To view a map, please consult http://atlas.nrcan.gc.ca/site/english/maps/reference/provincesterritories. (With permission of Natural Resources Canada 2008, courtesy of the Atlas of Canada)

Population
The population in 2012 was 8,054,800, over 50 per cent of the population is urban. Figures for 2002 show that the city of Montréal had the largest number of inhabitants at 3,548,800, Ottawa-Hull had a population of 1,128,900 and Québec a population of 697,800. Both French and English are spoken although the population is mainly French-speaking with figures from the 2001 census putting the number of French speakers at 5,761,765 compared to 557,040 English speakers. Other languages spoken include Italian, Arabic and Chinese. There are estimated to be 600,000 immigrants and 71,400 indigenous peoples, including 63,000 Amerindians and 8,000 Inuit who live in the northernmost regions of the state. (Source: Bureau de la statistique du Québec and Statistics Canada)

Births, Marriages, Deaths
In the year June 2011-July 2012 there were 88,500 births and 59,500 deaths. During the year June 2006-July 2007, 26,263 immigrants arrived from other Canadian provinces and 41,831 Quebecois left for other provinces, 45,082 foreign immigrants arrived and 6,687 people emigrated to foreign countries. Quebec. Provisional figures for 2008 show that 22,050 marriages took place and in 2005, 15,423 divorces were granted. (Source: Statistics Canada, www.statcan.ca)

Public Holidays 2014
In addition to the standard days celebrated in Canada, Quebec also celebrates the following:
2 January: New Year
19 May: Victoria Day
24 June: Saint-Jean-Baptiste Day
13 October: Thanksgiving Day

EMPLOYMENT

Of a population of over 8.0 million, Quebec had a labour force in 2012 of 4,320,300. The number of employed was 3,984,400, of whom 335,900 were unemployed, giving an unemployment rate of 7.8 per cent. The following table shows the distribution by industry of employed persons in recent years.

Industry	Dec. 2011	Dec. 2012
Agriculture	55,800	56,400
Forestry, fishing, mining, oil & gas	37,500	34,100
Utilities	57,500	25,300
Construction	228,600	250,300
Manufacturing	477,400	506,800
Trade	636,200	629,800
Transportation & warehousing	179,700	164,500
Finance, insurance, real estate & leasing	218,300	231,100
Professional, scientific & technical services	300,100	296,600
Business, building & other support services	139,600	153,100
Educational services	281,000	303,200
Health care & social assistance	490,900	571,200
Information, culture & recreation	157,400	186,700
Accommodation & food services	257,500	228,800
Other services	183,600	179,500
Public administration	238,000	226,700

Source: Statistics Canada CANSIM Table 282-0088, Feb. 2013

BANKING AND FINANCE

GDP/GNP, Inflation, National Debt
The following table shows Quebec's expenditure-based GDP in recent years.

Year	GDP in Can$ millions
2004	262,761
2005	272,049
2006	282,505
2007	306,317
2008	314,135
2009	316,276
2010	330,400
2011	345,842

Source: Statistics Canada, CANSIM, table 384-0038 Feb. 2013

In terms of GDP by sector, services (28 per cent), manufacturing (19 per cent), finance, insurance and real estate (14 per cent), and commerce (11.6 per cent) are the major sectors.

Foreign Investment
Major investors in the province include the US, Sweden, Germany, the Netherlands, the UK and France. Major industries include aerospace, information technology, petrochemical and health. (Source: Bureau de la Statistique du Québec)

Balance of Payments / Imports and Exports
The USA, the UK France and Germany are Quebec's largest foreign trade markets. Goods exported include telecommunication goods, aerospace parts, clothes, forestry products, electricity, leather goods and chemical goods. Imports include cars and car parts, electronic goods and semi-conductors, crude oil, chemical products, manufactured goods and clothing.

MANUFACTURING, MINING AND SERVICES

Primary and Extractive Industries
Quebec is among the world's top mineral producers. Over two thirds of its mining production comes from gold, iron, asbestos, copper, niobium and zinc. It is also one of the world's top producers of peat. It has roughly 30 mines, 158 exploration firms and 15 primary processing industries.

In 2011 it was announced that an area of 1.2 million sq km in the north of the province (Plan Nord) would be made available as an area to be developed for mining and renewable energy. It is believed that the area is rich in deposits of nickel, cobalt, platinum, zinc, iron ore and rare earth minerals.

The following table shows selected mineral and fuel production by value in 2007.

Mineral Production

Product	Can$ million
Copper	167.3
Gold	649.2
Nickel	994.6
Silver	85.7
Zinc	374.2
Sand & gravel	79.2

Source: Statistics Canada: www40.statcan.gc.ca/l01/cst01/envi38b-eng.htm Jan. 2012

Energy

Over the last two decades there have been major changes in the energy sector. In 1970 oil accounted for almost 75 per cent of the energy market. By 1993, electricity had become the main energy source with more than 50 per cent of the market share compared to 41.2 per cent for oil. Quebec is one of three main producers of crude oil. Recent figures show that the province's capacity is over 369,000 billion barrels per day.

Natural gas has increased its share to 16 per cent. Quebec could become a major gas exporter. Gaz Metropolitan and IPL Energy are currently building a Can$1.3 billion pipeline from Sable Island to the northeast of the US. The pipeline will extend the TransQuebec and Maritimes pipeline.

Alongside Ontario, Quebec produces more than 50 per cent of Canada's total electricity. Total sales of electricity were recently Can$6.8 billion, and over 40,000 jobs are based in this industry. Due to the number of waterways in Quebec more than 90 per cent of Quebec's electricity is produced by hydroelectric plants, the rest mainly coming from nuclear power. Most electricity is produced by a government corporation called Hydro-Quebec which together with Newfoundland and Labrador Hydro is planning a dam on the Churchill River along the boundaries of Quebec and Newfoundland which will cost US$4 billion and produce 3,000 MW. Hydro Quebec also owns a nuclear reactor situated at the Gentilly site. The province also has a wind power generation plant, Le Nordais, capable of producing 100 MW.

Manufacturing

Over 20 per cent of the work force is employed in this sector. Manufacturing sales in 2006 were $146,580.0 million rising to Can$144,342.3 million in 2007, Can$147,293.2 million in 2008 and Can$126,568.1 million.

Quebec's primary metal processing industry is strong on foreign markets; exports in this sector recently accounted for 80 per cent of all shipments. 14 per cent of the world's aluminium is produced in Quebec.

Other large manufacturing industries include the chemical and petrochemical industries, the aerospace industry, Information Technology and communications. 38,000 people are employed in the aerospace industry.

Manufacturing Shipments by Subsector, figures in Can$ millions

Industry	2010	2011
Food	19,466.8	20,217.4
Beverage & tobacco products	3,478.4	3,557.8
Textile mills	773.1	819.3
Textile mill products	441.4	420.9
Clothing	1,298.1	1,296.9
Leather & allied products	205.3	172.6
Wood products	5,554.8	5,149.1
Paper	8,758.2	8,638.1
Printing & related support activities	2,533.0	2,419.5
Petroleum & coal products	14,838.7	15,741.0
Chemicals	9,634.6	8,910.6
Plastics & rubber products	5,484.9	5,790.9
Non-metallic mineral products	3,302.9	3,392.9
Primary metals	19,283.1	21,982.3
Fabricated metal products	7,060.4	7,378.1
Machinery	5,474.5	6,150.2
Computer & electronic products	2,994.2	3,293.9
Electrical equipment appliances and components	3,438.8	3,380.0
Transportation equipment	12,585.1	15,006.4
Furniture & related products	3,230.3	3,208.7
Miscellaneous manufacturing	2,279.4	2,265.9

Source: Statistics Canada, www.statcan.gc.ca/tables-tableaux/sum-som/l01/cst01/manuf33f-eng.htm Feb. 2013

Service Industries

The service sector accounts for over 70 per cent of employment in Quebec mainly in services, commerce, government, finance and insurance, real estate, transportation and communications. These jobs are concentrated in Montreal and Quebec. Both Quebec and Montreal are major financial centres. The Montreal Stock Exchange is the second-ranking Canadian stock exchange and is in the top ten world-wide for price-earnings ratio.

Tourism

Over 20 million tourists visit Quebec each year.
Tourisme Québec, URL: http://www.tourisme.gouv.qc.ca / http://www.bonjourquebec.com

Agriculture

Quebec's broad range of agricultural products is based primarily on dairy, cattle (beef), grain and oilseed, hog and fruit. 58,000 people are involved in farming. Figures for 2010 show that Quebec had 23,075 farms.

Principal Field Crop Production, figures in Tonnes

Crop	2011	2012
Barley	196,000	234,000
Canola	36,000	33,000
Corn for grain	3,125,000	3,505,000
Oats	223,000	220,000
Soybeans	800,000	825,000
Wheat, all	116,000	160,000
Wheat, spring	106,000	142,500
Wheat, winter remaining	10,000	17,500

Source: Statistics Canada: CANSIM 001-0010 Feb. 2013

The following table shows number of livestock in July 2006.

Livestock	'000 head
Dairy cows	400.0
Beef cows	225.0
Calves	472.0
Pigs	4,060.0
Sheep	167.3
Lambs	112.7
Hens & chickens (2005)	162,642
Eggs (thousand dozen)	104,110

Source: Adapted from Statistics Canada www.statcan.ca, February 2007

Forestry plays an essential part in the province's economy - recent sales figures of wood and paper were over Can$12 billion, and make up 20 per cent of the territory's exports. Some 50 per cent of the land mass is taken with commercial forests. Most of the forest is under government jurisdiction and there are environmental regulations.

COMMUNICATIONS AND TRANSPORT

National Airlines
Air Inuit, URL: http://www.airinuit.com

International Airports
There are three international airports in Quebec: Montreal-Trudeau (formerly Dorval) (URL: http://www.admtl.com) and Montreal-Mirabel at Montreal and Jean-Lesage at Quebec (URL: http://www.aeroportdequebec.com), and some 100 local and regional airports. Some 9 million passengers use the airports each year.

Railways
Two Canadian companies operate 85 per cent of Quebec's rail system: the Canadian National operates 5,000 km and Canadian Pacific operates 2,200 km. Passenger transport in Quebec's main regions is managed by a government-owned company (Via Rail Canada).

Roads
There are over 164,000 km of roads of which some 2,000 km are main roads linking Quebec to Canada and the US. More than 4 million vehicles are registered.

Ports and Harbours
The main ports are Sept-Iles, Port-Cartier, Montreal and Quebec City. One third of Canada's maritime traffic uses Quebec's ports.
The following ports are administered by the Canadian Ports Corporation:
Port of Sept-Iles, URL: http://www.portsi.com
Port Saguenay/Baie des Ha Ha, URL: http://www.portsaguenay.ca/
Port of Trois-Rivières URL: http://www.porttr.com
The local port corporations are located at:
Montreal Port Corporation, URL: http://www.port-montreal.com
Port of Quebec Corporation, URL: http://www.portquebec.ca/

Total port traffic has increased at the port of Quebec by 11 per cent in the past year to almost 18 million tonnes. Higher volumes of dry bulk commodities and liquid bulk traffic were handled during this period. Total port traffic decreased at the Port of Montreal by 4 per cent to some 19 million tonnes.

HEALTH

Health services are provided free of charge throughout Quebec. Total spending on health in 2009 was put at Can$15,990,403 thousand. There are 18 regional boards that are responsible for the organisation of health care.

There are over 21,500 health care professionals practicing in Quebec, including over 16,000 physicians. Over 240,000 people are employed in the health and social services network. The population/physician ratio is over 400:1.

The approved beds in health care institutions ratio was recently 13.7 per 1,000 population. The hospital bed ratio is 4.4 per 1,000 population.

EDUCATION

Like the French-speaking majority English-speaking Quebecois have their own free public education system. Although the Charter of the French language stipulates that French must be the language of instruction in Quebec from kindergarten to the end of secondary school, children whose mother tongue is English are entitled to be educated in English.

CANADA

The education system is composed of four levels: primary (including pre-school), secondary, college and university. Although pre-school education is not compulsory, about 98 per cent of all children go to kindergarten. Education is compulsory from ages 6 to 16. The usual duration of primary school is six years. Secondary school, which lasts five years, is divided into the general stream, leading to further studies, and the vocational stream, which enables students to enter the labour market. Cegep (Colleges d'enseignement général et professionnel) programs leading to university studies last two years and those leading to vocational certification, three years.

Figures for recent years show a decline in the number of students enrolled in general education but for the first time in more than 10 years figures rose from 1,188,853 in the 2007-08 school year to 1,189,790 in the 2009-10 school year. Expenditure per student in public general education in 2009-10 was Can$11,404.

COMMUNICATIONS AND MEDIA

Newspapers
There are 12 daily papers and over 200 weeklies. Top newspapers include:
Le Journal de Montréal, URL: http://www.canoe.com/journaldemontreal/
La Presse, URL: http://www.cyberpresse.ca/actualites/regional/montreal/

Broadcasting
There are four major French-language networks (Radio-Canada, Radio-Québec, TVA and Télévision Quatre-Saisons) broadcasting through 30 stations across Quebec and three English-language stations. 90 per cent of Quebec households have access to cable television. There are 135 radio stations, the majority of which are publicly owned.
CFJP-TV Montreal, URL: http://www.tqs.ca/accueil/
CFAP-TV Quebec City, URL: http://www.tqs.ca/accueil/
Tele-Quebec, URL: http://www.telequebec.tv/ (educational)

SASKATCHEWAN

Capital: Regina (Population estimate: 179,000)

Lieutenant-Governor: Vaughn Solomon Schofield (page 1517)

Provincial Flag: Two horizontal bands of equal width, green and yellow, with the coat of arms in the top left corner and a flower on the right side.

CONSTITUTION AND GOVERNMENT

Constitution
Saskatchewan was admitted to the Dominion of Canada in September 1905.

Upper House
Although the province has no upper house, it is represented on the Canadian Senate. The following members of the Saskatchewan political parties are also Canadian Senators: Raynell Andreychuk, Lillian Eva Dyck, Pana Merchant, David Tkachuk and Pamela Wallin.

Legislature
The Assembly has 58 elected members.
Speaker: Hon. Dan D'Autremont
Legislative Building, 2405 Legislative Drive, Regina, Saskatchewan, S4S 0B3 Canada. Tel: +1 306 787 2376, fax: +1 306 787-1558, URL: http://www.legassembly.sk.ca

---

Cabinet (as at June 2013)
Premier, President of the Executive Council, Minister of Intergovernmental Affairs: Hon. Brad Wall
Deputy Premier and Minister of Finance: Hon. Ken Krawetz (page 1458)
Minister of Advanced Education; Labour Relations and Workplace: Hon. Don Morgan QC
Minister of Crown Investments: Hon. Donna Harpauer
Minister of Corrections and Policing: Hon. Christine Tell
Minister of Health: Hon. Dustin Duncan
Minister of Justice and Attorney General, Deputy Government House Leader: Hon. Gordon Wyant (page 1540)Q.C.
Minister of Government Relations, Minister of First Nation and Metis and Northern Affairs: Hon. Jim Reiter
Minister of Energy and Resources, Minister Responsible for Trade and Tourism Saskatchewan: Hon. Tim McMillan
Minister of Agriculture: Hon. Lyle Stewart
Minister of Environment: Hon. Ken Cheveldayoff
Minister of Highways and Infrastructure: Hon. Don McMorris
Minister of Social Services: Hon. June Draude
Minister of Parks, Culture and Sport: Hon. Kevin Doherty
Minister Responsible for Rural and Remote Health: Hon. Randy Weekes
Minister of Central Services: Hon. Nancy Heppner
Minister of Education: Hon. Russ Marchuk
Minister of the Economy: Hon. Bill Boyd

Ministries
Office of the Premier, Room 226, Legislative Building, Regina, SK, S4S 0B3, Canada. Tel: +1 306 787 9433, fax: +1 306 787 0885, URL: http://www.premier.gov.sk.ca/
Ministry of Agriculture, 3085 Albert Street, Regina, Saskatchewan, S4S 0B1, Canada. Tel: +1 306 787 5140, fax: +1 306 787 2393, URL: http://www.agriculture.gov.sk.ca/
Ministry of Advanced Education, URL: http://www.ae.gov.sk.ca/
Ministry of Central Services, URL: http://www.cs.gov.sk.ca/
Ministry of Education, 5th Floor, 2220 College Avenue, Regina, SK S4P 3V7, Canada. Tel: +1 306 787 7071, fax: +1 306 787 1300, URL: http://www.education.gov.sk.ca/
Ministry of Environment, 3211 Albert Street, Regina, Saskatchewan, S4S 5W6, Canada. Tel: +1 306 787 0393, fax: +1 306 787 0395, URL: http://www.environment.gov.sk.ca/
Ministry of Finance, 2350 Albert Street, Regina, SK, S4P 4A6, Canada. Tel: +1 306 787 6768, fax: +1 306 787 6544, URL: http://www.finance.gov.sk.ca/
Minister of Government Relations, URL: http://www.gr.gov.sk.ca/
Ministry of Health, T.C. Douglas Building, 3475 Albert Street, Regina, Saskatchewan, S4S 6X6, Canada. Tel: +1 306 787 3696, fax: +1 306 787 8310, URL: http://www.health.gov.sk.ca
Ministry of Highways and Transportation, 1855 Victoria Avenue, Regina, Sk. S4P 3V5, Canada. Tel: +1 306 787 4800, fax: +1 306 787 9777, URL: http://www.highways.gov.sk.ca

Ministry of First Nations and Métis Relations, 2nd Floor, 1855 Victoria Avenue Regina, SK, S4P 3V7, Canada. Tel: +1 306 787 6250 URL: http://www.fnmr.gov.sk.ca
Ministry of Justice and Attorney General's Office, 1874 Scarth Street Regina, Saskatchewan, S4P 3V7, Canada. Tel: +1 306 787 8971, fax: +1 306 787 5830, URL: http://www.justice.gov.sk.ca/
Ministry of Labour Relations and Workplace Safety, Room 345, Legislative Building, Regina, Saskatchewan, S4S 0B3, Canada. Tel: +1 306 787 1117, fax: +1 306 787 6946, URL: http://www.lrws.gov.sk.ca/
Ministry of Parks, Culture, and Sport, 4th floor - 1919 Saskatchewan Drive Regina, SK S4P 3V7, Canada. Tel: +1 306 787 5729, fax: +1 306 798 0033, URL: http://www.pcs.gov.sk.ca/
Ministry of Social Services, URL: http://www.socialservices.gov.sk.ca/

Elections
The most recent elections were held in November 2011. The Saskatchewan Party won 49 seats and the New Democratic Party won 9 seats.

LEGAL SYSTEM

Saskatchewan Court of Appeal Court House, 2425 Victoria Avenue, Regina, Saskatchewan S4P 3V7, Canada. Tel: +1 306 787-5382, fax: +1 306 787-5815, URL: http://www.sasklawcourts.ca
Chief Justice Hon. J. Klebuc
Saskatchewan Court of Queen's Bench sits in 13 communities of Saskatchewan as follows; Assiniboia, Battleford, Estevan, Humboldt, Melfort, Moose Jaw, Prince Albert, Regina, Saskatoon, Swift Current, Weyburn, Wynyard and Yorkton.
Chief Justice: Hon. M. D. Popescul
Provincial Court, situated in 13 main towns and cities as follows: Estevan, La Ronge, Lloydminster, Meadow Lake, Melfort, Moose Jaw, North Battleford, Prince Albert, Regina, Saskatoon, Swift Current, Wynyard and Yorkton. The court also travels to 78 communities.
Chief Justice: C.A. Snell

LOCAL GOVERNMENT

Saskatchewan has 13 cities, 145 towns, 358 villages, 35 northern municipalities and 296 rural municipalities. (Source: Gov't. of Saskatchewan)

AREA AND POPULATION

Area
The area of Saskatchewan is 651,900 sq. km. Situated in the west of Canada, it borders Alberta to the west, Manitoba to the east, the Northwest Territories and Nunavut to the North and the USA, (Montana and North Dakota) to the South.

To view a map, please consult http://atlas.nrcan.gc.ca/site/english/maps/reference/provincesterritories. (With permission of Natural Resources Canada 2008, courtesy of the Atlas of Canada)

Population
Saskatchewan had a population of 1,080,000 in mid 2012, the population in 2001 was 1,000,134 and had been falling until it reached 987,520 in 2006. The figures for 2007 showed the first increase since 2001. The most densely populated cities in 2003 in the province were Saskatoon, with 231,800 inhabitants and Regina, the capital, with 197,000 inhabitants. 76 per cent of the population lives in urban areas. In 2012, 206,100 of the population were aged 14 or under, 715,200 were aged 15 to 64 and 158,700 were aged over 64.

Births, Marriages, Deaths
In the year July 1, 2011 - 30 June 2012 there were 14,801 births and 9,235 deaths. During the period July 1, 2006 - 30 June 2007, 25,903 people from other Canadian provinces emigrated to Saskatchewan and 21,904 people left Saskatchewan for other Canadian provinces. Also during that period 3,086 foreign immigrants arrived and 579 people from Saskatchewan emigrated to foreign countries. (Source: Statistics Canada, URL: http://www.statcan.ca)

In addition to the standard days celebrated in Canada, Saskatchewan also celebrates the following:

Public Holidays 2014
17 February: Family Day
19 May: Victoria Day
4 August: Civic Holiday
13 October: Thanksgiving Day
11 November: Remembrance Day

EMPLOYMENT

Figures for 2012 put the labour force of Saskatchewan at 563,800 of whom 537,100 were employed. 26,700 were unemployed, giving an unemployment rate of 4.7 per cent. The following table shows how the labour force was recently employed.

Employment sector	Dec. 2011	Dec. 2012
Agriculture	38,100	42,000
Forestry, fishing, mining, oil & gas	23,100	26,000
Utilities	5,300	4,800
Construction	42,400	47,300
Manufacturing	26,000	30,100
Trade	84,200	81,900
Transportation & warehousing	25,800	25,500
Finance, insurance, real estate & leasing	30,900	28,200
Professional, scientific & technical services	26,200	24,900
Business building & other support services	12,300	12,900
Educational services	38,900	43,600
Health care & social assistance	70,500	72,200
Information, culture & recreation	17,400	19,300
Accommodation & food services	33,000	28,300
Other services	25,900	24,500
Public administration	27,600	32,900

Source: Statistics Canada CANSIM table 282-0088. Jan. 2013

BANKING AND FINANCE

GDP/GNP, Inflation, National Debt
The following tables show Saskatchewan's expenditure-based GDP in recent years:

Year	Can$ millions
2004	40,796
2005	43,996
2006	45,604
2007	51,964
2008	67,590
2009	60,938
2010	66,036
2011	74,738

Source: Statistics Canada: CANSIM, table 384-0038

Balance of Payments / Imports and Exports
Manufacturing Sales

Year	Can$ millions
2007	10,430.3
2008	13,181.1
2009	11,363.5
2010	10,911.5
2011	12,577.5

Source Statistics Canada, CANSIM, tables 304-0014 and 304-0015

Chambers of Commerce and Trade Organisations
Canada-Saskatchewan Business Service Centre, URL: www.entreprisescanada.ca/sask/

MANUFACTURING, MINING AND SERVICES

Primary and Extractive Industries
Potash, uranium, coal, gold, iron, copper, bentonite, salt, oil and natural gas can be found in Saskatchewan. There are 3,520 crude oil wells drilled producing in 2002 24.4 million cubit metres of oil. Saskatchewan now has 2,134 gas wells and figures for 2002 show that 390 million cubic metres of gas were produced. Major out-of-province crude oil markets include the US, Ontario and Alberta. Figures from 2009 show that Saskatchewan's crude oil reserves were; 152.4 million cubic metres, 81.0 billion cubic metres of natural gas and 271.400 thousand cubic metres of natural gas liquids.

The province has two thirds of the world's reserves of potash and is the leading exporter.

Manufacturing
The following table shows the value of manufacturing sales in millions of Can$ in recent years:

Industry	2010	2011
Food	2,167.6	2,774.5
Wood products	219.2	216.2
Paper	264.4	175.7
Printing & support activities	104.1	102.4
Plastics & rubber products	129.0	133.8
Non-metallic mineral products	166.8	165.9
- continued		
Fabricated metal products	598.5	830.6
Machinery	1,157.6	1,274.3
Chemicals	1,339.7	1,724.8
Furniture & related products	104.1	104.9
Miscellaneous manufacturing	86.0	86.6

Source: Statistics Canada, CANSIM, table 304-0015

Service Industries
Total receipts from foreign visitors in 2003 were Can$443 million, compared with Can$291 million in 1996. Can$294 million of this figure was contributed by Canadian visitors from other provinces whilst Can$149 million was generated by foreign tourists.

Agriculture
Recent statistics put the number of farms in the province at around 36,952, with an average size of 1,668 acres. Major farm products are wheat, other grains (oats, rye, barley) and livestock (cattle, calves, pigs, sheep and lambs).

Production of principal field crops in tonnes is set out in the following table:

Crop	2011
Wheat	11,525,800
Oats	1,557,600
Barley	2,438,500
Rye	81,300
Dry field peas	1,330,800
Flaxseed	279,400
Mustard seed	103,200
Canola (rapeseed)	7,019,300
Tame hay	6,078,100
Lentils	1,455,000
Canary seed	102,300
Triticale	10,200
Chickpeas	75,200

Source: Statistics Canada, CANSIM table 001-0010

Recent figures for farm animals are set out in the following table:

Livestock thousand head	2002	2003	2004
Milk cows	29	34	29
Calves	1,167	1,271	1,375
Other cattle	1,744	1,915	2,136
Hogs	1,230	1,250	1,350
Sheep & lambs	155	145	160

Source: Government of Saskatchewan

Forestry
Recent figures show that Saskatchewan had over 20,000 hectares of forest land.

COMMUNICATIONS AND TRANSPORT

National Airlines
Athabaska Airways, PO Box 100, Prince Albert, Saskatchewan S6U SR4, Canada. Tel: +1 306 764 1404

International Airports
In 2010 there were over 1.4 million passenger flights at Regina Airport (http://www.yqr.ca) which continues to expand. Saskatoon Airport (http://www.yqr.ca) is also undergoing expansion (due to complete in 2013) and currently has an annual passenger capacity of 1.4 million passengers.

Railways
Saskatchewan has a total rail network of 9,873 km.

Roads
2003 statistics put the length of the province's four-lane highways at 2,140 km, its two-lane highways at 11,520 km. Figures for 2004 show that there were 750,000 registered vehicles on the roads along with 115,000 licensed trailers. (Source: Saskatchewan Department of Highways and Transport)

HEALTH

The most recent figures available show that the approved bed within a health care institution ratio to 1,000 population is 19.6. The ratio within hospitals is 6.0 and within residential care facilities, 8.3. Figures for 2009 show that total expenditure on health care was Can$2.7 billion.

EDUCATION

Figures for recent years show a decline in the number of students enrolled in general education: 168,622 in the 2007-08 school year, falling to 167,553 in the 2008-09 school year, before rising in the 2009-10 school year to 168,194. Expenditure per student in public general education in 2008-09 was Can$11,678.

The University of Saskatchewan at Saskatoon and the University of Regina have a total enrolment of some 22,000. Recently, some 4,700 undergraduate and 650 graduate degrees were awarded.

CANADA

COMMUNICATIONS AND MEDIA

Newspapers
Saskatchewan has a total of five daily newspapers and over 90 weekly publications.

Broadcasting
Several television networks operate in the province including,: CIPA-TV, CKBI-TV Prince Albert, CBKFT-TV Regina, CBKT-TV Regina, CFRE-TV Regina, CKCK-TV Regina, CBKST-TV Saskatoon, CFQC-TV Saskatoon, CFSK-TV Saskatoon, CJFB-TV Swift Current, CICC-TV and CKOS Yorkton. Several stations are owned by CTV.
CTV, URL: http://www.ctv.ca/
CBC Saskatoon, URL: http://www.cbc.ca/sask/

Radio
Rawlco Communications Ltd, URL: http://www.rawlco.com

Telecommunications
The number of cellular phones is currently more than 135,620. Internet access is put at 30,844, compared with 12,796 the previous year.

ENVIRONMENT

Recent figures show that over 70 per cent of households have access to recycling programmes for paper, metal products, glass and plastics.

YUKON TERRITORY

Capital: Whitehorse (Population estimate: 26,418)

Commissioner: Douglas George Phillips (page 1495)

Provincial Flag: Vertically green, white, blue, in the proportions 2:3:2, charged in the centre with the coat of arms of the territory.

CONSTITUTION AND GOVERNMENT

Constitution
The Yukon is governed by a wholly-elected cabinet (Executive Council) and a federally-appointed commissioner who, under the Yukon Act, is designated as the head of government. The Commissioner now performs duties similar to those of a lieutenant governor in Canadian provinces. The day-to-day administration of government is in the hands of the cabinet which, as in other Canadian jurisdictions, must maintain the confidence of the elected legislative assembly. The Legislative Assembly consists of 18 members, who hold terms not to exceed four years. The Yukon Party currently holds power with 10 seats, The Liberal Party has five seats and The New Democrat Party three seats. The Yukon government consists of 12 departments, as well as a women's directorate and 4 crown corporations, each taking direction from a responsible cabinet minister. Government departments and agencies are responsible for a similar range of activities as found in Canadian provinces, including education, economic development, finance, government services, health and social services, justice, public service commission, renewable resources and tourism. The administration of certain programmes, mostly in the natural resources field, remain under federal to territorial jurisdiction. Negotiations have taken place for the transfer of oil and gas management, forestry and the delivery of health services to Yukon government control. Oil and gas management was recently transferred to Yukon's control.

The Yukon is represented in the federal House of Commons by one member of parliament.

Legislature
Yukon Legislative Assembly, Box 2703, Whitehorse, Yukon Y1A 2C6, Canada. Tel: +1 867 667 8683, e-mail: yla@gov.yk.ca, URL: http://www.gov.yk.ca/leg-assembly

---

Cabinet (as at June 2013)
Premier, Minister of Finance, Minister responsible for the Executive Council Office: Hon. Darrell Pasloski
Deputy Premier, Minister of Community Services, Minister responsible for Women's Direcorate, for the Public Service Commission, and for the French Language Directorate: Hon. Elaine Taylor (page 1523)
Minister of Energy, Mines and Resources: Brad Cathers
Minister of Economic Development, Minister of Environment: Hon. Currie Dixon
Minister of Justice, Minister of Tourism and Culture: Hon. Mike Nixon
Minister of Highways and Public Works: Hon. Wade Istchenko
Minister of Education: Hon. Scott Kent
Minister of Health and Social Services: Hon. Doug Graham

Ministries
Ministry of Education, Whitehorse, Yukon, Canada. Tel: +1 867 667 5141, fax +1 867 667 8424, URL: http://www.education.gov.yk.ca
Ministry of Finance, Yukon Government Administration Building, Whitehorse, Yukon, Canada. Tel: +1 867 667-5343, fax: +1 867 667 8424, http://www.finance.gov.yk.ca
Ministry of Economic Development, Yukon Government Administration Building, Whitehorse, Yukon, Canada. Tel: +1 867 667 3544, fax: +1 867 667 8424, URL: http://www.economicdevelopment.gov.yk.ca
Ministry of Community and Transportation, Yukon Government Administration Building, Whitehorse, Yukon, Canada. Tel: +1 867 667 8534, fax: +1 867 667 8424, URL: http://www.community.gov.yk.ca
Ministry of Tourism and Culture, Yukon Government Administration Building, Whitehorse, Yukon, Canada. Tel: +1 867 667 8262, fax: +1 867 667 8424, URL: http://www.tc.gov.yk.ca
Ministry of Health and Social Services, Yukon Government Administration Building, Whitehorse, Yukon, Canada. Tel: +1 867 667 8417, fax: +1 867 667 8424, URL: http://www.hss.gov.yk.ca
Ministry of Justice, Yukon Government Administration Building, Whitehorse, Yukon, Canada. Tel: +1 867 667 8417, fax: +1 867 667 8424, URL: http://www.justice.gov.yk.ca

Elections
The most recent general election was held on 11 October 2011. The result of which was as follows: Yukon Party, 11 seats, Yukon New Democratic Party, six seats, and the Yukon Liberal Party, two seats.

Political Parties
Yukon Party, URL: http://www.yukonparty.ca
Yukon New Democratic Party, URL: http://www.yukonndp.ca
Yukon Liberal Party, URL: http://www.liberal.ca

LEGAL SYSTEM

There are four levels of courts in the Yukon: Justice of the Peace Court, Territorial Court, Supreme Court and Court of Appeal.

AREA AND POPULATION

Area
The area of the Yukon Territory is 483,450 sq. km, which includes 4,480 sq. km of fresh water and 281,030 sq. km of forested lands. It is located in the extreme north-west of Canada and borders Alaska. The largest urban area and only city is Whitehorse where approximately 60 per cent of the population lives. The main rivers which run through Yukon are Donjek, Klondike, Liard, MacMillan, McQuesten, Nisutlin, Peel, Pelly, Porcupine, Ross, Snake, Stewart, White, Wind, and the Yukon. The main lakes are Aishihik, Bennett, Dezadeash, Frances, Kluane, Kusawa, Laberge, Little Salmon, Marsh, Mayo, Quiet, Tagish, and Teslin.

To view a map, please consult http://atlas.nrcan.gc.ca/site/english/maps/reference/provincesterritories. (With permission of Natural Resources Canada 2008, courtesy of the Atlas of Canada)

Population
The population in mid 2012 was 36,100. The following figures show a breakdown of the population: population aged under 15 years, 6,200; population aged 15 to 64, 26,500; population aged 65 years and over, 3,400.

Births, Marriages, Deaths
During the year 1 July 2011 - 30 June 2012 there were 383 births and 218 deaths. In the year 2006-07 1,597 people from other Canadian provinces emigrated to the Yukon and 1,967 people from the Yukon left for other Canadian provinces, 55 foreign immigrants arrived and 13 people from Yukon left for other countries. (Source: Statistics Canada) CANSIM, table 051-0001.

Public Holidays 2014
17 February: Heritage Day
19 May: Victoria Day
18 August: Discovery Day
13 October: Thanksgiving Day
11 November: Remembrance Day

EMPLOYMENT

Figures for 2006 show that the total labour force numbered 19,125. The following table shows how the workforce was employed that year:

Sector	Employed
Agriculture, forestry, fishing & hunting	200
Mining, oil & gas extraction	680
Utilities	80
Construction	1,305
Manufacturing	405
Wholesale trade	330
Retail trade	1,925
Transportation & warehousing	855
Information & cultural industries	570
Finance & insurance	310
Real estate, rental & leasing	240
Professional, scientific & technical services	815
Admin., support, waste management &	630

- continued
remediation services
Educational services 1,285
Health care & social assistance 1,725
Arts, entertainment & recreation 510
Accommodation & food services 1,680
Public administration 4,535
Other services 795

Source: Statistics Canada, Census of Population 2006

Figures for 2008 put the unemployment rate for Yukon at 5.0 per cent rising to 6.8 per cent in 2009, falling to 4.2 per cent at the end of 2010. Figures for the end of 2012 put the unemployment rate at 6.0 per cent.

BANKING AND FINANCE

GDP/GNP, Inflation, National Debt
Expenditure based GDP in recent years in shown in the following table:

Expenditure based GDP

Year	Can$ millions
2004	1,394
2005	1,497
2006	1,634
2007	1,812
2008	2,026
2009	2,134
2010	2,384
2011	2,660

Source : Statistics Canada CANSIM, table 384-0038

The largest contributor to GDP is the mining, quarrying and oil and gas extraction industries contributing around 22 per cent of GDP.

Balance of Payments / Imports and Exports
The value of retail trade in 2009 was Can$526.7 million, compared with the previous year with Can$534.5 million. Figures for 2010 estimated the retail trade value at $578.4 million rising to Can$662.2 nillion in 2011 (Source: Statistics Canada, CANSIM table 080-0020, Cat. no. 63-005-X)

Chambers of Commerce and Trade Organisations
The Whitehorse Chamber of Commerce, URL: http://www.whitehorsechamber.com
Canada-Yukon Business Service Centre, URL: http://www.cbsc.org/yukon

MANUFACTURING, MINING AND SERVICES

Primary and Extractive Industries
Mining is the main industry and accounts for about 30 per cent of the economy. Gold, silver, lead, natural gas, and zinc are all mined. Yukon also has deposits of copper, nickel, platinum, coal, tungsten, uranium, oil and gas. Figures for 2005 put the production value of gold mined at Can$33.6 million and silver at Can$139,000, figures from 2011 put the contribution to GDP of the mining, quarrying and oil and extraction industries at Can$541.7 million (2007 chained dollars).

Energy
Total power generation in 2006 was 359,031 megawatt hours, of which 335,187 MWh were hydro-produced and 23,884 MWh were internal combustion produced. (Source: Yukon Bureau of Statistics)

Manufacturing
Total manufacturing sales in 2011 were Can$37.4 million, up from Can$31.1 million in 2010.

Service Industries
There were 415,000 travelers to the Yukon in 2007, compared with 327,811 in 1997.

Agriculture
Figures for 2011 show that the agriculture sector contribed Can$3.7 million to GDP (at 2007 chained dollars). Forest production and the fur trade are key agricultural industries in the province. The value of fur production in the province in recent years was as follows: Can$281.6 thousand in 2003; Can$241.2 thousand in 2004; Can$428.8 thousand in 2005; Can$389.0 thousand in 2006. 4,000 pelts were produced in 2007. Pelt production fell in 2009 to 2,300.

COMMUNICATIONS AND TRANSPORT

National Airlines
Air North operates a scheduled and charter service between the Yukon, Alaska and the Northwest Territories. Era Aviation operates a scheduled service between Whitehorse and Anchorage.
Air North, URL: http://www.flyairnorth.com
Era Aviation, URL: http://www.flyera.com/

International Airports
Whitehorse International Airport, URL: http://www.gov.yk.ca/yxy/

Roads
There are 4,681.3 km of roads in the Yukon, of which 3,623.7 km are trunk highways. The Alaska Highway and branch highway systems connect Yukon's main communities with the rest of Canada and Alaska. The Klondike and Dempster Highways provide tidewater connections between Skagway, Alaska on the Pacific Ocean and Inuvik, Northwest Territories on the Arctic Ocean.

Recent figures show there are over around 25,500 registered vehicles on Yukon's roads, of which 8,000 were passenger cars and 16,000 were trucks and tractors.

HEALTH

Recent figures show that there are 282 hospital beds available. There is one major hospital located in Whitehorse, a cottage hospital located in Watson Lake and nine health centres located throughout the Yukon.

The number of health facilities and personnel are as follows: 2 hospitals; 71 staffed hospital beds; 4 nursing stations; 9 health treatment centres; 119 licensed physicians; and 34 licensed dentists. (Source: Yukon Bureau of Statistics)

EDUCATION

The Yukon government operates (with the assistance of elected school councils) 28 schools throughout the territory for students to attend, from kindergarten to grade 12. There are also three private schools. There is a French first language school in Whitehorse, offering kindergarten to Grade 10. French immersion schooling is also offered in Whitehorse, from Grades 1 to 12. The Yukon government also provides financial assistance to students wishing to pursue their post secondary education at universities, community colleges and technical institutions inside or outside the Yukon. Financial assistance is available to students of aboriginal decent from the federal Department of Indian Affairs and Northern Development.

Figures for recent years show a decline in the number of students enrolled in general education: 5,227 in the 2007-08 school year falling to 5,005 in the 2008-09 school year. Expenditure per student in public general education in 2008-09 was Can$20,374.

COMMUNICATIONS AND MEDIA

Newspapers
Several newspapers published in the province, including weekly, monthly and annual journals. Newspapers include the Whitehorse Star (http://www.whitehorsestar.com/) and Yukon News (http://www.yukon-news.com).

Broadcasting
In Whitehorse there are several TV channels operating. In Faro and Watson Lake there are private cable operations. CBC national television and Television Northern Canada (TVNC) is provided to all communities by satellite and over-the-air systems. CBC radio and Northern Native Broadcasting (CHON-FM) are received in all Yukon communities. Dawson city has its own community run radio station, CFYT-FM.748.
CBC, URL: http://www.cbc.com

Telecommunications
Yukon's telecommunications systems are provided by NorthwesTel Inc., a Bell Canada Enterprises Inc. company. NorthwesTel's operations include local telephone service, long distance communications by microwave radio and satellite, cellular service in Whitehorse and manual mobile radio and data communications.

ENVIRONMENT

Statistics show that the territorial government recently spent Can$3,212,000 on pollution abatement and control measures whilst the local government spent Can$6,432,000.

STATES OF THE WORLD

CAPE VERDE
Republic of Cape Verde
República de Cabo Verde

Capital: Praia (Population estimate: 116,000)

Head of State: Jorge Carlos Fonseca (President) (page 1426)

National Flag: Comprises three horizontal bands, the top one of which is double width and blue. The middle bank is white, with a horizontal red stripe through the middle, and the bottom strip is blue. A circle of 10 yellow five-pointed stars is centered on the hoist end.

CONSTITUTION AND GOVERNMENT

Constitution
Independence from Portugal was gained on the 5 July 1975. Until the constitution was amended in 1990 Cape Verde had one political party, the African Party for the Independence of Cape Verde (PAICV). Multi-party elections soon followed the constitutional amendment.

Under the terms of the September 1992 constitution, Cape Verde's executive branch of government is headed by the President, directly elected by universal adult suffrage for five years. The National Assembly nominates the Prime Minister who appoints, and is assisted by, the Council of Ministers.

To consult the constitution (in Portuguese), please visit: http://www.parlamento.cv/leisdarepublica.aspx.

International Relations
Cape Verde has an international outlook, due to the diaspora of its people and its history. The country has especially close relations with Portugal, its colonisers from the fifteenth century until independence. Cape Verde also has close ties to Africa; it is a member of the African Union, and joined the regional organisation ECOWAS in 1977. Cape Verde is a member of the CPLP (Organisation of Portuguese speaking countries) and actively pursues closer economic links with Brazil.

Recent Events
The World Trade Organization council approved the accession of Cape Verde to the organisation in December 2007, and the country officially joined on 23 July 2008. There was a major cabinet reshuffle in June 2008.

In November 2009, following an outbreak of Dengue fever a national emergency was declared.

Parliamentary elections took place in February 2011 and presidential elections in August 2011. Jorge Carlos Fonseca, a former foreign minister, won on the second round.

Legislature
The unicameral legislature is the 72-member National Assembly (Assembléia Nacional) whose deputies are elected by universal suffrage for a five-year term.

Cabinet (as at June 2013)
Prime Minister: Dr Jose Maria Pereira Neves (page 1494)
Deputy Prime Minister, Minister of Health: Cristina Lopes de Almeida Fontes Lima (page 1426)
Minister of Defence and Government Spokesperson: Jorge Tolentino
Minister of Tourism, Industry and Energy: Humberto Brito
Minister of Environment, Housing and Territorial Management: Sara Maria Duarte Lopes
Minister of Education and Sport: Fernanda Marques
Minister of Foreign Affairs: Jorge Borges
Minister of Infrastructure and Marine Economy: Maria Viega
Minister of Justice: José Carlos Lopes Correia
Minister of Labour and the Development of Human Resources, Minister of Youth: Jandira Fonseca Hopffer Almada
Minister of Finance and Planning: Cristina Duarte
Minister for Parliamentary Affairs: Rui Semedo
Minister of Internal Administration: Marisa Helena do Nascimento Morais
Minister for Rural Development: Eva Ortet
Minister of Higher Education, Science and Innovation: Antonio Leao Correia E. Silva
Minister of Culture: Mario Lucio Sousa
Minister of Communities: Fernanda Fernandes
Secretary of State for Public Administration: Dr Romeu Fonseca Modesto
Secretary of State for Foreign Affairs: José Luis Rocha
State Secretary for Marine Resources: Adalberto Viera

Ministries
Government portal, URL: http://www.governo.cv/
Office of the President, Presidência da República, CP 100, Plateau, Praia, São Tiago, Cape Verde. Tel: +238 2 61 26 69, fax: +238 2 61 43 56, URL: http://www.presidenciarepublica.cv
Office of the Prime Minister, Palácio do Governo, Várzea, CP 16, Praia, São Tiago, Cape Verde. Tel: +238 2 61 05 13, fax: +238 2 61 30 99, e-mail: gab.imprensa@gpm.gov.cv, URL: http://www.governo.cv

Ministry of the Economy, Growth and Competitiveness, 107 Avda Amílcar Cabral, Plateau, Praia, C.P. 107, São Tiago, Cape Verde. Tel: +238 2 61 58 46, fax: +238 2 61 38 97, URL: http://www.governo.cv
Ministry of Foreign Affairs, Co-operation and Communities, Praceta Instituto Superior de Educação, Praia, CP 123, São Tiago, Cape Verde. Tel: +238 2 61 61 61, fax: +238 2 61 62 62, e-mail: mne@gov.cv, URL: http://www.gov.cv/minnec
Ministry of Culture, Palácio do Governo, Av Cidade de Lisboa, Praia, São Tiago, Cape Verde. URL: http://www.governo.cv
Ministry of Defence and Parliamentary Affairs, Palácio do Governo, Av Cidade de Lisboa, Praia, São Tiago, Cape Verde. Tel: +238 2 61 05 11, fax: +238 2 63 12 86, URL: http://www.fa.xpu.cv
Ministry of Education Development and Human Resources, Palácio do Governo, Av Cidade de Lisboa, Praia, São Tiago, Cape Verde. Tel: +238 2 61 05 07, fax: +238 2 61 39 91, URL: http://www.minedu.cv
Ministry of the Environment, Agricultural Development and Marine Resources, Ponta Belém, Praia, CP 206, São Tiago, Cape Verde. Tel: +238 2 61 57 16, fax: +238 2 61 40 64, URL: http://www.governo.cv
Ministry of Finance, Planning and Regional Development, 107 Avda Amílcar Cabral, Praia, CP 30, São Tiago, Cape Verde. Tel: +238 2 61 43 50, fax: +238 2 61 31 97, e-mail: juliat@govl.gov.cv, URL: http://www.minfin.cv
Ministry of Health, Palácio do Governo, Av Cidade de Lisboa, Praia, C.P 47, São Tiago, Cape Verde. Tel: +238 2 61 05 01, fax: +238 2 61 39 91, URL: http://www.governo.cv
Ministry of Infrastructure, Transport and Marine Affairs, Palácio do Governo, Av Cidade Lisboa, Praia, São Tiago, Cape Verde. Tel: +238 2 61 56 99, fax: +238 2 61 69 29, URL: http://www.governo.cv
Ministry of Justice and the Interior, Praca 12 de Setembro, Plateau, Praia, São Tiago, Cape Verde. Tel: +238 2 61 56 87, fax: +238 2 61 56 78, URL: http://www.governo.cv
Ministry of Labour, Professional Training and Social Solidarity, Palácio do Governo, Av Cidade de Lisboa, Praia, São Tiago, Cape Verde. URL: http://www.governo.cv
Ministry of Public Administration, Palácio do Governo, Av Cidade de Lisboa, Praia, São Tiago, Cape Verde. Tel: +238 2 61 05 03, fax: +238 2 61 27 62, URL: http://www.governo.cv
Ministry of Youth and Sport, Palácio do Governo, Av Cidade de Lisboa, Praia, São Tiago, Cape Verde. Tel: +238 2 61 03 09, URL: http://www.juventude.cv

Political Parties
The main political parties are: African Party for the Independence of Cape Verde (PAICV); Independent and Democratic Cape Verdean Union (UCID); Movement for Democracy (MPD).

Elections
Suffrage is universal for adults over 18 years of age.

Presidential elections are held every five years. In June 2011, presidential elections took place. The PAICV nominated the former foreign minister Manuel Inocencio Sousa, but the speaker of the National Assembly, Aristides Lima, also ran for election with the support of some of the PAICV. The MPD nominated Jorge Carlos Fonseca, a former foreign minister. In the first round of voting Mr Fonseca won 37.3 per cent, followed by Mr Sousa with 32 per cent and Lima with 27.4 per cent. Mr Fonseca stressed his political independence in the second round and won with 54.6 per cent of the vote.

The last parliamentary election was held in February 2011. The incumbent PAICV party won 38 of the 72 seats, the Movement for Democracy won 32 and the Democratic and Independent Cape Verdean Union won two seats.

Diplomatic Representation
British Consulate, (British Embassy staff based at Dakar), Shell Cabo Verde, Sarl, Ave. Amilcar Cabral CP4, Sao Vincente, Praia, Cape Verde. Tel: +238 326625 / 26 / 27, fax: +238 326629, e-mail: antonio.a.canuto@scv.sims.com
Honorary Consul in Cape Verde: Antonio Canuto
British Embassy (all staff resident in Dakar: 20 Rue du Docteur Guillet, Boite Postale 6025, Dakar, Senegal. Tel: +221 823 7392 / 823 9971, fax: +221 823 2766, e-mail: britemb@sentoo.sn)
Ambassador (resident in Dakar, Senegal): Robert Marshall
Cape Verde Embassy, 3415 Massachusetts Ave., NW, Washington, DC 20007, USA. Tel: +1 202 965 6820, fax: +1 202 965 1207, e-mail: ambacvus@sysnet.net, URL: http://www.virtualcapeverde.net
Ambassador: Fatima Lima Veiga
US Embassy, Rua Abilio Macedo 81, CP 201, Praia, Ilha de Santiago, Cape Verde. Tel: +238 615616, fax: +238 611355, URL: http://praia.usembassy.gov/
Ambassador: Adrienne S. O'Neal
Permanent Representative of the Republic of Cape Verde to the United Nations, 27 East 69th Street, New York, NY 10021, USA. Tel: +1 212 472 0333, fax: +1 212 794 1398, e-mail: capeverde@un.int
Permanent Representative: Ambassador Antonia Lima Monteiro

LEGAL SYSTEM

Cape Verde's court system consists of the Supreme Court of Justice, Judicial Courts of First Appeal, the Court of Audit, Military Courts, Fiscal and Customs Courts. The Supreme Court has seven justices. In 2011, the Supreme Court of Justice set up three specialized sections (civil and administrative; criminal; tax, labour and administrative) in order to speed up the resolution of cases. Each section should have three judges. Other proposed reforms include the establishment of appeal courts (Relation Courts) on the islands of Sao Vicente and Santiago to reduce the number of cases going to the Supreme Court.

The government generally respects the human rights of its citizens; however, prison conditions are poor, there are lengthy pretrial detentions and trials can be delayed excessively. The death penalty was officially abolished in 1981.

LOCAL GOVERNMENT

For administrative purposes, Cape Verde is divided into 17 districts or councils (*Municipios*): Boa Vista, Brava, Calheta, Maio, Mosteiros, Paul, Praia, Porto Novo, Ribeira Grande, Sal, Santa Catarina, Santa Cruz, Sao Domingos, Sao Nicolau, Sao Filipe, Sao Vicente, Tarrafal. Councils are represented by members elected for a five-year term by universal suffrage.

AREA AND POPULATION

Area
The islands of Cape Verde cover an area of 4,033 sq. km and lie about 400 miles off the west coast of Africa, opposite the Senegal coast. Cape Verde consists of 10 main islands and some eight islets. The islands are divided into two groups: those lying to the north are called Barlavento (windward) and those to the south are called Sotavento (leeward). There are six islands in the first group: Santo Antao, Sao Vicente, Santa Luzia, Sao Nicolau, Boa Vista and Sal. The four in the southern group are Sao Tiago (Santiago), Fogo, Brava and Maio. The terrain is largely rugged, and the climate temperate; however, rainfall is meagre and unpredictable.

To view a map, consult http://www.lib.utexas.edu/maps/africa/cape_verde_pol_2004.pdf

Population
The population of the islands was estimated at 496,000 in 2010, with a growth rate of around 1.3 per cent over the period 2000-10. The majority of Cape Verde's population (59 per cent) is aged between 15 and 60 years, with 32 per cent aged under 15 years, and 7 per cent aged 60 years and over. The median age is 23 years. Approximately 61 per cent of the population lives in urban areas.

More Cape Verdeans (700,000 in 2005) now live abroad than live on the islands, due to recurrent droughts and few natural resources, leading to famines. Most emigrés have moved to the United States or to Portugal.

The official languages are Portuguese and Crioulo (Portuguese/West African). The main ethnic group is Creole (71 per cent), followed by African (28 per cent), and European (1 per cent).

Births, Marriages, Deaths
According to 2010 estimates, the birth rate is 20.7 births per 1,000 people. The death rate is 6.3 deaths per 1,000 people. Life expectancy at birth is around 71 years (66 years for men and 75 years for women). The infant mortality rate is fallen in recent years to 29 deaths per 1,000 live births, whilst the total fertility rate is around 2.4 children born per woman. (Source: http://www.who.int, World Health Statistics 2012)

Public Holidays 2014
1 January: New Year
20 January: National Heroes' Day
18 April: Good Friday
21 April: Easter Monday
1 May: Labour Day
5 July: Independence Day
15 August: Assumption
1 November: All Saints' Day
25 December: Christmas Day

EMPLOYMENT

Estimates put the unemployment rate at 21 per cent in 2000. The majority of the active population is engaged in agriculture, when drought conditions do not prevail, and fishing. The services sector, particularly commerce, transport and public services, is a significant employer. Figures for 2007 estimated the labour force to be 196,000.

BANKING AND FINANCE

Currency
One Cape Verde Escudo = 100 centavos

GDP/GNP, Inflation, National Debt
The Cape Verde islands have few natural resources. However, they have recently experienced economic growth and development, especially in the service sector areas of tourism and shipping; commerce, public services and the shipping sub-sector account for over 70 per cent of GDP. Although most of the population lives in rural areas, agriculture contributes less than 10 per cent towards GDP. Industry accounts for nearly 20 per cent of GDP, and money sent by expatriate Cape Verdeans contribute between 10 and 20 per cent of GDP. Other

major economic sectors are fishing, fish processing, salt mining, ship repairs, shoes and clothing. The government has recently started a privatisation programme. The economy is generally well managed.

GDP in 2009 was estimated at US$1,500 million with a real growth rate of 2.5 per cent. Growth has continued, reaching US$2 billion in 2011.

Inflation, based on consumer prices, in 2005 was 0.4 per cent. It rose to 6.0 per cent in 2006, dipping to 4.5 per cent in 2007 and 3.5 per cent in 2009. Inflation fell to 2.5 per cent in 2011.

Total external public debt was US$530.47 million in 2006. (Source: AFDB)

Foreign Investment
Foreign investment made or planned in Cape Verde totalled US$407 million over the period 1994-2000, of which 58 per cent was in the tourist industry, 21 per cent in fisheries and services, 17 per cent in industry, and 4 per cent in infrastructure. Cape Verde's high trade deficit is partly financed by foreign aid. Cape Verde received economic aid of US$92 million in 2002; the principal donors were Portugal ($11 million), Japan, Luxembourg and the United States. Aid funds are directed towards poverty alleviation, and infrastructure, especially water provision. The government is pursuing a privatisation programme.

Balance of Payments / Imports and Exports
Exports are mainly fish and shellfish, bananas, fuel, clothing and shoes. Portugal and Spain buy a large proportion of Cape Verde's exports (Spain, 60 per cent, Portugal 30 per cent) and Portugal supplies the Islands with 48 per cent of its imports. The United States is another important purchaser of merchandise, and the Netherlands supplies approximately 17 per cent of imports. Major import commodities include food, industrial products, fuel, and transport equipment.

External Trade, US$ million

	2005	2006	2007
Trade balance	-348.91	-462.71	-600.30
Exports	88.93	95.94	92.23
Imports	437.84	558.65	692.53

Source: African Development Bank

Exports were estimated to be US$36.7 million in 2009 and imports US$746 million.

Central Bank
Banco de Cabo Verde, URL: http://www.bcv.cv/vEN/Pages/Homepage.aspx

Chambers of Commerce and Trade Organisations
Chamber of Commerce, Industry and Services, Rue Serpa Pinto 160, C.P. 105, Praia, Cape Verde. Tel: +238 617234, fax: +238 617235
Chamber of Commerce, Agriculture and Services, Rue de Luz 31, Mindelo, Sao Vincente, Cape Verde. Tel: +238 328495, fax: +238 328496, e-mail: marktestcv@mail.cvtelecom.cv

MANUFACTURING, MINING AND SERVICES

Primary and Extractive Industries
Salt, pozzolana and limestone are mined in Cape Verde. The country has no fossil fuel resources and relies entirely on imports for its oil requirements. According to EIA statistics, Cape Verde consumed an estimated 2,000 barrels per day of oil in 2010, all of which was imported.

Energy
All of Cape Verde's electricity is produced from fossil fuel in thermal plants. Total energy consumption was 0.005 quadrillion Btu in 2009, with electricity generation at 0.29 million kilowatthours (kWh), and consumption at 0.27 million kWh.

Manufacturing
Industry contributes nearly 20 per cent towards Cape Verde's GDP. Main sectors include food and beverages, salt refining, shoes and clothing, fish canning, beverage bottling and ship repairs. Rum is distilled from locally grown sugar cane.

Service Industries
The service industry is Cape Verde's largest economic sector, contributing nearly 70 per cent towards GDP. Major sectors include commerce, transport and public services. Cape Verde has begun to take advantage of its location in the mid-Atlantic; improvements to Mindelo's harbour (Porto Grande) and at Sal's international airport encourage the use of the islands as a stop off. Ship repair facilities at Mindelo were opened in 1983.

Tourism is a growth area; the number of hotels increased from 88 in 2001 to 108 in 2004 and the number of visitors who stayed overnight increased from around 806,000 in 2001 to 865,000 in 2004. The number of people employed in the sector grew by over 100 over the same period.

Agriculture
Despite the fact that almost 70 per cent of the population lives in rural areas, around 82 per cent of food has to be imported. Droughts in the 1990s dramatically reduced crop yields. Maize, bananas, sugar cane, beans, sweet potatoes, peanuts and coffee are the main crops.

Agricultural Production in 2010

Produce	Int. $'000*	Tonnes
Indigenous pigmeat	12,759	8,300
Mangoes, mangosteens, guavas	3,895	6,500

CAPE VERDE

- continued

Goat milk, whole, fresh	3,859	11,500
Cow milk, whole, fresh	3,714	11,900
Bananas	2,507	8,900
Indigenous cattle meat	2,464	912
Indigenous goat meat	2,269	947
Tomatoes	2,033	5,500
Fruit fresh nes	1,885	5,400
Hen eggs, in shell	1,775	2,140
Chillies and peppers, dry	1,424	1,300
Beans, green	996	2,800

* unofficial figures

Source: http://faostat.fao.org/site/339/default.aspx Food and Agriculture Organization of the United Nations, Food and Agricultural commodities production

The fishing industry contributes about 1.5 per cent of GDP. Both marine fish and shellfish are in good supply and the islands export small quantities. Cape Verde has a few fish processing and canning factories and the fishing potential of the islands, mostly lobster and tuna, is not fully exploited.

COMMUNICATIONS AND TRANSPORT

Travel Requirements
Citizens of the USA, Canada, Australia and the EU require a passport valid for at least six months and a visa. Other nationals should contact the embassy to check visa requirements.

National Airlines
The national airline is Transportes Aéreas de Cabo Verde (TACV). URL: http://www.tacv.cv

International Airports
Praia's new international airport opened on October 6, 2005, from which Cape Verdean Airlines (TACV) now offers direct flights between Praia and Boston once or twice a week, depending on the season. Cape Verde has another international airport (Amilcar Cabral Airport) located on Sal Island, more than 100 miles northeast of the capital. Airports have been built on all of the inhabited islands, and all but the airport on Brava enjoy scheduled air service.

Roads
There are over 3,050 km of roads. Vehicles are driven on the right.

Ports and Harbours
Mindelo has the main port of Cape Verde, Porto Grande, which has recently been renovated, along with the port at Praia. All other islands have smaller port facilities. Daily ferry services run between Mindelo, São Vincente and Santo Antao.

HEALTH

Recent figures put the number of hospitals in Cape Verde at 20, the number of beds at 630. According to the latest WHO figures for 2005-11 there were 310 doctors (5.7 per 10,000 population), 714 nurses/midwives (13.2 per 10,000 population), 11 dentists, 43 pharmaceutical personnel, and 65 community health workers.

In 2009, the Cape Verdeans spent the equivalent of 3.9 per cent of GDP on health care, which equates to US$150 per capita. General government expenditure represents 74.1 per cent of the total spend on health. Private expenditure accounts for 25.9 per cent of total expenditure on health, of which nearly 100 per cent is out-of-pocket. An estimated 7.4 per cent of health expenditure is from external resources.

In 2009, an estimated 88 per cent of the population had access to improved drinking water. In the same year, 61 per cent of the population had access to improved sanitation.

In 2010, the infant mortality rate stood at 29 per 1,000 live births and the child mortality rate stood at 36 per 1,000 live births. The major causes of childhood deaths are: prematurity (15 per cent), congenital abnormalities (16 per cent), diarrhoea (8 per cent), pneumonia (1 per cent) and injuries (5 per cent). (Source: http://www.who.int, World Health Statistics 2012)

EDUCATION

Cape Verde's compulsory education system lasts for six years (ages 7 to 13 years) and is free. Primary education also lasts for six years, whilst secondary education lasts for three years.

According to 2004 UNESCO figures, the literacy rate for males was 87.8 per cent and for females 75.5 per cent. For the age group 15-24 years the respective rates were 95.8 per cent and 96.7 per cent. Recent figures show that 16.5 per cent of government spending goes on education.

RELIGION

Cape Verde is almost entirely Roman Catholic (90 per cent of the population) with a Protestant minority, (4.0 per cent), around 2.0 per cent of the population are Muslim.

Cape Verde has a religious liberty rating of 10 on a scale of 1 to 10 (10 is most freedom). (Source: World Religion Database)

COMMUNICATIONS AND MEDIA

Press freedom is guaranteed and is generally respected.

Newspapers
The major daily newspapers are Jornal Horizonte and Novo Jornal Cabo Verde. Main weeklies include Expresso das Ilhas (URL: http://www.expressodasilhas.cv/), and A Semana (URL: http://www.asemana.cv/).

Broadcasting
Televisao Nacional De Cabo Verde (TNCV) is the state-run television station, and Radio Nacional De Cabo Verde (RNCV) is the state-run radio station. There is a growing number of private broadcasters.

Portuguese public TV and radio services for Africa and Radio France Internationale are relayed across Cape Verde. Some radio and TV programmes are presented in the Crioulo tongue .

Telecommunications
The telephone system was partially privatised in 1995 and has been modernised in recent years. The islands have around 71,600 mainline telephones, and 270,000 mobile phones in use (2008). Cape Verde had 102,000 internet users in 2008.

ENVIRONMENT

Current environmental problems include over-fishing, deforestation caused by high demand for woodfuel, desertification, and soil erosion due to unsuitable agricultural practises. There is concern that the growing tourism industry poses a threat to the Cape Verde's rich marine life. The islands are an important nesting site for loggerhead turtles, and humpback whales feed in the islands' waters.

According to figures from the EIA, carbon dioxide emissions rose from 0.14 million metric tons in 2002 to 0.27 million metric tons in 2010. Per capita carbon dioxide emissions reached 0.68 metric tons in 2005, below the African average of 1.17 metric tons.

Cape Verde is a party to the following international environmental agreements: soil erosion; deforestation due to demand for wood used as fuel; water shortages; desertification; environmental damage has threatened several species of birds and reptiles; illegal beach sand extraction; and overfishing.

CENTRAL AFRICAN REPUBLIC
République Centrafricaine

Capital: Bangui (Population estimate: 690,000)

Head of State: General François Bozize (President) (in exile as of March 2013) (page 1393)

Head of State: Michel Djotodia (President Self-appointed as of March 2013) (page 1416)

National Flag: On a field divided by a crimson upright, and parti of four fesswise, blue, white, green, yellow; five-pointed yellow at the upper hoist

CONSTITUTION AND GOVERNMENT

Constitution
On 17 August 1960 the then prime minister, M. David Dacko, declared the Central African Republic's independence from France. On 20 September 1960 the country was admitted to the UN. An army coup overthrew the government of President Dacko, and Colonel Bedel Bokassa assumed power as Chief of State. In September 1979 a bloodless coup took place and the former president, M. David Dacko, became president again. However, another bloodless coup in September 1981 overthrew M. David Dacko in favour of General Kolingba. In 1986 a one-party state was formed which President Kolingba reversed in 1987.

According to the 2004 constitution the president heads the executive branch of government and is elected by universal adult suffrage, serving a maximum of two successive five-year terms of office. The president appoints the prime minister and can dissolve the Assemblée Nationale. The prime minister appoints the Council of Ministers. In 2010 the National Assembly approved amendments to the constitution to allow the president and legislature to remain in office at the end of their terms if elections had not been held.

To consult the constitution (in French), please visit: http://www.presidentrdc.cd/constitution.html.

Recent Events
François Bozize seized power in a coup in March 2003. He suspended the 1995 constitution and set up a 98-member National Transitional Council (NTC) to assist with legislation, draft a new constitution and to prepare for elections. The council includes former heads of state, representatives of political parties, regional representatives and representatives of various sections of the community. Mr Bozize appointed Abel Goumba prime minister who formed a government which included members of the army (FACA), the Central African Trade Union (USTC) and five political groupings: the Combination of Political Parties in Opposition (the Patriotic Front for Progress, the Party of National Unity, the Democratic Forum for Modernity, the Social Democratic Party, and the Movement for Democracy and Independence-Social party); the Movement for the Liberation of the People; the Co-ordinated Central African Movement for Unity and Development; and the Central Africa Democratic Rally.

A new constitution was approved in December 2004. In May 2005, Mr Bozize won the presidential election.

In June 2006, thousands of people began to flee north-west to escape rebel fighting and lawlessness. In December, French fighter jets attacked rebel positions, in support of government troops trying to regain control of areas in the northeast of the country, and in February, the rebel People's Democratic Front signed a peace agreement.

The prime minister, Elie Dotie, and his entire cabinet resigned in January 2008 - a day before parliament was to debate a censure motion. Faustin Touadera was appointed prime minister. Two of the main rebel groups, the Union of Democratic Forces for Unity (UFDR) and the Popular Army for the Restoration of Democracy (APRD), signed a peace agreement with the government in June 2008. Under the deal the rebels had to disarm and demobilise. Parliament adopted an amnesty law in September 2008, and, in January 2009 President Bozize formed a unity government which included leaders of the two main rebel groups.

In February 2009 it was reported that Ugandan Lords Resistance Army (LRA) rebels had crossed into the Central African Republic and in September the Ugandan army said they were in pursuit.

In April 2010 scheduled presidential elections were postponed and parliament extended president Bozize's term until new elections could be organised. Elections were eventually held in January 2011, President Bozize was re-elected.

In December 2011, the charity Medecins Sans Frontieres warned that the central area of the country was suffering a state of chronic medical emergency due to the prevalence of epidemic diseases, conflict, and an economic downturn coupled with a poor health care system.

In August 2012, the armed group, Convention of Patriots for Justice and Peace (CPJP), signed a peace deal.

In November 2012, the Seleka rebel coalition overran the north and centre of country. In January 2013 a ceasefire was agreed and under the agreement President Bozize dissolved the government. A National Unity Government was formed from the five groups which had signed the ceasefire or Libreville peace agreement, these were the presidential majority, the Seleka rebel coalition, the democratic opposition, the non armed political grouping and the civil society. In March the Seleka rebels captured the south-eastern town of Bangassou after accusing the government of violating the January peace deal and saying their demands had not been met. The rebels captured the capital and President Bozize fled abroad. The rebel leader Michel Djotodia announced that he was suspending the constitution and dissolved parliament. He proclaimed himself president and said that he would step down after elections to be held in 2016. The Unity Government was to remain in office.

The country's neighbours had sent a 500-strong multinational peacekeeping force called Fomac to restore security. In April 2013 they agreed to send a further 2,000 personel.

International Relations
The Central African Republic has good relations with its neighbours, Cameroon and the Republic of Congo. There have been disputes with Chad and the Democratic Republic of Congo. The Central African Republic maintains relations with France, especially in terms of support for aid negotiations and defence.

Legislature
According to the 2004 constitution the unicameral legislature consists of the 105-seat Assemblée Nationale (National Assembly), whose members serve terms of five years. In addition to the Assemblée Nationale, the legislature comprises the Economic and Regional Council, providing advice in economic and social legislative matters; the State Council, which advises on matters referred by the president of the Assemblée Nationale; and the Congress, which passes Constitutional amendments.

National Assembly (Assemblée Nationale), PO Box 1003, Bangui, Central African Republic. Tel: +236 619583, URL: http://www.rca-gouv.net/
Speaker: Celestin le Roi Gaoumbalet

Cabinet of the Unity Government (as at April 2013)
Prime Minister: Nicolas Tiangaye (page 1525)
Minister of Finance and Budget: Georges Bozanga
Minister of Foreign Affairs, Integration, Francophony and Central African Communities Abroad: Charles Armel Doubane
Minister of Economy, Planning and International Co-operation: Abdallah Hassan Kadre
Minister of Trade and Industry: Amalas Amias Haroun
Minister of Territorial Administration, Decentralisation and Regionalisation: Aristide Sokambi
Minister of Justice, Keeper of the Seals and Judicial Reform: Arsene Sende
Minister of Education and Scientific Research: Marcel Loudegue
Minister of Transport and Civil Aviation: Arnaud Djoubaye Abazen
Minister of Civil Service, Labour and Social Security: Sabin Kpokolo
Minister of Health, Population and the Fight against HIV/AIDS: Dr Aquide Sounk
Minister of Small and Medium-sized Enterprises: Maurice Yondo
Minister of Social Affairs, National Solidarity and Gender Promotion: Marie Madeleine Moussa-Yadouma
Minister of Rural Development: Jeremie Tchimanguere
Minister of Youth, Sports, Arts and Culture: Abdoulaye Hissen
Minister for Town Planning: Rizigala Ramadan
Minister of Youth, Sports, Arts and Culture: Abdoulaye Hissen
Minister of Tourism: Mahamat Abdel Yacoub
Government Secretary-General: Ahamat Arol Teya
Minister of State in Charge of Mines: Oil and Hydraulics: Hubert Gontran Djono-Ahaba
Minister of State in charge of Public Security, Immigration and Public Order: Nourredine Adam
Minister of State in Charge of Communication, Civil Education and National Reconciliation: Christophe Gazam-Betty
Minister of State in charge of Equipment, Public Works and Access, Government Spokesman: Crepin Mboli-Goumba
Minister in charge of Water Resources, Forestry, Hunting, Fisheries and the Environment: Mohamed Moussa Daffhane
Minister in charge of Posts and Telecommunication, Minister in charge of New Technologies: Henry Pouzer

Ministries
Government portal: URL: http://www.rcainfo.org/Gouv/
Office of the President, Palais de la Renaissance, Bangui, Central African Republic. Tel: +236 21 61 03 23, fax: +236 21 61 75 08, URL: http://www.presidence-rca.org
Office of the Prime Minister, Bangui, Central African Republic. URL: http://www.rcainfo.org
Ministry of the Built Environment and Housing, BP 941, Bangui, Central African Republic. Tel: +236 21 61 23 07, fax: +236 21 61 15 52
Ministry of the Civil Service, Labour, Social Security and the Inclusion of Youth in the Professions, Bangui, Central African Republic. Tel: +236 21 61 01 44
Ministry of Defence, Veterans, Victims of War, Disarmament and Restructuring of the Army, Bangui, Central African Republic. Tel: +236 21 61 46 11
Ministry of Education, BP 791, Bangui, Central African Republic.
Ministry of Energy, Mines and Hydraulics, Bangui, Central African Republic. Fax: +236 21 61 60 76
Ministry of Finance and Budget, BP 696, Bangui, Central African Republic. Tel: +236 21 61 45 71
Ministry of Foreign Affairs and Relations with Francophone Countries, Bangui, Central African Republic. Tel: +236 21 61 15 74
Ministry of the Interior and Public Security, BP 941, Bangui, Central African Republic. Tel: +236 21 61 23 07, fax: +236 21 61 15 52
Ministry of Justice, Bangui, Central African Republic. Tel: +236 21 61 16 44

CENTRAL AFRICAN REPUBLIC

Ministry of Planning, Economy and International Co-operation, Bangui, Central African Republic.

Ministry of Posts, Telecommunication and New Technologies, BP 1290, Bangui, Central African Republic.

Ministry of Public Health, Population and the Fight against AIDS, Bangui, Central African Republic. Tel: +236 21 61 29 01

Ministry of Transport and Civil Aviation, BP 941, Bangui, Central African Republic. Tel: +236 21 61 23 07, fax: +236 21 61 15 52

Ministry of Youth, Sports, Arts and Culture, Bangui, Central African Republic. E-mail: masseka_rcagouv@hotmail.com, URL: http://membres.lycos.fr/rcamasseka

Political Parties

The main political parties are: Central African Democratic Rally (RDC); Central African People's Liberation Movement (MLPC); National Convergence (Kwa Na Kwa) (CN-KNK).

Elections

The most recent legislative elections to the National Assembly took place in January and March 2011. The Kwa na Kwa (National Convergence Party) won 63 and independents won 12 seats.

The most recent presidential election was held in January 2011, President Bozize was re-elected.

Diplomatic Representation

British Embassy all staff reside in Yaoundé. (British High Commission, Avenue Winston Churchill, BP 547, Yaoundé, Cameroon. Tel: +237 222 0545, fax: +237 222 0148)
Ambassador: Bharat Joshi (page 1452)

Embassy of the Central African Republic, 30 Rue des Perchamps, 75016, Paris, France. Tel: +33 1 42 24 42 56

US Embassy, Avenue David Dacko, BP 924, Bangui, Central African Republic. Tel: +236 61 02 00, fax: +236 61 44 94, URL: http://bangui.usembassy.gov/
Ambassador: Laurence D. Wohlers

Embassy of Central African Republic, 1618 22nd Street, NW, Washington DC 20008, USA. Tel: +1 202 483 7800, fax: +1 202 332 9893
Ambassador: Estanislas Moussa-Kembe

Permanent Mission of the Central African Republic to the United Nations, 51 Clifton Avenue, Suite 2008, Newark, NJ 07104, USA. Tel: +1 973 482 9161, fax: +1 973 350 1174
Chargé d'Affaires: Fernand Poukre-Kono

LEGAL SYSTEM

The legal system is based on the French system of law. The Republic's court system consists of the Supreme Court, Constitutional Court, Court of Appeal, and Criminal Courts. The Constitutional Court is presided over by nine judges, three appointed by the president, three by the president of the National Assembly and three by fellow judges. There are provisions for a High Court of Justice to try political cases against the president, members of congress and government ministers, but it has never convened. The judiciary is inefficient and there is a shortage of trained personnel as well as a lack of material resources.

The government's record on human rights is very poor. Despite a peace agreement between government forces and rebels in the north of the country, the presidential guard continue to carry out extrajudicial executions and security forces torture, detain, and rape suspects and prisoners. Military impunity remains widespread. Security forces arrest large numbers of people arbitrarily, and conditions in prisons is life threatening. Prolonged pretrial detention, denial of a fair trial, and judicial corruption continue to be problems, as does government corruption. Central African Republic retains the death penalty for ordinary crimes including murder, assassination, treason and espionage, but has not executed anyone since before 1999.

LOCAL GOVERNMENT

Administratively, the Central African Republic is divided into 14 prefectures (*prefets*), two economic prefectures (Gribingui and Sangha), and one commune (Bangui). The prefectures are: Bamingui-Bangoran, Basse-Kotto, Haute-Kotto, Haute-Sangha, Haut-Mbomou, Kemo-Gribingui, Lobaye, Mbomou, Nana-Mambere, Ombella-Mpoko, Ouaka, Ouham, Ouham-Pende, and Vakaga.

The 14 prefectures are subdivided into more than 70 subprefectures (*sous-prefets*). Heads of the prefectures and subprefectures are appointed by the president.

AREA AND POPULATION

Area

The Central African Republic is a landlocked country. It borders Chad to the north, Sudan to the east, Democratic Republic of Congo (formerly Zaire) to the south and Cameroon to the west. The Oubangui river forms the southern border. It flows through the capital Bangui and then south to the Congo basin and is an important transport route. The Central African Republic has an area of 623,000 sq. km. The climate is tropical, with hot, dry winters and mild to hot, wet summers. The terrain is mainly rolling plans with some hills in the northeast and southwest.

To view a map, please visit: http://www.un.org/Depts/Cartographic/map/profile/car.pdf

Population

The estimated population of the Central African Republic in 2010 was approximately 4.40 million with a growth rate of 1.7 per cent. The population is young: 40 per cent aged below 15, and 6 per cent aged 60 or over. The median age is 19 years. Approximately 39 per cent of the population lives in urban areas. Principal ethnic groups are the Baya (33 per cent), the Banda (27 per cent) and the Mandja (13 per cent). The official language is Sangho, and French is still widely used.

Births, Marriages, Deaths

According to 2010 estimates, the birth rate is 35.0 births per 1,000 population, whilst the death rate is 16.2 deaths per 1,000 population. According to the World Health Organization the infant mortality rate was 105 deaths per 1,000 live births in 2008. The neonatal mortality rate was 42 per 1,000 live births in 2010 and the maternal mortality rate was an estimated 850 per 100,000 live births. The total fertility rate in 2010 was 4.6 children born per woman.

In 2009, life expectancy at birth was estimated at 48 years. Latest figures for healthy life expectancy (2007) are 43.0 years for males and 42 for females. (Source: http://www.who.int World Health Statistics 2012)

Public Holidays 2014

1 January: New Year
29 March: Boganda Day
21 April: Easter Monday
1 May: Labour Day
9 May: Whit Monday
30 June: National Prayer Day
13 August: Independence Day
15 August: Assumption Day
1 November: All Saints Day
1 December: Republic Day
25 December: Christmas Day

EMPLOYMENT

The economic workforce is estimated at just over 50 per cent of the population and is largely unskilled. 75 per cent of the work force work in the agriculture sector, 15 per cent in government, six per cent in industry, and four per cent in commerce and services. According to 2001 estimates, the unemployment rate is about eight per cent (rising to 23 per cent in the capital, Bangui). Estimated figures for 2007 put the labour force at 1.9 million.

BANKING AND FINANCE

Currency
CFA France (pegged to the Euro)

GDP/GNP, Inflation, National Debt
The Central African Republic is a very poor country. The Central African Republic has large natural resources including water, timber and diamonds but poor infrastructure and reported corruption means they have not been exploited. The CAR also has reserves of gold and uranium but again, these are as yet unexploited. Economic development is hindered by its poor infrastructure and periodic conflict.

In early 2006 the country signed its second IMF Emergency Post Conflict Assistance Loan and began negotiations with the IMF for a Poverty Reduction and Growth facility programme. The EU has formally re-started project aid, but disbursement has so far been minimal. CAR has adopted the Central African Economic and Monetary Community (CENAC) charter of investment. The government recently embarked on economic reform including the privatisation of many state-owned businesses. The IMF certified its attainment of the Heavily Indebted Poor Countries (HIPC) completion point in 2009. The Government has adopted the Central African Economic and Monetary Community (CEMAC) Charter of Investment. Other reforms include the process of adopting a new labor code.

The Central African Republic's economy is largely based on agriculture and forestry, which contributed nearly 56 per cent of GDP, according to 2009 estimates. The services sector contributed almost 30 per cent of GDP in the same year, with industry accounting for over 15 per cent of GDP. Fighting between government forces and opponents has slowed economic growth.

The economy has been rising since 2003 when GDP was an estimated US$1,195.27 million with an annual growth rate of -7.6 . Growth was estimated to be 1.3 per cent in 2004, rising to 2.2 per cent in 2005, and 4.1 per cent in 2006. GDP in 2010 was US$2 billion with a growth rate of 3.0 per cent. Per capita GDP was estimated to be US$450. In 2011, GDP was estimated to be US$2.3 billion with a GDP growth rate of 4 per cent.

Inflation (consumer prices) was 2.9 per cent in 2005, 6.7 per cent in 2006, and 3.1 per cent in 2007. In 2010, the rate was estimated to be 1.5 per cent, rising to 2.5 per cent in 2011.

According to figures from the AFDB, total external public debt was US$929.55 million in 2004, US$870.77 million in 2005 and US$862.82 million in 2006.

Foreign Investment
In 2001, the Central African Republic received US$213,000 from the US in development assistance and IMET. The Central African Republic was a recipient of economic aid of about US$73 million in 2000. Donors pledged an estimated US$600m at in 2007. France has traditionally been the largest bilateral donor. The Central African Republic remains dependent on loans.

Balance of Payments / Imports and Exports

Major export commodities include diamonds, coffee, cotton, timber, and tobacco. In 2002, diamonds accounted for 50 per cent of total export earnings, and timber accounted for some 30 per cent in the same year. Export trading partners are Belgium, Italy, France, Germany, Luxembourg, Egypt, Spain and Côte d'Ivoire.

Import commodities include food, textiles, petroleum products, machinery, electrical equipment, motor vehicles, chemicals, pharmaceuticals, and consumer goods. Import trading partners are France, United States, Cameroon, Côte d'Ivoire, Germany, and Japan.

External Trade, US$ million

	2005	2006	2007
Trade balance	-43.54	-26.61	-25.24
Exports	128.41	157.71	183.57
Imports	171.95	184.33	208.81

Source: African Development Bank

Total exports of goods and services were estimated to be US$200 million in 2010 and imports US$450 million. China has developed into a major export market. Belgium and France remain significant trading partners.

Central Bank

Banque des Etats de L'Afrique Centrale (BEAC), PO Box 1917, Rue du Docteur Jamot, Yaounde, Cameroun. Tel: +237 234030 / 2230511, fax: +237 233329 / 223 3380, e-mail: beacyde@beac.int, URL: http://www.beac.int/
Governor: Lucas Abaga Nchama

Chambers of Commerce and Trade Organisations

Chamber of Commerce, Industry and Handicraft, Chambre de Commerce, d'Industrie et de l'Artisanat, BP 252 ET 813, Bangui. Central African Republic. Tel: +236 614255 / 611668

MANUFACTURING, MINING AND SERVICES

Primary and Extractive Industries

Diamonds represent the Central African Republic's chief mineral wealth. The diamond industry accounted for almost 50 per cent of export earnings (2002). There are also unexploited natural resources such as gold, uranium, iron ore, manganese, and copper.

Although there may be oil deposits along the northern border with Chad, these are as yet undeveloped and so the country relies entirely on imports for its oil requirements. In 2011 estimated imports of 2,000 barrels per day of oil were consumed, most of it distillate, jet fuel, kerosene, and gasoline.

Energy

In 2010 the Central African Republic had an electricity generating capacity of 40,000 GWe, and generated 0.16 billion kilowatthours (kWh) of electricity. Over 80 per cent is produced by hydropower, and just over 20 per cent is produced by fossil fuels. The country consumed an estimated 0.15 billion kWh of electricity.

Manufacturing

Industry contributes nearly 15 per cent of GDP and employs about 6 per cent of the workforce. Manufacturing industries include artesian diamond mining, preparation of timber, brewing, textiles, bicycle and motorcycle assembly, footwear, soap, cigarettes, soft drinks, paint, bricks and the manufacture of utensils. In areas where cotton is grown, closth is produced. Refined sugar and palm oil are produced.

Service Industries

The services industry accounts for just over 27 per cent of GDP and, along with the commerce sector, employs about 4 per cent of the workforce. The services sector is limited by high transport costs due to limited access to sea and river transport.

Agriculture

The Central African Republic's economy is primarily dependent on the agriculture industry, which accounts for over half of GDP and three-quarters of the workforce.

Agricultural Production in 2010

Produce	Int. $'000*	Tonnes
Indigenous cattle meat	248,540	92,005
Yams	99,850	435,000
Cassava	70,926	678,958
Groundnuts, with shell	60,513	140,000
Indigenous goat meat	43,109	17,991
Game meat	42,865	19,700
Honey, natural	37,140	14,800
Bananas	35,486	126,000
Sesame seed	33,281	50,000
Taro (cocoyam)	25,026	118,000
Indigenous pigmeat	24,581	15,990
Cow milk, whole, fresh	23,405	75,000

Source: http://faostat.fao.org/site/339/default.aspx Food and Agriculture Organization of the United Nations, Food and Agricultural commodities production

COMMUNICATIONS AND TRANSPORT

Travel Requirements

Citizens of the USA, Canada, Australia and the EU require a passport valid for six months after entry and a visa, unless in transit with onward ticket and not required by all nationals not leaving the airport. Evidence of yellow fever vaccination may also be required for entry. Other nationals should contact the embassy to check visa requirements.

International Airports

The Central African Republic has a total of 52 airports, of which three have paved runways and 49 have unpaved runways. International air services are limited and domestic flights are only charters.

Roads

According to recent statistics, the country has a total of 24,000 km of roads, though only 650 km are paved. A bus service links the Central African Republic with Chad. Vehicles are driven on the right.

Ports and Harbours

There are ports at Bangui and Nola. Eight hundred km of waterways exist, of which Ubangi or Oubangui is the major river ferries run up river from Ubangi. The river is also used for commercial traffic, but it is impassable from December to May due to weather conditions.

HEALTH

In 2009, the government spent approximately 8.5 per cent of its total budget on healthcare, accounting for 34.2 per cent of all healthcare spending. Total expenditure on healthcare equated to 4.0 per cent of the country's GDP. Per capita expenditure on health was approximately US$18.

According to recent statistics the Central African Republic has three hospitals located in Bangui, 11 prefectoral hospitals and four regional hospitals. There are 410 health centres and five leprosy hospitals. According to 2011 figures from the WHO, in 2000-10 there were 331 doctors (0.08 per 1,000 population), 1,613 nurses (0.30 per 1,000 population), 519 midwives (0.13 per 1,000 population), 13 dentists, 17 pharmacists, 55 public and environmental health workers, and 99 community health workers.

In 2006, an estimated 66 per cent of the population (90 per cent urban and 51 per cent rural) had sustainable access to improved drinking water. An estimated 31 per cent of the population had sustainable access to improved sanitation (40 per cent urban and 25 per cent rural). In 2010, 67 per cent of the population had access to improved drinking water and 34 per cent to improved sanitation. An estimated 45 per cent of the population is undernourished.

The under-5 mortality rate in 2010 was 159 per 1,000 live births and the infant mortality rate (probability of dying by first birthday) was 106 per 1,000 live births. An estimated 40 per cent of children aged 5 have stunted growth. The most common causes of death in young children are pneumonia (16 per cent), prematurity (11 per cent), birth asphyxia (8 per cent), malaria (26 per cent), diarrhoea (11 per cent) and HIV/AIDS (3 per cent). In 2010 there were 179 reported cases of leprosy, 361 of meningitis, 4 of polio, and 6,643 of TB. In 2009, there were 175,210 reported cases of malaria; an estimated 15 per cent of children sleep under treated-insect-nets. (Source: http://www.who.int, World Health Statistics 2012)

EDUCATION

Primary/Secondary Education

First level education begins at six years and ends at eleven years. Second level education begins at 12 and ends at the age of 15. Second level second stage education begins at 16 and is completed at the age of 18. Education is free between the ages of 6 and 14. An estimated 1.4 per cent of GDP was spent on education in 2006, of which over 50 per cent was on primary, 24 per cent on secondary and 23 per cent on tertiary education.

In 2006 the gross enrolment rate for primary education for children of primary school age was 46 per cent (53 per cent for boys and 38 per cent for girls). Under 25 per cent of primary school children complete their primary education. The latest figures (1991) on primary pupil: teacher ration put it at 77: 1. The gross enrolment ratio for secondary education was around 25 per cent.

Higher Education

According to UNESCO 1 per cent of the population is enrolled in higher education.

The latest UNESCO statistics (2006) estimate the literacy rate to be 62 per cent (71 per cent for males and 53.7 per cent for females). This represents a substantial increase from 1998 when the rates were estimated at 48 per cent for males and 20.3 per cent for females. For the age group 15-24 years the rate was 71.8 per cent (76.8 per cent for males and 67 per cent for females).

RELIGION

18 per cent of the Republic's population subscribe to indigenous beliefs, 66 per cent is Christian, both Protestant and Roman Catholic, and 15 per cent is Muslim.

The Central African Republic has a religious liberty rating of 6 on a scale of 1 to 10 (10 is most freedom). (Source: World Religion Database)

CHAD

COMMUNICATIONS AND MEDIA

Most broadcasters are run by the state. Private newspapers do exist and do carry criticism of the government. A law was passed in 2004 to abolish custodial sentences for press offences. The press is limited by high costs and a high level of illiteracy.

Newspapers
The main newspapers include Centrafrique presse, URL: http://www.centrafrique-presse.com (state-owned), Le Cityoen, Le Confident (URL: http://www.leconfident.net/), L'Hirondelle and Le Démocrate.

Broadcasting
According to recent statistics nearly 20,000 televisions are in use (two households per 1,000), and just over 280,000 radios. The state broadcaster is the Television Centrafricaine. There is a private television station (Tropic RTV). The state-run radio station is Radio Centrafrique. Radio Ndeke Luka is a UN-backed radio station based in Bangui (URL: http://www.radiondekeluka.org). Its coverage includes international news.

Telecommunications
The telephone service is very limited. Recent figures put the number of main telephone lines at 12,000. There were an estimated 150,000 mobile phones in use in 2008. Most telephone services (both landline and cellular) are concentrated around the capital.

According to 2008 figures there were an estimated 19,000 internet users, representing one of the lowest per capita usages in the world.

ENVIRONMENT

Current environmental problems include a lack of potable water, the loss of wildlife by poaching, deforestation, and desertification.

According to figures from the EIA, in 2010 the Central African Republic's emissions from the consumption of fossil fuels totalled 0.23 million metric tons of carbon dioxide amongst the lowest in Africa.

The country is a party to the following international environmental agreements: Biodiversity, Climate Change, Climate Change-Kyoto Protocol, Desertification, Endangered Species, Hazardous Wastes, Ozone Layer Protection, Tropical Timber 94, and Wetlands. It has signed, but not ratified the Law of the Sea.

CHAD
Republic of Chad
République du Tchad

Capital: N'Djamena (Population estimate: 800,000)

Head of State: Gen. Idriss Deby (President) (page 1413)

National Flag: A tricolour pale-wise, blue, yellow, red.

CONSTITUTION AND GOVERNMENT

Constitution
Chad gained independence from France on 11 August 1960. The first prime minister, Ngarta Tombalbaye, was killed during a coup in 1975 and was succeeded by General Félix Malloum Ngakoutou Bey-Ndi. Chad was subsequently ruled by a Military Council until 1979, when a Government of National Unity under Hassan Habré assumed power. However, the difficulties in setting up a working government structure proved insurmountable and civil war broke out. A number of international attempts were made to establish peace, but it was not until the overthrow of Hassan Habré by the forces of Idriss Deby in December 1990 that the way was open to the introduction of a National Charter in February 1991.

In October 1991 an order regulating the establishment of political parties was promulgated. A new government was formed in 1994. A national referendum in March 1996 adopted a new constitution based on the French model which provides for a unified and presidential state.

The President heads the executive branch of government and is elected by universal adult suffrage. An amendment to the constitution which removed the limit on presidential terms (maximum of two consecutive five-year terms) was approved by referendum in 2005. The President appoints the Prime Minister who appoints the cabinet. Suffrage is universal at 18.

A referendum was held on 3 June 2005 on several constitutional changes. The changes included allowing a third presidential term, replacing the Senate with an Economic, Social and Cultural Council, and making constitutional change a presidential prerogative. The parliament approved the changes after opposition MPs walked out.

To consult the constitution, please visit: http://www.presidencetchad.org/Constitution_Tchad.pdf

International Relations
Chad's relations with the Central African Republic have improved since President Bozize took power in 2003. Relations with Libya have also improved. There have been recent clashes in the Chad-Sudan border area between Chadian troops and Sudanese militia. The border was closed for a time in 2008 after renewed violence. Chad also cut its economic ties with Sudan. France is Chad's main international ally.

Recent Events
In January 2006, the President supported a law to reduce the amount of oil money spent on development. The World Bank responded by suspending loans and ordering the oil revenues account to be frozen.

In March 2006, there was an attempted military coup, and in April hundreds of people were killed during battles on the outskirts of the capital. The Government accused Sudan of backing the rebels, and cut diplomatic ties.

Parliament approved the establishment of Chad's first state oil company, Société des Hydrocarbures du Tchad (SHT), in July 2006.

In November, a state of emergency was imposed in the areas bordering Sudan's Darfur region, following ethnic violence, and by February 2007, a UN refugee agency was warning that killing tactics from neighbouring Darfur were being used in eastern Chad, threatening a genocide. In May the governments of Chad and Sudan agreed to stop the cross border violence but it was feared that the agreement would have little effect. In January 2008 the European Union approved a peacekeeping force to be sent to protect refugees from Darfur. The EU peacekeepers handed over to a UN force (Minurcat) in March 2009.

Nourradine Delwa Kassire Coumakoye was appointed prime minister in March 2007; He formed a coalition government which included the United Front for Change (FUC), a rebel group which in 2006 had attacked the capital and attempted to depose the president before signing a peace agreement. In December 2007 two ministers from the FUC were dismissed from the cabinet; this and further rebel attacks on the capital led to the dismissal of the prime minister. Youssouf Seleh Abbas was appointed to the post in April 2008.

Diplomatic relations with Sudan were very strained in 2008; Sudan cut off diplomatic ties and Chad responded by closing its border. Relations were restored in November 2008.

A new alliance between rebel groups was formed in January 2009. The group, the Union of Resistance Forces, is headed by Timan Erdimi, the leader of the Rally of Democratic Forces.

In October 2010, a meeting of experts took place on how to protext Lake Chad, the lake has shrunk a great deal in the last 50 years.

In April 2012, President Deby called on the countries neighbouring northern Nigeria to set up a joint military force to tackle Boko Haram militants. President Deby feared that Islamists could destabilise the whole Lake Chad basin area.

In January 2013, Prime Minister Nadingar was dismissed from his post and Djimranga Dadnadji replaced him.

In the begining of 2013, Chadian troops helped France drive al-Qaeda allies out of northern Mali. In April 2013, Chad sent further troops to the Central African Republic to help stabilise the area after a coup.

Legislature
The legislature is unicameral. The sole chamber, the National Assembly (Assemblée Nationale), has 155 members, directly elected for a four-year term. Assembly members may introduce legislation. Once passed by the Assembly the president must take action (sign or reject) within 15 days.

Assemblée Nationale, Palais du 15 janvier, BP 01, N'djamema, Chad.
President of National Assembly: Kamougué W. Abdelkader

Cabinet (as at June 2013)

Prime Minister: Joseph Djimrangar Dadnadji (page 1411)
Minister Advising the President: Dr Bayom Mallo Adrien
Minitster Delegate to the President in charge of National Defence and Veterans. Benaindo Tatola
Minister of Justice and Holder of the Seal: Jean Bernard Padare
Minister of Foreign Affairs and African Integration: Moussa Faki Mahamat
Minister of Agriculture and Irrigation: Dangde Laoubele Damaye
Minister of Land Development, Urban Planning and Housing: Gata Ngoulou
Minister of Finance and Budget: Atteib Habib Doutoum
Minister of Economy, Planning and International Co-operation: Issa Ali Taher
Minister of Infrastructure and Transport: Hassan Soukaya
Minister of Public Health: Ahmat Djidda Mahamat

Minister of Commerce and Industry: Hamid Mahamat Dahalop
Minister of Basic Education and Literacy: Albatoul Zakaria
Ministry of Secondary Education: Abdelkerim Seid Bauche
Minister of Higher Education, Scientific Research and Vocational Training: Dr Adoum Goudja
Minister of the Environment and Marine Resources: Mahamat Issa Halikimi
Minister of Civil Service and Employment: Abakar Abdoulaya
Minister of Livestock and Animal Resources:
Minister of Mines and Geology: Oumar Adoum Sini
Minister of Oil and Energy: Djerassem Le Bemadjiel
Minister of Posts, Information Technology and Communication: Dr Abdoulaya Sabre Fadoul
Minister of Tourism and Craft Industries: Abderahim Younous Ali
Minister of Urban and Rural Water Resources: Ali Mahamat Abdoulaya
Minister of Culture: Dayang Menwa Enoch
Minister of Territorial Administration and Decentralization: Yokabdjin Mandigui
Minister of Public Security and Immigration: Tchonai Elimi Hassan
Minister of Social Action, National Solidarity and the Family: Baiwong Djiberqui Amane Rosine
Minister of Public Morality and Promotion of Good Governance: Hinsou Hara
Minister of Information and Communication; Government Spokesman: Hassane Silla Bakari
Minister of Youth and Sport: Mahamat Adoum
Minister of Livestock and Pastoral Development: Amir Adoudou Artine
Minister of Micro-Finance for the Promotion of Women and Youth: Martin Bagrim Kibassim
Minister of Transport and Civil Aviation: Dillo Adoum
Minister of Human Rights and Basic Liberties: Amina Kodjiyana
Secretary-Genera to the Government: Samir Adam Annour

Ministries

Office of the President, PO Box 74, N'Djamena, Chad. Tel: +235 514437, fax: +235 514501 / 514653, e-mail: presidence@tchad.td, URL: http://www.tit.td/presidence.html
Office of the Prime Minister, N'Djamena, Chad.
Ministry of the Interior, Security and Decentralisation, N'Djamena, Chad. Fax: +235 525885.
Ministry of Foreign Affairs and Cooperation, PO Box 746, N'Djamena, Chad. Tel: +235 518050, fax: +235 514585
Ministry of Defence, PO Box 916, N'Djamena, Chad. Tel: +235 523513 / 522233 / 525045, fax: +235 526544
Ministry of Public Works and Transport, PO Box 436, N'Djamena,Chad. Tel: +235 520660 / 522096, fax: +235 523935
Ministry of Justice, PO Box 426 N'Djamena, Chad. Tel: +235 522172 / 522139, fax: +235 525885
Ministry of Finance and the Economy, PO Box 816, N'Djamena, Chad. Tel: +235 523398, fax: +235 524908
Ministry of National Education, PO Box 743, N'Djamena, Chad. Tel: +235 519353 / 519265, fax: +235 514512
Ministry of Higher Education and Scientific Research, PO Box 743, N'Djamena, Chad. Tel: +235 516158 / 514243, fax: +235 519231
Ministry of Communications, PO Box 892, N'Djamena, Chad. Tel: +235 524097 / 526094, fax: +235 526560
Ministry of the Civil Service, Employment and Labour, PO Box 637, N'Djamena, Chad. Tel: +235 520223 / 522198, fax: +235 526834
Ministry of the Environment and Water Resources, N'Djamena, Chad. Tel: +235 522099 / 523255 / 526012, fax: +235 523839
Ministry of Agriculture, PO Box 441, N'Djamena, Chad. Tel: +235 526979 / 523752, 526566, fax: +235 525119
Ministry of Livestock, PO Box 750, N'Djamena, Chad. Tel: +235 529853
Ministry of Oil, PO Box 816, N'Djamena, Chad. Tel: +235 525087 / 525603, fax: +235 512565
Ministry of Public Health, PO Box 440, N'Djamena, Chad. Tel: +235 515800 / 515114, fax: +235 515800
Ministry of Social Action and the Family, PO Box 80, N'Djamena, Chad. Tel: +235 0323 / 522532, fax: +235 520323
Ministry of Post and Telecommunications, PO Box 154, N'Djamena, Chad. Tel: +235 521579, fax : +235 521530
Ministry of Industrial, Commercial and Handicraft, PO Box 424, N'Djamena, Chad. Tel: +235 522199, fax: +235 522733
Ministry of Culture, Youth and Sports, PO Box 519, N'Djamena, Chad. Tel: +235 516886 / 522658
Ministry of Tourism Development, PO Box 86, N'Djamena, Chad. Tel: +235 523255
Ministry of Mines and Energy, PO Box 816, N'Djamena, Chad. Tel: +235 522088, fax: +235 522565
Ministry of Planning and Territorial Development, PO Box 436, N'Djamena, Chad. Tel: +235 523189, fax: +235 523935
Ministry of Planning, Development and Co-operation, PO Box 286, N'Djamena, Chad. Tel: +235 514795 / 514587 / 518981, fax: +235 515185
Ministry of Public Security and Immigration, PO Box 916, N'Djamena, Chad. Tel: +235 520576 / 520577

Elections

Chad held its first free, multiparty presidential elections in June 1996. Idriss Deby was elected, having received 69 per cent of the vote, although opposition parties suggested that a government court had disregarded 250,000, mainly anti-Deby Idriss votes. On 20 May 2001 Deby was re-elected as president of Chad with 67 per cent of the vote and on 3rd May 2006 he was elected for his third term. Opposition parties boycotted the 2006 election, and said that turnout was low. The Election Commission said that turnout was over 60 per cent. President Deby was re-elected in April 2011.

The last parliamentary elections took place in April 2002 when President Deby's Mouvement Patriotique du Salut (MPS) party won 112 of the Assemblée Nationale's 155 seats. The RDP won 10 seats, FAR 9, RNDP 6, URD, 4, and UNDR 4. Elections were due to take place in April 2006, but were postponed. Elections eventually took place on February 13 2011. Provisional results showed that Patriotic Salvation Movement (MPS) and its aligned parties had won 133 of the 188 seats.

Political Parties

Mouvement Patriotique du Salut (MPS, Patriotic Salvation Movement), URL: http://www.tchad-mps.com/
Secretary General: Mahamat Hisseine
Union pour le Rénouveau et la Démocratie (URD, Union for Renewal and Democracy), Leader: Wadel Abdelkader Kamougué
Union Nationale pour la Démocratie et le Renouvellement (UNDR, National Union for Democracy and Renewal), Leader: Saleh Kebzabo Célestin Topona
Union pour la Démocratie et la République (UDR, Union for Democracy and the Republic), Leader: Jean A. Bawoyeu
Rassemblement pour la Démocratie et le Progrès (RDP, Rally for Democracy and Progress), Leader: Lol Mahamat Choua
Union Démocratique Tchadienne (UDT, Chadian Democratic Union), founded 1990. URL: http://www.maxpages.com/udt1tchad/

There are also rebel movements including Le mouvement pour la démocratie et la justice au Tchad (CMJDT) (URL: http://www.mdjet.net/) which has the support of the CMAP (Co-ordination des mouvements armés et politiques de l'opposition) which claims to represent various political and armed groups. The CMAP is not legally recognised.

Diplomatic Representation

US Embassy, Avenue Felix Eboue, PO Box 413, N'Djamena, Chad. Tel: +235 517009, fax: +235 515654, e-mail: paschallrc@ndjamenab.us-state.gov, URL: http://ndjamena.usembassy.gov
Ambassador: Mark Boulware
British High Commission (all staff reside at Yaounde)
Ambassador: Bharat Joshi (page 1452)
British Consulate, BP 1182, N'Djamena, Chad. Tel: +235 523970, fax: +235 523970, e-mail: econsit@hotmail.com
Embassy of Chad, Boulevard Lambermont 52, 1030 Brussels, Belgium. Tel: +32 2 215 1975
Ambassador: Abderahim Yacoub Ndiaye
Embassy of Chad, 2002 R Street, NW Washington DC 20009, USA. Tel: +1 202 462 4009, fax: +1 202 265 1937, e-mail: info@chadembassy.org, URL: http://www.chadembassy.org
Ambassador: Mahamoud Adam Bechir
Permanent Representative of the Republic of Chad to the United Nations, 211 East 43rd Street, Suite 1703, New York, N.Y. 10017, USA. Tel: +1 212 986 0980, fax: +1 212 986 0152, e-mail: chad@un.int
Ambassador: Ahmad Allam-Mi

LEGAL SYSTEM

The system of law is based on French civil law and Chadian customary law. The Supreme Court is Chad's highest judicial authority, followed by the Court of Appeal, Magistrate and Criminal Courts. The Constitutional Council presides over state matters. The president appoints most judicial officials. The Supreme Court is made up of a chief justice, named by the president, and 15 councillors chosen by the president and the National Assembly. The appointments are for life. The Constitutional Council is made up of nine judges, each serving a nine-year term. It has the power to review legislation and treaties before they are implemented.

In recent years, an estimated 185,000 Chadians have been internally displaced as a result of violence. Approximately 250,000 Sudanese refugees live in camps along the border. Civilian authorities have found it difficult to control the security forces effectively. Human rights abuses have included extrajudicial killings and politically motivated disappearances; security force torture and impunity; arbitrary arrest and life-threatening prison conditions as well as denials of fair public trials; executive interference in the judiciary; use of excessive force and other abuses in internal conflict, and limits on freedom of speech, press, and assembly. There is also widespread official corruption, and the work of nongovernmental organizations has been obstructed.

Chad retains the death penalty for murder. The last reported execution was in 1993.

Chief Justice: Abderahim Bireme Hamid

Chad National Human Rights Commission, BP 1522, N'djamena, Chad. Tel: +235 522484, fax: +235 522089

LOCAL GOVERNMENT

Chad's local government system was re-organised in 2003. Its 14 prefectures were abolished and were replaced by 22 regions. Each region is headed by a governor appointed by the president. The regions are divided into departments administered by prefects. The 61 departments are further sub-divided into 200 sub-prefectures, which are made up of 446 cantons. As part of ongoing reforms, the cantons will be replaced by rural communities. Under the terms of the constitution local elections should take place, but they have been repeatedly postponed.

CHAD

The regions are: Barh El Gazel, Batha, Borkou, Chari Baguirmi, Ennedi, Guéra, Hadjer-Lamis, Kanem, Lac, Logone OPWestern Logone, Eastern Logone, Mandoul, Mayo-Kebbi Est, Mayo-Kebbi Ouest, Moyen-Chari, OUaddai, Salamat, Sila, Tandjile, Tibesti, Wadi Fira and N'Djamena.

AREA AND POPULATION

Area
Chad has an area of 1,284,000 sq. km extending 1,700 km from north to south and 1,000 km. east to west. It is situated in what was previously known as French Equatorial Africa. It has borders with Libya, Niger, Cameroon, the Central African Republic and Sudan. The country is arid in the centre and largely desert in the mountainous north. The southern lowlands have a more tropical climate and are more fertile. The population is concentrated in the south.

To view a map, please visit: http://www.un.org/Depts/Cartographic/map/profile/chad.pdf

Population
Chad had an estimated population of 11.227 million in 2010. The annual growth rate was 3.1 per cent over the period 2000-10 and the population is expected to reach 12.6 million by 2025. Major ethnic groups include Arab, Fulbe, Kotoko, Hausa, Sara, and Ngambaye. Chad's major cities are N'Djamena (the capital, population est. 800,000), Sarh (population 135,000), Moundou, and Abeche. The trend is for urban migration; in 2010, approximately 28 per cent of the population was urban compared to 4.2 per cent in 1998. Population density is approximately 8.0 inhabitants per km².

In January 2004 thousands of Sudanese refugees began arriving in Chad, fleeing the fighting in the Darfur region of Sudan. By 2005 there were estimated to be approximately 225,000 refugees from Sudan and 30,000 from the Central African Republic.

The official languages of Chad are Arabic and French.

Births, Deaths, Marriages
Average life expectancy in 2009 at birth was 47.0 for males, 48.0 for females. Healthy life expectancy in 2007 at birth was 40 years. The population is very young: 1,698,000 are under 5 and 4,155,000 are under 15 years. Some 45 per cent of the people are 14 years old or younger and under 5 per cent are over 60. The median age is 17.

In 2010, the crude birth rate was 44.7 per 1,000 population and the crude death rate was 16.9 per 1,000 population. The infant mortality rate was 99 per 1,000 live births in 2010. In 2010 the fertility rate was 6.0 children per female. Only 1 per cent of the female population is thought to use contraception. The maternal mortality ratio was 1,200 deaths per 100,000 live births in 2009. (Source: http://www.who.int, World Health Statistics 2012)

Public Holidays 2014
1 January: New Year
14 January: Birth of the Prophet* (Mawlid al-Nabi)
21 April: Easter Monday
1 May: Labour Day
9 June: Whit Monday
25 May: Liberation of Africa
29 July: End of Holy Month of Ramadan* (Eid al Fitr)
11 August: Independence Day
5 October: Feast of the Sacrifice (Eid al-Adha)*
1 November: All Saints Day
4 November: Muharram (Islamic New Year)*
28 November: Proclamation of the Republic
1 December: Liberation and Democracy Day
25 December: Christmas
* Dependent on the Islamic lunar calendar

EMPLOYMENT

Estimated figures from 2007 put the labour force at 4.2 million. About 85 per cent of Chad's labour force works in agriculture, mainly subsistence agriculture. The workforce represents just under half the population. 80 per cent of the population lives below the poverty line.

BANKING AND FINANCE

Currency
The unit of currency is the Communauté Financière Africaine (CFA) franc (fixed to the euro)

GDP/GNP, Inflation, National Debt
Chad is one of the poorest countries in the world. Economic and structural reforms have been ongoing since 1995 and public finances have improved. The main constraints to the country's economic development are an unskilled labour force, lack of production diversification, poor transport infrastructure, climate and situation (Chad is landlocked). The government has committed to continuing economic reforms including the development of agriculture, livestock and oil sectors, including export markets, addressing regional balances, building national capacity and reducing poverty. The government is also attempting to develop the private sector; privatisation of the sugar industry (SONASUT) took place in 2000. Privatisation of the water, electricity and the telecommunications industries are also planned. In 2003 Chad became an oil-producing country and the development of the Cameroon-Chad pipeline has transformed the economy. There is significant Chinese and US investment in the oil industry.

Chad's economy was primarily dependent on agriculture, with cotton as the major cash crop. However the development of the Cameroon-Chad pipeline transformed the economy. Oil revenue started going into the government accounts in 2004 and the economy was further boosted by foreign investment and the impact of the Cameroon-Chad pipeline. GDP was put at 33.7 per cent in that year with GDP at US$4,414.98 million. However forecasts indicate that oil production may decline in the next few years. GDP growth fell to 7.9 per cent in 2005, with GDP reaching US$6,873.38 million. GDP growth dropped to 0.2 per cent in 2006 and -0.3 per cent. GDP was US$6,508.95 million in 2007. Estimated figures for 2010 put GDP at US$7.9 billion, giving a per capita figure of US$780. Over 40 per cent of the population still live below the poverty line.

Agriculture accounted for 38 per cent of GDP, industry 13 per cent, and services 49 per cent, but changes to the economy since the oil pipeline was built and Chad became an oil exporting nation are reflected in the make up GDP. In 2008, agriculture contributed 14 per cent, industry 49 per cent and the service sector 37 per cent.

The government has also imposed greater controls on public spending. The resulting deflationary tendency was also reversed, with consumer prices rising from -8.4 per cent in 1999, to 3.8 per cent in 2000, to 6.2 per cent in 2002. This compares to 1994 when inflation was over 40 per cent following the devaluation of the CFA. Inflation was 7.9 per cent in 2005, 8.0 per cent in 2006 and -4.2 per cent in 2007.

Total external debt was US$1.686.74 million in 2006. Chad receives financial aid from the IMF under the Poverty Reduction and Growth Facility and was scheduled to receive US$38m in a three-year programme from 2005-08. The EU also agreed on an aid program worth over €270 million. The World Bank temporarily suspended payments in 2006.

Balance of Payments / Imports and Exports
Major exports are oil, cotton, livestock, meat, textiles and fish. The main export markets are US (over 80 per cent), China and Portugal. The export market has been transformed by the construction of the Chad-Cameroon pipeline.

Main imports include food, petroleum products, machinery and industrial goods. Main import countries are France, Cameroon, US, Belgium, India, Portugal and the Netherlands.

External Trade, US$ million

	2006	2007
Trade balance	2,101.57	1,767.61
Exports	3,410.36	3,106.89
Imports	1,308.79	1,339.28

Source: African Development Bank

Exports were estimated to be US$4.9 billion in 2011 and imports US$3.9 billion.

Chad is a member of the Central African Economic and Monetary Community (CEMAC) and the Economic Community of the Central African States (CEEAC).

Central Bank
Banque des États de l'Afrique Centrale (BEAC), PO Box 1917, Rue du Docteur Jamot, Yaounde, Cameroun. Tel: +237 234030 / 234060, fax: +237 233329, URL: http://www.beac.int
Governor: Lucas Abaga Nchama

MANUFACTURING, MINING AND SERVICES

Primary and Extractive Industries
Chad has resources of oil, iron, gold, tin, tungsten, diamonds, bauxite, gypsum, sodium carbonate (natron). Only oil, natron and kaolin are at present being exploited. Although recoverable oil reserves have been estimated at 1,500 million barrels, the country did not have the facilities to produce or refine it until 2003 and was totally dependent on imports from Nigeria and Cameroon. Chad consumes an estimated 2,000 barrels per day. Chad's major oilfields are the Doba Basin (Bolobo, Kome and Miandoun), and the Lake Chad Basin (Kanem, Kumia and Sedigi).

In 2000 the World Bank gave approval for a pipeline project between Chad and Cameroon. The project supported the development of three oil fields in southern Chad and the construction of a 1,070 km pipeline between the oil fields and Kribi, Cameroon on the Atlantic coast. The project included three pumping stations built by Tchad Oil Transport Company (capable of producing 225,000 barrels per day) as part of a consortium with the government. The project was completed a year ahead of schedule. The project is expected to earn over US$9bn which, after loan repayments, will provide the Chadian government with revenue of US$2.5 bn. Oil revenue started going into government accounts in July 2004. The Chadian government agreed to set up a fund (10 per cent) from this income to be put towards health, education, social services and regional development.

The Chadian part of the pipeline is 105 miles (170 km) long. The Doha Basin wells are expected to produce 900 million barrels of low sulphur oil. Major foreign oil companies investing in Chad's oil industry are a consortium of Chevron, Exxon Mobil, and Petronas. Exxon has a controlling 40 per cent share in this consortium. Production began in 2003 and in 2003, 36,000 barrels of petroleum per day were produced. By 2011 Chad was producing over 123.66 thousand bbl/d.

Chad has negligible natural gas resources.

Energy
Chad's electric installed capacity in 2010 was 0.03 GWe, all of which was conventional thermal. Electricity generation, according to 2010 estimates, was 0.10 billion kWh. Consumption was 0.09 billion kWh. At present only 2 per cent of homes in Chad have

electricity. In N'Djamena 9 per cent of homes have electricity. Electricity is produced from imported petroleum products and prices are high. Wood is the primary source of energy for most households and deforestation is a major issue. The World Bank has granted a loan for the creation of sustainable and affordable household energy. Chad has attempted to use oil from the Sedigi field to generate electricity but this failed through poor pipelines. Libya and France recently supplied generators and in 2004 the French Development Agency agreed to a €4 million loan to improve the sector. The state-run Société Tchadienne d'Eau et d'Electricité (STEE) handles generation and distribution of electricity.

Manufacturing
Production concentrates on the processing of agricultural products, particularly cotton, beverages, some furniture, and building materials, textiles and some chemicals, cement, mopeds and bikes, radios and perfume. Construction is growing sector of industry. Industry contributed an estimated 47 per cent to GDP in 2007.

Service Industries
An estimated 29,000 tourists visited Chad in 2006.

Agriculture
The agricultural sector is the primary contributor to Chad's economy, and its main function is the supply of the domestic market. The sector is dependent on climatic conditions and thus varies greatly from year to year. The sector is seen as having great potential for expansion. In the arable sector, arable land covers 3.5 million hectares, and permanent crops 30,000 hectares. Only 1 per cent of arable land is irrigated.

Agricultural Production in 2010

Produce	Int. $'000*	Tonnes
Indigenous cattle meat	288,604	106,836
Groundnuts, with shell	162,002	394,400
Cereals, nes	125,934	490,000
Millet	104,007	600,000
Yams	100,527	414,900
Sorghum	100,352	680,000
Indigenous goat meat	64,982	27,120
Cow milk, whole, fresh	61,052	195,642
Rice, paddy	45,561	170,000
Indigenous sheep meat	43,183	15,860
Beans, dry	10,158	72,800
Cotton lint	36,445	25,500

* unofficial figures
Source: http://faostat.fao.org/site/339/default.aspx Food and Agriculture Organization of the United Nations, Food and Agricultural commodities production

The livestock sub-sector is also a key expansion target. 350,000 cattle are exported each year but the industry needs a better distribution infrastructure and development of basic facilities such as cold storage for it to expand.

30,000 people are involved in fishing in the Lake Chad, Lower Logme and Lower Chari regions. 40,000 tonnes of fish are caught each year. Most fish is preserved.

COMMUNICATIONS AND TRANSPORT

Travel Requirements
US, Canadian, Australian and EU citizens require a passport valid for at least six months (and evidence of parental responsibility may be requested if travelling alone with children), and a visa. Visitors must register at the Sûreté (immigration department) within 72 hours of arrival. Citizens of Benin, Burkina-Faso, Cameroon, Republic of Central Africa, Congo, Ivory Coast, Gabon, Equatorial Guinea, Mauritania, Niger and Senegal do not require a visa.

Other nationals should contact the embassy to check visa requirements.

National Airlines
Air Tchad, 27 avenue Charles de Gaulle, BP 168, N'Djamena, Chad. Tel: +235 515090. Air Tchad flies from N'Djaména to Maundou, Sarh and Mao.

International Airports
There are two international airports at N'djamena and Faya Largeau.

Roads
A rebuilding programme for roads is under way. This programme is of particular importance since Chad is land-locked and roads are used for 95 per cent of domestic and foreign trade. There are approximately 33,000 km of classified roads linking N'djamena to Cameroon, Nigeria, Sudan and the Central African Republic. Under 300 km are paved. Transport costs are high. There is an ongoing project with foreign aid to develop the Djermaya-Massaguet road. Vehicles are driven on the right.

Coopérative des Transporteurs Tchadiens (TCC), PO Box 336, N'Djamena, Chad. Tel: +235 514355

HEALTH

In 2008, the Chad government spent approximately 3.3 per cent of its total budget on healthcare, accounting for 19.7 per cent of all healthcare spending. Total expenditure on health care equated to 4.6 per cent of the country's GDP. Per capita health expenditure in 2009 was US$28 (compared to US$11 in 2000). There is one national hospital serving approximately 7.5 million people and four Prefectorate hospitals serving 950,000 people

each. There are a further 52 district hospitals and 791 health centres. In 2000-10, there were an estimated 345 doctors (less than 1 per 10,000 population), 2,499 nurses (3 per 10,000 population), 37 pharmaceutical personnel 154 community health workers and 15 dentists.

Although rates are improving, child mortality rates remain high. The infant mortality rate (probability of dying by age 1) (as of 2010) was 99 per 1,000 live births and the under-5 mortality rate was 173 per 1,000 live births. Malnutrition affects many children: 44.8 per cent of children aged less than 5 were estimated to be stunted (2000-09) and 33.9 per cent underweight. Vaccination coverage has risen but remains relatively low: as of 2010, the vaccination rates were measles 46 per cent (compared to 28 per cent in 2000), diptheria 60 per cent.

In 2010 there were estimated to be 1,322 cases of tuberculosis, 389 of leprosy, 194 cases of measles, 5,863 cases of meningitus, and 130 of polio. In 2008 there were 182,415 reported cases of malaria. The major causes of childhood deaths are: prematurity (11 per cent), malaria (20 per cent), pneumonia (19 per cent), diarrhoea (14 per cent) and HIV/AIDS (3 per cent). Official figures put the HIV rate at 4 per cent in rural areas and 10 per cent in urban. Tuberculosis is also prevalent and over 30 per cent of TB sufferers are also HIV positive.

Only 1 per cent of children are estimated to sleep under insecticide-treated nets. In 2010, 51 per cent of the population had sustainable access to potable water and an estimated 13 per cent of the population had sustainable access to improved sanitation. (Source: http://www.who.int, World Health Statistics 2012)

EDUCATION

Primary/Secondary Education
Chad's compulsory education lasts six years, from the age of six to the age of 12. First level education lasts six years, from six to 12. Second level, first stage, education, lasts for four years, from the age of 12 to 15, whilst second level, second stage, education lasts from 16 to 18.

Primary school enrolment in 2006 for primary school age children was estimated to be 70 per cent (73 per cent for boys, 67 per cent for girls). Figures for 2007 show that the pupil:teacher ratio in primary education was 60:1. Secondary school enrolment for secondary age children was estimated to be 10 per cent (14 per cent for boys, 5 per cent for girls). An estimated 5 per cent of children go onto tertiary education.

The quality of education is hindered by poorly qualified staff (nearly half are not qualified), dilapidated schools and equipment, and very high pupil: teacher ratios. The average rate is 63:1. Public expenditure on education was estimated at 1.9 per cent of GDP in 2005 (10 per cent of total government expenditure).

In 2006 the adult literacy rate was 62 per cent (71 per cent for males, 54 per cent for females). The youth literacy rate (15-24 years) was 72 per cent (77 per cent for boys and 67 per cent for girls). By comparison the adult literacy rate was 12.2 per cent in 1992. (Source: UNESCO)

RELIGION

Chad's religious community is largely Muslim, at 57 per cent of the population, with its Christian followers accounting for about 26 per cent, and followers of indigenous beliefs and animism making up the final 16 per cent.

Chad has a religious liberty rating of 4 on a scale of 1 to 10 (10 is most freedom). (Source: World Religion Database)

COMMUNICATIONS AND MEDIA

Radio is the most popular medium within the country and is dominated by state-controlled radio broadcasting. Private newspapers do exist and do publish criticism of the government but their circulation is limited.

Newspapers
N'Djamena Hebdo, BP 760, N'Djamena, Chad. Tel: +235 515314
Le Progres, BP 3055, Ave Charles De Gaulle. Tel: +235 515586, fax: +235 514256
Le Temps and **Le Contact**.

Broadcasting
There is one television station - the state-owned Telechad. In 1997 there were estimated to be 10,000 television sets. The state-run Radiodiffusion Nationale Tchadienne operates national and regional radio stations. A few private radio stations do exist despite high fees.

Telecommunications
The telephone system is very limited. In 2008 there were an estimated 13,000 main telephone lines and 1.8 million mobiles.

In 2008, there were an estimated 130,000 internet users.

ENVIRONMENT

Chad is a signatory to conventions on Biodiversity, Climate Change, Desertification, Endangered Species, Hazardous Wastes, Ozone Layer Protection, and Wetlands. It has signed, but not ratified the Law of the Sea, Marine Dumping. It is also a Non-Annex I country under the United Nations Framework Convention on Climate Change (ratified in June 1994). In 1999 Chad signed the Yaounde Declaration for the Protection and Management of Forest Resources in Central Africa.

STATES OF THE WORLD

Chad's major environmental problems include desertification, deforestation, soil and water pollution caused by improper waste disposal in rural areas, and inadequate supplies of potable water.

According to EIA figures, in 2010, Chad's total emissions from the consumption of fossil fuel were 0.29 million metric tons of carbon dioxide. Chad's oil industry contributes 100 per cer of carbon emissions.

CHILE
Republic of Chile
República de Chile

Capital: Santiago (Population estimate: 6 million)

Head of State: President: Sebastián Piñera (page 1496)

National Flag: Divided fesswise white and red; a canton blue charged with a five-pointed white star

CONSTITUTION AND GOVERNMENT

Constitution

A new constitution for Chile was approved by plebiscite on 11 September 1980 and was brought into force on 11 March 1981. The articles of the constitution provided for an eight-year non-renewable term for the President, for an independent judiciary and central bank, and for a bicameral congress, to function from 1989.

A plebiscite on 5 October 1988, called to confirm General Pinochet as sole presidential candidate for the 1989 election, was defeated; 55 per cent voted against the it, obliging the government to hold free elections within a year. Presidential and congressional elections took place in December 1989, following a series of constitutional reforms. In the presidential contest, the opposition united behind Patricio Aylwin of the Christian Democrats who gained 55.2 per cent of the vote and took office on 11 March 1990.

The Constitutional Reform of August 2005 reduced presidential terms to four years. Executive power is vested in the President who appoints the members of the Cabinet. The Reform of 2005 also put an end to designated senators and 'senators for life' (previously awarded to former Presidents), removed responsibility from the armed forces as 'institutional guarantors' and restored the president's power to remove the commanders-in-chief of the armed forces and the forces of order. The reforms were seen as a milestone in the country's transition to democracy.

To consult the full constitution (in Spanish), please visit: http://www.camara.cl/camara/camara_LOC.aspx

General Pinochet

In 1973, at the behest of the legislative and judicial branches of government, Pinochet helped to depose Marxist President Salvador Allende in a coup. The following year, the ruling military junta appointed Pinochet president. He ruled Chile until 1990. After stepping down, he remained a senator, in accordance with Chilean law. During his presidency, Pinochet implemented anti-communist security operations which left some 3,000 suspected terrorists and dissidents dead; according to reports, a further 30,000 people were tortured. He also implemented economic reforms which led to recovery from the hyperinflation suffered under Allende's presidency.

Chilean courts stripped Gen. Pinochet of his immunity from prosecution several times, but failed to bring him to trial. Pinochet resigned his senatorial seat on 20 August 2002. In December 2004, he was placed under house arrest on human rights abuse charges. In 2005, a US Senate investigation found that the General had hidden some $13 million in secret bank accounts. A Chilean Court ruled in July 2005 that Pinochet could stand trial for tax evasion, but not for human rights abuses. At the time of his death of a heart attack (aged 91) on 10th December 2006, around 300 criminal charges were pending against Gen. Pinochet for alleged human rights abuses and embezzlement during his rule. In June 2007, the Government agreed to pay compensation to the families of 12 of Pinochet's victims.

International Relations

Territorial disputes dating back to the War of the Pacific (1879-83) have been an enduring source of tension between Chile and her neighbours. It was not until 1999 that Chile and Peru signed an agreement which finally completed implementation of the peace settlement in respect of their land frontier. In January 2008, Peru filed a lawsuit at the International Court of Justice to settle a long-standing dispute with Chile over maritime territory. Chile and Bolivia have not had full diplomatic relations since 1978, when Bolivia broke them off in pursuit of her continuing claim for restoration of her sovereign access to the Pacific Ocean, lost in the war. On economic and political levels, relations are improving; in December 2005, Chile signed its first bilateral agreement with Bolivia.

Chile is a member of APEC (the Asia-Pacific Economic Cooperation organisation) - Asia accounts for a fifth of Chile's foreign trade - and an Associate Member of Mercosur, (the common market of Argentina, Brazil, Uruguay, Paraguay and Venezuela). The country is politically committed to Mercosur's strategic vision of regional political and economic integration. Chile is also a member of the Organisation of American States (OAS), and an active member of the United Nations, contributing armed forces to the Peacekeeping Forces in Cyprus and Haiti. In May 2007 Chile was officially invited to join the OECD (Organisation for Economic Cooperation) where it would be the only Latin American member after Mexico. The invitation has been seen as recognition of Chile's economic and political stability.

The EU and Chile signed an Association Agreement to liberalise trade and increase politica dialogue and co-operation in 2002, and that Agreement has now been fully ratified.

Recent Events

In January 2006, Michelle Bachelet won the presidential election and became Chile's firs woman president.

On 15 November 2007, a 7.7-magnitude earthquake hit northern Chile, causing the destructio of roads and buildings. Two people died and over 100 were injured. Some 15,000 peopl were left homeless. The quake was felt in the capital Santiago, 1,260 km to the south, a well as in Argentina, Peru and Bolivia. In early January 2008, the Llaima volcano erupted sending a column of smoke approximately 3,000m into the air, as lava flowed down it eastern slope.

On the 2nd May 2008, Chaiten volcano, in the southern Patagonia region, began eruptin for the first time in 450 years. Located on the edge of the South American and Nazca tectoni plates, Chile is in one of the most volcanically-active regions on Earth; it is thought tha around 20 of its more than 100 active volcanoes are in danger of erupting at any time. Mor than 4,000 people evacuated the town of Chaiten, 10km from the volcano, after the firs eruption.

In February 2010 central Chile was hit by a devastating 8.8 magnitude earthquake and mor than 700 people were killed. Chile was hit by aftershocks for some time afterward. Man people in coastal areas were killed after the quake triggered tsunami size waves.

On August 5, 2010, 33 Chilean miners became trapped 700 metres below ground when par of the San Jose mine collapsed. Seventeen days later it was discovered that they were sti alive and a huge rescue mission began with a rescue shaft having to be dug. On October 1 the first of the miners was winched to the surface in a special cage. The rescue mission wa a complete success with all 33 miners being safely rescued watched by the world's media.

In December 2010, a programme of penal reform was announced by President Pinera afte a fire at an overcrowded prison in Santiago led to the deaths of 81 prisoners.

In July 2011, thousands of school and university students took to the streets demanding more equal education system. That month copper miners went on strike in protests a government plans to restructure the industry.

In January 2012, the government sparked controversy when the designation of Genera Pinocht's government was changed from 'dictatorship' to 'regime' in school textbooks.

In April 2012, Congress passed a law stating that discrimination because of sexual orientatio is an offence. The law had been much debated before it was passed.

Legislature

Legislative power is vested in the National Congress (Congreso Nacional) which is divide into two houses: the Chamber of Deputies (Camara de Diputados) and the Senate (Senad de la República).
Congress of Chile, Avda Pedro Montt s/n, Valparaiso, Chile. Tel: +56 (0)32 230995, fax +56 (0)32 232651, URL: http://www.congreso.cl

Upper House

The Senate is composed of 38 directly elected senators, chosen by universal popular vote These serve eight-year terms, with half of them being replaced every fourth year. Amendmen to the Constitution, approved by Congress in August 2005, eliminated non-directly electe senators from March 2006; until then, nine additional Institutional Senators were appointe from the Supreme Court, the Army, Navy, Air Force, Police, a state university, and th government itself, and one of them was a former President of the Republic.
Senate, Avda Pedro Montt s/n, Valparaiso, Chile. Tel: +56 (0)32 230995, fax: +56 (0)3 232651, URL: http://www.congreso.cl

Lower House

The Chamber of Deputies comprises 120 deputies, who are elected to four-year terms, b direct universal suffrage, from 60 two-member electoral districts.
Chamber of Deputies, Avda Pedro Montt s/n, Valparaiso, Chile. Tel: +56 (0)32 504000 fax: +56 (0)32 230531, URL: http://www.camara.cl/

Cabinet (as at June 2013)
Minister of the Interior: Andres Chadwick
Minister of Foreign Affairs: Alfredo Moreno Charme (page 1403)
Minister of Defence: Rodrigo Hinzpeter Kirberg
Secretary General to the President: Cristian Larroulet Vignau
Secretary General of the Government: Cecilia Perez
Minister of the Economy: Pablo Longueira

Minister of Finance: Felipe Larrain Bascuñán (page 1461)
Minister of Justice: Patricia Perez Goldberg
Minister of Mining: Hernan De Solminihac Tampier
Minister of Energy: Jorge Bunster
Minister of the Environment: María Ignacia Benítez Pereira
Minister of Transport and Telecommunications: Pedro Pablo Errazuriz Dominguez
Minister of Public Works: Maria Loreto Silva
Minister of Agriculture: Luis Mayol
Minister of Housing and Town Planning: Rodrigo Perez Mackenna
Minister of Labour and Social Security: Evelyn Matthei Fornet
Minister of Education: Carolina Schmidt Zaldivar
Minister of Health: Jaime Mañalich Muxi
Minister of Culture and the Arts: Roberto Ampuero
Minister of Social Deelopment: Bruno Baranda
Minister of Women's Affairs: Loreto Seguel

Ministries

Office of the President, Palacio de la Moneda, Santiago, Chile. Tel: +56 (2) 690 4000, fax: +56 (0)2 4656, URL: http://www.presidencia.gob.cl/
Ministry of Foreign Affairs, Catedral 1158, Santiago, Chile. Tel: +56 (0)2 679 4200, URL:http://www.minrel.cl
Ministry of Agriculture, Teatinos 40, Santiago, Chile. Tel: +56 (0)2 696 5698, fax: +56 (0)2 671 6500, URL: http://www.agricultura.gob.cl/
Ministry of Planning, Ahumada 48, Santiago, Chile. Tel: +56 (0)2 675 1400, fax: +56 (0)2 672 1879, URL: http://www.mideplan.cl/
Ministry of Public Works, Transport and Telecommunications, Morandé 59 Piso 6, Santiago, Chile. Tel; +56 (0)2 361 3048/9, fax: +56 (0)2 672 7989, URL: http://www.moptt.cl/
Ministry of National Defence, Edificio Diego Portales, Villavicencio 364, Piso 22, Santiago, Chile. Tel: +56 (0)2 222 1202, fax: +56 (0)2 634 5339, URL: http://www.defensa.cl/
Ministry of Arts and Culture: Edificio Fray, Camilo Henriquez 262, Santiago, Chile. Tel: +56 (0)2 731 9950, URL:http://www.consejodelacultura.cl/
Ministry of Education, Alameda 1371, Santiago, Chile. Tel: +56 (0)2 390 4000, fax: +56 (0)2 698 7831, URL: http://www.mineduc.cl/
Ministry of Finance, Teatinos 120 Piso 12, Santiago, Chile. Tel: +56 (0)2 675 5800, fax: +56 (0)2 696 4798, URL: http://www.minhda.cl/castellano/inicio.html
Ministry of Housing and Urban Affairs, Av. Bernardo O'Higgins 924, Santiago, Chile. Tel: +56 (0)2 638 3366, URL: http://www.minvu.cl/
Ministry of the Interior, Palacio de la Moneda, Santiago, Chile. Tel: +56 (0)2 690 4000/671 7054, URL: http://www.interior.cl
Ministry of Justice, Morandé 107, Santiago, Chile. Tel: +56 (0)2 674 3100, fax: +56 (0)2 698 7098, URL: http://www.minjusticia.cl/
Ministry of Labour and Social Security, Huérfanos 1273 Piso 6, Santiago, Chile. Tel: +56 (0)2 695 5133, fax: +56 (0)2 671 2906, URL: http://www.mintrab.gob.cl/
Ministry of Mining, Teatinos 120 Piso 9, Santiago, Chile. Tel: +56 (0)2 671 4373, fax: +56 (0)2 698 9262, URL: http://www.minmineria.cl/
Ministry of National Assets, Juan Antonio Ríos 6, Santiago, Chile. Tel: +56 (0)2 633 4305, fax: +56 (0)2 633 6521, URL: http://www.bienes.cl/
Ministry of Health, Mac-Iver 541 Piso 3, Santiago, Chile. Tel: +56 (0)2 639 4001, fax: +56 (0)2 630 0272, URL: http://www.minsal.cl/
Ministry of Economy and Energy, Teatinos 120 Piso 10, Santiago, Chile. Tel: +56 (0)2 834 0487, fax: +56 (0)2 672 6040, URL: http://www.economia.cl/
National Women's Secretariat, Teatinos 950 Piso 5 al 9, Santiago, Chile. Tel: +56 (0)2 549 6100, fax: +56 (0)2 549 6248

Political Parties

Partido Demócrata Cristiano (PDC Party for Democracy), URL: http://www.pdc.cl
Leader: Ignacio Walker
Renovación Nacional (RN, National Renovation), URL: http://www.rn.cl
President: Carlos Larrain
Unión Demócrata Independiente (UDI, Independent Democratic Union), URL: http://www.udi.cl
Leader: Juan Antonio Coloma
Partido por la Democracia (PPD, Party for Democracy), URL: http://www.ppd.cl
Leader: Carolina Toha
Partido Socialista de Chile (PS, Socialist Party), URL: http://www.pschile.cl
Leader: Osvaldo Andrade
Partido Radical Socialdemócrata (Social Democrat Radical Partya), URL: http://www.partidoradical.cl/
Leader: José Antonio Gómez
Partido Comunista de Chile (Communist Party), URL: http://www.pcchile.cl
Leader: Guillermo Teillier

Elections

The first round of the most recent presidential election took place on December 13, 2009, as there was no clear winner a run off election was held on January 17, 2010 when Sebastián Piñera won 51.6 per cent of the vote.

Parliamentary elections were also held on December 13, 2009 as well as 18 seats in the Senate. The Coalition for Change, consisting of the National Renewal party, Independent Democratic Union, Chile First and three independents won 58 seats. The Concertación de Partidos por la Democracia (CPD) - an alliance of the PDC, PPD, PS, Communist Party and Social Democrat Radical Party won 57 seats.

Diplomatic Representation

Chilean Embassy, 1732 Massachusetts Avenue, NW, Washington, DC 20036, USA. Tel: +1 202 785 1746, fax: +1 202 887 5579, URL: http://www.chile-usa.org/
Ambassador: Felipe Bulnes (page 1396)

Chilean Embassy, 12 Devonshire Street, London W1G 7DS, United Kingdom. Tel: +44 (0)20 7580 6392, fax: +44 (0)20 7436 5204, e-mail: embachile@embachile.co.uk, URL: http://www.chileabroad.gov.cl/reino-unido/en
Ambassador: Tomás E. Müller Sproat
US Embassy, Avenida Andrés Bello 2800, Las Condes, Santiago, Chile. Tel: +56 (0)2 232 2600, fax: +56 (0)2 339 3710, e-mail: infous.state.gov, URL: http://santiago.usembassy.gov/
Ambassador: Alejandro D. Wolff (page 1539)
British Embassy, Avda. El Bosque Norte 0125, Las Condes, (Casilla 72-D or Casilla 16552) Santiago, Chile. Tel: +56 (0)2 370 4100, fax: +56 (0)2 335 5988, e-mail: chancery.santiago@fco.gov.uk (chancery), consulate.santiago@fco.gov.uk (consular), URL: http://www.britemb.cl
Ambassador: Jon Benjamin (page 1386)
Permanent Mission of Chile to the United Nations, 885 Second Avenue, 40th Floor, New York, NY 10017. USA. Tel: +1 212 832 3323, fax: +1 212 832 0236, e-mail: chile@un.int, URL: http://www.un.int/chile/
Ambassador: Octavio Errázuriz Guilisasti

LEGAL SYSTEM

The highest judicial authority in Chile is the Supreme Court, which has 21 members. Supreme Court justices can remain in office until the compulsory retirement age of 75. Each region and/or major city has a Court of Appeal. The members of these courts are chosen by the President of the Republic from a list submitted by the Supreme Court.

After the military coup in September 1973, the Chilean national police (Carabineros) were incorporated into the Defense Ministry. With the return of democratic government, the police were placed under the operational control of the Interior Ministry but remained under the nominal control of the Defense Ministry.

Whilst the government generally respects human rights, there have been occasional instances of excessive use of force and mistreatment by police forces, and generally substandard prison conditions. Some indigenous people suffer discrimination, and many children work within the informal economy. Chile abolished the death penalty in 2008.

Supreme Court of Chile, URL: http://www.poderjudicial.cl/
President: Ruben Ballesteros Caracamo

LOCAL GOVERNMENT

Chile is divided into 15 regions: Tarapacá, Antofagasta, Atacama, Coquimbo, Valparaiso, the Region of Libertador General Bernardo O'Higgins, the Greater Santiago Metropolitan Region, Maule, Biobio, Araucania, Los Lagos, Aysén, Arica Parinacota, Los Ríos and the Magallanes. These are further divided into 54 provinces which are in turn divided into 346 communes.

Each region has a government, at the head of which is the Intendent who is directly responsible to the President of Chile. This government has full autonomy, legal capacity and its own assets, and consists of the Intendent and the Regional Council. Each of the regions' provinces is headed by a Governor who is also directly answerable to Chile's President but ranks below an Intendent. The governor is assisted in his administration by a Provincial Social and Economic Council. Administration in each commune is carried out by a Municipality, a body with full legal capacity and its own assets. The Municipality is headed by a publicly-elected Mayor who consults with a Communal and Social Council and is assisted in legal and supervisory matters by the Mayoral Council.

AREA AND POPULATION

Area
The Republic of Chile lies in South America between the Andes Mountains and the South Pacific Ocean. It has borders with Argentina, Bolivia and Peru. The total area of continental Chile is 756,626 sq. km. The country's sovereign territory includes Easter Island (a world heritage site famous for its enigmatic moai statues) and the Sala and Gomez Islands in the South Pacific. It also has a claim to part of Antarctica. In the north is the Atacama Desert, the driest in the world and to the south are the ice-fields and glaciers of Chilean Patagonia. It has high mountains in the east (the Andes) with a high point of 6,880 m (Nevado Ojos del Salado). The central valley is fertile and there are also low coastal mountains.

There is a desert climate in the north, a Mediterranean climate in the central region and cool weather in the south.

Located on the edge of the South American and Nazca tectonic plates, Chile is in one of the most volcanically-active regions on Earth; it is thought that around 20 of its more than 100 active volcanoes are in danger of erupting at any time.

To view a map, please visit http://www.lib.utexas.edu/maps/cia08/chile_sm_2008.gif

Population
The population of Chile in 2010 is estimated at 17.114 million with a population growth rate of 1.0 per cent over the year. Population density was an estimated 21.9 persons per sq. km in 2007. The majority of the population is aged between 15 and 64, whilst 23 per cent of Chileans are aged up to 14 years, and 13 per cent are aged 65 years and over.

Around 14.4 million people now live in urban areas (2008), some 6.6 million now living in greater Santiago. Other major population centres are Concepción, Punta Arenas, Antofagasta and Puerto Montt. (Source: Chile en Cifras, 2009)

CHILE

The great majority of the population is of mixed Spanish and 'Indian' origin. Estimates of the size of the indigenous community vary; for the 2002 census, 692,192 people identified themselves as belonging to an ethnic group. The indigenous community is comprised of the following groups: Mapuche (87.3 per cent), Aymara (seven per cent), Atacamenos (three per cent), Quechua, Rapa Nui, Colla, Alacalufe and Yamana. The British community in Chile numbers about 10,000. There are also communities of German and Croatian descendants.

The official language is Spanish, but the indigenous community also speak Mapuche, Aymara and Quechua.

Births, Marriages, Deaths

In 2010, the crude birth rate was estimated at 14.3 births per 1,000 population, and the death rate at 5.6 deaths per 1,000 population. The infant mortality rate was estimated at 8 deaths per 1,000 live births in 2010. Average life expectancy at birth is estimated at 79 years (76 for men and 82 for women). (Source: http://www.who.int, World Health Statistics 2012)

Public Holidays 2014

1 January: New Year's Day
18 April: Good Friday
21 April: Easter Monday
5 May: Labour Day
21 May: Battle of Iquique
19 June: Corpus Christi
15 August: Assumption
6 September: National Unity Day
18 September: Independence Day
13 October: Dia de la Raza (Day of the Race), Columbus Day
1 November: All Saints' Day
8 December: Immaculate Conception
25 December: Christmas Day

EMPLOYMENT

In 2008, the labour force was estimated to be around 7,285,000, equivalent to 56.3 per cent of the population over 15 years old. Of these, some 6,740,000 were employed (4.2 million men and 2.5 million women). 555,700 people were unemployed, equivalent to a rate of 7.5 per cent. The services sector continues to be the largest employer, followed by industry and agriculture. Estimated figures for 2010 put the workforce at 6.940,000 of whom 6,450,000.

Employment by Activity

Sector	2008
Agriculture, Hunting, Forestry and Fishing	789,700
Mining and Quarrying	99,600
Manufacturing	865,400
Electricity, Gas and Water	38,200
Construction	583,600
Wholesale and Retail Trade and Restaurants and Hotels	1,330,700
Transport, Storage and Communication	561,500
Financing, Insurance, Real Estate and Business Services	626,500
Community, Social and Personal Services	1,845,300
Total	**6,740,400**

Source: International Labour Organisation

BANKING AND FINANCE

Currency

One Chilean Peso (Ch$, CLP) = 100 Centavos

The financial centre is Santiago.

GDP/GNP, Inflation, National Debt

Chile's economy is largely dependent on foreign trade. Copper and copper by-products constitute around 50 per cent of total exports, and trade in non-traditional products, such as forestry products, fresh fruit and seafood, has grown considerably over the past two decades.

Slow global economic growth and the devaluation of the Argentine peso stalled incipient economic recovery following the 1999 recession. However, GDP grew by 3.3 per cent in 2003, by 6.2 per cent in 2004 and by 6.3 per cent in 2005. The economy grew by 5.5 per cent in 2006, but record copper prices could not offset the negative factors of high energy prices and low consumer demand, and growth was recorded at just four per cent the following year, to reach US$162.5 billion. Figures for 2009 showed that Chile was feeling the effects of the global economic slowdown with GDP growth of -1.5 per cent giving a figure of US$150 billion. It is now harder for some companies to access capital from the Chilean banking system, and demand for the country's exports decreased towards the end of 2008. A sharp fall in copper prices in the second half of 2008 when they hit their lowest level in three years added to Chile's economic woes. Copper exports accounted for more than half of Chile's total exports in 2007.

GDP was estimated at US$204 billion in 2010 with a growth estimate of 5 per cent. Per capita GDP was an estimated US$15,000. Manufacturing accounts for 12 per cent of GDP, trade 9 per cent, mining 15 per cent and financial services 15 per cent. Agriculture accounts for 2 per cent of GDP.

The inflation rate rose to 9.9 per cent in October 2008, up from 8.5 per cent over 2007, and 3.2 per cent over 2006. Inflation was 3 per cent in 2011 but expected to rise over 2012. Chile's total external debt rose from US$43,068 million in 2003 to US$47.5 billion in 2005.

Foreign Investment

Foreign investment is encouraged in Chile and this attitude is exemplified in the country's Foreign Investment Law, which gives foreign investors the same treatment as Chileans. Registration is simple, and foreign investors are guaranteed access to the official foreign exchange market to repatriate their profits and capital. Most FDI goes into the electricity, gas, water and mining sectors. In 2010, FDI was estimated at over US$18 billion.

Balance of Payments / Imports and Exports

Chile's economy is highly dependent on international trade which currently accounts for around 39 per cent of GDP. Total revenues from the export of goods and services reached US$59 billion in 2006. Revenue from copper exports, traditionally the highest earning sector, has been inflated recently by high prices, and in 2006, copper exports earned a record US$33.3 billion. Imports cost the country US$36 billion in the same previous year. Non-copper exports have also enjoyed strong growth in recent years. Chile recorded a trade surplus of US$23 billion in 2006, up from US$10 billion in 2005. Figures for 2009 show that exports earned US$57.6 billion, rising to US$69 billion in 2010. The increase was driven by copper prices. China was Chile's largest export market in 2010, followed by Japan, the US, Brazil and the Netherlands.

Major imported commodities are raw materials, petroleum, capital goods, chemical products, vehicles, electronic equipment, machinery, and consumer durables. The top import trading partners are the US, China, Brazil, Argentina and South Korea. Import costs rose to US$54 billion in 2010.

The United States remains Chile's most important trading partner; since the implementation of the US-Chile Free Trade Agreement in 2004, trade has increased by 154 per cent and reached US$14.8 billion in 2006. Trade with Europe grew by 42 per cent in 2006, and trade with Asia grew by 31 per cent; China represented the most important partner in the East, accounting for around 66 per cent (US$8.8 million) of Asian trade.

Since 1996, Chile has been an associate member of the Southern Cone Common Market (Mercosur) along with Bolivia (also an associate), Uruguay, Argentina, Paraguay and Brazil. Chile is also a member of the Asia-Pacific Economic Co-operation (APEC). In 2002, Chile signed free trade agreements (FTAs) with the European Union and South Korea. Chile recently signed FTAs with New Zealand, Singapore, Brunei and China. The so-called P4 economic association agreement including Chile, New Zealand, Singapore and Brunei came into force in November 2006. In August 2006, Chile and Peru signed the first FTA between two South American countries, and agreements with Colombia, Ecuador and Panama are now before Congress. As of 2012, Chile and India were negotiating a free trade agreement.

Central Bank

Banco Central de Chile, Agustinas 1180, Santiago, Chile. Tel: +56 (0)2 6702000, fax +56 (0)2 6984847, e-mail: bcch@bcentral.cl, URL: http://www.bcentral.cl
Governor: Rodrigo Vergara

Chambers of Commerce, Trade and Financial Organisations
Chile Chamber of Commerce, URL: http://www.dicom.cl/infotrad/menucnc.html
British Chilean Chamber of Commerce, URL: http://www.prochile.cl
National Customs Services of Chile, URL: http://www.abif.cl/
Santiago Stock Exchange, URL: http://www.bolsantiago.cl
Chilean Electronics Stock Exchange, URL: http://www.bolchile.cl

MANUFACTURING, MINING AND SERVICES

Primary and Extractive Industries
Recoverable coal reserves were 1.3 billion short tons in 2004. Coal production in 2010 was an estimated 0.68 million short tons, with total consumption 8.55 million short tons. The shortfall was imported from Australia, Indonesia and Canada.

Chile is not a major producer of oil, and the industry is in decline, as existing wells have matured and exploration has proved fruitless. Oil production was 17.1 barrels per day in 2011. Consumption was estimated to be 322,000 barrels per day. The country's main source of oil imports is Argentina, followed by Brazil, Angola, and Nigeria.

Reserves of natural gas stood at 3.0 trillion cubic feet in 2011. Natural gas production in 2010 was estimated at 65 billion cubic feet, whilst consumption was an estimated 187 billion cubic feet. The shortfall is made up through imports from Argentina. The GasAndes pipeline stretches 290 miles from the Neuquen Basin in Argentina to Santiago in Chile. A second pipeline is being planned for northern Chile, with delivery capacity expected to be 600 million cubic feet per day. In 2004, Argentina suffered an energy crisis and cut natural gas exports to Chile. Since then, exports to Chile have failed to reach the contracted volumes, with supplies ceasing completely on some occasions causing disruption to industry and black outs. Argentina has also increased prices.

The government is looking at ways to diversify its gas sources. A feasibility study for a pipeline linking Peru's Camisea natural gas project with northern Chile is currently underway. This pipeline would form part of the natural gas "ring" proposed by Peru, Chile, Argentina, Uruguay, and Brazil, bringing greater energy integration in the Southern Cone.

Energy
Total energy consumption in 2009 was estimated at 1,210 quadrillion Btu. whilst production stood at 0.360 quadrillion Btu.

Recent EIA figures show that electricity generation reached 57.9 billion kilowatthours (kWh) in 2010, whilst consumption was 53.93 billion kilowatthours. That year the installed capacity was 16.21 gigawatts. Hydroelectricity supplies the largest share of Chile's electricity supply (43 per cent in 2004). The contribution of conventional thermal sources grew rapidly following the start of natural gas imports from Argentina in the late 1990s, but the continuing shortfall in imports has led the government to consider further development of hydroelectricity.

Manufacturing

The manufacturing sector accounted for 17 per cent of GDP in 2007. The sector exports foodstuffs, beverages, wood, printed articles and derivatives from paper, chemical products and oil derivatives, machinery, metal products and electrical goods.

The construction sector accounted for eight per cent of GDP in 2007.

Service Industries

Within the services sector, the financial services subsector accounted for 12 per cent of GDP in 2007; Commerce contributed 8 per cent, whilst transport and communications accounted for 7 per cent.

According to recent figures there are an estimated 989 hotels in Chile, and 1.01 million foreign tourists visit the country annually.

Agriculture

Forestry, agriculture, and fisheries accounted for six per cent of GDP in 2007.

Agricultural activity occurs mainly in the centre of the country. Here, both the soil and the climate are more favourable. The extreme north is mostly desert and the far south extremely wet and cold. Magallanes, however, lends itself to sheep-breeding. Wool and frozen lamb provide substantial sources of foreign exchange. In 2004 Chile farmed 39,247,593 chickens, 4,098,438 head of beef cattle, 1,695,062 sheep and 1,716,881 pigs. 2,753,300 kg of honey were produced. The most important crops are wheat, maize, potatoes, oats, barley, beans, beet, rape and rice. In the richer areas of the centre, vines and fruit are of great importance.

Agricultural Production in 2010

Produce	Int. $'000*	Tonnes
Grapes	1,575,205	2,755,700
Indigenous pigmeat	766,032	498,316
Cow milk, whole, fresh	738,024	2,530,000
Indigenous chicken meat	717,454	503,686
Indigenous cattle meat	569,315	210,750
Apples	465,205	1,100,000
Tomatoes	332,608	900,000
Avocados	228,677	330,000
Wheat	210,896	1,523,920
Peaches and nectarines	194,356	357,000
Kiwi fruit	186,793	229,000
Plums and sloes	177,837	298,000
*unofficial figures		

Source: http://faostat.fao.org/site/339/default.aspx Food and Agriculture Organization of the United Nations, Food and Agricultural commodities production

Fruit growing has been largely developed in the region north and south of Valparaiso and near Valdivia in the south and is an export industry. The land is particularly suited to the growing of grapes, and the wine produced is reputed to be the best in South America. Exports from the timber, cellulose and paper industries have been increasing, with 4.140 million cubic metres of timber produced annually. Chile has the largest fish catch in Latin America (2.7 million tonnes in 2010), and the fishing industry is the second largest export earner after copper.

COMMUNICATIONS AND TRANSPORT

Travel Requirements

US, Canadian, Australian and EU citizens require a passport valid for six months, and a return ticket. They do not require a visa for stays of up to 90 days, except Greek passport holders (who require a visa for over 60 days) and Romanians (who require a visa for over 30 days). Visas may be obtained at the port of entry upon payment of a fee. Nationals of Australia, Canada and the USA entering Chile for tourism purposes will be charged a processing fee payable on arrival. Travellers are advised to contact the embassy to check visa requirements.

National Airlines

Lan-Chile, PO Box 147D, Santiago, Chile. Tel: +56 (0)2 639 4411, fax: +56 (0)2 638 3976, URL: http://www.lanchile.com
There are 636 airports in Chile, though just 84 of them are paved. Domestic air travel is a convenient mode of transport in the country, there are also flights to Easter Island.

Railways

Chile constructed the first railway in Latin America and there is a railroad network with a total extension of 7,998 km; this includes four international lines. Recent figures show that 10.07 million passengers and 13.11 million metric tons of freight are carried every year.

Roads

There are 79,605 km of roads, including 407 km of expressway. Most of the roads are not paved. Chile has a comprehensive bus system and bus services connect Chile with Argentina, Bolivia, Brazil and Peru. Vehicles are driven on the right.

Shipping

Compañia Sud Americana de Vapores, Calle Blanco 895, Casilla 49-V, Valparaiso
Empresa Maritima Del Estado, Almirante Gomez Carreno 49, Casilla 105-V, Valparaiso
Compañía Chilena de Navegación Interoceanica, Edificio Interoceanica, Plaza de la Justicia 59; Casilla 1410, Valparaiso
Transmares Naviera Chilena Ltd A, Edificio Eurocentro, Calle Moneda 970, 18 Piso, Casilla 193-D, Santiago

Ports and Harbours

The state-controlled company of Emporchi owns 11 ports, which handle half of all Chile's international freight. The Chilean Government intends that Emporchi will eventually grant concessions to use and then run these ports to private businesses. In addition to the state-run ports there are 19 private ports handling more than 23 million metric tons of freight annually. Major ports include: Santiago, Puerto Montt, Concepción and Valparaíso.

Ferry services operate in the south of the country from Puerto Montt to Chacabuco and Puerto Montt to Puerto Natales. Boats are available to Easter Island.

HEALTH

In 2009, Chile spent approximately 16.2 per cent of its total budget on healthcare (up from 14.1 per cent in 2000), accounting for 47.6 per cent of all healthcare spending. Total expenditure on health care equated to 8.4 per cent of the country's GDP. Per capita total expenditure amounted to US$802 in 2009. Figures for 2005-10 show that there are 17,411 physicians (10.3 per 10,000 population) and 2,443 nurses& midwives (1.4 per 10,000 population). There are 21 hospital beds per 10,000 population.

The infant mortality rate (probability of dying by age one) in 2010 was estimated at 8 per 1,000 live births and 9 per 1,000 live births for the under-fives. The most common causes of death in the under-fives were: prematurity 22 per cent and congenital abnormalities 36 per cent and pneumonia 7 per cent. In 2010 there were 891 reported cases of mumps, 2,376 of TB and 794 of pertussis. Around 0.3 per cent of the adult population is living with HIV/AIDS, equivalent to around 26,000 people. In 2003, 1,400 people died of the disease.

According to the latest WHO figures, in 2010 approximately 96 per cent of the population had access to improved drinking water and to improved sanitation. (Source: http://www.who.int, Global Health Statistics 2012)

EDUCATION

Since 2003, a constitutional amendment has guaranteed free, compulsory primary education (lasting eight years) and secondary schooling (lasting four years) in Chile.

In 2007, some 56 per cent of small children attended a nursery school. Recent figures show that around 99 per cent of the primary scholars completed to year five, and 97 per cent went on to study at secondary school-aged population attended state schools, In 2006, 47 per cent of pupils went on to study at Higher Education level. There are 62 universities, 37 of which are privately run.

In 2007, 18.2 per cent of total government spending went on education: 38 per cent on secondary and 35 per cent on primary. The adult literacy rate in 2006 was estimated to be 96.4 per cent, increasing to 99 per cent among those aged between 15 and 24. (Source: UNESCO, UIS)

RELIGION

There is no state religion, but almost 70 per cent of the population is Roman Catholic. Other Christian churches make up over 17 per cent of the population, 4.55 per cent follow other religions, such as Jews and Muslims, and 8.3 per cent are atheists. There are 27 ecclesiasic jurisdictions.
Bishop's Conference (Conferencia Episcopal de Chile), URL: http://www.iglesia.cl
Archbishop of Santiago: Cardenal Francisco Javier Errazuriz Ossa

Chile has a religious liberty rating of 9 on a scale of 1 to 10 (10 is most freedom). (Source: World Religion Database)

COMMUNICATIONS AND MEDIA

The constitution guarantees freedom of speech and of the media. The media is able to critise the government and is generally independent. Many repressive media laws were removed in 2001.

Newspapers

Newspapers in Chile include: La Nacion, URL: http://www.lanacion.cl; La Tercera, URL: http://www.latercera.cl; El Mercuro, URL: http://www.emol.com; La Segunda, http://www.lasegunda.com

Broadcasting

The state-run *Televison Nacional*, broadcasts to 97 per cent of Chile. It is state-run but not under government control. In addition to domestic and regional terrestial channels, there are many cable stations. There are hundreds of radio stations.
TVN Chile, URL: http://www.tvn.cl

Telecommunications

The telecommunications infrastructure is well developed. Fixed-line connections have dropped in recent years as mobile-cellular usage continues to increase, reaching a level of 85 telephones per 100 persons; figures for 2008 indicate that there are over 3.5 million mainline telephone lines in use in Chile, and over 14 million mobile phones. Internet users exceeded 5.5 million in 2008.

ENVIRONMENT

Major environmental problems include desertification, deforestation and soil erosion as well as water and air pollution. Chile's emissions from the consumption of fossil fuels in 2010 totaled 68.76 million metric tons of carbon dioxide. (Source: EIA)

The country is increasingly turning to alternative sources of energy in the industrial sector, using natural gas and hydroelectric generation to limit pollution where possible.

Chile is party to the following environmental agreements: Antarctic-Environmental Protocol, Antarctic-Marine Living Resources, Antarctic Seals, Antarctic Treaty, Biodiversity, Climate Change, Climate Change-Kyoto Protocol, Desertification, Endangered Species, Environmental Modification, Hazardous Wastes, Law of the Sea, Marine Dumping, Ozone Layer Protection, Ship Pollution, Wetlands, and Whaling.

SPACE PROGRAMME

The Chilean Space Agency reports to the Ministry of National Defence. It faciliates the development of space based information and technology and promotes the use of such technologies for the economic and social development of the country.
Chilean Space Agency, URL: http://www.agenciaespacial.cl

CHINA
People's Republic of China
Zhonghua Renmin Gongheguo

Capital: Beijing (Peking) (Population estimate, 2012: 11.7 million)

Head of State: Xi Jinping (President) (page 1540)

Vice-President: Li Yuanchao (page 1464)

National Flag: Red, charged at the upper hoist with a star of five-gold points, representative of the Chinese Communist Party (CCP). Around it on the fly side in an arc are four smaller stars, representing the four classes (workers, peasants, petty bourgeoisie and national bourgeoisie) which constituted the four-class alliance during the 'New Democratic Period'

CONSTITUTION AND GOVERNMENT

Constitution
The first plenary session of the Chinese People's Political Consultative Conference (CPPCC) and the formal proclamation of the People's Republic of China (PRC) took place on 1 October 1949 (China's National Day).

In the early post-Liberation years the CPPCC was the supreme organ of government and under its aegis an interim system of administration was established. However, a more lasting, formal institutional framework of government in China was derived largely from the first Constitution of the PRC, adopted in September 1954. Under the constitution, the National People's Congress (NPC) became the highest organ of state power in China, with the CPPCC assuming a merely advisory role.

The NPC has remained the source of all legislation and is responsible for formulating laws and policy, delegating authority and supervising other government bodies. The NPC approves all economic plans, as well as the state budget and government reports on all aspects of its work. It also retains the right to appoint senior state and government officials. An NPC Standing Committee, composed of 153 members, is elected in order to oversee the day-to-day work of the government between the plenary sessions of the parent body. The NPC has 2,979 deputies who meet in the first quarter of each year to discuss government policy. Every five years they elect the president, prime minister and vice-premiers.

The most important executive organ of state power, subordinate to the NPC, is the State Council. If the NPC is regarded as China's Parliament, the State Council can be thought of as an enlarged Cabinet and consists of the Premier, Vice Premiers, State Councillors, ministers in charge of commissions or ministries, the Auditor-General, and the Secretary-General. It is responsible for the enforcement of the statutes and resolutions adopted by the NPC and its Standing Committee. A smaller secretariat, comprising the Premier, Vice-Premiers and Secretary-General, exists as a kind of 'inner cabinet'.

The balance of power between the centre and the provinces, the relative authority of the constituent parts of government machinery, the role and involvement of the CCP, and the very constitutional basis of government itself - all have been subject to change since the original constitution of 1954. The most significant changes occurred during the radical periods of China's post-1949 history: 'the Great Leap Forward' (1958-60) and the 'Cultural Revolution' (1966-76). During the Great Leap Forward, administration was decentralised and rural people's communes were established. The latter created a new institutional framework for economic, political and social administration.

The 1954 Constitution was set aside following the events of the Cultural Revolution. Although the formal institutional structure of government remained largely unchanged, the new constitution (not formalized until 1975) made explicit the major shift in political power away from the NPC towards the CCP.

Accordingly, the 1975 Constitution affirmed the supremacy of the Party in state affairs and underlined its leadership through the proclamation of 'Marxism-Leninism-Mao Zedong Thought' as the theoretical basis of the lives of the people. The office of state president was abolished and China was left without a titular head of state. The former National Defence Council was abolished and the Chairman of the CCP Central Committee assumed supreme command of China's armed forces. All the functions previously fulfilled by the head of state became the responsibility of the NPC, acting under the leadership of the CCP. Although it remained the highest executive and administrative organ of state, appointments to the State Council now took place through the NPC on the basis of proposals made by the Party Central Committee. The reduction in citizens' rights and freedoms was paralleled by greater concentration of power in the police and the security organs.

Following the death of Mao Zedong in September 1976, the Constitution was revised. The 1978 constitution restored some of the functions of the NPC and its Standing Committee and extended the role of the local people's congresses. The significance of these changes was, however, eclipsed by the adoption in 1982 of China's fourth State Constitution - referred to by many as the 'Deng Xiaoping Constitution'. It moved away from the more radical tenor of its two immediate predecessors towards that of the original parent document, the Constitution of 1954.

Amongst the most important changes in the 1982 document were the restoration of the post of President and Vice-President of the PRC (both abolished in 1975) and the creation of a State Central Military Commission, responsible for national defence policy. Further strengthening of the state machinery was provided for through an expansion of the legislative, judicial, supervisory, and investigative powers of the NPC and its Standing Committee, which guaranteed the NPC supremacy over all other central organs. The new constitution also sought to rationalise the division of power between central and local governments and to strengthen local autonomy by enhancing the role of people's congresses at lower levels. An aspect of the 1982 Constitution that deserves note is the stipulation that the state leaders should not serve more than two consecutive terms of office.

According to the 1982 Constitution, the head of the state is the president, indirectly elected by the NPC for a maximum of two five-year terms. The head of government (State Council) is the premier, who is responsible to the NPC. The State Council is nominated by the premier and elected by the NPC. It is composed of the General Affairs Office, 28 ministries and commissions, and many affiliated organs and working offices.

The most recent amendments to the Constitution were in 2004 when the protection of human rights was included.

To consult the full Constitution, please visit: http://www.npc.gov.cn/englishnpc/Constitution/node_2824.htm

International Relations
Taiwan (referred to by the Taiwanese as the Republic of China) is an island off the coast of China. The retreating Koumintang forces established themselves there in 1949 after fleeing from the Communists. Taiwan has claimed its independence for over 50 years. China views it as a rebel nation which should be re-united with mainland China.

As China's economy continues to grow, so does its international political and economic weight. It is a member of the World Trade Organisation, and sits on the UN Security Council. China is becoming more involved in African development, investing in infrastructure projects; trade with the continent has quadrupled over the last five years and is expected to double over the next five years. China has played a constructive role in international issues over Iran and North Korea, as well as becoming involved in UN Peace Support Operations. China played host to the Olympic Games in 2008. In the run-up to the Games, protesters used the presence of the western press to bring to the fore the struggle for Tibetan autonomy; this put strain on the Chinese authorities' relations with western democratic governments.

The border between China and Russia is 4,300 km (2,700 miles) long, and there were armed clashes over parts of it during the Cold War. Marking the end of a 40 year old dispute, Russia returned all of Yinlong island (known in Russian as Tarabarov) and half of Heixiazi island (Bolshoi Ussuriyasky) to China in 2008. The deal was seen as a sign of warmer ties developing between Russia - a big energy exporter - and China, a big energy consumer. In the first five months of 2008, bilateral trade grew by around sixty per cent.

Recent Events
In 2005, China became the world's fourth largest economy (based on GDP), overtaking the United Kingdom.

The Chinese government announced a rise in public disturbances in 2005, citing rapid economic growth as the cause of social unrest. Official corruption and high-profile land disputes between authorities and villagers have triggered uprisings and riots in rural areas. A key cause was land seizures by corrupt local officials who failed to give adequate compensation to villagers.

In March 2005, the Chinese government passed a new law allowing the use of force should Taipei declare independence from mainland China. Taiwan's National Party leader Lien Chan visited China for the first meeting between Nationalist and Communist Party leaders since 1949.

In May 2006, work on the main wall of the Three Gorges Dam, the world's largest hydropower project, was completed. The wall stretches for more than two kms across the Yangtze river. On completion, the dam will be the largest hydro-electric power project in the world. Over a million people were moved to make way for the dam and some 1,200 towns and villages submerged under the rising waters of the reservoir. In July 2006, the world's highest railway line (6,600 feet above sea level) was opened between Qinghai and Tibet. There were fears the railway would increase immigration of ethnic Chinese into Tibet, threatening its cultural and religious identity.

Early in March 2007 China announced a 17 per cent increase in the defence budget. This followed China's call on the USA to cancel a planned sale of hundreds of missiles to Taiwan, claiming that the sale would harm peace and stability in the region. In the same month, China criticised Taiwan's President Chen Shui-bian following a speech in which he urged his countrymen to pursue independence, write a new constitution and change its official name from "Republic of China" to Taiwan.

A protest staged by around 20,000 rural workers in Hunan province in mid-March 2007 ended in violent clashes. The riot was sparked by rising transport costs, and is thought to reflect the growing discontent felt by rural communities about the gap between rich and poor, and corruption among government officials. The Chinese government introduced a series of measures, including farm subsidies, reining in the seizures of farmland for development and tackling government corruption.

China announced plans to increase military spending by nearly 18 per cent in 2008, to some $59 billion. US authorities voiced concern over advances in space and cyberspace. The Chinese authorities said that most of the spending rise will be on increasing salaries and accommodating higher oil prices.

Some 600 Buddhist monks took part in protests in the Tibetan city of Lhasa on the 10th March 2008- the anniversary of the 1959 Tibetan uprising against Chinese rule - in what was claimed to be the biggest display of opposition to Chinese rule in Tibet since 1989. Beijing claims sovereignty over Tibet, but many Tibetans remain loyal to the Dalai Lama. US-based Radio Free Asia reported that dozens of monks were detained as the authorities sought to crack down on dissent, and that the demonstrations were dispersed by tear gas. Protests continued through the week. By the 16th March, the protests had spread to neighbouring regions, in Sichuan and Gansu provinces, and convoys of military vehicles were seen heading towards Tibet. China claimed that 19 people were killed in the Lhasa riots, but Tibetan exiles say that nearly 100 were killed by the Chinese security forces.

On 12th May 2008, a 7.9 magnitude earthquake struck; its epicenter was in the mountainous Wenchuan county, Sichuan province, and it was felt as far away as Beijing and the Thai capital, Bangkok. It was the most powerful earthquake to hit China in 30 years. 87,000 people were killed or went missing, and over 281,000 were injured. Some 5.47 million people were left homeless. At least eight schools were flattened in the earthquake, and over a thousand school children died; it is not known whether faulty design or poor construction was to blame for their collapse. China's leaders promised a 70bn yuan ($10bn; £5bn) reconstruction fund and instructed Chinese banks to forgive debts owed by uninsured survivors.

In June, the national meteorological service warned that the 5,500 km (3,400 mile)Yellow River was in danger of bursting its banks, following heavy rain in the north of China. In the south, over a million people had to evacuate their homes after heavy storms. Large areas of farmland were submerged and thousands of homes were destroyed in Guangdong and Jiangxi provinces in the worst flooding of the Pearl river delta for 50 years.

On the 4th August 2008, sixteen policemen were killed and a further 16 policemen were hurt in an attack on a border post in the region of Xinjiang (near the border with Tajikistan) which is home to the Muslim Uighur people. Uighur separatists have waged a low-level campaign against Chinese rule for decades. Muslim separatists launched a series of bomb attacks in Kuqa, in southern Xinjiang, on the 10th August, killing 11 people. A third attack in eight days took place in the region when assailants killed three security staff at a checkpoint near Kashgar.

The Beijing Olympics began on the 8th of August of 2008.

On the 14th September, 13 mine officials were arrested after a landslide engulfed the village of Taoshi in Shanxi province, killing at least 254 people. The head of the local Communist Party and other senior local officials were also arrested. A dam holding back sludge at the Tashan iron ore mine had burst after torrential rain. The mine's safety certificate had been revoked in 2006.

On the 16th September, China's Health ministry announced that over 6,200 Chinese children had fallen ill, a further 158 had been diagnosed as suffering from kidney stones, and three had died, after drinking contaminated milk powder. It was thought that as many as 10,000 infants may have drunk the contaminated Sanlu milk powder. The Chinese media reported that melamine, an industrial chemical rich in nitrogen, had been added to the milk to help the food appear rich in protein, but it caused babies to develop kidney stones. Chinese quality control inspectors found that ten per cent of liquid milk was also contaminated with melamine, and milk products from three Chinese companies were cleared from shelves in several Asian

countries. 18 people were arrested. Ultimately, over a quarter of a million children were made ill by food tainted with melamine, and six babies died. On the 27th December 2008, the Chinese authorities announced that 22 dairy firms involved in the tainted milk scandal would compensate the families of the nearly 300,000 affected children.

On the 6th October 2008, two earthquakes of 6.6 and 5.1 magnitudes struck Tibet, killing at least 30 people in a sparsely populated area some 50 miles west of Lhasa. Many houses collapsed near the epicentre in Damxung county, and more people were buried under debris.

In early November, as the effects of the global credit crunch began to be felt, it was reported that tens of thousands of migrant workers were leaving the southern manufacturing city of Guangzhou after the companies they worked for collapsed. The worst hit companies are toy, shoe, and furniture manufacturers. Officials were concerned that the sudden increase in unemployment could lead to social unrest; there were reports of demonstrations in the provinces of Zhejiang and Guangdong. It was feared that loss of remittances from migrant workers could have a major impact on the inner regions of China.

In December 2008, Hong Kong authorities reported that the toxic chemical melamine had been found in eggs from China's northeastern Jilin province. In December, over 370,000 chickens were culled in the eastern province of Jiangsu following an outbreak of the H5N1 strain of bird flu. It was thought that migrating birds might have been the source of the disease.

On the 25th December, it was reported that China had detained 59 people in Tibet for trying to stir up racial hatred and incite violence. The news report said they were acting under the influence of exiled Tibetan spiritual leader, the Dalai Lama.

In January 2009, as a result of the government increasing its estimate of how much the economy grew over 2007, China's economy overtook that of Germany to become the world's third largest that year. Gross domestic product grew by 13 per cent (up from an earlier estimate of 11.9 per cent), to 25.7 trillion yuan ($3.5 trillion). However, Germany's GDP per capita was $38,800, compared with $2,800 in China. China's economy has grown tenfold in the past 30 years, and there were predictions that it would overtake Japan as the world's second largest economy within five years. This happened in February 2011 following the publication of Japans GDP growth for 2010 at 4.0 per cent.

In February 2009, at least 70 people were treated for stomach ache and diarrhea in Guangdong province after eating pork products contaminated with an illegal animal feed additive. The tainted pig organs contained a steroid which is used to prevent animals gaining fat. Three people were arrested on suspicion of raising and selling the contaminated pigs.

At the opening of the annual session of the National People's Congress on 5th March 2009, Premier Wen Jiabao warned that the year ahead would be the most difficult the country has faced this century because of the global economic crisis, and announced a $585 billion investment programme to stimulate the economy. He declared an annual growth target of eight per cent. Mr Wen said the government would work to maintain social cohesion, amid fears that job losses for millions of migrant workers could spark unrest.

In April 2009, PM Wen Jiabao said that China's economy was showing some signs of recovery from the global financial crisis; the government had implemented a 4tn yuan ($585bn) stimulus package to boost economic activity. The Prime Minister cited improved investment, consumption and trade figures. In March, China's manufacturing sector grew for the first time in six months. However, some analysts believe China will continue to struggle during the global economic slowdown.

On the 5th June 2009, a landslide in an iron-ore mining area of the Chongqing region, south-western China buried around 70 people. Millions of cubic metres of rock flooded a valley, burying an iron ore plant and six houses in Tiekuang township, and cutting power and communication lines.

In July 2009 ethnic unrest broke out in the city of Urumqi in China's Xinjiang region. Clashes between Muslim Uighurs and Han Chinese resulted in 200 deaths, and troops were sent in to quell the violence. Over 1,500 people were arrested over the riots. Head of the World Uighur Congress, Mrs Kadeer, was blamed by the authorities for orchestrating the riots.

July 2009 also saw the first signs of a re-thinking of the one-child per couple policy. China has become increasingly concerned like many nations about the increasing numbers of the ageing population and in Shanghai parents were urged to consider having a second child.

In March 2010 Google the internet search engine was due to decide whether to pull out of China over censorship issues. The Chinese Government has accused Google of trying to influence Chinese values.

In April 2010 China was again hit by an earthquake this one measuring 6.9 on the richter scale the epicentre was the remote Yushu county in the Tibetan mountains. Initial reports thought some 791 people had been killed and 15,000 homes destroyed.

In October 2010 the jailed Chinese dissident Liu Xiaobo was awarded the Nobel Peace Prize. The award led to official protests from Beijing. Liu Xiaobo was sentenced to 11 years in prison for calling for political change.

In February 2011 China overtook Japan to become the second-largest economy in the world.

In March 2011 the exiled Tibetan spiritual leader the Dalia Lama announced a plan to devolve his political responsibilities to an elected figure. The Tibetan parliament in exile was due to have elections later in March. The Chinese press dismissed the announcement as tricks to gain publicity from the international press. Lobsang Sangay, an academic of Harvard University, won the election.

CHINA

In March 2012 Bo Xilai, the leader of the Chongqing Communist Party, was sacked on the eve of the Party's ten-yearly leadership change and suspended from the politburo. His wife, Gu Kailai, was later investigated over the death of a British businessman, Neil Heywood, who died in Chongqing in November 2011. His death was initially reported as unsuspicious but was later treated as murder. Gu Kailai was found guilty in August 2012 and given a suspended death sentence. Wang Lijun the ex police chief implicated in covering up the scandal was later jailed for 15 years.

In April 2012, China increased the limit within which the yuan currency can fluctuate to one per cent in trading against the US dollar, up from 0.5 per cent.

In May 2012 naval vessels from China and the Philippines confronted each other in the South China Sea off the Scarborough Reef. Both countries assert a claim to the reef which is believed to have reserves of oil and gas.

In July 2012, China pledged US$20 billion (£12.8 billion) of credit for Africa in exchange for closer ties and increased trade.

In April 2013, an earthquake measuring a magnitude of 6.6 hit the Sichuan province. Initial reports showed 188 people had been killed and 11,500 injured. Rescue efforts were hampered by aftershocks.

In July 2013, the former Minister of Railways, Liu Zhijun, was convicted of bribery and abuse of power and given a suspended death sentence.

Legislature
China's unicameral legislature, the National People's Congress (*Quanguo Renmin Daibiao Dahui*), is made up of 2,979 members elected by municipal, regional and provincial congresses for a five-year term.
National People's Congress, Great Hall of the People, 100805, Beijing, China. URL: http://www.npc.gov.cn
Chairman, Standing Committee of the National People's Congress (NPC): Wu Bangguo (page 1383)

Presidency (as at May 2013)
President: Xi Jinping (page 1540)
Vice-President: Li Yuanchao (page 1464)

State Council (as at May 2013)
Premier: Li Keqiang (page 1464)
Vice-Premier: Zhang Gaoli (page 1543)
Vice-Premier: Liu Yandong
Vice-Premier: Wang Yang
Vice-Premier: Ma Kai
State Councillor, Minister for Public Security: Guo Shengkun
State Councillor, Minister for National Defence: Chang Wanquan
State Councillor: Yang Jiechi
State Councillor, Secretary-General: Yang Jing
State Councillor: Wang Yong

Ministers (as at May 2013)
Minister of Human Resources and Social Security: Yin Weimin
Minister of Industry and Information Technology: Miao Wei
Minister of Environmental Protection: Zhou Shengxian
Minister of Housing and Urban-Rural Development: Jiang Weixin
Minister of Foreign Affairs: Wang Yi
Chair of the National Development Development and Reform Commission: Xu Shaoshi
Minister of Education: Yang Guiren
Minister of Science and Technology: Wan Gang
Minister of Supervision: Huang Shuxian
Minister of State Security: Geng Huichang
Minister of Civil Affairs: Li Liquo
Minister of Justice: Wu Aiying
Minister of Finance: Lou Jiwel
Minister of Land and Natural Resources: Jiang Daming
Minister of Water Resources: Chen Lei
Minister of Agriculture: Han Changfu
Minister of Culture: Cai Wu
Minister of Health and Family Planning Commission: Li Bin
Minister of Commerce: Gao Hucheng
Minister of Communications and Transport: Yang Chuantang
Governor of the People's Bank of China: Zhou Xiaochuan (page 1540)
Auditor General of the National Audit Office: Li Jiayi
Chair of the State Ethnic Affairs Commission: Wang Zhengwei

Ministries
Office of the President, URL: http://english.gov.cn/2008-03/15/content_921051.htm
Ministry of Agriculture, 11 Nonzhanguan Nanli, Hepinli, Beijing 100026, China. Tel: +86 (0)10 6419 3366, fax: +86 (0)10 6419 2468, URL: http://www.agri.gov.cn/
Ministry of Civil Affairs, 147 Belheyan Dajie, Beijing 100721, China. Tel: +86 (0)10 6513 5544, URL: http://www.mca.gov.cn/news/Reidx.html
Ministry of Communications, 21 Jianlei Daijie, Beijing 100736, China. Tel: +86 (0)10 6519 6224, fax: 86 (0)10 6529 2201, URL: http://www.moc.gov.cn/
Ministry of Construction, 9 San Li He Lu, Haidian Qu, Beijing 100853, China. Tel: +86 (0)10 6839 3883, fax: 86 (0)10 6083 13669, URL: http://www.cin.gov.cn/
Ministry of Culture, Jia 83, Donganmen Bei Jie, Beijing 100722, China. Tel: +86 (0)10 6401 2255, fax: +86 (0)10 6401 3149, URL: http://www.ccnt.gov.cn/
Ministry of Education, 35 Damucang Htong, Xi Dan, xicheng Qu, 100816 Beijing, China. URL: http://www.moe.edu.cn/

Ministry of Environmental Protection, URL: http://english.mep.gov.cn/
Ministry of Finance, 3 Nansanxiang, Sanlihe, Xicheng Qu, Beijing 100820, China. Te +86 (0)10 6855 1114, fax: +86 (0)10 6853 6985, URL: http://www.mof.gov.cn/
Ministry of Foreign Affairs, 225 Chaoyangmennei Daile, Dongsi, Beijing 100701, China Tel: +86 (0)10 6513 5566 / 6513 4521, fax: +86 (0)10 6513 0368, e-mai webmaster@FMPRC.gov.cn, URL: http://www.fmprc.gov.cn/eng/
Ministry of Foreign Trade and Economic Co-operation, 2 Dong Chang'an Avenu Beijing 100731, China. Tel: +86 (0)10 6512 1919, fax: +86 (0)10 6519 8173, e-mai moftec@moftec.gov.cn, URL: http://www.moftec.gov.cn/
Ministry of Health, 44 Houhaibeiyan, Xicheng Qu, Beijing 100725, China. Tel: +86 1 6403 4433, fax: +86 (0)10 6401 4331, e-mail: manage@chsi.moh.gov.cn, URI http://www.moh.gov.cn/
Ministry of Justice, 11 Xiaguangli, Sanyuanqiao, Chaoyang Qu, Beijing 100016, China Tel: +86 (0)10 6520 5114, URL: http://www.legalinfo.gov.cn/english/node_7590.htm
Ministry of National Defence, 25 Huangsi Avenue, Beijing, China. Tel: +86 (0)10 620 8356, URL: http://eng.mod.gov.cn/
Ministry of Human Resources, 12 Hepinglizhong Jie, Dongcheng Qu, Beijing 10071€ China. Tel: +86 (0)10 6421 3431, URL: http://www.mohrss.gov.cn/
Ministry of Railways, 10 Fuxing Lu, Haidian Qu, Beijing 100845, China. Tel: +86 (0)1 6324 0114, fax: +86 (0)10 6324 6150, e-mail: webmaster@ns.chinamor.cn.net, URL http://www.chinamor.cn.net/
Ministry of Science and Technology, 15B Fuxing Lu, Haidian Qu, 100015, Beijing China. URL: http://www.most.gov.cn/
Ministry of State Security, 14 Dongchangan Jie, Dongcheng Qu, Beijing 100741, China Tel: +86 (0)10 6524 4702, URL: http://english.gov.cn/index.htm
Ministry of Supervision, 35 Huayuanbei Lu, Haidian Qu, Beijing 100083, China. Tel +86 (0)10 6201 6655, URL: http://english.gov.cn/index.htm
Ministry of Transport, URL: http://www.moc.gov.cn/
Ministry of Water Resources, 1 Baiguang Lu, Ertiao, Xuanwu Qu, Beijing 100761 China. Tel: +86 (0)10 6327 3322, fax: +86 (0)10 6326 0365, URL: http://www.mwr.gov.cn/

Political Parties
The Chinese Communist Party (Zhongguo Gongchandang) is the ruling party. A total of nine political parties form the 10th CPPCC National Committee, all members of the China People's Political Consultative Conference: the Chinese Communist Party; Jiu San Xuehui (September 3 Association); Taiwan Minzu Zizhi Tongmeng (Taiwan Democratic Self-Government League); Zhongguo Guomindang Geming Weiyuanhui (Chinese Nationalist Party Revolutionary Committee); Zhongguo Minzhu Cujin Hui (Chinese Association for Promoting Democracy) Zhongguo Minzhu Jianguo Hui (Chinese National Democratic Construction Association); Zhongguo Minzhu Tongmeng (Chinese Democratic League); Zhongguo Nonggong Minzhudang (Chinese Peasants' and Workers' Democratic Party); and Zhongguo Zhi Gong Dang (Chinese Party for Public Interest).

The Politburo Standing Committee of the **Zhongguo Gongchan Dang** (Chinese Communist Party) is as follows (June 2013): Xi Jinping (page 1540) (General Secretary), Li Changchun, Zhang Dejiang, Yu Zhengsheng, Liu Yunshan, Ma Kai, Wang Huning, Liu Yandong, Liu Qibao, Xu Qiliang, Sun Chunlan, Wang Qishan, Zhang Gaoli (page 1543)

Chinese Communist Party (Zhongguo Gongchandang), URL: http://english.cpc.people.com.cn/
China Association for Promoting Democracy, http://www.jhmj.org/
China Democratic League, URL: http://www.dem-league.org.cn/
China Democratic National Construction Association, URL: http://www.cndca.org.cn/
Chinese Peasants' and Workers' Democratic Party, URL: http://www.ngd.org.cn/
China Revolutionary Committee of the Kuomintang, URL: http://www.minge.gov.cn/
China Zhi Gong Dang (Party for Public Interests), URL: http://www.zg.org.cn/
Jiu San Society, URL: http://www.93.gov.cn/
Taiwan Democratic Self-government League, URL: http://www.taimeng.org.cn/

Elections
The penultimate presidential election took place in March 2008, when Hu Jintao was formally re-elected by the National People's Congress, after a near-unanimous vote. The Congress also voted to re-elect Mr Hu as chairman of the Central Military Commission. Xi Jinping, a possible candidate for the presidency in 2013, won election as vice-president.

Legislative elections last took place from November 2012 to February 2013. The CPP approves all candidates.

The current leadership of the Chinese Communist Party was formally elected at the party congress in November 2012; members of the Standing Committee of the CCP Politburo are listed above.

The most recent presidential election was held in November 2012, Xi Jinping (page 1540) was elected to the post of President, he and the new Politburo Standing Committee were sworn in in March 2013.

Diplomatic Representation
British Embassy, 11 Guang Hua Lu, Jian Guo Men Wai, Beijing 100600, China. Tel: +86 (0)10 5192 4000, fax: +86 (0)10 6532 1937, e-mail: commercialmail.beijing@fco.gov.uk (Commercial), info@britishcentre.org.cn (Information Resources Centre), ukscience.beijing@fco.gov.uk (Science & Technology), beijingvisamail@fco.gov.uk (Visa), consularmailbeijing@fco.gov.uk (Consular), URL: http://ukinchina.fco.gov.uk/en
Ambassador: Sebastian Wood (page 1539)
Embassy of the People's Republic of China, 2300 Connecticut Avenue, NW, Washington, DC 20008, USA. Tel: +1 202 328 2500, fax: +1 202 495 2138, e-mail: chinaembassy_us@fmprc.gov.cn, URL: http://www.china-embassy.org/
Ambassador: Cui Tiankai

Embassy of the People's Republic of China, 49-51 Portland Place, London, W1N 4JL, United Kingdom. Tel: +44 (0)20 9375 / 5726, fax: +44 (0)20 7636 9756, URL: http://www.chinese-embassy.org.uk
Ambassador: Liu Xiaoming (page 1465)
Embassy of the United States of America, Xiu Shui Bei Jie 3, Chao Yang District, Beijing 100600, China. Tel: +86 (0)10 6532 3831, fax: +86 (0)10 6532 3178, e-mail: BeijingWebmaster@state.gov, URL: http://beijing.usembassy.gov/
Ambassador: Gary Locke (page 1466)
Permanent Mission of the People's Republic of China to the UN, 350 East 35th Street, New York, NY 10016, USA. Tel: +1 212 655 6100, fax: +1 212 634 7626, e-mail: chinamission_un@fmprc.gov.cn, URL: http://www.china-un.org/
Permanent Representative: H.E. Li Baodong

LEGAL SYSTEM

The Chinese court system is based on civil law. It comprises a Supreme People's Court, local people's courts, and special people's courts. The Special Administrative Regions of Hong Kong and Macau have their own separate legal systems.

Chinese courts are divided into a four-level court system: The Supreme People's Court is the highest judicial body. Based in Beijing, it is the court of last resort, and has overall responsibility for the administration of justice by all subordinate courts. The president of the Supreme People's Court is elected by the NPC and serves a maximum of two successive five-year terms.

Local people's courts (the courts of the first instance) handle criminal and civil cases. They comprise three levels of the justice system: High people's courts handle cases at the level of the provinces, autonomous regions, and special municipalities; Intermediate people's courts operate at the level of prefectures, autonomous prefectures, and municipalities; and basic people's courts function at the level of towns, and municipal districts.

There are also Courts of Special Jurisdiction, comprising the Military Court of China, Railway Transport Court of China, and Maritime Court of China.

State procuratorial bodies are headed by the Supreme People's Procuratorate, followed by local people's procuratorates, and special people's procuratorates. The people's procuratorates are the state organs for legal supervision, and exercise authority over treason, attempts to divide the country and important criminal cases. The Procuratorate is responsible for both prosecution and investigation in mainland China. It also oversees the public security organs, courts and the prison system.

The government's human rights record is poor. Citizens do not have the right to change their government. The government monitors, arrests, and imprisons journalists, writers, activists, and defense lawyers, as well as exercising strict political control of courts and judges. There are tight controls on freedom of speech, assembly, movement and use of the Internet. There have been recent extrajudicial killings, and the torture and use of forced labour of prisoners. There is severe cultural and religious repression of ethnic minorities in Tibet and the Xinjiang Uighur Autonomous Region (XUAR). The state birth limitation policy continues, sometimes resulting in forced abortion or sterilization. Official corruption is endemic.

In October 2006, the Government approved a law allowing only the Supreme People's Court to approve death sentences. This was in response to miscarriages of justice since lower courts were given the right to approve death sentences in the 1980s. The death sentence can be handed down for such crimes as corruption and robbery. Over 2010, China was known to have carried out over 2,000 executions, although Amnesty International believe the total figure was much higher. In 2009, a newspaper revealed that prisoners on death row provide around two-thirds of all transplant organs. The government has now launched a voluntary donation scheme, which it hopes will also curb the illegal trafficking in organs. In 2011, China removed 13 offences from the list of 68 capital crimes. The relevant offences mainly related to economic crimes where capital punishment was rarely applied. Thousands of executions are also belived to have been carried out in 2011 and 2012.

Supreme People's Court, URL: http://www.chinacourt.org
President of the Supreme People's Court: Wang Shengjun
Supreme People's Procuratorate,
URL: http://english.peopledaily.com.cn/data/organs/procuratorate.html
President of the Supreme People's Procuratorate: Jia Chunwang
Procurator-general: Cao Jinming

LOCAL GOVERNMENT

China's provinces (*sheng*), autonomous regions (*zizhiqu*), and municipalities (*shi*) are subordinate to central government. Provision is made for the establishment of local people's congresses, which carry out local administration. The election of delegates to these congresses on a popular basis has been cited as evidence of the constitutional fact that all power ultimately resides in the hands of the people. At the lowest level, such direct elections determine the composition of the hierarchy of local people's congresses, which in turn provide delegates to the full NPC.

The executive responsibilities of the local people's governments extend to the implementation of decisions made by the people's congresses and their standing committees. In administrative terms, they direct and manage work within their areas. All local government bodies are state organs, answerable ultimately to the State Council.

China is currently divided into 33 provinces, which include five autonomous regions and four city municipalities. China considers Taiwan to be a province.

The following table shows the divisions with their seat of government, area and end of 2007 population (area is shown in 10,000 sq. km):

China's Administrative Divisions

Name	Seat of Gov.	Area	Pop. (millions)
NORTHERN CHINA			
Beijing Municipality	Beijing	1.68	16.3
Tianjin Municipality	Tianjin	1.13	11.1
Hebei Province	Shijiazhuang	19	69.4
Shaanxi Province	Taiyuan	15.6	37.4
NORTHEASTERN CHINA			
Liaoning Province	Shenyang	4.57	42.9
Jilin Province	Changchun	18.7	27.2
Heilongjiang Province	Harbin	46.9	38.2
EASTERN CHINA			
Shanghai Municipality	Shanghai	0.62	18.5
Shandong Province	Jinan	15.3	93.6
Jiangsu Province	Nanjing	10.26	76.2
Zhejiang Province	Hangzhou	10.18	50.6
Anhui Province	Hefei	13.9	61.1
Jiangxi Province	Nanchang	16.66	43.6
Fujian Province	Fuzhou	12	35.8
Taiwan Province*	Taipei	3.6	22.8
CENTRAL SOUTHERN CHINA			
Henan Province	Zhengzhou	16.7	93.6
Hubei Province	Wuhan	18.74	56.9
Hunan Province	Changsha	21	63.5
Guangdong Province	Guangzhou	18.6	94.4
Hainan Province	Haikou	3.4	8.4
SOUTHWESTERN CHINA			
Chongqing Municipality	Chongqing	8.2	28.1
Sichuan Province	Chengdu	57	81.2
Guizhou Province	Guiyang	17	39.7
Yunnan Province	Kunming	39.40	45.1
NORTHWESTERN CHINA			
Shaanxi Province	Xi'an	20.5	37.4
Gansu Province	Lanzhou	45	26.1
Qinghai Province	Xining	72	5.5
AUTONOMOUS REGIONS			
Guangxi Zhuang A.R.	Nanning	23.77	47.7
Tibet A.R.	Lhasa	122	2.8
Inner Mongolia A.R.	Hohhot	119.75	24.0
Ningxia Hui A.R.	Yinchuan	6.64	6.1
Xinjiang Uygur A.R.	Urumqi	160	20.9
Hong Kong SAR	Hong Kong	0.1103	6.9
Macao SAR	Macao	0.0027	0.5

* Taiwan is considered a province by the People's Republic of China

AREA AND POPULATION

Area
China covers a vast area of eastern Asia with Russia and Mongolia to the north, North Korea and the Pacific Ocean to the east, India, Nepal, Bhutan, Myanmar, Laos and Vietnam to the south and Kazakhstan, Kyrgyzstan, Tajikistan, Afghanistan and Pakistan to the west. China's total area is 9,596,960 sq. km., with 14,500 km. of coastline.

China's sovereignty also extends to the Hong Kong Special Administrative Region, Macao, and Taiwan Province. Macao is situated in Guangdong Province, 40 miles to the west of Hong Kong. It covers an area of 17.5 sq. km., consisting of the Macao Peninsula, Taipa Island, and Coloane Island. China resumed sovereignty over Macao on 20 December 1999. Taiwan Province is located southeast of the Chinese mainland opposite Fujian Province, and covers an area of 36,000 sq. km.

The terrain is mostly mountainous with high plateaus. The east of the country is fertile and also has mountains, deserts, steppes and some areas are subtropical. The west of the country has mountainous areas as well rolling plateaus. The climate is very varied with tropical in the south, varying to very cold in the north. Two main rivers run through China , the Yellow River in the north, and the Yangtze (or Yangzi) River in the south.

To view a map, please consult http://www.lib.utexas.edu/maps/cia08/china_sm_2008.gif

Population
Mainland China has the world's largest population, which, at 2010, numbered 1,348 million (approximately one fifth of the total world population), and up from around 1,321.3 million at the end of 2007. The population grew by 0.6 per cent over the period 2000-10. Population density was 139 people per sq. km in 2009. According to 2007 figures, the population of Hong Kong SAR is 6.87 million; Macao SAR has 520,400 inhabitants (18,428 persons per sq. km, making it the most densely populated region in the world), and the population of Taiwan Province is 22.85 million.

The population of China grew by 132 million, or 11.6 per cent, over the ten-year period to the 2000 Census. However, from 2001 onwards, the growth rate slowed to average 0.6 per cent per annum. The country succeeded in its Tenth Five-Year Plan (2001-2005) whereby the average annual natural increase in China's population was not to exceed nine per thousand, and for the population by 2005 to be less than 1.33 billion. The goal for 2010 was for the population of China to remain below 1.4 billion.

CHINA

Of China's 1.3 billion inhabitants in 2006, 51.5 per cent were male and 48.5 per cent were female. A report by the state Population and Family Planning Commission in 2007 warned that there will be 30 million more men of marriageable age by 2020 than women, an imbalance that could lead to social instability. The report noted that the ratio of newborn boys to girls was 118 to 100 in 2005 (higher in areas of southern China where the figure was 130 boys to 100 girls). By 2006, the overall ratio was 119.25 newborn boys to 100 newborn girls.

The report estimated that the number of those over the age of sixty would increase from the current 143 million to 430 million by 2040, and account for some 30 per cent of the population. At the end of 20107, largest age group was 15-60 years, which accounted for 72 per cent of the population,. Approximately 14 per cent of the population were aged between 0-14 years (14 per cent) and 24 per cent over 60 years.

Average population density at the end of 2009 was 139 people per sq. km. However, population density varies enormously in China, with the most marked contrast being that between the eastern seaboard and the west and northwest. The high mountains, plateaux and arid basins of Tibet and the Xinjiang-Inner Mongolia region comprise about half of China's total surface area, but contain little more than five per cent of its population. By contrast, the availability of fertile land in the east and southeast is reflected in very high population densities of over 400 people per sq.km., especially on the alluvial plains where intensive agriculture has traditionally been practised.

Although the majority of China's population still lives in rural areas, the population is shifting towards the city. In 1952 around 12.5 per cent of the population lived in urban areas; in 2009 this percentage had increased to 46.6 per cent; some predictions put the urban population as high as 60 per cent of the total population by 2030. 20 Chinese cities have over two million inhabitants (including Hong Kong and Taipei); the most highly populated cities in mainland China are Shanghai (17.8 million), Beijing (17.4 million) and Tianjin (11.1 million).

The majority of China's population - 91 per cent - is Han Chinese. In addition, there are 55 Minority Nationalities, who make up around nine per cent of the total population, and who live in China's Autonomous Regions and other border areas. These include Zhuang, Uygur, Hui, Yi, Tibetan, Miao, Manchu, Mongol, Buyi, and Korean. The population of the Han nationality has increased by 11.2 per cent since the 1990 Census, while that of the national minorities has increased by 16.7 per cent. Languages spoken include standard Chinese or Mandarin, Yue (Cantonese), Wu, Minbei, Minnan, Xiang, Gan, and Hakka.

Births, Marriages, Deaths
According to 2010 statistics, the crude birth rate was 14.3 per 1,000 population, slightly up on the previous year, whilst the crude death rate was 5.6 per 1,000 inhabitants, slightly lower than previous years. Life expectancy at birth was estimated at 74 years in 2009 (72 years for males, 76 years for females).

Shanghai, the largest Chinese city, has witnessed negative population growth for more than 12 years in succession. In 2004, the city's birth rate was six per thousand and its natural population growth was -1.2 per thousand. However, the city has the fastest growing aged population; by the end of 2006, 20.2 per cent of its 13.68 million residents were aged 60 or above, equivalent to an increase of 6.9 per cent on 2005. The number of those aged 80+ increased by 30,100 people, (up 13.3 per cent on 2005). Meanwhile, the number of people of working age continues to fall as a result of the one child per couple policy.

Since the late 1970s, population growth control has been a cornerstone of social economic strategy. A 'One Child' policy is strictly implemented; urban couples should only have one child, rural couples can have a second child if their first is female. Many people go to great lengths to ensure that their child is male which has led to a significant gender imbalance. Estimated figures for 2004 show that of the 22.3 per cent of the population aged 14 and under, 153.4 million are male and 135.8 million are female. The effect of the One Child policy is reflected in the reduction of the rate of natural increase from 25.83 (1970) to 13.08 (1984) per 1,000. In the second half of the 1980s the rate of population expansion started to rise again; however, in the middle of the last decade, it fell to 10.55 per 1,000. Even so, the Chinese government was unable to accomplish its original target of keeping total population below 1.2 billion by the end of the century, and adjusted it to 1.3 billion.

Tibet is an area where the one child policy is only applied to the Han officials and workers. Population growth is encouraged amongst the Tibetans. The birth rate was 17.4 per cent in 2004, and the death rate was 6.2 per cent. Natural population growth was 11.2 per cent and overall population density was low at 2.2 per km. sq.

Public Holidays 2014
1-3 January: Solar New Year
31 January - 5 February: Spring Festival, Chinese New Year
24 February: Lantern Festival
8 March: International Women's Day
18-21 April: Easter
5 April: Ching Ming (Tomb Sweeping) Festival
1-3 May: Labour Day
4 May: National Youth Day
23 May: Tibet Liberation Day
1 June: International Children's Day
2 June: Dragon Boat Festival
1 August: Army Day
30 September: Mid-Autumn Festival
1-3 October: National Day
14 October: Cheung Yeung Festival
25 December: Christmas Day
26 December: Day after Christmas Day

EMPLOYMENT

The workforce was estimated to be 807.2 million in 2008 and 786.5 million in 2007, up 0.5 per cent on the previous year. In the same year, 769.9 million people were employed. The agriculture sector continued to contract: an estimated 397.1 million worked in the sector in 2008, down from 360 million in 2000 and from 389 million in 1990. The unemployment rate for the whole of China fell to its lowest level since 2002, at 4.0 per cent, affecting 8.3 million people in 2007, but rose to 4.2 per cent in 2008 and 4.3 per cent in 2009, (9.2 million people). (Asian Development Bank, ADB)

In November 2008, the Chinese authorities admitted that China's employment outlook was looking grim, amid worries that economic problems could lead to rising unemployment and social unrest. An estimated 20 million migrant workers also lost their jobs over the year 2008. The unemployment rate was 4.2 per cent in 2011. According to official figures from 2006-10, 55 million new jobs were created in urban areas. The country is expected to face increased employment pressure and forecasts that one million new jobs per year will be needed up to 2015. Job shortages in urban areas are expected to exceed 13 million each year between 2011-2015. The government has said it will keep the unemployment rate below 5 per cent and aims to invest in industries and enterprises that can create more jobs. Priority will also be given to the employment of college graduates. It has also said it will expand the social security system to all workers by 2015.

Total Employment by Economic Activity (thousands) (estimated figures)

Occupation	2007
Agriculture, hunting, forestry & fishing	120,044
Mining & quarrying	5,350
Manufacturing	34,654
Electricity, gas & water supply	3,034
Construction	10,508
Wholesale & retail trade, repairs	5,069
Hotels & restaurants	1,858
Transport, storage & communications	6,231
Financial intermediation	3,897
Real estate, renting & business activities	6,571
Public admin. & defence; compulsory social security	12,912
Education	15,209
Health & social work	5,428
Other community, social & personal service activities	1,250
Not classifiable by economic activity	4,011

Source: Copyright © International Labour Organization (ILO Dept. of Statistics, http://laborsta.ilo.org)

BANKING AND FINANCE

Since the late 1970s the authorities have aimed to transform the economy to a market-oriented system whilst maintaining Communist Party control. Significant reform measures have been undertaken in the fiscal and taxation systems, banking, investment, foreign exchange and foreign trade. The Chinese government aims to continue economic liberalisation and growth. China has joined the World Trade Organisation, and a private sector comprising both domestic and foreign interests compliments the state sector.

Currency
The domestic Chinese currency is the Renminbi Yuan (RMB).
One Renminbi Yuan = 100 fen

GDP/GNP, Inflation, National Debt
China is the world's fastest growing major economy. In 2005, it overtook the British economy to become the 4th largest economy in the world (following USA, Japan and Germany), and a revised estimate of 2007 GDP growth from 11.9 per cent to 13 per cent meant that it overtook the German economy in that year. In March 2005 the Government set targets for sustainable growth of 8.0 per cent; other targets included the creation of nine million new jobs in urban areas, the reduction of urban unemployment to under 4.6 per cent and keeping inflation at around 4 per cent. In February 2011 China overtook Japan to become the world's second-largest economy.

As the global credit crunch began to bite, Chinese exports were hit hard by falling world demand, with millions of rural migrants returning to their villages after the factories that employed them closed down. In November 2008, the government announced a 4 trillion yuan (US$586bn) stimulus package to support the economy; the money will be spent on new infrastructure investment, tax cuts, consumer subsidies and increased spending on health care. Investment in railways, roads and power grids has already begun. The government also promised measures to help struggling exporters and vehicle and steel makers. China plans to run a deficit of 3 per cent of GDP. The crisis has not affected China to the same extent as western economies, and China is one of the few countries in the world where credit has accelerated since the start of the global credit crunch. However, China's many migrant workers have suffered. In March 2009, ahead of the G20 Summit, Chinese officials said that they would argue for a new global reserve currency and reforms of international financial institutions, such as the IMF, to give developing nations more power. Growth figures for 2009 were 7.9 per cent for Q2 compared to 6.1 per cent in Q1.

China's GDP has been rising steadily by an average rate of 9 per cent per annum since economic reform began in the 1970. According to Asian Development Bank estimates, GDP grew by 11.9 per cent in 2007 (up from 10.7 per cent over the previous year) to 24,953.0 billion yuan. Per capita GDP was 18,885.3 Yuan ($2,800), up from 7,129.3 Yuan in 2000. Growth slowed to 9 per cent in 2008. The Government recognised some of the problems created by the high growth rate such as the rising wealth disparities between urban and rural communities, environmental concerns associated with rapid industrial growth and increased demand on a weakened social security sector. Despite the global economic crisis, GDP grew by 8.7 per cent in 2009 and by at least 10 per cent in 2010 and 2011.

GDP was estimated to be US$5.8 trillion (exchange rate based) in 2010. Per capita GDP (PPP) was US$7,600.

The following table shows Gross Domestic Product according to sector in recent years:

GDP by Sector (Bn. Yuan at current Market Prices)

Sector	2008	2009	2010
Agriculture	3,370.2	3,522.6	4,049.7
Mining, Manufacturing, Utilities	13,026.0	13,524.0	16,003.0
Construction	1,874.3	2,239.9	2,645.1
Trade	2,618.2	2,898.5	..
Transport & Communications	1,636.3	1,705.8	..
Finance, Public administration & Others	8,879.6	10,160.0	..
Total	**31,622.9**	**34,140.2**	**40,004.1**

Source: Asian Development Bank

In percentage terms, agriculture, forestry, fishing and hunting made up 10.3 per cent of GDP in 2009, down from 14.8 per cent in 2000, and continuing the downward trend of the last fifty years (in 1952, agriculture contributed over 50 per cent of GDP). Industry accounted for 46.3 per cent of GDP (down slightly on the 2008 figure of 47.4 per cent) and the services sector contributed 43.4 per cent, up from 41.8 per cent the previous year.

Total central government revenue in 2008 amounted to 6,131.7 billion yuan (up from 5,132.2 bn. yuan the previous year) whilst total government expenditure rose to 6 242.7 billion yuan, up from 4 978.1 which gave a surplus of 173.9 billion yuan (in 2006, the government had a deficit of 166.3 billion yuan).

The Consumer Price Index went up by 4.8 per cent over 2006, the highest level in a decade. The greatest increases were in the Food index, which increased by 13.6 per cent overall: the cost of meat, poultry and related products increased by 31.8 per cent; oil went up by 28.3 per cent and fresh eggs went up by 22.8 per cent. (Source: ADB)

Inflation was 4.5 per cent by the end of 2011.

Foreign Investment

The opening up of China and the creation of special economic zones has led to increased foreign investment. Foreign enterprises contribute nearly a quarter of industrial production and there are over 270,000 foreign-funded enterprises operating in China. Investment into the services sectors including banking, insurance and law remain relatively restricted although regulations are being lifted gradually. The government has designated a number of areas 'special economic zones' where foreign investors receive the benefit of reduced taxes and tariffs. China was officially admitted to the World Trade Organisation (WTO) in November 2001 and has opened a number of its economic sectors to greater foreign involvement.

Foreign direct investment (FDI) in China totalled approximately $124 billion in 2011.

Balance of Payments / Imports and Exports

China as been a member of the World Trade Organisation (WTO) since November 2001. In 2010 official figures from China suggested that the country had become the largest exporting nation in the world overtaking Germany.

The following table shows China's trade balance in recent years. Figures are in billion US$.

External Trade	2007	2008	2009	2010
Exports fob	1,217.8	1,430.7	1,201.7	1,577.9
Imports cif	956.0	1,132.6	1,005.6	1,394.8
Trade Balance	261.8	298.1	196.1	183.1
Trade Balance % change				
- Exports of Goods	25.7	17.5	-16.0	31.3
- Imports of Goods	20.8	18.5	-11.2	38.7

Source: Asian Development Bank

Principal trading partners in 2009-10 are listed below (US$million):

Direction of exports	2009	2010
Total	1,203,420	1,580,400
United States	221,384	283,679
HKSAR	166,261	218,205
Japan	98,045	120,602
Korea, Rep. of	53,639	68,811
Germany	49,943	68,069
Netherlands	36,693	49,711
United Kingdom	31,283	38,776
Singapore	30,089	32,333
India	29,683	40,880
Russia	17,518	29,592

Source: Asian Development Bank

Imports	2009	2010
Total	1,003,910	1,393,920
Japan	130,928	176,304
Korea, Rep. of	102,501	138,024
United States	77,773	101,959
Germany	55,916	74,378

- continued		
Australia	39,241	59,698
Malaysia	32,224	50,375
Brazil	28,311	38,038
Thailand	24,846	33,201
Saudi Arabia	23,582	32,862
Russia	21,103	25,811

Source: Asian Development Bank

Main export commodities are light industrial and textile products, mineral fuels, heavy manufactures, and agricultural items. Major import products are machinery, chemicals, steel, industrial materials, manufactured goods, and grain.

Principal Exported and Imported Commodities in 2007 (US$ million)

Commodity	Export	Import
Animal and animal products	7,397	4,663
Vegetable products	11,269	10,976
Animal or vegetable fats	327	3,921
Prepared foodstuffs	16,477	4,074
Mineral products	23,578	123,544
Chemical products	51,115	56,221
Plastics and rubber	36,523	46,277
Hides and skins	16,367	6,276
Wood and wood products	11,434	6,495
Wood pulp products	9,199	11,893
Textiles and textile articles	165,821	25,678
Footwear, headgear	30,583	775
Articles of stone, plaster, cement etc	18,296	3,963
Pearls, precious or semi-precious stones, metals	8,121	4,616
Base metals and articles thereof	115,526	59,795
Machinery, mechanical & electrical equipment	528,939	328,185
Transportation equipment	54,996	29,720
Instruments, measuring, musical	40,721	60,075
Arms and ammunition	59	2
Misc. manufactured articles	69,013	2,423
Works of art	75	12

Source: Asian Development Bank

Central Bank
People's Bank of China, Cheng Fang Street, West City, Beijing 32, China. Tel: +86 (0)10 601 6494, fax: +86 (0)10 66016707, e-mail: master@pbc.gov.cn, URL: http://www.pbc.gov.cn. Governor: Zhou Xiaochuan (page 1540)

Chambers of Commerce and Trade Organisations
State Administration for Industry and Commerce, URL: http://www.saic.gov.cn/english/default.htm
China Council for Promotion of International Trade (CCPIT), URL: http://www.ccpit.org/infosystem/home.jsp
Ministry of Foreign Trade and Economic Co-operation, URL: http://www.moftec.gov.cn/
Beijing Foreign Economic Relations & Trade Commission, URL: http://www.bjmbc.gov.cn/index_english.jsp
Guangzhou Foreign Economic Relations and Trade Commission, URL: http://www.investguangzhou.gov.cn/web/eng/jsp/index.jsp
Shanghai Foreign Economic Relations And Trade Commission, URL: http://www.smert.gov.cn/
Tibet Autonomous Region Foreign Economic Relations and Trade Department, URL: http://www.ipim.gov.mo

MANUFACTURING, MINING AND SERVICES

Primary and Extractive Industries
China has the third highest reserves of mineral resources in the world and has deposits of all known minerals. In 2007, China overtook the United States to become the world's second largest gold producer with an output of 270.491 tons, second only to South Africa. Over the year, five major gold mines were discovered, with a combined reserve of some 600 tons. The Shandong peninsular in east China is one of the country's most important gold producers, with a proved gold reserve of over 1,000 tons.

Coal
China is the world's largest producer and consumer of coal. Consumption in 2009 was 3.474 billion short tons (over 33 per cent of the world total). At present it accounts for 70 per cent of China's primary energy consumption and demand is rising rapidly with economic growth. Total recoverable coal reserves were estimated at 126.2 billion short tons in 2006 (the third largest reserves in the world) and production in 2010 was an estimated 3,522.9 million short tons up from 3,004.4 million short tons in 2008.

China has some 28,000 small local coal mines which suffer from inefficient management and lack of investment. China's mines are among the most dangerous in the world, with about 5,000 deaths reported every year. China is becoming increasingly open to foreign investment in the coal sector. Coal imports and exports are the responsibility of the China Coal Import and Export Group.

China became a net coal importer in 2009. Imports come mainly from Indonesia, Australia, Vietnam and Russia. Figures for 2010 put coal imports at 172.405 million short tons. In 2009 China signed a $6 billion loan-for-coal deal with Russia for 15-20 million tons of coal for 25 years. Domestic demand for coal is likely to double by 2020. (Source: EIA)

CHINA

Natural Gas

China's reserves of natural gas stood at an estimated 107 trillion cubic feet in 2011, a substantial increase on previous estimates. Production in 2011 reached an estimated 6,629 billion cubic feet and consumption was around 4,624 billion cubic feet. Consumption is expected to rise by 5 per cent per year. With a view to its environmental benefits, China has embarked on a major expansion of its gas infrastructure.

The natural gas industry is dominated by the three state-owned oil and gas holding companies: CNPC, Sinopec, and CNOOC. Exploration has led to the discovery of several large gas fields in recent years, the largest being the Puguang natural gas field in the southwestern province of Sichuan, which holds proven recoverable reserves of 8.9 Tcf. In June 2006, CNOOC and Husky Energy announced a new natural gas discovery with estimated possible reserves of 6 Tcf in the South China Sea.

Significant investment in pipeline infrastructure has begun; the country's largest reserves of natural gas are in western and north-central China, and construction of the "West-to-East Pipeline," was completed in January 2005. Another proposed pipeline project would link the Russian natural gas grid in Siberia to China and possibly South Korea via a pipeline from the Kovykta gas fields near Irkutsk, which hold reserves of more than 50 trillion cubic feet. The cost of the project has been estimated at $12 billion. The pipeline would have a capacity of 2.9 billion cubic feet per day, of which China would consume about 1.9 billion cubic feet per day. As of 2009, the pipeline network comprised approximately 21,000 miles. This should have expanded to approximately 35,000 miles by 2015. (Source: EIA)

Oil

In January 2012, China had estimated proven oil reserves of 20.4 billion barrels. China is the world's second largest oil consumer after the US, using an estimated 8.9 million barrels per day in 2011, up from 4.9 million barrels in 2001. Consumption is expected to reach 10.5 million barrels per day by 2020. China ranked fourth in the world in terms of oil production in 2011, producing at an estimated 4.3 million barrels per day (up from 3.3 million barrels per day in 2001). As the source of around 38 per cent of world oil demand growth over the past four years, Chinese oil demand is a key factor in world oil markets; it is the world's largest importer, taking 9.6 million barrels per day (2010), mostly from the Middle East and Africa. Saudi Arabia is the main supplier (1,005,000 bbl/d in 2011), Angola (623,000 bbl/d) and Iran (555,000 bbl/d).

Most of China's oil production (85 per cent) takes place onshore, although the most recent discoveries have been offshore. China's largest field is at Daqing, in the north-east of the country, which produces over 900,000 barrels per day (a quarter of China's total crude oil production). Major fields in the process of development include the Pearl River Mouth area and the Bohai Sea area. Major producing oil fields (2006 production) are: Daqing (929,268 bbl/d), and Shengli (535,531 bbl/d). As of 2011, China's refinery capacity was 11 million bbl/d. It is expected to rise to over 13 million bbl/d by 2015. Major oil refineries (January 2006 capacity) are: Zhenhai (403,000 bbl/d), Ningbo (320,000), Maoming (270,000), and Nanjing (270,000). China has an estimated 13,392 miles of total crude oil pipelines and approximately 8,250 miles of oil products pipelines in the domestic network. Several long-distance pipeline links are under construction.

In 1998, most of China's state-owned oil and gas institutions were re-organised into two corporations: the China National Petroleum Corporation (CNPC) and the China Petrochemical Corporation (Sinopec). Following asset transfers between the two, they became regional institutions: CNPC representing the north and west of China, and Sinopec representing the south. CNPC retains over two-thirds of the country's crude oil production capacity, whilst Sinopec owns over half China's refining capacity. Other state corporations include the China National Offshore Oil Corporation (CNOOC) and China National Star Petroleum. The Chinese are encouraging foreign investment in the oil industry subject to them retaining a controlling interest. Foreign investment comes mainly from ENI, BP, ExxonMobil, Phillips Petroleum, Shell, Texaco, and Mitsubishi.

With growing dependence on oil imports, the China has been acquiring interests in exploration and production abroad. CNPC has acquired exploration and production interests in 21 countries spanning four continents. Offshore production has increased in recent years. Recent exploration has focused on the offshore areas of Bohai Bay and the South China Sea. and also the interior provinces including Xinjiang, Sichuan, Gansu and Inner Mongolia. Territorial disputes in the East China Sea have limited development of the fields. (Source: EIA)

Energy

Overall, China's energy consumption accounts for approximately 53 per cent of East Asia's (excluding Japan) total energy consumption. China is set to become the world's largest consumer of energy, according to a study by the International Energy Agency, and demand for energy in China is expected to have doubled within 20 years. In 2001, China accounted for 9.8 per cent of world energy consumption; projections indicate that China will be responsible for approximately 14.2 per cent of world energy consumption by 2025.

Total energy consumption reached an estimated 90.2 quadrillion Btus in 2009. It was the world's largest energy producer in 2009 (81.887 quadrillion Btu). In 2008, coal accounted for 71 per cent of total energy consumption, oil 19 per cent, hydroelectric 6 per cent, natural gas 3 per cent, nuclear 1 per cent and other renewables 0.2 per cent. (Source: EIA)

Electricity

In 2010, China had total installed electricity generating capacity of 987.94 gigawatts (GWe). In the same year, 3,445.72 billion kWh were generated and 3,253.19 BkWh of electricity were consumed. Since 2000, both electricity generation and consumption have increased by over 60 per cent. China was the world's second largest consumer and producer of electricity in 2009. There has been significant development of the electric power sector in recent years to cope with increased demand. Installed capacity is expected to rise to over 1,600 GW by 2020 and total net generation to 10,555 billion kWh by 2035.

Conventional thermal sources are expected to remain the dominant fuel for electricity generation in the coming years, with many power projects under construction or planned that will use coal or natural gas.

Hydro-electric power

In 2009, China was the world's largest producer of hydroelectric power, generating 549 billion kWh of electricity from hydroelectric sources (16 per cent of total power production). Hydroelectric power is due to increase significantly, given the number of large-scale hydroelectric projects planned or under construction at present. The largest of these is the Three Gorges Dam; whilst the original plan was completed in October 2008, when the 26th generator became operational, six additional generators were then installed. The dam became fully operational in 2012 with a generating capacity of 22,500 MW. The reservoir created by the dam began to fill in June 2003, and it began operating the first of its 26 turbines in July 2003. The main wall of the dam, 2km long running across the Yangste, was completed in 2006. Nine provinces and two cities, including Shanghai, consume the power from the Three Gorges Dam.

The upper portion of the Yellow River is also being used to harness electric power; Shaanxi, Qinghai, and Gansu provinces have joined to create the Yellow River Hydroelectric Development Corporation. The combined capacity of its planned 25 generating stations will reach 15.8 GW. (Source: EIA)

Other Renewables

China is the world's fifth largest wind producer and generated 25 billion kWh in 2009, up from 12.5 billion kWh in 2008. Its installed wind capacity in 2010 was 16 GW and capacity should increase to 100 GW by 2020. (Source: EIA)

Nuclear

China's total installed capacity for nuclear power generation stood at an estimated 10.8 GW in 2011 by it is planned to increase this to 70 GW by 2020. As of 2011, China had 13 operating reactors and 27 reactors under construction. Following the Fukushima accident in 2011 the government suspended approvals for new nuclear plans until safety reviews had been performed on both existing plants and those under construction. (Source: EIA)

Manufacturing

In 2009, manufacturing, together with mining and construction accounted for 46.3 per cent of the Chinese GDP, a slight drop on the figure for 2006 when the sector recorded its highest level since 1990. The sector contributed 13,026.0 billion yuan to the 2008 national GDP. Growth of output remained steady at 11 per cent over 2004 and 2005, before rising to 12.5 per cent in 2006, and to 13.4 per cent in 2007. The manufacturing sector employed 89.57 million people in 2003. The construction sector employed some 255,790,000 people in 2004 and contributed 9,572,100 million yuan to GDP. China recorded its largest manufacturing growth figures for five years in 2009.

Major industries are mining and ore processing; iron, steel, aluminum and coal; machinery; textiles and apparel; armaments; petroleum; cement, chemicals and fertilizers; consumer products including footwear, toys, and electronics; cars and other transportation equipment including rail cars and locomotives, ships, and aircraft; and telecommunications. China is a preferred location for international manufacturing facilities.

Service Industries

The service sector has seen significant growth over the past few years, averaging annual growth of ten per cent over the period 2000-05. Output grew by 10.3 per cent in 2006. The sector's contribution towards national GDP increased from 34.1 per cent in 2001 to 41.5 per cent in 2003, before dropping to 39.5 per cent in 2006. Employment in the sector grew from 172.11 million in 1990 to 289.29 in 2003.

The service industries are still largely protected by the government with major regulatory constraints in the way of foreign investors. Foreign banks operations in Chinese currency are limited. Foreign law firms may not advise or interpret laws or represent clients in Chinese courts.

In 2007, visitors to China numbered 131.87 million, an increase of 5.5 per cent over the previous year. Of these, 26.11 million visitors were foreign (up 17.6 per cent) and 105.76 million were Chinese compatriots from Hong Kong, Macao and Taiwan (up 2.9 per cent). 54.72 million stayed overnight. Foreign exchange earnings from international tourism exceeded US$41.9 billion, up 23.5 per cent on 2006. 2007 saw 1.61 billion domestic tourists, and revenue from domestic tourism reached 777.1 billion yuan, up 24.7 per cent on 2006.

Agriculture

China has the world's largest agricultural economy; the country has to feed over 1.3 billion inhabitants using approximately seven per cent of the world's arable land. Due to intensive farming practices, China is among the world's largest producers of rice, corn, wheat, soybeans, vegetables, tea, and pork. Major non-food crops include cotton, other fibers, and oilseeds. The wide range of crops is due to the country's varied climate and agricultural zones.

The agriculture, forestry and fisheries sector continues to be the largest employer in China, employing almost 41 per cent, 397.1 million people, in 2009. This is a large reduction on the rate of 50 per cent in 2002, when the number of people employed in agriculture was 368.70 million. Chinese farmers have not seen the increases in personal wealth that are available to urban workers, leading to an increasing wealth gap between the cities and countryside, and a rise in migration to the cities. Whilst annual output grew by a healthy five per cent in 2006, the sector's share of GDP fell from 15.2 per cent in 2004 to 11.8 per cent in 2006.

Estimated land use is divided as follows: arable, 10 per cent; pasture, 43 per cent; forest and woodland, 14 per cent; other, 33 per cent.

Agricultural Production in 2010

Produce	Int. $1000*	Tonnes
Indigenous pig meat	79,435,198	51,673,874
Rice, paddy	48,759,651	197,212,010
Vegetables fresh nes	24,683,339	152,987,093
Hen eggs, in shell	19,762,175	23,827,390
Tomatoes	17,412,409	47,116,084
Indigenous chicken meat	16,807,139	11,799,394
Indigenous cattle meat	16,796,410	6,217,724
Wheat	16,169,704	115,181,303
Apples	14,068,313	33,265,186
Other bird eggs, in shell	12,038,594	4,173,950
Cow milk, whole, fresh	11,245,444	36,036,043
Potatoes	10,674,759	74,799,084

* unofficial figures

Source: http://faostat.fao.org/site/339/default.aspx Food and Agriculture Organization of the United Nations, Food and Agricultural commodities production

China leads the world in fish production. In 2010, some 15.4 million tonnes of fish were caught.

There is concern over food safety issues in China following several incidents of food poisoning over recent years. In one of the worst instances, three babies died and over 6,000 were made ill in 2008, by a baby formula milk that had been contaminated with melamine. The supplier of the milk, Sanlu Group, is thought to have known of the problem for months, but claimed the contaminant came from milk suppliers.

Food safety regulations are complex and the ten government departments that oversee and enforce policies have overlapping duties. China's agricultural system is composed mostly of subsistence agriculture, and farmers use fertilizers and pesticides to maintain high food production on small plots. Food is sold in both open air markets and urban supermarkets. In 2007, Zheng Xiaoyu, the former head of China's State Food and Drug Administration, was executed for taking bribes from various firms in exchange for state licenses related to product safety.

COMMUNICATIONS AND TRANSPORT

Travel Requirements

US, Canadian, Australian and EU citizens require a passport valid for at least six months for a single or double entry within three months of the date of visa issue. A visa is also required, with the following exceptions: UK subjects visiting Hong Kong for up to 180 days or Macao for up to six months; Visitors to Macao for up to 90 days (or up to 30 days for USA citizens); transit passengers leaving within 24 hours who hold valid onward documentation and do not leave the airport. Other nationals should contact the embassy to check visa requirements. It is important to note that China does not recognise dual nationality, and that HIV-positive travellers are not allowed to enter China.

Every foreigner going to Tibet needs to get a travel permit which can be done through local travel agents. Most areas in Tibet are not open for foreigners except Lhasa City and part of Shan Nan. Foreigners can be fined up to RMB 500, taken into custody, and removed for visiting restricted areas. Those wishing to visit Tibet are strongly advised to join a travel group. For further information, contact the nearest Chinese Consulate for details.

National Airlines

Air China, URL: http://www.airchina.com.cn
Air Great Wall, URL: http://www.gwairlines.com/en/index.asp
China Eastern Airlines, URL: http://www.chinaeasternair.com
China United Airlines, URL: http://www.cu-air.com/nyairweb/webIndex.action

International Airports

There are 502 airports in China, 442 of which have paved runways. International airports include Beijing, Shanghai, Shenyang and Guangzhou. There are also 48 heliports. More than 78.6 million passengers used Beijing Capital in 2011. International Airport in 2011.
Beijing Capital International Airport, URL: http://www.bcia.com.cn/
Civil Aviation Administration of China, URL: http://english.gov.cn/2005-10/22/content_81677.htm

Railways

The total length of railway is 86,000 km, of which 19,303 km is electrified. Recent figures show that the volume of freight carried is 1.64 billion tons per annum and 1.12 billion passengers.

The world's highest railway from Qinghai to Tibet (1,100 km) was opened by the Chinese President Hu Jintao in July 2006; travelling over hundreds of km of permafrost, the journey from Beijing takes 2.5 days. Carriages carry oxygen supplies as most of the journey is at between five and six thousand metres above sea level.

Many cities including Beijing, Chengdu, Shanghai, Tianjin, Guangzhou, Shenzhen and Nanjing have subway systems. Hong Kong has a Mass Transit System. Cities without a subway system usually have trams.

Roads

There are 3,860,000 km of roads, 3,056,000 km of which are paved roads (including 34,288 km of motorways). China had 159.8 million motor vehicles by the end of 2007, up 10.02 per cent from 2006. Private cars rose by 10.92 per cent and made up 76.09 per cent of China's total motor vehicles. Vehicles are driven on the right.

Shipping

The merchant marine fleet consists approximately 2,030 vessels.

Ports and Harbours

There are 20 major harbours which handle over 790 million tons of cargo per annum. These include: Dalian; Fuzhou; Guanghzou; Haikou; Lianyungang; Nanjing; Nantong; Ningbo; Qingdao; Qinhuangdao; Shanghai; Shantou; Tianjin; Xiamen; Yantain; Zhanjiang.

Waterways

Major rivers have ferry services. A system of coastal ferries operates between Dalian, Tianjin, Qingdao and Shanghai. There are also ferry services between mainland China and Hong Kong.

HEALTH

The system under Chairman Mao of providing near-universal access to basic healthcare has been dismantled, and the present government struggles to spread the cost of providing care for almost a quarter of the world's population. Government figures indicate that between 2000 and 2003, hospital profits increased 70 per cent, yet hospital visits fell by five per cent, evidence that the poor are avoiding medical treatment because of the cost, whilst the rich are paying more. In January 2008, the authorities announced a budget of more than $120bn to reform the healthcare system over the next three years. By 2011, the government target is for most of the population to be covered by basic health insurance, for the cost of services to be reduced and quality improved. The health system faces the growing challenge of an aging population; changes in diet and lifestyle mean a growing percentage of people have chronic diseases, like heart attacks, strokes and cancer.

The health service operates at three levels: province, county and township. In addition there are general hospitals, hospitals for the treatment of special diseases, traditional Chinese medicine hospitals and Western medicine hospitals. Traditional forms of healthcare are used alongside modern Western techniques and research is being undertaken in order to develop some of the basic techniques of Chinese medicine. Over 12 ministries or agencies administer the health service, including the Ministry of Health, the Ministry of Labour and Social Security, and the National Development and Reform Commission.

In 2009, China spent approximately 12.1 per cent of it total budget on healthcare (up from 10.9 per cent in 2000), accounting for 47.3 per cent of all healthcare spending. Total expenditure on health care equated to 5.1 per cent of the country's GDP. Per capita spending on healthcare was US$146 in 2009 (compared with US$43 in 2000). (Source: WHO).

In 2004 China had a total of 60,867 hospitals with 30,470,000 beds. There were also sanitation and anti-epidemic institutions (4,065 in 2000), and mother and child healthcare institutions (2,600 in 2000). In 2000-10, according to WHO figures, there were 1,905,436 doctors (14.2 per 10,000 population), 1,854,818 nurses and midwives (13.8 per 10,000 inhabitants), 51,020 dentists (0.4 per 10,000 people) and 341,920 pharmaceutical personnel.

A smoking ban in most of Beijing's public buildings came into effect on 1st May 2008. This was an attempt to discourage some of China's 320 million smokers and also part of wider efforts to clean up the city in the run up to the Olympics. Smoking is deep-rooted in Chinese culture and there is still a general lack of awareness about the impact on health. Almost a quarter of the Chinese people are smokers, and a third of all cigarettes smoked worldwide is smoked in China. Smoking is contributing to a rapid rise of cancer and heart disease in the country. Leading causes of death in China include cerebrovascular disease (including stroke), heart disease and cancer (accounting for approximately more than 50 per cent of all deaths). Road-traffic injuries, depression and suicide are leading causes of mortality in the young and economically active age groups.

In 2009, there were 14,491 reported cases of malaria, 52,461 of measles, 299,329 of mumps, 69,860 of rubella and 965,257 of tuberculosis. China has a low overall HIV prevalence but high prevalence in certain population groups, particularly drug injectors. The World Health Organisation estimated that in 2008 the prevalence of HIV/AIDS in the population group aged 15-49 years was 0.1 per cent. Immunization rates are high: measles 94 per cent, DTP3 97 and HepB3 95 per cent.

In 2010 the infant mortality rate (probability of dying by age one) was 16 per 1,000 live births (down from 27 per 1,000 live births in 2000 and 38 per 1,000 live births in 1990). The under-five mortality rate was 18 per 1,000 live births. In 2010 the distribution of causes of death among the under-fives were: pneumonia 17 per cent, prematurity 15 per cent, birth asphyxia 16 per cent, congenital abnormalities 11 per cent and injuries 10 per cent.

In 2005-11, 9.4 per cent of children under five-years-old were considered stunted and 3.4 per cent underweight. Approximately 6.6 per cent were consdiered obese.

In 2008, an estimated 98 per cent of the urban population and 82 per cent of the rural population had access to improved drinking-water sources. In 2010, 91 per cent of the total population had access to improved drinking-water sources. In 2008, 58 per cent of the urban population and 52 per cent of the rural population had access to improved sanitation. In 2010, 64 per cent of the total population had access to improved sanitation. (Source: WHO, 2012)

EDUCATION

Pre-school Education

According to UNESCO statistics, 39 per cent of children of the relevant age were enrolled in pre-school education in 2006.

CHINA

Primary/Secondary Education

Education is provided by the state and overseen by the Ministry of Education, although in 1980 the first private schools were allowed to open. Primary education is compulsory, beginning at seven years of age and lasting until 12 years of age. There were more than 609,000 primary schools in 2007, with 105.64 million students.

Secondary education begins at 12 years of age and lasts until the students are 17. There are two types of secondary education: general secondary and special/technical secondary school. General secondary education is divided into junior and senior high school, each having a study period of three years. There are approximately 77,800 general secondary schools. There were 57.36 million students enrolled in junior secondary schools in 2007, and regular senior secondary schools had 25.22 million students. Special/technical secondary schools offer a technical and vocational curriculum over a two or three year period. In 2007, there were more than 3,200 special education schools teaching 410,000 students.

According to the 2000 Census, across the 31 provinces, autonomous regions and municipalities of China, almost 452 million people had received primary education, nearly 430 million had received junior secondary education, and just over 141 million had received senior secondary education (including secondary technical school education). The number of children with a junior secondary education per 100,000 people rose from 23,345 in 1990 to 33,960 in 2000. The rate of children with a senior secondary education per 100,000 people rose from 8,040 in 1990 to 11,145 in 2000. (National Bureau of Statistics of China, Statistical Communique, 2007)

In 2004, the Central Government earmarked special funds for education in rural areas, amounting to 10 billion yuan. The Government also began a boarding school building program in areas of poverty, aimed at meeting the educational requirements of 2.03 million students. In 2009, the Government invested 1.2 trillion yuan on education. By 2012, China has said it will invest 4 per cent of its GDP in education.

According to latest (2010) UNESCO statistics, the adult literacy rate was 97.1 for males and 91.3 for females. For the age group 15-24 years the rate rises to 99.5 for males and 99.3 for females.

Higher Education

Entry to higher education in China is by way of an entrance examination (testing moral and physical suitability as well as academic), after which students go to one of the 1,022 universities and colleges. Degrees usually last four or five years and professional courses last two or three years. In 2007, students at institutions of higher learning numbered 18.85 million. Scholarships for university education are available.

Latest 2000 Census figures put the number of people having completed their university education at nearly 46 million. The rate of students with a university education increased from 1,420 per 100,000 people in 1990 to 3,610 per 100,000 people in 2000. An estimated 6.4 million students graduated from college in 2011. This was expected to rise to 6.6 million in 2012.

The number of Chinese students studying abroad dropped 2.2 per cent in 2004, to 114,663. 3,524 of the students were government sponsored, and 6,858 were sponsored by state-owned enterprises. An estimated 104,280 were self-supported.

Vocational Education

In addition to China's technical secondary schools there are teacher-training schools, agricultural and vocational schools, and special schools.

RELIGION

Although China is officially an atheist country, the freedom of religious belief is enshrined in China's State Constitution and many different religions are followed. Taoism (Daoism) and Buddhism are widely practiced, especially by older generations. 1.5 per cent of the population is Muslim.

The official Christian representative body in China is the 'Three-Self Patriotic Movement'. There are now over 4,000 Protestant churches in China and official statistics indicate that there are some three million Christians. The true figure is, however, likely to be higher, as many worship in so-called "house churches". The Roman Catholic Church in China is a schismatic body, which has no relations with The Vatican. Recent figures show that 8.6 per cent of the population are Christian.

China has a religious liberty rating of 4 on a scale of 1 to 10 (10 is most freedom). (Source: World Religion Database)

COMMUNICATIONS AND MEDIA

The Communist Party controls the media market. Independent coverage exists only if is not perceived as a threat to the Party. Access to foreign news is limited by restricting broadcasting and by blocking shortwave broadcasts and blocking websites. China has the world's largest online population.

Newspapers
There are more than 2,000 newspapers.
Renmin Ribao (People's Daily), URL: http://www.people.com.cn/english
Jiefangjun Bao (Liberation Army Daily), URL: http://english.chinamil.com.cn
Zhongguo Qinghian Bao (China Youth Daily), URL: http://www.cyol.net/node/index.htm
Zhongguo Jingji Shibao (China Economic Daily), URL: http://www.jjxww.com/
Fazhi Ribao (Legal Daily), URL: http://www.legaldaily.com.cn/

Broadcasting

China has over 1,200 radio stations, the largest being the national Central People's Broadcasting Station. There are hundreds of television stations and an estimated 1.2 billion viewers. The state-run Chinese Central Television is China's largest media company and provides over 2,000 channels.. The cable television industry is well developed; the largest station is Shanghai cable television station which has 1.8 million viewers.
Chinese Central Television, URL: http://english.cctv.com/index.shtml
Chinese National Radio, URL: http://www.cnr.cn/
Chinese Radio International, URL: http://english.cri.cn/

Telecommunications

China continues to develop its telecommunications infrastructure. In partnership with foreign providers, it is expanding its global reach. China Mobile is the largest mobile provider in China with a huge market share, the largest network, the largest infrastructure and the best brand recognition.

The fastest growing area of the industry is mobile phone technology. China now has more mobile phones than landlines; the number of fixed-line phones has been falling and as of 2011, there were an estimated 295 million land lines, whilst there are now some 850 million mobile phone users. Three state companies control the mobile phone market: China Mobile, China Telecom and China Unicom. China issued licenses for third-generation (3G) mobile phones to China Mobile, China Telecom and China Unicom in March 2009 enabling faster data transmission and services such as watching TV, playing online games, wide-area wireless calls and web surfing.

Some 390 million Chinese people were regular internet users in 2011. Internet use in rural areas is currently increasing faster than in the cities. Many people already access the internet through a mobile phone, and it is thought that the availability of 3G services will lead to massive growth in mobile internet use. The government maintains tight control over what is available on the web, blocking politically sensitive sites (such as the BBC's Chinese language news), as well as 'vulgar' sites.

ENVIRONMENT

According to EIA estimates, carbon emissions in China reached 8,320.96 million metric tons in 2010 (up from 4,753.33 million metric tons in 2004). Per capita carbon emissions in 2005 were 4.07 metric tons (up from 3.66 metric tons in 2004), compared with 20.14 metric tons in the US. China has not agreed to binding targets for reduction of carbon dioxide emissions under the Kyoto Protocol and, in recent years, overall energy-related carbon emissions have risen dramatically. In its first policy paper on climate change, published in 2008, the Chinese authorities acknowledged that its greenhouse gas emissions now equal those of the US. China is heavily reliant on highly polluting coal for its energy, and mines far more coal than any other country.

China is home to seven of the world's ten most polluted cities, according to a World Health Organization report. An estimated 178,000 people suffer premature death each year in China due to pollution and children in major cities have blood-lead levels 80 per cent higher than that thought dangerous to mental health. In June 2002, China enacted the Cleaner Production Promotion Law, which established demonstration programs for pollution remediation in ten major Chinese cities, and designated several river valleys as priority areas. According to the 2007 Environmental Monitoring of China report, the country's seven major water systems, including the Yangtze and Yellow rivers, were polluted, and over half the 500 cities and counties monitored reported cases of acid rain.

In the run up to the Olympic Games in Beijing, the authorities initiated unprecedented measures to cut air pollution and ensure that Beijing's air quality would be up to the standard laid down by the World Health Organisation by August 2008; a new standard for car emissions came into force in Beijing and the surrounding provinces. A new less-polluting petrol was brought onto the market, and from July private car use in Beijing and Tianjin was restricted. In July, Beijing Shougang Group, one of the capital's top polluters, announced it was cutting production, and so pollution, by 70 per cent over the following months, and other factories in nearby provinces cut production or closed temporarily to ensure clear skies above Beijing during the Olympics. The result was a far less polluted city, with blue skies and clear roads; air pollution was reduced by 50 per cent.

Other environmental issues include water shortages; water pollution from industrial effluents; insufficient potable water; water treatment (less than 10 per cent of sewage is treated); desertification and deforestation (one fifth of agricultural land has been lost since 1949 due to economic development); and trade in endangered species. In 2006, it was reported that ten per cent of the country's farmland was polluted, posing a threat to food production; excessive fertiliser use, polluted water, heavy metals and solid wastes were to blame, according to government officials. Concerns about water supplies in China have come to the fore as rivers in the north of the country have dried up due to overuse and the building of dams for hydroelectricity. An official pollution inspection report, published in 2006, found that 25.5 million tonnes of sulphur dioxide were emitted the previous year, mainly from coal-burning factories, and that the increased levels of sulphur dioxide meant that one third of China was affected by acid rain. The country is also investing in water control projects, in provinces such as Shandong and Hubei, to both ease water shortages and combat flooding.

China is party to the following international agreements: Antarctic-Environmental Protocol, Antarctic Treaty, Biodiversity, Climate Change, Climate Change-Kyoto Protocol, Desertification, Endangered Species, Environmental Modification, Hazardous Wastes, Law of the Sea, Marine Dumping, Ozone Layer Protection, Ship Pollution, Tropical Timber 83, Tropical Timber 94, Wetlands, and Whaling.

SPACE PROGRAMME

The first Chinese satellite was launched in 1970, and in 1975 China became the third country in the world to have successfully launched and recovered a satellite. In 1987 it began to launch satellites commercially for other countries. The rockets used for this purpose are of the Long March-2 and Long March-3 varieties. China plans to launch 100 satellites between 2011 and 2015.

The third nation after the United States and Russia to independently put a man in space, China launched its first manned spacecraft, the Long March 2F rocket in October 2003. This was followed, two years later, by a second manned space flight, with two astronauts circling Earth in the Shenzhou VI space capsule. In October 2007 the Chang'e-1 orbiter was sent on an unmanned mission to the Moon, and a year later China launched its third manned space mission - The Shenzhou VII capsule on a 70 hour flight which included the country's first spacewalk. Manufacturing has begun on China's first lunar lander, Chang'e 3, which is expected to launch in 2013. In 2012, China completed its first manual docking with another space module. China's first female astronaut, Liu Yang, took part.

China's space development programme envisages the construction of an independent space station. Also planned are a cargo transport system, which will link earth and space stations, and the development of artificial intelligence space technology and automatic docking equipment for use in future manned space projects.

It has been announced that China's manned space programme aims to build a space station by 2020.

China National Space Administration, URL: http://www.cnsa.gov.cn/n615709/cindex.html

HONG KONG

Hong Kong Special Administrative Region

Xianggang

Chief Executive, Executive Council: Chun-Ying Leung (page 1463)

Flag: Red, with a white bauhinia flower of five petals, each containing a red star.

CONSTITUTION AND GOVERNMENT

Hong Kong Island and the southern tip of the Kowloon peninsula were ceded by China to Britain after the first and second Anglo-Chinese Wars by the Treaty of Nanking 1842 and the Convention of Peking 1860 respectively. The New Territories were leased to Britain for 99 years by China in 1898. From then, Hong Kong was under British administration, except from December 1941 to August 1945 during the Japanese occupation. Talks began in September 1982 between Britain and China over the future of Hong Kong after the expiry of the lease in 1997. On 19 December 1984, the two countries signed a joint declaration whereby China resumed the exercise of sovereignty over Hong Kong (comprising Hong Kong Island, Kowloon and the New Territories) from 1 July 1997.

Under this Sino-British Joint Declaration, Britain agreed that the entire territory of Hong Kong would return to China with effect from 1 July 1997, in return for detailed and binding arrangements for Hong Kong's future. China is committed to ensure the preservation of Hong Kong's way of life and its social and economic systems for at least 50 years from 1 July 1997. This 'one country, two systems' principle - embodied in the Basic Law and enacted by the National People's Congress of the People's Republic of China in 1990 - was to become the constitution for the Hong Kong Special Administrative Region. Hong Kong has been a Special Administrative Region of China since 1 July 1997.

The main points of the agreement ensure:
- Continuation of the existing economic and social systems
- Free movement of goods and capital, and Hong Kong's status as a free port and separate customs territory
- The continuation of Hong Kong to determine its own monetary and financial policies. No taxes will be paid to China
- Retention of the English common law system and protection by law of all the fundamental human rights
- Independence of the judiciary
- Protection of property rights and foreign investment

Hong Kong is governed by people from Hong Kong. The Chief Executive must be from Hong Kong and must have lived in Hong Kong for 20 years. The top 23 Civil Service positions can be held by Chinese citizens who have lived in Hong Kong for 15 years and who do not have right of abode elsewhere. All public servants (including foreign nationals) were allowed to continue in their posts following the handover.

At the end of 2007, Donald Tsang, Chief Executive of Hong Kong, announced that the Chinese administration had agreed to allow the Special Administrative Region to directly elect its leader by 2017 and its legislators by 2020. The constitution provides for the development of universal suffrage as the "ultimate aim", but is vague about the date.

For further information on the basic law of Hong Kong, please consult: http://www.basiclaw.gov.hk/en/index/

International Relations

Hong Kong's foreign relations and defence are the responsibility of China. Hong Kong is an independent customs territory and economic entity and, as such, can enter into international agreements in commercial and economic matters. Hong Kong participates in many international economic organizations including the World Trade Organization (WTO), the Asia Pacific Economic Cooperation forum (APEC), and the Financial Action Task Force (FATF).

Recent Events

In November 2008 Hong Kong's economy officially fell into recession in response to the global economic downturn. In 2009 proposals for political reform were put forward in response to pressure for greater democracy, including an enlarged Legislative Council. Opponents said the plans did not go far enough.

In October 2011, Hong Kong became the world's first place to offer gold trading in yuan.

Executive Council

The Executive Council is appointed and presided over by the Chief Executive and, at present, consists of 14 Principal Officials and fourteen non-official Members. Its primary duty is to advise the Chief Executive in matters of policy making. Members must be Chinese citizens who are permanent members of the Hong Kong Special Administrative Region. Their period of office is no longer than the expiry of the term of office of the Chief Executive who appointed them. The Executive Council usually meets once a week. The Chief Executive is required by the Basic Law of Hong Kong SAR to consult the Council before making important decisions or introducing bills to the Legislative Council. He is not required to consult on the appointment or dismissal of officials; nor does he need to consult the council prior to the introduction of emergency measures.

Executive Council (as at June 2013)
Chief Executive: Chun-Ying Leung (page 1463)
Chief Secretary for Administration: Carrie Lam Cheng
Financial Secretary: John Chun-wah Tsung (page 1528)
Secretary for Justice: Rimsky Kwok-keung Yuen
Secretary for Education: Eddie Hak-kim Ng
Secretary for Commerce and Economic Development: Gregory So
Secretary for Constitutional and Mainland Affairs: Raymond Tam Chi-yuen
Secretary for Security: Lai Tung-kwok
Secretary for Health and Food: Dr Ko Wing-man
Secretary for the Civil Service: Paul Tang Kwok-wai
Secretary for Home Affairs: Tsang Tak-sing (page 1523)
Secretary for Labour and Welfare: Matthew Cheung Kin-chung (page 1456)
Secretary for Financial Services and the Treasury: Professor K.C. Chan
Secretary for Development: Chan Mo-po
Secretary for the Environment: Wong Kam-sing
Secretary for Transport and Housing: Anthony Bing-leung Cheung

Non-Official Members of the Executive Council:
Mr Cheng Yiu-tong
Laura M. Cha
Professor Anthony Cheung Bing-leung
Kong-wah Lau
Wong-fat Lau
Professor Lawrence Lau
Anna Wu
Arthur Li Kowk-cheung
Andrew Liao Cheung-sing
Chow Chung-kong
Cheung Hok-ming
Fanny Law Fan
Cheung Chi-kong
Franklin Lam fan-deung
Bernard Charnwut Chan
Starry Lee Wai-king
Regina Ip Lau Suk-yee
Jeffrey Lam Kin-fung

In September 2002, the Hong Kong government unveiled proposals for a new anti-subversion bill to be passed under article 23 of the Basic Law. The bill set out the following proposals:
- the protection of the 'sovereignty, territorial integrity, unity and national security' of the Hong Kong government and China;
- the outlawing of the expression or reporting of opinion that incites others 'to levy war or use force or other serious offences to sedition';
- emergency powers allowing a property to entered or an individual to be stopped and searched where treason, secession, sedition or subversion is suspected;
- the penalty for such crimes would be life imprisonment, or up to seven years for inciting violence or public disorder;

CHINA

- the penalty for the publication of 'seditious' material would be seven years in prison and a HK$500,000 fine.
Human rights groups saw the proposals as a move away from western-style freedoms enjoyed under the British administration, and, following street protests involving some half a million people, the draft legislation was withdrawn.

Legislative Council
The laws of Hong Kong are enacted by the Chief Executive with the advice and approval of the Legislative Council. In September 1995, for the first time, the Legislative Council was wholly elected, and comprised 60 members: 20 directly elected from geographical constituencies, 30 elected by 'functional constituencies', and 10 by an election committee composed of all elected members of the district boards. The 60 members of the Hong Kong Special Administrative Region's provisional Legislative Council were elected at a meeting in December 1996. Thirty-three members of the provisional legislative council had served on the outgoing legislative council. Following the handover of Hong Kong from Britain to China on 1 July 1997 a new Legislative Council was appointed by China.

The fourth term of the Legislative Council since the handover (2008-2012) consists of 30 members directly elected by geographical constituencies and 30 members elected by functional constituencies. All serve four years, with effect from 1 October 2008, before standing for re-election. The President of the Legislative Council is chosen from, and elected by, members of the Council, which also has the power to impeach the Chief Executive, and agree the appointment and dismissal of the Chief Judge of the High Court and the judges of the Court of Final Appeal. The Legislative Council is also empowered to enact, amend and repeal laws; approve Government budgets; approve taxation and public expenditure; raise questions on the work of government; debate concerns of public interest; and deal with complaints from Hong Kong residents.

The Legislative Council has three standing committees which scrutinise bills, control public expenditure, and monitor the government's performance. They are the Finance Committee, the Public Accounts Committee, and the Committee on Members' Interests.

Legislative Council, Legislative Council Building, 8 Jackson Road, Hong Kong. Tel: +852 2869 9200 (Secretariat), fax: +852 2537 1851 (Secretariat), e-mail: pi@legco.gov.hk, URL: http://www.legco.gov.hk/
President: Hon. Jasper Tsang (page 1528)

Ministries
Office of the Chief Executive, 5/F, Central Government Offices, Lower Albert Road, Hong Kong. Tel: +852 2878 3300, fax: +852 2509 0577, e-mail: ceo@ceo.gov.hk, URL: http://www.info.gov.hk/ce
Government Secretariat, Central Government Offices, Lower Albert Road, Hong Kong. Tel: +852 2810 2717, fax: +852 2845 7895, URL: http://www.info.gov.hk/info/cs.htm
Government Information Services, 3-8F Murray Building, Garden Road, Hong Kong. Tel: +852 2842 8777, fax: +852 2845 9078, URL: http://www.isd.gov.hk/index.htm
Office of the Commissioner of the Chinese Ministry of Foreign Affairs, 42 Kennedy Road, Central, Hong Kong. Tel: +852 2106 6304 / 2106 6303, fax: +852 2804 1373, e-mail: fmco_hk@mfa.gov.cn, URL: http://www.fmcoprc.gov.hk
Department of Agriculture, Fisheries and Conservation, Cheung Sha Wan Government Offices, 5th to 7th, 8th (part), 9th (part) floors, 303 Cheung Sha Wan Road, Kowloon, Hong Kong. Tel: +852 2708 8885, fax: +852 2311 3731 URL: http://www.afcd.gov.hk/index_e.htm
Education and Manpower Bureau, 16/F, Wu Chung House, 213 Queen's Road East, Wan Chai, Hong Kong. Tel: +852 2891 0088, fax: +852 2893 0858, e-mail: embinfo@emb.gov.hk, URL: http://www.emb.gov.hk/index.asp
Security Bureau, 6/F Central Government Offices, (East Wing) Central, Hong Kong. Tel: +852 2810 3017, fax: +852 2530 3502, URL: http://www.sb.gov.hk
Health, Welfare and Food Bureau, 19/F Murray Building, Garden Road, Hong Kong. Tel: +852 2973 8284, fax: +852 2541 3352, e-mail: enquiry@hwfb.gov.hk, URL: http://www.hwfb.gov.hk
Department of Environmental Protection, 24-28/F Southorn Centre, 130 Hennessy Road, Wan Chai, Hong Kong. Tel: +852 2835 1018, fax: +852 2838 2155, e-mail: enquiry@epd.gov.hk, URL: http://www.epd.gov.hk/epd/
Department of Justice, 23rd Floor, High Block, Queensway Government Offices, 66 Queensway, Hong Kong. Tel: +852 2867 2198, fax: +852 2877 2353, e-mail: dojinfo@doj.gov.hk, URL: http://www.info.gov.hk/justice/
Department of Trade and Industry, Trade and Industry Department Tower, 700 Nathan Road, Kowloon, Hong Kong. Tel: +852 2392 2922, fax: +852 2787 7422, e-mail: enquiry@tid.gov.hk, URL: http://www.tid.gov.hk/eindex.html
Department of Transport, Transport Department Headquarters, 41/F, Immigration Tower, 7 Gloucester Road, Wan Chai, Hong Kong. Tel: +852 2804 2600, fax: +852 2824 0433, e-mail: tdenq@td.gov.hk, URL: http://www.info.gov.hk/td/

Political Parties
The Civic Party, Unit 202, 2/F, Block B, Sea View Estate, 4-6 Watson Road, North Point, Hong Kong. Tel: +852 2865 7111, fax: +852 2865 2771, e-mail: contact@civicparty.hk, URL: http://www.civicparty.hk
Chairman: Audrey Eu Yuet-mee
Democratic Party of Hong Kong, URL: http://www.dphk.org/eng/
Democratic Alliance for the Betterment of Hong Kong, URL: http://www.dab.org.hk
Liberal Party, URL: http://www.liberal.org.hk
Chairman: Selina Chow
3L (Economic Energy), URL: http://www.economicsynergy.org
Association for Democracy and People's Livelihood, URL: http://www.adpl.org.hk
League of Social Democrats, URL: http://www.lsd.org.hk

Elections
In February 2003 Hong Kong's Chief Executive Tung Chee Hwa was nominated for re-election by 702 members of the 800-member election committee. Mr Tung was Hong Kong's first Chinese leader after the territory's return to Chinese rule. He was nominated for a second five-year term as Chief Executive without a challenge from any other candidate, but resigned in 2005, citing ill health. He was succeeded by Donald Tsang Yam-keun, who served until 2007 before winning the post by election. The most recent election was held in March 2012, when Chun-Ying Leung (page 1463) was elected to the post.

Legislative Council elections were last held on 7th September 2008, the fourth Legislative Council to be elected since Hong Kong was transferred to China. The pro-democracy parties won 23 of the 30 elected seats (retaining their power of veto), though the pro-government Democratic Alliance for the Betterment of Hong Kong remained the largest single party, with nine geographical constituency seats on the council, and four functional constituency seats. The pro-Beijing government parties won 24 of the 30 functional constituency seats. Analysts had thought that pro-government parties would make gains riding on a surge in Chinese patriotism sparked by the Beijing Olympics and the Sichuan earthquake, as well as China's promise of some form of universal suffrage by 2017.

Legislative Council of Hong Kong

Party	No. of Seats
PRO-DEMOCRACY:	
Democratic Party	8
Civic Party	5
League of Social Democrats	3
Hong Kong Assn. for Democracy and People's Livelihood	2
Hong Kong Confederation of Trade Unions	1
Neighbourhood and Workers Service Centre	1
The Frontier	1
Civic Act-up	1
Pro-democracy individuals and others	1
PRO GOVERNMENT:	
Democratic Alliance for the Betterment of Hong Kong	13
Liberal Party	7
The Hong Kong Federation of Trade Unions	1
Professional Forum	4
Pro-government individual and others	10
INDEPENDENTS	2
Total	**60**

District council elections last took place in 2011.

Diplomatic Representation
British Consulate General, No 1 Supreme Court Road, Central, Hong Kong (PO Box 528). Tel: +852 2901 3000, fax: +852 2901 3066, e-mail: political@britishconsulate.org.hk, commercial@britishconsulate.org.hk,
URL: https://www.gov.uk/government/world/organisations/british-consulate-general-hong-kong
Consul-General: Caroline Wilson (page 1538)
US Consulate, 26 Garden Road (PSC 461, PO Box 1, FPO AP 96521-0006), Hong Kong. Tel: +852 2523 9011, fax: +852 2845 1598, URL: http://hongkong.usconsulate.gov/
Consul-General: Stephen M. Young (page 1542)
Hong Kong Economic and Trade Office, 6 Grafton Street, London, WIS 4EQ. Tel: +44 (0)20 7499 9821, fax: +44 (0)20 795 5033, e-mail: general@hketolondon.gov.hk, URL: http://www.info.gov.hk/cib/ehtml/main.html
Hong Kong Economic and Trade Office,1520, 18th Street N.W., Washington DC 20036, USA. Tel: +1 202 331 8947, fax : +1 202 331 8958, e-mail: hketo@hketowashington.gov.hk, URL: http://www.hongkong.org
HK Commissioner for Economic and Trade Affairs: Donald Tong
Office of the Government of the Hong Kong SAR, Beijing, No. 71, Di'anmen Xidajie, Xicheng District, Beijing, 100009, China. Tel: +86 10 6657 2880, fax: +86 10 6657 2821, URL: http://www.bjo.gov.hk

LEGAL SYSTEM

The Basic Law of Hong Kong was enacted by the National People's Congress in accordance with the Constitution of the People's Republic of China. It is akin to a mini-constitution for the HKSAR. All the systems and policies practiced in the HKSAR must be based on the provisions of the Basic Law. The region has a Court of Final Appeal which is independent of that of mainland China, and English continues to be the official language of the courts.

The legal system consists of the Court of Final Appeal, the High Court, (which includes the Court of Appeal and the Court of First Instance), the Lands Tribunal, the District Court (including the Family Court), the Magistrates Court (which includes the Juvenile Court) and the Coroner's Court.

The High Court has unlimited jurisdiction in civil and criminal cases. Appeals from both these courts go to the Court of Final Appeal, Hong Kong's highest appellate court, which consists of a Chief Justice, three permanent judges, and one non-permanent judge. From July 1997 the Court of Final Appeal was established to replace the Judicial Committee of Her Majesty's Privy Council as Hong Kong's highest appellate court. The existing system continued after the changeover except for changes resulting from the establishment of this Court of Final Appeal. The District Courts hear claims up to HK$120,000. The Lands Tribunal deals with cases relating to compensation for compulsorily purchased land or land affected by public or private developments, landlord and tenant matters and building management matters.

Prior to the handover, much localisation of legislation took place to ensure that by 1 July 1997 there was a comprehensive body of law which owed its authority to Hong Kong. Many of these laws related to merchant shipping and civil aviation. Hong Kong also came to a series of bilateral agreements with other jurisdictions on legal and judicial issues such as the Transfer of Sentenced Persons.

The government of HKSAR respects the human rights of its citizens, though the police have occasionally been accused of being heavy-handed. The death penalty was abolished in Hong Kong in 1993, and continues to be abolished following the hand over to China where capital punishment continues. The last execution in Hong Kong was carried out in 1966.

Court of Final Appeal, URL: http://www.judiciary.gov.hk/en/index/index.htm
Chief Justice of the Court of Final Appeal: The Hon Chief Justice Geoffrey MA
Permanent Judges: Mr Justice Bokhary, Mr Justice Tang, Mr Justice Ribeiro
High Court, URL: http://www.judiciary.gov.hk/en/index/index.htm
Chief Judge of the High Court: Mr Justice Cheung

Equal Opportunities Commission, 19/F City Plaza Three, 14 Taikoo Wan Road, Taikoo Shing, Hong Kong. Tel: +852 2511 8211, fax: +852 2511 8142, e-mail: eoc@eoc.org.uk, URL: http://www.eoc.org.hk/

LOCAL GOVERNMENT

Hong Kong has 18 District Councils, nine in urban areas and nine for the New Territories, whose main function is to advise the government on matters affecting the well being or interests of the people living and working in the districts. There are 534 members of the 18 councils (405 elected, 102 appointed by the Chief Executive, and 27 ex-officio members who are chairmen of the rural committees in the New Territories). The term of office of council members is four years. The most recent election took place in November 2011.

The City District Councils are responsible for providing municipal services to over three million people in urban areas. They also manage sporting and recreation facilities and cultural institutions such as museums. There are 32 members who are elected from geographical constituencies and one representative member from one of the nine urban district boards. It meets once a month to pass by-laws. The councils are financially autonomous.

Hong Kong District Councils

District	Resident Population (approx.)	Area (Hectares)
Hong Kong Island:		
- Central and West	267,000	1,240
- Eastern	616,199	1,900
- Southern	290,000	4,000
- Wan Chai	170,000	976
Kowloon Island:		
- Kowloon City	380,000	1,000
- Kwun Tong District	565,000	1,130
- Sham Shui Po	353,000	1,047
- Wong Tai Sin	440,000	926
- Yau Tsim Mong	278,400	7 (km sq.)
New Territories:		
- Islands	72,800	20 islands S/SE of HK
- Kwai Tsing	504,500	23.2 (km sq.)
- North	300,000	14,000
- Sai Kung	300,000	12,680
- Sha Tin	637,000	6,940
- Tai Po	320,000	14,800
- Twuen Wan	290,000	6,000
- Tuen Mun	n/a	n/a
- Yuen Long	449,000	14,430

The Regional Council is responsible for environmental hygiene, public health, sanitation, liquor licensing and provision of recreational facilities and services for some 2.8 million people in the New Territories. The council is made up of 39 members, 27 elected from geographical constituencies, nine from district boards in each of the nine New Territories districts and three ex-officio members who are the chairman and the two vice-chairmen of the Heung Yee Kuk (a statutory advisory body which represents the indigenous population of the New Territories). Council policies are implemented by the Regional Services Department, which has over 10,000 employees. The council is financially autonomous - most of its revenues come from rates and rental incomes.

AREA AND POPULATION

Area
Hong Kong is situated on China's southeast coast and consists of more than 200 islands. The area of the territory in 2008, including reclaimed land, was 1,104.3 sq. km, of which 80.5 sq. km was Hong Kong Island, 46.9 sq. km Kowloon, and 976.9 sq. km New Territories and Islands. A large part of Hong Kong is unproductive hill country.

Hong Kong's climate is subtropical, with temperatures falling below 10°C in winter and rising to 31°C in summer. Most of Hong Kong's rainfall occurs between March and September.

To view a map of Hong Kong, please consult
http://www.lib.utexas.edu/maps/cia08/hong_kong_sm_2008.gif

Population
Hong Kong's total population was estimated at 7.182 million at mid 2013. Around 20 per cent of the total population live on Hong Kong Island, 30 per cent in Kowloon and slightly over 50 per cent live in the New Territories. Hong Kong is the third most densely populated state/territory in the world, after Monaco and Macau; population density in 2009 was estimated at 6,480 people per sq. km. In 2008 the density of residents on Hong Kong Island was 16,390 people per sq. km, Kowloon 43,290 people per sq. km and in the New Territories and Islands 3,810 per sq. km.

Population by age group, mid-2008 ('000)

Age Group	Number	% of total
Under 15	902.3	12.9
15-34	1,978.3	28.4
35-64	3,217.5	46.1
65 and over	879.6	12.6
Total	**6,977.7**	**100.0**

Source: Hong Kong Census and Statistics Department

Most of Hong Kong's population (95 per cent) is Chinese, with 1.9 per cent Filipino, 1.9 per cent Indonesian, and 0.3 per cent British. Hong Kong's official languages are Chinese (Cantonese and Putonghua) and English. English is widely used by the government, the legal system, and the business community.

Births, Marriages, Deaths
Estimated figures for 2008 put the annual number of births in that year at 78,700, (up from 70,900 in 2007). This is equivalent to a crude birth rate of 11.3 births per 1,000 inhabitants. The number of deaths in the same year was 41,300 (up from 39,500 in 2007), equivalent to a rate of 5.9 deaths per 1,000 population.

Life expectancy at birth in 2011 was estimated at 79.3 years for males and 85 years for females. The infant mortality rate in the same year was 2.9 per 1,000 registered live births. In 2008 marriages numbered an estimated 48,500, equivalent to 6.9 marriages per 1,000 inhabitants. The median age for a Hong Kong inhabitant to be married is estimated to be 31.1 years for men and 28.1 years for women. (Source: Hong Kong Census and Statistics Department)

Public Holidays 2014
1 January: New Year's Day
1-3 February: Chinese New Year
5 April: Ching Ming Festival (Tomb Sweeping Day)*
18 April: Good Friday
21 April: Easter Monday
1 May: May Day
6 May: Birth of Buddha*
2 June: Tuen Ng (Dragon Boat) Festival*
1 July: Hong Kong Special Administrative Region Establishment Day
23 September*: Chinese Mid-Autumn Festival
1 October: National Day
2 October: Chung Yeung Festival*
25 December: Christmas Day
26 December: Boxing Day
* Religious festivals are timed according to the lunar calendar and variations may occur.

EMPLOYMENT

The Hong Kong Census and Statistics Department estimated the total labour force at 3,668,000 over 2008, up by 1.0 per cent on 2007. The labour force comprised 1,955,000 men and 1,712,000 women. Unemployment stood at 129,000 (3.5 per cent) in 2008, down from 146,000 (4.0 per cent) the previous year, and the lowest level since 1998. Figures from the Asian Development Bank show that in 2009 the labour force numbered 3,680,000 of which 3,480,000 were employed and 200,000 were unemployed (5.4 per cent). That year 100,000 were employed in the agricultural sector, 150,000 in manufacturing, and 3,520,000 in other sectors the main one of which is services. The unemployment rate was 3.5 per cent in 2011, expected to rise to 3.8 per cent in 2012 before returning to 3.5 per cent in the first half of 2013.

In 2007 a total of 8,027 working days (man-days) were lost; all but 17 of these were lost due to a bar-tenders strike for increased pay.

Total Employment by Economic Activity

Occupation	2008
Agriculture, hunting, fishing & forestry	8,300
Manufacturing	191,200
Electricity, gas & water supply	14,100
Construction	268,600
Wholesale & retail trade, repairs, hotels & restaurant	1.145.500
Transport, storage & communications	377,900
Financial intermediation, real estate, business activities	580,000
Other community, social & personal service activities	933,100

Source: Copyright © International Labour Organization (ILO Dept. of Statistics, http://laborsta.ilo.org)

CHINA

BANKING AND FINANCE

Currency
The unit of currency is the Hong Kong Dollar. It has been linked since 17 October 1983 to the US dollar and is allowed to trade within a range between 7.75 and 7.85 Hong Kong dollars to one United States dollar.

GDP/GNP, Inflation, National Debt
Continuing the practice established under British administration, the government of Hong Kong follows a policy of positive non-interventionism in the economy. With limited natural resources, food and raw materials have to be imported, and Hong Kong is the world's eleventh largest trading entity; the value of imports and exports exceeds its gross domestic product. Hong Kong's free market economy has increasingly close trade and investment ties with China; the Special Administrative Region is the most important gateway for the Chinese mainland, and handles around 22 per cent of China's foreign trade.

Strong GDP growth averaging 5 per cent over the period 1989-97 was followed by the Asian financial crisis in 1998 and a global downturn in 2000-01. The outbreak of Severe Acute Respiratory Syndrome (SARS) further reduced economic growth. After almost doubling over the previous 10 years, GDP (current market prices) fell from HK$1,288,338 million in 2000 to HK$1,222,023 million in 2003. The economy showed signs of recovery in 2005; GDP at current market prices reached HK$1,382.1 billion, equivalent to an increase of 7.3 per cent on the previous year's figure. In 2006, the economy grew by 6.7 per cent, the third successive year of strong growth; the main contributing factors were increased exports and inbound tourism, and strong consumer spending. (Source: HK Census and Statistics Dept.)

In 2007, the economy grew by 6.3 per cent, driven by domestic demand. The property market revived, helped by lower mortgage interest rates and improved incomes. House prices rose by 11.5 per cent over 2007 and the number of residential property transactions rose sharply by around 50 per cent. GDP (current market prices) reached HK$1,612.6 billion. Per capita GDP reached HK$232,836 in the same year, an increase of 8.2 per cent on 2006. The slowdown in the USA and China slowed growth through 2008. Figures from the first quarter of 2009 showed that the economy had shrunk by 7.8 per cent, as export markets continued to be effected by the continuing global recession. GDP contracted between 5.5 and 6.5 per cent in 2009. By 2010 figures showed that the economy was recovering with growth of 6.8 per cent, growth was still being driven in part by the housing market and the government introduced measures to curb the risk of a housing market bubble arising from the low interest rates. Economic growth was also stimulated by the recovery of foreign trade with exports growing by over 17 per cent and a large Chinese fiscal stimulus programme. Growth was still relatively strong in 2011, although it did decline over the year, falling from 7.5 per cent to 4.3 per cent over the first three quarters of the year. GDP growth in 2012 was put at 2.4 per cent and forecast to be stronger in 2013. Estimated figures for 2012 put GDP at US$361 billion giving a per capita figure of US$50,000)

The services sector accounts for the largest proportion of GDP, contributing around 93.0 per cent in 2012, the agricultural sector contributed 0.1 per cent and industry 6.9 per cent. GDP according to industry is shown on the following table:

GDP by Economic Activity (HK$m at current prices)

Industry	2007	2008	2009
Agriculture	900	828	1,049
Mining	115	97	41
Manufacturing	31,719	30,993	28,227
Electricity, gas and water	40,685	39,585	34,961
Construction	40,611	48,357	50,146
Trade	423,441	447,510	414,667
Transport and Communications	170,601	146,503	145,856
Finance	451,326	421,180	409,164
Public Administration	254,391	269,601	279,453
Others	166,352	188,244	187,286
Total GDP	**1,615,574**	**1,677,011**	**1,622,322**

Source: Asian Development Bank

GDP and GNI in Million Hong Kong Dollars

Year	GDP	GNI
1990	598,950	na
1995	1,115,739	1,125,229
2000	1,317,650	1,326,404
2005	1,382,590	1,384,238
2007	1,615,574	1,660,011
2008	1,677,011	1,760,317
2009	1,622,322	1,665,188
2010	1,743,858	1,780,426

Source: Asian Development Bank

Hong Kong's Consumer Price Index (CPI) fell by 3.0 per cent in 2002 and by 2.6 per cent in 2003. In 2004, it fell again, by 0.4 per cent, but in 2005 the Composite CPI rose by 0.9 per cent. In 2006, the Composite CPI rose by two per cent, and this rise was repeated in 2007. In 2007, the Food Price index rose sharply by 4.3 per cent. (Source: HK Census and Statistics Dept.) Inflation in 2012 was put at 4.9 per cent.

Foreign Investment
Hong Kong's net international investment position totalled HK$4,029.7 billion in 2006 (up from HK$3,406.1 billion the previous year).

Direct investment in Hong Kong reached HK$5,771.9 billion in 2006; the British Virgin Islands and mainland China were the largest sources of direct investment in Hong Kong by a large margin. Investment holdings, real estate and business services are the recipients of most foreign investment, followed by retail and import/export trades, and banks and deposit-taking companies.

Hong Kong direct investment abroad reached HK$5,264.5 billion in 2006. Most of this amount was invested via the British Virgin Islands and mainland China, and the main sector for investment was the investment holdings, real estate and business services sector.

Balance of Payments / Imports and Exports
In line with most countries Hong Kong's economy was adversely effected by the 2008 global economic downturn. Hong Kong exports have traditionally been a major contributor the economy and with exports falling during 2008 and 2009. Exports began to rise again in 2010.

In 2009 the five major industries of Hong Kong all recorded a drop in exports. In 2009 the wearing apparel industry exports earned HK$4.5 billion, a fall of 79.9 per cent on the 2008 figure. The computer, electronic and optical industry earned HK$13.7 billion in 2009, a fall of 17.3 per cent on 2008 figures. The chemicals and chemical products industry earned HK$7.5 billion in 2009, a fall of 13.8 per cent on 2008 figures. The basic metals industry earned HK$3.8 billion in 2009, a fall of 50.0 per cent on 2008 figures and the paper and paper products, printing and reproduction of recorded media industry earned HK$3.6 billion in 2009, a fall of 21.9 per cent on the 2008 figure. (Source: Hong Kong Census and Statistics Department)

External Trade	2007	2008	2009	2010
Exports fob	2,687,513	2,824,151	2,469,089	3,031,019
Imports cif	2,868,011	3,025,288	2,692,356	3,364,840
Trade Balance	-180,497	-201,137	-223,268	-333,821
Trade Balance % change				
- Exports of Goods	9.2	5.1	-12.5	22.8
- Imports of Goods	10.3	5.5	-11.0	25.0

Source: Asian Development Bank

The following tables show Hong Kong's top ten merchandise export and import trading partners:

Merchandise trade with top ten main partners (figures in US$ million)

Exports	2008	2009	2010
Total	362,987.0	318,751.0	390,348.0
China	176,061.0	163,030.0	205,765.0
USA	46,289.9	35,897.3	42,821.4
Japan	15,555.5	14,066.3	16,483.5
United Kingdom	9,590.7	7,702.2	7,825.8
Germany	12,075.0	10,242.9	10,390.1
Korea, Rep. of	6,371.8	5,566.7	6,919.0
Singapore	7,115.8	5,453.1	6,577.6
Netherlands	5,834.2	4,808.5	5,686.0
India	6,704.8	6,750.7	9,586.8
France	4,841.8	3,702.9	..
Imports			
Total	388,947.0	347,675.0	433,516.0
China	181,325.0	161,287.0	197,087.0
Japan	38,263.0	30,521.9	39,710.0
Singapore	25,044.1	22,561.7	30,573.9
USA	19,541.1	18,550.3	23,322.6
Korea, Rep. of	15,176.0	13,310.2	17,214.9
Malaysia	8,501.9	8,783.3	10,913.1
Thailand	8,194.9	7,434.8	9,831.5
Germany	6,865.2	6,468.4	7,426.0
India	7,476.8	6,794.3	9,258.4
Philippines	6,220.3	4,209.1	5,114.0

Source: Asian Development Bank

The Closer Economic Partnership Agreement (CEPA), a form of free trade area between the mainland and Hong Kong, has helped develop closer economic ties with the mainland and fuel the economy through zero tariffs to all Hong Kong-origin goods and preferential treatment in 27 service sectors. Hong Kong and Macau are also participants in the new pan-Pearl River Delta trade block with nine Chinese provinces, which aims to lower trade barriers among members.

Trade and Currency Restrictions
Under the joint declaration, Hong Kong will remain a free port and a free trader for at least 50 years after the handover. Trade will continue to be governed by international law. The Hong Kong SAR is able to conduct its own external economic relations, and its separate membership of the World Trade Organization, APEC and other international economic organisations will continue. Free movement of goods and capital will continue. Few products need licenses to enter or leave Hong Kong.

The principal financial services regulators are the Hong Kong Monetary Authority (HKMA), the Securities and Futures Commission (SFC) and the Insurance Authority (IA).
Hong Kong Monetary Authority, URL: http://www.info.gov.hk/hkma/

Chambers of Commerce and Trade Addresses
Hong Kong Chamber of Commerce, URL: http://www.chamber.org.hk
Hong Kong Futures Exchange Ltd, URL: http://www.hkex.com.hk
Hong Kong Stock Exchange, URL: http://www.hkex.com.hk/

MANUFACTURING, MINING AND SERVICES

Primary and Extractive Industries
Hong Kong produces no oil of its own, importing all its requirements. In 2011, imports of oil reached an estimated 366 thousand barrels, most of which was distillate. (Source: EIA)

In 2010, consumption of natural gas was reached 113 billion cubic feet, all imported. The domestic sector was the highest consumer of natural gas.

Coal consumption reached 13.593 million short tons in 2009, all of which was imported. It fell to 11.380 million short tons in 2010, all of which imported. (Source: EIA)

Energy
In 2010 Hong Kong had installed electricity capacity of 12.62 GWe. It generated 36.00 billion kWh and consumed 39.57 billion kWh. The following table shows electricity consumption in recent years (terajoules):

Energy Consumption	2007	2008
Domestic	36,422	35,194
Commercial	97,155	90,434
Industrial	13,104	11,224
Street Lighting	391	355
Export to mainland of China	14,527	11,667
Total	161,598	148,874

1 terajoule = 10 ^{12} joules
Source: Hong Kong Census and Statistics Department

In 2009, Hong Kong consumed 1.099 quadrillion Btu of electricity (Source: EIA).

Manufacturing
The contribution of manufacturing to Hong Kong's GDP (current prices at factor cost) has fallen from 23.7 per cent in 1990 to 8.5 per cent in 2006. Manufacturing contributed an estimated HK$ million (2000 Constant prices) towards GDP in 2006, indicating a slight fall on the 2005 figure of HK$51,553 million. In 2010, manufacturing contributed an estimated 1.8 per cent of GDP.

Manufacturing accounting for 3.4 per cent of total employment in 2011. Approximately 80 per cent of goods are manufactured for export. The main industries are clothing, electronics, textiles, plastics, toys, watches and clocks. Hong Kong is the world's third largest exporter of clothing. According to the HK Index of Industrial Production (Year 2000=100), the clothing sector output fell by two points, textile production fell by 25 points and the electrical and electronic products, machinery, professional equipment and optical goods sector fell by 12.8 points over the first three quarters of 2007.

Gross Output of Selected Industry Groups in 2008

Industry	HK$ Million
Food	18,514
Wearing apparel except footwear	8,061
Textiles	12,275
Printing, publishing and allied industries	31,654
Chemicals & chemical products	9,038
Plastic products	1,493
Basic metal industries	46,730
Electronic parts & components	6,388
Machinery, equipment, apparatus, parts & components, n.e.c.	5,413
Transport equipment	13,643

Source: Hong Kong Census and Statistics Department

Service Industries
The service sector has expanded dramatically over the past two decades, with contribution to GDP having risen from 67.5 per cent in 1980 to 91.2 per cent in 2007. It rose further to an estimated 93 per cent in 2010. Exports of services amounted to US$106 billion.

During 2000-10, value-added of the services sector rose at an annual rate of 3.6 per cent to US$203 billion. The finance and insurance sector grew by about 19 per cent in 2007, reflecting strong expansion in banking and financial market activity. Real estate and business services also enjoyed strong growth, as did the hotels and restaurants sector. Retail trading benefited from healthy consumer and tourist spending.

Hong Kong is a major international financial centre with an integrated network of institutions and markets. The Hong Kong stock market is the sixth largest in the world and the third largest in Asia. Hong Kong is the eleventh largest trader in the world and, according to the United Nations Conference on Trade and Development (UNCTAD), it is the largest source of foreign direct investment amongst Asian economies.
Hong Kong Stock Exchange, URL: http://www.hkex.com.hk/eng/index.htm

Tourism
Tourism receipts, from hotels and restaurants, contributed HK$33,109 million to GDP in 2004 (up from HK$25,753 million in 2003). There were around 28.17 million visitors in 2007, of whom 15.48 million came from the mainland of China. In the same year, 2.23 million visitors came from Taiwan, 2.88 from South and Southeast Asia, 2.2 million from North Asia, 1.7 million from the Americas, 2.18 million from Europe, Africa and the Middle East, 626,000 from Macau, and 757,000 from Australia, New Zealand, and the South Pacific. In 2007, there were 650 hotels and guesthouses in Hong Kong, with 56,573 rooms. The occupancy rate was 86 per cent. (Source: Hong Kong Statistics Bureau)

The first Disneyland theme park to be built in China was opened in Hong Kong ahead of schedule in September 2005. It occupies more than 100 hectares of land and cost the Hong Kong government, who hold a majority share, over HK$3 billion. The Hong Kong Wetland Park and the Ngong Ping 360 cable car opened in 2006.

In 2011, visitor arrivals totaled almost 42 million, up 16 per cent on the previous year.

Commission for Tourism, URL: http://www.info.gov.hk/tc
Hong Kong Tourist Board, URL: http://www.discoverhongkong.com/eng

Agriculture
Hong Kong's small agricultural and fishing industry accounts for just 0.1 per cent of GDP (at current factor cost) and contributed HK$870 million (Constant 2000 cost) towards Hong Kong's GDP in 2006 (down from HK$899 million in 2005). Due to the geographical make-up of Hong Kong, small, intensive farming methods of vegetable and livestock production have taken over from traditional rice farming. Main products are fresh vegetables, poultry, pork and fish. Hong Kong's domestic needs far outstrip its production and the country depends heavily on imports; in 2005, foodstuffs imported cost the country HK$50.8 billion (up from HK$45.7 billion in 2000).

COMMUNICATIONS AND TRANSPORT

Travel Requirements
The change of sovereignty between Hong Kong and the United Kingdom brought to an end the visa arrangements between the two countries. With effect from 1 April 1997, British citizens may visit Hong Kong visa-free for up to 180 days. Extensions of stay are considered under the same terms that apply to other foreign nationals. Resident British citizens lost their status of resident British citizen and are now subject to the provisions of the Immigration Ordinance. Those who were in Hong Kong on 1 April 1997 were automatically given permission to remain without any condition of stay. However, their permission to remain lapses with any departure from Hong Kong. If the absence from Hong Kong is less than 12 months, they are able to resume residence without a visa.

Citizens of the USA, Canada, Australia and the EU (apart from Britain - see above) require a passport valid for six months from date of departure but do not need a visa for stays of up to 90 days. Other nationals should contact the embassy to check visa requirements. Tourists must provide evidence of return or onward travel.

National Airlines
Cathay Pacific, URL: http://www.cathaypacific.com
Dragon Air (Hong Kong Dragon Airlines), URL: http://www.dragonair.com
Operates scheduled services to destinations in Hong Kong and Asia.
AHK Air Hong Kong, URL: http://www.airhongkong.com.hk
Parent company, Cathay Pacific. Provides international and regional scheduled and chartered cargo.

International Airports
Hong Kong's international airport at Chek Lap Kok, Lantau Island, opened on 6 July 1998, replacing Kai Tak Airport as Hong Kong's international airport. A second runway was completed in 1999. The airport railway link from the airport via Tsing Yi and West Kowloon to Central, was completed in July 1998. The SkyPiers, a new cross-boundary ferry terminal was launched in 2010. A third runway is currently under consideration.

Hong Kong's Airport Authority is one of the world's busiest airports; in 2011, almost 54 million passengers used HKIA and approximately 3.9 million tonnes of cargo were transported. The airport is being developed as an airfreight hub. A new Cathay Pacific Cargo Terminal opened in 2012 which added an additional air cargo throughput of 2.6 million tonnes a year.
Hong Kong International Airport, URL: http://www.hkairport.com/
Airport Authority Hong Kong, URL: http://www.hkairport.com/

Railways
The Kowloon-Canton Railway (34 km) is fully double tracked and electrified. The track is 34 km long and carries 640,000 passengers daily. The KCR system is linked to the Mass Transit Railway at Kowloon Tong Station.

Hong Kong has mass transit rail (MTR) system that covers all major districts in the territory, and includes stops at the boundary with Mainland China (Lo Wu and Lok Ma Chau). The MTR consists of nine lines: Kwun Tong, Tsuen Wan, Island, Tseung Kwan O, Tung Chung, West Rail, East Rail, Ma On Shan, and Disneyland Resort. It also runs the Airport Express. The MTR carries approximately 4 million passengers per day (2011). The MTR also operates a Light Rail system which extends between Yuen Long and Tuen Mun in the New Territories, and an inter-city train service into mainland China.
MTR, URL: http://www.mtr.com.hk

As of 2012, there were six routes for electric trams extending 30 km. In total there are163 tram cars transporting on average 230,000 passengers per day.
Hong Kong Tramways Ltd, URL: http://www.hktramways.com/en/index.html

Roads
There are (2011) some 2,060 km. of roads in Hong Kong, with a total licensed vehicle count of 628,000 (2008). Vehicles drive on the left. The trunk road network is still growing throughout the territory. Hong Kong's road infrastructure includes eight twin tube road tunnels - Lion Rock, Aberdeen Airport, Shing Mun, Tseung Kwan O and Tate's Cairn Tunnels as well as the Cross Harbour Tunnel, and the Eastern Harbour Crossing. Two cross harbour tunnels connect Hong Kong Island to the Kowloon peninsula.

CHINA

Shipping

Passenger services operate between Hong Kong and Macau using jetfoils, catamarans and high-speed ferries. Catamarans and conventional ferries operate between Hong Kong and Pearl River Ports in China. The Hong Kong Shipowners' Association represents more than 85 shipowners and managers who control almost 1,880 ships with a total deadweight of over 110 million tonnes.

Hong Kong Shipowners' Association, URL: http://www.hksoa.org/

Ports and Harbours

Hong Kong possesses one of the most magnificent natural harbours in the world. Cross harbour ferries are in operation as well as ferry services to offshore islands. Hong Kong harbour has facilities for handling all types of vessels and cargoes. There are extensive privately-owned facilities for repairing, maintaining and dry-docking or slipping all types of vessels up to about 150,000 tonnes. Six floating drydocks are located off the west coast of Tsing Yi Island and north of Lantau Island, the largest of which has a lifting capacity of 150,000 tonnes. The Kwai Chung Container Terminal is one of the world's busiest container port and is located in the northwestern part of Victoria Harbour. It consists of nine container terminals. Container throughput in the port reached 24 million TEUs (twenty-foot equivalent units) in 2011. In 2011, 205,700 ships (both ocean-going and river trade vessels) for cargo and passenger traffic, visited the port. Regular cargo liner services link Hong Kong with every major port throughout the world.

Hong Kong Port Development Council, URL: http://www.pdc.gov.hk/eng/home/index.htm

HEALTH

The Department of Health advises the government on health and works in collaboration with the private sector and teaching institutions to provide a wide range of primary health care services. The Hospital Authority is an independent body responsible for the management and control of all public hospitals.

There are some 29,900 hospital beds, 9,100 doctors and 36,300 nurses. In 2007 it was estimated that, per 1,000 inhabitants, there were five hospital beds, 1.7 medical doctors, 0.3 dentists, 0.2 pharmacists and 5.3 nurses. There were also 0.8 registered Chinese medicine practitioners for every 1,000 people.

The leading cause of death is malignant neoplasms (182.4 per 100,000 population in 2007), followed by heart disease (88.1 per 100,000). In 2008 the prevalence rate for TB was 91 per 100,000 population. In 2009, the child mortality rate was 2 per 1,000 live births.

Hong Kong has an aging population and has a mandatory pension fund which will help finance retirement expenses. It has been projected that some 52 per cent of the population will be aged over 50 years old by the year 2050, raising the costs of subsidised health care to the detriment of other public spending areas. The government is hoping to limit future public health-care liabilities by encouraging subsidised private insurance. (Source: ADB)

EDUCATION

The government provides 12 years of free education.

Primary/Secondary Education

Kindergarten education is supervised by the Education Department. In 2005, there were 737 kindergartens with a total enrolment of 130,157 children. The average class size was 19.6 children and the teacher/pupil ratio was one to 10.1.

In 2011, primary school enrolment was approximately 265,600 at 457 public sector schools. Primary school education starts at age 6 and there are six years of schooling at primary levels. The language of instruction is mainly Cantonese but Mandarin is becoming more widespread. English is taught as a second language.

Secondary public school enrolment was 393,000 pupils at 400 schools in 2011. The curriculum was revised in 2009; the new senior secondary curriculum consists of a three-year course of study leading to one public examination at the end of Secondary 6 - the new Hong Kong Diploma of Secondary Education which replaces the former Hong Kong Certificate of Education examination and Hong Kong Advanced Level Examination.

Higher Education

In 2011 there were 26 post-secondary institutions offering accredited sub-degree, degree and top-up degree programmes with some 32,500 student places. Hong Kong has 16 degree-awarding higher education institutions including eight universities. In the 2011/12 academic year approximately 65,000 students were enrolled at publicly-funded undergraduate and postgraduate courses.

Public expenditure on education amounted to an estimated $68 billion in 2011/12.

As Hong Kong continues to become an increasingly knowledge-based economy, the education system is under close review to ensure that it produces enough skilled people to meet growing demand.

RELIGION

The majority of the population is Buddhist and Taoist, and there are more than 600 Buddhist and Taoist temples in Hong Kong. Confucianism and Daoism are also practised widely. The Christian Community is estimated to be about 536,000, of whom about 227,000 are Catholic. There are some 70,000 Muslims, 15,000 Hindus, 8,000 Sikhs and 1,500 Jews.

COMMUNICATIONS AND MEDIA

Hong Kong is a major media and broadcasting centre. Although official control is not as prevalent as in other parts of China, the media does practise self-censorship.

Newspapers

There are numerous newspapers including Chinese-language dailies, English dailies and other language papers. China has pledged to continue the system of free press.
Major newspapers include:
Asian Wall Street Journal, URL: http://www.wsj-asia.com
South China Morning Post, URL: http://www.scmp.com
Sing Tao Daily News, URL: http://www.singtao.com
Apple Daily, URL: http://www.appledaily.atnext.com
The Hong Kong Standard, URL: http://www.hkstandard.com
Tung Fang Jih Pao, URL: http://orientaldaily.on.cc/
Ta Kung Pao and **Wen Wei Po** (managed from Beijing, follows Communist Party line). URL: http://www.takungpao.com / URL: http://www.wenweipo.com

Business Journals

Hong Kong Economic Journal, URL: http://www.hkej.com/
Hong Kong Economic Times, URL: http://www.hket.com/
Far Eastern Economic Review, URL: http://www.feer.com/

Broadcasting

Financed by the government, the public broadcaster Radio Television Hong Kong (RTHK) produces radio and television programmes in both English and China. It operates seven radio stations. Other commercial free-to-air stations exist; Television Broadcasts Ltd (TVB) and Asia Television Ltd (ATV), provide separate Chinese and English-language services and broadcast to some six million viewers. TVB is one of the world's largest producers of Chinese language programming.

Radio Television Hong Kong (RTHK), URL: http://rthk.hk/about/index_e.htm
Television Broadcasts Ltd (TVB), URL: http://www.tvb.com
Asia Television Ltd (ATV), URL: http://www.hkatv.com
Commercial Radio, URL: http://881903.com/Page/ZH-TW/index.aspx
Metro Broadcast, URL: http://www.metroradio.com.hk/

Telecommunications

Hong Kong has one of the most sophisticated and successful telecommunications markets in the world. In 1993 the Office of the Telecommunications Authority (OFTA) was established; it had responsibility for regulating the telecommunications industry and its work covered three main areas: regulation of telecommunications services; radio frequency spectrum management; and advisory and planning services. It was superseded by the Office of the Communications Authority in April 2012.

In 2011 there were some 4.3 million fixed line telephones in use and 15 million mobile phones. In 2011, there were an estimated 4.8 million internet users in Hong Kong.

Office of the Communications Authority, URL: http://www.ofca.gov.hk/mobile/en/home/index.html

ENVIRONMENT

Hong Kong's environmental problems are mainly due to rapid growth of population, industry and commerce. Air pollution and water pollution are areas of concern. The air pollution regularly exceeds levels recommended by the World Health Organisation and areas often experience smog. Much of the air pollution stems from coal-fired power plants from China and the proximity of Hong Kong to China's Pearl Delta region which houses some 70,000 factories, but Hong Kong's own industrial emissions, tall buildings and traffic fumes also contribute. China agreed to substantially reduce four major air pollutants by 2010. As well as health worries, there are concerns that the high level of pollution may make it hard for companies to hire and retain international staff.

Carbon dioxide emissions from the consumption and flaring of fossil fuels totaled 75.06 million metric tons in 2005, down on the figure for 2004, but up on 2002 when emissions totaled 65.62 million metric tons. Per capita carbon dioxide emissions reached 10.88 metric tons, well above the Asia and Oceania regional average of 2.87 metric tons. Carbon dioxide emissions from fossil fuels had risen to 79.05 million metric tons by 2008 and had fallen to 83.78 million metric tons by 2010. (Source: EIA)

Hong Kong is party to the following international agreements: Marine Dumping (associate member), Ship Pollution (associate member).

MACAO
Macao Special Administrative Region
Macau

Capital: Macau (Population estimate, 2011, 553,000)

Head of State: (President of People's Republic of China): Hu Jintao

Chief Executive, Executive Council: Fernando Chui Sai-on (page 1405)

Flag: The flag is light green with a central white lotus above a stylised bridge and water and beneath an arc of five stars.

CONSTITUTION AND GOVERNMENT

Constitution
Macao was originally administered by Portugal, whose president appointed its governor. In the late 1970s, Portugal let it be known that it was willing to negotiate Macao's return to China. Following the signing of the Sino-British Joint Declaration in 1984 on the future of Hong Kong, China and Portugal held negotiations to agree Macao's future, and these led to the signing of a Joint Declaration in 1987. Macao became a Special Administrative Region of China on 20th December 1999. The Joint Declaration and Basic Law of the Macao SAR (Basic Law) provide that Macao's capitalist system and way of life will remain unchanged for 50 years. The Basic Law (promulgated in 1993) serves as a mini-constitution for Macao. It confers independent executive legislative, judicial and economic powers on the Macao SAR and guarantees the rights and freedoms of its residents.

The Macao Special Administrative Region (MSAR) has its own Government headed by the Chief Executive, who must be a Chinese Citizen resident in Macao for over 20 years, and is accountable to the Central People's Government. The Chief Executive's term of office is for a maximum of two five-year terms. The Chief Executive is assisted by the seven to 11-member Executive Council in policy-making decisions.

Recent Events
A rare protest took place on 1st May 2007, over alleged corruption and illegal labour. Protesters complained about the lack of local jobs due to the import of cheap foreign labour from mainland China, caused by the boom in the casino trade. Macao has a history of co-operation with the central government in Beijing.

In January 2008, former Transport and Public Works Minister Ao Man-long was convicted of receiving MOP 187 million in bribes from three real estate and construction companies, in return for offered preference in 20 government works projects between 2002 and 2006. He was also convicted of bribery, abuse of power and money-laundering. The Macau media was sceptical that corruption on such a scale could take place without anyone else knowing or being involved.

A new state security law came into effect in 2009.

Legislation
The Legislative Assembly consists of 29 members, 12 of whom are directly elected, 10 indirectly elected, and seven appointed by the Chief Executive. The President and Vice President are included in this number, and all members must be residents of Macao.

The Basic Law allows for the rules relating to the composition of the Legislative assembly to be altered in 2009 provided that any alterations are made with the endorsement of a two-thirds majority of all the members of the Council and with the consent of the Chief Executive.
President: Lau Cheok Va
Legislative Council, email: info@al.gov.mo, URL: http://www.al.gov.mo/

Executive Council (as at June 2013)
Chief Executive: Fernando Chui- Sai-on (page 1405)
Secretary for Administration and Justice: Florinda de Rosa Silva Chan (page 1402)
Secretary for Economy and Finance: Francis Tam Pak-yeun
Secretary for Security: Cheong Kuoc Va (page 1459)
Secretary for Transport and Public Works: Lau Si Io
Secretary for Social Affairs and Culture: Cheong U

Prinicpal Officials (as at June 2013)
Commissioner Against Corruption: Fong Man Chong
Audit Commissioner: Ho Veng On
Commissioner General of the Unitary Police Service: José Proença Branco
Director-General of the Macao Customs: Choi Lai Hang

Government Portal: URL: http://www.gov.mo
Government Directory: URL: http://www.safp.gov.mo/

Elections
There are no formal political parties in Macao. The most recent legislative election was held in September 2009.

British Honorary Consulate:
URL: http://ukinhongkong.fco.gov.uk/en/about-us/uk-in-macao/macao

US Consulate General (Hong Kong), URL: http://hongkong.usconsulate.gov/

LEGAL SYSTEM

The Joint Declaration and the Basic Law gave Macao independent judicial power, including the power of final adjudication. The MSAR is responsible for its own courts. Its legal system is based on the Portuguese civil law tradition with Primary Courts, Intermediate Courts and a Court of Final Appeal.

Legal Portal: URL: http://www.court.gov.mo
President, Court of Final Appeal: Sam Hou Fai

Prosecutor General, Public Prosecutions Office: Ho Chio Meng

AREA AND POPULATION

Macao is situated on the south-east coast of China, at the entrance to the Canton River. It is 60 kilometres from Hong Kong, and borders Guangdong Province. Macao has been growing as a result of land reclamation: in the 19th century it covered only 10.28 square kilometres; in 2008, it covered 28.2 square kilometres. The territory is made up of the peninsula of Macao, and the two islands of Taipa and Coloane, now linked by a strip of reclaimed land known as Cotai.

The climate is tropical with cool, humid winters followed by hot weather with monsoons in the spring and summer.

To view a map of Macao, please consult
http://www.lib.utexas.edu/maps/cia08/macau_sm_2008.gif

Population
The total population was estimated at 573,000, by mid-2011, assuming an annual growth rate of less than 1 per cent. Population density is around 16,921 per square km. Over 75 per cent of inhabitants are aged between 15 and 64. The median age is 36.2 years. Macau's population is 95.7 per cent Chinese, mainly Cantonese from the nearby Guangdong Province. The remainder are of Portuguese or mixed Chinese-Portuguese ancestry. Chinese (Cantonese) is the most commonly spoken language, but Portuguese is still spoken.

Births, Marriages, Deaths
The birth rate in 2010 was 8.9 per 1,000 people, whilst the death rate in the same year was 3.6 deaths per 1,000 inhabitants. Infant mortality fell to 3.2 deaths per 1,000 live births. Total fertility was estimated at 0.9 children per woman. The average life expectancy rose to 84.4 years.

Public Holidays 2014
1 January: New Year's Day
31 January: Chinese New Year
5 April: Ching Ming Festival
18 April: Good Friday
21 April: Easter Monday
1 May: Labour Day
6 May: Lord Buddha's Birthday
2 June: Tuen Ng (Dragon Boat) Festival
1 July: Hong Kong Special Administrative Region Establishment Day
September: Chinese Mid-Autumn Festival
1-2 October: National Day of the People's Republic of China
2 October: Chung Yeung Festival
2 November: All Souls' Day
8 December: Feast of the Immaculate Conception
20 December: Macau Special Administrative Region Establishment Day
22 December: Winter Solstice
24-25 Dec Christmas Day

EMPLOYMENT

In 2004, 218,000 of Macao's residents were employed. Almost 32 per cent worked in public administration or other services (such as the growing gambling industry). Over 25 per cent worked in the wholesale, retail, hotels and catering sectors. The third largest employment sector was manufacturing, employing over 16 per cent of the workforce. In the same year, 4.8 per cent of the population was unemployed (down from 6 per cent in 2003). Overall labour force participation rate was 62 per cent in 2004.

Macau's strong economic growth over recent years has put pressure its labour market and businesses have begun to meet their staffing needs by using foreign workers. By 2006, non-resident workers comprised around 20 per cent of the total workforce in 2006, fuelling tensions among some segments of the population.

CHINA

Estimated figures for 2008 put the labour force at 337,400 with 14 per cent engaged in the gambling sector, over 12 per cent in restaurants and hotels, nearly 28 per cent in other service sectors and agriculture, over seven per cent in manufacturing and six per cent in the public sector.

BANKING AND FINANCE

Currency
The unit of currency is the *pataca*. Pataca (MOP) = 100 Avos.

GDP/GNP, Inflation, National Debt
Macao's economy boomed following the expansion of its casino and tourism industry. Macao faces strong local competition from Hong Kong's highly developed services economy and from the low wages and abundant land across the border in mainland China.

Macao's GDP rose to an estimated US$21.5 billion, compared to US$19.2 billion in 2007. The growth rate was 27.3 per cent over the previous year. It fell to 13.2 per cent in 2008. Per capita GDP was estimated to be US$36,300. Figures for 2009 estimated GDP to be US$21.2 billion.

There has been an investment boom in Macau following deregulation of gaming laws in 2002. The only part of China where gambling is legal, almost 27 million tourists visited Macau in 2007, (up 23 cent on the previous year); 55 per cent of these were from mainland China or Hong Kong. The government imposed a 35 per cent rate of tax on the gaming industry, and taxes on gambling generate nearly 70 per cent of total government revenue. The industry contributed around 55 per cent of GDP in 2007, and has overtaken Las Vegas in term of revenues (estimated at $6.6 billion in 2006). More casinos are currently under construction.

Until recently, the textile and garment manufacturing industry was the most important component of the economy, earning around three quarters of total export earnings in 2005. However, competition from mainland China, together with an end to the Multi-Fiber Arrangement quotas in 2005, encouraged many manufacturers to relocate across the border, leaving Macao's low-end mass production industry to run down gradually. The government is encouraging diversification into other manufacturing such as footwear, and machinery and mechanical appliances.

Macau depends on China for most of its food, fresh water, and energy imports. The European Union and Hong Kong are the main suppliers of raw materials and capital goods.

Inflation was estimated at over 5 per cent in 2011.

Balance of Payments / Imports and Exports
Exports were an estimated US$1,000 million in 20109. The territory's main exports are textiles and garments, toys, footwear and machinery. Major export trading partners are the US (8 per cent), Hong Kong (45 per cent), mainland China (15 per cent), and the European Union.

Imports cost US$6.5 billion in 2010, the main commodities being consumer goods, foodstuffs, fuels and raw materials. Most goods came from China (31 per cent), the EU (21 per cent), Japan (8.5 per cent) and Hong Kong (11 per cent).

Central Bank
Autoridade Monetária de Macau (Monetary Authority of Macao), URL: http://www.amcm.gov.mo

MANUFACTURING, MINING AND SERVICES

Primary and Extractive Industries
Macao has no natural oil resources and figure from the EIA for 2011 show that Macau imported 19,000 barrels per day.

Energy
Macao generated 1.43 billion kilowatthours in 2010 and consumed 4.08 billion kilowatthours.

Manufacturing
Textile and garment manufacturing has long been an important industry in the territory, earning around 75 per cent of total export revenues in 2005. However, the end of the Multi-Fiber Arrangement quotas in 2005, together with competition from mainland China, has since had an impact on the future of this industry, and many manufacturing companies have relocated across the border. The textile industry provided about 66 per cent of export earnings in 2007, but total exports only made up around 13 per cent of Macau's total GDP.

The government has encouraged diversification into other manufacturing such as footwear, and machinery and mechanical appliances. Construction, and real estate development continue to be important industries, responding to the deregulation of gaming in Macao, and the demand for tourist facilities.

Service Industries
Macao is an important centre of commerce and finance. Its wealth largely depends on tourism and transit trade. Tourist arrivals rose 16.6 million in 2004 to over 18.7 million in 2005; most come from mainland China, to enjoy the burgeoning gambling industry on the island. Gambling is illegal in mainland China. The gambling industry has seen major investment over the last few years, and this is set to continue, with more hotels and casinos planned for the near future. In 2007, gaming alone contributed almost 55 per cent of Macao's GDP.

Agriculture
The region grows a small amount of rice and vegetables, but most foodstuffs and water are imported.

COMMUNICATIONS AND TRANSPORT

Travel Requirements
Citizens of the USA, Canada, Australia and the EU require a passport valid for one beyond the length of stay; the passport requirements of other countries in the region are for longer periods, and this should be taken into account if the visitor is planning to travel further afield A visa is not required for stays of up to 90 days by most EU citizens (UK subjects can stay for up to six months). USA, Canada and Australia can stay for 30 days without a visa. Other nationals should contact the embassy to check visa requirements.

Nationals not referred to above should contact the embassy to check visa requirements.

International Airports
Macao's international airport is located on Taipa Island. Around 40,000 passengers use the airport every year, and over 140,000 tonnes of cargo are freighted through it annually.

Helicopter flights available from Macau's Terminal Maritimo and the Hong Kong-Macau Ferry Pier.

Ports and Harbours
Macao's ferry terminal began operations in 1993. It handles up to 30 million passengers a year, most arriving from Hong Kong and China.

HEALTH

Macao has one doctor per 470 people and one nurse for every 444 people. There are three hospitals, the main one being the S. Januário Hospital which has 476 beds. The Kiang Wu Hospital is a privately run charitable organization. The Macau University of Science and Technology Hospital is based in Cotai. There are also 486 clinics providing primary healthcare, of which over 75 per cent are private clinics. There are also over 240 Chinese medicine clinics and treatment centres. Most medical services are provided by Government health centres are basically free of charge. In 2010 there were estimated to be over 1,100 hospital beds in total. There are an estimated 1,500 nurses and 1300 doctors.

In 2011, the government budget for health care was 3.78 billion patacas, up 27 per cent on 2010.

The infant mortality rate was 2.9 per 1,000 live births.

EDUCATION

Primary/Secondary Education
Macau provides its citizens with 15 years of free education which includes kindergarten. There were 134 schools or institutions providing regular education in Macao during 2006-07, comprising 12 institutions of higher education and 122 schools that offered pre-primary, primary and/or secondary education. The teacher/student ratio averaged 1 to 16.4.

Macau has three educational systems: the Chinese, the English, and the Portuguese, although there is currently only one school where the language of instruction is Portuguese. Students within the Chinese system attend six years at primary school, three years in junior secondary school and two years in senior high school. Those within the English system have a further 1-2 years for matriculation. Students within the Portuguese system have four years in primary education, five years for their junior secondary school education, and three years for their senior school education. With the return of Macau to China, the Portuguese schools plan to reform their curricula and incorporate Mandarin learning as a compulsory subject into their curricula.

Macau has ten higher education institutions, including the University of Macau. Over 23.5 per cent of the University of Macau students are from overseas. In recent years, the government has tried to unify the educational system, standardising the number of years attended by students. However, proposals to this effect have not been well received in educational circles.

During the 2006/2007 academic year, the number of students in higher education grew by 9.6 per cent over the previous period. However, the total number of students in non-tertiary education decreased by 4.7 per cent (to 87,115), with students in secondary education decreasing by 2.2 per cent to 44,988, marking the second consecutive year of decline. (Source: Macao Statistics and Census Service DSEC). Recent figures put the literacy rate at just over 93.0 per cent although those people who are illiterate are mainly in the elderly population.

RELIGION

Around 17 per cent of the population is Buddhist, whilst 6.7 per cent are Roman Catholic. The majority of the population does not follow a religion.

COMMUNICATIONS AND MEDIA

Local government runs the region's terrestrial TV and radio stations, and subsidises printed publications.

Newspapers
Main newspapers include:
Macao Daily News, URL: http://www.macaodaily.com/
Vakio Daily, URL: http://www.vakiodaily.com/
Jornal Tribuna de Macau, URL: http://www.jtm.com.mo/
Hoje Macau, URL: http://www.hojemacau.com/

Broadcasting
Macao has two state-run radio stations in operation and one private. There are two television stations including Teledifusao Macau (URL: http://www.tdm.com.mo/). Cable and satellite is also available.

Telecommunications
In 2001 a monopoly over mobile-cellular telephone services in 2001 ended, and there was a sharp increase in subscriptions. In 2008 there were around 856,200 mobile phones in use. Fixed-line subscribership has begun to decline; there were approximately 177,800 in use in 2008. Approximately 300,000 people are now regular internet users.

ENVIRONMENT

Figures for 2010 showed that Macao produced 2.54 million metric tons of carbon dioxide.

Macao is party to the following international agreements: Marine Dumping (associate member), Ship Pollution (associate member).

TAIWAN
Republic of China

Capital: Taipei (Population estimate 2011: 2.64 million)

Head of State: Ma Ying-jeou (President) (page 1541)

Vice President: Wu Den-yih

National Flag: On a field of crimson, a white sun with 12 rays on a blue rectangle at the upper hoist

CONSTITUTION AND GOVERNMENT

Constitution
When the Kuomintang forces of General Chiang Kai-shek were defeated by the Communist forces in 1949 they established themselves on the island of Taiwan and set up the official Chinese government there. This government was the only Chinese government to be recognised, and it was the only one to represent China at the United Nations until 1971. Several attempts on the part of mainland China to reach an agreement on reunification were rejected on the grounds that the Beijing regime was in a state of rebellion against the rightful government and that contacts would not be established until Communism was abolished on the mainland. This view was gradually modified as the People's Republic of China became recognised internationally and in particular by the agreement between the People's Republic of China and Britain on the future of Hong Kong.

The constitution which is based on Dr. Sun Yat-sen's 'Principles of People', namely Nationalism, Democracy and Social Well-being, came into effect on 25 December 1947. On 30 April 1991 President Lee Teng-hui signed a document "terminating the Period of National Mobilization for Suppression of the Communist Rebellion", thus accepting the fact that the Chinese Communist regime controls the mainland. Mainland China still views Taiwan as a renegade province and wants it to be re-united with the mainland; Taiwan has rejected this. Relevant amendments to the Constitution were made at the same time. The Government of the Republic of China has its provisional seat in Taipei, Taiwan.

Recent amendments to the constitution have paved the way for a unicameral system of government. In 1994 the constitution was amended so that future constitutional amendments would have to be put to referendum. In 1996 the constitution was amended so that the president was directly elected.

To consult the constitution, please visit:
http://english.president.gov.tw/Default.aspx?tabid=434

Recent Events
In March 2000 Chen Shui-Bain, the Democratic Progress Party candidate, won the presidential election. This was of particular significance as in the past the DPP has called for independence from mainland China.

In March 2005, a new law was passed in China, allowing Beijing the right to use force in the event that Taiwan declared itself independent. In February 2006 Taiwan scrapped the National Unification Council, an organisation set up to debate re-unification with the mainland.

In 2006 President Chen came under pressure following allegations of corruption against his son-in-law. He ceded some presidential powers to the prime minister, including control of the cabinet.

In February 2007 reports appeared that Taiwan has test-fired a cruise missile which had the capability of hitting capable of hitting Shanghai or Hong Kong.

On the 10th October 2007, Taiwan marked its National Day with a military parade for the first time in 16 years, in what observers interpret as a signal to China that the island could defend itself if necessary. Taiwan had discontinued military parades on National Day in a move to improve ties with China, and to underline its own transition to democracy. President Chen Shui-bian used the celebrations to denounce China's military intimidation and to pledge that he would pursue recognition of Taiwan's by the United Nations.

Legislative elections took place on 12th January 2008. The National Party of China (Kuomintang - KMT) won an overall majority in the Legislative Yuan. Prime Minister Chang Chun-hsiung and his Executive Yuan offered their resignations on 24 January but remained in office when the resignations were rejected on 28 January by President Chen Shui-bian, whose term was due to expire at the end of April. On 16th March, hundreds of thousands of people took part in rival political rallies across Taiwan, in advance of the presidential election. The events were also aimed at expressing public opposition to China's anti-secession law, which legalises the use of force against Taiwan if it formally declares independence. Elections for the presidency took place on the 22nd March; Ma Ying-jeou of the Kuomintang party (KMT) won, and took office in May.

On April 12th 2008, China's President Hu Jintao held an historic but short meeting with Taiwan's Vice-President-elect, Vincent Siew. It was the highest-level contact between the two governments since their post-civil war split in 1949. Towards the end of May, the head of Taiwan's ruling party, Kuomintang, met Chinese President Hu Jintao. Expectations were high that the meeting could mark a watershed in relations which had been severely strained during the eight-year administration of Taiwan's independence-leaning President Chen Shui-bian. Taiwan accepted an invitation from China to restart bilateral talks that had been suspended for a decade. In December 2008, daily passenger flights, new shipping routes and postal links between the two countries were established for the first time in six decades.

In September, Taiwan's former President Chen Shui-bian was sentenced to life in prison after being found guilty of corruption. He had been charged with embezzlement of $3.15m from a special presidential fund, taking bribes and money laundering, involving a total of $15m (£9m) while in office from 2000-2008. Mr Chen said that the charges were politically motivated. His wife, Wu Shu-chen, was also sentenced to life for corruption. Two former advisors were given sentences of 16 and 20 years in prison.

In January 2010, the USA approved the sale of air defence missiles to Taiwan. China was against the deal and suspended military and security contacts with the USA as well as imposing sanctions on American firms involved in the deal.

In June 2010, Taiwan and China signed a landmark free trade pact.

Presidential and parliamentary elections took place in January 2012. President Ma Ying-Jeou won a second term of office.

In August 2012, Taiwan and China signed an investment protection agreement, creating formal channels to settle disputes.

The prime minister, Sean Chen-Chun, resigned in February 2013. The deputy premier Jiang Yi-huah was nominated as prime minister and a reshuffled cabinet was appointed.

Legislature
The government is divided into the Office of the President, the National Assembly and five government branches called *Yuan*. These are the Executive Yuan, the Legislative Yuan, the Judicial Yuan, the Control Yuan and the Examination Yuan.

The National Assembly has 300 members who are appointed proportionally by the elected parties in the Legislative Yuan. National Assembly members only meet when required and is largely ceremonial.

The Legislative Yuan at present has 113 members, 73 of whom are directly elected, 34 elected proportionately by party and six elected by indigenous people to two constituencies. They serve a four-year term.

Office of the President, 122 Chungking Road, Section 1, Taipei, Taiwan. Tel: +886 2 311 3731, fax: +886 2 311 1604, URL: http://www.president.gov.tw/
Office of the Premier: http://www.ey.gov.tw
Kuo-Min Ta-Hui (National Assembly), 53 Chungwa Road, Section 1, Taipei, Taiwan. Tel: +886 2 331 1312, fax: +886 2 361 3565
Executive Yuan, 1 Chuanghsiao E. Road, Section 1, Taipei, Taiwan. Tel: +886 2356 1500, fax: +886 2 394 8727, URL: http://www.ey.gov.tw
Li-Fa Yuan (Legislative Yuan), 1 Chuanshan S. Road, Taipei, Taiwan. Tel: +886 2 321 1531, fax: +886 2 322 2558, URL: http://www.ly.gov.tw
National Security Council, 122 Chungking South Road, Section 1, Taipei, Taiwan. Tel: +886 2 371 8578, fax: +886 2 371 8599, URL: http://www.taiwan.gov.tw

---

Cabinet - Executive Yuan (as at June 2013)
Premier: Chen (Sean) Chun
Vice Premier: Wu Den-yih
Minister without Portfolio, also Minister of Mongolian and Tibetan Affairs Commission: Luo Ying-shay (page 1467)
Minister without Portfolio: Yang Chiu-hsing
Minister without Portfolio, also Minister, Council for Economic Planning & Development: Kuan Chung-ming (page 1459)
Minister without Porfolio, also Minister, Public Construction Commission: Chern Jenn-chuan

---

CHINA

Minister without Portfolio: Huang Kuang-nan
Minister without Portfolio: Schive Chi
Minister without Portfolio: Lin Jung-tzer
Minister without Portfolio, also Governor, Taiwan Province: Chang San-cheng (page 1465)
Minister without Portfolio, also Governor, Fujian Province: Chen Shyh-kwei
Secretary-General: Chen Wei Zen (page 1403)
Deputy Secretary-General of the Executive Yuan: Chen Ching-Tsai
Deputy Secretary-General of the Executive Yuan: Chien Tai-Lang
Spokesperson, Executive Yuan: Cheng Li-wun
Minister of the Interior: Lee Hong-yuan (page 1462)
Minister of Foreign Affairs: Lin Yung-lo (page 1465) (David Yung-lo Lin)
Minister of Defence: Kao Hua-chu
Minister of Finance: Chang Sheng-ford (page 1402)
Minister of Education: Chiang Wei-ling
Minister of Justice: Tseng Yung-fu (page 1528)
Minister of Economic Affairs: Chang Chia-juch (page 1402)
Minister of Transport and Communications: Yeh Kuang-shih
Minister of Culture: Lung Ying-tai
Minister of Overseas Chinese Affairs Commission: Wu Ying-yih
Governor, Central Bank of the Republic of China: Perng Fai-nan
Minister, Directorate General of Budget, Accounting and Statistics: Shih Su-mei
Minister, Directorate General of Personnel Administration: Huang Fu-yuan
Minister of Health: Chiu Wen-ta
Head of the Environmental Protection Administration: Dr Shen Shu-hung (Stephen Shu-hung)
Minister, Coast Guard Administration: Wang Ginn-wang
Director, National Palace Museum: Fung Ming-chu
Minister, Mainland Affairs Council: Wang Yu-chi
Minister, Financial Supervisory Commission: Chen Yuh-chang
Minister, Veterans Affairs Commission: Tseng Jing-ling
Minister, Atomic Energy Council: Dr Tsai Chuen-horng
Minister, National Science Council: Chu Ching-yi (Cyrus C.Y. Chu)
Minister, Research Development and Evaluation Commission: Sung Yu-hsieh
Minister, Council of Agriculture: Chen Bao-ji
Minister, Council of Labour Affairs: Pan Shih-wei
Chair, Fair Trade Commission: Dr Wu Shiow-Ming
Minister, Council of Indigenous Peoples: Sun Ta-chuan
Minister for Hakka Affairs: Huang Yu-cheng
Chair, Central Election Commission: Chang Po-ya
Minister, National Communications Commission: Shyr Shyr-hau

Ministries

Ministry of the Interior, 5 Huschow Road, Taipei, Taiwan. Tel: +886 2 2356 5005, fax: +886 2 2356 6201, URL: http://www.moi.gov.tw/
Ministry of Foreign Affairs, 2 Kaitakelan Boulevard, Taipei, Taiwan. Tel: +886 2 2348 2999, URL: http://www.mofa.gov.tw/
Ministry of Defence, Chiehshou Hall, Chungking S. Road, Taipei, Taiwan. Tel: +886 2 2311 6117, URL: http://www.mnd.gov.tw/
Ministry of Finance, 2 Aikuo West Road, Taipei, Taiwan. Tel:+886 2 2322 8000, fax: +886 2 2321 1205, URL: http://www.mof.gov.tw/
Ministry of Education, 5 Chungshan S. Road, Taipei, Taiwan. Tel: +886 2 2356 6051, URL: http://www.moe.gov.tw/
Ministry of Justice, 130 Chingking South Road, Section 1, Taipei, Taiwan. Tel: +886 2 2314 6772, fax: +886 2 2331 9102, URL: http://www.moj.gov.tw/
Ministry of Mongolian and Tibetan Affairs, URL: http://www.cpa.gov.tw/
Ministry of Economic Affairs, 15 Foochow Street, Taipei, Taiwan. Tel: +886 2 2321 2200, URL: http://www.moea.gov.tw/
Ministry of Transportation and Communications, 2 Changsa Street, Section 1, Taipei, Taiwan. Tel:+886 2 2349 2900, fax: +886 2 2389 6009, URL: http://www.motc.gov.tw/
Department of Health, 100 Ai Kuo East Road, Section 4, Taipei, Taiwan. Tel: +886 2 2321 0151, fax: +886 2 2312 2907, URL: http://www.doh.gov.tw/
Overseas Taiwanese Affairs Commission, 3 Paoching Road, Taipei, Taiwan. Tel: + 886 2 2316 5300, fax: + 886 2 2370 0415, e-mail: ocacinfo@mail.ocac.gov.tw, URL: http://www.ocac.gov.tw
Council for Economic Planning and Development, 9th Floor, 87 Nanking East Road, Section 2 Taipei, Taiwan. Tel: +886 2 2522 5300, fax: +886 2 2551 9011, URL: http://www.cepd.gov.tw/
National Youth Commission, 14th Floor, 5 Hsu Chou Road, Taipei, Taiwan. Tel: +886 2 2356 6271, fax: +886 2 2356 6290, URL: http://www.nyc.gov.tw/
Atomic Energy Council, 67 Lance 144, Kee Lung Road, Section 4, Taipei, Taiwan. Tel: +886 2 2363 4180, fax: +886 2 2363 5377, URL: http://www.aec.gov.tw/www/index.php
National Science Council, 17th-22nd Floors, 106 Ho Ping East Road, Section 2, Taipei, Taiwan. Tel: +886 2 2737 750, fax: +886 2 2737 7668, e-mail: nsc@nsc.gov.tw, URL: http://web1.nsc.gov.tw/
Central Personnel Administration, URL: http://www.cpa.gov.tw/
Commission of Research, Development and Evaluation, URL: http://www.rdec.gov.tw/
Environmental Protection Administration, URL: http://www.epa.gov.tw/

Political Parties

Kuomintang (KMT, Nationalist Party of China), http://www.kmt.org.tw/english/index.aspx
Democratic Progressive Party (DPP), URL: http://www.dpp.org.tw/
People First Party, URL: http://www.pfp.org.tw/
Taiwan Solidarity Union, URL: http://www.tsu.org.tw/

Elections

Presidential elections are held every four years and both the president and vice president are eligible for re-election for a second term. 1996 saw the first ever direct presidential election; over 76 per cent of voters turned out to re-elect Lee Teng-hui with 54 per cent of the votes cast. The next presidential election was held in March 2000, and was won by Chen Shui-Bian of the Democratic Progressive Party with 39.3 per cent of the vote. Chen Shui-Bian was elected for a second term in 2004, with a slim margin of 0.2 per cent.

The most recent presidential election took place on 14 January 2012. The incumbent candidate, Ma Ying-jeou of the Kuomintang party (KMT) won with 51 per cent of the vote, 5 percentage points over his closest rival, Tsai Ing-Wen of the DPP party.

The National Assembly was elected by popular vote for a four-year term. The last election for the National Assembly was in 1996. At the end of its term in 2000 the National Assembly voted to become more of a ceremonial body, proportionally appointed by the represented parties in the Legislative Yuan, and will sit when required.

The Legislative Yuan is elected for a three-year term. The most recent elections were held on 14 January 2012. The Pan-Blue coalition (Kuomintang (KMT) party and the People First Party (PFP) won 67 seats (64 and three respectively), the Pan-Green coalition (Democratic Progressive Party 40 seats, Taiwan Solidarity Union 3 seats); the Non-Partisan Solidarity Union 2 seats and independents one seat.

Diplomatic Representation

Taiwanese Economic and Cultural Representative Office, 3 F No 65 Sung Chiang Road, Taipei, Taiwan. Tel: +88 62 516 6626, fax: +88 62 516 6625, URL:http://ukintaiwan.fco.gov.uk/en/
Taipei Economic and Cultural Representative Office, 4201 Wisconsin Ave., N.W., Washington , DC 20016, USA. Tel: +1 292 895 1800, URL: http://www.roc-taiwan.org/US/mp.asp?mp=12
Representative: King Pu-tsung
Taipei Representative Office in the UK, 50 Grosvenor Gardens, London, SW1W 0EB, UK. Tel: +44 (0)20 7881 2650, fax:+ 44 (0)20 7730 7379, e-mail: tro@taiwan-tro.net, URL: http://www.roc-taiwan.org/uk/
Representative: Chang Siao-yue

LEGAL SYSTEM

The judicial system is based on civil law and Taiwan accepts compulsory jurisdiction of the International Court of Justice.

The judicial yuan is Taiwan's highest judicial organ. It interprets the constitution and other laws and decrees, adjudicates administrative suits, and disciplines public functionaries. The president and vice president of the judicial yuan are nominated and appointed by the president of the republic, with the consent of the legislative yuan. They, together with 15 grand justices, form the Council of Grand Justices, which is charged with the power and responsibility of interpreting the constitution, laws, and ordinances.

The Supreme Court is the highest tribunal in the three-level court system. It exercises appellate jurisdiction only, automatically reviewing all sentences to life imprisonment or death. The Supreme Court consists of both civil and criminal divisions, each of which is formed by a presiding judge and four associate judges. The judges are appointed for life. The High Court is located in Taipei with branches at Tainan, Taichung and Hualien. There are 18 district courts, which handle civil and criminal cases of the first instance. There is also an administrative court.

The Ministry of Justice is in charge of the administration and supervision concerning legal affairs, prosecution affairs, prison and detention house, rehabilitation, social protection and investigation. In cooperation with the Judicial Yuan, the Ministry trains judges, public prosecutors, and other legal officials. Judges are appointed by the president and approved by the Legislative Yuan.

The government respects the rights of the citizens, though there have been instances of police abuse of prisoners and official corruption. Taiwan retains the death penalty. Four people were reported to have been executed in 2010, five in 2011 and six in December 2012.

Judicial Yuan, URL: http://www.judicial.gov.tw/en/
President, Judicial Yuan & Chief Justice: Hau Min-Rai

LOCAL GOVERNMENT

The Provincial Government is the highest administrative organ of local self-government. There are 35 provinces designated by the Constitution of the Republic of China but only one province under complete control of the Republic of China (ROC): Taiwan Province. This was established in 1947 and had its own legislative power, the Taiwan Provincial Assembly. It is further divided into 14 counties (Changhua, Chiayi (county), Hsinchu (county), Hualien, Kinmen, Lienchiang, Miaoli, Nantou, Penghu, Pingtung, Taitung, Taoyuan, Yilan, Yunlin), three municipalities (Chiayi (city), Hsinchu (city), Keelung) and five special municipalities (Kaohsiung, New Taipei, Taichung, Tainan, Taipei). In 1997 elections at local government level were abolished and the governor is now appointed rather than elected. In 1998 most responsibilities were assumed by central government and county-level governments. The ROC currently administers two provinces and two provincial level cities.

AREA AND POPULATION

Area

The island of Taiwan is 90 miles east of the south China coast with an area of 13,899.7 square miles; or, including the Kinma Area, a total of 13,968.7 square miles. Most of the terrain is made up of rugged mountains, with undulating plains in the west. There are two groups of islands along the mainland coast. The Kinmen (or Quemoy) islands are situated in the Amoy Bay along the coast of Fukien Province. Kinmen is 68 square miles in area and has a population of 42,783. To its north-east lie the 19 islands of the Matsu groups, one of them being only five nautical miles from the mainland. Besides the military, there are about 5,558 people there.

The climate is tropical, with a rainy season during the southwest monsoon (June to August).

To view a map of Taiwan, please consult
http://www.lib.utexas.edu/maps/cia08/taiwan_sm_2008.gif

Population

In 2011, Taiwan was estimated to have a population of 23.7 million (not including foreign residents), giving a population density of 629 people per sq km. About 70 per cent live in the metropolitan area. The population growth rate is estimated at 0.2 per cent. The chief cities are Taipei, the provisional capital, which has a population of 2.64 million, Taichung, Kaohsiung, Tainan, Chilung (Keelung), Hsinchu and Chiayi. The ethnic breakdown is approximately 84 per cent Taiwanese, 14 per cent mainland Chinese and 2 per cent aborigine. The official language is Mandarin and other languages spoken include Taiwanese, which is the Southern Gujianese dialect, and Hakka Chinese dialects. Many of the older population speak Japanese, a legacy of 50 years of Japanese colonial rule ending in 1945.

Births, Marriages, Deaths

In 2009 the birth rate was estimated at 8.9 per 1,000 population and the death rate was 6.76 per 1,000 population. Just over 16 per cent of the population is under 15 years of age and over 10 per cent of the population is over 65 year of age. Average life expectancy is 75 years for men and 81 years for women. The median age is estimated at 37.5 years. Taiwan has one of the highest population densities in the world with an average figure of 612 people per sq. km. Taipei City has a density of 9,739 people per sq. km.

Public Holidays 2014

1-3 January: Founding of the Republic of China and New Year's Day
31 January: Chinese Lunar New Year
28 February: Peace Memorial Day
April: Tomb-Sweeping Day
3 May: Labour Day
May/June (5th day of the 5th moon): Dragon Boat Festival
Sept/Oct.(15th day, 8th moon): Mid-Autumn Moon Festival
10 October: National Day

EMPLOYMENT

Figures for 2005 show that the workforce consisted of 10, 371,000 people (rising from 9,832,000 million in 2001), of which around 300,000 were foreign workers mainly from Indonesia and the Philippines. Unemployment in 2007 was put at 3.9 per cent rising to 4.1 per cent in 2008. It was an estimated 4.2 per cent in Q1 2012.

Total Employment by Economic Activity

Occupation	2008
Agriculture, hunting, fishing & forestry	535,000
Mining & quarrying	6,000
Manufacturing	2,886,000
Electricity, gas & water supply	99,000
Construction	842,000
Wholesale & retail trade, repairs	1,770,000
Hotels & restaurants	687,000
Transport, storage & communications	617,000
Financial intermediation	411,000
Real estate, renting & business activities	622,000
Public admin. & defence; compulsory social security	343,000
Education	605,000
Health & social work	355,000
Other community, social & personal service activities	528,000
Other	98,000

Source: Copyright © International Labour Organization (ILO Dept. of Statistics, http://laborsta.ilo.org)

BANKING AND FINANCE

Currency

New Taiwan Dollar (NTD) = 100 cents

GDP/GNP, Inflation, National Debt

Taiwan has enjoyed strong growth over the last thirty years of approximately 8 per cent per year and has developed a strong economy initially based on manufacturing. Taiwan officially entered a recession in 2009. The economy has been hard hit by falling global demand in the electronics and export sectors. The government pledged to invest in the country's infrastructure, and the Central Bank cut interest rates several times in 2008 and 2009 in an attempt to stimulate the economy.

Since 1953, national economic planning has been carried out through a series of four-year plans. Taiwan entered a recession in 2009, GDP growth that year was put at -1.9 per cent. Per capita GDP in 2009 was Taiwanese US$16,420. The economy recovered in 2010 and growth was estimated to 10.8 per cent. Growth was led by the services sector which grew by over 24 per cent. The following tables show GNP and GDP in recent years and the industrial origin of GDP. Exports also recovered before slowing in 2011 as the financial crisis deepened in the eurozone economic crisis. The economy was expected to grow by 3.75 per cent in 2012, helped by trade with China.

GDP by Industrial Origin at current market prices, billion New Taiwan Dollars

Sector	2008	2009	2010
GDP by industrial orgin	12,620.2	12,477.2	13,614.4
-Agriculture	201.8	215.9	214.2
-Mining	20.7	51.7	63.0
-Manufacturing	3,132.3	2,960.3	3,578.5
-Electricity, gas and water	148.6	251.9	249.0
-Construction	363.3	322.7	377.4
-Trade	2,390.4	2,319.3	2,473.8
-Transport and communications	850.8	837.9	885.2
-Finance	2,211.1	2,118.0	2,237.3
-Public administration	945.2	950.3	987.3
-Others	1,997.3	2,058.9	2,137.3
Net factor income from abroad	314.6	413.6	429.7
GNI	12,934.8	12,890.8	14,044.2

Source: Asian Development Bank

GDP was estimated to be US$490 billion in 2011.

Inflation was estimated to be under 1 per cent in 2010, rising to 1.4 per cent in 2011. Taiwan is expected to rise to 2.1 per cent in 2013.

In 2011, Taiwan had no external debt.

Balance of Payments / Imports and Exports

Taiwan's foreign trade rapidly expanded in the early 1990s. Textile products, electrical machinery and apparatus are Taiwan's leading exports. Other major export items are machinery and metal products, plastic products and iron and steel. Principal imports are crude oil, electrical machinery and apparatus, machine tools, basic metals, chemicals and consumer goods.

The trade balance in recent years is as follows:

External trade, billion new Taiwan Dollars

	2008	2009	2010
Exports, fob	8,010.4	6,708.9	8,656.8
Imports, cif	7,551.1	5,757.2	7,943.5
Trade balance	459.3	951.7	713.3

Source: Asian Development Bank

Direction of Trade, million US $

	2009	2010
Exports, total	**203,675**	**274,601**
China	54,249	76,935
Hong Kong	29,445	37,807
US	23,553	31,466
Japan	14,502	18,006
Singapore	8,614	12,096
Imports, total	**174,371**	**251,236**
Japan	36,220	51,917
China	24,423	35,946
US	18,154	26,379
Korea, Republic of	10,507	16,059
Saudi Arabia	8,658	11,859

Source: Asian Development Bank

Central Bank

Central Bank of China (Taiwan), 2 Roosevelt Road, Section 1, Taipei City, Taiwan. Tel: +886 2 2393 6161, fax: +886 2 2357 1974, URL: http://www.cbc.gov.tw
Governor: Fai-Nan Perng

MANUFACTURING, MINING AND SERVICES

Primary and Extractive Industries

Oil reserves were estimated at 0.002 billion barrels in 2008. Production ran at 26,600 barrels per day, 800 of which were crude oil in 2011. Consumption of oil in that year was estimated at 920,000 barrels per day. Taiwan imports most of its oil from countries in the Persian Gulf and West Africa. The Chinese Petroleum Corporation is Taiwan's national oil company although recently private competition has emerged from companies such as the Tuntex Group and Formosa Petrochemical Group (part of the Formosa Plastics Group). There are four oil refineries: Kaohsiung, Ta-Lin, Taoyuan and Mailiao, which is owned by the Formosa Petrochemical Group. As of 2010, refinery capacity stood at 1,310,000 bbl/d.

CHINA

Natural gas reserves are estimated at 297 billion cubic feet. Annual production fell to 9 billion cubic feet (Bcf) in 2010 whilst consumption rose to 535 Bcf. The shortfall is satisfied by imports primarily from Indonesia, Qatar and Malaysia. Taiwan's only liquified-natural gas terminal is in Yungan, Kaohsiung. A liquified-natural gas terminal in the Taoyuan county has been planned by Tuntex, to import LNG from the Australian Northwest shelf.

Coal reserves were estimated at 1.1 million short tons (MMST) in 1996. Production was 0.1 MMSTm. Active coal mining ceased in 2000. Coal is used primarily for generation of electricity and in the steel, cement and petrochemical industries. The bulk of demand is met by imports coming from Australia, Indonesia, South Africa, China, the United States and Canada.

Energy

Oil is the main fuel used, accounting for nearly half of total primary energy consumption. Coal accounts for 34 per cent of consumption, nuclear power for 9 per cent, natural gas 7 per cent and hydroelectric power 2 per cent. Approximately 55 per cent of the demand for energy comes from industry while 25 per cent comes from the transportation sector. Privatization of energy related enterprises is currently underway.

Current electricity generating capacity is 41 gigawatts and electricity generation in 2010 was 226 billion kWh. Electricity is produced by Taipower, the Taiwan Power Company. Private companies are currently allowed to produce 20 per cent of Taiwan's electricity. 58 power plants are in operation (38 hydropower, 17 thermal, 3 nuclear). Taiwan has a fourth nuclear power plant under construction, but work was suspended under the new government.

Manufacturing

Recent figures show industry accounting for 28 per cent of the country's GDP, and the industries increasing in size are notably the chemical, petroleum, electrical, electronic and information industries. Main products include laptop computers, monitors, desktop computers and motherboards. Areas which have been affected by the relocation abroad of manufacturers are light industries such as textiles, garments, leatherware and food processing.

Manufacturing in 2007

Product	'000 Tonnes
Cement	18,957
Steel bars	7,970
Sugar refined	721
Cotton fabrics (million metres)	418
Paper	878
Wheat flour	811
Cotton yam	280

Source: Asian Development Bank

Service Industries

Visitor arrivals increased to over 6 million in 2011, up 9 per cent on the previous year. International visitors come mainly from Asia, the US, and Hong Kong.

Agriculture

Today agriculture in Taiwan only takes up about 11 per cent of the work force and produces an estimated 1.5 per cent of the country's GDP. It is a declining sector threatened by industrialisation, falling incomes, rising costs and increased foreign competition and produce imports. The government is encouraging farmers to increase the size of their farms, so that increased size and mechanisation would increase production. Currently some 865,723 hectares of land are under cultivation. For the past decade farmers have derived more than 60 per cent of their income from non-farming activities. The following table shows agricultural production of main crops in thousand metric tonnes.

Product	1999	2000	2007
Sugarcane	3,256	2,894	721
Rice, brown	1,559	1,540	1,098
Citrus fruits	486	440	473
Maize	201	178	85
Pineapples	348	358	477
Sweet potatoes	219	198	200
Bananas	213	198	242
Sorghum	34	26	5

Source: Asian Development Bank

The island's fishing industry produces about US$3.7 billion worth of fish per annum. Half of this comes from deep sea fishing. The biggest items are tuna and eel and 30 per cent of the catch is exported. The fishing fleet totals 30,000, approximately half of which are powered craft. Deep sea fishing has grown as pollution and industrial waste have added to the swift depletion of coastal and off-shore fish stocks.

COMMUNICATIONS AND TRANSPORT

Travel Requirements

Citizens of the USA, Canada, Australia and most of the EU require a passport valid for at least six months but do not need a visa for stays of up to 30 days as long as they do not have a criminal record and have a confirmed return air ticket. The exceptions are citizens of Bulgaria, Cyprus, Czech Republic, Estonia, Hungary, Latvia, Lithuania, Poland, Romania, Slovak Republic and Slovenia, who do require a visa. Nationals of Czech Republic, Hungary, Poland and Slovak Republic can apply for a landing visa on arrival at CKS International Airport or Kaohsiung International Airport, on condition that they are holding tickets for an onward destination, and have no criminal record. The landing visa is valid for 30 days and cannot be extended.

Passengers arriving at Kaohsiung International Airport, including passengers arriving from China (PR), may apply for a temporary entry permit at the Kaohsiung Station Aviation Police Bureau. They must convert the permit into a visa at the Bureau of Consular Affairs or it Kaohsiung Office within three days. Nationals holding British National (overseas) passports if born in Hong Kong or Macau or if having previously visited Taiwan, may obtain a 14 day visa on arrival.

Other nationals should contact the embassy to check visa requirements. Travellers intending to stay more than three months in Taiwan will have to take an AIDS test, and it this proves positive, they will be required to leave the country.

National Airlines

China Airlines operates domestic and international scheduled and chartered flights. Far Eastern Air Transport, Formosa and Taiwan Airlines make domestic scheduled and chartered flights. Current air services include flights between Taiwan and the off-shore islands and helicopter passenger and agricultural chartered flights. Recently, China Airlines announced the start of passenger services from Taipai to Penang, Malaysia and Medan, Indonesia Passenger traffic in Taiwan is increasing rapidly, and the ROC aviation industry is becoming more competitive. Several airlines have begun air transportation services.
China Airlines, URL: http://www.china-airlines.com
Mandarin Airlines, URL: http://www.mandarin-airlines.com
EVA Air, URL: http://www.evaair.com.tw
TransAsia Airways, URL: http://www.tna.com.tw

International Airports

There are four international airports in Taiwan, Taiwan Taoyuan International Airport (formerly Chiang Kai-shek), Taipei Songshan Airport, Kaohsiung International Airport and Taichung Airport. Taiwan Taoyuan International Airport handled more than 11.6 million arrivals and 11.5 million departures in 2011.
Taiwan Taoyuan International Airport, URL: http://www.taoyuan-airport.com/english/index.jsp
Kaohsiung International Airport, URL: http://www.kia.gov.tw/english/e_index.asp

Railways

Taiwan has a good railway system, and with completion of the final link of the East Coast Railway and a cross-island highway, will have an excellent high speed network connecting all the important cities and towns of the province. The high speed rail line covers 345 km. The total length of railways in Taiwan is 1,580 kilometres, including the Taiwan High Speed Rail line, a bullet train based on the Japanese model which runs on the West Coast from Taipei to Zuoying (Kaohsiung). The system is undergoing reform: the RRB Hualien-Taitung Electrification Project is due to be completed by 2014. The project extends for 166.1 km and includes four tunnels, the largest of which, the 5.3 km Shanli Tunnel, opened in March 2012 A mass rapid transit system is also under development. An estimated 179 million passengers used the railways in 2008.
Taiwan Railway Administration, URL: http://www.railway.gov.tw

Roads

The number of motor vehicles in Taiwan continues to increase and there were an estimated 21 million vehicles registered in 2008 which equates to approximately 500 vehicles per square kilometre. The total length of the road network is over 21,000 km. Vehicles are driven on the right.

Shipping

As an island, Taiwan's ocean transportation is vital to its economy. In 2008, freight traffic amounted to over 65 million metric tons.

Ports and Harbours

There are seven international harbours in Taiwan: Keelung, Mailiao, Taichung, Kaohsiung (one of the world's busiest container ports), Anping, Hualien and Su-ao. Container handling amounted to an estimated 12.96 million TEU in 2008 and cargo amounted to 668.28 million revenue tons. there were some 50,000 passenger arrivals and departures.
Kaohsiung Harbour, URL: http://www.khb.gov.tw/english/

A ferry service operates between Matsu and Fuzhou, China. A ferry service between Taiwan and Japan was suspended in 2008.

HEALTH

There is a National Health Insurance Programme, and this covers over 96 per cent of the population. Recent government figures show that there are 19,600 medical care establishments in Taiwan, ranging from hospitals to health rooms in small villages. The number of hospitals has declined: as of 2006 there were 547 hospitals (94 cent Western). Of these, there were 55 regional hospitals, 24 medical centres, 344 district hospitals and 52 psychiatric hospitals. The number of clinics has increased: as of 2006 there were over 19,000 clinics. Chinese medical clinics increased by 50 per cent in the period 1996-2006. As of 2006 there were 981 nursing institutions. As of 2008, there were approximately 131,000 hospital beds available, and 121,517 medical personnel. As of 2006, there were 50,054 physicians (22 per 10,000 population), 109,521 nurses and midwives, 7,457 medical technicians, 27,412 pharmacists, and 12,515 other medical personnel.

EDUCATION

Primary/Secondary Education

The Republic of China offers nine years of compulsory education, starting at six years old. Instruction is in Mandarin. Following junior high there are three options for students. Either they may attend senior high schools, senior vocational schools or junior colleges. There is also a system for special schools catering for the needs of physically or mentally handicapped children. Traditionally Taiwanese students have excelled in the areas of Maths and Science, in recent years education reforms have been debated to encourage the study of arts subjects.

Higher Education
As well as the five-year junior colleges there are also two-year junior colleges which specialise in subjects such as business and engineering. Most university courses are of four years duration, apart from medicine and law which last for five to seven years. Recent figures show that there are approximately 140 universities and higher education institutes. In 2010, almost 1 million of the population held a bachelor's degree and 925,000 a master's or doctorate.

The literacy rate is estimated at 98.4 per cent.

RELIGION

The predominant religion in Taiwan are Chinese Folk Religionists (43 per cent of the population), 27 per cent of the population are Buddhists. The remainder of religious believers follow either Taoism (13 per cent), Christianity (6 per cent). There are small communities of Muslims, Baha'is and New Religionists.

It is a constitutional right of any citizen of the Republic of China to be able to follow their own religion. Recent figures show that more than half the population of the country follow some form of religious belief. Taiwan has a religious liberty rating of 10 on a scale of 1 to 10 (10 is most freedom). (Source: World Religion Database)

COMMUNICATIONS AND MEDIA

The government has increased press freedom and reduced government, military and political party ownership of the broadcast media. Wide-ranging views are published and broadcasts and laws prohibiting the promotion of independence are rarely enforced.

Newspapers
The newspaper market is vibrant with hundreds of titles.
China Post (English), URL: http://www.chinapost.com.tw
China Times, URL: http://news.chinatimes.com/mainpage.htm

Broadcasting
There were an estimated 170 radio stations in 2008 and five free-to-air television networks and some 75 television stations. There are high subscription rates for multi-channel Cable TV. The government hopes to phase out terrestial anaolgue TV signals by 2012. The five

major commercial television stations are the Taiwan Television Enterprise (TTV) (URL: http://www.ttv.com.tw), the China Television Company (URL: http://www.chinatv.com.tw), the Chinese Television System (CTS), Formosa Television Corporation and the Public Television Service.

Telecommunications
The telecommunication system is modern and fully digitized. In 2010 there were estimated to be over 16 million landlines and 27 million mobile phone subscriptions. Figures for 2011 showed that Taiwan had over 16 million internet users.

ENVIRONMENT

Due to the rapid industrialisation and dense population of Taiwan, the major threat to the environment is pollution. Air pollution is largely caused by the large number of factories and motor vehicles. According to figures from the EIA, Taiwan's emissions from the consumption of fossil fuels rose to 305 million metric tons in 2010, up from 290.4 million metric tons in 2008.

Following efforts to encourage use of unleaded petrol, almost 70 per cent of the total amount of petrol sold is unleaded. The government is promoting the use of electric motorcycles as petrol ones (of which Taiwan has 9.5 million out of its total of 14.5 million motor vehicles) generate 10 times the amount of hydrocarbon produced by cars.

Other major issues include raw sewage, water pollution from industrial emissions, contamination of drinking water supplies and trade in endangered species. Mountain deforestation and land subsidence are also threats to the environment.

SPACE PROGRAMME

The National Space Organization of Taiwan is based in HsinChu. Its vision is to establish indigenous space technology and promote frontier space science research. It has developed a satellite development infrastructure, including a test facility, ground control system and several professional laaboratories. It launched three development satellites in the period 1999-2006. It is currently carrying out two major satellite programs (FORMOSAT-5 and -7). FORMOSAT-5 will be the Taiwan's first remote sensing satellite to be developed indigenously. FORMATOST -7 is a joint Taiwan/US program.
National Space Organization, URL: http://www.nspo.org.tw/

COLOMBIA
Republic of Colombia
República de Colombia

Capital: Santafé de Bogotá (Population estimate, 2011: 7.1 million)

Head of State: Juan Manuel Santos (President) (page 1508)

Vice President: Angelino Garzon

National Flag: A tricolour fesswise, yellow, blue, red, the yellow to half the depth of the flag

CONSTITUTION AND GOVERNMENT

Constitution
Elections were held for a 74 seat Constitution Assembly in December 1990 and the resulting Constitution (replacing the 1886 Constitution) was effective from 6 July 1991. The President, elected by direct vote, serves for four years and, originally, could not be elected for a consecutive presidential term. The President appoints the Cabinet. The Constitution guarantees freedom of speech, press, and assembly as well as all other basic rights.

A bill to amend Colombia's constitution to allow President Uribe to stand for a second consecutive four-year term was approved by the Senate on 14 May 2004 and approved by 92 votes to six in the fourth of eight votes in the House of Representatives. The bill was supported by about 80 per cent of Colombians, according to polls at the time. The Constitutional Court in March 2010 rejected the holding of a referendum to allow for the president to stand for a third consecutive term..

To consult the 1991 Constitution with amendments to 2005 (in Spanish), please visit: http://web.presidencia.gov.co/constitucion/index.pdf

International Relations
The civil war between the Revolutionary Armed Forces of Colombia (Farc) and the United Self Defence Forces of Colombia (AUC), now in its fifth decade, has had an impact on Colombia's relations with her neighbours. Whilst the policy of Ecuador, Brazil and Venezuela has been to avoid direct involvement in the war, there have been tensions. In June 2005, an attack by the Farc on an army base close to the border with Ecuador provoked a diplomatic row between the two countries, with Colombia alleging that the Farc had used Ecuadorean

territory as a base for the attack. Relations with Venezuela were damaged when Rodrigo Granda, a leading Farc member, was kidnapped in Caracas and taken to Colombia. Colombia has claimed that President Chavez harbours Farc members and allows guerrilla camps to operate on Venezuelan soil; Sr. Chavez claims to be neutral in the conflict, but appears reluctant to co-operate in the fight against the Marxist Farc, when President Uribe is such a strong ally of US President Bush. In November 2007, President Chavez threatened to freeze bilateral ties with Colombia following the decision by President Uribe to end Mr Chavez's role as a hostage negotiator with Farc rebels. President Uribe was annoyed by Sr. Chavez's disregard for the proper diplomatic channels, and his defiance of instructions not to be in direct contact with Colombia's army chief. In January 2008, Sr. Chavez said the Farc and the ELN guerrilla movements should been seen as insurgent forces not terrorist groups.

The US sponsored 'Plan Colombia' is a cause of concern with Colombia's neighbours because of the potential spill-over of drugs production, terrorists and refugees. There is evidence now of coca production in transit through neighbouring states and of heavily armed Colombians prepared to defend it. There are two million internally displaced Colombians as a result of the conflict, and the UNHCR estimates that over 100,000 Colombians have sought asylum overseas. Ecuador receives the highest number of asylum seekers.

Colombia is an active member of the UN and the Organization of American States. It is one of the original members of the Andean Community and has also joined the Rio Group and the Non-Aligned Movement.

Recent Events
The two main left-wing guerrilla groups operating an armed opposition to the government are the FARC (Revolutionary Armed Forces of Colombia) and the ELN (National Liberation Army). The main right-wing paramilitary group, the AUC (United Self Defence Forces of Colombia), operated against the guerrillas until 2005, when half of them disarmed.

In May 2002, independent candidate Alvaro Uribe Vélez won the presidential election following promises to take a hard line against guerrilla groups.

Peace talks between the AUC and the government began in July 2004 following the disarming of about 800 militants, In November 2004 a further 450 fighters disarmed. In June 2005, a law was passed allowing shorter jail sentences and protection from extradition for those rebels who handed in their weapons. Most rank-and-file combatants would be pardoned, be eligible for job-training and given a government grant for two years. In December 2005, a further 2,000 AUC combatants disarmed, together with their leader, Ivan Roberto Duque, and their commander, Carlos Mario Jimenez (aka Macaco). However, the force remains strong.

The Government then turned its attention to the second largest rebel group, the National Liberation Army (ELN). Farc continues its campaign, but high returns from drugs and kidnapping now dominate the rebels' agenda, and have largely replaced ideological motivation. In June 2007, the government released dozens of Farc guerrillas from jail, hoping that the rebels would release hostages in return, but Farc said that it would only free hostages if the government set up a demilitarised zone.

In February 2007, Maria Consuelo Araujo, the Foreign Relations Minister, announced her resignation four days after her brother, a senator, was jailed on charges of colluding with paramilitaries and the kidnapping of a potential political rival. The Supreme Court recommended that federal prosecutors investigate her father, a former provincial governor, federal lawmaker and agriculture minister, in the kidnapping case. President Alvaro Uribe appointed Fernando Araujo, who escaped from six-year rebel captivity six weeks earlier, to the Foreign Relations Ministry.

On 13 October 2007, 21 gold prospectors were killed when the sides of an open cast gold mine collapsed, causing a landslide of mud and rock. 16 of the victims were women. The mines in the region are often makeshift and safety regulations are not enforced, leading to frequent accidents.

In November 2007, President Chavez froze bilateral ties with Colombia; this followed the decision by Colombian President Uribe to end Mr Chavez's role as a hostage negotiator with Colombia's Farc rebels. President Uribe was annoyed by Sr. Chavez's disregard for the proper diplomatic channels, and his defiance of instructions not to be in direct contact with Colombia's army chief. In early December 2007, President Uribe offered to designate a limited safe area to enable talks to take place with Farc, aimed at exchanging rebel-held hostages for jailed rebels; however, the Farc want a larger zone in south-western Colombia to be demilitarised, a demand Mr Uribe rejected. Two hostages were released in December 2007. On 4th February 2008, hundreds of thousands of Colombians protested against the Farc in Bogota, and thousands more protested elsewhere in Colombia, and in almost 100 other cities around the world. Schools and businesses were closed in many cities, to allow workers to march. The anti-Farc movement was started through the networking website Facebook, and taken up by the media.

On 1st March 2008, Raul Reyes, a member of Farc's ruling secretariat, was killed with 16 other rebels, during an air raid by the Colombian air force on a rebel camp one mile over the border in Ecuador. The following day, Venezuelan President Chavez mobilised national troops on the border with Colombia, and closed the embassy in Bogota. Ecuador flew troops by helicopter towards the border area on the 3rd March. National police chief Oscar Naranjo accused both Ecuador and Venezuela of having ties with the Farc, saying that this information came from information found during the raid on the rebel camp in Ecuador. The following day, President Uribe said he would ask the International Criminal Court to bring genocide charges against President Chavez, accusing him of sponsoring and financing the Farc rebels. Venezuela denied the charge. Colombian officials claimed that a laptop found during the raid on the Farc camp in Ecuador held files indicating that Venezuela had given the rebels $300 million. Allegedly, evidence of plans to make a bomb using radioactive material was also found on the computer. The crisis was defused when the three leaders met at a Rio Group summit on 7th March. A 20-point declaration by the Organization of American States (OAS), including a promise by President Uribe that Colombia's forces would never again violate the territory of its neighbours, sealed the reconciliation.

On the 7th March 2008, the Colombian government announced the death of another senior commander of the Farc rebel group, Ivan Rios, who had been killed by his own men. It later emerged that the rebel who killed Sr. Rios was to be paid $2.5 million by the Colombian government. The government has made paying rewards to informants a key part of its fight against the left-wing rebels. Critics say the policy amounts to government approval for murder. On the 19th May, another leading commander of the rebels surrendered to the authorities; Nelly Avila Moreno, known as Karina, was blamed for a string of murders and abductions, and for extortion in the north-western Antioquia region. Karina was an example to the women in the rebel army, who make up more than a third of the ranks of Farc. On 24th May, the Farc confirmed the death of top commander and founder of the group, Manuel Marulanda, saying he died of a heart attack on the 26th March. The Farc announced that Marulanda would be replaced as overall commander by Alfonso Cano, regarded by some as the group's ideological leader.

On 3rd July 2008, French-Colombian politician Ingrid Betancourt and 14 other hostages were freed when the Farc rebels holding them were tricked into handing them over to Colombian soldiers posing as members of a non-government organisation. Ms. Betancourt had been held by Farc rebels for over six years; she had been campaigning for the presidency of Colombia when she was kidnapped. Three Americans and 11 members of the Colombian security forces were also rescued. The Farc still holds up to 700 people captive, over 40 of whom are high-profile hostages.

At the end of October, three generals, 11 colonels, four majors, a captain, a lieutenant, and seven non-commissioned officers were sacked; they are suspected of being involved in the deaths of 11 young men from Bogota, whose bodies were found in mass graves in the north-east of the country. Human Rights groups allege they were kidnapped or lured with the promise of work, then killed in combat zones to inflate army statistics on rebels killed. It is thought that hundreds of soldiers are under investigation in similar cases.

In early February 2009, Farc guerrillas released the politician Sigifredo Lopez whom they had held captive for almost seven years. His release came shortly after four members of the armed forces and a former governor were freed. Farc are believed to still be holding some 700

people for ransom. Mr Lopez was kidnapped in 2002 from Cali's state assembly, with eleven other politicians who were shot dead whilst in captivity. It is thought that the guerrillas are seeking to regain political relevancy with these unilateral releases.

At the beginning of March, Colombian security forces killed 10 members of Farc, and captured eight, in the central province of Cundinamarca. Among those captured was "El Negro Antonio", whom authorities had been seeking for over a decade. The operation forestalled Farc plans to reopen a movement corridor into the capital, Bogota.

In late July 2009, Sweden asked Venezuela to explain how Swedish-made anti-tank rocket launchers, sold to Venezuela in the 1980s, had ended up in the hands of Colombia's Farc rebels. Colombian troops had recovered the weapons in a raid on a Farc camp. Colombia has long claimed that Venezuela backs the left-wing rebels.

In February 2010 the Colombian constitutional court rejected a referendum which could have led to President Uribe running for a third term in office. The proposed vote would have amended the constitution to allow the president to stand for three terms.

In June 2010, three hostages held by FARC for 10 years were finally released. In the following September Farc increased its campaign of violence and senior Farc commander Mono Jojoy was killed by the Colombian army in an air strike. In February 2011 Farc released several hostages in what it said was a gesture of peace to the government.

In September 2011, a court sentenced a former head of the intelligence services, Jorge Noguera, to 25 years for collaborating with right-wing paramilitaries.

The government announced in November 2011 that the Farc leader Alfonso Cano had been killed. Farc said it would continue to fight. Later that month, four hostages were shot dead by their Farc captors as troops approached the camp where they were being held. One hostage survived. All were members of the security forces and had been held for between 12 and 14 years.

In May 2012, Farc rebels killed 12 Colombian soldiers in an ambush near the Venezuelan border.

In November 2012, Farc rebels declared a two month ceasefire against the backdrop of peace talks with the government which took place in Cuba. The ceasefire was still holding in May 2013 as talks continued although they stalled over the issue of land redistribution. The government has said that it will return millions of hectares of land to displaced peasants, but the rebels must put down their guns first.

Plan Colombia

It is estimated that Colombia is the source of around 80 per cent of the worldwide powder cocaine supply, as well as being a source of heroin. In an effort to combat the trafficking, the US backed the government's Plan Colombia financially, from 1999, contributing some US$3 billion of the US$7.5 billion costs over the first four years. The Plan aimed to eradicate coca crops, combat terrorism and drug-barons and improve the infrastructure, and hence the economy, of the country. Attacks conducted by illegally armed groups against rural towns decreased by 91 per cent from 2002 to 2005, and between 2002 and 2005 homicides fell by 37 per cent, victims of massacres by 63 per cent and kidnappings by 72 per cent. Aerial spraying of coca crops and cocaine and heroin led to an estimated 15 per cent reduction between 2001 and 2004, whilst opium poppy cultivation was estimated to have fallen by 68 per cent over the same period. Between 2004 and 2006, Colombian security forces seized 562 metric tons of cocaine, coca base, and heroin.

Terrorist groups in Colombia are engaged in narcotics production and trafficking; the FARC is believed to be responsible for more than half of the cocaine entering the United States.

In January 2006, 'Operation Macarena' was launched to eradicate coca plants and cocaine laboratories in the area of the Sierra Macarena National Park. However, the price and purity of the cocaine on sale in the USA suggests that the operation had little effect on supply.

In November 2008, a US Congressional report stated that, despite record aerial eradication, coca cultivation in Colombia had risen by 15 per cent between 2000 and 2006, and that Plan Colombia had failed to reach its target of halving drug production. The report also stated that the Plan had helped reduce Colombia's kidnapping and murder rates, and diminished the threat from left-wing rebels. The report concluded that aid should be trimmed due to the financial crisis. Despite Plan Colombia, the country remains the world's top cocaine producer and is reportedly the source of 90 per cent of the drug in the US. The UN reported that coca cultivation had increased by 27 per cent in 2007.

In April 2009, Colombian authorities arrested the country's most wanted drug lord, Daniel Rendon Herrera, aka "Don Mario". The government had offered a reward of up to $2m for information leading to his arrest. Daniel Rendon is accused of smuggling hundreds of tonnes of cocaine. He had allegedly offered his men almost $1,000 for each police officer they murdered.

Legislature

The bicameral Legislative Branch is composed of a 102-member Senate and a 161-member House of Representatives. Members of both chambers are chosen by direct vote of the electorate, for a four-year term, with at least two Representatives for each department. Congress meets in Bogotá every year for a session of at least 150 days.

Upper House

Senate, Capitolio Nacional 2 Piso, Santafé de Bogotá, Colombia. Tel: +57 1 283 8411, fax: +57 1 284 5560, URL: http://www.senado.gov.co/

Lower House
House of Representatives, Capitolio Nacional Edificio Nuevo de Congreso, Santafé de Bogotá, Colombia. Tel: +57 1 283 4666 / 243 0506, fax: +57 1 281 4323, URL: http://www.camara-de-representantes.gov.co/

Cabinet (as at June 2013)
Minister of Foreign Relations: Maria Angela Holguin (page 1443)
Minister of Finance and Public Credit: Mauricio Cardenas Santa Maria
Minister of Defence: Juan Carlos Pinzon Bueno
Minister of the Interior: Fernando Carrillo
Minister of Environment and Sustainable Development: Juan Gabriel Uribe
Minister of Culture: Mariana Garces Cordoba
Minister of Commerce, Industry and Tourism: Sergio Diaz Granados
Minister of Agriculture and Rural Development: Francisco de Paula Estupinan Heredia
Minister of Information and Communications: Diego Molana Vega
Minister of Education: Maria Fernanda Campo Savedra
Minister of Public Health: Alejandro Gaviria
Minister of Mines and Energy: Federico Renjifo
Minister of Transport: Cecelia Alvarez-Correa
Minister of Housing and Land Development: Luis Felipe Henao
Minister of Justice and Law: Ruth Stella Correa
Minister of Labour: Rafael Pardo Rueda
Minister of Sport: Andres Botero Phillipsborne

Ministries

Ministry of Agriculture and Rural Development, Avenida Jiménez No. 7-65, Santafé de Bogota. Tel: +57 1 334 1199, fax: +57 1 283 1285, URL: http://www.minagricultura.gov.co/
Ministry of Commerce, Industry and Tourism, Calle 28 No 13 A Bogotá, Colombia. Tel: +57 1 606 7676, fax: +57 1 696 7521, URL: http://www.mincomercio.gov.co/
Ministry of Communications, Edificio Murillo Toro, Carrera 7 & 8, Calles 12A & 13, Santafé de Bogotá, Colombia. Tel: +57 1 286 6911, fax: +57 1 286 1185, URL: http://www.mincomunicaciones.gov.co/
Ministry of Culture, Carrera 8 No. 8-09, Bogotá, Colombia. Tel: +57 1 342 4100, fax: +57 1 336 1007, URL: http://www.mincultura.gov.co/
Ministry of Economic Development, Carrera 13 No. 28-01, Santafé de Bogotá, Colombia. Tel: +57 1 287 4765, fax: +57 1 287 6025, URL: http://www.mindesa.gov.co/
Ministry of the Environment, Edificio Avianca, Calle 16, No. 6-66, Santafé de Bogota, Colombia. Tel: +57 1 336 1166, fax: 57 1 336 3984, URL: http://www.minambiente.gov.co/
Ministry of Finance and Public Credit, Carrera 7a, No. 6-45, Santafé de Bogotá, Colombia. Tel: +57 1 284 5400, fax: +57 1 284 5396
Ministry of Foreign Affairs, Palacio de San Carlos, Calle 10, No. 5-51, Santafé de Bogotá, Colombia. Tel: +57 1 282 7811, fax: +57 1 341 6777, URL: http://www.minrelext.gov.co/
Ministry of Foreign Trade, Calle 28 No. 13A - 15 Piso 7, Santafé de Bogotá. Tel: +57 1 286 9111 / 286 4600, fax: +57 1 283 6323
Ministry of Health, Calle 16, No. 7-39, Santafé de Bogotá, Colombia. Tel: +57 1 282 2851, fax: + 57 1 282 0003, URL: http://www.minsalud.gov.co/
Ministry of the Interior, Palacio Echeverry, Carrera 8a, No. 8-09, Santafé de Bogotá, Colombia. Tel: +57 1 284 0214, fax: +57 1 281 5884
Ministry of Justice and Law, Avenida Jiménez No. 8-89, Santafé de Bogotá, Colombia. Tel: +57 1 286 0211 / 286 5888 / 286 9711, fax: +57 1 281 6443
Ministry of Labour and Social Security, Carrera 7a No. 34-50, Santafé de Bogotá, Colombia. Tel: +57 1 287 7189, fax: +57 1 285 7091
Ministry of Mines and Energy, Centro Administrativo Nacional CAN, Santafé de Bogotá, Colombia. Tel: +57 1 222 4555, fax: +57 1 222 4680, URL: http://www.minminas.gov.co/
Ministry of National Defence, Avenida El Dorado Carrera 52 CAN, Santafé de Bogotá, Colombia. Tel: +57 1 266 9300, fax: +57 1 222 1874, URL: http://www.mindefensa.gov.co/
Ministry of National Education, Centro Administrativo Nacional CAN, Santafé de Bogotá, Colombia. Tel: +57 1 222 2800, fax: +57 1 222 4578, URL: http://www.mineducacion.gov.co/
Ministry of Transport, Avenida el Dorado, Centro Administrativo Nacional (CAN), Santafé de Bogotá. Tel: +57 1 324 0800, e-mail: mintrans@mintransporte.gov.co, URL: http://www.mintransporte.gov.co/

Political Parties

Colombian Conservative Party (PCC); Liberal Party (PL); National Integration Party (PIN); (PU, or Social National Unity Party, PUSN); Radical Change (CR); Alternative Democratic Pole; Colombian Green Party; Mira Movement

Elections

Presidentential elections took place on 28 May 2006 when Alvaro Uribe Velez was re-elected, winning a landslide victory with 62 per cent of the vote. A change to the constitution in 2004 allowed Mr Uribe to stand for a second term. Of the five other candidates, the closest rival, left-wing Sr. Carlos Gaviria Diaz, won 22 per cent of the vote. In February 2010 the Constitutional Court voted against the holding of a referendum on whether President Uribe should be able to stand for a third term.

The most recent presidential election was held on 30 May 2010. In the first round of voting the former defence minister Juan Manuel Santos of the U party just failed to gain a majority of the votes. A second round took place on 20 June when Juan Manuel Santos secured victory.

The most recent parliamentary election was held in March 2010. Parties supporting the president gained a majority in the 2010 legislative elections. The National Social Unity Party (PSUN or U party) became the largest party with 28 eight seats in Congress.

The two seats in the Senate reserved for the indigenous population were won by the Indigenous Social Alliance.

Gubernatorial and local elections took place in October 2011. Gustavo Petro, a former guerilla with the M-19 movement, was elected as mayor of the capital, Bogota.

Diplomatic Representation

Colombian Embassy, 2118 Leroy Place, NW, Washington DC 20008, USA. Tel: +1 202 387 8338, fax: +1 202 232 8643, e-mail: emwas@colombiaemb.org, URL: http://www.colombiaemb.org/
Ambassador: Carlos Urrutia
Colombian Embassy, Flat 3a, 3 Hans Crescent, London, SW1X 0LN, United Kingdom. Tel: +44 (0)20 7589 9177, fax: +44 (0)20 7581 1829, e-mail: mail@colombianembassy.co.uk, URL: http://www.colombianembassy.co.uk
Ambassador: Mauricio Rodriguez Munera
British Embassy, Carrera 9, No 76 - 49, Floor 8 and 9, Santafé de Bogotá, Colombia. Tel: +57 1 326 8300, fax: +57 1 326 8303 (Visa/Consular), e-mail: britain@cable.net.co, URL: http://ukincolombia.fco.gov.uk/en
Ambassador: Lindsay Croisdale-Appleby
US Embassy, Calle 22D Bis # 47-51 (Carrera 45 # 22D-45), Santafé de Bogotá, Colombia. Tel: +57 1 315 0811, fax: +57 1 315 2197, URL: http://bogota.usembassy.gov/
Ambassador: Michael McKinley (page 1475)
Permanent Mission of Colombia to the UN, 5th Floor, 140 East 57th Street, New York, 10022, USA. Tel: +1 212 355 7776, fax: +1 212 371 2813, e-mail: colombia@un.int, URL: http://www.colombiaun.org
Ambassador: Nestor Osorio Londono

LEGAL SYSTEM

Colombia's constitutional integrity is guaranteed by the Constitutional Court. The seven judges of this Court are elected by the Senate for a non-renewable period of eight years.

The judicial system comprises a Constitutional Court, Supreme Court of Justice, Council of State, the Higher Judiciary Council, and superior and municipal courts. The Supreme Court is composed of 24 justices selected for lifetime terms by justices already in office. The Supreme Court reviews state laws and and proposes reforms. It has original jurisdiction in impeachment trials and constitutional interpretation and appellate jurisdiction in ordinary judicial matters. The court is divided into four chambers - civil, criminal, labour and constitutional procedure.

In each judicial district, there is a superior court with three or more judges and a number of municipal courts. There are also special labour courts. In 1991, the government set up five regional jurisdictions to handle narcotics, terrorism, and police corruption cases in which anonymous judges and prosecutors handle the major trials of narcotics terrorists. The procedures in these courts have raised concerns over defendants' rights.

The government's record on human rights continues to improve; in 2008, the Supreme Court and prosecutor general's investigations of links between politicians and paramilitary groups implicated 70 representatives, 15 governors, and 31 mayors, many of whom were imprisoned by the end of the year. However, there have been recent reports of unlawful and extrajudicial killings, and insubordinate military collaboration with new illegal groups and paramilitaries who refuse to demobilize. Prisons are overcrowded and insecure, and there have been cases of torture and mistreatment of detainees. The judiciary is inefficient and subject to intimidation.

The death penalty was abolished in 1910.

President of the Supreme Court: Javier Zapata

Office of the Ombudsman, URL: http://www.defensoria.org.co/red/

LOCAL GOVERNMENT

The nation is divided into 32 departments, which are then subdivided into municipalities. There is also the Capital District, Santafé de Bogotá. The State Governors are elected by direct suffrage every three years. Local elections for governors, mayors, and members of provincial and municipal councils will be held throughout Colombia in October. At least 20 people were killed in the run up to October's elections.

Departments and their Capitals and Population

Department	Capital	Pop.
Amazonas	Leticia	37,764
Antioquia	Medellin	4,799,609
Arauca	Arauca	137,193
Atlantico	Barranquilla	1,667,500
Bolivar	Cartagena	1,439,291
Boyaca	Tunja	1,174,031
Caldas	Manizales	925,358
Caqueta	Florencia	311,464
Casanare	Yopal	158,149
Cauca	Popayan	979,231
Cesar	Valledupar	729,634
Choco	Quibdo	338,160
Cordoba	Monteria	1,088,087
Cundinamarca	Santafé de Bogotá	1,658,698
Guainia	Inirida	13,441
Guaviare	San Jose del Guaviare	57,884
Huila	Neiva	758,013
La Guajira	Rioacha	387,773
Magdalena	Santa Marta	882,571
Meta	Villavicencio	561,121

COLOMBIA

- continued

Nariño	Pasto	1,274,708
Norte de Santander	Cucuta	1,046,577
Putumayo	Mocoa	204,309
Quindio	Armenio	435,018
Risaralda	Pereira	744,974
San Andres y Providencia	San Andres	50,094
Santander	Bucaramanga	1,598,688
Sucre	Sincelejo	624,463
Tolima	Ibague	1,150,080
Valle	Cali	3,333,150
Vaupes	Mitu	18,235
Vichada	Puerto Carreño	30,336

AREA AND POPULATION

Area
Colombia lies in the far north-west of South America with the Caribbean Sea to the north and the Pacific Ocean to the west. It has borders with Venezuela and Brazil to the east and Ecuador and Peru to the south and is connected to Central America by its border with Panama. Three mountain chains (part of the Andes) run southwest to northeast; there are high moorlands in the centre of the country and flat grasslands to the east. The total area of Colombia is 1,138,910 sq. km. The climate is tropical on coast and plains but cooler in highlands. The physical geography means that large areas are sparsely populated.

To view a map, please consult http://www.lib.utexas.edu/maps/cia08/colombia_sm_2008.gif

Population
Colombia's population was estimated to be 45.295 million in 2010, with annual population growth rate of 1.5 per cent. The median age of the inhabitants is 27 years. An estimated 62 per cent of Colombia's inhabitants are aged between 15 and 60 years, with 29 per cent aged up to 14 years, and 9 per cent aged 60 years and over.

Colombia is the third-most populous country in Latin America and thirty cities have a population exceeding 100,000 people. Approximately 74 per cent of the population live in urban areas. Major cities are Santafé de Bogotá (7.1 million inhabitants), Cali (1.8m), Medellin (1.8m) and Barranquilla (1.4m). The eastern lowlands, on the other hand, constitute about 54 per cent of Colombia's area, but have a population density of two persons per sq. mile. Spanish is the official language of Colombia. Colombia's main ethnic group is mestizo (58 per cent of the population), followed by white (20 per cent), mulatto (14 per cent), black (4 per cent), black-Amerindian (3 per cent), and Amerindian (1 per cent).

Births, Marriages, Deaths
The birth rate for 2010 is estimated at 19.7 births per 1,000 inhabitants, and the death rate is 4.4 deaths per 1,000 people. Infant mortality, according to 2010 estimates, is 17 deaths per 1,000 live births, whilst the total fertility rate is 2.4 children born per woman. Average life expectancy is 76 (73 years for men and 80 years for women). Healthy life expectancy is 66 years. (Source: http://www.who.int, World Health Statistics 2012)

Public Holidays 2014
1 January: New Year's Day
6 January: Epiphany*
19 March: St. Joseph's Day*
17 April: Maundy Thursday
18 March: Good Friday
22 April: Easter Monday
29 May: Ascension Day
1 May: Labour Day
19 June: Corpus Christi
20 July: Independence Day
15 August: Feast of the Assumption
13 October: Dia de la Raza (Columbus Day)*
1 November: All Saints Day
11 November: Independence of Cartagena*
8 December: Immaculate Conception
25 December: Christmas Day
*If these holidays do not fall on a Monday then they are observed on the following Monday.

EMPLOYMENT

Colombia's labour force (over the age of 12 and excluding armed forces and conscripts) in 2006 was 20.14 million, representing around 46.1 per cent of the total population. Of these, 17.6 million were employed.

The estimated unemployment rate had been moving down, from a high of 20 per cent in 2000, to 15.1 per cent in 2002, 13.6 per cent in 2004 and 11.8 per cent in December 2005. In 2006, it had increased slightly to 12.7 per cent, before falling to an average of 7.0 per cent in 2007 and 7.7 per cent in 2008. Employment by economic sector is shown below:

Employment by Economic Activity, 2008

Sector	No. of Employees
Agriculture, hunting and forestry	3,054,500
Mining and quarrying	149,100
Manufacturing	2,335,600
Electricity, gas and water supply	78,700
Construction	878,500

- continued

Wholesale and retail trade, Repairs of vehicles and personal goods; Hotels and restaurants	4,605,300
Transport, storage and communications	1,467,400
Financial services	219,600
Real estate, renting and business activities	1,146,800
Health and social work	3,463,300
Not classifiable by economic activity	26,900
Total	**17,425,700**

Source: Copyright © International Labour Organization (ILO Dept. of Statistics, http://laborsta.ilo.org)

BANKING AND FINANCE

Currency
One Colombian Peso (Col$, COP) = 100 centavos

The financial centre is Bogotá.

GDP/GNP, Inflation, National Debt
Colombia is a free market economy, largely based on the services sector, which contributes 46 per cent of the country's GDP, followed by industry and mining (22 per cent), and agriculture (7.1 per cent).

Following economic reforms implemented by President Uribe, Colombia's economy has improved in recent years and has been growing for the last ten years; GDP (current prices) was US$285 billion in 2009 with a growth rate of 5 per cent. GDP was an estimated US$325 billion in 2011, in a growth rate of 5.9 per cent. Per capita GDP was estimated at US$7,150. The sustained growth of the Colombian economy has been attributed to a stable currency, maintaining low inflation and increased domestic security as well as to increases in petrol prices and trade liberalisation. Chile has many free trade agreements.

Since economic recovery began in 2003 inflation has been relatively stable, falling from 7.1 per cent in 2003 to 5.7 per cent in 2004 and to an estimated 5.1 per cent in 2005. It rose to approximately 7.9 per cent in 2008 before falling to 4 per cent in 2009. In 2011, it was estimated to be 5.5 per cent.

Colombia's total foreign debt was US$67 billion in 2011, approximately 20 per cent of GDP.

Foreign Investment
In 1996 the US stopped most of its investment when it decertified Colombia's programme of compliance with international drug controls. US investment subsequently dropped from 70 per cent of the total at the beginning of 1996 to approximately 25 per cent at the end of 1996. However, in August 2000, President Clinton gave his support to President Pastrana's 'Plan Colombia', set up to target the drug-traffickers, destroy the coca crop, and develop the economy. Between 2002 and 2006, new foreign direct investment in Colombia has grown by 294 per cent, totalling US$6.3 billion in 2006. Most of the new investment is in the manufacturing, mining, and petroleum sectors. Foreign investment in 2010 amounted to was US$6.8 billion.

Balance of Payments / Imports and Exports
In 2010, exports earned an estimated US$39 billion. Oil is a major commodity, generating 28 per cent of total export income in 2003. Coffee, coal, nickel, emeralds and gold are also major contributors, together with cut flowers, sugar and fruits. Principal export destinations in 2010 were the US, EU, China and Ecuador.

In 2010, imports cost an estimated US$41 billion. Major import goods are transport and industrial equipment, grains, mineral products, chemicals, consumer goods and metal and rubber products as well as oil and gas industry equipment. Import trading partners in 2010 were the US, China, Mexico, Brazil and Germany.

Colombia is a member of ALADI and the Andean community, organisations which aim to increase trade and economic co-operation amongst countries in the region. It is also seeking entry to the North American Free Trade Agreement (NAFTA), which at present includes the US, Canada, and Mexico. Colombia signed several free trade agreements including Canada, South Korea, Japan, Chile, Mexico, China, Venezuela & the EU. The US-Colombia Free Trade Agreement is due to be implemented in 2012.

Central Bank
Banco de la Republica de Colombia, Piso 5°, Carrera 7 14-78, Bogotá, Colombia. Tel: +57 1 3430190 / 1 3360200, fax: +57 1 2861686 / 1 3347128 URL: http://www.banrep.gov.co Director General: José Dario Uribe Escobar (page 1530)

Chambers of Commerce
Cámara de Comercio de Bogotá, URL: http://www.ccb.org.co/
Cámara de Comercio de Medellin, URL: http://www.caramed.org.co
Cámara de Comercio Colombia Británica, URL: http://www.colombobritanica.com
British-Colombian Chamber of Commerce, URL: http://www.britishandcolombianchamber.com

MANUFACTURING, MINING AND SERVICES

Primary and Extractive Industries
Colombia is rich in mineral wealth, with oil the country's top export product, accounting for 28 per cent of export revenues and ten per cent of government revenues in 2003. Coal is Colombia's second largest export product. Colombia is also rich in precious metals; gold production accounts for 1.5 per cent of world output and Colombia is the world's leading producer of emeralds, providing over 90 per cent of global yield; however, production fell

from 116.3 million carats in 2005 to 112.7 million carats in 2006. Platinum and silver are also produced and the country has large reserves of iron ore. Ferronickel, silver and platinum are also mined in Colombia.

Colombia had estimated proven oil reserves of 1.9 billion barrels in 2012, the fifth-largest in South America. The country produced an estimated 939,900 barrels per day (bbl/d) of oil in 2011, up from 529,000 bbl/d in 2004. This was against the recent trend of declining production due to the depletion of mature fields, a lack of sizable new reserve discoveries and pipeline sabotage by guerrillas. The country used 298,000 barrels per day in 2011, and exported the remaining, the bulk going to the United States. Colombia's crude refining capacity was an estimated 291,000 barrels per day at the beginning of January 2012.

The national oil company is Empresa Colombiana de Petróleos (Ecopetrol). In an effort to attract more foreign investment in the oil industry, Colombia has passed legislation aimed at the relief of royalties, faster environmental licensing, and a reduction in the state oil company Ecopetrol's involvement in exploration and development. The National Agency for Hydrocarbons was created and now administers all exploration and production contracts. Foreign investment was adversely affected by the battle against the illegal drugs industry; however, recent improvements in security have led to a renewed interest by international oil companies. Kidnappings in the country fell by 60 percent in 2004, and there was a substantial decline in the number of attacks against oil infrastructure. According to the Colombian central bank, the oil sector received US$2.86 billion in foreign direct investment in 2010.

In June 2010, Colombia's National Hydrocarbons Agency (ANH) organised a bidding round, which included 228 exploratory blocks. Some of the blocks featured known hydrocarbon-rich areas, there were also blocks in the frontier regions and in offshore blocks in the Caribbean Sea and the Pacific Ocean. About a third of the block received licences and a further bidding round took place in 2012. Empresa Colombiana de Petróleos (Ecopetrol), URL: http://www.ecopetrol.com.co

At the beginning of January 2011 Colombia had estimated natural gas reserves of 4.0 trillion cubic feet. Production has risen in recent years, from an estimated 218 billion cubic feet in 2003 to 398 billion cubic feet in 2010. The country used all natural gas internally. Plans have been outlined to extend the gas grid into Ecuador and Panama and, in time, to the rest of Central America. At present, however, Colombia does not have sufficient gas production to enable the project to go ahead. Colombia's natural gas industry is controlled by the state-owned Ecopetrol, the Energy and Gas Regulatory Commission (CREG), and the state-owned Empresa Colombiana de Gas (Ecogas)

Colombia had recoverable coal reserves of 7.4 million short tons in 2006, the second largest in Latin America (behind Brazil) and the 16th largest in the world, accounting for around one per cent of the total global annual production. Most of the coal is high-quality bituminous coal but there is also a small amount of metallurgical coal. In 2010, Colombia produced 81.9 million tons of coal. Colombia's coal is mainly found in the Guajira peninsula on the Atlantic coast. The Cerrejón Norte mine is the largest of its kind in Latin America and one of the world's largest open-pit coal mines. It contains more than 1,000 million tons of coal and produces over 1 million metric tons per month.

In terms of revenue, coal is Colombia's second largest export (after oil). Very little is consumed nationally, (5.5 million short tons in 2010) and Colombia was the fifth largest coal exporter in the world in 2003. Currently, Columbia exports to the USA, South America and Europe, but the government is planning the infrastructure to allow exports to Asia, China is a growing market taking seven per cent of Colombia's coal exports in 2010. In January 2004 the state-owned coal company, Carbones de Colombia (Carbocol), was sold to the foreign-owned Carbones del Cerrejon consortium, which includes South Africa's Anglo-American, the UK/Australian BHP Billiton, and Switzerland's Glencore.

Energy
Colombia's total energy consumption was estimated at 1.338 quadrillion Btu in 2009, up from 1.203 quadrillion Btu in 2003. Fuel share of energy consumption in 2004 is estimated as follows: oil, 45 per cent; hydroelectricity, 31 per cent; natural gas 17 per cent; coal, seven per cent.

Colombia had an estimated 13.5 gigawatts of installed electricity generating capacity in 2010 provided by around 90 power plants. In the same year, Colombia generated 55.2 billion kilowatthours of electricity while consuming 45.3 billion kwh. Most of Colombia's electricity generation (76 percent) comes from hydroelectricity, with conventional thermal (mostly coal and natural gas) and other renewables making up the remainder.

The privatisation of the electricity industry began in 1996 and currently the private sector owns 40 per cent of distribution and 50 per cent of generation capacity.

Manufacturing
Industry contributes over 36 of GDP. The main industries are textiles and garments, chemicals, petrochemicals, metal products, cement, cardboard containers, plastic resins and manufactures, beverages, wood products, pharmaceuticals, machinery, electrical equipment. Colombia imports a substantial amount of raw materials for use in industry.

Services
Within the services sector, financial services contribute around 17 per cent towards GDP and commerce accounts for 11 per cent; transportation and communications services contribute almost 8 per cent, whilst government, personal and other services account for over 18 per cent. Electricity, gas, and water supply contributes almost three per cent.

Agriculture
Agriculture is an important sector of the Colombian economy, contributing just over 7 per cent of GDP and employing around 18 per cent of the workforce. Approximately 8.2 per cent of the land is cultivated. With a large variety of soils and climates, the country produces a wide range of crops both for the home market and for export. Major cash crops are cotton,

sugar, flowers and bananas; however, the main agricultural product and export commodity is coffee. Colombian coffee has the highest selling price of all coffees in the international market area and apprximately two million Colombians make their living from coffee farming.

Agricultural Production in 2010

Produce	Int. $'000	Tonnes
Indigenous cattle meat	2,526,178	935,145
Cow milk, whole, fresh	2,246,835	75,00,000
Indigenous chicken meat	1,425,589	1,000,830
Sugar cane	1,238,533	38,500,000
Rice, paddy	652,761	2,412,220
Bananas	572,933	2,034,340
Coffee, green	552,359	514,128
Plantains	522,645	2,815,050
Hen eggs, in shell	423,338	510,421
Citrus fruit, nes	329,999	730,000
Palm oil	327,641	753,100
Potatoes	306,030	2,121,880

*unofficial figures
Source: http://faostat.fao.org/site/339/default.aspx Food and Agriculture Organization of the United Nations, Food and Agricultural commodities production

There are over 52.5 million hectares of forest but these have not been exploited to any extent. The trees are mostly hardwoods, unsuitable for building purposes, but a certain amount of lumber is produced for cabinet making. Various drugs and dye woods as well as rubber are collected from the forests.

COMMUNICATIONS AND TRANSPORT

Travel Requirements
Visitors from the USA, Canada, Australia and the EU require a passport valid for six months, and a return ticket. They do not require a visa for visits of under 180 days with the exception of the following people: Bulgarians, Estonians, Latvians, Poles and Slovenians. Visitors are issued with an entry stamp on arrival which may be valid for 30, 60 or 90 days; extensions for up to a further 120 days are available from the Department of Administration and Security in Colombia.

Nationals not referred to above are advised to contact the embassy to check visa requirements.

National Airlines
Avianca (Aerovias Nacionales de Colombia), URL: http://www.avianca.com.co
Aerolineas Centrales de Colombia (ACES Colombia), Calle 49, No 50-21, Piso 34, Ed del Cafe, Medellin 6503, Antioquia, AA6503, Colombia. Tel: +57 4 251 7500, fax: +57 4 251 1677
SAM Colombia (Sociedad Aeronautica de Medellin Consolidada), Apartado Aereo 1085, Calle 45-211, Piso 21, Medellin, Colombia. Tel: +57 4 251 5544, fax: +57 4 251 0711
Intercontinental Colombia - Intercontinental de Aviación, Avenida Eldorado, Entrada No.2, Interior 6, Santafé de Bogotá, Colombia. Tel: +57 1 413 8888, fax: +57 1 413 9753
AeroRepublica Colombia, CRA 10, No 27-51, Ofc 303, Terminal Aereo Simon de Bolivar Apto Eldorado, Santafé de Bogotá, Colombia. Tel: +57 1 342 7221, fax: +57 1 283 1680
ATC Airlines - Aero Transcolombiana de carga, Terminal de Carga International, Bogotá, AA81001, Colombia. Tel: +57 1 414 8070, fax: +57 1 414 5431

International Airports
There are over 900 airports in Colombia, but only 103 have paved runways, and two have runways over 3,047 metres. The main airports are Eldorado, Bogotá; Alfonso Bonilla Aragon, Cali; Rionegro, Medellin; Matecaña, Pereira; and Cartago.

There are two heliports.

Railways
The Colombian National Railways (a state owned enterprise) operates a unified network of lines totalling 3,386 km. This system has access to the Pacific at Buenaventura and to the Atlantic at Santa Marta and links all of the major regions of the country. Owing to the difficulties in maintaining track in mountainous terrain, financial losses and competition from road transport, the railways have been in decline since 1967. Since 1986, only one long-distance passenger route has been in operation, from Santafé de Bogotá to Santa Marta.

Roads
Recent estimates show Colombia to have some 112,988 km of roads, of which about 16,270 km are paved. There are bus services which link Colombia with Venezuela and Ecuador. Vehicles are driven on the right.

Ports and Harbours
The main ports are Barranquilla, Buenaventura, Cartagena, Leticia, Puerto Bolivar, San Andres, Santa Marta, Tumaco and Turbo.

HEALTH

The health sector was reformed in the 1990s and Law 100 of 1993 established a social security system, to ensure universal health coverage through a mix of contributory and subsidised health schemes, using both the public and private sectors. By the end of 2004, 14.7 million people were covered by the contributory scheme and 15.4 million under the subsidised programme. Total expenditure on health in 2009 was equivalent to 7.6 per cent of its GDP, equating to US$392 per capita. General government expenditure accounts for

STATES OF THE WORLD

71.7 per cent of the total expenditure on health. Social security expenditure makes up 70.1 per cent of government expenditure. Private expenditure accounts for 28.9 per cent of total health expenditure. Over 48.6 per cent of private expenditure on health is made up of private pre-paid plans.

Recent figures show that there are 4,834 public hospitals and 407 private hospitals. According to the latest WHO figures, in 2005-10, there were 7,198 doctors (1.5 per 10,000 population), 30,119 nurses and midwives (6.2 per 10,000 population), and 44,858 dentists (9.2 per 10,000 population). There are an estimated 10 hospital beds per 10,000 population) .

An estimated 0.7 per cent of the adult population (190,000) live with HIV/AIDS and 3,600 have died of the disease to date. The infant mortality rate in 2009 was 17 per 1,000 live births and the child mortality rate (probability of dying before age five) 19 per 1,000 live births. The main causes of childhood deaths (2010) are: prematurity (21 per cent), diarrhoea (4 per cent), pneumonia (10 per cent), birth asphyxia (8 per cent) and congenital abnormalities (21 per cent). Approximately 12.7 per cent of children aged under five are classified as stunted for their age.

In 2008, 99 per cent of the urban population and 77 per cent of the rural population had access to improved drinking water. In the same year, 81 per cent of the urban population and 55 per cent of the rural population had access to improved sanitation. In 2010, 92 per cent of the population had access to improved drinking water and 77 per cent had access to improved sanitation. (Source: http://www.who.int, World Health Statistics 2012)

EDUCATION

Pre-school Education
Pre-school or kindergarten education lasts for two years, and around 41 per cent of children attend.

Primary/Secondary Education
Primary education is free. Primary education lasts for five years, and 87 per cent of the relevant age group was enrolled in 2007. The pupil/teacher ratio at this level was 28 to one. Secondary education lasts for six years, and in 2007, 67 per cent of the relevant age group was registered. The Plan Colombia subsidises people who live in poverty to keep their children in school.

Higher Education
There are 235 higher education institutions, including 13 state universities. The National University of Colombia is based in Bogotá. The capital has 11 other universities. In 2007, 32 per cent of the relevant age group was enrolled.

The adult literacy rate was estimated to be 92.7 per cent in 2007, rising to 98 per cent among the 15-24 age group. The rate in rural areas is lower, at around 70 per cent. In 2007, 12.6 per cent of government spending went on education. (Source: UNESCO, UIS)

RELIGION

The majority of Colombians (82 per cent) are Roman Catholic. Approximate 10.8 per cent are Protestants.

Bishop's Conference (Conferencia Episcopal de Colombia), URL: http://www.cec.org.co
President: Monseñor Luis Augusto Castro Quiroga

Colombia has a religious liberty rating of 5 on a scale of 1 to 10 (10 is most freedom). (Source: World Religion Database)

COMMUNICATIONS AND MEDIA

The broadcast medi is part state-owned and part privately owned. Television is the most popular medium in Colombia. Journalists and broadcasters face threats from various sources including guerillas, drug traffickers and corrupt politicians. Several journalists have been killed for reporting on drug-related issues.

Newspapers
El Tiempo, national, URL: http://www.eltiempo.com
El Espectador, URL: http://www.elespectador.com/elespectador
El Colombiano, URL: http://www.elcolombiano.com
El Espacio, URL: http://www.elespacio.com.co

Broadcasting
There are over 500 radio stations in the country and around 60 television stations. Local TV channels cover the departments of Antioquia, Atlántico, Boyacá, Bolívar, Caldas, Cauca, Cundinamarca, Huila, Magdalena, Santander, Tolima and Valle. Senal Colombia is a state run broadcaster, URL: http://www.senalcolombia.tv

Telecommunications
Colombia has an estimated 6.8 million telephone main lines and 41 million mobile phones (2006). There were an estmated 17 million internet users in 2008.

ENVIRONMENT

Major environmental issues include air pollution in major towns caused by vehicle emissions, soil damaged by pesticides, and deforestation due to road construction and development.

Carbon emissions in 2010 from the consumtion of fossil fuels was 72.3 million metric tons, an increase on the 2005 figure of 58.8 million metric tons. (Source: EIA)

Colombia is a party to the following international environmental agreements: Antarctic Treaty, Biodiversity, Climate Change, Climate Change-Kyoto Protocol, Desertification, Endangered Species, Hazardous Wastes, Marine Life Conservation, Ozone Layer Protection, Ship Pollution, Tropical Timber 83, Tropical Timber 94, and Wetlands. It has signed, but not ratified: the Law of the Sea.

SPACE PROGRAMME

The Colombian Space Commission was set up in 2006. It is responsible for the development of space technology and communication satellites. It also works in the observation of the country's natural resources.
Colombian Space Commission (CSC), URL: http://www.cce.gov.co

COMOROS
Union of the Comoros
Union des Comores

Capital: Moroni (Population estimate: 30,000)

Head of State: Ikililou Dhoinine (President) (page 1415)

National Flag: Four equal horizontal bars of yellow, white, red and blue, with a green triangle to the hoist superimposed with a white crescent and four five-pointed white stars arranged vertically between the points of the crescent. The four stars represent the four main islands: Mwali, Njazidja, Nzwani, and Mayotte (this last being claimed by the Comoros from France)

CONSTITUTION AND GOVERNMENT

Constitution
Previously an administrative region of Madagascar, the archipelago was given the status of an Overseas Territory with administrative and financial autonomy on 1 January 1947.

On 6 July 1975 the territory declared itself independent and in November 1975 the Comoros State was accepted into the United Nations. The French Parliament adopted a law on 31 December 1975 which recognised the independence of the islands of Grande Comore, Anjouan and Moheli. In a referendum in 1976 the inhabitants of Mayotte cast 99.4 per cent of their votes in favour of the islands remaining a part of the French Republic.

On 1 October 1978 the populations of Anjouan, Grande Comore and Moheli voted in a referendum to accept a new constitution, making the Comoros a federal Islamic republic. Ahmed Abdallah, the first President, was assassinated in November 1989. In accordance with the Constitution, Mohamed Said Djohar, who had been President of the Supreme Court, took over as interim Head of State and was confirmed in office by presidential election held in March 1990.

On 30 April 1999 Assoumani Azzali, the Army Chief of Staff, seized power in a bloodless coup and announced a timetable to create a union giving each of the three islands autonomy, with a president to be inaugurated in April 2000. This would lead to a Union of Comoran Islands replacing the Islamic Republic of the Comoros.

A referendum was held on 17 March 2002 when the final version of the new constitution was agreed by Moheli (re-named Mwali) and Anjouan (re-named Nzwani), but rejected by the voters of Grand Comore (re-named Ngazidja). However, elections for the new president of the Union and for the presidents of the three islands went ahead in March and April 2002. The islands' name was changed from the Federal Islamic Republic of the Comoros to the Union of the Comoros.

Under the terms of the 2002 Constitution the head of state is the president, who is elected from each of the three islands in turn for a term of four years. Each island also has its own president, who serves as head of the island government, as well as its own assembly. A referendum was held in May 2009 on various changes to the constitution which would have the effect of all the islands holding elections at the same time. Each island will also have a governor rather than a president. The term of the president was also extended to 2011.

To consult the full constitution (in French), please visit: http://www.beit-salam.km/article.php3?id_article=34

International Relations

Comoros has an Islamic culture, and enjoys close links with the Gulf states. It is a member of the League of Arab States and OIC. China maintains a resident Embassy in the Comoros, and in November 2005 wrote off all Comoros' US$5 million debt.

The government has long argued for the return of Mayotte to Comoran control, but the people of Mayotte prefer to remain an overseas department of France.

Recent Events

Elections for the Island Presidencies took place in June 2007. Mohamed Ali Said and Mohamed Abdouloihabi were elected Presidents of Mwali and Ngazidja respectively, but the presidency of Anjouan remained in dispute; the federal government appointed Dhoihirou Halidi to office, but Col. Mohammed Bacar, the previous incumbent, refused to stand down. In March 2008, Comoron and African Union troops recaptured the island and Colonel Bacar fled to the French-run island of Mayotte. The Comoran government and the AU asked France to extradite him.

The presidency of Comoros rotates between the presidents of the three islands. The current President Ahmed Abdallah Mohamed Sambi is from Anjouan and should be succeeded by the president from Moheli, however a referendum held in May 2009 approved a change to the constitution to allow President Sambi to serve until 2011.

In June 2009 a plane crashed off the coast of Comoros killing all but one of the 153 passengers and crew.

Legislature

Under the terms of the 2002 Constitution each of the islands has a local parliament. The Union parliament is composed of 33 members, 18 elected through universal adult suffrage and five appointed by each of the three local parliaments. Members are elected for a five year term.

Cabinet (as at June 2013)

Vice President, Minister for Production, Environment, Energy, Industry and Handicrafts: Fouad Ben Mohadji

Vice President, Minister of Finance, Economy, Budget for Investment and Trade, Minister in charge of Privatisation: Mohamed Ali Soilihi

Vice President, Minister for Physical Planning, Urban Affairs and Housing: Nourdine Bourhane

Minister of Foreign Relations and Co-operation, Francophone and Arab Affairs: Mohamed Bakri ben Abdoulfatah Charif

Minister of Justice, Institutional Reforms, Islamic Affairs, Human Rights and Keeper of the Seals: Dr Anliane Ahmed

Minister of Posts and Telecommunications, Promotion of New Information Technology and Communication, Transport and Tourism: Mouhidine Bastami

Minister of National Education, Research, Culture and the Arts, Minister in charge of Youth and Sport: Mohammed Issimaila

Minister of Health, Solidarity, Social Cohesion and Promotion of Gender Equality: Dr Moinafouraha Ahmed

Minister of Employment, Labour, Professional Training and Women's Enterprises, Government Spokesperson: Siti Kassim

Minister of Interior, Information and Decentralization, Relations with Institutions: Abdallah Hamada

Governors of the Islands (as at June 2013)

Governor of Moheli: Mohamed Ali Said
Governor of Nzwani: Anissi Chamsidine
Governor of Ngazidja: Mouigni Bakara Said Soilihi

Ministries

Office of the President, PO Box 521, Moroni, Comoros. Tel: +269 774 4808, fax: +269 744 8821, URL: http://www.beit-salam.km

Office of the Prime Minister, B.P. 1028 Moroni, Comoros. Tel: +269 744412 / 744400, fax: +269 744432

Ministry of Agriculture, Fishing, Environment, Energy, Industry and Handicrafts, BP 474, Moroni, Comoros. Tel: +269 774 4630, fax: +269 774 4630

Ministry of Foreign Relations and Co-operation, Francophone and Arab Affairs, BP 428, Moroni, Comoros. Tel: +269 774 4101, fax: +269 774 1111

Ministry of Justice, Islamic Affairs, Institutional Reforms and Relations with Parliament, Moroni, Comoros. Tel: +269 774 4200, fax: +269 774 4668

Ministry of Finance, Budget and Privatisation, B.P. 324, Moroni, Comoros. Tel: +269 744161, fax: +269 744140

Ministry of Transport and Tourism, BP 97, Moroni, Comoros. Tel: +269 774 4242, fax: +269 774 4241

Ministry of Health and Promotion of Gender Equality, BP 42, Moroni, Comoros. Tel: +269 773 2277

Ministry of National Education and Research, BP 73, Moroni, Comoros. Tel: +269 774 4185, fax: +269 774 4180. e-mail: coordi-education3@snpt.km

Ministry of Economy and Commerce, Moroni, Comoros. Tel: +269 730951, fax: +269 731981

Ministry of the Interior and Decentralisation, B.P. 686, Moroni, Comoros. Tel: +269 744666, fax: +269 744668

Ministry of Equipment and Energy, Moroni, Comoros. Tel: +269 744500

Ministry of Culture, Youth and Sports, Moroni, Comoros. Tel: +269 744044

Ministry of Information, Moroni, Comoros.

Ministry of Industry, Labour and Mineral Research, PO Box 521, Moroni, Comoros. Tel: +269 744540

Political Parties

Political groups are based on personal loyalties to certain leaders. In the last election, the main groupings were:

Convention pour la renaissance des Comores (CRC), supporting former President Assoumani.

Rassemblement National pour le Developpement (RND), loose alliance of parties formed at the 2004 elections to oppose the CRC.

Elections

Assoumanai Azali, who came to power in 1999 after a coup, resigned the presidency in 2002 to call an election. The first presidential elections for the new Union were held on 17 March and 14 April 2002 and were won by Assoumani Azali, who was sworn in on 31 May.

A presidential election was held in May 2006; the Muslim cleric Ahmed Abdallah Mohamed Sambi, from Anjouan, won 58 per cent of the vote, and oversaw the first peaceful change of power since independence. The most recent election took place in December 2010, Ikililou Dhoinine from the island of Mwali, was elected.

Elections to the Union parliament took place on 18-25 April 2004 and elections to the island legislatures took place on 14 and 21 March 2004. The elections were held under the 2002 constitution. Supporters of the islands presidents won more votes than supporters of the federal president, thus enabling them to block legislation. The New Assembly was inaugurated on 4 June 2004. President Azali dissolved his government on 9 June and a new coalition government was named on 13 July 2004. Following changes to the constitution, legislative elections were postponed.

The most recent parliamentary elections took place in December 2009, supporter of President Sambi represented by the Presidential Movement group, won 20 of the 24 directly elected seats in the Assembly of the Union.

Elections for the Island Presidencies took place on the 10th and 24th of June 2007. Mohamed Ali Said and Mohamed Abdoulohabi were elected Presidents of Mwali and Ngazidja respectively. The presidency of Anjouan remained in dispute; the federal government appointed Dhoihirou Halidi to office, but the previous incumbent, Col. Mohammed Bacar, remained the self-proclaimed President until March 2007, when troops, backed by the African Union, recaptured the island. Following changes to the constitution, the presidents of the islands became governors.

Diplomatic Representation

US Embassy, (Staff resident in Madagascar), URL: http://www.antananarivo.usembassy.gov
Charge d'Affaires: Eric M. Wong
British Embassy. The British High Commission in Mauritius has responsibility for Comoros. British High Commission, Les Cascades Building, Edith Cavell Street, Port Louis, Mauritius. Tel: +230 202 9400, fax: +230 202 9408, URL: http://ukinmauritius.fco.gov.uk/en
Ambassador: Nick Leake (page 1461)
Comoros Embassy, 420 E 50th St. New York, NY 10022, USA. Tel: +1 212 972 8010, fax: +1 212 983 4712
Ambassador: Roubani Kaambi
Permanent Representative of the Union of the Comoros to the United Nations and Ambassador to the US, 866 United Nations Plaza, Suite 418, New York, NY 10017, USA. Tel: +1 212 750 1637, fax: +1 212 750 1657, 715 0699, e-mail: comoros@un.int, URL: http://www.un.int/comoros/
Ambassador: Roubani Kaambi

LEGAL SYSTEM

According to the Constitution, the Comorian judicial system is independent from the executive and legislature. The Comoros law comprises both the Islamic and French law. The President chairs the Higher Council of the Magistracy. Village elders or civilian courts settle most disputes. The Supreme Court is the highest court in the Comoros, and is composed of two members appointed by the president, two elected by the Federal Assembly, one elected by the Council of each island; the remaining members are former presidents of the union. The Supreme Court acts as a Constitutional Council in resolving constitutional questions and supervising presidential elections. As High Court of Justice, the Supreme Court also arbitrates in cases where the government is accused of malpractice.

The Union government generally respects the human rights of its citizens, but there are poor prison conditions, official corruption and restrictions on freedom of movement, press, and religion. Comoros retains the death penalty. The last reported execution was in 1997.

LOCAL GOVERNMENT

Each of the three islands (Njazidja, Nzwani, and Mwali) is regarded as autonomous, having its own president, who serves as head of the island government. Administrative power is given to a Governor and a Council. Each Governor is appointed by the President and each Council consists of the mayors of the communes. There are also four municipalities: Domoni, Fomboni, Moroni, and Moutsamoudou.

AREA AND POPULATION

Area

The Comoros archipelago consists of the mountainous islands of Nzwani (formerly Anjouan), Ngazidja (formerly Grande Comore) and Mwali (formerly Moheli), and is situated about 310 miles from Madagascar. The total area of the islands forming the archipelago is about 2,166 sq. km. Whilst Mayotte (374 sq. km) is geographically counted as part of the archipelago, politically it is considered a department of France.

The climate is tropical, and temperatures average 25°C (coastal) and 22°C (highlands). The hot and rainy season is from November-April. There are regular cyclones, and the Karthala volcano on Ngazidja erupted in August 2003, in April 2005, and again in November 2005.

COMOROS

To view a map, visit: http://www.un.org/Depts/Cartographic/map/profile/comoros.pdf

Population
The Union had an estimated population of 735,000 in 2010, with an annual growth rate of 2.7 per cent. The majority of the population (53 per cent) is aged between 15 and 60 years, with 43 per cent aged under 15 years, and 4 per cent aged 60 years or over. The median age is 19 years. Approximately 28 per cent of the population lives in urban areas.

Main ethnic groups are Antalote, Cafre, Makoa, Oimatsaha, and Sakalava.

The official languages of the Comoros are Arabic and French. Shikomoro, a dialect of Swahili, is also spoken by the majority of the population.

Births, Marriages, Deaths
According to 2010 estimates the birth rate is 37.5 births per 1,000 people, whilst the death rate is 9.1 deaths per 1,000 people. Infant mortality is 63 deaths per 1,000 live births, whilst the total fertility rate is 4 children born per woman. Average life expectancy at birth in 2009, was 58 years for males and 62 years for females. Healthy life expectancy was respectively 55 years and 58 years. (Source: http://www.who.int, World Health Statistics 2012)

Public Holidays 2014
14 January: Mouloud (Birth of the Prophet)*
27 May: Lailat al Miraj (Ascent of the Prophet)*
29 June: Ramadan begins*
6 July: Independence Day (National Day)
29 July: Eid al Fitr (end of Ramadan)*
5 October: Eid al Adha (Feast of the Sacrifice)*
25 October: Al Hijira (Islamic New Year)
27 November: Anniversary of President Abdullah's assassination
3 November: Ashura*

EMPLOYMENT

Approximately 80 per cent of the working population is engaged in subsistence farming activities, fishing and forestry. Estimated figures for 2007 put the labour force at 268,500.

BANKING AND FINANCE

Currency
The currency of the Comoros Islands is the Comorian franc of 100 centimes.

GDP/GNP, Inflation, National Debt
Comoros is among the world's poorest and least developed nations. The Comorian economy is based largely on agriculture which contributes 40 per cent of GDP. Around 80 per cent of the workforce is employed on plantations that produce cash crops for export - vanilla, ylang ylang and cloves. Its economy has suffered because of a decline in world prices for its export goods. GDP is boosted from remittances from abroad. There is a developing tourism industry. Comoros still depends on foreign grants and technical assistance. In September 2009 the IMF approved a three-year US$21 million loan. However, political instability continues to undermine development and the country has made little progress in structural reform.

GDP (ppp) was an estimated US$800 million in 2009, rising to US$820 million in 2010. GDP was estimated to be US$830 million (ppp) in 2011 with a growth rate of 2.2 per cent. The services sector contributes 40 per cent towards GDP, agriculture approximately 50 per cent and industry 10 per cent.

The inflation rate, at consumer prices, was 3 per cent in 2007, down from 3.4 per cent in 2006. Inflation was 3.2 per cent in 2005 and 4.5 per cent in 2004. External debt was US$259.82 million in 2006. (Source: African Development Bank) Inflation was estimated to be 5.7 per cent in 2011.

Balance of Payments / Imports and Exports
The agricultural industry provides most of Comoros' exports. Major export products are ylang-ylang, cloves, vanilla, copra, and perfume oil. Main export partners are France, USA, Singapore, and Germany. Import products include foods (including rice), consumer goods, petroleum products, transport equipment, and cement. Major import partners are France, South Africa, Kenya, and Pakistan.

External Trade, US$ million

	2005	2006	2007
Trade balance	-80.72	-86.80	-90.70
Exports	14.48	16.00	18.50
Imports	96.20	102.80	109.20

Source: African Development Bank

Imports were estimated to be US$175 million in 2010 and exports US$25 million.

Central Bank
Banque Centrale des Comores, BP 405, Place de France, Moroni, Comoros. Tel: +269 731814 / 731002, fax: +269 213231 / 730349, URL: http://www.banque-comores.km/

Chambers of Commerce and Trade Organisations
Chambre Nationale de Commerce d'Industrie et d'Agriculture des Comores, PO Box 8, Moroni, Comoros. URL: http://www.uccia-comores.com/

MANUFACTURING, MINING AND SERVICES

Energy
The people of Comoros consumed just 0.001 quadrillion Btu of energy in 2009, one of the lowest rates in the world. Electricity generating capacity in 2010 was 0.001 GWe. Electricity generation in the same year was 0.4 million kilowatthours (kWh). Consumption was 0 million kWh.

Comoros produces none of its own oil and is entirely reliant on imports. In 2011 oil imports totaled 1,000 barrels per day, most of which was distillate, gasoline, and kerosene.

Manufacturing
Industry contributed just 4 per cent towards GDP in 2004. Manufacturing industries include perfume distillation, using locally grown vanilla, jasmine and ylang ylang; textiles; furniture; jewelry

Service Industries
The services industry contributed 56 per cent of GDP in 2004. The government is aiming to promote tourism.

Agriculture
Whilst Comorian agriculture contributes 40 per cent of GDP, employs 80 per cent of the labour force and provides most of its exports, the country is not self-sufficient in the production of food, and foodstuffs constitute 32 per cent of total imports. Principal food crops are rice, cassava, corn, sweet potatoes and some European vegetables, such as egg plants and tomatoes. Tropical fruits such as bananas, oranges, tangerines, lemons and mangoes grow in abundance. The chief industrial crop is vanilla. Other crops include perfume plants - such as ylang ylang, jasmine, basil, and spices - as well as coffee and sisal. There are numerous coconut palms which provide copra. There is a small fishing industry, the total catch for 2010 was put at 52,000 tonnes.

Agricultural Production in 2010

Produce	Int. $'000*	Tonnes
Bananas	12,504	44,400
Coconuts	9,753	88,200
Cloves	6,206	2,800
Pulses, nes	6,203	12,000
Cassava	5,954	57,000
Rice, paddy	4,682	19,400
Indigenous cattle meat	3,090	1,140
Taro (cocoyam)	2,248	10,600
Cow milk, whole, fresh	1,623	5,200
Fruit fresh nes	1,187	3,400
Vanilla	1,096	6
Yams	1,071	4,200

*unofficial figures

Source: http://faostat.fao.org/site/339/default.aspx Food and Agriculture Organization of the United Nations, Food and Agricultural commodities production

COMMUNICATIONS AND TRANSPORT

Travel Requirements
US, Canadian, Australian and EU citizens require a passport valid for at least three months from the date of entry and a visa (unless in transit with onward tickets and not leaving the airport). Other nationals should contact the embassy to check visa requirements. All nationals are issued with a free 24-hour transit visa on entry, and should go the immigration office in Moroni the following day to change their visa status.

International Airports
Comoros has an international airport at Hahaya on Grande Comore, and each island has a small airport. Kenya Airways flies direct from Nairobi and Air Austral flies from Paris and Marseille,
Comores Aviation flies from Madagascar and Tanzania.

Roads
The Comoros Islands have a total of 435 miles of roads, 370 miles of which are passable during all the seasons of the year. Vehicles are driven on the right. Some villages are not linked to the main road system or can only be accessed by four-wheel-drive vehicles.

Ports and Harbours
Major ports and harbours are Fomboni, Moroni, and Moutsamoudou. Anjouan and Grande Comore have small artificial harbours. Regular ferry services run between the islands.

The islands' ports are rudimentary, although a deepwater facility functions in Anjouan. Only small vessels can approach the existing quays in Moroni on Grande Comore, despite improvements. Long-distance, ocean-going ships must lie offshore and be unloaded by smaller boats; during the cyclone season, this procedure is dangerous, and ships are reluctant to call at the island. Most freight is sent first to Mombasa, Kenya or the island of Reunion and transshipped from there.

HEALTH

In 2009, the government spent an estimated 7.3 per cent of its total budget on healthcare, accounting for 53.2 per cent of all healthcare spending. Total expenditure on healthcare equated to 3.2 per cent of the country's GDP. Per capita expenditure on health was approximately US$24. Figures for 2000-10 showed that there were 115 physicians (2 per 10,000 population), 588 nurses and midwives (7 per 10,000 population) and 29 dentists. There are 22 hospital beds per 10,000 population

HIV prevalence is still low at around 0.12 per cent of the adult population, despite steady expansion of the pandemic disease. Lymphatic filariasis (Elephantiasis) is a serious public health concern; work towards its elimination, along with leprosy, has begun. In 2007, there were 108 reported cases of leprosy. There were a reported 1,555 cases of cholera. In 2010, there were 36,3583 reported cases of malaria. According to WHO figures there were no reported cases of leprosy or cholera in 2010. The infant mortality rate is high at 63 per 1,000 live births. The child mortality rate is higher, at 86 deaths under five years per 1,000 live births. Maternal mortality stood at 400 deaths per 100,000 live births in 2000. The main causes of child mortality are: prematurity (15 per cent), birth asphyxia (11 per cent), malaria (14 per cent), diarrhoea (9 per cent), and pneumonia (18 per cent).

According to the latest WHO figures, in 2008 approximately 91 per cent of the urban population and 97 per cent of the rural population had access to improved drinking water. In the same year, 50 per cent of the urban population and 30 per cent of the rural population had access to improved sanitation. In 2010, 95 per cent of the population had access to improved drinking water and 36 per cent had access to improved sanitation. (Source: http://www.who.int, World Health Statistics 2012)

EDUCATION

Primary/Secondary Education
The majority of children from the age of five attend Quranic school for two or three years. The compulsory education system lasts for nine years, from the age of seven to 16. Primary education begins at seven and lasts until the age of 12. Secondary education starts at 13, the first stage ending at 16, the second stage ending at 19. It is estimated that around 45 per cent of primary school aged children do not attend school and only 34 per cent of secondary school aged children attend. There is a significant gender difference for attendance. In 2005, 24.1 per cent of government spending went on education.

Figures from UNESCO for 2007 show that the adult literacy rate was 75.1 per cent and the youth literacy rate was 89.5 per cent.

RELIGION

The majority of Comorians (98 per cent) are Sunni Muslim, with 2 per cent Roman Catholic.

Comoros has a religious liberty rating of 2 on a scale of 1 to 10 (10 is most freedom). (Source: World Religion Database)

COMMUNICATIONS AND MEDIA

There is tight media control and journalists risk prison and broadcasters face being taken off air if the government deems their output offensive. Most newspapers practice self-censorship.

Newspapers
The newspaper market is fairly weak, hindered by high poverty and poor distribution networks.
Al-Watan, http://www.comores-online.com/al-watwan/index.htm (weekly)
Kwezi, (published on Mayotte)

Broadcasting
Radio is the most popular medium. There are four FM, one AM, and one shortwave radio stations. Some 90,000 radio receivers and 1,000 television receivers are in use. There is a national TV service (Comoros National TV) and a national radio station (Radio Comoros). French public radio may also be received (RFO Mayotte, URL: http://mayotte.rfo.fr/).

Telecommunications
Telephone main lines number 23,000 and mobiles 42,000, according to 2008 statistics. Per capita mobile phone density is one of the lowest in the world. There were an estimated 23,000 internet users, according to 2008 statistics.

ENVIRONMENT

Current environmental problems include deforestation, and soil erosion and degradation due to inappropriate crop cultivation.

In 2010, Comoros' emissions from the consumption of fossil fuels totaled 0.15 million metric tons of carbon dioxide. (Source: EIA)

The Republic of Comoros is a party to the following international environmental agreements: Biodiversity, Climate Change, Climate Change-Kyoto Protocol, Desertification, Endangered Species, Hazardous Wastes, Law of the Sea, Ozone Layer Protection, Ship Pollution and Wetlands.

DEMOCRATIC REPUBLIC OF CONGO
République Démocratique du Congo

Capital: Kinshasa (Population estimate: 8,000,000)

Head of State: Maj.-Gen. Joseph Kabila (President) (page 1452)

National Flag: A new flag was adopted in 2006. It is sky blue with a yellow five pointed star in the upper left corner and a diagonal red band with narrow yellow borders crossing from the bottom left to the top right of the flag. The star symbolises the hope for a radiant future for the country, whilst the colours symbolise peace (blue), the blood of the martyrs (red) and the country's wealth (yellow).

CONSTITUTION AND GOVERNMENT

Constitution
In June 1960 the former Belgian Congo became an independent republic. The constitution was originally promulgated on 24 June 1967, with amendments in 1974, 1978 and 1990. A transitional constitution was then promulgated in April 1994.

The Constituent and Legislative Assembly, inaugurated in August 2000, prepared the draft constitution for submission to a referendum. However, due to the outbreak of the civil war, the referendum did not take place. In April 2003 the constitution was signed by President Kabila. Under the terms of the new constitution (inaugurated in August 2003), an interim government would rule for two years, prior to elections being held. In December 2005 voters supported the new constitution of the third republic, paving the way for elections in 2006. In February 2006, the new constitution came into effect. This limits the powers of the presidency. According to the 2006 constitution, the Parliament is bicameral.

The president, as the head of state and head of government, appoints the cabinet. Under the new constitution, a Prime Minister shares the leadership of the executive branch of government, with the President of the Democratic Republic of the Congo, the Head of State. The Prime Minister is appointed by the President, from the party or political group that has the majority in the National Assembly. Antoine Gizenga (2007-) is the first Prime Minister to hold the premiership since the position was abolished in 1997.

In January 2011, the constitution was amended and some felt the changes would increase President Kabila's election chances.

To consult the constitution, please visit: http://www.presidentrdc.cd/constitution.pdf.

International Relations
Relations with neighbouring Rwanda and Uganda have been strained in the past, due to allegations of support for Rwandan and Ugandan rebel groups based on Congolese territory. This led to Rwandan and Ugandan military operations inside the DRC in 1996 and 1998. However, in 2002 the DRC signed peace agreements with Rwanda and Uganda, and a tripartite commission was established to resolve regional peace and security issues. This improved relations to some extent, though the presence of rebel groups inside DRC continued to be a matter of concern to her neighbours, and the outbreak of fighting in the east of DRC has its roots in the use of the Congo as a base by various insurgency groups attacking neighboring countries.

The DRC is subject to arms embargos by the EU and the UN. The country is a member of the UN, the African Union (AU), the Southern African Development Community (SADC), and the Community of East and Southern African States (COMESA).

Recent Events
In 1971 Joseph Mobutu became President and renamed the country Zaire. The country remained a one party state until April 1990 when President Mobutu removed the ban on multi-party politics. A conference on the country's political future was held in the period 1991-92.

In 1997, following Laurent-Desire Kabila's installation as President, the country changed its name from Zaire to the Democratic Republic of Congo. In mid-1998 rebel forces backed by Uganda and Rwanda began a campaign against the Kinshasa government. President Kabila announced in 1998 that elections promised for April 1999 would be postponed indefinitely until foreign military forces withdrew from the country. A ceasefire was signed in July 1999. Despite a UN presence in Kisangani to monitor the unstable ceasefire the fighting continued, with Government forces receiving military assistance from Zimbabwe, Namibia, and Angola.

In January 2001, President Kabila was assassinated, following a souring of relations with the armed forces. His son, Joseph Kabila, was sworn in as President on 26 January 2001.

On 30 July 2002 a peace deal was signed between the Democratic Republic of Congo and Rwanda aimed at ending the four-year conflict in which three million people died, either as a result of fighting or through disease and malnutrition.

In July 2003, President Joseph Kabila announced the formation of a UN-supervised transitional government. The threat of civil war was ever present; in 2004 a coup was foiled in Kinshasa and in June rebel soldiers occupied the town of Bukavu for a short time. Six ministers were suspended in November 2004 for alleged corruption; they were among nine ministers sacked in January 2005. In March 2005, the UN peacekeeping force claimed the lives of over 50 militia in the North East of the country, following the killing of UN peacekeeping soldiers nine days earlier. In 2006, the International Court of Justice ruled that Uganda must compensate DR Congo for the plundering of resources and the abuse of human rights in the five years up to 2003.

The first presidential election since 1984 was held in July 2006, and the incumbent President, Joseph Kabila, won. His rival, Jean-Pierre Bemba, contested the result and there was some civil unrest following the election. However the decision stood. In March 2007, a large number of people (up to 600) died during violent clashes between the army and armed guards loyal to Jean-Pierre Bemba. President Joseph Kabila said his troops had put down an armed rebellion; Mr Bemba denied plotting military action to overthrow the president and accused the army of trying to kill him. Following three weeks in the South African embassy, Mr. Bemba left for Portugal.

At the end of August 2007, the government sent troop reinforcements to quell a rebellion in the east of the country. This followed attacks by hundreds of rebel soldiers allied to the Tutsi General, Laurent Nkunda, in North Kivu province; his troops have been implicated in numerous instances of murder, torture and rape. General Nkunda accused the government of forming an alliance with Hutus to attack his troops. The UN estimated that 6,000 Rwandan Hutu rebels - known as the Democratic Forces for the Liberation of Rwanda (FDLR) - were operating in the east. By October, around 370,000 people had fled the fighting between Gen Nkunda's forces, ethnic Hutu Rwandan rebels and the Congolese army. On the 18 October, President Kabila announced a plan to disarm Hutu militias, and said that preparations were in place for the forced disarmament of General Nkunda's fighters. On Monday 3rd December, the government offensive began when the army retook several rebel-held villages in the east. The UN mission in DRC (Monuc) stated that it would provide fire support to the army offensive against rebels if required. A peace pact was signed on 23rd January 2008. The pact agreed to an immediate ceasefire and the deployment of UN peacekeepers in 13 key locations, as well as an amnesty to Gen. Nkunda and his forces. The rebels stated that the full implementation of the pact is dependent on the disarming of the Hutu militia.

In March 2008, at least 68 people were killed in the west of the DR Congo during clashes between the police and members of Bundu Dia Kongo, a religious and political group that has its own militia. The group accuses the central government of corruption and mismanagement and is trying to establish its own authority in the west. The Congolese police started destroying the group's churches and many houses believed to belong to its members. The chief of Bundu Dia Kongo (BDK), an elected member of parliament, requested peace talks but these were rejected by the government. Over 200 armed UN peacekeepers have been deployed in the area. On 21st March, the BDK was banned by the government. UN sources estimated that around 70 people had been killed during fighting, with hundreds missing.

In October, President Kabila appealed for people in the east of the country to take up arms against rebel general Laurant Nkunda, who had earlier announced that he wanted to liberate the whole of the DR Congo. Forces loyal to General Nkunda had taken over Rumangabo army base earlier in the week, but later withdrew. Amid the renewed violence, DR Congo accused Rwanda of sending troops across the border to threaten the city of Goma. Around 200,000 people were displaced by the renewed fighting in the east of the country, and up to two million people are thought to have been displaced in the Kivu area since the end of 2007. Up to 50,000 displaced people poured into Goma following days of fierce fighting in the area. General Laurent Nkunda called a ceasefire, and urged government troops to follow suit. However, a refugee agency said that camps sheltering 50,000 refugees in Rutshuru, 90km (56 miles) north of Goma, had been forcibly emptied, looted and razed in the last week of October. Early in November, the rebels took the town of Kiwanja and ordered thousands of civilians to leave;. Gen. Laurent Nkunda accused the government of breaking the previous week's ceasefire. On the 19th November, the rebels withdrew 40 km from two fronts to create humanitarian corridors. Forty-four community groups in the region made an impassioned plea for European troops to be sent to halt atrocities there. The UN mission in DR Congo (Monuc), currently 17,000 soldiers and police - the biggest UN force of its kind - was increased to 20,000 by a vote by the UN Security Council on 20th November.

In December 2008, a draft report for the UN alleged that there was Congolese army support for the Democratic Forces for the Liberation of Rwanda (FDLR), some of whose leaders were involved in the Rwandan genocide 14 years ago. The Congolese government had previously denied working with the FDLR to exploit the region's rich mines. The UN report named the foreign companies that traded with the FDLR, and recommended that sanctions be imposed against them. In late December, The UN extended the mandate of its peacekeeping force by a year, and gave the force the authority to protect civilians not only from rebel groups but also from renegade Congolese government soldiers. On the 29th December, Uganda's army accused the Lord's Resistance Army rebels of hacking to death 45 civilians in a Catholic church in the Democratic Republic of Congo. The incident allegedly happened close to the border with South Sudan on 26th December. A LRA spokesman denied responsibility. The armies of Uganda, South Sudan and DR Congo carried out a joint offensive against the rebels in mid-December after LRA leader Joseph Kony again refused to sign a peace deal. The aid agency Caritas in DR Congo said that 400 people were killed by LRA fighters over the last week of December, and a further 20,000 people had fled to the mountains, and on the 1st January 2009, the UN said that the rebels were advancing towards the Central African Republic (CAR), setting villages alight, abducting children and raping women en route. Senior officers of the main Tutsi rebel group in the east of the Democratic Republic of Congo have announced a ceasefire with government forces. On the 17th January, a breakaway faction of the National Congress for the Defence of the People (CNDP) said its fighters would join the Congolese army. The ceasefire was announced by nine top rebel commanders, but General Nkunda was absent.

On the 20th-21st January, around 3,000 Rwandan troops entered eastern DRC for a joint operation with the Congolese army against the Rwandan Hutu militia, the FDLR, whose presence in DRC lies at the heart of the region's instability. Action against the Hutu group, which numbers around 6,000, has been a key demand of the CNDP. UN peacekeepers and aid workers were blocked by Congolese troops north of Goma. Having fled DR Congo, General Nkunda was arrested in Rwanda; human rights groups have accused his group the CNDP of numerous killings, rapes and torture. It was thought that an inter-governmental deal had been reached, under which DR Congo would allow Rwanda take action against the Hutu rebels based in DR Congo in return for the arrest of General Nkunda.

On the 13th February, it was reported that at least 40 Rwandan Hutu rebels had been killed in air strikes in the east of the country, during a joint offensive by the Congolese and Rwandan armies. One air strike targeted a meeting of rebel commanders belonging to the Hutu Democratic Forces for the Liberation of Rwanda (FDLR), some of whose leaders are accused of involvement in Rwanda's 1994 genocide. The numbers killed in the air raids make them the deadliest since the arrival of Rwandan forces in January. Human Rights Watch reported an increasing number of civilian deaths since Rwandan forces moved over the border into DR Congo's eastern provinces.

In January 2011, the constitution was amended and some felt the changes would increase President Kabila's election chances.

Voting in presidential and parliamentary elections opened on 29 November 2011. Results of the presidential election gave President Joseph Kabila 49 per cent of the vote against 32 per cent for opposition leader Etienne Tshisekedi. The result was met with widespead protest both at home and by communities abroad. International observers of the election said lacked credibility.

Conflict between the DRC and Rwanda broke out in April 2012 after a mutiny by some Congolese army officers. There are allegations that Rwanda is supporting the rebellion.

In August 2012 a shaft at a gold mine in the Orientale province collapsed killing around 6 miners.

In July 2012, the warlord Thomas Lubanga became the first person convicted by the International Criminal Court since it was set up 10 years before. Lubanga was sentenced to 14 years in jail for using child soldiers in his rebel army in 2002 and 2003.

In October 2012, The UN Security Council announced its intention to impose sanctions against leaders of the M23 rebel movement and violators of the DRC arms embargo. A UN panel said that both Rwanda and Uganda supplied M23 with weapons and support, both countries deny the accusations.

In February 2013, representatives of 11 African countries signed an accord in Ethiopia pledging to help end the conflict in DR Congo. The M23 rebel group declared a ceasefire ahead of the talks, however, after the meeting there was a power struggle between leader Jean-Mari Runiga and military chief Sultani Makenga of the M23.

Legislature

In August 2000 the Legislative and Constituent Assembly - Transitional Parliament was created, consisting of 300 members, all appointed by the president. In August 2003 a new interim parliament met for the first time. It was composed of 500 deputies, of which 12 were nominated by political parties, representatives of the former government, and rebel groups.

Upper House

The upper house, the Senate, has 120 members indirectly elected by the provincial assemblies for a five-year term. In addition, former elected presidents are to be senators for life. The provincial legislature provides for the election of 14 senators, including tribal leaders for each province.

Senate, (Sénat), Palais du Peuple, Coin avenue des huiliers et boulevard triomphale Commune de Lingwala, Kinshasa, DRC. Tel: +243 81 514 2489

Lower House

The lower house, the National Assembly, has 500 members directly elected for a five-year term.

National Assembly, (Assemblée Nationale), Palais du Peuple, Coin avenue des huiliers et boulevard triomphale, Commune de Lingwala, Kinshasa, DRC. Tel: +243 81 514 2489

Cabinet (as at March 2013)

Prime Minister, Minister of Finance: Augustin Matata Ponyo Mapon (page 1497)
Deputy Prime Minister, responsible for Budget: Daniel Mukoko Sambai
Deputy Prime Minister, responsible for National Defence and Veterans: Alexandre Luba Ntambo
Minister of Planning and Modernisation: Celestin Vunabandi Kanyamihigo
Minister for Foreign Affairs and International Cooperation: Raymond Tshibanda N;tunga Mulongo
Minister of Economy and Commerce: Jean Paul Nemoyato Begepole
Minister of Agriculture and Rural Development: Jean Chrysostome Vahamwiti Mukesyayira
Minister of Justice and Human Rights: Wivine Mumba Matipa
Minister of Energy and Hydropower Resources: Bruno Kapanji Kalala
Minister of Media and Relations with Parliament and Citizenship: Lambert Mende Omalanga
Minister of Health: Felix Babange Numbi Mukwampa
Minister of Primary, Secondary and Vocational Education: Maker Mwangu Famba
Minister of Mines: Martin Kabwelulu Labilo
Minister of Transport and Communications: Justin Kalumba Mwana Ngongo
Minister of Industry, Small and Medium Enterprises: Remy Musungayi Bampale
Minister of Lands: Robert Mbwinga Bila
Minister of Culture and Arts, Youth and Sport: Banza Mukalayi Nsungu
Minister of Civil Service: Jean Claude Kibala
Minister of Labour and Social Welfare: Modeste Bahati Lukwebo
Minister of the Interior, Security, Decentralization and Customary Affairs: Richard Muyej Mangez

Minister for Gender, Family and Children: Genvieve Kinagosi
Minister of Hydrocarbons: Crispin Atama Tabe
Minister without portfolio: Louise Munga Mesozi
Minister of Regional and Town Planning, Housing, Infrastructure, Public Works and Reconstruction: Fridolin Kasweshi Musoka
Minister of the Environment, Conservation of Nature and Tourism: Bavon N'sa Mputu Elima
Minister of Posts, Telecommunications and New Information Technologies and Communication: Tryphon Kin Kiey Mulumba
Minister of Higher and University Education and Scientific Research: Chelo Lotsima
Minister of Social Affairs, Humanitarian Actions and National Solidarity: Charles Nawej Mundele

Ministries Office of the President, Avenue de Lemera, Kinshasa, DRC. Tel: +243 12 31312
Ministry of the Interior and Security, 44 avenue de Lemera, Kinshasa-Gombe, DRC. Tel: +243 12 31147
Ministry of Planning, 4155 avenue des Coteaux, BP 9378, Kinshasa-Gombe, DRC. Tel: +243 81 030 6644, e-mail: miniplan@micronet.cd, URL: http://www.ministereduplan.cd
Ministry of Foreign Affairs and International Co-operation, Place de l'Indépendance, BP 7100, Kinshasa-Gombe, DRC. Tel: +243 12 31168
Ministry of Transport and Communications, Immeuble ONATRA, Boulevard du 30 Juin, BP 3304, Kinshasa-Gombe, DRC. Tel: +243 12 23913
Ministry of Justice and Human Rights, 228 avenue de Lemera, BP 3137, Kinshasa-Gombe, DRC. Tel: +243 12 32432
Ministry of Health, Boulevard du 30 Juin, BP 3088, Kinshasa-Gombe, DRC. Tel: +243 12 30147
Ministry of Civil Service, Building administratif, Avenue des Héros nationaux, Kinshasa-Gombe, DRC. Tel: +243 12 30209
Ministry of Post and Telecommunications, 4484 Avenue des Huileries, BP 7821, Kinshasa-Gombe, DRC. Tel: +243 12 23878, fax: +243 88 02332, e-mail: minptt@ic.cd
Ministry of Finance, Boulevard du 30 Juin, BP 12997, Kinshasa-Gombe, DRC. Tel: +243 12 31197, URL: http://www.ministeredubudget.cd
Ministry of National Economy and Trade, BP 7100, Kinshasa-Gombe, DRC. Tel: +243 12 32450
Ministry of Culture and the Arts, BP 8541, Kinshasa 1, DRC. Tel: +243 12 31005
Ministry of the Environment and Conservation of Nature, 15 ave de la Clinique, BP 1248, Kinshasa, DRC. Tel: +243 12 31252
Ministry of Education, Coin ave Batetela et Ambassadeurs, BP 32, Kinshasa-Gombe, DRC. Tel: +243 12 30368
Ministry of Agriculture, Building SOZACOM, Boulevard du 30 Juin, BP 8722, Kinshasa-Gombe, DRC. Tel: +243 12 23821
Ministry of Mines and Energy, 239 avenue de la Justice, BP 8500, Kinshasa-Gombe, DRC. Tel: +243 12 30104
Ministry of Youth, Sports and Leisure, 77 Avenue de la Justice, BP 8541 KIN I, Kinshasa-Gombe, DRC
Ministry of Industry and Small Businesses, Boulevard de 30 Juin, Building Onatra, BP 8500 KIN I, Kinshasa-Gombe, DRC.

Elections
The first parliamentary election since 1987 and the first presidential election since 1984 took place on 30 July 2006 (postponed from 2005 as preparations, including voter registration, were behind schedule). There were 33 candidates for the presidency and 9,707 candidates contesting parliamentary 500 seats.

The presidential election in July 2006 resulted in no clear winner, and there was a run-off in October, which was won by the incumbent president, Joseph Kabange Kabila, with 58.05 per cent of the vote. His main rival was Jean-Pierre Bemba (one of the vice-presidents in the transitional government, of the Congolese Liberation Movement). Mr Bemba won 41.95 per cent of the vote, and contested the result. There was some civil unrest after the result was announced, but the international monitors generally approved the poll.

In the Legislative elections, the President's People's Party for Reconstruction and Democracy won 111 of the 500 seats contested, becoming the largest party in the National Assembly. Their closest rivals were the Movement for the Liberation of Congo, with 64 seats. 67 parties won seats in the National Assembly (most just one or two) and 64 independent members were elected. In the elections to the Senate in January 2007, the People's Party for Reconstruction and Democracy won 22 of the 108 seats, and the Movement for the Liberation of won 14. Again, the remaining seats were split between many different parties and 26 independents.

Voting in presidential and parliamentary elections started on 29 November 2011. Eleven candidates are running for president. President Kabila is running for re-election. The strongest opposition candidate is seen as Etienne Tshisekedi (78). There were a reported 19,000 parliamentary candidates for the 500 parliamentary seats. Voting in some areas has been delayed because of a lack of ballot papers. Agencies have appealed for calm. UN peacekeepers are stationed around the country. Joseph Kabila claimed victory with 48 per cent of the vote. Mr Tshisekedi took 32 per cent. In the parliamentary elections, results were finally released on 1 February 2012, amidst several allegations of fraud and errors. The provisional results were: PPRD 63 seats, UDPS 41 seats, PPPD 27 seats, MLC 22 seats; Palu 19 seats , the UN 17 seats, others 294. Although the ruling PPRD lost support, it retained a majority.

Political Parties
Parti du Peuple pour la Reconstruction et la Démocratie (PPRD) (People's Party for Reconstruction and Democracy)
Leader: Vital Kamerhe
Mouvement pour la Liberation du Congo (Movement for the Liberation of Congo), Avenue du Port, 6, Commune de la Gombé, Kinshasa, DRC. URL: http://www.mlc-congo.net/
Leader: Jean Pierre Bemba

Union pour la Démocratie et le Progrès Social (UDPS, Union for Democracy and Social Progress], 12 Rue Kinshasa-Limete, Congo-Kinshasa. E-mail: udps@udps.org, URL: http://www.udps.org/
Opposition Leader: Etienne Tshisekedi
Nouveau Parti Patriotique du Peuple Congolais (NPPPC National People's Patriotic Party of the Congo
Mouvement National Congolais-Lumumba/MNC-L (Congolese National Movement-Lumumba)
Leader: François Lumumba
Rassemblement Congolais pour la Démocratie/RCD-G, Congolese Rally for Democracy-Goma
Leader: Azarias Ruberwa

Diplomatic Representation
Embassy of the Democratic Republic of the Congo, 38 Holne Chase, London, N2 0QQ, United Kingdom. Tel: +44 (0)20 8458 0254 fax: +44 (0)20 8458 0254
Ambassador: Barnabe Kikaya Bin Karubi
British Embassy, 83 Avenue du Roi Baudouin, Kinshasa, Democratic Republic of the Congo. Tel: +243 81 715 0761, fax: +243 81 346 4291, e-mail: ambrit@ic.cd
Ambassador: Neil Wigan
US Embassy, 310 Avenue des Aviateurs, Unit 31550, APO AE 09828, Kinshasa-Gombe, Democratic Republic of the Congo. Tel: +243 81 225 5872, fax: +243 88 301 0560, URL: http://kinshasa.usembassy.gov
Ambassador: James Entwistle
Embassy of the Democratic Republic of the Congo, 1726 M Street NW, Suite 601, Washington, DC 20036, USA. Tel: +1 202 234 7490, fax: +1 202 234 2609
Ambassador: Faida Mitifu
Permanent Representative of the Democratic Republic of the Congo to the United Nations, 866 United Nations Plaza, Suite 511, New York, NY 10017, USA. Tel: +1 212 319 8061, fax: +1 212 319 8232, e-mail: drcongo@un.int, URL: http://www.un.int/drcongo/
Ambassador: Atoki Ileka

LEGAL SYSTEM

The legal system is based on both Belgian and traditional tribal law. The Constitution of 2006 saw an end to the Supreme Court, which was divided into three new institutions. The constitutional interpretation prerogative of the Supreme Court is now held by the Constitutional Court, and the Court of Cassation (Cour de cassation) is the main court of last resort and is located in the Kinshasa Palace of Justice. Cases of administrative justice go before the Conseil d'État.

During the war (1998-2002), a provisional military court (la Cour d'Ordre Militaire) was set up. The judges were soldiers and the rights of the defendants were often ignored. The court was closed down in 2003.

Government control over many regions remains weak, particularly in North and South Kivu provinces, and civilian authorities cannot maintain effective control over the security forces, which act with impunity, committing many serious abuses including unlawful killings, disappearances, torture, and rape. Security forces also retain child soldiers. There are arbitrary arrests, and detentions in life-threatening conditions in prison. The judiciary is not independent, and government corruption remains pervasive. The Democratic Republic of Congo retains the death penalty. The most recent reported execution was in 2003.

National Human Rights Observatory, Ave. Sendwe 5058, Kinshasha, DRC. Tel: +243 98 31 37 40

LOCAL GOVERNMENT

The Democratic Republic of the Congo is divided into 10 provinces and one city (Kinshasa): Bandundu, Bas-Congo, Equateur, Kasai-Occidental, Kasai-Oriental, Katanga, Maniema, Nord-Kivu, Orientale, and Sud-Kivu. According to the Constitution adopted in December 2005, the current administrative divisions were to be subdivided into 26 new provinces by 2009 but this has yet to be implemented.

AREA AND POPULATION

Area
One of the largest countries in Africa, the Democratic Republic of Congo is situated in sub-Saharan Africa. It borders the Central African Republic to the north, the Congo to the west and, across Lake Tanganyika, Rwanda, Burundi and Tanzania. It has an area of 2,345,410 sq. km (905,562 sq. miles), of which 2,267,600 sq. km is land and 77,810 sq. km is water. The central region has an equatorial climate with high temperatures and heavy rainfall. There are different climatic cycles in the north and south.

To view a map of the DRC, please visit:
http://www.un.org/Depts/Cartographic/map/profile/drcongo.pdf

Population
The population in 2010 was estimated at 66.956 million, with an annual population growth rate of 2.8 per cent. An estimated 46 per cent of the population is below 15 years old and 4 per cent of the population is aged 60 years or more. The median age is 17 years. In 2005, around 43,000 Congolese refugees returned home from neighbouring countries; however, another 462,000 Congolese refugees continue to seek asylum in neighbouring countries.

The population is made up of around 200 tribes. The four largest tribes, Mongo, Luba, Kongo, and the Mangbetu-Azande, make up nearly half the population.

DEMOCRATIC REPUBLIC OF CONGO

French is the official language, while Lingala is spoken by much of the population. Kingwana (a dialect of Kiswahili or Swahili), Kikongo, and Tshiluba are also spoken.

Births, Marriages, Deaths

Estimates for 2010 put the birth rate at 43.5 births per 1,000 people and the death rate at 15.9 deaths per 1,000 inhabitants. According to World Health Organization figures, the fertility rate was 5.9 children born per woman. The average life expectancy at birth is 49 years (47 for males, 51 for females). Healthy life expectancy is 45 years. (Source: http://www.who.int, World Health Statistics 2012)

Public Holidays 2014

1 January: New Year's Day
4 January: Martyrs of Independence Day
1 May: Labour Day
24 June: Constitution Day and Day of the Fishermen
30 June: Independence Day
1 August: Parents' Day
14 October: Youth Day
27 October: Naming Day
17 November: Army Day
24 November: Anniversary of the Second Republic
25 December: Christmas Day

EMPLOYMENT

2007 estimates put the labour force at 23.4 million, 65 per cent of whom are employed in agriculture, 20 per cent in services, and 15 per cent in industry. Child labour is commonplace, with more than a quarter of children aged between five and 14 working in mines and other industries; there are over four million orphans in the country.

BANKING AND FINANCE

Currency

The unit of currency is the Congolese franc. The financial centre is Kinshasa.

GDP/GNP, Inflation, National Debt

The Democratic Republic of Congo has a wealth of natural resources, including copper, cobalt, gold and diamonds. However, years of war and mismanagement have led DRC to be one of the poorest countries in the world. Foreign businesses withdrew from the country because of uncertainty about the outcome of the conflict and the difficulty of operating in a war zone. However, the Joseph Kabila regime undertook a programme of reforms (fiscal and monetary policies and liberalisation of prices and exchange rates), and, after a decade of contraction, economic growth began to return in 2002. The global economic crisis adversely affected the economy in 2009 but growth returned in 2011.

GDP was US$13.1 billion in 2010, up by 6 per cent from 2009. Per capita GDP was US$189 in 2010. GDP was an estimated US$15 billion in 2011, with a growth rate of 6.5 per cent. Agriculture accounts for over 40 per cent of GDP, industry 28 per cent and services 29 per cent.

The inflation rate fell from 550 per cent in 2000, to 357.3 per cent in 2001 to 25.3 per cent in 2002, to 4.1 per cent in 2003. This in turn is encouraging outside investment in development projects. Inflation was 9.5 per cent in 2007. In 2010, inflation was estimated to be 15 per cent.

DRC is one of the world's most debt-laden countries, with an estimated total external debt of $10.1 million in 2003. DRC was granted Highly Indebted Poor Country status in 2003, with a common reduction factor of 80 per cent as long as there is sustained economic improvement.

Total public external debt was estimated to be US$3.5 billion in 2010.

In July 2010 a US$12 billion debt relief deal was approved by the World Bank and IMF. In November 2010 the Paris Club of creditor countries wrote off half of the Democratic Republic of Congo's debt.

Balance of Payments / Imports and Exports

The Democratic Republic of Congo is one of 14 southern African states that form the Southern African Development Community (SADC). In 2007 the DRC together with Rwanda and Burundi relaunched the economic bloc the Great Lakes Countries Economic Community.

The main export commodity (2006) was diamonds, which accounted for over half total export revenue. Other major exported goods were crude oil, copper, coffee, and cobalt. Main export trading partners were the Japan, European Union, the US, South Africa and China.

Main suppliers of imports were South Africa, EU, the USA and China. Food, transport equipment, mining and other machinery, and fuels were the major import commodities.

External Trade, US$ million

	2005	2006	2007
Trade balance	-402.00	-421.00	-64.88
Exports	2,071.00	2,319.00	2,537.05
Imports	2,473.00	2,740.00	2,601.93

Source: African Development Bank

Exports were an estimated US$8.5 billion in 2010 and imports US$8 billion.

Central Bank

Banque Centrale du Congo, 563 Boulevard Tshatshi, 2697 Kinshasa/Gombe, Democratic Republic of Congo. Tel: +243 88 20704, fax: +243 880 5152, e-mail: cabgouv@bcc.cd, URL: http://www.bcc.cd/
Governor: Jean-Claude Masangu Mulongo

Chambers of Commerce and Trade Organisations

Federation of Enterprises in Congo, URL: http://www.fec.cd

MANUFACTURING, MINING AND SERVICES

Primary and Extractive Industries

The Democratic Republic of Congo has extensive mineral resources which include petroleum, copper, cobalt, zinc, gold and diamonds. During the 1980s the DRC was the world's fourth largest producer of diamonds, and although the civil war has affected production, diamonds still accounted for over half all exports in 2003 ($642 million). Most of Congo's diamonds are exported to Belgium, Israel, and India.

Copper and cobalt reserves are mined by the state-owned mining company Gecamines. Production has been adversely affected by civil war, corruption, market trends and a failure to invest. Mining accounts for just over 6 per cent of GDP (2000). To attract more investment in the mining industry the Congolese government has approved new investment and mining codes.

The DRC had proven crude oil reserves of 180 million barrels in January 2012. Oil production in 2005 fell to an estimated 19,700 barrels per day but rose slightly to 20,160 barrels per day in 2011. Oil consumption also fell, from 21,600 barrels per day in 2001 to 6,000 barrels per day in 2005, but rose to 10,000 barrels per day in 2011 whilst oil exports were around 10,100 barrels per day.

The Democratic Republic of Congo is one of only three SADC countries that produce oil (Angola and South Africa being the other two). Plans are underway to import crude oil from Nigeria and a new state-run organisation has been set up to construct a refinery to process the oil.

The DRC has reserves of natural gas but no production industry. Proven natural gas reserves were estimated at 35 billion cubic feet in January 2007. The Democratic Republic of Congo and Rwanda are considering a joint development of the Lake Kivu methane deposits.

The Democratic Republic of Congo has one of the smallest coal industries in the SADC, with recoverable coal reserves estimated at 97 million short tons. Consumption in 2010 was 377,000 short tons. Coal production that year was 147,000 short tons.

Energy

The Democratic Republic of Congo has enormous energy resources; the Inga dam, on the Congo River, has a potential capacity of 40,000-45,000 megawatts, which could supply all of Southern Africa's electricity needs. However, continuing political unrest has discouraged investors and therefore a fraction of this amount has been developed. Total installed generating capacity was estimated at 2.44 gigawatts in 2009, but actual generation was just 7.80 billion kilowatthours. DRC consumed 6.20 billion kilowatthours in 2010. The DRC exports hydroelectricity to the Republic of Congo, Zambia and South Africa.

In November 2003, BPC, Eskom, ENE, NamPower and SNEL formed the Westcor Power Project in order to provide low-cost and environmentally friendly electricity to ensure the economic development of the region. The Project may eventually include the construction of hydropower stations in Angola and Namibia. Depending on the outcome of feasibility studies, the project was due to begin in 2010. However DR Congo decided to develop its part of the project with private investment and later proposed a new project with Mozambique, Zambia and Zimbabwe.

In May 2006, refurbishment and rehabilitation work on the Inga Dam began; the Dam has been operating at 40 per cent.

Manufacturing

In 2002, industry accounted for only 18.8 per cent of GDP, with only 3.9 per cent attributed to manufacturing. Important manufacturing areas include processed and unprocessed minerals, consumer products (textiles, batteries, plastics, footwear, cigarettes, metal products), processed foods and beverages, timber and cement. the main centres for manufacturing are Kinshasa and Lubumbashi.

Service Industries

The Democratic Republic of Congo has many national parks with some wildlife unique to the region. Tourism is potentially a growth industry. Services contributed nearly 25 per cent of GDP in 2002.

Agriculture

Agriculture plays an important part in the economy of the Democratic Republic of Congo. It can provide all the food for the native population with a substantial surplus, despite only three per cent of the land being given over to agriculture. The main cash crops include coffee, palm oil, rubber, cotton, sugar, tea, and cocoa. Food crops include cassava, plantains, maize, groundnuts, and rice. Timber is also a major product; some 77 per cent of the land is forest and woodland.

Agricultural Production in 2010

Produce	Int. $'000*	Tonnes
Cassava	1,556,395	15,049,500
Plantains	258,073	1,250,000
Game meat	239,563	110,100

continued		
Maize	155,409	1,156,410
Groundnuts, with shell	148,117	371,263
Mangoes, mangosteens, guavas	127,002	211,964
Roots and tubers, nes	119,195	820,000
Meat nes	96,342	72,900
Bananas	89,128	316,472
Rice, paddy	83,716	317,231
Palm oil	81,356	187,000
Vegetables fresh nes	69,723	370,000

* unofficial figures
Source: http://faostat.fao.org/site/339/default.aspx Food and Agriculture Organization of the United Nations, Food and Agricultural commodities production

COMMUNICATIONS AND TRANSPORT

Travel Requirements
US, Canadian, Australian and EU subjects require a passport valid for at least six months, plus proof of sufficient funds, evidence of yellow fever vaccination and a return ticket. Holders of passports with an immigration stamp from Rwanda or Uganda may experience difficulties on arrival, whilst those with an immigration stamp from Burundi will be denied admission to the DRC. A visa is required, except for passengers transitting within 48 hours, not leaving the airport. Other nationals should contact the embassy to check visa requirements.

National Airlines
Congo Airlines (formerly Zaire Airlines and Zaire Express), No. 210 bis, 6eme rue, Limete-Kinsrosa, PO Box 12847, Kinshasa, Democratic Republic of Congo. Tel: +243 8 43862, fax: +1 212 372 3157

International Airports
The DRC has a total of 237 airports, 26 of which have paved runways. There are international airports at Ndjili (Kinshasa), Luano (Lubumbashi), Mangboka (Kisangani) and Goma.

Railways
The railway system is operated by Société Nationale des Chemins du Fer du Congo, and consists of 5,138 km of rail. trains run from Lubumbashi to Ilébo, Kalemie to Kindu, and from Kinshasa to Matadi.

Roads
There are 153,500 km of roads, though only 2,794 km are paved.

Shipping
The national sea company is called Compagnie Maritime du Congo.

Waterways
Over 1,500km of the Congo River are navigable and ferry services run from Kinshasa upriver to Kisangani and Ilébo subject to local conditions.

Ports and Harbours
Matadi is the only major harbour.

HEALTH

The health system was severely disrupted by the civil war, and has not yet recovered. Hospitals are in a state of decay and neglect. Doctors and nurses are rarely paid, and most state hospitals are operating under a system of self-financing, requiring patients to pay for treatment and medicines.

In 2009, the DRC government spent approximately 12.5 per cent of its total budget on healthcare (up from 1.8 per cent in 2000), accounting for 44.7 per cent of all healthcare spending (compared to 4.1 per cent in 2000). External resources contribute almost 34.3 per cent of healthcare expenditure. Total expenditure on healthcare equated to 9.6 per cent of the country's GDP. Per capita expenditure on health was approximately US$17 in 2009. Figures for 2000-10 show that there are 5,827 physicians (1 per 10,000 population), 28,789 nurses and midwives (5 per 10,000 population) and 159 dentists. There are 8 hospital beds per 10,000 population.

Poor living conditions lead to outbreaks of diseases; in December 2004, typhoid fever broke out in Kinshasa, with a reported 13,400 cases, and in February 2005, pneumonic plague struck a diamond mine, with 57 deaths reported by March. In 2010, there were 13,884 reported cases of cholera, 5,049 of leprosy, 2.4 million of malaria, 5,407 of measles, 5176 of meningitis, 114,170 of TB and 941 reported cases of polio.

The infant mortality rate (probability of dying by first birthday) in 2009 was 112 per 1,000 live births. The child mortality rate (under 5 years) was 170 per 1,000 live births. The main causes of childhood mortality are: prematurity (10 per cent), diarrhoea (13 per cent), pneumonia (19 per cent), malaria (18 per cent), and HIV/AIDs (1 per cent). Just 6 per cent of children sleep under insecticide-treated nets. Immunization rates for common diseases are improving: in 2008, 67 per cent of children received the measles vaccination, compared to 38 per cent in 1990. In 2008, 80 per cent of the urban population and 28 per cent of the rural population had sustainable access to an improved water source. In 2010, 24 per cent of the population had sustainable access to improved sanitation. (Source: http://www.who.int, World Health Statistics 2012)

According to UNAIDS estimates, at least five per cent of the population is infected with the HIV/AIDS virus; the rate is believed to be significantly higher in areas of recent armed conflict, where sexual abuse and violence against women was widespread. In 2005, the reported number of people receiving antiretroviral therapy for AIDS/HIV was 6,695; in the same year, it was estimated that some 209,000 were in need of the therapy.

EDUCATION

Primary/Secondary Education
Primary education lasts for a total of six years. Secondary education also lasts for six years: two years in lower secondary and four years in upper secondary school. School enrolment rates have been falling over recent years; gross enrolment in primary schools was 72 per cent in 1996, falling to an estimated 42 per cent in 2004. Enrolment in secondary schools has fallen from 26 per cent in 1996 to 15.4 per cent in 2004. It is estimated that 41.7 per cent of the population have had no schooling. Education is not free or compulsory which leads many children to miss out on any formal education as their parents are unable to afford the fees.

Higher Education
There is one National University divided into three campuses: Kinshasa, Lubumbashi and Kisangani. Tertiary school gross enrolment ratio was 2.3 per cent in 1996, and has fallen to 0.7 per cent in 2004.

According to UNESCO, the literacy rate in the population over 15 was 54.1 per cent for women compared with 80.9 per cent for men from 2000-2004.

RELIGION

Most of the population has Christian beliefs (95 per cent) the majority of whom are Roman Catholic. A small number follow traditional beliefs and just over one per cent are Muslim.

DR Congo has a religious liberty rating of 7 on a scale of 1 to 10 (10 is most freedom). (Source: World Religion Database)

COMMUNICATIONS AND MEDIA

Although reporters face arrests, threats and violence, criticism of the government still appears in the media.

Newspapers
There are several daily newspapers, the main ones being:
Le Potential (URL: http://www.lepotentiel.com/)
L'Avenir (URL: http://www.groupelavenir.net/)
L'Observateur (URL: http://www.lobservateur.cd/)

Broadcasting
There are dozens of private TV stations, though only three TV channels have near-national coverage. Radio-Television National Congolaise (RTNC) is the state-run television broadcaster.

Radio is the dominant medium and there are over 100 private radio stations. La Voix du Congo is operated by RTNC and broadcasts in French and Swahili as well as other local languages. Radio Okapi (URL: http://radiookapi.net/) is a UN backed and politically independent broadcaster.

Telecommunications
In 2008, there were an estimated 37,000 mainline telephones and 9.2 million mobile phones in use. Internet users numbered around 230,400 in 2008, with over two thousand internet hosts.

ENVIRONMENT

Major environmental concerns include: water pollution, deforestation, the poaching of wildlife, and environment damage caused by mining. The DRC is home to 47 per cent of Africa's forest. UNESCO has listed five of Congo's national parks as 'world heritage sites in danger' because of threats from conflict and mining. The parks' wildlife include mountain gorillas, savannah giraffe and rare white rhino.

In 2010, the DRC's emissions from the consumption of fossil fuels totaled 2.80 million metric tons of carbon dioxide. (Source: EIA)

The Democratic Republic of Congo is a party to the following environmental agreements: Biodiversity, Climate Change, Climate Change-Kyoto Protocol, Desertification, Endangered Species, Hazardous Wastes, Law of the Sea, Marine Dumping, Ozone Layer Protection, Tropical Timber 83, Tropical Timber 94 and Wetlands. It has signed, but not ratified, the Environmental Modification agreement.

CONGO
Republic of the Congo
République du Congo

Capital: Brazzaville (Population estimate: 1.2 million)

Head of State: General Denis Sassou-Nguesso (President of the Republic and Head of Government) (page 1509)

National Flag: Two triangles, green and red, separated by a yellow diagonal bar

CONSTITUTION AND GOVERNMENT

Constitution
Formerly part of French Equatorial Africa, the Congo became an autonomous republic within the French Community in 1958 and fully independent in 1960.

A new constitution was approved in 1992 but was suspended in October 1997, when former president Denis Sassou-Nguesso took control of the capital by force and reassumed power. A new constitution was presented to the people, who approved it in a referendum on 20 January 2002. The 2002 Constitution makes the president the head of state, elected by universal adult suffrage for a seven-year term. The president is also the head of government, with the power to appoint the cabinet.

To consult the full constitution (in French), please visit: http://www.presidence.cg/files/my_files/constit200102.pdf

International Relations
The Republic of Congo currently maintains good relations with neighbouring Angola and Gabon. Strained relations with the Democratic Republic of Congo (DRC) have improved slightly. The Congo's closest relationships are within the CEMAC grouping although President Sassou-Nguesso has also built alliances across the continent, developing contacts with Egypt, Morocco, Nigeria and South Africa. Congo's main international partner is France; there is still a sizeable French ex-patriot community in the country, and French companies still have significant investments in most sectors.

Congo is a member of the UN, African Union, African Development Bank, World Trade Organization (WTO) and the Central African Economic and Monetary Community (CEMAC).

In 2004, Congo was expelled from the Kimberley Process, an international diamond trading initiative established to counter trade in illicit "conflict diamonds". At that time, Congo's declared domestic production was 55,000 carats but it exported 5.2 million carats. It can be readmitted to the process if reforms are made. Congo applied for readmission at the end of 2006.

Recent Events
In March 2002, Sassou-Nguesso won the presidential elections. He was unopposed; his main rivals had been barred from standing.

Fighting broke out between government forces and 'Ninja' rebels (named after the Japanese warriors) in March 2002, causing thousands of civilians to flee their homes in the Pool region. The rebels were loyal to former Prime Minister Bernard Kolelas and led by a renegade priest named Pastor Ntumi. By June 2002, the fighting had spread to the capital of Brazzaville and approximately 100 people were killed. The following March, Pastor Ntumi agreed to end hostilities; the peace accord included political representation for the Ninjas in the southern Pool region and a programme of disarmament, demobilization, and reintegration (DDR). Thomas Lubanga, leader of the UBC, was arrested in 2005. He is suspected of ordering several massacres and was indicated on charges of forcibly recruiting child soldiers. He was the first suspect to be tried by the ICC in The Hague.

In January 2006 the Republic of Congo was chosen to lead the African Union. In June 2007, former "Ninja" rebels led by renegade Pastor Frederic Ntoumi ceremoniously burnt their weapons to demonstrate a commitment to peace.

The President's Congolese Labour Party (PCT) won an overall majority in the August 2007 elections to the National Assembly; many of the opposition parties had boycotted the elections. The most recent presidential election took place in July 2009 and was won by President Sassou-Nguesso.

Two alleged FDLR leaders were arrested in November 2009 on suspicion of war crimes.

In March 2010, the Paris Club of creditor countries and Brazil agreed to cancel all the debt owed to them by Congo, the figure was in the region of $2.4 billion.

In November 2010, the UN Special Rapporteur on Indigenous Peoples urged the government to protect the rights of the Pygmy peoples, saying they are subject to discrimination.

On October 2012, the former Minister of Defence, Charles Zacharie Boeao was charged with responsibility for an accident in Brazzaville the previous March. An ammunition stockpile blew up killing over 200 people and injuring around 2,300. He accused the government of using him as a scapegoat.

Legislature
Under the terms of the 2002 Constitution, the bicameral legislature, or Parliament (*Parlement*), consists of the Senate (Sénat) and the National Assembly (Assemblée Nationale). President Sassou-Nguesso's Parti Congolais du Travail (PCT, Congolese Labour Party) holds the majority of seats in both houses.
National Assembly, Palais du Parlement, BP 2106, Brazzaville, Republic of Congo. Tel: +242 281 1727, URL: http://www.congo-site.net/v4x/instit/others/ass.php

Upper House
The Senate is composed of 66 members, indirectly elected for a term of six years (one third elected every two years).

Lower House
The National Assembly is composed of 153 members, directly elected for a term of five years.

Cabinet (as at June 2013)

Minister of State for Industrial Development and Promotion of the Private Sector: Isidore Mvouba (page 1483)
Minister of Equipment and Public Works: Emile Ouosso
Minister of Foreign Affairs and Co-operation: Basil Ikouebe
Minister of Civil Service and State Reform: Guy Brice Parfait Kolelas
Minister of Justice and Human Rights, and Keeper of the Seals: Aime Emmanuel Yok
Minister of State for Transport, Civil Aviation and Merchant Marine: Rodolphe Adad
Minister of Agriculture and Livestock: Rigobert Maboundou
Minister of Commerce, Consumption and Supplies: Claudine Munari
Minister of Forest Habitat and Environment: Henri Djombo
Ministry of Construction, Town Planning, Housing and Land Reforms: Claude Alphonse Ntsilou
Minister of Finance and Budget: Gilbert Ondongo
Minister of Posts and Telecommunications, with responsibility for new technologies: Thierry Moungala
Minister of Technical Education and Vocational Training: Serge Blaise Zoniaba
Minister of Higher Education: Georges Moyen
Minister of Land Reform and the Protection of Public Property: Pierre Mabiala
Minister of Energy and Hydraulics: Henri Ossebi
Minister of Communications, in charge of relations with Parliament, Government Spokesman: Bienvenu Okiemy
Minister of Health and Population: Francois Ibovi
Minister of Mines, Mining Industry and Geology: Gen. Pierre Oba
Minister of Tourism and Entertainment: Josue Rodrique Ngouonimba
Minister of Fishing and Aquaculture: Bernard Tchibambelela
Minister of Petroleum: Andre Louemba
Minister of Promotion and Integration of Women: Catherine Embondza
Minister of Small and Medium-sized Enterprises: Yvonne Adelaide Mougany
Minister of Labour and Social Security: Gen. Florent Ntsiba
Minister of Interior and Decentralisation: Raymond Zephyrin Mboulou
Minister of Primary and Secondary Education: Hellot Matson Mampouya
Minister of Scientific Research: Bruno Jean-Richard Itoua
Minister in the Office of the President responsible for Special Economic Zones: Alain Akouala Atipault
Minister of Civil Education and Youth: Anatole Collinet Makossa
Minister of Social Affairs, Humanitarian Action and Family Affairs: Emilienne Raoul
Minister of Primary and Secondary Education, in charge of Literacy: Hellot Matson Mampouya
Minister of Sports and Physical Education: Leon Alfred Opimbat
Minister of Culture and Arts: Jean-Claude Gakosso
Minister in the Office of the Prime Minister, in charge of Planning and Major Projects: Jean Jacques Bouya
Minister in the Office of the President in charge of Nationa Defence: Charles Richard Mondjo
Minister Delegate to the Minister of State for Economy, Planning and Territorial Development: Raphael Mokoko
Minister Delegate to the Minister of State for Transport, Civil Aviation and Merchant Marine: Martin Aime Parfait Coussoud-Mavounou
Minister Delegate to the Minister of State for Transport, Civil Aviation and Merchant Marine, responsible for Waterways and the Riverine Economy: Gilbert Mokoki

---

Ministries
Office of the President, PO Box 2006, Brazzaville, Republic of Congo. Tel: +242 812379, fax: +242 815864
Office of the Prime Minister, PO Box 2096, Brazzaville, Republic of Congo. Tel: +242 10 83 1124.
Ministry for State Control, Brazzaville, Republic of Congo.
Ministry of Defence, Brazzaville, Republic of Congo. Tel: +242 10 812620.
Ministry of Justice, Brazzaville, Republic of Congo. e-mail: minicom@cogonet.cg, URL: http://www.gouv.cg/gouv/justice/justice.htm
Ministry of the Interior, Brazzaville, Republic of Congo. Tel: +242 10 834157. e-mail: minicom@cogonet.cg, URL: http://www.gouv.cg/gouv/interieur/interieur.htm
Ministry of Foreign Affairs and Co-operation, PO Box 2070, Brazzaville, Republic of Congo. Tel: +242 814162 / 814161, fax: +242 10 836098 / 836200

Ministry of Construction, Town Planning and Housing, Brazzaville, Republic of Congo

Ministry of Social Amenities and Public Works, Brazzaville, Republic of Congo. Tel: +242 815907 / 815941

Ministry of Health and Social Affairs, PO Box 201, Brazzaville, Republic of Congo. Tel: +242 815746 / 811295

Ministry for Technical and Vocational Training, BP 169, Brazzaville, Republic of Congo.

Ministry of Culture and Art, Brazzaville, Republic of Congo.

Ministry of the Economy, Finance and the Budget, PO Box 2031, Brazzaville, Republic of Congo. Tel: +242 814143 / 814145 e-mail: minicom@cogonet.cg, URL: http://www.gouv.cg/gouv/finance/finance.htm

Ministry of Hydrocarbon Minerals, Brazzaville, Republic of Congo. Tel: +242 815614 / 815823

Ministry of Posts and Telecommunications, PO Box 114, Brazzaville, Republic of Congo. Tel: +242 814118 / 810470

Ministry of Agriculture and Livestock, Brazzaville, Republic of Congo. Tel: +242 814131 / 814133

Ministry of Transport and Civil Aviation, Brazzaville, Republic of Congo. Tel: +242 814550 / 814184

Ministry of Trade, Consumption and Small and Medium-Sized Enterprises, Brazzaville, Republic of Congo.

Ministry of the Forestry and the Environment, BP 98, Brazzaville, Republic of Congo. Tél: + 242 814137, fax: +242 814134, URL: http://www.minifor.com/

Ministry of the Civil Service, Administrative Reform and Women's Promotion, Brazzaville, Republic of Congo. e-mail: minicom@gogonet.cg, URL: http://www.gouv.cg/fonctpublique/fonctpublique.htm

Ministry of Territorial and Regional Development, Brazzaville, Republic of Congo.

Ministry of Communications, Brazzaville, Republic of Congo. Tel: +242 814129, fax: +242 814128, e-mail: minicom@cogonet.cg, URL: http://www.gouv.cg/gouv/communication/communication.htm

Ministry of National Education and Scientific Research, PO Box 169, Brazzaville, Republic of Congo. e-mail: minicom@cogonet.cg, URL: http://www.gouv.cg/gouv/ensprimaire/ensprimaire.htm

Ministry for Energy and Hydraulics, Brazzaville, Republic of Congo. Tel: +242 810264 / 810270

Ministry of Tourism, Brazzaville, Republic of Congo. Tel: +242 814031 / 814030

Ministry of Mines, Brazzaville, Republic of Congo. Tel: +242 810295

Ministry of Commerce and Handicraft, Brazzaville, Republic of Congo. Tel: +242 814157 / 814158

Ministry of Industry, Brazzaville, Republic of Congo. Tel: +242 814125

Elections

The last presidential election took place on 12 July 2009. The incumbent candidate, President Denis Sassou-Nguesso won after the opposition boycotted the vote. The main opposition candidate was also excluded from the vote.

In elections to the National Assembly held in August 2007, the President's Congolese Labour Party (PCT) won an overall majority; many of the opposition parties had boycotted the elections. In July 2002 President Sassou-Nguesso's PCT won 56 of the 72 seats in the Senate.

Political Parties

Parti Congolais du Travail (PCT, Congolese Labour Party)
Forces Démocratiques Unies (FDU, United Democratic Forces)
Union pour la Renouveau Démocratique/Mwinda (URD, Union for Democratic Renewal)
Union Panafricaine pour la Démocratie Sociale (UDAPS, Pan-African Union for Social-Democracy)
Convention pour la Démocratie et le Salut (Convention for Democracy and Health)
Union for Democracy and Republic (Union pour la Démocratie et la République-Mwinda)
Congolese Movement for Democracy and Integral Development (MCDDI)

Diplomatic Representation

Embassy of the Republic of Congo, 4891 Colorado Avenue, NW, Washington DC 20011, USA. Tel: +1 202 726 5500, fax: +1 202 726 1860
Ambassador: Serge Mombouli
British Embassy, Kinshasa (accredited to the Republic of the Congo), 83 Avenue du Roi Baudouin (ex Avenue Lemera), Gombe, Kinshasa, Democratic Republic of Congo. Tel: +243 88 44904, fax: +243 88 838543, e-mail: ambrit@ic.cd
Ambassador: Diane Corner
British Honorary Consulate, Brazzaville, Republic of Congo. Tel: +242 620893
US Embassy, 70-83 Section D, Maya-Maya Boulvard, Brazzaville, Congo. Tel: +242 06 612 2000, URL: http://brazzaville.usembassy.gov
Ambassador: Christopher Murray
Permanent Representative of the Republic of the Congo to the United Nations, Two Dag Hammarskjold Plaza, 866 Second Avenue, 2nd Floor, New York, NY 10017, USA. Tel: +1 212 832 6553, fax: +1 212 832 6558, e-mail: congo@un.int, URL: http://www.un.int/congo
Ambassador: H.E. Mr. Raymond Serge Bale

LEGAL SYSTEM

The Republic's legal system is based on the French civil law system and customary law. The highest court is the Cour Supreme. Auguste Iloki was appointed president of the court in September 2012.

There are serious human rights issues in Congo. There have been reports of killings and physical abuse of suspects and detainees by security forces, whilst harassment and extortion of civilians by unidentified armed elements are ongoing problems. Prison conditions are poor, and arrests can be arbitrary. The judiciary is seen as ineffective, there is official corruption and freedom of the press is limited.

The Republic of the Congo is largely composed of two major ethnic groups; the Pygmies live in servitude to the Bantus, who up the majority in this country of 3.7 million. Pygmies claim that discrimination limits their access to health centers, schools and often prevents them from voting and travelling. A law that would grant special protections to the Pygmy people is awaiting a vote by the Congo parliament.

The Republic of Congo is among those countries which retain the death penalty for ordinary crimes such as murder but has not executed anyone since before 1999. As of 2013, over 70 people were believed to be on death row.

LOCAL GOVERNMENT

The country is divided into 10 departments, subdivided into 76 sub-prefectures and one commune (Brazzaville). The departments are: Likouala (Impfondo), Sangha (Ouesso), Cuvette Ouest (Ewo), Cuvette (Owando), Plateaux (Djambala), Pool (Kinkala), Bouenza (Madingou), Lékoumou (Sibiti), Niari (Dolisie), Kouilou (Pointe-Noire).

AREA AND POPULATION

Area

The Republic of Congo is situated in west central Africa with an Atlantic coastline of about 160 km and an area of 342,000 sq. km (132,000 sq. miles). It is bordered to the east by the Democratic Republic of Congo and to the south by the Cabinda enclave of Angola. To the north-west and west is Gabon, and to the north are Cameroon and the Central African Republic. The country is covered mostly by rainforest. The climate is tropical, with a rainy season from March to June and a dry season from June to October.

To view a map of the Republic of Congo, please consult:
http://www.lib.utexas.edu/maps/cia08/congo_republic_sm_2008.gif

Population

The Republic of Congo had an estimated population of 4.02 million in 2010, with a population growth rate of 2.5 per cent over the year. The population density is 4.1 inhabitants per sq. km.; however, 70 per cent live in Brazzaville, Pointe-Noire or along the connecting railway, making it one of the most urbanised countries in Africa. The vast jungle in the north of the country is almost uninhabited.

There are fifteen main Bantu groups, the largest of which are Bacongo, Vili, Bateke, MBochi and Sangha. There are also some 100,000 Pygmies, the original inhabitants of the region.

The majority of Congolese (53 per cent) are aged between 15 and 60 years, with 41 per cent aged below 15 years, and 6 per cent aged 60 and over. The median age is 19.

French is the official language, although Lingala, Kikongo and Munukutuba are also spoken.

Births, Marriages, Deaths

Figures for 2010 indicate that there were 35.3 births per 1,000 people, and 12.5 deaths per 1,000 people. The World Health Organization estimates that life expectancy at birth was 55 years (53 years for men and 57 years for women) in 2009. Healthy life expectancy was 48 years. The fertility rate was 4.5 children per woman. (Source: http://www.who.int, World Health Statistics 2012)

Public Holidays 2014
1 January: New Year's Day
18 April: Good Friday
21 April: Easter Monday
1 May: Labour Day
9 June: Whit Monday
15 August: Independence Day
25 December: Christmas Day

EMPLOYMENT

The Republic's workforce represents about 40 per cent of the total population, two-thirds of whom work in the agriculture industry. High labour costs and a restrictive labour code have had an adverse effect on investment in the country. Recent figures show that unemployment in the 16-34 year age bracket is particularly high, around 42 per cent.

BANKING AND FINANCE

Currency
Co-operation financière en Afrique centrale franc (CFA) = 100 centimes (fixed to the euro)

GDP/GNP, Inflation, National Debt
Congo's economy is based largely on the oil industry, particularly the growing petroleum sector. The industry has provided the major share of government revenues and exports since the 1980s, accounting for approximately two-thirds of Congo's real gross domestic product (GDP). Thanks to oil revenues the country was able to finance infrastructure projects, However, it also has a large debt burden. Economic reforms were halted by the 1997 civil war and the economy badly affected by the conflict. It is estimated that around 70 per cent of the population live in poverty.

STATES OF THE WORLD

REPUBLIC OF CONGO

GDP growth has largely recovered from the effects of the civil war and reached US$7,670.26 million in 2006, with a growth rate of 6.2 per cent. Growth fell to -0.7 per cent in 2007. GDP was US$8,242.85 million. Figures for 2010 estimated GDP to be US$11.5 billion reflecting a growth rate of 10.0 per cent in 2009 and giving a per capita figure of US$2,700. GDP was estimated to be US$14 billion in 2011.

Inflation (consumer prices) fell from 3.6 per cent in 2004 to 2.5 per cent in 2005 before rising to 4.0 per cent in 2006 and 2007 and 3.0 per cent in 2009.

Total external debt stood at US$5,327.84 million in 2006. In November 2007 the London Club of private sector creditors canceled 80 per cent of Congo's debt. In March 2010 the Paris Club of creditor countries and Brazil agreed to cancel all the debt owed to them by Congo, this amounted to around US$2.4 billion.

Foreign Investment
In October 2004, Congo pledged to adhere to the Extractive Industries Transparency Initiative (EITI), a voluntary scheme designed to increase transparency in the oil and mining sectors. This, together with clearance of the country's outstanding external debt arrears, encouraged the IMF to approve a three-year, $84.4 million Poverty Reduction and Growth Facility (PRGF). In 2004, the World Bank approved a $30 million Economic Rehabilitation Credit (ERC) in December 2004, to be repaid over 40 years and the African Development Bank agreed a loan of $51.1 million.

Following satisfactory completion of the IMF PRGF programme, the World Bank and International Monetary Fund approved a Heavily Indebted Poor Countries (HIPC) decision point treatment for Congo in 2006. However, in order to qualify for irrevocable debt relief, the Congolese government must bring the internal controls and accounting system of the state-owned oil company (SNPC) up to internationally recognized standards; this proviso refers to irregularities in reporting oil revenues in the past. Those resources released through interim debt relief must be used for poverty reduction under a reform programme.

Balance of Payments / Imports and Exports
Exports were estimated to be US$10.35 billion in 2010 and imports US$3.7 billion. The hydrocarbon industry accounted for 89 per cent of total export revenue, and timber was the source of most of the rest. Sugar, cocoa, coffee and diamonds were also important export commodities. Most exports go to China (almost 40 per cent). USA, Brazil and India were major suppliers of import goods. Major import products are capital goods, food, machinery, vehicles and spare parts. The Republic's main suppliers were France, China, Italy, India, Brazil and the USA.

Central Bank
Banque des États de l'Afrique Centrale (BEAC), PO Box 1917, 736 Avenue Monseigneur Vogt, Yaounde, Cameroun. Tel: +237 234030 / 2230511, fax: +237 233329 / 223 3380, URL: http://www.beac.int
Governor: Lucas Abaga Nchama

MANUFACTURING, MINING AND SERVICES

Primary and Extractive Industries
The Republic of Congo is the sixth largest oil producer of sub-Saharan Africa. Oil accounts for around 90 per cent of the Congo's export earnings and contributes 80 per cent of government revenue. Estimated proven oil reserves in January 2009 were 1.6 billion barrels. Oil production peaked in 2000, when it reached 280,000 barrels per day. It declined due to lower production at mature fields and delays in bringing new fields online; crude oil production averaged 239.94 thousand barrels per day in 2008. Congo's first deepwater field came online in 2008 and this has boosted the declining oil production, figures for 2011 show that oil production had risen to 298.48 thousand barrels per day. Domestic consumption rose to 13,000 barrels per day in 2011, whilst 234,000 barrels per day of crude oil was exported in 2006. Most exports go to Asia, China purchasing around 46 per cent. Refining capacity was estimated at 21,000 barrels per day in 2012.

Most oil production is located offshore; however, the M'Boundi field is one of West Africa's biggest onshore oil fields, with estimated proven reserves of 1.3 billion barrels. In 2005, the field produced an average of 57,000 barrels per day. Exploration and production is overseen by the state-owned Société Nationale des Pétroles du Congo (SNPC). Congo's major oil refinery is the Congolaise de Raffinage (CORAF) plant at Pointe Noire, which has a capacity of 21,000 barrels per day. The two main oilfields are the 70,000 barrels per day N'Kossa field and the 60,000 barrels per day Kitina field. Leading foreign oil companies operating in the Congo are TotalFinaElf and Agip.

With natural gas reserves of 3.0 trillion cubic feet, Congo has the fifth largest gas resource in sub-Saharan Africa after Nigeria, Mozambique and Cameroon. However, due to a lack of infrastructure, there is very little production and much of it is flared or vented. Figures for 2010 show that 33 billion cubic feet were produced all of which was used domestically. Most of Congo's gas is associated with oil deposits, and is either vented or flared. The country itself does not use natural gas. (Source: Energy Information Administration)

Energy
Congo's per capita energy consumption in 2003 was 4.1 million Btu. Oil made up some 78 per cent of total energy, and hydroelectricity contributed 22 per cent.

Congo's electricity generation capacity was 0.15 GWe in 2010 and generation was 0.55 billion kWh. Electricity consumption was just 0.58 billion kWh in the same year; most people in rural areas rely on wood as their primary source of fuel. Electricity transmission links are non-existent in many parts of the country, and much of the infrastructure was destroyed during the civil war. The country's two main power plants are both hydroelectric: the 74-megawatt Bouenza and the 15-megawatt Djoué plant. Congo imports 25 per cent of its

electricity needs from the Democratic Republic of Congo; however, it plans to become more self reliant by expanding current plants and building new ones. Congo's electricity industry is run by the Société Nationale d'Electricité (SNE). (Source: Energy Information Administration)

Manufacturing
The manufacturing sector, whose contribution to GDP is amongst the highest in francophone Africa, is largely based on agricultural and forestry processing, as well as petroleum extraction, cement kilning, and textile printing. Footwear, soap and soft drinks are also produced.

A structural adjustment programme agreed with the IMF has led to the total or partial privatisation of a number of state corporations, and the closing down of some others.

Service Industries
Government and services are the largest contributors to GDP, earning over 40 per cent of GDP.

Agriculture
Whilst this sector is the largest employer, the agriculture industry earned just 4.2 per cent of GDP in 2011. It is estimated that 34 per cent of the population is undernourished. Only four per cent of the land is used for pasture, and none of it is irrigated.

Food production has not kept up with the needs of a highly urbanised and growing population. State farms have been poorly managed, overstaffed and in need of subsidies. However, a number of these have now been privatised. The main crops are manioc, sugar, rice, corn, peanuts, vegetables, coffee and cocoa.

Agricultural Production in 2010

Produce	Int. $'000*	Tonnes
Cassava	119,976	1,148,500
Game meat	86,165	39,600
Bananas	28,163	100,000
Sugar cane	21,344	650,000
Mangoes, amngosteens, guavas	16,777	28,000
Plantains	16,777	28,000
Indigenous cattle meat	16,614	6,150
Groundnuts, with shell	11,701	29,100
Palm oil	11,094	25,500
Fruit fresh nes	9,773	28,000
Roots and tubers, nes	9,406	55,000
Indigenous chicken meat	8,891	6,242

* unofficial figures
Source: http://faostat.fao.org/site/339/default.aspx Food and Agriculture Organization of the United Nations, Food and Agricultural commodities production

The major post-colonial export of the Congo was timber.

COMMUNICATIONS AND TRANSPORT

Travel Requirements
US, Canadian, Australian and EU citizens require a passport, visa and evidence of yellow fever vaccination. Other nationals should contact the embassy to check visa requirements.

National Airlines
Lina Congo (internal network and services to Gabon).

International Airports
There are international airports at Brazzaville and Pointe-Noire and 37 smaller airfields.

Railways
A rail line runs 510 km from Pointe-Noire to join the Congo river at Brazzaville. A 286 km spur runs from the main line to reach the Gabon border at M'binda where it joins with a cableway running to the Gabonese manganese mines at Moanda.

Roads
Recent statistics indicate that there are some 12,800 km of all-weather roads, 10 per cent of which are tarmacked. Vehicles are driven on the right.

Shipping
The Congo and Oubangui rivers and their tributaries are used for a well-developed river transport system, stretching some 4,385 km. Half the traffic passing through the port of Brazzaville goes to or comes from the Central African Republic.

Ports and Harbours
Brazzaville, Pointe-Noire, Ouesso and Djeno are the main harbours. The main port, Pointe Noire, is the centre of the offshore oil industry, linked to Brazzaville both by rail and road. Ferries run between Brazzaville and Kinshasa.

HEALTH

In 2009, the government spent approximately 5.3 per cent of its total budget on healthcare (up from 4.8 per cent in 2000), accounting for 47.5 per cent of all healthcare spending. Total expenditure on healthcare equated to 2.8 per cent of the country's GDP. Per capita expenditure on health was approximately US$67 in 2009, compared with US$22 in 2000. Figures for 2005-10 show that there are 401 physicians (1 per 10,000 population), 3,492 nurses and midwives (8.2 per 10,000 population), 63 pharmaceutical personnel and 12 dentists. There are 16 hospital beds per 10,000 population.

According to Unicef, in the wake of the civil war (1994-2003), less than half the population has access to clean water. As a result, diarrhoea and other water-borne diseases are prevalent, especially in the Pool region, where just 2 per cent of the population has access to modern sanitation and 8 per cent to clean water. According to the WHO, in 2008 approximately 95 per cent of the urban population and 34 per cent of the rural population had access to improved drinking water. In the same year, 31 per cent of the urban population and 29 per cent of the rural population had access to improved sanitation. In 2010, 71 per cent of the population had access to improved drinking water and 18 per cent had access to improved sanitation.

There is a very high maternal mortality rate, and the risk of dying in childbirth is 1 in 26; this is due to inadequate facilities and medical care. Malnutrition is common, with one in five children suffering from stunted growth. The infant mortality rate (probability of dying by first birthday) in 2009 was 61 per 1,000 live births. The child mortality rate (under 5 years) was 93 per 1,000 live births. The main causes of childhood mortality are: malaria (26 per cent), prematurity (13 per cent), diarrhoea (7 per cent), pneumonia (14 per cent), and HIV/AIDs (5 per cent). Just 6 per cent of children sleep under insecticide-treated nets.

There are over 90,000 adults with HIV/AIDS, over half of whom are women. Prevalence of the disease over the country averaged 4.9 per cent of the 15-49 age group in 2004; however, in some urban areas, such as Pointe Noire, it exceeds 10 per cent of the population. In 2008 it was recorded as 3.5 per cent. In 2003, around 9,700 deaths from the disease were recorded.

In 2008, there were 156 reported cases of cholera, 217 of leprosy and 3,371 of TB. A polio outbreak was reported in November 2010 with over 129 cases of acute flaccid paralysis and 58 deaths. An emergency vaccination campaign was launched. According to WHO figures in 2009, the measles vaccination rate in infants was 76 per cent, DTP3 90 per cent, HepB3 90 per cent and Hib3 90 per cent. (Source: http://www.who.int, World Health Statistics 2012)

EDUCATION

Primary/Secondary Education
Education at state schools is compulsory from the age of six to 12. Primary education lasts for six years, starting at the age of six and ending at 11. Secondary education begins at 12 and ends at 16. Entry into secondary education is dependent on passing the Secondary School Entry Test. During the decade of civil war that ended in 2003, the educational infrastructure was destroyed and many schools remain short of supplies and teachers. Many children are still two or three grades behind in their schooling.

UNESCO figures for the year 2005 indicate that 8.1 per cent of total government expenditure went on education. In 2004, 89 per cent of children enrolled in school, (including year repeaters) and sixty-six per cent of these reached grade five. 25 per cent of children had to re-take a year. In the same year, there were 83 primary school children for every teacher. 58 per cent of those children who completed primary school then went on to secondary education.

The adult literacy rate in 2005 was estimated to be 84.7 per cent, rising to 97.4 per cent among 15-24 year olds. This compares favourably to the regional averages of 59 and 69 per cent respectively. (Source: UNESCO, UIS, October 2007)

Higher Education
Higher education is provided by the Marien Ngouabi University, Brazzaville, which is state subsidized; the Institut Superieure des Sciences d'Education, Brazzaville; and the Institut Africain Monyondzi. An estimated six per cent of students enroll in tertiary education.

Vocational Education and Training
Vocational education and training are provided by the College Technique, Commercial et Industriel de Brazzaville; Ecole Superieure Africaine des Cadres des Chemins de Fer, Brazzaville; College d'Enseignement Technique Agricole, Sibiti; and Centre d'Etudes Administratives et Techniques Superieures, Brazzaville.

RELIGION

Around 89 per cent of the population are Christian, the majority being Catholic. Approximately 5 per cent hold traditional beliefs and 3.3 per cent are Muslim.

Congo has a religious liberty rating of 9 on a scale of 1 to 10 (10 is most freedom). (Source: World Religion Database)

COMMUNICATIONS AND MEDIA

There is increased freedom of expression following the 2001 abolition of a law which allowed for prison sentences for libel offences. However news coverage tends to reflect government views. Incitement to hatred or racism is punishable by prison.

Newspapers
The main newspapers in the Republic of Congo are Le Choc (http://www.lechoc.info/), L'Observateur, L'Humanitaire, Le Tam Tam and Les Echos du Congo. Many newspapers are privately owned and do publish criticism of the government.

Broadcasting
Radiodiffiusion Televison Congolaise, the state-run broadcaster, operates TV Congo and Radio Congo. Privately owned stations and satellite TV are available.

Telecommunications
The landline infrastructure is inadequate and centred around Brazzaville, Pointe-Noire and Loubomo. Mobile phone subscribership has increased dramatically in recent years. In 2008, there were 22,000 mainline phones, and over 1.8 million mobile phones. In the same year, 155,000 people were regular internet users.

ENVIRONMENT

Congo's main environmental problems are air pollution from cars, water pollution from raw sewage, the lack of potable water, and deforestation.

Energy related carbon emissions were estimated at 5.313 million metric tons in 2005, up from 2.98 million metric tons in 2002. Per capita carbon emissions were estimated at 1.47 metric tons in 2005. In 2006, Congo's emissions from the consumption of fossil fuels totaled 5.53 million metric tons of carbon dioxide. This figures had risen to 6.52 million metric tons by 2010. The natural gas industry produces the greatest proportion of carbon emissions. (Source: EIA)

Congo is a party to the following environmental agreements: Biodiversity, Climate Change, Climate Change-Kyoto Protocol, Desertification, Endangered Species, Hazardous Wastes, Law of the Sea, Ozone Layer Protection, Ship Pollution, Tropical Timber 83, Tropical Timber 94 and Wetlands.

STATES OF THE WORLD

COSTA RICA
Republic of Costa Rica
República de Costa Rica

Capital: San José (Population estimate: 1 million)

Head of State: Laura Chinchilla (President) (page 1404)

First Vice President: Alfio Piva Mesen (page 1496)

Second Vice President: Luis Liberman Ginsburg

National Flag: Parti of five fesswise, dark blue, white, red, white, dark blue, the red stripe being twice the width of the others, the coat of arms in a white elliptical disk is on the hoist side of the red band

CONSTITUTION AND GOVERNMENT

Constitution
Costa Rica formed part of the Spanish Empire until 1821 when the country gained independence. From 1824 to 1839 it belonged to the Confederation of Central America, but since that time has been an independent state.

The Constitution dates from 1871 but has been modified on several occasions since, most recently in 1949. Constitutional power is in the hands of the President who is elected for a non-renewable term of four years. The President is empowered by the constitution to appoint and remove cabinet ministers. The 1949 Constitution confirmed the total abolition of armed forces that had taken place in 1948.

To consult the full text of the constitution, please visit:
http://www.costaricalaw.com/constitutional_law/constitution_en.php

International Relations
Relations with Costa Rica's northern neighbour Nicaragua remain strained, due largely to a territorial dispute over navigation rights on the San Juan River and, in particular, the right of Costa Rican patrols to carry arms; in September 2005, the Costa Rican Government sent the case to the International Court in The Hague for arbitration. The number of Nicaraguans living and working in Costa Rica (mainly illegally) is estimated at about 500,000.

Costa Rica is a member of the Central American Integration System (SICA) but does not participate in the Central American Parliament -(PARLACEN). Negotiations to join the US CAFTA were completed in January 2004 and a referendum was held on its ratification in October 2007; 51.5 per cent of Costa Ricans voted in favour of joining the controversial agreement with Central American neighbours, the Dominican Republic and the U.S. after a year long battle. The pact has already taken effect in the Dominican Republic, Guatemala, Honduras, Nicaragua and El Salvador.

COSTA RICA

An FTA between Costa Rica and Caribbean Countries (CARICOM) was agreed in 2004 and is awaiting ratification by all the parties.

Costa Rica is an active member of the international community and supports efforts to protect the environment; promotes human rights and sustainable development, and advocates peaceful settlement of disputes. Costa Rica is host to the Inter-American Court of Human Rights and the UN University for Peace.

Costa Rica joined the Coalition on Iraq in 2003 but withdrew in September 2004 when the Constitutional Court ruled the decision unconstitutional. The country remains committed to the fight against terrorism. Costa Rica has been an active member of the United Nations Security Council since January 2008.

Recent Events
In October 2004, three former presidents - Jose Maria Figueres, Miguel Angel Rodriguez and Rafael Angel Calderon - were placed under house arrest pending investigations into corruption charges.

A two-day public workers' strike was held in October 2006, in protest against a free trade deal with the US. In a referendum held in October 2007, Costa Ricans voted in favour of implementing the controversial CAFTA agreement by a small majority.

In October 2009, former president Rafael Angel Calderon was sentenced to five years in jail following a conviction of corruption.

Laura Chinchilla, became Costa Rica's first female president in February 2010.

A disputed river border raised tensions between Costa Rica and Nicaragua in November 2010. In March 2011, the UN International Court of Justice ordered Nicaragua and Costa Rica to keep their troops back from the disputed river border.

In September 2012, the Nicoya peninsula west of San Jose was hit by an earthquake, two people were killed. The quake coincided with the eruption of the San Cristobel volcano in Nicaragua.

Legislature
Under the Constitution, legislative power is vested in a single Chamber of Representatives or Legislative Assembly (*Asamblea Legislativa*) made up of 57 Deputies who are elected for a single term of four years.

Asamblea Legislativa, Apartado postal 74-1013, San José, Costa Rice. Tel: +506 243 2441, fax: +506 243 2444, e-mail: alprensa@congreso.aleg.go.cr, URL: http://www.asamblea.go.cr/

Cabinet (as at June 2013)
Minister of Foreign Affairs, Minister of Religious Affairs: Enrique Castillo Barrantes
Minister of Environment, Telecommunications and Energy: Rene Castro Salazar
Minister of Foreign Trade: Anabel Gonzalez
Minister of Public Education: Leonardo Garnier Rimolo
Minister of Labour and Social Security: Olman Segura
Minister of Finance: Edgar Ayales
Minister of the Economy, Industry and Trade: Mayi Antillon
Minister of Health: Dr Daisy Corrales
Minister of Housing and Settlements: Guido Monge
Minister of Public Security and the Interior: Mario Zamora
Minister of Public Works and Transport: Pedro Castro
Minister of Culture and Youth: Manuel Obregon
Minister of Agriculture and Livestock: Gloria Abraham
Minister of Tourism: Allan Flores
Minister of Justice: Fernando Ferraro
Minister of the Presidency: Carlos Ricardo Benavides
Minister of Sport: William Corrales
Minister of Science and Technology: Alejandro Cruz Molina
Minister of National Planning and Political Economy: Roberto Gallardo
Minister of Decentralization and Local Government: Juan Marin Quiros
Minister of Social Welfare: Fernando Marin
Minister of Communications and Liaison with Public Institutions: vacant
Chair of the National Women's Institute: Maureen Clarke

Ministries
Ministry of Presidency and Planning, Apdo. 520 Zapote, San José, Costa Rica. Tel: +506 224 4092, fax: +506 253 6984
Ministry of Foreign Relations and Worship, Apdo. 10027-1000 San José, Costa Rica. Tel: +506 223 7555, fax: +506 223 9328, URL: http://www.rree.go.cr/
Ministry of Interior, Police and Public Security, Apdo. 10006-1000 San José, Costa Rica. Tel: + 506 223 8354, fax: +506 222 7726
Ministry of Justice, Apdo. 5685-1000 San José, Costa Rica. Tel: +506 223 9739, fax: +506 223 3879
Ministry of Finance, Ministerio de Hacienda, San José, Costa Rica. Tel: +506 222 2481, fax: +506 255 4874, URL: http://www.hacienda.go.cr/
Ministry for the Economy, Industry and Commerce, Apdo. 10216-1000 San José, Costa Rica. Tel: +506 222 1016, fax: +506 222 2305, URL: http://www.meic.go.cr/
Ministry of Foreign Trade, Apdo. 10216-1000, San José, Costa Rica. Tel: +506 222 5910, fax: +506 233 9176
Ministry of Public Works and Transport, Apdo. 10176-1000 San José, Costa Rica. Tel: +506 257 7798, fax: +506 255 0242
Ministry of Public Education, Apdo. 10087-1000 San José, Costa Rica. Tel: +506 222 0229, fax: +506 255 2868, URL: http://www.mep.go.cr/
Ministry of Public Health, Apdo. 10123-1000 San José, Costa Rica. Tel: +506 233 0683, fax: +506 255 8085, URL: http://www.netsalud.sa.cr/ms/

Ministry of Labour and Social Security, Apdo 10123-1000 San José, Costa Rica. Tel: +506 221 0238, fax: +506 222 8085
Ministry of Housing, Apdo. 222-1002 Paseo de los Estudiantes, San José, Costa Rica. Tel: +506 257 1415, fax: +506 255 1976
Ministry of Women's Affairs, San José, Costa Rica. Tel: +506 253 9772, fax: +506 253 8823
Ministry of Agriculture and Livestock, Science and Technology, Apdo 10094-1000 San José, Costa Rica. Tel: +506 231 5311, fax: +506 232 2103, URL: http://www.mag.go.cr/
Ministry of Culture, Apdo. 10227-1000 San José, Costa Rica. Tel: +506 223 1658, fax: +506 233 7066
Ministry of Environment and Energy, Apdo. 10104-1000 San José, Costa Rica. Tel: +506 233 9534, fax: +506 290 5091, URL: http://www.minae.go.cr/
Ministry of Energy and Mines:, San José, Costa Rica. Tel: +506 290 5091

Political Parties
Social Christian Unity Party (PUSC); National Liberation Party (PLN), URL: http://www.pln.or.cr; Partido Acción Ciudadana (PAC), (Citizen's Action Party), URL: http://www.pac.cr; Movimiento Libertario (ML) (Liberty Movement), URL: http://www.movimientolibertario.com; Partido Renovación Costariccense (PRC); Democratic Force (FD); Partido Integracion Nacional (PIN); Partido Unión Nacional (PUN), National Union Party; Partido de Unidad Socialcristiana (Social Christian Unity Party PUSC).

Elections
The presidential elections in February 2006 produced a close finish with a fraction of a percentage of votes separating the two leading candidates, former President Oscar Arias and former minister Otton Solis. Turnout was low, possibly due to political cynicism following bribe allegations against three former presidents. A recount was ordered and Sr. Arias was inaugurated on 9th May 2006. The most recent presidential election took place in February 2010. Former vice president Laura Chinchilla was elected to the post, becoming the country's first female head of state.

The last parliamentary election was held in February 2010 when the National Liberation Party, the party of newly elected President Chinchilla, failed to win a majority.

Diplomatic Representation
Embassy of Costa Rica, 2114 S Street, NW, Washington, DC 20008, USA. Tel: +1 202 234 2945, fax: +1 202 265 4795, e-mail: embassy@costarica-embassy.org, URL: http://costarica-embassy.org
Ambassador: Muni Figueres
Embassy of Costa Rica, Flat 1, 14 Lancaster Gate, London W2 3LH, UK. Tel: +44 (0)20 7706 8844, fax: +44 (0)20 7706 8655, e-mail: costaricanembassy@btconnect.com, URL: http://www.costaricanembassy.co.uk/
Ambassador: Pilar Saborio Rocafort
British Embassy, Apartado 815, Edifico Centro Colon (11th Floor), San José 1007, Costa Rica. Tel: +506 258 2025, fax: +506 233 9938, e-mail: britemb@racsa.co.cr, URL: http://ukincostarica.fco.gov.uk/en
Ambassador: Sharon Isabel Campbell (page 1399)
Embassy of the United States, Calle 120 Avenida 0, Pavas, San José, Costa Rica. Tel: +506 2519 2000, fax: +506 2519 2305, e-mail: info@usembassy.or.cr, URL: http://costarica.usembassy.gov
Ambassador: Anne Slaughter-Andrew
Permanent Representative of Costa Rica to the United Nations, 211 East 43rd Street, Room 903, New York, NY 10017, USA. Tel: +1 212 986 6373, fax: +1 212 986 6842, e-mail: costarica@un.int, URL: http://www.un.int/wcm/content/site/costarica
Ambassador: Eduardo Ulibarri

LEGAL SYSTEM

In addition to the Supreme Court of Justice, there are four Appeal Courts and a Court of Cassation. Minor crimes and misdemeanours are dealt with by provincial courts and local justices. Twenty-two Supreme Court justices are elected for eight-year terms. The Chief Justice is chosen from Supreme Court justices.

In general the government respects the human rights of its citizens. However, there are substantial delays in the judicial process, leading to prolonged pretrial detention.

Supreme Court, URL: http://www.poder-judicial.go.cr/
Acting President: Justice Zarella Villanueva

Office of the Ombudsman, URL: http://www.dhr.go.cr/

LOCAL GOVERNMENT

Administratively, Costa Rica is divided into seven provinces: San José, Alajuela, Cartago, Heredia, Puntarenas, Limón, and Guanacaste. The provinces are subdivided into 81 cantons, and the cantons into 421 districts. Municipal council members are elected for a term of four years. The most recent municipal elections took place in 2010.

AREA AND POPULATION

Area
The Republic of Costa Rica is located in Central America, south of Nicaragua and north of Panama, between the Caribbean Sea and the Pacific Ocean. It has an area of about 50,700 sq. km (19,738 sq. miles). A volcanic mountain range extends the length of the country; it comprises four volcanoes, two of which are active. There are coastal lowlands on either side of this range.

the climate varies from mild in the central highlands to tropical and subtropical in coastal areas.

To view a map, consult http://www.lib.utexas.edu/maps/cia08/costa_rica_sm_2008.gif

Population

The population in 2010 was an estimated 4.659 million with an annual growth rate of 1.7 per cent. Population density is around 84.1 inhabitants per sq. km. The majority of Costa Ricans (65 per cent) are aged between 15 and 60, with 25 per cent aged under 15, and 10 aged 60 years and over. The average age was 28 years in 2010. Nearly 64 per cent of the population lives in urban areas. The province of San José has the largest population, with over 1.2 million, followed by Alajuela, Cartago, Guanacaste, Heredia, Limón and Puntarenas. The official language of Costa Rica is Spanish.

Births, Marriages, Deaths

According to Instituto Nacional de Estadistica y Censos (INEC) estimates, there were 71,291 live births in 2006 and there were 16,766 deaths. The crude birth rate, in 2006 was 16.2 births per 1,000 people, whilst the death rate was 3.9 deaths per 1,000 people. The infant mortality rate was 10 deaths per 1,000 live births in 2009. In 2006, 26,575 weddings took place, 7,033 of which were Catholic and 19,542 civil; of the 24,436 weddings performed in 2000, 10,540 were Catholic and 13,896 civil. (Source: Instituto Nacional de Estadistica y Censo, INEC) According to figures from the WHO, the crude birth rate had fallen to 15.7 per 1,000 population in 2010 and the crude death rate had risen to 4.2 per 1,000 population.

Average life expectancy at birth in 2009 was 79 years (77 years for men and 81 years for women). Healthy life expectancy is 69 years. (Source: http://www.who.int, World Health Statistics 2012)

Public Holidays 2014

1 January: New Year's Day
17 April: Maundy Thursday
18 April: Good Friday
21 April: Easter Monday
11 April: Juan Santamaria Day
1 May: Labour Day
19 June: Corpus Christi
25 July: Annexation of Guanacaste Province
15 August: Assumption/Mother's Day
15 September: Independence Day
14 October: Columbus Day (non-mandatory)
8 December: Immaculate Conception
24 December: Christmas Eve (not banks)
25 December: Christmas Day

EMPLOYMENT

Costa Rica's total labour force numbered 2,018,444 in 2007 and the net participation rate was 57 per cent. 54.4 per cent of the workforce was employed (70.7 per cent of men and 38.7 per cent of women), while 4.6 per cent were unemployed and actively seeking work, and a further 7.4 per cent were underemployed. (Source: INEC)

Costa Rica attracts some half a million job-seeking Nicaraguans.

The services industry (particularly tourism) is the major source of employment, providing work for an estimated 64 per cent of the labour force. Industry (particularly the electronics sector) employs around 22 per cent and agriculture over 14 per cent. Foreign companies have provided major investments in Costa Rica, including Intel Corporation, which employs nearly 2,000 people.

Total Employment by Economic Activity

Occupation	2008
Agriculture, hunting & forestry	235,100
Fishing	6,600
Mining & quarrying	2,200
Manufacturing	239,500
Electricity, gas & water supply	28,000
Construction	152,400
Wholesale & retail trade, repairs	377,600
Hotels & restaurants	100,300
Transport, storage & communications	143,000
Financial intermediation	53,300
Real estate, renting & business activities	137,600
Public admin. & defence; compulsory social security	93,800
Education	112,300
Health & social work	64,700
Other community, social & personal service activities	81,100
Households with employed persons	119,000
Extra-territorial organisations & bodies	2,700
Other	8,300

Source: Copyright © International Labour Organization (ILO Dept. of Statistics, http://laborsta.ilo.org)

BANKING AND FINANCE

Currency

The unit of currency is the colón of 100 céntimos.

GDP/GNP, Inflation, National Debt

Costa Rica's major economic resources are its fertile land and frequent rainfall, a well-educated population, and its location which provides easy access to North and South American markets as well as ocean access to the European and Asian Continents. It is a popular tourist destination and attracts affluent retirees from the USA. Compared with its Central American neighbours, Costa Rica has a high standard of living. The government is pursuing moves towards regional economic integration in Central America. In 2007 the people voted by referendum to ratify the Central American Free Trade Agreement. The country continues to attract foreign investment.

Manufacturing and industry overtook agriculture during the 1990s in terms of contribution to GDP. Commerce, tourism, and services now contribute around 65 per cent of Costa Rica's GDP, with manufacturing industry accounting for 21 per cent, and agriculture around 12.5 per cent.

Until the current global economic crisis, Costa Rica had enjoyed a period of economic growth. In 2006, GDP grew by 8.8 per cent, before settling at 7.3 per cent in 2007. GDP was estimated at US$ 26.23 billion in 2007. In 2008, it was estimated at 35.1 billion with an annual growth rate of 3.5 per cent. Per capita GDP that year was estimated at US$6,700. Estimated figures for 2010 put GDP at US$38.3 billion with a growth rate of 3.5 per cent, rising to US$40 billion in 2011.

Inflation ran at an average of 10.81 per cent over 2007, slightly higher than the decade's average of around 10 per cent. The highest rises were seen in food and transport costs. In 2008, it fell slightly to 9.5 per cent and fell again in 2010 to an estimated 7.0 per cent.

Costa Rica has high levels of internal and external debt (US$7.2 billion in 2007), and the interest on this debt consumes around a third of the annual budget.

Foreign Investment

The stability of the country attracts foreign investment to Costa Rica. In 2011, foreign investment was estimated to be US$15.5 billion and was mostly directed into the tourism and construction sectors.

Balance of Payments / Imports and Exports

Costa Rica exports coffee, bananas, sugar, pineapples, textiles, medical equipment and electronic components. Exports in 2010 generated an estimated revenue of US$9,375 billion; the major markets (2009) were the USA (35.9 per cent), China (8.8 per cent), and the Netherlands (6.8 per cent). Exports were estimated to be US$10 billion in 2011.

Imports include petroleum, raw materials for industry, capital goods, and consumer goods. Imports in 2010 cost an estimated US$13.5 billion and most came from the USA (42.1 per cent), Mexico (6.5 per cent), China (6.2 per cent) and Japan (5.4 per cent). Imports rose to an estimated US$15 billion in 2011.

Costa Rica is a member of the World Trade Organization (WTO), the Central American Common Market and the US-Central American Free Trade Agreemeent (CAFTA). Exports to the US are not subject to CBI duties. Costa Rica has several Free Trade Agreements including Central America (apart from Panama), Mexico, Chile, the Dominican Republic, and Canada.

Central Bank

Banco Central de Costa Rica, Apartado Postal 10058-1000, Calle 2 y 4 av central y 1a, San José, Costa Rica. Tel: +506 243 3333, fax: +506 243 4566, e-mail: ulloasg@bccr.fi.cr, URL: http://www.bccr.fi.cr
President: Rodrigo Bolanos Zamora

Chambers of Commerce and Trade Organisations

Costa Rican-American Chamber of Commerce, e-mail: chamber@amcham.co.cr, URL: http://www.amcham.co.cr/
Costa Rica Foreign Trade Corporation, e-mail: info@procomer.com, URL: http://www.procomer.com/

MANUFACTURING, MINING AND SERVICES

Production is limited to gold, silver, sea salt and construction materials. Gold production in particular is encouraged by the government. Deposits of sulphur are estimated at 11 million tons. There are considerable deposits of bauxite and iron ore (400 million tons).

Costa Rica has oil deposits off its Atlantic Coast, but these have not been developed for environmental reasons. The country is therefore entirely reliant on imports of fossil fuels. Oil consumption in 2011 was 47,000 barrels per day, mainly gasoline and distillate. Costa Rica had a crude oil refining capacity of 24,000 barrels per day at the beginning of January 2011 from its Limon facility. Costa Rica, Nicaragua, and El Salvador are the only Central American countries with a crude oil refining capacity. Drilling for oil at the Talamanca fields, near the Panama border, has yielded positive results. It is estimated that output from these fields could be between 15,000-30,000 barrels per day, leading to self-sufficiency in oil for Costa Rica.
In 2006, as part of the Caribbean Basin Initiative, Costa Rica contributed to ethanol exports to the USA.

Costa Rica uses coal but has no resources of its own and so imports 0.115 million short tons in 2010.

Energy

Costa Rica consumed 0.185 quadrillion Btu of energy in 2009. This was below the Central and South American per capita average of 52.2 million Btu (Source EIA).

COSTA RICA

Costa Rica is self-sufficient in power. Its mild climate and trade winds make neither heating nor cooling necessary, particularly in the highland cities and towns where some 90 per cent of the population lives. The country's mountainous terrain and abundant rainfall have permitted the construction of a dozen hydroelectric power plants, and hydropower accounted for 84 per cent of power generation in 2002, followed by geothermal (15 per cent), and thermal (1 per cent). Electricity generation was around 9.47 billion kilowatthours (kWh) in 2010, with consumption at around 8.5 billion kWh. Costa Rica exports electricity to Nicaragua, and has the potential to become a major electricity exporter on the completion of new generating plants and the Sistema de Interconexion Electrica de los Paises America Central (SIEPAC - a regional distribution grid) due in 2008. In 2007, Costa Rica experienced nationwide blackouts resulting from a severe dry season (which limited hydroelectric resources).

The state-owned Instituto Costarricense de Electricidad (ICE) provides 97 per cent of Costa Rica's electricity. Distribution is controlled by Compañía Nacional de Fuerza y Luz, SA (CNFL), a subsidiary of ICE. Some 80 per cent of the population has access to electricity. A National Atomic Energy Commission was formed in September 1957 under the auspices of the University of Costa Rica. (Source: EIA)

Manufacturing

Industry contributed 26 per cent of GDP in 2008. Industrial activity in Costa Rica focuses on electronic components, food processing, textiles and apparel, construction materials, fertilizers, plastics and medical equipment. Foreign investment in the country's free trade zone has helped the sector grow in recent years; Intel Corporation's microprocessor plant and Proctor and Gamble's administrative center jointly employ over 3,000 people.

Service Industries

Costa Rica's services sector in total accounted for over 65 per cent of GDP in 2008. The main areas of activity revolve around the tourism sector, banking and insurance. Tourism is Costa Rica's main source of foreign exchange. 1.7 million tourists visited Costa Rica in 2006 generating earnings of US$1.8 millions.

Agriculture

The importance of the agricultural sector is diminishing as the service and manufacturing industries expand. However, agriculture still accounted for 6.4 per cent of GDP in 2011 and employed around 14 per cent of the workforce. The principal commodities and most important exports are bananas, pineapples, coffee, cocoa and sugar.

Government purchases of land, improved farming methods and good prices have raised formerly low production of cocoa. Rice, maize, beans and cotton are also important crops, grown mainly for the domestic market, while African palm, fresh fruits (e.g. pineapple, mango and strawberry) and macadamia are grown for export.

Agricultural Production in 2010

Produce	Int. $'000*	Tonnes
Pineapples	563,468	1,976,760
Bananas	493,964	1,803,940
Cow milk, whole, fresh	296,685	950,726
Indigenous cattle meat	263,600	97,580
Indigenous chicken meat	159,804	112,190
Sugar cane	121,439	3,734,730
Coffee, green	104,541	97,305
Fruit fresh nes	96,613	276,800
Palm oil	91,756	210,905
Indigenous pigmeat	82,403	53,605
Rice, paddy	72,481	264,756
Oranges	60,297	312,000

*unofficial figures

Source: http://faostat.fao.org/site/339/default.aspx Food and Agriculture Organization of the United Nations, Food and Agricultural commodities production

COMMUNICATIONS AND TRANSPORT

Travel Requirements

A passport valid for at least 30 days after the date of departure and a return ticket are required. US, Canadian and most EU citizens do not require a visa for stays of under 90 days. Australian, Bulgarian and Irish passport holders require a visa for stays over 30 days. Nationals not referred to above are advised to contact the embassy to check visa requirements.

Persons traveling to Costa Rica from countries with risk of yellow fever transmission must provide evidence of a valid yellow fever vaccination prior to entry. The South American countries include Bolivia, Brazil, Colombia, Ecuador and Venezuela.

National Airlines

Costa Rica has 19 passenger airlines of which the major one is Líneas Aéreas Costarricenses, SA - LACSA

SANSA - Servicios Aéreos Nacionales, URL: http://www.grupotaca.com/ing/sansa.html

International Airports

The Juan Santamaría international airport is at Alajuela, 10 miles from San José. Costa Rica has 110 airports around the country 39 of which have paved runways.

Railways

Costa Rica has 278 km of railways although none of it is currently in use.

Roads

There are almost 35,343 km of roads, mostly unpaved. The Costa Rican portion of the Pan-American Highway is about 665 km long. Bus services connect Costa Rica with Panama, Nicaragua, Honduras, El Salvador, Mexico and Guatemala. Vehicles are driven on the right.

Shipping

Among the shipping lines that serve Costa Rica are Hamburg Amerika, Horn Line, Royal Ma Lines, Fyffes and Marina Mercante Nicaraguense. The country has 8 cargo liners, 24 shippir companies and 115 shipping agencies.

Ports and Harbours

The chief ports are Puerto Limón on the Atlantic coast, and Puntarenas on the Pacific. The Pacific port of Caldera is being enlarged and improved. Ferrie services run between Los Chile in the north east of the country and San Carlos, Nicaragua. There are also small cruise boa services between Panama and Cost Rica.

HEALTH

Life expectancy at birth is an average of 77 years for men and 81 years for women.

According to the World Health Organization, total expenditure on health was equivalent 10.5 per cent of GDP on health care in 2009. Government expenditure accounted for 67 per cent of this, and private expenditure 32.6 per cent. Social security expenditure accounte for 84.6 per cent of government expenditure on health. Per capita total expenditure on healt was estimated to be US$667 in 2009.

In 2000-10, there were 5,204 doctors (13 per 10,000 population), 3,653 nurses and midwive (9 per 10,000 population) and 1,905 dentists (5 per 10,000 population). There were a estimated 4 beds per 10,000 population. In 2003, it is estimated that some 12,000 peopl were living with HIV, and the number of deaths caused by the disease had reached 900.

In 2010 there were reported to be 114 cases of malaria, 71 of pertussis, 490 of TB and seve cases of leprosy. An estimated 0.4 per cent of the population aged 15-49 is believed to b infected with HIV/AIDS. In 2009, the infant mortality rate (probability of dying by first birthday was 9 per 1,000 births. The under-fives mortality rate was 10 per 1,000 live births. Th most common causes of death for young children were: prematurity 20 per cent, congenita abnormalities 37 per cent, birth asphyxia 8 per cent, pneumonia 3 per cent and diarrhoea per cent.

In 2010, 97 per cent of the population had access to improved drinking water. An estimate 95 per cent of the population had access to improved sanitation. (Source: http://www.who.in World Health Statistics 2012)

EDUCATION

Primary/Secondary Education

Costa Rica's compulsory education system lasts for 10 years and is free. Primary educatio begins at the age of six and lasts for six years. Secondary education begins at the age of 1 and lasts for a total of five years (three years at lower school and two years at upper school Enrolment in pre-primary education ran at 70 per cent in 2006, above the regional average The Gross Enrolment Ratio percentage for primary school in the same year was 111, droppin to 86 for secondary education; both figures are slightly below the regional average.

Higher Education

Higher education is provided at four universities. The number of tertiary students per 100,00 inhabitants rose from 2,525 in 1990 to 2,830 in 1996.

Figures from UNESCO for 2007 show that 20.6 per cent of government spending went o education. That year the adult literacy rate was put at 95.9 per cent rising to 98.0 per cen for youth literacy.

RELIGION

Roman Catholicism is the state religion, with around 70 per cent of the population followinc it. Around 17 per cent of the population are Protestants. There is also freedom of worship for other faiths. Costa Rica has a religious liberty rating of 10 on a scale of 1 to 10 (10 i most freedom). (Source: World Religion Database)

COMMUNICATIONS AND MEDIA

Freedom of expression in the media is moderate with libel laws in force.

Newspapers

La Nacion, URL: http://www.nacion.com/; La Prensa Libre, URL: http://www.prensalibre.co.cr/; La Republica, URL: http://www.larepublica.net/; Al Dia, URL: http://www.aldia.co.cr/; El Heraldo, URL: http://www.elheraldo.net/; Tico Times (English language), URL: http://www.ticotimes.net/.

Broadcasting

There is one publicly-owned television station and numerous privately-owned television stations. Cable services are also widely available. There is a public radio network and more than 100 privately-owned radio stations.

Telecommunications

Whilst the country has a good domestic telephone service, the mobile service is restricted as the state provider cannot satisfy demand. The market is beginning to open up to competition. According to 2008 estimates, some 1.4 million telephone main lines were operating in Costa Rica, with a further 1.8 million mobile phones in 2008. There were 1.2 million internet users in 2006, and the number of hosts reached 13,792 in 2007.

ENVIRONMENT

over 25 per cent of Costa Rican territory is designated national park or reserve; however, problems such as illegal logging, pollution of rivers and destruction of maritime habitats and species continue due to insufficient funding and failure to enforce of protection policies. Costa Rica's current environmental problems include deforestation, soil erosion, air pollution, water pollution, the protection of fisheries, and the management of solid waste.

Carbon dioxide emissions in 2005 reached 5.69 million metric tons. Per capita carbon dioxide emissions reached 1.42 metric tons in 2005, up from 1.37 metric tons in 2002 but well below the Central American average of 2.45 metric tons. In 2006 Costa Rica's emissions from the consumption of fossil fuels totaled 5.76 million metric tons of carbon dioxide. In May 2007, the Costa Rican government announced that Costa Rica was on course to become the first voluntarily 'carbon neutral' country. However, figures from the EIA for 2010 show that carbon dioxide emissions from fossil fuels were 6.41 million metric tons.

The country is a party to the following international environmental agreements: Biodiversity, Climate Change, Climate Change-Kyoto Protocol, Desertification, Endangered Species, Environmental Modification, Hazardous Wastes, Law of the Sea, Marine Dumping, Ozone Layer Protection, Wetlands and Whaling. It as signed, but not ratified the Marine Life Conservation agreement.

CÔTE D'IVOIRE

République de Côte d'Ivoire

Capital: Yamoussoukro (Official/administrative capital); Abidjan (Commercial capital, population estimate, 2005: over 3 million)

Head of State: Alassane Ouattara (page 1491) (President)

Vice President: Guillaume Kigbafori Soro (page 1518)

National Flag: The flag consists of three vertical stripes in orange, white and green

CONSTITUTION AND GOVERNMENT

Constitution

The Ivory Coast, now the Côte d'Ivoire, was part of French West Africa from 1904 until 1960. It became independent in 1960 under President Félix Houphouët-Boigny, leader of the Parti Démocratique de la Côte d'Ivoire (PDCI). The country changed its name to Côte d'Ivoire in 1986. Houphouët-Boigny ruled the country for over 30 years until his death in 1993.

On 24 December 1999 the government of Côte d'Ivoire was overthrown in a coup d'état by a military regime known as the 'Committee for Public Salvation'. Led by General Robert Guéi, the regime announced the formation of an interim government, a 24-member cabinet, to hold power until fresh elections were held. The transitional government consisted of both military officers and civilians nominated by political parties. Henri Konan Bedie, the deposed president, went into exile.

A referendum on a new draft constitution took place on 23 July 2000 and nearly 90 per cent of voters agreed to constitutional change. One of the proposed amendments was the restriction of presidential candidates to those with Ivorian parents. This amendment was dropped in 2004.

According to the 2000 Constitution, the head of state is the President, directly elected for a single term of five years. The President appoints the Prime Minister and, with the advice of the Prime Minister, the Council of Ministers.

The Economic and Social Council (Conseil Économique et Social) consists of 105 members, appointed by the Head of State, who serve a term of five years. The Council advises on economic and social matters in relation to proposed legislation.

To consult the constitution, please visit: http://abidjan.usembassy.gov/ivoirian_constitution2.html.

International Relations

The civil war 2002-03 strained the Cote d'Ivoire's relations with neighbouring states, who previously provided migrant labour for the cocoa farms. Many of these workers returned to their home countries. This put pressure on their home states and resulted in a serious loss of remittances to those countries. The headquarters of the African Development Bank relocated from Abidjan, where it had been since 1966, to Tunis. The UN deployed a peace keeping operation to the country in 2004, and its mandate was renewed in 2007.

France is the country's principal trading partner, and several French citizens remain in the Cote d'Ivoire, though the number of expatriates has declined.

Recent Events

On 19 September 2002 some 750 troops mutinied. The soldiers, who were rebelling against their treatment by the government, had been recruited by former military ruler General Robert Guei, who was killed in the uprising. An agreement between the rebels and the government was reached in January 2003. Seydou Diarra was appointed prime minister and he formed a government which included members from all the warring parties. The war was officially declared over in July 2003 but by September the rebels pulled out of the government accusing President Gbagbo of not honouring the peace agreement. In March 2004, 120 people were killed during a rally opposing the rule of the President, and the first contingent of a UN peacekeeping force was deployed.

In November 2004, government planes bombed French positions, killing nine French peacekeepers. The French retaliated by destroying the Ivoirian airforce. Riots broke out across Abidjan, targeting French nationals and the French army. Foreign nationals were evacuated and between 20 and 60 Ivorians were killed in clashes with French soldiers. On 15 November, the UN Security Council imposed an arms embargo and threatened to impose sanctions on those responsible for blocking the peace process.

In December, key reforms were passed by parliament, including the abolition of the requirement for President's to have two Ivoirian parents. Following talks in South Africa, an end of hostilities was announced by both government and rebels in April 2005. However, three months later, 120 people were killed during a massacre in Duekoue, possibly caused by ethnic splits.

In October 2005, President Gbagbo postponed elections for a year; the UN extended his mandate for twelve months and the UN Security Council demanded that a new Prime Minister be appointed, with more powers.

In January 2006, UN-backed mediators recommended dissolving parliament, following the expiry of its mandate. President Gbagbo's Ivorian Popular Front (FPI) pulled out of the transitional government and peace talks, sparking anti-UN protests from his supporters, and fears among rebels of a resumption of military conflict. However, in February, the main political rivals met and agreed to negotiations. In June, the militias loyal to President Gbagbo missed the agreed disarmament deadlines, and by September the rebel leaders admitted that they had failed to agree on voter registration and disarmament, both pre-requisites to elections being held. A UN Security Council resolution passed in November extended the mandate of the transitional government for a further year.

The cabinet resigned in September 2006, over a scandal involving the dumping of toxic waste in Abidjan. Fumes from the waste killed three people and more than 1,500 people needed treatment.

In March 2007, the Ivory Coast government and the rebel movement agreed to form a new power-sharing government and to set up a joint army command. Guillaume Soro was appointed the new prime minister. The deal set a timetable for disarmament and for a mass identification programme, as well as for the removal of the buffer zone patrolled by French and UN troops. President Gbago declared the war officially over in April 2007. In June 2007, Prime Minister Soro survived a rocket attack on his plane. At the beginning of May 2008, the former rebels in Ivory Coast who control the northern half of the country started to disarm. They plan to rejoin civilian life or join a new joint national army.

Escalating food prices sparked protests in Abidjan in March and April 2008, and in July, the Ivory Coast increased diesel prices by 44 per cent and petrol prices by 29 per cent, attributing the rises to global oil prices. In August, the government halved the salaries of its ministers and of state company managers to pay for a ten per cent reduction in fuel prices.

In October 2008 voter registration for November parliamentary elections was suspended amid uncertainty about the validity of identity cards. The elections were postponed until early 2009. The UN extended its arms embargo and sanctions on Ivory Coast's diamond trade for another year, promising to review the embargo once the country holds a presidential election. Elections were later postponed until the end of 2009. The MFA withdrew from the government on 24 March 2009.

In February 2010 voter registration was suspended indefinitely following violent protests at the government's handling of process. President Gbagbo dissolved government and electoral commission, which led to more protests. Following mediation talks brokered by the Burkina Faso president, Blaise Compaore, a new coalition government was formed.

Presidential elections were then held in October and November 2010. On December 2 the electoral commission announced that Alassane Ouattara had won with 54.1 per cent of the vote compared with 45.9 per cent for President Gbagbo. The following day the Constitutional Council, run by allies of Laurent Gbagbo, rejected the result and declared Gbagbo the winner. The UN refused to accept this decision and endorsed Alassane Ouattara as the winner instead, a stance followed by the African Union, the West African ECOWAS bloc, the US and the EU. Later in December supporters of both men took to the streets and around 20 people were killed in the ensuing gun battles. Gbagbo demanded that UN and French forces should leave the country but UN Secretary-General Ban Ki-moon refused. Following this the West African ECOWAS bloc threatened military action if Gbagbo refused to cede power to Ouattara. Several presidents of African nations including President Goodluck Jonathan of Nigeria were involved in mediation talks. In January 2011 President Gbagbo announced he was ready to negotiate a peaceful end to the crisis without preconditions. The African Union gave Gbagbo until March 24 to stand down but the date passed. A few days later pro-Ouattara forces came down from northern strongholds towards Abidjan, fighting around the city continued for several days until UN and French troops launched air strikes against pro-Gbagbo supporters who they accused of using heavy weapons against civilians and UN headquarters. Mr Gbagbo was seized from his residence, originally it was reported that French troops had gained access to the residence and arrested him but this was denied by Paris, it was later reported that he was arrested by forces loyal to Mr Ouattara with the help of French troops and the UN. An estimated 3,000 people died in the post-election violence.

Mr Ouattara was formally sworn in as president on 21 May.

In November 2011, the International Criminal Court (ICC) issued an arrest warrant for the former president Laurent Gbagbo on charges of crimes against humanity. Mr Gbagbo was transferred on 30 November. He will be the first former head of state to be tried by the ICC since it was set up in 2002.

In June 2012, the interior minister announced that a plot organised by supporters of ex-president Gbagbo to overthrow the government had been foiled. The plot may have been linked to seven UN peacekeepers who had been killed at the end of the previous year, the accused killers were Liberian mercenaries and Ivorian militias. In September and October the Ivory Coast closed its borders with Ghana after an attack on the border town of Noe, again supporters of President Gbagbo were suspected.

In November 2012, President Ouattara dissolved the government following a row between the parties over a new marriage law.

Legislature
The unicameral legislature is known as the National Assembly (Assemblée Nationale) and consists of 225 members elected for a five year term by universal suffrage.
Assemblée Nationale, 01 BP 1381, Abidjan, Côte d'Ivoire. URL: http://www.anci.ci
President of the National Assembly: Mamadou Koulibaly

Cabinet
Following the disputed presidential election results, both presidential claimants named their Councils of Ministers. Mr Gbagbo named N'Gbo Gilbert Marie Aké as his prime minister and Mr Outtara named Mr Guillaume Kignafori Soro as his prime minister and minister of defence. Mr Ouattara was formally sworn in as president on 21 May.

Cabinet (as at June 2013)
Prime Minister, Minister of Justice, Keeper of the Seals: Daniel Kablan Duncan (page 1418)
Minister of Planning and Development: Dr Albert Toikeusse Mabri
Minister of the Interior and Security: Hamad Bakayoko
Minister of Foreign Affairs: Charles Koffi Diby
Minister of Mining and Energy: Adam Toungara
Minister of Livestock and Water Resources: Kobena Kouassi Adjoumani
Minister of Economic Infrastructure: Patrick Achi
Minister of National Education: Kandia Kamissoko Camara
Minister of Industry: Jean-Claude Brou
Minister of Health and AIDS Control: Raymonde Goudou Coffie
Minister of Civil Service and Administrative Reform: Konan Gnamien
Minister of the Craft Industry and Promotion of Small and Medium Enterprises: Jean-Louis Billon
Minister of Higher Education and Scientific Research: Ibrahima Cisse Bacongo
Minister of Agriculture: Mamadou Sangafowa Coulibaly
Minister of Human Rights and Public Liberties, Justice and Keeper of Seals: Gnenema Coulibaly
Minister of Culture and Francophonie: Maurice Kouakou Bandama
Minister of Family, Women and Children: Anne Desiree Ouloto
Minister of Post and Information Communications, Government Spokesperson: Bruno Kone
Minister of the Environment, Urban Development and Sustainable Development: Remi Allah Kouadio
Minister of Tourism: Roger Kacou
Minister of Construction, Sanitation and Town Planning: Mamadou Sanogo
Minister of State for Employment, Social Affairs and Solidarity: Moussa Dossa
Minister of Transport: Gaoussou Toure
Minister of African Integration: Ally Coulibaly
Minister of Youth and Civic Service Promotion: Alain Michel Lobognon
Minister of Water Resources and Forestry: Mathieu Babaud Darret
Minister of Communication, Assistant Government Spokesperson: Affoussiata Bamba-Lamine
Minister to the President in charge of Defence: Paul Koffi Koffi
Minister to the Prime Minister in Charge of Economy and Finance: Niale Kaba
Minister of State in the Office of the President: Jeannot Kouadio Ahoussou

Ministries
Office of the President, 01 BP 1354 Abidjan 01, Côte d'Ivoire. Tel: +225 2031 4000, fax: +225 2031 4540, e-mail: lepresident@pr.ci, URL: http://www.cotedivoirepr.ci
Prime Minister's Office, 01 BP 1533 Abidjan 01, Côte d'Ivoire. Tel: +225 20 22 00 20, e-mail: pm@primature.gov.ci, URL: http://www.primature.gov.ci
Ministry of Foreign Affairs, Bloc Ministériel, blvd Angoulvand, BP V109, Abidjan, Côte d'Ivoire. Tel: +225 20 32 71 50, fax: +225 20 33 23 08
Ministry of State and Ministry of Interior and Decentralisation:, BP V 121 Abidjan, Côte d'Ivoire. Tel: +225 2032 2343, fax:+225 2032 4735
Ministry of Defence and Civil Protection, 01 BP V 11 Abidjan 01, Côte d'Ivoire. Tel: +225 2029 0288, fax: +225 2022 2818
Ministry of Finance and Economy, Immeuble SCIAM, 16e étage, ave Marchand, BP V163, Abidjan, Côte d'Ivoire. Tel: +225 20 21 05 66, fax: +225 20 21 35 01
Ministry of Justice, Bloc Ministériel, blvd Angoulvandm A-17, BP V107, Abidjan, Côte d'Ivoire. Tel: +225 20 21 11 27, fax: +225 20 21 16 90
Ministry of Higher Education and Scientific Research, Cité Administrative Tour C, 20e étage, BP V151, Plateau, Abidjan, Côte d'Ivoire. Tel: +225 20 21 57 73, fax: +225 20 21 22 25

Ministry of National Education, BP V 120 Abidjan, Côte d'Ivoire. Tel: +225 2022 441 +225 226490, fax: +225 2022 6908
Ministry of Labour and Civil Service:, BP, V 93 Abidjan, Côte d'Ivoire. Tel: +225 202 0400, fax: +225 2022 8415
Ministry of Mines and Energy, Inn Sciam 15e Etage BP V 65 Abidjan, Côte d'Ivoire Tel:+225 2021 5003, fax: +225 2021 5302
Ministry of Public Health, Cité Administrative Tour C 16e Etage BP V 4 Abidjan, Côte d'Ivoire. Tel: +225 2021 4871, fax: +225 2021 1085
Ministry of Agriculture and Animal Resources, BP V 82, Côte d'Ivoire. Tel: +225 2021 0833, fax: +225 2021 4618
Ministry of Economic Infrastructure, BP V 6 Abidjan, Côte d'Ivoire. Tel: +225 202 6055, fax: +225 2034 7307
Ministry of Construction and Environment, Tour D 19e Etage, BP V 153 Abidjan Côte d'Ivoire. Tel: +225 2021 9406, +225 214408, fax: +225 2021 4561
Ministry of Transport, BP V 06 Abidjan, Côte d'Ivoire. Tel:+225 2021 6055, fax: +225 2034 7329
Ministry Social Security and National Solidarity, 01 BP V301 Abidjan 01, Côte d'Ivoire. Tel: +225 2022 0469, +225 2022 0488, fax: +225 2022 9077
Ministry of Culture and Communication, Tour C 22e Etage BP V 138 Abidjan, Côte d'Ivoire. Tel: +225 2021 1116, +225 2021 2985, fax: +225 2022 2297
Ministry of Environment, Water and Forests, BP V 153 Abidjan, Côte d'Ivoire. Tel +225 20 22 4662, fax: +225 2021 4561
Ministry of the Family, Women and Children, Cité Administrative Tour E 16e Etage BP V 200 Abidjan, Côte d'Ivoire. Tel: +225 2021 7626, fax: +225 2021 4461
Ministry of Youth, Imm Sogefia, 3e Etage BP V 136 Abidjan, Côte d'Ivoire. Tel: +225 2021 5251, fax: +225 2021 4821
Ministry of Sport, Imm Sogefia, 3e Etage BP V 136 Abidjan, Côte d'Ivoire. Tel: +225 2021 5251, fax: +225 2022 4821

Political Parties
Front Populaire Ivoirien (FPI); Mouvement des Forces d'Avenir (MFA); Parti Democratique de Côte d'Ivoire - Rassemblement Démocratique Africain (PDCI-RDA); Parti Ivoirien des Travailleurs (PIT); Rassemblement des Républicains (RDR); Union des Sociaux Democrate (USD), Union pour la Democratie et la Paix en Cote d'Ivoire (UDPCI); New Forces (FN).

Elections
When the leader of the military regime General Robert Guéi took power in 1999 he promised that democratic elections would take place. He later changed the constitution to allow only those with Ivorian parents to stand, thus preventing key opposition member Alassane Outtara from standing. The election was duly held on 19 October 2000. General Guéi initially refused to accept the vote, which gave 59 per cent of the vote to Laurent Gbagbo, leader of the Ivorian Popular Front. General Guéi sacked the electoral commission and attempted to remain in power. However, following civil unrest and loss of support from the military, he fled a few days later. Laurent Gbagbo was named president on 25 October 2000.

Elections took place for the National Assembly on 10 December 2000 and 14 January 2001 and resulted in Laurent Gbagbo's Front Populaire Ivorien (FPI) party winning 96 of the Assembly's 223 seats. The PDCI-RDA won 94 seats, and the RDR won 5.

The next presidential election was due to take place in October 2005 and the next parliamentary elections were due to take place in December 2005. These were initially postponed for a year; it was felt that elections could not be free and fair due to the continuing armed opposition in the north. In November 2006, the UN Security Council extended the mandate of the transitional government for a further year, pending militia disarmament and voter registration. Elections were then expected to take place in 2007. However, in October 2007, the Representative to the UN stated that elections would have to be postponed due to delays in registering voters around the country and by lack of progress on disarmament. The election was then scheduled for 30 November 2008, but it was again postponed due to lack of progress on voter registration. The presidential election was then re-scheduled for 29 November 2009. This was however postponed again and the first round was eventually held in October 2010 and the second round on 28 November. On December 2 the electoral commission announced that Alassane Ouattara had won with 54.1 per cent of the vote compared with 45.9 per cent for President Gbagbo. The following day the Constitutional Council, run by allies of Gbagbo, rejected the result and declared Gbagbo the winner. The UN refused to accept this decision and endorsed Alassane Ouattara as the winner instead, a stance followed by the African Union, West African ECOWAS bloc, US and the EU. Later in December supporters of both men took to the streets and around 20 people were killed in the ensuing gun battles. Gbagbo demanded that UN and French forces should leave the country but UN Secretary-General Ban Ki-moon refused, following this the West African ECOWAS bloc threatened military action if Gbagbo refused to cede power to Ouattara.

The repeatedly postponed elections took place on 11 December 2011. President Ouattara and his allies secured the majory of the vote, supporters of Laurent Gbagbo boycotted the vote.

Diplomatic Representation
Embassy of the Republic of Côte d'Ivoire, 2 Upper Belgrave Street, London SW1X 8BJ, United Kingdom. Tel: +44 (0)20 7201 9601, fax: +44 (0)20 7462 0087
Ambassador: Claude Stanislaus Bouah-Kamon
US Embassy, rue Jesse Owens, 01 BP 1712, Abidjan 01, Côte d'Ivoire. Tel: +225 2021 0979, fax: +225 2022 3259, e-mail: abidjancons@state.gov, URL: http://abidjan.usembassy.gov/
Ambassador: Phillip Carter III
Embassy of the Republic of Côte d'Ivoire, 2424 Massachusetts Avenue, NW, Washington DC 20008, USA. Tel: +1 202 797 0300
Ambassador: Daouda Diabate
British Embassy, Due to security risk, the British Embassy in Cote d'Ivoire has suspended operations within the country. Consular matters can be effected through the High Commission in neighbouring Ghana - Tel: +233 21 221665, e-mail: high.commission.accra@fco.gov.uk, URL: http://www.britishhighcommission.gov.uk/ghana

Ambassador: Peter Jones
Permanent Representative of Côte d'Ivoire to the United Nations, 46 East 74th Street, New York, N.Y. 10021, USA. Tel: +1 212 717 5555, fax: +1 212 717 4492, e-mail: ivorycoast@un.int, URL: http://www.un.int/cotedivoire/
Ambassador: Youssef Bamba

LEGAL SYSTEM

The Supreme Court oversees all aspects of Côte d'Ivoire's judicial system, including the Court of Appeals and lower courts. The Supreme Court (Cour Supreme) consists of four chambers: the Judicial Chamber for criminal cases, the Audit Chamber for financial cases, the Constitutional Chamber for judicial review cases, and the Administrative Chamber for civil cases. There is no legal limit to the number of members of the Supreme Court. The High Court of Justice can try government officials for major offenses, and there are military courts. There is also a Constitutional Council of seven members who are responsible for determining the eligibility of candidates running in presidential and legislative elections, announcing final election results, conducting referendums, and ensuring the constitutionality of legislation.

In rural areas, traditional institutions resolve domestic disputes and minor land questions in accordance with customary law. However, the formal court system is increasingly taking over these traditional mechanisms, and the current Constitution provides for a Grand Mediator, bridging the gap between traditional and modern methods of dispute resolution. The presidentially-appointed Grand Mediator settles disputes that cannot be resolved by traditional means.

The government's human rights record continues to be poor. There have been recent arbitrary and unlawful killings, including summary executions by security forces and progovernment militias, as well as cases of torture by security forces. Conditions in prison are life-threatening, and arrests can be arbitrary. There is official corruption, and there are restrictions on freedoms of speech, press, assembly, association, and movement. The death penalty was abolished in 2000.

LOCAL GOVERNMENT

Cote d'Ivoire is divided into 19 regions and 90 departments. The regions are Agneby, Bafing, Bas-Sassandra, Denguele, Dix-Huit Montagnes, Fromager, Haut-Sassandra, Lacs, Lagunes, Marahoue, Moyen-Cavally, Moyen-Comoe, N'zi-Comoe, Savanes, Sud-Bandama, Sud-Comoe, Vallee du Bandama, Worodougou and Zanzan. Each region and department is headed by a prefect appointed by the central government. There are also 196 communes, each headed by an elected mayor, plus the city of Abidjan with 10 mayors.

AREA AND POPULATION

Area

The total area of the country is 322,462 sq. km. The West African Republic of the Côte d'Ivoire is bordered by Liberia and Guinea to the west, Mali and Burkina Faso to the north, and Ghana to the east. A dozen rivers cross the Côte d'Ivoire, the three most important ones being the Cavally, the Bandama and the Comoé. The terrain is generally flat to undulating plains. There is a mountainous region in the north-west. There are two climatic zones: the southern or coastal climate, with a fairly even temperature the whole year around but with heavy rainfall; and the northern climate, with great variations in temperature, and a dry and rainy season.

To view a map of Côte d'Ivoire, please consult:
http://www.un.org/Depts/Cartographic/map/profile/cotedivoire.pdf

Population

The population of the Côte d'Ivoire was estimated at around 19,738 million in 2010, with an estimated annual growth rate of 1.7 per cent over the period 2000-10. Population density is about 51 people per sq. km (132 per sq. mile). The majority of the population (53 per cent) is aged between 15 and 60, with 41 per cent aged up to 14 years, and 6 per cent aged 60 years and over. The median age is 19 years. About 51 per cent of the population lives in urban areas. Abidjan, the economic capital, now has a population of over three million. Other large cities include Bouake, with a population of 329,850; Yamoussoukro (the official capital), 110,000; Aloa, 121,842; and Korhogo, 109,445.

There are over 60 ethnic groups in Cote d'Ivoire, the principal groups being: Baoule, Bete, Senoufou, Malinke and Agni. Of the more than five million non-Ivoirian Africans living in Cote d'Ivoire, between 33 and 50 per cent are from Burkina Faso; the rest are from Ghana, Guinea, Mali, Nigeria, Benin, Senegal, Liberia, and Mauritania. The non-African expatriate community includes around 10,000 French and possibly 60,000 Lebanese.

French is the official language but many ethnic languages are also spoken.

Births, Marriages, Deaths

In 2010 the birth rate was estimated at 34.0 births per 1,000 people, whilst the death rate was an estimated 14.6 deaths per 1,000. Average life expectancy at birth in 2009 was around 50 years (49 years for men and 52 years for women). Healthy life expectancy was 45 and 48 years respectively. Mortality is particularly high in the country due to the effects of AIDS, which affects more than seven per cent of the adult population; over 570,000 adults were suffering from AIDS in 2003, with the number of AIDS-related deaths at 47,000 in the same year. The total fertility rate was estimated to be 4.4 children per female. (Source: http://www.who.int, World Health Statistics 2012)

Public Holidays 2014

1 January: New Year's Day
18 April: Good Friday
21 April: Easter Monday
29 May: Ascension Day
9 June: Whit Monday
29 June: Ramadan begins*
29 July: Eid Al Fitr* (End of Ramadan)
7 August: Independence Day
15 August: Assumption Day
5 October: Eid al- Adha* (Festival of the Sacrifice)
1 November: All Saints' Day
7 December: Félix Houphouet-Boigny Remembrance Day
25 December: Christmas
*Islamic holidays: precise date depends upon sighting of the moon

EMPLOYMENT

The country's labour force was estimated at 7.2 million in 2008, with 68 per cent working in the agricultural sector. Unemployment was in the region of 13 per cent in urban areas but unofficially could be as high as 45 per cent.

BANKING AND FINANCE

Currency
The unit of currency is the Communauté Financière Africaine France (FCFA) fixed to the euro.

GDP/GNP, Inflation, National Debt
Côte d'Ivoire is the most developed country in French-speaking Africa. Its economy is primarily dependent on agriculture and export of aagricultural products, in particular coffee, cocoa and timber, employing up to 70 per cent of the workforce. The agriculture sector contributes about 23 per cent of GDP and 60 per cent of export earnings. The Côte d'Ivoire is the world's largest producer of cocoa (producing 40 per cent of global supply), and the fifth largest producer of robusta coffee. Some 650,000 farmers work solely in the cocoa sector. In recent years, the economy has expanded into the manufacture of consumer goods. The economy was badly affected by the conflict, especially industries based in the north such as cotton. Tourism collapsed and many foreign-owned businesses left. The economy has been boosted by the developing oil sector.

The services industry is the largest contributor to GDP, accounting for 51 per cent in 2007, whilst industry accounts for nearly 25 per cent. The country's nascent industrial growth was curtailed by the civil war but is now beginning to recover. The oil industry is growing and petroleum is now the country's largest foreign exchange earner. Earnings from oil and refined products were $1.3 billion in 2006.

Real GDP rose by 2.6 per cent in 2010, to US$22.8 billion, due in part to steady cocoa exports and increased oil and gas revenues. Strong economic growth is not expected until peace is firmly re-established. Per capita GDP was estimated at US$1,700 in 2008.

The estimated inflation rate (based on consumer prices) rose from 3.1 per cent in 2002 to 4.2 per cent in 2003 and to 3.9 per cent in 2005. In 2007, it fell to 2.1 per cent. Inflation was estimated to be 6.1 per cent in 2008.

Côte d'Ivoire reduced its external debt from US$16,200 million in 1997 to US$10,700 million in 2003, assisted by the rescheduling of the country's commercial bank and bilateral debts, as well as its inclusion in the IMF/World Bank debt forgiveness programme. In 2007 an emergency post conflict aid programme was agreed with the IMF. In April 2008, the World Bank announced that Cote d'Ivoire had fully paid its arrears. However, the government's application for HIPC status has been delayed since the beginning of the civil war, and aid from all donors was stopped or suspended in 2002/03 pending full implementation of the peace agreement. External debt was estimated to be US$8.5 billion in 2011.

Foreign Investment
Direct foreign investment accounts for about 40-50 per cent of total capital in Ivorian companies. France is the key foreign investor, accounting for about 25 per cent of total capital in Ivorian companies, and between 55 per cent and 60 per cent of the total stock of foreign investment capital.

Balance of Payments / Imports and Exports
Estimated export revenue rose from US$10.8 billion in 2008 to US$11.2 billion in 2011. Import costs were an estimated US8 billion in 2011. Major export products are cocoa, coffee, cotton, palm oil, bananas, pineapples, fish, timber and petroleum products, whilst the main imported products were food, fuel, consumer goods, industrial goods and machinery. Côte d'Ivoire's main export trading partners in 2011 were France, Netherlands, Nigeria, the USA and Germany. The major import trading partners in the same year were Nigeria, France and China.

Côte d'Ivoire is a member of the West African Economic and Monetary Union (UEMOA) and ECOWAS.

Central Bank
Banque Centrale des Etats de l'Afrique de l'Ouest, BPO Box 3108, Avenue Abdoulaye Fadiga, Dakar, Senegal Tel: +221 8 390500, fax: +221 8 239335, URL: http://www.bceao.int
Governor: Tiémoko Meyliet Kone

MANUFACTURING, MINING AND SERVICES

Primary and Extractive Industries
Côte d'Ivoire has reserves of natural gas and oil. Iron reserves exist on Mount Klahoyo but have not yet been exploited. There are also diamond and gold reserves.

STATES OF THE WORLD

CÔTE D'IVOIRE

Côte d'Ivoire had proven oil reserves estimated at 100 million barrels at the beginning of January 2012. Crude refining capacity is 64,000 barrels per day. Côte d'Ivoire's oil production increased from 56,000 barrels per day in 2005 to 59,000 bbl/d in 2008 and fell to 40,000 bbl/d in 2011. Consumption rose to 25,000 bbl/d and approximately 35,000 bbl/d were exported, mainly to Western Europe in 2005. Consumption in 2010 was put at 23,000 bbl/d. Oil exports represent around 28 per cent of the country's total export revenue. Côte d'Ivoire's national oil company is Petroci, established in 1975. Foreign companies involved in developing the Côte d'Ivoire's oil reserves include Addax, Apache, Canadian Natural Resources, Dana Petroleum, Energy Africa, ENI-Agip, ExxonMobil, Royal Dutch/Shell, Texaco, and TotalFinaElf.

Natural gas was first discovered in Côte d'Ivoire in the 1980s. Total reserves were estimated at 1 trillion cubic feet at the beginning of January 2011. Production reached an estimated 53 billion cubic feet in 2010, all of which was consumed by the domestic market. Consumption is predicted to rise sharply over the next three years.

Energy
Côte d'Ivoire consumed a total of 0.113 quadrillion Btu in 2005. Fuel share of energy consumption in 2004 was estimated as follows: oil, 42 per cent; natural gas, 42 per cent; and hydroelectricity, 16 per cent. Energy consumption was 0.130 quadrillion btu in 2009.

Côte d'Ivoire had a total electricity generating capacity of 1.22 GWe in 2010, electricity generation in the same year was 5.72 billion kWh and consumption was 3.87 billion kWh. 60 per cent of electricity is generated through conventional thermal stations, and 40 per cent using hydroelectricity. The privately-owned Compagnie Électricité Ivoirienne (CIE) handles the management and distribution of electricity in the country. The government has made rural electrification a priority, with the aim of connecting 200 rural districts to the national grid annually.

Manufacturing
The Côte d'Ivoire was the second French-speaking African country to become industrialised, but this sector has stagnated following the civil war. Prior to the conflict (2002/03) there were about 700 enterprises in the country, of which 240 were classified as large and 240 as small. There was a growing agro-industry and expansion in the manufacture of consumer goods. Some 8000 French nationals left in 2004, which led to the closure of businesses. Other foreign firms moved production facilities elsewhere. However, the industrial sector contributed around 21 per cent to GDP in 2004. There are large enterprises in the fields of food production including processing of cocoa, coffee, cotton, palm kernels, pineapples, and fish. Other manufactuing plants include wood, petroleum refining, chemical manufacturing, soap making, fertilizers, paints and mechanical and electrical engineering.

Agriculture
The economic development of the country depends mainly on agriculture. Around 70 per cent of inhabitants are engaged in agriculture, the sector generates about 70 per cent of the country's export earnings, and contributes about a third of GDP. Cocoa and coffee are the country's main cash crops. With harvests of more than 804,200 tonnes, Côte d'Ivoire is one of the world's largest producers of cocoa. Recent figures indicate that the country produces 240,000 tonnes of coffee, making it the world's fifth largest producer. Other cash crops produced are rubber, bananas, timber, logs, cotton, cotton fibre, pineapples, palm oil and palm kernels. There are about 1,145,000 cattle and 2,069,000 goats and sheep.

Agricultural Production in 2010

Produce	Int. $'000*	Tonnes
Cocoa beans	1,290,103	1,242,290
Yams	1,044,223	5,392,370
Cashew nuts, with shell	332,619	380,000
Plantains	318,270	1,541,570
Game meat	305,492	140,400
Natural rubber	264,742	231,451
Cassava	240,979	2,306,840
Rice, paddy	189,259	722,609
Palm oil	143,569	330,000
Cottin lint	115,766	81,000
Coffee, green	101,335	94,321
Bananas	88,508	314,270

*unofficial figures
Source: http://faostat.fao.org/site/339/default.aspx Food and Agriculture Organization of the United Nations, Food and Agricultural commodities production

Forestry
At the beginning of the century Côte d'Ivoire was covered by 15.5 million hectares of forest. Today, only 2.9 million hectares exist, of which 1.6 million hectares are in the south region and 1.3 million are in the savannah zone. A re-forestation programme is in operation. Each year the Société de développement des plantations forestières (Sodefor) replants 4,000 hectares. With the financial support of international sponsors the Ivorian authorities have launched a re-forestation programme to take the country to 2015. Financial contributors include the World Bank, France, Germany, and Canada. Forestry regulation has been implemented since 1991. In 2004, the forestry sector produced 8.6 million cubic metres of fuel wood, and 1.6 million cubic metres of industrial roundwood. (Source: FAOSTAT, Food and Agriculture Organization of the United Nations)

Fishing
Since 1980 the fisheries industry has been transformed and industrialized. The total catch in 2010 was 71,800 tonnes. (Source: FAOSTAT)

COMMUNICATIONS AND TRANSPORT

Travel Requirements
Citizens of the USA, Canada, Australia and the EU require a passport valid for six months after intended length of stay. Canadians, Australians and EU subjects require a visa, and US citizens must obtain a visa before arriving. Visas are not required by transit passengers leaving within 12 hours, provided they have onward documentation and do not leave the airport.

Other nationals should contact the embassy to check visa requirements.

An international health certificate showing current yellow fever immunisation is required; without it, visitors may be required to submit to vaccination at the airport health office.

National Airlines
The principal airlines are UTA and Air Ivoire, URL: http://www.airivoire.com

International Airports
The main airport is Abidjan-Port Bouet, about 10 miles from the capital, which is of international standard and provides the link with the principal towns in Côte d'Ivoire. There are also international airports at Bouaké and Yamoussoukro.

Railways
A railway line runs from Abidjan northwards into Burkina Faso. It is about 1,156 km in length. The system was originally run as one by the two countries, but now each is responsible for their respective section. In total there are 660 km of railway track in the country. Daily services run from Abidjan to Bouaké and Ferkessédougou.

Roads
Roads now total over 80,000 km, of which 6,500 km are asphalted. Vehicles are driven on the right.

Ports and Harbours
There are two large sea ports, at Abidjan (Port Autonome d'Abidjan) and San Pedro. Abidjan is the busiest port in Francophone Africa. It has 2,750 tonne container-handling gantry cranes to deal with annual traffic of about 14,000 containers. The port also serves Burkina Faso and also Mali to a lesser extent.

There are 980 km of navigable rivers and canals in Cote d'Ivoire, and numerous coastal lagoons.

HEALTH

The total national health expenditure in 2009 was 5.2 per cent of GDP according to figures published by the World Health Organization. This was equivalent to US$61 per capita. General government expenditure accounts for only 20.9 per cent of the total health spend. External resources account for 10.5 per cent. Health spending accounts for 5.1 per cent of the government expenditure. About 60 per cent of the population has access to local health care.

In 2008, an estimated 93 per cent of the urban population and 76 per cent of the rural population had access to improved drinking water. In the same year, 36 per cent of the urban population and 11 per cent of the rural population had access to improved sanitation.

In 2005-10, there were 2,746 doctors (1 per 10,000 population), 9,231 nurses (5 per 10,000 inhabitants), 274 dentists, 413 pharmaceutical personnel and 1,419 environment and public health workers. There were an estimated 4 hospital beds per 10,000 population.

Life expectancy at birth was 50 years in 2009, and health life expectancy was 47 years. The infant mortality rate (probability of dying by first birthday was 86 per 1,000 live births and the under-fives mortality rate was 123 per 1,000 live births. Most common causes of child deaths were: prematurity (13 per cent), pneumonia (15 per cent), diarrhoea (9 per cent), malaria (25 per cent) and HIV/AIDS (3 per cent). Only 6 per cent of children in Côte d'Ivoire sleep under treated mosquito nets.

Since 2001, there have been several outbreaks of Yellow Fever and Cholera in the Côte d'Ivoire. In 2009 there were 32 reported cases of cholera, 62,726 of malaria, 441 of measles, 126 of meningitis, 36 of polio, 22,708 of TB and 49 of yellow fever. The country had one of the highest HIV/AIDs prevalence in West Africa, at around 7 per cent in 2003 (570,000 people affected). In 2008 approximately 3.9 per cent of the population aged 15-49 were infected. Approximately 28 per cent of people with advanced HIV infections received anti-retroviral therapy. The rate was higher among HIV-infected pregnant women at 41 per cent. (Source: WHO, 2010) An estimated 300 000 women aged 15-19 years were living with HIV/AIDS at the end of 2003, and WHO/UNAIDS estimated that some 310,000 children had lost at least one parent to AIDS. (Source: http://www.who.int, Global Health Statistics 2012)

EDUCATION

Education is not compulsory, tuition is free but pupils are expected to pay for uniforms and an entrance fee. Around 75 per cent of children attended primary school in 2002, but this fell to 25 per cent at secondary school level. In 2000, spending on education accounted for about 21.5 per cent of total government expenditure, which was equivalent to 4.6 per cent of GDP. There is a university at Abidjan. The adult literacy rate was estimated to be 48.7 per cent in 2000 (60.8 per cent for men, 38.6 per cent for women), rising to 60.7 per cent among the 15-24 age group (70.8 per cent for men and 52.1 per cent for women). Both the rates are below the regional average.

RELIGION

A large proportion of the population is Muslim (approximately 39 per cent of the population) and 26 per cent of the population Christian, mainly Catholic. Approximately 17 per cent of the population subscribe to traditional beliefs.

COMMUNICATIONS AND MEDIA

Radio is the most popular medium. Both the government and rebels use the media for their own purposes and violent attacks against journalists and broadcasters have been reported.

Newspapers
Fraternite Matin, URL: http://www.fratmat.net; Soir Info, URL: http://www.soirinfo.com; Le Patriote, URL: http://www.lepatriote.net/main/lejournal.aspx

The country's news agency is Agence Ivoirienne de Presse, URL: http://www.aip.ci/

Broadcasting
The state-run broadcasting service is Radiodiffusion Television Ivorienne (RTI), and runs two TV channels and two national radio stations, URL: http://www.rti.ci. Canal Satellite Horizons provides a pay-TV service. Rebel groups launched their own radio station, Onuci FM, in 2005

Telecommunications
Côte d'Ivoire had an estimated 350,000 mainline telephones and over 10 million mobile phones in use in 2008. Internet users numbered about 600,000 in 2008.

ENVIRONMENT

Main areas of environmental concern are deforestation and water pollution.

The Côte d'Ivoire is a signatory to several international environmental agreements including: Biodiversity, Climate Change, Climate Change-Kyoto Protocol, Desertification, Endangered Species, Hazardous Wastes, Law of the Sea, Marine Dumping, Ozone Layer Protection, Ship Pollution, Tropical Timber 83, Tropical Timber 94, Wetlands and Whaling.

According to EIA figures, in 2010, Côte d'Ivoire's emissions from the consumption of fossil fuels totaled 5.94 million metric tons of carbon dioxide.

CROATIA
Republic of Croatia
Republika Hrvatska

Capital: Zagreb (Population estimate: 800,000)

Head of State: Ivo Josipovic (President) (page 1452)

National Flag: Three stripes, fesswise, red, white and blue, with the coat of arms in the centre

CONSTITUTION AND GOVERNMENT

Constitution
According to the Constitution of 22 December 1990 Croatia is a multiparty democratic republic headed by a president who is elected for a term of five years. State power in Croatia is divided into executive, legislative and judicial branches. Following constitutional amendments in 2000, Parliament appoints the Prime Minister, who then appoints the Cabinet. Government appointments are subject to confirmation by the Chamber of Representatives.

In the elections of May 1990, the Croatian Democratic Union, led by Dr. Franjo Tudjman, won a majority. A new Constitution was proclaimed in December 1990. In a referendum in May 1991 the citizens of the Republic of Croatia decided by an overwhelming majority of over 94 per cent to create a sovereign state of Croatia. This was followed by the proclamation of sovereignty and independence from Yugoslavia on 25 June 1991. In the meantime, war was waged against Croatia by the Yugoslav Army and the Serbian-led rump presidency of the former Yugoslavia. The process of international recognition of Croatia began at the end of 1991 and was widely recognized by January 1992.

In November 2000 the constitution was changed to move some power from the president to the parliament.

To consult the consolidated text of the constitution, please visit: http://www.sabor.hr/Default.aspx?art=2405.

International Relations
In October 2005 Slovenia declared an ecological zone in the Adriatic, with rights to use and protect the seabed, Croatia objected and asked for international mediation in the matter.

Recent Events
In June 1991 Croatia declared its independence from Yugoslavia. The Yugoslav army was sent in as a show of force. Croatian Serbs began to expel Croats and the following year the UN set up four protected zones to keep the factions apart. Those areas occupied by Croatian Serbs were declared autonomous regions and announced themselves to be the Republic of Serbian Krajina (RSK). In January 1992 the fighting between the Yugoslav army and Croatia ended, but Croatia still had the problem of what it considered to be illegal occupation by the RSK. In 1995 the Croatian army in two separate military offensives regained control of the areas claimed by the RSK and around 250,000 Croatian Serbs fled to Bosnia and Serbia. In December 1995 President Tudjman signed the General Framework for Peace which came to be known as the Dayton Agreement.

Croatia became a member of the World Trade Organisation in 2000.

In July 2001, the Croatian government decided to hand over two war crimes suspects to the international tribunal at the Hague. The decision prompted four government ministers to resign in protest: Deputy Prime Minister Goran Granic, Minister of Defence Jozo Rados, Minister of Economy Goranko Fizulic, and Minister of Science and Technology Hrvoje Kraljevic. At a press conference, Prime Minister Racan said that he would not be replacing them immediately, and was confident of surviving a vote of no confidence.

On 8 July 2002 Prime Minister Ivica Racan resigned following disagreements within the five-party coalition which he said were delaying economic reforms. However, on 16 July 2002, following a 15-hour debate in parliament, the Croatian government won a confidence vote by a margin of 93 votes to 36 and Racan retained his position as Prime Minister.

In February 2003 Croatia submitted a formal application to join the European Union and is hoping to become a full member by 2010. In March 2005 the EU delayed talks on membership because of Croatia's failure to hand over Gen. Ante Gotovino who was wanted for war crimes. Talks began again in October 2005. Gen. Gotovino was arrested in Spain in 2005. A report published by the European Commission in November 2006 stated that Croatia need to do more to tackle corruption and its attitude to non-Croats. Accession talks are now expected to end in 2090 with membership possible in 2011.

In March 2008 the trial of three Croatian former generals started at the Hague. Ante Gotovina, Ivan Cermak and Mladen Markac faced charges of killing Croatian Serbs in the 1990s.

In July 2009 the prime minister, Ivo Sanader unexpectedly resigned, parliament approved Jadranka Kosor in the post making her the country's first female prime minister. The deputy prime minister and co-ordinator for the economic sector resigned in October 2009.

In November 2010, the president of Serbia, Boris Tadic made what was viewed by many as a significant act of reconciliation between Croatia and Serbia, when he visited the country and apologised for the 1991 massacre of 260 Croat civilians by Serb forces.

In December 2011, Croatia signed a treaty that will make it the 28th member of the European Union. In January 2012, Croatian voters backed joining the EU in a referendum.

In July 2011, Goran Hadzic, commander of Serb rebel forces during Croatia's 1991-1995 civil war, went on trial at The Hague charged with war crimes.

In November 2011, former Prime Minister Ivo Sanader went on trial charged with corruption. The following year he was imprisoned for 10 years.

On July 1 2013, Croatia joined the EU becoming the 28th member.

Legislature
The Croatian Parliament (*Hrvatski Sabor*), which is the highest legislative body, now has just one chamber: the House of Representatives (*Zastupnicki Dom*). The House currently has 151 members (increased from 127 to a maximum of 160 in October 1999). A total of 140 deputies are elected from 10 constituencies, five are elected by ethnic minorities, and up to 15 represent Croatians abroad. All members are directly elected for a term of four years.

Prior to May 2001 Croatia's parliament was bicameral, consisting of the House of Counties (upper house) and the House of Representatives (lower house). Following the expiry of the upper house's mandate in May 2001, the House of Representatives voted in March 2001 to abolish it. The House of Counties was composed of 68 members elected every four years.

House of Representatives, Hrvatski Sabor, Trg Svetog Marka 6, 10 000 Zagreb, Croatia. Tel: +385 (0)1 456 9222 / +385 (0)1 630 3222, fax: +385 (0)1 630 3018, e-mail: sabor@sabor.hr, URL: http://www.sabor.hr
Speaker: Josip Leko

Cabinet (as at July 2013)
Prime Minister: Zoran Milanovic (page 1477)
First Deputy Prime Minister, Minister of Foreign and European Affairs: Vesna Pusic (page 1498)

CROATIA

Deputy Prime Minister, Minister of Domestic, Foreign and European Policy: Neven Mimica (page 1478)
Deputy Prime Minister, Minister of Social Welfare Policy and Youth: Milanka Opacic
Deputy Prime Minister, Minister of Regional Development and EU Funds: Prof. Branko Grcic
Minister of Finance: Slavko Linic (page 1465)
Minister of Defence: Dr Ante Kotromanovic
Minister of Economy: Ivan Vrdoljak
Minister of Interior: Ranko Ostojic
Minister of Justice: Orsat Miljenic
Minister of Science, Education and Sports: Dr Zeljko Jovanovic
Minister of Environment, Protection and Nature: Mihael Zmajlovic
Minister of Tourism: Darko Lorencin
Minister of Agriculture: Tihomir Jakovina
Minister of Culture: Prof. Andrea Zlatar Violic
Minister of Labour and Pension System: Prof. Mirando Mrsic
Minister of Maritime Affairs, Transport and Infrastructure: Zdenko Antesic (acting)
Minister of Construction and Spatial Planning: Anka Mrak-Taritas (acting)
Minister of Health: Prof. Rajko Ostojic
Minister of War Veterans: Predrag Matic
Minister of Public Administration: Arsen Bauk
Minister of Business and Trade: Gordan Maras

Ministries

Government of the Republic of Croatia, Trg Sv. Marka 2, 10000 Zagreb, Croatia. Tel: +385 (0)1 456 9222, fax: +385 (0)1 278483, URL: http://www.vlada.hr
Parliament of the Republic of Croatia, Trg Sv. Marka 6-7, 10000 Zagreb, Croatia. Tel: +385 (0)1 456 9222, fax: +385 (0)1 278483, URL: http://www.sabor.hr
Prime Minister's Office, Trg Sv. Marka 2, Zagreb, Croatia. Tel: +385 (0)1 456 9201, fax: +385 (0)1 630 3019
Ministry of Agriculture and Forestry, Ul. grada Vukovara 78, 10000 Zagreb, Croatia. Tel: +385 (0)1 610 6111, fax: +385 (0)1 610 9201, e-mail: office@mps.hr, URL: http://www.mps.hr/
Ministry of Croatian Homeland War Veterans, Park Stara Tresnjevka 4, 100000 Zagreb, Croatia. Tel: +385 (0)1 365 7800, fax: +385 (0)1 365 7852, e-mail: mhbdr@mhbdr.tel.hr, URL: http://www.mhbdr.hr
Ministry of Culture, Runjaninova ulica br. 2, 10000 Zagreb, Croatia. Tel: +385 (0)1 486 6666, fax: +385 (0)1 461 0489, e-mail: web@min-kulture.hr, URL: http://www.min-kulture.hr/
Ministry of Defence, Trga Kralja Petra Kresimira IV, br. 1, 10000 Zagreb, Croatia. Tel: +385 (0)1 456 7111 / 456 7412, fax: +385 (0)1 456 7963, e-mail: infor@morh.hr, URL: http://www.morh.hr
Ministry of Economy, Ulica grada Vukovara 78, 10000 Zagreb, Croatia. Tel: +385 (0)1 610 6111, fax: +385 (0)1 610 9110, e-mail: info@mingo.hr, URL: http://www.mingo.hr/
Ministry of Education and Sports, Trg hrvatskih velikana 6, 10000 Zagreb, Croatia. Tel: +385 1 456 9000, fax: +385 1 456 9087, e-mail: ured@mips.hr, URL: http://www.prosvjeta.hinet.hr
Ministry of Environmental Protection and Zoning, Ulica Republike Austrije 20, Zagreb, Croatia. Tel: +385 (0)1 378 2444, fax: +385 (0)1 377 2555, URL: http://www.mzopu.hr/
Ministry for European Integration, Ulica Grada Vukovara 62, 10000 Zagreb, Croatia. Tel: +385 (0)1 456 9335 / 456 9336, fax +385 (0)1 456 630 3183, e-mail: info@mei.hr, URL: http://www.mei.hr
Ministry of Finance, Katanciceva 5, 10000 Zagreb, Croatia. Tel: +385 (0)1 459 1333, fax: +385 (0)1 492 2583, URL: http://www.mfin.hr/
Ministry of Foreign Affairs, Trg Nikole Subica Zrinskog 7-8, 10000 Zagreb, Croatia. Tel: +385 (0)1 456 9964, fax: +385 (0)1 492 0149, URL: http://www.mvp.hr
Ministry of Health, Ksaver 200a, 10000 Zagreb, Croatia. Tel: +385 (0)1 460 7555, 467 7005, fax: +385 (0)1 467 7091, URL: http://www.miz.hr
Ministry of the Interior, Savska cesta 39, 10000 Zagreb, Croatia. Tel: +385 (0)1 612 2111, fax: +385 (0)1 612 2771, e-mail: pitanja@mup.hr, URL: http://www.mup.hr
Ministry of Justice, Administration and Local Self-Government, Ulica Republike Austrije 14, 10000 Zagreb, Croatia. Tel. +385 (0)1 371 0666, fax. +385 (0)1 371 0602, URL: http://www.pravosudje.hr/
Ministry of Labour and Social Welfare, Prisavlje 14, 10000 Zagreb, Croatia. Tel: +385 (0)1 616 9111, fax: +385 (0)1 619 6526, URL: http://www.mrss.hr
Ministry of Maritime Affairs, Transportation and Communications, Prisavlje 14, 10000 Zagreb, Croatia. Tel +385 (0)1 616 9111, fax +385 (0)1 619 6519, URL: www.mppv.hr
Ministry of Public Works, Reconstruction and Construction, Nazorova 61, 10000 Zagreb, Croatia. Tel. +385 (0)1 378 4500, fax. +385 (0)1 378 4550, e-mail: info@mjr.hr, URL: http://www.mjr.hr/
Ministry of Science and Technology, Strossmayerov trg 4, 10000 Zagreb, Croatia. Tel: +385 (0)1 459 4444, fax: +385 (0)1 459 4469, e-mail: ured@mzt.hr, URL: http://www.mzt.hr
Ministry of Tourism, Ul. grada Vukovara 78, 10000 Zagreb, Croatia. Tel: +385 (0)1 610 6300, fax. +385 (0)1 610 9300, e-mail: ministarstvo-turizma@zg.tel.hr, URL: http://www.mint.hr/
Ministry of Trades, Small and Medium Enterprises, Ksaver 200, 10000 Zagreb, Croatia. Tel: +385 (0)1 469 8300, fax: +385 (0)1 469 8308, URL: http://www.momsp.hr

Political Parties

Hrvatska Demokratska Zajednica (HDZ, Croatian Democratic Community) URL: http://www.hdz.hr
Socialdemokratska Partija Hrvatske (SDP, Social Democratic Party of Croatia) URL: http://www.sdp.hr
- Istarski Demokratski Sabor/Dieta Democratica Istriana (IDS, Istrian Democratic Assembly)
- Libra - Stranka Liberalnih Demokrata (LIBRA, Party of Liberal Democrats)
- Liberalna Stranka (LS, Liberal Party)
Hrvatska Narodna Stranka (HNS, Croatian People's Party), URL: http://www.hns.hr
- Primorski-Goranksi Savez (PGS, Littoral and Highland Region Alliance)
- Slavonsko-Baranjska Hrvatska Stranka (SBHS, Slavonian-Baranian Croatian Party)

Hrvatska Seljacka stranka (HSS, Croatian Peasant Party), URL: http://www.hss.hr
Hrvatska Stranka Prava (HSP, Croatian Right's Party)
- Zagorska Demokratska Stranka (ZDS, Zagorian Democratic Party)
- Medimurska Stranka (MS, Medimurian Party)
Hrvatska Socialna Liberalna Stranka-Demokratski Centar (HSLS-DC)
- Hrvatska Socialna Liberalna Stranka (HSLS, Croatian Social Liberal Party)
- Demokratski Centar (DC, Democratic Centre)
Hrvatska Stranka Umirovljenika (HSU, Croatian Pensioners' Party)
Samostalna Demokratska Srpska Stranka (SDSS, Independent Democratic Serbian Party), URL: http://www.sdss.hr
HDSS-HDC-DPZS (HDSS)
- Hrvatska Demokratska Seljacka stranka (HDSS, Croatian Democratic Peasant Party)
- Hrvatski Demokratski Centar (HDC, Croatian Democratic Centre)
- Democratska Prigorsko-Zagrebacka Stranka (DPZS, Democratic Prigorian Zagrebian Party)

Elections

The most recent presidential elections took place in January 2010 when Social Democrat, Ivo Josipovic won with over 60 per cent of the vote.

At the election held on 25 November 2007, the ruling Croatian Democratic Union (HDZ) won the most seats of any party but had to form a coalition with the Croatian Social Liberal Party, the Independent Democratic Serb Party and the Croatian Peasant Party. The most recent election was held in December 2011, the SDP-led Kukuriku coalition overtook the HDZ, winning 80 seats to secure an overall majority in the parliament. The HDZ coalition won 44 seats.

Diplomatic Representation

British Embassy, Ivana Lucica 4, Zagreb, Croatia. Tel: +385 (0)1 600 9100, fax: +385 (0)1 600 9111, e-mail: british.embassyzagreb@fco.gov.uk, URL: http://ukincroatia.fco.gov.uk/en
Ambassador: David Arthur Slinn (page 1516)
Embassy of Croatia, 21 Conway Street, London, W1T 6BN, United Kingdom. Tel: +44 (0)20 7387 2022, fax: +44 (0)20 7387 0310, e-mail: consular-dept@croatianembassy.co.uk (Consular Department), info-press@croatianembassy.co.uk (Information and Press Section), URL: http://uk.mfa.hr/?mh=38&mv=148
Ambassador: Ivan Grdešić
Embassy of the United States of America, Thomasa Jeffersona 2, 10010 Zagreb, Croatia. Tel: +385 (0)1 661 2200, fax: +385 (0)1 661 2373, e-mail: irc@usembassy.hr, URL: http://zagreb.usembassy.gov
Ambassador: Kenneth Merten
Embassy of Croatia, 2501 Porter Street NW, Washington, DC 20008, USA. Tel: +1 202 588 5899, fax: +1 202 588 8936, e-mail: webmaster@croatiaemb.org, URL: http://www.croatiaemb.org
Ambassador: Neven Jurica
Permanent Representative of the Republic of Croatia to the United Nations, 820 Second Avenue, 19th Floor, New York, NY 10017, USA. Tel: +1 212 986 1585, fax: +1 212 986 2011, e-mail: croatia@un.int, URL: http://un.mfa.hr/?mv=826&mh=150
Ambassador: Ranko Vilovic

LEGAL SYSTEM

There are three levels of justice consisting of the municipal courts, the county courts and the Supreme Court. The Supreme Court is the highest judicial body in the state, comprising 15 members elected by the Chamber of Provinces on the proposal of the Chamber of Representatives. It ensures the uniform application of law and equal position of citizens under the law. The High Commercial Court, as well as the county courts (20 courts), are generally courts of the second instance. In criminal matters, county courts investigate and try certain types criminal cases of the first instance. The Administrative Court decides on appeals against the final administrative acts. The Constitutional Court consists of 13 judges elected for a period of eight years.

The government respects the human rights of its citizens. However, the judicial system is overburdened and suffers from a case backlog.

Capital punishment was abolished in 1991.

Constitutional Court: URL: http://www.usud.hr/
President of the Constitutional Court: Jasna Omejec
Supreme Court: URL: http://www.vsrh.hr/

Office of the Ombudsman, URL: http://www.ombudsman.hr/

LOCAL GOVERNMENT

Croatia is divided into 20 counties and the City of Zagreb, which act as units of local administration. The counties are subdivided into 127 towns, 429 municipalities and 6,755 settlements. The counties are Bjelovarsko-Bilogorska Zupanija, Brodsko-Posavska Zupanija, Dubrovacko-Neretvanska Zupanija, Istarska Zupanija, Karlovacka Zupanija, Koprivnicko-Krizevacka Zupanija, Krapinsko-Zagorska Zupanija, Licko-Senjska Zupanija, Medimurska Zupanija, Osjecko-Baranjska Zupanija, Pozesko-Slavonska Zupanija, Primorsko-Goranska Zupanija, Sibensko-Kninska Zupanija, Sisacko-Moslavacka Zupanija, Splitsko-Dalmatinska Zupanija, Varazdinska Zupanija, Viroviticko-Podravska Zupanija, Vukovarsko-Srijemska Zupanija, Zadarska Zupanija, and Zagrebacka Zupanija.

AREA AND POPULATION

Area
Croatia lies between the Alps and the Adriatic and has borders with Slovenia, Hungary, Serbia and Montenegro. Its total area is 56,538 sq. km. There are three main geographical regions: Mediterranean coast, mountains, and the Pannonian Plain.

The climate is predominately continental: summers are mainly hot and dry with cold winters. Winters are milder along the coast.

To view a map, visit: http://www.un.org/Depts/Cartographic/map/profile/croatia.pdf

Population
Croatia's population was estimated at 4,416,000 in mid 2009, a decline of -0.3 per cent per year over the period 1999-2009. In 2011, it was estimated to have fallen to 4.403,000. Population density is 77.8 people per sq. km. Approximately 58 per cent of the population lives in urban areas. Of Croatia's 20 counties, Primorje-Gorskikotar has the highest number of inhabitants, 304,410 in 2001. The City of Zagreb had 691,724 inhabitants, according to the 2001 Census. Croatia's other major cities include Split (175,140), Rijeka (143,800), and Osijek (90,411). (Source: Croatian Bureau of Statistics), During the war in former Yugoslavia it is estimated that up to 350,000 ethnic Serbs left Croatia. Figures for 2006 show that around 120,000 have returned but in order for those still wishing to return to do so occupied homes need to be repossessed and the programme of repairing and building new homes needs to accelerated.

The majority of the population is Croat (89.63 per cent at the time of the 2001 Census). Serbo-Croat is the official language of Croatia.

Births, Marriages, Deaths
The following table shows the number and rate of births, deaths, marriages and divorces in recent years:

Births, deaths, marriages and divorces

	2004	2005	2011
Live births	40,307	42,492	41,197
Live births per '000 inhabitants	9.1	9.6	9.4
Deaths	49,756	51,790	51,019
Deaths per '000 inhabitants	11.2	11.7	11.6
Natural increase	-9,449	-9,298	-2.2
Marriages	22,700	22,138	20,211
Marriages per '000 inhabitants	5.1	5.0	4.6
Divorces	4,985	4,883	5,662
Divorces per '000 marriages	219.6	220.6	280.1

Source: Croatian Bureau of Statistics

Average life expectancy at birth in 2009, was 73 years for males and 79 years for males. Healthy life expectancy was respectively 66 years and 70 years. Approximately 15 per cent of the population is aged under 15 years and 23 per cent over 60 years. The median age is 42. According to figures from the WHO, the crude birth rate was 9.7 per 1,000 population in 2010 and the crude death rate was 12.2 per 1,000 population. (Source: http://www.who.int, World Health Statistics 2012)

Public Holidays 2014
1 January: New Year's Day
18 April: Good Friday
21 April: Easter Monday
1 May: Labour Day
19 June: Corpus Christi
22 June: Anti-Fascism Day
5 August: Statehood Day
15 August: Assumption Day
8 October: Croatian Independence Day
1 November: All Saints Day
25-26 December: Christmas

EMPLOYMENT

The following table shows Croatian labour force, employment and unemployment statistics in recent years:

	2009	2010	2011
Economically active population	1,765,000	1,747,000	1,724,000
No. of employed	1,605,000	1,541,000	1,492,000
No. of unemployed	160,000	206,000	232,000
Unemployment rate (%)	9.1	12.1	13.9

Source: Croatian Bureau of Statistics

Employment according to economic activity is shown on the following table:

Employment by activity

Employment	2008
Total	1,635,600
Agriculture, hunting and forestry	216,400
Fishing	5,300
Mining and quarrying	8,800

- continued

Manufacturing	316,100
Electricity, gas and water	28,600
Construction	145,000
Wholesale and retail trade, repairs	245,700
Hotels and restaurants	89,100
Transport, storage and communication	108,800
Financial intermediation	34,400
Real estate, renting and business activities	82,700
Public administration and defence	94,000
Education	91,500
Health and social work	92,300
Other services	69,900
Households with employed persons	5,400

Source: Copyright © International Labour Organization (ILO Dept. of Statistics, http://laborsta.ilo.org)

BANKING AND FINANCE

Currency
The unit of currency is the Kuna (HRK), introduced in May 1994.
One kuna = 100 lipa

GDP/GNP, Inflation, National Debt
Since independence, the economy has transformed into a market economy. Structural reform still needs to be completed to make the economy more competitive. Issues include pension reform, privatisation and health service reform. Croatia has been adversely affected by the world economic crisis and is forecast to enter into recession by 2014.

Croatia's economy is largely based on the services industry (particularly tourism), with services contributing an estimated 62 per cent towards GDP.. Industry accounted for 30 per cent of GDP in the same year, followed by agriculture at 8 per cent. Tourism revenue was primarily responsible for bringing the country out of recession in 2000.

Gross Domestic Product	2009	2010	2011
GDP, market prices (current) mln. kuna	328,672	326,980	333,956
GDP, market prices (current) mln EUR	44,781	44,876	44,922
GDP per capita EUR	10,111	10,158	10,203
Annual growth rate (%)	-6.9	-1.4	0.0

Source: Central Bureau of Statistics

Croatia's retail price index fell from 104.9 in 2000-01 to 102.2 in 2001-02 to 101.5 in 2002-03. It was estimated to be 106 in 2007/08. Inflation in 2009 was estimated to be 2.9 per cent. External debt rose from US$15,248.5 million in 2002 to US$23,672.0 million in 2003. In 2008, it was estimated to be €39,124.6 million. (Source: Croatian Bureau of Statistics)

Foreign Investment
Direct foreign investment totalled an estimated US$30 billion in 2011.

Balance of Payments / Imports and Exports
Foreign Trade Balance in Recent Years, figures in thousand Euros

Year	Exports	Imports	Balance
2007	9,004,144	18,832,981	-9,828,837
2008	9,585,134	20,817,147	-11,232,013
2009	7,529,396	15,220,090	-7,690,694
2010	8,905,242	15,137,011	-6,231,769
2011	9,582,161	16,281,147	-6,698,986

Source: Croatian Bureau of Statistics

Croatia's top international trading partners in 2008 (provisional figures) are shown on the following table. Figures are in million US$:

Country	Exports	Imports
Total	14,112	30,728
EU 27 Countries	8,594	19,709
- Austria	816	1,509
- Italy	2,694	5,258
- Germany	1,518	4,116
- Slovenia	1,098	1,712
EFTA Countries	171	530
Other Developed Countries	1,013	2,059
-CEFTA Countries	3,332	1,547
- Bosnia and Herzegovina	2,178	819
Other European Developing Countries	2,065	3,132
- Russia	186	3,204
Other Developing Countries	732	3,447

Source: Central Bureau of Statistics

The following table shows export and import revenue according to industry (in US$m):

Import and Exports, 2006* (US$million)

Commodity	Exports	Imports
Food and live animals	952	1,554
Beverages and tobacco	195	139
Crude materials except fuels	608	383

CROATIA

- continued

Mineral fuels & lubricants	1,567	3,405
Animal and vegetable oils	19	56
Chemical products	952	2,331
Manufactured goods	1,545	4,193
Machinery and transport	2,993	6,926
Miscellaneous manufactured goods	1,544	2,492
Commodities and transactions	1	10
Total	**10,376**	**21,488**

* provisional figures
Source: Croatian Bureau of Statistics

Central Bank
Hrvatska narodna banka (Croatian National Bank), Trg hrvatskih velikana 3, HR-10000 Zagreb, Croatia. Tel: +385 (0)1 4564555, fax: +385 (0)1 4550726 / (0)1 4550598, e-mail: webmaster@hnb.hr, URL: http://www.hnb.hr
Governor: Boris Vujcic (page 1532)

Chambers of Commerce and Trade Organisations
Croatian Chamber of Economy, URL: http://www2.hgk.hr/en/
Croatian Privatization Fund, URL: http://www.hfp.hr/
Zagreb Stock Exchange, URL: http://www.zse.hr/

MANUFACTURING, MINING AND SERVICES

Primary and Extractive Industries
Croatia has deposits of non-metal ores, such as barite and graphite, as well as bentonite, quartz, quartz rock and sand. Bauxite deposits are found in the Adriatic region.

Proven oil reserves were 70 million barrels at the beginning of January 2012. Croatia had a crude oil refining capacity of 250,000 barrels per day at the beginning of January 2011. Croatia led the Balkans region in 2005 in terms of oil production with an estimated 28,000 barrels per day (down from 33,000 barrels per day in 2000). Such low levels of production makes Croatia a net oil importer. In 2011 imports of 91,000 barrels per day were necessary to satisfy consumption of 113,000 barrels per day. Pipelines transport oil to the Balkans region from Russia and Greece, and there are port facilities on the Adriatic Sea.

Croatia had proven natural gas reserves of 1.0 trillion cubic feet at the beginning of January 2011. However, consumption outstrips production and imports are necessary. In 2010 natural gas production was 67,000 million cubic feet, whilst consumption was 100 million cubic feet, necessitating imports of 33,000 million cubic feet. Most of the Balkans' natural gas imports come from Russia.

Like Bosnia and Herzegovina and Albania, Croatia has minimal coal reserves. Reserves were 43 million short tons at the beginning of January 2003, no coal is produced and imports of 2.2 million short tons were necessary to satisfy consumption in 2010. Most imports are hard coal.

Energy
Energy Figures for 2007 in Peta Joules

Source	Production	Imports	Exports
Coal & coke		35.69	1.29
Fuel wood	15.11	1.92	1.86
Crude oil	37.27	191.32	-
Natural gas	100.13	35.87	25.56
Hydro power	42.22	-	-
Other renewables	.71	-	-
Petroleum products	-	50.86	85.42
Electricity	-	28.12	5.22

Source: Central Bureau of Statistics

Total Croatian energy consumption in 2009 was an estimated 0.399 quadrillion Btu. Oil heads primary energy consumption (48 per cent in 1999), followed by natural gas (24 per cent), hydroelectricity (14 per cent), and coal (2 per cent).

Croatia's electricity generating capacity is 13.54 billion kilowatts (kw) in 2010. However, electricity consumption exceeds domestic generation and Croatia is required to import supplies. In 2010 estimated consumption was 15.59 million kWh.

Manufacturing
The textile industry has traditionally been one of the most important industries. Croatia was at one time the third biggest ship building nation and this industry is being restructured. Other important industries are pharmaceuticals, machine tools, footwear and construction.

Value of Products Sold in Thousand Kuna

Product	2010	2011
Food products	21,085,197	22,263,133
Textiles	926,538	1,099,530
Wearing apparel	1,941,168	2,178,652
Leather & leather products	1,307,317	1,613,865
Wood & wood products	2,492,635	2,788,747
Paper & paper products	3,234,621	3,204,149
Printing & reproduction of recorded products	3,001,220	3,311,303
Coke & refined petroleum products	13,806,808	15,171,449
Chemicals & chemical products	6,206,170	6,551,248
Rubber & plastic products	2,806,346	3,075,051
Non metallic mineral products	5,438,539	5,682,355

- continued

Basic metals	2,225,201	2,504,450
Fabricated metal products	5,757,647	5,940,967
Electrical equipment	5,017,828	4,131,444
Manufacture of transport equipment excl. vehicles, trailers & semi-trailers	6,255,666	6,796,737

Source: Central Bureau of Statistics

Tourism
Foreign tourist arrivals rose from 8,694,000 in 2009 to 9,111,000 in 2010 and 9,927,000 in 20118. The majority of visitors to Croatia in 2008 were from Germany (1,546,000, followed by Italy (1,168,000) and Slovenia (1,043,000).

Agriculture
In 1999 Croatia had about 3,151,000 hectares of agricultural land, accounting for 57 per cent of its overall territory, of which 2,086,000 hectares were private farmsteads. Major crops and fruits include maize, wheat, grapes, apples and plums. Food products that are exported include beef, pork and fish.

Agricultural Production in 2010

Produce	Int. $'000	Tonnes
Cow milk, whole, fresh	239,975	769,000
Grapes	118,749	207,743
Indigenous pigmeat	115,626	75,217
Wheat	72,740	681,017
Maize	62,141	2,067,820
Sugar beet	53,731	1,249,150
Apples	45,195	106,865
Hen eggs, in shell	35,083	42,300
Indigenous chicken meat	33,094	23,233
Indigenous cattle meat	30,727	11,375
Olives	30,428	38,001
Soybeans	27,490	153,580

*unofficial figures
Source: http://faostat.fao.org/site/339/default.aspx Food and Agriculture Organization of the United Nations, Food and Agricultural commodities production

Figures for 2006 show that Croatia had 485,000 head of cattle, 1,230,000 pigs, 768,000 sheep, and 10,045,000 poultry.

Forest covers a third of the land area and are managed by a public company, Hrvatske sume. Wood products are exported. Figures for 2004 show that 2,021,129 hectares of land are given over to forestry reserves.

Total catch of fish, molluscs and crustaceans in 2010 was 52,800 tonnes.

COMMUNICATIONS AND TRANSPORT

Travel Requirements
Visitors from the USA, Canada, Australia and the EU require a passport valid for at least three months beyond length of stay (apart from those EU subjects with a vallid national photo ID card) but do not require a visa for stays of up to 90 days. Visitors must have proof of return or onward travel and sufficient funds for the length of stay.

Nationals not referred to above should contact the embassy to check visa requirements. Note also that all foreign citizens must register with the local police within 24 hours of arrival; this is usually done through the hotels.

National Airlines
Croatia Airlines, URL: http://www.croatiaairlines.hr

International Airports
There are international airports at Zagreb (URL: http://www.zagreb-airport.hr), Split, Dubrovnik, Rijeka, Pula, Zadar and Osijek.

Railways
Croatia has 2,726 km of railway lines, of which 36 per cent are electrified. Figures for 2011 show that over 49 million passenger journeys were made and over 11 million tonnes of freight were carried. Croatia has direct rail links to Austria, Czech Republic, Switzerland, Germany, Hungary, Slovenia, Italy, Bosnia and Herzegovina, Serbia, and Greece.
Croatian Railways: URL: http://www.hznet.hr

Roads
Croatia's road network extends over a length of 29,480km, 1,254 km of which is motorway. There is currently an extensive programme of road building. Figures for 2006 showed that there were 1,435,781 passenger cars on the roads. There are bus routes to Venice, Italy, Bosnia and Hercegovina and Montenegro, Hungary and Serbia. Vehicles are driven on the right.

Ports and Harbours
The main ports are Rijeka, Ploce, Split, Sibenik, Zadar, Dubrovnik and Pula. The main ports and offshore islands are connected by ferry services.

HEALTH

The Croatian health service comprises the public and private health sectors, and citizens are free to choose their health service unit and doctors for treatment and care. The health service is carried out at primary level (surgeries), poly-clinics and in-patient hospitals according to individual health care requirements and type of treatment as well as national and regional strategic planning. Health service units encompass community health service centres, infirmaries and surgery services as well as pharmacies. Each citizen has the right to health care. The necessary funds are provided through taxes and contributions as well as an allocation of government resources. In 2009, expenditure on health equated to 7.8 per cent of GDP, representing US$1,112 per capita. Government expenditure accounts for 84.9 per cent of the total expenditure. Private expenditure accounts for 15.1 per cent of total expenditure, mostly out-of-pocket expenditure.

The Croatian health service has a workforce of approximately 50,000 people. According to the WHO in 2000-10, there are 11,813 doctors (26 per 10,000 population), 24,201 (53.3 per 10,000 population), 2,673 pharmaceutical personnel (7.3 per 10,000 population) and 3,293 dentists (7.3 per 10,000 population).

In 2009 the infant mortality rate (probability of dying by first birthday) was 5 per 1,000 live births. The under-fives mortality rate was 6 per 1,000 live births. Approximately 13 per cent of deaths were caused by prematurity and 29 by congenital abnormalities.

In 2010, approximately 99 per cent of the population had access to improved water supplies and to improved sanitation. (Source: http://www.who.int, World Health Statistics 2012)

EDUCATION

Croatia's education system comprises pre-school education, primary schools, secondary schools, and higher education establishments, education in the main is free. The latest UNESCO figures (2007) put the literacy rate at 99.5 for males and 98.0 for males. For the age group 15-24 years this rises to 99.6 for males and 99.7 for females.

Pre-School Education
Nursery schools admit children aged 1-6 when they reach school age. The system of pre-school education is almost entirely supported by the state, although recently a number of independent (private) and church-supported schools have been established. Attendance is optional and depends on parental choice. In the academic year 2006-07, there were 1,244 kindergartens or other legal entities, with 109,508 children being taught by 8,079 teachers.

Primary/Secondary Education
Primary (or basic) schools in Croatia are state-supported. Attendance is compulsory for children between six and 15 years of age. During the academic year 2006-07, 382,441 pupils attended 2,146 basic schools. A total of 30,450 teachers were employed in that year.

Secondary schooling lasts from two to five years, depending on the type of school. These schools are run either by the state or privately. At present the secondary education system is undergoing structural changes from single-curriculum schools (grammar-type schools, technical, specialised schools) to multi-curricula schools. During the academic year 2006-07, 187,977 students attended 693 secondary schools, where a total of 22,573 teachers were employed.

Higher Education
Croatia has four university centres: Zagreb, Rijeka, Osijek, and Split. Founded in 1669, the University of Zagreb is the oldest and largest of Croatia's universities. Higher education institutions may be state-supported or private.

Croatia has four schools of medicine (Zagreb, Split, Osijek, Rijeka), two colleges of dental medicine (Zagreb and Rijeka), and a college of pharmacy and biochemistry in Zagreb.

Figures for 2004 from UNESCO show that spending on education was the equivalent of 4.5 per cent of GDP.

RELIGION

The predominant religion is Christianity, with Roman Catholicism being the state religion. (Roman Catholics, 76.5 per cent; Orthodox, 11.1 per cent; and Protestants, 1.4 per cent). Islam accounts for 2.4 per cent of the population.

Croatia has a religious tolerance rating of 8 on a scale of 1 to 10 (10 is most freedom). (Source: World Religion Database)

COMMUNICATIONS AND MEDIA

Newspapers
Recent figures indicate that over 50 weekly newspapers and more than 400 other newspapers are published in Croatia. The majority of newspapers are financed privately and include:
Vecernji List, URL: http://www.vecernji.hr/home/index.do
Jutarnji List, URL: http://www.jutarnji.hr
Glass Istre, URL: http://www.glasistre.hr
Novi List, URL: http://www.novilist.hr
Slobodna Dalmacija, URL: http://www.slobodnadalmacija.hr/20070706/index.asp

Broadcasting
The broadcasting company of Croatia is *Croatian Radio and Television (HTV)*, which broadcasts daily on two television and three radio channels. Radio programmes of HTV reach 96 per cent of the population and television programmes 93 per cent. There are about 1,002,398 TV subscribers.
Croatian Radiotelevision, URL: http://www.hrt.hr/htv
RTL Televizija (national, private) URL: http://www.rtl.hr
Nova TV (natioanl, private) URL: http://novatv.dnevnik.hr

Telecommunications
Croatia has an estimated 1.7 million telephone main lines in use (2011), with a further 5.1 million mobile phones (2011). Internet users numbered 2.2 million in 2009.

ENVIRONMENT

Croatia's environmental problems include air pollution from metallurgical plants which results in damaging acid rain and pollution along the coasts from domestic and industrial waste.

In 2006, Croatia's emissions from the consumption of fossil fuels totaled 21.43 million metric tons of carbon dioxide. Oil produces the greatest proportion of carbon emissions (70 per cent in 1999), followed by natural gas (26 per cent), and coal (4 per cent). According to the Kyoto Protocol, Croatia has agreed to reduce greenhouse gases to 5 per cent below 1990 levels by 2008-12. Figures for 2010 put carbon dioxide emissions at 23.43 million metric tons. (Source: EIA)

Croatia is a party to the following international environmental agreements: Air Pollution, Air Pollution-Nitrogen Oxides, Air Pollution-Persistent Organic Pollutants, Air Pollution-Sulfur 94, Air Pollution-Volatile Organic Compounds, Biodiversity, Climate Change, Climate Change-Kyoto Protocol, Desertification, Endangered Species, Hazardous Wastes, Law of the Sea, Marine Dumping, Ozone Layer Protection, Ship Pollution, Wetlands and Whaling.

STATES OF THE WORLD

CUBA

Republic of Cuba

República de Cuba

Capital: Havana (Population estimate: 2.2 million)

Head of State: General Raul Castro Ruz (page 1401) (President)

First Vice-President: Miguel Diaz-Canel Bermudez

Vice-Presidents of the Council of State: José R. Machado Ventura; Ricardo Cabrisas Ruiz; Div. Gen. Ulises Rosales del Toro; Ramiro Valdes Menendes; Marino Murillo Jorge; Antonio Enrique Lusson Batile; Abdel Izquierdo Rodriquez; Brig.-Gen. Jose Amado Ricardo Guerra

National Flag: Parti of five fesswise, alternately blue and white; at the hoist, pointing towards the fly, a triangle red charged with a star five-pointed white

CONSTITUTION AND GOVERNMENT

Constitution
On 1 January 1959 Fidel Castro defeated General Batista and took control of Cuba. In 1961, the US sponsored Bay of Pigs invasion was defeated, and Castro proclaimed Cuba a Socialist State, allying the country with the USSR.

A new constitution was proclaimed and a National Assembly of People's Power, *Asamblea Nacional del Poder Popular (ANPP)*, set up. According to the current, 1976, Constitution the head of state is the President, indirectly elected by Parliament for a five-year term. The Council of Ministers is appointed by the ANPP. The Council of Ministers is the government's highest executive body. Its Executive Committee comprises the President, the first vice-president, as well as the vice-presidents of the Council of Ministers.

On 28 June 2002 Cuba's parliament voted unanimously in favour of a constitutional amendment making the country's socialist system 'irrevocable'. Fidel Castro suggested that Cuba 'will never return' to capitalism.

To consult the full constitution, please visit:
http://www.cubaminrex.cu/english/LookCuba/Articles/AboutCuba/Constitution/inicio.html

International Relations
Cuba has relations with over 160 countries and has civilian assistance workers in over 20 foreign countries. Cuba is a member of the Organization of American States (OAS), although its present government has been excluded from participation since 1962 for incompatibility with the principles of the inter-American system. Cuba hosted the Non-Aligned Movement (NAM) summit in September 2006 and will hold the NAM presidency until 2009.

In 1961, the USA declared a trade embargo with Cuba, and this has never been lifted. On May 20, 2002, President Bush announced the Initiative for a New Cuba that called on the Cuban Government to undertake political and economic reforms and conduct free and fair elections for the National Assembly. Elections for the National Assembly were held in January 2003, with 609 government-approved candidates running for 609 seats. In October 2003, President Bush created the Commission for Assistance to a Free Cuba to help the Cuban people achieve the goal of a rapid, peaceful transition to democracy. Following Hurricanes Gustav and Ike in the autumn of 2008, US government offered up to $5 million in aid for Cuban hurricane victims; the Cuban authorities would not accept the gift while under a US embargo, and asked the US to lift the trade embargo for six months, to allow the country to buy materials needed for reconstruction. The USA said this was not possible, but offered aid through NGOs involved in the reconstruction.

The United Kingdom and Cuba have full diplomatic relations, unbroken since they were established in 1902 following Cuba's independence.

The European Union adopted a Common Position on Cuba, in December 1996; its objective is to encourage a process of transition to pluralist democracy and respect for human rights and fundamental freedoms, through dialogue with the Cuban authorities and sectors of Cuban society. Following the crackdown on the opposition in March 2003, the EU introduced restrictive measures such as invitations of the peaceful opposition to Embassy events and the limitation of ministerial visits. In response the Cuban Government 'froze' contact with EU embassies in 2003. In January 2005, the EU agreed to temporarily suspend these measures, while reaffirming the Common Position of 1996. The most recent review of the Common Position, in June 2008, recognised recent changes in Cuba and encouraged the government to introduce liberalising changes.

Canada and Spain maintain strong investment links with Cuba. The Cuban economy has benefited enormously from the "Integral Cooperation Accord" signed by Fidel Castro and Venezuelan President Hugo Chavez in October 2000; this laid the foundations for the exchange of Venezuelan oil for Cuban goods and services. Cuban exports of goods and services to Venezuela climbed to more than $150 million in 2003. Venezuela is also committed to sending more than $400 million in various products duty-free to Cuba and plans to open an office of state-owned commercial Venezuelan Industrial Bank (BIV) in Havana.

A series of economic agreements between Cuba and China have strengthened trade between the two countries. Sino-Cuban trade totalled more than $525 million in 2004, representing an increase of over 47 per cent over 2003. Most of China's aid involves in-kind supply of goods or technical assistance. During President Hu-Jintao's visit to Cuba in November 2004, China signed memorandums of understanding (MOUs) estimated at more than $500 million. The Russian prime minister visited Cuba in October 2006, signalling a new effort to expand trade and investment.

Recent Events
In November 2001, Hurricane Michelle killed five people and caused extensive damage, estimated at US$1.8 billion. Cuba was struck by two hurricanes in the autumn of 2002; both hurricanes caused widespread damage, affecting 10,000 people.

In April 2003, 75 Cuban dissidents were sentenced to up to 28 years in jail after being found guilty of various charges, ranging from aiding a foreign power to violating national security laws. The detainees were given summary trials and sentenced to prison terms ranging from six to 28 years. Amnesty International identified all 75 as "prisoners of conscience." As of August 2008, 55 of the original 75 prisoners remained incarcerated. The US President created the Commission for Assistance to a Free Cuba in October 2003; this aimed to help Cubans towards a peaceful transition to democracy. The US government committed $59 million to the Commission, over the following two years.

Some 200 dissidents held a public meeting in May 2005, possibly the first such gathering since the 1959 revolution. In July 2005, Hurricane Dennis caused widespread destruction and 16 people died. In October the same year, more than 600,000 people were evacuated from the path of Hurricane Wilma. Havana's sea defences were breached, and sea water penetrated up to half a mile inland.

President Castro underwent surgery in July 2006, and handed temporary control of the country to his brother Raul Castro. Once back in control of the country, the President missed a few notable events and there was speculation regarding his health. In May 2007 he missed the annual May Day parade. In February 2008, President Fidel Castro, leader of Cuba since the 1959 revolution, announced that he would not stand for another term as president and Raul Castro was appointed his successor. Over 70 per cent of Cubans were born after the revolution, so most of the population know no other leader than Fidel Castro, or any other system of government.

In April 2008, Raul Castro introduced a series of reforms. These included the lifting of some restrictions on the purchase of electrical goods such as mobile phones, microwave ovens and DVD players, and the lifting of the ban on Cubans staying in hotels previously reserved for foreigners. The biggest reforms were in the agriculture sector, giving farmers more scope to decide how to use their land, which crops to plant and supplies to buy. Unused state land can now be lent to private farmers as part of efforts to increase agricultural output. State workers can now own their homes and pass them on to their children; however, buying and selling property is still not allowed.

At the end of April, President Raul Castro lifted the death sentence on all but three people on death row, commuting their sentences to life imprisonment. Mr Castro also announced a Communist Party congress to take place in 2009, the first for more than a decade. The congress is expected to chart Cuba's future political and economic agenda. At the beginning of May, the first legalised home computers went on sale, though internet access remained restricted to certain workplaces, schools and universities. The desktop computers cost almost $800, in a country where the average wage is under $20 a month.

In July 2008, President Raul Castro announced that more state-controlled farm land will be put into private hands, in a move to increase the island's lagging food production. Since the 1959 revolution, most agriculture was under the control of large, state-owned enterprises which have proved inefficient. The President also announced that workers could earn productivity bonuses, doing away with the egalitarian concept that everyone must earn the same.

On the 31st August 2008, Hurricane Gustav, a Category 4 storm, lashed Cuba with torrential rain and winds of nearly 150mph. Cuba has one of the best organised disaster-preparedness systems in the region. Almost 250,000 people were evacuated from low-lying coastal regions and half a million sacks of valuable dried cigar tobacco leaves were moved into safe storage. The storm brought extensive flooding to the western, tobacco-growing province of Pinar del Rio and to Havana province. On the 8th September, Hurricane Ike (Category Two) struck the eastern end of the island with giant waves and torrential rain. Some 800,000 people were evacuated from homes along the coast. Winds of about 100mph tore the roofs off buildings, knocked down trees and destroyed crops. Together Gustav and Ike were the most destructive hurricanes ever to have hit Cuba; around 200,000 people were left homeless, hundreds of thousands needed temporary accommodation and the country's infrastructure, including its power grid, road network, schools and hospitals, was severely damaged. The US government offered up to $5 million in aid for Cuban hurricane victims, but the Cuban government said that it could not accept a gift while under a US embargo, and asked the US to consider lifting its trade embargo for six months, to allow the country to buy materials needed for reconstruction. The USA said this was not possible, but offered aid through NGOs involved in the reconstruction.

On the 8th November, Hurricane Paloma caused yet more destruction, flooding coastal areas, downing power lines and forcing the evacuation of half a million people. Paloma was the fifth hurricane in 2008 to hit Cuba, and the eighth hurricane of the Atlantic storm season.

In December, the Cuban authorities said that the country had suffered one of the most difficult financial years since the collapse of the Soviet Union. The economy had grown by just 4.3 per cent over 2008, instead of the eight per cent forecast by the government. This was largely due to hurricanes Gustav, Ike and Paloma (with estimated losses of almost $10 billion), and a rise in the cost of food imports. However, the authorities were confident that the centrally-controlled state run economy would escape the worst of the global financial crisis, and would grow by six per cent in 2009. Cuba calculates its Gross Domestic Product by including state spending on health care, education and food rationing; the figure reflects public spending, not just economic activity, as elsewhere in the world. President Raul Castro called for austerity measures including cutbacks in official travel and bonuses.

On the 1st January 2009, Cuba marked 50 years of the revolution that brought Fidel Castro to power. President Raul Castro predicted the revolution would survive another 50 years. AWhite House spokesman said the US continued to seek freedom for the Cuban people.

On the 3rd March, Raul Castro announced the first major cabinet reshuffle since coming to office; Cabinet Secretary Carlos Lage and Foreign Minister Felipe Perez Roque, seen as possible future candidates for the presidency, were among ten officials to leave. The shake-up coincided with Cuba and the US signalling that they would welcome the possibility of moving towards improved ties. In April, President Obama approved measures to allow Cuban Americans to travel more freely to Cuba, and to increase remittances from Cuban-Americans to relatives in Cuba.

On the 3rd June 2009, the Organization of American States (OAS) voted to lift Cuba's suspension, paving the way for it to be readmitted after nearly half a century. Cuba was suspended from the OAS in 1962 over its adherence to Marxism-Leninism. A diplomatic compromise which won the backing of the US in the final vote called for Cuba's readmission to be based on a "process of dialogue" in line with OAS pro-democracy "practices, proposals and principles".

In July 2010, Cuba agreed to release over 50 political prisoners, a move heralded by the international community as a new era for Cuba.

In December 2010 the government launched a debate on plans to transform the economy by boosting private enterprise.

In January 2011 US President Obama announced that travel restrictions to Cuba were to be relaxed although Cuba felt the changes didn't go far enough.

In November 2011, a law was passed allowing individuals to buy and sell private property for first time in 50 years.

In December 2011, 2,500 prisoners, including some convicted of political crimes, were released as part of an amnesty ahead of the papal visit due the following year.

In October 2012, the government abolished the requirement for its citizens to buy expensive exit permits when traveling abroad, although, educated professionals such as doctors and scientists would still be required to obtain permission to travel.

Legislature

Cuba's unicameral legislature is known as the National Assembly of the People's Power (*Asamblea Nacional del Poder Popular*). The National Assembly has constituent and legislative authority, and comprises 601 deputies (over 18 years of age) elected by direct ballot for five years. In 1991 the Constitution was changed to allow the direct election of National Assembly members by secret ballot.

The Council of State is elected by the National Assembly, contains elected members of the National Assembly and acts on behalf of the Assembly between sessions. Since the National Assembly meets only twice a year for a few days, the 31-member Council of State wields power. The Council of Ministers, through its 9-member executive committee, handles the administration of the economy. Raul Castro is President of the Council of State and Council of Ministers, and Jose Ramon Machado Ventura serves as First Vice President of both bodies. The President of the Council of State is both the Head of State and the Head of Government.

Council of Ministers (as at June 2013)

President, Council of State; President, Council of Ministers: General Raul Castro Ruz (page 1401)
First Vice President, Council of Ministers: Miguel Diaz-Canel Bermudez
Minister of the Revolutionary Armed Forces: Leopoldo Cintra Frias
Vice President of the Council of Ministers: Jose Ramon Machado Ventura
Vice President, Minister in charge of Foreign Trade: Ricardo Cabrisas Ruiz
Vice President, Minister in charge of Food Production: Div.-Gen. Ulises Rosales del Toro
Vice President, Chair of the Committee on the Implementation of the Guidelines of the Sixth Congress: Marino Murillo Jorge
Vice President: Antonio Enrique Lusson Batlle
Vice President, in charge of Information Science and Communications: Ramiro Valdés Menéndez
Vice President, Minister of Economy and Planning: Abdel Izquierdo Rodriquez
Secretary of the Executive Committee of Council of Ministers: Gen. Jose Amado Ricardo Guerra
Minister of Agriculture: Gustavo Rodriguez Rollero
Minister of Construction: Rene Mesa Villafana
Minister of Culture: Rafael Bernal
Minister of Domestic Trade: Mary Blanca Ortega Barredo
Minister of Education: Ana Elsa Velasquez Cobiella

Minister of Finance and Prices: Lina Pedraza Rodriguez
Minister of the Food and Fishing Industry: Maria del Carmen Concepcion Gonzalez
Minister of Foreign Relations: Bruno Rodriguez Parrilla
Minister of Foreign Trade and Investment: Rodrigo Malmierca Diaz
Minister of Higher Education: Rodolfo Alarcon Ortiz
Minister of Interior: Gen. Abelardo Colome Ibarra (page 1407)
Minister of Justice: Maria Esther Reus González
Minister of Labour and Social Security: Margarita Marlene Gonzalez Fernandez
Minister of Energy and Mines: Alfredo Lopez Valdez
Minister of Industries: Brig.-Gen. Salvador Perez Cruz
Minister of Public Health: Roberto Morales Ojeda
Minister of Tourism: Manuel Marrero Cruz
Minister of Science, Technology and the Environment: Elba Rosa Perez Montoya
Minister of Industries: Salvador Pardo Cruz
Minister of Transportation: Cesar Ignacio Arocha Masid
Minister of Information Science and Communication: Maimir Mesa Ramos
Minister of Auditing and Control: Gladys Maria Bejarano Portera
Chairman of the National Bank of Cuba: Ernesto Medina Vilaveiran

Ministries

Ministry of Culture: URL: http://www.ministerio.cult.cu
Ministry of Education: URL: http://www.cubagob.cu/des_soc/mined/mined.htm
Ministry of External Relations: URL: http://www.cubaminrex.cu/
Ministry of Finance, Calle Obispo #211 Esquina Cuba, Habana Vieja, Cuba.
Office of Industrial Property, Picota #15 entre Luz y Acosta, La Habana Vieja, CP 10100, Havana, Cuba. Tel: + 53 (0)7 610185 / 623602, fax: +53 (0)7 335610, e-mail: oniitem@ceniai.inf.cu
Ministry of Information and Communications: URL: http://www.cubagob.cu
Ministry of Justice: URL: http://www.minjus.cu/
Ministry of Public Health: URL: http://www.dne.sld.cu/
Ministry of Tourism: URL: http://www.cubatravel.cu/client/home/index.php
Ministry of Transport: URL: http://www.cubagov.cu/des_eco/mitrans/

Political Parties

Cuba's only authorised political party is the Partido Comunista de Cuba (PCC, Communist Party of Cuba)
First Secretary: Raúl Castro (page 1401)

Other parties include: Cuban American National Foundation (CANF). Leader: Jorge Mas Canosa (largest Cuban exile opposition group); Partido Demócrata Cristiano de Cuba (PDC, Christian Democratic Party of Cuba); Partido Solidaridad Democrática (PSD, Democratic Solidarity Party); Partido Social Revolucionario Democrático Cubano (PSRDC, Cuban Social Revolutionary Democratic Party); Coordinadora Social Demócrata de Cuba (CSDC, Social Democratic Coordination of Cuba); Unión Liberal Cubana (ULC, Cuban Liberal Union).

Elections

The most recent elections for the National Assembly of People's Power took place on 20 January 2008. The vote is an endorsement of pre-selected candidates rather than a choice between rivals. Half of the candidates are nominated at public meetings before gaining approval from electoral committees, while the other half are nominated by official mass organisations (such as trade unions, farmers organisations and students unions). Ailing leader Fidel Castro stood for his seat, even though he had not been seen in public for almost a year-and-a-half. On 22nd February, he announced his retirement. The new chamber met on 24th February, and unanimously appointed Raul Castro as president. In February 2013, the National Assembly re-elected Raul Castro as president. President Castro said he would stand down at the end of his second term which would be in 2018.

All Cubans aged 16 or over, with the exception of those mentally incapacitated or those having committed a crime, are eligible to vote for National Assembly candidates. Legislative elections take place every five years.

Diplomatic Representation

Embassy of Republic of Cuba, 167 High Holborn, London WC1 6PA UK. Tel: +44 (0)20 7240 2488 fax: +44 020 7836 2602, e-mail: embacuba.lnd@cubaldn.com, URL: http://www.cubadiplomatica.cu/reinounido/EN/Mission/Embassy.aspx
Head of Mission: HE Mrs: Esther G. Armenteros Cárdenas
British Embassy Calle 34, No. 702/4 entre 7ma Avenida y 17, Miramar, Havana, Cuba. Tel: +53 (0)7 204 1771, fax: +53 (0)7 204 9214, e-mail: embrit@ceniai.inf.cu, URL: https://www.gov.uk/government/world/organisations/british-embassy-havana
Ambassador: Timothy Cole
Cuba Interests Section, 2630 and 2639 16th Street, NW, Washington, DC 20009, USA. Tel: +1 202 797 8518, fax: +1 202 986 7283, e-mail: cubaseccion@igc.apc.org
US Interests Section, Calzada between L & M Streets, Vedado, Havana, Cuba. Tel: +53 (0)7 833 3551 / 3559, fax: +53 (0)7 833 2095, e-mail: infousis@pd.state.gov, URL: http://havana.usint.gov
Chief of Mission: John Caulfield
Permanent Representative of Cuba to the United Nations, 315 Lexington Avenue and 38th Street, New York, N.Y. 10016, USA. Tel: +1 212 689 7215, fax: +1 212 689 9073, e-mail: cuba@un.int, URL: http://www.un.int/cuba/
Permanent Representative: H.E. Ambassador Pedro Nunez Mosquera

There are no diplomatic relations between Cuba and USA.

LEGAL SYSTEM

This is made up of the People's Supreme Court, the People's Provincial Courts and the People's Municipal Courts. The People's Supreme Court is accountable to the National Assembly. Each tribunal at the Supreme Court is composed of one professional and two lay judges, or three professional and two lay judges depending on the importance of the issue.

CUBA

Cubans do not have the right to change their government. Many people have been detained without being charged with a specific crime. Prison conditions are very harsh, and a fair trial is often denied. There are limitations on freedom of speech, movement and the press, as well as monitoring of private communications. Citizens can be denied exit permits. Cuba retains the death penalty.

People's Supreme Court: URL: http://www.tsp.cu/
President: Dr. Rubén Remigio Ferro

LOCAL GOVERNMENT

Cuba is divided administratively into 15 provinces including the city of Havana and one special municipality, Isla de la Juventud (Isle of Youth), and 169 municipalities. The provinces are Artemisa, Camaguey, Ciego de Avila, Cienfuegos, Granma, Guantanamo, Holguin, La Habana, Las Tunas, Matanzas, Mayabeque, Pinar del Rio, Sancti Spiritus, Santiago de Cuba and Villa Clara. Any citizen over the age of 16 who is eligible can vote for delegates to the Municipal Assemblies, who serve for a two and a half year term. Each province has a court of appeal. All the provinces have courts for civil-administrative, labour and minor criminal offences and there are courts in 167 of the 169 municipalities in the country. The system of judging is as for the People's Supreme Court.

AREA AND POPULATION

Area
Cuba is the largest island in the Caribbean. Its total area is 110,860 sq. km (44,200 sq. miles). The terrain is largely flat, with hills and mountains of up to 2,000 metres to the south east. The climate is tropical, with a dry season from November to April, and a wet season from May to October.

To view a map, consult http://www.lib.utexas.edu/maps/cia08/cuba_sm_2008.gif

Population
The population has grown from 11.17 million at the last official census in 2002 to an estimated 11.258 million in 2010. The estimated growth rate in 2000-10 was 0.1 per cent per year, and overall population density is around 102.3 people per sq. km. Approximately 68 per cent of the population is aged between 15 and 64, with 17 per cent aged up to 15 years, and 17 per cent aged 60 years and over. The median age is 38 years. Around 75 per cent of the population lives in towns and cities. Cuba's major towns are: Havana, with a population of 2.2 million; Santiago de Cuba, with a population of just over a million; and Holguin, at just over a million.

Cuba is a multiracial society of mainly Spanish and African origins. Around 51 per cent of the people are of mixed race, and one per cent is Chinese. Spanish is the official language.

Births, Marriages, Deaths
According to 2010 estimates, the birth rate is 9.9 births per 1,000 people, whilst the death rate is 8.2 deaths per 1,000 people. Average life expectancy at birth in 2009 was 78 years (76 years for men and 80 years for women). Healthy life expectancy was respectively 68 years and 71 years. The infant mortality rate is 5 deaths per 1,000 live births, whilst the fertility rate is 1.5 children born per woman. (Source: http://www.who.int, World Health Statistics 2012)

Public Holidays 2014
1 January: National Liberation Day
2 January: Victory of Armed Forces Day
1 May: Labour Day
20 May: Independence Day
25-27 July: Anniversary of the 1953 Revolution
10 October: Anniversary of War of Independence 1868 Day
25 December: Christmas Day

EMPLOYMENT

In 2007, Cuba had an economically active population of 5,235,000 (up from 5,227,000 in 2006), equivalent to 57 per cent. Of these some 4,867,700 were employed (3,016,000), whilst around 88,600 (1.8 per cent) were unemployed. According to Cuban Government statistics, about 75 per cent of the labour force is employed by the state (though the figure may be as high as 93 per cent).

Total Employment by Economic Activity

Occupation	2007	2008
Agriculture, hunting, forestry & fishing	912,300	919,100
Mining & quarrying	25,700	26,700
Manufacturing	523,300	543,100
Electricity, gas & water supply	85,000	79,800
Construction	243,700	245,200
Wholesale & retail trade, repairs, hotels & restaurants	613,600	610,200
Transport, storage & communications	289,300	301,400
Financial intermediation, real estate & renting	111,400	123,000
Community, social & personal service activities	2,063,400	2,099,700
Total	4,867,700	4,948,200

Source: Copyright © International Labour Organization (ILO Dept. of Statistics, http://laborsta.ilo.org)

BANKING AND FINANCE

Currency
One Cuban Peso (CUP) = 100 centavos

Cuba currently has two currencies in circulation: the Cuban peso (CUP), and the convertible peso (CUC). (1 CUC = 25 Cuban Pesos)

GDP/GNP, Inflation, National Debt
Cuba's economy was strongly linked to the Soviet Union, and the collapse of the latter, together with US sanctions (in force since 1961), led to an economic downturn in the 1990s. Gross Domestic Product declined by 35 per cent over the period 1989-93 following the loss of Soviet aid. The US trade embargo and sanctions blocked medium and long-term loans, whilst the state of the economy discouraged aid from international financial institutions such as the World Bank. Droughts, hurricanes, power shortages, increased US economic restrictions and falling foreign investment added to the economic problems over the period 2001-04.

Since Raul Castro became the head of state in 2008, there have been several initiatives to increase state revenues: the government has begun to expand access to public land for private farmers, to allow some Cubans to own their homes and to increase wages and retirement pensions. It also intends to upgrade public transportation systems and to deregulate the construction industry. Previously restricted consumer goods, such as computers, cell phones, DVD players, motorcycles, air conditioners, electric ovens, and agricultural supplies and tools, are now available for purchase; previously they had been available only through the flourishing black market. The state remains dominant in the economy. In 2011 some relatively wide-ranging economic reforms were approved.

Cuba's main industries are tourism, sugar, nickel, and tobacco. In 2007, nickel was the leading export and top foreign exchange earner.

Traditionally, Cuba's economy was based on the sugar industry; however, following years of declining productivity, the government announced a comprehensive transformation of the sector in 2002, and almost half the sugar mills were closed. The sugar harvest continued to fall, reaching 2.1 million tons in 2003, the smallest since 1933, before falling further to 1.2 million tons in 2006.

Tourism took over as the mainstay of the economy in the 1990s and continues to be a primary source of foreign exchange (around $2bn in revenue). The effects of Hurricane Michelle (November 2001), Hurricane Isidore (September 2002) and Hurricane Lili (October 2002), as well as the negative effects on worldwide tourism caused by the 11 September 2001 terrorist attacks, caused a downturn in tourist revenue. However, figures for 2004 onwards have improved, boosted by medical tourists from other Latin American countries who undergo medical treatment at Cuban facilities. Cuba's growing biotechnology and medical expertise sectors are main contributors to GDP. In 2007, the pharmaceutical industry ranked second in foreign sales.

Remittances play an important role in the economy, and are estimated to amount to between $600 million to $1 billion per year, most coming from families in the United States.

The services sector was the largest GDP-producing industry, accounting for around 74 per cent of GDP in 2010. Industry contributed nearly 21 per cent and agriculture 4 per cent.

Estimates for 2010 put nominal GDP (Gross Domestic Product) at $57 billion, indicating a growth rate of 2.1 per cent. Estimated figures for 2009 put GDP at US$50.0 billion, a growth rate of 1.4 per cent down from 4.1 per cent in 2008. Per capita GDP averaged an estimated US$5,100 in 2010.

Inflation was estimated at 3 per cent over the same year. External debt is estimated at over US$20 billion.

Foreign Investment
Cuba passed its Foreign Investment Law in 1995 which allows 100 per cent foreign ownership in certain cases. However, in practice, majority ownership by the foreign partner is rare. Of the 540 joint ventures formed since 1995, 397 remained at the end of 2002, and 287 at the close of 2005. Foreign investors blamed a hostile investment climate characterized by dense regulations, impenetrable bureaucracy and an overpriced state-imposed workforce. Foreign direct investment flows decreased from $448 million in 2000 to $39 million in 2001 and were at zero in 2002.

Since 2004, the Cuban government has actively encouraged investment from China and Venezuela (especially in the nickel and energy sectors). Spain is the largest European investor.

Balance of Payments / Imports and Exports
Exports earned an estimated $6 billion in 2011, whilst imports cost an estimated $13 billion. Estimated figures for 2008 put export earnings at $3.6 billion and imports cost 14.2 billion.

Major export markets in 2011 were the China (25 per cent), Canada (20 per cent), Netherlands (7 per cent), Venezuela (7 per cent) and Spain (5 per cent). Cuba's chief exports are minerals, medical products, sugar, tobacco, fish, coffee, and citrus.

Major import suppliers in 2011 were Venezuela (35 per cent), China (10 per cent), Spain (9 per cent), and Brazil (5 per cent) and the USA (5 per cent). Major imports are mineral fuels, machinery and transport equipment, food and live animals.

The US imposed a trade embargo on Cuba in 1962.

Central Bank
Banco Central de Cuba, URL: http://www.bc.gov.cu/
President: Ernesto Medina Villaveirán

MANUFACTURING, MINING AND SERVICES

Primary and Extractive Industries
Cuba has reserves of nickel, cobalt and iron, as well as chromite, magnetite, manganese, copper, limestone, rock salt, gypsum, dolomite and, to a lesser extent, lead, zinc, gold, silver and tungsten. There are large kaolin and marble deposits on the Island of Pines.

Nickel became the leading export and the top foreign exchange earner in 2007, valued at approximately $2.7 billion. Extraction increased by 2.2 per cent in 2007 and exceeded 75,000 tons. The main market for nickel exports is China. The government predicts that nickel and cobalt production would reach a record 80,000 tons in 2008. Other major mining products are crushed stone, silica and sand, and crude oil.

According to recent EIA figures, Cuba had 120 billion barrels of oil reserves in January 2012. Production reached 55,000 barrels per day in 2011, whilst consumption was 165,000 barrels per day. Cuba's oil production more than tripled over the past two decades in response to severe energy shortages following the collapse of the Soviet Union.

Cuba is one of only three Caribbean countries (Barbados, Cuba, and Trinidad and Tobago) with oil and natural gas reserves. The country is reliant on imports, mainly from Venezuela and Mexico. Venezuela resumed supplies of oil to Cuba in September 2002. In 2005, nearly all Caribbean countries, including Cuba, signed the Venezuela-backed Petrocaribe initiative, under which Venezuela sells crude oil and refined products with favorable financing terms.

Cuba's crude oil refining capacity is 301,000 barrels per day, according to January 2012 EIA statistics, split between the following four companies/locations: Cienfuegos, 76,000 barrels per day; Ermonos Dia, Santiago, 101,000; Niko Lopes, Havana, 121,800; and Serhio Soto, Cabaiguan, 2,000. Cuba has the fourth largest crude oil refining capacity in the Caribbean (after the US Virgin Islands, Netherlands Antilles, and Aruba).

It is estimated that 4.6 billion barrels of oil and 9.8 trillion cubic feet of natural gas could lie in the North Cuba Basin. Cuba recently offered 59 offshore sites for oil exploration and, in addition to the six foreign companies already operating there, is attracting investments from a number of European countries. The 44-year-old US trade embargo bars American companies from bidding for exploration rights, but US oil companies want the embargo, and environmental laws, to be relaxed to allow them to benefit from the energy resources just 50 miles from Key West. In July 2009, Cuba signed an agreement with Russia permitting oil exploration in Cuban waters.

Cuba had proven natural gas reserves of 3,000 billion cubic feet at the beginning of January 2011. Gross natural gas production has increased considerably since the early 1990s, rising to 14 billion cubic feet in 2006, and 38 billion cubic feet in 2010, all of which was used domestically.

Cuba imports all of its coal requirements; in 2010 it consumed 0.030 million short tons of coal. The country also uses by-products of sugar-cane as a fuel source.

Energy
Cuba consumed 0.385 quadrillion Btu of energy in 2009, most of which was produced using petroleum.

Cuba has the second highest installed electricity capacity and the second highest net generation in the Caribbean after Puerto Rico. Electricity capacity was 5.86 gigawatts in 2010, whilst net electricity generation in the same year was 16.40 billion kilowatthours (kWh).

Construction of Cuba's first nuclear reactor was halted in 1992, following the collapse of the Soviet Union, and was finally abandoned in December 2000. In April 2001 the Cuban Energy Saving Program was launched to reduce energy consumption. In addition to the development of a 75 megawatt power plant and completion of a further three plants, many are in the process of being refurbished.

Tourism
In 2004, the number of tourists to Cuba crossed the two million mark, and it has remained above that figure since. In 2007, there were 2.1 million visitors. The numbers are boosted by medical tourists, who come for medical procedures; most of these are from parts of Central and South America. Gross revenues from the tourism sector are thought to exceed US$2.1 billion per annum. Most tourists came from the Americas and Europe; in 2004, Canadian visitors numbered 602,000, followed by the UK with 199,000 visitors. 194,000 came from Spain and 185,000 from Venezuela.(Oficina Nacional de Estadistica, 2005)
Cubatravel, e-mail: tourism@cubasi.info, URL: http://www.cubatravel.cu

Manufacturing
There are a number of factories manufacturing consumer goods for local consumption, including cotton and rayon textiles, rayon yarn, staple fibre and tyre yarn (the latter is also exported), leather and rubber footwear, tyres and tubes, cement, paint, soap, beer and mineral water, matches, leather goods, pharmaceuticals, aluminium ware and cardboard boxes. In 2007, the pharmaceutical industry generated $350 million in exports, ranking it second in foreign sales behind nickel and ahead of traditional products such as tobacco, rum, and sugar. The manufacture of cigars and cigarettes is the best-known export industry. 90 per cent of all industry is controlled by the government.

Agriculture
Cuba's soil is fertile and up to two annual crops can therefore be obtained. Of the total 10,988,600 hectares of land, 6,391,800 are state-owned, and 6,597,100 are used agriculturally.

In 2005, 1,335,800 hectares were dedicated to growing sugar cane, the island's principal crop. Since the collapse of Cuba's main sugar market, the Soviet Union, the harvest has fallen from 79 million tons in 1990 to fallen to its lowest level for 50 years. The government announced a streamlining of the industry in 2002, and closed almost half the sugar mills. Other major crops are potatoes, oranges, tobacco, grapefruit and pomelos.

In July 2008, the President announced that more state-controlled farm land would be placed in private hands, in order to increase lagging food production. Private farmers who do well will be able to increase their holdings by up to 99 acres for a renewable 10-year period that can be renewed, and co-operatives are also allowed to add an unspecified amount of additional land for 25 years, with the possibility of renewing the lease. The Presidential decree said that farmers would have to pay taxes on their production, but the amount was not specified.

Agricultural Production in 2010

Produce	Int. $'000	Tonnes
Sugar cane	371,058	11,300,000
Indigenous pigmeat	264,919	172,334
Cow milk, whole, fresh	196,442	629,500
Tomatoes	191,065	517,000
Indigenous cattle meat	171,567	63,511
Mangoes, mangosteens, guavas	121,985	203,591
Rice, paddy	116,851	454,400
Fruit fresh nes	99,739	285,758
Plantains	97,288	485,800
Hen eggs, in shell	88,678	106,920
Vegetables fresh nes	85,057	804,453
Yams	74,417	395,781

*unofficial figures
Source: http://faostat.fao.org/site/339/default.aspx Food and Agriculture Organization of the United Nations, Food and Agricultural commodities production

The forests (covering 3,055,000 hectares in 2005) contain many valuable cabinet woods such as mahogany and cedar, the latter being used locally for the manufacture of cigar boxes. Fuel wood provided about 2.5 million cubic metres, according to recent FAO estimates, whilst other industrial wood provided some 418,000 cubic metres.

There are about 500 different species and varieties of edible fish living around the island. Modern boats have recently increased the size of catches. Total catch in 2010 was put at 23,950 tonnes down from 54,660 tonnes in 2001.

Principal livestock in 2004 were cattle, at 3.9 million head, pigs, at 1.6 million head, and horses, at 499,800 head. Principal livestock products in the same year were cow milk, yielding 332,400 tons, pig meat, providing 146,500 tons, and poultry meat, providing 37,000 tons. In 2005, 86,400 beehives were kept, producing 3,800 tons of honey. (Source: Oficina Nacional de Estadisticas, 2005)

COMMUNICATIONS AND TRANSPORT

Travel Requirements
Travel by US citizens to Cuba is restricted by the Cuban Assets Control Regulations, enforced by the U.S. Treasury Department; tourist travel is not licensable under the Regulations, and this restriction includes tourist travel to Cuba from or through a third country such as Mexico or Canada. Travellers who fail to comply with the regulations could face civil penalties and criminal prosecution upon return to the United States. There are some exceptions to the travel restrictions, such as journalists, people on government or NGO business. Special licences to travel can be issued. For details, see http://travel.state.gov/travel/cis_pa_tw/cis/cis_1097.html.

Canadian, Australian and EU citizens require a passport valid for six months, a return ticket and a visa. Persons of Cuban origin who are nationals of other countries must travel with a Cuban passport if they left Cuba after 1970. Neither visa exemptions nor tourist visa card facilities are applicable to foreign passport holders born in Cuba, unless holding a document proving withdrawal of Cuban citizenship.

Nationals not referred to above are advised to contact the embassy to check visa requirements.

International Airports
Jose Martí International Airport is situated outside Havana.

National Airlines
The national airline is Cubana de Aviacion.

Railways
Cuba's national rail network has 12,605 km of track in operation, of which only 1,006 km are narrow gauge. The main route runs from Havana to Santiago de Cuba.

Roads
The highway network consists of approximately 18,932 km of which approximately 14,478 km are surfaced. The most important roads are the 1,444 km central highway and the White Road, which is 110 km long and connects Havana and Matanzas. About 800 km of roads are being built in Oriente Province. The construction of the country's largest marine causeway is underway, which will link Las Brujus, Ensenacho and Santa Maria cays to the mainland and with each other. Vehicles are driven on the right.

CUBA

HEALTH

Cuba's Social Security system provides free health care. In 2009, total expenditure was 12.1 per cent of GDP, equating to a per capita expenditure of US$672. Health represents 14.9 per cent of total government expenditure. General government expenditure accounts for 92.7 per cent of total health expenditure.

The healthcare sector is becoming an important foreign exchange earner through biotechnology joint ventures, vaccine exports and the provision of health services to other countries. In 2005, Cuba's health budget was increased by biotech exports (which earned $300 million), fees from foreign patients and exports of medicinal products and diagnostic equipment. Successful clinical trials in several countries have already established Cuba as a world leader in cancer research and treatment, and eye treatment clinics have restored the sight of many poor people in Latin America. Cuban doctors assisted in humanitarian missions such as the Boxing Day Tsunami and the earthquake in Pakistan, and their services are traded for other commodities, such as oil from Venezuela.

In 2005-10 there were 76,506 doctors (67.2 per 10,000 population), 103,014 nurses and midwives (90.5 per 10,000 population) and 18,578 dentistry personnel (16.3 per 10,000 population). There were 59 hospital beds per 10,000 population.

The infant mortality rate (likelihood of dying by age 1) was 5 per 1,000 live births. The child mortality rate (likelihood of dying between ages 1-5) was 6 per 1,000 live births. Prematurity is the cause of death in 11 per cent of cases, pneumonia 10 per cent and congenital abnormalities 23 per cent.

In 2008, 946 per cent of the population had access to improved drinking water. In the same year, 91 per cent of the population had access to improved sanitation. (Source: http://www.who.int, World Health Statistics 2012)

EDUCATION

Free education includes primary level between six and 11 years, secondary level between 12 and 17 years. In the 2005-06 academic year, there were 12,334 schools in Cuba, with 2,718,874 pupils registered. There were 261,003 teaching staff in the same year. The number of students entering tertiary education has increased dramatically, as shown below:

Number of students registered in Higher Education, per subject

Subject	2000/01	2005/06
Technical Sciences	14,514	34,117
Natural Sciences and Mathematics	3,828	3,838
Agricultural Sciences	5,125	7,487
Economics	13,569	50,897
Social Sciences and Humanities	15,546	112,720
Medicine	24,606	117,574
Teaching	38,892	113,821
Physical Education	11,269	45,668
Arts	1,054	1,417
Total	128,403	487,539

Source: Oficina Nacional de Estadisticas, 2005

In 2005, 599,405 students were registered as undertaking formal postgraduate education.

Recent statistics show that nearly 100 per cent of primary age children attend school, and 80 per cent of secondary age children enrol. The estimated adult literacy rate is over 99 per cent, rising to 100 per cent for youth literacy. Figures for 2007 show that the equivalent of 13.3 per cent of GDP. (Source: UNESCO)

RELIGION

Cuba has been an atheist state since 1962, when the government seized and shut down more than 400 Catholic schools, and the country officially became an atheist state. However the Communist Party lifted its prohibition against religious believers seeking membership in 1991, and the constitution was amended the following year to describe the state as secular instead of atheist. In 1998, Pope John Paul II visited Cuba. In 2007, Christmas Day was declared to be a public holiday for the first time since the revolution.

The Roman Catholic Church is the largest religious organisation, but protestant denominations are growing rapidly. Afro-Cuban religions, a blend of native African religions and Roman Catholicism, are widely practiced.

COMMUNICATIONS AND MEDIA

Pres freedom is extremely limited. The Cuban media are tightly controlled by the government, journalists have to operate within the confines of laws against anti-government propaganda. Private ownership of electronic media is forbidden.

Newspapers
The major newspapers include: Granma, URL: http://www.granma.cu; Trabajadores (Mondays), Juventud Rebelde (Sundays). All are based in Havana. Local newspapers are published in all provinces.

Broadcasting
Cuba has its own radio and television network. There are two television stations in Havana and a provincial one in Oriente. There are five national radio networks, one international network, 14 provincial radio stations and 31 municipal radio stations. The state-controlled broadcasting company is:
Instituto Cubano de Radio y Televisión (ICRT), URL: http://www.tvcubana.icrt.cu/
CubaVision, http://www.cubavision.cubaweb.cu/portada.asp

Telecommunications
Recent investment has improved the infrastructure. In 2007, there were an estimated 1.1 million mainline telephones in the country, and 330,000 mobile phones. Mobile phone usage is limited by high subscription costs.

The purchase of computers became officially sanctioned in 2008, though the cost is prohibitive for most citizens. Internet usage is very low, with less then 2 per cent of the population having access. It is estimated that there were 1.31 million internet users by 2007.

ENVIRONMENT

Current environmental problems include deforestation, the threat to wildlife by excessive hunting, and the pollution of Havana Bay.

In 2006 Cuba's emissions from the consumption of fossil fuels totaled 28.64 million metric tons of carbon dioxide. In 2007 Cuba produced 83.4 ODP tons of Ozone depleting CFCs. Figures for 2010 showed that total carbon dioxide emissions were 34.46 million metric tons (Source: EIA)

Cuba is a party to the following international environmental agreements: Antarctic Treaty, Biodiversity, Climate Change, Climate Change-Kyoto Protocol, Desertification, Endangered Species, Environmental Modification, Hazardous Wastes, Law of the Sea, Marine Dumping, Ozone Layer Protection, Ship Pollution, and Wetlands. The Marine Life Conservation agreement has been signed but not ratified.

CYPRUS

Republic of Cyprus

Kypriaki Dimokratia / Kibris Çumhuriyeti

Capital: Nicosia (Population estimate, 2011: 325,760)

Head of State: Nico Anastasiades (page 1378) (President)

National Flag: White, at the centre the shape of the island in orange/yellow above two green olive branches crossed

CONSTITUTION AND GOVERNMENT

Constitution

Cyprus was declared an independent sovereign state on 16 August 1960, having been annexed by Britain in 1914. Since 1974 the island has been divided into the Government-controlled area in the South and the 'Turkish Republic of Northern Cyprus', which is recognised only by Turkey.

Under the Constitution of the Republic of Cyprus, the island has a Greek President and a Turkish Vice-President, elected by universal suffrage for a five-year term of office by the Greek and Turkish communities respectively. Legislative power rests with the House of Representatives. The island is administered by an 11-member Council of Ministers originally seven Greek and three Turkish) appointed by the President.

Since the Turkish Cypriot rebellion in December 1963, however, there have been no members of Turkish community serving within the government. Following a coup in 1974 by the military against Archbishop Makarios, Turkey sent troops in to protect the Turkish Community. Although the coup collapsed the Turkish forces remained and occupied the northern third of the island. In 1983 this area was named the Turkish Republic of Northern Cyprus, but is only recognised by Turkey. At present the position of vice president is vacant and the Council of Ministers which is appointed by the president is entirely composed of Greek Cypriots.

For details on the constitution, please visit:
http://www.cyprus.gov.cy/portal/portal.nsf/0/C44572D7363776ACC2256EBD004F3BB3?OpenDocument

International Relations

Traditionally Cyprus has had very close ties with Greece and the UK, and is a member of the Commonwealth. Politically relations with Greece and Turkey are dominated by the division of Cyprus. Cyprus is host to the Sovereign Base Areas (SBAs) these are sovereign British territory and cover 98 square miles of the island of Cyprus. They are military areas and have their own legislation, police force and courts. The SBAs enjoy a close relationship with Cyprus and have a customs and currency union.

Recent Events

In January 2002 President Clerides and the Turkish Cypriot leader Rauf Denktash agreed to series of talks in the UN controlled buffer zone. The talks were prompted by the imminent entry of Cyprus to the EU, However, Greek Cypriots wanted the return of Cyprus to a single state, and Turkish Cypriots wanted Cyprus recognised as a two state nation. In 2002 secretary of the UN Kofi Annan presented a peace plan for Cyprus which set out the country as a federation with two parts with a rotating presidency. The deadline for agreement was set at March 2003; however, no agreement was reached. Greek Cypriots felt that not enough refugees would be able to return to their homes, while Turkish Cypriots felt they would have to concede too much land.

In April 2003 the line dividing Cyprus, known as the Green Line, was opened for the first time in 30 years allowing Cypriots from both sides to visit.

As entry to the EU became imminent both sides held a referendum in April 2004 on the proposed UN reunification plan, which both sides had to agree. The Turkish Cypriots voted for reunification, but the Greek Cypriots voted overwhelmingly against the plan. On 1 May 2004 Cyprus - without Turkish Northern Cyprus - became a member of the EU. In April 2005 Mehmet Ali Talat was elected Turkish Cypriot President and talks began in May 2005 on a new peace deal.

In November 2006, the EU-Turkey talks on Cyprus broke down over Turkey's continued refusal to open its ports to traffic from the Republic of Cyprus. Matters worsened the following February in a row over oil drilling rights off Cyprus.

Early in 2007 both Greek and Turkish Cypriots began dismantling obstacles in Nicosia; this was taken as a positive move in the possible opening of another official crossing point. In April 2008 the crossing point at Ledra Street was re-opened. The crossing point had become a symbol of the division over the years. In September 2008 both leaders of the Greek and Turkish Cypriot communities began negotiations aimed at bringing the division to an end. However in April 2009 the nationalist National Unity Party won parliamentary elections in northern Cyprus, leading to fears that peace talks would falter. Talks have continued intermittently but with little progress.

In April 2010, the Turkish Cypriot head of government Dervis Eroglu, of the pro-independence National Unity Party in the self-proclaimed state's presidential election, beat the pro-unity candidate Mehmet Ali Talat.

In July 2011 a cache of Iranian munitions which had been seized and were being held at a Naval base exploded. Several people were injured in what was Cyprus' worst peacetime military accident. The explosion led to serious power outages which had a detrimental affect on the economy. Fears over the economy were exacerbated by the fact that banks in Cyprus hold large Greek debts and so concerns began to rise that the Cypriot economy would not be robust enough to withstand this. In August Cyprus had its debt rating cut. Following the energy crisis triggered by the arms explosion, the cabinet resigned and on August 5 President Demetris appointed a new cabinet.

In September 2011, exploratory drilling for oil and gas began, this led to a diplomatic row with Turkey. In April 2012, Turkey's Turkish Petroleum Corporation began drilling for oil and gas onshore in northern Cyprus despite. The Cypriot Government claimed that the action is illegal.

In June 2012, Cyprus went to the EU for financial assistance to help shore up its banks which were failing in response to the financial crisis in Greece. In November an in principle agreement was reached with the European Commission, the European Central Bank and the IMF.

In March 2013, a €10 billion bank bailout was secured from the European Union and IMF, the bailout was subject to parliamentary approval. In order to secure the €10 billion the Cypriot government had to raise €5 billion itself. Cyprus agreed to a significant restructuring of its banking sector, along with other measures such as tax rises and privatisations. One very significant and controversial measure suggested was to take money from the bank accounts of customers with more than €100,000 in the bank. Although this levy was voted down by the government in effect this is where much of the €5 billion will come from, as the government cannot vote down the bank restructuring laws. Protesters took to the streets and several banks closed for several days to prevent a run on the banks. Measures were taken to ensure money could not be taken out of the country. In April 2013, Finance Minister Michalis Sarris resigned.

In May 2013, Cyprus received €2 billion as the first tranche of its €10 billion rescue package.

Legislature

The House of Representatives, *Vouli Antiprosopon* has 80 seats, 56 reserved for Greek-Cypriots and 24 for Turkish Cypriots. However, no Turkish-Cypriot has taken their seat in this House since the 1963 Turkish Cypriot rebellion. The President of this House becomes Acting-President of the country when the President is absent.

House of Representatives, Dyiavaharlal Nehrou, Omerou Avenue, 1402 Nicosia, Cyprus. Tel: +357 (0)2 303451, fax:+357 (0)2 366611, URL: http://www.parliament.cy
President: Yiannakis Omirou (page 1489)

Council of Ministers (as at July 2013)
Minister of Defence: Fotis Fotiou
Minister of Agriculture, Natural Resources and Environment: Nicos Kouyialis
Minister of Justice and Public Order: Ionas Nicolaou
Minister of Energy, Commerce, Industry and Tourism: Georgios Lakkotrypis
Minister of Foreign Affairs: Ioannis Kasoulides (page 1454)
Minister of Labour and Social Insurance: Zeta Emilanidou
Minister of the Interior: Socrates Hasikos
Minister of Finance: Charis Georgiades (page 1429)
Minister of Education and Culture: Kyriakos Kenevezos
Minister of Communications and Works: Tasos Mitsopoulos
Minister of Health: Petros Petrides

Ministries

Ministry of Foreign Affairs, Dem. Severis Avenue, 1477 Nicosia, Cyprus. Tel: +357 22 401000, fax: +357 22 661881, e-mail: minforeign1@mfa.gov.cy, URL: http://www.mfa.gov.cy
Ministry of the Interior, Dem. Severis Avenue, Ex Secretariat Offices, 1453 Nicosia, Cyprus. Tel: +357 22 867629, fax: +357 22 671465, e-mail: minint3@cytanet.com.cy, URL: http://moi.gov.cy
Ministry of Defence, 4 Emmanuel Roides Street, 1432 Nicosia, Cyprus. Tel: +357 22 807501, fax: +357 22 366225.e-,mail: defense@cytanet.com.cy, URL: http://www.mod.gov.cy
Ministry of Commerce, Industry and Tourism, 6 A. Araouzos Street, 1424 Nicosia, Cyprus. Tel: +357 22 867100, fax: +357 22 375120, e-mail: permsec@mcit.gov.cy, URL: http://www.mcit.gov.cy
Ministry of Health, Byron Avenue, 1448 Nicosia, Cyprus. Tel: +357 22 400103, e-mail: ministryofhealth@cytanet.com.cy, URL: http://www.moh.gov.cy
Ministry of Communications and Works, Dem. Severis Avenue, 1424 Nicosia, Cyprus. Tel: +357 22 800102, fax: +357 22 675024, URL: http://mcw.gov.cy
Ministry of Finance, Ex Secretariat Compound, 1439 Nicosia, Cyprus. Tel: +357 22 601149, fax: +357 22 602747, URL: http://www.mof.gov.cy
Ministry of Education and Culture, Corner Thoucydides and Kimon, 1434 Nicosia, Cyprus. Tel: +357 22 800607, fax: +357 22 305974, e-mail: moec@moec.gov.cy, URL: http://www.moec.gov.cy
Ministry of Labour and Social Insurance, Byron Avenue, 1463 Nicosia, Cyprus. Tel: +357 22 673580, fax: +357 22 670993, e-mail: min.of.labour@cytanet.com.cy, URL: http://www.mlsi.gov.cy
Ministry of Justice and Public Order, 12 Ilioupoleos Street, 1461 Nicosia, Cyprus. Tel: +357 22 805911, fax: +357 22 518349, URL: http://www.mjpo.gov.cy

CYPRUS

Ministry of Agriculture, Natural Resources and Environment, Loukis Akritas Avenue, 1411 Nicosia, Cyprus. Tel: +357 22 300817, fax: +357 22 781156, URL: http://www.mjpo.gov.cy

Political Parties

Dimokratikos Synagermos (DISY, Democratic Rally), Tymvion Building, 25 Pindarou Street, 1061 Nicosia, Cyprus. Tel: +357 22 883000, fax: +357 22 759894, e-mail: disy@disy.org.cy, URL: http://www.disy.org.cy
President: Nicos Anastasiades (page 1378)
Anorthotiko Komma Ergazomenou Laou (AKEL, The Progressive Party of the Working People), 4 Ezekias Papaioannou Street, 1075 Nicosia, Cyprus. Tel: +357 22 761121, fax: +357 22 761574, e-mail: k.e.akel@cytanet.com.cy, URL: http://www.akel.org.cy
Leader: Andros Kyprianou
Dimokratico Komma (DIKO, The Democratic Party), 50 Grivas Dighenis Avenue, 1687 Nicosia, Cyprus. Tel: +357 22 666002, fax +357 22 666488, e-mail: diko@logos.cy.net, URL: http://www.diko.org.cy
President: Marios Garoyian (page 1429)
Kinima Sosialdimokraton (KISOS, Movement of Social Democrats), 40 Byron Avenue, 1096 Nicosia, Cyprus. Tel: +357 22 670121, fax: +357 22 678894, URL: http://www.edek.org.cy
President: Yiannakis Omirou (page 1489)
Enomeni Dimokrates (EDI, United Democrats Movement), URL: http://www.edi.org.cy
Leader: Praxoula Antoniadou
Kinima Oikologoi Perivallontistoi (Ecological and Environmental Movement or Cyprus Green Party), URL: http://www.cyprusgreens.org
Leader: George Perdikis

Elections

The most recent legislative elections took place on 22 May 2011. The Democratic Rally (DISY) won 20 seats, the Progressive Party of the Working People (AKEL) won 19 seats.

Presidential elections took place on February 2008. They were won by Demetris Christofias who promised to work towards reunification. The most recent presidential election took place in February 2013, the result was inconclusive and a second round took place on February 24. Nicos Anastasiades of the Democratic Rally party was duly elected president with 57.5 per cent of the vote. Stavros Malos gained 42.5 per cent.

Diplomatic Representation

High Commission of the Republic of Cyprus, 13 St. James's Square, London, SWIY 4LB, United Kingdom. Tel: +44 220 7499 8272, fax: +44 22 7491 0691, URL: www.mfa.gov.cy/highcomlondon
High Commissioner: Alexandros Zenon (page 1543)
Embassy of the Republic of Cyprus, 2211 R. Street, N.W., Washington, DC 20008, USA. Tel: +1 202 462 5772/462083, fax: +1 202 483 6710, URL: http://www.cyprusembassy.net/home
Ambassador: Pavlos Anastasiades (page 1378)
British High Commission Alexander Pallis Street (PO Box 21978), 1587 Nicosia or BFPO 567, Cyprus. Tel:+357 22 861100, fax; +357 22 861125, e-mail : infobhc@cylink.com.cy URL: http://ukincyprus.fco.gov.uk/en/
High Commissioner: Matthew (John) Kidd
US Embassy, Metarchou and Ploutarchou Streets, 2406 Enkomi, Nicosia, Cyprus. Tel: +357 22 476100, fax:+357 22 465944, URL: http://cyprus.usembassy.gov
Ambassador: Frank Urbancic
Permanent Mission of the Republic of Cyprus to the United Nations, 13 East 40th Street, New York 10016, USA. Tel:+1 212 481 6023, fax:+1 212 685 7316
Permanent Representative: Nikolaos Emiliou
Permanent Mission to the United Nations Office (Geneva), 7th Floor, 34 Chemin-Francois Lehmann, 1218 Grand Saconnex, Geneva. Tel:+41 (0)22 798 2150/798 2175, fax: +41 (0)22 791 0084

LEGAL SYSTEM

Under the 1960 Constitution and other legislation, the island's independent judiciary consists of the Supreme Court, the Assize Courts (there is a permanent Assize Court for all the districts), the District Courts, the Military Court, the Rent Control Courts, Industrial Disputes Court and Family Courts.

The Supreme Court consists of a President and twelve other judges, all of whom currently are Greek Cypriots. The Supreme Court adjudicates on the constitutionality of legislation and any judicial proceedings concerning laws or decisions given either by the House of Representatives or in the Budget. It also interprets the Constitution in cases of ambiguity and arbitrates whenever there is any conflict of power between state organs. The Supreme Court is the final Appellate Court in the Republic and has jurisdiction to hear and determine appeals in civil and criminal cases from Assize Courts and District Courts as well as appeals from decisions of its own judges when sitting alone in the exercise of original and revisional jurisdiction of the Supreme Court. It functions as a Court of Admiralty, where it exercises original jurisdiction, and is the only Court which deals with proceedings concerning the issue of orders of *habeas corpus, mandamus, certiorari, quo warranto* and prohibition.

There is also a Supreme Council of Judicature which appoints, promotes and disciplines all judicial officers excepting the Judges of the Supreme Court.

The Permanent Assize Court has unlimited criminal jurisdiction and presides over all the districts of Cyprus. There is also a District Court for each district, which exercises original criminal and civil jurisdiction. There are separate Courts for Military, Industrial Dispute, Rent Control or Family cases.

There are 85 judges serving in all Courts of first instance and 13 Judges serving in the Supreme Court.

The government respects the human rights of its citizens. However, there have been instances of discrimination against members of minority ethnic and national groups.

Capital punishment was abolished in 1983.

Supreme Court of Justice: URL: http://www.supremecourt.gov.cy/
Cyprus Law Commissioner and Protector of Human Rights, URL: http://www.olc.gov.cy/

LOCAL GOVERNMENT

For purposes of administration, Cyprus is divided into six districts: Lefkosia, Ammochostos, Lemesos, Pafos, Larnaca and Kyrenia. Each district is headed by a District Officer who coordinates the activities of all the Ministries in that district, and is answerable to the Ministry of the Interior. In addition, each district is divided into municipalities. There are 33 municipalities in total, nine in the Turkish occupied area. Nicosia has the most municipalities with eight of Cyprus's 33 - each of which is headed by a Mayor. Municipal councils are elected bodies and are responsible for local government services and the administration of towns and rural areas. The administration of villages are the responsibility of elected Community councils. Municipalities may be abolished if the population falls below 4,000. Municipalities are further divided into communities of which there are currently 355.

AREA AND POPULATION

Area

Cyprus is situated in the eastern corner of the Mediterranean, and is close to all the three continents of Europe, Africa and Asia. Cyprus is 60 km south of Turkey and 300 km north of Egypt. The area of the island is 3,572 sq. miles (9,251 sq. km.), making it the third largest island in the Mediterranean. There are two mountain ranges: the Trodos massif in the central and south-western parts of the island, with a high point of Mount Olympus (1,953 m), and the Pentadaktylos range along the north coast. The Messaoria plain lies behind the mountains.

The climate is Mediterranean with hot, dry summers with changeable winters.

To view a map, visit: http://www.un.org/Depts/Cartographic/map/profile/cyprus.pdf

Population

The population of Cyprus (Cypriot Government contolled) was estimated at 862,000 million in 2011, showing a mid year growth rate of 2.6 per cent. Approximately 70 per cent of the population lives in urban areas. The most densely populated area is the district of Lefkosia which includes the city of Nicosia which has a population of 336,000.

The language of the Greek Cypriot community is Greek, and English is widely spoken. The religious minorities of Armenians, Maronites and Latins opted to belong to the Greek Cypriot Community. The language of the Turkish Cypriot Community is Turkish.

Births, Marriages, Deaths

In 2011 the crude birth rate was put at 11.3 births per thousand population. In 2011 the fertility rate was recorded at 1.4. The crude death rate in 2011 was 6.5 per 1,000 population. 2009 saw 12,769 marriages taking place of which 6,327 were amongst citizens of Cyprus that year 1,738 divorces were granted.

Average life expectancy at birth in 2009 was 78 years for males and 83 years for females. Healthy life expectancy was respectively 69 years and 71 years. Approximately 18 per cent of the population is aged under 15 years and 18 per cent over 60 years. The median age is 34. (Source: http://www.who.int, World Health Statistics 2012)

Public Holidays 2014

1 January: New Year's Day
6 January: Epiphany Day
3 March: Green Monday (beginning of Lent)
25 March: Greek Independence Day
1 April: Anniversary of Cyprus Liberation Struggle
18 April: Orthodox Good Friday
21 April: Orthodox Easter Monday
1 May: Labour Day
9 June: Pentecost
15 August: Assumption Day
1 October: Independence Day
28 October: Greek National Day (Ochi Day)
25 December: Christmas Day
26 December: Boxing Day

EMPLOYMENT

Most people work in the wholesale, retail, restaurant and hotel trades, followed by the community, social and personal services; manufacturing; the agriculture, forestry and fishing trades; construction; the finance, insurance, real estate and business services; and transport, storage and communication.

In 2010 the economically active population was put at 412,100 rising to a provisional figure of 420,200 in 2011. The number of people unemployed in 2010 was 24,400 giving an unemployment rate of 6.2 per cent. The number of unemployed people rose to 31,500 in 2011, giving an unemployment rate of 7.7 per cent. In the under-25 age group the rate is estimated to be 22 per cent.

Total Employment by Economic Activity

Occupation	2008
Agriculture, hunting & forestry	15,900
Fishing	600
Mining & quarrying	500
Manufacturing	37,500
Electricity, gas & water supply	3,100
Construction	44,900
Wholesale & retail trade, repairs	69,500
Hotels & restaurants	24,700
Transport, storage & communications	21,200
Financial intermediation	19,600
Real estate, renting & business activities	32,700
Public admin. & defence; compulsory social security	30,200
Education	27,100
Health & social work	16,200
Other community, social & personal service activities	18,400
Households with employed persons	16,900
Extra-territorial organisations & bodies	2,600

Source: Copyright © International Labour Organization (ILO Dept. of Statistics, http://laborsta.ilo.org)

BANKING AND FINANCE

Currency
Cyprus adopted the Euro on 1 January 2008. Prior to that, the currency was the Cyprus Pound (C£) = 100 cents.

GDP/GNP, Inflation, National Debt
Gross National Income at market prices was put at €16,857,7 million in 2010* and €17,155,7 million in 2011* (*provisional figures).

Gross Domestic Product at market prices was put at €9.756,0 million in 2000; €13.402,0 million in 2005; €17,333,6 in 2010* and €17,761,4 million in 2011* (*provisional figures). Cyprus's banks were badly hit by exposure to Greek debts, losing over 70 per cent of their investments, resulting in credit rating downgrades. The government has said that more austerity measures in 2012 were necessary if Cyprus were to meet its goal of meeting a deficit target of 2.5 per cent of GDP. The economy faced further difficulties in 2013 with a €10 billion bailout from the EU required to prevent the collapse of the banking industry, the mainstay of the Cypriot economy.

The following table shows Gross Domestic Product at current market prices by economic activity in € million:

Economic Activity	2005	2010*	2011*
Agriculture, forestry & fishing	346.7	381.4	389.5
Mining & quarrying	43.4	53.4	51.1
Manufacturing	1,014.7	1,003.6	988.5
Electricity, gas, steam & air conditioning supply	189.9	276,0	285,9
Water supply, sewerage, waste management & remediation activities	95.0	122.3	132.8
Construction	1,330.4	1,428.2	1,289.1
Wholesale & retail trade, repairs	1,499.5	1,879,8	1,928.0
Transport & storage	538,7	816,7	766,1
Accommodation & food services	882,3	967,4	1,047,9
Information & communication	542,0	623,8	659,9
Financial & insurance activities	825,8	1,314,3	1,411,5
Real estate activities	1,189,7	1,784,8	1,892,2
Professional scientific & technical activities	514,5	776,5	820,4
Admin. & support service activities	154,0	189,7	191,1
Public admin. & defence, compulsory social security	1,271,6	1,721,9	1,807,7
Education	705,9	1,020,9	1,083,4
Health & social work	452,2	636,9	674,8
Arts, entertainment & recreation	161,2	218,7	225,3
Other service activities	192,5	231,9	233,9
Private households with employed persons	96,7	170,3	200,1
Total gross value added	12,046,6	15,618,5	16,079,0
Plus: import duties	156,3	135,7	118,7
Plus: Value added tax (net)	1,199.0	1,579.4	1,563,7
GDP at current market prices	13,402,0	17,333,6	17,761,4

* = provisional
Source: Cyprus Statistical Service

The inflation rate has risen in recent years from 2.0 per cent in 2001, to 2.8 per cent in 2002 and 4.1 per cent in 2003. During 2000 VAT was raised from 8 per cent to 10 per cent bringing it closer into line with an EU average of 15 per cent. This, coupled with higher oil prices, meant that inflation was expected rise. More recent figures show that inflation has fallen to 2.6 per cent in 2005, 2.5 per cent in 2006 and 2.4 per cent in 2007. Inflation was 2.4 per cent in 2011 and 3.3 per cent in 2012. In the period Jan.-March 2013, inflation was 1.5 per cent.

Foreign Investment
In 2010, direct foreign investment was estimated to be €580 million.

Balance of Payments / Imports and Exports
Figures from the Cyprus Statistical Office show that total exports in 2000 were €1.011,3 million, rising to €1.228,7 million in 2005 before falling to €1.111,8 million in 2006 and €1.082,7 million in 2007. Total import figures for 2000 were €4.104,0 million, rising to €5.069,1 million in 2005, €5.513,5 million in 2006, and €6.353,7 million in 2007. In 2008, estimated export figures were €7.349 million and exports €1.167 million. The crude trade balance was -€6.181 million. Preliminary figures for 2011 showed that exports had increased by over 20 per cent from 2010 to €1.39 billion. Imports fell in 2011 to an estimated €6.25 million, down 4.2 per cent on 2010.

The following tables show total value of category earnings of imports and exports in recent years:

Imports. Category	2010 %	2011 %
Intermediate inputs	26,1	26,4
Consumer goods	30,1	30,9
Transport equipment	13,4	8,8
Fuels & lubricants	20,1	25,2
Capital goods	8,5	7,6
Unclassified	1,8	1,1
Total imports €mn	6,517,4	6,260,5

Exports

Category	2010 %	2011 %
Agricultural products	15,2	17,6
Minerals	0,8	0,9
Industrial products of agricultural origin	16,6	17,0
Industrial products of mineral origin	4,3	5,3
Industrial products of manufacturing origin	63,0	59,2
Unclassified	0,1,0	0,0
Total exports €mn	1.136,8	1.406,0

Source: Cyprus Statistical Service

Main Export Products in €mn

Product	2009	2010
Canned fruit, vegetables & juices	11,1	16,2
Dairy products	43,4	51,0
Pharmaceutical products & preparations	108,0	129,8
Cathodes of copper	8,8	13,4
Photovoltaic cells	57,4	83,4
Recycled metals	29,9	51,1
Tobacco	10,7	9,6

Source: Cyprus in Figures

Principal trading partners in 2011 in €mn

Country	Imports	Exports
Greece	1,337,3	334,1
Italy	509,2	42,0
United Kingdom	551,8	124,9
Germany	507,9	67,7
Israel	637,9	29,1
France	350,2	12,1
China	300,3	19,0
Netherlands	282,3	17,5
Spain	198,7	7,5
Japan	53,1	0,3
Thailand	32,3	4,3
USA	93,6	18,2

Source: Cyprus Statistical Service

Central Bank
Central Bank of Cyprus, 80 Kennedy Ave, CY-1395 Nicosia, Cyprus. Tel: +357 22 714100, fax: +357 22 378153, e-mail: cbcinfo@centralbank.gov.cy, URL: http://www.centralbank.gov.cy
Governor: Panicos O. Demetriades (page 1414)

Chamber of Commerce and Trade Organisations
Cyprus Chamber of Commerce and Industry, URL: http://www.ccci.org.cy
Cyprus Stock Exchange, URL: http://www.cse.com.cy
Cyprus Embassy Trade Centre, URL: http://www.cyprustradeny.org

CYPRUS

MANUFACTURING, MINING AND SERVICES

Primary and Extractive Industries

Quarrying in Cyprus produces sand, gravel, limestone, gypsum, clay and stone for local use and bentonite, umber, ochre, gypsum and stone for export. The opening of a copper mine in 1996 has led to an increase in prospecting for mineral resources. Estimated figures from 2008 show that production in the mining and quarrying sector was valued at €57.3 million. Due to an increase in construction there has been a related increase in the mining of sand, gravel and road aggregate in recent years.

Energy

The total generating capacity is 1.39 GWe and is installed at two oil-fired steam power stations. All electricity in Cyprus in generated from fossil fuels. A new law for the Promotion of Use of Renewable Energy Resources and Energy Saving was introduced in 2003. In 2007 1.404 Tj of energy was produced from solar thermal systems up from 1.359 Tj in 2006. Estimated figures from 2008 show that production in the electricity, gas and water supply sector was valued at €339,3 million. In 2010, 5.01 billion KWh of electricity was generated and 4.7 billion kWh was consumed. Electricity Authority of Cyprus (EAC), URL: http://www.eac.com.cy

Manufacturing

The most important sectors of manufacturing are food and beverages, clothing and footwear, furniture and metal products. Other expanding industrial sectors include printing and publishing, rubber and plastics, chemical and pharmaceutical products and machinery. The following table shows the gross output in current market prices in €million:

Industry	2009	2010
Food & beverages	437,9	431,7
Textiles wearing apparel & leather	30,4	26,4
Wood & wood products	80,6	69,8
Paper products & printing	68.5	68,5
Chemical, pharmaceutical, rubber & plastic products	123,0	131,0
Non-metalic mineral products	184,3	169,2
Basic metals & metal products	147,1	138,2
Electronic & electric products, machinery & transport equipment	53,1	53,1
Other manufacturing	86,1	79,9
Total manufacturing	1,211,0	1,167,8

Source: Cyprus in Figures

Service Industries

There is a thriving tourist industry in Cyprus, presided over by a statutory body, the Cyprus Tourism Organisation (CTO). In 2011 the total number of arrivals visiting Cyprus was 3,7881,200, slightly up on 2010. Tourist visitors were estimated to be 2.3 million. Visitors are mainly from the UK, Russia, Germany and Greece.
Cyprus Tourism Organisation (CTO), URL: http://www.visitcyprus.com/wps/portal

Agriculture

There is an estimated 134,700 hectares of land used for agriculture, of which 75,200 are for temporary crops, 29,900 are for permanent crops, 9,300 are fallow land, 2,100 are for grazing and 18,200 are uncultivated. An area of 175,200 hectares, or almost 19 per cent of the total area of Cyprus, is covered by forests. This is divided into main state forests (14,996 hectares) which consist of permanent forest reserves, national forest parks and nature reserves, and minor state forests (15,830 hectares) which are communal and municipal forests, nurseries and grazing grounds. A further 13,578 hectares are in private hands.

Principal agricultural products are potatoes, grapes, citrus fruits, vine products, cereals, carobs, olives, carrots and almonds. Cyprus fisheries produced 3,364 tons of fish in 1996 at a value of over C£12 m. In 2010, livestock consisted of 53,500 cattle, 305,400 sheep and lambs, 307,400 goats and kids and 464,200 pigs.

Agricultural Production in 2010

Produce	Int. $'000	Tonnes
Indigenous pigmeat	87,671	57,032
Indigenous chicken meat	38,101	26,749
Cow milk, whole, fresh	37,574	150,960
Grapes	15,925	27,860
Olives	12,555	15,680
Indigenous cattle meat	12,098	4,479
Potatoes	11,140	82,000
Tomatoes	9,897	26,780
Tangerines, mandarins, clem.	8,614	34,870
Goat milk, whole, fresh	8,406	25,050
Hen eggs, in shell	8,219	9,910
Oranges	8,128	42,060

*unofficial figures
Source: http://faostat.fao.org/site/339/default.aspx Food and Agriculture Organization of the United Nations, Food and Agricultural commodities production

COMMUNICATIONS AND TRANSPORT

Travel Requirements

USA, Canadian, Australian and EU citizens (apart from those carrying a valid national ID card, require a passport valid for three months after departure. They can stay for up to 90 days without a visa. People with stamps or visas from the 'Turkish Republic of Northern Cyprus' in their passports can only enter Cyprus after the visas/stamps are cancelled by the immigration authorities of the Republic of Cyprus. Cyprus is a member of the Schengen Agreement but it is not fully implemented yet.

Customs Restrictions

Cyprus has now abolished tariffs on most EU goods in accordance with its Customs Union Agreement.

National Airlines

Cyprus Airways operates out of Larnaca and Paphos Airports. Carrying over one million passengers a year, its destinations are the Middle East, Europe and the Gulf.
Cyprus Airways, URL: http://www.cyprusairways.com/main/default.aspx

International Airports

Larnaca International Airport, URL: http://www.hermesairports.com/
Larnaca Airport deals with over 4.5 million passengers a year.
Paphos International Airport, URL: http://www.hermesairports.com/
Paphos Airport deals with over 1.3 million passengers a year.

Roads

The road network in Cyprus consists of 11,009 km of paved and 4,300 km of unpaved roads. Figures for 2011 show that there were 651,671 licensed vehicles on the roads including 456,545 private cars, 1,823 taxis and 3,461 buses. Vehicles are driven on the left.

Shipping

In 2011 the international fleet consisted of 1,857 ocean-going vessels with a gross tonnage of over 21 million. The responsibility for the development of all maritime activities in Cyprus lies with the Department of Merchant Shipping.
Department of Merchant Shipping, http://www.mcw.gov.cy/

Ports and Harbours

The main ports which serve the island's maritime trade at present are the multi-purpose Larnaca and Limassol ports. Besides serving local traffic, both Limassol and Larnaca act as cargo distribution and consolidation centres for the Mediterranean area and as regional warehouse and distribution bases for Europe, the Middle East and the Arabian Gulf. There is an industrial port at Vassiliko, and three specialised petroleum ports at Larnaca, Dhekelia and Moni. All port facilities of the island are under the jurisdiction of the Cyprus Port Authority. Figures for 2011 show an estimated 4,300 ships arrived at Cypriot ports, also 303,000 passengers, 345,000 containers and 7 million metric tons of cargo.
Cyprus Port Authority, URL: http://www.cpa.gov.cy

HEALTH

Free health care is provided to people unable to afford private health care, and to all people attending Accident and Emergency Departments. Health care schemes are also provided by some trade unions and employer-sponsored schemes. Total expenditure on health in 2009 was 6.1 per cent of GDP, equating to a per capita expenditure of US$1,794. General government expenditure accounts for 41.5 per cent of total expenditure on health and private expenditure 58.6 per cent. Private pre-paid plans account for 9.4 per cent of the private expenditure on health.

According to WHO figures (2005-10), there were 2,230 doctors (25.8 per 10,000 population), 3,710 nurses and midwives (43 per 10,000 population), 210 pharmaceutical personnel and 792 dentists (9.2 per 10,000 population). There were 38 hospital beds per 10,000 population.

In 2009, the infant mortality rate was 5 deaths per 1,000 live births and the child mortality rate was 6 per 1,000 live births. The main causes of death for child mortality are prematurity (25 per cent) and congenital abnormalities (34 per cent). All the population has access to improved drinking-water and improved sanitation. (Source: http://www.who.int/, World Health Statistics 2012)

EDUCATION

Education in Cyprus is the responsibility of the Ministry of Education and Culture including the appointment, transfer, promotion and disciplinary matters of all teachers as well as the education of all minorities other than Turkish. Non-compulsory pre-school education is provided by Public Kindergartens (government supported), Community Kindergartens (established by parent associations) and Private Kindergartens. Turkish education remains under the control of the Turkish Community. In 2010, 8.1 per cent of GDP was spent on education.

Education in Cyprus begins at the age of five years and eight months and is compulsory until the age of 14. Elementary education is mainly funded by the public sector. For secondary education, approximately 12 per cent is provided by the private sector. Figures from 2010/11 show that 100 per cent of girls and boys were enrolled in primary school and 94 per cent of girls and boys were enrolled in secondary school. Recent figures show that the University of Cyprus has 4,000 students, 20 per cent of whom are foreign students.

The 2010 literacy rate was 99.0 per cent for males and 97 per cent for females. For the age group 15-24 years the rate rose to 99.9 for males and females. (Source: UNESCO)

RELIGION

Recent figures show that 78 per cent of the population belonged to the Greek Orthodox Church and 18 per cent were Turkish Muslims. The remainder comprised members of other religions including: Maronites, Armenians and Apostolics. The Cypriot Church is independent within the Eastern Orthodox Church.

Cyprus has a religious liberty rating of 6 on a scale of 1 to 10 (10 is most freedom). (Source: World Religion Database)

Archbishop of Nova Justiniana and all Cyprus, PO Box 1130, Archbishop Kyprianos Street, Nicosia, Cyprus. Tel: +357 (0)2 430696, fax: +357 (0)2 432470
Archbishop of Nova Justiniana and all Cyprus: His Beatitude the Archbishop Chrysostomos II (page 1405)

COMMUNICATIONS AND MEDIA

There are both privately-run and state radio and television services. The media reflects the island's division with the areas administered by Turkish Cypriots having their own press and broadcasters.

Newspapers
Simerini (Today) URL: http://www.simerini.com.cy
Cyprus Weekly (English) URL: http://www.cyprusweekly.com.cy
Cyprus Mail, URL: http://www.cyprus-mail.com/news
Politis, URL: http://www.politis-news.com
Kibris Gazete (Northern Cyprus - Turkish), URL: http://www.kibrisgazetesi.com

Broadcasting
The Cyprus Broadcasting Corporation (CyBC) is administered by a Board of Governors appointed by the Council of Ministers. It has two television channels (Channel 1 and Channel 2) and four radio channels broadcasting in English, Greek, Turkish and Armenian. Private radio stations also exist. Satellite and cable television stations also operate.
Cyprus Broadcasting Corporation (CyBC), URL: http://www.cybc.com.cy

Telecommunications
The telephone system is generally excellent throughout the island. Recent estimates put the number of mainlines in the area under government control as over 410,000 and over 85,000 within the area administered by Turkey. Estimated mobile subscriptions were respectively over 1 million and approximately 200,000. Figures for 2011 estimate that around 580,000 people are regular internet users.
Cyprus Telecommunications Authority (CYTA), URL: http://ww.cyta.com.cy

ENVIRONMENT

Environmental concerns include lack of water resources, water pollution from industry, and coastal degradation.

Cyprus is a party to the following international agreements; Air Pollution, Air Pollution-Nitrogen Oxides, Air Pollution-Persistent Organic Pollutants, Air Pollution-Sulfur 94, Biodiversity, Climate Change, Climate Change-Kyoto Protocol, Desertification, Endangered Species, Environmental Modification, Hazardous Wastes, Law of the Sea, Marine Dumping, Ozone Layer Protection, Ship Pollution, and Wetlands.

In 2010, Cyprus's emissions from the consumption of fossil fuels totalled 9.26 million metric tons of carbon dioxide. (Source: EIA)

SPACE PROGRAMME

Cyprus signed a co-operation agreement with the European Space Agency in 2009.

CZECH REPUBLIC
Česká Republika

Capital: Prague (Population estimate, 2011: 1.24 million)

Head of State: Milos Zeman (President) (page 1543)

National Flag: Divided fesswise, white and red. A full depth blue triangle appears point to the fly at the hoist

CONSTITUTION AND GOVERNMENT

Constitution
In September 1938 Czechoslovakia conceded part of its border areas to Germany, Hungary and Poland on the basis of the Munich agreement. Political life in the post-war Czechoslovak Republic was dominated by the Communist Party. Following the Soviet model, extensive nationalisation measures were introduced, and after 1948 private property gradually fell into the hands of the state. Czechoslovakia joined Comecom and the Warsaw Pact. In 1960 a new constitution was adopted, and the country was renamed the Czechoslovak Socialist Republic. In 1968, under Alexander Dubcek, an attempt was made to reform socialism in Czechoslovakia. In August 1968 the "Prague Spring", as it became known, was suppressed by the armies of the Soviet Union and the other member countries of the Warsaw Pact. Constitutional modification was effected in October 1968, when the Law on Federation was adopted, providing for the existence of both the Czech and Slovak Socialist Republics within the framework of the Czechoslovak Socialist Republic.

The playwright Václav Havel became a leading figure in the Charter 77 opposition movement, who united under the title Civic Forum in 1989. On 3 December 1989, shortly after the Communist Party of Czechoslovakia was forced to give up its leading role in society, the new Czechoslovak Government was appointed. On the same day President Gustáv Husák resigned from office and the opposition leader, Václav Havel, was elected as Czechoslovak president. The political system gradually underwent further restructuring during 1990. After the 1990 elections the country's name was changed to the Czech and Slovak Federal Republic. Discussions took place after the 1992 elections on dividing Czechoslovakia into a Czech Republic and a Slovak Republic. The date of the federation's dissolution was agreed on 1 January 1993 and became known as the 'Velvet Divorce'.

Under the terms of the December 1992 constitution the head of state is the president, indirectly elected by a joint session of both houses of Parliament for a maximum of two consecutive five-year terms. The constitution was amended in 2012 to allow for the presidential election to be by popular vote. The head of government is the prime minister, responsible to the Chamber of Deputies. The Council of Ministers is nominated by the prime minister and appointed by the president.

To consult the full constitution, please visit:
http://www.psp.cz/cgi-bin/eng/docs/laws/constitution.html

International Relations
The Czech Republic is a founding member of the Visegrad Group along with Hungary, Poland and Slovakia. The Czech Republic became a member of the OECD in 1995, a full member of NATO in 1999, and became a member of the EU on 1 May 2004.

The Czech Republic has sent troops to Afghanistan particularly the province of Logar. In November 2010 the Parliament voted to increase the country's contingent by 200 to 720 troops.

Recent Events
In June 2004, following a poor showing in the European elections, Vladimir Spidla resigned as prime minister and leader of the Social Democratic Party. He was later nominated for the position of the European Commissioner for the Czech Republic. In July 2004 Stanislav Gross became prime minister. He resigned in April 2005 after a crisis over the financing of a luxury apartment. The regional development minister and deputy leader of the CSSD, Jiri Paroubek, was appointed as his successor. A general election in June 2006 resulted in a hung parliament. In September, the president appointed Mirek Topolanek of the Civic Democratic Party to lead the centre-right government, but the government lost a vote of no confidence the following month. Mirek Topolanek was again appointed to the post of prime minister in November. In January 2007 parliament approved a three party coalition, made up by the Christian and Democratic Union-Czechoslovak People's Party, the Civic Democratic Party and the Green Party.

In June 2007, US President Bush visited the country sparking protests against the US plans to build a radar base near Prague which would form part of a missile defence shield.

In March 2009, Prime Minister Mirek Topolanek lost a vote of no-confidence when four rebel MPs voted with the opposition Social Democrat and Communists. Prime Minister Topolanek resigned and was replaced by Jan Fischer, a former economist, who formed a government in May. Legislataive elections were held in May 2010 and a caretaker cabinet was in place until coalition talks were finalised. In June Petr Necas of the ODS formed a coalition government with two smaller parties, the right-wing TOP 09 and the central Public Affairs Party.

In September 2010, the government proposed spending cuts which resulted in mass protests in Prague.

In December 2011, the former president Vaclav Havel died. A week of mourning was declared.

In February 2012, the Senate approved legislation permitting the presidential election to be by popular vote, not by parliament. This was passed into law in August and the first presidential elections took place in January 2013. After an inconclusive first round, the former premier Milos Zeman and the foreign minister Karel Schwarzenberg faced run-off elections on 25 and 26 January. The former prime minister, Milos Zeman, took 55 per cent of the votes in the second round.

In June 2013, Prime Minister Petr Nečas resigned his post, following a bribery and spying scandal.

Legislature
The Parliament (*Parlament*) consists of two chambers: the Chamber of Deputies (*Poslanecka Snemovna*) and the Senate (*Senat*). Parliament passes all legislation and approves international treaties.

Upper House
The Senate is made up of 81 senators, one for each constituency, elected for six year terms. Every two years one third of the seats come up for re-election. Bills, passed by the Chamber of Deputies, go to the Senate which may veto them, send them back with amendments or table them. The Senate is elected by a majority vote. The Civic Democratic Party (ODS) holds the majority of seats in the Senate. At the beginning of December 2012 the Senate was composed of the following parties: CSSD, 42 seats; independents, 18 seats; ODS, 14 seats; KDU-CSL, 3 seats; KSCM, 2 seat; others, 2 seats.

CZECH REPUBLIC

Senat, Valdstenejnské Namesti 4, 118 11, Prague 1, Czech Republic. Tel: +420 2 5707 1111, fax: +420 2 4499, URL: http://www.senat.cz
President of the Senate: Milan Štěch

Lower House

The Chamber of Deputies is made up of 200 deputies, directly elected for a four year term. The Chamber of Deputies is elected by proportional representation, where political parties must get at least five per cent of the vote in order to be represented in the chamber. As of December 2012, the Chamber was divided as follows: Czech Social Democratic Party (CSSD), 56 seats; Civic Democratic Party (ODS), 53 seats; TOP09, 41 seats; KSCM, 26 seats; LIDEM, 24 seats.
Poslanecká Snemovna, Snemovni 4, 118 29, Prague 1, Czech Republic. Tel: +420 2 5717 5111, fax: +420 2 5753 2361, URL: http://www.psp.cz/
Chairperson of the Chamber of Deputies: Miroslava Nemcova

Cabinet (as at June 2013)
Prime Minister, Acting Minister of Defence: vacant
Deputy Prime Minister, Minister in Charge of the Government Legislative Council and Minister for the Fight against Corruption: Karolina Peake (page 1493)
Minister of Foreign Affairs: Karel Schwarzenberg (page 1510)
Minister of Finance: Miroslav Kalousek (page 1453)
Minister of Industry and Trade: Martin Kuba
Minister of Health: Dr Leos Heger
Minister of Education, Youth and Sports: Dr Petr Fiala
Minister of Justice: Pavel Blazek
Minister of Environment: Tomáš Chalupa
Minister of Culture: Alena Hanakova
Minister of Regional Development: Kamil Jankovsky
Minister of Agriculture: Petr Bendl
Minister of Labour and Social Affairs: Ludmila Muellerova
Minister of Transportation: Zbynek Stanjura
Minister of the Interior: Jan Kubice
Minister without Portfolio, Head of the Government Legislative Council: Petr Mlsna

Ministries

Office of the Prime Minister, Nabr. Eduarda Benese 4, 118 01 Prague, Czech Republic. Tel: +420 2 2400 2224, fax: +420 2 2481 0231, URL: http://www.vlada.cz
Ministry of Agriculture, Tesnov 17, 117 05 Prague 1, Czech Republic. Tel: +420 2 2181 1111, fax: 420 2 2481 0475, URL: http://eagri.cz/public/web/en/mze/
Ministry of Defence, Tychonova 1, Prague 160 01, Czech Republic. Tel: +420 973 201111, e-mail: posta@army.cz, URL: http://www.army.cz/en/
Ministry of Education, Youth and Sports, Karmelitská 7, 118 12 Prague 1, Czech Republic. Tel: +420 2 5719 3111, e-mail: info@msmt.cz, URL: http://www.msmt.cz/
Ministry of Finance, Letenská 15, 118 10 Prague 1, Czech Republic. Tel: +420 2 5704 1111, fax: +420 2 5704 2788, e-mail: Podatelna@mfcr.cz, URL: http://www.mfcr.cz/cps/rde/xchg/mfcr/xsl/en.html
Ministry of Foreign Affairs, Loretánské námestí 5, 118 00, Prague 1, Czech Republic. Tel: +420 2 2418 1111, e-mail: info@mzv.cz, URL: http://www.mzv.cz/
Ministry of Health, Palackeho nam., 4 128 01 Prague 2, Czech Republic. Tel: +420 2 2497 1111, fax: +420 224 972 111, e-mail: mzcr@mzcr.cz, URL: http://www.mzcr.cz/
Ministry of Industry and Trade, Na Frantisku 32, 110 15 Prague 1, Czech Republic. Tel.: +420 224 851 111, e-mail: mpo@mpo.cz, URL: http://www.mpo.cz/
Ministry of the Interior, nad Stolou 3, 170 34 Prague 7, Czech Republic. Tel: +420 974 811111, e-mail: dotazy@mvcr.cz, URL: http://www.mvcr.cz/mvcren/
Ministry of Justice, Vysehradská 16, 128 10 Praha 2, Czech Republic. URL: http://www.justice.cz
Ministry of Labour and Social Affairs, Na Porícním právu 1, 128 01 Prague 2, Czech Republic. Tel: +420 2 2192 1111, fax: +420 2 2491 8391, e-mail: posta@mpsv.cz, URL: http://www.mpsv.cz/en/
Ministry of Regional Development, Staromestske nam. 6, 110 15 Prague 1, Czech Republic. Tel: +420 224 861 111, fax: +420 224 861 333, URL: http://www.mmr.cz/en/Ministerstvo
Ministry of the Environment, Vrsovicka 65, Prague 10, 100 10, Czech Republic. Tel: +420 2 6712-1111, fax: +420 2 6731-0308, e-mail: info@mzp.cz, URL: http://www.mzp.cz/en/
Ministry of Transport, PO Box 9, nab. Ludvika Svobody 12/22, 110 15 Prague 1, Czech Republic. Tel: + 420 2 514 31 111, fax: + 420 2 514 31 184, URL: http://www.mdcr.cz/
Ministry of Culture, Maltezske namesti 1, 118 11 Prague 1, Czech Republic. Tel: +420 257 085 111, fax: +420 224 318 155, URL: http://www.mkcr.cz/en/

Political Parties

Ceska Strana Sociálne Demokraticka (CSSD, Czech Social Democratic Party), Lidovy dum, Hybernska 7, 110 00 Prague 1, Czech Republic. Tel: +420 2 9652 2111, e-mail: info@socdem.cz, URL: http://www.cssd.cz
Party Chair: Jiï Paroubek
Krestanska a Demokraticka Unie-Ceskoslovenska Strana Lidova (KDU-CSL, Christian and Democratic Union-Czechoslovak People's Party), Karlovo namesti 5, 128 01 Prague 2, Czech Republic. Tel: +420 2 2491 4826 (Secretary General), fax: +420 2 2491 4826 (Secretary General), e-mail: press@kdu.cz (Party Spokesman), URL: http://www.kdu.cz
President: Pavel Bělobrádek
Komunisticka Strana Cech a Moravy (KSCM, Communist Party of Bohemia and Moravia), Politickych veznu 9, 110 00 Prague 1, Czech Republic. Tel: +420 2 2289 7111, fax: +420 2 2289 7207, URL: http://www.kscm.cz
Chairman: Vojtech Filip
Obcanska Demokraticka Strana (ODS, Civic Democratic Party), Snemovni 3, 110 00 Prague 1, Czech Republic. Tel: +420 257 534 920-2, fax: +420 257 530 378, e-mail: hk@ods.cz, URL: http://www.ods.cz
Chairman: Petr Nečas
Strana Zelených (SZ Green Party), Ostrovní 2063/7, Prague, Czech Republic. URL: http://www.zeleni.cz

Leader: Ondřej Liška
Unie Svobody - Demokratická Unie (US-DU, Freedom Union - Democratic Union), Malostranské nám. 266/5, 118 00 Prague 1, Czech Republic. Tel: +420 2 5701 1411, fax: +420 2 5753 0102, e-mail: info@unie.cz, URL: http://www.unie.cz
Leader: Jan Černý
Tradition Responsibility Prosperity 09 (TOP09), URL: http://www.top09.cz
Leader: Karel Schwarzenberg

Elections

Vaclav Klaus of the conservative Civic Democratic Party was elected president by parliament at the third attempt on February 28, 2003, and took office on 7 March. He retained power in presidential elections in February 2008. The mos trecent election took place on 11-12 January.

The most recent legislative election took place in May 2010. As a result the two largest parties in the parliament were the Czech Social Democratic Party (CSSD) and the Civic Democratic Party (ODS). In June Petr Necas of the ODS formed a coalition government with two smaller parties, TOP 09 and Public Affairs.

Elections to the Senate took place in October 2010. The opposition Social Democrats won control meaning they could obstruct the government's proposed austerity plans. Partial elections took place in 2012.

Diplomatic Representation

British Embassy, Thunovska 14, 118 00 Prague 1, Czech Republic. Tel: +420 2 5740 2111, fax: +420 2 5740 2296, e-mail: info@britain.cz, URL: http://ukinczechrepublic.fco.gov.uk/er
Ambassador: Sian MacLeod (page 1468)
US Embassy, Trziste 15, 118 01 Prague 1, Czech Republic. Tel: +420 2 5753 0663, e-mail: webmaster@usembassy.cz, URL: http://prague.usembassy.gov
Ambassador: Norman L. Eisen (page 1419)
Embassy of the Czech Republic, 3900 Spring of Freedom St., NW, Washington, DC 20008, USA. Tel: +1 202 274 9100, fax: +1 202 966 8540, URL: http://www.mzv.cz/washington
Ambassador: Petr Gandalovič
Embassy of the Czech Republic, 26 Kensington Palace Gardens, London W8 4QY United Kingdom. Tel: +44 (0)20 7243 1115, fax: +44 (0)20 7727 9654, e-mail: london@embassy.mzv.cz, URL: http://www.mzv.cz/london
Ambassador: Michael Zantovsky (page 1543)
Permanent Mission of the Czech Republic to the United Nations, 1109-1111 Madison Avenue, New York, NY 10028, USA. Tel: +1 212 535 8814, fax: +1 212 772 0586, URL: http://www.mzv.cz/un.newyork
Ambassador: Edita Hrda

LEGAL SYSTEM

The judiciary was completely reorganized under the 1992 Constitution and the system now includes a Supreme Court; a supreme administrative court; high, regional, and district courts; and a Constitutional Court. The Supreme Court is the highest appellate court. The 15-member Constitutional Court rules on the constitutionality of legislation. Constitutional court judges are appointed by the president, subject to Senate approval, for ten-year terms. Military courts were abolished in 1993 and their functions transferred to the civil court system.

The government respects the rights of its citizens. However, there are sometimes long delays in the court system, and there have been recent instances of corruption among the police and in the judiciary, as well as in the legislative and executive branches of government. There is discrimination against minorities, in particular the Roma.

The death penalty was abolished in 1990.

Constitutional Court of the Czech Republic, URL: http://www.concourt.cz
Chairman: Pavel Rychetsky
Public Defender of Human Rights, URL: http://www.ochrance.cz/en/

LOCAL GOVERNMENT

For administrative purposes the Czech Republic is divided into 13 administrative districts or *Kraj*: Jihocesky Kraj, Jihomoravsky Kraj, Karlovarsky Kraj, Kralovehradecky Kraj, Liberecky Kraj, Moravskoslezsky Kraj, Olomoucky Kraj, Pardubicky Kraj, Plzensky Kraj, Stredocesky Kraj, Ustecky Kraj, Vysocina, and Zlinsky Kraj.

The capital of the Czech Republic, Prague, is a self-governing municipality. It is divided into 57 city districts and 112 land areas. Prague is administered by the Prague City Assembly (70 representatives elected for a four-year term), the Prague City Council (11 members elected from the representatives), and the Prague City Hall. A Mayor heads Prague City Council. The most recent municipal elections took place in October 2010.

District Populations as at mid 2010

District	Population
City of Prague	1,251,726
Stredocesky	1,257,194
Jihocesky	637,910
Plzensky	572,023
Karolvarsky	307,619
Ustecky	835,796
Liberecky	439,483
Kralovehradecky	554,296
Pardubicky	516,776

- continued

Vysocina	514,800
Jihomoravsky	1,152,765
Olomoucky	641,661
Zlinsky	591,303
Moravskoslezsky	1,249,356

Source: Czech Statistical Office

AREA AND POPULATION

Area

The Czech Republic is situated in Central Europe and shares borders with Poland in the north, Slovakia in the east, Austria in the south and Germany in the west. It has an area of 78,866 sq. km. The west of the country known as Bohemia, is predominantly an area of rolling plains surrounded by low mountains; in the east the area known as Moravia, is more hilly. Principal rivers flowing through the Czech Republic are the Labe and the Vltava situated in Bohemia, the Morava and the Dyje are located in Moravia, the Odra and the Opava are in Silesia and northern Moravia.

The climate is temperate with warm summers and cold, humid winters.

To view a map of the Czech Republic, please consult:
http://www.un.org/Depts/Cartographic/map/profile/czech.pdf

Population

The population in mid 2010 was 10,517,247 with an average annual growth rate of 0.1 per cent over the period 1999-2009. Prague had a 2011 population of around 1.24 million. The ethnic composition is Czech 81.2 per cent, Moravian and Silesian 13.7 per cent, Slovak 3.1 per cent, Polish 0.6 per cent, German 0.5 per cent and Romany 0.3 per cent.

Births, Marriages, Deaths

The following table shows vital statistics for recent years:

Vital Statistics	2008	2009	2010	2011
Live births	119,570	118,348	117,446	108,673
Deaths	104,948	107,421	106,844	106,848
Marriages	52,457	47,862	46,746	45,137
Divorces	31,300	29,133	30,783	28,113
Net Migration	71,790	28,344	15,648	

Source: Czech Statistical Office

Average life expectancy at birth in 2011, was 74.7 years for males and 80.7 years for females. (Source: CSO) Healthy life expectancy was respectively 68 years and 72 years. Approximately 14 per cent of the population is aged under 15 years and 22 per cent over 60 years. The median age is 39. (Source: http://www.who.int, World Health Statistics 2012)

Public Holidays 2014

1 January: New Year's Day
18 April: Good Friday
21 April: Easter Monday
1 May: May Day
8 May: Liberation Day
5 July: Day of the Apostles St. Cyril and St. Methodius
6 July: Anniversary of the Martyrdom of Jan Hus
28 September: St. Wenceslas Day
28 October: Independence Day
17 November: Freedom and Democracy Day
24-25 December: Christmas
26 December: St. Stephen's Day
If a public holiday falls on a Saturday or Sunday the following Monday is not a holiday.

EMPLOYMENT

Total Employment by Economic Activity

Occupation	2010	2011
Agriculture, hunting & forestry	151,200	145,800
Industry	1,390,800	1,449,700
Construction	464,900	433,100
Trade	593,800	602,100
Financial & insurance activities	115,300	123,700
Education	295,600	296,800
Health	339,900	326,700
Total employed in the national economy	4,885,200	4,904,000
Total unemployed	383,700	353,600

Source: Czech Statistical Office

The unemployment rate was put at 5.3 per cent in 2007, 4.4 per cent in 2008, 6.7 per cent in 2009 and 7.3 per cent in 2010. It fell to 6.7 per cent in 2011.

BANKING AND FINANCE

Currency

The currency is the Czech Koruna or crown (CZK) of 100 Heller. The Czech Republic is working towards adopting the Euro in 2013.

GDP/GNP, Inflation, National Debt

The Czech Republic has one of the most stable economies of the former Communist states. It harmonized its laws and regulations to those of the EU prior to is accession to the EU in 2004. There are high levels of foreign investment and strong exports. Most trade is with the EU. These factors, however, lead to a downturn in 2009, and GDP growth that year was estimated to have been -4.2 per cent.

The following table shows GDP in recent years:

GDP, Production, Current prices, CZK million

	2008	2009	2010
Output	9,742,514	8,867,859	9,304,832
Intermediate consumption	6,262,592	5,497,382	5,900,177
Gross value added	3,479,922	3,370,477	3,404,655
Taxes on products	405,022	410,811	417,475
Subsidies on products	-36,533	-42,063	-46,893
GDP	3,848,411	3,739,225	3,775,237

Source: Czech Statistical Office

GDP was estimated to be 3779.5 CZK billion (current prices) in 2010 with a growth rate of 2.7 per cent. GDP was estimated to be 3841.4 CZK billion (current prices) in 2011. The economy was expected to stagnate or go into recession in 2012. Per capita GDP was 365,961 CZK in 2011.

Gross Value Added by Industry, constant prices in million CZK

Activity	2009	2010
Agriculture, hunting, forestry & fishing	174,325	172,922
Mining & quarrying	86,708	89,411
Manufacturing	2,997,480	3,392,491
Electricity, gas, steam & air conditioning supply	385,880	365,958
Water supply; sewerage, waste management & remediation activities	99,614	116,396
Construction	853,456	827,978
Wholesale & retail trade, repairs	772,995	826,078
Transport & storage	542,391	564,268
Accommodation & food service activities	170,110	164,081
Information & communication	363,451	361,659
Financial intermediation	286,606	289,507
Real estate activities	514,025	523,021
Professional, scientific & technical activities	450,109	451,508
Admin. & support service activities	186,473	176,738
Public admin. & defence, compulsory social security	380,805	377,907
Education	194,038	191,393
Health & social work	243,672	245,456
Arts, entertainment & recreation	94,433	94,103
Other service activities	70,799	73,467
Activities of households as employers & producers for own use	489	490
Total	8,867,859	9,304,832

Source: Czech Statistical Office

Inflation was 1.5 per cent in 2010, rising to 1.9 per cent in 2011.

The state debt was an estimated 1,344.1 billion CZK in 2010, 36.6 per cent of GDP compared to 25 per cent five years ago.

Balance of Payments / Imports and Exports

Czech Republic's foreign trade has changed considerably since 1990 with less trade with the former Soviet Union and more trade with European Union countries, particularly Germany (31 per cent), Slovakia, Italy, UK, France, Poland and Austria. Figures for 2009 put exports at US$136 billion and imports at US$141 billion. Estimates for 2010 put exports at US$136 billion and imports US$129 billion.

The following table shows imports and exports of selected commodities in 2011, figures are in CZK million

Exports and Imports, Selected Commodities 2011

Commodities	Exports	Imports
Food & live animals	91,355	123,162
Beverages & tobacco	17,120	16,345
Crude materials, inedible, except fuels	80,854	80,072
Mineral fuels, lubricants & related materials	109,595	286,233
Animal & vegetable oils, fats & waxes	4,752	5,904
Chemicals & related products, n.e.s.	180,176	293,700
Manufactured foods classified chiefly by material machinery & transport	507,775	490,123
Machinery & transport equipment	1,576,337	1,126,862
Miscellaneous manufactured articles	307,201	259,514
Commodities & transactions n.e.c. in SITC	3,536	5,648
Total	2,878,691	2,687,563

Source: Czech Statistical Office

Total exports of goods amounted to 2,878.7 billion CSK. Exports to developed market economies amounted to 2,576.9 bn in 2011, of which EU 2,389.0 CSK bn. Most exports go to Germany (927.1 billion CSK) followed by Slovakia (257.6 billion CZK). Exports to the value

CZECH REPUBLIC

of 29.5 billion CSK go to China. Imports amounted to (cif) 2,687.6 billion CSK in 2011. Of these, 1,715.9 billion CSK come from EU27, of which Germany 689.6 billion CSK and Slovakia 153.1 billion CSK. China supplies imports to the value of 334.5 billion CSK.

Central Bank
Ceská Národni Banka, Na Príkope 28, 11503 Prague 1, Czech Republic. Tel: +420 2 2441 1111, fax: +420 2 2441 3708, URL: http://www.cnb.cz
Governor: Miroslav Singer (page 1515)

Chambers of Commerce and Trade Organisations
Economic Chamber of Commerce of the Czech Republic, URL: http://www.komora.cz
Czech-German Chamber of Commerce and Industry, URL: http://www.dtihk.cz/
American Chamber of Commerce, URL: http://www.amcham.cz/
Confederation of Industry of the Czech Republic, URL: http://www.spcr.cz
Czechinvest, URL: http://www.czechinvest.com
Czech Trade, URL: http://www.tpo.cz

MANUFACTURING, MINING AND SERVICES

Primary and Extractive Industries
Domestic minerals and metals include coal, iron, graphite, silver, copper, lead and uranium. A uranium processing plant in Ceska Lipa was opened in 1979.

The coal industry has undergone some restructuring in recent years as natural gas begins to take on more importance as a fuel. In 2000 around 20 mines faced closure. Coal reserves in 2003 were estimated at 6,120 million short tons. Coal production fell to 60.9 million short tons in 2010 from 74.0 million short tons in 2003, and 94.0 million short tons in 1993. Coal consumption was 54.8 million short tons in 2010.

Domestic production of oil and natural gas is quite low. In 2012 proven oil reserves stood at 2 million barrels, with about 13,000 barrels per day produced in 2011. The Czech Republic had a crude oil refining capacity of 183,000 barrels per day at the beginning of January 2011. Oil imports come mainly from Russian via the Druzba pipeline and Germany through the Mero pipeline which enables the Czech Republic to import oil from the Italian port of Trieste.

Natural gas reserves are around 140 billion cubic feet, with 7,000 million cubic feet produced. Consumption in 2011 was 316 billion cubic feet. Dry imports were 323 billion cubic feet in the same year. The Czech Republic's natural gas consumption is supplied through the Transit gas pipeline from the CIS. Potential long term disruption of gas supplies presents less of a problem than oil since the western European gas pipeline system is also connected to the Transit pipe. The Czech Republic looked to increase its use of natural gas in order to meet environmental requirements prior to entry into the EU. As a result natural gas consumption rose by 28 per cent between 1993 and 1998.

Ostravsko-Karvinské Doly a.s. (Mining and agglomeration of lignite), URL: http://www.okd.cz

Energy
Natural energy sources in the Czech Republic are limited to solid fuels - lignite and black coal - which provide 70 per cent of all energy consumed.

The Czech Republic has an electricity generating capacity of 18.30 billion GWe (2009). Production was 11,466,000 kWh thermal, 2,760,000 kWh was nuclear, and 952,000 kWh was hydroelectric. Electricity generation in 2009 was 77.01 billion kWh. Electricity consumed in 2009 was 58.88 billion kWh.

In recent years thermal power stations, fuelled by brown coal, produced 78 per cent of all electrical energy, the Dukovany nuclear power station produced a further 19 per cent and some 2 per cent came from hydro-electrical sources. A further nuclear plant, Temelin, was re-opened in October 2000. Nuclear energy provides 25 per cent of energy needs, and this is predicted to rise. The Czech Republic is actively trying to reduce its energy generating dependence on brown coal and figures from 2003 show that fossil fuel plants generated 56 per cent of energy needs, 42.5 per cent came from the nuclear power stations and 1.5 per cent from liquid and natural gas provided by pipelines from Norway and Russia. The Czech Republic is committed to increasing the contribution of renewable sources and hopes to have 3.0 - 6.0 per cent of its total consumption generated by renewable sources by 2010, increasing to 4.0 - 8.0 per cent by 2020.

Manufacturing
In 1997 the main cause of economic growth was manufacturing with major increases in electrical machinery, optical equipment and transport equipment. Industries which declined were the leather industry and the textiles industry. Main manufacturing industries are food and beverages, basic metals and metal products and non-electric machinery and domestic appliance production, as well as vehicle production, iron and steel production, glass, ceramics, textiles and pharmaceuticals.

Selected Manufacturing Production in 2010

Product	Unit
Woven fabrics of cotton	51,683,000 m²
Paper & paperboard	117,855 t
Plastics	1,368,000 t
Building blocks & bricks of cement	4,833,000 t
Portland cement, aluminous cement & others	3,559,000 t
Hottrolled flat products of non-alloy steel	1,578,000 t
Wooden bedroom furniture	774,671 pcs
Wooden dining & living room furniture	519,136 pcs
Fresh of chilled swine meat	227,385 t
Wheat flour	764,122 t

- continued

Spirits, liquers & other spirits	17,500,000 litres
Transmission shafts & cranks	16,431 t

Source: Czech Statistical Office

Service Industries
The country is similar to smaller western European countries for example the Netherlands, Belgium, and Denmark, which derive the greatest profit from foreign visitors' shorter trips and from city and convention tourism. Prague is already one of the most visited cities in Europe. There has been rapid investment in new hotels and restaurants, and substantial renovation of tourist areas using foreign and domestic capital. In 2010 there were 6.5 million visitors to the Czech Republic. Visitors mainly come from Germany, Poland, Netherlands, Italy and Russia. Visitor numbers from Russia were up 27 per cent from the previous year.
Czech Tourist Authority, URL: http://www.czechtourism.com

Agriculture
More than half the arable land lies higher than 450m above sea level. In spite of this, some sectors - primarily the traditional cultivation of hops, grapes, and the breeding of fish - are very profitable. Hops, the best-known and most in demand of all Czech agricultural exports, take up 11,000 hectares of land, mainly in western central Bohemia. South Moravia is famous for its vineyards, and fish from the 51,000 hectares of ponds, built in south Bohemia in the Middle Ages, are also exported. Despite an abundance of highlands and foothills ideal for pasture, until recently the year-round housing of milk cows in large barns was encouraged. In 2011, there were 1.35 million head of cattle, 1.58 million pigs, 221,000 sheep, 33,000 horses, 20.69 million poultry.

Agricultural Production in 2010

Produce	Int. $'000	Tonnes
Cow milk, whole, fresh	804,795	2,683,030
Wheat	423,897	1,161,600
Indigenous chicken meat	408,722	286,942
Indigenous pigmeat	393,354	255,883
Indigenous cattle meat	327,963	121,406
Rapeseed	290,205	1,042,400
Sugar beet	131,838	3,065,000
Hen eggs, in shell	101,295	122,132
Barley	98,696	1,584,500
Potatoes	88,981	665,200
Indigenous rabbit meat	69,800	37,568
Apples	42,207	99,801

*unofficial figures
Source: http://faostat.fao.org/site/339/default.aspx Food and Agriculture Organization of the United Nations, Food and Agricultural commodities production

Recent figures show that the contributions of the agricultural sector to GDP has fallen from 8.0 per cent in 1990 to 3.5 per cent in 2002 and 1.6 per cent in 2010.

COMMUNICATIONS AND TRANSPORT

Travel Requirements
US, Canadian and Australian subjects require a passport valid for at least 90 days beyond the length of stay. British nationals require a passport valid for the length of stay, and EU subjects who have a valid national ID card do not require a passport. Visas should be obtained by by US, Canadian and Australian citizens for stays exceeding 90 days, and they must register with the Alien and Border Police within three days of arrival (normally arrranged through accommodation providers). EU subjects may stay for an unlimited period without a visa, but must register with the Alien and Border Police within 30 days of arrival.

The Czech Republic is a party to the Schengen Agreement. Nationals not referred to above should contact the embassy to check visa requirements.

National Airlines
CSA (Czech Airlines), URL: http://www.csa.cz

International Airports
The main airport in Prague (Ruzyňe) (URL: http://www.prg.aero/cs/) runs regular international flights. It handles 11-12 milion passengers annually. Other international airports are sited at Ostrava (URL: http://www.airport-ostrava.cz/en/), Brno (URL: http://www.brno-airport.cz/), Karlovy Vary and Pardubice.

Railways
The Czech Republic has a network of 9,500 km. Use of the railway system to transport freight traffic has declined in recent years. Prague has a subway as well as a tram system. International train services runs from most points in Europe including Slovakia, Poland, Germany, Netherlands, Switzerland, Austria, Slovenia, Hungary, Romania and Ukraine.
Czech Railways, URL: http://www.cdrail.cz

Roads
There are 128,000 km of roads including 546 km. of motorways in the Republic. CSDAD, the former road transport monopoly has been privatised and restructured. Figures for 2004 show that 466,034,000 tonnes of good were carried by road. Regular bus services connect the Czech Republic to Germany, Netherlands, Slovakia, Switzerland and Austria. Vehicles are driven on the right.

Shipping
The Czech Republic has a network of 663 km of navigable inland waterways which already transport goods in significant quantities. The Elbe is the main navigable river, the Vlatava and Oder rivers are also used. River ports include Prague, Usti, Decin and Labem.

HEALTH

According to the latest WHO statistics, in 2009 total expenditure on health was 6.3 per cent of GDP. This equated to a per capita spend of US$1,495. Government expenditure was 84.0 per cent of the total expenditure on health. Social security expenditure accounts for 90.2 per cent of the general government expenditure. Private expenditure on health amounts to 16.0 per cent of total expenditure on health.

According to the latest figures (2005-10), there were 37,351 doctors (36.7 per 10,000 population), and 88,874 nurses and midwives (87.4 per 10,000 population), 5,915 pharmaceutical personnel, and 7,092 dentistry personnel (7.0 per 10,000 population). There were an estimated 71 hospital beds per 10,000 population.

The infant mortality rate in 2009 was 3 per 1,000 live births and the under-five mortality rate was 4 per 1,000 live births. Major causes include prematurity (17 per cent), pneumonia (5 per cent), 14 per cent (birth asphyxia) and congenital abnormalities (22 per cent).

An estimated 100 per cent of the population have access to improved drinking water and 98 per cent to improved sanitation. (Source: http://www.who.int, World Health Statistics 2012)

EDUCATION

The Czech school system has been gradually reformed in recent years. Education is free and compulsory from the age 6 to 15. A large number of teachers of western languages are now working in Czech Republic schools, even at elementary level.

Selected Education Statistics, 2011

Schools	No. of schools	Pupils	Teachers
Nursery	4,931	342,521	27,781
Basic	4,111	794,642	57,815
Grammar	371	135,588	43,876
Secondary technical and vocational	1,082	366,255	1,121
Conservatoires	18	3,557	1,891
Higher professional	180	29,335	5,318
Universities	72	392,429	11,002

Source: Czech Statistical Office (CZSO)

State expenditure on education amounted to 41,341 CZK million. Local government budgets amounted to 114,723 CZK million. (Source: CZSO) Figures from 2007 show that 10.5 per cent of government spending goes to education, of which 49 per cent on secondary education, 26 per cent on tertiary education, 13 per cent on primary education and 9 per cent on pre-school education.

Additional short-term finance for students at foreign universities, new forms of co-operation in several programmes including Tempus, PHARE, USAID and Fulbright programmes, have all contributed to this educational exchange. Some 100,000 students are now enrolled at 23 colleges and universities throughout the Republic. These institutions enjoy full academic freedom. Charles University, in Prague, was founded in 1348. It was the first university in Europe north of the Alps and east of France. It has some 27,000 students and 3,539 permanent and visiting staff.

Literacy is estimated at 99.8 per cent.

RELIGION

The principal religion is Christianity, followed by 56 per cent of the population the majority of whom are Roman Catholic. 40 per cent are not religious.

The Czech Republic has a religious tolerance rating of 8 on a scale of 1 to 10 (10 is most freedom). (Source: World Religion Database)

COMMUNICATIONS AND MEDIA

A charter of basic rights protects press freedom.

Newspapers
Lidivé Noviny (People's News), URL: http://www.lidovky.cz
Právo (Right), URL: http://pravo.novinky.cz
Mlada Fronta Dnes, URL: http://idnes.cz
Blesk, URL: http://www.blesk.cz

Broadcasting
There are two state run television stations (CT1 and CT2), as well as a 24-hour news station. There are numberous private radio and TV stations. The country is in the process of digitising broadcasting and hopes to to switch off analogue signals by 2012.
Czech TV, URL: http://www.ceskatelevize.cz/ (public)
CT 24, URL: http://www.ct24.cz/ (news channel)
Ceský rozhlas (Czech Radio), URL: http://www.rozhlas.cz/portal/portal/
Radio Prague, URL: http://www.radio.cz/english/

Telecommunications
The telecommunications system has been updated in recent years and is now virtually fully digital. Figures for 2011 show that there were an estimated 1.7 million landlines in use and 14.25 million mobile phones. In 2011, an estimated 67.3 per cent of households had a PC and 65.4 per cent had an internet connection. In 2011, there 3.086 million fixed broadband internet subscribers. There were 881,000 registered domains. (Source: CZO)

ENVIRONMENT

Particular environmental concerns for the Czech Republic include air and water pollution caused by industry, mining and agriculture, in the regions of northwest Bohemia and in northern Moravia around Ostrava.

In 2010, the Czech Republic's emissions from the consumption of fossil fuels totaled 90.83 million metric tons of carbon dioxide, down from the 2006 figure of 116.30 million metric tons. (Source: EIA)

The Czech Republic is a party to the following international agreements: Air Pollution, Air Pollution-Nitrogen Oxides, Air Pollution-Persistent Organic Pollutants, Air Pollution-Sulfur 85, Air Pollution-Sulfur 94, Air Pollution-Volatile Organic Compounds, Antarctic-Environmental Protocol, Antarctic Treaty, Biodiversity, Climate Change, Climate Change-Kyoto Protocol, Desertification, Endangered Species, Environmental Modification, Hazardous Wastes, Law of the Sea, Ozone Layer Protection, Ship Pollution, Wetlands, and Whaling.

SPACE PROGRAMME

The Czech Space Office was founded in 2003 and acts as the central point for the coordination of space related activities in the Czech Republic Its aim is to increase the participation of the Czech Republic in European space programmes. The Czech Republic acceded to the ESA Convention in 2008.
Czech Space Office, URL: http://www.czechspace.cz

STATES OF THE WORLD

DENMARK
Kingdom of Denmark
Kongeriget Danmark

Capital: Copenhagen (Population estimate, 2011: 710,038)

Head of State: Queen Margrethe II (Sovereign) (page 1471)

National Flag: Red, with a white cross, the upright slightly towards the hoist.

CONSTITUTION AND GOVERNMENT

Constitution
Denmark's first free and democratic Constitution dates from 1849. It has been revised several times. The latest Constitution dates from 5 June 1953.

The form of government is a limited (constitutional) monarchy. The legislative authority rests jointly with the Crown and Parliament (Folketing). Executive power is vested in the Crown, and the administration of justice is exercised by the courts.

Constitutionally the Sovereign can 'do no wrong' and exercises her authority through the ministers appointed by her. The Sovereign acts on behalf of the State in international affairs. Except with the consent of the Parliament, she cannot, however, take any action which increases or reduces the area of the Realm or undertake any obligation, the fulfillment of which requires the co-operation of the Parliament or is of major importance. Nor can the Sovereign, without the consent of the Parliament, terminate any international agreement which has been concluded with the consent of the Parliament. Apart from defence against armed attack on the Realm or on Danish forces, the Sovereign cannot, without the consent of the Parliament, employ military force against any foreign power.

The ministers are responsible for the government of the country. The Constitution establishes the principle of Parliamentarianism under which individual ministers or the whole Cabinet must retire when defeated in Parliament by a 'vote of no confidence'. The prime minister can ask the Queen to dissolve Parliament and issue writs for an election.

Through the Constitution of 5 June 1953, the bicameral legislature was replaced by one chamber, the Folketing, consisting of not more than 179 members, two of whom are elected on the Faroe Islands and two in Greenland. Although part of the Danish Kingdom Greenland and the Faroe Islands enjoy home rule, the Danish Government retains jurisdiction over monetary, defence and foreign affairs. Danish nationals with permanent residence in Denmark have the franchise and are eligible. The age-limit is 18 years. The members of the Folketing are elected for four years by a system of proportional representation so that any party gaining over two per cent of the vote is represented. A bill adopted by the Folketing may be submitted to referendum when such referendum is claimed by not less than one-third of the members of the Folketing and not later than three days after the adoption. The bill is void if rejected by a majority of the votes cast, representing not less than 30 per cent of all electors.

To consult the full constitution, please visit: http://www.ft.dk/Dokumenter/Publikationer/

International Relations
Denmark has always had close links with the Nordic countries and is a member of the Nordic Council. Denmark joined the EEC in 1973. The Danes voted to reject the Maastricht Treaty in 1992 but after another referendum in May 1993 the Treaty was accepted after Denmark was granted certain opt-outs. A further referendum in 2000 saw Denmark reject the adoption of the Euro. In January 2003 the Foreign Minister announced that a further referendum might be held, but no date was given at that time. On becoming prime minister in 2009 Lars Løkke Rasmussen (page 1500)expressed his intention to hold a referendum in the future on the question of Denmark's opt outs and the possibility of adopting the Euro.

Denmark is an active supporter of international peacekeeping. Danish forces have been sent to the former Yugoslavia in the UN Protection Forces (SFOR and KFOR). Danish peacekeepers are now deployed in Kosovo, Southern Afghanistan and were based in Iraq but withdrew in August 2007.

Recent Events
In September 2005 the newspaper Jullands-Posten published cartoons depicting the Prophet Muhammad and linking him to terrorism. Pictures of Muhammad are banned by Muslims, and the cartoons were seen as deeply insulting. The cartoons were published along with an editorial against self censorship. By January 2006, as news of the cartoon spread, many anti Danish demonstrations were held in mainly Muslim countries leading to the deaths of several protestors in South Asia and Africa. In the Middle East several Danish Embassies were attacked and Danish goods boycotted. The Prime Minister apologised for the offence caused but not for the printing of the cartoons; he argued that Freedom of Expression is provided for in Danish law. Some newspapers in other European countries re-published the cartoons as a show of support for the principle of freedom of the press and freedom of speech. In February 2008 the Danish police discovered a plot to kill one of the cartoonists, and some Danish newspapers reprinted one of the cartoons in response, leading to further protests. Another attempt was made on the life of cartoonist Kurt Westergaard. In January 2010, a Somalian was arrested and charged.

In November 2008 a referendum held in Greenland approved plans to seek more autonomy from Denmark.

In April 2009 Lars Lokke Rasmussen took over as prime minister when Prime Minister Anders Fogh Rasmussen was elected as elected NATO secretary-general.

In December 2009 the UN Climate Change Summit took place in Copenhagen, representatives of 192 countries attended and many felt that this was best opportunity to make changes that would halt global warming. By the end of the summit, the US, China, India, Brazil and South Africa reached a last-minute agreement on a number of issues, such as a recognition to limit temperature rises to less than 2C (3.6F) but nothing was signed so agreements made are not legally binding. Before the summit began small island nations and vulnerable coastal countries had wanted a binding agreement that would limit emissions to a level that would prevent global temperatures rising more than 1.5C (2.7F) above pre-industrial levels.

The Immigration Minister, Birthe Roenn Hornbech, was sacked in March 2011 after 36 stateless Palestinians were wrongly refused citizenship.

In July 2011, Denmark reintroduced border controls in an effort to reduce illegal immigration. This led to questions about the legality of such a move given that under the 1995 Schengen agreement, internal borders with much of western Europe were abolished.

Legislative elections were held on 15 September 2011. The Venstre (Liberal Party) won most seats, followed by the Social Democrats. Helle Thorning-Schmidt, leader of the Social Democrats, is Denmark's first female prime minister.

Legislature
The Parliament is elected using proportional representation. There are 179 elected members, of which two are elected from Greenland and two from the Faroe Islands. 135 members are elected from constituencies and 40 do not represent constituencies but are party representatives, the number depending on the party's share of the vote. Members are directly elected for a four year term. A party must receive two per cent of the overall vote in order to have four members of parliament

Folketing, Christiansborg, 1240 Copenhagen K, Denmark. Tel: +45 3337 5500, fax: +45 3332 8536, e-mail: folketinget@folketinget.dk, URL: http://www.folketinget.dk

---

Cabinet (as at June 2013)
Prime Minister: Helle Thorning-Schmidt (SD) (page 1525)
Deputy Prime Minister, Minister for Economic Affairs, Minister of the Interior: Margrethe Vestager Hansen (RV) (page 1437)
Minister for Foreign Affairs: Villy Soevndal (SF) (page 1517)
Minister for Finance: Bjarne Fog Corydon (SD) (page 1409)
Minister for Employment: Mette Frederiksen (SD) (page 1427)
Minister for Justice: Morten Bødskov (SD) (page 1391)
Minister for Taxation: Holger K. Nielsen (page 1486)
Minister of Climate, Energy and Buildings: Martin Lidegaard (RV) (page 1464)
Minister for Education And Children: Christine Edda Antorini (SD) (page 1378)
Minister of Health and Prevention: Astrid Krag Kristensen (SF) (page 1458)
Minister for Science, Innovation and Higher Education: Morten Østergaard (RV) (page 1490)
Minister for Defence: Nick Hækkerup (SD) (page 1436)
Minister for Food, Agriculture and Fisheries: Mette Gjerskov (SD) (page 1431)
Minister for Transport: Henrik Dam Kristensen (SD) (page 1458)
Minister for Social Affairs and Integration: Karen Angelo Hækkerup SD)
Minister for Gender Equality, Ecclesiastical Affairs and Nordic Co-operation: Manu Sareen (RV)
Minister of the Environment: Ida Margrete Meier Auken (SF)
Minister of Business Affairs and Growth: Annette Vilhelmsen (SF)
Minister of Housing, Urban Affairs and Rural Affairs: Carsten Mogens Hansen (SD)
Minister of Trade and Investment: Pia Olsen Dyhr: (SF)
Minister for Development Co-operation: Christian Friis Bach (RV)
Minister of Culture: Marianne Jelved (RV) (page 1449)
Minister of European Affairs: Nicolai Halby Wammen (SD)

Ministries
Office of the Prime Minister, Christiansborg, Prins Jørgens Gård 11, 1218 Copenhagen K, Denmark. Tel: +45 3392 3300, fax: +45 3311 1665, e-mail: stm@stm.dk, URL: http://www.stm.dk
Ministry of Food, Agriculture and Fisheries, Holbergsgade 2, 1057 Copenhagen K, Denmark. Tel: +45 3392 3301, fax: +45 3314 5042, e-mail: fvm@fvm.dk, URL: http://www.fvm.dk
Ministry for Economic and Business Affairs, Slotsholmsgade 10-12, 1216 Copenhagen K, Denmark. Tel: +45 3392 3350, fax: +45 3312 3778, e-mail: oem@oem.dk, URL: http://www.oem.dk
Ministry for Culture, Nybrogade 2, 1015 Copenhagen K, Denmark. Tel: +45 3392 3370, fax: +45 3391 3388, e-mail:kum@kum.dk, URL: http://www.kum.dk
Ministry of Defence, Holmens Kanal 42, 1060 Copenhagen K, Denmark. Tel: +45 3392 3320, fax: +45 3332 0655, e-mail: fmn@fmn.dk, URL: http://www.fmn.dk
Ministry of Ecclesiastical Affairs, Frederiksholms Kanal 21, 1015 Copenhagen K, Denmark. Tel: +45 3392 3390, fax: +45 3392 3913, e-mail: km@km.dk, URL: http://www.km.dk
Ministry of Education, Frederiksholms Kanal 21-25, 1220 Copenhagen K, Denmark. Tel: +45 3392 5000, fax: +45 3392 5547, e-mail: uvm@uvm.dk, URL: http://www.uvm.dk

Ministry of the Environment, Højbro Plads 4, 1200 Copenhagen K, Denmark. Tel: +45 3392 7600, fax: +45 3332 2227, e-mail: mim@mim.dk, URL: http://www.mim.dk

Ministry of Finance, Christiansborg Slotsplads 1, 1218 Copenhagen K, Denmark. Tel: +45 3392 3333, fax: +45 3332 8030, e-mail: fm@fm.dk, URL: http://www.fm.dk

Ministry of Foreign Affairs, Asiatisk Plads 2, 1448 Copenhagen K, Denmark. Tel: +45 3392 0000, fax: +45 3254 0533, e-mail: um@um.dk, URL: http://www.um.dk

Ministry of the Interior and Health, Slotsholmsgade 10-12, 1216 Copenhagen K, Denmark. Tel: +45 72 26 9000, fax: +45 72 26 9001, e-mail: im@im.dk, URL: http://www.im.dk

Ministry of Justice, Slotsholmsgade 10, 1216 Copenhagen K, Denmark. Tel: +45 3392 3340, fax: +45 3393 3510, e-mail: jm@jm.dk, URL: http://www.jm.dk

Ministry of Employment, Ved Stranden 8, 1061 Copenhagen K, Denmark. Tel: +45 3392 5900, fax: +45 3312 1378, e-mail: bm@bm.dk, URL: http://www.bm.dk

Ministry for Family and Consumer Affairs, Stormgade 2-6, 1470 Copenhagen K, Denmark. Tel: +45 3395 1310, fax: +45 3395 1311, e-mail: minff@minff.dk, URL: http://www.minff.dk

Ministry for Refugee, Immigration and Integration Affairs, Holbergsgade 6, 1057 Copenhagen K, Denmark. Tel: +45 3392 3380, fax: +45 3311 1239, e-mail: inm@inm.dk, URL: http://www.inm.dk

Ministry of Science, Technology and Innovation, Bredgade 43, 1260 Copenhagen K, Denmark. Tel: +45 3392 9700, fax: +45 3332 3501, e-mail: vtu@vtu.dk, URL: http://www.vtu.dk

Ministry of Social Affairs and Gender Equality, Holmens Kanal 22, 1060 Copenhagen K, Denmark. Tel: +45 3392 9300, fax: +45 3393 2518, e-mail: sm@socialministeriet.dk, URL: http://www.social.dk

Ministry of Taxation, Nicolai Eigtveds Gade 28, 1402 Copenhagen K, Denmark. Tel: +45 3392 3392, fax: +45 3314 9105, e-mail: skm@skm.dk, URL: http://www.skm.dk

Ministry of Transport and Energy, Frederiksholms Kanal 27, 1220 Copenhagen K, Denmark. Tel: +45 3392 3355, fax: +45 3312 3893, e-mail: trm@trm.dk, URL: http://www.trm.dk

Political Parties

Venstre (Denmark's Liberal Party), Søllerødvej 30, 2840 Holte, Denmark. Tel: +45 4580 2233, fax: +45 4580 3830, e-mail: venstre@venstre.dk, URL: http://www.venstre.dk
Leader: Lars Løkke Rasmussen (page 1500)

Socialdemokraterne (Social Democrat Party), Danasvej 7, 1910 Frederiksberg C, Denmark. E-mail: partikontoret@net.dialog.dk, URL: http://www.socialdemokraterne.dk
Leader: Helle Thorning-Schmidt

Det Radikale Venstre (Radical Liberal Party), Christiansborg, 1240 København K, Denmark. URL: http://www.radikale.dk
Leader: Margrethe Vestager

Dansk Folkeparti (Danish People's Party), Christiansborg, DK-1240 Copenhagen K, Denmark. Tel: +45 3337 5199, fax: +45 3337 5191, e-mail: dfcceb@ft.dk, URL: http://www.danskfolkeparti.dk
Leader: Pia Kjaersgaard

Enhedslisten-De Rød-Grønne (The Danish Red-Green Alliance), Studiestræde 24, I, DK-1455 Copenhagen K, Denmark. Tel: +45 3393 3324, fax: +45 3332 0372, e-mail: enhedslisten@enhedslisten.dk, URL: http://www.enhedslisten.dk
Leadership: 21 member collective

De Konservative Folkeparti (The Danish Conservative Party), Nyhavn 4, Box 1515, DK-1020 Copenhagen K, Denmark. Tel: +45 3313 4140, fax: +45 3393 3773, e-mail: info@konservative.dk, URL: http://www.konservative.dk
Leader: Lars Barfoed

Socialistisk Folkeparti (Socialist People's Party), Christiansborg, 1240 København K, Denmark. URL: http://www.sf.dk
Leader: Villy Søvndal

Folkebevægelsen mod EF-Unionen (The Danish People's Movement against the European Union), Sigurdsgade 39 A, DK-2200 Copenhagen N, Denmark. Tel: +45 3582 1800, fax: +45 3582 1806, e-mail: katte-ud@post1.tele.dk, URL: http://www.inform.dk/sturm/folkenet

Kristendemokraterne (Christian Democrats), URL: http://www.kd.dk
Leader: Bjarne Hartung Kirkegaard

Fokus (Focus)
Leader: Christain H. Hansen

Elections

Parliament is elected using a system of proportional representation whereby any party receiving more than 2 per cent of the total national vote is afforded parliamentary representation. The voting age is 18 and voter turnout is traditionally quite high.

After 10 years of government by a liberal minority coalition led by Prime Minister Poul Schluter, the Social Democrats returned to power. On 25 January 1993, the leader of the Social Democratic Party, Poul Nyrup Rasmussen, formed a new coalition government with the Centre Democratic, Social Liberal and Christian People's parties. This was done without a general election. A general election was held in November 2001; the Social Democrats suffered their first defeat since 1924 and the Liberal Party formed a coalition government with the Conservative People's Party. An election was held in February 2005 when the liberal-led coalition was re-elected. New stricter immigration laws played an important part in the election. In the November 2007 legislative election, Prime Minister Anders Fogh Rasmussen's Liberal-Conservative coalition retained power.

The most recent legislative election took place on 17 September 2011. All 179 seats of the parliament were up for election. Turnout was put at approximately 85 per cent. Venstre/Liberals won 47 seats (26.73 per cent of vote), Social Democrats 44 seats (24.8 per cent of votes), Danish People's Party 22 seats, Radical Left/Social Liberals 17 seats, Unity 12 seats, Liberal Alliance 9 seats, Conservative People's Party 8 seats (down 10). The Christian Democrats won no seats.

Diplomatic Representation

US Embassy, Dag Hammarskjölds Allé 24, 2100 Copenhagen Ø, Denmark. Tel: +45 3555 3144, Fax: +45 3543 0223, e-mail: nivcpn@state.gov, URL: http://denmark.usembassy.gov

Ambassador: vacant
British Embassy, Kastelsvej 36/38/40, 2100 Copenhagen Ø, Denmark. Tel: +45 3544 5200, Fax: +45 3544 5293, e-mail: info@britishembassy.dk, URL: https://www.gov.uk/government/world/denmark
Ambassador: Vivien Life (page 1464)
Danish Embassy, 3200 Whitehaven St., NW, Washington, DC 20008-3683, USA. Tel: +1 202 234 4300, fax: +1 202 328 1470, URL: http://www.ambwashington.um.dk/en
Ambassador: Peter Taksoe-Jensen (page 1523)
Danish Embassy, 55 Sloane Street, London, SW1X 9SR, UK. Tel: +44 (0)20 7333 0200, fax: +44 (0)20 7333 0270, e-mail lonamb@um.dk, URL: http://www.denmark.org.uk
Ambassador: Anne Hedensted Steffensen (page 1440)
Permanent Mission of Denmark to the United Nations, One Dag Hammarskjold Plaza, 885 2nd Avenue, 18th Floor, New York, NY 10017, USA. Tel: +1 212 308 7009, Fax: +1 212 308 3384, URL: http://www.un.int/denmark
Ambassador Extraordinary & Plenipotentiary Representative: H.E. Carsten Staur

LEGAL SYSTEM

The legal system is based upon The Administration of Justice Act which originally came into force in 1919. The Supreme Court, *Højesteret* is the highest tribunal of the country and consists of a President and 19 other judges. Next are the two High Courts: The Eastern High Court and the Western High Court. These courts hold assizes in various places in their respective districts.

Below the two High Courts, Denmark is divided into Town Court districts, the Faroe Islands district and Greenland. Generally, each case is dealt with in two courts only. Civil cases of less importance and criminal cases in which juries are not compulsory are heard in the Town Courts and appeals go to the High Court. Cases of greater importance are heard in the High Court and may be carried up to the Supreme Court. Juries are compulsory for the more serious criminal cases, which are always tried before the High Court.

There are a few special courts of which the most important is the Maritime and Commercial Court in Copenhagen, which tries cases involving legal questions arising out of shipping and commerce. The court is formed by a professional judge and two to four non-legal experts. There is also a Permanent Arbitration Court for the settlement of disputes regarding labour agreements. Military courts have been abolished. Judges are appointed by the Queen.

The Court Administration was formed in 1999 following the Court Administration Act, 1998. Responsibility of administering the justice system was passed from the Ministry of Justice and given to a newly formed, independent Court Administration (Domstolsstyrelsen), thereby securing separation of the judicial and executive branches of government.

The government respects the rights of its citizens. The death penalty was completely abolished in 1978.

Supreme Court: URL: http://www.domstol.dk/hojesteret/

Danish Institute for Human Rights, Strandgade 56, 1401 Copenhagen K, Denmark. Tel: +45 3269 8800, URL: http://www.humanrights.dk/

LOCAL GOVERNMENT

A reorganisation of the structure of local government was implemented in 1970 resulting in a two-tier system. The number of counties was reduced from 86 to 14 and the number of municipalities from 1300 to 275. The reform created the basis for restructuring the distribution of tasks and cost burdens from the state to the counties and municipalities.

As of 2011, Denmark was divided into 98 local authorities (kommuner) and five regions (regioner), each covering several municipalities. Only the municipalities are considered local authorities.

The affairs of the five regions (Hovedstaden, Midtjylland, Nordjylland, Sjaelland and Syddanmark) are governed by five regional councils. Each council has 41 members. The councils are elected for a four year period in general regional elections, which are held on the same day as the local government elections. The regions are required by law to establish a business committee. The regional council must also establish a contact committee consisting of the chairperson of the regional council and the mayors of the municipalities in the region. The chairperson of the regional council is chairperson of the contact committee. The five regions are primarily responsible for the health care system. The regions are also responsible for a variety of specifically defined tasks, which are most appropriately solved at the regional level. These include tasks related to regional development and growth, and tasks related to specialised educational and social institutions. The number of regional council members was reduced from 357 to 205. The regions have no right to impose taxes. Instead, a special financing system has been established.

The supervision of the regions in Denmark is performed by five regional state administrations. The Minister for Welfare monitors the five regional state administrations.

All local councillors are elected for a four-year period in local government elections. All municipalities are required by law to appoint a Finance Committee, and one or more standing committees. The head of the local authority is the mayor, who chairs both the council and the Finance Committee. The mayor is elected by the council from amongst its members for a term of four years. The supervision of municipalities in Denmark is performed by five regional state administrations.

Local government elections are now held on the third Saturday of October, every two years.

DENMARK

AREA AND POPULATION

Area
Denmark is situated in Northern Europe between the North Sea, the Baltic Sea and the Scandinavian peninsula and Germany. It consists of the Jutland peninsula and more than 400 islands. The Faroe Islands and Greenland are also part of the Danish Kingdom although they have home rule. The total area of the Kingdom of Denmark is about 43,094 sq. kilometres, including the Faroe Islands in the Atlantic Ocean, which have an area of about 1,399 sq. kilometres. There are 7,313,93 kilometres of coastline. The terrain is generally low and flat. The highest point is 173 metres.

The climate is temperate: January and February are the coldest months with an average of 0°C. August is the warmest month.

To view a map of Denmark, please consult
http://www.lib.utexas.edu/maps/cia08/denmark_sm_2008.gif

Population
Copenhagen is the only large city and in 2011 it and its suburbs had a population of 710,038. Figures from 2011 put the populations of the largest towns as Aarhus 249,709, Odense, 167,615, Aalborg 103,545, Esbjerg 71,576.

On 1 January 2012 the population was put at 5,580,516. Approximately 78 per cent live in urban areas. Figures for 2012 put the population density at 1230.1 people per sq km. The average life expectancy for women is 82 years and 77 years for men. The official language is Danish.

Denmark has recently introduced strict laws on immigration and asylum seekers. Figures for 2000 show that Denmark had 31 per cent of applications for asylum from those applying to Scandinavian countries; this figure fell to nine per cent in 2003. In 2012, 10.4 per cent of the population were immigrants or their descendants.

Births, Marriages, Deaths
Figures for 2012 show that there were 59,226 live births and 52,489 deaths, 56,438 immigrants arrived and 41,265 people emigrated from Denmark. Figures for 2009 show that 32,934 marriages took place and 14,940 divorces was granted. (Source: Statistics Denmark-StatBank.dk)

Public Holidays 2014
1 January: New Year's Day
16 April: HM Queen Margrethe's Birthday
17 April: Maundy Thursday
18 April: Good Friday
21 April: Easter Monday
16 May: General Prayer Day
29 May: Ascension Day
5 June: Constitution Day
9 June: Whit Monday
24 December: Christmas Eve
25 December: Christmas Day
26 December: Boxing Day

EMPLOYMENT

Figures for 2007 put the average labour force (age 16-65) at 2,790,000 with on average 94,000 being unemployed, of whom 41,000 were men and 53,000 were women, giving an unemployment rate of 3.4 per cent. Unemployment for 2010 was put at 4.2 per cent. The number of unemployed in 2008 was put at 51,300 persons.

The following table gives an industry sector breakdown of those employed in recent years.

Employment of Economic Activity

Sector	2007	2008
Agriculture, hunting, & forestry	79,700	73,800
Mining & quarrying	5,200	3,600
Manufacturing	432,900	426,000
Electricity, gas & water supply	16,500	17,600
Construction	192,900	193,000
Wholesale & retail trade & repair	412,100	430,500
Hotels & restaurants	81,100	82,000
Transport, storage & communications	173,100	158,900
Financial intermediation	85,900	86,900
Real estate, renting & business activities	268,400	292,200
Public admin. & defence, compulsory social security	164,200	177,600
Education	215,200	210,600
Health & social work	499,900	516,200
Other community, social & personal service activities	145,700	148,800
Private households with employed persons	3,900	na
Extra-Territorial oranisations & bodies	1,900	na
Other	na	3,700
Total	2,778,600	2,827,400

Source: Copyright © International Labour Organization (ILO Dept. of Statistics, http://laborsta.ilo.org)

BANKING AND FINANCE

Currency
One Krone = 100 øre

Economic policy is aimed towards: sound public finances; maintaining low inflation and ■ surplus on the current account; increasing employment and respecting the environment.

In 1993 Denmark decided by referendum not to join the European single currency, b government, opposition and industry wanted to join. Another referendum was held on September 2000. The turnout of voters was 87.5 per cent, with 53.1 per cent voting again joining and 46.9 per cent in favour of joining. Following the vote, it was announced that t Krone would still be tied to the euro through the original co-operation agreement: the cent exchange rate is DKK 7.46038 to the euro and a 2.25 per cent fluctuation either way allowed for. The government announced the possibility of another referendum which mig include a vote on the adoption of the proposed EU constitution. Denmark has since postpon having a referendum on the adoption of the constitution until a definitive text has be agreed on.

Denmark has enjoyed economic growth for a while. Growth rates were high 2004-06, w a lower growth rate in 2007. Along with other economies around the world Denmark h been hit by the global economic downturn and in July 2008 experienced its second quar of negative growth putting the country officially in recession, the first eurozone country do so. The economy experienced negative growth of 1.1 per cent in 2008, the most significa downturn since 1975, and the first time since 1997 that Denmark had experienced negati growth. However, while the Danes enjoy low unemployment this has had an econom knock-on with businesses struggling to recruit employees; they have been forced to off higher rates of pay which has fuelled inflation. The housing market has also been affect by the credit crunch, house prices have fallen and the mortgage lender Roskilde had to bailed out by the central bank. The export market has also been affected and exports fell 20 per cent. In Q2 2010 the National Bank reported that the Danish economy was gradua recovering and moderate economic growth was expected to continue. Growth was put 2.1 per cent in 2010 and forecast to be 1.7 per cent in 2011 and 1.5 per cent in 2012.

GDP/GNP, Inflation, National Debt
Traditionally the Danish economy was based on the agricultural sector but began to chang during the latter half of the 20th century. Agriculture now accounts for only 4 per cent GDP but is still an important sector for export earnings. The service sector is now the large contributor of GDP at around 75 per cent.

The Danish economy experienced sustained growth following a downturn in 2002-200 However, the country was the first eurozone country to enter a recession after two quarte of negative growth in 2008. The Danish government has announced that it wants to mainta its budget surplus at around 2 per cent until 2010 in order to reduce the national debt fro 44 per cent to 26 per cent of GDP. Per capita GDP was DKK309.1 thousand in 2007.

GDP at market prices

Year	DKK million	% rea growt
2001	1,335,611	0.
2002	1,372,737	0
2003	1,400,689	0
2004	1,466,180	2
2005	1,545,257	2
2006	1,631,659	3
2007	1,695,264	1
2008	1,610,288	0.
2009*	1,516,348	-5.
2010*	1,535,994	1.
2011*	1,551,315	1.

* provisional figures
Source: Statistics Denmark

Gross National Income at current prices

Year	DKK millio
2000	1,266,60
2001	1,316,77
2002	1,356,52
2003	1,392,12
2004	1,472,91
2005	1,566,80
2006	1,662,10
2007	1,713,50
2008	1,780,88
2009*	1,694,63
2010*	1,795,60
2011*	1,843,87

*provisional figures
Source: Statistics Denmark

The following table shows GVA at current prices in recent years. Figures are provisional an in DKK million:

Sector	2010	201
Agriculture, forestry and fishing	19,619	22,96
Mining & quarrying	52,103	64,37
Manufacturing	174,063	167,37
Electricity, gas & water supply	38,043	35,72

- continued

Construction	70,684	73,852
Trade & transport etc.	289,408	294,516
Information & communication	68,611	69,115
Financial & insurance	94,496	93,645
Real estate; rent of non-res.b.	37,794	41,066
Dwellings	127,067	130,104
Other business services	112,804	117,213
Public admin. education & health	372,144	370,478
Arts, entertainment other services	53,535	54,697
Total	1,510,371	1,534,801

Source: Statistics Denmark

Denmark has had several years of low inflation. It ran at 2 per cent over the period of 1990-95. Inflation for 1999 was put at 1.8 per cent, falling to 0.1 per cent in 2000. The average inflation rate for 2002 was 2.4 per cent. It fell to 2.0 per cent in 2003 and 2005, and was estimated to be 1.8 per cent in 2007. However, in 2008 it reached 4.3 per cent, the highest level since 1989.

In 2005, Denmark had no foreign debt, the first time since the 1950s. Net debt has, however, increased since 2005, despite a surplus of the balance of payments, in part because of foreign exchange movements. In 2008, the national foreign debt reached 153 billion DKK. In 2010, the government budget deficit was expected to reach kr. 100 billion (5 per cent of GDP).

Balance of Payments / Imports and Exports

The following table shows the value of imports and exports in recent years. Figures are in DKK million.

Year	Imports	Exports
2000	358,870.1	408,238.9
2001	367,032.5	424,669.4
2002	384,709.4	442,753.7
2003	369,700.9	429,272.2
2004	400,124.6	452,399.8
2005	448,719.6	503,672.8
2006	506,494.6	543,848.8
2007	528,718.5	553,586.9
2008	553,294.5	587,601.8
2009	440,196.4	496,906.3
2010	475,117.1	542,483.8
2011	524,644.1	604,292.8

Source: Statistics Denmark

The following tables show the principal trading partners and exported commodities (in million Krone):

Principal Trading Partners (2010*) in DKK million	Imports	Exports	Trade Balance
Germany	98,192	91,528	-6,665
Sweden	63,656	73,288	9,632
UK	28,324	42,511	14,187
Netherlands	34,013	24,479	-9,534
Norway	18,612	34,245	15,633
France & Monaco	15,909	22,710	6,801
USA	15,147	35,624	20,477
Italy	16,211	15,531	-680
Belgium	16,012	7,720	-8,293
China	35,986	13,404	-22,582
Total all countries	474,295	543,487	69,195

Provisional figures*
Source: Statistics Denmark

The following tables show the value of selected principal imported and exported commodities in recent years. Figures are in DKK thousands.

Exports

Commodity	2007	2008*
Petroleum oils & oils	27,685,092	30,998,681
Medicaments containing insulin but not antibiotics	11,008,533	10,421,235
Generating sets, wind-powered	9,329,653	6,333,170
Medicaments put up for retail sale	9,212,645	10,142,258
Frozen boneless meat of domestic swine	6,792,821	6,662,272
Medicaments containing hormones	5,489,905	4,918,765
Fresh or chilled with bone in, domestic swine hams & cuts	4,803,172	4,656,055
Parts for electric motors & generators	4,452,623	2,965,593
Haemoglobin, blood globulins & serum globulins	4,574,113	5,497,127
Articles of non-textile glass fibres	4,369,396	5,752,248

* provisional figures
Source: Statistics Denmark

Imports

Commodity	2007	2008*
Motor cars, diesel capacity 1500-2500cc	8,515,700	7,718,927
Motor cars, motto cycle, 1500-3000 cc	8,269,981	6,668,404
Medicaments put up for retail sale	7,346,220	7,119,210
Gas oils of petroleum/bituminous minerals	5,211,081	8,749,229

- continued

Petroleum oils & oils from bituminous minerals	4,838,684	5,667,761
Parts for electric motors & generators	4,171,082	3,239,246
Mobile phones	4,190,305	3,097,513
Computers (portable)	3,900,516	4,478,755
Reception apparatus for television	3,317,518	3,407,028
Parts of airplanes or helicopters	2,992,764	2,723,650

* provisional figures
Source: Statistics Denmark

Central Bank

Danmarks Nationalbank, Havnegade 5, 1093 Copenhagen K, Denmark. Tel: +45 3363 6363, fax: +45 3363 7103, e-mail: nationalbanken@nationalbanken.dk, URL: http://www.nationalbanken.dk
Chairman of Board of Directors and Committee of Directors: Søren Bjerre-Nielsen (page 1389)

Chambers of Commerce and Trade Organisations

The Danish Chamber of Commerce, URL: http://www.handelskammaret.dk
Dansk Industri (Confederation of Danish Industries), URL: http://www.di.dk
Landsforeningen Dansk Arbejde (The National Association for Danish Enterprise), URL: http://www.danskearbejde.dk
Det Økonomiske Råd (Danish Economic Council), URL: http://www.dors.dk

MANUFACTURING, MINING AND SERVICES

Primary and Extractive Industries

Denmark lacks natural mineral deposits but export of oil and gas from the Danish sector of the North Sea started in 1991 and the country is now self sufficient in both these resources. Denmark has proven oil reserves of 1.2 billion barrels and production for 2008 was 287 thousand barrels per day. New fields have started producing including Halfdan, Siri, and Syd Anre, Nina, Cecilie and Nif, which have contributed to the increase in Denmark's production. Denmark has proven gas reserves of 2,542 billion cubic feet and figures for 2007 show a production rate of 326 billion cubic feet.

Extraction of raw materials in thousand m³ from land area

Material	2000	2009
Sand, gravel and stone	27,587	25,361
Quartz sand	479	332
Granite	199	156
Clay	788	364
Expanded clay	313	202
Moler	227	241
Chalk, limestone	3,405	4,431
Peat	247	242
Other raw materials	563	1,732

Source: Statistics Denmark

Energy

Since the oil price shock of the 1970s Denmark has encouraged energy conservation. There are no nuclear power plants and therefore more investment is made into alternative energy sources, such as wind. Although coal still remains the main fuel for electricity, wind power currently provides more than 10 per cent of Denmark's electricity production. In recent years, the consumption of renewable energy such as wind and solar power has increased as has the use of carbon neutral fuels such as hay and wood.

Energy consumption, gross, in thousand tons

Fuel	2000	2007
Hard coal etc	6,571	7,953
Coke & furnace coke	41	38
Brown coal etc	2	0
Waste	2,905	3,677
Fuel wood etc.	1,338	4,861
Straw	843	1,412
Kerosene	4	4
Jet fuel	535	338
Motor gasoline	1,965	1,788
Other petrol and oil products	1,251	12
Gas/Diesel oil	3,493	3,852
Fuel oil	596	595
Petroleum-coke	224	314
Liquid gas (LPG)	76	74
Refinery gas	294	306
Crude oil	17,780	15,169
Natural gas mio Nm³	4,205	3,630

Source: Statistics Denmark

Production of renewable energy in TJ

Source	2000	2009
Solar energy	335	586
Wind power	15,268	24,194
Hydro power	109	68
Straw	12,220	17,339
Wood chips	2,744	9,827
Firewood	12,432	23,054
Wood pellets	2,984	2,325
Wood wastes	6,895	5,641

DENKMARK

Biogas	2,912	4,171
Waste combustion	23,601	22,706
Biodiesel	-	3,268
Fish oil	49	1,622
Geothermal heat	3,702	6,831

Source: Statistics Denmark

Manufacturing

Main industries include the food and beverage industry including bacon, dairies, milling and breweries. The chemical industry is very successful particularly in the production of plastics, insulin and petrol. Other large manufacturing sectors include the metal and mechanical engineering sectors which produce motors, agricultural machinery telecommunications equipment and shipping. The main organisation of Danish industry is the Federation of Danish Industries. The Federation is concerned with all aspects of industrial activity in Denmark and with collective bargaining.

Around 45 per cent of Denmark's manufactured goods go for export and the export surplus for the manufacturing sector averages at around 23 per cent. The following table shows manufacturers' total turnover by selected kind of activity.

Manufactured Goods	2011
Food beverages & tobacco	158,331
Textiles & leather	8,464
Wood & paper products & printing	28,170
Chemicals & oil refineries etc.	73,816
Pharmaceuticals	39,665
Plastic, glass & concrete	39,714
Basic metals & fabricated metal products	46,147
Electronic components	27,554
Electrical equipment	17,477
Manufacture of machinery	109,389
Transport equipment	14,969
Furniture & other equipment	43,893

Source: Statistics Denmark

Agriculture

63 per cent of the total area of the country is agricultural land, although the importance of agriculture varies regionally. The number of agricultural holdings has decreased and many have become part-time farms. In 1990 there were 79,338 farms. By 2006 this had dropped to 47,385. Figures for 2002 show that 188,400 people were employed in agricultural activity. Also that year 3,595 agricultural holdings were authorised as producers of organic produce. The trend is now towards fewer but larger farms.

More than half the land is employed in cereal farming. During the 1990s the percentage of land under cereal increased and there is a tendency towards winter crops. Production has risen annually to date by approximately 5 per cent.

The following table shows cereal crop production.

Crop production in thousand tonnes

Crop	2010	2011*
Winter wheat	4,996	4,769
Spring wheat	64	72
Rye	255	294
Triticale	177	137
Winter barley	784	724
Spring barley	2,198	2,540
Oats & mixed grain	274	227
Rape	580	508
Pulses	34	25
Roots	3,990	na
Grass & green fodder	25,1	na

* provisional figures
Source: Statistics Denmark

Livestock farming is centralised in the west and the rearing of milking cows has decreased in recent years to the advantage of the pig and broiler populations. There is a tendency towards specialisation, concentration and increasing herd size. Figures for 2008 show that Denmark had 1.5 million cattle, 12.7 million pigs, 136,000 sheep, 13.2 million chickens and 60,029 horses.

The following table shows livestock production.

Livestock Production in million kgs

Product	2008	2009
Whole milk and cream powder	95	111
Butter	38	37
Cheese	332	324
Beef & veal	138	137
Pork	1,985	1,898
Horse meat	1	1
Mutton & lamb	2	2
Poultry meat	205	197

Source: Statistics Denmark

After two decades of thriving production of mink fur pelts, low sales prices reduced output in the late 1980s. However, since the mid-1990s output and sales have begun to increase before dipping again in 2006-07.

Forestry

Recent figures show that around 486,000 hectares of land is covered by forest. Timber production for 2003 was 1.8 million cubic metres.

Fishing

Figures for 2008 show that Denmark has just over 1,815 commercial fishing vessels of a length of six metres or over. The total catch for 2010 was over 798,000 tonnes and was worth DKK 2.90 billion. The fish caught are chiefly cod, mackerel, haddock, flatfish, herrings, lobsters and shrimps. Danish fishermen also catch fish used in the production of fish meal and fish oil. The main fishing ports are Esbjerg, Thyborøn, Hanstholm, Hirshals and Sagen. Over 80 per cent of catches come from the North Sea and the Skagerrak.

COMMUNICATIONS AND TRANSPORT

Travel Requirements

Visitors from the USA, Canada and Australia require a passport valid for at least three months. They do not require a visa for stays of up to three months. EU citizens with a valid National Identity Card do not require a passport, and can stay indefinitely without a visa, though they require a residence permit if staying for more than 90 days. Nationals not referred to above should contact the embassy to check visa requirements.

Denmark is a signatory to the Schengen Agreement; with a Schengen visa, a visitor can travel freely throughout the Schengen zone, and there are few border stops and checks. See http://www.eurovisa.info/SchengenCountries.htm for details.

National Airlines

There are regular air services between Copenhagen Airport and most of the larger cities of Europe and other continents except Australia.
DDL-Det Danske Luftfartselskab A/S (Danish Air Lines), http://www.sasgroup.net/SASGroup/default.asp
SAS-Scandinavian Airlines System, URL: http://www.sasgroup.net/SASGroup/default.aspm
Cimber Aur Denmark URL: http://www.cimber.com

There are also major Danish charter operators such as Sterling Airways, Premiair and Maersk Air as well as a number of private companies providing internal services. (Source: The Ministry of Transport).

International Airports

Copenhagen airport has an estimated 700 arrivals and departures daily. Aviation is regulated by the following bodies.
Ministry of Transport (Trafikministeriet), URL: http://www.trm.dk
Civil Aviation Administration (Luftfartshuset), URL: http://www.slv.dk
Aarhus Airport, URL: http://www.aar.dk/
Copenhagen Airports, URL: http://www.cph.dk

Railways

There are 2,644 kilometres of railway (including rail ferry crossings) in Denmark of which 85 per cent belong to the State (DSB) and 15 per cent (mostly branch lines of small importance) are owned by private companies. Nearly all the shares of the private companies belong to the state and local authorities. Trains and cars cross the Great Belt between Funen and Zealand on ferries belonging to DSB.

There are also rail and car ferry services connecting Denmark with Sweden via Elsinore-Helsingborg and with the Continent via Rodby Faerge-Puttgarden. In addition a rail and car ferry service operates between Denmark and Germany (Gedser-Warnemunde). Denmark and Sweden are linked by a 10-mile tunnel and bridge, the Oresund Link, providing direct road and rail communication between the Danish capital, Copenhagen, and Malmo in Sweden.

Recent figures show that around 7 per cent of passenger transport is carried on the railway system and around 8 per cent of goods traffic.

Copenhagen has a subway system and an urban railway system.

DSB (Danish State Railways), URL: http://www.dsb.dk

Roads

Denmark had as of 2010 an extensive road system of 73,574 km including around 1,130 km of motorway. Figures for that year show that there were 178,8060 registered vehicles on the roads. Vehicles are driven on the right.

In February 2011 plans for an underwater tunnel running form Lolland island to the German island of Fehmarn were approved. The tunnel is forecast to cost around $5.9 billion and is scheduled to be built in 2014-2020. The tunnel would speed up transport links between Scandinavia and continental Europe.

Shipping

In view of Denmark's location and its peculiar geographic structure, shipping has always played a major role in the Danish economy and in the communication system. The Danish industry employs about 20,000 people on the ships and shore. On 1 January 2011 Danish ships of at least 20 gross tonnage number 1,768. Gross foreign earnings of Danish shipowners amounted to 26,600 million in 1993. Ninety-three per cent of earnings derived from world-wide trading (cross-trade). Figures from 2002 showed that 10.2 million passenger journeys were taken and 82.2 million tonnes of freight were carried by sea. Denmark has a total of 118 ports, 74 of which accommodate passenger ferries.

The main organisation of the shipping industry is:
Danish Shipowners' Association, (Danmarks Rederiforening), URL: http://www.danishshipping.com

The association is an employer's organisation making wage agreements with seafarers' unions and dealing with all matters of employment and safety in shipping. Furthermore, the association is a trade organisation representing Danish shipowners in dealings with government, parliament, EU and various authorities and cooperating with shipowners organisations abroad and participating in the works of international maritime organisations.

Ports
Most Danish ports are operated by the local municipalities as separate economic units. However, a few important ports are state-owned, and refineries, power stations, and some other industries usually own and operate the adjacent port facilities. The Port of Copenhagen handles about 10 per cent of the total cargo traffic through Danish ports. Other important seaports are the Kalundborg port region (including the refinery and the power station), Stigsnaes (refinery and power station), Fredericia (including the refinery), Aarhus, the Aalborg port region (including the cement works and the power station) Aabenraa (including the power station) and Esbjerg (owned and operated by the State).

Ferry services operate between Kalundborg and Århus, Ebeltoft and Sjællands Odde, Rønne and Copenhagen.

HEALTH

Denmark was one of the first countries to introduce state welfare providing a range of benefits including those for sickness and disability. Denmark has a very comprehensive welfare system often referred to as the Scandinavian Model. Danes do pay high taxes and as a result the state subsidizes the system and so services such as education and health services are provided free. The Ministry of Health remains the primary health authority in Denmark and legislative power lies with the *Folketing*. 85 per cent of health care is financed through taxes.

According to latest figures from the WHO, total expenditure on health in 2009 was equivalent to 11.5 per cent of GDP. General government expenditure accounted for 85.0 per cent of this. The remainder (15.0 per cent) was private expenditure, almost all out-of-pocket expenditure (88 per cent). Pre-paid plans accounted for 11.5 per cent. General government expenditure on health accounted for 16.8 per cent of its total expenditure. Per capita expenditure was US$6,452 in 2009.

In 2005, there were 49 general hospitals and 10 psychiatric hospitals. Figures for the period 2000-10 show that there were 18,797 physicians (34.2 per 10,000 population), 88,395 nurses and midwives (160.9 per 10,000 population), 4,438 dentistry personnel (8.1 per 10,000 population) and 2,593 pharmaceutical personnel (4.8 per 10,000 population). In the same period there were 35 hospital beds per 10,000 population.

In 2009, the infant mortality rate (probability of dying by first birthday) was 3 per 1,000 births and the under-fives mortality rate was also 4 per 1,000 births. Approximately 34 per cent of these deaths were caused by prematurity and 28 per cent by congenital anomalies. There were 5 reported cases of measles, 32 of mumps, 77 of pertussis and 313 of TB. (Source: http://www.who.int, World Health Statistics 2012)

EDUCATION

Primary/Secondary Education
Education has been compulsory since 1814, and state education is free. The *folkeskole* (public primary and lower secondary school) comprises a pre-school class *børnehaveklasse*, a nine-year basic school corresponding to the period of compulsory education, and a one-year voluntary tenth form. Compulsory education may be fulfilled either through attending the *folkeskole* or private schools or through home instruction on the condition that the instruction given is comparable to that given in the *folkeskole*. The *folkeskole* is mainly a municipal school and no fees are paid. Approximately 18 per cent of schools are private schools.

The nine-year basic school is in practice not streamed. However, a certain differentiation may take place in the eight and ninth forms. On completion of the ninth form, the pupil may sit for the leaving examination (*folkeskolens afgangsprøve*). On completion of the tenth form, the pupil may sit for either the leaving examination or the advanced leaving examination (*folkeskolens udvidede afgangsprøve*). Under certain conditions, the pupil may continue school in either the three-year gymnasium (upper secondary school) ending with the *studentereksamen* (upper secondary school leaving examination) or the two-year higher preparatory examination course ending with the *højere forberedelseseksamen*. Beside the basic education system Denmark has a well-developed system of adult and voluntary education.

Higher Education
Denmark has five universities, some of them founded hundreds of years ago, such as the University of Copenhagen. Other tertiary colleges include the two dental colleges, the Danish School of Librarianship, the Danish School of Journalism, and the Royal Danish School of Educational Studies.

Primary and secondary schools come under municipality and county control for financing and running. Higher education comes under the responsibility of central government. Since the early 1990s the financing of further education has undergone some reforms and introduced the *taximeter system* whereby grants are paid to institutions based on number of students attending.

The following table shows number of students in education in 2008.

Total Students	1,171,164
Basic school/preparatory	656,129
General upper Secondary Schools	118,666
Vocational Training	125,137
Institutions of Further Education	206,019

Source: Statistics Denmark

Literacy is estimated at 100 per cent.

RELIGION

The Evangelical Lutheran Church is the national church with 87 per cent of the entire Danish population as members. The Sovereign must belong to this church.

Recent figures from Statistics Denmark show the numbers of people belonging to religious communities in Denmark as: Lutherans, 4,541,650; Muslims, 84,000; Catholics, 32,367; Jehovah's Witnesses, 16,329; Baptists, 5,641; Pentecostals, 5,134; Mormons, 4,204; Jews, 3,320; Apostolics, 2,268; Methodists, 1,470; Reformed Churches, 360.

In Denmark there is complete freedom of religion, and no civil liabilities attached to dissenters.

Det Økumeniske Faellesraad i Danmark (Ecumenical Council of Denmark), URL: http://www.klf.dk
Chairman: Bishop Karsten Nissen
Associate council of the World Council of Churches, founded in 1939.
The National Church
Den Evangelisk-Lutherske Folkekirke i Danmark (Evangelical Lutheran Church in Denmark), URL: http://www.folkekirken.dk/
The Roman Catholic Church
Bishop of Copenhagen, URL http://www.katolsk.dk

COMMUNICATIONS AND MEDIA

The constitution provides for freedom of expression.

Newspapers
As of 2007, the average daily circulation of newspapers was 1.2 million (excluding free newspapers), a decline of 6.2 per cent from 2006.
B.T., URL: http://www.bt.dk
Berlingske Tidende, URL: http://www.berlingske.dk
Ekstra Bladet, URL http://www.ekstrabladet.dk
Jydske Vestkysten, URL: http://www.jv.dk
Jyllands-Posten, URL: http://www.jp.dk
Politiken, URL: http://www.politiken.dk
Information, URL: http://www.information.dk/
Kristeligt Dagblad, URL: http://www.kristeligt-dagblad.dk/tilbud

Broadcasting
The regulation of broadcasting in Denmark is the responsibility of the Ministry of Culture. The public broadcaster, Danmarks Radio (DR) operates two TV networks and national and regional radio statuions. TV2 is a government-owned commercial broadcaster. Private stations are available through cable. There are numerous regional radio stations. As of 2007, an estimated 97 per cent of households had access to a television, most with access to DR1 or TV2. The average viewing rates were 2 hours 28 minutes per day in 2007. In addition to the two national TV channels and four national radio stations there are numerous local TV and radio stations.

Radio
DR Radio, URL: http://www.dr.dk Independent corporation.

Television
DR TV, URL http://www.dr.dk/
TV 2/Danmark, URL: http://www.tv2.dk
Denmark's first commercial television station which began in 1988. 20 per cent of its finances come from licence fees, with the rest in advertising.
TV 3, URL: http://www.tv3.dk/
Reaches 60 per cent of the country via cable and satellite.
TV Danmark, URL: http://www.kanal4.dk/

Telecommunications
The Minister for Communication and Tourism is responsible for the overall telecommunications sector in Denmark. The Ministry for Communication and Tourism (The General Directorate of Posts and Telegraphs) attends to the departmental functions of the sector and is responsible for relations to the public telecommunications sector. The National Telecom Agency is in charge of administrative and regulatory activities of the telecommunications sector. The administration of frequencies, type approval and control, is also handled by the Agency.

In 2011, nearly 7.2 million mobile phones were in use. Recent figures show that Denmark has approximately 4.7 million internet users. In 2007, 78 per cent of families had access to the internet at home, compared to 48 per cent in 2001. (Source: Statistics Denmark)

DENMARK

ENVIRONMENT

Environmental protection is an important issue for the Danish and there has been a concerted effort towards recycling and the use of unleaded petrol. In industry, advanced systems have been developed for water purification and disposal of chemical waste.

There has also been a drive to reduce the levels of sulphur dioxide in the air, and the levels in Copenhagen over the last twenty years have fallen from 450,000 tonnes per year to 250,000 tonnes per year. Figures for 2010 show that total carbon dioxide emissions were 45.9 million metric tons, down from 49.6 million metric tons.

Denmark is a party to the following international environment agreements: Air Pollution, Air Pollution-Nitrogen Oxides, Air Pollution-Persistent Organic Pollutants, Air Pollution-Sulfur 85, Air Pollution-Sulfur 94, Air Pollution-Volatile Organic Compounds, Antarctic Treaty, Biodiversity, Climate Change, Climate Change-Kyoto Protocol, Desertification, Endangered Species, Environmental Modification, Hazardous Wastes, Law of the Sea, Marine Dumping, Marine Life Conservation, Ozone Layer Protection, Ship Pollution, Tropical Timber 83, Tropical Timber 94, Wetlands, Whaling.

SPACE PROGRAMME

Denmark joined the European Space Agency (ESA) in 1977. In 1996, the Minister for Research and Information Technology set up a Space Research Advisory Board to advise on Danish participation in international projects. Danish co-operation is focused on areas which serve commercial interests. It launched the satellite Oersted in 1999. Space research is carried out at the National Space Institute.
DTU Space, National Space Institute, URL: http://www.space.dtu.dk/english.aspx

FAROE ISLANDS
Føroyar - Færøerne

Capital: Torshavn (Population estimate: 18,000)

Head of State: Queen Margrethe II (Sovereign) (page 1471)

Flag: White, charged with a pale blue-bordered red cross, the upright one-third from the hoist

CONSTITUTION AND GOVERNMENT

Constitution
The Faroe Islands has been a self governing territory with the Kingdom of Denmark since 1948. The *Rigsombudsmand* is the highest representative of the Danish state in the islands. The islanders elect two members to the Danish parliament to represent them.

After the 1998 elections the resulting coalition government initiated talks with Denmark to instigate full sovereignty for the Faroe Islands. The plans under discussion would mean the islands would form a commonwealth with Denmark keeping the joint monarchy and having monetary union. A referendum on independence was to be held in 2001 but was abandoned after Denmark announced an end to subsidies if the islands voted in favour.

Denmark is a member of the European Union but the Faroe Islands are not, although special trade and fishing agreements exist.

Legislature
Local legislation and administration are carried out by an elected assembly, called the *Lagting*, which comprises 32 members.
Parliament Office, Løgtingið, PO Box 208, 110 Tórshavn, Faroe Islands. Tel: +298 363900, fax: +298 363901, Mail: logting@logting.fo, URL: http://www.logting.fo

---
Cabinet (as at June 2013)
Prime Minister: Kaj Leo Johannesen (page 1450)
Minister for Trade, Industry and Fisheries: Johan Dahl
Minister of Finance: Jørgen Niclasen
Minister of Interior: Kari P. Højgaard
Minister of Health Affairs: Karsten Hansen
Minister of Social Affairs: Annika Olsen
Minister of Education, Reseach and Culture: Bjørn Kalsø
Minister of Fisheries: Jacob Vestergaard

Political Parties
The political parties are: The People's Party; Self Rule Party; The Republicans; Unionist Party; Faroese Social Democratic Party; Independence Party; Centre Party

Elections
The last election was held in October 2011. This resulted in a coalition government formed by the Unionist Party, the People's Party, the Centre Party and the Independence Party.

Diplomatic Representation
British Consulate, Yviri vid Strond 19, PO Box 49, FR-110 Tórshavn, Faroe Islands. Tel: +298 313510, fax: +298 311318
Honorary Consul: Mr J. Mortensen

LOCAL GOVERNMENT

For administrative purposes the Faroe Islands are divided into 34 municipalities.

AREA AND POPULATION

Area
The Faroes are a group of islands in the Atlantic Ocean, north-west of Scotland, which form a separate Danish territory and enjoy a wide degree of home rule. The total area of the islands is 1,400 sq. km. There are 18 inhabited islands. Winters are mild, often foggy. Summers are cool and often cloudy.

To view a map of the islands, please consult
http://www.lib.utexas.edu/maps/cia08/faroe_islands_sm_2008.gif

Population
In 2012 the estimated total population was an estimated 48,372The population density in 2009 was 35 people per km^2. Approximately 21 per cent of the population is aged under 15 and 19 per cent over 60 years. Faroese and Danish are spoken.

Births, Marriages, Deaths
In 2007 there were 672 births and 380 deaths recorded. Net migration was -186. In 2007, the marriage rate was 5.3 per 1,000 people and the divorce rate was 1.1 per 1,000 people. Life expectancy from birth in 2008 was 77 years for males and 82 years for females. (Source: Statistics Faroe Islands)

Public Holidays 2014
1 January: New Year's Day
17 April: Maundy Thursday
18 April: Good Friday
21 April: Easter Monday
16 May: General Prayer Day
29 May: Ascension Day
5 June: Constitution Day
9 June: Whit Monday
24 December: Christmas Eve
25 December: Christmas Day
26 December: Boxing Day

EMPLOYMENT

Figures from Statistics Denmark show that, in 2010, the Faroe Islands had a labour force of 28,9700, with an unemployment rate of 6.8 per cent. In 2008 one of the largest sectors of employment was fishing which employed 1,836 people and a further 1,482 in the fish processing industry and 632 in aquaculture

BANKING AND FINANCE

Currency
1 Danish krone = 100 ore

GDP/GNP, Inflation, National Debt
Over the years, the Faroe Islands have become less financially dependent on Denmark, but still receive some financial support. In 2007, they received grants of DKK 616 million. The economy is highly dependent on the fishing industry.

In 2008, GDP was an estimated US$1.5 billion. Growth was an estimated 0.5 per cent compared with 14 per cent the previous year. Due to its reliance on a single industry, the economy is often subject to strong fluctuations in growth. Figures for 2010 show that GDP at current prices was DKK 12,942 million giving a per capital figure of DKK 267,551.

Inflation is high in the Faroe Islands, compared to Denmark in Greenland. Denmark and Greenland have had an average rate of inflation of respectively 2.5 per cent and 2.3 per cent since 1995. By comparison, the Faroe Islands' rate of inflation averaged 3.6 per cent for the same period.

Balance of Payments / Imports and Exports
Figures for 2011 show that exports earned DKK 5,359 million. Imports for 2011 cost DKK 5,3252 million. In 2008, the exports had increased to DKK 4,318 million, of which 12 per cent went to Denmark. Exports of fish and fish products accounted for 81 per cent of exports. Imports for 2008 cost DKK 5,005 million of which 31.8 per cent came from Denmark. (Source: Statistics Denmark)

Central Bank
National Bank of Denmark, URL: http://www.nationalbanken.dk

MANUFACTURING, MINING AND SERVICES

Oil
Some exploratory drilling took place in 2001 and some oil deposits were found. Further research is underway to determine if these deposits are of commercial value.

Energy
Net electricity production in 2010 was 0.27 billion kilowatthours and consumption was 0.25 million kilowatthours.

Agriculture
Figures from FAOSTAT estimate the main agricultural products for 2010 were indigenous sheep meat of 521 tonnes, worth Int$1,419,000; 1,400 tonnes of potatoes, worth Int$236,000 and 78 tonnes of indigenous cattle meat worth Int$211,000.

Fishing
The economic life of the islands depends primarily on fishing; 26 per cent of the economically active population live directly on the proceeds of this industry. In 2006, the Faroe Islands had 158 fishing vessels and the total catch that year was 623,000 tonnes. The Faroese fish for whales, which are eaten during the winter. In 2006, the Faroe Islands began buying whalemeat from Iceland. Figures for 2010 put the total catch at 393,875 tonnes.

COMMUNICATIONS AND TRANSPORT

National Airlines
Atlantic Airways is the national airline for the Faroe Islands. Air services are also provided by Maersk Air and Air Iceland. Helicopter travel is also available between the islands. The airport is situated on the island of Vágar.

Shipping
A passenger and car ferry operates between Denmark and the Faroe Islands all year round. During the summer months ferry travel is available between the islands, Norway, Iceland and the Shetland Islands.

Roads
There are 264 private cars and taxis per 1,000 capita. All communities are connected by road and Streymoy and Eysturoy. The largest islands are connected by a bridge.

HEALTH
In 2007, there were 230 physicians and general practitioners, 45 dentists and 672 hospital beds. Public health care expenditure in 2006 was DKK862. (Source: ArcticStat)

EDUCATION
The education system in the Faroe Islands is similar to that of Denmark and is overseen by the Faroese Ministry of Education and Culture. Education is compulsory for nine years. Figures for 2009 put spending on education at 9.4 per cent of GDP. Primary education starts at age 7, the language of instruction is Faroese, in the third grade students begin to learn Danish and English in the fifth grade.

RELIGION
The majority of the population belong to the Evangelical Lutheran Church of Denmark. There is also a community of Plymouth Brethren.

COMMUNICATIONS AND MEDIA

Newspapers
The Faroe Islands produce two daily newspapers, Dimmalaetting (URL: http://www.dimma.fo) and Sosialurin (URL: http://www.http://www.sosialurin.fo/).

Broadcasting
The main national radio and TV services are publicly-funded. The public television broadcaster is Sjonvarp Foroya and Radio Utvarp Foroya (URL: http://www.kringvarp.fo/).

ENVIRONMENT
Figures for 2010 show that total carbon dioxide emissions from fossil fuels was 0.74 million metric tons. (Source: EIA)

The Faroe Islands is a party to the Marine Dumping international agreement and is an associate member to the London Convention and Ship Pollution.

GREENLAND
Grønland - Kalaalit Nunaat

Capital: Nuuk (Population estimate, 2004: 14,350)

Head of State: H.M. Queen Margrethe II (Sovereign) (page 1471)

National Flag: Two equal horizontal bands of white (top) and red with a large disc slightly to the hoist side of centre - the top of the disc is red and the bottom half is white.

CONSTITUTION AND GOVERNMENT

Constitution
Greenland, Denmark's former colony, was incorporated as an integral part of the Danish Realm by the Constitution of 5 June 1953, which also gave Greenland two representatives in the Folketing. In 1979 Greenland achieved home rule within the framework of the unity of the realm, which has gradually meant a considerable administrative independence from Denmark, but not economic or human separation. Greenland receives subsidies from Denmark and Greenlanders benefit from free education, hospital care and other services.

International Relations
The USA has a radar base at Thule in the north of the country.

Recent Events
Greenland held a referendum in December 2008, the vote was in favour of greater control over energy resources and granting Kalaallisut or Western Greenlandic status of official language in place of Danish.

Legislature
Greenland is administered by a *Landsting* (parliament) with 31 members and a *Landsstyre* (government) with up to seven members. Ministers do not have to be Members of Parliament. Home rule has meant the gradual assumption of control over all areas of government, with the exception of the administration of justice, the police service, foreign relations and defence, which continue to be administered by the Danish authorities. Greenland also elects two representatives to the Danish Parliament (Folketing). Denmark is represented in Greenland by the High Commissioner. Elections are held every four years.

High Commissioner for Greenland, P.O. Box 1030, DK 3900, Nuuk, Greenland. Tel: +299 321001, fax: +299 324171,
URL: http://www.stm.dk/Index/mainstart.asp?o=4&n=3&s=4
High Commissioner: Søren Hald Møller (2005-)

Cabinet (as at June 2013)
Prime Minister, Minister of Foreign Affairs: Aleqa Hammond (page 1437)
Deputy Prime Minister, Minister of Health and Infrastructure: Steen Lynge
Minister of Fishing, Hunting and Agriculture: Karl Lyberth
Minister of Finance and Domestic Affairs: Vittus Qujaukitsoq
Minister of Industry and Mineral Materials: Jens-Erik Kirkegaard
Minister of Culture, Education, Gender Equality and the Church: Nick Nielsen
Minister of Housing, Nature, Environment and Nordic Cooperation: Miiti Lynge
Minister for Family and Legal and Justice Department: Martha Lund Olsen

Ministries
Government portal, URL: http://naalakkersuisut.gl/
Office of the Prime Minister, P.O.Box 1015, 3900 Nuuk, Greenland. Tel: +299 345000, URL: http://naalakkersuisut.gl/
Ministry of Finance and Trade, P.O. Box 1037, DK 3900, Nuuk, Greenland. Tel: +299 345000, fax: +299 324614
Ministry of Taxation, P.O. Box 1605, DK 3900, Nuuk, Greenland. Tel +229 345000, fax: +299 322042
Ministry of Housing and Infrastructure, P.O. Box 909, DK 3900, Nuuk, Denmark. Tel: +299 345000, fax: +299 345410
Ministry of Industry, P.O. Box 269, DK 3900, Nuuk, Denmark. Tel: +299 345000, fax: +299 324704
Ministy of Health, P.O. Box 1160, DK 3900, Nuuk, Greenland. Tel: +299 345000, fax: +299 325505, URL: http://www.dsk.gl
Ministry of Environment and Nature, P.O. Box 1614, DK 3900, Nuuk, Greenland. Tel: +299 345000, fax: +299 325286
Ministry of Culture, Education, Research and Church, P.O. Box 1029, DK 3900, Nuuk, Greenland. Tel: +299 344000, fax: +299 322073
Ministry of Social Affairs and Labour Market, P.O. Box 260, DK 3900, Nuuk, Greenland. Tel: +299 345000, fax: +299 324547, URL: http://www.isp.gl

Political Parties
Siumut, - Social Democratic Party, URL: http://www.siumut.gl. Leader: Aleqa Hammond
Atassut, - Solidarity, URL: http://www.atassut.gl. Leader: Finn Karlsen
Inuit Ataqatigiit, - The United Inuit, URL: http://www.ia.gl. Leader: Kuupik Kleist (page 1457)
Demokraatit, -Democrats, URL: http://www.demokrat.gl. Leader: Jens B. Frederiksen
Kattusseqatigiit, Association of Candidates, URL: http://www.kattusseqatigiit.gl. Leader: Anthon Frederiksen

DENMARK

Elections

An election was held in June 2009. This was the first election to be held following the referendum resulting in greater home rule. The left-wing Inuit Ataqatigiit party won 7 seats and announced it would form a coalition with democrats and the independents.

The most recent election was held on 12 April 2013 amid fears that the country was surrendering its interests to foreign multinationals. The Siumut party in Greenland, led by Aleqa Hammond won 42 per cent of the vote and formed a coalition government.

LEGAL SYSTEM

The administration of justice is widely based on lay people: district judges, lay judges and defence counsel are ordinary citizens while the local police handle the prosecuting function. It is only when a case goes before the High Court that legally trained people become involved. Each town in Greenland has its own District Court presided over by a judge. Cases of a very serious nature are heard in the High Court in Denmark.

LOCAL GOVERNMENT

Greenland's local administration was revised in 2009 moving from three regions (Avannaa (the North), Tunu (East), and Kitaa (West)) subdivided into18 municipalities (one in the North, two in the East and 15 in the West) to four municipalities: Kujalleq, Qaasuitsup, Qeqqata and Sermersooq. The North East Greenland National Park is unincorporated. Kujalleq comprises the former districts of Nanortalik, Narsaq and Qaqortoq and includes some uninhabited territory on the east coast which was formerly part of Tasiilaq. The Thule Air Base is within the Qaasuitsup municipality but is also an unincorporated area and does not belong to any muncipality.

The municipalities are :
Kujalleq, Municipal centre: Qaqortoq, URL: http://www.nanortalik.gl/english/index-english.htm
Qaasuitsup, Municipal centre: Ilulissat, URL: http://www.qaasuitsup.gl/
Qeqqata, Municipal centre: Sisimiut, URL: http://www.qeqqata.gl/
Sermersooq, Municipal centre, Nuuk (the capital), URL: http://www.sermersooq.gl/kl

AREA AND POPULATION

Area

Greenland is the largest island in the world, with a total area of about 840,000 sq. miles. Of these, 114,600 sq. miles are made up of coastal tracts. The islands along the coast cover a total area of 17,300 sq. miles, while the inland ice covers 708,100 sq. miles. The ice can be as thick as four kilometres in places.

To view a map, please consult http://www.lib.utexas.edu/maps/cia08/greenland_sm_2008.gif

Population

In 2012 the population was estimated to be 56,749, down from 56,780 in 2010. The capital Nuuk had a population in 2009 of 15,105. Figures for 2009 put the population density of Greenland at 0.14 people per sq km (ice-free area). An estimated 89 per cent of the population are Inuit with the remaining 11 per cent being mainly Danish. In 2008, immigration was estimated at 2,387 people, emigration at 1,073, leaving a net migration figure of 695. Major municipalities (2011) include: Sermersooq (21,600), Qaasuitsup (17,750) and Qeqqata (9,700).

Greenland has its own official language - *Kalaallisut or Western Greenlandic*. Danish and Kalaallisut are used in public administration.

Births, Marriages and Deaths

The total fertility rate was estimated to be 2.23 live births per woman aged 15-49 years. Figures for 2007 show that there were 8.0 deaths per 1,000 population. Average life expectancy as of 2007 was 66 years for males and 71 years for females. In 2011, 6,017 men and 6,608 women were registered as married, 1,445 men and 1,516 women registered as divorced and 519 men and 1,346 women registered as widowed. (Source: Statistics Greenland)

Public Holidays 2014

1 January: New Year's Day
17 April: Maundy Thursday
18 April: Good Friday
21 April: Easter Monday
16 May: General Prayer Day
29 May: Ascension Day
5 June: Constitution Day
9 June: Whit Monday
21 June: National Day (Ullortuneq)
24 December: Christmas Eve
25 December: Christmas Day
26 December: Boxing Day

EMPLOYMENT

Figures for 2012 put the labour force at 40,156 with an unemployment rate of 8.8 per cent.

BANKING AND FINANCE

Currency
1 Danish krone (DKK) = 100 øre

GDP/GNP, Inflation, National Debt

The economy is highly dependent on the fishing industry, and as such, is vulnerable to fluctuations in the industry, such as the prices of the catch. Figures for 2010 put GDP at DKK 12,295 million, giving a growth rate of 1.2 per cent. Per capita GDP was estimated at 271,80 DKK. Inflation was estimated at 5 per cent in 2007, and 4.8 per cent in 2008.

Imports and Exports

Figures for 2008 put import costs at DKK4.421 million and export revenue at DKK2.48 million. The trade balance was -1.941 million, the highest trade deficit since the 1960s. In 2007 imports cost DKK 3.642.5 million and exports earned DKK 2.332 million, resulting in a trade deficit of -DKK1.3 million. Figures for 2011 show that import costs were DKK 4,82 million and exports earned DKK 2,541 million. Import costs have risen primarily because of the increase in prince of minerals, fuels and lubricants. The deficit is covered by a subsidy from Denmark. Exports revolve around the fishing industry. Main trading partners are Denmark, UK, the Faroe Islands, Iceland, Norway, Germany, Sweden, France, Japan, Canada and USA.

Major Bank

Grønlandsbanken, PO Box 1033, DK-3900 Nuuk, Greenland. Tel: +299 347700; fax +299 347720, e-mail: grbank@greennet.gl, URL: http://www.webbanken.gl

Chambers of Commerce and Trade Organisations

Aasiaat Trade Council, niels Egedesvej 6, DK 3950 Aasiaat, Greenland. Tel: +299 892540
Nuuk Chamber of Commerce, Nuuk Handelsstandsforening, P.O. Box 1311, DK 3900 Nuuk, Greenland.
The Trade Council of Greenland, P.O. Box 1037, DK 3900, Nuuk, Greenland. Tel: +299 345235

MANUFACTURING, MINING AND SERVICES

Primary and Extractive Industries
Greenland has natural reserves of cryolite, marble, zinc, silver, gold, diamonds and uranium. In 2001 a licensing round for petroleum exploration licences was launched.

Manufacturing
The majority of the inhabitants live by fishing, hunting, processing of fish products, construction, commerce, and transport. Other articles for export are frozen fish and shrimps and other fishery products, hides and furs. Some communities of hunters of Arctic animals have, during the last 50 years, become fishing villages where the inhabitants now fish for shrimps, cod and salmon. Greenland's fishing catch is sold on the world markets. Freezing plants for shrimps and fish exist in many localities on the West coast. While fishing is the main industry, there is some sheep farming. Hunting of marine mammals is still of importance, especially in the small settlements in the northern part of Greenland and in Eastern Greenland. Greenland has six shipyards which maintain and repair ships and produce industrial tanks, containers and steel constructions for building.

Service Industries
Tourists total about 16,000 per year.

Agriculture
Figures from FAOSTAT estimate the main agricultural production for 2010 as 926 tonnes of indigenous sheep meat worth Int$340,000, 38 tonnes of wool (greasy), worth Int$20,000 and 278 tonnes of meat nes, worth Int$210,000.

Fishing
The main industry of Greenland employs around 6,500 people and accounts for over 85 per cent of exported goods. Fishing is carried out under a licence and quota system in order to preserve fish stocks. Figures for 2006 show that Greenland had 863 fishing vessels and in 2004 the total catch was 192,000 tonnes over 70 per cent of which was prawn. Whaling is also carried out. The total catch in 2010 was put at 210,000.

COMMUNICATIONS AND TRANSPORT

National Airlines
Greenlandair, Box 1012, DK-3900 Nuuk, Greenland. Tel: +299 328888, fax: +299 327288, e-mail: glsales@greennet.gl, URL: http://www.greenlandair.gl
Operates services to Denmark, Iceland and Canada (Frobisher Bay). Icelandair and SAS also provide services to Greenland.

Greenland has two international airports at Kangerlussuaq (Søndre Strømfjord) and Narsarsuaq (URL: http://iserit.greennet.gl), as well as 18 local airports and heliports.

Roads
There are 150 km of roads of which 60 km are paved. No roads run between towns. In 2002 there were a total of 4,211 registered vehicles.

Ports and Harbours
The main ports are Kangerluarsoruseq, Kangerlussuaq, Nanortalik, Narsarsuaq, Nuuk, Saamiut and Sisimiut. Cargo services operate between Denmark, Iceland and Canada (St. John's).

HEALTH

A free medical service is provided. Greenland has one central hospital in the capital Nuuk, and 15 smaller district hospitals. In 1998 there were 84 doctors. Figures for 2010 show that 10.5 per cent of GDP was spent on healthcare. In 2008 the infant mortality rate was 9.6 deaths per 1,000 live births. Life expectancy is 66.6 years for men and 71/6 years for females. In 2005, there were six cases of HIV/AIDS. (Source: Greenland Statistics)

EDUCATION

Compulsory education is from six to 15 years of age, followed by an optional three years of schooling. In the academic year 2002-03 there were 11,350 pupils attending pre-primary and primary school, with 1,222 teachers, and there are three secondary schools. Some students who live a long way from school can live in student residences which house students in the municipality.

Figures for 2006 show that DKK 1,477 million was spent on education.

RELIGION

Around 99 per cent of the population are Evangelical Lutherans. Figures for 1998 show that there were 17 parishes, 81 churches and 22 ministers.

COMMUNICATIONS AND MEDIA

Media legislation is controlled by the Greenlandic government. Press freedom is guaranteed but there have been some reports of alleged political pressure.

Newspapers
The Atuagagdloitit/Gronlandsposten(Greenland Post) (URL: http://sermitsiaq.ag/) is published twice a week and the Sermitsiaq (URL: http://www.sermitsiaq.gl/) is published weekly.

Broadcasting
The Greenland National Broadcasting Company (Kalaallit Nunaata Radio (KNR) provides public radio and TV services. It broadcasts in Greenlandic and Danish. Private local TV and radio stations also operate.
Greenland National Broadcasting Company, URL: http://knr.gl

Telecommunications
Recent figures show that there are 22,000 telephone subscribers, approximately 50,000 cellular phone users and 36,000 internet users.

ENVIRONMENT

The most important environmental issues for Greenland include preservation of the arctic environment. Observations from space show that the thickness of the ice cover is depleting by 239 cubic kilometres per year. This has serious implications for rising sea levels. Preservation of the Inuit way of life is also a major concern. During the international Copenhagen Conference on Climate Change held in December 2009, one of the many environmental changes brought to the attention of the conference was the Greenland ice sheet which is thought to be 'vanishing at an alarming rate'. In November 2010 a study found that the ice sheet is shrinking faster and making a bigger contribution to rising sea levels than originally thought.

DJIBOUTI

Republic of Djibouti

Jumhuriyat Jibuti

Capital: Djibouti (Population estimate: 550,000)

Head of State: Ismael Omar Guelleh (President) (page 1434)

National Flag: Two equal horizontal bands of light blue (top) and light green with a white triangle with its point towards the fly containing a red star

CONSTITUTION AND GOVERNMENT

Constitution
Formerly French Somaliland, Djibouti became independent from France on 27 June 1977 following a referendum in May of that year. A new constitution was approved in September 1992 which allowed the existence of up to four political parties. In 2002 this ruling expired to allow full multi party elections to be held. The president, elected by universal adult suffrage for a term of six years, holds executive power. In 2010 the constitution was changed to allow the president to stand for three terms.

To consult the constitution (in French), please visit: http://www.adi.dj/constitut/constitut_dj.htm.

International Relations
As a former French colony, Djibouti retains strong links with France; nearly 3,000 French troops are based in the country under the agreed terms of independence. France also provides significant aid and financial support. Relations with Eritrea have suffered over the disputed Ras Doumeira border area.

Recent Events
A UN report published in November 2006 stated that Djibouti (among other countries) has supplied arms to the Islamist administration in Mogadishu, despite the 1992 arms embargo on Somalia; Djibouti denied the claim.

Drought conditions affected inland areas of Djibouti in spring 2007, and the UN World Food Programme estimated that 53,000 people could be affected.

Parliamentary elections took place on 8th February 2008 but were boycotted by the opposition; the ruling coalition therefore won all the seats.

In December 2009 the UN Security Council approved sanctions against Eritrea for supplying weapons to Somali insurgents and for its refusal to solve the border problem with Djibouti.

In July 2011 Djibouti and other horn of Africa countries began to feel the effects of the region's worst drought for 60 years; thousands of animals died and crops withered in fields. Western aid agencies were fearful that the drought would escalate into a full blown famine. In February 2012 the IMF approved a $14 million loan to help the drought hit finances.

Legislature
The legislature is unicameral. The National Assembly controls legislative power and consists of 65 members elected for five years. The prime minister presides over the Council of Ministers, which is responsible to the president.
National Assembly, BP 138, Djibouti. Tel: +253 352037, e-mail: assnatdji@intnet.dj, URL: http://www.presidence.dj/assemblee.htm

Cabinet (as at June 2013)
Prime Minister: Mohamed Kamil Abdoulkader (page 1453)
Minister of Agriculture, Fisheries, Livestock and Fishery Resources: Mohamed Ahmed Awaleh
Minister of Eonomy and Finance, Industry and Planning: Ilyas Moussa Dawaleh (page 1413)
Minister of Communications, Post and Telecommunications: Ali Hassan Bahdon
Minister of National Defence: Hassan Darar Houffaneh
Minister of National Education and Vocational Training: Djama Elmi Okieh
Minister of Employment: Abdi Houssein Ahmed
Minister of Energy and Water: Dr Ali Yacoub Mahamoud
Minister of Equipment and Transport: Moussa Ahmed Hassan
Minister of Foreign Affairs and International Co-operation: Muhammad Ali Youssouf
Minister of Muslim Affairs, Culture and Endowment: Aden Hassan Aden
Minister of Health: Dr Kassim Issak Osman
Minister of Housing, Urban Planning and Environment: Mohamed Moussa Ibrahim Balala
Minister of the Interior: Hassan Omar Mohamed Bourhan
Minister of Justice and Prison Affairs, Human Rights: Ali Farah Assoweh
Minister of Higher Education and Research: Dr Nabil Mohamed Ahmed
Minister of Promotion of Women and Family Planning, Relations with Parliament: Hasna Barkat Daoud
Minister of the Budget: Bodeh Ahmed Robleh

Ministries
Office of the Prime Minister, BP 2086, Djibouti. Tel: +253 351494, fax: +253 355049
Secrétariat Général du Gouvernement, B.P. 06, Djibouti. Tel: +253 351145 / 352481, fax: +253 358296, e-mail: sggpr@intnet.dj, URL: http://www.presidence.dj/
Djibouti Information Agency, 1 Rue de Moscou, B.P. 32, Djibouti. Tel: +253 354013, fax: +253 354037, e-mail: adi@intnet.dj
Ministry of National and Higher Education, Cité ministérielle, Djibouti. Tel: +253 350997, fax: +253 354234, e-mail: education.gov@intnet.dj
Ministry of Communication, Culture, Post and Telecommunications, 1 Rue de Moscou, BP 32, Djibouti. Tel: +253 355672 / 353928, fax: +253 353957, e-mail: mccpt@intnet.dj, URL: http://www.mccpt.dj/
Ministry of the Interior and Decentralisation, Djibouti. Tel: +253 352542, e-mail: elections@intnet.dj, URL: http://www.elec.dj/
Ministry of Economy, Finance, Planning and Privatisation, B.P. 13, Djibouti. Tel: +253 353331, e-mail: cabmefpp@intnet.d, URL: http://www.ministere-finances.dj
Ministry of Foreign Affairs, BP 1863, Djibouti. Tel: +253 353342, fax: +253 353840
Ministry of the Interior and Decentralisation, BP 33, Djibouti. Tel: +253 350791, fax: +253 354862, URL: http://www.elec.dj
Ministry of Port and Maritime Affairs, BP 2107, Djibouti. Tel: +253 350105, fax: +253 356187
Ministry of Trade and Industry, BP 1846, Djibouti. Tel: +253 351682
Ministry of Health and Social Affairs, BP 1974, Djibouti. Tel: +253 351491, fax: +253 356300
Ministry of Justice and Religious Affairs, BP 12, Djibouti. Tel: +253 351506, fax: +253 354012
Ministry of Labour, BP 2107, Djibouti. Tel: +253 350105, fax: +253 356187
Ministry of Defence, BP 42, Djibouti. Tel: +253 352034, fax: +253 35425
Ministry of Energy and Natural Resources, BP 175, Djibouti. Tel: +253 350340, fax: +253 354423

DJIBOUTI

Political Parties
l'Union pour la Majorite Presidentielle, (Union for a Presidential Majority, UMP), made up of Rassemblement Populaire pour le Progres (RPP) and Front pour la Restauration de la Democratie (FRUD). The Union for a Democratic Alternative (UAD) is made up of three opposition parties

Elections
Under the Electoral system in Djibouti the party or coalition which wins the most votes wins all 65 seats in parliament. The penultimate parliamentary elections were held in January 2003 and were won by the four party l'Union pour la Majorite Presidentielle. Legislative elections then took place on 8th February 2008, but were boycotted by the opposition; the ruling coalition therefore won all the parliamentary seats. The most recent election took place in February 2013, opposition parties took part this time but contested the result which gave the Union for the Presidential Majority 49 of the 65 seats.

The most recent presidential elections were held in April 2011 when President Guelleh was re-elected for a third term.

Diplomatic Representation
US Embassy, Plateau du Serpent, Blvd. Marechal Joffre, PO Box 185, Djibouti. Tel: +253 353995, fax: +253 353940, URL: http://djibouti.usembassy.gov/
Ambassador: Geeta Pasi
Embassy of Djibouti, Suite 515, 1156 15th Street NW, Washington, DC 20005, USA. Tel: +1 202 331 0270, fax: +1 202 331 0302
Ambassador: Roble Olhaye
British Embassy (All Staff resident at Addis Ababa), URL: http://ukinethiopia.fco.gov.uk/en/
Ambassador: Gregory Dorey (page 1417)
British Consulate, PO Box 169, Rue de Djibouti, Djibouti. Tel +253 385007, fax: +253 352543, e-mail: martinet@intnet.dj
Embassy of Djibouti, 26 Rue Emile Ménier, 75116 Paris, France. Tel: +331 47 274922, URL: http://www.ambdjibouti.org
Head of Mission: Rachad Farah
Permanent Representative of the Republic of Djibouti to the United Nations, 866 United Nations Plaza, Suite 4011, New York, NY 10017, USA. Tel: +212 753 3163, fax: +212 223 1276
Ambassador to the US and UN: Roble Olhaye

LEGAL SYSTEM

The legal system is a mix of Islamic law, and French civil law based on Napoleonic code, and consists of courts of first instance, a High Court of Appeal, and a Supreme Court. Each of the five administrative districts also has a traditional court. A state security court hears political trials and cases involving threats to national security. Political trials may be heard by the Supreme Court, and the Constitutional Council rules on the constitutionality of laws.

The government's human rights record is poor. There is corruption, official impunity, arbitrary arrest and severe prison conditions. The government applies restrictions on the freedom of the press, assembly, and association. The death penalty was abolished in 1995.

LOCAL GOVERNMENT

Djibouti is divided into six administrative districts: Ali Sabieh, Arta, Dikhil, Djibouti, Obock and Tadjourah.

AREA AND POPULATION

Area
Djibouti is situated on the north-east coast of Africa with Eritrea to the north-west, Ethiopia to the west and south and Somalia to the south. It has an area of 23,200 sq. km. . The terrain is coastal plain, mountains or plateaus. Its coast on the Red Sea linking to the Gulf of Aden and the Indian Ocean and north to Mediterranean Sea through Suez makes Djibouti an ideal centre for trans-shipment of goods for other landlocked African nations.

The climate is hot and very dry, with an average rainfall less than 150mm per year

To view a regional map, please consult
http://www.lib.utexas.edu/maps/cia08/djibouti_sm_2008.gif

Population
The population in 2010 was estimated at 889,000. The average annual growth rate was for the period 2000-10 was estimated to be 1.9 per cent. The Issa make up 60 per cent of the population, the Afar, 35 per cent the rest are mainly French, Arab, Ethiopian and Italian. There are three major groups of languages: Afar and Issa (Somali), French and Arabic are the official languages. Approximately 76 per cent of the population lives in urban areas. Nearly two thirds of the population live in the capital.

Births, Marriages, Deaths
In 2010, the crude birth rate at 28.9 per 1,000 population, and the average annual death rate at 96.1 per 1,000. The average life expectancy in 2009 was 58 years for males and 62 years for females. Healthy life expectancy was 47 years for males and 50 years for females (2007). The median age is 21 years. An estimated 36 per cent of the population is aged less than 15 and 10 per cent over 60 years. The total fertility rate for women was 3.8. (Source: http://www.who.int, World Health Statistics 2012)

National Day
27 June: Independence Day

EMPLOYMENT

Recent estimates put the labour force at 280,000, the majority of whom are employed in the agricultural sector. Unemployment has been estimated at 57 per cent with some source putting as high as 60 per cent. The Government is a large employer including sectors such as telecommunications, electricity, the port and airport.

BANKING AND FINANCE

Currency
One Djibouti Franc = 100 centimes.

GDP/GNP, Inflation, National Debt
Djibouti's economy largely derives from its port which handles 90 per cent of Ethiopia's trading. It is also a free-trade zone. It also generates income from foreign soldiers. It has no significant natural resources. Djibouti's finances have improved in recent years and it currently receives some US$200 million from private sector investment per annum. A new port is currently being developed and there are possibilities of foreign aid to develop the railway line.

Djibouti's economy is dependent on the service sector, earned from the strategic location of the country as a free trade zone for land locked north-east Africa. It also earns revenue from agreements with French military bases situated there and the US Task Force based there.

GDP/GNI

	2005	2006	2007
GDP, US$ million	708.84	768.87	833.35
GDP growth rate, %	3.2	4.8	4.8
GNI per capita	1,010	1,060	..

Source: African Development Bank

GDP was estimated to be US$1.1 billion in 2010.

Djibouti's average annual inflation rate has been low for several years. In 2005, it was 3.1 per cent, rising to 3.6 per cent in 2006, then dipping to 3.5 per cent in 2007 and 2.0 per cent in 2009.

Total external public debt was US$426.42 million. (Source: AFDB)

Balance of Payments / Imports and Exports
Principal countries providing exports to Djibouti are France, Ethiopia, Saudi Arabia, Italy and the UK. Principal countries receiving Djibouti exports are Somalia, Ethiopia and Yemen. Major imports are livestock, food, machinery and electrical appliances, and petroleum products. Main exports are livestock and food, machinery and transport equipment, and coffee and coffee substitutes. Djibouti benefits from its geographical location by being a re-export centre for several landlocked nations, particularly Ethiopia, allowing goods to be flown in and sent out from its ports.

External Trade, US$ million

	2005	2006	2007
Trade balance	-237.82	-296.30	-365.99
Exports	39.50	49.54	145.75
Imports	277.32	345.85	511.74

Source: African Development Bank

Central Bank
Banque Centrale de Djibouti, PO Box 2118, Ave Saint Laurent du Var, Djibouti, Djibouti. Tel: +253 352751, fax: +253 356288, e-mail: bndj@intnet.dj, URL: http://www.banque-centrale.dj/
Governor: M. Djama M. Haid

MANUFACTURING, MINING AND SERVICES

Energy
Djibouti has no oil reserves and relies on imports to meet its needs. Figures for 2011 show that Djibouti imported 13,000 barrels per day.

In 2010, 33 million kWh of electricity was generated and 30 million kWh consumed. All of Djibouti's electricity is generated from fossil fuels.

Manufacturing
Djibouti has very limited industry, mainly restricted to dairy products.

Service Industries
Djibouti benefits from its geographical location and its status as a free trade zone, it is able to act as the major re-export centre for several landlocked nations, particularly Ethiopia, allowing goods to be flown in and sent out from its ports. Djibouti is the home port of the Ethiopian Shipping Lines. The port is to be expanded with the help of investment for the United Arab Emirates, and the first phase of re-development was hoped to be in place by the end of 2008.

The number of tourists recorded in 1998 was 20,000, down by over half compared with visitors in 1994.

Agriculture

Agriculture generated less than 3 per cent of Djibouti's GDP in 2006. Goats are the main livestock bred, some 507,000 head being bred in 1996, followed by sheep at 470,000 head and cattle at 190,000 head. Estimates put Djibouti's total fishing catch in 2010 at 1,060 metric tons.

Agricultural Production in 2010

Produce	Int. $'000*	Tonnes
Indigenous camel meat	18,127	8,649
Indigenous cattle meat	16,719	6,189
Indigenous sheep meat	5,947	2,184
Vegetables fresh nes	5,748	30,500
Indigenous goat meat	5,631	2,350
Cow milk, whole, fresh	2,862	9,170
Camel milk, whole, fresh	2,237	6,560
Beans, dry	902	1,500
Lemons and limes	634	1,600
Tomatoes	444	1,200
Mangoes, mangosteens, guavas	390	650
Fruit, tropical fresh nes	352	860

* unofficial figures
Source: http://faostat.fao.org/site/339/default.aspx Food and Agriculture Organization of the United Nations, Food and Agricultural commodities production

COMMUNICATIONS AND TRANSPORT

Travel Requirements
Visitors from the USA, Canada, Australia and the EU require a passport valid for six months (with three blank pages), a return ticket and a visa (except transit passengers not disembarking and continuing their journey by the same aircraft or ship). Nationals not referred above should contact the embassy to check visa requirements.

National Airlines
Air Djibouti is the national airline, providing international services to the Middle East and Europe.
Air Djibouti, BP499, Place Lagarde, Rue de Bruxelles, Djibouti, Republic of Djibouti. Tel: +253 356723, fax: +253 356734

International Airports
Djibouti's international airport, Djibouti-Ambouli International Airport is located at Ambouli, six km from Djibouti. In addition there are 11 other airports which provide services within the country.

Railways
Djibouti's rail service, Chemin de Fer Djibouti-Ethiopien (CDE), is jointly owned by the Governments of Djibouti and Ethiopia. There is a railway running inland from Djibouti to Addis Ababa.

Roads
Estimates put the total length of roads in 1996 at 2,890 km. Of those, 1,090 km were main highways and 1,800 km were regional roads. The Grand Bara road joins the capital with the south of the country. The Saudi Arabian-financed Djibouti-Tadjourah road links the capital with the north. Vehicles are driven on the right.

Ports and Harbours
Port Autonome International de Djibouti was established as a free port in 1981 and handled 736,000 metric tons of freight in 1995. During the conflict between Ethiopia and Eritrea, the port of Djibouti increased in importance as it became the port for Ethiopia. In order to create more ease of access to the port a new bridge has been inaugurated crossing the River Gelba. This also makes it possible to bypass the Gobi Desert. Foreign investment in Djibouti aims to increase port capacity, improvements will include a new container terminal at Doraleh.

Ferry services are available between L'Escale (Djibouti), Tadjoura and Obock.

HEALTH

In 2009, the government spent approximately 14.1 per cent of its total budget on healthcare (up from 12 per cent in 2000), accounting for 69.3 per cent of all healthcare spending. Total expenditure on healthcare equated to 7.8 per cent of the country's GDP. Per capita expenditure on health was approximately US$94, compared with US$44 in 2000. Figures for 2005-10 show that there are 185 physicians (2.3 per 10,000 population), 666 nurses and midwives (8 per 10,000 population) and 99 dentistry personnel. According to the latest WHO figures, in 2008 approximately 98 per cent of the urban population and 52 per cent of the rural population had access to improved drinking water. In the same year, 63 per cent of the urban population and 10 per cent of the rural population had access to improved sanitation. In 2010, 88 per cent of the total population had access to improved drinking water and 50 per cent of the population had access to improved sanitation. Diarrhoea accounts for 11 per cent of childhood deaths. Other primary causes of death are pneumonia (20 per cent), prematurity (14 per cent), HIV (4 per cent) and malaria (1 per cent). The infant mortality rate was 73 per 1,000 live births and the childhood mortality rate was 91 per 1,000 live births. (Source: http://www.who.int, World Health Statistics 2012)

EDUCATION

Recent UNESCO statistics put the number of pre-primary schools at two, and the number of primary schools in the country at 72. Pre-primary education lasts for two years from the age of four. Primary education lasts for six years from age six and secondary schooling lasts for seven years from age 12. Primary education is free although parents may have to pay for books which can put off poorer families. In 1996, 247 students attended pre-primary school, 36,896 students attended primary school, 13,311 students attended secondary school (26 per cent of children of school age) and 161 students were in further education. Djibouti has no university of its own but students can apply for grants to study abroad.

An average of 22.0 per cent of total expenditure is spent by the government each year on education. The adult literacy rate was recently estimated at 62 per cent.

RELIGION

The majority of the population (97 per cent) are Muslim, there is a small Christian community (1.6 per cent). Djibouti has a religious liberty rating of 6 on a scale of 1 to 10 (10 is most freedom). (Source: World Religion Database)

COMMUNICATIONS AND MEDIA

There are no private broadcasters but private newspapers exist. Self-censorship is common. The government controls the electronic media.

Newspapers
Principal newspapers published in Djibouti are: La Nation de Djibouti. state-owned. (URL: http://www.lanation.dj/); La Republique; La Renouveau. Journalists tend to practise self-censorship.

Broadcasting
Recent figures show that there are in the region of 52,000 radio receivers and 28,000 television receivers in use. Djibouti's state-controlled broadcasting company produces programmes in French, Afar, Somali and Arabic. There are no private broadcasters.
Radiodiffusion-Télévision de Djibouti (RTD), URL: http://www.rtd.dj/

The state press agency is the Agence Djiboutienne d'Information (URL: http://www.adi.dj/)

Telecommunications
Both landline and mobile phone services are currently limited and mainly concentrated around the capital. As of 2008 there were estimated to be more than 10,500 telephone lines and 44,000 mobile phones. Coverage is generally limited to the city of Djibouti and its environs. In 2008 it was estimated that Djibouti had 13,000 internet users.

ENVIRONMENT

Main environmental concerns for Djibouti are lack of potable water, desertificaton and the increasingly limited availability of arable land. Djibouti is a party to the following international agreements: Biodiversity, Climate Change, Climate Change-Kyoto Protocol, Desertification, Endangered Species, Hazardous Wastes, Law of the Sea, Ozone Layer Protection, Ship Pollution, Wetlands.

According to figures from the EIA, in 2010 Djibouti's emissions from the consumption of fossil fuels totaled 2.3 million metric tons of carbon dioxide. In 2007, Djibouti produced 2.0 ODP tons of ozone depleting CFCs.

DOMINICA
Commonwealth of Dominica

Capital: Roseau (Population estimate: 20,000)

Head of State: Eliud Williams (President) (page 1537)

National Flag: Green ground with a cross overall of yellow, black and white stripes. A red disc in the centre charged with a Sisserou Parrot perched on a twig within a ring of green stars

CONSTITUTION AND GOVERNMENT

Constitution
The island was a British colony until 1967, when it obtained the status of a self-governing Associated State. Full independence was granted in 1978. Today Dominica is a Republic within the Commonwealth. The Republic has a non-executive president and parliamentary government. The President is elected by the House of Assembly for not more than two terms of five years. The President then appoints the Prime Minister who consults the President in appointing other ministers.

To consult the constitution, please visit: http://www.dominica.gov.dm/laws/chapters/chap1-01.pdf.

International Relations
Through its geographical position Dominica has a close relationship with the French Departments of Martinique and Guadeloupe.

Recent Events
On 1 October 2000 Prime Minister Douglas died. The then communications and works minister, Pierre Charles, became prime minister, but died suddenly in January 2004. Roosevelt Skerrit, the education minister, took over the post. He was re-elected in the May 2005 elections.

In 2004, Dominica cut off diplomatic ties with Taiwan in favour of ties with China. China pledged US$100 million of aid in the following five years.

In August 2007 Dominica was hit by Hurricane Dean; it was estimated that 99 per cent of the island's banana crop was damaged.

Eliud Williams was elected to the post of president by the House of Assembly in September 2012, following the resignation of President Nicholas Liverpool on the grounds of ill health.

Legislature
Dominica's unicameral legislature is known as the House of Assembly, and has 21 directly elected members and nine senators. Members serve a five year term.
House of Assembly, Victoria Street, Roseau, Commonwealth of Dominica. Tel: +1 767 448 2401, fax: +1 767 449 8353, e-mail: parldominica@marpin.dm, URL: http://www.dominica.gov.dm/cms

Cabinet (as at June 2013)
Prime Minister and Minister for Finance, Foreign Affairs and Social Security: Hon. Roosevelt Skerrit (page 1516)
Minister of Tourism, Legal Affairs, and Civil Aviation: Hon. Ian Douglas
Minister of State in the Ministry of Foreign Affairs: Alvin Bernard (page 1387)
Minister of Public Utilities, Energy, Ports and Public Service: Rayburn Blackmoore
Minister for Education and Human Resource Development: Peter St. Jean
Minister of Trade, Industry, Employment and Diaspora Affairs: John Colin McIntyre
Minister for Information and Community Development: Ambrose George
Minister for Agriculture and Forestry: Hon. Matthew Walter (page 1533)
Minister for Housing, Lands and Telecommunications: Hon. Reginald Austrie (page 1380)
Minister for Health: Hon. Julius Timothy
Minister of Caribbean Affairs: Ashton Graneau
Minister of Culture, Youth and Sports: Justina Charles
Minister of Environment, Natural Resources, Physical Planning and Fisheries: Kenneth Darroux
Minister of Social Services, Community Development and Gender Equality: Gloria Shillingford
Minister of National Security, Labour and Immigration: Charles Savarin (page 1509)
Attorney General: Levi Peter

Ministries
All ministries can be reached at: Government Headquarters, Kennedy Avenue, Roseau, Commonwealth of Dominica. URL: http://www.government.dm

Political Parties
Dominica Labour Party, URL: www.dlp.dm. Leader: Roosevelt Skerrit
United Workers Party, URL: http://www.unitedworkersparty.com. Leader: Hector John

Elections
The most recent election took place in December 2009 when the Dominica Labour Party which has been in power since 2000 won an overall majority.

Diplomatic Representation
Embassy of Dominica, 3216 New Mexico Avenue NW, Washington, DC 20016, USA. Tel: +1 202 364 6781, fax: +1 202 364 6791
Ambassador: Hubert John Charles
High Commission of Dominica, 1 Collingham Gardens, London, SW5 0HW, United Kingdom. Tel: +44 (0)20 7370 5194, fax: +44 (0)20 7373 8743, e-mail: highcommission@dominica.co.uk, URL: http://www.dominicahighcommission.co.uk
High Commissioner: Francine Baron
British High Commission (Resident in Bridgetown), URL: http://ukinbarbados.fco.gov.uk/en: .
High Commissioner: Paul Brummel (page 1396)
British Consulate, PO Box 2269, Roseau, Dominica. Tel: +1 767 448 7655, fax: +1 767 448 7817
US Embassy (Resident in Bridgetown)
Ambassador: Larry Leon Palmer (page 1492)
Permanent Representative of the Commonwealth of Dominica to the United Nations 800 Second Avenue, Suite 400H, New York, N.Y. 10017 USA. Tel +1 212 949-0853, fax: +1 212 808 4975
Permanent Representative: Crispin Gregoire

LEGAL SYSTEM

The legal system is based on English common law, and is exercised by the Eastern Caribbean Supreme Court of Justice (comprising a High Court and a Court of Appeal), which has a puisne judge resident in Dominica. For lesser cases there are three magistrate's courts. The Eastern Caribbean also has provision for appeal to the Privy Council in London.

The government respects the human rights of its citizens. Dominica retains the death penalty, though the last execution was carried out 1983. In early 2009, Prime Minister Roosevelt Skerrit stated that the death penalty would not be removed from the laws of Dominica.

Eastern Caribbean Supreme Court of Justice, URL: http://www.eccourts.org/about.html
Chief Justice: Justice Janice Mesadis Pereira

LOCAL GOVERNMENT

For administrative purposes Dominica is divided into ten parishes: St Andrew, St David, St George, St John, St Joseph, St Luke, St Mark, St Patrick, St Paul and St Peter. There are currently 41 local authorities: three municipal Councils (the Roseau City Council, the Portsmouth Town Council and the Canefield Urban Council); the Carib Council; and 37 Village Councils. The Roseau and Portsmouth Councils comprise thirteen members, eight of whom are elected and five appointed by the Minister for Local Government. They serve a term of three years. The Carib Council has a five year tem. It is composed of seven elected members including the Carib Chief for whom separate elections are held. The Canefield Urban and Village Councils serve for three years at a time. They comprise eight members each; five are elected and three are appointed by the Minister.

AREA AND POPULATION

Area
Dominica is situated in the Caribbean Sea between the French islands of Guadeloupe and Martinique, being about 30 miles away from each. It is northernmost of the group of islands known as the Windward Islands and also forms part of the group of islands is known as the Lesser Antilles. It has an area of approximately 290 sq. miles. The island is mountainous with a high point of 4,747 ft (Mome Diabotin).The mountains are volcanic in origin and there are many craters including Boiling Lake, the second-largest thermally active lake in the world. Its flora and fauna are varied, with many forests.

The climate is tropical with heavy rain. The driest months are February to June. The wettest month is August.

To view a map of Dominica, please consult http://www.lib.utexas.edu/maps/cia08/dominica_sm_2008.gif

Population
The population was estimated at 68,000 in 2010 with an annual average growth rate of -0.3 per cent in the period 2000-10. Over 67 per cent of the population lives in urban areas. The capital, Roseau (population 20,000), is a port of registry. The other main town is Portsmouth to the north-west of the island in Prince Rupert's Bay. The population is mainly of Afro-West Indian origin and includes about 3,000 Caribbean Indians mainly based in the east of the island. The official language is English, with a French-based Creole being widely used by the locals.

Births, Marriages, Deaths
In 2010 the crude birth rate was an estimated 16.00 births per 1,000 population and the crude death rate was 7.0 per 1,000 population. Figures for that year also estimate a migration rate of 11 people per 1,000 population leaving the island, most people leave to find work on other Caribbean Islands, the UK, the USA and Canada. Life expectancy from birth in 2009 was 72 years for males and 76 years for females. Healthy life expectancy in 2007 was 65

years and 67 years respectively. Approximately 24 per cent of the population is aged under 15 years and 10 per cent over 60 years. (Source: http://www.who.int, World Health Statistics 2012)

Public Holidays 2014
1 January: New Year's Day
3-4 March: Carnival
18 April: Good Friday
21 April: Easter Monday
1 May: Labour Day
9 June: Whit Monday
4 August: August Monday
3 November: Independence Day
4 November: Community Day of Service
25 December: Christmas Day
26 December: Boxing Day

EMPLOYMENT

Recent figures show the labour force of Dominica is about 24,500 with unemployment estimated to be 13 per cent. The following table shows how the working population was employed in 2001:
Employment by Economic Activity

Activity	Employed
Agriculture, forestry, hunting & fishing	5,222
Mining & quarrying	160
Manufacturing	1,930
Electricity, gas & water	410
Construction	2,420
Wholesale & retail trade, restaurants & hotels	5,120
Transport, storage & communication	1,560
Financial services, real estate	1,140
Community, social & personal services	6,770

Source: International Labour Organisation

BANKING AND FINANCE

Currency
The unit of currency is the Eastern Caribbean dollar (EC$), which is tied to the US dollar at a rate of US$1.00 = EC$ 2.70.

GDP/GNP, Inflation, National Debt
Despite its mountainous terrain Dominica's economy is based principally on agriculture, especially bananas. Faced with difficult challenges in this market especially the ending of preferential EU trade tariffs, the government has made efforts to diversify the economy, identifying eco-tourism and offshore finance as potential sectors. Dominica's GDP has declined in recent years mainly due to difficulties in the agriculture sector. Dominica's agriculture-based economy has been adversely affected by the loss of preferential access to EU markets and the devastation of the banana crop by Hurricane Dean in 2007. The global economic crisis has also hit its tourism sector.

Estimated figures for 2011 put GDP at US$490 million with a growth rate of 1 per cent. Per capita GDP was an estimated US$13,500.

In 2010 breakdown of GDP by sector was as follows: agriculture 20 per cent; industry 23 per cent; services 56 per cent.

Inflation was estimated at 1.7 per cent in 2005, 3.1 per cent in 2007 and 6.2 per cent in 2008.

Foreign debt was estimated to be US$650 million in 2012. Total debt was estimated to be almost US$900 million.

Balance of Payments / Imports and Exports
The primary export crop is bananas which are sold mainly to Europe but, since losing preferential access to European markets, banana exports have fallen. Other exports include soap, fruit, fruit preparations and fruit juices, essential oils, coconuts, vegetables, garments, shoes, housing components, bottled water and alcoholic drinks. In 2011, exports were estimated to be worth US$33 million and imports that year were estimated to cost US$190 million. Main exports were bananas, soap, oranges, grapefruit, vegetables and cocoa. Main export partners are Japan (40 per cent), Jamaica, Antigua and Barbuda, Trinidad and Tobago and Guyana. Main imports are manufactured goods, machinery and equipment, foodstuffs and cement. Japan, the US, Trinidad and Tobago and China are the main import partners.

Dominica is a member of the Caribbean Common Market, CARICOM; the Organization of Eastern Caribbean States, OECS; the Association of Caribbean States, ACS; the African Caribbean and Pacific States, ACP; and the World Trade Organization, WTO.

Central Bank
Eastern Caribbean Central Bank, PO Box 89, Basseterre, St. Kitts, Leeward & Windward Islands. Tel: +1 869 465 2537-9, fax: +1 869 465 5615, URL: http://www.eccb-centralbank.org Governor: K. Dwight Venner

MANUFACTURING, MINING AND SERVICES

Primary and Extractive Industries
Pumice stone is mined on a small scale.

Energy
Much of the country's electricity is generated from imported oil, but renewable forms of energy such as hydro-electricity are beginning to take over. There are plans to build coal fired plants and three hydropower plants are currently under construction. Dominica imports 1,000 barrels of oil per day.

Manufacturing
Products include soap, coconut oil, copra, cement blocks, wooden furniture, cardboard boxes, paint, gloves, shoes and candles. In recent years the soap and detergent sector has grown with the introduction of toothpaste manufacture.

Service Industries
According to recent figures, tourists number approximately 450,000, of which 350,000 are cruise liner passengers. Following the downturn in the banana trade, Dominica is now promoting itself as the nature island of the Caribbean, with the emphasis on eco-tourism. However it will need to make improvements to its infrastructure to achieve this. The number of cruise passengers visiting has increased since improvements were made to docking facilities in Roseau.

In an effort to diversify the economy plan have been discussed to develop Dominica as an offshore financial sector.

Agriculture
Agriculture still accounts for the largest part of Dominica's output, the main products being tropical and sub-tropical fruit, ground provisions and coconuts. It accounts for around 18 per cent of the GDP (down from 25 per cent in 1990), and employs 26 per cent of the labour force. Figures for 1997 show that 34,911 tonnes of bananas and 12.000 tonnes of coconuts were harvested. Dominica and St Lucia exported the bulk of their bananas to the EU, but the US lodged a complaint in 1999 with the WTO against favourable EU tariff duties and quotas to Caribbean producers at the expense of Latin American producers. As a result, preferential tariffs for bananas were phased out. Dominica has subsequently had to diversify its agricultural products. Some new products have been introduced including coffee, cut flowers, and exotic fruits such as mangoes and papayas. In 2007 Dominica was hit by Hurricane Dean which destroyued 99 per cent of the islands banana crop.

Agricultural Production in 2010

Produce	Int. $'000	Tonnes*
Bananas	5,773	21,000
Grapefruit (inc. pomelos)	3,597	16,000
Cow milk, whole, fresh	2,341	7,500
Yams	2,097	15,300
Indigenous cattle meat	1,459	540
Oranges	1,411	7,300
Mangoes, mangosteens, guavas	1,318	2,200
Taro (cocoyam)	1,297	17,100
Yautia (cocoyam)	1,144	5,500
Coconuts	1,036	9,365
Cocoa beans	831	800
Plantains	650	5,000

* unofficial figures
Source: http://faostat.fao.org/site/339/default.aspx Food and Agriculture Organization of the United Nations, Food and Agricultural commodities production

A National Development Corporation has been set up to encourage industry and tourism. The forestry division of the Ministry of Agriculture has undertaken to preserve the forest and wildlife of the country by setting up national parks, where the felling of trees and hunting are closely monitored.

Fishing makes an important contribution to local food production, with the government encouraging and training personnel in the fishing industry in modern fishing methods. The industry is also expected to receive a substantial boost from the construction of the new fishing port, which has been constructed with the aid of Japan. Total fish catch in 2006 was 694 tonnes.

COMMUNICATIONS AND TRANSPORT

Travel Requirements
Visitors from the USA, Canada, Australia and the EU require a passport valid for at least six month, except Canadian nationals who hold proof of citizenship bearing a photograph and return or onward tickets and French citizens with National Identity Cards (Carte d'Identité) for stays of up to two weeks. Visas are not required by nationals of Belgium, Denmark, France, Germany, Greece, Ireland, Italy, Luxembourg, Malta, The Netherlands, Portugal, Spain, Sweden, the UK and the USA for stays of up to six months; and visas are not required by citizens of Australia, Austria, Bulgaria, Canada, Cyprus, the Czech Republic, Estonia, Finland, Hungary, Latvia, Lithuania, Poland, Romania, Slovak Republic and Slovenia for tourist stays of up to 21 days. For an extension, visitors should apply to the Immigration Department at the Police Headquarters in Roseau, Dominica. A visa is not required for transit passengers.

Nationals not referred above should contact the embassy to check visa requirements.

DOMINICAN REPUBLIC

International Airports
There are two airports on Dominica, Melville Hall and Canefield. Links to international airlines exist through a number of regional airports in Puerto Rico, Antigua, Guadeloupe and others. In 2001 an airport capable of taking jet aircraft was under construction.

Roads
The road network comprises more than 500 km. of paved roads. Vehicles drive on the left. All towns and villages are connected by bus services.

Shipping
Dominica has regular and reliable shipping links in all major ports in North America, Europe and the Caribbean as well as a regular ferry service to Guadeloupe, Martinique and St. Lucia.

Ports and Harbours
The country's primary ports are those at Roseau and Portsmouth, with the former being a deep water harbour for vessels with a draft of 30ft up to 500ft. Modern container facilities allow handling of 20ft (nominal) 20 ton containers as well as 20ft or 40ft roll on, roll off containers. All cargo ships (except tankers) discharge alongside berth. Woodbridge bay also has a deep-water harbour and cruise ships can berth at Roseau and Portsmouth. A new fishing port is under construction.

HEALTH

The health system operates through local clinics, health centres and a polyclinic at the Princess Margaret Hospital in Roseau. The main hospital, the Princess Margaret, has 136 beds, and there are hospitals at Grand Bay, Portsmouth and Marigot. In 2009, the government spent approximately 8.3 per cent of its total budget on healthcare (down from 6.6 per cent in 2000), accounting for 65.2 per cent of all healthcare spending. Total expenditure on health care equated to 6.2 per cent of the country's GDP. Per capita expenditure on health was US$342.

According to WHO figures (2000-07) there were 35 doctors, 317 nurses and midwives (42 per 10,000 population), and 4 dentists. There are an estimated 40 hospital beds per 10,000 population. In 2006, 97 per cent of the population had access to an improved water supply and 83 per cent to improved sanitation.

In 2010, the infant mortality rate was 11 per 1,000 live births and the under-five mortality rate was 12 per 1,000 live births. The most common causes of childhood deaths are prematurity 10 per cent, birth asphyxia 48 per cent, congenital anomalies 7 per cent and pneumonia 3 per cent. (Source: http://www.who.int, World Health Statistics 2012)

EDUCATION

Education is compulsory up to the age of 16 years and free of charge. Primary education starts at age five and lasts for seven years. Secondary education starts at age 12 and lasts for five years. Recent figures show that Dominica has 73 nursery schools, 64 primary schools

with over 14,000 pupils and 641 teachers, and 14 secondary schools, some of which are subsidised by the government, and cater for nearly 5,000 pupils. There are two colleges and the University of the West-Indies School of Continuing Studies. The average literacy rate for the Republic is 95 per cent.

Figures from 2007 show that the equivalent of 5.1 per cent of GDP was spent on education. (UNESCO)

RELIGION

The majority of the population belong to the Christian faith (94.2 per cent) with Roman Catholics being the majority. Anglican and Methodists are the other main denominations in addition to Bah'ai (1.8 per cent), Spiritulist (2.7 per cent), Jewish and Muslim minorities.

Dominica has a religious tolerance rating of 4 on a scale of 9 to 10 (10 is most freedom). (Source: World Religion Database)

COMMUNICATIONS AND MEDIA

Newspapers
Dominica has four newspapers all of which are published weekly: The Chronicle (URL: http://www.news-dominica.com/), The Times (URL: http://www.thetimes.dm/), The Sun and the Weekly Star.

Broadcasting
There are five radio stations broadcasting on both FM and AM frequencies. Two cable TV stations provide a multi-channel service, with regular US programming. There is no national television service. The state broadcaster Dominica Broadcasting Corporation operates DBS Radio.
DBS, URL: http://news.dbcradio.net/

Telecommunications
In 2008, it was estimated that there were 17,5000 main lines and over 100,000 mobile cellular phones. Around 27,500 Dominicans are regular internet users.

ENVIRONMENT

Dominica is a party to the following international agreements: Biodiversity, Climate Change, Climate Change-Kyoto Protocol, Desertification, Endangered Species, Environmental Modification, Hazardous Wastes, Law of the Sea, Ozone Layer Protection, Ship Pollution and Whaling.

In 2010, Dominica's emissions from the consumption of fossil fuels totaled 0.14 million metric tons of carbon dioxide. (Source: EIA)

DOMINICAN REPUBLIC
República Dominicana

Capital: Santo Domingo (Population estimate: 2,500,000)

Head of State: Danilo Medina (page 1476)

Vice-President: Margarita Cedeño de Fernández

National Flag: Quarterly, first and fourth blue, second and third red; over all a white cross charged at the centre with the national coat of arms

CONSTITUTION AND GOVERNMENT

Constitution
The constitution now in force was passed by President Balaguer's Government in 1966. It has been amended several times; the 38th version was passed in 2009. Executive power is vested in the President who is elected by direct vote of the people for a term of four years. The President appoints the members of his cabinet without reference to Congress. Congress is composed of Upper and Lower Chambers.

The new constitution provides for referenda and plebiscites; the establishment of the sanctity of life from the time of conception; the inclusion of multiple guarantees for the exercise of fundamental rights; a ban on consecutive presidential reelection; the creation of the Constitutional Court, the Council of the Judiciary and the Supreme Electoral Court; and the change in the names of government officials from 'secretaries of state' to 'ministers'.

To consult the constitution, please visit:
http://www.comisionadodejusticia.gob.do/phocadownload/Actualizaciones/Libros/libro%20constitucion%20abril2011.pdf.

Foreign Relations
The Dominican Republic has good relations with the USA and the other states of the inter-American system. It has Consular relations with Cuba. It is a founding member of the UN and participates in many of its specialised and related agencies, including the World Bank, the International Labor Organization and the International Atomic Energy Agency. It is also a member of the OAS and of the Inter-American Development Bank. In July 2005, the

Dominican Republic formally requested full membership of CARICOM. The Venezuelan and Dominican Republic leaders have signed two oil agreements, which assist the Dominican Republic with increasing world oil prices.

There is a long history of friction between the DR and Haiti over illegal immigration by Haitian agricultural and construction workers, conservatively estimated at 500,000 people. It is thought that there are a further 40,000 Haitians working in the Dominican sugar plantations.

Recent Events
In September 2005, a free trade agreement was proposed between the USA and Central American Nations including the Dominican Republic. The Dominican Republic entered the agreement in March 2007.

On the 26th August 2008, Hurricane Gustav hit Hispaniola, and caused the deaths of eight people in a landslide in the Dominican Republic. Two persons were injured. Government authorities evacuated some 6,255 people and over 1,239 homes were damaged. 50 communities were isolated by the flooding. Two weeks later, Hurricane Ike hit the island with heavy winds and rain, but neighbouring Haiti took the brunt of the impact.

In October 2010, following the devastating earthquake that had hit neighbouring Haiti, the Dominican Republic tightened its border restriction to prevent cholera spreading from Haiti.

Upper House
The Upper Chamber, or Senate, has 32 senators (one for each of the 31 provinces and one for the national district of Santo Domingo). Members are elected for a term of four years.
Senate, Congreso Nacional de la Republica, Centro de los Heroes, Santo Dominico. Tel: +1 809 532 7012, fax: +1 809 532 7012, URL: http://www.senado.gov.do

Lower House
The Chamber of Deputies is made up of 183 deputies also directly elected for a term of four years. However, members of both houses elected in 2010 will serve a six year term in order to synchronise parliamentary and presidential elections to be held in 2016.
Chamber of Deputies, Congreso Nacional de la Republica, Centro de los Heroes, Santo Domingo. Tel: +1 809 535 2626, fax: +1 809 532 7012, URL: http://www.congreso.gov.do

Cabinet (as at June 2013)

Minister of Foreign Affairs: Carlos Morales Troncoso (page 1527)
Minister of Finance: Simon Lizardo Mezquita
Minister of the Interior and Police: Jose Ramon Fadul
Minister of Agriculture: Luis Ramon Rodriguez
Minister of the Armed Forces: Vice Admiral Sigfrido Pared Perez
Minister of Trade and Commerce: Jose del Castillo Savinon
Minister of Labour: Maritza Hernandez
Minister of Public Health: Freddy Hidalgo
Minister of Public Works: Gonzalo Castillo
Minister of Sport: Jaime David Fernandez Mirabal
Minister of Tourism: Francisco Javier Garcia
Minister of Youth: Jorge Minaya
Minister of Environment and Natural Resources: Bautista Rojas Gomez
Minister of Women's Affairs: Alejandrina German
Minister of Culture: José Antonio Rodriguez
Minister of Higher Education, Science and Technology: Ligia Amada Melo
Minister of Education: Josefina Pimentel
Minister of Economy, Planning and Development: Juan Temistocles Montas Dominguez
Minister to the President: Gustavo Montalvo
Attorney General, Minister of Justice: Francisco Dominquez Brito
Administrative Secretary of the Presidency: Jose Ramon Peralta
Minister of Public Administration, Ventura Camejo
Presidential Legal Advisor: Dr Cesar Pina Toribio
Minister without portfolio in charge of Citizen Safety Programs: Franklin Almeyda
Minister without portfolio: Antonio Isa Conde
Minister without portfolio, in charage of Regional Intergration Affairs: Miguel Mejia
Controller General: Haivanjoe N.G. Cortinas

Ministries

Office of the Presidency, Calle Moisés García, Santo Domingo, Dominican Republic. Tel: +1 829 695 8000, fax: +1 829 688 2100, e-mail: prensa@presidencia.gov.do, URL: http://www.presidencia.gov.do

Ministry of Finance, Avda México 45, Santo Domingo, Dominican Republic. Tel: +1 829 687 5131, fax: +1 829 688 6561, URL: http://www.finanzas.gov.do/

Ministry of the Economy, Planning and Development, Palacio Nacional de la Presidencia, Avda México esq. Doctor Delgado, Distrito Nacional, Santo Domingo, Dominican Republic. Tel: +1 829 695 8588, e-mail: informacion@economia.gob.do, URL: http://www.economia.gob.do

Ministry of Foreign Affairs, Avda Independencia 752, Santo Domingo, Dominican Republic. Tel: +1 829 535 6280, fax: +1 829 533 5772, e-mail: correspondencia@serex.gov.do, URL: http://www.serex.gov.do

Ministry of Industry and Commerce, Edif. de Oficinas Gubernamentales 7, Avda Francia, esq. Leopoldo Navarro, Santo Domingo, Dominican Republic. Tel: +1 829 685 5171, fax: +1 829 686 1973, e-mail: ind.comercio@codetel.net.do, URL: http://www.seic.gov.do

Ministry of Defence, Avda 27 de Febrero, esq. Luperón, Santo Domingo, Dominican Republic. Tel: +1 829 530 5149, fax: +1 829 531 1309, URL: http://www.secffaa.mil.do

Ministry of Labour, Centro de los Héroes, Jiménez Moya 9, Santo Domingo, Dominican Republic. Tel: +1 829 535 4400, fax: +1 829 535 4590, URL: http://www.set.gov.do

Ministry of Agriculture, Autopista Duarte Km 6.5, Los Jardines del Norte, Santo Domingo, Dominican Republic. Tel: +1 829 547 3888, fax: +1 829 227 1268, e-mail: sec.agric@codetel.net.do, URL: http://www.agricultura.gov.do

Ministry of Education, Avda Máximo Gómez, Santo Domingo, Dominican Republic. Tel: +1 829 689 9700, fax: +1 829 689 8907, URL: http://www.see.gov.do

Ministry of Higher Education, Avda Jiménez Moya, esq. Juan de Dios Ventura Simó, Centro de los Héroes, 5to. Piso, Santo Domingo, Dominican Republic. Tel: +1 809 533 3381, fax: +1 809 535 4694, e-mail: info@seescyt.gov.do, URL: http://www.seescyt.gov.do

Ministry of Culture, Av. George Washington, Santo Domingo, Dominican Republic. URL: http://www.cultura.gov.do

Ministry of Public Health and Social Welfare, Avda Tiradentes, esq. San Cristóbal, Ensanche La Fe, Santo Domingo, Dominican Republic. Tel: +1 829 541 3121, fax: +1 829 540 6445, URL: http://www.saludpublica.gov.do

Ministry of Public Works and Communications, Avda Tiradentes, esq. San Cristóbal, Ensanche La Fe, Santo Domingo, Dominican Republic. Tel: +1 829 565 2811, fax: +1 829 562 3362, URL: http://www.seopc.gov.do

Ministry of Sports, Avda Ortega y Gasset, Centro Olímpico, Santa Domingo, Dominican Republic. Tel: +1 829 540 4010, fax: +1 829 563 6586, URL: http://www.sedefir.gov.do

Ministry of Tourism, Bloque D Edif. de Oficinas Gubernamentales, Avda México, esq c/30 de Marzo, Santo Domingo, Dominican Republic. Tel: +1 829 221 4660, fax: +1 829 682 3806, URL: http://www.sectur.gov.do / URL: http://www.domincana.com

Ministry of the Environment, Local 28, Plaza Naco, AvdaTiradentes Esquina Fantino Falco, Ensanche Naco, Santo Domingo, Dominican Republic. Tel: +1 829 567 4300, fax: +1 829 540 2667, e-mail: contacto@medioambiente.gob.do, URL: http://http://www.medioambiente.gov.do

Ministry for Women's Affairs, Bloque D, Edif. de Oficinas Gubernamentales, Avda México, esq c/30 de Marzo, Santo Domingo, Dominican Republic. Tel: +1 829 605 3755, fax: +1 829 686 0911, e-mail: info@sem.gov.do, URL: http://www.sem.gov.do

Ministry of Youth, Plaza Metropolitana, Avda John F. Kennedy esq. Ortega y Gasset, Santo Domingo, Dominican Republic. Tel: +1 829 689 2842, fax: +1 829 686 8620, e-mail: juventud@verizon.net.do, URL: http://www.juventudom.gov.do

Political Parties

Dominican Revolutionary Party (PRD), URL: http://www.prd.partidos.com/; Dominican Liberation Party (PLD); Reformist Social Christian Party (PRSC)

Elections

Elections for the presidency and for members of Congress are held every four years. All Dominicans over the age of 18 are eligible to vote, with the exception of members of the Armed Forces and police force. Married people are eligible to vote regardless of age. Voting is compulsory.

In May 2000 Hipólito Mejía's PRD coalition won 49.87 per cent of the votes on a platform of education reform, development of the economy, reduced poverty and increased agricultural production. Mejía replaced Leonel Fernández Reyna as president, and was sworn into office in August 2000. At the presidential elections held in May 2004, Mejía was defeated by Leonel Fernández.

The most recent parliamentary elections were held in May 2010 when the PLD again won a majority in both houses of parliament. The most recent presidential election took place in May 2012. The previous president, Leonel Fernandez, was constitutionally barred from seeking a third term. Danillo Medina was elected to the post with 51 per cent of the vote. He was sworn in as president in August 2012.

Diplomatic Representation

Embassy of the Dominican Republic, 1715 22nd Street, NW, Washington, DC 20008, USA. Tel: +1 202 332 6280, fax: +1 202 265 8057, URL: http://www.domrep.org
Ambassador: Aníbal de Castro (page 1413)
British Embassy, Ave 27 de Febrero No 233, Edificio Corominas Pepin, Santo Domingo, Dominican Republic. Tel: +1 809 472 7111, +1 809 472 7190, e-mail: brit.emb.sadom@codetel.net.do, URL: http://ukindominicanrepublic.fco.gov.uk/en/
Ambassador: Steven Mark Fisher
US Embassy, César Nicolàs Pensòn, esq Leopoldo Navarro, Santo Domingo, Dominican Republic. Tel: +1 809 221 2171, URL: http://santodomingo.usembassy.gov
Ambassador: Raúl H. Yzaguirre
Embassy of the Dominican Republic, 139 Inverness Terrace, Bayswater, London W2 6JF. Tel: +44 (0)20 7727 6285, fax: +44 (0)20 7727 3693, e-mail: embassy@dominicanembassy.org.uk, URL: http://www.dominicanembassy.org.uk
Ambassador: Federico Alberto Cuello Camilo

LEGAL SYSTEM

The Dominican judicial system is based on the French system. There is a Court of Justice in each of the state's 72 municipal districts, and these handle minor cases. The 26 provincial courts deal with more serious civil and criminal cases. There are three Courts of Appeal, each with five judges, which review the judgements of the provincial courts. There are also various specialised courts dealing with matters such as judicial administration, property disputes and registration, traffic accidents, juveniles, and labour disputes. Military courts try military personnel charged with extrajudicial killings.

The Supreme Court is made up of nine judges appointed by the Senate, and deals with constitutional issues as well as serving as the last court of appeals. It appoints the judges of the lower and special courts. The Supreme Court has jurisdiction over the highest officials of the state and resolves disputes between the state and the municipalities.

The National Judicial Council has seven members including the president and legislators from both houses of Congress, the president of the Supreme Court, and a second Supreme Court justice.

Whilst the government's human rights record continues to improve, there have been recent cases of unlawful killings and abuse of detainees, and prisoners by security forces. Prison conditions are poor and arrests can be arbitrary. There is widespread corruption, and some human rights groups have been harassed. Although the constitution provides for an independent judiciary, in practice the executive branch as well as public and private entities exert pressures on the courts. The death penalty was abolished in 1966.

Supreme Court of Justice: URL: http://www.suprema.gov.do/
President: Justice Mariano German Mejia

LOCAL GOVERNMENT

The Dominican Republic is divided for administrative purposes into 31 provinces and one district (the National District of Santo Domingo) whose administration is the responsibility of a civil governor appointed by the President.

Each province consists of two or more *comuns* governed by a locally elected county council, *ayuntamiento de regidores.* The people of the *comun* elect the chief administrative officer, the *alcade,* who acts as the local justice. Local government officials are elected every two years. The provinces are Azua, Baoruco, Barahona, Dajabon, Duarte, Elias Pina, El Seibo, Espaillat, Hato Mayor, Independencia, La Altagracia, La Romana, La Vega, Maria Trinidad Sanchez, Monsenor Nouel, Monte Cristi, Monte Plata, Pedernales, Peravia, Puerto Plata, Salcedo, Samana, Sanchez Ramirez, San Cristobal, San Jose de Ocoa, San Juan, San Pedro de Macoris, Santiago, Santiago Rodriguez, Santo Domingo, Valverde.

AREA AND POPULATION

Area

The Dominican Republic is situated in the West Indies occupying the eastern two thirds of the island of Hispaniola with Haiti to the west. The total area is estimated at 48,442 sq. km. It is the second largest nation in the Caribbean. The land is mountainous, and the climate is tropical.

To view a map of the Dominican Republic, please consult http://www.lib.utexas.edu/maps/cia08/dominican_republic_sm_2008.gif

Population

The population was estimated to be 9,927 million in 2010, with an average annual growth rate of 1.4 per cent over the period 2000-10. The median age is 25 years. Approximately 31 per cent of the population is aged 15 years or less and 9 per cent over 60 years old.

DOMINICAN REPUBLIC

Approximately 69 per cent of the population lives in rural areas. The principal cities are Santo Domingo (2.5 million inhabitants), Santiago de los Caballeros (908,302), La Vega (225,000), San Francisco de Macoris (175,000), San Cristóbal (160,000), San Pedro de Macoris (150,000), La Romana (140,000), Puerto Plata (130,000), and San Juan de la Maguana (130,000).

Spanish is the official language.

Births, Marriages, Deaths
In 2009 life expectancy for men was 71 years and for women was 72 years. Healthy life expectancy was 62 and 64 years respectively. The infant mortality rate was 22 per 1,000 births in 2010. The maternal mortality rate was 100 per 100,000 live births. In 2010 the birth rate was estimated to be 21.8 births per 1,000 population and the death rate was put at 6.9 deaths per 1,000 population. (Source: http://www.who.int, World Health Statistics)

Public Holidays 2014
1 January: New Year's Day
6 January: Epiphany
21 January: Day of the Virgin of Altagracia
26 January: Birthday of Juan Pablo Duarte
27 February: Independence Day (National Day)
18 April: Good Friday
1 May: Labour Day
19 June: Corpus Christi
16 August: Independence Restoration Day
24 September: Day of the Virgin of Mercedes
6 November: Constitution Day
25 December: Christmas Day

EMPLOYMENT

In 2004, the labour force was estimated at 3,933,000, of whom 2,938,000 were men and 1,534,000 were women. 3,209,900 were employed and 723,700 (18.4 per cent) were unemployed. Just over 30 per cent were employed in the services and government sector, just over 12 per cent in industry, and 28 per cent in agriculture. In 2004 the unemployment rate was estimated at 17 per cent. (Source: International Labour Organisation, September 2008) In 2012, more than 30 per cent of the population were believed to be below the poverty line.

Total Employment by Economic Activity

Occupation	2007
Agriculture, hunting & forestry	502,300
Fishing	12,800
Mining & quarrying	6,000
Manufacturing	494,500
Electricity, gas & water supply	30,800
Construction	246,900
Wholesale & retail trade, repairs	732,400
Hotels & restaurants	222,300
Transport, storage & communications	257,500
Financial intermediation	73,500
Real estate, renting & business activities	94,000
Public admin. & defence; compulsory social security	152,600
Education	169,900
Health & social work	96,400
Other community, social & personal service activities	263,000
Households with employed persons	194,600
Extra-territorial organisations & bodies	1,500

Source: Copyright © International Labour Organization (ILO Dept. of Statistics, http://laborsta.ilo.org)

BANKING AND FINANCE

Currency
One Dominican peso (RD$) = 100 centavos

GDP/GNP, Inflation, National Debt
The Dominican Republic is a middle-income developing country. Its economy is mainly reliant on agriculture, trade and services, especially tourism which is the fastest-growing sector and is now the leading employer. Agriculture continues to be foremost in terms of domestic consumption. Telecomunications is a growth sector. The economy has been helped by the development of Free Trade Zones.

GDP is currently composed of 65 per cent service sector (tourism and the Free Trade Zones), 22 per cent industry and 6 per cent agriculture. GDP growth for the years 1998-2000 averaged at 7.0 per cent. However the Dominican Republic was badly hit by the global economy downturn as nearly 90 per cent of its exports were destined for the US market. In 2002, economic growth was recorded at -0.4 per cent and estimated at -1.2 per cent in 2004. In 2003 one of the Dominican Republic's major banking groups, Banco Intercontinental (Baninter), collapsed resulting in an economic slide that led to high inflation, strikes and demonstrations against rising prices and power cuts. As a result of the crisis, the Dominican Republic entered into a Stand-By Agreement with the IMF. Against this background President Fernandez came to power and promised to get the economy back on track. In 2007 the Dominican Republic implemented a Free Trade Agreement between the USA and Central American countries.

Figures for 2010 put GDP at an estimated US$51 billion. Growth was estimated at 7 per cent. GDP is boosted by remittances from abroad, estimated at US$3.5 million per annum. Per capita GDP was US$5,200. Growth was estimated at 4.5 per cent in 2012. An estimated 30 per cent of the population remain below the poverty line.

Inflation was estimated to have fallen to five per cent in 2005, before rising to 8.2 per cent in 2006 and to 5.9 in the first six months of 2007.

The Dominican Republic is a major recipient of foreign aid from the World Bank, the IMF, the IADRD and the EU. In 2009, the IMF approved a US$1.7 billion arrangement to support the Dominican Republic through the economic crisis.

Foreign Investment
The Industrial Free Trade Zones offer incentives for foreign investment in areas such as textiles and electronics. The DR has a low cost and flexible workforce.

The main reason behind ratification of the Free Trade Agreement in 2007 was to enhance trade between the DR, the Central American countries and the US, abolishing trade restrictions, and promoting fair trade in a duty free zone. Investment opportunities are another major element of the Agreement, which includes multiple guarantees and incentives for foreign investors.

Balance of Payments / Imports and Exports
The Dominican Republic's main exports are clothing and other goods manufactured in the duty free industrial zones, as well as ferronickel, sugar, coffee, cocoa, tobacco, meats and medical supplies. Exports in 2010 were estimated at US$6.5 billion (f.o.b.). The main imports were foodstuffs, petroleum, industrial and agricultural raw materials, capital goods, vehicles, wood and pharmaceuticals, and were valued at US$10.9 billion (f.o.b.). The US is the largest trading partner, followed by Canada and western Europe, Japan, Mexico and Venezuela. As of January 2009, all exports in goods and services from the Dominican Republic received duty-free and quota-free access in Europe.

Central Bank
Banco Central de la Republica Dominicana, PO Box 1347, Calle Pedro Henriquez Ureña, esq Leopoldo Navarro, Santo Domingo, Distrito Nacional, Dominican Republic. Tel: +1 809 2219111, fax: +1 809 6867488, e-mail: webmaster@bancentral.gov.do, URL: http://www.bancentral.gov.do
Governor: Héctor Valdez Albizu

MANUFACTURING, MINING AND SERVICES

Primary and Extractive Industries
There are commercial deposits of gold, silver, ferro-nickel, bauxite, copper, marble, salt and gypsum. There are estimated to be 100 million tons of sulfide ore reserves. These reserves are being explored. Exploration is under way for oil deposits at Azua, Bonao and Salcedo.

There have been sharp increases in nickel, marble and plaster production (at 11 per cent, 10 per cent and 60 per cent respectively), and the sector has been further assisted by an increase in international nickel prices.

In common with many Caribbean countries, the Dominican Republic imports oil and refined products from Mexico and Venezuela under the favorable terms of the San Jose Pact. In 2005, the Dominican Republic signed the Venezuela-backed Petrocaribe initiative, under which Venezuela will sell crude oil and refined products to these countries under favorable financing terms. Figures from the EIA showed that an estimated 120,000 barrels per day were imported.

Energy
Three regional electricity distribution systems were privatised in 1998, with the sale of half the shares going to foreign operators companies; however, the government repurchased all foreign-owned shares in two of these systems in 2003. The third system, serving the eastern provinces, is operated by U.S. companies. Due to low collection rates, theft, infrastructure problems, and corruption, distribution losses remain high, exceeding 38 per cent in 2005, and the sector is heavily subsidized. Congress passed a law in 2007 that criminalizes the act of stealing electricity. Debts in the sector, including government debt, amount to more than U.S. $500 million. Some generating companies are undercapitalized and at times unable to purchase adequate fuel supplies. During 2010 the net generation of electricity was 14.7 billion kWh and consumption was 13.1 billion kWh.

Manufacturing
Most of the manufacturing takes place in the industrial free zones. Companies in the free zones manufacture clothing, footwear, electronics, sporting goods, pharmaceuticals, furniture and other goods. Clothing makes up 60 per cent of the production in the free zones, and the Dominican Republic is the fourth largest supplier of textiles to the USA after Mexico, Hong Kong and Taiwan. The type of company within the free zones is now diversifying so this should help to ensure the growth of the industry. Outside of the free zones export goods include beer, rum, fruit, vegetables, clothing, leather goods, fertilizer, furniture and batteries.

Service Industries
Tourism is the Dominican Republic's primary industry and is the largest foreign exchange earner, with visitor numbers steadily growing. In 2006 there were 3.9 million visitors, compared to 3.2 million in 2002. The majority of overseas visitors come from the US and Canada but the Dominican Republic is also a popular holiday destination for the French, British and Spanish. Recent figures show that tourism accounts for more than US$3 billion of earnings. Investment in the sector has led to developments in Puerto Plata in the North, Punta Cana to the east and Bayahibe in the South. After an absence of some years, Caribbean cruise ships are again calling at ports in the Dominican Republic.

Agriculture

The traditional export crops were sugar, coffee, cocoa and tobacco, but the country's agricultural sector has diversified its produce, with increased production and exports of organic bananas, pineapples, citrus, melons, and mangoes. Other crops include rice, corn, potatoes, spices and nuts. Cattle are bred for domestic use. The government is committed to attracting new investment to this sector.

Agricultural Production in 2010

Produce	Int. $'000	Tonnes
Indigenous chicken meat	447,691	314,300
Indigenous cattle meat	305,066	112,930
Papayas	257,826	908,462
Bananas	207.012	735,045
Avocados	184,043	288,684
Cow milk, whole, fresh	162,575	520,971
Rice, paddy	152,901	567,329
Sugar cane	150,299	4,577,120
Indigenous pigmeat	133,705	86,977
Plantains	101,476	491,509
Hen eggs, in shell	87,691	105,730
Cocoa beans	60,579	58,334

* unofficial figures
Source: http://faostat.fao.org/site/339/default.aspx Food and Agriculture Organization of the United Nations, Food and Agricultural commodities production

COMMUNICATIONS AND TRANSPORT

Travel Requirements

Visitors from the USA, Canada, Australia and the EU require a passport that is valid for twice as long as the intended stay. Tourists do not require a visa, (the exceptions being Bulgarian, Cypriot, Estonian, Latvian, Maltese and Romanian citizens), but need to apply for a tourist card, valid for up to 30 days from entry. Visas for four months are required for business purposes.

Nationals not referred to above should contact the embassy to check visa requirements.

International Airports

There are seven international airports in the Dominican Republic: Las Américas and Herrera in Santo Domingo, Puerto Plata, La Romana, Punta Cana, Santiago and Barahona. A new international airport in Samana has recently opened.

Railways

There are about 1,700 km of railway lines on the sugar estates but there are no passenger services.

Roads

The Government has invested in the road network and is constructing new roads to improve the connection between the capital city and the east of the country, including links between Santo Domingo and Santiago, and Santo Domingo and San Cristóbal. Vehicles drive on the right.

Ports and Harbours

Santo Domingo and other cities have modern port facilities. Haina, near the capital, has a 2,600 foot long, 35 foot draft wharf, a 40 ton container crane, and a 60 acre container yard. There are other ports at La Romana, Boca Chica, San Pedro de Macoris and Puerto Plata. A ferry service runs between Santo Domingo and Mayagüez in Puerto Rico.

HEALTH

Figures for 2009 showed that total expenditure on health amounted to 5.9 per cent of GDP, and 12.4 per cent of total government expenditure went on health. Per capita expenditure on health was estimated at US$279 in the same year. There is a national insurance scheme to help cover welfare costs but payments are on a voluntary basis. Within the private sector, which funds around 58.6 per cent of total healthcare, 65.7 per cent is paid out-of-pocket and 22.5 per cent is financed through pre-paid plans.

Figures for 2000-10 show that there are 15,670 physicians (19 per 10,000 population), 15,532 nurses (18 per 10,000 population) and 7,000 dentistry personnel. There are approximately 10 hospital beds per 10,000 population. An estimated 86 per cent of the population had access to improved drinking water. An estimated 83 per cent of the population had access to improved sanitation. The infant mortality rate is 22 per 1,000 live births and the under-five mortality rate was 27 per 1,000 live births. The most common causes of childhood deaths

are prematurity (25 per cent), pneumonia (11 per cent), birth asphyxia (11 per cent), diarrhoea (4 per cent), birth asphyxia (13 per cent), congenital anomalies (18 per cent), and HIV/AIDS (2 per cent). (Source: http://www.who.int, World Health Statistics 2012)

EDUCATION

Education is free and compulsory up to the age of 14. There are public and private schools and universities. The Universidad Autónoma de Santo Domingo, the state university, was the first university in the New World.

In 2007, around 32 per cent of small children attended a nursery school (lower than the regional average of 65 per cent). In the same year, 83 per cent of girls and 82 per cent of boys were registered in their appropriate year group at primary school (below the regional average of 94 per cent overall) and 68 per cent of girls and 55 per cent of boys were in secondary school, again below the regional average of 70 per cent. The pupil: teacher ratio was 24:1 in primary school.

In 2007, 11.0 per cent of government expenditure was directed towards education, 55 per cent going into primary education.

In 2007, the adult literacy rate was estimated at 88.8 for males and 89.5 for females. For the age group 15-24 years, the rate was 95.0 per cent for males and 97.0 per cent for females. All figures were slightly below the regional average. (Source: UNESCO, 2009)

RELIGION

Over 93 per cent of the population are Christians. The state religion is Roman Catholic followed by 78 per cent of the population. There is freedom of worship. Other religions include Evangelical, Seventh Day Adventist, Baptist and Mormon.

The Dominican Republic has a religious tolerance rating of 9 on a scale of 1 to 10 (10 is most freedom). (Source: World Religion Database)

COMMUNICATIONS AND MEDIA

Press freedom is guaranteed by the constitution but self-censorship is exercised over some matters. Criticsim of the government does appear. Media and broadcasting ownership is dominated by a small number of people.

Newspapers

El Caribe, URL: http://www.elcaribecdn.com; Hoy, URL: http://www.hoy.com.do/; Listin Diaro, URL: http://www.listin.com.do; Diaro Libre, URL: http://www.diariolibre.com; El Nacional, URL: http://www.elnacional.com.do

Broadcasting

There is one government television and radio station (Corporacion Estatal de Radio y Television, URL:http://www.certvdominicana.com/) and a number of private television and radio stations throughout the country. Cable provides access to over 50 US, Latin American and European channels including the major US networks.

Telecommunications

The Dominican Republic has an advanced telecommunications system. Competition between the principal companies ensures that the country has all the latest telecommunication services. Mobile telephones far exceed fixed line phones at approximately 7 million to 985,000 respectively. Around 2 million people are regular internet users.

ENVIRONMENT

Main environmental concerns for the Dominican Republic include hurricane damage including, most recently, Hurricane Georges in 1998 and Hurricane Gustav in 2008. Deforestation and coral reef damage are also major concerns. Severe floods hit the Dominican Republic and Haiti in May 2004, and around 2,000 people were killed. In May 2003, the government voted to pass a bill that would reduce the size of some of the national parks and open up areas for mining and beach resorts.

The Dominican Republic is a party to the following international agreements: Biodiversity, Climate Change, Climate Change-Kyoto Protocol, Desertification, Endangered Species, Hazardous Wastes, Marine Dumping, Marine Life Conservation, Ozone Layer Protection, Ship Pollution, and Wetlands. It has signed, but not ratified the Law of the Sea agreement.

In 2010, the Dominican Republic's emissions from the consumption of fossil fuels totaled 19.60 million metric tons of carbon dioxide and, in 2007, it produced 47.0 ODP tons of ozone-depleting CFCs. (Source: EIA)

ECUADOR
Republic of Ecuador
República del Ecuador

Capital: Quito (Population estimate, 2011: 2 million)

Head of State: Rafael Correa, President (page 1409)

Vice President: Lenin Moreno

National Flag: A tricolour fesswise, yellow, blue, red, the yellow half the depth of the flag, which bears at its centre the national coat of arms: a condor, Mount Chimborazo and four signs of the zodiac.

CONSTITUTION AND GOVERNMENT

Constitution

Guayaquil became the first city in Ecuador to gain its independence from Spain in October 1820; it was not until May 24, 1822 (the Glorious May Revolution) that the rest of Ecuador gained its independence following the defeat of Spanish forces at the Batalla de Pichincha (Battle of Pichincha) near Quito. Ecuador joined Simón Bolívar's Republic of Gran Colombia, before becoming an independent republic in 1830.

The President of the Republic presides over the executive branch and represents the State. He is elected for a four-year term by popular vote - one ballot for President and Vice-President. The President determines the number and functions of the ministries that comprise the executive branch and appoints the ministers of each bureau that he creates. He is also the Commander-in-Chief of the Armed Forces.

A new Constitution was written in 1998. It included: social policy to be directed toward the poor; measures to reduce poverty and provide free education for primary and secondary levels; free health care to be available only to those who could not afford to pay; measures to combat corruption; the setting up an independent judicial system and measures to ensure that the state work towards sustained economic growth. In February 2007, President Rafael Correa called for a referendum on whether to form a national assembly. He argued that Congress was corrupt and the referendum would be a first step in the process of by-passing its power. The motion was passed in the 100-seat Congress after protests and negotiations; however, Congress stopped its support after President Correa made revisions to the text. In March 2007, 57 Congressmen were sacked for trying to block the referendum; 21 new legislators were quickly appointed so that Congress had a quorum. Constituent Assembly elections took place in October 2007, and a new constitution was drafted. The country's 20th Constitution was put to a national referendum at the end of September 2008, and was passed by around 65 per cent of the voters.

To consult the constitution, please visit: http://www.corteconstitucional.gov.ec

Foreign Relations

Ecuador is a member of the United Nations and most of its specialized agencies. It is also a member of the Organization of American States (OAS), the Rio Group, the Latin American Economic System, the Latin American Energy Organization, the Latin American Integration Association, and the Andean Pact.

For 50 years, there was tension between Peru and Ecuador due to a dispute over a large part of rain forest which resulted in three wars. In October 1998 President Mahuad and Peru's President Fujimori signed the Acta de Brasilia, bringing a permanent solution to the problem.

The Ecuadorian army has deployed troops to the border with Colombia in an effort to combat intimidation of the local population by Colombian guerillas. The guerrillas extort money, practice vigilante justice on the villagers, and kidnap foreign oil workers from the nearby oil fields. There is also concern over the large number of displaced Colombians entering Ecuador, fleeing the violence in their country. The UDENOR organisation was created to tackle the northern border issues.

Relations with the USA, Ecuador's principal trading partner, have deteriorated recently. In May 2004, Ecuador entered into negotiations for an Andean free trade agreement with the U.S., Colombia, and Peru, but negotiations between the US and Ecuador have not resumed since the Government of Ecuador announced controversial reforms to hydrocarbons legislation in April 2006. In 1999, Ecuador and the U.S. came to a 10-year arrangement whereby U.S. military surveillance aircraft could use the airbase at Manta, as a Forward Operating Location to detect drug trafficking flights through the region; President Correa has stated that he will not to renew the agreement. The U.S and Ecuador also have fundamental differences concerning the recognition of territorial waters.

Recent Events

In 1998 the economy was badly affected by the effects of devastating floods, mudslide damage, high inflation and falling oil prices. Protests by the army and the indigenous population led to the resignation of President Mahuad. His vice president, Gustavo Noboa, replaced him. Ecuador adopted the US Dollar, in lieu of the Sucre, in an attempt to stabilise the economy. In 2002 the indigenous people of Ecuador brought oil production to a halt, demanding that a larger proportion of the revenue should be invested in their communities, and in January 2003, a Leftist leader, Lucio Gutierrez, was elected President. In April 2005 Congress sacked President Gutierrez, whose attempts to reform the judiciary had made him very unpopular, and replaced him with the vice-president Alfredo Palacio.

In August 2005, protesters brought oil production to a halt and a state of emergency was declared in two oil-producing provinces, ending only when the oil companies agreed to mend roads and pay local taxes. Protests broke out in March 2006 over a proposed free trade agreement with the US which the poorer sectors of the society believe would harm the economy and only benefit the wealthy.

Voters in a referendum held in April 2007 supported President Correa's plan to form a citizens' assembly to rewrite the constitution. His supporters won the Constituent Assembly elections at the beginning of October 2007, and the drafting of a new constitution began.

On 1 March 2008, Colombian military forces crossed the border and raided a Farc rebel camp one mile within Ecuador. Raul Reyes, a member of Farc's ruling secretariat, was killed with 16 other rebels. Colombian President Alvaro Uribe had advised President Rafael Correa of the operation by telephone. The following day, Ecuador withdrew its ambassador from Bogota, and flew troops by helicopter towards the border area. The Colombian national police chief Oscar Naranjo accused both Ecuador and Venezuela of having ties with the Farc, saying that this information had come from documents found during the raid on the rebel camp in Ecuador. As the crisis threatened to deepen, UN Secretary General Ban Ki-moon called for restraint. The situation was defused when the three leaders met at a Rio Group summit on 7th March. A 20-point declaration by the Organization of American States (OAS), including a promise by President Uribe that Colombia's forces would never again violate the territory of its neighbours, sealed the reconciliation. However, Ecuador said that it would take time before diplomatic relations were fully restored.

On 2nd April 2008, a constitutional change outlawing foreign military bases in Ecuador was approved. The US has a base in the town of Manta, its only base in South America. The approval of the new Constitution in September 2008 signals the end of joint US/Ecuadorian efforts in the fight against drug cartels.

On the 24th September, President Correa ordered troops to seize the assets of a major Brazilian construction company, following a dispute over the country's second largest dam, which was built by the Odebrecht company but shut down just a year after it was opened. The government demanded large sums in compensation. A national emergency was declared to recover the operational capacity of the San Francisco hydro-electric dam and to avoid internal unrest as a result of power blackouts across the country.

On the 28th September 2008, around 65 per cent voters approved the nation's 20th constitution. President Correa said the new constitution will help bring about a more just society, but critics fear it will give the president too much power. The package contains some of the most wide-ranging proposals the country - or any country in the region - has seen. As well as allowing the president to dissolve Congress within the first three years of its term, the new constitution will allow the president to stand for a second four-year term. It tightens state control over vital industries such as oil and mining, and allows the state to expropriate and redistribute idle farm land. The government can also declare some foreign loans illegitimate, and therefore non-repayable. The constitution allows civil marriages for gay partners, and gives free health care to older citizens.

In December 2008, President Correa said that Ecuador would default officially on billions of dollars of foreign debt; he argued that some of Ecuador's $10bn debt was contracted illegally by a previous administration. The decision follows a government audit which concluded that former officials and bankers had profited irresponsibly from bond deals. The country's foreign debt amounts to about a fifth of its Gross Domestic Product. It was the first debt default by a country in Latin America since 2001.

Presidential and legislative elections took place on 26th April 2009. Rafael Correa retained the presidency, with preliminary official results giving him around 49 per cent of the vote.

A new law came into effect in July 2010 which means that the state will own all of the oil and gas produced. Ecuador also pledged to not drill for oil in virgin rainforest in return for international financial compensation.

A state of emergency was declared in September 2010 after President Correa was besieged by policemen. He was freed by the army.

In February 2011, the US oil company Chevron was fined £5.3 billion for polluting the Amazon.

In May 2011, President Correa proposed a wide-ranging package of reforms, which the electorate approved in a referendum.

In June 2012, Wikileaks founder Julian Assange, took refuge in the Ecuadorian Embassy in London in order to escape extradition to Sweden where he is wanted on rape charges.

Legislature

Ecuador has a unicameral legislature, the National Congress, *Congreso Nacional*, made up of 121 elected members who serve a four-year term. Congressmen are elected during multi-party elections and represent one of Ecuador's 21 provinces. The President of the Congress is chosen by the Party that received the highest percentage of the national vote. The President of Congress ranks after the President and Vice-President of the Republic.

National Congress, Palacio Legislativo, Av. 10 de Agosto y Briceño, Edificio Centenario de Banco, Central del Ecuador, Quito, Ecuador. Email: info@congreso.gov.ec, URL: http://www.congreso.gov.ec/

Cabinet (as at June 2013)
Co-ordinating Minister for Social Development: Richard Espinosa
Co-ordinating Minister for Economic Policy: Patricio Rivera Yanez
Co-ordinating Minister for Policy and Autonomous Governments: Betty Tola
Co-ordinating Minister for Cultural and Natural Heritage: vacant
Co-ordinating Minister for Internal and External Security: Homero Arellano
Co-ordinating Minister for Production, Employment and Competition: Santiago Leon
Co-ordinating Minister for Strategic Sectors: Jorge Glas Espinel
Minister of Foreign Relations, Trade and Integration: Ricardo Patiño Aroca (page 1492)
Minister of Finance: Fausto Herrera
Minister of Justice and Human Rights: Johana Pesantez
Minister of Agriculture, Livestock and Fisheries: Javier Ponce Cevallos (page 1497)
Minister of Environment: Lorena Tapia
Minister of Electricity and Renewable Energy: Esteban Albornoz
Minister of Transport and Public Works: Maria de los Angeles
Minister of Urban Development and Housing: Pedro Jaramillo
Minister of Education: Gloria Vidal
Minister of Public Health: David Chiriboga
Minister of Tourism: Freddy Ehlers
Minister of Culture: Erika Silva
Minister of Sport: José Francisco Cevallos
Minister of Economy and Social Inclusion: Doris Soliz
Minister of Labour: Juan Francisco Vacas
Minister of National Defence: Maria Fernanda Espinosa
Minister of Industry and Competition: Veronica Sion
Minister of Telecommunications and Information: Jaime Guerrero Ruiz
Minister of Mines and Oil: Pedro Merizalde
Minister at the National Secretariat for Migrants: Lorena Escudero
Minister of Human Resources: Augusto Espinosa
Minister of Government, Religious Affairs, Police and Local Government: Jose Serrano

Ministries
Office of the President, Palacio de Gobierno, García Moreno 1043, Quito, Ecuador. Tel: +593 (0)2 210300, fax: +593 (0)2 580735, URL: http://www.presidencia.gov.ec/
Office of the Vice President, Benancazar Centre Chile y Espejo, Quito, Ecuador. Tel:+593 (0)2 503093, fax: +593 (0)2 584639, URL: http://www.presidencia.gov.ec/
Ministry of Foreign Affairs, Carrión 10-40, Avienda 10 de Agosto y Carrión, Quito, Ecuador. Tel: +593 (0)2 299 3284 / 3285, fax: +593 (0)2 227025, e-mail: webmaster@mmrree.gov.ec, URL: http://www.mmrree.gov.ec
Ministry of Finance, Avenida 10 de Agosto 1661 y Bolivia, Quito, Ecuador. Tel: +593 (0)2 503328 fax: +593 (0)2 500702, URL: http://www.mef.gov.ec/
Ministry of Energy and Mining, Av. Orellana N26-220 y Juan León Mera, Edificio MOP, Quito, Ecuador. Tel: +593 (0)2 2550 018 / 041, e-mail: subsecm@ecnet.ec, URL: http://www.menergia.gov.ec/
Ministry of Electricity and Renewable Energy, URL: http://www.mer.gov.ec/
Ministry of Industry and Competitiveness, Avenida y Eloy Alfaro, Quito, Ecuador. Tel: +593 (0)2 529076 / 529079, fax: +593 (0)2 504922, URL: http://www.mic.gov.ec/
Ministry of Agriculture, Avenida Amazonas y Eloy Alfarom, Quito, Ecuador. Tel: +593 (0)2 504433, fax: +593 (0)2 504922, e-mail: rtipan@sica.gov.ec, URL: http://www.magap.gov.ec/
Ministry of Tourism, Eloy Alfaro N32-300 Carlos Tobar, Quito, Ecuador. Tel: +593 (0)2 2507 559 / 560, fax: +593 (0)2 229330, e-mail: mtur1@ec-gov-net, URL: http://www.vivecuador.com/
Ministry of Environment, Avenida Eloy Alfaro y Amazonas, Quido, Ecuador. Tel: +593 (0)2 3429 / 3430, fax: +593 (0)2 255172, e-mail: mma@ambiente.gov.ec, URL: http://www.ambiente.gov.ec/
Ministry of Public Works, Avenida Orellana y Juan León Mera, Quito, Ecuador. Tel: +593 (0)2 222749, fax: +593 (0)2 223077, URL: http://www.mop.gov.ec/
Ministry of Housing and Urban Development, Avenida 10 de Agosto 2270 y Cordero, Quito, Ecuador. Tel: +593 (0)2 238060, fax: +593 (0)2 566785, URL: http://www.miduvi.gov.ec/
Ministry of Education, Calle San Salvador E6-49 y Eloy Alfaro, Quito, Ecuador. Tel: +593 (0)2 2528355, fax: +593 (0)2 580116, URL: http://www.educacion.gov.ec/
Ministry of Health, Juan Larrea 445, Quito, Ecuador. Tel: +593 (0)2 529 163, fax: +593 (0)2 569092, URL: http://www.msp.gov.ec/
Ministry of Labour, Luis Felipe Borja y C. Ponce, Quito, Ecuador. Tel: +593 (0)2 566148, fax: +593 (0)2 503122, URL: http://www.mrl.gov.ec/
Ministry of the Interior and Police, Benalcázar y Espejo, Quito, Ecuador. Tel.: +593 (0)2 955666, fax: +593 (0)2 95360, e-mail: informacion@mingobierno.gov.ec, URL: http://www.mingobierno.gov.ec/
Ministry of Defence, Exposición 208, Quito, Ecuador. Tel: +593 (0)2 512803, fax: 569386, URL: http://www.midena.gov.ec/
Ministry of Social Welfare, Robles 850 Y Amazonas, Quito, Ecuador. Tel: +593 (0)2 227975, fax:+593 (0)2 563497
Ministry of Justice and Human Rights, Av. Amazonas 4545 y Pereira. Edf. Centro Financiero. Piso 10. Of. 1010, Quito, Ecuador. URL: www.minjusticia-ddhh.gov.ec
Ministry of Coastal Affairs, URL: http://www.minlitoral.gov.ec
Ministry of Culture, URL: http://www.ministeriodecultura.gov.ec
Ministry of Government, Religious Affairs, Police and Local Government, URL: http://www.mingobierno.gov.ec/
Ministry for Natural Heritage, URL: http://www.ministeriopatrimonio.gov.ec/
Ministry for the Co-ordination of Internal and External Security, URL: http://www.micsie.gov.ec/
Ministry for the Co-ordination of Politics, URL: http://www.mcpolitica.gov.ec/
Minister for Production, Employment and Competition, URL: http://www.mcpec.gov.ec

Major Political Parties
Partido Sociedad Patriótica 21 de Enero, January 21 Patriotic Society Party (PSP); Democratic People's Movement (MPD); Institutional Renewal Party of National Action (PRIAN); Municipalist Movement for National Integrity (MMIN); Proud and Sovereign Fatherland (PAIS) Alliance; Social Christian Party (PSC).

Elections
The last Presidential elections took place in October 2006, with a run-off in November. The two main contenders were the Conservative Alvaro Noboa (a billionaire who ran for the Presidency in 2002) and the left-wing Rafael Correa, who promised a referendum on the Constitution and a restructuring of Congress. Sr. Correa won. In October 2007, his supporters won elections to a Constituent Assembly, giving the President a mandate to re-write the Constitution.

On the 28th September 2008, some 65 per cent of voters approved the nation's 20th constitution; among the clauses was one which allowed the President to run for a second term in office.

Presidential and legislative elections took place on 26th April 2009. President Correa retained his position, with preliminary official results giving him around 49 per cent of the vote. His main rival was former president Lucio Gutierrez.

The most recent presidential election took place in February 2013. Under the terms of the new constitution President Correa was eligible for re-election and won the election with over 50 per cent of the vote.

Diplomatic Representation
Embassy of the United States of America, Avenida 12 de Octubre y Avenida Patria, APO AA 34039, Quito, Ecuador. Tel: +593 (0)2 256 2890, fax: +593 (0)2 250 2052, URL: http://ecuador.usembassy.gov/
Ambassador: Adam E. Namm
British Embassy, Citiplaza Building, Naciones Unidas Ave and Republica de El Salvador 14th Floor (Consular Section 12th Floor), PO Box 17-17-830, Quito, Ecuador. Tel: +593 (0)2 2970800/970801, fax: +593 (0)2 2970809, e-mail: britemq@uio.satnet.net, URL: https://www.gov.uk/government/world/ecuador
Ambassador: Patrick Mullee (page 1481)
Embassy of Ecuador, 2535 15th St. NW, Washington, DC 20009, USA. Tel: +1 202 234 7200, fax: +1 202 667 3482, URL: http://www.ecuador.org
Ambassador: Saskia Nathalie Cely Suarez
Embassy of Ecuador, Flat 3, 3 Hans Crescent, Knightsbridge, London, SW1X 0LS, United Kingdom. Tel: +44 (0)20 7584 2648 / 8084, fax: +44 (0)20 7823 9701, URL: http://www.ecuadorembassyuk.org.uk
Ambassador: Ana Alban Mora
Mission to The United Nations, 886 UN Plaza, 5th Floor, Suite 516, New York 10017, NY, USA. Tel: +1 212 935 1680, fax: +1 212 935 1835, URL: http://www.un.int/wcm/content/site/ecuador/
Ambassador: vacant

LEGAL SYSTEM

The judicial system is comprised of administrative courts, trial courts, appellate or Provincial Superior Courts and a Supreme Court. A parochial judge handles minor civil cases. Cantonal courts, at least one in each canton, try minor civil and criminal actions. Provincial courts handle all but a few of the criminal cases and the more serious civil and commercial suits. Provincial Superior Courts handle appeals from the lower courts and have other administrative duties in the district; they may try original cases only if these relate to the affairs of their district. The Supreme Court has 31 justices and three alternates chosen by the National Chamber of Representatives for six-year periods.

The government respects the human rights of its citizens. However, there have been occasional cases of unlawful killings and use of excessive force by security forces. Prison conditions are poor, and arrests can be arbitrary. There is corruption within the judiciary system. Capital punishment was abolished in 1906.

Defensor del Pueblo de la Republica de Ecuador, URL: http://www.dpe.gob.ec/

LOCAL GOVERNMENT

The country is divided into 24 provinces, each of which is administered by a Governor. Their subdivisions, or cantons, are administered by Political Chiefs and elected Cantonal Councillors. The cantons are divided into parishes administered by Political Lieutenants. The 24 provinces are Azuay, Bolivar, Canar, Carchi, Chimborazo, Cotopaxi, El Oro, Esmeraldas, Galapagos, Guayas, Imbabura, Loja, Los Rios, Manabi, Morona-Santiago, Napo, Orellana, Pastaza, Pichincha, Santa Elena, Santo Domingo de los Tsachilas, Sucumbios, Tungurahua and Zamora-Chinchipe.

AREA AND POPULATION

Area
Ecuador lies on the west coast of South America, bounded in the north by Colombia, in the south and east by Peru and has a Pacific Ocean coastline of over 2000 km to the west. It has a total area of 276,840 sq. km. The equator lies a few kilometres north of the capital city of Quito. The Andes mountain range runs through the centre of Ecuador; there is jungle to the east of the mountains and a fertile coastal plain to the west. The territory includes the Galapagos Islands, an archipelago of volcanic islands in the Pacific Ocean lying some 1,000 km off the coast. The climate varies from tropical on the coast, to humid in the Amazon region and dry on the Galápagos Islands.

ECUADOR

To view a map, consult: http://www.un.org/Depts/Cartographic/map/profile/ecuador.pdf

Population

The total population reached around 14,465,000 in 2010, with an annual growth rate of 1.6 per cent per annum. Approximately 67 per cent of the population now lives in urban areas, Quito having a population of around two million. The most populous city is Guayaquil, with around 2.4 million inhabitants. Just 3 per cent of the population lives in the jungle areas east of the Andes. Overall the population density is approximately 43 per sq. km.

Around 77 per cent of the population is of mixed indigenous and Spanish race (mestizo). 6.8 per cent are indigenous, whilst 10.8 per cent are Caucasian. Africans make up almost 5 per cent of the population. It is estimated that there are around one million Ecuadorians currently residing in the US, most of them unofficially. The country's official language is Spanish but Quechua is also widely spoken.

In 2009, average life expectancy was 73 years for males and 78 years for females. Healthy life expectancy was 64 years. The median age was 26 years. Approximately 30 per cent of the population is aged under 15 years and 9 per cent over 60 years. Total fertility per woman is 2.5 children. In 2010, the crude birth rate was 20.7 per 1,000 population and the crude death rate was 4.9 per 1,000 population. (Source: http://www.who.int, World Health Statistics 2012)

Public Holidays 2014

1 January: New Year's Day (Año Nuevo)
6 January: Epiphany
3-4 March: Carnival (Carnaval)
17 April: Holy Thursday
18 April: Good Friday (Viernes Santo)
21 April: Easter Monday
1 May: Labour Day (Día del Trabajo)
24 May: Battle of Pichincha (Batalla del Pichincha)
19 June: Corpus Christi
24 July: Simon Bolivar Day
10 August: Independence Day (Día de la Independencia)
9 October: Independence of Guayaquil (Independencia de Guayaquil)
1 November: Day of the Faithful Dead (Día de los Fieles Difuntos)
3 November: Day of the Valley (Día de Cuenca)
6 December: Foundation of Quito (Fundación de Quito)
25 December: Christmas (Navidad)

EMPLOYMENT

The labour force in Ecuador numbered an estimated 4.28 million people in 2006, equivalent to 67.9 per cent of the population over 15 years old. In the same year, 4.031 million people were employed (aged 10+, urban), of whom 2.4 million were men. 341,800 people were unemployed. (Source: International Labor Organisation, ILO). Estimated figures for 2010 put the labour force at 4,645,000 with an unemployment rate of 7.5 per cent.

Total Employment by Economic Activity

Occupation	2006
Agriculture, hunting & forestry	285,000
Fishing	48,900
Mining & quarrying	15,800
Manufacturing	555,500
Electricity, gas & water supply	19,400
Construction	290,100
Wholesale & retail trade, repairs	1,151,800
Hotels & restaurants	225,400
Transport, storage & communications	292,300
Financial intermediation	47,900
Real estate, renting & business activities	200,700
Public admin. & defence; compulsory social security	170,300
Education	281,000
Health & social work	116,000
Other community, social & personal service activities	162,900
Households with employed persons	167,700
Extra-territorial organisations & bodies	900
Total	4,031,600

Source: Copyright © International Labour Organization (ILO Dept. of Statistics, http://laborsta.ilo.org)

BANKING AND FINANCE

Currency

One US Dollar = 100 cents (Previously One Sucre = 100 centavos)

The US Dollar became the official currency of Ecuador on 9 September 2000.

GDP/GNP, Inflation, National Debt

The economy is largely dependent on oil export revenues. Recession hit Ecuador in the late 1990s, caused by the El Nino weather phenomenon in 1997, instability in international markets and low oil prices. Ecuador's economy emerged from a recession over the five years to 2005. High oil prices have been a determining factor in the economic growth of recent years. The economy is based on petroleum production (which accounted for more than 59 per cent of total export earnings in 2006), and the export of banana and shrimps, coffee and cocoa. Ecuador is the world's largest exporter of bananas, a trade that earned the country some US$1.2 billion in 2006. The economy was also helped by growing remittances (amounting to around $3 billion in 2007) from Ecuadorians living abroad.

President Correa defaulted in December 2008 on Ecuador's US$3.2 billion sovereign debt which, represented about 80 per cent of Ecuador's private external debt. In May 2009 Ecuador bought back over 90 per cent of its defaulted. President Correa also announced in 2009 he was planning to end 13 bilateral investment treaties causing economic uncertainty. The Ecuadorian economy contracted 0.4 per cent in 2009 due to the global financial crisis and to the decline in world oil prices and remittance flows. Growth was estimated to have recovered to 3.7 per cent in 2010 and GDP was estimated to be US$56.9 billion. Per capita GDP was estimated to be US$4,000 in 2010. GDP was estimated to be US$60 billion in 2011. The government has revised downwards its growth forecasts for 2012 due to instability of oil prices. Growth is now forecast to be 4.8 per cent over 2012, mainly driven by the construction sector.

In 2010 the agriculture sector, including seafood, accounted for 6.4 per cent of GDP; in the same year, industry accounted for 36 per cent, and services contributed 55 per cent.

In 2000, Ecuador adopted the U.S. dollar as its official currency; the inflation rate, which had reached over 96 per cent in 2000, dropped dramatically over the following years, falling to 1.9 per cent in 2004, before rising to 3.32 per cent in 2007. Inflation was estimated at 8.8 per cent in 2008.

Foreign Investment

Following economic problems in the 1990s, the International Monetary Fund (IMF) provided financial assistance, conditional upon the establishment of certain reforms, including social programmes. Implementation of these reforms led to a plummeting in the popularity of President Gutierrez, who was dismissed in 2005.

Commercial disputes as well as judicial and contractual uncertainties have deterred private oil and other companies from investing in the country. The electricity and telecommunications sectors also have similar significant problems. Ecuador was in the final stages of negotiating a free trade agreement with the U.S. but this stalled following the 2006 hydrocarbons law mandating revisions in contract terms, and the May 2006 seizure of the assets of Occidental Petroleum, at the time the country's largest US investor. President Correa has announced his opposition to resumption of FTA talks, arguing that Ecuador is not yet sufficiently competitive.

In October 2007 the Correa administration decreed that many foreign oil companies operating in Ecuador pay 99 per cent of extraordinary income to the government. The government increased income transfers to the poor and spending on health, education, and basic infrastructure. As of January 2008, Ecuador had met its external debt obligations.

In 2011, Ecuador signed a US$2 billion loan with the China Development Bank and announced plans for further funding from China in 2012. China is now Ecuador's largest foreign bilateral lender.

Balance of Payments / Imports and Exports

Ecuador is part of the Andean Free Trade Zone, which has helped exports in recent years. Talks with the US on a free trade agreement have been halted as President Correa does not believe they are in the best interest of Ecuador. Ecuador will continue to benefit from tariff free trade with the US on some goods until December 2009. To try and reduce its reliance on the US, Ecuador is trying to establish new trading partners especially in Asia.

Major exports include petroleum and petroleum by-products, bananas, shrimp, coffee and coffee products, cocoa beans and cocoa products, tuna and other fish and cut flowers. 42 per cent of exports go to the USA, 26 per cent to Latin America, 20 per cent to the Andean Community and 13 per cent to the EU. Main imports include industrial raw materials and consumer goods. The main suppliers are Latin America (40 per cent), the Andean Community (24 per cent), US (21 per cent), Asia (20 per cent) and the EU (9 per cent).

Estimated figures for 2010 show that export earnings were $17.4 billion, down from the 2008 figure of $18.4 billion. The estimated cost of imports in 2010 was US$13.8 billion in 2010. Main trading partners include the USA, Colombia, Brazil, Chile, Japan, Germany and Venezuela.

Central Bank

Banco Central del Ecuador, Casilla 339, Plaza Bolivar, Av. 10 de Agosto y Briceño, Quito, Ecuador. Tel: +593 (0)2 2572522, fax: +593 (0)2 955458, URL: http://www.bce.fin.ec President: Pedro Delgado

Chambers of Commerce and Trading Organisations
Chamber of Commerce of Quito, URL: http://www.ccq.org.ec/

MANUFACTURING, MINING AND SERVICES

Primary and Extractive Industries

Ecuador had an estimated 7.21 billion barrels of proven oil reserves in early 2012 (the third largest in South America) and ranks fifth in crude oil production in South America. Oil production during 2011 reached 498.99 barrels of oil per day, 99 per cent of which was crude. Domestic consumption reached an estimated 166,000 barrels per day. Net exports reached 298,000 barrels per day. The oil sector dominates the economy, and accounts for nearly 50 per cent of total export earnings and a third of all tax revenues.

Petroecuador, the state-owned company, controlled around 37 per cent of Ecuador's oil production in 2005. Former President Gutierrez tried to reform the sector to attract more private investment and to re-organize Petroecuador, but met with opposition from unions and indigenous groups. In 2004, Congress vetoed the proposal that would have seen these reforms put into practise. Petroecuador's share of national production jumped to 46 per cent in 2006, following the company's takeover of the former production assets of Occidental.

Petroleum; the government claimed that Occidental had violated its production contract by transferring some assets to another oil company. Occidental launched an arbitration claim against the Ecuadorian government seeking compensation for the takeover.

In 2007, President Correa signed a decree establishing a 99 per cent windfall tax on oil company profits (up from the 50 per cent rate established in 2006). The tax comes into effect whenever Ecuador's oil export basket exceeds $24 per barrel; it was well above this threshold level in 2007.

Indigenous groups object to development of the oil industry and have obstructed exploration and production activities. They have taken ChevronTexaco to court over Texaco's former oil operations in Ecuador and it is feared that a decision in their favor could jeopardise foreign oil operators.

Ecuador has three oil refineries, the largest being Esmeraldas on the Pacific coast. Total capacity is 176,000 barrels per day. However, the country is a net importer of refined oil products so the Government aims to increase refining capacity by building a fourth refinery. In 2008, the Ecuadorian government announced that it had reached an agreement with Venezuela to build a 300,000-bbl/d refinery in Manabi province; it was expected to come online in 2012 but only a small part of it has been completed, financial backing is being sought to complete the project and it has been reported that China may become an investor.

Ecuador has two major oil pipelines, the SOTE, which suffers from natural disasters which disrupt oil production, and the OCP, completed in 2003 and the reason for the large increase in production over the period 2002-2004.

Ecuador has natural gas reserves of 267 billion cubic feet. Production and consumption reached an estimated 12 billion cubic feet in 2010. The Amistad field, is the only significant natural gas producer, and it is used to fire a power plant in the Guayaquil region.

Gold, silver, copper, lead, zinc, limestone, pumice, marble and salt are also mined. (Source: Energy Information Administration - EIA)

Energy
Total energy consumption was 0.5 quadrillion Btus in 2009. Oil is the main source of energy, representing 70 per cent of the country's total energy consumption in 2010. Hydroelectric power represented 15 per cent of energy consumption, and is the largest source of electricity generation. Other renewable energy sources produce 12 per cent and natural gas, three per cent.

In 2010, Ecuador has an estimated 5.2 gigawatts of installed electricity capacity. 17.3 billion kWh were produced, exceeding the 16.0 billion kWh required domestically. Whilst the country has a surplus capacity of electricity, the dry season can lead to shortages, when power is imported from Colombia.

Manufacturing
Wool, woollen goods and handicrafts are produced, mainly for the tourist trade. Petroleum by-products, chemicals and pharmaceuticals, wood by-products, canned seafood, processed coffee and cocoa and automobile assembly are amongst Ecuador's industrially manufactured goods. Software is an industry of growing importance to the country's economy.

Service Industries
Tourism is an important source of revenue, and employs some 56,000 people.

Visitor numbers rose gradually to 913,000 in 2004. Over 60 per cent of visitors came on holiday and nearly 20 per cent came to visit relatives. Ecuador benefits from varied landscapes which attract tourists: coast, mountains, Amazon rainforest and the Galapagos Islands. The country protects its enormous wealth of different species within over twenty parks and reserved areas. (Source: Ministry of Tourism)

Agriculture
Produce includes bananas, coffee, cocoa beans, natural flowers, vegetables, fresh fruits and timber. Shrimp, prawns and tuna are fished. Figures show the total fishing catch for 2010 was 392,000 tonnes. The sector employs some eight per cent of the workforce.

Agricultural Production in 2010

Produce	Int.$'000	Tonnes
Bananas	2,233,632	7,931,060
Indigenous cattle meat	642,306	237,770
Cow milk, whole	497,026	5,709,460
Indigenous chicken meat	477,813	335,447
Rice, paddy	463,748	1,706,190
Indigenous pigmeat	281,793	183,311
Sugar cane	270,156	8,347,180
Cocoa beans	137,184	132,100
Palm oil	126,123	289,900
Mangoes, mangosteens, guavas	112,584	187,900
Plantains	96,044	547,291
Fruit fresh nes	88,096	252,400
*unofficial figures

Source: http://faostat.fao.org/site/339/default.aspx Food and Agriculture Organization of the United Nations, Food and Agricultural commodities production

COMMUNICATIONS AND TRANSPORT

Travel Requirements
US, Canadian, Australian and EU citizens require a passport valid for at least six months, and must carry it with them at all times. They do not require a visa for stays of up to 90 days. People travelling from Germany and Italy must show a measles vaccination certificate on arrival. Nationals not referred to above should contact the embassy to check visa requirements. In June 2008 the president announced that citizens of any nationality can enter Ecuador without a visa and stay for a period of ninety days, the move was to promote the principle of free movement and to strengthen relations between Ecuador and all countries and to promote tourism, Colombian citizens must still present their valid passport to enter Ecuador.

National Airlines
Ecuador's main airlines are
TAME - Linea Aérea del Ecuador, URL: http://wwwpub4.ecua.net.ec/tame/
SAN Ecuador, PO Box 7138, Km2 1/2 Guayaquil, Ecuador. Tel: +593 (0)4 200277, fax: +593 (0)4 201153
Ecuatoriana de Aviacion, URL: http://www.ecuatoriana.com.ar/

International Airports
Ecuador has two international airports:
Mariscal Sucre, Quito. Tel: +593 (0)2 440083
Simón Bolívar, Gauyaquil. Tel: +593 (0)4 282100

There are daily flights to the Galápagos Islands from Quito and Guayaquil.

Railways
The railways are under state management and cover a total length of 1,064.9 kms.

Roads
There are 10,935 miles of asphalted roads crossing the country in all directions. There are also 51,000 miles of dirt roads. Vehicles are driven on the right.

Ports and Harbours
Ecuador's major ports are at Guayaquil, Manta, Machala, La Libertad, San Lorenzo and Esmeraldas. The port of Guayaquil is the largest on the South American coastline.

HEALTH

Under the 1998 constitution, free health care is provided for those who cannot afford to pay. Approximately 70 per cent of the population lives in poverty. In 2008, Ecuador spent approximately 7.7 per cent of its total budget on healthcare (up from 6.4 per cent in 2000), accounting for 34.9 per cent of all healthcare spending. Total expenditure on health care equated to 8.8 per cent of the country's GDP. Per capita expenditure on health amounted to US$321.

Figures for 2005-10 show that there are 23,614 physicians (16.9 per 10,000 population), 27,764 nurses (19.8 per 10,000 population) and 3,363 dentistry personnel. There are 15 hospital beds per 10,000 population.

Infant mortality (probability of dying aged less than 1 year old) was estimated to be 18 per 1,000 live births in 2009 and among under-five-year-olds was around 20 deaths per 1,000 children. The most common causes of death in children aged less than five are: prematurity (16 per cent), congenital abnormalities (25 per cent), diarrhoea (4 per cent), and pneumonia (10 per cent). HIV/AIDS causes 1 per cent of deaths in this age bracket. According to figures published by the World Health Organization (WHO), average life expectancy for Ecuadorian men at birth stood at 73 years in 2009, and for women at 78 years.

In 2010 approximately 94 per cent of the population had access to improved drinking water. In the same year, 92 per cent of the population had access to improved sanitation. (Source: http://www.who.int, World Health Statistics 2012)

EDUCATION

Education in Ecuador is free and compulsory. In 2007, 100 per cent of young children were enrolled in pre-primary school. That same year 97 per cent of girls and 96 per cent of boys were enrolled in primary schools where the pupil:teacher ratio was 23:1. The figure for secondary school attendance then falls to a 2007 figure of 60 per cent of girls and 59 per cent of boys, well below the regional average of 70 per cent. On average eight per cent of total government spending went on education, equivalent to one per cent of GDP.

Ecuador has 17 advanced educational institutions, including music schools, 14 universities and 3 technical institutes.

The adult literacy rate is estimated to be 84.2 per cent, rising to 95.4 per cent among the 15-24 years group. (Source: UNESCO)

RELIGION

There is no state religion. Around 95 per cent of the population, however, are practising Roman Catholics.

Ecuador has a religious liberty rating of 10 on a scale of 1 to 10 (10 is most freedom). (Source: World Religion Database)

ECUADOR

COMMUNICATIONS AND MEDIA

Freedom of speech is guaranteed under the constitution. There is some self-censorship over politically sensitive issues and the army. By law, the government may also require the media to give the government free air time or space.

Newspapers
El Comercio, URL: http://www.elcomercio.com
HOY, URL: http://www.hoy.com.ec/home.htm
El Telegrafo, URL: http://www.telegrafo.com.ec
El Universo, URL: http://www.eluniverso.com
El Tiempo, URL: http://www.eltiempo.com.ec

Broadcasting
There is one government controlled station and numerous commercial channels and networks. There are more than 400 radio stations.

Telecommunications
The telecommunications infrastructure is under expansion. Mainline density is currently about 13 per 100 persons whilst mobile phone usage has surged and over 75 out of every 100 persons has one. Estimates for 2008 suggest that there are now over 11 million mobile phone users in Ecuador and 1.8 million landlines in use. Ecuador has over 1.3 million internet users.

ENVIRONMENT

Ecuador is one of the most bio-diverse countries in the world. The Galapagos Islands and the waters surrounding it are both World Heritage Sites of major ecological importance. However, the biodiversity of Ecuador is threatened with destruction; Ecuador has the second highest deforestation rate in South America. Forestry and bio-diversity laws have still to be passed through government.

Other environmental issues include desertification and wastes in ecologically sensitive area of the Amazon and the Galapagos Islands. Ecuador is a key supporter of the Kyoto Protocol and environmental forums. It is party to the following environmental agreements: Antarctic-Environmental Protocol, Antarctic Treaty, Biodiversity, Climate Change, Climate Change-Kyoto Protocol, Desertification, Endangered Species, Hazardous Wastes, Ozone Layer Protection, Ship Pollution, Tropical Timber 83, Tropical Timber 94, and Wetlands.

Figures EIA for 2010 show that emissions of carbon dioxide amounted to 24.43 million metric tons, down from 57.55 million metric tons in 2009.

SPACE PROGRAMME

The Ecuador Civilian Space Agency was founded in 1997. Its aims are to conduct scientific research on space and planetary sciences and to develop the role of science in education. The agency developed Latin America's first microgravity plane and has undertaken micro-gravity research. Its first satellite (NEE-01 Pegasus) was built in 2011. It has the capability to send live video from space and has its own anti-radiation shield. It is scheduled to be launched into orbit by the end of 2012.
Ecuador Civilian Space Agency, URL: http://www.exa.ec/index-en.html

GALAPAGOS ISLANDS

Capital: Puerto Baquerizo Moreno (Population estimate, 2006: 30,000)

Head of State: Rafael Correa, President (page 1409)

Flag: A horizontal tricolour, green, white then blue

CONSTITUTION AND GOVERNMENT

It is probable that the first visitors to the Galapagos Islands were South American Indians from the coastal regions of Ecuador and northern Peru. The recorded discovery of the islands did not come until 1535, however, when Tomas de Berlanga, Bishop of Panama, accidentally landed there on his way to Peru. Finding their climate unwelcoming, he left without giving them a name. Subsequent visitors were Diego de Rivadeneira, leader of a group of renegade Spaniards, who wrote about the islands in the mid 1600s, followed by, in the 17th and 18th centuries, pirates, who found the islands ideal for use as their hide-outs. In 1793, a period of exploitation of the islands' whale population began under the helm of an English Captain, James Colnett. It was to last until around 1870. The whalers, and later sealers, were to do irreparable damage to the islands' abundant wildlife. Greater and greater numbers of English and then American vessels arrived, turning their attention in time to the giant tortoises which they removed from the islands in vast quantities. The introduction of goats, pigs, cattle and even rats was almost as destructive in depleting the animal populations, and even after the islands were claimed by Ecuador in 1832, it was a hundred years before laws governing and protecting the wildlife were passed.

In 1835, the Galapagos received their most famous visitor, the great naturalist Charles Darwin, who used his study of the rare fauna and flora to perfect his theory on the origin of species. In 1959, the Galapagos National Park (covering 97 per cent of the archipelago) was set up by the Government to protect the natural environment, and the commemorative laboratories of the Charles Darwin Foundation were installed, aided by UNESCO, so that scientists, naturalists and others interested in the islands would be able to study and research some of their rarest biological species. The Charles Darwin Research Station is currently working on the rehabilitation and conservation of the islands' fragile ecology.

AREA AND POPULATION

Area
The islands' name is derived from the Spanish word *galapagos*, meaning giant tortoise. The islands lie in the dry zone of the Equatorial Pacific, 1,120 km (622 miles) from the coast of Ecuador. There are 13 major islands, 6 small islands and 24 islets. The three main islands are Isabela, San Cristóbal and Santa Cruz. Of volcanic origin, the islands were formed by uplifting of the sea bed and are characterised by large black rocks, lava formations and multi-coloured sands in the lowlands, and denser vegetation in the highlands. The oldest island is thought to have formed between five and ten million years ago; the youngest islands, Isabela and Fernandina, are still being formed, with the most recent volcanic eruption in 2007.

The islands cover an area of 8,010 sq. km.

Owing to the position of the islands and the influence of ocean currents, the climate of the Galapagos is hot and dry in the low-lying areas and moist and temperate in the higher ones, manifesting itself rather as a variety of microclimates. From May to December the air and sea are coolest and at this time a mist called the *garua* is often present. There is rarely any rainfall and little plant life exists, other than trees which grow on the larger islands where there is sufficient cloud cover.

To view a map, please consult http://www.lib.utexas.edu/maps/cia08/ecuador_sm_2008.gif

Population
Five of the islands are inhabited: Baltra, Floreana, Isabela, San Cristobal and Santa Cruz. The islanders, or *galapageños*, are of mixed origin. Some are descendants of the European colonists of the 1930s but most come from the coasts and mountains of Ecuador, attracted over the last twenty years by the profits from tourism. By 1960, 1,000 to 2,000 people lived on the islands; this figure had grown to 3,488 by the time of the 1972 census. Over the next thirty years, the population grew to over 15,000 people, and it is estimated that, in 2006, the population was around 30,000 people.

The official language of the islanders is Spanish. The time is one hour behind Ecuador, or GMT minus 6 hours.

Of the creatures living on the Galapagos around 90 per cent of reptiles, 50 per cent of birds and 40 per cent of insects are only found on the islands.

MANUFACTURING, MINING AND SERVICES

The islanders farm the highlands to produce bananas, avocados, sugar and yucca. Coffee and cattle are the sole exports. Fishing for sea bass and grouper and diving for lobster also brings in some income. Although on the direct route from Panama to Australia and New Zealand, the islands are of little commercial importance.

Ecotourism is the main industry of the Islands and has earned the following designations: Natural Bioshpere Reserve, Marine Resource Reserve, World Heritage and Whale Sanctuary. In 2000, 17 per cent of visitors to Ecuador visited the Galapagos, representing some 105,000 tourists.

COMMUNICATIONS AND TRANSPORT

Airport
Flights to the islands from Quito and Guayaquil land at Isla Baltra airport.

ENVIRONMENT

The Galapagos Islands are still struggling with the effects of the 1982 El Nino weather system which destroyed much of the coral reefs which weakened the marine ecosystem. In January 2001, the Galapagos Islands were hit by a potential environmental disaster when the oil tanker 'Jessica' ran aground on the island of San Cristóbal spilling over 200,000 gallons of fuel. Although much of the oil was moved northwards away from the islands by the wind, the Ecuadorian government estimated that a clean-up operation would cost more than US$2 million.

In 2006, scientists were alarmed to find foreign species of animals including an iguana and a foreign turtle on the island, probably from South America. Ecologists fear that a rapid increase in the human population and the gradual introduction of external species of flora and fauna are threatening the entire ecosystem on the islands. In 2007, UNESCO put the Galápagos Islands on their World Heritage in Danger List.

EGYPT

Arab Republic of Egypt
Jumhuriyat Misr al-Arabiya

Capital: Cairo (Population estimate, 2008: 17 million)

Interim Head of State: Adly Mahmud Monsour (page 1470)

National Flag: Horizontal tricolour, red, white and black; the white stripe is charged with the national emblem, a gold Eagle of Saladin facing the hoist side with a shield superimposed on its chest above a scroll bearing the name of the country in Arabic.

CONSTITUTION AND GOVERNMENT

Constitution

Egypt gained independence from Britain on 22 February 1922. Following the July 1952 Revolution, Egypt proclaimed the end of its monarchy, dissolved all political parties and declared a republican regime. Muhammad Najib became President and Prime Minister. In 1956, under President Gamal Abdul Nasser, the Suez Canal was nationalised resulting in an invasion by Britain, France and Israel. A ceasefire was agreed at the end of the year. Also in 1956 the Constitution was proclaimed, and a year later the National Assembly was formed. This assembly lasted until 1958 and then with each successive leader a new replacement constitution and legislature was formed.

Two main national documents were compiled which defined the framework of the social, economic and political system of the state as well as the system of government. The Charter of National Action, proclaimed on 21 May 1962, is considered the basic document expressing the philosophy of national action in all home and foreign affairs. The Provisional Constitution, issued on 25 March 1964, defines the form of government, the rights of citizens and the competence of the State organs.

Under the 1971 Constitution, the Egyptian Parliament became known as the 'People's Assembly'. In 1980 the Shoura (Consultative) Council, a body offering advice and consultation in accordance with the Constitution, was established. In March 2007 amendments to the constitution were proposed giving more power to the president; the amendments also brought about the end of the state of emergency which had been in force since 1981. The changes were approved by a referendum. Under this constitution, the president was nominated by a two thirds majority of the Assembly and then needed a majority of the following referendum. The term was six years with successive terms possible. The president appoints the prime minister and the cabinet.

Following the ousting of President Hosni Mubarak in February 2011, the constitution dating from 1971 was amended. The leader of the Supreme Council of the Armed Forces (SCAF) charged eight jurists with drawing up a new constitution within ten days. Proposals for amendments included reducing the presidential term from six to four years, and making it renewable once only. A referendum held on 20 March 2011 approved by a substantial majority the changes to the constitution.

To consult the full 2011 constitution, please visit:
http://www.egypt.gov.eg/english/laws/constitution/default.aspx

International Relations

Egypt is an active member of the Arab League. In 2004 the EU-Egypt Association Agreement came into force. The agreement includes plans for initiating free trade between the EU and Egypt.

Recent Events

In February 2005 President Mubarak put forward constitutional amendments which would allow multi-candidate presidential elections and a referendum vote in May backed this reform, although a ban remains on overtly religious political parties. President Mubarak has been unopposed since 1981. In March 2005 the opposition leader, Ayman Nour, was charged with forging signatures needed to establish his party.

Egypt extended its emergency laws to arrest and detain people in March 2006. The government said the laws were needed in the wake of recent bombings including those in April in Dahab which killed 24 people. In November 2007 the National Democratic Party voted to retain President Mubarak as party leader.

In January 2008, UN Secretary General, Ban Ki-moon, called for urgent measures to end the escalating violence in the Gaza Strip, and for the borders to be re-opened. Following the violence in Gaza the border wall between Gaza and Egypt at Rafah was breached, and tens of thousands of Gaza residents surged through to buy food and other supplies made scarce by the blockade. Egypt resealed the border after 12 days, succumbing to Israeli and US pressure to clamp down on potential arms smuggling routes. Since then the border has been opened periodically to allow people needing medical attention to cross into Egypt.

The military courts sentenced 25 members of the Muslim Brotherhood to jail in April 2008 and arrested over 800 members in a month. The Brotherhood boycotted municipal elections after the majority of their candidates were not allowed to stand.

Another terrorist attack occured in February, when a bomb exploded in a tourist area of Cairo, killing three and injuring 24. A small Islamist cell connected to al-Qaeda was thought to be responsible. Arrests were made later in the year in connection to the attack.

In March 2009, Egypt hosted talks between the rival Palestinian factions, Fatah and Hamas.

Construction of a church in Giza led to clashes between Coptic Christians and police in November 2010 and in January 2011, 21 people were killed when a bomb exploded at a church in Alexandria where Christians had gathered to celebrate the new year.

In January 2011 street protests took place in Tunisia leading to President Ben Ali leaving the country. Anti-government demonstrators also took to the streets of Egypt, driven by high unemployment amongst the young, rising prices and increasing anger at the corruption and enrichment of the ruling elite. In response President Mubarak reshuffled his cabinet; he named the intelligence chief Omar Suleiman as vice-president, a new position, and the aviation minister Ahmed Shafiq was appointed prime minister. The reshuffle did not stop the protests and increasing numbers of demonstrators took to the streets demanding that President Mubarak stand down. President Mubarak called on the army to suppress the demonstrations but in the event the army announced it would not use force against the people. In early February the leaders of the governing National Democratic Party resigned including President Mubarak's son Gamal Mubarak, who many believed was being groomed to succeed his father. On February 10 rumours began to circulate that President Mubarak was about to resign, instead he appeared on national television announcing his intention to stay in office until elections due in September. Street protests continued and on February 11 President Mubarak finally bowed to pressure and resigned.

Following the resignation of President Mubarak, the army took over power, led by Field Marshal Mohammad Hussein Tantawi, who has been the minister of defence and commander in chief of the armed forces. The People's Assembly was dissolved on 13 February 2011. A transitional government was announced in March; it remained in place until elections could be held. A reshuffle of the transitional cabinet took place in July 2011 during which foreign minister Mohammed al-Orabi resigned. In November 2011 former Prime Minister Dr Kamal El-Ganzouri was appointed to the post of Prime Minister-designate, he was charged with the job of forming a new cabinet after the existing cabinet resigned following protests against military rule.

In April the prosecutor general ordered that former President Mubarak and his sons Alaa and Gamal should be detained following allegations of corruption and violence. Mr Mubarak had been admitted to hospital at the time suffering from heart problems. Mr Mubarak and his sons will be tried over the deaths of anti-government protesters, his family has been banned from leaving Egypt and the family's assets have been frozen while investigations are ongoing. Mr Mubarak denied the charges against him.

The army oversaw the transition to democracy and elections are expected later in the year. The opposition Muslim Brotherhood group was expected to do well.

In May 2011 the first trial of an official from Mr Mubarak's regime took place. The former Interior Minister Habib al-Aldil was charged and found guilty of money laundering and profiteering and was sentenced to 12 years in prison. He faces a further charge of ordering troops to fire on demonstrators. The trial of Mr Mubarak commenced in August.

Estimated figures put the number of people killed during the uprising at 846 with more than 6,400 people injured.

In September 2011, protestors broke into the Israeli embassy in Cairo.

Voting in the first elections since President Mubarak's fall from power began on 28 November 2011. The voting continued until March 2012. Elections to the 508-member People's Assembly took place between 28 November 2011 and January 2012 and Islamist parties emerged as the winners. Elections to the 270-strong Shural Council took place from 29 January - 11 March 2012.

In November 2011 violence broke out in Tahrir Square in Cairo as protesters accused the military of continuing their grip on power. Prime Minister Essam Sharaf resigned his post.

In early February 2012 clashes took place at a football match between Cairo's al-Ahly team, and Port Said side al-Masry, in which 74 fans were killed. Conspiracy theories abounded after people accused the police of negligence and others blamed outside forces for provoking the violence.

Pope Shendouda III, the head of the Coptic Church died in March 2012.

In April 2012 Egypt's ruling generals approved an amendment to the law which would prevent senior officials from President Mubarak's era from standing for president.

In May 2012, five Egyptian police officers were sentenced in absentia to 10 years in prison for their part in the deaths of protesters during the 2011 uprising. Several other officers were aquitted. Witnesses had said that police fired live ammunition, rubber bullets and tear gas during the uprising. The trials of several of former President Mubarak's closest aides began to draw to an end. His chief of staff, Zakaria Azmi, was found guilty of corruption, fined US$6 million and jailed for seven years. Also that month, military leaders announced the end of the state of emergency as its last renewal expired. Egypt had been under a state of emergency since Anwar al-Sadat's assassination in 1981.

EGYPT

In June 2012, ex-President Mubarak was sentenced to life in prison for complicity in the killing of protesters during the 2011 uprising. Four senior interior ministry officials were acquitted at the trial leading to widespread anger.

Just before the run-off Presidential election in June 2012, the Supreme Court declared that the parliamentary elections had been invalid. The military government issued two decrees dissolving the Islamist-dominated parliament and claimed legislative power itself.

Muslim Brotherhood candidate Mohammed Mursi was declared the winner of the first free presidential elections, which were held in June 2012. He then re-instated the dissolved parliament. In August 2012 August Hisham Kandil, was appointed Prime Minister and announced a new government.

In September 2012, violent protests took place in several Middle East countries following the release of an amateur anti-Islam video made in the USA. In Egypt a mob attacked the US embassy, replacing the American flag with an Islamic banner.

In November 2012 Bishop Tawadros was chosen as the new Pope of Egypt's Coptic Christians.

Later that month President Morsi issued a decree that stripped the judiciary of the right to challenge his decisions. Top judges denounced the decree accusing him of undermining the independence of the judiciary. Protestors took to the streets against what it feared was the increase of presidential powers. The Islamist dominated assembly approved a draft constitution that boosted the role of Islam, the same session was boycotted by the liberals and Christian members. Following increased protests President Morsi cancelled his decree on judicial powers but insisted that a referendum on the draft constitution would still go ahead.

On June 30 2013, millions of people took to the streets, including thousands of protesters on the streets of Cairo, demanding the resignation of President Morsi (page 1481). The protestors claimed that after a year in power he had not made promised changes and demanded that he step down and fresh elections be held. Thousands of his supporters also took to the streets. The military issued an ultimatum following the days of protest, the ultimatum ran out on the afternoon of July 3. On July 3, the military moved in and removed President Morsi and Prime Minister Kandil were put under arrest, in response most of the ministers of the Freedom and Justice Party (FJP, the party founded by the Muslim Brotherhood), immediately resigned in protest. On July 4, Adly Mansour, leader of the Constitutional Court was sworn in as interim leader. It is believed that around 50 people were killed in the days of protest. Interim president Mansour began having talks to form a technocrat caretaker government.

Following the ousting of President Morsi it was believed he was being held at the Presidential Guard Club in Cairo, many of his supporters including members of the Muslim Brotherhood staged a sit-in demanding that he be reinstated to his post. On July 8 it was reported that the protesters had been fired on and up to 34 people had been killed. As a result the Salafist Nour party who had supported Mr Morsi's removal said it would be withdrawing from talks to choose an interim prime minister, after what it said was a 'massacre'.

On July 8 there were rumours that the former head of the UN nuclear watchdog, Mohamed El Baradei was to be appointed as the interim prime minister, but at the time of going to press these reports were unconfirmed.

Legislature
Egypt's Legislature in unicameral, the People's Assembly has 444 directly elected members plus ten members appointed by the president, all members serve a five year term. There is a Shoura Council or Consultative Council which consists of 264 members, 176 of whom are directly elected and 88 are appointed by the president. The Council acts in an advisory capacity and members serve a six year term.

Shoura Council, URL: http://www.shoura.gov.eg
People's Assembly, Magles El Shaab Street, Cairo, CA104, Egypt. Tel: +20 (0)2 794 3130, e-mail: parli@idsc.gov.eg, URL: http://www.assembly.gov.eg

Cabinet (as at July 2013)
Prime Minister: vacant
Minister of Finance: Dr Fayed Abdel-Moneim Hassanein Ibrahim
Minister of Foreign Affairs: vacant
Minister of Industry and Foreign Trade: Hatem Saleh
Minister of the Interior: Gen. Mohamed Ibrahim
Minister of Justice: Judge Mohamed Ahmed Soliman
Minister of Education: vacant
Minister of Higher Education: Mostafa Mosaad
Minister of Agriculture and Land Reclamation: Dr Ahmed Mahmoud Ali El-Gizawi
Minister of People's Assembly and Shura Council Affairs: vacant
Minister of Manpower and Immigration: vacant
Minister of International Co-operation and Planning: vacant
Minister of Culture: Alaa Abdel-Aziz El-Sayed Abdel-Fattah
Minister of Tourism: vacant
Minister of Housing and Urban Development: Tarek Wafiq
Minister of Religious Affairs and Waqfs: Dr Talaat Mohamed Afifi Salem
Minister of Health and Population: Dr Mohamed Mostafa Hamed
Minister of Irrigation and Water Resources: Mohamed Bahaa El-Din
Minister of Drinking Water and Sanitation: vacant
Minister of Supplies and Domestic Trade: vacant
Minister of Civil Aviation: Wael Al-Maaddawi
Minister of Transport: vacant
Minister of Electricity and Energy: Ahmed Imam
Minister of Petroleum and Mineral Resources: Sherif Hassan Ramadan Hadarra
Minister of the Environment: vacant
Minister of Antiquities: Dr Ahmed Eissa
Minister of Scientific Research: Dr Nadia Eskndar Zkhary

Minister of State for Local Development: vacant
Minister of State for Military Production: Lt.-Gen. Reda Mahmoud Hafez Abdel-Mequid
Minister of Defence: Gen, Abdel Fattah Al-Sisi (page 1377)
Minister of Investment: vacant
Minister of Communication and Information Technology: vacant
Minister of Sport: Farouk El-Amry
Minister of Insurance and Social Affairs: Dr Nagwa Hussein Khalil
Minister of Youth: vacant
Minister of Information: vacant

Ministries
Office of the Prime Minister, Sharia Majlis ash-Sha'ab, Cairo, Egypt. Tel: +20 (0)2 355 3192, e-mail: primemin@idsc.gov.eg, URL: http://www.egyptiancabinet.gov.eg/Cabinet/Cabinet.asp
Ministry of Foreign Affairs, Corniche en-Nil, Maspiro CAI 02, Cairo, Egypt. Tel: +20 (0)2 574 9816, e-mail: minexter@idsc1.gov.eg, URL: http://www.mfa.gov.eg
Ministry of Finance, Justice and Finance Building, Sharia Majlis ash-Sha'ab, Lazoughli Square, CAI 04 Cairo. Egypt. Tel: +20 (0)2 354 1055, fax: +20 (0)2 355 1537, e-mail: mofinance@idsc1.gov.eg, URL: http://www.salestax.gov.eg
Ministry of Agriculture and Land Reclamation, Sharia Nadi es-Sayed, Dokki, Giza, Cairo, Egypt. Tel: +20 (0)2 337 3388 / (0)2 749 8128, fax: +20 (0)2 349 8128, e-mail: sea@idsc.fov.eg, URL: http://www.agri.gov.eg
Ministry of Defence and Military Production, Sharia 23 July, Kobri el Kubba, CAI 36, Cairo, Egypt. Tel: +20 (0)2 419 2183 / 260 2566, fax: +20 (0)2 290 6004 / 291 6227, e-mail: mod@idsc.gov.eg, URL: http://www.mmc.gov.eg
Ministry of the Economy and Foreign Trade, 9 Sharia Adly, Down Town Cairo, Egypt. Tel: +20 (0)2 391 9661, fax: +20 (0)2 390 3029, e-mail: mineco@idsc.gov.eg, URL: http://www.economy.gov.eg
Ministry of Emigration and Egyptians Abroad, URL: http://www.emigration.gov.eg
Ministry of Information, Radio and TV Building, Corniche en-Nil, Maspiro CAI 02, Cairo, Egypt. Tel: +20 (0)2 574 8984, e-mail: rtu@idsc.gov.eg, URL: http://www.sis.gov.eg
Ministry of Justice, Justice and Finance Building, Sharia Majlis ash-Sha'ab, Lazoughli Square, CAI 15 Cairo, Egypt. Tel: +20 (0)2 759 1176 / 8108, fax: +20 (0)2 759 8103 / 5700, e-mail: mojeb@idsc.gov.eg
Ministry of Culture, 2 Sharia Shagaret ed-Dor, Zamalek, CAI 03 Cairo, Egypt. Tel: +20 (0)2 738 0761 / 0762, fax: +20 (0)2 735 6449, e-mail: mculture@idsc.gov.eg, URL: http://www.ecm.gov.eg
Ministry of Education, 4 Sharia Ibrahim Naguib, Garden City, Cairo, Egypt. Tel: +20 (0)2 578 7643, e-mail: moe@idsc.gov.eg, URL: http://www.emoe.edu
Ministry of Foreign Trade, 8 Adly St., Cairo, Egypt. Tel: +20 (0)2 391 9661 / 6629, fax: +20 (0)2 390 3029, e-mail: minecon@idsc1.gov.eg, URL: http://www.moft.gov.eg
Ministry for the People's Assembly and the Shura Council Affairs, Sharia Majlis ash-Sha'ab, Lazoughli Square, Cairo, Egypt. Tel: +20 (0)2 759 7750 / 3855, fax: +20 (0)2 759 7681, e-mail: parli@idsc.gov.eg
Ministry of Tourism, Misr Travel Tower, Abbassia Square, CAI 24 Cairo, Egypt. Tel: +20 (0)2 682 8439, fax: +20 (0)2 285 9551, e-mail: mol@idsc.gov.eg, URL: http://www.touregypt.net
Ministry for Administrative Development, Sharia Salah Salem, Nasr City, Cairo, Egypt. Tel: +20 (0)2 402 4152 / 4167, fax: +20 (0)2 402 4152, e-mail: zamer@idsc.gov.eg, URL: http://www.edara.gov.eg/
Ministry of Housing, Utilities & Urban Communities, 1 Ismail Abaza, Qasr el-Eini, Cairo, Egypt. Tel: +20 (0)2 792 1384 / 1385, fax: +20 (0)2 795 7836, e-mail: mhuuc@idsc1.gov.eg, URL: http://www.nuca.com.eg
Ministry of Manpower and Immigration, 3 Sharia Yousuf Abbas, Nasr City, Abbassia, Cairo, Egypt. Tel: +20 (0)2 404 2910 / 2911, fax: +20 (0)2 260 9891, e-mail: mwlabor@idsc1.gov.eg, URL: http://www.emigration.gov.eg
Ministry of Endowments, Sharia Sabri Abu Alam, Bab el-Luk, Cairo, Egypt. Tel: +20 (0)2 392 9403, fax: +20 (0)2 390 0362, e-mail: mawkaf@idsc1.gov.eg
Minister of Health and Population, Cairo, Egypt. Tel: +20(0) 2 794 1507 / 0526, fax: +20 (0)2 795 3966 / 9422, e-mail: moh@idsc.gov.eg
Ministry of Higher Education and the State for Scientific Research, 101 Sharia Kasr el Aini, CAI 04, Cairo, Egypt. Tel: +20 (0)2 795 6962, fax: +20 (0)2 794 1005, e-mail: mheducat@idsc1.gov.eg, URL: http://www.egy-mhe.gov.eg
Ministry of Public Works and Water Resources, Sharia Corniche en-Nil, Imbaba, Cairo, Egypt. Tel: +20 (0)2 544 9446 / 9447, fax: +20 (0)2 544 9449, e-mail: mpwwr@idsc.gov.eg, URL: http://www.starnet.com.eg/mpwwr
Ministry for the Environment Affairs, 30 Misr Helwan El-Zyrae Road, Maadi, Cairo, Egypt. Tel: +20 (0)2 525 6463 / 6472, fax: +20 (0)2 525 6461, e-mail: eeaa@eeaa.gov.eg, URL: http://www.eeaa.gov.eg
Ministry of Interior, Sharia Al-Sheikh Rihan, Bab Al-Louk, CAI 06 Cairo, Egypt. Tel: +20 (0)2 795 7500 / 7511, fax: +20 (0)2 579 2031, e-mail: moi1@idsc.gov.eg, URL: http://www.moiegypt.gov.eg/
Ministry of Local Development, Sharia Nadi es-Seid, Dokki, Cairo, Egypt. Tel: +20 (0)2 749 7470 / 7656, fax: +20 (0)2 761 6383, e-mail: mlocmng@idsc1.gov.eg, URL:http://www.mold.gov.eg
Ministry of Social Affairs, Sharia Sheikh Rihan, Bab el-Louk, CAI 06 Cairo, Egypt. Tel: +20 2 337 0039, e-mail: msi@idsc.gov.eg, URL: http://www.misaegy.com
Ministry of Industry and Technological Development, 2 Sharia Latin America, Garden City, CAI 04 Cairo, Egypt. Tel: +20 (0)2 795 7034, fax: +20 (0)2 795 5025, e-mail: moimw@idsc1.gov.eg, URL: http://msht.tripod.com
Ministry of Electricity and Energy, Sharia Ramses, Abbassia, Nasr City, CAI 01 Cairo, Egypt. Tel: +20 (0)2 261 6514 / 6317, fax: +20 (0)2 261 6302, e-mail: moimw@idsc1.gov.eg, URL: http://msht.tripod.com
Ministry for Military Production, 5 Sharia Ismail Abaza, Kasr el Aini, Cairo, Egypt. Tel: +20 (0)2 795 2428, fax: +20 (0)2 794 8739, e-mail: mmpiscc@idsc.gov.eg
Ministry of Transport, 105 Sharia Qasr el-Eini, CAI 04 Cairo, Egypt. Tel: +20 (0)2 795 7149 / 5566, fax: +20 (0)2 795 5564, e-mail: garb@idsc.gov.eg
Ministry of Youth, Cairo, Egypt. Tel: +20 (0)2 346 1113, fax: +20 (0)2 346 9025, e-mail: info@alshabab.gov.eg

Ministry of Trade and Supply, 99 Sharia Qasr el-Eini, CAI 04 Cairo, Egypt. Tel: +20 (0)2 355 7598, fax: +20 (0)2 354 4973, e-mail: msit@idsc.gov.eg
Ministry of Planning, Sharia Salah Salem, Nasr City, Cairo, Egypt. Tel: +20 (0)2 401 4615 / 4719, fax: +20 (0)2 401 4733 / 4705, e-mail: miceu@idsc.gov.eg, URL: http://www.mop.gov.eg
Ministry of Public Enterprise, Cairo, Egypt. Tel: +20 (0)2 795 8026 / 0164, fax: +20 (0)2 795 5882, e-mail: mops3@idsc.gov.eg
Ministry of Communications and Information, Ramses Square, Cairo, Egypt. Tel: +20 (0)2 577 0000, e-mail: anazif@mcit.gov.eg, URL: http://www.mcit.gov.eg
Ministry of Petroleum, Sharia el-Mokhayem ed-Dayem, Nasr City, Cairo, Egypt. Tel: +20 (0)2 263 1010, fax: +20 (0)2 263 6060, e-mail: mopm@idsc1.gov.eg, URL: http://www.emp.gov.eg

Political Parties

The National Democratic Party; The National Progressive Unionist Grouping Party, URL: www.al-ahaly.com; The Socialist Liberals; The Socialist Labour Party; The Neo Wafd (New Wafd Party), URL: http://www.alwafd.org; Egyptian Socialist Arab Party; The Egyptian Khodhr (Greens); Adala Igtimiya (Social Justice Party); The Democratic Union Party; Al-Ummah (The Nation Party); The Nasserist Democratic Party; The Democratic People's Party; Al-Takaful (Social Solidarity Party); Al-Wifak al-Kawmi (National Concordance Party); Egypt 2000; Misr Al-Fatah (Young Egypt Party - currently suspended). The Muslim Brotherhood is one of the main opposition parties but under the constitutional ban on religious political parties were not able to stand. Members of the party stood as independents in the November 2005 election. The Freedom and Justice Party is the political party linked with the Muslim Brotherhood, in 2012, the former Egyptian parliamentary speaker Saad al-Katatni was elected as party leader. The party is still nominally independent.

Elections

Presidential elections took place in September 2005 when Hosni Mubarak was re-elected to his fifth term of office. Mr Mubarak originally came to power in October 1981 following the assassination of Anwar al-Sadat. Following Mr Mubarak's fall from power the next presidential election took place in 2012. The first round took place in May 2012, the Muslim Brotherhoold candidate Mohammed Mursi came first in the first round although the turnout was low. The final round was held in June 2012 and it was announced the Mohammed Mursi had won. Just before the run-off election, the Supreme Court declared that the parliamentary elections were invalid. The military government issued two decrees dissolving the Islamist-dominated parliament and claimed legislative power itself.

Parliamentary elections took place in November 2005 and were won by the governing National Democratic Party who won 311 seats. The banned party, the Muslim Brotherhood whose candidates stood as independents, won 88 seats. Elections for both the People's Assembly and the Advisory Council took place in November 2010 and the governing National Democratic Party won with an overwhelming majority.

Following President Mubarak's fall from power, it was agreed that parliamentary elections would take place in 2011. Elections to the 508-member People's Assembly took place between 28 November 2011 and January 2012. The FJP won 235 seats, Al-Nour Party won 121 seats, NWP won 38 seats. Elections to the 270-strong Shural Council took place from 29 January - 11 March 2012. The Democratic Alliance for Egypt, led by the FJP won 105 seats, the Islamic Bloc led by the Al-Nour Party won 45 seats. An estimated 50 million people are eligible to vote. There are 50 registered parties and more than 10,000 candidates. Just before the presidential run-off election in June 2012, the Supreme Court declared that the parliamentary elections were invalid. The military government issued two decrees dissolving the Islamist-dominated parliament and claimed legislative power itself.

Diplomatic Representation

US Embassy, North Gate, 8 Kamal El-Din Salah Street, Garden City, Cairo, Egypt. Tel: +20 (0)2 797 3300, fax: +20 (0)2 797 3200, URL: http://cairo.usembassy.gov
Ambassador: Anne W. Patterson (page 1493)
British Embassy, 7 Ahmed Ragheb Street, Garden City, Cairo, Egypt. Tel: +20 (0)2 794 0850, fax:+20 (0)2 794 0859, e-mail: information.cairo@fco.gov.uk, URL: http://ukinegypt.fco.gov.uk/en
Ambassador: James Watt (page 1534)
Egyptian Embassy, 3521 International Court, NW, Washington DC, 20008, USA. Tel: +1 202 895 5400, fax: +1 202 244 4319, URL: http://www.egyptembassy.net
Ambassador: Mohamed Tawfik
Egyptian Embassy, 26 South Street, London W1Y 6DD, UK. Tel +44 (0)20 7499 2401 / 3304, fax: +44 (0)20 7491 1542, e-mail: etembuk@hotmail.com, URL: http://www.egyptembassy.net
Ambassador: Ashraf Elkholy
Permanent Representative of the Arab Republic of Egypt to the United Nations, 304 East 44th Street, New York, NY 10017, USA, Tel: +1 212 503 0300, fax: +1 212 949 5999, URL: http://www.un.int/egypt
Permanent Representative to the UN: Amabassador Mootaz Ahmadein Khalil

LEGAL SYSTEM

The judicial system is based on the Islamic and civic systems, the legal code stems mainly from the Napoleonic code. The system is comprised of the following: the Courts of Justice, the administrative judiciary and the Supreme Constitutional Court. A Supreme Council presided over by the president supervises the judiciary.

The Personal Status Law was passed in March 2000 which allows women to apply for a divorce. The new law is based on a legal right under Sharia Islamic law. Much family law is primarily based on the religous law of the individual. Thus, there are three forms of family law in Egypt: Islamic, Christian, and secular (based on the French family laws).

There have been cases of serious human rights abuses over recent years. A state of emergency has been in place almost continuously since 1967. Security forces have tortured and abused prisoners and detainees, often with impunity. Prison conditions are poor. Security forces arbitrarily arrest individuals, and sometimes hold them in prolonged pretrial detention. The government restricts civil liberties, particularly freedom of speech and freedom of assembly. Egypt retains the death penalty for various crimes including certain cases of rape, murder, treason and organised drug trafficking. The four executions were reported to have been carried out in 2010 and one in 2011.

Although reforms to the legal system are expected following the Arab Spring comprehensive legal changes have not yet taken place. A draft law is under discussion to reassign powers of the Minister of Justice to the Supreme Judicial Council, with the aim of protecting judges from political interference and protecting their independence.

National Council for Human Rights, URL: http://www.nchregypt.org/en/

LOCAL GOVERNMENT

The current local administration system was introduced in 1960 with a view to giving the people an active share in running and organising their own affairs in a concerted effort with the central government. Accordingly, local councils were set up at gubernatorial, city and village levels. Each of these governorates (Muhafazat) is a legal entity, and is financially autonomous. Within the borders of his governate, a governor has much of the powers of the President of the Republic, but all affairs are run in co-ordination with the central government. The most recent municipal election were held in 2008.

The 29 governorates are: Ad Daqahliyah, Al Bahr al Ahmar (Red Sea), Al Buhayrah (El Beheira), Al Fayyum (El Faiyum), Al Gharbiyah, Al Iskandariyah (Alexandria), Al Isma'iliyah (Ismailia), Al Jizah (Giza), Al Minufiyah (El Monofia), Al Minya, Al Qahirah (Cairo), Al Qalyubiyah, Al Uqsur, Al Wadi al Jadid (New Valley), As Suways (Suez), Ash Sharqiyah, Aswan, Asyut, Bani Suwayf (Beni Suef), Bur Sa'id (Port Said), Dumyat (Damietta), Helwan, Janub Sina' (South Sinai), Kafr ash Shaykh, Matruh (Western Desert), Qina (Qena), Shamal Sina' (North Sinai), Sittah Uktubar and Suhaj (Sohag).

AREA AND POPULATION

Area

Egypt is located in north east Africa and has borders with Israel, Libya, the Sudan and the Mediterranean Sea to the north and the Red Sea to the east. It controls the Suez canal. The area of the country is estimated at 1,002,000 sq. km of which some 55,039 sq. km are inhabited. There are four broad regions: the Western Desert, which occupies over 60 per cent of the total area; the Eastern desert; the Sinai Peninsula; and the Nile Valley and Delta. The river Nile flows for over 1,000 miles through Egypt. 96 per cent of the population lives along its banks and in inhabited regions the population density is estimated at 1,096 people per square km. Over 90 per cent of the population is dependent on the Nile to meet their water needs. Most of the rest of the land is arid desert.

The climate is mild in the winter with rainfall increasing near the coast. Summers are hot and dry.

To view a map, visit: http://www.un.org/Depts/Cartographic/map/profile/egypt.pdf

Population

The population at the 2006 census was put at 76.5 million. 2010 estimates put it at 81.121 million with an annual growth rate of 1.8 per cent over the period 2000-10. In 2010 the median age of the population was 24 years. An estimated 8 per cent of the population was over 60 years old and an estimated 32 per cent under 15 years old. An estimated 43 per cent of the population lived in urban areas in 2010. In 2008, an estimated 17 million people lived in the capital, Cairo. Other major cities include Alexandria, Port Said, Suez, Ismailia, Aswan and Asyut.

The Arabic is the official language although English and French are widely spoken.

Births, Marriages, Deaths

In 2009 the average life expectancy was 69 years for males, 73 years for females. Healthy life expectancy was 60 years in 2007. In 2010, the crude birth rate was estimated to be 23.23 per 1,000 compared to 38.03 per 1,000 in 1986. The 2010 total fertility rate per woman was 2.7. The maternal mortality rate was estimated to be 82 per 100,000 live births in 2009 although other agencies estimated different rates. The crude death rate in 2010 was 5.9 per 1,000. (Source: http://www.who.int, World Health Statistics 2012)

Public Holidays 2014

1 January: New Year's Day
14 January: Mawlid al-Nabi (Muhammad's Birthday)*
25 April: Sinai Liberation Day
1 May: Labour Day
23 July: Revolution Day
29 July: Eid al-Fitr (Ramadan ends)*
6 October: Armed Forces Day
24 October: Suez Day
5 October: Eid al-Adha (Festival of Sacrifice)*
25 October: Al Hijira (Islamic New Year)
23 December: Victory Day (schools, universities)

The annual flooding of the Nile is a national holiday which varies each year but normally occurs mid to late August.

EGYPT

Islamic holidays including the Islamic New Year (Muharram), Id al-Adha, Birth of Muhammad, Ascension of Muhammad and Id al-Fitr are all national holidays but dates vary each year and rely on the sighting of the moon.

Coptic Christians celebrate Christmas on 7 January and New Year on 11 September.

EMPLOYMENT

The largest area of employment is the services sector, which employs around 51 per cent of the working population. The agricultural sector employs around 32 per cent and industry 17 per cent. Estimated figures for 2007 put the unemployment rate at 8.9 per cent. In 2000 it was estimated that over 16.5 per cent of the population was below the poverty line. The following table shows how the population was employed in 2008. The estimated unemployment rate in 2010 was 9.0 per cent.

Employment of Economic Activity

Sector	2008
Agriculture, hunting, & forestry	6,965,000
Fishing	151,000
Mining & quarrying	37,000
Manufacturing	2,567,000
Electricity, gas & water supply	297,000
Construction	2,268,000
Wholesale & retail trade & repair	2,387,000
Hotels & restaurants	462,000
Transport, storage & communications	1,575,000
Financial intermediation	166,000
Real estate, renting & business activities	448,000
Public admin. & defence, compulsory social security	1,890,000
Education	2,042,000
Health & social work	583,000
Other community, social & personal service activities	574,000
Private households with employed persons	66,000
Extra-Territorial oranisations & bodies	3,000
Other	26,000
Total	22,507,000

Source: Copyright © International Labour Organization (ILO Dept. of Statistics, http://laborsta.ilo.org)

BANKING AND FINANCE

Currency
The unit of currency is the Egyptian pound of 100 piastres. The financial centre is Cairo.

In mid-2001 Egypt devalued the pound. Following the events of September 11th Egypt further devalued the pound in order to encourage tourism and boost the economy. In January 2003 the government floated the pound in an attempt to increase its foreign currency reserves.

GDP/GNP, Inflation, National Debt
The Egyptian economy has developed from being very centralised to much more open. President Mubarak pushed through much economic reform in an attempt to attract foreign investment and to stimulate the economy. Despite this living conditions for many Egyptians remained poor which contributed to the civil unrest in 2011. The government increased social spending but the political uncertainty caused economic growth to slow dramatically. Tourism has been especially hard it. The economy is not expected to begin to recover until 2013.

The economy is heavily dependent on agriculture, tourism and cash remittances sent home from Egyptians working abroad. The increasing population is putting a strain on the agricultural sector and therefore the economy.

Egypt introduced a series of five year development plans in 1982 and these are scheduled to run continuously until 2016. The aims of these development plans include the raising of the standard of living of Egyptians, raising economic performance and reducing dependence on other countries. The plan set to run from 2007-2012 aims to get annual GDP growth to 8 per cent through a reduction in the national debt and rapid economic growth, building on economic reform including a continuing privatisation programme and the investment in infrastructure and communications in recent years. Reform of the education sector is necessary to maintain strong growth. The reforms produced strong growth in 2005-08, although it fell in 2009.

Tourism provides 11 per cent of the GDP and this sector has been adversely affected by terrorist attacks, including an attack on Luxor in 1997 when 58 tourists were killed and the attack on the USA on September 11 2001. However figures for 2003 showed an improvement in the sector.

GDP was estimated at US$230 billion in 2011 (per capita US$5,900) with a growth rate of 1.7 per cent.

After a period of relatively stable inflation rate in the 1990s when inflation was below 4 per cent, inflation is currently high which has caused some social tension with rising food prices. It reached 10 per cent in 2004, fell to 4.3 per cent in 2005. Inflation was 14.1 per cent in 2008, falling to 11 per cent in 2010.

In 2010 total foreign debt was put at US$32 billion.

In 2010, government debt amounted to almost 85 per cent of GDP.

Balance of Payments / Imports and Exports
Estimated figures put export earnings at US$27 billion in 2011, the same year import costs were an estimated US$55 billion. The major export products are crude oil and petroleum products, cotton yarn and textiles, engineering and metallurgical goods, agricultural goods and raw cotton. The major import products are machinery and transport equipment, livestock, food and beverages. Egypt's major trading partners are the United States, Italy, Germany and Japan.

Central Bank
Central Bank of Egypt, 31 Kasr El-Nil Street, Cairo, Egypt. Tel: +20 (0)2 3931 514, fax: +20 (0)2 3926361 / 3925045, e-mail: research@cbe.org.eg, URL: http://www.cbe.org.eg
Governor & Chairman of the Board: Dr Farouk Abd El Bakry El Okdah

Chambers of Commerce and Trade Organisations
Federation of Egyptian Industries, URL: http://www.fei.org.eg
American Chamber of Commerce in Egypt, URL: http://www.amcham.org.eg

MANUFACTURING, MINING AND SERVICES

Primary and Extractive Industries
Egypt is the second largest producer of refined oil products. In 2011 the average production of oil was 725.09 bbl/d. Domestic consumption was around 697,000 barrels per day. Net oil exports for 2011 were around 28,000 barrels per day. Figures for 2011 show that 51 per cent of crude oil exports went to India, 22 per cent to Italy and six per cent to China. The bulk of Egypt's oil comes from the Western Desert, the Eastern Desert, the Gulf of Suez and the Sinai Peninsula. It is estimated that with new finds Egypt's crude oil reserves stand at around 4.4 billion barrels. Exploration of new reserves is ongoing, and there have been new finds in the Mediterranean deepwater offshore and in mature areas in the Gulf of Suez and Nile. Currently there is exploration going on in the Western Desert area; if successful this would provide Egypt with oil that is cheaper to exploit. Egypt's nine refineries can process more than 700,000 barrels per day and there are plans to build another five refineries and petrochemical plants. Recent geological surveys have discovered the presence of iron, magnesite, titanomagnetite and gold.

Egypt has an estimated 77 trillion cubic feet of natural gas reserves (2011). By 2010 production had reached an estimated 2.6 trillion cubic feet, exceeding domestic consumption which is estimated at 1.6 trillion cubic feet. Currently major foreign companies including British Gas, BP-Amoco, ENI-Agip and Shell are involved in gas exploration and production in Egypt. There have been new discoveries offshore the Nile Delta and in the Western. Over 80 percent of Egypt's natural gas reserves and 70 percent of its production is located in the Mediterranean and Nile Delta. In 2000 an agreement was signed to build pipelines that would eventually carry gas from Egypt to Tripoli in Lebanon and to Turkey.

Coal production came into effect in 1995 at the El-Maghara mine, which exports coal to Turkey. The government intends expanding the port of El-Arish to accommodate coal exports from the mine. In 2005 Egyptian coal reserves were estimated at 23 million short tons. Figures for 2010 show that production stood at 0.03 million short tons while consumption that year stood at 1.00 million short tons.

Energy
In 2010 Egypt produced 138 billion kWh of electricity and consumption that year was 122 billion kWh. Approximately 79 per cent of electricity is thermal, which is generated by gas turbines, and 21 per cent is hydroelectric, mainly generated from the Aswan High Dam. Oil fired generating plants have all been converted to run on natural gas. A new part-solar plant is planned to be built in Kureimat. Recently all oil-fired plants were converted to run on natural gas and Compressed Natural Gas (CNG) is being utilised as fuel for over 20,000 taxis in Cairo which have been converted to use CNG. These taxis are serviced by 17 CNG filling stations which were recently built. Solar heating is becoming increasingly popular, especially in remote areas, with 400,000 domestic heating units in operation, saving more than 120,000 tons of oil. There are currently 30,200 km of power lines which have enabled Egypt to supply electricity to almost all of its applicants. In 2001 Egypt signed an agreement with Syria and Jordan that would link the electricity grids of those countries.

Total energy consumption was estimated at 7.8 quadrillion Btus in 2009. (Source: EIA)

Manufacturing
The industrial sector is now one of the largest in the Egyptian economy. It is also regarded as one of the most important because of its role in economic and social development, as well as its contribution to other sectors such as agriculture, electricity and transport. Successive development plans have provided for greater co-ordination between the development of the heavy, medium and consumer industries in relation to each other and also in relation to the requirements of the market, both domestic and foreign. In the past 25 years this sector increased its production and executed a wide range of projects which had the effect of increasing the national income. These efforts were aided by an extensive electrification programme. Industry has benefited from the general trend towards privatisation. Companies remaining within the public sector will profit from new legislation, aimed at improved organisation and flexibility. The main manufactured goods are textiles, furniture, chemicals, petrochemicals, iron and steel products, aluminium, cement, ceramics, pharmaceuticals, military equipment and food processing.

Service Industries
In the early 1990s tourism was a growth industry and is Egypt's largest foreign currency earner. There were 3.1 million visitors in 1995/96. However, the tourist industry was badly hit in 1997 by terrorist activity at Luxor. There has been increased government and private spending in this sector and an increase in the domestic market. During the period 1999-00, 5.3 million tourists visited Egypt, generating revenues of US$4,313.8 million. Tourism directly employs around 150,000 people. Following the terrorist attacks on 11 September 2001 in the USA, tourism suffered world wide but the Middle East was particularly hit. In an effort to make Egypt a more attractive proposition to foreign travellers the Egyptian pound was

devalued. In 2003 the tourism sector showed signs of recovery with over 6 million visitors. This rose to over 8.5 million in 2006. Over 65 per cent of visitors come from Europe, approximately 25 per cent from the Middle East and 11 per cent from the US.

Agriculture

The cultivatable area of Egypt is comparatively small in proportion to the whole, just 2,801,000 hectares being confined to the Nile valley and delta and the oases. The development of agriculture depends almost entirely on irrigation from the flood waters of the Nile. Barrages have been erected at several places to conserve flood water and to ensure adequate supplies during the growing season. The benefits accruing from the Aswan High Dam project, now completed, are an expansion of the cultivatable area by 1.3 million acres, to a total of 7.8 million acres. The project has also converted 700,000 acres from the basic irrigation system to perennial irrigation. Other benefits are an adequate supply of water for the irrigation of the present and newly cultivated areas, as well as the land under reclamation; an increase in the productivity of the cultivated land, and a major expansion in the cultivation of the rice crop for export. In 1997 Egypt became self-sufficient in rice, vegetables, fruits, poultry, fish, milk and eggs, and had a surplus for export. Sugar production increased to around 11 million tons. Recent figures show that agriculture employs 4,820,000 people directly and in food processing industries. Main exported produce is rice, onions, other vegetables and peanuts. Recently fruit and flowers have begun to be grown for export.

Agricultural Production in 2010

Produce	Int. $'000	Tonnes
Tomatoes	3,157,921	8,544,990
Rice, paddy	1,152,330	4,329,500
Buffalo milk, whole, fresh	1,102,360	2,763,700
Indigenous buffalo meat	1,076,797	400,038
Indigenous cattle meat	1,014,472	375,539
Indigenous chicken meat	975,895	685,124
Cow milk, whole, fresh	898,517	2,879,300
Wheat	842,335	7,169,000
Grapes	777,452	1,360,250
Dates	690,957	1,352,950
Potatoes	546,044	3,643,220
Olives	489,950	611,900

*unofficial figures
Source: http://faostat.fao.org/site/339/default.aspx Food and Agriculture Organization of the United Nations, Food and Agricultural commodities production

Fishing

Figures for 2010 put the total fishing catch atfor pelagic fish at 35,000 tonnes, freshwater fish at 574,000 tonnes and demersal fish 216,000 tonnes.

COMMUNICATIONS AND TRANSPORT

Travel Requirements

US, Canadian, Australian and EU citizens require a passport valid for at least six months. Visitors from all countries except the USA and the EU must register with the police within a week of arrival (this is usually done through the hotels). Visas are required by the aforementioned nationals, except EU citizens travelling to Sharm el Sheikh, Dahab, Newiba or Taba for visits of up to 14 days, (who receive an entry permission stamp on arrival), and those continuing their journey to a third country within 24 hours and remaining in the airport.

Proof of yellow fever immunization is required if arriving from an infected area. Evidence of an AIDS test is required for everyone staying over thirty days, for the purpose of studying or working in Egypt. Visit the Egyptian Ministry of Foreign Affairs web site at http://www.mfa.gov.eg for the most current visa information. Nationals not referred to above should contact the embassy to check visa requirements.

National Airlines

Egyptair, URL: http://www.egyptair.com.eg

International Airports

There are international airports in Cairo (URL: http://www.cairo-airport.com/), Luxor, Sinai, Hurghada and Alexandria, as well as many domestic airports.

In 2007, there were an estimated 125,000 aircraft departures from Cairo International Airport. An estimated 12.6 million passengers passed through the airport. A third terminal is due to be completed in 2009.

Railways

The state railway system covers 8,600 km and more than 460 million passenger journeys (excluding underground journeys). 13 million tons of freight are also transported annually. The main line travels from Alexandria to Aswan. Recent work has been done to the rail infrastructure including upgrades to the following lines: Qalyoub-Menouf-Tanta, New Valley-Red Sea.

Cairo now has its own underground system, the first in Africa. It links the governorates of Cairo, Qaliobiya and Giza. The final phase of the second line, Shubra el-Kheima-Giza, was recently completed. Alexandria has a tramway system.

Roads

The total length of paved roads is 50,000 km. There are seven bridges over the Nile. Vehicles are driven on the right.

Shipping

The Suez Canal plays an important role in the transport of oil which is exported from the Persian Gulf but competition from oil pipelines and alternative routes have caused a decline in tanker traffic. In an attempt to revive the industry the canal has been deepened to accommodate large bulk carriers, transit fees were not increased for four years and discounts have been offered to tankers carrying liquified natural gas and oil. The Suez Canal Authority is presently continuing with enlargement projects to enable the canal to accommodate fully laden very large crude carriers. In 2004 approximately 16,850 vessels passed through the Suez Canal with receipts of over US$300 million.

Waterways

In addition to the Suez Canal, Egypt has around 3,300 km of waterways. Much of the Nile is navigable as is Lake Nasser and the Alexandria-Cairo waterway. There is also a system of small canals in the Nile Delta. A ferry service runs from Aqaba across to Nuweiba on Egypt's Sinai peninsula another service runs from Aswan to Wadi Halfa in Sudan.

Pipelines

The alternative for the transport of oil is the Sumed pipeline, which is owned by the Arab Petroleum Company, a joint venture between Egypt (50 per cent), Saudi Arabia (15 per cent), Kuwait (15 per cent), the UAE (15 per cent), and Qatar (5 per cent).

Ports and Harbours

The main ports are Alexandria, Port Said, Al Adabia, Safaga, Damietta, Dekheila and Nowaba. The port capacity is 50.7 million tons.

HEALTH

Egypt has a state scheme which includes provision for sickness benefits and health insurance. In 2009, Egypt spent approximately 5.6 per cent of its total budget on healthcare, accounting for 39.5 per cent of all healthcare spending. External resources contributed 1.5 per cent of total expenditure. Total expenditure on health care equated to 4.8 per cent of the country's GDP. Per capita total expenditure was estimated at US$114 in 2009.

In 2005-10, there were 225,565 doctors (density per 10,000 population, 35.2), 280,561 nurses and midwives (density per 10,000 population, 35.2), 133,107 pharmaceutical personnel (density per 10,000 population, 16.7), 9,531 environment and public health workers (density per 10,000 population 1.00), 26,553 laboratory health workers (density 3 per 10,000 population) and approximately 33,476 dentists (density per 10,000 population, 4.2). Latest estimates in 2009 put the number of bed places as at 17 per 10,000 population.

In 2010 the infant mortality rate (probability of dying before first birthday) was 19 per 1,000 live births and under-fives mortality rate was 22 per 1,000 live births. The most common causes of death for children aged five years or less were: prematurity 30 per cent, congenital anomalies 21 per cent, diarrhoeal diseases 7 per cent and pneumonia 11 per cent. An estimated 6.8 per cent of children were thought to be underweight in 2009 and over 30.7 per cent were classified as stunted.

In 2010, an estimated 95 per cent of the population had sustainable access to improved sanitation and an estimated 99 per cent of the population had sustainable access to improved drinking water. (Source: http://www.who.int, World Health Statistics 2012)

EDUCATION

The Egyptian government is committed to improving the education system and education is free at all levels. According to the latest UNESCO figures, an estimated 17 per cent of children were enrolled in pre-primary school in 2007.

Primary education was made compulsory in 1952. An estimated 94 per cent of girls and 98 per cent of boys attended primary school in 2007, the pupil:teacher ratio was 27:1. An estimated 98 per cent of children complete primary education. An estimated 4 per cent repeat some primary education.

Secondary education takes place at general and technical levels. An estimated 86 per cent of pupils progress from primary to secondary education. Figures for 2006 showed that 78 per cent of girls and 82 per cent of boys of secondary school age attended secondary school. Recently computer science became a topic in 2,000 schools, 175 schools were linked on the internet, computerised physics laboratories were downloaded for 700 secondary schools, and an e-mail service was introduced for 2,136 schools.

An estimated 22 per cent of pupils go onto higher education.

In 1995 the adult illiteracy rate was 49 per cent which led to a large programme of adult education and in 1998 the Egyptian Authority for Combating Illiteracy and Adult Education was awarded the UNESCO prize for work in this field. According to 2006 UNESCO figures, the adult literacy rate has now reached 83.3 per cent for males and 59.7 per cent for females. For the group aged 15-24 years the rates are 90.3 for males and 80.3 for females.

An estimated 12 per cent of government spending is allocated to education. (Source: UNESCO)

RELIGION

Islam is the state religion and Egyptians are predominantly Sunni Muslims. Around 12 per cent of the population are Christians, mainly Coptic Christians.

Egypt has a religious liberty rating of 2 on a scale of 1 to 10 (10 is most freedom). (Source: World Religion Database)

EL SALVADOR

COMMUNICATIONS AND MEDIA

The Egyptian press is one of the most influential in the region. There is media criticism of the government but libel and 'insults' can result in imprisonment. Internet access was cut for a time in early 2011 in an effort to end political unrest. Social networks were used to organise anti-government demonstrations.

Newspapers
Al Ahram, Cairo. State-owned. Circ: 1,228,281, URL: http://www.ahram.org.eg
Al Gomhuria, Cairo. State-owned. Circ: 650,000, URL: http://www.algomhuria.net.eg/
Al Wafd, Circ: 360,000, Semi state-owned. URL: http://www.alwafd.org/
Al Akhbar, Circ: 250,000, URL: http://www.elakhbar.org.eg/
Al Missa, Cairo. Circ: 105,000, URL: http://www.almessa.net.eg/
Middle East Times, URL: http://www.metimes.com/

Broadcasting
Broadcasting is a mixture of state and private operators. There are two main state-run television stations and six provincial stations. Domestic television broadcasting is state-owned (ETV). (URL: http://www.ertu.org/). Egypt has its own satellite, Nilesat 101. Private TV stations first aired in 2001. The state monopoly on radio stations ended in 2003. There are now some 70 state-run radio stations and two privately owned stations.

Telecommunications
The telephone system was upgraded in the 1990s. In 2008 there were approximately 9.6 million telephone lines, compared to 5.25 million in 1997. In 1996 mobile phone services were introduced with 100,000 lines. By 2009 an estimated 55 million mobile phones were in use.

Figures for 2009 show that Egypt had over 16 million internet users.

ENVIRONMENT

The rapidly growing population and economic sector have led to an increased consumptio of energy which has resulted in increased air pollution. Air quality monitoring an pollution-control technology have been implemented. Further environmental problems bein experienced by Egypt are loss of agricultural land due to urbanisation and windblown sand increasing soil salinisation, desertification, oil pollution threatening coral reefs, beaches an marine life, water pollution from agricultural pesticides, raw sewage and industrial effluent and limited natural fresh water supplies from the Nile.

Egypt is a party to the following international agreements: Biodiversity, Climate Change Climate Change-Kyoto Protocol, Desertification, Endangered Species, Environmenta Modification, Hazardous Wastes, Law of the Sea, Marine Dumping, Ozone Layer Protectio Ship Pollution, Tropical Timber 83, Tropical Timber 94, and Wetlands.

In 2010, Egypt's emissions from the consumption of fossil fuels totaled 195.55 million metr tons of carbon dioxide. In 2007, Egypt produced 242.0 ODP tons of ozone depleting CFC (Source: EIA)

SPACE PROGRAMME

Egypt's space programme is focussed on research and the building of remote sensing satellite for the peaceful and sustainable development of the country. The EgyptSat-1 satellite Egypt's first experimental satellite for remote sensing. It was launched in 2007. A secon which much greater Egyptian input into the engineering, is due to be launched in 2012 an a third in 2017. Egypt has a satellite control station near Cairo, and data receiving station near Cairo and Aswan. The data coverage of the Aswan station includes south Europe, Middl East and part of Africa.
National Authority for Remote Sensing and Space Sciences, UR http://www.narss.sci.eg/

EL SALVADOR
Republic of El Salvador
República de El Salvador

Capital: San Salvador (Population estimate: 1.8 million)

Head of State: Mauricio Funes (President) (page 1427)

Vice-President: Salvador Sanchez Ceren (page 1508)

National Flag: A tricolour fesswise, blue, white, blue, the centre stripe charged with the national coat of arms.

CONSTITUTION AND GOVERNMENT

Constitution
El Salvador became an Independent Republic in 1841 when the Central American Federation, which had comprised the states of Guatemala, El Salvador, Honduras, Nicaragua and Costa Rica, was dissolved.

The Constitution was revised in 1962 to include universal male and female suffrage and provides for a unicameral legislative assembly consisting of 84 members elected for a three-year term. The current constitution dates from 1983.

Civil war prevented any political progress throughout the 1980s and after intensive negotiations by the United Nations a peace plan was signed in January 1992 by the government and the left-wing Farabundo Marti National Liberation Front.

To consult the full constitution, please visit:
http://www.asamblea.gob.sv/recursos-visuales/imagenesportlets/portlet-constitucion-vigente.png/view

International Relations
El Salvador is a member of the United Nations and several of its specialised agencies; the Organisation of American States (OAS), the Central American Common Market (CACM), The Central American Parliament (PARLACEN) and the Central American Integration System (SICA). El Salvador is a member of the World Trade Organisation (WTO) and is pursuing regional free trade agreements. Together with its neighbours, El Salvador negotiated a Political Dialogue and Co-operation Agreement with the EU in 2004.

In 2004, El Salvador was the first country to ratify the Central American Free Trade Agreement (CAFTA) with the USA, the other countries being Guatemala, Honduras, Nicaragua, Costa Rica and the Dominican Republic. During 2004 and early 2005 several Central American countries signed bilateral border agreements to simplify customs procedures.

El Salvador and Honduras fought a 100-hour Soccer War in 1969 over disputed border areas and friction arising from the 300,000 Salvadoreans who had emigrated to Honduras in search of land and employment. The catalyst was a series of soccer matches between the two countries. They formally signed a peace treaty on 30 October 1980, putting the border dispute before the International Court of Justice (ICJ). In September 1992, the Court awarded most of the disputed land to Honduras. In December 2003 the ICJ declined El Salvador's applicatio for a revision of its ruling. El Salvador has allegedly refused to put into effect the ICJ' judgement, and Honduras has raised the issue with the UN Security Council.

Recent Events
Recovery from the civil war has been hampered by natural disasters. In 1998, Hurricane Mitc struck Central America, leaving 239 San Salvadoreans dead and 500,000 homeless. In Januar 2001, two earthquakes killed some 1,200 people and left a million homeless, and in Octobe 2005, many people had to leave their homes after the volcano Ilamatepec (also known a Santa Ana) erupted. Two days later, Tropical Storm 'Stan' hit the region, causing floodin and landslides. An estimated 31 people died, and 8,500 were left homeless.

El Salvador was the first Central American country to implement a regional free trad agreement with the US, in March 2006.

The former rebel movement, Farabundo Marti Liberation Front (FMLN), won parliamentar elections on the 18th January 2009, but failed to win an outright majority. Their leader, th moderate former television journalist Mauricio Funes, won the 15 March presidential elections

In November 2009, El Salvador was hit by severe floods causing mudslides and an estimate 140 people were killed and thousands more were left homeless. Torrential rains struck agai in October 2011 leading to flooding and the deaths of several people.

In October 2011, Central America was hit by devastating floods, several people in El Salvado lost their lives.

Legislature
The legislature is unicameral and its 84 members are elected for a three-year term.
Legislative Assembly, (Asamblea Legislativa), Palacio Legislativo, Centro de Gobierno, Apartado Postal 2682, San Salvador, El Salvador. URL: http//www.asamblea.gob.s

---

Cabinet (as at June 2013)
Minister of Foreign Affairs: Hugo Martínez Bonilla (page 1472)
Minister of Security and Justice: David Victoriano Munguia Payes
Minister of Economy: Hector Dada Hirezi
Minister of Defence: Jose Atilio Benitez Parada
Minister of Education: Vice President Salvador Sanchez Ceren
Minister of Livestock and Agriculture: Guillermo Lopez Suarez
Minister of Health and Social Assistance: Dr Maria Isabel Rodriguez
Minister of Public Works, Transport, Housing and Urban Development: Manue Quinteros Gerson Martinez
Minister of the Environment: Herman Rosa Chavez
Minister of Labour and Social Welfare: Humberto Centeno
Minister of Tourism: José Napoleon Duarte
Minister of Finance: Carlos Caceres
Minister of the Interior: Gregorio Zelayandia

Ministries
Office of the President, Alameda Nauel Enrique Araujo 5505, El Salvador. Tel: +503 48 9000, fax: +503 243 9947, e-mail: casapres@casapres@gob.sv, URL: http://www.casapres.gob.sv/
Office of the Vice-President, Alameda Nauel Enrique Araujo 5505, El Salvador. Tel: +503 248 9108/10, fax: +503 243 9951, e-mail: casapres@casapres@gob.sv, URL: http://www.casapres.gob.sv/
Ministry of Foreign Affairs, Colonia San Benito. Calle Circunvalación, No.227, San Salvador, El Salvador. Tel: +503 243 9648 / 9649, fax: +503 243 9656, e-mail: webmaster@rree.gob.sv, URL: http://www.rree.gob.sv/
Ministry of Finance, Diagonal Centroamérica y Av. Alvarado, Edificio las Tres Torres, El Salvador. Tel: +503 244 3000, fax: +503 244 6408, e-mail: webmaster@mh.gob.sv, URL: http://www.mh.gob.sv/
Ministry of the Treasury, Edificio Las Tres Torres, San Salvador, El Salvador. Tel:+503 244 3000, fax: +503 2244 6408, URL: http://www.mh.gob.sv
Ministry of the Interior and Justice, Centro de Goberno, El Salvador. e-mail: desarrollo.tecnologico@gobernacion.gob.sv, URL: http://www.gobernacion.gob.sv/
Ministry of Public Works, Transport, Housing and Urban Development, Plantel la lechuza, Carretera a Santa Tecla. Km 5 1/2, San Salvador C.A., El Salvador. Tel: +503 223 8040 / 279 3723, e-mail: ministro@mop.gob.sv, URL: http://www.mop.gob.sv/
Ministry of the Economy, Alameda Juan Pablo II y Calle Guadelupe, C1-C2, Centro de Gobierno, San Salvador, El Salvador. Tel: +503 281 1122, fax: +503 221 5446, e-mail: marzel@minec.gob.sv, URL: http://www.minec.gob.sv/
Ministry of Education, Alameda Juan Pablo II y Calle Guadelupe, Plan Maesiro, Centro de Gobierno, San Salvador, El Salvador. Tel: +503 281 0259, fax: +503 281 0261, URL: http://www.mined.gob.sv/
Ministry of National Defence, Alameda Manual Enrique Araujo 5 1/2, Carretera a Santa Tecla, San Salvador, El Salvador. Tel: +503 263 6388, fax: +503 298 2005, e-mail: fuerzaarmada@saltel.net, URL: http://fuerzaarmada.gob.sv/
Ministry of Labour and Social Security, Paseo General Escalon Número 4122, San Salvador, El Salvador. Tel: +503 264 7510 / 7515, fax: +503 263 5427, e-mail: mestrada@mtps.gob.sv, URL: http://www.mtps.gob.sv/
Ministry of Agriculture and Livestock, Final 1a Avenida Norte y Avenida Manuel Gallardo, Nueva San Slavador, El Salvador. Tel: +502 288 4443, fax: +503 229 9271, e-mail: alabi@mag.gob.sv, URL: http://www.mag.gob.sv/
Ministry of Public Health and Social Welfare, Calle Arce 827, San Salvador, El Salvador. Tel: +503 221 0966, fax: +503 221 0991, e-mail: webmaster@mspas.gob.sv, URL: http://www.mspas.gob.sv/
Ministry of the Environment, Calle y Colonia Las Mercedes, Edificio Marn anexo al edificio Ista No. 2, San Salvador, El Salvador. Tel: +503 260 8876, fax: +503 223-0444, e-mail: medioambiente@marn.gob.sv, URL: http://www.marn.gob.sv/

Political Parties
Christian Democratic Party (PDC), URL: http://www.pdc.org.sv/index.htm; Democratic Change (CD), http://www.cambiodemocratico.com.sv; Farabundo Martí National Liberation Front (FMLN), http://www.fmln.org.sv; National Conciliation Party (PCN), URL: http://www.pcn.com.sv; Nationalist Republican Alliance (Arena), URL: www.arena.com.sv.

Elections
The most recent presidential elections were held in March 2009, and were won by Mauricio Funes of the former Marxist rebel FMLN party. With 51.3 per cent of the vote, he defeated the Arena party's Rodrigo Avila, who garnered 48.7 per cent of the vote. Opponents fear he may become a puppet of Venezuela's President Hugo Chavez. Arena had won every presidential election since the end of El Salvador's civil war 18 years previously.

Parliamentary elections were held on 18 January 2009. The former rebel movement, Farabundo Marti Liberation Front (FMLN), won by a slim margin of 35 seats against 32 seats for the governing conservative party Arena. Either of the major parties will be able to block legislation requiring a two-thirds (56 vote) supermajority. The most recent election was held in March 2012, Arena won 33 seats and the FMLN 31 seats.

Diplomatic Representation
Embassy of the USA, Boulevard Santa Elena, Antiguo Cuscatlán La Libertad, El Salvador. Tel: +503 2278 4444, fax: +503 2278 6011, URL: http://sansalvador.usembassy.gov/
Ambassador: Mari Carmen Aponte (page 1379)
British Embassy, Honorary British Consulate, P. O. Box 242, San Salvador, El Salvador. The embassy closed in 2003 and embassy staff are now resident in Guatemala City. Tel: +503 281 5555, e-mail: embassy@intelnett.com; URL: http://www.ukinguatemala.fco.gov.uk
Ambassador: Sarah Dickson (page 1415)
Embassy of El Salvador, 2308 California Street NW, Washington, DC 20008, USA. Tel: +1 202 265 9671, fax: +1 202 234 3834, e-mail: correo@elsalvador.org, URL: http://www.elsalvador.org/embajadas/eeuu/home.nsf/home
Ambassador: Francisco Altschul
Embassy of El Salvador, 8 Dorset Square, London NW1 6PU, UK. Tel: +44 (0)20 7224 9800, fax: +44 (0)20 7224 9878, e-mail: elsalvadorembassy@rree.gob.sv
Head of Mission: Werner Matias Romero
Permanent Representative of El Salvador to the United Nations, 46 Park Avenue, New York, NY 10016, USA. Tel: +1 212 679 1616 / 1617, fax: +1 212 725 3467
Ambassador: Joaquin Alexander Maza Martelli

LEGAL SYSTEM

There is a Supreme Court of Justice, several courts of first and second instance, a court of third instance and some minor courts. There are also special courts, appointed by the National Assembly, and military tribunals, selected by the Supreme Court. The Supreme Court appoints judges of the first instance, whilst judges of second and third instance are elected by the National Assembly. There are 13 justices on the Supreme Court. All judges serve renewable terms of three years.

The 12-year civil war, which ended in 1992, left 75,000 dead and 1 million displaced. Since then, the country has made considerable progress in reconciling the one-time warring factions and in moving forward the democratic process. There is no longer any systemic abuse of human rights. However, there is now a high level of violent crime and public security is in need of improvement. There are high levels of impunity from prosecution, and judicial corruption. Prison conditions are harsh and violent. The death penalty is retained only for exceptional crimes, such as crimes under military law or crimes committed in exceptional circumstances

Corte Suprema de Justicia, URL: http://www.csj.gob.sv
President of the Supreme Court: Dr. José Salomon Padilla

Commission of Human Rights for El Salvador, URL: http://www.cdhes.org.sv/

LOCAL GOVERNMENT

El Salvador is divided into 14 departments for administrative purposes: Ahuachapán, Cabanas, Chalatenango, Cuscutlán, La Libertad, La Paz, La Unión, Morazán, Santa Ana, San Miguel, San Salvador, San Vicente, Sonsonate, Usulután. The most recent municipal elections were held in 2009.

AREA AND POPULATION

Area
El Salvador is the most densely populated state in the continent of America (around 298 people per sq. km.) It is located on the Pacific coast of Central America bordered by Guatemala in the west and Honduras in the north and east. It is the smallest Central American country (total area - 21,073 sq. km.), and is the only one without a coastline on the Caribbean Sea. Mountains divide the country into three distinct regions - the southern coastal belt, the central valleys and plateaus, and the northern mountains. The climate is semitropical, with wet and dry seasons.

To view a map of El Salvador, please consult:
http://www.un.org/Depts/Cartographic/map/profile/elsalvad.pdf

El Salvador's location on the Pacific Ring of Fire makes the country vulnerable to seismic activity and storms. In 2001 it was hit by devastating earthquakes resulting in the deaths of 1,200 people and over a million homeless. The Ilamatepec volcano (also known as Santa Ana) erupted in October 2005, forcing 5,000 people to leave their homes permanently.

Population
The estimated population in 2010 was 6.193 million, with an annual average growth rate of 0.4 per cent in the period 2000-10. In 2010, 58 per cent of the population were aged between 15 and 60, 32 per cent were under the age of 15 and 10 per cent were over the age of 60. The median age was 23 years.

Approximately 64 per cent of inhabitants live in rural areas. The population of San Salvador is around 2.2 million; Santa Ana is the second most popular city with around 136,000 people and San Miguel is the third most populated with some 87,000. Almost 90 per cent of the population is of mixed Indian and Spanish extraction; around one per cent is indigenous, though very few Indians have retained their customs and traditions.

Spanish is the official language although indigenous minorities speak Nahuatl.

Births, Marriages, Deaths
Estimates for 2010 put the birth rate at 20.3 per 1,000 population and the death rate at 6,7 per 1,000 inhabitants. The infant mortality rate was 20 per 1,000 live births. The average fertility rate was 2.3 per woman in 2010. Life expectancy at birth was estimated at 75 years (68 years for males and 76 years for females). Healthy life expectancy is 61 years. (Source: http://www.who.int, World Health Statistics 2012)

Public Holidays 2014
1 January: New Year's Day
17 April: Maundy Thursday
18 April: Good Friday
21 April: Easter Monday
1 May: Labour Day
August: Festivities of El Salvador (first week in August)
15 September: Independence Day
14 October: Discovery of America Day
2 November: All Souls' Day
24 December: Christmas Eve
25 December: Christmas Day
31 December: New Year's Eve

EMPLOYMENT

Figures for 2007 indicate a workforce of 2.5 million with an unemployment rate of 6.4 per cent down from 6.6 per cent in 2006 before rising to 7.1 per cent in 2010.

Employment by economic sector in 2007

Sector	No. of employees
Agriculture	422,300
Fishing	13,500
Mining and quarrying	3,700
Manufacturing	403,600

EL SALVADOR

- continued

Electricity, gas and water supply	10,200
Construction	148,400
Wholesale and Retail Trade; Repair of vehicles, motorcycles and personal goods; Hotels and restaurants	720,600
Transport, Storage and Communications	103,200
Financial Services; Real Estate, renting and business activities	114,400
Public Administration and Defence; Compulsory Social Security	98,700
Education	90,000
Health and Social Work; Other community, social and personal service activities	178,400
Private household employees	117,700
Not classifiable by economic activity	400
Total	**2,419,200**

Source: Copyright © International Labour Organization (ILO Dept. of Statistics, http://laborsta.ilo.org)

The textile and apparel (maquila) sector directly provides 70,000 jobs and the services sector, including retail and financial, have also shown strong employment growth, with about 49.8 per cent of the total labour force now employed in the sector.

BANKING AND FINANCE

Currency
One Colón = 100 centavos
In 2001, the US Dollar became legal tender in El Salvador; it has now replaced the Colón.

GDP/GNP, Inflation, National Debt
The economy has been growing steadily since the end of the civil war in 1992, moving from an agricultural economy, centred around coffee production, to a largely services-based economy focusing on commerce and financial services. Manufacturing has also grown, with the development of offshore assembly for re-export industries. A commitment to free markets and careful fiscal management has benefited and helped to diversify the economy. Privatisation of the banking system, telecommunications, public pensions, electrical distribution and some electrical generation has been a spur to economic growth, as have the reduction of import duties, the elimination of price controls and the enforcement of intellectual property rights.

Remittances from Salvadorans working abroad are an important source of income; these were estimated to total $3.7 billion in 2007.

GDP was estimated at US$22.3 billion in 2008, and the annual real growth rate was 3.2 per cent this was predicted to fall to a rate of -3.4 per cent in 2009 is response to the global economic downturn. The agriculture sector contributed 11.2 per cent to GDP and industry approximately 20.6 per cent. GDP was estimated to be US$21.2 billion in 2010 with growth of over 1 per cent.

Total external debt as at 2010 was about $11 billion, approximately 50 per cent of GDP. Inflation remains low and stable; it was estimated to be 1.1 per cent in 2010.

In September 2007, a five year anti-poverty Compact between the government and the Millennium Challenge Corporation (MCC) came into effect; its aim is to stimulate economic growth and reduce poverty in the country's northern region, through investment in education, public services, enterprise development, and the transport infrastructure.

Foreign Investment
Laws now encourage and protect foreign investments. Special grants are given to industries which export their output to the Central American Common Market.

Balance of Payments / Imports and Exports
El Salvador has pursued economic integration with its Central American neighbours and negotiated trade agreements with the Dominican Republic, Chile, Mexico, Panama, Taiwan, Colombia, and the United States. Central American countries began negotiating an Association Agreement with the EU in 2007.

Exports in 2007 grew 7.4 per cent while imports grew 13.1 per cent. As in previous years, the large trade deficit was offset by family remittances.

El Salvador's major exports are coffee, garments (maquila) and textiles, medicines, sugar and shrimp. Whilst coffee used to account for over 50 per cent of export earnings, by 2002 revenue had dropped steeply due to the worldwide slump in coffee prices. In 2010, total export revenues totalled US$4.5 billion. Major export destinations are the US (48 per cent in 2010) and members of the Central American Common Market (CACM, 35 per cent).

Imports cost El Salvador an estimated US$8.5 billion in 2010, the main commodities being consumer goods, capital goods, raw industrial materials, crude oil, petroleum and food. The US was the main supplier (36 per cent), with the CACM (19 per cent) being the major supplier.

Central Bank
Banco Central de Reserva de El Salvador, PO Box (01) 106, Alameda Juan Pablo II y 17 Avenida Norte, San Salvador, El Salvador. Tel: +503 2281 8400, fax: +503 2281 80113, e-mail: info@bcr.gob.sv, URL: http://www.bcr.gob.sv
President: Carlos Acevedo

Chambers of Commerce and Trade Organisations
Chamber of Commerce and Industry El Salvador, URL: http://www.camarasal.com/

MANUFACTURING, MINING AND SERVICES

Primary and Extractive Industries
Mining and raw material extraction accounts for less than 0.2 per cent of El Salvador's GDP. Its activities were severely curtailed by the civil war, with production limited to gold, silver, sea salt and limestone.

Because of the lack of oil reserves, El Salvador is dependent upon imports, which totalled 49,440 barrels per day in 2011; it receives oil under preferential terms and pricing from Mexico and Venezuela. Under the San Jose Pact, Mexico and Venezuela supply El Salvador with crude oil and petroleum products. Furthermore, Venezuela provides oil under the Caracas Energy Accord. El Salvador has one refinery, with capacity of 22,000 barrels per day.

In 2006, under the Caribbean Basins Initiative (CBI), El Salvador exported 7,500 barrels per day of ethanol to the U.S. The American Renewable Fuel Suppliers (ARFS) operates a 3,900 barrels per day ethanol plant near the port of Acajutla.
The country does not at present use natural gas.

Energy
El Salvador is the largest producer of geothermal energy in the region. In 2010, the country produced an estimated 6.07 billion kwh of electricity, and used around 5.39 billion kwh. There are two geothermal facilities in El Salvador, both operated by the state-owned company LaGeo. There are also seven thermal plants and four hydropower plants in El Salvador.

Manufacturing
Manufacturing industry contributes around 24 per cent of GDP. With the fall worldwide of coffee prices, El Salvador has tried to diversify its economy; the maquila industry (cutting and assembling of clothes for export to the US) has been particularly successful. Food, beverages, chemicals, medicines and electronics are also produced.

Services
El Salvador has a growing tourism industry with 1.1 million visitors in 2006. Another growing area is that of call centres.

Agriculture
Agriculture is an important economic sector, contributing some 11 per cent of GDP in 2007. The major cash crop grown is coffee, and shrimp and honey are now being produced for the export market. Other staples of the agriculture sector are maize, rice, beans and millet. Following the falling price of coffee in 2000 and the devastating earthquakes in 2001, coffee production has fallen.

Agricultural Production in 2010

Produce	Int. $'000*	Tonnes
Cow milk, whole, fresh	173,691	556,594
Indigenous chicken meat	169,403	118,929
Sugar cane	163,295	5,126,690
Coffee, green	104,506	97,273
Indigenous cattle meat	86,795	32,130
Mangoes, mangosteens, guavas	58,479	97,600
Hen eggs, in shell	53,666	64,705
Beans, dry	49,634	87,514
Papayas	20,150	71,000
Yautia (cocoyam)	19,480	40,000
Plantains	18,275	96,500
Sorghum	17,570	166,009

*unofficial figures
Source: http://faostat.fao.org/site/339/default.aspx Food and Agriculture Organization of the United Nations, Food and Agricultural commodities production

Fishing
The total catch for 2010 was put at 36,000 tonnes.

COMMUNICATIONS AND TRANSPORT

Travel Requirements
US, Canadian, Australian and EU citizens require a passport valid for at least six months to enter El Salvador. They do not require a visa for stays of up to 30 days. Citizens of Canada, Greece and the USA must buy a Tourist Card on entry. Other nationals should contact the embassy to check entry requirements.

In June 2006, El Salvador joined the Central America-4 (CA-4) Border Control Agreement, which allows the citizens of Guatemala, Honduras, Nicaragua and El Salvador to travel freely across the borders of the four countries. US citizens and other eligible foreign nationals entering one of the four countries may travel among the four without having to apply for additional visas or tourist entry permits. Foreigners expelled from any one of the countries are excluded for the entire CA-4 region. For further information on this, contact the El Salvador embassy.

Nationals not mentioned above should contact the embassy to check entry requirements.

National Airlines
TACA International Airlines, Altos Edificio Caribe 2 Piso, Segunda Planta, Colonia Escalón, San Salvador, El Salvador. Tel: +503 239 9155, fax: +503 223 3757, URL: http://www.taca.com

International Airports
Cuscatlán Airport, Comalapa

Railways
El Salvador has two rail systems whose combined network length is 674 km. The Salvador Railway connects the capital with Acajutla and Santa Ana, while the American-owned International Railways of Central America has a line from the part of La Unión via San Salvador to Zacapa (Guatemala) and Puerto Barrios. Rail services were suspended in 2002 but a commuter link between San Salvador and Apopa was reopened in 2007.

Roads
There are 12,164 km of roads in El Salvador of which 14 per cent are asphalt including the Salvadoran Section A of the Pan-American highway. Vehicles are driven on the right.

Ports and Harbours
The principal ports are Acajutla, La Liberatad and La Unión.

HEALTH

Health services are not readily accessible to a majority of the population. In the more isolated regions of El Salvador, there are almost no physicians, and government clinics often lack adequate personnel, equipment and medicines. Health care is provided by the state, funded by insurance contributions from the workforce, employers and the state.

In 2008, El Salvador spent approximately 12.3 per cent of its total budget on healthcare, accounting for 60.3 per cent of all healthcare spending. Total expenditure on health care equated to 6.8 per cent of the country's GDP. Per capita total spend equated to US$228. Figures for 2005-10 show that there are 11,542 physicians (16 per 10,000 population), 2,929 nurses (4.1per 10,000 population) and 4,669 dentistry personnel. There are an estimated 11 hospital beds per 10,000 population.

The infant mortality rate in 2010 was estimated at 14 per 1,000 live births and the child mortality rate was 16 per 1,000 live births. Around 0.5 per cent of the adult population is living with HIV/AIDS. In 2003, 1,400 people died of the disease. In 2010, HIV/AIDS accounted for 4 per cent of childhood deaths. Other major causes of death amongst young children (<5) were: diarrhoea (5 per cent), pneumonia (11 per cent), prematurity (15 per cent), congenital abnormalities (24 per cent) and injuries (11 per cent). Approximately 20 per cent of children aged less than five years old are classified as stunted.

According to the latest WHO figures, in 2010 approximately 88 per cent of the population had access to improved drinking water. In the same year, 87 per cent of the population had access to improved sanitation. The number of childhood deaths from diarrhoea has fallen substantially and now accounts for 4 per cent of childhood deaths, compared to over 13 per cent in 2006. (Source: http://www.who.int, World Health Statistics 2012)

EDUCATION

Primary education is free and obligatory, starts at age seven and lasts for nine years. Figures for 2007 indicate that just under half very young children attended a nursery school and 92 per cent of the relevant age group were enrolled in primary school. Secondary education lasts for three years and figures for 2007 show that 54 per cent of students of secondary school age were enrolled; this is below the regional average of 70 per cent (in 2006). There is a National University, and 13 private or church-affiliated universities. In 2007, 22 per cent of students went on to enroll in tertiary education, below the regional average of 31 per cent.

Some 13 per cent of government expenditure currently goes on education, equivalent to around three per cent of GDP.

Adult literacy was estimated to be around 82.0 per cent in 2007, though within the age group of 15-24 year olds the rate rose to 93.6 per cent. (Source: UNESCO, UIS)

RELIGION

Roman Catholicism is the dominant religion, with some 47 per cent of the population adhering to this faith. Protestantism is the second most popular faith in the country (29 per cent).

El Salvador has a religious liberty rating of 9 on a scale of 1 to 10 (10 is most freedom). (Source: World Religion Database)

COMMUNICATIONS AND MEDIA

Press freedom is guaranteed by the constitution.

Newspapers
Newspapers include:
El Diaro de Hoy, URL: http://www.elsalvador.com
La Prensa Grafica, San Salvador, URL: http://www.laprensagrafica.com/portada

Broadcasting
Broadcasting is dominated by the private sector. There are hundreds of radio stations. Cable television is also widely available.

Telecommunications
Mobile-cellular service providers are expanding services rapidly and in 2008 mobile-cellular density stood at nearly 100 per 100 people; growth in fixed-line services has slowed in the face of mobile-cellular competition, and there were 1.08 million lines in use in 2008. Mobile phone subscriptions were estimated to be 6.9 million in 2008.

Figures for 2008 indicate that some 800,000 Salvadorans were regular internet users.

ENVIRONMENT

El Salvador is known as the Land of Volcanoes, and is liable to frequent and sometimes destructive earthquakes and volcanic activity. It is also susceptible to hurricanes. Environmental concerns include deforestation, soil erosion, water pollution and the contamination of soils from disposal of toxic wastes.

El Salvador is party to the following international agreements: Biodiversity, Climate Change, Climate Change-Kyoto Protocol, Desertification, Endangered Species, Hazardous Wastes, Ozone Layer Protection and Wetlands. It has signed, but not ratified, the Law of the Sea.

In 2010, El Salvador's emissions from the consumption of fossil fuels totaled 6.48 million metric tons of carbon dioxide. (Source: EIA)

STATES OF THE WORLD

EQUATORIAL GUINEA

Republic of Equatorial Guinea

República de Guinea Ecuatorial

Capital: Malabo (formerly Santa Isavel) (Population estimate: 100,000)

Head of State: Brig. Gen. Teodoro Obiang Nguema Mbasogo (President) (page 1473)

Vice President: Ignacio Milam Tang (page 1477)

Second Vice President: Teodoro Nguema Obiang Manque

National Flag: Three horizontal stripes, green, white and red, with a triangle of blue on the staff side and the national coat of arms in the centre

CONSTITUTION AND GOVERNMENT

Constitution
Previously part of Spain's overseas territories, the colony was made an integral part of Spain as the Equatorial Region in 1959. Independence was granted on 12 October 1968.

Lt. Col. Teodoro Obiang Nguema Mbasogo came to power in 1979 by leading a military coup in which he overthrew his uncle, Francisco Nguema. He reshuffled the military council in 1986 and in 1987 formed a new governing political party, to which all wage earners were expected to contribute 3 per cent of their incomes. Parliamentary elections were last held in March 1999 but were denounced by the opposition. President Mbasogo has survived several attempted coups.

The Constitution was approved in November 1991 by a national referendum and was amended in January 1995. The President holds executive power and has a seven-year term of office, which is renewable indefinitely. Reforms to the constitution were discussed in 2011 including limiting the number of presidential terms to two and the creation of the post of vice-president. The reforms were approved in a referendum in November 2011.

To consult the full constitution, please visit:
http://www.wipo.int/wipolex/fr/details.jsp?id=7988

International Relations
Equatorial Guinea and Gabon are in dispute over the ownership of three islands in the Gulf of Guinea.

Recent Events
The election in 1999 saw a victory for the ruling Democratic Party of Equatorial Guinea. Opposition parties criticised the elections as fraudulent and many of the opposition party, Popular Union, were arrested. In 2001 some of the exiled opposition parties set up a coalition in Spain hoping to influence the political situation at home. In August 2003 they announced themselves as a government-in-exile.

In March 2004 a planned coup attempt against President Obiang Nguema was uncovered, 70 mercenaries were arrested in Zimbabwe and another 15 were arrested in Equatorial Guinea. Among those charged was Sir Mark Thatcher, son of former British Prime Minister Margaret Thatcher. He received a 3 million rand fine and a four-year suspended sentence

EQUATORIAL GUINEA

for his part in the plot. In June 2005 six Armenians convicted of taking part in the 2004 coup were given amnesties. In September 2005, 23 people, mainly military officers, were jailed for plotting the coup.

The government resigned en masse in August 2006 following the President's criticism that it was corrupt and had poor leadership. Ricardo Mangue Obama Nfubea was named prime minister, but was dismissed by the president on 9 July 2008, and replaced by Ignacio Milam Tang. A reshuffled cabinet was appointed on 14 July, composed entirely of PDGE members.

In February 2009, 15 people were arrested over an attack on the presidential palace. The government accused Nigeria of involvement, a claim denied by Nigeria. In August 2010 four alleged coup plotters were executed just hours after being found guilty.

In November 2010 a French appeal court authorised an investigation into corruption charges against President Obiang who has been accused of using state money to buy luxury homes in France. The US authorities are in the process of trying to seize some of the assets of the president's son, Teodoro Neguema Obiang Mangue. The assets amount to an estimated US$71 billion which they believe were bought using funds taken from the country. The assets include real estate, luxury cars and a private jet.

In May 2012 the government resigned and Vincente Ehate Tomi was appointed prime minister. The president's son, Teodorio Neguema Obiang Mangue, was promoted to vice president. In July France issued an arrest warrant for Teodoro following investigations into the misspending of public funds.

The ruling PDGE maintained its dominance in parliamentary elections held in May 2013.

Legislature

The 80-member House of Representatives holds legislative power and serves for a five-year term. The President nominates a Council of Ministers, headed by the Prime Minister.

House of Representatives of the People, (Camara de Representantes del Pueblo), PO Box 51, Malabo, Equatorial Guinea. Tel: +240 92539, fax: +240 9 3313, URL: http://guinea-equatorial.com/

Cabinet (as at June 2013)

Prime Minister: Vincent Ehate Tomi (page 1526)
First Deputy Prime Minister, in charge of Political and Democracy Affairs: Clemente Engonga Nguema Onguene
Second Deputy Prime Minister, in charge of Social and Human Rights Affairs: Alfonso Nsue Mokuy
Minister of State to the Presidency in charge of Missions: Alejandro Evuna Owono Asangono
Minister in charge of relations with Parliament: Angel Masie Mibuy
Minister of State in charge of Civil Cabinet: Braulio Ncogo Abegue
Minister of State to the Presidency, in charge of Regional Integration: Baltasar Engonga Edjo
Minister of State for National Defence: Gen. Antonio Mba Nguema
Minister of State for Justice & Religious Affairs: Francisco Javier Ngoma Mbengono
Minister Secretary General: Tomas Esona Ava
Minister of Foreign Affairs & International Co-operation: Agapito Mba Mokuy
Minister of Finance and Budgets: Marcelino Owono Edu
Minister of National Security: Nicholas Obama Nchama
Minister of Economy and Trade: Celestino Bacale Obiang
Minister of Transport, Technology, Posts and Telecommunications: Francisco Mba Ola Bahamonde
Minister of Plannning, Economic Development and Investment: Conrado Okenve Ndoho
Minister of Health and Social Welfare: Tomas Fernandez Galilea
Minister of Youth and Sports: Francisco Obama Asue
Minister of Education, & Science: Maria del Carmen Ekoro
Minister of Mines, Industry and Energy: Gabriel Mbega Obiang Lima
Minister of Labour and Social Security: Miguel Abia Biteo Borico
Minister of Public Service: Purificacion Lasaquero
Minister of Agriculture and Forestry: Miguel Oyono Ndong Mifumu
Minister for Social Affairs and Promotion of Women: Maria Epam Biribe
Minister of Fisheries and Environment: Cresencio Tamarite Castano
Minister of Information, Press & Radio: Augustin Nze Nfumu
Minister of Public Works and Infrastructure: Juan Nko Mbula

Ministries

Government Portal: URL: http://guinea-equatorial.com/
Ministry of Information, Tourism and Culture, Barrio Nzalang (antiguo Africa 2000), Malabo, Equatorial Guinea. Tel: +240 98221, fax: +240 92444, e-mail: nkat_fuen@hotmail.com
Ministry of Mines, Industry and Energy, Calle 12 de Octubre, Malabo, Eqatorial Guinea. Tel: +240 09 35 67, fax: +240 09 33 53, e-mail: d.shaw@ecqc.com, URL: http://www.equatorialoil.com/
Ministry of Finance, BP 404, Malabo, Equatorial Guinea. Tel: +240 93105, fax: +240 92043
Ministry of Agriculture and Forests, Apartado 504, Malabo, Equatorial Guinea.
Ministry of Finance and Budget, BP 404, Malabo, Equatorial Guinea. Tel: +240 09 31 05, fax: +240 09 20 43
Ministry of Economy, Commerce and Business Development, BP 404, Malabo, Equatorial Guinea. Tel: +240 09 31 05, fax: +240 09 20 43
Ministry of Foreign Affairs, International Co-operation, Malabo, Equatorial Guinea. Tel: +240 93220, fax: +240 9 3132
Ministry of Information, Culture and Tourism, Malabo, Equatorial Guinea. URL: http://www.ceiba-guinea-ecuatorial.org
Ministry of Public Works and Infrastructure, Malabo, Eqatorial Guinea. Tel: +240 09 34 60

Political Parties

Partido Democrático de Guinea Ecuatorial (PDGE); Convergencia para la Democracia Social (CpDS); Unión Democrática Nacional de Guinea Ecuatorial; Party for Progress of Equatorial Guinea (PPGE). There are also many small minor parties.

Elections

The President and the House of Representatives are elected by universal adult suffrage. Presidential elections took place on 15 December 2002. President Mbasogo was re-elected with over 90 per cent of the vote. Voting irregularities were alleged. The most recent elections were held in November 2009 having been brought forward from 2010. President Mbasogo was declared the winner with over 90 per cent of the vote but opponents complained of voting irregularities. The main opposition candidate, Placido Mico Abogo, gained just 3.6 per cent of the vote.

The most recent parliamentary election was held on 26 May 2013. The president's Democratic Party of Equatorial Guinea and its allies won 99 of the 100 seats; the sole legal opposition party, Convergence for Social Democracy, won the remaining seat.

Diplomatic Representation

British Embassy, (based in Nigeria), URL: http://ukinnigeria.fco.gov.uk/en/
Ambassador: Dr Andrew Pocock (page 1496)
Embassy to the UK, (based in France), 6 rue Alfred de Vigny, 75008 Paris, France. Tel: +33 (0)1 47 66 44 33
Ambassador: Agustin Nze Nfumu
Embassy of the Republic of Equatorial Guinea, 2020 16th St., NW, Washington, DC 20009, USA. Tel: +1 202 518 5700, fax: +1 202 518 5252
Ambassador: P. Angue Ondo
US Embassy, Rue Nachtigal, PO Box 817, Yaounde, Cameroon. Tet:+237 223 05 12, URL: http://malabo.usembassy.gov
Ambassador: Mark L. Asquino
Permanent Representative of Equatorial Guinea to the United Nations, 242 East 51st Street, NY 10022, USA. Tel: +1 212 223 2324, fax: +1 212 223 2366, e-mail: e q u a t o r i a l g u i n e a m i s s i o n @ y a h o o . c o m ,   U R L : http://www.un.int/wcm/content/site/equatorialguinea
Permanent Representative: H.E. Lino Sima Ekua Avomo

LEGAL SYSTEM

The judicial system, set up in 1981, consists of the Supreme Tribunal, Territorial High Courts, courts of first instance and local courts. The Supreme Tribunal, the highest court of appeal, comprises a President, Presidents of the three chambers (civil, criminal and administrative) and two magistrates from each chamber. Most courts are situated in Malabo and Bata.

The government has tried to improve its human rights record over recent years. However, there are still reports of unlawful killings by security forces. Furthermore, there have been cases of torture of prisoners and detainees, arbitrary arrest and life threatening conditions in prisons. There has been both government and judicial corruption, and there are restrictions on freedom of speech, on the rights of assembly, association, and discrimination against ethnic minorities. Equatorial Guinea retains the death penalty. Four executions were reported to have been carried out in 2010.

LOCAL GOVERNMENT

For administrative purposes Equatorial Guinea is divided into seven provinces. Bioko Norte and Bioko Sur on the island of Bioko (formerly Fernando Póo then, from 1973 until 1979, Macías Nguema Byogo), the capital of the province Bioko Norte is also the country capital Malabo. The capital of Bioko Sur is Luba. The Annobón Province is also an island province, the capital is San Antonio de Palé. The other five provinces are located on what is known as the Continental Region, they are The Litoral Province, capital Bata; The Kie-Ntem Province, capital Ebebiyín; The Wele-Nzás Province, capital Mongomo; The Centro-Sur Province, Capital Evinayong. The provinces are further divided into thirty municipalities, which are administered by elected councillors.

AREA AND POPULATION

Area

Equatorial Guinea consists of several islands in, or close to, the Gulf of Guinea, and territory on the west coast of the mainland of Africa bordering the Gulf of Guinea. This mainland territory (Rio Muni) forms an enclave between Cameroon and Gabon. The total area is 28,021 km sq. The islands are volcanic. The mainland territory is mainly forested, rising to mountains further inland.

Bioko including Pagalu (17 km sq.) is 2,034 km sq. in area. The Bubi are the indigenous ethnic group of Bioko. The area of Río Muni (Mbini) is 26,017.5 km sq. including Corisco (15 km sq.) and the Elobeys islands (2.5 km sq.) The main city on the mainland, and the capital of Río Muni province is Bata, where a new harbour was built by Macías. Most of the inhabitants of the province are of the Fang ethnic group. Other main urban centres are Malabo, the national capital, Luba (on Bioko) and various Río Munian harbours such as Mbini (Rio Benito) or inland administrative centres such as Mikomeseng, Niefang, Ebebiyin and Evinayong.

The climate is tropical and this area is subject to violent windstorms.

To view a map of Equatorial Guinea, please visit http://www.un.org/Depts/Cartographic/map/profile/eqguinea.pdf

Population

The total population, according to 2010 estimates, is 700,000. The annual growth rate was an estimated 3.0 per cent over the period 2000-10. 80 per cent of the population live on the mainland or Continental Region. Approximately 40 per cent of the population live in urban areas. The official languages are Spanish and French. Pidgin English, Fang, Bubi and Ibo are also spoken

In 2009, life expectancy was 53 years for males and 54 years for females. Healthy life expectancy was estimated at 45 and 46 years respectively. Total fertility per woman is 5.2 children. The crude birth rate is 36.7 per 1,000 population and the crude death rate is 13.3 per 1,000 population. (Source: http://www.who.int, World Health Statistics 2012)

National Day

2 October: Independence Day

EMPLOYMENT

Agriculture (including hunting, forestry and fishing) is Equatorial Guinea's largest employment sector, with 59,390 actively employed, according to the last census. Trade, restaurants and hotels make up the next highest sector, employing 3,059 people, whilst construction employed 2,929. Estimated figures for 2007 put the labour force at 195,200 with an unemployment rate of 22.0 per cent, unemployment in 2009 was put at 22.3 per cent.

BANKING AND FINANCE

Currency

Co-opération financière en Afrique centrale (CFA) franc = 100 centimes

GDP/GNP, Inflation, National Debt

In the mid-1990s large oil and gas deposits were discovered off Bioko leading to a large growth in the economy, turning it into one of the fastest growing economies in the world in the early 2000s. Since the discovery of oil, allegations have been made against the government of misappropriation of oil revenues, although recently the government has announced that some oil revenues will be used for social projects. The economy dipped in 2009 with falling oil production and falling oil prices. Prices have since recovered. The economy has been further stimulated by public spending on infrastructure.

GDP/GNI

	2005	2006	2007
GDP, US$ million	7,520.42	8,563.23	9,730.79
GDP growth rate, %	8.8	5.3	9.8
GNI per capita	5,410	8,250	..

Source: African Development Bank

Estimated figures for 2009 put GDP growth at 5.0 per cent. Growth fell to -0.5 per cent in 2010 before returning to growth in 2011. GDP was estimated to be US$19 billion in 2011. Industry contributes around 92 per cent of GDP, the service sector contributes 5.0 per cent and agriculture 3.0 per cent.

The average inflation rate in 2007 was 4.9 per cent and 4.5 per cent in 2009 rising to an estimated 6.1 per cent in 2012.

Total external debt in 2011 was estimated to be US$1 billion.

Balance of Payments / Imports and Exports

Principal imports are foodstuffs and beverages, clothing, iron and steel, machinery and equipment, consumer goods. Principal exports are oil (97 per cent), timber (2 per cent), methanol, cocoa and coffee. Oil contributed some US$6,500 million to export earnings in 2006. There are an estimated 10 to 20 years worth of reserves. Main trading partners are Cameroon, Spain, UK, USA, Italy, France, China and Japan.

External Trade, US$ million

	2005	2006	2007
Trade balance	4,866.38	5,598.64	6,225.27
Exports	6,966.22	8,220.71	9,098.60
Imports	2,119.84	2,622.07	2,873.33

Source: African Development Bank

Exports were estimated to be worth US$10 billion and imports US$5.7 billion in 2010.

Foreign Investment

France and Spain are the highest contributors of development aid. The USA is the leading foreign investor, largely due to the oil industry. China also provided US$2 billion to help fund infrastructure projects.

Central Bank

Banque des États de l'Afrique Centrale (BEAC), PO Box 1917, Rue du Docteur Jamot, Yaounde, Cameroon. Tel: +237 234030 / 2230511, fax: +237 233329 / 223 3380, e-mail: beacyde@beac.int, URL: http://www.beac.int
Governor: Lucas Abaga Nchama

MANUFACTURING, MINING AND SERVICES

Primary and Extractive Industries

There are known reserves of iron, tantalum and manganese ores, and these have been systematically explored by geological and mining research stations from France and other foreign countries, although work is hampered by the dense forests and lack of roads. There are believed to be deposits of gold, diamonds and uranium.

Oil was discovered near the coast and along the river Rio Muni, and natural gas deposits are known to exist 3,800 m below sea level, 36 km northwest of Malabo. Estimated figures for 2012 show that there are proven oil reserves of 1.1 billion barrels and in 2011 an average of 302,000 barrels of oil per day are produced. Consumption stands at around 1,000 barrels a day, leaving the surplus available for export. Equatorial Guinea is now the third largest exporter of oil in Sub-Saharan Africa after Nigeria and Angola. Further exploration is underway. New deposits have been found at the Aseng oil and gas-condensate field as well as the Alen gas-condensate field which is expected to to come on line at the end of 2013. Figures for 2010 show that 29 per cent of exported oil went to the United States, 14 per cent to Spain, 13 per cent to Italy, 10 per cent to Canada and seven percent to China.

Natural gas reserves are estimated to be 1.0 trillion cubic feet with production estimated at 231 billion cubic feet in 2010 all of which 23 billion cubic feet is consumed domestically and 175 billion cubic feet was exported as LNG. That year 33 per cent of exports of LNG went to SOuth Korea, 30 Per cent to China, 15 Per cent to Japan and six per ent to Taiwan.

Energy

Electricity generation in 2010 was 0.10 billion kilowatthours, with consumption was 0.09 billion kilowatthours, with Malabo and Bata accounting for roughly equal shares. In addition, the hydro-electric project on the island of Bioko has been completed, with a capacity of 3.6 MW. Around 20 per cent of Equatorial Guinea's electricity is generated by hydroelectric the rest is from thermal sources.

Manufacturing

The manufacturing sector contributes over 90 per cent of GDP, the vast majority of which comes from petroleum and natural gas production. Products from the timber and fishing sectors are also important contributors, there is also a water-bottling plant at Bata.

Agriculture

Approximately 11 per cent of the country's total area is used for agriculture and the sector contributes just under three per cent of GDP. Production of cocoa, was the most important agricultural product, but production has fallen considerably since independence, from 38,000 metric tons in 1967 to 1,200 metric tons in 2010, mainly as a result of the departure of Spanish and Turkish workers. The Bioko region has a highly fertile volcanic soil which, coupled with abundant rain, makes it particularly suitable for cocoa growing. However, of the total area of plantations, less than one third is suitable for cocoa production.

Agricultural Production in 2010

Produce	Int. $'000*	Tonnes
Plantains	8,671	42,000
Bananas	7,660	27,200
Sweet potatoes	6,813	90,200
Cassava	6,717	64,300
Roots and tubers, nes	5,746	33,600
Coffee, green	4,512	4,200
Palm oil	2,175	5,000
Cocoa beans	1,246	1,200
Coconuts	785	7,100
Palm kernels	645	2,500
Hen eggs, in shelf	348	420
Indigenous chicken meat	331	232

* unofficial figures

Source: http://faostat.fao.org/site/339/default.aspx Food and Agriculture
Organization of the United Nations, Food and Agricultural commodities production

Forestry

Equatorial Guinea has great potential as a producer and exporter of wood, with forests covering 46.2 per cent of the country's area. Progress is impeded because there is little infrastructure. While the potential output is in excess of 300,000 cubic metres, actual output figures were 714,000 cubic metres in 1994. In 2002 output was a more sustainable output of 530,000 cubic metres. Most timber production takes place in the Okoumu region. The island of Bioko has been permanently damaged as a result of over exploitation.

Fishing

Commercial fishing takes place at artisan level and on an industrial scale, the latter being carried out by foreign fishing boats, especially those from EC countries. Equatorial Guinea extends a 300,000 sq km exclusive maritime fishing zone around the island of Annabón. The total catch in 2010 was put at 7,400 tonnes.

COMMUNICATIONS AND TRANSPORT

Travel Requirements

US, Canadian, Australian and EU citizens require a passport valid for at least six months to enter Equatorial Guinea, and these should be carried at all times. They also require a visa, apart from US citizens who can stay for up to 30 days without a visa. Proof of vaccination against yellow fever, small pox and cholera is also a requirement. Citizens of other countries should refer to the embassy to check entry requirements.

ERITREA

National Airlines
EGA - Ecuato Guineana Apartado 665, Malabo, Equatorial Guinea. Tel: +240 9 2325, fax: +240 9 3313. (operates two services, Malabo - Douala and Malabo - Libreville)

International Airports
There are two international airports Malabo and Bata, daily domestic flights operate between the two.

Railways
There are no railways in Equatorial Guinea.

Roads
Equatorial Guinea has around 2,880 km of roads and tracks. As a result of the poor road system, economic growth has been slow as movement of goods proves difficult. In 2002 the IMF and the African Development Bank agreed funds to build a motorway system which will link Equatorial Guinea to Cameroon and Gabon. Local roads from Malabo to Luba and Riaba were also to be improved. Vehicles are driven on the right.

Ports and Harbours
The main port is Bata and mainly handles timber. Other ports are situated at Luba (bananas, timber), Bioko, Malabo, Evinayong and Mbini (timber). A ferry service operates between Malabo, Bata and Douala.

HEALTH

Health care is limited. In 2009, the government of Equatorial Guinea spent approximately 7.0 per cent of its total budget on healthcare (down from 7.8 per cent in 2000), accounting for 76.0 per cent of all healthcare spending. Total expenditure on healthcare equated to 4.5 per cent of the country's GDP. External resources accounted for 2.8 per cent of healthcare expenditure (compared to 8.8 per cent in 2000). Per capita expenditure on health was approximately US$804, compared to US$46 in 2000. Figures for 2000-10 show that there were an estimated 153 physicians (3 per 10,000 population), 271 nurses and midwives (5 per 10,000 population), 15 dentists, 121 pharmaceutical personnel, 18 environment and public health workers and 308 community health workers (6 per 10,000 population). There were an estimated 19 hospital beds per 10,000 population.

Several diseases are endemic including malaria, hepatitis and whooping cough. HIV/AIDS is estimated to affect 3.4 per cent of the adult (15-49 years) population. In 2008 there were 63,147 reported cases of malaria, 436 of measles, 27 of leprosy, 541 of TB and 10 of yellow fever. The infant mortality rate (probability of dying before first birthday) in 2010 was 81 per 1,000 live births. The child mortality rate (under 5 years) was 121 per 1,000 live births. The main causes of childhood mortality are: malaria (21 per cent), prematurity (13 per cent), diarrhoea (7 per cent), pneumonia (14 per cent), and HIV/AIDs (8 per cent). The number of children sleeping under insecticide-treated nets is an estimated 42 per cent. Immunization rates are estimated to be low: just 51 per cent of one-year-olds were immunized against measles in 2010 and 33 had received the DTP3 vaccine. An estimated 35 per cent of young children were classified as stunted in 2000-09 and 10.6 per cent as underweight.

In 2006, 43 per cent of the population had sustainable access to an improved water source and 51 per cent had sustainable access to improved sanitation. (Source: http://www.who.int, World Health Statistics 2012)

EDUCATION

The country's education system is officially compulsory. Education is free, beginning at years of age and ending at 11. Secondary education begins at 12 and lasts for seven year Spain and France provide some financial assistance. Net enrolment rates at primary an secondary levels were approximately 65 per cent and 24 per cent respectively in 2004. 4 per cent of students repeat primary education. The pupil: teacher ratio at primary level wa 43:1 in 2004. Expenditure as a percentage of GDP is estimated to be 0.6 per cent.

The 2004 literacy rates were 93.4 for males and 80.5 for females. (Source: UNESCO)

RELIGION

The population of the islands is mainly Christian (89 per cent) and predominantly Roma Catholic. Traditional African beliefs can be found in Río Muni and there is also a Muslir community numbering around 28,000.

Equatorial Guinea has a religious tolerance rating of 8 on a scale of 1 to 10 (10 is mos freedom). (Source: World Religion Database)

COMMUNICATIONS AND MEDIA

The media is closely controlled by the government.

Newspapers
Ebano (state-owned), La Opinion, La Nacion, La Gaceta.

Broadcasting
Both radio and television stations operate in Equatorial Guinea and are run by the state There is one private radio statio, Radio Asonga, run by the president's son. Satellite televisio is available. Radio France Internationale and Africa No 1 (Gabon) are available.
Televisión Nacional, Malabo
Radio Nacional de Guinea Ecuatorial, Bata

Telecommunications
According to 2010 statistics there were 13,000 main telephone lines and in 2011, 425,00 mobile phones in use. Around 14,000 users have internet access.

ENVIRONMENT

Equatorial Guinea's major environmental problems are deforestation and wildlife destructior both of which require forest management. Figures from the EIA for 2010 show that carbo dioxide emissions from the consumption of fossil fuels was 5.24 million metric tons whic fell to 5.0 million metric tons in 2009.

Equatorial Guinea is party to the following environmental agreements: Biodiversity, Climate Change, Climate Change-Kyoto Protocol, Desertification, Endangered Species, Hazardou Wastes, Law of the Sea, Marine Dumping, Ozone Layer Protection, Ship Pollution an Wetlands.

ERITREA
State of Eritrea
Hagere Ertra

Capital: Asmara (Population estimate: 500,000)

Head of State: Issaias Afewerki (President) (page 1372)

National Flag: A red isosceles triangle, base to the hoist side, divides the flag into two right triangles, the upper triangle is green, the lower one is blue, a gold wreath encircling a gold olive branch is centred on the hoist side of the red triangle

CONSTITUTION AND GOVERNMENT

Constitution
A former colony of Italy, and also ruled by Britain and Ethiopia, now an independent state. In 1962 Emperor Haile Sellassie (emperor of Ethiopia) annexed Eritrea, dissolved the parliament and the fight for independence began. Sellassie was ousted in a coup in 1974 and in 1977 the Marxist leader Mengistu Haile Miriam took control. The Eritrean People's Liberation Front (EPLF) took control of the country from the Mengitsu Government in 1991. In April 1993 an internationally monitored referendum was held. The result was an overwhelming vote for independence. A four year transitional government was announced in May 1993, known as the Government of Eritrea, and included legislative, executive and judicial bodies.

The President is Head of the Government and Commander-in-Chief of the armed forces. He nominates individuals to head the various ministries and the legislative body ratifies the nominations. Made up of 16 ministers and chaired by the President, the Cabinet is the

country's executive branch. It has the highest authority between sessions of the Nationa Assembly and implements the policies, resolutions and laws of the government and is accountable to the National Assembly.

During the four year transition period, the drafting and ratifying of a constitution, the preparation of laws on political parties, the preparation of a press law, and the preparatior for election of a permanent government were all proposed. The constitution was adopted ir May 1997.

International Relations
In 1998 relations deteriorated with Ethiopia as the two countries fought over a disputec area, Badme, whose frontier has not been properly demarcated. In May 2000 Ethiopia launched an offensive and captured large areas of Eritrean territory. In June 2000 the twc countries signed a ceasefire accord brokered by the Organisation of African Unity. The plar allows for a United Nations peace-keeping force in a buffer zone until the border is demarcated. In April 2001 the buffer zone was established. In April 2002 the Boundary Commission came up with the new boundaries which Ethiopia disputed as the border towr of Badme was designated as being in Eritrea. In November 2004 Ethiopia said that it acceptec 'in principle' the Boundary Commission's ruling. Tension rose again later in the year. The UN Security Council threatened Ethiopia and Eritrea with sanctions unless they returned to the 2000 peace plan. Eritrea banned UN peacekeepers from the US, Europe and Russia ir December 2005. The Hague ruled that Eritrea had broken international law when it attackec Ethiopia in 1998. In November 2006 both Ethiopia and Eritrea rejected the proposed boundary put forward by an independent boundary commission.

Recent Events

In the autumn of 2006, Eritrean relations with the UN deteriorated when Eritrea expelled five UN staff as spies, and UN Secretary General Kofi Annan urged Eritrea to pull back the troops from within the buffer zone on the Ethiopian border, a major ceasefire violation. In November, a UN report listed seven countries - including Eritrea - which had been providing arms and supplies to the rival Islamist administration in Somalia. Eritrea denied the charge.

In November 2007 Eritrea accepted the border line proposed by the international boundary commission. However Ethiopia rejected it. In January 2008 the mandate of UN peacekeepers on the Eritrea-Ethiopia border was extended for six months despite Eritrean opposition. Eritrea later withheld fuel supplies and in February 2008 the UN began to pull its peacekeeping troops out. In May 2008 Eritrea asked the UN to end its mission. Fighting broke out between Eritrea and Djibouti in the disputed Ras Doumeira border area. Eritrea denied launching an attack. The UN Security Council voted to end the UN peacekeeping mission on the border in July 2008. In April 2009 the UN accused Eritrea of failing to withdraw its troops from the disputed area, a claim denied by Eritrea.

In August 2009, Eritrea and Ethiopia were ordered to pay each other compensation for the 1998-2000 border war. In December 2009 the UN imposed sanctions on Eritrea for its alleged support for Islamist insurgents in Somalia.

In December 2009 the UN imposed santions on Eritrea for the alleged support for Islamist insurgents in Somalia.

In June 2010, Eritrea and Djibouti agreed to try to resolve their border dispute peacefully.

In April 2011 Ethiopia announced it would support Eritrean rebel groups to overthrow President Isaias Afewerki.

In December 2011 the UN Security Council increased sanctions against Eritrea in response to its continuing support of Islamists in Somalia.

In March 2012, troops from Ethiopia attacked positions in south-eastern Eritrea aying they believed they were the training grounds for subversive groups.

In January 2013, dissident soldiers briefly took over the Ministry of Information building in Asmara and demanded the release of political prisoners.

Legislature

The legislative body, the National Assembly, includes 75 members of the People's Front for Democracy and Justice's Central Committee and 75 additional representatives elected by the population. The National Assembly outlines the internal and external policies of the government, regulates their implementation, approves the budget and elects a president for the country. The 1997 Constitution sets out that assembly members should serve a four year term of office.

National Assembly, (*Hagerawi Baito*), P.O. Box 242, Asmara, Eritrea. Tel: +291 1 119701, fax: +291 1 125123, URL: http://www.netafrica.org/eritrea/national.html

Cabinet (as at June 2013)

Minister of Defence: Gen. Sebhat Ephrem Emmanuel (page 1421)
Minister of Justice: Foazia Hashim
Minister of Foreign Affairs: Osman Saleh (page 1507)
Minister of Information: Ali Abdu Ahmad
Minister of Finance and Development: Berhane Abrehe
Minister of Trade and Industry: Estifanos Habte
Minister of Agriculture: Arefaine Berhe
Minister of Labour and Human Welfare: Salema Hassan
Minister of Fisheries: Tewelde Kelati
Minister of Public Works: Asfaha Abraha
Minister of Energy and Mines: Ahmed Hajj Ali
Minister of Education: Semere Russom
Minister of Health: Amna Nur Husayn
Minister of Transport and Communication: Woldemichael Abraha
Minister of Tourism: Askalu Menkorios
Minister for National Development: Giorgis Teklemichael
Minister for Local Government: Woldenkial Ghebremariam
Minister of Land, Water and Environment: Tesfai Ghebresselassie

Ministries

Office of the President, P.O. Box 257, Asmara, Eritrea. Tel: +291 (0)1 122132, fax: +291 (0)1 125123
Ministry of Agriculture, P.O. Box 1048, Asmara, Eritrea. Tel: +291 (0)1 181499, fax: +291 (0)1 181415
Ministry of Finance & Development, P.O. Box 895, Asmara, Eritrea. Tel: +291 (0)1 118131, fax: +291 (0)1 127947
Ministry of Labor & Human Welfare, P.O. Box 5252, Asmara, Eritrea. Tel: +291 (0)1 182886 / 181846, fax: +291 (0)1 181649
Ministry of Foreign Affairs, P.O. Box 190, Asmara, Eritrea. Tel: +291 (0)1 127108 / 127838 / (0)116967, fax: +291 1 123788 / 12124
Ministry of Fishery , P.O. Box 923, Asmara, Eritrea. Tel: +291 (0)1 1114271, fax: +291 1 112185
Ministry of Culture, Asmara, Eritrea. Fax: +291 1 126368
Ministry of Health, P.O. Box 212, Asmara, Eritrea. Tel: +291 (0)1 117549 / 120297, fax: +291 1 122899
Ministry of Construction, P.O. Box 841, Asmara, Eritrea. Tel: +291 (0)1 119077 / (0)114588, fax: +291 (0)1 120661
Ministry of Defense, P.O. Box 629, Asmara, Eritrea. Tel: +291 (0)1 115493, fax: +291 (0)1 124920
Ministry of Justice, P.O. Box 241, Asmara, Eritrea. Tel: +291 (0)1 117603 / 127739, fax: +291 (0)1 126422

Ministry of Land Water & Environment, P.O. Box 976, Asmara, Eritrea. Tel: +291 (0)1 118021, fax: +291 (0)1 123285
Ministry of Transport and Communication, Asmara, Eritrea. Tel: +291 (0)1 114307 / 115847, fax: +291 (0)1 127048 / 126966
Ministry of Information, P.O. Box 242, Asmara, Eritrea. Tel: +291 (0)1 117111, fax: +291 (0)1 124647, URL: http://shabait.com/
Ministry of Tourism, PO Box 1010, Asmara, Eritrea. Tel: +291 (0)1 126997, fax: +291 (0)1 126949, e-mail: eritrea_tourism@cts.com.er, URL: http://www.shaebia.org/
Ministry of Energy, Mining and Water Resources, PO Box 5285, Asmara, Eritrea. Tel: +291 (0)1 116872, fax: +291 (0)1 117652
Ministry of Trade and Industry, PO Box 1844, Asmara, Eritrea. Tel: +291 (0)1 117717 / 113910, fax: +291 (0)1 120586

Elections

The last presidential election took place in 1993. The presidential term should last for five years but no elections have been held since 1993. Legislative elections last took place in 1997. Legislative elections scheduled for December 2001 have been postponed indefinitely.

Political Parties

The Eritrean People's Liberation Front came into existence in the 1970s and was headed by Isaias Afewerki. Following his election to president in 1993 the party changed its name to People's Front for Democracy and Justice. No other political parties are permitted.

Diplomatic Representation

US Embassy, 179 Alaa Street, PO Box 211, Asmara, Eritrea. Tel: +291 (0)1 120004, fax: +291 (0)1 127584, URL: http://eritrea.usembassy.gov
Charge d'Affaires: Sue Bremner
Embassy of Eritrea, 1708 New Hampshire Ave., NW, Washington, DC, 20009, USA. Tel: +1 202 319 1991, fax: +1 202 319 1304, URL: www.embassyeritrea.org
Charge d'Affaires: Berhane G Solomon
British Embassy, 66-68 Mariam Ghimbi Street, Asmara, Eritrea. Tel: +291 (0)1 120145, fax: +291 (0)1 120104, e-mail: Asmara.Enquiries@fco.gov.uk, URL: http://ukineritrea.fco.gov.uk/en
Ambassador: Dr Amanda Susannah Tanfield
Embassy of Eritrea, 96 White Lion Street, London N1 9PF, United Kingdom. Tel: +44 (0)20 7713 0096, fax: +44 (0)20 7713 0161, URL: http://www.eriembassyuk.com/
Ambassador: Tesfamicael Gerahtu Ogbaghiorghis
Permanent Representative of Eritrea to the United Nations, 800 Second Avenue, 18th Floor, New York, NY 10017, USA. Tel: +1 212 687 3390, fax: +1 212 687 3138, e-mail: eritrea@un.int, URL: http://www.un.int/eritrea
Ambassador: Araya Destra

LEGAL SYSTEM

The legal system is a civil law system, with its origins in the Napoleonic Code. The court system consists of courts of first instance, courts of appeals composed of 5 judges, and military courts. Traditional courts play a major role in rural areas, where village elders determine property and family disputes under customary law or in the case of Muslims, Sharia law.

The government continues to postpone presidential and legislative elections, and the border dispute with Ethiopia is used by the government to justify severe restrictions on civil liberties. Security forces carry out unlawful killings and torture of prisoners. There are cases of arbitrary arrests, including of national service evaders and their family. Prison conditions are life-threatening. The government restricts freedoms of speech, press, assembly, association, and religion. The government also limited freedom of movement for personnel of humanitarian and development agencies, and employees of the UN Mission to Eritrea and Ethiopia (UNMEE). Eritrea retains the death penalty, but no-one has been executed since before 1999.

LOCAL GOVERNMENT

The country is divided into six regions: Anseba, Debub. Debubawi Kayih Bahri, Gash-Barka, Zoba-Ma'akel and Semenawi Keyih Bahri. Each is headed by a regional administrator.

AREA AND POPULATION

Area

Eritrea is situated in north-east or horn of Africa to the south of the Red Sea, bordering Sudan to the east and Ethiopia to the south. It has an area of 125,000 km sq. The terrain is varied with coastal desert plains on the east, more hilly in the north, highlands in the centre, and rolling plains in the southwest. The climate also varies from dry arid desert conditions on the coast, and cooler and wetter in the central highlands. The climate is semi-arid in the western hills.

To view a map, please consult http://www.lib.utexas.edu/maps/cia08/eritrea_sm_2008.gif

Population

In 2010, the population was estimated at 5.254 million with an average density of about 28 people per square km. Almost 78 per cent of the population reside in rural areas and of those about 20-30 per cent are nomadic or semi-nomadic. The average annual population growth rate was 3.6 per cent over the period 2000-10. Asmara, the capital, has an estimated population of 500,000. Other large cities include Assab, with a population of 28,000, Massawa 25,000, Keren, 57,000, Afabet, 25,000 and Tessenie, 25,000. Ethnic groups found in the country include Tigrinya who make up 50 per cent of the population, Tigre, 31 per cent, Afar, Bilen, Hadareb, Kunama, Nara, Rashaida and Saho. Many languages are spoken in Eritrea of which Tigrinya is the predominant one. Other languages include Arabic, Tigre, Kunama, Afar and Amharic. English is taught in schools.

ERITREA

Births, Marriages, Deaths
Life expectancy is currently 64 years for males and 68 years for females. Healthy life expectancy is 54 and 56 years respectively. The median age was 19 years in 2010. Approximately 42 per cent of the population was less than 15 years old. Just 4 per cent was aged over 60 years old. In 2010 the birth rate was estimated at 36.2 births per 1,000 population and the death rate was 5.8 deaths per 1,000 population. The total fertility rate was 4.5 children per woman. (Source: http://www.who.int, World Health Statistics 2012)

National Holiday: 24 May: Independence Day

EMPLOYMENT

In 2007 the workforce was put at 1.9 million. Around 80 per cent of the labour force is employed in agriculture, and 20 per cent in industry and commerce. In 2003, 66 per cent of the population were living below the poverty line, rising to 80 per cent in rural areas. The country is dependent on foreign aid.

BANKING AND FINANCE

Currency
1 Nakfa = 100 cents

GDP/GNP, Inflation, National Debt
The economy of Eritrea is largely based on agriculture. The sector employs around 80 per cent of the population mainly on subsistence level, but only contributes around 12 per cent of GDP. The sector is particularly vulnerable to the erratic rainfall of the area and the recent war with Ethiopia has also had an impact. Since the war with Ethiopia ended in 2001, Eritrea has not been able to recover as it has been hit by four successive droughts. Eritrea has now become heavily reliant on remittances sent home from Eritreans living and working abroad. Some estimates put these remittances as contributing as much as 32 per cent of GDP. Mineral extraction started in 2010.

Most Eritreans are extremely poor. Contributing factors include thirty years of war, the demobilising of ex-soldiers and the retrenchment of thousands of workers from the public sector.

GDP/GNI

	2005	2006	2007
GDP, US$ million	962.20	1,084.49	1,084.49
GDP growth rate, %	4.8	2.0	1.3
GNI per capita, US$	170	200	..
Source: African Development Bank			

GDP was estimated at US$2.5 billion in 2011.

In 2005, inflation was 12.4 per cent, 17.3 per cent in 2006, 22.7 per cent in 2007, 18 per cent in 2008 and 20 per cent in 2011.

External public debt was US$781.37 million in 2006. (Source: AFDB)

Foreign Investment
In 1994 the government issued a new investment code to encourage investors by offering them lower tax rates, 100 per cent foreign exchange retention and ownership, guarantees against nationalisation, confiscation or any other non commercial risks and approval time for new businesses reduced to a maximum of 10 days. Further, foreign employees may remit 40 per cent of their net earnings abroad per month. Exporters may also retain 100 per cent of their proceeds and no negative list is maintained for imported goods except for internationally prohibited goods.

Balance of Payments / Imports and Exports
Main exports are skins, live sheep and cattle, gum arabic and meat. Main imports are food, fuel, manufactured goods, machinery and transportation equipment and military material. Eritrea's main trading partners are Saudi Arabia, UAE, Yemen, Italy, Belgium, Germany, Djibouti and Sudan.

External Trade, US$ million

	2005	2006	2007
Trade balance	-423.93	-387.51	-443.65
Exports	11.32	12.27	13.22
Imports	435.25	399.78	456.88
Source: African Development Bank			

Imports were estimated to be US$680 million in 2010 and exports US$29 million.

Central Bank
Bank of Eritrea, PO Box 849, 21 Victory Avenue, Asmara, Eritrea. Tel: +291 (0)1 123033 / (0)1 123036, fax: +291 (0)1 123162 / (0)1 122091, URL: http://www.boe.gov.er/ Governor: Y Gebreselassie

MANUFACTURING, MINING AND SERVICES

Primary and Extractive Industries
Potentially profitable deposits of gold, copper, potash, iron ore, nickel, gypsum, barite, marble feldspar, rock salt, silica, asbestos, granite and other minerals exist. Oil exploration is now being planned with negotiations taking place with major companies. Figures for 2011 show that Eritrea imports 6,000 barrels of oil per day.

Energy
Production, distribution and development of power is controlled by the Eritrean Energy Authority. Energy is acquired from wood fuel (70 per cent), oil products (16 per cent), animal waste (8 per cent), crop residue (4 per cent), charcoal (1 per cent) and electricity (1 per cent). Electricity is generated by thermal power plants driven by diesel engines. Currently only about 10 per cent of the population has access to electricity.

Manufacturing
The industrial sector's contribution to the GDP was 11 per cent in 2003. Light manufacturing industries are predominantly producing food, beverages, textiles, leather goods, chemical products, construction materials, glass, ceramics, marble, recylced plastiscs, rubber goods and metal products.

Tourism
Eritrea should be popular tourist destination but suffers from a lack of infrastructure, there are only a few hotels in existance all in the Asmara area. Plans have been discussed for foreign investment in a casino and several hotels on the Dahlak archipelago.

Agriculture
In 2003 the agricultural sector is estimated to have accounted for 12 per cent of the GDP, 80 per cent of export earnings and employed about 70-80 per cent of the work force. Approximately 26 per cent of the total land is arable but only about 10 per cent is cultivated. The major crops are sorghum, sesame, cotton, maize, beans, barley, millet, teff, vegetable and fruit. Although crop production is dominated by small scale farmers, commercial farms are being developed in the less densely populated areas.

Livestock includes sheep, goats, cattle and camels. This sector has been severely affected by the war and drought, which is evident from the 1987-91 estimates of livestock numbers falling by 75 per cent for sheep and goats and 50 per cent for cattle. Figures for 2000 show that Eritrea had 1.9 million head of cattle and 3.8 million sheep and goats. Eritrea suffered a severe drought in 2000. Continued drought conditions led the World Food Programme in 2005 to warn of a dire food situation and to extend its emergency operations. Figures for 2003 estimate that more than 70 per cent of the population depended on foreign assistance for all or some of their food supply. Similar numbers were said to need food aid in 2005.

Agricultural Production in 2010

Produce	Int. $'000*	Tonnes
Indigenous cattle meat	68,607	25,397
Cow milk, whole, fresh	32,844	105,250
Indigenous sheep meat	29,000	10,651
Indigenous goat meat	14,445	6,029
Pulses, nes	12,459	24,300
Cereals, nes	11,494	45,000
Roots & tubers, nes	11,116	65,000
Sorghum	9,490	66,700
Vegetables fresh nes	8,160	43,300
Camel milk, whole, fresh	7,883	23,120
Barley	7,454	67,000
Indigenous camel meat	5,197	2,480

* unofficial figures
Source: http://faostat.fao.org/site/339/default.aspx Food and Agriculture Organization of the United Nations, Food and Agricultural commodities production

Marine fishing is an important form of revenue for Eritrea, with the Red Sea being abundant with marine life. Current fish catch is estimated at 3,285 tonnes per annum.

COMMUNICATIONS AND TRANSPORT

Travel Requirements
US, Canadian, Australian and EU citizens require a passport valid for three months beyond the intended departure date, and a visa, obtained prior to arrival. People who stay beyond the time for which thieir visa is valid may be subject to fines or imprisonment. Since 1 June 2006, all foreign nationals (including resident diplomats) are required to have a travel permit to visit areas outside Asmara.

Nationals not listed above should contact the embassy to check visa requirements.

International Airports
Eritrea has one international airport at Asmara and another airport at Assab. A new airport has recently opened at Massawa. Around 17 airstrips are also operational.

Railways
Eritrea has 305 km of railtrack, the Asmara-Massawa track but services are not regular.

Roads
Eritrea has 875 km of asphalted roads, 375 km gravel roads and 4,535 km of rural earth roads. Vehicles are driven on the right.

Shipping
There are two seaports, Massawa and Assab.

HEALTH

The health care system is poor and has suffered due to years of war and droughts. Most medical facilities including hospitals and birthing centres are in either the capital, Asmara, or the cities of Keren and Massawa. Hospitals are generally under-equipped. The government is trying to decentralised health care and health care facilities. Private health care is available but is expensive.

In 2000-10, there were 215 doctors (0.05 per 1,000 population), 2,505 nurses (0.58 per 1,000 population), 16 dentistry personnel and 107 pharmaceutical personnel. Total expenditure on healthcare equated to 2.8 per cent of the country's GDP in 2009. In 2009, the government spent approximately 3.6 per cent of its total budget on healthcare, accounting for 47.7 per cent of all healthcare spending. External resources accounted for 61 per cent of total healthcare expenditure. Per capita expenditure on health was approximately US$11 in 2009.

In 2010 there were 35,982 reported cases of malaria, 2,410 of mumps, 11 of leprosy and 2,870 of TB. The most common causes of death for children aged 5 or less (2010) are prematurity (14 per cent), HIV/AIDS (2 per cent), diarrhoeal diseases (11 per cent), malaria (1 per cent), and pneumonia (19 per cent). Almost 40 per cent of children aged 5 are underweight. In 2008, 74 per cent of the urban population and 57 per cent of the rural population had sustainable access to improved water supply. In the same year, 52 per cent of the urban population and 14 per cent of the rural population had sustainable access to improved sanitation. (Source: http://www.who.int, World Health Statistics 2012)

EDUCATION

Primary education lasts for five years. Attendance in 2007 was 50 per cent of girls and 60 per cent of boys. Secondary education lasts for 6 years and attendance in 2007 was 24 per cent of girls and 34 per cent of boys. Between the ages of 7 and 13 education is officially compulsory, fees are payable for enrollment and books. The adult literacy rate stands at approximately 60 per cent. (Figures from UNESCO) Eritrea currently has two universities, the University of Asmara and the Eritrea Institute of Technology. In addition, there are several small colleges and technical schools.

RELIGION

There are roughly equal numbers of Christians and Sunni Muslims, as well as some animists. The majority of Christians belong to the Orthodox Church.

Eritrea has a religious tolerance rating of 5 on a scale of 1 to 10 (10 is most freedom). (Source: World Religion Database)

COMMUNICATIONS AND MEDIA

The press in Eritrea is wholly government-owned. The government closed down the private press in 2001 for 'endangering national security'. Journalists have been arrested after publishing dissenting views.

Newspapers
The main newspapers are **Hadas Eritrea**, which is published three times a week, and the weekly **Eritrea Profile**, which is published in English.

Broadcasting
The television broadcaster **TV Eri** is government-owned as is the radio station **Voice of the Broad Masses of Eritrea**. There are no private broadcasters.

Telecommunications
The telephone system is very limited. Estimated figures from 2008 show that there are 40,000 telephone lines in use and around 108,000 mobile phones. Figures from 2009 estimated the number of regular internet users as 200,000.

ENVIRONMENT

In order to protect and conserve the environment the government has implemented certain regulations, action plans and councils. The Environmental Impact Assessments was introduced to protect marine life. To deal with land, forest and water issues the National Environmental Action Plan was formulated and the Eritrean Environmental Agency, which is accountable to the National Environmental Council, was established. Deforestation, desertification, soil erosion and overgrazing are all of particular environmental concern for Eritrea.

Eritrea is a party to the following international agreements: Biodiversity, Climate Change, Climate Change-Kyoto Protocol, Desertification, Endangered Species, Hazardous Wastes, and Ozone Layer Protection.

According to the EIA, in 2010, Eritrea's emissions from the consumption of fossil fuels totalled 0.80 million metric tons of carbon dioxide.

ESTONIA
Republic of Estonia
Eesti Vabariik

Capital: Tallinn (Population estimate: 411,600)

Head of State: Toomas Hendrik Ilves (President) (page 1446)

National Flag: A fesswise tricolour of blue, black and white.

CONSTITUTION AND GOVERNMENT

Constitution
Estonia had been part of Russia when it declared its independence in 1918 which resulted in a short war. In 1940 it was invaded by Soviet troops resulting in its absorption in the USSR. In 1941 Estonia came under German occupation before returning to Soviet Russia in 1944.

Following Estonia's independence from the former Soviet Union in 1991, a new Constitution was introduced by referendum in June 1992. This Constitution delineated a new relationship between the state and its people and included provisions on human rights and responsibilities, the parliament, the president's powers, foreign relations, finance, the legal system and local government.

To consult the full constitution, please visit: http://www.eesti.ee/eng/riik/pohiseadus/

Recent Events
In November 2002 Estonia was formally invited to join NATO and became a member in March 2004. In December 2000 she was invited to join the EU. A referendum was held in September 2003 when 63 per cent of eligible voters cast their votes and 67 per cent of those voted for Estonia to join the EU. Full membership came in May 2004.

In March 2005 the prime minister, Juhan Parts, resigned after a vote of no-confidence in an anti-corruption programme led by his justice minister, Ken-Marti Vaher. Andrus Ansip of the Reform Party was confirmed as his successor the following month.

In May 2005, following 10 years of negotiations, Russia and Estonia signed a border treaty agreeing land and sea borders. In June Russia ruled against ratifying the agreement as Estonia had made references in the agreement to 'Soviet Occupation'. Russia objected to the use of political statements in the accord.

Parliament ratified the EU constitution in June 2006. In February 2007, the Estonian Parliament passed a law prohibiting the display of monuments glorifying Soviet rule, and in April, a controversial Red Army war memorial in Tallinn was removed; Russia warned of consequences, and there were protests by ethnic Russians.

At midnight on December 31 2010, the Euro became the official currency of Estonia, replacing the Kroon.

In October 2012, Estonia and Russia resumed talks on a border treaty. The previous agreement was signed in 2005 but Russia withdrew from it following a dispute over treatment of the Soviet past.

Legislature
The legislature of Estonia is unicameral. The parliament or *Riigikogu* consists of 101 members, elected in free elections on the basis of proportionality. The Riigikogu elects the president. Members of the Riigikogu are elected for a four-year term.

Riigikogu, Lossi plats 1A, 15165 Tallinn, Estonia. Tel: +372 631 6331, fax: +372 631 6334, e-mail: riigikogu@riigikogu.ee, URL: http://www.riigikogu.ee
President: Ene Ergma

Cabinet (as at June 2013)
Prime Minister: Andrus Ansip (page 1378)
Minister for Education and Research: Jaak Aaviksoo (page 1371)
Minister of Justice: Hanno Pevkur
Minister of Defence: Urmas Reinsalu
Minister of the Environment: Keit Pentus
Minister of Culture: Rein Lang (page 1460)
Minister of Economic Affairs and Communications: Juhan Parts (page 1492)
Minister of Agriculture: Helir-Valdor Seeder
Minister of Finance: Jürgen Ligi
Minister of Internal Affairs: Ken-Marti Vaher
Minister of Social Affairs: Taavi Roivas
Minister of Foreign Affairs: Urmas Paet (page 1491)
Minister of Regional Affairs: Siim Valmar Kiisler

ESTONIA

Ministries

Office of the President, A. Weizenbergi 39, 15050 Tallinn, Estonia. Tel: +372 631 6202, fax: +372 631 6250, e-mail: vpinfo@vpk.ee, URL: http://www.president.ee

Office of the Prime Minister, Stenbock House, Rahukohtu 3, 15161 Tallinn, Estonia. Tel: +372 693 5555, fax: +372 693 5554, e-mail: valitsus@rk.ee, URL: http://www.valitsus.ee

Ministry of Finance, Suur Ameerika 1, 15006 Tallinn, Estonia. Tel: +372 611 3558, fax: +372 696 6810, e-mail: info@fin.ee, URL: http://www.fin.ee

Ministry of Foreign Affairs, Islandi Väljak 1, 15049 Tallinn, Estonia. Tel: +372 637 7000, fax: +372 637 7099, e-mail: vminfo@vm.ee, URL: http://www.vm.ee

Ministry of Agriculture, Lai 39-41, 15056 Tallinn, Estonia. Tel: +372 625 6101, fax: +372 625 6200, e-mail: pm@agri.ee, URL: http://www.agri.ee

Ministry of Culture, Suur Karja 23, 15076 Tallinn, Estonia. Tel: +372 628 2250. fax: +372 628 2200, e-mail: min@kul.ee, URL: http://www.kul.ee

Ministry of Defence, Sakala 1, 15094 Tallinn, Estonia. Tel: +372 717 0022, fax: +372 717 0001, e-mail: info@kmin.ee, URL: http://www.mod.gov.ee

Ministry of Economic Affairs and Communications, Harju 11, 15072 Tallinn, Estonia. Tel: +372 625 6342, fax: +372 631 3660, e-mail: info@mkm.ee, URL: http://www.mineco.ee

Ministry of Education and Research, Munga 18, 50088 Tartu, Estonia. Tel: +372 735 0222, fax: +372 735 0250, e-mail: hm@hm.ee, URL: http://www.hm.ee

Ministry of the Environment, Narva mnt 7a, 15172 Tallinn, Estonia. Tel: +372 626 2802, fax: +372 626 2801, e-mail: min@ekm.envir.ee, URL: http://www.envir.ee

Ministry of Internal Affairs, Pikk 61, 15065 Tallinn, Estonia. Tel: +372 612 5008, fax: +372 612 5010, e-mail: min@siseministeerium.ee, URL: http://www.sisemin.gov.ee

Ministry of Justice, Tõnismägi 5a, 15191 Tallinn, Estonia. Tel: +372 620 8100, fax: +372 620 8109, e-mail: info@just.ee, URL: http://www.just.ee

Ministry of Regional Affairs, Pikk 61, Tallinn, Estonia. Tel: +372 612 5009, fax: +372 612 5010, e-mail: min@siseministeerium.ee, URL: http://www.eesti.ee

Ministry of Social Affairs, Gonsiori 29, 15027 Tallinn, Estonia. Tel: +372 626 9301, fax: +372 699 2209, e-mail: info@sm.ee, URL: http://www.sm.ee

State Chancellery, Stenbock House, Rahukohtu 3, 15161 Tallinn, Estonia, Tel: +372 693 5860, fax: +372 693 5914, email: riigikantselei@rk.ee, URL: http://www.riik.ee/riigikantselei/

Political Parties:

Eesti Keskerakond (K, Estonian Centre Party), Toom-Ruutli 3/5, 10130 Tallinn, Estonia. Tel: +372 627 3460, fax: +372 627 3461, URL: http://www.keskerakond.ee
Leader: Edgar Savisaar

Eesti Reformierakond (RE, Estonian Reform Party), Tõnismäe 9, 10119 Tallinn, Estonia. Tel: +372 640 8740, fax: +372 640 8741, URL: http://www.reform.ee
Leader: Andrus Ansip

Isamaa ja Res Publica Liit (RPPPU, Union of Pro Patria and Res Publica), URL: http://www.isamaajarespublicaliit.ee
Leader: Mart Laar

Sotsiaaldemokraatlik Erakond, (SDE, Social Democratic Party), Ahtri 10a, V floor, Tallinn 10151, Etonia. URL: http://www.sotsdem.ee
Leader: Sven Mikser

Elections

In January 2002 Prime Minister Mart Laar ended the coalition which had dated from the 1999 elections, citing irreconcilable differences. A new coalition was formed from the Centre party, with eight ministers, and the Reform party, with six ministers, headed by Siim Kallas. Legislative elections took place in March 2003. The Centrist Party (KP) and the Union for the Republic-Res Publica (RP), a new political party, each won 28 seats. Juhan Parts, leader of the RP, was asked to form a government. He formed a coalition with the Reform Party (RE) and the Estonian People's Union. The cabinet took office in April 2003. In early 2004, eight MPs from the Centre Party left to form the new parliamentary group the Social Liberals.

Parliamentary elections took place in March 2007; the Reform Party led by Prime Minister Andrus Ansip became the largest party in the parliament and formed a coalition government with the Union of Pro Patria and Res Publica and the Estonia Social Democratic Party. The most recent election took place in March 2011, the Reform Party and its coalition partner IRL retained their majority winning 56 of the 101 seats.

The most recent presidential elections were held in September 2006 and were won by Toomas Hendrik Ilves.

Local elections were held in October 2005 and for the first time voters were able to vote using the internet. Estonians carry national identity cards, which contain a microchip and by using these cards, the electorate can vote electronically.

Diplomatic Representation

British Embassy, Wismari 6, 10136 Tallinn, Estonia. Tel: +372 667 4700, fax: +372 667 4724, e-mail: information@britishembassy.ee, URL: http://ukinestonia.fco.gov.uk/en
Ambassador: Christopher Holtby OBE (page 1443)

US Embassy, Kentmanni 20, 15099 Tallinn, Estonia. Tel: +372 631 2021, fax: +372 631 2025, URL: http://estonia.usembassy.gov/
Ambassador: Jeffrey D. Levine

Estonian Embassy, 16 Hyde Park Gate, London, SW7 5DG, United Kingdom. Tel: +44 (0)20 7589 3428, fax: +44 (0)20 7589 3430, e-mail: london@mfa.ee, URL: http://www.estonia.gov.uk
Ambassador: Aino Lepil von Wiren (page 1462)

Estonian Embassy, Suite 503, 1730 M Street, NW, Washington, DC 20036, USA. Tel: +1 202 588 0101, fax: +1 202 588 0108, URL: http://www.estemb.org
Ambassador: Marina Kaljurand

Permanent Mission of Estonia to the UN, 600 Third Avenue, 26th Floor, New York, NY 10016-2001, USA. Tel: +1 212 883 0640, fax: +1 212 883 0648, e-mail: Mission.NewYork@mfa.ee, URL: http://www.un.estemb.org/
Ambassador: Marcus Kolga

LEGAL SYSTEM

The country's highest court is the Supreme Court, which also reviews the constitution. It ha 19 justices and the Chief Justice is appointed by parliament on the nomination of the president The Chief Justice nominates the other justices. Below this are circuit courts of appeal, rural city and district courts. Judges are appointed for life. They cannot hold any other elected o appointed office and can only be recalled by a court decision.

The government respects the human rights of its citizens and of the large ethnic Russian noncitizen community. There have been up-held allegations of excessive force by police during arrests. Long pre-trial detention is a problem, and conditions in detention centers i poor.

The death penalty was abolished in 1998.

Supreme Court, URL: http://www.nc.ee
Chief Justice: Märt Rask

LOCAL GOVERNMENT

Under the Constitution introduced in 1992 the local government units are districts and towns The representative body of local government is the *Volikogu* which is elected for a term o three years. Local governments have their own budgets and the right to impose and collec taxes. There are 15 counties, 193 municipalities and 33 cities. The 15 counties are Harju Hiiu, Ida-Viru, Jogeva, Järva, Lääne, Lääne-Viru, Polva, Pärnu, Rapla, Saare, Tartu, Valga Viljandi and Voru. Municipal elections took place in October 2005 and for the first time voters were able to vote electronically. The most recent elections took place in 2009.

AREA AND POPULATION

Area

Estonia lies in northern Europe at the eastern end of the Baltic, on the Finnish Gulf. It is bordered in the east by the Russian Federation and in the south by Latvia. Its total area (excluding territorial waters) is 45,227 sq. km, almost half of which is forested. There are four major islands: Saaremaa, Hiiumaa, Muhu and Vormsi. Estonia's Baltic coast has numerous bays, straits and islets and there are over 1,400 natural and man-made lakes including Peipsi, the largest, Vortsjärv and Narva reservoir.

The climate is maritime with cool summers and wet, moderate winters.

In May 2005 Estonia and Russia signed a treaty delimiting their border, but this has not been ratified.

To view a map of Estonia, please visit:
http://www.un.org/Depts/Cartographic/map/profile/estonia.pdf

Population

Estonia's population was estimated to be 1,341,000 in 2010, down from 1,345,000 as at January 1 2006 but up from 1,300,000 at the beginning of 2005. The population density is approximately 30 inhabitants per sq. km. Nearly 69 per cent of the population live in urban areas. The population of the main cities in 2004 was: Tallinn (397,150), Tartu (101,190), Narva (67,750), Kohtla-Ja'rve (46,760) and Pa'rnu (44,780). In 2010 the median age was 40 years. An estimated 23 per cent of the population was over 60 years old and 15 per cent under 15 years old.

In 2002 the ethnic composition of Estonia was 67.9 per cent (930,000) Estonian, 25.6 per cent (351,000) Russian, 2.1 per cent (29,000) Ukrainian, 1.3 per cent (17,000) Belarussian and 0.9 per cent (12,000) Finnish.

The official language is Estonian, belonging to the Baltic-Finnic group of the Finno-Ugric languages. It is closely related to Finnish and distantly related to Hungarian. It uses the Latin alphabet in its written form. Russian, Finnish, English and German are all widely spoken. A large proportion of Russian speakers, were workers brought into Estonia from the Soviet Union and have ended up living in Estonia but do not enjoy Estonian citizenship. In order to acquire citizenship they must pass an Estonian language test.

Births, Marriages, Deaths

In 2010, the total fertility rate was 1.7 per woman. The maternal mortality rate in 2009 was 12 deaths per 100,000 live births. The crude birth rate in 2010 was 12.1 per 1,000 population and the crude death rate was 12.2 per 1,000 population.

In 2009 life expectancy at birth was 80 years for females and 70 years for males. In 2007 healthy life expectancy was 71 years for females and 61 years for males. (Source: http://www.who.int, World Health Statistics 2012)

Public Holidays 2014

1 January: New Year's Day
24 February: Independence Day
18 April: Good Friday
20 April: Easter Sunday
1 May: Labour Day
8 June: Pentecost
23 June: Victory Day (anniversary of Battle of Vonnu, 1919)
24 June: Midsummer Day
20 August: Day of Restoration of Independence
25-26 December: Christmas

EMPLOYMENT

The following table shows the employed working population (656,500 persons) by sector of employment for 2008.

Sector of employment	2008
Agriculture, hunting & forestry	24,400
Fishing	1,100
Mining & quarrying	6,000
Manufacturing	138,500
Electricity, gas & water supply	8,900
Construction	79,900
Wholesale & retail trade, repairs	93,500
Hotels & restaurants	24,200
Transport, storage & communication	55,700
Financial intermediation	10,400
Real estate, renting & business	51,900
Public admin. & defence, compulsory social security	38,400
Education	59,600
Health & social care	31,600
Other	32,400

Source: Copyright © International Labour Organization (ILO Dept. of Statistics, http://laborsta.ilo.org)

The unemployment rate in 2000 was 13.7 per cent, falling to 12.7 per cent in 2001, 10.3 per cent in 2002, 10.0 per cent in 2003 and 9.7 per cent in 2004. Estimated figures for 2010 showed that the unemployment rate had risen to 16.5 per cent.

BANKING AND FINANCE

Currency
In June 1992 the Estonian kroon (crown) of 100 sents was introduced. The Kroon is pegged to the euro € at 1 € = 15.65 kroon. Estonia has been working towards adopting the Euro as its currency and as a result of the global economic downturn has had to introduce austerity measures to keep the economy in line for adoption of the Euro. At midnight on December 31 2010, the Euro became the official currency of Estonia, replacing the Kroon.

GDP/GNP, Inflation, National Debt
Estonia has a very free market-based economy. It has enjoyed economic stability in recent years, although under the current economic crisis growth has fallen by some 4 per cent. The telecommunications sector remains very strong.

In 2000, GDP at current prices was €5.5 billion, rising to €6.1 billion in 2001. Growth for 2001 was put at 6.5 per cent, 7.3 per cent in 2002 and 7.8 per cent in 2003. Figures for 2004 showed that the economy grew, which disproved the fears of some that joining the EU would result in a downturn in growth, although the predicted rise in inflation proved correct. Since membership of the EU, the economy has grown by 7.8 per cent in 2004, 9.7 per cent in 2005 and 11.3 per cent in 2006. The small labour market coupled with such strong growth led to high wage inflation as the available labour was in demand to fuel the continued economic growth. Growth slowed in 2007 to 5 per cent. Figures for 2009 estimated that economic growth in line with the global economic downturn had shrunk to -13 per cent. GDP growth recovered to 2.3 per cent in 2010 with nominal GDP of €14.3 billion. Growth continued in 2011 with GDP rising to €16 billion. Modest growth is expected to continue in 2012 despite the eurozone crisis. Growth was estimated at 3.4 per cent in 3Q 2012.

Per capita GDP was estimated at US$15,500 per annum in 2007 and US$14,075 in 2009.

Inflation stood at 3.6 per cent in 2002, falling to 1.3 per cent in 2003 before rising again to 3.0 per cent in 2004 and 6.4 per cent in 2006. It was estimated at -0.1 per cent in 2009. Inflation was estimated at 3 per cent in 2010, rising to an estimated 5 per cent in 2011.

The following table shows the value of GDP at current prices and real growth in recent years.

Year	GDP (million kroon)	Growth (%)
2004	151,541.6	7.2
2005	174,956.2	9.4
2006	206,996.0	10.0
2007	244,503.6	7.2
2008	251,492.8	-3.6

Source: Bank of Estonia

Manufacturing accounts for approximately 19 per cent of GDP, real estate accounts for 16 per cent, transport 14 per cent, wholesale and retail trade 12 per cent, construction 7 per cent, education 5 per cent, finance 4 per cent, and agriculture 2.5 per cent.

Foreign Investment
Foreign direct investment amounted to €4,034.1 million in 2002, 40 per cent of which came from Sweden and nearly 30 per cent from Finland.

Balance of Payments / Imports and Exports
Estonia became a full member of the European Union on 1 May 2004. Estonia is also a member of the World Trade Organisation.

The following table shows the balance of payments in recent years. Figures are in million kroon.

Foreign Trade	2006	2007	2008
Exports	120,775.6	125,702.3	132,456.1
- continued			
Imports	167,597.3	178,990.4	170,510.9
Trade balance	-46,821.7	-53,288.2	-38,054.8

Source: Bank of Estonia

Exports were estimated to be US$11.5 billion in 2010 and imports cost over US$12 billion.

Estonia's main trading partners are Finland, Sweden, Germany, Russian Federation, Japan, US and Latvia. Nearly 80 per cent of exports go to Europe.

Central Bank
Bank of Estonia, Estonia bld. 13, 15095 Tallinn, Estonia. Tel: +372 668 0719 / 668 0900, fax: +372 668 0836 / 668 0954, e-mail: info@epbe.ee, URL: http://www.eestipank.info
Governor: Ardo Hansson (page 1438)

Chambers of Commerce and Trade Organisations
The Estonian Chamber of Commerce and Industry, URL: http://www.koda.ee/

MANUFACTURING, MINING AND SERVICES

Primary and Extractive Industries
The bedrock of northern Estonia contains deposits of limestone and clay, which is used in the manufacture of cement, lime building stone and bricks and drainage pipes. Other raw materials include silica sand, building sand and gravel sand, peat, granite, glass dolomite, lake chalk and brick clay. Oil shale is Estonia's most valuable mineral resource and is used for generating electric power, as well as producing petrol, oil and chemical products.

In 2009, total estimated oil production was 7.60 thousand barrels per day. Consumption was estimated at 29,700 bbl/d. There are no recorded oil reserves. Most of the oil production comes from oil shale. Most imported oil comes from Russia. The Tallinn port complex is (URL: http://www.portoftallinn.com/) made up of six harbours (Old City Harbour, Old City Marina, Muuga, Stareema, Paljassaare and Paldiski). In 2005 the port had oil flows of 537,000 bbl/d. Expansion of the port is planned. Estonia has no natural gas reserves of its own and in 2010 imported 25 billion cubic feet to meets its needs.

In 2010, an estimated 19.78 million short tons of coal were produced. Consumption was estimated at 19.76 million metric tons. (Source: EIA)

Energy
Oil shale is the primary energy source and over 95 per cent of electric power is generated by oil shale fired power plants It is estimated that there are reserves of 4 billion tonnes. Estonia has no natural gas supplies of its own; all natural gas is imported from Russia. In February 2006 Lithuania, Latvia and Estonia signed an agreement to build a new nuclear power plant in Lithuania. They are also committed to drawing up a pan-Baltic energy policy. In 2007 gas consumption was estimated at 52 billion cubic feet.

In 2010, 12.2 billion kWh of electricity was generated and 7.95 billion kWh consumed. Estonia exports electricity to Latvia and Russia. Most of the electricity is generated by the oil shale-fired power plants. The installed capacity was 2.66 billion GWe. Total primary energy produced was 0.136 quadrillion Btu and total consumption was 0.244 Quadrillion Btu. (Source: EIA)

Manufacturing
Food processing is the most important sector of manufacturing followed by machinery, wood processing and light industry. The food processing industry is dominated by milk and fish processing. The machinery sector includes the manufacture of industrial and laboratory equipment, parts for mobile phones, computer parts and parts for lifting and loading equipment. Light industry consists mainly of textiles, clothing and footwear. The following table shows the gross output of industries at current prices in million kroons:

Industry	2006	2007
Mining	3,124	4,457
Manufacturing	103,696	119,369
of which:		
Food products and beverages	15,867	17,777
Textiles	4,180	4,283
Wearing apparel	2,484	2,462
Leather & footwear	436	459
Wood & wood products	16,554	18,826
Pulp & paper	2,200	3,031
Publishing, printing & reproduction of recorded media	4,549	5,074
Chemicals & chemical products	5,388	5,933
Rubber & plastic products	4,768	5,053
Machinery & equipment	3,759	4,693
Electrical machinery & apparatus	5,372	6,582
Radio, television & communication equipment & apparatus	3,715	4,169
Medical, precision & optical instruments, watches & clocks	1,555	1,815
Transport equipment	2,456	3,191
Furniture & other manufactured goods	6,455	6,899
Other manufacturing	2,538	2,870

Service Industries
In 2001 there were 1,231,620 visitors to Estonia of whom 1,058,386 came from Finland, 17,664 from Sweden, 12,022 from CIS, 11,243 from Latvia and Lithuania and 54,541 from USA and Canada. Overall visitors were down from the 2000 figure of 1,369,159. Figures from 2003 show that Estonia had 1,462,000 visitors, generating receipts of US$886 million. Figures from 2006 show that visitor figures had risen to 1,940,000 in 2006.

ESTONIA

Agriculture

Agriculture and hunting contributed 3.5 per cent of GDP in 2011. An estimated 843,000 hectares are arable land, 12,000 hectares permanent crop land and 131,000 hectares pasture.

Agricultural Production in 2010

Produce	Int. $'000*	Tonnes
Cow milk, whole, fresh	185,741	675,344
Indigenous pigmeat	87,921	57,194
Indigenous cattle meat	52,977	19,611
Rapeseed	35,613	131,022
Potatoes	24,199	163,373
Wheat	23,792	327,600
Indigenous chicken meat	20,180	14,167
Hen eggs, in shell	9,427	11,366
Carrots & turnips	5,693	22,817
Vegetables fresh nes	2,787	14,787
Rye	2,493	25,100
Cabbages & other brassicas	2,436	16,280

*=unofficial figures

Source: http://faostat.fao.org/site/339/default.aspx Food and Agriculture Organization of the United Nations, Food and Agricultural commodities production

According to the latest FAO figures, in 2004 there were 257,000 head of cattle and buffaloes and 34,000 sheep and goats.

Forestry

About 40 per cent of the country's area is covered by forests. The main species of trees are conifers (pine and shrub) as well as a variety of deciduous varieties, among them ash and maple. The following tables shows timber production in 2004.

Timber Production

Product	'000 cubic metres
Roundwood	8,100
Log: saw & veneer	3,360
Wood fuel	2,200
Sawnwood	2,000
Wood charcoal*	3
Paper, Paper Board	66
Wood-based panels	388

*'000 tonnes

Source: FAOSTAT, Food & Agriculture Organization of the UN

Fishing

In 2010, the total catch was put at 95,400 tonnes.

COMMUNICATIONS AND TRANSPORT

Travel Requirements

US, Canadian and Australian citizens require a passport but not a visa for stays of up to three months. EU nationals holding a national Identity Card do not require a passport or a visa for visits of up to three months. Other visitors should contact the embassy to check visa requirements. Estonia joined the Schengen Agreement in June 2007 for borders and seaports, and in March 2008 for airports. Evidence of health and travel insurance is required, as well as sufficient funds for the visit.

National Airlines

Estonian Air, URL: http://www.estonian-air.ee
Aviation is regulated by the following bodies.
Civil Aviation Administration, URL: http://www.ecaa.ee
Ministry of Economic Affairs and Communications, http://www.mkm.ee

International Airports

Tallinn Airport, URL: http://www.tallinn-airport.ee
Kärdla Airport, http://www.airport.hiiumaa.ee
Kuressaare Airport, http://www.eeke.ee

Railways

The total length of the railway system is 967 km of which 131 km is electrified. Figures for 2001 show that 64.7 million tons of goods were transported by rail of which 33.5 million tons were international traffic, and 5.5 million passenger journeys were made. The state railway company, AS Eesti Raudtee was restructured in 2009. A rail connection runs between Estonia and Moscow, Russia.
Estonian State Railway, Pikk 36, 15073 Tallinn, Estonia. Tel: +372 615 8610, fax: +372 615 8710, URL: http://www.evr.ee

Roads

Recent figures show that there are 56,860 km of roads, of which around 13,000 km were paved. Vehicles are driven on the right. Tallin has a tram system. Bus routes link Estonia to many international cities including Moscow, Saint Petersburg, Kiev, Kaliningrad, and Warsaw.

Waterways

Estonia has 320 km of navigable inland waterways with boat services on the Emajõgi River and Lake Peipsi. Ferries run from the mainland to the larger islands.

Shipping

Shipping has gained in importance since the opening of the new harbour at Tallinn. Th Estonian Merchant Shipping Agency, the country's main shipping agent, has recently acquire several modern vessels. Regular ferry connections operate from Tallinn to Stockholm an Helsinki by the Tallink, Inreko, Estline and Silja Line companies. There are also other por in the vicinity of Tallinn, including Muuga, Tallinn City and Kopli. The Tallinn City Port i mainly a passenger terminal and the Muuga Port deals with various cargoes. Figures fo 2001 show that 4.5 million passenger journeys were made by sea and that 1.5 million ton of goods were transported by sea, all of which was international traffic.
Estonian Shipping Company (ESCO), URL: http://www.eml.ee/

Ports and Harbours

The main ports are Tallin, Muuga, Paldiski, Parnu, Haapsalu and Kunda.

HEALTH

In 2008, Estonia spent approximately 11.7 per cent of its total budget on healthcare accounting for 78.4 per cent of all healthcare spending. Total expenditure on health car equated to 6.7 per cent of the country's GDP. External resources accounted for 67 per cent of total expenditure. Per capita total expenditure on health in 2009 was US$967 (compare to US$250 in 2000). In 2005-10, there were 4,378 doctors (33.3 per 10,000 population) 8,605 nurses and midwives (65.5 per 10,000 population), 1,196 dentists (9.1 per 10,00 population) and 857 pharmacuetical personnel. There were 56 hospital beds per 10,00 population.

An estimated 1.3 per cent of the population aged 15-49 have HIV/AIDS. In 2008, the estimate infant mortality rate (probability of dying by first birthday) was 4 per 1,000 live births. Th under-fives mortality rate was 5 per 1,000 live births. The most common causes of deat among young children were congential abnormalities 24 per cent, prematurity 5 per cer and birth asphyxia 19 per cent, pneumonia 3 per cent and HIV/AIDs 2 per cent.

In 2008, an estimated 99 per cent of the urban population and 97 per cent of the rura population used improved drinking water sources. An estimated 96 per cent of the populatio and 94 per cent of the rural population had access to improved sanitation. (Source http://www.who.int, World Health Statistics 2012)

EDUCATION

Education is compulsory and free. The present school system comprises pre-school educatio (crèches, nursery education), general education, vocational training, secondary specialise education and higher education. Specialised schools cater for handicapped children an those with particular needs.

In 2009 it was estimated that 96 per cent of children were enrolled in pre-primary educatio and an estimated 94.5 per cent of children were enrolled in primary education. An estimate 100 per cent of children completed their primary education. The pupil/teacher ratio in primar education was 12:1.

Secondary enrolment is estimated at 92 per cent and tertiary enrolment at 63 per cent Institutes of Higher Education include Tartu University (founded in 1632), Tallinn Art Universit Tallinn Conservatoire, Tallinn Technical University, Tallinn Teacher Training Institute, th Estonian Lutheran Church Theological Institute, and the Estonian Agricultural Academy.

Government expenditure was estimated at 5.7 per cent of GDP in 2008 (14.2 per cent o total government expenditure). The distribution was as follows: pre-primary 9 per cent primary 25 per cent, secondary 44 per cent and tertiary 21 per cent.

The adult literacy rate is estimated at 99.8 per cent. (Source: UNESCO)

RELIGION

The 1992 Estonian Constitution states that all persons can freely belong to a church o religious group. Consequently, there are a number of different faiths and denomination represented in Estonia. Around 73 per cent of the population are Christian, including Protestantism, Lutheran, the Eastern Orthodox Church, and the Roman Catholic Church. Small Muslim and Jewish communities also exist. There is a Jewish community of around 1,500 and the first synagogue to be built in Estonia since the Holocaust opened in Tallinn in 2007. There are an estimated 4,000 Muslims in the country.

Estonia has a religious tolerance rating of 9 on a scale of 1 to 10 (10 is most freedom). (Source: World Religion Database)

COMMUNICATIONS AND MEDIA

Newspapers

Postimees (Postman), daily, URL: http://www.postimees.ee
Vesti Dnya, Russian language, URL: http://www.vesti.ee/
Eesti Paevaleht (Estonian Daily), URL: http://www.postimees.ee
Maaleht, weekly, URL: http://www.maaleht.ee
Aripaev, business daily, URL: http://www.ap3.ee/

Broadcasting

Estonian Television has one channel but channels from Finland and the Russian Federation can also be received in certain areas. Many Estonians have cable TV. Radio transmissions are broadcast in eight languages. Many privately-owned TVs are owne by Swedish and Norwegian media groups.
Eesti Televisioon, public broadcaster, URL: http://www.etv.ee

TV3, private, URL: http://www.tv3.ee/
Kanal 2, URL: http://www.kanal2.ee/
Eesti Radio, public, four stations, URL: http://www.er.ee/

Telecommunications
Foreign investment has improved the telephone service in recent years. Interent services are widely available. In 2010 it was estimated that there were 480,000 main lines. Foreign investment helped improved the mobile communications network and by 2010 it was estimated that there were 1.6 million mobile phone subscriptions.

Estonia has a developed internet set up. All schools are connected to the internet and online voting in a parliamentary election has taken place. An estimated 990,000 people used the internet in 2011.

ENVIRONMENT

Environmental issues include air pollution and waste water pollution. Air quality has been improved; sulphur dioxide emissions fell 20 per cent between 1980 and 2000. In 2009, Estonia's total emissions from the consumption of fossil fuels were 16.87 million metric tons of carbon dioxide, dbut this had risen to 20.56 million metric tons in 2010. (Source: EIA).

Estonia is a party to the following international agreements: Air Pollution, Air Pollution-Nitrogen Oxides, Air Pollution-Persistent Organic Pollutants, Air Pollution-Sulfur 85, Air Pollution-Volatile Organic Compounds, Antarctic Treaty, Biodiversity, Climate Change, Climate Change-Kyoto Protocol, Endangered Species, Hazardous Wastes, Law of the Sea, Ozone Layer Protection, Ship Pollution and Wetlands.

SPACE PROGRAMME

Since independence, Estonia's main area of space research has been cosmology. Estonian companies are involved in the production of antennas and have contributed to the Mars mission. In 2012 Estonia launched a research satellite with Finland. Its mission was to gather data on solar winds.

Estonia signed a co-operation agreement with the European Space Agency in 2007.

ETHIOPIA
Federal Democratic Republic of Ethiopia
Ityop'iya Federalawi Demokrasiyawi Ripeblik

Capital: Addis Ababa (Population estimate: 2.6 million)

Head of State: H.E. Ato Girma Wolde Giorgis (page 1538)

National Flag: A horizontal tricolour of green, yellow and red with a yellow pentagram and single yellow rays emanating from the angles between the points on a light blue disc centred on the three bands

CONSTITUTION AND GOVERNMENT

Constitution
Until 1974 the country preserved the tradition of Imperial rule. The last emperor, Haile Selassie, came to the throne in 1930. Although he introduced elements of constitutional rule, including provision for an elected Chamber of Deputies, the political system was in practice feudal. Following military intervention in 1974 and the deposition of Emperor Haile Selassie on 12 September of that year, the constitution was abolished. Ethiopia was then governed by a Provisional Military Administrative Council (PMAC) which ruled by decree. From 1962, Eritrea was incorporated into Ethiopia as a province. A secessionist movement was active in the region until independence in 1993.

Lt. Col. Mengistu Haile Mariam took power in 1977 and ruled until 1991 when, due to increasing pressure from the Ethiopian People's Revolutionary Democratic Front (EPRDF), he fled the country. The EPRDF leader Meles Zenawi announced the formation of a provisional government. A new constitution was promulgated in December 1994, which allows for a federal style of government. The first democratic elections took place in Ethiopia in May 1995.

To consult the full constitution, please visit:
http://www.wipo.int/wipolex/en/details.jsp?id=7438

International Relations
In 1998 relations deteriorated with Eritrea as the two countries fought over a disputed area, Badme, whose frontier has not been properly demarcated. In May 2000 Ethiopia captured large areas of Eritrean territory. In June 2000 the two countries signed a ceasefire accord, which allowed for a United Nations peace-keeping force in a buffer zone until the border is demarcated. In December 2000 the two countries signed a peace treaty, and an international commission was set up to draw up a new border between the two countries. In April 2001 the buffer zone was established. In April 2003 the Boundary Commission came up with the new boundaries, which Ethiopia disputed because the border town of Badme was designated as being in Eritrea. In November 2004 Ethiopia announced that it accepted UN's ruling on the boundary 'in principle'.

In October 2006 the UN called on Eritrea to withdraw troops from the buffer zone on the Ethiopian border. Tension rose between Ethiopia and the militia who control part of Somalia and in December, the Ethiopian authorities confirmed that they were fighting Islamic militia in Somalia, in support of the Somali transitional government. The militia were defeated. Over the six months to February 2007, some 50,000 Somalis sought refuge in Ethiopia according to the UNHCR. In June 2008 the Somali peace deal provided for the withdrawal of Ethiopian troops within three months. The troop withdrawal was completed in January 2009.

In September 2007 the UN warned that the conflict between Eritrea and Ethiopia could resume. The following month Eritrea accepted the International Boundary Commission's proposed border demarcation. Ethiopia however rejected it. In July 2008 the UN Security Council voted to end its peace-keeping mission on the disputed border.

Recent Events
Elections in May 2005 were marred by allegations of electoral fraud, and ended in protests in which forty people were killed. Further protests broke out in November, and 46 people died. Thousands of people were detained, and in May 2006, eighty people were charged with genocide and treason. In May 2006, an oppostion alliance (the Alliance for Freedom and Democracy) was formed by six political parties and armed groups.

In May 2008, Ethiopia's Supreme Court sentenced former ruler Mengistu Haile Mariam, in absentia, to death. Colonel Mengitsu came to power in 1977 as leader of the Provisional Military Administrative Council known as The Derg; under his rule civil war had raged, the economy had failed and many Ethiopians were subjected to human rights abuses. He was overthrown in 1991 after the Ethiopian People's Revolutionary Democratic Front captured Addis Ababa. He has since been in exile in Zimbabwe.

In September 2008, Ethiopia held celebrations to mark the completion of the reassembly of 1700 year old Axum Obelisk, the obelisk had been looted in 1937 during the Italian conquest, Italy returned the obelisk in three parts.

In January 2009, the Ethiopian parliament passed a bill which banned foreign agencies from work related to human rights or conflict resolution, it also severely restricted foreign funding for local agencies, the bill was seen as a way of restricting unwanted foreign interference.

In August 2009, Ethiopia and Eritrea were ordered to pay each other compensation following their 1998-2000 border war.

In September 2009, Chinese firms secured agreements to build several hydro-power dams and wind farms.

In October 2009, Ethiopia was hit by severe drought conditions the government said around six million needed food aid.

In December 2009, Ogaden National Liberation Front rebels claimed they had captured several towns in the east following heavy fighting.

In June 2010, talks were held in Addis Ababa between countries sharing the River Nile, the talks failed to resolve their differences on how to use the waters.

In October 2010, clashes between government forces and rebels of the Ogaden National Liberation Front were reported.

In July 2011 Ethiopia and other Horn of Africa countries began to feel the effects of the region's worst drought for 60 years. It is believed that 500,000 cattle in Ethiopia alone have died and crops have withered in fields. The crisis has been further fueled by food shortages following a drought in 2009 of which most countries are still feeling the effects. Western aid agencies are fearful that the drought will escalate into a full blown famine.

In August 2012, Prime Minister Meles Zenawi died in Brussels after 21 years in power. Hailemariam Desalegn became acting prime minister and was sworn in as prime minister in September.

Legislature
The legislature of Ethiopia is bicameral. The lower house is the House of People's Representatives, *Yehizb Tewokayoch Mekir Bet*, consisting currently of 547 directly elected members who serve a five year term. There is provision for 550 members. The upper house is the Federal Council or *Yefedereshn Mekir Bet*, consisting of 110 indirectly elected members who also serve a five year term. The members represent the nations and nationalities of Ethiopia and are elected by the government councils of Ethiopia's nine states.

ETHIOPIA

House of People's Representatives, P.O. Box 80001, Addis Ababa, Ethiopia. Tel: +251 (0) 55 30 00, fax: +251 (0)1 55 09 00, e-mail: national.parliament@telecom.net.et, URL: http://www.ethiopar.net
House of the Federation, P.O. Box 80001, Addis Ababa, Ethiopia. Tel: +251 (0)1 55 63 95, fax: +251 (0)1 55 07 22, URL: http://www.ethiopar.ent

---

Cabinet (as at March 2013)
Prime Minister, Commander in Chief of the National Armed Forces: Hailemariam Desalegn (page 1436)
Minister of Foreign Affairs: Dr Tewodros Adhanom
Deputy Prime Minister, Minister of Education: Demeke Mekonnen
Deputy Prime Minister for Good Governance and Reforms, Minister for the Civil Service: Muktar Kedir
Deputy Prime Minister for Finance and Economy, Minister of Information and Communication Technology: Gebremichael Debretsion
Minister of Defence: Siraj Fegesa
Minister of Federal Affairs: Shiferaw Tekle-Mariam
Minister of Trade: Kebed Chane
Minister of Industry: Mekonnen Manyazewal
Minister of Finance and Economic Development: Sofian Ahmed
Minister of Justice: Berhan Hailu
Minister of Water and Energy: Alemayehu Tegenu
Minister of Transport: Diriba Kuma
Minister of Labour and Social Affairs: Abdulfeta Abdoulrahman
Minister of Health: Keseteberhan Admassu
Minister of Culture and Tourism: Amin Abdulkadir
Minister of Women and Youth Affairs: Zenebu Taddesse
Minister of Agriculture and Rural Development: Tefera Deribew
Minister of Mines: Sinkinesh Ejigu
Minister of Science and Technology: Desse Balke
Minister of Urban Development and Construction: Mekuria Haile
Government Whip: Aster Mamo

Ministries

Office of the President, PO Box 1031, Addis Ababa, Ethiopia. Tel: +251 11 155 0224, fax: +251 11 155 2041
Office of the Prime Minister, PO Box 1031, Addis Ababa, Ethiopia. Tel: +251 11 155 2044, fax: +251 11 155 2020
Ministry of Finance and Economic Development, PO Box 1037, Addis Ababa, Ethiopia. Tel: +251 11 122 6698, fax: +251 11 155 3844, e-mail: medac2@telecom.net.et, URL: http://mofaed.org
Ministry of Foreign Affairs, PO Box 393, Abbis Ababa, Ethiopia. Tel: +251 11 551 7345, fax: +251 11 551 4300, e-mail: mfa.addis@telecom.net.et, URL: http://www.mfa.gov.et
Ministry of Agriculture and Rural Development, PO Box 63247, Addis Ababa, Ethiopia. Tel: +251 11 551 8040, fax: +251 11 551 2984, e-mail: moard@ethionet.et, URL: http://www.moard.gov.et
Ministry of Capacity Building, PO Box 1082, Addis Ababa, Ethiopia. Tel: +251 11 123 9911, fax: +251 11 123 9872, e-mail: mocb5@ethionet.et, URL: http://www.mocb.gov.et
Ministry of Culture and Tourism, PO Box 2183, Addis Ababa, Ethiopia. Tel: +251 11 551 2310, fax: +251 11 551 2889, e-mail: info@tourismethiopia.org, URL: http://www.tourismethiopia.org
Ministry of Education, PO Box 1367,Addis Ababa, Ethiopia. Tel: +251 11 155 3133, fax: +251 11 155 0877
Ministry of Health, PO Box 486, Addis Ababa, Ethiopia. Tel: +251 11 551 7011, fax: +251 11 551 9366, e-mail: moh@ethionet.et, URL: http://www.moh.gov.et
Ministry of Justice, PO Box 1370, Addis Ababa, Ethiopia. Tel: +251 11 551 2288, fax: +251 11 551 7775, e-mail: ministry-justice@telecom.net.et, URL: http://www.mojet.gov.et
Ministry of Labour and Social Affairs, PO Box 2056, Addis Ababa, Ethiopia. Tel: +251 11 551 7080, fax: +251 11 551 8396,
Ministry of Mines and Energy, PO Box 486, Addis Ababa, Ethiopia. Tel: +251 11 646 3166, fax: +251 11 646 6134, e-mail: mme@ethionet.et, URL: http://www.mom.gov.et
Ministry of National Defence, PO Box 1373, Addis Ababa, Ethiopia. Tel: +251 11 551 1777, fax: +251 11 551 6053
Ministry of Revenue Collection, PO Box 2559, Debrezeit Road, near Global Hotel, Abbis Ababa, Ethiopia. Tel: +251 11 466 7466, fax: +251 11 466 2628, e-mail: mor@ethionet.et, URL: http://www.mor.gov.et
Ministry of Science and Technology, PO Box 2490, Addis Ababa, Ethiopia. Tel: +251 11 551 1344, fax: +251 11 552 4400, e-mail: comm@estc.gov.et
Ministry of Trade and Industry, PO Box 704, Addis Ababa, Ethiopia. Tel: +251 11 551 3900, fax: +251 11 551 4288, e-mail: moi@moi.gov.et, URL: http://www.moi.gov.et
Ministry of Transport and Communications, PO Box 1238, Addis Ababa, Ethiopia. Tel: +251 11 551 6166, fax: +251 11 155 5665, e-mail: moi@moi.gov.et, URL: http://www.moi.gov.et
Ministry of Water Resources, PO Box 5744, Addis Ababa, Ethiopia. Tel: +251 11 661 1111, fax: +251 11 661 0885, e-mail: mowr@mowr.com.et, URL: http://www.mowr.gov.et/
Ministry of Women, Children and Youth Affairs, PO Box 1293, Addis Ababa, Ethiopia. Tel: +251 11 416 6362
Ministry of Works and Urban Development, PO Box 1238, Addis Ababa, Ethiopia. Tel: +251 11 551 6166, fax: +251 11 551 5665, e-mail: publicrelation@moi.gov.et, URL: http://www.moi.gov.et

Elections
Parliamentary elections were held on 15 May 2005. They were marred by allegations of election fraud and, in the ensuing protests 40 people were killed. In September it was announced that the ruling Ethiopian People's Revolutionary Democratic Front had been re-elected but with a reduced majority, winning 360 seats. In November there were fresh protests over the election; 46 protesters died and thousands of people were detained. Over eighty people were later charged with treason and genocide over the clashes. The most

recent parliamentary elections were held in May 2010, the ruling Ethiopian People's Revolutionary Democratic Front won with a large majority. Opposition parties asked for a rerun.

The most recent presidential elections were held in October 2007. The President is elected for a six year term, whilst the Prime Minister is elected for a five year term.

Political Parties
The government is run by the Ethiopian People's Revolutionary Democratic Front (EPRDF), which is an alliance of four parties: the Tigrayan People's Liberation Front (TPLF), Amhara National Democratic Movement (ANDM), Oromo People's Democratic Organisation (OPDO) and Southern Ethiopian People's Democratic Movement (SEPDM). Other parties include the United Ethiopian Democratic Forces (UEDF), the Coalition for Unity and Democracy (CUD) and the Oromo National Congress (ONC). The Oromo Liberation Front is an outlawed party.

Diplomatic Representation
British Embassy, Fikre Mariam Abatechan Street, Addis Ababa (PO Box 858), Ethiopia. Tel: +251 (0)1 612354, fax: +251 (0)1 610588, e-mail: BritishEmbassy.AddisAbaba@fco.gov.uk, URL: http://ukinethiopia.fco.gov.uk/en
Ambassador: Gregory Dorey (page 1417)
US Embassy, Entoto Street, Addis Ababa (PO Box 1014), Ethiopia. Tel: +251 (0)1 550666, fax: +251 (0)1 551328, e-mail: usemaddis@state.gov, URL: http://ethiopia.usembassy.gov
Ambassador: Donald E. Booth (page 1391)
Ethiopian Embassy, 17 Prince's Gate, London, SW7 1PZ. Tel: +44 (0)20 7589 72125, fax: +44 (0)20 7584 7054, URL: http://www.ethioembassy.org.uk
Ambassador: Berhanu Kebede (page 1454)
Ethiopian Embassy, 3506 International Drive, NW Washington, DC 20008, USA. Tel: + 202 364 1200, fax: +1 202 686 9551, URL: http://www.ethiopianembassy.org
Ambassador: Girma Birru (page 1389)
Permanent Representative of the Federal Democratic Republic of Ethiopia to the United Nations , 866 Second Avenue, Third Floor, New York, NY 10017, USA. Tel: +1 212 421 1830, fax: +1 212 754 0360, URL: http://www.ethiopianmission-ny.org
Permanent Representative: Tekeda Alemu Wolde Mariam

LEGAL SYSTEM

Ethiopia's judicial system has two parallel court structures; federal courts and state courts with their independent structures.

The Constitution states that supreme federal judicial authority is vested in the Federal Supreme Court. The Federal Supreme Court sits in Addis Ababa with national jurisdiction and Federal High Courts, previously limited to Addis Adaba and Dire Dawa, have now been established in five States. Federal Courts has a civil, criminal and labour division with a presiding judge and two other judges in each division. The Federal Supreme Court includs a cassation division to review decision issued by lower federal courts.

There are three levels of State courts; the State Supreme Court, High Courts and First Instance Courts. State Supreme Courts sit in the capital cities of the respective states and have final judicial authority over matters of State law and jurisdiction.

There are also local Shari'ah courts which hear religion and family cases involving Muslims.

In 1994, a special prosecutor's office began trying defendants charged with crimes against humanity during the Mengistu regime; over 5,000 people had been charged with war crimes by the end of 1999. The former dictator Mengistu Haile Mariam was found guilty in absentia of genocide in 2007.

The current judiciary suffers from a lack of trained personnel as well as financial constraints.

In 1999, the Council of People's Representatives passed legislation enabling the creation of a human rights commission. Human rights abuses include unlawful killings, torture, and abuse by security forces, usually with impunity. There are many instances of arbitrary arrest and detention, police and judicial corruption, and infringement of citizens' privacy rights including illegal searches. Prison conditions are harsh. There are restrictions on freedom of the press, and on freedom of assembly and association, as well as government interference in union activities. Ethiopia retains the death penalty.

Supreme Court of Ethiopia, URL: http://www.fsc.gov.et/

Ethiopia Human Rights Commission, PO Box 1165, Addis Ababa, Ethiopia. Tel: +251 11 618 0040, fax: +251 11 618 0041, URL: http://www.ehrc.org.et/

LOCAL GOVERNMENT

In 1994 the new constitution established nine regional governments, each responsible for administering their own areas. These local governments are: Afar, Amhara, Benishangul/Gumuz, Gambella, Harari, Oromiya, Southern Nations Nationalities and Peoples', Somali and Tigray. There are also two chartered cities, Addis Ababa and Dire-Dawa.

AREA AND POPULATION

Area
Ethiopia is a landlocked country situated on the east side of Africa, in the area known as the Horn of Africa. It is above the equator, lying between the White Nile and the Red Sea. It is bounded on the north and west by the Sudan, on the north and east by Eritrea and the

Republic of Djibouti, on the south-east by the Somali Republic, and to the south by Kenya. The country is mountainous, with high plateaux and deep ravines. The total area is approximately 395,000 sq. miles.

The climate varies significantly throughout the country. The low-lying areas are the hottest areas with both tropical and arid conditions. Temperatures can reach 50°C. There is a temperate zone and then a cool zone in the highest areas above 2,400 metres. The rainy-season is generally from June to September. The remainder of the year is generally dry and droughts can occur when the rains fail.

To view a map, please consult
http://www.lib.utexas.edu/maps/cia08/ethiopia_sm_2008.gif

Ethiopia never adopted the Gregorian calendar, but has always used the Julian calendar. Therefore the Ethiopian year has twelve 30-day months and a thirteenth month of five or six days, depending on whether the year is a leap year or not. The first month of the year is Meskerem (September) and New Year's Day is the 12th September. Years in the Julian calendar are seven or eight years behind the Gregorian calendar, so year 2000 would be 1992 in Ethiopia. Ethiopia also uses its own time, based on 12 hours of daylight, starting at 6.00am, and 12 hours of darkness, starting at 6.00pm. Therefore 7.00am GMT is 1.00am Ethiopian time.

Population
Ethiopia is home to over eighty ethnic groups; Around 60 per cent of the population is Amhara, Tigre and Oromo. Amharic is the official language; other languages spoken include Arabic, Tigrinya, Oromifa, Somali and English as well as many local languages.

In 2010 the population was estimated to be approximately 82.95 million. It is estimated that 83 per cent of the population lives in rural areas, and that the annual population growth was 2.3 per cent over the period 2000-10. Addis Ababa, the capital, has a population of around 2.6 million. Other cities include Dire Dawa with a population of 238,000, Harar with a population of 138,000, Dessie with a population of 142,000 and Nazret with a population of 190,000. In 2004 the government began a drive to move people away from the arid areas in the east of the country in an attempt to ease food shortages. The plans accounted for the movement of 2 million people

Births, Marriages, Deaths
In 2010, the crude birth rate was an estimated 31.4 births per 1,000 population and 11.7 deaths per 1,000 population. Average life expectancy in 2009 was 53 years for males and 56 years for females. Healthy life expectancy at birth would be 50 years. The infant mortality rate is estimated at 68 per 1,000 live births. (Source: http://www.who.int, World Health Statistics 2012)

National Day
21 March: Proclamation of the Republic.

EMPLOYMENT

Agriculture accounts for 85 per cent of employment. Approximately 9.5 per cent are employed in manufacturing. Some 23 per cent of the population live on under $1 a day. Figures for 2007 estimated the work force to number 38 million.

Employment by Economic Activity in July 2006

Activity	Employed
Agriculture, hunting, forestry & fishing	3,310,000
Mining & quarrying	134,000
Manufacturing	5,856,000
Electricity, gas & water supply	386,000
Construction	2,090,000
Wholesale & retail trade, repairs	8,726,000
Hotels & restaurants	3,691,000
Transport, storage & communications	1,545,000
Financial intermediation	444,000
Real estate, renting & business	564,000
Public admin. & defence	2,686,000
Education, health & social work	3,144,000
Other community, social & personal service activities	3,495,000
Households with employed persons	2,017,000
Extra-territorial orgs. & bodies	251,000
Other	31 000
Total	38,368,000

Source: Copyright © International Labour Organization (ILO Dept. of Statistics, http://laborsta.ilo.org)

BANKING AND FINANCE

Currency
The unit of currency is the Birr. Each Birr is divided into 100 cents. The Birr was devalued in 1992.

GDP/GNP, Inflation, National Debt
Ethiopia is a very poor country. The economy is dominated by agriculture; it accounts for around 50 per cent of GDP, 80 per cent of employment and 60 per cent of export earnings, particularly from coffee. The agriculture sector is heavily reliant on rainfall, and droughts in recent years have led to a loss of earnings and dependence on food aid. However, Ethiopia is now benefiting from HIPC debt relief (Heavily Indebted Poor Countries). The new

government of Ethiopia has set out to make economic reforms which will include the privatisation of some state enterprises. The government has attracted some foreign investment.

Estimated figures for 2008-09 put GDP at around US$32 billion with an estimated growth rate of 9.8 per cent. Figures for 2007 put GDP at US$15,068.95 million with a growth rate of around 8.2 per cent. In 2006, GDP was put at US$14,022.25 million with a growth rate of 6.4 per cent. Per capita income in 2009-10 was an estimated US$350. Inflation was 17 per cent in 2007, up from 12.83 per cent in 2006 and 6.8 per cent in 2005. It was estimated to be 8 per cent in 2010.

Total external public debt was US$8 billion in 2011.

Balance of Payments / Imports and Exports
Main export goods are gold, leather goods and coffee. Coffee represents some 50 per cent of exports. Main imported goods are food and animals, petroleum and machinery including vehicles. Main trading partners include Japan, UK, USA, Germany and Italy.

External Trade, US$ million

	2005	2006	2007
Trade balance	-2,786.76	-3,383.17	-3,716.40
Exports	847.20	1,000.29	1,066.79
Imports	3,632.96	4,383.46	4,782.19

Source: African Development Bank

Exports were estimated to be worth US$2 billion in 2010 and imports cost US$8 billion.

Central Bank
National Bank of Ethiopia, PO Box 5550, Addis Ababa, Ethiopia. Tel: +251 (0)1 517430, fax: +251 (0)1 514588, e-mail: nbe.vgov@telecom.net.et, URL: http://www.nbe.gov.et
Governor: HE Ato Teklewold Atnafu

Chambers of Commerce and Trade Organisations
Ethiopian Chamber of Commerce and Industry, URL: http://www.ethiopianchamber.com/
Ethiopian Investment Office, URL: http://www.ethiomarket.com/eic/
Addis Ababa Chamber of Commerce, URL: http://www.addischamber.com/

MANUFACTURING, MINING AND SERVICES

Primary and Extractive Industries
Gold is exploited in commercial quantities. A new mine was inaugurated at Legadembi in February 1991. An initial annual output of 3,000 kg was anticipated. The country is rich in minerals. There is traditional exploitation of salt and platinum and deposits of zinc, potash, copper and titanium. Very small reserves of oil have been found and exploration in ongoing, natural gas has been found in Harar but has yet to be exploited, reserves are estimated at 1.0 billion cubic feet. Figures from the EIA showed that in 2011 Ethiopia imported 44,000 barrels of oil per day to meet its needs. The government wants to develop the mining industry and its objective is for mining to contribute up to 10 per cent of GDP within 10 years.

Energy
Ethiopia has six hydro electric plants. The Gelgal Gibe hydro electric plant came online in 2010 and currently generates 400 MW of electricity. The next stage of the Gilgel Gibe plant is under construction and when completed is expected to generate 1,800 MW of power. Ethiopia expects exports of electricity to outstrip exports of coffee in the future. In 2010 Ethiopia produced 4.93 billion kWh of electricity and consumed 4.45 billion kWh.

Manufacturing
Industrial development has taken place in Addis Ababa, Asmara and Dire Dawa. Manufacturing now accounts for nearly 10 per cent of GDP and employs nearly 10 per cent of the labour force. The general policy is of import substitution but there is a growing proportion of goods available for export and the leather industry is key industry here. The largest areas of capital investment are the railways, sugar factories, beverages, cement, cotton, flour, oil crushing mills, meat canning, pharmaceuticals, pulp and paper, tyres and textile mills (cotton and wool). A small steel rolling mill is also in operation. Main manufactured goods which are exported include textiles, tobacco, beverages, foodstuffs, cement, leather and leather products, wood, paper, metallic and non-metallic products, plastic and tiles.

Service Industries
Tourism is increasing in Ethiopia; figures for 2001 show 125,000 visitors, rising to 290,000 in 2006 and earning US$639 million.
Ethiopian Tourism Commission, URL: http://www.tourismethiopia.org

Agriculture
Agriculture provides approximately 50 per cent of GDP (coffee), 65 per cent of total exports and employment for 85 per cent of the population. Coffee is the main export crop and the economy has been affected in recent years by the downturn worldwide in coffee prices. Barley, wheat, peas and beans grow at altitudes of 5,000 to 9,000 feet and maize and millet at lower altitudes. Teff, a grass-like grain peculiar to the country, is used, and the flour baked in flat cakes used as bread. Wheat, millet and other cereals are similarly used. Large scale growing of cotton is well established and expanding, and Ethiopia is now self sufficient in cotton. Fruit is grown on the lower slopes, principally bananas and citrus fruits. Grapes do well at somewhat higher altitudes. Soft fruit is grown in the neighbourhood of Addis Ababa. The main products are coffee, tea, oilseeds, cotton, tobacco, fruits, pepper, sugar cane, fish and livestock. The main exports are coffee, oilseeds, hides and livestock.

ETHIOPIA

Certain areas have been severely affected by drought in recent years. Output has fallen and this has resulted in a heavy dependence on food aid. Figures for 2003 showed that over 13 million people were dependent of food aid. The problem has been exacerbated by poor infrastructure, soil erosion, deforestation and guerrilla activity which has killed off much of the country's livestock. The government is now focusing on agriculture in its development plans. In 1995-96 the government launched Agricultural Development Led Industrialisation (ADLI), a five-year-plan to enhance productivity and use agriculture as the base of future industrial development. Intensive farming was encouraged with the supply of fertiliser, improved seed supply and distribution, and development of small scale irrigation. Conservation of natural resources and environment and research were also part of the plan. Nearly 3 million farmers are now beneficiaries of the programme. In 2000 another drought threatened another famine and the lives of many. Ethiopia has two rainy seasons, in February and June. In 2002 both seasons were very light and Ethiopia again faced drought and famine. In 2004 the rain fall was good and growth in the agricultural sector for 2004-05 was put as high as 6.6 per cent. In spring 2008 it became clear that Ethiopia was facing another agricultural crisis, the rains the previous year failed resulting in fewer crops planted and with the worldwide increase in food prices many Ethiopian families are facing shortages and starvation.

Coffee is the main export crop and the economy has been affected in recent years by the downturn worldwide in coffee prices. Barley, wheat, peas and beans grow at altitudes of 5,000 to 9,000 feet and maize and millet at lower altitudes. Teff, a grass-like grain peculiar to the country, is used, and the flour baked in flat cakes used as bread. Wheat, millet and other cereals are similarly used. Large scale growing of cotton is well established and expanding, and Ethiopia is now self sufficient in cotton. Fruit is grown on the lower slopes, principally bananas and citrus fruits. Grapes do well at somewhat higher altitudes. Soft fruit is grown in the neighbourhood of Addis Ababa. The main products are coffee, tea, oilseeds, cotton, tobacco, fruits, pepper, sugar cane, fish and livestock. The main exports are coffee, oilseeds, hides and livestock. In March 2009 the government revoked the licences of six of the largest coffee exporters following accusations the exporters had hoarded stocks in the hope that coffee prices would rise.

Agricultural Production in 2010

Produce	Int. $'000*	Tonnes
Indigenous cattle meat	1,052,472	389,606
Roots & tubers, nes	930,197	5,439,400
Cereals, nes	821,423	3,207,300
Maize	528,815	3,897,160
Wheat	466,686	3,075,640
Sorghum	452,014	2,971,270
Cow milk, whole, fresh	436,885	1,400,000
Coffee, green	290,077	270,000
Indigenous sheep meat	201,128	606,800
Broad beans, horse beans, dry	201,128	606,800
Barley	198,195	1,750,440
Game meat	184,296	84,700

*=unofficial figures
Source: http://faostat.fao.org/site/339/default.aspx Food and Agriculture Organization of the United Nations, Food and Agricultural commodities production

Cattle herding is carried on jointly with agriculture on the plateaux. Sheep and goats are also kept, but the wool is of poor quality. Horses are found all over the uplands, as are mules, which are used mainly for transport in broken country. Figures for 2004 show that there were over 38 million head of cattle and more than 26 million sheep and goats. In the damp sub-tropical regions of the south-west the forest areas are a potential source of wealth. Cedar is found, as well as other hardwoods. Eucalyptus is planted near most of the big towns and is an important source of fuel.

Fishing
The total catch in 2010 was put at 18,060.

COMMUNICATIONS AND TRANSPORT

Travel requirements
US, Canadian, Australian and EU nationals require a passport valid for six months and a visa, unless in transit within 12 hours and not leaving the airport. Other nationals should contact the embassy to check entry requirements. Foreign nationals coming from a country where there is no Ethiopian mission, or from Australia, Austria, Canada, Denmark, Finland, France, Germany, Greece, Ireland, Italy, Luxembourg, The Netherlands, Poland, Portugal, Spain, Sweden, UK and USA can be issued with a tourist visa on arrival at Bole International airport. An exit permit is required by visitors staying over 30 days.

International Airports
International scheduled services by jet aircraft are operated from Addis Ababa, Asmara and Dire Dawa to major cities. Airports at Arba Minch, Lalibela, Mekele, Axum and Gondar have recently been upgraded. Bole International airport is undergoing expansion including construction of a new runway. Airport capacity will rise from 500,000 passengers per annum to approximately 7 million. The government hopes it will become one of the continents most important airports.
Bole Airport, P.O. Box 978, Addis Ababa, Ethiopia. Tel: +251 (0)1 187827, fax: +251 (0)1 612533

National Airlines
Ethiopian Airlines (EAL), URL: http://www.flyethiopian.com. Ethiopian Airlines, operating since 1946, runs services to more than 40 destinations worldwide as well as domestic routes.

Railways
Addis Ababa is linked by rail to Dire Dawa and the port of Djibouti in the Republic of Djibouti. The distance is 680 miles. More than half of Ethiopia's trade is moved by rail.

In 2009 the government announced it was to construct 5,000km (3,000 miles) of new railway track, which will mainly be used for carrying goods.

Roads
Many areas of the country are poorly served due to road closure during military activity and bad terrain. The road network however is expanding under rural development programmes. In 1997 the government launched the Road Sector Development Programme (RSDP) to build 3,833 km of asphalt roads, 1,390 km of feeder roads and 5,399 km of gravel roads, as well as upgrading and repairing existing roads. As well as a levy on fuel prices, and government investment of $940 million, funding has also come from the World Bank ($309 million), the EU ($300 million) and the African Development Bank ($104 million). Most of the money is being spent on main roads leading from Addis Ababa to Jimma, Awassa, Adigrat and Djibouti. Vehicles drive on the right.

Ports and Harbours
Ethiopia is landlocked but by agreement with Eritrea used the ports of Assab and Massawa. During the border conflict with Eritrea this was suspended, and Ethiopia has had to use the port of Djibouti.

HEALTH

In 2008, Ethiopia spent approximately 13.3 per cent of its total budget on healthcare (up from 8.5 per cent in 2000), accounting for 53.6 per cent of all healthcare spending. External resources accounted for 38 per cent of healthcare expenditure. Total expenditure on health care equated to 4.4 per cent of the country's GDP. Per capita total expenditure on health was US$16 in 2009. Figures for 2005-10 show that there are 1,806 physicians (less than 1 per 10,000 population), 19,158 nurses (2 per 10,000 population), 1201 pharmaceutical personnel, 1,109 environmental and public health workers, 24,571 community health workers (3 per 10,000 population) and 93 dentists. There are 63 hospital beds per 10,000 population.

Ethiopia like many African nations has a high incidence of HIV/AIDS infection. Recent figures suggest 1.5 million are infected with the virus, making it the fifth highest infection rate in Africa. An estimated 2.1 per cent of the population aged 15-49 are believed to be infected (2007). The infant mortality rate(proability of dying before first birthday) in 2009 was estimated at 68 per 1,000 live births and the under-5 mortality rate was 106 per 1,000 live births. The most common causes of child/infant deaths were: prematurity (15 per cent), birth asphyxia (10 per cent), diarrhoea (14 per cent), measles (4 per cent), pneumonia (21 per cent), malaria (2 per cent), HIV/AIDS (2 per cent). Approximately 33 per cent of children now sleep under insecticide-treated nets and 10 per cent received treatment for malaria. Vaccination rates have increased recently to 81 per cent for measles and 86 per cent for diptheria and hepatitis.

In 2010, 44 per cent of the population had sustainable access to an improved water source and 22 per cent had sustainable access to improved sanitation. (Source: http://www.who.int, World Health Statistics 2012)

EDUCATION

In recent years there has been a large increase in the literacy rate. This has been achieved by a series of mass literacy campaigns in various rural organisations and resettlement areas, as well as increased government spending on education. In 1990 the adult literacy rate among males was 37 per cent and 20 per cent among females. By 2002 this had risen to 49 per cent among males and 34 per cent among females, but children in rural areas are still less likely to have any education as working is considered more essential than education.

Primary/Secondary Education
Figures from 2007 show that just 3 per cent of young children attended pre-school education. Primary education commences at 7 years, continuing with secondary education at 13, which lasts for six years. Figures for 2007 show that 68 per cent of girls and 74 per cent of boys were enrolled in primary school and an estimated 30 per cent went onto secondary school. English is taught in all secondary schools. That year, 3 per cent of students were enrolled in tertiary education.

Higher Education
Ethiopia has two universities in Addis Ababa and Alemaya, with a polytechnic institute in Bahir Dah.

Figures for 2007 show that 23.3 per cent of total government expenditure went on education, the equivalent of 5.5 per cent of GDP. 51 per cent of spending went on primary education, 16 per cent on secondary education and 20 per cent on tertiary education.

In 2007, the adult literacy rate was 35.9 per cent and youth literacy rate was 49.9 per cent.

RELIGION

The Ethiopian Orthodox Church, a Christian Church of Monophysite belief, is the main church, accounting for 45 per cent of the population. Islam is also practised and 34 per cent of the population are Sunni Muslims. Other religions followed include traditional animist beliefs (7 per cent), Hinduism and Sikhism. The majority of the small Jewish community were evacuated in 1991 by the Israeli government; some of the remaining Jews are still awaiting permission to enter Israel.

Traditionally the Christian communities live in the highland areas whilst Muslims and those of traditional beliefs live in the lowland areas.

Ethiopia has a religious liberty rating of 5 on a scale of 1 to 10 (10 is most freedom). (Source: World Religion Database)

COMMUNICATIONS AND MEDIA

Radio is the most popular medium. Most radio stations and the TV network are state controlled but the print and broadcast media are freer and offer criticism of the government. There are allegations of repressive behaviour against journalists. Self censorship is frequent.

Newspapers
Circulation is limited by the high level of illiteracy. Press circulation is mainly in urban areas.
Addis Zemen, URL: http://www.ethpress.gov.et/zemen/
Ethiopian Herald, URL: http://www.ethpress.gov.et/Herald/
Capital, business weekly, URL: http://www.capitalethiopia.com/

Broadcasting
The Ethiopian Broadcasting Service operates a radio service 'Radio Ethiopia', primarily in Amharic, but also in English, French, Somali and other local languages and is state owned. The state-controlled television network broadcasts to most of the country, in Amharic, English, Tigrigna and Oromigna.

Telecommunications
A telecommunications system operates throughout the country. International services are available from Addis Ababa and Asmara. Recent figures show that 880,000 land line phones are in use and over three million mobile phones. There are am estimated 380,000 internet users.

The Ethiopian Telecommunications Authority regulates the industry and the Ethiopian Telecommunications Corporation (ETC) is responsible for expanding and improving the service.

ENVIRONMENT

The main environmental concerns of Ethiopia include desertification, soil erosion and overgrazing. Soil degradation is being caused by inappropriate agricultural practices.

Ethiopia is a party to the following international agreements: Biodiversity, Climate Change, Climate Change-Kyoto Protocol, Desertification, Endangered Species, Hazardous Wastes, Ozone Layer Protection, it has signed, but not ratified agreements on Environmental Modification and Law of the Sea.

According to the EIA, in 2010, Ethiopia's emissions from the consumption and flaring of fossil fuels totalled 6.74 million metric tons of carbon dioxide.

FIJI
Republic of Fiji
Matanitu ko Viti

Capital: Suva (Viti Levu) (Population estimate, 2009: 88,270)

Head of State: Ratu Epeli Nailatikau (page 1483)

Vice President: currently vacant

National Flag: Azure blue, with the Union Jack in the top left hand corner and the shield of the Fiji coat-of-arms in the fly

CONSTITUTION AND GOVERNMENT

Constitution
A former British colony, Fiji has been independent since 1970. Its membership of the Commonwealth lapsed on 7 October 1987 when it was declared a republic. The President, Ratu Sir Penaia Ganilau, proclaimed and decreed a new constitution for Fiji on 25 July 1990. Under this constitution, Fijians were allocated 37 seats, Indians 27, General Electors 5, and Rotumans 1. The current constitution dating from 1997, dispensed with the provision that guaranteed the political dominance of ethnic Fijians, and as a result Fiji was re-admitted to the Commonwealth. In July 2009 Commodore Frank Bainimarama announced plans for a new constitution to be in place by 2013. He said 'The new constitution must include provisions that will entrench common and equal citizenry, it must not have ethnic-based voting'.

For further details on the constitution please visit:
http://www.parliament.gov.fj/publications/viewResearch.aspx?research=22

International Relations
Fiji is an active member of the Pacific Islands Forum and, as a member of the UN, has supplied peacekeeping troops to many destinations including Iraq. Fiji has a close relationship with New Zealand and Australia although relations came under some pressure during the 2006 government takeover. Fiji is a member of the Commonwealth, but membership from the Councils of the Commonwealth was suspended following the events of 2006. It has been suspended several times. On September 1 2009 Fiji was fully suspended from the Commonwealth. Fiji had said it would hold elections by 2010 but then reneged on this agreement, Commodore Frank Bainimarama has said that elections cannot take place until 2014 after reforms have been made. Others see this as preventing the democratic process.

Recent Events
On the 19 May 2000 nationalist rebels stormed parliament and held 27 people hostage, including the prime minister Mahendra Chaudhry. On 23 May Fiji's Great Council of Chiefs called for the prime minister to be replaced by an indigenous prime minister, and on 27 May the president, Ratu Mara, dismissed the Chaudhry government. On the 3 July an interim government, comprising 17 ministers and a new prime minister, Laisenia Qarase, was set up by Fiji's military rulers to remain in place for three years and prepare for new elections. Although the interim government had an all indigenous membership without any ethnic Indian members, a demand made by the rebels' leader George Speight, it was rejected. The hostages were released on 13 July 2000 when the Great Council of Chiefs issued an ultimatum to the rebels stating that a new president and interim government would not be elected until the coup was over. On 26 July George Speight and three of his aides were arrested on suspicion of making threats against the president. He was charged with treason at the beginning of August 2000. In 2002 he was found guilty and sentenced to death. This was subsequently commuted to life imprisonment.

In March 2001 Ratu Iloilo, the acting president, was re-appointed by the Council of Chiefs for a further five years. He then swore in Ratu Tevita Momoedonu as prime minister, replacing Laisenia Qarase who had been in power since the coup. Momoedonu then resigned after 24 hours and Laisenia Qurase was reinstated. This was seen as a legal requirement after the interim government had been declared illegal by an international appeals court.

In September 2001 elections took place and Laisenia Qarase's SDL party won 31 seats and Mahendra Chaudhry's FLP party won 27 seats. Laisenia Qarase formed a government with no ethnic Indians being given ministerial posts; this was seen as unconstitutional since a party with more than eight seats is entitled to cabinet positions. In August 2002 the High Court ruled that the elections were flawed and that the FLP should have as many cabinet seats as the SDL. The cabinet was subsequently reshuffled; no new ministers were appointed but ministries were re-organised. In August 2003 the courts ruled that it was illegal for no opposition MPs to be included in the cabinet. Subsequently 14 members of the FLP were invited to join the cabinet. However, the list did not include ousted prime minister, Mahendra Chaudhry, and this led to the named MPs refusing to join.

In June 2005 the opposition walked out of parliament in protest against proposed legislation to allow coup plotters to seek amnesties if they could prove they had acted for political reasons. In July, the military chief warned he may be forced to remove the government if the amnesty was granted. In May 2006, the former PM, Sitiveni Rabuka, was charged with orchestrating a failed army mutiny in November 2000. In late October, the military chief, Commodore Frank Bainimarama, threatened to topple the government after it tried to replace him, and in December, he took over executive powers and dismissed the PM. In January 2007, Commodore Bainimarama restored powers to the President, and took on the role of interim prime minister. He promised elections in 2010, but in April, he sacked the Great Council of Chiefs, when the chiefs refused to endorse his government and his nomination for vice president. The state of emergency was lifted in June 2007 but re-imposed in September before being lifted again in October. Commodore Bainimarama appointed himself to the position of Chairman of the Great Council of Chiefs in February 2008. In July Commodore Bainimarama announced that election which had been promised for early 2009, would be postponed as electoral reforms would not be completed in time. In April 2009 Frank Bainimarama was reinstated as prime minister in spite of the fact of a court ruling that is government was illegal. Australia and New Zealand called for sanctions against Fiji after some of their journalists were deported. Bainimarama said that elections would now not take place until 2014.

The Commonwealth fully suspended Fiji in September 2009 over its refusal to call elections by 2010.

In November 2009, Fiji expelled the High Commissioners of Australia and New Zealand, accusing them of interfering in the continuing dispute over the judiciary. New Zealand and Fiji reappointed their main envoys in January 2010.

In March 2010, eight men were jailed by a court for the attempted killing of Commodore Bainimarama in 2007, critics said that the accused did not have a fair hearing.

In February 2011, Fiji officially changed its name from the Republic of the Fiji Islands to the Republic of Fiji.

In November 2010, the American owned company Fiji Water, closed its operations in Fiji, saying the country has become "increasingly unstable."

In March 2011, Amnesty International announced that it felt the human rights situation was worsening particularly against critics of the government.

FIJI

In January 2012, Commodore Frank Bainimarama announced that martial law was to be lifted and that consultations on a new constitution would begin.

In July 2012, Australia and New Zealand agreed to resume diplomatic relations with Fiji after Commodore Bainimarama agreed to call an election before 2014.

In December 2012, a draft constitution was produced ahead of the proposed free elections to be held in 2014. The new constitution was designed to get away from the race-based political system of the old constitution where indigenous Fijians were favoured over the Indian minority.

Legislature

The system of parliament is based on the British system, with lower and upper houses. The Lower House or House of Representatives has 71 elected members, and the Upper House or Senate has 32 members. A term of government lasts five years unless dissolved early, the term of the Senate ending at the same time as that of the House of Representatives.
House of Representatives, Parliament Chambers, Government Buildings, P.O. Box 2352, Suva, Fiji. Tel: +679 330 5811, fax: +679 330 5325, e-mail: fijparlib@undp.org.fj, URL: http://www.fiji.gov.fj/parliament/house_representatives.shtml
Senate
Parliament Chambers, Government Buildings, P.O. Box 2352, Suva, Fiji. Tel: +679 330 5811, fax: +679 330 5325, e-mail: fijparlib@undp.org.fj, URL: http://www.fiji.gov.fj/parliament/senate.shtml

---

Interim Cabinet (as at June 2013)
Prime Minister, Minister for Finance and National Planning; Sugar; Public Service, People's Charter for Change, Information, Foreign Affairs and International Cooperation; Civil Aviation; Provincial Development; Indigenous and Multi-Ethnic Affairs: Commodore Josaia Voreqe (Frank) Bainimarama (page 1381)
Minister of Justice; Attorney General; Minister of Tourism, Electoral Reform, Public Enterprises; Industry; Trade and Commerce: Aiyaz Sayed-Khaiyum
Minister for Defence, Primary Industries, National Security and Immigration (acting): Joketani Cokanasiga
Minister for Foreign Affairs: Ratu Inoke Kubuabola
Minister for Women and Social Welfare, Minister for Poverty Alleviation: Dr Jiko Luveni
Minister for Education, National Heritage, Culture and Arts: Filipe Bole
Minister of Youth and Sports: Viliame Naupotp
Minister of Labour, Industrial Relations and Employment: Jone Usumate
Minister for Works, Transport and Public Utilities: Capt. Timoci Lesi Natuva
Minister of Health: Dr Neil Sharma
Minister for Local Government, Urban Development, Housing and Environment: Col. Samuela Saumatua
Minister of Agriculture, Fisheries and Forests: Lt.-Col. Inia Batikoto Seruiratu

---

Ministries
Government portal: URL: http://www.fiji.gov.fj
Office of the President, P.O. Box 2513, Government Buildings, Suva, Fiji. Tel: +679 3314 244, fax: +679 3301 645, e-mail: info@fiji.gov.fj, URL: http://www.fiji.gov.fj
Office of the Prime Minister, P.O. Box 2353, Government Buildings, Suva, Fiji. Tel: +679 3211 201, fax: +679 3306 034, e-mail: Email: pmsoffice@connect.com.fj, URL: http://www.fiji.gov.fj/publish/pm_office.shtml
Office of the Attorney-General, P.O. Box 2213, Government Buildings, Suva, Fiji. Tel: +679 3309 866, fax: +679 3305 421, e-mail: nnand@govnet.gov.fj
Ministry of Agriculture, Sugar & Land Resettlement, Robinson Complex, Grantham Road, (Private Mail Bag), Raiwaqa, Fiji. Tel: +679 3384 233, fax: +679 3385 048, e-mail: maffinfo@is.com.fj
Ministry of Defence, National Security and Immigration, Government Buildings, PO Box 2349, Suva, Fiji. Tel: +679 3211 401, ax: +679 3300 346, e-mail: infohomaff@govnet.gov.fj, URL: http://www.immigration.gov.fj
Ministry of Commerce, Business Development and Investment, Naibati House, 9 Goodenough Street, (P.O. Box 2131, Government Buildings), Suva, Fiji. Tel: +679 3305 411, fax: +679 3301 741
Ministry of Communication, 1st floor Colonial Bank Building, (Private Mail Bag), Samabula, Fiji. Tel: +679 3384766, fax: +679 3386310, e-mail: jturaganivalu@connect.com.fj
Ministry of Education, National Heritage, Culture and Arts, Youth and Sports, Marela House, Thurston Street, Suva, Fiji. Tel: +679 3314 477, fax: +679 3303 511, URL: http://www.youth.gov.fj
Ministry of Finance and National Planning, Ro Lalabalavu House, Victoria Parade, (P.O. Box 2212, Government Buildings), Suva, Fiji. Tel: +679 3307 011, fax: +679 3300 834, e-mail: psfinance@govnet.gov.fj, URL: http://www.mfnp.gov.fj
Ministry of Foreign Affairs & External Trade, 8th & 9th Floor, Suvavou House, (P.O. Box 2220, Government Buildings), Suva, Fiji. Tel: +679 3309 631, fax: +679 3301 741, e-mail: info@foreignaffairs.gov.fj, URL: http://www.foreignaffairs.gov.fj
Ministry of Health, 3rd Floor Dinem House, 88 Amy Street, (P.O. Box 2223, Government Buildings), Suva, Fiji. Tel: +679 3306 177, fax: +679 3306 163, e-mail: info@health.gov.fj, URL: http://www.health.gov.fj
Ministry of Home Affairs and Immigration, 1st Floor, New Wing Government Buildings, (P.O. Box 2349, Government Buildings), Suva, Fiji. Tel: +679 3211 401, fax: +679 3300 346, e-mail: infohomaff@govnet.gov.fj
Ministry of Labour, Industrial Relations & Productivity, 414 Victoria Parade, (P.O. Box 2216, Government Buildings), Suva, Fiji. Tel: +679 3211640, fax: +679 3304701, e-mail: minilabour@is.com.fj
Ministry of Lands & Mineral Resources, 1st Floor, Government Buildings, (P.O. Box 2222, Government Buildings), Suva, Fiji. Tel: +679 3211 556, fax: +679 3302 730, e-mail: mbaravilala@lands.gov.fj
Ministry of Local Government, Housing & Environment, 2nd Flr, Fiji FA House, Gladstone Rd, (P.O. Box 2131, Government Buildings), Suva, Fiji. Tel: +679 3304 364, fax: +679 3303 515

Ministry of Primary Industries, Government Buildings, PO Box 2218, Suva, Fiji. Tel: +679 3301 611, fax: +679 3301 595, e-mail: maffinfo@connect.com.fj, URL: http://www.fisheries.gov.fj
Ministry of Provincial Development, I-Taukei Affairs and Multi-Ethnic Affairs, Government Buildings, PO Box 2219, Suva, Fiji. Tel: +679 3311 774, fax: +679 3314 717, URL: http://www.fijianaffairs.gov.fj/
Ministry of Information and Archives, Government Buildings, PO Box 2225, Suva, Fiji. Tel: +679 3211 250, fax: +679 3303 146, e-mail: info@fiji.gov.fj, URL: http://www.info.gov.fj
Ministry of Tourism, 3rd Floor, Civic Towers Bldg., (P.O. Box 1260), Suva, Fiji. Tel: +679 3312 788, fax: +679 3302 060, e-mail: infodesk@fijifvb.gov.fj, URL: http://www.bulafiji.com/
Ministry of Women, Social Welfare & Poverty Alleviation, 5th Floor, Civic Towers, (P.O. Box 14068), Suva, Fiji. Tel: +679 3312 199, fax: +679 3303 829, URL: http://women.fiji.gov.fj
Ministry of Youth, Employment Opportunities & Sports, Rev. John Hunt Building, Saint Fort Street, (P.O. Box 2448, Government Buildings), Suva, Fiji. Tel: +679 3315 960, fax: +679 3305 348
Ministry of Fisheries and Forests, 46 Knolly Street, (PO Box 2218, Government Buildings), Suva, Fiji. Tel: +679 3301 611, fax: +679 3301 595, e-mail: Forestry-HQ@msd.forestry.gov.fj
Ministry of National Reconciliation and Unity, PO Box 2645, Government Buildings, Suva, Fiji. Tel: +679 309720 / 309721 / 309723, fax: +679 309719
Ministry of Public Enterprise & Public Sector Reform, 3rd Floor, Civic Towers, (PO Box 2278, Government Buildings), Suva, Fiji. Tel: +679 315577, fax: +679 315035
Ministry of Regional Development, Regional House, 1 Knolly Street, (PO Box 2219, Government Buildings), Suva, Fiji. Tel: +679 3313 400, fax: +679 3313 035
Ministry of Public Utilities, Works and Transport, Government Buildings, PO Box 2493, Suva, Fiji. Tel: +679 3384 111, fax: +679 3383 198, e-mail: svatucawaqa@govnet.gov.fj, URL: http://www.fiji.gov.fj
Ministry of Works and Energy, Nasilivata House, Samabula, (PO Box 2493, Government Buildings), Suva, Fiji. Tel: +679 3384 111, fax: +679 3383 198
Ministry of Industry and Trade, Government Buildings, PO Box 2118, Suva, Fiji. Tel: +679 3305 411, fax: +679 3301 741, URL: http://www.commerce.gov.fj
Ministry of Women's Affairs, Social Welfare and Poverty Alleviation, Government Buildings, PO Box 14068, Suva, Fiji. Tel: +679 3312 199, fax: +679 3303 829, URL: http://www.health.gov.fj
Ministry of Local Government, Urban Development, Housing and Environment, Government Buildings, PO Box 2131, Suva, Fiji. Tel: +679 3304 364, fax: +679 3303 515, e-mail: callcentre@labour.gov.fj, URL: http://www.labour.gov.fj

Elections
The most recent presidential election was on 8 March 2006. The incumbent president, Ratu Josefa Iloilo, won a second term of office. He was unopposed. The most recent legislative election was held on 13 May 2006 and was narrowly won by the incumbent Soqosoqo Duavatu Lewnivanuo (SDL) party. They took 36 of the 71 seats. The SDL party leader and incumbent PM Laesenia Qarase retained the premiership for a second term. Voting was mainly along racial lines.

In December 2006, Commodore Frank Bainimarama led a military coup and took over as interim Prime Minister. His interim cabinet was sworn into office on 8 and 9 January 2007, and included Mahendra Chaudhry, former prime minister and leader of the Fiji Labour Party (FLP), a second FLP member, one member of the United People's Party (UPP), and one member of the SDL government ousted in the December 2006 coup.

Elections are not expected to take place before 2014.

Political Parties
Soqosoqo Duavata ni Lewenivanua (United Fijian Party) SDL, URL:
Fiji Labour Party (FLP), URL: http://www.flp.org.fj
United People's Party (UPP)

Diplomatic Representation
British High Commission, Victoria House, 47 Gladstone Road, Suva, Fiji. Tel: +679 311033, fax: +679 301406, e-mail: ukinfo@bhc.org.fj, URL: http://ukinfiji.fco.gov.uk/en
High Commissioner: Martin Fidler
Embassy of the United States of America, 31 Loftus Street, P.O. Box 218, Suva, Fiji. Tel: +679 3314466, fax: +679 3300081, e-mail: usembsuva@is.com.fj, URL: http://suva.usembassy.gov
Ambassador: Frankie Annette Reed
Delegation of the European Commission for the Pacific, 4th Floor, Fiji Development Bank Building, Private Mail Bag, Suva Fiji. Tel: +679 313633, fax:+679 300370, e-mail: eudelfiji@eu.org.fj
High Commission of the Republic of Fiji, 34 Hyde Park Gate, London, SW7 5DN, United Kingdom. Tel: +44 (0)20 7584 3661, fax: +44 (0)20 7584 2838, e-mail: fijirepuk@compuserve.com, URL: http://www.fijihighcommission.org.uk
High Commissioner: Solo Mara
Embassy of the Republic of Fiji, 2233 Wisconsin Avenue, N.W., Suite 240, Washington, DC 20007, USA. Tel: +1 202 337 8320, fax: +1 202 337 1996, e-mail: fijiemb@earthlink.net, URL: http://www.fijiembassydc.com/
Ambassador: Winston Thompson
Permanent Mission of Fiji to the UN, 630 Third Avenue, 7th Floor, New York, NY 10017. Tel: +1 212 687 4130, fax: +1 212 687 3963, URL: http://www.fijiprun.org/
Permanent Representative: Peter Thomson

LEGAL SYSTEM

The judiciary is independent. The court system includes Magistrate Courts in each of the main towns, a High Court, a Court of Appeals, and the Supreme Court - the final appeal court. Military courts try only members of the armed forces. The appellate courts, including the High Court, can review the constitution and has unlimited original jurisdiction to head and determine any civil or criminal proceedings. It also hears and determines any questions relating to the protection of fundamental rights and freedom of the individual. The Court of Appeal consists of three specially appointed Justices of Appeal, one resident Justice of Appeal, and an *ad hoc* Justice of Appeal. Judges are appointed by the President after consultation with the independent Judicial and Legal Services Commission. Members of the judiciary cannot be removed except under a complicated system of checks and balances.

In January 2007, the interim military government was replaced by a nominally civilian interim government. Prime Minister Bainimarama and his Military Council control the security forces. The judiciary is subject to political interference, and there is government corruption. The interim government restricts the right to assemble, and there have been cases of media intimidation. Incommunicado and arbitrary detention are illegal in Fiji. The criminal law permits corporal punishment as a penalty for certain criminal acts, but this provision is seldom invoked. Fiji retains the death penalty only for exceptional crimes such as those committed under military law or in other exceptional circumstances. There have been no executions since independence.

Judiciary portal, URL: http://www.judiciary.gov.fj
President, Supreme Court: Hon. Mr Justice Anthony H.C.T. Gates
Court of Appeal, Resident Justice of Appeal: Hon. Mr Justice William Robert Marshall

Fiji Human Rights Commission, URL: http://www.fhrc.org.fj/

LOCAL GOVERNMENT

Fiji has four administrative divisions; central, eastern, northern, and western. Each province is under the charge of a divisional commissioner, all of whom are senior military officers. Ethnic Fijians have their own administration in which councils preside over a hierarchy of provinces, districts, and villages. The 14 provincial councils deal with all matters affecting ethnic Fijians. There is also a Rotuma Island Council for the island of Rotuma. The provinces are Ba, Bua, Cakaudrove, Kadavu, Lau, Lomaivit, Macuata, Nadroga-Navosa, Naitasiri, Namosi, Ra, Rewa, Serua, and Tailevu each with its own provincial council. The provinces are divided into approximately 109 Tikinas. Tikinas are composed of village units headed by a locally appointed chief. There are over 1,170 villages and 480 Fijian settlements. The number of tikina councils in a province varies from four - twenty two. Tikina councils have wide powers to make by-laws and levy rates to raise revenue. 50 per cent of the rates collected are credited to the provincial council treasury for the running of the council and the other half is used for the financing of the tikina and village projects.

AREA AND POPULATION

Area
Fiji is situated in the Pacific Ocean, 2,100 km north of Auckland, New Zealand. It has a total land area of 18,333 sq. km consisting of 332 islands, including atolls and reefs. About 100 of these islands are permanently inhabited and many more used for planting crops. The largest island, Viti Levu, is 10,429 sq. km and the second largest, Vanua Levu, is 5,556 sq. km. Other islands include Taveuni, Kadavu, Gau and Koro. Fifji has two cities both on the island of Viti Levu, they are Suva, the capital, and Lautoka.

The climate is a maritime climate. Average temperatures range from 28°C in the cooler months (May to October) rising to 32°C in the warmer, wetter months (November-April). This period may be subject to heavy downpours and tropical cyclones.

To view a map of Fiji, please consult http://www.lib.utexas.edu/maps/cia08/fiji_sm_2008.gif

Population
In 2010 the population was estimated at 861,000 of which about 60 per cent are Fijians and 40 per cent of Indian Descent. The annual growth rate was estimated at 0.6 per cent over the period 2000-10. Approximately 52 per cent of the population live in urban areas. The official language is English, Fijian, Rotuman, Urdu and Hindi are also spoken.

Births, Marriages, Deaths
The birth rate is 21.6 per thousand population and the death rate is 6.6 per thousand. Infant mortality rate was 16 per thousand live births and the fertility rate was 2.7 children per women in 2010. The average life expectancy at birth in 2009 was 69 years, 66 years for males and 73 years for females. Healthy life expectancy was 60 years and 64 years respectively. Approximately 29 per cent of the population is aged under 15 years and 8 per cent over 60 years. The median age was 26. (Source: http://www.who.int, World Health Statistics 2012)

Public Holidays 2014
1 January: New Year's Day
14 January: Prophet Mohamed's Birthday*
22 March: National Youth Day
18 March: Good Friday
19 March: Easter Saturday
21 April: Easter Monday
28 May: Ratu Sir Lala Sukuna Day
8 June: Queen's Birthday (2nd Saturday in June)
12 October: Fiji Day/Independence Day
23 October: Diwali**
25 December: Christmas Day
26 December: Boxing Day
*varies according to Islamic calendar
**varies according to Hindu calendar

EMPLOYMENT

Figures for 2007 show that the workforce numbered 376,700, up from 369,300 in 2006. Estimated figures for 2009 put the unemployment rate at 8.5 per cent. The following table shows number of employees by sector in 2007.

Sector	No. employed '000
Agriculture	1.8
Manufacturing	37.4
Services	80.6
Unemployed	26.0
Unemployment rate	6.9%

Source: Asian Development Bank

BANKING AND FINANCE

Currency
The unit of currency is the Fiji Dollar (F$) of 100 cents. The financial centre is Suva.

GDP/GNP, Inflation, National Debt
Following the political and civil unrest in Fiji the economy contracted by 9 per cent in 2000 and the tourism, manufacturing and the construction sectors were particularly badly hit. Although Fiji's economy is developing, the subsistence agricultural sector is still very large. The sector has been hit a decline in the sugar industry following the end of preferential tariffs with the EU. The EU has promised aid but it is dependent on Fiji returning to democracy and improving its human rights situation following the 2006 coup. In recent years, tourism has become a developing industry.

The following table shows GDP by industrial origin in recent years.

GDP by industrial origin, F$ Million

Industry	2007	2008	2009
GDP current factor cost	4,370.0	4,379.2	4,248.8
Agriculture	607.7	638.3	562.1
Mining	-5.4	14.1	12.3
Manufacturing	619.3	606.7	594.5
Utilities	57.4	33.3	33.6
Construction	120.4	126.1	121.9
Trade	733.3	705.2	673.4
Transport & communications	659.5	626.1	643.5
Finance	839.7	888.2	794.2
Public admin.	738.1	741.2	813.1

Source: Asian Development Bank

GDP was estimated at US$3.8 billion in 2011.

Growth was predicted at 5.2 per cent in 2004, 0.6 per cent in 2006, 3.4 per cent in 2006 and it fell to -6.6 per cent in 2007. Growth was estimated to be -3 per cent in 2009. In 2008, inflation rose to over 9 per cent due to rising food prices and high oil prices. It was estimated at 5 per cent in 2010, rising to over 8 per cent in 2011.

External debt was estimated at US$250 million in 2010.

Balance of Payments / Imports and Exports
Principal exports are sugar, gold, molasses, cement, fish, garments and apparel, coconut oil and textile yarn. Principal imports include fuel, crude materials, food, beverages and tobacco, animal and vegetable fats, machines and chemicals.

The following tables show external trade, export earnings and import spending:

External Trade in Million Fiji Dollars

External Trade	2008	2009	2010
Exports, fob	1,471.0	1,230.3	1,175.2
Imports, cif	3,601.4	2,808.0	2,438.8
Trade balance	-2,130.4	-1,577.6	-1,263.7

Source: Asian Development Bank

Selected Overseas Merchandise Trade, 2007

Commodity	Exports F$ mil.	Imports F$ mil.
Animals & animal products	115.8	130.2
Vegetable products	61.7	164.9
Prepared foodstuffs	391.6	120.9
Mineral products	297.4	977.0
Chemical products	28.8	149.5
Plastics & rubber	6.7	142.9
Wood & wood products	52.7	12.4
Wood pulp products	18.8	96.1
Textiles & textile articles	112.8	153.2
Pearls, precious or semiprecious stones, metals	3.9	20.1
Base metals & articles	28.1	163.7
Transportation equipment	30.4	170.7

Source: Asian Development Bank

Main export destinations in 2008 were Israel (US$513.3 million), the USA (US$178.7million), the UK (US$136.2 million) and Australia (US$119.2 million). The main importers were Singapore (US$576.7 million), Australia (US$392.4 million) and New Zealand (US$290.0 million).

Central Bank
Reserve Bank of Fiji, Private Mail Bag, Suva, Viti Levu Island, Fiji. Tel: +679 313611, fax: +679 301688, e-mail: rbf@reservebank.gov.fj, URL: http://www.reservebank.gov.fj
Governor: Barry Whiteside

Chambers of Commerce and Trade Organisations
Suva Chamber of Commerce, 29 Ackland Street, Vatuwara, P.O. Box 337, Suva, Fiji. Tel: +679 303854, fax: +679 300475
Fiji Chamber of Commerce, PO Box 299, Suva, Tel: +679 313122, fax: +679 300953
US Fiji Chamber of Commerce, URL: http://www.fijiamcham.com/
Fiji Trades and Investment Bureau, PO Box 299, Suva, Tel: +679 313122, fax: +679 300953, e-mail: ftibinfo@ftib.org.fj, URL: http://www.ftib.org.fj/

MANUFACTURING, MINING AND SERVICES

Primary and Extractive Industries
Fiji has a variety of mineral resources and exploration activity on the two large islands of Viti Levu and Vanua Levu is quite intense. Large areas of land are under licence to many companies. The most interesting exploration is being carried out in the Namosi area of Viti Levu where over 70 diamond drill holes have been completed so far to explore a low grade porphyry copper deposit.

Two offshore areas are being actively explored for oil in the northern and eastern shores of Viti Levu under establishment agreements between the Government and two oil companies. Extensive seismic and aero-magnetic surveys have so far been carried out and it is hoped that a decision will be made in the near future on drilling. Figures for 2011 show that Fiji imports 13,000 barrels of oil per day to meet its needs.

Gold is mined at the Emperor Goldmine at Vatukoula. This makes up 10 per cent of Fiji's exports and employs 1,700 people. Figures for 2006 show that 1,403 kilograms of gold was produced down from 2,793 kg in 2005 and 4,033 kg in 2004.

Energy
In 2010, 0.87 billion kilowatt hours of electricity were generated and 0.81 billion kWh consumed. The electricity was generated by plants powered by fossil fuels and hydro plants. The use of wind and geothermal power is being investigated.

Manufacturing
Fiji produces a range of industrial products. Apart from traditional items like raw sugar and copra oil, it has other processing facilities for rice and flour milling, steel rolling, saw milling and building materials.

It has built up facilities for production of coaches, boats, steel tanks, copra dryers and other steel fabrications, including solar heaters and tanks. It produces various food items as well as cigarettes and tobacco. Besides a variety of consumer items like clothing, household goods, and detergents, various types of handicrafts are also produced.

Manufacturing output was expected to fall in 1998 due to a fall in sugar production. However the clothing and footwear sectors were set to raise production in that period. Exports of textile goods has begun to fall now that special access agreements that Fiji enjoys with the US have come to an end.

In order to encourage investment in industry a Tax Free Factory/Tax Free Zone TFF/TFZ has been established.

The following tables shows the volume of manufactured production in recent years:

Commodity	Weight	2003	2004
Sugar	000 tonnes	308	311
Coconut oil	tonnes	7,523	8,242
Sharps	tonnes	1,083	714
Flour	tonnes	63,559	88,310
Butter	tonnes	1,839	1,442
Cigarettes	tonnes	473	516
Saw log	000 cubic metres	129	101
Stock feed	tonnes	41,095	40,264
Gold	kilogram	3,517	4,033
Silver	kilogram	1,247	1,523
Cement	000 tonnes	100	111
Beer	mega litres	15	20
Paint	000 litres	3,096	3,140
Soap	tonnes	3,192	4,023
Matches	000 gross boxes	132	133
Electricity	million kwhs	812	816
Ice-cream	000 litres	3,290	2,321
Non-alcoholic drinks	000 litres	79,401	94,335
Toilet paper	000 rolls	22,926	20,109
Garment	F$ 000	140,700	178,038

Source: Fiji Islands Bureau of Statistics

Tourism
Figures for 1997 show that Fiji had 359,000 international visitors. This figure rose to 410,000 in 1999. Although tourism was hit by the coup in 2000, figures for 2001 show numbers of visitors to be increasing. Figures for 2003 show that Fiji had 430,800 visitors, of whom 20,058 arrived on cruise ships. Most visitors come from Australia, New Zealand, USA, Japan and Europe.

Agriculture
Some 600,000 acres (243,000 hectares) of land in Fiji are in agricultural use, or 16 per cent of land. The cultivable land is confined to major river valleys, deltas and coastal flats. This sector plays a vital role in the country's economy. It contributes nearly a quarter of GDP.

Sugar cane is the principal cash crop, accounting for more than two-thirds of Fiji's export earnings. About one quarter of the population depend on it directly for their livelihood. Sugar cane crops have declined in recent years but a 2003 government reform initiative hopes to reverse that trend. Coconuts, Fiji's second major cash crop, provide coconut oil and other products for export and the industry employs nearly as many workers as the sugar industry. Coconut oil is also used in the domestic manufacture of food products, soaps and detergents. Ginger is the third major export crop. The bananas industry, which used to be the third most important crop, has declined recently because of disease and hurricanes. Other agricultural products include cocoa, maize, kava, tobacco and a variety of fruit and vegetables.

Efforts are being made to develop the production of rice. Three production areas, Rewa, Navua and Dreketi, are being developed for double-cropped irrigated rice.

There is a small but developing livestock industry. Efforts are being made to improve goat production to meet demand and to substitute mutton imports. Fiji is nearly self-sufficient in goat meat.

Forestry has an important place in the economy because it supplies the bulk of local needs for timber and timber products. The main objectives of the government's forestry policy are to ensure the best possible use of indigenous species of timber and to plant other species to meet future domestic needs, as well as supplying a surplus for export. Forestry contributes around 2.5 per cent of GDP.

Although there is no large-scale fishing industry, plans are in hand to exploit the substantial skip-jack tuna resources for the local market and for canning. Seaweed production is now a growth area. Figures for 2010 put the total catch at 41,350 tonnes.

Agricultural Production in 2010

Produce	Int. $'000	Tonnes
Sugar cane	57,498	1,751,000
Coconuts	22,806	206,250
Indigenous cattle meat	22,584	8,360
Indigenous chicken meat	20,403	14,324
Cow milk, whole, fresh	19,129	61,300
Taro (cocoyam)	12,785	60,283
Indigenous pigmeat	6,122	3,983
Cassava	4,860	51,590
Hen eggs, in shell	4,733	5,707
Fruit fresh nes	3,246	9,300
Rice, paddy	2,070	7,684
Vegetables fresh nes	1,602	8,500

*=unofficial figures
Source: http://faostat.fao.org/site/339/default.aspx Food and Agriculture Organization of the United Nations, Food and Agricultural commodities production

COMMUNICATIONS AND TRANSPORT

Travel Requirements
Visitors from the USA, Canada, Australia and the EU require a passport valid for at least six months beyond intended period of stay, as well as a return ticket and sufficient funds for the stay. Most of the above nationals are issued with a visitor's permit on arrival, and do not require a visa for stays of up to three months. The exceptions to this are Lithuanians (who need a visa) and passengers in transit, leaving within 3 hours and not leaving the airport. Nationals of other countries should contact the embassy to check visa requirements.

National Airlines
There are 24 airports of which four have paved airstrips. There are airstrips at Ovalau, Lakeba, Bua, Gau, Koro, Vanuabalavu, Ono-i-lau, Ba and Vatukoula, Kadanu, Rotuma and Seqani Cicia. The National carrier is Air Pacific, Commercial domestic air operators include Sunflower Airlines Limited, Air Fiji Limited, URL: http://www.airfiji.com.fj, Vanua Air Limited, Air Wakaya Limited, Turtle Airways Limited and Pacific Crown Aviation Limited (Helicopter Operator).
Air Pacific Limited, URL: http://www.airpacific.com

International Airports
An increasing number of international and regional air services are operated through Nadi International Airport, situated on the west coast of Viti Levu, connecting Fiji with Australia, New Zealand, North and South America, Europe and other parts of the world.

Railways
The Fiji Sugar Cane Corporation runs 600mm gauge railways at four of its mills on Viti Levu and Vanue Levu, totalling about 595 km.

Roads

There are almost 5,300 km of roads, of which 1,692km are paved. A multi-million dollar highway has been constructed between Badi and Suva. Figures for 2004 show that there were 4,858 private cars on the road, 295 taxis, 36 buses and 987 goods vehicles. Vehicles are driven on the left.

Ports and Harbours

Fiji's four ports of entry are Suva, Lautoka, Levuka and Savusavu. In 1988, Suva Port handled a total of 585,245 tonnes of cargo. This represents 501,733 tonnes of foreign cargo and 83,522 tonnes of local products. A total of 1,259 vessels called at Suva with a gross registered tonnage of 1,088,508.

Lautoka handled a total of 984,840 tonnes of cargo in 1988. This represents 939,428 tonnes of foreign cargo and 45,412 tonnes of local cargo. A total of 1,256 vessels called at Lautoka Port with a gross tonnage of 2,522,975.

Levuka Port serves as a base for Fiji's only fish canning industry. In 1988 a total of 848 vessels called at the port with a total gross registered tonnage of 219,153.

Savusavu has been declared Fiji's fourth port of entry. Local shipping plays an important role in Fiji and provides services to scattered outer islands of the group. Government and private companies operate ferries between the islands. Some routes use roll on roll off ferries.

HEALTH

In 2009, Fiji spent approximately 10.1 per cent of its total budget on healthcare, accounting for 69.4 per cent of all healthcare spending. External resources accounted for 6.1 per cent. Total expenditure on health care equated to 4.9 per cent of the country's GDP. Per capita total expenditure on health was US$144 in 2009. Figures for 2005-10 show that there are 372 physicians (4.3 per 10,000 population), 1,957 nurses (22.4 per 10,000 population) and 171 dentists. There are 21 hospital beds per 10,000 population. There are approximately 25 hospitals and 74 health centres.

The infant mortality rate in 2008 was estimated at 15 per 1,000 live births and the child mortality rate 17 per 10,000 population. Major causes of childhood deaths include diarrhoea 4 per cent, pneumonia 10 per cent, prematurity 20 per cent, birth asphyxia 8 per cent, neonatal sepsis 3 per cent and congenital anomalies 24 per cent. Around 0.3 per cent of the adult population is living with HIV/AIDS.

According to the latest WHO figures, in 2010 approximately 98 per cent of the population had access to improved drinking water and 83 per cent to improved sanitation. (Source: http://www.who.int, World Health Statistics 2012)

EDUCATION

School attendance is not compulsory in Fiji although compulsory education is gradually being phased in. The past two decades have seen great improvements both in the quality and quantity of Fiji education. Nearly 100 per cent of primary school-age children attend school with classes one to seven receiving free education. However in recent years attendance in recent years has begun to fall mainly because of the cost of fees and the cost of transport to and from school.

2003 figures show that there were 451 pre-schools, 17 special schools with 1,108 students, 712 primary schools with 142,781 students, 157 secondary schools with 68,178 students and 47 technical or vocational schools with 2,319 students. The number of primary school teachers is 5,127 and the number of secondary school teachers is 3,935.

Vocational Education

The Government is giving special attention to increasing the provision of vocational and technical training at all levels and to encouraging secondary and higher education. Full-time vocational education is provided by the Fiji Institute of Technology, Ratu Kadavulevu School and the Ba Technical Institute.

A three-year post-secondary course for Diploma in Tropical Agriculture is provided at the Fiji College of Agriculture, which qualifies students for services in general agriculture, fisheries or animal science. A number of secondary schools offer courses in field husbandry and animal husbandry. Navuso Agricultural School provides a two-year general residential course in Tropical Agriculture and runs a three-year Student Farmer Scheme. The Agricultural College at the Marist Training Centre on Taveuni also provides a course in general agriculture for adults. There is a forestry training school at Lololo, Lautoka. There are three teacher-training colleges.

Tertiary/Higher

The University of the South Pacific (USP) opened in February 1968 at Laucala Bay, Suva, to meet the needs for higher education of the communities of the South Pacific. There are about 2,000 students enrolled in courses on Campus, but there are 6,000 further enrolments in extension courses. These are about 260 academic and comparable staff at USP. The university offers six degree courses, six diploma courses, three certificate programmes and two pre-degree programmes. Its budget in 1991 was $20 million.

Medical training is provided at the Fiji School of Medicine, founded in 1883. It has been reorganised and extended a number of times and now serves as a regional centre for medical training in the Pacific area, providing a five-year diploma course in medicine, a three-and-a-half year diploma course in dentistry and ancillary courses in such subjects as public health inspection, physiotherapy, dietetics and laboratory technology.

There is also provision for post-graduate training at universities overseas. Basic nursing training is given at the Central Nursing School in Suva, which also accepts some students from other Pacific Islands. The School has a branch at Lautoka.

The literacy rate is 93.0 per cent.

RELIGION

Religion is an important facet of life in Fiji. Indian temples, mosques and Christian churches are common sights in the towns and it is rare to find a Fijian village without a church. More than half of Fiji's population are Christian (62 per cent). Other religious communities include Hindus (30 per cent), Muslims (6 per cent), Sikh (0.5 per cent) and others.

Fiji has a religious liberty rating of 8 on a scale of 1 to 10 (10 is most freedom). (Source: World Religion Database)

COMMUNICATIONS AND MEDIA

A new press law, enforcing strict censorship, came into force in 2009. Media ownership requirements also changed and allowed for prison terms for journalists, threatening the hitherto free private press.

Newspapers
The Daily Post, Suva, Fiji. (Weekly). URL: http://www.fijidailypost.com/
The Fiji Times, private, URL: http://www.fijitimes.com/
The Fiji Sun, URL: http://www.sun.com.fj/
Nai Lalakai is in Fijian and is published weekly
Shanti Dut in Hindi, published weekly

Broadcasting
The state-owned commercial radio company is the Fiji Broadcasting Company (URL: http://www.radiofiji.com.fj/). There are two major radio stations - Island Network Corporation Ltd and Communication Fiji Ltd. The Fiji Television Company (URL: http://www.fijitv.com.fj/) has one free and two pay channels.

Telecommunication Systems
Improvements to postal and telephone services, particularly in the rural areas, have been made in recent times. There are over 120,000 installed lines and over 600,000 mobile phones in circulation.

Figures for 2008 show that Fiji had over 100,000 internet users.

ENVIRONMENT

Fiji has played a role on an international level in conferences and is party to the following international agreements: Biodiversity, Climate Change, Climate Change-Kyoto Protocol, Desertification, Endangered Species, Law of the Sea, Marine Life Conservation, Ozone Layer Protection, Tropical Timber 83, Tropical Timber 94 and Wetlands. Main environmental concerns for Fiji are soil erosion and deforestation.

In 2010, Fiji's emissions from the consumption of fossil fuels totalled 2.50 million metric tons of carbon dioxide. (Source: EIA)

FINLAND

Republic of Finland

Suomen Tasavalta - Republiken Finland

Capital: Helinski (Population estimate, 2012: 592,400)

Head of State: Sauli Niinisto (President) (page 1486)

National Flag: Ultramarine cross on a white-field. The upright slightly to the hoist. The Finnish Standard, used only by the President of the Republic and State Institutions, bears the Finnish coat of arms in the middle of the blue cross.

CONSTITUTION AND GOVERNMENT

Constitution

From 1154 to 1809, Finland formed a part of the Kingdom of Sweden. It then became an autonomous Grand Duchy connected with Russia until 6 December 1917, the date of its declaration of independence. A republican constitution was laid down by the Form of Government Act promulgated at Helsinki on 17 July 1919, along with other constitutional laws.

Sovereign power belongs to the people represented by the delegates assembled in Parliament, who hold legislative power in conjunction with the President. Supreme executive power is vested in the President of the Republic, who is assisted in the general government of the State by a Council of State (Cabinet) consisting of a Prime Minister and the necessary number of ministers. The president is elected by direct popular vote. In the event of no candidate winning an absolute majority, a second round is held between the two most successful candidates. The president's term of office is six years and he has extensive power which enables him to control foreign policy and dissolve parliament.

A new Constitution came into force on 1 March 2000. The main reforms under the new Constitution are that the president's powers are reduced in the formation of governments; the prime minister is now elected by the parliament rather than being appointed by the president and, whilst the president still leads foreign policy, this is now with close co-operation with the Council of States.

Finland became a member of the Nordic Council and the United Nations in 1955 and a member of the European Union in 1995.

To consult the full constitution, please visit:
http://www.om.fi/Etusivu/Perussaannoksia/Perustuslaki?lang=en

International Relations

Finland enjoys close relations with her nordic and baltic neighbours and is a member of the Nordic Council. Finland is a member of the UN and has consistently been involved in peacekeeping activities.

Recent Events

In March 2003 the Centre Party led by Anneli Jaatteenmaki, beat the incumbent Social Democrats at the general election. In June Ms Jaatteenmaki resigned as prime minister and leader of the Centre Party following allegations that she had used confidential material to aid her election campaign. Following the resignation defence minister Matti Vanhanen was appointed prime minister. In March 2004 Ms Jaatteenmaki was officially cleared.

In March 2006 the Finnish parliament voted in favour of the European constitution.

In September 2008 a gunman opened fire in a college killing 11 people including himself. The incident led to the government introducing stricter rules on gun ownership. In December 2009 another gunman went on a shooting spree in the city of Espoo resulting in the death of five people.

In June 2010 Prime Minister Matti Vanhanen retired due to ill health and was replaced by Mari Kiviniemi. Parliamentary elections took place in April 2011; no single party gained an absolute majority.

In July 2010, Finland became the world's first country to give its citizens a legal right to broadband internet.

Legislature

Parliament consists of a single chamber of 200 members elected for four years. Parliament elects its own Speaker and two Deputy Speakers who, together with the chairmen of the various committees, form the Speaker's Council. As a substitute for an upper chamber there is a Grand Committee of at least 25 members, chosen by parliament. It may consider and express an opinion on bills coming up before parliament in full session.

Parliament of Finland (Eduskunta), FIN - 00102 Helsinki, Finland. Tel: +358 (0)9 4321, fax: +358 (0)9 432 2642, URL: http://www.eduskunta.fi

Speaker: Eero Heinäluoma

Cabinet (as at June 2013)
Prime Minister: Jyrki Katainen (page 1454)
Deputy Prime Minister, Minister for Finance: Jutta Urpilainen (page 1530)
Minister for Foreign Affairs: Erkki Tuomioja (page 1528)
Minister for European and Foreign Affairs: Alexander Stubb (page 1521)

Minister for International Development: Heidi Hautala (page 1439)
Minister of Justice: Anna-Maja Henriksson (page 1441)
Minister of the Interior: Päivi Räsänen (page 1500)
Minister of Defence: Stefan Wallin (page 1533)
Minister of Public Administration and Local Government: Henna Virkkunen (page 1532)
Minister of Education and Science: Krista Kiuru (page 1457)
Minister of Culture and Sport: Paavo Arhinmaki (page 1379)
Minister of Agriculture and Forestry: Jari Koskinen (page 1458)
Minister of Transport: Merja Kyllonen (page 1459)
Minister of Economic Affairs: Jyri Häkämies (page 1436)
Minister of Labour: Lauri Ihalainen (page 1446)
Minister of Social Affairs and Health: Paula Risikko (page 1503)
Minister of Health and Social Services: Susanna Huovinen
Minister of the Environment: Ville Niinistö (page 1487)
Minister of Housing and Communication: Pia Viitanen

Ministries

Office of the President, Mariankatu 2, 00170 Helsinki, Finland. Tel: +358 (0)9 661133, fax: +358 (0)9 638247, e-mail:presidentti@tpk.fi, URL: http://www.president.fi

Office of the Prime Minister, P.O. Box 23, 00023 Government, Finland. Tel: +358 (0)9 160 2001, fax: +358 (0)9 160 2225, e-mail: name.surname@vnk.vn.fi, URL: http://www.vn.fi

The Information Unit of the Council of State, Snellmaninkatu 1A, P.O.Box 23, 00023 Government, Finland. Tel: +358 (0)9 1601, fax: +358 (0)9 160 4006, e-mail: name.surname@vnk.vn.fi, URL: http://www.vn.fi

Ministry of Agriculture and Forestry, Hallituskatu 3A, P.O.Box 30, 00023 Government, Helsinki, Finland. Tel: +358 (0)9 1602299, fax: +358 (0)9 1602190, e-mail: name.surname@mmm.fi, URL: http://www.mmm.fi

Ministry of Defence, Fabianinkatu 2, P.O.Box 31, 00131 Helsinki, Finland. Tel: +358 (0)9 1608 8200, fax +358 (0)9 653254, e-mail: name.surname@plm.vn.fi, URL: http://www.defmin.fi/plm

Ministry of Education, Meritullinkatu 10, P.O.Box 380 Helsinki, 00023 Government, Finland. Tel: +358 (0)9 1341 7407, fax: +358 176191, URL: http://www.minedu.fi

Ministry of Employment and the Economy, Eteläesplanadi 4, Helsinki, PO Box 32, FI-00023 Government, Finland. URL: http://www.tem.fi

Ministry of the Environment, Kasarmikatu 25, P.O.Box 380, 00131 Helsinki, Finland. Tel: +358 (0)9 1991 9308, fax: +358 (0)9 1991 9323, e-mail: name.surname@vyh.fi, URL: http://www.environment.fi

Ministry of Finance, Snellmaninkatu 1A, P.O.Box 28, 00023 Government, Helsinki, Finland. Tel: +358 (0)9 160 3099, fax: +358 (0)9 160 4755, e-mail: name.surname@vm.vn.fi, URL: http://www.ministryoffinance.fi/vm

Ministry of Foreign Affairs, Merikasarmi, PO Box 176, 00161 Helsinki, Finland. Tel: +358 (0)9 160 05, URL: http://formin.finland.fi

Ministry of the Interior, Kirkkokatu 12, P.O. Box 26 00023 Government, Finland. Tel: +358 (0)9 160 2812, fax: +358 (0)9 160 2927/ 2936, e-mail: name.surname@intermin.fi, URL: http://www.intermin.fi

Ministry of Justice, Eteläesplanadi 10, P.O. Box 1, 00131 Helsinki, Finland. Tel: +358 (0)9 1825 7605, fax: +358 (0)9 1825 7630, e-mail: name.surname@om.fi, URL: http://www.om.fi

Ministry of Labour, Eteläesplanadi 4, P.O.Box 524, 00101 Helsinki, Finland. Tel: +358 (0)9 1845 8042, fax: +358 (0)9 1856 8059, e-mail: name.surname@mol.fi, URL: http://www.mol.fi

Ministry of Social Affairs and Health, Meritullinkatum 8, 00171 Helsinki, P.O.Box 33, 00023 Government, Finland. Tel: +358 (0)9 160 4182, fax: +358 (0)9 160 4328, e-mail: name.surname@stm.vn.fi, URL: http://www.stm.fi

Ministry of Trade and Industry, Aleksanterinkatu 4, P.O. Box 32, 00023 Government, Helsinki, Finland. Tel: +358 (0)9 160 3641, fax: +358 (0)9 160 2665, e-mail: name.surname@ktm.vn.fi, URL: http://www.vn.fi/ktm

Ministry of Transport and Communications, Eteläesplanadi 16, PO Box 31, 00023 Helsinki, Finalnd. Tel: +358 9 16002, fax: +358 9 1602 8596, e-mail: kirjaamo@mintc.fi, URL: http://www.mintc.fi/

Political Parties

Kansallinen Kokoomus (KOK, The National Coalition Party), Kansakoulukuja 3, 00100 Helsinki, Finland. Tel: +358 (0)9 69381, fax: +358 (0)9 694 3736, URL: http://www.kokoomus.fi
Leader: Jyrki Katainen

Svenska Folkpartiet (SFP, Swedish People's Party), Simonsgatan 8a, Post Box 430, 00101, Helsinki, Finland. Tel: +358 (0)9 693070, fax: +358 (0)9 693 1968, URL: http://www.sfp.fi
Party Leader: Carl Haglund

Suomen Keskusta (KESK, Centre Party), Apollonkatu 1a, 00100 Helsinki, Finland. Tel: +358 (0)9 751 44200, fax: +358 (0)9 751 44240, URL: http://www.keskusta.fi
Party Leader: Carl Haglund

Kristillinen Demokraatit (KD, Christian Democrats), Kargalankatu 2c 7th Floor, 00520 Helsinki, Finland. Tel: +358 (0)9 348 82200, fax: +358 (0)9 348 82228, URL: http://www.Kristillisdemokraatit.fi
Chairman: Paivi Rasanen

Vasemmistolitto (Left-Wing Alliance), Viherankatu 5, 2nd Floor, 00530 Helsinki, Finland. Tel: +358 (0)9 774741, fax: +358 (0)9 7747 4200, URL: http://www.vasemmistoliitto.fi/html/
Chairman: Paavo Arhinmaki
Socialdemokratic (Social Democratic Party), Saariniemendatu 6, 00530 Helsinki, Finland. Tel: +358 (0)9 773 2816, fax: +358 (0)9 712752, URL: http://www.sdp.fi
Chairman: Jutta Urpilainen
Vihrea Liitto (Green League), URL: http://www.greens.fi
Leader: Ville Niinisto
Perussuomalaiset (True Finns), URL: http://www.perussuomalaaiset.fi
President: Timo Soini

Elections
Voting at a general election is by secret ballot and is based on a system of proportional representation. All persons of 18 years and over are entitled to vote.

The most recent presidential election took place in February 2012; former Minister of Finance Sauli Niinisto was elected to the post.

The most recent parliamentary elections took place on 17 April 2011. The KOK party did well, becoming the largest party in parliament. The former ruling KSEK fared badly, finishing in fourth, beaten by the far-right PS. The breakdown of seats is as follows: KOK 44 seats; SDP 42 seats; PS 39 seats; KESK 35 seats; VL 14 seats; Greens 10 seats; SFP 9 seats; KD 6 seats; reserved for Åland Islands 1 seat. On 22 June 2011, the President of the Republic appointed Finland's 72nd government, that of Prime Minister Jyrki Katainen. The government is a majority coalition formed by the National Coalition Party, the Social Democratic Party, the Left Alliance, the Swedish People's Party in Finland, the Green League and the Christian Democratic Party. The Government has 19 ministers.

Diplomatic Representation
Embassy of the United States of America, Itäinen Puistotie 14b, 00140 Helsinki, Finland. Tel: +358 (0)9 171931, fax: +358 (0)9 174681, URL: http://finland.usembassy.gov
Ambassador: Bruce J. Oreck (page 1490)
Finnish Embassy, 3301 Massachusetts Ave., NW, Washington, DC 2008, USA. Tel: +1 202 298 5800, fax: +1 202 298 6030, URL: http://www.finland.org/Public/Default.aspx
Ambassador: Ritva Koukku-Ronde
British Embassy, Itäinen Puistotie 17, 00140 Helsinki, Finland. Tel: +358 (0)9 2286 5100, fax: +358 (0)9 2286 5262, e-mail: info@ukembassy.fi, URL: http://ukinfinland.fco.gov.uk/en
Ambassador: Matthew Lodge (page 1466)
Finnish Embassy, 38 Chesham Place, London, SW1X 8HW, United Kingdom. Tel: +44 (0)20 7838 6200, fax: +44 (0)20 7235 3680, URL: http://www.finemb.org.uk
Ambassador: Pekka Huhtaniemi (page 1445)
Permanent Mission of Finland to the UN, 866 UN Plaza, Suite 222, New York, NY 10017, USA. Tel: +1 212 355 2100, fax: +1 212 759 6156, URL: http://www.finlandun.org
Ambassador: Jarmo Viinanen

LEGAL SYSTEM

Ordinary Courts
City Courts located in 28 of the oldest cities are the courts of the first instance, followed by the District Courts in the rest of country. These courts handle civil and criminal cases except when they belong to the jurisdiction of one of the special courts. There are also ten housing courts of the first instance.

The District Court is chaired by a judge with legal training who is assisted by five to seven laymen jurors. The jurors are appointed by the local municipal council and can only overrule the judge by unanimous vote, on both the law and the facts.

The City Court consists of three members. Their chairman is a judge with legal training. The other two members may be laymen although the majority of City Court members today have legal training. Each member has an independent vote.

The decisions of the ordinary courts can be reviewed by the Courts of Appeal, *hovioikeus*. In addition to reviewing appeals, the six Courts of Appeal act as courts of the first instance in cases of treason and criminal charges against higher civil servants. They also exercise control of the courts of first instance. They sit in divisions of three judges.

The highest instance of the ordinary courts is the Supreme Court. It may review the decisions of the Courts of Appeal and some of the special courts. The Supreme Court also exercises control over the lower courts, and participates in the appointment of lower judges. The Supreme Court is headed by a president (appointed by the President of Finland) and has at least 15 members. There are currently 18 members.

Special Courts
The Land Courts have been established to settle disputes arising from land partition and surveying. The Water Rights Courts handle civil and criminal cases concerning waterways. A considerable number of Water Court cases refer to applications in connection with the use of water. The Water Rights Appeal Court acts as an appellate instance for decisions of the Water Rights Courts.

The Insurance Court deals with disputes in social matters such as industrial accidents, military invalidity, appeals against the decisions of pensions institutions and unemployment compensation. The decisions of the Land Courts, and, in some cases, of the Water Rights Appeal Court and the Insurance Court can be reviewed by the Supreme Court. Other decisions of the Water Rights Appeal Court may be reviewed by the Supreme Administrative Court (see below).

The Labour Court is a special court established to settle certain disputes concerning collective bargaining in private as well as in public service. The decision of the Labour Court is final.

The Market Court deals with disputes arising from marketing and consumer protection. No appeals are allowed against the decisions of the Market Court.

All special courts are collegiate courts chaired by a judge with legal training. Members may be specialists in different areas such as engineers, doctors or representatives of interest groups. The composition of the courts has been defined by law.

The Prison Court deals with juvenile crime.

Administrative Courts
The highest court in matters relating to the legality of administrative decisions is the Supreme Administrative Court. It may review the decisions of the Province Courts, which are general courts in administrative matters, the decisions of the Turnover Tax Court, some decisions of the Water Rights Appeal Court as well as the decisions of numerous administrative authorities such as ministries and administrative central boards. The Supreme Administrative Court is divided into four divisions. The court is normally competent to pass judgement when five members of the bench are present. The Supreme Administrative Court supervises the application of administrative law by lower authorities.

There is a Regional Administrative Court previously known as the Province Court in each of the 12 provinces. These courts may be separated into divisions. The majority of cases dealt with by the Province Courts concern taxation. The Turnover Tax Court is a special administrative court with jurisdiction in appeals on turnover tax matters. The administrative courts are collegiate courts.

Legal Aid
The municipalities can obtain state funds for establishing legal aid bureaus, employing an attorney with legal training to counsel people either free of charge or for a reduced fee. Poor citizens may also engage a private attorney for a court case and have the attorney's fees, as fixed by the court, paid by the state.

A general control is exercised over the administration by the *oikeuskansleri* or Chancellor of Justice and the *Eduskunnan oikeusasiamies* or Parliamentary Ombudsman. The Chancellor of Justice is the chief public prosecutor and acts as counsel for the government. The Parliamentary Ombudsman, appointed by parliament, exercises supervision over the general administration of justice. There are also other ombudsmen, such as the Consumer Ombudsman and the Equality Ombudsman. They are not, however, appointed by parliament.

Human Rights
The government respects the human rights of its citizens.

Capital punishment was abolished on civilian crimes in 1949 and on all crimes in 1972.

Supreme Court, URL: http://www.kko.fi/27080.htm

Parliamentary Ombudsman of Finland, Arkadiankatu 3, Helsinki, Finland. URL: http://www.oikeusasiamies.fi/Resource.phx/eoa/english/index.htx

LOCAL GOVERNMENT

The country is divided into six provinces, Southern Finland, Western Finland, Eastern Finland, Oulu, Lapland and Åland. The central administrative authority of each province is the Provincial Government headed by a Governor. There is also a large number of separate district authorities. Reform of the intermediate level of government is under preparation.

Finland's many inter-municipal federations also belong to the intermediate level of government. These partly statutory, partly voluntary federations are set up to carry out social welfare and health care work, along with vocational training and physical planning. In reforming intermediate government, special attention will be paid to making the network of inter-municipal federations more compact.

Local government was reorganised most recently in 2011. There are currently 336 municipalities, 16 of which are in the Åland Islands. In 2011 there was some further re-organisation: six municipal mergers involving 12 municipalities took place. Akaa and Kylmäkoski formed the new town of Akaa; Kangasala and Kuhmalahti formed the new municipality of Kangasala; Kuopio and Karttula formed the new city of Kuopio; Lapinlahti and Varpaisjärvi formed the new municipality of Lapinlahti; Orimattila and Artjärvi formed the new town of Orimattila; Vöyri-Maksamaa and Oravainen formed the new municipality of Vöyri. One regional change also took place: Eastern Uusimaa became part of the Uusimaa region, making the municipalities of Askola, Lapinjärvi, Loviisa, Myrskylä, Porvoo, Pukkila and Sipoo part of the Uusimaa region.

The following table shows the largest municipalities and their populations at the end of December 2011.

Municipality	Population	Change %
Helsinki	595,384	1.2
Espoo	252,439	1.8
Tampere	215,168	0.9
Vantaa	203,001	1.5
Turku	178,630	0.7
Oulu	143,909	1.6
Jyväskyla	132,062	1.0
Lahti	102,308	0.7
Kuopio	97,433	0.7
Kouvola	87,567	-0.6
Pori	83,133	0.1

Source: Statistics Finland

FINLAND

Municipalities enjoy extensive autonomy. Most of the municipalities' tasks are compulsory by law but the municipalities can undertake what they see to be in the interests of the population. They do not need the approval of central government for this, and central government authorities cannot require the municipalities to do anything except by law.

One of the most important tasks concerns education and culture. The municipalities have to provide primary, secondary and senior secondary education and public vocational education.

The health and medical services are almost entirely municipal (though the health insurance system is national). Physical planning and building supervision, sharing in housing production and its control, the building of streets, water supply, sewage, energy and the fire and rescue services are also provided by the municipalities. Under the Municipal Act of 1977 a comprehensive municipal plan is compulsory. In every municipality, supreme authority is vested in a council elected by universal, secret, proportional and direct elections for a period of four years. All citizens resident in the municipality who have reached the age of 18 before the beginning of the election year are eligible to vote, and the poll is usually 60-80 per cent. Depending on the population the number of council members is 13-85. It is also possible for the municipal council to set up a system of municipal sub-area administration with limited powers. The municipal board is subordinate to the council and is set up for a period of two years. It is responsible for seeing to the preparation and execution of administrative tasks and day-to-day routine. The municipal board is assisted by specialised boards elected by the council which look after various sectors of the administration. Some of these are required by law, others are set up voluntarily.

In the inter-municipal federations, authority is exercised by a council whose members are elected by the councils of the member municipalities. This council in turn elects the federation board which plays the same role as the municipal board in a municipality. The municipalities have the right to collect taxes on the income of their inhabitants. The amounts of taxable income are endorsed by law according to principles laid down but the percentage that has to be paid to the municipality on taxable income is decided according to how much is needed to cover the expenses in the municipality's budget, taking other income sources into account. Neither the budget nor the tax percentage is submitted to central government for approval. The tax percentage is proportional.

A very important asset for the citizens to control the local government is the right not only of the person(s) concerned but of every member of the municipality to appeal against the lawfulness of a decision made by a municipal authority to the Province Court, and then to appeal against this court's decision to the Supreme Administrative Court if necessary. Only a few decisions made by municipal authorities must be submitted to the Provincial Government or the relevant central agency or ministry for ratification. On the other hand, the development of planning systems has meant increasing the control to which local government is subject in many sectors of its administration, such as social services and health.

The Åland Islands, with a predominantly Swedish-speaking population of about 23,000, have an unusual position in that they enjoy a certain amount of autonomy including legislative powers within limits specified in the Åland Self-government Act. The population of Åland elects its own Parliament (Lagting) with 30 members. The Parliament appoints the members of the Province Government (Landskapsstyrelse) which is the central administrative body of the province. The legislative power of the Ålandic Parliament extends to the cultural, social and economic fields, whereas civil and penal laws as well as laws relating to legal procedure fall within the exclusive competence of the National Parliament. The President of the Republic has a limited veto with regard to laws passed by the Ålandic Parliament.

AREA AND POPULATION

Area
Finland is situated with the Gulf of Bothnia to the west and the Gulf of Finland to the south. It has borders with Sweden in the north-west, Norway in the north and the Russian Federation in the east. The area is 338,145 sq. km, of which inland waters form 10 per cent, forests 69 per cent, and cultivated land 8 per cent. The coastline is approximately 1,100 km long. The terrain is generally low-lying with rolling plains and low hills. Land is distributed among different classes of owner approximately as follows: 59.5 per cent private, 31.6 per cent state, 7.0 per cent joint stock companies and similar, 1.9 per cent municipalities and parishes. A quarter of the country is within the Arctic Circle, which means that for 10 weeks in the summer in that northern quarter the sun does not drop below the horizon, making Finland the land of the midnight sun. In winter the sun does not rise above the horizon for around eight weeks keeping that area in darkness.

Finnish Lapland has an area of 92,662 sq km and had a population of 183,330 in December 2012. In 2005 it generated a GDP of €4,621 million.

Winters are long and cold. The average temperature ranges from 0°C to -15°C, and often reach much lower temperatures. Average summer temperatures range from 16°C to 25°C.

To view a map, consult http://www.lib.utexas.edu/maps/cia08/finland_sm_2008.gif

Population
Finland's total population at the end of 2011 was estimated to be 5,401,000 (2,652,000 males and 2,749,000 females) compared to 5,256,000 in 2005. The capital, Helsinki, had a population in 2011 of 595,384. Population density is approximately 17 persons per square kilometre. Approximately 35 per cent of the population inhabit rural areas and 65 per cent the urban areas. There is a Sami (Lapp) population of around 6,500.

There were over 1.460 million families in Finland in 2011 of which 580,547 had children aged 0-17.

Finnish and Swedish are the official languages. Sami (Lappish) and Russian are also spoken. In 2011, 90.04 per cent of the population spoke Finnish and 5.3 per cent Swedish. The Swedish-speaking population is concentrated in the central part of the West coast, on the South coast and on the Åland Islands. 0.03 per cent spoke Lappish and 1.08 per cent spoke Russian.

Births, Marriages and Deaths
In 2011, there were 59,961 recorded live births (compared to 60,980 live births in 2010), in Finland. The infant mortality rate is 0.5 per cent. The fertility rate for women was estimated at 1.8 per woman. In 2011, 50,585 deaths were recorded. This trend is expected to reverse by 2030 with deaths outnumbering births. However the population is expected to continue to increase because of continued immigration.

In 2011, 29,481 immigrants arrived in Finland, up from the 2007 figures of 26,029. Figures for 2007 show that the largest group of foreigners in Finland were Russian (26,211). Other significant groups were 20,006 Estonians, 8,349 Swedes and 4,852 Somalians. At the end of 2006 there were an estimated 5,155,216 Finnish citizens in permanent residence and 121,739 foreign citizens. The number of people who were born abroad but who live in Finland is estimated at 187,910. In 2005 there were 3,574 asylum-seekers. In 12 cases, asylum was granted and 585 residence permits were also given.

The number of older people in Finland is increasing. In 2006, 17.1 per cent of the population was aged 14 or under, compared with 30 per cent in the 1950s. Likewise, the proportion of people aged 65 and over has increased from 7 per cent in the 1950s to 16.5 per cent in 2006. The average life-expectancy of Finnish women in 2006 is estimated at 83 years, and of men 76. The most common causes of death are cardio-vascular diseases, cancer and respiratory diseases.

In 2011, there were 28,408 marriages and 13,469 divorces compared to 29,952 and 13,619 respectively in 2010. In 2006, 322 same sex partnerships were registered. In 2005 there were a total of 949,475 married couples, 293,437 cohabiting heterosexual couples. In total there were 398 registered male couples and 430 registered female couples.

Public Holidays 2014
1 January: New Year's Day
6 January: Epiphany
18 April: Good Friday
20 April: Easter Sunday
21 April: Easter Monday
30 April-1 May: May Day Eve & Day
29 May: Ascension Day
08 June: Whit Sunday
21-22 June: Midsummer's Eve and Day
1 November: All Saints Day
6 December: Independence Day
24-25 December: Christmas Eve and Day
26 December: Boxing Day

EMPLOYMENT

Employment Sector	2009	2010	2011
Agriculture & forestry	119,000	115,000	110,000
Manufacturing	406,000	388,000	384,000
Construction	175,000	172,000	176,000
Wholesale & retail trade, repairs	296,000	298,000	303,000
Transport & storage	153,000	156,000	147,000
Accommodation & food service activities	85,000	83,000	83,000
Information and communication	64,000	95,000	99,000
Financial, insurance and real estate activities	70,000	71,000	75,000
Professional, scientific & technical activities, admin. & support	244,000	250,000	253,000
Public admin. & defence, compulsory social security	116,000	117,000	116,000
Education	164,000	174,000	179,000
Human health & social work activities	388,000	379,000	396,000
Arts, entertainment & recreation; other service activities	138,000	139,000	141,000
Industry unknown	9,000	12,000	11,000
Mean population	5,339,000	5,363,000	5,388,000
Labour force	2,678,000	2,672,000	2,682,000
Employed	2,457,000	2,447,000	2,474,000
Unemployed	221,000	224,000	209,000
Not in labour force	1,347,000	1,372,000	1,376,000
Labour force %	66.5	66.1	66,100
Unemployment rate %	8.2	8.4	7.8

Source: Statistics Finland

Like many western countries Finland has a fast growing ageing population. In order to combat the problems that a labour shortage would bring, Finland in 1998 introduced a plan called 'Work Ability'. Workers are encouraged to remain in the workforce rather than taking early retirement and are offered a 4.5 per cent increase to their pensions for every year they remain working after the age of 63 up to a maximum age of 68. Employers are encouraged to tailor jobs to the individuals' health and skills and offer training in new skills. Figures for 2003 showed that the employment rate for those in the workforce aged 55 to 64 had grown by 13 per cent since the introduction of the Work Ability scheme.

BANKING AND FINANCE

Currency
On 1 January 2002 the euro became legal tender. Prior to that the currency was the Markka (mark, mk, FIM) = 100 penni.
1 euro (€) = 100 cents
€ = 5.94573 Finnish markka (European Central Bank irrevocable conversion rate)

GDP/GNP, Inflation, National Debt
Traditionally the Soviet Union was Finland's largest trading partner and its collapse in 1991 severely affected the Finnish economy; GDP fell by 10 per cent and unemployment grew to a record 20 per cent. Finland successfully changed its economic focus to producing high technology products aimed at the Western market. Finland became a full member of the EU in 1995. In 2007, Germany was Finland's largest export market with 57 per cent of all exports going to the EU. Russia is the largest source of imported goods to Finland with 14.1 per cent originating from there. Finland still exports large amounts of goods and services to Russia and it is estimated that one in four mobile phones made in Finland are destined for Russia. To help guard against future economic shocks such as the collapse of the Russian economy or the present global economic crisis, Finland has developed a 'Buffer Fund' whereby funds are set aside to be used in any such future event. Finland has also been affected by the 2009 global economic crisis. GDP fell by almost 8 per cent in 2009 and there were substantial declines in outputs. Growth was expected to remain below 2 per cent for several years but rallied to an estimated 3.1 per cent in 2010.

The following table shows GDP at current prices in recent years:

Year	Billion Euro	€ per capita
1995	95.9	18,778
2000	132.1	25,524
2001	139.2	26,831
2002	143.5	27,599
2003	145.4	27,895
2004	152.1	29,106
2005	157.3	29,991
2006	165.6	31,453
2007	179.7	34,003
2008	185.7	34,944
2009*	172.3	32,276
2010*	179.7	33,336
2011*	189.4	35,173

*preliminary figures
Source: Statistics Finland

GDP annual change in volume

Year	Percentage
2000	5.3
2001	2.3
2002	1.8
2003	2.0
2004	4.1
2005	2.9
2006	4.4
2007	5.3
2008	0.3
2009	-8.5
2010*	3.3
2011*	2.8

* preliminary figures
Source: Statistics Finland

The following table shows the percentage composition of GDP by industry in recent years:

Industry	2008	2009	2010*	2011*
Agriculture, forestry, hunting & fishing	2.7	2.8	2.9	2.9
Mining & quarrying	0.4	0.4	0.5	0.5
Manufacturing	21.5	16.8	17.4	17.2
Electricity, gas, steam & air conditioning supply	2.0	2.4	2.7	2.3
Water supply, sewerage, waste management & remediation activities	0.7	0.8	0.9	0.9
Construction	7.3	7.1	6.7	6.8
Wholesale & retail trade: repairs	10.2	10.0	9.8	10.3
Transportation & storage	5.4	5.4	5.4	5.3
Accommodation & food service activities	1.6	1.7	1.7	1.7
Information & communication	4.8	5.1	5.0	5.0
Financial & insurance activities	2.8	2.9	2.8	2.8
Real estate activities	10.8	11.9	11.8	11.9
Professional, scientific & technical activities	4.3	4.5	4.4	4.5
Admin. & support service activities	3.2	3.3	3.4	3.5

- continued

Public admin. & defence; compulsory social security	5.8	6.4	6.2	6.1
Education	4.7	5.3	5.3	5.2
Human health & social work activities	8.7	9.9	9.8	9.9
Arts, entertainment & recreation	1.2	1.3	1.3	1.3
Other service activities	1.7	1.9	1.9	1.9
GDP at basic prices	100	100	100	100
Primary production	2.7	2.8	2.9	2.9
Secondary production	32.0	27.5	28.2	27.8
Services	65.3	69.6	69.0	69.3

*preliminary figures
Source: Statistics Finland

Average inflation in 2002 was 1.6 per cent, falling slightly in 2003 to an average of 1.3 per cent. Figures for 2005 put inflation at 0.8 per cent, rising to 2.0 per cent in 2006. It was estimated at 2.6 per cent in 2007 and 4.1 per cent in 2008.

Preliminary figures for 2011 put general government debt at €93 billion or 48.6 of cent of GDP.

Foreign Investment
In 2010 preliminary figures showed investment by Finland in foreign countries (in direct investments and investment stock) amounted to €94.5 billion, and foreign investment in Finland amounted to €58.3 billion. In the same year, Finnish investments in foreign securities amounted to an estimated €207.0 billion (compared to an estimated €130.6 billion in 2005) and foreign investment in Finnish securities amounted to an estimated €224.6 billion (compared to €185.2 billion in 2005).

Balance of Payments / Imports and Exports
The following shows a breakdown of Finland's import / export figures:

Finland's Foreign Trade by Country in 2010 in million €

Main Trading Partners	Imports	Exports
Russia	9,163	4,689
Germany	6,836	5,264
Sweden	5,220	5,987
China	3,776	2,687
Netherlands	2,798	3,545
United States	1,767	3,672
United Kingdom	1,603	2,504
France	2,012	1,775
Italy	1,429	1,365
Belgium	1,223	1,518
Other countries	15,675	19,366
TOTAL	51,500	52,372

Source: Statistics Finland

Foreign Trade € million

Year	Imports	Exports	Trade Balance
2000	36,837	49,484	12,647
2001	35,891	47,800	11,910
2002	35,611	47,245	11,634
2003	36,775	46,378	9,604
2004	40,730	48,917	8,187
2005	47,027	52,453	5,426
2006	55,253	61,489	6,237
2007	59,616	65,688	6,072
2008	62,402	65,580	3,178
2009	43,655	45,063	1,409
2010*	51,500	52,372	873

* preliminary figures
Source: Statistics Finland

Imports & Exports by Product in 2010*

Product	€ million	%
Imports		
Chemicals & chemical products	9,238	17.9
Electrical & electronics industry products	7,413	14.4
Products from mining & quarrying	8,312	16.1
Machinery & equipment	4,124	8.0
Transport equipment	4,114	8.0
Other	18,298	35.5
Exports		
Electrical & electronics industry products	7,974	15.2
Forestry industry products	10,687	20.4
Chemical industry products	10,390	19.8
Machinery & equipment	7,034	13.4
Metal & metal products	7,793	14.9
Other	8,495	16.2

* preliminary figures
Source: Statistics Finland

FINLAND

Central Bank
Suomen Pankki-Finlands Bank (Bank of Finland), PO Box 160, FIN-00101 Helsinki, Finland. Tel: +358 (0)9 1831, fax: +358 (0)9 174872, e-mail: info@bof.fi, URL: http://www.bof.fi
Governor: Erkki Liikanen (page 1464)

Chambers of Commerce and Trade Organisations
Finnish Foreign Trade Association (now: FINPRO), URL: http//www.finpro.fi
Central Chamber of Commerce of Finland, URL: http://www.keskuskauppakamari.fi
Helsinki Chamber of Commerce, URL: http://www.helsinki.chamber.fi
Helsinki Stock Exchange, URL: http://omxgroup.com/nordicexchange/
Invest in Finland Bureau, URL: http://www.investinfinland.fi

MANUFACTURING, MINING AND SERVICES

Primary and Extractive Industries
A number of useful minerals are found in Finland. The main metallic deposits are copper, nickel, zinc and chromium ore. There were seven ore mines operating in 1991. In 2009 there were 948 establishments involved in mining and quarrying. The sector employed 4,608 personnel. Value added in production was €481 million.

Energy
Due to the fact that increased exploitation of hydro-electric power resources is impossible, and consumption increase must be covered by thermal capacity, the use of nuclear energy is of particular interest to the Finnish power economy.

A special Law on Atomic Energy was issued in October 1957 and a Law on Protection Against Radiation has been in force since 1 July 1957. This legislation is under total revision. The main regime of the present law is designed to cover and control the nuclear substances and facilities, as well as, to ensure safety, protect the public interest, and enforce the international safeguard regulations. A licence is required for all kind of handling, possession, import and export of fissionable material, utilisation of a reactor, or facilities designed to produce materials of this kind. Prospecting and mining are excluded from the provisions of this law. The licensing authority is the Ministry of Trade and Industry assisted by the Institute of Radiation Protection as a control authority. Finland has also entered into agreement with the International Atomic Energy Agency on the application of safeguards in accordance with the Treaty on Non-Proliferation of Nuclear weapons and put all her peaceful activities under the control of the Agency. Finland has also entered into the Paris and Brussels Conventions on third party liability in the field of nuclear energy.

The Atomic Energy Commission was established in October 1958. It acts as an advisory body to the Ministry of Trade and Industry, follows development in the field of atomic energy, makes appropriate proposals to the Ministry of Trade and Industry and maintains contact with foreign organisations. There are several enterprises working in the nuclear field.

The state-owned Imatran Voima Oy (Imatra Power Company) owns a nuclear power plant at Loviisa on the south coast of Finland. The first unit started in 1977 and the second in 1980.

TVO Power Company, Teollisuuden Voima Oy, has two identical nuclear power plant units, each with a capacity of 660 MW (BWR), located on the south-west coast of Finland, on Olkiluoto island. The first unit, TVO I, started in 1979 and TVO II in 1980. For equipment and machinery production eight big metal industry enterprises have formed a joint company, Oy Finnatom Ab. The Technical Research Centre of Finland has one Triga Mk. II research reactor and the Helsinki University of Technology has in addition a subcritical assembly for training purposes. In 2000 Teollisuuden Voima put forward proposals to build a fifth reactor and construction was approved in 2002. The Green Party left the governing coalition in protest. The new reactor is seen as a way to cut Finnish imports of energy; Finland currently imports 70 per cent of her energy needs from Russia. In May 2009 it was announced that the start-up date for OL3 nuclear reactor was to be postponed until 2012. This has been further postponed to 2015.

Finland is a member of the International Atomic Energy Agency and participates in the OECD NEA work and Halden Reactor Project. As one of the Scandinavian countries Finland participates in several joint Scandinavian undertakings like information services, research, safety and other co-operative arrangements. Nuclear engineering is taught at the Helsinki University of Technology, and nuclear physics, chemistry, etc., at the Helsinki University. A training simulator for Loviisa Nuclear Power Plant was planned and built by Oy Nokia Ab Electronics and Imatran Voima Oy in 1980.

Prospecting for uranium, thorium and other ores which are used in reactors is done by the state and private enterprises.

The following table gives the preliminary figures for total energy consumption in 2011:

Source	Petajoule	%
Oil	334	24.1
Wood fuels	309	22.2
Nuclear energy	243	17.5
Coal	150	10.8
Natural gas	134	9.6
Peat	87	6.3
Hydro power	44	3.2
Wind power	2	0.1
Other energy sources	36	2.6
Net imports of electricity	50	3.6
Total	1,389	100

Source: Statistics Finland

Some 50 per cent of energy is consumed by industry.

In 2011, 10,000 barrels of day of oil were produced. Finland has a refining capacity of 261,000 bbld. There are no reserves. Finland has no reserves of natural gas and figures for 2011 show that 145 billion cubic feet were imported to satisfy demand. In 2010, 77 billion kWh of electricity were generated. Finland has a capacity of 17 GWe.

Manufacturing
Some 22 per cent of the total labour force are engaged in industry. Although the forest industry still leads in exports (including pulp and paper), the metal and shipbuilding industries have become more important and the electrical equipment sector has grown in recent years, the largest contributor being Nokia, the world's largest manufacturer of mobile phone sets. Figures for 2000 showed that the electronics industry accounted for 27 per cent of Finland's exports, this had fallen to 15.2 per cent by 2010.

The following table shows manufacturing value added in production for 2010 for selected products:

Industry	Labour force	€ million
Total industry	344,000	32,102
Mining & quarrying	5,000	626
Manufacturing	321,000	23,190
-food	29,000	2,071
-beverages	3,000	371
-textiles	2,000	176
-wood & wood products	21,000	1,161
-paper & paper products	21,000	2,984
-printing & reproduction of recorded media	10,000	558
-coke & refined petroleum products	2,000	698
-chemicals & chemical products	12,000	1,791
-Basic pharmaceutical products & pharmaceutical preparations	4,000	807
-Rubber and plastic products	13,000	920
-Electrical equipment	15,000	1,315
-non-metallic mineral products	14,000	894
-basic metals	14,000	1,386
-fabricated metal products, except machinery & equipment	36,000	2,120
-machinery & equipment	43,000	3,550
-computer, electrical & optical equipment	32,00	3,153
-motor vehicles, trailers & semi-trailers	6,000	349
-other transport equipment	9,000	311
-furniture	7,000	350
-other manufacturing	4,000	250
-repair & installation of machinery & equipment	19,000	1,133
Electricity, gas & water supply	11,000	3,396

Source: Statistics Finland

Figures from the end of 2008 show that some manufacturing sectors were in negative growth such as manufacture of basic metals, wood and pulp and textiles. The energy sector, fabricated metals and the food sectors continued to grow.

Service Industries
Tourism accounts for about 3 per cent of total Finnish exports of goods and services and provides some 70,000 people with full-time employment. In 2006 there were 3.3 million tourist arrivals generating receipts of US$54,033 million.

Agriculture
In 1991 approximately 8 per cent of the labour force was employed in agriculture, which, however, only accounted for 3.3 per cent of GDP. By 1998 this had fallen to 6 per cent employed and a contribution of 1.2 per cent of GDP. In 1990 Finland had a total of 129,114 arable farms and this number had fallen to 65,802 by 2008.

Low productivity is mainly due to climate. The cereal crops, especially in the northern part of the country, are not entirely safe owing to frosts in late summer, but as agricultural production is mostly based on fodder crops, the climate does not form an obstacle to rational production.

The opportunities for horticulture are limited owing to the cold climate. Apples are the only fruit grown on a large scale. Pears, plums and cherries can only be grown in the very southern-most parts of the country. In 2009 the livestock population included 72,000 horses, 918,000 cattle, 122,000 sheep (2008 figure), 1,381,000 pigs, 3,785,000 poultry and 193,000 reindeer.

The following tables show the 2009 figures for produce:

Principal field crops

Crop	Yield (kg per hectare)	Yield (mil. kg)
Wheat	3,430	724
Rye	2,720	69
Barley	3,210	1,340
Oats	2,910	810
Potatoes	26,210	659
Sugar beets	37,120	542

Source: Statistics Finland

Other produce in 2010

Produce	mil. kg
Butter	45

- continued

Cheese	101
Beef	83
Pork	203
Poultry meat	96
Eggs	62
Milk	2,222 mil. lt

Source: Statistics Finland

Forestry

The forests of Finland cover an area of 19.7 million hectares which is 65 per cent of the total land area. Pine, spruce and birch are the most important trees with respectively 46 per cent, 36 per cent and 18 per cent of the total growing stock. Of the forest land 54 per cent is in private ownership, 33 per cent is owned by the state, 8 per cent by forest industry enterprises, and 5 per cent by smaller communities such as communes and parishes. In 2008 21,500,000 cubic metres of logs and 30,100,000 cubic metres of pulpwood were produced.

Forest management in Finland is carried out on the basis of a sustained yield. There is a special law concerning private forestry which prohibits destructive cuttings and a law of forest improvement which provides state subsidies for improvement of the production of wood. The state forest service takes care of the government owned forests. The promotion of private forestry is carried out mainly by voluntary organisations of forest owners. The University of Helsinki has a faculty of forestry and there are 29 forestry schools in the country. The Forest Research Institute does extensive research work including a general survey of forest resources and of the use of wood. There are many other organisations dealing with different aspects of forestry.

Fishing

The type of fish caught around the coast of Finland is conditioned by the unusual freshness of the Baltic which in the Gulf of Bothnia and the Gulf of Finland is of insignificant salinity. The most important fish from the economic point of view is the little Baltic herring. Another important salt water fish is the sprat, used mainly for the canning industry.

COMMUNICATIONS AND TRANSPORT

Travel Requirements

US, Canadian and Australian citizens require a valid passport, but do not require a visa for visits not exceeding 90 days in a six-month period. EU citizens holding a valid national ID card do not require a passport or a visa for stays of up to 90 days, but should apply for a residence permit if staying longer.

Finland is a signatory to the Schengen Agreement; With a Schengen visa, a visitor can travel freely throughout the Schengen zone, and there are few border stops and checks. See http://www.eurovisa.info/SchengenCountries.htm for details.
Other nationals should refer to the Finnish embassy to check entry requirements.

National Airlines

International air services are provided by most international airlines to major destinations. In 2006 a total of 16.3 million passengers used Finnish airports (compared to 15.1 million in 2005). Freight in the same year amounted to 145,000 tons.
Finnair, URL: http://www.finnair.fi
President: Jukko Heinonen
Total revenue achieved in 2006 was €2 billion.

International Airports

Helsinki-Vantaa Airport, URL: www.helsinki-vantaa.fi
Civil aviation is regulated by the following bodies.
Ministry of Communications and Transport, URL: http://www.mintc.fi
Civil Aviation Administration, URL: http://www.ilmailulaitos.com

Railways

In 2010 the Finnish State Railways operated a network with 5,919 km of routes of which 3,073 km were electrified line. Freight traffic in the same year amounted to over 35.7 million tons (9.8 billion freight tonne km) and 68 million passenger traffic journeys (4.0 billion passenger km). Helsinki has a subway system.

Roads

The total length of Finland's road network is 78,162 km, of which approximately 49,800km are paved. According to 2006 figures, the number of registered motor vehicles is 2.9 million, including 2.5 million passenger cars (475 per 1,000 population), 376,092 lorries and vans, other 24,780. In the same year there were also 172,283 motorcycles, 353,941 tractors and 106,562 snowmobiles (excluding Åland) registered. (Source: Statistics Finland), Vehicles drive on the right.

Shipping

Owing to the improvement of road networks and transport equipment, inland waterways transport on the chain of lakes and rivers has become less important, there is a system of ferries and waterbuses. In 2010, 25,373 vessels entered Finland. 51.488 million tonnes of imports were brought in and 41,786 million tonnes were exported. There were 8.7 million passenger arrivals and 8.6 million passenger departures.

Ports and Harbours

In total there are 60 ports and loading berths in Finland. The largest cargo ports are located in Helsinki, Kotka, Hamina and Kokkola, and the largest passenger ports are at Helsinki, Mariehamm and Turku.

HEALTH

Public health services include both primary and specialised health care and cover the whole population. Expenditure breaks down thus: Public financing: state 20 per cent; local authorities 40 per cent; social insurance institutions16 per cent; Private financing: households 18 per cent; other 5 per cent. According to the WHO, total expenditure on health amounted to 9.0 per cent of GDP. General government expenditure accounts for 74.7 per cent of total expenditure and amounts to 12.1 per cent of its total expenditure. Private expenditure amounts to 25.3 per cent and social services expenditure 19.5 per cent. Out-of-pocket expenditure amounts to 72.2 per cent of private expenditure and private prepaid plans 19.3 per cent. Per capital total expenditure was US$144 in 2009. (Source: WHO)

Figures for 2010 show that there were 20,306 doctors (one per 265 inhabitants), 69,817 nurses, 87,006 practical nurses, 4,699 dentists, 618 pharmacies, 2,473 chief dispensers and 6,588 pharmacists. (Source: Statistics Finland)

According to the latest WHO figures, in 2010 the infant mortality rate was 2 per 1,000 live births and the under-five mortality rate was 3 per 1,000 live births. Approximately 36 per cent of childhood deaths are caused by congenital anomalies, 17 per cent to prematurity and pneumonia 4 per cent. The childhood vaccination rates for common diseases are high at 98 per cent.

All the population has access to improved drinking water and sanitation. (Source: http://www.who.int, World Health Statistics 2012)

EDUCATION

The pre-primary system has recently been reformed and pre-primary education is available free of charge for children one year before they start actual compulsory schooling. Pre-primary education is not compulsory but local authorities have statutory duty to provide it. About 59 per cent of children attend pre-primary school.

Compulsory education starts at the age of seven and consists of the full nine-year comprehensive school course. Tuition is free and students are also provided with free meals. The language of instruction is either Finnish or Swedish (the two national languages).

The comprehensive school is divided into a six-year lower level and a three-year upper level. In 2009 the number of students in the comprehensive school system was 553,329. In 2006 there were also 65,783 leaving certificates from comprehensive schools.

After comprehensive school the student may transfer either to a senior secondary school or to vocational and professional education institutions. The senior secondary school provides a three-year course of general education. At the end of the senior secondary school the students take the so-called matriculation examination. Having passed this examination they are qualified to seek admission to universities or vocational and professional education institutions with similar entrance requirements. In 2009 the number of senior secondary general school students was 112,088 and 33,034 matriculation examinations were attained.

Finland no longer has a national system of school inspections but schools are encouraged to follow a policy of self-evaluation.

Secondary Education

Vocational and professional education is mainly provided in specialised institutions. Teaching is organised into 25 basic branches and further into more than 200 lines of specialisation. Vocational education at the upper secondary level usually takes 2-3 years and technical and professional education at the tertiary level 4-6 years. Students must previously have completed either the comprehensive school or the senior secondary school. Some courses providing education for specialised professions are open to matriculated students only. In 2005, there were 256,782 people in vocational and professional education. In the same year 60,280 qualifications were attained.

The comprehensive and senior secondary schools are, with some exceptions, run by the municipalities. The vocational and professional education institutions are either municipal (50 per cent), State-run (34 per cent) or private (16 per cent). The State covers the greater part of the recurrent costs of the comprehensive schools (74 per cent), the senior secondary schools (70 per cent) and the vocational and professional education institutions (60 per cent).

Higher Education

The Finnish university system consists of 20 institutions, of which 10 are multi-faculty universities, three technical universities, three schools of economics and business administration, one is a veterinary college and three are academies of art. In addition there are 34 Polytechnics. Students must as a rule have matriculated before they can enter a university, although a vocational and professional education institution provides them with the same eligibility as a matriculation examination. It takes 6-8 years to complete the first degree (candidate = masters degree), while a post graduate degree (licenciate, doctorate) takes several more years. In 2005, the total student population was 309,115 (polytechnic 132,560; university 176,555). In 2006, 21,006 polytechnic degrees were awarded and 19,410 university degrees. (Source: Statistics Finland)

Literacy is almost 100 per cent.

RELIGION

The National Churches are the Evangelical-Lutheran Church of Finland, to which about 83.1 per cent of the people belong, and the Greek Orthodox Church (1.1 per cent). The Greek Orthodox Church, in spite of its comparatively few adherents (about 52,800), is also a National Church with the same rights as the Evangelical-Lutheran Church. The bishops of both churches are appointed by the President of the Republic from among the candidates put forward by

FINLAND

the church authorities. Entire freedom is allowed to other religions and denominations. The minority groups are small. The various Free Churches (Free Church of Finland, Methodist, Baptist, Adventist, Jehovah's Witnesses etc) number about 40,800. The membership of the Catholic Church in Finland is 4,500.

Finland has a religious liberty rating of 9 on a scale of 1 to 10 (10 is most freedom). (Source: World Religion Database)

COMMUNICATIONS AND MEDIA

Newspapers
Helsingen Sanomat, URL: http://www.hs.fi.
Aamulehti, URL: http://www.aamulehti.fi
Iltalehti, URL: http://www.iltalehti.fi/etusivu/ (evening daily)
Kauppalehti, URL: http://www.kauppalehti.fi
Ilta-Sanomat, URL: http://www.iltasanomat.fi/
Talous Sanomat, URL: http://www.taloussanomat.fi/
Turun Sanomat, URL: http://www.taloussanomat.fi/
Hufvudstadsbladet (Swedish language) URL: http://hbl.fi

Broadcasting
YLE (The Finnish Broadcasting Association) is the largest national radio and television service provider and is a non-commercial, public service broadcaster and is state owned. The only other nationwide broadcaster is MTV3 which is privately owned and only operates one channel. YLE operates two television channels, YLE1 and YLE2. The pan-Nordic operator Canal+ runs Pay-TV channels.

The Finnish Broadcasting Company also operates four national radio channels transmitted in both Finnish and Swedish, and various regional channels, one of which is transmitted in Lapp for the Lapland region. In addition to several private radio stations there are also some 60 local radio stations operated privately and many newspapers, associations and public corporations.
Yleisradio Oy (Finnish Broadcasting Company), URL: http://www.yle.fi/bc

Telecommunications
The total number of landline subscriber lines in the country was 1.08 million in 2011 (down from 2,140,000 in 2005) and there were an estimated 9 million mobile phone connections. In 2009 there were over 4 million internet users. In July 2010 Finland became the first country where access to broadband internet became a legal right.

ENVIRONMENT

Finland's forests and inland waters are threatened by acid rain originating from neighbouring countries.

As at 1 January 2007, Finland had 5,692 protected areas covering 1,784,100 hectares which included national parks, nature reserves and animal protection areas. Approximately 13.8 per cent of the area is covered by water. There are also 12 wilderness areas covering 1,489,00 hectares, of which approximately 7.4 per cent is water.

In 2006, air emissions were as follows: greenhouse gas emissions, CO_2 equivalent: 80.2 million tonnes; carbon dioxide: 64.1 million tonnes; sulphur (as SO_2): 84,000 tonnes; nitrogen oxides: 193,000 tonnes; particles: 41,000 tonnes. (Source: Statistics Finland). Figuures from the EIA show that in 2010 total carbon dioxide emission from fossil fuels was 54.40 million tonnes up from 52.29 million tonnes in 2009.

Finland is party to the following international agreements: Air Pollution, Air Pollution-Nitrogen Oxides, Air Pollution-Persistent Organic Pollutants, Air Pollution-Sulfur 85, Air Pollution-Sulfur 94, Air Pollution-Volatile Organic Compounds, Antarctic-Environmental Protocol, Antarctic-Marine Living Resources, Antarctic Treaty, Biodiversity, Climate Change, Climate Change-Kyoto Protocol, Desertification, Endangered Species, Environmental Modification, Hazardous Wastes, Law of the Sea, Marine Dumping, Marine Life Conservation, Ozone Layer Protection, Ship Pollution, Tropical Timber 83, Tropical Timber 94, Wetlands, Whaling.

SPACE PROGRAMME

Finland's space activities are focused on environmental monitoring, navigation, telecommunications, space technology and scientific research. Its space activities are conducted through ESA programmes, national programmes and bilateral international agreements. Finland became an associate member of the European Space Agency in 1987 and a full member in 1995. The Finnish Funding Agency for Technology and Innovation (Tekes) is responsible for coordinating and financing Finland's participation in ESA. The Finnish satellite Aalto-1 is due to launch in 2013. The device uses Cubesat technology.

ÅLAND ISLANDS

Capital: Mariehamn (Population estimate: 10,600)

Head of State: Sauli Niinisto (President of Finland) (page 1486)

Governor: Peter Lindbäck (page 1465)

National flag: Rectangular blue background with a red cross with a gold border. The vertical bar of the cross is off centre towards the hoist

CONSTITUTION AND GOVERNMENT

Constitution
The Åland Islands belonged to Sweden up until the war in 1808-09, when Sweden was forced to give up Finland and the Åland Islands to Russia. The Islands then became part of the Duchy of Finland. During the Russian Revolution in 1917, the Ålanders expressed their wish for a reunion with Sweden during a meeting at the Folk High School on 20 August. On 6 December, Finland proclaimed itself independent, but was reluctant to cede the islands to Sweden. Instead, in 1920, the Finnish Parliament passed an act of autonomy, which the islanders were reluctant to accept. In June 1921 the matter was referred to the League of Nations which ruled that the islands would remain under Finnish sovereignty. The ruling was then supplemented by guarantees that the Åland Islands be autonomous, would keep their Swedish language and customs, and would become a demilitarized area.

The first elections to the new parliament, the *Lagting*, were held on 9 June 1922.

Parliament
The Lagting is the Åland Islands' Parliament. It has 30 members elected every four years by a secret ballot, and is overseen by the speaker *Talaman*. Only those over 18 and with regional citizenship in Åland are eligible to vote or stand for election. A system of proportional representation is used. The Lagting then elects the government, *Landskapsstyrelse*, which consists of five to seven members.

There are seven standing committees in the parliament. There are six special standing committees are responsible for a specific area: Legal; Finance; Industry, Trade and Agriculture; Culture; Social and Environment. These committees are made up of five members and five deputy members. There is also a Review Committee made up of three members and three deputy members. The Review Committee ensures that the wording of any parliamentary resolutions is correct. There is also a Grand Committee which examines legal matters or international treaties after they have been before a special Committee. The Grand Committee has ten members.

Ålands' Lagting, PB 69, 22101 Mariehamn, Åland. Tel: +358 (0)18 25000, fax: +358 (0)18 13302, URL: http://www.lagtinget.ax

Speaker: Barbro Sundback

Legislature
The current Autonomy Act was adopted in January 1993 and defines the areas in which the Lagting can pass laws. These include education, health and medical services, promotion of industry, municipal administration, police, postal service, culture and preservation of ancient monuments, and the adoption of its budget. New laws are submitted to the President of Finland who has power of veto.

The areas of foreign affairs, some aspects of civil and penal law, courts of justice and monetary services come under Finnish jurisdiction. To safeguard its interests in these matters Åland has a representative in the Finnish Parliament. The Finnish Government is represented in Åland by a Governor who is appointed by the Finnish President in agreement with the Åland speaker.

Cabinet (as at June 2013)
Head of Åland Government: Camilla Gunell (page 1435)
Deputy Head, Minister of Finance: Roger Norlund
Minister: Johan Ehn
Minister: Carina Aaltonen
Minister: Gun-Mari Lindholm
Minister: Fredrik Karlstrom
Minister: Veronica Thornroos

Government portal: URL: http://www.government.ax/

Elections
The most recent elections were held on 16 October 2011. The composition of the parliament is as follows: Åland Centre 7 seats; Liberals 6 seats; Åland Social Democrats 6 seats; Moderates of Åland 4 seats; Non-aligned Coalition 4 seats; Future of Åland (Independent) 3 seats.

The present government is a coalition between Åland Social Democrats; Åland Centre Party; The Independent Group; The Moderates of Åland

Political Parties
Liberalerna, URL: http://www.liberalerna.ax
Centern, URL: http://www.centern.ax/
Obunden Samling, URL: http://www.obs.ax/
Ålands Socialdemokrater, URL: http://www.socialdemokraterna.ax/
Frisinnad Samverkan, URL: http://www.fs.ax/
Ålands Framtid, URL: http://www.alandsframtid.ax/

LOCAL GOVERNMENT

For administrative purposes Åland is divided into 16 municipalities. Each has its own council which is elected every four years.

The following table shows the municipalities and their populations in 2010:

Municipality	Population 2000	2010
Brändö	514	488
Eckerö	830	943
Finström	2,299	2,502
Föglö	595	580
Geta	478	475
Hammarland	1,351	1,508
Jomala	3,328	4,098
Kumlinge	405	364
Kökar	296	259
Lemland	1,585	1,814
Lumparland	377	394
Mariehamn	10,488	11,190
Saltvik	1,679	1,802
Sottunga	129	119
Sund	1,013	1,019
Vårdö	409	452

Source: ASUB - Dept. of Statistics & Economic Research in Åland

AREA AND POPULATION

Area
The Åland Islands are situated at the mouth of the Gulf of Bothnia between Finland and Sweden. It is an archipelago of some 6,500 islands of which around 65 are inhabited. It covers an area of 6,784 sq. km. The largest island is *Fasta Island*, which is home to 90 per cent of the population and Åland's only town, Mariehamn.

The winters are relatively mild with temperatures above freezing during the day, commonly falling below zero at night and the summers fairly warm with average daily highs of 18°C.

Population
In 2012, the population was estimated to be 28,335. The population is expected to reach 31,104 by 2020 and 36,177 by 2040. The population density is 18.0 per km². The municipalities with the highest populations are Hammarland 4,022, Finstrom 2,486, and Mariehamn 11,123. The official language is Swedish.

Births, Marriages, Deaths
Figures for 2010 show that there were 286 births and 233 deaths. Also that year there were 873 immigrants and 649 emigrants. Average life expectancy from birth was 81.5 years (males 79.7 years, females 83.1 years) in 2010. In 2010, 16.4 per cent of the population was aged less than 15 years old, 65.3 per cent were aged between 15-64 years and 18.4 per cent were aged 65 years or older. In 2009, 9,957 people were married, 2,178 were divorced and 1,533 were either widows or widowers.(Source: Åland Statistics)

Public Holidays 2014
1 January: New Year's Day
6 January: Epiphany
18 April: Good Friday
21 April: Easter Monday
29 May: Ascension Day
8 June: Whitsun
9 June: Autonomy Day
1 November: All Saints Day
24 December: Christmas Eve
25 December: Christmas Day
26 December: Boxing Day

EMPLOYMENT

In 2008, the workforce was 14,247 (out of a total population of 27,456). Of this, 13,960 were employed and 287 unemployed.

BANKING AND FINANCE

Currency
One euro (€) = 100 cents
€ = 5.94573 Finnish markka (European Central Bank irrevocable conversion rate)
On 1 January 1999 the euro was launched as an electronic currency across the 12 member states of the EU. On 1 January 2002 the euro became legal tender in Finland and the Åland Islands, replacing the Finnish markka. Euro banknotes come in denominations of 5, 10, 20, 50, 100, 200, and 500. Euro coins come in denominations of 2 and 1 euros, 50, 20, 10, 5, 2, and 1 cents.

GDP/GNP, Inflation, National Debt
Figures for 2008 put GDP at 1,044.7 million, a per capita figure of €38,300. The following table shows the make-up of GDP by economic activity in 2008 (figures are in million euros):

Industry	Million Euros	%
Agriculture	27	2.8

- continued

Industry	Million Euros	%
Industry	70	7.1
Construction	51	5.2
Trade, hotels	87	8.9
Shipping	259	26.4
Other Transport	39	4.0
Information and communication	34	3.5
Finance & real estate	133	13.6
Professional, scientific & techn.	20	2.0
Public Services	7	0.7
Pers. Services	51	5.2
Unallocated banking services	-30	-3.1
Industries, total	749	76.4
Government services	216	22.0
Non-profit institutions	15	1.6
GDP at basic prices	**980**	**100**

Source: ASUB

Imports/Exports
Total Imports and exports 2007-09, €1,000

	2007	2008	2009
Total Imports	450.905	366,950	395,882
Total Exports	145,864	142,556	127,466
Trade balance	-305,041	-224,394	-268,416

Source: Statistical Year Book of Åland

Main imports included machinery and equipment (€35,618,000), pulp, paper (€20,104,000), textile articles (€17,581,000), vehicles, ships and transport equipment (€17,824,000), live animals and animal products (€16,646,000), and plastics (€9,772).

Exports included plastics & rubber (€15,549,000), wood and wood products (€7,475,000), machinery (€5,812,000), and products from the chemical industry (€4,104,000).

MANUFACTURING, MINING AND SERVICES

Manufacturing
Manufacturing on the islands is on a small scale and includes fish processing, food processing, and some plastic, metal, electronics and technology industries. In 2008, the value of the gross output manufacturing industry amounted to €199 million, up from €180 million the previous year. The food industry was the largest contributor (€97 million).

Tourism
Tourism plays a large part in the economy with arrivals growing from 39,500 in 1958 to some 208,000 overnight visitors in 2009. Visitors stayed an average of two nights. In 2009, there were 14 registered camping sites, 34 hotels, guesthouses etc and 65 holiday villages. (Source: Åland Statistics)
Åland Islands Tourist Office, URL: http://www.visitaland.com/en

Agriculture
In 2009, there were a total of 551 farms. Total farmland was 14,103 hectares. Average farm size was 25.6 hectares. There were 199 livestock farms, and 370 crop and other production farms. In 2009, there were 7,694 cattle, 294 pigs, 12,780 hens, 13,124 sheep, and 257 horses.

Agricultural Production 2008-09

Product	Production ,Tonnes 2008	Prod. Tonnes, 2009	Gross income 2008 €'000	Gross income € '000
Meat	625	698	1,333	1,520
Milk	13,611	13,861	6,284	6,302
Eggs	236	236	378	378
Grain	9,440	10,507	1,709	1,139
Sugar beets	7,846	5,013	176	132
Potatoes	15,509	18,642	2,843	3,001
Vegetables	7,586	6,539	3,370	2,897
Apples	2,819	2,794	2,855	2,792
Other			525	352
Total			**19,475**	**18,513**

Source: ASUB, Åland Statistical Yearbook

Forestry
According to Åland Statistics, in 2007, Åland a total of 67,400 hectares were forested (52 per cent pine, 20 per cent spruce, 27.8 per cent broad leaves). In 2009, 176,787 m³ of timber was produced, with a delivery value of €4.019 million.

Fishing
The total catch is in a period of decline: 2,090 tonnes in 2009 (gross value €1,716,000), 2,485 tonnes (gross value €2,130,000) in 2008 and 3,390 tonnes (gross value €2,888,000) in 2007. The main fish are: cod (468 tonnes, €611,000), whitefish (54 tonnes, €332,00), Baltic herring and sprat (468 tonnes, €611,000) and perch (81 tonnes, €206,000).

There are 29 fish culture firms. In 2007, 4257 tonnes were sold with a production value of €14,950,000. (Source: Åland Statistics)

Hunting
In 2009, 4330 hunting licences were issued. In 2009, 186 elks and 4,162 deer were shot. Approximately 145 seals were shot. (Source: Åland Statistics)

FRANCE

COMMUNICATIONS AND TRANSPORT

International Airports
The Åland Islands have an airport at Mariehamn, with flights to Finland and Sweden. In 2009, there were 3,521 landings. Total passengers amounted to 56,193. In the same year, 13.0 tonnes of cargo were carried and 311 tonnes of mail.
Air Åland, URL: http://www.airaland.com

Roads
Figures for 2008 show that there were over 918 km of roads. According to Åland Statistics, in 2009, there were 777 new vehicle registrations (348 cars), down on 1,076 in 2008. Total vehicle registrations amounted to 18,373 cars, 3,683 vans, 629 lorries, 1,286 motorcycles, 1,655 mopeds, 3,570 tractors, 6,489 trailers.

Shipping
In 2009, 1,101,222 passengers travelled on the archipelago ferry service. An estimated 596,013 vehicles also used the ferry service. Ferries run from Sweden and Tallinn in Estonia.
Viking Line, URL: http://www.vikingline.fi/index.asp?lang=en
Tallink Silja, URL: http://www.tallinksilja.com

The merchant fleet amounted to 33 vessels, compared to 76 in 1975. Gross freight amounted to €599.3 million in 2007.

HEALTH
There are a reported 176 hospital beds and 23 psychiatric care beds. Government health care expenditure was an estimated MEUR 118 in 2010. The most common cause of death was diseases of the circulation system. (Source: Aland Statistics)

EDUCATION
The system of education is similar to that in Finland, except that the language of instruction is Swedish and the islands have autonomy over the education system. Education is free and compulsory for nine years between the ages of 7 and 16 years. Local districts are responsible for providing basic education, which means that some schools are relatively small. According to Åland Statistics, in 2009 there were 25 comprehensive schools with 2,887 pupils. In the same year, there were 1,300 students registered at the upper secondary level. In 2008, there were 392 teachers in comprehensive schools, 169 at upper secondary level, 37 at the Åland university of Applied Science and 19 in other education. Students wishing to study at university have to go to Finland or Sweden.

RELIGION
Recent figures show that over 92 per cent of the population belong to the Lutheran National Church.

COMMUNICATIONS AND MEDIA

Newspapers
Two newspapers are produced: *Tindningen Åland* comes out five days a week, and *Nya Åland* comes out four days a week (URL: http://www.nyan.ax/nyheter/). According to Åland Statistics, in 2009, circulation of daily newspapers amounted to 16,611.

Broadcasting
The province of Åland owns Ålands' Radio and TV Am, and has been broadcasting since 1996. There is also a commercial radio station.

FRANCE

French Republic

République Française

Capital: Paris (Population estimate, 2010: 2,43,833)

Head of State: François Hollande (President) (page 1443)

National Flag: A tricolour pale-wise, blue, white, red

CONSTITUTION AND GOVERNMENT

Constitution
The Constitution of 4 October 1958 provides the institutional basis for the Fifth Republic. It has been amended several times; key changes include the election of the President of the Republic by direct universal suffrage (1962) and enlarging the application of the referendum (1995). It was amended in March 2003 to devolve wide-ranging powers to the regions and departments. It was most recently modified in July 2008.

The President is the supreme authority of the Fifth Republic. The Constitution stipulates that the President of the Republic is elected by an absolute majority of votes (direct universal suffrage) for a five-year term. If an absolute majority is not obtained in the first round of voting then a second round must be held. The president determines the broad direction of political strategy and is vested with wide powers. Since 1958 it has been accepted that, in practice, tenure of the office of prime minister is contingent upon the continuing confidence of the Head of State. The president of the Republic appoints the prime minister and, with the recommendation of the prime minister, appoints and presides over the *Conseil des Ministres* (Cabinet), promulgates laws, makes appointments to high-ranking civilian and military posts, signs the most important decrees, accredits ambassadors, and negotiates and ratifies treaties. The president also chairs the Higher Council of the Judiciary, and the higher national defence councils and committees.

As Head of the Armed Forces, the president alone can authorise use of nuclear weapons. In the event of a severe crisis posing a threat to the nation's institutions, the president is empowered to take such measures as are necessary to restore order (subject to certain constitutional safeguards). The president can dismiss the prime minister, dissolve the National Assembly (there have been three dissolutions since 1958), or, acting on a proposal from the Government or Parliament, hold a national referendum on any Bill concerned with organisation of the public authorities or ratification of a treaty (for example, the referendum on the Maastricht Treaty in 1992).

The Government, headed by the prime minister, sets national policy and carries it out. The prime minister reports regularly on the Government's programme to Parliament, before which he is accountable on the Government's behalf. He is also responsible for his own stewardship before the National Assembly, but only a motion of censure signed by one tenth of the Deputies and passed by an absolute majority of their number can oblige him to resign.

There are several main Constitutional bodies. The Constitutional Council (*Conseil constitutionnel*) has a two-fold role. It rules on the regularity of presidential and parliamentary elections and referenda, is the arbiter of the constitutionality of legislation, and performs a fundamental role in the protection of public freedom. The nine members of

the Constitutional Council are appointed for a non-renewable nine year term (one third re-appointed every three years) by the president of the Republic, the president of the Senate and the president of the National Assembly.

To consult the full constitution, please visit:
http://www.conseil-constitutionnel.fr/

Constitutional Council (Conseil Constitutionnel), 2 rue de Montpensier, 75001 Paris, France. Tel: + 33 (0)1 40 15 30 00, fax: +33 (0)1 40 20 93 27, URL: http://www.conseil-constitutionnel.fr/
President: Jean-Louis Debré (page 1413)
Ex officio Members: Valéry Giscard d'Estaing (page 1431), Jacques Chirac (page 1404), Nicholas Sarkozy (page 1508)
Members: Pierre Steinmetz, Jacqueline de Guillenchmidt, Renaud Denoix-de-Saint-Marc, Guy Canivet, Michel Charasse, Hubert Haenel, Jacques Barrot, Claire Bazy-Malaurie

The *Council of State* is both an advisory and a judicial body. There are approximately 300 members who are senior public servants enjoying great independence from the Government. The Council of State is consulted on all Government Bills and most draft decrees. It is also the supreme court in the system of administrative courts which hear disputes between citizens and administrative authorities. The Conseil d'Etat may be presided over by either the prime minister or the minister of foreign affairs.
Council of State (Conseil d'Etat), 1 place du Palais-Royal, 75100 Paris, France. Tel: +33 (0)1 40 20 80 50, fax: +33 (0)1 40 20 80 08, URL: http://www.conseil-etat.fr/
President: François Hollande (page 1443)
Vice President: Jean-Marc Sauvé (page 1509)
Secretary-General: François Séners

The *Economic and Social Council* is a body existing to reflect the opinions of a broad range of economic and social interests. It is independent of both the executive and parliament. Of its 231 members, 68 are appointed by decree on the basis of their special competence and the other 163 are nominated by organisations representing business, farming, employees, families and the self-employed. The Government is obliged to consult the Council on draft economic or social planning legislation and on each five-year plan.
Conseil économique et social, 9 Place d'Iéna, 75775 Paris Cedex 16, France. Tel: +33 (0)1 44 43 60 00, e-mail: secgen@ces.fr, URL: http://www.lecese.fr/
President: Jean-Paul Delevoye

The *Auditor General's Department (Cour des Comptes)* monitors implementation of the budget and, with assistance from 24 regional audit offices, audits the accounts of all the public accountants up and down the country. Its annual report, which receives wide coverage in the press, draws attention to errors or instances of poor management and helps, by constructive criticism, to improve the efficiency of the administration. Its members are appointed by the Government and cannot be removed from office. There are seven chambers. Each chamber has jurisdiction over a defined range of central government activity.
Auditor General's Department, 13 rue Cambon, 75100 Paris cedex 01, France. Tel: +33 (0)1 42 98 95 00, fax: +33 (0)1 42 60 01 59, URL: http://www.ccomptes.fr/
President: Didier Migaud

Public Prosecutor: Gilles Johanet
President of the first chamber: Raoul Briet
President of the second chamber: Gilles-Pierre Lévy
President of the third chamber: Patrick Lefas
President of the fourth chamber: Jean-Pierre Bayle
President of the fifth chamber: Anne Froment-Meurice
President of the sixth chamber: Antoine Durrleman
President of the seventh chamber: Evelyne Ratte

The *Ombudsman* is an administrative official who deals with complaints passed on to him by Members of Parliament from citizens who have experienced difficulties with public authorities. Since the establishment of a network of local mediators under his authority, he has been able to handle many more cases, settling the majority of the problems brought to his attention. His annual report draws the Government's attention to areas where administrative reforms are required.
Office of the Ombudsman, 7 rue St. Florentin, 75008 Paris, France. Tel: +33 (0)1 55 35 24 24, fax: +33 (0)1 55 35 24 25, URL: http://www.defenseurdesdroits.fr/
Ombudsman: Jean-Paul Delevoye

Recent Events
The French people rejected the European Constitution in a referendum held in May 2005. President Chirac, a strong supporter of the Constitution, recognised the vote in part as a rejection of his government and its policies. Prime Minister Raffarin resigned, and there were major changes in the Cabinet line-up. The President promised to tackle high unemployment in France.

The autumn of 2005 saw street riots. The riots, which started in deprived, largely immigrant communities in north-east Paris, spread to other cities, and the Government had to introduce emergency measures to bring the situation under control. The following year, there were mass protests over the government's privatisation and pension reform plans. New legislation giving employers greater freedom to hire and fire young people sparked street demonstrations across the country in spring 2006. The authorities said the new rules were intended to improve job prospects for the young. As protests and strikes continued, the legislation was abandoned.

Nicholas Sarkozy, a former interior minister and leader of the ruling UMP, was elected president in May 2007. The UMP won parliamentary elections in June 2007. However in November 2007 there was further unrest with demonstrations against proposed reform of pension benefits and reform of some parts of the public sector.

In February 2008 France formally ratified the Lisbon Treaty.

In October 2008, the French government announced an injection of €10.5 billion in to France's six largest banks in response to the global financial crisis. In December 2008 President Sarkozy presented a €26 billion recovery plan to stimulate the French economy. The government later said it would issue a decree banning bonuses in banks that had received public money.

In March 2009 France said it would offer compensation to people who had suffered health problems as a result of nuclear weapons testing. France carried out more than 200 tests in Algeria and then French Polynesia between 1966 and 1996.

President Sarkozy announced in March 2009 that France was to return to NATO's military command. France withdrew from the military command under the presidency of Charles de Gaulle who said that France's sovereignty was being undermined.

In June 2010, the government announced public spending cuts of €45bn aiming to reduce high level of public debt. The following month two junior ministers resigned after becoming involved in financial scandals. Both Overseas Development Minister Alain Joyandet and Greater Paris Minister Christian Blanc resigned over their expense claims.

In August 2010, France started to dismantle illegal Roma camps and Roma or gypsies were then deported. This move was seen as controversial and the European Parliament called for deportations to be halted.

On September 15, 2010, France's lower house of parliament passed a bill which will raise the minimum pension age from 60 to 62 by 2018. The proposed bill had seen thousands of people of people on streets in protest. By the middle of October strikes had spread to nearly all sectors. The bill will now go to the Senate.

A military and nuclear accord was signed between the UK and France in November 2010. The two countries will cooperate in testing nuclear warheads.

In March 2011, France played a significant part in imposing and enforcing a no-fly zone over Libya. France was one of the first countries to recognise as legitimate a transitional council in Libya.

On April 2011 a law was passed, making it an offence for a Muslim woman to conceal her face behind a veil when out in public, punishable by a fine of €150. Anyone found guilty of forcing a woman to wear a veil in public would be subject to a larger fine and a prison sentence of up to two years.

In May 2011, the head of the IMF and potential French presidential candidate, Dominique Strauss-Kahn, was arrested in the USA and charged with attempted rape. He subsequently resigned as head of the IMF. The French finance minister, Christine Lagarde (page 1459), was announced as his successor in June 2011. A minor cabinet reshuffle followed. Criminal charges against Mr Strauss-Kahn were dropped but in May 2012 diplomatic immunity was dropped meaning the civil lawsuit filed by his alleged victim may now proceed.

In September 2011, the former prime minister Dominique de Villepin, was acquitted on appeal over allegations that he had allowed false rumours to be spread about Nicholas Sarkozy. However, subsequently further allegations have been made over illegal donations to Dominique de Villepin and Jacques Chirac.

Senate elections took place in France on 25 September 2011. The Left gained control of the Upper House. Early results from the indirect elections showed that left-wing candidates (from the Socialist Party, the Communist Party and the Greens) gained enough seats for an outright majority.

In October 2011 François Hollande was elected the Socialist Party's candidate for the 2012 presidential election.

In November 2011, further budget savings were announced of €7 bn in 2012 and €11.6 bn in 2013. Measures including pension reform, a rise in VAT and corporation tax. The government has already announced it intends to save €12 billion over the next two years. The retirement age will rise by two years to 62 in 2017, not 2018 as originally planned and VAT will be raised from 5.5 per cent to 7 per cent. Corporation tax on companies with an annual turnover of more than €250 million will be temporarily raised by 5 per cent. France is determined to protect its AAA credit rating.

The first round of presidential elections took place on 22 April 2012. The incumbent candidate, Nicholas Sarkozy, came second with 27.1 per cent of the vote whilst the Socialist candidate François Hollande took 28.6 per cent. Marie Le Pen of the far right National Front, came third with 18 per cent, the largest share of the vote the NF has ever won. A second round of voting took place on 6 May when the opposition candidate François Hollande defeated the incumbent candidate Nicholas Sarkozy.

Parliamentary elections took place in June 2012 and were won by the Socialist Party. France lost its triple AAA credit rating when the ratings' Agency Moody's downgraded it, citing stalled economic growth and contagion from the eurozone. Economic growth was put at zero in Q4 2012, better than forecast.

In January 2013, French troops intervened in Mali to help the government in its fight against Islamist insurgents who had seized the north of the country.

Legislature
Legislative power is exercised by the bicameral Parliament, which consists of the *Assemblée Nationale* (National Assembly) and the *Sénat* (Senate). Parliament passes legislation and monitors the Government's administration. Parliament does not sit continuously throughout the year. Under the Constitution, there are only two sessions: the first, starting in October and lasting for 90 days, is devoted largely to the Finance Bill; the second runs from April to June. Parliament may be recalled for extraordinary sessions to adopt the reforming legislation formulated by the Government. A Bill can become law only if it is approved, in the same wording, by both Chambers. Parliament has developed the role of 'watchdog' over the Government's activities.

Upper House
The Senate has been undergoing reform aimed at modernising the senate and better representing local bodies and their population. The reforms were completed in 2011. The number of senators has gradually increased: prior to 2004 there were 321 Senators elected for nine years in indirect elections. One third of their number was renewable every three years. The number increased to 331 in 2004 and to 343 after the 2008 elections. The number rose to 348 in the 2011 elections to reflect increases in population. From 2011 onwards, half the membership will be elected every three years for six-year terms.

The speaker of the Senate presides over the debates. He is elected for a three-year term after the renewal of Senate membership. The Speaker chairs the Managing Committee which is made up of 25 senators and which is responsible for all major decisions on the workings of the Senate. The Senators are affiliated to various political groups. The groups must be composed of at least 15 members.

There are 12 seats taken by representatives for French citizens overseas. Currently, there are currently 10 senators representing overseas territories: two senators for Martinique, two for French Polynesia, two for Guyana, three for Guadeloupe, one for Wallis and Fortuna, one Saint-Barthemly, one Saint-Martin, and one for Saint-Pierre et Miquelon.

Partial elections took place in 25 September 2011 elections for 170 seats The Senate now breaks down thus: PS and allies (including PCF and EELV) 177 seats; UMP and allies (including NC) 171 seats.

Le Sénat, 15, rue de Vaugirard, 75291 Paris Cedex 06, France. Tel: +33 (0)1 42 34 20 00, fax: +33 (0)1 42 34 26 77, e-mail: communication@senat.fr, URL: http://www.senat.fr
President: Jean-Pierre Bel

Lower House
The 577 Deputies in the National Assembly are elected for a five-year term by direct universal suffrage in a two-ballot system. Its main functions are to adopt statutes and to supervise government. The constituencies were redrawn in 2009 and the number of constituencies and seats for French residents overseas increased to 11. In the event of a dispute between the Senate and the National Assembly over a law, the National Assembly is empowered to make the final decision. According to the constitution there can be no more than six standing committees. No deputy may serve on more than one standing committee. There are also six parliamentary delegations which are responsible for keeping Parliament informed in particular areas.

Elections for the chairs of the permanent committees took place on 28 June 2012:
National Defence and Armed Forces: Patrician Adam
Cultural Affairs and Education: Patrick Bloche
Social Affairs: Catherine Lemorton

FRANCE

Economic Affairs: François Brottes
Foreign Affairs: Elisabeth Guigou
Finance, the Economy and Budgetary Control: Gilles Carrez
Constitutional Law, Legislation and General State Administration: Jean-Jacques Urvoas
Sustainable Development and Land Management: Jean-Paul Chanteguet

In the June 2012 elections the opposition PS (with their allies) gained control of the Assemblée Nationale. The house now breaks down thus: Parti Socialist 280 seats; UMP 194 seats; various left wing seats 22; EELV 17 seats; various right 15 seats; NC 12 seats; Radical Party of the Left 12 seats; Left Front 10 seats; Radical Party 6 seats; Front National 2 seats; others 7 seats.

L'Assemblée Nationale, 126 rue de l'Université, 75355 Paris 07 SP, France. Tel: +33 (0)1 40 63 60 00 / 99 99, fax: +33 (0)1 45 55 75 23, e-mail: infos@assemblee-nationale.fr, URL: http://www.assemblee-nationale.fr
President of the Assemblée Nationale: Claude Bartolone

Cabinet (as at June 2013)

Prime Minister: Jean-Marc Ayrault (page 1380)
Minister of Foreign Affairs: Lauren Fabius (page 1422)
Minister of National Education: Vincent Peillon (page 1493)
Keeper of the Seals: Christiane Taubira (page 1523)
Minister of the Economy & Finance: Pierre Moscovici (page 1481)
Minister of Social Affairs and Health: Marisol Touraine (page 1527)
Minister of Land Management and Housing: Cécile Duflot
Minister of the Interior: Manuel Valls (page 1530)
Minister of Foreign Trade: Nicole Bricq (page 1394)
Minister of Productive Recovery: Arnaud Montebourg (page 1479)
Minister of Ecology, Sustainable Development and Energy: Delphine Batho
Minister of Labour, Employment, Professional Training and Social Dialogue: Michel Sapin (page 1508)
Minister of Defence: Jean-Yves Le Drian (page 1461)
Minister of Culture and Communication: Aurélie Filippetti
Minister of Higher Education and Research: Mme Geneviève Fioraso
Minister of Women's Rights, Government Spokesperson: Naja Vallaud-Belkacem
Minister of Agriculture, Food & Forestry: Stéphane Le Foll (page 1462)
Minister of State Reform, Decentralisation and Public Service: Marylise Lebranchu (page 1461)
Minister for Overseas France: Victorin Lurel
Minister of Decentralization: Anne-Marie Escoffier
Minister of Sports & Youth: Valérie Fourneyron
Minister of Apprenticeship and Professional Training: Thierry Repentin
Minister of Food Processing: William Garo
Minister for French Nationals Abroad: Helen Conway
Minister of Craft, Commerce and Tourism: Sylvia Pinel

Deputy Ministers (as of June 2013)

Deputy Minister to the Prime Minister, with responsibility for relations with Parliament: Alain Vidalies
Deputy Minister to the Minister of Foreign Affairs, with responsibility for European Affairs: Thierry Repentin
Deputy Minister to the Minister of Foreign Affairs, with responsibility for Development: Pascal Canfin
Deputy Minister to the Minister of Foreign Affairs, with responsibility for Francophony: Yamina Benguigui
Deputy Minister to the Minister of Foreign Affairs, with responsibility for French Citizens Abroad: Hélène Conway-Mouret
Deputy Minister to the Minister of Education, with responsibility for the Academic Success: George Pau-Langevin
Deputy Minister to the Minister of Economy & Finance, with responsibility for the Budget: Bernard Cazeneuve
Deputy Minister to the Minister of Economy & Finance, with responsibility for the Social Economy & Consumer Affairs: Benoit Hamon
Deputy Minister to the Minister of Social Affairs and Health, with responsibility for Older People and Autonomy: Michèle Delaunay
Deputy Minister to the Minister of Social Affairs and Health, with responsibility for the Family: Dominque Bertinotti
Deputy Minister to the Minister of Social Affairs and Health, with responsibility for Disabled People and the fight against exclusion: Marie-Arlette Carlotti
Deputy Minister to the Minister of Equality of Territories and Housing, with responsibility for towns: François Lamy
Deputy Minister to the Minister of Productive Recovery, with responsibility for SMEs, innovation and economy: Fleur Pellerin
Deputy Minister to the Minister of Ecology, Sustainable Development and Energy, with responsibility for Transport, the Sea and Fishing: Frédéric Cuvillier
Deputy Minister to the Minister of Defence, with responsiblity for Veterans: Kader Arif
Deputy Minister to the Minister of Agriculture, Food & Forestry, with responsibility for food: Guillaume Garot
Deputy Minister to the Minister of State Reform, Decentralisation and Public Service: Anne-Marie Escoffier

Ministries

Office of the President, Palais de l'Elysée, 55-57 rue du Faubourg, Saint Honoré, 75008 Paris, France. Tel: +33 (0)1 42 92 81 00, fax: +33 (0)1 47 42 24 65, URL: http://www.elysee.fr
Office of the Prime Minister, Hôtel Matignon, 57 rue de Varenne, 75700 Paris, France. Tel: +33 (0)1 42 75 80 00, fax: +33 (0)1 42 75 75 04, URL: http://www.gouvernement.fr/premier-ministre
Ministry of Agriculture and Food, 78 rue de Varenne, 75349 Paris. Tel: +33 (0)1 49 55 49 55, fax: +33 (0)1 49 55 40 39, URL: http://agriculture.gouv.fr

Ministry for the Civil Service, Reform of the State and Decentralisation, Hotel de Castries, 72 rue de Varenne, 75007 Paris, France. Tel: +33 (0)1 42 75 80 00, URL http://www.fonction-publique.gouv.fr
Ministry of Culture and Communication, 3 rue de Valois, 75001 Paris Cedex 01, France. Tel: +33 (0)1 40 15 80 00, fax: +33 (0)1 42 61 35 77, e-mail point.culture@culture.gouv.fr, URL: http://www.culture.gouv.fr
Ministry of Defence, 14 rue Saint Dominique, 00452 Armees, France. Tel: +33 (0)1 42 19 30 11, fax: +33 (0)1 47 05 40 91, e-mail: courrier-defense@defense.gouv.fr, URL: http://www.defense.gouv.fr
Ministry of the Economy & Finance, 139 rue de Bercy, 75012 Paris Cedex 12, France. Tel: +33 (0)1 40 04 04 04, fax: +33 (0)1 43 43 75 97, URL: http://www.minefi.gouv.fr/
Ministry of Economic Recovery, 139 rue de Bercy, 75012 Paris Cedex 12, France. Tel: +33 (0)1 40 04 04 04, URL: http://www.redressement-productif.gouv.fr
Ministry for the Budget, Public Accounts and the Civil Service, 139, rue de Bercy, 75572 Paris Cedex 12, France. Tel: +33 (0)1 40 04 04 04, fax: +33 (0)1 53 18 96 48, URL: http://www.bercy.gouv.fr
Ministry of National Education, 110 rue Grenelle, 75317 Paris cedex 07, France. Tel: +33 (0)1 55 55 10 10, URL: http://www.education.gouv.fr
Ministry of Higher Education and Research, 1 rue Descartes, 75005 Paris, France. Tel: +33 (0)1 55 55 10 10, URL: http://www.enseignementsup-recherche.gouv.fr/
Ministry of Employment, Labour Relations and Social Dialogue, 127, rue de Grenelle, 75007 Paris, France. Tel: +33 (0)1 44 38 38 38, URL: http://travail-emploi.gouv.fr
Ministry for Ecology, Energy and Sustainable Development, Hotel de Roquelaure, 246 Boulevard Saint-Germain, 75007 Paris, France. Tel: +33 (0)1 42 19 20 21, URL: http://www.developpement-durable.gouv.fr/
Ministry of Foreign Affairs, 37 quai d'Orsay, 75351 Paris Cédex 07, France. Tel: +33 (0)1 43 17 53 53, fax: +33 (0)1 43 17 53 53, URL: http://www.diplomatie.gouv.fr
Ministry of Social Affairs and Health, 14 avenue Duquesne, 75007 Paris, France. Tel: +33 (0)1 40 56 60 00, URL: http://www.social-sante.gouv.fr
Ministry of the Interior, Place Beauvau, 75800 Paris, France. Tel: +33 (0)1 40 07 60 60, URL: http://www.interieur.gouv.fr
Ministry of Justice and Keeper of the Seals, 13 place Vendôme, 75042 Paris Cedex 01, France. Tel: +33 (0)1 44 77 61 15, fax: +33 (0)1 44 77 70 20, URL: http://www.justice.gouv.fr
Ministry of Housing and Regional Equality, 5 rue Pleyel, 93283 Saint Denis, France. Tel: +33 (0)1 73 60 39 39, URL: http://www.logement.gouv.fr/
Ministry for Overseas France, 27 rue Oudinot, 75358 Paris Cedex 07, France. Tel: +33 (0)1 49 17 46 46, URL: http://www.outre-mer.gouv.fr/
Ministry for Transport, 246 bld Saint-Germain, 75007 Paris Cedex, France. URL: http://www.equipement.gouv.fr
Ministry for Youth, Sport & Community Life, 95 ave de France, 75650 Paris, France. Tel: +33 (0)1 40 45 90 00, URL: http://www.sports.gouv.fr

Political Parties

Union pour un Mouvement Populaire (UMP), 55, rue La Boétie, 75384 Paris Cedex 08, France. Tel: +33 (0)1 40 76 60 00, URL: http://www.u-m-p.org/
President: Jean-François Copé
Mouvement Democrate (formerly the UDF, Union for French Democracy), 133 bis rue de l'Université, 75007 Paris, France. Tel: +33 (0)1 53 59 20 00, fax: +33 (0)1 53 59 20 00, URL: http://www.mouvementdemocrate.fr/
Chairman: François Bayrou (page 1385)
Parti Socialiste (PS, Socialist Party), 10 rue de Solférino, 75333 Paris Cédex 07, France. Tel: +33 (0)1 45 56 77 00, fax: +33 (0)1 45 56 15 78, URL: http://www.parti-socialiste.fr
First Secretary: Martine Audry
Parti Communiste Français (PCF, French Communist Party), 2 place du Colonel Fabien, 75940 Paris Cédex 19, France. Tel: +33 (0)1 40 40 12 12, fax: +33 (0)1 40 40 13 56, e-mail: pcf@pcf.fr, URL: http://www.pcf.fr
National Secretary: Pierre Laurent
Parti Radical de Gauche (PRG, Radical Socialist Party), 13 rue Duroc, 75007 Paris, France. +33 (0)1 45 66 67 68, URL: http://www.planeteradicale.org
President: Jean-Michel Baylet (page 1385)
Mouvment Republicain et Citoyens (MRC, Republicans' and Citizens' Movement), 9 rue du Faubourg Poissonnière, 75009 Paris, France. Tel: +33 (0)1 44 83 83 00, fax: +33 (0)1 44 83 8320, e-mail: contact@mrc.org, URL: http://www.mrc-france.org
Pres: Jean-Luc Laurent
L'Ecologie les Verts (EELV) (The Greens), 247 rue du Faubourg Saint-Martin, 75010 Paris, France. Tel: +33 (0)1 53 19 53 19 01, fax: +33 (0)1 53 19 03 93, e-mail: verts@les-verts.org, URL: http://www.lesverts.fr
National Secretary: Cécile Duflot
Front National (FN, National Front), 4 rue Vauguyon, 92210 Saint-Cloud, France. Tel: +33 (0)1 41 12 5000, fax: +33 (0)1 41 12 1099, URL: http://www.frontnational.com
Chairman: Marine le Pen
Mouvement Pour la France, URL: http://www.pourlafrance.fr
Secretary General: Philippe de Villiers
Le Front de Gauche (Left Front), election coalition, URL: http://www.placeaupeuple2012.fr/

Elections

Elections include: legislative elections (577 deputies who sit in the National Assembly are elected by direct universal suffrage); senatorial elections; presidential elections; European elections (87 deputies are elected by direct universal suffrage).

The electorate involved in direct universal suffrage elections is composed of 40 million voters. The age for eligibility is 18. The electorate may also be called upon to vote in a referendum submitted by the President (for example, the 1992 referendum on the ratification of the treaty of the European Union).

The most recent presidential election took place in 2012. The first ballot was held on 22 April; no candidate obtained an absolute majority (François Hollande (PS) 29 per cent; Nicholas Sarkozy (UMP) 27 per cent; Marine Le Pen 18 per cent; Jean-Luc Mélenchon (Front de Guache)

1 per cent; François Bayrou (Democrat Movement) 9 per cent. A second ballot took place on 6 May. François Hollande of the PS won around 51.5 per cent of the vote, defeating the incumbent Nicholas Sarkozy who received approximately 48 per cent of the vote. President Hollande appointed Jean-Marc Ayrault as Prime Minister.

The most recent Senate elections took place 25 September 2011. The elections are for 170 seats, of which 112 were elected by proportional representation and 58 by majority after two rounds. The Senate now breaks down thus: PS and allies (including PCF and EELV) 177 seats; UMP and allies (including NC) 171 seats.

Elections for the National Assembly were held on 10 and 17 June 2012. In the June 2012 elections the opposition PS (with their allies) gained control of the Assemblée Nationale. The house now breaks down thus: Parti Socialist 280 seats; UMP 194 seats; various left wing seats 22; EELV 17 seats; various right 15 seats; NC 12 seats; Radical Party of the Left 12 seats; Left Front 10 seats; Radical Party 6 seats; Front National 2 seats; others 7 seats.

Local elections took place in March 2010. President Sarkozy's UMP party suffered heavy defeats, keeping control of just one of 22 regions. The Socialist-led opposition won approximately 54 per cent of the vote.

Diplomatic Representation

French Embassy, 58 Knightsbridge, London, SW1X 7JT, United Kingdom. Tel: +44 (0)20 7073 1000, fax: +44 (0)20 7201 1004, e-mail: press@ambafrance.org.uk, URL: http://www.diplomatie.gouv.fr / http://www.ambafrance-uk.org
Ambassador: Bernard Emié (page 1421)
French Embassy, 4101 Reservoir Road, NW, Washington, DC 20007, USA. Tel: +1 202 944 6000, fax: +1 202 944 6166, URL: http://www.ambafrance-us.org/
Ambassador: François Delattre (page 1414)
British Embassy, 35 rue de Faubourg Saint Honoré, 75383 Paris Cedex 08, France. Tel: +33 (0)1 44 51 31 00, fax: +33 (0)1 44 51 41 27, URL: http://www.ukinfrance.fco.gov.uk/en/
Ambassador: Sir Peter Ricketts (page 1503)
American Embassy, 2 avenue Gabriel, 75008 Paris, France. Tel: +33 (0)1 43 12 22 22, fax: +33 (0)1 42 66 97 83, URL: http://france.usembassy.gov/
Ambassador: Charles Rivkin (page 1503)
Permanent Mission to the United Nations, One Dag Hammarskjöld Plaza, 245 East 47th Street, 44th Floor, New York, NY 10017, USA. Tel: +1 212 308 5700, fax: +1 212 421 6889, e-mail: france@un.int, URL: http://www.franceonu.org
Ambassador and Permanent Representative to the UN: Gérard Araud (page 1379)

LEGAL SYSTEM

The judiciary is independent of the executive and the legislature. The President of the Republic, assisted by the *Conseil supérieur de la magistrature* (High Council of Judges and Public Prosecutors), is the guarantor of the independent administration of justice.

The judicial system has two types of court: civil courts and criminal courts. Civil courts are either ordinary (Regional Court) or specialised (district courts, commercial courts, social security courts and the *conseils des prud'hommes* (industrial relations). Criminal courts distinguish three types of offences: contraventions (which are dealt with by police courts); misdemeanours (dealt with by criminal courts); and crimes (dealt with by the Assizes). The Youth Court deals with both civil and criminal cases.

The core of the system is represented by the judicial courts (*l'ordre judiciaire*) (civil and criminal), with courts of first instance and police courts, higher courts, 35 courts of appeal and the Court of Cassation (*Cour de Cassation*), which is the supreme court and adjudicates on the law involved in cases referred to it, but never questions the lower courts' final judgements on substantive issues. A distinction is made between the *magistrature debout* or *Parquet*, the body of public prosecutors who represent the State in the courts, safeguarding the public interest, and the *magistrature assise* or Bench, made up of judges, with security of tenure, who deliver judgements and sentences.

Hearings are held in open court, except in special circumstances calling for cases to be held *in camera*. The accused are represented by barristers and can apply for legal aid. All judgments are subject to appeal, before a higher court. Except in the lowest courts, several judges sit on each case and deliver their judgements or sentences jointly. In criminal cases, the verdict is given by nine jurors whose names have been drawn at random from the electoral roll, and, if the verdict is guilty, the court passes sentence.

A particular feature of the French system is the network of administrative courts which judge cases brought against the Administration. The appeal court here is the *Conseil d'Etat* Council of State, the supreme administrative court, which acts as both a court, ruling on the legality of important administrative acts, and a consultative body, acting as the government's legal advisor. In addition, there are the *conseils de prud'hommes*, elective arbitration boards for disputes between employers and employees, and commercial courts.

Since 1981 special courts like the Court of State Security and the Armed Forces' standing tribunals have been abolished.

In 2009, there were an estimated 72,749 people involved in the legal system, including 29,295 people in judicial justice, 33,020 in prison administration and 8,951 in youth protection. The prison population was approximately 66,178 people (including 15,933 awaiting trial). In 2011, provisional figures showed there were 603,994 infractions. (Source: INSEE)

In the face of increasing terrorism and violent crime, the Government maintains the full legality of police checks and sanctions the keeping of computer files on terrorists. The Commission Nationale de L'Informatique et des Libertés (CNIL) monitors all data banks in which personal records are stored and ensures that the total number of national data banks and the extent of cross-referencing between them is kept within limits.

The government respects the rights of its citizens. There are, however, problems of protracted trial proceedings, overcrowded prisons and lengthy pretrial detention. The death penalty was abolished by the Law of 9 October 1981.

Conseil d'Etat, URL: http://www.conseil-etat.fr/fr/
Vice President of the Conseil d'Etat: Jean-Marc Sauvé (page 1509)
Cour de Cassation, URL: http://www.courdecassation.fr/
President of the Cour de Cassation: Vincent Lamanda
Conseil Superieur Magistrature,
URL: http://www.conseil-superieur-magistrature.fr/index.php

National Consultative Commission on Human Rights, URL: http://www.cncdh.fr/

LOCAL GOVERNMENT

France has a three-tier local government structure: the basic administrative unit is the *commune* (municipality) followed by the *département*, and finally the region. The French Constitution of 4 October 1958 recognises the *communes*, *départements* and overseas territories as local government structures. It also states that local authorities can be created either by the Constitution or by law, - as in the cases of the French regions Paris, Mayotte, Saint Pierre and Miquelon and New Caledonia.

There are now five overseas departments (DOM): Guadeloupe, Martinique, Guyane (French Guiana), Réunion and most recently Mayotte. There are six overseas territories: French Polynesia, Wallis and Futuna, Saint Pierre and Miquelon, the French Southern and Antarctic Territories, Saint-Barthélémy and Saint-Martin. Mayotte, formerly an overseas territory, voted in a referendum in favour of becoming a DOM. This came into effect on 31 March 2011. It is the fifth DOM and the101st French department. There is also one territory with a special status: New Caledonia. A referendence on independence for New Caledonia is expected to take place before 2020.

There are currently 36,564 communes in mainland France (including 112 in the overseas collectivities), 80 per cent of which have less than 1,000 inhabitants. They are administered by the municipal council (*conseil municipal*), whose number is in proportion to that of the population, the decision making body, and the Mayor, assisted by one or several deputies responsible for executing the council's decisions. The municipal council is elected by direct universal suffrage for a six-year period and in turn elects the Mayor and deputies, also for a six-year term, on the basis of a two-round absolute majority vote.

The Mayor has a dual role - that of 'municipal officer' (*agent de la commune*) representing the interests of the local community and promoting its development, and secondly that of state official, administering duties on behalf of the state such as the registration of births, deaths and marriages and local policing. The commune is responsible for town planning regulations, schooling including school transport, household refuge collection, yachting harbours and other matters.

The *département* is the intermediary level of local government in France and is independent from central government. Today France has 95 départements, as well as five overseas (Guadeloupe, Martinique, French Guyana, Réunion and Mayotte). Paris has dual status as both a commune and a département. They are relatively homogenous in terms of area whilst population density can show considerable differences. The département is administered by the *Conseil Général* headed by its president. Councillors are elected for six years by universal suffrage. The president is then elected by the councillors and holds an executive role within the council assisted in his or her duties by a committee of four to ten vice-presidents and in some cases other councillors. The responsibilities of the Conseil Général include social affairs, construction and maintenance of *collèges*, middle schools, roads, fire services, housing, fishing and commercial ports among others. The départments are sub-divided into 3,879 Cantons (as well as a further 156 overseas: Guadeloupe, Martinique, French Guyana and Réunion) which act as constituencies during elections.

The third and most recent level of government is the region. It was not until the 1982 reform that the region was fully recognised as a local authority. Today there are 26 regions in France, including the four overseas départements which also have regional status. The region is administered by a regional council made up of councillors elected for a six-year period on the basis of a proportional representation list system by département. Election of the leader of the council (the president) takes the form of a two-round absolute majority vote. The regional council is responsible for economic development, professional training, the construction and maintenance of secondary schools, regional town and country planning and river ports. Each region has its own economic or social committee consulted by the council on matters falling within these fields.

The regions are Alsace, Aquitaine, Auvergne, Basse-Normandie, Bourgogne, Bretagne, Centre, Champagne-Ardenne, Corse (Corsica), Franche-Comte, Guadeloupe, Guyane, French Guiana), Haute-Normandie, Ile-de-France, Languedoc-Roussillon, Limousin, Lorraine, Martinique, Reunion, Midi-Pyrenees, Nord-Pas-de-Calais, Pays de la Loire, Picardie, Poitou-Charentes, Provence-Alpes-Cote d'Azur and Rhone-Alpes.

In March 2009 President Sarkozy presented a controversial plan to revise the structure of local government including the merging of some regions, the creation of a larger Paris, and metropolitan status for 11 of France's largest cities. A single Assembly for France's overseas departments and regions has also been proposed.

The most recent local elections took place in March 2010. President Sarkozy's UMP party suffered heavy defeats, keeping control of just one of 22 regions. The Socialist-led opposition won approximately 54 per cent of the vote.

FRANCE

AREA AND POPULATION

Area

France is the largest country in the European Union and has the longest coastline in Europe. It has an area of 544,000 sq. km. and shares borders with Belgium and Luxembourg to the north, Germany and Switzerland to the east, Italy to the south east and Spain to the south west. France is divided into 22 regions which are subdivided into 96 departments, 3,876 cantons, and 36,566 communes.

In addition there are four overseas departments (Guadeloupe, Martinique, Guyane (French Guiana) and Réunion), six overseas collectivities (French Polynesia, Mayotte, Saint Pierre et Miquelon, Wallis and Futuna, Saint Martin and Saint Barthélmy), one sui generis collectivity (New Caledonia), and overseas territories (French Southern and Antarctic Lands). French Polynesia has a designation of overseas country (pays d'outre mer) but the Constitutional Court ruled this was not a particular status. Mayotte voted in a referendum for 2009 in favour of becoming a DOM and this came into effect on 31 March 2011. It is the fifth DOM and the101st Department. New Caledonia has a unique status and is not an overseas territory. A referendum on independence is expected to take place before 2020 on whether it becomes an overseas collectivity or an independent nation.

The four largest rivers are the Rhône (812 km.), the Loire (1,020 km.), the Seine (776 km.) and the Garonne (573 km.). Terrain is varied: a large proportion of the country consists of fertile plains from the south west of France up to the Belgian border. There are also vast mountain ranges: the Alps, of which Mont Blanc (4,810 m) is the highest in Europe, and the Pyrenees, which rise to 3,404 m.

The climate in metropolitan France is generally cool winters and mild summers, hotter in the south.

To view a map, please visit: http://www.lib.utexas.edu/maps/cia08/france_sm_2008.gif

Population

According to the 2004 census the total population of France including overseas departments and territories was 62 million (metropolitan France, 60.2 million). The population of metropolitan France increased by 1.7 million in the period 1999-2003. The increase is mainly due to a higher birth rate than death rate (1.13 million people), and immigration (410,000). This represents a growth rate of 0.6 per cent. According to the latest figures from INSEE, as of 2008, an estimated 2.2 million people live in Paris, 851,420 in Marseille, 474,946 in Lyon and 439,553 in Toulouse.

In 2013 the population of metropolitan France was estimated to be 65.6 million. The total population including overseas departments and territories was estimated to be 66.2 million.

Those French citizens living abroad number 1.5 million, whilst approximately 6 per cent of the population of France are foreign residents. In 2006 the French Senate approved a tough immigration bill. The bill makes it harder for unskilled migrants to settle in France and abolishes the rights of illegal immigrants to remain after 10 years

The following table gives a recent breakdown of the metropolitan population of France by region:

Population 2010

Regions	Area (sq. km)	Pop. in '000s	Regional Capital
Alsace	8,280	1,845.7	Strasbourg
Aquitaine	41,309	3,232.4	Bordeaux
Auvergne	26.013	1,347.4	Clermont-Ferrand
Basse-Normandie	17,589	1,473.5	Caen
Bourgogne	31,582	1,642.1	Dijon
Bretagne	27,209	3,199.1	Rennes
Centre	39,151	2,548.1	Orléans
Champagne-Ardenne	25,606	1,335.9	Chalons-en-Champagne
Corse	8,680	309.7	Ajaccio
Franche-Comté	16,202	1,171.8	Besancon
Haute-Normandie	12,318	1,836.95	Rouen
Île de France	12,011	11,786.2	Paris
Languedoc-Roussillon	27,376	2,636.4	Montpellier
Limousin	16,942	742.7	Limoges
Lorraine	23,542	2,350.9	Metz
Midi-Pyrénées	45,348	2,881.8	Toulouse
Nord-Pas-de-Calais	12,414	4,038.2	Lille
Pays de la Loire	32,082	3,566.7	Nantes
Picardie	19,399	1,914.8	Amiens
Poitou-Charentes	25,809	1,770.3	Poitiers
Provence-Alpes-Côte-d'Azur	31,400	4,899.2	Marseille
Rhône-Alpes	43,698	6,230.7	Lyon
Metropolitan France	543,965	62,765,235	

Source: INSEE

The following table provides the latest figures for the population of overseas departments:

Population of Overseas Departments (2010)

Overseas Department	Area (sq. km)	Population in '000s	Principal Town	2010 '000 E
Guadeloupe	1,702	403,355	BasseTerre	405
French Guiana	83,534	229,040	Cayenne	221

- continued

Martinique	1,128	394,173	Fort-de-France	402
Réunion	2,512	821,136	St. Denis	802

Source: INSEE

According to the latest INSEE figures, the population of Mayotte is 186,452 (2007), New Caledonia 245,580 (2009), French Polynesia 259,596 (2007), Saint Pierre and Miquelon 6,072 (2007), Wallis and Futuna 13,484 (2008).

Births, Marriages, Deaths

According to estimates from INSEE the birth rate dropped slightly in the period 2010-11: the number of births in 2011 was estimated at 827,000. The birth rate was 12.7 per 1,000 population. The average age of the mother was 30.0 years. The number of births in 2012 was estimated at 822,000, with a birth rate of 12.6 per 1,000 population. An estimated 56.6 per cent of children were born outside of marriage. The number of deaths in 2011 rose to an estimated 555,000 from an estimated 551,218 the previous year. The 2011 death rate was estimated at 8.5 per 1,000 habitants and the infant mortality rate was 3.5 per 1,000 live births. In 2009, for approximately 79.9 per cent of births both parents were French, for 13.1 per cent of births one parent was French and the other foreign and for 7 per cent of births, both parents were of foreign nationality.

Life expectancy for men and women continues to rise: in 2012 it was estimated to be 84.8 years for females and 78.4 years for males (metropolitan France). Healthy life expectancy (2007) was estimated at 64.2 years for females and 63.1 years for males.

According to 2009 estimates (France) 18.5 per cent were under 15, 12.7 per cent between 15-24, 52.2 per cent between 25-64, and 7.9 65-74, and 8.7 per cent aged 75 years old or more. By comparison in 1970 the breakdown was: under 20, 33.1 per cent; 20-59, 48.8 per cent; 60+, 18 per cent. By 2050 it is estimated that over 35 per cent of people will be aged 60 or over compared to 20.6 per cent in 2003. By 2050, 1 in 5 people will be over 80.

In the last two decades the number of marriages has fallen by a third, due to a gradual increase in age before marriage and the number of couples who live together without marrying. For the first half of the 1990s over 20 per cent of women over 35 had never married, compared with only 10 per cent in the early 1980s. In 2006 the average age for marriage was 31.1 for males and 29.1 for females. Estimates for 2009 show that 40.9 per cent of males were single, 49.7 per cent married, 2.8 per cent widowered and 6.6 per cent divorced. For females, the rates were 33.8 per cent single, 45.3 per cent married, 12.4 per cent widowed and 8.5 per cent divorced. The marriage rate in 2010 was estimated to be 3.9 marriages per 1,000 population and 251,654 marriages took place. The number of marriages taking place in 2011 fell to an estimated 241,000. In 2010, 133,909 divorces took place, a rate of 10.9 per 1,000 marriages.

In 1999 the civil solidarity pact was introduced to give two people (hetero- or homosexual) the rights of married couples in housekeeping laws, taxes etc. Since that date some 350,000 pacts have been registered. There were 77,362 registered pacts in 2006. In the first quarter of 2007 there were an estimated 73,000 pacts. In July 2012, the government announced that it would legalise gay marriage and adoption rights.

The structure of the family is also changing. The number of households has increased dramatically, rising from 14.6 million in 1960 to 28.7 million in 1999. Of that 10 per cent are second homes. The average number of occupants of the main home is 2.4. Single parent families have also increased dramatically. The current estimate is that there are over one million single parent families. Approximately 55 per cent of children are now born outside of marriage. (Source: INSEE)

Public Holidays 2014

1 January: New Year's Day
21 April: Easter Monday
1 May: May Day
8 May: Anniversary of 1945 Victory
10 May: Slavery Memorial Day
29 May: Ascension
9 June: Whit Monday
14 July: Bastille Day
15 August: Assumption Day
1 November: All Saints Day
11 November: Anniversary of 1918 Armistice
25 December: Christmas Day

EMPLOYMENT

Labour force figures are shown on the following table.

Working Population, 2007-2050

	2007	2011*	2050*
Workforce (1,000s)	27,843	26,888	24,364
Percentage female	46.9	46.4	46.5
Percentage male	53.1	53.6	53.5
Aged 15-24 (%)	8.8	8.4	8.1
Aged 25-54 (%)	81.3	79.2	77.9
Aged 55+ (%)	9.9	12.4	14.0

Source: INSEE (* projection)

In 2011Q4 the unemployment rate was 9.4 per cent (2.7 million), up by 0.1 per cent from the previous quarter. The unemployment rate is much higher for the age group 15-24 years (22.4 per cent, 2011Q4). In 2012 Q3, the unemployment rate was estimated at 10.5 per cent, rising to 10.6 per cent in Q4.

Male economic activity has fallen in recent years, mainly due to an ageing population, and female economic activity has increased. In 2009 it was estimated that 5.5 per cent of the population (1.4 million) were underemployed. With both genders unemployment was highest in the 15-24 years old age bracket (22.3 per cent for females and 25.3 per cent for males).

Unemployment remains a major problem. The National Assembly approved a bill cutting the French working week from 39 hours to 35 hours in 1998. In June 2001 the National Assembly passed new employment legislation designed to give employees greater protection against mass redundancies. In 2005 the National Assembly approved a bill allowing private firms to increase working hours to maximum 48-hour week. Private sector workers will be able to convert extra days off into wage rises of pension contributions. The 35-hour week still applies to France's public sector. In 2006 the government was forced to abandoned proposed new legislation giving employers greater power to hire and fire young people after widespread protests and rioting.

France's economy has undergone many changes in recent years, with a dramatic decline in employment in agriculture and the goods-producing industries, and a corresponding upturn in services employment. Employment by sector in 2011 was as follows:

Paid Employment by sector, '000s

Sector	2010	2011 (e)
Agriculture, forestry, fishing	221,3	217,8
Production of food, beverages and tobacco goods	553,3	547,7
Refining	11,1	10,5
Equipment electrical and electronic goods	450,6	449,7
Production of transport materials	361,1	367,9
Production of other industrial goods	1531,6	1520,3
Extractive industries, energy, water, waste, depollution	361,7	367,1
Construction	1439,4	1427,4
Trade, vehicles and motorcyles	3016,4	3036,0
Transport	1348,3	1351,6
Accomodation	917,1	929,9
Information and communication	689,8	704,1
Finance and insurance	824,0	704,1
Real estate	235,9	235,9
Scientfic and technical services	2882,4	2906,2
Public administration, teaching, health & social action	7609,5	7577,4
Other services	1338,3	1319,3

Source: INSEE

France's minimum wage was €9.22 an hour in 2012.

In 2009, there were an estimated 14.7 million retired people in France. An estimated 40 per cent of the population aged 55-64 are retired.

Approximately 1.4 million people are members of trade unions. The main trade unions are:
Confédération Générale du Travail, URL: http://www.cgt.fr/internet/
Confédération Française Démocratique du Travail, URL: http://www.cfdt.fr/edito.htm
Force Ouvrière, URL: http://www.force-ouvriere.fr/
Confédération Française des Travailleurs Chrétiens, URL: http://www.cftc.fr/
Fédération Syndicale Unitaire, URL: http://actu.fsu.fr/

BANKING AND FINANCE

Currency
One euro (€) = 100 cents
€ = 6.55957 francs (European Central Bank irrevocable conversion rate)
On 1 January 1999 the euro was launched as an electronic currency across the 12 member states of the EU. On 1 January 2002 the euro became legal tender in France and the 11 other member states of the EU. France's old currency, the franc, ceased to be legal tender from midnight on 17 February 2002. Euro banknotes are issued in denominations of 5, 10, 20, 50, 100, 200, and 500. Euro coins are issued in denominations of 2 and 1 euros, 50, 20, 10, 5, 2, and 1 cents.

GDP/GNP, Inflation, National Debt
The French gross domestic product increased in 2003 by 0.5 per cent in volume, the lowest rate since 1993; GDP increased by 1.2 per cent in 2002, and by 1.8 per cent in 2001. The downturn at the beginning of the century was due in part to a fall in French exports and falling company profits, both linked to the worldwide slowdown. Annual GDP rose from €1,594.8 billion in 2003 to €1,659.0 billion in 2004, and by 2005 it had risen to €1,710.0 billion (value added at basic price). Real GDP grew by a relatively modest 2.2 per cent in 2006 (one of the slowest rates in the EU27), and again by 2.2 per cent in 2007. GDP was estimated at €1,892.2 billion in 2007.

France has also been affected by the global economic crisis. Although the overall growth for 2008 was positive at just under 1 per cent, the last quarter had negative growth of -1.5 per cent. In October 2008, the government said it would inject €10.5 billion into its six largest banks. President Sarkozy announced a further €26 billion initiative in February 2009 to stimulate the economy. Financial support has been offered to French industry, including the car industry. Although this has been welcomed in France, other European governments have accused France of protectionism. There has been some social unrest in response to the economic crisis. The first quarter of 2009 also showed negative growth (-1.4 per cent), but GDP grew by 0.3 per cent in the second and third quarters. In August 2010, France cut its growth expectations to 2.0 per cent for 2011. GDP growth in Q1 of 2011 was estimated to be 1.0 per cent, higher than expected. However, in 2011 it announced that growth for the whole of 2011 and 2012 was expected to be 1.75 per cent, lower than forecast. Concerns over growth meant that financial reforms are to be brought in earlier than expected. VAT is to be increased from 5.5 per cent to 7 per cent and there will be an increase of corporation tax of 5 per cent on companies with a turnover greater than €250 million. Growth in the second quarter of 2012 was put at 0.0 per cent. In November 2012, the ratings agency Moody's downgraded France's triple AAA rating to Aa1. Growth in 2012 as a whole was expected to be 0.3 per cent, rising to 0.4 per cent for 2013.

GDP value added, by industry, in volume, (current prices) is shown on the following table (€ billion).

GDP (€ billion)

Titles	2009	2010	2011 (p)
Agriculture, forestry, fishery	26.2	31.8	32.8
Construction	109.2	106.4	110.1
Mainly market services	960.6	987.1	1,017.2
-Transport	82.4	84.0	84.9
-Financial activities	75.8	83.7	83.3
-Information & communication	84.6	86.5	86.1
-Real estate / renting	227.9	229.1	236.7
Mainly non-market services	383.7	393.3	404.3
Total	**1,701.2**	**1,741.5**	**1,789.0**

Source: INSEE, National Accounts
(p): provisional

Inflation was 1.8 per cent in 2005 falling to 1.5 per cent in 2006. In 2007 it was estimated at 1.5 per cent, rising to 2.8 per cent in 2008. It was estimated to be 2.3 per cent in Q1 2012, falling to 1.3 per cent in Q1 2013.

In 2011, the government presented an austerity budget with an emphasis on deficit reduction. The public deficit was forecast to reach 5.7 per cent of GDP in 2011, before falling to 4.5 per cent in 2012 and then to the EU limit of 3.0 per cent in 2013.

Foreign Investment
France offers a variety of incentives to foreign investors and has an investment promotion agency called Invest in France Agency which operates from offices worldwide. There are various sectoral investment restrictions and non-EU nationals may be denied national treatment in the following sectors: agriculture, financial services, accounting, legal services, air transport, maritime transport, road transport, publications, telecommunications and tourism. These restrictions have been reduced as a reflection of the government's aim to attract new investment. The government announced in 2013 that it was aiming to attract 1,000 foreign investment decisions and 300 new companies to France by 2017.

In 2011 an estimated €29.5 billion was invested, substantially down on the €70 billion invested in 2007. Investment was estimated to be over €50 billion in 2012. French investment abroad amounted to €700 bn in 2009. (Source: INSEE)

Balance of Payments / Imports and Exports
In 2009, both imports and exports contracted sharply. Exports fell by an unprecedented 12.4 per cent in 2009, following a fall of 0.5 per cent in 2008. Imports fell by 10.7 per cent in 2009, and 0.6 per cent in 2008. Trade in manufactured goods and petroleum products both contracted significantly. Exports of goods and services rebounded in 2010 by 9.7 per cent to €389.4 billion (fab). Imports also rose by 8.8 per cent to €438.8 billion (fab).

Imports and exports according to industry are shown on the following table.

Imports and Exports by Sector, 2009 (€ billion of CIF-FOB)

Sector	Imports CIF (09)	Exports FOB(09)
Agriculture, forestry, fishery	9.9	11.5
Industry	387.9	331.6
-Food industries	29.8	34.0
-Consumer goods	72.5	61.3
-Automobiles	39.2	33.9
-Capital goods	82.3	88.7
-Intermediate goods	107.4	97.6
-Energy	56.7	16.1
Merchant Services	65.8	62.2
-Trade	4.4	4.6
-Transportation	24.5	17.4
-Financial Activities	3.6	9.4
-Business Services	31.2	29.0
-Services for Individuals	2.1	1.8
Education, health, social	0.2	0.8
Correction CIF-FOB	-12.7	-
Correction territorial	25.5	33.5
Total FOB-FOB	**476.6**	**439.6**

Source: INSEE

Over 50 per cent of trade is with euro area countries.

Export Trade, 2008-11, Major Clients, € bn

Destination	2008	2009	2011
Germany	59.5	55.5	70.0
Spain	34.2	27.0	30.9
Italy	35.9	28.4	34.6
UK	32.0	24.5	28.1

FRANCE

- continued

Belgium	31.2	25.7	31.2
USA	23.9	19.7	23.4
Netherlands	17.1	13.8	18.2
Switzerland	12.1	10.1	13.1
China	9.0	7.9	13.1
Poland	6.8	5.2	6.8
Russia	7.0	5.1	7.5

Source: INSEE

Import Trade, 2008-11, Top Ten Suppliers, € bn

Country	2008	2009	2011
Germany	78.8	71.5	87.7
Italy	39.2	31.6	38.2
Belgium	40.9	32.6	40.3
Spain	31.1	25.0	31.2
UK	23.1	18.3	22.5
USA	26.4	25.1	29.6
China	31.6	29.9	42.1
Netherlands	19.5	16.7	22.3
Japan	9.5	7.8	9.8
Russia	13.7	9.3	14.5
Switzerland	..	9.7	11.9

Source: INSEE

In 2011, it was estimated that 1,498 French businesses were controlled by the state, compared to 1,230 in 2010 and 2,636 in 1995.

France's key public enterprises by turnover, 2009, in € million

Rank	Corporation	Sales (turnover) net	No. employees
1	GDF-SUEZ	79,908	242,700
2	EDF	66,336	164,300
3	France Telecom	45,944	178,400
4	EADS	42,822	119,500
5	Renault	33,712	121,400
6	SNCF	24,882	200,100
7	AirFrance-KLM	20,994	104,700
8	Groupe La Poste	20,527	287,200
9	Thales	12,882	64,300
10	Safran	10.559	54,900

Source: INSEE

Central Bank
Since 1993 the central bank of France has been independent of the government. It is unable to authorise the granting of credit to the Treasury or any other Public body. It still maintains the current accounts of the Treasury and Treasury Bonds, draws up the balance of payments for the state and plays a role in managing the national debt.
Banque de France, 1 rue la Vrillière, 75001 Paris, France. Tel: +33 (0)1 42 92 42 92, fax: +33 (0)1 42 92 45 00, URL: http://www.banque-france.fr
Governor: Christian Noyer (page 1487)

Supervisory Bodies
Association Française des Etablissements de Crédit et des Entreprises d'Ivestissement (AFECEI), URL: http://www.afecei.asso.fr/
Association Française des Banques, URL: http://www.afb.fr/
Federation Bancaire Française, URL: http://www.fbf.fr

Chambers of Commerce and Trade Organisations
Chamber of Commerce et d'Industrie de Paris, URL: http://www.acfci.cci.fr/
Assemblée des Chambres Françaises de Commerce et d'Industrie, URL: http://www.acfci.cci.fr/
Bourse de Paris, URL: http://www.euronext.com
Autorité des Marchés Financiers (AMF), URL: http://www.cob.fr/
Fédération Nationale des Associations de Clubs d'Investissement, URL: http://www.ffci.fr

MANUFACTURING, MINING AND SERVICES

Primary and Extractive Industries
France is not rich in mineral resources and consumes a far greater quantity of fossil fuels than it produces. As well as small quantities of oil and gas, France's mineral resources include iron, potassium, sulphur and bauxite.

Oil
Proven oil reserves were an estimated 90 million barrels in January 2012. Oil production in 2011 was estimated at 94,580 barrels per day. Consumption was an estimated 1.791 million barrels per day. Consequently, France had to import an estimated 1.696 million barrels per day in 2011. France also imported 760,000 bbl/d of refined petroleum products in 2008. Imports mainly come from Norway (256,000 bbl/d), Russia (186,000 bbl/d) and Saudi Arabia (166,000 bbl/d). Crude oil refining capacity was an estimated 1.986 million barrels per day of crude oil in 2009. The largest refinery was the Gonfreville l'Orcher facility (Total) which has a capacity of 331,000 bbl/d. (Source: EIA)

France's Total SA (http://www.total.com) is one of the world's largest oil companies, and was formed as TotalFinaElf in 2000 from the merger of Total, Petrofina (Belgium) and Elf Aquitaine. In February 2004 Total, in partnership with the National Iranian Oil Company and Petronas of Malaysia, created Pars LNG which will source its natural gas from Iran.

Over 40 per cent of unrefined petroleum products come from the Middle East. The rest comes from Europe (UK, Norway, Russian Federation) and Africa. The imported crude oil is processed in 12 refineries, mainly near the major ports Dunkirk, Rouen, Le Havre, Nantes and Marseilles. (Source: EIA)

Natural Gas
Reserves of natural gas are extremely limited. Production in 2011 was an estimated 21 bcf. Consumption in 2011 was estimated at 1,466 trillion cubic feet, all imported. Natural gas has increased its share of primary energy to 15.7 per cent.

The major gas company is Gaz de France (GdF) (URL: http://www.gdf.fr/) is majority-government-owned and dominates the import, transport, and distribution of natural gas. Following EU legislation in August 2000 requiring competition in the energy sectors, GdF had to beome partially privatised and will ultimately lose its monopoly. GdF operates 19,000 miles of natural gas pipelines in France. France is becoming a hub for Western European gas supplies. At the end of 1998 it was linked via the 521 mile NorFra pipeline to Norway's Troll gas field. Gas from the pipeline will ultimately provide one third of France's total gas consumption. In 2005 France inaugurated the 48-Mmcf/d Euskadour natural gas pipeline between Bilbao, Spain and France. The GdF-constructed Les Marches du Nord-Est pipeline supplies 6 billion cubic metres of Norwegian gas.

Coal
In recent years France has produced and consumed very little coal. France has coal reserves estimated at 39 million short tons. The last coal mine, La Houvre, closed in April 2004. In 2010 consumption was estimated at 20.5 million short tons, all imported. In 2010 coal was imported from Australia (18.4 per cent), the USA (17.6 per cent), the EU (16 per cent), Colombia (15.8 per cent), Russia (15.5 per cent) and South Africa (12.7 per cent). (Source: INSEE)
Charbonnages de France (CDF), URL: http://www.groupecharbonnages.fr/

Energy
France's total energy consumption in 2009 was estimated at 10.658 quadrillion Btu and total production was 4.785 quadrillion Btu. In 2010 of primary energy consumed, 4.9 per cent was coal, 30.9 per cent was from oil, 15.1 was from gas, 43.3 per cent was from primary electricity (nuclear, hydraulic, wind), and 6.4 per cent from thermal renewable energies (wood, woodwaste, solar thermal, biogas, biofuels). (Source: INSEE)

Electricity
Electricity generation in 2009 was estimated at 510.23 bn kWh, of which approximately 78 per cent was nuclear, 14 per cent hydro, and 8 per cent thermal. Electricity consumption shows a continuous upward trend and has virtually increased tenfold since the 1950s. Consumption in 2009 was 451.3 million kWh. The state-owned company Electricité de France (EdF) (URL: http://www.edf.fr/) produces, transports and distributes over 95 per cent of France's electricity. France is the largest net exporter of electricity in the EU and exported 100 BkWh to the EU in 2004. Following recent EU directives the French government has started to privatise EdF. Compagnie Nationale du Rhone is the second largest electricity company in France and operates 19 hydro-electric plants on the River Rhone. There are also a small number of electricity distributors who buy their electricity from EdF.

Nuclear Energy
France has shifted its reliance on fossil fuel electricity generation (which accounted for 80 per cent of generation in 1973) to nuclear generation (currently 80 per cent of generation). France ranks first for per capita nuclear power generation, and is second (after the US) for total installed nuclear capacity. However, initial plans to develop nuclear power to 100 per cent of electricity generation have recently been modified, due in part to environmental concerns as well as Germany's decision to phase out nuclear power. The nuclear industry was reorganised in December 2000. A single holding company, Areva (URL: http://www.areva-np.com/, now owns two companies: the first based on the fuels group Compagnie Genérale des Matières Nucléares (Cogema) and nuclear construction company Framatome SA; the second based on FCI, a subsidiary of Framatome making connection material for the nuclear and electricity industries.

Of France's 58 nuclear power plants, there are four natural uranium/graphite-gas cooled reactors (MAGNOX type); two fast breeder reactors (FBR) and 49 pressurised water reactors (PWR). The scope of the nuclear program led those in charge of operations to design standardised and mass-produced units, but adaptable to different sites. Standardisation is based on the selection of one single technology - pressurised water reactors (PWRs) - which helped reduce construction time and costs.

France planned to expand its nuclear industry. With Germany, France is developing a European Pressurized Reactor (EPR) which is designed to be safer and more efficient. It would be used to upgrade existing plants. Each EPR reactor should produce around 1,600 MW of electricity (compared to 900 MW for the current second generation of reactors). EdF announced in 2004 that it would build the first EPR. The project should have been completed by 2012 at a cost of US$3.8 billion, but completion has been delayed until 2016. The plans were approved by France's nuclear safety agency in 2007. France is also playing a leading role in the development of the International Thermonuclear Experimental Reactor (ITER) in a consortium of the EU, the US, Japan, Russia, China and South Korea. The consortium is aiming to have a working fusion reactor at a testing site in France by 2015. In 2009, France and Italy agreed to work together to build four nuclear power stations in Italy. Following the 2011 Fukushima crisis, it is possible that new safety requirements for nuclear power will be required worldwide. Several countries have halted their plans for nuclear energy. Following the 2012 presidential election, President Hollande has suggested that he would like to see France's older reactors phased out by 2025, this could affect 24 reactors.

Alternative Energy

Alternative sources of energy are also being developed, including geothermal and solar energy, and count for under 2 per cent of the nation's total. The EU is providing aid to help develop other sources such as grain surpluses. A new hydroelectric project was announced in 2005. The site is at Gavet, Isere and should be operational by 2013. Annual production should be 540 million kWh.

Primary Energy production from renewable sources (ktoe)

	2010	2011 (p)
Wood energy	10,229	8,873
Hydraulic	5,406	3,924
Biofuels	2,256	2,055
Renewable municipal waste	1,222	1,252
Heat pumps	1,427	1,298
Wind	858	1,052
Agricultural residues and IAA	343	350
Biogas	334	350
Geothermal	92	94
Solar thermal	57	64
Solar photovoltaic	53	173
Total	**22,277**	**19,487**

Source: INSEE

Manufacturing

Industrial growth has slowed with the global recession and the manufacturing sector has been hard hit (-12 per cent in 2009). Employment in industry continues to decline. However, the number of new businesses reached a record high in 2009, with 580,200 creations. This is across virtually all industries and regions.

Principal Agregates of the Manufacturing Industry 2011 (evolution 2011/10 in volume in %)

Industry	Production (€000 million)	Production	Value added +/-	Imports	Exports
Extractive energy, energy, water, waste	148.0	-3.9	-0.6	21.0	1.2
Electrical & electronic goods	91.2	5.1	6.4	8.7	6.8
Production of transport materials	127.0	5.6	-15.6	0.6	6.9
Production of other industrial productions incl.:	361.7	2.8	2.6	4.1	5.6
-textiles	16.6	-2.3	-1.2	7.5	3.4
-chemical industry	66.1	4.8	-11.3	3.2	6.3
-pharmaceutical industry	26.2	1.2	3.5	6.1	8.0
-metallurgy and production of metal products excl. machinery	98.6	2.8	9.4	6.2	8.3
Total	**727.9**	**2.3**	**1.1**	**4.5**	**6.3**

Source: INSEE

The steel industry produces approximately 17 million tonnes of steel per year. Steel is produced by Usinor. Most steel production takes place in the Nord-Pas-de-Calais region. France has a large non-ferrous metal industry, of which the main sector is the production of aluminium, produced by Péchiney. Saint-Gobain is the world's largest producer of glass. The annual turnover of materials processing is almost €43bn.

The manufacturing of basic chemical products takes place primarily in the former mining areas and near oil refineries. Turnover is approximately €70bn per year with a workforce of 236,000. Major companies include Rhodia, Hutchinson and Atofina.

The construction industry and public works industry covers a wide range of sectors, from heavy engineering products to precision mechanics and earns approximately €93bn and employs 1.4 million people. Major firms include Bouygues, SGE-Vivendi, the GTM group, Eiffage and Colas.

France is the third most important exporter of vehicles in the world. There are two large companies of international stature: PSA (owners of Peugeot and Citroën) and Renault. Over 5.6 million French vehicles were produced worldwide in 2010. More than 60 per cent are exported although in recent years the domestic market has declined.

After the USA and the former USSR, France is one of the most important countries in aerospace construction and the arms industry, producing civil aircraft, helicopters, military aircraft and satellite equipment. The aeronautic industry is centred around Paris and in the south-west (Bordeaux and Toulouse) with a workforce of about 95,000. The major firms are Matra-Aérospatiale, Dassault-Aviation and Snecma.

The annual turnover of the telecommunications, information and communication technology sector is €67.23bn. Alcatel is one of the world's leading manufacturers of telecommunications equipment. E-commerce has an annual turnover of €2.3bn.

On the basis of its diversified agricultural output, France has built up a highly sophisticated food and beverages industry. The industry is spread throughout the country, and consists of small to medium sized companies to internationally known large enterprises that export luxury items from champagne and cognac to mineral water and cheeses to all parts of the world. (Source: INSEE).

Leading Companies:

Air Liquide, URL: http://www.airliquide.com
Bouygues, URL: http://www.bouygues.fr/
Dassault-Aviation, URL: http://www.dasssault-aviation.com/
Total, URL: http://www.total.com
Group Bull, URL: http://www.bull.com./
PSA, URL: http://www.psa-peugeot-citroen.com/
Renault, URL: http://www.renault.fr
Saint Gobain, URL: http://www.saint-gobain.com/
Sanofi-Aventis, URL: http://en.sanofi.com/
Société Nationale d'Etude et de Construction de Moteurs d'Aviation (SNECMA), URL: http://www.snecma.com/
Thales (formerly Thomson-CSF), URL: http://www.thalesgroup.com/

Service Industries

The French bank system plays an important role in the economy and accounts for 3.56 per cent of the country's economy. There are now some 1,600 credit institutions and over 25,000 bank branches in France. Over 200,000 people are employed in the insurance sector. Its worldwide turnover is over €155.5 billion.

Tourism

In 2009, turnover in the tourism sector amounted to an estimated €130.9 million. In 2009 France's 248,810 tourist enterprises employed approximately 916,504 people. 2009 figures show that the number of foreign visitors continued to fall with 76.8 million registered visitors from abroad. Visitor numbers rose to 77.1 million in 2010, mainly the USA, China and Spain. Top tourist attractions include Disneyland, Paris (15 million visitors, 2010), the Louvre (8.3 million visitors), and the Eiffel Tower (6.7 million visitors).
Maison de la France, URL: http://www.franceguide.com

Agriculture

More than half of France's territory is devoted to farming. The greater part of the land used for farming consists of arable land amounting to some 28 million hectares, and is used for growing cereals, forage or industrial crops (sugar beets, oilseeds). The number of holdings has more than halved in the last twenty-five years due to advances in technology and mechanisation (567,000 in 2006, compared with over 1.5 million in 1970), while the average size of holdings is rising. As a result of these changes the agricultural working population is in decline and now accounts for 4.1 per cent of the total working population.

Crops accounted for some 50 per cent of the country's agricultural production. France is Europe's top grain-producer and produced an estimated 70.2 million tonnes in 2009 including 36.2 million tonnes of soft wheat, 2.1 million tonnes of hard wheat and 15.5 million tonnes of grain maize. France is also the leading producer of sugar beet and oilseeds: estimated figures for 2008 were 31 million tonnes of sugar beet and 6.4 million tonnes of oilseeds. 12 per cent of Europe's vegetable production comes from France, with the main vegetable crops being tomatoes, carrots, cauliflower and salads.

Estimates for 2011 put the number of sheep at 8.1 million, cattle at approximately 19.1 million, pigs at 14.0 million and goats at 1.4 million. Over 23 billion litres of cows' milk and 1.5 million tons of cheese are produced annually. Approximately 19.7 million eggs were produced.

Production (value added)

	Value 2011 € 'billion	Volume % change 2011/10	Price % change 2011/10	Value % change 2011/10
Crop production	42.2	3.3	1.6	5.0
-cereals	11.8	-2.5	2.9	0.4
-oil seeds & protein crops	3.3	7.0	3.6	10.9
-sugar beet	1.0	15.2	5.6	21.6
-other industrial crops*	0.4	-8.8	-6.6	-14.8
-fruit, veg., potatoes	7.1	5.5	-13.0	-8.2
-wine	10.9	11.3	4.2	16.0
-feed crops, plants, flowers	7.7	-2.2	11.7	9.2
Animal production	25.4	1.9	8.5	10.6
-livestock	10.9	0.3	8.0	8.3
-poultry, eggs	4.6	0.3	12.0	12.3
-milk & other products	9.9	4.6	7.5	12.5
Agricultural services	3.8	0.0	1.4	1.4
Production (excl. grant)	71.4	2.7	4.0	6.7
Subsidies on products	1.1	-4.9	-1.7	-6.5
Intermediate consumption (excl. VAT)	43.7	0.3	8.2	8.5
Gross value added	28.8	5.8	-2.1	3.6
Fixed capital consumption	10.6	-0.3	1.1	0.8
Net value added	18.2	9.4	-3.8	5.2

Source: INSEE

In 2011, 51.1 million hectolitres of wine were produced, up 12.8 per cent from the 2010 harvest. Production is distributed throughout ten different areas and is divided into three categories: quality wines, ordinary wines, and wines distilled for the manufacture of spirits.

FRANCE

Forestry
A quarter of France (about 16 million hectares) is covered by woodland. Woodlands increase by over 50,000 hectares per year. Three-quarters of the forest is privately owned and the rest is owned by state or local authorities. The most densely wooded areas are in the mountain regions (Alps, Pyrenees, Massif Central, Jura, Vosges) and coastal areas (Mediterranean). French forests produce some 53 million cubic metres of timber.

Fishing
The maritime catch was an estimated 440,000 tonnes of fish in 2010, with a value of €893 million. In 2009, the maritime catch was 437,000 tonnes with a value of €930 million. The most important species are sardines, whiting and anchovies. It also imports roughly 300,000 tonnes per annum. Main fishing ports include Boulogne, Lorient and Concarneau. There were 4,979 fishing vessels registered to metropolitan France in 2008. Aquaculture produced 237,500 tonnes in 2007.

COMMUNICATIONS AND TRANSPORT

Travel Requirements
US, Canadian and Australian citizens require a passport valid for at least three months beyond the length of stay, but do not require a visa for visits not exceeding 90 days. EU nationals who hold a valid Identity Card do not require a passport or a visa. Citizens of other countries should contact the French embassy to check entry requirements. France is a signatory to the Schengen Agreement. With a Schengen visa, a visitor can travel freely throughout the Schengen zone, and there are few border stops and checks. See http://www.eurovisa.info/SchengenCountries.htm for details.

Customs Restrictions
Import duties are calculated on the value of the goods imported and the costs of importing them. Duty rates range from 0% (e.g. on books) to 17 per cent. Certain goods may be subject to additional duties depending on the country of manifacture. The standard VAT rate for importing items is 19.6 per cent, although some goods have reduced rates.

Air
Air freight and mail transport (Paris airports) amounted to approximately 2.4 million tonnes in 2011. Approximately 130.370 million passengers were also transported.

National Airlines
Air France, URL: http://www.airfrance.fr
Passengers carried 2007/08: 73.5 million. Freight transported: 1.5 million tons

International Airports
The following are the main airports:
Lyon-Satolas Airport, URL: http://www.lyon.aeroport.fr
Marseille-Provence Airport, URL: http://www.marseille.aeroport.fr
Nice Côte d'Azur Airport, URL: http://www.nice.aeroport.fr
Paris (Charles de Gaulle) Airport, URL: http://www.adp.fr/
Paris (Orly) Airport, URL: http://www.adp.fr/
Toulouse (Blagnac) Airport, URL: http://www.toulouse.aeroport.fr
Bordeaux-Mérignac Airport, URL: http://www.bordeaux.aeroport.fr/en

In 2010, there were 95.3 million international passenger flights and 225.3 million domestic flights within metropolitan France.

Civil Aviation Authorities
Direction Générale de l'Aviation Civile (DGAC, Civil Aviation Authority), URL: http://www.dgac.fr/

Railways
The French railway network totals 31,385 km, of which 45 per cent is electrified. The railway system is operated by the state-controlled SNCF, with a workforce of over 230,000 and a turnover of some €22.5 thousand million (2003). SNCF currently operates more than 13,500 trains. The high-speed trains (TGV), which run at speeds of up to 320 km/h, run on 1,540 km of special track. In 2006 108 million tonnes of freight were transported by train and 1 billion passengers. Goods to the value of €34.3 million were transported in 2011. Passenger-km of domestic rail passengers amounted to €72.624 billion in 2011.

France's fastest train link was inaugurated in June 2007. Trains should travel at 200 mph (320 k/ph). The new 185 mile (300 km) LGV-Est line links Paris to 23 destinations in eastern France and 10 international destinations. It is estimated that passenger levels will rise by 65 per cent with the opening of TGV Est Européen with a projected 11.5 million passengers per year. Three new stations have been built to meet expected demand. Rail traffic between France and Germany is expected to double. Journey times have dramatically reduced. The journey time between Paris-Strasbourg has been cut from 4 hours to 2 hours 20 minutes, and Paris-Munich from 8 hours 30 minutes to 6 hours 15 minutes. The total cost of TGV Est Européen was over €5 billion, split thus: French government 30 per cent, SNCF 24 per cent, French Regional Councils 18 per cent, Réseau Ferré de France 17 per cent, Europe 8 per cent and Luxembourg 3 per cent.

In 1994 the channel tunnel opened connecting France and Britain by a direct rail link. In 2007 new international stations opened in the UK, cutting international travel time. The journey from Gare du Nord in Paris to St. Pancreas International takes around 2 hours 15 minutes (compared to 2 hours 35 minutes to London Waterloo). Ebbsfleet International in Kent also opened. In 2007 there were approximately 8.2 million passengers (Eurostar) and over 3.5 million vehicles carried. In 2005 1.6 million tonnes of freight were transported.

In the Paris region the SNCF services are linked with the RATP (Régie Autonome des Transports Parisiens) which carries more than 1.5 billion passengers on the underground metro system and 800 million on buses. The three networks interconnect to form the RER (Réseau Express Régional). The underground is currently undergoing expansion. There are plans to build a

130 km super metro to open by 2017, which extends round outer Paris. The extension of line 14 to Quartier des Olympiades became operational in June 2007. Line 13 reached Asnières-Gennevillers-Le-Luth in 2008. M12 should be extended by 3 km to Mairie d'Aubervilliers. The first stage of this to Proudhon-Gradinoux opened in December 2012.

There are now four tram lines operating in Paris. T1 between Gare de Saint-Denis and Noisy-le-Sec, T2 between La Défense and Issy-Val de Seine, T3 between Point du Garigliano and Porte d'Ivry, and T3 between Bondy RER and Aulnay Sous Bois. T3 line opened in December 2006 and cost €300 million. Further lines are under construction.

Paris, Lyon and Marseille have subway systems.

In 2009 railways carried 9.3 per cent of goods being transported domestically.

In 2011 work started on a high speed rail link through the Alps between Italy and France, linking Turin and Lyon and reducing journey times by upto 50 per cent. The project is forecast to cost $21 billion.

Société Nationale des Chemins de fer Français (SNCF), URL: http://www.sncf.com
Régie Autonome des Transports Parisiens (RATP), URL: http://www.ratp.fr/
Eurotunnel, URL: http://www.eurotunnel.com

Roads
France has an extensive road network with over 965,000 km of local, secondary and main roads and motorways. There are over 9,000 km of motorways. This is planned to increase to over 12,000 km by 2010. Tolls operate on the motorways. According to INSEE, in 2006 private vehicle road traffic amounted to 724 billion passenger-kilometres (83 per cent of domestic transport). French roads carried 310.5 billion ton /kilometres of goods in the same year. In 2009, 83.2 per cent of goods were transported by road.

As of January 2002, there were 28.7 million cars (37.9 per cent diesel), and 80.2 per cent of households had at least one car, with over 30.2 per cent of households having two or more cars. In 2010, 2.251 million new cars were registered of which 1.593 million were diesel, 567,900 were petrol, 75,600 were bi-fuel and 9,700 were hybrid (electricity and gas). Vehicles drive on the right.

In 2009 a new system of car registration plates was introduced to try to combat registration fraud and make stolen cars easier to trace. The plates will have the format AA-111-AA. After a public outcry, regional numbers will still appear on the plates, but will be smaller and will appear on a small strip on the right-hand side.

Fédération Nationale des Transports Routiers (FNTR), URL: http://www.fntr.fr

Shipping
Roughly 92 million tonnes of freight is transported per annum. France's fleet is ranked 27th in the world in tonnage. French shipping is overseen by the Compagnie Générale Maritime (CGM), a state owned company.
Compagnie Générale Maritime, URL: http://www.cma-cgm.com/

Inland waterways, of which there are nearly 6,000 km in use, carried 6,890 million ton/km of freight in 2003. In 2009, 2.2 per cent of goods were transported by inland waterways. Most canals are too small for large vessels to navigate. The main river ports are Paris, Strasbourg, Thionville and Rouen. In 2011, goods to the value of approximately €4,627 million were transported on domestic waterways (excluding transit).

Ports and Harbours
Sea traffic is handled by a number of ports, of which 40 deal with over one million tonnes. In 2011, goods to the value of €198.14 million were transported through France's seven ports.Marseilles is France's largest and Europe's fourth largest port (94.1 million tonnes, 2004). The main freight ports are Marseilles (96.5 million tonnes, 2006), Le Havre (70.0 million tonnes, 2006) and Dunkerque (51.0 million tonnes, 2004). The main passenger ports are Calais (1.8m passengers) and Cherbourg (1.5m).
Port Autonome de Marseille, URL: http://www.marseille-port.fr

HEALTH

The public health insurance programme in France was established in 1945. It has since undergone many changes. The French Social Security system is based on a 'pay as you go' system. All legal residents are covered by health insurance. Contributions from employees and employers finance 84 per cent of the total expenditure. The benefit breakdown is: pensions, 50 per cent; health, 27 per cent; family allowance, 13 per cent; and unemployment, 10 per cent. A new tax, generalised social contribution (CSG) has been recently introduced, which replaced national insurance, to try to counterbalance the budget deficit which has cumulated since 1993. This has in part been caused by an ageing population and the cost of medical advances. In 2000, CMU (Covuverture maladie universelle, universal health care coverage) was implemented. This gives the possibility to all people who legally reside in France for more than three months to have health expenses reimbursed by Social Security. CMU also offers a complementary health protection of 100 per cent for people on low incomes, which adds to the standard Social Security.

In 2011, the amount of current health expenditure amounted to €240.3 billion, up 2.6 per cent from 2010, equating to 12.0 per cent of GDP. Approximately €15.1 billion was spent on elderly care facilities and prevention €12.9 bn in 2011. Some €7.6 bn was spent on training.

The workforce within the medical sector in the public sector is made up of some 86,000 men and some 32,000 women. In the private sector the workforce is more evenly split with just over 29,000 men and 25,000 women. In 2012, there were an estimated 216,762 doctors (334 per 100,000 population), 40,599 dental surgeons (63 per 100,000 inhabitants), 19,128 midwives (132 per 100,000 women between ages of 15-49), 72,811 pharmacists (112 per

100,000 inhabitants). In 2011, there were 534,378 nurses (855 per 100,000 inhabitants), 70,780 physiotherapists (113 per 100,000 inhabitants) and 19,963 speech therapists (32 per 100,000 inhabitants).

Estimated figures for 2009 show the following number of medical establishments: 2,751 medical establishments provide 488,006 patient beds. This breaks down to 966 public establishments (307,455 beds); and 1,785 private establishments (180,551 beds). The trend is to reduce stays within hospital.

The most medical common causes of death in 2009 were cancers (30 per cent) and cardiovascular diseases (27 per cent). There were 37,368 deaths by external causes (7.0 per cent), of which 4,306 were transport accidents and 10,464 were suicides. One in six deaths in men aged 15 to 49 years is suicide. In 2010, 618 cases of HIV/AIDS were diagnosed, bringing the cumulative total to an estimated 66,387. (Source: INSEE)

Life expectancy for men and women continues to rise: in 2010 it was estimated to be 84.8 year for females and 78.1 years for males (metropolitan France). The gender gap is one of the largest in Europe.

By 2009, an estimated 62,279 (males 51,795, females 13,484) people in France had been diagnosed with AIDS, the second highest total in the EU behind Spain. There were a reported 596 new cases in 2009 .

A survey in 1999-2000 found that 14 per cent of six-year-olds were overweight, of whom 4 per cent were obese. Asthma affects 6-12 per cent of children. (Source: INSEE)

Main health agencies include:
L'Institut national de veille sanitaire (INVS), National Institute for Public Health Surveillance, URL: http://www.invs.sante.fr/
L'Agence française de sécurité sanitaire des aliments (AFSSA), French Food Safety Agency, URL: http://www.afssa.fr/
L'Etablissement français du sang, French Blood Agency, URL: http://www.dondusang.net/afficherAccueil.do
Agence de la Biomédicine, Biomedicine Agency (formerly French Transplant Agency), URL: http://www.agence-biomedecine.fr/?lang.fr

EDUCATION

Education is compulsory from the age of 6 to 16 years, and is provided either by the free and non-sectarian schools controlled by the State (approximately four-fifths of the total school population), or by private schools, which are either completely independent or helped in some measure by the State. In 2011, €137.4 billion was spent on education (primary €39.6 billion, secondary €57.1 billion, higher €28.0 billion, other €10.0 billion). Per pupil expenditure on education was €7,990 in 2009.

Approximately 12 per cent of adults aged 18-65 have literacy problems; of these, 7 per cent are born in France with French as their mother tongue.

In order to safeguard secularism in schools, a law was passed in 2004 which banned the wearing of religious symbols in schools. The law includes headscarves, skullcaps and turbans.

Pre-school Education
An estimated 100 per cent of three-five year olds attend nursery school. Education at this level is the responsibility of local communes. In the school period 2009-10, approximately 2.218 million pupils attended public pre-elementary institutions and 314,020 attended private institutions.

Primary/Secondary Education
There are seven grades, starting with the sixth, finishing with the first. *Colléges* give tuition at the first level, from sixth to third grade, *lycées* from third grade up to the final one. At the end of this pupils sit the *baccalauréat*, a preparatory examination for higher education. In 2007, 83.3 per cent of those taking the *baccalauréat* passed.

In 2011, approximately 6,658,000 pupils were enrolled in pre-school and primary education; 5,384,000 in secondary education; 223,000 in other schools (e.g. miscellaneous training programs) and 2,348,000 in higher education. An estimated 443,000 people were in apprenticeships.

In 2009/10 there were 16,497 nursery schools, 37,783 elementary schools and 11,377 secondary schools (7,017 colleges, 1,653 lycées, 2,627 technical secondary schools, 80 regional or adapted schools).

The pupil/teacher ratio was estimated at 13.9 to 1. In public education for the period 2009-10, average nursery class size is 25.5 and in elementary schools 22.6. In secondary education, the class size is 24.1.

Higher Education
The annual student intake for higher education is around 6 per cent. The student/teacher ratio is approximately 31 to one. There are now 90 universities and university centres in France. The university population is distributed in the main between the following disciplines: law, 13.9 per cent; economics, 6.8 per cent; literature and social studies, 35.1 per cent; science, 19.4 per cent; and physical education. Foreign students make up approximately 10 per cent of the total. As of 2011-12, university enrolment was estimated at 1.269 million. Total enrolment in higher education was estimated at 2.347 million.

Vocational Training
The expansion of the vocational high schools system or *lycées d'enseignement professionel* has been crucial in achieving the goal of getting 80 per cent of students to the *baccalauréat* level. There are now over 1,500 of these institutions.

RELIGION

France is a secular state. The Church and the State have been separate since the Act of 1905. Everyone is free to practise the religion of his/her choice without any restriction. In May 2001 the About-Picard law came into force. The law was designed to protect vulnerable individuals from sects who violate Human Rights and fundamental freedoms.

In 2004 a law was passed which banned the wearing of conspicuous religious symbols in public schools. The law includes headscarves, skullcaps and turbans. The law was overwhelming endorsed by parliament (494 for, 36 against and 31 abstentions). The law was primarily passed to safeguard secularism in schools. In 2011, wearing the burkha and niquab in public became illegal.

France has a religious liberty rating of 6 on a scale of 1 to 10 (10 is most freedom). (Source: World Religion Database)

Religious affiliation breaks down thus: Catholic: 47,000,000 (81.4 per cent of the population); Muslim: 4,000,000 (6.89 per cent); Protestant: 950,000 (1.64 per cent); Jewish: 750,000 (1.29 per cent); Buddhist: 400,000 (0.68 per cent); Orthodox: 200,000 (0.34 per cent); Other: 4,700,000 (8.12 per cent)

Bishops' Conference (Conférence des Evêques de France),
URL: http://www.eglise.catholique.fr/accueil.html
Permanent Council
President: Mgr André Vingt-Trois, Archbishop of Paris
Vice-Presidents: Mgr Laurent Ulrich, Mgr Hippolyte Simon

COMMUNICATIONS AND MEDIA

Freedom of expression is a right in France. In 1944 three decrees were announced to protect the press from government interference. In 1984 and 1986 further laws were passed to guarantee the plurality of the press and prevent ownership monopolies. A single press group is not allowed to control more than 30 per cent of the total circulation of France's newspapers. There is also legislation to protect the independence and status of journalists, and rights of the individual.

As of 2009 there were an estimated 65 daily newspapers (11 national, 54 regional). Recent figures estimate that there are approximately 30,000 journalists in France. 30 per cent of French people read a newspaper each day. Advertising represented almost 44 per cent of revenue. Circulation of the main newspapers was estimated in 2002 at: Le Figaro (345,000), Le Monde (361,200), Libération (156,000), Le Parisien (360,500). The paid press is continuing to decline faced with the challenges of the internet and free daillies.

Newspapers National
Le Figaro, URL: http://www.lefigaro.fr
Libération (France), URL: http://www.liberation.fr
Le Monde, URL: http://www.lemonde.fr
Les Echos, URL: http://www.lesechos.fr
L'Humanité, URL: http://www.humanite.presse.fr
La Tribune, URL: http://www.latribune.fr
La Croix, URL: http://www.la-croix.com

Regional Daily Press
Le Bien Public (Dijon), URL: http://www.bienpublic.com
Le Dauphiné Libéré (Grenoble), URL: http://www.dauphine-libere.com
La Dépêche du Midi, URL: http://www.ladepeche.fr
Les Dernières Nouvelles d'Alsace, URL: http://www.dna.fr
Nice-Matin, URL: http://www.nice-matin.fr
Le Parisien, URL: http://www.leparisien.fr
Le Progrès, URL: http://www.leprogres.fr
La Provence, URL: http://www.laprovence-presse.fr/
Ouest France, URL: http://www.france-ouest.fr
Le Républicain Lorrain, URL: http://www.republicain-lorrain.fr
Sud-Ouest, URL: http://www.sudouest.com
La Voix du Nord, URL: http://www.lavoixdunord.fr

Business Journals
L'Express, URL: http://www.l'express.fr/express
L'Entreprise, URL: http://www.l'entreprise.com
Le Point, URL: http://www.lepoint.fr

Television
Television in France has changed radically in recent years. Laws passed in 1981, 1982 and 1986 ended the state monopoly. There are currently seven national public channels: France2, France3, France4, France5 (educational), RFO (All part of the France Television group), Arte (a Franco-German cultural channel) and La Chaine parlémentaire. There are numerous private channels including TFI, M6 and Canal+ (subscription). The public channels have approximately 46 per cent of the viewing audience, and the private channels, just over 50 per cent. To protect the public service channels the group France Télévision (France 2, France 3, La Cinquième (now France 5) was formed in 2000. RFO joined in 2004 and France 4 in 2005. Most of the financing of the public service television comes from the licence fee paid by households. There are some 180 channels including pay-TV and cable and. In 2007 an estimated 10 million households had subscriptions for pay television. Digital terrestrial tv is being rolled out.

France's first 24-hour news service, France 24, launched in December 2006.

France Télévision (France 2 / France3 / La Cinquième), URL: http://www.francetelevisions.fr/

FRANCE

President: Patrick de Carolis
France 2: URL: http://www.france2.fr/
France 3: URL: http://www.france3.fr/
France 4: URL: http://www.france4.fr/
France 5: URL: http://www.france5.fr/
RFO: URL: http://www.rfo.fr/
Arte, URL: http://www.arte-tv.com
La Chaîne Parlémentaire, URL: http://www.lcpan.fr/
Canal+, URL: http://www.canalplus.fr
Télévision Française 1 (TF1), URL: http://www.tf1.fr
M6, URL: http://www.m6.fr/
France 24, URL: http://www.france24.com

Radio

A law was passed in 1982 to end the state monopoly on radio broadcasting. The national radio company, Radio France, is comprised of several networks: France Inter, France Info, France Culture, Radio Bleue, France Musique, Le Mouv'. There are also a number of private stations, including Europe 1, Europe 2 and RTL. France has nearly 1,200 local radio stations. France broadcasts throughout the world through Radio France Internationale.

Société Nationale de Radiodiffusion (Radio France), URL: http://www.radiofrance.fr
Radio France Internationale (RFI), URL: http://www.rfi.fr/
Europe 1, URL: http://www.europe1.fr/
RTL, URL: http://www.rtl.fr/
NRJ, URL: http://www.nrj.fr/

Post and Telecommunications

Since 1990 the Ministry of Posts and Telecommunications has run this sector through two separate companies: La Poste (the Post Office) and France-Telecom (Telecommunications). Approximately 25 million items are handled by La Poste every year. The telecommunications sector has expanded rapidly. There are now over 40 million telephone lines, over one million fax terminals and nearly 2 million card-operated phone booths. The Minitel network enables telephone subscribers to be connected with a range of data banks, and there are about 7 million Minitel-sets in service. In 2009, an estimated 19,500 million items of correspondence were sent throught the mail and some 19,000 million items of unaddressed advertising.

In 2011 there were an estimated 68.6 million cell phone subscribers (penetration rate over 90 per cent). In 2011 it was estimated that there were 50 million internet users (95 per cent penetration rate) with over 17 million broadband subscriptions. (Source: INSEE)

France Télécom-Orange, URL: http://www.francetelecom.com
La Poste, URL: http://www.laposte.fr/

The Telecommunications Act of 26 July 1996 changed the regulatory framework for telecommunications by creating an independent authority - the Authorité de Régulation des Télécommunications (ART). Its main responsibilities include settling disputes about interconnection and infrastructure sharing, approving the interconnection reference for public network operators, allocating resources (e.g. radio frequencies), processing licence applications, authorising establishment of independent networks and regulating and supervising competition. A new organisation structure was adopted in 2004 to respond to the technical challenges of the sector.

Regulatory Bodies
Authorité de Régulation des Télécommunications (ART), URL: http://www.art-telecom.fr/
Conseil Supérieur de l'Audiovisuel (CSA), URL: http://www.csa.fr
The CSA was an independent administrative body created in 1989 to guarantee broadcasting freedom.

ENVIRONMENT

France's major environmental problems include forest damage caused by acid rain, air pollution caused by vehicle and industrial emissions, water pollution from agricultural run-off and urban wastes, and marine pollution.

France has had recent marine pollution problems with two major oil tanker spills, the Erika in 1999 (90,000 barrels), and the Prestige in 2002 (77,000 barrels). In March 2003 the EU agreed to ban single-hull tankers carrying heavy-duty oil between European ports. The ban came into effect in 2005. In 2003 the French government passed a law establishing a 90-mile ecological zone to deter ships from dumping dirty ballast in its coastal areas.

France contributed approximately 415.3 million metric tons of energy-related carbon dioxide emissions in 2005. Of France's energy sources, oil generates the largest carbon emissions, 65 per cent in 2004, followed by natural gas (23 per cent), and coal (12 per cent). Per capita emissions were estimated to be 6.7 metric tons in the 2004. In January 2000 the government's Inter-Ministerial Greenhouse Effect Mission (MIES) launched a plan for 2000-2010 to reduce its carbon emissions. Industry is also required to reduce its emissions by 20-30 per cent. Overall emissions of greenhouse gases reduced by 2 per cent between 1990 and 2005. However emissions from transport increased by over 22 per cent in the same period and in 2006 accounted for 26.5 per cent of greenhouse emissions. The increase has been offset by reductions in other sectors including industry and agriculture. A Climate Plan was launched in 2004 to help France meet its objectives.

Emissions of greenhouse gases under the Kyoto Protocol, 2010

Gas emissions	2009	2010	1990/2010 +/-
CO2	373	383	-3.2
CH4	65	62	-0.8
N20	62	60	-35.0
HFC	15.4	16.9	352.5
PFC	0.4	0.4	-91.1
SF6	0.6	0.6	-72.0
Global warming potential	517	522	-7

Source: INSEE

CO^2 emissions from transport were estimated as follows in 2009: air 4.5 million tonnes, road 120.4 million tonnes, train 0.5 million tonnes, and maritime 2.8 million tonnes.

Many targets have been set with the aim of protecting the atmosphere. These include increased research into the possibility of an electric car to reduce sulphur dioxide emissions and the installation of an automatic air pollution measuring system. In 2004 agglomerations with more than 100,000 inhabitants experienced an average of 24 days on which air quality was either mediocre or bad.

Since 1993 businesses have been required to contribute to finance recycling or to be responsible for eliminating the packaging they market. Each department has to draw up a plan to eliminate household waste products, there is a ban on importing household waste into France for disposal, and in 1993 a tax on storage of waste products was introduced. In 2010, 355 million tonnes of waste were produced, 5.5 tonnes per inhabitant. In 2010, 91.9 per cent of paper/cardboard was recycled, 69.8 per cent of glass and 23.7 per cent of plastics. France has met all of the EU's 2008 Packaging Waste directives except for plastics. In 2008, 16.9 million tonnes of raw materials for recycling were used to produce 39.5 million tons of materials (metals, paper and cardboard, plastics and glass).

Since the ratification of the 1983 law providing for decentralising of urban planning decisions, local bodies also play a key role in environment issues. The mayor is responsible for matters such as drinking water, sewage treatment, household waste treatment and traffic. An interministerial committee for the environment was set up in the same year to promote environmental policies.

Total expenditure on the protection of the environment was an estimated €43.8 billion in 2010 (2 per cent of GDP) and total expenditure on the environment was estimated at €61.6 billion in the same period.

France is a party to the following international environmental agreements: Air Pollution, Air Pollution-Nitrogen Oxides, Air Pollution-Persistent Organic Pollutants, Air Pollution-Sulfur 85, Air Pollution-Sulfur 94, Air Pollution-Volatile Organic Compounds, Antarctic-Environmental Protocol, Antarctic-Marine Living Resources, Antarctic Seals, Antarctic Treaty, Biodiversity, Climate Change, Climate Change-Kyoto Protocol, Desertification, Endangered Species, Hazardous Wastes, Law of the Sea, Marine Dumping, Marine Life Conservation, Ozone Layer Protection, Ship Pollution, Tropical Timber 83, Tropical Timber 94, Wetlands, Whaling.

SPACE PROGRAMME

France is a member of the European Space Agency (ESA). The European space industry has an annual turnover of €6 billion and employs 40,000 people. France is the largest contributor to the ESA budget (29 per cent) and has the highest investment in military space applications (€450 million). France is very competitive in telecommunication and observation satellites research and launched its first military spy satellite in 1995.

France's national space research centre, Centre National d'Etudes patiales (CNES), was founded in 1961. Its role is to suggest directives to the government and then carry them out. Its activities include access to space, earth observation, telecommunications, study and exploration of the universe, and manned space flights. A key aim is independent access to space. France's space programme suffered a setback in 1996 when Ariane 501 crashed. Ariane 5 was successfully re-launched in October 1997. The Ariane programme is still ongoing. The most recent launch took place in August 2012. Its launch vehicles (Société Européen de Propulsion, SEP) are fired from French Guiana.

France is currently developing new space-balloon launch site in Ontario in partnership with Canada. Canada will provide $10 million for construction and flights and France will provide expertise and balloons. Space balloons carry equipment into the stratosphere. The balloons can hover for several months, allowing the collection of data for research. A launch of a balloon that can expand to 800,000 square metres will be take place in 2013, and should carry a telescope 42 km into the sky. France has participated in over 3,000 balloon launches to date.

In 2010 the CNES budget was €1,865 million. Approximately €685 million is allocated to ESA. CNES currently employs 2,400 people.

Centre National d'Etudes Spatiales, URL: http://www.cnes.fr/

FRENCH GUIANA
French Overseas Department
La Guyane

Capital: Cayenne (Population estimate, 2012: 61,500)

Head of State: François Hollande (President of France) (page 1443)

CONSTITUTION AND GOVERNMENT

Constitution
Previously a colony, the status of French Guiana was changed to that of a French Overseas Department (Département d'Outre-Mer) on 19 March 1946, and Guiana thus became an integral part of the French Republic. The administrative structure is the same as in any department of metropolitan France: it is administered by a prefect (in Cayenne), assisted by an Under-Prefect (in Saint-Laurent-du-Maroni). They are appointed by the Government. Guiana has a General Council of 19 members as well as a Regional Council of 31 members elected by universal suffrage since 1974 when Guiana was granted the additional status of a Region. Councillors serve a term of six years. Since the Decentralization Law of March 1982, the executive power of the Government-appointed Prefect has been transferred to the locally-elected General Council.

There are two District Councils: Cayenne and Saint-Laurent-du-Maroni, which in turn cover 21 communes. Guiana has representatives in metropolitan France, namely two Deputies in the National Assembly and one Senator in the Senate. Guiana is also represented at the Economic and Social Council. As a French département, Guiana belongs to the European Union and thus has representatives at the European Parliament in Strasbourg. However, in order to adapt Community Law to its specific conditions and its economic development, Guiana is entitled to specific measures.

In January 2010, French Guiana voted against plans for increased autonomy. There was a 48 per cent turnout in the referendum and 69.8 per cent voted against the plans.

In June 2010, the first French overseas interministerial council (CIOM) took place in Guyana. The Council agreed to establish a regional council of export and co-operation (COREC).

Administration (as at April 2013)
Prefect: Denis Labbé (page 1371)
President of General Council: Alain Tien-Liong
President of Regional Council: Rodolphe Alexandre
Deputy to the French National Assembly: Gabriel Serville (PS)
Deputy to the French National Assembly: Chantal Berthelot (PS)
Senator in French Senate: Georges Patient (DVG)
Senator in French Senate: Jean-Etienne Antoinette (DVG)

French Overseas Economic and Social Council (Outre-Mer du Conseil Economique et Social) (as at April 2013)
Representative for French Guiana: Rémy Budoc

Ministries
Préfecture, Rue Fiedmont, BP 7008, 97307 Cayenne, Guyane. Tel: +594 39 45 00, fax: +594 30 02 77, e-mail: secretariat-president@cr-guyane.fr, URL: http://www.guyane.pref.gouv.fr
Sous-Préfecture, 4 bd du Général-de-Gaulle, 97320 St-Laurent-du-Maroni, Guyane. Tel: +594 39 04 04, fax: +594 34 15 30, URL: http://www.guyane.pref.gouv.fr
General Council, Hôtel du Département, Place Léopoid-Héder, BP 5021, 97305 Cayenne, Guyane. Tel: +594 29 55 00, fax: +594 29 55 25, e-mail: communication@cg973.gf, URL: http://www.cg973.fr
Regional Council, 66 avenue du Général de Gaulle, BP 7025, 97307 Cayenne Cedex. Tel: +594 29 20 20, fax: +594 31 95 22, URL: http://www.cr-guyane.fr
Department of Agriculture and Forestry, Parc Rebard, BP 5002, 97305 Cayenne Cedex, Tel: +594 29 63 74, fax: +594 29 63 63, URL: http://daf.guyane.agriculture.gouv.fr/
Department of Health and Social Affairs, 19 rue Victor Schoelcher, 97336 Cayenne Cedex. Tél: +594 25 53 00, fax: +594 25 53 29
Department of Youth, Sport and Social Cohesion, URL: http://www.guyane.drjscs.gouv.fr/
Department of Infrastructure, URL: http://www.guyane.developpement-durable.gouv.fr/
Department of Enterprise, Employment, Consumer Affairs, URL: http://www.guyane.diecte.gouv.fr/-guyane-.html
Department of Culture and Communication, URL: http://www.guyane.culture.gouv.fr/

Elections
The most recent Regional Council elections took place on 14 and 21 March 2010. Rodophe Alexandre became the new leader. His party, LMAJ, Guyane 73, took 21 seats and the LDVG led by Christiane Taubira (LDVG) took 10 seats. The most recent elections to the General Council took place in 2008.

LEGAL SYSTEM

French law applies. French Guiana's court system is headed by the Court of Appeals (*Cour d'Appel*). A new Court of Appeals was created in January 2012, based in Cayenne.

LOCAL GOVERNMENT

French Guiana is divided into arrondissements, 19 cantons and 22 communes. The largest communes (2004) were Cayenne (population: 50,395), Saint-Laurent-du-Maroni (19,167), Kourou (19,074), Matoury (18,037) and Rémire-Montjoly (15,538).

AREA AND POPULATION

Area
Guiana is located in the north east of South America, between Suriname and Brazil. The total area is 91,000 sq. km. The climate is tropical with little seasonal variation in temperature. The landscape largely consists of low coastal plains with some hills and mountains.

To view a map of Guiana, please consult http://www.lib.utexas.edu/maps/cia06/french_guiana_sm_2006.gif

Population
In 1954 the population was 27,900; by 1999 it had risen to 157,000. According to the 2004 census, the population as at 1 January 2004 was 185,000. The annual growth rate for the period 1999-2003 was 3.48 per cent. In 2009, the population was estimated to be 229,000. The steep increase in population is mostly due to immigration resulting from the development of the space programme. There is also a high birth rate. The population is projected to rise to 261,000 by 2015 and 425,520 by 2030. Population density is approximately 5 persons per sq. km. Approximately 75 per cent of the population lives in urban areas and approximately 90 per cent live in a strip alongside the Atlantic coast.

An estimated 44 per cent of the population is aged 20 and just 4 per cent of the population is aged 65 or more.

The population of the three main urban areas in 2006 was: Cayenne (75,740), St-Laurent-du-Maroni (33,707) and Matoury (24,583)

Births, Marriages, Deaths
The birth rate was estimated to be 27.7 per 1,000 inhabitants in 2008, down from 29.4 per 1,000 inhabitants in 2007. The death rate was 3.4 per 1,000 inhabitants in 2008. Average life expectancy at birth in 2011 was 73 years for males and 81 years for females. The infant mortality rate in 2002 was14.2 deaths per 1,000 live births compared to 19.2 per 1,000 live births in 1990. In 2002, there were 530 marriages (compared to 553 in 2001).

Public Holidays 2014
1 January: New Year's Day
4 March: Mardi Gras
5 March: Ash Wednesday
18 April: Good Friday
20 April Easter Sunday
21 April: Easter Monday
29 May: Ascension
9 June: Whit Monday
14 July: National Day
25 December: Christmas Day

EMPLOYMENT

French labour laws apply in Guiana but regulations on income vary. In French Guiana an analysis of the labour market must take into account that one-third of the population are migrants who are often there illegally. In addition to a 'legal' labour market reflected by the statistics, there is a clandestine market, the size of which cannot be exactly determined.

The unemployment rate was estimated to be 20.5 per cent in 2009. (Source: INSEE)

Paid Employment by Economic Activity

Occupation	2005
Agriculture, hunting, forestry & fishing	974
Manufacturing	2,705
Electricity, gas & water supply	643
Construction	2,698
Wholesale & retail trade, repairs	3,920
Hotels & restaurants	1,029
Transport, storage & communications	2,308
Financial intermediation	527
Real estate, renting & business activities	4,062
Public admin. & defence; compulsory social security	9,827
Education	6,728
Health & social work	4,484

FRANCE

- continued

Other community, social & personal service activities	1,908
Households with employed persons	1,461

Source: Copyright © International Labour Organization (ILO Dept. of Statistics, http://laborsta.ilo.org)

BANKING AND FINANCE

Currency
The currency of French Guiana is the euro which, on 1 January 2002, replaced the French franc.
€ = 6.55957 French francs (European Central Bank irrevocable conversion rate)
1 euro (€) = 100 cents

GDP/GNP, Inflation, National Debt
The Kourou Space Centre is French Guiana's most important economic activity, followed by the fishing and forestry industries. Growth was estimated to 4 per cent in 2011. GDP was €3,212 million in 2009, up from €3,095 million in 2008. Per cpaita GDP was €14,028 in 2009. GDP fell in 2007 to an estimated €2,696 million, down from €2,805 million in 2006. The inflation rate, according to recent figures, is 2.5 per cent. External debt was US$1.2 billion, according to recent statistics. The consumer price index went up by 3.5 per cent in 2008 from 2007.

Gross value (€ million) added by sector

Sector	2006	2007
Agriculture	116	111
Agricultural and food industries	26	25
Manufacturing	197	221
Energy	53	63
Construction	226	239
Trade	241	259
Transport	161	159
Services	1,607	1,672
-of which education, health & administration	923	990
Total	2,576	2,696

Source: INSEE

Balance of Payments / Imports and Exports
Guiana imports consumer goods (food, textiles, clothing, tourism, vehicles), production goods (construction materials, machines, service and utility vehicles) and crude oil. Exports include timber, rum gold, shrimp, clothing, and rosewood essence. Imports (cif) in 2006 were €1,3485 million, whilst exports (fob) were €1,195 million. Gold accounts for nearly 50 per cent of exports.

External trade

	2005	2006
Exports of goods	**93.7**	**122.1**
Agriculture, forestry, fishing	0.6	1.2
Agricultural and food products	13.2	12.9
Consumer goods	1.2	1.0
Vehicles	11.2	19.7
Equipment goods	20.6	28.9
Intermediate foods	46.8	58.2
Imports of goods	**734.8**	**749.7**
Agriculture, forestry, fishing	8.8	9.5
Agricultural and food products	147.8	143.8
Consumer goods	131.9	131.6
Vehicles	103.0	100.8
Equipment	125.5	138.4
Intermediate goods	121.9	131.4
Combustibles and fuels	94.9	92.8
Various products	1.4	1.3

Source: INSEE

The main import sources in 2009 were France €352 million, EU countries excl. France (€99 million), of which Germany (€24 million), Guadeloupe (€65 million), Martinique (€64 million), Caribbean (€78 million), and US (€17 million).

Principal export markets in 2009 were France (€49.5 million), EU excl. France (€22.7 million), of which Germany (€9.7 million), Guadeloupe (€6.1 million), Martinque (€7.6 million), Caribbean (€2.2 million), US €3.7 million. (Source: INSEE)

Chambers of Commerce and Trade Organisations
French Guiana Chamber of Commerce and Industry, URL: http://www.guyane.cci.fr

MANUFACTURING, MINING AND SERVICES

Primary and Extractive Industries
Although French Guiana once experienced a gold rush similar to the California gold rush of 1849, panning activity steadily decreased until 1965, when it ceased completely. There are about 40 mines of which only one is an industrial mine. There are five small companies and around 50 small enterprises employing a total of 300 people. A mining inventory has established the existence of several sites containing gold deposits with a potential yield of several tons. French Guiana's other natural resources are bauxite, kaolin, silica, zinc, diamonds, silver, lead, manganese, copper and platinum.

French Guiana imports all of its oil requirements. In 2011 a total of 8,000 barrels per day of oil were imported and consumed. (Source: EIA)

Energy
Electricité de France produces and distributes French Guiana's electrical energy. In 2009 electrical generation was 0.79 billion kWh and consumption was 0.74 billion kWh in 2009. Installed capacity GWe was 0.14 billion kWh. (Source: EIA)

Manufacturing
There are over estimated 200 plant/factories making consumer goods, 400 making capital goods, 840 making intermediate goods. There are an estimated 1,300 construction plants. Mechanical equipment is a major industry.

Service Industries
The hotel attendance of the département is estimated at 30,000 tourists a year. Activity in the space sector plays a key role in the tourism industry and so this sector suffered a decline in 2003. Hotel occupation was an estimated 48 per cent in 2010, down -6 per cent on the year.

Agriculture
Although the land is fertile, local production accounts for a mere 10 per cent of consumption - most food is imported to the EU, Latin America, the US, Canada and Japan. The recent extension of the land area devoted to agriculture (23,478 ha in 2005) has boosted agriculture and export oriented products such as rice and sugar cane.

Use of agricultural area (hectares)

Land use	2000	2004	2005
Agricultural area	23,195	22,769	23,478
Arable land, of which:	13,005	12,525	13,224
-Cereal	4,600	4,635	5,066
-Vegetable cultivation	6,165	6,369	6,428
incl. -roots & tubers	5,545	5,744	..
-fresh vegetables	620	625	..
Industrial cultivation	480	388	410
-sugar cane	240	146	161
Semi-permanent fruit cultivation	540	548	565
-bananas	345	352	355
Fallow	870	235	..
Permanent fruit cultivation	3,180	3,232	3,244
Floral cultivation	35	38	40
Various vegetable cultivation	35	35	30
Permanent grassland	6,940	6,940	6,940

Source: INSEE

Production remains poor compared to potential but several food processors are settling in French Guiana, mainly to produce rum (2,753 hectolitres in 1998) and fruit juice. The level of production is good, with a livestock of 16,500 head of cattle and 9,500 pigs. French Guiana is now self sufficient in its requirements of pigs, poultry, vegetables and fruit.

Agricultural Production in 2010

Produce	Int. $'000*	Tonnes
Cassava	2,998	28,700
Rice, paddy	2,298	8,500
Tomatoes	1,478	4,000
Fruit, tropical fresh nes	1,430	3,500
Bananas	1,070	3,800
Vegetables fresh nes	1,055	5,600
Pineapples	998	3,500
Indigenous cattle meat	783	290
Cabbages and other brassicas	733	4,900
Indigenous chicken meat	684	480
Plantains	647	3,300
Indigenous pigmeat	630	410

* unofficial figures

Source: http://faostat.fao.org/site/339/default.aspx Food and Agriculture Organization of the United Nations, Food and Agricultural commodities production

In 2003, there were 9,702 heads of cattle (of which 3,816 were cows), 6,928 pigs, 1,547 sheep,1,604 goats, 827 horses and 486 poultry.

Meat production (tonnes)

Animal	2003	2004
Cattle	252	247
Veal	26	12
Pork	1,037	882
Sheep	14	9
Goat	2	2
Poultry	411	436
Rabbit	25	25
Other production		
Cow's milk (hl)	1,200	1,140
Eggs (1000s)	5,566	7,023

Source: INSEE

Forestry

Due to its immense size (7.5 million hectares in 2002, corresponding to 94 per cent of the département's surface area), the French Guianese forest is difficult to develop. Infrastructures such as ports and routes remain insufficient, and the local workpower is both scarce and expensive. However, French Guiana's development plan aspires to stimulate greater forest cultivation by improving the infrastructure of the roads and tracks as well as by planning new harbours. Public authorities have supported this economic sector since 1966, favouring the installation of high efficiency companies. These companies conduct 70 to 80 per cent of the forestry activities of logging and wood processing, of soft, hard or inlaid wood (amarante, wacapou, courbaril, amourette, rosewood).

Fishing

Fishing is one of the region's leading activities, since French Guiana has a vast continental shelf with extensive stocks of shrimp and fish. Industrial and prawn fishing are undertaken by the Guianese company Pêcheries Internationales de Guyane (PIDEG) of Larivot near Cayenne, by the Compagnie Française de Pêche (CFP) and by the Société Armement et Mareyage de Guyane (ARMAG). Local fishing, an activity that is yet to be modernised, nevertheless contributes to the Guianese, Antillan and metropolitan French markets. An extensive program of aquaculture, notably for fresh-water shrimp, is currently being developed. Kourou's experimental station, which in 1987 had 2.1 hectares of basin area, has been operating since 1986. In 2010, 4,000 tonnes were landed in 2010, (compared to 3,100 in 2002). In 2005, there were 99 registered fishermen.

COMMUNICATIONS AND TRANSPORT

Travel Requirements

A passport valid for at least three months after departure is required by US, Australian and Canadian nationals. They do not require a visa for stays of up to three months, unless they receive a salary during their stay. US citizens need a visa if they are crew members, journalists on assignment or students enrolled at schools and universities in any of the French Overseas Departments. EU nationals holding a valid national ID card do not require a passport or a visa, unless receiving a salary. Other nationals should contact the French embassy to check visa requirements.

International Airports

French Guiana is linked by air to metropolitan France, the United States, South America and the French Antilles. The main airport is Cayenne Rochambeau. Passenger traffic (arrivals, departures and transit) was estimated to be 400,555 in 2009, up from 385,142 in 2008. The main airline companies are Air Guyane (URL: http://www.airguyane.com/), Air France, PENTA and Surinam Airways. Air freight fell by over 20 per cent in 2003. Over €4 million was invested in the airports in 2003.

Roads

There are almost 1,820 km of roads, 725 km of which are paved. Bus routes connect French Guiana with Brazil and Suriname.

Waterways

Inland waterways are the most common means of accessing the interior of the country, especially in Maroni. Almost 400 pirogues are registered for the waterways between Saint-Laurent and Maripasoula.

Shipping

The main shipping companies are CGM, Marfret and Chargeurs Réunis. The shipping sector is also unstable. In 2003, 252 ships entered Guiana's ports compared to 420 in 2002 and 366 in 2001. In 2006 there were 540,362 tonnes of freight (down 1.1 per cent on 2005).

Ports and Harbours

There are ports and harbours at Degrad des Cannes, Cayenne, and Saint-Laurent du Maroni.

HEALTH

French Guiana has a modern hospital in Cayenne and another one in Saint-Laurent du Maroni. There is also a medical centre at the space centre in Kourou. Each of French Guiana's townships has its own community dispensary. A centre for tropical medicine run by the Pasteur Institute is located in Cayenne. Since its opening in 1940, this centre has done much to improve health conditions in the département, conducting research in tropical diseases, spraying to kill mosquitoes and mounting a large-scale vaccination campaign against smallpox. Cayenne also has several private clinics. Nurses are trained locally.

Health care officials have developed a modern system of patient transportation using, in addition to ambulances, planes and helicopters to cope with the lack of roadways to many parts of the interior.

Metropolitan legislation applies to social programs concerning health insurance, workmen's compensation, retirement benefits and social security. Various other options regarding social allocations, offered notably by an important collective action undertaken by the Funds for Health and Social projects (FASSO), are available. As in the rest of France, social aid (for example, medical aid for families and the elderly) has been decentralised.

In 2010, per 100,000 inhabitants there were 41 general practitioners, 23 specialists, 20 dentists, 97 nurses, 27 physiotherapists and 45 pharmaceutical personnel. In 2011, in public hospitals there were 471 short stay beds. In the private sector there were 260 short stay beds and 44 rehabilitation places. There were 84 psychiatric places and 215 maternity beds.

There were 441 registered deaths in 2006. Of these 141 were attributed to injury or poisoning, 128 to diseases relating to circulation, 85 to cancer, and 27 to AIDS. (Source: INSEE)

EDUCATION

French Guiana's educational services are administered by the Antilles-Guiana Directorate of Education set up in September 1974 at Fort-de-France in Martinique. Schools follow the same calendar as in metropolitan France. Education is compulsory and free, there are currently 41 infant schools and 106 primary and specialised schools. There are 128 public colleges and 9 secondary schools. Higher education covers law, economics, literature and technical subjects in the form of the French baccalauréat, in which there is a 63.68 per cent pass rate. The Kourou Institute of Superior Education has 269 students, whilst the Technical Institute in Kourou has 48. Vocational facilities exist for the building-trade, agriculture, mechanics, electricity and electronics.

In 2008 there were an estimated 4,742 teachers (all levels) in the public sector and 270 in the private sector.

RELIGION

The majority of the population belong to the Catholic Church. Hinduism is also practised.

COMMUNICATIONS AND MEDIA

Newspapers
Most metropolitan French newspapers can be found in French Guiana. In addition, there are several local newspapers.
Journal France-Guyane, URL: http://www.franceguyane.fr/

Broadcasting
RFO (Radio France Outremer) has two television channels, one with regional programmes, the other with the French public channel Antenne 2. RFO also has a radio frequency, with productions proposed and taken from the programmes of France Inter. Commercial and pay TV are also available.
RFO, URL: http://guyane.rfo.fr/
Canal+ Guyane, URL: http://www.canalguyane.com/
Radio Caraibes International, URL: http://www.rci.fm/
Tele Guyane, URL: http://www.franceguyane.fr/

Telecommunications
According to recent figures there are nearly 50,000 telephone lines in use. In 2000 there were approximately 2,000 internet users and two ISPs.

ENVIRONMENT

In 2009, French Guiana's emissions from the consumption of fossil fuels totalled 1.12 million metric tons of carbon dioxide. (Source: EIA)

SPACE PROGRAMME

The Space Centre was created in 1964, and in 1968 France's National Centre for Space Studies (CNES) moved its rocket launching operations from the Algerian Sahara to French Guiana. Currently, it is used primarily by the European Space Agency (ESA) for its Ariane program. The site chosen, near Kourou, is close to the equator. Rockets launched there are able to carry a payload 17 per cent heavier than rockets launched from Cape Canaveral because of the slightly weaker gravitational pull. Since the site opens eastward to the Atlantic Ocean, rockets also have the advantage of being launched in the direction of the natural rotation of the earth. Therefore, in the event of a mislaunch, there is the 'safety net' of more than 2,400 miles of ocean. The complex is composed of the launching site and a town of 3,500 inhabitants, built on the mouth of the River Kourou. The growth of the space centre has a direct bearing on the centre itself as well as indirect consequences on every aspect of Guiana's economy.

A satellite receiving station (SEAS) was officially opened in February 2012; its aim is to increase the understanding and monitoring of the Amazon and Caribbean environments. A launch for Russian-built Soyuz rockets has also been built. The first Soyuz launch took place in 2011.

Two telecommunications satellites were launched in September 2012. The satellites will provide telecommnications services to the eastern hemisphere. Both satellites will have a lifespan of 15 years.

CNES, URL: http://www.cnes.fr/

GUADELOUPE AND ITS ISLANDS

French Overseas Department

Capital: Basse-Terre (Population estimate, 2011: 50,000)

Head of State: François Hollande (President) (page 1443)

CONSTITUTION AND GOVERNMENT

Constitution

Previously a colony, Guadeloupe changed its status to that of a French Overseas Territory on 19 March 1946, thus becoming an integral part of the French Republic. The administrative structure is the same as any *département* of metropolitan France: it is administered by a Prefect in Basse-Terre appointed by the Government.

Guadeloupe has a 42-member General Council as well as a 41-member Regional Council. All are elected by universal suffrage for terms of six years. There are also two consultative chambers: the Regional Social and Economic Council and the Culture, Education and Environment Council. The council system was introduced in 1974 when Guadeloupe was granted the additional status of a Region, as with the other Overseas Departments. In February 2006 a Regional Council for Young People was set up and people aged 16-21 could vote or present themselves as candidates for the Council. The Regional Council for Young People is presided over by the president of the Regional Council or his representative. Decisions made by the Regional Council for Young People must be ratified by the permanent commission of the Regional Council.

Since the Decentralization Law of March 1982, the executive power of the government-appointed Prefect has been transferred to the locally-elected General Council. Guadeloupe has the following representatives in metropolitan France: four deputies in the National Assembly and two Senators in the Senate, as well as a representative at the Economic and Social Council. As a French département, Guadeloupe belongs to the European Community and thus has representatives at the European Parliament in Strasbourg. However, in order to adapt Community law to its specific conditions and its economic development, Guadeloupe is entitled to specific measures.

Recent Events

In 2003 the people of Saint Barthélemy and Saint Martin voted to secede from Guadeloupe. This was passed by the French legislature in 2007. Their new status is that of French overseas collectivities.

Administration (as at June 2013)
Prefect: Marcelle Pierrot (page 1495)
Deputy Prefect, Secretary General: Charles Brenard
President of the General Council: Dr Jacques Gillot
President of the Regional Council: Josette Borel-Lincertin
Deputy to the French National Assembly: Éric Jalton
Deputy to the French National Assembly: Gabrielle Louis-Carabin
Deputy to the French National Assembly: Ary Chalus
Deputy to the French National Assembly: Hélène Vainqueur-Christophe
Representative in the French Senate: Jacques Gillot
Representative in the French Senate: Félix Desplan
Representative in the French Senate: Jacques Cornano

French Overseas Economic and Social Council (Outre-Mer du Conseil Economique et Social)
Representative for Guadeloupe: Eustase Janky

Ministries

Prefecture, Palais d'Orléans, rue Lardenoy, 97109 Basse-Terre, Guadeloupe. Tel: +590 99 39 00, fax: +590 81 58 32, URL: http://www.guadeloupe.pref.gouv.fr/
General Council, bd Félix-Eboué, Petit Paris, 97109 Basse-Terre Cedex, Guadeloupe. Tel: +590 99 77 77, fax: +590 99 76 00, e-mail: info@cg971.com, URL: http://www.cg971.com
Regional Council, rue Paul Lacavé, 97109 Basse-Terre. Tel: +590 80 40 40, fax: +590 81 34 19, URL: http://www.cr-guadeloupe.fr

Elections

The most recent Regional Council elections were held on March 14 2010 when the incumbent Victorin Lurel (PS-PPDG) was re-elected in the first round of voting. The UMP came in second. The most recent General Council elections took place on 27 March 2011.

LEGAL SYSTEM

The laws of France, where applicable, apply. Justice is administered by a Court of Appeal (*Cour d'Appel*), an Assize Court and a Court of First Instance at Basse-Terre and a Court of First Instance at Pointe-à-Pitre.

AREA AND POPULATION

Area

Guadeloupe is the largest island of the French Antilles with a total area of 1,780 sq. km. It is composed of two main islands: Basse-Terre and Grande-Terre (linked by a bridge) and five other islands which are dependencies: Marie-Galante, les Saintes, la Désirade, la Petite-Terre Islands and Tintamarre. Two other islands (Saint-Martin (French part) and Saint-Bartélemy)

seceded from Guadeloupe in 2007. NB Figures cited in this profile include these two islands. The terrain of Basse-Terre is rough volcanic relief; Grande Terre is composed of flat plains and rolling hills. Guadeloupe is subject to hurricanes.

To view a map of Guadeloupe, please consult
http://www.lib.utexas.edu/maps/cia06/guadeloupe_sm_2006.gif

Population

According to the 2004 Census the population at 1 January 2004 was 443,000, an increase of 1.0 per cent from 1999. In 2009 the population was estimated to be 404,000, with an annual average increase of 0.5 per cent. The population is expected to reach 548,000 by 2030. The population density is estimated to be 248.7 per km².

An estimated 35.8 per cent of the population is aged less than 25 years and 12.1 per cent of the population is over 60. Ninety per cent of Guadeloupe's population is black, 5 per cent white, and less than 5 per cent East Indian, Lebanese, or Chinese. The official language of Guadeloupe is French, although Creole patois is also spoken.

Births, Marriages, Deaths

According to 2007 estimates, the birth rate is 16 per 1,000 population, whilst the death rate is 6 per 1,000. In 2006 there were an estimated 7,193 births and 2,800 deaths. The total fertility rate in 2007 was 2.3 children per female. The fertility rate is 1.9 children born per woman. Average life expectancy at birth in 2007 was 79.7 years (76.2 years for males and 83.2 years for females). The infant mortality rate is 6.9 per cent (deaths of infants / total live births). The population is an ageing population. As of 2007, there were reported to be approximately 163,500 single people aged 15 years or older, 112,150 were married, 16,532 were widows/widowers, and 17, 316 were divorced. In 2008 the marriage rate was reported to be 3.3. per cent (number of marriages / total population). In 2008 there were 989 divorces.

EMPLOYMENT

The total number of employed in 2005 was just over 115,000. In 2006 the total number of unemployed people was 43,980 of whom nearly 50 per cent had been unemployed for over a year. The unemployment rate fell from just under 30 per cent in 1999 to nearly 26 per cent in 2000. It rose again to 26.9 per cent in 2003 (24.6 per cent males, 29.4 per cent females). In 2Q 2009 the rate had fallen to 23.5 per cent. 45 per cent of people under 30 are unemployed, and 55 per cent of people under 25.

Electricité de France (EDF) remains the island's largest employer. Sixty-two per cent of the estimated 12,000 enterprises on the island are shops. French labour laws apply in Guadeloupe but the minimum salary differs because of the economic environment.

Paid Employment by sector

Sector	2008 (provisional)
Agriculture	1,741
Extractive industries	171
Manufacturing	5,896
Utilities	1,635
Construction	4,826
Commerce; Vehicle repairs	11,482
Transports	4,909
Lodging and catering	3,521
Information and communication	1,823
Financial and insurance	2,720
Property	576
Specialised activity, scientific and technical	2,183
Administrative and upkeep services	7,053
Public administration	21,526
Teaching	10,783
Health and social services	14,186
Other	1,520

Source: INSEE

BANKING AND FINANCE

Currency

One euro (€) = 100 cents
€ = 6.55957 francs (European Central Bank irrevocable conversion rate)
On 1 January 1999 the euro was launched as an electronic currency across the 12 member states of the EU. On 1 January 2002 the euro became legal tender in France and the 11 other member states of the EU. France's old currency, the franc, ceased to be legal tender from midnight on 17 February 2002.

GDP/GNP, Inflation, National Debt

Guadeloupe's economy is based largely on the agriculture industry, with contributions from tourism, light industry and services. GDP is beginning to move back towards the highs of 2009. GDP fell to €7,683 million in 2010, recovering to €7,910 million in 2011. In 2009 GDP was €8,160 million compared to €8,375 million in 2008. Per capita GDP was €18,170 in 2008 compared to €18,680 in 2009. In 2007, GDP breakdown by sector was as follows: agriculture

€241 million, agricultural industries €99 million, manufacturing €254 million, energy €43 million, construction €678 milllion, trade €986 million, transport €486 million, services €4,976 million.

Inflation has risen in recent years, by 3 per cent in 2001 and 2002, and by 1.6 per cent in 2003. Food went up by 4.6 per cent in 2003 and tobacco by 20.7. Manufactured products fell by 1.7 per cent, energy by 2.6 per cent. Services rose by 2.3 per cent. National debt stands at approximately €1,800 million.

Balance of Payments / Imports and Exports

Guadeloupe's main export products are fresh bananas, wheat flour, sugar and rum. Agricultural exports represent 30 per cent of exports, agribusiness 30 per cent (sugar 60 per cent, rum 20 per cent), equipment 25 per cent, and consumer goods 5 per cent. Major export trading partners are France (60 per cent of exports), Guyane and Martinique. In 2008, 444,570 tonnes of bananas were exported and 41,246 hectolitres of alcohol.

Guadeloupe imports foodstuffs and industrial and energy products, vehicles, clothing, and construction materials. Major import and export trading partners are France (€1,160 million, 72.6 per cent), EU excluding France (€259 million, 16.7 per cent) of which Germany (€74 million, 1.8 per cent), US (€141 million, 3.9 per cent), Martinique (€99 million), Caribbean (€117 million), and Guyana (€6 million).

Export revenue, according to 2011 estimates, was €889 million, up from €798 million in 2010. Import costs were an estimated €2,664 million, up from €2,554 million in 2010. (Source: INSEE)

Chambers of Commerce and Trade Organisations

Pointe-a-Pitre Chamber of Commerce and Industry, URL: http://www.cci-pap.org/
Basse-Terre Chamber of Commerce and Industry, URL: http://www.basse-terre.cci.fr

MANUFACTURING, MINING AND SERVICES

Primary and Extractive Industries

Guadeloupe has no significant minerals and has to import its oil requirements. In 2011, a total of 17 thousand barrels per day of oil were imported and consumed. Guadeloupe does not consume natural gas or coal.

Energy

Total electricity capacity in 2009 was 0.41 billion kWh. Electricity generation was 1.64 billion kWh, with consumption at 1.52 billion kWh. Total primary production was 0.001 quadrillion Btu and consumption was 0.037 quadrillion Btu. (Source: EIA)

Manufacturing

The industry sector contributes about 17 per cent towards Guadeloupe's GDP and employs nearly 8 per cent of the workforce, according to 1997 figures. The manufacturing sector is mainly composed of small and medium enterprises. Agrobusiness is the largest and accounts for some 52 per cent of total employment in this sector. Consumer-oriented industries account for the rest of the sector, with the building industry providing 11 per cent and printing 7 per cent of jobs. Main industries are sugar refining, rum distilling, cement and brick manufacture and mineral water bottling. There is an industrial free-port at Jarry which has tax and import duty exemptions to encourage businnesses.

Service Industries

About 87,550 people are employed in the service industries, accounting for nearly 82 per cent of the island's workforce (65 per cent in 1980), enabling the level of employment to remain stable.

Tourism

This has been the main activity since the mid 1970s. The sector has developed rapidly although it was affected by the world events of 2001. It is the only source of income for Saint-Martin and Saint-Barthelemy islands. In 2001 2.1 million passengers passed through the Guadeloupe Pôle Caraïbes, dropping to 1.75 million in 2003. Port passengers (including cruises) fell from 1.3 million in 2000 to 1 million in 2003. The northern islands focus on luxury tourism and that sector has grown: 130,000 tourists in 2003 compared to 105 in 2000-01.
Office of Tourism, URL: http://www.antilles-info-tourisme.com/guadeloupe/
St-Martin Tourist Office, URL: http://www.st-martin.org/

Agriculture

This sector employs just 3.6 per cent of the working population, contributes 15 per cent towards GDP and 90 per cent towards the island's exports. Agricultural land covers 43,709 hectares, of which arable land covers 22,443 hectares. Sugar production covers 12,300 hectares and employs over 4,200 people. Approximately 7.5 million quintals were produced in 2010. Approximately 79,500 quintals of melon are produced of which 66 per cent are exported. The banana industry has been affected adversely by the phasing out of EU preferential quotas.

Agricultural Production in 2010

Produce	Int. $'000*	Tonnes
Sugar cane	28,568	870,000
Bananas	18,165	68,000
Indegenous cattle meat	7,834	2,900
Vegetables fresh nes	3,957	21,000
Indigenous pigmeat	2,306	1,500
Pineapples	2,195	7,700
Indigenous chicken meat	1,994	1,400
Hen eggs, in shell	1,659	2,000
Lettuce and chicory	1,590	3,400
Tomatoes	1,440	3,900

- continued		
Plantains	1,321	6,400
Other melons (inc. cantaloupes)	1,289	7,000

* unofficial figures
Source: http://faostat.fao.org/site/339/default.aspx Food and Agriculture Organization of the United Nations, Food and Agricultural commodities production

In 2003 livestock head figures were 54,940 cattle (of which cows 21,369), 24,675 pigs (of which sows 5,946), sheep 1,689 (ewes 737), goats 34,216 (females 14,445), 124 horses and 489,313 poultry.

There are two types of rum: agricultural rum obtained by the distillation of fermented sugar juice, and agricultural rum prepared from molasses and light rum. In 1998 output of agricultural rum was 19,019 hectolitres of pure alcohol, making 29,048 hectolitres of sugar juice and 14,612 hectolitres of light rum.

Fishing activity remains undeveloped because of a lack of maritime resources in the area. It meets only 75 per cent of the local requirements. In 2005 there were a total of 871 registered boats (10 large scale), and 1109 registered fishermen. On the other hand, aquaculture, which has been aided during recent years, offers interesting prospects. Estimated figures for 2010 put the total catch at 10,000 tonnes.

In 2004, 70,000 hectares of Guadeloupe were wooded.

COMMUNICATIONS AND TRANSPORT

Travel Requirements

US, Canadian and Australian citizens require a passport valid for at least three months beyond applicant's last day of stay, but do not require a visa for tourism purposes, for up to three months. EU nationals do not require a passport if they carry a national identity card, and do not normally require a visa for tourism purposes. US nationals need a visa if they are crew members, or journalists on assignments, or students enrolled at schools and universities in any of the French Overseas Departments.

Other nationals should contact the embassy to check visa requirements.

International Airports

Guadeloupe is linked by air to Metropolitan France, the United States and South America. The largest airfield is in Pointe-a-Pitre (Aéroport Pôle Caraïbe) which handled over 2 million passengers in 2011. There are secondary airfields in Saint-Barthelemy (170,000 passengers), Marie-Galante, Les Saintes and St Martin Grand Case (176,000 domestic passengers). Both Pointe-a-Pitre and Saint-Barthelemy handle international flights.

The main airline company is Air France (697,600 passengers). CorsAir transported 412,800 passengers. Air Antilles Express and Air Caraï are the main regional airlines. 10,400 tonnes of freight passed through the airport in 2011.

Roads

Guadeloupe has over 2,080 km of roads, 1,750 km of which are paved. The number of registered new vehicles (private and commercial) was 17,300 in 2005. Car ferries run between the islands.

Ports and Harbours

Ports and harbours exist at Basse-Terre, Gustavia (Saint Barthelemy), Marigot, and Pointe-a-Pitre. In 2006 3,136,676 tonnes of maritime goods (gross) were transported through the ports (up 5 per cent from 2005). Imports represent almost 80 per cent of the traffic. Ferries run between the islands and connect with Martinique, Dominica and Saint Lucia.

HEALTH

There are eight general hospitals, six maternity units, a psychiatric hospital and a sanatorium. In addition, community clinics serve the main communes. Numerous clinics operate in the private sector. Sanitary conditions are good, but aid from metropolitan France is important.

According to 2011 figures there are 1,111 short-stay beds in the public sector, and about 592 in the private sector. In the same year there wree 204 re-hab (medium stay) beds in the public sector and 384 in the private sector. Thre are an estimated 224 public sector psychiatric beds and 50 within the private sector.

In 2010 there were 1066 doctors in total (584 general practitioners and 482 specialists) giving a density of 94 general doctors and 69 specialist doctors per 100,000 people. There were an estimated 81 pharmacists, 48 dentists, 87 phsyiotherapists, 254 nurses per 100,000 people.

The main causes of death in 2009 were diseases of the circulation (823) and tumours (669). There were 18 deaths caused by AIDS. (Source: INSEE)

EDUCATION

Education is compulsory from the ages of six to 16. Schools follow the same calendar and the same programmes as metropolitan France. The pass rate of the general French baccalauréat was 73.8 per cent in 2005. The University of the Antilles is located in Pointe-à-Pitre.

FRANCE

Numbers in education (2005-06)

Establishment	No of pupils
Public education	
Pre-elementary	20,108
Elementary	33,402
Special education	1,041
Middle school	27,493
Upper school general & technical	11,928
Upper school professional	7,757
Special education	1,379
Higher education	8,379
Private education	
Pre-elementary	2,022
Elementary	3,898
Special production	212
Middle school	2,953
Upper school general & technical	872
Upper school professional	1,342
Special education	0

Source: INSEE

RELIGION

Most of the population belongs to the Catholic Church, with about 5 per cent Hindu and about 1 per cent Protestant.

COMMUNICATIONS AND MEDIA

Newspapers
Most metropolitan French newspapers can be purchased in Guadeloupe. Guadeloupe itself publishes a local daily and many weeklies, often politically-oriented. France Antilles (URL: http://www.franceantilles.fr/ (owned by Groupe Hersant Média) is the regional daily.

Broadcasting
RFO (Radio France Outremer) has two television channels, one transmitting regional programmes, the other the French public channel Antenne 2. RFO has a radio frequency with productions proposed and taken from the programmes of France Inter. The local station, Radio Caraibes Internationale, broadcasts 24 hours a day. Private local radios are numerous and express the wealth of Guadeloupe's music and culture.
RFO Guadeloupe, URL: http://guadeloupe.rfo.fr/
Radio Caraibes, URL: http://www.rciguadeloupe.fm/

ENVIRONMENT

In 2010, Guadeloupe and its Islands' emissions from the consumption of fossil fuels totalled 2.10 million metric tons of carbon dioxide. (Source: EIA)

MARTINIQUE

French Overseas Department

Capital: Fort de France (Population, 2011: 90,500)

Head of State: François Hollande (President of France) (page 1443)

CONSTITUTION AND GOVERNMENT

Constitution
The status of Martinique, a large island in the West Indies, was changed from that of a colony to a French *département* on 19 March 1946, thus making it an integral part of the French Republic. The administrative structure is the same as in any *département* of metropolitan France. It is administrated by a Commissaire de la République in Fort-de-France, assisted by two under-prefects in Trinité and in Le Marin. They are appointed by the Government.

Martinique has a General Council of 45 members and a Regional Council of 41 members, all elected by universal suffrage for terms of six years. Like other Overseas Departments Martinique was granted the additional status of a Region in 1974. Since the Decentralization Law of March 1982, the executive power of the government-appointed Commissaire de la République has been transferred to the locally elected General Council. There are three District Councils, Fort-de-France, Trinité and Le Marin which in turn cover 34 communes. Martinique's representatives in metropolitan France are four Deputies in the National Assembly, two Senators in the Senate and one Counsellor in the Economic and Social Council. As a French *département*, Martinique belongs to the European Union and thus has representatives in the European Parliament in Strasbourg. However, in order to adapt Community law to its specific conditions and its economic development, Martinique is entitled to specific measures.

In January 2010, Martinique voted against plans for increased autonomy. There was a 55 per cent turnout in the referendum and 80 per cent voted against the plans.

Regional Council, 20 av des Caraibes, BP 679, 97262 Fort-de-France, Martinique. Tel: +596 55 26 00, fax: +596 75 59 32, URL: http://www.cr-martinique.fr/
General Council, URL: http://www.cg972.fr/

Administration (as at June 2013)
Prefect: Laurent Prévost
Deputy Prefect, Marin: Patrick Naudin
Deputy Prefect, Trinité and Acting Deputy Prefect, Saint-Pierre: Jean Almazan
President of the General Council: Josette Manin
President of the Regional Council: Serge Letchimy
Deputy to the French National Assembly: Bruno Nestor Azerot
Deputy to the French National Assembly: Alfred Marie-Jeanne
Deputy to the French National Assembly: Serge Letchimy
Deputy to the French National Assembly: Jean-Philippe Nilor
Senator in the French Senate: Serge Larcher
Senator in the French Senate: Maurice Antiste

Ministries
Government portal, URL: http://www.martinique.pref.gouv.fr/
Préfecture, 82 rue Victor-Sévere, 97262 Fort-de-France, Martinique. Tel: +596 39 36 00, fax: +596 71 40 29, URL: http://www.martinique.pref.gouv.fr/
Sous-Préfecture, Quartier Mondésir, 97290 Le Marin, Martinique. Tel: +596 74 92 90, fax: +596 74 95 26
Sous-Préfecture, Rue Lagrosillière, 97220 Trinité, Martinique. Tel: +596 58 21 13, fax: +596 58 31 40

Sous-Préfecture, Rue Domaines, 97250 Saint-Pierre, Martinique. Tel: +596 78 29 50, fax: +596 78 29 48
Department for Agriculture and Forests, Jardin Desclieux, 97200 Fort-de-France: Tel: +596 71 20 40, URL: http://daaf972.agriculture.gouv.fr
Department for the Environment, Pointe de Haham, BP 7212, 97233 Schoelcher Cedex. Tel:+596 59 5700, URL: http://www.martinique.developpement-durable.gouv.fr / http://www.martinique.ecologie.gouv.fr
Department for Enterprise, Competition, Consumers, Work and Employment (DIECCTE), Pointe de Sables, 97200 Fort-de-France. URL: http://martinique.dieccte.gouv.fr
Department of Youth, Sport and Social Cohesion, URL: http://www.drjscs.gouv.fr
Department of Culture, 54 Rue du Prof Raymond Garcin, 97200 Fort-de-France. Tel: +596 600536
Department of Health, URL: http://www.martinique.sante.gouv.fr

Elections
The most recent Regional Council elections took place in March 2010. The political group Ensemble pour une Martinique Nouvelle led by Serge Letchimy gained 26 seats (63 per cent of the vote), the grouping Patriotes et Sympathisants led by Daniel Marie Sainte gained 12 seats (29 per cent of the vote), and Rassembler la Martinique led by André Lesueur took 3 seats (7 per cent of the vote).

The most recent elections for the General Council took place in 2012.

LEGAL SYSTEM

The French legal system applies. Justice is administered by a Court of Appeal, a Court of Assize, a Commercial Court and a Court of First Instance. These are located at Fort-de-France. There are five Justices of the Peace in the principal communities of the island.
Justice portal, URL: http://www.cdad-martinique.justice.fr/juridiction1.php

AREA AND POPULATION

Area
Martinique, situated in the Windward Islands group of the West Indies, is the smallest French Overseas Department (*Départment d'Outre Mer*). It has a total area of 1,100 km. sq. The climate is tropical, tempered by sea breezes and trade winds. The average annual temperature is 25 degrees Centigrade. Intermittent rain is experienced in September and October.

To view a map of Martinique, please consult
http://www.lib.utexas.edu/maps/cia06/martinique_sm_2006.gif

Population
The 2004 census put the population at 393,000, a growth rate of 0.62 per cent for the period 1999-2003. By 1 January 2007 it was estimated at 403,000, an annual growth of 0.67 per cent. The population density is approximately 357 inhabitants per sq. km. As of 2007, the majority of the population (57.5 per cent) was aged between 20 and 64 years, with 28.6 per cent aged 19 years or under, and 14 per cent aged 65 or over. Forty-seven per cent of the population was male. The population was estimated at 395,953 in 2010.

The main towns are Fort-de-France (94,050 inhabitants), Le Lamentin (35,450) and Schoelcher (20,850). The varied ethnic population contains Caribbeans, Lebanese and Indians. The official language is French, although a Creole dialect is also spoken.

Births, Marriages, Deaths
Estimates for 2009 put the birth rate at 13.1 per 1,000 population, with 4,888 registered births in 2009. In 2010, there were 2,843 registered deaths and the death rate at 7.0 per 1,000 population in 2009. Average life expectancy at birth is 81 years, according to 2009 estimates (77.9 years for men and 84.3 years for women). The infant mortality rate was an estimated 8.3 deaths per 1,000 live births in 2010. In 2009 there were 1,357 registered marriages, 163 civil pacts and 563 divorces. (Source: INSEE)

EMPLOYMENT

French labour laws apply in Martinique but the regulations on minimum income vary. The unemployment rate is high: it was estimated at 22.0 per cent in 2Q 2009 (down from 25.2 per cent in 2006). In mid-2006 there were 42,155 job-seekers (down from 38,179 in 2004). An estimated 48 per cent of those aged under 30 were unemployed. The rate among women is 27.3 per cent. In 2003 the employed workforce was estimated to be 122,621. In January 2004 there were estimated to be 27,607 business enterprises in operation.

Paid Employment by Economic Activity

Occupation	2008
Agriculture, forestry & fishing	4,113
Extractive industries	157
Manufacturing industries	7,158
Utilities	1,957
Construction	7,962
Wholesale & retail trade, repairs	15,349
Hotels & restaurants	4,398
Transport, storage & communications	5,676
Financial intermediation	3,139
Real estate	837
Research	4,158
Administrative services	7,918
Public admin.	21,925
Education	11,367
Health & social work	16,905
Arts and recreations	1,318
Other community, social & personal service activities	4,407
Households with employed persons	5,255

Source: Copyright © International Labour Organization (ILO Dept. of Statistics, http://laborsta.ilo.org)

BANKING AND FINANCE

Currency
The currency of Martinique is the euro, which, on 1 January 2002, replaced the French Franc.
€ = 6.55957 French francs (European Central Bank irrevocable conversion rate)
1 euro (€) = 100 cents

GDP/GNP, Inflation, National Debt
GDP (at purchasing power parity) was €7,702 million in 2009 (compared to €5,496 million in 2000). GDP per capita (at purchasing power parity) fell from €20,070 in 2008 to €19,160 in 2009. The breakdown of GDP contributions per sector in 2007 was as follows: agriculture €159 million, food industry €112 million, manufacturing €274 million, energy €218 million, construction €462 million, trade €831 million, transport €396, services €5,039 million. (Source: INSEE)

Balance of Payments / Imports and Exports
In 2006, export revenue was an estimated €489.1 million (up 29.5 per cent from 2005). Martinique exports mainly refined petroleum products (60 per cent of exports), bananas (14 per cent), rum (9 per cent), and pineapples. Agricultural exports are in decline. Major export destinations by region as of 2006 are Guadeloupe and Guyana (€179 million, 36.7 per cent), the EU (€116 million, 23.7 per cent), North America (€83 million, 17.0 per cent), the Caribbean (€78 million, 15.9 per cent) and Africa (€29 million, 5.9 per cent). The most significant export countries are Guadeloupe (€161 million, 32.9 per cent) and France (€107 million, 21.8 per cent). Almost 100 per cent of banana exports go to France and over 40 per cent of rum. Exports amounted to €701 million in 2011, down from €727 million in 2010.

Main import commodities are crude oil, petroleum products, food, construction materials, clothing, and vehicles. Major import trading partners by region are the EU (€2,105 million, 84.1 per cent), Asia (€120 million, 4.8 per cent), the Caribbean (56 million, 2.2 per cent), Guadeloupe and Guyana (€55 million, 2.2 per cent), Central and South America (€52 million, 2.1 per cent) and North America (€50 million, 2.0 per cent). Of these, significant individual supplier countries are France (€1,393 million, 55.6 per cent) and the UK (€382 million, 15.2 per cent). In 2006 estimated import costs were €2,5 million (up 8.9 per cent from 2005) of which consumer goods were €991 million. The UK provides over 60 per cent of energy imports. Imports amounted to €2,925 million in 2011, up from €2,652 million in 2010. The increase was mainly driven by rising oil costs. (Source: INSEE)

Chambers of Commerce and Trade Organisations
Martinique Chamber of Commerce and Industry, URL: http://www.martinique.cci.fr

MANUFACTURING, MINING AND SERVICES

Primary and Extractive Industries
Martinique produces none of its own oil but has a refinery capacity of 17,000 barrels per day in 2011. Imports in the same year were 18.08 thousand barrels per day. Total oil consumption in 2011 was 18 thousand barrels per day.

Energy
Total installed capacity (GWe) in 2010 was 0.4 billion kEh. Electricity generation in the same year was 1.6 billion kWh, whilst consumption was 1.49 billion kWh. (Source: EIA)

Manufacturing
The industrial sector is mainly composed of small and medium companies in the building and public works sectors, agrobusiness and the chemical industry. Two companies are of an industrial size: Electricité de France and the Société Anonyme de Raffinage des Antilles (created in 1962 to refine and distribute petroleum products to Martinique and Guadeloupe) with a throughput capacity of 550,000 tonnes per year. There are also establishments producing cement, rum, dairy produce, a fruit canning plant, a mineral water bottling plant and a polyethylene plant. Martinique has five established industrial zones which offer tax and duty exemptions in the hope of promoting the area.

Service Industries
A work force of some 7,000 people are employed in numerous branches such as building, mechanics and electricity. Tourism has been a sector that has shown rapid growth during recent years. This expansion has resulted in a large investment effort from Martinique companies. Business tourism is in expansion due to international meetings to promote its growth. It currently accounts for approximately 8 per cent of tourism. An estimated 450,000 tourists visited Martinique in 2009. Tourist receipts were an estimated €242.5 million.

Tourist Board, URL: http://www.touristmartinique.com/

The tertiary sector represents 75 per cent of employment, almost half of it is in the non-merchant public sector. The main activities are import and export, wholesale and retail trade (90 per cent of the tertiary sector companies), banks, tourism and transport.

Agriculture
The main products are bananas, pineapples, sugar and rum, although production of all is in decline. Harvests were hit by poor weather in 2006.

In 2006 the total area planted with bananas declined from 7,350 ha in 2005 to 6,980 in 2006. Exports of bananas were down 5 per cent. The banana trade has also been affected by changes in international banana export rules, although the full impact is not yet known. The price also reduced sharply in 2006 from €432.70 per tonne in 2005 to €264.80 in 2006. Total banana exports were 216,827 net tonnes in 2006.

The sugar cane crop was the worst for 24 years, falling 23 per cent from 2005 to 165,100 tonnes. Such a drop will impact on other industries. The crop overs 3,800 hectares. There is one sugar factory, le Galion, which extracts sugar from cane for the domestic market (82,600 tonnes in 2006). Around 14 cane distilleries produced 80,754 HAP (hl of pure alcohol) in 2006. Some 4,400 tonnes of sugar were also produced.

Martinique is the only Overseas Department to produce tinned pineapple for export. Ranking fourth in terms of exports, pineapple is cultivated to be consumed both fresh, in juice, or tinned. Production is concentrated in the north of the island. The area planted declined by 25 per cent in 2006 to 176 ha (compared to 235 in 2005). In 2006 only 2,700 tonnes were produced of which 1,270 tonnes were lost or too poor to be used. A new trade group has been set up to try to rescue the industry. The sector of market gardening and flowers represents 32 per cent of agricultural output. In 2006 the melon sector covered 220 ha. and produced 3,380 tonnes.

In 2006 1,245 tonnes of beef were produced, 895 tonnes of pork, 874 tonnes of poultry and 67 tonnes of goat/ovine meat were produced. Martinique has to import meat.

Fishing is carried out locally along the coasts. With around 5,000 tonnes of fish caught each year, Martinique still has to import about 63 per cent of its annual consumption. Aquaculture is recording good growth figures.

Agricultural Production in 2010

Produce	Int. $'000*	Tonnes
Bananas	45,906	192,000
Sugar cane	7,336	223,393
Indigenous cattle meat	3,241	1,200
Lettuce and chicory	3,226	6,900
Plantains	2,829	13,700
Vegetables fresh nes	2,393	12,700
Hen eggs, in shell	2,239	2,700
Tomatoes	1,996	5,400
Indigenous chicken meat	1,709	1,200
Indigenous pigmeat	1,476	960
Cucumbers and gherkins	1,122	5,650
Other melons (inc. cantaloupes)	957	5,200

* unofficial figures
Source: http://faostat.fao.org/site/339/default.aspx Food and Agriculture Organization of the United Nations, Food and Agricultural commodities production

The total number of fishing boats was estimated at 1,071 in 2010.

COMMUNICATIONS AND TRANSPORT

Travel Requirements
Citizens of the USA, Canada and Australia require a passport valid for three months beyond the length of stay, whilst EU citizens need a passport valid for the duration of the stay. A visa is required by Australians, but not required by USA and Canadian subjects for tourism

FRANCE

stays of up to three months; if the purpose of their visit is other than tourism, they should contact the embassy for further information. EU subjects do not require a visa. Visitors, except French subjects, must carry sufficient funds or a lodging certificate.

Other nationals should contact the embassy to check visa requirements.

International Airports
Martinique is linked by air to metropolitan France, the United States, South America and Canada. There is an international airport in Lamentin, 8 km from Fort-de-France (URL: http://www.martinique.aeroport.fr/). It changed its name in 2007 to the Martinique Aimé Césaire International Airport. The main airlines are Air France, Minerve, Aeromaritime, Air Martinique, Air Guadeloupe and Corse Air International. In 2010 there were 20,993 commercial aircraft movements flights. In 2006, there were 1.636 million passengers (up 1.2 per cent from 2005) and approximately 13,500 tons of freight (up 3.8 per cent from 2005) passed through Martinique.

Roads
In 2010, there were estimated to be 7km of highways and a general road network of 290 km. In 2010, 15,250 new cars were registered. A tramway project is underway.

Shipping
The main shipping companies are CGM, Chargeurs Réunis, and Marfret. In 2004 an estimated 2.073 million tons of goods were unloaded and 851,000 tons loaded.

Ferries run between Martinique and her neighbouring islands, the main ferry companies are Express des Iles and Brudey Frères.

HEALTH

According to 2007 statistics there were 548 general doctors (84 per 100,000 inhabitants compared to 111 per 100,000 in France) and 465 specialist doctors (a density of 46 per 100,000 inhabitants compared to 86 per 100,000 in France). In 2007 there were 37 dentists per 100,000 population (compared to 61 per 100,000 in metropolitan France), 212 nurses per 100,000 population (compared to 112 in metropolitan France), and 66 physiotherapists per 100,000 population (compared to 81 in metropolitan France). The total number of short-term hospital beds was 1,455, of which 1,397 were public and 258 were private. In addition there were 561 medium stay beds (public sector 395, private 134 and day beds 31). There were 153 maternity beds. There are a further 290 beds in psychiatric wards. There are 11 general hospitals, five maternity units, a psychiatric hospital and a sanitarium. In addition, community clinics serve the main communes. Numerous clinics operate in the private sector, of which five are maternity units. The training of midwives and nurses takes place locally in public professional schools. French legislation applies to all social services.

The main causes of death in Martinique are circulatory diseases and cancer. (Source: INSEE)

In 2008, an estimated 98 per cent of households had indoor sanitation, 60 per cent had hot water and 98 per cent had electricity.

EDUCATION

Education is compulsory from the age of six to 16. According to figures for 2009-10 there were 262 pre-primary and primary schools. Recent figures show that there were 49,920 pupils in pre-primary schools. According to the 2009-10 figures there were 79 secondary education schools. Secondary education covers 43,287 pupils and there is a vocational secondary school for agriculture, fishery and the hotel business. In 2006, 5,727 students were registered for the baccalauréat, with a pass rate of 70 per cent. In 2009, there were 5,323 students registered at university. The University of Antilles-Guyane covers Martinique and Guadeloupe. In Martinique, the Schoelcher campus counted 2,600 students of literature, human sciences, law and economics. Teachers are trained locally in vocational schools. There were 6,861 public teaching professionals registered in 2010 of which women accounted for 67.9 per cent. There were also 613 private teachers.

RELIGION

Some 95 per cent of Martinique's population is Roman Catholic, whilst 5 per cent is pagan, African and Hindu.

COMMUNICATIONS AND MEDIA

Newspapers
Most metropolitan French newspapers can be found. There is one regional daily and a few weekly papers.

Broadcasting
RFO, the national radio and TV broadcasting company for overseas territories, broadcasts on two television channels. One is allocated to RFO and transmits programmes from metropolitan French channels, the other is reserved for the metropolitan channel Antenne 2, transmitting by satellite. RFO radio programmes, broadcasting on FM and medium waves, cover local programmes and productions taken from France Inter. Since their establishment, private local radios have expanded. Radio Caraibes Internationale, created in 1960, broadcasts local news and programmes taken from Europe 1.
Radio France Outremer, URL: http://www.rfo.fr
Radio Caraibes Internationale, URL: http://rci.fm/
Antilles TV, private, URL: http://www.antillestelevision.com/

ENVIRONMENT

Martinique has rich and varied flora and fauna. There are thought to be some 1,000 indigenous species on Martinique, of which 400 are only found on the Antilles and 30 only on Martinique. Threats to the flora and fauna include colonisation from non-native species and urbanisation which threatens especially Martinique's mangroves. Martinique's two nature reserves are La Caravelle and the Ilets of Saint-Anne. Several research organisations are active including the Volcanic Observatory of the Montagne Pelée, the Institute for Research and Development (IRD), IFREMER, CIRAD and INRA.

In 2010, according to the EIA, Martinique's emissions from the consumption of fossil fuels totalled 2.77 million metric tons of carbon dioxide. In 2010, 295 days were reported to have had excellent or good air quality, 24 of average and 46 days of poor air quality.

MAYOTTE
French Overseas Department

Capital: Dzaoudzi (Population estimate, 2007: 15,500)

Head of State: François Hollande (President of France) (page 1443)

CONSTITUTION AND GOVERNMENT

Mayotte became the responsibility of France in 1843. It voted to keep its link with France in a referendum in 1974, unlike the rest of the islands in the Comoros archipelago. Mayotte changed its status to that of a *Collectivité Territoriale* in 1976. In 2001 Mayotte changed its status to that of a *Collectivité Départementale*.

In March 2009, Mayotte held a referendum on changing its status to overseas department in 2011. The population voted overwhelmingly in favour. Its status was officially changed on 31 March 2011.

Mayotte consists of 17 communes and is administered by a representative of the French Government. Each commune is administrated by a municipal council presided over by a mayor who is elected by universal suffrage. Decisions of the municipal council are subject to approval by the Government representative.

The General Council, consisting of 19 councillors, is elected directly every three years by the island's population. Its decisions are implemented by the Government representative, who nominates a Council of Ministers and is assisted by a General Secretary. The Council of Ministers is the executive body of the *collectivité* and is responsible for national interests, administrative control and law and order. It also ensures that the decisions made by the General Council are implemented. Mayotte sends three representatives to France: a Deputy to the National Assembly and two Senators to the Senate.

Administration (as at June 2013)
Prefect: Jacques Witkowski (page 1538)
Vice-Prefect and Secretary General: François Chauvin
Vice-Prefect, Director of the Cabinet: Jean-Pierre Frederic Debons
Secretary General for Economic and Regional Affairs: Philippe Laycuras
Deputy Prefect with responsibility for Youth and Social Cohesion: Sylvie Especier
President of General Council: Daniel Zaidani
Deputy to the French National Assembly: Ibrahim Aboubacar
Deputy to the French National Assembly: Boinali Said
Senator in the French Senate: Thani Mohamed Soilihi
Senator in the French Senate: Abdourahamane Soilhi

Ministries
Government portal, URL: http://www.mayotte.pref.gouv.fr/
Prefecture, BP 20, 97610 Dzaoudzi, Mayotte. Tel: +262 60 10 54, fax: +262 61 95 15, URL: http://www.mayotte.pref.gouv.fr/
General Council, 8 rue de l'Hôpital, 97600 Mamoudzou, Mayotte. Tel: +262 61 12 33, fax: +262 61 95 15, URL: http://www.cg976.fr/

Elections
The most recent elections for the General Council were held in March 2011.

LEGAL SYSTEM

The laws of France apply. Mayotte has a Court of First Instance, a Superior Court of Appeal and an Administrative Court. Between 1989 and 1998, Parliament authorised an appeal procedure in Mayotte, with amendments to laws on justice, the environment, health, town planning, employment code insurance amongst others.

AREA AND POPULATION

Area
The island of Mayotte is situated in the Indian Ocean just north of the Mozambique Canal. It is the southern-most of the four islands which make up the Comores archipelago. Its total area is 375 sq. km. This *collectivité territoriale* is situated 8,000 km. from mainland France and consists of two main islands *Grande Terre* and *Petite Terre*, and about thirty islets. Mayotte's terrain is largely undulating, although ravines and volcanic mountains exist in some areas. The climate is hot and humid, with a rainy season from November to May, and a dry season from May to November.

To view a map of Mayotte, please consult
http://www.lib.utexas.edu/maps/cia08/mayotte_sm_2008.gif

Population
The population of Mayotte was 160,025, according to 2002 estimates, with a population density of 351 people per sq. km. It was estimated to have risen to over 225,000 by 2010. The population growth rate was an estimated 3.2 per cent in 2009. Nearly half of the population are under the age of 14, with just over half the population aged between 15 and 64. The population consists mainly of Arabs, Anatolians, and Africans.

Principal towns (approximate 2002 populations) are Mamoutzou, with a population of 45,485, Koungou (15,400), Dzaoudzi (12,300), Dembini (7,800), Tsingoni (7,700), Pamanzi (7,500) and Bandraboua (7,500). The majority of the population lives in villages along the coast. Most government administration takes place at Dzaoudzi whilst economic activity centres around Mamoutzou.

Births, Marriages, Deaths
There were more than 37,250 births registered in Mayotte in 2006, compared to 27,900 in 2002. The average age of the mother was 26.2 years (compared to 29.4 for metropolitan France). Almost 70 per cent of mothers who gave birth were not from Mayotte; almost 63 per cent were from the Comores. Mayotte's birth rate was 38.7 births per 1,000 people, according to 2004 estimates. The average fertility rate was 4.7 children per woman. In 2009, there were 1,357 marriages registered.

In 2006, 4,150 deaths were registered, compared to 2,555 in 2002. The mortality rate was 3 per cent. Infant mortality was 71.3 deaths per 1,000 live births.

Estimated life expectancy in 2010 was 61 years for men and 66 years for women.

EMPLOYMENT

In 2007 the total workforce was 37,910, of which males 24,157 and females 13,753. By sector, education, health, social services, 19 per cent; public administration, 17 per cent; small business, 15 per cent; transport, 13 per cent; trade, 12 per cent; agriculture/fishing 8 per cent; construction, 8 per cent; industry, 5 per cent; hotels & restaurants, 2 per cent.

The unemployment rate fell to 27 per cent in 2007 (women, 35.9 per cent, men 19.7 per cent). Youth unemployment is high at 41.5 per cent. (Source: INSEE)

In 2005, 20 per cent of the population lived on the poverty line, compared to 25 per cent in 1995. In 2005, one person out of 10 lived on less then €838 per annum. One person in ten had an income of €8,142 per annum. The average income was €3,728 per annum.

BANKING AND FINANCE

Currency
One euro (€) = 100 cents
€ = 6.55957 francs (European Central Bank irrevocable conversion rate)
On 1 January 1999 the euro was launched as an electronic currency across the 12 member states of the EU. On 1 January 2002 the euro became legal tender in France and the 11 other member states of the EU. France's old currency, the franc, ceased to be legal tender from midnight on 17 February 2002.

GDP/GNP, Inflation, National Debt
Mayotte's economy is based mainly on agriculture. It is heavily dependent on financial assistance from France. GDP (purchasing power parity) was an estimated €950 million in 2005. Per capita GDP (purchasing power parity) was an estimated €4,900 in 2005. GDP was estimated to be US$3.8 billion in 2007.

Industry contributions to the economy, break down thus:

Portrait of eight large sectors

Sector	No. of enterprises	Turnover 2005 million €	Value added million €
Agriculture	7	3.1	0.9
Industry, energy	65	141.6	38.1
Construction	99	105.5	37.0
Commerce	192	400.3	61.5

- continued			
Transport	39	52.2	19.4
Finance	12	20.9	17.8
Business, construction	90	101.4	46.4
Health, education, social	51	26.3	14.7

Source: INSEE

Inflation was estimated at 1.27 per cent in Mayotte in 2011 and 1.7 per cent over 2010.

Balance of Payments / Imports and Exports
Major export commodities are ylang-ylang, copra, vanilla, coffee, coconuts, and cinnamon. Major import commodities are food, machinery and equipment, metals, chemicals, and transport equipment. Mayotte's main trading partners are France, Comoros, and Africa. Exports in 2004 were an estimated €3.9 million, of which vanilla was €0.1 million, and ylang-ylang €0.2 million. Imports in the same year were an estimated €206.4 million, of which foodstuffs were €47.3 million, transport material was €35.1 million, machines and electrical equipment was €34.1 million and chemical products were €17.5 million. Source: INSEE

MANUFACTURING, MINING AND SERVICES

Primary and Extractive Industries
Mayotte has no mineral or energy resources, and the island's economy is almost entirely based on agriculture.

Energy
In 2005, electricity consumption was 139,161 (compared to 122,609 million kWh in 2004). There were 29,968 registered users. Source: Electricité de Mayotte.

Service Industries
Building and public works is an important sector, employing 15.3 per cent of the active population. More recently efforts have been made to develop the tourist sector, but not much progress has been made to date, mainly because of a lack of infrastructure. In 2006 there were 31,100 tourist visitor, down from 38,800 in 2005. Like Réunion, the tourist industry suffered because of the chikungunya epidemic. However, although there were fewer visitors, tourist receipts were up to €16.3 million. Over half of Mayotte's tourists come from France, with 40 per cent arriving from Reunion. Business tourism is a growth market.

The main countries of destination for commercial goods are France and the other Comoros Islands.

Agriculture
The soils are volcanic in origin, well watered and therefore very fertile. Forest covers 20,000 ha and the cultivatable area is estimated at 24,000 hectares. Currently, only about 11,000 ha is cultivated, but this is nearly twice as much as was in use in 1988. Most are smallholdings of under 1 hectare. Exports consist mainly of ylang-ylang, used for making essential oils and perfume (accounting for three-quarters of all exports), vanilla and cinnamon. Other products include coffee, bananas, cassava and coconuts.

Agricultural products used for domestic consumption are rice and animal products.

Fishing is primarily aimed at the local market. Its economic and export potential remains undeveloped.

COMMUNICATIONS AND TRANSPORT

International Airports
Mayotte's airport is located at Dzaoudzi-Pamandzi. Réunion Air-Service and Air Comores operate on routes to Réunion and Grande-Comore. Kenya Airways opperates flights from Nairobi to Mayotte. In 2004 there were 166,128 air passengers and 3,575 aircraft movements. In the same year 1,143 tonnes of commercial freight were transported. The most recent figures for military freight date from 2000 when 307 tonnes were transported.

Roads
Mayotte has almost 95 km of roads, 70 km of which are surfaced. One household in five has a car.

Shipping
Merchandise brought onto the island in 2004 totalled 260,263 tonnes, whilst over 70,000 tonnes left the island by ship. In the same year there were 34,283 passenger journeys. Source: INSEE

HEALTH

There are two hospitals on the island. In 1997 there were 57 doctors (4 per 10,000 of the population), 131 nurses, 62 midwives, 186 hospital beds, two pharmacists and four dental surgeons. There was a total of 45,199 days of hospitalisation in 1997.

An estimated 22 per cent of homes had neither water or electricity in 2002.

EDUCATION

In 2003 there were 9,966 pupils registered in nursery school, 29,195 in primary school, 12,289 at college and 4,219 at lycées. Almost 1,800 were registered on training places. In 2001, almost 50 per cent of children leaving school left without qualifications. An academic action plan was adopted in February 2003 in an attempt to improve the situation.

FRANCE

RELIGION

The main religion in Mayotte is Islam, and is practised by about 99 per cent of the population.

Mayotte has a religious liberty rating of 1 on a scale of 1 to 10 (10 is most freedom). (Source: World Religion Database)

COMMUNICATIONS AND MEDIA

Broadcasting

Radio France Outremer (RFO) (URL: http://mayotte. rfo.fr/) in Mayotte has broadcast since 1986.

Telecommunications

Mayotte has an automatic telephone network for local calls and a semi-automatic network for international calls. As of 2008, an estimated 10,000 landlines were in use and 48,000 mobile phones.

REUNION ISLAND
French Overseas Department
La Réunion

Capital: Saint Denis (Population estimate: 131,600)

Head of State: François Hollande (President of France) (page 1443)

CONSTITUTION AND GOVERNMENT

Constitution

The status of Réunion was changed from that of a colony to a Department of France on 19 March 1946, and Réunion thus became an integral part of the French Republic. The administrative structure is the same as in any *département* of metropolitan France: it is administered by a Prefect in Saint-Denis, assisted by three government-appointed under-Prefects in Saint-Pierre, Saint-Paul and Saint-Benoît.

Réunion has a General Council of 49 members, as well as a Regional Council of 45 members, all elected by universal suffrage for terms of up to six years. This system came into effect in 1974 when Réunion was granted the additional status of a region. Since the Decentralization Law of March 1982, the executive power of the government-appointed Prefect has been transferred to the locally elected General Council.

There are four District Councils which in turn cover 24 communes. Réunion's representatives in metropolitan France are five Deputies in the National Assembly, three Senators in the Senate and one Councillor in the Economic and Social Council. As a French *département*, Réunion belongs to the European Union and thus has representatives in the European Parliament in Strasbourg. Moreover, in order to adapt Community Law to its specific conditions and its economic development, Réunion is entitled to specific measures.

Administration (as at June 2013)
Prefect: Jean-Luc Marx
President of the General Council: Nassimah Dindar
President of the Regional Council: Didier Robert
Deputy in the French National Assembly: Ericka Bareigts
Deputy in the French National Assembly: Huguette Bello
Deputy in the French National Assembly: Jean-Claude Fruteau
Deputy in the French National Assembly: Patrick Lebreton
Deputy in the French National Assembly: Monique Orphé
Deputy in the French National Assembly: Thierry Robert
Deputy in the French National Assembly: Jean Jacques Vlody
Senator in the French Senate: Jacqueline Farreyrol
Senator in the French Senate: Michel Fontaine
Senator in the French Senate: Paul Vergès
Senator in the French Senate: Michel Vergoz

Ministries

Préfecture, Avenue Victoire, 97405 St-Denis, Réunion. Tel: +262 40 77 77, fax: +262 41 73 74, URL: http://www.reunion.pref.gouv.fr
Sous-Préfecture, 7 avenue François Mitterrand, 97470 St-Benoit, Réunion. Tel: +262 50 77 10, fax: +262 50 34 88
Sous-Préfecture, Rue Evariste de Parny, 97460 St-Paul, Réunion. Tel: +262 45 38 45, fax: +262 45 53 41
Sous-Préfecture, Rue Augustin Archambaud, 97410 St-Pierre, Réunion. Tel: +262 35 71 00, fax: +262 25 97 83
Regional Council, Avenue René Cassin, Le Moufia, 97494 Sainte-Clotilde, Réunion. Tel: +262 48 70 00, fax: +262 48 70 71, URL: http://www.regionreunion.com
General Council: http://www.cg974.fr
Department of Agriculture and Forestry, Parc de la Providence, 97489 Saint-Denis Cedex. Tel: +262 48 61 00, fax: +262 48 61 99
Department of Cultural Affairs, 18 rue Rontaunay, 97400 Saint-Denis, BP 224, Réunion. Tel: +262 21 91 71, fax: +262 41 61 93
Department of Health and Social Affairs, 28 bis, avenue Georges Brassens, BP 199, 97400 Saint-Denis, Réunion. Tel: +262 48 60 60, fax: +262 48 60 08
Department of Labour, Employment and Professional Training, 112 rue de la République, 97488 Saint Denis Cedex, Réunion. Tel: +262 94 46 46, fax: +262 94 46 33

Political Parties

Front National (FN); Mouvement des Radicaux de Gauche (MRG); Mouvement pour l'Indepenance de la Réunion (MIR); Parti Communiste Réunionnais (PCR); Parti Socialiste (PS) - Féderation de la Réunion; Rassemblement des Socialistes et des Démocrates (RSD); Rassemblement pour la République (RPR); Union pour la Démocratie Français (UDF).

Elections

In the most recent regional elections in 2010, Didier Robert's Presidential Majority took 27 seats, the Communist Party of Réunion led by Paul Vergès took 12 seats and the Parti Socialist 6 seats.

The most recent General Council election took place in 2011 when the Socialist coalition retained power with an increased majority.

LEGAL SYSTEM

French law applies. Réunion's court system is headed by the Court of Appeals (*Cour d'Appel*).

The prison population was estimated to be 1,194 in 2009 (of which women accounted for 32). (Source: INSEE)

LOCAL GOVERNMENT

For administrative purposes, Réunion is divided into four District Councils which are themselves subdivided into 24 communes.

AREA AND POPULATION

Located in the Indian ocean off the coast of southern Africa, east of Madagascar, Réunion has a total area of 2,512 km sq. Réunion's terrain is mountainous, with lowlands along the coast. Its climate is tropical, with a dry season from May to November, and a wet season from November to May.

To view a map of Réunion, please consult http://www.lib.utexas.edu/maps/cia06/reunion_sm_2006.gif

Population

According to the 2004 census the population was 763,000, an annual increase of 1.63 per cent for the period 1999-2003. The population was estimated at 784,000 in 2006 and 805,500 in 2008. The population is expected to continue to increase with a projected population of over 1 million by the year 2030.The majority of the population (62) are aged between 15 and 64, with 32 per cent aged under 15 years and nearly 6 per cent aged over 65. The main towns are Saint-Denis (1999: 131,557 inhabitants), Saint-Paul (87,712), Saint-Pierre (68,915) and Le Tampon (60,323). French is the official language, although a local dialect of Creole is also spoken.

Since the colonisation of the island by the Companie des Indes in the 17th century, the composition of Réunion's population has undergone great changes with population groups coming from Europe, Africa, Asia and Madagascar. It is estimated that 130,000 inhabitants are descendants of the former settlers from Europe. One fifth of the actual population consists of Malabars, descendants of workers from the sugar plantations in the 19th century. The rest of the population is composed of Chinese, Indians and half-castes from different ethnic groups.

Births, Marriages, Deaths

According to 2008 estimates the birth rate is 18.5 per 1,000 of the population, whilst the death rate is 5 per cent (deaths/total population). In 2008 there were 14,927 births (up from the 2002 figure of 14,261). The average fertility rate per women was 2.5 children in 2008.

There were 3,149 marriages and 634 civil partnerships registered on Réunion in 2008. There were more than 1,350 divorces in 2008.

In 2008 there were an estimated 4,115 deaths (down from 4,255 in 2005). Average life expectancy at birth in 2007 was 74.6 years for men and 81.8 years for women. The infant mortality rate was 8 per cent (deaths of infants/total live births).

EMPLOYMENT

The active population numbered 323,200 in 2006 (180,969 males and 142,231 females). The unemployment rate was 27.2 per cent in 2Q 2009 compared to 24.5 in 2Q 2008. Approximately 77,500 were looking for work.

According to 2008 estimates, the majority (187,978, 76 per cent) of Réunion's population are employed in the services sector, 7.8 per cent (19,479) in construction with 6.7 per cent (16,599) in industry, and 1 per cent (2,679) in agriculture. (Source: INSEE)

Metropolitan French laws apply in Réunion but the regulations on minimum income vary.

Estimated Paid Employment by Economic Activity

Occupation	2007
Agriculture, hunting, forestry & fishing	3,300
Manufacturing	12,600
Electricity, gas & water supply	1,800
Construction	18,700
Wholesale & retail trade, repairs	17,100
Hotels & restaurants	5,100
Transport, storage & communications	10,900
Financial intermediation	4,000
Real estate, renting & business activities	18,800
Public admin. & defence; compulsory social security	41,900
Education	23,500
Health & social work	18,300
Other community, social & personal service activities	9,500
Households with employed persons	11,270

Source: Copyright © International Labour Organization (ILO Dept. of Statistics, http://laborsta.ilo.org)

BANKING AND FINANCE

Currency
The currency of Réunion is the euro, which replaced the French Franc on 1 January 2002. (Due to its position in the Indian Ocean, Réunion was the first country to begin using the euro.)
One euro (€) = 100 cents
€ = 6.55957 francs (European Central Bank irrevocable conversion rate)

GDP/GNP, Inflation, National Debt
Réunion's economy is largely based on agriculture, with sugarcane the primary crop. The economy also relies heavily on investment from France. GDP in 2008 was €14.70 thousand million with an estimated growth rate of 3.7 per cent. It was estimated to be €14.416 million in 2009. The economy was particularly strong in 2005 with a growth rate of 4.9 per cent. The main sectors are services (administrative) 37.0 per cent, consumer services 46.9 per cent, industry 7.3 per cent, construction 6.5 per cent and agriculture including fishing, 2.3 per cent. Tourism receipts were down almost 30 per cent in 2006.

GDP per capita was €18,220 in 2008, falling to €17,520 in 2009.

Inflation was an estimated 2.9 per cent in 2008, compared to 2.6 per cent in 2006.

Balance of Payments / Imports and Exports
Major export commodities include sugar, rum, fish and crustaceans, fruits perfume essences. Major import commodities include food, beverages, tobacco, machinery and transport equipment, and petroleum products. Réunion's main trading partner is France.

Main trading partners, 2009, €million

Imports	Value €m	Exports	Value €m
Metropolitan France	2,262	Metro. France	108.9
EU excl. France	499	Indian Ocean Isles	50.6
- of which, Germany	130	-Mayotte	25.3
USA	306	-Madagascar	16.2
Singapore	293	-Mauritius	7.2
China	234	EU excl. France	36.2
South Africa	115	Hong Kong	9
Indian Ocean islands	51	India	7.9
		USA	7.3

Source: INSEE

Imports cost €3,86 thousand million in 2008, an increase of 6.0 per cent from the previous year. In 2009 they were estimated at €4,176 million. Exports amounted to €260 million in 2008, a decrease of 6.9 per cent from 2007. They fell to an estimated €251 million in 2009. (Source: INSEE)

Chambers of Commerce and Trade Organisations
Reunion Chamber of Commerce and Industry, URL: http://www.reunion.cci.fr

MANUFACTURING, MINING AND SERVICES

Energy
Réunion has no fossil fuels of its own and relies entirely on imports. In 2006 it imported 1,231,450 tonnes of coal and fuel (486,837 tonnes and 744,613 tonnes respectively). Fuel consumption in the same year was also 595,110 tonnes (excluding electricity).

Total electricity capacity in 1998 was 305,000 kilowatts. Electrical generation in 2006 was 2,365 GWh, an increase of 4.1 per cent from 2005. Hydrolectric energy makes up 25 per cent. In 2006, energy by production broke down thus: Oil/Gaz 525 Gwh, coal 983 Gwh, bagasse 273 Gwh, hydro 576 Gwh, thermal and wind power 5.7 Gwh. By the end of 2006, 75,00 solar-powered water heaters had been installed.

Manufacturing
Industry as a whole employs about 20 per cent of the workforce. In 1988 the total workforce in industry was 6,683. The manufacturing sector is mainly composed of small and medium enterprises in the textile, tobacco, wood, printing, chemicals, food and works sectors. Electric energy, produced by Eléctricité De France, sugar factories, distilleries, building companies and public works enterprises are among larger companies.

Service Industries
This sector has developed during the last few years and now numbers a workforce of 14,000 people in many branches such as the food industry, building and textiles. The tertiary sector accounts for 73 per cent of the working population, and, through distribution and commerce, is important to the local economy. About 81,076 people are currently employed in commerce and services. In recent years tourism has become an expanding sector but there was a sharp decline in the number of visitors in 2006 (278,800 compared to 410,000 tourists in 2005). The decline was due to an epidemic. That figure represents the lowest total of visitors since 1995. Most visitors are from France. Other main nationalities include German, Swiss and Italians.
Comité de Tourisme: URL: http://www.la-reunion-tourisme.com

Agriculture
Réunion's agriculture industry employs about 8 per cent of the workforce. Sugar cane is the main product and is grown on 26,000 hectares of land. In 2005 sugar cane production represented over 39 per cent of the total value of agricultural production. In that year sugar production amounted to 1,864,300 tonnes, an increase of 3.5 per cent from 2005. Sugar factories and distilleries process the sugar cane crop into sugar or rum. Other traditional crops are vanilla, perfume oils and tobacco.

Use of agricultural area (hectares)

Land use	2004	2005
Land area of Reunion	252,000	252,000
Land used for agriculture	49,922	47,286
Cereals	757	850
Fresh vegetables	1,322	1,310
Dried vegetables and pulses	133	135
Market gardens and orchards	3,095	3,095
Fruit cultivation	2,201	2,006
Fodder cultivation	1,000	1,505
Semi-permanent fruit	596	872
Vines and floral cultivation	167	171
Permanent grassland	9,300	9,300
Fallow	750	826
Sugar cane	26,403	25,988

Source: INSEE

Agricultural Production in 2010

Produce	Int. $'000*	Tonnes
Sugar cane	63,375	1,930,000
Indigenous chicken meat	23,930	16,800
Indigenous pigmeat	18,442	11,997
Cow milk, whole, fresh	9,299	29,800
Fruit fresh nes	5,703	17,200
Hen eggs, in shell	5,557	6,700
Indigenous duck meat	5,416	3,287
Pineapples	5,017	17,600
Indigenous cattle meat	4,593	1,700
Tomatoes	4,361	11,800
Indigenous rabbit meat	3,913	2,106
Fruit, tropical fresh nes	2,779	6,800

* unofficial figures
Source: http://faostat.fao.org/site/339/default.aspx Food and Agriculture Organization of the United Nations, Food and Agricultural commodities production

Fish is the fourth most important product exported (after sugar, rum and perfume oils). In 2010 an estimated 3,050 tonnes of fish were caught. Local fishing along the coastline is underdeveloped (there were only 344 fishermen in 1988) because of the lack of a continental shelf around the island. By contrast, open sea fishing (crayfish) and industrial fishing are active.

Forests covered 85,921 hectares in 2004, compared to 87,220 hectares in 2002 (approximately 30 per cent).

COMMUNICATIONS AND TRANSPORT

Travel Requirements
Citizens of the USA, Canada, Australia and the EU require a passport valid for three months beyond the length of stay (except EU citizens who carry a valid national identity card), but do not need a visa for holidays up to three months. Visas are required by people who are visiting for purposes other than tourism, and by Romanians. but do not need a visa for stays of up to 90 days. Other nationals should contact the embassy to check visa requirements.

FRANCE

International Airports
The principal airport on the island is St Denis Roland Garros (URL: www.reunion.aeroport.fr/), which handled 796,403 passenger arrivals and 790,102 passenger departures in 2004. The other major airport is Pierrefonds which handled 44,759 passenger arrivals and 49,887 passenger departures in 2004. In 2006 there were a total of 1,422,384 (arrivals and departures and transit). Some 20,700 tonnes of goods arrived by air and approximately 7,800 tonnes were sent out by air.

Roads
There are 2,780 km of roads, of which 2,180 are surfaced. New vehicle registrations numbered 29,805 in 2006. The total number of registered vehicles was 438,357 in 2007.

Shipping
Shipping links are maintained on a daily basis with Europe, Madagascar, South Africa, the Far East and Japan. In addition, there are two pleasure ports: Saint-Gilles-les-Bains and Saint-Pierre. The main shipping companies are Consortium and Capricorne.

Ports and Harbours
Ports and harbours exist at Le Port and Pointe des Galets. 716 ships entered the ports in 2006. Approximately 3.5 million tonnes of goods were disembarked and 469,00 tonnes of goods were shipped out.

HEALTH

There are nine hospitals with one psychiatric unit and nine maternity units. Eight clinics operate in the private sector, and community clinics serve each commune. Nurses and midwives are trained locally. French legislation applies to all social services.

In 2007, there were 1,388 short stay beds and 101 rehabilitation beds in the public sector. In the private sector there were 639 short stay beds and 159 rehabilitation beds. There were 260 public sector beds for psychiatric patients and 292 private sector beds. There were an estimated 284 maternity beds. According to 2008 figures, there were 1,203 general practitioners (105 per 100,000 population) and 993 specialists (54 per 100,000 population). There were an estimated 432 dentists (53 dentists per 100,000 population), 345 midwives (13 per 100,000 population), 4115 nurses (151 per 100,000 population), and 867 physiotherapists (100 per 100,000 population).

The main causes of death in 2007 were cancer (929out of 4,009 total deaths), circulatory diseases (1,139 deaths) and injury and poisoning (356 deaths). There were 6 AIDS-related deaths. (Source: INSEE)

EDUCATION

The curriculum is the same as in metropolitan France but holidays take place at different times. Secondary education takes the form of the French baccalauréat.

No. of pupils/students in education

Establishment	2002-03	2003-04
Primary	41,910	42,545
Elementary	69,466	68,830
Special education	1,680	1,429
Middle school	56,620	57,564
Upper school: professional	14,493	14,625
Upper school: general & technological	20,652	20,829
Private		
Pre-elementary	3,060	3,118
Elementary	5,806	5,867
Special education	0	39
Middle school	3,881	3,985
Upper school: professional	616	657
Upper school: general & technological	1,452	1,466

Source: INSEE

In the period 2001-02 there were 15,900 pupils in higher education, and in 2002-03, there were 16,552. In 2002 the pass rate for the general baccalauréat was 86.9 per cent (compared to 83.7 per cent in France as a whole), 78.9 per cent for the technological baccalauréat, 80.4 per cent for the technical agricultural baccalauréat and 80.2 per cent for the professional baccalauréat. In the period 2008-09 there were estimated to be 10,838 students registered at university in Reunion. In 2010 there were estimated to be 15,513 teaching professionals.

RELIGION

Just over 85 per cent of Réunion's population is Roman Catholic, with the balance of the population Muslims, Hindus, and Buddhists.

Réunion has a religious liberty rating of 10 on a scale of 1 to 10 (10 is most freedom). (Source: World Religion Database)

COMMUNICATIONS AND MEDIA

Newspapers
Most metropolitan French newspapers can be found. In addition, there are three regional dailies, numerous weeklies and a monthly magazine.
Le Journal de l'Ile, URL: http://www.clicanoo.re/

Broadcasting
RFO (RéseauFrance Outremer) - the national radio and television broadcasting for overseas - broadcasts on two television channels. Private television also exists. RFO radio programmes, broadcasting on FM and medium waves, cover local programmes as well as productions taken from France Inter.
RFO, URL: http://www.rfo.fr
Antenne Réunion, URL: http://www.antennereunion.fr/

NEW CALEDONIA AND DEPENDENCIES
French Territorial Collectivity
La Nouvelle-Calédonie

Capital: Nouméa (Population estimate, 2012: 96,000)

Head of State: François Hollande (President of France) (page 1443)

High Commissioner: Jean-Jacques Brot (page 1395)

CONSTITUTION AND GOVERNMENT

Constitution
In accordance with the terms of the Constitution of the Fourth Republic, New Caledonia became a French Territory in 1946. New Caledonia later ratified this choice in the referendum of 28 September 1958, where 98 per cent of New Caledonians chose to remain French, eventually leading to the adoption of the Constitution of the Fifth Republic. New Caledonia therefore remains an integral part of the French Republic and its inhabitants are French citizens in every respect. It was granted special status in 1988.

New Caledonia is administered by a High Commissioner, appointed by the French Government and resident in Nouméa, who is responsible for external relations, law and order, defence, finance and secondary education. He is advised by a Territorial Congress whose 54 members are also members of regional councils elected by universal suffrage and assisted by an Executive Council. The Executive Council is composed of the President and the Vice-President of the Territorial Congress and the Presidents and Vice-Presidents of the administrative regions of New Caledonia. Administratively, New Caledonia is divided into three provinces, each with their own Provincial Assembly: North Province, with the capital Koné; South Province, with the capital Noumea; and Loyalty Islands Province, with the capital Wé.

Members from the three provinces form the Territorial Congress, which is responsible for the territory's budget and fiscal affairs, infrastructure and primary education. The Territory is represented in the French Parliament by two Deputies and one Senator. In addition, it has a seat in the Economic and Social Council. Since 1983 the Territory has experienced political unrest and tension resulting from pressures - especially from many of the indigenous Melanesian/Kanak population - for independence from France against the desire of others to remain French. During a referendum conducted by the French Government on the Territory's future in September 1987, a majority of electors (57 per cent) expressed the wish to remain French, but it was boycotted by pro-independence political groups.

A further referendum on the future status of New Caledonia was due to take place in 1998, but this was postponed and is now expected to take place by 2014. France has been discussing with Kanaks, the island's natives who give the Front de Libération Nationale Kanak Socialiste (FLNKS) most of its support, and pro-France loyalists from Rassemblement pour la Calédonie dans la République (RPCR) on how the island's future can best be settled without necessarily resorting to a referendum. Until a referendum is held, the jurisdiction of the assembly and the executive of New Caledonia will be strengthened. By that time, the French state should only control matters such as justice, security, currency and foreign affairs.

Recent Events
Talks took place in Paris aimed at amending the 1999 election law which states that elections have to be held two weeks after a collapse of a government. The law change is aimed at the Caledonia Together Party which resigned from the coalition government three times within a month to try to precipitate fresh general elections. In response, the Congress has suspended any elections. The Caledonia Together party wants to chose a new flag for New Caledonia but the majority of Congress and the French government support the joint use of the Kanak flag and the French national flag. Following this period of instability, the number of ministers within the collegial government has been fixed at 11. The French overseas minister, Marie-Luce Penchard ruled out early general elections.

Legislature
Congress, URL: http://www.congres.nc/

Economic and Social Council, URL: http://www.ces.nc/

Administration (as at June 2013)
President of Cabinet with responsibility for Regional Co-operation, Foreign Relations, Customs, Agriculture, Livestock, Fishing and International Air Transport: Harold Martin
Vice-President with responsibility for Mining, Infrastructure, Domestic and Maritime Transport: Gilbert Tyuienon
Cabinet Member with responsibility for Finance, Fiscal Policy, the Budget, & Energy: Sonia Backes
Cabinet Member with responsibility for Civil Function: Frédéric de Greslan
Cabinet Member with responsibility for Economy, Foreign Trade & Sustainable Development: Anthony Lecren
Cabinet Member with responsibility for Youth & Sports & Social Dialogue: Jean-Claude Briault
Cabinet Member with responsibility for Citizenship, Culture & the Status of Women: Déwé Gorodey
Cabinet Member with responsibility for Health, Social Security, Solidarity, the Disabled and Professional Training: Sylvie Robineau
Cabinet Member with responsibility for Traffic and Road Safety: Philippe Dunoyer
Cabinet Member with responsibility for Labour & Employment: Georges Mandaque
Cabinet Member with responsibility for Primary Education, Teaching and Conservation of Natural Resources: Hélène Iekawe

Province Administration (as of June 2013)
President of South Province: Cynthia Ligeard
President of North Province: Paul Neaoutyne
President of the Island Province: Néko Hnepeune

Republic Administration (as of June 2013)
Deputy in the French National Assembly: Philippe Gomes
Deputy in the French National Assembly: Sonia Lagarde
Deputy in the Senate: Pierre Frogier (UMP)
Deputy in the French Senate: Hilarion Vendegou (UMP)

Economic and Social Council for Overseas Territories (as of June 2013)
Representative on the Economic and Social Council for Overseas Territories: Mme Marie-Claude Tjibaou

Ministries
Government portal, URL: http://www.gouv.nc/
Prefecture (High Commission of the Republic), 1 avenue Maréchal Foch, BP C05, 98844 Nouméa Cedex. Tel: +687 26 63 00, fax: +687 27 28 28, URL: http://www.etat.nc/
Presidency of the Government, Centre ville, 19 avenue Foch, BP M2, 98849 Nouméa Cedex. Tel: +687 24 65 65, fax: +687 24 65 50, URL: http://www.gouv.nc/
Secretary-General of New Caledonia, Immeuble administratif Jacques Iekawe, 18, avenue Paul Doumer, BP C5, 98844 Nouméa Cedex. Tel: +687 25 60 00, fax: +687 28 68 48, URL: http://www.gouv.nc

Political Parties
Alliance pour la Calédonie (APLC); Fédération des Comités de Coordination des Indépendantistes (FCCI); Front de Libération Nationale Kana Socialist (FLKNS); Front National (FN); Libération Kanak Socialiste (LKS); Parti de Libération Kanak (PALIKA); Rassemblement pour la Calédonie dans la République (RPCR); Union Nationale pour l'Independence (UNI).

Elections
The most recent general elections took place on 9 May 2009. The main loyalist parties gained 31 seats in the Congress and pro-independence parties gained 23 seats (up from18). Elections for the provincial assemblies take place every five years.

LEGAL SYSTEM

The law is based on French civil law; the 1988 Matignon Accords grant substantial autonomy to the islands.

There is a Court of Appeal at Nouméa, an Assize Court and a Court of First Instance, as well as Justices of the Peace.

LOCAL GOVERNMENT

Administratively, New Caledonia is divided into three provinces, each with their own Provincial Assembly: North Province, with the capital Koné; South Province, with the capital Noumea; and Loyalty Islands Province, with the capital Wé.
Loyalty Islands, URL: http://www.loyalty.nc/
North Province, URL: http://www.province-nord.nc/
South Province, URL: http://www.province-sud.nc/

AREA AND POPULATION

Area
New Caledonia, also known as Grande Terre, is the main island of the Territory, an island some 240 miles long by almost 40 miles wide, situated in the West Pacific 700 miles east of Queensland. The Territory also includes a number of groups of small islands, the chief of which being the Loyalty Islands. The whole Territory has an area of approximately 19,000 sq. km.

To view a map of New Caledonia, please consult

http://www.lib.utexas.edu/maps/cia08/new_caledonia_sm_2008.gif

Population
In 2006, the estimated population was 240,390 with a population growth rate of over 12 per cent. Population density is approximately 12.4 inhabitants per km^2. The majority of New Caledonia's inhabitants (65 per cent) are aged between 15 and 64, with just over 30 per cent aged up to 14 years. The population is made up of Melanesians, Europeans, Polynesians and Wallisians, as well as Indonesians and Vietnamese. Melanesians, the original population, live mainly on the East Coast of Grande Terre and on Loyalty Islands. The main towns are (population 2004): Nouméa (91,386); Mont Dore (24,195); Dumbea (18,602); and Paita (12,062). In 1996, almost 30 per cent of the people lived in one of 342 tribes. (Source: URL: http://www.isee.nc)

Births, Marriages, Deaths
According to 2006 estimates, the birth rate is 17.7 per 1,000 people. The death rate is 4.7 per 1,000 people. Infant mortality is an estimated 5.7 deaths per 1,000 live births. Fertility is an estimated 2.5 children born per woman. The average life expectancy is 75.2 years. In 2004, there were 895 marriages and 246 divorces. (Source: URL: http://www.isee.nc)

EMPLOYMENT

In 2007 the labour force was estimated at 102,500. The unemployment rate in 2006 was 16.3 per cent. Approximately 30 per cent of the population is employed in the public sector.

BANKING AND FINANCE

Currency
As an overseas département, New Caledonia is not legally part of the European Union and therefore its official currency remains the Franc Pacifique (CFP) of 100 cents. The Franc Pacifique is linked to the euro by a fixed rate of 1,000 CFP = 8.38 euro. One euro = 119.33 CFP.

GDP/GNP, Inflation, National Debt
New Caledonia's economy, heavily dependent on nickel, has suffered recently due to falling international demand. Tourism also provides a substantial contribution to the economy; however, New Caledonia is still reliant on France financially. GDP (purchasing power parity) was estimated at CFP728,500 million in 2008, compared to CFP 652,000 million in 2006. The real growth rate is estimated at 0.2 per cent. Per capita GDP was estimated at €2,953 in 2008.

The inflation rate was estimated at 0.9 per cent in 2004. It had risen to 1.4 per cent in 2006. Inflation was estimated to be 2.3 per cent in 2011.

National debt was nearly US$80 million according to 1998 estimates.

Balance of Payments / Imports and Exports
New Caledonia's main export trading partners are Japan, France, the US, and Taiwan. Major import trading partners are France, Australia, New Zealand, and Japan. Main export commodities include nickel ore, ferronickels, and fish. Major import commodities are machinery and equipment, food, and fuels. In 2011 export revenue was an estimated 146,000 million F.CFP. Imports cost 316,000 million F.CFP in the same year. (Source: http://www.insee.nc)

Chambers of Commerce and Trade Organisations
New Caledonia Chamber of Commerce and Industry, URL: http://www.cci.nc

MANUFACTURING, MINING AND SERVICES

Primary and Extractive Industries
New Caledonia has rich mineral deposits. Of these, the most important are: nickel (25 per cent of the world's reserves are in New Caledonia); chrome; and other minerals including iron, cobalt and zinc. In 2006 6.18 million tonnes of nickel were extracted (compared to almost 7 million tonnes in 2004).

Energy
In 2010, approximately 1.98 billion kWh of electricity was produced, of which 1.71 billion kWh were consumed. The 2010 installed capacity is 0.50 GWe. Total primary energy production was 0.005 quadrillion Btu in 2005, and consumption was 0.043 quadrillion Btu. In 2010, 15.00 thousand barrels of oil per day were consumed, all imported. An estimated 0.331 million short tons of coal were consumed, all imported. (Source: EIA)

Manufacturing
Smelting products, especially nickel, now account for an important part of New Caledonia's industrial activity, apart from tourism, services and agriculture.

Tourism
In 2010, there approximately 99,500 visitors, mainly from France and Japan.

Agriculture
In 2002, livestock figures were as follows: 111,308, 25,447 pigs, 8,130 goats, 2,297 ovines, 7,512 horses, 382,838 poultry, 1,971 beehives. In 2006, 2,992 tonnes of beef meat, 1,962 tonnes of pork, 248 tonnes of deer meat, and 903 tonnes of poultry meat were produced.

In addition to fishing for local consumption, industrial fishing has been developed in recent years. The territory's fishing area covers 7,000 sq. km. In 2006 2,278 tonnes of prawns were caught. An estimated 1,786 tonnes of prawns and 626 tonnes of tuna were exported. Source: http://www.isee.nc, Figures for 2010 put the estimated total fish catch at 3,770 tonnes.

FRANCE

Agricultural Production in New Caledonia 2010

Produce	Int. $'000*	Tonnes
Indigenous cattle meat	9,247	3,423
Indigenous pigmeat	3,465	2,254
Hen eggs, in shell	2,482	2,992
Coconuts	1,880	17,000
Indigenous chicken meat	1,303	915
Yams	1,303	7,300
Vegetables fresh nes	980	5,200
Fruit fresh nes	663	1,900
Bananas	297	1,089
Honey, natural	151	60
Cassava	124	1,700
Potatoes	104	868

* unofficial figures

Source: http://faostat.fao.org/site/339/default.aspx Food and Agriculture Organization of the United Nations, Food and Agricultural commodities production

COMMUNICATIONS AND TRANSPORT

International Airports
The Territory's airport is at Tontouta (URL: http://www.tontouta-aeroport.nc/). Intercontinental flights go to France and a number of Asian countries. The airport has been undergoing expansion. In 2006 there were approximately 414,990 international passenger flights and 297,257 domestic passengers. Almost 5,440 tonnes of goods were transported internationally and some 950 tonnes domestically. New Caledonia is served by several international airlines including Qantas. Air Caledonie (URL: http://www.air-caledonie.nc/) operates on international and domestic routes.

Roads
There were 5,620 km of roads in 2008. In 2006 approximately 12,200 new vehicles were registered.

Shipping
Shipping connections with France exist through Cie Générale Maritime Sotramat. In 2006, 5.3 million tonnes of goods were transported internationally and 3.4 million nationally.

Ports and Harbours
Ports and harbours exist at Mueo, Nouméa, and Thio.

HEALTH

All basic medical care is available from 25 medical centres. In 2009 there were 260 general practitioners and 282 specialists, 120 dentists, 1,103 nurses. In 2008, there were 106 midwives and 141 pharmacists. In 2008, there were a total of 710 short-term hospital beds (2.9 per 1,000 inhabitants) and 261 full-time public medium and long-term psychiatric beds and 83 part-time. In 2008, health spending amounted to €575 million, 9.2 per cent of GDP. (Source: URL: http://www.isee.nc)

EDUCATION

Education is free and compulsory for students aged between six and 16. In 2010 there were approximately 36,000 pupils enrolled in the primary and junior school system, and 33,500 in secondary education. Approximately 3,800 pupils were enrolled in higher education in 2009.

RELIGION

The majority of the population are Christians, with both the Catholic and Protestant churches represented. There is also a Muslim community.

COMMUNICATIONS AND MEDIA

The press is generally able to operate freely.

Newspapers
The publishing company *Les Nouvelles Calédoniens* (URL: http://www.info.lnc.nc/) publishes dailies and weeklies.

Broadcasting
Most broadcast services are provided by the French public overseas broadcaster RFO. Private radio stations do exist. The private radio station Radio Nouméa broadcasts for New Caledonia, Wallis and Futuna, and Vanuatu.
RFO Nouvelle Caledonie (operated by Reseau France Outre-mer), URL: http://nouvellecaledonie.rfo.fr/
Canal+ Caledonie, subscriber, URL: http://www.canalcaledonie.com/index2.htm
Radio Djiido, private, URL: http://www.radiodjiido.nc/forum/portal.php (Kanak)

Telecommunications
An underwater cable network connection between New Caledonia and Australia was completed in 2007. In 2011 there were estimated to be over 75,000 land lines in use and over 225,000 mobile phones. There were estimated to be over 85,000 internet users in 2009

ENVIRONMENT

In 2010, New Caledonia's from the consumption of fossil fuels totalled 3.027 million metric tons of carbon dioxide. (Source: EIA)

SAINT-BARTHÉLEMY
French Overseas Territorial Collectivity

Capital: Gustavia (Population estimate: 2,500)

Head of State: François Hollande (President of France) (page 1443)

Prefect: Philippe Chopin (page 1404)

Flag: The tricolour of France is used.

CONSTITUTION AND GOVERNMENT

Christopher Colombus first discovered the island in 1493 and named it after his brother Bartolomeo. The island was first settled by the French in 1648. They sold the island to Sweden in 1784 who renamed the largest town Gustavia, after the Swedish King Gustav III. Gustavia was made a free port. France repurchased the island in 1878 under the administration of Guadeloupe.

In 2003 a referendum was held on St. Barthélemy and the people voted to secede from Guadeloupe. The motion was passed by the French legislature and in 2007 the island became a French overseas collectivity. France is still the mother country, the constitution is still the French constitution, but Saint-Barthélemy now has greater independence.

Legislature
There is a unicameral 19-seat Territorial Council. Members are elected by popular vote for five-year terms.

The first elections took place on 1 and 8 July 2007. The Saint-Barth d'Abord (SBA) party led by Bruno Magas, won 16 of the 19 seats. Other parties represented in the Territorial Council are the Action-Equilibre-Transparence party, the Ensemble pour Saint-Barthélemy, and the Tous Unis pour Saint-Barthélemy. These parties all hold one seat on the council. The Territorial Council is headed by a president.

Mr Magras, the leader of the SBA party, was himself elected president of the Territorial Council for a five-year-term.

On 15 July 2007 elections took place for the Executive Council. The seven council members are chosen from members of the Territorial Council. Elections took place most recently on 18 March 2012.

Saint-Barthélemy has one seat in the French Senate and as of 2012 one seat in the French Assembly. The deputy to the French Assembly also represents Saint Martin.

Administration (as at June 2013)
President of Territorial Council: Bruno Magras
Deputy to the National Assembly: Daniel Gibbes (UMP)
Deputy in the French Senate: Michel Magras (UMP)

LEGAL SYSTEM

Where applicable, the laws of France of apply.

AREA AND POPULATION

Area
The Isle of St Barthélemy is a small island of approximately 8 square miles. The island is hilly and each valley is distinctive. The climate is arid tropical maritime.

To view a map of the island, please consult:
http://www.lib.utexas.edu/maps/cia08/saint_barthelemy_sm_2008.gif

Population
According to the 1999 census, the population was 6,852. By 2012, it had risen to an estimated 9,000, with a density of 393.1 inhabitants per km^2. The birth rate was put at 12.9 per cent in 2006 and the death rate at 4.5 per cent. The median age was 40 years.

French is the primary language.

14 July, Bastille Day (French National Day)
24 August: St. Barthélemy Day

BANKING AND FINANCE

The economy is based on tourism. The sector targets the luxury market as its location is too remote for mass-market tourism. Construction related to the tourism sector is also a major earner. Most visitors come from the US.

MANUFACTURING, MINING AND SERVICES

The main industry is tourism, mainly aimed at the luxury market. Some 200,000 visitors come to the island each year. A large percentage of food must be imported. Energy and most manufactured goods are also imported. Employment is high.
Tourism Office: http://www.st-barths.com/people.html

COMMUNICATIONS AND TRANSPORT

Airports
There is one airport on the island with a paved runways. The nearest international airport is on the island of Saint Marten

COMMUNICATIONS AND MEDIA

A local newspaper, **Le Journal de Saint-Barth**, is published weekly. URL: http://www.journaldesaintbarth.com/

There are no local TV broadcasters. There are three radio channels, two received by repeater.
Radio Saint-Barth, URL: http://radiostbarth.com.pagesperso-orange.fr/
Radio Transat, URL: http://www.radiotransat.com/

The telephone system operates on both fixed and wireless systems.

ENVIRONMENT

There are no natural rivers on the island so shortage of fresh water is a major concern. Water supply is currently provided by rain water, desalinization of sea water and water imports.

SAINT MARTIN
French Overseas Territorial Collectivity

Capital: Marigot (Population (E): 5,800

Head of State: François Hollande (President) (page 1443)

Prefect: Philippe Chopin (page 1404)

Flag: The flag of France is used.

CONSTITUTION AND GOVERNMENT

The island was noted by Christopher Colombus for Spain in 1493 but it was occupied by the Dutch in 1931. The Spanish reclaimed the island in 1633, against Dutch will. Spain relinquished the island to France and the Netherlands in 1648. The two countries subsequently divided the island between themselves.

In 2003 a referendum was held on whether to secede from Guadeloupe. The people voted overwhelmingly in favour and the motion was passed by the French parliament in 2007. The northern part of the island is now a French overseas collectivity.

The constitution is the French constitution.

As France remains the mother nation the head of state is the French president. He is represented on the island by a prefect.

Legislature
The unicameral legislature is called the Territorial Council. The 23-seat council members are elected by popular vote. The Council members elect their president for a five-year term. The cabinet is called the Executive Council. Saint-Martin has one seat in the French senate.

Administration (as of June 2013)
President, Territorial Council: Aline Hanson
Senator to the National Senate: Loius-Constant Fleming (UMP

Elections
The most recent elections for the Territorial Council took place on 18 and 25 March 2012. The Rassemblement Responsabilité Réussite Party won 17 seats and the Team Daniel Gibbs party won 6. The next elections are due to take place in 2017.

LEGAL SYSTEM

The French legal system is used.

AREA AND POPULATION

Area
Saint Martin is situated in the Caribbean Sea, approximately 187 miles southeast of Puero Rico. The island is volcanic. The average temperature is 80 degrees all year long. The hurricane season is July-November. It shares a border with Sint Maarten of the Netherlands Antilles. The French part of the island is the northern part of the island and includes the mountain Pic du Paradis (424 m). Total land area is 54.4 sq. km.

To view a map of Saint Martin, please consult:
http://www.lib.utexas.edu/maps/cia08/saint_martin_sm_2008.gif

Population
According to the October 2004 census the population was 33,102. By 2010, it was put at an estimated 30,000, with a population density of 665.3 per km^2. The annual growth rate is approximately 2.6 per cent. The birth rate was put at 26.6 per cent and the death rate 3.1 per cent. (Source: INSEE)

French is the official language. English, Dutch, French Patois, Spanish and the Papiamento dialect are also spoken.

National Day
12 July: Schoalcher Day (Slavery Abolition Day)
14 July: Bastille Day

EMPLOYMENT

Estimated figures show that 85 per cent of the working population are directly or indirectly employed in the tourist industry.

BANKING AND FINANCE

The island is supported by financial injections from France, most recently €18 million in January 2012. The economy centres around tourism. Approximately 85 per cent of the workforce works in the tourism sector. Over 1 million tourists visit the islands each year. The international airport, the Princess Juliana International Airport, is in the Dutch part of the island. There is little agriculture and most food must be imported. Energy resources and manufactured goods must also be imported. Main suppliers are Mexico and the US.

MANUFACTURING, MINING AND SERVICES

Tourism
The many beaches and interesting bird and sea life make Saint-Martin a popular tourist destination.
Tourist Office: URL: http://www.st-martin.org/

COMMUNICATIONS AND TRANSPORT

International Airports
Saint Martin is served by Princess Juliana International Airport which is located in the Dutch part of the Island.

Ports and Harbours
Inter island ferries use the harbour of Marigot.

RELIGION

Due to its multi-cultural population, there are several different religious communities including Catholic, Anglican, Baptist, Methodist, Rastafarian and Hinduism.

COMMUNICATIONS AND MEDIA

Broadcasting
There is one local television station. Broadcasts can also be received from the islands of the former Netherlands Antilles. Saint-Martin also has access to some 20 radio stations including RFO Guadeloupe.

Telecommunications
The system is integrated and uses both fixed and wireless systems.

ENVIRONMENT

Lack of fresh water is a problem and the population is dependent on desalinisation of sea water.

SAINT PIERRE AND MIQUELON
Territorial Overseas Collectivity of Saint Pierre and Miquelon
Saint-Pierre et Miquelon

Capital: Saint-Pierre (Population estimate: 5,600)

Head of State: François Hollande (President) (page 1443)

CONSTITUTION AND GOVERNMENT

Constitution
The former French Overseas Department became a *Collectivité Territoriale* in 1985, but has been French since 1816. It consists of two communes: Saint-Pierre and Miquelon-Langlade. It is administered by a Prefect in Saint-Pierre who is appointed by the French Government, and a Territorial Council of 19 members elected by the public (Saint-Pierre has 15 councillors, Miquelon-Langlade has four). The Economic and Social Committee is in charge of taxation, customs duties, town planning and housing. The *Collectivité Territoriale* is represented in the French Parliament by one Deputy and one Senator, both elected. It also has one councillor in the Economic and Social Council.

Elections for the Territorial Council (formerly the General Council) took place most recently on 18 March 2012.

> **Administration (as at June 2013)**
> *Prefect:* Patrice Latron (page 1461)
> *President of Territorial Council:* Stéphane Artano
> *Deputy in the French National Assembly:* Annick Girardin
> *Senator in the French Senate:* Karine Claireaux

Ministries
Government portal: URL: http://www.saint-pierre-et-miquelon.pref.gouv.fr/
Préfecture, pl. du Lieutenant-Colonel-Pigeaud, BP 4200, 97500 St-Pierre. Tel: +508 41 10 10, fax: +508 41 47 38, e-mail: prefepm@cancom.net, URL: http://www.saint-pierre-et-miquelon.pref.gouv.fr/
Territorial Council, 2 place Msgnr Francois Maurer, BP 4208, 97500, St-Pierre-et-Miquelon. Tel: +508 41 01 02, fax: +508 41 22 97, URL: http://www.cg975.fr/

LEGAL SYSTEM

The laws of France, where applicable, apply. The judicial administration consists a Court of First Instance, a Superior Court of Appeal and a Litigation Council.

LOCAL GOVERNMENT

On the local level, the Department is divided into two communes, the commune of Saint-Pierre, which includes Ile aux Marins, and the commune of Miquelon-Langlade. Elected municipal councils administer both communes.

AREA AND POPULATION

Area
The archipelago of Saint Pierre and Miquelon, situated about 25 km. off the south coast of Newfoundland, Canada, comprises three main islands, Saint-Pierre (26 sq. km), Langlade and Miquelon. The latter two have in fact been united during the last 75 years by a low sandy isthmus (216 sq. km). There are also about a dozen small islets. The total area is about 242 sq. km. The terrain is largely barren rock, whilst the climate is maritime and cool. Annual rainfall is above 1,000 mm and annual annual snowfall is 300 cm.

To view a map of Saint Pierre and Miquelon, please consult http://www.lib.utexas.edu/maps/cia08/saint_pierre_miquelon_sm_2008.gif

Population
Saint Pierre and Miquelon had a total population of 6,600 in 1996, which rose to an estimated 6,900 in 2000, with a growth rate of just 0.5 per cent. According to the 2006 census, total population was 6,125. In 2012 the population was estimated to have fallen to 5,800. Saint Pierre is the most populated island and the base of economic activity. The main towns are Saint-Pierre, with a population of 5,509 and Miquelon with 616 inhabitants (2006). About 100 families reside on the island of Miquelon, living on local fishing and agriculture. Thirty per cent of the population is under 20 years of age and the last three censuses have shown a tendency towards an ageing population. The population is also in decline.

The language spoken on the islands is French.

Births, Marriages, Deaths
The birth rate was estimated at 8.065 per 1,000 people in 2012. The death was an estimated 8.9 per 1,000 people in 2005. The infant mortality rate was 7.3 deaths per 1,000 live births, whilst the fertility rate was 1.5 children born per woman. Average life expectancy at birth in 2012 was estimated to be 77 for men and 82 for women.

EMPLOYMENT

In 2006 the active population of Saint-Pierre was 2,854 (out of a population of 5,509). The unemployment rate was 8.7 per cent. On Miquelon the active population was 330 (out of a total population of 616). The unemployment rate was 21.7 per cent.

The labour force breaks down thus: industry (mainly fish processing) 41 per cent; services 41 per cent; fishing 18 per cent.

The labour laws are the same as those in France.

BANKING AND FINANCE

Currency
One euro (€) = 100 cents
€ = 6.55957 francs (European Central Bank irrevocable conversion rate)
On 1 January 1999 the euro was launched as an electronic currency across the 12 member states of the EU. On 1 January 2002 the euro became legal tender in France and the 11 other member states of the EU. France's old currency, the franc, ceased to be legal tender from midnight on 17 February 2002.

GDP/GNP, Inflation, National Debt
The economy of Saint-Pierre and Miquelon depends largely on the fishing industry; however, due to a recent dispute with Canada over fishing quotas, the economy has declined and now relies on subsidies from France which provides some US$60 million of grants per annum. GDP (purchasing power parity) was estimated at almost US$108.3 million in 2003 (US$60 million supplement from France). In 2005 the inflation rate was estimated at 8 per cent.

Balance of Payments / Imports and Exports
Major export commodities are fish and fish products, crustaceans and molluscs, mink and fox pelts. Major import commodities include clothing, food, fuel, electrical equipment, building materials, and machinery. The islands' main trading partners are the US, France, Canada, Belgium, Spain, Italy and Ireland. Export revenue was an estimated US$5.5 million in 2005; imports were US$68 million. Main import commodities are meat, clothing, fuel, machinery and electrical equipment.

MANUFACTURING, MINING AND SERVICES

Energy
In 2007 an estimated 45 million kWh of electricity was produced and 46.5 million kWh consumed. Miquelon now has wind turbines. In 2007 renewable energy produced 3 per cent of the archipelago's total electricity production. In 2007, the islands imported 25,000 tonnes of oil. In 2005, France and Canada signed a unified agreeement on oil and gas.

Manufacturing
The industrial sector employs 41 per cent of the active population. It comprises three main areas of activity: the fish industry (producing frozen cod fillets etc.); electricity production from two power stations, (43 million kWh in 2002) and public works, which has kept a sustainable level of activity since the beginning of the construction of the new airport in 1994.

Service Industries
Tourism is on the increase because of the islands' proximity to Canada. Visitor numbers were estimated to be 12,000 in 2007, over 50 per cent of whom were from Canada.
Tourism Office, URL: http://www.st-pierre-et-miquelon.info

Agriculture

Because of the adverse climate and its poor soil, the territory's agriculture industry (covering an area of 700 hectares) remains limited. In recent years market gardening, using glass houses, has been developed. Livestock production, both pork and poultry, now meets about two thirds of domestic demand.

Agricultural Production in 2010

Produce	Int. $'000*	Tonnes
Hen eggs, in shell	12	14
Vegetables	8	40
Indigenous chicken meat	5	4
Tomatoes	2	6
Strawberries	2	1
Carrots and turnips	0	1
Pumpkins, squash and gourds	0	1

* unofficial figures
Source: http://faostat.fao.org/site/339/default.aspx Food and Agriculture Organization of the United Nations, Food and Agricultural commodities production

Fishing is the territory's main economic activity and takes place both on an industrial scale and for local consumption. Because of a conflict with Canada over fishing rights in 1987 and 1988, the volume of fish caught, and subsequently fish exports, have fallen by 45 per cent (value and volume). An agreement was reached with Canada in 1989, under which the fishing areas and quotas were defined for three years. A further agreement was signed in December 1994. The terms of this agreement were that 70 per cent of the queen scallops found in both Canadian and French waters would be reserved for the French territory. Islanders would also keep the right to fish cod in Canadian waters. The local fishing season is about five months long, from May to September. The total local catch was 2,040 tonnes in 2010. The main products are frozen fish and fish meal. In an effort to sustain the fishing industry fish farming and fishing for crabs has increased.

COMMUNICATIONS AND TRANSPORT

Travel Requirements
All arrivals must have a valid passport.

Flights from the Saint-Pierre Airport to Montréal provide connections to and from other destinations. The main airlines operating from the island are Air France and Air St Pierre.
Air Saint-Pierre, URL: http://www.airsaintpierre.com

There are approximately 69 km of paved roads and 45 km unpaved.

Passenger ferries operate from Fortune Newfoundland.

SPM Express, URL: http://www.spmexpress.net

HEALTH

There is one hospital for general medical cases. Specialist treatment is provided in Canada or France. Metropolitan French social laws apply.

EDUCATION

Education is free and compulsory for students aged between six and sixteen. In 1999, 782 pupils were enrolled in primary schools and 703 in secondary schools. The literacy rate is 99 per cent.

RELIGION

Most of Saint Pierre and Miquelon's population is Roman Catholic, there is a small Bahai community.

Saint Pierre and Miquelon has a religious liberty rating of 10 on a scale of 1 to 10 (10 is most freedom). (Source: World Religion Database)

COMMUNICATIONS AND MEDIA

Newspapers
Newspapers from metropolitan France are available. Only one local paper is produced, the weekly *L'Echo des Caps*. (URL: http://www.mairie-stpierre.fr/)

Broadcasting
Radio France Outremer (RFO) (URL: http://www.rfo.fr/) transmits on two television channels, one being a local channel, the other for French programmes from Antenne 2. There is cable access to several US and Canadian stations. RFO radio programmes originate from France-Inter and local programmes. In addition, one private local radio station has operated since 1984. AM receivers may pick up US and Canadian stations.

Telecommunications
In 2010 there were an estimated 4,800 telephone lines in place.

ENVIRONMENT

In 2006, Saint Pierre and Miquelon's emissions from the consumption of fossil fuels totalled 0.08 million metric tons of carbon dioxide.

FRENCH POLYNESIA
Overseas Country
Pays d'outre-mer de la Polynésie Française

Capital: Papeete (Population estimate, urban area, 2007: 131,000)

Head of State: François Hollande (President of France) (page 1443)

President: Gaston Flosse (President of French Polynesia) (page 1425)

High Commissioner: Jean-Pierre Laflaquière (page 1459)

CONSTITUTION AND GOVERNMENT

Constitution
Polynesia became a French Overseas Territory in 1946. Its autonomy has increased in recent years and in 2003 its status was changed to that of overseas lands of France.

Polynesia has the following representatives in metropolitan France: two deputies to the National Assembly, one senator to the Senate, and one councillor to the Economic and Social Council.

The chief of state is the president of France who is represented in French Polynesia by a High Commissioner. He resides at Papeete, the seat of the Territorial Assembly. The Head of the Government is a president, elected by popular vote for a five-year term. The High Commissioner is appointed by the French president on the advice of the French Ministry of the Interior. The President's Council of Ministers is made up of members of the Territorial Assembly and must be approved by the Territorial Assembly. There is one chamber (Assemblée Territoriale) composed of 57 seats. Members are elected by popular vote for five-year terms.

Each of the four administrative sub-divisions, which correspond with the main archipelagos, has a Chief.

The French state retains responsibility for justice, monetary policy, education, defence, foreign affairs and immigration.

Recent Events
Following his election as president in May 2013, Gaston Flosse, announced he wanted to hold a referendum on self determination. French Polynesia is one of several territories on the UN's decolonization list.

Cabinet (as at June 2013)
President: Gaston Flosse (page 1425)
Vice President, Minister of the Economy, Finance & Budget; Civil Service: Nuihau Laurey
Minister of Tourism; Ecology; Culture; Land Management; Air Transport: Geffry Salmon
Minister of Marine Resources; Mines; Research: Tearii Alpha
Minister of Housing; Financial Matters; Economics; Communication; Handicrafts; Government spokesperson: Marcel Tuihani
Minister of Health; Employment: Béatrice Chansin
Minister of Education; Higher Education; Youth; & Sport: Michel Leboucher
Minister of Equipment; Town Planning; Energy; Land & Maritime Transport: Bruno Marty
Minister of Agriculture; Livestock; Crops; Equality; Development of the Archipelago: Thomas Moutane

Legislature (as at June 2013)
Deputy to the French National Assembly: Edouard Fritch
Deputy to the French National Assembly: Jonas Tahuaitu
Deputy to the French National Assembly: Jean-Paul Tuaiva
Senator in the French Senate: Gaston Flosse
Senator in the French Senate: Richard Tuheiava

Ministries
Prefecture, Avenue Bruat, BP 115, Papeete, French Polynesia. Tel: +689 46 86 86, fax: +689 46 86 89, URL: http://www.polynesie-francaise.pref.gouv.fr/

FRANCE

Presidency of the Government of French Polynesia, BP 2551, Papeete, French Polynesia. Tel: +689 54 34 50, fax: +689 41 02 71, URL: http://www.presidence.pf
Vice-President's Office, URL: http://www.vp.gov.pf
Ministry of Solidarity, Housing and Family, Immeuble Papineau, 6eme etage, French Polynesia. URL: http://www.msf.gov.pf
Ministry of the Economy and Finance, URL: http://www.mef.gov.pf
Ministry of Equipment, Town Planning and Transport, URL: http://www.mut.gov.pf
Ministry of Tourism, URL: http://www.mte.gov.pf
Ministry of Public Works, Energy and Mines, URL: http://www.mgt.gov.pf
Ministry of Health, URL: http://www.msp.gov.pf
Ministry of Labour and Employment, URL: http://www.mtf.gov.pf
Ministry of the Archipelago Development, URL: http://www.mda.gov.pf
Ministry of Marine Resources, URL: http://www.mrm.gov.pf
Ministry of the Environment, URL: http://www.mev.gov.pf
Administrative Subdivision of the Iles sous-le-Vent, Centre ville, BP 1, 98735 Uturoa-Raiatea, French Polynesia. Tel: +689 60 00 50, fax: +689 66 23 78
Administrative Subdivision of the Iles du Vent, Rue des Poilus Tahitiens, BP 6, Papeete, French Polynesia. Tel: +689 46 86 11, fax: +689 46 86 19
Administrative Subdivision of Tuamotu-Gambier, Rue des Poilus Tahitiens, BP 115, Papeete, French Polynesia. Tel: +689 46 86 21, fax: +689 46 83 29
Administrative Subdivision of the Iles Marquises, BP 11, Taiohae Nuku Hiva, French Polynesia. Tel: +689 92 03 32, fax: +689 92 03 05
Administrative Subdivision of the Iles Australes, Rue des Poilus Tahitiens, Papeete, French Polynesia. Tel: +689 46 86 76, fax: +689 46 86 79
National Assembly, BP 28, Papeete, French Polynesia. Tel: +689 41 61 00, fax: +689 41 61 60, URL: http://www.assemblee.pf

Political Parties

Parties include: Union pour La Democratie (UPLD), a coalition led by Oscar Temaru and the pro-autonomy Tahoera'a Huira'atira Party led by Gaston Flosse. Others include the Alliance pour une Democratie Nouvelle (ADN), a centrist party, the To Tatou ai'a party led by Gaston Ton Sang, another pro-autonomy party and the Te Mana o te Mau Motu party.

Elections

A new electoral system was approved in France on 26 November 2007, in order to stabilise the French Polynesian political scene. Under the new system, there are two rounds, and candidates need at least 12.5 per cent of the vote to enter the second round of voting.

France called an early general election for February 2008. No party gained an overall majority. The To Tatou Ai'a (Our Home) coalition won 27 seats, the Union for Democracy coalition won 20, and the Tahoeraa Huiraatira (Popular Rally) won 10 seats.

In October 2007, veteran pro-independence leader, Oscar Temaru, was elected president for the third time in three years; he replaced President Gaston Tong Sang, who lost a no-confidence vote in parliament on 31 August. A presidential election took place in February 2008, and Gaston Flosse (former president, and the founder of Tahoeraa Huiraatira) was returned to power despite the fact that his party came third in the election. Oscar Temaru was re-elected president in February 2009. Following a vote of no confidence, Gaston Tong Sang acceded to the presidency for the third time on 24 November 2009. Oscar Temaru of the Union pour La Democratie became president again in April 2011, following a no-confidence vote against Gaston Tong Sang.

Elections took place in May 2013. The Tahoeraa Huiraatira party won elections with over 45 per cent of the vote. The French Polynesian Assembly duly elected veteran politician and party leader, Gaston Flosse, 81, as the president of French Polynesia for a five year term. Mr Flosse took 38 of the 57 Assembly votes, defeating the two other candidates, Antony Geros of the Union for Democracy and Teva Rohfritsch of the A Tia Porinetia. Mr Flosse was convicted of corruption in 2013 and is currently appealing a custodial sentence.

LEGAL SYSTEM

French Polynesia's constitutional status ('Statut') defines its institutions, legal powers and relationship with France. The laws of France apply in most instances, though French Polynesia can pass "country laws", and now has jurisdiction over commercial and labour law.

AREA AND POPULATION

Area
French Polynesia comprises approximately 188 islands which are volcanic or coralline in origin, covering a land area of 4,220 sq. km., dispersed over 2.5 million sq. km. of the eastern Pacific Ocean. The land is a mixture of volcanic peaks or low lying coral reefs. The Territory consists of five archipelagos: l'archipel de la Société which includes les Iles du Vent and les Iles Sous le Vent, l'archipel des Marquises, l'archipel des Australes and l'archipel des Tuamotu et des Gambier. The climate is moderately tropical.

To view a map of French Polynesia, please consult http://www.lib.utexas.edu/maps/cia07/french_polynesia_sm_2007.gif

Population
According to the 2007 census, the population stood at 260,000, up by 15,000 since 2002. The growth is due natural increase with births outnumbering deaths. Fertility and mortality rates have decreased and the population growth is slowing. In 2007, the population was distributed as follows: Îles du Vent, 13 communes with a total population of 196,520; Îles Sous-le-Vent, 7 communes, total population of 333,949; Îles Marquises, 6 communes, total population 9,281; Îles Australes, 5 communes, total population 6,669; Îles Tuamotu-Gambier 17 communes, 18,317 population. (Source: INSEE)

French Polynesia's ethnic composition is as follows: 82.8 per cent are Polynesians, 4.7 per cent are Asian and 11.9 per cent are European. The territory is characterised by its young population: 43.1 per cent are under the age of 20. French and Tahitian are the official languages.

Births, Marriages, Deaths
In 2012, per 1,000 inhabitants the estimated crude birth rate was 15.9 per 1,000 population and the death rate was 4.7. The infant mortality rate was 4.8. The population is young but ageing. In 2007, 36 per cent of the population was aged less than 20 years and 9 per cent over 60 years old. In 2010 there were an estimated 1,330 marriages.

EMPLOYMENT

In 2007 the workforce numbered an estimated 166,000. The main employment sectors are services (68 per cent), industry (19 per cent), and agriculture. (13 per cent). In 2007 the unemployment rate was 11.7 per cent.

BANKING AND FINANCE

Currency
As an overseas département, French Polynesia is not legally part of the European Union and therefore its official currency remains the Franc Pacifique (CFP) of 100 cents. The Franc Pacifique is linked to the euro by a fixed rate of 1,000 CFP = 8.38 euro. One euro = 119.33 CFP.

GDP/GNP, Inflation, National Debt
On 27 January 1993 a ten-year economic and social stimulus package called the Pacte de Progres was agreed upon by the terrestrial Government and Metropolitan France to help revitalise the Polynesian economy. To cushion the impact of a decrease in military spending due to the cessation of French nuclear testing, the French Government, through the Pacte de Progres granted $193 million a year for ten years. A Contrat de Developement, signed in May 1994 for a five-year period, outlined the share of public financing for projects that had to be undertaken in leading economic sectors, infrastructure upgrades, as well as improvement of health and welfare coverage.

French Polynesia's economy has developed from one based on subsistence agriculture to one based on tourism and the military sector. According to recent figures, nearly 80 per cent of GDP comes from the services sector, whilst nearly 20 per cent comes from industry, and almost 5 per cent from agriculture. Tourism currently contributes a quarter of French Polynesia's GDP.

In 2005, GDP was F.CFP525,957 compared to CFP 511,90 million in 2004. Per capita GDP was CFP 2.1 million in the same year. Growth was estimated at 2.7 per cent. GDP was estimated to be US$4,530 million in 2009, with a growth rate of 2.1 per cent.

Balance of Payments / Imports and Exports
French Polynesia main export trading partners include Hong Kong, Japan and France. Main export commodities include cultured pearls, mother of pearl, coconuts, shark meat, and vanilla. Export revenue was an estimated 22,380 million CFP in 2006, compared to 20,800 million F.CFP in 2005. Of this figure, cultured pearls made up over 12,000 million F.CFP in 2006. Import trading partners include France (over 30 per cent) and the US, who sell French Polynesia such commodities as fuels and foodstuffs, and Singapore. Imports cost 157,492 million F.CFP in 2006. The balance of trade in 2006 was -CFP 135,112 million. (Source: http://www.ispf.pf)

Imports were estimated to be US$1,720 million in 2009 and exports US$148 million.

MANUFACTURING, MINING AND SERVICES

Primary and Extractive Industries
It is believed that the waters around the islands are rich in deposits of nickel, cobalt, manganese, and copper, although extraction may prove to be prohibitively expensive.

Energy
In 2009, 725 million kWh were produced, of which approx 225 million kWh were hydroelectric.

Manufacturing
The craft industry employs around 12,000 people. A wide range of products is produced such as objects and jewellery from shellfish, coral or mother-of-pearl, bags, hats, wallets, wooden sculptures, beer, sandalwood oil, sandals and patchwork.

Industry is concentrated on the island of Tahiti, and employs over 5,000 people.

Service Industries
Tourism is Polynesia's prime source of external income. Ten per cent of the population earns its living from visitors, and tourism accounts for 25 per cent of GDP. There were 239 hotels in 1998 offering 3,961 rooms. In 2006 there were approximately 221,500 tourists, compared to 212,767 in 2003. The average stay lasted 13 nights. Almost 50 per cent of visitors come from Europe, over 25 per cent from America and over 25 per cent from Asia. (Source: http://www.ispf)

Agriculture
The main agricultural product is copra, whose oil is exported to make perfume. Other agricultural products include coconuts, vanilla pods, coffee, and tropical fruit. Agriculture only employs 10 per cent of the active population and only produces 20 per cent of local

consumption demand. Agricultural exploitation occurs on a small scale with a limited area of land being cultivated, 18,524 ha in 1995. Wooded area is 5,000 ha. Livestock is kept for domestic use and consumption, but is not enough to meet local demand.

Agricultural Production in 2010

Produce	Int. $'000*	Tonnes
Coconuts	14,828	134,100
Hen eggs, in shell	2,488	3,000
Fruit fresh nes	2,478	7,100
Indigenous pigmeat	1,876	1,220
Pineapples	998	3,500
Vanilla	996	60
Fruit, tropical fresh nes	899	2,200
Roots and tubers, nes	800	5,500
Tomatoes	628	1,700
Indigenous chicken cattle meat	605	425
Indigenous cattle meat	459	170
Cow milk, whole, fresh	375	1,200

* unofficial figures
Source: http://faostat.fao.org/site/339/default.aspx FAOSTAT, Statistics Division, Food and Agriculture Organization of the UN

Most of the fishing is still used for local consumption or sold to restaurants, although efforts are now under way to develop fishing on an industrial scale. The total catch is estimated at being around 13,000 tonnes per annum. The cultivation of pearls (400 kg per annum) and related products (mother of pearl) make a significant contribution to the economy, the main source of foreign income after tourism. French Polynesia is the second largest producer and exporter of pearls in the world, 80 per cent of the production going to Japan. Recently the pearl market has suffered from the availability of cheaper cultivated pearls and Japan has been buying increasingly fewer pearls from French Polynesia. The industry has recently turned its attention to the American market.

COMMUNICATIONS AND TRANSPORT

International Airports
The main airport is Tahiti-Faaa. Smaller airfields for domestic flights are on a number of islands. A number of major international airlines operate into and out of Tahiti. There were 677,817 international passengers in 2006 and 13,827 tonnes of goods were disembarqued. In the same year there were 855,550 internal passenger flights made and 3,555 tonnes of goods were transported.

Roads
French Polynesia has nearly 800 km of roads, all of which are surfaced. In 2006 7,829 vehicles were registered, including 4,602 cars. In 2007, 75 per cent of households had at least one car, and 25 per cent had at least two.

Shipping
There are frequent international links with Europe, the United States, Canada and Australia from the port of Papeete. The main shipping lines are: *Cie. Générale Maritime* from Le Havre and Marseille, and *Bankline Ltd.* from North Sea harbours. In 2005, 1,020,662 tonnes of merchandise arrived by ship and over 33,792 tonnes was taken from the islands by ship. According to recent estimates, French Polynesia has one cargo ship, two passenger/cargo ships, and one refrigerated cargo ship. Small ferries run between most of the islands.

Ports and Harbours
Ports and harbours include Mataura, Rikitea, Papeete, and Uturoa. (Source: http://www.ispf)

HEALTH

Health is the responsibility of the Territory, which has its own Minister of Health. In 2004 there were 178 doctors per 100,000 population), 40 pharmacists per 100,000 population) and 41 dentists per 100,000 population. There were also an estimated 81 midwives and 724 nurses.

According to figures from INSEE, an estimated 91.6 per cent of households had running water.

EDUCATION

Primary and secondary education are now the responsibility of the territory. Compulsory education lasts for 10 years from age 6 to 16 years of age. Vocational training is offered by 14 institutions, while higher education is provided by the University of the Pacific. In 2007, 68 per cent of the population aged 15 or more is increasing, up to 68 per cent in 2007, compared to 59 per cent in 1996. An estimated 23 per cent of the population had obtained the Bac, compared to 15 per cent in 1996. (Source: INSEE)

RELIGION

Most of the population are Christian (94 per cent). There are some Mormons and Seventh Day Adventists as well as small communities of Baha'is, new religionists and those that follow traditional beliefs.

COMMUNICATIONS AND MEDIA

Newspapers
The two daily newspapers are: La Depeche de Tahiti (URL: http://www.ladepeche.pf/) and Les Nouvelles de Tahiti (URL: http://www.lesnouvelles.pf/).

Broadcasting
Radio and television broadcasting is mainly in the hands of Radio France Outremer (URL: http://www.rfo.fr). A government-owned television station also operates. Multi-channel TV is available. In addition, there are many local private radio stations. Ninety per cent of households have a television.
RFO Polynesie, URL: http://polynesie.rfo.fr/
Tahiti Nui TV, government run, URL: http://www.tntv.pf/interface.html

Telecommunications
The number of telephone lines in French Polynesia was estimated at 55,000 in 2011, whilst the number of mobile phones is estimated at 220,000. There are an estimated 120,000 internet users.

ENVIRONMENT

In 2010, French Polynesia's emissions from the consumption of fossil fuels totalled 1.2 million metric tons of carbon dioxide. (Source: EIA)

FRENCH SOUTHERN AND ANTARCTIC TERRITORIES
Overseas Territory
Territoire des Terres Australes et Antarctiques Françaises

CONSTITUTION AND GOVERNMENT

Constitution
The French Southern and Antarctic Territories became a territory on 6 August 1955. The Chief Administrator, appointed by the French Government, is assisted by a Consultative Council of seven members. They are appointed by the Ministry of Overseas Departments and Territories and by a Scientific Committee of 12 members which is in charge of approving scientific programmes on the Antarctic, as determined by the Scientific Committee on Antarctic Research. There are four districts - St. Paul and Amsterdam, Kerguelen, Crozet and Terre Adélie - each with a District Chief. France exercises full sovereignty over the Southern Islands, while, concerning the lands forming part of the Antarctic continent itself, she has accepted the terms of the Washington Treaty of the Antarctic. There are no permanent inhabitants. In 1997 the administrative seat was moved from France to Reunion.

Since January 2005 the prefect (chief administrator) of the French Southern and Antarctic Territories has also been responsible for the administration of certain islands in the Indian Ocean (Tromelin, Glorieuses, Juan de Nova, Europa, and Bassas da India). The islands have permanent military garrisons and research personnel in residence.

Administration (as at June 2013)
Prefect: Pascal Bolot (page 1391)

Government portal, URL: http://www.taaf.fr/

AREA AND POPULATION

Area
At the southern extremity of the Indian Ocean, France possesses a number of islands that, together with the French portion of the Antarctic continent, are grouped into one administrative framework. These territories have been given the overall name of *Territoire des Terres Australes et Antarctiques Françaises* and cover a total area of 7,780 sq. km. These lands, which are more than 15,000 km away from France, have in common their Antarctic and sub-Antarctic fauna, the fact that they were uninhabited until very recent times, and their extremely limited economic activity. Since the end of the Second World War, however, they have served as a base for scientific activities and the population of all these territories is mainly composed of scientists (currently approximately 200).

The islands and territories involved are:

Saint-Paul and Amsterdam
Saint-Paul, situated at 38°S. latitude and 77°E. longitude is a small island of about seven sq. km. Amsterdam lies at 37°S. latitude and 70°E. longitude with an area of 54 sq. km. Like Saint-Paul, it is a volcanic island. The central peak of its volcanic cone is Mont Dives (881 m).

FRANCE

The Crozet Archipelago
This archipelago is formed by two groups of islands, some 100 km apart, between 50 and 53°E. longitude and at 46° latitude, with a total area of 115 sq. km.

Kerguelen
Kerguelen consists of one large island, called Grande Terre, closely surrounded by 85 smaller islands, and countless islets and rocks. Grand Terre has an area of 6,675 sq. km. The group total area is 7,215 sq. km. Kerguelen is situated at a mean latitude of 49° 1511, and a mean longitude of 69° 3011.

Terre Adélie
The French Antarctic territory is a narrow section of a circle covering some 432,000 sq. km of that continent. In the absence of natural frontiers, it can only be determined by reference to the order of 1 April 1938, whereby 'The islands and territories situated south of the 60th Parallel of latitude and between the 136th and 142nd meridians east of Greenwich are under French Sovereignty'.

To view a map, please consult:
http://www.lib.utexas.edu/maps/cia08/french_antarctic_sm_2008.gif

BANKING AND FINANCE

Currency
One euro (€) = 100 cents
€ = 6.55957 francs (European Central Bank irrevocable conversion rate)
On 1 January 2002 the euro became legal tender in France and the French Southern and Antarctic Territories. France's old currency, the franc, ceased to be legal tender from midnight on 17 February 2002. Euro banknotes are issued in denominations of 5, 10, 20, 50, 100, 200, and 500. Euro coins are issued in denominations of 2 and 1 euros, 50, 20, 10, 5, 2, and 1 cents.

Economy
The French Southern and Antarctic Territories' economy is restricted to the provision of services to the scientific research stations, as well as French and foreign fishing fleets.

MANUFACTURING, MINING AND SERVICES

Fishing
The small economy is based on fishing by refrigeration vessels. Main marine catches include salmon, krill, and seaweed. Approximately 340 metric tonnes of fish were caught in 1998 consisting mainly of crayfish. In 2004-05 eight vessels had permission to fish.

A number of scientific programmes exist with the aim of developing geophysical and geographic features of the area, as well as meteorological research.

COMMUNICATIONS AND TRANSPORT

Shipping
The territories have a fleet of just over 70 ships, including chemical, liquified gas and petroleum tankers, refrigerated cargo vessels, and roll on/roll off vessels. Two shipping vessels call about five times each year to bring provisions and relieve personnel. A small number of tourists are allowed to visit.

ENVIRONMENT

The area has a unique and unspoilt ecosystem. France signed the Rio Convention in 1992, thereby committing itself to preserving the area's biological diversity for future generations.

WALLIS AND FUTUNA

Overseas Territory of Wallis and Futuna

Territoire d'outre-mer des Îles Wallis-et-Futuna

Capital: Mata-Utu (Wallis) (Population estimate: 1,100)

Head of State: François Hollande (President of France) (page 1443)

CONSTITUTION AND GOVERNMENT

Constitution
Wallis and Futuna has been a French Overseas Territory since July 1961 and is administered by a Prefect appointed by the French Government. The Prefect is in charge of external affairs, defence, law and order, financial and educational affairs. The Territorial Council is only a consultative body. It has six members, three are traditional chiefs or kings of Wallis and Futuna, the other three are appointed by the Prefect with the agreement of the Territorial Assembly. The latter consists of 20 members (13 for Wallis and seven for Futuna), elected for five years.

The social structure remains traditional: in Wallis, a King, assisted by a Prime Minister and five ministers, is in charge of customary laws, administered through district and village chiefs. In Futuna the island is divided into two kingdoms, Siave and Alo. Each of these is ruled by a King, assisted by five ministers and village chiefs. The King of Alo abdicated in 2010.

Wallis and Futuna sends the following representatives to metropolitan France: one Deputy to the National Assembly, one Senator to the Senate and one representative to the Economic and Social Council.

International Relations
Wallis and Futuna participates in the Franc Zone, is a permanent member of the Secretariat of the Pacific Community and is an observer member of the South Pacific Forum.

Administration (as at June 2013)
High Administrator (Prefect): Michel Aubouin (page 1380)
President of the Territorial Assembly: Nivaleta Iloa
King of Uvea: Kapeliele Faupala
King of Alo: currently vacant
King of Sigave: Polikalepo Kolivai
Deputy to the French National Assembly: David Vergé
Deputy to the French Senate: Robert Laufoaulu

French Overseas Economic and Social Council (Outre-Mer du Conseil Economique et Social)
Representative from Wallis and Futuna: Patalione Kanimoa

Ministries
Administration Superieure, Havelu, BP 16, 98600 Mata-Utu, Ile de Wallis, Wallis and Futuna. Tel: +681 722403, fax: +681 72 0512, email: adsupwf@wallis.co.nc, URL: http://www.wallis-et-futuna.pref.gouv.fr/

Territorial Assembly, Havel, BP 3, 98600 Mata-Utu, Ile de Wallis, Wallis and Futuna. Tel: +681 72 25 04, fax: +681 72 20 54, e-mail: cab-pres.at@wallis.co.nc
Cabinet: email: cabinet@adsupwf.org
Department of Customs and Maritime Affairs, Aka'aka, District de Hahake, BP 06, 98600 Mata-Utu, Wallis and Futuna. Tel: +681 72 25 71, fax: +681 72 29 86
Department of Health, District de Hahake, 98600 Mata-Utu, Wallis and Futuna. Tel: +681 72 17 72, fax: +681 72 23 99, URL: http://www.wallis.co.nc/sante.wf
Department of Agriculture, Forestry and Fisheries, ABP 19, 98600 Uvea, Ile de Wallis, Wallis and Futuna. Tel: +681 72 04 00, e-mail: bivap@mail.wf

Political Parties
Lua Kae Tahi, Mouvement des Radicaux de Gauche (MRG), Rally for the Republic (RPR) allied to France's UMP, Socialist Party (PS), Taumu'a Lelei, Union Poulaire Locale (UPL), Union Pour la Démocratie Française (UDF)

Elections
Territorial Assembly elections took place on 25 March 2012. Elections for the Territorial Assembly in Alo took place in 2013. Partial legislative elections took place in March 2013.

LEGAL SYSTEM

The French legal system applies to Wallis and Futuna. The Tribunal of Great Instance and the Court of Appeal is situated at Nouméa and the Tribunal of Instance and the Tribunal Administrative at Mata'Uta.

LOCAL GOVERNMENT

The territory is divided into three chiefdoms - Uvea, on Wallis; Sigave, western Futuna; and Alo on the island of Alofi and on the eastern part of the island of Futuna.

AREA AND POPULATION

Area
The Territory of Wallis and Futuna is an archipelago of three main islands, Wallis, Futuna and Alofi, situated between Fiji in the west and Samoa and Tonga to the south east in the Pacific Ocean. Their combined area is 274 sq. km, of which Wallis accounts for 96 sq. km, and Futuna 64 sq. km. Wallis lies 200 km to the north-east of Futuna and Alofi, which are separated by a channel of 2 km. The islands are volcanic in origin. Mount Singavi is the highest point (765 m).

The climate is tropical with a hot rainy season between November and April and a cool dry season from May to October. Rainfall averages some 2,700 mm per year (80 per cent humidity).

To view a map of the islands, please consult

Population

The population, which is Polynesian, was estimated at 13,455 in 2008, 34 per cent of whom were living on Futuna. There is a high rate of immigration to the French territory of New Caledonia, 2,000 km away. Within the five-year period preceeding the 2008 census, the population decreased by 1,500 or roughly 10 per cent. The population is aging and the birth rate slowing down. According to latest figures (2008), 41 per cent of the population is aged 0-19 years, 45 per cent aged 20-59 years, and 11 per cent aged 60 years or older.

As of 2008, the population was spread thus: Futuna 4,238, down 13 per cent on 2003 (Alo 2,655; Sigave 1,583); Wallis 9,207, down 10 per cent on 2003, (Hahake district 3,748; Hihifo district 2,197; Mua district 3,262). Population density was approximately 130 population per km sq. on Wallis and 75 people per km sq. on Futuna. The average size of households has decreased from 4.7 per household to 4.2. The trend is for the younger generations to live apart from the older generation. (Source: INSEE)

Polynesian languages are also spoken.

Births, Marriages, Deaths

In 2006 there were 220 registered births and 77 registered deaths. In 2008, the fertility rate was estimated to 2 children per female, compared to 2.7 per in 2003. Figures from 2008 put the birth rate at 16.0 per 1,000 population and the death rate at 5.4 per 1,000 population. The child mortality rate was 5.5 per 1,000 population and the infant mortality rate was1.6 per 1,000 population. Average life expectancy is 74.3 years. (Source: INSEE)

Public Holidays

As for France, plus:
28 April: Saint Pierre Chanel
29 June: Saint Pierre and Saint Paul
29 July: Territory Day

EMPLOYMENT

The majority of the population are engaged in agriculture and fishing. The employment situation has improved in the period 2003-08, with reforms to local industry. In 2008 the unemployment rate was estimated at over 12.8 per cent (Futuna , 19.5 per cent, Wallis 10.8 per cent). The rate is much higher for young people. For the age group 15-24 years the rate is 42 per cent. (Source: INSEE)

BANKING AND FINANCE

Currency

As an overseas département, Wallis and Futuna is not legally part of the European Union and therefore its official currency remains the Franc Pacifique (CFP) of 100 cents. The Franc Pacifique is linked to the euro by a fixed rate of 1,000 CFP = 8.38 euro. One euro = 119.33 CFP.

GDP/GNP, Inflation, National Debt

Wallis and Futuna's economy is largely based on subsistence agriculture, livestock and fishing, with additional sums coming from French subsidises, import taxes, and fishing rights to South Korea and Japan. A development contract between France and Wallis and Futuna was signed in 2012 which should mean Wallis and Futuna receives almost €42 million for firstly, health, education, employment, sport and culture; and secondly, sustainable land management and the environment. Subsidies amounted to approximtely €104 million in 2010. GDP (purchasing power parity) in 2004 was estimated at almost US$60 million. Per capita GDP (purchasing power parity) was US$3,800 in the same year.

Inflation was 2.8 per cent in 2005.

Balance of Payments / Imports and Exports

Exports are mainly limited to locally grown food which is sold to New Caledonia. Export value in 2004 was estimated at €38,000. Imports consist of raw materials, industrial products, food, and petroleum products. Imports were estimated at over €49.2 million in 2004 and come mainly from Australia, China, France and Fiji.

MANUFACTURING, MINING AND SERVICES

Service Industries

Tourism is under-developed. Currently, there are four hotels with a total of 26 rooms and bungalows, all situated in Mata-Utu. In 2006 approximately 5,300 tourists visited Wallis and Futuna. Most foreign visitors are from New Caledonia and France.

Agriculture

Agriculture accounts for 80 per cent of the islands' economic activities. Bananas, breadfruit, yams, taro, manioc, arrowroot and coconuts are the main crops. Arable crops account for some 40 per cent of land use. Pig livestock is also important, with a recent count of 10,000 to 15,000 pigs, compared with about 50 cattle. All agricultural output is used locally. Since 1992 one sector that has been expanding is that of egg-laying hens. The production of eggs is therefore rising, but still does not meet demand.

The development of agriculture is subject to constraints such as the small area of the islands, the relief of the land and the traditional methods of cultivation which alternates between two or three years of exploitation and a long period of fallow. Each family has around 0.25 to 0.5 hectares of land to grow what it needs to be self-sufficient. Any other fruit and vegetables are imported by sea or air from Australia, New Zealand or New Caledonia.

All fishing takes place on a local basis and is not enough to serve local demand. It is estimated that the amounts are in the region of 800 tonnes per annum. The forest has been over-exploited in the past, but is now undergoing a reafforestation programme.

Agricultural Production in 2010

Produce	Int. $'000*	Tonnes
Fruit, tropical fresh nes	1,799	5,300
Bananas	1,546	6,100
Indigenous pigmeat	484	315
Coconuts	409	3,700
Taro (cocoyam)	272	1,600
Cassava	197	2,100
Roots & tubers, nes	132	1,100
Yams	114	560
Vegetables fresh nes	104	550
Indigenous chicken meat	68	48
Fruit fresh nes	53	160
Hen eggs, in shell	42	50

* unofficial figures
Source: http://faostat.fao.org/site/339/default.aspx Food and Agriculture Organization of the United Nations, Food and Agricultural commodities production

COMMUNICATIONS AND TRANSPORT

International Airports

There are regular domestic flights between the two groups of islands; links to international flights exist through New Caledonia. In 2002 there were over 25,300 international passengers and almost 13,000 domestic passengers.

Roads

Wallis and Futuna has a total of 120 km of roads, 100 km on Ile Uvea and 20 km on Futuna. Only 16 km of Ile Uvea's roads are surfaced. In 2006, 255 cars were registered. There were also 7 heavy goods lorries, 14 motor cycles and 6 buses.

Shipping

This constitutes the main means of transport, especially for commercial purposes. Recent figures show that Wallis and Futuna have a total of eight registered ships, all foreign-owned. In 2001 almost 30,640 tonnes of goods were unloaded and 17.3 tonnes were loaded.

Ports and Harbour

Ports and harbours exist at Leava and Mata-Utu. The port at Matu'Uta is currently undergoing significant expansion including the construction of a new quay. The work, which is financed by the EU, should finish in 2013.

HEALTH

There is one hospital (60 beds) in Wallis. In Futuna there is a 21-bed hospital and two dispensaries which cater for maternity and non-serious illnesses. Patients with more serious illnesses are transferred to Wallis, New Caledonia and Australia. In 2004 there were 13 doctors (9.2 per 10,000 population) and 12 nurses. There were 4 dentists (2.83 per 10,000 population). Source: INSEE

An estimated 81 per cent of the population has sustainable access to drinking water (Wallis 87 per cent, Futuna 67 per cent). An estimated 68.5 per cent of the population has sustainable access to improved sanitation (Wallis 76 per cent, Futuna 51.5 per cent).

No vaccination is required to enter the territory.

EDUCATION

Education is supported by the French Government. Over 90 per cent of children (5,200) receive primary education (2008). There are currently six primary schools on Futuna and 12 on Wallis. There are currently four colleges on Wallis and two at Futuna and two secondary schools on Wallis (one general education, one specialising in agriculture). There were approximately 230 primary teachers in 2003 and 215 secondary school teachers. Approximately 40 per cent of pupils attain a diploma.

The adult literacy rate was in the region of 79 per cent according to 2003 figures.

RELIGION

Catholicism is the main religion.

COMMUNICATIONS AND MEDIA

Newspapers

The daily 'Les Nouvelles Caledoniennes', includes articles on the territory. URL: http://www.lnc.nc

Broadcasting

Reseau France Outremer (URL: http://www.rfo.fr) transmits on the islands' television and radio stations. Services include TFI, France 2, France 3 and Arte. In addition, there is a radio service (RFO Radio).

STATES OF THE WORLD

GABON

Telecommunications

In 2008 there were an estimated 2700 main lines in use. In the same year there were an estimated 1,700 internet users. An estimated of 20 per cent of households in Futuna and 35 per cent of households in Wallis had a computer and 12 per cent of households in Futuna and 22 per cent in Wallis were connected to the internet. The ADSL network became operative in Wallis and Futuna in 2007.

ENVIRONMENT

Deforestation is the main environmental issue for the islands; traditionally wood is used as the main energy source resulting in the loss of forests and subsequent to soil erosion.

GABON

Gabonese Republic

République Gabonaise

Capital: Libreville (Population estimate: 673,995)

Head of State: Ali Ben Bongo Ondimba (President) (page 1391)

National Flag: Three horizontal stripes, green, yellow and blue

CONSTITUTION AND GOVERNMENT

Constitution

Gabon, a former part of the French territory of Equatorial Africa, became independent on 17 August 1960. A new constitution creating a multiparty political system was introduced in 1991. It was amended in 1995 to include the 1994 Paris Accord agreements.

Executive power rests with the President, elected by universal suffrage for a seven year term (increased from five years in 1997). He appoints the Prime Minister who, with the President, names the Council of Ministers and takes special powers in times of 'grave danger or menace to the country'. In 2003 the constitution was amended to allow President Bongo to serve an indefinite number of terms.

To consult the full constitution, please visit: http://www.assemblee.ga/rubrique.php3?id_rubrique=27

Recent Events

In May 2009, President Bongo was one of three African leaders accused of embezzlement by the French arm of the anti-corruption watchdog Transparency International. It was alleged that the amount of real estate owned by Mr Bongo's family in France (33 properties in Paris and Nice worth an estimated $190 million) could not have been purchased with official salaries alone. In 1999, an investigation by the American senate into Citibank estimated that the Gabonese president held $130 million in the bank's personal accounts. Mr Bongo, who temporarily stepped down from his post on health grounds, denied any wrongdoing.

President Omar Bongo died of a heart attack on the 10th June 2009. He had led Gabon since 1967, and was Afrca's longest serving president. The defence ministry, headed by Mr. Bongo's son Ali-Ben Bongo, said it was closing Gabon's air, land and sea borders. In accordance with the constitution, leader of the Senate, Rose Francine Rogombe, became the interim leader and must organise elections within 45 days. However, since it will be necessary to update the voter roll, it is widely thought impossible to hold the election within the constitutional 45-day timeframe. Ali-Ben Bongo won the subsequent presidential election.

In August 2010, Gabon signed agreements with India and Singapore for major infrastructure projects.

In December the parliament approved constitutiona changes which allowed the government to delay caling an electoral college. The opposition National Union said that the changes would allow for a dictatorship.

Legislature

Gabon's bicameral legislature consists of the National Assembly (Assemblée Nationale) and the Senate (Sénat).

Upper House

As a result of the implementation of the 1995 Paris Accords, an upper legislative house, the 91-member Senate, was created. Senators are elected by regional and municipal councillors for a term of six years.
Senate, BP 7513, Libreville, Gabon. Tel: +241 762053, fax: +241 721864, e-mail: senatgabonais@assala.com, URL: http://www.senat-gabon.org/
President of the Senate: Georges Rawiri

Lower House

The National Assembly comprises 120 deputies elected by universal suffrage for a five-year period.
National Assembly, Palais de l'Assemblée nationale, BP 29 Libreville, Gabon. Tel: +241 74 00 60 / 74 92 47, fax: +241 72 61 96, e-mail: assemblee_gabon@yahoo.fr, URL: http://www.assemblee.ga/
President of the National Assembly: Guy Nzouba-Ndama

Cabinet (as of June 2013)
Prime Minister: Raymond Ndong Sima (page 1485)
Minister for the Economy, Employment and Sustainable Developmen: Luc Oyoubi
Minister of Foreign Affairs, International Co-operation, Francophone Affairs and Regional Integration: Emmanel Issozet Ngondet

---

Minister of Justice, Keeper of the Seals, Minister for Human Rights and Relations with Constitutional Institutions: Ida Reteno Assonquet
Minister of Health: Leon Nzouba
Minister of Mines, Oil and Hydrocarbons: Etienne Ngoubou
Minister of National Defence: Pacome Rufin Ondzounga
Minister of the Interior, Public Security, Immigration and Decentralization: Jean-Francois Ngongou
Minister of Agriculture, Livestock, Fisheries and Rural Development: Julien Nkoghe Bekale
Minister of National Education, Higher Education, Minister of Technical Education and Professional Training, and responsible for Youth and Sports: Séraphin Moungounga
Minister of Housing, Transport, Tourism and Investment Promotion: Magloire Ngambia
Minister of Small and Medium-sized Enterprises and Handicrafts: Fidele Mengue M'engouang
Minister of Digital Economy, Communications and Post: Blaise Loumbe
Minister of Water and Forests: Gabriel Ntchango
Minister of Family and Social Affairs: Honorine Nzet Biteghe
Minister of Industry and Mines: Regis Immongault Tatagani
Minister of Budget, Public Finance and Civil Service: Christiane Rose Ossoucah Raponda

Ministries

Office of the President, BP 546, Libreville, Gabon. Tel: +241 172 2030
Office of the Prime Minister, BP 546, Libreville, Gabon. Tel: +241 177 8981
Ministry of Agriculture, Livestock, Fisheries and Rural Development, BP 551, Libreville, Gabon. Tel: +241 176 2943
Ministry of Communications, Post and Digital Economy, BP 2280, Libreville, Gabon. Tel: +241 176 1692
Ministry of the Economy, Commerce, Industry and Tourism, BP 3906, Libreville, Gabon. Tel: +241 176 3055, URL: http://www.gabontour.com
Ministry of Energy and Hydraulic Resources, BP 576, Libreville, Gabon. Tel: +241 176 3558, fax: +241 172 4990
Ministry of Equipment, Infrastructure and Planning, BP 49, Libreville, Gabon. Tel: +241 176 3856, fax: +241 174 8092
Ministry of Finance, Budget, Civil Service and State Reform, BP 165, Libreville, Gabon. Tel: +241 172 1210, fax: +241 176 5974, URL: http://www.finances.gouv.ga
Ministry of Foreign Affairs, Co-operation, Francophone Affairs and NEPAD, BP 2245, Libreville, Gabon. Tel: +241 173 9465
Ministry of Health, Social Affairs, Solidarity and the Family, BP 50, Libreville, Gabon. Tel: +241 173 2086
Ministry of Housing, Urban Development, Ecology and Sustainable Development, BP 512, Libreville, Gabon. Tel: +241 177 3102
Ministry of the Interior, Public Security, Immigration and Decentralization, BP 2110, Libreville, Gabon, Tel: +241 172 0075, URL: http://www.primature.gouv.ga/primature/interieur/index.html
Ministry of Justice, BP 547, Libreville, Gabon. Tel: +241 174 6628, fax: +241 172 3384
Ministry of Labour, Employment and Social Insurance, BP 4577, Libreville, Gabon. Tel: +241 174 3218
Ministry of Mines, Oil and Hydrocarbons, BP 576, Libreville, Gabon. Tel: +241 176 3558, fax: +241 172 4990
Ministry of National Defence, BP 13493, Libreville, Gabon. Tel: +241 177 8694
Ministry of National Education, Higher Education, Scientific Research, Innovation and Culture, BP 1007, Libreville, Gabon. Tel: +241 176 3233, fax: +241 172 3688, URL: http://www.primature.gouv.ga/enseigne
Ministry of Small and Medium-sized Enterprises and Handicrafts, BP 3096, Libreville, Gabon. Tel: +241 174 5921
Ministry of Technical Education and Professional Training, BP 2258, Libreville, Gabon. Tel: +241 144 4743
Ministry of Transport and Civil Aviation, BP 803, Libreville, Gabon. Tel: +241 174 7196, fax: +241 717 3331
Ministry of Water, Forests, Environment and Sustainable Development, BP 3974, Libreville, Gabon. Tel: +241 176 0109, fax: +241 176 6133
Ministry of Youth, Sport and Leisure, BP 2150, Libreville, Gabon. Tel: +241 174 0019, fax: +241 174 6589

Major Political Parties

Gabonese Democratic Party (PDG); Gabonese Party for the Independent Centre (PGCI); Gabonese People's Rally (RPG); Gabonese Union for Democracy and Development (UGDD); Union of the Gabonese People (UPG)

Elections

Omar Bongo first came to power in 1967 and was the second longest serving head of state in Africa until his death in June 2009. Presidential elections took place on 27 November 2005 when Omar Bongo was re-elected president for a further seven years, with 79 per cent of the vote. The next presidential election was supposed to take place within 45 days of the death of the President and took place on 3 September 2009. Omar Bongo's son Ali Ben Bongo was elected to the position but opposition leaders denounced the election as fraudulent.

National Assembly elections were last held in December 2011; the President's Gabonese Democratic Party (PDG) and its allies won 114 seats. Senate elections were last held on 18 January 2009.

Diplomatic Representation

Embassy of the Republic of Gabon, 27 Elvaston Place, London SW7 5NL, United Kingdom. Tel: +44 (0)20 7823 9986, fax: +44 (0)20 7584 0047, URL: http://gabonembassyuk.org/
Ambassador: Omer Piankali (page 1495)
Embassy of the Republic of Gabon, 2034 20th Street, NW, Suite 200, Washington, DC 20009, USA. Tel: +1 202 797 1000, fax: +1 202 332 0668, e-mail: info@ambagabonusa.net, URL: http://gabonembassyusa.org
Ambassador: Michael Moussa-Adamo
US Embassy, Blvd. du Bord de Mer, BP 4000, Libreville, Gabon. Tel: +241 762003, fax: +241 745507, URL: http://libreville.usembassy.gov
Chargé d'Affaires: Dante Paradiso
British Consulate, (All British Embassy staff are resident at Yaounde) c/o Brossette, BP 486, Libreville, Gabon. Tel: +241 762200, fax: +241 765789; URL: http://ukincameroon.fco.gov.uk/en
Ambassador: H.E. Bharat Joshi (page 1452)
Permanent Representative of the Gabonese Republic to the United Nations, 18 East 41st Street, 9th Floor, New York, NY 10017, USA. Tel: +1 212 686 9720, fax: +1 212 689 5769, e-mail: gabon@un.int, URL: http://www.un.int/gabon/
Ambassador: Noel Nelson Messone

LEGAL SYSTEM

The judiciary is independent, and the President is the guarantor of that independence, assisted by the Conseil Supérieur de la Magistrature. The civil court system consists of trial courts, appellate courts, and a Supreme Court. The Supreme Court has three chambers: judicial, administrative, and accounts. The 1991 constitution established a Constitutional Court to consider constitutional matters.

The judiciary also consists of a military tribunal, a state security court, and a special criminal court for cases of fraud and corruption involving government officials. Village chiefs continue resolve local disputes though traditional law is no longer recognised.

The government's human rights record is poor. The security forces use excessive force, including torture. Prison conditions are harsh, and arrests can be arbitrary. The judiciary is susceptible to government influence, and there is widespread government corruption. There are restrictions on freedom of speech, association, and movement. Gabon abolished the death penalty in 2010.

National Human Rights Commission, BP 546, Libreville, Gabon. Tel: +241 727857, fax: +241 702096

LOCAL GOVERNMENT

Gabon is divided administratively into nine provinces: Estuaire, Haut-Ogooue, Moyen-Ogooue, Ngounie, Nyanga, Ogooue-Ivindo, Ogooue-Lolo, Ogooue-Maritime, Woleu-Ntem. Each has an appointed governor. The provinces are subdivided into 36 prefectures and eight subprefectures.

AREA AND POPULATION

Area

Gabon lies in West Africa, on the continent's Atlantic coast. It is bordered by the Republic of Congo to the east and south, Cameroon and Equatorial Guinea to the north, and the Atlantic Ocean to the west. The area of the country is 267,667 sq. km. Around 80 per cent of the country is forested. The interior is hilly, there are plains in the east and south, and there is a narrow coastal strip. The weather is hot and humid, with two rainy seasons, and two dry seasons per year; the main dry season lasts from June to August, and the main rainy season is from October to May.

To view a map, visit http://www.un.org/Depts/Cartographic/map/profile/gabon.pdf

Population

The population in 2010 was estimated at 1.505 million, with an annual population growth rate estimated at 2.0 per cent over the period 2000-10. The majority of Gabonese (57 per cent) are aged between 15 and 60 years, with 35 per cent aged up to 14 years, and 6 per cent aged 60 years and over. Approximately 86 per cent of the population live in urban areas. Principal towns are Libreville, with a population of about 673,995, and Port-Gentil. Ethnically, Gabon is composed of about 40 Bantu tribes, of which there are four major tribal groups: Fang, Bapounou, Nzebi, and Obamba. The population also includes about 154,000 expatriates from Europe and Africa.

The official language is French. Fang is spoken in the north, Bantu languages along the coast and other local dialects throughout the rest of the country.

Births, Marriages, Deaths

In 2010, the estimated birth rate was 27.1 births per 1,000 inhabitants and the death rate was 9.3 deaths per 1,000 people. The median age is 22 years. Average life expectancy at birth in 2009 was 60 years for males and 64 years for females. The infant mortality rate is estimated at 54 deaths per 1,000 live births, whilst the total fertility rate is an estimated 3.3 children born per woman. (Source: http://www.who.int, World Health Statistics 2012)

Public Holidays 2014

1 January: New Year's Day
14 January: Birth of Muhammad (Mouloud)*
12 March: Renovation Day
21 April: Easter Monday
1 May: Labour Day
6 May: Martyrs' Day
9 June: Whit Monday
29 July: End of Ramadan (Eid al-Fitr)*
15 August: Assumption
16/17 August: Independence Days
5 October: Feast of the Sacrifice (Eid al-Adha)*
1 November: All Saints' Day
25 December: Christmas Day
* Islamic holiday: precise dates depend on a sighting of the moon

EMPLOYMENT

Gabon had an estimated labour force in 2010 of 600,000, of which an estimated 52 per cent is employed in agriculture, 32 per cent in government and services, and 16 per cent in commerce and industry. The unemployment rate, according to recent reports, could be as high as 21 per cent.

Gabon is a member of the International Labour Organisation (ILO).

BANKING AND FINANCE

Currency

The unit of currency is the Franc de la Coopération Financière en Afrique Centrale (CFA) of 100 centimes. Gabon's CFA has been pegged to the euro since 1998.

The financial centre is Libreville.

GDP/GNP, Inflation, National Debt

Gabon's economy relies largely on revenues from oil exports. Oil exports currently account for around 51 per cent of GDP and around 70 per cent of export revenues. However, the country is facing declines in both oil production and reserves and is attempting to diversify its economy. Gabon's public expenditures from the years of significant oil revenues were not spent efficiently and the country earned a poor reputation for the management of its debt and revenues. Timber is Gabon's second largest export, accounting for 5 per cent of GDP and 12 per cent of total exports. Exports of manganese also make significant contributions to the country's GDP, and in recent years, Gabon begun to market itself as a high end ecotourism destination.

Gabon's Gross Domestic Product (GDP) rose by 2.2 per cent in 2003, up from 1.7 per cent in 2001. High oil prices helped to offset the drop in production. GDP grew by 1.2 per cent in 2006, to an estimated US$9,546.94 million. In 2007 it reached US$10,651.51 million. In 2007 it reached US$10,651.51 million. Estimated figures for 2010 put GDP at US$14 billion, showing a growth rate of 5.5 per cent. Estimated figures for 2010 put GDP at US$14 billion, showing a growth rate of 5.3 per cent, rising to US$15 billion in 2011. Per capita GDP was $8,500 in 2010, well above most of sub-Saharan Africa. However, the richest 20 per cent of the population receives over 90 per cent of the income, and about a third of Gabonese live in poverty. Industry makes the largest contribution to Gabon's GDP (an estimated 64 per cent in 2007), followed by services (32 per cent), and agriculture (4.0 per cent).

Inflation was 4.8 per cent in 2007, up from 4.0 per cent in 2006, up from -0.2 per cent in 2005 and 0.4 per cent in 2004. Estimated inflation for 2010 was 5.0 per cent. Gabon's total external debt was US$2.5 billion in 2011.

Foreign Investment

Part of the Gabonese government's plan to increase economic growth is the encouragement of foreign investment in a number of parastatal industries, including fisheries, port development and transport, and light industry.

Recent IMF recommendations have been a speeding up of Gabon's privatisation programme and further development of the private sector. In May 2007, the IMF approved a new US$ 117 million standby loan to support government efforts to expand the non-oil sectors.

Balance of Payments / Imports and Exports

Merchandise export revenue rose from an estimated US$3.7 billion f.o.b. in 2004 to an estimated US$6.677 billion in 2006. Export commodities are mainly crude oil, timber, manganese, and uranium. Gabon's major export trading partners in 2006 were the US (53 per cent), China (8.5 per cent) and France (7.4 per cent). Export revenue was estimated to be US$9.5 billion in 2011.

Estimated merchandise import costs rose from US$1.2 billion f.o.b. in 2004 to US$1.607 billion f.o.b. in 2006. Import commodities consisted largely of machinery, food, manufactured goods, cars and construction equipment. Main import trading partners in 2006 were France (43 per cent), the US (6 per cent), and the UK (5 per cent). Imports were estimated to cost US$3 billion in 2011.

GABON

Gabon is a member of the African Development Bank (AFDB), African Union, Central African Economic and Monetary Community (CEMAC), International Monetary Fund (IMF), and World Trade Organisation (WTO).

Central Bank

Banque des Etats de l'Afrique Centrale (BEAC), PO Box 1917, Rue du Docteur Jamot, Yaounde, Cameroun. Tel: +237 234030 / 234060, fax: +237 233329, URL: http://www.beac.int
Governor: Lucas Abaga Nchama

MANUFACTURING, MINING AND SERVICES

Primary and Extractive Industries

Gabon is rich in mineral resources, of which oil and manganese are the most important. Along with political stability, such mineral wealth has increased the country's per capita GDP to one of the highest in Africa. Gabon's oil industry contributes about 45 per cent of GDP, and over 60 per cent of export revenues. Proven oil reserves are the largest in sub-Saharan Africa at an estimated 2 billion barrels at the beginning of 2012, down from 2.5 billion barrels in 2006.

Gabon is now the sixth largest producer of oil in sub-Saharan Africa; production is falling to the point where reserves were expected to be seriously depleted by 2012 unless new fields are discovered, so far only modest reserves have been found. In recent years international interest has grown inn exploiting Gabon's pre-salt reserves. Oil production was estimated at 244,400 barrels per day in 2011, down from 289,700 barrels per day in 2003 and an significant drop on the 1997 high of 371,000 barrels per day. Domestic oil consumption was an estimated 14,000 barrels per day in 2011; most of the oil produced was exported to the USA, Europe, China and India. Gabon had a January 2012 crude oil refining capacity of 24,000 barrels per day.

Gabon's state oil company is Société Nationale Petrolière Gabonaise. Major foreign oil companies involved in exploration and development in Gabon include Total, Shell, Amerada Hess, and Eni.

Most of Gabon's natural gas is used in the generation of electricity or to fuel its refineries. Natural gas reserves were estimated at 1 trillion cubic feet at the beginning of January 2011. Gas production was an estimated 3.0 billion cubic feet in 2010, with gas consumption at the same volume.

Manganese has been produced since the early 1960s. Extraction takes the form of open-cast mining from deposits that comprise 35 per cent of the world's known deposits. Recent output amounted to 663,000 metric tons.

Although it is known that Gabon has other mineral resources, among them barytes and talc, none are currently being exploited. The chemical, metal processing and metallurgy industries are also important. (Source: Energy Information Administration, EIA)

Energy

Figures for 2010 show that 49 per cent of energy consumption came from biomass and waste, 37 per cent from petroleum, nine per cent from hydroelectricity and three per cent from gas. Gabon's total energy consumption in 2009 was estimated at 1.145 quadrillion Btu, less than 0.1 per cent of world total energy consumption.

Gabon's electricity generation capacity was an estimated 0.4 gigawatts at the beginning of January 2010; officially, 59 per cent was thermally generated whilst the remaining 41 per cent was hydroelectric, but more recent sources show that up to 70 per cent is hydroelectric. Electricity production was estimated at 1.78billion kilowatthours (kWh) in the same year and consumption was 1.45 billion kWh. Plans to expand hydroelectricity generation capacity, some in conjunction with future mining developments, are under consideration, and additional electricity is being generated through a recent project providing solar panels to remote villages. Low levels of rainfall in early 2007 led to blackouts in Libreville, and the authorities are planning an increase in dam storage capacities to allow for fluctuations in water supply. Figures for 2009 show that 55 per cent of electricity came from hydroelectricity the rest from conventional thermal supplys.

Approximately 20 per cent of households in Gabon are not yet connected to the grid. Gabon's electricity and water utility is the Société d'Electricité et d'Eaux du Gabon (SEEG), 51 per cent of which is owned by the French company Veolia. The rest of the shares are owned by employees and the public. Major hydro-electric power stations are situated at Tchimbele (68 megawatts), Kinguele (58 megawatts), and Poubara.

A recently launched plan was to develop the electricity sector with the construction of six power plants and 5,000 kilometer transmission lines. It was hoped that the first stage of the plan would come online in 2013, this would be the 160-MW Poubara hydroelectric dam on the Ogooué River, this has been built by built by China's Sinohydro company. Gabon has recently released plans to build a 180-MW hydroelectric dam in the south. (Source: EIA)

Manufacturing

This sector consists mainly of petroleum refining, mineral processing, timber preparation and other agro-industrial processes.

Services

The service sector accounted for around 25 per cent of GDP in 2006.

In 2002, some 10 per cent of Gabon's land area was designated a National Park - the highest proportion of any state in the world. The country has enormous potential as a destination for eco-tourism.

Agriculture

Agriculture and forestry accounted for 5.9 per cent of GDP in 2006. Although only 1 per cent of the country's area is cultivated, 44.3 per cent of the economically active population is involved in agriculture and animal husbandry. In addition to the food crops that are intended for domestic consumption, Gabon produces coffee, cocoa, sugar, pineapples and rubber, all of which are exported. Cattle, pigs, and poultry are now being reared in Gabon for the domestic market; however, output falls far short of demand, and more than half the food requirements of the country are met by imports.

Agricultural Production in 2010

Produce	Int. $'000*	Tonne
Plantains	55,168	296,90
Game meat	54,614	25,10
Yams	32,110	167,90
Cassava	20,579	270,00
Natural rubber	15,671	13,70
Taro (cocoyam)	10,392	55,00
Groundnuts, with shell	7,413	17,70
Sugar cane	6,633	240,00
Vegetables fresh nes	6,633	35,20
Indigenous chicken meat	4,955	3,478
Indigenous pigmeat	4,864	3,164
Fruit fesh nes	4,293	12,30

*=unofficial figures
Source: http://faostat.fao.org/site/339/default.aspx Food and Agriculture Organization of the United Nations, Food and Agricultural commodities production

Timber products are Gabon's second largest export, accounting for 15 of total exports and over 5 per cent of GDP. Marketing and production of timber is the responsibility of the parastatal National Timber Corporation (SNBG).

In 2010 the total catch of fish was estimated to be 32,000 tonnes.

COMMUNICATIONS AND TRANSPORT

Travel Requirements

US, Australian, Canadian and EU citizens require a passport valid for at least six months, and a visa. Proof of yellow fever vaccination is also required. Other nationals should contact the Gabon embassy to check entry requirements

International Airports

The main international airport is Libreville, built in 1988. In addition there are international airports at Port-Gentil and Franceville. Gabon has a relatively dense network of air routes, with 210 airfields of varying sizes.

Railways

The Trans-Gabon Railway has been extended in recent years. It now runs between Owendo, Booué and Franceville. In the region of 181,000 passengers and three million tons of freight are transported by rail annually. The Transgabonais railway company, OCTRA, is currently in the process of being privatised as part of a government plan to increase economic growth in the country.
Office du Chemin de Fer Transgabonais (OCTRA), Libreville, Gabon.

Roads

Gabon's road system is presently being developed, with plans to extend it some 1,851 km. Total length is 7,800 km, of which 30 km are motorways, 3,780 km are main roads and 2,420 km are secondary roads. Some 24,750 passenger cars and 16,500 lorries are in use. Vehicles are driven on the right.

Shipping

The merchant shipping fleet has a total displacement of 32,178 grt, a decrease of more than 66,000 grt 10 years earlier.
Société Nationale de Transports Maritimes (SONATRAM), Libreville, Gabon.

Ports and Harbours

There are two main port complexes, Libreville-Owendo (barge traffic) and Port Gentil (petroleum). Annual throughput is some 12.8 million metric tons of goods loaded and 0.21 million metric tons unloaded. A ferry service operates along the coast from Libreville to Port Gentil,
Office des Ports et Rades du Gabon (OPRAG), Libreville, Gabon.

HEALTH

In 2009, Gabon spent approximately 6.6 per cent of its total budget on healthcare, accounting for 47.9 per cent of all healthcare spending. Private expenditure accounted to 52.1 per cent. Total expenditure on health care equated to 3.6 per cent of the country's GDP. Per capita expenditure on health in 2009 was US$266. All private expenditure on health is out-of-pocket. According to WHO figures, in 2000-10 there were 395 doctors (three per 10,000 inhabitants) and 6,778 nursing and midwifery staff (50 per 10,000 people). There was less than one dentist per 10,000 people.

Despite the relative wealth of Gabon, the majority of the people are extremely poor. The United Nations estimated in 2006 that between 60 and 70 per cent of the population lived below the poverty line, with less than US$1 per day to spend. The infant mortality rate was 54 per 1,000 live births in 2009 and the under-five mortality rate was 74 per 1,000 live births. The main causes of child mortality are: prematurity (16 per cent), malaria (15 per cent),

HIV/AIDS (8 per cent), pneumonia (11 per cent), and diarrhoea (7 per cent). An estimated 26.3 per cent of children under five were deemed to be stunted and 8.8 per cent under-weight in 2000-09. Approximately 5.2 per cent of adults are infected with HIV/AIDs.

According to the latest WHO figures, in 2010 approximately 87 per cent of the population had access to improved drinking water and 33 per cent had access to improved sanitation. Source: http://www.who.int, World Health Statistics 2012)

EDUCATION

Education is compulsory between the ages of 6 and 16. Primary education begins at six years of age and finishes at 11. Subsequent schooling can take the form of academically oriented secondary education or vocational training. Secondary education begins at 12 years and lasts up to seven years.

Primary education provides 1,147 schools. According to 2004 statistics, the primary pupil-teacher ratio was 36 to one. Secondary education provides 99 schools. In 2002, around 60 per cent of children attended.

University level education is carried out in two higher education institutions - Université Nationale Omar Bongo, Libreville, and Université des Sciences et des Techniques de Masuku (USTM) - with 299 teachers and 3,000 students. Around 8 per cent of students go on to tertiary education.

In 2004, 9.6 per cent of total government expenditure went on education. The literacy rate in 2007 was 08 per cent for males and 82.2 per cent for females. In the age group 15-24 years this rose to 98 per cent for males and 95.9 per cent for females. (Source: UNESCO, UIS)

RELIGION

About 90 per cent of the population are Christian, predominantly Roman Catholic, whilst 2 per cent are animists and 4 per cent Muslim. Gabon has a religious liberty rating of 9 on a scale of 1 to 10 (10 is most freedom). (Source: World Religion Database)

COMMUNICATIONS AND MEDIA

Most of the media is state controlled. Some newspapers are privately owned, some controlled by opposition parties.

Newspapers
L'Union, Libreville, Gabon.
Gabon-Matin, Libreville, Gabon.

Broadcasting
The state-controlled RTG broadcasts two national radio and television channels as well as provincial services. In addition there is a commercial radio station. There are over 51,000 television receivers currently in use.

Telecommunications
Estimates put the number of mainline telephones in use in 2008 at 26,500. Mobile telephones sales have quickly exceeded that number, and by 2008 there were 1.3 million in use (over 50 per cent of the population now has one). Internet users numbered over 90,000 in 2008.

ENVIRONMENT

Gabon's main environmental problems are poaching, deforestation and resultant wildlife destruction.

Gabon is a party to a number of international environmental agreements including Biodiversity, Climate Change, Climate Change-Kyoto Protocol, Desertification, Endangered Species, Hazardous Wastes, Law of the Sea, Marine Dumping, Ozone Layer Protection, Ship Pollution, Tropical Timber 83, Tropical Timber 94, Wetlands, and Whaling.

In 2012 Gabon's emissions from the consumption of fossil fuels totalled 4.59 million metric tons of carbon dioxide. (Source: EIA)

GAMBIA
Republic of The Gambia

Capital: Banjul (Population estimate: 50,000)

Head of State: H.E. Dr Alhaji Yahya A.J.J. Jammeh (President) (page 1448)

Vice-President: Dr Isatou Njie-Saidy (page 1487)

National Flag: Three horizontal stripes, red, blue and green, the blue stripe bordered by two narrow white stripes.

CONSTITUTION AND GOVERNMENT

Constitution
The Gambia was a British colony from the late 19th century. Self-government was conceded in 1962, when elections were won by the People's Progressive Party (PPP), whose leader, Dawda Kairaba Jawara, became prime minister. The country became independent in 1965 and in April 1970 it was declared a republic with Jawara as president. Although the Gambia retained multiparty democracy throughout Sir Jawara's 29 year leadership, there were allegations of corruption. After re-election on five occasions Jawara was deposed in a bloodless coup by junior army officers in July 1994. Captain Yahya Jammeh set up the Armed Forces Provisional Ruling Council (AFPRC).

The Constitution of the Second Republic of the Gambia was agreed in a national referendum on 8 August 1996 and came into effect on 16 January 1997. It makes the President of the Republic the head of state and the head of government. The President is directly elected for a five-year term by universal adult suffrage and appoints the members of the government.

To consult the full constitution, please visit http://www.wipo.int/wipolex/en/details.jsp?id=7439

International Relations
The Gambia has good relations with other African countries and is a member of the African Union. President Jammeh has mediated in West African peace processes. Relations with Senegal have been recently strained by trade and transport issues, and they were exacerbated by President Jammeh's accusation that Senegal was habouring the instigators of an attempted coup in April 2006.

The Gambia is a member of the Commonwealth, and has developed links with Islamic countries; the Islamic development bank and OPEC have offered financial support.

Recent Events
In December 2004, a law was passed allowing the government to jail journalists found guilty of libel or sedition. A prominent newspaper editor and critic of the law, Deyda Hydara, was shot dead shortly afterwards.

In March 2006 the government said a military coup had been foiled and in September of the same year, President Jammeh won a third term in office. In February 2007 the UN development envoy, Fadzai Gwaradzimba, was expelled from the country for criticizing the president's assertion that he could cure AIDS. In April 2007 ten army officers were jailed for plotting a coup.

In May 2008, President Yahya Jammeh told a political rally that gay people had 24 hours to leave the country, saying he would behead any gay person found in The Gambia. The Gambia is the host country for the African Commission on Human and People's Rights. A number of homosexual men had fled to The Gambia from neighbouring Senegal following a crackdown there. In March 2009 Amnesty International voiced concern saying that hundreds of people have been kidnapped following a government campaign against witchcraft.

In August 2009 six journalists were imprisoned for criticising the president, they were later pardoned.

In June 2012, former justice minister Fatou Bensouda was sworn in as the new Chief Prosecuter at the International Criminal Court in The Hague.

In August 2012, nine prisoners were executed by firing squad. The following month President Jammeh suspended future executions following international criticism.

Legislature
The Gambia's unicameral legislature is known as the National Assembly. Of the National Assembly's 53 members, 48 are directly elected by universal adult suffrage, whilst the remaining five members are nominated by the President. All serve terms of five years.
National Assembly, Parliament Buildings, Independence Drive, Banjul, The Gambia. Tel: +220 228305, fax: +220 225123

Cabinet (as at June 2013)
Commander in Chief of the Armed Forces: President Col. Yahya Jammeh (page 1448)
Secretary of State for Women and Social Affairs: Vice President Isatou N'jie-Saidy (page 1487)
Secretary of State for Finance and Economic Affairs: Abdou Kolley
Secretary of State for Foreign Affairs, International Co-operation and Gambians Abroad: Susan Waffa-Ogoo (page 1532)
Attorney General and Secretary of State for Justice: Justice Amie Joof
Secretary of State for Trade, Regional Integration and Employment: Kebba S. Touray
Secretary of State for Culture and Tourism: Fatou Mas Jobe-Njie
Secretary of State for Interior: Ousman Sonko
Secretary of State for Youth and Sports: Alieu K. Jammeh
Secretary of State for Primary and Secondary Education: Fatou Faye
Secretary of State for Health and Social Welfare, Minister of National Assembly Affairs: Bala Garba-Jahumpa
Secretary of State for Parks and Wilflife and Environment: Fatou Gaye

---

GAMBIA

Secretary of State for Higher Education and Research, Science and Technology: Mambury Njie
Secretary General, Heald of Civil Service: Momodou Sabally
Secretary of State for Energy: Teneng Mba Jaiteh
Secretary of State for Agriculture: Solomon Owens
Secretary of State for Transport, Works and Infrastructure: Francis Liti Mboge
Secretary of State for Fisheries and Water Resources: Mass Axi Gai
Secretary of State for Information and Communication Infrastructure, Deputy Secretary-General: Nana Grey-Johnson
Secretary of State for Lands and Regional Government: Momodou Aki Bayo

Ministries

Government Portal: URL: http://www.statehouse.gm
Office of the President, Private mail bag, State House, Banjul, Gambia. Tel: +220 4223 811, fax: +220 4227 034, e-mail: info@statehouse.gm, URL: http://www.statehouse.gm
Ministry of Agriculture, The Quadrangle, Banjul, Gambia. Tel: +220 4221 47, fax: +220 4229 546, e-mail: jammeh2@hotmail.com, URL: http://www.agrigambia.gm
Ministry of Basic and Secondary Education, Gambia Technical Training Institute Building, PO Box 989, Banjul, Gambia. Tel: +220 4228 232, fax: +220 4224 180, e-mail: dosy-s@qanet.gm
Ministry of Defence, State House, Banjul, Gambia. Tel: +220 4227 208, fax: +220 4227 034
Ministry of Energy, Second floor Futurelec Building, Bertil Harding Highway, Kotu, Banjul, Gambia. Tel: +220 8905 105, fax: +220 4466 560
Ministry of Finance and Economic Affairs, The Quadrangle, Banjul, Gambia. Tel: +220 4228 291, fax: +220 4227 954, URL: http://www.dosfea.gm
Ministry of Fisheries and Water Resources, 6 Marina Parade, Banjul, Gambia. Tel: +220 4201 400, fax: +220 4223 987
Ministry of Foreign Affairs, International Co-operation and Gambians Abroad, 4 Marina Parade, Banjul, Gambia. Tel: +220 4228 291, fax: +220 4228 060
Ministry of Forestry and the Environment, 5C Marina Parade, Banjul, Gambia. Tel: +220 4227 307, fax: +220 4224 765, URL: http://www.crdfp.org/fd.htm
Ministry of Health and Social Welfare, The Quadrangle, Banjul, Gambia. Tel: +220 4227 872, fax: +220 4228 505, URL: http://www.dosh.gm
Ministry of Higher Education, Research, Science and Technology, Willy Thorpe Building, Banjul, Gambia. Tel: +220 4224 505, URL: http://www.edugambia.gm
Ministry of Information and Communication Infrastructure, GRTS Building, MDI Road, Kanifing, Gambia. Tel: +220 4378 028, fax: +220 4378 029, URL: http://www.doscit.gm
Ministry of the Interior, 21 OAU Boulevard, Banjul, Gambia. Tel: +220 4228 611, fax: +220 4201 320
Ministry of Justice, Marina Parade, Banjul, Gambia. Tel: +220 4228 181, fax: +220 4225 352, e-mail: sukamie@yahoo.com
Ministry of Local Government and Lands, The Quadrangle, New Administrative Building, Banjul, Gambia. Tel: +220 4228 291, fax: +220 4225 261
Ministry of Petroleum and Mineral Resources, 7 Marina Parade, Banjul, Gambia. Tel: +220 4224 122, fax: +220 4225 009
Ministry of Tourism and Culture, The Quadrangle, New Administrative Building, Banjul, Gambia. Tel: +220 4228 496, fax: +220 4227 753
Ministry of Trade, Regional Integration and Employment, Independence Drive, Banjul, Gambia. Tel: +220 4228 229, fax: +220 4229 220, URL: http://www.gambia.gm
Ministry of Women's Affairs, State House, PO Box 83, Banjul, Gambia. Tel: +220 4227 605, fax: +220 4201 463, e-mail: dibbapsave@qanet.gm
Ministry of Works, Construction and Infrastructure, MDI Road, Kanifing, Gambia. Tel: +220 4395 024, fax: +220 4378 015
Ministry of Youth and Sports, The Quadrangle, Banjul, Gambia. Tel: +220 4496 386, fax: +220 4495 621

Political Parties

Alliance for Patriotic Reorientation and Construction (APRC); National Alliance for Democracy and Development (NADD); United Democratic Party (UDP)

Elections

Presidential elections took place on 22nd September 2006 when the incumbent president, Yahya Jammeh, was re-elected for a third term, with 67.3 per cent of the vote. Oussainou Darboe was the main opposition candidate for the second time. Mr Jammeh has been in power since the 1994 military coup.

The most recent presidential elections took place on 24 November 2011. The incumbent President Yahya Jammeh won a fourth term in office taking 72 per cent of the vote. The opposition candidate Ousainou Darboe won 17 per cent and Hamat Bah 11 per cent. Turnout was estimated to be 72 per cent. The opposition has alleged fraud and Ecowas has said the elections would not be free and fair because of intimidation in the run-up to the election by the government.

Parliamentary elections were held in Gambia on 29 March 2012; the Ruling Alliance for Patriotic Reorientation and Construction (APRC) won 43 of the 48 elected seats.

Diplomatic Representation

The Gambia High Commission, 57 Kensington Court, London W8 5DG, United Kingdom. Tel: (0)20 7937 6316/7/8, fax: (0)20 7937 9095, URL: http://gambia.embassyhomepage.com
High Commissioner: H E Mrs Elizabeth Ya Eli Harding
British High Commission, 48 Atlantic Road, Fajara (PO Box 507), Banjul, The Gambia. Tel: +220 449 5133, fax: +220 449 6134, e-mail: bhcbanjul@gamtel.gm, URL: http://ukingambia.fco.gov.uk/en
High Commissioner: David Morley
Embassy of the Gambia, Suite 1000, 1155 15the Street, NW Washington DC 20005, USA. Tel: +1 202 785 1399, fax: +1 202 785 1430, e-mail: gamembdc@gambia.com, URL: http://www.gambiaembassy.us
Ambassador: H. E. Alieu Ngum

US Embassy, Fajara, Kairaba Avenue, PMB 19, Banjul, The Gambia. Tel: +220 439 2856 fax: +220 439 2475, URL: http://banjul.usembassy.gov
Ambassador: Edward M. Alford
Permanent Representative of the Gambia to the United Nations, 800 Secon Avenue, Suite 400F, New York, NY 10017, USA. Tel: +1 212 949 6640, fax: +1 212 808 4975 e-mail: gambia@un.int
Ambassador: vacant

LEGAL SYSTEM

The legal system is based on English common law, Islamic law and customary law. Shari'a law is applied in certain cases involving Muslim people, whilst tribal chiefs rule on customar law and local affairs. The Gambia's court system is headed by the Supreme Court, unde which is the Court of Appeal. The lower courts comprise Khadis' courts, district tribunals an magistrate courts. The Supreme Court has unlimited jurisdiction and comprises the chie justice and puisne judges. Appeals from subordinate courts and the Islamic courts go to the Supreme Court.

The constitution and law provide for the protection of human rights. However, the securit forces arbitrarily arrest and detain people, and harass opposition members and journalists Prison conditions are poor, and detainees can be held without charge for long periods without access to lawyers. The government restricts freedom of speech and press through intimidation and restrictive legislation.

Although permitted under the 1996 constitution, death sentences in Gambia are rare an require the signature of President Yahya Jammeh. Only one person has been executed since independence from Britain in 1965. However, in 2007, two people were handed the death sentence, and Guinean man and a Senegalese women; the magistrate said the sentence had been harsh in order to curtail a rising tide of violent crime by foreigners which he said was alien to Gambian culture. In 2010, the death penalty was introduced for possession o cocaine or heroin, this was in a bid to discourage international drug trafficking. Nine executions were carried out in 2012.

LOCAL GOVERNMENT

Administratively, the Gambia is divided into three main areas: the capital territory (containing the seat of government), the Kombo St. Mary area, and the provinces. The provinces are themselves divided into five divisions - Lower River, Central River, North Bank, Upper River, and Western - and one city, Banjul. All are governed by a commissioner. Each council has its own treasury and is responsible for local government services. Each division is subdivided into districts administered by tribal chiefs who retain traditional powers authorized by customary law in some instances.

AREA AND POPULATION

Area

With a total area of 11,295 sq. km, The Gambia is the smallest country in Africa. It is located in West Africa on the Atlantic coast, surrounded by Senegal. The country forms a narrow strip along the river Gambia, about 50 km wide at the river's mouth, but less than 24 km across for most of its length. The landscape is principally one of flood plain along the length of the Gambia River, flanked by low hills. The Gambia's climate is tropical, with a hot wet season (June to November) and a cooler dry season (November to May).

To view a map, consult http://www.lib.utexas.edu/maps/cia08/gambia_sm_2008.gif

Population

Gambia's population was estimated at 1.728 million in 2010, with an annual population growth rate of 3.0 per cent over the period 2000-10 and a population density of 104 people per sq. km. The majority of Gambians (53 per cent according to 2010 estimates) is aged between 15 and 60, with 44 per cent aged up to 14 years, and nearly 3 per cent aged 60 years and over. The median age is 18 years. The population is now predominately urban (57 per cent), as more and more young people are now coming to the capital in search of work and education. More areas have also been declared urban.

The principal ethnic groups are the Mandinka (42 per cent), Fula (18 per cent), Wolof (16 per cent), Jola (10 per cent) and Serahula (9 per cent). There are also significant numbers of Europeans, Lebanese and Mauritanians, and substantial seasonal migration from Senegal, Guinea and Mali. English is the official language. Local languages spoken are Wolof, Mandingo and Fulani.

Births, Marriages, Deaths

According to 2010 estimates, the birth rate was 38.1 per 1,000 people, whilst the death rate was 8.5 per 1,000 people. The average life expectancy in 2009 was 59 years (58 years for men and 61 years for women). Healthy life expectancy was put at 51 years. Infant mortality fell to 57 deaths per 1,000 live births in 2010, and the fertility rate rose to 4.9 children born per woman. (Source: http://www.who.int, World Health Statistics 2012)

Public Holidays 2014

1 January: New Year's Day
14 January: Birth of the Prophet*
18 February: Independence Day
18 April: Good Friday
21 April: Easter Monday
1 May: Labour Day
22 July: Anniversary of the Second Republic
29 July: Eid Al Fitr* (Ramadan ends)
15 August: Assumption Day

5 October: Eid al-Adha, Festival of the Sacrifice
25 December: Christmas
*Islamic holidays: precise date depend upon sighting of the moon

EMPLOYMENT

Unemployment is high in urban areas and in rural areas the fragile agricultural sector is highly dependent on the weather. Of Gambia's 777,000 labour force, some 75 per cent work in agriculture, mainly at a subsistence level. Around 19 per cent are employed in industry and 6 per cent work within the service sector.

BANKING AND FINANCE

Currency
Dalasi (GMD) = 100 Butut
Decimalized currency, the *dalasi*, was introduced in 1971. It replaced the Gambian pound which had been in use since 1965. The dalasi has undergone successive devaluations.

GDP/GNP, Inflation, National Debt
The Gambian economy relies principally on traditional subsistence agriculture, and the export of peanuts. Growth areas are the re-export trade and the tourism industry. The economy is also boosted by remittances from abroad.

GDP was estimated to be US$1.1 billion in 2011, with a growth rate of 3.3 per cent. GDP was estimated to be US$789 million in 2009 (compared to US$511.4 million in 2006), indicating a growth rate of 5.7 per cent. Per capita GDP was estimated at US$515 in 2009 (compared to US$356 in 2006). Agriculture contributed over 24 per cent of GDP in 2009 and employed three-quarters of the work force. Industry contributed almost 12 per cent of GDP, whilst the service sector accounted for around 60 per cent of GDP. Total external debt stood at US$550 million in 2011.

The inflation rate peaked in 2003 at 17 per cent before falling to 14 per cent in 2004 and 3.2 per cent in 2005. Inflation was estimated at 6.0 per cent in 2010.

Foreign Investment
The Gambia is heavily dependent on external assistance for its development finance. It also relies on responsible economic management as proposed by IMF and other donor organisations, and on expected growth in the construction sector.

Direct foreign investment was an estimated US$35 billion in 2011.

Balance of Payments / Imports and Exports
Export revenue in 2011 was estimated at US$100 million, the main export commodities being re-exports (82 per cent), peanuts and peanut products, fish products, cotton lint and palm kernels were also exported. The major export trading partners in 2011 were China (35 per cent), India, and France. Import costs in the same year were US$325 million with food, minerals, fuel, and machinery and transport equipment the main import commodities. In 2011, the main suppliers were China (25 per cent), Senegal and Brazil.

Central Bank
Central Bank of the Gambia, 1/2 Ecowas Avenue, Banjul, Gambia. Tel: +220 228103, fax: +220 226969, e-mail: centralbank.gambia@ganet.gm, URL: http://www.cbg.gm
Governor: Momodou Bamba Saho

Chambers of Commerce and Trade Organisations
Gambia Chamber of Commerce and Industry, URL: http://www.gambiachamber.gm/

MANUFACTURING, MINING AND SERVICES

Primary and Extractive Industries
To date, Gambia has no significant mineral resources and has to import all of its oil requirements. Oil consumption in 2011 reached an estimated 2,000 barrels per day. No natural gas or coal is imported or consumed. Seismic studies indicate the possible presence of oil and gas offshore.

Energy
Gambia had a 2010 electricity capacity of 0.06 gigawatts, entirely thermal generated. Production reached 0.23 billion kWh in 2010 and consumption was 0.21 billion kWh in the same year. Gambia is entirely dependent on imported oil for its energy needs, although hydroelectric generation is under development. Along with Senegal, Guinea and Guinea-Bissau, Gambia is a participant in the Gambia River Development Organisation, but progress on irrigation and hydropower schemes has been held up for lack of funding.

Manufacturing
The manufacturing sector accounted for 14 per cent of GDP in 2006, and, along with commerce and services, employed around 19 per cent of the labour force. The main manufacturing industries are agricultural machinery assembly, peanut products, brewing and soft drinks, woodworking, metalworking, and clothing.

Re-export trade to neighbouring countries makes a significant contribution to the economy. This sector has been helped recently by a stable currency, an efficient port, the relative lack of bureaucracy and improved relations with Senegal.

Service Industries
The services industry was the main contributor towards GDP in past years, accounting for 53 per cent in 2004. Tourism revenues fell at the beginning of the millennium, but there has been a recent upturn in the sector; the number of tourists arriving by charter flight increased from 78,500 in 2000 to 110,815 in 2005. A large proportion of visitors came from the UK.
Gambia National Tourist Office, URL: http://www.gambiatourism.info

Agriculture
Gambia has a limited agricultural base. Nonetheless, agriculture is a major source of economic revenue, contributing about 32 per cent of GDP and employing three-quarters of the workforce. Major crops include peanuts, millet, sorghum, rice, corn, sesame, cassava, and palm kernels. Groundnuts are the most important crop, usually accounting for about four fifths of exports, and 6.9 per cent of GDP; the country's economic health is heavily dependent on the movement of world groundnut prices. About a third of the crop is produced by seasonal immigrants from Senegal, Guinea and Mali. Other crops account for around 8 per cent of GDP, livestock contributes 5 per cent, fishing almost 2 per cent and forestry, around 0.5 per cent.

In 2004, 45 per cent (459,000 hectares) of the total land was used for pasture, and 29 per cent (285,000 hectares) was arable, but not irrigated. There were 412 sheep and goats, and 328 head of cattle. There were no tractors or harvesters. (Source: FAO Statistical Yearbook, 2005-06)

Agricultural Production in 2010

Produce	Int. $'000*	Tonnes
Groundnuts, with shell	57,896	137,631
Millet	26,863	158,018
Rice, paddy	26,372	99,890
Indigenous cattle meat	11,022	4,080
Sorghum	5,675	39,000
Maize	5,652	66,000
Cow milk, whole, fresh	2,911	9,328
Game meat	2,611	1,200
Fruit fresh nes	2,583	7,400
Indigenous goat meat	2,504	1,045
Vegetables fresh nes	2,299	12,200
Sesame seed	2,099	3,100

* unofficial figures
Source: http://faostat.fao.org/site/339/default.aspx Food and Agriculture Organization of the United Nations, Food and Agricultural commodities production

COMMUNICATIONS AND TRANSPORT

Travel Requirements
US, Australian, Canadian and EU subjects require a passport valid for at least three months following departure, a return or onward ticket and sufficient funds for their stay. Some nationals require a transit visa. Australians and some EU citizens do not require a visa for stays of up to 28 days; nationals of the USA, Canada, Austria, Bulgaria, Cyprus, Czech Republic, Estonia, France, Hungary, Latvia, Lithuania, Malta, Poland, Portugal, Romania, Slovak Republic, Slovenia and Spain do require a visa. Other nationals should contact the embassy to check entry requirements.

Evidence of vaccination against yellow fever is required from travellers coming from areas with risk of yellow fever transmission. This is particularly relevant for those travelling to the Gambia from neighbouring African countries.

International Airports
Improvements have been made to the airport at Yundum near Banjul, from which Air Gambia, Gambia Airways and several other international airlines operate.
Gambia Civil Aviation Authority, Banjul National Airport, Yundum, Gambia. Tel: +220 472831 / 472172, fax: +220 472190

Roads
All-weather roads have been developed considerably since the 1960s. According to recent figures there are nearly 3,742 km of roads, about 723 km of which are paved. Vehicles drive on the right.

Ports and Harbours
The Gambia River has been a major conduit of trade and transport. The port at Banjul has been modernised and enlarged. 394 vessels docked in Banjul in 1999, and shipping tonnage reached 1,115,067 net registered tonnage. Ferry services operate across the Gambia River.
Gambia Ports Authority, URL: http://www.gambiaports.com

HEALTH

In 2009, Gambia spent approximately 11.3 per cent of its total budget on healthcare, accounting for 43.4 per cent of all healthcare spending. External resources accounted for 25.4 per cent of expenditure. Total expenditure on health care equated to 6.1 per cent of the country's GDP. Per capita total expenditure on health was US$27. Figures for 20050-10 show that there are 62 physicians (less than 0.4 per 10,000 population), 927 nurses and midwives (6 per 10,000 population) and 23 dentistry personnel. There are 11 hospital beds per 10,000 population.

The under 5 mortality rate in 2009 was 57 deaths per 1,000 live births and the under-five mortality rate was 98 per 1,000 live births. Major causes were: HIV/AIDS 3 per cent, diarrhoea 9 per cent, malaria 20 per cent, pneumonia 15 per cent, prematurity 14 per cent and birth asphyxia 10 per cent. An estimated 49 per cent of children now sleep under treated mosquito nets. Approximately 8,000 adult Gambians are living with HIV/AIDS, over half of whom are women.

According to the latest WHO figures, in 2010 approximately 89 per cent of the population had access to improved drinking water and 68 per cent had access to improved sanitation. (Source: http://www.who.int, World Health Statistics 2012)

EDUCATION

Primary/Secondary Education
Education is free and compulsory in the Gambia, but poor infrastructure and lack of resources means that not all children are able to attend school. Attendance in primary education in 2007 was put at 73 per cent of girls and 69 per cent of boys, falling to 38 per cent of girls and 39 per cent of boys in secondary school. In primary schools, there are approximately 41 pupils per teacher, and around 10 per cent of pupils have to repeat years.

A distance learning project was developed in Gambia in 2003, within the framework of reinforcing teaching capabilities. The project aims to improve teaching programmes in matters such as mathematics, science, technology and languages.

Higher Education
Higher education, including courses in teacher training, agriculture and health, is limited to the Gambia College and a number of technical training schools. In 2004, one per cent of the relevant age group went on to study at tertiary level.

In 2004, 8.9 per cent of government spending went on education. The most recent figures available (2002) put the adult literacy rate at just 49.9 per cent, though this improves to 67.5 per cent among the 15-24 age group. Both figures are below the regional average. (Source: UNESCO, UIS)

RELIGION

The Gambia is predominantly Muslim (86 per cent of the population). About 5 per cent of the population is Christian, of variety of different denominations. Gambians officially observe the holidays of both religions and practice religious tolerance. Gambia has a religious liberty rating of 10 on a scale of 1 to 10 (10 is most freedom). (Source: World Religion Database)

COMMUNICATIONS AND MEDIA

The media is severely restricted with broadcasters and the press having to pay for expensive license fees. Recent laws have provided for jail terms for journalists found guilty of libel or sedition.

Newspapers
The Gambia's newspapers include the Observer (URL: http://observer.gm/), The Independent, The Point, URL: http://www.maaleht.ee, The Gambia Times, Banjul (fortnightly), and The Gambia Weekly, Banjul. There is also an internet news service, Gambia News (URL: http://http://www.gambianow.com/news).

Broadcasting
The national television station, Gambia Television and radio station, Radio Gambia are both government run. There is one private satellite channel.

Telecommunications
In 2008, there were an estimated 49,000 mainline telephones and 1.6 million mobile phones in use. There are around 110,000 internet users in The Gambia.

ENVIRONMENT

The Gambia's main environmental problems are desertification, deforestation, and water-borne diseases. In addition, rainfall has dropped by almost a third over the past 30 years.

In 2010 carbon dioxide emissions from the comsumption of fossil fuels was put at 0.29 million metric tons, down from the 2009 figure of 0.44 million metric tons. (Source: EIA)

The Gambia is a party to the following international environmental agreements: Biodiversity, Climate Change, Climate Change-Kyoto Protocol, Desertification, Endangered Species, Hazardous Wastes, Law of the Sea, Ozone Layer Protection, Ship Pollution, Wetlands and Whaling.

GEORGIA
Republic of Georgia
Sakartvelos Respublika

Capital: Tblisi (Population estimate 2011: 1,106,700)

Head of State: Mikhail Saakashvili (President) (page 1507)

National Flag: White, with a red cross creating quarters with a smaller red cross in each quarter

CONSTITUTION AND GOVERNMENT

Constitution
At the end of the 1980s, internal tension caused by pro-Georgian and pro-Abkhaz independence movements pressed the Georgian Supreme Soviet to initiate the Republic's right to secede from the Soviet Federation. A series of constitutional amendments slowly granted the Republic greater autonomy and control of its resources. In 1990, the newly named Republic of Georgia abolished the monopoly of the Communist party, and complete independence was declared on 9 April 1991. In the same month, the Supreme Soviet elected Zviad Gamsakhurdia as President.

Opposition to the elected President from internal opposition forces, led to the creation of the breakaway republic of South Ossetia. Presidential power was then lost and internal conflict continued until August 1993, when a joint peace-keeping force made up of Russians, Georgians and Abkhazians was installed.

EC recognition of Georgia's independence came in March 1992 and UN membership was accorded on 31 July 1992. Georgia joined the Alma Ata Agreement for membership of the Commonwealth of Independent States on 2 March 1994. In April 1996, Georgia, with Azerbaijan and Armenia, signed an agreement with the EU for increased partnership and cooperation.

According to the August 1995 Constitution, (which replaced the Decree on State Power of November 1992) the President takes on the roles of Head of State, head of the executive and Commander-in-Chief of the Armed Forces. The President is elected for five years and may not hold more than two consecutive terms in office. The Government advises the President to whom it is directly accountable.

A new draft constitution was proposed in June 2010. It includes a reduction of presidential powers with increased authority to parliament and the prime minister.

To consult the full constitution, please visit: http://www.parliament.ge

International Relations
Georgia's relationship with close neighbour Russia has deteriorated in recent years. Traditionally Russia was a large market for Georgia's exports but recently agricultural products, particularly wine and mineral water, have been banned apparently on health grounds. Georgia has also accused Russian of shutting off gas supplies. In 2006 Georgia publicly humiliated Russians suspected of being spies; Russia retaliated by deporting many Georgians. Relations further deteriorated over the question of the Georgian breakaway regions of South Ossetia and Abkhazia, whose claims for independence have been supported by Russia; the situation escalated in August 2008, when Georgian troops entered South Ossetia to re-establish Georgian control, and Russian troops invaded Georgia in response.

In 2006 Georgia was granted Intensified Dialogue status by NATO in a step towards membership.

Recent Events
Parliamentary elections were held in November 2003 and were criticised by independent observers. Thousands of people took to the streets to protest about the elections, and the president, Eduard Shevardnadze, declared a state of emergency. Shortly afterwards he resigned, in what became known as the velvet revolution. The speaker of the parliament, Nino Burjanadze, took over the role of president until elections could be held. In January 2004 Mikhail Saakashvili was elected president.

In February 2005 the prime minister, Zurab Zhvania, died apparently from accidental gas poisoning. Mr Saakashvili's nominee, Zurab Noghaideli, the former finance minister, was approved as his successor.

In July the Baku-Tbilisi-Ceyhan Caspian oil pipeline was opened.

In September 2007 President Saakashvili was accused of corruption, sparking large street protests, the anti government protests carried on into November when President Saakashvili declared a state of emergency, he then resigned to concentrate on his election campaign after bringing forward the date of presidential election to January 2008.

In April 2008 Russia announced its wish to form closer ties with Abkhazia and South Ossetia. In May 2008 Georgia accused Russia of planning a military intervention after it sent troops to Abkhazia ostensibly to help with repairs to the railway system.

Tensions between Moscow and Tbilisi are never far from the surface and in August 2008 flared up into an armed conflict triggered by clashes between Georgian troops and South Ossetian separatist forces. Russia said it would intervene if conflict erupted and duly sent in armoured units into the region. Fierce clashes ensued. Both Russians and Georgians accused the other side of attacks. Georgian president Mr Saakashvili said Georgia had shot down several Russian planes and accused Moscow of bombing Georgian air bases and towns. Russian President Dmitry Medvedev said he had to act to defend South Ossetia's civilians, most of whom have been given Russian citizenship. On August 9 Georgia declared a State of War. Russian planes attacked military targets in the Georgian town of Gori, killing around 60 people, mainly civilians. Russia claimed to have wrested control of the South Ossetian capital Tskhinvali from Georgian forces. Meanwhile in Abkhazia, Georgia's other breakaway region, separatists claimed to have launched air and artillery strikes on Georgian forces in the Kodori Gorge. A delegation of European and US envoys traveled to Georgia, in the hope of brokering a truce.

On August 11th European diplomats persuaded Georgia's president Mikhail Saakashvili to sign a draft ceasefire agreement, however, Russia rejected it and continued to send troops to Abkhazia. On August 12 European diplomats led by French President Nicolas Sarkozy again tried to broker a ceasefire agreement. President Medvedev later announced that Russia had agreed to a six point peace deal which agreed neither side would use force and troops would return to the positions they held before the conflict. President Sarkozy then travelled to Georgia where President Saakashvili announced that Georgia would accept the terms of the ceasefire.

On the 25th August, the Russian government announced its recognition of the independence of the breakaway regions of South Ossetia and Abkhazia. President Medvedev said that Russia had been obliged to act because of Georgia's "genocide" of separatists. The separatist authorities in Abkhazia and South Ossetia, which have had de facto independence since the early 1990s, thanked Russia. On the 29th August, Georgia cut diplomatic ties with Russia. By September 9th Russia had withdrawn her troops from Georgia apart from 7,600 who Russia said would be stationed at military bases in Abkhazia and South Ossetia. Meanwhile a meeting of EU foreign ministers took place to discuss the deployment of some 200 ceasefire monitors in buffer zones around South Ossetia and Abkhazia.

In January 2010 direct passenger flights resumed between Russia and Georgia for the first time since 2008 and in March a border crossing between the two countries was re-opened. It is the only crossing which does not go through Abkhazia and South Ossetia.
In October 2010, the parliament approved changes to the constitution which would curb the powers of the president and increase the role of the prime minister and government.

In May 2011, police were called in to disperse protestors who had held a five day rally calling for the resignation of President Saakashvili. In October 2011 billionaire Bidzina Ivanishvili had his Georgian citizenship cancelled a week after he announced he would form a political party and stand in elections. In May 2012 tens of thousands of protestors took to the streets and attended an anti-government rally.

Abkhazia
Capital: Sukhumi
President: Sergei Bagapsh
Abkhazia is an area in north east Georgia that was a popular Black Sea resort for the Soviet elite. At the beginning of the 19th Century Russia declared that Abkhazia was a protectorate and in 1864 went on to annexe it. In 1931, under Stalin, the region was incorporated into Georgia and given the status of autonomous region. Following Georgian independence in 1991, Abkhazia made a bid to break away from Georgia, who responded by sending in troops. In 1993 following fierce fighting Georgia's troops were expelled and around quarter of a million Georgians left the area as refugees. In 1999 Abkhazia declared its independence, but was given no international recognition. As a result, Abkhazia has become isolated. A CIS peacekeeping force is stationed in the region. The UN has tried to mediate between the two sides but with Georgia saying it will never recognise Abkhazia as an independent state and Abkhazia insisting on independence and turning more toward Russia, an agreement seems a distant prospect.

Presidential elections were held in January 2005; the two leading contenders had both previously held the post of prime minister. Sergei Bagapsh became president and Raul Khadzhimba took the post of vice president.

In March 2008 the separatist government approached the UN asking it to recognise its independence. The following month Russia said it would form closer ties with Abkhazia and South Ossetia. Georgia accused Russia of attempting to annexe the two regions. In May Russia sent troops to Abkhazia to help with repairs to the railway system, the troops were unarmed but Georgia accused Russia of planning a military intervention.

Ajaria
Capital: Batumi
Leader of the Regional Government: Levan Varshalomidze
Ajaria is a semi-autonomous region on the border with Turkey in the south west. The port of Batumi is an important transshipment point for oil coming from Kazakhstan and Turkmenistan, as well as being the main port for goods destined for Georgia, Azerbaijan and Armenia. Ajaria has a population estimated at 400,000.

The president of Ajaria from Georgian independence until 2004 was Aslan Abashidze. He failed to recognise the authority of Mikhail Saakashvili after the overthrow of Georgian president Eduard Shevardnadze, and ordered bridges linking Ajara and Georgia to be blown up saying he feared an invasion by Georgian troops. Street demonstrations were held in Ajaria and President Abashidze resigned; the post of president was subsequently abolished. Ajaria has an elected government consisting of an assembly of 30 members. The Georgian president nominates the government leader.

South Ossetia
Capital: Tskhinvali

President: Eduard Kokoiti
South Ossetia is situated in the north of Georgia and is referred to as the Samachablo or Tskinvali region, in order to distance it from North Ossetia which is situated across the border in Russia. In 1990 South Ossetia announced that it wished to be independent of Georgia. Violence broke out between Georgian troops and South Ossetian separatists. In 2004 South Ossetia held parliamentary elections which were not recognised by Georgia. The region has a population of around 70,000. President Saakashvili has opened talks with South Ossetia and has offered the region autonomy within Georgia, something that the separatists have refused. A referendum on independence was held in November 2006; over 98 per cent of South Ossetians voted for independence from Georgia, a result that was disregarded by the Georgian government.

A presidential election held on 27 November 2011 for South Ossetia was annulled. Preliminary results gave the opposition leader Alla Dxhioyeva a surprise victory over Russia's preferred candidate, Anatoly Bibilov. Mr Bibilov accused Mr Dzhioyeva of fraud and the result was declared invalid.

Legislature
The Georgian Parliament is the supreme legislative body and is made up of 230 members in a single legislative chamber, 85 members are elected from constituencies and the remainder from party lists. The Constitution, however, makes provisions for two chambers, made up of a Senate and a Council of the Republic.
Parliament of Georgia, 8 Rustaveli Avenue, Tbilisi 380018, Georgia. Tel: +995 (8)32 935113, URL: http://www.parliament.ge
Speaker: Nino Burjanadze

Cabinet (as at June 2013)
Prime Minister: Bidzina Ivanishvili (page 1447)
First Deputy Prime Minister, Minister for Education and Science: Giorgi Margvelashvili
Deputy Prime Minister, Minister of Energy: Kakha Kaladze
Minister of European Integration: Alexi Petriashvili
Minister of State for the Diaspora: Kote Surguladze
Minister of Refugees and Housing: David Darakhvelidze
Minister of Finance: Nodar Khaduri
Minister of Foreign Affairs: Maia Panjikidze
Minister of the Economy and Sustainable Development: Giorgi Kvirikashvili
Minister of Internal Affairs: Irakli Garibashvili
Minister of Labour, Health and Social Welfare: Dr David Sergienko
Minister of Agriculture: Shalva Pipia
Minister of Justice: Tea Tsulukiani
Minister of Culture: Guram Odisharia
Minister of Environment: Khatuna Gogoladze
Minister of Regional Development and Infrastructure: David Narmania
Minister of Sports and Youth: Levan Kipiani
Minister of Corrections, Probation and Legal Assistance: Sozar Subari
Minister Re-intergration: Paata Zakareishvili
Minister of Defence: Irakli Alasania

Ministries
Office of the Prime Minister and Government, Ingorovka Street 7, Tbilisi 380018, Georgia. Tel: +995 (8)32 935907, fax: +995 (8)32 982354, URL: http://www.government.gov.ge/eng
Ministry of Education, 52 Uznadze Street, Tbilisi 380002, Georgia. Tel: +995 (8)32 958386, fax: +995 (8)32 770073, URL: http://www.mes.gov.ge
Ministry of Environmental Protection and Natural Resources, 68A Kostava Street, Tbilisi 380015, Georgia. Tel: +995 (8)32 230664, fax: +995 (8)32 943420
Ministry of Economics, Industry and Trade, 12 Chanturia Street, Tbilisi 380008, Georgia. Tel: +995 (8)32 921929, fax: +995 (8)32 982367
Ministry of Economic Development and Infrastructure, Vazha Pshavela 16, Tbilisi, Goergia. Tel: +995 (8)32 374276, fax: +995 (8)32 220541
Ministry of Defence, 2 University Street, Tbilisi 380007, Georgia. Tel: +995 (8)32 983930, fax: +995 (8)32 983929
Ministry of Justice, 30 Rustaveli av, Tbilisi 380008, Georgia. Tel: +995 (8)32 932721, fax: +995 (8)32 930225, URL: http://www.justice.gov.ge
Ministry of Culture, 37 Rustaveli Avenue, Tbilisi, 380008, Georgia. Tel: +995 (8)32 932255, fax: +995 (8)32 999037, e-mail: info@mc.gov.ge
Ministry of Refugees and Placement, 30 Dadiani Street, Tbilisi 380080, Georgia. Tel: +995 (8)32 941611, fax: +995 (8)32 921427
Ministry of Foreign Affairs, 4 Chitadze Street, Tbilisi 380018, Georgia. Tel: +995 (8)32 989377, fax: +995 (8)32 997248, e-mail: listsrv@mfa.gov.ge, URL: http://www.mfa.gov.ge
Ministry of Fuel and Energy, 10 Lermontov Street, Tbilisi, Georgia. Tel: +995 (8)32 996098, fax: +995 (8)32 933542, e-mail: webmaster@georgia-gateway.org, URL: http://www.georgia-gateway.org/energy/
Ministry of Police and Social Order, 49 April Street, Tbilisi 380008, Georgia. Tel: +995 (8)32 995784, fax: +995 (8)32 932791
Ministry of State Property Management, 64 Chavczhavadze Avenue, Tbilisi 380062, Georgia. Tel: +995 (8)32 294875, fax: +995 (8)32 225209, e-mail: lchitanava@access.sanet.ge, URL: http://web.sanet.ge/mospm
Ministry of Agriculture and Products, 41 Kostava Street, Tbilisi 380023, Georgia. Tel: +995 (8)32 990272, fax: +995 (8)32 999444
Ministry of Transport and Communications, 12 Kazbegi Street, Tbilisi 380060, Georgia. Tel: +995 (8)32 986385, fax: +995 (8)32 990461, e-mail: mintrans@iberiapac.ge, URL: http://www.iberiapac.ge/mintrans/
Ministry of Urbanisation and Construction, 16 V. Pshavela Avenue, Tbilisi 380060, Georgia. Tel: +995 (8)32 374276, fax: +995 (8)32 220541
Ministry of Finance, 70 Abashidze Street, Tbilisi 380062, Georgia. Tel: +995 (8)32 226805, fax: +995 (8)32 292368, e-mail: minister@mof.ge, URL: http://www.mof.ge
Ministry of the Internal Affairs, 10 Gulua Street, Tbilisi 380014, Georgia. Tel: +995 (8)32 996296, fax: +995 (8)32 986532, URL: http://www.police.ge

GEORGIA

Ministry of Healthcare, Labour and Social Security, 30 Gamsakhurdia Avenue, Tbilisi 380060, Georgia. Tel: +995 (8)32 387071, fax: +995 (8)32 370086
Ministry of Post and Telecommunications, 9th April Street, Tbilisi, Georgia. Tel: +995 (8)32 997777 / 988682, e-mail: esakia@iberiapac.ge, URL: http://www.iberiapac.ge/mincom

Political Parties
Joint Opposition (JO); United National Movement - For Victorious Georgia (UNM-FVG), URL: http://www.unm.ge. Leaders: Mikheil Saakashvili and David Bakradze; Democratic Movement, United Georgia, URL: http://www.democrats.ge, Leader: Nino Burjanadze.

Elections
In 1992, Eduard Shevardnadze was elected Chairman of Parliament. Shevardnadze lost power to the Military Council led by Tengiz Kitovani and Djabu Loselliani on 6 January 1992, but was reinstated at elections held in October 1992. After the adoption of the new constitution in 1995 Shevardnadze was elected to the newly restored post of President.

Presidential elections were held on 9 April 2000 and parliamentary elections in November 2003. International observers recorded irregularities in the voting and street protests were held following the election which resulted in what became known as the Velvet Revolution and the resignation of the president. Another presidential election followed in January 2004. President Mikhail Saakashvili won 96.3 percent of the vote. In the parliamentarian elections, Natshhiakhun Modraoba Demokrathebi NMD won 67 percent of the vote, and 135 of the 235 seats.

The most recent presidential election was held in January 2008. Mikhail Saakashvili was re-elected in the first round with over 52 per cent of the vote. Although opposition groups protested that the vote was rigged, official observers declared them to be fair.

Parliamentary elections were held in May 2008. Mikhai Saakashvili's United National Movement won 120 of parliament's 150 seats and he pledged to work closely with opposition parties. The opposition alleged intimidation and vote rigging, and said that they would not work in the new parliament. Saakashvili dismissed Lado Gurgenidze as prime minister on 27 October 2008, and nominated Grigol Mgaloblishvili to replace him. Mgaboloshvili resigned on 30 January 2009. The Deputy Prime Minister Nika Gilauri was nominated as his successor.

The most recent election took place on 1 October 2012, the opposition Georgian Dream party won, marking the first peaceful election and transfer of power since independence.

Diplomatic Representation
American Embassy, 11 George Balanchine Street, 0130 Tbilisi, Georgia. Tel: +995 (8)32 227000, fax: +995 (8)32 532310, URL: http://georgia.usembassy.gov
Ambassador: Richard B. Norland (page 1487)
British Embassy, GMT Plaza, 4 Freedom Square, Tbilisi, 0105, Georgia. Tel: 995 32 274747, fax: +995 32 274792, e-mail: British.Embassy.Tbilisi@fco.gov.uk, URL: http://ukingeorgia.fco.gov.uk/en
Ambassador: David Moran
Embassy of Georgia to USA, Canada and Mexico, 1101 15th Street NW, Suite 602, Washington, DC 20005, USA. Tel: +1 202 387 2390, fax: +1 202 393 4537, e-mail: embassy@georgiaemb.org, URL: http://usa.mfa.gov.ge/index.php?lang_id=GEO&sec_id=38&lang_id=ENGsec_id=38
Ambassador: Dr. Archil Gegeshidze
Embassy of Georgia, 4 Russell Gardens, London, W14 8EZ, United Kingdom. Tel: +44 (0)20 7603 7799, fax: +44 (0)20 7603 6682, e-mail: geoemb@dircon.co.uk, URL: http://www.geoemb.org.uk
Ambassador: Giorgi Badridze (page 1381)
Permanent Representation of Georgia in the UN, One UN Plaza, 26th Floor, New York, NY 10017, USA. Tel: +1 212 759 1949, fax: +1 212 759 1832, email: georgia@un.int, URL: http://embassy.mfa.gov.ge/
Permanent Representative: Alexander Lomaia

LEGAL SYSTEM

Georgia has a three-tier court system. At the first level are the District courts, which hear minor criminal and civil cases. At the second level are the Regional courts of appeal, which have both original and appellate jurisdiction, trying major criminal and civil cases, and reviewing cases. The Supreme Court is the highest appellate court; it also hears some cases, and some appeals from the Central Electoral Commission.

A constitutional court arbitrates constitutional disputes and rules on individual claims of human rights abuses.

Administration of the court system is the responsibility of the Council of Justice, which consists of four members from each of the three branches of government.

The constitution provides for an independent judiciary. However, the judiciary is sometimes influenced by government and by extensive clan networks. The main human rights issues are the use of excessive force by law enforcement officers, intimidation of suspects and abuse of prisoners. Prison conditions are poor. There are reports of politically motivated detentions and of corruption among senior officials.

The death penalty was abolished for most offenses in 1997 and for all crimes in 2006.

The Supreme Court of Georgia, URL: http://www.supremecourt.ge
Chairman: Konstantine Kublashvil

Public Defender of Georgia, http://www.ombudsman.ge/

LOCAL GOVERNMENT

Georgia is divided into the autonomous Republics of Ajaria and Abkhazia, nine regions and one city. The capital city also has the status of a district. The regions are: Guria, Imereti, Kakheti, Kvemo Kartli, Mtskheta-Mtianeti, Racha-Lechkhumi and Kvemo Svaneti, Samegrelo and Zemo Svaneti, Samtskhe-Javakheti, Shida Kartli. The city is T'blisi. The largest units are further divided into regions (65), district towns, small towns and villages. The President appoints the heads of the larger units of local government and then the District Governor recommends the appointment of the heads of towns and villages. All levels of local government are run by boards of administration. The most recent local elections took place in May 2010.

AREA AND POPULATION

Area
The Republic of Georgia occupies the central and western parts of Transcaucasia. It is bounded in the north by the Russian Federation (Chechen Republic), in the south by Turkey and Armenia, in the east by Azerbaijan and in the west by the Black Sea. The total area of Georgia is 69,700 sq. km. The terrain is largely mountainous, with sub-tropical weather in the west and a moderate climate in the east. Forests cover 40 per cent of the country.

Georgia includes two autonomous Republics: Abkhazia and Ajaria and the South Ossetian Autonomous Region. After almost ten years of conflict between Abkhazia and Georgia, an agreement was signed in 2001 that neither side would use force against the other.

To view a map of Georgia, please visit:
http://www.un.org/Depts/Cartographic/map/profile/georgia.pdf

Population
The total population in 2010 was put at 4.352million. Approximately 17 per cent are aged under 15 years and 19 per cent over 60. The median age is 37 years. The population has been in decline for 20 years; for the period 2000-10 the average annual growth rate was -0.9 per cent.

The country has 51 towns; the capital city is Tbilisi, with an estimated population of 1,106,700 in 2011. Large towns include Kutaisi, Batumi Sukhumi and Rustavi, each has a population of more than 100,000.

Just over 70 per cent of the population are ethnic Georgians, 8 per cent are Armenian, 6.5 per cent Russian, nearly 6.0 per cent Azeri, 3 per cent Ossetian, and nearly 2 per cent Abkhaz.

Georgian is the official language. Russian and Abkhazian are also spoken.

Births, Marriages, Deaths
Estimated figures for 2010 put the crude birth rate as 11.9 per 1,000 population and the crude death rate at 12.3 per 1,000 population. The average fertility rate was 1.6 per woman in 2010. Life expectancy from birth at 2008 was put at 67 years for males and 75 years for females. Healthy life expectancy was 64 years in 2007. (Source: http://www.who.int, World Health Statistics 2012) Figures for 2005 show that 18,012 marriages took place and 1,928 divorces were recorded. (Source: Statistics Department of Georgia)

Public Holidays 2014
1 January: New Year
6-7 January: Orthodox Christmas
6 January: Orthodox Epiphany
3 March: Mother's Day
8 March: Women's Day
20 April: Orthodox Easter Sunday
21 April: Orthodox Easter Monday
26 May: Independence Day
28 August: St. Mary's Day
14 October: Svetitskhovloba (Georgian Orthodox Festival)
23 November: St. George's Day

EMPLOYMENT

Figures for 2005 show that the workforce numbered 2,023,900, of which 1,744,600 were employed and 279,300 were unemployed giving an unemployment rate of 13.8 per cent. (Source: Department of Statistics Georgia). It is estimated that 40 per cent of the workforce is employed in the agriculture and forestry sector, 6 per cent in industry and 10 per cent in trade, and 34 per cent in the service sector.

Estimated figures for 2010 put the workforce at 1.94 million. Unemployment in April 2011 was recorded at 16.6 per cent.

Employment by occupation, 2007

Sector	Employed
Agriculture, forestry & hunting	910,500
Mining & quarrying	4,700
Manufacturing	82,700
Electricity, gas & water supply	18,200
Construction	71,200
Wholesale, retail trade, repairs	168,800
Hotels & restaurants	18,000
Transport, storage & communications	71,700
Financial intermediation	17,300
Real estate, renting and business activities	34,700

continued

Public administration & defence	64,300
Education	124,200
Health & social work	59,900
Other community, social & personal service activities	43,900
Households with employed persons	11,100
Extra territorial Organisations & bodies	2,900

Source: Copyright © International Labour Organization (ILO Dept. of Statistics, http://laborsta.ilo.org)

BANKING AND FINANCE

Currency
The Georgian coupon was replaced by the Georgian Lari (GEL) in October 1995. One Lari is equivalent to 1,000,000 coupons. The coupons were introduced in 1993 but their value rapidly decreased and the transition from coupon to Lari took only one week.
1 Lari = 100 Tetri.

GDP/GNP, Inflation, National Debt
Following independence from the Soviet Union, George implement major strucutral reform to establish a free market economy. Georgia was badly affected by the Russian financial crisis of 1998 but since 2003 the economy has been recovering. The government of Mikheil Saakashvili implemented tax and economic reforms and addressed corruption. Agriculture is the biggest industry although exports have been affected with the deterioration in relationships with its main market, Russia. Georgia has been trying to diversify and expand its trade relations. Following the 2008 conflict with Russia many countries and international organisations pledged aid to assist the country with its post-conflict reconstruction. Georgia is working to overcome its energy shortages by relying less on nautral gas imports from Russia, working instead with Azerbaijan and also by investment in its hydropower plants.

The following table shows the value of Gross National Income (GNI) and Gross Domestic Product (GDP) in recent years. Figures are in million GEL at current prices.

National Accounts

Year	GNI	GDP
2001	6,741.3	6,674.0
2002	7,435.9	7,456.0
2003	8,550.5	8,564.1
2004	9,701.8	9,824.3
2005	11,483.3	11,591.8
2006	14,102.5	13,789.9
2007	17,060.5	16,993.8
2008	18,818.0	19,074.9

Source: Department of Statistics Georgia

The Asian Development Bank put GDP at current market prices at 13,789.9 million GEL in 2006, rising to 16,993.8 million GEL in 2007 and 19,060.5 million GEL in 2008. Growth was 9.4 per cent in 2006 and 12.3 per cent in 2007. It fell to 2.1 per cent in 2008.

GDP by industrial origin at current market prices, million GEL

	2008	2009	2010
GDP at current market prices	19,074.9	17,986.0	20,791.3
-Agriculture	1,551,1	1,457.1	1,518.3
-Mining	128.9	123.3	192.2
-Manufacturing	1,992.0	1,785.7	2,330.2
-Electricity, gas and water	434.3	490.8	533.9
-Construction	1,058.3	1,004.3	1,139.2
-Trade	2,680.9	2,344.1	3,006.0
-Transport & communications	1,813.0	1,746.3	2,097.2
-Finance	442.0	452.7	476.7
-Public administration	2,850.1	2,457.6	2,343.1
Others	3,794.8	3,908.8	4,661.0

Source: ADB

Inflation was estimated at 2 per cent in 2011, rising to 6 per cent in 2012.

Total foreign debt in inQ3 2011 was estimated at US$10.8 billion; much of this is owed to Turkmenistan and Russia for supplies of fuel. The IMF recently approved a three year loan to Georgia under its poverty reduction and growth facility.

Foreign Investment
Georgian production lost its market with the collapse of the Soviet Union. Foreign investment was hindered by the near destruction of the economic infrastructure as a result of the civil war and ethnic conflicts. The Georgian economy therefore suffered a depression between 1992 and 1995. Higher input of foreign investment began again in 1995 with the strengthening of central authority and the introduction of privatisation. Most of the foreign investment is in the areas of oil and gas extraction, manufacturing, banking, agriculture, telecommunications and light industry. FDI amounted to US$980 million in 2011.Countries investing include Denmark, Cyprus, Turkey, Russia and the UK.

Balance of Payments / Imports and Exports
Russia and Turkey were Georgia's main trading partners, but in recent years deteriorating relations with Russia has seen exports cut. Major import products are oil and oil products (16 per cent), cigars and cigarettes (11.5 per cent), natural gas (9 per cent), wheat and rye-wheat mix (6 per cent), and cars (4.7 per cent). Major export products are mineral water (7.2 per cent), ferrous metal pipes (7 per cent), ferro-alloys (6.2 per cent), and tea (5.5 per cent) and other agricultural produce including wine and citrus fruit.

External Trade, US$ million

	2008	2009	2010
Exports	1,495.3	1,133.6	1,583.4
Imports	6,301.5	4,366.1	5,095.1
Trade balance	-4,806.2	-3,232.5	-3,511.7

Source: Asian Development Bank

Main export destinations in 2010 were Turkey (US$264 million), Bulgaria (US$188 million), and the US (US$182 million). Main importers were Azerbaijan (US$386 million), China (US$302 million) and Bulgaria (US$207 million).

Central Bank
National Bank of Georgia, 3/5 Leonidze Street, 380005 Tbilisi, Georgia. Tel: +995 (8)32 996505 / (8)32 982203, fax: +995 (8)32 999346, e-mail: nbg@access.sunet.ge, URL: http://www.nbg.gov.ge
Chairman of the Board: Giorgi Kadagidze

Chambers of Commerce and Trade Organisations
American Chamber of Commerce in Georgia, URL: http://www.amcham.ge/

MANUFACTURING, MINING AND SERVICES

Primary and Extractive Industries
Coal and manganese ore are mined. Estimates for 2010 put coal production at 0.235 million short tons, but consumption was 0.257 million short tons. Other significant plants include an oil refinery, ferro-alloy works and a metallurgical plant. Foreign investment should lead to rapid expansion of oil production especially in oil fields in the Black Sea. Proven oil reserves stand at 0.04 billion barrels. In 2011 Georgia was producing around 0.98 thousand barrels per day but was consuming 14,000 barrels per day. Georgia is also seen as an important transit point for oil and gas pipelines from the Caspian Sea, Azerbaijan and Kazakhstan, and is planned to be part of the Eurasian Transport Corridor, bringing oil and gas from the Caspian and Caucasus region. The majority of Georgia's oil imports come from Russia and Azerbaijan. There are also reserves of natural gas of 300 billion cubic metres, around 27 per cent of Georgia's energy needs comes from natural gas. Figures for 2011 show that no natural gas was produced but 58 billion cubic feet was consumed all of which was imported.

Energy
Only 30-40 per cent of demand was satisfied by domestic resources, the rest being supplied from outside the country, but even then a large part of demand was not met, and this led to protests. In theory Georgia should have enough hydroelectric power for domestic needs and for export but due to poor maintenance of power plants there had been energy rationing. A privatisation programme was put into practice and after much improvement in recent years Georgia is now self sufficient in electricity production with 80 per cent coming from hydropower stations and the rest from thermal power stations. Georgia is now in a position to export electricity. Figures for 2010 show that Georgia generated 9.98 billion kWh of electricity of which 7.62 billion kWh were consumed.

Manufacturing
Industry has a 12 per cent share of GDP, a 108 per cent increase compared to 1996. Georgia has a varied manufacturing industry which includes the production of aircraft, trucks, tractors, steel, textiles and shoes, machinery, machine tools, textiles, bottled water and wine, chemicals and wood products. There has been some privatisation by the Government. Heavy industry has generally been more successful than light industry although all industries have been affected by the poor and high-cost energy supply.

Service Industries
The share of services and trade in GDP is around 39.0 per cent.

Tourism
Tourism is a growing sector in Georgia and figures for 2006 show that there were 983,000 visitors to the country.

Agriculture
Agriculture has a 9.0 per cent share of GDP and employs 55 per cent of the active population. Soil and climate are good for the cultivation of subtropical crops. Watermelons, citrus and other fruits are grown, while poultry farming and silk worm breeding are well developed. Tea, tobacco and grapes are produced and Georgia has the potential to be a major wine exporter, as it was under the Soviet system.

Agriculture is now in the process of being restructured. The products requiring further technical processing and previously orientated to Russian markets are diminishing. The production of products considered necessary and orientated to the local markets is increasing. Despite this only viticulture, tea growing and citrus growing completely satisfy demand. Fruit growing can satisfy 60-70 per cent of demand, stockbreeding 40 per cent and grain growing 10-15 per cent. In recent years, bee-keeping has been developing as one of the most important branches of agriculture and honey and honey materials are significant export products.

The privatisation of agricultural land, which began in 1992 and is implemented in several stages, was an important event for transition from social economy to market relations.

Agricultural Production in 2010

Produce	Int. $'000*	Tonnes
Cow milk, whole, fresh	179,435	575,000
Indigenous cattle meat	79,952	29,597
Grapes	68,994	120,700
Hazelnuts, with shell	46,164	28,800

GEORGIA

- continued

Potatoes	31,866	228,800
Tomatoes	20,696	56,000
Hen eggs, in shell	20,403	24,600
Indigenous pigmeat	19,691	12,809
Indigenous sheep meat	18,132	6,659
Indigenous chicken meat	14,456	10,149
Maize	12,478	141,100
Tangerines, mandarins, clem.	12,005	48,600

*unofficial figures
*Source: http://faostat.fao.org/site/339/default.aspx Food and Agriculture
Organization of the United Nations, Food and Agricultural commodities production*

COMMUNICATIONS AND TRANSPORT

Travel Requirements
Citizens of the USA, Canada, Australia and the EU need a passport valid for at least six months from the date of application, and all visitors must register with the police within three days of arrival. US, Canadian and EU nationals do not require a visa for stays of up to 90 days but Australians do. Other nationals should contact the embassy to check visa requirements. Cruise ship passengers staying in Georgian ports for less than 72 hours do not require a visa.

National Airlines
Orbi Airline, 380058 Tbilisi Airport, Georgia. Tel: +995 (8)32 931623
Air Georgia, 49A, Chavchavadze Avenue, 380062 Tbilisi, Georgia. Tel: +995 (8)32 235407, fax: +995 (8)32 233423

International Airports
Airports are situated in Sukhumi, Batumi and Tbilisi. Airspace is controlled by the following authorities:
Department of Air Transportation, 36 Rustaveli Avenue, 380004 Tbilisi, Georgia. Tel: +995 (8)32 933092/997728, fax: +995 (8)32 989639
Ministry of Transport, 12 Kazbegi Street, 330060 Tbilisi, Georgia. Tel: +995 (8)32 364555

Railways
There is approximately 1,500 km of rail track in Georgia. Much of this is in need of repair. The railway is being modernised with the help of a US$20 million loan from the EBRD. The Transcaucasian railway main line connects two railway branches, from Baku in Azerbaijan and from Yerevan in Armenia, on Georgian territory. The line has been blocked due to the conflict in Abkhazia and mainly serves domestic purposes, i.e. the transportation of cargo within the country as well as from the Batumi port to different parts of Georgia and other Caucasian countries. Tbilisi has a subway system.

Roads
Recent figures reveal the total length of motor roads to be approximately 35,000 km. of which 31,000 km. was hard surfaced. The motor highways connect Georgia and Russia in the north via the Abkhazian coast and through the Caucasian Range tunnel to Oseti, and via the Georgian Military Highway running through the Dariali gorge to Turkey, Armenia and Azerbaijan in the south. Vehicles are driven on the right.

Ports and Harbours
The principal sea ports are Batumi, Poti and Sukhumi. These Black Sea ports provide a transit point to European ports from Azerbaijan and Iran, and also the central Asian states. Container traffic is increasing quickly through the ports of Poti and Batumi.

HEALTH

The health care system has been reformed since independence in 1991. Mandatory social health insurance was introduced but was abolished in 2004. Health care and health insurance are now privatised.

In 2009, Georgia spent approximately 6.1 per cent of its total budget on healthcare (down from 6.9 per cent in 2000), accounting for 22.3 per cent of all healthcare spending. Private expenditure accounts for 77.7 per cent of healthcare expenditure, almost all (85 per cent) paid for out-of-pocket. Total expenditure on health care equated to 10.2 per cent of the country's GDP. Per capita health expenditure was US$251 in 2009 (compared to US$45 in 2000). Figures for 2005-10 show that there are 20,609 physicians (47.6 per 10,000 population), 13,925 nurses and midwives (32.2 per 10,000 population) and 1,219 dentistry personnel. There are 31 hospital beds per 10,000 population.

In 2009, the infant mortality rate was 20 per 1,000 live births and the under-fives mortality rate was 22 per 1,000 live births. Main causes of death were prematurity (24 per cent), pneumonia (11 per cent) and diarrhoea (1 per cent). Immunization rates for common diseases

have improved and are now over 90 per cent. In 2010, 98 per cent of the population has access to improved drinking water sources. In the same year, 95 per cent of the population had access to improved sanitation. (Source: http://www.who.int, World Health Statistic 2012)

EDUCATION

Pre-school education consists of nursery schools for babies aged 1-2 and kindergarten for children aged 3-6. Education is free and compulsory from the age of 6 to16. There is primary, secondary and higher education in Georgia. Primary education starts at age six, secondary education starts at age 10 and lasts for six years. Figures for 2007 show that 57 per cent of young children were attending pre school. Also that year 92 per cent of girls and 95 per cent of boys were enrolled primary school and 82 per cent of girls and 82 per cent of boys were enrolled in secondary school.

Figures for 2007 show that 7.8 per cent of total government spending went on education the equivalent of 2.7 per cent of GDP. (Source: UNESCO)

RELIGION

According to the Constitution of Georgia, every individual in Georgia has the right to choose religion and belief, and persecution of people by the religion is prohibited. The dominant religion is Christianity (followed by 86 per cent of the population), and the Georgian Orthodox Church is by far the largest. Jewish communities currently numbering 11,500 have existed throughout the country, with major concentrations in Tbilisi and Kutaisi. Azerbaijani groups have practiced Islam in Georgia for centuries, the community currently numbers around 440,000.

Georgia has a religious liberty rating of 4 on a scale of 1 to 10 (10 is most freedom). (Source: World Religion Database)

COMMUNICATIONS AND MEDIA

The constitution provides for freedom of speech but there are allegations of political pressure. In 2007, the government suspended the news on private television stations under a state of emergency.

Newspapers
According to recent data, 149 newspapers are published, 128 of which are in Georgian. Total circulation is 3.7 million copies, of which 3.2 million are in Georgian. In addition 75 periodicals are published, including 61 in Georgian. Russian newspapers are also available. Ciculation figures are low.
Georgian News (English), URL: http://www.geotimes.ge/
Svobodnaya Gruzia, URL: http://www.svobodnaya-gruzia.com/

Broadcasting
The state-owned public television station operates from Tbilisi and operates two networks. Several privately-owned TV stations and numerous cable TV operators and commercial TV stations also operate. Stations include: Georgian Channel I and Channel II, Rustavi 2, Iberia, Evrika, 1st Stereo, Sakartvelos) and also two Russian channels (Ostaniko and Public Television). Satellite programmes can be received through Ayety TV company. Local radio stations operate in Tbilisi and other cities. Nationwide radio stations broadcast mainly in Georgian. FM musical radio stations also broadcast.

Telecommunications
The landline network has limited coverage outside the capital. Multiple mobile phone suppliers provide services throughout the country. Estimated figures for 2008 show that there were over 600,000 telephone lines in use and more than 2.7 million mobile phones.

Figures for 2008 show that more than 1,000,000 people were regular internet users.

ENVIRONMENT

Georgia is party to: Air Pollution, Biodiversity, Climate Change, Climate Change-Kyoto Protocol, Desertification, Endangered Species, Hazardous Wastes, Law of the Sea, Ozone Layer Protection, Ship Pollution and Wetlands international environment agreements.

Among the environmental concerns of Georgia are soil pollution from industry and toxic chemicals, air pollution, and pollution of the Mtkvari River and the Black Sea.

According to the EIA, in 2010, Georgia's emissions from the consumption of fossil fuels totalled 5.30 million metric tons of carbon dioxide.

GERMANY

Federal Republic of Germany

Bundesrepublik Deutschland

Capital: Berlin (Population estimate, 2012: 3,515,473)

Seat of Government: Moved from Bonn to Berlin in 1999

Head of State: Joachim Gauck (page 1429)

National Flag: Three equal horizontal bands of black, red and yellow

CONSTITUTION AND GOVERNMENT

Constitution

After the unconditional surrender of Germany at the end of World War II, the country was split into areas occupied by USA, UK, France and the then Soviet Union. The Federal Republic of Germany (FRG) was created out of the zones occupied by the three western nations. The communist eastern Germany was known as the German Democratic Republic (GDR). In 1961 the Berlin Wall was built, separating the conflicting western and eastern-occupied areas of the city, and preventing people from the eastern bloc defecting to the west.

The Federal Republic gradually became more integrated with the western powers, whilst the GDR became a satellite state of the Soviet Union. In 1970, the signing of the Treaty of Warsaw and the Quadripartite Agreement started to improve the ties between the eastern and western sectors, and the Federal Republic continued to better relations.

Political transformation accelerated in the 1980s. Hungary opened its border in September 1989, which allowed people from the GDR to enter the Federal Republic via Austria. This resulted in mass demonstrations within the GDR. Erich Honecker resigned as head of state in October 1989, followed by his council of ministers and the SED Politburo. Border crossings in Berlin were opened on 9 November 1989; the Berlin Wall was finally breached and the communist government collapsed.

Economic and currency union was announced on 1 July 1990. A treaty was signed between the Federal Republic, the GDR and the four occupying powers the same year, and Germany was unified in October 1990. The first all-German elections took place in December 1990.

The Basic Law was adopted by the Federal Republic of Germany in 1949, and agreed by the Democratic Republic during reunification. It is based on the principle of representative democracy, and its constitutional character is laid down in Article 20:
1. The Federal Republic of Germany is a democratic and social federal state.
2. All state authority emanates from the people. It shall be exercised by the people by means of elections and voting and by specific legislative, executive and judicial organs.
3. Legislation shall be subject to the constitutional order; the executive and the judiciary shall be bound by law and justice.
4. All Germans shall have the right to resist any person or persons seeking to abolish that constitutional order, should no other remedy be possible.

The Basic Law may only be amended with a majority of two-thirds of the members of the *Bundestag* (Federal Parliament) and two-thirds of the votes cast in the *Bundesrat* (Federal Council). However some laws may not be changed at all (mainly the rules concerning democracy and the federal system).

The head of state is the Federal President, who is elected by the Federal Convention, a body created primarily for this purpose. The Federal President is elected for a five-year term, and may only be re-elected once. He nominates to the Bundestag a candidate for the position of Federal Chancellor, and if the Chancellor should gain a vote of no confidence, the President can dissolve the Bundestag.

In accordance with the Bundestag's longstanding desire that Berlin be restored as the capital of Germany, and following the reunification of Germany in 1989, the German Parliament has been moved from Bonn to Berlin. The Bundestag was re-located in 1999, while the Bundesrat transferred with effect from 1 August 2000.

To consult the full constitution, please visit:
http://www.gesetze-im-internet.de/gg/BJNR000010949.html

International Relations

Germany was a founding member of the EU, and since the end of the second world war has had a close relationship with France. Germany has set out to strengthen relations with Russia and countries in Eastern Europe since the reunification of Germany. As well as the EU, Germany is a member of, The European Bank for Reconstruction and Development, the G8, The World Trade Organisation, The UN , NATO, IMF, The International Bank for Reconstruction and Development, The Organisation for Co-operation and Security in Europe, and The Organisation for Economic Cooperation and Development. In recent years Germany has sent peacekeeping forces to the Balkans and Afghanistan, but German troops have not been involved in the US led operations in Iraq.

Recent Events

Former Chancellor Helmut Kohl, architect of German reunification, resigned as honorary party chairman of the CDU in January 2000 after admitting illegally accepting party contributions. In March 2001 the former East German leader Egon Krenz and two other East German Communist leaders had their jail terms ruled lawful by the European Court of Human Rights in response to the shooting of escapees at the Berlin Wall. Following the government's decision to deploy 4,000 troops in the US-led campaign in Afghanistan, Chancellor Schroeder survived a confidence vote in parliament. In January 2002 the German government's attempt to ban the far-right National Democratic Party suffered a setback when the Constitutional Court postponed a hearing following revelations that a key witness had been an informer for German intelligence.

Germany, France and Russia did not support the war on Iraq led by US and UK coalition forces.

Chancellor Schroeder resigned as party leader of the Social Democrats in March 2004, amid criticism within his party of his welfare reforms. Franz Muentefering took over as party leader. Regional elections were held in May 2005; the Social Democratic Party lost control of North RhineWestphalia, prompting Chancellor Schroeder to announce early elections. These were held in September, but there was no clear leader. Following extensive coalition negotiations, the leader of the CDU, Angela Merkel, was elected Chancellor of a government made up of CDU, CSU and SPD members.

Unemployment figures released in November 2006 show that unemployment had fallen below four million for the first time in four years.

In common with many economies, Germany has experienced the global downturn in the economy and the banking crisis; in October 2008 one of the countries largest banks Hypo Real Estate received a US$68 billion boost to save it from collapse. In November 2008 Germany suffered two quarters of negative economic growth and was officially in recession. In February 2009 the government approved a stimulus package worth US$63 million to help bolster the economy. In April 2009 the government launched a takeover offer for lender Hypo Real Estate.

The most recent parliamentary elections were held on 27 September 2009. Angela Merkel and her Christian Democrats party were re-elected to power. Results showed that the CDU/CSU took 33.8 per cent of the vote, the SPD 23 per cent, and the FDP 14.6 per cent, 11.9 per cent to the Die Linke and 10.7 per cent to the Grune. The CDU/CSU formed a new coalition government with the FDU. In November 2009 labour Minister Franz Josef Jung resigned amid allegations of a cover-up relating to a deadly Nato air strike in Afghanistan which took place while he was minister of defence.

In May 2010, despite widespread resistance, the parliament voted to approve a €22.4bn German contribution to bail out Greece. Chancellor Angela Merkel's governing centre-right was defeated in regional elections in North-Rhine Westphalia, losing its majority in the upper house of parliament.

President Horst Koehler resigned in May 2010 after making controversial remarks on overseas missions by the German army. An election had to be held within 30 days to elect his successor. Two inconclusive rounds of voting meant that a third round was required. Christian Wulff, the candidate of Chancellor Merkel, finally triumphed in the third round of voting on 30 June.

In September 2010, the cabinet approved a plan to extend the life of Germany's nuclear reactors, this reversed a previous ruling in 2001 to phase out nuclear energy by 2021. However, in May 2011 Chancellor Angela Merkel announced plans to phase out nuclear power by 2022 and become more reliant on renewable energy.

In January 2011 around 4,700 German farms were closed after is was discovered that animal feed being used was contaminated with dioxin.

Regional elections took place in May 2011. Following poor results for the FPD party the cabinet was reshuffled. The Christian Democrats led by Angela Merkel lost the state of Baden-Württemberg for the first time in approximately 60 years. Angela Merkel defended her position on the eurozone crisis, saying it was Germany's duty to save the euro. In July 2011 Germany backed a second large bailout.

In February 2012 President Christian Wulff resigned following a scandal over financial favours. In March, former Lutheran pastor Joachim Gauck was elected to the position.

Poor July 2012 local election results for the FPD in North-Rhine Westphalia were seen as a further sign of the people's hostility towards the government's austerity programme.

In September 2012, the Constitutional Court rejected a call to block the European Stability Mechanism permanent eurozone rescue fund and the European fiscal treaty, instead it imposed a cap on Germany's contribution, this cap can only be overruled by parliament.

In December 2012, following a steep decline in industrial output, the Bundesbank cut its growth forecast for 2013 from 1.6 per cent to 0.4 per cent.

Lower House

The *Bundestag* (House of Representatives) is Germany's parliamentary assembly which represents the people and enacts the country's laws. Currently, there are 603 members. This number was reduced from 669 in 2002. Members are elected for a four-year term. Members are elected in the constituencies and further seats are allocated using a system of proportional representation. The principal functions of the Bundestag include legislation, election of the Federal Chancellor, election of the President of the Federal Republic (within the Federal Assembly) and parliamentary control of the Federal Government. It is split into committees which correspond with Government ministries and departments. Committee meetings are not open to the public.

As the Bundestag is the only constitutional body elected by the people, it is the supreme authority within the state, making the president of the Bundestag second in rank only to the Federal President. The Bundestag's president/speaker and vice presidents are elected by the strongest parliamentary group for a maximum of one electoral term.

Bundestag, Platz der Republik 1, D-11011 Berlin, Germany. Tel: +49 (0)30 227-0, fax: +49 (0)30 227 36979, e-mail: mail@bundestag.de, URL: http://www.bundestag.de

Upper House
The 69 members of the *Bundesrat* (Federal Council) represent the 16 Federal States (*Länder*). The members are not elected by the people but by members of the state governments or their representatives and their terms of office vary. Members of the Bundesrat are restricted to state premiers and ministers (or mayor and senators of Berlin, Hamburg, and Bremen). The number of members representing a state depends on the size of the state's population. Those states with populations of between 2 and 6 million have four votes; those with populations of between 6 and 7 million have five votes; and those with populations of more than 7 million have six votes. An absolute majority requires 35 votes, whilst a two-thirds majority requires 46 votes. Bills which hold particular interest to the Federal States (for example administrative powers) must be passed by the Bundesrat. Any objection of the Bundesrat can be overruled by the Bundestag. The President of the Bundesrat is the current premier and is elected for a 12-month term by the minister-presidents of the states.
Bundesrat, Leipzigerstrasse 3-4, 10117 Berlin, Germany. (Mailing address: Bundesrat, 11055 Berlin, Germany.) Tel: +49 1 8889 1000, fax: +49 1888 9100 400, URL: http://www.bundesrat.de
President: Winfried Kretschmann

Cabinet (as at June 2013)
Federal Chancellor: Angela Merkel (CDU) (page 1476)
Deputy Federal Chancellor and Federal Minister of Economics and Technology: Philipp Rosler (FDP) (page 1505)
Federal Minister of Foreign Affairs: Guido Westerwelle (FDP) (page 1535)
Federal Minister of the Interior: Hans-Peter Friedrich (CSU) (page 1427)
Federal Minister of Justice: Sabine Leutheusser-Schnarrenberger (page 1463)
Federal Minister of Finance: Wolfgang Schäuble (CDU) (page 1509)
Federal Minister of Health: Daniel Bahr (page 1381)
Federal Minister of Labour and Social Affairs: Ursula von der Leyen (CDU) (page 1532)
Federal Minister of Consumer Protection, Food and Agriculture: Ilse Aigner (CSU) (page 1373)
Federal Minister of Defence: Thomas de Maizière (CDU) (page 1414)
Federal Minister of Family Affairs, Senior Citizens, Women and Youth: Kristina Schröder (page 1510)
Federal Minister of Transport, Building and Urban Planning: Peter Ramsauer (CSU) (page 1500)
Federal Minister of Environment, Nature Conservation and Nuclear Safety: Peter Altmaier (page 1377)
Federal Minister of Education and Research: Johanna Wanka (CDU)
Federal Minister of Economic Co-operation and Development: Dirk Niebel (FDP) (page 1486)
Head of Federal Chancellery: Ronald Pofalla (CDU) (page 1496)

Ministers of State
Minister of State in the Federal Chancellery and in charge of Federal-State Coordination: Eckart von Klaeden
Minister of State in the Federal Chancellery, Federal Government Commissioner for Migration, Refugees, and Integration: Maria Böhmer (page 1391)
Minister of State to the Federal Chancellor, Federal Government Commissioner for Culture and Media: Bernd Neumann (page 1485)

Ministries
Office of the Federal President, Bundespraesidialamt, Spreeweg 1, 10557 Berlin, Germany.Tel: +49 (0)30 2000 0, fax: +49 (0)30 2000 1999, e-mail: posteingang@bundespraesident.de, URL: http://www.bundespraesident.de
Federal Chancellery, Bundeskanzleramt, Willy-Brandt Str. 1, 10557 Berlin, Germany. Tel: +49 (0)18884000, fax: +49 (0)18888400 2357, e-mail: internetpost@bundesregierung.de, URL: http://www.bundeskanzler.de
Federal Press and Information Office Dorotheenstrasse 84, 10117 Berlin, Germany. (Mailing address: Presse- und Informationsamt, 11044 Berlin, Germany), Tel: +49 (0)1888 2720, fax: +49 (0)1888 2721365, e-mail: InternetPost@bundesregierung.de, URL: http://www.bundesregierung.de
Ministry for Foreign Affairs, Auswärtiges Amt, Werderscher Markt 1, 10117, Berlin, Germany. (Mailing address: Auswaertiges Amt, 11013 Berlin), Tel: +49 (0)30 5000, fax: +49 (0)1888 173402, e-mail: poststelle@auswaertiges-amt.de, URL: http://www.auswaertiges-amt.de
Ministry of the Interior, BM des Innern, Alt-Moabit 101, 10559 Berlin, Germany. Tel: +49 (0)1888 6810, fax: +49 (0)1888 681 2926, e-mail: poststelle@bmi.bund.de, URL: http://www.bmi.bund.de
Ministry of Justice, BM der Justiz, Mohrenstr. 37, 10117 Berlin, Germany. (Mailing address: Justizministerium, 11015 Berlin), Tel: +49 (0)30 202 570, fax: +49 (0)30 2025 9525, e-mail: poststelle@bmj.bund.de, URL: http//www.bmj.bund.de
Ministry of Finance, BM der Finanzen, Wilhelmstraße 97, 10117 Berlin, Germany. Tel: +49 (0)30 22420, fax: +49 (0)30 2242 3260, e-mail: oststelle@BMF.bund.de, URL: http://www.bundesfinanzministerium.de

Ministry of Economics and Technologies, Scharnhorststraße 34-37, 10115 Berlin, Germany. Tel: +49 (0)1888 6150, fax: +49 (0)1888 615 7010, e-mail: info@bmwi.bund.de, URL: http://www.bmwi.bund.de
Ministry of Defence, BM der Verteidigung, Stauffenbergstraße 18, 10785 Berlin, Germany. Tel: +49 (0)30 200400, fax: +49 (0)30 2004 8333, e-mail: postelle@bmvg.bund400.de, URL: http://www.bmvg.de
Ministry of Labour and Social Affairs, Wilhelmstraße 49, 10117 Berlin, Germany. Tel: +49 (0)30 18 5270, fax: +49 (0)30 18 5271830, e-mail: postelle@bmas.bund.de, URL: http://www.bmas.bund.de
Ministry for Family Affairs, Senior Citizens, Women and Youth, BM fü Familie, Senioren, Frauen und Jugend, Alexanderstraße 3, 10178 Berlin, Germany. (Mailing address: BM für Familie, Senioren, Frauen und Jugend, 11055 Berlin), Tel: +49 (0)30 18 5550, fax: +49 (0)30 18 555-1145, e-mail: poststelle@bmfsfj.bund.de, URL: http://www.bmfsfj.de
Ministry of Transport, Building and Urban Affairs, BM für Verkehr, Bau und Wohnungswesen, Invalidenstrasse 44, 10115 Berlin, Germany. Tel: +49 (0)30 20080, fax: +49 (0)30 2008 1920, e-mail: buergerinfo@bmvbs.bund.de, URL: http://www.bmvbs.de
Ministry for the Environment, Nature Conservation and Nuclear Safety, BM für Umwelt, Naturschutz und Reaktorsicherheit, Alexanderstrasse 3, 10178 Berlin, Germany. Tel: +49 (0)1888 3050, fax: +49 (0)1888 305 4375, e-mail: service@bmu.de, URL: http://www.bmu.de
Ministry for Economic Co-operation and Development, BM fü wirtschaftliche Zusammenarbeit und Entwicklung, Europahaus, Stresemannstraß 94, 10963 Berlin, Germany. Tel: +49 (0)30 25030, fax: +49 (0)18888 535 3500, e-mail: postelle@bmz.bund.de, URL: http://www.bmz.de
Ministry of Consumer Protection, Food and Agriculture, BM fü Verbraucherschutz, Ernährung und Landwirtschaft, Wilhelmstrasse 54, 10117 Berlin, Germany. (Mailing address: BM für Verbraucherschutz, Ernährung und Landwirtschaft 11055 Berlin), Tel: +49 (0)30 20060, fax: +49 (0)30 2006 4262, e-mail: postelle@bmelv.bund.de, URL: http://www.bmelv.de
Ministry of Health, BM für Gesundheit, FriedrichStr. 108, 10117 Berlin, Germany. (Mailing address: BM für Gesundheit, 11017 Berlin), Tel: +49 (0)30 206400, fax: +49 (0)30 206 404974, e-mail: postelle@bmg.bund.de, URL: http://www.bmg.bund.de
Ministry for Education and Research, BM für Bildung und Forschung, Hannoversche Straße 28-30, 10115 Berlin, Germany. (Mailing address: PO Box 229, 10106 Berlin), Tel: +49 (0)1888 570, fax: +49 (0)1888 578 3601, e-mail: bmbf@bmbf.bund.de, URL: http://bmbf.de

Political Parties
Christlich Demokratische Union (CDU, Christian Democratic Union) Klingelhöferstr.8, 10785 Berlin, Germany. Tel: +49 (0)30 220700 fax: +49 (0)30 22070111, e-mail: redaktion@cdu.de, URL: http://www.cdu.de
Chairman: Angela Merkel (CDU) (page 1476)
Christlich Soziale Union Deutschlands (CSU, Christian Social Union) Franz-Josef-Strauß-Haus, Nymphenburger Straße 64, 80335 Munich, Germany. Tel: +49 (0)89 12430, fax: +49 (0)89 124 3299, e-mail: info@csu-bayern.de, URL: http://www.csu.de
Chairman: Horst Seehofer
Sozialdemokratische Partei Deutschlands (SPD, Social Democratic Party of Germany), Wilhelmstr. 141, 10963 Berlin, Germany. Tel: +49 (0)30 259910, fax: +49 (0)30 25991410, e-mail: parteivorstand@spd.de, URL: http://www.spd.de
Chairman: Sigmar Gabriel
Head of the Parliamentary Group: Dr. Frank-Walter Steinmeier (page 1520)
Bündnis 90/Die Grünen (Alliance 90/The Green Party), Bundesgeschäftsstelle, Platz vor dem Neuen Tor 1, 10115 Berlin, Germany. (Mailing address: Postfach 040609, 10063 Berlin, Germany.), Tel: +49 (0)30 28442 0, fax: +49 (0)30 28442 210, e-mail: info@gruene.de, URL: http://www.gruene.de
Leaders: Claudia Roth and Cem Özdemir
Freie Demokratische Partei (FDP, Free Democratic Party), Thomas-Dehler-Haus, Reinhardtstraße 14, 10117 Berlin, Germany. Tel: +49 (0)30 2849 580, fax: +49 (0)30 2849 5822, e-mail: fdp-point@fdp.de, URL: http://www.fdp-bundesverband.de
Chairman: Philipp Rösler
Die Linke (The Left), Karl-Liebknecht-Haus, Kleine Alexanderstraße 28, 10178 Berlin, Germany. Tel: +49 (0) 3024 0090, fax: +49 (0)30241 1046, URL: http://www.die-linke.de
Chairman: Katya Kipping and Bernd Riexinger

Elections
The age of voting in Germany is 18. Voters have two votes: the first is for a candidate in their constituency, and the second is given to a list of candidates put up by the parties.

In the presidential election held on 23 May 2004 Horst Koehler was elected. He resigned in May 2010. Elections were held within 30 days as required by the constitution. Christian Wulff, the candidate of Chancellor Merkel, failed to win outright victories in both first and second rounds of voting falling short of the required margin of victory by 8 votes. In total he had 600 votes compared to his rival Joachim Gauck's 499 votes. Mr Wulff won the third round.

The most recent presidential election was held in March 2012 following the resignation of Christian Wulff. Joachim Gauck was elected to the post.

The parliamentary election to elect the 16th Bundestag was held in September 2005. The result was extremely close with the CDU and its ally the CSU winning 226 seats, and the SPD winning 222 seats. Lengthy talks took place before a Grand Coalition was formed between the CDU, CSU and SPD. Angela Merkel of the CDU became chancellor and a cabinet was made up of six members of the CDU including the post of chancellor, two posts to the CSU and seven posts to the SPD, including four members of the previous administration.

The most recent parliamentary elections were held on 27 September 2009. Angela Merkel and her Christian Democrats party were re-elected to power. Results showed that the CDU/CSU took 33.8 per cent of the vote, the SPD 23 per cent, and the FDP 14.6 per cent, 11.9 per cent to the Die Linke and 10.7 per cent to the Grune. The CDU/CSU formed a new coalition government with the FDU.

The following table shows the seats won in the 2005 and 2009 elections.

Election Results

Party	Seats 2005	Seats 2009
Social Democrats (SPD)	222	146
Christian Democratic Union (CDU)	180	194
Christian Social Union (CSU)	46	45
Alliance 90/The Greens	51	68
Free Democrats (FDP)	61	93
Democratic Socialists (PDS)	-	-
The Left Party	54	76

Diplomatic Representation
British Embassy, Wilhelmstrasse 70-71, 10117 Berlin, Germany. Tel: +49 (0)30 20457-0, fax: +49 (0)30 20457 574, e-mail: info@britischebotschaft.de,
URL: http://ukingermany.fco.gov.uk/en
Ambassador: Simon McDonald CMG (page 1474)
Embassy of the United States of America, Neustädtische Kirchstraße 4-5, 10117 Berlin, Germany. Tel: +49 (0)30 830 50, fax: +49 (0)30 238 6290, URL: http://www.usembassy.de
Ambassador: Philip D. Murphy (page 1482)
Embassy of the Federal Republic of Germany, 4645 Reservoir Road NW, Washington, DC 20007-1998, USA. Tel: +1 202 298 4000, fax: +1 202 298 4249, URL: http://www.germany.info/Vertretung/usa/en/Startseite.html
Ambassador: Niels Peter Georg Ammon (page 1377)
Embassy of the Federal Republic of Germany, 23 Belgrave Square, London SW1X 8PZ, United Kingdom. Tel: +44 (0)20 7824 1300, fax: +44 (0)20 7824 1435, e-mail: m a i l @ g e r m a n - e m b a s s y . o r g . u k , URL: http://www.london.diplo.de/Vertretung/london/en/Startseite.html
Ambassador: Georg Boomgaarden (page 1391)
Permanent Mission of the Federal Republic of Germany to the United Nations, 871 UN Plaza (First Avenue, 48/49 Street), NY 10017 USA. Tel: +1 212 940 0400, fax: +1 212 940 0402, e-mail: germany@un.int, URL: http://www.new-york-un.diplo.de/Vertretung/newyorkvn/en/Startseite.html
Ambassador: Peter Wittig
Mission Permanente de la Republique federale d'Allemagne auprès de l'Office des Nations Unies et des autres Organisations Internationales, 28C, Chemin du Petit-Saconnex 28C, 1209 Geneva, Switzerland. (Postal address: Case postale 171, 1211 Geneva 19, Switzerland.) Tel: +41 (0)22 730 1111, fax: +41 (0)22 734 3043, e-mail: mission.germany@itu.ch, URL: http://www.itu.ch

LEGAL SYSTEM

The legal system is based on the Basic Law for the Federal Republic of Germany, the principles of which are enshrined in the constitution.

Federal law includes approximately 4,000 laws, and states can pass laws concerning regional matters such as policing, education and broadcasting.

The country's supreme court is known as the Federal Constitutional Court which adjudicates on:

(i) the interpretation of the Basic Law in disputes concerning the extent of the rights and obligations of any one of the highest federal organs;
(ii) the constitutionality of laws;
(iii) the compatibility of land legislation with federal legislation;
(iv) disputes between the Federation and Länder;
(v) the constitutionality of political parties; and
(vi) constitutional complaints.

The Federal Constitutional Court, which sits at Karlsruhe, consists of two Chambers. Each federal state also has a Constitutional Court.

There are five basic categories of court:
(i) 'ordinary' courts - those responsible for civil matters, criminal matters and non-contentious legal proceedings. These courts have the four levels of Amtsgericht (local court), Landgericht (regional court), Oberlandesgericht (higher regional court) and the Bundesgerichtshof (Federal Court of Justice);
(ii) labour courts, dealing with employment disputes. The levels here are local, higher, i.e.: state, and federal;
(iii) administrative courts, dealing with administrative law proceedings which do not involve social or finance matters. Levels here are also local, higher and federal;
(iv) social courts, handling social security disputes, with the local, higher and federal levels;
(v) finance courts, with levels of higher and federal.

Most professional judges, who number some 21,000, work within the ordinary courts. Judges are appointed for life and may not on principle be removed from office. Non-contentious local court cases are dealt with by judicial officers, a profession within the civil service. There are over 4,000 public prosecutors mainly involved with criminal court hearings.

The government respects the rights of its citizens, though it restricts the freedoms of speech, press, assembly, and association for groups it considers extremist. The death penalty was abolished in 1949 in West Germany, but not abolished in the German Democratic Republic until 1987.

Bundesverfassungsgericht (Federal Constitutional Court), URL: http://www.bundesverfassungsgericht.de
President: Prof. Dr. Andreas Voßkuhle
Bundesgerichtshof (Federal Supreme Court of Justice), URL: http://www.bundesgerichtshof.de
President: Prof. Dr. Klaus Tolksdorf
Bundesverwaltungsgericht (Federal Administrative Court), URL: http://www.bverwg.de
Bundesfinanzhof (Federal Financial Court), URL: http://www.bundesfinanzhof.de

German Institute for Human Rights,
URL: http://www.institut-fuer-menschenrechte.de/en/home/homepage.html

LOCAL GOVERNMENT

Germany is divided into 16 *Länder*, or Federal States: Baden-Wurttemberg, Bavaria, Berlin, Brandenburg, Bremen, Hamburg, Hesse, Lower Saxony, Mecklenburg-Western Pomerania, North Rhine-Westphalia, Rhineland-Palatinate, Saarland, Saxony, Saxony-Anhalt, Schleswig-Holstein and Thuringia.

Each state has its own powers and can pass local laws, while keeping within the country's Basic Law and principles of its constitution. Any laws they pass must not already be covered by federal law. State laws usually cover areas such as police, education, environment, regional planning, regional water supply and landscape.

Regional elections took place in May 2011.

For further information on these states, please see their separate entries after Germany's main listing.

AREA AND POPULATION

Area
The Federal Republic of Germany lies in the heart of Europe and shares borders with nine countries: Denmark in the north, the Netherlands, Belgium, Luxembourg and France in the west, Switzerland and Austria in the south and the Czech Republic and Poland in the east. Germany has a total area of 357,028 sq. km, of which 193,136 sq. km is agricultural land, 104,915 sq. km is forest, 21,937 sq. km is built-up land, 16,785 sq. km is used for traffic, and 7,940 sq. km is water. The Federal Republic is divided into the following geographical areas: the North German Plain, the Central Upland Range, the Southwest German Central Upland Scarps, the South German Alpine Foreland and the Bavarian Alps. The highest point is Zugspitze (2,963 metres). Germany's coastline runs to 2,389 km. The rivers Rhine, Danube and Elbe run through Germany.

The climate is temperate with cool, cloudy, wet winters and mild/warm summers.

To view a map of Germany, please consult:
http://www.lib.utexas.edu/maps/europe/germany.pdf

Of Germany's 16 Länder (Federal States), Bavaria is the largest at 70,551 sq. km.
The following table shows the area and population at December 31 2010 of each of Germany's 16 Länder:

Lander	Area (sq. km)	Population
Baden-Wurttemberg	35,751	10,754,000
Bavaria	70,550	12,539,000
Berlin	888	3,461,000
Brandenburg	29,483	2,503,000
Bremen	419	661,000
Hamburg	755	1,786,000
Hesse	21,115	6,067,000
Mecklenburg-Western Pomerania	23,191	1,642,000
Lower Saxony	47,613	7,918,000
North Rhine-Westphalia	34,092	17,845,000
Rhineland-Palatinate	19,854	4,004,000
Saarland	2,569	1,018,000
Saxony	18,420	4,149,000
Saxony-Anhalt	20,450	2,335,000
Schleswig-Holstein	15,799	2,834,000
Thuringia	16,172	2,235,000

Source: © Statistisches Bundesamt, Wiesbaden 2013

Population
The population of Germany rose for the first time in eight years in 2011. It was estimated to be 81.8 million in 2011, up 50,000 on 2010. On December 31 2009 Germany's population was 81,802,257, down from the December 2008 figure of 82,002,356. The population was 82,437,995 in December 2005 and 82,531,700 in December 2003. Germany has the largest number of inhabitants of any EU country (followed by Great Britain and Northern Ireland, France, and Italy). Germany is also the fourth most densely populated country in Europe (after the Netherlands, Belgium, and Great Britain and Northern Ireland), with 229 people per sq. km.

STATES OF THE WORLD

GERMANY

In common with many western countries, Germany's birth rate is falling. The result is an increasingly aged population; projected figures for 2050 show that half of the population will be aged over 48 and one third be age 60 or older.

Nearly one third of the population live in Germany's 84 cities (of more than 100,000 inhabitants). The remaining majority live in villages and small towns.

The following table gives recent figures for the population of Germany's principal cities in 2010:

Population of Germany's Principal Cities

City	Population
Berlin	3,460,725
Hamburg	1,786,448
Munich	1,353,186
Cologne	1,007,119
Frankfurt am Main	679,664
Stuttgart	606,588
Dusseldorf	588,735
Dortmund	580,635
Essen	574,635

At the end of December 2004, the number of foreign residents in the Federal Republic of Germany was just over 6.7 million. Figures from December 2008 show that the largest foreign community was Turkish (1.68 million). Other large foreign communities include those from: Italy (523,162), Greece (287,187), Bosnia and Herzegovina (156,804), Poland (393,848), Croatia (223,056), Austria (175,434), Serbia and Montenegro (177,330), Russian Federation (188,253), 2007 follow: Ukraine (126,960), Portugal (114,552), Spain (106,301), Netherlands (128,192), France (106,549), United Kingdom (97,070), United States (99,891). In 2011, it was estimated that net immigration was 240,000.

Births, Marriages, Deaths

Estimates for 2011 indicate that there were 660,000-680,000 live births. This compares to 678,000 live births in 2010, and 665,126 in 2009. The birth rate is estimated at 1.4 children per woman. Estimated deaths for 2011 were put at 835,000-850,000 deaths. Recorded deaths in 2009 were 854,544 up from 844,439 in 2008. Marriages and divorces in 2009 numbered 378,439 and 185,817 respectively. Average life expectancy is 79 years for men and 84 years for women. (Source: https://www.destatis.de)

Public Holidays 2014

1 January: New Year's Day
6 January: Epiphany*
18 April: Good Friday
21 April: Easter Monday
5 May: Labour Day
29 May: Ascension Day
9 June: Whit Monday
19 June: Corpus Christi**
15 August: Assumption***
3 October: Day of Unity
31 October: Day of Reformation****
1 November: All Saints' Day*****
22 November: Repentance Day (Saxony only)
25 December: Christmas Day
26 December: Christmas Holiday
31 December: New Year's Eve

Holidays marked with asterisks are observed only in the following areas:
*Baden-Württemberg, Bavaria, Saxony-Anhalt
**Baden-Württemberg, Bavaria, Hesse, North Rhine Westphalia, Rhineland-Palatinate, Saarland
***Saarland, Catholic areas of Bavaria
****Brandenburg, Mecklenburg-W. Pomerania, Saxony, Saxony-Anhalt, Thuringia
*****Baden-Württemberg, Bavaria, Hesse, North Rhine Palatinate, Saarland, Catholic areas of Thuringia

EMPLOYMENT

Following the unification of Germany, employment initially went through a boom period. This soon declined in response to a recession in the west. The old eastern states also lost many jobs in the transition from a system of central planning to a market economy. In 1996 the number of unemployed increased considerably, to nearly 4.2 million, prompting the Government to introduce a scheme entitled the Alliance for Jobs and a Competitive Germany. This set a goal for the country to halve the number of unemployed over the following ten years. Despite this, unemployment rose to 4.82 million in February 1998, a total of 12.6 per cent of the work force. The average unemployment rate over the whole year was 11.1 per cent.

The following table shows how the working population was employed on June 30 2012

Employment Sector	Employed
Agriculture, forestry & fishing	230,576
Mining & quarrying	85,889
Manufacturing	6,509,473
Electricity, gas, steam & air conditioning supply	237,519
Water supply, sewerage, waste management	227,424
Construction	1,662,200
Wholesale & retail trade, repair of vehicles	4,162,072

- continued	
Transportation & storage	1,485,268
Accommodation	901,459
Information & communication	881,516
Financial & insurance activities	1,004,033
Real estate activities	221,140
Professional, scientific & technical activities	1,726,883
Administrative & support service activities	2,013,079
Public admin. & defence; compulsory social security	1,670,722
Education	1,101,675
Human health & social work activities	3,678,296
Arts, entertainment & recreation	244,765
Other service activities	789,322
Households	41,788
Extraterritorial organisations & bodies	23,885
Total	28,920,588

Copyright: Statistisches Bundesamt. Weisbaden (2013)

Chancellor Schroeder made employment and job creation a big part of his 2002 election campaign, but high unemployment and worries over job security led consumers to hold back, which in turn had an adverse effect on economic growth. As part of the unemployment reforms, benefits were cut in an effort to encourage people to seek work, which led in 2004 to large demonstrations and protests. People who had been unemployed for over a year were offered very low paid jobs known as 'one Euro jobs' in the public sector.

In March 2002 the German government passed a controversial immigration bill through the Bundesrat, allowing a small number of skilled EU workers into Germany.

By April 2003 the number of people unemployed had reached 4.46 million, a rate of 10.8 per cent. Figures for April 2004 put unemployment at 4.3 million registered unemployed. By March 2005 seasonally adjusted figures put the number of unemployed at 4.97 million. The non-seasonally adjusted figure was 5.17 million, an unemployment rate of 12 per cent. This was the highest recorded unemployment figure since the end of the WWII. Unemployment was still higher in the former East Germany, with an unemployment rate of 18.8 per cent. Towards the end of 2005 unemployment showed signs of dropping slightly. In April 2006 unemployment was recorded at 11.5 per cent and was still higher in former East Germany where an unemployment rate of 17 per cent was recorded. By March 2008, unemployment had fallen to 3.507 million, giving an unemployment rate of 8.4 per cent. Figures for March 2009 put unemployment at 3.586 million, giving an unemployment rate 8.6 per cent. The average unemployment rate over 2009 was 8.2 per cent. As unemployment rose due to the global economic downturn. The government introduced a scheme whereby employers were encouraged to keep employees on by employing them on reduced hours usually four days a week and the government would make up the shortfall from a special fund.

Figures for the last quarter of 2010 showed that the number of people employed had risen by 422,000 to 41.04 million, taking the number of employed over 41 million for the first time since reunification. In March 2010 the unemployment rate was 8.5 per cent, falling to 7.6 per cent in March 2011 (2.9 million persons). Figures from February 2013 show that 41.415 million people were in employment, with 2.54 million unemployed giving an unemployment rate of 6.0 per cent.

Unemployment insurance is mandatory for all employees, and is paid equally by employer and employee. Unemployment benefit may be paid, for a maximum of a year, to anyone who previously paid the insurance for a certain amount of time. If a person is out of work for longer than the stipulated period of time in which they can draw benefit, they can apply for assistance whereby various sources of income are taken into account.

Employment according to Länder is shown on the following table (in '000s). Figures are from 2010:

Lander	No. of employed ('000s)	Unemployed ('000s)
Germany	40,483	3,238
Baden-Wurttemberg	5,594	273
Bavaria	6,694	299
Berlin	1,685	231
Brandenburg	1,229	149
Bremen	389	39
Hamburg	1,136	76
Hesse	3,132	198
Mecklenburg-Western Pomerania	728	110
Lower Saxony	3,705	299
North Rhine-Westphalia	8,712	799
Rhineland-Palatinate	1,864	120
Saarland	507	38
Saxony	1,951	253
Saxony-Anhalt	1,013	151
Schleswig-Holstein	1,282	107
Thuringia	1,022	117

Copyright: © Statistisches Bundesamt, Wiesbaden 2011

BANKING AND FINANCE

Currency

One euro (€) = 100 cents
On 1 January 1999 the euro was launched as an electronic currency across the 12 member states of the EU. On 1 January 2002 the euro became legal tender in Germany and the 11 other member states of the EU. Germany's old currency, the Deutsche Mark, ceased to be

legal tender from 28 February 2002. Euro banknotes come in denominations of 5, 10, 20, 50, 100, 200, and 500. Euro coins come in denominations of 2 and 1 euros, 50, 20, 10, 5, 2, and 1 cents.

GDP/GNP, Inflation, National Debt

Germany has the highest Gross Domestic Product (GDP) in western Europe and the third highest in the world (after USA and Japan), with exports accounting for approximately one-third of GDP. The economy slowed following reunification and as an export-based economy was particularly hit by the global slowdown in economic growth in 2001. GDP growth was recorded at 2.8 per cent in 2000, falling to 0.8 per cent in 2001, 0.1 per cent in 2002 and contracting to -0.1 per cent in 2003, before rising to 1.6 per cent in 2004. The rise was mainly driven by exports. Growth in 2005 was put at 0.9 per cent; although the export market did well the high cost of oil meant that growth was not as strong as had been hoped. Forecast figures for 2006 put growth at 1.6 per cent; it was expected that exports would continue to do well and that the domestic consumer market would pick up following Chancellor Angela Merkel's announcement that VAT would be raised in 2007, prompting consumers to spend sooner rather than later. The hosting of the World Cup in June and July 2006 also added to the growth of the economy. Provisional figures for 2006 put economic growth at 2.7 per cent with forecasts predicting a fall to 1.9 per cent in 2007 mainly due to the increase in VAT rates and a growth of 2.7 per cent in 2008. In fact, the economy grew by 2.6 per cent in 2007 but growth was still led by exports as domestic private consumption remained low.

Germany has also suffered as part of the global economic crisis. As the global economy slowed, growth fell in 2008 to 1.5 per cent as a result of a fall in exports. Projected figures for 2009 estimated economic growth to be 0.2 per cent. In October 2008 one of Germany's largest banks, Hypo Real Estate, was bailed out by the government with US$68 billion to save it from collapsing. In a Europe wide agreement European governments pledged up to €1.8 trillion to bolster the financial sectors and Germany's contribution alone was to be €500 billion. By November 2008 Germany had experienced two consecutive quarters of negative growth, thus officially going into recession. In February 2009 the government approved a stimulus package worth US$63 billion to boost the economy. Germany officially came out of recession in 2009, after returning to positive growth. Growth was 0.3 per cent in the period April-June 2009. The quick recovery was attributed to government stimulus packages, strong exports and consumer spending. However, in January 2010 exports fell by 6.3 per cent compared to December 2009 and imports increased by six per cent. The cold weather at the beginning of the year was said to be a contributing factor; trade surplus that month narrowed to €8.7 billion euros. In 2009 Germany was overtaken by China as the largest exporter. The economy grew by 1.8 per cent in 2010 and by 3 per cent in 2011. Growth was strongest in the early part of the year, and the economy contracted by 0.25 per cent in Q4. There were fears in 2012 that the German economy would be dragged down by the eurozone crisis. The economy grew by 0.5 per cent in Q1 2012, compared to the eurozone as a whole which contacted by 0.1 per cent. Final figures for 2012 put economic growth at 0.7 per cent, exports were up by 4.1 per cent and imports grew by 2.3 per cent, the industrial sectors and construction contracted but household and government expenditure was up. Forecast figures for 2013 put economic growth at 0.4 per cent.

Per capita GDP was estimated to be €30,420 in 2011.

GDP (Current Prices) €bn

Year	GDP	GNI
2000	2,062.50	2,043.16
2001	2,113.16	2,092.15
2002	2,143.18	2,116.64
2003	2,161.50	2,145.77
2004	2,221.2	2,226.3
2005	2,243.2	2,270.8
2006	2,321.5	2,362.4
2007	2,432.4	2,475.2
2008	2,481.2	2,520.9
2009	2,397.1	2,430.9
2010	2,496.2	2,546.6
2011	2,592.6	2,640.9
2012	2,643.9	2,695.3

Copyright: Statistisches Bundesamt. Weisbaden 2013

Provisional figures for gross value added by industries is shown on the following table (at current prices, €bn):

Gross Value Added by Industry (€bn)

Industry	2010	2011	2012
Agriculture, hunting, forestry and fishing	17.83	21.57	23.04
Industry excl. construction	564.89	607.44	614.70
inc. manufacturing	481.74	524.51	527.64
Construction	100.43	106.05	107.57
Trade, transport , accommodation & food services	354.79	269.73	378.89
Information & communication	90.03	88.96	91.40
Financial & insurance services	101.41	101.55	94.38
Real estate activities	263.22	264.17	269.92
Business services	236.26	242.92	252.77
Public services, education, health	405.72	412.43	426.78
Other services	102.05	102.61	105.06
Total	2,224.8	2,140.6	2,239.9

Copyright: Statistisches Bundesamt. Weisbaden (2013)

Production of GDP in 2010

Sector	Percentage
Financial, real estate, renting and business activities	30.4
Industry inc. energy	23.7
Other business activities	23.6
Trade, transport & communications	17.2
Construction	4.1
Agriculture, hunting, forestry and fishing	0.9

Source: Federal Statistics Office 2011

Following reunification, increased wages and taxes caused higher inflation, the rate reaching 4 per cent in 1994. Since then, inflation has fallen, to 3 per cent at the end of 1994, 1.8 per cent at the end of 1998, and 1.9 per cent in 1999 and 2002. Inflation for 2006 was 1.7 per cent and 0.9 per cent in 2009. It was estimated to be 2.1 per cent in March 2012, partly due to rising energy costs.

The German government has warned of a dramatic increase in public debt in Germany because of the global economic crisis. Public debt was estimated to be €1.7 trillion in 2009. Provisional figures put new borrowings at €86 billion for 2012. Total federal public expenditure is expected to reach €328 billion in 2012.

Foreign Investment

Trade fairs are an important part of German commercial life and attract both domestic and international firms. The UK Department of Trade and Industry (DTI) has identified the following sectors as being good opportunities for foreign firms: biotechnology; telecommunications; vehicle components; textiles, clothing and footwear; jewellery. Direct foreign investment stood at US$630 billion in 2007.

Bundesagentur für Außenwirtschaft, (Federal Foreign Trade Office), URL: http://www.bfai.de

Balance of Payments / Imports and Exports

Germany's export surplus declined drastically after reunification, following a constant rise in the 1980s. However, more recently, export revenue has risen due to the weak euro and the recovery of some Asian economies. Since the 1950s, exports have usually exceeded imports, although imports rose just after reunification due to higher demand for goods in the former East Germany. The following table shows the value of foreign trade in recent years:

Balance of Exports and Imports in billion €

Year	Exports	Imports	Balance
2010	1,173.34	1,034.44	138.90
2011	1,300.81	1,169.15	131.66
2012	1,362.59	1,210.96	151.63

Copyright: Statistisches Bundesamt. Weisbaden (2013)

A highly developed industrial base provides Germany with a number of excellent export products of which the principal groups are machinery, chemical and electrical engineering products, motor vehicles and iron and steel products.

Main Trading Partners 2012 (preliminary figures)

	€ Millions
Imports	
Netherlands	86,595.9
China	77,313.3
France	64,759.5
United States	50,575.3
Italy	49,160.0
Exports	
France	104,476.1
United States	86,831.1
United Kingdom	72,162.6
Netherlands	70,957.2
China	66,628.5

Copyright: Statistisches Bundesamt. Weisbaden (2013)

Germany's lack of raw materials and natural energy sources, however, means that it cannot be self-sufficient in foodstuffs; these therefore make up much of its imports from abroad. Germany is also Europe's largest importer of clothing.

The following table shows principal import and export commodities in 2012:

Product	€ millions
Imports	
Crude petroleum & natural gas	97,395
Computer, electronic & optical products	87,699
Motor vehicles, trailers & semi-trailers	81,193
Chemicals & chemical products	71,872
Machinery & equipment	68,566
Basic metals	55.112
Exports	
Motor vehicles, trailers & semi-trailers	190,192
Machinery & equipment	164,233
Chemicals & chemical products	104,673
Computer, electronic & optical products	86,012
Electrical equipment	65,825
Basic metals	58,064

Copyright: © Statistisches Bundesamt, Wiesbaden 2013

GERMANY

Trade or Currency Restrictions
The Foreign Trade and Payments Regulation shows restrictions of imports/exports and contains foreign trade rules. A licence is required for goods which have restrictions of import volume, such as textiles, as well as agricultural products. The following office issues import/export licences for commercial goods:
Bundesamt für Wirtschaft und Ausfuhrkontrolle (Federal Export Office), URL: http://www.bafa.de

Central Bank
Deutsche Bundesbank (German Federal Bank), Wilhelm Epstein Straße 14, 60431 Frankfurt am Main, Germany. Tel: +49 (0)69 9566 3511, fax: +49 (0)69 9566 4679, e-mail: presse-information@bundesbank.de, URL: http://www.bundesbank.de
President: Dr Jens Weidmann (page 1535)

Major Banks
Germany has over 300 commercial banks, as well as further savings banks, giro institutions, credit co-operatives, mortgage banks and building and loan associations. The European Central Bank is based in Germany.
European Central Bank, URL: http://www.ecb.int

Banking Associations
Bundesverband deutscher Banken EV (Association of German Banks), URL: http://www.bdb.de
Bundesverband öffentlicher Banken Deutschlands eV (Association of German Public-Sector Banks), URL: http://www.voeb.de
Deutscher Sparkassen- und Giroverband eV (German Savings Banks Association), URL: http://www.dsgv.de

Trade Organisations and Chambers of Commerce
Deutscher Industrie- und Handelskammertag (Association of German Chambers of Industry and Commerce), URL: http://www.dihk.de
Invest in Germany (Foreign Direct Investment), URL: http://www.fdin.de
Arbeitsgemeinschaft Hessischer Industrie- und Handelskammern, URL: http://www.frankfurt-main.ihk.de
Arbeitsgemeinschaft Norddeutscher Industrie- und Handelskammern, URL: http://www.hamburg.ihk.de
Representative of German Industry and Trade (BDI/DIHT Office), URL: http://www.rgit-usa.com
Messe Berlin GmbH (Berlin Trade Fair), URL: http://www.messe-berlin.de
Berlin Chamber of Commerce (Industrie und Handelskammer Berlin), URL: http://www.berlin.ihk.de
Bonn Chamber of Commerce (Industrie und Handelskammer Bonn), URL: http://www.ihk-bonn.de
German American Chamber of Commerce Inc., URL: http://www.gaccny.com
Bundesverband der Deutschen Industrie eV (Federation of German Industry), URL: http://www.bdi-online.de
Bundesverband der Deutschen Luft- und Raumfahrtindustrie eV (BDLI) (German Aerospace Industries Association), URL: http://www.bdli.de
Verband der Elektrizitätswirtschaft eV (Electricity), URL: http://www.strom.de
Gesamtverband kunststoffverarbeitender Industrie eV (GKV) (Plastics), URL: http://www.gkv.de
Mineralölwirtschaftsverband eV (Petroleum), URL: http://www.mwv.de
Verband der Chemischen Industrie eV (Chemical Industry), URL: http://www.vci.de
Verband für Schiffbau und Meerestechnik eV (Shipbuilding), URL: http://www.vsm.de
Wirtschaftsverband Erdöl- und Erdgasgewinnung eV (Association of Crude Oil and Gas Producers), URL: http://www.erdoel-erdgas.de
Wirtschaftsverband Stahlbau und Energietechnik (SET) (Steel and Energy), URL: http://www.set-online.de
Wirtschaftsvereinigung Bergbau eV (Mining), URL: http://www.wv-bergbau.de
Deutscher Gewerkschaftsbund (DGB) (Federation of German Trade Unions), URL: http://www.dgb.de/index_html?-C=

Stock Exchanges
Frankfurt am Main: URL: http://deutsche-boerse.com
Berlin: URL: http://www.berlinerboerse.de
Düsseldorf: URL: http://www.boerse-duesseldorf.de
Hamburg: URL: http://www.boerse-hamburg.de
Munich: URL: http://www.bayerische-boerse.de

MANUFACTURING, MINING AND SERVICES

Primary and Extractive Industries
While Germany has deposits of coal, salt and lignite, it depends largely on imports for main supplies of raw materials and energy. The extraction of hard coal, principally from the Ruhr and Saarland regions, is expensive due to the fact that the coal is located deep underground. The German hard coal industry has been viable only because of considerable subsidies. Following an agreement between the German government, the mining industry, and the unions, subsidies to the coal industry were cut from DM10 billion in 1997 to DM5.5 billion by 2005. Year 2000 subsidies totalled DM8.5 billion. Additionally, as a result of an agreement to close seven to eight of Germany's 19 hard coal mines, the coal mining industry is also expected to decline in employment, from 76,000 in 1997 to an estimated 36,000 in 2005. Coal reserves have been estimated at 72.8 billion short tons, with 2010 production an estimated 200 million short tons and consumption estimated at 255 million short tons. Coal mining is expected to cease in 2018.

As a consequence of the decline in production, coal imports have risen. Germany's largest supplier is Poland, with significant quantities also coming from Australia, South Africa and Colombia. Coal imports are expected to double in the next 20 years as production declines and nuclear power is phased out. Figures for January 2010 show that 45 million short tons of coal were imported.

Germany's major coal producer is Deutsche Steinkohle (DSK), recently formed from Saarberger and Ruhrkohle Bergbau, and accounts for 96 per cent of German production.

Due to limited fossil fuel resources (proven oil reserves were 0.28 billion barrels at the beginning of 2012), Germany imports almost all of its oil requirements. Oil consumption was 2,400 thousand barrels per day in 2011, whilst net oil imports were 2,235.05 million barrels per day.. Germany is the fourth largest oil importer in the world, with supplies coming primarily from Russia (35 per cent), as well as Norway (21 per cent), the United Kingdom (11 per cent), and Libya (8 per cent). Domestic oil production in 2011 was an estimated 165.09 thousand barrels per day, of which 54,920 barrels per day was crude oil. Oil deposits are located in the German North Sea (accounting for 25 per cent of crude production), the North German Plain, the Upper Rheinish Lowlands, and the Alpine foothills. Because of limited oil reserves, the German government has sought to limit consumption by increasing federal taxes.

Germany produces little natural gas, relying on imports to satisfy demand. Germany is the EU's second and world's fifth largest consumer of natural gas. In 2011, just 420 billion cubic feet of gas was produced, whilst consumption was an estimated 2,740 billion cubic feet. At present, natural gas consumption represents 21 per cent of Germany's total energy consumption, and demand is expected to rise in the coming decade, particularly for power generation. Just over half of natural gas demand is accounted for by residential and non-commercial consumers. Industry accounts for 38 per cent and power stations 9 per cent. Ruhrgas is Germany's major gas transmission company (accounting for 60 per cent of natural gas sales), followed by Wingas. Germany's second largest utility, E.On, owns about 60 per cent of Ruhrgas.

Energy
Germany energy consumption was an estimated 13.461 quadrillion Btu in 2009, ranking it sixth in the world. Total energy production was 4.705 quadrillion Btu in 2009.

Germany's electricity market is the largest in Europe, generating 546.78 billion kilowatthours in 2009, with total electricity generation capacity at 146.87 GWe.

Nuclear power currently accounts for 9 per cent of electricity generation. Germany ranks fourth in the world for installed nuclear capacity, after the United States, France, and Japan. In 2009, energy policy was reviewed, resulting in a planned phasing out of nuclear power. Following the nuclear disaster in Fukushima in Japan, the eight oldest of the 17 nuclear power stations in operation were immediately shut down. The remaining nine reactors are to be decommissioned by 2022. Renewable energy will be brought to the fore.

Renewable energy makes up for more than 10 per cent of all German energy consumption. By 2020, 35 per cent of Germany's energy requirements should be met by solar, wind, biomass, hydro and geothermal sources, and by 2050 this should be 80 per cent. As of 2011, green electricity accounted for 20 per cent of its electricity. Germany currently has an installed capacity of 17,300 MW of photovoltaic technology. Germany has a major investment in the Desertec initiative; by 2050 the energy produced by solar power stations in North Africa should cover 15 per cent of European electricity requirements. Germany currently has 14 per cent of global wind energy output.

Primary Energy Production in 2008

Energy source	Percentage
Coal and lignite	37.8
Crude oil	2.3
Natural gas	8.5
Nuclear energy	28.9
Renewable energy	22.4
Total (1,000 tons oil equivalent)	132,488

Copyright: Statistisches Bundesamt, Wiesbaden (Germany 2011)

Gross Electricity Production in 2012

Fuel	Billion kWh	Percentage
Gross electricity production, total	617.0	100
Lignite	158.0	25.7
Nuclear energy	99.0	16.0
Hard coal	118.0	19.1
Natural gas	70.0	11.3
Mineral oil products	10.0	1.6
Renewable energy products	135.0	21.9
Water power	20.5	3.3
Wind power	45.0	7.3
Biomass energy	36.0	5.8
Photovaltaic energy	28.5	4.6
Geothermal energy	0.0	0.0
Household waste	5.0	0.8
Other energy sources	27.0	4.4

Copyright: Statistisches Bundesamt Wiesbaden, (Germany 2013)

Manufacturing
The manufacturing industry provides nearly 35 per cent of the country's GDP. The most significant industry is car manufacturing. Companies include VW, Porsche (VW), Audi, BMW, and Mercedes-Benz (DaimlerChrysler). Germany is the world's third largest producer,

manufacturing approximately 5.1 million vehicles per annum, of which 70 per cent are exported. The chemical industry and electrical engineering / electronics industry are also important in Germany.

Index of Orders Received (Volume) in Manufacturing, 2000 = 100

Sector	2005	2006
Textiles & textile products	82.2	83.1
Pulp, paper & paper products, publishing & printing	102.9	106.8
Chemicals, chemical products & manmade fibres	109.5	112.6
Rubber & plastic products	107.0	115.9
Other non metallic mineral products	88.1	96.4
Basic metals & fabricated metal products	102.9	115.5
Machinery & equipment n.e.c.	108.3	121.7
Electrical & optical equipment	112.0	128.1
Transport equipment	120.5	127.7

Copyright: Statistisches Bundesamt. Wiesbaden (Germany 2007)

Figures for 2010 show that 6,923,521 people were employed in manufacturing. Manufacturing turnover that year was €147,947 billion.

Exports by Selected Branches of Production (% shares of non-domestic turnover in total turnover 2008)

Branch	Percentage
Transport equipment	61.2
Machinery & equipment	58.5
Chemical products	56.0
Office machinery & electrical equipment	48.7
Textiles & clothing	42.7

Copyright: Statistisches Bundesamt. Wiesbaden (Germany 2011)

Tourism

Germany's tourist industry employs nearly 1.5 million people. The number of overnight stays by foreigners was estimated at 61.8 million in 2011 and 330.3 million overnight stays by Germans in Germany. In 2010, tourism contributed €185 billion to GDP. Most visitors come from Russia/Northeast Europe (14 per cent).

German National Tourist Board (Deutsche Zentrale fur Tourismus, DZT), URL: http://www.germany-tourism.de

Agriculture

Germany's total area is nearly 36 million hectares, with about half of this used for agriculture. Of Germany's agriculturally used area of 17.13 million hectares, arable land accounts for 11.89 million hectares, permanent grassland 4.9 million hectares, and vineland 98,000 million hectares. There are just over 290,000 farms in Germany, compared with 1.6 million farms in 1950. Figures for 2010 show that Germany had 16,532 organic farms. The majority of farms are smaller than 50 hectares. Employment in the agriculture, forestry and fisheries industry was 856,000 in 2008. When the country was reunited in 1990, farmland in the former East Germany was returned to private ownership. Most of those are still privately owned.

Main agricultural products are milk, pork, beef, cereals and sugar beets, although livestock farms are relatively small. Germany is the world's largest importer of agricultural products. The following table shows harvested quantities of selected crops in recent years, figures are in 1,000 t.

Crop	2011	2012
Wheat	22,783	22,432
Rye & mixed winter cereals	2,521	3,893
Barley	8,734	10,422
Oats	627	758
Triticale	2,004	2,306
Potatoes	11,837	10,586
Sugar beets	29,578	na
Winter rape	3,830	1,805
	2010	2011
White cabbage	471	507
Red cabbage	133	138
Cauliflower	124	119
Carrots	554	534
Asparagus	92	103
Iceberg lettuce	101	133

Copyright: Statistisches Bundesamt. Wiesbaden (Germany 2013)

Figures for 2011show that Germany had a total of 27,400,000 pigs and 12,500,000 cattle.

Recent figures show that 102,500 hectares were under vine cultivation with annual production of approximately 9 million hl. Germany is the eighth largest wine-producer in the world. Over 60 per cent is white wine.

Forestry

A third of Germany's area is covered by forest. Just over 40 per cent of the Rhineland-Palatinate is forest, the largest proportion of any German state. Nearly 40 million cubic metres of timber are felled every year, which is two-thirds of domestic demand. The country has a Forest Preservation and Forestry Promotion Act which protects forest areas and lays down rules concerning forest clearing and reforesting harvested areas. Germany produced over 50 million m^3 of roundwood in 2010 and 22 million m^3 of sawnwood.

Fishing

Germany's principal fishing areas are the North Sea, the Baltic, and the Atlantic off the British Isles. Traditional stocks have been greatly depleted in recent years, mainly due to the excessive use of modern catching methods which result in overfishing. In 2009, total production (all fishery products) was approximately 289,254 tonnes. Aquaculture production amounted to an estimated 39,000 tonnes. Total live fishing catch amounted to 250,347 tonnes (live weight). The fishing fleet comprised over 2,800 vessels in 2009.

German Farmers' Association (Deutscher Bauernverband e.V.), URL: http://www.bauernverband.de
Consumer Protection, Food, Agriculture Information Service (Informationsdienst Verbraucherschutz, Ernährung, Landwirtschaft eV), URL: http://www.aid.de

COMMUNICATIONS AND TRANSPORT

Travel Requirements

Citizens of USA, Australia and Canada need a passport that is valid for the length of their stay in Germany. EU citizens holding a national Identity Card do not require a passport or a visa. Nationals of EU countries intending to stay for three months or more must register with the German authorities within seven days of arrival.

Germany is a signatory to the Schengen Agreement; With a Schengen visa, a visitor can travel freely throughout the Schengen zone, and there are few border stops and checks. See http://www.eurovisa.info/SchengenCountries.htm for details. Canadian, US and Australian visitors do not require a visa for visits that do not exceed 90 days starting from entry into the first Schengen country. For further information, go to http://www.schengenvisa.cc/

National Airlines

Deutsche Lufthansa AG (Lufthansa German Airlines), URL: http://www.lufthansa.com
Hapag-Lloyd, http://www.hapag-lloyd.com
Eurowings Luftverkehrs AG, URL: http://www.eurowings.com
Aero Lloyd Flugreisen GmbH & Co, http://www.aerolloyd.de
Air Berlin, URL: http://www.airberlin.com/site/start.php?LANG=deu

International Airports

Over 108 million passengers pass through Germany's 660 airports every year. The airports operate as private companies under public control.
Frankfurt am Main, URL: http://www.frankfurt-airport.de
Düsseldorf, URL: http://www.duesseldorf-airport.de
München, URL: http://www.munich-airport.de
Berlin Airports, URL: http://www.berlin-airport.de
Hamburg, URL: http://www.ham.airport.de
Bremen, URL: http://www.airport-bremen.de
Köln/Bonn, URL: http://www.airport-cgn.de
Dresden, URL: http://www.dresden-airport.de
Hannover, URL: http://www.hannover-airport.de
Leipzig/Halle, URL: http://www.leipzig-halle-airport.de
Nürnberg, URL: http://www.airport-nuernberg.de

DFS Deutsche Flugsicherung GmbH (Air Traffic Control Authority), URL: http://www.dfs.de
Luftfahrt Bundesamt LBA (Federal Office of Civil Aviation), URL: http://www.lba.de

Railways

In 1993 the Federal Government introduced the Federal Transport Plan, a programme whereby over DM 450 billion was to be spent on German transport networks (road, rail and waterways).

The rail authorities of the former West Germany and East Germany (Deutsche Bundesbahn and Deutsche Reichsbahn respectively) were merged in 1994 to form the Deutsche Bahn AG. With new high-speed routes now available, more being planned and money constantly being spent on railways, the Government hopes to keep rail travel as a favourable, more environmentally-friendly alternative form of transport for the public, as well as for freight transport.

New routes include Hannover-Wurzburg-Mannheim-Stuttgart-Munich; Metz, France to Ludwigshafen, as part of the planned Paris-Frankfurt am Main-Berlin project; Cologne-Frankfurt am Main high-speed link; Transrapid magnetic levitation train with a route of Berlin-Schwerin-Hamburg. The aim for this last route, a distance of 285 km, is to have a journey time of under one hour.

Metropolitan rail networks are known as the *S-Bahn*, and in heavily populated cities these trains are linked to trams, buses and underground services, as another attempt by the Government to encourage people to use public transport and ease road congestion and car pollution. The total length of railway track in Germany is 43,800 km. Berlin and Munich have subway systems.

Deutsche Bahn (German Railways), URL: http://www.bahn.de
Berliner Verkehrsbetriebe (Berlin Transport Authority), URL: http://www.bvg.de

Roads

Germany had over 49 million cars on its roads in 2009. Figures for 2008 show that there were 12,594 km of *autobahns* or motorways, part of 230,000 km of Germany's road network. 49.0 million passenger cars were on the road in 2008.

GERMANY

Rather than building new roads, the German Government's current concern is to re-structure problem areas in existing roads, hopefully helping congestion and accident-prone areas. With regard to environmental issues, buyers of low-pollutant cars are entitled to tax concessions. Recent figures show that Germany had 12,037 km. of motorways (autobahns), 40,969 km. of federal highways, 86,736 km. of ordinary roads and 91,588 of district roads. Vehicles drive on the right.

Shipping

Recent figures showed that Germany's merchant fleet totalled 774 vessels. With regards to inland shipping, the country has a large network of waterways, with approximately six million inland water craft. The river Rhine ships over 80 per cent of all goods transported via inland waterways. The country plans improvement work on the rivers and canals in eastern Germany. The main inland ports are Duisburg and Magdeburg.

Wasser- und Schifffahrtsverwaltung des Bundes (Federal Ministry of Transport, Inland Waterways Department), URL: http://www.wsv.de
Verband Deutscher Reeder eV (German Shipowners' Association), URL: http://www.reederverband.de
Zentralverband der Deutschen Seehafenbetriebe eV (Federal Association of German Seaport Operators), URL: http://www.zds-seehafen.de

Ports and Harbours

The largest German seaports are Hamburg, Bremen/Bremerhaven, Wilhelmshaven, Lubeck and Rostock. Although foreign North Sea ports such as Rotterdam are closer to the West European industrial centres, the German ports have tried to combat this disadvantage by investing heavily in infrastructure and port facilities. They are now "fast ports" which can turn even large vessels around in a short time. Germany's largest port is Hamburg; it handles almost 63 per cent of container cargo. Container shipments amounted to 72 million tons in 2011. In total, 114 million tons were handled by Hamburg port in 2011.

HEALTH

90 per cent of Germans are part of the statutory health insurance scheme. This is compulsory for the employed, and also encompasses pensioners, students and the unemployed. Payment depends on the level of earnings. Public health insurance paid out approximately €128 865m in 2001 for health services. In 2009, according to WHO figures, total expenditure on health as a percentage of GDP was 11.7 per cent. General government expenditure on health was 76.9 per cent of the total health expenditure. Private expenditure accounts for 23.1 per cent of the total expenditure on health. General government expenditure on health accounts for 18.7 per cent of the total government expenditure on health. Social security accounts for 88.7 per cent of the total general government expenditure. Some 40.3 per cent of private expenditure is made up of prepaid plans. Per capita total expenditure on health was US$4,723 in 2009.

Figures for 2011 show that Germany had a total of 342,000 doctors, 826,000 nurses, 21,000 midwives, 69,000 dentists and 61,000 pharmaceutical personnel. In the same period there were 502,000 hospital beds. The state maintains 42 per cent of hospitals, the remainder being maintained by local authorities, charities and private enterprises.

Average life expectancy is 78 years for men and 83 years for women. The infant mortality rate was 3 per 1,000 live births and the under-fives mortality rate was 4 per 1,000 live births. The main causes of death in infants were prematurity (33 per cent), birth asphyxia (7 per cent) and congenital abnormalities (28 per cent). Approximately 0.1 per cent of the population (aged 15-49 years old) have HIV/AIDS. (Source: WHO, 2012)

EDUCATION

Under the Basic Law the entire schooling system, including private education, is under state supervision. The federal states are responsible for school administration, which is why the systems vary across the country, but the Government ensures a basic structure throughout. Education policy was reviewed after reunification to ensure that the new states were included in this country-wide structure.

School attendance is compulsory between the ages of six and 18, and is free at public schools. Attendance must be full-time for the first nine years, but may be part-time vocational after this time, or continued full-time education at college.

Private schools must be approved by the state, and receive some financial help from the educational authority. Approximately 9.7 million pupils attended schools of general education in 2003/04. (Source: Statistisches Bundesamt)

Pre-school Education

There is no compulsory education before the age of six; however, morning kindergartens are common. In 1996 it was ruled that children have a legal right to attend pre-school, and as a result more kindergartens are being constructed. Payment is calculated on family income.

Primary /Secondary Education

Primary school is mandatory for children from the age of six, and is known as *Grundschule*. In most states this lasts four years (six years in Berlin and Brandenburg). General secondary schools, or *Hauptschule*, are attended by approximately a quarter of Germany's children. Compulsory subjects for pupils to cover are German, mathematics, science and a foreign language. *Realschule*, or intermediate school, is the step after the general secondary school.

The nine-year *Gymnasium* (5th to 13th school years) is the traditional grammar or senior high school in Germany. It leads to an intermediate school certificate, qualifying the pupil for higher or vocational education. This certificate is gained by approximately 40 per cent of pupils.

Gesamtschule is a comprehensive school which offers another type of the first stage of secondary schooling. Some of these schools also offer the final stage of secondary school, with the same structure as the Gymnasiums.

The following table shows enrolments in a selection of Germany's schools of general education in school year 2008/09:

School	No. of pupils
Primary schools	29,997,000
Secondary general schools	826,000
Intermediate schools	1,263,000
Grammar schools	2,469,000
Integrated comprehensive schools	503,000
Special schools	394,000
Other school types	573,000

Copyright: © Statistisches Bundesamt, Wiesbaden 2010

Figures for 2006-07 show that 9,355,900 students were enrolled in general education schools and 2,781,875 pupils attended vocational schools. Also that academic year 1,372,893 students attended university, 31,327 students attended art or music colleges and 570,712 students were at specialised colleges of further education.

Higher Education

Admission to higher education courses is usually based on entrance qualification (*Abitur* examination), and there are some national restrictions, due to increasing competition for places. Approximately one third of pupils in Germany apply for higher education.

Most places of study for higher education are traditional universities, where pupils can study for a Master's degree (*Magister*), a Diploma or a state examination, leading on if desired to a doctorate. Germany also offers *Fachhochschulen* where the length of study is shorter than a traditional university course, and subjects are usually of a scientific nature.

The main body for higher education and its future is the Bund-Länder Commission for Educational Planning and Research Promotion. Higher education establishments are self-governing but owned by the state. Germany has 102 general universities, as well as universities of applied sciences, theology and administration. Germany's oldest university is Ruprecht Karls University in Heidelberg which was founded in 1386. The largest is Cologne University which has 47,000 students.

Vocational Education

In theory, everyone starting work should have had some kind of vocational training, which, in Germany, is a mixture of work-training and part-time education at a vocational school. As this benefits industry, private businesses as well as the state are responsible for the country's vocational training. Those pupils under the age of 18 not wishing to continue with higher education must attend a vocational school, which is a year of full-time theory before on-the-job training. *Berufsfachschule* is a full-time vocational school which can enhance or replace an apprenticeship. *Fachoberschule* courses last two years and the school only accepts students with an intermediate school certificate. This school qualifies pupils for the *Fachhochschule*.

The literacy rate in Germany is almost 100 per cent.

RELIGION

The majority of Germans (over 55 million) are Christians. Over 28 million are Protestant and 27 million are Roman Catholic. Germany has no state church; however, churches are looked upon as independent public-law corporations. The state finances many church establishments, such as kindergartens, and the church works in many establishments such as hospitals, training centres and schools.

Germany has a Jewish community of around 150,000, many of whom are immigrants from the former Soviet Union. In 2007, Germany's largest Synagogue was reopened after extensive restoration. The Synagogue in Berlin was destroyed in 1938. Around 3.2 million Muslims live in Germany, a large proportion originally coming from Turkey.

Germany has a religious liberty rating of 6 on a scale of 1 to 10 (10 is most freedom). (Source: World Religion Database)

Evangelical Church in Germany, URL: http://www.ekd.de
Arbeitsgemeinschaft Christlicher Kirchen in Deutschland (Council of Christian Churches in Germany), URL: http://www.oekumene-ack.de
Deutsche Bischofskonferenz (Bishops' Conference), URL: http://www.dbk.de
Zentralrat der Juden in Deutschland (Central Council of Jews in Germany), URL: http://www.zentralratdjuden.de

COMMUNICATIONS AND MEDIA

Newspapers

Approximately 25 million copies of daily newspapers are sold per day. Press rights are governed by each state, and any reports of misconduct or unethical behaviour are looked into by the German Press Council. Most papers are regional and there are relatively few national titles. Germany's major dailies are:
Bild, URL: http://www.bild.de
Frankfurter Allgemeine Zeitung, URL: http://www.faz.net/s/homepage.html
Die Welt, URL: http://www.welt.de
Frankfurter Rundschau, URL: http://www.fr-online.de
Sueddeutsche Zeitung, URL: http://www.sueddeutsche.de
Die Zeit, URL: http://www.zeit.de/index

Handelsblatt, URL: http://www.handelsblatt.com

Business Journals
The largest journals are:
Der Spiegel, URL: http://www.spiegel.de
Focus, URL: http://www.focus.de
Stern, URL: http://www.stern.de
Bunte, URL:http://www.bunte.t-online.de

Broadcasting
Private and public radio and television networks exist under state laws. There is one broadcasting organisation under federal law (ARD), 11 regional broadcasting corporations, a second national television network (ZDF) and the public radio broadcasting corporation Deutschlandradio. The main TV stations are RTL, RTL II, ARD and ZDF.

The regional corporations make up an association which operates a national television programme (Erstes Deutsches Fernsehen - Channel One), and which separately produces regional Channel Three programmes. Channel Two is the largest television-only station in Europe and reaches nearly all German homes. The regional corporations each broadcast up to five programmes on a wide variety of subjects. In 1995, satellite broadcasting began in Germany with the launch of SAT1. There are now another nine satellite stations currently broadcasting. Over 24 million households are connected to the cable network.

ARD, URL: http://www.ard.de
ZDF, URL: http://www.zdf.de
RTL, URL: http://www.rtl.de
N-TV, URL: http://www.n-tv.de
N-24, URL: http://www.n24.de

Association of Public Law Broadcasting Organisations (ARD), URL: http://www.ard.de
Zweites Deutsches Fernsehen (ZDF), URL: http://www.zdf.de

Deutschlandradio, formed in 1993, runs two information programmes with no advertising. The federal radio station, Deutsche Welle, is for foreign broadcast. There are approximately 170 private radio stations.
Deutschland Radio, URL: http://www.dradio.de
Deutsche Welle, URL: http://www.dw-world.de/
British Forces Broadcasting Service, Germany, URL: http://www.bfbs.com

Postal Service
Until 1995 the postal service was run by the state. The privatisation formed three companies, Deutsche Telekom, Deutsche Post and Deutsche Postbank (URL: http://www.postbank.com/), which are linked, being stock corporations, but are run as private enterprises. Deutsche Post AG (URL: http://www.deutschepost.de/) employs around 320,000 people, and delivers approximately 20 billion letters and freight items world-wide each year.

Telecommunications
Figures for 2011 show that there were over 51 million telephone land lines in use and nearly 108 million mobile phones.

Recent figures show that Germany has over 65 million regular internet users.

ENVIRONMENT

Under previous coalition between Gerhard Schroeder's SPD and the Greens had meant a greater emphasis on environmental issues. Amongst a range of ecologically focused policies currently in force are the phasing out of nuclear power for the generation of energy, the development of renewable power, and the reduction of carbon emissions through a system of eco-taxes.

Germany ranks sixth in the world for carbon emissions. In 2008, 823.07 million metric tons of carbon were emitted from the burning of fossil fuels, representing 2.7 per cent of world carbon emissions. In accordance with the Kyoto Protocol agreed in December 1997 Germany will have to reduce carbon emissions to 8 per cent below 1990 levels by the period 2008 to 2012. Since 2007, Germany has reduced its emissions by 24 per cent, above the 21 per cent set by the Kyoto Agreement. In 2009, 765.56 million metric tons of carbon were emitted from the consumption of fossil fuels, this figure had risen to 793.66 million metric tons by 2010. (Source: EIA)

Greenhouse gas emissions from road traffic have decreased since 1999 despite the increase in traffic and are now below the 1990 level. Nitrous oxide emissions have reduced by approximately 50 per cent partly due to the introduction of catalytic converters. A mandatory flue gas desulfurization process has reduced sulfur dioxide emissions from coal and lignite power stations by 90 per cent.

Responsibility for environmental protection in Germany is shared between the Federal Government (sole legislative power), the Länder (by monitoring implementation) and the local authorities. The Federal Environmental Agency (Umweltbundesamt, UBA) was set up to support the Federal Ministry of Environment, particularly for public enquiries and education, involvement in a 'Blue Angel' environmental label, collection of data and assistance in governmental research.

Germany is a party to the following environmental agreements: Air Pollution, Air Pollution-Nitrogen Oxides, Air Pollution-Persistent Organic Pollutants, Air Pollution-Sulfur 85, Air Pollution-Sulfur 94, Air Pollution-Volatile Organic Compounds, Antarctic-Environmental Protocol, Antarctic-Marine Living Resources, Antarctic Seals, Antarctic Treaty, Biodiversity, Climate Change, Climate Change-Kyoto Protocol, Desertification, Endangered Species, Environmental Modification, Hazardous Wastes, Law of the Sea, Marine Dumping, Ozone Layer Protection, Ship Pollution, Tropical Timber 83, Tropical Timber 94, Wetlands, Whaling.

Federal Environmental Agency (Umweltbundesamt, UBA), URL: http://www.umweltbundesamt.de
Federal Office for Nature Conservation (Bundesamt fur Naturschutz, BfN), URL: http://www.bfn.de
Federal Office for Radiation Protection (Bundesamt fur Strahlenschutz, BfS), URL: http://www.bfs.de

SPACE PROGRAMME

The DLR is Germany's national research centre for aeronautics and space. It does extensive research and development work in aeronautics, space, transportation, energy and defence.As the Germany National Space Agency it also has responsibility for the strategy and implementation of the German space programme. The DLR has approximately 32 institutes and facilites at 16 locations in Germany, and an estimated 7,000 employees.The annual DLR budget for in-house research and development work is approximately €745 million (2010). DLR also administers the space budget of the German government, approximately €1033 million. An estimated 63 percent of this amount is the German contribution to ESA, 22 per cent is allocated to the national space program and 15 per cent is the Centre's own space research.

Deutsches Zentrum für Luft- und Raumfahrt eV (DLR) (German Space Agency), URL: http://www.dlr.de

BADEN-WÜRTTEMBERG

Capital: Stuttgart (Population estimate: 585,400)

CONSTITUTION AND GOVERNMENT

The state of Baden-Württemberg came into being in 1952 following a referendum in three south-western states that had been formed in 1945. It is the third-largest state of the Federal Republic. It is divided into four counties, 12 regional associations, 35 rural districts, nine county boroughs, and about 1,000 local authorities.

The current Parliament of the state of Baden-Württemberg (2011-16) comprises a total of 138 members, elected for five years. Each member of parliament represents approximately 77,900 constituents. There are currently 70 constituencies. The rightist Christian Democratic Union of Germany (CDU), has led all but one of Lower Saxony's governments since the establishment of the state in 1952.

State Parliament: http://www.landtag-bw.de
President: Guido Wolf

Cabinet (as at May 2013)
Minister-President: Winfried Kretschmann (Grüne)

Deputy Minister of State and Minister of Finance and Economics: Dr Nils Schmid (SPD)
Minister in the Ministry of State: Silke Krebs (Grüne)
Minister for Parliament, Europe and International Affairs: Peter Friedrich (SPD)
Minister of the Interior: Reinhold Gall (SPD)
Minister of the Environment, Climate Protection and Energy: Franz Untersteller (Grüne)
Minister of Education, Youth and Sport: Gabriele Warminski-Leitheußer (SPD)
Minister of Rural Affairs and Consumer Protection: Alexander Bonde (Grüne)
Minister of Justice: Rainer Stickelberger (SPD)
Minister of Science, Research and the Arts: Theresia Bauer (Grüne)
Minister of Transport and Infrastructure: Winfried Hermann (Grüne)
Minister of Labour and Social Affairs, Families, Women and Senior Citizens: Katrin Altpeter (SPD)
Minister of Integration: Bilkay Öney (SPD)
State Secretary in the Ministry of Transport and Infrastructure: Dr. Gisela Splett (Grüne)
State Counsellor for Civil Society and Civic Participation: Gisela Erler (Grüne)

Elections
The most recent parliamentary elections took place on 27 March 2011 and resulted in a Green and SPD coalition government. The State Government formed by Minister President Winfried Kretschmann took office on 12 May 2011. Elections are due in 2016.

GERMANY

LOCAL GOVERNMENT

There are four Administrative Districts: Freiburg, Karlsruhe, Stuttgart, and Tübingen. These are divided into 35 districts (Landkreise) and 9 independent cities (Stadtkreise).

AREA AND POPULATION

Baden-Württemberg is a highly industrialised region in the southwestern part of Germany, to the east of the Upper Rhine. Well-known landmarks include the Black Forest and the Rhine, Danube, Neckar and Tauber rivers.

It has an area of 35,752 sq. km and a population of 10.749 million. Population density is around 300 people per square km. 1.3 million inhabitants are not of German origin; there are an estimated 323,000 Turks, 248,000 people from former Yugoslavia and around 188,000 Italians.

Municipalities with a population of more than 100,000 are Stuttgart, 590,429; Mannheim, 307,000; Karlsruhe, 284,000; Freiburg im Breisgau, 214,000; Heidelberg, 143,000; Heilbronn, 121,000; Ulm, 120,000; Pforzheim, 119,000; Reutlingen, 112,000. Stuttgart lies at the centre of a heavily populated area, circled by a ring of smaller towns; with a population of 2.7 million, 'greater Stuttgart' is the fifth biggest city region in Germany.

The dialects of Swabian (Schwäbisch) and 'Badisch'/Allemanic are spoken in many regions, both of which are considered almost unintelligible to northern Germans.

EMPLOYMENT

The total number of employees was estimated at 5.5 million in 2007. Baden-Württemberg has enjoyed the lowest unemployment levels in Germany over recent years; in 2007, unemployment had fallen to 4.3 per cent, the lowest in Germany. In 2012, the unemployment rate was estimated to be 4.1 per cent (down from 4.5 per cent in 2011), compared to the national rate of 7.4 per cent.

The manufacturing industry continues to be an important sector, providing work for some 1.3 million people (2012). Around 100,000 people were employed in the agriculture sector in 2007. The strongest job growth over the decade has been in the business services sector. (Source: EU)

BANKING AND FINANCE

Baden-Württemberg is among the most prosperous states in Germany and is one of the wealthiest regions in Europe. The economy is dominated by small and medium-sized innovative enterprises, but some of the largest manufacturing companies are also based in the region.

In 2010, GDP was estimated at €362 billion (14.5 per cent of the national total). This represents a growth rate of 5.5 per cent, compared to a fall of 7 per cent in 2009. Growth was estimated to be over 5.5 per cent in 2011. Per capita GDP was estimated to be €32,900 in 2007.

MANUFACTURING, MINING AND SERVICES

Manufacturing
Industry is largely concentrated around the river Neckar, the main centres being Stuttgart, Esslingen and Plochingen (motor cars, mechanical engineering, electronics, chemicals). Baden-Württemberg also produces furniture, textiles, musical instruments, shoes, surgical instruments, and optical equipment. Precision engineering and the automotive industry are the most traditional bases of Baden-Württemberg's industrial activity, however. Software, biotechnology and environmental technology sectors are key growth areas. The region also provides the headquarters to many world famous firms such as Mercedez Benz, Bosch, IBM and Porsche.

Services
Growth in business services has fuelled economic development over the last decade.

Agriculture
Almost half of Baden-Württemberg is used for agriculture and some 38 per cent of the state remains forested. The sector employs less than two per cent of the workforce.

Many small and medium-sized farms specialise in wine growing, tobacco, fruit, asparagus, hop and vegetable production.

COMMUNICATIONS AND TRANSPORT

Stuttgart airport (URL: http://www.stuttgart-airport.com/) carried 10.3 million passengers in 2007.

Baden-Württemberg has a network of over 1,500 km of motorways and over 5,000 km of main roads, 9,980 km of state roads and over 12,100 km of district roads.

The Deutsche Bahn AG rail neworks amounts to approximately 3,800 km. A further 900 km is owned privately. The network is being developed; a new rail route between Stuttgart and Ulm is being developed as part of the Stuttgart 21 project.

There are some 550 km of waterways used for inland commercial shipping. The River Rhine flows for 28 4km between Mannheim and Basle. The Rhine is used as a transport route to the ports of Amsterdam, Rotterdam and Antwerp. Mannheim port handled 6.6 million tones in 2011.

EDUCATION

In 2007, there were some 1.7 million pupils registered in the state's primary and secondary schools.

Baden-Württemberg has three universities: Heidelberg (founded in 1386), Freiburg (1457), and Tubigen (1477). In 2004, there were around 238,000 students.

BAVARIA

Capital: Munich (Population estimate: 1.4 million)

CONSTITUTION AND GOVERNMENT

Bavaria has been a political and cultural entity for a thousand years. It is the only state of the Federal Republic to have retained its borders after 1945. It comprises seven counties, 25 town boroughs, and 71 rural districts.

Legislature
Bavaria's legislature consists of the unicameral *Lantag*. The 187 members are elected for five years.

For details of the Bavarian constitution, please consult: http://www.bayern.landtag.de/en/bayer_verfassung.html
Landtag: URL: http://www.landtag-bayern.de/
President of the Landtag : Barbara Stamm

Cabinet (as at May 2013)
Minister-President: Winfried Kretschmann
Deputy Minister President and Minister of Finance and Economic Affairs: Dr Nils Schmid
Minister of the Interior: Reinhold Gall
Minister in the Ministry State: Silke Krebs
Minister of Federal, European and International Affairs: Peter Friedrich
Minister for the Environment, Climate and Energy Policy: Frank Untersteller
Minister of Education, Youth and Sport: Gabriele Warminski-Leitheußer
Minister of Rural Development and Consumer Protection: Alexander Bonde
Minister of Justice: Rainer Stickelberger
Minister of Science, Research and the Arts: Theresia Bauer
Minister of Transport and Infrastructure: Winfried Hermann
Minister of Employment, Social Affairs, Families, Women and Senior Citizens: Katrin Altpeter

---

Minister of Integration: Bilkay Öney
State Secretary in the Ministry of Transport and Infrastructure: Dr Gisela Splett
State Council for Civil Society and Civic Participation: Gisela Erler

Ministries
Office of the Minister-President, Franz-Josef-Strauß-Ring 1, 80539 Munich, Germany. Tel: +49 (0)89 21650, fax: +49 (0)49 294044, URL: http://www.bayern.de/Staatsregierung-.2920/index.htm
Ministry for Home Affairs, Odeonsplatz 3, 80539 Munich, Germany. Tel: +49 (0)89 219201, fax: +49 (0)49 282090, URL: http://www.innenministerium.bayern.de/
Ministry of Justice, Justizpalast, 80333 Munich, Germany. Tel: +49 (0)89 55971, fax: +49 (0)89 896091, URL: http://www.justiz.bayern.de/
Ministry of Education and Culture, Salvatorplatz 2, 80333 Munich, Germany. Tel: +49 (0)89 21860, fax: +49 (0)89 2186 2800
Ministry of Scientific Research and Arts, Salvatorplatz 2, 80333 Munich, Germany. Tel: +49 (0)89 21860, fax: +49 (0)89 2186 2800, URL: http://www.stmwfk.bayern.de/
Ministry of Finance, Odeonsplatz 4, 80539 Munich, Germany. Tel: +49 (0)89 23060, fax: +49 (0)89 280 9313, URL: http://www.stmf.bayern.de/
Ministry of Transportation, Economy and Technologies, Prinzregentstraße, 80538 Munich, Germany. Tel: +49 (0)89 21820, fax: +49 (0)89 2182 2677
Ministry of Food, Agriculture and Forestry, Ludwigstraße 2, 80539 Munich, Germany. Tel: +49 (0)89 21820, fax: +49 (0)89 2182 2677
Ministry of Development and the Environment, Rosenkavalierplatz 2, 81925 Munich, Germany. Tel: +49 (0)89 92140, fax: +49 (0)89 9214 2266

Elections
The conservative Christian Social Union of Bavaria (CSU) has won every election since 1957. However, in the 2008 elections, the CSU lost its absolute majority for the first time in 46 years, and was obliged to form a coalition with the Free Democratic Party.

Results of the last state elections (28 September 2008): CSU: 49.2 per cent (92 seats- down by 32); SPD: 20.9 per cent (39 seats); Free Voters: 11.2 per cent (21 seats); Alliance 90/Green Party: 10.2 per cent (19 seats); Free Democratic Party: 8.6 per cent (16 seats).

Elections are due to take place on 15 September 2013. At the time of going to press, results were not known.

In 1995 Bavaria introduced direct democracy on the local level in a referendum. Bavaria has the most advanced regulations on local direct democracy in Germany, resulting in 835 referenda from 1995 to 2005.

LOCAL GOVERNMENT

Bavaria is divided into 7 administrative regions (Regierungsbezirke): Upper, Middle and Lower Franconia; Swabia; Upper Palatinate; Upper and Lower Bavaria. The regions are in turn divided into 71 administrative districts (Landkreise) and 25 independent cities. There are also 2,031 local authorities.

AREA AND POPULATION

Bavaria is in the southeast of Germany and, at 70,549.21 km. sq., it is the largest state of Germany in terms of area. The region has international borders with Austria and the Czech Republic as well as with Switzerland (across Lake Constance). Two major rivers flow through the state, the Danube (Donau) and the Main, and the upper Rhine forms part of the southwest border of the state. The Bavarian Alps define the border with Austria.

Its population of approximately 12.5 million can be divided into three main groups, which differ from each other with regard to dialect and culture: the 'old' Bavarians in the south and east (numbering approx. 6.4 million), the Franconians in the north (4.1 million), and the Bavarian Swabians in the south-west (1.8 million). Population density is estimated to be 177 inhabitants per square km. Approximately 15.5 per cent is aged under 15 years and 16.5 per cent over 65 years.

Towns with a population of over 100,000 are: Munich, 1.35 million; Nuremberg, 503,500; Augsburg, 264,000; Regensburg, 135,000; Wurzburg, 133,000; Furth, 114,500 and Ingolstadt, 125,000, Furth 115,000, and Erlangen 105,400. Munich is the third largest city in Germany, after Berlin and Hamburg. Its population is expected to rise to 1.5 million by 2030.

EMPLOYMENT

Official estimates indicated that there were 6.35 million employees in 2010. The region had an unemployment rate of 4.5 per cent in 2010. Almost half of those employed work in the service sector.

BANKING AND FINANCE

Bavaria has long enjoyed one of the healthiest economies of any region in Germany. Its GDP in 2007 exceeded €423 billion, making it one of the largest economies in Europe. Its real GDP rose to over €443 billion in 2010. Large companies headquartered in Bavaria include BMW, Siemens, Munich Re, Allianz, Infineon, MAN, Wacker Chemie, Puma AG and Adidas AG.

In the past, Bavaria's economy was largely agrarian, but the agriculture sector has now dwindled to represent just one per cent of the region's Gross Value Added (GVA). The economy is now fuelled by high-tech industry and service providers.

The sectors of greatest growth are: laser-based technologies; electronics and microelectronics; genetic engineering and biotechnologies; information and communication; automation, environment technologies and automation.

MANUFACTURING, MINING AND SERVICES

Energy
Bavaria hosts one of the world's largest solar energy complexes in the world. The photovoltaic power station opened in 2006 and has a maximum output of 110 MW.

Manufacturing
Industry has developed rapidly since 1945, and Bavaria now has an aerospace and automobile industry, oil refineries and a petrochemical industry. Motor car, electronics, textile and chemical companies have settled around Munich. Nuremberg focuses on engineering and toy manufacture; its annual International Toy Fair is the most important of its kind.

Service Industries
The service sector is the largest sector of the Bavarian economy, contributing some 67 per cent of the state's GDP and employing around 60 per cent of the workforce. The services industry continues to grow, and the great majority of new companies setting up are in this sector.

Agriculture
Bavaria is the most important state in the Federal Republic of Germany in terms of agricultural produce. It accounts for around 20 per cent of Germany's arable land, and over 86 per cent of land in Bavaria is used for agriculture, forestry and fish farming. However, farming and forestry now contributes just one per cent towards GDP.

Main products include milk, beef, pork and grain as well as maize, potatos, sugar beet and rye. Hops, grapes and asparagus are also grown.

COMMUNICATIONS AND TRANSPORT

There are two international airports in Munich (URL: http://www.munich-airport.de/) and Nuremberg (URL: http://www.airport-nuernberg.de/english/). In 2011, approximately 37.8 million passengers used Munich airport in 2011, ranking it as Germany's second-busiest passenger airport and sixth in Europe. It is also one of the busiest cargo hubs. Approximately 4 million passengers used Nuremberg airport in 2010 and 110,000 tonnes of cargo were transported.

The road network comprises 87,000 miles of which 1,430 miles are motorways. The road network covers approximately 4,200 miles.

The Rhine-Main Danube canal isapproximately 106 miles long. Approximately 7 billion tons of goods are transported via the canal per year.

EDUCATION

The annual state expenditure on education amounts to approximately €8 billion. Approximately 250,000 people are enrolled in further education institutions, approximately 10 per cent from abroad. There are nine-state-run universities and 17 state-run universities.

RELIGION

Most Bavarians (an estimated 56 per cent) are Catholic. Pope Benedict XVI is from Bavaria, and was previously Archbishop of Munich and Freising. Lutheranism has a significant presence in large parts of Franconia.

BERLIN

Capital: Berlin (Population estimate: 3.5 million)

CONSTITUTION AND GOVERNMENT

On 3 October 1990, the day of German unification, the city-state of Berlin ceased to be divided and became a full state of the Federal Republic. After 1945 it was initially divided into four sectors, of which the three western sectors were eventually integrated into the Federal Republic and afforded restricted rights, whilst the eastern sector became the capital of the German Democratic Republic. In 2001, the 23 boroughs of Berlin were amalgamated to form 12 boroughs - administrative units with political rights comparable to incorporated communities in the rest of Germany (although they are not separate legal entities from the city).

The seat of the federal government moved from Bonn to Berlin in 1999.

Legislature
Berlin's House of Representatives (*Abgeordnetenhaus*), consists of 149 members. They serve a five-year term in office. One of their duties is to elect the Governing Mayor.
Abgeordnetenhaus: URL: http://www.parlament-berlin.de/
President, House of Representatives: Ralf Wieland

Cabinet (as at May 2013)
Governing Mayor: Klaus Wowereit (SPD)
Senator for Economics, Technology and Research: Cornedia Yzer
Senator for Justice and Consumer Protection: Thomas Heilman (CDU)
Senator for Education Youth and Science: Sandra Scheeres (SPD)
Mayor and Senator for the Interior and Sport: Frank Henkel (CDU)
Se nator for Health and Social Services: Mario Czaja (CDU)
Senator for Integration, Labour and Women's Issues: Dilek Kolat (SPD)
Senator for Finance: Dr Ulrich Nussbaum (Ind.)
Mayor and Senator for Urban Development and the Environment: Michael Müller (SPD)

Government portal: URL: http://www.berlin.de

Elections
Elections were last held on 18 September 2011; the SPD won 47 seats (down 7), the CDU won 39 (up 2) and the Greens won 29 seats (up 6). The Left Party (Linke, PDS) also won 19 seats (down 5), and the Pirate Party won 15. The FDP lost all its 15 seats. The SPD formed a coalition with the Left Party.

The next state elections are due to take place in 2016.

GERMANY

LOCAL GOVERNMENT

Berlin is subdivided into 12 boroughs (Bezirke), which were combined from the earlier 23 boroughs on January 1, 2001.

AREA AND POPULATION

Berlin covers an area of 892 sq. km and has a population of around 3.5 million. The population density is 37 people per hectare. Over 14 per cent of the population are foreign nationals, mainly Turkish. It is Germany's largest city and, as the Federal Capital, is a cultural and tourist centre.

EMPLOYMENT

The work force comprises around 53 per cent of the population. The unemployment rate remains significantly higher than the national average. Figures for 2008 indicate that 14 per cent of the workforce was unemployed over the year, down from 19 per cent in 2005. Most of the unemployed have low skills or come from immigrant backgrounds. Approximately 20 per cent of the population is believed to be dependent on state aid.

The service sector is the largest employer (approximately 85 per cent in 2010), followed by the industrial sector. The health services sector accounts for 180,000 people. Less than one per cent work in the agricultural sector. Although downsized since unification, the public sector remains an important employer.

BANKING AND FINANCE

Gross Domestic Product was estimated at €83,600 million at the end of 2007. Growth was estimated at 1.6 per cent in 2008 and 1.7 per cent in 2009 (compared to -3.5 per cent in Germany as a whole). GDP was estimated at €90 billion in 2009 and €94.5 billion in 2011.

Berlin's debt was estimated at over €60 billion in 2009.

MANUFACTURING, MINING AND SERVICES

Because of its special geographic position, the western part of Berlin had formerly been greatly dependent on the Federal Government, although efforts were made to develop industry. After reunification, the Berlin government aimed to establish financial independence from the Federal Government and to develop the eastern part of the city.

The reinstatement of Berlin as the German capital gives new impetus to economic development. Its economy is based on the service sector, encompassing a range of media corporations, convention venues, research and life science institutes, and creative industries. Berlin is one of Germany's main R&D locations. Approximately 40,000 people work in R&D. Berlin spends 4.2 per cent of its GDP in R&D, the highest percentage of the German states.

Berlin has a busy tourist industry; 9.7 million people visited the city in 2011 and there were over 22 million overnight stays. The number of tourists has risen recently thanks to budget airlines.

COMMUNICATIONS AND TRANSPORT

The public road network covers 5,490 km, and the rest of the transport system (subway, suburban rail, streetcar and buslines) cover 1,700 km. Millions of passengers use the S-Bahn and the BVG transport options every day. Berlin's new main train station cut travel times to many destinations. In 2011, there were an estimated 1.33 million registered cars in the city.

A new airport, the Berlin Brandenburg Airport (URL: http://www.berlin-airport.de) should be completed by 2013. Telgel Airport will be then be closed.

HEALTH

At the end of 2010, there were 79 hospitals, staffed by 7,600 doctors. The city has approximately 140 dentists.

EDUCATION

Around 440,878 children were registered at the 1,180 primary or secondary schools in the city in 2005. There are 14 public and 22 private institutions in Berlin's higher education system. In 2008, there were approximately 135,000 students at university or college level in the same year, approximately 70 per cent of them in research. Universities include three research-intensive universities: Free University of Berlin, Humboldt University and the Technical University of Berlin.

BRANDENBURG

Capital: Potsdam (Population estimate: 150,000)

CONSTITUTION AND GOVERNMENT

Brandenburg, formerly one of the provinces of Prussia, became Land Mark Brandenburg in 1947 but lost its identity as a political entity in 1952. The present State of Brandenburg was re-established after German reunification in 1990. In 1995, there was a referendum on whether to merge the state with Berlin, to form a new state with the name of "Berlin-Brandenburg". Although West Berliners were in favour of the merger, East Berliners and Brandenburgers voted against it.

Brandenburg's state Assembly consists of 88 members and is currently led by a coalition of the SPD and CDU.
URL: http://www.brandenburg.de/
President: Gunther Fritsch

Cabinet (as at June 2013)
Prime Minister: Matthias Platzeck (page 1496)
Deputy Prime Minister and Finance Minister: Dr Helmuth Markov
Home Secretary: Dr Dietmar Woidke
Minister of Justice: Dr Volkmar Schoneburg
Minister of Economy and European Affairs: Ralf Christoffers
Minister of Infrastructure and Agriculture: Jorg Vogel
Minister for Health, Consumer Affairs and the Environment: Anita Tack
Minister for Education, Youth and Sports: Dr Martina Münch
Minister of Labour, Social Affairs, Women and Family: Günter Baaske
Minister for Science, Research & Culture: Prof. Dr.-Ing. Dr. Sabine Kunst

---

Elections
The most recent elections took place in September 2009. Prime Minister Matthias Platzeck retained power. The seats are divided thus: SPD 5; Die Linke 6; CDU 5; FDP 2; Grüne / B90 1 seat.

The next elections are due to take place in 2014.

LOCAL GOVERNMENT

Brandenburg surrounds but excludes the national capital Berlin. The region is divided into fourteen administrative districts and four district free towns.

AREA AND POPULATION

Brandenburg has an area of 29,479 sq. km and is known for its Ice Age landscape of lowlands and valleys, rivers, lakes and swamps. The state has a population of 2,567,220. The principal towns are: Potsdam, 141,000; Cottbus, 129,000; and Brandenburg, 93,000.

EMPLOYMENT

An estimated 1.3 million people were employed in 2010 with an unemployment rate of 11.1 per cent.

BANKING AND FINANCE

The Brandenburg economy has undergone considerable structural change since reunification, and there has been a clear shift away from industrial manufacturing towards the services sector. In 2010, GDP amounted to €55.8 billion, approximately 2.2 per cent of the national total. Per capita is substantially lower than the national average (€22,260 compared to €30,570).

Exports from the region reached a new annual record 2003, exceeding €5 billion. This represented a ten per cent increase on 2002. Pharmaceuticals accounted for almost 16 per cent of exports; other important exports included aircraft, plywood, chipboard and fibreboard, sheets of iron or steel, and plastics. The main destinations were the USA, Poland, the Netherlands, the UK and Italy.

Imports cost the region €5.5 billion in 2003, a reduction of 6 per cent on 2002. Crude oil and natural gas were the main import goods (38 per cent of the total), followed by aircraft, electrical machinery and apparatus, ferrous waste and scrap, and furniture. Over 90 per cent of these goods were imported from Europe, the main import partner being the Russian Federation.

MANUFACTURING, MINING AND SERVICES

Primary and Extractive Industries
Lignite is mined in the areas of Niederlausitz and Furstenberg.

Manufacturing

After 40 years of central planning, Brandenburg's industries are in the process of modernisation. Iron smelting takes place around Brandenburg, Henningsdorf, Finow and Eisenhuttenstadt. Textiles are produced in the Guben, Forst, and Luckenwalde areas. A petrochemical centre is located at Schwedt on the Oder. Alongside the traditional motor vehicle and rail vehicle manufacturing industries, a modern aerospace industry has been built up in recent years.

Around 87,000 people were employed on average in 2003 in the industrial sector, (including mining and quarrying). 12 per cent worked in the agri-food industry, and 14 per cent were employed in the manufacture of transport equipment.

Agriculture

Brandenburg's farmers and foresters farm, tend and cultivate about 85 per cent of the land. The agriculturally rather infertile region is characterised by sandy soil and numerous lakes. Agricultural products are rye, oats, sugarbeet and potatoes. Dairy farming takes place in the lower lying regions. The sandy soil is ideal for the cultivation of extensive pine forests.

COMMUNICATIONS AND TRANSPORT

Brandenburg's infrastructure has been greatly improved since reunification. There are approximately 900 km of motorways, 1,500 km of rail roads and 900 km of water ways.

BREMEN

Capital: Bremen (Population estimate: 547,500)

CONSTITUTION AND GOVERNMENT

The Free Hanseatic City of Bremen is a combination of two cities, Bremen and Bremerhaven, in one state. The state parliament elects the Senate, the federal state government, which comprises seven senators. The President of the Senate (comparable to the minister presidents of Germany's other federal states) is also a mayor of the city of Bremen together with another senator.

Legislature

Bremen's unicameral legislature consists of the City Council (*Bremische Bürgerschaft*). The state parliament (2011-15) currently has 83 members (68 from the city of Bremen and 15 from Bremerhaven).
City Council: http://www.bremische-buergerschaft.de/
Senate: URL: http://www.bremen.de

State Senators (as at June 2013)
President of the Senate, Senator for Culture and Religious Affairs: Mayor Jens Böhrnsen (SPD)
Senator for Finance: Mayor Karoline Linnert (Alliance 90 /Die Grüne)
Senator of the Interior and Sport: Ulrich Mäurer (SPD)
Senator for Education, Science and Health: Renate Jürgens-Pieper (SPD)
Senator of Building, Environment and Transport: Dr. Joachim Lohse (Alliance 90 /Die Grüne)
Senator of Social Affairs, Children, Yout and Women: Anja Stahmann (Alliance 90 /Die Grüne)
Senator for Justice & Constitutional Affairs; Economy, Labour and Ports: Martin Güthner (SPD)
Representative of the Free Hanseatic City of Bremen to the Federation: Prof. Dr. Eva Quante Brandt (SPD)

Elections
The most recent state elections took place in May 2011. The SPD won most seats with 38.78 per cent of the vote, up two per cent. The CDU had its worst result since 1959 losing 5.3 per cent to finish with 20.4 per cent of the vote. The Greens increased their share of the vote by 4 per cent to 22.5 per cent. The Left Party retained a 5.6 per cent share. The FDP fell to 2.4 per cent and will not be represented in the city state parliament. Turnout was low at 56.6 per cent. For the first-time 16-year-olds were able to vote in the state election.

The next state elections are due to take place in 2015.

AREA AND POPULATION

Located on the River Weser, the state of Bremen consists of two separated cities: Bremen, officially the 'City' which is the state capital, and the city of Bremerhaven, which serves as a North Sea harbour. At 60 km from the sea, the ports of the city of Bremen comprise the furthest inland transshipment centre in Germany, with corresponding fast connections to the hinterland. Both cities of Bremen are individually surrounded by the State of Lower Saxony. The state has a total area of 400 sq. km, making it the smallest of the German states.

The population currently numbers 660,740 (547,340 in Bremen and 113,400 in Bremerhaven).

EMPLOYMENT

Employment in Bremen was estimated at 294,000 in 2010 with an unemployment rate of 12 per cent.

BANKING AND FINANCE

Bremen contributes just over 1 per cent of the national GDP. In 2009, GDP was estimated at €24.9 billion, rising to €26.7 billion in 2010. In 2010, GDP grew by 3.5 per cent, rising to an estimated €28 billion. It has a high GDP per capita rate of €42,500, reflecting its status of city-state.

MANUFACTURING, MINING AND SERVICES

Bremen's ports form the foundation of the city's trade and industry. Much of the imported tobacco is processed by Bremen's cigar and cigarette factories. Coffee beans are roasted and marketed locally and throughout Germany. Cornmills, wool-carding and jute spinning factories, timberyards, wine importers, warehouses, as well as the docks and all related installations, depend on Bremen's importance as a seaport.

Car manufacturing, conventions and trade fairs, engineering and electronics firms are more recent developments as is the newly established aerospace industry. These new industries are intended to make Bremen less dependent on maritime trade and shipbuilding. Bremen is Europe's leading port for car import and export. Mercedes-Benz is the city's largest single employer, with a workforce of 13,500.

COMMUNICATIONS AND TRANSPORT

Approximately 2.5 million passengers used Bremen Airport (URL: http://www.airport-bremen.de) in 2008.

Bremen is Germany's second largest port after Hamburg, and an important transshipment centre. Bremen's ports account for a third of its state product, and more than 75,000 jobs are connected directly or indirectly with port activities. Over a thousand ships use the ports per year, transporting approximately 40 million tonnes of goods.

HAMBURG

Capital: Hamburg (Population estimate: 1.8 million)

CONSTITUTION AND GOVERNMENT

The Free and Hanseatic City of Hamburg, under a constitution adopted in 1952, regards itself as one of Germany's gateways to the world. It is one of three German City States. The city is governed by the Senate. The President of the Senate is at the same time First Mayor but, as *primus inter pares*, cannot lay down policy guidelines. Hamburg's senators, judges and civil servants are not permitted to accept orders and decorations.

Legislature
Hamburg's legislature consists of the City Council (*Burgerschaft*) which is composed of 121 members. The head of government is the First Mayor (Erster Bürgermeister). He determines the political guidelines. The ministers of Hamburg are known as senators (Senatoren). Currently the Hamburg government consists of ten ministries each headed by a senator.
URL: http://www.hamburg.de/
President of the Parliament: Carola Veit

Cabinet (as at June 2013)
First Mayor and President of the Senate: Olaf Scholz
Second Mayor and Minister of Science and Research: Dr Dorothee Stapelfeldt
Minister of Urban Development and Environment: Jutta Blankau
Minister of Economics, Transport and Innovation: Frank Horch
Minister of Finance: Dr Peter Tschentscher
Minister of Justice: Jana Schiedek
Minister of the Interior and Sport: Michael Neumann
Minister of Culture: Prof. Dr. Barbara Kisseler
Minister of Social Affairs, Family, Health and Consumer Protection: Detlef Scheele
Minister of Education: Ties Rabe
Minister of Health: Cornelia Prufer-Storck

Elections
State elections were most recently held in March 2011, the Social Democratic Party gained an overall majority. The next state elections are due to take place in 2015.

AREA AND POPULATION

The City of Hamburg is located on the southern point of the Jutland Peninsula, directly between Continental Europe to the south, Scandinavia to the north, the North Sea to the west, and the Baltic Sea to the east. It is the meeting point of the Rivers Elbe, Alster and Bille. The island of Neuwerk and two other islands in the North Sea form part of Hamburg. The state covers an area of 750 sq. km, including a water surface of 62 sq. km.

Hamburg is the second-largest city in Germany (after Berlin), and the second-largest port in Europe (ninth-largest port in the world). It is the most populous city in the European Union that is not a national capital.

Its population was around 1,774,000 inhabitants in 2007. It has a foreign population of around 257,060 resident (14.8 per cent of the population). The largest group of these are Turks who constitute 22.6 per cent of the foreign residents. There are an estimated 20,740 Polish residents, 4,040 people from the United Kingdom and 4,370 from the United States.

EMPLOYMENT

In 2010, 884,000 people were employed with an unemployment rate of 8.2 per cent.

BANKING AND FINANCE

The gross domestic product of Hamburg totalled €94 billion in 2011. GDP per capita was €50,000.

MANUFACTURING, MINING AND SERVICES

Hamburg (URL: http://www.hafen-hamburg.de/en) is Germany's largest seaport and principal trading and transshipment centre. Although situated 68 miles up the Elbe, it is considered a sea port due to its ability to handle large ocean-going vessels. The port dominates sea trade with eastern and northern Europe. Situated on the river Elbe, as a container port, it ranks first in Europe and ninth in the world. The port handled some 9 million single unit containers and over 130 million tonnes of goods in 2011 and is regarded as one of the fastest transshipment harbour in the world. The port's industrial area encompasses shipyards, refineries and processing plants for raw materials from abroad. Numerous factories and warehouses are situated near the docks, handling products such a grain, rubber, chemicals, oil, canned foods, cocoa and cigarettes. The aerospace, electronics, precision engineering, optical and chemical industries play an increasingly important role in Hamburg. The city-state is also an important banking, insurance and services centre.

HESSE

Capital: Wiesbaden (Population estimate: 276,000)

CONSTITUTION AND GOVERNMENT

Hesse's present boundaries were drawn after the Second World War, but the state combines areas with a common ethnic, historical and cultural identity. It comprises three counties, five county boroughs, 21 rural districts and some 430 local authorities.

Legislature
Hesse's legislature is the unicameral Assembly, composed of 110 members.
President of the Assembly: Norbert Kartmann
URL: http://www.hessen.de

Cabinet (as at June 2013)
Minister President: Volker Bouffier
Minister of State, Head of the State Chancellery: Axel Wintermeyer
Minister for Science and Arts: Eva Kühne-Hörmann
Deputy Prime Minister, Minister of Justice, Integration with Europe: Jörg-Uwe Hahn
Minister of Social Affairs: Stefan Gruttner
Minister of Culture: Nicola Beer
Minister of Economics, Transport, and Land Development: Florian Rentsch
Minister of Interior and Sport: Boris Rhein
Minister for the Environment, Energy, Agriculture and Consumer Protection: Lucia Puttrich
Minister of Finance: Thomas Schafer

Elections
In the Hesse state election of January 2008, the Prime Minister, Roland Koch (CDU), lost his majority in the state parliament (Landtag of Hesse). The CDU and SPD won 42 seats each, the Greens won nine seats and the FDP, eleven seats. Roland Koch formed a coalition government, he resigned in May 2010 and was succeeded by Volker Bouffier.

Elections are due to take place on 22 September 2013. At the time of going to press, results were not known.

LOCAL GOVERNMENT

Local elections took place in March 2011.

AREA AND POPULATION

Hesse covers an area of 21,110 sq. km and had an estimated population of 6,073,000 in 2007. It has three counties, five county boroughs, 21 rural districts, and some 430 local authorities.

Towns with a population of over 100,000 are: Frankfurt, 646,400; Wiesbaden, 274,000; Kassel, 198,000; Darmstadt, 139,000; Offenbach, 118,000.

EMPLOYMENT

The number of employed people was estimated at 2.9 million in 2010 with an unemployment rate of 6.4 per cent.

BANKING AND FINANCE

Frankfurt-am-Main is Hesse's most important city, though not the capital. A major banking centre, it is the home of the European Central Bank, which is charged with overseeing the euro.

The estimated state GDP was € 216,515 million in 2009. Services contributed almost 40 per cent and the production industry 17.5 per cent, transport 19.5 per cent. Agriculture contributed just 0.5 per cent.

MANUFACTURING, MINING AND SERVICES

Manufacturing

Manufacturing plays a major role in the economy of Hesse. The main industrial centre is the Rhine-Main area around Frankfurt, the second largest industrial region after the Ruhr area. The principal branches of industry are chemicals (Darmstadt, Frankfurt-Hoechst), motor cars (Ruesselsheim, Kassel), optical instruments (Wetzlar), leather (Offenbach), electronics, and engineering.

Agriculture

Agriculture and forestry together account for about 6 per cent of the state's workforce. The main crops are sugarbeet, vegetables, fruit wine, tobacco and, in the hilly regions, rye, barley, oats, and potatoes. Almost two fifths of Hesse is covered by woodland.

COMMUNICATIONS AND TRANSPORT

The transport infrastructure is undergoing expansion. The Frankfurt/Main International Airport has expanded and there is increased development of the rail road network. Frankfurt-am-Main train station is Germany's primary rail hub. Hesse's road network extends over 16,000 km.

Over 56 million passengers used Frankfurt/Main International Airport (URL: http://www.frankfurt-airport.de/) in 2011. Its new runway opened in 2011.

EDUCATION

Approximately 668,500 pupils were enrolled in school in the academic year 2009-10 and 186,000 in higher education.

LOWER SAXONY

Capital: Hanover (Population estimate: 523,000)

CONSTITUTION AND GOVERNMENT

Lower Saxony was formed in 1946 when previously autonomous regions in the area were merged with the former province of Hanover.

Legislature

Lower Saxony's unicameral legislature is the state Assembly and is composed of 155 members. 100 of the members are directly elected, 55 are elected through proportional representation. As of 2012, there were 152 members and 87 constituencies.
President of the Assembly: Herman Dinkla
URL: http://www.landtag-niedersachsen.de/

> **Cabinet (as at March 2013)**
> *Minister President:* Stephan Weil
> *Minister for Economics, Labour and Transport:* Olaf Lies
> *Minister of Finance:* Peter Jurgen Schnieder
> *Minister of Internal Affairs and Sport:* Boris Pistorius
> *Ministry for Regional Development, Food, Agriculture and Consumer Protection:* Gert Lindderman
> *Minister of Education:* Franke Heligenstadt
> *Minister of the Environment and Climate Protection:* Stefan Wenzel
> *Minister for Social Affairs, Women, the Family and Health:* Cornelia Rundt
> *Minister of Justice:* Antje Niewisch-Lennartz
> *Minister for Science and Culture:* Gabriele Heinen-Kljajic

The former prime minister of Lower Saxony, Christian Wulff, was elected president of Germany in June 2010.

Ministries

State Chancellery, URL: http://www.stk.niedersachsen.de
Ministry of Economy, Labour and Transport, URL: http://www.mw.niedersachsen.de
Ministry of Home Affairs, Sport & Integration, URL: http://www.mi.niedersachsen.de
Ministry of Finance, URL: http://www.mf.niedersachsen.de
Ministry of Social Affairs, Women, Family and Health, URL: http://www.ms.niedersachsen.de
Ministry of Justice, URL: http://www.mj.niedersachsen.de
Ministry of Food and Agriculture, URL: http://www.ml.niedersachsen.de
Ministry of the Environment, URL: http://www.mu.niedersachsen.de

Elections

The most recent election was held in January 2013. The CDU led government failed to regain power by one seat. They were replaced by a SPD-Green coalition which had a one seat majority. The CDU won 68 seats, the SPD won 48 seats and the Greens won 12 seats.

The next state elections are due to take place in 2017.

LOCAL GOVERNMENT

For administrative purposes Lower Saxony is divided into four districts: Braunschweig, Hannover, Lunegurg, and Weser-Ems. These are sub-divided into nine county boroughs, 38 rural districts, and about 1,000 local authorities.

AREA AND POPULATION

Located in north-western Germany with an area of 47,618 sq. km and a population of almost 7.95 million in 2011, Lower Saxony is thinly populated with just 167 inhabitants per km. sq. It is the second largest state, the largest being Bavaria. It accounts for approximately 9.6 per cent of Germany's total population. Approximately 6.7 per cent of the population is of foreign birth.

Towns with a population of more than 100,000 are: Hanover, 515,000; Brunswick, 246,000; Osnabruck, 164,000; Oldenburg, 158,000 and Göttingen, 122,000.

EMPLOYMENT

In 2012, the unemployment rate was 7.1 per cent, compared to the national rate of 7.4 per cent. Manufacturing is the main employment sector, with a workforce of some 575,500. Just four per cent of the population is involved in agriculture.

BANKING AND FINANCE

State GDP was estimated at €214.4 billion in 2008, approximately 8.6 per cent of Germany's total. Per capita GDP was estimated at €26,000. GDP fell in 2009 by an estimated 4.4 per cent. It grew by 3.4 per cent and reached €214 billion. Growth was an estimated 3 per cent in 2011.

MANUFACTURING, MINING AND SERVICES

Primary and Extractive Industries

Silver ore became a foundation of notable economic prosperity in the Harz Mountains as early as the 1100s. There are rock salt and potassium deposits in the foothills of the Harz mountains and Germany's largest iron ore deposits near Salzgitter and Brunswick. Significant quantities of oil and gas are extracted; approximately 90 per cent of Germany's natural gas and 30 per cent of its oil is produced in Lower Saxony.

Energy

Lower Saxony hopes to produce 90 per cent of its electricity comsumption from renewables by 2020 and has approximately 6.6GW installed wind power capacity (around 25 per cent of Germany's total). Offshore wind capacity is planned to reach 25GW by 2030 using sites in the North Sea off Lower Saxony.

Manufacturing

Manufacturing is another large part of the regional economy. The car industry is the largest sector in the Lower Saxony economy. Volkswagen, with five production plants within the state, remains the single biggest private-sector employer; its headquarters are based in Wolfsburg. There are chemical factories and oil refineries in the coastal area around Wilhelmshaven.

Other mainstays of the Lower Saxon industrial sector include aviation, shipbuilding, biotechnology, and steel.

Services

Important service sector branches are the tourism industry, trade and telecommunications.

Agriculture

The agricultural and food industry has always occupied a central role in Lower Saxony: it is the state's second-largest business sector. The food industry as a whole employs around 80,000 people.

Nearly two-thirds of the region is given over to farming. Around half of Germany's production of potatoes and poultry comes from Lower Saxony, as well as more than a third of the eggs, a third of all the pork and a quarter of the sugar.

COMMUNICATIONS AND TRANSPORT

Lower Saxony has a well established road and rail infrastructure plus good waterways. Its sea ports represent a major transport hub for international goods flow. Germany's only deep-water port (JadeWesterPort) is currently under construction at Wilhelmshaven.

MECKLENBURG-WESTERN POMERANIA

Capital: Schwerin (Population estimate: 96,000)

CONSTITUTION AND GOVERNMENT

Mecklenburg, which came into being in 1934, and parts of the former Western Pomerania, were merged in 1945 to form the new state of Mecklenburg-Western Pomerania. In 1947 the words 'Western Pomerania' were deleted from the name, and the state - like all others in the then German Democratic Republic - was dissolved in 1952. It was restored in 1990 under the name Mecklenburg-Western Pomerania before reunification.

Legislature
The legislature consists of the Assembly, currently composed of 71 members.
President of the Assembly: Werner Kuhn

Cabinet (as at June 2013)
Minister-President: Erwin Sellering (SPD)
Deputy Minister-President and Minister for Internal Affairs and Sports: Lorenz Caffier (CDU)
Minister of Justice: Uta-Maria Kuder (CDU)
Minister of Finance: Heike Polzin (SPD)
Minister of Economic Affairs, Construction and Tourism: Harry Glawe (CDU)
Minister for Agriculture, Environment and Consumer Protection: Dr Till Backhaus (SPD)
Minister of Education, Science and Culture: Mathias Brodkorb (SPD)
Minister for Energy, Infrastructure and Regional Development: Volker Scholtmann (SPD)
Minister of Labour, Social Affairs and Equal Opportunities: Manuela Schwesig (SPD)

Government portal: URL: http://www.mv-regierung.de

Elections
Results of the state elections in September 2011: SPD, 35.7 per cent (28 seats); CDU, 23.1 per cent, (18 seats); Die Linke (the Left Party), 18.4 per cent (14 seats); Green 8.4 per cent (6 seats), National

The next state elections are due to take place in 2016.

LOCAL GOVERNMENT

There are currently six administrative districts and two self-administrating cities. The districts are divided into communities. They have their own directly-elected respresentatives. The state districts are: Landkreis Rostock, Ludwigslust-Parchim, Mecklenburgische Seenplatte, Nordwest-Mecklenburg, Vorpommern-Greifswald and Vorpommern-Rugen. The two self-administrating cities are Rostock and Schwerin.

AREA AND POPULATION

The state of Mecklenburg-Western Pomerania covers an area of 23,174 sq. km but has a population of just 1,683,000 (giving a density of 73 people per square kilometre). No other German state is as rural or has such a varied coastline. Its area includes the Mecklenburger Seenplatte with 650 lakes as well as two islands in the Baltic, Rugen (926 sq. km.) and parts of Usedom (a third of which belongs to Poland).

The principal towns are: Rostock, 200,400; Schwerin, 95,800; Neubrandenburg, 67,500; Strasund, 57,600; Greifswald, 53,400.

The Low German language is still used in Mecklenburg-Western Pomerania. It is protected by the state's constitution and is taught at school and university level, and is recognised by the Netherlands and by Germany as a regional language according to the European Charter for Regional or Minority Languages.

EMPLOYMENT

Total employment was estimated at 780,000 in 2010 and the unemployment rate was estimated to be 12.7 per cent.

BANKING AND FINANCE

State GDP was estimated to be €35.8 billion in 2010 (1.4 per cent of total German GDP). Per capital GDP was €21,730, substantially down on the national average.

MANUFACTURING, MINING AND SERVICES

The region, although principally agricultural (farming and animal husbandry), also has a shipbuilding industry around Rostock. Food, computer, telecommunications, and electronic industries are also in existence. The state is Germany's most popular tourist location, the main attractions being the Baltic Sea coastline, spa towns, castles and manor houses, and the Mecklenburg Lake District.

COMMUNICATIONS AND TRANSPORT

There are five regional airports (Barth, Heringsdorf, Neubrandenburg, Rostock-Laage and Schwerin-Parchim). The most important sea ports are Rostock, Sassnitz and Wismar. The road network has been undergoing expansion.

EDUCATION

Two of Germany's oldest universities are sited in the state: University of Greifswald (1456) and University of Rostock (1419).

NORTH RHINE-WESTPHALIA

Capital: Dusseldorf (Population estimate: 588,000)

CONSTITUTION AND GOVERNMENT

North Rhine-Westphalia did not acquire its present political form until 1946, when the former Prussian provinces of Rhineland and Westphalia were merged. In 1947 the previously autonomous state of Lippe was added.

Legislature
The unicameral legislature consists of the state Assembly, composed of 187 members. In May 2012, the parliament elected Carina Goedecke (SPD) as president of the 16th NRW State Parliament.
President of the Assembly: Carina Goedecke (SPD)
URL: http://www.landtag.nrw.de

Cabinet (as at June 2013)
Prime Minister: Hannelore Kraft (page 1458)
Deputy Prime Minister, Minister for Schools and Further Training: Sylvia Löhrmann
Minister of Finance: Dr. Norbert Walter-Borjans
Minister of Economic Affairs, Energy and Industry: Garrelt Duin
Minister of Home Affairs & Local Government: Ralf Jager
Minister of Work, Social Integration and Welfare: Guntram Schneider
Minister of Justice: Thomas Kutschaty
Minister for Climate Change, Environment, Agriculture, Nature, and Consumer Protection: Johannes Remmel
Minister for Building, Housing, City Development & Transport: Michael Groschek
Minister for Innovation, Science and Research: Svenja Schulze
Minister of Family, Children, Youth, Culture and Sport: Ute Schaefer
Minister for Health: Barbara Steffens

Minister for Federal Affairs, Europe and the Media: Dr. Angelica Schwall Düren

---

Elections
The result of the state elections on 9 May 2010 were as follows: CDU (67 seats); SPD (67 seats); FDP (13 seats); Bundnis90/Greens (23 seats); and Die Linke (11 seats). Parliamentary chairmen are as follows: Karl-Joself Laumann, CDU; Norbert Romans, SPD; Dr. Gerhard Papke, FDP; Reiner Priggen, Alliance 90/The Greens; Bärbel Beuermann and Wolfgang Zimmermann for the Left.

Another state election took place in May 2012 and the Social Democrats won approximately 39 per cent of the vote. Support for the Christian Democrats fell to just 26 per cent. The Greens won 12 per cent. The result was seen as a rejection of Chancellor Merkel's austerity policies.

The next state elections are due to take place in 2017.

LOCAL GOVERNMENT

The region is divided administratively into five counties, 23 urban districts, 31 rural districts, and some 396 local authorities.

AREA AND POPULATION

The state of North Rhine-Westphalia was established by the British military administration in 1946. It is situated in the Western part of Germany and shares borders with Belgium and the Netherlands. With an area of 34,071 sq. km and a population of 18 million is the most densely populated German state, at 530 people per sq.km. Of the 71 cities in the Federal Republic with more than 100,000 inhabitants, 30 are located in North Rhine-Westphalia. Of hese, the ten largest are: Cologne: 976,000; Essen: 585,000; Dortmund: 584,000; Dusseldorf: 575,000; Duisburg: 503,000; Bochum: 387,000; Bielsfeld: 327,000; Gelsenkirchen: 269,000; Bonn: 314,000; Munster: 270,000.

EMPLOYMENT

An estimated 8.05 million people were in employment in 2011 and the unemployment rate was estimated to be 8.7 per cent.

BANKING AND FINANCE

North Rhine-Westphalia's GDP amounted to €569 billion, representing 22 per cent of national GDP, and the top federal state. Per capita GDP is approximately €32,000. Many of Germany's top companies are based in the state, including Bayer, Deutsche Post DHL and Deutsche Telekom. Over two-thirds of the economic output is generated by service providers.

MANUFACTURING, MINING AND SERVICES

North Rhine-Westphalia contains the largest industrial agglomeration on the European continent. Its rich coal deposits led to the dynamic growth of its heavy industry in the 19th century. Following the oil boom the state needed to restructure its industries. Key manufacturing sectors include: the automotive industry, biotechnology, chemicals, energy, environmental technology, healthcare, food, IT, mechanical engineering, and nanotechnology.

The automotive industry remains significant: approximately 800,000 vehicles are produced each year providing employment for over 200,000 people. The three largest automobile manufacturers in NRW are Daimler AG, Ford Werke and Adam Opel.

NRW has a leading reputation in the biotechnology industry, and is ranked ninth worldwide for its number of biotech patent applications. Some 340 life science firms are linked to the state including international companies such as as Protagen and Ai Curis.

Agriculture
More than half of the state's total land is occupied with commercial farming as well as gardens and orchards, although these enterprises amount to only a small portion of the area's gross annual product.

COMMUNICATIONS AND TRANSPORT

There are two major international airports in the state: Düsseldorf International Airport (URL: http://www.dus-int.de/dus_en/) and Cologne Bonn Airport (URL: http://www.koeln-bonn-airport.de/).

There are approximately 2,200 km of motorways, 4,800 km of federal highways, 9,700 km of local district roads and 12,800 km of country roads.

The rail infrastructure extends over 6,000 km. Approximately 280,000 people and over 1,200 trains passthrough Cologne station per day.

The state has no coastline but the Rhine flows through the state. The state's waterways tota approximately 720 km. Duisberg is the world's largest inland port (URL: http://www.duisport.de). In 2011, total cargo handled rose to 125.6 million tonnes and container volumes grew to 2.5 million TEU.

EDUCATION

There are 69 universities and technical colleges within the state.

RHINELAND-PALATINATE

Capital: Mainz (Population estimate: 197,000)

CONSTITUTION AND GOVERNMENT

Rhineland-Palatinate was formed in 1946 through the merger of a number of small territories. It shares borders with France, Luxembourg and Belgium.

Legislature
The Assembly is composed of 101 members and has the power to elect the Minister-President. Rhineland-Palatinate is the only German Bundesland to have a cabinet minister for winegrowing.
URL: http://www.landtag.rlp.de

Cabinet (as at June 2013)
Minister-President: Malu Dreyer (page 1418)
Minister for the Economy, Climate, Energy and Planning: Eveline Lemke
Minister for Integration, Families, Children, Youth and Women: Irene Alt
Minister for Infrastructure, the Interior and Sport: Roger Lewentz
Minister for Finance: Dr Carsten Kühl
Minister of Justice and Consumer Protection: Jochen Hartloff
Minister for Labour, Social Affairs, Health, and Demographics: Alexander Schweitzer
Minister for Education, Science, Youth and Culture: Doris Ahnen (SPD)
Minister for the Environment, Forests, Agriculture, Food & Viticulture: Ulrike Höfken
Head of the State Chancellery: Martin Stadelmaier (SPD)

Ministries
Government portal, URL: http://www.rlp.de/
Ministry of the Interior, Sports & Infrastructure, URL: http://www.isim.rlp.de/
Ministry of Finance, URL: http://www.fm.rlp.de/
Ministry of Justice and Consumer Affairs, URL: http://www.mjv.rlp.de/Startseite
Ministry for Labour, Social Affairs, Health & Demographics, URL: http://msagd.rlp.de/
Ministry for the Economy, Climate, Energy and Planning, URL: http://www.mwkel.rlp.de/Startseite/
Ministry for Education, Science, Youth and Culture, URL: http://www.mbwwk.rlp.de/
Ministry for the Environment, Forests, Agriculture, Food & Viticulture, URL: http://www.mulewf.rlp.de/
Ministry for Integration, the Family, Women and Children, URL: http://www.mifkjf.rlp.de/

Elections
The most recent state parliament election took place on 27 March 2011. The ruling Social Democrats remained the strongest party but lost 10 per cent of their votes. The Christian Democrats made gains and became the second largest party, just behind the Social Democrats. The Green party doubled its vote. The FDP lost their representation in the state parliament. Seats are as follows: SPD 42, CDU 41, Greens, 18.

The next state elections are due to take place in 2016.

LOCAL GOVERNMENT

The state is divided into three districts (Koblenz, Rheinhessen-Pfalz, and Trier), 24 rural districts (formerly grouped into the three districts of Koblenz, Rheinhessen-Pfalz and Trier) and 12 urban regions. There are around 2,300 local authorities.

AREA AND POPULATION

The state of Rheinland-Pfalz was formed after the end of World War II, by the French military government. The population was 4,049,000 in 2007, in an area of 19,846 sq. km., giving a density of 204 inhabitants per square km. Eighty per cent of the population live in the 'Rhine axis', the 290 km section of the river which constitutes the region's main economic artery. One of the smaller German states, Rhineland-Palatinate is the country's biggest wine-producing region, comprising the Rhine, the Ahr and the Mosel vineyards.

Towns with a population of more than 100,000 are: Mainz, 199,000; Ludwigshafen, 165,000; Koblenz, 109,000, Kaiserlautern 102,000 and Trier, 100,000.

EMPLOYMENT

Approximately 1.9 million people were employed in 2010 and the unemployment rate was 6.7 per cent, one of the lowest rates among the German states.

BANKING AND FINANCE

GDP amounted to €107.6 billion in 2010, accounting for 4.3 per cent of the total German GDP. Growth was estimated at 4.8 per cent for 2010 and approximately 4 per cent in 2011.

MANUFACTURING, MINING AND SERVICES

When it was founded, Rhineland-Palatinate had hardly any industry, and its agricultural land was fragmented and infertile. The state lost its isolated position at the border with France when the European Economic Community (now EU) came into being in 1957, and is now at the centre of the EU. The proportion of the population engaged in farming and forestry has decreased steadily, and many new jobs have been created in industry and the service sectors. The state's main industries are the chemical industry (around Ludwigshafen and Mainz), engineering, shoe, brickmaking and cement industries and the timber, printing, textiles and clothing industries. Famous jewellery and precious stones factories are located at Idar-Oberstein. Most businesses within the state are SMEs.

Six out of the thirteen regulated production areas in Germany (Rheinhessen, Pfalz, Mosel-Saar-Ruwer, Nahe, Middle Rhine and Ahr) are located in Rhineland-Palatinate. They grow around 70 per cent of German wine grapes and produce between 80 and 90 per cent of wine exports.

Wood is another significant product of the region.

COMMUNICATIONS AND TRANSPORT

The state's main airport is Frankfurt-Hahn (URL: http://www.hahn-airport.de) which is the fifth largest cargo airport in Germany. There are also five freight transport centres and 13

public inland ports. The inland ports at Wörth, Germersheim and Mainz are among the top ports win Germany.

The state has approximately 870 km of motorways and 2,960 km of main routes.

SAARLAND

Capital: Saarbrucken (Population estimate: 181,200)

CONSTITUTION AND GOVERNMENT

Because of its economic importance, Saarland was separated from Germany after the Second World War and formed a customs and currency union with France. After a referendum in 1955, carried out in agreement with France, Saarland became a state of the Federal Republic of Germany. The customs and currency union with France continued until 1959.

Legislature
Saarland's 1957 Constitution set up a legislative Assembly composed of 51 representatives.
URL: http://www.saarland.de
President of the Assembly: Hans Ley (Christian Democrat)

Cabinet (as at June 2013)
Prime Minister: Annegret Kramp-Karrenbauer (CDU) (page 1458)
Head of State & Plenipotentiary to the Federal Government to Berlin: Jurgen Lennartz (CDU)
Miister of Internal Affairs and Sports: Monika Bachmann (CDU)
Minister of Economy, Labour, Energy & Transport & Deputy Prime Minister: Heiko Maas (SPD)
Minister of Finance and Europe: Stephan Toscani (CDU)
Minister of Education and Culture: Ulrich Commerçon (SPD)
Minister of Justice, Minister of Environment and Consumer Protection: Anke Rehlinger (SPD)
Minister of Social Affairs, Health, Women and Family: Andreas Storm (CDU)

Elections
Since Saarland joined the Federal Republic of Germany, the CDU has governed the state except during the period 1985-1998 when the SDP was the ruling party.

The most recent elections took place in March 2012. The CDU won 19 seats, the SPD led by Heiko Mass won 17 (up from 13 seats), the Left, led by Oskar Lafontaine won 9 seats (down 2), the Pirates party won 4 (up 4), and the Green Party won two seats, down one. The FDP lost all their five seats.

The next state elections are due to take place in 2017.

LOCAL GOVERNMENT

The state's administrative sub-divisions are the city of Saarbrucken and five urban districts consisting of 52 local authorities.

AREA AND POPULATION

Named after the Saar River, a tributary of the Moselle, the state of Saarland borders France and Luxembourg. Following World War II, the Saarland remained under French administration as the Saar Protectorate, until 1957, when the Saar Treaty established that Saarland should be allowed to join the Federal Republic of Germany, which it did on January 1, 1957. This was the last international border change in Europe until the Fall of Communism in 1989.

It has an area of 2,570 sq. km and a population of around one million. The only major city is Saarbrucken, with a population of 181,200. One third of the land is covered by forest, one of highest percentages in Germany. People in the Saarland speak the Rhine Franconian an Moselle Franconian dialects of German. Most of the population is able to speak French which is a compulsory subject at many schools.

Over 65 per cent of the population are Catholic, making it one of only two states (the other being Bavaria) that has a majority Catholic population.

EMPLOYMENT

Approximately 455,000 people were in employment in 2010 and the unemployment rate was estimated at 7.5 per cent.

BANKING AND FINANCE

In 2010, GDP in the state was €30 billion, approximately 1.2 per cent of national GDP. Per capita GDP was approximately €29,5000. The services sector contributed approximately 70 per cent of GDP and industry 30 per cent.

MANUFACTURING, MINING AND SERVICES

Industrial and commercial activity in the Saarland is determined by the extensive coal deposits, which were initially used for the processing of imported iron ore and formed the basis of the iron and steel industry. Downstream industries, such as steel construction and machinery subsequently moved into the area, as did other branches of industry that rely on energy. This diversification, which now includes entirely different sectors, proved to be a positive counterbalance to the downgrading of coal and steel industries. Today, in addition to the metal processing and engineering industries, cables, glass, textiles, shoes, cement, ceramics, paper and timber are also manufactured. The automotive industry is an important part of the engineering sector.

COMMUNICATIONS AND TRANSPORT

The state's main airport is Saarbrücken-Ensheim (URL: http://www.flughafen-saarbruecken.de/).

Saarland has one of the most concentrated road networks in Germany. The network includes 240 km of motorwys an, 320 km of trunk roads and 1,340 km of main roads. The river Saar is a tributary of the river Mosel and is a major water way with connections to the ports of Antwerp and Rotterdam through the Mosel and Rhine rivers.

EDUCATION

The university, polytechnic, art college and music academy of Saarland are situated in Saarbrucken, the state capital. The university has encouraged the growth of science and technology in the city, through a local science park.

SAXONY

Capital: Dresden (Population estimate, 2011: 530,500)

CONSTITUTION AND GOVERNMENT

The Kingdom of Saxony became the Free State of Saxony in 1919. After 1945 it formed part of the German Democratic Republic. The state was dissolved in 1952 but was re-established in 1990 before the reunification of Germany.

Legislature

Saxony's state parliament is composed of members appointed in general and secret elections for five-year terms. As a result of the 2009 election, two compensatory mandates had to be allocated to list applicants from other parties to compensate for two additional direct mandates of a party. Accordingly, the 5th Saxon State Parliament (2009-14) has 132 members.

Saxon State Assembly, Public Relations Department, Visitor's Service, Bernhard-von-Lindenau-Platz 1, 01067 Dresden, Germany. Tel: +49 (0)351 493 5131, fax +49 (0)351 493 5478, URL: http://www.landtag.sachsen.de
President of the Land Parliament: Dr Matthias Rößler

Cabinet (as at June 2013)

Prime Minister: Stanislaw Tillich (page 1525)
Deputy Prime Minister and State Minister for Economic Affairs, Employment and Transport: Sven Morlok
Minister for Finance: Prof. Dr. Georg Unland
State Minister for the Interior: Markus Ulbig
State Minister for Justice & European Affairs: Jürgen Martens
State Minister for Education: Brunhild Kurth
State Minister of Science and the Arts: Prof. Dr. Dr. Sabine Freifrau von Schorlemer
State Minister of Social Affairs and Consumer Protection: Christine Clauss
State Minister of Environment and Agriculture: Frank Kupfer
State Minister and Head of State Chancellery: Dr. Johannes Beerman

Government portal, URL: http://www.sachsen.de/en/index.html

Elections

Following the 2009 election, the parties received the following percentages of votes: CDU (Christian Democratic Union) 40.2 per cent; Die Linke (Party of Democratic Socialism) 20.6 per cent; SPD (Social Democratic party of Germany) 10.4 per cent; FDP (Liberal Democratic Party) 10.0 per cent; Grüne (Alliance 90 / The Green Party) 6.4 per cent; NPD (The National Democratic Party of Germany) 5.6 per cent. As a result of the election, two compensatory mandates had to be allocated to list applicants from other parties to compensate for two additional direct mandates of a party. Accordingly, the 5th Saxon State Parliament has 132 members. Seats are divided accordingly: CDU 58; Die Linke 29 seats; SPD 14; FDP 14 seats; Grüne 9 seats; NPD 8 seats.

The next elections are due to take place in 2014.

LOCAL GOVERNMENT

Sachsen is divided into three regions (Direktionsbezirk), Chemnitz, Dresden and Leipzig, which are subdivided into 10 districts. There are also the three urban districts of Chemnitz, Dresden and Leipzig.

AREA AND POPULATION

Saxony, with an area of 18,413 sq. km and a population of 4.226 million, has borders with Poland and the Czech Republic. It is the most densely populated and the most industrialized German state, with an average population density of 229 inhabitants per square km. More than one fifth of its inhabitants live in Leipzig and Dresden. The principal towns are: Leipzig, 520,000; Dresden, 530,500; Chemnitz, 243,000; Zwickau, 98,000.

EMPLOYMENT

In 2010, 1.94 million residents were employed; the unemployment rate remained high at 11.8 per cent. Approximately 66 per cent of the workforce was employed in the services sector.

BANKING AND FINANCE

Saxony has a vibrant economy. In 2010, the state GDP was estimated to be €95 billion. Per capita GDP was higher than the national average at €48,500 billion.

The service sector has grown rapidly since integration with the West. This is partly due to the establishment of a chip producing economy near Dresden, giving rise to the region's nickname of "Silicon Saxony". Banking and insurance are significant industries, together with the food industry. However, unemployment remains high and there is little investment. Saxony, along with the rest of the east (excluding Berlin) qualifies as an "Objective 1" development region within the European Union, and receives investment subsidies of up to 30 per cent until 2013.

MANUFACTURING, MINING AND SERVICES

Primary and Extractive Industries

Saxony has extensive lignite deposits in the Leipzig area and hard coal in the Zwickau region. Uranium, tungsten, bismuth, and zinc ores were mined in the Erzgebirge during the GDR period. As a result, great environmental damage has been caused, both through radioactive contamination and pollution resulting from the use of lignite.

Manufacturing

The traditional and largest branches of industry are mechanical engineering, precision tools and optical instruments, textiles, chemicals, motor vehicles, and porcelain (Meissen). The states is now well known for its microelectronics and biotechnology industry. Toy manufacturing has a long tradition in the Erzgebirge, as has the production of musical instruments.

Agriculture

The northern part of Saxony has fertile soil, suitable for sugarbeet and wheat, and the region between Pirna and Meissen on the river Elbe is well known for its market gardening.

Saxony is one of the northernmost wine regions in Europe. The Elbe Valley wine-growing area covers just 416 hectares. Wines produced include Muller-Thurgau, Riesling and Pinot Blanc (Weissburgunder).

COMMUNICATIONS AND TRANSPORT

The state has two international airports: Dresden (URL: http://www.dresden-airport.de/homepage.html) and Leipzig (URL: http://www.leipzig-halle-airport.de/en/index.html). The road network extends for approximately 14,500 km including 530 federal highways. The railway network comprises 2,580 km of track. There are three main ports on the river Elbe: Dresden, Reisa and Torgau.

EDUCATION

The state includes seven universities, 26 universities of applied sciences, art and vocational academies. The state includes six Max-Planck Institutes.

SAXONY-ANHALT

Capital: Magdeburg (Population estimate: 230,000)

CONSTITUTION AND GOVERNMENT

Saxony-Anhalt has a short history as a political entity. It was formed after the Second World War from parts of the former Prussian province of Saxony, and Anhalt, an independent state until 1946. Between 1952 and 1990 the state was abolished, but was reinstated before unification.

From 1990 to 2003 Saxony-Anhalt was divided into three districts: Dessau, Halle and Magdeburg. In 2004 these were abolished, and 24 counties were constituted the primary divisions of the state. As of July 2007, the number of counties was reduced to 11, and three independent cities were constituted.

Legislature
The legislature is formed by the Assembly, and composed of 116 members.
President of the Assembly: Detlef Gurth (CDU)
URL: http://www.landtag.sachsen-anhalt.de

Recent Events
Saxony-Anhalt was hit with severe flooding in 2013.

> **Cabinet (as at June 2013)**
> *Prime Minister:* Dr. Reiner Haselhoff (CDU) (page 1439)
> *State Minister:* Rainer Robra
> *Government Spokesman:* Dr Matthias Scale
> *State Secretary for Federal and European Affairs:* Dr Michael Schneider
> *Representative to the EU:* Dr Henrike Franz
> *Minister of the Internal Affairs and Sport:* Holger Stahlknecht
> *Minister of Justice & Equality:* Prof. Dr. Angela Kolb
> *Minister of Finance:* Jens Bullerjahn
> *Minister for Labour and Social Affairs:* Norbert Bischoff
> *Minister of Culture:* Stephan Dorgerloh
> *Minister of Science and Economics:* Hartmut Mollring
> *Minister for Agriculture and Environment:* Dr Hermann Onko Aeikens
> *Minister of Regional Development and Transport:* Thomas Webel

Ministries
Government portal, URL: http://www.sachsen-anhalt.de/index.php?id=20800
Ministry of the Interior, URL: http://www.mi.sachsen-anhalt.de
Ministry of Justice, URL: http://www.mj.sachsen-anhalt.de
Ministry of Health, URL: http://www.ms.sachsen-anhalt.de
Ministry of Education and Cultural Affairs, URL: http://www.mk.sachsen-anhalt.de
Ministry of Employment and Economic Affairs, URL: http://www.mw.sachsen-anhalt.de
Ministry of Agriculture and Environment, URL: http://www.mlu.sachsen-anhalt.de
Ministry of Regional Development and Transport, URL: http://www.mlv.sachsen-anhalt.de

Elections
The most recent elections to the State Parliament were held on 20 March 2011. The Assembly is currently formed by the following political parties: CDU (41 seats); The Left Party (29 seats); SPD (26 seats); Alliance 90/ Greens (9 seats). A coalition of the CDU and the SPD now leads the government.

The next state elections are due to take place in 2016.

LOCAL GOVERNMENT

From 1994 to 2003, Saxony-Anhalt was divided into 21 districts ("Landkreise"). Following reform effective from July 2007, the number of rural districts was reduced to eleven. There were also 219 administrative communities in 2011. The three urban districts are: Madeburg, Halle and Dessau-Roßlau.

AREA AND POPULATION

Saxony-Anhalt covers an area of about 20,447 sq. km and has a population of 2,320,000 people in 2011. The region is only thinly populated (121 inhabitants per sq. km.), particularly in the northern parts Altmark and Magdeburger Börde. Nearly one in five of the state's inhabitants live in Halle, Magdeburg and Dessau, the principal towns. Populations in 2011 were as follows: Halle, 233,000; Magdeburg, 231,500; Dessau, 87,000. The population is in decline.

EMPLOYMENT

There were estimated to be 1.091 million people in employment in 2010 and the unemployment rate was estimated to be 12.5 per cent. The main source of employment is manufacturing, followed by business services, health care and trade.

BANKING AND FINANCE

GDP was estimated at €52.2 billion in 2010, amounting to approximately 2.1 per cent of the national total. Growth was estimated at 2.4 per cent in 2011, with growth in 2011 amounting to 4.5 per cent in 2011.

MANUFACTURING, MINING AND SERVICES

Primary and Extractive Industries
Deposits of copper slate, lignite, limestone, rock salt and potassium salt form the basis of extensive industries.

Manufacturing
The state's mineral deposits were used widely during the GDR regime as the basis for chemicals, building materials and engineering products. Much of the chemical and engineering industries produced heavy pollution, and many of the obsolete factories had to be closed down. Funds for restructuring and privatisation projects, from the state government, the Federal Government and the EU, amounted to around 7.2 billion. Saxony-Anhalt now has the largest chemical industry in Germany, employing over 12,000 people. Since 1990, new industries such as the automotive industry, biotechnology, information and communication technology and the service sector have become established alongside more traditional sectors such as the chemical industry, mechanical engineering and the food industry.

Services
The service sector accounts for around 70 per cent of the state's gross domestic product, and is a high employment sector. Skilled workers and competitive labour costs had made Saxony-Anhalt a popular location for call centres. There is also a large student population at the state's many colleges and universities available for employment.

Agriculture
The food industry is the most important sector in Saxony-Anhalt, in turnover and employment terms. Sugarbeet and wheat are grown in the fertile regions of the Magdeburger Börde, while less fertile areas produce potatoes, rye and oats. Animal breeding takes place in some hilly regions.

COMMUNICATIONS AND TRANSPORT

The state's most significant airport is Leipzig-Halle airport (URL: http://www.leipzig-halle-airport.de/en/index.html). The airport is currently undergoing expansion.

The road network currently extends 11,000 km. The rail network is 3,000 km long. Its most important inland waterways are part of the River Elbe. There are 17 ports operating in the state.

EDUCATION

The state's higher education institutes include two universities (Martin Luther University, Otto von Guericke University and the Universtiy of Art & Design at Burg Giebichenstein), four universities of applied science (Anhalt University of Applied Sciences, Harz University of Applied Sciences, Magdeburg-Stendal University of Applied Sciences and Merseburg University of Applied Sciences) and a college of art.

SCHLESWIG-HOLSTEIN

Capital: Kiel (Population estimate: 239,000)

CONSTITUTION AND GOVERNMENT

Legislature
The legislature is the unicameral Assembly, currently consisting of 69 members.
URL: http://www.sh-landtag.de/
President: Joachim Gauck

Cabinet (as at June 2013)
Prime Minister: Torsten Albig (SPD) (page 1374)
Deputy Prime Minister, Minister of Energy, Environment, Agriculture and Rural Areas: Dr Robert Habeck (Green)
Second Deputy Prime Minister, Minister of Justice, Europe and Culture: Anke Spoorendonk (SSW)
Minister of the Interior: Andreas Breitner (SPD)
Minister of Finance: Monika Heinold (Green)
Minister of Economy, Labour, Transport and Technology: Reinhard Meyer (SPD)
Minister of Social Affairs, Health, Family and Equality: Kristin Alheit (SPD)
Ministry of Education and Science: Prof. Dr. Waltraud Wende (Ind)

Elections
The most recent state election took place on 6 May 2012. The CDU did badly, losing 12 seats, ending with 22. The SPD won 22 seats, the Greens 10, the FDP 14, the Pirate Party 6, and the SSW 3. It was the worst result for the CDU in the state in 50 years. A coalition is expected to be formed by the SPD, the Greens and the SSW. Torsten Albig was voted in as the new prime minister with 37 out of the 69 parliamentary votes.

The next state elections are due to take place in 2017.

LOCAL GOVERNMENT

Schleswig-Holstein comprises four county boroughs, eleven rural districts and about 1,100 local authorities.

AREA AND POPULATION

Lying at the base of the Jutland peninsula between the Baltic Sea and the North Sea, Schleswig-Holstein is the most northern of Germany's states. It has an area of 15,729 sq. km and a population of 2.82 million. Its coastline of 500 km (920 km including the islands) plays an important part in the state's history and life; the Kiel Canal which connects the North Sea and Baltic Sea is located in Schleswig-Holstein.

The area is sparsely populated, with a density of 180 people per square km. The principal towns are: Kiel, 230,000, and Lubeck, 212,000.

EMPLOYMENT

Approximately 1.4 million people are in employment in the state and the unemployment rate was estimated to be 7.5 per cent in 2010. The major employment sectors are services (80 per cent), industry (20 per cent) and agriculture (2 per cent).

BANKING AND FINANCE

The state GDP was estimated at €75.6 billion in 2010, approximately 3 per cent of the national total. Per capita GDP was €26,000.

MANUFACTURING, MINING AND SERVICES

Manufacturing
Industries include shipbuilding and the maritime industry, the food industry, mechanical engineering, alternative energy technology and the health care sector.

Services
Tourism is one of the state's most important industry sectors. The islands of Sylt and Föhr and the southern Baltic coast are popular tourist resorts, while Eutin, Lübeck, and Schleswig are historic centers. There are approximately 70 million overnight stays per year.

Agriculture
The fertile marsh-land is widely used for the farming of crops and livestock. As of 2010 there were over 14,000 agricultural holdings in the state with an average farm size of 79 ha. There were over 440 organic farms. Approximately 674,300 ha of land are used for arable farming and 314,00 for grassland. There are over 1 million head of cattle. Coastal fishing has led to the establishment of an important industry.

COMMUNICATIONS AND TRANSPORT

Schleswig-Holstein has important ports both in the North Sea and the Baltic with Lubeck-Travemunde one of Germany's principal ferry ports. They are connected by the Kiel Canal, one of the world's most heavily travelled stretches of navigable water, which saves the 520 km needed to sail around the Jutland peninsula. Approximately 65 per cent of goods passing though Germany's Baltic ports are handled in Schleswig-Hostein. The state has 30 ports and harbours with an annual cargo turnover of 50 million tonnes. More than 15 million ferry passengers use the ports per year.

EDUCATION

There are nine public institutions of higher education in the state including three universities, located in Kiel, Lubeck and Flensburg. The oldest university in the state is the Christian-Albrechts-University of Kiel, established in 1665. Approximately 50,000 sutudents are currently in higher education in the state.

THURINGIA

Capital: Erfurt (Population estimate: 205,000)

CONSTITUTION AND GOVERNMENT

Thuringia came into being in 1920 through the merger of a number of principalities. The then Free State of Thuringia had Weimar as its capital, the venue of Germany's constituent national assembly, which gave its name to the Weimar Constitution and the Weimar Republic. Thuringia was re-established in 1945 and retained its status until 1952, when all states of the then GDR were dissolved. It was reinstated in 1990 before German unification.

Recent Events
In March 2009, Dieter Althaus, governor of Thuringia, was accused of failing to observe regulations while skiing at high speed, and charged with manslaughter over a collision on an Austrian ski slope in which a woman died. Mr. Althaus took responsibility of the accident, and, was fined. He remained a party leader and governor until his resignation in September 2009 following poor election results.

Legislature
Thuringia's unicameral legislature is the Assembly, consisting of 88 members.
URL: http://www.thueringer-landtag.de/tlt/
President of the Assembly: Birgit Diezel

Cabinet (as at May 2013)
Prime Minister: Christine Lieberknecht (page 1464) (CDU)
Deputy Prime Minister and Minister for Education, Science and Culture: Christoph Matschie (SPD)
Minister of the Interior: Jorg Geibert (CDU)
Minister of Justice: Dr Holger Poppenhäger (Social Democratic Party)
Minister of Finance: Dr Wolfgang Voss (CDU)

Minister of Economy, Labour and Technology: Matthias Machnig (SPD)
Minister for Social Affairs, Family and Health: Heike Taubert (SPD)
Minister for Agriculture, Forestry, Environment and Conservation: Jürgen Reinholz (CDU)
Minister of Construction, Development and Transport: Christian Carius (CDU)
Minister for Federal and European Affairs and Head of the State Chancellery: Marion Walsmann (CDU)

Government portal, URL: http://www.thueringen.de

Elections
The most recent election was held on 30 August 2009. The CDU won 31.8 per cent of the vote (28 seats), the Left 27.7 per cent (14 seats), and the SPD 19 per cent (2 seats). Turnout was estimated at 56.2 per cent.

Elections are next due to take place in 2014.

LOCAL GOVERNMENT

Administratively, Thuringia is divided into 17 rural districts and six urban districts.

AREA AND POPULATION

Thuringia has no international borders, and is surrounded by other German states. It is known as 'Germany's green heartland' due to its extensive forests. It has an area of 16,251 sq. km and a population of 2,335,000. The population of the capital Erfurt, named a 'garden city',

GHANA

is 205,000. Other major cities include Gera, with 199,500 inhabitants and Jena with 104,500 inhabitants. 77 per cent of the population lives in towns of less than 2,000 people. Population density is approximately 138 people per km².

EMPLOYMENT

Approximately 1.1 million people were in employment in 2010 and the unemployment rate was 9.8 per cent. Approximately 30 per cent of the population work in manufacturing and 68 per cent in services.

BANKING AND FINANCE

Regional GDP was estimated to be €49.9 billion accounting for 2.0 per cent of the national GDP. Average per capita GDP is approximately €22,250.

MANUFACTURING, MINING AND SERVICES

Primary and Extractive Industries
Potash and uranium deposits used to be mined in the Werra valley and Harz mountains, respectively. This has resulted in heavy contamination and pollution.

Manufacturing
Manufacturing is one of the biggest employment sectors in Thuringia. Jena has long been famous for its optical and glass industries, while there is a long-established motor industry in Eisenach. There is also a long tradition of toy making. Other industries include: precision components for the aerospace industry; electronic components; biotechnology; software technology industries; and food processing.

Agriculture
Wheat and sugarbeet are grown in the highly fertile lowlands, while the region around Erfurt is well known for vegetables, commercial flowers, and seeds. Approximately 50 per cent of of the state's land is used for agriculture.

COMMUNICATIONS AND TRANSPORT

The road system consists of 667 km including motorway junctions and the federal highway network extends over 1,732 km.

The railway network is 1,509 km long, of which 1,263 km is public federally owned.

GHANA
Republic of Ghana

Capital: Accra (Population estimate: 1.7 million)

Head of State: John Dramani Mahama (page 1469)

Vice-President: Kwesis Amissah-Arthur

National Flag: On a tricolour fesswise, red, gold, green, a star five-pointed centred black

CONSTITUTION AND GOVERNMENT

Constitution
Ghana (formerly the Gold Coast) became independent of Great Britain in 1957. The first president, Kwame Nkrumah, was overthrown in 1966. A Supreme Military Council (SMC) came to power in 1972 but was in turn overthrown by Flight-Lieutenant Jerry Rawlings in 1979. Although a timetable for a return to civilian rule was established, Rawlings again seized power in 1981. Political parties were banned and the 1979 Constitution was suspended. However, Rawlings was elected president for a four-year term in democratic elections held in November 1992. A new constitution was also approved in that year. Rawlings was re-elected in December 1996 for a second term, having received 57 per cent of the vote. President Rawlings stepped down from office in December 2000, as required by the constitution, and was replaced by John Agyekum Kufour.

According to the 1993 Constitution, the head of state is the President who is directly elected by universal adult suffrage for a maximum of two four-year terms. The President appoints the Cabinet and the 25-member Council of State, and chairs the 20-member National Security Council. The two Councils play an advisory role.

To consult the full constitution, please visit: http://www.judicial.gov.gh/constitution/chapter/chap_4.htm

International Relations
Ghana is a member of the West African States (ECOWAS) and the African Union. Through the UN, Ghana has peacekeeping troops deployed in Côte d'Ivoire, Liberia, Sierra Leone and the Democratic Republic of Congo. Ghana is a member of the Commonwealth and has close ties with the UK.

Recent Events
In 2006 Chinese Premier Wen Jiabao made a tour of African nations. He visited Ghana in June and promised to lend the country around US$66 million to help fund development projects.

In June 2007, oil deposits were found off the coast of Ghana. They are believed to contain three billion barrels.

In September 2007 Ghana was hit by devastating floods, the worst for over 30 years, and much of the annual crop was lost. The floods were in the north of the country and around 400,000 people were made homeless.

The 2008 presidential election was narrowly won by the opposition National Democratic Congress candidate, John Atta Mills.

In July 2009, Ghana secured a three year loan from the IMF worth $600 million. Also that month US President Barack Obama visited the country.

In July 2012 President John Atta Mills died, former Vice-President John Dramani Mahama was sworn in as president and promised stability.

Legislature
Ghana's unicameral legislature is known as the Parliament and consists of 230 members elected from single-seat constituencies for a four-year term.
Parliament, Parliament House, Accra, Ghana. Tel/fax: +233 21 665597, URL: http://www.ghana.gov.gh
Speaker of Parliament: Ebenezer Sekyi-Hughes

Cabinet (as at June 2013)
Minister of the Interior: Kwesi Ahwoi
Minister of Chieftancy and Culture: Dr Henry Seidu Danaa
Minister of Communications: Dr Omane Boamah
Minister of Defence: Mark Owen Woyongo
Minister of Education: Prof. Jane Nana Opoku Agyemang
Minister of Finance: Seth Tekper
Minister of Trade and Industry: Haruna Iddrisu
Minister of Food and Agriculture: Clement Kofi Humado
Minister for Foreign Affairs and Regional Integration: Hannah Tetteh
Minister of Health: Hanny-Sherry Ayitey
Minister of Information: Mahama Ayariga
Minister of Lands and Natural Resources: Inusah Fusani
Minister of the Environment, Science and Technology: Dr Oteng Agyei
Minister of Local Government and Rural Development: Akwasi Oppong-Fosu
Minister of Energy and Petroleum: Emmanuel Kofi Buah
Minister of Employment and Social Welfare: Nil Armaah Ashitey
Minister of Youth and Sports: Elvis Afriyie Ankrah
Attorney General and Minister of Justice: Marietta Brew Appiah Oppong
Minister of Roads and Highways: Alhaji Amin Amidu Sulemani
Minister of Tourism, Culture and Creative Arts: Elizabeth Ofosu Agare
Minister for Transport: Dzifa Ativor
Minister of Water Resources, Works and Housing: Alhaji Collins Dauda
Minister of Women and Children's Affairs: Nana Oye Lithur
Minister of Fisheries and Aquaculture: Nayon Bilijo
Minister of Presidential Affairs in Parliament: Dr Benjamin Kunbuor
Minister of State in the Office of the President: Fifi Kwetey
Minister of State in the Office of the President: Alhaji Abdul Rashid Hassan Pelpuo
Minister of State in the Office of the President: Alhaassan Azong
Minister of State in the Office of the President: Dr Mustapha Ahmed
Minister of State in the Office of the President: Mrs Comfort Doyoe Cudjoe Ghansah

Ministries
Ministry of Communication and Technology, PO Box M42, Accra 228011, Ghana. Tel: +233 21 685606, fax: +233 21 667114, e-mail: moct@ghana.gov.gh
Ministry of Defence, Burma Camp Accra, 776111 Accra, Ghana. Tel: +233 21 7761115, fax: +233 21 776111
Ministry of Education, Youth & Sports, PO Box M45, Accra, Ghana. Tel: +233 21 662772, fax: +233 21 664067
Ministry of Employment and Manpower Development, PO Box M84, Ministries, Accra, Ghana. Tel: +233 21 665421, fax: +233 21 667251
Ministry of Finance, PO Box M40, Accra, Ghana. Tel: +233 21 665441, fax: +233 21 667069 / 66385, URL: http://www.finance.gov.gh
Ministry of Food and Agriculture, PO Box MB.37, Accra, Ghana. Tel: +233 21 663036 / 6171360, fax: +233 21 668245, e-mail: info@mofa.gov.gh, URL: http://www.mofa.gov.gh
Ministry of Foreign Affairs, PO Box M.53, Ministries, Accra, Ghana. Tel: +233 21 664951, fax: +233 21 665363 / 667823, e-mail: ghmfaoo@ghana.com, URL: http://www.mfa.gov.gh
Ministry of Health, PO Box M44, Accra, Ghana. Tel: +233 21 662014, fax: +233 21 663810, URL: http://www.moh-ghana.org
Ministry of the Interior, PO Box M42, Ministries, Accra, Ghana. Tel: +233 21 662688 / 684407, fax: +233 21 667450

Ministry of Justice and Attorney General, PO Box M60, Ministries, Accra, Ghana. Tel: +233 21 665051 / 682102, fax: +233 21 667609, e-mail: attorneygeneral@ghana.com

Ministry of Information and Presidential Affairs, PO Box 745, Accra, Ghana. Tel: +233 21 228059 / 228054, fax: +233 21 235800, e-mail: mipa@ghana.gov.gh

Ministry of Roads and Transport, PO Box M 38, Accra, Ghana. Tel: +233 21 669986, fax: +233 21 667114, e-mail: info@mrt.gov.gh, URL: http://www.mrt.gov.gh

Ministry of Science and Environment, PO Box 232, Ministries, Accra, Ghana. Tel: +233 21 666049 / 662626, fax: +233 21 666828

Ministry of Tourism, PO Box 4386, Accra, Ghana. Tel: +233 21 666701, fax: +233 21 666182, e-mail: motgov@hotmail.com, URL: www.ghanatourism.gov.gh

Ministry of Trade and Industry, PO Box M.47, Accra, Ghana. Tel: +233 21 663188, fax: +233 21 664776 / 662428, e-mail: mis-moti@africaonline.com.gh, URL: http://www.moti-ghana.com

Ministry of Energy, PO Box MB40 Stadium, Accra, Ghana. Tel: +233 21 667151-3, fax: +233 21 668262, e-mail: energy1@ncs.com.gh, URL: http://www.energycom.gov.gh

Ministry of Mines, PO Box 40 Stadium, Accra, Ghana, Tel: +233 21 672337, fax: +233 21 666801

Ministry of Local Government and Rural Development, PO Box M50, Accra, Ghana, Tel: +233 21 664763 / 663668, fax: +233 21 668071

Ministry of Works and Housing, PO Box M43, Accra, Ghana. Tel: +233 21 665940, fax: +233 21 667689

Ministry of Lands and Forestry, PO Box M212, Accra, Ghana, Tel: +233 21 665949, fax: +233 21 666896, e-mail: motgov@hotmail.com

Ministry of Regional Co-operation and NEPAD, PO Box CT 633, Accra, Ghana, Tel: +233 21 771777 / 773011, fax: +233 21 771778

Environmental Protection Agency of Ghana, PO Box M.326, Accra, Ghana. Tel: +233 21 664697-8, fax: +233 21 662690, e-mail:epainfo@ghana.com, URL: http://www.epa.gov.gh

Political Parties

New Patriotic Party; National Democratic Congress; People's National Convention; Convention People's Party; Every Ghanaian Living Everywhere Party; Ghana Democratic Republic Party; Reform Movement; Traditional Congress Party; United Ghana Movement.

Elections

The most recent parliamentary elections took place on 7 December 2008. Local and international observers praised Ghana for setting a good example on how to conduct an election.

The most recent presidential election took place in December 2012. President Mahama was re-elected but the opposition alleged the elections had not been free or fair.

Diplomatic Representation

Embassy of Ghana, 3512 International Drive, NW, Washington, DC 20008, USA. Tel: +1 202 686 4520, fax: +1 202 686 4527, e-mail: ghtrade@cais.com, URL: http://www.ghanaembassy.org

Ambassador: Daniel Ohene Agyekum (page 1489)

US Embassy, Ring Road East, PO Box 194, Accra, Ghana. Tel: +233 21 775348, fax: +233 21 776008, e-mail: accra_office_box@mail.doc.gov, URL: http://accra.usembassy.gov

Ambassador: Gene A. Cretz

British High Commission, Osu Link, off Gamel Abdul Nasser Avenue (PO Box 296), Accra, Ghana. Tel: +233 21 221665 / +233 21 701 0650 (24hr), fax: +233 21 701 0655, e-mail: high.commission@accra.mail.fco.gov.uk, URL: http://ukinghana.fco.gov.uk/en

High Commissioner: Peter Jones (page 1451)

Ghana High Commission, 13 Belgrave Square, London SW1X 8PN. Tel: +44 (0)20 7235 4142, fax: +44 (0)20 7245 9552, e-mail: enquiries@ghana-com.co.uk, URL: http://www.ghanahighcommissionuk.com

High Commissioner: Prof. Kwaku Danso-Boafo (page 1412)

Permanent Mission of Ghana to the United Nations, 19 East 47th Street, New York, NY 10017, USA. Tel: +1 212 832 1300, fax: +1 212 751 6743, e-mail: ghana@un.int URL: http://www.un.int/ghana

Ambassador: Kenneth Kweku Kanda

LEGAL SYSTEM

Ghana's court system consists of the Supreme Court (the highest court in Ghana), the Court of Appeal, the High Court, and Regional Tribunals. The Supreme Court, the final court of appeal, has jurisdiction over matters relating to the enforcement or the interpretation of constitutional law and comprises the Chief Justice and not less than nine Justices. At present the Supreme Court has ten Justices. The Court of Appeal has a Chief Justice and not less than five other Justices, and has jurisdiction to hear and to determine appeals from any judgment, decree, or High Court of Justice order. The High Court consists of a Chief Justice and no fewer than twelve other justices, has jurisdiction in all matters, civil and criminal, other than those involving treason. Fast Track Courts have been introduced as a way of speeding up trials.

In general, the government respects human rights. However, some problems persist, including the excessive use of force by police; government and police corruption and impunity; life-threatening prison conditions, and prolonged pretrial detention. Ghana retains the death penalty for ordinary crimes but no executions have been carried out since before 1999.

Supreme Court of Ghana:

URL: http://www.ghanaweb.com/GhanaHomePage/republic/supreme_court.php
Chief Justice of the Supreme Court: Chief Justice Mrs. Georgina Theodora Wood

Commission on Human Rights and Administrative Justice, National Headquarters, Old Parliament House, High Street, Accra, Ghana, Tel: +233 21 668839, fax: +233 21 660020, URL: http://www.chrajghana.com

LOCAL GOVERNMENT

Ghana is divided into 10 regions and 138 districts. The regions are: Greater Accra Region, Central Region, Western Region, Eastern Region, Ashanti Region, Brong Ahafo Region, Northern Region, Upper East Region, Upper West Region and Volta Region.

There are 170 metropolitan, municipal and district assemblies. Local elections were postponed in eight regions in Decemer 2010 as not all districts were ready because of the number of candidates involved in local elections. District assembly elections should take place every four years.

AREA AND POPULATION

Area

Ghana is located on the west coast of Africa. It is bounded on the south by the Gulf of Guinea, on the east by Togo, on the north by Burkina Faso and on the west by Côte d'Ivoire. Its area is 238,537 sq. km. Major cities include Accra (the capital) which has a population of around 1.7 million, Kumasi 1.0 million, Sekondi-Takoradi, 370,000 and Tema 500,000. The south and west of the country are covered by rain forest, the north is hilly with forests and further north dry savannah and woodland. The Black and White Volta rivers both run into Ghana from Burkina Faso and run into the world's largest man-made lake, Lake Volta in the south east of the country.

Ghana's climate is varied. It is hot and dry in the north, hot and humid in the southwest and cooler along the coast.

To view a map, visit: http://www.un.org/Depts/Cartographic/map/profile/ghana.pdf

Population

Latest, 2010, estimates put the population of Ghana at 24.3 million, with an average annual population growth rate of 2.4 per cent for the period 2000-10. The majority of Ghanaians (55 per cent) are aged between 15 and 60 years, whilst 39 per cent are aged up to 14 years. The median age is 20 years. Around 70 per cent of the population is located in the southern half of the country. An estimated 51 per cent of the population live in urban areas.

Ghana has five main ethnic groups: Akan, Ewe, MoleDagbane, Guan, and Ga-Adangbe. English is the official language. The main native language is Ga although a number of other languages - including Akan, Ewe, Nzemea, Dagbane, and Kasena - are also spoken, French and Hausa and quite widely spoken.

Births, Marriages, Deaths

According to 2010 estimates the crude birth rate is 31.5 births per 1,000 population, whilst the death rate is 9.5 deaths per 1,000. Average life expectancy at birth is estimated at 62.0 years (60 years for men and 64 years for women). Healthy life expectancy is put at 50 years. The infant mortality rate is an estimated 50.0 deaths per 1,000 live births. The fertility rate is estimated at 4.2 children born per woman. (Source: http://www.who.int, World Health Statistics 2012)

Public Holidays 2014

1 January: New Year's Day
14 January: Birth of the Prophet*
6 March: Independence Day
18 April: Good Friday
20 April: Easter Sunday
21 April: Easter Monday
1 May: Labour Day
1 July: Republic Day
29 July: Eid al Fitr (end of Ramadan)*
5 October: Eid al Adha (Feast of the Sacrifice)*
6 December: Farmers' Day
25 December: Christmas Day
26 December: Boxing Day
*Islamic holiday; precise date depends upon sighting of the moon

EMPLOYMENT

Ghana's labour force was estimated at 11.1 million in 2011. The economy is largely based on subsistence agriculture, which employs about 48 per cent of the labour force. The industry and transport sectors employ around 16 per cent, professionals make up around 9.0 per cent, and sales and clerical workers and those in the service sector make up around 25 per cent. The unemployment rate in 2000 was 11 per cent.

BANKING AND FINANCE

Currency
Cedi (GHC) = 100 Pesewas

The financial centre is Accra.

GDP/GNP, Inflation, National Debt
Agriculture and mining are the mainstays of Ghana's economy, with gold and cocoa the largest contributors to foreign exchange and government revenue. Agriculture, forestry and fishing make up over 38 per cent of GDP, whilst industry contributes 24 per cent. Off shore deposits of oil were discovered in 2007 and production (85,000 barrels) began in 2010. Oil production is expected to transform Ghana's economy. The economy has also been boosted by reforms in the agricultural sector.

GHANA

GDP was estimated to be US$35 billion in 2011 with a growth rate of 14 per cent.

Inflation fell from 74.4 per cent in 1995 to 20.5 per cent in 1998. Estimates put the 2000 inflation rate at 25.2 per cent, and although forecasts put the 2001 inflation rate at 27.7 per cent it was actually recorded at 22.8 per cent and 15.2 per cent in 2002. Inflation in 2003 rose to an average of 23.5 per cent before coming down to 14.1 per cent in 2004 and 14.7 per cent in 2005. Figures for 2006 put inflation at 10 per cent. It rose to over 16 per cent by 2008. By July 2009 it had reached 20 per cent, pushed upwards by several factors including a 30 per cent rise in petroleum prices. The inflation target for 2012 is 9.5 per cent.

Ghana's total external debt was estimated at US$9.2 billion in 2011.

Foreign Investment
Ghana is party to a number of economic aid agreements. In 2001 Ghana applied to the IMF for the status of Heavily Indebted Poor Country. In 2004 having successfully met the criteria set, Ghana's debt was reduced from US$5 billion to US$2.4 billion. In July 2009 Ghana secured a $600 million loan for three-years from the IMF.

Balance of Payments / Imports and Exports
Estimated figures for 2010 show that exports earned US$7.3 billion (compared to US$5.7 billion in 2009) of which around US$1.25 million came from cocoa. Ghana's major export products are gold, cocoa, diamonds and timber. Imports in 2010 cost an estimated US$10 billion (compared to US$8.4 billion in 2009). Main import products are machinery and transport equipment, food, petroleum, consumer and industrial goods. Key trading partners are the UK, China, the Netherlands, France, and Nigeria.

Ghana is a member of the Economic Community of West African States (ECOWAS). A free trade area was due to be implemented by ECOWAS in 2000, organised primarily by Ghana and Nigeria.

Central Bank
Bank of Ghana, PO Box GP 2674, High Street, Accra, Ghana. Tel: +233 30 266 6174, e-mail: bogsecretary@bog.gov.gh, URL: http://www.bog.gov.gh
Governor & Chairman: Kwesi B. Ammissah-Arthur

Chambers of Commerce and Trade Organisations
Association of Ghana Industries, URL: http://agighana.org/
Ghana National Chamber of Commerce, http://www.ghanachamber.org/website/

MANUFACTURING, MINING AND SERVICES

Primary and Extractive Industries
Mining is one of Ghana's primary industries, contributing a major proportion of government revenue and foreign exchange. Gold, diamonds and manganese ore have been major export earners in recent years. Gold makes up 30 per cent of Ghana's export revenues, whilst the industrial sector (which includes mining) accounts for 25 per cent of the country's GDP. However, production of all mining products significantly declined in the late 1970s and the first years of the 1980s. All are industries requiring substantial foreign exchange inputs for current expenditure, maintenance, and development, and all suffered particularly badly from the lack of foreign exchange in the 1970s and early 1980s. Gold in particular suffered from falling world market prices in 1999. Bauxite is exported but the industry has been hampered by the deterioration of the western railway and its rolling stock. Ghana also produces trioxide arsenic, hydraulic cement, kaolin, salt, sand, gravel, silica sand, silver and lime.

Ghana had proven oil reserves estimated at 0.66 billion barrels at the beginning of January 2012. All reserves are located in five sedimentary basins: Tano, Saltpond, Accra/Keta, Voltaian, and Cape Three Points. Ghana consumed an estimated 64,000 barrels of oil per day in 2011, and produced 74,000 barrels per day. Offshore oil deposits were discovered in 2007. Ghana had an oil refining capacity of 45,000 barrels per day at the beginning of January 2012. The Ghana National Petroleum Company (GNPC) has overall responsibility for importing crude oil and petroleum products. Major foreign oil companies operating in Ghana include Elf TotalFina, Exxon Mobil, Royal Dutch/Shell, Dana Petroleum, Energy Africa, and Unipetrol.

Reserves of natural gas were estimated at 1.0 trillion cubic feet at the beginning of January 2011, located primarily in the Tano fields. Ghana's gas industry has only recently gone into production figures for 2010 show that Ghana produced 2 billion cubic feet but consumed 4 billion cubic feet.

Energy
Ghana consumed 0.185 quadrillion Btu of energy in 2009, equivalent to less than 0.1 per cent of world energy consumption. The residential sector uses the greatest proportion of energy (56 per cent in 1998), followed by the industrial (30 per cent), transport (13 per cent), and commercial (0.4 per cent) sectors.

Most of Ghana's electricity is generated by hydro-electric plants. Total electric generation capacity is estimated at 1.9 gigawatts. Ghana has two hydro-electric power stations, at Akosombo and Kpong, which together generate 1,072 mW of power to almost every region of Ghana, Togo and Benin. Thermal generation plants exist at Tema and Takoradi. Electricity generated in 2010 was an estimated 1.99 billion kWh.

The Volta River Authority (VRA) has responsibility for the generation and transmission of electricity in Ghana, whilst its subsidiary, the Northern Electricity Department (NED), is responsible for distribution in northern Ghana. Distribution in all other areas is dealt with by the Electricity Company of Ghana (ECG).

Ghana's government intends to reform the power sector to enable the supply of electricity to all parts of Ghana. It also intends to reduce dependence on hydropower, following reductions in rainfall in the recent past. Plans are underway for the installation of diesel and gas turbine generators. Ghana's electricity industry is in receipt of significant foreign investment, including a US$29 million loan from the China International Water and Electric Corporation (CWE) for electrification of towns along the Volta Lake; a US$165,000 loan from the US Trade and Development Agency (TDA) for a feasibility study on the construction of a gas turbine power station in western Ghana; a US$100 million project financed by the Spanish power utility Union Fenosa for the improvement of the supply to the industrial region of Tema; and a €10 million loan from the European Development Fund for the completion of Ghana's electrification by 2020.

Manufacturing
Ghana's industry sector contributes about 24 per cent of GDP and employs about 15 per cent of the workforce. Manufacturing industries include cocoa processing, brewing and distilling, vehicle assembly, radio and TV assembly, soft drinks, cigarettes, cement, petroleum refining and textiles. Government corporations were established in the early 1960s in such fields as meat processing, steel-making (from scrap), sugar refining, flour-milling and glass-making but most were ill-planned, high cost ventures which under-utilised their plants and are now often moribund. Industry has been moving away from the traditional export of logs to high quality wood products.

Service Industries
Ghana's services sector accounts for just under 40 per cent of GDP and employs about 20 per cent of the labour force.

Tourism
Tourism is seen by the government as a potential growth area. Figures for 1995 show that Ghana had 286,000 visitors. This had risen to an estimated 429,000 visitors generation $910 million in 2006.
Ghana Tourist Board (GTB), URL: http://www.ghanatourism.com

Agriculture
Agriculture makes up almost 41 per cent of Ghana's GDP and employs 50 per cent of the workforce. Cocoa and timber account for almost 35 per cent of exports. Figures for 2008 show that cocoa production was 700,000 tonnes, making Ghana the second largest producer in the world. Since the colonial period Ghana has been heavily dependent on cocoa, grown entirely by peasant enterprise. For a variety of reasons production has declined since a peak in the early 1960s. Producers experienced steadily declining real income from cocoa and a corrupt and inefficient state-run purchasing system delayed payments to farmers.

Subsistence crops grown in Ghana include rice and maize. Production of both crops has been hit by poor transport infrastructure, high fuel costs, a lack of incentives to producers, and bad weather conditions. Other agricultural exports include Shea butter, oranges, pineapples, kila nuts, yams, pepper and bananas.

Agricultural Production in 2010

Produce	Int. $'000	Tonnes
Yams	1,520,187	5,960,490
Cassava	1,410,679	13,504,100
Plantains	730,393	3,537,730
Cocoa beans	656,363	632,037
Taro (cocoyam)	287,336	1,354,800
Maize	246,773	1,871,700
Groundnuts, with shell	226,752	530,887
Game meat	161,232	74,100
Chillies and peppers, green	138,450	294,100
Rice, paddy	134,213	491,603
Tomatoes	129,347	350,000
Oranges	107,471	556,100

*unofficial figures
Source: http://faostat.fao.org/site/339/default.aspx Food and Agriculture Organization of the United Nations, Food and Agricultural commodities production

Figures for 2004 show that Ghana had 1.3 million head of cattle, and 6.7 head of sheep and goats. The total fish catch for 2010 was put at 351,200.

Severe floods in September 2007 caused widespread damage and destroyed much of that year's harvest.

COMMUNICATIONS AND TRANSPORT

Travel Requirements
US, Canadian, Australian and EU subjects require a passport valid for six months, and a visa unless in transit to another country. For exact requirements contact the Ghana High Commission or Embassy. Other nationals should contact the embassy or high commission to check visa requirements. Evidence of a yellow fever vaccination is also required.

National Airlines
There is currently no national airline after Ghana International Airlines ceased operating. The establishment of a national airline is not a priority according to President Mills.

International Airports
Ghana's main international airport is the Kotoka International Airport in the capital, Accra.

Railways
The routes mainly link mining centres to the ports. The system (1,000 km) forms a letter 'A' with Kumasi at the apex and Accra and Takoradi at the feet. The cross-piece consists of the line from Huni Valley near Tarkwa to Kotoku, some 30 km north of Accra. There are in addition a number of branch lines radiating from the main lines, with an important extension to Tema and thence to Shai Hills.

Roads
Ghana has about 30,000 km. (18,000 miles) of classified roads. The trunk roads linking the main town and cities are paved. Vehicles are driven on the right.

Shipping
The Ghana National Shipping Corporation (the Black Star Line) operates between Ghana and many European and Far East countries, as well as the Americas. About 29 shipping companies operate services into and out of the country giving direct connections with all continents.

Ports and Harbours
The main sea ports include Tema and Takoradi. The Volta River is navigable for light draught launches as far as Akuse, and with the exception of the Krachi rapids, can be used for canoe traffic during certain seasons of the year as far as Yeji. The Akosombo Dam, completed in 1965, has greatly increased its river transport potential. The Ankobra River is navigable for many months of the year by surf boats and light draught launches for a distance of 80 km. The Tano, connected with Half Assini by the main lagoon, is navigable for light draught launches and canoes as far as Tanoso, a distance of about 100km. Ferries run at Yeji for Buipe and Makongo.

HEALTH

In 2009, Ghana spent approximately 12.4 per cent of its total budget on healthcare, accounting for 56.7 per cent of all healthcare spending. Total expenditure on health care equated to 5.0 per cent of the country's GDP. Private expenditure amounted to 51.3 per cent. External resources accounted for 14.4 per cent. Social security expenditure amounted to 27 per cent of general government expenditure on health. Per capita expenditure amounted to $54. In 2004 the government added a 2.5 per cent national Health Insurance levy on top of VAT.

Each of the regional capitals has a hospital and there are many district hospitals. Figures for 2005-10 show that there are 2,033 physicians (0.9 per 10,000 population), 24,974 nurses and midwives (10.5 per 10,000 population) and 148 dentistry personnel. There are 9 hospital beds per 10,000 population.

As well as suffering from malaria and TB, Ghana's population has been badly affected by HIV/AIDS. According to recent figures there are nearly 320,000 adults with HIV/AIDS (3 per cent of the population), just over half of whom are women and most of whom are under 50 years of age. It is feared that this figure may be higher due to the stigma attached to admitting to the disease. The infant mortality rate in 2009 was 50 per 1,000 live births and the child (under five years) mortality rate was 74 per 1,000 live births. The most common causes of child mortality were: prematurity (16 per cent), malaria (18 per cent), pneumonia (13 per cent), diarrhoea (7 per cent) and HIV/AIDS (3 per cent). The World Bank extended Ghana a $25 million loan which the Ghanaian Aids Commission is using to fund HIV/AIDS projects. The UK's Department for International Development (DFID) pledged £20 million over five years to support Ghana's fight against HIV/AIDS, mainly through the supply of condoms. Approximately 28 per cent of children sleep under insecticide-treated nets.

In 2010, an estimated 86 per cent of the population used improved drinking water sources. In the same year 14 per cent of the population used improved drinking water sources. (Source: http://www.who.int, World Health Statistics 2012)

EDUCATION

Primary/Secondary Education
The Ghana education system operates at three levels: primary, middle and secondary. Primary and middle education systems are free but not yet mandatory. Primary education begins at the age of six and lasts for six years. Junior secondary school lasts for three years, as does senior secondary school. Currently there are over 12,100 primary schools, nearly 5,500 junior secondary schools, and over 500 senior secondary schools. Figures from UNESCO for 2007 show that 60 per cent of young children attend pre school, 71 of girls and 73 of boys were enrolled in primary school and 43 per cent of girls and 47 per cent of boys were enrolled in secondary school.

Higher Education
Beyond this there is a higher education system consisting of teacher training colleges and the five universities: the University of Ghana at Legon, near Accra; the University of Science and Technology, Kumasi; the University of Cape Coast; the University of Development Studies; and the University College of Education. There are more than 18,000 students enrolled in the university system.

The literacy rate was estimated in 2007 at 71.7 per cent for males and 58.3 per cent for females. For the age group 15-24 years this rose to 79.7 for males and 75.8 for females. (Source: UNESCO).

RELIGION

Over 62 per cent of the population are Christian, whilst 19 per cent are Muslim, and 18 per cent subscribe to traditional and indigenous beliefs.

Ghana has a religious liberty rating of 7 on a scale of 1 to 10 (10 is most freedom). (Source: World Religion Database)

COMMUNICATIONS AND MEDIA

There is a high level of media freedom in Ghana. Radio remains the most significant medium for news.

Newspapers
There are two national dailies published in Accra, The privately owned Ghanaian Chronicle, URL: http://www.ghanaian-chronicle.com and the state owned Ghanaian Times, URL: http://www.newtimesonline.com. Weeklies include The Mirror, The Independent and the Ghana Palaver. The Pioneer is published in Kumasi. The circulation of most other weekly newspapers is limited to Accra.

Broadcasting
The Ghanaian Broadcasting Corporation (GBC) (URL: http://www.gbcghana.com/ operates two national networks - Radio 1 and Radio 2 broadcasting from Accra. There is also an FM station in Accra, a regional FM station at Bolgatanga and a community FM station at Apam (in the Central Region) as well as an external service which broadcasts in English and French. The first network, Radio 1, broadcasts in six Ghanaian languages - Akan, Dagbani, Ewe, Ga, Nzema and Hausa. GBC Radio 2 is the English network.

The television service, which started in July 1965, has colour transmitters serving the country. These are located at Adjankote (Greater Accra Region), Jamasi (Ashanti Region), Bolgatanga (Upper East Region), Han (Upper West Region), Tamale (Northern Region), Amadjofe and Akatsi (both Volta Region). There is a state-owned TV station and several privately-owned TV stations. Cable and satellite is also available.

Telecommunications
Direct international dialling is now operative to and from Ghana, especially in Accra and the other regional capitals. There are telephone services to all urban areas of economic and industrial importance. Estimated figures for 2008 show that 150,000 phone lines were in use as well as 11.6 million mobile phones.

According to 2008 figures there were nearly 1,000,000 internet users. Ghana's internet country code is '.gh'.

ENVIRONMENT

Ghana's main environmental problems include drought, overgrazing, deforestation, soil erosion, water pollution, and the threat to wildlife by poaching and the destruction of the natural habitat.

Figures from 2006 show Ghana's emissions from the consumption of fossil fuels totalled 7.29 million metric tons of carbon dioxide, rising to 10.58 million metric tons in 2010. (Source: EIA)

Ghana is a party to the following international environmental agreements: Biodiversity, Climate Change, Climate Change-Kyoto Protocol, Desertification, Endangered Species, Environmental Modification, Hazardous Wastes, Law of the Sea, Ozone Layer Protection, Ship Pollution, Tropical Timber 83, Tropical Timber 94, and Wetlands. It has signed, but not ratified, the Marine Life Conservation agreement.

Environmental Protection Agency of Ghana, URL: http://www.epa.gov.gh

SPACE PROGRAMME

Ghana launched its space centre, the Ghana Space Science and Technology Centre, in May 2012. Its mission is to develop programmes in space technology and science that relate to the state's development, including natural resource management and weather forecasting.

GREECE
Hellenic Republic
Elliniki Dhimokratia

Capital: Athens (Population estimate: 3.7 million)

Head of State: Karolos Papoulias (President) (page 1492)

National Flag: A white cross through a blue canton with nine horizontal stripes, five blue and four white.

CONSTITUTION AND GOVERNMENT

Constitution
In 1974 the people of Greece voted to abolish the monarchy and establish a non-monarchical republic. The constitution was revised in 1975. The basic principles enshrined in the constitution include sovereignty of the people through their elected representatives, rule of law, equality, social state, human dignity, liberty and the separation of powers into executive, legislative and judicial.

The Head of State is the President but he does not hold complete executive power as much of the executive responsibilities were vested in the legislature when the Constitution was amended in March 1986. The President appoints the Prime Minister and the Cabinet, on the recommendation of the Prime Minister. The President is elected every five years only by a two-third majority or a three-fifths majority on a third ballot. If he still does not hold a majority, parliament is dissolved and the President can be elected by a majority of votes by the deputies in the new parliament.

To consult the full constitution, please visit:
http://www.hellenicparliament.gr/en/Vouli-ton-Ellinon/To-Politevma/Syntagma/

International Relations
Greece joined Nato in 1952 and the EU in 1981. An ongoing dispute exists between Greece and Turkey over the island of Cyprus. Since 1974 the island has been divided into the Cypriot Government-controlled area in the South and the 'Turkish Republic of Northern Cyprus', which is recognised only by Turkey, in the North. Relations between the two countries have generally improved and in 2004 Greece supported the European Council decision to open accession negotiations with Turkey. Greece supports the UN over the Cyprus issue. Relations with the Balkan states are generally good, but Greece has a dispute with Macedonia over its name (which is the name of a region in northern Greece). In March 2008 Greece blocked Macedonia's effort to become a member of NATO because of the continuing dispute over the name. Relations between Greece and the FYROM are friendly but talks are being held over the disputed name by the UN.

Recent Events
In September 2006, Greece, Russia and Bulgaria agreed a deal to build an oil pipeline from Russia to Europe via Alexandropoulis in Greece.

Over the summer of 2007, around 170 wildfires swept through forests both on the mainland and on the islands, killing 63 people. In August, the government appealed for EU assistance, and a state of emergency was declared in two provinces. Despite criticism of his government's handling of the fires, Mr Karamanlis won a narrow majority in the poll held in September, giving him a mandate for further reforms.

In March 2008, the government passed a controversial pension reform bill. The bill was only narrowly passed and was met with mass protests. It brought in pension reforms and ceilings on pay as well as privatisation plans. The following October, unrest continued with thousands of public-sector employees and professionals going on strike.

In December 2008, a 15 year old student was shot by police. Although the police officers involved were arrested, the incident sparked protests which quickly spread through Athens and other large cities. Many buildings including banks and shops were set on fire and protestors called for Prime Minister Costas Karamanlis and his government to resign.

In December 2009 international concern about Greece's growing debt led to the country's credit rating being downgraded and Prime Minister Papandreou announced a package of austerity measures. The following January a second round of cuts were announced and EU leaders said that they would offer Greece help but failed to agree a plan. The continued austerity measures led to strikes and in March a series of tax rises and spending cuts were introduced. In April 2010 it was feared that Greece would default on its debts and so the Eurozone countries agreed a $146.2 billion rescue package. More cuts were announced by Prime Minister Papandreou and trade unions called a general strike in protest. In August the European Commission announced that Greece had met the conditions for it to receive the second part of the EU/IMF loan. The Government announced further tougher austerity measure which would include new taxes and a higher rate of sales tax this measure would be introduced in the 2011 draft budget. In November 2010 the EU and IMF approved a third tranche of funding. In February 2011 international observers said that the austerity packages did not go far enough. Further street protests took place.

In September 2011 there was further international concern that Greece was about to default on its debts. France and Germany reaffirmed their commitment to Greece. The IMF and Eurozone countries agreed to lend a further €109 billion ($155 billion), but Greece will only receive the money if it proves it is acting to sort out the crisis. In October, Greece said that although parliament had voted in favour of the new austerity budget its 2011 deficit was likely to be 8.5 per cent of GDP, down on the 10.5 per cent of 2010 but higher than the 7.6 per cent target set by the EU and IMF. It blamed the shortfall on the worsening of the global economy.

The situation worsened in November 2011 after the prime minister George Papandreau announced he would hold a referendum on whether to accept the bailout. After several days of confusion he revoked the decision. He tried to build a national unity government but on 6 November he agreed to stand down after the opposition refused to negotiate whilst he remained in power. The country has been warned that it must accept the bailout or go bankrupt before the end of the year.

An interim government was sworn in on November 11 headed by former Vice President of the European Central Bank, Lucas Papedemos. The interim coalition cabinet is expected to sit until elections are held in February 2012.

Talks held in January 2012 with Greece's private creditors faltered which meant that Greece was in danger of not meeting its debt repayment deadline in March 2012, meaning the €130 billion EU rescue package was also in danger. In February the Greek government approved a new round of austerity measures agreed with the EU which meant that the EU would approve the €130 billion bailout. These new measures led to widespread demonstrations and violence on the streets and much anger was directed an the German Chancellor, Angela Merkel.

In March 2012 a 'debt swap' deal was agreed between Greece and its private-sector lenders which meant that the debt load could be halved, this arrangement had been insisted on by the EU as a condition of its signing off the €130 billion bailout.

A general election was held on 6 May 2012. The electorate did not vote in great numbers for the main parties but turned instead to those parties who promised an end to the austerity measures or said that they would 'rip up' the bailout agreement with the EU and the IMF. No one party won enough seats to form a majority government and so coalition talks began. An agreement was not found and so a second election was held in June. The New Democracy party became the dominant party but they did not get enough votes for an outright majority and so a coalition was formed with Pasok, and the Democratic Left. The finance minister resigned in June because of ill health.

In July 2011, in his first major speech to parliament, the new prime minister, Antonis Samaras, said his priority was restoring economic growth Greece.

In September 2012 it was announced that a further €11.5 billion of spending cuts were to be made, these savings were a pre-condition to be made by Greece before it received the next tranche of bailout funds. Without the bailout the country faced imminent bankruptcy. The announced cuts led to a fresh outbreak of demonstrations. In November the government passed a €13.5 billion austerity plan, this plan included tax rises and pension cuts. That month the Eurozone and IMF agreed to release the next installment of the bailout loan, it was feared that Greece may leave the Euro. In April 2013 Greece agreed to further austerity measures in order to receive the next tranche of bailout funds. Parliament also passed a bill sanctioning 15,000 civil service job cuts, this new bill brought to an end the constitutional guarantee of a job for life.

Legislature
Legislative and most executive power is held by the Unicameral *Vouli*. It has 300 members who are directly elected for a term of four years.

Vouli, Palais du Parliament, Palaia Anactora, Syntagma Square, 100-21, Athens, Greece. Tel: +30 (0)1 370 7000, fax: +30 (0)1 369 2170, URL: http://www.parliament.gr

---

Cabinet (as at June 2013)
Prime Minister: Antonis Samaras (page 1507)
Minister of Finance: Yannis Stournaras (page 1520)
Minister of Administrative Reform and e-Governance: Antonios Manitakis (page 1470)
Minister of Interior: Evripidis Stylianidis (page 1521)
Minister of Foreign Affairs: Dimitris Avramopoulos (page 1380)
Minister of Defence: Panos Panagiotopoulos (page 1492)
Minister of Development, Competitiveness, Infrastructure, Transport and Networks: Kostis Chatzidakis (page 1403)
Minister of the Environment, Energy and Climate Control: Evangelos Livieratos
Minister of Education, Religious Affairs, Culture and Sport: Constantinos Arvanitopoulos
Minister of Labour, Social Security and Welfare: Ioannis Vroutsis (page 1532)
Minister of Health: Andreas Lykourentzos
Minister of Agricultural Development and Food: Athanasios Tsaftsaris (page 1528)
Minister of Justice, Transparency and Human Rights: Antonis Roupakiotis (page 1505)
Minister of Public Order and Citizen's Protection: Nikolaos Dendias (page 1414)
Minister of Tourism: Olga Kefalogianni (page 1455)
Minister of Merchant Marine and Aegean: Constantinos Mousouroulis (page 1481)
Minister for Macedonia and Thrace: Theodoros Karaoglou (page 1454)
Minister of State: Dimitris Stamatis
Government Spokesperson: Simos Kedikoglou

Ministries

Presidency, URL: http://www.presidency.gr
Ministry to the Prime Minister, 15 Vassilissis Sophias Ave, 106 74 Athens, Greece. Tel: +30 (0)10 338 5372, 228 5344, fax: +30 (0)10 645 0658, e-mail: mail@primeminister.gr, URL: http://www.primeminister.gr
Ministry of the Aegean, 2 Mikras Asias Str, 81100 Mytilini, Greece. Tel: +30 (0)251 020796, fax: +30 (0)251 041175, e-mail: webmaster@ypai.gr, URL: http://www.ypai.gr
Ministry of Agriculture, 2-6 Acharnon Str., 10438 Athens, Greece. Tel: +30 (0)10 529 2111, fax: +30 (0)10 524 0475, e-mail: webmaster@minagric.gr, URL: http://www.minagric.gr
Ministry of Culture, 20-22 Bouboulinas str., 106 82 Athens, Greece. Tel: +30 (0)10 820 1100, fax: +30 (0)10 820 1373, e-mail: generalenquiries@noc.culture.gr, URL: http://www.culture.gr
Ministry of Development, 80 Michalacopoulou str., 115 28 Athens, Greece. Tel: +30 (0)10 748 2770, fax: +30 (0)10 778 8279, e-mail: grammatia@ypan.gr, URL: http://www.ypan.gr
Ministry of Education and Religious Affairs, 15 Mitropoleos str., 105 57 Athens, Greece. Tel: +30 (0)10 323 0461, fax: +30 (0)10 324 8264, e-mail: edu_ref@ypepth.gr, URL: http://www.ypepth.gr
Ministry of the Environment, Physical Planning and Public Works, 17 Amaliados str., 115 23 Athens, Greece. Tel: +30 (0)10 643 1641, fax: +30 (0)10 643 4470, e-mail: service@dorg.minenv.gr, URL: http://www.minenv.gr
Ministry of Economy and Finance, 5-7 Nikis str., 105 63 Athens, Greece. Tel: +30 (0)10 333 2000, fax: +30 (0)10 323 8657, e-mail: info@mnec.gr, URL: http://www.ypetho.gr/
Ministry of Foreign Affairs, 1 Acadimias str., 106 71 Athens, Greece. Tel: +30 (0)10 368 1000, fax: +30 (0)10 362 4195, e-mail: mfa@mfa.gr, URL: http://www.mfa.gr
Ministry of Health and Welfare, 17 Aristotelous str., 104 33 Athens, Greece. Tel: +30 (0)10 523 2820, fax: +30 (0)10 523 1707, URL: http://www.mohaw.gr
Ministry of the Interior, 27 Stadiou str., 10183 Athens, Greece. Tel: +30 (0)10 322 3521, fax: +30 (0)10 339 3500, e-mail: info@ypes.gr, URL: http://www.ypes.gr
Ministry of Justice, 96 Mesogeion str., 115 27 Athens, Greece. Tel: +30 (0)10 771 1019, fax: +30 (0)10 775 8759, e-mail: minjust@otenet.gr, URL: http://www.ministryofjustice.gr
Ministry of Labour and Social Security, 40 Pireos str., 104 37 Athens, Greece. Tel: +30 (0)10 529 5000, fax: +30 (0)10 524 9805, e-mail: info@labor-ministry.gr, URL: http://www.ypakp.gr
Ministry of Macedonia and Thrace, Administration Building, 54123 Thessaloniki, Greece. Tel: +30 (0)310 379000, fax: +30 (0)310 235109, e-mail: minister@mathra.gr, URL: http://www.mathra.gr
Ministry of the Merchant Marine and Island Policy, 150 Gregoriou Lambraki str., 18535 Piraeus, Greece. Tel: +30 (0)1 412 1211, fax: +30 (0)1 411 7286, e-mail: egov@mail.yen.gr, URL: http://www.yen.gr
Ministry of National Defence, Pentagon, Mesogeion, Athens, Greece. Tel: +30 (0)10 555 5911, fax: +30 (0)10 646 5584, e-mail: minister@mod.gr, URL: http://www.mod.gr
Ministry of Public Order, 4 P. Canellopoulou Str., 10177 Athens, Greece. Tel: +30 (0)10 692 8510, fax: 30 (0)10 692 1675, e-mail: ydt@otenet.gr, URL: http://www.ydt.gr
Ministry of Rural Development and Food, e-mail: info@minagric.gr, URL: http://www.minagric.gr
Ministry of Tourism, e-mail: info@mintour.gr, URL: http://www.mintour.gr
Ministry of Transport, Infrastructure and Communications, 13 Xenofontos str., 10557 Athens, Greece. Tel: +30 (0)10 325 1211, fax: +30 (0)10 323 9039, e-mail: yme@yme.gr, URL: http://www.yme.gr
Ministry of Administrative Reform and e-Governance, Vas Sofias 15, 10674 Athens, Greece. Tel: +30 213 131 3000

Political Parties

Main political parties are:
Nea Demokratia (New Democracy), Odos Rigillis 18, 106 74 Athens, Greece. Tel: +30 (0)10 729 0071, fax: +30 (0)10 723 6429, URL: http://www.nd.gr
President: Antonis Samaras (page 1507)
Panellinion Socialistikon Kinema (PASOK Panhellenic Socialist Movement), Odos Charilaou Trikoupi, 10680 Athens, Greece. Tel: +30 (0)10 360 1875, fax: +30 (0)10 364 5219, URL: http://www.pasok.gr
Leader: Evangelos Venizelos
Synaspismos Rizospastikís Aristerás (Coalition of the Radical Left) (Syriza), 1 Eleftherias Sq., 10553 Athens, Greece. Tel: +30 (0)10 337 8400, fax: +30 (0)10 321 9914, URL: http://www.syriza.gr
Leader: Alexis Tsipras
Kommunistiko Komma Ellados KKE(Communist Party of Greece), Leoforos Irakliou 145, 142 31 Nea Ionia-Athens, Greece. Tel: +30 (0)10 259 2111, fax: +30 (0)10 259 2298, e-mail: cpg@int.kke.gr, URL: http://www.kke.gr
General Secretary: Aleka Papariga
Independent Greeks, URL: http://www.anexartitoiellines.gr
Leader Panos Kammenos
Golden Dawn, URL: /http://xryshaygh.wordpress.com
Leader: Nikolaos Michaloliakos
Democratic Left, URL: http://www.dimokratikiaristera.gr
Leader: Fotis Kouvelis
LAOS, Popular Orthodox Rally, URL: http://www.laos.gr
Leader: Georgios Karatzaferis
Democratic Alliance, URL: http://www.dimsim.gr
President: Dora Bakoyannis
Ecologist Greens, URL: http://www.ecogreens.gr
Leader: Six member Committee
Syriza, URL: http://www.syriza.gr
Leader: Alexis Tsipras

Elections

Parliamentary elections are held every four years. There is universal direct suffrage for all citizens over the age of 18. Members are elected by proportional representation.

The most recent presidential elections were held in February 2010 and Karolos Papoulias, a former government minister, was re-elected for a further five year term.

In February 2004 the prime minister, Costas Simitis, announced he would step down as leader of PASOK at the elections to be held in March 2005. George Papandreou was elected as the new party leader. PASOK lost the elections and the New Democracy Party led by Costas Karamanlis were elected to power for the first time since 1993. New Democracy won 165 seats, PASOK, 117, The Communist Party of Greece, 12 seats and Synaspismos, 6 seats. In August 2007 Prime Minister Karamanlis called a snap election which was held on September 16; his party was re-elected with a narrow majority.

In September 2009 Prime Minister Karamanlis called a snap election to be held on October 4; his party was trailing in opinion polls and had a majority of just one seat. PASOK won the elections with 43 per cent giving them an outright majority.

A parliamentary election was held on 6 May 2012. The electorate, having had enough of austerity measures, did not vote in great numbers for the main parties but turned instead to those parties who promised an end to the austerity measures or said that they would 'rip up' the bailout agreement with the EU and the IMF. No one party won enough seats to form a majority government and so coalition talks began. This proved to be inconclusive so a second election was held on June 17. This time the electorate chose the pro-bailout New Democracy party, they did not get enough votes for an outright majority and so coalition talks began again. After three days it was announced that New Democracy would form a coalition with Pasok, and the Democratic Left.

Seats won in May and June 2012

Party	May	June
New Democracy	108	129
Syriza	52	71
Pasok	41	33
Independent Greeks	33	20
KKE (Communist)	26	12
Golden Dawn	21	18
Democratic Left	19	17

Diplomatic Representation

Embassy of the United States of America, 91 Vassilissis Sophias Blvd, 10160, Athens, Greece. Tel: +30 (0)10 721 2951, fax: +30 (0)10 645 6282, e-mail: AthensAmEmb@state.gov, URL: http://athens.usembassy.gov
Ambassador: Daniel B. Smith (page 1516)
British Embassy, Ploutarchou 1, 106 75 Athens, Greece. Tel: +30 (0)10 727 2600, fax: +30 (0)10 7272734, e-mail: britania@hol.gr, URL: http://ukingreece.fco.gov.uk/en/
Ambassador: John Kittmer (page 1457)
Embassy of Greece, 1A Holland Park, London, W11 3TP, United Kingdom. Tel: +44 (0)20 7229 3850, fax: +44 (0)20 7229 3850, URL: http://www.mfa.gr/uk/en
Ambassador: Konstantinos Bikas
Embassy of Greece, 2221, Massachusetts Ave N.W., Washington DC 20008, USA. Tel: +1 202 667 3169, fax: +1 202 939 5824, URL: http://www.mfa.gr/www.mfa.gr/AuthoritiesAbroad/North+America/USA/EmbassyWashington/en-US
Ambassador: Christos P. Panagopoulos
Permanent Mission of Greece to the United Nations, 13th Floor, 866 Second Avenue, New York, NY 10017, USA. Tel: +1 212 888 69000, fax: +1 212 888 4440, e-mail: greece@un.int, URL: http://www.un.int/greece
Permanent Representative: Anastassis Mitsialis

LEGAL SYSTEM

The law is based on Roman law. Greece has three kinds of courts: civil and criminal courts for civil and criminal matters; administrative courts for administrative issues; and special courts.

There are three types of civil and criminal courts: district courts (Justice of the peace, one-member district courts, and three-member District Courts); twelve Courts of Appeal and the Supreme Court (*Areios Pagos*). The Supreme Court is the Areios Pagos and may review the decisions of the lower criminal courts. The president has the constitutional right, with certain exceptions, to commute and reduce sentences.

Administrative courts have jurisdiction over administrative disputes. The Supreme Administrative Court is the Council of State (*Symvoulion Epikrateias*), which assesses administrative disputes, administrative violations of laws, and revision of disciplinary procedures affecting civil servants. It also reviews the legality of administrative acts and has the power to annul them. It reviews the decisions of the administrative courts of appeal.

The Auditors' Court has jurisdiction over issues such as pensions, accounts, liability of public officers, fraud disputes with the government.

The Supreme Special Tribunal reviews the constitutionality of laws, and is the final arbiter in disputes arising over general elections and referenda. It also deals with matters of international law.

Judges of the Supreme Court, the courts of appeal, and the courts of first instance are appointed for life on the recommendation of the Ministry of Justice. For lawyers to be appointed to the higher courts (Courts of Appeal and Supreme Court), they must be a member of a Greek Bar Association. The position of Ombudsman was created in 1997.

The government respects the rights of its citizens. However, there have been recent reports of excessive use of force by security forces. There is a degree of discrimination against Roma children in education, and many Roma lack access to housing, medical care, public services,

GREECE

and employment opportunities. Prisons can be overcrowded and conditions can be harsh. The last execution in Greece was carried out in 1972. The death penalty was abolished in 1994 for all crimes except for crimes of high treason in time of war. It was completely abolished in 2001.

Areios Pagos Hellenic Supreme Court of Civil and Penal Law, URL: http://www.areiospagos.gr

National Commission for Human Rights, 6 Neofytou Vamva, 10674 Athens, Greece. Tel: +30 210 7233 221, fax: +30 210 7233 217, e-mail: info@nchr.gr, URL: http://www.nchr.gr/index.php?category_id=3

LOCAL GOVERNMENT

Greece is divided into 13 administrative regions: Eastern Macedonia and Thraki, Central Macedonia, Western Macedonia, Thessalia, Ipiros, Ionian Islands, Western Greece, Central Greece, Peloponnissos, Attiki, Northern Egeo, Southern Egeo and Kriti. Nine regions are on the mainland. The regions are subdivided into a system of 51 self-governing Prefectural Self Administrations, Nomoi. A Prefectural council is elected by universal suffrage every four years. The Prefectural Self Administrations are further divided into municipalities which are headed by an elected mayor and communities.

Mount Athos situated on the Halkidiki peninsular is an autonomous region, home to 20 monasteries all of which govern their own territory.

Following reforms in 1997, the regions implement domestic and European policies for economic and social development within their own geographic region, and have an important role in regional planning. Further executive powers are being transferred from central government to the regions.

Each region is headed by a Secretary General, appointed by the Council of Ministers. The Secretary General is the representative of the central government at regional level. Regional administration is organised in a General Directorate. Each region has a Regional Council, composed of the Secretary General, elected Prefects, representatives of local government associations, and representatives of professional groups such as Chambers of Commerce. Main areas of responsibility include planning, regional development, public works, health, environment and forest and agriculture management. The Secretary General offers support to both tiers of local government (departmental and municipal).

AREA AND POPULATION

Area

Greece is situated in the south-east of Europe. On its northern borders lie Albania, the Former Yugoslav Republic of Macedonia and Bulgaria. The Ionian Sea is to the west and Turkey lies to the east across the Aegean Sea. The country consists of the mainland and several island groups including the Kikladhes and the Dodecanese. Altogether there are over 2,000 islands. It has a total area of 131,944 sq. km. The climate is temperate, with mild, wet winters and hot, dry summers.

Greece is in an earthquake prone zone, its worst quakes in recent years being 1953 and 1981. The most recent large quake was in September 1999, the epicentre being just north of Athens, when 52 people were reported killed. Southern Greece was hit by a quake in June 2008, two people were killed and several injured when the quake struck the area near Patras in the Peloponnese.

Athens is the capital of Greece and has an estimated population of 4 million. Other major cities include Thessaloniki, which has an estimated population of 1 million, Piraeus and Patras.

To view a map, consult: http://www.un.org/Depts/Cartographic/map/profile/greece.pdf

Population

Estimated figures for 2011 put the population at 10,787,090, over 61 per cent of which lives in urban areas (almost 40 per cent of the population lives in Athens). Population density in Greece is around 80 persons per sq. km. Projections suggest that the population will begin to decrease after reaching a peak in 2030, declining to 10,778,997 by 2050. The number of foreign nationals in 2006 was estimated at 695,979 of which 605,758 came from European countries. Approximately 70 per cent (481,66) came from Albania. Figures from January 2005 show that 604,215 foreign nationals were living in Greece. Largest groups by nationality were: Albania 448,152; Bulgaria 33,469; Romania 17,546; Ukraine 13,249; Georgia 10,431; Pakistan 9,945; India 7583.

The official language is Greek.

Births, Marriages, Deaths

Figures for 2010 show there were an estimated 114,766 live births (10.2 per 1,000 population) compared to 107,545 (9.69 per 1,000 population) in 2005. In 2008 there were 392 still births and 314 infant deaths. The number of marriages in 2010 was 56,338 (5.0 per 1,000 population), compared to 58,491 in 2000. There were 13,607 divorces in 2009. The number of recorded deaths in 2010 was 108,310 (9.8 per 1,000 population) compared to105,170 in 2000. (Source: http://www.statistics.gr)

According to WHO figures the child mortality rate (under years) in 2010 was 3 per 1,000 live births. The neonatal mortality rate was three per 1,000 live births. In 2010, the maternal mortality rate was 3 per 100,000 live births. The total fertility rate was estimated at 1.5 in 2010.

Life expectancy in 2009 was estimated at 78 years for males and 83 years for females. Health life expectancy was estimated in 2007 at 71.0 years for males and 44.0 years for females (Source: http://www.who.int, World Health Statistics 2012)

Public Holidays 2014

1 January: New Year's Day
6 January: Epiphany
3 March: Shrove Monday (Orthodox)
25 March: Independence Day
18 April: Orthodox Good Friday
21 April: Orthodox Easter Monday
1 May: May Day
9 June: Orthodox Whit Monday
15 August: Assumption Day
28 October: Ohi Day (rejection of Mussolini's ultimatum)
25 December: Christmas Day
26 December: St Stephen's Day

EMPLOYMENT

In 2011 the labour force numbered 4,967,200 in 2011 down from 5,021,000 in 2010. In 201 4,156,300 of the labour force was employed and 810,800 were unemployed, an unemployment rate of 16.3 per cent.

The unemployment rate has risen steadily in the last few years from7.9 per cent in the fourth quarter of 2008 to 10.3 per cent in the fourth quarter of 2009, 14.2 per cent in the fourth quarter of 2010 and 20.7 per cent in the fourth quarter of 2011 and 26.0 per cent in the fourth quarter of 2012. (Source: http://www.statistics.gr)

The largest employer is the trade, restaurant and hotel sector, followed by other service industries, agriculture and fishing, and manufacturing. The following table shows how the working population was employed in recent years.

Employment Sector	2011	2012*
Agriculture, forestry and fishing	517,804	498,90
Mining & quarrying, manufacturing & utilities	489,659	428,81
Construction	249,554	207,17
Wholesale and retail trade; repair of motor vehicles, transportation & storage, accommodation & food service activities	828,855	749,18
Information & communication	68,412	67,00
Financial & insurance activities	109,947	108,50
Real estate activities	4,036	3,84
Professional, scientific & technical activities, admin. & support service activities	319,657	312,38
Public admin. & defence; compulsory social security	946,136	893,55
Arts, entertainment & recreation, repair of household goods & other services	237,405	201,89

* provisional
Source: National Statistical Service of Greece

Greece introduced an austerity budget sparking mass strikes in May 2010. Measures include pay freezes, pension cuts and tax rises. Bonus payments have been banned for public sector workers, as have increases in public sector salaries and pensions for at least three years. The pension age is also to be raised.

BANKING AND FINANCE

Currency

On January 1st 2002 the euro, € became legal tender. Prior to that the currency was the drachma of 100 lepta. 1 euro = 100 cents. The notes are in denominations of 5, 10, 20, 50 100, 200 and 500 euro and the coins are 1, 2, 5, 10, 20 and 50 cent and 1 and 2 euro.

Since being accepted into the Eurozone, it transpired that not all the facts regarding Greece's public finances had been correctly reported. In 2004 the deficit had reached 6.1 per cent o GDP and 4.5 per cent in 2005, above the 3 per cent limit for Eurozone members. A case can be made for extraordinary circumstances in hosting the 2004 Olympic Games. Government spending also increased with increasing in public spending and public sector wages. The New Democracy Party, who came to power in 2004, announced its intent to make economic reforms. GDP growth slowed dramatically to 2.9 per cent in 2009, and the high levels o public debt discouraged foreign investment. In an effort to balance its budget the government announced unpopular reforms to the social security system including increased pension contributions by workers, tax rises and the sales of government stakes in some ports and telecommunications.

In December 2009 the European Central Bank warned that the situation in Greece was very difficult. In January 2010 the government announced tough austerity measures including the raising of the retirement age but international concern continued amidst fears that Greece would be unable to pay off its €300 billion (US$419 billion) government debt. In March 2010 the EU agreed a rescue plan in conjunction with the IMF worth €22 billion but the euro continued to fall. In April the Eurozone leaders agreed a further emergency loan package worth €30 billion. . In May 2010 the IMF and the EU announced a €110 billion rescue package over three years, on condition that Greece drastically reduce its public spending and increases its tax revenue. In August the second tranche of the EU/IMF loan was paid as Greece had met the conditions. In October the Government announced further austerity measures in its 2011 draft budget including new taxes and a higher rate of VAT. In November the third tranche of the EU/IMF loan was paid. In February 2011 international lenders felt that the austerity measures introduced by the government did not go far enough and the process eeded to be speeded up. There are worries that if Greece were to default there would be risk of contagion to other economies. Greece projected that the 2011 deficit would be 8.5 er cent of GDP, down from 10.5 per cent in 2010 but higher than the 7.6 per cent target et by the EU and IMF. In the latest proposed deal private banks have accepted a loss of 50 er cent on their loans to Greece. Fears remain that the country will default.

he 2010 rescue package was not enough to rescue Greece's financial crisis, a further bailout f €130 billion was paid in 2011 in order to stop Greece from defaulting on her debts. Figures or 2012 showed that the economy had continued to contract. Greece agreed to further usterity measures in April 2013.

GDP/GNP, Inflation, National Debt

rowth in recent years has been driven by construction of the infrastructure and foreign nvestment in preparation for Athens hosting the 2004 Olympic Games. Estimates for 2006 howed that contributions to GDP were as follows: 5.5 per cent from agriculture, 22 per cent om industry and 73 per cent from the service sector. GDP growth in 2006 was estimated t 4.2 per cent, falling to 4.0 per cent in 2007 and 2.8 per cent in 2008. Greece's economy as suffered in the global credit crisis. GDP was -3.5 per cent in 2010. Its deficit had increased o 12.7 per cent; four times higher than European rules permit. GDP growth rates were stimated at -6/9 per cent in 2011 and -6 per cent in 2012. The recession is forecast to ontinue with projected growth of -3.5 per cent in 2013.

Deficit and Debt of General Government in million Euro

	2008	2009	2010
GDP at market prices	236,917	235,017	230,173
Government deficit	-23,121	-136,305	-24,193
% of GDP	-9.8	-15.4	-10.5
Government debt	262,318	298,706	328,588
% of GDP	110.7	127,1	142,8

Source: National Statistical Service of Greece

Gross Value Added by Industry in million € (current prices)

Industry	2010*	2011*	2012*
Agriculture, forestry & fishing	6,300	6,175	5,751
Mining & quarrying, manufacturing, electricity, gas & water supply	26,371	24,402	24,404
Construction	6,772	4,561	3,616
Wholesale & retail trade, transportation & storage, accommodation & food service activities	49,980	45,723	39,801
Information & communication	9,464	8,894	8,309
Financial & insurance activities	9,245	8,958	8,326
Real estate activities	27,371	28,929	28,456
Professional, scientific & technical activities, admin. & support service activities	11,050	8,834	8,227
Public admin. & defence, compulsory social security, education, human health & social work activities	39,628	37,469	35,520
Arts, entertainment & recreation, repairs	9,041	9,191	8,110
Total	195,222	183,137	170,521
Taxes less subsidies on products	26,930	25,395	23,228
Gross Domestic Product	222,151	208,532	193,749

* provisional data
Source: National Statistical Service of Greece

nflation ran at an estimated 3.5 per cent in 2002 , falling to 2.9 per cent in 2004 before rising to an estimated 3.3 per cent in 2006. It fell to 3.0 per cent in 2007. Inflation was estimated to be 4.3 per cent in 2008, falling to 3.0 per cent in 2009. Figures for February 2011 showed that inflation was running at 4.2 per cent, down from the previous month of 4.9 per cent.

Foreign Investment

On 1 January 2001, Greece entered the European Monetary Union (EMU) and it was hoped that this would lead to more foreign investment. Direct foreign investment stood at US$985 million in 1998.

Greece has 24 industrial estates, divided into five development zones, each with their own level of incentives. Depending on the amount of investment, cash grants are given by the government ranging from 10 per cent to 65 per cent of the investment, while tax allowances or interest rate subsidies for bank loans can go up to 100 per cent. Minimum industry investment to qualify for these grants is US$165,000, and although there is a limit on the grants paid (approximately US$14 million), grants to tourism or industrial investments over US$85 million are considered on a case-by-case basis.

Balance of Payments / Imports and Exports

Principal exports are manufactured goods, food and beverages, petroleum products, minerals, tobacco, cotton and handicrafts. Imports include vehicles, food and drink, crude oil, iron and steel, pharmaceuticals, machinery and equipment. Figures for 2002 show 51.6 per cent of exports went to EU countries, particularly Germany, Italy and the UK. 5.7 per cent went to the US. In 2002, 66.2 per cent of imported goods came from the EU, particularly Italy, Germany, France and the Netherlands. Main imports are manufactured consumer goods, capital goods, food, and raw materials.

External Trade in Recent Years in Million Euro at Current Prices

	2010*	2011*	2012*
Imports	70,020	69,119	62,053
-Goods	57,382	57,655	51,336
-Services	12,638	11,464	10,718
-Expenditures of residents in the rest of the world	2,156	2,267	1,850
Exports	49,414	52,247	52,309
-Goods	23,345	26,286	27,761
-Services	26,069	25,962	24,548
-Expenditures of non-residents on the economic territory	9,611	10,505	10,024
Balance of trade	-20,606	-16,871	-9,744

Source: Statistical Office of Greece

Exports by SITC in Million €

Product	2005	2006
Food & live animals	2.076	2.336
Beverages & tobacco	559	509
Crude materials inedible, except fuels	692	865
Mineral, fuels, lubricants, etc.	1.323	2.171
Animal & vegetable oils & fats	399	486
Chemicals	2.044	2.180
Manufactured foods classified by raw material	2.874	3.421
Machinery & transport equipment	1.786	2.093
Miscellaneous manufactured articles	1.931	1.974
Commodities & transactions, not classified by category	362	450
Total	14.046	16.485

Source: National Statistical Service of Greece

Imports by SITC in Million €

Product	2005	2006
Food & live animals	4.000	4.420
Beverages & tobacco	682	719
Crude materials inedible, except fuels	1.103	1.229
Mineral, fuels, lubricants, etc.	7.885	9.713
Animal & vegetable oils & fats	129	167
Chemicals	6.364	6.934
Manufactured foods classified by raw material	5.917	7.194
Machinery & transport equipment	12.619	14.386
Miscellaneous manufactured articles	5.165	5.804
Commodities & transactions, not classified by category	78	164
Total	43.942	50.729

Source: National Statistical Service of Greece

Central Bank

Bank of Greece, 21 E Venizelos Avenue, GR-102 50 Athens, Attiki, Greece. Tel: +30 210 320 1111 / 320 2052 / 320 2048, fax: +30 210 323 2816, e-mail: secretariat@bankofgreece.gr
URL: http://www.bankofgreece.gr
Governor: Georgios A. Provopoulos (page 1498)

Chambers of Commerce and Trade Organisations

Union of Hellenic Chamber of Commerce, URL: http://www.acci.gr
Thessaloniki Chamber of Commerce & Industry, URL: http://www.ebeth.gr

Stock Exchange

Athens Stock Exchange, URL: http://www.ase.gr

MANUFACTURING, MINING AND SERVICES

Primary and Extractive Industries

More than 30 kinds of minerals and ores are produced in Greece. Estimates of their total reserves range between 5 and 10 billion tonnes. The most important minerals and ores extracted are bauxite, lignite, nickel ore, manganese magnesite, chromium, iron pyrites, emery, gypsum, asbestos, lead, zinc, marble, limestone, baryte, bentonite, kaoline, perlite and pumice stone.

Figures for 2012 show that Greece has very limited oil reserves. just 0.01 million barrels. Oil production stood at 7.58 thousand barrels per day in 2011, all from the Prinos fields in the Aegean sea. Greece consumes around 343,000 barrels a day and is therefore heavily reliant on imports, mainly from Iran, Russia, Saudi Arabia and Libya. Greece has the capacity to refine 423,000 barrels per day of crude oil. There are major refineries at Aspropyrgos, Aghi Theodori, Elefsis and Thessaloniki. The state oil company is HP (Hellenic Petroleum) is being privatised. A pipeline is planned between the Black Sea and the Aegean Sea port of Alexandroupoulis.

Greece has no reserves of natural gas. In 2011 consumption stood at around 167 billion cubic feet, mostly imported from Russia via Bulgaria. Greece is trying to reduce its dependency on Russia and was to be connected to the European natural gas network by 2010. It aims to be become a regional transit hub for natural gas from the Caspian sea. There is now an

GREECE

operational gas inter-connector with Turkey. A gas link with Italy is also planned. Liquified natural gas is imported from Algeria. Gas consumption is expected to increase by 2.8 per cent between 2010 and 2030.

Coal (lignite) reserves were estimated at 4.3 million short tons in 2008 and coal production was around 62.2 million short tons in 2010, consumption that year was 61.1 million short tons,.

Bauxite (whose deposits are estimated at more than 500 million tonnes) is used for the production of alumina and aluminium. Other minerals industrially processed in Greece include nickel-bearing deposits, magnesite (making dead-burned magnesite and caustic magnesia), bentonite and parlite. Figures for 2005 show that 2,484,000 tons of bauxite was produced and 68,531,000 tons of lignite.

Energy

In 2006 the Greek government passed a bill to deregulate the energy industry.

Lignite is used locally as fuel for thermo-electric power plants and crude oil is imported. Over 50 per cent of the Greek Islands are provided with electricity from diesel fired units.

A ten year electric power development plan, which was running from 1994-2003, called for 28 hydroelectric plants and some solar and wind powered plants to be built, as well as three natural gas and four lignite-fired power stations.

Greece has linked its electrical grid system to neighbouring countries including the Former Yugoslav Republic of Macedonia, Albania and Bulgaria allowing it to export some of its electricity. It is hoped that eventually Greece will be able to supply power through these links to Kosovo.

Figures for 2009 show that Greece had an installed electricity capacity of 14.36 billion kWh. Altogether Greece produced 57.57 billion kWh and consumed 58.71 billion kWh. (Source: EIA)

In total, 1.4 Quadrillion Btu (Quad) of total energy was consumed, of which 64 per cent was petroleum, 34 per cent was coal, 8 per cent was dry natural gas and 5 per cent was hydroelectric and renewable energy. The EU expects Greece to be able to develop its renewable energy sector.

Manufacturing

Manufacturing constitutes the principal single sector in the formation of the country's gross domestic product contributing around 23 per cent.

The principal manufacturing sectors are food, beverages, tobacco, textiles, metals and metal products, manufacturing, chemicals, clothing and footwear. It was also in these sectors that the biggest increases in output were registered in recent years. The construction sector had been stimulated in recent years with projects for the 2004 Athens Olympic Games. The following table shows the index of manufacturing in recent years with the base year as 2005 = 100.0

General Index	2009	2010	2011
Food	100.8	96.7	95.8
Beverages	104.2	96.3	87.4
Tobacco products	90.4	74.6	82.4
Textiles	52.9	41.9	32.7
Wearing apparel	62.9	48.3	36.1
Leather & footwear	79.2	50.0	42.2
Wood & cork	57.0	60.4	75.5
Paper & paper products	97.4	94.1	85.7
Printing & recording services	87.9	75.7	57.2
Coke & refined petroleum products	104.8	110.8	94.7
Chemical & chemical products	84.9	84.7	81.0
Basic pharmaceutical preparations	149.9	153.5	152.9
Rubber & plastic products	91.8	85.4	78.8
Other non-metallic mineral products	69.3	59.4	38.2
Basic metals	82.7	92.6	98.5
Fabricated metal products	79.7	79.7	76.2
Computers, electronic & optical products	27.7	30.6	23.4
Electrical equipment	82.4	79.1	70.4
Machinery & equipment n.e.c.	72.1	64.9	59.7
Motor vehicles, trailers & semi-trailers	76.1	71.6	49.8
Other transport equipment	91.0	54.8	37.0
Furniture	77.6	62.9	49.0
Other manufactured goods	70.5	64.5	55.9
Repair & installation services of machinery & equipment	82.1	58.0	57.2

Source: National Statistical Service of Greece

Tourism

Figures for 2010 show that Greece had 13.9 million visitors from abroad, down from 14.1 million in 2008 and 16.1 million in 2007. Over 90 per cent of foreign visitors are from Europe. Almost 70 per cent arrived by air. In 2003 tourism receipts were an estimated €7.3 billion. In 2004 Athens hosted the Olympic Games and as a result of this improvements were made to the infrastructure, including an underground railway line to the Maroussi district, where the stadium is located, to cope with the large influx of tourists the games generated.

Greek National Tourism Organisation: http://www.mintour.gr

Agriculture

Greece is mainly an agricultural country, the agricultural sector employs around 12 per cent of the workforce and most farms are quite small. According to 2007 figures, there were 860,153 holdings with a total agriculturalised area of 854,123 thousand stremma (one stremma equals 1,000 sq. metres). The total number of permanent agricultural workers in 2007 was 29,582. There were an estimated 1,164,354 seasonal workers. In 2007 agricultural crops covered 32,331,000 stremma. Crops covered 19,929,000 stremma, vegetables 1,057,000 stremma, vines 1,248,000 stremma, areas under trees 10,097,000 stremma. Greece has over 127 million olive trees. Olive groves occupy 14 per cent of Greece's cultivated land, producing 200,000 to 300,000 tons of olive oil annually. Agriculture accounts for 8 per cent of GDP.

Agricultural Production in 2010

Produce	Int. $'000*	Tonnes
Olives	1,449,112	1,809,800
Grapes	573,275	1,002,900
Tomatoes	519,681	1,406,200
Peaches and nectarines	348,099	639,400
Sheep milk, whole, fresh	332,949	855,000
Cotton lint	280,124	196,000
Cow milk, whole, fresh	241,723	774,600
Indigenous sheep meat	230,893	84,800
Wheat	200,383	1,600,000
Indigenous cattle meat	160,462	59,400
Indigenous pigmeat	158,425	103,058
Oranges	148,809	770,000

*unofficial figures

Source: http://faostat.fao.org/site/339/default.aspx Food and Agriculture Organization of the United Nations, Food and Agricultural commodities production

Greece has very little pasture and this is reflected in the livestock being mainly goats and sheep. In 2008, there were 115,748 holdings with goats and 115,350 holdings with sheep, mainly in Western Greece, Crete, Central Greece and the Peloponnese. In 2008, there were 20,094 holdings with cattle, predominantly in Eastern Macedonia and Thrace (4,318 holdings) and Central Macedonia (4,150).

Head of Livestock 2006-08

Livestock	'000 Head 06	'000 Head 08
Cattle	629	634
Pigs	902	1,087
Sheep	8,830	9,064
Goats	5,402	4,779
Beehives (in '000s)	1,331	..

Source: National Statistical Office of Greece

Animal Production in thousand tons

Produce	2006	2007
Meat	461	450
Milk	2.077	2.043
Cheese, hard	38	10
Cheese, soft	120	121
Honey	16	15

Source: National Statistical Office of Greece

Fishing

Recent figures show that Greece has 6,187 fishing vessels of 20 hp or above and a total annual catch (sea fishing) of 70,000 tons in 2010 (worth €289,619.7 thousand). This compares to a total sea catch in 2004 of 21,000 tons (worth €291,913.7 thousand). A further 106,200 tonnes (worth €346,846.1 thousand) were caught through aquaculture and pisciculture (compared to 97,100 tonnes in 2004). Fish farming has become a large industry and Greece now produces 58,000 tons of sea bass and sea bream, the majority of which is exported to European markets. (Source: Statistics Greece)

Forestry

Forests cover approximately 22,411,600 stremmas. In 2007 forest fires covered 2.257.746 stremmas. An estimated 10.920 stremmas were reforested.

COMMUNICATIONS AND TRANSPORT

Travel Requirements

A passport is required by all nationals apart from EU citizens holding a valid national ID card. British and EU citizens (excluding Bulgaria, Cyprus, Czech Republic, Estonia, Hungary, Latvia, Lithuania, Malta, Poland, Romania, Slovak Republic and Slovenia) who do not have an ID card require a passport valid for the length of stay, whilst Australian, USA, Canadian and excluded EU passports must be valid for at least 3 months beyond the length of stay.

Greece is a signatory to the 1995 Schengen Agreement. With a Schengen visa, a visitor can travel freely throughout the Schengen zone, and there are few border stops and checks. See http://www.eurovisa.info/SchengenCountries.htm for details.

Visas are not required by USA, Canadian, Bulgarian, Romanian and Australian nationals for stays of up to 90 days. Other EU citizens can stay for an unlimited period without a visa, but must apply for a national visa if staying for employment reasons, or if staying for over 90 days. Greece refuses admission and transit to holders of travel documents issued by the area of Cyprus not controlled by the Government of Cyprus, and holders of UN laissez-passers.

nationals not referred to above should contact the embassy to check visa requirements.

National Airlines
Olympic Air, URL: http://www.olympicair.com
The national airline Olympic Airways was privatised in 2009.

International Airports
There are 39 airports on the mainland and islands including 15 international airports:
Athens International Airport SA, (Eleftherios Venizelos), URL: http://www.aia.gr
Alexandroupolis, URL: http://www.alexandroupolisairport.gr/
Chania, URL: http://www.hcaa-eleng.gr/hania.htm
Corfu, URL: http://www.hcaa-eleng.gr/kerk.htm
Heraklion, URL: http://www.hcaa-eleng.gr/irak.htm
Kalamarta, URL: http://www.hcaa-eleng.gr/kalam.htm
Kavala, URL: http://www.hcaa-eleng.gr/kavala.htm
Kephalonia, URL: http://www.hcaa-eleng.gr/kefalonia.htm
Kos, URL: http://www.hcaa-eleng.gr/kos.htm
Lemnos, URL: http://www.hcaa-eleng.gr/limnos.htm
Mytilene International Airport, URL: http://www.hcaa-eleng.gr/mitilin.htm
Rhodes, URL: http://www.hcaa-eleng.gr/rhod.htm
Samos, URL: http://www.hcaa-eleng.gr/samos.htm
Thessaloniki, URL: http://www.hcaa-eleng.gr/thes.htm
Zakynthos, URL: http://www.hcaa-eleng.gr/zakinth.htm

Total passenger numbers in 2010 were 19.0 million arrivals and 19.2 million departures. Altogether there were 428,859 aircraft movements. A total of 116,774 tons of freight and mail were loaded and unloaded. (Source: Statistics Greece)

Aviation Authorities
Civil Aviation Authority, URL: http://www.hcaa.gr/home/index.asp
Air Traffic Safety Electronic Engineers Assn, URL: http://www.hcaa-eleng.gr/

Railways
As of 2006, the country's total railway network is 2,509 km long. Of this, 1,652 km is of standard international width, (Athens-Thessaloniki network), 106 km are of electrified standard line, 7,008 km are of metric width (Pireas-Peloponnissos and Volos-Kalabaka), and there are 43 kms of other lines. Recent investment in Greek railways has included an extra line connecting Athens and Piraeus and an extension of the Athens - Thessaloniki line to the Bulgarian border.

There is one main railway network operating in Greece, the Greek Railways Organisation (OSE). It is the outcome of a merger of the Greek State Railways, connecting Athens with Thessaloniki, and the main towns in central and northern Greece and the Piraeus-Athens-Peloponnese Railways (SPAP), connecting the capital with the main towns in the Peloponnese. The length of the OSE network is 2,479 km.

Figures for 2006 show that 9.233 million domestic passengers and 288,000 foreign passengers were carried. A total of 1.811 million passenger km were traveled. In the same year 564,000 tons of domestic freight and 2.347 million tons of international freight were carried. A total of 517 million freight ton-km were traveled. (Source: Statistics Greece)

Organismos Sidirodromon Ellados (OSE), URL: http://www.ose.gr

Athens has its own metro system which was extended in recent years to include links to the new Athens airport and accommodate the increased passenger journeys for the 2004 Athens Olympics. (URL: http://www.ametro.gr). Total length is 26 km. In 2006, 168.7 million passengers were transported. There are also 26 km of tramways.

Roads
The road network has been greatly improved in recent years. The total length of the network is 8,945 km of national highways and 29,161 km of provincial roads. Currently under construction is the Via Egnatia a route across northern Greece which will link the ports of Igoumenitsa and Thessaloniki. Provisional figures for 2010 show that 8,062,085 vehicles were on the road including 5.2 million passenger cars, 27,311 buses, 1.31 million trucks and 1.49 million motorcycles. There were 15,032 registered road accidents with 20,366 casualties including 1,258 fatalities. Vehicles are driven on the right.

Waterways
Greece has no navigable rivers and just one canal, the Corinth canal.

Shipping
In 2011 there were 2,014 vessels in Greece's merchant fleet with a capacity of 43,398,000 GRT. There were 40,481,000 passengers (38,512,000 domestic and 1,964,000 foreign). In 2011, 104,128,000 tonnes were transported (28,954,000 domestic and 75,174,000 foreign). Ferries run from Piraeus to islands in the Argo-Saronic, Cyclades, Dodacanese and the Northeast Aegean as well as Crete and some mainland ports. Ferries also run between some of the islands.

Ports and Harbours
Greece has 123 cargo or passenger ports. The major ports are Piraeus, Patras and Thessaloniki.

HEALTH

Under the Greek healthcare system established in 1983, all citizens receive free healthcare. Consultations with a GP are free of charge and visit to outpatient clinics are cheap. Primary health care services are provided through rural health centres and surgeries in rural areas, the outpatient departments of regional and district hospitals, the polyclinics of the social insurance institutions and specialists in urban areas. Secondary care is provided by public

hospitals, private for-profit hospitals and clinics or hospitals owned by social insurance funds. With the crisis in the Greek economy, healthcare budgets were slashed in 2010 by up to 40 per cent. The number of hospitals is expected to be reduced by 50 per cent

In 2009, Greece spent approximately 12.1 per cent of its total budget on healthcare (up from 10.1 per cent in 2000 but down from 13.1 per cent in 2007), accounting for 61.7 per cent of all healthcare spending. Social security expenditure accounts for 51.8 per cent of general government expenditure. Private expenditure amounts to 38.3 per cent of health expenditure, largely out-of-pocket. Total expenditure on health care equated to 10.6 per cent of the country's GDP. Per capita total expenditure on health was US$3,015 in 2009 (compared to US$917 in 2000).

Figures for 2000-10 show that there are 69,030 physicians (61.7 per 10,000 population), 2,626 nurses and midwives (2.4 per 10,000 population), 9,837 pharmaceutical personnel and 14,744 dentistry personnel (13.2 per 10,000 population). There are 48 hospital beds per 10,000.

The infant mortality rate (likelihood of dying by first birthday) in 2009 was estimated at 3 per 1,000 live births and and the child mortality rate (likelihood of dying by fifth birthday) was 4 per 1,000 live births. Approximately 35 per cent of the deaths among children aged less than 5 years were prematurity 34 per cent, congenital anomalies 44 per cent and pneumonia 7 per cent.

In 2010, 100 per cent of the population used improved drinking water sources. In the same year, 98 per cent of the population used improved sanitation. (Source: http://www.who.int, World Health Statistics 2012)

HIV infections appear to be on the increase. There were forecast to be over 925 cases of HIV infections in 2011, up from 505 reported cases in 2010. Most infections are believed to be through drug use.

EDUCATION

Education is provided free of charge in Greece from nursery to university level. This includes both tuition and textbooks. Up to the age of 15 education is compulsory. According to Unesco 2007 figures, the literacy rate for adults was 97.1 per cent. In the age group 15-24 years this rises to 99.3 per cent.

The education system is divided into Kindergarten, Primary School (Dimotikó) from age 6, from age 12 pupils go on to Lower Secondary Education (Gymnasio) for 3 years, then at 15 students enter Upper Secondary Education (General Lyceum) for three years. Some of these offer technical or vocational education.

Pre-school Education
In the year 2009/10, there were 6,103 nursery schools, with 13,488 kindergartens and 157,908 infants.

Primary/Secondary Education
There were 5,460 elementary schools with 64,268 teachers and 633,406 pupils.

In the same year there were 3,348 high schools, with 69,413 teaching staff and 584,529 pupils, also that year there were 641 schools of secondary technical, vocational or ecclesiastic with 19,042 teachers and 110,567 pupils.

Higher Education
Higher education in Greece is divided into technical colleges (vocational and ecclesiastic) and universities. There are 77 technical colleges with 11,165 teachers and 173,256 pupils. There are 21 universities with 13,336 teachers and 173,256 pupils. (Source: Statistics Greece). Greece currently does not recognise private universities but this is currently under debate; the state universities can't cope with the demand for places which is leading some students no option but to study abroad.

RELIGION

It is estimated that over 92 per cent of the people adhere to the Greek Orthodox Church which is the established religion. In spiritual matters the Greek Church is subject to the authority of the Ecumenical Patriarch at Constantinople but its government is vested in a permanent council, the Holy Synod, under the presidency of the Archbishop of Athens and all Greece.

Other religions are tolerated and freedom of worship is guaranteed by the constitution. Proselytising and any other intervention against the established religion is prohibited. Greece has a religious liberty rating of 4 on a scale of 1 to 10 (10 is most freedom). (Source: World Religion Database). Approximately 4.3 per cent of the population is Muslim.

The Orthodox Church of Greece, Odos Ioannou Gennadiou 14, 115 21 Athens, Greece. Tel: +30 (0)10 724 8680, fax: +30 (0)10 721 2839, e-mail: contact@ecclesia.gr, URL: http://www.ecclesia.gr/english/EnIndex.html
Archbishop of Athens and Greece: Archbishop Hieronymos II

COMMUNICATIONS AND MEDIA

Newspapers
Eleftheria, URL: http://www.eleftheria.gr
Eleftherotypia, URL: http://www.enet.gr/online/online
Ethnos, URL: http://www.ethnos.gr/
Kathimerini, http://www.ekathimerini.com/

GRENADA

Patris, URL: http://www.patris.gr/
Rizospastis, URL: http://www.rizospastis.gr/
Ta Nea, URL: http://ta-nea.dolnet.gr/
Athens News, http://www.athensnews.gr/

Business Journals
Express (Greece), URL: http://www.express.gr/

Broadcasting
Radio and television services come under ERT, *Ethnicon Idryma Radiophonias-Tileoraseos*, the Hellenic National Radio-Television, which is an organisation sponsored by the state. An estimated 99.7 per cent of the population have access to terrestial TV, an estimated 6.78 per cent to digital terrestrial TV and an estimated 5.38 per cent have access to satellite or cable TV (2005).

Radio Athens has three medium-wave transmitters (150 kW, 50 kW and 15 kW) and two short-wave transmitters (100 kW each), for external broadcasting. There are also 37 FM transmitters of 3 or 10 kW (ERP) throughout Greece. Regional AM stations are at Thessaloniki, Corfu, Zakynthos (50 kW each), Rhodes, Chania (Crete), Komotini (5 kW each), Volos, Amalias (1 kW each) and Patrai (0.25 kW). For television programmes, broadcast from Athens, there are 17 transmitters of 30/6 or 10/2 kW (ERP). There is a licence fee, for radio receivers only.

After 1990 private commercial stations were allowed to operate, there are independent broadcasting companies and TV stations in various parts of the country.

Television
ERT, URL: http://www.ert.gr
Ant 1, URL: http://www.antenna.gr
Mega TV, URL: http://www.megatv.com
Alpha TV, URKL http://www.alphatv.gr/index.asp?a_id=45

Radio
Elliniki Radiophonia Tileorassi (ERT, SA), URL: http://www.ert.gr/en/

Antenna FM, URL: http://radio.antenna.gr/
Athina 9.84 FM Stereo, URL: http://www.athina984fm.gr/

Telecommunications
In 2011 there were an estimated 5.7 million landlines. In 2011 an estimated 12.2 millio people had a mobile phone. In 2009 there were an estimated 4.9 million internet users.

ENVIRONMENT

Major environmental concerns include air and water pollution. In 2006, total energy-relate carbon dioxide emissions were 103.2 million metric tonnes of CO^2 of which oil (62 per cen coal (33 per cent) and natural gas (6 per cent). In 2006, per capita energy-related carbo dioxide emissions totalled 10 metric tons. Figures for 2010 put total carbon dioxide emission at 92.99 million metric tons down from 101.02 million metric tons in 2009. (Source: EIA)

In 2005, total renewable water resources were estimated at 72 cu km.

Greece is party to international environmental agreements including Air Pollution, A Pollution-Nitrogen Oxides, Air Pollution-Sulfur 94, Antarctic-Environmental Protoco Antarctic-Marine Living Resources, Antarctic Treaty, Biodiversity, Climate Change, Climat Change-Kyoto Protocol, Desertification, Endangered Species, Environmental Modificatior Hazardous Wastes, Law of the Sea, Marine Dumping, Ozone Layer Protection, Ship Pollutior Tropical Timber 83, Tropical Timber 94, Wetlands. Greece has signed, but not ratified: Ai Pollution-Persistent Organic Pollutants, Air Pollution-Volatile Organic Compounds.

SPACE PROGRAMME

The Hellenic National Space Committee began co-operating with ESA in the early 1990s an it signed its first cooperation agreement in 1994. Greece became the 16th member of th European Space Agency in 2005.

GRENADA

Capital: St. George's (Population estimate, 2010: 34,000)

Head of State: H.M. Queen Elizabeth II (page 1420)

Governor General: Carlyle Arnold Glean (page 1431)

National Flag: A red border around the outside edges of the flag, with three small gold stars on the upper and the lower border. The rectangle inside the border is split into four triangles, the right and left ones being green and the upper and lower ones being gold. In the centre of the rectangle there is a red circle with a gold star inside. Inside the left hand triangle is a small nutmeg.

CONSTITUTION AND GOVERNMENT

Constitution
The former British colony became an independent member of the Commonwealth in 1974.

In 1979 Grenada's government was overthrown by the People's Revolutionary Government led by Maurice Bishop, the leader of the left-wing New Jewel Movement, who suspended the 1974 Constitution. Following internal disagreements in October 1983 Bishop was executed and the government was replaced by the Revolutionary Military Council (RMC). At the request of the Organisation of Eastern Caribbean States (OECS), the US, along with member countries of the OECS, invaded Grenada and ultimately detained the leaders of the RMC. An interim government was set up and elections followed in December 1984.

Under the 1974 Constitution, Grenada's head of state is the British sovereign represented by the Governor-General. The Cabinet is appointed by the Governor-General in consultation with the head of government, the Prime Minister.

To consult the constitution, please visit:
http://www.gov.gd/egov/docs/legislations/constitution/grenada_constitution_draft.pdf

Recent Events
In September 2004, Grenada was severely hit by Hurricane Ivan. Around 90 per cent of the island was damaged, including buildings, crops and infrastructure. In 2005, Hurricane Emily hit, causing yet further damage to homes and crops.

In January 2005, Grenada re-established diplomatic ties with China.

Legislature
Grenada has a bicameral parliament consisting of a Senate and House of Representatives.

Upper House
Grenada's 13 senators are appointed by the Governor-General in consultation with the Prime Minister (seven senators), the Leader of the Opposition (three senators) and other interested parties after consultation with the Prime Minister (three senators).
Senate, Houses of Parliament, PO Box 315, St George's, Grenada. Tel: +1 473 440 3456, fax: +1 473 440 4138

Lower House
The House of Representatives' 15 members are elected one from each of the country's 1 constituencies. The Parliament is elected for a five year term.
House of Representatives, Houses of Parliament, PO Box 315, St George's, Grenad Tel: +1 473 440 3456, fax: +1 473 440 4138

Cabinet (as at March 2013)
Prime Minister, Minister of Finance, Energy, National Security, Public Administratior Disaster Preparedness, Home Affairs and Information: Dr Keith Mitchell (page 1478
Deputy Prime Minister, Attorney General, Minister for Legal Affairs, Labour, Loca Government, Carricou and Martinique Affairs: Elvin Nimrod (page 1487)
Minister of Communications and Works, Physical Development, Public Utilitie and Information Commuications: Gregory Bowen (page 1393)
Minister of Education and Human Resource Development: Anthony Boatswain (pag 1390)
Minister of Health and Social Security: Dr Claris Modeste-Curwen (page 1479)
Minister of Youth Empowerment, Sports and Ecclesiastical Affairs: Emmalin Pierre
Minister of Tourism, Civil Aviation and Culture: Alexandria Otway-Noel
Minister of Social Development, Housing, and Community Development: Delm Thomas
Minister of Agriculture, Lands, Forestry, Fisheries and the Environment: Roland Bhol
Minister of Foreign Affairs and International Business: Nickolas Steele
Minister of Economic Development, Trade, Planning and Co-operatives: Oliver Josep

---

Ministries
Government portal, URL: http://www.gov.gd/
Office of the Prime Minister, Ministerial Complex, 6th Floor, Botanical Gardens Tanteen, St George's, Grenada. Tel: +1 473 440 2255, fax: +1 473 440 4116, e-mail pmsec@gov.gd, URL: http://pmoffice.gov.gd/
Ministry of Foreign Affairs, Ministerial Complex, 4th Floor, Botanical Gardens, Tanteen St George's. Grenada. Tel: +1 473 440 2640, fax: +1 473 440 4184, e-mail foreignaffairs@gov.gd, URL: http://www.gov.gd/ministries/foreign_affairs.html
Ministry of Education and Human Resources Development, Ministerial Complex Botanical Gardens, Tanteen, St George's, Grenada. Tel: +1 473 440 2737, fax: +1 473 44 6650, e-mail: mail@mined.edu.gd, URL: http://www.grenadaedu.com
Ministry of Carriacou and Petite Martinique Affairs, Beausejour, Carriacou Grenada. Tel: +1 473 443 6026, fax: +1 473 443 6040, e-mail: minccoupm@spiceisle.com URL: http://www.gov.gd/ministries/carriacou_pm_affairs.html
Ministry of Finance, Trade and Industry, Financial Complex, The Carenage, S George's, Grenada. Tel: +1 473 440 2731, fax: +1 473 440 4115, e-mail: finance@gov.gc URL: http://www.gov.gd/ministries/finance.html
Ministry of Legal Affairs, Communal House, 414 H A Blaize Street, St George's, Grenad Tel: +1 473 440 2962, fax: +1 473 435 2964, e-mail: legalaffairs@spiceisle.com, URL http://www.gov.gd/ministries/legal_affairs.html
Ministry of Health, Ministerial Complex, Southern Wing 1st and 2nd Floors, Botanica Gardens, Tanteen, St George's, Grenada. Tel: +1 473 440 2649, fax: +1 473 440 4126, e-mail min-healthgrenada@spiceisle.com, URL: http://www.gov.gd/ministries/health.html
Ministry of Agriculture, Land, Forestry and Fisheries, Ministerial Complex, 3r Floor, Botanical Gardens, Tanteen, St George's, Grenada. Tel: +1 473 440 2708, fax: +1 47: 440 4191, e-mail: agriculture@gov.gd, URL: http://www.gov.gd/ministries/agriculture.html

Ministry of Tourism and Civil Aviation, Ministerial Complex, Tanteen, St George's, Grenada. Tel: +1 473 440 0366, fax: +1 473 440 0443, e-mail: tourism@gov.gd, URL: http://www.gov.gd/ministries/tourism.html

Ministry of Youth Empowerment and Sports, Ministerial Complex, 3rd Floor, Botanical Gardens, Tanteen, St George's, Grenada. Tel: +1 473 440 6917, fax: +1 473 440 6924, e-mail: sports@gov.gd, URL: http://www.gov.gd/ministries/youth_sports.html

Ministry of Housing, Lands and Community Development, Ministerial Complex, 2nd Floor, Botanical Gardens, Tanteen, St George's, Grenada. Tel: +1 473 440 6917, fax: +1 473 440 6924, e-mail: mofhlcd@gov.gd, URL: http://www.gov.gd/ministries/housing.html

Ministry of the Environment, Foreign Trade and Export Development, Financial Complex, Carenage, St George's, Grenada. Tel: +1 473 440 2731, fax: +1 473 440 4115, URL: http://www.gov.gd/ministries/environment.html

Ministry of Labour, Social Security and Ecclesiastical Affairs, Ministerial Complex, Botanical Gardens, Tanteen, St George's, Grenada. Tel: +1 473 440 2269, fax: +1 473 440 7990, URL: http://www.gov.gd/ministries/labour.html

Ministry of Works, Physical Development and Public Utilities, Ministerial Complex, 4th Floor, Botanical Gardens, Tanteen, St George's, Grenada. Tel: +1 473 440 2271, fax: +1 473 440 4122, e-mail: ministryofworks@gov.gd, URL: http://www.gov.gd/ministries/works.html

Political Parties

New National Party (NNP), URL: http://www.nnpnews.com. Leader: Keith Mitchell
National Democratic Congress (NDC), URL: http://www.ndcgrenada.org. Leader: Tillman Thomas
Grenada United Labour Party/United Labour, Gladstone Road, Grenville, St. Andrew's, Grenada.

Elections

At the elections held in July 2008; the National Democratic Congress (NDC) won a small overall majority, defeating the New National Party (NNP), in power since 1995. The most recent election was held in February 2013 the NNP won all 15 seats.

Diplomatic Representation

British High Commission (based in Barbados), Lower Collymore Rock, PO Box 676, Bridgetown, Barbados. Tel: +1 246 430 7800, e-mail: britishhhc@sunbeach.net, URL: http://ukinbarbados.fco.gov.uk
High Commissioner: Paul Brummell (page 1396)
Honorary Consul: John Albanie ('Hard Landings', Pointe Salines, PO Box 38, St George's, Grenada. Tel: (473) 440 8844
Grenada High Commission, The Chapel, Archel Road, West Kensington, London W14. Tel: +44 (0)20 7385 4415, fax: +44 (0)20 7381 4807, e-mail: grenada@high-commission.demon.co.uk,
URL: http://www.grenadahclon.co.uk/high-commission.php
High Commissioner: Ruth Rouse (page 1505)
Embassy of Grenada, 1701 New Hampshire Avenue, NW, Washington, DC 20009, USA. Tel: +1 202 265 2561, fax: +1 202 265 2468, URL: http://www.grenadaembassyusa.org/
Ambassador: Gillian Bristol
Embassy of the United States, Lance Aux Epines, St. George's, Grenada. Tel: +473 444 1173 / 6, fax: +473 444 4820, e-mail: usemb-gd@caribsurf.com
Ambassador: Larry Leon Palmer
Permanent Mission of Grenada to the UN, 800 Second Avenue, Suite 400 K, New York, NY 10017, USA. Tel: +1 212 599 0301, fax: +1 212 599 1540, e-mail: grenada@un.int
Permanent Representative: Dessima Williams

LEGAL SYSTEM

The legal system in Grenada is based on the English common law. The Eastern Caribbean Supreme Court (ECSC) is the region's final court of appeal, and Grenada has a resident puisne judge. Magistrate's Courts deal with the lesser cases. The High Court and the Court of Appeal is above them. Until 2003, appeals could be heard by the Judicial Committee of Her Majesty's Privy Council in the United Kingdom. Grenada was among the eight nations (Barbados, Belize, Dominica, Guyana, Jamaica, St. Lucia, St. Vincent and the Grenadines, and Trinidad and Tobago) who ratified a treaty to establish the Caribbean Court of Justice (CCJ) to hear cases formerly taken to the Privy Council.

The government respects the human rights of its citizens. There have been allegations of corruption. Grenada retains the death penalty for ordinary crimes but no executions have been carried out since before 1999.

Eastern Caribbean Supreme Court, URL: http://www.eccourts.org/
Caribbean Court of Justice, URL: http://www.caribbeancourtofjustice.org/

LOCAL GOVERNMENT

Grenada is divided into six parishes and one dependency, Carriacou and Petite Martinique. The parishes are Saint Andrew, Saint David, Saint George, Saint John, Saint Mark and Saint Patrick. The constitution does not provide for local government but does provide for a council for Carriacou and Petite Martinique which would be the principal organ of local government.

AREA AND POPULATION

Area

Grenada, the most southerly of the Windward Islands, lies about 110 km south-west of St. Vincent and about 145 km north of Trinidad, and has a surface area of 344.5 sq. km. Grenada consists of three volcanic islands (Grenada and the smaller islands of Carriacou and Petit Martinique). Tropical rainforests and mangrove swamps contribute to its diverse vegetation. It has a tropical climate.

To view a map, consult http://www.lib.utexas.edu/maps/cia08/grenada_sm_2008.gif

Population

Grenada's population is 104,000 according to 2010 estimates, with around 34,000 in St George's. The annual growth rate is thought to be 0.3 per cent and population density is around 687 people per sq. mile. Approximately half of Grenada's population is under the age of 30. Just under 90 per cent of Grenadians is of African descent, and a further 8.2 per cent is of mixed East Indian, African, and/or Caucasian ancestry. This reflects Grenada's history of African slaves, East Indian servants, and European settlers. English is the official language and some people still speak French patois.

Births, Marriages, Deaths

The crude birth rate is 19.4 per 1,000 inhabitants, according to 2010 estimates, whilst the death rate is 6.5 per 1,000 people. Life expectancy at birth in 2009 was about 73 years (69 years for men and 77 years for women). Healthy life expectancy was 61 years and 62 years respectively. The infant mortality rate was 9 deaths per 1,000 live births, whilst the fertility rate was 2.2 children born per woman. (Source: http://www.who.int, World Health Statistics 2012)

Public Holidays 2014

1 January: New Year's Day
7 February: Independence Day
18 April: Good Friday
21 April: Easter Monday
1 May: Labour Day
9 June: Whit Monday
19 June: Corpus Christi
6 August: Emancipation Day
August: Carnival Monday and Tuesday
25 October: Thanksgiving Day
25 December: Christmas Day
26 December: Boxing Day

EMPLOYMENT

The main sources of employment in Grenada are agriculture, construction and tourism. Grenada had a total labour force of about 47,600 in 2008; over 60 per cent is employed in the services sector, 24 per cent in agriculture, and 14 per cent in industry. Recent figures show that the unemployment rate fell from 15.2 per cent in 1998 to 13 per cent in 2001, before rising to 18 per cent in 2005 and 25 per cent in 2008. Unemployment is particularly high amongst the Grenadian youth.

Following the devastation wrought by Hurricane Ivan, despite initial high unemployment in the tourist and other sectors, Grenadians benefited from job opportunities in the surging construction sector. Agricultural workers were hit harder; Ivan destroyed or significantly damaged a large percentage of Grenada's tree crops, and Hurricane Emily further damaged the sector. In the period following the hurricane, there was a surge of migration to the towns, and a reduction of young people taking up agricultural jobs.

BANKING AND FINANCE

Currency

The currency is the Eastern Caribbean Dollar (EC$). The US dollar is also accepted as legal tender.

Grenada is a member of the Eastern Caribbean Currency Union (ECCU) along with Anguilla, Antigua and Barbuda, Dominica, Grenada, Montserrat, St. Kitts and Nevis, St. Lucia, and St. Vincent and the Grenadines.

GDP/GNP, Inflation, National Debt

Grenada's economy is largely based on tourism, agriculture and construction. The tourism industry has been boosted by the building of an international airport but hurricanes including Ivan in 2004 mean the industry is subject to fluctuations. The service industry as a whole contributes about three-quarters of Grenada's GDP and employs nearly two-thirds of the labour force. Agriculture accounts for over 50 per cent of merchandise exports, just under 10 per cent of GDP, and 24 per cent of the labour force. The economy contracted in 2009-10 due to a fall in remittances and a decline in the tourism industry.

Economic growth for 2005 was estimated to be 1.5 per cent and 1.6 per cent in 2006. The main growth areas were the construction industry and cruise tourism. Preparations for the Cricket World Cup aided the construction sector, but also meant that capital spending rose to over 20 per cent of GDP in 2006. The main agriculture sector declined sharply (by 38 per cent) in 2005 due to Hurricane Ivan, but rebounded in 2006 (by 20.5 per cent). GDP grew by 4.3 per cent in 2007 and by an estimated 4.0 per cent in 2008. The global economic crisis was expected to lead to a downturn for the tourism sector in 2009 and this was reflected in the estimated growth figure for -5.5 per cent. Growth remained negative in 2010 at -1 per cent. GDP was estimated at US$800 million in 2011 with a growth rate of 0.5 per cent.

The average inflation rate for 2005 stood at 3.55, and in 2006 it was 3.8 per cent, driven by increases in fuel prices over the period. It was estimated at 3.9 per cent in 2007 inflation had fallen to an estimated -2.3 per cent in 2009. Inflation was estimated to be 3 per cent in 2011. Total external debt was US$525 million in 2011.

Foreign Investment

Various fiscal incentives encourage foreign investment particularly in areas involving export and high employment. Foreign investors are permitted to own 100 per cent of businesses.

GRENADA

Balance of Payments / Imports and Exports
Principal agricultural exports are bananas, cocoa, nutmegs, mace, fruit and vegetables, and fish. However, the importance of agriculture has been reduced over the last decade with natural disasters, declining international prices and disease affecting this sector. It is, however, establishing itself as a fair trade supplier. The main manufactured exports are flour, wheat bran, clothing, paints and varnish, paper products, malt, and animal feed.

Grenada's main trading partner for exports is Santa Lucia, accounting for 20 per cent. Other main partners include the US and Caribbean countries. Export revenue was an estimated to be US$30 million in 2010.

Principal imports are food, fuel and lubricants, animal and vegetable oils, chemicals, machinery, transport equipment, and manufactured material. Trinidad and Tobago is Grenada's main import trading partner, accounting for over 40 per cent of imports, followed by the USA. Estimates put import costs at US$300 million in 2011.

Grenada is a member of Caribbean Community and Common Market (CARICOM), along with other Caribbean islands and South American states.

Chambers of Commerce and Trade Organisations
Grenada Chamber of Commerce, URL: http://www.grenadachamber.org/

MANUFACTURING, MINING AND SERVICES

Primary and Extractive Industries
Grenada has no mineral resources and relies entirely on imports for its fuel requirements. It has expressed an interest in looking for oil and natural gas, and may consider Trinidad and Tobago as a potential partner in joint exploration operations. Imports/consumption of oil totalled 4.0 thousand barrels per day in 2011. Grenada neither imports nor uses natural gas or coal.

Energy
Grenada consumed a total of 0.005 quadrillion Btu in 2009, all of which was produced by petroleum.

Grenlec generates and distributes electricity from imported oil. Electricity is also generated for private use. The electricity on the island is 220/240 volts AC, 50Hz. Installed electricity capacity in 2010 was 0.05 GWe, with net generation at 0.20 billion kilowatthours (kWh). Electricity consumed that year was 0.18 billion kWh.

Manufacturing
Main manufacturing activities revolve around agricultural processing, including canning, spice grinding and distilling rum. There is also some garment manufacturing and production of electronic components.

Service Industries
Grenada's service industries contribute over three-quarters of GDP and employ nearly two-thirds of the labour force.

Tourism
Tourism is Grenada's main foreign exchange earner. Declining passenger confidence following the events of 11 September 2001 led to a fall in visitor numbers (123,351 total visitors of which 28,488 were from the UK), and Hurricane Ivan in September 2004 badly damaged the tourist infrastructure. The number of hotel rooms is an impediment to further growth, At the beginning of the 2005-06 tourist season, most of the sector had been rebuilt. Although cruise ships have since returned to Grenada and many hotels have reopened, slowdowns in the US, UK and Canadian economies in 2008 may delay a full recovery of the industry.
Grenada Board of Tourism, URL: http://www.grenada.org

Agriculture
The importance of this sector has declined over the last decade due to natural disasters, declining international prices and disease affecting the banana crop. Overall, agriculture is likely to remain weak for the foreseeable future. A National Strategy has recently been implemented, to address a decline in the number of people working in the sector.

Major crops include bananas, cocoa, sugar cane, and nutmeg. Grenada produces a third of the world's nutmeg. Banana growers have benefited by a growing niche market for Fair Trade crops within the UK market. Other crops are grown for local consumption, and there are plans for diversification. There are also forestry and fishing industries in Grenada.

Agricultural Production in 2008

Produce	Int. $'000	Tonnes
Nutmeg, mace & cardamoms	4,018	2,800
Avocados	1,028	1,600
Hen eggs, in shell	771	920
Coconuts	587	6,500
Mangoes, mangosteens, guavas	486	2,000
Indigenous chicken meat	449	385
Citrus fruit, nes	404	1,125
Grapefruit (inc. pomelos)	358	2,100
Vegetables fresh nes	356	1,900
Fruit fresh nes	319	2,000
Chillies & peppers, dry	267	90
Indigenous pigmeat	202	199

Source: http://faostat.fao.org/site/339/default.aspx FAOSTAT, Statistics Division, Food and Agriculture Organization of the UN

Grants and training by Japan are helping to expand Grenada's fisheries sector. The export earnings on this sector are currently in the region of EC$6 million.

COMMUNICATIONS AND TRANSPORT

Travel Requirements
USA, Australian and EU citizens require a passport valid for six months from date of departure but do not require a visa for stays of up to three months. Canadians who can provide proof of citizenship do not need a passport or a visa for stays of up to three months. Nationals not referred to above should contact the high commission or embassy to check visa requirements.

National Airlines
The main airline is Leeward Islands Air Transport, which operates on regional routes.
Airlines of Carriacou, Point Salines International Airport, Point Salines, St. George's, Grenada, W.I. Tel: +809 444 3549 / 1475, fax: +809 444 2898

International Airports
The international airport of Point Salines is suitable for large aircraft. There is also a small airport at Lauriston on Carriacou.
Point Salines International Airport, Point Salines, St. George's, Grenada, W.I.

Roads
Grenada has a well developed road system of around 1,127 km. (or 700 miles), two thirds of which is paved. The roads in the mountainous areas are often narrow and winding. Vehicles are driven on the left.

Ports and Harbours
St. George's is the island's principal port which can be used by ocean-going vessels and small craft. It has a sheltered harbour with a maximum depth of 30 feet, an 800-foot pier with space for about 3 vessels, 27,500 sq. feet of warehouse facilities, and a 250-foot schooner berth with a depth of 18 feet. Anchorage and facilities for yachts are also offered at Prickly Bay on the south-east coast and at Secret Harbour which is situated south of St George's. There is a port at Hillsborough in Carriacou which is currently being expanded. There are passenger and cargo services between Grenada and neighbouring islands, water taxis and charter yachts available for hire. A ferry service between the islands of Grenada, Carriacou and Petite Martinique.

HEALTH

There are three hospitals on Grenada: General Hospital in St George's, Princess Alice Hospital in St Andrew's and Princess Royal Hospital in Carriacou. Six health centres and 30 district medical stations undertake maternity and child welfare work under the charge of a nurse or midwife. Government hospitals and clinics provide free medical and dental treatment. The are also care homes for the disabled and elderly. In 2009, Grenada spent approximately 9.5 per cent of its total budget on healthcare, accounting for 49.2 per cent of all healthcare spending. Private out-of-pocket expenditure accounts for almost all the rest. Total expenditure on health care equated to 6.2 per cent of the country's GDP. Per capita expenditure on health amounted to US$462, compared to US$3391 in 2000.

According to 2000-07 WHO figures there are 80 doctors (10 per 10,000 population), 326 nurses and midwives (40 per 10,000 population), and 20 dentists. There are an estimated 26 hospital beds per 10,000 population.

In 2008, approximately 97 per cent of the urban population had access to improved drinking water and 96 per cent to improved sanitation. In the same year, 97 per cent of the rural population had access to improved sanitation.

The infant mortality rate in 2009 was put at 9 per 1,000 live births and the child mortality rate (under fives) was 11 per 1,000 live births. The main causes of childhood mortality are: prematurity 6 per cent & congenital anomalies 44 per cent. (Source: http://www.who.int, World Health Statistics 2012)

EDUCATION

Primary and secondary education is free and compulsory on the island for 6-14 year olds. There are 57 primary schools and 19 public secondary schools. Further education is provided at the Grenada National College, the Technical and Vocational Institute and three technical centres: St. Patrick's, St. David's and St. John's. There is also a School of Medicine and a branch of the Extra-Mural Department of the University of the West Indies in St George's. Grenada also has 24 centres around the country, teaching housecrafts and handicrafts. Adult literacy in Grenada is 96 per cent.

In 2007, some 80 per cent of small children attended a pre-primary school and 76 per cent went to primary school (below the regional average of 95 per cent). Recent figures show that 78 per cent of students of the relevant age attended secondary school, which was above the regional average of 67 per cent. In 2004, 12.9 per cent of government expenditure was spent on education.

RELIGION

Grenada is a predominantly Christian island and there is freedom of worship. Grenada has a religious liberty rating of 10 on a scale of 1 to 10 (10 is most freedom). (Source: World Religion Database)

Recent figures show 53 per cent of the island as being Roman Catholic, 13.8 per cent Anglican, 2 per cent Methodist, 8 per cent Seventh Day Adventist and 1.3 per cent spiritualists.

COMMUNICATIONS AND MEDIA

Freedom of media expression is provided for by law.

Newspapers
There are no daily newspapers.
The Barnacle (monthly); The Consumer (monthly); The Grenada Guardian (weekly); The Grenada Today (weekly, URL: http://www.belgrafix.com/); The Grenadian Voice (weekly); The Informer (weekly, URL: http://www.belgrafix.com/).

Broadcasting
GBC television is jointly owned by the government of Grenada and the Caribbean Communications Network of Trinidad and Tobago. CBC operates a television station and two radio stations. Several private stations also operate. Cable is also available. It is estimated that there are 54,700 radios and 31,000 television sets on the island.
Grenada Broadcasting Commission, URL: http://www.klassicgrenada.com/

Telecommunications
Recent estimates show there are 28,500 main telephone lines in use, and an estimated 60,000 mobile telephones (2008).

Internet users numbered about 24,000 in 2008.

ENVIRONMENT

Grenada is a party to the following international environmental agreements: Biodiversity, Climate Change, Climate Change-Kyoto Protocol, Desertification, Endangered Species, Law of the Sea, Ozone Layer Protection, and Whaling.

According to the EIA, in 2010, Grenada's emissions from the consumption of fossil fuels totalled 0.43 million metric tons of carbon dioxide.

GUATEMALA
Republic of Guatemala
República de Guatemala

Capital: Guatemala City (Population estimate - metropolitan area: 2.5 million)

Head of State: Otto Perez Molina (President) (page 1494)

Vice-President: Roxanna Baldetti Elias (page 1382)

National Flag: A tricolour pale-wise, blue, white, blue, charged with the coat of arms centred and inscribed 'Libertad 15 de Setiembre 1821'

CONSTITUTION AND GOVERNMENT

Constitution
Guatemala became independent of Spanish colonial rule in 1821. The following year it joined the Mexican empire. Guatemala became a fully independent nation in 1839. There then followed a series of civilian and military governments. Civil war broke out in the 1960s and lasted for 36 years, ending in 1996 when the government and the Unidad Revolucionaria Nacional Guatemalteca (URNG) signed a definitive peace treaty. A new constitution came into effect in January 1986. It was briefly suspended in 1993 and amended in the same year.

To consult the constitution (in Spanish), please visit: http://200.12.63.122/Pdf/Normativa/Constitucion.PDF

International Relations
Guatemala's claim on territory in Belize:
An area covering the southern half of Belize has always been claimed by Guatemala and is the reason for a continuing British Army presence in the country. Whilst Guatemala recognised Belize's independence in 1991, it never formally relinquished its claim, and in 2000 the claim was renewed. Talks were held in Washington to try to resolve the situation and, in 2002, the two nations agreed a draft settlement. This was due to be the subject of referenda in both countries, but in 2003 Guatemalan officials notified the OAS (Organization of American States who were acting as facilitators) that they could not accept the recommendations for constitutional reasons. Discussions continue under the auspices of the OAS.

Guatemala's 36 year long civil war ended in 1996 with the signing of a series of 'Peace Accords', aimed at redressing longstanding injustices and modernising the country. The international community undertook to monitor the implementation of these 'Peace Accords'.

Guatemala participates in several regional groups, particularly those related to trade and the environment. Guatemala also originated the idea for, and is the seat of, the Central American Parliament (PARLACEN)

Guatemala has deployed its troops to UN peacekeeping operations in Haiti and the Congo.

Recent Events
Efrain Rios Montt, a military leader under whom the army committed atrocities during the civil war, was put under house arrest in 2004. In July, the state admitted guilt in human rights crimes, and paid damages amounting to $3.5 million to victims of the civil war. Sr. Rios Montt became a congressman in July 2007.

In March 2005, the Guatemalan Government ratified the Central American Free Trade Agreement with the United States, to facilitate access to the US market. There were protests in the capital.

Tropical Storm Stan hit Guatemala in October 2005, causing major flooding and landslides, and sweeping away two villages. Flood waters reached two metres in Quetzaltenango, the second most important city in Guatemala. The official death toll reached 652, but the real figure could be as high as 2,000, as whole communities were engulfed by landslides.

In May, Guatemala ratified an international adoption treaty, to ensure babies are not bought or stolen. International election monitors voiced concern over the high murder rate among political candidates and activists in the approach to elections in September. The presidential election was won by Alvaro Colom of the National Unity of Hope Party in November 2007.

The former president Alfonso Portillo was extradited from Mexico in October 2008 to face corruption charges. It is alleged that US$15 million of government defence money was misappropriated.

In May 2009, tens of thousands of Guatemalans took to the streets when a video emerged in which a lawyer, Rodrigo Rosenberg, accused the President Alvaro Colom and three others of murder and corruption. Mr. Rosenberg, who was shot dead on May 10, recorded the video days earlier. Mr. Colom denied involvement and said that the accusations were a right-wing political conspiracy designed to bring down his government.

In 2010 a state of emergency was declared after the Pacaya volcano erupted.

The first round of presidential elections took place in September 2011. Otto Perez Molina gained most votes but not enough for an outright majority necessitating a second round of voting in November 2011 which Mr Perez Molina duly won.

The former military leader Efrain Rios Mott, now 85, was charged in January 2012 on separate counts of genocide and crimes against humanity, charges relating to the massacres of an estimated 1,770 indigenous people and the forced displacement of 29,000 others. As a congressman Mr Mott had immunity from prosecution; this ceased when his term of office ended in January. The trial began in January 2013.

In March 2012, President Perez Molina proposed the decriminalisiation of drugs as a way of combatting the illegal narcotics trade.

In November 2012, Guatemala was his by two major earthquakes, more than 50 people were killed.

Legislature
The Constitution provides for a unicameral National Congress of 113 members representing the legislative authority - 75 elected directly, the remainder by proportional representation, all members serve a four year term. Executive authority is exercised by the president, assisted by the vice-president and cabinet. The term of office for a president lasts for four years and is non-renewable. Suffrage is universal and obligatory for the literate population; for those who are illiterate, suffrage is optional.
National Congress, 9a Av9-44, Guatemala City, Guatemala. Tel: +502 232 1260, URL: http://www.congreso.gob.gt
President 2008-2012: Aristides Baldomero Crespo Villegas

Cabinet (as at March 2013)
Minister of Foreign Affairs: Luis Fernando Carrera Castro
Minister of Defence: Maj. Gen. Ulises Noe Anzueto Giron
Minister of Public Health: Dr Jorge Alejandro Villavicencio Alvarez
Minister of Economy: Sergio De La Torre
Minister of Energy and Mining: Erick Archila Dehesa
Minister of Communications: Alejandro Sinibaldi
Minister of Agriculture, Livestock and Food: Elmer Lopez Rodriquez
Minister of Cultural Affairs and Sport: Carlos Batzin
Minister of Labour and Social Provision: Carlos Contreras
Minister of the Environment and Natural Resources: Roxana Sobenes
Minister of Education: Cynthia Del Aguila
Minister of Public Finance: Pavel Centeno
Minister of Social Assistance: Luz Lainfiesta
Minister of the Interior: Mauricio Lopez Bonilla

GUATEMALA

Ministries

Office of the President, Palacio Nacional, 6a calle y 7a avenida, Zona 1, Guatemala City, Guatemala. Tel: +502 2221 4428, URL: http://www.guatemala.gob.gt

Ministry of the Economy, 8a avenida 10-43, Zona 1, Guatemala City, Guatemala. Tel: +502 2412 0200, fax: +502 2412 0200, URL: http://www.mineco.gob.gt

Ministry of Foreign Affairs, 2a avenida 4-47, Zona 10, Guatemala City, Guatemala. Tel: +502 2410 0000, fax: +502 2410 0011, e-mail: webmaster@minex.gob.gt, URL: http://www.minex.gob.gt

Ministry of Agriculture, Livestock and Food, Edificio Monja Blanca, 7a avenida 12-90, Zona 13, Guatemala City, Guatemala. Tel: +502 2413 7000, fax: +502 2413 7006, e-mail: infoagro@maga.gob.gt, URL: http://www.maga.gob.gt

Ministry of Communications, Transport, Public Works and Housing, 8a avenida y 15 calle, Zona 13, Antiguo Edificio COCESNA, Guatemala City, Guatemala. Tel: +502 2223 4000, fax: +502 2223 4000, e-mail: relpublicas@micivi.gob.gt, URL: http://www.micivi.gob.gt

Ministry of Culture and Sport, 12 avenida 11-11, Zona 1, Guatemala City, Guatemala. Tel: +502 2253 0545, fax: +502 2253 0544, URL: http://www.mcd.gob.gt

Ministry of Defence, avenida "La Reforma" 1-45, Zona 10, Antigua Escuela Politécnica, Guatemala City, Guatemala. Tel: +502 2414 7000, fax: +502 2362 0115, URL: http://www.mindef.mil.gt

Ministry of Education, 6a calle 1-87, Zona 10, Guatemala City, Guatemala. el: +502 2411 9595, fax: +502 2411 9595, URL: http://www.mineduc.gob.gt

Ministry of Energy and Mines, Diagonal 17, nos. 29-78, Zona 11, Guatemala City, Guatemala. Tel: +502 2476 0679, fax: +502 2476 0679, e-mail: informatica@mem.gob.gt, URL: http://www.mem.gob.gt

Ministry of the Environment and Natural Resources, Edificio MARN, 20 calle 28-58, Zona 10, Guatemala City, Guatemala. Tel: +502 2423 0500, URL: http://www.marn.gob.gt

Ministry of the Interior, 6a avenida 13-71, Zona 1, Guatemala City, Guatemala. Tel: +502 2413 8888, fax: +502 7926 1035, URL: http://www.mingob.gob.gt

Ministry of Labour and Social Provision, 7a avenida 3-33, Zona 9, Edificio Empresarial, Guatemala City, Guatemala. Tel: +502 2422 2500, fax: +502 2422 2500, URL: http://www.mintrabajo.gob.gt

Ministry of Public Finance, 8a avenida y 21a calle, Zona 1, Centro civico, Guatemala City, Guatemala. Tel: +502 2248 5120, fax: +502 2248 5127, URL: http://www.minfin.gob.gt

Ministry of Public Health and Social Assistance, 6a avenida 3-45, Zona 11, Escuela de Enfermeriam Guatemala City, Guatemala. Tel: +502 2475 4682, fax: +502 2475 4682, e-mail: info@mspas.gob.gt, URL: http://www.mspas.gob.gt

Political Parties

Union Democratica (UD), Gran Alianza Nacional; Unidad Revolucionaria Nacional Guatemalteca; Frente Republicano Guatemalteco, Partido de Avazada Nacional; Unidad Nacional de la Esperanza (UNE), Union del Cambio Nacionalista, Partido Patriota, Centro de Accion Social, Partido Unionista

Elections

Suffrage is universal for adults 18 and over who are not serving on active duty with the armed forces or police. In the past, several procedural obstacles reduced participation by poor, rural, and indigenous people; however, the implementation in 2007 of voting reform legislation nearly doubled the number of polling places, resulting in higher participation in rural areas.

The most recent presidential election took place in September 2011. A second round took place on 5 November after Otto Perez Molina failed to achieve an outright win. Mr Perez Molina won 36 per cent of the vote and Manuel Baldizon 23 per cent. In the second round, Mr Perez Molina won over 54 per cent of the vote.

Legislative elections were held on 11 September 2011. The PP won most votes with 26.7 per cent of the vote (up 11 per cent from 2007) but fell short of an overall majority. The governing UNE-GANA fell to 22.63 per cent of the vote and the LIDER party 8.9 per cent.

Diplomatic Representation

US Embassy, Avenida Reforma 7-01, Zona 10, Guatemala City, Guatemala. Tel: +502 2326 4000, fax: +502 2334 4000 / 1549, URL: http://guatemala.usembassy.gov
Ambassador: Arnold A. Chacon

British Embassy, Edificio Torre Internacional, Nivel 11, 16 Calle 00-55, Zona 10, Guatemala. Tel: +502 2380 7300, fax:+502 2380 7339, e-mail: embassy@intelnett.com; URL: http://ukinguatemala.fco.gov.uk/en
Ambassador: Sarah Dickson (page 1415)

Embassy of Guatemala, 13 Fawcett Street, London, SW10 9HN, United Kingdom. Tel: +44 (0)20 7351 3042, fax: +44 (0)20 7376 5708
Ambassador: HE Mr Alfonso Roberto Jose Matta Fahsen

Embassy of Guatemala, 2220 R St. N.W., Washington, DC 20008, USA. Tel: +1 202 745 4952, fax: +1 202 745 1908, URL: http://www.guatemala-embassy.org/
Ambassador: Francisco Villagran de Leon

Permanent Representative of Guatemala to the United Nations, 57 Park Avenue, New York, NY 10016, USA. Tel: +1 212 679 4760, fax: +1 212 685 8741, URL: http://www.guatemalaun.org
Ambassador & Permanent Representative: Gert Rosenthal (page 1505)

LEGAL SYSTEM

The independence of the judiciary is guaranteed under the 1985 Constitution. The legal system comprises a Supreme Court consisting of 13 members, ten Courts of Appeal, 33 civil courts of first instance and 10 penal courts of the first instance. Supreme Court and Court of Appeal justices are elected for a five-year terms by Congress from nominations submitted by the bar association, law school deans, a university rector, and appellate judges. The judges of courts of first instance are appointed by the Supreme Court. Courts of private jurisdiction deal with labor disputes, administrative litigation and military affairs.

There is a separate Constitutional Court, composed of five judges, each elected for five-yea terms. One is elected by Congress, one by the Supreme Court of Justice, one is appointed b the President, one is elected by Superior Council of the Universidad San Carlos de Guatemala and one by the Bar Association (Colegio de Abogados). The Attorney General is the lega representative of the State of Guatemala.

Violence is now a major problem in Guatemala. In 2006, the country had a national homicide rate of 47 per 100,000 inhabitants, rising to 108 per 100,000 in Guatemala City - rates tha position Guatemala as one of the world's most violent countries. According to official police figures, some 5,885 Guatemalans died violently in 2006, a 60 per cent increase on the figure for 2003. Guatemala has a single-digit conviction rate for murder; the judiciary suffers from inefficiency and intimidation. In recent years Guatemala has become a transit point fo cocaine shipments, and there has been rapid growth of youth gangs known as maras.

In December 2006, the government and the UN agreed to the creation of the joint Internationa Commission Against Impunity in Guatemala (CICIG). In 2007, three Salvadoran parliamentarians were assassinated by senior members of the Guatemalan National Civiliar Police, including the head of the organized crime unit. The mandate of CICIG is to promote the prosecution of illegal security organizations - powerful clandestine groups allegedly responsible for attacks on human rights defenders, as well as involved in corruption, organized crime, drug trafficking and political violence. The Commission began to function in 2008.

Guatemala retains the death penalty.

Attorney General: Claudia Paz y Paz
Office of the Attorney General: URL: http://www.pgn.gob.gt/
International Commission Against Impunity in Guatemala, URL: http://cicig.org
Procurador de los Derechos Humanos, URL: http://www.pdh.org.gt/

LOCAL GOVERNMENT

The country is divided for administrative purposes into 22 departments: Guatemala, Sar Marcos, Hueuetenango, Alta Verapaz, Baja Verapaz, Quezaltenango, Quiché, Jutiapa, Escuintla, Suchitepéquez, Chimal-tenango, Chiquimula, Santa Rosa, Totonicapán, Sololá, Jalapa, Zacapa, Retalhuleu, Sacatepéquez, Izabal, Progreso and El Péten. Each has a governor appointed by the President. The departments are divided into 331 municipalities, each of which has an elected mayor and council.

The most recent local and municipal elections took place on 11 September 2011.

AREA AND POPULATION

Area

Guatemala is situated in Central America, bounded in the north and west by Mexico, in the south by the Pacific and El Salvador, and in the east by Honduras, the Gulf of Honduras and Belize (formerly British Honduras). The total area of Guatemala is 108,889 sq. km. Mountains run through the country from north to south and from east to west. There are lowlands to the north and to the south of the mountains. The high plateau in the centre is volcanic.

The climate is tropical on the coasts but temperate in the highlands.

To view a map of Guatemala, please visit:
http://www.un.org/Depts/Cartographic/map/profile/guatemal.pdf

Population

Population was estimated in 2010 at 14.389 million, with an annual growth rate of around 2.5 per cent for the period 2000-10. The median age is 19 years. An estimated 41 per cent of the population are under 15 years old and six per cent over 60 years old. Most of Guatemala's population is rural, though urbanisation is accelerating; 49 per cent of the population now live in urban areas. The largest cities have populations as follows: Guatemala City, 2,500,000; Quezaltenango, 268,000; Escuintla, 62,500.

Mayan Indians make up approximately 66 per cent of the population. There is also a small community of 'Garifuna' (of Caribbean descent). The remainder are Guatemalans of Spanish and European descent. Spanish is the official national language but most of the population speak one of the 22 Mayan dialects. The peace accords signed in December 1996 provided for the translation of some official documents, including voting information.

Births, Marriages, Deaths

In 2010, the crude birth rate was 32.3 births per 1,000 inhabitants, whilst the death rate was 5.8 per 1,000 people. Life expectancy at birth in 2009 was 66 years for males and 73 years for females. Healthy life expectancy was 60 years. Infant mortality in the same year stood at 25 deaths per 1,000 children. The fertility rate is around 4.0 children per woman. (Source: http://www.who.int, World Health Statistics 2012)

Public Holidays 2014

1 January: New Year
17 April: Holy Thursday
18 April: Good Friday
20 April: Easter Sunday
1 May: Labour Day
30 June: Army Day
15 August: The Assumption of the Virgin Mary
15 September: Independence Day (National Day)
20 October: Revolution Day
1 November: All Saints Day
24- 25 December: Christmas
31 December: New Year's Eve

EMPLOYMENT

The Guatemalan work force numbered around 5.65 million people in 2006, equivalent to an activity rate of 42.8 per cent. 5.3 million people over the age of 10 were employed; of these, 3.3 million were men. 100,100 people were unemployed. (Source: International Labour Organisation, November 2008).

Around 15 per cent of the labour force is employed in the agricultural sector (though around half the population is involved in some form of farming, mainly subsistence and outside the official economy); 37 per cent of the workforce is engaged in industry and commerce, 40 per cent in the service sector, and about four per cent work in mining, construction and utilities. Around 74,000 children aged up to 9 years old were working in 2006.

Total Employment by Economic Activity

Occupation	2006
Agriculture, hunting, forestry & fishing	1,791,400
Mining & quarrying	7,500
Manufacturing	854,800
Electricity, gas & water supply	12,400
Construction	354,900
Wholesale & retail trade, repairs, hotels & restaurants	1,226,900
Transport, storage & communications	160,700
Financial intermediation, real estate, renting & business activities	176,100
Public admin. & defence; compulsory social security	115,500
Education	219,800
Health & social work, other community, social & personal service activities	457,400
Extra-territorial organisations & bodies	13,200

Source: Copyright © International Labour Organization (ILO Dept. of Statistics, http://laborsta.ilo.org)

BANKING AND FINANCE

Currency
One quetzal (Q) = 100 centavos

GDP/GNP, Inflation, National Debt
According to the World Bank, Guatemala has one of the most unequal income distributions in the hemisphere. The wealthiest 10 per cent of the population receives almost one-half of all income, and the top 20 per cent receives two-thirds of all income. Around 70 per cent of the population lives below the poverty line. Guatemala's economy is dominated by the private sector, which generates about 90 per cent of GDP. The government plans financial sector restructuring and reforms to boost growth and reduce poverty. Natural resources include oil, timber and nickel. Remittances from a large expatriate community have become the primary source of foreign income, exceeding the total value of exports and tourism combined.

Growth was slow over the first three years of the century, but the economy picked up in 2004. By 2007, GDP had reached US$24.16 billion, with average growth over the year of 5.7 per cent. In 2008, GDP was estimated at US$25.65 billion with a growth rate of 4 per cent estimated figures for 2009 show GDP growth dropped to 0.6 per cent. In 2009, the manufacturing sector accounted for 18.3 per cent of GDP, whilst the agricultural sector accounted for around 13.4 per cent of GDP and 24 per cent of exports. Around half the population is involved in farming, most of it subsistence. The main products are coffee, bananas and sugar. Per capita income was estimated at US$4,690. In 2011, GDP was estimated to have risen to US$40 billion. Per capita GDP was estimated at US$5,000.

Inflation in 2003 ran at 5.8 per cent rising to an estimated 9.23 per cent in 2004 and 2005, before falling to around 6.5 per cent in 2006. Inflation was estimated at 5.9 per cent in 2007.

Foreign Investment
Since the end of the civil war, international financial organisations and countries such as France, Italy, Germany, Spain, Japan and the USA have increased financing in development projects. However, their continued support is dependant upon reforms taking place.

The Berger administration (2004-2007) made promotion of foreign investment and competitiveness a priority. In March 2005, the government ratified the Central American Free Trade Agreement (CAFTA) with the USA. The Agreement became operational in July 2006, and foreign direct investment (FDI) inflows increased from $591.6 million in 2006 to $723.5 million in 2007.

Balance of Payments / Imports and Exports
Exports of goods earned an estimated US$10 billion in 2011 (compared to US$7.8 billion in 2008). The main agricultural exports were coffee, cotton, sugar, bananas, flowers and plants, timber and rice. Crude oil and chemical products were also exported. Guatemala's major trading partners for exports are the US (38 per cent) and the Central American Common Market (30.4 per cent).

Imports of goods and services cost US$15 billion in 2011 (compared to US$14.5 billion in 2008). Imports included machinery and equipment, fuels, mineral products, chemical products, vehicles and transport materials, plastic materials and products. Major suppliers were the USA (40 per cent), Central American Common Market (10.7 per cent) and Mexico (10 per cent) and China (8 per cent).

Central Bank
Banco de Guatemala, PO Box 365, 7a Avenida 22-01, Zona 1, 01001 Guatemala City, Guatemala. Tel: +502 230 6222 / 230 6232, fax: +502 253 4035, URL: http://www.banguat.gob.gt

President: Lic. Edgar Baltazar Barquin Duran

Chambers of Commerce and Trade Organisations
Guatemalan Chamber of Commerce, URL: http://www.camaradecomercio.org.gt/

MANUFACTURING, MINING AND SERVICES

Primary and Extractive Industries
The mining sector now accounts for only 0.4 per cent of GDP. Many types of mineral deposits, both metal and non-metal, are present, but remain almost completely unexploited. Copper is the principal hard mineral. Other minerals extracted include lead, zinc, silver, antimony and tungsten.

Guatemala has proven oil reserves of 0.08 billion barrels, and current production is at 11,200 barrels a day. Consumption is currently 91,000 barrels a day and so imports around 79,980 barrels per day. There is no refining capacity at present.

Guatemala has small reserves of natural gas (109 billion cubic feet), although these are not being exploited at present.

Energy
Overall energy consumption rose to 0.216 quadrillion Btu in 2009, whilst production stood at 0.064 quadrillion Btu. The country had installed electricity capacity of 2.75 gigawatts, and generated 8.62 billion kilowatthours over 2010. Consumption was 7.95 billion kilowatthours over the same year.

In 2001, the Central American countries agreed to integrate their electricity grids, creating a regional wholesale electricity market (Mercado Eléctrico Regional - MER). The first stage of the project is construction of the Sistema de Interconexión Eléctrica de los Países América Central (SIEPAC), a transmission line connecting Panama, Costa Rica, Honduras, Nicaragua, El Salvador, and Guatemala.

Under the Puebla-Panama Plan, interconnectors are planned to link SIEPAC with the electricity grids of southern Mexico and Belize. It is hoped that SIEPAC will increase security of supply, reduce the cost of electricity and attract foreign investment

Manufacturing
Manufacturing accounted for 18.5 per cent of GDP in 2007. Most manufacturing is light assembly and food processing, geared to the domestic, U.S., and Central American markets. Recent figures show that production of manufactured goods included 2.4 billion cigarettes, 83,000 cubic metres of sawnwood, 17,000 tonnes of paper and paperboard, 790,000 tonnes of cement, 100 tonnes of lead, 10,000 tonnes of nitrogen fertilizer and 10,000 metric tons of phosphate fertilizer. Pharmaceuticals, chemicals, soap, sugar, electrical machinery, plastics, tyres and textiles are also produced.

Service Industries
The Guatemalan Institute of Tourism is responsible for the development of a tourist policy. An increase in the number of tourists arriving in Guatemala has been observed over the past few years. In 2006, there were 1,502,000 visitors to Guatemala.
Guatemala Tourist Commission, URL: http://www.visitguatemala.com

Agriculture
Guatemala is predominantly an agricultural country and production accounts for 24 per cent of exports. Over half the population is involved in subsistence farming, though only 13 per cent are officially employed in the sector. Much of the soil is fertile, and climatic conditions allow a variety of crops to be grown. Coffee, sugar, and banana exports are an important source of foreign exchange. Cardamoms, vegetables, flowers and plants, timber, rice and rubber are also grown.

Agricultural Production in 2010

Produce	Int. $'000*	Tonnes
Sugar cane	728,545	22,216,700
Bananas	714,658	2,637,570
Coffee, green	273,871	254,915
Indigenous chicken meat	229,837	161,356
Indigenous cattle meat	202,093	74,811
Hen eggs, in shell	182,255	219,746
Cow milk, whole, fresh	140,428	450,000
Beans, dry	112,638	198,113
Natural rubber	111,981	97,900
Tomatoes	110,941	300,193
Indigenous pigmeat	90,550	58,904
Other melons (inc. cantaloupes)	88,444	480,434

*unofficial figures
Source: http://faostat.fao.org/site/339/default.aspx Food and Agriculture Organization of the United Nations, Food and Agricultural commodities production

Sardines and red snapper are found in abundance in Guatemala's territorial waters. Natural and artificial lagoons in Guatemala's South Coast area have led to rapid development of shrimp farming, which has become a principal export to the USA and Europe. Figures for 2010 put the total catch at 21,850 tonnes.

20,000 tons of rubber are produced each year. There are 383 plantations which plant 38,800 hectares. Mexico is a major importer of Guatemalan rubber.

Guatemala has 4.4 million hectares of forest - large areas of which contain precious woods - supplying the wood working and furniture industries.

GUATEMALA

COMMUNICATIONS AND TRANSPORT

Travel Requirements
US, Canadian, Australian and EU citizens need a passport valid for at least six months, but do not require a visa for stays of up to 90 days.

Other nationals should contact the embassy to check visa requirements.

In June 2006, Guatemala entered a "Central America-4 (CA-4) Border Control Agreement" with El Salvador, Honduras, and Nicaragua. Under the terms of the agreement, U.S. citizens and other eligible foreign nationals, who legally enter any of the four countries, may travel for up to 90 days among the four without obtaining additional visas or tourist entry permits for the other three countries. For further information, travelers should contact the Guatemalan Embassy.

International Airports
There are two international airports at Santa Elena Petén and *La Aurora* in Guatemala City. There are 12 airports with paved runways in total.

Railways
There are 886 km of railway track, most of which is operated by the Government-owned Ferrocarril de Guatemala (FEGUA).

Roads
The Ministry of Communications, Transport and Public Works estimates that 43 per cent of the 3,425 km paved road system is in poor condition. Guatemala is linked by the Pan-American Highway toMexico, Honduras and El Salvador. Vehicles are driven on the right.

Shipping
There are sailings to Puerto Barrios from New York, New Orleans and the Gulf ports by United Fruit Co. and to the US West Coast by Grace Lines. Ferries also link Puerto Barrios and Livingston, with Punta Gorda, Belize.

Ports and Harbours
The chief ports are Puerto Barrios, Santo Tomás de Castilla (formerly Matías de Gálvez), Livingston on the Atlantic and San José and Champerico on the Pacific.

HEALTH

In 2009, Guatemala spent approximately 17.09 per cent of its total budget on healthcare, accounting for 37.0 per cent of all healthcare spending. Total expenditure on health care equated to 6.9 per cent of the country's GDP. Per capita GDP was US$184 in 2009, compared to US$95.

Figures for 2000-07 show that there are 9,965 physicians (9 per 10,000 population), 44,986 nurses and midwives (41 per 10,000 population) and 2,046 dentists. There are an estimated 7 hospital beds per 10,000 population.

Approximately 80 per cent of Guatemalans live in poverty, and around 7.6 million live in extreme poverty. There is chronic malnutrition among the poor. The infant and child mortality rates (respectively 25 deaths per 1,000 live births and 32 deaths per 1,000 live births) are among the highest in the Central American region. Rural indigenous women have an average of 6.2 births per 1000 (highest rate in Latin America), and the estimated maternal mortality rate in 2009 was 120 per 100,000 live birth, with the figure for the indigenous population three times higher than for the non indigenous population. The HIV/AIDS epidemic is growing and there is low antiretroviral coverage. The male/female ratio is 1:1. Guatemala reports around 60 per cent of all the malaria cases in Central America. In 2010 there were 7,198 reported cases of malaria, 3 of leprosy, and 3,322 of TB. (Source: http://www.who.int, World Health Statistics 2012)

EDUCATION

Education is free at elementary level. In urban areas it is compulsory between seven and 14 years. Guatemala has recently undertaken moves to improve its educational services and the enrolment rate at primary school has increased from 89 per cent in 2002 to 95 per cent in 2007. In 2006, 37 per cent of girls and 40 per cent of boys enrolled in secondary school, and 9 per cent of tertiary-aged students registered for in higher education.

According to UNESCO figures, in 2007, 73.2 per cent of adults and 85.5 per cent of 15-24 year olds were literate. However, in some regions, 87 per cent of the female indigenous population is illiterate and less than 1 per cent receives secondary education. Most only speak a Mayan dialect. In comparison with the regional literacy rates, the Guatemalan rates continue to be low. (Source: UNESCO, UIS)

RELIGION

The predominant religion is Roman Catholicism (followed by 54 per cent of the population), although there are a number of Protestant groups. Other religions also have freedom of worship. Guatemala has a religious liberty rating of 8 on a scale of 1 to 10 (10 is most freedom). (Source: World Religion Database)

COMMUNICATIONS AND MEDIA

Freedom of expression is guaranteed by the constitution. Newspapers are able to publish criticism of the government but there are reports of threats against reporters who tackle corruption issues.

Newspapers
Guatemala's main newspapers are Prensa Libre (URL: http://www.prensalibre.com/), La Hora (URL: http://www.lahora.com.gt/), El Periodico (URL:http://www.elperiodico.com.gt/l), Siglo Veintiuno (URL: http://www.sigloxxi.com/). All are located in Guatemala City.

Broadcasting
Broadcasting is dominated by four terrestial stations under the same ownership. There are licences for two state television stations but they are not currently broadcasting. There are hundreds of broadcasting stations in Guatemala. The state radio station is La Voz de Guatemala (URL: http://www.radiotgw.gob.gt/).

Telecommunications
It is estimated that there were 1.4 million main line telephones and approximately 15 million mobiles in use in 2008. An estimated 1.9 million people have regular access to the internet.

ENVIRONMENT

Major environmental issues include soil erosion, deforestation, water pollution, and the effects of Hurricane Mitch. Major environmental agreements signed by Guatemala include Antarctic Treaty, Biodiversity, Climate Change, Climate Change-Kyoto Protocol, Desertification, Endangered Species, Environmental Modification, Hazardous Wastes, Law of the Sea, Marine Dumping, Ozone Layer Protection, Ship Pollution, Wetlands and Whaling.

In 2005, Guatemala had carbon dioxide emissions of 10.96 million metric tons, equivalent to 0.90 metric tons per capita. This was well below the regional average of 2.45 metric tons per capita. In 2010 emissions from the consumption of fossil fuels totalled 12.97 million metric tons of carbon dioxide. (Source: EIA)

GUINEA

Republic of Guinea

République de Guinée

Capital: Conakry (Population estimate, 2010: 2.4 million)

Head of State: Alpha Conde (President) (page 1408)

National Flag: A tricolour pale-wise, red, gold, green

CONSTITUTION AND GOVERNMENT

Constitution

Guinea became independent from France on 2 October 1958. Lansana Conté took power in 1984 after the death of Ahmed Sekou Touré.

In a referendum in December 1990, 95 per cent of eligible voters approved a new constitution containing provisions for a transition to civilian rule. This came into force in February 1991. The first democratic elections took place in 1993 when the current president, Lansana Conté (who led the military government), was elected.

The 1990 Constitution makes the president the head of the executive branch of government. The president is directly elected by universal adult suffrage for a maximum of two successive five-year terms, and is responsible for appointing the Council of Ministers. The president is able to stand for a third longer term following a constitutional amendment approved by referendum on 11 November 2001.

The constitution was suspended in 2008. A new constitution was presented to the National Assembly in April 2010.

Recent Events

Up to half a million refugees fleeing fighting in Sierra Leone and Liberia have settled in Guinea, creating a strain on the economy and increasing ethnic tension. These factors, together with attacks on the borders, have led the International Crisis Group to believe that Guinea may become a "failed state". In 2005, the President survived an alleged assassination attempt, when someone shot at his motorcade. In April 2006, the Prime Minister Cellou Dalein Diallo was sacked and the President announced a new cabinet.

In January 2007, around 60 people were killed in protests during an 18-day strike, called by the unions who believed that President Conte was too sick and corrupt to continue running the country. The President agreed to hand over powers to a Prime Minister, but on 10 February the strike was renewed when the President named Eugene Camara, a close colleague, to the post. The unions demanded the President's resignation, and violent protests ensued. The President declared martial law and imposed an 18-hour curfew to curb demonstrations. Guineans returned to work on 27 February, when ex-diplomat Lansana Kouyate was chosen as a new prime minister. 110 people had been killed during the weeks of strike and protest.

In May 2007, soldiers rioted in the capital, Conakry, in support of improved working conditions and the re-instatement of military leaders sacked after a coup. After ten days of violence, President Lansana Conte sacked the defence minister and army chief of staff, along with five other top commanders.

In August 2007, significant deposits of the nuclear fuel uranium were discovered. The government announced its intention to create nuclear power. Power cuts are a major setback to development in Africa.

In May 2008, the president sacked Lansana Koutate as prime minister and appointed the former minister of mines Ahmed Tidiane Souaré in his place.

On the 23rd December, President Lansana Conte died, and within hours, a faction of the army announced that it had dissolved the country's government and suspended the constitution. A body called the National Council for Democracy and Development (CNDD) was set up in place of the government. The junior army officer who led the coup, Capt. Moussa Dadis Camara, told journalists he was now President of the Republic. The coup leaders enjoyed considerable public support. The CNDD announced a curfew from 2000 to 0600, and warned forces loyal to the government against using mercenaries to restore themselves to power.

The African Union, Ecowas, the EU and the USA all condemned the coup, and the parliament speaker, Aboubacar Sompare, who should have been in charge of the government until elections were held, called for the international community to intervene. Capt Camara said that free and transparent elections would be held in December 2010. On the 25th December, Guinea's prime minister and some 30 other ministers submitted to the leaders of the coup. The following day, the African Union suspended Guinea's membership until the return of constitutional order. The coup leaders sacked more than 20 generals, and suspended mining operations in the country pending renegotiation of agreements with mining companies. More than a third of the world's bauxite reserves are in Guinea, making it the second-largest producer internationally. It also has large reserves of gold, diamonds, iron and nickel.

In March 2009 the military authorities arrested three former ministers including ex-prime minister Ahmed Tidiane Souare. No charges were immediately announced.

Riots broke out in September 2009 when it was thought that Moussa Dadis Camara would run for president in the election scheduled for January 2010. During the riots several opposition supporters were kiilled. The African Union asked Captain Camara to confirm that he would not stand for election. In December 2009 Camara survived an assassination attempt when he was shot during a gun battle between rival army factions. Gen. Sékouba Konaté has since been acting as head of state.

It was agreed on 20 January 2010 that Jean-Marie Doré who had been nominated by the opposition would head an interim government until the expected elections in March 2010. He took office on 26 January and members of the interim government were then announced.

The first round of the presidential elections took place in June 2010 the second round was held in November. Alpha Conde was declared the winner, but a state of emergency had to be called after the result was declared as supporters of defeated candidate Cellou Dalein Diallo and security forces clashed. The state of emergency was to remain in place until the Supreme Court declares the definitive results. In November, Alpha Conde was declared the winner of the run-off presidential race. A state of emergency was declared after security forces and supporters of defeated candidate Cellou Dalein Diallo clashed.

Legislature

Guinea's unicameral legislature is the National Assembly whose 114 members are directly elected for a five-year term.

National Assembly (Assemblée Nationale), Palais du Peuple, BP 414, Conakry, Guinea. Tel: +224 452156, fax: +224 451700, e-mail: webmaster@assemblee.gov.gn, URL: http://www.assemblee-nationale.gn
President of the National Assembly: El Hadj Aboubacar Sompare

Cabinet (as at June 2013)

Prime Minister: Mohamed Said Fofana (page 1426)
Minister of State in charge of Energy: Papa Koly Kourouma
Minister of State in charge of Public Works and Transport: Ousmane Bah
Minister of Security, Civil Protection and Reform of the Security Services: Madifing Diane
Minister of Economy and Finance: Kerfalla Yansane
Minister of Foreign Affairs and Guineans Overseas: Francois Lounceny Fall
Minister of Telecommunications and New Information Technologies: Oye Guilavogui
Minister of Social Affairs, Women and Children's Promotion: Diaka Diakite
Minister of Urban Affairs, Construction and Housing: Ibrahima Bangoura
Minister of Youth, Youth Employment and Sports: Sanoussy Bantam Sow
Minister of Industry and Small and Medium Enterprises: Ramatoulaye Bah
Minister of Tourism, Hotels and Crafts Industry: Hadja Mariame Balde
Minister of Employment and Technical and Professional Education: Damantang Albert Camara
Minister of the Environment, Water and Forests: Saran Mady Toure
Minister of Territorial Administration and Political Affairs: Alhassane Conde
Minister of Agriculture: Emile Yombouno
Minister for Trade: Mohamed Dorval Doumbouya
Minister of Higher Education and Scientific Research: Teliwel Bailo Diallo
Minister of Culture and Heritage: Ahmed Tidiane Cisse
Minister of Health and Public Sanitation: Edouard Gnankoye Lama
Minister Delegate in charge of Budget: Mohamed Diarre
Minister Delegate in charge of Social Affairs: Mimi Koumbassa
Minister Delegate in charge of Guineans Overseas: Rougui Barry
Minister of State, Minister of Justice, Keeper of the Seals: Christian Sow
Minister of Mines and Geology: Mohamed Lamine Fofana
Minister of Planning: Sekou Traore
Minister of International Co-operation: Dr Mustafa Koutoubou Sanoh
Minister of Pre-University Education: Ibrahima Kourouma
Minister of Fisheries and Aquaculture: Moussa Conde
Minister Delegate for National Defence: Abdoul Kabele Camara
Minister Delegate for Health: Dr Naman Keita
Minister of Trade: Mohamed Dorval Doumbouya
Minister of Human Rights and Civil Liberties: Kalifa Gassama Diaby
Minister of Communications: Toqba Cesaire Kpoghomou
Chief of Staff of the Presidency: Dr Mohamed Diane
Minister Delegate for Transport: Elhadj Tidiane Traore

Ministries

Office of the Prime Minister, BP 5141, Conakry, Guinea. Tel: +224 415119, fax: +224 415282
Ministry of Economy and Finance, face au collège Boulbinet, BP 279, Conakry, Guinea. Tel: +224 30 45 17 95, fax: +224 30 42 21 02
Ministry of Foreign Affairs, face au Port, ex-Primature, BP 2519, Conakry, Guinea. Tel: +224 30 41 16 33, fax: +224 30 41 16 21
Ministry of Justice, face Immeuble La Paternelle, Conakry, Guinea. Tel: +224 30 45 29 06
Ministry of National Defence, BP 1000, Conakry, Guinea. Tel: +224 30 45 11 91
Ministry of Natural Resources and Energy, Immeuble CBG/OFAB, 3, blvd. du Commerce, BP 295, Conakry, Guinea. Tel: +250 415001

GUINEA

Ministry of Health and Public Sanitation, BP 585, Conakry, Guinea. Tel: +224 3041 2032, fax: +224 3041 4138

Ministry of Fishery and Aquaculture, face à la Cité du Port, BP 307, Conakry, Guinea. Tel: +224 3041 1258, fax: +224 3041 3528, e-mail: minipaq.jpl@eti-bull.net, URL: http://www.fis.com/guinea

Ministry of Territorial Administration and Decentralisation, BP 3495, Conakry, Guinea. Tel: +224 411510, fax: +224 454507

Ministry of Geology and Environment, BP 295, Conakry, Guinea. Tel: +224 413833, fax: +224 414913

Ministry of Commerce, Industry and Small and Medium-Sized Enterprises, BP 468, Conakry, Guinea. Tel: +224 415222 / 442606, fax: +224 413990

Ministry of Agriculture and Livestock, BP 576, Conakry, Guinea. Tel: +224 411181, fax: +224 411169

Ministry of Public Works and Transport, BP 715, Conakry, Guinea. Tel: +224 413639, fax: +224 413577

Ministry of Urbanisation and Housing, BP 846, Conakry, Guinea. Tel : +224 414687, fax: +224 414681

Ministry of Tourism, Hotels and Handicrafts, Conakry, Guinea. Tel: +224 414994

Ministry of Higher Education and Scientific Research, BP 2201 Conakry, Guinea. Tel: +224 411901, fax: +224 453217

Ministry of Technical Education and Professional Training, BP 2201, Conakry, Guinea. Tel: +224 453217

Ministry of Pre-University Teaching and Civil Education, BP 2201, Conakry, Guinea. Tel: +224 411960

Ministry of Employment and Civil Service, Conakry, Guinea. Tel: +224 415965

Ministry of Communication, BP 317, Conakry, Guinea. Tel: +224 415001, fax: +224 414797

Ministry of Youth, Sports and Culture, BP 262, Conakry, Guinea. Tel: +224 411959, fax: +224 411926

Ministry of Social Affairs, Promotion of Women and Children, BP 527, Conakry, Guinea. Tel: +224 454539, fax: +224 414660

Ministry of International Co-operation, BP 2519, Conakry, Guinea. Tel: +224 3041 1633, fax: +224 3041 1621

Political Parties

Parti de l'Unité et du Progrès (PUP, Party of Unity and Progress)
Union pour le Progrès et le Renouveau (UPR, Union for Progress and Renewal)
Union pour le Progrès de la Guinée (UPG, Union for the Progress of Guinea)
Parti Démocratique de Guinée (PDG, Democratic Party of Guinea)
National Alliance for Progress (ANP)
Parti de l'Union pour le Développement (PUD)

Elections

On 14 December 1998, in the first multiparty elections, the PUP's Lansana Conté was reaffirmed as president with 56 per cent of the vote. Conté was re-elected for a third term, with 95.6 per cent of the vote, on 21 December 2003, although the elections were boycotted by the opposition. The most recent elections for the National Assembly took place on 30 June 2002 when the PUP won with 61.5 per cent of the vote and 85 of the National Assembly's 114 seats. The UPR won 20 seats, the UPG three, the PDG three, the ANP two, and the PUD one.

In April 2006, the President dismissed Prime Minister Cellou Dalein Diallo and appointed a new cabinet.

Elections due in 2007 did not take place. Following the 2008 coup, the junta leader, Captain Moussa Dadis Camara said that elections due for 2009 would be held in 2010, after a two-year transitional period. Presidential elections held in June 2010 proved inconclusive and a second round was scheduled for September 2010. Former prime minister Cellou Dalein Diallo and opposition leader, Alpha Conde were the front runners. The run off election was eventually held in November 2010. Alpha Conde was declared the winner, but a state of emergency was then declared following clashes between security forces and supporters defeated candidate, Cellou Dalein Diallo.

Elections have continually been postponed, a date was set for the end of June 2013 but at the time of going to press this had not been confirmed.

Diplomatic Representation

British Embassy, BP 6729, Conakry, Guinea. Tel: +224 30 455807, fax: +224 30 456020, e-mail: britcon.oury@biasy.net, URL: https://www.gov.uk/government/world/organisations/british-embassy-conakry (All consular and visa services are centralised at the British High Commission in Freetown, and are referred accordingly)
Ambassador: Graham Styles
US Embassy, rue KA 038, BP 603, Conakry, Republic of Guinea. Tel: +224 30 420861, fax: +224 30 420873, URL: http://conakry.usembassy.gov
Ambassador: Alexander Mark Laskaris
Embassy of the Republic of Guinea, 2112 Leroy Place, NW, Washington, DC 20008, USA. Tel: +1 202 483 9420, fax: +1 202 483 8688
Ambassador: Blaise Cherif
Consulate General of Guinea, 48 Onslow Gardens, London SW7 3PY, United Kingdom. Tel: +44 (0)20 7594 4809, fax: +44 (0)20 7078 6086
Ambassador: Dondo Sylla
Permanent Representative of the Republic of Guinea to the United Nations, 140 East 39th Street, New York, NY 10016, USA. Tel: +1 212 687 8115 / 8116 /8117, fax: +1 212 687 8248, e-mail: guinea@un.int, URL: http://www.un.int/guinea/
Ambassador: Mr. Mamadi Toure

LEGAL SYSTEM

Guinea's legal system is based on the French civil law system. There are Courts of the First Instance (Tribunal de Première Instance), two Courts of Appeal (Cour d'Appel) and the Supreme Court (Cour Supreme). There is also a State Security Court (Cour de Sûreté de l'Etat) and a military court handles criminal cases involving military personnel. At village level, there is a traditional system which resolves minor disputes, though this system discriminates against women.

A discipline council for dealing with civil servants who abuse their positions in the government was established in 1996, and a special arbitration court was set up in 1998 to resolve business disputes.

The constitution guarantees the independence of the judiciary, but it is influenced by the government. Police and paramilitary personnel often ignore constitutional legal protections of the citizens. Guinea's constitution was suspended following a military coup on December 23 2008, after the death of former President Lansana Conte, and there have since been serious human rights abuses. Security forces have tortured and abused detainees, and killed and abused civilians. Prison conditions are life threatening. Perpetrators of these abuses act with impunity. The judiciary is subject to corruption and outside influence. The government restricts freedoms of speech, press, assembly, association, and movement. Guinea retains the death penalty. Nineteen people are believed to be on death row.

Supreme Court (Cour Supreme), BP 2260, Conakry, Guinea. Tel: +224 46 29 52 / 41 29 28

LOCAL GOVERNMENT

Guinea is divided into seven administrative regions and the city of Conakry. Each region is headed by a Governor. The administrative regions are subdivided into 34 prefectures, including one special zone (Conakry). Conakry is further divided into five communes. The prefectures are Beyla, Boffa, Boke, Coyah, Dabola, Dalaba, Dinguiraye, Dubreka, Faranah, Forecariah, Fria, Gaoual, Gueckedou, Kankan, Kerouane, Kindia, Kissidougou, Koubia, Koundara, Kouroussa, Labe, Lelouma, Lola, Macenta, Mali, Mamou, Mandiana, Nzerekore, Pita, Siguiri, Telimele, Tougue and Yomou.

AREA AND POPULATION

Area

Guinea is situated in West Africa, north and north-west of Sierra Leone and south-east of Senegal. Its area is 245,857 sq. km. The geography is varied: the north-west is hilly, the central area is savannah, the south east is rain forest and there is a narrow coastal belt. There are two main seasons; the months June-November are hot and humid, with some monsoons, and a dry season (December-May).

To view a map, please consult: http://www.un.org/Depts/Cartographic/map/profile/guinea.pdf

Population

Guinea's estimated population in 2010 was 9,982 million, with an average annual population growth rate of 1.8 per cent in the period 2000-10. Due to neighbouring conflicts, Guinea now has around 60,000 refugees from Liberia and Sierra Leone, down from between 180,000 and 200,000 at the height of the conflicts in those countries. Just over 52 per cent of Guineans are aged between 15 and 60, with 43 per cent aged up to 14 years, and just over 5 per cent aged 60 or over. The median age is 18 years. Over 51 per cent of Guinea's population is female.

Thirty-five per cent of the population lives in urban areas, with most concentrated in the capital, Conakry. The second largest city is Kankan with 100,000 inhabitants.

The population consists of three major tribes: the Peuhls (40 per cent), the Malinkes (30 per cent), and the Soussous (20 per cent). The remaining tribes include the Kissi, the Tomas, the Guerze and the Manos.

Although French is the official language, the principal languages are Pular, Mandigue and Soussou. Each ethnic group has its own language.

Births, Marriages, Deaths

The high death rate (13.9 per 1,000 in 2004), especially of infants and juveniles, counteracts the high birth rate (38.8 per 1,000 in 2010). Life expectancy at birth in 2009 was 54 years (49 years for men and 55 years for women). Healthy life expectancy is 47 years (46 years for females and 48 years for males). (Source: http://www.who.int, World Health Statistics 2012)

Public Holidays 2014

1 January: New Year's Day
14 January: Birth of the Prophet*
3 April: Anniversary of the Second Republic
18 April: Good Friday
21 April: Easter Monday
1 May: Labour Day
29 June: Beginning of Ramadan*
29 July: Eid al Fitr, End of Ramadan*
15 August: Assumption
2 October: Independence/Republic Day
25 December: Christmas Day
*Islamic holiday: precise date depends on appearance of the moon

EMPLOYMENT

Figures for 2007 indicate that 76 per cent of Guinea's 4.3 million labour force is employed in the agriculture industry (mainly subsistance farming), with 18 per cent in industry and commerce, and 6 per cent in services. Over 54 per cent of the population is estimated to be under the poverty threshold.

BANKING AND FINANCE

Currency
One Guinean Franc = 100 centimes

GDP/GNP, Inflation, National Debt
Despite mineral resources, Guinea remains a poor country. Its economy is hindered by political uncertainty, poor infrastructure and corruption. High inflation is an ongoing problem. The government proposed a new mining code in 2011; a successful mining industry with foreign investment would transform its economy.

Guinea's economy experienced a crisis in 2005, caused by the suspension of aid by major donors (the IMF, African Development Bank and the EU) as well as inflation (due in part to high oil prices) and mismanagement. Under IMF policy, Guinea adopted a floating exchange rate on 1 March 2005; as a result the Guinean Franc lost 38 percent of its value against currencies such as the dollar. GDP (at current prices) was estimated at US$4,743.23 billion in 2007 with a growth rate of 1.5 per cent in 2007. The economic growth rate for 2008 was estimated to be 2.9 per cent. GDP was estimated to be US$5 billion in 2011 with a growth rate of 3.5 per cent.

The inflation rate rose dramatically from just under 15 per cent in 2003 to 31.4 per cent in 2005, following increased money generation. It rose again to 34.7 per cent in 2006 but fell to 23.4 per cent in 2007 before rising again to30 per cent in 2008. It was estimated to fall to 15 per cent in 2010 before rising to over 20 per cent in 2011.

GDP by sector broke down thus: agriculture 15.6 per cent, industry 24 per cent (including manufacturing 2.6 per cent), and services 60.5 per cent. The agricultural sector was estimated to have grown by 2.5 per cent in 2007, industry by 4 per cent (of which manufacturing by 1 per cent), and the service sector was estimated to have declined by 0.7 per cent.

External debt was estimated to be US$2.980.42 billion in 2006, over 60 per cent of GDP. This compares to an average of US$3.2 billion in the period 2000-06, 95.6 per cent of GDP. Servicing of the debt accounted for 13.34 per cent of GDP in 2006. (Source: AFDB)

Foreign Investment
In 2002, the IMF suspended the country's Poverty Reduction and Growth Facility, since the Guinean government had failed to meet performance criteria. Whilst the World Bank noted that targets had been achieved with regard to spending on social sectors, spending on defence had contributed heavily to a significant overall deficit. In December 2004, the government began to address this through various reforms, such as a curb on government spending, more rigorous tax collection, and the loosening of price controls.

Balance of Payments / Imports and Exports
Guinea's major export commodities are bauxite, gold, alumina, diamonds as well as agricultural products such as bananas, pineapples, palm products and coffee. Major markets are the European Union, US, South Korea, Russia, Cameroon, Cote d'Ivoire and China.

Imported commodities include petroleum products, machinery, metals, textiles, transport equipment, textiles, grain, and other foods. Import trading partners include France, China, Belgium, Italy, the Netherlands, and the UK.

External Trade, US$ million

	2005	2006	2007
Trade balance	86.45	69.17	-87.91
Exports	841.35	1,011.14	1,074.51
Imports	754.91	941.97	1,162.43

Source: African Development Bank

In 2011, export revenue was estimated to be US$1.4 billion and import costs US$1.9 billion.

Central Bank
Banque Centrale de la Républic de Guinée, PO Box 692, 3 Boulevard du Commerce, Conakry, Guinea. Tel: +224 412651 / 415072, fax: +224 414898, URL: http://bcrg-guinee.org/

Chambers of Commerce and Trade Organisations
Chamber of Commerce, PO Box 545, Conakry, Guinea. Tel: +224 454516, fax: +224 454517
Chamber of Mines, BP 2773, Coléah, Conakry, Guinea. Tel: +224 465190

MANUFACTURING, MINING AND SERVICES

Primary and Extractive Industries
Guinea has a third of the world's bauxite reserves and is its second largest producer. The country also has 1,800 million metric tons of high grade iron ore, and extensive reserves of gold, diamonds and uranium. The mining sector accounts for three-quarters of total export receipts and nearly two thirds of the government's revenues. Mining accounts for about 75 per cent of exports, contributes 21 per cent of GDP and employs 8 per cent of the working population. In March 2010 the Anglo-Australian mining company Rio Tinto announced it had signed a deal with China to develop an iron ore mine in Samandou.

Bauxite provides about 90 per cent of Guinea's foreign exchange. It is mined from high-grade deposits near Boke. Annual production capacity is nearly 20 million metric tons. The Compagnie des Bauxites de Guinea (CBG), owned by the Guinean government and a consortium of largely US and Canadian interests, exported over 14 million metric tons of Bauxite in 2000. The Compagnie des Bauxites de Kindia (CBK), a joint venture between the Guinean government and Russki Alumina, produces 2 million metric tons. Dian Dian, a Guinean/Ukrainian venture, is to produce 1 million metric tons per year, and the Alumina Compagnie de Guinée (ACG) produces just under 2.5 million metric tons.

Industrial mining of diamonds produces about 150,000 - 200,000 carats per year, of which 93 per cent is gem quality. Companies operating in Guinea include AREDOR, a joint venture between the Guinean government and an Australian, British and Swiss consortium; HYMEX; and the South African De Beers Corporation.

About 1.4 tonnes of gold is produced each year from mines in Siguiri. Gold and diamonds are also mined by artisans in small quantities, and efforts are now under way to turn this industry to national economic benefit.

In August 2007 the government announced that commercially viable reserves of uranium had been found in the southern region of Kissidougou. The government hoped that extraction of the valuable mineral would be undertaken quickly as a boost to the economy.

Guinea has no oil reserves and imports all of its requirements. In 2011 oil imports/consumption was 9,000 barrels per day (up from 8,230 barrels per day in 2002), most of it residual, gasoline and distillate.

Neither natural gas nor coal are produced or consumed in Guinea.

Energy
Guinea has massive hydroelectric power potential, only a small part of which has yet been tapped. In 2010 installed electricity capacity was 0.4 GWe, that year 0.97 billion kilowatthours of electricity was produced and 0.90 billion kilowatthours consumed. (Source: EIA)

Manufacturing
Main industrial activity is based on alumina production, as well as sugar and wood products. Food and beverage production includes fruit canning and fruit juice production, rice mills, peanut and palm oil factories. Cement, textiles and plastics are also produced.

Service Industries
The services sector is Guinea's largest contributor to GDP at around 45 per cent, according to 2005 estimates. Along with industry, the sector employs 20 per cent of the labour force.

Agriculture
A total of 1.6 million hectares are used for agriculture, of which an estimated 95,000 are irrigated. Guinea's agricultural output is dominated by palm kernels, coffee, bananas, citrus fruit, and cereals. The industry contributes almost 17 per cent of GDP, according to 2011 estimates. Exports of coffee have risen 26.7 per cent per year since 1990, but only represent 9 per cent of export receipts. 35 per cent of land is arable, with just 4.5 per cent being cultivated at present. About 80 per cent of Guineans rely on subsistence agriculture for a living, which consists largely of paddy rice, potatoes and fruit. Free market policies introduced as a result of constitutional changes have aided growth of agricultural output.

Agricultural Production in 2010

Produce	Int. $'000*	Tonnes
Rice, paddy	405,658	1,498,960
Indigenous cattle meat	150,834	55,836
Fonio	134,877	388,600
Groundnuts, with shell	1126,749	291,700
Maize, green	122,904	297,000
Cassava	107,681	1,030,800
Citrus fruit.nes	106,866	236,400
Mangoes, mangosteens, guavas	98,204	163,900
Plantains	95,322	461,700
Bananas	56,749	201,500
Vegetables fresh nes	49,748	264,000
Cow milk, whole, fresh	35,874	114,959

*unofficial figures
Source: http://faostat.fao.org/site/339/default.aspx Food and Agriculture Organization of the United Nations, Food and Agricultural commodities production

Guinea has rich wood resources. About 10 per cent of the total cut is used for building and industrial purposes each year. The remainder is intended for fuel. Forestry contributes 3.5 per cent of GDP.

Deep-sea fishing catches exceed 200,000 tonnes per annum, contributing 0.9 per cent of GDP. Because of a lack of equipment and boats, fishermen catch only one-eighth of the estimated potential. However, the fishing industry is growing rapidly. In recent years, foreign commercial fleets have competed with local fishermen.

COMMUNICATIONS AND TRANSPORT

Travel Requirements
US, Canadian, Australian and EU subjects require a passport valid for six months, and a visa unless in transit to another country. They also require a return ticket or sufficient funds and proof of accommodation, as well as an international vaccination record (WHO card), and current yellow fever vaccination. For exact requirements contact the Guinea High Commission or Embassy. Other nationals should contact the embassy or high commission to check visa requirements.

GUINEA

International Airports
The country's only international airport is G'Bessia at Conakry. Guinea Airlines operates internal services to the main towns, though schedules are erratic.

Railways
Guinea's railway network runs for a total of 1,100 km. The main railway line links Conakry with Kankan over a distance of 660 km. Whilst there are plans to upgrade the system, at present there are no rail services in Guinea. Rail services carry cargo only.

Roads
Total road length exceeds 30,000 km, of which 5,000 km are paved and 25,500 km are unpaved. Vehicles drive on the right. Despite the opening in 2005 of a new road connecting Guinea and Mali, most major roadways connecting the country's trade centres remain in poor repair, slowing the delivery of goods to local markets. There are road links with the Cote d'Ivoire, Mali, Senegal and Sierra Leone, and there are bus services to these countries, though these can be unreliable.

Ports and Harbours
The country's main port is that of Conakry, which not only serves international lines but also has deep-water docking and loading facilities for commercial traffic, including containers. The port of Kammar is predominantly used for the shipping of bauxite.

There is a hydrofoil service from Conakry to Freetown, and a ferry to Mali when the river is high enough.

HEALTH

According to 2009 estimates, the government of Guinea spent around 1.8 per cent of its total budget on health care. Total expenditure on health equated to 5.3 per cent of GDP. Government expenditure accounts for 8.2 per cent of the total health expenditure. Out-of-pocket private expenditure accounts for some 90 per cent of the total expenditure. Total per capita expenditure on health is estimated at US$25. According to 2000-10 estimates, there are 940 doctors (1 per 10,000 population), 33 dentistry personnel and 4,01 nurses and midwives (0.4 per 10,000 population).

Mortality rates are high, with poor drinking water quality and sanitary conditions resulting in parasitic and infectious diseases. Cases of yellow fever occur regularly, and September 2005 saw an outbreak of cholera, with close to 2,000 cases and 72 fatalities. In 2006, it was estimated that over 54 per cent of the population were living below the poverty threshold. In 2010 it was estimated that 74 per cent of the population had sustainable access to improved drinking water sources. An estimated 18 per cent of the population had sustainable access to improved sanitation. The infant mortality rate was 81 per 1,000 live births in 2009 and the child mortality rate (under 5 years old) was 130 per 1,000 live births. The most common causes of death in infants and young children are: prematurity (22 per cent), pneumonia (15 per cent), diarrhoea (7 per cent), injuries (2.5 per cent) and HIV/AIDS (2 per cent). The immunization rates are still relatively low: 51 per cent for measles and 57 per cent for diptheria and hepatitis B. Approximately 1 per cent of young children sleep under insecticide-treated nets. (Source: http://www.who.int, World Health Statistics 2012)

EDUCATION

In 2007, enrolment in primary schools reached 74.0 per cent, (female 69.0 per cent). In 2004, 48 per cent of children completed a full course of primary education. Pupil:teacher ratios in primary school averaged 45:1. Secondary school enrolment in 2007 stood at 13 per cent (6.4 per cent for girls). Two per cent of students went on to tertiary education (four per cent of men and one per cent of women).

The literacy rate among adult Guineans (15+) during the period 2000 to 2004 was 29.5 per cent; 42.6 per cent of men can read and write, but only 18.1 per cent of women can do so. The regional average for adult literacy is 62.5 per cent. Among those Guineans aged between 15 and 24, the literacy rate is better, at 46.6 per cent. In 2004, 25.6 per cent of total government expenditure was spent on education.

RELIGION

Guinea is predominantly Muslim (70 per cent of the population), although 4 per cent of the population follow Christianity and 26 per cent traditional beliefs. There are small communities of Buddhists and Baha'is.

COMMUNICATIONS AND MEDIA

There is little press freedom. By law, the government is allowed to censor publications. Most broadcasters and newspapers are strate controlled.

Newspapers
Newspapers include La Nouvelle Tribune, L'Observateur (URL: http://www.observateur-guinee.com/, Le Populaire (URL: http://www.lepopulaire-guinee.info/, Le Lynx (satirical, weekly), L'Independent and the Lance (weekly) and L'Evenement de Guinea (monthly). Publishing of newspapers is limited by high printing costs.

Broadcasting
Three private radio stations were given authorisation to operate in 2006, ostensibly ending a government monopoly on the broadcast media. Recent figures put the number of television stations at six, with the number of television receivers exceeding 80,000. The state broadcaster is Radiodiffusion-Television Guineenne (RTG).

Telecommunications
With the exception of the capital, the telecommunications infrastucture is poor. The number of telephones in use is estimated at about 50,000, according to 2008 estimates (5.8 per 1,000 population). In 2008 there were an estimated 3 million mobile phones, approximately 40 per 1,000 population. Mobile use is expanding rapidly.

Internet users numbered 90,000 in 2008.

ENVIRONMENT

Heavy mining is degrading soils and destroying vegetation cover, as well as causing noise, air and water pollution. Soils are also being over-exploited by agriculture. Forests are being destroyed at the rate of 36,000 ha per year, leading to desertification which is exacerbated by drought. Fish stocks are also over-exploited.

Guinea is a party to the following international environmental agreements: Biodiversity, Climate Change, Climate Change-Kyoto Protocol, Desertification, Endangered Species, Hazardous Wastes, Law of the Sea, Ozone Layer Protection, Ship Pollution, Wetlands and Whaling.

According to figures from the EIA, in 2010, Guinea's emissions from the consumption of fossil fuels totalled 1.39 million metric tons of carbon dioxide.

GUINEA-BISSAU
Republic of Guinea-Bissau
República da Guiné-Bissau

Capital: Bissau (Population estimate: 365,000)

Head of State: Manuel Serifo Nhamadjo (interim president)

National Flag: Horizontal stripes, coloured yellow then green, with a black star on a vertical red stripe in the hoist

CONSTITUTION AND GOVERNMENT

Constitution

Guinea-Bissau gained its independence from Portugal on 24 September 1974. The current constitution, approved in May 1984 and last amended in July 1999, provides for a President, directly elected by universal adult suffrage for a term of five years. As the head of government, the president appoints the Council of Ministers, including the prime minister. The president's term of office was extended to a maximum of two terms following a constitutional amendment in July 1999.

To consult the constitution, please visit: http://www.wipo.int/wipolex/en/details.jsp?id=7611

International Relations

Relations with neighbouring Senegal have been strained in the past due to the Senegalese army's fight against Casamance separatists, but Guinea-Bissau has now made efforts to expel the separatists from the country. Guinea-Bissau and Senegal also had a land and maritime border dispute, which was resolved in 1995. Relations with other neighbours have generally been good. Guinea-Bissau has enjoyed close relations with Portugal since independence, and looks for Portuguese support within the international donor community.

In October 2007, the UN Security Council referred Guinea Bissau to the UN Peace Building Commission.

Recent Events

In 1980, Luis Cabral was ousted from the Presidency following a coup led by Joao Bernardo Vieira. President Vieira introduced reforms, including allowing political parties, and was elected President in the first free election of the country, in 1994. In 1998, he sacked General Ansumane Mane for allowing weapons to be smuggled to Senegal, and was toppled by the General one year later.

In January 2000, Kumba Yala was elected President, but deposed in September 2003 in a military coup. An interim civilian administration was headed by President Henrique Rosa and Prime Minister Antonio Artur Rosa, and the PAIGC won the general election in 2004. In July 2005, the former military ruler Joao Bernardo Vieira won the presidential elections. He dismissed the government under the PAIGC premiership of Carlos Gomes, and appointed a close ally, Aristides Gomes, as prime minister.

In April 2007, the President appointed Martinho N'Dafa Cabi as the new prime minister following three weeks of political uncertainty stemming from the national assembly's passage of a no-confidence motion against Aristides Gomes. In December 2007 the government passed a law guaranteeing amnesty for violence committed between 1980 and 2004.

On 26 July 2008, the PAIGC announced that it was withdrawing co-operation from the unity government. The President dissolved parliament; Carlos Correia became prime minister and took office on 6 August and named a reshuffled cabinet pending elections in November 2008.

Over the summer of 2008, there were several media reports of a growing drug trafficking problem in Guinea Bissau. The country is used as a staging post between Latin America and Europe; smugglers benefit from the mangrove swamps and jagged coastline, as well as the country's poor capacity to deal with the problem. Both the justice minister and the attorney-general claimed to have received death threats in July and August over the arrest of three Venezuelans, the head of air traffic control and his deputy on suspicion of drugs trafficking.

According to the National Electoral Commission, the African Party for the Independence of Guinea-Bissau and Cape Verde (PAIGC) won 67 of the 100 National Assembly seats in legislative elections held on 16th November. The party allied to the president, the Republican Party for Independence and Development (PRID), won just three seats in the ballot. The result was contested, but Carlos Gomes Jr of the PAIGC took office as prime minister with a new Council of Ministers on 7 January 2009.

President Joao Bernardo Vieira survived a gun attack on his home by mutinous soldiers, in an attempted coup on the 23rd November 2008. The soldiers stormed Mr Vieira's compound during a three-hour battle.

On the 2nd March 2009, renegade soldiers shot President Vieira dead, possibly in revenge for ordering the killing of the army chief of staff, General Kagme, hours earlier. The armed forces said the military would respect the constitutional order, and National Assembly speaker, Raimundo Pereira, took control of a transitional government pending presidential elections.

On the 5th June, in the run-up to presidential elections at the end of June, presidential candidate, Baciro Dabo, and former Defence Minister Helder Proenca were killed by soldiers who accused them of plotting a coup. Former PM Faustino Fudut Imbali was taken away by the military, and was detained on suspicion of involvement in the alleged coup plot.

In August 2010, the EU announced it was to end it mission to reform Guinea Bissau's security forces, it sited that a lack of respect for rule of law made it an impossible task. In October the EU threatened to suspend development aid unless democratic norms were restored.

In April 2013 it was reported that soldiers had taken control of much of the capital in a coup led by Gen. Mamadu Ture Kuruma. A transitional government led by Manuel Serifo Nhamadjo was formed and elections are to be held within a year.

Legislature

Guinea-Bissau's unicameral legislature is known as the National People's Assembly (*Assembleia Nacional Popular*), which currently has 102 members directly elected for a term of four years. The National Assembly selects a Council of State composed of 15 members. The President of the Council is automatically Head of State.

Transitional Cabinet (as at June 2013)
Prime Minister: Rui Duarte De Barros
Minister of National Defence, Veteran's Affairs: Col. Celestin De Carvalho
Minister of Education, Culture and Science, Youth and Sport: Alfredo Gomes
Minister of Foreign Affairs, Minister of International Co-operation and Community Affairs: Fernando Delfim Da Silva
Minister of Finance: Gino Mendes
Minister of the Economy and Regional Integration: Soares Sambu
Minister of the Interior: Antonio Suka Ntchama
Minister of Justice: Dr Mamadu Saido Balde
Minister of Infrastructure: Rui Araujo Gomes
Minister of Agriculture: Nicholau Santos
Minister of Natural Resources: Certorio Biote
Minister of Public Health: Dr Agostinho Ca
Minister of Regional Administration and Local Government: Dr Baptista Te
Minister of Trade and Industry, Tourism and Handicrafts: Dr Abubacar Balde
Minister of Civil Service, Labour and Modernisation: Aristides Ocante Da Silva
Minister of the Presidency and Council of Ministers, Social Communication and Parliamentary Affairs: Fernando Vaz
Minister of Fisheries and Rishery Resources: Mario Lopes Da Rosa
Minister of Women, Family ad Social Solidarity: Gabriela Fernandes

---

Ministries

Office of the President, Bissau, Guinea-Bissau. Tel: +245 205005 / 204777
Office of the Prime Minister, Bissau, Guinea-Bissau. Tel: +245 204484 / 205661
Ministry of Economy and Finance, Bairro de Ajuda, 2 Fase, B.P. 742, Bissau, Guinea-Bissau. Tel: +245 254807, fax: +245 254809, e-mail: info@mail.guine-bissau.org, URL: http://www.guine-bissau.org/
Ministry of Internal Administration, Bissau, Guinea-Bissau. Tel: +245 203781 / 203626
Ministry of National Defence, Bissau, Guinea-Bissau. Tel: +245 223646
Ministry of Foreign Affairs and International Co-operation, Bissau, Guinea-Bissau. Tel: +245 204301
Ministry of Justice, Bissau, Guinea-Bissau. Tel: +245 202185
Ministry of Public Works, Bissau, Guinea-Bissau. Tel: +245 204532
Ministry of Agriculture, Forests and Livestock, Bissau, Guinea-Bissau. Tel: +245 221200 / 223028
Ministry of Natural Resources and Energy, BP 399, Bissau, Guinea-Bissau. Tel: +245 223149
Ministry of National Education, Bissau, Guinea-Bissau. Tel: +245 201400 / 202244
Ministry of Public Administration and Labour, Bissau, Guinea-Bissau. Tel: +245 202625 / 215119
Ministry of Fisheries, Bissau, Guinea-Bissau. Tel: +245 203749
Ministry of Health, Bissau, Guinea-Bissau. Tel: +245 204438
Ministry of Commerce, Tourism and Handicrafts, BP 85 Bissau, Guinea-Bissau. Tel: +245 202195
Ministry of Youth, Culture and Sports, Bissau, Guinea-Bissau. Tel: +245 205372

Political Parties

Partido para a Renovaçao Social (PRS, Party for Social Renewal), Leader: Mohamed Ialá Embaló
Resistencia da Guiné-Bissau - Movimento Bah-Fatah (RGB-MB, Resistance of Guinea-Bissau - Bafatá Movement)
Partido Africano da Independencia da Guiné e Cabo Verde (PAIGC, African Independence Party of Guinea and Cape Verde)
Uniao Eleitoral (Electoral Union Party)
Uniao para a Mudança (UM, Union for Change)
Plataforma Unida (United Platform)
Uniao Nacional para a Democracia e o Progresso (UNDP, National Union for Democracy and Progress)

GUINEA-BISSAU

Elections

President Yala dissolved parliament in November 2002 and scheduled elections for February 2003. These elections were never held, and President Yala was removed from power in September 2003. Parliamentary elections finally took place in March 2004, and the PAIGC won. In 2005, the newly elected President Vieira dismissed the Government under the PAIGC premiership of Carlos Gomes, and appointed a new Government made up of the Social Renovation Party, the United Social Democratic Party, the Electoral Union, the Democratic Convergence Party and the PAIGC. In July 2008, the PAIGC withdrew support for the unity government, precipitating a political crisis. Carlos Correia became prime minister and appointed a reshuffled cabinet pending elections in November 2008.

The African Party for the Independence of Guinea-Bissau and Cape Verde (PAIGC) won 67 of the 100 National Assembly seats in legislative elections held on 16th November. The party allied to the president, the Republican Party for Independence and Development (PRID), won just three seats in the ballot. The result was contested.

Presidential elections were held in July 2005 but the result was disputed. In the run off election, former ruler Joao Bernardo Vieira won 55 per cent of the vote. The other candidate, Malam Bacai Sanha, challenged the result, citing alleged election fraud. However, international observers judged the elections to have been fair, and the result stood. Following the assassination of President Vieira, presidential elections were held in June and July 2009. Malam Bacai Sanha won the second round with 63 per cent of the vote.

The most recent presidential election was held in March 2012 triggered by the death in January of President Malam Bacai Sanha. Only the first round took place and the second round has been postponed indefinitely.

Diplomatic Representation

Embassy for the Republic of Guinea-Bissau, 94 Rue St Lazare, Paris 9, France. Tel: +33 1 45 26 18 51
Ambassador: vacant
British Consulate, Mavegro Int., CP100, Bissau, Guinea-Bissau. Tel: +245 2012 24 / 16, fax: +245 201265, e-mail: mavegro@gtelecom.gw, mavegro@hotmail.com
Ambassador (to Senegal): Robert Marshall
Honory Consul: Jan van Maanen
US Embassy, C.P. 297, 1067 Bissau Codex, Guinea-Bissau. +245 25 22 73 / 76, fax: +245 25 22 82, URL: http://dakar.usembassy.gov/
Ambassador: Lewis Alan Lukens
Embassy of the Republic of Guinea-Bissau, PO Box 33813, NW, Washington, DC 20033, USA. Tel: +1 301 947 3958 , fax: +1 301947 3958
Ambassador: vacant
Permanent Representative of the Republic of Guinea-Bissau to the United Nations, 211 East 43rd Street, Room 704, New York, NY 10017, USA. Tel: +212 661 3977, Fax: +1 914 636 3007, e-mail: guinea-bissau@un.int
Permanent Representative: vacant

LEGAL SYSTEM

At the head of the court system is the Supreme Court (*Supremo Tribunal da Justica*), comprising nine judges appointed by the president. In addition to the Supreme Court are final courts of appeal (civil and criminal), nine Regional Courts (one for each region), and 24 Sectoral Courts, whose judges are not necessarily trained lawyers. These courts hear civil cases and minor criminal cases, and their judgements can be reviewed by a first Court of Appeals, which also hears all felony cases and original civil cases valued at over $1,000.

There is a culture of impunity in the country. There are arbitrary killings, arrests and detentions. Prison conditions are poor. Corruption is widespread, and there is a lack of judicial independence. Guinea-Bissau is a source country for children trafficking to other West African countries, it has recently enacted comprehensive anti-trafficking laws but prosecution is extremely rare.

Guinea-Bissau abolished the death penalty in 1993.

LOCAL GOVERNMENT

Guinea-Bissau is divided into the autonomous sector of Bissau and eight regions, or *regioes*: Bafata, Biombo, Bissau, Bolama (or Bijagos), Cacheu, Gabu, Oio, Quinara, and Tombali.

AREA AND POPULATION

Area

Guinea-Bissau is situated on the west coast of Africa, to the south of Gambia. It borders Senegal and the Republic of Guinea. Guinea-Bissau is small, at just 13,948 sq miles, and includes the island of Bolama, and the archipelago of Bissangos (Bijagos). The terrain is mostly low coastal plain rising to savannah in the east. The coastline is indented with many creeks and mangrove swamps. The climate is generally hot and humid.

To view a map, consult: http://www.un.org/Depts/Cartographic/map/profile/guineabi.pdf

Population

The population of Guinea-Bissau was estimated at 1.515 million in 2010, assuming an annual growth rate of 2.0 per cent over the period 2000-10. Almost 54 per cent the population is aged between 15 and 64 years, with 41 per cent aged up to 14 years, and 5 per cent 60 and over. The median age is 19 years. Some 70 per cent of the people live in rural areas.

Ninety-nine per cent of the population is African, of which 30 per cent are Balanta, 20 per cent Fula, 14 per cent Manjaca, 13 per cent Mandinga, and 7 per cent Papel.

Portuguese is the official language, but Creole and French are also spoken widely. There are many indigenous languages.

Births, Marriages, Deaths

According to 2010 estimates, the crude birth rate is 38.3 births per 1,000 of the population whilst the death rate is 16 deaths per 1,000 population. Average life expectancy in 2009 was 49 years (47 years for males, 51 years for females). Healthy life expectancy was 42 years. The fertility rate was 5.1 children born per woman, whilst the infant mortality rate was 92 deaths per 1,000 live births. The maternal mortality rate was also high at a reported 790 deaths per 100,000 live births in 2010. (Source: http://www.who.int, World Health Statistics 2012)

Public Holidays 2014

1 January: New Year's Day
8 March: International Women's Day
1 May: Labour Day
29 July: Korité (end of Ramadan)*
3 August: Martyrs' Day
24 September: Independence Day
14 November: Anniversary of the Movement of Readjustment
5 October: Tabaski (Feast of Sacrifice)*
25 December: Christmas Day
* Islamic holidays depend on the sighting of the moon and so dates can vary. Korité and Tabaski may last from two to 10 days, depending on the region.

EMPLOYMENT

Of an estimated labour force of 632,500, around 86 per cent are employed in the agricultural sector, 2 per cent are government employees, and the remaining 12 per cent work in industry, services or commerce. Amongst the unemployed, 60 per cent are either unskilled or semi-skilled, whilst a significant number of low-skill jobs are occupied by qualified professionals.

BANKING AND FINANCE

GDP/GNP, Inflation, National Debt

The civil war in 1998/99 caused major damage to the country's economic infrastructure and left Guinea-Bissau one of the poorest nations of the world. The country's economy is dependent on low value-added agricultural products (mainly cashew nuts), subsistence crops and fishing.

After a bad year in 2006, Guinea-Bissau's economy bounced back in 2007, due in part to good growth in the tourism sector and a sharp increase in the sale of the country's main cash crop, cashews. Other crops include peanuts, palm kernels and rice. Fishing licenses is another source of revenue. Economic growth was forecast to be 3.0 per cent in 2009, with support from new international donors, Angola's planned investment in a bauxite mining project and continued strong exports of cashews. There has been some oil prospecting but there are not yet enough signs to encourage significant investment.

Guinea-Bissau was due to benefit from the Heavily Indebted Poor Countries initiative in 2000, but the progamme was suspended due to off-programme expenditure by the Yala regime. The relative stability of the current government brought some improvements; the country signed an IMF monitored programme early in 2005, which was renewed in March 2006. In January 2008 the IMF announced its approval for $2.8 million in emergency post-conflict assistance. In 2010, the World Bank and the IMF announced support for over US$1 billion of debt relief. The Paris Club also voted to cancel much of Guinea-Bissau's debt obligations.

In 2007, GDP reached US$367.09 million (up from US$307.68 million in 2006), with an estimated annual growth rate of 2.5 per cent. The greatest contributor to GDP is agriculture (62 per cent), followed by services (26 per cent) and industry (12 per cent). GDP was estimated to have risen to US$970 million in 2011.

Inflation (consumer prices) has been under 4 per cent since 2001. It reached its lowest point of 0.9 per cent in 2004. It rose to 3.3 per cent in 2005, dipped to 2.0 per cent in 2006 and then rose again to 3.0 per cent in 2007. (Source: AFDB) Inflation was estimated to be 5.4 per cent in 2011.

Balance of Payments / Imports and Exports

Guinea-Bissau's main export commodities are cashew nuts (US$110 million in 2006), fish and shrimp, peanuts, sawn timber, and palm kernels. Major export trading partners include India (70 per cent in 2011) and Nigeria (15 per cent).

Guinea-Bissau imports mainly from Senegal (15), Portugal (25 per cent) and China (5 per cent). Food costs represent almost 50 per cent of imports, petroleum and energy products some 20 per cent and capital good approximately 5 per cent.

External Trade, US$ million

	2005	2006	2007
Trade balance	-16.52	-69.37	-34.88
Exports	89.64	61.53	92.19
Imports	106.16	120.90	127.08

Source: African Development Bank

Imports were estimated to be US$200 million in 2010 and export revenue US$125 million.

Central Bank
Banque Centrale des Etats de l'Afrique de l'Ouest, PO Box 3108, Avenue Abdoulaye Fadiga, Dakar, Senegal. Tel: +221 8 390500, fax: +221 8 239335, e-mail: webmaster@bceao.int, URL: http://www.bceao.int
Governor: Tiémoko Meyliet Kone

Chambers of Commerce and Trade Organisations
Chamber of Commerce, Avenida Amilcar Cabral 7, P.O. Box 361, Bissau, Guinea-Bissau. Tel: +245 212844, fax: +245 201602

MANUFACTURING, MINING AND SERVICES

Primary and Extractive Industries
Geological surveys have indicated that there is potential for the production of bauxite, phosphates and offshore oil. However, due to high costs, Guinea-Bissau has not been able to develop petroleum and other mineral resources to date. The national oil company of Guinea-Bissau, Petroguin, is planning to offer the country's new deep-water acreage to prospective investors. Angola plans to invest in a bauxite mining project.

In June 2002, an American oil company, Amerada Hess (Hess), acquired a majority interest in the Croix du Sud Block, located in jointly-administered waters offshore Guinea-Bissau and Senegal. In 1995 Guinea-Bissau and Senegal established the Agence de Gestion et de Cooperation (AGC) for the joint-development of maritime resources located in the area.

Guinea-Bissau consumed 9,000 barrels of oil per day in 2011, all of which was imported. The country does not have any gas reserves, nor does it use this commodity.

Energy
Although the country has a large hydrographic network, this has not been used for hydroelectric power, and electricity is generated solely from imported oil. Figures for 2010 show that Guinea-Bissau generated 0.97 billion kilowatthours and consumed 0.90 billion kilowatthours.

The electricity network only provides for a small sector of the population and even in the regional capital electricity is only available for an average of 14 hours a day. (Source: Energy Information Administration).

Manufacturing
The 1998 civil war left little in the way of industrial capacity in Guinea-Bissau. The manufacturing sector is severely hindered by a lack of trained labour and experience in management and finance. The industrial sector contributes about 12 per cent of GDP. Major industries are the processing of agricultural products, particularly cashew nuts, beer and soft drinks. Agricultural processing accounts for 62.2 per cent of production, wood processing 10.8 per cent, non-ferrous and mineral processing 5.8 per cent, and metallurgic, mechanical and equipment 5 per cent.

Service Industries
The services sector contributes about 26 per cent of Guinea-Bissau's GDP, according to recent estimates.

Agriculture
Around 43 per cent of the land is arable, and the agricultural sector accounts for 62 per cent of GDP and 78 per cent of employment. Main agricultural products are cashews, groundnuts, coconuts, sugar cane, palm oil and rice. Crops of cashews have increased considerably in recent years, with Guinea-Bissau ranked sixth in cashew production. About 46,000 tonnes of groundnuts and about 14,000 tonnes of coconuts are produced annually. Palm oil production is about 2,700 tonnes a year and rice 128,349 tonnes (Guinea-Bissau could potentially be self-sufficient in rice). Tropical fruits such as mangos could also be developed to provide more income. Timber, wax and hides are also produced. The poor transport infrastructure prevents farmers from delivering their crops to the markets on time.

In 2006, the government raised the price of cashews; foreign dealers declined to buy them and tens of thousands of tonnes rotted. The country's cashew industry went into crisis. The government lowered the cashew price, and in 2007 exports soared.

Agricultural Production in 2010

Produce	Int. $'000*	Tonnes
Cashew nuts, with shell	79,741	91,100
Rice, paddy	47,368	177,022
Groundnuts, with shell	30,316	69,651
Indigenous pigmeat	19,664	12,792
Indigenous cattle meat	17,161	6,353
Roots and tubers, nes	12,501	73,100
Cassava	9,275	88,786
Plantains	8,754	42,400
Fruit fresh nes	7,225	20,700
Vegetables fresh nes	6,445	34,200
Cow milk, whole, fresh	5,411	17,340
Millet	4,814	28062

*unofficial figures
Source: http://faostat.fao.org/site/339/default.aspx Food and Agriculture Organization of the United Nations, Food and Agricultural commodities production

Small farmers keep livestock for subsistence farming and the generation of cash through sales at local markets. However, due to shortages of pastures and lack of water, veterinary services and a structured market, there is little scope to develop livestock farming.

Guinea Bissau has abundant offshore and coastal fish resources. The fisheries sector is made up of two sections: industrial fishing carried out by foreign companies, and small scale fishing. Although there has been an increase in catches in the fishing industry, this has mainly benefited foreign fishing fleets. Industrial fishing licenses account for 45 per cent of government revenue and are an important source of foreign exchange. Figures for 2010 put the total catch at 6,800 tonnes.

Guinea Bissau has extensive forestry resources covering nearly 2 million hectares of land. Commercial logging is concentrated on the two species with the highest market value, and logging is performed at over 100 per cent of their regeneration capacity. Deforestation, due to commercial exploitation, uncontrolled bush fires, and charcoal and firewood export, has caused concerns about the sustainability of the country's forestry resources. The government intends to raise the taxes for logging by charging the loggers for the whole tree and not just the log portion, which should increase the tax revenue by approximately 20 per cent.

COMMUNICATIONS AND TRANSPORT

Travel Requirements
US, Canadian, Australian and EU visitors require a passport valid for six months and a visa (except transit passengers not leaving the airport, with onward or return documentation). Other nationals should contact the embassy to check visa requirements.

International Airports
Guinea Bissau has one international airport in Bissau and around 20 small domestic airports.

Roads
There are 2,636 km of roads in Guinea-Bissau consisting of 735 km of paved road, 480 km laterite roads and 1,537 km of earth roads. The roads are in a poor condition due to a lack of maintenance. Vehicles are driven on the right.

Ports and Harbours
The capital, Bissau, has a deep water port and another is situated at Caboxanque. There are approximately a dozen other inland ports. Ferries operate from Bissau, Bolama, Bubaque Island, Catio and Enyudé, and from Bissau to Bafatá.

HEALTH

The majority of health care facilities in Guinea Bissau are unable to provide even basic health care due to a lack of equipment, water, fuel and electricity. Latest available statistics indicate that Guinea Bissau spent approximately 4.1 per cent of its total budget on healthcare in 2009 (up from 2.3 per cent in 2000), accounting for 10.6 per cent of all healthcare spending. Total expenditure on health care equated to 8.6 per cent of the country's GDP. Private expenditure accounts for 89.4 per cent of health care spending. Per capita total expenditure on health is US$48. According to the latest estimates (2005-10) there are 78 physicians (0.5 per 10,000 population), 953 nurses (5.5 per 10,000 population) and 6 dentistry personnel. Many of the healthcare workers are under-qualified and many of the qualified nurses and physicians leave the public sector or emigrate due to low salaries and poor working conditions.

The main causes of mortality and morbidity are malaria, acute diarrhoeal diseases, respiratory infections and tuberculosis. Child malnutrition affects about 30 per cent of children between the ages of 12-59 months. The mortality rates are high. The infant mortality rate in 2009 was 92 per 1,000 live births and the child (under 5) rate was 152 per 1,000 live births. The most common causes of deaths of infants and young children are: prematurity (11 per cent), pneumonia (18 per cent), malaria (18 per cent), diarrhoea (12 per cent) and HIV/AIDS (3 per cent).

Between 16,000 and 23,000 of the adult population is infected with the HIV/AIDS virus, of whom nearly 7,500 are women. In 2007, around 1,000 people died of AIDS. Tuberculosis is growing in Africa and there were 2,183 reported cases in 2010.

In 2010 approximately 64 per cent of the population had access to improved drinking water. In the same year, 20 per cent of the population had access to improved sanitation. (Source: http://www.who.int, World Health Statistics 2012)

EDUCATION

Many of Guinea-Bissau's schools are housed in temporary structures. There is a scarcity of qualified teachers due to poor salaries and working conditions. The enrolment figure for boys is considerably higher than that for girls in both primary and secondary education. Only 15 per cent of children complete two cycles of basic education, and in the rural areas where there is extreme poverty 84 per cent have no formal education and 14 per cent have only attended primary school. The adult literacy rate is estimated to be just 62.8 per cent of the population and has shown marked improvement over the last few years. In the 15-24 year age-group, the overall literacy rate stood at 71.8 per cent in 2006 (93.1 per cent for males), considerably higher than the average literacy rates of the region.

In 2006, 11.9 per cent of government spending went on education, which represented approximately 5 per cent of GDP. This was a considerable improvement on previous years, when just 2 per cent of GDP was spent on education and healthcare. (Source: UNESCO, September 2008, http://stats.uis.unesco.org/)

RELIGION

Nearly half of Guinea-Bissau's population holds indigenous beliefs, while 45 per cent are Muslim, and 11 per cent Christian.

GUYANA

Guinea-Bissau has a religious liberty rating of 9 on a scale of 1 to 10 (10 is most freedom). (Source: World Religion Database)

COMMUNICATIONS AND MEDIA

There has been more freedom of media expression since the 2003 coup. Broadcasting and the media is hindered by poverty and the country's poor infrastructure and power supply.

Broadcasting
There is one state-owned TV station. Another station, RTP Africa, run by the Portuguese public broadcaster RTP also opersates. There is one state-owned radio station and several private stations. International broadcasters also operate.

Telecommunications
There are approximately 4,500 landlines in operation as of 2008 and 500,000 mobile phones. Approximately 37,000 people had internet access in 2008.

ENVIRONMENT

Exploitation of Guinea-Bissau's forestry and fishing resources is a concern. The increased demand for coal to supply energy and for export has put severe pressure on the forest areas, a situation which has been compounded by desertification. The government has indicated that reforms are to be implemented in the legal system to provide incentives for forestry conservation and to strengthen the monitoring of fishing.

Guinea-Bissau is a party to the following international environmental agreements: Biodiversity, Climate Change, Climate Change-Kyoto Protocol, Desertification, Endangered Species, Hazardous Wastes, Law of the Sea, Ozone Layer Protection andWetlands.

According to figures from the EIA, in 2010, Guinea-Bissau's emissions from the consumption of fossil fuels totalled 1.39 million metric tons of carbon dioxide.

GUYANA
Co-operative Republic of Guyana

Capital: Georgetown (Population estimate: 250,000)

Head of State: Hon. Donald Ramotar (President) (page 1500)

National Flag: Red triangle with black border pointing from hoist to fly on a yellow triangle with white border all on a green field

CONSTITUTION AND GOVERNMENT

Constitution
Guyana, formerly the colonial territory of British Guiana, was ceded to Great Britain by the Dutch in 1814. On 26 May 1966 Guyana became independent and the 23rd member of the Commonwealth. On 20 September 1966 it became the 199th member of the United Nations. The country became a Cooperative Republic on 23 February 1970.

Guyana's Peoples' New Constitution was enacted on 6 October 1981. The Constitution is the Supreme Law of Guyana and provides for the fundamental rights and freedom of the individual irrespective of race, place of origin, political opinions, colour, creed or sex.

To consult the full constitution, please visit:
http://www.parliament.gov.gy/constitution/constitutionindex.php

Recent events
Guyana has a long-running offshore border dispute with its neighbour, Suriname, over a potentially oil-rich marine area. In September 2007, the UN made its ruling and gave both parties a share of the territory.

The capital, Georgetown, was declared a disaster zone in January 2005, following severe flooding and the consequent loss to the economy of $500 million.

In April 2006 during the run up to elections, agriculture minister Satyadeow Sawh was shot dead. The elections went ahead as scheduled in August and President Bharrat Jagdeo was re-elected. Samuel Hinds was re-appointed prime minister.

In September 2007, a UN tribunal ruled in a dispute between Guyana and Surinme over a maritime territory issue, the UN ruled that both will have a share of the potentially oil-rich offshore basin.

In October 2008, President Jagdeo signed a trade agreement with EU.

In October 2010, the parliament abolished the death penalty for murder, the only exception is for those convicted of murdering a member of the security forces.

Presidential and parliamentary elections took place on 28 November 2011.

Legislature
The Executive President and the National Assembly make up the Parliament of Guyana. Under the electoral system of proportional representation, 53 of the 65 members are elected. Twelve other MPs are selected by regional authorities. The life of parliament is five years. The House of Parliament is presided over by the Speaker. The president appoints the prime minister and cabinet which is responsible to parliament. The Constitution makes definite provision for a minority leader, who is an elected member of the National Assembly, appointed by the president as most capable of commanding the support of the majority of those elected members who do not support the Government.
National Assembly, Parliament Office, Public Buildings, Brickdam, Stabroek, Georgetown, Guyana. Tel: +592 226 8456, fax: +592 225 1357, e-mail: fnarain@parliament.gov.gy, URL: http://www.sdnp.org.gy/parliament/

Cabinet (as at June 2013)
Prime Minister: Hon. Samuel A. A. Hinds (page 1442)
Minister of Finance: Dr Ashni Singh
Minister of Home Affairs: Hon. Clement J. Rohee (page 1505)
Minister of Agriculture: Hon. Dr Leslie Ramsammy

Minister of Foreign Affairs, Foreign Trade and International Co-operation: Carolyn Rodrigues-Birkett (page 1504)
Minister of Education: Ms. Priya Devi Manickchand (page 1470)
Minister of the Public Service, Public Service Management: Hon. Jennifer Westford
Minister of Culture, Youth and Sport: Hon. Dr. Frank Anthony
Minister of Amerindian Affairs: Pauline Campbell-Sukhai
Minister of Tourism, Industry and Commerce: vacant
Attorney General and Minister of Legal Affairs: Mohabir Anil Nandlall
Minister of Labour: Hon. Dr Nanda Kissore Gopaul
Minister of Local Government and Regional Development: Hon Ganga Persaud
Minister of Health: Hon. Dr Bheri Ramsaran
Minister of Housing and Water: Mohamed Irfaan Ali
Head of the Presidential Secretariat: Dr Roger Luncheon
Minister of Public Works: Robeson Benn
Minister of Natural Resources and Environment: Robert Montgomery Persaud
Mnister of Human Services and Social Security: Jennifer Webster
Minister in the Ministry of Finance: Juan Edghill
Minister in the Ministry of Local Government and Regional Development: Norman Whittaker
Minister in the Ministry of Agriculture: Alli Baksh

Ministries
Government portal: http://gina.gov.gy
Office of the President, New Garden Street, Georgetown, Guyana. Tel: +592 225 13308 / 227 1574, e-mail: opjagdeo@guyana.net.gy, URL: http://www.op.gov.gy/
Office of the Prime Minister, Wights Lane, Kingston, Georgetown, Guyana. Tel: +592 226 6955, fax: +592 226 7573, URL: http://gina.gov.gy
Ministry of Finance, Main and Urquhart Streets, Georgetown, Guyana. Tel: +592 227 1114 / 225 6088, fax: +592 226 1284
Ministry of Foreign Affairs, Takuba Lodge, 254 South Road and New Garden Streets, Georgetown, Guyana. Tel: +592 226 1607 / 225 6467, fax: +592 225 9192, e-mail: minfor@sdnp.org.gy, URL: http://www.minfor.gov.gy/
Ministry of Agriculture, Regent and Vlissengen Roads, PO Box 1001, Georgetown, Guyana. Tel: +592 226 7863, fax: +592 225 0599, e-mail: guyagri@hotmail.com, URL: http://www.sdnp.org.gy/minagri/
Ministry of Public Service, 164 Waterloo Street N/Cummingsburg, Georgetown, Guyana. Tel: +592 226 6528, fax: +592 225 7899, e-mail: psm@sdnp.org.gy, URL: http://www.sdnp.org.gy/psm/
Ministry of Culture, Youth and Sport, 71-72 Main Street, Georgetown, Guyana. Tel: +592 227 7860 / 3576, fax: +592 225 5067
Ministry of Transport and Hydraulics, Wights Lane, Kingston, Georgetown, Guyana. Tel: +592 226 1875, fax: +592 225 6954
Ministry of Information, Office of the President, New Garden Street, Georgetown, Guyana. Tel: +592 226 8849, fax: +592 226 8883
Ministry of Amerindian Affairs, Office of the President, New Garden Street, Georgetown, Guyana. Tel: +592 227 5067
Ministry of Tourism, Industry and Commerce, 229 South Road, Georgetown, Guyana. Tel: +592 226 2505 / 2392 / 3182, fax: +592 225 4310 / 9898, e-mail ministry@mintic.gov.gy, URL: http://www.mintic.gov.gy/
Ministry of Education, 21 Brickdam, Georgetown, Guyana. Tel: +592 223 7900, fax: +592 225 5570, e-mail: moegyweb@yahoo.com, URL: http://www.sdnp.org.gy/minedu/
Ministry of Legal Affairs, Carmichael Street, Georgetown, Guyana. Tel: +592 225 3607, fax: +592 227 5419
Ministry of Agriculture, Department of Forestry, Fisheries, Crops and Livestock, Regent and Vlissengen Roads, Georgetown, Guyana. Tel: +592 2 61565, Fax: +592 2 73638
Ministry of Labour, Human Services and Social Security, 1 Water and Cornhill Street, Stabroek, Georgetown, Guyana. Tel: +592 225 0655 , fax: +592 227 1308, e-mail: nrdocgd@sdnp.org.gy, URL: http://www.sdnp.org.gy/mohss/
Ministry of Local Government, DeWinkle Buildings, Fort Street, Georgetown, Guyana. Tel: +592 225 8639, fax: +592 225 8619
Ministry of Health, Lot1, Brickdam, Georgetown, Guyana. Tel: +592 226 1560, fax: +592 225 4505, e-mail: moh@sdnp.org.gy, ministerofhealth@hotmail.com, URL: http://www.sdnp.org.gy/moh

Ministry of Housing and Water, Homestretch Avenue, Georgetown, Guyana. Tel: +592 226 0489, fax: +592 225 3477
Ministry of Home Affairs, Brickdam, Georgetown, Guyana. Tel: +592 225 7270, fax: +592 226 2740
Ministry of Foreign Trade and International Co-operation, Takuba Lodge, 254 South Road & New Garden Street, Georgetown, Guyana. Tel: +592 226 1607 - 9, fax: +592 226 8426, e-mail: minister@moftic.gov.gy, URL: http://www.moftic.gov.gy

Political Parties
People's Progressive Party (PPP), URL: http://www.ppp-civic.org
Leader Elect: Donald Ramotar
People's National Congress (PNC), URL: http://www.guyanapnc.org
Leader: Robert Corbin
People's Unity Party, URL: http://www.peoplesunityparty.com/;
Rise Organise and Rebuild Guyana; Alliance for Change; The United Force (TUF)

Elections
Voting tends to be on racial lines with Indo-Guyanese traditionally supporting the PPP and Afro-Guyanese supporting the PNC. The ruling party, the PPP (People's Progressive Party), came to power in 1992 after 28 years of rule by the PNC.

The President is not directly elected but nominated by a party and elected by the assembly. In 1999 Janet Jagan resigned due to ill health and Bharrat Jagdeo became president. Parliamentary elections were held in August 2006. The People's Progressive Party (PPP) retained the presidency of Bharrat Jagdeo, and maintained its position as the largest party in the National Assembly.

The most recent parliamentary elections took place on 28 November 2011. The People's Progressive Party - Civic Party won with 32 seats, the Partnership for National Unity (alliance led by PNC-R) won 26 seats.

President Bharrat Jagdeo could not stand for a third term in office. His successor was Donald Ramotar of the ruling PPP-C.

Diplomatic Representation
Guyana High Commission, 3 Palace Court, Bayswater Road, London, W2 4LP, UK. Tel: +44 (0)20 7229 7684 - 8, fax: +44 (0)20 7727 9809, URL: http://www.guyanahclondon.co.uk
High Commissioner: Mr Laleshwar K.N. Singh
Embassy of Guyana, 2490 Tracy Place NW, Washington, DC, 20008, USA. Tel: + 1 202 265 6900, fax: +1 202 232 1297, e-mail: GuyanaEmbassy@hotmail.com, URL: http://www.guyana.org/govt/embassy.html
Ambassador: Bayney Karran (page 1454)
British High Commission, 44 Main Street, PO Box 10849, Georgetown, Guyana. Tel: +592 22 65881, fax: +592 22 53555, URL: http://ukinguyana.fco.gov.uk/en
High Commissioner: Andrew Ayre
US Embassy, 100 Young and Duke Streets, Georgetown, Guyana. Tel: +592 226 3938, fax: +592 227 0240, e-mail: usembassy@hotmail.com, URL: http://georgetown.usembassy.gov
Ambassador: Dr Brent Hardt (page 1438)
Permanent Representative of the Republic of Guyana to the United Nations, 801 Second Avenue, 5th Floor, New York, NY 10017, USA. Tel: +1 212 573 5828, fax: +1 212 573 6225, email: guyanan@un.int, URL: http://www.un.int/wcm/content/site/guyana/
Ambassador: vacant

LEGAL SYSTEM

The legal system is based on English common law. The highest court is the Supreme Court, which has two divisions: the High Court which consists of the chief justice of the Supreme Court and 10 puisne justices and has both original and appellate jurisdiction; and the Court of Appeal, which consists of a chancellor, the chief justice of the Supreme Court, and as many justices as the National Assembly may prescribe. The chancellor of the court of appeal is the country's chief judicial officer. Magistrates' courts exercise summary jurisdiction in lesser civil and criminal matters. An ombudsman can investigate governmental wrongdoing, but lacks the authority to investigate allegations of police misconduct.

The government respects the human rights of its citizens, but there have been instances of unlawful killings by police, government corruption, lengthy pretrial detention in poor prison conditions, and the mistreatment of suspects and detainees by the security forces. Guyana retains the death penalty for crimes including terrorist acts, rape, murder, treason and torture. It is not a mandatory punishment.

Guyana is a member of the Caribbean Court of Justice.

Caribbean Court of Justice: URL: http://www.caribbeancourtofjustice.org/default.htm

Office of the Ombudsman, 39 Brickdam, Georgetown, Guyana. Tel: +592 226 2294

LOCAL GOVERNMENT

Guyana is divided into ten regions administered by Regional Democratic Councils. Local communities are administered by village or city councils. Included in the regions are five municipal districts (cities) each with a mayor and council. Regional Councils are elected for a term of up to five years and four months. Elections are due in 2011. The following table shows local government regions and their populations:

Region	Population
Barimi - Waini	18,755
Pomeroon - Supernaam	43,147
Essequibo Island & West Demerara	92,139

- continued	
Mahaica - West Berbice	49,937
East Berbice - Corentyne	144,107
Cuyuni - Mazaruni	15,478
Potaro - Siparuni	5,788
Upper Takutu - Upper Essequibo	15,221
Upper Demerara - Berbice	39,453
Demerara - Mahaica	na

AREA AND POPULATION

Area
Guyana lies on the mainland of the South American continent. Its northern coastline, about 270 miles long, borders the Atlantic Ocean from the eastern mouth of the Orinoco river to the west, and the Corentyne river to the east. Guyana is bounded on the south and south-east by Brazil, on the east by Suriname (Dutch Guiana), and on the north-west by Venezuela. The area of Guyana is 216,000 sq. km (83,000 sq. miles). The interior of the country is savannah, the highlands are forested and the coastal area is low coastal plains.

The climate is tropical but moderated by trade winds. There are two rainy seasons (November to January and May to August).

To view a map, consult: http://www.lib.utexas.edu/maps/cia08/guyana_sm_2008.gif

Population
In 2010 the population was estimated at 754,000 with an annual growth rate of about 0.3 per cent for the period 2000-10. Approximately 90 per cent of the population lives on Guyana's narrow coastal plain. The population density here is 115 people per square km. Georgetown, the capital, has a population of 250,000. An estimated 29 per cent of the population live in urban areas.

Indians account for over 49 per cent of the population, Africans over 35 per cent, Amerindians over six per cent, mixed race seven per cent, and Europeans and Chinese less than one per cent each. The official language is English. Hindi and Urdu are used in religious rites.

Births, Marriages, Deaths
The crude birth rate for 2010 is estimated at 18.1 births per 1,000 people, and the death rate is an estimated 6.6 deaths per 1,000 in the same year. The infant mortality rate was 25 per 1,000 live births in 2010. The maternal mortality rate in 2010 was 280 per 100,000 live births. The fertility rate in 2010 stood at 2.3 children per woman.

The median age of the population is 24 years. An estimated 34 per cent of the population is aged under 15 years, and an estimated 6 per cent of the population is aged over 60 years. The average life expectancy at birth is 65 years (64 years for males and 70 years for females). Healthy life expectancy is estimated at 53 years (55 years for females and 52 years for males). (Source: http://www.who.int, World Health Statistics 2012)

Public Holidays 2014
1 January: New Year's Day
23 February: Proclamation of the Republic Day
18 April: Good Friday
21 April: Easter Monday
1 May: Labour Day
29 June: Beginning of Ramadan*
29 July: End of Ramadan*
7 August: Freedom Day
5 October: Feast of the Sacrifice*
25-26 December: Christmas
* Islamic holidays depend on the sighting of the moon and so dates can vary

EMPLOYMENT

Recent figures estimate the workforce to number 334,000 of whom 45 per cent are involved in the industry and commerce sector, 33 per cent in agriculture and 22 per cent in services. Recent figures put the unemployment rate at around 9 per cent.

The following table shows breakdown of employment by industry.

Employment in Guyana, 2002

Sector	Employed
Total	239,610
Agriculture, hunting and forestry	45,615
Fishing	5,587
Mining and quarrying	9,471
Manufacturing	30,631
Utilities	2,262
Construction	16,220
Wholesale and retail trade	37,907
Hotels and restaurants	5,601
Transport, storage and communications	16,954
Financial intermediation	3,101
Real estate, renting and business affairs	7,440
Public administration	15,092
Education	13,075
Health and social work	5,555
Other community, social & personal service activities	9,683
Households with employed persons	6,191

GUYANA

- continued

Extra-territorial organisations & bodies 8,734
Not classifiable by economic activity 8,734
Source: Copyright © International Labour Organization (ILO Dept. of Statistics, http://laborsta.ilo.org)

BANKING AND FINANCE

Currency
The unit of currency is the Guyana dollar, 1G$ = 100 cents.

The financial centre is Georgetown.

GDP/GNP, Inflation, National Debt
The economy is based mainly on agriculture and extractive industries. The country has experienced several years of moderate growth. The Takatu Bridge, connecting Guyana to Brazil, opened in 2009 meaning that Brazil may now export goods to the US, Caribbean and European markets through Guyana. Markets in the south of the country will also be opened and is it hoped that the economic benefits of the bridge for Guyana will be substantial.

Agriculture accounts for around 38 per cent of GDP, services for 42 per cent and industry for around 20 per cent. Traditionally sugar has been a large contributor of GDP, averaging an 18 per cent contribution. In January and February 2003 Guyana was hit by devastating floods which had an adverse effect on agriculture and business; as a result GDP grew by just 1.1 per cent in 2003 and by an estimated 1.7 per cent in 2004 (down from 2.3 per cent in 2002). Since the EU agreed to reform its sugar buying from preferential markets in 2005, Guyana has been working hard to diversify its economy to offset any potential downturn in the economy. The fishing sector had strong growth in 2007 following the launch of the Fisheries Management Plan. In 2007, GDP grew by an estimated 5 per cent, 3.1 per cent in 2008 and 2.3 per cent.

GDP was approximately US$2.5 billion in 2011 with an estimated growth rate of 5.2 per cent. GDP per capita was an estimated US$7,500.

Inflation between 1990 and 1997 averaged around 25 per cent but fell to an estimated six per cent in 2001 and to 4.5 per cent in 2004. In 2006, it stood at 4.2 per cent. In 2007 it was estimated to be over 12 per cent. The substantial increase is due to rising global food prices and energy costs.

Total external debt in 2002 amounted to some US$1.2 billion. During the G8 summit in 2005, it was agreed that US$336 million of Guyana's debt would be cancelled. Guyana no longer receives aid through the Heavily Indebted Poor Country Initiative. Debt service payments stand at an estimated US$19 million.

Foreign Investment
The government is keen to attract foreign investment. GO-INVEST, a quasi-governmental organisation, provides information and assistance to investors.

Balance of Payments / Imports and Exports
In 2007, total exports earned Guyana over US$680 million (f.o.b.), a growth of over 15 per cent from the previous year. The increase is due mainly to increased commodity prices and greater supply. Major export products are sugar, bauxite, rice, gold, shrimp, rum, timber and molasses to markets in Canada, the US, the UK, Portugal and Jamaica. The agricultural and mining industries are responsible for 75-80 per cent of export earnings. Estimated figures for 2009 put export earnings at US$769 million.

Imports cost the country around US$1.6 billion (f.o.b.) in 2007. The major import suppliers are the US, Trinidad and Tobago, the UK, Cuba and China. Main imported goods are manufactured goods, machinery and petroleum. Estimated figures for 2009 put import costs at US$1.2 billion.

In October 2008, Guyana signed a trade agreement with the European Union.

Central Bank
Bank of Guyana, PO Box 1003, 1 Church Street and Avenue of the Republic, Georgetown, Guyana. Tel: +592 2 263250-9 / 263261-5, fax: +592 2 272965, e-mail: communications@bankofguyana.org.gy, URL: http://www.bankofguyana.org.gy
Governor: Lawrence Williams

Chambers of Commerce and Trade Organisations
Georgetown Chamber of Commerce and Industry, URL: http://www.georgetownchamberofcommerce.org

MANUFACTURING, MINING AND SERVICES

Primary and Extractive Industries
Guyana is rich in mineral resources. Bauxite is the major export earner, with proven reserves of approximately 350 million tons. Open-cast mining of this resource began during the first quarter of this century. In 2002, the country produced over 62,000 tonnes of calcinated bauxite and 1.5 million tonnes of dried bauxite.

Other minerals found include gold (453,000 ounces mined in 2002), diamonds and high-quality kaolin, which is suitable for the production of paper coatings, paper fillers and paints. In addition, there are significant deposits of copper, iron, laterite, nickel, magnesite, talc, manganese, phosphates, uranite and silica sand. Offshore oil exploration is currently being considered.

Energy
The country is dependent on imported oil from Venezuela and Trinidad, amounting to 11,000 barrels per day in 2011. Figures for 2010 show that Guyana produced 0.70 billion kWh of electricity and consumed 0.51 kWh, most of which was produced from fossil fuels and a small amount from hydro sources.

Manufacturing
This sector contributes around 10 per cent of GDP. The majority of production consists of processing mineral and agricultural goods including rice milling, sugar, shrimp, bauxite, timber and gold, although there are small factories making products such as clothing, footwear and cigarettes. Industrial growth is hampered by a shortage of skilled workers and a deficient infrastructure.

Tourism
In 2000 there were 105,000 visitors to Guyana. This figure had grown to almost 122,000 by 2004. Guyana is looking to expand its tourism industry to become a substantial contributor to the economy.

Agriculture
This sector contributed around 31.5 per cent of GDP in 2003, sugar production forming a large part. Guyana's other main agricultural products include rice (over 12 per cent of agricultural GDP), wheat, livestock (four per cent of agricultural GDP), poultry, vegetable oils and shrimps. Fishing as a whole contributed over nine per cent of the agricultural GDP in 2003. Guyana is almost self-sufficient in food. An estimated 480,000 hectares are used for arable farming and 30,000 for permanent crops. Twenty-five per cent of the land is irrigated.

Agricultural Production in 2010

Produce	Int. $'000*	Tonnes
Rice paddy	149,418	556,200
Sugar cane	83,153	2,762,300
Indigenous chicken meat	35,367	34,829
Cow milk, whole, fresh	13,450	43,100
Coconuts	7,895	71,400
Indigenous cattle meat	4,863	1,800
Beans, green	4,541	12,771
Plantains	3,964	21,335
Tomatoes	3,134	8,481
Fruit, tropical fresh nes	2,248	5,500
Chillies and peppers. green	2,030	4,312
Bananas	1,802	6,400

*unofficial figures
Source: http://faostat.fao.org/site/339/default.aspx Food and Agriculture Organization of the United Nations, Food and Agricultural commodities production

An estimated 1,230,000 hectares of land are used for pasture.

Guyana's forests contain over 1,000 different varieties of trees. About 70 species of timber are exploited on a regular basis. Several plants have constituents which may be used to produce medicines and essential oils. Approximately 360,000 ha (1.45 million acres) of land has been allocated for the Rain Forest Project, which seeks to establish guidelines for sustainable development of tropical forests. A third of the area, almost uninhabited, is to be preserved as virgin forest. The rest is to be developed on an environmentally sustainable basis for the benefit of the population.

Forestry Production 2004

Product	Thousand Cubic Metres
Roundwood	481
Sawn wood	36
Wood fuel	866
Wood charcoal	22
Wood-based panels	54

Source: FAOSTAT, Food & Agricultural Organization of the United Nations

COMMUNICATIONS AND TRANSPORT

Travel Requirements
US, Canadian, Australian and EU subjects require a passport valid for the duration of stay but do not require a visa for tourist stays of up to 90 days. The exceptions are citizens of Austria, Bulgaria, Cyprus, the Czech Republic, Estonia, Hungary, Latvia, Lithuania, Malta, Poland, Romania, Slovak Republic, Slovenia and Sweden who do need a visa. Transit passengers leaving within seven hours and not leaving the airport do no require a visa. Other nationals should contact the embassy/high commission to check visa requirements.

Travellers for purposes other than tourism should check with the Ministry of Home Affairs for information about requirements for work permits and extended stays.

International Airports
Cheddi Jagan is Guyana's international airport. It is situated 40 km south of Georgetown. Other smaller airfields include Ogle, Kaieteur, Lethem, Mainstay and Mahdia Airstrip.

Railways
The rail system is used solely for the transportation of goods, such as ore. There are 187 km of mainly standard gauge railways.

Roads

Guyana's roads network is approximately 8,000 km of which 600 km are paved. Vehicles are driven on the left. The Takatu Bridge is currently under construction which will connect Brazil with Guyana, opening up new markets. Bus services connect Guyana with Suriname and Brazil.

Waterways

The Berbice, Demerara and Essequiblo rivers are navigable by ocean vessels for up to 150 km, 100 km and 80 km respectively.

Ports and Harbours

Georgetown, New Amsterdam and Springlands are the main ports.

HEALTH

Health care is provided by the state and some private facilities are available. Health facilities consist of 39 local health posts, 194 health centres and 18 district hospitals. Four regional hospitals provide accident and emergency care and the Public Hospital at Georgetown is the national referral hospital. In addition there are 10 private hospitals and some large companies provide health care and hospital facilities for their employees.

In 2009, Guyana spent approximately 10 per cent of its total budget on healthcare, accounting for 54.9 per cent of all healthcare spending. External resources accounted for 36 per cent of expenditure. Total expenditure on health care equated to 5.6 per cent of the country's GDP. Per capita total expenditure on health was US$152 in 2009, compared with US$56 in 2000. Figures for 2000-10 showed that there were 366 physicians (5 per 10,000 population), 1,738 nurses (23 per 10,000 population) and 30 dentists. There are 25 hospital beds per 10,000 population.

The infant mortality rate (probability of dying by age one) was 25 per 1,000 live births and the childhood mortality rate (probability of dying by age five) was 30 per 1,000 live births. The most common causes of death for children under five are: diarrhoea 3 per cent (compared to 80 per cent in 2000), malaria 7 per cent, prematurity 25 per cent and HIV/AIDS 1 per cent (compared with 5 per cent in 2000). Immunization rates against common diseases such as measles has risen and is now over 95 per cent.

In 2010, an estimated 94 per cent of the population had sustainable access to improved drinking water and an estimated 84 per cent of the population had sustainable access to improved sanitation. (Source: http://www.who.int, World Health Statistics 2012)

EDUCATION

The Government is responsible for education, from primary to tertiary level. In 2007, government expenditure on education as a percentage of total government expenditure was 12.5 per cent (6.3 per cent of GDP). This broke down to 13 per cent pre-primary, 33 per cent primary, 34 per cent secondary and 5 per cent tertiary.

The total adult literacy rate is estimated at 91.3 per cent (92 per cent for males and 90.87 per cent for females). The youth literacy rate (15-24 years) is estimated at 97 per cent (males 96.5 per cent, females 97.4 per cent). (Source: UNESCO)

Primary/Secondary Education

Primary enrolment is estimated at 89 per cent of primary school age children. The ratio of pupil to teacher is estimated at 28:1. An estimated 68 per cent of primary school children go onto secondary education.

Students are offered places at the secondary schools on the basis of marks gained at secondary school entrance examinations. At the better equipped schools, places are severely limited, and competition is correspondingly high. Secondary and community high schools provide academic and pre-vocational training. The curricula offered in secondary schools are based on the British Grammar School system. Students are prepared for external examinations such as the General Certificate of Education at Ordinary and Advanced levels and the Caribbean Examinations Council (CXC) Examinations. Community High Schools place greater emphasis on pre-vocational subjects. Secondary school attendance is estimated at 70 per cent. Recent figures show that there are 894 schools and 7,453 teachers.

Higher Education

An estimated 12 per cent of the population attend higher education. Higher education is provided by the University of Guyana, established in 1963. The University offers training in many disciplines, including natural sciences, social sciences, art, technology, education, health sciences, agriculture and the First Year law programme. Students are, however, required to complete the additional two years at the University of the West Indies. The University also offers Masters degrees in the fields of education, political science, and history.

Technical and vocational training is provided at six technical institutions including the Government Technical Institute, the Industrial Training Centre and the Carnegie School of Home Economics. Private vocational schools exist which provide teaching in computing, accountancy and business, electronics and mechanics.

RELIGION

Freedom of worship is guaranteed by the Constitution. Christianity, Hinduism and Islam are followed. Of the total population, 52.6 per cent are Christians, 31.6 per cent are Hindus, 8.1 per cent are Muslim, 2.3 per cent follow traditional beliefs and 1.7 per cent are Baha'is.

Guyana has a religious liberty rating of 10 on a scale of 1 to 10 (10 is most freedom). (Source: World Religion Database)

COMMUNICATIONS AND MEDIA

The press and broadcasters have freedom of expression but self-censorship is also practised.

Newspapers

Guyana Chronicle, Georgetown, (Daily, government owned), URL: http://www.guyanachronicle.com
Stabroek News, Lacytown, (Daily), URL: http://www.stabroeknews.com
Mirror, (Bi weekly), URL: http://www.mirrornewsonline.com
Kaieteur News, URL: http://www.kaieteurnews.com/

Broadcasting

The National Communications Network operates two radio stations: Voice of Guyana and Radio Roraima. They broadcast daily in English. Guyana Television (Government News Service) provides three hours of programmes on a weekly basis. Additional provisions exist for a 15-minute nightly news broadcast. Local television channels are WRHM and VCT; both televise daily in English. The government has imposed limits on the number of private licenses available.

National Communications Network, URL: http://www.ncnguyana.com/

Telecommunications

Many areas still do not have access to landlines. In 2008 there were an estimated 125,000 main lines in operation and an estimated 280,000 mobile phones.

Recent figures show that Guyana has around 200,000 internet users.

ENVIRONMENT

Forests are an important resource to Guyana, hence the implementation of the Iwokrama Rainforest Programme. The program involved setting aside one million acres of virgin forest for preservation and scientific study. Environmental concerns include climate change and the rising of the sea level, as flooding would greatly affect the low-lying plains where 90 per cent of the population lives.

Guyana is a party to international environmental agreements on Biodiversity, Climate Change, Climate Change-Kyoto Protocol, Desertification, Endangered Species, Hazardous Wastes, Law of the Sea, Ozone Layer Protection, Ship Pollution, Tropical Timber 83, and Tropical Timber 94.

In 2010, Guyana's emissions from the consumption of fossil fuels totalled 1.52 million metric tons of carbon dioxide. (Source: EIA)

HAITI
Republic of Haiti
République d'Haïti

Capital: Port-au-Prince (Population estimate: 2,000,000)

Head of State: Michel Martelly (President) (page 1471)

National Flag: Horizontal blue and red bands: palm tree centre with drum at base, and cannon at each side, all over a ribboned motto: 'L'union fait la force'

CONSTITUTION AND GOVERNMENT

Constitution

In 1804 the former French colony, Saint Domingue, was declared an independent republic named Haiti, making it the first black republic.

In 1956 Dr. François Duvalier (Papa Doc) seized power in a coup and was elected president in 1957. On 14 June 1964, after a national referendum, Dr. Duvalier was elected President for Life. Dr. Duvalier died on 21 April 1971. He was succeeded as President for Life on the same day by his son, Jean-Claude Duvalier (Baby Doc), whom he had nominated as his successor under the constitution. Duvalier was ousted on 7 February 1986 and the army leader Gen. Henri Namphy headed a new National Governing Council. A new constitution was approved and elections scheduled for 1987. These were aborted and were replaced by military controlled elections resulting in the election of Leslie Manigat as president in January 1988. Only four months later Gen. Namphy ousted Manigat before himself being ousted by General Prosper Avril, who took office as president. By 1990 he had declared a state of siege before resigning later in the year. Democratic elections took place later in the year and Jean-Bertrand Aristide was elected president in December 1990 with over 60 per cent of the vote. He took office on 7 February 1991. He was sent into exile on 30 September 1991 following a coup by the army, led by Gen. Raoul Cedras.

With the exception of the Vatican, all countries continued to recognise Aristide as the president, and worldwide embargoes against the coup regime were declared. Under the coup regime the human rights situation continued to deteriorate and in 1994 the UN Security Council passed a resolution authorising the member states to facilitate the departure of the military regime. This culminated in a multi-national force landing in Haiti after the coup leaders stepped down. On 15 October 1994 President Aristide and his government in exile returned to Haiti.

For further information on the constitution, please visit:
http://www.haiti.org/index.php?option=com_content&view=article&id=60&Itemid=108

Recent Events

President Aristide was elected for a second term in 2000. In January 2004 a series of uprisings began against his rule, and he went into exile in February. The chief justice of the Supreme Court, Boniface Alexandre, took over as interim president. In June UN peacekeepers arrived to deal with the security situation and flood victims. Violence continued with armed groups and former soldiers still loyal to former president Aristide carrying out sporadic attacks. In April 2005 police killed a rebel leader, Ravix Remissainthe, who had been involved in the ousting of President Aristide and was wanted by the police in connection with the murders of four policemen.

Democratic elections took place in 2006; René Preval was declared the winner of the presidential vote after a deal was reached over spoiled ballot papers. In September 2006, the UN began a scheme to disarm gang members in return for grants and job training, and in January 2007, UN troops launched an offensive against armed gangs in Cite Soleil, one of the capital's largest and most violent shantytowns.

In April 2008 there were riots over the high cost of food. The prime minister, Jacques-Édouard Alexis, was dismissed and the government announced an emergency plan to cut the price of rice in order to quell the violence.

The 2008 hurricane season hit Haiti hard. Hurricane Hanna at the beginning of September was particularly bad with the city Gonaives suffering the brunt; more than 500 people were believed to have died in the storms and up to a million people were left homeless. Hurricane Ike followed, and again Gonaives was the worst affected, with widespread damage and flooding. Overall, nearly 800 people were killed in the four major storms which devastated the country over the season, and a further 300 went missing.

After several attempts to appoint a successor to Mr Alexis, Michele Pierre-Louis was appointed as prime minister. Her cabinet took office in September 2008. However, Ms Pierre-Louis lost a vote of confidence in October 2009. The president named Jean-Max Bellerive, the then minister of planning, as the new prime minister. After approval by both the Senate and the Chamber of Deputies on 6 and 7 November respectively, Mr Bellerive announced a reshuffled cabinet on 8 November.

On 12th January 2010 Haiti was hit by a devastating earthquake; the capital Port-au-Prince was particularly badly hit and initial reports put the number of dead anything from 50,000 to 200,000. Providing access to clean water and food became the immediate focus for foreign aid agencies. The number of fatalities as a result of the earthquake was later revised to 300,000, with 1.5 million made homeless. Government buildings suffered severe damage.

In October and November Haiti suffered a Cholera outbreak. More than 1,000 people died, the outbreak started north of the Port-au-Prince and many of the victims were among those still homeless from the earthquake.

In February 2012, Prime Minister Garry Conille announced he was resigning from the post following power struggles with the government. Foreign Minister Laurent Lamothe was appointed to the position in May 2012.

In November 2012, Haiti was hit by Hurricane Sandy, more than 20,000 people were made homeless and there was extensive crop damage.

Legislature

Haiti's bicameral legislature consists of the Senate and the House of Deputies.

Upper House

The Senate comprises three senators per Department, all elected by universal suffrage for a term of six years. One third of the Senate must be replaced every two years. There are currently 30 senators.
Senate, (Sénat), Avenue Marie Jeanne, Cité de l''Exposition, Port-au-Prince, Haiti. Tel: +509 222 3903, fax: +509 222 8541, e-mail: senat@acn2.net

Lower House

The House of Deputies consists of a minimum of 70 Deputies elected by direct suffrage for a term of four years. The entire House of Deputies must be replaced every four years. There are currently 99 members.
Chamber of Deputies, (Chambre des Députés), Palais législatif, Port-au-Prince, Haiti. Tel: +509 222 3363, fax: +509 222 4129, e-mail: info@haitiparlement.org

Cabinet (as at June 2013)

Prime Minister, Minister of Planning and External Co-operation: Laurent Lamothe (page 1460)
Minister of Foreign Affairs and Religious Affairs: Pierra Richard Casimir
Minister of Finance and Economy, Trade and Industry (acting): Wilson Laleau
Minister of the Interior and Territorial Collectives: David Bazile
Minister of Justice and Public Security: Jean Sanon
Minister of Public Works, Transport and Communications: Jacques Rousseau
Minister of National Education and Professional Training: Vanneur Pierre
Minister of Public Health and Population: Florence Duperval Guillaume
Minister of Agriculture, Natural Resources and Rural Development: Thomas Jacques
Minister of Women's Affairs and Rights: Yanick Mezile
Minister of Social Affairs and Labour: Charles Jean-Jacques
Minister of Haitians Abroad: Bernice Fidelia
Minister of Tourism: Stephanie Balmir Villedrouin
Minister of Culture, Minister of Communications (acting): Josette Darguste
Minister of the Environment: Jean Francois Thomas
Minister of Youth, Sport and Civil Action: Magalie Racine
Minister of National Defence: Jean Rodolphe Joazile
Minister Delegate to the Prime Minister with Relations with Parliament: Ralph Ricardo Theano
Minister Delegate to tohe Prime Minister for Human Rights and the Fight against Extreme Poverty: Marie Carmelle Auguste
Minister Delegate to the Prime Minister for Promoting the Peasantry: Marie Mimose Felix
Minister Delegate to the Prime Minister responsible for Energy Security: Rene Jean-Jumeau

Ministries

Office of the President, Rue Champ-de-Mars, Port-au-Prince, Haiti. Tel: +509 2228 2128, fax: +509 2228 2320, URL: http://www.palaishaiti.net
Office of the Prime Minister, Villa d'Accueil, Musseau, Port-au-Prince, Haiti. Tel: +509 2245 0025, fax: +509 2298 3900
Ministry of Agriculture, Natural Resources and Rural Development, Rte Nationale 1, Damien, Port-au-Prince, Haiti. Tel: +509 2298 3010
Ministry of Commerce and Industry, 8 rue Légitime, Champ-de-Mars, Port-au-Prince, Haiti. Tel: +509 2222 2499, fax: +509 2223 8402
Ministry of Culture and Communication, 31 Ruelle Roy, Ave Christophe, Port-au-Prince, Haiti. Tel: +509 2221 1721, fax: +509 2221 7318
Ministry of the Environment, Haut de Turgeau 181, Turgeau, Port-au-Prince, Haiti. Tel: +509 2245 7572, fax: +509 2245 7572, e-mail: dgmde@rehred-haiti.net, URL: http://www.rehred-haiti.net
Ministry of Finance and Economy, Palais des Ministères, Champ-de-Mars, Port-au-Prince, Haiti. Tel: +509 2299 1722, fax: +509 2299 1732
Ministry of Foreign Affairs, Blvd Harry S. Truman, Bicentaire, Port-au-Prince, Haiti. Tel: +509 2222 8484, fax: +509 2298 3772
Ministry for Haitians Living Abroad, 87 Ave Jean Paul II, Port-au-Prince, Haiti. Tel: +509 2245 1116, fax: +509 2245 3400
Ministry of the Interior and Territorial Collectives, Palais des Ministères, Champ-de-Mars, Port-au-Prince, Haiti. Tel: +509 2222 3347, fax: +509 2222 4429
Ministry of Justice and Public Security, 18 ave Charles Summer, Bois Verna, Port-au-Prince, Haiti. Tel: +509 2245 0474, fax: +509 2245 0474

Ministry of National Education and Vocational Training, rue Dr Audain, Port-au-Prince, Haiti. Tel: +509 2223 4716, fax: +509 2223 7887
Ministry of Planning and External Co-operation, Palais des Ministères, Champ-de-Mars, Port-au-Prince, Haiti. Tel: +509 2222 0226, fax: +509 2223 4222
Ministry of Public Health and Population, Palais des Ministères, Champ-de-Mars, Port-au-Prince, Haiti. Tel: +509 2222 1248, fax: +509 2222 1248
Ministry of Public Works, Transport and Communications, Palais des Ministères, Champ-de-Mars, Port-au-Prince, Haiti. Tel: +509 2223 3240, fax: +509 2223 4798
Ministry of Social Affairs and Labour, Rues du Champ-de-Mars et Magasin de l'Etat, Centre-Ville, Port-au-Prince, Haiti. Tel: +509 2222 1244, fax: +509 2223 2899
Ministry of Tourism, rue Légitime a coté Ministère du Commerce, Champ-de-Mars, Port-au-Prince, Haiti. Tel: +509 2223 0723, fax: +509 2223 7350, URL: http://www.haititourisme.com
Ministry of Women's Affairs and Rights, Angle rue Geffoprard et Piquant, Port-au-Prince, Haiti. Tel: +509 2223 4797, fax: +509 2223 4797
Ministry of Youth, Sports and Civic Action, 11 rue Garoute, Pacot, Port-au-Prince, Haiti. Tel: +509 2245 5794, fax: +509 2245 4568

Elections

In the February 2006 presidential election René Préval won 51 per cent of the vote and began his second term as president. General elections were held in February 2006, the first since former President Aristide was overthrown in 2004, and in June a new government took office, headed by Prime Minister Jacques-Edouard Alexis. Parliamentary elections were due in February 2010 but were postponed due to the previous month's earthquake. Elections were eventually held on 28 November 2010. The election was inconclusive and a run-off election was held in March 2011. Former musician Michel Martelly was elected with 67.6 per cent of the vote he then appointed and in October he appointed UN development expert Garry Conille as prime minister.

The most recent legislative elections were held in November 2010, Inite won 46 seats, AAA, won eight seats, Alternativ, seven seats.

Political Parties

Alternative for Progress and Democracy (Alternativ); Haiti in Action (AAA); Lavalas; Organization of the Future (Lavni); Peasants' Response (Repons Peyizan); Unity (Inité).

Diplomatic Representation

Haitian Embassy, 2311 Massachusetts Ave., N.W., Washington, DC 20008, USA. Tel: +1 202 332 4090, fax: +1 202 745 7215, e-mail: embassy@haiti.org, URL: http://www.haiti.org
Ambassador: Paul Getty Altidor
US Embassy, 5 Boulevard Harry S Truman, Port-au-Prince, Republic of Haiti. Tel: +509 222 0200 / 0354, fax. +509 223 9038, URL: http://haiti.usembassy.gov/
Ambassador: Pamela White
British Consulate, Hotel Montana, (P O Box 1302), Port-au-Prince, Haiti. Tel: +509 257 3969, fax: +509 257 4048, (Ambassador resides at Santo Domingo).URL: http://ukindominicanrepublic.fco.gov.uk/en/
Ambassador: Steven Fisher
There is no diplomatic representation in the UK.
Permanent Representative of Haiti to the United Nations, 801 Second Avenue, Room 600, New York, NY 10017, USA. Tel: +1 212 370 4840, e-mail: haiti@un.int, URL: http://www.un.int/wcm/content/site/haiti/
Ambassador: Leo Merores

LEGAL SYSTEM

Haitian law is based on the French Napoleonic Code. Justice is administered by a Supreme Court, or *Cour de Cassation,* Courts of Appeal, Civil Courts and magistrates' courts. Supreme Court judges are appointed by the President of Haiti for 10 years, whilst judges of the Courts of First Instance are appointed for seven years. There are also specialist children's courts and land and labour courts, as well as military courts.

Haiti accepts the compulsory jurisdiction of the International Court of Justice, and has agreed to use the Caribbean Court of Justice (CCJ) for resolution of trade disputes.

The human rights situation in Haiti is poor. There have been recent alleged unlawful killings by police officers, as well as possible police involvement in kidnappings. Prisons are overcrowded and unhealthy. The judiciary is inefficient and subject to pressure from the government, and there is severe corruption in all branches of government.

The death penalty was abolished in 1987.

Office for the Protection of Citizens, 80 Rue Bois Patate, Port-au-Prince, Haiti. Tel: +509 244 3594

LOCAL GOVERNMENT

The country is divided into 10 Departments: Artibonite, Centre, Grand'Anse, Nippes, Nord, Nord-Est, Nord-Ouest, Sud and Sud-Est. In turn these Departments are divided into arrondissements, which are in turn divided into communes. In each commune there is a Mayor who takes care of communal interests. The most recent municipal elections took place in December 2010.

AREA AND POPULATION

Area

The area of the Republic, including offshore islands, is estimated at 10,714 sq. miles (27,750 sq. km). Mountains make up 76 per cent of the country, plains and plateaux 24 per cent. Haiti occupies the western side of the island of Hispaniola (around a third of the total area), whilst the Dominican Republic occupies the eastern two thirds. The climate is generally warm and semi-arid, but with high humidity along the coast. The hurricane season can run from June to November and the 2008 season hit Haiti particularly hard.

To view a map, please visit http://www.un.org/Depts/Cartographic/map/profile/haiti.pdf

Population

The population, recently estimated at 9,933 million (2010), is predominantly of African descent (95 per cent). The growth rate is 1.4 per cent per annum. Approximately 52 per cent of the population lives in urban areas. Chief towns are Port-au-Prince, with 2,000,000 inhabitants and Cap Haitian, 800,000. There are 259 inhabitants per sq. km. but the majority of people live in urban areas. It is estimated than one in eight Haitians have left to live abroad, popular destinations are the US, Canada and other Caribbean islands particularly the Dominican Republic. A major earthquake hit Port-au-Prince in January 2009, killing an estimated 200,000 people.

The official languages are French and Creole.

Births, Marriages and Deaths

In 2009, life expectancy was estimated at 60 years for males and 63 years for females. Healthy life expectancy was 53 and 55 years respectively. Approximately 36 per cent of the population is aged under 15 years and 7 per cent over 60 years. The median age is 22. In 2010 the infant mortality rate was 70 deaths per 1,000 live births. The maternal mortality rate was an estimated 350 per 100,000 population. Over 5 per cent of the population is estimated to have HIV/AIDS. The total fertility rate for women in 2009 was 3.4. The crude birth rate was estimated to be 26.6 per 1,000 population and the crude death rate was 8.8 per 1,000 population. (Source: http://www.who.int, World Health Statistics 2012)

Public Holidays 2014

1 January: Independence Day
2 January: Ancestors' Day
3-5 March: Carnival (Monday to Ash Wednesday)
18 April: Good Friday
20 April: Easter Sunday
1 May: Agriculture and Labour Day
18 May: Flag and University Day
29 May: Ascension Day
19 June: Corpus Christi
15 August: Feast of the Assumption
17 October: Anniversary of the Death of Jean-Jacques Dessalines
24 October: United Nations Day
1 November: All Saints Day
2 November: All Souls Day
18 November: Battle of Vertières' Day
25 December: Christmas Day

EMPLOYMENT

Recent figures put the labour force at around 4.8 million with around 66 per cent employed in agriculture, mainly subsistence farming, and 10 per cent in industry. About 80 per cent of the population live in extreme poverty. Unemployment was estimated in 2010 to be 41 per cent. Workers are protected by a labour code. Mass emigration is a problem.

BANKING AND FINANCE

Currency

US currency, along with the *gourde* (HTG) of 100 centimes, is legal tender in Haiti.

GDP/GNP, Inflation, National Debt

Comparative social and economic indicators show that Haiti has been falling behind other low-income developing countries for over 20 years. The economic decline has been caused by mismanagement, political instability, lack of investment, lack of good arable land, and environmental deterioration including deforestation.

Haïti's GDP was an estimated US$6.5 billion in 2008. Agriculture contributed 24 per cent, industry, 8 per cent, and services 43 per cent. Figures for 2009 put the growth rate at 2.0 per cent. Per capita average annual income is estimated at US$733 (a decline of over 40 per cent from the 1980s).

Figures for early 2003 put the inflation rate at 29 per cent; in March 2004 this had fallen to 20 per cent. In 2008 it was estimated at 8.7 per cent and -4.6 per cent in 2009. Following the ousting of President Aristide, foreign governments pledged US$1,000 million of aid. External aid is essential to the future economic development of Haiti.

Balance of Payments / Imports and Exports

In July 1999 Haiti became a full member of CARICOM. The main commercial partner of Haiti is the United States, followed by the EU. Trade with the US accounts for about 60 per cent of exports and imports. Haiti's main exports include coffee, mangoes, leather, sisal, apparel, seafood and essential oils. Its main imports are petroleum products, foods, plastics, beverages and machinery and transport equipment. Figures for 2006 show the total of exports (fob)

HAITI

and imports (cif) as, respectively, US$494 million and US$1,548 million. Estimated figures for 2009 showed that exports (fob) earned US$550 million and imports cost (fob) US$2.02 billion.

Central Bank
Banque de la République d'Haiti, PO Box 1570, Angle rue des Miracles & Magasin de l'Etat, Port-au-Prince, Haiti. Tel: +509 299 1200 (10 lines), fax: +509 299 1045 / 1145, e-mail: webmaster@brh.net, URL: http://www.brh.net
Governor: Charles Castel

Chambers of Commerce and Trade Organisations
Association Professionnelle des Banques, URL: http://www.apbhaiti.org/
Haitian-American Chamber of Commerce, URL: http://www.haitianamericanchamber.com/

MANUFACTURING, MINING AND SERVICES

Primary and Extractive Industries
Production of copper in the Terre Neuve area began in 1960 but was suspended as uneconomic at the end of 1971. Deposits of copper were recently discovered and are now being investigated by test drilling. There are some brown coal deposits but they are not considered viable. Bauxite, marble and gold also exist.

Energy
Main towns and some rural areas have electricity but the majority of the country has none. Because of the shortage of electricity generating capacity in the area power cuts are regularly experienced. There are three electric plants which serve the Port-au-Prince area. Electricity production was 300 million kWh in 2006. Haiti uses a 110 Volt, 60 cycle system. Just over 40 per cent of electricity is hydro produced. Electricity generation in 2010 was 0.26 billion kilowatthours and consumption was 0.22 billion kilowatthours. Oil consumption was estimated at 12,000 barrels per day in 2011 all of which is imported.

Manufacturing
Over the past twenty-five years, a manufacturing sector has grown in and around the capital although still on a small scale. However, the last few years have seen a steady and considerable expansion of light industry using cheap labour. Main manufactured goods include textiles, cement, light assembly goods, flour milling, sugar refining, baseballs, underwear and electronic equipment.

Service Industries
Tourism has been adversely affected by political instability. In 2006 Haiti had around 112,000 visitors. By comparison, the Dominican Republic (occupying two thirds of the island) had 3.9 million visitors.

Agriculture
Haiti is almost entirely an agricultural country. Around 70 per cent of the population rely on subsistence farming. Coffee accounts for about one-third of the total exports and is still a mainstay of the country's economy. Other important crops are sisal, sugar, cocoa, cotton and various kinds of oil seed. Exports have been restricted since 1991 because of the trade embargo.

Agricultural Production in 2010

Produce	Int. $'000*	Tonnes
Mangoes, mangosteens, guavas	130,858	218,400
Indigenous cattle meat	121,562	45,000
Bananas	94,346	335,000
Yams	90,031	353,000
Cassava	56,880	599,500
Indigenous pigmeat	53,759	34,971
Plantains	38,355	238,500
Beans, dry	35,100	62,300
Rice, paddy	33,542	124,600
Avocados	32,846	47,400
Maize	28,961	233,700
Coffee, green	28,685	26,700

* estimated figures
Source: http://faostat.fao.org/site/339/default.aspx Food and Agriculture Organization of the United Nations, Food and Agricultural commodities production

Haiti's forest cover is less than 5 per cent and timber is no longer exported. Charcoal is still used for more than 70 per cent of fuel needs.

Caribbean waters have been over-fished. Haiti has no large-scale fishing industry. The local fishermen fish for domestic consumption using small craft. A small amount of shellfish is exported. Estimated figures for 2010 put the total catch at 8,300 tonnes.

COMMUNICATIONS AND TRANSPORT

Travel Requirements
Citizens of the USA, Canada, Australia and the EU require a passport valid for six months from date of entry but do not need a visa for stays of up to 90 days. Other nationals should contact the embassy to check visa requirements. Visas are required by citizens of China, Colombia, Dominican Republic and Panama.

International Airports
Haiti is well served by air from New York and Miami, Kingston, Puerto Rico, the French Antilles, with daily services to the north and the south. The international airport is Port-au-Prince International Airport (URL: http://www.aanhaiti.com). The airport handles approximately 700,000 passengers per annum and 15,000 tonnes of cargo.

Railways
There are about 100 miles of railway track, which is privately owned and used exclusively for the transport of sugar cane.

Roads
Existing roads have long been in a poor state of repair. Vehicles are driven on the right. Roads in the south of the country are sometimes impassable for light vehicles during the rainy season. The IADB is financing the construction of an all-weather road to Cayes (capital of the south), and the World Bank has financed a similar road to Cap Haitien (capital of the north). The French government has financed a new road from Port-au-Prince to Jacuel. There is a border crossing at Ouanaminthe with Dajabón, Dominican Republic which is very busy.

Shipping
Freight sailings to North and South America, Europe and the West Indies (except Cuba) are frequent. There are ports at Cap-Haiten, Port-au-Prince, Port-de-Paix, Saint-Marc, Gonaives and Les Cayes.

HEALTH

The rural population has limited access to health care. Urban dwellers fare slightly better. There are private and public centres, but patients must bear at least some of the cost of medication and treatment. Before the 2009 earthquake there an were 50 hospitals, 66 centres with beds and 143 centres without beds and over 370 dispensaries. However the 2009 earthquake decimated the capital and at least eight hospitals were reported to have been destroyed.

In 2009, the government of Haiti spent approximately 6 per cent of its total budget on healthcare, accounting for 21.8 per cent of all healthcare spending. Total expenditure on healthcare equated to 6.1 per cent of the country's GDP. Per capita expenditure on GDP was US$40 in 2009, compared with US$26 in 2000. The latest WHO figures estimate that in 2000-07 there were 1,949 doctors (0.25 per 1,000 population), 834 nurses (0.11 per 1,000 population) and 94 dentistry personnel.

Poverty is a major problem and 50 per cent of people live below minimum dietary requirements. In 2010, 69 per cent of the population had sustainable access to an improved water source and an estimated 17 per cent had sustainable access to improved sanitation.

The infant mortality rate in 2009 was 70 per 1,000 live births. The child (under-five) mortality rate was 165, compared to 109 in 2000 and 152 in 1990. The major causes of child mortality in 2010 were: prematurity (7 per cent), birth asphyxia (9 per cent), pneumonia (10 per cent), diarrhoea (7 per cent), and HIV/AIDS (1 per cent). (Source: WHO)

EDUCATION

Primary education is free and theoretically compulsory, and lasts for six years, but the enrolment rate is estimated at under 70 per cent. Secondary education is also in theory compulsory and lasts for three years. Enrolment is estimated at 15 per cent. Parents have to provide their children with uniforms, textbooks and other extras the cost of which many Haitians find prohibitive. Higher education is provided by the University of Haiti, the Polytechnic School, the Institute of Ethnology and the School of International Studies. There are also two teacher training colleges and a military academy.

The literacy rate is estimated at 46 per cent, well below the regional average of 91.0 per cent.

RELIGION

Haiti is a Roman Catholic country. Many Protestant denominations, such as the Episcopal, Baptist and Methodist churches, have their adherents. The folk religion is Voodoo and in 2003 it became an official religion of Haiti.

Haiti has a religious liberty rating of 8 on a scale of 1 to 10 (10 is most freedom). (Source: World Religion Database)

COMMUNICATIONS AND MEDIA

Press freedom has improved substantially since the fall of Jean-Bertrand Aristide. Self-censorship is common.

Newspapers
Access to the press is limited by the country's high level of illiteracy. Local daily newspapers include: Le Matin, and Le Nouvelliste (URL: http://www.haitiprogres.com/). Haiti Progress is a weekly publication (URL: http://www.haitiprogres.com/).

Broadcasting
The main television stations are Television Nationale d'Haiti (government owned, broadcasts in Creole, Spanish and French), PVS Antenne and Trans-America. There are over 250 radio stations. Radio Nationale d'Haiti is government-run. Cable-TV subscription is available.
Television Nationale d'Haiti, URL: http://www.tnh.ht/

Telecommunications
The domestic service is poor. As of 2008 there were estimated to be 100,000 landlines and over 3 million mobile phones. Figures for 2005 estimated that there were 1 million internet users.

ENVIRONMENT

Environmental concerns include the deforestation as forests are cleared for fuel and to extend land available for agriculture. The deforestation has led to greater devastation when the island is hit by hurricanes. Soil erosion is a big problem.

Haiti is party to the following international agreements: Biodiversity, Climate Change, Climate Change-Kyoto Protocol, Desertification, Law of the Sea, Marine Dumping, Marine Life Conservation and Ozone Layer Protection. It has signed, but not ratified, the agreement on Hazardous Wastes.

In 2010, Haiti's emissions from the consumption of fossil fuels totalled 1.46 million metric tons of carbon dioxide. (Source: EIA)

HONDURAS
Republic of Honduras
República de Honduras

Capital: Tegucigalpa (Population estimate, 2005: 1.15 million)

Head of State: Porfirio Lobo Sosa (page 1466)

First Vice President: Maria Antonieta Guillen de Bogran

Second Vice President: Sr Samuel Reyes

Third Vice President: Sr Victor Barnica

National Flag: A tricolour fesswise, blue, white, blue. Five blue five-pointed stars on central band.

CONSTITUTION AND GOVERNMENT

Constitution
Originally discovered by the Spanish in the early 16th century, Honduras formed part of the Spanish-American dominions for close to three centuries. It became an independent republic on 15 September 1821.

A constitution was enacted by a Constitutional Assembly on 6 June 1965 which provided for executive power to be vested in the President. The 1982 constitution provides for a strong executive, a unicameral National Congress, and a judiciary appointed by the National Congress. The president is directly elected to a 4-year term by popular vote and is assisted by a Cabinet of Ministers.

To consult the constitution (in Spanish), please visit: http://www.honduras.com/honduras-constitution.html

International Relations
Honduras is a member of the UN, the World Trade Organization (WTO), the Organization of American States (OAS), the Central American Parliament (PARLACEN), the Central American Integration System (SICA), the Conference of Central American Armed Forces (CFAC), and the Central American Security Commission (CASC). The country is a strong supporter of Central American cooperation and integration.

In 1969, El Salvador and Honduras fought the brief "Soccer War" over disputed border areas. The two countries formally signed a peace treaty in 1980, putting the dispute before the International Court of Justice (ICJ). The Court awarded most of the disputed territory to Honduras in 1992, and a border demarcation treaty was signed in 1998, though delays continue due to technical difficulties. Honduras and El Salvador maintain normal diplomatic and trade relations. Honduras also has unresolved maritime border disputes with El Salvador, Jamaica, and Cuba.

Recent Events
In 2003, the Honduran government announced a special commission (The Permanent Commission on the Physical and Moral Integrity of Children) to investigate the deaths of 1,569 street children over the previous five years. The commission was formed as Amnesty International began a campaign to stop the deaths of street children in Honduras.

The Honduran Congress approved the Central American Free Trade Agreement (Cafta) with the United States, in March 2005; the deal became effective in April 2006.

In May 2007, President Zelaya ordered all the country's radio and TV stations to carry government propaganda for two hours a day for 10 days to counteract 'a campaign of misinformation'. In October 2007, the International Court of Justice in the Hague settled a long-running territorial dispute between Honduras and Nicaragua.

In August 2008, Honduras joined the Bolivarian Alternative for the Americas (ALBA), an alliance of leftist leaders in Latin America headed by Venezuelan President Hugo Chavez. President Manuel Zelaya said that a lack of international support to tackle chronic poverty had forced him to seek aid from Venezuela.

On the 28 June 2009, troops forcibly removed the President from his home and put him on a plane to Costa Rica. The speaker of Congress, Roberto Micheletti, was sworn in as interim leader. Mr Zelaya had planned to hold a public consultation on possible changes to constitution, which would have led to a referendum at the same time as the presidential election in November. It was thought that the consultation was aimed at removing the current one-term limit on the presidential term, paving the way for Mr. Zelaya's possible re-election. The consultation was ruled illegal by the Supreme Court and Congress, and was opposed by the army. Mr Zelaya had been moving the country leftwards, enjoying the support of Venezuelan President Hugo Chavez. Mr Zelaya's expulsion was criticised in Europe, Washington and Latin America. The UN General Assembly approved a resolution calling for his reinstatement. Costa Rican President Oscar Arias agreed to lead mediation talks between Manuel Zelaya and Roberto Micheletti in an effort to resolve the crisis.

Mr Micheletti named ministers for his six-month tenure. President Zelaya returned to the country but was forced to take refuge in the Brazilian embassy when faced with violent opposition to his return. A suggested unity government was rejected by Mr Zelaya. Both presidential and parliamentary elections took place in November. The Supreme Court finally debated whether President Zelaya could be reinstated on 2 December, after the presidential election had taken place. The court voted aganist his reinstatment. The winner of the presidential election, Porrfirio Lobo, was inaugurated on 27 January 2010 and a new cabinet was appointed.

In November 2011, at least 175 police officers were arrested in a purge against corruption and organised crime. Charges include murder, kidnap and drug dealing. Honduras had the highest reported murder rate in the world in 2010. In December 2011, the Honduras Congress voted to allow the military to take on police duties including making arrests and conducting searches.

In December 2011, Congress took a vote which allowed troops to take on police duties in an effort to tackle the high murder rate.

In February 2012, a fire in the overcrowded Comayagua prison killed 358.

Legislature
Under a new constitution, promulgated in 1982, Honduras has three branches of government: executive - headed by a president, whose term was reduced from six to four years; legislative - a 128 member unicameral Congress elected for a four year term; and judicial - an independent judiciary headed by a nine member Supreme Court elected for a four year term by Congress. Voting is by proportional representation and there is universal adult suffrage. **National Congress**, PO Box 3682, Palacio Legislativo, Tegucigalpa D.C., Honduras. E-mail: webmaster@congreso.gob.hn, URL: http://www.congreso.gob.hn

Cabinet (as at March 2013)
Minister of Foreign Affairs: Arturo Corrales Alvarez
Minister of Agriculture and Livestock: Jacobo Regalado
Minister of Culture, Arts and Sports: Tulio Mariano Gonzalez
Minister of Defence: Marlon Pascua
Minister of Education: Dr Marlon Escoto
Minister of Finance: Wilfredo Cerrato
Minister of Interior and Justice: Africo Madrid
Minister of Public Health: Arturo Bendana
Minister of Labour: Felicito Avila
Minister of Natural Resources and Environment: Rigoberto Cuellar
Minister of Tourism: Nelly Jerez
Minister of Planning and International Co-operation: Julio Raudales
Minister of Public Works, Transport and Housing: Miguel Angel Gamez
Minister for Security: Pompeyo Bonilla
Minister for Women's Affairs: Antonieta Botto
Minister of Family Support: Maria Elena Zepeda
Minister of Social Development: Hilda Hernandez
Minister of Industry and Commerce: Adonys Lavaide
Director of the National Institute for Agriculture: Cesar Ham
Director of the Honduran Fund for Social Investment: Miguel Edgardo Martinez Pineda

Ministries
Government portal, URL: http://www.gov.hn
Office of the President, Casa Presidencial, Blvd Juan Pablo II, Tegucigalpa, Honduras. Tel: +504 232 1527, fax: +504 232 1666, e-mail: ministerio@sdp.gob.hn, URL: http://www.presidencia.gob.hn

HONDURAS

Ministry of Agriculture and Livestock (SAG), Blvd Miraflores Avenida FAO, Tegucigalpa, Honduras. Tel: +504 232 4105, fax: +504 231 0051, e-mail: infoagro@sag.gob.hn, URL: http://www.sag.gob.hn

Ministry of Culture, Arts and Sports, Colonia Palmira, Edificio Castillo y Poujol, Tegucigalpa, Honduras. Tel: +504 235 4700, fax: +504 235 6717, e-mail: binah@sdnhon.org.hn, URL: http://www.sdnhon.org.hn

Ministry of Education, la Avenida, 2a y 3a Calle 201, Comayagüela, Tegucigalpa, Honduras. Tel: +504 238 4325, fax: +504 222 8571, e-mail: webmaster@se.gob.hn, URL: http://www.se.gob.hn

Ministry of Finance, Avenida Cervantes, Barrio El Jazmin, Edificio SEFIN, Tegucigalpa, Honduras. Tel: +504 222 0111, fax: +504 238 2309, URL: http://www.sefin.gob.hn

Ministry of Foreign Relations, Centro Cívico Gubernamental, Antigua Casa Presidencial, Blvd Fuerzas Armadas, Tegucigalpa, Honduras. Tel: +504 234 3998, fax: +504 234 1484, e-mail: consultas.sre@gmail.com, URL: http://www.sre.hn

Ministry of Health, 2 Calle, Avenida Cervantes, Tegucigalpa, Honduras. Tel: +504 222 8518, fax: +504 238 6787, URL: http://www.salud.gob.hn

Ministry of Industry and Commerce, Edif. San José, Boulevard José Cecilio del Valle, Tegucigalpa, Honduras. Tel: +504 235 3699, fax: +504 235 3686, e-mail: info@sic.gob.hn, URL: http://www.sic.gob.hn

Ministry of the Interior and Justice, Boulevard La Hacienda, Calle La Estancia, Tegucigalpa, Honduras. Tel: +504 232 1373, fax: +504 232 0226, e-mail: encionalpublico@gobernacion.gob.hn, URL: http://www.gobernacion.gob.hn

Ministry of Labour, Boulevard La Hacienda, frente a Auto Excell, Tegucigalpa, Honduras. Tel: +504 232 3918, fax: +504 235 3456, e-mail: upeq@trabajo.gob.hn, URL: http://www.trabajo.gob.hn

Ministry of the Merchant Marine, Avenida La Paz 2930, Tegucigalpa, Honduras. Tel: +504 236 8880, fax: +504 236 8866, e-mail: mercadeo@marinamercante.hn, URL: http://www.marinamercante.hn

Ministry of National Defence, Barrio Concepción, Paseo El Obelisco, Comayagüela, Tegucigalpa, Honduras. Tel: +504 238 2890, fax: +504 238 0238

Ministry of Natural Resources and the Environment (SERNA), 100 mts al sur del Estadio Nacional, Apdo. Postal 1389, Tegucigalpa, Honduras. Tel: +504 232 1386, fax: +504 239 2011, e-mail: sdespacho@serna.gob.hn, URL: http://www.serna.gob.hn

Ministry of Planning and International Co-operation, Blvd. San Juan Bosco, Edificio El Sol, contiguo a Ministerio de Trabajo, Tegucigalpa, Honduras. Tel: +504 239 5545, fax: +504 239 5277, e-mail: correo@setco.gob.hn, URL: http://www.setco.gob.hn

Ministry of Public Works, Transport and Housing (SOPTRAVI), Barrio La Bolsa, Comayagüela, Tegucigalpa, Honduras. Tel: +504 225 0994, fax: +504 225 5003, e-mail: soptravi@soptravi.gob.hn, URL: http://www.soptravi.gob.hn

Ministry of Science and Technology, Edificio CAD, contiguo a Chiminike, Boulevard Fuerzas Armadas, Tegucigalpa, Honduras. Tel: +504 230 7673, fax: +504 230 1664, e-mail: memejia@cohcit.gob.hn, URL: http://www.cohcit.gob.hn

Ministry of Tourism, Colonia San Carlos, Edif. Europa, Apdo. Postal 3261, Tegucigalpa, Honduras. Tel: +504 222 2124, fax: +504 238 2102, e-mail: tourisminfo@iht.hn

Political Parties

Partido Nacional de Honduras, (National Party of Honduras), URL: http://www.partidonacional.hn
Leader: Ricardo Álvarez

Partido Liberal de Honduras, (Liberal Party of Honduras), URL: http://www.partidoliberaldehonduras.hn
Leader: Roberto Micheletti

Partido Innovación y Unidad, Innovation and Unity Party, URL: http://www.pinusd.com

Partido Demócrata Cristiano de Honduras, Christian Democratic Party of Honduras, URL: http://www.pdch.hn
Leader: Lucas Evangelisto Aguilera Pineda

Partido Unificación Democrática, Democratic Unification Party

Elections

The most recent elections were held on 27th November 2005. Manuel Zelaya Rosales of the Liberal Party of Honduras won the closely fought Presidential election, winning 49.98 per cent of the vote. His National Party rival, Porfirio Pepe Lobo, won 46.2 per cent.

In the elections for the National Congress, the Liberal Party won 62 of the 124 seats, whilst the National Party won 55 seats. Turnout was 46 per cent.

Parliamentary and presidential elections were held on 30 November 2009. Porfirio 'Pepe' Lobo Sosa of the National Party won the presidential election, beating Elvin Santos, the Liberal Party candidate.

Diplomatic Representation

Embassy of Honduras, 3007 Tilden St. NW, Washington, D.C. 20008, USA. Tel: +1 202 966 4596, fax: +1 202 966 9751, URL: http://www.hondurasemb.org
Ambassador: Jorge Ramón Hernández Alcerro

Embassy of Honduras, 115 Gloucester Place, London, W1H 2PJ, United Kingdom. Tel: +44 (0)20 7486 4880, fax: +44 (0)20 7486 4550
Ambassador: HE Mr Ivan Romero-Martinez

Embassy of the United States, Avenida La Paz, Apartado Postal No. 3453, Tegucigalpa, Honduras. Tel: +504 236 9320, fax: +504 236 9037, URL: http://honduras.usembassy.gov
Ambassador: Lisa Kubiske

British Embassy, Edificio Torre Internacional, Nivel 11, 16 Calle 0-55, Zona 10, Guatemala City, Guatemala. Tel: +502 2367 5425, URL: http://ukinguatemala.fco.gov.uk/enSa
Ambassador: Sarah Dickson

Permanent Representative of Honduras to the United Nations, 866 United Nations Plaza, Suite 417, New York, N.Y. 10017, USA. Tel: +1 212 752 3370 / 3371, fax: +1 212 223 0498 / 751-0403, e-mail: mihonduras@worldnet.att.net, URL: http://www.un.int/wcm/content/site/honduras/
Ambassador: Mary Elizabeth Flores Flake

LEGAL SYSTEM

The judiciary includes a Supreme Court of Justice (with nine members elected by the National Assembly for a four-year term), 10 courts of appeal, 67 courts of first instance and over three hundred justice of the peace courts, which have limited jurisdiction. of original jurisdiction (labour, tax, and criminal courts). The Supreme Court can declare laws unconstitutional, and ousted President Zelaya in 2009, when he attempted to change the constitution to allow himself to run for a second term in office.

There is also a military court of first instance from which appeals can be taken to the civilian judicial system.

The constitution provides for an independent judiciary and the right to a fair trial. However, due to underfunding and corruption, resolution of legal disputes in courts is often the product of influence and political pressure. The human rights situation in the country remains poor. There have been recent unlawful killings by the police as well as arbitrary killings by former members of the security forces. Prison conditions are harsh, and there are lengthy pretrial detentions. The judiciary is highly politicized and corruption is widespread in all branches of government.

The death penalty was abolished in 1956.

Honduras has a partly autonomous Public Ministry which is headed by an Attorney-General who is elected for five years.

Supreme Court, URL: http://www.poderjudicial.gob.hn/Paginas/InicioCorteSuprema.aspx
Supreme Court President: Jorge Alberto Rivera Avilés

National Commission for Human Rights in Honduras, URL: http://www.conadeh.hn/

LOCAL GOVERNMENT

Administratively, Honduras is divided into 18 provinces, or *departamentos*, and 293 municipalities (from cities to villages). Each province is led by a Governor appointed by the Executive Branch. Each municipality elects its own mayor. The provinces are Atlantida, Choluteca, Colon, Comayagua, Copan, Cortes, El Paraiso, Francisco Morazan, Gracias a Dios, Intibuca, Islas de la Bahia, La Paz, Lempira, Ocotepeque, Olancho, Santa Barbara, Valle and Yoro.

AREA AND POPULATION

Area
Honduras is situated in Central America and has borders with Guatemala, El Salvador and Nicaragua. Its total area is approximately 112,088 sq. km and for the large part is very mountainous with vast areas of forest. The climate varies from tropical to subtropical.

To view a map, please visit: http://www.un.org/Depts/Cartographic/map/profile/honduras.pdf

Population
The estimated population in 2010 was 7.6 million with an annual growth rate in the region of 2.0 per cent for the period 2000-10. The population of Honduras is young with a median age of 21 years in 2009. Approximately 37 per cent of the population is aged less than 15 years old and 6 per cent over 60 years old.

Around 90 per cent of the inhabitants are of mixed Spanish and Indian blood and speak various languages, although Spanish is the official language of the country. The estimated populations of the chief towns are: Tegucigalpa 1,150,000, San Pedro Sula 850,000, La Ceiba 77,100 and the Bay Islands 26,000. The population of Tegucigalpa is expected to reach 2 million by 2030.

Life expectancy at birth was approximately 69 years in 2009 (67 years for males and 73 for females). The fertility rate is 3.1 per female. The birth rate in 2010 was estimated at 26.7 per 1,000 inhabitants, whilst the death rate was 6.1 per 1,000 people. Infant mortality is relatively high at 20 deaths per 1,000 live births. (Source: http://www.who.int, World Health Statistics 2012)

Public Holidays 2014
1 January: New Year's Day
17 April: Holy Thursday
18 April: Good Friday / Day of the Americas
21 April: Easter Monday
1 May: Labour Day
15 September: Independence Day
3 October: Day of the Soldier
13 October: Columbus Day
21 October: Armed Forces Day
25 December: Christmas

EMPLOYMENT

Total Employment by Economic Activity

Occupation	2007
Agriculture, hunting, forestry & fishing	979,900
Mining & quarrying	7,100
Manufacturing	421,200

- continued

Electricity, gas & water supply	12,400
Construction	189,200
Wholesale & retail trade, repairs	603,600
Transport, storage & communications	106,100
Financial intermediation, real estate & business activities	94,900
Public admin. & defence; compulsory social security	249,500
Community, social & personal service activities	419,400
Extra-territorial organisations & bodies	500
Total	2,836,100

Source: Copyright © International Labour Organization (ILO Dept. of Statistics, http://laborsta.ilo.org)

BANKING AND FINANCE

Currency
The unit of currency is the Lempira of 100 centavos.

GDP/GNP, Inflation, National Debt
Honduras remains one of the poorest countries in the Western Hemisphere. It took the economy almost a decade to recover from the effects of Hurricane Mitch (1998), which crippled certain key sectors of the economy, causing over $3 billion worth of damage in Honduras alone. Growth fell by 3 per cent in 2009 due to the global economic crisis. Domestic demand has contracted and political stability is adversely affecting foreign investment.

GDP grew by an estimated 6.3 per cent in 2007, to US$12.3 billion. It was the fourth consecutive year of growth over 6 per cent. In 2008, it was estimated at US$14.32 billion with a growth rate of 4 per cent. Per capita GDP was estimated at US$1,859. Estimated figures for 2009 showed that GDP in response to the global economic downturn had shrunk by -2.1 per cent, giving a figure of US$14.7 billion. That year the service sector's contribution to GDP had grown to 58 per cent, and industry's contribution to 28 per cent, while the contribution of the agriculture sector fell to 14 per cent. GDP was estimated to be US$15 billion in 2010 with a growth rate of 2.8 per cent. In 2011, GDP was estimated at US$17 billion with a growth rate of 3.5 per cent.

Until recently, Honduras was dependent on the export of coffee and bananas for its economic wellbeing. Over the past two decades, however, the government has pursued a policy of diversification and the development of other exports, such as shellfish and melons. It has promoted the growth of tourism and the establishment of the maquila industry, which now employs approximately 130,000 people. Family remittances from abroad are also an important source of revenue, rising to an US$2.56 billion in 2007. This is the equivalent of around a fifth of total GDP.

Inflation (consumer price index), was estimated at approximately 6.2 per cent in 2006, but rose to 8.9 per cent in 2007, largely due to the rise in global oil and grain prices. Inflation was estimated to be 10.8 per cent in 2008, 4.5 per cent in 2010 and 6 per cent in 2011. International reserves, which were $1.16 billion at end of 2003, rebounded to an estimated $2.23 billion in 2005.

In 2005, Honduras reached completion point under the Heavily Indebted Poor Countries (HIPC) initiative, qualifying the country for multilateral debt relief. Since then, Honduras has received nearly $4 billion in debt relief from bilateral and multilateral donors. The government committed to apply the funds to poverty alleviation, as laid out in the Poverty Reduction Strategy; however, a large proportion of the ensuing rise in government spending went into public sector salaries and fuel subsidies. In April 2008, Honduras signed a new deal with the IMF. In 2008, fuel subsidies were phased out, and electricity subsidies were targeted towards the poor. The current government has worked to gain more foreign investment.

Balance of Payments / Imports and Exports
Revenue from the export of goods reached around US$7 billion in 2011, up from an estimated US$5.5 billion in 2010. The main goods exported are clothing, coffee, shrimp, bananas, palm oil, gold, zinc/lead concentrates, soap/detergents, melons, lobster, pineapple, lumber, sugar, and tobacco. The United States was the main recipient of Honduran goods, purchasing some 30 per cent. Other main export destinations are Germany (10 per cent), El Salvador (7 per cent), and Belgium.

Imported goods cost the country an estimated US$10.1 billion in 2011, up from an estimated US$7.6 billion in 2009. Most goods were imported from the USA (45 per cent), and the main imports were: fabrics and yarn (for the clothing industry), machinery, chemicals, petroleum, vehicles, processed foods, metals, agricultural products, plastic articles, and paper articles.

Honduras is a member of the Central American Common Market (CACM), which it joined in 1993 along with El Salvador, Guatemala and Nicaragua. This free trade area is subject to mutually agreed common external tariffs, and members' goods are exempt from import and export duties. Ultimately, the CACM wants to eliminate tariffs and restrictions on trade, as well as providing unrestricted movement of capital and labour, and the harmonisation of fiscal and monetary policies within the free trade area. In March 2005 the Honduran parliament ratified a Central American free trade pact with the US.

Central Bank
Banco Central de Honduras, PO Box 3165, 1a Calle, Tegucigalpa, Honduras. Tel: +504 237 2270 (10 lines), fax: +504 237 1876, URL: http://www.bch.hn
President: Maria Elena Mondragon

Chambers of Commerce and Trade Organisations
Honduran-American Chamber of Commerce, URL: http://www.amchamhonduras.org/

MANUFACTURING, MINING AND SERVICES

Primary and Extractive Industries
There are mineral reserves of tin, iron, copper, coal, antimony, silver, gold, lead and zinc. The mining sector accounts for a negligible part of GDP (less than 2 per cent). The primary mineral exports are silver, lead, and zinc.

Honduras imports all its oil requirements, 68,000 barrels per day in 2011. Under the San Jose Pact, Mexico and Venezuela supply all of Central America and four Caribbean islands with crude oil and petroleum products. In addition, Venezuela provides oil to the region under the Caracas Energy Accord. (Source: Energy Information Administration, EIA)

Energy
In response to surging power demand and possible power shortages caused by underperforming hydropower plants, the Honduran government has been trying to diversify its power supply. In October 2003, the Honduran government approved a contract with Luz y Fuerza de San Lorenzo to build a new thermal power plant (Pavana). The diesel-fired Choloma III power plant has also been expanded to an installed electric generating capacity of 230 MW. (Source: EIA)

Over 65 per cent of Honduran electricity is now generated from hydro power, the rest from fossil fuels. Figures for 2010 show that Honduras generation 6.49 billion kilowatthours and consumed 4.85 billion kilowatthours.

Manufacturing
Manufacturing accounts for almost 20 per cent of GDP and has grown in response to greater domestic demand. The manufacture of food and beverage products is the largest sector, while other main items include wood products, textiles, cement and cigars. The manufacturing industry recently diversified into 'maquila', (re-assembly for export), which has become a significant employer and export revenue earner, particularly in the textile and garment fields.

Services
The services sector is the largest contributor to GDP, at over 54 per cent in 2007.

Tourism
Tourism is now an important contributor to the Honduras economy. In 2003, 886,600 people visited the country, rising to 1,056,600 in 2004. In 2005, an estimated 1,194,100 people visited, 444,600 of whom were day visitors, many off cruise ships. Most visitors to Honduras are from other parts of Central America (433,400); around 227,600 come from North America and around 54,100 come from Europe. In 2005 there were an estimated 908 hotels, with 20,453 rooms. The industry directly employs some 48,500 people, and a further 56,500 jobs are indirectly connected to tourism.

Agriculture
Agriculture currently represents just under 14 per cent of GDP. The main agricultural exports are bananas (although export figures for this crop have declined over the years), coffee, sugar, fruit, lobster and shellfish. The sector was hard hit by Hurricane Mitch in 1998 and by drought in 2001, when a state of emergency was announced in some provinces and food aid was received from the UN.

Agricultural Production in 2010

Produce	Int. $'000*	Tonnes
Coffee, green	246,424	229,368
Cow milk, whole, fresh	230,723	739,351
Indigenous chicken meat	213,286	149,737
Bananas	203,560	750,788
Sugar cane	164,766	7,818,920
Indigenous cattle meat	161,994	59,967
Palm oil	119,641	275,000
Tomatoes	58,364	157,926
Oranges	51,449	266,221
Beans, dry	38,830	68,543
Hen eggs, in shell	36,661	44,202
Pineapples	35,551	124,719

*unofficial figures

Source: http://faostat.fao.org/site/339/default.aspx Food and Agriculture Organization of the United Nations, Food and Agricultural commodities production

Honduras has extensive forests; some 40 per cent of the land is forested. However, slash-and-burn agricultural methods and illegal logging are destroying them.

COMMUNICATIONS AND TRANSPORT

Travel Requirements
Citizens of the USA, Canada, Australia and the EU require a passport valid for three months from date of entry but do not need a visa for stays of up to 90 days. Tourists must provide evidence of return or onward travel. Other nationals should contact the embassy to check visa requirements.

Honduras is party to the Central America Border Control Agreement (CA-4), under which tourists may travel within any of the CA-4 countries (Honduras, Nicaragua, El Salvador and Guatemala) for a period of up to 90 days, without completing entry and exit formalities at border immigration checkpoints. This period begins at the first point of entry in to any of the CA-4 countries.

HONDURAS

International Airports
There are international airports at Tegucigalpa (at Toncontín, 6.5 km from the centre), San Pedro Sula and La Ceiba. A new US$200m airport is planned for Tegucigalpa. Inland communications are maintained by improved air services. There are altogether nearly 200 airports or air-strips in the larger and smaller towns of which only 35 are fully serviced commercially and 25 can take twin-engine passenger aircraft.

Railways
There is 595 km of railway track in operation in the Northern Region, owned by Ferrocarril Nacional de Honduras and used, principally, for the transportation of bananas. Other companies operate 360 km of track.

Roads
Prior to the devastation of Hurricane Mitch, total road length was 18,494 km, of which 2,262 km was paved. The asphalted roads included: the Northern Highway linking Tegucigalpa, San Pedro Sula and Puerto Cortés; the Inter American Highway between El Salvador and Nicaragua, linked to Tegucigalpa by the Southern Highway; the North Coast Highway joining San Pedro Sula with Progreso, Tela, La Ceiba and Trujillo; the Western Highway running from San Pedro Sula to the Guatemalan and El Salvadorean frontiers; and the Eastern Highway linking Tegucigalpa, Danli and the Nicaraguan frontier. However, Hurricane Mitch destroyed nearly 90 bridges and most major roads. Vehicles are driven on the right.

Shipping
Among the shipping lines that serve Honduras are Fyffes, Italian Line, French Line, Royal Netherlands, N.G. Lloyd, Hamburg-Amerika, Johnson, United Brands Ltd, Standard Fruit Co., Marina Mercantil Nicaraguense.

Ports and Harbours
The major ports in Honduras on the Caribbean are Puerto Cortés, Tela and La Ceiba. The main port on the Pacific is Puerto San Lorenzo, which has replaced Amapala. Ferries operate between La Ceiba and Puerto Cortés to the Bay Islands.

HEALTH

Recent figures show that Honduras has 62 hospitals, about half of which are private, as well as a network of health centres and clinics. In 2009, Honduras spent approximately 17.7 per cent of its total budget on healthcare, accounting for 66.3 per cent of all healthcare spending. External resource amounted to 6.9 per cent of the total. Total expenditure on healthcare equated to 7 per cent of the country's GDP. Per capita total expenditure on health was US$134 in 2009. According to latest WHO figures (2000-10) there were 3,676 doctors (6 per 10,000 inhabitants), 8,528 nurses and midwives (13 per 100,000 inhabitants), and 1,371 dentistry personnel. There were approximately 7 beds per 10,000 inhabitants.

There are high maternal and infant mortality rates due to high rates of adolescent pregnancies, low levels of education, and limited access to services, as well as a high prevalence of child malnutrition. The infant mortality rate was 20 deaths per every 1,000 births in 2009 (compared to 45 in 1990) and the child mortality rates were 24 per 1,000 live births (compared to 58 in 1990). There were estimated to be 280 maternal deaths per 100,000 live births in 2005. Honduras accounts for 60 per cent of HIV/AIDS cases in Central America. and 2 per cent of childhood deaths. Life expectancy is 69 years. In the period 2000-10, approximately 29.9 per cent of children under-five were classified as stunted and 8.6 per cent underweight.

According to the latest WHO figures, in 2010 approximately 87 per cent of the population had access to improved drinking water and 77 per cent of the population had access to improved sanitation. Diarrhoea accounts for 5 per cent of childhood deaths. (Source: http://www.who.int, World Health Statistics 2012)

EDUCATION

Primary education is free and nominally compulsory for children from the age of seven. In 2006, it was estimated that 38 per cent of small children attended a pre-primary school. In 2007 94 per cent of girls and 93 per cent of boys were enrolled in primary school. In 2002, 65 per cent of children enrolled in secondary education, which lasts for five years, and 17 per cent of students went on to tertiary education. All the attendance rates were below the average for the region.

In 2007, 83.6 per cent of the adult population was considered to be literate; this figure rose to 93.9 per cent among the 15-24 age group. The regional average for adult literacy is 91.0 per cent.

The National University is based in Tegucigalpa with departments in San Pedro Sula and La Ceiba. Also in Tegucigalpa is the Universidad José Cecilio del Valle and there is a university in San Pedro Sula.

RELIGION

The constitution guarantees freedom to all religious sects. The majority of the population are Christian with 49 per cent following the Roman Catholic Church and 39 per cent are Protestant.

Honduras has a religious liberty rating of 9 on a scale of 1 to 10 (10 is most freedom). (Source: World Religion Database)

COMMUNICATIONS AND MEDIA

There are extremely restrictive media laws in operation. and self-censorship is also common. There are also reports of violence against journalists.

Newspapers
El Heraldo, URL: http://www.elheraldo.hn
La Tribuna, URL: http://www.latribuna.info
La Prensa, URL: http://www.laprensahn.com
Other newspapers include: El Cronista, Tegucigalpa; El Tiempo, URL: http://www.tiempo.hn, San Pedro Sula; and Honduras This Week.

Broadcasting
There are over 300 radio broadcasting stations in Honduras and eleven television stations. In 2007 President Zelaya ordered all Honduras's television and radio stations to broadcast government propaganda for two hours a day for 10 days in response to what he called a campaign of misinformation.
Televicentro, URL: http://www.televicentrotv.net/home/home.php

Telecommunications
As from 2003, private sub-operators were allowed to provide fixed-lines in order to expand telephone coverage, and main line usage has since increased to 825,000 subscriptions. In the meantime, the use of mobile telephones has soared to over 6 million.

In 2008, there were approximately 650,000 internet users in Honduras.

ENVIRONMENT

Honduras suffers frequent, but generally mild, earthquakes. The country is susceptible to hurricanes and floods along the Caribbean coast. Hurricane Mitch (1998) ruined almost three-quarters of the year's crops and 700,000 hectares of land were destroyed. Other environmental concerns of Honduras are pollution of the largest source of fresh water - the Lago de Yojoa- through mining activities; deforestation through logging and the clearing of land for agricultural purposes; and the expansion of the urban population.

The Río Plátano Biosphere Reserve, (525,100-hectare surface area) is one of the few remaining areas of tropical rainforest in Central America. It has been included on the World Heritage Danger List since 1996 as a result of massive logging of precious wood, particularly mahogany, as well as the illegal hunting and fishing for exotic animals.

Honduras is party to the following environmental agreements: Biodiversity, Climate Change, Climate Change-Kyoto Protocol, Desertification, Endangered Species, Hazardous Wastes, Law of the Sea, Marine Dumping, Ozone Layer Protection, Ship Pollution, Tropical Timber 83, Tropical Timber 94 and Wetlands.

In 2010, emissions from the consumption of fossil fuels totalled 8.29 million metric tons of carbon dioxide.

HUNGARY
Magyarország

Capital: Budapest (Population estimate, 2010: 1,721,560)

Head of State: Janos Ader (President) (page 1372)

National Flag: A fesswise tricolour of red, white and green

CONSTITUTION AND GOVERNMENT

Constitution

Following the break up of the Austro-Hungarian Empire after the WWI, the Communists briefly came to power before the Kingdom of Hungary was restored in 1920. After the Second World War Hungary came under Soviet control. The constitution dates from 1949, but many amendments were added in the 1980s, resulting in a gradual move away from a Communist administration and Hungary experienced what has been described as the quiet revolution. A special conference held by the ruling Hungarian Socialist Workers' Party in 1988 accepted the need for a multi-party democracy. New parties were established and the previously dissolved parties re-founded. Formerly the Hungarian People's Republic, the Parliament adopted the name Republic of Hungary in October 1989. Initially, the duties of the Head of State were carried out by a Presidium. This has now been replaced by a President. The constitution was amended in 2003 to allow for Hungary's accession into the EU. Further revisions were agreed on and on 18 April 2011 parliament approved the draft of a new constitution. In December 2011 further amendments were approved; the number of MPs is to be halved and electoral boundaries changed. The new constitution came into force in January 2012. In March 2013, controversial amendments to the new constitution were approved by the Hungarian parliament. The new provisions include limiting the power of the Constitutional Court.

To consult the full current constitution, please visit: http://net.jogtar.hu/jr/gen/getdoc.cgi?docid=94900020.tv&dbnum=62.

International Relations

Hungary became a member of NATO in 1999. At the EU Copenhagen summit held in December 2002, Hungary was formally invited to join EU. A referendum was held in April 2003 and Hungary became a member state on May 1 2004. Parliament ratified the EU constitution in December 2004.

Recent Events

Hungary played a pivotal role in the fall of communism and bringing down the Berlin Wall. In 1989 Hungary opened its borders which allowed East Germans to enter Western Europe.

Following the end of World War I, Hungary lost nearly two thirds of its territory under the terms of the Treaty of Trianon, with the result that over 2.5 million ethnic Hungarians found themselves living outside Hungary, in Romania, Slovakia, Serbia, Montenegro and Ukraine. In December 2004 Hungary held a referendum on whether ethnic Hungarians living outside of the country should be offered citizenship but a low turnout invalidated the result.

In October 2006 Prime Minister Ferenc Gyurcsany survived a vote of no confidence following admissions that he had lied during the general election held in April. Gyurcsany campaigned on a platform of tax cuts but then increased taxes on being elected in an effort to reduce the budget deficit. The admission of lying led to protests which threatened to overshadow events planned to commemorate the 50th anniversary of the Hungarian uprising against Soviet rule.

On December 31 2007 Hungary became a member of Schengen Area, the common European area without internal borders.

Prime Minister Ferenc Gyurcsany announced his resignation in March 2009 amid the global financial crisis and the falling in popularity of his party. Minister of economy Gordon Bajnai was elected the post of prime minister by parliament and was sworn in in April.

In May 2010, the Hungarian Parliament passed a law which allowed ethnic Hungarians living abroad to apply for Hungarian citizenship. Slovakia protested the law and accused Hungary of revisionism, it threatened to strip any Slovak who applies for dual nationality of their Slovak citizenship.

In October 2010 an aluminium plant's reservoir burst its banks in the western county of Veszprem. Toxic sludge then flooded an area of about 40 sq km an area including six villages and a town. The sludge contains mining waste and heavy metals including lead, cadmium and arsenic. Efforts were made to contain the spill before it reached the river Danube. Top soil in the affected areas will have to be removed and houses destroyed, the initial spill killed four people and injured 120.

Controversial amendments to the constitution were passed in 2011. Another law was passed giving the government greater control over monetary matters, prompting the IMF to withdraw from loan negotiations fearing potential political influence on the central bank. In January 2012 demonstrations were held against the controversial changes to the constitution and the austerity measures imposed by the government. The government announced revisions to the law in April 2012, moving the EC to start discussing possible aid talks again.

On January 1 2012, a new constitution came into force, in it the country's name changed from the Republic of Hungary to Hungary.

The president, Pal Schmitt, resigned on 2 April 2012 after admitting he had plagarised some of his doctoral thesis. The presidential election took place in May 2012.

In March 2012, the EU suspended aid payments to Hungary because of the country's budget deficit. The following month Hungary made small changes to the Central Bank law, resulting in the European Commission agreeing to resume talks with the IMF on a large bailout.

In September 2012, the Government rejected conditions attached by the IMF to a new 15 billion Euro loan as unacceptable. Prime Minister Orban said the government would present an alternative negotiation proposal. The following month in a speech Mr Orban attacked the EU accusing it of interfering in Hungary's domestic affairs.

In November 2012, MP Marton Gyongyosi caused outrage when he called for a list of officials of Jewish origin to be compiled, he said they could pose a national security risk. His remarks were condemned by the government.

In March 2013, Parliament approved a fourth amendment to the 2012 constitution. The amendment which was controversial curbs the powers of the constitutional court. Critics of the amendment say it undermines democracy by removing a number of checks and balances. Parliament later said it might be ready to amend further the constitution to allay criticism from the EU that the previous amendment was anti-democratic.

In May 2013, the European Commission released Hungary from the EU's excessive deficit procedure (EDP) mechanism after Hungary reduced its budget deficit to below the permitted threshold of 3 per cent.

Figures from the beginning of 2013 showed that Hungary had emerged from recession in the first quarter of the year.

Legislature

Hungary's unicameral Parliament consists of 386 members elected for a four-year term. In order to form a parliamentary faction a political party must win five per cent of the vote at a general election. The Hungarian Parliament has important scope within the Government structure. Parliament elects the President of the Republic, a largely ceremonial role; the Prime Minister and the members of the Constitutional Court; the Ombudsmen for national and ethnic minority rights; the president and vice-president of the State Audit Office; the president of the Supreme Court; and the Chief Prosecutor.

Orszaggyules, (National Assembly), Kossuth ter 1 - 3, 1357 Budapest, Hungary. Tel: +36 (0)1 441 4000, e-mail: webmaster@mkogy.hu, URL: http://www.mkogy.hu

---

Cabinet (as at June 2013)
Prime Minister: Victor Orban (page 1490)
Deputy Prime Minister, Minister of Justice and National Administration: Tibor Navracsics (page 1484)
Deputy Prime Minister, Minister of General Affairs: Zsolt Semjen (page 1511)
Minister of Foreign Affairs: Janos Martonyi (page 1472)
Minister of National Economy, Chief Negotiator on the EU Budget: Mihaly Varga (page 1531)
*Mi*nister *of Human Resources, Minister of Cultural Heritage and Youth, Education and Health:* Zoltan Balog
Minister of Defence: Csaba Hende
Minister of Rural Development: Sandor Fazekas
Minister of the Interior: Sandor Pinter
Minister of National Development Zsuzsanna Nemeth

Ministries

Országgyulés (National Assembly), Kossuth Lajos tér 1-3, 1055 Budapest, Hungary. Tel: +36 (0)1 268 4000, URL: http://www.mkogy.hu/
Speaker: Dr. Katalin Szili

Office of the Prime Minister, Kossuth Lajos tér 4, 1055 Budapest, Hungary. Tel: +36 (0)1 268 3000, fax: +36 (0)1 268 3050, URL: http://www.kancellaria.gov.hu

Ministry of Defence, Balaton u. 7-11, 1055 Budapest, Hungary. Tel: +36 (0)1 332 2500, fax: +36 (0)1 311 0182, URL: http://www.h-m.hu

Ministry of Finance, József Nádor tèr 2-4, 1051 Budapest, Hungary. Tel: +36 (0)1 318 2066, fax: +36 (0)1 318 2570, URL: http://www2.pm.gov.hu

Ministry of Local Government and the Regions, Jószef Attila u. 2-4, 1051 Budapest, Hungary. Tel: +36 (0)1 441 1000, fax: +36 (0)1 318 2870, URL: http://www.b-m.hu

Ministry of Foreign Affairs, Bem. rakpart 47, 1027 Budapest, Hungary. Tel: +36 (0)1 458 1000, fax: +36 (0)1 155 9693, URL: http://www.mfa.gov.hu

Ministry of Agriculture and Rural Development, Kossuth Lájos tér 11, 1055 Budapest, Hungary. Tel: +36 (0)1 302 0000, fax: +36 (0)1 302 0402, URL: http://www.f-m.hu

Ministry for Environmental Protection, Fö u.44-50, 1011 Budapest, Hungary. Tel: +36 (0)1 457 3300, URL: http://www.ktm.hu

Ministry of Justice, Szalay u. 16, 1055 Budapest, Hungary. Tel: +36 (0)1 441 3003, fax: +36 (0)1 268 3702, URL: http://www.lm.hu

Ministry of Economic Affairs and Transport, Honvéd u. 13-15, 1055 Budapest, Hungary. Tel: +36 (0)1 374 2700, fax: +36 (0)1 374 2925, URL: http://www.gm.hu

Ministry of Education, Szalay u. 10-14, 1055 Budapest, Hungary. Tel: +36 (0)1 302 0600, fax: +36 (0)1 302 2002, URL: http://www.om.hu

Ministry of Health, Arany János u. 6-8, 1051 Budapest, Hungary. Tel: +36 (0)1 332 3100, fax: +36 (0)1 302 0925, URL: http://www.nepjoleti.gov.hu

HUNGARY

Ministry for National Cultural Heritage, Wesselenyi U. 20-22, 1077 Budapest, Hungary. Tel: +36 (0)1 484 7100, URL: http://www.nkom.hu
Ministry of Labour and Social Affairs, Alkotmány utca 3, 1054 Budapest, Hungary. Tel: +36 (0)1 473 8100, fax: +36 (0)1 473 8101, URL: http://www.fmm.gov.hu
Ministry of Information Science and Telecommunications, Dob utca 75-81, 1077 Budapest, Hungary. Tel: +36 (0)1 461 3401, fax: +36 (0)1 461 3406, URL: http://www.ihm.hu
Ministry for Children, Youth and Sport, Hold u. 1, 1054 Budapest, Hungary. Tel: +36 (0)1 311 9080, fax: +36 (0)1 269 0118, URL: http://www.ism.hu

Minority Government
A National Office for National and Ethnic Minorities was set up in the early 1990s, which operates under a minister without portfolio, to ensure that the rights of minority groups are observed. An important act of 1993 recognised the various minorities and made provisions for their recognition in terms of local government and education. It also allowed for the establishment of minority self-governments at a national and local level which are legitimately elected representative bodies. Elections were held in 1994 and 1995. Each self-government receives a transfer of assets from the government budget and operates from an allocated headquarters. The autonomy and influence of the minority self-governments is under constant development.

Office for National and Ethnic Minorities, Kossuth tér 4, 1055 Budapest, Hungary. Tel: +36 (0)1 268 3801, fax: +36 (0)1 268 3802, e-mail: nekh.titkarsag@mail.datanet.hu, URL: http://www.meh.hu/nekh
German National Self-Government, Julia u.9, 1026 Budapest, Hungary. Tel: +36 (0)1 212 9151, fax: +36 (0)1 212 9153
Roma/Gypsy National Self-Government, Rákóczi ùt 80, 1074 Budapest, Hungary. Tel: +36 (0)1 322 1502
Romanian National Self-Government, Vár u. 16, 5700 Gyula, Hungary. Tel: +36 66 463 951
Slovak National Self-Government, Fadrusz u.11, 1114 Budapest, Hungary. Tel: +36 (0)1 166 9463, fax: +36 (0)1 186 4077

Political Parties
Magyar Socialistá Párt (Hungarian Socialist Party MSZP), 1081 Budapest, Köztártaság tér 26, Hungary. Tel: +36 (0)1 210 0046, fax: +36 (0)1 210 0011, URL: http://www.mszp.hu
Leader: Attila Mesterházy
Magyar Demokrata Néppárt (Hungarian Democratic Forum MDF), 1538 Budapest, POB 579, Hungary. Tel: +36 (0)1 212 4601, fax: +36 (0)1 156 8522, URL: http://www.mdf.hu
Leader: Ibolya Dávid
Fuggetlen Kisgazda, Földmunkás és Polgári Párt (Independent Smallholders' and Peasants' Party FKGP), Belgrád rkp. 24, 1056 Budapest, Hungary. Tel: +36 (0)1 118 0976, fax: +36 (0)1 118 1824, URL: http://www.fkgp.hu
Leader: Péter Hegedüs
Szabad Demokraták Szövetsége (Alliance of Free Democrats SZDSZ), 1051 Budapest, Mérleg u. 6, Hungary. Tel: +36 (0)1 117 6911, fax: +36 (0)1 118 7944, URL: http://www.szdsz.hu
Leader: Attila Retkes
Keresztény Demokrata Néppárt (Christian Democratic People's Party KDNP), 1126 Budapest, Nagy Jenö u.5, Hungary. Tel: +36 (0)1 175 0333, fax: +36 (0)1 155 5772
Leader: Zsolt Semjén
Fidesz (Hungarian Civic Union), 1088 Budapest, VIII. Visi Imre Street 6, Hungary. URL: http://www.fidesz.hu
Leader: Viktor Orbán
Jobbik Magyarországért Mozgalom, (Movement for a Better Hungary), URL: http://www.jobbik.com
Leader: Gábor Vona
Lehet Más a Politika, Politics Can Be Different, URL: http://lehetmas.hu
Leader: Committe of 13
Together 2014, URL: http://www.egyutt2014.hu
Leader: Gordon Bajnai (page 1382)

Elections
The first free elections were held in spring 1990 and were won by a wide margin by the Hungarian Democratic Forum. The MDF was heavily defeated in the 1994 elections as the former communist Hungarian Socialist Party (MSzP) won an overall majority of seats. The 1998 elections were won by FIDESZ; however, no party gained absolute power so a coalition government was formed. Another coalition was formed following the elections of 2002, by the Hungarian Socialist Party and the Alliance of Free Democrats (SzDSz). During a reshuffle in 2004, the Minister of Economy lost his post and his party, the SzDSz, threatened to leave the coalition. In August 2004, the MSzP withdrew its support for Prime Minister Medgyessy, who resigned. Ferenc Gyurcsány (MSzP) was elected Prime Minister by Parliament on September 30. Parliamentary elections were held in April 2006. Prime Minister Gyurcsany and his Socialist-led coalition were re-elected.

The most recent parliamentary election took place April 2010, initial results showed that the conservative opposition party, Fidesz, had won ousting the socialists, a second round was held on April 25, Fidesz won over 68 per cent of the vote giving them 263 seats with the Socialists came in second place with 59 seats, the far-right Jobbik won 47 seats and a new Green party called Politics Can Be Different won 16 seats.

The most recent presidential elections were held in May 2012 and Janos Ader was elected president by the National Assembly. The election followed the resignation of Pat Schmitts. The presidential term lasts for five years.

Diplomatic Representation
British Embassy, Harmincad Utca 6, Budapest 1051, Hungary. Tel: +36 (0)1 266 2888, fax: +36 (0)1 266 0907, e-mail: info@britemb.hu, URL: http://ukinhungary.fco.gov.uk/en

Ambassador: Jonathan Knott (page 1457)
US Embassy, 1054 Szabadság tér 12, H-1050 Budapest, Hungary. Tel: +36 (0)1 475 4400, fax: +36 (0)1 475 4764, e-mail: usembudapest@pronet.hu, URL: http://hungary.usembassy.gov
Ambassador: Eleni Tsakopoulos Kounalakis
Embassy of the Republic of Hungary, 35 Eaton Place, London, SW1X 8BY, United Kingdom. Tel: +44 (0)20 7235 5218, fax: +44 (0)20 7823 1348, URL: http://www.huemblon.org.uk/front.htm
Ambassador: János Csák
Embassy of the Republic of Hungary, 3910 Shoemaker Street, NW, Washington, DC 20008, USA. Tel: +1 202 362 6730, fax: +1 202 686 6412, URL: http://washington.kormany.hu
Ambassador: Dr. György Szapáry
UN Representation, 227 East 52nd Street, New York 10022, USA. Tel: +1 212 752 0209, fax: +1 212 755 5395, URL: http://www.mfa.gov.hu/newyork_unmission
Ambassador: Csaba Korosi

LEGAL SYSTEM

Justice is administered by the Supreme Court of the Republic of Hungary, the Budapest Metropolitan Court, regional appeal courts, county (municipal) and district (municipal district) courts.

The President of the Supreme Court is elected by Parliament under the proposal of the President of the Republic. The deputy presidents are appointed by the President of the Republic under the proposal of the President of the Supreme Court. The Court Judges are also appointed by the President of the Republic. Judges are independent and subject only to the law. They are forbidden to engage in political activity or join any political party.

The Chief Public Prosecutor and the public prosecutors provide for the protection of citizens' rights and for the consistent prosecution of acts violating or endangering constitutional order and the country's security and independence. The public prosecutor's office may investigate certain affairs, it exerts supervision over the legality of investigations and the implementation of sentences, and acts as public prosecutor in court procedure.

The Constitutional Court examines the constitutionality of laws, both prior and after enactment, acts on judges' complaints about the violation of constitutional rights and interprets the constitution. Should the Court judge a law or other regulation unconstitutional, it has the right of repeal. Any citizen may initiate proceedings by the Constitutional Court in the event that rights protected by the constitution have been violated. The 15 members of the Constitutional Court are elected by the Parliament for a term of nine years.

There are currently five regional appeal courts (in Budapest, Debrecen, Győr, Pécs and Szeged), 20 County Courts, 20 Labour Courts and 111 Local Courts.

The government respects the human rights of its citizens, but the police occasionally use excessive force, particularly against Roma people. There is discrimination against Roma, in access to all services. There is also some degree of government corruption.

Following the end of WWI, millions of Hungarians found themselves outside the newly designated area of Hungary. In 2001, the Status Law was introduced, giving ethnic Hungarians living in neighbouring countries the right to work, study and claim health care within Hungary. The law was criticised by the neighbouring countries who feared it would interfere with their sovereignty and could be seen as discriminating against other ethnic groups. The law was amended in 2003.

The death penalty was abolished in 1990.

Supreme Court of Hungary: URL: http://www.lb.hu/english/index.html
President of the Curia: Dr. Péter Darák
Office of the Commissioner for Fundamental Rights, URL: http://www.obh.hu/indexen.htm

LOCAL GOVERNMENT

Recent reforms, which began in 1995, mark a decentralisation process whereby many of the 30 regional state administration organs now fall under the responsibility of local government authorities. The increased autonomy of local government has increased the level of decision making at regional level. The system of hierarchy has also been legally abolished.

The principal powers and duties of local government include: the administration of local government affairs; the exercise of ownership rights over local government property; the levying of local taxes and legislation. At the same time, local governments also have responsibilities such as ensuring primary education, providing basic health care and social welfare services and asserting the rights of the national and ethnic minorities. Each local government has an elected mayor.

There are 19 counties, 23 urban counties and one capital city (Budapest). The counties are: Bacs-Kiskun, Baranya, Bekes, Borsod-Abauj-Zemplen, Csongrad, Fejer, Gyor-Moson-Sopron, Hajdu-Bihar, Heves, Jasz-Nagykun-Szolnok, Komarom-Esztergom, Nograd, Pest, Somogy, Szabolcs-Szatmar-Bereg, Tolna, Vas, Veszprem, Zala. The urban counties are: Bekescsaba, Debrecen, Dunaujvaros, Eger, Erd, Gyor, Hodmezovasarhely, Kaposvar, Kecskemet, Miskolc, Nagykanizsa, Nyiregyhaza, Pecs, Salgotarjan, Sopron, Szeged, Szekesfehervar, Szekszard, Szolnok, Szombathely, Tatabanya, Veszprem, Zalaegerszeg.

The governing Fidesz party won municipal elections in October 2010, winning most major country towns and also the mayor's office in the capital for the first time.

AREA AND POPULATION

Area
Hungary is situated in lowlands, within the Carpathian Basin of Central Europe. It extends over an area of 93,033 sq. km and is landlocked, bounded by the countries of Slovakia, Ukraine, Romania, Serbia, Croatia, Slovenia and Austria. The land is mainly low-lying with low mountains to the north and north-east, and also to the north west of Lake Balaton in western Hungary. The highest point is Kekes at 1,014 metres. The climate is temperate with cold winters and warm summers.

To view a map of Hungary, please consult:
http://www.lib.utexas.edu/maps/cia08/hungary_sm_2008.gif

Population
Since the 1970s there has been a natural drop in the population. By January 2012, the population was estimated to be 9,958,000 down from 10,014,000 in 2010 with a density of 106 people per sq. km. This represents over a 600,000 decrease on figures from the late 1970s. A trend of rural desertion means that an estimated 68 per cent of the population are now town-dwellers.

Hungarian is the official language.

Foreign minorities in Hungary account for approximately 10 per cent of the population compared to the 30 per cent of the Hungarian community who live as minorities in surrounding countries. Due to earlier border revisions, there is a large Hungarian speaking community in Transylvania. Germans make up 2.6 per cent of the population and Gypsy communities make up around 4.0 per cent. Germans and Gypsies have been present in the country at least since the nineteenth century. Other minorities, particularly from the former socialist states, expanded during and after the political changes of the late 1980s, Slovaks make up around 1 per cent of the population. Though not recognised as official minorities, there are considerable American and British communities concentrated in Budapest.

Births, Marriages, Deaths
The following table shows vital statistics in recent years.

Denomination	2010	2011
Population	10,014,000	9,986,000
Live births	90,335	88,049
Deaths	130,456	128,795
Natural decrease	-40,121	-40,746

Source: Hungarian Central Statistical Office

The total fertility rate per woman was estimated at 1.4 in 2009. In 2011, the crude birth rate was 8.8 per 1,000 population and the crude death rate was 12.9 per 1,000 population. In 2010 the median age was estimated to be 35.0 years. An estimated 23 per cent of the population was aged 60 or over and 15 per cent was aged under 15 years. Average life expectancy at birth was estimated to be 74 years in 2009 (70 years for males and 78 years for females). Healthy life expectancy was estimated at 66 years (62 years for males and 69 years for females). (Source: http://www.who.int, World Health Statistics 2012)

Public Holidays 2014
1 January: New Year's Day
15 March: National Day
18 April - 21 April: Easter
1 May: Labour Day
9 June: Whit Monday
15 August: Assumption
20 August: Constitution Day
23 October: Republic Day
1 November: All Saints Day
25-26 December: Christmas

EMPLOYMENT

Economic restructuring has resulted in the loss of many jobs, most from agriculture and industry. Despite fears that the privatisation programme might contribute to an increasing unemployment rate with new owners streamlining staff structures, the rate stabilised after the drastic increase of 1990-92. In 1998 the registered unemployment rate was 9.1 per cent (401,000 people). In 1999 the unemployment rate had fallen to 7 per cent, or 285,000 people, and fell again to 5.7 per cent or 238,000 people by December 2000. Unemployment has since risen to 5.9 per cent in 2003 and an estimated 8.0 per cent in 2004 before falling to 7.3 per cent in 2005. It was estimated at 8.4 per cent in 2009 and 11.1 per cent in 2010. Figures for the fourth quarter of 2012 put the unemployment rate at 10.7 per cent.

Total Employment by Economic Activity

Occupation	2008
Agriculture, hunting, forestry & fishing	174,100
Mining & quarrying	9,000
Manufacturing	870,800
Electricity, gas & water supply	57,400
Construction	309,500
Wholesale & retail trade, repairs	585,000
Hotels & restaurants	157,200
Transport, storage & communications	287,400
Financial intermediation	94,700
Real estate, renting & business activities	306,600
Public admin. & defence; compulsory social security	288,600
Education	310,700

- continued

Health & social work	249,100
Other community, social & personal service activities	176,900
Households with employed persons	1,900
Extra-territorial organisations & bodies	500
Total	3 879,400

Source: Copyright © International Labour Organization (ILO Dept. of Statistics, http://laborsta.ilo.org)

BANKING AND FINANCE

Some alterations to the strict Soviet-style planned economy had already been made in the early 1970s, but the reforms were not sufficient to enable Hungary to keep abreast of western market economies. The already poor infrastructure declined further in the 1980s and gross debt accumulated to 20,000 million dollars. Privatisation of state property and the move towards a market economy were initiated in the early 1990s and after eight years the privatisation programme was successfully completed. Around 80 per cent of GDP is now generated by the private sector. A series of austerity measures (the Bokros package) were implemented in 1995 following a large rise in inflation and the government deficit. As a result of these measures, the Hungarian economy has performed well.

The Hungarian economy faced a series of setbacks at the end of the 1990s: the collapse of the Russian economy badly affected exports, particularly agricultural products, and the continued unrest in neighbouring Yugoslavia meant that tourism was affected, as was transport; the Danube was blocked between 1999 and 2001 following NATO bombing of Yugoslav bridges. In spite of this, the economy grew through a developing export market to the EU and continued foreign direct investment.

Hungary became an associate member of the EU in 1994 and a full member on 1 May 2004. Hungary hoped to adopt the Euro by 2008, postponed to 2011 but as of January 2012, no date has been set. In 1996 Hungary became a member of the Organisation for Economic Co-operation and Development (OECD), and in 1999, the country joined NATO.

Prime Minister Gyurcsany introduced a package of austerity measures in June 2006 with the aim of cutting the budget deficit to 8 per cent in 2006, 5 per cent in 2007 and 3 per cent in 2008. This would help clear the way for Hungary to join the Eurozone. He planned to raise taxes and cut waste in the public sector as well as bringing in wide-ranging reforms to the healthcare sector, state administration, local government and education.

Hungary has been badly affected by the global economic crisis and the value of the forint fell sharply in 2008. The IMF, the EU and the World Bank granted a rescue package worth £15.5 billion (US$25 billion) to Hungary in October 2008. The government was forced to approach the IMF and EU again in November 2011 for a second rescue package. The IMF withdrew from discussions amidst concern over reforms to central bank.

Currency
One forint = 100 filler
In June 2001 the forint became fully convertible.

GDP/GNP, Inflation, National Debt
In 2000 GDP grew by 5.1 per cent, falling slightly to 3.8 per cent in 2001, 3.4 per cent in 2002 and 2.8 per cent in 2003. GDP grew in 2004 by 4.0 per cent and by 4.1 per cent in 2005. In 2007, growth was estimated at 1.7 per cent, less than its European neighbours. It was 0.3 per cent in 2008. Estimated figures for 2009 put GDP at US$129 billion and for 2011 at US$135 billion. In response to the global economic downturn, growth in 2009 was put at -6.2 per cent. Growth was estimated to be 1.2 per cent in 2010 and 1.7 in 2011. Figures for 2011 put value added GDP at HUF 27,886,401 million. Growth was expected to remain weak through 2012. GDP by sector is as follows: services 65 per cent; industry 32 per cent; agriculture 3 per cent.

Inflation in 1995 was at 28 per cent. It had fallen to 10 per cent by 1999. In 2007, it was estimated at 6.3 per cent. In 3Q2012 it was running at 6 per cent, higher than the government target of 3 per cent.

Total external debt was estimated to be US$180 billion in 2011.

Foreign Investment
Foreign investment has played an important role in the growth of Hungary's economy. It was estimated to be €60 billion in 2009.

Balance of Payments / Imports and Exports
Seventy per cent of goods are exported to the European Union, which in turn provides nearly 60 per cent of Hungary's imported goods. The recovery of the export market helped the economy to grow in 2010. Figures for 2011 put the cost of imports of goods and services at HUF 23,601,098 million and earnings from the export of goods and services at HUF 25,649,995 million.

Central Bank
Magyar Nemzeti Bank (National Bank of Hungary), Szabadság tér 8-9, H-1850 Budapest V, Hungary. Tel: +36 (0)1 428 2600, fax: +36 (0)1 428 2500, URL: http://www.mnb.hu
Governor: Dr Matolcsy György (page 1435)

Chambers of Commerce and Trade Addresses
Hungarian Chamber of Commerce, URL: http://www.tradepartner.eu/commerce/hungary
Budapest Chamber of Commerce and Industry, URL: http://www.bkik.hu/

HUNGARY

MANUFACTURING, MINING AND SERVICES

Primary and Extractive Industries
Coal production, which declined in favour of oil and natural gas, has revived since the increased oil and gas prices of the mid-1980s. Recent figures show that recoverable reserves of hard coal are around 650 million short tons, lignite 3,000 million short tons, and brown coal 1,000 million short tons. Hungary is trying to move away from coal fired power plants to cleaner fuels such as gas. Figures for 2010 show that coal production was at 10 million short tons, down from 15.5 million short tons in 2000.

Resources of the ore, bauxite, used in the production of aluminium are estimated 18-20 per cent of the world total. Mining is carried out in the Bakony and Vértes mountain regions. Hungary's aluminium industry was previously aided by an agreement whereby alumina was exported to Russia for processing and returned in ingot form. Copper, lead and zinc have also been found.

Oil and natural gas fields near Szeged provide the greatest output, others include Lispe and Lovászi. Extra oil and gas are supplied by pipeline from Russia and from the Adria pipeline running through the former Yugoslavia. Figures for 2011 show that Hungary produced 37,640 barrels per day and consumed around 141,000 barrels per day. The shortfall was made up of imports, mainly from Russia. Its oil refinery capacity was 161,000 bbl/d.

Hungary has natural gas reserves of an estimated 75 billion cubic feet. Gross production of natural gas in 2011 was 98 billion cubic feet and consumption was 408 billion cubic feet. (Source: EIA)

Energy
Hungary's first and only nuclear power plant stands at Paks on the Danube. It provides approximately 40 per cent of the country's electric energy. Total net generation of electricity was estimated to be 35.4 billion kWh with consumption estimated at 37 billion kWh. Installed capacity was 9.0 GWe.

Total primal energy production in 2009 was 0.406 quadrillion Btu and total energy consumption was 1.033quadrillion Btu. (Source: EIA)

Manufacturing
Light industry and food processing developed in the 1980s though production still tended to show a bias towards heavy industry. Extensive steel and iron production is carried out at the plant at Duaujváros. In the early 1990s the loss of some industrial markets caused a steep decline in production. The economy recovered with investment from abroad aimed at using Hungary as a base for the manufacture of consumer products including Philips, Samsung, Sony, TDK, IBM, Suzuki, Ford, General Motors and Scania. The pharmaceutical industry and food production sector were key growth areas. However, Hungary has been badly affected by the global economic downturn.

The following table shows gross output at current prices by branch of industry in 2000:

Branch	Billion forints
Food, beverages & tobacco	1,602
Textiles, apparel, leather & fur products	410
Wood, paper, printing, & publishing	570
Chemicals & chemical products	1,765
Non-metallic mineral products	280
Basic metals and fabricated metals	849
Machinery & equipment	4,929
Other manufacturing & recycling	133

Source: Hungarian Central Statistical Office

Service Industries
Tourism is a growing industry and one of the most significant hard currency earners. Major cultural festivals in Budapest are the result of government and commercial injection of funds into the tourist industry. Established tourist attractions outside Budapest include Lake Balaton and the puszta region where folk culture and equestrian shows are a traditional theme. Figures for 2011 show that 18.6 million Hungarians travelled abroad and 3.4 million foreigners travelled to Hungary. Revenue was estimated at Hf 245 billion. Most visitors are from Europe, especially Germany, and the USA.
Hungarian National Tourist Board, URL: http://www.hungary.com

Agriculture
70 per cent of the country's land is under cultivation making agriculture a significant part of the economy. Grains (wheat and maize), sunflowers, sugarbeet and rapeseed are the main arable crops. Products such as beef, pork and poultry remain important despite falling production and viticulture also forms an important part of the economy. Figures for 2011 show that Hungary had 694,000 head of cattle, 3,025,000 pigs, 1,080 sheep amd 41,488,000 poultry.

In recent years, the exchange of land from the hands of large working co-operatives to private entrepreneurs together with the decrease in subsidies has had a large effect on the various aspects of the farming industry. Re-organisation programmes and institutions such as the Agrarian Entrepreneurial Credit Guarantee Foundation provide aid and guidance for the development of the industry today.

Agricultural Production in 2010

Produce	Int. $'000*	Tonnes
Indigenous pigmeat	631,050	410,508
Maize	607,930	6,967,170
Cow milk, whole, fresh	510,195	1,684,920

- continued		
Indigenous chicken meat	382,720	268,687
Wheat	367,825	3,763,680
Sunflower seed	260,826	969,718
Apples	209,645	496,916
Grapes	168,496	194,771
Indigenous cattle meat	153,333	56,761
Rapeseed	143,267	530,619
Maize, green	125,287	302,757
Hen eggs, in shell	124,216	151,804

*unofficial figures
Source: http://faostat.fao.org/site/339/default.aspx Food and Agriculture Organization of the United Nations, Food and Agricultural commodities production

Forestry
In 2004 an estimated 2.9 million m³ of roundwood and 2.6 million m³ were produced.

COMMUNICATIONS AND TRANSPORT

Travel Requirements
Citizens of the USA, Canada, Australia and the EU require a valid passport valid but do not need a visa for stays of up to 90 days. EU citizens carrying a valid national Identity Card do not require a passport. Visitors staying for longer than 30 days, who are not staying in a hotel, must register with the local police. Other nationals should contact the embassy to check visa requirements.

Hungary is a member of the Schengen Agreement.

National Airlines
Hungary's international airline, Malév, operated in Europe, the Middle East and Scandinavia. In February 2012, Malev was declared bankrupt.
Malév Hungarian Airlines, URL: http://www.malev.com/bp/eng/index.asp

International Airports
Hungary has three international airports, situated in Budapest, are Ferihegy 1 and Ferihegy 2. Airport Debrecen in Debrecen and FlyBalaton Airport in Sármellék. There are several other airfields located regionally.
Budapest, Ferihegy, URL: http://www.bud.hu/english
Airport Debrecen, URL: http://www.airportdebrecen.hu
FlyBalaton Airport, URL: http://www.flybalaton.com

Roads
The road network consists of nearly 200,000 km of roads of which 75,000 are paved. Figures for 2003 show that nearly 27 million tonnes of freight were carried by road. In 2000 there were 2.3 million passenger cars on the roads, 17,855 buses and 342,007 lorries. Vehicles drive on the right. The cities of Budapest, Debrecen, Szeged and Miskolc all have tram systems.

Railways
Budapest has over 9,000 km of track. In 2003 around 8.1 million tons of freight was carried by rail. The former Hungarian State Railways became part of the MAV Group in 2007, and the different branches of the business operate as separate companies.
MAV Group, URL: http://www.mav.hu/english/index.php

Waterways
Although Hungary has no sea-board, her shipping company MAHART operates both river transport on the Danube and sea-going ships which transport goods to ports throughout the world. MAHART was privatised in 2008.
MAHART (Hungarian Shipping Co.), http://www.mahartpassnave.hu/

HEALTH

All employers and employees pay into a national insurance scheme for health care and pensions. Private health care is also available.

In 2009, Hungary spent approximately 10.3 per cent of its total budget on healthcare, accounting for 69.7 per cent of all healthcare spending. Total expenditure on healthcare equated to 7.6 per cent of the country's GDP. Per capita total expenditure on health was US$957 in 2009, compared to US$326 in 2000.

Statistics for 2005-10 show that there were 30,276 doctors (30.3 per 10,000 population), 63,980 nurses and midwives (64 per 10,000 population), 5,731 pharmacists (5.7 per 10,000 population), and 4,920 dentists (4.9 per 10,000 population). There were an estimated 71 hospital beds per 10,000 population.

In 2009, the infant mortality rate (likelihood of dying before age 1) was 5 per 1,000 live births. The child mortality rate (under fives) was 6 per 1,000 live births. In 2010 the main causes of death among children aged less than 5 years were pneumonia 4 per cent, prematurity 28 per cent, 5 per cent birth asphyxia, 28 per cent congenital abnormalities and 4 per cent injuries. All of the population has access to improved drinking water and sanitation. (Source: http://www.who.int, World Health Statistics 2012)

EDUCATION

Education is compulsory for all children aged six to sixteen. The development of education at all levels is aided by the World Bank and PHARE project. Literacy is estimated at 98.9 per cent. Recent figures (2008) show that almost 10.1 per cent of government spending (5.4 per ent of GDP) goes on education. Of that, 44 per cent is allocated to secondary education, 17 er cent on primary education, 19 per cent on tertiary education and 14 per cent pre-primary ducation. (Source: UNESCO)

re-school Education

here are over 35,000 nursery schools called *bölcsöde* or *óvada*. An estimated 85 per cent f children attended pre-primary school in 2009.

rimary/Secondary Education

n estimated 92 per cent of girls and 93 per cent of boys attended primary school in 2009. he pupil to teacher ratio was 10:1. An estimated 96 per cent of pupils completed primary ducation. Those completing the eight grades of primary school or *általános iskola* approximately 99 per cent) went on to secondary or vocational schools. In 1999-00 there ere 1,054 secondary schools or *gimnázium*. In addition to the existing religious schools, number of new church schools opened recently in Budapest and in the country.

ocational Education

ocational training declined at the end of the 1980s as it was formerly geared to the needs f heavy industry and large scale farming which at that time were affected by economic ansformation. Considerable aid from the PHARE programme and the World Bank has nabled redevelopment. Vocational middle schools are called *szakközep iskola*.

ligher Education

here are over 140 colleges and universities in Hungary called *föiskolák* or *egyetemek*. An stimated 62 per cent of the tertiary age population are in tertiary education.

he Hungarian Academy of Sciences (MTA after the Hungarian initials) has cooperation rojects with several foreign academies or large research institutions. In addition, a Sörös oundation funded university, the Central European University, is based in Budapest. The niversity brings together post-graduate students from central European countries with a cholarship system and aims to further scholarly exchange and understanding in the region.

RELIGION

iplomatic relations between the Vatican and Hungary were severed in 1945 and the perations of the church in Hungary were closely monitored for the next four decades. After he political changes at the end of the 1980s, the number of religious movements and sects nultiplied.

he population of Hungary remains largely Catholic (45 per cent) and Protestant (18 per ent). Baptists, Methodist and Adventist free churches number 40-80,000 followers. The ewish community concentrated in Budapest has decreased steadily since the Second World Var, currently the community is around 98,000. The Muslim community numbers around 5,000. There is a rapidly growing interest in cult groups, and eastern world religions have 0-12,000 followers. Simultaneously, however, there is a tendency towards atheism, with 4 per cent of the population professing a lack of faith.

total of US$7 million was allocated by the state towards the construction and renovation f church buildings in 1998. The majority of this went to the Catholic church.

lungary has a religious liberty rating of 8 on a scale of 1 to 10 (10 is most freedom). (Source: Vorld Religion Database)

COMMUNICATIONS AND MEDIA

rivate and state broadcasters operate. The state broadcaster has struggled in recent years. controversial new media law was introduced in 2011 and has been criticised for increasing overnment control over the media.

Jewspapers

lungary's newspapers are privately-owned, some by foreign investors.
Népszabadság, URL: http://www.nol.hu
Népszava, URL: http://www.nepszava.hu

Magyar Hirlap (Hungarian News), URL: http://www.magyarhirlap.hu
Magyar Nemzet, URL: http://www.mno.hu/
Budapest Times, URL: http://www.budapesttimes.hu/ (English language)

Broadcasting

State-run broadcasting competes against private media. The state broadcaster has faced allegations of political influence and its audience share has declined. Television stations include MTV (Hungarian public television, operates two stations), Duna TV, TV2 and Hir TV (News TV). There are also several hundred cable TV channels available. Transformation to digital television has been postponed until 2014.
MTV, URL: http://www.mtv.hu (state-run)
Duna TV, URL: http://www.dunatv.hu (state-run)
TV2, URL: http://tv2.hu/Nyitooldal
Hir TV, URL: http://www.hirtv.net/

Magyar Rádió (Hungarian Radio) is joined by a growing number of commercial radios, including Rádió Juventus and Rádió Bridge. Commercial radio stations are also emerging in provincial areas.
Magyar Rádió, , URL: http://www.english.radio.hu
Danubius Radio, URL: http://www.danubius.hu/
Rádió Juventus, URL: http://www.juventus.hu/

Telecommunications

At the beginning of the 1990s, Hungary stood well behind the rest of Europe in terms of telecommunications. Recent steps forward have included the privatisation of the former nationally owned telecommunications company, MATÁV. Hungary was the first East Central European country to be upgraded by the International Telecommunications Union. MATÁV has improved the network by introducing 100 per cent automation and increased the rate of digitalization. The number of telephone lines in Hungary has doubled, from 1.5 million in 1993 to an estimated 2.9 million in 2010. Figures from that year estimated that over 12 million mobile phones were in use.

Recent figures show that Hungary has over 6 million regular internet users.

ENVIRONMENT

The capital suffers dangerous smog levels in the summer months and citizens are guided by pollution level indicators situated in the cities' tube stations. In 1998 the government passed a resolution to eliminate environmental damage caused by the previous regime by 2002. The cost is estimated at several hundred billion HUF. Much of the damage is at former Soviet military bases. The river Tisza was polluted by cyanide from a leakage at a gold mine in Romania in January 2000.

Hungary is a party to the following international agreements: Air Pollution, Air Pollution-Nitrogen Oxides, Air Pollution-Persistent Organic Pollutants, Air Pollution-Sulfur 85, Air Pollution-Sulfur 94, Air Pollution-Volatile Organic Compounds, Antarctic Treaty, Biodiversity, Climate Change, Climate Change-Kyoto Protocol, Desertification, Endangered Species, Environmental Modification, Hazardous Wastes, Law of the Sea, Marine Dumping, Ozone Layer Protection, Ship Pollution, Wetlands and Whaling.

In 2010, Hungary's emissions from the consumption of fossil fuels totalled 50.39 million metric tons of carbon dioxide, down on 56.05 million metric tons in 2008. (Source: EIA)

SPACE PROGRAMME

Hungarian scientists have been responsible for the development of various instruments and equipment for use in international space exploration projects since the 1940s and were involved in the former socialist countries COSMOS agreement in the 1960s. The Government of Hungary established the Hungarian Space Office in January 1992. It was integrated into the Ministry of National Development in 2010.

Hungarian Space Research Agency, URL: http://www.hso.hu/page.php?page=215

ICELAND
Republic of Iceland
Lydveldid Island

Capital: Reykjavik (Population estimate, 2012: 118,840)

Head of State: Ólafur Ragnar Grímsson (President) (page 1434)

National Flag: Blue, bearing a red cross bordered white, the upright slightly towards the hoist

CONSTITUTION AND GOVERNMENT

Constitution

Iceland was settled between the years AD 874-1000, mostly by Norwegians and some Celts from Britain. A Republic was established in 930, when a central parliament for all Iceland, the *Althing*, was established at Thingvellir. The Republic came to an end in 1262-64, when the Icelanders made a Treaty of Union with the Crown of Norway in which they accepted its supremacy. In 1380 Iceland came under the Danish Crown as a result of the Chalmar Union. The Icelandic people maintained that they had accepted the supremacy of the King of Norway but not that of the Danish Government. In spite of this they had no more than provincial autonomy far into the 19th century.

In 1874 Iceland was granted a constitution by which the people were allowed a say in the management of some of their own affairs, but this did not satisfy national aspirations and there was a long struggle for constitutional freedom which at last came to an end in 1918. In that year an Act of Union was passed, the Parliament of both countries acknowledging Iceland to be a sovereign state having the King in common with Denmark. It also provided that after 25 years either party could request negotiations regarding its future and, if no agreement be concluded within three years, either Parliament might, by a two-thirds majority, resolve that the Act be cancelled, subject to confirmation by plebiscite. Denmark being under German occupation in 1940, no negotiations were possible and Iceland adopted a temporary regency. A plebiscite for the purpose of determining a form of government was held in 1944 and as a result the Republic of Iceland was declared on 17 June 1944.

Under the Constitution executive power is exercised by the President and other government authorities specified by the Constitution, whilst judicial power is exercised by the Judiciary. The President acts through his ministers. He is not answerable for his official actions, whereas the Cabinet, headed by the Prime Minister, is responsible for all acts of government. The president has power to appoint and dismiss ministers, to make appointments to all the more important official posts, to make treaties with other nations and to summon Parliament. He can dissolve Parliament if he thinks fit. All legislation passed by Parliament has to have the consent of the president before it becomes law. He may refuse to ratify a law passed by Parliament but it does not become void thereby. Ratification lies with a plebiscite to whose judgement the law must be submitted as soon as circumstances permit.

The ministers forming the Government are appointed by the president but they must have the confidence of Parliament, and if they are unable to command a parliamentary majority the Government must resign. Ministers need not necessarily be elected members of Parliament but they have seats in the house according to their office and have freedom of speech there and the right of introducing bills. They have, however, no right to vote unless they are also members of the Parliament.

The constitution was most recently amended in 1999. To consult the constitution, please visit: http://government.is/constitution

International Relations

Iceland is a member of the following international organisations, Arctic Council; Barents Euro-Arctic Council; Council for Baltic Sea States; Council of Europe; European Bank for Reconstruction and Development; European Economic Area; European Free Trade Area; International Bank for Reconstruction and Development; International Civil Aviation Authority; International Criminal Court; International Monetary Fund; International Maritime Organisation; Interpol; Intelsat; International Whaling Commission; NATO; OSCE; OSPAR; Convention for the Protection of the Marine Environment of the North East Atlantic; Nordic Council of Ministers; Schengen; UN; Western European Union (associate); World Trade Organisation. As yet Iceland has not become a member of the EU and there are not plans for membership to be come part of a national debate. It is felt that membership of the EEC and EFTA fulfills its needs. Under the terms of a bilateral defence agreement between Iceland and the USA, the USA agrees to defend Iceland should the need arise, until 2006 the USA had personnel and aircraft based a base at Keflavik.

In July 2009 Iceland formally applied for membership of the European Union, formal talks began in July 2010.

Recent Events

In 1985 Iceland declared itself a nuclear free zone.

In August 2003 Iceland held its first whale hunt for 15 years; the hunt was a scientific catch to study the impact whales have on fish stocks. In October 2006 Iceland announced that it would resume commercial whaling despite the international moratorium.

Following poor results by his Progressive Party in the local elections in May 2006, Prime Minister Halldor Asgrimsson resigned and Geir Hilmar Haarde of the Independence Party, member of the coalition government, became Prime Minister.

In September 2006, US troops left Iceland; troops from America had been stationed in Iceland continually since the end of World War II. Iceland broke its 21-year moratorium on commercial whaling in October 2006; catches of 30 minke and nine fin whales were authorised by the government.

In October 2008 Iceland became the first western country to apply for help from the IMF since 1976. Icelandic banks had expanded in recent years and held foreign assets around 1 times the value of Iceland's GDP but following the global financial crisis the government had to take control of three of the largest banks. At the end of September, the government announced it was nationalising the Glitnir bank, and the following week took control of Landsbanki which together with Glitnir were handed over to the receivers and the week after that the Financial Supervisory Authority (FME) put Kaupthing, Iceland's largest bank into receivership. The Icesave Bank also collapsed, the bank had many foreign savers especial from the Netherlands and Britain. Iceland applied to the IMF for help and was granted US$5. billion loan package made up from the IMF and other countries. Unemployment ros dramatically from below two per cent to over 10 per cent as many businesses closed or were declared bankrupt, at one point around 5,000 jobs were being lost per month. The Krona then fell sharply in value, and the Icelandic stock exchange dropped by more than 90 per cent. In November inflation was reported to have reached 17.1 per cent.

Following the deepening financial crisis and lack of confidence in the government Prime Minister Geir Haarde announced on January 23 2009 that he was calling an early election for May 9, he also said he would not be standing for re-election on medical grounds. Iceland's coalition government had collapsed under the strain of an escalating economic crisis. On 2 January talks between the coalition parties broke down, Prime Minister Haarde said he could not accept the Social Democrats' demand to lead the country. Following the breakdown the government resigned. On February 1 a new government was announced led by Johann Sigurdardottir of the Social Democratic Alliance. Elections took place in April 2009 and were won by Johanna Sigurdadottir who continued the existing coalition. The Minister of Health resigned in September 2009 over negotiations on the repayment of debts from the Icelandic banking crisis.

In January 2010 President Olaf Ragnar Grimsson vetoed an unpopular plan which would have seen Iceland repaying British and Dutch savers €3.8bn euros in compensation after the 2008 collapse of the Icesave bank. A referendum was held in March and voters overwhelmingly rejected the proposals to pay back debts to the UK and the Netherlands.

In March 2010 a volcano 75 miles east of Reykjavik that had been dormant for over 200 years erupted causing widespread disruption to air traffic in northern Europe. Disruption continued into May.

In July 2010, formal talks began on Iceland's accession to the EU.

In December 2010 the government agreed a new deal to repay the UK and the Netherland the €4bn. Under the terms of the agreement Iceland will begin repayments in 2016 and repayments should be completed by 2046. In February the parliament approved a new deal to settle the banking dispute with the UK and the Netherlands but a referendum held the following April again resulted in a rejection to repay Britain and the Netherlands. In September 2011 former prime minister Geir Haarde appeared in court accused of failure to handle the 2008 financial crisis. In January 2013 a European court cleared the Icelandic government of failing to guarantee minimum levels of compensation for British and Dutch savers.

In January 2013, Iceland awarded two oil exploration and production licences to Faroe Petroleum and Valiant Petroleum, with Norway having a 25 per cent share in each.

Legislature

Parliament consists of one House. The 63 seats are divided between eight constituencies and members serve a four year term. The largest is Reykjavik with 19 seats. South-West Iceland has 12 and the remaining six have five-six seats each. Three quarters of the seats are allocated to the parties on the basis of the local election outcome in each constituency. The allocation of the remaining seats takes into account the national outcome to ensure overall proportionality in the allocation.
Althingi, 150, Reykjavik, Iceland. Tel: +354 563 0500, fax: +354 563 0550, URL http://www.althingi.is
Speaker: Ásta R. Jóhannesdóttir
Head of State: Ólafur Ragnar Grímsson

Cabinet (as at June 2013)
Prime Minister: Sigmundur Gunnlaugsson (page 1435)
Minister for Foreign Affairs: Gunnar Braqi Sveinsson (page 1522)
Minister of the Interior: Hanna Kristhansdottir (page 1458)
Minister of Finance and Economic Affairs: Bjarni Benediktsson (page 1386)
Minister of Fisheries and Agriculture, Minister of Environment and Natural Resources: Sigurdur Jonsson (page 1450)
Minister of Social Affairs and Housing: Eyglo Hardardottir (page 1438)
Minister of Education, Science and Culture: Illugi Gunnarsson

---

Minister of Industry and Trade: Ragnheidur Arnadottir (page 1379)
Minister of Health: Kristjan þor Juliusson (page 1452)

The government is a coalition of the Social Democratic Alliance and the Green-Left Party.

Ministries

Office of the President, Stadastadur, Sóleyjargata 1, 150 Reykjavík, Iceland. Tel: +354 540 4400, fax: +354 562 4802, e-mail: forseti@forseti.is

Office of the Prime Minister, Stjórnarrádshúsinu v/Laekjartorg, 150 Reykjavík, Iceland. Tel: +354 545 8400, fax: +354 562 4014, e-mail: postur@for.stjr.is, URL: http://www.stjr.is/for

Ministry of Economic Affairs, Solvholsgotu 7, 150 Reykjavík, Iceland. Tel: +354 545 4800, fax: +354 511 1161, e-mail: postur@vrn.stjr.is, URL: http://eng.vidskiptaraduneyti.is

Ministry of Education, Science and Culture, Sölvhólsgötu 4, 150 Reykjavík, Iceland. Tel: +354 545 9500, fax: +354 562 3068, e-mail: postur@mrn.stjr.is, URL: http://www.mrn.stjr.is

Ministry of the Environment, Vonarstraeti 4, 150 Reykjavík, Iceland. Tel: +354 545 8600, fax: +354 562 4566, e-mail: postur@umh.stjr.is, URL: http://www.stjr.is/umh

Ministry of Finance, Arnarhváli, 150 Reykjavík, Iceland. Tel: +354 545 9200, fax: +354 562 8280, e-mail: mail@fjr.stjr.is, URL: http://www.fjr.stjr.is

Ministry of Fisheries and Agriculture, Skúlagöta 4, 150 Reykjavík, Iceland. Tel: +354 545 8300, fax: +354 562 1853, e-mail: postur@hafro.is, URL: http://www.stjr.is/sjr

Ministry of Foreign Affairs, Raudarárstígur 25, 150 Reykjavík, Iceland. Tel: +354 545 9900, fax: +354 562 2373, e-mail: external@utn.stjr.is, URL: http://www.mfa.is

Ministry of Industry, Energy and Tourism, Arnarhváli, 150 Reykjavík, Iceland. Tel: +354 545 8500, fax: +354 562 1289, e-mail: postur@id.stjr.is, URL: http://eng.idnadarraduneyti.is

Ministry of the Interior (Justice), Skuggasundi, 150 Reykjavík, Iceland. Tel: +354 545 9000, fax: +354 552 7340, e-mail: postur@irr.is, URL: http://www.stjr.is/dkm

Ministry of the Interior (Transport and Communications), Hafnarhúsinu vid Tryggvagötu, 150 Reykjavík, Iceland. Tel: +354 545 8200, fax: +354 562 1702, e-mail: postur@irr.is, URL: http://www.stjr.is/sam

Ministry of Welfare, Hafnarhusinu vid Tryggvagotu, 150 Reykjavík, Iceland. Tel: +354 545 8100, fax: +354 551 9165, e-mail: postur@vel.is, URL: http://www.stjr.is/htr

Elections

Election to the Parliament is by universal suffrage every four years. In May 2006 Halldor Agrimsson resigned as Prime Minister following the poor showing of his party in local elections; Geir Hilmar Haarde of the Independence Party took over the post of Prime Minister. In the May 2007 General Elections, the governing coalition of the Independence Party and the Progressive Party held onto its majority in parliament by a single seat. The leaders of the coalition parties announced that the coalition would discontinue, due to the narrow majority, and Prime Minister Geir H. Haarde, leader of the Independence Party, formed a new government with the Social Democratic Alliance.

In June 1996 Olafur Ragnar Grimsson began his first term as president. This was followed by a second term without an election and he was re-elected in June 2004. The next presidential election took place in June 2008, President Grimsson was re-elected unopposed. The most recent presidential election took place in July 2012, President Grimsson was again re-elected making him the longest serving president in Iceland's history.

In response to the deepening financial crisis and lack of confidence in the government, Prime Minister Geir Haarde announced on January 23 2009 that he was calling an early election for May 9, he did not stand for re-election himself due to medical issues. Iceland's coalition government had collapsed under the strain of an escalating economic crisis. On 26 January talks between the coalition parties broke down, Prime Minister Haarde said he could not accept the Social Democrats' demand to lead the country and following the breakdown the government resigned. On February 1 a new government was announced led by Johanna Sigurdardottir of the Social Democratic Alliance. Elections took place in April 2009 and were won by Johanna Sigurdadottir who continued the existing coalition.

The most recent election was held in April 2013, the opposition Progressive and Independence parties won the most seats and formed a coalition.

Political Parties

Social and Democrataic Alliance (Samfylkingin), Hallveigarstíg 1 101 Reykjavík, Iceland. Tel: +354 414 2200 fax: +354 414-2201, URL: http://www.samfylking.is
Leader: Jóhanna Sigurðardóttir

Independence Party (Sjálfstaedisflokkurinn), Háaleitisbraut 1, 105 Reykjavík, Iceland. Tel; +354 515 1700, e-mail: xd@xd.is, URL: http://www.xd.is
Leader: Bjarni Benediktsson

Progressive Party (Framsóknarflokkurinn), Hversisgata 33-2, 101 Reykjavík, Iceland. Tel: +354 540 4300, URL: http://www.framsokn.is, e-mail: framsokn@framsokn.is
Leader: Sigmundur Davið Gunnlaugsson

The Liberal Party (Frjálslyndi flokkurinn), Aðalstræti 9, 101 Reykjavík, Iceland. URL: http://www.xf.is
Leader: Sigurjón Þórðarson

Left-Green Movement (Vinstrihreyfingin - grænt framboð), Suðurgata 3, 101 Reykjavík, Iceland. URL: http://www.vg.is
Leader: Steingrímur J. Sigfússon

The Movement, (Hreyfingin), URL: http://www.hreyfingin.is
Leader: Þór Saari

Diplomatic Representation

US Embassy, Laufásvegur 21, 101 Reykjavík, Iceland. Tel: +354 562 9100, fax: +354 562 9139, URL: http://www.usa.is
Ambassador: Luis E. Arreaga (page 1379)
British Embassy, Laufásvegur 31, 101 Reykjavík, Iceland. Tel: +354 550 5100-2, fax: +354 550 5105, e-mail: britemb@centrum.is, URL: http://ukiniceland.fco.gov.uk/en
Ambassador: Stuart Gill (page 1430)

Embassy of Iceland, 2a Hans Street, London, SW1X 0JE, United Kingdom. Tel: +44 (0)20 7259 3999, fax: +44 (0)20 7245 9649, e-mail: icemb.london@utn.stjr.is, URL: http://www.iceland.is/iceland-abroad/uk
Ambassador: Benedikt Jonsson (page 1451)
Embassy of Iceland, 1156 15th St., NW, Suite 1200, Washington, DC 20005, USA. Tel: +1 202 265 6653, fax: +1 202 265 6656, e-mail: icemb.wash@utn.stjr.is, URL: http://www.iceland.is/iceland-abroad/us
Ambassador: Gudmundur A. Stefansson (page 1520)
Permanent Mission of Iceland to the United Nations, 800 Third Avenue, 36th Floor, New York, NY 10022, USA. Tel: +1 212 593 2700, fax: +1 212 593 6269, e-mail: icecon.ny@utn.stjr.is, URL: http://www.iceland.is/iceland-abroad/un/nyc/
Ambassador: Gréta Gunnarsdóttir

LEGAL SYSTEM

The highest court in Iceland is called Haestiréttur, which is a Supreme Court of Appeal of eight judges. One of these is the Chief Justice and elected by the other Justices for a period of two years. There are eight lower courts that are district courts for the country. They are called héradsdómur. There are 38 district court judges, called héradsdómari. All judges are appointed by the president and cannot be removed apart from in exceptional circumstances such as misconduct in the performance of their duties.

The government respects the rights of its citizens. The death penalty was abolished in 1928, and the 1995 revision of the constitution forbids its reintroduction.

Supreme Court, URL: http://www.haestirettur.is
President: Markus Sigurbjornsson
Justices: Arne Kolbeinsson, Gudrun Erlendsdóttir, Gardar Gíslason, Gunnlaugur Claessen, Hrafn Bragason, Ingibjorg Benediktsdottir, Jon Steinar Gunnlaugsson and Olafur Borkur Thorvaldsson

LOCAL GOVERNMENT

Iceland is divided into 8 provinces, 26 districts and 77 municipalities. There are eight urban municipalities, Austurland, Hofudhborgarsvaedhi, Nordhurland Eystra, Nordhurland Vestra, Sudhurland, Sudhurnes, Vestfirdhir, and Vesturland which are governed by town councils. Each locality has an elected local council. The number of elected members on the council is always uneven and ranges in number according to the population it is representing, for example, Reykhavik has the largest town council as it is the area with the largest population and is represented by 15 members; the smallest localities with a population of around 200 would have a council of 3 members.

Population by Province in January 1 2011

Province	Population
Hofudhborgarsvaedhi	202,341
Nordhurland Eystra	29,006
Nordhurland Vestra	7,393
Sudhurland	23,802
Sudhurnes	21,088
Vestfirdhir	7,137
Vesturland	15,379
Austurland	12,306

Source: Statistics Iceland

AREA AND POPULATION

Area

Iceland is situated in the North Atlantic Ocean. It has an area of 39,756 sq. miles (103,000 km sq) with a coastline of 3,700 miles. Much of this area consists of high terrain, glaciers cover 11,922 sq km. and lava fields, there are also 2,757 sq km of lakes. Cultivable land numbers some 20,000 sq. km. Greenland is the nearest land surface, 287 km to the east. During the summer Iceland becomes a land of the midnight sun, when the sun does not dip below the horizon. The land is temperate for its latitude. The south coast tends to be warmer and wetter, inland areas more arid. Snowfall is more common in the north. The central region is the coldest part of the country.

To view a map, please consult http://www.lib.utexas.edu/maps/cia08/iceland_sm_2008.gif

Population

The population at January 2012 was 319,575, up from the January 2008 figure of 313,376. In 2011 the population of Reykjavik, the capital, was 118,840. Life expectancy for men is 75.9 years and for women it is 80.8 years. Figures for 2011 show that 5,625 people immigrated to Iceland and 2,754 people migrated from Iceland. Iceland is the most sparsely populated country in Europe with just 3 people per sq km. Icelandic belongs to the North Germanic branch of the Indo-European family of languages.

Icelanders follow the patronymic system for names; that is, each Icelander's name is derived from the first name of their father, so each name is the forename followed by døttir (daughter of) or son (son of) and the father's name. A woman keeps her name even after marriage.

Births, Marriages, Deaths

Figures for 2011 show that there were 4,492 live births and 1,986 deaths, in that year 1,458 marriages took place and 516 divorces.

Public Holidays 2014

1 January: New Year's Day

579

ICELAND

17 April: Maundy Thursday
18 April: Good Friday
20 March: Easter Sunday
21 April: Easter Monday
24 April: First Day of Summer
1 May: Labour Day
29 May: Ascension Day
8 June: Whit Sunday
9 June: Whit Monday
17 June: National Day
4 August: Shop and Office Workers' Holiday
24 December: Christmas Eve**
25 December: Christmas Day
26 December: Boxing Day
31 December: New Year's Eve**

* Holidays falling on Sundays are not observed on the following Monday.
** Christmas Eve and New Year's Eve are half working days (until 12 noon).

EMPLOYMENT

Towards the end of 2008, Iceland felt the effects of the global economic downturn and banking crisis; unemployment rose dramatically from below 2 per cent to over 10 per cent as many businesses closed or were declared bankrupt. At one point around 5,000 jobs were being lost per month.

Figures for 2011 show that of a labour force of 180,000, 167,300 people were employed and 12,700 were unemployed, giving an unemployment rate of 7.1 per cent.

Employment and unemployment figures Q1

Sector	2008	2009	2011
% activity rate	81.0	79.5	79.2
% unemployment rate	2.3	7.1	7.8
Labour force est. number	178,100	178,200	176,000
Employed	174,000	165,500	162,300
Unemployed	4,200	12,700	13,700
Employed full-time, est. number	133,500	123,500	118,600
Employed part time, est. number	40,500	42,000	43,800
Average hours of work	40.8	38.9	39.5
Full-time hours of work	46.2	44.7	45.4
Part-time hours of work	22.0	21.4	22.5

Source: Statistics Iceland

The following table shows how the working population in 2011 was employed by sector.

Employment sector	Employed persons
Agriculture	4,800
Fishing	5,200
Fish processing	3,800
Manufacturing (except fish processing)	15,400
Electricity & water supply	1,600
Construction	10,000
Wholesale, retail trade & repairs	21,800
Hotels, restaurants	8,800
Transport, communication	11,300
Financial intermediation	8,300
Retail estate & business activities	18,000
Public administration	7,200
Education	18,300
Health services, social work	20,500
Other services	12,400

Source: Statistics Iceland

BANKING AND FINANCE

Currency
One Icelandic Króna (ISK) = 100 aurar

GDP/GNP, Inflation, National Debt
The economy of Iceland showed strong growth during the 1990s but suffered a recession in 2001. Traditionally the Icelandic economy is heavily reliant on the fishing industry which accounts for around 60 per cent of exports, and contributes around eight per cent of GDP. In recent years the government has explored other industries in order to be less dependent on fishing. As Iceland has access to clean and cheap fuel, industries which are energy intensive are a possibility and Iceland now has two expanded aluminium smelters with a third and larger one being built.

In October 2008 Iceland became the first western country to apply for help from the IMF since 1976. Icelandic banks have expanded in recent years and held foreign assets around 10 times the value of Iceland's GDP but following the global financial crisis the government had to take control of three of the largest banks. At the end of September, the government announced it was nationalising the Glitnir bank, a week later it took control of Landsbanki and Glitnir were handed over to the receivers and the week after that the Financial Supervisory Authority (FME) put Kaupthing, Iceland's largest bank into receivership. Iceland applied to the IMF for help and was granted US$5.1 billion loan package made up from the IMF and

other countries. The Krona has fallen sharply in value, and the Icelandic stock exchange dropped by more than 90 per cent. In November 2008 inflation was reported to have reached 17.1 per cent. In March 2010 the IMF released a further US$160 million from its original 2008 aid package. Payment had been delayed over compensation claims for the collapse of Icesave.

Figures for 2008 put GDP growth at 0.3 per cent in real terms. This was down from the 2005 figure of 5.5 per cent and 4.5 per cent in 2006. Figures for 2008 put growth at -6.8 per cent. Economic growth for 2010 was put at -4.0 per cent.

Forecast figures for 2011 put GDP growth at 2.6 per cent and 2.7 per cent in 2012.

GDP

Year	Million ISK
2004	956,58.
2005	1,025,74.
2006	1,074,04.
2007	1,138,32.
2008	1,151,84.
2009	1,076,06.
2010	1,032,89.
2011	1,059,29.

Source: Statistics Iceland

Gross National Income at market Prices

Year	Million ISK
2004	891,14.
2005	989,76.
2006	1,100,39.
2007	1,236,75.
2008	1,196,40.
2009	1,205,83.
2010	1,267,05.
2011	1,382,75.

Source: Statistics Iceland

The following table shows a percentage breakdown of GDP in recent years:

Industry	2000	2005	2010*
Agriculture	2.0	1.5	1.4
Fishing	57.1	4.8	5.3
Mining & quarrying	0.1	0.1	0.0
Manufacturing	13.9	10.5	16.5
of which fish processing	2.8	2.1	na
Electricity & water supply	3.4	3.3	4.9
Construction	8.7	10.5	4.0
Wholesale & retail trade	22.0	18.9	18.4
Hotels & restaurants	1.9	1.6	na
Transport, storage & communication	8.7	6.1	7.3
Financial, real estate, renting & business activities	18.9	25.5	25.3
Other service activities	23.9	25.0	24.2

* = provisional figures
Source: Statistics Iceland

Foreign Investment
Areas that attract investment include automotive components, construction materials, textiles and apparel, telecommunications and healthcare products. Foreign investment in the fishing industry is not allowed.

Balance of Payments / Imports and Exports
Iceland's main export is fish and fish products, and around 70 per cent of export earnings come from this sector. Other main exports include animal feed, oils and fats, non-ferrous metals, industrial machinery and transport equipment. Main imports include petroleum, transport equipment and vehicles, medicines, fruit and vegetables.

Balance of Trade in Million ISK

Year	Exports fob	Imports fob	Balance
2001	196,582	202,518	-5,936
2002	204,303	190,221	14,082
2003	182,580	198,480	-15,900
2004	202,373	238,920	-36,547
2005	194,355	288,895	-94,540
2006	242,740	401,202	-158,462
2007	305,096	397,241	-92,145
2008	466,860	473,525	-6,665
2009	500,855	410,575	90,280
2010	561,032	440,820	120,211
2011	620,127	522,985	97,142

Source: Statistics Iceland

The following table shows imports and exports by selected economic categories for 2011 million ISK.

Foreign Trade

Economic category

Economic category	Exports fob	Imports cif
Live animals	777.6	106.1
Meat & meat preparations	3,685.0	1,265.7
Fish, crustaceans, molluscs etc.	227,208.7	11,414.2
Animal feeds, excl. unmilled cereals	17,665.1	2,601.4
Petroleum, petroleum products	11,986.5	76,746.3
Iron & steel	24,281.0	7,492.5
Non-ferrous metals	245,487.2	14,710.0
Gen. industr. machinery & equipm.	4,746.8	17,616.7
Road vehicles	4,124.0	21,372.5
Other transport equipment	8,713.9	22,126.3

Source: Statistics Iceland

Iceland is a member of the European Free Trade Association (EFTA) and most of its trade is done between other member countries and the rest of Europe. Iceland's main trading partners for exports are the United Kingdom, Germany, Netherlands, the United States and Spain. The main trading partners for imports are Germany, the United States, Sweden, Denmark, Norway, the United Kingdom and Netherlands.

Central Bank

Sedlabanki Islands, Kalkofnsvegur 1, 150 Reykjavik, Iceland. Tel: +354 569 9600, fax: +354 569 9605, e-mail: sedlabanki@sedlabanki.is, URL: http://www.sedlabanki.is Governor: Már Gudmundsson (page 1434)

Chambers of Commerce and Trade Organisations

Iceland Chamber of Commerce, URL: http://www.chamber.is
The Trade Council of Iceland, URL: http://www.icetrade.is

MANUFACTURING, MINING AND SERVICES

Energy

Iceland has no proven resources of oil, natural gas or coal, figures for 2009 show that Iceland consumed 0.127 million short tons of coal of which was imported and 20.77 thousand barrels of oil per day, again all of which was imported.

The energy resources in Iceland, i.e. hydro and geothermal reserves, are vast in relation to the size and population of the country, and make it one of Europe's richest nations in terms of hydro-electric potential. This vast source of power has attracted many power-intensive industries and aluminium production is now a major industry for the country. Potential electric power from rivers and geothermal sources is estimated to be at least 64,000 GWh per annum, taking into account economic and ecological considerations. Research has being carried out in Iceland to produce energy from its renewable energy forms, that is to produce electricity from hydrogen and oxygen to power its transport systems thus making herself self sufficient in energy production. In April 2003 the first filling station for hydrogen-powered vehicles opened in readiness for the first of the hydrogen powered bus fleet to come into use.

Today, the entire population has access to electricity. All towns and villages and virtually all farms are connected to public power supplies and around 90 per cent of the population live in houses heated with geothermal power.

Figures from 2009 show that 85.0 per cent of energy used was produced domestically, 18.6 per cent from hydro sources and 66.4 per cent from geothermal sources, 15.0 per cent of energy used that year was from imported sources, 13.4 per cent from oil and 1.6 per cent from coal.

Annual Generation of Electricity in Public Power Plants

GWh	2003	2011
Annual generation of electricity	8,495	17,210.4
Hydro energy	7,084	12,506.8
Geothermal energy	1,406	4,701.5
Fuel	5	2.1

Source: Statistics Iceland

Gross Energy Consumption by Source in 2011

Source	Percentage
Domestic energy total	85.8
Hydro-energy	19.2
Geothermal energy	66.6
Imported energy total	14.2
Oil	12.5
Coal	1.7

Source: Statistics Iceland

Manufacturing

In order to reduce dependence on the marine sector and to broaden further the productive base of the economy, successive governments have followed a policy of encouraging the manufacturing sector and of seeking the co-operation of foreign enterprises in the development of power intensive industries.

Excluding fishing and fish processing, manufacturing has become the most important single sector in the economy. In 2010 it employed 15,400 people and in 2010 contributed 16.5 per cent of GDP. The main enterprises to date are two aluminium smelting plants with a third one planned and factories for fertilizers, cement, rockwool and seaweed meal. The following table shows the total value of sold manufactured products in recent years, figures are in Million ISK.

Sector	2009	2011
Food products & beverages	278,529	339,433
Textiles	2,897	3,415
Wearing apparel & leather goods	1,050	1,524
Wood & of products of wood	1,940	2,551
Paper & paper products	2,560	3,281
Printing & reproduction of recorded media	8,412	9,134
Chemicals & chemical products	11,967	15,156
Rubber & plastic products	6,025	6,725
Other non-metallic mineral products	9,726	8,059
Basic metals	190,794	255,786
Fabricated metal products, except machinery & equipment	11,284	11,056
Computer, electronic & optical products & equipment	3,479	16,008
Machinery & equipment n.e.c.	12,297	15,987
Transport equipment	1,744	1,852
Furniture	3,288	4,015
Other manufacturing	6,179	7,140
Repair & installation of machinery & equipment	20,039	24,581

Source: Statistics Iceland

Service Industries

Recent trends in ecotourism and whale watching have shown an increase in tourism. In 2000, there were close to 303,000 visitors to the country, and in 2005, an estimated 400.000 tourists arrived. Figures show that most tourists come from Denmark, Germany, Sweden, USA and the UK.
Iceland Tourist Board. URL: http://www.icetourist.is

Agriculture

Only one per cent of Iceland is suitable for cultivation and only 20 per cent is suitable for grazing. The main crops are hay, potatoes, turnips, carrots, cabbage and vegetables. The agricultural population is mainly engaged in the rearing of livestock, especially sheep. Figures for 2010 show that Iceland had 2,592 farms.

The following table shows selected agricultural output for 2011:

Produce	Yield
Total hay yield	1,958,749.0 cubic metres
Potatoes	7,222.0 tonnes
Cereal grains	9,600.0 tonnes
Tomatoes	1,605.0 tonnes
Cucumbers	1,582.0 tonnes
Big-bale silage	1,807,314.0 cubic metres

Source: Statistics Iceland

Number of livestock

Livestock	2011
Cattle	72,773
Sheep	474,759
Horses	78,277
Pigs	34,281
Hens	221,167

Source: Statistics Iceland

Fishing

The share of fishing and fish processing in total employment - 5 per cent and 6 per cent respectively - does not properly convey the importance of this sector in the Icelandic economy. Almost the entire output is exported and the industry accounts for around 10 per cent of GDP. On 1 January 2005 registered fishing vessels were 70 stern trawlers and 873 other fishing vessels. The share of fish products has now declined to about three quarters owing to considerable 'new exports' of aluminium (122.3 thousand tonnes in 1997) and other manufacturing products.

The following table shows the value of the catch of major species, values are in ISK thousand:

Fish	2011
Cod	46,387,130
Saithe	9,139,463
Haddock	11,992,052
Redfish	14,972,974
Oceanic redfish	4,027,868
Greenland halibut	7,634,615
Plaice	1,068,157
Herring	5,632,364
Monk	1,589,168
Capelin	8,884,771
Capelin roe	1,531,658
Blue whiting	257,451
Norwegian spring spawning herring	8,862,640
Catfish	2,713,657
Lobster	993,798
Shrimp	1,901,576

Source: Statistics Iceland

In 1989 Iceland gave up whale hunting following the international moratorium concerned with commercial whaling in 1986. In 2003, amid some controversy, the government allowed scientific whaling to resume, to investigate the impact whales have on fish stocks.

ICELAND

COMMUNICATIONS AND TRANSPORT

Travel Requirements
Citizens of the USA, Canada, Australia and most of the EU require a passport valid for three months beyond the length of stay, but do not need a visa for stays of up to 90 days. Other nationals should contact the embassy to check visa requirements. Nationals of Austria, Belgium, Denmark, Finland, France, Germany, Greece, Italy, Luxembourg, the Netherlands, Portugal, Spain and Sweden can use national identity cards instead of passports.

Iceland is a signatory to the 1995 Schengen Agreement. See http://www.eurovisa.info/SchengenCountries.htm for details.

National Airlines
There are regular external air services between Iceland, Britain, Continental Europe and the USA. Keflavík and Reykjavik are ports of call for airliners on the trans-Atlantic air routes. Civil aviation in Iceland is controlled by the Aeronautic Board. There are Customs Airports at Reykjavík and Keflavík.

The air company *Icelandair* is a private company which serves both domestic and international routes, with direct flights to a number of European cities as well as transatlantic flights between several US and European cities. The airline handles about 80,000 passengers a year.
Icelandair: URL: http://www.icelandair.is

International Airports
International services are operated from Keflavík Airport (URL: http://www.kefairport.is/english/). Total passenger movements in 2009 were 854,521.

Railways
There are no railways in Iceland. Internal travel is entirely by road or air services. Recently a rail link between the airport at Keflavik and Reykjavik has been proposed.

Roads
There are approximately 12,700 km of roads in the country. In 2011 there were 1.5 inhabitants per vehicle, including 206,112 registered passenger cars, 1,972 buses, 30,209 lorries and vans, and 9,922 motorcycles. Vehicles are driven on the right.

Shipping
Iceland has numerous harbours including Reykjavik, Akureyri, Straumscik, Keflavik, Hornafjordhur and Isafjordhur, all of which are ice free throughout the year. The two main shipping companies, *Icelandic Steamship Company and Samband Line*, operate regular shipping routes to the major ports of Europe and the United States. In 2003 there were 1,135 seafaring vessels, of which 871 were fishing boats, 76 were trawlers, 4 were whalers and 42 belonged to the merchant fleet. Ferries operate around the coast to islands and fjords.

HEALTH

Iceland's health care system is publicaly financed. Iceland is divided into 7 health districts (which provide specialized care, primary care and elderly care) and 76 municipalities (of which some provide elderly care). About 14 per cent of the care is privately provided. There are currently two main hospitals, 6 regional hospitals and 16 health institutions.

In 2009, Iceland spent approximately 15.7 per cent of its total budget on healthcare (down from 18.5 per cent in 2000), accounting for 82.2 per cent of all healthcare spending. Social security spending made up 35.2 per cent of the government expenditure. Total expenditure on healthcare equated to 9.8 per cent of the country's GDP. Per capita total expenditure on health was US$3,692 in 2009. Iceland has cut its healthcare expenditure because of the economic crisis.

Figures for 2000-10 show that there are 1,146 physicians (37.3 per 10,000 population), 4,875 nurses and midwives (158.8 per 10,000 population), 313 dentistry personnel and 595 pharmaceutical personnel. There are 58 hospital beds per 10,000 population. The infant and childhood mortality rates are low at 2 per 1,000 live births. The most common causes of death in the under-fives were 41 per cent prematurity, 10 per cent birth asphyxia, and 22 per cent congenital anomalies. All of the population have access to improved drinking-water and sanitation. (Source: http://www.who.int, World Health Statistics 2012)

EDUCATION

Education is compulsory for all from 6-16 years of age. Education provided by the state is free. There are primary schools and secondary schools (grammar, integrated comprehensive and vocational). Upper Secondary Schools or Gymnasia are available but not compulsory, although the education here is free, students are expected to pay an enrollment fee and buy text books. Students can also attend, agricultural, technical, and seamen's schools and there are nine universities in total. Literacy is almost 100 per cent.

Figures for 2011 show that 107,741 pupils were enrolled at schools, of which 19,159 were at Pre-primary level, 42,365 at Compulsory school, 26,153 at Upper Secondary level and 18,647 in Tertiary education. The number of licensed teachers employed in 2003 was 3,545 there were also 188 headmasters and 140 assistant headmasters.

Figures from UNESCO for 2006 show that 18.1 per cent of total government expenditure went on education, 34 per cent of which went on primary education and 34 per cent on secondary education, 19 per cent went on tertiary education.

RELIGION

The Evangelical Lutheran Church is the established church of Iceland with about 90 per cen of the population as followers. Other denominations include the Congregational Church Independent Congregation and the Roman Catholic Church which is attended by about one per cent of the population. There are small communities of Muslims, Baha'is and Buddhists.

Iceland has a religious liberty rating of 9 on a scale of 1 to 10 (10 is most freedom). (Source World Religion Database)

COMMUNICATIONS AND MEDIA

The constitution guarantees press freedom.

Newspapers
In 2007, there were 197 newspapers.
Frettabladid, URL: http://www.visir.is
Morgunbladid, URL: http://www.mbl.is
DV, URL: http://www.dv.is
Icelandreview, URL: http://www.icelandreview.com
The National Union of Icelandic Journalists, URL: http://www.press.is

Broadcasting
The Public Broadcasting System operates two radio channels and one TV channel, reaching virtually the whole country. Several private radio stations and TV stations are operated. The Icelandic National Broadcasting Service (RUV) is obliged to promote the Islandic language, history and heritage. It is funded partly by a licence fee and partly by advertising funding. In 2008, there were 21 channels in total.
Icelandic National Broadcasting Service (Rikissjonvarpid), URL: http://www.ruv.is
Channel 2 (Stog 2), URL: http://www.stod2.visir.is
Syn, URL: http://www.syn.visir.is

Radio
Icelandic National Broadcasting Service, URL: http://www.ruv.is
Bylgjan, URL: http://www.bylgjan.is/

Telecommunications
The telephone system is both extensive and modern, with satellite stations, optical fibre cables and an extensive cellular mobile telephone system. Every home in the country is now equipped with a telephone and around 330,000 mobile phones were in use in 2008. Recent figures show that Iceland has around 301,500 internet users. An estimated 92 per cent of households have a home computer and 90 per cent an internet communication. Approximately 2,400 people are employed in the telecommunication and postal industry.

ENVIRONMENT

The greatest deterioration to the land has been to the vegetation, accompanied by soil erosion. Only about one-quarter of the country has continuous plant cover which is threatened by the unfavourable climate, volcanic activity, glacier movements and overgrazing. Efforts have been made to halt erosion by reforestation schemes which also prevent livestock from grazing the land. As at 2003, 9,985 square kilometres were designated 'protected areas', comprising of country and national parks and reserves.

Iceland is a party to the following international agreements: Air Pollution, Air Pollution-Persistent Organic Pollutants, Biodiversity, Climate Change, Climate Change-Kyoto Protocol, Desertification, Endangered Species, Hazardous Wastes, Kyoto Protocol, Law of the Sea, Marine Dumping, Ozone Layer Protection, Ship Pollution, Transboundary Air Pollution, Wetlands and Whaling. Iceland has signed but not ratified agreements on Environmental Modification and Marine Life Conservation.

Figures for 2010 show that the total carbon dioxide emissions from the consumption of fossil fuels was 3.36 million metric tons. (Source: EIA)

INDIA
Republic of India
Bharatiya Ganarajya

Capital: New Delhi (Population estimate, 2008: 17 million)

Head of State: Pranab Mukherjee (page 1481)

Vice President: Mohammad Hamid Ansari (page 1378)

National Flag: A tricolour fesswise, saffron, white, green, the white charged with the chakra of Asoka, the wheel of law, in dark blue centred.

CONSTITUTION AND GOVERNMENT

Constitution

India became an independent State as the result of the Indian Independence Act, 1947, which provided for the setting up of two independent Dominions, to be known as India and Pakistan. The Act declared that, from the 15 August 1947, His Majesty's Government of the United Kingdom should have no responsibility as respects the governing of any of the territories, which immediately before that date were included in British India. As a consequence of this Act the old Indian legislature ceased to function, and its powers were taken over by the Indian Constituent Assembly.

The most important function of the Constituent Assembly was the drafting of a new Constitution, which was finally adopted on 26 November 1949. By this Constitution India became a sovereign independent republic on 26 January 1950. The conference of Commonwealth Prime Ministers had previously reached a unanimous agreement regarding Indian relations with the Commonwealth. It was agreed that India should be accepted as a full member of the Commonwealth. India, although a republic, accepted the Sovereign as the symbol of the free association of its independent member nations, and as such the head of the Commonwealth'.

The chief features of the new Constitution are the disappearance of Princely India, and the creation of a President and a Cabinet system of government, sovereignty of the people, adult suffrage, joint electorates, the abolition of Privy Council jurisdiction and the substitution of that of the Supreme Court, the abolition of titles and 'untouchability', and civil equality irrespective of religion. India is a Union of 28 States and seven Union Territories. The executive of each State consists of a Governor appointed by the President and the Council of Ministers. The Union Territories are administered by the President acting through an administrator.

The President is the head of the executive, and the supreme commander of the defence forces of the Union. He is elected by an Electoral College consisting of the elected members of both Houses of Parliament and the Legislative Assemblies of the States. He holds office for five years and is eligible for re-election. The President is constitutionally the head of the Union, and is not expected to govern. His functions are similar to those of the Governor-General in the former regime. He summons, prorogues and dissolves the Lok Sabha; he appoints all the higher officials, consents to bills, proclaims emergencies and promulgates ordinances.

There is also a Vice-President who is *ex-officio* Chairman of the Council of States. He is elected by members of both Houses of Parliament and holds office for five years. Actual executive power is in the hands of the Council of Ministers with the Prime Minister at the head. His position is similar to that of the Prime Minister in Great Britain; in fact the constitution follows closely the model of the British parliamentary system.

To consult the constitution, please visit: http://indiacode.nic.in/coiweb/welcome.html

International Relations

India enjoys both close cultural and economic ties with the United Kingdom; it is estimated that over a million people of Indian descent live in the UK and figures for 2005 show that bilateral trade amounted to nearly £8.0 billion. India is a member of the Commonwealth; United Nations and the United Nations Human Rights Council; World Trade Organisation; South Asian Association for Regional Co-operation (SAARC); ASEAN, and G4.

Relations with neighbouring Pakistan are still strained over the disputed area of Jammu and Kashmir which has led the countries to war three times. India claims that Jammu and Kashmir was legally acceded to it, whereas Pakistan claims that Kashmiris were never allowed to choose which state to belong to.

Recent Events

In 1992 religious unrest broke out between Hindus and Muslims over the disputed site at Ayodhya, in Uttar Pradesh. A Muslim Mosque dating from the 16th century was demolished by Hindu's who believe it covered the site of the birthplace of the Hindu God Ram. The violence came to a head in 2002 when a train carrying Hindu pilgrims returning from the Ayodhya site was set on fire, in revenge attacks carried out against Muslims around 800 people are believed to have been killed. An archaeological dig is currently underway to establish what was on the site before the Mosque.

In September 2004 India applied for a permanent seat on the UN Security Council. During 2005 India was hit by several natural disasters including heavy Monsoon rains in July which resulted in flooding and the deaths of over 1,000 people. On the 8th October, there was a powerful earthquake, with its epicentre in Pakistan administered Kashmir; over 1,000 people in Indian administered Kashmir were killed.

US President George W. Bush visited India in March 2006. An agreement was reached whereby the US would grant India access to civilian nuclear technology in return for India allowing more open scrutiny of its nuclear programme. The following December, President Bush approved a controversial law which allowed India to buy US nuclear reactors and fuel. In February 2007 an agreement was signed between India and Pakistan which was designed to reduce the risk of an accidental nuclear war.

India suffered very heavy monsoon rains in August and September 2008; Bihar and Assam were particularly affected when the rivers Kosi and Brahmaputra burst their banks. In Bihar more than 250,000 people were displaced by the floods and the government expected the flood refugees to spend at least six months in relief camps until flood waters receded.

On the evening of 28th November 2008, Mumbai suffered a serious terrorist attack when several sites were attacked simultaneously by gunmen. At the Chhatrapati Shivaji railway station, shots were fired indiscriminately and there were several deaths. Gunmen also attacked the Cama and Albless Hospital, and took control of the Nariman House business complex, home to the Jewish Chabad Lubavitch outreach centre. The Cafe Leopold, a popular place with visiting western tourists, was also attacked. The main attacks were centred on two prestigious hotels - the Oberoi-Trident and the Taj Mahal Palace. There were reports that the gunmen tried to identify any guests from Britain or the USA leading to speculation as to the identity of the terrorists. By early on Thursday morning, the Indian army was involved in running battles with several of the gunmen and fires had broken out at the Taj Mahal Palace hotel. A group calling itself Deccan Mujahedeen claimed responsibility for the attacks and were believed to have arrived by sea from Pakistan. Islamabad denied any involvement but tensions between India and Pakistan were raised. An estimated 173 people were killed in the attacks, including all but one of the gunmen, and a further 308 people were injured. In February 2009 the Pakistan admitted that the attacks had been partly planned on its soil. The sole surviving gunman, Ajmal Amir Qasab, was convicted and sentenced to death in May 2010 and was executed in Pune Prison in December 2012.

In December 2009 plans for a new state were announced. The new state, to be called Telangana, would be made out of the southern state of Andhra Pradesh and will probably include Hyderabad which is currently the capital of Andhra Pradesh. Many people feel the creation of the new state is a mistake as it might fuel demands by protesters for other states. Protests both in support and against the new state broke out. An official report on the creation of the state was issued in January 2011 and was submitted to parliament.

In March 2011 the census put the the population at 1.21 billion, an increase of 181 million since the 2001 census.

On July 13 2011, three bombs exploded in Mumbai, 21 people were killed and 113 injured.

In September 2011 more than two million people were affected by floods in the states of Orissa, Uttar Pradesh and Bihar. More than 80 people are believed to have died following heavy monsoon rains.

A wide-ranging corruption trial opened in November 2011. A government minister is one of the 14 people charged with offences relating to the alleged telecommunications fraud.

In March 2012, Minister of Railways Dinesh Trivedi resigned following protests after he announced the cost of rail fares was to be raised.

In September 2012, the government announced plans to allow foreign supermarket giants to operate in India which would bring foreign investment to the country. In protest at the move the West Bengal left-wing All India Trinamool Congress withdrew from the coalition government, there had been widespread protests by shopkeepers.

In December 2012, a young medical student was attacked and gang-raped on a bus in Delhi. The attack was so savage that she later died of her injuries. The attack led to widespread condemation and protests about the attack and the prevailing negative attitude to women. Five men and one juvenile were arrested over the attack but the Bar Association of India said none of its members were willing to defend the suspects. In light of the widespread condemnation it has been announced that police stations in Delhi will always have a female officer on duty and a helpline was set up.

In February 2013 there were two explosions in central Hyderabad which killed 16 people. The Indian Mujahideeen Islamist group were suspected of being responsible.

Legislature

The Indian Parliament consists of the President and two Houses: Lok Sabha (House of the People) and Rajya Sabha (Council of States). The Constitution provides that the Council of States has not more than 250 representatives of the States who serve a six year term. At present it has 224 members including 12 nominated by the president. The nominated members represent literature, science and social services. The Council of States is not subject to dissolution, but one-third of the members retire every second year. The House of the People consists of 545 members elected from the States and Union Territories on the basis of adult franchise, the constituencies being so demarcated that there is not less than one member for every 75,000 of the population, and not more than one member for every 50,000, members serve a five year term. Two Anglo-Indian members are nominated by the President. The states and territories are represented by the following number of elected members, Andhra Pradesh,

STATES OF THE WORLD

INDIA

42; Arunachal Pradesh, 2; Assam, 14; Bihar, 54; Chhattisgarh, 11; Goa, 2; Gujarat, 26; Haryana, 10; Himachal Pradesh, 4; Jammu and Kashmir, 6; Jharkhand, 14; Karnataka, 28; Kerala, 20; Madhya Pradesh, 40; Maharashtra, 48; Manipur, 2; Meghalaya, 2; Mizoram, 1; Nagaland, 1; Odisha, 21; Punjab, 13; Rajisthan, 25; Sikkim, 1; Tamil Nadu, 39; Tripura, 2; Uttar Pradesh, 85; Uttarakhand, 5; West Bengal, 42; Andaman and Nicobar Islands, 1; Chandigarh, 1; Dadra and Nagar Haveli, 1; Daman and Diu, 1; Delhi, 7; Lakshadweep, 1; Puducherry, 1.

The first Indian General Election was held on varying dates between October 1951 and February 1952, the spread over being necessary owing to the huge area of the country, the size of the electorate, the varied climatic conditions and the desire to avoid interference with agricultural operations. As of 2010, 10.8 per cent of parliamentary seats were held by women.

Lower House

Lok Sabha (House of the People), Parliament House, Parliament Street, New Delhi 110001, India. Tel: +91 11 3017 465, fax: +91 11 3015 518, e-mail: lokmail@parlis.nic.in; URL: http://www.parliamentofindia.nic.in
Speaker: Smt. Meira Kumar (page 1459)

Upper House

Rajya Sabha (Council of States), Parliament House, Parliament Street, New Delhi 110001, India. Tel: +91 11 3034 695; fax: +91 11 3792 940; email: tripathi@sansad.nic.in, URL: http://rajyasabha.nic.in
Chairman: Mohammad Hamid Ansari (page 1378)

Cabinet (as at June 2013)

Prime Minister, Minister for Personnel, Public Grievances and Pensions, Minister of Atomic Energy, Minister of Planning, Minister of Space: Dr. Manmohan Singh (page 1515)
Minister of Finance: Palaniappan Chidambaram (page 1404)
Minister of Defence: A.K. Anthony (page 1378)
Minister of External Affairs: Salman Khursheed
Minister of Agriculture, Food and Civil Supplies, Consumer Affairs and Public Distribution: Sharad Pawar Yadav (page 1493)
Minister of Home Affairs: Sushil Kumar Shinde (page 1514)
Minister of Chemicals and Fertilizers: vacant
Minister of Tribal Affairs, Minister of Panchayati Raj: V. Kishore Chandra Deo
Minister of Road Transport and Highways, Minister of Railways: C.P. Joshi (page 1452)
Minister of Commerce and Industry, Minister of Textiles: Anand Sharma (page 1513)
Minister of Law and Justice, Minister of Communications and Information Technology: Kapil Sibal (page 1514)
Minister of Rural Development, Drinking Water and Sanitation: Jairam Ramesh
Minister of Social Justice and Empowerment: Kumari Selja
Minister of Human Resource Development: Dr M Mangapati Pallam Raju
Minister of Heavy Industries and Public Enterprises: Praful Patel
Minister of Overseas Indian Affairs, Minister of Micro, Small and Medium Enterprises: Vayalar Ravi (page 1500)
Minister of Civil Aviation: Chaudhary Ajit Singh
Minister of Urban Development, Minister of Parliamentary Affairs: Kamal Nath (page 1484)
Minister of Science and Technology, Minister of Earth Sciences: Jaipal Reddy (page 1501)
Minister of New and Renewable Energy: Dr Farooq Abdullah (page 1371)
Minister of Labour and Employment: Mallikarjun Kharge (page 1456)
Minister of Shipping: G.K. Vasan (page 1531)
Minister of Water Resources: Harish Rawat
Minister of Health and Family Welfare: Ghulam Nabi Azad (page 1380)
Minister of Housing and Urban Poverty Alleviation: Ajay Maken
Minister of Culture: Chandresh Kumari Katoch ; Kumari Selja
Minister of Coal: Sriprakash Jaiswal
Minister of Steel: Beni Prasad Verma
Minister of Minority Affairs: K Rahman Khan
Minister of Mines: Dinsha J. Patel
Minister of Petroleum and Natural Gas: M. Veerappa Moily
Ministers of State with Independent Charge
Minister of State with Independent Charge for Women and Child Development: Krishna Tirath
Minister of State with Independent Charge for Statistics and Programme Implementation, Chemicals and Fertilizer: Dr Srikanta Jena
Minister of State with Independent Charge for Environment and Forests: Jayanthi Natarajan
Minister of State with Independent Charge for Youth Affairs and Sport: Jitendra Singh
Minister of State with Independent Charge for Development of North Eastern Region: Paban Singh Ghatowar
Minister of State with Independent Charge for Consumer Affairs, Food and Public Distribution: Prof. Kuruppassery V. Thomas
Minister of State with Independent Charge for Information and Broadcasting: Manesh Tewari
Minister of State with Independent Charge for Tourism; Dr K. Chiranjeevi
Minister of State with Independent Charge for Drinking Water and Sanitation: Bharatsinh Madhavsinh Solanki
Minister of State for Independent Charge for Power; Jyotiraditya Madhavrao Scindia
Minister of State with Independent Charge for Micro, Small and Medium Enterprises; K.H. Muniyappa
Minister of State with Independent Charge for Corportae Affairs: Sachin Pilot

---

Ministries

Office of the President, Rashtrapati Bhavan, New Delhi 110 004, India. Tel: +91 1 2301 5321, fax: +91 11 2301 7290, e-mail: poi_gen@rb.nic.in, URL http://presidentofindia.nic.in
Prime Minister's Office, Room No. 152, South Block, New Delhi 110 011, India. Te +91 11 2301 2312, fax: +91 11 2301 6857, URL: http://pmindia.nic.in
Ministry of Agriculture, Krishi Bhavan, Dr Rajendra Prasad Rd., New Delhi 110 011 India. Tel: +91 11 2338 2651, fax: +91 11 2338 6004, e-mail: secy.icar@nic.in, URL http://dare.nic.in
Ministry of Agro and Rural Industries, Room 275-D, Udyog Bhawan, Rafi Marg New Delhi - 110011, India. e-mail: atmishra@ub.nic.in, URL: http://www.ari.nic.in
Ministry of Atomic Energy, Anushakti Bhavan, Chatrapathi Shivaji, Maharj Marg Mumbai 400 001, India. Tel: +91 22 2202 6823, fax: +91 22 2204 8476, e-mai webmaster@dae.gov.in, URL: http://www.dae.gov.in
Ministry of Chemicals and Fertilisers, Shastri Bhavan, New Delhi 110 001, India. Te +91 11 2338 6519, fax: +91 11 2338 4020, e-mail: mincf.cpc@sb.nic.in, URL http://chemicals.nic.in
Ministry of Civil Aviation, Rajiv Ghandi Bhavan, New Delhi 110 003, India. Tel: +9 11 2463 2991, fax: +91 11 2461 0354, e-mail: mos_mdy@hub.nic.in, URL: http://civilaviation.nic.in
Ministry of Coal, Shastri Bhavan, Rafi Marg, New Delhi, India. Tel: +91 11 2338 4887 fax: +91 11 2338 4893, e-mail: jsla@sb.nic.in, URL: http://coal.nic.in
Ministry of Commerce and Industry, Udyog Bhavan, New Delhi 110 011, India. Tel +91 11 2301 0008, fax: +91 11 2301 9947, e-mail: sdash@ub.nic.in, URL: http://commin.nic.in
Ministry of Communications and Information Technology, Sanchar Bhavan 20 Asoka Road, New Delhi 110 001, India. Tel: +91 11 2436 9345, fax: +91 11 2436 9179 e-mail: ashourie@nic.in, URL: http://www.moc.gov.in
Ministry of Culture, Room No. 334-C Wing, Shastri Bhawan, New Delhi 110 011, India Tel: +91 11 2338 1198, fax: +91 11 2338 2907, e-mail: K_ jayakumar@email.com, URL http://indiaculture.nic.in
Ministry of Defence, South Block, New Delhi 110 011, India. Tel: +91 11 2301 2380 URL: http://mod.nic.in
Ministry of Energy, Shram Shakti Bhavan, Raffi Marg, New Delhi 110 001, India. Te +91 11 371 0071
Ministry of Environment and Forests, Paryavaran Bhavan, CGO Complex, Lodh Road, New Delhi 110 003, India. Tel: +91 11 2436 1727, fax: +91 11 2436 0678, e-mai secy@menf.delhi.nic.in, URL: http://envfor.nic.in
Ministry of External Affairs, South Block, New Delhi 110 011, India. Tel: +91 11 230 2318, fax: +91 11 2301 0700, URL: http://www.meaindia.nic.in
Ministry of Finance and Planning, North Block, New Delhi 110 001, India. Tel: +91 1 2301 2611, fax: +91 11 2301 4420, e-mail: jsdea@finance.delhi.nic.in, URL: http://finmin.nic.in
Ministry of Food and Civil Supplies, Consumer Affairs and Publi Distribution, Krishi Bhavan, Dr Rajendra Prasad Road, New Delhi, 110 001, India. Tel: +9 11 338 5723, fax: +91 11 378 2213
Ministry of Food Processing Industries, Panchsheel Bhavan, Khelgaon Marg, Nev Delhi 110 049, India. Tel: +91 11 2649 3012, fax: +91 11 2649 3228, e-mail anpsinha@mofpi.delhi.nic.in, URL: http://mofpi.nic.in
Ministry of Health and Family Welfare, Nirman Bhavan, New Delhi 110 011, India Tel: +91 11 2649 3012, fax: +91 11 2649 3228, e-mail: anpsinha@mofpi.delhi.nic.in, URL http://mofpi.nic.in
Ministry of Home Affairs, Room 26, North Block, New Delhi 110 001, India. Tel: +9 11 2309 2462, fax: +91 11 2309 2113, e-mail: mhaweb@mhant.delhi.nic.in, URL http://mha.nic.in
Ministry of Human Resource Development, Shastri Bhavan, De Rajendra Prasa Road, New Delhi 110 001, India. Tel: +91 11 2378 2698, fax: +91 11 2338 2365, e-mail hrm@sb.nic.in, URL: http://www.education.nic.in
Ministry of Heavy Industries and Public Enterprises, Udyog Bhavan, New Delh 110 001, India. Tel: +91 11 2301 2207, fax: +91 11 2301 1770, e-mail: d.dar@ub.nic.in URL: http://dhi.nic.in
Ministry of Information and Broadcasting, Shastri Bhavan, Dr Rajendra Prasa Road, New Delhi 110 001, India. Tel: +91 11 2338 2639, fax: +91 11 2338 3513, URL http://mib.nic.in
Ministry of Labour and Employment, Shram Shakti Bhavan, Rafi Marg, New Delh 110 001, India. Tel: +91 11 2371 0240, fax: +91 11 2379 4788, e-mail labour@lisd.delhi.nic.in, URL: http://labour.nic.in
Ministry of Law and Justice, Shastri Bhavan, Dr Rajendra Prasad Rd, New Delhi 11 001, India. Tel: +91 11 2338 4777, fax: +91 11 2338 7259, e-mail lawmin@caselaw.delhi.nic.in, URL: http://lawmin.nic.in
Ministry of Micro, Small and Medium Enterprises, Udyog Bhavan, Rafi Marg New Delhi 110 011, India. Tel: +91 11 2301 6566, fax: +91 11 2301 3141, e-mail cpthakur@sansad.nic.in, URL: http://www.ssi.nic.in
Ministry of Mines, 3rd Floor, Shastri Bhavan A-wing, New Delhi 110 011, India. Tel: +9 11 2338 3082, fax: +91 11 2338 6402, e-mail: dom@sb.nic.in, URL: http://mines.nic.in
Ministry of New and Renewable Energy, Block 14, CGO Complex, New Delhi 11 003, India. Tel: +91 11 2436 1481, fax: +91 11 2436 2272, e-mail: secymnes@hub.nic.in URL: http://mnes.nic.in
Ministry of Overseas Indian Affairs, 9th Floor, Akbar Bhawan, Chanakya Puri, New Delhi 110 021, India. Tel: +91 11 2419 7900, fax: +91 11 2301 3386, e-mail: info@moia.nic.in URL: http://moia.gov.in
Ministry of Panchayati Raj, Krishi Bhavan, Dr. Rajendra Prasad Road, New Delhi 110 001, India. Tel: +91 11 2378 2373, fax: +91 11 2464 3534, e-mail: minoffice@nic.in, URL http://panchayat.nic.in
Ministry of Parliamentary Affairs, 8 Parliament House, New Delhi 110 001, India Tel: +91 11 2301 7663, fax: +91 11 2301 7726, e-mail: secympa@sansad.nic.in, URL http://mpa.nic.in/
Ministry of Personnel, Public Grievances and Pensions, North Block, New Delh 110 001, India. Tel: +91 11 2301 4848, fax: +91 11 2301 2432, e-mail pgweb@arpg.delhi.noc.in, URL: http://persmin.nic.in

Ministry of Petroleum and Natural Gas, Shastri Bhavan, Dr Rajendra Prasad Road, New Delhi 110 001, India. Tel: +91 11 2338 6622, fax: +91 11 2338 1462, e-mail: mopng.png@sb.nic.in, URL: http://petroleum.nic.in

Ministry of Power, Shram Shakti Bhavan, New Delhi 110 001, India. Tel: +91 11 2371 7474, fax: +91 11 2371 0065, URL: http://powermin.nic.in

Ministry of Railways, Rail Bhavan, Parliament Street, New Delhi 110 001, India. Tel: +91 11 2338 4010, http://www.indianrailway.gov.in

Ministry of Rural Development, Krishi Bhavan, New Delhi 110 001, India. Tel: +91 11 2378 2373, fax: +91 11 2338 5876, e-mail: krana@sansad.nic.in, URL: http://rural.nic.in

Ministry of Science and Technology, Technology Bhavan, New Mehrauli Road, New Delhi 110 016, India. Tel: +91 11 2656 7373, fax: +91 11 2686 4570, e-mail: dstinfo@alpha.nic.in, URL: http://mst.nic.in

Ministry of Shipping, Jahaj Bhavan, Walchand H. Marg, Mumbai 400 001, India. Tel: +91 22 2261 3651, fax: +91 22 2261 3655, e-mail: dgship@dgshipping.com, URL: http://shipping.nic.in

Ministry of Social Justice and Empowerment, Shastri Bhavan, Dr Rajendra Prasad Road, New Delhi 110 001, India. Tel: +91 11 2338 4918, fax: +91 11 2338 4918, e-mail: secywel@sb.nic.in, URL: http://socialjustice.nic.in

Ministry of Statistics, S.P. Bhavan, Parliament Street, New Delhi 110 001, India. Tel: +91 11 2301 2312, fax: +91 11 2334 0138, e-mail: pmo.sb@pmo.nic.in, URL: http://mospi.nic.in

Ministry of Steel, Udyog Bhavan, New Delhi 110 011, India. Tel: +91 11 2301 5486, fax: +91 11 2301 3236, e-mail: tripatblc@sansad.nic.in, URL: http://steel.nic.in

Ministry of Textiles, Udyog Bhavan, New Delhi 110 011, India. Tel: +91 11 2301 1320, fax: +91 11 2301 3711, e-mail: textiles@ub.delhi.nic.in, URL: http://texmin.nic.in

Ministry of Tourism, Transport Bhavan, Parliament Street, New Delhi 110 001, India. Tel: +91 11 2371 5054, fax: +91 11 2371 0518, e-mail: contactus@incredibleindia.org, URL: http://www.tourismofindia.com

Ministry of Tribal Affairs, Shastri Bhavan, New Delhi 110001, India. Tel: +91 11 2338 1499, e-mail: dirit@tribal.nic.in, URL: http://tribal.nic.in

Ministry of Urban Affairs and Employment, Nirman Bhavan, New Delhi 110 011, India. Tel: +91 11 2306 3495, fax: +91 11 2306 2089, e-mail: secyurban@nic.in, URL: http://urbanindia.nic.in

Ministry of Water Resources, Shram Shakti Bhavan, Rafi Marg, New Delhi 110 001, India. Tel: +91 11 2371 4200, fax: +91 11 2371 0804, e-mail: acsethi@sansad.nic.in, URL: http://wrmin.nic.in

Ministry of Women and Child Development, Nirman Bhavan, New Delhi 110 001, India. Tel: +91 11 2307 4052, fax: +91 11 2465 4849, e-mail: secy.wcd@nic.in, URL: http://wcd.nic.in

Ministry of Youth Affairs and Sport, Shastri Bhavan, Dr Rajendra Prasad Road, New Delhi 110 001, India. Tel: +91 11 2338 4183, fax: +91 11 2338 7418, e-mail: minister.yas@sb.nic.in, URL: http://www.yas.nic.in

Political Parties

Bharatiya Janata Party (BJP, Indian People's Party), 11 Ashok Road, New Delhi 110001, India. Tel: +91 11 2338 2234, fax: +91 11 2378 2163, URL: http://www.bjp.org
President: Rajinath Singh

India National Congress (INC), 24 Akbar Road, New Delhi 110 011, India. Tel: +91 11 2338 2234, URL: http://www.congress.org.in
President: Sonia Gandhi.

Bahujan Samaj Party, (Majoritarian Society Party, BSP) 12, Gurudwara Rakabganj Road, New Delhi 11000, India. URL: http://www.bahujansamajp.com
Leader: Mayawati Kumari

Nationalist Congress Party (NCP), 10 Bishambhar Das Marg, New Delhi 110001, India. URL: http://www.ncp.org.in
Leader: Sharad Pawar

Communist Party of India, Ajoy Bhawan, Kotla Marg, New Delhi 110002, India. URL: http://www.cpindia.org
Leadership: Auravaram Sudhakar Reddy

Communist Party of India (Marxist), 27-29, Bhai Vir Singh Marg, New Delhi 110001, India. URL: http://www.cpim.org
Leader: Prakash Karat

Telugu Desam Party (TDP); Samajwadi Party (SP); Shiv Sena (SS); Bahujan Samaj Party (BSP); Dravida Munnetra Kazhagam (DMK); All India Anna Dravida Munnetra Kazhagam (AIADMK); Biju Janata Dal (BJD); All India Trinamool Congress (AITC); Nationalist Congress Party (NCP); Rashtriya Janata Dal (RJD); Independent (Ind.); Janata Dal (United) (JDU); Indian National Lok Dal (INLD); Jammu & Kashmir National Conference (J&KNC); Pattali Makkal Katchi (PMK); Lok Jan Shakti Party (LJSP); Marumalarchi Dravida Munnetra Kazhagam (MDMK); Communist Party of India (CPI); Revolutionary Socialist Party (RSP); Akhil Bharatiya Lok Tantrik Congress (ABLTC); All India Forward Bloc (FBL); Janata Dal (Secular) (JDS); Muslim League Kerala State Committee (MLKSC); Rashtriya Lok Dal (RLD); Shiromani Akali Dal (SAD); All India Majlis-E-Ittehadul Muslimmen (AIMIM); Bharipa Bahujan Mahasangha (BBM); Communist Party of India (Marxist-Lennist Liberation) CPIMLL); Himachal Vikas Congress (HVC); Kerala Congress (KEC); Kerala Congress (M) (KECM); Manipur State Congress Party (MSCP); Peasants And Workers Party of India (PAWPI); Shiromani Akali Dal (Simranjit Singh Mann) (SADM); Sikkim Democratic Front (SDF); Samajwadi Janata Party (Rashtriya) (SJPR).

Elections

Elections were held in September and October 1999, after the government of Atal Bihari Vajpayee was forced to resign when it lost a vote of confidence held by the Council of Ministers on 17 April 1999. These were the third elections in three years. Nearly 600 million citizens were eligible to vote and polling was spread over several days to help man the polling booths. The Bharatiya Janata Party (BJP) won 182 of the 543 seats in the Lok Sabha and formed a coalition government, again with Atal Bihari Vajpayee as Prime Minister.

Elections held in May 2004 were was won by the Congress Party, in what was seen as a surprise victory. Sonia Ghandi, the leader of the party, then turned down the post of prime minister. This was done to protect the party as she had come under personnel attack during the election campaign because of her Italian birth. Dr Manmohan Singh was appointed to the post. The Congress Party and its allies won 219 seats with the BJP and its allies winning 186 seats. Other parties won 131 seats. The Congress Party formed a coalition government called the United Progressive Alliance. The most recent election was held in May 2009. The Congress Party retained power.

Pratibha Patil was elected as the first female president of India in July 2007. The most recent presidential elections were held in July 2012, former finance minister Pranab Mukherjee was elected to the post.

Diplomatic Representation

Embassy of the United States of America, Shanti Path, Chanakyapuri 110021, New Delhi 110 021, India. Tel: +91 11 2419 8000, fax: +91 11 2419 0017, URL: http://newdelhi.usembassy.gov
Ambassador: Nancy Powell (page 1497)

British High Commission, Chanakyapuri, New Delhi 110021, India. Tel: +91 11 2687 2161, fax: +91 11 2687 2882, e-mail, postmaster.NewDelhi@fco.gov.uk, URL: http://ukinindia.fco.gov.uk/en
High Commissioner: James Bevan CMG (page 1388)

Embassy of India, 2107 Massachusetts Ave, NW, Washington, DC 20008, USA. Tel: +1 2202 939 7000, fax: +1 2202 939 7027, URL: http://www.indianembassy.org
Ambassador: Nirupama Rao

Indian High Commission, India House, Aldwych, London, WC2B 4NA, United Kingdom. Tel: +44 (0)20 7836 8484, fax: +44 (0)20 7836 4331, URL: http://hcilondon.in
High Commissioner: Dr J. Bhagwati (page 1388)

Permanent Representative to the UN in New York: 235 East 43rd Street, New York, NY 10017, USA.
Permanent Representative: Hardeep Singh Puri

LEGAL SYSTEM

Article 124 provides for the establishment of a Supreme Court of India consisting of a Chief Justice of India and of not more than 25 judges. Judges are appointed by the President, and hold office until the age of 65. The Supreme Court has exclusive final jurisdiction in any dispute between (a) the Government of India or one or more of the States, (b) the Government of India and one or more of the States on one side or one or more of the States on the other and (c) between two or more States.

The Appellate jurisdiction of the Supreme Court extends over all appeals from judgement, decree or final order of the High Court in civil, criminal or other proceedings if the High Court certifies that the case involves a substantial question of law as to the interpretation of the Constitution. Appeals also lie in other specified civil and criminal cases.

There are High Courts and subordinate courts in each of the States. Judges of the High Courts are appointed by the President and hold office until they reach the age of 62. The High Courts supervise all subordinate courts within their respective jurisdiction.

Civil courts are competent to try cases and to administer any punishment authorised by law, though sentences of death are subject to confirmation by the highest court of criminal appeal in the States. There are magistrate's courts for the trial of petty offences, family courts and courts of small causes for the trial of money cases up to Rs. 500. Lok Adalat is a voluntary arbitration agency for the resolution of disputes.

In general, the government respects the rights of its citizens. However, there is corruption at all levels of government and police. People have died in custody, and the security forces have been implicated in disappearances and cases of brutality, with apparent impunity in most instances. Special anti-terrorism legislation has led to the excessive use of force. Prison conditions are poor and pretrial detentions can be lengthy.

In 1983, the Supreme Court ruled that the death penalty should only be imposed in "the rarest of rare cases". Capital crimes are murder, gang robbery with murder, abetting the suicide of a child or insane person, waging war against the government, and abetting mutiny by a member of the armed forces. The death penalty has recently been imposed for people convicted of terrorist activities. At least 100 people were sentenced to death in 2007, according to Amnesty International. The last execution took place in 2004, ending a de facto moratorium since 1997.

Supreme Court of India, URL: http://supremecourtofindia.nic.in/
Chief Justice: Hon. Mr. Justice Altamas Kabir

National Human Rights Commission, Faridkot House, Copernicus Marg., New Delhi, India. URL: http://www.nhrc.nic.in

LOCAL GOVERNMENT

India is divided into 28 States, each of which is overseen by a governor and each has its own Legislative Assembly, and seven Union Territories, which are governed by the President acting through an administrator.

At the end of 2000, three new states were created using some districts of existing states. Chhattisgarh, the 26th state, came into existence at midnight on October 31 2000, created out of Madhya Pradesh. Uttaranchal, later known as Uttarakhand, the 27th state, came into existence at midnight on November 8 2000, created from Uttar Pradesh, and Jharkhand, the 28th state, came into existence at midnight on November 14, 2000, created from Bihar. In December 2009 the government agreed in principal to a new state called Telangana being created, the state would be carved out of Andhra Pradesh, there have been protests both for and against the new state and negotiations are ongoing.

The following table shows the States and Union Territories of India and their populations following the 2011 census.

INDIA

State	Population
Andhra Pradesh	84,655,533
Arunachal Pradesh	1,382,611
Assam	31,169,272
Bihar	103,804,637
Chhattisgarh	25,540,196
Goa	1,457,723
Gujarat	60,383,628
Haryana	25,353,081
Himachal Pradesh	6,856,509
Jammu & Kashmir **	12,548,926
Jharkhand	32,966,238
Karnataka	61,130,704
Kerala	33,387,358
Madhya Pradesh	72,597,565
Maharashtra	112,372,972
Manipur	2,721,756
Meghalaya	2,964,007
Mizoram	1,091,014
Nagaland	1,980,602
Odisha	41,947,358
Punjab	27,704,236
Rajasthan	68,621,012
Sikkim	607,688
Tamil Nadu	72,138,958
Tripura	3,671,032
Uttar Pradesh	199,581,477
Uttarakhand	10,116,752
West Bengal	91,347,736
Union Territories	
Andaman & Nicobar Islands	379,944
Chandigarh	1,054,686
Dadra & Nagar Haveli	342,853
Daman & Diu	242,911
Delhi	16,753,235
Lakshadweep	64,429
Puducherry	1,244,464

AREA AND POPULATION

Area

India is situated in Southern Asia, bordering the Arabian Sea and the Bay of Bengal, and shares borders with Afghanistan (through the disputed Kashmir region) and Pakistan in the North East, China, (Tibet), Bhutan, and Nepal in the North and Myanmar to the East, Bangladesh is almost completely surrounded by India in the North East. India covers an area of approximately 3,287,590 sq. km. Features of the south of the country is upland plain, flat to rolling plain along the Ganges, the west of the country feature desert and in the north of the country are the Himalayas. Major river systems of India include the Indus, the Ganga and the Brahmaputra. The coastline of India including the Lakshadweep islands and Andaman and Nicobar islands measures 7,516.6 km.

Apart from the very north of the country the climate is tropical and the monsoon season is June - September.

To view a map of India, please consult http://www.un.org/Depts/Cartographic/map/profile/seasia.pdf

Kashmir

The border with Pakistan in the Kashmir area is currently under dispute between the two nations and part of Kashmir is under Chinese control. Following Indian independence in 1947 Kashmir was free to join India or Pakistan. Hari Singh the Maharaja had wanted to be independent but in exchange for military aid ceded Kashmir to India. India wishes Kashmir to remain one of her states but Pakistan argues that since the majority of Kashmir's population are Muslim, Kashmir should have become part of Pakistan. Following the first Kashmiri war in 1947-48 a demarcation line was established. War broke out again in 1965 which resulted in the Simla Agreement in 1972 under which the Line of Control was established; this divides Kashmir into Indian administered Jammu and Kashmir and Pakistan administered Kashmir. Violence has continued to break out sporadically.

In July 2001 Indian Prime Minister Atal Behari Vajpayee met with Pakistani President Pervez Musharraf but the meeting failed to bring an agreement on Kashmir. Further violence over Kashmir resulted in India imposing sanctions against Pakistan in December 2001, followed by Pakistan imposing sanctions on India. Tensions came to a head in 2002 when India showed its military capabilities by successfully test firing a ballistic missile. A raid on an Indian army camp in Kashmir resulted in the deaths of over 30 people and Prime Minister Vajpayee announced to the front line soldiers that the time for a decisive fight had come. Pakistan then tested missiles capable of carrying nuclear warheads. By the middle of 2002 diplomatic moves were being made to avert full scale war and in October India announced it was withdrawing its troops from the border. Early 2003 saw relations failing again when tit-for-tat expulsions of diplomats began. Further talks took place in December 2004; although no settlement was reached both sides agreed to talks in the future. In 2005 India and Pakistan agreed to a landmark bus service over the ceasefire line. The first bus crossed the line in April 2005. On October 8 2005 an earthquake hit the Kashmir region. Its epicenter was in Pakistan administered Kashmir and around 1,000 people died in Indian Kashmir; rescue efforts were hampered by the terrain and the Kashmiri winter.

Population

After China, India is the most densely populated country in the world, and the population is rapidly increasing. In May 2000 it was estimated that the population had reached 1 billion with the birth of a baby girl in New Delhi. The population of India grows by over 15.5 million each year. A census was taken in March 2001 which gave the population as 1,027,015,247, giving an average density of 324 people per sq. km. Nearly 70 per cent of the population live in rural areas. Figures from the 2011 census put the population at 1,210,193,422, an increase of 181 million over ten years. Population density was recorded at 382 people per sq km. The predicted life expectancy for years 2010-15 was 66.9 years for females and 63.7 years for males.

The sex ratio of the population has been generally adverse to females; that is, the number of males has exceeded that of the females. The only State that shows a sex ratio exceeding 1,000 in favour of females is Kerala (1,034). Following the 2001 census, figures showed the ratio of females per 1,000 males to be 933. But recent figures estimate the ratio to be as low as 1,000 males to 927 females. Indian society has traditionally favoured boys over girls, with boys being able to help physically and financially and girls having to have an expensive dowry provided for them. In 1994 clinics were banned from revealing the sex of a foetus during ultra sound scans in the hope that this would lead to fewer abortions of female foetuses but it is believed that the practice is still widespread resulting in such a marked difference in the sex ratio. Figures taken from the 2001 census showed that males outnumbered females by 35 million. In March 2011 the census showed the female to male ratio as 940 females for every 1,000 males.

The most heavily populated cities of the country are Kolkata (formerly Calcutta), Chennai, Greater Mumbai (formerly Bombay), Hyderabad, Delhi, Chandigarh, Mahe, Howrah, Kanpur City and Bangalore, all of which have a population density of over 2,000 people per sq km. (Source: India 2000). Figures from the 2011 census show that the most densely populated states are Delhi with 11,297 people per sq. km., Chandigarh with 9,252 people per sq. km., Pondicherry with 2,598 people per sq. km., Daman and Diu with 2,169 people per sq. km. and Lakshadweep with 2,013 people per sq. km. The population of India is predominantly rural with figures from the 2001 census showing that 72.2. per cent of the population lived in rural areas. Figures for 2009 put the rural population at 71 per cent.

The official language of the Indian Union is Hindi, in Devanagari script, and is spoken by around 45 per cent of the population. All forms of numerals are in international form. English, however, will continue to be used for official purposes for the transaction of business in Parliament and is classed as an 'associated language' . The language of the Supreme Court and the High Court and all Acts, regulations, rules and orders is English, with translations into Hindi.

A number of additional languages and dialects are spoken in India. Of these, 15 languages have been specified in the Eighth Schedule of the Constitution. These are: Assamese, Bengali, Gujarati, Hindi, Kannada, Kashmiri, Malayalam, Marathi, Odia, Punjabi, Sanskrit, Sindhi, Tamil, Telugu and Urdu. Another 24 languages are spoken along with 720 dialects and 23 tribal languages.

Births, Marriages, Deaths

Estimated figures for 2010 put the birth rate at 22.2 per 1,000 population and the death rate at 8.4 per 1,000 population. By 2009, the average life expectancy was 63 years for males and 66 years for females. Healthy life expectancy was 56 years and 57 years respectively. Approximately 31 per cent of the population is aged under 15 years and 8 per cent over 60 years. The median age was 25. The total fertility rate per woman was 2.6 children. (Source: http://www.who.int, World Health Statistics 2012)

Public Holidays 2014

1 January: New Year's Day
13 January: Birth of the Prophet (Islamic festival)*
17 March: Holi, celebrates the coming of Spring
8 April: Ram Navami (Hindu festival, birth of Lord Ram)
13 April: Mahavir Jayanthi, (Jain festival)
18 April: Good Friday (Christian Festival)
13 May: Buddha Purnima (Buddha's Birthday)
28 June: Ramadan begins (Muslim Festival)*
28 July: Eid al Fitr (Ramadan ends, Muslim Festival)*
15 August: Independence Day.
2 October: Mahatma Gandhi's Birthday
23 October: Diwali (Hindu festival of Lights also observed by Jains and Sikhs)
25 October: Muharram (Islamic New Year)*
6 November: Guru Nanak's Birthday (Sikh Festival)
25 December: Christmas Day (Christian Festival)

* Islamic holidays depend on the sighting of the moon and so dates can vary.
Religious holidays are observed by the many religions in India including Hindu, Muslim, Christian, Buddhist, Parsi and Sikh holidays.

EMPLOYMENT

Total Employment by Economic Activity

Occupation	2005
Agriculture, hunting, forestry & fishing	1,479,000
Mining & quarrying	1,093,000
Manufacturing	5,619,000
Electricity, gas & water supply	910,000
Construction	960,000
Wholesale & retail trade, repairs	559,000
Transport, storage & communications	2,837,000
Financing, Insurance, Real Estate and Business Services	1,931,000

- continued

Community, social & personal services	11,072,000
Total	26,458,000

Source: Copyright © International Labour Organization (ILO Dept. of Statistics, http://laborsta.ilo.org)

Estimated figures for 2010 put the work force at 467 million, with 52 per cent employed in agriculture, 34 per cent in the service and government sector and 14 per cent in industry and commerce. The unemployment rate was 9.4 per cent in 2009-10. Estimated figures for 2012 put the work force at 499 million with an unemployment rate of 9.9 per cent.

BANKING AND FINANCE

Currency
One Indian rupee (Rs) = 100 paisa

GDP/GNP, Inflation, National Debt
India has one of the six fastest economies in the world. Figures for 2007 showed that India now has the 12th largest economy in the world and the third largest in Asia, behind Japan and China. Agriculture remains an important part of the economy but in recent years the service sector has become increasingly important and India has become popular with international companies seeking to outsource work. The economy has remained relatively strong despite the world economic crisis.

GDP had begun an acceleration in GDP growth in the period 1998-99 due to improvement in the agricultural industries. Growth for 2002 was estimated to be 4.7 per cent and 5.6 per cent for 2003. The monsoon season in 2003 was very successful, leading to increased production in the agricultural and industry sectors. Growth of GDP was put at 8.8 per cent in 2005, 2006 and 2007. GDP fell in the year to March 2009 to 6.7 per cent. The government has pledged to return growth to 9 per cent, but forecast figures for the year April 2009-March 2010 put GDP growth at 7.2 per cent. Following the global economic downturn the Indian government introduced a stimulus package for the economy but in 2010 it was felt that government attention would focus on tackling rising inflation which was predicted to be 8.5 per cent in March 2010. Growth was 8.5 per cent in 2010. Per capita GDP was 66,405 rupees in 2010. Economic growth continued to slow and was put at an estimated 6.8 per cent in 2011 and 6.5 per cent in 2012. GDP was put at US$1,847 billion in 2011.

Industry makes up just over 28 per cent of GDP, agriculture, 17 per cent and the service and transport sector nearly 55 per cent.

GNI and GDP at Current Market Prices in Bn. Rupees

Year	GNI	GDP
2000	22,585.8	19,250.2
2002	24,378.7	22,614.1
2003	27,339.1	25,381.7
2004	32,198.3	29,714.6
2005	36,663.7	33,895.2
2006	42,604.4	39,522.4
2007	49,659.1	45,581.2
2008	55,497,0	52,820.9
2009	65,122.7	61,332.3
2010	78,235.8	73,069.9

Source: Asian Development Bank

The following table shows the make up of GDP in recent years by industrial origin at current factor cost.

Industrial Origin, Billion Rupees	2008	2009	2010
GDP by industrial origin	52,820.9	61,332.2	73,069.9
Agriculture	9,289.4	10,893.0	13,868.8
Mining	1,386.5	1,542.7	1,915.7
Manufacturing	8,162.2	9,052.2	10,341.5
Utilities	841,6	926.7	1,031.7
Construction	4,514.1	5,017.1	5,918.6
Trade, transport & communications	13,086.4	15,021.6	17,254.9
Finance	8,491.9	10,271.6	12,329.0
Public administration & others	7,048.7	8,854.5	10,409.8

Source: Asian Development bank

The average rate of inflation, which was 6.7 per cent at the start of 1997-98, rose to 8.8 per cent in September 1998. By 2004 it had fallen to an average of 3.9 per cent and averaged around 6.4 per cent in 2005 and 5.6 per cent in 2006. Inflation was predicted to have reached 8.5 per cent in March 2010 and reached 8.8 per cent in 2011.

Estimated figures for 2005 put the total outstanding debt of India at approximately US$123,145 million, rising to an estimated US$175,540 million in 2006 and US$220,956 million in 2007.

Foreign Investment
In recent years India has encouraged foreign investment by lowering tariffs on imported goods particularly on equipment relating to the power generation sector. Some foreign ownership laws have also been relaxed in an effort to attract more foreign investment. Majority foreign equity (or even 100 per cent) is allowed in several sectors, and foreign investment of up to 51 per cent in 35 designated sectors (including hotels and tourism) is eligible for automatic approval from the Reserve Bank of India within two weeks of application. It is planned that foreign direct investment be increased to US$10 billion per year. In recent years Foreign Direct Investment has average US$5-6 billion per year. India receives assistance from other countries around US$3.8 billion in the year 2005-06 of which approximately US$125 million was from the USA. The World Bank has plans for aid of around US£ billion a year for India for use in projects such as infrastructure, education, health and help to rural communities. Figures for 2010 show that foreign direct investment fell by 22 per cent on the previous year.

Balance of Payments / Imports and Exports
India has trade links with practically all the countries of the world. Exports cover over 7,500 commodities to about 180 countries while imports from about 135 countries account for over 6,800 commodities.

Exports cover a wide range of items from the agricultural and industrial sectors and various handicrafts, handloom, cottage and craft articles, and more recently software and software workers, ores and minerals, chemicals and chemical products, gems and jewellery. Project exports which include consultancy, civil construction and turn-key contracts have also made a significant progress in recent years.

Similarly, there has been a substantial increase in imports on account of development and economic needs. The bulk of imports comprises sophisticated machines, scarce raw materials, lubricants, oils and fertilisers essential for industrial and agricultural development, petroleum products, newsprint and pharmaceutical products. In the last few years, the country has experienced a large adverse balance of trade due to the need for heavy imports on the one hand and the steep hike in global prices of major imports on the other.

Following India's nuclear tests in May 1998, certain countries including the US, Canada, Denmark, Germany, Japan and Sweden imposed economic sanctions on India although most countries, including the US, had ended restrictions by the end of July 1998. In July 2005 India and the US signed a nuclear co-operation deal.

Major exports include gems and jewellery, clothing and cotton textiles, engineering goods, leather and leather goods, iron ore, chemical and software and agricultural products. Major imports included petroleum and related products, iron and steel, machinery, edible oils, fertilizers and chemicals.

The following tables shows the value of foreign trade in recent years. Figures are in million Rupees.

Year	Exports, fob	Imports, cif	Trade Balance
1990	325,576	431,929	-106.4
1995	1,063.5	1,226.8	-163.2
2000	2,035.7	2,308.7	-273.1
2005	4,564.2	6,604.1	-2,039.9
2010	11,188.2	15,968.7	-4,780.5

Source: Asian Development Bank

Direction of Export Trade, Million US$

Country	2009	2010
United States of America	18,280	27,469
UAE	20,667	25,049
China, People's Rep. of	10,155	17,700
Singapore	6,721	8,684
Hong Kong, China	6,938	8,874
UK	6,183	6,423
Germany	5,451	6,423
Netherlands	6,407	4,529
Belgium	3,450	4,410
Italy	3,238	4,408
Total	165,204	207,898

Source: Asian Development Bank

Direction of Import Trade, US$ million

Country	2009	2010
People's Republic of China	28,840	44,012
United States of America	16,644	20,394
Saudi Arabia	14,603	19,562
UAE	15,418	22,046
Iran	10,574	13,301
Germany	10,722	12,354
Australia	10,744	15,947
Switzerland	10,222	7,411
Singapore	6,047	13,305
Kuwait	7,535	9,507
Total	257,665	342,046

Source: Asian Development Bank

The main exports of India are cotton yarn and fabrics; drugs, pharmaceuticals and fine chemicals; manufactures of metals; machinery and instruments; manmade yarn, fabrics, madeups; transport equipment; primary and semi finished iron and steel; plastic and linoleum products; inorganic, organic and agro chemicals. Major imports are gold; coal, coke and briquettes; inorganic chemicals; metalifers ores, metal scrap; pearls, precious and semi precious stones; fertilizers.

Central Bank
Reserve Bank of India, PO Box 10007, Central Office Building, Shahid Bhagat Singh Road, Mumbai 400 001, Maharashtra, India. Tel: +91 2022 266 1602, fax: +91 2022 265 8269, e-mail: rbiprd@giasbm01.vsnl.net.in, URL: http://www.rbi.org.in

INDIA

Governor (2008-13): Dr Duvvuri Subbarao (page 1521)

Trade Organisations and Chambers of Commerce
Associated Chambers of Commerce and Industry of India, URL: http://www.assocham.org/
Federation of Indian Chambers of Commerce and Industry, URL: http://www.ficci.com/
Securities and Exchanges Board of India (SEBI), URL: http://www.sebi.gov.in/
Confederation of Indian Industry, URL: http://www.cii.in/

MANUFACTURING, MINING AND SERVICES

Primary and Extractive Industries

India is rich in mineral deposits, ranking first for mica, and fourth for bauxite and fifth for coal in the world. Other natural resources include iron ore, manganese, chromite, gas, diamonds, limestone, copper ore, phosphorite, dolomite and petroleum. The following table shows figures for production and value of selected minerals in the year 2004-05:

Mineral	Unit	Value Rs million
Coal	383 mil. tonnes	304,335
Petroleum (crude)	34 mil. tonnes	189,464
Bauxite	12 mil. tonnes	2,517
Copper Conc.	137,000 tonnes	2,131
Gold	3,526 kg.	1,943
Iron ore	146 mil. tonnes	74,029
Manganese ore	20 mil. tonnes	5,549
Gypsum	4 mil. tonnes	502
Limestone	166 mil. tonnes	17,942

Source: adapted from India Statistical Pocket Book

Oil accounts for 24 per cent of Indian energy needs. India had oil reserves in 2012 in the region of 8.9 billion barrels situated mainly in the Mumbai High oilfield which produces around 275,000 barrels per day. Figures for 2011 show that India produced 942.7 thousand barrels per day from more than 3,600 wells. In order to meets its oil needs India has to import around 2.4 million barrels per day, mostly from Saudi Arabia. Iran, Kuwait, Iraq and the United Arab Emirates.

India had estimated natural gas reserves of 38 trillion cubic feet in 2011 Natural gas production in 2011 was 1,682 billion cubic feet, mostly from reserves in the Bombay High basin, India uses all the natural gas it produces. Use of natural gas was estimated to have reached 2,261 billion cubic feet in 2011. Investment is currently underway building liquid natural gas terminals and pipelines. Reserves have recently been discovered in Adhra Pradesh, Orissa and Gujarat. These new finds are not expected to be enough to keep pace with the increasing demand.

Consumption of coal was 622.818 million short tons in 2010. The main coalfields are in Bihar, West Bengal and Madhya Pradesh but they cannot fulfill domestic demand with the quantity or quality of coal required, which makes India the third largest importer of coal in the world. Recent figures show that India has coal reserves of around 328 million tonnes.

Energy

At present about 80 per cent of the population has electricity. In 2009 generating capacity was around 1847.43 billion kilowattthours. There are plans to create a national power grid and a state company (Powergrid) has been set up to oversee this. This would involve unifying the nine state electricity boards currently in existence. Rules on foreign investment in the power sector have been relaxed to encourage investment. The government want to encourage the building of larger power plants and amongst those planned are a 21,000 MW hydroelectric project in Arunchal Pradesh, a coal fired 1,072 MW plant at Bhadrawati and a 1,886 MW liquid natural gas fired plant at Ennore.

Total Energy Consumption by Type in 2009

Energy	Percentage
Coal/peat	42
Combustible renewables & waste	24
Oil	24
Natural gas	7
Nuclear	1
Other renewables	2

Source: International Energy Agency

Manufacturing

Progress of industrialisation over the last 43 years has been a striking feature of Indian economic development. The process of industrialisation was launched as a conscious and deliberate policy in the early 1950s. In pursuance of this policy, large investment has been made in building up capacity over a wide spectrum of industries.

Industrial production has made rapid strides in terms of variety, quality and quantity. There is substantial diversification of the industrial base and as a result India produces a very broad range of industrial goods. Self-reliance has been achieved in basic and capital goods. Indigenous capabilities have now been established to the point of virtual self-sufficiency so that further expansion in various sectors such as mining, irrigation, power, chemicals, transport and communication can be based primarily on indigenous equipment.

Figures for 2008 show that manufacturing contributed 8,162.2 billion rupees to GDP, rising to 9,052.2 billion rupees in 2009 and 10,341.5 billion rupees in 2010.

Textiles are the largest single industry in India, accounting for about 14 per cent of industrial production and the industry contributes an average of three per cent of GDP. It provides direct employment to around 35 million people. Textile and clothing exports account for about 38 per cent of the total value of exports from the country. India is the world largest producer of jute. Average annual production of silk is 18,000 tonnes, accounting for 20 per cent of the world's production. Cotton is another large commodity accounting for nearly 60 per cent of all fibre consumption in spinning mills.

Around 6.5 million people are employed in the handloom sector, and produce around 14 per cent of all cloth in India, 5,524 million sq. metres in 2002-03.

India is the fifth largest cement manufacturer in the world, accounting for about 4 per cent of the world's production. In 2003 India exported nearly 7.0 million tonnes of cement. It is well endowed with raw materials such as lime gypsum and coal for the industry.

India is the world's second largest producer of two-wheelers. Recent figures put the turnover of the automotive industry at Rs 810 billion. Automobile and automobile component manufacture is now rising and India hopes to be global centre for car production by 2016. Other main manufactured items include leather goods, rubber, leather, steel, paper and newsprint, steel, soaps, fertilisers, chemicals, chemicals and petrochemicals, drugs and pharmaceuticals.

A growing area of manufacturing is the electronics and software sector, estimated figures for the year 2006-07 put software exports at US$29 billion.

The Indian economy has been performing well in recent years with the manufacturing sector growing. Several government initiatives have been introduced to foster and expand the manufacturing sector. The Industrial Infrastructure Upgradation Scheme has been set up to reduce transaction costs. In order to increase exports the Department of Commerce has set up the Assistance to States for Infrastructure Development for Exports project, Market Access Initiatives and Special Economic Zones.

The following table shows selected industrial production in 2005:

Product	Thousand Metric Tonnes
Cement	140,512
Sugar	18,486
Finished steel	43,205
Paper & paper board	5,885
Jute manufactures	1,449
Tea	928

Source: Asian Development Bank

Services

The tourist industry directly employs over 16 million people. Figures for 2000 show that around 210 million domestic tourist trips were made and in 2005 3,915,000 foreign tourists arrived.

Information technology has expanded in India in recent years and with a large and skilled workforce many international companies now outsource work to India particularly in the field of call centre work.

Agriculture

Economic regeneration attempted in successive Five Year Plans has made agriculture the backbone of the national economy. The sector provides the livelihood of about 70 per cent of the labour force, contributes nearly 35 per cent of net national product and accounts for a sizeable share of the total value of the country's exports. It supplies the bulk of wage goods required by the non-agricultural sector and raw material for a large section of industry. Around 124 million hectares are under cultivation.

Figures for 2008 show that agriculture contributed 9,289.2 billion rupees to GDP, rising to 10,893.0 billion rupees in 2009 and 13,868.8 billion rupees in 2010.

In terms of gross fertiliser consumption, India ranks fourth in the world after the US, Russia and China. The country has the largest area in the world under pulse crops. India was the first country to evolve a cotton hybrid.

Figures from the Statistical Year Book of India for 2008-09 show that India produced 22,276,000 bales of cotton.

Sugar is one of the major agricultural industries in India. It is the single largest employer in rural India and employs about 350,000 people.

The agriculture sector contributes around 25 per cent of GDP and provides employment for nearly 70 per cent of the population. The sector is dependent of the monsoon rains and is thus subject to fluctuations.

Agricultural Production in 2010

Produce	Int. $'000*	Tonnes
Rice, paddy	38,424,912	143,963,000
Buffalo milk, whole, fresh	24,869,607	62,350,000
Cow milk, whole, fresh	17,133,085	54,903,000
Wheat	12,146,402	80,800,000
Mangoes, mangosteens, guavas	9,003,503	15,026,700
Sugar cane	8926,377	292,300,000
Bananas	8,386,971	29,780,000
Cotton lint	8,139,317	5,695,000
Vegetables fresh nes	5,978,102	31,724,000
Potatoes	5,677,931	36,577,300

- continued		
Tomatoes	4,594,863	12,433,200
Indigenous buffalo meat	4,009,154	1,489,430

*unofficial figures

Source: http://faostat.fao.org/site/339/default.aspx Food and Agriculture Organization of the United Nations, Food and Agricultural commodities production

In early 2008 India and some other Asian countries began experiencing rice shortages; poor weather had led to failed crops in some countries and so the price of staples such as wheat, rice and pulses had risen. It has been estimated that between March 2007 and March 2008 the price of rice rose by 74 per cent. In April 2008 inflation in India was put at 7.0 per cent, the rise being driven by rising food prices. The Indian government responded by freezing rice exports. However, since exports account for just a small percentage of rice production, it is thought that this will make little difference. The government also announced a waiver on agricultural loans. Early figures for 2008 showed that the monsoon was good and that crop production could reach record levels.

Fisheries play an important role in the economy of India. They help augment food supply, generate employment, raise nutritional levels and earn foreign exchange. The Fisheries Division of the Department of Agriculture undertakes various production-oriented programmes, input supply programmes and infrastructure development programmes as well as formulating and initiating appropriate policies to increase production and productivity in the fisheries sector. The Division has also established a number of institutes for the development of the fishing industry.

The main objectives of the fisheries development programme are: enhancing production and productivity of fishermen, fish farmers and the fishing industry; increasing food production and thereby raising people's standard of nutrition; earning foreign exchange from export of marine products; improving the socio-economic conditions of traditional fishermen; employment generation; conservation of depleted species of fish.

Apart from four major fishing harbours, Cochin, Chennai (Madras), Vishakhapatnam and Roychowk, 18 minor fishing harbours and 93 fish landing centres have been constructed to provide landing and berthing facilities to fishing craft, and a major fishing harbour is under construction at Sasson Dock in Bombay. The government is providing subsidy to poor fishermen for the motorisation of their traditional craft which reduces physical strain on the part of the fishermen and increases the area and frequency of operation with consequent increase in catch and earnings. Figures for 2010 put the total catch at 4,695,000 tonnes.

COMMUNICATIONS AND TRANSPORT

Travel Requirements
Citizens of the USA, Canada, Australia and the EU require a passport valid for 190 days, and a visa. Other nationals should contact the embassy to check visa requirements. Certain parts of the country are designated protected or restricted areas that require special permits and in some cases prior government authorisation.

Customs Restrictions
The export or import of Indian currency is expressly prohibited without permission from the Reserve Bank of India. Please contact an Indian Consulate for further details.

National Airlines
Air India, URL: http://www.airindia.com
Indian Airlines, URL: http://www.indian-airlines.org provides domestic routes to more than 40 destinations.
Jet Airways, URL: http:// www.jetairways.com
Air Sahara, URL: http://www.airsahara.org

International Airports
The National Airports Authority formed under the National Airports Authority Act, 1985 started functioning from 1 June 1986. There are 16 international airports, (Ahmedabad, Amritsar, Bangalore, Kolkata, Chennai, Cochin, Delhi, Goa, Guwahati, Hyderabad, Mumbai, Thiruvananthpuram, Agra, Jaipur, Varanasi and Port Blair) and 250 domestic airports and airfields. Some domestic airports can take international flights if they have customs and immigration facilities. India also has 40 heliports.

Railways
Indian Railways virtually form the lifeline of the country, servicing its needs for large scale movement of traffic, both freight and passenger. In 1853 the railway network covered a distance of 34 km, it now covers a total of 63,970 km., connecting over 7,000 stations and served by over 7,700 locomotives. To make administration easier the system is divided into 16 zones: Central, which has its head office in Mumbai; Northern, head office New Delhi; North Eastern, head office Gorakhpur; Northeast Frontier, head office Maligoan; Southern, head office Chennai (Madras); South Central, head office Secunderabad; South Eastern, head office Kolkata (Calcutta); Western, head office Church Gate, Mumbai; and Eastern, head office Kolkata; East Central Railway, Hajipur; East Coast Railway, Bhubaneshwar; North Central Railway, Allahabad; North Western Railway, Jaipur; South East Central Railway, Bilaspur; South Western Railway, Hubli and West Central Railway which has its headquarters in Jabalpur. Indian Railways are now Asia's largest and the world's second largest railway system under single management. Over 5,000 million passengers are carried each year and 518.7 million tonnes of freight was carried in 2002-03. The railways are the biggest employer, employing 1.6 million workers. In 2008 railways services resumed between India and Bangladesh after an absence of more than 40 years; trains stopped running between Calcutta and Dhaka following the Indo-Pakistan war in 1965.

The rail link between the Kashmir valley and the rest of India is due to be completed in 2014. The tunnel is one of the world's longest (11 km) and deepest. It is below the snowline on the Pir Panjal mountain range and will mean that Kashmir and Jammu will be able to be connected throughout the year.. The only other link is the Jawahar road tunnels which is often blocked by snow.
Indian Railways: URL: http:// www.indianrail.gov.in

The Delhi metro became the world's first railway network to earn carbon credits from the UN-run scheme called the Clean Development Mechansim (CDM). The scheme gives firms in developing countries financial incentives to cut greenhouse gas emissions. The transport system which carries 1.8 million people daily has helped to reduce pollution levels in the city by an estimated 630,000 tonnes a year. It will now get $9.5 million in carbon credits annually for seven years. The hi-tech railway system was introduced in 2002.

Roads
India has the third largest road network in the world. Vehicles are driven on the left. There is a large motorway or National Highway system, which is the responsibility of central government, this network covers over 58,000 km. The country's total road length is approximately 3.32 million km. Estimated figures for 2004 showed that there were nearly 52 million vehicles on the roads. In 1999 a four times a week bus service started between India and Pakistan, the first such service since Partition. The service runs between Delhi and Lahore, along the Grand Trunk Road. In April 2005 a service began between Srinagar in Indian-controlled Kashmir and Muzaffarabad in Pakistani administered Kashmir.

Shipping
Around 90 per cent of trade volume is carried by sea As of July 2004 India's shipping fleet consisted of 211 overseas vessels and 441 coastal vessels. Figures for 2001-02 show that 274.76 millions tonnes of overseas cargo was handled and India's ports. The country has the largest merchant shipping fleet among developing countries and ranks 19th in the world in shipping tonnage with approximately 500 ships.

Waterways
India has a system of rivers and canals which the government is currently considering developing into National Waterways to compliment the internal transport systems. Areas currently under consideration include the Ganga between Allahabad (Uttar Pradesh) and Haldia (West Bengal), the Brahmaputra river between Sadiya and Dhuburi (Assam), the West Coast Canal, the Champakara Canal and the Udyogmandal Canal (Kerala). India currently has 14,500 km. of navigable rivers and 485 km of canal network.

Ports and Harbours
There are 12 major ports in the country as well as roughly 180 minor working ports on the coast. Major ports are the direct responsibility of central government. Kandla, Mumbai, Marmugao, New Mangalore, Cochin and Jawaharlal Nehru Port of Mumbai are the major ports on the west coast. Jawaharlal Nehru Port is equipped with modern facilities having mechanised container berths for handling dry bulk cargo and service berths. On the east coast, Tuticorin, Chennai, Visakhapatnam, Paradip, Ennore, Kolkata-Haldia are the major ports. The major ports handle around 15,000 cargo ships and 315 million tonnes of cargo each year.

HEALTH

Health care is primarily the responsibility of Central and State Governments. The broad objectives of the health programmes so far have been to control and eradicate communicable diseases; to provide curative and preventive health services in rural areas through the establishment of a primary health centre in each community development block; and to augment programmes for the training of medical and para-medical personnel. India currently has over 15,500 hospitals.

In the overall health development programmes, emphasis is being laid on preventive and promotive aspects by organising effective and efficient health services. There are now a number of training centres for different categories of health workers, i.e. nurses, sanitary inspectors, para-medical workers, non-medical supervisors, physiotherapists and so on. The plan of action on the report of the Group on Medical Education and Support Manpower for a three-tier reconstruction of entire health care system has been worked out. The scheme of involvement of community level workers is also being implemented.

The government is extending financial assistance to voluntary organisations/institutions under grant-in-aid schemes i.e. schemes for the improvement of medical services, special health schemes for setting up new hospitals/dispensaries in rural areas, extensions for existing hospital buildings and equipment purchase schemes. Apart from this, financial assistance is also given to voluntary organisations for voluntary blood donation programmes. According to the WHO, in 2009 India spent 4.2 per cent of GDP on healthcare. General government expenditure accounted for 4.5 per cent of total expenditure. Private expenditure accounted for 69.7 per cent of total expenditure on health, social security expenditure for 17.4 per cent and 1.1 per cent was spent by external resources. Per capita total expenditure on health was US$44.

Diseases like malaria, tuberculosis and cholera, which used to take a heavy toll of life, have been controlled to varying degrees. No case of plague has been reported in the country since 1967. Smallpox has been eradicated. The National Leprosy Eradication Programme was set up in 1983. Anti-leprosy drugs are supplied to all states and territories free of charge however there were still 133,717 cases of leprosy in 2009. There were 1,563,344 reported cases of malaria, and 43 cases of polio. Life expectancy at birth has increased from 32 in 1941-51 to 65 in 2009. Health life expectancy was 56 years in 2007.

In 1992 in response to growing concern of the threat of AIDS, the National AIDS Control Organisation was established, with an emphasis on education, and improving blood safety. Recent estimates put the number of HIV positive people between 3 and 5 million.

INDIA

Figures for 2002 show that there were 15,393 General Hospitals in India and 3,844 hospitals specializing in Homeopathy and Indian Medicine. Health care in rural areas is generally provided by Primary Health Centres of which there were 137,311 in 2004. Each Primary Health Centre covers and approximate population of 30,000 in plain areas and 20,000 in tribal areas or areas with difficult terrain. According to latest figures from the WHO, in the period 2000-10 there were 660,801 doctors (6 per 10,000 inhabitants), 1,430,555 nurses and midwives (13 per 10,000 people), 78,096 dentistry personnel (less than 1 per 10,000 people) and 578,179 pharmacists (5.2 per 10,000 population).

Rural Medical Infrastructure

In order to provide rural communities with health care services India has a system of Community Health Centres which are staffed by up to 30 medical staff including a medical specialist, a surgical specialist, a paediatrician and a gynaecologist. They are usually equipped with a laboratory, x-ray facilities and up to 30 beds, and are designed to serve up to 120,000 people.

Primary Health Care Centres are staffed by a medical officer, a pharmacist, and staff nurse, a laboratory technician and a health educator and provide care for up to 30,000 people. Health Care Sub-Centres are staffed by two multi-purpose workers, usually one male and one female, and provide care for up to 5,000 people.

Family Planning

Family Planning as an official programme was adopted in 1952. A fully-fledged Department of Family Planning was created in 1966 within the Ministry of Health, Family Planning and Urban Development. Health and Family Welfare is now a separate Ministry. The operational goals of the Ministry are the adoption of family planning by the people as a way of life through group acceptance of a small family norm, personal knowledge of family planning methods and ready availability of supplies and services. The programme is implemented through the State Governments as a centrally sponsored scheme.

Voluntary organisations and private medical practitioners are also used in the family planning campaign. The Programme is implemented through 1,230 community health centres, 13,893 primary health centres and 100,031 sub-centres. A further 5,780 other institutions also provide health services.

IUCD and sterilisation services are offered through both mobile and static units. Nirodh (condoms) are presently distributed over the country by three methods, namely, a Free Supply Scheme, a Depot Holder Scheme and a Commercial Distribution Scheme. Conventional contraceptives are distributed free to interested couples under the Free Supply Scheme through family planning centres and sub-centres numbering about 40,000. In addition, family planning field workers also distribute conventional contraceptives free during their field visits.

The oral contraception pill was introduced as a pilot project in the family planning programme in 1967. Some 319 Oral Contraception Projects have been commissioned so far. The pill is now being distributed through 23,775 centres in the country, and is estimated that 42.7 per cent of eligible couples whose wives are in the reproductive age-group of 15-44 years were using an approved family planning method.

EDUCATION

Education is an integral part of the country's development process and thus has been accorded a high priority. Concerted efforts during the last 40 plus years have seen a four-fold increase in the total number of literates. The number of schools has also more than doubled and universities increased by more than five times. With quantitative expansion of educational facilities, there is now a greater emphasis on qualitative improvement. Before 1976 education was exclusively the responsibility of states while the central government was only concerned with certain areas like co-ordination and determination of standards in technical and higher education. In 1976, through a constitutional amendment, education became their joint responsibility. In 2002 a further constitutional amendment was made to make elementary education a fundamental right of all children aged 6-14.

The overall aim is to eradicate illiteracy and spread universal elementary education in the age group of 15-35. For this, meticulously formulated strategies based on micro-planning are being applied at grass root levels. A major strategy to overcome various obstacles in achieving this goal focuses on detailed block and school level planning with community participation and effective linkages with local environment and development activities. A programme named 'Operation Blackboard' is already in operation to provide basic amenities in education in primary schools and a second teacher in single teacher schools. Education of castes and tribes and people from hill areas is being specially promoted as well as women's education, which is an area of special importance. Necessary reforms will be initiated to make vocational education more attractive. Degrees will not be insisted upon as an essential qualification or pre-condition for jobs even if not directly relevant.

Figures for 2005-10 showed that government expenditure on education was the equivalent of 3.1 per cent of GDP.

Primary/Secondary Education

Primary education lasts until the age of 14, in order to encourage education among children education is free and child labour has been banned although in some areas this has been difficult to enforce. In 1994 the state funded District Primary Education Programme was launched with the mandate to reform the existing system and bring uniformity to the curriculum, under the programme around 160,000 new schools have opened. Primary school enrollment figures are rising and the enrollment of female students is encouraged.

In the Secondary school system, students can choose to follow vocational training which is often aimed at the more disadvantaged students hoping to gain skills for future employment.

India currently has 407 universities, over 800 medical schools and more than 1,000 teacher training colleges as well as over 2,400 other professional colleges or university level institutions.

School Education Figures for 2004-05

Institution	Number	Students '000
Primary School	767,500	130,760
Middle School	274,700	51,240
High/Higher Schools	152,000	37,000

According to the latest UNESCO figures (2006), the literacy rate for males was 76.4 per cent and 53.4 per cent for females. For the age group 15 to 24 years, the rate was 86.3 per cent for males and 75.3 for females.

National Council of Educational Research and Training, URL: http://www.ncert.nic.in/index.htm
Central Board of Secondary Education, URL: http://www.cbse.nic.in

RELIGION

India has a religious liberty rating of 2 on a scale of 1 to 10 (10 is most freedom). (Source: World Religion Database).

The following table shows the number and percentage of membership to different religions in India according to the 2001 census.

Religion	Millions	%
Hindus	827.6	80.5
Muslims	138,2	13.4
Christians	24,.1	2.3
Sikhs	19.2	1.9
Buddhists	8.0	0.8
Jains	4.2	0.4
Others	6.6	0.6

COMMUNICATIONS AND MEDIA

Newspapers

The Times of India, URL: http://timesofindia.indiatimes.com
India Today, URL: http://www.asianage.com/
The Hindu, URL: http://www.thehindu.com
The Hindustan Times, URL: http://www.hindustantimes.com/
The Pioneer, URL: http://www.dailypioneer.com
The Indian Express, URL: http://www.indianexpress.com
The Statesman, URL: http://www.thestatesman.net
The Asian Age, URL: http://www.asianage.com/
Deccan Herald, URL: http://www.deccanherald.com

Broadcasting

There are approximately 306 radio station broadcasting and over 110 million radios are in use.
All India Radio, public broadcaster, URL: http://allindiaradio.org
Radio Mirchi, commercial network, Radio City, Red FM

Over 560 television stations are broadcasting and around 50 million television sets are in use.
Doordarshan Television, (public TV), URL: http://www.ddindia.gov.in
Zee TV, (satellite), URL: http://www.zeetelevision.com
Star TV, (satellite), URL: http://www.starnews.indya.com
Aaj Tak, (24-hour news), URL: http://www.aajtak.com
New Delhi TV (NDTV), URL: http://www.ndtv.com

Postal Service

India has the largest postal system in the world and recent figures show that there were more than 153,000 post offices.

Telecommunications

By 2010 it was estimated that nearly 336 million land lines were in use and 752 million mobile phones.

Figures for 2008 indicate that 80 million people regularly use the internet.

ENVIRONMENT

Threats to the environment include soil erosion, deforestation (23 per cent of the land is presently covered by forest and woodland), air pollution, water pollution and an ever increasing population which places a heavy strain on natural resources.

A scheme of wildlife conservation has been implemented and there are currently 89 national parks and 490 wildlife sanctuaries, including 27 tiger reserves.

India was badly affected by the Asian tsunami disaster, caused by a huge undersea earthquake in the Indian Ocean in December 2004. The southern part of the country was hit, with nearly 8,000 people killed in Tamil Nadu and almost 600 in Pondicherry. Thousands of people, mainly from fishing villages, were never found. In the Andaman and Nicobar Islands, nearly

2,000 of the 400,000 population were killed and many others remain missing. The islands were almost covered by salt water leading to long-term problems of contamination of soil and fresh water supplies.

In July 2005, India suffered a particularly heavy monsoon; over 800 people were believed to have been killed in floods and landslides, mainly in the Mumbai and Maharashtra region.

In December 2009 the World Bank granted India a US$1 billion loan to help clean up the River Ganges which is now one of the most heavily polluted rivers in the world.

India is party to the following environmental agreements: Antarctic-Environmental Protocol, Antarctic-Marine Living Resources, Antarctic Treaty, Biodiversity, Climate Change, Climate Change-Kyoto Protocol, Desertification, Endangered Species, Environmental Modification, Hazardous Wastes, Law of the Sea, Ozone Layer Protection, Ship Pollution, Tropical Timber 83, Tropical Timber 94, Wetlands, and Whaling.

According to the figures from the EIA, figures for 2009 showed that total carbon dioxide emissions from the consumption of fossil fuels was 1,622.70 million metric tons. This rose to 1,695.62 million metric tons.

SPACE PROGRAMME

The Indian National Committee for Space Research (INCOSPAR) was formed by the Department of Atomic Energy in 1962. The first rocket was launched from the Thumba Equatorial Launching Station (TERLS) in 1963. In 1972 the Government set up the Space Commission and Department of Space. INCOSPAR has been superceded by the Indian Space Research Organisation, one of the largest space agencies in the world. Its principal aim is to develop space technology. It has put into operation two major satellite sysystems; the Indian National Satellites (INSAT) for communication and the Indian Remote Sensing (IRS) satellite for management of natural resources. It has also developed launch vehicles.
Indian Space Research Organisation, URL: http://www.isro.org/

ANDAMAN AND NICOBAR ISLANDS

Capital: Port Blair (Population estimate: 100,100)

Head of State: Lt General (Retd) Bhopinder Singh, PVSM, AVSM (Lieutenant Governor)

CONSTITUTION AND GOVERNMENT

Legislature
There is no elected or nominated legislature. Government is administered by the President of the Union of India acting through a Lt. Governor. Andaman and Nicobar Islands are a Union Territory of India.

The Islands are represented in the Lok Sabha by one MP, Shri Bishnu Pada Ray (BJP)

Chief Secretary: Shri Anand Prakash, IAS

Recent Events
India was badly affected by the Asian tsunami disaster, caused by a huge undersea earthquake in the Indian Ocean in December 2004. In the Andaman and Nicobar Islands nearly 2,000 of the estimated 400,000 population were killed and many others remain missing. Most of the islands jetties were washed away. Due to the presence of a military base situated on one of the islands, and the isolation of some indigenous tribes the Indian government refused international aid agencies access to the islands.

In 2012 concern was expressed about tourist interaction with members of the Jarawa tribe. The worry is that interaction with outsiders may bring disease to them and that the tribe is on the verge of extinction.

LEGAL SYSTEM

The islands come under the jurisdiction of the Calcutta High Court.

LOCAL GOVERNMENT

The islands are divided into three districts, North and Middle Andaman District, South Andaman Dictrict and Nicobar District. The districts are sub-divided into seven sub-districts.

AREA AND POPULATION

Area
The Andaman Islands lie in the Bay of Bengal, 193 km from Cape Negaris in Burma, 1,255 km from Calcutta and 1,190 km from Madras. The five islands grouped together are called the Great Andamans and to their south lies the island of Little Andaman. There are some 204 islets, the two principal groups being Ritchie Archipelago and Labyrinth Islands. The Nicobar Islands are situated to the south of the Andamans, 121 km from Little Andaman. They comprise 19 islands, 7 of which are the uninhabited chief islands of Great Nicobar, Camotra with Noncowire and Car Nicobar.

The Andoman and Nicobar Islands cover an area of approximately 8,249 sq. km, 6,408 sq. km. in the Andaman group and 1,841 sq. km. in the Nicobar group. Forests cover around 80-90 per cent of the islands, and have been categorised as one of the highest potential productivity zones in India, although much of the area is protected. The topography is undulating, with flat land only found in narrow valleys or at the coast. It rains for almost 200 days of the year, being exposed to both the south-west and the north-east monsoons. The average relative humidity is 80 per cent.

The total number of islands and islets is 572.

To consult a map, please visit:
http://www.lib.utexas.edu/maps/islands_oceans_poles/andaman_nicobar_76.jpg

Population
Population figures from the 2001 census put the population at 356,152, giving a population density of 34 persons per sq. km. Figures for 2011 put the population at 379,944. Original inhabitants of the Andaman group of islands are the Great Andamanese, Onge, Jarawa,

Shompens and Sentinales. Following more contact with outsiders these indigenous tribes are now under threat and in particular the Jarawa are estimated to only number a few hundred (2001 figures). Contact from outsiders is now being discouraged. Indigenous tribes of the Nicobar Islands are the Nicobarese and Shompens.

Recent figures show that 25 islands in the Andaman group are inhabited and 13 in the Nicobar group.

The principal languages are Bengali, Hindi, Nicobares, Malayalam, Tamil and Telugu.

EMPLOYMENT

Figures from the 2001 census show that the islands have a workforce of 136,254.

MANUFACTURING, MINING AND SERVICES

Primary and Extractive Industries
In 1998 the Indian Government issued permits for oil exploration around the Andaman Islands.

Manufacturing
Products comprise sawn timber, commercial plywood, match splints and veneers and fish processing. Small scale and handicraft units are engaged in shell crafts, furniture making, bakery products, rice milling, wheat grinding and oilseeds crushing. Two small factories are engaged in fish processing. Recently the manufacture of polythene bags, PVC pipes and fittings, soft drinks and fibre glass has begun on a small scale.

Tourism
Tourism is a growing economic sector for the islands which have promoted the idea of eco-friendly tourism. Since the December 2004 Asian tsunami brought the islands to the attention of a greater number of people, tourism looks set to expand with several companies beginning to build hotels. The islands are being promoted as a centre for water sports including scuba diving as well as adventure tourism. Recent figures show that the islands have around 180,000 visitors per year.

Agriculture
Of the total area of 8,249 sq. km, only 52,000 hectares are available for agricultural use, and only 12,000 hectares are flat. Paddy is the main food crop cultivated in the Andaman group of islands whereas the Nicobar Islands cultivate coconut and arecanut as the main cash crops. Other crops such as sugarcane, red oil palm, fruits including mango, pineapple, guava, jackfruit and citrus fruits, oilseeds, pulses and vegetables are also cultivated. Many spices are cultivated including pepper, nutmeg, cinnamon and cloves. Fruits grown include bananas, mangos, papaya and pineapples. Rubber and cashew are smaller agricultural products.

Intensification of cropping systems with greater use of chemical fertilisers and highly toxic pesticides have resulted in the undermining of the soil, leading to deficiencies of macronutrients in the soil. This has also led to pollution of the environment, creating health hazards both to animals and humans. Since agricultural development cannot subsist on a deteriorating natural resource base, the state Department of Agriculture has given emphasis on effectively implementing an Integrated Intensive Farming System, based on environment friendly technologies for sustainable agriculture. In the islands the agricultural sector is particularly dependent on rainfall and unpredictable weather or failure of rainfall adds to the farmers difficulties. In order to overcome this and to sustain productivity, the Department is encouraging rain water conservation management.

Recent figures show that the islands produce nearly 24,000 metric tons of rice, 5,800 metric tons of aercanut, 2,332 metric tons of sugarcane. The land that was submerged by the tsunami waves became full of salt and it was feared that the agricultural sector would be badly affected. Fortunately, in the months following the disaster, the islands were subjected to heavy rains which washed the salt from the soil.

Fishing
Recent figures show that the islands' fishermen catch around 27,000 tonnes of fish. This figure may fall following the 2004 tsunami as coral reefs that attracted fish were damaged resulting in fish moving out to deeper waters.

INDIA

Forestry
Over 7,000 sq km of the islands are covered in forests which include valuable timbers such as paduak and gurjan.

COMMUNICATIONS AND TRANSPORT

Entry Restrictions
Indian nationals need no permit to visit the Andamans except to the reserve area; however, a permit is required to visit Nicobar and other restricted areas. The permit is granted only in special cases. The Andaman and Nicobar Islands are restricted under the Foreigners (Restricted Areas) Order 1963, so no foreigner can enter or stay in the Islands without obtaining a permit from the competent authority. All foreign nationals can stay in the islands for 30 days after obtaining a permit on arrival at Port Blair from the immigration authorities. Permits can also be obtained from Indian Missions Overseas, Foreigner Registration Offices at Delhi, Mumbai, Chennai and Calcutta, and the immigration authorities at airports in Port Blair, Delhi, Bombay, Calcutta and Chennai.

Roads
The Andoman and Nicobar Islands have a total of 333 kms of highways and 180 kms of district roads.

Air
Alliance Air operates flights that connect Port Blair to Chennai, Visakhapatnam and Calcutta, the journey time being approximately two hours. Jet Airways have also started to operate services between Chennai and Port Blair.

Shipping
Regular passenger ship services are available to Port Blair from Chennai, Calcutta and Vishakhapatnam. There are three to four sailings every month from Chennai and Calcutta to Port Blair and from Vishakhapatnam once every two months. The voyage takes about three days and the ships normally berth at Port Blair for about two days. There are also regular inter-island ferries.

HEALTH

2005 figures show the islands have three hospitals and four Community Health Centres, there were also around 20 primary health care centres. There are 137 doctors serving the islands and 357 nurses. The main diseases suffered from on the islands are acute respiratory infections, gastro-intestinal disorders, nutritional diseases including anaemia and vitamin deficiency, and malaria. More recently, outbreaks of leptospirosis have occurred after monsoons, a disease not previously known on the islands. 2006 saw an outbreak of measles on the islands.

EDUCATION

Until 1947 there was no Education Department in the islands and the Deputy Commissioner also oversaw education in his capacity as the President of the Educational Advisory Committee. The spread in education has led to a noticeable rise in literacy over the decades. It has more than doubled since 1961, when it was only 33.63 per cent, to 73.02 per cent in 1991. According to the 2001 census it was 81 per cent, the eighth highest in the country.

In 1946, there were only 12 schools, including one Karen school and one Burmese school. In the year 2009/10 the islands had 207 primary schools with 34,242 pupils, 67 middle schools, with 22,323 pupils, 46 secondary schools and 53 senior secondary schools with a combined student enrolment of 22,581. Education is free to all in the islands, and highly subsidised with free text books and uniforms to all tribal students and to those living below the poverty line. Free travel is provided to those living beyond 4 km. from the nearest school. Figures for 2011 put the literacy rate at 86 per cent.

Figures for 2005 show that the islands had a total of 213 primary schools, and 49 secondary schools. There are two polytechnics and two government colleges.

ENVIRONMENT

India was badly affected by the Asian tsunami disaster, caused by a huge undersea earthquake in the Indian Ocean in December 2004. In the Andaman and Nicobar Islands, nearly 2,000 of the estimated 400,000 population were killed and many others remain missing. The islands were almost covered by salt water which it was feared would lead to long term problems of contamination of soil and fresh water supplies. In the weeks following the Tsunami, the islands experienced very heavy rainfall and the salt was washed from the soil.

The natural environment is important to the survival of the islands and the promotion of tourism. The islands now have 96 Wildlife Sanctuaries, 9 National Parks and a Biosphere Reserve.

ANDHRA PRADESH

Capital: Hyderabad (Population estimate: 3.5 million)

Head of State: Shri Ekkadu Srinivasan Lakshmi Narasimhan (Governor)

CONSTITUTION AND GOVERNMENT

Andhra Pradesh became a state on 1st November 1956 under the States' re-organisation scheme.

In December 2009 Government plans for a new state were announced. The new state to be called Telangana would be made out of the southern state of Andhra Pradesh and will probably include Hyderabad which is currently the capital . The new state would have a population of around 35 million and would be a predominantly agricultural area although Hyderabad is home to many software companies including Microsoft and Google.

Legislature
Number of seats in legislative council: 90
Number of seats in legislative assembly: 295 including one for the Anglo-Indian community
Chief Minister, Shri Nallari Kiran Kumar Reddy

LEGAL SYSTEM

In addition to the High Court, Andhra Pradesh has 63 District Courts and around 100 subordinate judges courts, it also has several mobile courts.

LOCAL GOVERNMENT

For administrative purposes Andhra Pradesh is divided into 23 districts.

AREA AND POPULATION

Area
Andhra Pradesh is bounded on the north by the states of Orissa and Madhya Pradesh, on the west by Maharashtra and Karnataka, on the south by Tamil Nadu and on the east by the Bay of Bengal. It has an area of 275,068 sq. km. The sea coastline is about 974 km in length.

In December 2003 Andhra Pradesh was hit by a cyclone which led to the deaths of around 50 people and many homes and crops were lost. Cyclone Laila hit in May 2010, it was believed that 23 people were killed and the state suffered severely disrupted transport links.

Population
The census for 2001 gave the population as 75,727,541 making it the fifth most highly populated state with a density of 275 people per sq. km. There is a sex ratio of 933 females to every 1,000 males. Just over 27 per cent of the population lives in urban areas. Population estimates for 2007 put the population at 81,800,000 rising to 84,665,533 in 2011.

Language
The chief languages are Telugu and Urdu.

EMPLOYMENT

There is a working population of approximately 34 million, which is around 45 per cent of the total population. Cultivators and agricultural labourers make up 62 per cent of the main workers.

Andhra Pradesh did have a ruling that five per cent of jobs in government and education should be reserved for the Muslim minority, this law however has been challenged and a hearing in the High Court ruled that it was unconstitutional. In 2005 the case was taken to India's Supreme Court which refused to block the High Court's decision. The State Governemnt is the largest single employer.

BANKING AND FINANCE

In 2006 the World Bank announced it would be giving assistance loan worth US$1billion in view of the state's successful economic reforms. Half of the money will go on irrigation projects the other half will be spent on structural adjustments and urban reforms. Estimated figures for the period 2004-05 put the per capita state domestic product at Rs12,350.

MANUFACTURING, MINING AND SERVICES

Primary and Extractive Industries
The state has large resources of minerals, including oil and natural gas, bauxite, mica, dolomite, ochres, quartz, fire clay limestone, gold, diamonds and coal. The coal mines at Singareni supply coal to the whole of Southern India.

Energy
Andhra Pradesh has the third largest installed power capacity in the country.

Power generation

Source of power	Megawatts
Thermal	2953
Gas	696
Hydro	2683
Wind	57
Cogeneration	44
Total	6433
Share from central generating stations	897
Grand total	7330

Manufacturing

Several major industries are in operation around Hyderabad and Vishakhapatnam. Weaving was formerly a large employment sector, employing around 233,000, but this industry is now in decline. Other industries include the manufacture of machine tools, synthetic drugs, pharmaceuticals, heavy electrical machinery, ships, fertilisers, aeronautical parts, cement and cement products, chemicals, asbestos, glass and watches, and information technology and electronic equipment. Hyderabad is fast becoming a centre for information technology; it is now home to the Hyderabad Information Technology, Engineering Consultancy (HITEC) city, a large IT park and the Indian Institute of Information Technology (IIIT).

Figures from mid-2005 show that the state had 4,220 large and medium scale industries which employed around 973,055 people. There were also 495,892 small scale industries which employed 3,575,563 people.

Agriculture

Agriculture is the main occupation of about 69 per cent of people. Nearly 75 per cent of the territory is covered by the basins of three large rivers (the Godavari, Krishna and Pennarand), as well as 17 shorter rivers providing water for irrigation. Andhra Pradesh was the first state to involve farmers in the management of irrigation systems. There are now nearly 10,000 water associations and in 2002-03 a large investment was made to make them economically viable.

The state is the largest producer of rice in India, as well as wheat, jowar and bajra and is also the leading producer of cash crops such as tobacco, groundnut, chillies, turmeric, oilseeds, cotton, sugar and jute. Varieties of mango, grape, guava, sapota, papaya and banana are also produced.

Since 2001 Andhra Pradesh has suffered from drought, leading to the suicide of many farmers. In 2004, Indian Prime Minister Manmohan Singh announced plans for assistance packages to areas hit by drought. The aid was to help build water tanks and improve and supply piped water. as well as building schools and roads.

Forestry

Over 20 per cent of Andjra Pradesh is covered by forests. Main products of the forestry industry include teak, bamboo, cashew, casuarina and eucalyptus.

COMMUNICATIONS AND TRANSPORT

Air

Regular air services to Hyderabad, Visakhapatnam, Vijayawada and Tirupathi are provided by regional airlines. Hyderabad is a customs airport, with an air cargo complex having customs clearance facilities. It is also now an international airport following expansion work. The State Government also intends to set up an international airport at Visakhapatnam. Direct flights have been introduced between Hyderabad and Singapore, Kuwait and Sharjah.

Railways

The state is serviced by a 5,055km. railway route. A thousand kilometres of the older metric gauge railway are being converted into broad gauge. 35 million tonnes of cargo are handled annually by railways.

Roads

The length of roads in the state is 199,900 km. A total of 150,000 km of road are maintained by the State, of which state highways comprise 50,000 km, national highways. The State Government has set up a Roads Development Corporation and has identified 10,266 km of high density traffic roads for improvement. 38.04 billion rupees have been set aside for improving the road infrastructure in the state. In 1953 there were 70,080 registered vehicles, rising to 2,071,050 in 1994 and 8,230,000 in 2010. The growth rate of the number of vehicles is 16 per cent, the highest in the country.

Ports and Harbours

There is one major port at Visakhapatnam and two intermediate ports at Kakinada and Machilipatnam. There are further minor ports at Krishnapatnam, Gangavaram, Mutyalampalem, Bhvanapadu, Kalingapatnam, Bhimunipatnam, Narsapur, Nizamapatnam and Vodarevu. The Government has taken a major initiative for the development of the port infrastructure in the state. Three ports, Krishnapatnam, Kakinada and Vodarevu, have been privatised and Gangavaram is also in the process of being privatised.

HEALTH

Recent figures show that there are 2,319 hospitals and dispensaries with nearly 40,000 beds. Andhra Pradesh has over 9,800 doctors.

EDUCATION

Recent figures show that there were 65,900 primary schools with 5,300,000 students and 8,661 higher secondary schools with 3,713,000 students. The literacy rate for males in 2005 was 61.0 per cent and 45.0 per cent for females, the overall literacy rate being 53.0 per cent.

ENVIRONMENT

Andhra Pradesh has set up several sanctuaries to protect wildlife particularly tigers, but figures for 2005 showed that the number of tigers was still falling.

SPACE PROGRAMME

Andhra Pradesh is home to the Sriharikota base, which in April 2001 saw the successful launch of the Geosynchronous Satellite Launch Vehicle (GSLV).

ARUNACHAL PRADESH

Capital: Itanagar

Head of State: H.E. General (Rtd.) Nirbhay Shama (Governor)

CONSTITUTION AND GOVERNMENT

Constitution

Arunachal Pradesh became the 25th State of the Union of India on 20th February 1987. Arunachal Pradesh is represented by one seat in the Rajya Sabha and two seats in the Lok Sabha.

Legislature

Number of seats in Legislative Assembly, 60

Chief Minister, Shri Nabam Tuki

LEGAL SYSTEM

Arunachal Pradesh comes under the jurisdiction of the Guwahati High Court.

LOCAL GOVERNMENT

For administrative purposes Arunachal Pradesh is divided into 16 districts: Tawang, West Kameng, East Kameng, Papumpare, Lower Subansiri, Upper Subansiri, East Siang, West Siang, Upper Siang, Dibang Valley, Lower Dibang Valley, Lohit, Changlang, Tirap, Kurung Kumey, Anjaw.

AREA AND POPULATION

Area

Arunachal Pradesh was declared a state on 20 February 1987, prior to this it became a Union Territory in 1972 and before that when it was still part of Assam it was known as the North East Frontier Agency. It is skirted by Bhutan in the west, Tibet and China in the north and north-east, Myanmar (Burma) to the east, Assam and Nagaland in the south. Geographically it is made up of the submontane and mountainous ranges which then slope to the plains of Assam. It is the largest state in the north-east region with an area of 83,743 sq. km.

In 2008 Arunachal Pradesh was hit by severe monsoon rains and suffered a series of mudslides

Talks took place between India and China in 2012 about the disputed border between the two nations the disputed area includes Arunachal Pradesh, both countries have previously claimed the other is occupying parts of its land.

Population

Figures from the 2001 census gave the population as 1,091,117 with a density of 13 people per sq. km., the lowest in the country. Estimated figures for 2007 put the population at 1,188,000, rising to 1,382,611 in 2011 giving a density figure of 119 people per sq km.

Language

The principal languages of the state are Monpa, Miji, Aka, Sherdukpen, Bangni, Nisni, Apatani, Tagin, Hill Miri, Adi, Gallong, Digaru Mishmi, Idu-Mishmi, Miju-Mishmi, Khampti, Nocte, Tangsa and Wancho.

INDIA

EMPLOYMENT

Figures from the 2001 census show that Arunachal Pradesh had a workforce of 482,902. Over 60 per cent of the population is employed in the agricultural sector.

BANKING AND FINANCE

Estimated figures for the period 2004-05 put the per capita state domestic product at Rs10,345.

MANUFACTURING, MINING AND SERVICES

Primary and Extractive Industries
Arunachal Pradesh has many proven natural resources, including oil, gas and coal, dolomite, limestone, marble, yellow ochre, lead, zinc and graphite.

Energy
A 2,000 megawatt hydro electric plant is currently being constructed in the Lower Subansiri District. Recent figures show that of 3,649 villages, 2,597 have electricity.

Manufacturing
Important industries are a light roofing-sheet factory at Pasighat, a fruit processing plant at Nigmoi in the West Siang district, a cement plant at Tezu, a lemon grass oil expeller unit at Tawang, and a citronella distillation plant at Pasighat. There are also many crafts and weaving centres.

Agriculture
Ecological conditions in Arunachal Pradesh are favourable for horticulture. Besides pineapple, orange, lemon, lychee, papaya, banana and guava, temperate fruits such as apples, plums, pears, peaches, cherries, walnuts and almonds are grown in about 1,390 horticulture gardens.

Principal crops are rice, maize, millet, wheat, pulses, potato, sugarcane and oilseeds. Figures for the 1998-99 season show that food grain production was 203,287 metric tonnes.

COMMUNICATIONS AND TRANSPORT

Roads
The state has a transport system including 330 km of national highways.

HEALTH

Arunachal Pradesh has three general hospitals as well as 11 district hospitals.

EDUCATION

There is one university and one polytechnic based in the state. Three Industrial Training Institutes based at Roing and Daporijo train craftsmen in different trades and there are colleges specialising in agriculture and forestry. There are over 1,200 primary schools, and more than 420 secondary level high schools.

The literacy rate was estimated at 60 per cent in 2005.

ENVIRONMENT

Arunachal Pradesh has two National Parks at Namdapha and Mouling.

ASSAM

Capital: Dispur

Head of State: Shri Janaki Ballav Pattanaik (Governor)

CONSTITUTION AND GOVERNMENT

Legislature
Number of seats in Legislative Assembly: 126

Chief Minister: Tarun Gogoi

Recent Events
The North-East of India has more than 20 groups fighting for some degree of independence either on a national or tribal level. One of the largest groups is the United Liberation Front of Assam (ULFA); it has been fighting for independence for Assam for over 25 years and it is estimated that over 10,000 people have lost their lives in the struggle. In December 2004 Indian Prime Minister Manmohan Singh called on rebel groups to hold talks. ULFA said that they would only attend talks that did not demand any preconditions. The Prime Minister held talks in October 2005 but both sides refused to say what had been discussed. Talks were again held the following year but broke down in September 2006 and since then there has been an escalation in violence. In 2008 there were several bomb attacks at a cement factory and at busy markets. A breakaway faction known as Black Widow (fighting for an independent homeland for the Dimasa) has claimed responsibility for some of the attacks.

LEGAL SYSTEM

Chief Justice: B. Sudershan Reddy

LOCAL GOVERNMENT

For administrative purposes Assam is divided into 27 districts.

AREA AND POPULATION

Area
Assam is situated in the north-east corner of India and surrounded by Bhutan and Arunachal Pradesh in the north, Nagaland and Manipur in the east, Meghalaya and Mizoram in the south and Bangladesh, Tripura and West Bengal in the west. The area of the state is 78,438 sq. km.

Population
Population figures from the 2001 census gave the population as 26,638,407 with a density of 340 people per sq. km. The majority of people live in rural areas. Population estimates for 2007 were 29,180,000, rising to 31,169,272 in 2011 giving a density figure of 397 people per sq km.

Language
The principal languages are Assamese, Bodo and Karbi.

EMPLOYMENT

Figures from the 2001 census put the workforce at 9,538,591, nearly 60 per cent of whom are employed in the agricultural sector.

BANKING AND FINANCE

Estimated figures for the period 2004-05 put the per capita state domestic product at Rs 6,720,000.

MANUFACTURING, MINING AND SERVICES

Primary and Extractive Industries
Assam has reserves of oil and gas, coal and limestone. Assam has four oil refineries.

Energy
Estimated figures for 2006 show that Assam has an installed electricity generating capacity of 622 MW. Electricity is mainly supplied by thermal power stations.

Manufacturing
Assam has established six industrial growth centres with another two planned at Balipara and Matia.

Agriculture
The economy of Assam is based on agriculture. The principal food crop is rice. Several cash crops are grown including jute, tea, cotton, oilseeds, sugarcane and potato. Fruits grown include citrus fruits, pineapple, mango, guava and banana.

Ever since wild tea bushes were first located in Upper Assam during the early 19th century, the tea industry has contributed a good share of the state economy . Assam leads the country's tea producing states, both in terms of quantity and labour force. There are around 850 teas estates in the state and Assam had the highest tea output in the country, producing about 55 per cent of the entire tea output of India, and 15 per cent of the world's tea production. It is estimated that the tea industry employs around 17 per cent of the workforce.

Forests cover some 22 per cent of Assam.

Cottage industries include hand loom, sericulture, cane and bamboo articles, carpentry and brass and metal crafts. Assam also produces several types of silk including Muga, a non-Mulberry silk only produced in Assam.

In August 2000 Assam was badly hit by widespread floods after heavy rains. This was expected to affect adversely the agricultural output of the state. In 2002 Assam was again hit by severe flooding. July 2004 saw extensive flooding in the region with nearly 470,000 hectares of agricultural land under water.

COMMUNICATIONS AND TRANSPORT

Airports
Airports are located Guwahati, Dibrugarh, Tezpur, Lakhimpur, Silchar and Jorhat.

Railways
Assam has a rail network consisting of 243,513 km of track. This includes a broad gauge section connecting Guwahati and Dibrugarh.

Roads
The road network covers over 69,000 km and includes 2,000 km of national highway and 2,000 km of state highway. The government is currently undertaking a road building scheme to connect the industrial areas.

Waterways
The river Brahmaputra is a major national waterway and carries passengers and goods. Some remote areas of Assam can only be reached by water. The internal waterway network connects Assam with Bangladesh and West Bengal, therefore accessing the ports of Chittagong, Kolkatta and Haldia.

EDUCATION

Literacy rates in 2005 were put at 71 per cent.

Assam has six universities, four engineering colleges aad four medical schools.

ENVIRONMENT

Assam has set up five National Parks and 15 wild life and bird sanctuaries to preserve its diverse wildlife, including the Manas Tiger Project.

BIHAR

Capital: Patna (Population estimate: 1.5 million)

Head of State: Shri DnyandeoYashwantrao Patil (Governor)

CONSTITUTION AND GOVERNMENT

Legislature
Number of seats in Legislative Council: 96
Number of seats in Legislative Assembly: 243

Chief Minister, Shri Nitish Kumar

Elections
Elections held in 2010 resulted in the Chief Minister led Janata Dal (United) party winning 206 seats.

LOCAL GOVERNMENT

For administrative purposes Bihar is divided into 38 districts. Before the creation of the new state Jharkhand, Bihar had 52 districts.

AREA AND POPULATION

Area
Bihar is one of the main states of the Indian Union and is bounded in the north by Nepal, in the east by West Bengal, in the west by Uttar Pradesh and Madhya Pradesh and in the south by Jharkhand. It covered an area of 173,877 sq. km until November 14 2000 when the new Indian state of Jharkhand came into existence made up of some 18 districts in the south of Bihar. Bihar now covers an area of 94,163 sq km. Bihar has a number of important rivers including the Ganga, Sone, Poonpoon, Kosi, Gandak, Ghaghara, Karmanasa and Falgu

Population
Figures from the 2001 census show the population of Bihar as 82,878,796, the third most populous state in India, with a density of 880 people per sq. km. Estimated figures for 2011 put the population at 103,804,000 giving a population density figure of 1,102 people per sq km.

Language
The principal language is Hindi.

EMPLOYMENT

Figures from the 2001 census show that Bihar had a workforce of 27,974,606, of which over 75 per cent were engaged in the agricultural sector.

BANKING AND FINANCE

Estimated figures for 2005 put per capita state domestic product at Rs 8,020.

MANUFACTURING, MINING AND SERVICES

Primary and Extractive Industries
Bihar has rich mineral resources - coal, mica, copper ore, iron, uranium, limestone, china clay, fire clay, pyrite, bauxite and kyanite. It has been the pioneer producer of important industrial minerals and is still the sole producer in India of coking coal, pyrites and uranium.

Energy
Bihar has several state owned power plants including Pataratu Thermal Power Station (840 MW), Barauni Thermal Power Station (320 MW), Muzaffarpur Thermal Power Station (220 M) and the Subarnrekha Power Station (130 MW).

Manufacturing
Bihar has steel plants at Bokaro and Jamshedpur, a sponge iron project at Chandil, a copper complex at Ghatsila, coal mining industries, heavy engineering, oil refining and a number of other manufacturing plants including cement plants, cable manufacturing, jute, cotton and sugar mills, distilleries, fertilizer and leather tanning plants. There are also large railway carriage plants at Muzaffarpur and Mokamah.

Agriculture
Principal food grain crops are paddy, wheat, maize and pulses. Main cash crops are sugarcane, potato, tobacco, oilseeds, onion, chillies, jute and mesta.

Forestry
Bihar has around 2.9 million hectares of forest, around 7 per cent of its area.

COMMUNICATIONS AND TRANSPORT

Airports
As well as landing strips in the larger districts, Bihar has airports at Gaya, Jamshedpur and Ranchi. There is an international airport at Patna.

Railways
Bihar has a relatively good railway network which connects Muzaffarpur, Samastipur, Barauni, Katihar and Muzaffarpur, Chapra and Siwan. Main junctions are located at Patna, Dhanbad, Gaya, Muzaffarpur, Katihar, Samastipur, Jamshedpur and Ranchi. The expansion of the network is hampered by the terrain although bridges over the rivers Ganga and Burhi Gandah are currently under construction.

Roads
The road network covers a total of nearly 30,000 km including national and state highways.

EDUCATION

Bihar has 13 universities and several colleges specializing in engineering, pharmacy, medicine, law and agriculture.

Figures for 2005 show the adult literacy rate for Bihar is 46 per cent, the lowest in India.

CHANDIGARH

Capital: Chandigarh (Population estimate: 900,110)

Head of State: Shri Shivraj V. Patil (Administrator)

CONSTITUTION AND GOVERNMENT

Chandigarh became a Union Territory on 1 November, 1966. It serves as the joint capital of both Punjab and Haryana states.

LEGAL SYSTEM

Chandigarh comes under the jurisdiction of the Punjab and Haryana High Court.

AREA AND POPULATION

Area
Chandigarh is bounded in the north and west by Punjab and in east and south by Haryana. As a result of the Punjab Reorganization Act 1966, the City of Chandrigah became a Union Territory. The city is also joint capital of the States of Punjab and Haryana. The territory covers an area of approximately 114 sq. km. nearly 80 per cent of which is urban.

Population
Figures from the 2001 census put the population at 900,914 up from the 1991 figure of 642,015. The gender ratio is 790 females per 1,000 males. Population density is 7,903 persons per sq. km., the second highest in the country. Estimated figures for 2007 put the population at 1,180,000. Figures for 2011 put the population at 27,704,236 giving a population density figure of 550 people per sq km.

The infant mortality rate is high - 37.69 per 1,000.

Language
The principal languages are Hindi, Punjabi and English.

EMPLOYMENT

Figures from the 2001 census show that Chandigarh had a workforce of 340,422.

BANKING AND FINANCE

Figures for 2005 estimate the per capita state domestic product to have been Rs 35,450.

Trade Organisations and Chambers of Commerce
PHD Chamber of Commerce, K. No. 107, Sector 18-A, Chandigarh - 160018, India. Tel: +91 781665, fax: +91 781665

Chandigarh Industrial & Tourism Development Corporation, SCO 121, Sector 17B, Chandigarh. Tel: +91 704761

MANUFACTURING, MINING AND SERVICES

Primary and Extractive Industries
Coal, coke, lime and limestone, cement, iron and steel are all exported from Chandigarh.

Energy
Chandigarh gets its electricity supply from neighbouring states.

Manufacturing
Large and medium scale units produce hosiery and knitting machine needles, wooltops, electric meters, cycle free wheels and rims, antibiotics, soft drinks and card boards. Recent figures show that there are over 145 factories operating in Chandigarh employing around 16,340 workers. As a result of the large industrial sector in comparison to the size of land available and small population, Chandigarh has the highest per capita income in India.

Agriculture
Wheat, maize and fodder are the major crops grown in Chandigarh. In recent years the total cropped area was 680 hectares. Recent figures show that Chandigarh produces around 450 tonnes of paddy, 300 tonnes of maize and 3,200 tonnes of wheat. Potatoes and onions are also grown. Forests cover 24.15 per cent of its area.

COMMUNICATIONS AND TRANSPORT

Roads
The Union Territory of Chandigarh has around 1,489 km of roads and is connected to the neighbouring states (Punjab and Haryana) by rail and air services.

HEALTH

Recent figures show that Chandigarh has 5 hospitals, 44 dispensaries and an estimated 560 doctors.

EDUCATION

Figures for 2005 put the adult literacy level at 84 per cent, one of the highest rates in India.

There are several universities and colleges in Chandigarh including Panjab University and the Post-Graduate Institute of Medical Research & Education. In 1996 almost 78,000 students were enrolled at Panjab University.

CHHATTISGARH

Capital: Riapur (Population estimate: 700,000)

Governor: Shri Shekhar Dutt

CONSTITUTION AND GOVERNMENT

Chhattisgarh, the 26th state of India, came into existence at midnight on 31 October 2000, having been created from districts formerly in Madhya Pradesh.

Chhattisgarh has 90 seats in the legislative assembly.

Chief Minister: Dr. Raman Singh

Recent Events
Maoist rebels have called for the creation of a communist state to be made up of tribal areas in the states of Andhra Pradesh, Maharashtra, Orissa, Bihar and Chhattisgarh. In recent years this insurgency has led to attacks on railways, electricity and power supplies and has resulted in the deaths of many civilians. In over 30 years of attacks thousands of people have been killed. In April 2010 rebels launched a major attack against paramilitary soldiers in the state, and around 76 were killed.

LEGAL SYSTEM

The High Court of Chhattisgarh is located at Bilaspur.

LOCAL GOVERNMENT

Chhattisgarh is divided into 16 districts, Raipur, Dhamtari, Mahasamund, Durg, Rajnandgaon, Kawardha, Bilaspur, Korba, Janjgir, Raigarh, Jashpur, Surguja, Koriya, Bastar, Dantewada and Kanker.

AREA AND POPULATION

Area
Chhattisgarh covers an area of some 135,194 sq km and was created out of Madhya Pradesh. It is bordered on the north by Uttar Pradesh, Jharkhand in the north east, Orissa in the east, Andhra Pradesh to the south and south east and Madhya Pradesh to the west and north west.

Population
According to recent census figures the population of Chhattisgarh is around 20,833,803, of which only about 18 per cent live in urban areas. Estimated figures for 2007 put the population at 23,050,000. Figures for 2011 put the population at 25,510,196 giving a population density figure of 189 people per sq km. The main languages are Hindi and Chhattisgarhi.

EMPLOYMENT

Figures from the 2001 census show that Chhattisgarh had a workforce of 9,679,871 of which over 75 per cent were engaged in the agricultural sector.

MANUFACTURING, MINING AND SERVICES

Primary and Extractive Industries
Mineral resources found in Chhattisgarh include limestone, iron ore (reserves of 2,000 million tonnes), copper-ore, rock phosphate, manganese ore, asbestos, mica, granite, coal (reserves of 29,000 tonnes), bauxite (reserves of 73 million tonnes) and dolomite (reserves of 525 million tonnes). Reserves of diamonds have been found in Deobogh in Raipur and extraction is expected to commence soon. Deposits of gold, garnet, rock crystal, beryl, amethyst, base metal and alexandrite also exist.

Energy
Chhattisgarh's large coal deposits means it generates nearly 50 per cent of the additional power required by the rest of the country.

Manufacturing
Main industries in the state include rice mills, cement plants, steel works including 133 steel re-rolling mills, iron works and food processing, chemical and plastics factories as well as factories producing construction material and forest based products.

Agriculture
Around 17,600,000 are employed in the agriculture sector and around 43 per cent of the state is cultivated. Chhattisgargh is referred to as the rice bowl of India and food grain is supplied to 600 rice mills. Apart from rice other crops grown include grains, groundnut, wheat, pulses and oilseeds. Fruit production includes mango, banana, pomegranate, papaya, guava, custard apple and tomato. Vegetables grown include cabbage, okra, cauliflower, leafy vegetables and potato.

Forestry
Chhattisgarh holds 12 per cent of all India's forest. Over 40 per cent of Chhattisgarh is covered by forest which include bamboo, saja and teak.

COMMUNICATIONS AND TRANSPORT

International Airports
Raipur airport is being enlarged to take larger aircraft and may be designated as an international airport. It currently services daily flights to New Delhi and Nagpur and flights to Mumbai and Bhubaneswar take place three times a week.

Railways
The rail network of Chhattisgargh covers 1,300 km. The capital, Raipur, is on the main route between Mumbai (formerly Bombay) and Kolkata (formerly Calcutta).

Roads
Chhattisgarh has a road network covering over 3,538,854 km and is on the main National Highway between Mumbai and Kolkata.

HEALTH

Infant mortality in Chhattisgargh is above the national average recording 84 deaths per 1,000 live births compared to an Indian average of 71 deaths per 1,000 births. Hospitals include a specialist heart hospital in Raipur. Chhattisgarh has six district hospitals and over 500 primary health centres.

EDUCATION

Recent figures show around 3 million children enrolled in pre-primary and primary schools, 860,000 in middle schools and 661,000 at secondary and higher schools. Chhattisgarh has four universities and several polytechnics and colleges.

Chhattisgarh had one of the highest literacy rates in India, but figures show that it has fallen from 65 per cent in 2001 to 57 per cent in 2005 (68 per cent for males and 47 per cent for females).

COMMUNICATIONS AND MEDIA

Telecommunications
Phone connections in Chhattisgarh are good and it was hoped that all villages would be connected to a phone system by 2003. There is also a high usage of mobile phones in the state.

DADRA AND NAGAR HAVELI

Capital: Silvassa (Population estimate: 22,000)

Head of State: Shri B.S. Bhalla, IAS (Administrator)

CONSTITUTION AND GOVERNMENT

Until 1954 Dadra and Nagar Haveli came under Portuguese rule and became a Union Territory in 1961.

Legislature
Dadra and Nagar Haveli is represented by one seat in the Lok Sabha and as a Union Territory has no legislature of its own.

LEGAL SYSTEM

Dadra and Nagar Haveli comes under the jurisdiction of the Mumbai High Court

LOCAL GOVERNMENT

For administrative purposes, the territory is under an administrator with Panchayats at village level. There are 70 villages in total. Before the construction of the Damanganga Irrigation Project there were 72 villages.

AREA AND POPULATION

Area
Dadar and Nagar Haveli was integrated with the Union of India on 11 August 1961 and is surrounded by Gujarat and Maharashtra. The territory consists of two areas, namely Dadra and Nagar Haveli. Forests cover 40 per cent of the total geographical area which is 491 sq. km. The territory is crossed by the major river Damanganga and its tributaries. Nagar Haveli is home to 69 villages including the capital Silvassam Dadra is 3 kms away separated by a piece of Gujarat and consists of two villages and the Dadra Islet.

Population
Figures from the 2001 census put the population at 220,451 and the population density at 449 persons per sq. km. The population is predominantly rural, 78 per cent are tribal people the main tribes being Dhodia, Kokna and Varli. Estimated figures for 2007 put the population at 286,000. Figures from 2011 showed that the population had reached 342,853 giving a population density of 698 people per sq km.

Language
The principal languages are Gujarati, Hindi, Bhilli, Marathi and Bildoli.

EMPLOYMENT

Figures from the 2001 census put the workforce at 114,122, nearly half of which are engaged in the agricultural sector.

MANUFACTURING, MINING AND SERVICES

Energy
Electricity in purchased from the Gujarat State Electricity Board. All villages have electric power.

Manufacturing
There are small industrial estates at Silvassa, Masat and Khadoli. There are also cottage, village and small scale industries in existence producing chemicals, pharmaceuticals, plastics, textiles and electronics.

Agriculture
Dadra and Nagar Haveli is a predominantly rural and tribal area. Its major crop is paddy (khariff). Nagali and other hill-millets are the second important crops of the area with sugarcane slowly developing. Fruits grown include banana and mango.

Tourism
Tourism is seen as a growth area and the territory is actively trying to market itself with reference to the various festivals held there.

COMMUNICATIONS AND TRANSPORT

Airports
The nearest airport is Mumbai.

Railways
The Mumbai to Ahmedabad railway links Vapi to the system, Vapi is 18 km. from the capital Silvassa.

Roads
Total road length is around 580 km, 68 villages are connected by the road system.

HEALTH

There is a hospital based in the capital Silvassa, the territory also has three dispensaries a mobile health unit and a community health centre.

EDUCATION

Figures from the 2001 census put the average adult literacy rate at 60 per cent. Recent figures show the territory has 215 schools and one college.

RELIGION

95 per cent of the population are Hindu.

DAMAN AND DIU

Capital: Daman (Population estimate: 36,000)

Head of State: Shri Bhupinder S. Bhalla (Administrator)

CONSTITUTION AND GOVERNMENT

Daman and Diu along with Goa were formerly a colony held by the Portuguese even after Indian independence. In 1961 it was integrated into India. It was part of the former union territory of Goa, Daman and Diu. After conferring statehood on Goa on 30 May 1987, Daman and Diu became a separate union territory.

LEGAL SYSTEM

Daman and Diu comes under the jurisdiction of the High Court in Mumbai.

AREA AND POPULATION

Area
Daman lies about 160 km north of Mumbai. It is bounded in the north by the Kolak river, in the east by Gujarat, by the Kalem river in the south and in the west by the Gulf of Cambay. Diu is an island, and is connected by a two bridges, one near Tad village the other at Ghoghla village in Gujarat. Daman covers an area of 72 sq. km. and Diu covers an area of 40 sq. km.

Population
Figures from the 2001 census put the population at 158,204 with a density of 1,411 persons per sq. km., the fifth highest in the country. Daman has a population of 113,949 and Diu, 44,110. Estimated figures for 2007 put the population at 230,000. Figures from 2011 show that the population had risen to 242,911 giving a population density of 618 people per sq km.

Language
The principal languages are Gujarati and Marathi. English is spoken and Portuguese by some of the older generation.

EMPLOYMENT

Figures from the 2001 census put the workforce at 72,791.

MANUFACTURING, MINING AND SERVICES

Energy
All villages in the territory have electricity.

Manufacturing
Industrial areas are located at Daman, Dabhel, Bhimpore and Kadaiya.

Agriculture
Important field and garden crops are paddy, ragi, bajra, jowar, groundnut, pulses and beans, wheat, banana, sapota, mango, coconut and sugarcane.

Fishing
Fishing is the largest industry.

COMMUNICATIONS AND TRANSPORT

Airports
There are airports at both Daman and Diu. There are daily flights between Diu and Mumbai.

Railways
Daman and Diu has no railway of its own, the nearest connection is at Vapi on the Mumbai-Delhi route.

Roads
The total road network in Daman is 191 km. and 78 km. in Diu.

EDUCATION

Figures from the 2005 census put the average adult literacy rate at 76 per cent.

DELHI

Capital: New Delhi (Population estimate: 13 million)

Head of State: Tejendra Khanna (Lieutenant Governor)

CONSTITUTION AND GOVERNMENT

Constitution
Under the constitution Delhi has had its own legislative assembly since 1991.

Recent Events
Delhi hosted the 2010 Commonwealth Games.

Legislature
Number of seats in the legislative assembly: 70

Chief Minister: Sheila Dikshit

Cabinet (as at May 2013)
Minister of Public Works, Welfare, Development: Shri Raj Kumar Chauhan
Minister of Health & Family Welfare, Higher Education, Training and Technical Education, Labour, Irrigation & Flood Control: Dr Ashok Kumar Walia
Minister of Education, Social Welfare, Women & Children, Languages: Prof. Kiran Walia
Minister of Urban Development, Revenue, Local Bodies, Gurudwara Election and Gurudwara Administration: Arvinder Singh Lovely
Minister of Power, Food & Civil Supplies, Industries, Employement : Haroon Yusuf
Minister of Transport, Law & Justice, Legislative Affairs, Elections: Ramakant Goswami

---

LEGAL SYSTEM

Delhi has its own High Court and District Courts.

Chief Justice, Justice D. Murugesan

LOCAL GOVERNMENT

For administrative purposed Delhi is divided into nine districts, 27 tehsils, 59 census towns, 165 villages and three statutory towns.

AREA AND POPULATION

Area
The National Capital Territory of Delhi comprises the cities of Old and New Delhi and the areas immediately surrounding them. Lying in the northern part of the country it is bordered by Haryana on all sides except in the east where it has borders with Uttar Pradesh. It covers an area of some 1,483 sq. km.

The climate is very hot in summer, cold in winter. The winter months are December - February.

Population
Figures from the 2001 census put the population at 13,850,507 giving a population density of 9,294 persons per sq. km, the highest in the country. Since then census the population density has risen to 9,340 per sq. km. The majority of the population live in urban areas. Estimated population figures for 2011 put the population at 16,753,235, giving a density of figure of 11,297 people per sq km.

Births, Marriages, Deaths
Figures from 2008 put the birth rate at 18.4 births per thousand population and the number of deaths at 4.8 per thousand population, that year the infant mortality rate was 35 per thousand births.

Language
The principal languages are Hindi, Punjabi, Urdu and English.

EMPLOYMENT

Figures from the 2001 census put the workforce at 4,545,234. In recent years the service sector of Delhi has become a major employer. A large proportion of English speakers has made Delhi an attractive place for many multinational companies. Key service industries include information technology, telecommunications, hotels, banking, media and tourism.

BANKING AND FINANCE

GDP/GNP, inflation, National Debt
The Gross State Domestic Product (GSDP) of Delhi (current prices) was put at Rs. 144,303 crore in the financial year 2007-08 rising to Rs.165,948 crore in 2008-09. (1 crore = 10 million)

The finance and business sectors are the biggest contributors followed by manufacturing.

MANUFACTURING, MINING AND SERVICES

Manufacturing
The modern city of Delhi is the largest commercial centre in northern India and also an important industrial centre. Since 1947 a large number of industrial concerns have been established. These include factories for the manufacture of razor blades, sports goods, radio and television parts, bicycles and parts, plastic and PVC goods including footwear, textiles, chemicals, fertilisers, medicines, hosiery, leather goods, soft drinks, hand and machine tools. There is also metal forging, casting, galvanising and electro-plating, printing and warehousing. Delhi has produced a Millennium Industrial Policy to attract high-tech industries to the capital, such as telecommunications and software manufacturers. These are seen as non-polluting industries and employers of a skilled labour force. Recent figures show that Delhi has 6,865 factories.

Agriculture
The cultivated area is fast diminishing due to urbanisation of rural areas and increased housing demand. Wheat and maize are major food crops although emphasis is shifting from food grains to fruit and vegetables, dairy and poultry products which offer better financial return. Figures for 2008-09 showed that Delhi produced 31,000 tonnes of rice and 74,000 tonnes of wheat.

COMMUNICATIONS AND TRANSPORT

International Airports
Indira Gandhi International, which has both international and domestic flights.

Other airports include Safdarjung and Palam.

Railways
Delhi has a comprehensive rail network including three major junctions at Delhi, New Delhi and Nizamuddin.
Railway Enquiries: +91 (0)11 331 3535, URL: http://www.indianrailway.com
Road Enquiries: +91 (0)11 252 3145

Because Delhi has a high population and is a centre for commerce its roads are often crowded. Recent figures show that there are more than 4,809,010 registered vehicles on the road. To combat the congestion a Mass Rapid Transit System is being built phase one is completed and phase two is expected to be ready in time for the 2010 Commonwealth Games.

Roads
Delhi has a comprehensive road system, and has invested in subways and flyovers in an effort to reduce congestion. Recent figures show that around 4.8 million vehicles are registered in Delhi.

HEALTH

Delhi has 65 General Hospitals with over 19,000 beds.

EDUCATION

Figures for 2005 put the literacy rate at 80 per cent. Figures for the year 2004-05, showed that there were 2,515 primary school, 635 middle schools, 504 secondary schools and 1,208 senior secondary schools in Delhi. Tertiary education consists of 165 colleges, including five medical colleges and eight engineering colleges, Delhi also has six universities and nine institutions with university status.

GOA

Capital: Panaji (Population estimate: 95,000)

Head of State: Shri. B.V. Wanchoo (Governor)

CONSTITUTION AND GOVERNMENT

Constitution
Previously in the hands of the Portuguese, Goa was liberated on 19 December 1961 and was made a composite union territory with Daman and Diu. On 30 May 1987 Goa was conferred statehood and Daman and Diu made a separate union territory.

Legislature
Number of seats in legislative assembly: 40

Chief Minister: Shri. Manohar Parrikar

LEGAL SYSTEM

Goa comes under the jurisdiction of the Panaji Bench of the Mumbai High Court.

LOCAL GOVERNMENT

For administrative purposes Goa is divided into two districts, North Goa and South Goa.

AREA AND POPULATION

Area
Goa is situated on the western coast of the Indian Peninsula. The Terekhol river separates it from Maharashtra in the North. The north district of Karnataka lies to the south, the Western Ghats to its east and the Arabian Sea to its west. Goa covers an area of approximately 3,702 sq. km.

Population
The census taken in 2001 gave the population of Goa as 1,347,668 with a density of 363 people per sq. km. Approximately 60 per cent live in rural areas. Figures for 2011 put the population at 1,457,723 giving a population density of 394 people per sq km.

Language
The principal languages are Konkani and Marathi. Hindi, English and Portuguese are also spoken.

Births, Marriages, Deaths
Figures from the nic Statistical Year Book 2011 put the birth rate of Goa in 2008 as 13.6 per 1,000 population, the lowest of all the Indian states. The death rate that year was 6.6 per 1,000 population, the infant mortality rate in 2008 was 10 per 1,000 births.

EMPLOYMENT

Figures form the 2001 census put the workforce at 522,855.

BANKING AND FINANCE

Estimated figures for 2005 put per capita state domestic product at Rs 24,797, one of the highest in the country.

MANUFACTURING, MINING AND SERVICES

Primary and Extractive Industries
Mineral products are ferromanganese, bauxite and iron ore, which make a substantial contribution to the economy of the state via export.

Manufacturing
Goa has 16 industrial estates witharound 670 factories and an electronic city. Recent figures estimate there to be over 5,900 industrial units employing around 58,400 people.

Tourism
Goa has long been established as a tourist destination and has an average of 1.2 million visitors per year. It is estimated that some 12 per cent of foreign visitors to India travel to Goa.

Agriculture
Goa is a mainly agricultural state. Rice is the principal food crop and recent figures put annual production at 123,000 tonnes. Pulses, ragi and other food crops are also grown. The main cash crops are coconut, with around 121 million nuts produced annually, cashew nut, sugarcane, with around 64,000 tonnes produced annually, and fruits like pineapple, mango and banana.

The average yield for the main crops per hectare is: cashew nuts, 310 kg and rice, 3,000 kg.

Around 40 per cent of the land is cultivated. Approximately 46,400 hectares are paddy fields. 1,400 hectares are used for sugarcane. Approximately 35 per cent of the land is forested.

INDIA

Fishing
The fishing industry is an important contributor to the economy particularly fishing for prawns. Goa accounts for 40 per cent of India's total prawn exports, worth around US$15 million per year. In order to preserve the breeding grounds of prawns and fish, deep sea fishing is banned each year for 70 days between May and July. Recently the government extended this period into August.

COMMUNICATIONS AND TRANSPORT

Airports
There is one airport, Dabolim Airport, served by Indian Airlines with flights to Mumbai, Bangalore, Cochin, Delhi, Chennai, Mangalore and Trivandrum. Private airlines also provide flights to Delhi and Mumbai.

Railways
There are railway links to Mumbai, Mangalore and Thiruvananthapuram.

Roads
The road network covers a total of 1,271 km, of which 224 km is National Highway.

Ports and Harbours
The main port of Goa is Mormugao which handles cargo vessels. There are also smaller ports located at Panaji, Tiracol, Talpona and Chapora Betul.

HEALTH

Goa has a total of 14 hospitals as well as 123 private hospitals and clinics.

EDUCATION

The official figures put the 1991 literacy rate at 75.51 per cent. The gender analysis is 83.43 per cent for males, 67.09 per cent for females. The urban rate is higher than the rural rate: 80.10 per cent compared to 72.31 per cent. Figures from the 2001 census showed that the literacy rate had risen to 82 per cent, although figures for 2005 showed that the rate had fallen to 75 per cent.

Recent figures show that Goa had 1,241 primary schools, 4,325 middle schools, 363 secondary schools, 81 higher secondary schools and 45 colleges and universities.

RELIGION

The main religions in Goa are Hinduism and Christianity (predominantly Catholicism).

ENVIRONMENT

Goa has several wildlife sanctuaries.

GUJARAT

Capital: Gandhinagar (Population estimate: 195,000)

Head of State: Dr. Kamla Beniwal (Governor)

CONSTITUTION AND GOVERNMENT

Constitution
Gujarat became a state on 1st May 1960.

Legislature
Number of seats in Legislative Assembly: 182

Chief Minister: Narendra Modi

LEGAL SYSTEM

Gujarat has its own High Court.

LOCAL GOVERNMENT

For administrative purposes Gujarat is divided into 26 districts.

AREA AND POPULATION

Area
Established on 1 May 1960, following the division of the bilingual Bombay State, Gujarat comprises the former States of Saurashtra and Kutch and the Gujarati-speaking area in the north of the former Bombay State.

It is situated on the west coast of India. The state is bounded by the Arabian Sea in the west, Pakistan and Rajasthan in the north and east, Madhya Pradesh in the south-east and Maharashtra in the south. It covers an area of approximately 196,024 sq. km.

On the morning of 26 January 2001, Gujarat was hit by a devastating earthquake, measuring 6.9 on the Richter scale. The epicentre was the town of Bhuj. In total 30,000 people lost their lives.

Population
According to the census taken in 2001 the population of Gujarat was 50,671,017 (a density of 258 per sq. km.). The figure included estimates for those districts affected by the earthquake. Estimated figures for 2007 put the population at 56,085,000. Figures from the 2011 census put the population at 60,383,628, giving a population density of 308 people per sq km. The principal language is Gujarati.

Births, Marriages, Deaths
Figures for 2008 put the birth rate at 22.6 per 1,000 population and the death rate at 6.9 per 1,000 population, that year the infant mortality rate was recoded at 50 per 1,000 births.

EMPLOYMENT

Figures from the 2001 census put the workforce of Gujarat at 21,255,521 of which around 50 per cent worked in the agricultural sector.

BANKING AND FINANCE

National State Domestic Product/NSDP for 2004-05 was estimated at 107,033 crore Rupees, up from 101,794 crore Rupees in the previous year. Figures are at factor cost at 1993-94 prices. (Crore = ten million), Per capita state domestic product in 2005 was put at Rs 16,875. Estimated figures for NSDP in 2009-10 was estimated at Rs. 331,364 crore, figures at factor cost at 2004-05 prices.

MANUFACTURING, MINING AND SERVICES

Primary and Extractive Industries
Figures for 2007 show that around 15,500 people are employed in the mining sector. Minerals mined include limestone and lignite.

Energy
In January 2007 the controversial Sardar Sarovar dam on the Narmada river was inaugurated. This will generate 1450 MW of hydro-electricity for the region. Water from the dam is also expected to irrigate around two million hectares of land.

Nearly all villages in Gujarat have electricity.

Manufacturing
Gujarat is dominant in the textiles industry and is recognised as one of the leading industrialised states in the country. Recent figures show that there were nearly 21,000 working factories and over 230,000 small industrial units in operation. The industry sector has recently diversified into the manufacture of chemicals, fertilizer, petrochemical and electronics. Large industrial estates are located at Jhagadia, Savli and Vagra. A further industrial estate is being constructed at Dahej.

Agriculture
Gujarat ranks first in the country in the production of tobacco, cotton and groundnut which have found good markets and provide a foundation for important industries like textiles, oil and soap. Cash crops grown include rice and wheat.

Crop production for 2008-09 included over 1.3 million tonnes of rice, 2.5 million tonnes of wheat, 200,000 tonnes of Jower, 961,000 tonnes of Bajara, 2.6 million tonnes of groundnut, 8.7 million bales of cotton and 15.5 million tonnes of sugar cane.

Recent figures show that over 9.5 per cent of Gujarat is forest including teak.

COMMUNICATIONS AND TRANSPORT

International Airports
The main airport for Gujarat is Ahmadabad which has daily flights to Mumbai and Delhi as well as international destinations. Other airports include Bhavnagar, Bhuj, Jamnagar, Kandla, Keshod, Porbandar, Rajkot, Surat and Vadidara.

Railways
As of 2002 Gujarat had over 5,300 km of railway system.

Roads
Gujarat's road system covers a total of 74,031 km. 8,622,000 vehicles were registered in 2006

Ports and Harbours
The main port of Gujarat is Kandla which is currently undergoing expansion to include ten deep water berths. There are more than 30 other ports in the state.

EDUCATION

Figures for 2005 put the literacy rate at 66 per cent, 75 per cent for males and 56 per cent for females.

RELIGION

In recent years religious tension between the Muslim and Hindu communities has increased in Gujarat. In 2002, 56,000 people were living in refugee camps having fled the violence following Hindus returning from the disputed holy site in Ayodhya in Uttar Pradesh. Hindus believe the site is the birthplace of the Lord Rama; however in the sixteenth century a mosque was built on the site which was destroyed 1992, leading to rioting between Hindus and Muslims. In 2002 work being done on a shrine to Lord Rama led to a fresh outbreak of violence.

COMMUNICATIONS AND MEDIA

Recent figures show that Gujarat has around 9,000 post offices, 2,000 telegraph offices and 1.5 million telephone connections. As of 2003 over 1,045,000 mobile phones were in use in Gujarat.

HARYANA

Capital: Chandigarh (Population estimate: 900,100)

Head of State: Shri Jagannath Pahadia (Governor)

CONSTITUTION AND GOVERNMENT

Legislature
Number of seats in Legislative Assembly: 90. The most recent elections took place in 2009.

In an effort to curb population growth, Haryana introduced a scheme in 1994 whereby people with more than two children would not be able to vote in local elections. This was abandoned in 2006 as it was unworkable.

Chief Minister: Shri Bhupinder Singh Hooda

Government portal: http://www.haryana.gov.in/

LEGAL SYSTEM

Haryana comes under the jurisdiction of the Punjab and Haryana High Court.

LOCAL GOVERNMENT

Haryana is divided into 19 districts with 94 towns and over 6,700 villages.

AREA AND POPULATION

Area
Under the Punjab Reorganization Act 1966, the State was formed on 1 November 1966 out of the Hindi-speaking areas of Punjab. It is bounded by Uttar Pradesh in the east, Punjab in the west, Himachal Pradesh in the north and Rajasthan in the south; the Union Territory of Delhi juts into Haryana. The area of the state is 44,212 sq. km, approximately 1.4 per cent of the total area of India.

Population
Population figures from the 2001 census put the population at 21,144,564, up from 16,750,000 in 1991. This gives a population density figure for 2001 of 477 people per sq. km. Estimated figures for 2004 put the population at 22,513,000 and 23,885,000 in 2007. Figures from the 2011 census put the population figure at 25,353,081 giving a population density of 573 people per sq km. The principal language is Hindi.

Births, Marriages, Deaths
Figures from nic, Statistical Year Book of India show that in 2008 Haryana recorded a birth rate of 23 births per 1,000 population and 6.9 death per 1,000 population, that year the infant mortality rate was 54 per 1,000 births.

EMPLOYMENT

Figures from the 2001 census put the workforce at 8,377,466. Recent figures estimated that over 80 per cent of the population as a whole is engaged in agriculture.

BANKING AND FINANCE

Estimated figures for 2005 put Domestic State Product per capita at Rs 16,870.

MANUFACTURING, MINING AND SERVICES

Energy
In 1970 Haryana became the first state in India to provide electricity to all rural locations.

Manufacturing
The state has a very sound industrial base. Haryana produces four-fifths of passenger cars, half the tractors, two thirds of motor cycles, a quarter of all bicycles and 50 per cent of refrigerators manufactured in the country. Scientific instruments and stoves also made in Haryana. Panipat is famous for its carpet weaving. Figures for 2000 show that there were over 80,000 industrial units in operation.

Haryana is fast becoming a centre for the IT industry. A Cyber City and a Cyber Park have been established in Gurgaon and the state government provides incentives to encourage IT companies to set up in the state. Recent figures show that software exports account for 45 per cent of the states total exports.

Figures from 2005 show that Haryana had over 9,240 working factories employing 575,000 workers

Tourism
Haryana has a well established tourist industry and has over six million visitors a year.

Agriculture
Haryana is primarily an agricultural state. About 75 per cent of its people depend on agriculture for their livelihood. Principal cash crops are cotton, sugar cane, potatoes and oilseeds, other major crops include rice, wheat, barley and pulses, with new crops being introduced such as sunflowers, soybean, fruits and vegetables. Four Food Parks have been established in the state to develop agro and food based industries. Haryana has Asia's biggest agricultural university - the Chaudry Charan Singh Haryana Agricultural University at Hisar. Haryana produces around 11 million tonnes of food grain annually, it meets it own needs and contributes 45 lakh tonnes to the Indian Central Pool each year. Figures for 2008-09 show that Haryana's agricultural production included 3,298,000 tonnes of rice, 1,079,000 tonnes of bajra, 10,808,000 tonnes of wheat, 802,000 tonnes of rapeseed and mustard and 1,814,000 tonnes of cotton. Livestock is very important in the agriculture sector of Haryana and there are around 9.8 million livestock mainly buffalo and dairy cows.

COMMUNICATIONS AND TRANSPORT

Airports
Haryana has five small airports at Bhiwani, Hisar, Karnal, Narnaul and Pinjore.

Railways
Haryana is crossed by lines from Delhi to Agra, Amritsar, Chandigargh, Jammu, Ajmer and Ferozepur with stations at Panipat, Ambala and Jakhal.

Roads
There are approximately 29,500 km of metalled roads. All villages in the state have road connections. Figures for 2006 show that Haryana had 3,087,000 registered figures on the road.

HEALTH

Figures for 2004 show that there were 3,220 health institutions. All villages have safe drinking water.

EDUCATION

In 2003-04 there were 11,400 primary schools, 2,171 middle schools, 5,120 high and senior secondary schools, 257 colleges and four universities, including the Chaudhry Charan Singh Haryana Agricultural University at Hisar. Figures from 2005 show that the adult literacy rate was 62 per cent.

Due to the increase of IT companies being based in the state, the setting up of an Indian Institute of Information Technology has been proposed which would train the skilled workforce required.

HIMACHAL PRADESH

Capital: Shimla (Population estimate, 2011: 813,384)

Head of State: Smt. Urmila Singh (Governor)

CONSTITUTION AND GOVERNMENT

Legislature
Number of seats in Legislative Assembly: 68. Nationally Himachal Pradesh is represented in the Lok Sabha by four seats and the Rajya Sabha by three seats.

Chief Minister: Virbhadra Singh

Government portal, URL: http://himachalrajbhavan.nic.in/

LEGAL SYSTEM

Himachal Pradesh has its own High Court.

LOCAL GOVERNMENT

Himachal Pradesh is divided into 12 districts, Bilaspur, Chamba, Hamirpur, Kangra, Kinnaur, Kullu, Lahaul and Spiti, Mandi, Shimla, Sirmaur, Solan and Una.

AREA AND POPULATION

Area
Himachal Pradesh became a Union Territory in 1949. Under the Punjab Reorganization Act 1966, the Hill areas of Punjab were transferred to Himachal Pradesh, doubling its size and it became state in 1971. It is bordered by Jammu and Kashmir in the north, Punjab in the west and south-west, Haryana in the south, Uttar Pradesh in the south-east and Tibet in the east. It covers an area of approximately 55,673 sq. km.

Population
Figures from the 2001 census show the population as 6,077,900, up from the figure from the 1991 census of 5,170,877. Estimated figures for 2007 put the population at 6,550,000. The majority of the population live in rural areas and the density is 109 people per sq. km. Figures from the 2011 census put the population at 6,856,509 giving a population density at 123 people per sq km. The principal languages are Hindi and Pahari.

Births, Marriages, Deaths
Figures from The Statistical Year Book of India 2011, show that in 2008 the birth rate was put at 21.8 births per 1,000 population and 5.2 deaths per 1,000 population, that year the infant mortality rate was put at 32 per 1,000 births.

EMPLOYMENT

Figures from the 2001 census put the work force at 2,992,461. Nearly 70 per cent of the working population are directly employed in the agricultural sector.

BANKING AND FINANCE

The per capita state domestic product in 2005 was estimated to be 13,470 rupees.

MANUFACTURING, MINING AND SERVICES

Primary and Extractive Industries
Important minerals of the state are rock salt, gypsum, limestone, baryte, silca, dolomite and pyrite. Himachal Pradesh has three cement plants.

Energy
In 2003, the largest hydropower plant in India came online. The plant, situated in Himachal Pradesh, can generate up to 1,500 MW of power and, as well as providing electricity to Himachal Pradesh, will also serve Rajasthan, Delhi, Haryana and Punjab.

Manufacturing
The ready availability of electrical power has boosted the development of the industrial sector in Himachal Pradesh in recent years and the sector now contributes around 15 per cent of state domestic product. Manufacturing in Himachal Pradesh is closely related to the agricultural sector, producing such goods as fruit processing, sericulture and wool production and a packaging plant for produce. The manufacture of electronic goods is a growth area. Cottage industries including handloom and handicrafts also play an important part in the economy.

Recent figures show that Himachal Pradesh now has 10 industrial estates, over 30 industrial areas and an export promotion park. Annual turnover of the industrial sector is in the region of R4,500 crore (1 crore = 10 million). To attract industry an industrial policy was set up in 2004 whereby incentive packages are offered to entrepreneurs setting up in the state.

The government is also keen to encourage the growth of the information technology industry within the state and the setting up of an Information Technology Park has been proposed.

Agriculture
The agriculture sector provides employment for the majority of the population, nearly 70 of the working population and contributes over 22 per cent of state domestic product. Himachal Pradesh produces fruit, vegetables, foodgrains and tea. Mushroom production has recently been introduced. A programme of diversification has been introduced in order to produce out of season vegetables including potato, ginger, oilseeds, pulses and soya bean and the number of hectares dedicated to vegetable production has increased. Many fruits are grown in the state including plum, cherry, pear, peach, citrus fruits, mango, guava and litchi. Figures from 2008-09 show that the state produced 118,000 tonnes of rice, 677,000 tonnes of maize, 547,000 tonnes of wheat531,000 tonnes of sugar cane.

Over 60 per cent of the state is covered by forest.

COMMUNICATIONS AND TRANSPORT

Airports
Himachal Pradesh has three airports at Kangra, Kullu Valley and Jubbarhatti.

Railways
The current railway system connects Pathankot with Joginder Nagar and Kalka to Shimla, some expansion of the system is planned.

Roads
Himachal Pradesh has over 23,000 km of roads. There are eight National Highways crossing the state totaling 1,235 km. In 2008 there were 334,000 registered vehicles on the road.

HEALTH

Recent figures show that Himachal Pradesh has over 630 hospitals and clinics.

EDUCATION

In 1997-98 there were 10,484 primary schools, 1,056 middle schools and 1,339 high schools and higher secondary schools. There are also three universities and 64 colleges, including two medical schools. The literacy rate in 2005 was estimated to be 72 per cent (79 per cent for males and 65 per cent for females).

COMMUNICATIONS AND MEDIA

Telecommunications
Recent figures show that the state has around 145,505 telephones.

JAMMU AND KASHMIR

Capital: Srinagar (Summer, May-Oct.) (Population estimate, 2011: 1,269,751); Jammu (Winter, Nov.-April) (Population estimate, 2011: 503,000)

Head of State: N.N. Vohra (Governor)

CONSTITUTION AND GOVERNMENT

In 1947 both India and Pakistan became independent of the United Kingdom. Under the partition plan Kashmir was able to decide whether to join India or Pakistan. Originally the Maharaja, Hari Singh, wished to remain independent, but later ceded the territory to India. Ever since then the territory has been disputed between the two countries, India believes that it has the right to administer Kashmir under the agreement with the Maharaja. Pakistan believes that Kashmir should belong to it as the majority of the population are Muslim.

Recent Events

In November 2000 India declared a unilateral ceasefire, which was due to end in May 2001. There were hopes that this would be extended, although the ceasefire had not been recognised by all groups. In July 2001 the Indian prime minister, Atal Behari Vajpayee met with the president of Pakistan, Pervez Musharraf, but the meeting failed to bring an agreement on Kashmir. Further violence over Kashmir resulted in India imposing sanctions against Pakistan in December 2001, followed by Pakistan imposing sanctions on India. This action was followed by both sides sending troops to the border area. By May 2002 violence had escalated to the point where the Indian prime minister, Mr Vajpayee, warned his troops that the time for a decisive fight was at hand. Pakistan responded to this by testing Ghauri missiles, capable of carrying nuclear warheads. In June 2002 Britain and the USA engaged in diplomatic talks with both sides in an effort to stop war breaking out, and in October India announced it was withdrawing its troops from the border. Early 2003 saw relations failing again when tit for tat expulsions of diplomats began. At the beginning of 2004 talks took place between the government and some of the Kashmiri separatists. In November 2004 India began withdrawing some of her troops from Kashmir. Both sides agreed to a ceasefire and to try and find a solution through negotiation. Pakistan would like to see a referendum of Kashmiri's to decide their future; India feels a referendum is unnecessary. Internationally the dispute is of concern as both countries have nuclear capabilities. Talks between India and Pakistan are still ongoing.

Indian Kashmir has a population of nine million. Pakistani administered Kashmir, now known as Azad or Free Kashmir, has a population of around three million.

The UN which monitors the Line of Control has been a presence in the area since 1949.

On April 7 2005 bus services between Srinigar in Indian Kashmir and Muzaffarabad in Pakistan administered Kashmir began for the first time in 60 years.

On the 8th October 2005, an earthquake hit the Kashmir region. Its epicenter was in Pakistan administered Kashmir and around 1,000 people died in Indian Kashmir. Rescue efforts were hampered by the terrain and the Kashmiri winter.

The Indian-administered area of Kashmir was put under federal rule in July 2008 after the state government collapsed following rows over a land transfer deal for a Hindu shrine. Elections were held in November but were marred by violence. Results were as follows: JKNC 28; PDP 21; INC 17; BJP 11; Others 10.

In September 2011, three Pakistani soldiers were killed by Indian forces who fired across the line of control. The Indian soldiers accused the Pakistani soldiers of firing first.

In August 2012, Omar Abdullah the Chief Minister said that the security situation was not conducsive yet to revoke the Armed Forces Special Powers Act.

In September 2012, despite protests from separatists newly appointed Indian President Pranab Mukherjee made a vist to Jammu and Kashmir, the visit passed without serious incident.

Legislature
Number of seats in Legislative Council: 36
Number of seats in Legislative Assembly: 87

Chief Minister: Omar Abdullah

Office of the Governor, URL: http://jkrajbhawan.nic.in/His%20Excellency/present1.htm

LEGAL SYSTEM

Jammu and Kashmir comes under the jurisdiction of the Jammu, Kashmir and Ladakh High Court.

LOCAL GOVERNMENT

Jammu and Kashmir is divided into 14 districts. The headquarters of these districts are based in the cities and towns of Jammu, Srinagar, Anantnag, Pulwama, Budgam, Baramulla, Kupwara, Udhampur, Kathua, Rajouri, Poonch, Doda, Leh and Kargil.

AREA AND POPULATION

Area
Jammu and Kashmir is situated between 32° 17' and 36° 58' north latitude and 73° 26' and 83° 30' east longitude. Its boundaries extend to Turkmenistan in the north, Tibet in the east, Punjab in the south and Pakistan in the west and it covers an area of 222,236 sq. km. (including areas occupied by China and Pakistan). The climate varies greatly in the state form tropical in Jammu to almost arctic conditions in Ladakh, the Himalayas form part of the state and the highest point is 28,250 above sea level. Today the state is divided three ways. In the west the population is predominantly Muslim and this area is under Pakistan control and calls itself Free Kashmir. In the east the population is predominantly Buddhist and is under Chinese control. The rest of Kashmir and Jammu is under Indian control and here the population is predominantly Hindu.

To view a map of the area, please consult:
http://www.un.org/Depts/Cartographic/map/profile/kashmir.pdf

Population
The 2001 census gave the population as 10,143,700 (excluding occupied areas). Figures from the 2011 census put the population at 12,548,926, giving a population density of 124 people per sq km. The principal languages are Urdu, Kashmiri, Dogri, Pahari, Balti, Ladakhi, Punjabi, Hindi, Gujri, and Dadri.

Births, Marriages, Deaths
Figures for 2008 put the birth rate at 18.8 births per 1,000 population and the death rate at 5.8 per 1,000 population. That year the infant mortality rate was put at 49 per 1,000 births.

EMPLOYMENT

Figures from the 2001 census put the workforce at 3,753,815, nearly 50 per cent of whom are engaged in the agricultural sector.

MANUFACTURING, MINING AND SERVICES

Primary and Extractive Industries
Jammu and Kashmir has mines producing, limestone, coal and gypsum.

Manufacturing
Handicrafts, being the traditional industry of the state, receive top priority in view of their large employment potential and also the demand for hand-crafted goods both within and outside the country. Handicraft production mainly covers papier-maché, wood carving, carpets and shawl making (pashminas). The number of people using handlooms has been steadily increasing in recent years. Figures for 2001 show that handicraft production was worth Rs 704 crore (1 crore = 10 million). An export development park has opened at Kartholi. Food processing is becoming an important part of the manufacturing economy especially.

Agriculture
About 80 per cent of the population of the state depends on agriculture. Paddy, wheat and maize are the major crops although barley, *bajra* and *jowar* are cultivated in some parts and fruit production is on the increase. The state is an Agri Export Zone for apples and walnuts. Figures for the year 2008-09 show that amongst the states agricultural production was 563,000 tonnes of rice, 633,000 tonnes of maize and 484,000 tonnes of wheat.

COMMUNICATIONS AND TRANSPORT

Airports
There are three airports providing flights to other parts of India, they are at Jammu, Leh, and Srinagar.

Railways
A railway line exists to Jammu, but plans are underway to extend the network to Udhampur and Srinagar.

Roads
There are over 13,500 km of roads in the state. In 1999 a four times a week bus service started between India and Pakistan, the first such service since Partition. The service runs between Delhi and Lahore, along the Grand Trunk Road. In April 2005 a service began between Srinagar in Indian controlled Kashmir and Muzaffarabad in Pakistani administered Kashmir. In 2006 an estimated 524,000 registered vehicles were on the road.

HEALTH

Recent figures show that there are 100 hospitals, over 340 primary health care centres and more than 3,300 medical sub centres. These provide more that 10,000 beds.

INDIA

EDUCATION

Jammu and Kashmir has around 15,000 schools catering for around 1.5 million students. There are also 32 colleges as well as four medical colleges, two engineering colleges and four polytechnics and nearly 40 industrial training institutes. There are three universities one in Jammu and two in Kashmir.

RELIGION

The majority of the population is Muslim.

JHARKHAND

The state came into existence at midnight on 14 November 2000 and is India's 28th state.

Capital: Ranchi (Population estimate: 850,000)

Governor: Dr. Syed Ahmad

CONSTITUTION AND GOVERNMENT

Legislature
Number of seats in the legislative assembly: 82.

Chief Minister: vacant

Recent Events
Jharkhand is at the centre of what is often called the Red Corridor, an area where Maoist rebels have a heavy presence, in 2010 several state politicians received death threats from rebels if they didn't oppose the government's military offensive against the guerrillas.

Office of the Governor, URL: http://jharkhand.nic.in/governor.htm
Government portal, URL: http://jharkhand.gov.in/

LEGAL SYSTEM

Jharkhand has its own High Court.

LOCAL GOVERNMENT

Jharkhand is divided into 24 districts.

AREA AND POPULATION

Area
The state of Jharkhand came into existence at midnight on 14 November 2000 and was created from 18 districts of Bihar. It has an area of 74,677 sq km. and is bordered by Bihar, Madhya Pradesh, Orissa and West Bengal. Tribes in Jharkhand had been campaigning for their own state for decades.

Population
The population at the 2001 census was put at 26,945,829 people with a density of 274 per sq km. Estimated figures for 2007 put the population at 29,895,000. Figures from the 2011 census put the population at 32,966,238 giving a population density of 414 people per sq km. Languages spoken in Jharkhand include Hindi, Urdu, Karmali, Malto, Nagpuria, Sadri, Khortha, Kurukh, Mundari and Santhali

Births, Marriages Deaths
Figures from 2008 put the birth rate at 25.8 per 1,000 population and the death rate at 7.1 per 1,000 population. That year the infant mortality rate was put at 46 per1,000 births.

EMPLOYMENT

Figures from the 2001 census put the workforce at 10,109,03. Nearly 70 per cent of the workforce is engaged in the agricultural sector.

BANKING AND FINANCE

Prior to 2000, 63 per cent of the state of Bihar's revenue was made up of earnings from what is now Jharkhand. Estimated figures for the year 2004-05 put the state domestic product per capita at Rs 8,025.

MANUFACTURING, MINING AND SERVICES

Primary and Extractive Industries
Jharkhand is rich in natural minerals including coal, bauxite, lime stone, pyrite, quartz, china clay, fire clay, gold, silver and graphite. Jharkhand ranks first in the country for production of coal, iron ore, copper ores, micca, kainite, uranium and asbestos

Manufacturing
Jharkhand is home to the two largest steel plants in India, the privately owned Tata Iron and Steel Company in Jamshedpur and a public sector plant in Bokaro. Jharkhand has around 5,415 factories altogether.

Agriculture
Figures for the year 2008-09 showed thta Jharkhand produced 3,420,000 tonnes of rice, 304,000 tonnes of maize, 154,000 tonnes of barley, 237,000 tonnes of pulses, and 349,000 tonnes of sugar cane.

COMMUNICATIONS AND TRANSPORT

Airports
The airport at Ranchi has connections to Delhi, Mumbai and Patna. There are airstrips at Jamshedpur, Bokaro, Deoghar, Daltonganj, Noamundi, Giridih and Hazaribagh.

Railways
Jharkhand has a well developed rail network. Main stations include Ranchi, Bokaro, Jamshedpur and Dhanbad.

Roads
The road system of Jharkhand covers over 4,300 km., of which 1,600 km is National Highway. Figures for 2006 estimated the number of registered vehicles on the road as 1,505,000.

HEALTH

Jharkhand has three hospitals and over 500 health centres.

EDUCATION

According to figures from the 2001 census, Jahrkhand had among the worst literacy rates in India at 54.1 per cent. Estimated figures for 2005 put the literacy rate at 52 per cent, 64 per cent for males and 40 per cent for women.

Jharkhand has five universities and 18 colleges.

KARNATAKA

Capital: Bangalore (Population estimate: 4.3 million)

Head of State: Shri H.R. Bhardwaj (Governor)

CONSTITUTION AND GOVERNMENT

Legislature
Number of seats in Legislative Council: 75
Number of seats in Legislative Assembly: 224

Chief Minister: Shri. K. Siddaramaiah

Recent Events
In January 2006 Chief Minister Dharam Singh resigned from his post. Political upheaval was triggered when the Janata Dal (Secular) party, split from the coalition. H.D. Kumaraswamy who led the split of the Janara Dal was asked by the governor to form a new government.

Governor's Office, URL: http://:www.kar.nic.in/kla/governor.htm
Government portal, URL: http://www.karnataka.gov.in/Pages/Default.aspx

LEGAL SYSTEM

There are, besides the High Court, 74 Criminal and 45 Civil Courts.

LOCAL GOVERNMENT

For administrative purposes Karnataka is divided into 27 districts.

AREA AND POPULATION

Area
The State of Karnataka, comprising the former Princely State of Mysore, more than doubled in size in 1956 by the addition of the Kannada-speaking area of Bombay, Hyderabad, Madras and Coorg. It was originally known as Mysore State and became known as Karnataka in 1973. It lies to the south of Goa and Maharashtra, to the west of Andhra Pradesh, to the north-west of Tamil Nadu and to the north of Kerala. It has a sea coast of nearly 260 km. Almost parallel to the coast are the Sahyadri ranges of the Western Ghats. The state covers some 191,791 sq. km.

Population
Figures from the 2001 census showed the population to be 52,850,562, the majority of which live in rural areas. Estimated figures for 2007 put the population at 57,125,000. Figures from the 2011 census put the population at 61,130,704 giving a population density figure of 319 people per sq km.

The principal language is Kannada. English, Hindi, Urdu, Tamil, Telegu and Malayalam are also spoken.

Births, Marriages, Deaths
Figures from the Statistical Year Book of India put the birthrate in 2008 at 19.8 per 1,000 population and the death rate at 7.4 per 1,000 population. The infant mortality rate that year was 45 per 1,000 births.

EMPLOYMENT

Figures from the 2001 census show that Karnataka has a workforce of 23,534,791, more than half of whom are engaged in the agricultural sector.

BANKING AND FINANCE

Estimated figures for 2005 put the state domestic product per capita at Rs 13,810.

Balance of Payments / Imports and Exports
Recent figures show that exports from Karnataka were valued at 11,250 million Rupees. 35 per cent of India's software exports come from Karnataka as well as around 70 per cent of India's coffee and silk.

Foreign Investment
Karnataka attracts nearly 8 per cent of India's total foreign investment.

MANUFACTURING, MINING AND SERVICES

Primary and Extractive Industries
Important minerals found in the state include high grade iron ore, copper, manganese, chromite, china clay, limestone and magnetite. The state is the main producer of gold. Silver, granite and bauxite are also mined.

Energy
Karnataka had the first hydro-electric power station in India. Total potential is estimated at more than 7,500 MW. All cities, towns, and villages have electricity. Local rivers such as the Cauvrey, Sharavathi, and Ghataprabha are used to generate hydro electric power. The Karnataka Power Corporation Ltd (KPCL) oversees a system of 18 power stations. Some private power corporations also exist in the state.

Manufacturing
Bangalore is known as the 'electronic city' of India, and a third of India's software exports originate from Karnataka. The state stands first in production of raw silk (mostly multi-voltine) accounting for about 53 per cent of country's production and is famous in world markets for its sandal soap and sandal wood oil. It is one of the leading industrialised states in India and major activities include iron and steel production, cement, chemicals and fertilizers, textiles, bio-technology, information technology and vehicles. Karnataka has over 10,000 factories employing around 1,000,000 people.

Agriculture
Karnataka is predominantly rural and agrarian. About 69 per cent of its population lives in rural areas with 71 per cent of the work force engaged in agriculture and other allied activities. Figures from the Statistical Year Book of India show that in the year 2008-09 Karnataka produced 3,802,000 tonnes of rice, 1,629,000 tonnes of jower, 187,000 tonnes of bajra, 3,029,000 tonnes of maize, 1,394 tonnes of small millets and 247,000 tonnes of barley. it also produced 972,000 tonnes of pulses, 501,000 tonnes of ground nuts, 610 000 tonnes of cotton and 23,328,000 tonnes of sugar cane. Sunflowers are important crops. Tobacco, cashews and spices such as cardamom and cloves are also grown. Many fruits are grown including mango, banana, guava, pineapple, papaya, pomegranate and citrus fruits.

COMMUNICATIONS AND TRANSPORT

Airports
The main airport is situated at Bangalore. There are also airports at Belgaum, Hubli and Mangalore.

Railways
There are nearly 4,000 km of railway. The track between Bangalore and Madras is electrified.

Roads
Karnataka has over 117,000 km of roads, including 2,355 km of national highways and nearly 18,000 km of state highways.

Ports and Harbours
Karnataka has around 20 ports, the most important being Mangalore and Karwar. Mangalore is predominately a cargo port.

EDUCATION

Estimated figures for 2005 put the literacy rate at 61 per cent: 68 per cent for males and 54 per cent for females.

RELIGION

There are many faiths followed in Karnataka including Hinduism, Christianity, Islam, Buddhism, Jainism and Sikhism. In recent years some churches have been attacked by militant Hindu groups such as Bajrang Dal who accuse the Christian Church of illegally converting Hindus to Christianity, a charge the church denies.

COMMUNICATIONS AND MEDIA

It is estimated that there are over 9,650 post offices.

ENVIRONMENT

Karnataka has five national parks and 21 wildlife sanctuaries, including two particularly concerned with the preservation of the tiger population.

KERALA

Capital: Thiruvananthapuram (Population estimate: 850,000)

Head of State: Nikhil Kumar (Governor)

CONSTITUTION AND GOVERNMENT

Legislature
Number of seats in Legislative Assembly: 140

Chief Minister: Oommen Chandy

Government portal, URL: http://www.kerala.gov.in/
Governor's Office, URL: http://www.rajbhavan.kerala.gov.in/

Elections
The most recent elections took place in 2011. The Congress party won 72 seats and the left 68.

LEGAL SYSTEM

The highest court in Kerala is the High Court of the State. There are also District Courts, Sub Courts, and Magistrates Courts.

LOCAL GOVERNMENT

Kerala is divided into 14 districts: Kannur, Waynad, Kozhikode, Malappuram, Palakkad, Thrissur, Ernakulam, Idukki, Alappuzha, Kottayam, Pathanamthitta, Kollam, Kasaragode and Thiruvananthapuram.

AREA AND POPULATION

Area
The State of Kerala was formed in 1956 out of most of the former Malayalam-speaking State of Travancore-Cochin, together with the Malabar District of Madras. It covers an area of 38,863 sq km in between the high Western Ghats on the east and the Arabian Sea on the west. The width of the state varies from 35 km. to 120km.

Population
The population according to the 2001 census was 31,841,374. Most of the population live in rural areas. The population density is 819 persons per sq. km. Figures from the 2011 census put the population at 33,387,677 giving a density figure of 859 people per sq. km.

The chief language is Malayalam.

Births, Marriages, Deaths
Figures from the Statistical Year Book of India put the birth rate in 2008 at 14.6 per 1,000 population and the death rate at 6.6 per 1,000 population. The infant mortality rate that year was 12 per 1,000 births.

EMPLOYMENT

Figures from the 2001 census show that Kerala had a workforce of 10,283,887.

BANKING AND FINANCE

GDP/GNP, Inflation, National Debt
Gross state domestic product at current prices for 2005-06 was 132,739 crore showing a growth rate on the previous year of 11.5 per cent. (a crore equals 10 million). Figures for 2003-04 show that the agricultural sector contributes around 13 per cent of gross state income. Estimated figures for 2005 put per capita state domestic product at 13,320 rupees.

Imports and Exports
Main exports of Kerala include cashew nuts, tea, rose wood, coir, tea, coffee and spices.

MANUFACTURING, MINING AND SERVICES

Primary and Extractive Industries
Kerala has natural resources including clay, limestone, ilmenite, rutile, monazite, zircon, sillimanite and quartz sand.

Manufacturing
Kerala is rich in industrial potential and infrastructure facilities such as hydro-electric power and has an efficient system of transport and communications. It also has rich forests and rare minerals like ilmenite and monazite. Traditional industries are handloom, coir and handicrafts. Other important industries are rubber, tea, ceramics, electric and electronic appliances, telephone cables, transformers, bricks and tiles, drugs and chemicals, general engineering, plywood splints and veneers, beedi and cigars, soaps, oils, fertilisers, khadi and village industry products. The industrial sector grew by 7.18 per cent during 1998-99. Recent figures show that Kerala had over 18,000 factories. Traditional industries employ around 1 million people. There are over 500 industrial enterprises in the state.

Agriculture
Agriculture forms the mainstay of the people. About 50 per cent of the population depends upon agriculture for its livelihood and the state contributes a major share of the country's sea-fish production. Kerala has the highest gross income per net-cropped area. The state accounts for 92 per cent of India's rubber production, 70 per cent of coconut, 60 per cent of tapioca and almost 100 per cent of lemon grass oil. Kerala is the single largest producer of a number of other crops such as banana and ginger, as well as abundant production of tea and coffee. Other cash crops grown include the famous Malabar pepper, cardamom, cocoa, arecanut and in recent years vanilla. Rice, nutmeg, cinnamon and cloves are also cultivated, as are fruits and vegetables. In recent years the cultivation of cheaper pepper in other Indian states and Sri Lanka has threatened the traditional pepper production in Kerala and many farmers have suffered as a result.

COMMUNICATIONS AND TRANSPORT

International Airports
Kerala has two international airports at Thiruvananthapuram and Kochi. There is a third domestic airport at Kozhikode.

Railways
There are 13 railway routes in Kerala covering a total of 1,050 km.

Roads
The state has a total road network of more than 219,805 km and is crossed by three national highways. Figures for 2005 show that there were 3,122,000 registered cars on the road.

Ports and Harbours
Kerala has 16 ports, the largest of which is Kochi.

EDUCATION

The literacy rate was estimated to be 83 per cent in 2005, the second highest in the country, with figures of 86 per cent and 81 per cent for males and females respectively. School education is free and compulsory. There are 12,330 schools, seven universities and 186 colleges of science and art. Women are more highly educated here than in any other part of India and enjoy a high level of respect in society.

LAKSHADWEEP

Capital: Kavaratti (Population estimate, 10,100)

Head of State: H. Rajesh Prasad, IAS (Administrator)

LEGAL SYSTEM

Lakshadweep comes under the jurisdiction of the Kerala High Court.

AREA AND POPULATION

Area
This archipelago of small islands lies between 100 and 200 miles off the southwest coast of India in the Arabian Sea. It includes 12 atolls and three reefs. Only 11 of the islands are inhabited. In 1956 the islands were made a single union territory and since then have been directly administered by the Union government through an administrator. The islands cover an area of approximately 32 sq. km. The inhabited islands are Kavaratti, Agatti, Amini, Kadmat, Kiltan, Chetlat, Bitra, Andrott, Kalpeni and Minicoy.

Population
Figures from the 2001 census put the population at 60,650, the lowest in the country, but has a population density of 1,894, the fourth highest in the country. Figures from the 2011 census put the population at 64,429 giving a density figures of 2,013 people per sq. km.

Language
The principal languages are Jesri, Mahal and Malayalam.

Births, Marriages, Deaths
Figures from the Statistical Year Book of India put the birth rate in 2008 at 14.3 per 1,000 population and the death rate at 7.1 per 1,000 population. The infant mortality rate that year was 31 per 1,000 births.

EMPLOYMENT

Figures from 2003 show that Lakshadweep had a workforce of 10,335.

MANUFACTURING, MINING AND SERVICES

Energy
Solar power is gradually being introduced to the islands although the majority of power still comes from diesel generators.

Manufacturing
The main industry of the islands is centred around the coconut industry. There are seven coir fibre factories in operation as well as six coir production centres. Lakshadweep also has one handicraft centre.

Tourism
Lakshadweep has an active tourist industry based around Bangaram. Recent figures show that tourism is increasing and the islands have nearly 5,000 visitors a year, mostly travelling from other parts of India.

Agriculture
More than 90 per cent of the population depend on agriculture for their livelihood. Coconut is the only major crop and over 27 million tonnes of it are produced per year. The conversion of its fibres is the main industry on the islands.

Fishing is gradually taking over from coconut production as the main source of income on the islands, fishing for Skipjack Tuna is the main source of income. Recent figures show there were around 8,060 fishermen.

COMMUNICATIONS AND TRANSPORT

Shipping
Ferry services run between the islands and the mainland. Regular helicopter flights also provide transport links.

HEALTH

The islands have three community health centres and four primary health centres, there are around 21 doctors working in the islands.

EDUCATION

Figures from the 2001 census show that the average adult literacy rate was 88 per cent, the third highest in the country. All children of school age have access to a school. Recent figures show that the islands have 20 junior schools and 4 senior schools, 9 high schools and 4 senior secondary schools. Students wishing to undertake higher education must travel to the mainland.

RELIGION

Over 90 per cent of the population are Muslim.

MADHYA PRADESH

Capital: Bhopal (Population estimate: 1.5 million)

Head of State: Ram Naresh Yadav (Governor) (page 1484)

CONSTITUTION AND GOVERNMENT

Legislature
Number of seats in Legislative Assembly: 230

Chief Minister: Shri Shivraj Singh Chouhan (page 1404)

Government Portal: URL: http://www.mp.gov.in/

Recent events
In 1984 Madhya Pradesh and India suffered one of the world's worst industrial accidents, following a leak of 40 tonnes of a toxin called methyl isocyanate at the US owned Union Carbide plant in Bhopal. It was estimated that 3,500 people died within days of the leak and subsequently another 15,000 died. In June 2010 eight people were sentenced to two years imprisonment for death by negligence.

LEGAL SYSTEM

Madhya Pradesh has its own High Court

LOCAL GOVERNMENT

For administrative purposes Madhya Pradesh was formerly divided into 61 districts, 347 tehasils and 459 blocks. There were 465 towns and 71,526 uninhabited villages.

At midnight on 1 November 2000, 16 of the districts were used to form the new state of Chhattisgarh and therefore Madhya Pradesh is now divided into 45 districts, 260 tehasils and 313 blocks.

AREA AND POPULATION

Area
Madhya Pradesh is bounded by seven states; in the north-west by Rajasthan, in the north by Uttar Pradesh, in the north-east by Bihar, in the east by Orissa, in the south by Andhra Pradesh and Maharashtra and in the west by Gujarat. Madhya Pradesh covers and area of 308,000 sq. km. Making it the second largest state in India. The principal language is Hindi. Other languages spoken include Urdu, Punjabi, Gujarti, Marathi and Sindhi.

At midnight on 1 November 2000, the new state of Chhattisgarh was created, formed from 16 states of Madhya Pradesh.

Population
Figures from the 2001 census put the population at 60,348,023 giving a population density of 196 people per sq. km. Estimated figures for 2007 put the population at 67,965,000. Figures from the 2011 census put the population at 72,597,565 giving a population density figure of 236 people per sq km. Over 75 per cent of the population live in rural areas.

Births, Marriages, Deaths
Figures from the Statistical Year Book of India put the birth rate in 2008 at 28.0 per 1,000 population and the death rate at 8.6 per 1,000 population. The infant mortality rate that year was 70 per 1,000 births.

EMPLOYMENT

Figures from the 2001 census put the workforce at 25,793,519, over 70 per cent of which were engaged in the agricultural sector.

INDIA

BANKING AND FINANCE

Estimated figures for 2005 put the per capita State Domestic Product at Rs 8,235. Gross state domestic product at current prices for 2006-07 was 128,202 crore showing a growth rate on the previous year of 10.2 per cent. (a crore equals 10 million).

MANUFACTURING, MINING AND SERVICES

Primary and Extractive Industries

Madhya Pradesh produces diamonds and tin. Other minerals include coal, iron ore, copper ore, manganese ore, bauxite and limestone. Recent figures show that Madhya Pradesh produced 26,100 metric tonnes of limestone, 191,000 metric tonnes of bauxite, 109,000 metric tonnes of iron ore, 124,000 metric tonnes of dolomite and 71,259 carats of diamonds. Excluding oil and gas, Madhya Pradesh produces nearly 25 per cent of India's minerals.

Energy

Madhya Pradesh has a commercial wind farm located near Dewas, and currently the Maheshwar hydro electric dam is being built across the Narmada River. This construction has led to some protests about the number of villages which will be lost. Figures for 2006 put installed generating capacity of electricity at 9,795 MW.

Manufacturing

Madhya Pradesh has high technology industries like electronics, telecommunications, petro-chemicals, food processing and automobiles. It was the first state in the country to start producing optical fibre for purposes of telecommunications. A large number of automobile industries are located in Pithampur. The state also has papers mills and a newsprint factory as well as a bank note press at Dewas. The state is also leading in soyabean processing and the manufacture of cement, production of steel and cloth. Figures for 1998-99 show that 65 million metres of cloth were produced by the handloom sector and 325 million metres by the powerloom sector. 8.6 million metric tonnes of cement was produced in 2003-04 and 22.0 thousand metric tonnes of newsprint. The government has developed an IT policy to encourage the development of the IT sector. Figures for 2005 show that there were nearly 8,000 factories operating in the state.

Agriculture

The economy of Madhya Pradesh is primarily agriculture-based. 43 per cent of the area is cultivated and 78 per cent of the population is engaged in agriculture. It is the third largest foodgrains-producing state in India, main crops being paddy, wheat, maize, jowar, gram, linsead, pulses, oilseeds, mustard, soyabean and cotton. Figures from the Statistical Year Book of India show that in the year 2008-09 Madhya Pradesh produced 1,560,000 tonnes of rice, 574,000 tonnes of jowar, 1,144,000 tonnes of maize, 6,522,000 tonnes of wheat, 3,683,000 tonnes of pulses, 228,000 tonnes of groundnuts, 693,000 tonnes of rapeseed and mustard, 829,000 bales of cotton and 2,975,000 tonnes of sugar cane.

COMMUNICATIONS AND TRANSPORT

Airports

Madhya Pradesh has five airports located at Bhopal, Indore, Raipur, Gwalior and Khajuraho.

Railways

The rail network covers nearly 6,000 km. The main route joining northern and southern India passes through the state. Main railway junctions are Bhopal, Bina, Gwalior, Indore, Itarsi, Jabalpur, Katni, Ratlam, Ujjain and Khandwa.

Roads

The road network covers around 70,000 km. Figures from 2006 show that there were 4,609,000 registered vehicles on the road.

HEALTH

In 2008 a report by the International Food Policy Research Institute showed that 12 states in India had alarming levels of hunger. Madhya Pradesh was ranked as Extremely Alarming. This was partly attributable to the large rise in food prices particularly of rice in India that year.

EDUCATION

Estimated figures for 2005 showed that the average adult literacy rate stood at 54 per cent, 64 per cent for males and 43 per cent for females. Madhya Pradesh has nine universities.

COMMUNICATIONS AND MEDIA

Postal Service

In 1994, 5,901 people were served by each post office on average.

Telecommunications

The landline system has improved in recent years. Mobile use is widespread. Reliance Telecommunication Ltd is one of the telecommunication companies operating in the state.

ENVIRONMENT

Madhya Pradesh has set up some wild life sanctuaries.

SPACE PROGRAMME

In September 2004 India launched a satellite that will be used exclusively for education, and will link teachers and pupils across India. The launch took place from Sriharikota island in Andhra Pradesh.

MAHARASHTRA

Capital: Mumbai (formerly Bombay) (Population estimate: 18 million)

Head of State: Shri Kateekal Sankaranarayanan (Governor)

CONSTITUTION AND GOVERNMENT

Legislature

Number of seats in Legislative Council: 78
Number of seats in Legislative Assembly: 288

Chief Minister: Prithviraj Chavan

Recent Events

July 2005 saw the worst flooding in the state's history when 990mm (38 inches) of rain fell. It was estimated that 1,000 people lost their lives and around 5,000 families were made homeless as whole villages were swept away. In response to this disaster, the state government pledged to build 100 new villages as well as markets, schools and hospitals. The state was again hit by heavy rains in August 2006 and around 35 people were believed to have died in flooding.

On the evening of 28th November 2008, Mumbai suffered serious terrorist attacks when several sites were targeted simultaneously by gunmen. At the Chhatrapati Shivaji railway station, shots were fired indiscriminately and there were several deaths. Gunmen also attacked the Cama and Albless Hospital, and took control of the Nariman House business complex, home to the Jewish Chabad Lubavitch outreach centre. The Cafe Leopold, a popular place with visiting western tourists, was also attacked. The main attacks were centred on two prestigious hotels - the Oberoi-Trident and the Taj Mahal Palace. A group calling itself Deccan Mujahedeen claimed responsibility for the attacks and were believed to have arrived by sea from Pakistan. Islamabad denied any involvement but tensions between India and Pakistan were raised. An estimated 172 people had been killed in the attacks, including all but one of the gunmen.

India's Home Minister, Shivraj Patil, resigned following the attacks and national security adviser, M.K. Narayanan, also offered his resignation but this was turned down. The chief minister of Maharashtra also offered his resignation.

In July 2009 following disappointing monsoon rains Mumbai faced water rationing for the first time in living memory. In 2010 monsoon rains led to the deaths of 46 people due to flooding and landslides.

In March 2012 a landmine explosion in the state killed 15 policeman, the device was blamed on Maoist rebels.

Elections

The most recent state elections were held in 2009. The Indian National Congress won most seats (82) followed by the Nationalist Congress Party (620), the BJP (46), Shiv Shena (45), Maharashtra Navnirman Sena (13), Samajwad Party (3), the PWPI (4), the BCA, (2), and the Communicat Party of India (1).

The next state elections are due to take place in 2014.

LEGAL SYSTEM

Maharashtra comes under the jurisdiction of the Maharashtra and Goa High Court.

LOCAL GOVERNMENT

For administrative purposes Maharashtra is divided into 35 districts.

AREA AND POPULATION

Area

Established on 1 May 1960 following the division of the bi-lingual Bombay State, Maharashtra comprises the area of the former Bombay State south and east of the Surat District. The Arabian Sea forms the western boundary while Gujarat and Madhya Pradesh are its neighbours on the northern side. Karnataka and Andhra Pradesh are on its southern side. The state covers an area of approximately 307,690 sq. km. It is the third largest Indian state.

Population

At the time of the census in 1991, the population was 78,937,197. The 2001 census gave the population as 96,878,627, making it the state with the second highest population. Approximately 60 per cent live in rural areas. The population density per sq. km is 314. The ratio of female to males is 935:1000. In May 2001 the state government introduced a law which it hoped would restrict the size of families, anyone now seeking a job in the civil service must undertake not to have more than two children, and there will be no welfare cover for families with more than two children. It also hoped to bring in a law that girls must be 18 years of age or older when they marry. Estimated figures for 2007 put the population at 106,920,000. Figures from the 2011 census put the population at 112,372,972 giving a population density of 365 people per sq. km.

Figures for 2003 show that the birth rate had fallen to 19.9 live births per 1,000 population down from 26.2 live births per 1,000 population in 1991, figures for 2008 put the birth rate at 17.9 births per 1,000 population. The death rate in 2003 was recorded at 7.2 per 1,000 population falling to 6.6 per 1,000 population in 2008. The infant mortality rate in 2003 was put at 42 per 1,000 live births falling to 33 per 1,000 live births in 2008.

The principal language is Marathi.

EMPLOYMENT

Figures from the 2001 census put the workforce at 41,173,351. Agriculture is the largest employer with over 50 per cent of the working population engaged in this sector.

In 2008 the government sought to implement a law which had been brought in in 1968, whereby all businesses should should give priorty to people applying for jobs who have lived in the state for at least 15 years. There have been outbreaks of violence in recent years over the number of migrants to the state who have arrived in search of work, it is estimated that 37 per cent of the population of the capital Mumbai are migrants who have arrived in search of jobs.

BANKING AND FINANCE

The financial and corporate sectors are well-established. 12 per cent (Rs 156bn) of India's total foreign investment is through Maharastra. Mumbai is identified as the centre point of India's financial and commercial markets.

Estimated figures for 2005 show that the per capita State Domestic Product was Rs 106.920, the second highest in the country after Uttar Pradesh. Figures from the financial year 2005-06 put Gross State Domestic Product at Rs 432,413 crore (1 crore equals 10 million)

MANUFACTURING, MINING AND SERVICES

Energy

The total installed power capacity in 2001 was over 15,144 megawatts. Its transmission network is connected to the national grid and every village has electricity. Independent power producers are developing new power sources, including a gas-based project at Dabhol. The American energy giant Enron owned the power plant in Maharashtra through its Indian subsidiary but the plant closed following the collapse of Enron in 2002.

Manufacturing

Important industry groups are food products (mainly sugar); beverages, tobacco and tobacco products; cotton textiles; textile products; paper, paper products and printing; rubber, plastic, petroleum and coal products; chemicals, chemical products and pharmaceuticals; metal products; machinery; electrical machinery, apparatus and appliances, and transport equipment. Figures for 2005 show that there were over 30,460 working factories, employing around 1.3 million people.

Agriculture

Poor soil and a difficult climate result in difficult agricultural conditions and a lower than average agricultural yield. However about 70 per cent of the population in the state depends on agriculture for their livelihood. Principal crops grown are rice, jowar, bajra, wheat, soya bean, groundnut and a variety of pulses. The state produces 6.3 per cent of the country's total food grains. The state is also an important producer of oilseeds, including groundnut, sunflower and soya bean. Important cash crops are cotton, sugarcane, tobacco, turmeric and a variety of vegetables. Approximately 35m tons of sugarcane were produced in the 1997-98 agricultural year, which represents over 30 per cent of the national sugar production. The state also produces fruits and has a substantial area of orchards of orange, banana, mango, grape, cashew nut and sweet lime.

Figures from the Statistical Year Book Inida show that agricultural production in the year 2008-09 included 2,284,000 tonnes of rice, 3,587,000 tonnes of jowar, 1,560,000 of maize, 1,516,000 tonnes of wheat, 1,656,000 tonnes of pulses, 355,000 tonnes of groundnuts, 3,410,000 bales of cotton, 4,618,000 bales of jute, and 60,648,000 tonnes of sugar cane. Over 2000 state run irrigation projects are in operation. There are currently approximately 950 operational agricultural holdings, the average size of which is 221 hectares.

Recent figures show that the state has nearly 37,000,000 livestock and nearly 62,000 sq km of forest. The potential catch for fish is estimated at 630,000 tonnes per year.

COMMUNICATIONS AND TRANSPORT

International Airports
There are 24 airports in the state not all of which operate commercial flights.

Railways
The rail network covers around 5,500 km.

Roads
The state has 299,302 km of roads 200,430 km of which is paved. Over 10.9 million registered vehicles are on the road. In June 2009 a toll bridge across the sea was opened, it has eight lanes and is 5.6 km long and cost US$400 million. The bridge links the western suburbs of Mumbai with Worli. It is hoped that the bridge will have a big impact on reducing congestion in Mumbai.

Ports and Harbours
Maharashtra has over 50 ports the main one being the port of Mumbai. A large amount of India's imports and exports are handled here.

HEALTH

Recent figures show that the state has 1,028 hospitals and 2,058 dispensaries.

EDUCATION

Figures for 2004 show that Maharashtra had 68,644 primary schools and 19,480 secondary schools. There are 1,405 higher education establishments with 870,000 students, including one university exclusively for women. The literacy rate in 2005 was estimated to be 70 per cent.

COMMUNICATIONS AND MEDIA

In Mumbai there are 1.4m direct telephone lines, and Pune has approximately 200,000. Mumbai is also linked via Subscriber Trunk Dialling (STD) to over 1,390 cities world-wide. Over 120 towns in the state have International Subscriber Dialling (ISD) which gives them good global linkage. Most villages have a telegraph office. Cellular telephone services began in Mumbai in 1996.

ENVIRONMENT

In July 2005 Maharashtra suffered a particularly heavy monsoon and over 800 people were believed to have been killed in floods and landslides. In 2005 the state banned the sale and use of plastic bags in response to research that suggested discarded plastic bags have been clogging up the drainage and sewer systems, particularly in the capital Mumbai, and the blocked drains may have contributed to the severe flooding suffered in the state that year.

MANIPUR

Capital: Imphal (Population estimate: 240,000)

Head of State: Shri Gurbachan Jagat (Governor)

CONSTITUTION AND GOVERNMENT

Manipur became an Indian state on January 21, 1972.

Legislature
There are 60 seats in the Legislative Assembly, of which 20 are reserved for Scheduled Tribe and 1 is reserved for Scheduled Caste. Manipur is represented in the Lok Sabha by two members and by one member in the Rajya Sabha. Rajkumar Meghen, leader of the United National Liberation Front, the oldest separatist group in the north-east, was arrested in Bangladesh in 2010 and handed over to India to stand trial for sedition.

Recent Events
Manipur has suffered violent attacks from Naga rebels, including a recent blockade of the main road connecting Manipur to the rest of India. The rebels want some of the northern districts of Manipur, home to a predominantly Naga population, to join with the neighbouring state of Nagaland.

Chief Minister: Okram Ibobi Singh

LEGAL SYSTEM

Manipur falls under the jurisdiction of the Guwahati High Court.

LOCAL GOVERNMENT

For administrative purposes Manipur is divided into nine districts: Bishnupur; Chandel; Churachandpur; Imphal East; Imphal West; Senapati; Tamenglong; Thoubal; Ukhrul.

AREA AND POPULATION

Area
Geographically the state is divided into two tracts - the hills comprising five districts and the plains with four districts. It has borders with Myanmar to the east, Nagaland in the north, Assam in the west and Mizoram in the south and south-west. The state covers an area of some 22,327 sq. km.

Population
Figures from the last census in 2001 put the population at 2,3166,788 giving a population density of 82 persons per sq. km. Estimated figures for 2007 put the population 2,345,000. The 2011 census put the population at 2,721,756 giving a population density of 122 people per sq. km. The principal language is Manipuri.

Figures from the Statistical Year Book, India put the birthrate in 2008 at 15.8 per 1,000 population and the death rate at 5.0 per 1,000 population the infant mortality rate that year was 14 per 1,00 births.

Festivals
Ningol Chakouba - the social festival of Manipuries
Yaoshang - the premier festival of Manipur Hindus
Ramjan ID- the festival of Manipuri Muslims
KUT - the festival of Kuki-Chin-Mizo
Gang-Ngai - festival of Kabui Nagas

Chumpha - festival of Tanghui Nagas
Christmas
Cjeriaoba - the Manipur New Year
Kang - the RathaJatra of Manipur
Heikru Hitongba

EMPLOYMENT

Figures from the 2001 census put the workforce at 945,213, over 50 per cent of whom are engaged in the agricultural sector.

BANKING AND FINANCE

Estimated figures for 2005 put the per capita State Domestic Product at Rs 2,345. Figures from the financial year 2006-07 put Gross State Domestic Product at Rs 6,348 crore (1 crore equals 10 million)

MANUFACTURING, MINING AND SERVICES

Manufacturing
Manipur is an industrially backward state although it has been taking steps to progress in this area. Recent figures show that around 46,000 people are employed in industry. A government sponsored Export Promotion Industrial Park is to be set up at Khunuta Chingjin and money has been invested into an existing cement plant and some spinning mills. The central government has also provided investment for two Trade Centres and an Industrial Growth Centre and in 2005 announced plans to build a Food Park at Imphal. Handloom work is still the largest industry in the state and this is carried out almost exclusively by women.

Agriculture
Agriculture is the single largest source of livelihood for the majority of the Manipur population and is the basis of the state's economy. Under the 2006-07 plan, the government sought to increase agricultural production by increasing mechanisation, improving infrastructure in state farms and introducing high yield varieties of crops including paddy, pulses and oil seeds.

Figures from the Statistical Year Book India show that agricultural production in the year 2008-09 included 397,000 tonnes of rice and 21,000 tonnes of sugar cane.

Forest
Over 77 per cent of the state of Manipur is covered by forest.

COMMUNICATIONS AND TRANSPORT

Airports
There is an airport located at Imphal.

Railways
Manipur became connected to the railway network in 1990 with a junction at Jiribam.

Roads
The road system in Manipur covers just over 7,500 km.Figures from 2006 show that there were 124,000 registered vehicles on the roads.

EDUCATION

The literacy rate in 2005 was put at 76 per cent, 82 per cent of males and 69 per cent for females.

MEGHALAYA

Capital: Shillong (Population estimate: 265,000)

Head of State: Ranjit Shekhar Mooshahary (Governor)

CONSTITUTION AND GOVERNMENT

Meghalaya became a state of India on January 21 1972.

Legislature
The state has a unicameral legislature called the Meghalaya Legislative Assembly. The Assembly has 60 seats, 29 from Khasi Hills, 24 from Garo Hills, and 7 from Jaintia Hills. Members are elected for periods of five years. The Assembly must meet at least once every six months. The Assembly is responsible for the legislation of the state according to the powers vested in it.

Chief Minister: Dr. Mukul Sangma

Government portal: http://www.meghalaya.nic.in

LEGAL SYSTEM

Meghalaya falls under the jurisdiction of the Guwahati High Court. Shillong houses a High Court Bench.

LOCAL GOVERNMENT

Meghalaya is divided into seven districts. There are three autonomous district councils: Garo Hills, seated at Tura covering the East Garo Hills and West Garo Hills districts; Khasi Hills, seated at Shillong covering the East Khasi Hills and West Khasi Hills districts; and Jaintia Hills seated at Jowai covering the Jaintia Hills.

AREA AND POPULATION

Area
Meghalaya is a land-locked state bounded in the north by the Gopalpur, Kamrup, Nowgong and Karby Anglong districts of Assam and in the east by the districts of Cachar and the North Cachar hills, also part of Assam. In the south and west lies Bangladesh. It covers an area of 22,429 sq. km.

Population
The most recent census taken in 2001 put the population of Meghalaya at 2,318,822 with a density of 103 per sq. km. Estimated figures for 2007 put the population at 2,510,000. Figures from the 2011 census put the population of Meghalaya at 2,964,007 giving a population density of 132 people per sq. km. Figures from Statistical Year Book, India show that in 2008 the birth rate was 25.2 per 1,000 population and the death rate was 7.9 per cent per 1,000 population and an infant mortality rate of 58 per 1,000 births.

The principal languages are Khasi, Garo, Jaintia and English.

EMPLOYMENT

Figures from the 2001 census put the workforce at 970,146, nearly 70 per cent of whom were employed in the agricultural sector.

BANKING AND FINANCE

Estimated figures for 2005 put per capita State Domestic Product at Rs 11,275. Figures from the financial year 2006-07 put Gross State Domestic Product at Rs 7,052 crore (1 crore equals 10 million).

MANUFACTURING, MINING AND SERVICES

Primary and Extractive Industries
The mineral wealth of the Khasi Hills, Jaintia Hills and Garo Hills districts includes coal, sillimanite, limestone, dolomite, fire clay, felspar, quartz and glass sand. Coal and limestone are exported to Bangladesh. In 1997-98 the mineral sector generated revenue of Rs. 3980.32 lakh. The state's coal reserve is estimated to be around 640 million tonnes, most of which is in the Garo Hills. The projected limestone reserve is approximately 5,000 million tonnes. In late 2000 permission was granted to start a uranium mine in the Domiosiat-Wakhyn area, but, due to local opposition concerned with health related issues, mining has not yet started.

Energy
The state possesses a hydro-electric potential of nearly 1,200 MW and it has a surplus in power generation. Over 2,500 villages now have electricity. 120 bio-gas plants and 16,000 LPD of solar water heater system have also been set up.

Manufacturing
In order to promote industry, several industrial estates have been built at Shillong, Tura, Jowai, Williamnager and Nongstoin. Some manufacturing industries in Meghalaya include a plywood factory, a chemical oils factory, and steel and concrete factories. A large cement factory exists at Cherrapunjee. Smaller industries include furniture making, steel fabrication and tyre retreading. Figures from 2005 show that Meghalaya had 82,000 working factories.

Agriculture
Meghalaya is basically an agricultural state. 83 per cent of the total population depends primarily on agriculture for their livelihood. Rice and maize are the principal food crops and wheat has also recently been introduced. The state produces oranges, peaches, pineapples, pears, guavas, plums, bananas, potatoes, tapioca, bay leaves, ginger, black pepper, mustard and jackfruit. Non traditional crops are also being cultivated, including flowers especially orchids, medicinal plants, coffee and mushrooms. Figures from the Statistical Year Book India show that agricultural production in the year 2008-09 included 204,000 tonnes of rice, 26,000 of maize, 35,000 bales of jute and 20,000 bales of mesta.

Silk production is another important industry and 57,000 kg of mulberry silk is now produced.

COMMUNICATIONS AND TRANSPORT

Airports
Meghalaya has one small airport at Umroi, which is not yet operating.

Railways
At present there are no railway connections in Meghalaya.

Roads
There are 350 km of national highways which connect Shillong and West Garo Hills to other parts of the state and to Guwahati. There are approximately 950 km of state highways and 5,620 km of district roads.

HEALTH

In 1997 there were five state government hospitals - three at Shillong, one at Turan and one at Jowai, and seven private hospitals - five at Shillong, one at Tura and one at Jowai.

There are also 20 state government dispensaries, 81 primary health centres, 379 sub-centres and 10 community health centres. In 1995 there were 378 doctors, 81 pharmacists and 337 staff nurses.

The government has launched a programme for the treatment of tuberculosis, leprosy, cancer, and mental diseases. 95 per cent of children below the age of three have been immunised against polio.

A sanitation programme is in progress. Its aims include drinking water in every village and mass construction of sanitary latrines.

EDUCATION

The literacy rate in the 2001 census was 63 per cent. There is currently a literacy campaign taking place to raise this level and in 2005 literacy rates had risen to an estimated 78 per cent. The structure of the education system has also been overhauled and in recent years over 2,000 primary school places have been created. Almost 1,000 primary schools have also been built.

COMMUNICATIONS AND MEDIA

The state is served by the North-Eastern Telecommunications Circle. STD facilities are available at the seven district headquarters. Internet facilities and an ISDN line are available at Shillong and at the district headquarters.

The postal service covers the state. There is one General Post Office, one Head Post Office and 495 other post offices.

Meghalaya has several newspapers including, The Shillong Times, Mawphor, and the North East Telegraph.

ENVIRONMENT

Meghalaya has abundant wildlife including elephant, tiger, leopard and deer. Many animals and birds are protected by law and the state has two wildlife parks and two sanctuaries.

MIZORAM

Capital: Aizawl (Population estimate: 230,000)

Head of State: Vakkom B. Purushothaman (Governor)

CONSTITUTION AND GOVERNMENT

Mizoram became the 23rd state of India in February 1987

Legislature
Number of Seats in Legislative Assembly: 40. Mizoram is represented by one seat in the Lok Sabha and one seat in the Rajya Sabha.

Chief Minister: Pu Lalthanhawla

Government portal: URL: http://www.mizoram.nic.in

LEGAL SYSTEM

Mizoram comes under the jurisdiction of the Guwahati High Court.

LOCAL GOVERNMENT

For administrative purposes Mizoram is divided into eight districts, Aizawl, Champhai, Chhimtuipui, Kolasib, Lawngtlai, Lunglei, Mamit, and Serchhip.

AREA AND POPULATION

Area
Sandwiched between Myanmar in the east and south and Bangladesh in the west, the state occupies an area of strategic importance in the north-eastern corner of India covering an area of 21,087 sq. km. The Indian states of Tripura, Assam and Manipur are on the northern border. Mizoram became a Union Territory in 1972 and was granted statehood in 1987. The state is predominantly hilly, characterized by hill ranges and deep river gorges.

Population
Figures from the 2001 census put the population at 891,058, giving a density of 42 people per sq. km., one of the lowest in the country. Estimated figures for 2007 put the population at 960,000. Figures from the 2011 census put the population at 1,091,014 giving a population density figures of 52 people per sq. km.

Births Marriages, Deaths
Figures from the Statistical Year Book of India put the birth rate in 2008 at 17.8 per 1,000 population and the death rate at 5.1 per 1,000 population. The infant mortality rate that year was 37 per 1,000 births.

Language
The principal languages are Mizo and English.

EMPLOYMENT

Figures from the 2001 census put the workforce at 469,597. Around 80 per cent of the workforce are employed in the agricultural sector.

BANKING AND FINANCE

Figures from the financial year 2006-07 put Gross State Domestic Product at Rs 2,985 crore (1 crore equals 10 million).

MANUFACTURING, MINING AND SERVICES

Energy
A 60 MW power plant in currently under construction.

Manufacturing
There is no major industry in Mizoram. Handloom and handicrafts are cottage industries. Rice-milling, oil and flour-milling, mechanised carpentry workshops, saw-milling, brick making and furniture workshops are small scale industries. Under the government industrial policy, new industries are being encouraged including a fruit juice concentrate plant, a fruit preservation factory and a ginger dehydration plant. Development of the tea industry is currently being explored and two tea factories are planned.

Agriculture
The people of Mizoram are mainly engaged in agriculture. The main pattern of agriculture followed is *jhum* or shifting cultivation, but the government is trying to stop this type of agriculture as it can be harmful to the environment. A new contour system has been introduced, which uses trenches and hedges, which should lead to permanent farmland. Main crops grown include wet-rice cultivation, maize, sesame, mustard and potatoes, sugarcane, cotton, ginger and fruit such as orange, lemon, lime, papaya, pineapple and passion fruit. A growing area of importance is sericulture. Medicinal and aromatic plants are also being cultivated.

Figures from the Statistical Year Book India show that agricultural production in the year 2008-09 included 46,000 tonnes of rice, 9,000 tonnes of maize, 4,000 tonnes of pulses, 5,000 bales of cotton and 14,000 tonnes of sugar cane.

COMMUNICATIONS AND TRANSPORT

Airports
There is an airport at Aizawl and an airfield at Lunglei.

Roads
Total road length has been put at 4,064 km of which 2,222 km is paved, there are over 30,000 registered vehicles on the road.

HEALTH

Recent figures show that Mizoram had seven hospitals, nine community health centres and 45 primary health centres.

EDUCATION

Recent figures show that Mizoram had 1,280 primary schools, 770 middle schools and 377 high schools. Figures from the 2001 census show that Mizoram has the second highest adult literacy rate in the county at 88 per cent, 90 per cent for males and 86 per cent for females. Figures for 2005 estimate the literacy rate to be 90 per cent, 90 per cent for males and females making it the highest literacy rate in the country.

RELIGION

The predominant religion in Mizoram is Christianity. Mizoram is also home to the Bnei Menashe Jewish community, believed by many to be decended from the lost tribe of Menashe. In recent years many of the community have relocated to Israel.

NAGALAND

Capital: Kohima (Population estimate: 78,500)

Head of State: Dr. Ashwani Kumar (Governor)

CONSTITUTION AND GOVERNMENT

Nagaland gained full statehood from 1 December 1963, although since Indian independence Nagaland militants have fought for a separate Nagaland. To preserve the cultural and social identity of the Nagas, the state has been given special status. No central law relating to customary laws, social, religious practices, or land, will apply to it unless the State Legislature, made up of elected representatives of the Nagas, have approved it. The tribes of Nagaland are the Angami, Ao, Sema, Lotha, Rengma, Chakhesang, Sangtam, Konyak, Phom, Chang, Yimchunger, Khiamungan, Zeliang, Kuki and Pochury.

Recent Events

Since becoming a state, separatist Naga rebels have campaigned to enlarge the state, to make it the homeland for Naga tribes people living in adjoining states and to have greater autonomy. In 2003 on a visit to Nagaland Prime Minister Vajpayee said there was no consensus to enlarge the state. Further talks were held in December 2004. Talks between the Indian government and The Nationalist Socialist Council of Nagaland (NSCN) reconvened in 2006, and a ceasefire that came into effect in 1997 was extended.

In January 2008 presidential rule was imposed on Nagaland and the coalition government dismissed.

Legislature

Number of seats in Legislative Assembly: 60

Chief Minister: Shri. Neiphiu Rio
Chief Secretary: Shri. Alemtemshi Jamir

Government portal: http://www.nagaland.nic.in/

LEGAL SYSTEM

Nagaland comes under the jurisdiction of the Guwahati High Court and there is a bench at Kohima.

LOCAL GOVERNMENT

For administrative purposes Nagaland is divided into eight districts: Kohima, Mokokchung, Mon, Phek, Tuensang, Wokha, Zunheboto and Dimapur.

AREA AND POPULATION

Area

Under the Constitution (Thirteenth Amendment) Act 1962, the areas comprising the Naga Hills-Tuensang area, known by the name of Nagaland, became a separate State of the Union. Situated in the extreme northeast, Nagaland is bounded in the west and north by Assam, in the east by Burma and in the south by Manipur and covers an area of 15,579 sq. km.

Population

Figures from the 2001 census put the population at 1,990,036 with a population density of 120 people per sq.km. Figures from the 2011 census put the population at 1,980,602 giving a population density figure of 19 people per sq. km.

Births Marriages, Deaths

Figures from the Statistical Year Book of India put the birth rate in 2008 at 17.5 per 1,000 population and the death rate at 4.6 per 1,000 population. The infant mortality rate that year was 26 per 1,000 births.

Language

The official language in English, principal languages are Ao, Konayak, Chakhesang, Chang, Sangtam, Angami, Sema and Lotha.

EMPLOYMENT

Figures from the 2001 census put the workforce at 847,796, nearly 70 per cent of the population is employed in the agriculture sector.

BANKING AND FINANCE

In its 1997-98 annual plan the government of India allocated 3064.80 million rs. to Nagaland. The state also receives government funding to aid the development of its infrastructure.

Figures from the financial year 2004-05 put Gross State Domestic Product at Rs 5,346 crore (1 crore equals 10 million).

MANUFACTURING, MINING AND SERVICES

Primary and Extractive Industries

Minerals found in the state are clay, coal, limestone, glass, and sand.

Manufacturing

Industry in Nagaland includes a sugar mill at Dimapur which has a production capacity of 1,000 tonnes per day, a plywood factory at Tizit and a paper and pulp mill at Tuli. There is also a fruit and vegetable processing plant, a small cement plant and cottage industries including handloom and handicrafts. A brick factory has recently been commissioned.

Energy

A major hydro electric project was completed in 1999. All villages now have electricity.

Agriculture

Agriculture is the main occupation of the majority of the population in the state. Rice is the important food grain, figures from the Statistical Year Book India show that agricultural production in the year 2008-09 included 315,000 tonnes of rice, 116,000 tonnes of maize, 40,000 tonnes of pulses and 186,000 tonnes of sugar cane.

Rubber and tea are also grown. Fruit and vegetables are cultivated including bananas, pineapples, oranges, passion fruit, pears, plums, ginger, garlic, potatoes and cabbages. 21 per cent of the land is covered by forest.

COMMUNICATIONS AND TRANSPORT

Airports

In 1997 the new air terminal at Dimapur was completed. Air India operates to the airport.

Railways

Dimapur in Nagaland is an important railway point in the state. Its track has been converted to broad gauge to make it faster and more economical.

Roads

There are now 2,900 metalled kms of road in the state, which has a total road network of 9,800 km. The Nagaland State Transport buses provide services on 97 routes covering 20,696 km per day. The Nagaland National Highway 39 connects the state to Assam and Manipur.

HEALTH

There are 29 hospitals, 65 dispensaries, 199 health sub-centres, and 27 public health centres. There are a further two hospitals specialising in tuberculosis. Four drug addiction centres have also been established. Nagaland has one mental health hospital.

EDUCATION

Figures from the 2001 census give the average literacy rate of 67 per cent. The female literacy rate is 62 per cent. Estimated figures from 2005 show the literacy rate has risen to 78 per cent, 82 per cent for males and 75 per cent for females.

Nagaland has one university, 40 colleges, 236 high schools, 418 middle schools, 2 polytechnics, and 5 industrial training institutes.

RELIGION

The main religions followed in Nagaland are Christianity, Hinduism and Islam.

ODISHA

Capital: Bhubaneswar (Population estimate: 660,000)

Head of State: S.C. Jamir (Governor)

CONSTITUTION AND GOVERNMENT

Recent Events

In October 1999 Odisha was hit by a massive cyclone. Twelve districts were affected, over 9,000 people died and much livestock and many houses and fishing boats were lost. Autumn and winter crops were completely destroyed and more than 80 per cent of coconut trees were lost. In 2001 Odisha was hit by severe flooding in which more than 15,000 villages were affected. Heavy flooding during the monsoon season in 2003 again hit the state and around three million people were affected.

On November 2011, the name of the state was changed. The state is now called Odisha, rather than the English influenced pronounciation of Orissa.

Legislature

Number of seats in Legislative Assembly: 147. The most recent elections took place in 2009.

Chief Minister: Shri Naveen Patnaik

Government portal, URL: http://www.odisha.gov.in/portal/default.asp
Governor's Office, URL: http://www.rajbhavanorissa.gov.in/governorbioadata.htm

LEGAL SYSTEM

The state of Odisha has its own High Court.

LOCAL GOVERNMENT

For administrative purposes Odisha is divided into 30 districts.

AREA AND POPULATION

Area

Odisha is situated in the northeastern section of the Indian Peninsula between 17° 48' and 22° 34' north latitude and 81° 24' and 87° 28' east longitude, with the Bay of Bengal to the east. Odisha is bounded in the north by Bihar and in the west by Madhya Pradesh and covers an area of 155,707 sq. km.

Population

Figures from the 2001 census put the population at 36,804,660, giving a population density of 236 people per sq. km. Estimated figures for 2007 put the population at 39,405,000. Figures from the 2011 census put the population at 41,947,358 giving a population density figure of 269 people per sq. km.

Births, Marriages, Deaths

Figures from the Statistical Year Book of India put the birth rate in 2008 at 21.4 per 1,000 population and the death rate at 9.0 per 1,000 population. The infant mortality rate that year was 69 per 1,000 births

Language

The principal languages are Odia and Bengali.

EMPLOYMENT

Figures from the 2001 census put the working population at 14,276,488. Around 65 per cent of the population is engaged in the agricultural sector.

BANKING AND FINANCE

Agriculture contributes an average of 28 per cent of net state domestic product. Figures for 2005 estimated per capita State Domestic Product to be Rs 7,175. Figures from the financial year 2006-07 put Gross State Domestic Product at Rs 91,151 crore (1 crore equals 10 million).

MANUFACTURING, MINING AND SERVICES

Primary and Extractive Industries

Odisha has many mineral resources, including iron ore, limestone, magnesite coal and chromite. Industrialization plans for Odisha include steel factoring, which produces an estimated 25,000 tonnes of steel annually, and an improved infrastructure including an airport, hospital, schools and new housing. One new factory costing US$12 billion has been proposed by the South Korean firm Posco. This would be the single largest direct foreign investment in India. Many local people who will be affected by the plans have objected as they feel they won't benefit financially or the proposed jobs won't materialize. Several demonstrations have taken place resulting in the deaths of some protesters. In December 2006, Arcelor Mittal, the world's largest steel company, signed a deal in principle, agreeing to build a US$9 billion steel plant north west of the capital.

Energy

As of 2001, 35,362 of Orissa's 46,989 villages had electricity.

Manufacturing

The pace of industrial progress has quickened in recent years, and the electronics industry has developed. Figures for 2003-04 show that there were 361 larger and medium industries and nearly 60,000 small industries in operation, with a further 4,400 set up in 2003-04.

Agriculture

Cultivation of rice is the principal occupation of nearly 76 per cent of the state population. Rice is the main crop grown. Cash crops grown include sugarcane and oilseeds. Vegetable crops are being introduced, particularly onions. Fruit is also grown. Figures from the Statistical Year Book India show that agricultural production in the year 2008-09 included 6,813,000 tonnes of rice, 135,000 tonnes of maize, 387,000 tonnes of pulses, 97,000 tonnes of groundnuts, 108,000 bales of cotton and 646,000 tonnes of sugar cane.

COMMUNICATIONS AND TRANSPORT

Airports

There is an airport at Bhubaneswar for domestic flights including flights to Delhi, Calcutta. Chennai and Hyderabad. The airport is currently under expansion. There are also several air fields in the state.

Railways

There are over 2,000 km of railway line in Odisha.

Roads

In total there are almost 45,000 km of roads.

Waterways

Recently the Government announced its intention to set up transport services using motorised launches to more inaccessible areas.

Ports and Harbours

The main port is Paradeep, ports at Gopalpur and Dhamara are currently being improved. There are plans to build a large port at Dhamara funded by private investment.

HEALTH

Recent figures show that Odisha has 180 hospitals with 9,512 beds. Odisha also has a system of community health centres and mobile health centres.

EDUCATION

Recent figures put the average adult literacy rate at 57 per cent, 65 per cent for males and 49 per cent for females. Odisha has 10 universities.

RELIGION

In recent years there have been tensions between the Christian and Hindu communities of Odisha. There have been several violent attacks on both sides. The Hindu community accuses the Christian community of bribing Hindus to convert. The Christian community argue that many lower caste Hindus voluntarily convert to escape the caste system.

ENVIRONMENT

In 2001, Odisha suffered some its worst flooding for years. Experts are concerned that this will become a more regular occurrence due to global warming and localised deforestation.

PUDUCHERRY

Capital: Puducherry (Population estimate: 221,000)

Head of State: Shri Iqbal Singh (Lieutenant Governor)

CONSTITUTION AND GOVERNMENT

Constitution
The Government of India, in agreement with the Government of France, took over the administration of the French Establishments in India (Pondicherry, Karaikal, Yamam and Mahe) in 1954. A Treaty ceding these territories to India was signed in 1956 and ratified by the French Assembly in 1962.

Legislature
Number of seats in Legislative Assembly: 30

Recent Events
In September 2006, the name of the territory was changed from Pondicherry to Puducherry, the original Tamil name which had been changed by the French. Puducherry means new village.

Chief Minister: N. Rangasamy

Elections
In the most recent elections in 2011, the All India NR Congress (AINRC), led by Mr Rangasamy, won 15 seats, its ally the AIADML won five seats, Congress seven seats and the DMK two. There is also one independent which is supporting AINRC.

LEGAL SYSTEM

Puducherry comes under the jurisdiction of the Madras High Court.

LOCAL GOVERNMENT

Puducherry is divided into four districts, Puducherry, Karaikal, Mahe and Yanam.

AREA AND POPULATION

Area
Puducherry is one of the Union Territories of India. The present Puducherry is comprised of the former French India-Karaikal, Mahe and Yanam and the capital Puducherry, formerly the French headquarters in India. Karaikal is geographically inside Thanjavur district of Tamil Nadu. Mahe is within Kerala situated on the mouth of the Mahe river. Yanam is in the East Godavari district of Andhra Pradesh. The Bay of Bengal forms the eastern boundary of Puducherry, and on the other three sides by the south Arcot district of Tamil Nadu. Puducherry covers an area of approximately 492 sq. km.

Population
Figures from the 2001 census put the population at 974,345 giving a density of 2,029 persons per sq. km., the third highest in the country. Estimated figures for 2007 put the population at 1,160,000. Figures from the 2011 census put the population at 1,244,464 giving a population density figure of 2,598 people per sq.km. the second highest density figure after Chandigarh. The principal languages are Tamil, Telugu, Malayalam, English and French.

Births, Marriages, Deaths
Figures from the Statistical Year Book of India put the birth rate in 2008 at 16.4 per 1,000 population and the death rate at 7.5 per 1,000 population. The infant mortality rate that year was 25 per 1,000 births.

EMPLOYMENT

Almost 45 per cent of the population is engaged in the agricultural sector. Figures for 2002 show that the industrial sector provides employment for around 80,000 people.

BANKING AND FINANCE

Estimated figures for 2005 put State Domestic Product per capita at Rs 29,892. Figures from the financial year 2006-07 put Gross State Domestic Product at Rs 6,299 crore (1 crore equals 10 million).

MANUFACTURING, MINING AND SERVICES

Manufacturing
Manufactured goods in Puducherry include textiles, computers, electronic products, leather goods, washing machines, bio-polymers, pharmaceuticals, car parts, roof sheets, sugar and yarn. There are two sugar factories and eight textile mills. Recent figures show that there were 55 large scale, 147 medium scale and 7,126 small industries operating in Puducherry.

Agriculture
Nearly 45 per cent of the population is involved in agriculture and related activities. Ninety per cent of the cultivated area is irrigated. The main food crops are rice, pulses and sugarcane. Groundnut and cotton are principal cash crops. Figures for 2003 show that over 36,380 hectares of land was under cultivation. In 2005, 24,200 hectares of land were being used for rice cultivation.

Figures from the Statistical Year Book India show that agricultural production in the year 2008-09 included 51,000 tonnes of rice, 1,000 tonne of pulses, 2,000 tonnes of groundnut and 162,000 tonnes of sugar cane.

Recent figures show that 42,800 metric tonnes of marine fish were caught annually.

Service Industries
Figures for 2003 show that Puducherry had 525,698 tourist arrivals.

COMMUNICATIONS AND TRANSPORT

Airports
Puducherry has no main airport of its own, the nearest is in Chennai (formerly Madras).

Railways
Puducherry has a rail link to Chennai.

Roads
Total road length is 606 km with 384,000 registered vehicles on the road.

HEALTH

There are eight hospitals and 39 primary health care centres in Puducherry.

EDUCATION

Figures from the 2005 estimate the literacy rate to be 74 per cent, 82 per cent for males and 67 per cent for females.

COMMUNICATIONS AND MEDIA

There are 100 post offices and 23,168 telephone connections.

ENVIRONMENT

India was badly affected by the Asian tsunami disaster caused by a huge undersea earthquake in the Indian Ocean in December 2004. The southern part of the country was hit with nearly 8,000 people killed in Tamil Nadu and almost 600 in Puducherry.

PUNJAB

Capital: Chandigarh (Population estimate: 900,500)

Head of State: Shivraj Patil (Governor)

CONSTITUTION AND GOVERNMENT

Recent Events
In 2006 bus services to Pakistan resumed for the first time since partition in 1947. The route goes from Amritsar in Punjab to Lahore in Pakistan.

The governor of Punjab, Salman Taseer, was assassinated in Islamabad in January 2011.

Legislature
Punjab has a unicameral legislature called *Vidhan Sabha* or The House of the People, consisting of 117 seats. The Upper house was abolished in the 1960s. Nationally Punjab is represented by 13 seats in the Lok Sabha and 7 seats in the Rajya Sabha.

Chief Minister: Parkash Singh Badal

LEGAL SYSTEM

Punjab comes under the jurisdiction of the Punjab, Haryana and Chandigarh High Court.

LOCAL GOVERNMENT

For administrative purposes Punjab is divided into 17 districts: Amritsar, Bhatinda, Faridkot, Fatehgarh, Ferozepur, Gurdaspur, Hoshiarpur, Jalandhar, Kapurthala, Ludhiana, Mansa, Moga, Muktsar, Nawanshahr, Patiala, Ropar and Sangrur.

AREA AND POPULATION

Area
By the Punjab Reorganization Act, 1966, the Punjab became a unilingual state. The predominantly Hindi-speaking areas were formed into the new state of Haryana, while the Hill areas merged with the contiguous state of Himachal Pradesh. The state is situated in the north-western corner of the country. It is bounded in the west by Pakistan, in the north by Jammu and Kashmir, in the northeast by Himachal Pradesh and in the south by Haryana and Rajasthan. It covers an area of 50,362 sq. km.

Population
Figures from the 2001 census put the population at 24,358,999 giving a population density of 482 persons per sq. km. Estimated figures for 2007 put the population at 26,500,000. Figures from the 2011 census put the population at 27,704,236 giving a population density figures of 550 people per sq. km. The principal language is Punjabi. Hindi, Urdu and English are also spoken.

Births, Marriages, Deaths
Figures from the Statistical Year Book of India put the birth rate in 2008 at 17.3 per 1,000 population and the death rate at 7.2 per 1,000 population. The infant mortality rate that year was 41 per 1,000 births.

EMPLOYMENT

Figures from the 2001 census put the workforce at 9,127,474. The agriculture sector is the main employer.

BANKING AND FINANCE

Gross State Domestic Product was estimated to be Rs.123,397 crore in 2006-07 up from Rs.109,735 crore in 2005-06, (one crore = 10 million).

MANUFACTURING, MINING AND SERVICES

Manufacturing
Important industrial items produced in the state are bicycle parts, sewing machines, hand-tools, machine tools, auto parts, electronic items, sports goods, surgical and leather goods, hosiery, knitwear, fasteners, nuts and bolts, textiles, paper and paper packaging, pharmaceuticals and leather goods and food and agro products including sugar and vegetable oils. Electronic software is a particular growth area. Information technology including software is becoming an important part of the economy as more companies move to Punjab. Mohali is to be the home of a new IT park. Recent figures show that there were 14,102 working factories in Punjab employing 460,166 people. In June 2006, the German car manufacturer Volkswagen was given the go-ahead to build a factory in Punjab. The factory is expected to employ 5,000 people with a possible further 50,000 employed to make components. Recent figures show that Punjab has around 204,000 small scale manufacturing units.

Agriculture
About 83.5 per cent of the total geographical area of Punjab is under cultivation. Three-quarters of the population is engaged in agriculture. The state has surplus foodgrains especially wheat and rice. Other main foodgrains are maize, grain, barley and pulses. Figures from the Statistical Year Book India show that agricultural production in the year 2008-09 included 11,000,000 tonnes of rice, 514,000 tonnes of maize, 15,733,000 tonnes of wheat, 22,000 tonnes of pulses, 46,000 tonnes of rapeseed and mustard, 2,678,000 bales of cotton and 4,670,000 tonnes of sugar cane. Fruits grown include grape, pear, peach, lichi, lemon and mango. Vegetables include potatoes, other root crops, cauliflowers, tomatoes, onions and cabbages. Many food products are exported from Punjab particularly honey, potato crisps, mushrooms, tomato paste and chillies. Recent figures showed that Punjab had 8,608,000 head of livestock. Forests cover 3,084 sq km of Punjab.

COMMUNICATIONS AND TRANSPORT

International Airports
Amritsar has an international airport and a domestic airport is located at Chandigarh. Aerodromes are located at Patiala and Sahnewal.

Railways
All major towns and district headquarters have good rail links for both passengers and freight and rail links to Pakistan run from Punjab. Total length of railtrack in Punjab is over 3,700 km.

Roads
There are 1,198 km of national highways, 1,485 km of state highways and 41,559 km of provincial highways. 4,035 registered vehicles were on the road in 2005.

HEALTH

Figures for 2004 show that Punjab had 219 hospitals and 1,479 dispensaries.

EDUCATION

Education is provided by 13,212 primary schools, 2,493 middle schools, 3,977 senior and high schools. Punjab has 209 colleges and six universities. Figures for 2001 put the average adult literacy rate at 70 per cent falling slightly to 68 per cent in 2005.

RELIGION

Sikhism is the main religion of Punjab. The main religious centre, Harmiandir Sahib (the Golden Temple), is located at Amritsar.

RAJASTHAN

Capital: Jaipur (Population estimate: 2.3 million)

Head of State: Margaret Alva

CONSTITUTION AND GOVERNMENT

Legislature
Number of seats in Legislative Assembly: 200. The most recent elections took place in 2008. The INC have 96 seats, the BJP 79, the BSP 6, and others 20.

Chief Minister: Shri Ashok Gehlot

Government portal: http://rajasthan.gov.in/

LEGAL SYSTEM

Rajasthan has its own High Court.

LOCAL GOVERNMENT

For administrative purposes, Rajasthan is divided into 32 districts.

AREA AND POPULATION

Area
Rajasthan shares its western border with Pakistan while Punjab, Haryana, Uttar Pradesh and Madhya Pradesh surround Rajasthan in the north, northeast and southeast and Gujarat in the southwest. The state covers an area of 342,239 sq. km.

Population
Figures from the 2001 census put the population at 56,507,188 giving a population density of 165 persons per sq. km, the majority of which live in rural areas. Estimated figures for 2007 put the population at 63,790,000. Figures from the 2011 census put the population at 68,621,012 giving a population density figure of 201 people per sq. km.

Births, Marriages, Deaths
Figures from the Statistical Year Book of India put the birth rate in 2008 at 17.3 per 1,000 population and the death rate at 7.2 per 1,000 population. The infant mortality rate that year was 41 per 1,000 births.

Language
Principal languages are Rajasthani and Hindi.

EMPLOYMENT

Figures from the 2001 census put the workforce at 23,766,655. Over 60 per cent of the working population are engaged in the agricultural sector.

BANKING AND FINANCE

Gross State Domestic Product was estimated to be Rs.142,036 crore in 2006-07 up from Rs.124,224 crore in 2005-06, (one crore = 10 million).

MANUFACTURING, MINING AND SERVICES

Primary and Extractive Industries
Minerals found in Rajasthan include zinc, silver ore, copper, rock phosphate, asbestos, felspar, limestone, gypsum, selenite, salt and green marble. Precious stones include emerald and garnet. In 2001 oil was discovered in the border area of Barmer, and reserves of lignite have been found.

Manufacturing
Major industries are textiles, rugged and woollen goods, sugar, cement, glass, sodium plants, oxygen and acetylene, vegetable dyes, pesticides, insecticides, zinc ingots and sheets, fertilisers, railway wagons, ball bearings, water and electric meters, sulphuric acid, television sets, synthetic yarn and insulating bricks, polished and unpolished precious and semi-precious stones, spirits and wines.

Service Industries
Rajasthan is a popular destination for both domestic and foreign tourists. Recent figures show that nearly 7.0 million tourists travel there each year.

Agriculture
Over two million hectares are under cultivation. Principal crops cultivated in the state are *jowar*, *bajra*, maize, gram, wheat, oilseeds, cotton, pulses and tobacco. Cultivation of vegetables and citrus fruits like oranges and malta has grown in recent years. Commercial crops are red chillies, methi, hing, mustard and cuminseed. Figures from the Statistical Year Book India show that agricultural production in the year 2008-09 included 241,000 tonnes of rice, 1,828,000 tonnes of maize, 7,287,000 tonnes of wheat, 1,826,000 tonnes of pulses, 3,806,000 tonnes of rapeseed and mustard, 747,000 bales of cotton and 388,000 tonnes of sugar cane.

COMMUNICATIONS AND TRANSPORT

Airports
Rajasthan has airports located at Jaipur, Jodhpur and Udaipur and has regular connections to Mumbai and Delhi.

Railways
Rajasthan has good railway connections with main junctions at Jaipur, Bharatpur, Sawai Madhopur, Kota, Bikaner and Jodhpur.

Roads
Rajasthan has a road network of over 158,000 km.

HEALTH

Recent figures show that Rajisthan has 215 hospitals, over 200 dispensaries and over 1,800 primary health centres.

EDUCATION

Figures from the 2001 census put the average adult literacy rate at 61 per cent, 76 per cent for males and 44 per cent for females.

ENVIRONMENT

Rajistan is home to several National Parks and a tiger sanctuary is located at Alwar.

Shortage of water in a problem for Rajasthan; the fact that it is quite a dry state is exacerbated by the large use of water in the marble industry, used to cool the marble down when being cut.

SIKKIM

Capital: Gangtok (Population estimate: 98,600)

Head of State: Shri Balmiki Prasad Singh (Governor)

CONSTITUTION AND GOVERNMENT

Legislature
Number of seats in the Legislative Assembly: 32. The most recent elections took place in 2009; all seats were won by the SDF.

Chief Minister: Dr. Pawan Chamling

Recent Events
Sikkim was a disputed territory, as China had never recognised that it belonged to India. Until 1975 Sikkim was an independent principality which then acceded to India. In 2003 China and India agreed to talks, and in June of that year special envoys were employed to look into ways of settling the dispute. In 2005 China accepted that Sikkim belonged to India and relations were further advanced between the two nations when in June 2006 the Nathu La pass, an old trade route in the Himalayas, was re-opened after a period of more that 40 years.

LEGAL SYSTEM

Sikkim has its own High Court.

LOCAL GOVERNMENT

Sikkim is divided into four districts, North, South, East and West.

AREA AND POPULATION

Area
A mountain state in the eastern Himalayas, Sikkim is bounded in the west by Nepal, in the north by Tibet, in the east by Bhutan and in the south by West Bengal. Sikkim is strategically important for India as it lies astride the shortest route from India to Tibet. The state is almost entirely mountainous with only 20 per cent being habitable and covers 7,096 sq. km.

Population
The census for 2001 put the population at 540,851, giving a population density of 76 persons per sq. km. Estimated figures for 2007 put the population at 585,000. Figures from the 2011 census put the population at 607,688 giving a population density figure of 86 people per sq. km. The majority of the population lives in rural areas. Languages spoken include Nepali, Bhutia, Lepcha, Limboo, Magar, Rai, Gurung, Sherpa, Tamang, Newari, Hindi and English.

Births, Marriages, Deaths
Figures from the Statistical Year Book of India put the birth rate in 2008 at 18.4 per 1,000 population and the death rate at 5.2 per 1,000 population. The infant mortality rate that year was 33 per 1,000 births.

EMPLOYMENT

Figures from the 2001 census put the workforce at 263,043, over 50 per cent of whom are employed in the agricultural sector.

BANKING AND FINANCE

Gross State Domestic Product was estimated to be Rs.2,040 crore in 2006-07 up from Rs.1,803 crore in 2005-06, (one crore = 10 million).

MANUFACTURING, MINING AND SERVICES

Primary and Extractive Industries
Mineral resources in Sikkim include coal, graphite, quartzite, dolomite, talc, limestone and material for porcelain. Only copper, lead and zinc exist in quantities worth mining.

Energy
Sikkim produces around 70 per cent of the electricity it needs from hydroelectric sources; the rest it imports from neighbouring states.

Manufacturing
Industry does not exist on any large scale in Sikkim. Training is given in skills for handloom and handicrafts and small scale units have recently been set up to manufacture watches and precision measuring instruments.

Agriculture
The state's economy is basically agrarian. Maize, rice, wheat, potato, large cardamom, ginger and orange are principal crops. Sikkim has the largest area and the highest production of cardamom in India. Ginger, potato, orange and off-season vegetables are other cash crops. Flowers are now beginning to be grown commercially. Tea is grown commercially and is exported to Russia and Germany, and a coffee plantation has been planted at Majitar.

Figures from the Statistical Year Book India show that agricultural production in the year 2008-09 included 22,000 tonnes of rice, 58,000 tonnes of maize, 8,000 tonnes of wheat, 12,000 tonnes of pulses and 4,000 tonnes of rapeseed and mustard.

Forestry
Over 80 per cent of Sikkim is covered in forest.

COMMUNICATIONS AND TRANSPORT

Airports
Sikkim has no airport of its own. The nearest is Bagdogra in West Bengal.

Railways
The nearest rail links are at Siliguri and New Jalpaiguri, rail links are also based in West Bengal.

Roads
Sikkim has a total of 2,375 km of roads. In 2005 there were an estimated 22.000 registered vehicles on the road.

HEALTH

Sikkim has six hospitals and 24 primary health centres.

EDUCATION

Recent figures show that there are 84,986 primary school pupils, 23,949 high school pupils, 3,331 senior secondary school pupils and 1,484 students studying for degrees. The state has one medical college and one college of law. Figures from the 2001 census put the average adult literacy rate at 70 per cent rising to an estimated 75 per cent in 2005. Sikkim has one medical school, one law school, one teacher training college and 50 Monastic schools.

TAMIL NADU

Capital: Chennai (formerly Madras) (Population estimate: 4.3 million)

Head of State: Dr. K. Rosaiah (Governor)

CONSTITUTION AND GOVERNMENT

Legislature
The legislature has 234 members plus one nominated Anglo Indian member

Nationally Tamil Nadu is represented by 39 seats in the Lok Sabha and by 18 seats in the Rajya Sabha.

Recent Events
India was badly affected by the Asian tsunami disaster, caused by a huge undersea earthquake in the Indian Ocean in December 2004. The Southern part of the country was hit with nearly 8,000 people killed in Tamil Nadu. The state suffered heavy flooding in 2005, following heavy rainfall. The government pledged US$100 million to help flood-affected areas.

Chief Minister: Selvi Jayaram Jayalalithaa

Government portal: URL: http://www.tn.gov.in/

Elections
The most recent elections for the Tamil Nadu Legislative Assembly were held in 2011. The ADMK won 203 seats and the DMK 31.

LEGAL SYSTEM

Tamil Nadu has its own High Court which also has jurisdiction over Pondicherry.

LOCAL GOVERNMENT

Tamil Nadu is divided into 30 districts, which includes 16,317 villages.

AREA AND POPULATION

Area
The state of Tamil Nadu comprises the Tamil-speaking remnant of the former Province of Madras. It is bounded in the north by Andhra Pradesh and Karnataka, in the west by Kerala, in the east by the Bay of Bengal and in the south by the Indian Ocean and covers 130,058 sq. km.

Population
Figures from the 2001 census put the population at 62,405,679, making it the sixth most populous state in India and giving it a population density of 478 persons per sq. km. 34 per cent of the population live in urban areas. Estimated figures for 2007 put the population at 65,795,000. The principal language is Tamil.

Births, Marriages, Deaths
Figures from 2003 put the birth rate at 18 per 1,000 population and the death rate at 8 per 1,000 population the infant mortality rate was recorded at 43 per 1,000 live births.

EMPLOYMENT

Figures from the 2001 census put the workforce at 27,878,282, nearly 50 per cent of whom are employed in the agricultural sector.

BANKING AND FINANCE

GDP/GNP, Inflation, National Debt
Gross State Domestic Product was estimated to be Rs. 245,266 crore in 2006-07 up from Rs. 223,528 crore in 2005-06, (one crore = 10 million).

Balance of Payments / Imports and Exports
Principal exports of the state include leather and leather goods, ready made garments, cotton textiles, engineering goods, and granites. Figures from 2002-03 show that exports earned Rs. 25,039 crores amd imports cost Rs. 35,697 crores.

MANUFACTURING, MINING AND SERVICES

Primary and Extractive Industries
Tamil Nadu has many mineral reserves including granite, limestone, lignite, magnasite, psyrite, china clay, fireclay, mica, gypsum, quartz, ilumenite and iron ore.

Energy
Currently two nuclear power plants are in the initial stages of construction at Koodankulam. This is a joint project with Russia.

Manufacturing
Main industries are cotton textiles, leather goods, chemical fertilisers, paper and its products, printing and allied industries, diesel engines, automobiles, bicycles, cement, sugar, iron steel, railway wagons and coaches. An electronics industry is now developing and there is a software technology park and an institute of excellence in IT in Chennai. An oil refinery at Chennai has led to petro-based manufacturing. Figures for 2005 show that TAmil Nadu had 28,342 working factories.

Car manufacturers Hyundai, Ford, Hindustan Motors and Mitsubishi all have manufacturing plants in Tamil Nadu.

Agriculture
Agriculture is the mainstay of Tamil Nadu's economy. Main food crops are rice, maize, jowar, bajra, ragi and pulses. Important commercial crops are tapioca, coconuts, sugarcane, oilseeds, cardamom, cashew nuts, cotton, chillies, banana, coffee, tea and rubber. Around 5,000 hectares of farmland was affected by flooding from seawater as a result of the Asian Tsunami in 2004.

Figures from the Statistical Year Book India show that agricultural production in the year 2008-09 included 5,182,000 tonnes of rice, 214,000 tonnes of jowar,, 1,258,000 tonnes of maize, 165,000 tonnes of pulses, 975,000 tonnes of groundnuts, 1,043,000 bales of cotton and 32,804,000 tonnes of sugar cane.

Recent figures show that Tamil Nadu had 24,562,293 head of livestock and over 86 million poultry.

With over 1,070 km of coastline, the fishing industry plays an important part in Tamil Nadu. Recent figures put the annual marine fish production at over 300,000 tonnes and inland fish production at over 77,000 tonnes.

Tamil Nadu has nearly 23,000 sq km of forest from which timber including teak and sandalwood is produced.

COMMUNICATIONS AND TRANSPORT

International Airports
There is an international airport at Chennai.

There are six domestic airports at Salem, Tiruchirapalli, Madurai, Tuticorn, Chennai and Coimbatore.

Railways
There are 4,113 km of rail track. Tamil Nadu has a total of 626 railway stations including main juctions at Chennai, Madurai, Tiruchirapalli and Coimbatore.

Roads
There are 136,727 km of surfaced roads. Estimated figures for 2005 put the number of registered vehicles on the road at 10,054,000.

Ports and Harbours
There are ports at Chennai, and Tuticorin. Smaller ports include Cuddalore and Nagapattinam.

HEALTH

Recent figures show that Tamil Nadu has 323 hospitals, over 200 dispensaries and a system of health centres.

EDUCATION

Tamil Nadu has 129 engineering colleges, 184 polytechnics and 19 universities. Figures from the 2005 census show that the average adult literacy rate was 70 per cent.

COMMUNICATIONS AND MEDIA

Postal Service
There are over 12,000 post offices in the state, nearly 4,000 of which are registered as telegraph offices as well.

Telecommunications
Tamil Nadu currently has 1,603 telephone exchanges and 1.2 million telephone lines.

ENVIRONMENT

Tamil Nadu has several wildlife and bird sanctuaries.

India was badly affected by the Asian tsunami disaster, caused by a huge undersea earthquake in the Indian Ocean in December 2004. The southern part of the country was hit with nearly 8,000 people killed in Tamil Nadu.

TRIPURA

Capital: Agartala (Population estimate: 365,000)

Head of State: Devanand Konwar (Governor)

CONSTITUTION AND GOVERNMENT

Legislature
Number of seats in Legislative Assembly: 60

Chief Minister: Manik Sarkar

Elections
The most recent assembly elections took place in 2008. The CPI won 46 seats, the INC 10, the CPI two, and the INPT and the RSP one seat each.

LEGAL SYSTEM

Tripura comes under the jurisdiction of the Guwahati High Court, with a Bench at Agartala.

LOCAL GOVERNMENT

For administrative purposes, Tripura is divided into four districts, North Tripura, South Tripura, West Tripura and Dhalai, 15 subdivisions and 38 rural development blocks which are further subdivided.

AREA AND POPULATION

Area
Tripura is located between the river valleys of Myanmar (Burma) and Bangladesh. Encircled almost on three sides by Bangladesh, it is linked with Assam only in the northeast and covers 10,486 sq. km.

There are occasional violent incidents mainly involving rebels demanding independence for Tripura.

Population
Figures for the 2001 census put the population at 3,199,203, giving Tripura a population density of 304 persons per sq. km. Estimated figures for 2007 put the population at 3,462,000. Figures from the 2011 census put the population at 3,671,032 giving a population density figure of 350 people per sq. km. The large majority of the population lives in rural areas. Principal languages are Bengali, Kokborak and Manipuri.

EMPLOYMENT

Figures from the 2001 census put the workforce at 1,159,561 of which, 50 per cent are employed in the agricultural sector, only around 5 per cent of the work force is employed in industry.

BANKING AND FINANCE

Gross State Domestic Product was estimated to be Rs.9,124 crore in 2005-06, (one crore = 10 million).

MANUFACTURING, MINING AND SERVICES

Primary and Extractive Industries
Tripura has large reserves of natural gas.

Energy
At present Tripura generates 56 MW of electricity from its own power plants. A new 500 MW thermal power project at Melaghar is planned which will mean that Tripura will produce more than enough power to meet its needs. The majority of villages have electrical power.

Manufacturing
Tea is the major industry in Tripura and handloom is the single largest industry. Weaving is essentially a tribal household activity. Figures from 2005 show that Tripura had 1,575 working factories.

Tourism
Figures for 2001-02 show that Tripura had 257,989 domestic and 2,564 foreign visitors.

Agriculture
In Tripura, principal crops are paddy, wheat, jute, mesta, potato, sugarcane and oilseeds. There are also several government orchards and nurseries . Fruits grown include pineapple, orange, jackfruit, coconut, lemon, lime and litchi. Rubber is grown and plans are underway for rubber processing plants in the state. Around 6 million kg of tea is produced annually. Other crops include cashew nut, coconut, banana, mango, ginger, turmeric and chili. Agriculture employs over 60 per cent of the population and contributes nearly 50 per cent of the state domestic product.

Figures from the Statistical Year Book India show that agricultural production in the year 2008-09 included 627,000 tonnes of rice, 4,000 tonnes of pulses, 2,000 bales of cotton, 4,000 bales of Jute and 52,000 tonnes of sugar cane.

COMMUNICATIONS AND TRANSPORT

Airports
There is an airport with domestic connections at Agartala.

Railways
Tripura only has 44 km of rail track which extends to Kumarghat in the north.

Roads
Tripura has a road system of over 12,500 km. In 2003 a new bus service was launched connecting Agartala to Dhaka in Bangladesh. Estimated figures from 2005 show that 106,000 registered vehicles were on the road.

EDUCATION

Figures from the 2005 put the average adult literacy rate at 74 per cent, 79 per cent for males and 69 per cent for females.

ENVIRONMENT

Tripura is home to several wildlife sanctuaries.

UTTAR PRADESH

Capital: Lucknow (Population estimate: 2.4 million)

Head of State: Shri B.L. Joshi (Governor)

CONSTITUTION AND GOVERNMENT

Constitution
Under the Constitution of India, Uttar Pradesh has a Governor and a bicameral Legislature. The Lower House (Vidhan Sabha) has 403 elected members and one Anglo-Indian member nominated by the Governor. The Upper House (Vidhan Parishad) has 108 members, of which 12 are nominated by the Governor. Executive power is vested in the Governor.

Recent Events
In 2008 Uttar Pradesh was hit by severe storms; around 130 people died and much of the mango crop was lost.

Legislature
Number of Seats in Legislative Council: 108
Number of seats in Legislative Assembly: 425

Chief Minister: Sri Akhilesh Yadav

Office of the Governor, URL: http://upgovernor.gov.in/
Government portal, URL: http://upgov.nic.in/

Elections
The most recent assembly elections were held in 2012, The Samajwadi Party won 224 seats

LEGAL SYSTEM

Uttar Pradesh has its own High Court.

LOCAL GOVERNMENT

Uttar Pradesh is divided into 70 districts (83 districts pre October 2000).

AREA AND POPULATION

Area
The State comprises the former United Provinces and the Princely States of Benares, Tehri-Garhmal and Rampur. It is bounded by Tibet and Nepal in the north, Himachal Pradesh in the northwest, Haryana in the west, Rajasthan in the southwest, Madhya Pradesh in the south and southwest and Bihar in the east and covers an area of 238,566 sq. km. The main rivers running through Uttar Pradesh are the Ganga, Yamuna, Gomti, Ramganga and Ghaghara.

At midnight on November 2000 a new state, Uttaranchal, was created from several districts of Uttar Pradesh.

Population
Figures from the 2001 census put the population at 166,052,859 which makes it the highest populated state in India and gives it a population density of 689 persons per sq. km. Estimated figures for 2007 put the population at 187,930,000. Figures from the 2011 census put the population at 199,581,477 giving a population density figure of 828 people per sq. km. The principal languages are Hindi and Urdu.

Births, Marriages, Deaths
Figures from the Statistical Year Book of India put the birth rate in 2008 at 29.1 per 1,000 population and the death rate at 8.4 per 1,000 population. The infant mortality rate that year was 67 per 1,000 births.

EMPLOYMENT

Figures from the 2001 census put the workforce at 53,983,824. Nearly 70 per cent of the population are engaged in the agriculture sector.

BANKING AND FINANCE

Gross State Domestic Product was estimated to be Rs.312,832 crore in 2006-07 up from Rs.279,762 crore in 2005-06, (one crore = 10 million).

MANUFACTURING, MINING AND SERVICES

Primary and Extractive Industries
Among the minerals found are limestone, dolomite, magnesite, gypsum, glass-sand, marble, granite, fireclay, phosphorite and bauxite.

Manufacturing
While the handloom industry is the largest cottage industry, cotton and woollen textiles, leather and footwear, distilleries and breweries, paper and chemicals, agricultural implements and glass products are some of the other flourishing industries. The state does now have several cement plants. Recent figures show Uttar Pradesh has 68 textile producing units and 32 automobile units.

Plans are underway to develop the New Okhla Industrial Development Authority, which will include industrial and housing sectors and is hoped to be completed in 2011.

Kanpur is home to a Software Technology Park and plans are being made for five further such parks.

Agriculture
Uttar Pradesh is the largest producer of foodgrains, particularly wheat and rice, sugarcane, pulses and oilseeds. It is also one of the principal sugar producing states in the country. Mango and guava are also grown.

Figures from the Statistical Year Book India show that agricultural production in the year 2008-09 included 13,097,000 tonnes of rice, 1,302,000 tonnes of bajra, 1,198,000 tonnes of maize, 28,554,000 tonnes of wheat, 376,000 tonnes of barley, 1,998,000 tonnes of pulses, 874,000 tonnes of rapeseed and mustard and 109,048,000 tonnes of sugar cane.

COMMUNICATIONS AND TRANSPORT

Airports
Uttar Pradesh has airports located at Agra, Allahabad, Bareilly, Dehradun, Ghaziabad, Gorakhpur, Jhansi, Kanpur, Lucknow, Pantnager, Varanasi, Rae Bareli and Sarsawa.

Railways
Uttar Pradesh has a comprehensive railway network and has main junctions at Lucknow, Agra, Allahabad, Bareilly, Faizabad, Gonda, Gorakhpur, Jhansi, Kanpur, Moradabad, Mughalsarai, Sitapur, Tundla and Varanasi.

Roads
There are over 121,000 km of roads. Figures for 2005 show that there were 7,989,000 registered vehicles on the road.

EDUCATION

Uttar Pradesh has 26 universities, 89 polytechnics, 12 engineering colleges and 9 medical colleges.

In 2000 Uttar Pradesh launched a literacy drive to encourage children into schools. The scheme includes free textbooks and free lunches for poorer children.

Figures from the 2001 census give the average adult literacy rate as 57 per cent.

RELIGION

Many religions are catered for in Uttar Pradesh, but it is most well known for its six-week Hindu festival, the Kumbh Mela, which takes place in Allahabad on the banks of the Ganges. It takes place every 12 years, most recently in January 2001 when it was attended by some 70 million people. In January 2007, there was an Ardh or Half Kumbh Mela.

UTTARAKHAND

Capital: Dehradun (Population, approx.: 510,000)

Governor: Aziz Qureshi

CONSTITUTION AND GOVERNMENT

Uttaranchal, the 27th state, came into existence at midnight on 8 November 2000. While discussions were underway regarding the creation of the new state, the name used was Uttarakhand. Central government chose the Uttaranchal, but in 2006 the name was officially changed back to Uttarakhand, following public pressure.

Uttarakhand is divided into two main regions, Garhwal and Kumaon, both of which put forward their largest towns to be the state capital. Dehradun in Garhwal was chosen over Nanital in Kumaon.

Legislature
Number of seats in the Legislative Assembly: 70. Nationally, Uttarakhand is represented by five seats in the Lok Sabha and three seats in the Rajya Sabha.

Chief Minister, Shri Vijay Bahuguna

Office of the Governor, URL: http://www.governoruk.gov.in/
Government portal, URL: http://uk.gov.in/

Elections
The most recent assembly elections took place in January 2012. Breakdown of seats was as follows: BJP 31; INC 32; BSP 3; Ind. 3; Others 4.

LEGAL SYSTEM

Uttarakhand has its own High Court

LOCAL GOVERNMENT

Uttarakhand is divided into 13 districts.

AREA AND POPULATION

Area
Uttarakhand is the 27th state of India and came into existence at midnight on 8 November 2000. Situated in the Himalayas it includes the hill regions of Kumaon and Garhwal. It was created out of Uttar Pradesh and shares borders with Tibet, Nepal and Himachal Pradesh. It covers an area of 53,483 sq km.

Population
The population at the 2001 census was put at 8,489,349. Estimated figures for 2007 put the population at 9,415,000. Figures from the 2011 census put the population at 10,116,752 giving a population density figure of 189 people per sq. km.

Births, Marriages, Deaths
Figures from the Statistical Year Book of India put the birth rate in 2008 at 20.1 per 1,000 population and the death rate at 6.4 per 1,000 population. The infant mortality rate that year was 44 per 1,000 births.

EMPLOYMENT

Figures from the 2001 census put the workforce at 3,134,036, with nearly 60 per cent being engaged in the agricultural sector.

621

INDIA

BANKING AND FINANCE

Gross State Domestic Product was estimated to be Rs.29,881 crore in 2006-07 up from Rs.25,776 crore in 2005-06, (one crore = 10 million).

MANUFACTURING, MINING AND SERVICES

Primary and Extractive Industries
There are deposits of dolomite, magnesite, limestone, copper graphite and soapstone.

Energy
A dam to provide hydro-electric power is currently under construction on the Bhagirathi river at Tehri. There have been protests against the environmental impact of the dam but the Supreme Court has ruled against these.

Manufacturing
Uttarakhand has very little industry and most is forest based. Recent figures show that there are 670 factories of varying sizes employing around 27,590 people.

Agriculture
Although agriculture provides a living for some 90 per cent of the population the majority of this is carried out on small holdings of less that one hectare. Around 1,261,900 hectares are under cultivation. 35,395 sq km of the state is covered in forest. Main crops are rice, wheat, barley, maize, pulses, oil seeds, and sugarcane.

Figures from the Statistical Year Book India show that agricultural production in the year 2008-09 included 582,000 tonnes of rice, 43,000 tonnes of maize, 193,000 tonnes of ragi, 787,000 tonnes of wheat, 22,000 tonnes of barley, 39,000 tonnes of pulses and 5,590,000 tonnes of sugar cane.

COMMUNICATIONS AND TRANSPORT

Airports
Some airstrips exist including one at Dehradun.

Railways
Uttarakhand has stations located at Dehradun, Hardwar, Roorkee, Kotdwar, Kashipur, Udhamsingh Nagar, Haldwani and Kathgodam.

Roads
The total road system covers 33,304 km.

HEALTH

Recent figures show that Uttarakhand has 17 hospitals, 224 public health centres, and 49 community health centres.

EDUCATION

Recent figures put the male literacy rate at 83.3 per cent and the female literacy rate at 59.6 per cent.

WEST BENGAL

Capital: Kolkata (formerly Calcutta) (Population estimate, urban agglomeration: 13 million)

Head of State: Shri M.K. Narayanan (Governor)

CONSTITUTION AND GOVERNMENT

Legislature
Number of seats in Legislative Assembly: 294

Chief Minister: Mamata Banerjee

Office of the Governor, URL: http://rajbhavankolkata.gov.in/
Chief Minister's Office, URL: http://wbcm.gov.in/Htmlpage/index.aspx
Government portal, URL: http://www.wbgov.com/

Elections
Elections took place most recently in 2011. The TMC gained an absolute majority and Mamata Banerjee became the state's first female chief minister.

LEGAL SYSTEM

West Bengal has its own High Court which also has jurisdiction of the Andaman and Nicobar Islands.

LOCAL GOVERNMENT

West Bengal is divided into 18 districts.

AREA AND POPULATION

Area
West Bengal borders Bangladesh in the east, the Bay of Bengal in the south, Orissa in the south west, Bihar to the west and Sikkim, Bhutan and Assam in the north. The entire state covers 88,752 sq. km.

Population
Figures from the 2001 census put the population at 80,176,197, the fourth most populated state in the country. The population density is 904 persons per sq. km. Estimated figures for 2007 put the population at 86,430,000. Figures from the 2011 census put the population at 91,347,736 giving a population density figure of 1,029 people per sq. km. The principal language is Bengali.

Births, Marriages, Deaths
Figures from the Statistical Year Book of India put the birth rate in 2008 at 17.5 per 1,000 population and the death rate at 6.2 per 1,000 population. The infant mortality rate that year was 35 per 1,000 births.

EMPLOYMENT

Figures from the 2001 census put the workforce at 29,481,690. Nearly 50 per cent of the working population is engaged in the agricultural sector.

BANKING AND FINANCE

Gross State Domestic Product was estimated to be Rs.236,044 crore in 2005-06 up from Rs.208,578 crore in 2004-05, (one crore = 10 million).

Chambers of Commerce and Trade Organisations
Bengal National Chamber of Commerce and Industry, URL: http://www.bncci.com/

MANUFACTURING, MINING AND SERVICES

Primary and Extractive Industries
Coal and china clay are two important minerals found in large quantity. Limestone, manganese, silica, dolomite, lead and iron ore are also found.

Manufacturing
West Bengal is one of the larger industrial states in the country with over 11,000 registered working factories in 1998. Major industries, among others, are engineering, automobiles, cement, beverages, chemicals, petrochemicals, pharmaceuticals, aluminium, ceramics, cotton textiles, paper, glass, leather, footwear, bonemeal, bicycles, dairy and poultry produce, and timber processing. In recent years there have been some protests at what some people believe is the unnecessary use of agricultural land being used for industrial development.

Agriculture
Agriculture contributes just over 50 per cent of the state's income and between 70 and 80 per cent of the population is directly or indirectly involved in the sector. West Bengal is the largest producer of rice in India. Other important crops are jute, tea, fruit, potato, oilseeds, tomato, mango and wheat. Recent figures show that 5,548,000 hectares of land is under cultivation. Figures from the Statistical Year Book India show that agricultural production in the year 2008-09 included 15,037,000 tonnes of rice, 343,000 tonnes of maize, 765,000 tonnes of wheat, 129,000 tonnes of pulses, 118,000 tonnes of groundnuts, 339,000 tonnes of rapeseed and mustard, 8,415,000 bales of jute and 1,638,000 tonnes of sugar cane.

In January 2008 thousands of chickens were culled after an outbreak of bird flu.

COMMUNICATIONS AND TRANSPORT

Airports
There are airports at Kolkata (Dum Dum), which is an international airport, Bagdogra, Siliguri and Coochbehar.

Railways
The total length of railway track is 3,867 km and serves 813 stations. Main junctions are at Asansol, Bandel, Bardhaman, Howrah, Kharagpur, New Jalpaiguri and Sealdah.

Roads
West Bengal has a total of 85,388 km of roads. Figures from 2005 put the number of registered vehicles on the road at 2,872.

Ports and Harbours
There are ports at Kolkata, Haldia and Kulpi.

HEALTH

Recent figures show that there are 413 hospitals with a total of 54,000 beds, 551 dispensaries, and nearly 42,000 registered practitioners.

EDUCATION

Recent figures show that there are 61,091 schools, 364 colleges and 11 universities. Figures from the 2001 census put the average adult literacy rate at 69 per cent.

ENVIRONMENT

The East Calcutta Wetland Association was set up in 2005 to preserve 12,500 hectares of urban marshland that was under threat.

INDONESIA

Republic of Indonesia

Republik Indonesia

Capital: Jakarta (Population estimate: 13.23 million)

Head of State: Susilo Bambang Yudhoyono (President) (page 1542)

Vice President: Prof. Dr Boediono (page 1391)

National Flag: Divided fesswise, red and white, in the proportion two to three.

CONSTITUTION AND GOVERNMENT

Constitution

From the early seventeenth century until the Second World War, much of Indonesia was a Dutch colony. Following the Japanese occupation during WWII, Indonesia proclaimed independence in 1945, and Sukarno was declared the country's first president. Independence was formally recognised on 17 August 1950 and the country became known as the Republic of Indonesia.

Indonesia is a republic with sovereignty vested in the people to be fully exercised by an elected People's Consultative Assembly which holds the power in the state. The 1945 Constitution decrees six organs of state: the People's Consultative Assembly, the Presidency, the House of Representatives, the Supreme Advisory Council, the Supreme Audit Board, and the Supreme Court. The Assembly has the responsibility to sanction the Constitution, decree guidelines of state policy and elect the president and vice president for terms of five years.

The provisional constitution of 1945 became the constitution, by presidential decree, in 1959. Further amendments to the constitution were made in August 2002, including the direct election of the president and the abolition of parliamentary seats previously reserved for the military.

According to the constitution, the president is both head of state and chief executive, holding office for a term of five years and eligible for re-election. As mandatory leader of the People's Consultative Assembly (*MPR, Majelis Permusyawakilan Rakyat*), the president must execute duties in compliance with the guidelines of state policy as decreed by the Assembly. Under the terms of the constitution the president cannot dissolve the legislature, whilst the legislature cannot dismiss the president.

The People's Consultative Assembly is the supreme holder of power in Indonesia, and can sanction the Constitution, decide the guidelines of state policy, and elect the president and vice president. The president is accountable to the Assembly for the conduct of government. The membership of the Assembly was reduced from 1,000 to 700 in 1999, made up of the 500 members of the House of Representatives and 200 members appointed by the government (165 delegates of regional assemblies and 65 party representatives). The constitution was amended in 2002 regarding the abolition of parliamentary seats reserved for members of the military.

People's Consultative Assembly (MPR), Jl. Jendral Gatot Soebroto no.6 senayan, Jakarta 10270, Indonesia. Tel: +62 21 572 5965 / 571 5644 / 571 5268, URL: http://www.mpr.go.id/

The functions of the Supreme Advisory Council are to answer any questions that the President may ask in relation to affairs of state, and to recommend or express views on matters of national importance. The council is made up of a chairman, four vice-chairmen and 45 members who are nominated by the House and appointed by the President for a term of five years.

To consult the full constitution, please visit: http://www.embassyofindonesia.org/about/pdf/IndonesianConstitution.pdf

International Relations

Following East Timor's UN administered independence from Indonesia in 1999, Indonesia has worked to improve relation between the two countries.

Indonesia is a founding and strong member of ASEAN, although in recent years relations have been strained with fellow member Malaysia over the number of Indonesian illegal immigrants in Malaysia and a territorial dispute over the Amblat Islands.

Recent Events

On 12 October 2002 bombs exploded outside two nightclubs in the beach resort of Kuta on the island of Bali killing over 180 people, mainly tourists. Muslim militants with links to Osama Bin Laden's al-Qaeda were suspected of carrying out the attack. Four suspects were found guilty in August to October 2003, three of whom were sentenced to death and one to life imprisonment.

In December 2002 the Indonesian government signed a peace deal with the separatist Free Aceh Movement (GAM). Following thirty years of violence, the agreement, signed in Geneva, allows for autonomy and free elections in the oil-rich province on the northern tip of Sumatra island in exchange for an end to the conflict. However, in May 2003, the peace talks broke down and the Indonesian government launched a military offensive against Gam rebels in Aceh, imposing martial law on the province.

Violence by Muslim extremists has continued in Indonesia: in August 2003 a car bomb exploded outside a luxury hotel in Jakarta, killing 14 people; four died on 10 January 2004 following a bomb in a crowded cafe on the island of Sulawesi; whilst ten people were killed in a bomb blast at a New Year concert in the troubled province of Aceh. In September 2004 a car bomb exploded outside the Australian Embassy in Jakarta, killing nine.

In December 2004 Indonesia was hit by a massive tsunami that devastated countries around the Indian Ocean. The earthquake that triggered the wave occurred off the coast of Sumatra, More than 170,000 people were killed in Indonesia, the worst affected area was the Aceh region of Sumatra.

Following the tsunami, the government lifted the state of emergency in the Aceh region in May 2005. In August, the Helsinki peace deal was reached between the Government and the Free Aceh Movement; the rebels gave up a demand for independence in return for autonomy and the right to fully democratic elections. The rebels began disarming in September 2005. Some 15,000 people died in the 30 year conflict. Gubernatorial and local elections took place in December 2006; ex-rebel Irwandi Yusuf, became the first directly-elected governor of Aceh province.

In October 2005, Bali was again the target for Muslim extremists; three suicide bombers killed 23 people. Early January 2006 saw flash floods and landslides in East and Central Java. An estimated 180 people were buried in the landslides. Environmentalists claimed that deforestation in the area had exacerbated the effects on seasonal heavy rainfall.

There were protests at a US-owned gold and copper mine in Papua province in March 2006, following attempts to remove illegal prospectors from the site. There is an underlying discontent in Papua; in 2001, the Indonesian government granted the province increased autonomy, but there have been few material benefits and the Papuans are losing faith in the political process.

At sunrise (5.45 a.m) on 28th May 2006, the island of Java was struck by an earthquake of magnitude 6.3. Initial estimates indicated a death toll of between 4,900 and 5,100 people, with a further 20,000 injured and 200,000 left homeless. The worst affected area was south of the ancient royal city of Yogyakarta. A major relief operation was quickly put into effect, and countries and international aid organisations pledged financial support. There were reports of heightened activity on the neighbouring Mount Merapi volcano, which had shown signs of imminent eruption earlier in the month. On 17th July, Java was hit by a tsunami triggered by an undersea earthquake of 7.7 magnitude. The wave, some 2 metres high, killed over 500 people. Around 53,000 people were displaced. The Pacific Tsunami Warning Center in Hawaii had issued tsunami warnings for parts of Indonesia but the warning communication system to Java was not yet operational.

In January 2007, at least 20 people were killed and 340,000 made homeless by massive floods that swept through the Indonesian capital, Jakarta. Three days of torrential rain caused rivers to burst their banks. In early March, landslides on the island of Flores killed around seventy people; it was thought that deforestation exacerbated the seasonal problem. On the 6th March, a powerful earthquake (6.3 magnitude) struck close to the Sumatran city of Padang, killing around 70 people and flattening hundreds of houses. The quake was felt as far away as Malaysia and Singapore. The following day, a plane crashed on landing at Yogyakarta airport in Java, killing 22 people. In December 2007, the worst landslides and floods for 25 years hit the central island of Java; at least 120 people were reported dead or missing, and tens of thousands forced to flee their homes. Environmentalists blamed the disaster on intensive deforestation.

INDONESIA

The former President, Haji Muhammad Suharto, who ruled Indonesia with an iron fist for thirty two years, died in January 2008. During his rule, the economy thrived, but thousands were killed in the provinces of Papua, Aceh and East Timor (invaded in 1975). Suharto left office in 1998 amid mass protests over corruption and human rights abuses.

In January 2008, the human death toll from bird flu reached one hundred, almost half the total worldwide fatalities. Indonesia has struggled to contain the virus.

Two earthquakes hit the island of Sumatra in February 2008. Although a Tsunami warning was issued, it was later lifted. There was no damage but an earthquake in the same area in September 2007 left an estimated 25 people dead.

At the end of September 2009 the island of Sumatra was hit by an earthquake killing 1,100 people. The earthquake also affected the Samoan islands and Tonga which were hit by a Tsunami triggered by the quake. The death toll was expected to rise as more remote areas were searched.

Several suspected militants have been arrested recently in a series of raids on alleged terrorist training camps. In March 2010, an alleged leader and member of Jemaah Islamiah, was shot dead in Jakarta. He was the last main suspect of the 2002 Bali bombings.

Following heavy rains in September and October 2010, rivers burst their banks. At least 86 people lost their lives as a result of ensuing flash floods and landslides in the eastern province of West Papua.

In December 2011, a three month strike by workers at copper and gold mines owned by the US company Freeport-McMoran ended when a pay deal was reached.

In June 2012, Umar Patek who had been involved in the Bali bomb attacks was sentenced to 20 years in prison, he had been extradited from Pakistan the previous year.

East Timor
East Timor's new president, Xanana Gusmao, was inaugurated on 20 May 2002, ending 27 years of unofficial rule by Indonesia. East Timor had been ruled by Portugal for more than 400 years when Indonesia took control of the province in 1975. Since then the island had fought for independence. The 1999 referendum showed that over 78 per cent of East Timorese wanted independence from Indonesia and, following violence from anti-independence militias, a UN Transitional Administration for East Timor (UNTAET) was set up. Elections for the island's 88-member Legislative Assembly took place in August 2001, and a presidential election took place on 14 April 2002. In January 2006, an East Timorese report held the government of Indonesia responsible for the deaths of more than 100,000 people during its occupation.

Legislature
Indonesia's legislature in bicameral, the House of Representatives (*Dewan Perwakilan Rakyat*), is currently 550 directly elected members. Members serve a five year term. The House operates on a system of majority voting. The annual session of the House runs from 16 August to 15 August the following year. The number of members is determined by the size of the population. Each member of the House represents some 400,000 people. Consequently, if the population increases significantly, more members are elected to the House.

For laws to be passed bills have to be submitted, either by the Government or by members of the House of Representatives, to the Speaker of the House. There are generally four readings and a bill becomes law when it has obtained the signature of the President. The bill is then published in the State Gazette of the Republic of Indonesia.

The upper house, the House of Representatives of the Regions (*Dewan Perwakilan Daerah*), came into being following constitutional amendments passed in 2001. This house deals with regional matters and is made up of 128 directly elected members, four from each province.

House of Representatives, Jalan Jenderai Gatot Subroto, 10270 Jakarta, Indonesia. Tel: +62 21 572 5965, URL: http://www.dpr.go.id
House of Representatives of the Regions, Jalan Jenderal Gatot Subroto, 10270 Jakarta, Indonesia, URL: http://www.dpd.go.id

---

Cabinet (as at June 2013)
Co-ordinating Minister for Political and Security Affairs: Djoko Suyanto (page 1522)
Co-ordinating Minister for Economy: Hatta Rajasa (page 1499)
Co-ordinating Minister for People's Welfare: Agung Laksono (page 1459)
Minister of Home Affairs: Gamawan Fauzi (page 1423)
Minister of Foreign Affairs: Raden Mohammad Natalegawa (page 1484)
Minister of Finance: Dr Muhammad Chatib Basri
Minister of Defence: Purnomo Yusgiantoro (page 1542)
Minister of Justice and Human Rights: Amir Syamsuddin
Minister of Energy and Mineral Resources: Ir Jero Wacik
Minister of Industry: Mohamad Suleman Hidayat
Minister of Trade: Gita Wirjawan
Minister of Agriculture: Ir H. Suswono
Minister of Forestry: Zulkifli Hasan
Minister of Health: Nafsiah Mboi
Minister of Transport: Evert Ernest Mangindaam
Minister of Maritime Affairs and Fisheries: Syarif Cicip Sutardjo
Minister of Manpower and Transmigration: Muhaimin Iskandar
Minister of Public Works: Djoko Kirmanto
Minister of Education and Culture: Muhammad Nuh
Minister of Social Affairs: Salim Segaf Al-Jufrie
Minister of Religious Affairs: Dr H Suryadharma Ali
Minister of Tourism and Creative Economy: Dr Mari Elka Pangestu
State Secretary: Lt. Gen. (Ret'd) Sudi Silalahi

Minister for Communication and Information: Tifatul Sembiring
Minister for Youth and Sports: Roy Suryo
Attorney General: Jaksa Agung
Minister of State for the Development of Disadvantaged Regions: Helmy Faishal Zaini
State Minister for the Environment: Baltazar Kambuaya
State Minister for National Development Planning: Prof. Armida Alisjahbana
State Minister for Public Housing: Suharso Djan Faridz
State Minister for Research and Technology: Prof. Gusti Muhammad Hatta
State Minister for State Administrative Reform: Azwar Abubakar
State Minister for State-Owned Enterprises: Dahlan Iskan
State Minister for Women and Child Protection: Linda Amalia Agum Gumelar
State Minister for Co-operatives and Small and Medium Sized Enterprises: Syarifuddin Hasan

Ministries
Office of the President, Istana Merdeka, Jakarta, Indonesia. Tel: +62 (0) 21 331097, URL: http://www.indonesia.go.id/
Office of the Vice-President, Jalan Merdeka Selatan 6, Jakarta, Indonesia. Tel: +62 (0)21 363539, URL: http://www.indonesia.go.id/
Ministry of Administrative Reform, Jalan Taman Suropati 2, Jakarta, Indonesia. Tel: +62 (0)21 334811, URL: http://www.menpan.go.id/
Ministry of Agriculture, Jl. Harsono RM No.3, Gedung D-Lantai 4, Ragunan-Jakarta 12550-Indonesia. Tel: +62 (0)21 782 2638, 781 5380, fax: +62 (0)21 781 6385, e-mail: webadmin@deptan.go.id, URL: http://www.deptan.go.id
Ministry of Communications, Jalan Merdeka Barat 8, Jakarta 10110, Indonesia. Tel: +62 (0)21 381 1308, URL: http://www.dephub.go.id/index.asp
Ministry of Co-operatives and Small and Medium Enterprises, Jl. H.R. Rasuna Said Kav. 3-5 Kuningan Jakarta 12940, Indonesia. Tel: +62 (0)21 5299 2885, fax: +62 (0)21 527 2742, e-mail: pusdatin@depkop.go.id, URL: http://www.depkop.go.id
Ministry of Defence and Security, Jalan Merdeka Barat 13-14, Jakarta 10110, Indonesia. Tel: +62 (0)21 345 6184, URL: http://www.hankam.go.id/
Ministry of National Education, Jalan Jenderal Sudirman, Senayan, Jakarta Pusat, Indonesia. Tel: +62 (0)21 581665, URL: http://www.depdiknas.go.id/
Ministry of Finance, Jalan Lapangan Banteng Timur 4, Jakarta Pusat, Indonesia. Tel: +62 (0)21 372758, URL: http://www.depkeu.go.id/Ind/
Ministry of Foreign Affairs, Jalan Taman Pejambon 6, Jakarta 10410, Indonesia. Tel: +62 (0)21 3441 508, e-mail: guestbook@dfa-deplu.go.id, URL: http://www.deplu.go.id/
Ministry of Forestry and Estate Crops, Jalan Jenderal Gatot Subroto, Jakarta 10270, Indonesia. Tel: +62 (0)21 583034, URL: http://www.dephut.go.id/
Ministry of Health, Jalan H.R. Rasuna Said, Block X5, Kav. 4-9, Jakarta 12950, Indonesia. Tel: +62 (0)21 520 4395, URL: http://www.depkes.go.id/
Ministry of Home Affairs, Jalan Merdeka Utara 7, Jakarta Pusat, Indonesia. Tel: + 62 (0)21 377392, URL: http://www.otonomi.gol.go.id/
Ministry of Industry and Trade, Jalan Jenderal Gatot Subroto Kav. 52-53, Jakarta, Indonesia. Tel: +62 (0)21 515198, URL: http://indag.dprin.go.id/
Ministry of Information & Communication, Jalan Merdeka Barat 9, Jakarta 10110, Indonesia. Tel: +62 (0)21 377392, URL: http://www.kominfo.go.id/
Ministry of Justice, Jalan H.R. Rasuna Said, Kav. 4-5, Jakarta Pusat, Indonesia. Tel: +62 (0)21 520 2391, URL: http://www.depkehham.go.id/
Ministry of Manpower, Jalan Jenderal Gatot Subroto 51, Jakarta Pusat, Indonesia. Tel: +62 (0)21 515622, URL: http://indonesia.go.id/
Ministry of Mining and Energy, Jalan Merdeka Selatan 18, Jakarta 10110, Indonesia. Tel: +62 (0)21 380 4242, e-mail: pulahta@setjen.dpe.go.id, URL: http://www.dpe.go.id/
Ministry of National Development Planning, Jalan Taman Suropati 2, Jakarta Pusat 10310, Indonesia. Tel: +62 (0)21 336207, fax: +62 (0)21 314 5375, e-mail: admin@bappenas.go.id, URL: http://www.bappenas.go.id/
Ministry for Population and the Environment, Jalan Medan Merdeka Barat 15, Jakarta Pusat, Indonesia. Tel: +62 (0)21 371295, URL: http://www.bkkbn.go.id/
Ministry for Public Works, Jl Rd., Patah I No.1 Kebayoran Baru, Jakarta Selatan, Indonesia. Tel: +62 (0)21 739 5588, URL: http://www.pu.go.id/
Ministry of Religious Affairs, Jalan Lapangan Banteng Barat 3-4, Jakarta, Indonesia. Tel: +62 (0)21 362018, URL: http://www.indonesia.go.id/
Ministry of Research and Technology, Gedung Menara Patra, 3rd Floor, Jalan M.H. Thamrin 8, Jakarta, Indonesia. Tel: +62 (0)21 324767, URL: http://www.ristek.go.id/
Ministry of Tourism, Art and Culture, Jalan Kebon Sirih 36, Jakarta, Indonesia. Tel: +62 (0)21 366705, URL: http://www.deparsenibud.go.id/
Ministry of Transport, Jl. Medan Merdeka Barat No. 8, Jakarta 10110, Indonesia. Tel: +62 (0)21 3811 308, URL: http://www.dephub.go.id/index.asp
Ministry of Transmigration and Forest Settlements, Jalan Lethenderal Haryono MT, Cikoko, Jakarta Selatan, Indonesia. Tel: +62 (0)21 794 682, URL: http://www.deptrans.go.id/
Ministry of Youth Affairs and Sports, Jalan Gerbang Pemuda 3, Senayan, Jakarta Pusat, Indonesia. Tel: +62 (0)21 573 8310, URL: http://www.indonesia.go.id/

Main Political Parties
Golongan Karya (Golkar, Functional Group), Jalan Anggrek Nelimurni, Jakarta 11480, Indonesia. Tel: +62 21 530 2222, fax: +62 21 530 3380, URL: http://www.golkar.or.id
Chairperson: Aburizal Bakrie
Partai Demkrasi Indonesia Perjuangan (PDIP, Indonesia Democratic Party of Struggle), Jalan Diponegoro 58, Jakarta, Indonesia 10310, India. Tel: +62 21336331, URL: http://www.pdiperjuangan.or.id
Leader: Megawati Soekarnoputri
Partai Persatuan Pembangunan (PPP, United Development Party), Jalan Diponegoro 60, Jakarta 10310, Indonesia. Tel: +62 21 336338, fax: +62 21 3908070, URL: http://www.ppp.or.id
Leader: Suryadharma Ali
Partai Kebangkitan Bangsa (PKB, National Awakening Party), URL: http://www.dpp-pkb.or.id
Leader: Muhaimin Iskandar

Partai Demokrat (PD, Democrat Party), Jalan Pemuda No. 712 Jakarta Timur 13220, Indonesia. URL: http://www.demokrat.or.id
Chairman: Anas Urbaningrum

Partai Keadilan Sejahtera (PKS, Prosperous Justice Party), e-mail: partai@pks.or.id, URL: http://pk-sejahtera.org
Chairman: Luthfi Hasan Ishaaq

Partai Amanat Nasional, (National Mandate Party), URL: http://pan.or.id
Chairman: Hatta Rajasa

Partai Hati Nurani Rakyat, (People's Conscience Party), URL: http://www.hanura.com
Sec. Gen.: Yus Usman Sumanegara

Partai Gerakan Indonesia Raya, (Great Indonesia Movement Party), URL: http://www.partaigerindra.or.id
Sec. Gen.: Ahmad Muzani

Elections

In 1993, the People's Consultative Assembly re-elected President Suharto to his fifth term of office. President Suharto was first elected to office in 1968. In the midst of a financial crisis, and following widespread civil unrest, President Suharto was forced to resign in May 1998. Vice-president Bacharuddin Jusuf Habibie became president until elections took place. The 1999 Presidential elections resulted in victory for Abdurrahman Wahid, head of an alliance of Muslim parties. In April 2001 he was dismissed by the Indonesian parliament following allegations of corruption and incompetence. Vice President Mrs. Megawati Sukarnoputri replaced him as president.

In September 2004, Susilo Bambang Yudhoyono of the Democratic party, beat the incumbent President, Mrs Megawati Sukarnoputri, in the second round of the presidential election, and became the first democratically elected president of Indonesia.

The most recent presidential elections took place on 8 July 2009 and President Yudhoyono was re-elected with over 60 per cent of the vote, winning in one round of voting. The opposition candidate Megawati Sukarnoputri won 27 per cent of the vote and the third candidate, Yusuf Kalla, the vice-president, gained 12 per vent of the vote.

The most recent election was in April 2009. The Democrat Party won the most seats but not enough for an overall majority. Presidential elections were also held in April 2009; Susilo Bambang Yudhoyono of the Democratic Party won.

Diplomatic Representation

Embassy of the Republic of Indonesia, 38 Grosvenor Square, London, WIK 2HW, UK. Tel: +44 (0)20 7499 7661, fax: +44 (0)20 7491 4993, e-mail: kbri@btconnect.com., URL: http://www.indonesianembassy.org.uk
Ambassador: Teuku Mohammad Hamzah Thayeb

Embassy of the Republic of Indonesia, 2020 Massachusetts Avenue, NW, Washington, DC 20036, USA. Tel: +1 202 775 5200, fax: +1 202 265 5365, URL: http://www.embassyofindonesia.org
Ambassador: Dino Patti Djalal (page 1415)

British Embassy, Jalan M.H. Thamrin 75, Jakarta 10310, Indonesia. Tel: +62 21 315 6264, fax: +62 21 315 4061 (Commercial) / +62 21 392 6263 (Chancery/Economic), URL: http://ukinindonesia.fco.gov.uk/en
Ambassador: Mark Canning (page 1400)

Embassy of the United States of America, Jl. Merdeka Selatan 4-5, Jakarta 10110, Indonesia. Tel: +62 21 3435 9000, fax: +62 21 3435 9922, URL: http://jakarta.usembassy.gov
Ambassador: Scot Marciel

Embassy of Singapore, Jalan H.R Rasuna Said, Blok X14, Kav.2, Kuningan, Jakarta 12950, Indonesia. Tel: +62 (0)21 520 1489, fax: +62 (0)21 520 1486, URL: http://www.mfa.gov.sg

Permanent Mission of Indonesia to the United Nations, 325 East 38th Street, New York, NY 10016, USA. Tel: +1 212 972 8333, fax: +1 212 972 9780, e-mail:ptri@indonesiamission-ny.org, URL: http://www.indonesiamission-ny.org
Ambassador: Hasan Kleib

Indonesian Mission to the United Nations in Geneva, 16 rue de St.-Jean, Geneva 1203, Switzerland. Tel: +41 (0)22 338 3350, fax: +41 (0)22 345 5733, e-mail: indonesia@ties.itu.int

LEGAL SYSTEM

The constitution decrees that the Supreme Court be independent and free from government intervention. In 1970 a law was enacted that laid down the basic principles of Indonesian law. In 1989 the Islamic Judicature Bill was approved by the Dewan Perwakilan Rakyat (House of Representatives), giving the Muslim sharia courts authority over civil matters such as marriage and divorce.

The judicial system comprises various distinct courts under the oversight of the Supreme Court (Mahkamah Agung). The court of first instance is the State Court (Pengadilan Negeri). There are around 250 State Courts in Indonesia. Appeals from the State Court are heard by the country's 20 High Courts (Pengadilan Tinggi). Appeals from the High Court and, in some instances from the State Court, are heard by the Supreme Court in Jakarta. The Supreme Court can also conduct re-trials when new evidence comes to light.

In 1998, the Commercial Court (Pengadilan Niaga) was established to rule on bankruptcy applications and other commercial matters. The State Administrative Court (Pengadilan Tata Usaha Negara) judges on law cases filed against the government. The Constitutional Court (Mahkamah Konstitusi) was established as part of the 2001 constitutional amendments in order to judge the constitutionality of legislation. It also has the power to dismiss a President from office.

In general, the government respects the human rights of its citizens. However, there is a degree of corruption in the judiciary, and impunity among prison authorities. In recent years, there have been killings by security forces. Freedom of speech is limited. The government is taking action to improve human rights, and has recently prosecuted officials found guilty of corrupt practises. In 2008, President Yudhoyono accepted the conclusion and recommendations of the Indonesia/Timor-Leste Commission on Truth and Friendship that Indonesian security forces bore responsibility for 1999 human rights abuses and should undergo enhanced human rights training.

Indonesia retains the death penalty for terrorism, premeditated murder, grave human rights violations, narcotics offences and corruption. The most recent reported execution took place in 2013. In 2013, 114 people were reported to be on death row including 40 foreigners mostly convicted of drug crimes.

Supreme Court of Indonesia, URL: http://www.mahkamahagung.go.id/ (not in English)
National Commission for Human Rights, URL: http://www.komnasham.go.id/

LOCAL GOVERNMENT

The Unitary State of the Republic of Indonesia is divided into 30 provinces, 2 special regions (Aceh and Yogyakarta) and one special capital city district (Jakarta). These are futher are sub-divided into 243 districts, 55 municipalities, 16 administrative municipalities, 35 administrative cities and 3,841 sub-districts (or kecamatans).

Each province has a governor who is the chief executive of the province. There are provincial legislatures with whom the regional government meets to decide regional legislation and budgetary decisions. Districts are able to act autonomously but levels below this cannot. Most national government departments have branch offices in provinces and districts.

The Republic of Indonesia is divided into 22 first level autonomous regions: East-, Central- and West-Java; Aceh; North- and West-Sumatra; Riau; Djambi; South-Sumatra; Central-, West-, South- and East- Kalimantan; North, Central, South, South-West and South-East Sulawesi; Bali; West-Nusa Tenggara; East-Nusa Tenggara; Maluku; Irian-Jaya; the special Territory of Jakarta Raya; and the special Territory of Yogyakarta.

Population figures by Province

Province	Population 2000	Population 2010*
Nanggroe Aceh Darussalam	3,930,905	4,494,410
Sumatera Utara	11,649,655	12,982,204
Sumatera Barat	4,248,931	4,846,909
Riau	4,957,627	5,538,367
Jambi	2,413,846	3,092,265
Sumatera Selatan	6,899,675	7,450,394
Bengkulu	1,567,432	1,715,518
Lampung	6,741,439	7,608,405
Kep. Bangka Belitung	900,197	1,223,296
Kepulauan Riau	-	1,679,163
DKI Jakarta	8,389,443	9,607,787
Jawa Barat	35,729,537	43,053,732
Jawa Tengah	31,228,940	32,382,657
DI Yogyakarta	3,122,268	3,457,491
Jawa Timur	34,783,640	37,476,757
Banten	8,098,780	10,632,166
Bali	3,151,162	3,890,757
Nusa Tenggara Barat	4,009,261	4,500,212
Nusa Tenggara Timur	3,952,279	4,683,827
Kalimantan Barat	4,034,198	4,395,983
Kalimantan Tengah	1,857,000	2,212,089
Kalimantan Selatan	2,985,240	3,626,616,
Kalimantan Timur	2,455,120	3,553,143
Sulawesi Utara	2,012,098	2,270,596
Sulawesi Tengah	2,218,435	2,635,009
Sulawesi Selatan	8,059,627	8,034,776
Sulawesi Tenggara	1,821,284	2,232,586
Gorontalo	835,044	1,040,164
Sulawesi Barat	-	1,158,651
Maluku	1,205,539	1,533,506
Maluku Utara	785,059	1,038,087
Papua Barat	-	760,422
Papua	2,220,934	2,833,381

Source: Statistics Indonesia

AREA AND POPULATION

Area

Situated between South East Asia and Australia, Indonesia comprises a total of 17,508 islands, stretching 5,120 km from east to west, and 1,760 km from north to south. Around 6,000 of the islands are inhabited. The largest islands are Sumatra, Java, Kalimantan (Indonesian Borneo), Sulawesi (Celebes) and Papua (the Indonesian half of New Guinea, also known as Irian Jaya). Indonesia has a total land area of 1,919,317 sq. km. Indonesia sits on the seismically active Pacific Ring of Fire, and experiences frequent earthquakes and tsunamis, which are triggered by underwater earthquakes. The highest point is Puncak Jaya at 5,030 metres.

The climate is tropical, hot and humid, cooler in the highlands.

INDONESIA

To view a map, please visit http://www.un.org/Depts/Cartographic/map/profile/indonesi.pdf

Population
The population of Indonesia reached an estimated 239.87 million in 2010, up from 225.6 million in 2007. It is the fourth most highly populated country in the world (after the People's Republic of China, India and the United States of America). Indonesia's population grew at an average annual rate of 1.2 per cent over the period 2000-10.

The population is concentrated on six main islands: Java, Sumatra, Bali, Kalimantan (the Indonesian portion of the island of Borneo), Sulawesi and Irian Jaya (the western part of New Guinea). Java is home to 60 per cent of the Indonesian population and is one of the most densely populated areas in the world. Urbanisation in Indonesia is increasing, leading to some social problems.

Population density for the whole of Indonesia in 2008 was 120 people per sq. km. up from 101 per sq. km. in 1995. The most densely populated province is DKI Jakarta, with over 12,635 people per sq. km in 2000. The least densely populated province is Papua, with 6 people per sq. km in 2000.

The vast majority of Indonesians are of Malay origin. Major ethnic groups include Javanese (45 per cent), Sundanese (14 per cent), Madurese (7.5 per cent), and coastal Malays (7.5 per cent).

The official language is Bahasa Indonesia, similar to Malay. There are over 550 languages and dialects spoken in the archipelago. English is the language of instruction.

Births, Marriages, Deaths
The birth rate is currently in decline, falling from 21.8 per 1,000 inhabitants in 2002 to 18.2 in 20103. The rate has been influenced by various factors, including rising living standards, improved health standards and more widespread contraception. Life expectancy has risen steadily over the last 30 years; it is currently 68 years (2009) compared with 57.9 in 1985. Healthy life expectancy is 60 years. The median age is 28 years. Approximately 27 per cent of the population is aged under 15 years and 8 per cent over 60 years. The crude death rate has decreased, from 8.3 deaths per 1,000 population in 1997 to 7.1 per 1,000 population in 2010. Better nutrition, a rising standard of living, better working conditions, better education and smaller nuclear families are among the factors influencing this trend. (Source: http://www.who.int, World Health Statistics 2012)

Public Holidays 2014
1 January: New Year's Day
14 January: Prophet Muhammad's Birthday*
31 January: Chinese New Year*
18 April: Good Friday
21 April: Easter Monday
27 May: Ascent of the Prophet Muhammad*
29 May: Ascension (Christian)
29 July: Eid al Fitr* (end of Ramadan)
17 August: Independence Day
5 October: Eid al-Adha* (Festival of the Sacrifice)
25 December: Christmas Day
*Precise dates depend upon sighting of the moon

EMPLOYMENT

Indonesia's total labour force rose from 106,388,935 in August 2006 to 111,947,265 in August 2008. Those in employment numbered 102,552,750 in August 2008, whilst those unemployed numbered 9,394,515. The unemployment rate rose from 9.9 per cent in 2004 to 11.2 per cent in 2005 before falling to 10.4 per cent in 2006, 8.39 per cent in 2008, 7.9 per cent in 2009 and 7.1 per cent in 2010.

Employment by Industry, February 2009

Employment sector	No. employed
Agriculture, forestry, fisheries	43,029,493
Mining and quarrying	1,139,495
Manufacturing	12,615,440
Electricity, gas, and water	209,441
Construction	4,610,695
Wholesale/retail trade, restaurants and hotels	21,836,768
Transportation, storage and communication	5,947,673
Finance, insurance, real estate	1,484,598
Community, social and personal services	13,611,841
TOTAL	104,485,444

Source: Statistics Indonesia

BANKING AND FINANCE

Currency
One Rupiah (Rp) = 100 sen

GDP/GNP, Inflation, National Debt
Over the last 30 years Indonesia's economic situation has changed dramatically; it used to be ranked one of the poorest countries in the world, with a per capita income of US$70, but is now the largest economy in South East Asia and is forecast to be the tenth largest by 2030. It is predicted that by 2015, it will be a middle-income country with a per capita income of US$4,000. However, despite agrowing middle class, poverty remains widespread. The economy is hindered by poor education, weak infrastructure and corruption. Indonesia is one of the largest carbon emitters in the world.

In December 2004 Indonesia was badly hit by a tsunami which occurred after an underwater earthquake just off the coast of the island of Sumatra. The overall economy was not badly hit, as the main area to be affected by the disaster, Aceh, was not crucial to economic growth.

Indonesia's economy, unlike others in the region, is not export based, foreign trade making up around 25 per cent of GDP with the main export earning coming from the hydrocarbon, mining and agricultural sectors while main imports are manufactured goods. This high reliance on domestic consumption has helped it in the global economic crisis and although growth dipped in 2009, it recovered in 2010. Economic reform is still required and the high poverty rates are in danger of increasing because of high inflation.

Gross domestic product (GDP) at constant 2000 prices grew at a rate of 4.3 per cent in 2002 by 4.8 per cent in 2003, 5.0 per cent in 2004 and by 5.7 per cent in 2005, 5.5 per cent in 2006 and 6.3 per cent in 2007 before falling slightly to 6.1 per cent in 2008. (Source: Asian Development Bank, ADB). Indonesia's economy suffered as its exports fell sharply in Q4 of 2008. In response to the global economic crisis, the Indonesian government passed a US$6 billion fiscal stimulus. GDP was estimated at US$1 trillion in 2011, with a growth rate of 6 per cent.

GNP and GDP at Current Market Prices in Recent Years (billion Rupiah)

Year	GNP	GDP
1995	441,148	454,514
2001	1,623,229	1,684,280
2002	1,808,762	1,863,275
2003	1,936,261	2,013,675
2004	2,190,476	2,295,826
2005	2,639,281	2,774,281
2006	3,196,948	3,339,217
2007	3,786,837	3,949,321
2008	4,778,164	4,954,029

Source: Asian Development Bank

GDP at Current Market Prices by Industrial Origin, Billion Rupiahs

Origin	2008	2009	2010
Agriculture	716.7	857.2	985.1
Mining	541.3	591.9	716.4
Manufacturing	1,376.4	1,477.7	1,594.3
Electricity, gas & water supply	40.9	47.2	50.0
Construction	419.7	555.2	661.0
Trade	691.5	744.1	881.1
Transport & communication	312.2	352.4	417.5
Finance	368.1	404.0	462.8
Public Administration	257.5	318.6	354.2
Others	224.3	255.5	300.5
Total Gross Domestic Product	4,948.7	5,603.9	6,422.9

Source: Statistics Indonesia

Per capita GDP (current market prices) rose from 12,414,000 in 2005 to 14,991,000 in 2006, 17,503,000 in 2007 and 21,678,000 in 2008. Per capita GNI (current market prices) rose from 12,002,000 rupiahs in 2005 to 14,352,000 in 2006, 16,7852,000 in 2007 and 20,909,000 in 2008. (Source: ADB)

Although inflation had stabilised and was on average roughly 10.0 per cent during the 1980s and 1990s, the Asian economic crisis of 1998 forced it up to an estimated 74.5 per cent in 1998. There was a sharp drop following the crisis to just 2.01 in 1999. The rate remained below 12.5 per cent until 2005, when it rose to 17.11 per cent. The main increase was in the Transport, Communications and Financial Services sector, where there was a 44.75 per cent increase in prices. Inflation was put at 5 per cent in 2010 and 4 per cent in 2011.

Indonesia's total external debt in 2003 was estimated at US$134,389 million, down from the 2000 peak of US$144,407 million. US$101,205 million (around 75 per cent) of the debt was long term. The debt represents over 67 per cent of Indonesia's Gross National Income. External debt was estimated at US$185 billion in 2011.

Foreign Investment
Following Indonesia's economic collapse in 1998, and with about three-quarters of businesses in technical bankruptcy, the government was forced to turn to the International Monetary Fund (IMF) for emergency debt-relief assistance of US$43,000 million. After initial delays in economic reform, including privatization of a number of economic sectors, greater transparency in the issuing of government loans and subsidies, and stricter enforcement of laws and regulations for government procurement, the IMF released US$395 million in September 2001. A further US$469 million was released by the IMF in March 2003 following Indonesia's increased economic growth, lower inflation rates, and a stronger banking sector. By the end of 2003 Indonesia had graduated from IMF support.

Indonesia is committed to attracting foreign investment. It rose 30 per cent on an annual basis to US$11.9 billion in the first half of 2012. The top investors are Japan, Singapore, South Korea, the UK and the US.

Balance of Payments / Imports and Exports
External Trade in Million US$

Year	Exports, fob	Imports, cif	Trade Balance
2008	137,020	129,197	7,823
2009	116,510	96,829	19,681
2010	157,779	135,663	22,116

Source: Asian Development Bank

Exports increased by 35 per cent in 2010 and imports by 40 per cent.

Indonesia's primary exports are petroleum and natural gas, which accounted for 22.4 per cent of total exports in 2003. Export revenue from oil and gas over the year 2003 was US$13,651.7 million (an increase on 2002 revenue of US$ 12,112.7), of which US$5,621.0 million was from crude oil, US$1,553.8 million from oil products, and US$6,476.9 million from gas. (Source: Statistics Indonesia)

The following table shows the current top ten export trading partners, according to export revenue:

Exports by top trading partners, 2009-2010 (US$m)

Country	2009	2010
Exports total	116,510	157,791
Japan	18,575	25,782
US	10,889	14,302
China	11,499	15,693
Singapore	10,263	13,723
Rep. of Korea	8,145	12,575
India	7,433	9,915
Malaysia	6,812	9,362
Australia	3,264	4,244
Thailand	3,234	4,567
Netherlands	2,909	3,722

Source: Asian Development Bank

Top non-oil and gas imports are machinery and mechanical appliances, chemicals, base metals and vehicles and accessories.

Cost of selected Imports, US$million

Commodity	2007
Mineral products	22,667
Machinery, mechanical and electrical equipment	14,174
Chemical products	8,269
Base metals and articles thereof	7,633
Transportation equipment	4,958
Plastics & rubber	2,985
Prepared foodstuffs	3,090
Vegetable products	3,520

Source: Asian Development Bank

The following table shows the top ten import trading partners according to import cost:

Imports by top ten trading partners, 2009-10 (US$m)

Country	2009	2010
Total	96,968	135,691
Singapore	15,550	20,241
China	14,002	30,424
Japan	9,844	16,966
United States of America	7,094	9,416
Malaysia	5,688	8,649
Thailand	4,613	7,471
Korea, Rep. of	4,742	7,703
Saudi Arabia	3,136	4,361
Australia	3,436	4,099
Germany	2,374	3,007

Source: Asian Development Bank

Imports decreased by 18 per cent in the year 2009-10, but exports rose by 22 per cent.

Central Bank
Bank Indonesia, Jalan M. H. Thamrin 2, Pusat, Jakarta 10110, Java, Indonesia. Tel: +62 21 381 7187, fax: +62 21 350 1867, URL: http://www.bi.go.id
Governor: Darmin Nasution

Chambers of Commerce and Trade Organisations
Indonesian Chamber of Commerce and Industry, URL: http://www.bsd-kadin.org/
Jakarta Stock Exchange, URL: http://www.idx.co.id/

MANUFACTURING, MINING AND SERVICES

Primary and Extractive Industries
The mining sector is Indonesia's prime foreign exchange earner, oil and gas exports accounted for 21.1 per cent of total export revenue in 2008. The government actively encourages private domestic and foreign investment in the mining and energy sectors. Main products mined are crude oil and natural gas, coal, iron sand, tin concentrate, nickel ore, bauxite, copper concentrate, gold, silver, and manganese. Top exported mining products are copper ore, coal, nickel ore, natural sands, bauxite. The mining and quarrying industries employed around 1.1 million people in 2009 and contributed 716,400 billion rupiahs to the GDP.

There is rising local anger at foreign mining interests in Indonesia, which led to protests and attacks on US owned mines in the spring of 2006. Local activists targeted mines in Papua, Java and Sumbawa. The Government sees foreign investment as essential to strengthening the economy.

As of January 2012, Indonesia had proven oil reserves of 3.8 billion barrels. Indonesia has substantial, but falling, oil production. Indonesia's OPEC production quota is 1.45 million barrels per day, well above its production capacity. Indonesia became a net oil importer in 2004, when consumption exceeded 1.2 million barrels per day. It suspended its OPEC membership in 2004. Oil production was estimated at 994.69 thousand barrels per day in 2011, of which 917.92 thousand barrels per day was crude. It produced 1.045 million bbl/d in 2009, of which crude oil was 969 million bbl/d. Consumption was estimated at 1.11 million bbl/d. There are seven refineries in the country, with a combined capacity of 1,012 bbl/d.

Indonesia has significant reserves of natural gas and was the world's sixth largest exporter of natural gas in 2009 and the third largest exporter of LNG. Proven reserves of natural gas in January 2011 were an estimated 106 trillion cubic feet. Production in 2011 reached 2,693 billion cubic feet, and domestic consumption in the same year was an estimated 1,327 billion cubic feet. About 68 per cent of Indonesia's LNG exports go to Japan, 19 per cent to South Korea, and the remainder to Taiwan. As oil production has begun to decline in recent years, the Indonesia has sought to use its natural gas resources for power generation. However, the distribution infrastructure is inadequate. Main domestic customers for natural gas are fertilizer plants and petrochemical plants, followed by power generators.

Indonesia has considerable coal reserves and in recent years coal production has increased through the intensification of exploration, rehabilitation and the expansion of the state mines, as well as by providing opportunities for foreign and domestic investments. Most recent estimates (2004) indicate total reserves of 5.47 billion short tons, 58.6 per cent is lignite, 26.6 per cent is sub-bituminous, 14.4 per cent is bituminous, and 0.4 per cent anthracite. Sumatra contains roughly two-thirds of Indonesia's total coal reserves; the rest is located in Kalimantan, West Java, and Sulawesi. Coal production was an estimated 370 million short tons in 2010 and domestic consumption during the same year was 54 million short tons. Power plants accounted for nearly two-thirs of of 2009 total coal sales. Indonesia is now the world's second-largest coal exporter. (Source: Energy Information Agency, EIA)

Minerals apart from coal, petroleum and natural gas mined in Indonesia include, asphalt, bauxite, nickel ores, gold, silver, granite, manganese, iron sand, copper and tin. Tin is one of the most important commodities of Indonesia's hard mineral exports. Tin mining in Indonesia takes place on the islands of Singkep, Bangka, Belitung, Karimun and Bengkalis.

Mineral Production in 2007 (estimated)

Product	Weight
Coal	178,930,188 tons
Bauxite	1,251,147 tons
Nickel ores	7,122,870 tons
Gold	117,854 kg
Silver	268,967 kg
Granite	1,793,440 tons
Iron sand	124,610 tons
Tin concentrate	64,127 metric tonnes
Copper concentrate	796,899 metric tonnes

Source: Statistics Indonesia

Energy
In 2009, Indonesia consumed an estimated 6.052 quadrillion Btu. of energy. Per capita energy consumption in 2004 was 19.7 million Btu. Industry consumes most of Indonesia's energy, followed by the residential, transport and commercial (2 per cent) sectors. Fuel share of energy consumption in 2004 was as follows: oil, 53 per cent; natural gas, 30 per cent; coal, 12 per cent; hydroelectricity, 2 per cent and other renewables, 3 per cent.

Recent figures show that Indonesia now has an installed capacity of 34.07 billion GWe (January 2010). Net generation was 161.05 billion kWh in 2010. Consumption of electricity increased from 89.1 billion kWh in 2001 to 145.10 billion kWh in 2010. Prior to the Asian economic crisis, Indonesia was initiating a programme of rapid expansion of the power industry, opening up the country's power market to independent producers. However, the state-owned Perusahaan Listrik Negara (PLN) suffered financially and was left with over $5 billion in debts. As a consequence, Indonesia now faces an electricity supply crisis, due to underinvestment in power generation capacity, at a time when demand for electrical power is expected to grow by 6-7 per cent per annum. In 2003, the World Bank approved a $141 million loan to Indonesia to be used for improving the power sector on Java and Bali, which use approximately 80 per cent of Indonesia's power generation capacity. PLN's monopoly on distribution ended in 2009. The electricity infrastructure remains poor; as of 2009 only 65 per cent of the population had access to electricity. The government is currently expanding capacity. An additional 10 GW should be available by 2013 and a further 10 GW by 2014. (Source: EIA)

Indonesia currently has geothermal power capacity of 1 GW although the government estimates it has resources to generate 28 GW. The government plans to increase the use of renewable energy to 15 per cent of the electricty portfolio by 2025 based on the development of goethermal resources. Geothermal capacity is planned to be increased to 4 GW by 2014. (Source: EIA)

Manufacturing
Industrial development is one of the main priorities for the Indonesian government with emphasis on the following sectors: agro-industry; mineral processing; machinery, capital goods and electronic industries and export-concentrated industries such as textiles. Manufacturing is Indonesia's top GDP-contributing industry.

Value Added by Selected Subsector in Billion Rupiahs

Subsector	2007	2008*
Food products & beverages	94,643	115,928
Tobacco	58,941	77,952
Textiles	39,336	49,093

INDONESIA

- continued

Wearing apparel	21,165	26,743
Paper & paper products	32,579	42,722
Chemicals & chemical products	79,776	100,128
Rubber & plastics products	34,433	38,718
Basic metals	24,779	32,095
Electrical machinery & apparatus n.e.c	12,113	10,320
Radio, television & communication equipment	18,331	31,223
Motor vehicles, trailers & semi-trailers	40,919	49,035
Other transport equipment	37,853	24,746
Furniture & manufacturing n.e.c	14,735	18,441

* estimated figures
Source: Statistics Indonesia

Service Industries

The services industry contributed 40.8 per cent of Indonesia's GDP in 2005. In the 3rd Quarter 2005, the trade, hotel and restaurant sectors contributed 15.79 per cent of GDP, whilst financial, property and business services contributed 6.34 per cent. Other services contributed 9.94 per cent. The sector employed some 37,540 in 2003.

Tourism

Tourism is a key component of the government's economic plans. The number of foreign tourists visiting Indonesia stood at over 5 million in 2007. 1.3 million came from Singapore, 891,353 from Malaysia, 508,820 from Japan and 314,432 from Australia. Some 796,730 tourists travelled from Europe, mainly from Germany and the UK. Despite recent bomb attacks, in 2005, Bali remained the most popular resort with foreign visitors.

There are some 1,039 hotels, with around 104,600 rooms, in Indonesia. The average amount spent by each visitor is US$901.66, though the biggest spenders are the Canadians and the Dutch at over US$1,365 per visit.
Indonesia Tourism Promotion Board, URL: http://www.tourismindonesia.com

Agriculture

Agriculture currently contributes around 13.4 per cent of Indonesia's GDP and has shown steady decline in its economic importance over the past fifteen years relative to other economic sectors. Financially, however, the sector continues to grow; in 2004 agriculture earned 354,435 billion rupiahs, an increase on the previous year's figure of 325,654 billion rupiahs. Most Indonesians still depend on agriculture and agro-industries for their livelihoods. Principal crops are rice, cereals, sugarcane, pulses, jute, tea and cotton, cassava (tapioca), peanuts, rubber, cocoa, coffee, palm oil and copra. Under the 1993 Guidelines of State Policy, the government is trying to implement plans to develop agriculture with more effective agricultural systems, more product diversity, greater food price stability and more land care.

Rice production was hit by droughts and floods in recent years (possibly caused by the El Nino weather system), leading to a slight fall in production. However, figures for 2003 were the highest for over a decade at 52,137 thousand metric tons, and rose by 3.74 per cent in 2004 to 54,088 thousand metric tons. The government is trying to promote more self-sufficiency in rice farmers by encouraging farmers to plant higher quality rice.

Recent efforts to increase the production of vegetables and fruits have put emphasis on the use of high quality plant seeds and modern cultivation technology.

Agricultural Production in 2010

Produce	Int. $'000*	Tonnes
Rice, paddy	17,951,110	66,469,400
Palm oil	8,596,726	19,760,000
Natural rubber	2,964,752	2,591,940
Cassava	2,448,414	23,918,100
Indigenous chicken meat	2,350,172	1,649,930
Coconuts	1,990,314	18,000,000
Maize	1,793,139	18,327,600
Bananas	1,620,806	5,755,070
Palm kernals	1,388,680	5,380,000
Indigenous pigmeat	1,026,251	667,593
Fruit, tropical fresh nes	948,548	2,321,050
Hen eggs, in shell	927,091	1,117,800

*unofficial figures
Source: http://faostat.fao.org/site/339/default.aspx Food and Agriculture Organization of the United Nations, Food and Agricultural commodities production

Reared livestock in Indonesia are shown on the table below:

Livestock (000 head)

Livestock	2004	2005
Dairy cows	10,533	10,680
Buffaloes	2,403	2,428
Horses	397	406
Goats	12,781	13,182
Sheep	8,075	8,307
Pigs	5,980	6,267
Local chickens	276,989	286,690
Layer chickens	93,416	98,491
Broiller chickens	778,970	864,246
Ducks	32,573	34,275

Source: Statistics Indonesia

An estimated 1.45 million metric tons of meat were produced in 2001, mainly beef, pork and chicken.

The development of the forestry industry is directed to meeting domestic and export needs and preserving the natural forest. Indonesia is the world's largest producer of plywood and supplies around 85 per cent of the word's needs. According to Statistics Indonesia, there were an estimated 413 Forest Concession Estates in 2001, covering some 37 million hectares. In the same year, over around 15.8 million cubic metres of logs were felled.

Recent figures show that around 5.3 million tonnes of fish were caught in 2010.

COMMUNICATIONS AND TRANSPORT

Travel Requirements

Citizens of the USA, Canada, Australia and the EU require a passport valid for six months beyond the length of stay and a visa. A 30 day visa can be obtained on arrival, but are not extendable. Other nationals should contact the embassy to check visa requirements. Visitors who exceed the term of their visa may be fined or imprisoned.

National Airlines

Air transport in Indonesia is served by Garuda Indonesia, Merpati Nusantara Airlines (MNA) and Pelita Air Service, as well as private-owned companies. Garuda Indonesia flies international routes.
Garuda Indonesia Airways (PT Garuda Indonesia), URL: http://www.garuda-indonesia.com/
Merpati Nusantara Airlines, URL: http://www.merpati.co.id/
Pelita Air Service, URL: http://www.pelita-air.com/

International Airports

In 2010 there were an estimated 49 million domestic passenger departures and 50.5 million passenger domestic arrivals. In the same year there were an estimated 9.5 million international passenger departures and 9.56 million international passenger arrivals. Total cargo loaded in 2010 was approximately 555,000 tons and 514,000 tons were unloaded.
Jakarta Airport (Soekarno-Hatta), URL: http://www.jakartaairportonline.com/

Railways

There are currently a total of 5,000 km of railway in Indonesia. During the first nine months of 2005, there were 125,086,000 passengers on the railway (an increase of 0.38 per cent on the same period in 2004). 14,542, 000 tons on merchandise was transported by rail during the first nine months of 2005, representing a fall of 7.13 per cent on the same period in 2004.

Roads

According to Statistics Indonesia, the number of vehicles on the roads has more than doubled over the decade to 2002, from 10,197,955 to 22,985,193. By 2010 the number was over 70 million. The road network has an approximate total length of 435,000 km (260,000 km asphalted). Vehicles drive on the left.

Shipping

The development of sea transportation is focused on access to all regions, stimulation of economic growth, expansion of inter-regional trade and increased competitiveness of domestic products in domestic and foreign markets. The capabilities and role of the national shipping companies engaged in domestic sea transportation are being promoted. Cooperation among national shipping lines has been strengthened in order to create a cohesive and strong transportation fleet. PELNI is the state-owned shipping company and this runs ships between the islands, URL: http://www.pelni.com

In 2001, some 163,687,000 tons of cargo was shipped between the Indonesian islands (a large increase on the figures of 127,740,000 the previous year) and 143,750, 000 was shipped abroad (up from 141,528,000). 46,659,000 tons of cargo was unloaded from abroad in 2001 (up from 45,040,000).

Ports and Harbours

The Indonesia Port Corporations (I-IV) manage the ports in Indonesia. Jakarta's international container port, Tanjung Perak is crucial to this transport sector and container trade is increasing. There are also container ports in Surabaya and Rambipuji. A state-owned company, Indonesia Port Corporation III, manages commercial ports in provinces including Tanjung Perak.
Tanjung Perak, URL: http://www.perakport.co.id/main/index.php

HEALTH

The government has been trying to improve the country's health care system, with some health care decentralised. There are 33 provinces and each provinces is sub-divided into districts and each district into sub-districts. Each sub-district has at least one health centre headed by a doctor. There may be further sub-centres (puskemas), headed by nurses. At the village level the integrated Family Health post provides preventative services. The posts are established and managed by the community. This care includes midwife care.

In 2009, the government of Indonesia spent approximately 6.8 per cent of its total budget on healthcare (up from 4.5 per cent in 2000), accounting for 53.9 per cent of all healthcare spending. Total expenditure on healthcare equated to 2.5 per cent of the country's GDP. Per capita expenditure on health was US$56 in 2009. Figures for 2005-10 show that there are 65,722 physicians (2.9 per 10,000 population), 465,662 nurses and midwives (20.4 per 10,000 population) and 13,709 dentistry personnel. There are 6 hospital beds per 10,000.

There have been recent vaccination campaigns. In 2005 a second mass vaccination against polio was carried out, following an outbreak of the disease. Over 6 million children were given the vaccine. There have been no cases of polio since 2007. Although the average rate of vaccination is 90 per cent, in the West Java region it is approximately 55 per cent. Indonesia was the nation worst affected by bird flu and struggled to contain the virus. Almost all infected people were thought to have contracted the disease from poultry. In 2010, there were 385 reported cases of diphtheria, 12 of H5N1 influenza, 17,012 of leprosy, 229,819 of malaria, 16,529 of measles, 300,659 of TB and 1,308 of rubella. The vaccination rate for measles is now over 80 per cent, as it is for diptheria.

The infant mortality rate (likelihood of dying before first birthday) is 27 per 1,000 live births and the childhood mortality rate (likelihood of dying before fifth birthday) is 35 per 1,000 live births. Major causes of deaths are: diarrhoea 5 per cent, measles 5 per cent, malaria 2 per cent, pneumonia 14 per cent, prematurity 25 per cent and birth asphyxia 11 per cent.

According to the latest WHO figures, in 2010 approximately 82 per cent of the population had access to improved drinking water and 54 per cent of the population had access to improved sanitation. (Source: http://www.who.int, World Health Statistics 2012)

EDUCATION

Pre-school/Primary/Secondary Education
There are six levels of education in Indonesia: nursery school (for children under 5), kindergarten (between the ages of 5 and 6), primary school (for children between 6 and 12 or 7 and 13), lower secondary school (3 years), upper secondary school (3 years), higher education. There are also special schools for handicapped children. Education is compulsory for nine years from the age of seven. Recent figures show that over 97 per cent of 7-12 year olds were enrolled in school, 85 per cent of 13-15 year olds were enrolled and 55.5 per cent of 16-18 year olds were registered at a school. (Source: Statistics Indonesia)

The literacy rate (for those aged over 10 years old) stands at 93 per cent for young people, falling to just over 80 per cent for the population aged 45 or older. The tsunami of December 2004 destroyed between 700 and 1,100 primary schools, mainly in Aceh province on Sumatra; over 1,700 teachers were killed and 180,000 children were left without a school. In 2005, Unicef pledged US$90 million for school rebuilding and re-staffing.

Higher Education
An estimated 13 per cent of the tertiary age population went onto higher education in 2010.

Figures for 2008 show that 17.8 per cent of total government expenditure went on education.

RELIGION

87 per cent of the population are Muslim, 6 per cent are Protestant, 3 per cent are Roman Catholic, 2 per cent are Hindu, 1 per cent are Buddhist and the remaining 1 per cent follow other religions. However, the inhabitants of Bali are predominantly Hindu. Freedom of religion is protected by the Indonesian Constitution, although Indonesia has a religious liberty rating of 3 on a scale of 1 to 10 (10 is most freedom). (Source: World Religion Database).

Majelis Ulama Indonesia (Indonesian Ulama Council), central Muslim organisation, URL: http://www.mui.or.id

COMMUNICATIONS AND MEDIA

Press freedom is limited by legal restrictions and defamation may be punishable by imprisonment. Broadcasters frequently self-censor. Television is the main medium followed by the internet.

Newspapers
There are numerous Indonesian daily newspapers.
Kompas, URL: http://kompas.com
Jakarta Post, URL: http://www.thejakartapost.com/headlines.asp

Media Indonesia, URL: http://www.mediaindonesia.com/
Pos Kota, URL: http://www.poskota.co.id

Business Journals
Bisnis Indonesia, URL: http://web.bisnis.com/

Broadcasting
The state-owned Radio Republik Indonesia has six national networks and 50 broadcasting stations. There are also over 650 non-RRI broadcasting stations throughout the country. Television has been available in Indonesia since the 1960s and is the dominant medium. There the state-owned Televisi Republik Indonesia - TVRI operates two networks. Private television also exists but may not broadcast live news broadcasts from international stations.
Radio Republik Indonesia, URL: http://www.rri.co.id/
Televisi Republik Indonesia, URL: http://www.tvri.co.id/

Telecommunications
The national telecommunication system has improved with the application of digital technology. Two services - International Network Services and International Service Digital Network (ISDN) have been launched. In 2010, there were an estimated 37 million landlines and 220 million mobile phones. Figures for 2010 estimate that 20 million Indonesians are regular internet users.

ENVIRONMENT

Indonesia has the world's largest reef system in its waters, and one of the world's largest rain forests, both of which are home to thousands of unique species.

Illegal logging is one of the gravest problems facing Indonesia. The country contains ten percent of the world's forest cover, and has the third largest tropical rain forest. Laws aimed at protecting the forest have been difficult to enforce, and the consequent deforestation has been linked to floods and landslides which seasonally destroy villages and drown inhabitants. Furthermore, the slash and burn methods used by illegal loggers exacerbate already high levels of emissions from industry and motor vehicles, leading to high levels of air pollution that have affected neighbouring countries.

Air pollution, caused mainly by motor vehicles, is a major environmental problem. The main mode of transport is motorcycles and scooters, which do not have catalytic converters. Hardly any vehicles in Indonesia use unleaded petrol.

Indonesia's energy related carbon emissions were estimated at 414 million metric tons in 2009. In 2008 it was ranked 18th in the world for its carbon emissions. Emissions had fallen to 389.43 million metric tons in 2010 making Indonesia 14th in the world for carbon emissions. (Source: EIA)

Indonesia is a party to the following international environmental conventions: Biodiversity, Climate Change, Climate Change-Kyoto Protocol, Desertification, Endangered Species, Hazardous Wastes, Law of the Sea, Marine Life Conservation, Ozone Layer Protection, Ship Pollution, Tropical Timber 83, Tropical Timber 94, and Wetlands.

SPACE PROGRAMME

Indonesia's National Space and Aeronautics Institute (LAPAN) was established in 1963. It organises research and development of remote sensing, aerospace technology, atmospheric knowledge and develops aerospace systems.

National Institute of Aeronautics and Space (LAPAN, Lembaga Penerbangan dan Antariksa Nasional), URL: http://www.lapan.go.id/

STATES OF THE WORLD

IRAN

Islamic Republic of Iran
Jomhuri-e Eslami-e Iran

Capital: Tehran (Population estimate, 2011: 12 million)

Spiritual Leader (Commander in Chief of the Armed Forces): Ayatollah al-Udhma Sayyid Ali Khamenei (page 1456)

Head of State: Hassan Rouhani (President Elect) (page 1505)

First Vice-President: Mohammed Reza Rahimi
Vice President (Environment Protection): Mohammad Javad Mohammadizadeh
Vice President (International Affairs): Alia Saidlu
Vice President (Atomic Energy Organisation): Fereidoun Abbasi
Vice President (Management, Development and Human Resources): Lotfollah Faruzandesh Dehkardi
Vice President (Executive Affairs): Hamid Baqaei
Vice President (Martyrs and War Veterans Affairs): Massoud Zaribafan
Vice President (Legal and Parliamentary Affairs): Mohammad Reza Mir Tajodini
Vice President (Planning and Strategic Supervision): Ehrahim Azizi
Vice President (Scientific and Technological Affairs): Nasrin Soltankhah
Vice President (Foreign Affairs): Ali Akbar Salehi
Vice President (Head of the Centre for Women and Family Participation Affairs): Maryam Mojtahed Zadeh
Vice President (Public Affairs): Abdolreza Sheikholeslami

National Flag: A fesswise tricolour of green, white, and red, with the emblem of the Islamic Republic in the centre of the white band. Bordered with the words 'Allah-o-Akbar' ('Allah is Great') in white Arabic script repeated 11 times along the bottom edge of the green bank and 11 times along the top edge of the red band.

CONSTITUTION AND GOVERNMENT

Constitution
After World War II, Mohammad Reza Pahlavi, son of the former constitutional monarch, became the ruler of Iran. Dissatisfaction with the Shah's regime led to civil disruption and the Shah was forced to flee the country on 16 January 1979. The exiled religious leader Ayatollah Khomeini returned to Iran and a provisional government was then formed under Mr. Mehdi Bazargan. In March 1979 Iran was declared an Islamic Republic after a national referendum and in December 1979 a new constitution was approved.

Under the 1979 constitution the Supreme Leader, at present Ayatollah Ali Khamenei, holds overall power in Iran, and appoints the Head of the Judiciary, six clergy from the 12-member Council of Guardians, Armed Forces commanders, leaders of Friday prayers, and the heads of radio and television. The Supreme Leader is elected by the 86-member Assembly of Experts who are themselves elected for an eight-year term. The president heads the executive branch of government and is elected by universal adult suffrage for a maximum of two consecutive four-year terms. As the head of government, the president appoints the Council of Ministers, subject to the approval of parliament.

Recent amendments to the constitution abolished the post of prime minister and gave increased powers to the president. To consult the constitution, please visit: http://www.iranonline.com/iran/iran-info/government/constitution.html.

International Relations
Iran has had an uneasy relationship with Iraq since the Iran-Iraq war of the 1980s. However, the country remained neutral during the US-Iraq conflict. Iran promotes stability in Afghanistan, having suffered from the Afghan civil war and the Taliban, and has pledged some $560 million for the reconstruction of the country. Iran also co-operates in the fight against the drugs trade.

Iranian leaders have taken a vehement anti-Israeli position, arguing that the state of Israel is illegitimate; they do not accept a two-state solution for Israel and the Palestinians. President Ahmadinejad has made several provocative statements, and government is critical of the Middle East Peace Process.

Iran-US relations have not been restored since they were broken off in 1980, and 1995 executive orders prohibit U.S. companies and their foreign subsidiaries from conducting business with Iran. The US has accused Iran of destabilising Iraq and Afghanistan, blaming the Iranian Revolutionary Guards for supplying and training insurgents. In January 2002, President Bush referred to the country as part of an 'Axis of Evil'. Concern over Iran's uranium enrichment programme has further strained relations with the USA and Europe. However, in 2007 the US and Iranian Ambassadors in Iraq met on three occasions to discuss Iraq; these were the first official meetings between the US and Iranian governments since 1980. The incoming US administration of Barack Obama hope to improve relations with Iran.

UK-Iran relations were fully restored after Iran gave assurances in 1998 that it had no intention to threaten the life of Salman Rushdie against whom a fatwah had been issued. The UK and Iran exchanged Ambassadors in 1999. Prince Charles visited in 2004 in his capacity as the Patron of the British Red Cross following the earthquake in Bam.

Recent Events
In January 1980 Dr Abol Hassan Bani Sadr was elected President, and in August 1980 a new prime minister, Mr Mohammad Ali Rajai, was appointed following the establishment of a new National Assembly *Majles*. On 21 June 1981 Bani Sadr was impeached by the *Majles*, following a period of conflict with the Islamic Republican Party, and was given political asylum in France. In October 1981, Seyed Ali Khamenei was elected President.

War with Iraq began with the Iraqi invasion of Iran in September 1980. A ceasefire and process of negotiation was established in August 1988 and settlement of the conflict came in August 1990.

Ayatollah Khomeini died in June 1989 and was succeeded as Spiritual leader by Ayatollah Sayyid Ali Khamenei (President of Iran, 1981-89). Ali Akbar Hashemi-Rafsanjani was sworn in as the new president.

In June 1990, 35,000 people died in an earthquake affecting the Caspian regions of Gilan and Zanjan.

In 1995, the US imposed oil and trade sanctions, alleging that Iran was sponsoring terrorism, seeking to acquire nuclear arms and demonstrating a hostility to the Middle East process. The reformist Mohammad Khatami became President in 1997. Following the adoption of a new press law, the publication of 16 reformist newspapers was banned by the judiciary in 2000.

In 2002, US President Bush described Iraq, Iran and North Korea as part of an "axis of evil" in a speech that outraged both reformists and conservatives in Iran.

In December 2003, some 25,000 people were killed in an earthquake measuring 6.7 in south-east Iran. The city of Bam was devastated. Iran is the most earthquake prone country in the world, with an average of one minor earthquake every day. There were destructive earthquakes in 2004 and 2006. In March 2006, scientists urged the government to move out of Tehran, which is built on over a hundred fault lines.

In February 2004, the conservatives regained control of parliament in elections. Thousands of reformist candidates were disqualified by the hardline Council of Guardians before the polls. Following eight years of moderate government, conservative Mahmoud Ahmadinejad beat his reformist rival in the presidential elections of June 2005.

In February 2007, the US administration said that there was evidence that Iran was providing weapons to Shia militias in Iraq who were attacking the US military. President Mahmoud Ahmadinejad said that no peace would come with foreign troops in Iraq.

On 23rd March, the day before a UN debate on what further sanctions to impose on Iran to halt its nuclear programme, 15 British Royal Navy personnel were seized by Iranian forces and imprisoned on charges that they were in Iranian territorial waters. The British Foreign Office disputed this, and sought international support for its stand from the UN Security Council and the EU. The sailors were released after thirteen days.

In April 2007, the US military accused Iran of arming Sunni militants fighting in Iraq, and of training unspecified groups fighting the coalition and Iraqi government forces. In August 2007, US officials announced that the government was preparing to designate Iran's Revolutionary Guards force as a foreign terrorist unit. If implemented, this would be the first time official armed units of a sovereign state are included in the list of banned terrorist groups. The classification would allow the US to target the force's finances. The US has repeatedly accused the Revolutionary Guards of supplying and training insurgents.

In January 2008, in the run-up to March elections, almost 3,000 reformist candidates were disqualified from standing by the Guardian Council. The interior ministry's chief electoral officer said candidates could challenge their disqualification by legal means. A reformist coalition was formed, consisting of 21 pro-reform groups, including Islamic Iran Participation Front (IIPF) and the Islamic Revolution Mojaheddin organisation (IMRO). By 19th February, around 1,100 reformist candidates had been reinstated.

Conservative candidates kept control of parliament following the general elections on 14th March, doing particularly well in Tehran. The reformists saw a small increase in their representation, despite the disqualification of many of their proposed candidates. Following run-off elections in 82 districts in April, the conservatives increased their lead, though many of them are critical of President Ahmadinejad.

On the 8th July, Iran test-fired nine missiles, including a Shahab-3 which has a range of 2,000km (1,240 miles) and is capable of reaching Tel Aviv. Israel and the US condemned the missile firing. The following month, Iranian authorities announced that the country had launched a test rocket capable of carrying a satellite into space.

On the 10th September 2008, the southern city of Bandar Abbas was struck by an earthquake measuring 6.1. Most casualties occurred on the Gulf island of Qeshm where a number of buildings collapsed. Seven people were killed and up to 40 injured.

Police raided and closed the office of a human rights group led by the Nobel Peace Prize winner, Shirin Ebadi in December 2008; the authorities claimed that the centre was acting as an illegal political organisation.

In April 2009, diplomats from least 30 countries walked out of a UN anti-racism conference during a speech by President Ahmadinejad in which he described Israel as "totally racist". The US, Israel, Canada, Australia, Germany, Italy, the Netherlands, Poland and New Zealand had already boycotted the conference in protest at Mr Ahmadinejad's appearance.

Presidential elections were held on 12th June 2009. There were four candidates, the favorites being the incumbent Mr. Ahmadinejad and the more reformist Mr Mousavi. The official results gave Mr. Ahmadinejad almost 63 per cent of the vote, and Mr. Mousavi 33.8 per cent. Mr. Mousavi alleged fraud and his supporters clashed with police in Tehran. All three opposition candidates called for the election to be annulled and re-run. Reformist political groups in Iran claimed that up to a hundred people were arrested on the 13th June, and eight people were killed in the violent confrontations that continued over the next few days. On the 16th June, the Guardian Council announced a recount of votes in some areas. On the 18th June, over 100,000 people attended a day of mourning for the eight protesters who were killed in the post-election violence. Ayatollah Khamenei endorsed Mahmoud Ahmadinejad's landslide win, appealed to candidates who had doubts about the election result to pursue any challenges through legal avenues and accused foreign powers of trying to foment unrest in the country. The following day, in defiance of the President, protests continued and the police responded with water cannon, batons, tear gas and live rounds. It was thought that ten people were killed and over 450 were arrested. Protests continued over the following days, amid increasing calls by the international community for an end to the Iranian authorities' repressive actions.

In late July, Mir Hossein Mousavi confirmed plans to form a new broad-based political front, giving the opposition a legal framework. On the 29th July, around 140 Iranians detained during protests were released from prison. According to the authorities, about 200 others, accused of more serious crimes, remain in prison. Supporters of the protesters say the true number of people detained may be in the thousands. Iran's prisons are notorious for their poor conditions.

On the 30th July, police clashed with mourners holding memorials for those killed in post-election violence. They used teargas to disperse crowds of 3,000 people from the grave of Neda Agha Soltan, whose death has become a symbol of post-election unrest. Several hundred people defied a heavy police presence to gather at the Grand Mossala prayer area in central Tehran. On the 14th August, a group of former Iranian MPs appealed to the powerful Assembly of Experts to investigate whether the Ayatollah Ali Khamenei was fit to rule, following his crackdown on protests following the elections. At the same time, Ayatollah Ahmad Khatami called for reformist leader Mehdi Karroubi to be prosecuted for alleging that protesters had been raped whilst in prison.

In February 2011, following on from demonstrations in the Middle East a mass opposition demonstration took place in Iran. The two main opposition parties had called on people to protest in a show of support and solidarity for the pro-democracy protests going on across the Arab world. Security forces cracked down on the protest. Two people were killed and many more injured. Rallies held in the days following, as well as on 20 February, were also suppressed. In further demonstrations on 1 March, the opposition claimed that 200 people were arrested.

In May 2013, a constitutional body ruled that women could not run in the forthcoming presidential election that was scheduled to take place on June 14. Thirty women had registered as candidates.

Nuclear Capability

Confirmation of the existence of a large uranium enrichment plant at Natanz and a heavy water plant at Arak in December 2002 marked the beginnings of international concern over the possibility of Iran creating a nuclear bomb. In the summer of 2003, traces of highly enriched weapons-grade uranium were discovered. In October, the Iranian government agreed to stop producing enriched uranium, and in December, Iran signed an Additional Protocol, allowing tougher inspections.

In February 2004, Abdul Qadeer Khan, creator of Pakistan's nuclear bomb, is alleged to have sold nuclear weapons technology to Iran. Uranium enrichment continued, and the IAEA ordered Iran to stop preparations for enrichment. In April 2005, Iran announced its plans to resume uranium conversion.

By August 2005, Iran had resumed fuel cycle work at its uranium conversion facility near Isfahan. The IAEA declared that Iran was in non-compliance with the nuclear Non-Proliferation Treaty. In January 2006, Iran broke the IAEA seals at its Natanz nuclear research facility and announced its intention to enrich uranium at the plant. Russia proposed that it carry out Iran's enrichment programme, shipping nuclear fuel to Iran, but talks to this end were put on hold when, on the 31st January, the US, Britain, Russia, China, France and Germany agreed that the IAEA should report Iran to the Security Council. In April 2006, Iran announced that it had succeeded in enriching uranium. The UN Security Council started discussing a resolution calling on Iran to suspend enrichment or face further action. The Iranian President promised that his government would respond to a UN package of incentives in August. The incentives offered included: the purchase of spare parts for civilian aircraft made by US manufacturers; the lifting of restrictions on the use of US agricultural technology; the provision of light water nuclear reactors and enriched fuel and support for Iranian membership of World Trade Organisation. The August deadline for a response from Iran passed.

In December 2006, the UN Security Council voted to impose sanctions on Iran's trade in sensitive nuclear materials and technology. On 24th March 2007, further sanctions were imposed on Iran, blocking Iranian arms exports and freezing the assets of anyone involved in nuclear and missile work. In April, President Ahmadinejad announced that Iran could now produce nuclear fuel on an industrial scale and in May, the IAEA estimated that Iran would be able to develop a nuclear weapon in three to eight years. In July 2007, Iranian officials

agreed to allow IAEA inspectors into the Arak heavy water plant and agree safeguards at its Natanz uranium enrichment plant; however, Iran continued to enrich uranium in defiance of the UN Security Council. In October 2007, the USA imposed new sanctions on Iran, accusing the country of pursuing technologies "that can lead to a nuclear weapon", building ballistic missiles, and supporting militants in Iraq and "terrorists" in Iraq, Afghanistan, Lebanon and the Palestinian territories. The new measures targeted the finances of Iran's Islamic Revolution Guards Corps and three state-owned banks.

At the end of November 2007, the declassified summary of a US National Intelligence Estimate concluded that Iran stopped its nuclear weapons programme in 2003 but continues to enrich uranium. The authors further concluded that the country is not likely to have enough highly enriched uranium to build a bomb until 2010-2015. Russia started delivering enriched uranium fuel to the Bushehr power plant in December 2007, but Tehran said it would not stop its own uranium enrichment process.

At the beginning of March 2008, the UN Security Council voted in favour of a third set of sanctions against Iran over its nuclear programme. The sanctions called for a ban of the sale of dual-use items (which can have either a military or civilian purpose); the freezing of the foreign assets of 13 Iranian companies; and the imposition of travel bans on five Iranian officials. In April 2008, Iran began installing 6,000 new centrifuges at its nuclear plant in Natanz; it is thought that there are already 3,000 centrifuges there. In June, the EU imposed an asset freeze on Iran's largest bank and added more names to a list of Iranians who are banned from travelling to the EU. Iran condemned the new sanctions as illegal.

At the end of July 2008, President Mahmoud Ahmadinejad announced that Iran now possessed 6,000 centrifuges for enriching uranium. The UN Security Council passed a new resolution in September, demanding that Iran stop enriching uranium, but without imposing new sanctions, as Russia refused to support further sanctions.

In February 2010 Iran announced it was ready to send enriched uranium abroad for further enrichment under a deal agreed with the West. The following May a deal was reached following mediation talks with Turkey and Brazil. In June 2010 the UN Security Council imposed a fourth round of sanctions against Iran over its nuclear programme. In August, Iranian engineers began loading fuel into the Bushehr nuclear power plant, Iran said this was a milestone in its drive to produce nuclear energy. Talks were held in Geneva in December between Iran and other world powers to discuss Iran's nuclear programme but were inconclusive.

In November 2011, Britain said it was to impose further sanctions on Iran over its nuclear programme. In response the Iranian parliament voted to reduce its diplomatic relations with the UK. The UK embassy was later attacked and all diplomatic staff withdrawn.

In May 2012, UN nuclear inspectors found traces of enriched uranium at the Fordo Nuclear site. Iran said the uranium enriched at the plant was for civilian use. Uranium enriched for civilian use should give a maximum reading of 20 per cent: the samples found readings of 27 per cent.

In June 2012, in an effort to stop countries importing oil from Iran the USA announced it would exempt seven countries from economic sanctions if they cut Iranian imports. The countries concerned were India, South Korea, Malaysia, South Africa, Sri Lanka, Taiwan and Turkey.

Legislature

Iran's unicameral legislature is known as the Islamic Consultative Council (*Majlis ash Shoura*), which has 290 members (to be increased to 293) directly elected for four years, renewable once only. The 12-member Council of Guardians of the Constitution (*Shura-ye Negahban-e Qanun-e Assassi*) is responsible for the approval of legislation passed by parliament, and consists of six theologians and six jurists. It can also veto prospective parliamentary candidates. The Assembly of Experts (*Majlis-e Khobregan*) comprises 83 clerics, elected by universal adult suffrage, who decide on religious matters.
Consultative Council, Imam Khomeini Avenue, Tehran, Iran. E-mail: mellat@majlis.ir, URL: http://www.majlis.ir
Speaker: Ali Ardeshir-Ahmadinejad

Outgoing Cabinet (as at July 2013)
Minister of Economic Affairs and Finance: Shamseddin Hosseini (page 1443)
Minister of Oil: Brig. Gen. Rostam Gasemi
Minister of Agricultural Jihad: Sadeq Khalilian
Minister of Trade, Industries and Mines: Mehdi Ghazanfari
Minister of Energy: Majid Namjou
Minister of Roads and Urban Development: Ali Nikzad
Minister of Labour and Social Affairs, Minister of Co-operatives: vacant
Minister of Communications and Information Technology: Gen. Mohammad Hassan Nami
Minister of Science Research and Technology: Kamran Daneshjoo
Minister of Education: Hamidreza Hajibaba'i
Minister of the Interior: Mostafa Mohammad Najjar
Minister of Intelligence: Heyder Moslehi
Minister of Culture and Islamic Guidance: Mohammad Sharif Malekzadeh
Minister of Defence: Ahmad Vahidi
Minister of Health (acting): Nohammad Hassan Tarigat Monfared
Minister of Sports and Youth: Mohammad Abbasi

Ministries
Office of the President, Pasteur Avenue, 13168-43311, Tehran, Iran. Tel: +98 21 614451, URL: http://www.president.ir
Ministry of Agriculture, 20 Malaei Avenue, Vali-e-Asr Square, Tehran, Iran. Tel: +98 21 8889 5354, fax: +98 21 8890 4357, e-mail: payam@asid.moa.or.irURL: http://www.agri-jahad.org

IRAN

Ministry of Commerce, Ave Vali-Asr 492, Tehran, Iran. E-mail: minister@irtp.com. URL: http://www.moc.gov.ir
Ministry of Science, Research and Technology, 7th Floor, Central Building, Ave. Ostad Nejatollahi 170, Sepand Crossing, Tehran, Iran. Tel: +98 21 8889 1065, fax: +98 21 8882 7234, URL: http://www.msrt.ir
Ministry of Defence and Armed Forces, Sayed Khandan Area, Tehran, Iran. Tel: +98 21 21401, fax: +98 21 864008, URL: http://www.fatehnet.net
Ministry of Economic Affairs and Finance, Sour Israfil Street, Babe Homayoon Avenue, Tehran, Iran. Tel: +98 21 3391 6791, fax: +98 21 390528, e -mail: info@mofir.com, URL: http://www.mefa.gov.ir
Ministry of Education, Si-e-Tir Street, Emam Khomeini Square, Tehran, Iran. Tel: +98 21 32421, fax: +98 21 675503, e-mail: info@medu.ir, URL: http://www.medu.ir
Ministry of Energy, Ave Felestine Shomali 47, Tehran, Iran. Tel: +98 21 891081, URL: http://www.moe.org.ir
Ministry of Foreign Affairs, Ebn.e Sina Street, Imam Komenini Square, Tehran, Iran. Tel: +98 21 6673 9191, URL: http://www.mfa.gov.ir
Ministry of Health and Medical Education, Avenue Azadi, Tehran, Iran. Tel: +98 21 6643 4606, fax: +98 21 3385 3947, e-mail: webmaster@hbi.ir, URL: http://www.hbi.ir
Ministry of Justice, Panzdah-e-Khordad Square, Tehran, Iran. URL: http://www.justice.ir
Ministry of Labour and Social Affairs, Ave Azadi, near Behboudi Street, Tehran, Iran. Tel: +98 21 930050, e-mail: mlmh@irimlsa.org, URL: http://www.irimlsa.ir
Ministry of Oil, Ave Taleghani, Hafez Intersection, Tehran, Iran. Tel: +98 21 6615 2215, URL: http://www.nioc.org.ir
Ministry of Culture and Islamic Guidance, Baharestan Square, Sepand Crossing, Tehran, Iran. Tel: +98 21 32411, URL: http://www.molavi.mche.gov.ir
Ministry of the Interior, Jahad Square, Fatemi Street, Tehran, Iran. Tel: +98 21 61311, URL: http://www.moi.ir
Ministry of Industries and Mines, Avenue Ostad Nejatollahi 30, Shahid Kalantari Street, Tehran, Iran. Tel: +98 21 81061, URL: http://www.mim.gov.ir
Ministry of Co-operatives, Bozorgmehr Street 16, Vali-e-Asr Avenue, Tehran, Iran. Tel: +98 21 6640 0938, fax: +98 21 6641 0938, URL: http://www.icm.gov.ir
Ministry of Housing, Shahid Khodami Street, Vanak Square, Tehran, Iran. Tel: +98 21 877711, fax: +98 21 8877 6634, e-mail: minister@icic.gov.ir, URL: http://www.mhud.gov.ir
Ministry of Road and Transport, Avenue Taleghani 49, Spahbod Gharani Street, Tehran, Iran. Tel: +98 21 6646 0583, fax: +98 21 6640 7991, URL: http://www.mrt.ir
Ministry of Telecommunications, PO box 11365-931, Avenue Dr Shariati, Tehran, Iran. Tel: +98 21 864796, Fax: +98 21 866023, URL: http://www.iranpac.net.ir
Ministry of Communications and Information Technology, PO box 11365-931, Avenue Dr Shariati, Tehran, Iran. Tel: +98 21 864796, fax: +98 21 866023, e-mail: motamedi@imail.dci.or.ir, IRL: http://www.iranpac.net.ir
Ministry of Culture and Islamic Guidance, Baharestan Square, Sepand Crossing, Tehran, Iran. Tel: +98 21 32411, fax: +98 21 3117535, e-mail: ershad@neda.net, URL: http://www.molavi.mche.gov.ir
Ministry of Housing and Urban Development, Shahid Khodami Street, Vanak Square, Tehran, Iran. Tel: +98 21 877711, fax: +98 21 8877 6634, e-mail: minister@icic.gov.ir, URL: http://www.mhud.gov.ir
Ministry of Welfare and Social Security, Avenue Azadi, near Behboudi Street, Tehran, Iran. Tel: +98 21 930050, fax: +98 21 931066, e-mail: mlmh@irimlsa.org, URL: http://www.irimlsa.ir

Political Parties
Although a number of political parties are registered in Iran, their activities for election purposes are still in their infancy. An alliance of reformist candidates, the Islamic Iran Participation Front (IIPF) gained a majority of parliamentary seats in the 2000 elections, but this was lost in the elections of 2004. Broad Principalists Coalition (anti-Ahmadinejad conservatives) (BPC); Unified Principalists Front (pro-Ahmadinejad conservatives) (UPF).

Elections
Mahmoud Ahmadinejad, was declared the winner of the 2009 election with almost two-thirds of the votes after a very high turnout. He was sworn in for second term as president in August 2009. He then presented his cabinet, the first since 1979 to include women.

The most recent presidential election was held in June 2013, reformist-backed cleric Hassan Rouhani was elected with over 50 per cent of the vote

The most recent election for the Majlis al-Shoura took place on 2 March and 4 May 2012. Conservatives won, although with a reduced majority: Conservatives 182 seats; reformists 75; independents 19; religious minorities 14 seats.

Elections for the Assembly of Experts were held in October 2006. The Iranian City and Village Councils elections last took place on December 15, 2006; people elected representatives for City and Village Councils, who in their turn elected the mayors.

Iranians are allowed to vote from the age of 15 years.

Diplomatic Representation
British Embassy, 198 Ferdowsi Avenue (PO Box No 11365-4474), Tehran 11344, Iran. Tel: +98 21 6670 5011, fax: +98 21 6670 8021, e-mail: BritishEmbassyTehran@fco.gov.uk, URL: http://ukiniran.fco.gov.uk/en/
Ambassador: vacant. (As of November 2011, Iran was debating the explusion of the Ambassador after the UK imposed sanctions on Iranian banks accusing them of facilitating Iran's nuclear programme. All staff were withdrawn in December 2011)
Iranian Embassy, 16 Prince's Gate, London SW7 1PT. Tel: +44 (0)20 7225 3000, fax: +44 (0)20 7589 4440, URL: http://www.iran-embassy.org.uk
Ambassador: vacant
Iranian Interests Section, Embassy of Pakistan, 2209 Wisconsin Avenue, NW, Washington DC 20007, USA. Tel: +1 202 965 4990, fax: +1 202 337 7984, e-mail: yaaliali@aol.com, URL: http://www.embassyofpakistanusa.org
Ambassador: Mostafa Rahmani

Permanent Representative of the Islamic Republic of Iran to the United Nations, 622 Third Avenue, 34th Floor, New York, NY 10017, USA. Tel: +1 212 687 2020, fax: +1 212 867 7086, e-mail: iran@un.int, URL: http://www.un.int/iran/
Ambassador: Mohammad Khazaee

LEGAL SYSTEM

The Supreme Court revoked all laws which did not conform to Islam in August 1982. The legal system consists of two kinds of court, public and special. Public courts include the high and low penal courts, high and low civil courts. Criminal courts fall into two categories: the first level courts have jurisdiction over prosecution for felony charges, while the second level courts try cases that involve lighter punitive action. Special courts include clerical tribunals, revolutionary tribunals, and the Court of Administrative Justice. Clerical courts try misdeeds by the clergy. Revolutionary tribunals hear charges of terrorism and offenses against national security. The Court of Administrative Justice investigates complaints or objections by people with respect to government officials, organs and statues.

The Supreme Court ensures the implementation of laws by the courts as well as uniformity in judicial procedures. The head of the judiciary nominates the Chief of the Supreme Court and the Attomey-General who must be specialists in Islamic Law. All judges are certified in Islamic law, and most, but not all, are members of the ruling clergy. The judge serves not only as judge but as prosecutor, jury, and arbiter.

Iran's record on human rights is poor. The government continues to apply the death penalty to juveniles - a practice banned by the International Convention on the Rights of the Child, which Iran has signed and ratified. Over 250 people were reported to have been executed in 2010, 360 in 2011 and 314 in 2012. Over 1,660 people are believed to be on death row. Security forces have been implicated in custodial deaths and torture, and the government administered severe punishments, such as death by stoning, amputation and flogging. Prison conditions remain poor. Security forces arbitrarily arrest people, and often hold them incommunicado. There is a lack of judicial independence and civil liberties, such as freedom of speech and assembly are severely restricted.

LOCAL GOVERNMENT

For the purposes of local government, Iran is divided into 31 provinces (*Ostan*): Alborz, Ardabil, Azarbayjan-e Gharbi, Azarbayjan-e Sharqi, Bushehr, Chahar Mahal va Bakhtiari, Esfahan, Fars, Gilan, Golestan, Hamadan, Hormozgan, Ilam, Kerman, Kermanshah, Khorasan-e Jonubi (North Khorasan), Khorasan-e Razavi (Razavi Khorasan), Khorasan-e Shomali (South Khorasan), Khuzestan, Kohgiluyeh va Bowyer Ahmad, Kordestan, Lorestan, Markazi, Mazandaran, Qazvin, Qom, Semnan, Sistan va Baluchestan, Tehran, Yazd and Zanjan. Each province is sub-divided into 282 sub-provinces (*Shahrestan*) and 742 counties (*Bakhsh*).

The first ever local elections took place in 1999.

AREA AND POPULATION

Area
The Islamic Republic of Iran is situated in the west of Asia, with Azerbaijan and Turkmenistan to the north, Pakistan and Afghanistan to the east, the Persian Gulf and the Gulf of Oman to the south and Iraq and Turkey to the west. It has a total area of 1,648,195 sq. km, making it the 16th largest country in the world. The centre and east of Iran is mainly desert. To the north and west there are mountain ranges. The climate is mostly arid or semiarid, though it is subtropical along the Caspian coast.

To view a map, please visit http://www.un.org/Depts/Cartographic/map/profile/iran.pdf

Population
Iran's total population was estimated to be 73.97 million in 2010. The annual population growth rate was an estimated 1.2 per cent over the period 2000-10. Approximately 70 per cent of the population is aged between 15 and 60, whilst 23 per cent is aged under 14 years, and 7 per cent is aged over 60 years. The median age is 27 years. Population density is approximately 35 persons per sq. km. and some 71 per cent of the population now lives in urban areas; 12 million people live in Tehran, which has doubled its population over the last twenty years. Other major cities are Isfahan, Tabriz, Mashhad, Shiraz, Yazd and Qom.

Just over half the population is of Persian origin, with 24 per cent Azeri, eight per cent Gilaki and Mazandarani, seven per cent Kurd, three per cent Arab, two per cent Lur, one per cent Baluch, and one per cent Turkmen. The official language is Farsi (Persian); Persian and Arabic scripts are written throughout. The Turkish, Kurdish, Arabic, Lori, Guilani, Mazandarani and Baluchi dialects are in use as local languages.

Births, Marriages, Deaths
Estimates for 2010 put the birth rate at 17.1 births per 1,000 inhabitants, and the death rate at 5.5 deaths per 1,000 people. Average life expectancy at birth was estimated at 72 years (70 years for men and 75 years for women) in 2009. The child mortality rate was 22 deaths per 1,000 live births, whilst the fertility rate was 1.7 children born per woman. (Source: http://www.who.int, World Health Statistics 2012)

Public Holidays 2014
14 January: Arbaeen
22 January: Martyrdom of Imam Reza
14 January: Birth of the Prophet
11 February: Victory of Islamic Revolution
19 March: Nationalisation of Oil Industry Day
20 March: Navruz
27 May: Prophet Mohammad receives his calling

16 July: Birthday Imam Ali
29 July: Eid-e Fitr (Ramadan Ends)
10 August: Martyrdom of Iman Ali
12 September: Martyrdom Imam Jafar Sadegh
5 October: Eid-e Ghorbani (Feast of the Sacrifice)
25 October: Al-Hijira (Islamic New Year)
3 November: Eid-e Ghadir Khom
24 November: Tassoua
25 November: Ashura

A substantial number of unofficial holidays are added each year to the national holidays. The problem of too many public holidays is currently being considered by the Majlis, and there is a plan to remove six days from the holiday calendar, and add one. Islamic holiday dates depend on the sighting of the moon, so dates can vary.

EMPLOYMENT

Iran had a labour force estimated at about 22.3 million in 2005, representing around 33.3 per cent of the total population. 17.7 million of the workforce were men, whilst just 4.5 million were women. 19.76 million people were employed (15.9 million men and 3.8 million women). According to official estimates, unemployment ran at 11.5 per cent in 2005 (10 per cent for men and 17 per cent for women), but was significantly higher among young people. The service sector is the largest employer, using about 45 per cent of the workforce, followed by agriculture (30 per cent), and industry (25 per cent). Employment by economic activity is shown below:

In 2007, the work force was estimated to number 23.5 million people. 25 per cent worked in the agricultural sector, 31 per cent in industry and 45 per cent in services. The official estimate of unemployment was 12.1 per cent over the year; the IMF estimated unemployment at 20 per cent.

Iran has an educated population, and economic inefficiency and insufficient investment have prompted a significant and increasing number of Iranians to seek employment overseas.

Total Employment by Economic Activity

Occupation	2008
Agriculture, hunting & forestry	4,266,000
Fishing	78,000
Mining & quarrying	128,000
Manufacturing	3,512,000
Electricity, gas & water supply	180,000
Construction	2,791,000
Wholesale & retail trade, repairs	2,981,000
Hotels & restaurants	211,000
Transport, storage & communications	2,067,000
Financial intermediation	284,000
Real estate, renting & business activities	521,000
Public admin. & defence; compulsory social security	1,332,000
Education	1,219,000
Health & social work	448,000
Other community, social & personal service activities	443,000
Households with employed persons	19,000
Extra-territorial organisations & bodies	1,000
Other	19,000
Total	20,500,000

Source: Copyright © International Labour Organization (ILO Dept. of Statistics, http://laborsta.ilo.org)

BANKING AND FINANCE

Currency
The unit of currency is the rial.

GDP/GNP, Inflation, National Debt
Iran's economy is reliant on oil export revenues, and is a mix of central planning, state ownership of large enterprises, village agriculture, and smallscale private enterprises. Oil provides around 80 per cent of export earnings and 85 per cent of government revenues. Presidents Rafsanjani and Khatami planned wide ranging reforms in an attempt to diversify the economy, but these were hampered by high inflation and ideological infighting.

Although the Supreme Leader issued a decree in July 2006 to privatize 80 per cent of the shares of most government-owned companies, private sector activity is limited to small-scale workshops, farming, and services. However, to date, not much progress has been made. Price controls and subsidies continue in force, and, together with administrative controls, undermine the potential for private-sector-led growth. There is a significant informal market activity. Earnings from oil exports soared following price increases in 2003; however, high unemployment and inflation continue.

GDP was estimated to be US$330 billion in 2010. It was estimated to reach US$410 billion in 2011. The services sector was the largest contributor to GDP, at 44.0 per cent; industry accounted for 45 per cent and agriculture, 11.0 per cent.

According to official figures, inflation fell from 19.2 per cent in 2000 to around 16 per cent in 2005; however, other estimates put the figure at over 40 per cent. Inflation was estimated at 11.2 per cent in 2006. Inflation was estimated at 10 per cent in 2010.

Iran's total external debt was estimated at US$16.9 billion at the end of 2005. (Source: Energy Information Administration, EIA)

Balance of Payments / Imports and Exports
Export revenues reached an estimated US$78 billion in 2010 (compared to US$70 billion in 2009). Non-oil exports have enjoyed a rapid growth in recent years. Various minerals, copper bullions, caviar, canned fish, pistachio nuts and carpets are significant non-oil exports. Major export trading partners in 2009 were China (17 per cent), Japan (12), India (10.5 per cent), South Korea (7.5 per cent), and Turkey (4 per cent).

Imports cost the country US$58 billion in 2010 (compared to US$57.1 billion in 2009), most being spent on food, machinery, technical services, military supplies and raw materials. The main suppliers in 2008 were UAE (15 per cent), China (13 per cent), Germany (9.5 per cent), South Korea (7 per cent), Russia (5 per cent), and Italy (5.0 per cent).

Central Bank
Bank Markazi Jomhouri Islami Iran (The Central Bank of Iran), Miramad Blvd., 144, Tehran, Iran. Tel: +98 21 29951, 21 64461 fax: +98 21 3115674, e-mail: g.secdept@cbi.iranet.net, URL: http://www.cbi.ir
Governor: Mahmud Bahmani

Chambers of Commerce and Trade Organisations
Iran Chamber of Commerce, Industries and Mines, URL: http://www.iccima.ir/fa/

MANUFACTURING, MINING AND SERVICES

Primary and Extractive Industries
Iran is rich in minerals. Principal exports are lead, zinc and chromite. There are extensive reserves of copper and iron ore and coal deposits are used for Iran's iron and steel industries. Mercury, molybdenum and gold are found, and the geology also favours tin. Limestone, marble, travertine and phosphate deposits occur widely.

Iran's oil generates 80 per cent of total export earnings ($54 billion in 2006), and 85 per cent of total government revenue. Iran is the world's fifth largest producer and crude oil exporter, and has the fourth largest reserves in the world, behind Saudi Arabia and Canada; proven oil reserves at the beginning of January 2012 were estimated at 151 million barrels, equivalent to around 10 per cent of the world's proven oil reserves.

Total oil production in 2011 was an estimated 4.2 million barrels per day, of which 4.0 million barrels per day was crude oil. Iran is a member of the Organisation of the Petroleum Exporting Countries (OPEC), with a crude oil production quota of 4.11 million barrels per day from July 2005. The government had plans to increase production to over 5.8 million barrels per day by 2015; however, investment in Iran's energy sector has fallen following the election of a conservative government in 2005 and economic sanctions imposed due to the Iranian uranium enrichment and nuclear program. Oil consumption was estimated at 2,028 million barrels per day in 2011 (up from 1.679 million barrels per day in 2006). Iran is a major exporter of oil and in 2010 20 per cent of exported oil went to China, 17 per cent to Japan, 16 per cent to India and 10 per cent to Italy.

Iran has a shortage of refining capacity to produce petroleum, and imports around a third of its requirements. Figures for 2008 showed that Iran's refining capacity was 1.5 nillion barrels per day and plans were being made to increase this to 3.0 million barrels per day by 2012. In 2006, imported petroleum amounted to 150,000 barrels per day. In volume terms, Iran is the second largest importer of petrol in the world after the United States. Petrol costs are heavily subsidised; in 2005, energy subsidies accounted for 12 per cent of GDP, according to the IMF. This has contributed to a rapid rise in consumption.

Overall, Iran has 40 producing fields - 27 onshore and 13 offshore. Major onshore fields are: Ahwaz-Asmari (700,000 million barrels per day), Bangestan (158,000 barrels per day), Marun (520,000 barrels per day), Gachsaran (480,000 barrels per day), Agha Jari (200,000 barrels per day), and Karanj-Parsi (250,000 barrels per day).

The National Iranian Oil Company (NIOC) is in charge of all oil operations. The oil refineries of Tehran, Tabriz, Bakhtaran, Shiraz and Esfahan meet the bulk of internal demand. In 1999 Iran was beginning to re-open its oil sector to foreign investment. An agreement was signed in March with Elf Aquitaine (France) and Eni (Italy) to refurbish the offshore Doroud field. The deal meant that the field's recoverable reserves are boosted from 600 million barrels to 1.5 billion barrels. This has led to more that 30 foreign companies from 18 different countries submitting proposals to take part in future projects, including BG, ENI, Gazprom, Petronas, Royal Dutch/Shell, and TotalFinaElf.

Iran has the world's fourth largest gas reserves. In January 2012, reserves of natural gas were estimated at 1,046 trillion cubic feet (Tcf). Around 62 per cent of Iranian natural gas reserves are located in non-associated fields and have not been developed. Production in 2011 was 5,361 billion cubic feet up from 5,161,billion cubic feet in 2010. Natural gas accounts for nearly half of Iran's total energy consumption and consumption is expected to grow. Figures for 2010 show that Iran consumed 4,106 billion cubic feet, this figure rose to 5,415 billion cubic feet in 2011. The price of natural gas to residential and industrial consumers is state-controlled at extremely low prices, encouraging rapid consumption growth and replacement of fuel oil, kerosene and LPG demand.

The industry is managed by the National Iranian Gas Company (NIGC). Iran's major non-associated gas fields are South Pars (280-500 Tcf of gas reserves), North Pars (50 Tcf), Kangan (29 Tcf), Nar (13 Tcf), and Khangiran (11 Tcf).

IRAN

In 2002, a natural gas pipeline was opened between Turkey and Iran, with the potential to export 350 Bcf per year to Turkey. Iran hopes to extend the pipeline to Greece, Bulgaria and Romania. In March 2007, the 87-mile long Iran-Armenia pipeline was completed in Agarak, and will transport 200 Mcf/d to Armenia in exchange for electricity. (Source: Energy Information Administration)

Recoverable coal reserves are estimated at 462 million short tons (2007). Coal production rose from an estimated 1.6 million short tons in 2006 and to 1.7 million short tons in 2007 before falling to 1.3 million short tons in 2010. Consumption fell from 2.3 million short tons in 2001 to 1.3 million short tons in 2010.

Energy
According to 2006 EIA estimates, Iran has an estimated total energy consumption in 2009 of 9.01 quadrillion Btu (up from 5.18 quadrillion Btu in 2001). Natural gas and oil were the two main fuels used; hydroelectricity contributed 2 per cent to the energy mix, and coal made up the balance of 1 per cent. Per capita energy consumption in 2004 was estimated at 95.5 million Btu (up from 80.3 million Btu in 2001).

Iran had a 2004 electricity generation capacity estimated at 34.3 gigawatts, of which over 75 per cent was gas-fired. The remainder was either hydroelectric (7 per cent) or oil-fired. Installed capacity in 2010 was put at 62.09 GWe. Currently, around 94 percent of Iran's rural population has access to electricity. Electricity production in 2010 was 219.46 billion kilowatthours and consumption was 182.70 billion kilowatthours. Though the electricity industry is currently run by the state-controlled Tavanir organisation, some limited privatisation is likely. Iran is building significant new generation capacity, with the goal of adding 18 GW over the next five years. (Source: EIA)

Iran has several small nuclear reactors and a large-scale nuclear power plant under construction at the southern town of Bushehr. Iran has said that this plant will provide domestic power and allow oil and natural gas to be exported for additional hard currency revenues. In September 2003 the International Atomic Energy Agency (IAEA) asked Iran for guarantees that its nuclear programme was for peaceful purposes only and requested inspection of the facilities. In October of that year Iran threatened to withdraw from the Nuclear Non Proliferation Treaty (NNPT) if pressure from the West continued. Finally, on 18 December 2003, Iran signed a protocol to the NNPT allowing the IAEA access to nuclear sites and, despite further threats to bar nuclear inspectors in March 2004, has continued to allow inspections. In November 2004 Iran agreed to suspend most of its uranium enrichment programme following discussions with the EU, but the following April, the Government announced plans to resume uranium conversion. By August, Iran had resumed fuel cycle work at its uranium conversion facility near Isfahan. In September 2005, President Ahmadinejad argued that Iran has a right to produce nuclear fuel. The IAEA declared that Iran was in non-compliance with the nuclear Non-Proliferation Treaty. By December 2006, the UN Security Council were discussing what sanctions to apply to Iran, in view of the country's continuing uranium enrichment programme. In December 2007, Russia began to ship enriched uranium fuel to the Bushehr power plant, which is still under construction (Jan. 2009), but Tehran said it would not stop its own uranium enrichment process, arguing that fuel is needed for a reactor under construction in Darkhovin, south-west Iran. International sanctions have affected other arieas of energy production. Sanctions imposed in 2010 have led to less foreign investment which has slowed upstream investment in both oil and natural gas projects.

Manufacturing
The economic activities of strategic importance include both large scale and basic industries such as steel mills, metallurgic industries, marine industries, road construction, manufacture of farming machinery, car industries and the production of various household appliances. All are at present controlled by the government. There is large scale production of textiles, food, chemicals and cement. Petrochemicals and steel are being given particular attention in the current plan. Several petrochemical complexes, such as that of Shiraz, are currently producing various chemicals, including different kinds of chemical fertilizers.

Agriculture
Iran is not self-sufficient in food. Ten per cent of the land is used for arable farming, and 53 per cent of this is not irrigated. Irrigation methods used to consist only of ditches cut on gentle slopes to bring water from higher ground, animal lifts from wells and, where the slopes are steep, tunnels carrying water from the heights. A great deal of dam building, both for irrigation and electricity generation, has recently taken place.

The main cereals are wheat, barley and rice. Cotton, sugarbeet and tobacco are the main commercial crops, cotton being the most important. Fruit grown includes apricots, mulberries, plums and grapes. Vegetables grown include cucumbers, tomatoes, melons, pumpkins and gourds.

Agricultural Production in 2010

Produce	Int. $'000*	Tonnes
Indigenous chicken meat	2,368,390	1,662,720
Cow milk, whole, fresh	1,994,507	6,391,400
Tomatoes	1,942,469	5,256,110
Wheat	1,886,514	15,028,800
Pistachios	1,466,850	446,647
Grapes	1,189,379	2,255,670
Indigenous cattle meat	1,045,865	387,160
Indigenous sheep meat	1,004,313	368,853
Fruit fresh nes	757,194	2,169,400
Apples	703,065	1,662,430
Potatoes	659,627	4,054,490
Hen eggs, in shell	614,577	741,000

*unofficial figures

Source: http://faostat.fao.org/site/339/default.aspx Food and Agriculture Organization of the United Nations, Food and Agricultural commodities production

Livestock in the country is estimated at: cattle, 9.7 million; sheep and goats, 80.3 million; donkeys and horses, 2.5 million; camels, 200,000.

The forests of Iran, which cover a total area of 180,200 sq. km, play a significant role in the economy through the wood and paper industries.

The Iranian Fisheries Company is responsible for the fishing industry in the Caspian Sea and fish from the Persian Gulf, including caviar from the Caspian Sea and shrimps from the Persian Gulf are a large export earner. The total catch was an estimated 444,000 tonnes.

COMMUNICATIONS AND TRANSPORT

Travel Requirements
Citizens of the USA, Canada, Australia and the EU require a passport valid for six months beyond the length of stay and a visa.

Transit passengers continuing their journey within 12 hours provided holding valid onward or return documentation and not leaving the airport do not require a visa.

Nationals of Israel or holders of passports containing a visa for Israel (either valid or expired) will be refused entry. Women judged to be dressed immodestly will be refused entry. Women over nine years old should wear a headscarf in their visa application photo in accordance with Islamic custom.

Other nationals should contact the embassy to check visa requirements.

National Airlines
There are 39 airports in Iran. The Airline of the Islamic Republic of Iran (Iran Air) conducts most of the domestic and international flights. Asseman Airlines, with its small and medium-sized planes, also flies passengers and goods on domestic routes. There is direct communication between Tehran and the chief European capitals by Iran Air and several European airlines. Internal services are operated by Iran Air.
Iran Air (*Homa*), URL: http://www.iranair.com

International Airports
Imam Khomeini International Airport is situated just outside Tehran, Iran has 70 other airports and airfields situated in the country.

Railways
The Trans-Iranian railway was built on the orders of Reza Shah. It extends from Bandar Khomeini on the Persian Gulf to Bandar Turkman and Gorgan on the Caspian Sea via Ahwaz, Arak, Qum, Tehran and Savi, a distance of 1,427 km. It has 93 stations and rises 2,176 metres above sea level in the mountains. At present, the Iranian State Railways have a network of 6,688 km. The main routes being Tehran to Jolfa, Tehran to Gorgan, Tehran to Bandar-e-Abbas, Tehran to Mashhad, and Tehran to Khorramshahr.

There is an underground system in Tehran, carrying up to 600,000 passengers across the city every day.

Roads
There are now around two million cars in Tehran, causing congestion and serious levels of pollution. The cars are generally inefficient and do not use lead-free petrol. The government has set targets to phase out cars without catalytic converters, and to improve air quality levels. Vehicles drive on the right.

Shipping
The carrying capacity of the shipping lines of the Islamic Republic of Iran has increased fourfold since the Islamic Revolution, with a fleet of around 88 ships representing a total tonnage of more than 3,000,000 tons. In addition, the Indo-Iranian Joint Shipping Company, in which the Islamic Republic holds 51 per cent of the shares, has a considerable fleet of cargo vessels which move goods mainly between the Islamic Republic of Iran and the Indian Subcontinent.

HEALTH

In 2009, the equivalent of 5.7 per cent of GDP was spent on health care. In the same year, 10.5 per cent of total government expenditure went on health. The state paid for 41.1 per cent of all healthcare, whilst 58.9 per cent was paid privately, over 96 per cent of which was in the form of out-of-pocket expenditure. Per capita expenditure on health care was US$287 in 2009.

Figures for 2005-10 show that there are 61,870 physicians (9 per 10,000 population), 98,020 nurses and midwives (16 per 10,000 population) and 13,210 dentistry personnel. There are 14 hospital beds per 10,000 population.

In 2009, the infant mortality rate stood at 22 per 1,000 live births and the under-fives mortality rate stood at 26 deaths per 1,000 children. The fertility rate was 2 children per woman in the same year. Major causes of childhood deaths are: diarrhoea 4 per cent, pneumonia 13 per cent, prematurity 28 per cent, birth asphyxia 11 per cent and congenital anomalies 18 per cent.

It is estimated that about 66,000 adults were living with HIV/AIDS in 2005 (11,000 of whom were women), and an estimated 1,600 had died from the illness. Intra-venous drug use and needle sharing account for an estimated 62 per cent of transmissions. Drug-related deaths have increased over recent years.

An estimated 100 per cent of the population have access to improved drinking-water and 96 per cent to improved sanitation. (Souce: http://www.who.int, World Health Statistics 2012)

EDUCATION

The educational system has been reformed along Islamic principles under the revolutionary system. Free education is provided for all children and young adults up to the end of high school level. The Iranian educational programme is divided into the following stages: preparatory school, primary school, orientation school, high school and university.

The education system has five years of elementary education, three years of intermediate or guidance school and then four years at secondary or high school level. Graduation from high school is at 18 years. Special schools are provided for exceptionally gifted children.

In 2006, 94 per cent of primary school-aged children attended a school, and 78 per cent of children were enrolled in a secondary school. In the same year 27 per cent of students went on to higher education. 18.6 per cent of total government spending went on education in 2006. (Source: UNESCO, UIS)

University admission requires a high school diploma. It is also necessary to pass an entrance examination. Universities also offer vocational courses.

According to figures published by UNESCO, in 2006 the adult literacy was 89 per cent for men and 78 per cent for women. These figures rise to 98.1 per cent and 97 per cent respectively among the 15-24 year old age group. All figures are well above the literacy rates of the region.

RELIGION

Most Iranians are Muslims; 89 per cent belong to the Shi'a branch of Islam, the official state religion, and around 9 per cent are Sunni Muslims, notably the Kurds and Baluchis. The remaining 2 per cent of the population are Zoroastrians, Jews, Baha'is, and Christians.

Iran has a religious liberty rating of 1 on a scale of 1 to 10 (10 is most freedom). (Source: World Religion Database)

COMMUNICATIONS AND MEDIA

The press has traditionally had more freedom than broadcasters. However, conservatives have recently targeted the press and several operations have closed down.

Newspapers
There are some 20 major national dailies, including:
Ettela'at, URL: http://www.ettelaat.com/today/
Kayhan, URL: http://www.kayhanintl.com
Jomhuriye Eslami, URL: http://www.jomhourieslami.com/
Tehran Times, URL: http://www.tehrantimes.com
Iran Daily, URL: http://www.iran-daily.com/1387/3311/html/
Iran News, URL: http://www.irannewsdaily.com/home.asp?home=true

Broadcasting
The state-run Islamic Republic of Iran Broadcasting (IRIB) operates four national and provincial television networks. Launched in 2007, Press TV is IRIB's English-language satellite channel, and its Jaam-e Jam international TV channels are available worldwide via satellite. Despite a ban on owning dishes, foreign satellite TV channels are widely watched, and this tends to be tolerated by the authorities.

IRIB also operates eight radio channels, including a parliamentary network, Radio Qur'an and the Voice of the Islamic Republic of Iran, an external radio service.

Telecommunications
By 2008, there were over 24.8 million mainline telephones in use in Iran, and more than 43 million mobile phones. The telephone system is being expanded and modernised to improve the efficiency and increase the volume of the urban service, and also to bring telephone services to several thousand villages which are not currently connected. Overall, main line availability has more than doubled since 2000, and mobile service subscription has soared.

By early 2008 there were around 23 million internet users in Iran. Service providers cannot provide access to sites deemed to be anti-Islamic, but the web is a forum for dissident views and access is easy for middle-class households. It is thought that there are tens of thousands of weblogs; government officials, including President Ahmadinejad, have launched blogs under their own names.

ENVIRONMENT

The Environment Protection Organisation is the body in charge of environmental matters. There is also a forestry commission responsible for the protection of forests and green areas in the country. Iran is a party to the following international environmental agreements: Biodiversity, Climate Change, Climate Change-Kyoto Protocol, Desertification, Endangered Species, Hazardous Wastes, Marine Dumping, Ozone Layer Protection, Ship Pollution and Wetlands. Iran has signed, but not ratified the following agreements: Environmental Modification, Law of the Sea and Marine Life Conservation.

Iran's environmental problems include air pollution from motor vehicles, industry and refineries; deforestation; desertification; overgrazing; oil pollution in the Persian Gulf; and insufficient potable water.

Tehran is one of the most polluted cities in the world. Located in a valley surrounded by mountains, the pollutants hang in the air until cleared by winds. According to Iranian officials, air pollution killed nearly 10,000 people in Tehran over the year to March 2006; most of the deaths were caused by heart attacks and respiratory illnesses brought on by smog. Cheap fuel encourages car use in Iran, and many vehicles do not meet global emissions standards.

Energy related carbon dioxide emissions were estimated at 450.68 million metric tons in 2005, (up from 403.91 million metric tons the previous year). Per capita carbon dioxide emissions in the same year were estimated at 6.96 metric tons, up from 6.01 metric tons in 2003. Carbon dioxide emissions are generated mainly by the industry sector, followed by the transport, residential and commercial sectors. In 2010, Iran's emissions from the consumption and flaring of fossil fuels totalled 560.33 million metric tons of carbon dioxide. (Source: EIA)

SPACE PROGRAMME

Iran has a major satellite launch complex near Semnan and a satellite monitoring facility near Mahdash, near Tehran. A third space centre is under construction. Iran launched its first commercial satellite in 2005 in a joint project with Russia. Its first independent space mission took place in 2009 and in 2010 Iran announced it had launched several animals into space on a research rocket. It aims to send a manned mission into space by 2020.

IRAQ

Iraqi Republic

Al Jumhuriyah al-Iraqiyah

Capital: Baghdad (Population estimate: 5.8 million)

Head of State: Jalal Talabani (Kurdish) (page 1523)

First Vice President: Tariq al-Hashimi (Sunni) (page 1374)

Second Vice President: Khodair Al-Khozaei (page 1375)

National Flag: A tricolour pale-wise, red, white, black; on the white band in green Arabic script appear the words Allahu Akbar (God is Great).

In January 2008, Iraq's parliament voted to change the flag, removing the three stars from the white band that represented the Baath Party. The Iraqi Kurds had refused to fly the flag because of its close association with a regime that repressed and killed their people. The new temporary flag will retain the three colours of the old one - red, white and black - and the Arabic inscription Allahu Akbar in green will also remain. A design for a new flag will be sought after one year.

CONSTITUTION AND GOVERNMENT

Constitution

Iraq was freed from Turkish rule during the later stages of World War I. Its independent status was recognised by the Allied powers, and the League of Nations appointed Great Britain as the mandatory power. A provisional Arab Government was set up in 1920 to administer the country. Faisal, the first son of King Hussain of the Hedjaz, was chosen as the King of Iraq in 1920. A constitution of 1925 stated that Iraq should be a constitutional hereditary monarchy with a parliamentary form of government. On 30 June 1930 a treaty was concluded between the UK and Iraq which provided that the UK should renounce the mandate and recommend Iraq for admission to the League of Nations. This came about on 4 October 1932.

In July 1958 a revolution led by the army took place in Iraq, the first results of which were the ending of the monarchy and the proclamation of a republic. A government was formed in which the nationalist movement was represented. This government was headed by Brigadier Abdul Karim Qassem with a Council of Sovereignty consisting of General Najib Rubai, Mohammed Mahdi Kubba and Khalid Nakshabandi. The UK and the United States gave recognition at the beginning of August. In September 1961 a Kurdish rebellion erupted in the north of Iraq. That revolt, the failure of the claim made by Qassem's Government upon Kuwait, the deterioration of the political and economic situation and Iraq's isolation from the Arab countries, all led to the creation of difficulties for the government.

On 8 February 1963 the Arab Ba'ath Socialist Party led an armed popular revolution. Abdul Karim Qassem was executed the following day. The post of president was assumed by Abdul Salam Aref who later reneged against the Ba'ath Party on 18 November 1963 by leading a military *coup d'etat*. On 13 April 1966 Abdul Salem Aref was killed in a helicopter crash near Basra. Three days later his brother, Abdul Rahman Aref, was chosen as President.

On 17 July 1968 the Arab Ba'ath Socialist Party carried out a revolution which put an end to the unpopular rule of Abdul Rahman Aref. President al-Bakr became President of the Republic and Prime Minister. In July 1979 the Vice-Chairman of the Revolutionary Command Council, Saddam Hussein, took over as its Chairman and as President of Iraq. In May 1994 Hussein sacked his prime minister and assumed the role himself.

Following the end of Saddam Hussein's regime and the setting up of the Transitional National Assembly, a draft Constitution was written. A referendum for its approval was held in October 2005 and a yes vote was passed. A Constitutional Review Committee was then set up to look into amendments to the constitution. This will be put before the Council of Representatives for approval, prior to a referendum.

To consult the constitution, please visit: http://www.uniraq.org/documents/iraqi_constitution.pdf

Recent Events

Following Iraqi accusations that Kuwait violated Iraq's border to obtain petroleum, and its criticism of Kuwait and the United Arab Emirates for exceeding their OPEC oil quotas, Iraq invaded Kuwait on 2 August 1990. The UN Security Council condemned the invasion and a UN-authorised multinational force was mobilised. A cease-fire was agreed on 28 February 1991 and Iraq subsequently renounced its claim to Kuwait.

On 18 November 2002 UN weapons inspectors arrived in Iraq, more than four years after the country ended all co-operation with the UN Special Commission to Oversee the Destruction of Iraq's Weapons of Mass Destruction (Unscom) (which became the UN Monitoring, Verification and Inspection Commission (Unmovic) in 1999). The inspections followed months of pressure on Iraq from the US, the UK and the UN, resulting in Iraq's agreement in October 2002 to allow in the UN inspectors.

In early 2003 diplomatic efforts to resolve the arms issue ended and US-led forces began an assault on Iraq on 20 March 2003 to oust Saddam Hussein's regime. The regime collapsed in April 2003 and, following the cessation of military action, was replaced by a Coalition Provisional Authority led by Ambassador L. Paul Bremer III. Immediate priorities for the

Authority were the reconstruction of Iraq's infrastructure and the re-establishment of Iraqi rule. General Jay Garner heads the Office of Reconstruction and Humanitarian Assistance for Iraq, responsible for humanitarian assistance, reconstruction, and civil administration. Although an interim Iraqi administration was proposed, Mr Bremer said that the Iraqi constitution would be re-written to allow for democratic elections.

A 25-member Iraqi Governing Council was chosen by the US administration in Iraq, and was first convened on 14 July 2003. Its members were all Iraqi nationals and represented a broad range of ethnic and religious backgrounds. The Council consisted of 13 Shia Muslims, five Sunni Muslims, five Kurds, one Christian, and one Turkmen. The Council's first decision was to send a delegation to the UN Security Council.

Iraq's first post-war cabinet was announced on 1 June 2004. Its 24 members were nominated by the US-appointed Governing Council, and included Iyad Allawi as prime minister and Ghazi Yawer as president. The US Coalition Provisional Authority formally handed over sovereignty to the interim Iraqi government on 28 June 2004. Elections for the National Assembly took place on 30 January 2005. Full elections for an Iraqi government took place in December 2005.

On December 14 2003, US forces captured Saddam Hussein in Tikrit, and in June 2004 he was handed over to Iraq legal custody to await his trial. In October 2005 the trial of Saddam Hussein began; he was charged with seven counts of crimes against humanity. In November 2006 he was found guilty and sentenced to death; he was executed by hanging on December 30.

Despite the establishment of an Iraqi government, the guerrilla war against the US presence in Iraq has continued unabated since the initial assault by US-led forces in March 2003. By November 2003, six months after the war was officially declared over, more US soldiers had been killed than died during the war against Saddam Hussein. Since then, insurgent attacks by armed rebels, guerrilla groups and increased sectarian tensions between the Sunni and Shia communities have led to almost daily reports of casualties.

On 14th August 2007, four bombs devastated two villages of the Yazidi, a Kurdish religious sect, near the city of Mosul, leaving 344 people dead and around 400 people injured. It was the deadliest attack on a single area since the 2003 war. The US military blamed al-Qaeda for the attacks. The Yazidi sect is due to vote alongside other Kurds outside the Kurdish autonomous region in a referendum on joining the grouping; the planned referendum makes northern Iraq's Kurds a target for politically-motivated attacks.

On the 16th August, four Iraqi political parties announced an alliance in an effort to break the deadlock which has severely weakened the Shia-led unity government. The Moderates Bloc of Shia and Kurdish politicians is made up of the Daawa Party, the Supreme Islamic Council of Iraq, the Patriotic Union of Kurdistan and the Kurdistan Democratic Party. The main Sunni Arab party - the Iraqi Islamic Party - declined to join; in the weeks preceding the formation of the alliance, almost all Sunni members of the cabinet had quit, leaving 17 seats empty.

In mid-October 2007, Turkey's parliament gave permission to its government to launch military operations into Iraq in pursuit of Kurdish rebels. Iraq's parliament condemned Turkey's threat of force, but also called for the PKK to leave Iraq. On 21 October, at least 12 Turkish soldiers were killed following an ambush by the PKK guerillas near the Iraqi border. Iraq closed down the offices of the Kurdistan Workers Party (PKK).

On 10 November, the Sunni Islamic Army of Iraq, (previously part of the insurgency against US-led forces) attacked a compound near Samarra, Iraq. 18 al-Qaeda militants were killed and around 16 militants are thought to have been captured. The faction is one of several Sunni insurgent groups that have turned against al-Qaeda. The previous day, a suicide bomber had killed Sunni anti-al-Qaeda tribal leader Sheikh Faez al-Obeidi and other members of the Diyala Salvation Council. Diyala province is now at the fore in the struggle to drive al-Qaeda from Iraq; many in the Sunni community dislike al-Qaeda's austere form of Islam.

On December 16, British forces transferred control of Basra province to the Iraqi authorities. The 4,500 British troops still in Iraq will now focus on training Iraqi forces. Basra was the ninth of Iraq's 18 provinces to resume responsibility for its own security. On the same day, up to 50 Turkish fighter jets bombed suspected Kurdish rebel bases in Northern Iraq, targeting 10 villages.

On 2nd March 2008, the Iranian President Mahmoud Ahmadinejad became the first Iranian president to visit Iraq. The visit marked the culmination of a process of normalisation between the two countries after the long war of the 1980s. The number of United States military personnel killed in Iraq passed the 4,000 mark on the 22nd March, days after the 5th anniversary of the US-led invasion. Roadside bombs accounted for 44 per cent of deaths in 2007.

In the deadliest bombing in the capital for weeks, a car bomb explosion at a bus stop in northern Baghdad killed 51 people and left another 75 wounded on the17th June. On the 15th July, a double suicide bombing at an army recruitment camp in the city of Baquba left 35 dead. Baquba is the capital of Diyala province - one of the most dangerous parts of Iraq.

Provincial elections were held at the end of January 2009, and allies of Prime Minister Nouri Maliki won in Baghdad and key provinces.

In March 2009 the British army in southern Iraq formally handed over to a US general, marking the beginning of the withdrawal of British troops from Iraq. Also that month a US soldier was sentenced to 35 years in prison for murdering four Iraqi detainees in 2007. He was earlier convicted by a court martial of premeditated murder and conspiracy to commit premeditated murder. The detainees had been shot and dumped in a Baghdad canal in retribution for an attack on an US patrol in the Iraqi capital in which two soldiers had died.

In April, a suicide bomber attacked as militiamen from an Awakening council were waiting to collect their salaries at an army post in Iskandariyaa, killing at least nine people and wounding 31 others. The US-sponsored Sunni Awakening councils have helped cut violence in Iraq after turning against al-Qaeda. Relations between the councils and Iraq's Shia-led government had worsened over recent weeks. In one of the worst bomb attacks of the year, almost 70 people were killed and 130 injured in the Sadr City area of Baghdad, on 24th June. Most of the 133,000 US troops in Iraq withdrew to military bases in Iraq on 30 June, and were to finish combat operations by September, before leaving the country by the end of 2011. As the withdrawal took place on June 30 a public holiday, National Sovereignty Day was declared.

There was an upsurge of violence in July and August. On the 10th August, a series of bomb blasts killed more than 40 people and wounded at least 200. The prime minister Nouri Maliki warned that insurgents would try to create the impression that the government was not in control, ahead of January's elections. However, many Iraqis believe that the army (perceived to be corrupt) is incapable of protecting them. There was a series of bomb attacks in Baghdad on the 19th August, in which over 95 people were killed and some 560 more injured. Two of the bombs exploded close to the protected Green Zone. In October 2009 Iraq suffered its worst bomb attack when two car bombs were detonated in Baghdad near the Green Zone killing at least 155 people.

Ali Hassan al - Majid (Chemical Ali) was executed in January 2010.

Parliamentary elections took place in March 2010. No coalition won enough votes for an outright majority. The political uncertainty led to an increase in violence. In April several suicide car bombings near embassies killed at least 40 people. Another series of suicide bombs and attacks killed 100 in May 2010 including 45 in Hilla. A further 30 were killed in a car bomb attack in a market in Khalis. In June 2010 Baghdad was again targeted with 26 killed in suicide car bombings. In July 2010 more than 40 people were killed in a suicide bomb attack on Shia pilgrims. The parliament finally convened in June, three months after the elections, but then was suspended indefinitely. The various political blocks wanted more time to elect a speaker. In November 2010 parliament was reconvened and Jalal Talabani was re-appointed as president and Nouri al-Maliki as prime minister. The following month parliament approved a new government which was to include all major factions.

In February 2011 oil exports resumed from Iraqi Kurdistan.

In March 2011 troops from Iraqi Kurdistan moved into position around the disputed city of Kirkuk; this raised tensions between Iraqi Kurdistan and the central government.

In the autumn there was a resurgence of violence; in October at least 250 people were killed nationwide. There were several bomb attacks in Baghdad. Despite increased security ahead of celebrations for Eid al-Adha, a bomb killed at least eight people in a market in Baghdad. The last of the US troops left in December 2011.

In March 2012 the Arab League summit was held in Baghdad for the first time since the fall of Saddam Hussein. In the lead up to the summit there was a spate of attacks resulting in many deaths.

In May 2012 the trial began of the fugitive former vice president Tareq a-Hashemi who is accused of organising death squads which targeted Shia officials.

In 2013, car bomb and suicide attacks continued throughout the country, in February a suicide bomber attacked an anti-al-Qaeda milital north of Baghdad, around 35 people were believed killed and more than 16 people were killed in an attack on a police station in Kirkuk. Baghdad was again targeted in a series of car bombs in March with around 24 people dead. al-Qaeda were believed to be behind attacks on mainly Shia neighbourhoods around Baghdad killing 50 people, the attacks coincided with the 10th anniversary of the US-led invasion. In April more than 30 people were killed and over 200 injured during explosions across the country, and in May 2013, several car bombs went off in central and southern Iraq, Baghdad was particularly badly hit, around 26 people were reported to have been killed and many more injured. In July a Shia Mosque in Baghdad was targeted by a suicide bomber, at least 15 people were reported to have been killed.

Legislature

Prior to the ousting of Saddam Hussein's regime, Iraq's legislature consisted of the unicameral 250-seat National Assembly (*Majlis Watani*). Following the December 2005 election Iraq's legislature the Council of Representatives, (*Majlis al-Nuwab*) has 275 members, the government consists of a Prime Minister, two Deputy Prime Ministers, 27 Ministers and up to ten Ministers of State. Members are elected for a four year term and must include 69 women. Following changes made to electoral law at the end of 2009 the number of seats was increased to 325.

Council of Representatives, Baghdad International Zone, Convention Centre, Baghdad, Iraq. Tel: +964 1 7433 3077, e-mail: webmaster@na-iraqi.com, URL: http://www.na-iraqi.com
Speaker: Ayad al-Samarrai

Elections were held in March 2010 but no overall majority was won. On May 6 it was announced that the State of Law coalition had agreed to form a governing coalition with the Iraqi National Alliance, although the coalition would still be four seats short of a majority in the Council of Representatives. It took nine months to approve the new cabinet; all major factions are included, some of the posts remained unconfirmed.

Cabinet (as at June 2013)

Prime Minister; Interim Interior, and National Security Minister: Nouri Jawad al-Maliki (page 1376)(Shia)
Deputy Prime Minister for Economic Affairs: Roj Nuri Shawis
Deputy Prime Minister for Energy Affairs: Dr Hussain Al-Shahristani (Shia) Saleh
Deputy Prime Minister: Saleh Mutlaq
Interim Minister of Defence: Saadun Al-Dulaimi
Minister of Agriculture: vacant
Minister of Communications (acting): Torurhan Mudhir Hassan Al-Mufti
Minister of Reconstruction and Housing: Mohamad Sahib Al-Darraj
Minister of Higher Education: Ali Al-Adib
Minister of Emigration and Immigration: Din Dar Najman Shafiq
Minister of Planning Minister of Finance (acting): Dr Ali Youssef Abdel Nabi
Minister of Foreign Affairs: Hoshyar al-Zebari (page 1377)
Minister of Health: Majid Mohamad Amin
Minister of Trade: Khairalla Hassan Babker
Minister of Industry and Minerals: Ahmad Nasser al-Dali Karbuli
Minister of Justice: Hassan Al-Shummari
Minister of Labour and Social Affairs: Nassar Al-Rubae
Minister of Oil: Abul Kareem Al-Luaibi
Minister of Science and Technology: vacant
Minister of Transport: Hadi Al-Ameri
Minister of Youth and Sports: Jassim Mohammed Jaafar (page 1448)
Minister for Human Rights: Mohamad Al-Soudani
Minister of Municipality and Public Works: Adel Mhoder
Minister of Environment: Sargon Lazar Sulaywah
Minister of Civil Society Affairs: Dakheel Kassem
Minitser of Culture: vacant
Minister of Tourism and Antiquities: Liwaa Smaissem
Minister of Electricity: Raad Shallal Al-Ani
Minister of Education: vacant
Minister of Water Resources and Irrigation: Muhannad Salman As-Saadi

Ministries

Ministry of Agriculture, Khulafa Street, Khullani Square, Baghdad, Iraq. Tel: +964 1 887 3251Baghdad, Iraq. E-mail: Min_of_agriculture@orha.centcom.mil
Ministry of Culture, Baghdad, Iraq. E-mail: culture@cultureiraq.org, URL: http://www.cultureiraq.org
Ministry of Education, PO Box 258, Baghdad, Iraq. URL: http://www.moeiraq.info
Commission of Electricity, Baghdad, Iraq. URL: http://www.iraqelectric.org
Ministry of Finance and Banking, Khulafa Street, Nr ar-Russafi Square, Baghdad, Iraq. Tel: +964 (0)1 887 4871, e-mail: Min_of_finance@orha.centcom.mil
Ministry of Foreign Affairs, Baghdad, Iraq. E-mail: contact@iraqmofa.net, URL: http://www.iraqmofa.net
Ministry of Health, Khulafa Street, Khullani Square, Baghdad, Iraq. Tel: +964 (0)1 887 1881, e-ail: info@mohiraq.org, URL: http://www.mohiraq.org
Ministry of Higher Education and Scientific Research, E-mail: min_of_higher_edu@orha.centcom.mil, URL: http://www.moheiraq.org
Ministry of Industry and Materials, Baghdad, Iraq. E-mail: info@iraqiindustry.com, URL: http://www.iraqiindustry.com
Ministry of the Interior, Baghdad, Iraq. E-mail: Min_of_interior@orha.centcom.mil
Ministry of Justice, Baghdad, Iraq. E-mail: Min_of_justice@orha.centcom.mil
Ministry of National Defence, North Gate, Baghdad, Iraq. Tel: +964 (0)1 888 9071, e-mail: Min_of_defense@orha.centcom.mil
Ministry of Oil, Oil Complex Building, Port Saeed Street, Baghdad, Iraq. Tel: +964 (0)1 817 7000, e-mail: oil@uruklink.net. URL: http://www.uruklink.net/oil
Ministry of Planning, Karradat Mariam, ash-Shawaf Square, Baghdad, Iraq. E-mail: Min_of_planning@orha.centcom.mil
Ministry of Religious Affairs, North Gate, Baghdad, Iraq. E-mail: Min_of_religious_affrs@orha.centcom.mil
Ministry of Trade, Baghdad, Iraq. E-mail: Min_of_trade@orha.centcom.mil, URL: http://www.motiraq.org
Ministry of Transport and Telecommunications, Baghdad, Iraq. E-mail: moc1@uruklink.net, URL: http://www.motiraq.org
Ministry of Water Resources, Baghdad, Iraq. E-mail: info@iraqi-mwr.org, URL: http://www.iraqi-mwr.org
Ministry of Youth and Sport, Baghdad, Iraq. E-mail: markjmclark@hotmail.com
Ministry of Displacement and Migration, URL: http://www.modm-iraq.com
Ministry of Communications, URL: http://www.iraqimoc.net

Elections

Elections took place for the 275 seat Transitional National Assembly and Transitional Government on 30 January 2005. 58 per cent of the electorate turned out to vote, many of those who chose not to vote were from the Sunni Muslim community. The United Iraqi Coalition won 140 seats, the Kurdistan Alliance, 75 seats, the Iraqi List, 40 seats and the Iraqijun, five seats. Presidential elections were held on 6 April 2005. A Kurd, Jalal Talbani, was elected president assisted by two vice presidents, one a Sunni and one a Shia.

Following the approval of the new constitution in December 2005, a general election was held and 76 per cent of the electorate turned out to vote. The United Iraqi Alliance ((a Shia coalition), won 128 seats, the Kurdish Alliance, 53 seats, the Iraqi Tawafuq (Sunni Arab), won 44 seats, the National Iraqiya List won 25 seats, the Iraqi Front for National Dialogue (Sunni Arab) won 11 seats, the Kurdish Islamic Union won five seats, Al Risaliyun (Shia Arab) won two seats and seven seats were divided between five other political parties.

IRAQ

Local elections were held at the end of January 2009. Preliminary results showed that PM Maliki's State of Law coalition had made spectacular gains in southern Shia areas. The coalition won 38 per cent of votes in Baghdad and 37 per cent in Basra. The once-dominant Sunni Arabs, who boycotted the regained power in other parts of the country - having boycotted the 2005 election.

A general election was scheduled to take place on 30 January 2010, but in December 2009 a much debated electoral law was signed which had been holding up plans elections were then scheduled to take place on February 27 2010. The new law is seen as being fairer to Iraq's minorities and the number of parliamentary seats would rise from 275 seats to 325. The election was eventually held on March 7. President Jalal Talabani and Prime Minister Nouri Maliki both backed calls for a recount of the results and many people felt the delay in announcing the results were due to corruption. International observers had largely approved of the way the election was carried out. The result was eventually announced three weeks after the election, the former premier Iyad Allawi's secular Al-Iraqiya bloc was declared the winner having beaten Prime Minister Nouri al-Maliki's State of Law alliance by two seats. Mr Maliki refused to accept the result and announced he would be challenging the result through the courts. However on May 6 it was announced that the State of Law coalition had agreed to form a governing coalition with the Iraqi National Alliance, although the combination would still be four seats short of a majority in the Council of Representatives.

The most recent presidential election took place on 11 November 2010. The election had been held up because of stalemate in the Council of Representatives. Jalal Talabani was re-elected.

Political Parties
Until it was banned in mid-May 2003 by the US-led interim Iraqi administration, Saddam Hussein's Arab Ba'ath Socialist Party held the Presidency of Iraq, as well as a majority in the National Assembly. In May 2001 Saddam Hussein's son Qusay was elected as leader of the Ba'ath Party. The formation of other political parties had been allowed under Iraqi law, although no other party had completed the necessary registration procedure in time for the March 2000 elections.

The principal parties are now the Iraqi National Alliance (INA); Iraqi National Movement (al-Iraqiya) (INM); Kurdistan Alliance (KA, led by the Patriotic Union of Kurdistan (PUK)); State of Law (SL).

Diplomatic Representation
Britain resumed diplomatic relations with Iraq in June 2004
British Embassy, International Zone, Baghdad, Iraq. E-mail: lonemb@iraqmofamail.net, URL: http://ukiniraq.fco.gov.uk/en
Ambassador: Simon Collis (page 1407)
Embassy of Iraq, 169 Knightsbridge, London SW7 1DW, United Kingdom. Tel: +44 (0)20 7581 2264
Chargé d'Affaires: Abdulmuhaimen Al-Oraibi
US Embassy, Baghdad, Iraq. URL: http://iraq.usembassy.gov
Ambassador: Robert Stephen Beecroft (page 1386)
Embassy of the Republic of Iraq, 3421 Massachusetts Avenue, NW, Washington DC, 2007, USA. URL: http://www.iraqembassy.us/
Ambassador: Lukman Faily
Permanent Representative of Iraq to the United Nations, 14 East 79th Street, New York, N.Y. 10021, USA. Tel: +1 212 737 4433, fax: +1 212 772 1794, URL: http://www.iraqi-mission.org
Permanent Representative: Hamid al-Bayati

LEGAL SYSTEM

No law may be enacted or enforced that violates the "undisputed" teachings of Islam.

Iraqi courts are divided into two major divisions: Civil and Criminal. Litigation usually progresses through the courts of first instance, to a court of appeal and finally to a court of cassation. Personal Status courts deal with matters of personal status such as marriage, divorce, custody of children, inheritance and endowments. State security matters and serious criminal offences are usually referred to special courts.

Judges are usually appointed, assigned and promoted by the Ministry of Justice.

The constitution and law provide a strong framework for human rights. However, insurgent and extremist violence, together with a weak government, has led to widespread human rights abuses and its criminal justice system is the subject of international concern. Widespread corruption affects all levels of government. There are poor conditions in prisons, arrests can be arbitrary, and newly-established judicial institutions lack the capacity to cope. Most convictions are based on confessions. There are limitations on freedoms of speech, press and assembly due to sectarianism and extremist threats and violence.

Iraq retains the death penalty.

LOCAL GOVERNMENT

For administrative purposes Iraq is divided into 18 *Mahafdha* (governorates), Anbar, Al Basrah, Al Muthanna, Al Qadisiyah, An Najaf, Arbil, As Sulaymaniyah, At Ta'mim, Babil, Baghdad, Dahuk, Dhi Qar, Diyala, Karbala, Maysan, Ninawa, Salah ad Din and Wasit. Each *Mahafdha* is administered by a *Muhafdh* and is subdivided into smaller administrative units, *Qadhas*, which in turn are subdivided into units called *Nahiyas*. There is also one region: Karbala.

Under the current administration most of Iraq's towns and cities have functioning local governments. Baghdad is divided into 89 neighbourhoods, each of which is divided into a local governing council. Representatives of each local governing council nominate members of nine District Councils, and a 37-member City Council.

AREA AND POPULATION

Area
Iraq is situated in the Middle East. It is bordered by Syria and Jordan to the west, Iran to the east, Saudi Arabia to the south and west, Kuwait to the south, and Turkey to the north. Iraq has a total area of 537,072 sq. km, of which 432,162 sq. km is land, and 4,910 sq. km is water. There are three distinct areas: desert plains in the north-west and south; the Mesopotanian plain south of Baghdad, and the uplands and Kurdistan Mountains of the north east.

The climate is mostly desert with hot, dry summers and mild to cool winters. The winters in the mountainous areas are much colder with occasional heavy snows.

To view a map, please visit http://www.un.org/Depts/Cartographic/map/profile/iraq.pdf

Population
The estimated population in 2010 was estimated to be 31.67 million, with an annual population growth rate of 2.8 per cent over the period 2000-10. Most of the population (52 per cent) is aged between 15 and 60 years, with 43 per cent aged up to 14 years, and 5 per cent aged 60 years or over. Ethnically, Iraq is predominantly Arab (75-80 per cent), with Kurdish people accounting for 15-20 per cent of the population, and Turkmen or Assyrians representing about 5 per cent. The official language is Arabic, although Kurdish is the official language in Kurdish regions. Assyrian and Armenian are also spoken.

Births, Marriages, Deaths
According to 2010 estimates the birth rate is 35.4 births per 1,000 population, whilst the death rate is 6.4 deaths per 1,000 population. Average life expectancy at birth in 2009 was 66 years (62 years for males and 70 years for females). Healthy life expectancy was 50 years and 58 years respectively. The total fertility rate is estimated at 4.7 children born per woman. (Source: http://www.who.int, World Health Statistics 2012)

Public Holidays 2014
1 January: New Year's Day
6 January: Army Day
14 January: Birth of the Prophet (Mouloud)*
8 February: Anniversary of the 1963 Revolution
27 May: Lailat al Miraj (The Ascent of the Prophet)
14 July: Republic Day
29 July: End of Ramadan (Eid Al Fitr)*
5 October: Feast of Sacrifice (Eid al Adha)
25 October: Islamic New Year*
*Islamic holiday: precise date depends upon sighting of the moon

EMPLOYMENT

The labour force in 2008 was estimated at 7.7 million with an estimated unemployment rate of 18.1 per cent.

Total Employment by Economic Activity

Occupation	2008
Agriculture, hunting & forestry	1,759,900
Fishing	21,700
Mining & quarrying	32,400
Manufacturing	369,400
Electricity, gas & water supply	161,600
Construction	823,500
Wholesale & retail trade, repairs	1,167,200
Hotels & restaurants	62,600
Transport, storage & communications	608,100
Financial intermediation	20,800
Real estate, renting & business activities	35,100
Public admin. & defence; compulsory social security	1,003,300
Education	686,700
Health & social work	218,200
Other community, social & personal service activities	618,500
Households with employed persons	9,700
Extra-territorial organisations & bodies	7,300
Total	7,606,100

Source: Copyright © International Labour Organization (ILO Dept. of Statistics, http://laborsta.ilo.org)

BANKING AND FINANCE

Currency
The unit of currency is the Iraqi Dinar.

GDP/GNP, Inflation, National Debt
As a result of three wars (the Iran-Iraq war, the Kuwait war, and the March 2003 US-led military campaign) and over ten years of economic sanctions, Iraq's infrastructure, environment, health care system, and economy have suffered accordingly. Unemployment

s high. The economy is oil-based and traditionally accounts for some 90 per cent of foreign-exchange earnings. Revenues fluctuate depending on the price of oil. The improvement in the political situation in 2008-09 has been reflected in improvements in the economy.

In October 2003 donors at a conference in Madrid pledged $33 billion; to date, only a small fraction of the money pledged has been disbursed. Iraq's total external debt could be as high as US$250 billion if compensation payment arising from Iraq's invasion of Kuwait and debts to Gulf states and Russia are taken into account. Iraq's oil export earnings were immune from legal proceedings, such as debt collection, until the end of 2007. In November 2004, a group of 19 creditor nations agreed to write off up to 80 per cent ($42 billion) worth of loans, on condition that Iraq agrees a stabilization program with the IMF. In March 2009 Iraq agreed a Stand-By-Agreement with the IMF which allows for an 80 per cent reduction of Iraq's debt to Paris Club creditor nations in return for economic reforms. The Central Bank has managed to bring inflation under control by appreciation of the dinar against the US dollar. For the economy to continue to grow, Iraq's political situation must continue to stabilise, structural reforms must be made and corruption tackled. In February 2010, the IMF approved US3.6 billion and the World Bank, US$250 million of support to Iraq. Recent figures show that around 23 per cent of the population live below the poverty line.

GDP was estimated at US55.4 billion in 2007 with an estimated growth rate of 5 per cent. Per capita GDP was estimated at US$3,500. Figures for 2009 estimated GDP at US$65.7 billion with a growth rate of 4.0 per cent, per capital GDP (ppp) was put at US$2,107. Figures for 2010 estimated GDP at US$82.2 billion with a growth rate of 0.7 per cent. GDP is expected to grow strongly in the medium term with increased production in the oil industry and higher oil prices.

Figures for the year August, 2005 to August 2006 put average inflation at 76.5 per cent. Inflation was reported to fall dramatically to approximately 5 per cent in 2006, rising to an estimated 8 per cent in 2008 before falling to -4.0 per cent in 2009. Inflation was estimated at 4.5 per cent in 2012.

Public debt at the end of 2008 was estimated to be between US$46 and US$86 billion.

Balance of Payments / Imports and Exports

Estimated figures for 2010 put export earnings at US$39 billion (compared to US$50 billion in 2009) and the cost of imports at US$45 billion (compared to US$41 billion in 2009). The USA is the main export partner accounting for nearly 30 per cent of trade, followed by India (14.0 per cent) and Italy (10.0 per cent). Main trading partners for imported goods are Turkey (25.0 per cent), Syria (17.0 per cent, the USA (9.0 per cent and China (7.0 per cent).

Iraq's oil export revenues represent about 90 per cent of total export revenues. Oil production is currently around 2.4 million barrels per day of which around 1.9 million barrels per day go for export. Food and live animals are also important to the export trade. Main imported goods include food, medicine and manufactured goods.

Trade or Currency Restrictions

In May 2003 the UN Security Council passed Resolution 1483 lifting the sanctions imposed on Iraq since 1990-91, following the country's invasion of Kuwait. In addition the 'Oil-for-Food' programme was phased out over a period of six months. In the same month the US Treasury Department lifted most of the US sanctions on Iraq, including an embargo on goods and services imported from or exported to Iraq.

Central Bank

Central Bank of Iraq, PO Box 64, Rashid Street, Baghdad, Iraq. Tel: +964 1 8165171, fax: +964 1 8165725, e-mail: cbi@uruklink.net; URL: http://www.cbi.iq/ Governor and Chairman of the Board of Administration: Dr. Sinan Al-Shibibi

MANUFACTURING, MINING AND SERVICES

Primary and Extractive Industries

Oil was first discovered in Iraq in 1927, in the Kirkuk area, which today has proven reserves of 10 million barrels. At the beginning of January 2012 proven oil reserves were estimated at 143 billion barrels. Iraq has the fifth largest proven reserves in the world; over 65 per cent of these reserves are located in southern Iraq. 75,000 million barrels of Iraq's oil reserves has yet to be developed and the country has potential reserves estimated as high as 220,000 million barrels.

Oil production in 2011 was an estimated 2,634 thousand barrels per day (down from 2.45 million barrels per day in 2001), of which 95 per cent was crude oil. Oil consumption was an estimated 818,000 barrels per day in 2011, up from 300,000-350,000 barrels per day by August 2003. Net oil exports have risen from 1.58 million barrels per day in 2002 to 1.81 million barrels per day in 2011 according to latest EIA estimates. Iraq had a crude oil refining capacity of 638,000 barrels per day at the beginning of January 2011.

International Energy Agency (IEA) figures for 2007 show that Iraqi oil production exceeded the levels seen before the US-led invasion of the country in 2003. By mid 2007, Iraqi crude production was running at 2.3 million barrels per day, compared with 1.9 million barrels at the start of the year. The IEA put the increase down to improved security on the main oil pipeline from Iraq's northern oilfields to the port of Ceyhan in Turkey. The pipeline had been out of action for long periods due to sabotage attacks.

There are seven oil refineries in Iraq: Baiji (150,000 barrels per day crude refining capacity), Basra (140,000), Daura (100,000), Khanakin (12,000), Haditha (7,000), Muftiah (4,500), and Qayarah Mosul (2,000). Prior to the March 2003 conflict, the state undertook the distribution and marketing of refined oil products, which in the past were the responsibility of the Khanaqin Oil Company.

At the beginning of January 2011 Iraq had estimated natural gas reserves of 112 trillion cubic feet; there are a further 150 trillion cubic feet of probable reserves. About 70 per cent of Iraq's natural gas is produced in conjunction with oil (associated), while the balance is made up from non-associated gas and dome gas. In 2004, production was estimated at 62 billion cubic feet, down from 215 Bcf in 1989, this figure had fallen to 31 billion cubic feet in 2011. All natural gas produced is domestically. Around 60 per cent of all natural gas production is flared off, and large amounts are used for power generation and reinjection for oil recovery. Iraq plans to increase production, reducing dependence on oil and possibly for export.

Geological exploration and prospecting work have discovered large deposits of copper and sulphur in the northern parts of Iraq. Production of sulphur has already commenced.

Energy

In 2006, total Iraqi energy consumption was estimated at 1.2 quadrillion Btu, of which oil made up 94 per cent and natural gas contributed six per cent. Per capita energy consumption was 38.8 million Btu in 2003. Total energy consumption in 2009 was 1.4 quadrillion Btu, production that year was 5.1 quadrillion Btu.

Most of Iraq's national power grid (90 per cent) was destroyed during the course of the Gulf War. The December 1990 generating capacity of 9,000 megawatts fell to just 34 megawatts in March 1991. Some 85 per cent of Iraq's power plants were damaged as a result of the conflict. By the beginning of 1992, according to Iraq, three-quarters of the national grid had been restored, and by 2002 it was estimated that maximum available electricity generation capacity was 4.3-4.4 gigawatts, 90 per cent of which was thermal. Electricity production rose from 27.3 billion kWh in 2000 to 36 billion kWh in 2001. By 2004, following the downfall of Saddam Hussain's regime, capacity had again fallen, to 2.76 gigawatts; production over the same year fell to 29.3 billion kWh, and consumption was down to an estimated 27.3 billion kWh. Figures for 2006 showed electricity generation to be 29.9 billion kWh and consumption at 29.2 billion kWh. Figures for 2010 show that electricity generation had grown to 47.4 billion KWh and consumption was 35.1 billion kWh.

Iraq's shortage of electric generating capacity has been caused by sabotage, looting and lack of security for workers. Disruptions in fuel supplies for the plants and problems in finding replacement parts for the aging stations have exacerbated the problem. The World Bank has estimated that restoring the power sector will require about $12 billion in investment, whilst Iraq's power ministry has cited $35 billion as the overall cost of rebuilding the sector.

Agriculture

The main crops of Iraq are classed under two groups: winter crops, including wheat, barley, flax, vetch, broad beans, berseam (Egyptian clover), onions, turnips and lentils; and summer crops, including dates, cotton, rice, tobacco, maize, sesame, millet, alfalfa, green gram, potatoes and ground nuts. As its main horticultural crops, Iraq produces citrus fruits, truck crops, dates, fruit crops and nuts.

Agricultural Production in 2010

Produce	Int. $'000*	Tonnes
Tomatoes	374,435	1,013,180
Dates	234,837	566,829
Wheat	195,467	2,748,840
Indigenous cattle meat	133,463	49,406
Indigenous sheep meat	127,691	46,897
Grapes	121,554	212,649
Okra	96,704	151,219
Cucumbers and gherkins	85,871	432,500
Eggplants (aubergines)	82,834	387,435
Barley	81,724	1,137,170
Indigenous chicken meat	69,753	48,970
Cow milk, whole, fresh	56,772	191,500

* unofficial figures
Source: http://faostat.fao.org/site/339/default.aspx Food and Agriculture Organization of the United Nations, Food and Agricultural commodities production

COMMUNICATIONS AND TRANSPORT

Travel Requirements

Citizens of the USA, Canada, Australia and the EU require a passport valid for at least six months beyond the length of stay and a visa. Other nationals should contact the embassy to check visa requirements.

At the time of publication, visas were being restricted. For a list of those allowed entry visas, consult the website of the Embassy of the Republic of Iraq in the UK. For stays exceeding ten days, visitors must obtain a residency stamp at the main residency office in Baghdad.

National Airlines

Iraqi Airways, Saddam International Airport, Baghdad, Iraq. Tel: +964 1 887 2400, fax: +964 1 887 5808, URL: http://www.iraqiairways.co.uk

International Airports

The only international airport is Baghdad International Airport (formerly the Saddam International Airport), although there are three other civil airports: Basrah airport, Mosul airport and Bamerni Airport.

Railways

The track and freight are operated by Iraq State Railways. The total length of track is 2,032 km, some of which has been damaged and is currently under repair. Before the conflict in Iraq the main rail routes ran between the Syrian border at Tel-Kotchek to Mosul, Baghdad and Al Basrah; Baghdad to Kirkuk and Arbil; and Baghdad and Al Basrah.

IRELAND

Roads
The total length of the roads in Iraq is 46.500 km, of which 39,990 km is paved. Vehicles are driven on the right.

Ports and Harbours
The main harbours are Umm Qasr, Khawr az Zubayr and Al Basrah.

HEALTH

In 2009, total expenditure on healthcare amounted to 7.0 per cent of its total budget on healthcare (up from 0.1 per cent in 2000), accounting for 78.1 per cent of all healthcare spending. Total expenditure on healthcare equated to 8.4 per cent of the country's GDP. Per capita expenditure on health was US$200 in 2009 (compared to US$34 in 2000).

Figures for 2005-10 show that there are 21,925 physicians (6.9 per 10,000 population), 43,850 nurses (13.8 per 10,000 population) and 4,766 dentistry personnel. There are 13 hospital beds per 10,000 population.

In 2009 the infant mortality rate (probability of dying by age one) was 31 per 1,000 live births. The child (aged under-five) mortality rate was 39 per 1,000 live births. The most common causes of death were diarrhoea 6 per cent, pneumonia 18 per cent, prematurity 20 per cent, birth asphyxia 15 per cent and congenital anomalies 14 per cent. Approximately 27.5 per cent of children under-five were classified as stunted in the period 2005-11.

In 2010, approximately 79 per cent of the population used improved drinking water. In the same year, 73 per cent of the population had access to improved sanitation. (Source: http://www.who.int, World Health Statistics 2012)

EDUCATION

Free education is offered at schools and universities operated by the Iraqi government, including those specialising in medicine and law. There are also private schools and colleges.

Prior to the war literacy was put at 100 per cent. Latest figures from UNESCO (2000) put the literacy rate at 84.1 per cent for males and 64.2 per cent for females. For the age group 15-24 years the rate was 88.9 per cent for males and 80.5 per cent for females.

RELIGION

The majority of Iraq's population is Muslim (97 per cent), with Christians representing 1.7 per cent. The predominant Muslim sects are Shi'a, with up to 65 per cent of Muslims, and Sunni, with up to 37 per cent. There are very small communities of Baha'is, Buddhists, Hindus and Sikhs.

Iraq has a religious liberty rating of 2 on a scale of 1 to 10 (10 is most freedom). (Source World Religion Database)

COMMUNICATIONS AND MEDIA

Freedom of expression is protected under the constitution but in reality there are often sectarian and violent attacks against journalists and broadcasters. There are numerous newspapers and radio and TV stations. Many operations are controlled by religous or politica movements.

Newspapers
Newspapers include:
Al-Sabah, URL: http://www.alsabaah.com/
Al-Zaman, URL: http://www.azzaman.com/english/
Al-Mashriq, URL: http://www.al-mashriq.net/

Broadcasting
The number of private radio and television stations has increased since 2003. Most private operators are linked to political, religious or ethnic factions. The Iraqi Public Broadcasting Service operates government-owned TV and radio stations. Satellite TV is widely availalbe There are an estimated 4.02 million radios and 1 million televisions.

Telecommunications
The government is trying to rebuild domestic and international communications through fiber optic links. As of 2008, there were over 1 million landlines in use and 20 million mobile cellular phones. There were an estimated 300,000 internet users in the same year.

ENVIRONMENT

Iraq's main environmental problems include the drainage of marsh areas east of An Nasiriyah due to government water control projects; the destruction of the area's natural habitat and consequent threat to its wildlife; insufficient potable water; air and water pollution; desertification; and soil salination and erosion.

Iraq is a party to the following international environmental agreements; Biodiversity, Law of the Sea and Ozone Layer Protection. The Environmental Modification agreement has been signed but not ratified.

Energy related carbon emissions were estimated at 20.0 million metric tons in 2001, equivalent to 0.3 per cent of world emissions. Per capita carbon emissions were an estimated 0.85 metric tons in the same year, compared with 5.5 metric tons in the US. Transport contributes the greatest proportion of carbon emissions with an estimated 61.1 per cent in 1998, whilst industry contributed 28.9 per cent and the residential sector 9.9 per cent. Fuel share of carbon emissions in 2001 has been estimated as follows: oil (90 per cent), natural gas (10 per cent). In 2006 Iraq's emissions from the consumption and flaring of fossil fuels totalled 98.95 million metric tons of carbon dioxide this figure had risen to 118.31 million metric tons in 2010.

IRELAND

Eire

Capital: Dublin (Population at 2011: 525,383)

Head of State: Michael D. Higgins (President) (page 1441)

National Flag: A tricolour pale-wise, green, white, orange.

CONSTITUTION AND GOVERNMENT

Constitution
Ireland is a parliamentary democracy. It has an elected President who is Head of State, a Prime Minister (the Taoiseach) who is Head of Government, and two Houses of Parliament.

The basic law of the State is Bunreacht na hÉireann (Constitution of Ireland) was enacted by the people on 1 July 1937. It sets out the form of government and defines the powers of the President, Parliament and the Government. It also defines the structure and powers of the Courts, sets out the fundamental rights of citizens and contains a number of directive principles of social policy for the general guidance of the Oireachtas. The Constitution can be amended only as a result of a bill passed by the Houses of the Oireachtas (Parliament). Any bill passed must subsequently be approved by a referendum. Any citizen has the right to petition the courts to secure his rights under the Constitution. To date 27 amendments to the Constitution have been put to the people, of which 23 have been approved; the 12th, 22nd, 24th and 25th were rejected. The last amendment was approved on 24th June 2004.

The Courts have the jurisdiction to rule on the validity of any law having regard to the provisions of the constitution. The President may refer a Bill refer to the Supreme Court for a decision on its compatibility with the Constitution.

The President of Ireland (Uachtarán na hÉireann) is elected by direct vote of the people for not more than two terms, each of seven years. The President acts on the advice of the Government in relation to powers and functions conferred by law, but performs some constitutional functions in consultation with an advisory Council of State. Subject to the Constitution and the law, supreme command of the Armed Forces is vested in the President. The President also receives and accredits Ambassadors on the advice of the Government.

The President signs and promulgates Bills passed by the Houses of the Oireachtas. On the advice of the Taoiseach (Prime Minister), the President summons and dissolves Dáil Éireann and summons Seanad Éireann. He may refuse to dissolve Dáil Éireann on the advice of a Taoiseach who has ceased to retain the support of a majority in the Dáil.

To consult the constitution, please visit: http://www.taoiseach.gov.ie/attached_files/Pdf%20files/Constitution%20of%20Ireland.pdf

International Relations
Ireland's diaspora extends all over the world and diplomatic relations are maintained with more than 100 countries. Emigration declined with Ireland's economic boom in the 1990s, and, for the first time in modern history, the country has recently enjoyed high levels of inward migration. The Irish continue to spend time overseas for work or study, mainly in the U.S. and the U.K., before returning to establish careers in Ireland. It is thought that the recession that hit the Irish economy in Autumn 2008 may lead to another wave of long-term emigration.

Ireland has close links with the USA where there is a large Irish American population. Relations with the British Government improved following the signing of the Good Friday Agreement in 1998; the governments of both countries co-operated to implement the Agreement and achieved a settlement in Northern Ireland.

Ireland is a member of the United Nations and the Organization for Security and Cooperation in Europe, as well as being an important contributor to international peacekeeping missions, such as in Lebanon (UNIFIL), Liberia (UNIMIL), and the Balkans (KFOR and EUFOR). Membership of the EU has transformed the Irish economy.

The Northern Ireland Peace Process
On the 10th April 1998, The Good Friday Agreement was signed by the governments and major political parties of Ireland and the United Kingdom. Its aim was to devolve parts of central government power to a Northern Ireland assembly. A referendum was held in May 1998 in the Republic of Ireland and Northern Ireland to decide whether the Agreement should be implemented; it was supported by around 94 per cent of voters in the Republic and approximately 71 per cent of voters in Northern Ireland.

The Agreement provided for the devolution to a 108-member Northern Ireland Assembly of a range of executive and legislative powers, the creation of a North/South Ministerial Council (accountable to both the Assembly and the Oireachtas), and a British-Irish Council representing the Irish Government, the British Government, and the devolved assemblies of Northern Ireland, Scotland and Wales. Elections for the Assembly were held on 25 June 1998, each member representing a constituency and elected by proportional representation.

The Irish government removed from its constitution the Republic's territorial claim to Northern Ireland in December 1999.

Legislation to formally establish the Northern Ireland Assembly and transfer real power was due to be passed in January 1999, but the issue of arms decommissioning remained unresolved. The IRA's reluctance to decommission its weapons until Sinn Féin had seats in the Assembly, and the Ulster Unionists' subsequent refusal to sit in the Assembly with Sinn Féin until decommissioning occurred, meant that the process stalled. In February 2000 the Assembly and Executive were suspended. They were reinstated in May 2000 amidst renewed talks on decommissioning.

On 23rd October 2001, the decommissioning body confirmed it had witnessed a 'significant' disposal of arms. On 8 April 2002, the IRA announced a second move to put arms 'beyond use' and, in July 2002 the IRA apologised to 'non-combatant' victims of its campaign.

In October 2002, Sinn Fein's Stormont offices were raided as part of a police enquiry into republican intelligence-gathering. Four people were arrested on charges of possessing documents useful to terrorists, but all charges were later dropped without explanation. On 14 October 2002 John Reid announced the suspension of devolution and the resumption of direct rule from London. In December 2002, a leaked Irish government paper suggested that the IRA were still active.

On 1 May 2003, UK Prime Minister Tony Blair announced the postponement of Assembly elections until the autumn due to the lack of clarity over the IRA's position. However, the delayed Good Friday Agreement blueprint was finally published; it included plans to repeal the power to suspend the Northern Ireland Assembly, a scaling back of the military, and plans to begin devolving policing and justice to Northern Ireland.

On 17 June 2003 David Trimble won the backing of the Ulster Unionist Party for British and Irish government plans. In September, David Trimble held talks with the Irish Prime Minister about the restoration of the Northern Ireland Assembly and an end to paramilitarism. The November 2003 elections saw Ian Paisley's DUP overtake the Ulster Unionists as Northern Ireland's largest party. Sinn Fein also took more seats than its nationalist rival, the SDLP.

On 28 July 2005 the IRA leadership formally ordered an end to the armed campaign. In September 2005, Gen. John de Chastelain, head of the independent decommissioning body, said that he was satisfied that the IRA's arms had been put beyond use.

In March 2006 the British Government proposed emergency legislation that allowed the recall of the Assembly in May and set a deadline of November 24 2006 for the formation of a power-sharing executive. A transitional government was established in November, and elections took place on 7th March 2007; the DUP won 36 seats and Sinn Féin won 28 seats. Direct rule from London ended at midnight. The leaders of the main parties agreed to a coalition and the new government took office on May 8 2007.

Recent Events
In April 2008, Irish Prime Minister Bertie Ahern announced his intention to resign on 6 May. The announcement came a day after Mr. Ahern began a court challenge to limit the work of a public inquiry probing planning corruption in the 1990s. Brian Cowen was confirmed as the new Fianna Fáil leader.

In June 2008, the Irish voted against the EU Lisbon Treaty in a referendum.

In October, Ireland was first country in western Europe to officially enter a recession, defined as two consecutive quarters of negative economic growth, as a result of the global financial crisis. The economy was heavily reliant on the construction sector, and a collapse in property prices impacted on Ireland's banks with large property-related debt. The government stepped in to guarantee the main banks' liabilities, and recapitalised them; however, the banks remained fragile, and subject to bad debts as the recession deepened. In February 2009, around 100,000 people rallied in Dublin in protest at the government's handling of the economic crisis.

On 7th April, the government unveiled its second budget in six months to deal with its contracting economy; the Finance Minister forecast that the economy would contract by eight per cent over 2009, down from three per cent in 2008. Ireland lost its AAA debt rating. The budget includes a large tax rises and spending cuts, to deal with the worst deficit in Europe. An independent agency would take over banks' bad assets to restore lending.

In October 2009 Ireland held a second referendum on the Lisbon treaty, the vote was in favour.

November 2009 saw a damning report published which criticised the Catholic Church's handling of allegations of child abuse against 46 priests. In March 2010 Pope Benedict XVI sent a pastoral letter apologising to victims of child sex abuse by Catholic priests in Ireland. The pastoral letter is the first of its kind sent by the Vatican on the sexual abuse of children.

The financial crisis continued and in September 2010 the banks had to be bailed out to the tune of €45 billion, resulting in a budget deficit around a third of GDP. Speculation began on whether the EU would have to bail out the Irish economy and in November it was announced that the EU and IMF would loan Ireland in the region of €85 billion. The UK also agreed to loan Ireland £7 billion. In return, the government will put together a four-year economic plan and draw up an austerity budget. Demonstrators took to the streets to protest about the government handling of the situation and the Green Party who hold the balance of power in the government called for a general election to be held in March 2011, Prime Minister Brian Cowen agreed. On January 16 Brian Cowen won a vote of confidence at a Fianna Fail Party meeting but Foreign Minister Michael Martin who voted again Mr Cowen resigned, in the following few days five more minister resigned and Mr Cowen announced he would be having a major reshuffle of the cabinet in order to fill the vacant posts while also continuing with plans to enact the Finance Bill, this bill would make law the measures announced in the budget. On January 23 the Green Party announced it was pulling out of the Fianna Fail-led ruling coalition, thus depriving it of its majority. Mr Cowen resigned as leader of the Fianna Fail party but said he would stay on as prime minister until the general election. The election took place on 25 February 2011. The opposition party Fine Gael won most seats, 76, but not enough for an overall majority. Labour won 37 seats and the two parties agreed to form a coalition government headed by Fine Gael's Enda Kenny.

In May 2011 the Queen made a four day visit to Ireland, the first reigning monarch for 100 years to do so. The visit went ahead amidst tight security and was seen as a success.

The following week US President Obama visited Ireland on route to a Group of Eight (G8) meeting in France.

In July 2011, following the financial crisis the ratings agency Moody's downgraded Ireland's debt rating to junk status.

In June 2012, a referendum was held, Irish voters approved the EU fiscal treaty by 60 per cent, this endorsed the government's commitment to an EU-backed austerity programme.

In February 2013, the European Central Bank approved a deal to liquidate the former Anglo Irish Bank, the bank had previously been nationalised in January 2009. Under the terms of the deal Ireland was able to defer by decades the bill for the bank bailout.

In April 2013, the International Monetary Fund delivered a harsh assessment of the Irish economy. In a review of Ireland's bailout programme, the IMF warned that Ireland's debt burden may become unsustainable if economic growth continues to be weak.

Legislature
The Oireachtas consists of two Houses: the House of Representatives (Dáil Éireann) and the Senate (Seanad Éireann).
Houses of the Oireachtas, Leinster House, Kildare Street, Dublin 2, Ireland. Tel: +353 (0)1 618 3000, fax: +353 (0)1 618 4118, e-mail: info@oireachtas.ie, URL: http://www.oireachtas.ie/

Upper House
The Seanad is made up of 60 senators who serve a five-year term. 11 of the senators are nominated by the Taoiseach, 43 are elected by five vocational interests panels (Culture and Education, Agriculture, Labour, Industry and Commerce, and Public Administration), and six are elected by graduates of the National University of Ireland and the University of Dublin (Trinity College). The primary function of the Seanad is to revise legislation sent by the Dáil; increasingly, however, it is used to initiate legislation.

Seanad Éireann (Senate), Leinster House, Kildare Street, Dublin 2, Ireland. Tel: +353 (0)1 618 3333, fax: +353 (0)1 618 4101, e-mail: Cathaoirleach@oireachtas.ie, URL: http://www.oireachtas.ie
Chairman: Paddy Burke (page 1397)

Lower House
The Dáil consists of 166 members, known as Teachtaí Dála (usually abbreviated to TD), who are elected by adult suffrage in secret ballot under a system of proportional representation for a five-year term. Each of Ireland's constituencies elects three, four, or five members according to the size of the constituency. According to the Constitution, each member must represent no fewer than 20,000 and no more than 30,000 people. Currently, the 166 members represent 41 constituencies. The constituencies are revised at least once every 12 years, usually following the five-year census.

Dáil Éireann (House of Representatives), Leinster House, Kildare Street, Dublin 2, Ireland. Tel: +353 (0)1 618 3000, fax: +353 (0)1 618 4100, http://www.oireachtas.ie
Chairman: Seán Barrett
Deputy Chairman: Michael P. Kitt

Cabinet (as of June 2013)
Taoiseach (Prime Minister): Enda Kenny (FG) (page 1455)
Minister of Tánaiste (Deputy Prime Minister) and Minister of Foreign Affairs and Trade: Eamon Gilmore (Lab) (page 1430)
Minister for Health: Dr James Reilly (FG) (page 1502)
Minister for Finance: Michael Noonan (FG) (page 1487)
Minister for Social Protection: Joan Burton (Lab) (page 1397)
Minister for Transport, Tourism and Sport: Leo Varadkar (FG) (page 1531)
Minister for Education and Skills: Ruairi Quinn (Lab) (page 1499)
Minister for Agriculture, Fisheries and Food: Simon Coveney (FG) (page 1409)
Minister for Environment, Heritage and Local Government: Phil Hogan (FG) (page 1442)
Minister for Arts, Heritage and Gaeltacht: Jimmy Deenihan (FG) (page 1414)
Minister for Justice, Equality and Defence: Alan Shatter (FG) (page 1513)
Minister for Communications, Energy and Natural Resources: Pat Rabbitte (Lab) (page 1499)

IRELAND

Ministries

Office of the President, Áras an Uachtaráin, Phoenix Park, Dublin 8, Ireland. Tel +353 (0)1 617 1000, fax: +353 (0)1 617 1001, e-mail: webmaster@aras.irlgov.ie, URL: http://www.irlgov.ie/aras/
Department of the Taoiseach, Government Buildings, Upper Merrion Street, Dublin 2, Ireland. Tel: +353 (0)1 619 4000, fax: +353 (0)1 619 4258, URL: http://www.taoiseach.gov.ie
Department of Agriculture, Fisheries and Food, Kildare Street, Dublin 2, Ireland. Tel: +353 (0)1 607 2000, fax: +353 (0)1 661 6263, e-mail: info@agriculture.gov.ie, URL: http://www.agriculture.gov.ie
Department of Arts, Sport and Tourism, 23 Kildare Street, Dublin 2, Ireland. Tel: +353 (0)1 631 3800, fax: +353 (0)1 661 1201, e-mail: webmaster@dast.gov.ie, URL: http://www.arts-sport-tourism.gov.ie
Department of Community, Rural and Gaeltacht Affairs, Dún Aimhirgin, 43-49 Mespil Road, Dublin 4, Ireland. Tel: +353 (0)1 647 3000, fax: +353 (0)1 6473051, e-mail: eolas@pobail.ie, URL: http://www.pobail.ie
Department of Defence, Infirmary Road, Dublin 7, Ireland. Tel: +353 (0)1 804 2000, fax: +353 (0)1 804 5000, e-mail: info@defence.irlgov.ie, URL: http://www.defence.ie
Department of Education and Science, Marlborough Street, Dublin 1, Ireland. Tel: +353 (0)1 889 6400, fax: +353 (0)1 878 6712, e-mail: info@education.gov.ie, URL: http://www.education.ie
Department of Enterprise, Trade and Employment, Kildare Street, Dublin 2, Ireland. Tel: 353 (0)1 631 2121, fax: 353 (0)1 631 2827, e-mail: info@entemp.ie, URL: http://www.entemp.ie
Department of the Environment, Heritage and Local Government, The Custom House, Dublin 1, Ireland. Tel: +353 (0)1 888 2000, fax: +353 (0)1 888 2888, e-mail: press-office@environ.ie, URL: http://www.environ.ie
Department of Finance, Government Buildings, Upper Merrion Street, Dublin 2, Ireland. Tel: +353 (0)1 676 7571, fax: +353 (0)1 678 9936, e-mail: webmaster@finance.ie, URL: http://www.finance.gov.ie
Department of Foreign Affairs, 80 St. Stephen's Green, Dublin 2, Ireland. Tel: +353 (0)1 478 0822, fax: +353 (0)1 478 1484, URL: http://www.dfa.ie
Department of Health and Children, Hawkins House, Hawkins Street, Dublin 2, Ireland. Tel: +353 (0)1 635 4000, fax: +353 (0)1 635 4001, e-mail: info@health.gov.ie, URL: http://www.dohc.ie
Department of Justice, Equality and Law Reform, 72-76 St. Stephen's Green, Dublin 2, Ireland. Tel: +353 (0)1 602 8202, fax: +353 (0)1 661 5461, e-mail: info@justice.ie, URL: http://www.justice.ie
Department of Communications, Energy and Natural Resources, 29-31 Adelaide Road, Dublin 2, Ireland. Tel: +353 1 678 2000, fax: +353 1 678 2449, e-mail: webmaster@dcmnr.gov.ie, URL: http://www.dcmnr.gov.ie
Department of Social and Family Affairs, Aras Mhic Dhiarmada, Store Street, Dublin 1, Ireland. Tel: +353 (0)1 704 3000, fax: +353 (0)1 704 3868, URL: http://www.welfare.ie/
Department of Tran sport and the Marine, Transport House, 44 Kildare St., Dublin 2, Ireland. Tel: + 353 (0)1 670 7444, e-mail: info@transport.ie, URL: http://www.transport.ie/

Parties

Fianna Fáil (Republican Party), 65-66 Lower Mount Street, Dublin 2, Ireland. Tel: +353 (0)1 676 1551, fax: +353 (0)1 678 5690, e-mail: info@fiannafail.ie, URL: http://www.fiannafail.ie/
Leader: Micheál Martin
Fine Gael (United Ireland Party), 51 Upper Mount Street, Dublin 2, Ireland. Tel: +353 (0)1 619 8444, fax: +353 (0)1 662 5046, e-mail: finegael@finegael.com, URL: http://www.finegael.ie/
Leader: Enda Kenny (page 1455)
Labour Party, 17 Ely Place, Dublin 2, Ireland. Tel: +353 (0)1 678 4700, fax: +353 (0)1 661 2640, e-mail: head_office@labour.ie, URL: http://www.labour.ie/
Leader: Eamon Gilmore (page 1430)
Sinn Féin, 44 Parnell Square, Dublin 1, Ireland. Tel: +353 (0)1 872 6100 / 872 6932, fax: +353 (0)1 873 3441, e-mail: sfadmin@eircom.net, URL: http://www.sinnfein.ie/
President: Gerry Adams (page 1372)
Green Party/Comhaontas Glas, 16/17 Suffolk Street, Dublin 2, Ireland. Tel: +353 (0)1 679 0012, fax: +353 (0)1 679 7168, e-mail: info@greenparty.ie, URL: http://www.greenparty.ie/
Party Leader: Eamon Ryan (page 1507)
Socialist Party, 141 Thomas Street, Dublin 8, Ireland. Tel: +353 (0)1 677 2686, fax: +353 (0)1 677 2592, e-mail: info@socialistparty.net, URL: http://www.socialistparty.net/
Leader: Joe Higgins
People Before Profit Alliance, 26 Elmwood Avenue, Ranelagh, Dublin 6, Ireland. URL: http://www.peoplebeforeprofit.ie

Elections

A general election is held at least every five years. There are at present 41 electoral areas or constituencies, each of which elects from three to five members according to its population.

The most recent presidential election took place on 29 October 2011. The former MP and cabinet member Michael D. Higgins was elected with almost 40 per cent of the vote. The favourite Sean Gallagher came second and Martin McGuiness of Sinn Fein third.

The most recent election to the Dail Eireann was held on 25 February 2011: Fianna Fáil won 20 of the Dáil's 166 seats. Fine Gael won 76 seats, the Labour Party 37, People Before Profit Alliance 2, Sinn Féin 14 and independents 15 seats. The last Seanad Éireann elections took place in April 2011.

Nice Treaty

In June 2001, Ireland's electorate voted in a referendum to determine whether or not European Union (EU) membership should be extended to other countries. On 7 June 2001, 54 per cent of Ireland's voters decided against ratification of the Nice Treaty; they were asked to vote again on the 19 October 2002, and passed the treaty.

Lisbon Treaty

The Lisbon treaty was designed to help EU expansion, making it more streamlined and leading to the removal of national veto votes in some areas. Ireland had to hold a referendum on the Treaty, as acceptance would have led to amendments having to be made to the Irish constitution. On June 12 2008, Irish voters rejected the treaty. The treaty can only be implemented if all EU member countries approve it. In October 2009 Ireland held a second referendum on the Lisbon treaty, the vote was in favour.

Diplomatic Representation

British Embassy, 29 Merrion Road, Ballsbridge, Dublin 4, Ireland. Tel: +353 (0)1 205 3700, fax: +353 (0)1 205 3880 (Commercial) / +353 (0)1 205 3893 (Press and Public Affairs) / +353 (0)1 205 3890 (Consular / Passport / Visa), e-mail: publicaffairs.dubli@fco.gov.uk (Press and Public Affairs), URL: http://www.britishembassy.ie/
Ambassador: Dominick Chilcott (page 1404)
Embassy of the Holy See, 183 Navan Road, Dublin 7, Ireland. Tel: +353 (0)1 838 0577, fax: +353 (0)1 838 0276, e-mail: nuncioirl@eircom.net
Embassy of Ireland, 2234 Massachusetts Ave, NW, Washington, DC 20008, USA. Tel: +1 202 462 3939, fax: +1 202 232 5993, e-mail: http://www.irelandemb.org/feedback.html, URL: http://www.embassyofireland.org/home/index.aspx?id=30782
Ambassador: H.E. Michael Collins (page 1407)
Embassy of Ireland, 17 Grosvenor Place, London, SW1X 7HR, United Kingdom. Tel: +44 (0)20 7235 2171, fax: +44 (0)20 7245 6961, URL: http://www.embassyofireland.co.uk/home/index.aspx?id=33706
Ambassador: Bobby McDonagh (page 1474)
Embassy of the United States of America, 42 Elgin Road, Ballsbridge, Dublin 4, Ireland. Tel: +353 (0)1 668 8777, fax: +353 (0)1 668 9946, e-mail: webmasterireland@state.gov, URL: http://dublin.usembassy.gov/
Chargé d'affaires: John Hennessey-Niland
Economic Department: Tel: +353 (0)1 678 9811
Permanent Representative of Ireland to the United Nations, One Dag Hammarskjöld Plaza, 885 Second Avenue, 19th Floor, New York, NY 10017, USA. Tel: +1 212 421 6934, fax: +1 212 752 4726, e-mail: ireland@un.int, URL: http://www.irelandunnewyork.org
Ambassador and Permanent Representative: Anne Anderson

LEGAL SYSTEM

Irish law is based on Common Law, modified by subsequent legislation and by the Constitution of 1937. Statutes passed by the British parliament before 1921 have the force of law unless they have been repealed by the Irish Parliament.

There are Courts of First Instance and a Court of Final Appeal called the Supreme Court. The Courts of First Instance are the High Court with full original jurisdiction and the Circuit and District Courts with local and limited jurisdiction.

The High Court, which consists of the President of the High Court (who is *ex officio* an additional judge of the Supreme Court) and 17 ordinary judges, has full original jurisdiction in and power to determine all matters and questions, whether of law or fact, civil or criminal. In all cases regarding the validity of any law with reference to the Constitution, the High Court alone exercises original jurisdiction. The High Court on Circuit acts as an appeal court from the Circuit Court.

The Supreme Court, which consists of the Chief Justice (who is *ex officio* an additional judge of the High Court) and seven ordinary judges, has appellate jurisdiction from all decisions of the High Court, except where otherwise provided by law.

The President may, after consultation with the Council of State, refer a Bill passed by both Houses of the Oireachtas, to the Supreme Court for a decision on whether such a Bill should be disallowed under the Constitution.

The Court of Criminal Appeal consists of at least three judges, one of whom is the Chief Justice or an ordinary Judge of the Supreme Court together with the President of the High Court and an ordinary judge of the High Court, or two ordinary judges of the same. It deals with appeals by persons convicted on indictment where the appellant obtains a certificate from the trial judge that the case is a fit one for appeal, or, in case such certificate is refused, where the Court itself, on appeal from such refusal, grants leave to appeal.

The Central Criminal Court consists of a Judge or Judges of the High Court. The Court sits at such times and in such places as the President of the High Court may direct and tries criminal cases which are outside the jurisdiction of the Circuit Court.

There are 26 Circuit Courts in Ireland, one in each county. The President of the Circuit Court is *ex officio* an additional judge of the High Court. In criminal matters the Court has jurisdiction in all cases except murder, treason, piracy and allied offences. The Circuit Court acts as an appeal court from the District Court.

The District Court has summary jurisdiction in a large number of criminal cases where the offence is not of a serious nature. In civil matters the Court has jurisdiction in contract and tort (except slander, libel, seduction, slander of title, malicious prosecution and false imprisonment) and in some hire-purchase and credit-sale agreement proceedings. All criminal cases, except those dealt with by a Judge in the District Court, are tried by a judge and jury of 12.

A judge may not be removed from office except for stated misbehaviour or incapacity and then only on resolutions passed by both Houses of the Oireachtas. Judges of the Supreme, High and Circuit Courts are appointed from among practicing barristers. Judges of the District Court may be appointed from among practicing barristers or practicing solicitors.

The government respects the rights of its citizens. There have been occasional reports of police abuse of authority and inadequate care for prisoners with mental disabilities. Capital punishment still existed up to 1990 for the murder of police officers but was abolished completely in 1990, and has been prohibited by the Constitution of Ireland since 2002.

In December 2006 the Government established a Working Group on a Court of Appeal, which is considering the need for a general Court of Appeal.

Attorney General: Máire Whelan SC

The Supreme Court/An Chúirt Uachtarach, URL: http://www.supremecourt.ie/
Chief Justice: Justice Susan Gageby Denham
Ordinary Judges: The Hon. Mr. Justice John L. Murray, The Hon. Mr. Justice Adrian Hardiman, The Hon. Mr. Justice Nial Fennelly, The Hon. Mr. Justice Donal O'Donnell, The Hon. Mr. Justice William McKechnie, The Hon. Mr. Justice Frank Clarke, The Hon. Mr. Justice John Mac Menamin.

The High Court, URL: http://www.courts.ie/Home.nsf/Content/Courts+Opening

Irish Human Rights Commission, Fourth Floor, Jervis House, Jervis Street, Dublin 1, Ireland. Tel: +353 (0)1 858 9601, e-mail: info@ihrc.ie, URL: http://www.ihrc.ie/home/default.asp

LOCAL GOVERNMENT

At present the elected local authorities comprise 29 County Councils, five City Councils, five Borough Councils and 75 Town Councils. The range of services for which local authorities are responsible is broken down into eight main programme groups as follows: Housing and Building; Road Transportation and Safety; Water Supply and Sewerage; Development Incentives and Controls; Environmental Protection; Recreation and Amenity; Agriculture, Education, Health and Welfare; and Miscellaneous Services.

The local authorities have a system of government which combines an elected council and a full-time manager. The elected members determine the policy framework within which the manager exercises his executive functions. The major policy decisions of the local authority are reserved to the elected members, including the levying of rates (local tax), the borrowing of money, the adoption of development plans, the making, amending or revoking of bye-laws and the nomination of persons to other bodies.

The revenue expenditure of local authorities is financed by a local tax on the occupation of certain property (called rates), by grants and subsidies from the central government and payments for certain services which they provide. Capital expenditure is financed mainly by means of capital grants from the Exchequer and by loans from banking institutions.

There are also eight Regional Authorities which co-ordinate some of the county/city and sub-county activities and monitor the use of EU structural funds.

The 29 counties are, Carlow, Cavan, Clare, Cork, Donegal, Dun Laoghaire-Rathdown, Fingal, Galway, Kerry, Kildare, Kilkenny, Laois, Leitrim, Limerick, Longford, Louth, Mayo, Meath, Monaghan, North Tipperary, Offaly, Roscommon, Sligo, South Dublin, South Tipperary, Waterford, Westmeath, Wexford, and Wicklow. The five cities are Cork, Dublin, Galway, Limerick and Waterford.

Department of the Environment, Heritage and Local Government, URL: http://www.environ.ie/

AREA AND POPULATION

Area
The whole island of Ireland is 8,301,465 hectares in area, whilst the Republic of Ireland covers 6,889,456 hectares, or 84,412 sq. km, exclusive of lakes, rivers and tideways. The coastline of the Republic of Ireland covers a total distance of 3,170 km. The climate is temperate maritime.

To view a map, please consult http://www.lib.utexas.edu/maps/cia08/ireland_sm_2008.gif

Population
Ireland's total population as at 10 April 2011 (the last census) was put at 4,581,269 up from 4,239,848 in April 2006 representing an increase of 8.1 per cent in five years. The number of inhabitants is now the highest since 1871. The following table shows Ireland's estimated annual population in April in recent years according to gender ('000s):

Year	Total	Male	Female
1996	3,626.1	1,800.2	1,825.9
2000	3,789.5	1,882.9	1,906.6
2003	3,978.9	1,977.2	2,001.7

- continued

2004	4,043.8	2,011.2	2,032.6
2005	4,130.7	2,059.0	2,071.8
2006	4,239.8	2,121.2	2,118.7
2007	4,375.8	2,191.3	2,184.6
2008	4,485.1	2,238.6	2,246.5
2009	4,533.4	2,257.3	2,276.1
2010	4,554.8	2,262.2	2,292.6
2011*	4,574.9	2,270.5	2,304.4
2012*	4,585.4	2,269.6	2,315.8

*provisional
Source: CSO

The largest age group is 25-44 years, of which there were 1,450,140 in 2011. Ireland's major cities (2011 figures) are Dublin (527,612), Cork (119,230), Galway (75,529), Limerick (57,106), and Waterford (46,732).

The number of emigrants from Ireland fell steadily from 31,500 in 1999 to 16,600 in 2005, but rose in the year ending April 2009 to 65,100 nearly half of those were European nationals returning to their country of origin while around 18,000 were Irish nationals. The number of immigrants to Ireland rose from 39,200 in 1996 to an estimated 70,000 in 2005, and reached a high of 109,500 in 2007 before declining in 2008 to 83,800 and 27,300 in year ending April 2009. This confirmed predictions that recent immigration flows to Ireland would slow or be reversed following the economic recession that began in the autumn of 2008.

The languages spoken are Irish and English. Ireland's Constitution stipulates that Irish, as the national language, is the first official language, whilst English is the second official language and in 2006 the Irish language was officially recognised as a working language by the European Union. The total number of Irish speakers rose from 789,430 in 1971 (28 per cent of the population) to 1,570,894 in 2002 (42 per cent), and there are areas in western Ireland where Irish is spoken by more than 80 per cent of the people. (Source: CSO)

Births, Marriages, Deaths
The following table gives the components of population change in recent years (years ending in April):

	2010	2011	2012
Births	77,200	75,100	74,000
Deaths	28,400	27,700	29,200
Natural Increase	48,800	47,500	44,900
Immigrants	41,800	53,300	52,700
Emigrants	69,200	80,600	87,100
Net migration	-27,500	-27,400	-34,400
Population change	21,400	20,100	10,500

Source: CSO

In recent years when the Irish economy was strong Ireland saw an increase in immigrants coming to the country, following the economic crisis figures have shown a decrease in immigrants arriving and an increase in those leaving. Figures for 2005 indicate that, of the population over the age of 15 years (3,277,400 people), 1,363,600 were single, 1,607,890 were married, 115,300 were divorced or separated and 190,800 were widowed. There were 20,635 marriages in 2010. The number of divorces has decreased in recent years from a high of 3,684 in 2007 to 3,113 in 2010. Contraception has been legalized in Ireland, but abortion remains illegal except in the most extraordinary circumstances.

Public Holidays 2014
1 January: New Year's Day*
17 March: St. Patrick's Day*
18 April: Good Friday
21 April: Easter Monday
5 May: May Day
2 June: Bank Holiday (first Monday in June)
4 August: Bank Holiday (first Monday in August)
27 October: Bank Holiday (last Monday in October)
25 December: Christmas Day**
26 December: St. Stephen's Day

* Celebrated on the following Monday if falling on a weekend
**Celebrated on the following Tuesday if falling on a weekend

EMPLOYMENT

The population of 15 years and above totaled 3,455,300 over 2007, and the labour force numbered 2,202,100. Over the same year, those in employment numbered 2,101,600. There were 100,300 unemployed, up on the previous year. The annual average unemployment rate remained stable at 4.4 per cent from 2004 to 2006, before rising to 4.5 per cent in 2007 and 6.4 per cent in 2008 before rising considerably in response to the economic downturn. Average unemployment in 2009 was 12.0 per cent rising to 13.8 per cent in 2010, 14.6 per cent in 2011 and 14.7 per cent in 2012, the construction sector particularly badly hit. (Source: CSO)

The following table shows employment according to economic sector in recent years (the period covers April -June).

Sector	2010	2011	2012
Agriculture, forestry & fishing	85,100	85,700	87,100
Industry	244,700	239,500	231,700
Construction	126,500	106,400	99,600
Wholesale, retails trade & repairs	278,400	274,500	268,200

IRELAND

- continued

Transportation & storage	90,800	95,700	90,900
Accommodation & food services	127,200	114,400	120,000
Information & communication	76,600	77,900	81,200
Financial, insurance & real estate	104,200	105,100	99,300
Professional, scientific & technical	101,900	103,800	102,600
Admin. & support services	63,800	69,300	63,000
Public admin. & defence; compulsory social security	106,700	99,100	99,600
Education	149,400	146,100	146,300
Human health & social work activities	237,100	243,300	244,400
Other NACE activities	92,400	96,300	100,62
Total in employment	1,893.6	1,861.3	1,836.2
Total unemployed	305.0	317.4	323.0
Total labour force	2,198.7	2,178.7	2,159.1
Not in labour force	1,399.5	1,420.4	1,431.9
Population 15 years & over	3,598.2	3,599.1	3,591.0

Source: Central Statistics Office Ireland

Ireland's economic success up to 2008 was assisted by a "Social Partnership" between the state, employers, unions and civil society representatives. This partnership comes to periodic agreements covering minimum standards in pay, employment conditions, social welfare provision and specific parts of infrastructural development. The latest of these agreements, entitled "Towards 2016", came into effect in 2006, and set the agenda for social and economic development until 2016. The number of industrial disputes has fallen steadily from a high of 39 in 2000 to six in 2007.

Employers' Organisations

Irish Business and Employers' Confederation (IBEC), URL: http://www.ibec.ie/
Irish Exporters Association, URL: http://www.irishexporters.ie/

BANKING AND FINANCE

Currency
One euro (€) = 100 cents
€ = 0.787564 punts (European Central Bank irrevocable conversion rate)
On 1 January 1999 the euro was launched as an electronic currency across the 12 member states of the EU. On 1 January 2002 the euro became legal tender in Ireland and the 11 other member states of the EU. Ireland's old currency, the punt, ceased to be legal tender from 9 February 2002. Euro banknotes come in denominations of 5, 10, 20, 50, 100, 200, and 500. Euro coins come in denominations of 2 and 1 euros, 50, 20, 10, 5, 2, and 1 cents.

GDP/GNP, Inflation, National Debt
Ireland enjoyed the "Celtic Tiger" period of economic growth during the mid to late 1990s when GDP grew by over 10 per cent per annum, driven by an industrial policy that boosted large-scale foreign direct investment and exports. The economy dipped following the post 9/11 global slowdown, but between 2003 and 2008, the Irish economy expanded at a steady 3-6 per cent per annum. The main reasons for this growth were a strong construction sector, and consumer spending. House prices in parts of Dublin rose rapidly over the period, often by 25 per cent per annum. The influx of migrant workers provided a workforce for the sector, and boosted the residential property market. Over 2006 and 2007, however, there were signs of a slow-down in the housing market, the property boom had been fuelled by huge amounts of banks loans, and when the housing boom collapsed, lenders were unable to pay and the banks were plunged into crisis. Consumer spending grew over 2003-08, but the Central Bank became concerned about increases in the levels of personal debt. As the recession, fuelled by the global financial crisis hit in the autumn 2008, consumer spending also fell. The government stepped in to guarantee the main banks' liabilities, and recapitalised them; however, the banks remained fragile, and subject to bad debts as the recession deepened. The economy contracted 10 per cent in 2009. Widespread public cuts were enforced. GDP grew by 0.3 per cent in Q3 of 2009 and by the end of 2009 the economy came out of recession. In September 2010 it was revealed that the cost of bailing out the Irish banking system had risen to €45 billion and in November the Irish government agreed a rescue package with the EU of €85 billion. As part of the package the government had to prepare an austerity programme which included four years of tax rises and spending cuts. In February 2013, Ireland agreed a deal with the European Central Bank. In order to ease the country's debt burden, arrangements were made to underwrite the bankrupt institutions such as the Anglos Irish Bank, these banks are now know as 'Zombie Banks'.

The service sector accounted for around 58 per cent of GDP. Industry and construction together contributed around 38.8 per cent. The following table shows annual economic aggregates, Gross Domestic Product (GDP), Gross National Product (GNP), Gross National Income (GNI) and Gross National Disposable Income (GNDI) at current market prices in € million:

GDP, GNI and GNP (€million)

Gross Product	2008	2009	2010	2011
GDP	179,882	161,275	156,487	158,993
GNP	153,565	132,911	130,202	127,016
GNI	154,878	134,271	131,295	128,301
GNDI	152,411	131,488	128,788	125,858

Source: CSO

Per capita GDP, GNP and GNI are shown on the following table (current market prices):

Per capita figures at constant market prices(€)

Gross Product	2008	2009	2010	2011
GDP per capita	37,719	35,363	35,003	35,696
GNP per capita	31,731	28,926	29,123	28,317
GNI per capita	31,927	29,200	29,368	28,557
GNDI per capita	31,293	29,032	28,807	27,112

Source: CSO

The following table shows Gross Value Added by Sector of Origin, (€m, constant factor cost, chain linked annually and referenced to year 2010.):

Gross Value Added by sector, at constant factor cost (€million)

Sector	2008	2009	2010	2011
Agriculture, forestry and fishing	3,651	3,437	3,222	3,049
Industry including Construction	39,835	35,852	36,525	37,168
Distribution, transport, communication	31,146	32,219	33,733	35,041
Public administration and defence	8,685	8,291	7,831	7,551
Other services (inc. rent)	62,057	61,026	59,808	59,252
Gross Value Added at constant factor cost	146,683	141,335	140,538	142,957

Source: CSO

Ireland's wage rates rose quicker than the EU average over 2003-08, though they were tempered by the wages paid to immigrants working in the construction industry from 2006 onwards. Growth in the economy was accompanied by a rise in inflation, as measured by the Consumer Price Index (CPI). Annual inflation rose to a high of 5.6 per cent in 2008 before averaging 3.4 per cent over 2003-07. Over 2007, the inflation rate was 4.9 per cent; the highest increase was in the Housing, Water, Electricity, Gas and Other Fuels sector, at 20.4 per cent. March 2010 saw 3.1 per cent inflation. At the beginning of 2009, Ireland's inflation fell into negative figures but rose again in the middle of 2010. By January 2011 it was running at 1.7 per cent and 3.2 per cent in April.

External debt rose to €973 billion at the end of 2005, although much of this debt is offset by holdings of foreign financial assets by Irish residents. Figures for 2008 put national debt at €50,398 million equivalent to 28.2 per cent of GDP, this figures had risen to €75,152 million, 46.6 per cent of GDP in 2009. 2010 figures put national debt at €3,445 million, 59.7 per cent of GDP and €19,082 million equivalent to 74.9 per cent of GDP. (Source: CSO)

Foreign Investment
Irish Foreign Direct Investment (FDI) abroad increased from €30,011 million in 2000 to €8,196 million in 2005. Foreign direct investment in Ireland rose from €136,581 million in 2000 to €176,531 million in 2003, before falling to €140,909 million in 2005.

Balance of Payments / Imports and Exports
Net export revenue fell from a high of €38,047 million in 2002 to €25,740 million in 2008, largely due to a significant increase in imports over recent years. The following table shows imports, exports, and trade surplus (€m):

Balance of Trade, (€million)

Year	Imports	Exports	Balance
2002	55,628	93,675	38,047
2003	47,865	82,076	34,211
2004	51,105	84,409	33,304
2005	57,465	86,732	29,267
2006	60,857	86,772	25,915
2007	63,486	89,226	25,740
2008	57,585	86,394	28,810
2009	45,061	84,805	40,742
2010	45,764	89,703	43,940
2011	48,315	91,228	42,913
2012	49,219	92,123	42,905

Source: CSO

Imports and exports according to commodity are shown on the following table (€m):

Imports and Exports by Commodity (SITC), Jan. & Feb. 2012 (€m)

Commodity	Imports	Exports
Food and live animals	838	1,187
Beverages and tobacco	99	170
Crude materials	112	274
Mineral fuels, lubricants	1,172	353
Animal and vegetable oils	42	9
Chemicals & related products	1,554	9,284
Manufactured goods	601	259
Machinery and transport equip.	2,541	1,583
Miscellaneous manufactures	942	1,752
Unclassified commodities and transactions	176	55
Unclassified estimates	159	260
TOTAL	8,336	15,084

Source: CSO

In 2011, Ireland imported €49,219.0 million worth of goods, most of which came from the United Kingdom (€16,410.4 million). other EU countries supplied €13,800.6 million worth of goods, and €6,479.1 million worth of goods came from the USA. Ireland's exports amounted to €92,123.0 million; the main destination was the EU, which accounted for €39,141.9 million. The USA was the largest individual importer of Irish goods (€18,159.8 million), followed by the United Kingdom, (15,307.9 million).

Top international trading partners, Jan. & Feb. 2012 (€million)

Country of Origin	Imports
Great Britain	2,542
USA	1,419
Germany	585
China	482
Netherlands	329
France	329
Northern Ireland	172
Belgium	131
Norway	131
Japan	130
Spain	119
Italy	116

Destination Country	Exports
USA	2,830
Belgium	2,566
Great Britain	2,445
Germany	1,045
Switzerland	753
France	738
Netherlands	512
Italy	504
Spain	453
China	383
Japan	301
Northern Ireland	222

Source: CSO

Central Bank
Central Bank of Ireland, PO Box 559, Dame Street, Dublin 2, Co Dublin, Ireland. Tel: +353 (0)1 434 4000, fax: +353 (0)1 671 6561, e-mail: enquiries@centralbank.ie, URL: http://www.centralbank.ie
Governor: Patrick Honohan (page 1443)

Banking Associations
The Institute of Bankers in Ireland, URL: http://www.instbank.ie/
Irish Bankers' Federation, URL: http://www.ibf.ie/
Irish Brokers Association (IBA), URL: http://www.irishbrokers.com/

Chambers of Commerce and Trade
The Chambers of Commerce of Ireland (CCI), URL: http://www.chambersireland.ie
Irish Stock Exchange, URL: http://www.ise.ie
Enterprise Ireland, URL: http://www.enterprise-ireland.com/

MANUFACTURING, MINING AND SERVICES

Primary and Extractive Industries
Proven coal reserves stood at 15 million short tons in 2003. Figures for 2010 show that production of coal was nil and consumption was 2.140 million short tons. (Source: EIA)

Ireland has no oil reserves and therefore relies on imports to satisfy domestic demand. US Energy Information Administration (EIA) figures show that oil consumption in 2011 was 144 thousand barrels per day, mainly distillate, residual, gasoline, and jet fuel.

Ireland had proved natural gas reserves of 350 billion cubic feet in 2006. Gross production in 2011 was 12 billion cubic feet. Consumption reached 171 billion cubic feet. Imports totalled 159 billion cubic feet. (Source: EIA)

Energy
In 2009, Ireland's primary energy consumption reached 0.632 quadrillion Btu., up from 0.615 Btu in 2009.

Electricity capacity in 20010 according to EIA statistics, was 8.32 GWe. Generation that year was 26.83 billion kWh and consumption was 8.32 billion kWh. Most of this was thermal athough there was a small capacity for hydroelectric, geothermal and other forms.

Bord Gáis Éireann (BGE) (Irish Gas Board), URL: http://www.bge.ie/
Bord na Móna (Irish Peat Board), URL: http://www.bnm.ie
Electricity Supply Board (ESB), URL: http://www.esb.ie/

Manufacturing
In 2007, the industry contributed €41,381 million of GVA. The greatest Value Added came from basic pharmaceutical products and preparations €9,779 million, followed by food products (€4,892 million), electrical and optical engineering (€4,653 million) and the chemicals industry (€3,085 million), followed by electrical and optical engineering (€4,653 million).

In 2009 there were around 5,029 units of industrial enterprises, employing some 195,542 people.

The total value of products manufactured and sold in 2010 are shown in the following table:

Sector	€'000
Mining & quarrying (except energy producing materials)	779,595

- continued	
Food products	17,188,573
Beverages	2,073,748
Textiles, wearing apparel, leather & related products	422,820
Paper & paper products; printing & reproduction of recorded media	1,494,020
Chemicals & chemical products	7,449,264
Basic pharmaceutical products & preparations	34,667,425
Rubber & plastic products	925,453
Basic metals & fabricated metal products, machinery & equipment n.e.c	3,135,333
Computer, electronic, optical & electrical equipment	9,135,039
Wood & wood products & non-metallic mineral products, furniture	3,032,251
Transport equipment	651,588
Other	6,768,804
Total	88,453,913

Source: CSO

Service Industries
Ireland's services industry (including rent) is the largest contributor to GDP. In 2005, Gross Value Added was €45,870,934,000. There were 83,988 service providing businesses in 2005, most of which were in the Retail trade (16,664) and Other Business sectors (18,521). Employment in the services sector in 2005 totalled around 740,400, most being employed in Retail, Hotels and Restaurants, and Other Business Activities.

Tourism
According to CSO figures there were 6,505,000 visitors from overseas to Ireland in 2011, down from 6,977,000 in 2005. Estimated earnings from tourism reached an estimated €4,693 million in 2006, up from €4,272 million in 2005. Most visitors came from the United Kingdom (4,060,000) or the rest of Europe (2,281,000), and most came on holiday, though 2,323,000 came to visit relatives.
Bord Fáilte Éireann (Irish Tourist Board), URL: http://www.ireland.travel.ie/
Irish Tourist Industry Confederation, URL: http://www.itic.ie/

Agriculture
The agriculture, fishing and hunting sector had a Gross Value Added of €3,998 million in 2006, up from €3,594 million in 2005. Employment in the sector has been falling since 1994 when it stood at a high of just under 142,500. In 2009 97,200 people were employed in the sector. This figure fell to 84,900 in 2010 before rising again in 2011 by 85,800.

The estimated value of agricultural output, in recent years, is shown on the following table (€m):

Product Groups	2011	2012
All Livestock	2,662.0	3,131.8
All Livestock Products	1,894.0	1,704.8
All Crops	1,751.8	1,778.2
Total	6,307.8	6,614.8

Source: CSO

The following table shows selected livestock numbers :

Livestock ('000s)

	Dec. 2011	Dec. 2012
Cattle	5,925.3	6,253.2
Sheep	3,321.3	3,430.3
Pigs	1,552.9	1,493.0

Source: CSO

The number of agricultural holdings fallen from 263,600 in 1980 to 1239,800 in 2010. The following table shows crop yield by type of crop and 2011:

Crop Yield

Area	Wheat	Oats	Barley	Potatoes
Area under Crops 000 hectares	94.2	21.4	180.6	10.4
Crop yield per hectare (tonnes)	9.9	7.9	7.8	34.4
Crop yield 000 tonnes	929.0	168.1	1,412.0	356.1

Source: CSO

Fishing is an important part of the Irish economy. The cod catch has shrunk significantly; in 2002, 2,503 tonnes were caught and in 2004 just 1,246 tonnes were landed. There were reductions in all deep sea fish landing over the same period. Conversely, there were increases in the pelagic catch, (especially the Blue Whiting - from 14,268 tonnes to 61,470) and in shellfish landings, resulting in an overall increase in the catch. This was not reflected in the value of the catch, which fell some €30,000 over the same period. The following table shows principal sea fish landings in weight and value in recent years:

Sea fish landings by weight and value

Species	2003 tonnes	2004 tonnes	2003 €'000	2004 €'000
Demersal				
Cod	1,694	1,246	5,126	3,702
Haddock	2,788	2,257	5,215	4,379
Plaice	876	564	1,678	1,087
Whiting	5,351	4,799	4,468	4,026
Pelagic				

IRELAND

- continued

Blue Whiting	22,586	61,470	3,244	8,346
Herring	28,839	33,178	6,036	7,139
Horse Mackerel	36,960	37,431	8,981	8,845
Mackerel	67,480	72,345	27,411	32,241
Shellfish				
Blue Mussel	422	412	339	343
Crab	12,441	14,429	12,744	15,409
Lobster	657	853	8,241	10,705
Whelk	8,752	7,560	5,798	3,332
Other	75,535	72,788	91,049	81,353
Total	**264,381**	**309,332**	**180,330**	**180,907**

Source: CSO

COMMUNICATIONS AND TRANSPORT

Travel Requirements
Citizens of the USA, Canada, Australia and the EU require a passport valid for three months beyond the length of stay, but do not need a visa for stays of up to 90 days. Other nationals should contact the embassy to check visa requirements.

National Airlines
The national airline is Aer Lingus and comprises two companies - Aer Lingus plc and Aer Linte Eireann plc. There are subsidiary and associated companies reporting to both. The Aer Lingus Group is wholly owned by the Irish Government. Aer Lingus plc was incorporated in 1936 and operates services both within Ireland and between Ireland and the UK and Europe. Aer Linte Eireann plc was incorporated in 1947 and operates transatlantic services from Shannon to Boston, and New York in the USA. Although separate legal entities the two companies share a common management and Board of Directors.

Aer Lingus Commuter Ltd., a subsidiary of Aer Lingus, operates Irish domestic services and international services from Dublin to Bristol, Edinburgh, East Midlands, Leeds / Bradford, Newcastle, Birmingham, Glasgow, Brussels, Manchester and from Cork to Bristol, Manchester and Paris. Ryanair, a privately owned airline, operates scheduled air services on a number of routes between Ireland and the UK. Translift Airways, a privately owned airline based at Shannon, operates international passenger and cargo services.

There are also a small number of other air transport and helicopter companies operating within Ireland. A number of UK, Continental and US carriers provide competing services on the main air routes to and from Ireland.

Aer Lingus Group plc, URL: http://www.aerlingus.com
Ryanair, URL: http://www.ryanair.ie
Aer Arann, URL: http://www.aerarann.com

International Airports
In 2010 there were 39 airports in Ireland, 16 with paved runways. The principal airports are Dublin Airport, Shannon Airport, and Cork Airport, all of which are owned by the state and managed on behalf of the Minister by the State-sponsored company Dublin Airport Authority plc.

Shannon Airport is a customs-free airport. The development and promotion of industrial and tourist activity in the region of the Airport are the responsibility of the Shannon Free Airport Development Company Limited.

Dublin Airport Authority plc (formerly Aer Rianta), URL: http://www.aer-rianta.ie/
Shannon Airport, URL: http://www.snn.aero/
Dublin Airport, URL: http://www.dub.aero/
Cork Airport, URL: http://www.cork-airport.com/

Railways
Passenger and freight rail services are provided by Iarnród Eireann (Irish Rail) - a subsidiary company of Coras Iompair Éireann (The Irish Transport Co). The present railway network consists of approximately 3,312 km.
Coras Iompair Éireann (CIE) (The Irish Transport Co.), URL: http://www.cie.ie/home/
Iarnród Eireann (Irish Rail), URL: http://www.irishrail.ie/home/

Roads
There are 96,602 km of public roads in Ireland. In 2010, there were 2,416,387 vehicles on the road, 1,872,715 of which were private cars. Vehicles are driven on the left.

The national roads network in Ireland is overseen by the National Roads Authority which has overall responsibility for planning and supervising the construction, improvement and maintenance of the network.
National Roads Authority, URL: http://www.nra.ie

Shipping
Cork, Dublin, New Ross, Shannon Foynes and Waterford are the main ports in Ireland. In 2009, some 41,836,000 tons of cargo passed through Irish ports. The Irish Continental Group operates multipurpose ferry services on the Dublin/Holyhead and Rosslare/Pembroke routes. They also operate a freight service on the Dublin/Liverpool route in conjunction with Pandoro and a European container service from Dublin to Cork, Le Havre, Antwerp and Rotterdam.

Irish Continental Group http://www.irishferries.co.uk/plc, URL: http://www.icg.ie
Irish Ferries, URL: http://www.irishferries.co.uk/
Irish Ship Agents' Association, URL: http://www.irishshipagents.com/

HEALTH

Most hospitals in Ireland are owned and funded by Health Boards, but there are an increasing amount of private hospitals which operate independently of the Department of Health. According to World Health Organization figures for 2009, expenditure on health was split as follows: 75.0 per cent was public expenditure and 25.0 per cent was private spending, of which 49 per cent was out-of-pocket rather than pre-paid health plans. The Irish spent 9.4 per cent of GDP on healthcare in 2009. Per capita total expenditure on health was US$4,719 in 2009.

In 2009, there were 51 publicly funded acute hospitals in Ireland, with 11,369 in-patient beds and 1,172 day-care beds. (Source: CSO)

In 2000-10, according to the WHO, there were 13,763 physicians (31.9 per 10,000 population), 68,483 nurses and midwives (156.7 per 10,000 population), 2,702 dentistry personnel (6 per 10,000 population) and 4,451 pharmaceutical personnel.

In 2009 the infant mortality rate (probability of dying by age 1) was 3 per 1,000 live births. In the same year the under-fives mortality rate was 4 per 1,000 live births. The most common causes of death among children aged under 5 years were congenital abnormalities 48 per cent and prematurity 15 per cent. (Source: WHO)

EDUCATION

Education in Ireland is compulsory between the ages of six and 16 and is provided free even up to university level.

Elementary Education
Elementary education is delivered through around 3,396 national schools (including 130 special schools). The total number of pupils registered in 2009-10 was 505,998, taught by 31,709 teachers. The average pupil/teacher ratio was around 16.0 pupils to each teacher. The average class size was 4.1 pupils. (Source: CSO)

Special Needs
Special provision is made for handicapped and deprived children in special schools, as well as within special classes within the ordinary school system. There are also part-time teaching facilities in hospitals, clinics, rehabilitation workshops and at home. In 2003-04, there were 128 special needs schools with 6,718 pupils, and a further 9,340 children with special needs attended ordinary schools. There is a National Education Officer for traveling children.

Secondary Education
In 2010-11, there were 359,653 pupils registered in secondary schools, and there were 26,185 teachers.

Voluntary secondary schools are the most populated schools. They are under private control and are administered in most cases by religious orders. These schools receive grants from the state and are open to inspection by the Department of Education and Science.

The number of Gaelscoileanna schools is on the rise where the language of instruction is Irish, these schools are run by voluntary organisations.

Comprehensive Schools are financed by the State and combine academic and technical subjects in one broad curriculum. Community schools are being created through an amalgamation of existing voluntary secondary and Vocational Education Committee schools; they make facilities available to voluntary organisations and to the adult community generally.

Vocational schools are controlled by local Vocational Education Committees, and are financed mainly by state grants and also by contributions from local rating authorities and by VEC receipts. Pupils are prepared for State examinations and for entrance to universities and institutes of further education.

Higher Education
In the year 2009-10, 156,973 people were in full-time higher education.

University education is provided by the National University of Ireland, founded in Dublin in 1908, by the University of Dublin (Trinity College - founded in 1592), and by the Dublin City University and the University of Limerick (established in 1989).

The National University comprises three constituent colleges - University College, Dublin; University College, Cork; and University College, Galway. St. Patrick's College, Maynooth, Co. Kildare, is a national seminary for Catholic priests and a pontifical university with the power to confer degrees up to a doctoral level in philosophy, theology and canon law. It also admits lay students (both men and women) to the courses in arts, science and education that it provides as a recognised college of the National University.

Besides the University medical schools, the Royal College of Surgeons in Ireland (a long-established independent medical school) provides medical qualifications that are internationally recognised. Courses to degree level are available at the National College of Art and Design, Dublin.

Institutes of Technology in 13 centres (Athlone, Carlow, Cork, Dublin, Dundalk, Dun Laoghaire, Galway, Letterkenny, Limerick, Sligo, Tallaght, Tralee, and Waterford) provide vocational education and training for trade and industry from craft to professional level, operating under the aegis of the Vocational Education Committees (VECs) for their areas. These colleges were established on a statutory basis on 1 January 1993, except for Dun Laoghaire, which was designated under the RTC Act (1992) on 1 April 1997. There are also four agricultural colleges administered by the Agricultural and Food Development Authority (Teagasc), and seven Teagasc-aided agricultural colleges.

There are five Colleges of Education for training primary school teachers. For degree awarding purposes, three of these colleges are associated with Trinity College, one with Dublin City University and one with the University of Limerick. There are also two Home Economic Colleges for teacher training, one associated with Trinity College and one with the National University of Ireland in Galway.

In 2011, it was estimated that over a third of those aged 15-64 had a third level qualification.

Literacy is estimated at 99 per cent.

RELIGION

It is estimated that around 87 per cent of the population is Roman Catholic. A further 3 per cent follow the Church of Ireland. Approximately 1 per cent of the population are now Muslim, and less than 1 per cent are Presbyterian, or Jewish. The remaining 8.35 per cent follow a different religion.

Ireland has a religious liberty rating of 10 on a scale of 1 to 10 (10 is most freedom). (Source: World Religion Database)

Irish Council of Churches, URL: http://www.irishchurches.org
President (20130-15): Fr Godfrey O' Donnell

The Roman Catholic Church, URL: http://www.catholic-church.org.uk
Archbishop of Armagh and All Ireland: His Grace the Most Reverend Sean Brady (page 1393)
Archbishop of Dublin and Primate of Ireland: Diarmuid Martin D.D (page 1471)
Church of Ireland (The Anglican Communion)
Central Office of the Church of Ireland, URL: http://www.ireland.anglican.org
Archbishop of Armagh and Primate of All Ireland: The Most Revd Dr Richard Clarke
Archbishop of Dublin and Primate of Ireland: The Right Reverend Michael Jackson
URL: http://www.dublin.anglican.org/archbishop/archbishop/neill/neill-john.html

COMMUNICATIONS AND MEDIA

Newspapers
The Irish Examiner, URL: http://www.irishexaminer.com
Irish Independent, URL: http://www.unison.ie/irish_independent
The Irish Times, URL: http://www.ireland.com

Broadcasting
The national television and radio services are operated by Radio Telefís Éireann (RTE), an autonomous statutory corporation created by the Broadcasting Authority Act 1960 and funded by advertising and license fee revenue. The RTE Authority comprises nine members appointed by the Government.

RTE's television service (RTE 1) was inaugurated on 31 December 1961 and provides national coverage. On 2 November 1978 RTE inaugurated its second television channel (Network 2). Programmes are broadcast in both Irish and English. Teilifíis na Gaelige, Ireland's third national television channel, began transmitting in October 1996.

The national radio service began operations on 1 January 1926. RTE introduced its second national radio service (now 2FM) on 31 May 1979, and Raidió na Gaeltachta, a radio network to serve the scattered Irish-speaking communities in the western half of Ireland, was inaugurated on 2 April 1972. Independent privately operated broadcasting services are established under the aegis of the Independent Radio and Television Commission which is a statutory body in the Radio and Television Act 1988.

Radio Telefís Éireann (RTE), URL: http://www.rte.ie
Raidió na Gaeltachta, URL: http://www.rnag.ie
Independent Radio and Television Commission (IRTC), URL: http://www.irtc.ie

Postal Service
An Post, a state-owned company since 1984, operates the national postal service. Employing some 9,600 people, the company operates an extensive retail network using its 2,000 post office counters throughout the country. These are mostly on behalf of the Departments of Social Welfare (pensions and other welfare benefits), Finance (savings services) and Communications (television licenses) and of Telecom Eireann (telephone accounts).
An Post, URL: http://www.anpost.ie

Telecommunications
Telecom Eireann was established on 1 January 1984 under the Postal and Telecommunications Services Act 1983. Following privatisation in 1999, it became Eircom plc.

It is estimated that, in 2011, there were some 2.0 million mainline telephones and around 4.9 million mobile phones in use. There were around 3.0 million internet users.

Office of the Director of Telecommunications Regulation, URL: http://www.odtror.ie
Eircom plc., URL: http://www.eircom.net/

ENVIRONMENT

Ireland is a party to the following international agreements: Air Pollution, Air Pollution-Nitrogen Oxides, Air Pollution-Sulfur 94, Biodiversity, Climate Change, Climate Change-Kyoto Protocol, Desertification, Endangered Species, Environmental Modification, Hazardous Wastes, Law of the Sea, Marine Dumping, Ozone Layer Protection, Ship Pollution, Tropical Timber 83, Tropical Timber 94, Wetlands and Whaling. It has signed but not ratified the agreements on Air Pollution-Persistent Organic Pollutants, and Marine Life Conservation.

Carbon dioxide emissions continue to rise, whilst emissions of other gases have been reduced over recent years, as shown below:

Greenhouse gas emissions in kilotonnes

Emission	2000	2005	2010
Carbon Dioxide	44,974	47,673	41,268
Methane	644	610	553
Nitrous Oxide	32	26	25
Total	45,652	48,309	41,846

Source: CSO

Per capita carbon dioxide emissions have also risen, from 10.39 metric tons in 2003 to 10.98 metric tons in 2005. This is above the European average of 7.93 metric tons per capita. (Source: EIA)

The Irish government has declared the surrounding sea to be a whale and dolphin sanctuary.

ISRAEL
State of Israel
Medinat Yisrael

Capital: Tel Aviv, population estimate: 384,400. Although Jerusalem is used as the administrative capital of Israel and has the highest population (733,300 residents), it is not recognised as such by the UN and international law.

Head of State: Shimon Peres (President) (page 1494)

National Flag: White, charged with a star six-pointed centred blue, composed of two interlaced equilateral triangles, between two blue fesswise stripes.

CONSTITUTION AND GOVERNMENT

Constitution
The State of Israel's independence was proclaimed on 14 May 1948 with the termination of the British Mandate over Palestine. It followed a resolution agreed by the United Nation's General Assembly on 29 November 1947 recommending the partition of Mandatory Palestine into independent Jewish and Arab States.

The State of Israel is a Republic headed by a president elected by a secret Knesset ballot. Until 21 December 1998 the president was elected for a maximum of two five-year terms; however, a Knesset-approved act extended the term to a non-renewable period of seven years. The president appoints senior officials, including the prime minister, the state comptroller, the governor of the Bank of Israel, and the president and deputy president of the Supreme Court. The prime minister is responsible to Parliament and appoints the Cabinet.

The Government of Israel consists of the prime minister and a number of ministers who may or may not be members of the Knesset. Deputy ministers may also be appointed from among the members of the Knesset. The president entrusts a member of the Knesset with the formation of a government, which then must obtain a vote of confidence from the Knesset. The government is directly responsible to the Knesset. It may be removed from office by a parliamentary vote of censure and may also resign by its own decision as a result of the resignation of the prime minister.

Israel has no written constitution. In 1949 a proposal to create a written constitution was rejected by a majority vote of the Knesset. Instead it was decided to enact from time to time fundamental laws which would form a constitution. To date, eleven such laws have been enacted: 'The Knesset' (1958), 'State Lands' (1960), 'The President of the State' (1964), 'The State Economy' (1975), 'Israel Defence Forces' (1976), 'Jerusalem, Capital of Israel' (1980), 'The Judiciary' (1984), 'The State Comptroller' (1988), 'Human Dignity and Liberty' (1992), 'Freedom of Occupation' (1994) and 'The Government' (2001). Some aspects of the laws can only be changed by votes from at least two-thirds of the Knesset.

ISRAEL

There are a number of ordinary laws dealing with constitutional matters such as the Law and Administration Ordinance (1948), the State Comptroller Law (1949), the Knesset Elections Law (1955) and the Protection of Holy Places Law (1967). The Law of Return (1950) providing that 'Every Jew shall be entitled to come to Israel as an immigrant,' the Nationality Law (1952) and the Women's Equal Rights Law (1951) also belong to this type of constitutional legislation.

On 7 March 2001 the Knesset passed an amendment to the Basic Law under which the president appoints the prime minister, who is responsible to parliament.

For further information on the basic laws, please visit: http://www.knesset.gov.il/description/eng/eng_mimshal_yesod.htm

International Relations
At present, Israel maintains over 100 diplomatic missions and has diplomatic ties with a further 61 countries. Within the Middle East, Israel has diplomatic relations with Jordan, Mauritania and Egypt. Israel has diplomatic relations with nine non-Arab Muslim states and with 32 of the 43 Sub-Saharan states that are not members of the Arab League.

Golan Heights
The Heights are part of a plateau, rising between 400 and 1,700 feet above sea level. They are bordered on the west by an escarpment of 1,700 feet that drops to the Sea of Galilee and the Jordan River. On the south, they are bordered by the Yarmouk River; on the north by the international border with Lebanon, and on the east by a largely flat plain, called the Hauran.
After the 1948-49 Arab-Israeli War, the Golan Heights were partly demilitarised by the Israel-Syria Armistice Agreement, but there were many violations by both sides. The major causes of the conflict were a dispute over the disposition of the demilitarized zone between Israel and Syria, competition over water resources, and the Israeli-Palestinian conflict. The strategic Heights were frequently used by Syria to bombard Israeli farming settlements below. During the Six-Day War of 1967, the Israeli army captured the Golan Heights; the area came under Israeli military control, and Israeli settlements were quickly established. During the War, between 80,000 and 109,000 of the Golan's inhabitants, mainly Druze Arabs and Circassians, fled the region and have not been permitted to return.

During the Yom-Kippur War in 1973, Syrian forces attempted to re-take the Golan Heights, but were repelled. Israel and Syria signed a ceasefire agreement in 1974 that left almost all the Heights under Israeli control, while returning a narrow demilitarized zone to Syrian control. In November 1981, Israel unilaterally annexed the Golan Heights, but this has not been recognised internationally. The tiny Shebaa Farms area of the Golan Heights is claimed by both Lebanon and Syria.

In 1999-2000, talks were held between Ehud Barak, the Israeli Prime Minister, and the Syrian Foreign Minister. Israel offered withdrawal from the Golan Heights in return for peace, recognition and full normalisation of relations. However, Israel insisted on the pre-1948 border while Syria insisted on the 1967 frontier, which would give Syria access to the Sea of Galilee, Israel's only freshwater lake and a major water resource. The talks failed. In 2003, the Syrian President announced that he was willing to hold peace talks with Israel. However, Israel demanded Syria first disarm Hezbollah, who launched many attacks on northern Israeli towns and army posts from Lebanese territory. Israeli public opinion was not in favour of returning the Heights to Syria, believing them to be too strategically important. Peace talks began in April 2008, sparking outrage in the Israeli parliament; several MPs said they would try to accelerate the passage of a bill requiring any withdrawal from the Golan to be backed by a referendum. Further indirect peace talks took place in Turkey, in June 2008.

In 2005, the Golan Heights had a population of approximately 38,900 people, comprising approximately 19,300 Druze, 16,500 Jews, and 2,100 Muslims. The Jewish villages are administered by the Golan Regional Council, and are inhabited by Israeli citizens. The Golan Muslims (who accepted Israeli citizenship in 1981) live in the Israel-Lebanon border-straddling village of Ghajar. The Druze live in the villages of Ein Qinya, Buq'ata, Majdal Shams, and Mas'ada. The land is fertile, with the volcanic soil being used to cultivate vineyards and orchards and to raise cattle. The Golan Heights has tourist attractions, such as skiing on Mount Hermon, the crater lake of Birkat Ram and the mineral springs of Hamat Gader.

Israeli-Palestinian Conflict
A peace summit took place in July 2000 at Camp David, between Ehud Barak and Palestinian leader Yasser Arafat. Negotiations broke down after three weeks with no agreement, the main sticking point being the future of Jerusalem.

In July 2000 Israel withdrew its troops from the security zone in Southern Lebanon they had occupied since 1985. A 15 km buffer zone was set up to protect Israel from cross-border attacks by Islamic militants. The UN began patrols along the Israeli-Lebanese border from 26 July 2000.

In September 2000, Ariel Sharon, visited the Temple Mount, a site sacred to Muslims. The incident sparked off violent clashes between Palestinians and Israelis that caused over 300 deaths by the end of the year. The violence subsequently became known as the al-Aqsa intafada or uprising.

In response to suicide bombings, Israeli troops moved into Ramallah on 31 March 2002, entering the Palestinian settlements of Jenin, Salfit and Nablus and inflicting heavy Palestinian casualties. Israel blocked a UN fact-finding mission to Jenin, and on 8 May the UN General Assembly passed a motion condemning the Israeli military occupation of the town. Yasser Arafat was released from house arrest following the handover of six suspect Palestinian militants wanted by Israel.

In May 2003 a 'roadmap' for peace was put forward by the United States, Russia, the United Nations and the EU. It demanded a cessation of violence, the rebuilding of Palestinian security apparatus and Palestinian political reforms. The second stage of the roadmap would be the creation of a neutral Palestinian state with borders by December 2003, and the final stage was to be the negotiation of a permanent agreement by 2005.

However, violence and suicide attacks continued. In August 2003 President Bush called on Israel to halt work on its 245-km security fence in the West Bank. The fence was designed to reduce terrorist attacks, but Palestinians claimed it was annexing more land for Israeli settlements. The UN considered the barrier illegal.

An Israeli military operation, codenamed Days of Penitence, took place in northern Gaza in October 2004; 70 Palestinians were killed over in six days.

In October 2004 Israel's Knesset voted to withdraw Jewish settlers from Gaza and four settlements on the West Bank. Opposition to the Disengagement Plan led to dismissals and resignations of Israeli Government Ministers, and to the threat of civil disobedience by Gaza settlers.

Leader of the PLO, Yasser Arafat, died in early November 2004. Mahmoud Abbas was immediately elected head of the Palestine Liberation Organisation, and following elections in January 2005, Mahmoud Abbas was elected President of the PLO.

At the end of September 2005, Israel left its settlements in the Gaza Strip, but retained control over the Strip's links with the outside world: the airspace, the sea and the route to Egypt. Within a week, hostilities between Hamas and the Israelis had recommenced.

Having won the Palestinian Legislative Council elections in January, leaders of Hamas were sworn into government in March, amid threats of diplomatic and financial alienation from the governments of Israel, the US and Canada. Hamas refuses to recognise the state of Israel. On May 28th 2006, Israeli jets attacked an alleged Palestinian militant base in Lebanon, and air strikes were launched against Palestinian targets in Beirut.

On 25th June 2006, an Israeli soldier, Cpl. Gilad Shalit, was captured by three groups of militants, and demands were made for the release of some 1,500 prisoners. The Israelis responded by launching air strikes on Gaza; their tanks then moved into Gaza, and border crossings were closed. The UN warned the leaders of the two factions that they may be found personally responsible for 'disproportionate' actions. The EU delivered emergency aid through a temporary funding mechanism that by-passed the Hamas government and the civil service, which supports 25 per cent of the population, became impoverished. Following protests over unpaid wages and the storming of government headquarters, the Hamas led administration announced the closure of all government offices on 2nd October. In October 2011 Cpl. Gilad Shalit was released in exchange for 1,000 Palestinian prisoners.

The UN's Human Rights Council announced a fact-finding mission to the Gaza town of Beit Hanoun, where 19 Palestinians died during an Israeli shelling offensive on 8 November. The council had already approved a resolution that condemned "gross and systematic" human rights violations by Israel in the occupied Palestinian territories; the Israelis said the strike was due to a technical failure. A ceasefire in Gaza came into effect on 28th November 2006. The West Bank remained under Israeli military occupation, and was not included in the ceasefire agreement.
In December 2007, the US criticised Israel over its decision to build 300 homes on occupied land in East Jerusalem. Israel does not regard the area as occupied, since it was annexed in 1967. In March 2008, Prime Minister Ehud Olmert approved a plan to build up to 750 new homes in a Jewish settlement in the West Bank, provoking an angry reaction from Palestinian leaders. On 9th April, Palestinian militants carried out a raid on the Nahal Oz fuel depot, killing two Israeli workers. Israel shut the terminal, which supplies fuel to the 1.5m residents of the Gaza Strip, and sent tanks and bulldozers into the Gaza Strip. Eight Palestinians were killed in the four-day operation.

In mid-December 2008, a six-month truce ended and was allowed to lapse. Hamas said Israel had not respected its terms, including the lifting of the blockade; Israel said that Hamas failed to fulfill what Israel says were agreed conditions, including ending all rocket fire and halting weapons smuggling. Rocket and air strikes resumed with high casualties. On the 3rd January, Israeli ground forces entered the Gaza Strip and engaged in heavy clashes with Hamas fighters in northern Gaza. On the 6th January, at least 40 people were killed (including a number of children) and 55 injured when Israeli artillery shells landed outside the UN-run al-Fakhura school in the Jabaliya refugee camp in Gaza. On the 12th day of the offensive, Israel halted military operations in Gaza for three hours to allow supplies and fuel into Gaza for the first time since operations began. Fierce fighting continues and the UN compound in Gaza City was shelled by Israeli troops; around 700 people were sheltering there at the time. Israel eventually called a ceasefire on the 18th January, (22 days after the beginning of their offensive) having received assurances from the USA that it would take steps to halt the flow of arms into the Gaza Strip. Hamas rejected Israel's ceasefire in advance, and continued to fire rockets into Israel after the ceasefire had begun, triggering an Israeli air strike in response. Hamas then announced its own immediate one-week ceasefire. Israel began withdrawing troops on 20th January. Palestinian medical sources in Gaza said that at least 1,300 Palestinians were killed during the conflict; thirteen Israelis, including three civilians, were killed.

The army later announced an investigation into claims it had used white phosphorus illegally during its offensive in Gaza. White phosphorus, though legal for making smokescreens on a battlefield, burns through human skin, and can cause death if inhaled.

On the 19th March, Israel arrested ten senior Hamas leaders in the West Bank two days after talks on a possible prisoner swap collapsed. It is thought that the detentions were an attempt to pressure Hamas to release the captured soldier Gilad Shalit; Hamas is demanding the release of over 400 of the thousands of Palestinian prisoners held by Israel. Outgoing Israeli Prime Minister Ehud Olmert had hoped to secure the release of Sgt Shalit before he left office.

On March 20 2010, Palestinian officials said that 11 people had been injured by Israeli air strikes which were aimed at Gaza's airport. Israel said the attacks had been aimed at militants. Also in March Israel announced planning permission for 1,600 new homes in East Jerusalem. It is feared by the international community that any building in Jerusalem will undermine Israeli-Palestinian relations and hamper efforts to broker talks.

A fresh offensive broke out in November 2012; rockets had been fired from both sides with Israel saying it was particularly targeting Hamas officials. More than 90 Palestinians and three Israelis died in the first few days of the attacks. Egypt was trying to broker a peaceful end to the offensive amid international fears of a ground invasion by Israeli troops.

Other Recent Events

In November 2005, Amir Peretz defeated Shimon Peres to the leadership of the Labour Party. Ariel Sharon announced his resignation as leader of the Likud Party, formed the Kadima Party, and won the parliamentary elections in March 2006. The new party's main goals were peace with the Palestinians and Israeli security. However, Mr. Sharon suffered a major stroke in January 2006, and went into a coma from which he has yet to emerge (June 2011). Ehud Olmert took over the leadership of Kadima.

On 12th July 2006, the Lebanon-based Hezbollah group captured two Israeli soldiers, and demanded the release of prisoners in exchange. In retaliation, Israel imposed a sea blockade on Lebanon and launched jet strikes on Hezbollah targets. Further conflict ensued despite international condemnation. The UN's Kofi Annan attacked Israel's excessive use of force. Following an attack on Qana in which 54 Lebanese civilians (including over 30 children) were killed, the Israel agreed to a 48 hour ceasefire to allow for the evacuation of civilians from Southern Lebanon. A ceasefire came into force on the 14th August. During the conflict, around 1,109 Lebanese civilians died, together with 28 Lebanese soldiers. Figures for Hezbollah fatalities differ widely. 43 Israeli civilians were killed and 116 soldiers, according to official sources.

In November 2007, investigations into corruption charges against PM Olmert led to searches of government and private offices. The Kadima party agreed to hold leadership elections in September.

In July 2008, the bodies of the two Israeli soldiers whose capture sparked the 2006 war with Lebanon were returned to Israel, in exchange for five Hezbollah militants and the bodies of 200 Lebanese and Palestinian fighters. A Hezbollah official said that the soldiers had been captured alive, but had been injured during the cross-border attack and later died of their injuries.

At the end of July, Prime Minister Ehud Olmert announced that he would not stand in a leadership race for his Kadima Party; Tzipi Livni replaced him as leader of Kadima, and began negotiating a new coalition government with the Labour Party. At the end of October, having failed to form a coalition, Tzipi Livni called a general election for February 2009.

Early elections took place on 10th February 2009. The governing centre-left Kadima won 28 seats and the right-wing Likud opposition won 27; both were well short of the 61 seats needed to form a government. President Shimon Peres asked Benyamin Netanyahu of Likud to form a government. In April, the new ultra-nationalist foreign minister, Avigdor Lieberman, said that Israel is not bound by the Annapolis conference agreement of 2007. The agreement was for further discussions aimed at creating an independent Palestinian state. Palestinian officials described Mr Lieberman as an "obstacle to peace".

In June 2010 a flotilla of ships carrying aid to Gaza and manned by people of various nationalities from the group calling themselves Free Gaza, were boarded by Israeli troops, at least nine people died, and 30 were wounded. There was widespread condemnation of the violence and Turkey withdrew its ambassador from Israel.

In November 2010 Israel began work on a 250 km (155 mile) barrier along its border with Egypt. The barrier is being built to stop illegal immigrants entering the country.

In October 2011, Israel published the names of 477 Palestinian prisoners who are to be released in the first stage of an exchange for the captured Israeli soldier, Gilad Shalit. Mr Shalit was finally released the same month.

Following UNESCO's decision to give membership to Palestinians, Israel announced it was to accelerate settlement building in the West Bank and East Jerusalem.

In the first attacks since 2009, rockets were fired from Lebanon into Israel in November 2011. There were no casualties.

Legislature

Israel's unicameral legislature is known as the Knesset: the house of representatives of the State of Israel. The Knesset consists of 120 members, elected by the people for a single four-year term. The two arms of the Knesset are the plenum, in which all members take part, and the committees (12 permanent committees, two special committees, three functional committees, and parliamentary committees). The Knesset holds two sessions a year: the Winter session and the Summer session.

Bills can be presented by individual members of the Knesset, groups of members, ministers or government as a whole. After such bills have been examined by first the Ministry of Justice and then the Ministry of Finance, they are passed on to the rest of the Ministries for comment. If approved they are presented to the plenary arm of the Knesset for four readings, during which time the bill is debated and voted on before being refined and modified by the appropriate Knesset committee.

The Knesset, Qiryat Ben-Gurion, 91950 Jerusalem, Israel. Tel: +972 2 675 3333, URL: http://www.knesset.gov.il
Speaker of the Knesset: Reuven Rivlin (page 1503) (Likud)

Cabinet (as at July 2013)

Prime Minister, Minister of Economic Strategy, Pensioners and Health, Minister of Foreign Affairs: Benjamin Netanyahu (page 1485)
Minister of for Regional Development, the Negev and Galilee: Silvan Shalom (page 1512)
Minister of Strategic Affairs: Yuval Steinitz
Minister of Internal Affairs: Gideon Sa'ar
Minister for Defence: Lt.-Gen. Moshe Ya'alon
Minister of Transport, National Infrastructure and Road Safety: Yisrael Katz (page 1454)
Minister of Justice: Tzipi Livni (page 1465)
Minister of the Environmental Protection: Amir Peretz (page 1494)
Minister of Finance: Yair Lapid
Minister of Communications and Home Front Defence: Gilad Erdan
Minister of Housing and Construction: Uri Ariel
Minister of Public Security: Yitzhak Aharonovitch
Minister of Education: Shai Piron
Minister of Industry, Trade and Labour; Minister for Jerusalem Affairs and athe Diaspora: Naftali Bennett
Minister of Culture and Sport: Limor Livnat (page 1465)
Minister of Science and Technology: Yaakov Perry
Minister of Tourism: Uzi Landau (page 1460)
Minister of Immigrant Absorption: Sofa Landver
Minister of Agriculture and Rural Development: Yair Shamir
Minister for Senior Citizens: Uri Orbach
Minister of Health: Yael German
Minister of Social Affairs and Social Services: Meir Cohen

Ministries

Office of the President, Hanassi Street, Jerusalem 92188, Israel. Tel: +972 2 670 7211, fax: +972 2 561 0037, URL: http://www.president.gov.il
Office of the Prime Minister, 3 Kaplan Street, PO Box 187, Kiryat Ben-Gurion, Jerusalem 91919, Israel. Tel: +972 2 670 5555, fax: +972 2 651 2631, e-mail: doar@pmo.gov.il, URL: http://www.pmo.gov.il/
Ministry of Science and Technology, Kiryat Hamemshala Hamizrahit Building No. 3, Jerusalem 91181, Israel. Tel: +972 2 541 1111, URL: http://www.most.gov.il/
Ministry of Public Security, Kiryat Hamemshala, PO Box 18182, Jerusalem 91181, Israel. Tel: +972 2 530 9999, fax: +972 2 584 7872, URL: http://www.mops.gov.il
Ministry of Justice, 29 Salah A-din Street, Jerusalem 91010, Israel. Tel: +972 2 670 8511, fax: +972 2 628 8618, URL: http://www.justice.gov.il/
Ministry of Welfare and Social Affairs, 2 Kaplan Street, Kiryat Ben-Gurion, PO Box 915, Jerusalem 91008, Israel. Tel: +972 2 675 2311, fax: +972 2 675 2803, URL: http://www.molsa.gov.il
Ministry of Finance, 1 Kaplan Street, Kiryat Ben-Gurion, Jerusalem 13195, Israel. Tel: +972 2 531 7111, URL: http://www.mof.gov.il
Ministry of the Interior, 2 Kaplan Street, PO Box 6158, Kiryat Ben-Gurion, Jerusalem 91061, Israel. Tel: +972 2 670 1411, fax: +972 2 670 1628, URL: http://www.moin.gov.il
Ministry of Immigrant Absorption, 1 Kaplan Street, Kiryat Ben-Gurion, PO Box 13061, Jerusalem 91130, Israel. Tel: +972 2 675 2696, fax: +972 2 561 8138, URL: http://www.moia.gov.il/
Ministry of Transport, 97 Yaffo Street, Jerusalem 91000, Israel. Tel: +972 2 622 8211, fax: +972 2 622 8693, URL: http://portal.mot.gov.il/
Ministry of Defence, Kaplan Street, Hakirya, Tel-Aviv 67659, Israel. Tel: +972 3 569 2010, fax: +972 3 691 6940, URL: http://www.mod.gov.il/
Ministry of Environmental Protection, PO Box 34033, Jerusalem 95464, Israel. Tel: +972 2 655 3777, URL: http://www.environment.gov.il
Ministry of Construction and Housing, Kiryat Hamemshala, PO Box 18110, Jerusalem 91180, Israel. Tel: +972 2 584 7211, fax: +972 2 581 1904, URL: http://www.moch.gov.il/
Ministry of Health, 2 Ben-Tabai Street, PO Box 1176, Jerusalem 91010, Israel. Tel: +972 2 670 5705, fax: +972 2 623 3026, URL: http://www.health.gov.il/
Ministry of Religious Affairs, 236 Yaffo Street, PO Box 13059, Jerusalem 91130, Israel. Tel: +972 2 531 1171, fax: +972 2 531 1183, URL: http://www.religions.gov.il/
Ministry of Foreign Affairs, Hakirya, Romema, Jerusalem 91950, Israel. Tel: +972 2 530 3111, fax: +972 2 530 3367, URL: http://www.mfa.gov.il/
Ministry of Education, 34 Shivtei Israel Street, PO Box 292, Jerusalem 91911, Israel. Tel: +972 2 560 2222, fax: +972 2 560 2223, URL: http://www.education.gov.il/
Ministry of Energy and Water, Deerekh Petah Tikva 48, Tel Avivi 61171, Israel. Tel: +972 3 638 8113, URL: http://www.mni.gov.il
Ministry of Agriculture & Rural Development, 8 Arania Street, Hakirya, Tel-Aviv 61070, Israel. Tel: +972 3 948 5555, URL: http://www.moag.gov.il
Ministry of Tourism, 24 King George Street, PO Box 1018, Jerusalem 91009, Israel. Tel: +972 2 675 4909, fax: +972 2 673 3592, URL: http://www.tourism.gov.il
Ministry of Industry and Trade, 30 Agron Street, PO Box 299, Jerusalem 91002, Israel. Tel: +972 2 622 0220, fax: +972 2 624 5110, URL: http://www.moit.gov.il
Ministry of Communication, 23 Yaffo Street, Jerusalem 91999, Israel. Tel: +972 2 670 6320, fax: +972 2 670 6372, URL: http://www.moc.gov.il/
Ministry of Culture and Sport, URL: http://www.mcs.gov.il

Political Parties

Kadima. Tel: +972 (0)3 929 8600, URL: http://www.kadimasharon.co.il
Leader: Tzipi Livni (page 1465)
Labour Party, 110 Hayarkon Street, Tel Aviv, Israel. Tel: +972 (0)3 520 9272/63, fax: +972 (0)3 527 1744, URL: http://www.avoda2006.org.il/
Leader: Eitan Cabel
Likud (Consolidation), 38 King George Street, Tel Aviv, Israel. URL: http://www.likudnik.co.il/
Leader: Benjamin Netanyahu (page 1485)
Shas (International Organization of Torah-observant Sephardic Jews) URL: http://www.shasnet.org.il/index.asp
Leader: Eliyahu Yishai

ISRAEL

Yisrael Beytenu, URL: http://beytenu.org
Leader: Avigdor Lieberman
National Union, URL: http://www.leumi.org.il
Leader: Ya'akov Katz
Meretz (Energy Together), URL: http://www.meretz.org.il/HomePage.htm
Leader: Haim Oron
Independence, URL: http://www.haatzmaut.org.il
Leader: Ehud Barak
United Torah Judaism,
Leader: Yaakov Litzman
Hazit Democratit le-Shalom ve-Shivayon (Hadash, Democratic Front for Peace and Equality), URL: http://www.hadash.org.il/
Leader: Mohammad Barakek
Al Tahammu al-Watani al-Dimuqrati (Balad, National Democratic Alliance),
URL: http://www.balad.org/
Leader: Jamal Zahalka
United Arab List
Leader: Ibrahim Sarsur
The Jewish Home
Leader: Daniel Hershkowitz
Whole Nation
Leader: Haim Amsalem
Yesh Atid URL: http://www.yeshatid.org.il
Leader: Yair Lapid

Elections

A system of proportional representation is used in Israel's elections and there is universal suffrage for those over the age of 18. As no party has so far commanded an absolute majority all cabinets have been coalition cabinets between the major parties.

The latest presidential election took place on the 13th June 2007. Shimon Peres of the Kadima party was voted into the office by the Knesset, and was sworn into office on July 15, 2007 for a seven-year term. He is the ninth President of Israel. His predecessor, Moshe Katsav, began a leave of absence due to police investigations in January 2007, and resigned on 1st July 2007.

Elections for Prime Minister and the Knesset took place 10th February 2009. The election was called early after Ms Livni failed to form a new government following Prime Minister Ehud Olmert's decision to step down amid a corruption investigation. The governing centrist Kadima won 28 seats and the right-wing Likud opposition won 27; both were well short of the 61 seats needed to form a government. The ultra-nationalist Yisrael Beiteinu won15 seats, and the Labour Party were pushed into an unprecedented fourth place. The President asked Mr. Netanyahu to form a coalition government. The centre-left Labour party narrowly voted to join the coalition government; the far right Yisrael Beiteinu and ultra-Orthodox Jewish party Shas also agreed to join.

The most recent election was held in January 2013. Benjamin Netanyahu's Likud-Beiteinu remained the largest grouping in parliament but lost a quater of its seats. The newly formed Yesh Atid party came second and Mr Netanyahu offered Yesh Atid a place in his government.

Parties in the Knesset (following 2013 election)

	No. of Seats
Likud Yisrael Beytenu	31
Yesh Atid	19
Labor Party	15
The Jewish Home	12
Shas (Sephardi Religious Party)	11
United Torah Judaism	7
Hatnuah	6
Meretz	6
Ra'am Ta'al (United Arab List)	4
Hadash	4
Balad (National Democratic Assembly)	3
Kadima	2
Total	**120**

Diplomatic Representation

Embassy of Israel, 2 Palace Green, Kensington, London W8 4QB, United Kingdom. Tel: +44 (0)20 7957 9500, fax: +44 (0)20 7957 9555, e-mail: info-assist@london.mfa.gov.il, URL: http://www.embassyofisrael.co.uk
Ambassador: Daniel Taub
Embassy of Israel, 3514 International Drive, NW, Washington, DC 20008, USA. Tel: +1 202 364 5542, fax: +1 202 364 5423, e-mail: ask@israelemb.org, URL: http://www.israelemb.org/
Ambassador: Michael Oren (page 1490)
British Embassy, 192 Hayarkon Street, Tel Aviv 63405, Israel. Tel: +972 3 725 1222, fax: +972 3 524 3313 (commercial), e-mail: webmaster.telaviv@fco.gov.uk, URL: http://ukinisrael.fco.gov.uk/en
Ambassador: Matthew Gould (page 1432)
US Embassy, 71 Hayarkon Street, Tel Aviv 63903, Israel. Tel: +972 3 519 7575, fax: +972 3 517 3227, e-mail: webmaster@usembassy-israel.org.il, URL: http://telaviv.usembassy.gov
Ambassador: Daniel B. Shapiro
Permanent Representative of Israel to the United Nations, 800 Second Avenue, New York, NY 10017, USA. Tel: +1 212 499 5510, fax: +1 212 499 5516, e-mail: israel-un@newyork.mfa.gov.il, URL: http://www.israel-un.org/
Ambassador: Ron Prosor

LEGAL SYSTEM

The Basic Law provides for three levels of courts: the Supreme Court (an appellate court which also functions as the High Court of Justice); district courts, and magistrates' courts (both trial courts), including the Court of Traffic Offenses, Family Courts and Juvenile Courts. There are also National and Regional Labour Courts.

There is judicial autonomy for the main religious communities in all matters affecting personal status (such as marriage or divorce), where cases are heard by the relevant religious authority, Jewish, Christian, Druze or Muslim. Municipal courts exist in certain of the municipal areas, magistrate's courts in the districts and sub-districts and district courts in Jerusalem, Tel Aviv, Haifa, Beersheba and Nazareth.

The Supreme Court sits as a Court of Civil Appeal, Criminal Appeal and a High Court of Justice. The number of Supreme Court justices is determined by a resolution of the Knesset. Usually, there are twelve Justices, but at present there are fourteen Supreme Court Justices. At the head of the Supreme Court and of the whole judicial system is the President of the Supreme Court.

The government generally respects the human rights of the Israeli citizens. However, there have been some high-profile cases involving corruption by political leaders. There is institutional and legal discrimination against Arabs, and the government maintains unequal educational systems for Arab and Jewish students. Israeli law provides for the death penalty only for exceptional crimes such as those committed under military law or in exceptional circumstances. The most recent execution took place in 1962.

Supreme Court of Israel, URL: http://elyon1.court.gov.il/eng/home/index.html
President of the Supreme Court: Asher Grunis
Attorney General: Yehuda Weinstein

LOCAL GOVERNMENT

Israel is divided into six administrative districts: Jerusalem, Tel Aviv, Haifa, Northern (Tiberias), Central (Ramle), and Southern (Beersheba). The administration of these is coordinated by the Ministry of Interior. The Ministry of Defense is responsible for the administration of the Occupied Palestinian Territories. The occupied Golan Heights is a subdistrict of the Northern District. Each district is governed by a commissioner appointed by the central government.

There are three types of local authorities: municipalities (with populations over 20,000); local councils (with populations between 2,000 and 20,000); and regional councils (with populations up to 2,000). Individual local authorities are governed by a mayor or chairperson in addition to a council. The Ministry of the Interior allocates the number of council members according to the population of each authority. As of 2011, there were 73 municipalities, 124 local councils and 54 regional councils.

Local government elections are held every five years by secret ballot and any permanent resident from the age of 18, regardless of nationality, is eligible to vote.

AREA AND POPULATION

Area

Israel (as defined by the 1949 armistice boundaries) covers an area of 21,000 sq. km. However, in 1967 it occupied the West Bank, East Jerusalem and Gaza, and in 1981, it unilaterally annexed the Golan Heights. In 2005, the Israelis withdrew from Gaza. Israel's borders and the status of Jerusalem continue to be disputed.

Israel has four main regions: a central mountainous area; coastal plains; lowlands in the West; and the Negev desert. The Dead Sea is the lowest point on earth at 423 metres below sea level. The highest point in Israel is Mount Hermon at 2,224 m. The climate is temperate, with hot, dry conditions in southern and eastern desert areas. The Jordan river is the only river in Israel (approx. 250 km).

To view a map, please visit http://www.un.org/Depts/Cartographic/map/profile/israel.pdf

Population

Israel's population in 2010 was 7.695 million, with an annual increase of around 2.1 per cent for the period 2000-10. The population density per sq. mile was 334.5 at the end of 2010, the highest density being in Tel Aviv District (7,470 persons per sq. mile). Jerusalem District had a population density of 1,447 persons per sq. mile. The largest cities, according to 2010 figures, are: Jerusalem (788,100), Tel-Aviv-Yafo (404,300), Haifa (268,200), Rishon LeZiyyon (231,000) and Petah Tiqwa (211,100). Over 92 per cent of Israel's population lives in urban areas. (Source: http://www1.cbs.gov.il)

Approximately 79.5 per cent of the population were Jews and others, whilst 20.5 per cent were Arab.

Hebrew and Arabic are the official languages of the State.

Births, Marriages, Deaths

The number of live births rose from 148,170 in 2006 to 166,255 in 2010, whilst the number of deaths rose from 38,666 to 39,950 over the same period. In 2010, the crude birth rate was 21.8 per 1,000 population and the crude death rate was 5.2 per 1,000 population. The fertility rate was 3.03 children born per woman. Life expectancy at birth in 2010 for men was 79.7 years, and for women, it was 83.4 years. Healthy life expectancy was 72 years and 74 years respectively. Approximately 34 per cent of the population is aged 18 years or less, 55.8 per cent between 19-64, and 9.9 per cent over 65 years. The median age was 30. In 2009, 48,997 marriages took place (a crude mariage rate of 6.5 per 1,000 population) and 13,233 divorces took place. (Source: CBS, Statistics Abstract of Israel)

Public Holidays 2014
15-16 March: Purim
15-22 April: Passover (Pesach)
27 April: Holocaust Memorial Day (Yom HaShoah)
27 April: Independence Day (Yom Ha Atzmaut)
4 June: Pentecost (Shavuot)
5 August: The Fast of Av (Tish'a B'av)
25-26 September: Jewish New Year (Rosh Hashanah)
4 October: Day of Atonement (Yom Kippur)
8 October: Tabernacles (Sukkot)
16 October: Shmini Atzeret / Simchat Torah
17 November: Chanukah (Festival of Lights)
NB: The Jewish year runs from the equivalent of September to September.

EMPLOYMENT

In 2011, there was a total estimated workforce of 3,147,100. The total number of employed people was 2.642 million in 2011.The civilian unemployment rate in 2010 was 6.6 per cent in 2010.

Employment by Sector, 2008

Sector	No. employed
Agriculture, hunting & forestry	46,500
Mining & quarrying	5,000
Manufacturing	421,000
Electricity and water	19,900
Construction	150,700
Wholesale and retail trade, repairs	377,900
Hotels and restaurants	129,900
Transport, storage and communication	174,500
Financial intermediation	99,200
Real estate and business activities	388,900
Public administration and defence	130,600
Education	349,300
Health and welfare	274,600
Community, social, personal services	130,300
Households with employed persons	46,200
Not classifiable	29,000
Total employment	2,776,700

Source: Copyright © International Labour Organization (ILO Dept. of Statistics, http://laborsta.ilo.org)

BANKING AND FINANCE

Currency
One New Israeli Shekel (NIS) = 100 agorot

GDP/GNP, Inflation, National Debt
Israel's economy is still relatively strong despite the global financial crisis This is largely due to its technological research and development sector. Israel is in the process of applying to join the OECD. The long-term outlook depends on the conflict with the Palestinians, and the political and security situation in the region.

Assisted by growth in the high-technology sector and tourism, together with higher direct foreign investment and increased exports, Israel's economy turned from a recession in 2001-02 to growth of 5.2 per cent in 2005 and 4.8 per cent in 2006. GDP reached $170.3 billion in 2006, whilst per capita GDP was an estimated $26,800 in the same year. GDP growth was estimated to grow by 5.3 per cent in 2007 and by 4.1 per cent in 2008. Growth began to slow in the last quarter of 2008. Figures for 2009 show that GDP was NIS 768 billion, reflecting a growth rate that year of 0.8 per cent. GDP was US$217.8 billion (ppp) in 2010 with a growth rate of 4.8 per cent. Per capita GDP in 2010 was US$28,571. (Source: CBS) Despite the global economic crisis, Israel's GDP was reported to have grown by 4.8 per cent in 2011. It is forecast to fall to 3.6 per cent in 2012.

Major industries are information technology, electronics, telecommunications, biotechnology and tourism. Israel is a world leader in software development and is an important centre for diamond cutting. The services sector is Israel's largest contributor towards GDP, accounting for around 59 per cent, whilst industry contributes 38 per cent, and agriculture 3 per cent.

Gross Domestic Product at Basic Prices (2005 prices) Figures in NIS million

Industry	2008	2009
Finance & business services	177,098	181,610
Transport, storage & communications	50,552	49,358
Trade accomodation services & restaurants	61,188	60,008
Construction	30,383	30,105
Manufacturing	98,774	92,255
Total	441,119	441,550

Source: Central Bureau of Statistics

Inflation was estimated to be 3.5 per cent in 2011.

Israel's total external debt was estimated to be US$84 million at the end of 2009, approximately 45 per cent of GDP.

Israel's 2008 budget totalled NIS314 billion. The budget was set at NIS 245 billion in 2009. Debt repayment and military spending are the main components of budget spending. As of 2010, government liabilities was equivalent to 74.6 per cent of GDP.

Balance of Payments / Imports and Exports
Israel's major trading partners are the European Union and the United States. Figures from 2009 show that exports cost US$ 45.9 billion and imports earned US$ 46.0 billion.

Exports of Selected Commodities (excluding Palestinian Authority) 2009

Destination	% of all exports
Diamonds	24.2
Pharmaceutical products	8.9
Electronic integrated circuits	7.5
Electrical apparatus for line telephony	4.6
Mineral or chemical fertilizers	4.1
Aircraft parts	3.5
Mineral or chemical fertilizers	2.1
Tools & equipment for medical sciences	1.8
Implements and tools for measuring	1.2
Pesticides and herbicides	1.2

Source: Central Bureau of Statistics

Imports of Selected Commodities (excluding Palestinian Authority & direct defense Imports) 2009

Destination	% of all imports
Diamonds	11.2
Crude oils	10.8
Passenger vehicles	5.2
Petroleum oils	2.9
Electronical apparatus for line telephony	2.5
Coal	2.4
Pharmaceutical products	2.4
Computers	2.0
Electronic integrated circuits	1.6
Relevisions	1.1

Source: Central Bureau of Statistics

Central Bank
Bank of Israel, PO Box 780, Qiryat Ben-Gurion, Jerusalem 91007, Israel. Tel: +972 2 6552211, fax: +972 2 6528805, URL: http://www.boi.org.il/he/Pages/Default.aspx
Governor: Prof. Stanley Fische (page 1425)r

Chambers of Commerce and Trade Organisations
Tel Aviv Stock Exchange, URL: http://www.tase.co.il/taseeng
Federation of Israeli Chambers of Commerce, URL: http://www.chamber.org.il

MANUFACTURING, MINING AND SERVICES

Primary and Extractive Industries
There are large deposits of phosphates, copper, bitumen, manganese, iron, granite, marble, clay, feldspar, and silicate sand in Israel. Most activity is in the Negev and Dead Sea area.

Israel exported around US$6,364 million worth of polished diamonds and US$2,921.9 million worth of rough diamonds in 2004, indicating increases of 13 and 31 per cent respectively over the previous year.

Proven oil reserves fell from 3.8 million barrels at the beginning of 2004 to below 1 million barrels in 2012. Israel produced around 4,000 barrels of oil per day in 2011, and imported most of its requirements of 237,000 barrels per day. Most imports come from Russia and the Caspian area. Israel has begun to import larger quantities of Azeri oil. There are two major refineries, located at Haifa (130,000 bbl/d) and Ashdod (90,000 bbl/d). Oil Refineries Ltd (ORL) is one of Israel's largest energy companies and operates the country's largest oil refining and petrochemical complex.

The major pipeline is Tipline, which runs from Eilat to Ashkelon, and has a capacity of 800,000 barrels per day.

Natural gas reserves were estimated at 7 billion cubic feet in January 2011. This figure includes reserves from a major field recently found 12 miles offshore. The field contains reserves estimated at 274 billion cubic feet and was the third offshore gas field found in 2000. Natural gas production in 2011 was estimated at 92 billion cubic feet, all of which was used domestically. Consumption was 117 billion cu ft.

Coal consumption was an estimated 13 million short tons in 2010, all of which was imported. (Source: EIA)

Energy
Israel's total energy consumption has been stable since 2000, and was estimated at 0.9 quadrillion Btu. in 2009. Total energy production was 0.043 quadrillion Btu.

In 2009, installed electricity capacity was an estimated 12.07 GWe from 17 power stations. Electricity generation stood at 51.46 billion kWh in 2009, and consumption rose to 45.49 billion kWh. The government is in the process of converting its coal and oil-fired generators to natural gas, and hoped to generate 50 per cent of its electricity from gas by 2010.

ISRAEL

Israel uses solar energy for water heating and is a major exponent of solar technology. Around 80 per cent of Israeli homes have solar water heaters. In July 2006, construction began on a solar energy plant, in the Negev desert. It is expected to start producing power in 2013. Israel's first commercial solar field (Ketura Sun) was built in 2011 and is expected to produce 9GWh of electricity per year. Israel has two nuclear research centres: the Nahal Sorek Nuclear Research Centre and the Negev Nuclear Research Centre. The main areas of research and study are nuclear physics and chemistry, reactor engineering, radiation research, application of isotopes, metallurgy, electronics, radiobiology, nuclear medicine, nuclear power and desalination. (Source: EIA)

Manufacturing

The industrial sector is dynamic and widely diversified, producing both for domestic consumption and export. Israel has developed high technology products in the fields of medical electronics, agrotechnology, telecommunications, fine chemicals and solar energy. It also is a world leader in software development and diamond cutting and polishing. Traditional industrial activities include metal products, processed foods, textiles and fashion, fertilizers, chemicals, and transport equipment.

In recent years the kibbutz system, traditionally based on agriculture, has undergone a rapid process of industrialization, with industrial output accounting for about half of its total revenue. This production represents a growing proportion of Israel's total industrial output and around 6 per cent of industrial exports (excluding diamonds). Products of the 330 kibbutz factories range from processed foods, advanced irrigation systems and agricultural machinery to plastics, furniture and optical equipment, among many others.

Tourism

Israel was a major tourist destination prior to the violence that began in 2000. Numbers dipped from 2,416,800 in 2000 to 1,505,500 in 2004 before rising to 1,825,200 in 2006. In 2010 there were 3.4 million visitors to Israel, mostly from the USA and Europe.

Agriculture

Israel's agricultural industry employs just 3 per cent of people. Total area under cultivation is about 1.1 million acres with 0.6 million acres of irrigated land. Most of Israel's food needs are met domestically though some products are imported; however, these are funded by food exports. Production consists mainly of dairy and poultry products and fruits and vegetables.

Agricultural Production in 2010

Produce	Int. $'000*	Tonnes
Indigenous chicken meat	640,177	449,434
Cow milk, whole, fresh	401,579	1,292,060
Inidigenous cattle meat	193,661	71,690
Tomatoes	165,044	446,592
Chillies and peppers, green	138,544	294,300
Indigenous turkey meat	117,547	89,941
Potatoes	89,969	548,650
Hen eggs, in shell	84,996	548,650
Olives	58,852	73,500
Carrots and turnips	58,448	234,261
Apples	55,602	131,474
Grapes	54,347	95,075

* unofficial figures

Source: http://faostat.fao.org/site/339/default.aspx Food and Agriculture Organization of the United Nations, Food and Agricultural commodities production

In 2010, the total catch of fish was put at 2,500 tonnes. 142,000 hectares were dedicated to pasture, and livestock consisted of some 400,000 head of cattle and 454,000 sheep and goats.

COMMUNICATIONS AND TRANSPORT

Travel Requirements

Citizens of the USA, Canada, Australia and the EU require a passport valid for six months beyond the length of stay but do not need a visa for stays of up to 90 days (apart from Romanians who do need a visa). Visitors should also have an onward or return ticket, and proof of sufficient funds are required for entry. Other nationals should contact the embassy to check visa requirements.

Former Israeli citizens holding a foreign passport must have written proof of having given up Israeli identity, otherwise they may be required to obtain a new Israeli passport or renew their original one. Tourists continuing to Arab countries excluding Egypt and Jordan are recommended to request that an Israeli stamp does not appear in their passport.

National Airlines

El Al Israel Airlines, URL: http://www.elal.co.il/ELAL/English/States/General/ Established in 1948 as the national Israel Airlines.

International Airports

There are international airports at Tel-Aviv, Jerusalem and Eilat. Israel's main international airport, Ben-Gurion Airport, handled over 11 million passengers in 2008. In 2010, 11.57 million air passengers were transported.
Israel Airports Authority, URL: http://www.iaa.gov.il/Rashat/en-US/Rashot

Railways

There are an estimated 975 km of track. The state owned Israel Railways provides passenger services between Tel Aviv, Jerusalem, Haifa and Nahariya. Freight services also operate further south serving the port of Ashdod, and the towns of Ashkelon, Be'er Sheva and the mineral quarries south of Dimona. A small subway service is in operation in Haifa. A long-delayed light railway system finally opened in Jerusalem in 2011. Work began on a light-railway systemTel Aviv in 2011 and is scheduled to begin operating in 2017. Trains do not run on the Jewish sabbath. In 2010, there were 35.88 million passengers and 7.023 million tons of freight were transported. (Source: http://www1.cbs.gov.il)

Roads

In Israel vehicles are driven on the right. There are over 18,000 km of roads. In 2010, 2.053 million private vehicles and 347,152 trucks and commercial vehicles were reigstered. There were 14,762 buses. There were 3.538 million licenced drivers.

Ports and Harbours

The main ports are Haifa, Eilat and Ashdod. Israel's seaports handle 98 per cent of the country's import and export cargo.
Haifa Port, URL: http://www.haifaport.co.il/english.aspx

HEALTH

In 2009, 7.6 per cent of Israel's GDP was spent on healthcare. Approximately 60.3 per cent of healthcare costs were covered by the state, and 39.7 being paid for privately. Social security expenditure on health was 64.1 per cent of government expenditure. Out-of-pocket expenditure accounted for 73.5 per cent of private healthcare spending, and pre-paid plans accounted for 16.6 per cent. (Source: WHO)

Israel's medical infrastructure comprises hospitals, outpatient clinics and centers for preventive medicine and rehabilitation. In 2004, there were nearly 40,000 hospital beds available: 15,000 were for general care, 17,000 for long term patients and around 6,000 for psychiatric patients.

In 2005-10, there were approximately 26,700 doctors (36.5 per 10,000 population), 6,400 dentistry personnel, 37,898 nurses and midwives (51.8 per 10,000 population) and 4,900 pharmaceutical personnel (6.7 per 10,000 population).

In 2009, the infant mortality rate (probability of dying by age 1) was 4 per 1,000 live births and the child (under-fives mortality rate) was 5 per 1,000 live births. In 2010 the distribution of causes of death among children aged under 5 years was 38 per cent congenital abnormalities and 21 per cent prematurity.

All of the population has sustained access to drinking water and to improved sanitation. (Source: http://www.who.int, World Health Statistics 2012)

EDUCATION

The state education system comprises one year each of nursery school and kindergarten, six years of elementary school and three years each of junior high and high school.

Two school systems are maintained; the Jewish system, with instruction in Hebrew; and the Arab/Druze system, with instruction in Arabic. Both systems are financed by and accountable to the Ministry of Education and Culture, but enjoy a large measure of internal independence.

The Jewish education system consists of state schools, state-religious schools and government-recognised independent religious schools. The state and state-religious schools offer similar academic curricula, with the latter placing special emphasis on Jewish studies, tradition and observance. State schools are co-educational, while in the state-religious school network children may either attend mixed or separate schools. The independent schools, affiliated with various Orthodox Jewish trends, offer more intensive religious instruction and provide separate premises for girls and boys.

The Arab/Druze education system, with separate schools for Arab and Druze pupils, provides the standard academic and vocational curricula, adapted to emphasize Arab or Druze culture and history. Religious instruction in Islam or Christianity is provided by Arab schools, while in Druze schools it is the prerogative of the community elders.

Pre-School

Israel has one of the highest rates of pre-school attendance in the world with 98 per cent of young children attending some form of pre-school programme.

Primary/Secondary Education

Figures for 2007 show enrollment in primary education at 98 per cent for girls and 97 per cent for boys. Pupil:teacher ratio in primary schools was 13:1. In the academic period 2009-10, an estimated 1,978,927 pupils were enrolled and there were 132,578 teaching staff were registered. Of this, 470,025 pupils in pre-primary education, 884,685 in primary education, 259,834 in lower secondary education and 364,383 in upper secondary education. In the same period, there were an estimated 132,747 teachers in pre-primary education, 67,283 in primary education, 24,215 in lower seocndary education and 40,815 in upper secondary education. (Source: http://www1.cbs.gov.il)

Vocational Education

At secondary school level, students have the following options: the academic track, leading to matriculation and university admission; the technological/vocational track, leading to various technicians' certificates with or without matriculation; agricultural schools, usually residential and matriculation optional. There are also military preparatory schools, combining general studies with military subjects.

Military service is compulsory for both sexes at 18 years of age for Jews and Druze, and voluntary for Christians, Muslims and Circassians. Conscript service last 36 months for enlisted men, 21 months for enlisted women and 48 months for officers.

Higher Education

Post-secondary education in Israel is under the authority of the Council for Higher Education, headed by the Minister of Education and Culture. Members of the Council - which include academics as well as community representatives and at least one student - are appointed by the president, on recommendation of the government, for five-year terms.

By law, Israel's universities enjoy full academic and administrative freedom, including faculty appointments, student admissions, formulation of curricula and conduct of research programmes. In addition to the universities, there are institutes of higher education specialising in such fields as fine arts, music, graphic design, teaching, nursing, advanced technology, and fashion design.

In the academic period 2009/10 there were 33,419 university degrees awarded in total.

In 2010, the government spent 15.9 per cent of its budget on education. (Source: http://www1.cbs.gov.il)

RELIGION

In 2006, of the Jewish and other population, 94.6 per cent were Jews, 4.9 per cent were not classified by religion and 0.5 per cent were non-Arab Christians. Of the Arab population, Muslims make up 83 per cent, Druze, 8.3 per cent and Arab Christians, 8.5 per cent (Source: Central Bureau of Statistics)

There is a Ministry for the supervision of religious affairs, with separate departments for Jewish, Christian, Muslim and Druze religions. The religious affairs of each community are otherwise under the full control of the religious order concerned.

Israel has a religious liberty rating of 4 on a scale of 1 to 10 (10 is most freedom). (Source: World Religion Database)

Ministry of Religious Affairs, URL: http://www.religions.gov.il

Sephardic Chief Rabbi: Rabbi Shlomo Amar
Ashkenazi Chief Rabbi: Rabbi Yona Metzger

COMMUNICATIONS AND MEDIA

The press and broadcasters offer wide and varied views. There is freedom of expression but also some military censorship.

Newspapers

Numerous publications exist, both dailies and weeklies. Many are available online. All are privately owned.
The Jerusalem Post, URL: http://www.jpost.com
Maariv, URL: http://www.nrg.co.il/online/HP_0.html
Ha'aretz, URL: http://www.haaretz.com/

Broadcasting

The Israel Broadcasting Authority (URL: http://www.iba.org.il/) governs both the state-run television Channel 1 and public radio. Channel 2 and Israel 10 are the main commercial TV networks. Most Israeli households subscribe to cable or satellite packages.

Telecommunications

Israel is fully integrated into international communications systems by means of underwater cables and communications satellites. According to 2010 CBS figures, there were 3.14 million mainline telephone subscribers. There were an estimated 9.5 million mobile phone users.

According to 2009 estimates, over 4.5 million people had internet access.

ENVIRONMENT

Israel's environmental problems include limited freshwater resources and arable land, desertification, industrial and vehicle air pollution, and groundwater pollution.

Energy-related carbon emissions in 2010 were estimated at 70.32 million metric tons (up from 66.85 million metric tons in 2008). Industry accounts for the highest proportion of carbon emissions, followed by the transport, residential and commercial sectors. Per capita carbon emissions in 2006 were an estimated 10.36 metric tons. (Source: EIA)

Israel is a party to the following international environmental agreements: Biodiversity, Climate Change, Climate Change-Kyoto Protocol, Desertification, Endangered Species, Hazardous Wastes, Ozone Layer Protection, Ship Pollution, Wetlands, and Whaling. Israel has signed, but not ratified, the Marine Life Conservation agreement.

SPACE PROGRAMME

The Israel Space Agency (ISA) was established in in 1983 and Israel's first satellite was launched in 1988. It has an annual budget of US$6 million. It has signed co-operation agreements with the space agencies of the USA, France, Canada, India, Germany, Ukraine, Russia, the Netherlands and Brazil.
Israel Space Agency, URL: http://www.most.gov.il/

OCCUPIED PALESTINIAN TERRITORIES
West Bank and Gaza

Capital: East Jerusalem (although the status of Jerusalem is still under discussion) (Population estimate: 360,000)

Administrative Capital: Gaza City (Population estimate: 500,000)

Head of State: Mahmoud Abbas (President) (page 1371)

National Flag: Three horizontal stripes - black, white and green - with a red triangle with its base at the hoist (Palestinian National Authority flag).

CONSTITUTION AND GOVERNMENT

The Occupied Palestinian Territories refers to the West Bank and the Gaza Strip; information on the Golan Heights can be found within the Israel entry.
On 29 November 1947, the United Nation's General Assembly recommended the partition of Mandatory Palestine into independent Jewish and Arab States. The State of Israel's independence was proclaimed on 14 May 1948 with the termination of the British Mandate over Palestine. The Palestine Liberation Organization (PLO) was set up in 1964 and is internationally recognised as the representative body of the Palestinian people. In 1998 the Palestinian National Council, its highest body, declared the existence of an independent state of Palestine, under Israeli occupation. The capital is East Jerusalem. A peace deal was signed in 1993 in Washington, USA, between Israel and the PLO, which would create a Palestinian authority. The plan gave the PLO initial internal control of the Gaza Strip and Jericho. This control would spread as Israeli troops withdrew. A five-year transition period was agreed during which time the status of East Jerusalem was to be agreed; likewise the structure and boundaries of Palestine.

The Oslo B Accord set out the political structure for a Palestinian state. Executive authority is vested in the Palestinian National Authority which is headed by an elected leader. Yasser Arafat was elected Executive President on 20 January 1996 and the position is regarded as the head of state internationally. In March 2003 the position of prime minister was created when Mahmoud Abbas was nominated by Yasser Arafat. The president's executive powers were reduced as a result. The prime minister is the head of government, and appoints the executive authority subject to the approval of the PLO.

Recent Events

In September 2000 the US President Bill Clinton hosted a summit at Camp David: Yasser Arafat and the Israeli Prime Minister, Ehud Barak discussed the future of a Palestinian state and its people. The talks broke down over the sovereignty of the city of Jerusalem.

Later the same month, Ariel Sharon, leader of Israel's right-wing opposition party, visited the Temple Mount (Haram al-Sharif), a site sacred to Muslims. The incident sparked violent clashes between Palestinians and Israelis that caused over 300 deaths.

In February 2002, Israel attacked Yasser Arafat's headquarters in Gaza City. A summit of Arab leaders took place in Beirut on 27 March 2002 to discuss the new Middle East peace initiative, but Yasser Arafat could not attend as Israel refused to let him leave the country.

In response to suicide bombings, Israeli troops moved into Ramallah on 31 March 2002, and into the settlements of Jenin, Salfit and Nablus on 3 April 2002. They inflicted heavy Palestinian casualties. The UN General Assembly passed a motion condemning the Israeli military occupation of Jenin.

In response to two Palestinian suicide bombings in two days Israeli troops laid siege to Yasser Arafat's headquarters from19th to the 29th September 2002. Palestinian attacks and Israeli military responses continued into 2003.

In May 2003 a 'roadmap' for peace was put forward by the USA, Russia, the UN and the EU. It demanded a cessation of violence, the rebuilding of Palestinian security apparatus and Palestinian political reforms. The second stage of the roadmap would be the creation of a neutral Palestinian state with borders by December 2003. The final stage would be the negotiation of a permanent agreement by 2005. However, violence and suicide attacks continued. In August 2003 President Bush called on Israel to halt work on its 245-km (150-mile) security fence in the West Bank. Palestinians claim that it has annexed more land for Israeli settlements. The US government expressed concern that the fence would become an obstacle to peace. In September 2003 the UN condemned the barrier as illegal.

An Israeli military operation, codenamed Days of Penitence, took place in northern Gaza in early October 2004; 79 Palestinians were killed in six days.

In October 2004 Israel's Knesset voted by 67 votes to 45 in favour of a plan to withdraw Jewish settlers from Gaza.

ISRAEL

Leader of the Palestinians for 40 years, Yasser Arafat died aged 75 on 11 November 2004. Mahmoud Abbas was immediately elected head of the Palestine Liberation Organisation, and then President, following elections on 9th January 2005.

At the end of September 2005, Israel left its settlements in the Gaza Strip, but retained control over the Strip's links with the outside world in order to prevent weapons smuggling and to ensure that long-range rockets did not reach the hands of Palestinian terrorist groups within Gaza. Hostilities between the militant group Hamas and the Israelis recommenced within a week.

In the January 2006 Palestinian parliamentary elections, the Islamic militant group Hamas won a surprise victory. The EU, US Russia and the UN called for Hamas to commit to renouncing violence and to recognise the state of Israel, or to face the prospect of future cuts in global aid amounting to over $1 billion. Israel suspended payment of monthly tax revenues to the Palestinian Authority. Hamas leader, Ismail Haniya, promised that all foreign aid would be spent on the needs of the people, but the EU and US froze donations. The UN and EU sought ways to allow humanitarian aid to reach the Palestinians without going through the Hamas government.

On 25 June 2006 an Israeli soldier, Cpl. Gilad Shalit, was captured, and demands were made for the release of some 1,500 prisoners. The Israelis responded by launching nightly air strikes against militant targets and infrastructure in Gaza. Militants in Gaza fired rockets into the Israeli city of Ashkelon, demonstrating that they now had weapons capable of travelling some 15km. In response, Israeli troops crossed the border, with the declared intention of creating a 'buffer-zone'. On 20 July 2006 the UN warned the leaders of both sides that they may be found personally responsible for 'disproportionate' actions. In September, delegates at the Stockholm conference learnt that some 200 Palestinians had been killed since late June, and many more injured.

The EU and America continued to prevent funds reaching the Hamas government and the civil service. Following protests over unpaid wages and the storming of government headquarters, the Hamas-led administration announced the closure of all government offices on 2nd October and the suspension of government work. Protests the previous day had led to clashes between Hamas militias and those of the Fatah movement. Violence between the two factions continued into 2007. In January 2007, Israel paid the owing tax revenues directly to the moderate President Mahmoud Abbas, not the Hamas government.

The violence between the Hamas and the Fatah factions in Gaza escalated in January 2007. A unity government was formed, but violence again flared. By 14th June, Hamas gunmen had taken control of the Gaza strip whilst Fatah retained control of the West Bank. President Abbas declared a state of emergency, and dismissed the unity government. He appointed a new prime minister and Council of Ministers, most of whom were not members of Fatah or Hamas. The President issued a decree enabling the new government to rule without the approval of the Hamas-dominated parliament. In October 2007, Amnesty International reported that the fighting between Hamas and Fatah was leading to human rights abuses, stating that illegal detentions and torture had become commonplace in both Gaza and the West Bank. Also in October, the Israeli government approved sanctions against Gaza, including cuts in the supply of electricity and fuel as punishment for rocket attacks. Israel had declared Gaza a "hostile entity" in September, and argued that, as such, the Israeli state was not bound to supply utilities to the civilian population. The international community disagreed since Israel remains legally responsible for the coastal strip because it still controls Gaza's borders, airspace and territorial waters.

A new Middle-East peace initiative was launched at Annapolis, Maryland, in November; Israeli President Ehud Olmert and President Mahmoud Abbas agreed to start talks aimed at reaching a full peace deal by the end of 2008. There were no representatives of Hamas. In December 2007, foreign aid of at least $7 billion was pledged to the Palestinians at a donors' conference in Paris, to be used to create a viable Palestinian state.

On 14th January 2008, Israeli and Palestinian negotiators discussed the most intractable issues in the peace process: the status of Jerusalem, the borders of a Palestinian state, settlements in the West Bank, refugees, security and water resources. The following day, around 18 Palestinians were killed and 48 were injured when Israeli tanks entered the eastern suburbs of Gaza City. Israel closed the border crossings on 17th January. A few days later, the border wall between Gaza and Egypt at Rafah was breached, and tens of thousands of Gaza residents surged through to buy food and other supplies made scarce by the blockade; Egypt resealed the border after 12 days, succumbing to Israeli and US pressure to clamp down on potential arms smuggling routes.

The first half of 2008 saw many rocket attacks from Gaza into Israel, and responses by the Israelis, including air strikes and incursions into Gaza. The international community urged both sides to show restraint. On the 10th May 2008, there were widespread electricity blackouts in the Gaza Strip after the territory's only power plant shut down due to a blockade of fuel supplies by the Israelis. On the 17 June, Israel and Hamas agreed to end months of clashes with a six-month truce. As well as a halt to hostilities, the deal (brokered by Egypt) envisaged a partial reopening of Gaza's borders. The agreement included the return of captured Israeli soldier Gilad Shalit and the reopening of the main Rafah crossing into Egypt at a later date. The truce only applied to Gaza, and under its terms militants could not respond to any Israeli action in the West Bank. On the 24th June, two rockets were fired from the Gaza into Sderot, Israel. Although there were no injuries, Israel declared the attack to be a "grave violation" of the truce.

Hamas forces in Gaza arrested 160 Fatah supporters following an explosion which killed six people on 25th July. Seven people were killed and at least 18 others were injured during one of the bloodiest days in Gaza since Hamas and Israel agreed a ceasefire in June.

In early October 2008, a senior Israeli commander in the West Bank said that hundreds of settlers were engaged in violence against Palestinians and Israeli soldiers, diverting military resources away from operations against militants. A UN report recorded 222 acts of settler violence in the first half of 2008. Defence Minister Ehud Barak urged tougher penalties for settlers who attack Palestinian property. All settlements are considered illegal under international law, though Israel disputes this.

In mid-December, the six-month ceasefire between Hamas and the Israeli government ended. The truce had been under strain and was allowed to lapse when it expired. Hamas blamed Israel, saying it had not respected its terms, including the lifting of the blockade under which little more than humanitarian aid has been allowed into Gaza. Israel said it initially began a staged easing of the blockade, but this was halted when Hamas failed to fulfill what Israel says were agreed conditions, including ending all rocket fire and halting weapons smuggling.

Over 50 rockets were fired from the Gaza Strip over the week following the end of the ceasefire. On the 26th December, Israel opened crossings into the Gaza Strip to allow the delivery of humanitarian aid following requests from the international community.

On the 27th December, Israeli F-16 bombers pounded key targets across the Gaza Strip, killing over 225 people. About 700 other people were wounded as missiles struck security compounds and militant bases as well as Gaza City, Khan Younis and Rafah. The high numbers of casualties made the 27th December the single deadliest day in the Gaza Strip since Israel's occupation of the territory in 1967. Israel said it was responding to an escalation in rocket attacks from Gaza, and aimed to create a new security environment, to protect Israelis who live within range of rocket fire from Gaza. The exiled leader of Hamas, Khaled Meshaal, called for a new intifada against Israel, in response to the attacks. UN Secretary-General Ban Ki-moon condemned what he called Israel's "excessive use of force leading to the killing and injuring of civilians". The following day, Israel bombed over 40 supply tunnels in the southern Gaza Strip, claiming that the militants had fired 110 rockets into Israel since the beginning of the Israeli air raids. Thousands of people in the Arab world protested Israel's actions. Israeli air strikes continued despite UN calls for an immediate ceasefire.

On the 1st January 2009, the Israeli air strikes targeted the homes of over 20 leading Hamas figures and a mosque, believed to be a Hamas command post. Palestinian militants continued to fire on Israel, launching more than 60 missiles in 24 hours. On the 3rd January, Israeli ground forces entered the Gaza Strip and engaged in heavy clashes with Hamas fighters in northern Gaza. On the 6th January, at least 40 people were killed (including a number of children) and 55 injured when Israeli artillery shells landed outside the UN-run al-Fakhura school in the Jabaliya refugee camp in Gaza. On the 8th January, Israel carried out heavy bombardment on Gaza, with 60 air strikes targeting Hamas facilities. At least three rockets were fired into Israel from Lebanon, raising fears the Israeli offensive in Gaza may spread. Both Israel and Hamas ignored a UN resolution calling for an immediate end to the conflict. On the 11th January, a leaflet drop warned Gazans of 'phase three' of the operations, and forces entered the suburbs of Gaza City two days later.

On the 14th January, medical sources in Gaza said that over 1,000 Palestinians had died during the Israeli offensive, and a further 4,500 had been injured. Over 300 of those killed were children. Thirteen Israelis had died, three civilians and one soldier from rocket fire from Gaza. Egypt tried to broker a ceasefire. Hamas said any ceasefire agreement would have to entail a halt to Israeli attacks, a complete withdrawal of Israeli forces and the opening of border crossings to end the blockade of Gaza. The following day, Gaza saw one of the fiercest days of fighting since the conflict began and international condemnation of the Israeli operation grew. The UN compound in Gaza City was shelled by Israeli troops; around 700 people were sheltering there, and the ensuing fire burnt through stocks of food and medicine. Mr Olmert apologised for the attack. Israel eventually called a ceasefire on the 18th January, (22 days after the beginning of their offensive) having received assurances from the USA that it would take steps to halt the flow of arms into the Gaza Strip. Hamas continued to fire rockets into Israel after the ceasefire had begun, triggering an Israeli air strike in response, but then announced its own immediate one-week ceasefire.

On the 27th January, an Israeli soldier was killed by an explosive device planted on the Israel side of the border. Israel responded with an air attack on Gaza and a tank incursion into the Strip. On 31st January, Israeli aircraft bombed a Hamas security target in Gaza City and tunnels used by the militant group along the border with Egypt. The Egyptians led efforts to broker a permanent ceasefire.

On the 6th February, UNRWA suspended all aid shipments, accusing the Hamas government of seizing hundreds of tonnes of food supplies. It was the second such incident in three days; blankets and food parcels had been seized at gunpoint from a distribution centre in Gaza. Hamas said it would return the goods, but the aid agency said deliveries would not restart until it had assurances that such seizures would not happen again. Later, a stockpile of unexploded Israeli munitions, fired into Gaza during the recent conflict, went missing; the Israelis accused Hamas of taking them.

On the 18th February, Israel's security cabinet said that there would be no truce in Gaza until an Israeli soldier captured in 2006 was freed. Israel closed Gaza's borders, allowing only essential supplies in. Hamas said the border crossing and prisoner issues cannot be linked, and accused Mr Olmert of trying to block Egyptian-mediated truce efforts.

International donors pledged almost $4.5bn in aid to the Palestinians, mainly to rebuild Gaza after the Israeli offensive. The Palestinian Authority had requested only $2.8bn. It is estimated that some 14,000 homes, 220 factories and 240 schools were destroyed. All but essential supplies are subject to Israeli blockades, and Israel refuses to allow building materials into Gaza. In April, the UN appointed South African judge and former war crimes prosecutor Richard Goldstone to lead an investigation into alleged violations of international law during the recent conflict.

On the 14th August, Hamas fighters and policemen surrounded the Ibn-Taymiyah mosque in Gaza, where followers of the radical al-Qaeda-linked Islamist group Jund Ansar Allah had declared Gaza an "Islamic emirate". The mosque's imam, Abdul-Latif Moussa, and his armed supporters vowed to fight to the death rather than hand over authority of the mosque to Hamas. 24 people were killed and some 120 injured in the ensuing gun battle. Abdul-Latif Moussa died in an explosion; it was not clear whether he blew himself up.

In September, Israel strongly criticised a UN human rights report into alleged war crimes during the Gaza conflict. The report said both the Israeli army and Palestinian militants committed war crimes and possible crimes against humanity during fighting in January, and that Israel used disproportionate firepower against the densely populated Gaza Strip and disregarded the likelihood of civilian deaths. The Israeli spokesman said that the Human Rights Council which commissioned the report had an anti-Israeli agenda, and that the report was biased.

In May 2010 aid ships bound for Gaza were raided by Israel and nine Turkish activists were killed. The raid was condemned internationally. In June 2010 Israel said it would ease its blockade of Gaza and allow more civilian goods to enter the Palestinian territory.

The Obama administration relaunched direct Israeli-Palestinian peace talks in September 2010.

In September 2011, Palestinian officials launched a campaign to join the United Nations as a full member state. Currently the Palestine Liberation Organisation (PLO) only has observer entity status. They will ask for international recognition on 1967 borders with East Jerusalem as a capital. Both Israel and the US oppose the plan. If full-member-status were granted the Palestinians would be able to become party to international treaties and join UN agencies. The UN Security Council began consultations in September. In November 2012 it voted overwhelmingly to recognise Palestine as a non-member observer state. The assembly voted 138-9 in favour, 41 nations abstained.

After talks failed to decide on a government it was agreed in February 2012 that Mahmoud Abbas would head the unity government. However Hamas and Fatah were unable to agree on the composition of the cabinet and a cabinet lead by Salem Khaled Fayyad was sworn in on May 2013. In March 2013 the Minister of Finance resigned. The resignation was accepted by Fayyad but Mahmoud Abbas asked him to stay on. The ensuing political crisis led to the resignation of Fayyad. Fayyad agreed to stay on in a caretaker capacity. In June 2013 Abbas instructed non-partisan Rami Hamdallah to form the next government. However, Mr Hamdallah resigned after only two weeks, claiming that his two deputies, both advisors to President Abbas, were undermining his authority. His resignation was accepted and he agreed to stay on in a caretaker capacity until a new prime minister could be found.

Legislature

Legislative authority rests with the 133 member Palestinian Legislative Council (*al Majlis al Tashri'i*) which is elected on a first past the post system. Members are elected for a five-year term. One seat is reserved for the President. The remainder are elected from party lists.
Palestinian Legislative Council, Al Bireh. URL: http://www.pal-plc.org/

Palestinian National Authority Transitional Government (as at June 2013)
President: Mahmoud Abbas (page 1371)
Outgoing Prime Minister (Acting in caretaker capacity): Rami Hamdallah (ind) (page 1437)
Deputy Prime Minister: Ziad Abu Amr
Deputy Prime Minister for Economic Affairs: Muhammad Mustafa
Minister of Finance: Shukri Bishara
Minister of Foreign Affairs: Riyad Najib Abd-al-Rahman al Maliki
Minister of the Interior: Sa'id Abu Ali
Minister of the Environment: Yousef Abu Safieh
Minister of Health: Jawad Awad
Minister of Education: Lamis Alami
Minister of Higher Education: Ali Jarbawi
Minister of Justice: Ali Muhanna
Minister of Tourism: Rula Maayeh
Minister of Waqf and Religious Affairs: Sheikh Mahmud Sidqi al Habbash
Minister of Women's Affairs: Rubayha Dhiyab
Minister of Local Government: Saed Al-Kuni
Minister of the Economy: Jawad Naji
Minister of Transport: Nabil al-Dumeidi
Minister of Agriculture: Walid Assaf
Minister of Prisoner Affairs: Isa Qaraqi
Minister of Culture: Siham Al Barghouthi
Minister of Labour: Ahmad Al Majdalani
Minister of Telecommunications: Safa Nasser El-Din
Minister of Social Affairs: Kamal Ah-Shirafi
Minister of Planning: Mahmoud Abu Ramadan
Minister of Public Works and Housing: Naher Ghneim
Minister of Jerusalem Affairs: Adnan Husseini

Ministries

Office of the Prime Minister, URL: http://www.pmo.gov.ps/
Ministry of Agriculture, Al Balua, PO Box 197, Ramallah. Tel: +970 (0)2 296 1090
Ministry of Civil Affairs, Green Tower Building, An Nuzha Street, PO Box 2074, Ramallah. Tel: +970 (0)2 298 7336, fax: +970 (0)2 298 7335
Ministry of Culture, Ar Rayan Building, Irsal Street, PO Box 147, Ramallah. Tel: +970 (0)2 298 7336, URL: http://www.moc.gov.ps/
Ministry of Education, PO Box 576, Ramallah. Tel: +970 (0)2 298 3200, fax: +970 (0)2 298 3222, URL: http://www.moe.gov.ps/
Ministry of Finance, Beirut Street, Tel Al Hawa, PO Box 4007, Gaza. Tel: +970 (0)8 282 6188, URL: http://www.mof.gov.ps/
Ministry of Foreign Affairs, PO Box 1336, Ramalla, West Bank. Tel: +970 (0)2 574 7045, fax: +970 (0)2 574 7046, URL: http://www.mofa.gov.ps/
Ministry of Health, Abu Khadra Building, PO Box 1035, Gaza. URL: http://www.moh.gov.ps/
Ministry of Environmental Affairs, PO Box 3841, Ramallah, West Bank. URL: http://www.mena.gov.ps
Ministry of Information, Acre Street, Al-Bireh, PO Box 244, Ramallah. Tel: +970 (0)2 298 6465, fax: +970 (0)2 295 4043, URL: http://www.minfo.gov.ps/

Ministry of the Interior, An Nasser Street, Gaza. Tel: +970 (0)7 282 9090
Ministry of Justice, Gaza. Tel: +9702 (0)8 282 9118, fax: +970 (0)8 286 7109
Ministry of Labour, PO Box: 351, Industrial Zone, Ramallah. Tel: +970 (0)2 290 0375, fax: +970 (0)2 290 0607, URL: http://www.mol.gov.ps/
Ministry of Local Government, Kitf Al Wad, PO Box 98, Jericho. Tel: +970 (0)2 232 2619
Ministry of Planning and International Cooperation, PO Box 4017, Gaza. URL: http://www.mopic.gov.ps/
Ministry of Public Works, Sateh Marhaba, Al Bireh, PO Box 29, Ramallah. Tel: +970 (0)2 298 0206
Ministry of Social Affairs, Old Housing Building, Rimal, Gaza.
Ministry of Telecommunications, Gaza. Tel: +970 (0)2 282 2822, URL: http://www.mosa.gov.ps
Ministry of Tourism, Old Municipal Building, Al Mahed Square, PO Box 534, Bethlehem. Tel: +970 (0)2 274 1581
Ministry of Trade and Economy, Charles de Gaulle Street, Rimal, PO Box 4023, Gaza. URL: http://www.moet.gov.ps/
Ministry of Transport, PO Box 399, Ramallah. Tel: +970 (0)2 298 6944
Ministry of Waqf and Religious Affairs, Al Yarmuk Street, PO Box 283, Gaza.
Ministry of Youth and Sport, Ash Shifa Street, Southern Rimal, PO Box 1416, Gaza.

Political Parties

Fatah (Palestinian National Liberation Movement), PFLP, DFLP, FIDA, the People's Party, and Hamas. All parties, with the exception of Hamas, are members of the PLO.

Elections

Following the death of Yasser Arafat in November 2004, presidential elections took place on 9 January 2005; interim Palestinian leader Mahmoud Abbas won a landslide victory with 62.3 per cent of the vote, beating Mustafa Barghouti who received 19.8 per cent. Turnout was about 66 per cent.

The first Legislative elections in ten years were held on 26 January 2006. The Islamic militant group Hamas (Islamic Resistance Movement) won a surprise victory, gaining 76 of the 132 seats in the Palestinian parliament. Voters cited corruption within the Fatah government as the main cause for support for Hamas, a party committed to the destruction of the Jewish state. The Fatah party refused to be included in a Hamas-led Government. Results of the election can be seen in the table below:

Party	Seats won
Hamas	76
Fatah	43
PFLP	3
Badil	2
Independent Palestine	2
Third Way	2
Independent/Other	4

77 per cent of those eligible voted.

Both presidential and legislative elections were scheduled for 24 January 2010 but both have been postponed. Elections are currently expected to take place in 2013.

Diplomatic Representation

British Consulate-General, (Represented by the Consulate-General in Jerusalem) 19 Nashashibi Street, Sheikh Jarrah Quarter, PO Box 19690, East Jerusalem 97200, Occupied Territories. Tel: +972 (0)2 541 4100, fax: +972 (0)2 628 3021, URL: http://ukinjerusalem.fco.gov.uk/en/
Consul-General: Sir Vincent Fean
Palestinian Diplomatic Mission in the UK, 5 Galena Road, Hammersmith, London, W6 0LT, United Kingdom. Tel: +44 (0)208 563 0008, fax: +44 (0)208 563 0058, URL: http://palestinemissionuk.com/
Ambassador: Manuel Hassassian
Palestine Liberation Organization Office USA, 1730 K Street NW, 1004, Washington DC 20006, U.S.A. Tel: +1 202 785 8394, fax: +1 202 887 5337, URL: http://plodelegation.us/
Chief Representative: Maen Rashid Areikat
US Consulate General, Jerusalem, 18 Agron Road, Jerusalem 94190, 27 Nablus Road, Jerusalem 94190. Tel: 972 2 622 7230 / 972 2 625 3288, fax: 972 2 625 9270, e-mail: uscongenjerusalem@state.gov, URL: http://jerusalem.usconsulate.gov
Consul General: Michael Ratney
Permanent Observer Mission of Palestine to the United Nations, 115 East 65th Street, New York, NY 10021, USA. Tel: +1 212 288 8500, fax: +1 212 517 2377, e-mail: palestine@un.int, URL: http://www.un.int/wcm/content/site/palestine/pid/12363

LEGAL SYSTEM

Presidents Abbas and Fatah control Palestinian Authority (PA) security forces in the West Bank. There have been reports of torture at the hands of the PA, as well as arbitrary and prolonged detentions. There is official corruption and impunity. Prison conditions are poor. Five people were reported to be executed during 2010 and six during 2011.

In Gaza, Hamas has established its own security forces. There have been reports that these have killed, tortured, kidnapped and harassed Fatah members with impunity. Hamas and other Palestinian factions in Gaza continue to shell civilian targets in Israel.

Israeli authorities use excessive force, abuse civilians and torture Palestinian detainees. Prison conditions are overcrowded, and the Israelis impose severe restrictions on internal and external movement by Palestinians.

Independent Commission for Human Rights, URL: http://www.ichr.ps/

ISRAEL

LOCAL GOVERNMENT

The Palestinian Authority had a policy of intensive municipilization in its early years.There are three levels of government in the Occupied Palestinian Territories: central, regional and municipal. At the central level, the Ministry of Local Government was founded in 1994, It has a presence in every regional capital. The regional level is made up of governorates (muhafazat). under the supervision of the Ministry of the Interior and led by nominees from the President of the Palestinian Authority. Fourteen governorates were founded in 1995, nine in the West Bank (Nablus, Qalqilya, Tulkarm, Jenin, Jericho, Ramallah, Bethlehem, Hebron and Jerusalem) and five in the Gaza Strip (North Gaza, Gaza City, Deir el-Balah, Khan Yunis and Rafah). They replaced the eight regions set up by the Israeli administration. Two regions (Tubas and Salfit) have the status of separate 'autonomous district'. The local level consists of municipalities and village councils.There are currently 121 municipalities (96 in the West Bank and 25 in the Gaza Strip) and 355 village councils.

Local elections were held for the first time since 1976 in 2005. Four rounds of voting were held throughtout 509 local authorities (municipalities or village districts). Hamas dominated.

AREA AND POPULATION

Area
The Occupied Palestinian Territories consist of the West Bank and Gaza Strip. The area of the West Bank is 5,860 sq. km, of which 5,640 sq. km is land and 220 sq. km is water. The Gaza Strip has a total area of 360 sq. km. The Israeli Government withdrew all Israeli settlers from the Gaza Strip in 2005. The Palestinian Authority controls just under 40 per cent of the West Bank, where a number of Israeli settlements are located.

To view a map, please consult http://www.lib.utexas.edu/maps/cia08/west_bank_sm_2008.gif

Population
The total world population of Palestinians in 2007 was estimated to be 9.7 million by the Central Bureau of Statistics, of which 2.4 live in the West Bank and 1.4 live in the Gaza Strip.

The population within Occupied Palestinian Territories grew by 2.2 per cent over 2008. Around 1.1 million Palestinians live in the non-occupied areas of Israel, and there is a diaspora of 4.8 million. The largest number of Palestinians living outside the Territories is in Jordan, where 2.5-2.8 million live, over 1.93 million of them in ten refugee camps. The Lebanon has twelve official refugee camps, where 416,608 Palestinian refugees have settled. According to UNRWA statistics, the total number of registered Palestinian refugees rose from 870,000 in 1953 to over 4.6 million in 2008, and continues to rise due to natural population growth. (Palestine refugees are defined as persons who lost both their homes and means of livelihood as a result of the 1948 Arab-Israeli conflict, and their descendants through the male line).

The population of the Gaza Strip increased by almost 40 per cent over the decade to 2007, indicating an average annual growth rate of 3.3 per cent. At this rate, the population could double in 21 years, according to the Palestinian Central Bureau of Statistics. A large proportion of the population, (over 20 per cent in 2008) is aged below 15 years, and the median age is 20.2 years.

Births, Marriages, Deaths
Estimates for 2008 put the birth rate at 25.9 births per 1,000 inhabitants and the death rate at 3.7 deaths per 1,000 people. Life expectancy at birth in 2008 was estimated at 74 years. The fertility rate was 3.3 children per woman of childbearing age.

Public Holidays 2014
1 January: New Year's Day/Fateh Establishment Day
14 January: The Prophet's Birthday (Mawlid an Nabi)*
7 May: Labour Day
27 May: Isra al-Miraj*
29 June: Beginning of Ramadan
29 July: End of Ramadan (Eid al Fitr)*
5 October: Feast of the Sacrifice (Eid al Adha)*
25 October: Islamic New Year*
15 November: National Day
*Islamic holy day: precise date depends upon appearance of the moon.

EMPLOYMENT

Figures from the International Labour Organisation put the labour force at 871,900 for the whole of the Palestinian Territory over the year 2006, equivalent to 41.3 per cent of the population aged 15 years and over. Those in employment numbered 666,000 over the same period, while those unemployed numbered 206,000 (23.2 per cent of the labour force).

BANKING AND FINANCE

GDP/GNP, Inflation, National Debt
The economy is severely hindered by restrictions of the movement of Palestinian people and goods. The infrastrucutre has also been destroyed by Israeli bombing raids. The Occupied Palestinian Territory also depends on foreign aid. There have been some easing of the restrtictions in 2010 and 2011. The economy was also boosted by increased aid and improved security. The economic situation has improved more in the West Bank than Gaza; in the West Bank per capita income has returned to its 1999 level whereas in Gaza it is substantially lower.

GDP was estimated to be US$5 billion in 2006, rising to an estimated US$11 billion in 2008 with growth of 0.8 per cent. GDP per capita was estimated at US$1,764 in the same year. Per capita was estimated to have risen to US$2,900 by 2008. GDP was US$12 billion in 2009, reflecting a growth rate of 7 per cent.

The services sector accounts for 80 per cent of GDP; industry contributes 23 per cent and agriculture accounts for 12 per cent of GDP.

The Consumer Price Index (CPI) (base year 1996 = 100) for the Occupied Palestinian Territories (all items) rose from 148.58 in December 2005, to 153.46 in December 2006 reflecting an annual increase of 2.51 per cent. Price rises were greatest in Gaza (4.63 per cent), whilst Jerusalem and the Remaining West Bank showed increases of 1.61 per cent and 2.08 per cent respectively. Commodities showing the largest rise over the year were food (4.32 per cent) and transport and communications (3.53 per cent). Inflation was estimated to be 11 per cent in 2008.

Balance of Payments / Imports and Exports
The following table shows exports, imports and trade balance (US$ current prices):

Exports, Imports and Trade Balance, (US$'000)

Area	2003	2005
Exports	279,680	335,443
Imports	1,800,268	2,666,772
Trade Balance	1,520,588	2,331,329

Source: Palestinian Central Bureau of Statistics

The Occupied Territories export mainly to Jordan and Israel and import most of their requirements from the same region. Exports amounted to US$500 million in 2009 and imports US$3.7 million.

Value of imports and exports by SITC (2002) is shown on the following table:

Value of imports and exports by SITC, 2002 (US$'000)

Section	Exports	Imports
Food and live animals	27,036	261,172
Beverages and tobacco	13,657	52,965
Crude materials inedible except fuels	14,375	29,501
Mineral fuels lubricants and related materials	2,481	360,092
Animal and vegetable oils fats and waxes	5,720	9,706
Chemicals and related products	20,263	94,026
Manufactured goods	94,954	185,006
Machinery and transport equipment	12,042	89,593
Misc. manufactured articles	49,834	35,480
Other commodities and transactions	505	9
TOTAL	240,867	1,117,550

Source: Palestinian Central Bureau of Statistics

Banking
Bank of Palestine Ltd, P.O. Box: 471, Ramallah. Tel: +970 (02) 296 5010, fax: +970 (02) 296 4703, e-mail: info@bankofpalestine.com, URL: http://www.bankofpalestine.com Chairman and General Manager: Dr. Hashim Shawa

Chambers of Commerce and Trade Organisations
Palestine Trade Center (PALTRADE), URL: http://www.paltrade.org/

MANUFACTURING, MINING AND SERVICES

Energy
Most electricity is imported from Israel; East Jerusalem Electric Company buys and distributes electricity to Palestinians in East Jerusalem and its concession in the West Bank; the Israel Electric Company directly supplies electricity to most Jewish residents and military facilities; some Palestinian municipalities, such as Nablus and Janin, generate their own electricity from small power plants. In 2007, the Israeli government approved cuts in the supply of electricity and fuel as punishment for rocket attacks from Gaza. Israel argued that is it not bound to supply utilities to the civilian population of a 'hostile entity'. The international community held that Israel remains legally responsible for the coastal strip because it still controls Gaza's borders, airspace and territorial waters. Israel supplies 60 per cent (120 megawatts) of the Gaza's electricity requirements, 17 megawatts are supplied by Egypt and the Gaza produces the balance of 65 megawatts. The UN said that the sanctions punish an entire population and are therefore unacceptable.

Service Industries
According to 2003 statistics, the Occupied Territories has a total of 11,925 services enterprises, employing a total of 41,153 people, with an output of US$302,234,600. The largest sector is education, with a 2003 output of US$80,459,400 and 9,766 employees.

Agriculture
12 per cent of the male labour force and 33 per cent of the female workforce are active in the agriculture sector. Most of the men are self employed, whilst over 80 per cent of the women are unpaid family members. Cereals and olives are produced in the Occupied Territories. In terms of livestock, sheep are the main animals reared, followed by cattle and goats. Poultry is also reared.

Agricultural Production in 2010

Produce	Int. $'000*	Tonnes
Olives	79,270	99,000

- continued

Tomatoes	74,726	202,200
Indigenous chicken meat	69,794	48,999
Cucumbers and gherkins	49,081	247,200
Hen eggs, in shell	33,590	40,500
Grapes	32,525	56,900
Cow milk, whole, fresh	30,676	98,300
Indigenous sheep meat	27,746	10,190
Almonds, with shell	21,247	7,200
Sheep milk, whole, fresh	16,706	42,900
Anise, badian, fennel, corian	14,891	2,700
Indigenous goat meat	11,591	4,838

* unofficial figures
*Source: http://faostat.fao.org/site/339/default.aspx Food and Agriculture
Organization of the United Nations, Food and Agricultural commodities production*

Fishing
In 2010, almost 1,700 tonnes of fish were caught; a large proportion of which were sardines.

COMMUNICATIONS AND TRANSPORT

International Airports
There are three paved airports in the Occupied Territories.

Roads
Road network length in the Palestinian Territory by region and road type is shown on the following table (km):

Area	Paved Roads	Unpaved Roads	Total
West Bank	5,196.8	2,121.2	7,318
Gaza Strip	701.3	290.7	992.0
Palestinian Territory	5,898.1	2,411.9	8,310

Source: Palestinian Central Bureau of Statistics

However, the road network has been severely damaged by successive Israeli airstrikes and military incursions.

HEALTH

The Palestinian territories benefit from generous medical aid and highly skilled doctors and nurses. According to 2004 statistics, there were a total of 74 hospitals in the Occupied Territories, with 5,108 beds. 24 of the hospitals were government-run, whilst 50 were privately administered. However, restrictions on movement caused by checkpoints and by the new security barrier erected by the Israelis often means that medical supplies do not arrive at their destination. The World Health Organisation warned that the health situation in the West Bank and Gaza had reached a critical point in 2004, and could collapse if further assistance was not forthcoming. Malnutrition was rising and vaccination levels were falling, whilst diseases such as diabetes were not being adequately treated. With the election of Hamas in 2006, the situation worsened; funding cuts by Israel and donor countries led to shortages of drugs and unpaid salaries for clinical staff. After three months, the USA, the EU, the UN, Russia and Israel agreed to release emergency aid through a trust fund.

Since the closure of crossings into Gaza, prices of staple foods have increased, and around 70 per cent of Gazans rely on food assistance. Chronic malnutrition and dietary-related disease such as iron-deficiency anaemia are increasing, according to the World Health Organization. In January 2008, UNRWA believed Gaza to be on the brink of a public health disaster. Power cuts in Gaza after Israel bombed the only power plant in late June 2006 mean that hospitals and sewage treatment plants rely on diesel generators. Hospitals and pharmacies in Gaza are dangerously short of drugs and medical equipment. Restrictions have been tightened on patients needing to leave Gaza for treatment. In 2011, the Ministry of health warned of unprecedented shortages of medicines.

According to figures from WHO, as of 2009, GDP per capita was US$1,949. Total expenditure on health amounted to 6.4 per cent of GDP. General government expenditure on health was approximately 38.3 per cent of total health expenditure. In 2009, per 10,000 population, there were 28.3 doctors, 35.2 nurses and midwives, 16.7 pharmacists and 4.2 dentists. There were 0.7 hospital beds per 10,000 population. Approximately 88 per cent of the population have access to health care.

In 2008, the average infant mortality was 17 per 1,000 who survived their first year. Child mortality (under-fives) was 21.8 per 1,000. The figures increase with regard to Palestinian children in refugee camps.

EDUCATION

The UN have estimated that up to 330,000 school-children have their education disrupted regularly. Israeli military closures, curfews, and the West Bank wall and fencing restrict access to Palestinian academic institutions. Israeli authorities have at times shut universities, and schools have been damaged during military operations.

In the 2003-04 school year the Occupied Territories' schools numbered 2,192, of which 1,497 were basic primary, and 695 were secondary. 1,662 were government-run, 273 were UNRWA-run, and 258 were private.

Students in the same year numbered 931,260 in Primary education and 112,675 going on to secondary schools. In 2007 73 per cent of children of the relevant age attended a primary school, and 89 per cent of the relevant age group attended secondary school.

Higher Education
The Occupied Territories' universities include: Al-Quds University, Birzeit University, AN-Najah University, Bethlehem University, Hebron University, and Al-Azhar University, Gaza.

In June 2008, Palestinian human rights groups in Gaza said hundreds of students would miss deadlines to pursue studies at universities abroad if Israel did not relax travel restrictions. This followed the reinstatement by the US state department of Fulbright grants to seven Palestinians in Gaza. The scholarships had been withdrawn because Israel would not provide exit permits to the students. Human right groups and some Israeli politicians have described the policy of not letting the students out as "collective punishment".

RELIGION

The majority of Palestinians (80 per cent) are Muslim (mainly Sunni), whilst 12 per cent are Jewish, and two per cent are Christian.

Pope Benedict XVI visited the West Bank in May 2009, and offered his support for the Palestinians' right to a homeland.

The Occupied Territories have a religious liberty rating of 4 on a scale of 1 to 10 (10 is most freedom). (Source: World Religion Database)

COMMUNICATIONS AND MEDIA

Seen as one of the most dangerous places in the world for journalists, violence against journalists is relatively common, and kidnappings of journalists in Gaza were frequent in 2006, although in most cases the reporters and photographers were freed quickly.

Newspapers
Al Quds, URL: http://www.alquds.com/
Al-Ayyam, URL: http://www.al-ayyam.ps/
Palestinian News Agency (WAFA), URL: http://www.wafa.pna.net/

Broadcasting
In 2008, there were 30 television stations and 25 radio stations in the Territories. The Palestinian Broadcasting Corporation (PBC) runs the Voice of Palestine (VOP) radio station, which broadcasts in Arabic, English and Hebrew.
Voice of Palestine Ramallah. E-mail: bailasan@bailasan.com, URL: http://www.bailasan.com/pinc/voice.htm
Al-Aqsa, Hamas operated, URL: http://www.alaqsavoice.ps/arabic/

Telecommunications
The Israeli company BEZEK and the Palestinian company PALTEL are responsible for fixed line services, whilst the Palestinian JAWAL company provides cellular services. It is estimated that there were 350,000 mainline telephones in use in the Occupied Palestinian Territories in 2007, and 1.095 million mobile phones. In the same year, there were an estimated 255,500 internet users.

ENVIRONMENT

Current environmental problems include the inadequacy of fresh water and the treatment of sewage.

STATES OF THE WORLD

ITALY
Italian Republic
Repubblica Italiana

Capital: Rome (Population estimate, 2011: 2,777,000)

Head of State: Georgio Napolitano (President) (page 1484)

National Flag: A tricolour pale-wise, green, white, red.

CONSTITUTION AND GOVERNMENT

Constitution
Following the referendum on 2 June 1946 Italy became a republic and, on 13 June, King Umberto left the country, bringing to an end the reign of the House of Savoy. The first elections held concurrently with the referendum brought the Christian Democrats to power with the Communists and the Socialists. The first government was a coalition of the three parties under the premiership of Christian Democrat Alcide de Gasperi. In July 1947 de Gasperi dissolved the government and reformed it, leaving out the parties of the Left.

The first republican constitution was adopted by the Constituent Assembly on 22 December 1947, and came into force on 1 January 1948. The constitution describes Italy as 'a democratic republic founded on work, with sovereignty vested in the people, to be exercised in the forms and within the framework of the Constitution'. Although the constitution provides for the separation of the executive, legislative, and judicial branches of government, the government has the power to approve laws under decree in special circumstances.

The President of the Republic is elected by an electoral college consisting of the two legislative chambers sitting in joint session, to which are added three delegates from each Regional Council (58 delegates in all). The successful candidate must poll a two-thirds majority but, after three inconclusive ballots, an absolute majority is decisive. The President can dissolve Parliament, except in the course of the last six months of his seven years' tenure of office. The President appoints the government which is headed by the President of the Council of Ministers (Cabinet).

Article 94 of the constitution asserts the principle of cabinet responsibility. The newly constituted cabinet must obtain a vote of confidence within ten days of its coming to office. An adverse vote in parliament does not suffice to unseat a government. It can only be forced to resign by a deliberate vote of censure. Ministers are responsible collectively for the policy of the government, and individually for the actions of their departments. Legislative power is vested in the government, both chambers and such other bodies on whom it has been conferred by the constitution. The President promulgates laws, but his acts are only valid if counter-signed by the minister concerned.

The constitution is notable for certain features designed to bar the way to unconstitutional developments and the abuse of power. Thus it provides for a Constitutional Court, not unlike the US Supreme Court, whose duty it is to pronounce on the constitutionality of laws and decrees. Allowance is made for a referendum on controversial issues and for considerable local autonomy, aimed at avoiding excessive centralisation. In April 1993 a series of referenda were held on constitutional reform. Amongst other issues, Italians voted by 82.7 per cent to abolish the proportional representation system of voting, and by 90.3 per cent to end party funding by the state. Carlo Ciampi formed a government and pledged commitment to introducing a first-past-the-post electoral system. From 1994 to 2001, Italy had a mixed electoral system, with 75 per cent of the seats being assigned through a plurality voting system, and the other 25 per cent being allocated according to a proportional system.

In December 2005, Mr. Berlusconi's government pushed through electoral reform, returning Italy to a system of full proportional representation. The system grants a working majority of at least 340 seats in the lower house to the winning coalition, irrespective of the size of its electoral majority. Critics of the system feared that this could lead to a return to the unstable governments that characterized Italian politics in post-war years; the new legislation attempts to allay these fears by reducing the number of minor parties and their disproportionate political power within Italian politics through the introduction of a rule that parties must win two per cent of the vote before they are allocated a seat. Seats in the two houses are allocated according to candidates' position on their party lists, with those at the top of the list having a better chance of winning a seat than those at the bottom.

To consult the full constitution, please visit:
http://english.camera.it/cost_reg_funz/345/346/listaarticoli.asp

International Relations
Italy was a founding member of the European Community (now the European Union), and was admitted to the UN in 1955. It is also a member of NATO, the OECD, the World Trade Organization, the OSCE, and the Council of Europe.

Italy has deployed troops in support of UN peacekeeping missions in Lebanon, Somalia, Mozambique, and Timor-Leste as well as providing support for NATO and UN operations in Afghanistan, Bosnia, Kosovo, and Albania. The country maintains approximately 2,500 troops and a Provincial Reconstruction Team in Herat, western Afghanistan province of Herat. Italy continues to support reconstruction and development assistance of the Iraqi people through humanitarian workers and other officials.

Recent Events
In May 2003 the trial began of the prime minister Silvio Berlusconi on corruption charges relating to business dealings in the 1980s. The trial was stopped the following month after a law was passed granting him immunity from prosecution. In December 2003, following the passage through Parliament of a bill which would give Mr. Berlusconi more influence over the Italian media, President Ciampi refused to sign the legislation into law. At the beginning of 2004, Italy's Constitutional Court rejected a law granting Mr. Berlusconi and other top political figures immunity from prosecution and the trial of Mr Berlusconi was resumed. He was cleared on one count of corruption in December 2004, and acquitted definitively by the Italian Supreme Court in October 2007.

In April 2005 the Italian parliament ratified the EU constitution. A political crisis was triggered in April 2005 when Mr. Berlusconi's Forza Italia party did badly in regional elections. The coalition government collapsed and Mr. Berlusconi resigned. He formed a new government a few days later.

Elections on 12-13th April 2006 resulted in a very small majority for the centre-left Union coalition (L'Unione), headed by Romano Prodi. Mr. Berlusconi, leader of the centre-right House of Freedoms coalition (Casa delle Liberta) and of the Forza Italia party, refused to accept defeat, citing irregularities in overseas voting. For the first time, six seats in the Senate were allocated to Italians living abroad. On the 26th of April, the Supreme Court confirmed the narrow victory of the centre-left coalition and Mr. Prodi took office on 17th May 2006.

In February 2007, Mr. Prodi resigned as Prime Minister following opposition within the coalition to the government's foreign policies (specifically additional funding for troops in Afghanistan and enlarging the US military base at Vicenza), as well as to the policy of giving full rights to gay and unmarried couples. Mr. Prodi took up the Premiership again following a vote of confidence in both houses of parliament.

In January 2008, Mr. Prodi again faced votes of confidence in both houses; this was forced by the resignation of Clemente Mastella and the withdrawal of his Udeur party's support of the coalition, costing Mr Prodi his Senate majority of one. He won the vote of confidence in the Chamber of Deputies, but lost in the Senate, and resigned. He remained as caretaker PM whilst discussions over whether to appoint an interim government to carry out electoral reform took place. Former PM Silvio Berlusconi, ahead in the polls, opposed such an interim government but promised electoral reform if reelected. Italians went to the polls on 12-13th April; some 158 different parties contested the regional and national polls, including Mr Berlusconi's new conservative People of Freedom (PDL) and Mr Veltroni's recently formed Democratic Party (PD). Silvio Berlusconi was returned to power for a third term.

In August, Prime Minister Berlusconi apologised to Libya for damage inflicted by Italy during the colonial era, and signed a five billion dollar investment deal by way of compensation. In the same month, Alitalia filed for bankruptcy; the national airline had suffered serious financial problems for years. Attempts were made to sell the government's 49.9 per cent stake in the airline in 2006, but investors were discouraged by working restrictions in place. With losses of around $1 million per day, the airline seemed doomed to liquidation; but a €1 billion rescue package was put together by an Italian consortium in September 2008.

Around 1,700 migrants from Africa arrived on the Italian island of Lampedusa, on the 27-28 December. There was a sharp rise in the number of illegal migrants from Africa in 2008, many risking the dangerous Mediterranean crossing to enter Europe from Libya. Over 24,000 migrants arrived in Italy from January to September, compared to about 14,000 in the same period in 2007. Italy and Libya agreed to step up naval patrols to try to reduce the flow of migrants. Italy also offered to help Libya improve security on its southern desert frontier.

In November 2008, Italy was declared officially to be in a recession, following two consecutive quarters of negative growth. In March 2009, the government approved a massive 17.8bn-euro public works programme to create new jobs and boost the economy. The programme includes the construction of a two mile bridge from mainland Italy to Sicily, new urban railway networks, motorway expansion, prison and school construction, and a flood barrier system in Venice. Funding will come from public and private resources. Critics fear that huge amounts of taxpayers' money may be siphoned off by the Sicilian and Calabrian mafias, which control most public works projects in the south of Italy.

In March 2009, around 100,000 Italians marched through Naples in one of the largest anti-mafia protests of recent years. Organised crime is dominated by four mafia clans: Sicily's Cosa Nostra; the Camorra around Naples; Calabria's 'Ndrangheta; and the Sacra Corona Unita, in Puglia.

On the 6th April, around 293 people were killed and over 1,000 injured when an earthquake of 6.3 magnitude struck close to L'Aquila city, central Italy. Some 3,000 to 10,000 buildings in the medieval city were damaged. Italy lies on two fault lines and has been hit by powerful earthquakes in the past, mainly in the south of the country.

In October 2009, the Constitutional Court overturned a law which gave serving prime ministers immunity from prosecution while in office.

Mr Berlusconi's coalition did well in regional lections in March 2010. However in July, the speaker of parliament, Gian Franco Fini, split from Mr Berlusconi and set up a new centre-right political party, Future and Freedom for Italy (FLI). In August, more than 30 deputies in the

Lower House left Mr Berlusconi's Party of Freedom to join the FLI, causing Mr Berlusconi to lose his majority in the house. In November, four ministers resigned from the coalition government. Mr Berlusconi survived two confidence votes in December 2010.

In February 2011, Mr Berlusconi was order to stand trial on 6 April for abuse of power and for paying for sex with an under-age prostitute.

In July 2011 the IMF urged the Italian government to implement an austerity budget amid fears that the economy was failing which might lead to Italy having to be bailed out like Greece, Portugal and Ireland. In September, the parliament passed a much amended austerity budget worth €54 billion ($74 billion). In September, Standard & Poor downgraded Italy's sovereign debt rating from A+ to A. In September 2011 the country approved an austerity budget which should balance the budget by 2013 but the head of the central bank has since urged the government to introduce more measures to stimulate growth.

In October 2011, the Italian parliament failed to back a key part of the budget triggering a vote of no-confidence. Most of the opposition boycotted the first round of the vote but Mr Berlusconi won the vote in the lower house by 316 votes to 301. Concerns both home and abroad about Italy's debt crisis continued into November and Prime Minister Berlusconi resigned following his government's failure to gain a majority during a budget vote. Former EU commissioner Mario Monti was appointed and formed a new government.

In December 2011 Prime Minister Monti presented his package of austerity measures which amounted to €33 billion of spending cuts, as well as plans to raise taxes and to cut down on tax evasion; the measures were approved by parliament. The following month the Government issued a de-regulation decree which was designed to encourage competition and make it easier for young people to find employment. The following January the US ratings agency Fitch downgraded Italy's credit rating to A-.

In May 2012 the Emilia area of Northern Italy was hit by two earthquakes, a total of 15 people were killed.

In March 2013, Silvio Berlusconi was sentenced to a year in prison over an illegal wiretap. He announced he would appeal the decision and remains at liberty while this process is ongoing. In June the same year, he was found guilty of paying for sex with an underage prostitute and sentenced to seven years in jail. Again he remains at liberty during the appeals process.

Legislature
Parliament (*Parlamento Italiano*) is bicameral and consists of the *Senato della Repubblica* (Senate) and the *Camera dei Deputati* (Chamber of Deputies).

Upper House
The Senate consists of 315 senators, (aged 40 and over), elected by proportional representation following the constitutional reforms of December 2005. Single parties which win less than eight per cent of the vote in a region do not get a seat in the Senate; nor do coalitions that fail to win 20 per cent of the vote. A senator has to win 55 per cent of regional votes in order to obtain a seat. In the event of a close result, the coalition with most votes is given the extra seats to obtain 55 per cent. Six seats are allocated for Italians living abroad. In addition the President of the Republic can nominate 'senators for life' from among men eminent in the public, scientific and cultural life of the country. At present, there are six life senators. Most senators are elected for a term of five years.

Senate, Via del Salvatore 12, 00186 Rome, Italy. Fax: +39 (0)6 6706 3513, URL: http://www.senato.it
President of the Senate: Renato Giuseppe Schifani

Lower House
The Chamber of Deputies comprises 630 deputies, elected by proportional representation for five years. Various thresholds are set for winning seats: single parties with less than two per cent of the national vote do not get a seat, but their votes are counted as part of the coalition tally; parties with less than four per cent of the vote do not get a seat and coalitions which do not win at least ten per cent of the national vote are not given seats in the Chamber. In the event that the winning coalition does not gain the 340 seats necessary for a majority, the unallocated seats of the coalition tally (from parties gaining less than two per cent of the vote) are given to them.

Chamber of Deputies, Palazzo Montecitorio, 00186 Rome, Italy. Tel: +39 (0)6 6760 3316 / 9929, e-mail: attivita_amministrativa@camera.it, URL: http://www.camera.it
President and Speaker: Gianfranco Fini

Cabinet (Council of Ministers) (as at July 2013)
Prime Minister: Enrico Letta (page 1463)
Deputy Prime Minister, Minister for the Interior: Angelino Alfano (page 1374)
Minister of the Environment: Andrea Orlando
Minister of Foreign Affairs: Emma Bonino (page 1391)
Minister of Justice: Anna Maria Cancellieri (page 1400)
Minister of Labour and Social Policy: Enrico Giovannini (page 1430)
Minister of Defence: Mario Mauro (page 1472)
Minister of Education, Universities and Research: Maria Chiara Carrozza
Minister of Agricultural Policy, Food and Forestry: Nunzia de Girolamo
Minister of Health: Beatrice Lorenzin
Minister of Infrastructure and Transport: Maurizio Lupi
Minister of Cultural Activities, Heritage and Tourism: Massimo Bray
Minister without portfolio responsible for European Affairs: Enzo Moavero Milanesi
Minister of the Economy and Finance: Fabrizio Saccomanni (page 1507)
Minister of Economic Development: Flavio Zanonato (page 1543)
Minister without portfolio responsible for European Affairs: Enzo Moavero Milanesi
Minister without portfolio responsible for Equal Opportunities, Sport and Youth Policy: vacant
Minister without portfolio responsible for Regional Affairs and Autonomy: Graziano Delrio

Minister without portfolio, responsible for Relations with Parliament and Co-ordination of Government Activities: Dario Franceschini
Minister without portfolio: responsible for Integration: Cecile Kyenge Kashetu
Minister withut portfolio, responsible for Public Administration and Simplication: Giampiero D'Alia
Undersecretary of State to the President of the Council and Secretary of the Council of Ministers: Filippo Patroni Griffi
Minister without portfolio, responsible for Territorial Cohesion: Prof. Carlo Trigilia
Minister without portfolio, responsible for Constitutional Reforms: Prof. Gaetano Quagliariello

Ministries
Office of the President, Palazzo del Quirinale, 00187 Rome, Italy. Tel: +39 06 46991, fax: +39 06 4699 3125, URL: http://www.quirinale.it/
Office of the Prime Minister, Palazzo Chigi, Piazza Colonna 370, 00187 Rome, Italy. Tel: +39 06 67791, fax: +39 06 678 3998 / 679 6894, e-mail: redazione.web@governo.it, URL: http://www.palazzochigi.it, http://www.governo.it
Ministry of Agriculture and Forestry Resources, Via XX Settembre 20, 00187 Rome, Italy. Tel: +39 06 46651, fax: +39 06 474 6168, e-mail: stampa@politicheagricole.it, URL: http://www.politicheagricole.gov.it
Ministry of Communications, Viale America 201, 00144 Rome, Italy. Tel: +39 06 54441, fax: +39 06 679 6641, e-mail: ufficio.stamp@comunicazioni.it, URL: http://www.comunicazioni.it/
Ministry of Culture Heritage, Via del Collegio Romano 27, 00186 Rome, Italy. Tel: +39 06 67231, fax: +39 06 679 1905, e-mail: urp@beniculturali.it, URL: http://www.beniculturali.it/
Ministry of Defence, Gabinetto, Via XX Settembre, 8, 00187 Rome, Italy. Tel: +39 06 488 2126/7, fax: +39 06 474 7775, e-mail: ministro@difesa.it, URL: http://www.difesa.it/
Ministry of Economy and Finance, Via XX Settembre, 97, 00187 Rome, Italy. Tel: +39 06 59971, e-mail: ufficio.stampa@tesoro.it, URL: http://www.finanze.it/export/finanze/index.htm
Ministry of Economic Development, Via Molise, 2, 00186 Rome, Italy. Tel: +39 06 42043486, fax: +39 06 47887964, URL: http://www.sviluppoeconomico.gov.it
Ministry of Education, University and Scientific Research, Piazzale Kennedy, 20, 00144 Rome, Italy. Tel: +39 06 58491, URL: http://www.miur.it
Ministry of the Environment, Land and Sea, Viale Cristoforo Colombo, 44, 00147 Rome, Italy. Tel: +39 06 57221, fax: +39 06 5728 8323, e-mail: segr.ufficiostampa@minambiente.it, URL: http://www.minambiente.it
Ministry of Foreign Affairs, Piazzale della Farnesina 1, 00189 Rome, Italy. Tel: +39 06 36911, fax: +39 06 322 2850, e-mail: relazioni.pubblico@esteri.it, URL: http://www.esteri.it
Ministry for Foreign Trade, Viale Boston 25, 00144 Rome, Italy. Tel: +39 06 59931, URL: http://www.mincomes.it
Ministry of Health, Eur, Piazzale dell'Industria, 20, 00144 Rome, Italy. Tel: +39 06 59941, fax: +39 06 5994 5328, e-mail: ufficiostampa@sanita.it, URL: http://www.salute.gov.it/
Ministry of Transport, Piazza delle Croce Rossa 1, 00187 Rome, Italy. Tel: +39 06 44267206, fax: +39 06 4412 4308, e-mail: stampa.bianchi@trasporti.gpv.it, URL: http://www.trasporti.gov.it
Ministry for the Interior, Palazzo Viminale, Via Agostino Depretis, 00184 Rome, Italy. Tel: +39 06 4651, fax: +39 06 482 7630, e-mail: info@interno.it, URL: http://www.interno.it/
Ministry of Justice, Via Arenula 70, 00186 Rome, Italy. Tel: +39 06 68851, fax: +39 06 5227 8550, e-mail: callcentre@giustizia.it, URL: http://www.giustizia.it/
Ministry of Employment and Social Welfare, Via Veneto 56, 00187 Rome, Italy. Tel: +39 06 36751, e-mail: ufficiostampa@lavoro.gov.it, URL: http://www.lavoro.gov.it
Ministry of Infrastructure and Transport, Piazzale Porta Pia, 1, 00198 Rome, Italy. Tel: +39 06 44121, URL: http://www.mit.gov.it
Ministry of Social Welfare, Via Fornovo, 8, 00192 Rome, Italy. Tel: +39 06 36751, URL: http://www.solidarietasociale.gov.it

Political Parties
Il Popolo della Libertta (PdL) (Power of the People), (merger of **Forza Italia (FI)** and **Alleanza Nazionale**), URL: http://www.pdl.it/
Leader: Silvio Berlusconi
Lega Nord-Italia Federale (Northern League-Federal Italy), Via Carlo Bellerio, 41, 20161 Milan, Italy. Tel: +39 02 662341, fax: +39 02 6621 1298, URL: http://www.leganord.org
Secretary: Umberto Bossi
Partito della Rifondazione Comunista (PRC, Communist Re-establishment Party), Via del Policlinico 131, 00161 Rome, Italy. Tel: +39 06 441821, fax: +39 06 4418 2286, URL: http://www.rifondazione.it
Leader: Paolo Ferrero
Partito Liberale Italiano (PLI, Liberal Party), Via del Corso 117, 00187 Rome, Italy. Tel: +39 06 6954 9041, fax: +39 06 678 7511, URL: http://www.partitoliberale.it
Leader: Stefano de Luca
Partito Democratico, (PD, Democratic Party), URL: http://www.partitodemocratico.it
Leader: Enrico Letta
Unione dei Democratici Cristiani e di Centro/Unione di Centro, (UDC, Union of Christian and Centre Democrats/Union of the Centre), URL: http://www.udc-italia.it
Leader: Pier Ferdinando Casini
Futuro e Libertà per l'Italia (FLI, Future and Freedom for Italy), URL: http://www.futuroeliberta.com
Vice President: Italo Bocchino
Italia dei Valori (IDV, Italy of Values), URL: http://www.italiadeivalori.it
Leader: Antonio Di Pietro
Scelta Civica (SC,Civic Choice), URL: http://www.sceltacivica.it

ITALY

Elections

Both chambers of Parliament are elected for five year terms by adult suffrage (people over the age of 25) under a system of proportional representation. In April 1996 the centre-left Olive Tree alliance won a historic victory in the general election, ending 50 years of rule by the right-wing alliance. The then prime minister, Romano Prodi, resigned in October 1998, following the Communist Party's refusal to pass the Government budget.

The penultimate general election took place in April 2006. The results for both the Chamber of Deputies and the Senate were so close that Mr. Berlusconi called for a recount and would not concede defeat. The ruling of the supreme court Corte di Cassazione on 19th April stated that Romano Prodi and the centre-left coalition had won the election for the Chamber of Deputies by just 24,755 votes. In the Senate, Mr. Prodi's coalition won 158 seats, Mr. Berlusconi's coalition won 156 seats, and there was one independent senator. In the Chamber of Deputies, the centre-left won 348 seats whilst the centre-right won 281 seats.

Following a Senate vote of no confidence in his government, Mr. Prodi resigned in January 2008. Italians went to the polls on 12-13th April; 158 different parties contested the regional and national polls, which were won by Mr Berlusconi's new conservative People of Freedom (PDL). Silvio Berlusconi was returned to power for a third term.

The most recent elections took place in February 2013. The result was inconclusive: it left Pier Luigi Bersani's centre-left bloc in charge of the lower house but blocked from a Senate majority by Mr Berlusconi's PdL. A protest movement led by comedian Beppe Grillo won 25 per cent of the vote, this left Prime Minister Mario Monti's centre bloc in fourth place with 10 per cent of the vote.

He remained in office in a caretaker capacity in the run-up to and aftermath of elections in February 2013. The foreign minister resigned on 26 March 2013; Monti took over the portfolio temporarily. The mandate to form a government was given by the president to Pier Luigi Bersani of the PD (Democratic Party) on 22 March, but he returned the mandate on 28 March. Following coalition discussions the mandate was then given to Enrico Letta on 24 April, who formed a coalition with Berlusconi's PdL, the SC, the Union of Christian and Centre Democrats (UDC) and the Italian Radicals (Rad). The government also included four technocrats. The government was named on 27 April and was sworn in the following day.

The following table shows the main parties in the Senate following the April 2013 elections:

Coalition and Party	No. of Seats
Italy Common Good	123
Centre-right coalition	117
Five Star Movement	54
Monti for Italy	19
Others	2

The following table shows the political composition of the Chamber of Deputies following the April 2013 election:

Coalition and Party	No. of Seats
Italian Common Good (led by the Democratic Party)	345
Centre-right coalition (led by Alliance of People of Freedom)	125
Five Star Movement	109
Monti for Italy (led by Civic Choice)	470
Others	4

The most recent presidential election took place in April 2013, Giorgio Napolitano was re-elected, he became the first Italian president to be re-elected for a second term.

Diplomatic Representation

Italian Embassy, 14 Three Kings Yard, Davies Street, London W1K 4EH, United Kingdom. Tel: +44 (0)20 7312 2200, fax: +44 (0)20 7312 2230, e-mail: emblondon@embitaly.org.uk, URL: http://www.amblondra.esteri.it
Ambassador: Pasquale Terracciano (page 1524)
Italian Embassy, 3000 Whitehaven Street, NW, Washington, DC 20008, USA. Tel: +1 202 612 4400, fax: +1 202 518 2154, URL: http://www.ambwashingtondc.esteri.it
Ambassador: Claudio Bisogniero (page 1389)
US Embassy, via Vittorio Veneto 121, 00187 Rome, Italy. Tel: +39 06 46741, fax: +39 06 488 2672, URL: http://rome.usembassy.gov
Ambassador: David Thorne (page 1525)
British Embassy, Via XX Settembre 80a, 00187 Rome, Italy. Tel: +39 06 4220 0001, fax: +39 06 487 3324, e-mail: InfoRome@fco.gov.uk, URL: http://ukinitaly.fco.gov.uk/en
Ambassador: Christopher Prentice (page 1498)
Permanent Representative of Italy to the United Nations, 2 United Nations Plaza, 24th Floor, New York, NY 10017, USA. Tel: +1 212 486 9191, fax: +1 212 486 1036, e-mail: info.italyun@esteri.it, URL: http://www.italyun.org/
Ambassador: Cesare Maria Ragaglini

LEGAL SYSTEM

Italian law is based on Roman law, particularly its civil law, and on French Napoleonic law. Italy's courts of ordinary civil and criminal justice are: *Corte di cassazione* (Court of Cassation), the highest court of appeal; *Corte di appello* (Court of Appeal); *Tribunale per i minorenni* (Juvenile Court); *Tribunale di sorveglianza* (Court responsible for the enforcement of sentences); *Tribunale ordinario* (Trial Court).

The court system consists of a series of courts and a body of judges who are civil servants. The system is headed by the Court of Cassation, located in Rome, which has 10 Divisions: six criminal, three civil, and one for employment disputes. In addition, there are 26 Appeal

Court Districts and 159 Tribunals. The 628 *Mandamenti* each has its own magistracy or *Pretura*. There are also 90 Assize Courts and a number of *Uffici Conciliatori*, which deal with petty complaints connected with civil business.

The National Anti-Mafia Bureau (Direzione Nazionale Antimafia) was set up in January 1992, and falls within the scope of the General Public Prosecutor at the Court of Cassation. The office is responsible for coordinating investigations into organised crime throughout Italy. District Anti-Mafia Bureaux are based at the offices of the Public Prosecutor in the regional capitals.

The government respects the rights of its citizens, although there are lengthy pretrial detentions and excessively long court proceedings. The Italian Constitution on 1948 abolished the death penalty for all common military and civil crimes during peacetime. In 2007 Article 27 of Italian Constitution was changed to fully ban the death penalty. The last execution took place in 1945. There is no national ombudsman.

Corte Suprema di Cassazione (The Supreme Court of Cassation), URL: http://www.cortedicassazione.it
Consiglio Superiore della Magistratura (CSM), URL: http://www.csm.it
Corte Costituzionale (Constitutional Court), URL: http://www.cortecostituzionale.it
Consiglio di Stato, URL: http://www.giustizia-amministrativa.it
Corte dei Conti (Court of Accounts), URL: www.corteconti.it/English-co/index.asp
Direzione Nazionale Antimafia (National Anti-Mafia Bureau). Tel: +39 06 682821, fax: +39 06 689 2611, URL: http://www.giustizia.it

LOCAL GOVERNMENT

Italy's constitution specifically promotes local autonomy and the decentralisation of national services. The Republic is divided into 20 regions, 110 provinces and 8,100 municipalities. The functions of the 20 autonomous regions are defined by the constitution, and they enjoy certain legislative and administrative rights in local matters as well as a degree of financial autonomy. A government commissioner maintains national control, co-ordinating regional administration with the policy of the Republic. For geographic, linguistic and cultural reasons five regions have particular autonomy: Sicily, Sardinia, Valle d'Aosta, Trentino Alto Adige and Friuli-Venezia-Giulia. The elected regional Councils have administrative authority in each region, with powers to pass laws and issue administrative regulations. In addition, each region has a regional Committee and a President usually known as a governor, both directly elected by the people.

Local elections were held in May 2013. In what was seen as a protest against the Government's austerity measures, left-wing parties prospered.

AREA AND POPULATION

Area

Italy is situated in southern Europe and is bordered in the north by Switzerland and Austria, in the east by Slovenia and the Adriatic Sea, in the south by the Mediterranean Sea and in the west by France. The Republic of Italy consists of a peninsula, the islands of Sicily, Sardinia and Elba, and some 70 other small islands. The area of Italy is 301,336 sq. km. Over a third of the land is mountainous and over a further third is hilly. The climate is generally mild Mediterranean but there are cold northern winters.

To view a map, please consult http://www.lib.utexas.edu/maps/cia08/italy_sm_2008.gif

Population

The total population at January 2011 was estimated at 60,626,442. The average annual rate of increase in the population since 1970 has been approximately 0.3 per cent. The average population density in 2007 was 196 people per sq. km. Figures for December 2010 show that a large part of the population is located in the north with 27,763,261 residents, followed by the south of the country and Islands with 20,912,859. The centre is the least populated, with 11,950,322 residents. The population is ageing. The average age of the population was 43.5 years in 2010; 14.0 per cent were aged up to 14 years and 20.3 per cent were over the age of 65. (Source: Italian National Statistical Institute)

The following table shows the population by region at the beginning of 2011:

Region	Res. Pop.
Piemonte	4,457,335
Valle d'Aosta	128,230
Lombardia	9,917,714
Trentino-Alto Adige/Südtirol	527,699
Veneto	4,937,854
Friuli-Venezia Giulia	1,235,808
Liguria	1,616,788
Emilia-Romagna	4,432,418
Toscana	3,749,813
Umbria	906,486
Marche	1,565,335
Lazio	5,728,688
Abruzzo	1,342,366
Molise	319,780
Campania	5,834,056
Puglia	4,091,259
Basilicata	587,517
Calabria	2,011,395
Sicilia	5,051,075
Sardegna	1,675,411

- continued
Total   60,626,442
Source: ISTAT

The number of those born outside Italy, but permanently resident there reached 4,279,000 in January 2010, up 388,000 compared to January 2009. The foreign resident population makes up 7.5 per cent of the total population, compared to 6.5 per cent in 2008. The top five places of origin are: Albania, Morocco, Romania, China and the Ukraine. Permanent residents from the United Kingdom numbered around 22,300, whilst those from the US numbered approximately 14,150.

Italian, the official language, comprises a number of regional dialects.

Births, Marriages, Deaths
In 2010, 557,000 births were registered, down from 576,659 in 2008. The estimated birth rate in 2010 fell slightly to 9.2 live births per 1,000 inhabitants, whilst the estimated number of deaths was 587,000 with a death rate of 9.7 deaths per 1,000 people. The natural population balance was -30,200. The immigration rate fell from 10.6 per 1,000 inhabitants in 2003 to an estimated 3.9 in 2006. The total migration rate in 2009 and 2010 was 6.0 and was the main factor in population growth. In 2010, the migration balance was 365,000. Other contributing factors to the rising birth rate include: continuous increase older mothers giving birth, increase of births to foreign couples. In 2008, foreign female citizens had on average 2.31 children per female. The fertility rate for Italian women in 2010 was (1.41). The age at which an Italian woman has her first child increased from 25.2 in 1981 to 31.3 in 2009.

The low birth rate and its implications for the economy in the future continue to be a source of concern. Italy has the third lowest fertility rate in Europe (after Greece, 1.29 and Spain, 1.32). This is below the European population replacement rate of 2.1 children per woman. Reasons cited for the low birth rate have been that there are more women working (47 per cent of the workforce are now women); the university courses are long and therefore the start of a career and family life are late, and Italy has inflexible working conditions and low government spending on child-related issues, neither of which encourage women to combine raising a family and working outside the home.

Estimates for 2008 indicate that there were 246,613 marriages over the year (a rate of 4 marriages per 1,000 population), generally in line with the overall decline in marriages which began in the 1970s (7.7 per 1,000 population). The age of a first marriage continued to rise; in 2008, the average age for men to first marry was 33 years, and for women, 29.9 years. 34.4 per cent of marriages in 2007 were civil ceremonies, rising to over 74 per cent in Siena and 67 per cent in Florence. Latest figures indicate that divorces continue to rise; in 2005, there were around 47,000 divorces and some 82,000 separations.

The population is aging. As of January 2010, 14 per cent of the population was aged 0-14 years (14.3 per cent in 2000), 65.8 per cent was aged between 15 to 64 years, and some 20.32 per cent (18.1 per cent in 2000) of the population was aged 65 years and over. The mean age of the population was 43.3.

Life expectancy at birth in 2010 was estimated at 79.1 years for men and 84.3 years for women. (Source: Istituto Nazionale di Statistica, ISTAT)

Public Holidays 2014
1 January: New Year's Day (Capodanno)
6 January: Epiphany (Epifania)
18-20 April: Easter (Pasqua)
21 April: Easter Monday (Lunedì di Pasqua)
25 April: Anniversary of the Liberation (Liberazione)
1 May: Labour Day (Festa del Lavoro)
2 June: Anniversary of the Republic
15 August: Assumption of the Virgin (L'Assunzione)
1 November: All Saints Day (Tutti i Santi)
8 December: Immaculate Conception (Festa dell'Immacolata)
25 December: Christmas Day (Natale)
26 December: St. Stephen (Santo Stefano)

If a public holiday falls on a weekend that holiday is not moved to a weekday instead.

In addition, the following holidays are celebrated in major cities:
24 June: St. John's Day (Florence)
29 June: St. Peter's and St. Paul's Day (Rome)
19 September: St. Gennaro's Day (Naples)
7 December: St. Ambrogio's Day (Milan)

EMPLOYMENT

Provisional figures for the first quarter of 2011 show that 22.9 million people were employed. The employment rate was 56.8 per cent, the number of people unemployed was 2.2 million giving an unemployment rate of 8.6 per cent. In January 2012 provisional figures showed that 22.9 million people were employed, the employment rate was 57.0 pr cent, the unemployment rate was 9.2 per cent. Figures for January 2013 put unemployment at an all time high of 11.7 per cent, in February 2013 the unemployment rate fell slightly to 11.5 per cent and remained the same in March. Forecast figures for 2013 as a whole put the unemployment rate at 11.9 per cent rising to 12.3 per cent in 2014.

The unemployment rate was 8.5 per cent in 2010. The average number of unemployed people in 2009 was 2.1 million (equivalent to a rate of 8.6 per cent). However, unemployment among those under 25 is considerably higher, at 20.3 per cent. Unemployment is higher in the south (10.8 per cent) than in the north of the country (3.4 per cent). The inactivity rate was 37.6

per cent in May 2010. Inadequate infrastructure, corruption, and organised crime act as disincentives to investment and job creation in the south. A significant underground economy absorbs substantial numbers of people. (Source: ISTAT)

Employment according to area, 2007

Area	Workforce	Employed	Unemployed	Unemployed %
North	12,353,000	11,921,000	432,000	3.5
Centre	5,052,000	4,785,000	267,000	5.3
South	7,324,000	6,516,000	808,000	11.0
Total	**24,728,000**	**23,222,000**	**1,506,000**	**6.1**

Source: ISTAT

Employment by Economic Activity ('000s)

Sector	2007	2008
Agriculture	888,000	860,000
Mining & quarrying	39,000	36,000
Manufacturing, fuel and power products	4,870,000	4,805,000
Electricity, gas & water supply	139,000	144,000
Building and construction	1,955,000	1,970,000
Wholesale & retail trade & repairs	3,541,000	3,450,000
Hotels & restaurants	1,154,000	1,179,000
Transport, storage & communications	1,257,000	1,294,000
Financial intermediation	664,000	653,000
Real estate, renting & business activities	2,542,000	2,618,000
Public admin. & defence, compulsory social security	1,418,000	1,436,000
Education	1,606,000	1,584,000
Health & social work	1,575,000	1,659,000
Other community, social & personal service activities	1,167,000	1,136,000
Households with employed persons	349,000	419,000
Extra-territorial organisations & bodies	22,000	36,000

Source: Copyright © International Labour Organization (ILO Dept. of Statistics, http://laborsta.ilo.org)

Unions represent 40 per cent of the workforce and are grouped into three major confederations: the Italian General Confederation of Labour (CGIL) (URL: http://www.cgil.it/), the Italian Confederation of Labour Unions (CISL) (URL: http://www.cisl.it/) and the Union of Italian Labour (UIL) (URL: http://www.uil.it/).

BANKING AND FINANCE

Currency
One euro (€) = 100 cents
€ = 1,936.27 lire (European Central Bank irrevocable conversion rate)
On 1 January 1999 the euro was launched as an electronic currency across the 12 member states of the EU. On 1 January 2002 the euro became legal tender in Italy and the 11 other member states of the EU. Italy's old currency, the lire, ceased to be legal tender from 28 February 2002. Euro banknotes come in denominations of 5, 10, 20, 50, 100, 200, and 500. Euro coins come in denominations of 2 and 1 euros, 50, 20, 10, 5, 2, and 1 cents.

GDP / GNP, Inflation, National Debt
Italy is a land of few natural resources. Economic strength lies in the processing and manufacturing of goods, mainly in small and medium sized family-owned firms. The economy grew by only 0.66 per cent per annum over the five years ending in 2005, lower than the euro-zone average. It grew by 1.9 per cent in 2006, and, in 2007, GDP at current prices reached €1,535,540 billion, indicating annual growth of 1.7 per cent. The North-west and North-east of the country contributed 31.8 per cent and 22.6 per cent of GDP respectively; the centre produced 21.6 per cent of GDP, whilst the south accounted for 24 per cent. Growth slowed again as world economies moved into recession and Italy was officially declared to be in recession in November 2008 after two consecutive quarters of negative growth. Italy remained in recession in 2009 as negative growth continued. Italian GDP fell slightly in the last quarter of 2009 and growth for the year was estimated to be -5.2 per cent. Investment, particularly in construction, continued to contract and consumption was stagnant. GDP was put at €1,520,870 millions in 2009, down 3 per cent from 2008. GDP growth was estimated at 1.3 in 2010. Estimated figures for 2011 put GDP growth (at current prices) at 1.7 per cent, giving a figure of €1,580,220 million. The growth was attributed to a growth in exports of 5.6 per cent. Forecast figures for 2013 showed that the economy would shrink by a further 1.4 per cent but would show a small growth of 0.7 per cent in 2014. The fall in the economy was put down to a fall in private consumption and import growth remaining sluggish.

Italy was one of the first countries to approve a stimulus programme in response to the global financial downturn. In November, the government approved an €80bn emergency package that included tax breaks for poorer families, public works projects and mortgage relief.

Italy has the world's third-highest debt burden, over 110 per cent of GDP in 2009. There is a large 'black' economy in Italy, worth some 27 per cent of national GDP. In 2011, its financial rating was cut amidst fears over its high levels of debt. In 2011, its government debt stood at 118 per cent of GDP however levels of individual debt are relatively low. Italy's financial problems are mainly caused by low levels of growth (average of 0.75 per cent economic growth over the last 15 years) rather than over spending on public services. The financial ratings agency S&P downgraded Italy's financial rating to AAA in 2011, and warned it might downgrade it further unless the growth rate improved. Eurozone leaders have been pressing for structural reform to stimulate growth. In January 2012, the US ratings agency Fitch, downgraded Italy's credit rating to A-.

ITALY

Since the end of the World War II, the Italian economy has changed from an agriculture-based to a services-based economy. The service sector contributes approximately 73 per cent, industry 20 per cent, construction 6.0 per cent and agriculture just 2 per cent.

The following table shows Italy's supply and uses account in recent years (€million at current prices):

Resources & Uses	2008	2009	2010
GDP at market prices (€ million)	1,567,761	1,519,702	1,548,816
Imports of goods & services (fob)	461,273	368,682	442,163
TOTAL RESOURCES	2,029,034	1,888,384	1,990,979
Domestic consumption	1,245,527	1,238,548	1,263,509
Gross fixed capital formation	325,507	289,680	301,286
Changes of inventories	5,086	-4,424	8,845
Valuables	2,370	2,131	2,611
Exports of goods & services (fob)	450,543	362,449	414,728
TOTAL USES	2,029,034	1,888,384	1,990,979

Source: ISTAT

The inflation rate (as measured by Italy's Consumer Price Index) rose by 1.8 per cent in 2007. The greatest annual rises were seen in alcoholic beverages and tobacco (3.4 per cent), and food and beverages (2.9 per cent). There was a drop of 8.4 per cent in the cost of communications. (Source: ISTAT). Inflation was put at 1.3 per cent in 2009. For the period April 2010-11 it was estimated at 2.9 per cent.

Foreign Investment

Total direct investment in Italy amounted to an estimated €218,035 million as at June 2006, whilst investment abroad reached €170,120 million, giving a net position of € 47,915 million. However, the overall investment position at June 2006 indicated more outward investment (€1.4 million) than inward (€1.6 million). (Source: ISTAT)

Balance of Payments / Imports and Exports

Italy's imports traditionally exceed its exports, and to make up the adverse balance of trade it has relied on invisible exports such as receipts from tourists, shipping and the substantial remittances from Italian emigrants. In 2007, earnings on exports of goods (fob) reached €358,633 million. However, the cost of imports of goods (cif) increased to €368,080 million, resulting in a trade deficit of €9,447 million. Italy struggles with the effects of globalisation; countries such as China have eroded the Italian lower-end industrial product sector. The world wide recession has had a dramatic adverse effect on Italy's foreign trade. In 2009, imports were €370,582 million, down 19.7 per cent from 2008. Exports were €364,539 million, down 19.5 per cent from 2008. However, there foreign trade improved in 2010; exports of goods and services grew by 9.1 per cent (although growth dropped to 1.9 per cent in Q4) and imports of goods and services rose to 10.5 per cent.

Chief imports are raw materials (including energy products) for industry, mechanical products, transportation equipment, wool, cotton and basic food-stuffs. Principal exports are engineering products, textiles, machinery, motor cars, chemicals, fruit and vegetables. The following table shows imports and exports by branch, for 2010. Figures are provisional and in € million:

Branch	Imports	Exports
Agriculture & fishing	11,099	5,597
Mining & quarrying products	57,842	1,306
Food, beverages & tobacco	25,248	22,189
Textiles & clothing, leather & leather products	25,543	37,284
Wood & wood products, paper & printing	9,977	7,145
Coke & refined petroleum products	8,301	14,667
Chemicals & man made fibres	31,882	22,527
Pharmaceutical, medicinal chemical & botanical products	17,151	14,010
Rubber & plastics & other non-metallic mineral products	11,278	20,815
Basic metals & fabricated metal products excluding machinery & equipment	35,964	39,325
Computer, electronic & optical equipment	32,057	11,585
Electrical equipment	13,176	19,380
Machinery & equipment n.e.c.	22,252	60,089
Transport equipment	37,737	34,411
Other manufactured products	10,461	18,912
Electricity, gas, steam & air conditioning supply	3,959	1,055
Other products	11,023	7,285
TOTAL	364,950	337,584

Source: ISTAT

Most trade (some 58 per cent) is within the European Union; other major trading partners are the USA, China, Japan, Turkey, Russia. Top trading partners are shown on the following table:

Top trading partners in 2010 (provisional data) €millions

Country	Exports
Germany	43,815
France	39,055
United States	20,408
Spain	19,606
	Imports
Germany	58,234
France	30,382

- continued

China	28,572
Netherlands	19,473
Spain	16,306

Source: ISTAT

Central Bank
Banca d'Italia, Via Nazionale 91, 00184 Rome, RM Italy. Tel: +39 06 47921, fax: +39 06 4792 2983, URL: http://www.bancaditalia.it
Governor: Ignazio Visco (page 1532)

Stock Exchanges
Commissione Nazionale per le Società e la Borsa (CONSOB), URL: http://www.l-sparenta.it
Italian Stock Exchange/Derivatives Market, URL: http://www.borsaitalia.it

Chambers of Commerce and Trade Organisations
Istituto Nazionale per il Commercio Estero (National Institute for Foreign Trade), URL: http://www.ice.it
Milan Chamber of Commerce, URL: http://eng.mi.camcom.it/
Rome Chamber of Commerce, URL: http://www.rm.camcom.it
Venezia Chamber of Commerce, URL: http://www.ve.camcom.it/
Italy-America Chamber of Commerce Inc, URL: http://www.italchamber.org/

MANUFACTURING, MINING AND SERVICES

Primary and Extractive Industries
Italy is a large importer of coal, oil and petroleum products, iron ore, pyrites and iron, and steel scrap. To make up for its lack of domestic fuel sources, Italy has developed one of the largest hydro-electric industries in western Europe.

Italy relies almost completely (91 per cent) on imports for its oil requirements, about 70 per cent of which come from the Middle East and North Africa. In 2006, Italy's major suppliers were Russia (16 per cent), Libya (27 per cent), and Saudi Arabia (12 per cent).

Italy is increasing domestic oil production to reduce reliance on imports. Proven oil reserves at the beginning of January 2009 were estimated at 400 million barrels (the third-largest in the EU), and production was estimated at 146,500 barrels per day. Oil consumption was an estimated 1,527 million barrels per day. In 2009, Italy had the seventh largest refining capacity in the world, at 2.3 million barrels per day. A net exporter of refined petroleum products, Italy imported 260,000 bbl/d of petroleum products in 2006, and exported 560,000 bbl/d. (mainly to Spain, Belgium and the USA).

Italy's main oil and gas company is Ente Nazionale Idrocarburi (ENI). Previously a wholly state-owned company, the company has been largely privatised, and 35 per cent of shares are now owned by the Government. ENI's chief subsidiaries are Agip (hydrocarbons exploration and production), Snam (gas supplies and hydrocarbon transportation), and ENIchem (petrochemicals).

Italy's natural gas reserves were 2 trillion cubic feet at the beginning of January 2011. Natural gas production was estimated at 283 billion cubic feet in 2009, with consumption an estimated 2.75 trillion cubic feet. Italy is the third largest gas market in Europe, after Germany and the UK, relying heavily on natural gas imports for about 84 per cent of its requirements.

Following liberalisation in accordance with EU requirements, ENI's share of total natural gas delivered to the national grid has declined from almost 100 per cent to 68 per cent in 2003. In November 2005, the governments of Italy and Greece signed an agreement to build a 500 mile natural gas pipeline running from northern Greece to south-eastern Italy, under the Strait of Otranto. The system will be an extension of a pipeline currently being built between Greece and Turkey, and will therefore give Italy potential access to natural gas supplies in Central Asia and the Middle East.

Italy closed its last coal mine in 2001; in 2003, coal was used for just 7.3 per cent of the country's primary energy requirements, one of the lowest levels in the EU. In 2010, 23.3 million short tons were consumed, mainly by the power generation industry. Major coal suppliers are South Africa, Colombia and the United States. (Source: Energy Information Administration, EIA)

Energy
Italy's total energy consumption was estimated at 7.320 quadrillion Btu in 2009. Per capita energy consumption in 2005 was an estimated 138.9 million Btu, compared with 340.5 million Btu in the US, and with 146.4 million Btu over Europe.

In 2010, Italy had electricity generating capacity of 106.1 gigawatts, over 80 per cent of which was from conventional thermal sources. Hydroelectricity provided around 13 per and 4 per cent was from renewable energy sources. In the same year, 283.2 billion kilowatthours (Bkwh) of electricity was generated, but this was outstripped by consumption, which was 306.83 BkWh. The shortfall was met by imports from Switzerland, France and Slovenia. Blackouts in 2003 due to reliance on foreign imports and the lack of domestic reserve capacity, led the Government to encourage investment in the industry and to look at other sources of power generation.

The high cost of oil, used in most of Italy's conventional thermal plants, has meant that Italians currently pay much higher rates than the rest of Europe for its electricity. The country has increased its use of gas-fired plants and, in February 2009, the power company, ENEL agreed a deal with its French counterpart, EDF, to study the feasibility of building four power stations in Italy. They will replace those closed in accordance with a referendum held after the Chernobyl nuclear accident in 1986. Plans to build nuclear power plants were shelved after the disaster at the Fukushima reactor in Japan. The situation will be reassessed in the future. Italy is the only European member of the G8 not to have nuclear plants. It is subject to earthquakes.

A programme of building wind turbines was initiated in 2005, and Italy has the fourth largest installed geothermal capacity in the world.

Manufacturing

Italy's manufacturing industries include electronics, chemicals, computers, aerospace, robotics, steel, cars, machinery and textiles, leather, shoes, furniture and ceramics.

Official statistics (Istat) for 2005 include mining and utilities as part of the figures for manufacturing industry. In that year, there were 525,447 industrial enterprises, 488,711 of which had fewer than 20 employees. Some 4,770,000 people were employed in industry in 2005, as follows: mining and quarrying 42,400; manufacturing - 4,610,000; utilities - 117,800.

In 2005, there were 584,449 construction companies, 576,525 of which employed fewer than 20 people. Around 1,809,800 people worked in the construction industry.

Manufacturing industry's 'value added' in 2006 amounted to an estimated €218,775 million, whilst that of the construction sector was an estimated €63,257 million. The largest sectors were metalworking, processing foods, textiles, woods and other, and building construction.

Service Industries

The services industry is Italy's main source of revenue. The estimated 'value added' for the sector in 2005 was €340,668 million. The table below shows the estimated 'value added' per sector of the services industry in 2005 (€million):

Sector	Value added
Wholesale and retail trade	108,783
Hotels and restaurants	18,984
Transport, storage and communications	71,508
Real estate, information technologies, professional activities	99,684
Education	1,411
Health and other social services	21,479
Other public, social and personal services	18,820
Total Services	**340,668**

Source: ISTAT

There were an estimated 3.192 million services industry companies in 2005, 3.158 million of which employed fewer than twenty people. Wholesale and retail trade companies numbered 1,255,112 in 2005, whilst there were 1,030,922 real estate, information technology, research and professional activities companies. The sector employed around 65.6 per cent of the workforce in 2006. Over half of these were based in the north of Italy.

Tourism

In 2009, around 54,375,000 Italians travelled to and around Italy, and 41,125,000 foreigners visited. The north received most visitors. The average stay lasted 3-4 days. Most foreigners (2006 figures) came to visit towns of artistic interest (33.8 per cent) or the seaside (24.2 per cent). 18.5 per cent of Italians visited the 'art towns', most preferring a beach holiday. In 2009, it was estimated that Italian residents made 113 million trips (corresponding to 674.2 million nights), down 8 per cent from 2008. Approximately 86.6 per cent were for pleasure.

There were 134,707 accommodation places, some 96,500 of which were located in the Northern part of Italy.

Ente Nazionale Italiano per il Turismo-ENIT (National Tourist Board), URL: http://www.enit.it

Agriculture

Agriculture, forestry, fishing and hunting contributed less than 10o per cent of Italy's GDP in 2007. Employment within the sector has been declining since the 1970s; in 1971, 20.1 per cent of the Italian workforce worked on farms and in 2007 only four per cent of the workforce worked in agriculture. The agriculture sector employs most people in the South (456,000), compared with 346,000 in the North, and 122,000 in the Centre.

Approximately 12.7 million hectares of land is under cultivation, the largest areas dedicated to rotation forage (2,005,000 hectares), wheat (2,390,000 hectares), maize (916,000 hectares) and olive trees (1,147,000 hectares). In 2007, there were 1,679,000 agricultural holdings, down from 2,153,724 in 2000. The north of Italy produces grains, sugar beets, soybeans, meat and dairy products while the south specialises in producing fruits, vegetables, olive oil, wine and durum wheat.

60.3 millions of quintals of wine grapes and 13.5 millions of quintals of table grapes were harvested in 2007, and 42.6 million hectolitres of wine and must were produced. The largest wine grape growing area in 2007 was Veneto (10,446,000 quintals), followed by Puglia (7,953,000) and Sicily (7,161,000 quintals). In terms of livestock, Italy had 13.5 million swine, 7 million sheep and 4.2 million head of cattle in 2004.

The following table shows the production of main crops in 2009:

Crop	'000 quintals
Wheat	65,347
Maize	81,430
Tomato	68,781
Sugar beet	33,077
Olive trees	30,900
Citrus and fruit trees	100,922

Source: ISTAT

COMMUNICATIONS AND TRANSPORT

Travel Requirements

Citizens of the USA, Canada and Australia require a passport valid for at least three months beyond the length of stay, but do not need a visa for stays of up to 90 days. EU citizens do not require a passport if carrying a valid National Identity Card, and do not need a visa. Other nationals should contact the embassy to check visa requirements.

Italy is a signatory to the Schengen Agreement; with a Schengen visa, a visitor can travel freely throughout the Schengen zone, and there are few border stops and checks. See http://www.eurovisa.info/SchengenCountries.htm for details.

National Airlines

Alitalia, URL: http://www.alitalia.it
Air Dolomiti, URL: http://www.airdolomiti.it
Air One, URL: http://www.flyairone.it
Meridiana, URL: http://www.meridiana.it

International Airports

There are a total of 133 airports in Italy, the main ones being:
Rome (Leoanardo da Vinci - Fiumicino) Airport, URL: http://www.adr.it/fiumicino
Milan (Malpensa) Airport, URL: http://www.seamilano.eu/landing/index_en.html
Naples (Capodichino) Airport, URL: http://www.portal.gesac.it/

Aviation Authorities

Directorate General of Civil Aviation, URL: http://www.trasportinavigazione.it

Railways

There is a total of 19,459 km of track in Italy, 16,030 km of which are state owned. Rome and Milan both have small subway systems.
Ferrovie dello Stato SpA, URL: http://www.ferroviedellostato.it/

Roads

The total length of Italy's road network is 484,688 km, including 6,621 km of motorways. Vehicles are driven on the right.

Shipping

In 2006, 2,400 km of inland waterways were used for commercial shipping. The main Italian ports are Augusta, Genoa, Livorno, Melilli Oil Terminal, Ravenna, Taranto, Trieste and Venice. The Italian merchant marine comprises 604 vessels (18th largest in the world). Regular ferry services run to Regular boat and hydrofoil services run to Capri, Sardinia, Sicily and the Aeolian Islands.

Shipping Association

Confederazione Italiana Armatori-CONFITARMA, URL: http://www.confitarma.it

HEALTH

Italy's National Health Service (*Servizio Sanitario Nazionale*) was set up in 1978 to replace the state insurance system which had been in existence from the end of the Second World War. The current health service is funded by contributions from individuals and employers, and provides free health care. The health service is divided into three tiers: the State, which sets out the administrative framework for the scheme and employs the appropriate health staff; the 20 health regions which control the services in their area; and 660 local health boards (*Azienda Sanitaria Locale*).

According to the WHO, in the period 2000-10 there were 246,834 doctors (42.4 per 10,000 population), 379,213 nurses & midwives (65.2 per 10,000 population), 28,566 dentists (4.9 per 10,000 population) and 59,580 pharmacists (10.2 per 10,000 population). According to government figures, in 2007, the Italians spent a total of €130.9 billion current euros on health care, (up from €104 billion in 2002). Of this, €102.3 billion was public sector expenditure, whilst €28.6 billion was private sector spending. According to the latest WHO estimates Italy spent 9.4 per cent of GDP on health in 2009.

The following table shows the national health structure by activity and geographical area in 2007:

Category	Italy	North	Centre	South
Hospitals	1,197	409	279	509
Beds	248,776	114,445	51,526	82,605
General practitioners	46,961	20,199	10,010	16,752
National health service peadiatricians	7,657	3,141	1,494	3,022
Medical prescriptions ('000)	521,715	203,288	112,579	205,848
Non-emergency medical on-call services	3,042	768	408	1,866
Local health authorities	171	83	29	59

Source: ISTAT

According to ISTAT figures, the number of abortions, having peaked in 1982 (following legalisation in 1978) has gradually fallen; in 2003, there were 9.1 abortions per 1,000 women aged between 15 and 49, whereas in 1982 the rate was 16.7 abortions per 1,000 women. Likewise, the overall number of smokers (over 14 years) has fallen from 25.3 per cent in 1995 to 22 per cent in 2005. In 2004, an estimated 3.84 per 1,000 deaths were caused by circulatory system diseases (down from 4.46 in 1971) and 2.83 per 1,000 deaths were caused by cancer (up from 1.9 in 1971). The number of people who are obese is on the increase in 1994, 32.8 per cent of the population were overweight with 7.3 per cent classed as obese, in 2009 36.1 per cent of the population were overweight with 10.3 per cent classed as obese.

ITALY

The demographic changes in Italy, (ageing population and high immigration levels) are placing a heavier burden on the social services sector.

EDUCATION

Pre-school Education
Children from the age of three can attend a crèche or nursery school (*Asilo Nido* or *Scuola Materna*).

Primary/Secondary Education
Italy's state education system is compulsory and free of charge. It usually starts from the age of six and ends at fourteen. Nearly all state schools are the responsibility of the Ministry of Education, as is the teaching and examining at private schools. The school year lasts from September to June with holidays at Christmas and Easter.

Children spend five years from the age of six at the *Scuola Elementare*, followed by three years at the Middle School or *Scuola Media* from the age of 11 or 12. Those who pass the appropriate exams are awarded the Middle School Diploma or *Diploma di Licenza Media*. The Liceo (Upper Secondary School) prepares students for university, allowing them to specialise in a specific area of study. Courses at the Liceo last for five years and successful students are awarded the Diploma di Maturità, equivalent to A-levels.

Numbers of Schools, Pupils and Teachers, 2009-10

Type of School	No. of Schools	No. of Pupils	No. of Teachers*	Students per teacher*
Nursery school	24,221	1,680,987	82,432	12.0
Primary School	17,845	2,822,146	220,142	11.7
Lower Secondary	7,924	1,777,834	134,875	12.4
Upper Secondary	6,826	2,687,094	3214,598	11.6

* data refers to states schools
Source: ISTAT

At the end of October 2008, school pupils, university students and teachers demonstrated against a new school reform law which is expected to cut the education budget. In primary schools, there will be one all-purpose teacher per class and a grade system for pupils' behaviour which authorities say is aimed at curbing bullying. The opposition Democratic Party (PD) vowed to push for a national referendum to get the decree repealed.

Higher Education
Italy has 39 state universities as well as a number of private ones. Following recent reforms, courses can now last from three to six years depending on the subject studied.

The following table shows number of university students enrolled in 2008-09 by subject group:

Areas of Study

Subject	2008-09
Mathematics and physical science	55,306
Chemical and pharmaceutical	70,369
Life & natural sciences	85,286
Health	150,586
Engineering	204,349
Architecture	103,113
Business	238,850
Political & social sciences	197,626
Law	215,774
Humanities	158,877
Languages	96,084
Education	96,058
Psychology	68,990
Physical training	27,888
Army	2,006
Total Number of Students	**1,812,454**

Source: ISTAT

The literacy rate is estimated at 98 per cent.

RELIGION

Article 7 of the Constitution states that both State and Church are independent and sovereign in their respective spheres. Their relations are still governed by the Lateran Pact of 1929, according to which the Roman Catholic religion is recognised as the state religion, though the Constitution affirms the freedom of worship and equality before the law of all creeds. The great majority of the Italian population is Roman Catholic (80 per cent).

Italy has a religious liberty rating of 8 on a scale of 1 to 10 (10 is most freedom). (Source: World Religion Database)

Bishops' Conference, (Conferenza Episcopale Italiana), URL: http://www.chiesacattolica.it
Catholic Action, URL: http://www.azionecattolica.it

COMMUNICATIONS AND MEDIA

Newspapers
The press is very regionalised. Most newspapers are privately owned and often linked to a political party.
Corriere della Sera, URL: http://www.corriere.it/
Il Giornale, URL: http://www.ilgiornale.it/
Il Giorno, URL: http://ilgiorno.quotidiano.net/
Il Messagero di Roma, URL: http://www.ilmessaggero.it/
La Nazione, URL: http://lanazione.ilsole24ore.com/firenze/
La Repubblica, URL: http://www.repubblica.it (owned by L'Espresso Group)
Il Sole 24 Ore, URL: http://www.ilsole24ore.com/
La Stampa, URL: http://www.dariocorradino.it (owend by the Fiat Group)

Broadcasting
Radiotelevisione Italiana (RAI-TV) is a public share capital company and it was decreed that RAI would have political independence in 1975. However the Mr Berlusconi's Mediaset group operates Italy's main private TV stations. RAI-TV is also alleged to have been subject to political influence. A new media law was passed in 2004 which partially privatised Rai and created new digital TV stations. Opponents to the plan feared that the revisions gave increased potential influence to Mr Berlusconi. The pay-TV sector is dominated by the Murdoch-owned Sky Italia. There are approximately 2,500 commercial radio stations.
Radiotelevisione Italia (RAI), URL: http://www.rai.it
Mediaset, URL: http://www.mediaset.it/
La7, URL: http://www.la7.it/

Telecommunications
There are approximately 22 million fixed line telephones in Italy and by 2011 there were approximately 96 million mobile phones in use. In 2012, approximately 35 million Italians were internet users.

ENVIRONMENT

The greatest threats to the environment come from industrial emissions causing air pollution, as well as industrial and agricultural effluents which pollute rivers and lakes. Italy's total carbon dioxide emissions were estimated in 2010 at 416.37 million metric tons, ranking it 17th in the world. This was down from 449.75 million metric tons in 2008. Carbon dioxide emissions per capita in 2006 were estimated at 8.03 metric tons, lower than the US per capita emissions of 20.12 metric tons, but slightly above the European average of 7.93 metric tons. (Source. EIA) In 2009, nitrous oxide emissions were estimated to be 95,117.7 tonnes, methane emissions were estimated to be 1,713,668 metric tons, nitrogen oxides 1,167,132 metric tons and sulphur oxides 359,510 metric tons. (Source: ISTAT)

The illegal hunting and killing of wild birds remains a problem in Italy. In the north of the country hundreds of thousands of birds are trapped for sale to restaurants or as caged birds. Italy has derogated from the EU Birds Directive, allowing the netting of thrushes, lapwings, quails and skylarks in some areas. In 2002, Italy passed a hunting law giving regions the right to prolong the hunting season and allow the shooting of protected species. However, the Lega Italiana Protezione Uccelli (LIPU) had approval of the law delayed, and took action against a number of regions which had already implemented the law.

Italy is a party to the following international environmental agreements: Air Pollution, Air Pollution-Nitrogen Oxides, Air Pollution-Persistent Organic Pollutants, Air Pollution-Sulfur 85, Air Pollution-Sulfur 94, Air Pollution-Volatile Organic Compounds, Antarctic-Environmental Protocol, Antarctic-Marine Living Resources, Antarctic Seals, Antarctic Treaty, Biodiversity, Climate Change, Climate Change-Kyoto Protocol, Desertification, Endangered Species, Environmental Modification, Hazardous Wastes, Law of the Sea, Marine Dumping, Ozone Layer Protection, Ship Pollution, Tropical Timber 83, Tropical Timber 94, Wetlands, Whaling. As a member of the European Union, Italy has agreed under the terms of the 1998 Kyoto Protocol to reduce greenhouse gases 6.8 per cent below 1990 levels by 2008-12.

SPACE PROGRAMME

The Italian Space Agency (ASI - Agenzia Spaziale Italiana) was founded in 1988 and is responsible for the promotion and co-ordination of Italian space activities. Italy joined the following European space organisations: European Launch Development Organization (ELDO) in 1964; European Space Research Organization (ESRO) in 1975; and the European Space Agency (ESA), which was founded following the fusion of ELDO and ESRO. Italy is the third largest contributor to ESA's space programmes after France and Germany.

Agenzia Spaziale Italiana (ASI - Italian Space Agency), URL: http://www.asi.it

JAMAICA

Capital: Kingston (Population estimate, 2010: 930,000)

Head of State: Queen Elizabeth II, Queen of England (page 1420)

Governor General: The Hon. Dr. Patrick Linton Allen (page 1375)

National Flag: On a field quartered wedge-wise green and black, a gold saltire

CONSTITUTION AND GOVERNMENT

Constitution
Jamaica was discovered by Christopher Columbus on 4 May 1494. It remained a Spanish possession until 1655, when it came under British rule. On 6 August 1962 Jamaica became independent after over 300 years as a British colony and the Constitution established a parliamentary system based on the UK model. As chief of state, Queen Elizabeth II appoints a governor-general, on the advice of the prime minister, as her representative in Jamaica. The governor-general's role is largely ceremonial. Executive power is vested in the cabinet, led by the prime minister.

To consult the constitution, please visit: http://www.moj.gov.jm/law.

International Relations
Jamaica is a member of the UN, the Organisation of American States, the Commonwealth, CARICOM and the Association of Caribbean States.

Recent Events
In September 2004, Jamaica was badly hit by Hurricane Ivan; 20 people were killed and damage to homes and infrastructure was severe. The agriculture sector was badly affected, particularly the banana crop.

In April 2003 Prime Minister Patterson stood down from his position; he had been prime minister since 1992. Portia Simpson Miller was elected as head of the ruling People's National Party and became Jamaica's first female prime minister in March 2006.

Jamaica has a growing crime problem particularly with violent gangs. The island is a major trans-shipment point for drugs; cocaine arrives from South America and is shipped on to North America and Europe. Jamaica has one of the highest murder rates in the world with recent figures putting the murder rate at 50 per 100,000 population. In November 2008 Jamaica voted to retain the death penalty.

In May 2010 dozens of people were killed in fighting when security forces attempted to arrest an alleged drug lord Christopher "Dudus" Coke who was wanted in the USA. Many Kingston residents who regarded him as a benefactor fought against police to protect him. A state of emergency was in place in some areas of the capital. He was finally arrested in June 2010.

In September 2011 the Jamaica Labour Party announced that the prime minister Bruce Golding was to step down in November. Andrew Holness took over the post, before losing a snap election held in December.

In January 2012 on taking office as Prime Minister, Portia Simpson-Miller said that it was time for Jamaica to break from the United Kingdom and become a republic.

Legislature
Parliament is composed of an appointed Senate and an elected House of Representatives. The member of the House who, in the opinion of the Governor-General, can best command the confidence of a majority of the members of that Chamber, is appointed prime minister.

General control and direction of Government policy rests in the hands of the Cabinet, which is collectively responsible to Parliament. The Cabinet consists of the Prime Minister and not less than eleven other Ministers appointed from both Houses by the Governor-General on the advice of the Prime Minister. Between two and four Ministers may be appointed from the Senate. At present the cabinet consists of the Prime Minister and 16 other ministers. There are also three Parliamentary Secretaries.

Upper House
The Senate consists of 21 people, 13 of whom are appointed by the Governor-General on the advice of the prime minister and the remaining eight on the advice of the Leader of the Opposition. The Senate functions mainly as a review chamber and reviews legislation passed by the House of Representatives.
The Senate, Houses of Parliament, 81 Duke Street, PO Box 636, Kingston, Jamaica. Tel: +1 876 922 0200, fax +1 876 967 0064.

Lower House
The House of Representatives is elected at least once every five years by universal adult suffrage and consists of 60 members.
House of Representatives, Gordon House, 81 Duke Street, Kingston, Jamaica. Tel: +1 876 922 0200, fax: +1 876 967 0064, URL: http://www.mct.gov.jm/parliament.htm

Cabinet (as at June 2013)
Prime Minister and Minister of Defence, Development, Information and Sports: Hon. Portia Simpson-Miller (page 1515)
Deputy Prime Minister, Minister of Finance, Planning and Public Service: Hon. Dr Peter Phillips (page 1495)
Minister of Agriculture and Fisheries: Hon. Roger Clarke (page 1405)

Minister of Water, Land, Environment and Climate Change: Hon. Robert Pickersgill (page 1495)
Minister of Health: Hon. Dr Fenton Ferguson
Minister of Justice: Hon. Mark Golding
Minister of National Security: Hon. Peter Bunting
Minister of Industry, Investment and Commerce: Hon. Anthony Hylton (page 1446)
Minister of Labour and Social Security: Hon. Derrick Kellier
Minister of Culture and Youth: Hon. Lisa Hanna
Minister of Tourism and Environment: Hon. Dr Wykeham McNeill
Minister of Energy, Mining and ICT: Hon. Phillip Paulwell (page 1493)
Minister of Transport, Works and Housing: Hon. Dr Omar Davies
Minister of Foreign Affairs and Foreign Trade: Senator the Hon. Arnold Nicholson (page 1486)
Minister of Education: Hon. Rev. Ronald Thwaites
Minister of Local Government and Community Development: Hon. Noel Arscott
Minister without portfolio in the Office of the Prime Minister with responsibillity for Sports: Hon. Natalaie Neita-Headley
Minister without portfolio in the Ministry of Transport, Works and Housing with responsibility for Housing: Hon. Dr Marais Guy
Minister without Portfolio, in the Office of the Prime Minister with responsibility for Information: Senator the Hon. Sandrea Falconer
Minister without portfolio in the Ministry of Finance, Planning and Public Service: Hon. Horace Dalley

Ministries
Office of the Prime Minister, 1 Devon Road, Kingston 6, Jamaica. Tel: +1 876 927 9941- 3, fax: +1 876 929 0005, e-mail: cablib@cwjamaica.com, URL: http://www.cabinet.gov.jm
Office of the Deputy Prime Minister, 1 Devon Road, Kingston 10, Jamaica. Tel +1 876 926 1590 / 7008, fax: +1 876 927 99413, cablib@cwjamaica.com, URL: http://www.cabinet.gov.jm
Ministry of Finance and Planning, 30 National Heroes Circle, Kingston 4, Jamaica. Tel: +1 876 922 8600, fax +1 876 922 7097, e-mail: info@mof.gov.jm, URL: http://www.mof.gov.jm
Ministry of Local Government, Community Development and Sport, 85 Hagley Park Road, Kingston 10, Jamaica. Tel +1 876 754 0994, fax:+1 876 960 0725, URL: http://www.mlgycd.gov.jm
Ministry of Foreign Affairs and Foreign Trade, 21 Dominica Drive, Kingston 5, Jamaica. Tel: +1 876 926 4220-8, fax: +1 876 929 5112, URL: http://www.mfaft.gov.jm
Ministry of Transport and Works, 138h Maxfield Avenue, Kingston 10, Jamaica. Tel: +1 876 754 1900, fax: +1 876 927 8763, e-mail: ps@mtw.gov.jm, URL: http://www.mtw.gov.jm
Ministry of National Security, Mutual Life North Tower, 2 Oxford Road, Kingston 5, Jamaica. Tel: +1 876 906 4908-33, fax +1 876 906 1724, e-mail: inform@infochan.com URL: http://www.mns.gov.jm
Ministry of Information, Youth, Sport and Culture, 2 National Heroes Circle, Kingston 4, Jamaica. Tel:+1 876 922 1400-19, fax: +1 876 967 1837, e-mail: webmaster@moec.gov.jm, URL: http://www.moec.gov.jm
Ministry of Agriculture, Hope Gardens, Kingston 6, Jamaica. Tel: +1 876 927 1731-45, fax +1 876 927 1904, URL: http://www.moa.gov.jm
Ministry of Health & Environment, Oceana Hotel Complex, 2 King Street, Kingston, Jamaica. Tel: +1 876 967 1092, fax: +1 876 967 7293, e-mail: palmerr@moh.gov.jm, URL: http://www.moh.gov.jm
Ministry of Local Government and Community Development, 85 Hagley Park, Kingston 10, Jamaica. Tel: +1 876 754 09929, fax: +1 876 960 0725
Ministry of Water and Housing, 25 Dominica Drive, The Towers, Jamaica. Tel: +1 876 926 1691, fax: +1 876 754 2855, URL: http://www.mtw.gov.jm
Ministry of Industry, Commerce, and Investment, PCJ Building, 36 Trafalgar Road, Kingston 10, Jamaica. Tel: +1 876 754 5501, fax: +1 876 960 1623, e-mail: communications@mct.gov.jm, URL: http://www.mct.gov.jm
Ministry of Labour and Social Security, 1F North Street, Kingston, Jamaica. Tel: +1 876 922 9500, fax: +1 876 922 6902, URL: http://www.lmis-elel.org.jm
Ministry of Justice and Attorney General's Dept., Mutual Life Bldg., North Tower, 2 Oxford Road, Kingston 5, Jamaica. Tel: +1 876 906 4908, URL: http://www.moj.gov.jm
Ministry of Tourism, 64 Knutsford Boulevard, Kingston 5, Jamaica. Tel: +1 876 920 4926, fax: +1 876 920 4944, email: mts@cwjamaica.com
Ministry of Energy and Mining, PCJ Building, 36 Trafalgar Road, Kingston 10, Jamaica. Tel: +1 876 929 8990, fax: +1 876 960 1623, e-mail: info@mem.gov.jm

Political Parties
People's National Party, URL: http://www.pnp.org.jm
Leader: Portia Simpson-Miller
Jamaica Labour Party, URL: http://www.jlpteam.com
Leader: Bruce Golding
National Coalition (merger of the New Nation Coalition and the National Democratic Party), URL: http://www.nnc.org.jm
Leader: Betty Ann Blaine

Elections
The most recent parliamentary elections were held on 29 December 2011. The People's National Party won 42 seats ousting the Jamaica Labour Party who won 21 seats.

Diplomatic Representation
US Embassy, Jamaica Mutual Life Centre, 2 Oxford Road, 3rd Floor, Kingston 5, Jamaica. Tel: +1 876 935 6053, fax: +1 876 9293637, e-mail: opakgn@pd.state.gov, URL: http://kingston.usembassy.gov

JAMAICA

Ambassador: Pamela Bridgewater (page 1394)
British High Commission, PO Box 575, Trafalgar Road, Kingston 10, Jamaica. Tel: +1 876 510 0700, fax: +1 876 511 5304, e-mail: bhckingston@cwjamaica.com,
URL: https://www.gov.uk/government/world/jamaica
High Commissioner: David Fitton CMG
Jamaican Embassy, 1520 New Hampshire Avenue NW, Washington, DC 20036, USA. Tel: +1 202 452 0660, fax, +1 202 452 0081, URL: http://www.embassyofjamaica.org
Ambassador: Stephen Vasciannie
Jamaican High Commission, 1-2 Prince Consort Road, London, SW7 2BZ, UK. Tel: +44 (0)20 7823 9911, fax: +44 (0)20 7589 5154, e-mail: jamhigh@jhcuk.com, URL: http://jhcuk.org/
High Commissioner: Aloun Ndombet-Assamba
Permanent Mission of Jamaica to the United Nations, 767 Third Avenue 9th and 10th Floors, New York, NY 10017, USA Tel: +1 212 935 7509 fax: +1 212 935 7607, e-mail: jamaica@un.int, URL: http://www.un.int/jamaica
Permanent Representative: Raymond Wolfe

LEGAL SYSTEM

The Jamaican judiciary and legal system are based on English common law and practice.

Justice is administered through a Supreme Court, a Court of Appeal, and Magistrates' Courts as well as through Traffic Courts, Courts of Petty Sessions, a Gun Court, a Family Court, a Juvenile Court and a Revenue Court. Judges of the Supreme Court include the Chief Justice, a Senior Puisne Judge and 16 Puisne Judges. The Court of Appeal consists of a President, appointed by the Governor-General on recommendation of the Prime Minister, and Justices of Appeal.

In the past, certain cases could be appealed to the Privy Council of the UK. However, in 2003, Jamaica was one of a number of Caribbean countries who joined the Caribbean Court of Justice, which dispenses with the need for referral of cases to London.

While the government respects the human rights of its citizens, there have been unlawful killings committed by members of the security forces. There have also been reports of abuse of prisoners by prison guards, poor jail conditions. The judicial system is overburdened and trials can be delayed. Jamaica retains the death penalty although this has not been used since 1988. Jamaican MPs voted to keep the death penalty in 2008.

Supreme Court of Jamaica, URL: http://www.supremecourt.gov.jm/
Chief Justice: The Hon. Zaila McGalla

Office of the Public Defender, URL: http://www.opd.gov.jm/

LOCAL GOVERNMENT

Jamaica is divided into three counties, Cornwall, Middlesex and Surrey. These are divided into 14 parishes, St. Thomas, Portland, St. Mary, St. Ann, Trelawny, St. James, Hanover, Westmoreland, St. Elizabeth, Manchester, Clarendon, and St. Catherine, Kingston and St. Andrew (known as the Kingston and St. Andrew Corp.(KSAC) for local government purposes). The Department of Local Government carries out its functions through local authorities made up of 12 parish councils, the Portmore Municipal Council and the KSAC. The political side of the local authority is composed of councillors headed by a mayor.

AREA AND POPULATION

Area
Jamaica is the third largest of the Caribbean islands, situated in the Caribbean Sea 965.4 km. south of Florida, 160.9 km. southwest of Haiti and 144.81 km. south of Cuba. The total area is 10,991 sq. km and is mostly mountainous. The climate is tropical at sea level, but more temperate in the mountainous areas.

To view a map of Jamaica, please consult:
http://www.lib.utexas.edu/maps/americas/jamaica_pol_2002.pdf

Population
The population is approximately 2.741 million according to 2010 estimates, with an average annual growth rate of 0.6 per cent in the period 2000-10. An estimated 52 per cent of the population live in urban areas. The population of the capital, Kingston, is around 930,000. Other large cities include Montego Bay with a population of over 100,000 and Spanish Town with a population of some 150,000. The official language is English but Patois and regional dialects are common.

Ethnic groups are made up of African 90.9 per cent, East Indian 1.3 per cent, Chinese 0.2 per cent, Caucasian 0.2 per cent, mixed 7.3 per cent and others 0.1 per cent.

Births, Marriages, Deaths
Estimated figures for 2010 put the crude birth rate at 18.4 births per 1,000 population and the death rate at 7.9 deaths per 1,000 population. The infant mortality rate was estimated at 26 per 1,000 births in 2009 and the neonatal mortality rate at 12 per 1,000 live births in 2009. The maternal mortality rate was estimated by the government at 89 per 100,000 live births in 2009 although other agencies put the figure as some 40 per cent higher. The total fertility rate for women was estimated at 2.3 in 2010.

In 2009, life expectancy was estimated at 69 years for males and 74 years for females. Healthy life expectancy was estimated at 62 years for males and 66 years for females (2007). Approximately 29 per cent of the population is aged under 15 years and 11 per cent over 60 years. The median age was 27. (Source: http://www.who.int, World Health Statistics 2012)

Public Holidays 2014
1 January: New Year's Day
5 March: Ash Wednesday
18 April: Good Friday
21 April: Easter Monday
23 May: National Labour Day
31 July: Emancipation Day (Thursday preceding first Monday in August)
6 August: Independence Day
17 October: National Heroes' Day
25 December: Christmas Day
26 December: Boxing Day

EMPLOYMENT

The service sector is the largest employer, employing an estimated 65 per cent of the work force. Agriculture employs 18 per cent and industry 17 per cent. Estimated figures for 2006 put the unemployment rate at 11 per cent falling to an estimated 9.5 per cent in 2007. Figures for 2008 put the workforce at 1,167,800, with 10.3 per cent unemployed.

Employment by Economic Activity

Sector	2008
Agriculutre, hunting, forestry & fishing	222,600
Mining & quarrying	9,200
Manufacturing	68,000
Electricity, gas & water supply	9,000
Construction	106,100
Wholesale & retail trade & repairs	265,200
Hotels & restaurants	265,200
Transport, storage & communications	81,300
Financial, insurance, real estate & business services	77,800
Other community, social & personal service activities	326,600
Other	1,400
Total	1,167,800

Source: Copyright © International Labour Organization (ILO Dept. of Statistics, http://laborsta.ilo.org)

BANKING AND FINANCE

Currency
The unit of currency is the Jamaican dollar of 100 cents. The financial centre is Kingston.

GDP/GNP, Inflation, National Debt
The development of Jamaica's economy has been obstructed by longstanding external debt and trade deficit. In early 2010, the Jamaican government created the Jamaica Debt Exchange (JDX) to try to reduce annual debt servicing. Despite loans from multilaterals debt servicing costs remain high and hinder the government's ability to spend on infrastructure and social programs. Although the government's continuing tight controls on the economy has kept inflation down, it has led to a slowdown in economic growth which has caused hardship amongst the poor. There has been civil unrest and a rising crime rate; Jamaica has one of the highest murder rates in the world. The crime rate threatens to undermine Jamaica's economy with fears that it may affect tourism, one of the country's biggest earners. The economy has also been affected by hurricanes. The country is still suffering the effects of Hurricane Sandy which damaged its infrastructure.

Jamaica derives most of its foreign exchange from the tourism sector, remittances from Jamaicans living and working abroad and the bauxite industry. However in 2009 three of the four bauxite firms had to suspend operations due to the global downturn in demand; operations have since resumed.

At the beginning of 2010 the Government signed a US $1.27 billion, 27-month Standby Arrangement with the IMF to support the country's economic reforms. The government has also privatized Air Jamaica and is considering selling of former sugar estates.

The government is actively seeking foreign investment as a way of boosting the economy and generating employment. Annual growth rate was 1.8 per cent in 2005/06. In 2008, the growth rate was -0.6 per cent. Estimated figures for 2009 put GDP at US$12.6 billion, with a growth rate of -3.0 per cent. In 2010 GDP was estimated to be US$13 billion with a growth rate of -1.5 per cent. Positive growth returned in 2011 (estimated at over 1 per cent), and GDP was estimated to be US$14 billion. Per capita GDP was US$4,500 in 2010. Growth is expected to be neglible or even negative in 2013.

The average annual inflation rate over the period 1990-96 was 36 per cent, but has fallen since. It fell into single digits in 2011: 7.5 per cent compared to over 12 per cent in 2010. Jamaica's total external debt in 2011 was an estimated US$14 billion. Public debt is estimated to be over 125 per cent of GDP.

Foreign Investment
More than 80 US firms have operations in Jamaica, and total US investment is estimated at more than US$1 billion. To encourage trade and investment there is a Free Zone at Kingston as well as fiscal conditions beneficial to foreign investors. Jamaica joined the IMF in a Staff Monitored Programme (SMP) in 2000 with a view to increasing foreign investment. Jamaica is a founder member of CARICOM (the Caribbean Community and Common Market) and the Inter-American Development Bank. Direct foreign investment was an estimated US$735 million in 2007.

Balance of Payments / Imports and Exports

Jamaica suffers a balance of payments deficit. Figures for 2010 show exports earning US$1.4 billion. Exported goods include alumina, bauxite (53 per cent of the export trade), sugar, bananas, garments, citrus fruits, rum and cocoa. Main export partners are the US (over 35 per cent), the UK (15 per cent) and Canada. Imports cost an estimated US$4.6 billion in 2010. Imported goods consist mainly of machinery, transportation and electrical equipment, food, fuels and fertiliser. The US is Jamaica's most important trading partner (35 per cent). Other significant trading partners are Canada, Trinidad and Tobago, Venezuela, the Netherlands, China and the UK.

Trade or Currency Restrictions

Under the Caribbean Basin Initiative, products originating in Jamaica can enter the US on a duty-free basis. Textile and apparel, watches and watch parts, footwear, tuna and petroleum products are excluded from this agreement. Jamaica enjoys duty-free access into the Canadian market, excluding textiles and clothing, footwear, luggage and handbags, leather garments, lubrication oils and methanol. Under the Lomé Convention, member countries of the EU grant zero duty or a reduced rate of duty to goods originating from Jamaica. They can also enter the markets of other CARICOM territories on a duty free basis.

Central Bank

Bank of Jamaica, PO Box 621, Nethersole Place, Kingston, Jamaica. Tel: +1 876 9220 750, fax: +1 876 9220 828 / 854, e-mail: info@boj.org.jm, URL: http://www.boj.org.jm
Governor: Bryan Wynter

Chambers of Commerce and Trade Organisations

Jamaica Chamber of Commerce, URL: http://www.jcc.org.jm/
American Chamber of Commerce of Jamaica, URL: http://www.amchamjamaica.org/
The Jamaica Manufacturers' Association, URL: http://www.jma.com.jm/
Jamaica Exporters Association, URL: http://www.exportjamaica.org/

MANUFACTURING, MINING AND SERVICES

Primary and Extractive Industries

Jamaica's deposits of alumina and bauxite are exported without treatment or refining. The discovery of bauxite in the 1940s and the subsequent establishment of the bauxite-alumina industry shifted Jamaica's economy from sugar and bananas. By the 1970s, Jamaica had emerged as a world leader in export of these minerals and foreign investment increased. Other industrial minerals are limestone, gypsum, silica and marble. Although production of bauxite and alumina increased significantly during the late 1990s, international market prices were consistently poor.

The mining sector contributed heavily to the Jamaican economy by providing just over one half of total foreign exchange earnings, and an annual average of 9 per cent of GDP for the 1990 to 1996 period. The sector recorded an average annual growth of 4.8 per cent, recovering from the 0.8 per cent growth during the 1980s. Increased capacity and high levels of utilisation have been the source of this growth. Alumina production peaked at 3.4 tonnes in 1997. As a capital-intensive industry, it provided jobs for approximately 6,000 people, less than 1 per cent of the employed labour force.

Energy

Jamaica is dependent on imported hydrocarbon for its fuel. Its petroleum needs are serviced by Mexican and Venezuelan imports. In 2005 Venezuela signed a deal with Jamaica to supply it with oil at preferential rates; initially the agreement is for 22,000 barrels a day and Jamaica can pay in goods and services or low interest loans. Figures for 2011 show that Jamaica imported 80,000 barrels per day

Manufacturing

Jamaica's manufacturing industries are primarily based on the country's bauxite and agricultural produce and raw materials. Efforts are being made to diversify the range of manufactured products and to increase the number of regions to which they are exported. The majority of production is for domestic use, but the government is attempting to improve the export market. The manufacturing and export of garments contributed a significant proportion of total export earnings (17 per cent in 1997). In recent years although the introduction of free trade zones stimulated investment in the garment industry and light manufacturing, the garment industry is declining mainly due to cheaper products and labour in Mexico and Asia. Other industrial products include processed foods, sugar, rum, cement, tobacco, construction materials, metal, paint, paper, chemical products and assembled electrical appliances.

The manufacturing sector is a relatively large employer of the country's workforce. Foreign exchange earnings averaged US$430 million per year over the 1990 to 1997 period, a quarter of total merchandise exports. The sector has remained a major contributor to GDP contributing around 30 per cent.

Service Industries

Tourism is a growing industry, increasing annually by an average of 4.5 per cent, and is the major source of foreign exchange. The majority of tourists come from the USA. Jamaica had more than 1.6 million visitors in 2006. Tourism receipts have increased from US$1,199 million in 1995 to US$1,621 in 2003. Trade from cruise passengers has more than doubled in the past ten years. The service sector contributes around 63 per cent to GDP.

Agriculture

Estimated figures for 2011 showed that agriculture contributed nearly 6.0 per cent of GDP, 17 per cent of the population were engaged that year in the agriculture sector. Jamaica's traditional export crops are sugar, bananas, citrus fruits, pimento, cocoa, coffee and coconuts. The entire sector was badly affected by Hurricane Gilbert during the 1988/89 season, and by Hurricane Ivan in September 2004.

In 2001 the Jamaican government embarked on a programme of citrus replanting. Approximately 2,800 hectares of citrus were planned to be replanted within five years in an effort to eliminate the tristeza virus which had been badly affecting the crop. Farmers are being encouraged to grow vegetables and rice for the domestic market to cut down on imports of these basic foodstuffs.

Agricultural Production in 2010

Produce	Int. $'000*	Tonnes
Indigenous chicken meat	145,560	102,190
Goat milk, whole, fresh	59,733	178,000
Sugar cane	43,824	1,334,600
Yams	34,886	136,785
Coconuts	21,661	195,900
Oranges	20,945	108,376
Bananas	17,766	63,850
Indigenous cattle meat	14,220	5,264
Fruit, tropical fresh nes.	12,301	30,100
Chillies and peppers, dry	12,275	11,206
Indigenous pigmeat	12,246	7,966
Lemons and limes	10,348	26,100

* unofficial figures
Source: http://faostat.fao.org/site/339/default.aspx Food and Agriculture Organization of the United Nations, Food and Agricultural commodities production

Livestock and livestock products as well as fishery products are primarily intended for the domestic market. Estimated figures for 2010 put the total catch of fish at 15,440 tonnes.

COMMUNICATIONS AND TRANSPORT

Travel Requirements

Citizens of the USA, Canada, Australia and the EU require a passport valid for six months beyond the length of stay but do not need a visa for stays of up to 90 days. The exceptions are citizens of Bulgaria, Czech Republic, Estonia, Hungary, Latvia, Lithuania, Poland, Romania, Slovak Republic and Slovenia who do need a visa. Other nationals should contact the embassy to check visa requirements. Visitors must have evidence of sufficient funds and a return or onward-bound ticket.

National Airlines

Air Jamaica, URL: http://www.airjamaica.com
The government reclaimed control of Air Jamaica in 2004 in an attempt to solve its financial crisis.

International Airports

There are two international airports, Norman Manley International Airport (NMIA) (URL: http://www.manley-airport.com.jm/) and Donald Sangster International Airport (SIA) (URL: http://www.mbjairport.com/). In 2006 an estimated 1.7 million passengers 16 million kg of cargo were transported at NMIA. There were over 45,000 flights in and out of SIA in 2006/07 and an approximate 3.4 million passengers. A new terminal is also being constructed. Once complete it will have the capacity to handle 8 million passengers per annum.

Railways

The Jamaica Railways Corporation (JRC), a statutory body, operates the railway system, having a total track mileage of 182.5 miles. The main line is from Kingston to Montego Bay, a distance of 113 miles. One of JRC's main sources of income is freight and mining services for Alcan. Alcan have now formed Middlesex Railway Services, which will take over the operation of alumina trains. Currently the railway only carries freight but there have been talks about investing in new stations and re-introducing passenger trains.

Roads

The island has 3,000 miles of main roads. There are also 7,000 miles of subsidiary roads, of which more than half are suitable for light motor traffic. Around 70 per cent of the total distance of roads is paved. Vehicles are driven on the left.

Shipping

The two main ports, Kingston, which is situated near the Kingston Free Zone, and Montego Bay, (Montego Bay Free Port), cater for cargo ships as well as cruise ships. Kingston is currently undergoing expansion with a projected total capacity of 1.5 million TEUs.
Jamaican Port Authority, URL: http://www.portjam.com

HEALTH

Medical services are provided by 16 government general hospitals. Six hospitals specialise in treatment for mental illness, polio, respiratory illness, pre-and post-natal care and children. Among the health training facilities, there is one teaching hospital, one poly-clinic and a Dental Auxiliary School which trains nurses and assistants in dentistry. In addition, there are approximately 360 health centres and several private hospitals and nursing homes.

In 2009, Jamaica spent approximately 5.4 per cent of its total budget on healthcare (down from 6.6 per cent in 2000), accounting for 55.4 per cent of all healthcare spending. Total expenditure on healthcare equated to 4.9 per cent of the country's GDP. Per capita expenditure on health was US$228 in 2009.

In 2000-10, there were 2,253 doctors (9 per 10,000 population), 4,374 nurses (16 per 10,000 population), and 212 dentistry personnel.

JAPAN

An estimated 1.5 per cent of the adult population has HIV/AIDs. The infant mortality rate in 2009 was 20 per 1,000 live births. The child mortality rate (under 5 years) was 24 per 1,000 live births. The main causes of childhood mortality are: congenital anomalies (20 per cent), prematurity (16 per cent), diarrhoea (4 per cent), pneumonia (13 per cent), and HIV/AIDs (3 per cent).

In 2010, 93 per cent of the population had sustainable access to improved drinking water sources and 80 per cent of the population had sustainable access to improved sanitation. (Source: http://www.who.int, World Health Statistics)

EDUCATION

Education at primary level is compulsory to the age of 14 and free. There are 790 primary schools, and 493 all age schools (up to grade 9), 57 secondary high schools and 64 new secondary schools.

Figures for 2007 from UNESCO show that 87 per cent of young children were enrolled in pre-primary school, 87 per cent of girls and 86 per cent of boys were enrolled in primary school and 79 per cent of girls and 74 per cent of boys were enrolled in secondary school. In 2005 the pupil:teacher ratio in primary schools was 28:1.

Jamaica also has six vocational schools, and 11 technical high schools. Tertiary education is available through the University of the West Indies, The University of Technology, The Edna Manley College for the Visual and Performing Arts, as well as 12 teacher training colleges, and colleges for agriculture, physical education, teacher training and dentistry.

Adult literacy was estimated at 80.5 per cent for males and 91.1 per cent for females in 2007.

RELIGION

The great majority of Jamaicans are Christians (84 per cent of the population). Almost every Christian denomination and sect is represented in the country. There are also Jewish, Hindu, Muslim and Baha'i communities. Rastafarianism, advocating racial equality and non-violence, is practised by an estimated 1 per cent of the population in Jamaica. Due to its use of marijuana as a sacrament, its church, the Royal Ethiopian Judah Coptic Church, is not officially recognised. Religious freedom is safeguarded by the country's constitution.

Jamaica has a religious tolerance rating of 9 on a scale of 1 to 10 (10 is most freedom). (Source: World Religion Database)

COMMUNICATIONS AND MEDIA

The press is free and criticism of the government is allowed.

Newspapers
The main newspapers are privately owned.
Jamaica Gleaner, URL: http://www.jamaica-gleaner.com
Jamaica Observer, URL: http://www.jamaicaobserver.com/
Sunday Herald, URL: http://www.sunheraldjamaica.com/index.htm
Jamaica Star, URL: http://www.jamaica-star.com/

Broadcasting
Jamaica has two Atlantic Ocean Intelstat earth stations. There are several radio stations (two AM and seven FM) including the Television Jamaica Ltd (formerly Jamaica Broadcasting Corporation (JBC) until privatisation in 1997) (URL: http://www.televisionjamaica.com/), Radio Jamaica Ltd (RJR), KLAS FM, Radio Waves, Irie FM, Power 106 and Love FM. The TVJ operates a television service and there is a second TV station called CVM TV (URL: http://www.cvmtv.com/)

Telecommunications
A fully automatic digital domestic network with over 300,000 main lines is in operation. In 2008, there were an estimated 2.7 million mobiles in use.

In 2008 it was estimated that there were approximately 1.5 million regular internet users.

ENVIRONMENT

Main environmental concerns for Jamaica include the polluting of coastal waters and damage to coral reefs by industrial waste, sewage and oil spillages. Deforestation is also an issue. Hurricanes are a hazard in the period July-November.

Jamaica is a party to the following international agreements: Biodiversity, Climate Change, Climate Change-Kyoto Protocol, Desertification, Endangered Species, Hazardous Wastes, Law of the Sea, Marine Dumping, Marine Life Conservation, Ozone Layer Protection, Ship Pollution and Wetlands.

According to figures from the EIA, in 2010, Jamaica's emissions from the consumption of fossil fuels totaled 9.22 million metric tons of carbon dioxide, down from 12.04 million metric tons in 2009.

JAPAN

Nippon-koku - Nihon-koku

Capital: Tokyo (Population estimate, 2012: 13,216,220)

Head of State: H.M. Emperor Akihito (Sovereign) (page 1373)

National Flag: White, with a red circle in the centre, representing a rising sun

CONSTITUTION AND GOVERNMENT

Constitution
The present Constitution which was passed in the Japanese Congress in October 1946, was promulgated by the Emperor the following month and came into force on 3 May 1947.

The Constitution deprived the Emperor of all executive power and proclaimed that the sovereign power resided in the people. He performs only those acts that are laid down in the constitution, such as appointing the Prime Minister and the Chief Justice of the Supreme Court as designated by the Diet and the Cabinet. It abolished the peerage, renounced war (although a military force is kept for defence), granted votes to women and established many other democratic rights.

To consult the full constitution, please visit: http://www.sangiin.go.jp/eng/law/tcoj/index.htm

International Relations
Japan has been active diplomatically in many situations in recent years including Iraq, Indonesia/East Timor, the Middle East Peace Process and Afghanistan. Japan had troops on the ground in Iraq until July 2006. Talks have been taking place between Japan and her neighbour China regarding ownership of oil and gas reserves in some areas of the East China Sea, and in April 2007, Wen Jibao became the first Chinese prime minister to address the Japanese parliament.

In September 2012, China cancelled a ceremony to mark the 40th anniversary of restored diplomatic relations with Japan due to a escalation in the dispute over ownership of the Senkaku Islands which are administered by Japan but claimed by China (where they are known as the Diaoyu Islands), Taiwan also lays claim to the islands. In February 2013 a Chinese frigate locked radar on a Japanese navy ship, Prime Minister Shinzo Abe called it a 'dangerous act' and said that the act could lead to an 'unpredictable situation'. China said that Japan should stop 'illegal' activities near the islands.

Recent Events
In September 2006, Prime Minister Junichiro Koizumi stepped down as prime minister. He had announced his intention of doing so a year previously and was succeeded by Shinzo Abe. In December of that year a Ministry of Defence was established; this is the first time since the end of World War II that the institution has existed. In April 2007, the Agriculture Minister, Toshikatsu Matsuoka, was found dead in his flat, having allegedly killed himself; he was facing an investigation into his possible links to a political funding scandal. Following the defeat of his party in the elections to the Upper House in July 2007, Prime Minister Shinzo Abe resigned; he had been prime minister for less than a year. Yasuo Fukuda took over the post but resigned in September 2008 as confidence levels in his handling of domestic issues fell. Former Foreign Minister Taro Aso (page 1380) was appointed to the post of prime minister in September 2008.

In February 2009 industrial production dropped 9.4 per cent following a fall of 10.2 per cent in January. Car production alone dropped by over 56 per cent in February. The export market which Japan relies heavily on has constricted following the global economic downturn. Industrial production rallied in March and grew by 1.6 per cent. Difficult conditions remained throughout the year and growth was less than expected in the fourth quarter of 2010, 3.8 per cent compared to initial forecasts of 4.6 per cent.

In June 2010 Prime Minister Yukio Hatoyama announced he was resigning his post. His resignation came after he broke an election pledge to move a US military base away from the southern island of Okinawa. Naoto Kan was elected as the new prime minister two days later. In September 2010 Prime Minister Naoto Kan survived a leadership challenge from Ichiro Ozawa.

In September 2010 a diplomatic row erupted with China over Japan's arrest of a Chinese trawler crew in disputed waters in East China Sea.

Japan's central bank cut interest rates to almost zero in October 2010 in an effort to stimulate the economy.

In March 2011 Foreign Minister Seiji Maehara resigned from his post and was replaced by Takeaki Matsumoto.

Also that month a massive earthquake, measured at a magnitude of 8.9 on the Richter scale, hit the north-east of Japan, triggering a tsunami that caused extensive damage. The tsunami left a trail of destruction 2 km inland from the port town of Minami Sanriku. The official death toll was put at 14,340 with 5,282 people injured. More than 11,000 people remain listed as missing and more than 500,000 people were left homeless. The Fukushima Daichi nuclear power plant was damaged in the quake. By 15 March, three out of the four reactors had exploded and radiation from the plant reached harmful levels. One of the containment chambers was believed to be damaged. A danger zone currently at 18 miles was established with residents either evacuated or told to stay indoors. Radiation levels in the capital Tokyo were slightly higher than normal and seawater near the reactor was believed to be contaminated. In April Japan's Nuclear and Industrial Safety Agency raised the severity of the crisis at the Fukushima plant to level seven, this is the highest rating and was last used at the Chernobyl plant in Ukraine. In July it was announced that engineers were still working to shut down the Fukushima plant, which was still leaking radioactive material. Japan said it would stress test all its nuclear reactors to see if they could withstand any other disasters.

Japan has estimated that the cost of rebuilding the affected area of the earthquake and tsunami at 25 trillion yen (US$309bn; £189bn). The prime minister Naoto Kan resigned in March 2011 following criticism of his handling of the earthquake.

In August 2011 Yoshihiko Noda was backed by the parliament to become the new prime minister following his election as leader of the Democratic Party. The trade minister Yoshio Hachiro resigned as trade minister in September 2011 following criticism of his comments about Fukushima. He was replaced by Yukio Edano.

In May 2012 the third reactor at the Tomari Nuclear Plant was switched off, this was the last working reactor in Japan to be switched off as part of a safety drive following the tsunami in 2011 and leaves Japan without energy generated from atomic power for the first time in 40 years. Following the tsunami all reactors were to be switched off and stringent safety checks carried out before they could be switched back on. In July, the No 3 reactor at Ohi, in Fukui prefecture on the west coast of the country was the first reactor to be switched back on amid some protests.

In November 2012 Prime Minister Noda dissolved the parliament and called for snap elections following reports that money set aside for rebuilding projects following the 2011 tsunami had been spent on unrelated projects. The election took place in December 2012 and was won by the Liberal Democratic Party.

In January 2013, Japan posted a record high trade deficit of $78 billion for 2012, this was due to falling exports to Europe and China.

Legislature

The legislative power in the Diet, *Kokkai* rests with a bicameral Congress, consisting of a House of Representatives, *Shugiin* with 480 seats, and the House of Councillors, *Sangiin* with 242 seats.

Members of the House of Representatives (the lower chamber) are elected for a four-year term but the House can be dissolved before that period expires. Members of the House of Councillors (the upper chamber) are elected for six-year terms, with half the seats being filled in an election every three years. The House of Representatives takes precedence over the other chamber in the prior deliberation of the budget bill, designating a new prime minister and in consideration of treaties. Its most important power is to submit motions of no confidence in the cabinet. If the House of Representatives has been dissolved, the House of Councillors temporarily assumes the Diet's functions.

Under the present election system, members of the House of Representatives are elected from medium-sized constituencies, except for one one-member district, with one to six seats allotted to each district depending on the size of the population. There are now 130 constituencies, last redistributed in 1975.

For the House of Councillors, 48 members are elected under a nationwide proportional representation system and 73 from prefecture based multimember constituencies; for the national constituency voters cast their ballots for a party. Seats are allocated to each party in proportion to its share of the votes, and parties select winning candidates according to lists submitted prior to the election.

The Cabinet has executive power. It consists of the Prime Minister and 20 state ministers and is responsible to the Diet. The Prime Minister is chosen by the Diet. A majority of the cabinet must, like the Prime Minister, be members of the Diet. The Prime Minister has the power to appoint and dismiss ministers of state.

Upper House

House of Councillors, 7-1 Nagata-cho, 1-chome, Chiyoda-ku, Tokyo 100-8961, Japan. Tel: +81 (0)3 3581 3111, fax: +81 (0)3 5512 3895, URL: http://www.sangiin.go.jp

Lower House

House of Representatives, 7-1 Nagata-cho, 1-chome, Chiyoda-ku, Tokyo 100-8960, Japan. Tel: +81 (0)3 3581 5111, fax: +81 (0)3 3581 2900, e-mail: jpndiet@shugiinjk.go.jp, URL: http://www.shugiin.go.jp

Cabinet (as at July 2013)
Prime Minister: Shinzo Abe (page 1371)
Deputy Prime Minister, Minister of Finance, Overcoming Deflation and Counting Yen Appreciation, Minister of State for Financial Services: Taro Aso (page 1380)
Minister of Internal Affairs and Communications, Minister of Regional Revitalization, Minister for Regional Government: Yoshitaka Shindo
Minister of Justice: Sadakazu Tanigaki (page 1523)
Minister of Foreign Affairs: Fumio Kishida (page 1457)
Minister of Education, Culture, Sports, Science and Technology, Minister in charge of Rebuilding Education: Hakubun Shimomura
Minister of Health, Labour and Welfare: Norihisa Tamura
Minister of Agriculture, Forestry and Fisheries: Yoshimasa Hayashi

Minister of Economy, Trade and Industry, Minister of State for the Corporation in support of Compensation for Nuclear Damage, Minister for Nuclear Incident Economic Countermeasures, Minister in charge of Industrial Competitiveness: Toshimitsu Motegi
Minister of Land, Infrastructure and Transport, Minister for Ocean Policy: Akihiro Ohta
Minister of Environment, Minister of State for the Nuclear Emergency Preparedness: Nobuteru Ishihara (page 1447)
Minister of Defence: Itsunori Onodera
Chief Cabinet Secretary, Minister in charge of Strengthening National Security: Yoshihide Suga (page 1521)
Minister for Reconstruction, Minister in charge of Comprehensive Policy Coordination for Revival from the Nuclear Accident at Fukushima: Takumi Nemoto
Chairman of the National Public Safety Commission, Minister in Charge of the Abduction Issue, Minister of State for Disaster Management, Minister in Charge of the Nation's Infrastructure Resilience: Keiji Furuya
Minister of State for Ikinawa and Northern Territories Affairs, Minister of State for Science and Technology Policy, Minister in Charge of Information Technology Policy, Minister in Charge of Ocean Policy and Territorial Issues: Ichita Yamamoto
Minister in charge of Support for Women's Empowerment and Child-Rearing, Minister of State for Consumer Affairs and Food Safety, Minister of State for Measures for Declining Birthrate, Minister of State for Gender Equality: Masako Mori
Minister in charge of Economic Revitalization, Minister in charge of Total Reform of Social Security and Tax, Minister of State for Economic and Fiscal Policy: Akira Amari (page 1377)
Minister in charge of Administrative Reform, Minister in charge of Civil Service Reform, Minister in charge of 'Cool Japan' Strategy, Minister in charge of 'Challenge Again' Initiative, Minister of State for Regulatory Reform: Tomomi Inada

Ministries
Imperial Household Agency, 1-1, Chiyoda, Chiyoda-ku, Tokyo 100, Japan. Tel: +81 3 3213 1111, URL: http://www.kunaicho.go.jp/eindex.html
Prime Minister's Office, 1-6-1, Nagata-cho, Chiyoda-ku, Tokyo, Japan 100. Tel: +81 (0)3 3581 3111, fax: +81 (0)3 3593 1784, URL: http://www.kantei.go.jp
Ministry of Agriculture, Forestry and Fisheries, 1-2-1, Kasumigaseki, Chiyoda-ku, Tokyo 100, Japan. Tel: +81 3 3502 8111, fax: +81 3 3592 7697, URL: http://www.maff.go.jp
Ministry of Economy, Trade and Industry, 1-3-1, Kasumigaseki, Chiyoda-ku, Tokyo 100, Japan. Tel: +81 (0)3 3501 1511, fax: +81 (0)3 3501 2081, URL: http://www.meti.go.jp
Ministry of Education, Culture, Sport, Science and Technology, 3-2-2-, Kasumigaseki, Chiyoda-ku, Tokyo 100, Japan. Tel: +81 (0)3 3581 4211, fax: +81 (0)3 3591 8072, URL: http://www.mext.go.jp
Ministry of the Environment, 5 Godochosha, 1-2-2 Kasumigaseki, Chiyoda-ku, Tokyo 100, Japan. Tel: +81 3 3581 3351, e-mail: moe@env.go.jp, URL: http://www.env.go.jp
Ministry of Finance, 3-1-1, Kasumigaseki, Chiyoda-ku, Tokyo 100, Japan. Tel: +81 3 3581 4111, fax: +81 3 3592 1025, URL: http://www.mof.go.jp
Ministry of Foreign Affairs, 2-2-1-, Kasumigaseki, Chiyoda-ku, Tokyo 100 , Japan. Tel: +81 3 3580 3311, fax: +81 3 3581 9675, URL: http://www.mofa.go.jp
Ministry of Health, Labour and Welfare, 1-2-2, Kasumigaseki, Chiyoda-ku, Tokyo 100, Japan. Tel: +81 3 3503 1711, fax: +81 3 3501 4853, URL: http://www.mhlw.go.jp
Ministry of Justice, 1-1-1, Kasumigaseki, Chiyoda-ku, Tokyo 100, Japan. Tel: +81 (0)3 3580 4111, fax: +81 (0)3 3592 7011, URL: http://www.moj.go.jp
Ministry of Public Management, Home Affairs, Posts and Telecommunications, 1-3-2, Kasumigaseki, Chiyoda-ku, Tokyo 100, Japan. Tel: +81 (0)3 3504 4411, fax: +81 (0)3 3504 0265, URL: http://www.soumu.go.jp
Ministry of Land, Infrastructure and Transport, 2-1-3, Kasumigaseki, Chiyoda-ku, Tokyo 100, Japan. Tel: +81 (0)3 3580 3111, fax: +81 (0)3 3580 7982, URL: http://www.mlit.go.jp
Defence Agency, 9-7-45, Akasaka, Minato-ku, Tokyo 107, Japan. Tel: +81 (0)3 3408 521, URL: http://www.jda.go.jp

Political Parties
Liberal Democratic Party, (LDP), 1-11-23 Nagata-cho, Chiyoda-ku, Tokyo, Japan. URL: http://www.jimin.jp/index.html
President: Shinzo Abe
Democratic Party of Japan, (DPJ), 1-11-1 Nagata-cho, Chiyoda-ku, Tokyo 100-0014, Japan. URL: http://www.dpj.or.jp
Oresident: Yoshihiko Noda
New Komeito Party, 17 Minamimoto-machi, Shinjuku-ku, Tokyo 160-0012, Japan. URL: http://www.komei.or.jp/en/index.html
Chief Representative: Natsuo Yamaguchi
Social Democratic Party, 1-8-1 Nagata-cho, Chiyoda-ku, Tokyo 100-8909, Japan. URL: http://www5.sdp.or.jp
President: Mizuho Hukushima
Japanese Communist Party (JCP), 4-26-7 Sendagaya, Shibuya-ku, Tokyo 151-8586, Japan. URL: http://www.jcp.or.jp
President: Kazuo Shii
People's New Party, URL: http://www.kokumin.or.jp
Leader: Shizuka Kamei
Sunrise Party, URL: http://www.tachiagare.jp
Leader: Takeo Hiranuma
Your Party, URL: http://www.your-party.jp
Leader: Yoshimi Watanabe
New Renaissance Party, URL: http://shintokaikaku.jp
Leader: Yōichi Masuzoe

JAPAN

Elections

Japan has universal adult suffrage: all men and women over the age of 20 are eligible to vote in all elections. Women have had the vote since 1945. Japanese citizens over 25 are eligible for election to the House of Representatives and those over 30 to the House of Councillors.

Elections to the House of Councillors took place on July 29 2007. Half the house was up for election and the ruling LDP party lost control of the house for the first time in its history. At the time Prime Minister Abe announced he would not resign from his post, although loss of control of the upper house could hamper his reforms, but he announced his resignation on September 12. Yasuo Fakuda was named as leader of the ruling Liberal Democratic Party in September 2007 and was subsequently elected to the post of prime minister by the House of Representatives. Taro Aso was elected leader of the LDP on 22 September 2008; he automatically became Prime Minister, and named a new cabinet. Mr Aso fared badly in local elections in 2009 and called a general election.

The general election took place on 30 August 2009. The opposition Democratic Party of Japan won a landslide victory over the Liberal Democratic Party who had been in power almost continually since 1955. A snap election was called and took place in December 2012, the Liberal Democratic Party won 294 seats taking power back from the Democratic Party of Japan, which won 57 seats.

Diplomatic Representation

US Embassy, 10-5, Akasaka 1-chome, Minato-ku (107-8420), Tokyo, Japan. Tel: +81 (0)3 3224 5000, fax: +81 (0)3 3505 1862, URL: http://japan.usembassy.gov
Ambassador: John V. Roos (page 1505)
British Embassy, 1, Ichiban-cho, Chiyoda-ku, Tokyo 102-8381, Japan. Tel: +81 (0)3 5211 1100, fax: +81 (0)3 5211 3164, e-mail: embassy.tokyo@fco.gov.uk, URL: http://ukinjapan.fco.gov.uk/en
Ambassador: Tim Hitchens (page 1442)
Embassy of Japan, 2520 Massachusetts Avenue NW, Washington, DC 20008, USA. Tel: +1 202 939 6700, URL: http://www.us.emb-japan.go.jp/english/html/index.html
Ambassador: Kenichiro Sasae (page 1508)
Embassy of Japan, 101-104 Piccadilly, London W1V 9FN, United Kingdom. Tel: +44 (0)20 7465 6500, URL: http://www.uk.emb-japan.go.jp
Ambassador: Keiichi Hayashi (page 1439)
Permanent Mission of Japan to the United Nations, 866 United Nations Plaza, 2nd Floor, New York, N.Y. 10017, USA. Tel: +1 212 223-4300, fax: +1 212 751-1966, URL: http://www.un.emb-japan.go.jp/index.htm
Permanent Representative: H.E. Mr Tsuneo Nishida
Deputy Permanent Representative: H.E. Mr Kazuo Kodama
Ambassador: H.E. Mr Jun Yamazaki

LEGAL SYSTEM

The judiciary is independent of the executive and legislative branches of government. The highest court is the Supreme Court, then there are eight High Courts with six branch offices and an Intellectual Property High Court, 50 district courts (or one in each of the prefectures except Hokkaido, which has four), 50 family courts and 438 summary courts.

The Supreme Court is the highest court in the land, and exercises appellate jurisdiction. In addition, it has initial and final jurisdiction in the proceedings involving the impeachment of commissioners of the National Personnel Authority. Every case on appeal is first assigned to one of the three Petty Benches. If a case proves to involve an issue of the constitutionality of any law, order, rule, or disposition, the Grand Bench inquires and adjudicates on it. The Supreme Court is also the highest authority of judicial administration, and as such, considers and determines of matters of rule-making and judicial administration.

High Courts are located in eight cities in Japan: Tokyo, Osaka, Nagoya, Hiroshima, Fukuoka, Sendai, Sapporo, and Takamatsu. Each High Court consists of a President and other high court judges. Apart from the Intellectual Property High Court, High Courts have jurisdiction over appeals filed against judgments rendered by district courts in the first instance or family courts. In addition, High Courts have original jurisdiction over administrative cases on election, insurrection cases, etc. The district court is generally the court of the first instance. It also has appellate jurisdiction over appeals in civil cases lodged against judgments of summary courts. The summary courts have original jurisdiction over civil cases involving claims for amounts not exceeding 1,400,000 yen and criminal cases for offenses punishable by fines or lighter punishment.

The Supreme Court is composed of a chief justice and 14 other justices. The chief justice is appointed by the Emperor (and must retire at 70 years) and the other justices are appointed by the cabinet. The lower court judges are appointed from a list of people nominated by the Supreme Court. All lower court judges are appointed for ten years although they may be re-appointed.

The government respects the rights of its citizens. Japan retains the death penalty for murder and treason. Two people were executed in 2010. No executions were reported in 2011, three in 2012 and three to date in 2013.

Supreme Court of Japan, URL: http://www.courts.go.jp/english/system/index.html
Chief Justice: Hironobu Takesaki

LOCAL GOVERNMENT

The functions and responsibilities of administration are divided between the national government and local (prefectural and municipal) governments. The Local Autonomy Law came into effect in 1947. It enshrined the principle of self-government at local level.

The country is divided for administrative purposes into 47 prefectures: Aichi, Akita, Aomori, Chiba, Ehime, Fukui, Fukuoka, Fukushima, Gifu, Gunma, Hiroshima, Hokkaido, Hyogo, Ibaraki, Ishikawa, Iwate, Kagawa, Kagoshima, Kanagawa, Kochi, Kumamoto, Kyoto, Mie, Miyagi, Miyazaki, Nagano, Nagasaki, Nara, Niigata, Oita, Okayama, Okinawa, Osaka, Saga, Saitama, Shiga, Shimane, Shizuoka, Tochigi, Tokushima, Tokyo, Tottori, Toyama, Wakayama, Yamagata, Yamaguchi, and Yamanashi

The prefectures are divided into municipalities, towns, and villages. Each of these has an elected representative assembly. Each of the prefectures has a governor who is elected by the people in the area comprised by the prefecture, and each town and village has a mayor and an assembly elected in the same way.

People 30 years and over are eligible for election to governorship of a prefecture. The mayor of a city, town, or village must be 25. Local residents also have the right to make a range of appeals to local government bodies.

Local government is responsible for land preservation and development, disaster prevention, pollution control, labour, education, social welfare, and health. Responsibilities are divided between the prefectures and municipal governments.

AREA AND POPULATION

Area

Japan consists of four large and around 3,000 small islands situated in the North Pacific Ocean. The large islands from north to south are Hokkaido, or Yezo, 78,511 sq. km; Honshu (or Mainland), 230,531.9 sq. km; Shikoku, 18,765.80 sq. km and Kyushu, 41,969 sq. km. The cities of Tokyo and Osaka are located on the island of Honshu. The various parts of China which throughout the years of Japanese expansion and aggression have been leased or annexed - e.g. Formosa (now Taiwan) and the Kwantung Province - reverted to Chinese sovereignty after the War of 1939-45. Japan has a total area of 378,000 sq. km of which 66.5 per cent comprises forest, woodland and mountains and the remaining 33.5 per cent basins and plains. The highest mountain is Mount Fuji standing at 3,776 metres. Just 17 per cent of the land in cultivable. The general climate is temperate.

Japan is situated in a volcanic zone on the Pacific Ring of Fire and has over 100 active volcanoes as well as being susceptible to earthquakes. Recent major events include the 1995 Great Hanshin earthquake and the 2011 Tōhoku earthquake, this measured 9.0 on the Richter scale and triggered a large tsunami.

To view a map, please consult http://www.lib.utexas.edu/maps/cia08/japan_sm_2008.gif

Population

The population was estimated at 127.7 million in 2011 giving a population density of 343 persons per sq km. Figures for 2008 show that Tokyo had an estimated population of 8,663,751, Yokohama had a population of 3,631,200 and Osaka had an estimated population of 2,645,300.

Japan has a rapidly ageing population; over 20 per cent of the population is aged over 65 years, one of the highest rates in the world. Figures for 2005 showed that 20.1 per cent of the population was aged 65 or over, this had increased to 23.3 per cent in 2011 and was forecast to be 29.1 per cent in 2020. Some forecasts have shown the working age population set to decrease by 20 per cent over the next 20 years, and therefore creating problems for future pension and health care provision. There is very little immigration.

The Japanese language comprises the Chinese written characters (some 1,800 of them).

The following table shows the population of Japan in recent years.

Year	Population '000
1990	123,611
1995	125,570
2000	126,926
2005	127,768
2006	127,770
2007	127,771
2008	127,692
2010	128,057
2011	127,799
Projected Figures	
2020	124,100
2030	116,618
2040	107,276
2050	97,076

Source: Japan Statistics Bureau MIC

Births, Marriages, Deaths

Estimated figures from the Ministry of Health, Labour and Welfare for 2011 show that there were 8.3 births per 1,000 population, down from the 2000 figure of 9.5 live births per 1,000 population. The average age that women are having their first child has grown in recent years from 27.0 in 1990 to 28.9 in 2004 and an estimated 30.1 in 2011. The birth rate is in decline and is predicted to be as low as 1.35 children per female by 2060. The death rate was estimated at 9.9 per 1,000 population in 2011, up from 7.7 deaths per 1,000 population in 2000. Figures from 2011 show that 662,000 marriages took place and there were 236,000 divorces. (Source: Japan Statistical Yearbook).

Japan has one of the highest life expectancies in the world with the average being 79.4 years for men and 85.9 years for women (2011). This is predicted to continue to rise, reaching 90 years for females and 85 years for males by 2060.

Public Holidays 2014

1 January: New Year's Day (Ganjitsu)
13 January: Coming-of-Age Day (Seijin no Hi)
11 February: National Foundation Day (Kenkoku Kinen no Hi)
21 March: Vernal Equinox Day (Shumbun no Hi)
29 April: Birthday of Emperor Showa (Showa no Hi)
3 May: Constitution Memorial Day (Kempo Kinembi)
4 May: Greenery Day (Midori no Hi)
5 May: Children's Day (Kodomo no Hi)
21 July: Marine Day (Umi no Hi)
15 September: Respect for the Aged Day (Keiro no Hi)
23 September: Autumnal Equinox Day (Shubun no Hi)
13 October: Sports Day (Taiku no Hi)
3 November: Culture Day (Bunka no Hi)
23 November: Labour Thanksgiving Day (Kinro Kansha no Hi)
23 December: Emperor's Birthday (Tenno Tanjobi)
If a holiday falls on a Sunday the following Monday is a holiday.

EMPLOYMENT

Figures for February 2012 show that 62.26 million people were employed (down 0.6 per cent on the previous year) and 2.89 million were unemployed, giving an unemployment rate of 4.6 per cent. Although the unemployment rate remains low, it has risen slightly. The manufacturing sector has been adversely affected by the global economic crisis and key employers including Panasonic and TDK announced wide-ranging job cuts.

Employed Persons by Major Industries (figures in '000)

Industry	2010	2011*
Agriculture & forestry	2,110	2,170
Fisheries	170	160
Mining & quarrying of stone & gravel	30	30
Construction	4,730	4,730
Manufacturing	10,040	9,970
Electricity, gas, heat supply & water	320	290
Information & communications	1,920	1,850
Transport & postal activities	3,350	3,340
Wholesale & retail trade	10,090	10,060
Finance & insurance	1,570	1,550
Real estate & goods rental & leasing	1,060	1,080
Scientific research, professional technical services	1,930	1,990
Accommodation, eating & drinking services	3,720	3,650
Living related & personal services & amusement services	2,290	2,310
Education, learning support	2,740	2,800
Medical, health care & welfare	6,250	6,480
Compound services	420	400
Services (n.e.c.)	4,360	4,350
Government (n.e.c.)	2,090	2,100
Total	59,700	59,770

* Iwate, Miyagi, and Fukushima prefectures not included due to the impact of the 2011 earthquake
Source: Statistical Handbook of Japan 2012

BANKING AND FINANCE

Currency
One yen = 100 sen

During the 1960s, 70s and 80s, Japan had one of the world's highest economic growth rates. However, the country was badly affected by the Asian economic crisis during the mid 1990s, and in 1997 the Japanese economy went into a severe recession. By 1998, Far Eastern currencies were falling and the Japanese recession continued; large debts were accrued and many of the larger Japanese banks began to fail. The government injected public money into the system. The continuing economic crisis contributed to the fall of prime minister Mr. Hashimoto. In March 2001 Prime Minister Mori cut interest rates to zero in an attempt to boost the economy, but was forced to resign in April 2001 as the economy continued to fail. Figures for the fiscal year of 2001 show that there were 20,052 bankruptcy cases. Prime Minister Koizumi, who came to power in 2001, introduced structural reforms in both the corporate and public sectors. Figures from 2003 showed that the rate of bankruptcies was slowing and the investment and export sectors were improving. By early 2005 unemployment figures were showing signs of improvement and consumer spending was beginning to grow. Economic growth is now driven by the domestic private sector rather than exports.

The 2008 global economic crisis resulted in a dramatic fall in Japan's exports. In April 2009 the governing coalition announced it would be bringing in front of parliament a 15.4 trillion yen stimulus package to boost the economy. The package included plans to boost the fuel efficient vehicle and consumer electronics sectors. The package was the third within a year which included tax breaks and help for regional economies. Also in April Japan announced it first annual trade deficit for 28 years; exports in March were down 16 per cent on the previous year. Japan came out of recession in Q2 2009 when its economy grew by 0.9 per cent. However, there are fears that the recovery is fragile and growth in the Q4 of 2009 was down on expectations. The economy suffered further in March 2011 when Japan was hit by a huge earthquake and tsunami; the export sector was particularly badly hit and following the earthquake the Bank of Japan offered to put 15 trillion yen into the banking system in order to normalise market conditions. In April 2011 the Japanese economy slipped back into recession. The economy was expected to rebound in 2012, fuelled partly by rebuilding. Sustainable long-term growth was expected to be just over 1 per cent. Reports showed that money set aside for rebuilding following the 2011 tsunami had been spent on other projects,

this led to an election and continued unease about the Japanese economy. In January 2013, Japan posted a record high trade deficit of $78 billion for 2012, the deficit was due to falling exports to Europe and China. Japan's domestic economy has been struggling with deflation and plans drawn up in 2013 hoped that inflation would rise above 2 per cent. In order to raise inflation, Prime Minister Abe planned an aggressive ultra-easy monetary policy which would put more money into the economy and also weaken the yen. This would then boost exports and act as a catalyst for economic growth. There is a risk that the deliberate weakening of the Japanese yen could spark a currency war, if other countries trading or competing with Japan also take steps to devalue their currency in order to gain a trade advantage.

GDP/GNP, Inflation, National Debt

Figures for 2002 record GDP growth at -0.3 per cent, 1.4 per cent in 2003, 2.7 per cent in 2004 and 2.6 per cent in 2005. The growth was led by increased demand for exports (particularly from China), and confidence in the domestic private sector. Japan's exports almost halved as the global financial crisis took hold. By June 2009 the government was reporting some signs of a recovery with the pace of decline slowing, and a rise in factory output. Estimated figures for 2009 put growth of GDP at -5.2 per cent. Modest growth was forecast for 2010. In March 2010, economic growth was reported to be 3.8 per cent, lower than expected. The government fell back into recession following the tsunami. Over the whole of 2011, GDP fell by 0.9 per cent. GDP was estimated at $4.38 trillion in 2011. Per capita GDP was estimated at $34,300.

The following table shows GNI and GDP (exprenditure appraoch) in recent years (figures are in billion yen):

Year	GNI	GDP
2008	518,292.6	518,230.9
2009	497,366.3	489,588.5
2010	513,923.2	511,359.0
2011	505,565.2	507,613.1

Source: Statistical Handbook of Japan 2012

GDP contributions break down thus: agriculture 1.4 per cent, industry 27.3 per cent and services 71.3 per cent.

GDP by Economic Activities at Current Prices in billions of yen

Industry	2009	2010	2011
Total	471,138.7	482,384.4	470,623.2
Agriculture, forestry & fishing	5,440.1	5,655.6	5,449.8
Mining	283.3	301.0	298.0
Manufacturing	83,351.2	94,333.1	87,086.7
Construction	26,948.4	26,197.7	26,448.0
Utilities	11,131.8	11,007.8	8,609.7
Wholesale & retail trade	64,135.5	65,980.5	66,922.6
Finance & insurance	23,741.6	23,766.0	22,854.4
Real estate	56,879.2	56,890.0	56,727.7
Transport	22,973.9	23,465.3	22,779.4
Information & communications	26,188.6	25,978.2	25,551.4
Service activities	91,540.8	91,266.4	90,993.5

Source: Statistics Japan

The average inflation rate over the period 1990-96 was 0.7 per cent. Inflation for 1998 was estimated to be 1.1 per cent, and forecast at -0.7 per cent for 2000, -0.6 per cent in 2001 and -1.1 per cent in 2002. Figures for 2003 put inflation at -0.3 per cent. Figures for 2006 put inflation at 0.3 per cent and 1.4 per cent in 2008. Forecast figures for 2009 put inflation at 1.2 per cent before prices fell once more. After two years of deflation, inflation was estimated at 0.6 per cent in April 2011. The central bank, the Bank of Japan had set a target of 1.0 per cent inflation but said this might only be reached in the fiscal year 2014-15. However in early 2013 the Prime Minister asked the Bank of Japan to set the inflation target at 2.0 per cent.

Japan's national debt reached a record 960 trillion yen ($12 trillion) in Q4 2011.

Balance of Payments / Imports and Exports

Japan is the world's third largest trading country in both exports and imports, after the United States and Germany.

Figures for April 2011 showed that exports fell by 12.5 per cent that month, this was in response to the devastating earthquake and tsunami that hit Japan the previous month. Many factories were damaged and production particularly in the car manufacturing sector had to be suspended. The April figures also showed a 8.9 per cent rise in imports; this was mainly due to fuel having to be imported following disruption to electricity generating plants following the disaster.

The following table shows foreign trade in recent years.

Foreign Trade in billion yen

Year	Exports fob	Imports cif	Balance
2001	48,979	42,416	6,564
2002	52,109	42,228	9,881
2003	54,548	44,362	10,186
2004	61,170	49,217	11,953
2005	65,657	56,949	8,707
2006	75,246	67,344	7,902
2007	83,931	73,136	10,796
2008	81,018	78,955	2,063
2009	54,171	51,499	2,671

JAPAN

- continued

2010	67,400	680,765	6,635
2011	65,546	68,111	-2,565

Source: Statistical Handbook of Japan 2012

The following tables show the value, in billion yen, of the principal commodities for exports and imports for recent years:

Value of Exports

Commodity	2009	2010	2011
Foodstuffs	366	406	359
Raw materials	826	946	972
Mineral fuels	948	1,105	1,247
Chemicals	5,780	6,925	6,798
Manufactured goods	7,017	8,785	8,786
-Iron & steel	2,906	3,675	3,709
General machinery	9,669	13,317	13,803
-Power generating Machinery	1,839	2,327	2,317
Electrical machinery	10,771	12,650	11,600
-Semiconductors & other electronic parts	3,419	4,153	3,565
Transport equipment	11,850	15,258	14,033
-Motor vehicles	6,693	9,174	8,204
Others	6,944	8,007	7,948
-Scientific & optical instruments	1,578	2,014	2,109
Total	54,171	67,400	65,546

Source: Statistical Handbook of Japan 2012

Value of Imports

Commodity	2009	2010	2011
Foodstuffs	4,999	5,199	5,854
-Fish & shellfish	1,208	1,260	1,350
Raw materials	3,395	4,766	5,270
Mineral fuels	14,202	17,398	21,816
-Petroleum, crude & partly refined	7,564	9,406	11,415
Chemicals	4,583	5,379	6,098
-Medical & pharmaceutical products	1,329	1,523	1,725
Manufactured goods	4,345	5,379	6,069
-Non-ferrous metals	1,013	1,606	1,813
General machinery	4,225	4,826	4,970
Electrical machinery	6,509	8,101	7,989
- Semi-conductors & other electronic parts	1,758	2,136	1,762
Transport equipment	1,501	1,681	1,738
-Motor Vehicles	916	929	750
Others	7,742	8,036	8,307
-Clothing & clothing accessories	2,358	2,328	2,598
Total	51,499	60,765	68,111

Source: Statistical Handbook of Japan 2012

Japan's main trading partners are Southeast Asian countries, the US, Western Europe and Germany. Figures show that over the last few years Japan has invested an average of US$41.1 billion per year abroad.

The following tables shows the destination, origin and value of exported and imported goods in recent years (in billion yen):

Exports by Destination and Value	2010	2011
Total	67,400	65,546
Asia	37,827	36,686
-China	13,086	12,902
-Rep. of Korea	5,460	5,269
-Taiwan	4,594	4,058
USA	10,374	10,018
EU 27	7,616	7,619
Middle East	2,216	1,955
Oceania	1,955	1,778

Source: Statistical Handbook of Japan 2012

Imports by Area of Origin and Value	2007	2008
Total	60,765	68,111
Asia	27,511	30,391
-China	13,413	14,642
-Rep. of Korea	2,504	3,170
-Taiwan	2,025	1,852
USA	5,911	5,931
EU 27	5,821	6,411
Middle East	10,387	12,832
Oceania	4,327	4,893

Source: Statistical Handbook of Japan 2012

Central Bank

Bank of Japan (Nippon Ginko), 2-1-1 Hongoku-cho, Nihonbashi, Chuo-ku, Tokyo 103-0021, Honshu, Japan. Tel: +81 (0)3 3279 1111, fax: +81 (0)3 5200 2256 / 5201 5661, e-mail: prd@info.boj.or.jp, URL: http://www.boj.or.jp
Governor: Haruhiko Kuroda (page 1459)

Chambers of Commerce and Trade Organisations

The Japan Chamber of Commerce and Industry (Nippon Shoko Kaigi-sho), URL: http://www.jcci.or.jp
JETRO (Japan External Trade Organisation), URL: http://www.jetro.go.jp

MANUFACTURING, MINING AND SERVICES

Primary and Extractive Industries

Japan lacks most of the mineral resources necessary to sustain a modern industrial structure, having to import such basic materials as oil, iron ore, coking coal and non-ferrous metal ores such as copper, nickel, bauxite. Japan's main mineral resource is coal with reserves estimated at about 8.5 billion short tons. However, production came to end in 2002 with the closure of Japan's last operating mine in Kushiro, the coal mining industry had been heavily subsidized. Steam coal is used mainly for power generation, and in some manufacturing, coking coal is used in the steel industry. Japan is now the world's second largest importer of coal, importing 205,983 million short tons in 2010.

Seven other types of minerals are mined on a fairly wide scale, but most of them are in quantities barely sufficient to meet minimum domestic demand. These seven are lead, zinc, pyrites, sulphur, limestone, feldspar and dolomite. Figures for 2007 show that Japan produced 165,965 thousand tones of limestone, 12,258,000 tonnes of quarzites, 3,655,000 tonnes of dolomite, 4,314,000 tonnes of silica, and over 11,000 kg of silver (2006) and 7,169,000 tonnes of zinc (2006). Silver production has fallen dramatically from 103,781 kg in 2000, to 54,098 kg in 2000 and then again in 2006.

Japan is the third largest consumer of oil in the world. Domestic output of petroleum is so limited (134,96 bbl/d in 2011) that Japan must import practically all the crude oil it needs; of an estimated oil consumption of 4.4 million barrels per day, Japan, with oil reserves of only 44 million barrels (as of 1 January 2011), imports 4.3 million barrels a day, making Japan the third largest importer of oil. As of 2011, approximately 80 per cent of its imports came from Persian Gulf countries such as Saudi Arabia (33 per cent), the United Arab Emirates (23 per cent), Qatar (10 per cent), Kuwait and Iran. It also imports from Russia. The Japan National Oil Company is government-owned. As of January 2011, Japan had 30 refineries with a capacity of 4.7 million barrels a day.

As of 1 January 2011, Japan had proven gas reserves of 1.0 trillion cubic feet, mostly along the western coastline. Liquified natural gas (LNG) is Japan's sixth largest imported commodity. Annual consumption is roughly 3.5 trillion cubic feet, while annual domestic production is only 116 billion cubic feet. Imports have increased to cover the outages caused by the situation with the nuclear power industry. Japan is now the world's largest importer of LNG. Development of the renewable energy industry is also expected. Figures for imports of LNG for 2011 show that 19 per cent came from Malaysia, 18 per cent from Australia, 15 per cent from Qatar, 12 per cent from Indonesia, nine per cent from Russia, eight per cent from Brunei, and seven per cent from the United Arab Emirates. (Source: US EIA)

Energy

Dependence on nuclear power has increased, with output nearly doubling between 1985 and 1996. Despite opposition to the use of nuclear power in the country, Japan was the third largest consumer of nuclear power in the world. As of 2011, Japan had 54 operating nuclear power plants and ranks behind only the US and France in terms of installed nuclear capacity (49 GW as of 2011). The government-run company that oversees the nuclear industry is the Power Reactor and Nuclear Fuel Development Corporation (PNC). Many oppose the development of nuclear power on safety grounds: in 2007 an earthquake hit causing a shut down of the Kashiwazaki-Kariwa nuclear plant. Following the March 2011 earthquake and tsunami a state of emergency was declared over the failure of the cooling systems at Fukushima nuclear power plant, an exclusion zone was set up around the plant and radiation levels inside the plant were reported to be 1,000 times the normal levels. The government had had plans to expand the nuclear power industry; following the tsunami these plans were on hold and many other countries around the world also halted their own development plans. It is expected that following the earthquake and tsunami Japan's energy wil increasingly come from gas.

As of 2009, Japan generated an estimated 948.8 billion kWh of electricity; 65.0 per cent of electricity came from thermal plants, 26.1 per cent from nuclear reactors, 8.4 per cent from hydroelectric stations and 0.5 per cent from geothermal, solar and wind. Consumption was an estimated 934.28 billion kWh, ranking it third in the world. Installed capacity was 284.49 billion kWh. Energy prices in Japan are among the highest in the OECD.

In 2009, the Japan had installed hydroelectric generating capacity of 48 GW, up from 22 GW in 2008. A number of large hydro power projects are under development including the 2,350 MW Kannagawa plant which is due to come online in 2017. The Omarugawa plant came online in 2012.

New legislation is due to come into force in July 2012 requiring utilities to buy power produced by renewable sources at feed in tariffs set by the government in order to increase investor and business partnerships. A consortium of seven companies is looking at the development of a large solar plan on the island of Honshu. The project includes a 50 MW PV plant and 6 MW wind plant. Wind, solar, and tidal power are being actively pursued, installed capacity from these sources has increased in recent years from around 0.8 GW in 2004 to 4.6 GW in 2009. However, they still only account for a small share of electricity generation.

In 2006, the total primary energy production in Japan was 3.953 quadrillion Btu in 2009 and consumption was 20.598 quadrillion Btu. Total energy consumption in 2008 broke down as: oil 46 per cent, coal 21 per cent, natural gas 17 per cent, nuclear 11 per cent, hydro 3 per cent and other renewables 1 per cent. (Source: EIA)

Manufacturing

The electronics industry has overtaken more traditional industries such as steel and chemicals to become the leading industry in Japanese manufacturing. Figures for 2010 show that Japan had over 224,000 manufacturing establishments, of these 28,974 related to the manufacture of fabricated metal products, 14,085 plastic products, 11,055 ceramic, stone and clay products, 4,742 chemicals and related products, while 4,486 were concerned with the manufacture of iron and steel. Figures for the same year show that over 4,907 establishments were concerned with the production of electronic parts, devices and circuits, and 4,907 with electrical machinery, information and communication electronics equipment. In 2010 the electrical machinery, equipment and supplies sector employed over 212,000 people (down from 583,000 in 2002) and shipped products were worth over 12 billion yen. In the electrical parts and devices sector over 450,000 people were employed and shipped products were worth 16.6 billion yen. Japan leads the world in the production value of electric appliances, exporting TVs and DVD players, audio equipment and other products. Industrial equipment has also been steadily expanding. The market has also expanded for Japanese language word-processors, and telecommunications equipment. The manufacturing sector has been hit by the global economic crisis and several of Japan's largest electronic companies including Panasonic and TDK announced job losses.

Domestic production of automobiles was 10,800,000 vehicles in 2005. In 2007, production had risen to 11,596,000. Of these, 9,945,000 were passenger cars. Toyota is the world's biggest carmaker but its business has suffered in the recession. In March 2009 Toyota announced its first ever loss in response to the global economic downturn which has hit the demand for new vehicles. Its problems increased when it was forced to recall vast numbers of cars because of safety concerns. Car production was hit in March 2011 when several factories were damaged in the devastating earthquake that month and production had to be suspended for a while.

Japan's machinery industry is now dominated by the production of machine tools and industrial robots. Recent production levels have been the highest in the world. The industry has shifted its focus to equipment which includes electronic devices, and has invested heavily in plant and equipment.

The steel industry continues to be of significance in Japan, but aluminium manufacturing was hit by the recession, and all but one of the country's aluminium refining plants has been shut down.

Other significant industries are shipbuilding, chemicals and textiles. Shipbuilding has improved its position after a period of decline. The chemical industry has expanded into areas which use new technology. Textiles has switched its focus to complete garments and fashion.

The following table shows the value of manufactured foods in shipments in billion yen.

Goods Shipments of the Manufacturing Industry

Industries	2010
Food	24,114
Beverages, tobacco & feed	9,613
Textile mill products	3,790
Lumber & wood products	2,134
Furniture & fixtures	1,575
Pulp, paper & paper products	7,111
Printing & allied industries	6,045
Chemical & allied products	26,212
Petroleum & coal products	14,992
Plastic products	10,903
Rubber products	3,029
Leather tanning, leather products & fur skins	362
Ceramic, stone & clay products	7,101
Iron & steel	18,146
Non-ferrous metals & products	8,911
Fabricated metal products	12,292
General-purpose machinery	10,100
Production machinery	13,646
Business oriented machinery	6,873
Electronic parts, devices & electronic circuits	16,633
Electrical machinery, equipment & supplies	15,120
Information & communication electronics equipment	12,585
Transport equipment	54,214
Miscellaneous manufacaturing industries	3,607
Total	289,108

Source: Statistical Handbook of Japan 2012

Service Industries

Provisional figures for 2009 showed that sales from the service industry amounted to 291,467,811 million yen, of which 40,456,400 million yen came from the information and communications industry, transport and postal activities 6,806,813 million yen; Real estate and goods rental and leasing 34,724,476 million yen; scientific research, professional and technical services 30,174,422 million yen; living related and personal services and amusement services 41,233,119 million yen; medical , health care and welfare 42,215,493 million yen.

Tourism

Figures for 2002 show that 5.24 million overseas visitors travelled to Japan, a larger than average figure due in part to the normalisation of relations with China and Japan acting as co-host with South Korea of the World Cup Football Tournament. Figures for 2004 show that foreign visitors numbered 6.1 million; the largest group of visitors were from the Republic of Korea, 6.7 visitors arrived in 2005. In 2009 visitor numbers rose to 6.78 million.

Agriculture

The number of people employed in the agriculture sector has fallen over the years. According to the Japanese Statistics Handbook, the number of workers has fallen from 14.3 million in 1960 (32.7 per cent of the total workforce) to 4.9 million in 2008 (4.8 per cent of the total workforce). The GDP share of the industry fell from 12.8 per cent in 1960 to 1.4 per cent in 2005.

In 2007 around 1.7 million hectares of land was under cultivation as compared with 6.08 million hectares in 1960. Much of the cultivatable land in Japan has been used for other purposes such as the building of factories and housing. Farmers have also left the sector for jobs elsewhere.

Rice is the most important crop grown in Japan. Figures for 2007 show that paddy fields covered 1.6 million hectares and Japan produced 8.7 million tons of rice. Total vegetable production in Japan (2005) was 13.7 million tons. There has been growing demand for lighter vegetables. A wider variety of vegetables is now available due to an increase in the number of hothouses.

Amongst the fruit available in Japan are oranges, apples, pears, and grapes. There is an increasing demand for milk used to make dairy products, particularly cheese.

There is outside pressure on Japan to import more agricultural products. In April 1999 Japan removed its ban on rice imports. Over 30 per cent of food imports came from the USA and over 10 per cent came from China.

The following tables show agricultural output in recent years. Figures are in units of 1,000 tons.

Agricultural Production in 2010

Produce	Int. $'000*	Tonnes
Rice, paddy	2,940,699	10,600,000
Cow milk, whole, fresh	2,394,276	7,720,460
Hen eggs, in shell	2,085,913	2,515,000
Indigenous chicken meat	1,993,116	1,399,260
Indigenous pigmeat	1,984,440	1,290,910
Indigenous cattle meat	1,368,204	506,484
Vegetables fresh nes	493,602	2,619,400
Potatoes	387,482	2,450,000
Apples	337,570	798,200
Cabbages and other brassicas	336,350	2,247,700
Tomatoes	255,258	690,700
Lettuce and chicory	251,429	537,800

* unofficial figures

Source: http://faostat.fao.org/site/339/default.aspx Food and Agriculture Organization of the United Nations, Food and Agricultural commodities production

Fruit Production (selected crops, '000 tons)

Produce	2005	2009	2010
Mandarin oranges	1,132	1,003	786
Apples	819	846	787
Grapes	220	202	185
Japanese pears	362	218	259

Source: Statistical Handbook of Japan 2012

Industrial Crops

Produce	2005	2009	2010
Crude tea	100	86	84
Sugar beets	4,201	3,649	3,090

Source: Statistical Handbook of Japan 2012

Meat, Milk and Eggs in Tons

Produce	2005	2009	2010
Pork	1,244,963	1,309,910	1,292,451
Beef	498,428	515,908	514,078
Veal	1,042	1,113	881
Horse meat	7,129	5,734	5,880
Mutton & lamb	126	143	na
Goat meat	73	41	na
Broilers	1,702,001	1,826,543	1,835,091
Cow milk	8,285,215	7,910,413	7,720,456
Eggs	2,481,000	2,507,542	2,515,323

Source: Statistical Handbook of Japan 2012

Forestry

Total forested area in Japan is 250,282 sq. km or about two-thirds of the country's area. However, the import of lumber has increased as demand has risen. Japan imports 72.7 million cubic metres of timber a year, whilst domestic production amounts to around 19.3 million cubic metres a year. The government has stepped up its forestation programme. Around 80 million cubic metres of growing stock is planted each year.

JAPAN

Fishing

The seas surrounding Japan have always been rich in all forms of marine life and the Japanese have always taken a substantial proportion of their food supply from this fertile source. Thus, Japan has been one of the major fishing nations in the world. The industry can be divided into three broad categories: coastal fishing, offshore fishing and pelagic or distant water fishing.

A number of restrictions have been introduced which bar Japanese fleets from some fishing grounds which include the areas around the former Soviet Union, the United States, Canada and New Zealand. The Japanese government is encouraging coastal fishing and other forms of marine enterprise such as the breeding of shrimp, yellowtail fry, scallops, and oysters. The following table shows fishery type and selected products in recent years in units of 1,000 tons.

Fishery Type & products	2010	2011*
Marine fisheries	4,121	3,797
-Tunas	208	198
-Mackerels	492	386
-Squids	267	287
Marine culture	1,111	863
-Oysters	200	164
-Lavers	329	291
-Pearl (tons)	21	20
Inland water fisheries	40	34
-Salmon & trout	14	12
-Shellfish	14	13
Inland water culture	39	39
-Eel	21	22
-Common carp	4	3

Source: Statistical Handbook of Japan 2012

COMMUNICATIONS AND TRANSPORT

Travel Requirements

Citizens of the USA, Canada, Australia and the EU require a passport valid for the length of stay, an onward ticket and proof of sufficient funds for their stay. They do not need a visa for stays of up to 90 days. Citizens of Austria, Germany, Ireland and the UK may apply, while in Japan, to the local immigration department for an extension of up to a further 90 days. Other nationals should contact the embassy to check visa requirements.

Foreign nationals entering Japan are routinely required to provide fingerprint scans and be photographed at the port of entry.

National Airlines

Japan Airlines (JAL), URL: http://www.jal.com
Services are international regional and domestic scheduled passenger and cargo.
All Nippon Airways (ANA), URL: http://www.ana.co.jp/eng/
Services are international, regional and domestic scheduled and charter passenger and cargo.
Nippon Cargo Airlines, URL: https://www.nca.aero/

International Airports

Major airports include:
Tokyo International, URL: http://www.narita-airport.jp/en/
Kansai International Airport, URL: http://www.kansai-airport.or.jp/en/index.asp
Central Japan Airport (also known as Chubu Airport), Nagoya, Japan. URL: http://www.centrair.jp/en
Fukuoka Airport, URL: http://www.fuk-ab.co.jp/english/frame_index.html
Kobe Airport, URL: http://www.kairport.co.jp/. Built on reclaimed land, the airport opened in 2006 for domestic flights only.

In 2010, approximately 82 million passengers were carried by air on domestic scheduled flights. (Source: Japan Statistical Handbook)

Railways

Recent figures show that the total length of railtrack is approximately 27,327 km. In 1987 the government privatised Japanese National Railways; the group was then divided into six regional passenger companies and one freight company, and renamed the Japan Railways group. Fast trains operate on various routes including the Shinkansen ('bullet train') which runs on five lines, the Tokaido, San'yo, Tohoku, Joetsu and the Hokuriku, which opened in time for the winter Olympics in 1998. Approximately 177 private railways provide a regional service. Recent figures show that rail transport accounts for 30 per cent of Japan's total passenger transportation. Figures for 2007 show that 22.86 billion passenger journeys were made by rail. Figures for 2007 show that 405,544 million passenger kilometres were travelled by rail. In 2007, approximately 50,850,000 tonnes were transported, 23,334 million ton-kilometres were carried. In 2006, railway freight revenue was 1,365 hundred million yen.

Most large cities in Japan have their own subway system including Tokyo, Fukuoka, Kobe, Kyoto, Osaka, Nagoya, Sapporo, Sendai and Yokohama.

Roads

Recent figures show that the total length of express roads in Japan is over 6,000 km and a total road network of 1,203,770 km. In 2010 there were over 78 million vehicles on the roads. Vehicles are driven on the left.

Ports and Harbours

Japan has over 4,000 ports, used mainly for fishing. There are 112 major ports, of which 21 are specially designated, 961 local ports and 2,944 fishing ports.

Traffic volume by type of transport

Frieght (million tonnes)	2004	2005
Motor vehicles	5,076	4,966
Railways	52	52
Coastwise vessels	440	426
Domestic aviation	1.1	1.1
Total	5,569	5,446
Passengers (million)		
Motor vehicles	65,991	65,947
- Buses	5,995	5,889
- Passenger cars	52,311	52,722
Railways	21,686	21,963
Maritime	101	103
Domestic aviation	101	103

Source: Japan Statistical Yearbook 2008

There is a ferry terminal in Tokyo from which there are services to Hokkaido, Okinawa and Japan's islands. URL: http://ww.tptc.or.jp/eng/ferry.htm

HEALTH

All Japanese citizens must have health insurance. In 2000, a new long term health insurance plan was introduced to help combat the problems faced of an increasingly ageing population and falling birth rate. The new plan has been designed to help meet the needs of the aging population providing health and social care for a greater number of people over a longer period of time. In 2009, the government spent approximately 18.4 per cent of its total budget on healthcare (up from 15.9 per cent in 2000), accounting for 82.3 per cent of all healthcare spending. Total expenditure on healthcare equated to 9.5 per cent of the country's GDP. Per capita expenditure on health was approximately US$3,754.

Figures for 2000-10 show that there are 274,992 physicians (21.4 per 10,000 population), 531,210 nurses and midwives (41.4 per 10,000 population) and 94,882 dentistry personnel. There are an estimated 137 hospital beds per 10,000 population.

Life expectancy is estimated at 83 years. The infant mortality rate in 2009 was 2 per 1,000 live births. The child mortality rate (under 5 years) was 3 per 1,000 live births. The main causes of childhood mortality are: congenital anomalies (40 per cent), injuries (11 per cent), diarrhoea (2 per cent), prematurity (8 per cent) and pneumonia (6 per cent). The measles immunization rate was 94 per cent in 2010. There were 450 reported cases of measles in 2010, 179,635 of mumps, 5,406 of pertussis, 89 of rubella, 104 of tetanus, and 22,693 of TB. All of the population has access to improved drinking-water and improved sanitation. (Source: http://www.who.int, World Health Statistics 2012)

EDUCATION

The education system is divided into five stages: kindergarten (1-3 years), elementary school (six years), lower secondary school (three years), upper secondary school (three years) and university (four years). Education for six to 15 year olds is compulsory but most students carry on through upper secondary level.

Japan spends approximately 3.5 per cent of its GDP on education.

Pre-school Education

As of May 2011 there were 13,299 kindergartens, of which 49 were national, 5,024 were public and 8,226 were private, a total of 1,597,000 children attended kindergarten and were taught by 110,000 teachers.

Primary/Secondary Education

As of 2011 there were 21,721 elementary schools, of which 74 were national, 21,431 were public and 216 were private, that year there were 6,887,000 pupils attending school and 419,000 teachers. That year there were 10,751 lower secondary schools of which 73 were national, 9,915 were public and 763 were private, they were attended by 3,574,000 pupils who were taught by 253,000 teachers. That year there were also 5,060 upper secondary schools of which 15 were national, 3,724 were public and 1,322 were private, they were attended by 3,349,000 pupils who were taught by 238,000 teachers.

A new curriculum was introduced in 2002 to kindergartens, primary and junior high schools, which was less regimented and created a regular five day school week.

Higher Education

In the academic year 2007 Japan had 64 Technical Colleges, of which three were three private, six were public and the rest were national schools. These colleges were attended by 59,000 students, taught by 4,000 teachers. Also in 2007 there were 434 Junior Colleges (398 private, 34 public and 2 national) with 187,000 students, and 11,000 teachers. As of 2007 Japan had 756 universities (580 private, 89 public and 87 national), attended by 2,829,000 students, with 168,000 teachers. Figures for 1997 showed that 180,086 Japanese students were studying abroad, mainly in North America and Europe.

Vocational Education

Recent figures show that Japan has 3,565 vocational schools (3,206 private, 218 public and 141 national), with 753,740 students, and 37,463 teachers. That year there were also 2,361 miscellaneous schools, 2 national, 45 public and 2,314 private schools catering for 230,502 students, with 14,084 teachers. (Source: Japanese Statistical Handbook)

RELIGION

The Japanese constitution guarantees religious freedom. The two major religions in Japan are Buddhism (35 per cent of the population) and Shintoism although the numbers of Shinto followers has fallen in recent years to around 2.6 million. There are 2.9 million Christians in Japan and 180,000 Muslims.

Japan has a religious liberty rating of 9 on a scale of 1 to 10 (10 is most freedom). (Source: World Religion Database)

COMMUNICATIONS AND MEDIA

Newspapers
Major newspapers include:
Asahi Shimbun (Tokyo), URL: http://www.asahi.com/english/english.html
Chunichi Shimbun, URL: http://www.chunichi.co.jp/
Mainichi Shimbun, URL: http://mdn.mainichi.jp/
Nihon Keizai Shimbun, URL: http://www.nni.nikkei.co.jp/
Nikkan Gendai, URL: http://gendai.net/
Sankei Shimbun, URL: http://www.sankei.co.jp
Tokyo Shimbun, URL: http://www.tokyo-np.co.jp/
Yomiuri Shimbun, URL: http://www.yomiuri.co.jp/dy/

Broadcasting
The broadcasting system in Japan is divided into the public sector, represented by NHK, (Japan Broadcasting Corporation) and the commercial sector. NHK has three radio channels, two TV channels, an overseas radio broadcasting service and two satellite stations. There are five national terrestial TV companies. Japan Satellite Broadcasting Inc., Japan's first private satellite broadcasting company, was launched in April 1991. There are an estimated 211 stations. Recent figures show that roughly 14.5 million Japanese households have cable television. Japan has been a pioneer of television technology and NHK has a channel dedicated to high-definition TV (HDTV).

NHK, URL: http://www.nhk.or.jp/nhkworld/index.html
Tokyo Broadcasting System, URL: http://www.tbs.co.jp/eng/
TV Asahi, URL: http://www.tv-asahi.co.jp/
Fuji TV, URL: http://www.fujitv.co.jp/en/index.html
Nippon Television Network, URL: http://www.ntv.co.jp/english/index.html

Telecommunications
Recent figures indicate that there are 35 million landline telephones in the country. Nippon Telegraph and Telephone Corporation (NTT) was privatised in 1985 and the domestic industry was liberalised. NTT owns one telecommunications satellite. Figures for 2011 estimate 123 million mobile phones are in use.

Estimated figures for 2011 show that Japan has over 99 million regular internet users.

ENVIRONMENT

The major threats to the environment of Japan are caused by the high consumption of fish which threatens marine and aquatic life, as well as air pollution caused by toxic emissions from power plants which results in acid rain.

Earthquakes are a regular occurrence in Japan as it lies on the borders of at least three tectonic plates. A huge offshore earthquale caused a major tsunami. The Fukushima nuclear plant was damaged and radiation leaked contaminating food supplies and leaving large areas uninhabitable.

Regulations controlling the emission of automobile exhausts are strict and emission controls on sulphur, nitrogen and carbon dioxides in factory waste gases have been strengthened. As a result the volume of sulphur oxides in the atmosphere in urban areas has decreased steadily. With the growth in the volume of rubbish produced by private households and factories, the promotion of recycling and the expansion and improvement of waste treatment facilities are urgent issues.

Discharge of greenhouse gases, million tons of CO_2

	1990	2000	2007
Total	1,207.8	1,346.0	1,347.3
Carbon dioxide	1,143.2	1,254.6	1,303.8
Methane	32.6	26.4	22.6
Nitrous oxide	32.0	29.3	23.8
Hydrofluorocarbons	-	18.8	13.2
Perfluorocarbons	-	9.7	6.5
Sulphur hexafluoride	-	7.3	4.4

Source: Japan Statistical YearBook

Emissions from the consumption of fossil fuels fell to 1,104.60 million metric tons of carbon dioxide in 2009 but rose to 1,164.47 million metric tons in 2010.

Japan in a party to the following international agreements: Antarctic-Environmental Protocol, Antarctic-Marine Living Resources, Antarctic Seals, Antarctic Treaty, Biodiversity, Climate Change, Climate Change-Kyoto Protocol, Desertification, Endangered Species, Environmental Modification, Hazardous Wastes, Law of the Sea, Marine Dumping, Ozone Layer Protection, Ship Pollution, Tropical Timber 83, Tropical Timber 94, Wetlands, and Whaling.

SPACE PROGRAMME

In 2003, the Institute of Space and Astronautical Science (ISAS), the National Aerospace Laboratory of Japan (NAL) and the National Space Development Agency of Japan (NASDA) were merged into one independent institution, the Japan Aerospace Exploration Agency (JAXA), enabling a systematic and effective approach to space exploration. Its vision for the next 20 years is to: build a secure and prosperous society through the use of aerospace technology; become the leading science centre through space observation and asteroid exploration; implement world-class space transportation; develop aerospace as the next key industry; and establish Japan's aviation industry and develop supersonic aircraft.

Japan's space agency launched its first lunar probe in September 2007. The orbiter, called Selene, will gather information on the Moon's origin and evolution over the course of a year. In 2009, a Japanese astronaut, Koichi Wakata, attached the exposed facility of the Japanese experiment Module to the International Space Station. In 2010, its Venus climate orbiter and a small solar power sail demonstrator were launched. A quazi-Zenith satellite was also launched. The Hayabusa Asteroid Explorer (NUSES-C) returned to Earth in 2010 after completing a 7-year navigation in deep space, bringing back particles from an Asteroid to earth for the first time. A H-II transfer Vehicle (HTV2) was launched in 2011.

Japan Aerospace Exploration Agency, URL: http://www.jaxa.jp/index_e.html

JORDAN

Hashemite Kingdom of Jordan

El Mamlaka el Urduniyah el Hashimiyah

Capital: Amman (Population estimate: 2,027,000)

Head of State: King Abdullah II bin al-Hussein (page 1371)

National Flag: A fesswise tricolour of black, white and green. A full-depth red triangle, base at the hoist, is charged with a seven-pointed white star

CONSTITUTION AND GOVERNMENT

Constitution
Following the end of World War I, the League of Nations awarded the areas of Jordan, the West Bank, Gaza and Jerusalem to the United Kingdom. It was agreed that the Transjordan Emirate, as it was known, would be ruled by the Hashemite Prince Abdullah. This mandate ended in May 1946 and Jordan became the independent Hashemite Kingdom of Transjordan. Jordan backed the Palestinians against the creation of Israel in 1948, took control of the West Bank, and renamed itself the Hashemite Kingdom of Jordan. In 1950, the formal union of Jordan and the West Bank was declared. Following the 1967 war, Israel occupied the West Bank and, although Jordan handed responsibility for the West Bank to the Palestine Liberation Organisation, it did not renounce sovereignty over the occupied territories until 1999. Jordan is now home to around 1.7 million Palestinian refugees.

Jordan's constitution was written in 1949, promulgated in 1952, and amended several times (notably in 1974 and 1976). Jordan's 1952 constitution declared the country a hereditary monarchy with a parliamentary system. Several constitutional provisions define the rights and duties of the Jordanian citizen, including those of worship, opinion and association. The constitution outlines the powers and functions of the state, enforcement of the laws, interpretation of the constitution, emergency powers and constitutional amendments. It also separates the executive, legislative and judicial branches.

The constitution allows the king to appoint, release or accept the resignation of the prime minister and of cabinet ministers upon the recommendation of the prime minister. In the event of the king's illness, the crown prince is empowered to appoint and dismiss the prime minister.

The cabinet (Council of Ministers) presides over and controls the government through ministers, heads of statutory bodies attached to the prime minister, administrative governors and local government councils. The constitution requires that the Council of Ministers should submit its policies and plan of action for the approval of Parliament within a month of assuming office. A vote of no confidence by the House results in the resignation of the Cabinet or the minister(s) in question.

King Abdullah II has named his half brother Hamzah crown prince of the Hashemite Kingdom of Jordan.

JORDAN

To consult the constitution, please visit: http://www.kinghussein.gov.jo/constitution_jo.html

International Relations

Jordan supports the establishment of a Palestinian State as a way of bringing to a satisfactory end the Middle East Peace Process. Israel and Jordan signed a peace treaty in 1994 and in January 1998 land was returned to Jordan. Jordan seeks the restoration of stability in Iraq and has a diplomatic presence there.

Jordan is the only Arab nation to have a Free Trade Agreement with the USA.

Recent Events

In April 2005 a new cabinet was announced, led by Prime Minister Adnan Badran. The previous government had resigned amid reports that the King was unhappy about the pace of reform.

In November 2005, Jordan suffered a terrorist attack when suicide bombers detonated explosives at three international hotels in Amman; 56 people were killed. Al-Qaeda in Iraq claimed responsibility. Jordan is one of two Arab nations who have made peace with Israel, and it has been criticised by some organisations for its close ties with the USA.

In August 2008 King Abdullah became the first Arab leader to visit Iraq since the US invasion in 2003.

In December 2009 King Abdullah dissolved parliament midway through its term and appointed Samir al-Rifat as prime minister in an effort to push through economic reforms.

Elections were held in November 2010, opposition party Islamic Action Front boycotted the elections. There were riots after it was announced that pro-government candidates had won a landslide victory.

In January 2011 street protests in Tunisia ousted President Ben Ali, street protests then broke out in Egypt and Jordan. The protesters were demonstrating against the rise in unemployment and demanding food and fuel costs to be cut, they also wanted electoral reforms, resulting in the direct election of the prime minister and more powers being given over to parliament. As a result King Abdullah accepted the resignation of the Prime Minister and his cabinet. Marouf Al-Bakhit was asked to form a new government and look into making political reforms.

King Abdullah gave a speech on the 12th anniversary of his accession to the throne; he promised to give up his powers to appoint the prime minister and cabinet although he did not give a date for when this would take place.

In October 2011 following continued protests King Abdullah replaced Prime Minister Bakhit with Dr Awn al-Khasawneh, a judge at the International Court of Justice. In April 2012 Dr Awn al-Khasawneh resigned, he had been unable to satisfy demands for reform. King Abullah appointed the former prime minister Fayez al-Tarawneh to the post.

In early October 2012, King Abdullah called for early parliamentary elections, to be held on 23 January 2013. The Muslim Brotherhood's political wing, the Islamic Action Front, called for a broader political representation. Early in October the House of Represetatives was dissolved and on October 11 a new caretaker government was sworn in headed by an independent politician, Abdullah Ensour.

In November 2012, protesters and supporters of the king clashed following demonstrations in Amman. The demonstration was over the lifting of fuel subsidies, during the demonstrations calls were made for the end of the monarchy.

Legislature

Legislative power resides with the king and parliament. The bicameral National Assembly (Majlis al-Umma) comprises the Senate (Majlis al-Aayan) and the House of Deputies (Majlis al-Nuwaab).
National Assembly, House of Parliament, PO Box 72, Amman, Jordan. Tel: +962 2 569 0455, fax: +962 6 568 5970, URL: http://www.parliament.gov.jo

Upper House

The 55 members of the Senate (or House of Notables) are appointed by the king for a four-year term. The number of senators cannot exceed half of the number of elected representatives.
Senate, House of Parliament, PO Box 72, Amman, Jordan. Tel: +962 6 566 4121, fax: +962 6 562 1782, URL: http://www.parliament.gov.jo

Lower House

In 1974 the Lower House of Parliament was prorogued. It was replaced by a National Consultative Council whose members were appointed by the king. Parliament was recalled in 1984 and elections were held for East Bank seats which had become vacant since 1974.

The House of Deputies, as it is currently known, is composed of 110 elected members who serve a four year term. In 2001 the King approved a law to increase the number of members from 80 to 108, later amended to 110. Some seats are reserved for various religious factions, ethnic groupings and there is a quota of at least six women's seats.

The House of Deputies approves the prime minister and cabinet, and has the power to vote any individual minister out of office.

Caretaker Cabinet (as at June 2013)
Prime Minister, Minister of Defence: Abdullah Ensour (page 1421)
Minister of Finance: Dr Umayyah Touqan
Minister of Foreign Affairs: Nasir Judah
Minister of Planning and International Co-operation, Minister and Antiquities: Dr Ibrahim Saif
Minister of Religious Endowments and Islamic Affairs: Dr Mohammad Nouh Qudah

---

Minister of Industry and Trade, Minister of Information and Communications: Dr Hatem Al-Halawani
Minister of Energy and Mineral Resources: Malek Atallaj Al-Kabariti
Minister of Justice, Minister of State for Cabinet Affairs: Dr Ahmed Zeyadat
Minister of Health and the Environment: Dr Mjalli Mheilan
Minister of Agriculture, Minister of Water and Irrigation: Dr Hazem Al-Nasser
Minister of Education: Dr Mohammad Al-Wahsh
Minister of Higher Education and Scientific Research: Dr Amin Mahmoud
Minister of Public Works and Housing: Walid Al-Masri
Minister of Social Development: Reem Mamdouh Abu Hassan
Minister of Public Sector Development: Dr Khleif Al-Khawaldeh
Minister of Municipal Affairs, Minister of the Interior: Hussein Hazza Majali
Minister of Labour and Transport: Dr Nidal Qatamin
Minister of Political Development and Parliamentary Affairs, Minister of Media Affairs: Dr Mohammad Hussein Moumani
Minister of Culture: Dr Barakat Awajan
Minister of State for Prime Ministry Affairs and Legislation: Nofan al-Aweel Al-Ajarmah

Ministries

Office of the Prime Minister and Ministry of Defence, POB 80, Amman, Jordan. Tel: +962 6 4644361 / 4641211, fax: +962 6 5695541, e-mail: info@pm.gov.jo, URL: http://www.pm.gov.jo
Ministry of Interior, POB 100, Amman, Jordan. Tel: +962 6 5691141 / 5702811, fax: +962 6 5606908, e-mail: info@moi.gov.jo, URL: http://www.moi.gov.jo/i
Ministry of Justice, POB 6040, Amman, Jordan. Tel: +962 6 4653533 / 5663101, fax: +962 6 4643197 / 5680238, URL: http://www.nis.gov.jo/justice/
Ministry of Economic Affairs and Administrative Development, POB 1577, Amman, Jordan. Tel: +962 6 4641211 fax: +962 6 4642520
Ministry of Foreign Affairs, King Hussein Street, POB 85, Amman 11118, Jordan. Tel: +962 6 4642359, fax: +962 6 4648825, URL: http://www.mfa.gov.jo/
Ministry of Finance, POB 85, Amman, Jordan. Tel: +962 6 4636321 fax: +962 6 4618528, e-mail: webmaster@mof.gov.jo, URL: http://www.mof.gov.jo
Ministry of Communications and Information Technology, 8th Circle, Bayader Wadi Al Seer, POB 9903, Amman 11191, Jordan. Tel: +962 6 5859001, fax: +962 5861059, e-mail: cio@moict.gov.jo, URL: http://www.mopc.gov.jo/
Ministry of Industry and Trade, Queen Noor St, POB 2019, Amman 11181, Jordan. Tel: +962 6 5629030, fax: +962 6 5684892, e-mail: info@mit.gov.jo, URL: http://www.mit.gov.jo
Ministry of Planning, POB 555, Amman 11118, Jordan. Tel: +962 6 4644466, fax: +962 6 4649341, e-mail: webadmin@mop.gov.jo, URL: http://www.mop.gov.jo/
Ministry of Tourism and Antiquities, POB 224, Amman, Jordan. Tel: +962 6 4642311, fax: +962 6 4648465, URL: http://www.mota.gov.jo
Ministry of Transport, POB 35214, Amman, Jordan. Tel: +962 6 5518111, fax: +962 6 5527233, e-mail: mot1@go.com.jo, URL: http://amon.nic.gov.jo/trans/
Ministry of Information, Amman, Jordan. Tel: +962 6 4641467, fax: +962 6 4648895
Ministry of Energy and Mineral Resources, POB 140027, Amman, Jordan. Tel: +962 6 5863326 / 5817900, fax: +962 6 5865714 / 5818336, e-mail: memr@memr.gov.jo, URL: http://www.memr.gov.jo/
Ministry of Public Works and Housing, POB 1220, Amman, Jordan. Tel: +962 6 5850470 / 5607481, fax: +962 6 5857590 / 5684759, e-mail: mpwh@nic.net.jo, URL: http://www.mpwh.gov.jo/
Ministry for Culture, Amman, Jordan. Tel: +962 6 5697359, fax: +962 6 5696598, URL: http://www.culture.gov.jo/
Ministry of Health, POB 86, Amman, Jordan. Tel: +962 6 5665131, fax: +962 6 5688373, URL: http://www.moh.gov.jo/
Ministry of Water and Irrigation, Amman, Jordan. Tel: +962 6 5683100 / 5689400, fax: +962 6 4649341 / 5642520, URL: http://www.mwi.gov.jo/
Ministry of Municipal and Rural Affairs, POB 1766, Amman, Jordan. Tel: +962 6 4646541 / 4641393, fax: +962 6 4640404 / 4649341
Ministry of Education and Scientific Research, POB 1646, Amman, Jordan. Tel: +962 6 5607181 / 847671, fax: +962 6 5666019, e-mail: moe@moe.gov.jo, URL: http://www.moe.gov.jo
Ministry of Labour, POB 9052, Amman, Jordan. Tel: +962 6 5698186 / 5607481, fax: +962 6 5667193, URL: http://www.mol.gov.jo/
Ministry of Agriculture, POB 2099, Amman 11180, Jordan. Tel: +962 6 5686151, fax: +962 6 5601924 / 5686310, e-mail: agri@moa.gov.jo, URL: http://www.moa.gov.jo/
Ministry of Parliamentary Affairs, Amman, Jordan.
Ministry of Youth and Sport, POB 6140, Amman, Jordan. Tel: +962 6 5604701, fax: +962 6 5604717
Ministry of Religious Affairs, POB 659, Amman, Jordan. Tel: +962 6 5666141, fax: +962 6 5602254, URL: http://www.awqaf.gov.jo/
Ministry of the State and Judicial Affairs, Amman, Jordan. Tel:+962 6 4641211, fax: +962 6 4642520
Ministry for Social Development, POB 6720, Amman, Jordan. Tel: +962 6 5931391, fax: +962 6 5932645 / 5673198, e-mail: mosd@mosd.gov.jo, URL: http://www.mosd.gov.jo/
Ministry of Environment, POB 1408, Amman 11941, Jordan. Tel: +962 6 5350149, fax: +962 6 5355487, e-mail: info@gcep.gov.jo, URL: http://www.moenv.gov.jo/
Office of the Chief of the Royal Court, POB 80, Amman, Jordan. Tel: +962 6 4637341 / 4641211, fax: +962 6 4631452

Political Parties
Jabhat al-'Amal al-Islami (IAF, Islamic Action Front)

Elections
Men and women over the age of 18 are eligible to vote.

In 1988, Jordan disengaged legally and administratively from the West Bank and elections were held. It was the first time that women were allowed to vote and had the right to run for election. Elections were held in 1993 and 1997. The main opposition groups boycotted the ballot in 1997. The next elections were postponed from 2001, eventually taking place in 2003.

Elections to the Chamber of Deputies were held on November 20th 2007. The Parliament guarantees a minimum of six seats for women, nine for Christians, and three for the Circassian and Chechen minorities. Independents loyal to the king continue to hold the majority, having won 98 of the Chamber's 110 seats. The main opposition party, the Islamic Action Front, won six seats, a fall on the 17 seats they won in 2003.

The most recent election took place in January 2013. Pro-government candidates won although the election was boycotted by the main opposition Islamic Action Front. Prime Minister Abdullah Ensour resigned ready for the the new prime minister to take over. The prime minister will be elected by MPs.

Diplomatic Representation

British Embassy, (PO Box 87) Abdoun, Amman 11118, Jordan. Tel: +962 6 592 3100, fax: +962 6 592 3759, e-mail: becommercial@nets.com.jo, URL: http://ukinjordan.fco.gov.uk
Ambassador: Peter Millett (page 1477)
US Embassy, PO Box 354, Amman 11118 Jordan. Tel: +962 6 592 0101, fax: +962 6 592 0121, e-mail: Webmaster@usembassy-amman.org.jo, URL: http://jordan.usembassy.gov
Ambassador: Stuart E. Jones
Embassy of the Hashemite Kingdom of Jordan, 6 Upper Phillimore Gardens, London W8 7HB, United Kingdom. Tel: +44 (0)20 7937 3685, fax: +44 (0)20 7937 8795, e-mail: lonemb@dircon.co.uk, URL: http://www.jordanembassyuk.org
Ambassador: Mazen Kemal Homoud (page 1443)
Embassy of the Hashemite Kingdom of Jordan, 3504 International Drive, NW, Washington, DC 20008, USA. Tel: +1 202 966 2664, fax: +1 202 966 3110, e-mail: HKJEmbassyDC@aol.com, URL: http://www.jordanembassyus.org
Ambassador: Dr Alia Bouran (page 1392)
Permanent Representative of the Hashemite Kingdom of Jordan to the United Nations, 866 United Nations Plaza, 4th Floor, New York, NY 10017, USA. Tel: +1 212 752 0135 / 0136, fax: +1 212 826 0830, e-mail: missionun@jordanmissionun.com, URL: http://www.un.int/jordan/testj
Permanent Representative: Prince Zeid Ra'ad Al-Hussein

LEGAL SYSTEM

Jordan's constitution guarantees the independence of the judiciary. The king approves the appointment and dismissal of judges through the Higher Judicial Council. The courts fall into three categories: civil, religious and special.

Civil courts include Magistrate Courts, Courts of First Instance, Courts of Appeal, High Administrative Courts and the Court of Cassation (Supreme Court). The civil legal system in Jordan has its foundations in the Code Napoléon.

Religious courts include shari'a (Islamic law) courts and tribunals of other religious communities. These courts have primary and appellate courts and deal with only personal law such as marriage, divorce, inheritance and child custody. The Council of Religious Communities has jurisdiction over analogous cases among non-Muslims.

The State Security Court, composed of both military and civilian judges, tries both military and civilians for offenses against the external and internal security of the state as well as drug-related and other offenses. The findings of the court can be appealled before the High Court.

There are some human rights abuses. The government restricts the right to change the government, and there have been cases of arbitrary arrest, and torture. Prison conditions are poor. The government restricts freedom of speech, press, assembly and movement. Jordan retains the death penalty. The most recent execution took place in 2006.

Judiciary of Jordan: http://www.kinghussein.gov.jo/government4.html

National Centre for Human Rights, URL: http://www.nchr.org.jo/

LOCAL GOVERNMENT

The country is divided into 12 regional Governorates: Al Balqa', Al Karak, Al Mafraq', Amman, At Tafilah, Az Zarqa', Irbid, Ma'an, Madaba, Jerash, 'Ajloun, and Aqaba. Each is headed by a governor and is subdivided into administrative sub-regions. The governorates are an extension of the central government, and are appointed by the King through the Ministry of the Interior who are also responsible for supervising them. Governors enjoy wide administrative authority, and in specific cases they exercise the powers of ministers. Municipal councils within a governorate are elected by local residents for a four-year term. The mayor and half of the council of the Greater Amman Municipality are appointed by the government, and the other half elected. At the village level, each village has a council appointed by the governor, and councils are changed as the governor deems necessary.

The following table shows the estimated population of each Governorate in 2010.

Governorate	Population
Amman	2,367,000
Balqa	409,500
Zarqa	910,800
Madaba	152,900
Irbid	1,088,100

- continued

Mafraq	287,300
Jarash	183,400
Ajloun	140,600
Karak	238,400
Tafielah	85,600
Ma'an	116,200
Aqaba	133,200

Source: Jordan Department of Statistics

AREA AND POPULATION

Area

The Hashemite Kingdom of Jordan lies between Israel and Iraq, with Syria to the north and Saudi Arabia to the south. The total area of the country is 96,188 sq. km, similar in size to Austria or Portugal.

The climate of Western Jordan is comparable to the Mediterranean climate. It has hot, dry summers and cool, wet winters with two short transitional seasons. Almost 75 per cent of the country, however, has a desert climate with less than 200 mm of rain per year. The three main geographic and climatic areas to be found within Jordan are the Jordan Valley, the Mountains Heights Plateau, and the eastern desert, the Badia region.

The lowest point in Jordan is the Dead Sea which is 408 metres below sea level, the highest point is Jabal Ram at 1,734 metres.

To view a map, please visit http://www.lib.utexas.edu/maps/cia08/jordan_sm_2008.gif

Arabic is the official language but English is also spoken.

Population

The population of Jordan was estimated to be 6,187,000 in 2010 (up from 5,180,000 in 2001), with an annual growth rate of 2.5 per cent over the period 2000-10. Jordan has a population density of 56.4 people per sq km. Nearly 79 per cent of the population lives in urban areas. The capital Amman has a population of around of 1,210,000. Following the occupation of the West Bank after the 1967 war, Jordan received a huge influx of Palestinian refugees.

Births, Marriages, Deaths

The crude birth rate was estimated to be 25.0 per 1,000 population and the crude death rate was 4.7 per 1,000 population. Life expectancy from birth in 2009 was estimated at 72 years, 69 years for males and 74 years for females. Healthy life expectancy was estimated at 63 years. The median age was 21. Approximately 38 per cent of the population was aged under 15 years and 6 per cent over 60 years. The total fertility rate per woman was 3.1 children. (Source: http://www.who.int, World Health Statistics 2012) Marriages in 2004 numbered 53,800 (equivalent to a rate of 10.0 per 1,000 population), whilst divorces numbered 9,800 (1.8 per 1,000).

Public Holidays 2014

1 January: New Year's Day
14 January: Mouloud (Birth of the Prophet)*
30 January: King Abdullah's Birthday
1 May: Labour Day
25 May: Independence Day
9 June: King Abdullah's Accession
29 July: Eid al-Fitr (end of Ramadan)*
14 November: HM King Hussein's Birthday
5 October: Eid al Adha (Feast of the Sacrifice)*
25 October: Islamic New Year*
25 December: Christmas
*Islamic holiday: precise date will depend upon appearance of the moon

EMPLOYMENT

Those in employment (over 15 years of age) in 2005 numbered 42,120, of which the largest age group was 25-39 (20,993).

The following table shows employment according to industry in 2005:

Economic Activity	Percentage
Agriculture, hunting and forestry	3.63.4
Mining and quarrying	1.1
Manufacturing	11.6
Utilities	1.7
Construction	6.3
Wholesale and retail trade	17.9
Hotels and restaurants	2.4
Transport, storage and communications	9.8
Financial intermediation	1.7
Real estate, renting and business activities	3.6
Public administration	18.1
Education	11.3
Health and social work	4.9
Other community activities	5.6
Private households with employed persons	0.3
Extra-territorial organisations and bodies	0.4

Source: Jordan Department of Statistics

JORDAN

Those unemployed numbered 7,298 of which 5,360 were male and 1,937 were female.

BANKING AND FINANCE

Currency
One Jordanian Dinar (JOD, JD) = 1,000 fils

The exchange rate of the Jordanian Dinar is linked to a basket of major foreign currencies at weights proportionate to the importance of each currency in Jordan's external economic relations.

GDP/GNP, Inflation, National Debt
Jordan has limited natural resources and has particularly scarce water supplies. Its economy rlies on external energy sources. Jordan has long received foreign aid. Traditionally the economy has relied on phosphates, tourism, potash and overseas remittances. The government is now trying to diversify by developing the information technology sector. Its economy has suffered because of problems in its neighbours. Sanctions against Iraq, Jordan's main export market, hindered Jordan's economy and the poor security situation in Iraq also affected trade between the two countries. King Abdullah is supporting economic reform and economic growth has begun to improve. There has been some privatisation of state companies. The government approved economic relief deals in 2011 and Jordan has also received foreign aid. Jordan is likely to continue to need foreign assistance to finance its deficit in 2012-13. There have been several protests against increasing unemployment, corruption and poor living standards.

GDP was estimated to be in US$28 billion in 2011 with a growth rate of 2.4 per cent. Per capita GDP was estimated to be US$5,900.

Services account for over 65 per cent of GDP, industry 30 per cent, and agriculture 5 per cent.

Inflation was estimated at 6.4 per cent in 2011. Total external debt in 2006 was estimated at US$8,000 million.

Total external debt was estimated to be over US$7.5 billion in 2011.

Direct foreign investment was estimated to be US$22 billion in 201.

Balance of Payments / Imports and Exports
Exports earned an estimated US$7.8 billion in 2011 and imports that year cost an estimated US$16.1 billion. The main export markets are India, US, Iraq, Saudi Arabia, EU, the UAE, Syria and Israel. Tariff free export areas, including the Qualified Industrial Zone and Aqaba Special Economic Zone, have been introduced to promote economic growth.

Main imports are foodstuffs, chemicals, rubber, textiles, iron and steel, machinery, electrical equipment and crude oil. Main exports are agricultural products, phosphates, potash and chemicals. Major import suppliers are Saudi Arabia, the EU, China, the US Egypt and South Korea.

Central Bank
Central Bank of Jordan, PO Box 37, 11118 Amman, Jordan; Tel: +962 6 463 0301/10, fax: +962 6 463 8889, e-mail: redp@CBJ.gov.jo, URL: http://www.cbj.gov.jo
Governor: H.E. Dr Ziad Fariz

Chambers of Commerce and Trade Organisations
The American Chamber of Commerce in Jordan, URL: http://www.amcham.jo
Amman Chamber of Commerce, URL: http://www.ammanchamber.org.jo
Jordan Chamber of Commerce, URL: http://www.jocc.org.jo/

MANUFACTURING, MINING AND SERVICES

Primary and Extractive Industries
One of the main industries is phosphate mining. Potash and phosphate exports account for nearly 25 per cent of Jordan's export earnings.

Jordan has no real oil reserves of its own, and used to import most of its requirements from Iraq under a special UN agreement. However, following the war in Iraq, supplies were disrupted. In 2003, Jordan received oil from Kuwait, Saudi Arabia and the United Arab Emirates. Jordan has an oil refinery at Zarqa with a refining capacity of 90,000 barrels per day. Figures for 2011 show that Jordan imported 114.000 barrels per day. There are natural gas reserves estimated at 213 billion cubic feet and in 2011 production was eight billion cubic feet, consumption that year was 37 billion cubic feet of which 29 billion cubic feet was imported.

Energy
Figures for 2010 show that Jordan generated 13.90 billion kWh of electricity and consumed 12.57 billion kWh.

Manufacturing
In addition to a petroleum refinery at Zarqa (producing around 90,000 billion barrels per day) fertilizer production and a cement plant, there are many small manufacturing industries, mainly in the Amman district, producing goods including pharmaceuticals, paper, sugar and glass. The government has set up several Free Trade Zones in recent years to promote growth in the manufacturing sector.

Tourism
Figures for 2003 show that Jordan had 5.3 million visitors, the majority from other Arab countries. This figure fell slightly in 2004 to 5.0 million visitors and was down to 3.2 million in 2006.

Agriculture
Due to Jordan's aridity, agricultural policy has focused on investing heavily in intensive irrigated farming of fruit and vegetables in the Jordan valley, while developing rain-fed agriculture in the highlands, and expanding fruit tree cultivation (olives, figs, apricots and almonds) in the hillier regions. The agriculture sector contributes 4.5 per cent to GDP and employs nearly 3.0 per cent of the work force.

Agricultural Production in 2010

Produce	Int. $'000*	Tonnes
Tomatoes	272,465	737,261
Indigenous chicken meat	241,575	169,597
Olives	137,458	171,672
Cow milk, whole, fresh	79,014	253,200
Hen eggs, in shell	38,898	46,900
Cucumbers and gherkins	34,980	176,179
Indigenous sheep meat	28,842	10,593
Potatoes	27,079	174,931
Chillies and peppers, green	25,957	55,138
Sheep milk, whole, fresh	23,976	61,570
Indigenous cattle meat	23,009	8,517
Lettuce and chicory	22,534	48,200

* unofficial figures
Source: http://faostat.fao.org/site/339/default.aspx Food and Agriculture Organization of the United Nations, Food and Agricultural commodities production

In 2004 there were 2.0 million sheep and goats and 69,000 cattle.

COMMUNICATIONS AND TRANSPORT

Travel Requirements
Citizens of the USA, Canada, Australia and the EU require a passport valid for six months and a visa. A one month, single-entry visa can be obtained on arrival at any point of entry except the King Hussein Bridge at the Jordan/Israel border. Passengers in transit within 24 hours with valid onward or return documentation and not leaving the airport do not require a visa. Other nationals should contact the embassy to check visa requirements.

National Airlines
Royal Jordanian Airlines, URL: http://www.rja.com.jo
The Royal Jordanian Airline was established in 1963. At present it covers most of the world's cities.

International Airports
Queen Alia International Airport: Location: 30 km south of Amman; Grade: ILS CAT II; Area: 23 million sq. m; Terminals area: 6,500 sq. m.; Aircraft types: all types; Airport Capacity: 3 million passengers a year
Amman Civil Airport: Location: 30 km south of Amman; Grade: ILS CAT I; Area: 2.275 million sq. m.; Terminal area: 5,700sq. m.; Aircraft types: all types; Airport Capacity: 1.5 million passengers a year
Aqaba International Airport: Location: 10km north of Aqaba; Grade: ILS CAT I; Area: 3 million sq. m.; Terminals area: 2,200 sq. m.; Aircraft types: all types; Aircraft Capacity: 1 million passengers a year

In total Jordan has 19 airports and aerodromes, 14 of which have a permanent surface runway.

Railways
There are 789 km of railway in the country. The system is operated by the Aqaba Railway Corporation and the Hijaz Railway. There are proposals for over 1,300 km of new railway including a line to run between Amman and Aqaba. Services was suspended in 2006 due to damaged tracks.

Roads
Jordan's classified road network covers approximately 7,200 km, 41 per cent of which are primary. 5,500 km are asphalt roads and 2,000 km are of gravel and crushed stone. In 2004 there were 614,600 registered vehicles on Jordan's roads. Bus services link Jordan with Damascas is Syria and Tel Aviv and Israel. Vehicles are driven on the right.

Shipping
The port of Al 'Aqaba plays an important role as a transshipment centre for neighbouring countries of the region. In 2004 it handled approximately 2,888 vessels.

Ferries run from Aqaba to Nuweibah in Egypt.

HEALTH

In 2009, Jordan spent approximately 18.6 per cent of its total budget on healthcare (up from 10.9 per cent in 2000), accounting for 70.3 per cent of all healthcare spending. Total expenditure on healthcare equated to 9.6 per cent of the country's GDP. Per capita expenditure on health was US$373 in 2009. Figures for 2005-10 show that there are 15,226 physicians (24.5 per 10,000 population), 25,046 nurses (40.3 per 10,000 population), 4,536 dentistry personnel, 8,763 pharmaceutical personnel, and 1,412 environment and public health workers. There are 18 hospital beds per 10,000 population.

In 2009, the infant mortality rate (probability of dying by first birthday) was 18 per 1,000 live births) and the child mortality rate (probability of dying by fifth birthday) was 22 per 1,000 live births. Major causes include diarrhoea (4 per cent), pneumonia (13 per cent), birth asphyxia (12 per cent), congenital anomalies (21 per cent) and prematurity (22 per cent).

According to the latest WHO figures, in 2010 approximately 97 per cent of the population had access to improved drinking water. In the same year, 98 per cent of the population had access to improved sanitation. Following improved sanitation diarrhoea accounts for just 4 per cent of childhood deaths. (Source: http://www.who.int, World Health Statistics 2012)

EDUCATION

Most education in Jordan is organised by the government. Today there are 2,770 government schools, 1,473 private schools, 55 community colleges, and 19 universities. Jordan has a very young population with approximately 30 per cent enrolled in educational facilities. Education is free for all primary and secondary school students, and compulsory up to the age of 15. Today Jordan has an estimated 95 per cent enrolment for its school age children. This represents a massive improvement from 1960 where the figure was only 47 per cent.

Figures from UNESCO show that 32 per cent of young children were enrolled in pre-primary school, 89 per cent of girls and 88 per cent of boys were enrolled in primary school and 87 per cent of girls and 86 per cent of boys were enrolled in secondary school.

According to 2005 UNESCO figures, the literacy rate was 95.2 per cent for males and 87.0 per cent for females. For the age group 15-24 years the rate was 98.9 per cent for males and 99.0 per cent for females.

RELIGION

The official religion is Muslim (Sunni) 92 per cent and there is a Christian minority of 2.8 per cent.

Jordan has a religious liberty rating of 3 on a scale of 1 to 10 (10 is most freedom). (Source: World Religion Database)

COMMUNICATIONS AND MEDIA

Traditionally all media is under rigorous state control. Criticism of the monarchy, religion and state institutions is not permitted.

Newspapers
Ad-Dustour, URL: http://www.addustour.com/
Jordan Times, URL: http://www.jordantimes.com/
Al Ghad, http://www.alghad.jo/
Al Rai, URL: http://www.alrai.com/

Broadcasting
Jordan Radio and Television, is the state run broadcaster, operating TV station and radio (URL: http://www.jrtv.gov.jo/jrtv/arabic/index.php). The first independent operator started up in 2007. International satellite stations are also available. Approximately 30 radio stations are also operating through JRT. Transmissions of international broadcasts are available.

Telecommunications
The service has improved recently with increased digitalisation. Fixed line useage has reduced wtih mobile phone subscriptions increased. In 2009 there were an estimated 500,000 land lines and 5.9 million mobile phones in circulation

Internet penetration is modest. In 2009, over 1.7 million of Jordanians had internet access, and there were some twenty servers in the country. The government aims to give 50 per cent of the population access to the internet by 2012.

ENVIRONMENT

Jordan was the first country in the Middle East to adopt a national environmental strategy. The National Environment Strategy for Jordan, drafted by over 180 Jordanian specialists is a document with long term plans for the environment based on the principle of sustainable development.

Institutions involved in implementing environmental policies are: the Ministry of Municipal Rural Affairs and the Environment; the Ministry of Health; the Ministry of Trade and Industry; the Ministry of Agriculture; The Royal Scientific Society (who help to monitor water quality) and the Jordanian Society for the Control of Environmental Pollution. The Gulf of Aqaba Environmental Action Plan (GAEAP), supported by the World Bank carefully regulates industrial growth in the sensitive marine environment of the Gulf of Aqaba. The plan is complimented by the Egypt Red Sea Coastal Zone Management and the Yemen Marine Ecosystem Protection Projects.

Jordan is a party to the following international agreements: Biodiversity, Climate Change, Climate Change-Kyoto Protocol, Desertification, Endangered Species, Hazardous Wastes, Law of the Sea, Marine Dumping, Ozone Layer Protection and Wetlands.

According to figures from the EIA, in 2006, Jordan's emissions from the consumption of fossil fuels totalled 19.89 million metric tons of carbon dioxide, amongst the lowest in the Middle East. This figure had fallen slightly by 2010 to 19.07 million metric tons..

Water Shortage
The most significant single environmental problem facing Jordan is the dearth of water. A high rate of population growth and periodic influxes of refugees have increased the imbalance between water supply and demand. The problem is intensified by the fact that Jordan has to share most of its surface water resources with neighbouring countries, whose control gives them a disproportionate share of the water.

With already one of the lowest levels of water resources in the world, if the current population trend continues, Jordan's per capita water supply will fall from the current less than 200 cubic metres per person to only 91 cubic metres. This will put Jordan in the category of absolute water shortage.

The 1994 Jordan Israel peace treaty guaranteed Jordan its right to an additional 215 MCM of water annually but this, though significant, is barely enough to maintain the current position. Talks with Syria are also hoped to help the situation by securing a share in the upper catchment of the Yarmouk River. Sixty-one projects at home are also hoped to yield a further 500 MCM per year.

KAZAKHSTAN
Republic of Kazakhstan
Qazaqstan Respublikasy

Capital: Astana (called Akmola until May 1998). Almaty was the capital until a presidential declaration in November 1998. (Population estimate, 2011: 775,000)

Head of State: Nursultan Abisevich Nazarbayev (President) (page 1484)

National Flag: A gold sun with 32 rays above an eagle in the centre of the flag on a sky blue background and a nation ornamentation on the hoist side in yellow.

CONSTITUTION AND GOVERNMENT

Constitution
The population of what is today Kazakhstan were initially a Sunni Muslim nomadic people who came under Russian influence, both culturally and in terms of their religion in the 18th century. On 5 December 1936 the republic was proclaimed a constituent republic of the USSR under the name Kazakh Soviet Socialist Republic.

A national language law was adopted in September 1989. The country declared itself a sovereign state in October 1990. Following the August 1991 coup President Nazarbayev declared the State Committee for the State of Emergency, which took over the running of the USSR, illegal. On 28 August 1991 the Communist Party of Kazakhstan dissolved itself and Nazarbayev resigned his post as First Secretary. The Independent Socialist Party of Kazakhstan, non-aligned to the Communist Party of the Soviet Union, was formed in September.

The Republic of Kazakhstan appointed its own defence minister in October 1991. President Nursultan won presidential elections on 1 December 1991 and appointed Yerik Asanbayev as his Vice-President, and on 10 December the Supreme Soviet renamed the country the Republic of Kazakhstan. On 21 December 1991 the country became a signatory to the Commonwealth of Independent States (CIS). This move was ratified by the Supreme Soviet on 23 December, together with an agreement to centralise control over nuclear weapons.

In August 1995 the Republic adopted a new constitution. This outlined the powers of the President, who can appoint the Prime Minister, senior ministers, diplomats and the chairman of the National Security Council. The Parliament consists of two chambers. The Majilis (Assembly) has 77 seats, 67 of them directly elected, and ten seats allocated proportionally, for a five-year term. The Senate has 39 members. 32 are indirectly elected, and seven appointed, for six-year terms, with half elected every three years.

The constitution was amended in April 2005 when the legislature passed amendments to the country's electoral law that banned political rallies in the period between the end of electoral campaigns and the declaration of official results. In May 2007, Kazakhstan's parliament voted overwhelmingly to allow President Nursultan Nazarbayev to stand for an unlimited number of terms in office, instead of the maximum two consecutive terms. In May 2010 deputies in Kazakhstan approved a bill granting more power to President Nazarbayev and gave him the title Leader of the Nation. He was also given immunity from prosecution.

To consult the constitution, please visit: http://www.akorda.kz/

KAZAKHSTAN

Recent Events

In 1997 the capital city was moved from Almaty in the south of the country to Akmola (formerly Tselinograd) in the north. The following year, the new capital was renamed Astana.

President Nazarbayev was re-elected in 1999 but the elections were criticised by outside observers and main rival, former prime minister Akezhern Kazhegeldin, was barred from standing. In November 2001 President Nazarbayev removed from government those officials who were members of a group calling for reform, Democratic Choice. In 2002 co-founders Mukhtar Ablyazov and Galymzhan Zhakiyanov were jailed on charges of 'abuse of office'. Ablyazov was pardoned in May 2003 and Zhakiyanov was released in August 2004 but was sent into exile; he was allowed to return in 2006. September 2004 saw President Nazarbayev's Otan party winning the legislative elections but again observers criticised the elections. The reformist group Democratic Choice was dissolved by the courts in 2005 and opposition groups formed For A Just Kazakhstan movement.

In 2001 an oil pipeline carrying oil from the Tenzig oil field to the Russian port of Novorossiysk was opened. Also that year Kazakhstan along with China, Russia, Kyrgystan, Uzbekistan and Tajikistan launched the Shangair Co-operation Organisation (SCO) to fight ethnic and religious militancy and to promote trade.

In May 2007, Kazakhstan's parliament voted overwhelmingly to allow President Nursultan Nazarbayev to stand for an unlimited number of terms in office, instead of the maximum two consecutive terms under the Constitution. Mr Nazarbayev has been in power since 1989 and his current term is due to end in 2012.

The former son-in-law of President Nazarbayev was sentenced to 20 years imprisonment in absentia, after being found guilty of plotting a coup. Rakhat Aliyev, who lives in exile, denied the charges.

President Nazarbayev announced that Kazakhstan was prepared to build a nuclear fuel bank to ensure other countries do not need to develop their own fuel. The idea had been proposed by the International Atomic Energy Agency in 2005.

In May 2010, parliament approves a bill granting more powers to President Nazarbayev; it gave him the title of "leader of the nation" and immunity from prosecution. He called early presidential elections in February 2011 and won the April election. Opposition groups boycotted the election.

In December 2011, during a strike in the oil town of Zhanaozen, clashes between striking miners and the poice resulted in 16 deaths. The government declared a state of emergency.

In October 2012 Vladimir Kozlov, leader of an unofficial Alga opposition party, was jailed for seven and a half years, he was found guilty of 'attempting to overthrow the government' he was accused of inciting violence during the Zhanaozen protests. Mr Kozlov responded by saying the sentence was politically motivated.

International Relations

Kazakhstan has stable relations with its neighbours.

Legislature

Kazakhstan has a bi-cameral system of government, the upper house, The Senate is composed of 32 indirectly elected members and seven appointed members, senators serve a six year term. The lower house, the Assembly or *Majlis*, has 67 directly elected members, and ten members whose seats are allocated proportionately, all members serve a five year term. **House of Parliament**, 473000 Astana, Kazakhstan. Tel: +7 3172 153430, fax: +7 3172 327102, URL: http://www.parlam.kz/, e-mail: parliament@kaznet.kz

---

Cabinet (as at March 2013)
Prime Minister: Serik Akhmetov (page 1373)
First Deputy Prime Minister, Minister of Regional Development: Bakhytzhan Sagintayev
Second Deputy Prime Minister: Yerbol Orynbayev
Third Prime Minister, Minister of Macro-Economic Issues, Minister of Integration: Kairat Kelimbetov
Fourth Deputy Prime Minister, Minister of Industry and New Technologies: Asset Issekeshev
Minister of Culture and Information: Dr Mukhtar Kul-Muhammed PhD
Minister of Foreign Affairs: Yerlan Idrisov
Minister of Economic Development and Budget Planning: Yerbolat Dossayev
Minister of Agriculture: Asylzhan Mamybetov
Minister of Economic Integration: Zhanar Aitzhanova
Minister of Energy and Mineral Resources: Sauat Mynbayev PhD
Minister of Finance: Dr Bolat Zhamishev (page 1543)
Minister of Defence: Dr Adilbek Dzhaksybekov PhD
Minister of Interior Affairs: Maj.-Gen. Kalmukhanbet Kassymov
Minister of Education and Science: Dr Bakytzhan Zhumagulov PhD
Minister of Labour and Social Security: Serik Abdenov PhD
Minister of Justice: Berik Imashev
Minister of Transport and Communications: Askar Zhumagaliyev
Minister of Health: Dr Salidat Qayirebekova
Minister of Emergencies: Dr Vladimir Bozhko PhD
Minister of Environmental Protection: Nurlan Kapparov
Head of the President's Administration: Dr Karim Massimov
Secretary of State for Cultural Affairs, Information and the National Language: Marat Tazhin

---

Ministries

President's Office, Akorda Building, Left Bank of the Ishim River, 010000 Astana, Kazakhstan. Tel: +7 7172 745684, fax: +7 7172 741869, e-mail: press@akorda.kz, URL: http://www.akorda.kz

Prime Minister's Office,Government House, 010000 Astana, Kazakhstan. Tel: +7 7172 745400, URL: http://www.government.kz
Ministry of Foreign Affairs, 31 Tauelsizdik Street, 010000 Astana, Kazakhstan. Tel: +7 7172 720518, fax: +7 7172 720516, e-mail: midrk@mid.kz, URL: http://www.mfa.kz
Ministry of Culture and Religious Affairs, House of Ministries, Entrance 15, 8 No 35 Street, 010000 Astana, Kazakhstan. URL: http://www.mki.gov.kz
Ministry of Defence, SEZ apt 2, Left Bank of the Ishim River, 010000 Astana, Kazakhstan. Tel: +7 7172 721591, URL: http://www.mod.kz/
Ministry of Education and Science, 8 Orenburskaya Street, 010000 Astana, Kazakhstan. Tel: +7 7172 742428, fax: +7 7172 742416, e-mail: pressa@edu.gov.kz, URL: http://www.edu.gov.kz
Ministry of Finance, 11 Pobeda Street, 010000 Astana, Kazakhstan. Tel: +7 7172 717764, fax: +7 7172 717785, e-mail: administrator@minfin.kz, URL: http://www.minfin.kz
Ministry of Energy and Mineral Resources, 37 Mira Street, 473002 Astana, Kazakhstan. Tel: +7 3172 337133, fax: +7 3172 337164, URL: http://www.minenrgo.kz
Ministry of Agriculture, 49 Abai Street, 010000 Astana, Kazakhstan. Tel: +7 7172 323763, fax: +7 7172 298559, e-mail: info_kam@minagri.kz, URL: http://www.minagri.kz
Ministry of Health, 66 Moskovskaya Street, 010000 Astana, Kazakhstan. Tel: +7 7172 317327, fax: +7 7172 317327, e-mail: info@mz.gov.kz, URL: http://www.mz.gov.kz
Ministry of Industry and New Technologies, Transport Tower, Kabanbai Batyr Avenue, 010000 Astana, Kazakhstan. Tel: +7 7172 241642, fax: +7 7172 241901, e-mail: pressa@mit.kz, URL: http://www.mit.kz/
Ministry of Internal Affairs, 4 Manas Street. 010000 Astana, Kazakhstan. Tel: +7 7172 722493, e-mail: press@mvd.kz, URL: http://www.mvd.kz
Ministry of Justice, House of Ministries, Entrance 13, 8 No 35 Street, 010000 Astana, Kazakhstan. Tel: +7 7172 740737, fax: +7 7172 740954, e-mail: news@minjust.kz, URL: http://www.minjust.kz
Ministry of Labour and Social Protection, House of Ministries, 35 Street, 010000 Astana, Kazakhstan. Tel: +7 7172 742851, e-mail: mintrud@enbek.kz, URL: http://www.enbek.gov.kz
Ministry of Oil and Gas, 22 Kabanbai Batyr Avenue, 010000 Astana, Kazakhstan. Tel: +7 7172 976883, e-mail: ayan@memr.kz, URL: http://www.memr.gov.kz
Ministry of Tourism and Sports, 33 Abai Street, 010000 Astana, Kazakhstan. Tel: +7 7172 753010, URL: http://www.mts.gov.kz
Ministry of Transport and Communications, 47 Kabanbai Batyr Avenue, 010000 Astana, Kazakhstan. Tel:+7 7172 241312, fax:+7 7172 241419, URL: http://www.mtk.gov.kz
Ministry of Emergencies, 22 Beybitshilik Street, 010000 Astana, Kazakhstan. Tel: +7 7172 944829, fax: +7 7172 934832, e-mail: mchs@emer.kz, URL: http://www.emer.kz
Ministry of Environmental Protection, House of Ministries, Entrance 14, 8 No 35 Street, 010000 Astana, Kazakhstan. Tel: +7 7172 740816, URL: http://www.eco.gov.kz

Political Parties

Nur OTAN (Fatherland) Party, URL: http://www.otan.kz
Leader: Nursultan Nazarbayev

In January 2005 one of the main opposition parties, the Democratic Choice Party of Kazakhstan was dissolved by the courts; it was accused of breaching the security of the state by calling for protests against election results. Opposition groups have since formed a movement called For A Just Kazakhstan.

Elections

Presidential elections took place on 3 April 2011 and were won by the incumbent candidate, Nursultan Nazarbayev with approximately 95 per cent of the vote.

Elections to the Majlis took place on 18 August 2007; all 98 seats were won by the Otan party. Partial indirect elections to the Senate took place in October 2008. The most recent election took place in January 2012, Otan won 83 seats, AK Zhol eight seats, and CPPK, seven seats..

Diplomatic Representation

Embassy of the Republic of Kazakhstan, 1401 16th Street, NW, Washington, DC 20036, USA. Tel: +1 202 232 5488, fax: +1 202 232 5845, email: kasak@intr.net, URL: http://www.kazakhembus.com/
Ambassador: Kairat Umarov (page 1529)
Embassy of the Republic of Kazakhstan, 33 Thurloe Square, London SW7 2SD, United Kingdom. Tel: +44 (0)20 7581 4646, fax: +44 (0)20 7584 8481, URL: http://www.kazembassy.org.uk
Ambassador: Kairat Abusseitov (page 1372)
British Embassy, Renco Building 6 Floor, 62 Kosmonavtov street, Astana 010010, Kazakhstan. Tel: +7 7172 556200, e-mail: british-embassy@online.kz, URL: http://ukinkz.fco.gov.uk/en
Ambassador: Carolyn Browne (page 1395)
Embassy of the United States, Building 3, Ak Bulak 4, Str. 23-22, Astana 010010, Republic of Kazakhstan. Tel: +7 7172 702100, e-mail: info@usembassy.kz, URL: http://kazakhstan.usembassy.gov/
Ambassador: Kenneth J. Fairfax
Permanent Mission of the Republic of Kazakhstan to the United Nations, 866 UN Plaza, Suite 586, New York, NY 10017, USA. Tel: +1 212 230 1900, fax: +1 212 230 1172, e-mail: kazakhstan@un.int, URL: http://www.kazakhstanun.org/
Permanent Representative to the UN: Amb. Byrganym Aitimova

LEGAL SYSTEM

The system is based on Islamic and Roman Law. The judiciary came under the control of the president and the executive branch following a referendum on a new Constitution in 1995. The Constitutional Council is the supreme law court of Kazakhstan. It has seven members (three appointed by the president) and decides the conduct of elections, the accuracy of parliamentary laws and the constitutionality of international treaties as well as appeals from the lower courts of law. There is also a Supreme Court, which hears appeals from the regional (oblast) courts. Local level courts serve as courts of first instance for less serious crimes such as theft whilst oblast courts hear more serious criminal cases as well as cases in rural areas where no local courts have been established. An arbitration court hears disputes between state enterprises, and there is a military court system.

The human rights situation remains poor. There have been recent cases of arbitrary arrests and prisoner abuse. Conditions in prisons are unhealthy. Corruption is widespread and the judiciary is not independent. There are restrictions on freedom of speech, the press, assembly, and association. Kazakhstan does not accept compulsory ICJ jurisdiction. The death penalty has been abolished for most crimes.

Supreme Court of Kazakhstan, URL: http://www.supcourt.kz/en/

Commissioner of Human Rights in Kazakhstan, URL: http://www.ombudsman.kz/en/

LOCAL GOVERNMENT

For purposes of administration Kazakhstan is divided into 14 regions (*Oblasts*), two cities, Almaty and Astana, and the territory of Bayqongyr (now leased by Russia). These areas are administered by a council which is elected for four years and headed by an *Akim*, a provincial governor. The regions are Almaty Oblysy, Aqmola Oblysy, Aqtobe Oblysy, Atyrau Oblysy, Batys Qazaqstan Oblysy, Mangghystau Oblysy, Ongtustik Qazaqstan Oblysy, Pavlodar Oblysy, Qaraghandy Oblysy, Qostanay Oblysy, Qyzylorda Oblysy, Shyghys Qazaqstan Oblysy, Soltustik Qazaqstan Oblysy and Zhambyl Oblysy.

In 1995, Kazakhstan and Russia agreed that Russia would lease for a period of 20 years an area of 6,000 sq km enclosing the Baykonur space launch facilities and the city of Bayqongyr (Baykonur, formerly Leninsk), in 2004 the agreement was extended to 2050.

AREA AND POPULATION

Area
The Republic of Kazakhstan is a landlocked state bounded on the west by the Caspian Sea and the Russian Federation, on the east by China, on the north by the Russian Federation and on the south by the Republics of Turkmenistan, Uzbekistan and Kyrgyzstan. The country's land area is 2,717,300 sq. km, equal to the size of Western Europe. Kazakhstan is the second largest of the former Soviet republics (after Russia) and includes large areas of grassland, some semi desert areas and mountains.

The climate is continental with cold winters and hot summers.

To view a map, please visit:
http://www.un.org/Depts/Cartographic/map/profile/kazakhst.pdf

Population
The population was estimated to be 16.062 million in 2010. The median age of the population is 29 years, with an estimated 10 per cent of the population aged over 60 years and 24 per cent under 15 years old. The annual growth rate was put at 0.7 per cent for the period 2000-10.

An estimated 59 per cent of the population live in urban areas. Towns with populations over 250,000 are: Astana (750,000), Almaty (1.2 million), Karaganda (440,000), Chimkent (370,000), Taraz (340,000) Ust-Kamenogoorsk (310,000), Pavlodar (300,000).

There are nearly 120 different nationalities comprised of Kazakhs (53.5 per cent), Russians (30.0 per cent), Ukrainians (2.4 per cent), Germans (2.5 per cent), Tatars (0.7 per cent) and the remaining minorities (9 per cent). Population density is 6 people by km sq. (2006).

The official language is Kazakh, while Russian is used for business purposes.

Births, Marriages, Deaths
Estimates for 2010 put the birth rate at 21.5 per 1,000 population and the death rate at 11.6 per 1,000 population. In 2009 the infant mortality rate was 26 per 1,000 live births. Neonatal mortality was an estimated 15 per 1,000 live births. Maternal mortality was an estimated at 45 per 100,000 births in 2009. The adolescent fertility rate was 31 per 1,000 girls. The total fertility rate was estimated at 2.6 per woman.

Life expectancy at birth in 2009 was estimated at 59 years for males and 70 years for females. Healthy life expectancy from birth was estimated at 53 years for males and 60 years for females in 2007. (Source: http://www.who.int, World Health Statistics 2012)

Public Holidays 2014
1-2 January: New Year's Holiday
7 January: Orthodox Christmas
8 March: International Women's Day
21 March: Nauryz (Traditional Spring Holiday)
1 May: Kazakhstan People's Unity Day
9 May: Victory Day
30 August: Constitution Day
25 October: Republic Day
16-17 December: Independence Day

EMPLOYMENT

Total Employment by Economic Activity

Activity	2008
Agriculture, hunting & forestry	2,349,000
Fishing	20,000
Mining & quarrying	200,300
Manufacturing	572,900
Electricity, gas & water supply	164,800
Construction	548,900
Wholesale & retail trade, repairs	1,150,300
Hotels & restaurants	103,100
Transport, storage & communications	588,900
Financial intermediation	96,200
Real estate, renting & business activities	378,200
Public administration and defence	352,500
Education	754,300
Health & social work	347,300
Other community, social and personal service activities	205,400
Private households with employed persons	24,400
Extra-territorial organisations & bodies	100
Total	7,857,200

Source: Copyright © International Labour Organization (ILO Dept. of Statistics, http://laborsta.ilo.org)

Figures from 2006 show that the unemployment rate was 7.6 per cent. (Source: ADB)

BANKING AND FINANCE

Currency
1 Tenge = 100 tien

GDP/GNP, Inflation, National Debt
Kazakhstan has plentiful reserves of fossil fuels and minerals and mining is the mainstay of its economy. Its economy is hindered by its poor but improving infrastructure. As a landlocked country it is dependent on its neighbours to export its oil. The financial crisis of 2008 caused a major drop in demand for oil and the economy went into recession although it has since recovered. The government is currently following a programme of diversificiation to try and reduce its reliance on oil. Kazakhstan is expected to join the World Trade Organization in 2013.

GDP had grown steadily in recent years, due to increased domestic production, stable economic policies and, more recently, high world oil prices. The economy dipped in 2008/09 but has since recovered. Kazakhstan's growing oil industry accounts now for approximately 30 per cent of its GDP and over 50 per cent of export revenues. GDP was an estimated US$210 billion in 2011 with a growth rate of 7.5 per cent. Per capita GDP is estimated at US$12,500.

Make-up of GDP in recent years is shown in the following table. Figures are in billions of Tenge and are at current market prices:

GDP by Industrial Origin

Sector	2008	2009	2010
GDP	16,052.9	17,007.6	21,647.6
Agriculture	853.3	1,045.4	945.4
Mining	3,003.6	3,036.3	4,174.6
Manufacturing	1,890.1	1,849.1	2,469.7
Utilities	268.9	309.4	457.5
Construction	1,298.7	1,341.5	1,677
Trade	1,965.6	2,076.0	2,834
Transport & communications	1,769.1	1,874.4	1,746.6
Finance	848.5	844.0	853.9
Public administration	272.3	348.6	417.1
Others	3,508.8	4,040.4	5,378.5

Source: Asian Development Bank

The inflation rate averaged 8.3 per cent in 2008, 7 per cent in 2010 and over 8 per cent in 2011. External debt for 2011 was estimated at US$101 billion. International reserves in 2007 were US$19 million.

Foreign Investment
Kazakhstan is a full member of the IMF, and entered into an Extended Fund Facility of US$450 million in 1996. As of August 1997 the Republic had signed more than 70 treaties to promote and protect investments as well as double taxation treaties with 20 countries. Special economic zones such as the new capital Astana have been established since 1996. Among other incentives to foreign investment, companies operating in these zones are exempt from customs duties and pay corporation tax of 20 per cent (compared to the usual 30 per cent). Foreign direct investments amounted to an estimated US$28 billion in 2011.

Balance of Payments / Imports and Exports
Major exports are petroleum, chemicals, wool, coal, ferrous and non-ferrous metals, meat and grain. Major imports are industrial materials, consumer goods, machinery and equipment.

The value of external trade in recent years is shown in the following table.

STATES OF THE WORLD

KAZAKHSTAN

External Trade (million US dollars, calendar year)

	2008	2009	2010
Exports, fob	71,183.5	43,195.8	57,244.1
Imports, cif	37,889.0	28,408.7	24,023.6
Trade balance	33,294.5	14,787.1	33,220.5

Source: Asian Development Bank

Main trading partners are as follows:

Direction of Trade, Million US Dollars, calendar year

	Exports 2010	Imports 2010
Total	47,601.4	35,812.6
China	10,031.3	10,207.1
Germany	4,497.6	1,932.4
Russian Federation	4,007.9	12,061.8
France	3,545.3	357.5
Italy	2,053.7	1,424.7
Romania	1,621.9	n/a
Ukraine	776.7	1,347.4
Turkey	2,246.3	901.9
United States	1,758.6	810.7
Austria	1,045.2	n/a
Poland	n/a	450.3
Netherlands	n/a	533.1

Source: ADB

Central Bank
National Bank of Kazakhstan (NBK), 21 Koktem-3, 480090 Almaty, Kazakhstan. Tel: +7 3272 504701, fax: +7 3272 506090, e-mail: hq@nationalbank.kz, URL: http://www.nationalbank.kz
Chairman: Grigoriy Marchenko

Chambers of Commerce
Chamber of Commerce and Industry of the Republic of Kazakhstan, URL: http://www.cci.kz/

MANUFACTURING, MINING AND SERVICES

Primary and Extractive Industries
Kazakhstan has substantial mineral resources. These include 90 per cent of the total former USSR reserves of chrome and nearly half those for lead, copper and zinc. There is large-scale mining of certain metals including copper, zinc, lead and gold (second largest reserves in the world) as well as iron ore, (20,300 thousand metric tons produced in 2004). An estimated 91 million metric tons of coal were produced in 2006. Of this, 63.7 million metric tons were consumed locally. 28.1 million metric tons were exported and 300,000 metric tons were imported. The country has coal reserves of an estimated 34 billion metric tons, of which 31 billion are hard coal. The mining industry is centred on Karaganda and Ekibastuz. Kazakhstan also produces beryllium, tantalum, barite, uranium, cadmium, and arsenic

Oil
The country also has proven oil reserves estimated to be 30 billion barrels, and is the largest producer of oil of the former Soviet republics after the Russian Federation. These have attracted interest from western investors. Kazakhoil, the state oil and gas company, is partner in nearly three quarters of this production. However, under the law of 28 June 1995 exploration rights may now be put out to competitive tender; China won a contract to develop an oil field in Kazakhstan and to pipe the oil to Xinjiang, 2,000 miles away. Other countries involved in the oil industry include the Russian Federation and the US. An international consortium struck oil in the area of the Caspian Sea belonging to Kazakhstan in 2000.

Figures for 2011 show that 25 per cent of Kazadhstan's liquid fuels exports went to Italy, 16 per cent to China, 12 per cent to the Netherlands, eight per cent to France, Seven percent to Austria and Switzerland six per cent.

In 2011, 1.6 million bbl/d of oil were produced (of which 1.55 million bbl/d crude petroleum). An estimated 263,000 barrels per day were consumed. Major oil production growth is expected in the next 10 years.Kazakhstan exported 1.3 million barrels per day in 2011. Kazakhstan exports to the world markets by pipelines to the Black Sea via Russia; by barge and pipeline to the Mediterranean via Azerbaijan and Turkey; by barge and rail to Batumi, Georgia on the Black Sea; and by pipeline to China, (the Kazakhstan-China oil pipeline spans 1,384 miles). In order to mazimise export revenues Kazakhstan has to improve and expand its export infrastructure. Projects under consideration inculde the Kazakhstan Caspian Transportation System (KCTS), which includes the construction of an 830-kilometre, 600,000 bbl/d capacity onshore pipeline from Eskene in west Kazakhstan to Kuryk on the Caspian near Aktau. Aktau is the construction site of a 760,000-bbl/d oil terminal.. The KCTS system will also include a maritime link to Baku, Azerbaijan.

Gas
As of 2011, Kazakhstan also has natural gas reserves of an estimated 85 trillion cubic feet. Production in 2011 was estimated to be 401 billion cubic feet compared to 25,178 million cubic feet in 2005. 1,354 billion cubic feet were consumed and 35 billion cubic feet were imported. As yet there is no large gas pipeline available outside the Russian system to export the gas; the Soviet Union intended for the gas be exported via Russia, but their company, Gazprom, left the project after being unable to reach agreement with its partners. Construction of a new processing plant is underway and this should increase production. There have been plans to build a pipeline from Turkmenistan through Uzbekistan and Kazakhstan to China.

This is currently a priority for the government, the Beineu-Bozoi-Akbulak pipeline, would Kazakhstan's demand centres with its supply and to allow for exports to China. The pipeline is expected to be completed by the end of 2015 and will have a capacity of 1 Bcf.

Energy
There are five hydro-electric power stations. The nuclear-power plant at Aktau is being dismantled but other nuclear stations are planned. Wind energy is also being developed. As of 2003 the system had the electric-generation capacity of 17 gigawatts. In 2010, Kazakhstan produced 78.09 billion kWh annually. Electricity consumption was 72.61 billion kWh. Industry was responsible for 58.3 per cent of energy consumption, transportation 35.7 per cent and residential 6 per cent. (Figures from the EIA).

In April 2009, Kazakhstan proposed building a nuclear fuel tank so that other countries need not develop their own fuel. The plan is backed by the IAEA and the US.

Manufacturing
A number of industrial sectors are well-developed in Kazakhstan. These include metallurgy, particularly aluminum, copper, steel, uranium, and zinc, heavy machinery and machine tools, petrochemicals, agro-processing and textiles.

Production (thousand metric tonnes)

	2004	2005	2006
Steel	5,372	4,452	4,170
Rolled steel	4,040	3,195	3,006
Acid, sulphuric	745	751	758
Sugar	543	525	491

Source: Asian Development Bank

Service Industries
The government of Kazakhstan is keen to encourage tourism. From 1991 to 1996 the share of tourism in the national income grew from 0.06 per cent to 0.23 per cent. Figures for 2006 show that Kazakhstan had 3.1 million visitors.

Agriculture
Agriculture is the traditional centre of the economy, although this has recently been hit by droughts. The government is undertaking a review of irrigation and land reclamation policies. Kazakhstan is also hit by a yearly locust plague. Although Kazakhstan is a large producer of grain and meat, the food-processing industry is not well-developed; the Republic exports some grain,but is still reliant on food imports.

Agricultural Production in 2010

Produce	Int. $'000*	Tonnes
Cow milk, whole, fresh	1,463,111	5,347,540
Indigenous cattle meat	1,098,547	406,662
Wheat	968,529	9,638,400
Indigenous sheep meat	334,559	122,873
Potatoes	328,887	2,554,600
Indigenous pigmeat	316,658	205,991
Tomatoes	219,307	293,420
Indigenous chicken meat	140,318	98,510
Hen eggs, in shell	138,757	207,300
Cotton lint	132,133	92,452
Indigenous horse meat	113,846	73,088
Rice, paddy	100,638	373,150

* unofficial figures
Source: http://faostat.fao.org/site/339/default.aspx Food and Agriculture Organization of the United Nations, Food and Agricultural commodities production

COMMUNICATIONS AND TRANSPORT

Travel Requirements
Citizens of the USA, Canada, Australia and the EU require a passport valid for three months beyond the length of stay and a visa. All foreigners are required to register with the local police within five days of arrival except UK citizens staying less than 30 days. Other nationals should contact the embassy to check visa requirements. Long-term visitors require an HIV/AIDS free certificate.

National Airlines
Air Astana, URL: http://www.airastana.com
Aeroservice Air Company, Tel: +7 3272 366926, fax: +7 3272 529345
Sayakhat Air Company, e-mail: sayakhat@asdc.kz, URL: http://www.asdc.kz/sayakhat

International Airports
There are airports situated in eighteen locations regionally as well as in the former capital Almaty. Airspace is controlled by the following authority:
Ministry of Transport, Communications and Transport, Tel: +7 3172 326277, fax: +7 3172 321696

Railways
There is an extensive railway network in Kazakhstan of some 14,400 km administered in three regions: North (Astana), Western (Aktyubinsk) and South-East (Almaty). A new line between Almaty-Chimkent is under construction. A recent addition to the rail network is a link to Ürümqi, China. There are also rail links to Novosibirsk and Moscow, Russia.

Roads

The total length of motor roads is over 164,900 km, of which 99,000 km are hard-surfaced. According to recent figures the person-to-car rate is 11.9 people per motor vehicle. A bus route links Kazakhstan with Ürümqi, China. Vehicles are driven on the right.

Ports and Harbours

Kazakhstan has harbours at Shevchenko, Gur'yev, Oskemen, Pavlodar and Semipalatinsk.

HEALTH

Kazakhstan provides medical care for its citizens which is funded through health insurance. Figures for 2009 show that 4.5 per cent of the value of GDP was spent on healthcare (per capita US$326). General government expenditure on health accounts for approximately 59.2 per cent of total expenditure on health. External resources account for 0.3 per cent of expenditure. The remaining private expenditure is out of pocket.

According to the World Health Organisation, in 2000-10 there were 60,656 physicians (41 per 10,000 population). In the same year, there were an estimated 122,453 nurses and midwives (82.8 per 10,000 inhabitants), 12,230 pharmaceutical personnel (8.3 per 10,000 population) and 5,691 dentistry personnel (3.9 per 10,000 population). There are an estimated 76 hospital beds per 10,000 population.

In 2010, an estimated 95 per cent of the population had access to improved water sources and an estimated 97 per cent of the population had sustainable access to improved sanitation.

In 2009, the infant mortality rate was 29 per 1,000 live births and the under-five mortality rate was 33 per 1,000 live births. In 2008, the main causes of deaths of children aged under five years were: congenital anomalies, 14 per cent, diarrhoeal diseases 6 per cent, pneumonia 13 per cent, prematurity 22 per cent, birth asphyxia 10 per cent and neo-natal sepsis 7 per cent. In 2005-11, an estimated 14.8 per cent of children were overweight for their age, 4.9 per cent underweight and 17.5 per cent were stunted for age. In 2010, there were 19,703 reported cases of TB. (Source: http://www.who.int, World Health Statistics 2012)

EDUCATION

Education is free and compulsory up to secondary level. In 2005, public expenditure on education was 2.3 per cent of GDP and 12 per cent of total government expenditure.

The state-owned schools of general education provide both primary and secondary education. There are a number of specialised schools including those that teach in other languages. Recent figures show that of the total number of schools, 3,291 teach in Kazakh, 2,406 in Russian, and 2,138 in Russian and Kazakh. A small number of schools teach in Uzbek, Uigur, Tajik, Ukrainian and German. There are 292 vocational schools, attended by 117,000 students, which provide training in over 300 professions. Higher education is provided by 126 institutions of which 53 are state-owned.

Figures for 2007 from UNESCO show that 38 per cent of young children were enrolled in pre-primary school, 90 per cent of girls and 90 per cent of boys were enrolled in primary school where the pupil to teacher ratio was 17 to 1, 86 per cent of girls and 86 per cent of boys were enrolled in secondary school and 51 per cent of the population of tertiary age students were enrolled in tertiary education. Government figures say that 100 per cent of children complete their primary education.

Adult literacy was put at 99.6 per cent in 2007 which rose the level of 99.8 per cent among the 15-24 age group.

RELIGION

Islam is the dominant religion in Kazakhstan with 52 per cent, followed by the Russian Orthodox Church 44 per cent, Protestant 2 per cent, and other 7 per cent.

Kazakhstan has a religious liberty rating of 4 on a scale of 1 to 10 (10 is most freedom). (Source: World Religion Database)

COMMUNICATIONS AND MEDIA

The constitution guarantees a free press but there are reports of harrassment and censorship of opposition and private media. Insulting the president is a criminal offence. The government controls the printing presses and also most television and radio transmission facilities. In 2010, a court overturned a ruling that banned the media from publishing criticism of President Nazarbayev's son-in-law, Timur Kulibayev.

Newspapers

There are numerous print and online newspapers, including:
Kazakhstanskaya Pravda, (government backed), URL: http://www.kazpravda.kz/
Ekspress-K, private, Russian language, URL: http://www.express-k.kz/
Zhas Alash, private, Kazakh language, URL: http://www.zhasalash.kz/
Vremya, private, oppostion weekly, URL: http://www.time.kz/

Broadcasting

The main state run broadcasting company is Television and Radio of Kazakhstan Corporation which was set up in 1920. The state owns most networks but there are several private radio and TV stations.
Kazakh TV, URL: http://www.kazakh.tv/
Kharbar TV, URL: http://www.khabar.kz/, state-run, in Russian and Kazakh.
Kazakh Commercial TV, URL: http://www.ktk.kz/, private in Russian and Kazakh.
Caspionet TV, URL: http://www.caspionet.kz/, satellite channel, Russian, Kazakh, English.

Telecommunications

Figures from 2008 estimated that there were 3.4 million main telephone lines and an estimated 14 million mobile phone subscribers (approx. 80 per cent). In 2008, an estimated 1.8 million people were internet users.

ENVIRONMENT

Industrial pollution is severe in some cities and there are radioactive and/or toxic sites (left over from the Soviet defence industry) scattered around the country.

The country has also been subject to toxic dust storms since the two main rivers feeding the Aral Sea were diverted for irrigation purposes in the late 1960s. By the 1990s, the world's fourth largest inland body of water had shrunk to a quarter of its size. A recently constructed dam is helping to reverse one of the world's worst man-made environmental disasters and bring back the sea. The 13 km dam (financed by loans from the World Bank) split the sea, and allows the river to feed the northern Aral; the sea has been pushing back into the desert and Kazakh officials claim that 40 per cent of the water has returned so far.

In 2003, energy related carbon dioxide emissions were estimated to be 150 million metric tons (of which coal 64 per cent). Per capita energy related carbon dioxide emissions were estimated to be 9.7 metric tons. In 2006, Kazakhstan's emissions from the consumption of fossil fuels totalled 213.50 million metric tons of carbon dioxide; this figure fell to 184.47 million metric tons by 2010. (Source: EIA)

On an international level Kazakhstan has signed conventions on: Air Pollution, Biodiversity, Climate Change, Desertification, Endangered Species, Environmental Modification, Hazardous Wastes, Ozone Layer Protection, Ship Pollution, and Wetlands.

SPACE PROGRAMME

The Baikonur space centre, in north Kazakhstan, was the prime location for the former USSR space programme and is the largest operational space launch facility. This area, including the city of Bayqongyr, is now leased by the Russian Federation, currently until 2050. Numerous missions are launched annually. However, Russia has recently said it may decrease usage of the facility. Kazakhstan has its own space agency, Kazcosmos, which launched its first satellite in 2006. Its current strategic plan (2011-15) called for the development of a comprehensive terrestial infrastucture including increased satellite launch facilities and further development of space technologies.

STATES OF THE WORLD

KENYA
Republic of Kenya
Jamhuri y Kenya

Capital: Nairobi (Population estimate, 2010: 3.18 million)

Head of State: Uhuru Kenyatta (page 1455)

Vice-President: William Samoei arap Ruto

National Flag: Three horizontal stripes of green, black and red, the red having white edging, and in the centre a black and white African shield in front of two crossed spears

CONSTITUTION AND GOVERNMENT

Constitution

On 12 December 1963 Kenya became an independent state and a member of the Commonwealth. It was proclaimed a republic in December 1964. Jomo Kenyatta, head of the Kenya African National Union (KANU), was the first president of the republic. KANU became the sole political party after 1969. After President Kenyatta's death in 1978, Vice-President Daniel Arap Moi became president.

In 1991 there were changes to the constitution to allow multi-party politics. In 1997 President Moi agreed to enact his own package of reforms. Certain repressive rules dating from British colonial times were amended or repealed, and state radio and television were to give equal

KENYA

coverage to the opposition. 10 opposition nominees were added to the electoral commission. A Constitutional review committee was set up and announced that a draft new constitution would be ready to go before parliament in mid-September 2002. The then president Daniel Arap Moi dissolved parliament on 25 October 2002 before it could approve the changes. His successor, President Mwai Kibaki, confirmed that he intended to introduce the new constitution in mid-2004. Talks on the constitution stalled in mid-2004 over the exact powers of the president. The first draft constitution called for the dividing up of the presidential power, between the president and a newly created post of Prime Minister. There would also be devolved power on a four tier basis, national, provincial, district and rural; the parliament would also become a bi-cameral legislature. This draft was known as the Bomas draft. Following long and protracted political wrangling, the original amendments were scaled down. In what was seen as a protest against President Kibaki and allegations of corruption against the government, the new constitution was rejected. President Kibaki responded by replacing his cabinet.

In November 2009 a draft constitution which would cut the president's powers and put the prime minister in charge of routine government business was published. It was approved by referendum in 2010. To consult the new constitution, please visit: http://www.kenya-information-guide.com/kenya-constitution.html.

International Relations

Kenya is a member of the Commonwealth and therefore has close ties with the UK. Kenya is also a member of several international organisations including the UN, the African Union, the East African Community and the Common Market for Western and Southern Africa.

Recent Events

Kenya has been suffering the effects of a long drought and, in January 2006, the government estimated that four million people in the north of the country were in need of food aid. In April 2006 Kenya entered an agreement with China which allows China to explore for oil off the Kenyan coast.

Presidential and Parliamentary elections were held in December 2007. President Kibaki claimed victory, leading to widespread protests and accusations of vote rigging. The opposition party, Orange Democratic Movement (ODM), won the most seats in the parliamentary election. More than 250,000 people were displaced by the violence which subsequently erupted. President Kibaki began announcing his government in January 2008 and left several posts open, after proposing power sharing as a solution. This offer met with a lukewarm response. In February Ban Ki-moon General Secretary of the UN travelled to Kenya to assess the situation and look for a peaceful solution. Former UN Secretary General Kofi Annan acted as mediator. The first round of talks were adjourned on February 21 but it was understood that a newly created post of Prime Minister would be filled by a member of the opposition, forming the basis of a grand coalition. Talks resumed at the end of February and resulted in agreement over a coalition consisting of the Party of National Unity and the The Orange Democratic Movement. The new post of Prime Minister was filled by Raila Odinga, leader of ODM, and two new posts of Deputy Prime Minister were also created. The cabinet was finally sworn in April 2008. In June 2008 Minister of Roads Kipkalya Kones, was killed in a plane crash.

Following severe droughts the government said in August 2009 that at least one third of the population were in need of food aid, and moved to begin distributing food and medical aid to affected areas.

President Mwai Kibaki suspended several senior officials following corruption scandals in the education and agriculture ministries. In February 2010 the coalition government came under strain when President Kibaki overturned a decision by Prime Minister Raila Odinga to suspend the country's agriculture and education ministers over alleged corruption.

In July 2010 Kenya and its neighbours approved the forming of a new East African Common Market, with the intention of integrating the region's economy.

In July 2011 Kenya and other horn of Africa countries began to feel the effects of the region's worst drought for 60 years; thousands of animals have died and and crops have withered in fields. The crisis has been further fuelled by food shortages following a drought in 2009 of which most countries are still feeling the effects. Western aid agencies are fearful that the drought will escalate into a full blown famine. At the Dadaab refugee camp in northern Kenya around 1,000 refugees were arriving each day, mainly escaping the drought and fighting in Somalia.

In May 2012, more than 30 people are injured in an attack on a shopping centre in Nairobi. The police accused Somalia's Al-Shabab Islamist militia of being responsible. Al-Shabab was also thought to be responsible for an attack on a church near the Somali border in July 2012 in which 15 people were killed.

In July 2012, Britain acknowledged that under its colonial administration, detainees were tortured during the Mau Mau uprising in the 1950s, veterans then claimed damages through the High Court in London.

In August - September 2012, there were serious outbreaks of violence in the Coast Province. Over 100 people were killed in clashes over land and resources in Tana River District. The government imposed an overnight curfew.

In June 2013 the British Government gave a statement regretting the torture during the suppression of the Mau Mau, and promised to pay £20 million in compensation.

Legislature

The Cabinet consists of the President and Ministers who are collectively responsible to the National Assembly. The president appoints the cabinet. There are 224 seats in the National Assembly, 210 of which are directly elected for a five-year term. A further 12 members representing special interests are nominated by the president. In addition there are two ex-officio members - the speaker and the Attorney-General. Suffrage is universal at 18.

National Assembly, Parliament Buildings, Parliament Road, Nairobi, Kenya. Tel: +254 20 222 1291, fax: +254 20 233 6589, e-mail: bunge@swiftkenya.com, URL: http://www.parliament.go.ke

Cabinet (as at June 2013)

Cabinet Secretary for the Interior and Co-ordination of the National Government: Joseph Ole Lenku
Minister of Defence: Raychelle Omamo
Minister for Foreign Affairs: Amina Mohamed
Minister for the National Treasury: Henry Rotich
Minister of State for Devolution and Planning: Anne Waiguru
Minister for Mining: Najib Balala
Minister for Education: Prof. Jacob Kaimenyi
Minister for Lands, Housing and Urban Development: Charity Ngilu
Minister of Transport and Infrastructure: Michael Kamua
Minister of Education: Jacob Kaimemyi
Minister of Health: James Wainana Macharia
Minister of Water and Natural Resources, Minister for the Environment: Judy Wakhungu
Minister of Agriculture, Livestock and Fisheries: Felix Kosgey
Minister of Energy and Petroleum: Davis Chirchir
Minister of East African Affairs, Commerce and Tourism: Phyllis Kandie
Minister for Information, Communication and Technology: Dr Fred Okengo Matiang'i
Minister of Industrialisation and Enterprise Development: Adan Abdulla Mohammed
Minister for Sports, Culture and Arts: Dr Hassan Wario
Minister for Labour, Social Security and Services: Kazungu Kambi

Ministries

The Office of the President, Harambee House, Harambee Avenue, PO Box 30510, Nairobi, Kenya. Tel: +254 20 227411, fax: +254 20 210150, URL: http://www.officeofthepresident.go.ke
Office of the Prime Minister, Treasury Building 14th floor, Harambee Avenue, PO Box 74434, Nairobi, Kenya. Tel: +254 20 252 299, e-mail: info@primeminister.go.ke, URL: http://www.primeminister.go.ke
Ministry of Finance, Treasury Building, Harambee Avenue, PO Box 30007, Nairobi, Kenya. Tel: +254 20 2338111, fax: +254 20 2330 426, e-mail: info@treasury.go.ke, URL: http://www.treasury.go.ke
Ministry of Foreign Affairs, Old Treasury Building, Harambee Avenue, PO Box 30551, Nairobi, Kenya. Tel: +254 20 2334 433, e-mail: press@mfa.go.ke, URL: http://www.mfa.go.ke
Ministry of Education, Jogoo House B, Harambee Avenue, PO Box 30040, Nairobi, Kenya. Tel: +254 20 2334 411, e-mail: info@education.go.ke, URL: http://www.education.go.ke
Ministry of Labour, NSSF Building, Bishop Road, PO Box 40326, Nairobi, Kenya. Tel: +254 20 2729 800, e-mail: admin@labour.go.ke, URL: http://www.labour.go.ke
Ministry of Energy, Nyayo House, Kenyatta Avenue, PO Box 30582, Nairobi, Kenya. Tel: +254 20 2333 551, e-mail: ps@energy.go.ke, URL: http://www.energy.go.ke
Ministry of Environment, Natural Resources and Wildlife, NHIF Building 12th Floor, Ngong Road, PO Box 30126, Nairobi, Kenya. Tel: +254 20 2730 808, fax: +254 20 2713 654, e-mail: mec@nbnet.co.ke, URL: http://www.environment.go.ke
Ministry of Roads, Public Works and Housing, Ministry of Works Building, Ngong Road, PO Box 30260, Nairobi, Kenya. Tel: +254 20 723101 / 723188 / 723155 / 713135, URL: http://www.publicworks.go.ke/
Ministry of Health, Medical HQ, Afya House, Cathedral Road, PO Box 30016, Nairobi, Kenya. Tel: +254 20 2717 077, fax: +254 20 2713 234, e-mail: enquiries@health.go.ke, URL: http://www.health.go.ke/
Ministry of Home Affairs, Jogoo House, "A" Taifa Road, PO Box 30520, Nairobi, Kenya. Tel: +254 20 228411, URL: http://www.homeaffairs.go.ke/
Ministry of Planning and National Development and Vision 2030, Treasury Building, Harambee Avenue, PO Box 30005, Nairobi, Kenya. Tel: +254 20 2338 111, fax: +254 20 2218 475, e-mail: psplanning@treasury.go.ke, URL: http://www.planning.go.ke
Ministry of Justice, National Cohesion and Constitutional Affairs, Sheria House, Harambee Avenue, PO Box 56057, Nairobi, Kenya. Tel: +254 20 2224 029, fax: +254 20 2316 317, e-mail: ps-justice@africaonline.co.be, URL: http://www.attorney-general.go.ke
Ministry of Water Resources Management and Development, Maji House, Ngong Road, PO Box 49720, Nairobi, Kenya. Tel: +254 20 2716 103, fax: +254 20 2727 622, URL: http://www.water.go.ke/
Ministry of Co-operative Development, Kencom House, Moi Avenue, PO Box 30547, Nairobi, Kenya. Tel: +254 20 2340 081, URL: http://www.cooperative.go.ke
Ministry of Gender, Sports, Culture and Social Services, Jogoo House, "A" Taifa Road, PO Box 30520, Nairobi, Kenya. Tel: +254 20 228411, URL: http://www.kenya.go.ke/gender
Ministry of Finance, Treasury Building, Harambee Avenue, PO Box 30007, Nairobi, Kenya, Tel: +254 20 2338 111, fax: +254 20 2330 426, e-mail: info@treasury.go.ke, URL: http://www.treasury.go.ke
Ministry of Labour, NSSF Building, Bishop Road, PO Box 40326, Nairobi, Kenya. Tel: +254 20 2729 800, e-mail: admin@labour.go.ke, URL: http://www.labour.go.ke
Ministry of Gender and Children's Affairs, NSSF Building Bishop Road, Block A, Eastern Wing 6th Floor, Milimani, PO Box 16936, Nairobi, Kenya. Tel: +254 20 2727 980, fax: +254 20 2734 417, URL: http://www.gender.go.ke
Ministry of Higher Education, Science and Technology, Jogoo House A, Taifa Road, PO Box 30520, Nairobi, Kenya. URL: http://www.scienceandtechnology.go.ke
Ministry of Housing, Ardhi House, Ngong Road, PO Box 30119, Nairobi, Kenya. Tel: +254 20 2710 451, e-mail: pro@housing.go.ke, URL: http://www.housing.go.ke
Ministry of Immigration and Registration of Persons, Nyayo House, Off Kenyatta Avenue, PO Box 30191, Nairobi, Kenya. Tel: +254 20 2222 022, URL: http://www.immigration.go.ke
Ministry of Industrialization, Telposta Towers 18th floor, Kenyatta Avenue, PO Box 30418, Nairobi, Kenya. Tel: +254 20 315 001, fax: +254 20 2215 815, e-mail: hkosgey@industrialization.go.ke, URL: http://www.tradeandindustry.go.ke

Ministry of Information and Communications, Teleposta Towers, Kenyatta Avenue, PO Box 30025, Nairobi, Kenya. Tel: +254 20 2221 376, URL: http://www.information.go.ke

Ministry of Lands, Ardhi House, Ngong Road, PO Box 30450, Nairobi, Kenya. Tel: +254 20 2718 050, URL: http://www.ardhi.go.ke

Ministry of Livestock and Fisheries Development, Kilimo House, Cathedral Road, PO Box 30028, Nairobi, Kenya. Tel: +254 20 2718 870, fax: +254 20 2711 149, URL: http://www.livestock.go.ke

Ministry of Local Government, Jogoo House A, Taifa Road, PO Box 30004, Nairobi, Kenya. Tel: +254 20 2217 475, fax: +254 20 2217 869, URL: http://www.kenya.go.ke

Ministry of Nairobi Metropolitan Development, Kenya International Conference Centre 25th Floor, Harambee Avenue, PO Box 30130, Nairobi, Kenya. Tel: +254 20 317 224, fax: +254 20 317 226, e-mail: nairobimetro@kenya.go.ke, URL: http://www.nairobimetro.go.ke

Ministry of National Heritage and Culture, Jogoo House A, Taifa Road, PO Box 30520, Nairobi, Kenya. Tel: +254 20 228 411, fax: +254 20 2218 811, URL: http://www.vp.go.ke

Ministry of Public Health and Sanitation, Medical HQ, Afya House, Cathedral Road, PO Box 30016, Nairobi, Kenya. Tel: +254 20 2717 077, fax: +254 20 2713 234, e-mail: enquiries@health.go.ke, URL: http://www.health.go.ke

Ministry of Public Service, Harambee House, Harambee Avenue, PO Box 30050, Nairobi, Kenya. Tel: +254 20 227 411, fax: +254 20 243 620, URL: http://www.dpm.go.ke

Ministry of Public Works and Roads, Ministry of Works Building, Ngong Road, PO Box 30260, Nairobi, Kenya. Tel: +254 20 2723 101, fax: +254 20 2713 135, e-mail: info@publiworks.go.ke, URL: http://www.publicworks.go.ke

Ministry of the Regional Development Authorities, Social Security House, Bishops Road Block A 20th Floor, PO Box 10280, Nairobi, Kenya. Tel: +254 20 2733 824, fax: +254 20 2737 694, e-mail: mrd@nbinet.co.ke, URL: http://www.regional-dev.go.ke

Ministry of Special Programmes, Comcraft House 5th Floor, Haile Selasie Avenue, PO Box 40213, Nairobi, Kenya. Tel: +254 20 247 880, fax: +254 20 227 622, e-mail: info@sprogrammes.go.ke, URL: http://www.sprogrammes.go.ke

Ministry of Tourism, Forestry and Wildlife, Utalii House, Off Uhuru Highway, PO Box 30027, Nairobi, Kenya. Tel: +254 20 2333 555, fax: +254 20 2318 045, e-mail: pstourism@wananchi.com, URL: http://www.tourism.go.ke

Ministry of Trade, Teleposta Towers, Kenyatta Avenue, PO Box 30430, Nairobi, Kenya. Tel: +254 20 2331 030, fax: +254 20 2213 508, URL: http://www.trade.go.ke

Ministry of Transport, Transcom House, Ngong Road, PO Box 52692, Nairobi, Kenya. Tel: +254 20 2729 200, fax: +254 20 2726 326, URL: http://www.transport.go.ke

Ministry of Water and Irrigation, Maji House, Ngong Road, PO Box 49720, Nairobi, Kenya. Tel: +254 20 2716 103, fax: +254 20 2727 622, URL: http://www.water.go.ke

Ministry of Youth and Sports, Kencom House 3rd Floor, Moi Avenue/City Hall Way, PO Box 34303, Nairobi, Kenya. Tel: +254 20 2240 068, fax: +254 20 312 351, e-mail: infor@youthaffairs.go.ke, http://www.youthaffairs.go.ke

Elections

Presidential and parliamentary elections took place on 27 December 2002. The National Rainbow Coalition (NARC) won 125 seats. The main parties of the coalition were the National Alliance Party of Kenya and the Liberal Democratic Party. The Kanu party, which had been in power for forty years, won just 64 seats. Daniel Arap Moi had to stand down as president for constitutional reasons. Mr Kibaki gained over 60 per cent of the vote, easily defeating the new leader of Kanu, Uhuru Kenyatta.

Parliamentary and presidential elections took place in December 2007. President Kibaki claimed victory, leading to street protests and violence as the opposition claimed the vote was rigged. In January 2008 power sharing talks took place resulting in an agreement at the end of February; a coalition was formed consisting of the Party of National Unity and the The Orange Democratic Movement. The post of Prime Minister and two new posts of Deputy Prime Minister were created, to be held by MPs nominated by each of the coalition members.

The most recent presidential election was held in April 2013, Uhuru Kenyatta was elected president with 50.07 per cent. His main rival, Raila Odinga, vowed to challenge the result in court.

Political Parties

There are currently over 40 political parties, the main ones being, Kenya African National Union (KANU, affiliated to the PNU); National Rainbow Coalition (NARC, affiliated to the ODM); National Rainbow Coalition - Kenya (NARC-K); Orange Democratic Movement (ODM); Orange Democratic Movement - Kenya (ODM-K); Party of National Unity (PNU).

Diplomatic Representation

US Embassy, Mombasa Road, PO Box 30137, Unit 64100, Nairobi, Kenya. Tel: +254 2 537800, fax +254 2 537863, e-mail: ircnairobi@state.gov, URL: http://nairobi.usembassy.gov
Ambassador: Robert F. Godec (page 1431)

British High Commission, Upper Hill Road, PO Box 30465, Nairobi, Kenya. Tel: +254 2 284 4000, fax: +254 2 284 4077, e-mail: bhcinfo@iconnect.co.ke, URL: http://www.ukinkenya.fco.gov.uk
High Commissioner: Dr Christian Turner (page 1528)

Kenya High Commission, 45 Portland Place, London W1N 4AS. Tel: +44 (0)20 7636 2371/5, fax: +44 (0)20 7323 6717, URL: http://www.kenyahighcommission.net/khccontent/index.php
High Commissioner: Ephraim Waweru Ngare

Kenyan Embassy, 2249 R Street, NW, Washington DC 20008, USA. Tel: +1 202 387 6101, fax: +1 202 462 3829, URL: http://kenyaembassy.com/
Ambassador: Elkana Odembo

Kenyan Mission to the United Nations, 866 UN Plaza, Room 486, New York 10017 NY, USA. Tel: +1 212 421 470, fax: +1 212 486 1985, e-mail: kenya@un.int, URL: http://www.un.int/kenya
Ambassador: H.E. Macharia Kamau

LEGAL SYSTEM

The legal system is based on Kenyan statutory law, Kenyan and English common law, as well as tribal and Islamic laws. Justice is administered by the High Court, which consists of the Chief Justice and up to 50 puisne judges. The Chief Justice is appointed by the president. The court sits in Nairobi, Mombasa and other centres. The Appeal Court only hears appeals from the High Court; it is composed of the Chief Justice and up to eleven judges. Kadhi's Courts (of which there are 17 nationwide) have jusidiction over questions of Muslim Law relating to personal matters, where all parties are Muslims. There are also traffic courts and anti-corruption courts.

In general, the government upholds the human rights of its citizens. However, over 2008, there were instances of excessive use of force by police as well as police corruption, arbitrary arrest and prolonged pretrial detention. There was also official corruption. Following the presidential election of December 2007, violence erupted in parts of Nairobi and the Nyanza, Rift Valley, and Coast provinces; approximately 1,500 persons were killed and more than 500,000 displaced. While civilian authorities generally maintained effective control of the security forces, there were many instances in which the police acted independently.

Kenya retains the death penalty for ordinary crimes such as murder but no death sentences have been carried out in over two decades. Since then more than 4,000 people have been on death row in the country's overcrowded, underfunded prisons. In August 2009, President Kibaki announced that the prisoners on death row would have their sentences commuted to life imprisonment. He added that a life sentence meant that the prisoners could work, and thus prison discipline would be improved. The Kenyan government has long promised judicial and prison reform.

High Court of Kenya: URL: http://www.judiciary.go.ke/
Chief Justice: Hon. Mr. Chief Justice Willy Mutunga

Kenya National Commission on Human Rights (KNCHR), URL: http://www.knchr.org

LOCAL GOVERNMENT

Kenya is divided into eight provinces including the Nairobi area which has special status, the provinces are Central, Coast, Eastern, North, Rift Valley, Western and North Eastern. The August 2010 constitution designates 47 counties as administrative units. These counties are yet to be defined.

AREA AND POPULATION

Area

The Republic of Kenya lies across the Equator on the eastern seaboard of Africa. It is bounded on the north by the Sudan and Ethiopia, on the east by the Indian Ocean and Somalia, on the south by Tanzania and on the west by Uganda and Lake Victoria. From the narrow, tropical, coastal belt the land rises towards the great plateau of East Africa. The Highlands, which include some of the best agricultural land in Africa, rise from the plateau at about 5,000 feet. The country is divided by the Rift Valley which runs from Lake Turkana in the north southwards to where it splits the Highlands. Kenya's arid northern region stretches from near the coast to the foothills of Mount Kenya and to Lake Turkana. This region, which covers more than half the country, is sparsely populated and hot, with a low rainfall. The total area of Kenya is approximately 582,646 sq km or 224,960 sq. miles including 5,171 sq. miles of inland water.

To view a map, please visit http://www.un.org/Depts/Cartographic/map/profile/kenya.pdf

Population

Most of the population is concentrated into a relatively small portion of the country in the south-west.

The population at the 1999 census was 28,686,607 of which 14,205,589 were male and 14,481,018 were female. In 2010 the population was estimated to be 40.513 million with an annual growth rate of 2.6 per cent for the period 2000-10. Around 22 per cent of the population live in urban areas. Generally Kenya's population is young: approximately 42 per cent of the population is under 15 and 4 per cent over 60. The median age is 19 years old. Many Somali refugees are in camps in Kenya escaping drought and conflict, estimates of numbers vary between 35,000 and 100,000.

English is the official language and Swahili is widely spoken. Around 40 local languages are also spoken. The main ethnic groups of Kenya are Kikuyu, Luhya, Luo, Kelenjin, Kamba, Kisii and Meru.

More than half the population live below the poverty line.

Births, Marriages, Deaths

In 2010 the child mortality rate was 85 per 1,000. In 2010 the crude birth rate was estimated to be 37.6 per 1,000 population and the crude death rate was 8.8 per 1,000 population. Just over 30 per cent of women are estimated to use contraception. In 2009, the total fertility rate was estimated to be 4.7 per cent. By 2009, the average life expectancy was 58 years for males and 62 years for females. Healthy life expectancy was 48 years and 48 years respectively. (Source: http://www.who.int, World Health Statistics 2012)

Public Holidays 2014

1 January: New Year's Day
18 March: Good Friday
21 April: Easter Monday
1 May: Labour Day

KENYA

1 June: Responsibility Day
10 October: Moi Day
29 July: End of Ramadan*
20 October: Kenyatta Day
12 December: Independence Day
25 December: Christmas Day
26 December: Boxing Day
*Islamic holidays depend on the sighting of the moon and so can vary. Any public holiday which falls on a Sunday is observed on the following Monday.

EMPLOYMENT

The labour force was estimated at 17.8 million in 2010, with agricultural labour accounting for 75 per cent of the figure. The unemployment figure in 2008 was estimated at 40 per cent. An estimated 50 per cent of people live below the poverty line. Most people are involved in subsistence farming.

BANKING AND FINANCE

Currency
The currency is the Kenya shilling which was introduced in 1966. There are 100 cents in a shilling. The financial centre is Nairobi.

GDP/GNP, Inflation, National Debt
After years of poor economic performance the government began a series of economic reforms in 1993 with help from the World Bank and IMF. Reforms included elimination of price controls and foreign exchange controls, privatisation, and reduced bureaucracy. Because of the country's continued dependence on agriculture, its economic performance remains tied to weather conditions and thus vulnerable. Aid has been supplied by various governments, the IMF and World Bank, but continued corruption has meant that it has sometimes been withheld. Tourism is increasingly seen as a sector to expand to reduce dependency on agriculture.

The 2008 post-election violence adversely affected the economy. The tourism and agricultural sectors were both badly hit. Since then the tourism sector has rebounded and in 2009 earned US$807 million an increase of nearly 20 per cent on 2008 and in the first quarter of 2010 growth was 19 per cent up on the same quarter the previous year.

GDP was US$29,859.97 million in 2007, compared to US$22,779.29 million in 2006 and US$19,131.69 million in 2005. Growth rates were respectively 6.6 per cent, 6.1 per cent and 5.7 per cent. Per capita income was US$680 in 2006. Figures for 2009 put GDP at US$29.3 billion, the service sector contributed around 60 per cent of GDP, industry and commerce, 16.5 per cent and agriculture, 23.5 per cent. GDP was estimated to be US$32 billion in 2010, reflecting a growth rate of 5.4 per cent. GDP was estimated to be US$33 billion in 2011 with an estimated growth rate of 4.1 per cent.

The inflation rate in 1993 was 40.8 per cent, falling to 28.8 per cent in 1994. It fell rapidly to 1.8 per cent in 1995 before beginning an generally upward trend. In 2005, it was 10.3 per cent, 14.5 per cent in 2006. Inflation remains volatile, rising from 4 per cent in 2010 to 14 per cent in 2011.

External debt was estimated to be US$8 billion in 2011. Foreign aid was also made during the late 1990s to aid famine relief due to lack of rain.

Foreign Investment
In 2011, foreign direct investment amounted to an estimated US$2,500 million. In January 2011, the IMF approved a three-year $508 million arrangement for Kenya under the Fund's Extended Credit Facility.

Kenya's largest source of foreign exchange comes from remittances sent by Kenyans living and working abroad. 2009 figures estimated that recorded remittances were worth US$609 million.

Balance of Payments / Imports and Exports
Main export markets are Uganda, Tanzania, South Africa, Ethiopia, Rwanda, Egypt, UK, Germany, Netherlands, Japan, the UAE, Italy, India, France and Saudi Arabia. In March 2004 the presidents of Kenya, Tanzania and Uganda signed a customs pact designed to harmonise external tariffs and boost trade.

External Trade, US$ million

	2005	2006	2007
Trade balance	-2,147.16	-3,266.43	-4,488.39
Exports	3,454.62	3,602.01	4,790.08
Imports	6,601.67	6,768.44	9,278.47

Source: African Development Bank

Exports were estimated to be US$4.96 billion in 2010 and imports US$11.5 billion. Tea was the top export in 2010.

Central Bank
Central Bank of Kenya, PO Box 60000, Haile Selasie Avenue, Nairobi, Kenya. Tel: +254 2 226431 / 2 246000, fax: +254 2 340192, e-mail: info@centralbank.go.ke, URL: http://www.centralbank.go.ke
Governor: Prof. Njuguna S. Ndung'u

Chambers of Commerce and Trade Organisations
Kenya National Chamber of Commerce and Industry, URL: http://www.knccimaragua.com/

MANUFACTURING, MINING AND SERVICES

Primary and Extractive Industries
Kenya's mineral mining has been growing steadily in the last few years and includes cement, soda ash, diatomite, flour spar, and baryte. Petroleum dominates Kenya's external trade not only in imports of crude oil but also in exports of refined products to neighbouring countries from the Mombasa refinery. Figures for 2011 show that Kenya imported 82,000 barrels of oil per day and had a refining capacity of 90,000 barrels per day. Kenya also imports coal 114,000 short tons in 2010.

Energy
Imported petroleum provides the largest source of energy, followed by electricity. Petroleum provides over 70 per cent of all energy requirements. The coastal area is supplied by a modern steam generating station at Mombasa with an installed capacity of about 40 MW. The area from Nairobi westward to the Uganda boundary (a distance of about 300 miles) is principally supplied from a comprehensive transmission system fed from a capacity of over 100 MW. Kenya has developed hydro-generation plants, the main plants are situated along the River Tana. In 2010 Kenya generated 7.33 billion kWh and consumed 6.15 billion kilowatthours. Around 80 per cent of Kenya's electricity is produced by hydro power and over 8 per cent from fossil fuels. Following a severe drought in 1999 Kenya introduced electricity rationing. This prompted the government to build two diesel generating plants and to expand the storage capacity of the Masinga Dam. In 2006 Kenya agreed to let China explore for oil off the Kenyan coast.

Manufacturing
Manufacturing accounts for about 10 per cent of GDP. More than half of the manufacturing industry is based on processing of primary agricultural products. The manufacture of cement for export and local consumption is important although production fell in the year to July 2000 to 1.1 million tonnes from 1.3 million tonnes in the previous twelve months. In addition, there are garment, plastics, textiles and blanket manufacturing and food product industries.

Nairobi remains the chief industrial centre and it is still the headquarters of many commercial organisations operating throughout East Africa. Among the more important industries established in Nairobi are brewing, soft drinks, flour milling, pharmaceuticals, small textile and knitwear factories, cigarette manufacture, clothing and footwear, foodstuffs manufacture, light engineering and soap-making.

Mombasa also has a big industrial complex and the port itself has ship-repairing facilities. The first oil refinery in East Africa is at Mombasa. There are good prospects for industries in western Kenya where there is a high population density. Several small industries exist at Nakuru, Kisumu, Eldoret and Thika.

Production of Selected Manufactures June 2004/05

Product	Output	Output Growth %
Processed sugar	507,306 million tonnes	-.38
Cement production	1,985,996 million tonnes	17.41
Soda ash	357,521 million tonnes	0.56
Milk	281,336 '000 litres	17.37
Beer	257,124 '000 litres	21.84
Cigarettes	8,590,015 sticks	17.02

Source: Central Bank of Kenya

Service Industries
Tourism from North America and western Europe constitutes an important form of foreign exchange and employment, which accounts for 14 per cent of GDP. Tourism has been targeted as a growth area for the economy. Tourism in the year 2004 earned an estimated US$808 million, with 927,000 visitors. Figures for 2005 show that visitor numbers had risen to 1.2 million, generating earnings of US$969 million and rose again in 2006 to 3.1 million visitors generating earnings of US$973 million. Most visitors were from the UK and Germany. Safari holidays are particularly popular.

Agriculture
Agriculture is the mainstay of Kenya's economy. More than 80 per cent of the population is engaged on the land, while agriculture and livestock provide over 80 per cent of the country's export earnings, or 16 per cent of GDP.

Promising results have been achieved from irrigation schemes, in particular the Mwea Tebere scheme in Embu district where rice is the chief cash crop. On the Lower Tana River a three-year pre-investment survey of the irrigation potentialities of the area is being undertaken.

Owing to the variation of altitude from sea level to over 9,000 feet, Kenya lends itself to the production of a wide range of crops. In the areas of 5,000 feet and above, coffee, tea, pyrethrum, maize, wattle bark and wheat, barley and oats are the principal crops. At the lower altitudes sisal, cotton and oilseeds are most important. Other crops grown in various parts of the country include beans, potatoes, sorghum, millets, pulses, coconuts, cashew nuts, sugar cane, vegetables, fruit and essential oil plants. Kenya has an expanding livestock industry. Much of the country is suited to ranching and there is an important dairy industry in the areas of higher rainfall. Dairy products such as butter, cheese, milk, ghee and eggs are exported. Rearing of sheep and of pigs is being expanded to provide all local requirements as well as for export.

Agricultural Production in 2010

Produce	Int. $'000*	Tonnes
Indigenous cattle meat	1,251,191	463,168
Cow milk, whole, fresh	1,238,196	3,967,800
Maize	434,912	3,222,000
Tea	424,327	399,000
Mangoes, mangosteens, guavas	331,765	553,710
Beans, dry	234,904	390,598
Bananas	222,931	791,570
Tomatoes	199,251	539,151
Sugar cane	187,486	5,709,590
Plantains	163,426	791,570
Indigenous goat meat	117,742	49,139
Indigenous sheep meat	113,342	41,627

* unofficial figures
Source: http://faostat.fao.org/site/339/default.aspx Food and Agriculture Organization of the United Nations, Food and Agricultural commodities production

A wide variety of forest trees are found in Kenya varying from the coastal mangroves to coniferous mountain forest with limited areas of tropical rain forests.

There is a substantial fishing industry on Lakes Victoria, Baringo and Naivasha. The coastal fisheries and those of Lake Turkana are being developed. Figures for 2010 show that the total catch was 143,000 tonnes.

COMMUNICATIONS AND TRANSPORT

Travel Requirements
Citizens of the USA, Canada, Australia and the EU require a passport valid for three months beyond the date of entry, with at least one blank page, and a visa. Citizens of Cyprus do not need a visa. Other nationals should contact the embassy to check visa requirements.

National Airlines
Kenya Airways, Jomo Kenyatta International Airport, URL://www.kenyaairways.com
African Airlines International (AIK), PO Box 74772, Nairobi, Kenya. Tel: +254 2 501319, fax: +254 2 506101
African Safari Airways, PO Box 81443, Mombasa, Kenya. Tel: +254 11 485522 / 485523, fax: +254 11 485909 / 485032

International Airports
There are three international airports: Jomo Kenyatta International Airport, Nairobi; Moi International Airport, Mombasa; Moi International Airport, Eldoret.
In total there are 19 airports with paved runways.

Railways
There are about 2,700 km of railway operated by the Kenya Railways and Harbours. The main railway line runs from Mombasa, through Kenya to Uganda.

Roads
Kenya has about 64,000 km of public roads of which approximately 7,740 km are bitumen-surfaced. The main roads, where not bitumen-surfaced, are gravel-surfaced and usually 'all-weather' roads, except during excessive rains. In 1994 a special levy on motor fuel was implemented in order to assist with the funding of road maintenance. The Kenya Roads Board has been established to oversee the building and maintenance of the road system of Kenya. Kenya are linked by bus routes from Nairobi, Kenya to Arusha, Tanzania; Nairobi to Kampala, Uganda; Mombasa and Dar-es-Salaam, Tanzania; Kisumu and Kampala, Uganda. Vehicles are driven on the left.

Ports and Harbours
Mombasa is the largest port in East Africa, serving not only Kenya but also Uganda and parts of Tanzania. There are 18 deep water berths together with an oil berth and a new oil jetty for the modern larger tankers. There are also ports at Kisumu and Lamu.

Kenya is also part of the Lake Victoria waterway system.

HEALTH

According to the latest WHO figures, in 2009, the Kenyan government spent approximately 7.3 per cent of its total budget on healthcare (down from 9.1 per cent in 2000), accounting for 43.3 per cent of all healthcare spending. Total expenditure on healthcare equated to 4.8 per cent of the country's GDP and equated to US$33 per capita. Approximately 76.7 per cent of private expenditure on health is out-of-pocket. External resources accounted for 34 per cent of total expenditure on health in 2009 compared to 8.0 per cent in 2000.

Recent figures indicate that Kenya's free health service consists of over 3000 hospitals, with 50,000 beds, 522 health centres and 2,868 sub-centres and dispensaries. According to the latest WHO figures (2000-10), medical personnel include 4,506 doctors (1 per 10,000 population), 37,113 nurses and midwives (12 per 10,000 population), 3,094 pharmaceutical personnel and 1,340 dentistry personnel.

The infant mortality rate in 2010 was 55 per 1,000 live births and the child mortality rate (under five years old) was 85 per 1,000 live births. The main causes of childhood mortality are: prematurity (15 per cent), diarrhoea (9 per cent), pneumonia (17 per cent), malaria (3

per cent) and HIV/AIDs (7 per cent). Imunization rates have risen and now over 95 per cent of infants receive a vaccination against measles. The number of children sleeping under insecticide-treated nets has risen dramatically to approximately 46 per cent by 2005-09. In 2005-11, approximately 35.2 per cent of children under 5 were classified as stunted and 16.4 per cent as underweight.

The country is currently faced with an AIDS epidemic and the Government has launched education programmes countywide. In 2001, the official estimates were that 2.5 million people were living with HIV/AIDS and, in the same year, 190,000 deaths due to AIDS/HIV were recorded. The Government has set up the National AIDS Control Programme (NASCOP), which aims to prevent and manage the spread of HIV/AIDS.

According to the latest WHO figures, in 2008 approximately 59 per cent of the population had access to improved drinking water. In the same year, 32 per cent of the population had access to improved sanitation. (Source: http://www.who.int, World Health Statistics 2012)

In 2001, President Moi outlawed the practice of female circumcision.

EDUCATION

Recent statistics put the number of schools in Kenya as follows: 27,573 pre-primary schools, 18,901 primary schools, 3,621 secondary schools, 32 teacher-training schools, 20 technical institutes, three polytechnics, six state and four private universities. Figures from UNESCO for 2007 show that 48 per cent of young children were enrolled in pre-primary school and 86 per cent of girls and 86 per cent of boys were enrolled in primary school where the pupil:teacher ration was 46:1. Kenya introduced free primary school education in 2003 which is reflected in the high enrollment figures. Enrollment figures in 2007 for secondary school pupils was 43 per cent of girls and 47 per cent of boys.

In 2004 the adult literacy rate was estimated to be 65.5 per cent.

RELIGION

Recent figures show that Kenya is predominantly Christian with around 29 per cent belonging to the Catholic Church and 39 per cent to Protestant churches. Islam accounts for 6.0 per cent of the population.

Kenya has a religious liberty rating of 6 on a scale of 1 to 10 (10 is most freedom). (Source: World Religion Database)

COMMUNICATIONS AND MEDIA

The media has enjoyed relative freedom but recent legislation has introduced greater controls. In 2007, a ban was introduced on some live broadcasts and in 2009 a law was passed allowing official censorship on the grounds of national security.

Newspapers
Newspapers publishing is dominated by two publishing houses, the Nation and the Standard.
Daily Nation, largest circulation, URL: http://www.nation.co.ke/
The Standard, URL: http://www.standardmedia.co.ke/

Broadcasting
The Voice of Kenya operates a National Sound Service in Swahili and a general service in English, which are transmitted from Nairobi on the medium- and short wave bands. An additional 15 vernacular languages are also transmitted from the new medium wave transmitter station sited at Ngong, near Nairobi. Kenya Broadcasting Corporation is state owned and broadcasts in English and Swahili. There are a large number of private stations.
Kenya Broadcasting Corporation, Nairobi, Kenya. URL: http://www.kbc.co.ke
Kenya Television Network, privately owned by Standard Group, URL: http://www.ktnkenya.tv/
Communications Commission of Kenya, URL: http://www.cck.go.ke

Telecommunications
The landline system is inadequate. In 2008 there were approximately 245,000 telephone lines in use and 16 million mobile phones in use. Recent figures show that over 3 million Kenyans are regular internet users.

ENVIRONMENT

Environmental problems are being experienced in the arid and semi-arid lands due to the rapid growth of the population and industrial developments. This rapid growth rate has led to land shortages and the resettlement of people into areas where there are poor management practices and environmental conservation is not promoted. Kenya is prone to droughts.

Recently over 50,000 pink flamingos have died in Kenya's Rift Valley lakes. It is believed that industrial and agricultural pollution is the cause of the deaths. There is also a water hyacinth infestation in Lake Victoria.

In 2010, Kenya's emissions from the consumption of fossil fuels totalled 12.25 million metric tons of carbon dioxide. (Source: EIA)

In October 2004, the Kenyan ecologist Wangari Maathai became the first African woman to win the Nobel Peace Prize.

Kenya is party to the following treaties: Biodiversity, Climate Change, Climate Change-Kyoto Protocol, Desertification, Endangered Species, Hazardous Wastes, Law of the Sea, Marine Dumping, Marine Life Conservation, Ozone Layer Protection, Ship Pollution, Wetlands and Whaling.

SPACE PROGRAMME

Italy operates a tracking station at Malindi in Kenya. The station and inter-government co-operation agreement gives Kenya access to geospatial data and training in satellite systems.

KIRIBATI
Republic of Kiribati
Ribaberikin Kiribati

Capital: Tarawa (Population estimate: 25,000)

Head of State: H.E. Anote Tong (President) (page 1526)

Vice President: Teima Onorio

National Flag: Red with blue and white wavy lines representing the ocean towards the bottom, a gold sun in the centre with a bird flying above it.

CONSTITUTION AND GOVERNMENT

Constitution
On 12 July 1979 the Republic of Kiribati (formerly known as the Gilbert Islands) became independent of the United Kingdom. The Independence Constitution outlined a 35 member House of Assembly, protection of fundamental human rights and special provisions for the Banabans.

The president is directly elected from candidates selected from members of the legislature for a four-year term. The president may serve no more than three terms. The president appoints the cabinet. The House of Assembly (Maneaba) now has 40 members directly elected for a four-year term, a Banaban representative, and an Attorney-General. The Speaker of the Legislature is elected by the House of Assembly from outside of the Assembly. The Speaker has no voting rights. Suffrage is universal at 18.

For further information, please visit: http://www.parliament.gov.ki/content/constitution-kiribati.

Recent Events
The people of Banaba Island campaigned to be placed under the protection of Fiji. Most Banabans left the island in the 1940s, after it had been devastated by phosphate farming, and moved to the island of Raba, Fiji. They now have full Fiji citizenship. The Kiribati government made provisions in the constitution including the return of land previously acquired for phosphate farming and including a Banaban representative in parliament. Approximately 300 people remain on Banaba.

The atolls of Kiribati used to straddle the International Date Line, but in 1995 the government moved the line eastwards to ensure that the day was the same all over the country. Kiribati was therefore the first inhabited place on Earth to greet the new millennium on 1 January 2000. Caroline Island was re-named Millennium Island and revenue from tourism at that time soared.

In March 2002, Kiribati joined Tuvalu and the Maldives in their decision to take legal action against the USA for its refusal to sign the Kyoto Protocol. The three states are low-lying and concerned that global warming will lead to a rise in sea-levels. Two of Kiribati's atolls have already disappeared beneath the sea.

China severed diplomatic relations with Kiribati in November 2003, in protest at the establishment of ties with Taiwan. The Chinese removed their satellite tracking station from Kiribati's main island.

Kiribati created the world's third-largest marine reserve in March 2006; fishing is banned in the Phoenix Islands Protected Area, home to hundreds of species of fish and coral.

Legislature
The legislature of Kiribati is unicameral. The House of Assembly has 40 members who are elected for a four year term.
House of Assembly, (Maneaba ni Maungatabu), PO Box 52, Bairiki, Tarawa, Kiribati. Tel: +686 21880

State Administration (as at June 2013)
Minister of Foreign Affairs and Immigration: Anote Tong (page 1526)
Vice-President, Minister of Internal Affairs: Teima Onorio
Minister of Education: Maere Tekanene
Minister of Communications, Transport and Tourism Development: Taberannang Timeon
Minister of the Environment, Lands and Agricultural Development: Tiarite Kwong
Minister of Finance and Economic Development: Tim Murdoch
Minister of Labour and Human Resources Development: Boutu Bateriki
Minister of Health and Medical Services: Dr Kautu Tenaua
Minister of Public Works and Utilities: Kirabuke Teiaua
Minister of Fisheries and Marine Resources Development: Tinian Reiher
Minister of Line and Phoenix Islands Development: Tawita Tomoku

---

Minister of Commerce, Industry and Co-operatives: Pinto Katia
Attorney General: Tiitabu Taabane

Ministries
Office of the President and Ministry of Foreign Affairs, PO Box 68, Bairiki, Tarawa. Tel: +686 21183, fax: +686 21145
Ministry of Home Affairs and Rural Development, PO Box 75, Bairiki, Tarawa. Tel: +686 21092, fax: +686 21133
Ministry of Finance and Economic Planning, PO Box 67, Bairiki, Tarawa. Tel: +686 21805, fax: +686 21307
Ministry of Natural Resource Development, PO Box 64, Bairiki, Tarawa. Tel: +686 21099, fax: +686 21120
Ministry of Education, Training and Technology, PO Box 263, Bikenibeu, Tarawa. Tel: +686 28101, fax: +686 28222
Ministry of Health and Family Planning, PO Box 268, Bikenibeu, Tarawa. Tel: +686 28100, fax: +686 28152
Ministry of Information, Communications and Transport, PO Box 487, Betio, Tarawa. Tel: +686 26003/004, fax: +686 26193
Ministry of Labour, Employment and Cooperatives, PO Box 69, Bairiki, Tarawa. Tel: +686 21097/071, fax: +686 21452
Ministry of Works and Energy, PO Box 498, Betio, Tarawa. Tel: +686 26192, fax: +686 26172
Ministry of Line and Phoenix Development, London, Kiritimati Island. Tel: +686 81215, fax: +686 81278
Ministry of Environment and Social Development, PO Box 234, Bikenibeu, Tarawa. Tel: +686 28000/071, fax: +686 28202/334
Ministry of Commerce, Industry and Tourism, PO Box 510, Betio, Tarawa. Tel: +686 26158/157, fax: +686 26233

Political Parties
Political parties are not formally organised but the following groups do exist: Boutokaan Te Koaavu (Pillars of Truth), Maneaban Te Mauri (Protect the Maneaba), National Progressive Party, United Coalition Party.

Elections
The most recent presidential election was held in January 2012. The incumbent president Anote Tong was re-elected.

Legislative elections were held in Octoober 2011. Independent candidates won 17 seats, the President's Pillars of Truth party won 15 and the United Coalition Party won 11 seats.

Diplomatic Representation
US Embassy (based in Suva): 31 Loftus Street, Suva, Fiji. Mailing address: P.O. Box 218, Suva, Fiji. Tel: +679 331 4466, fax: +679 330 0081, URL: http://suva.usembassy.gov/
Ambassador: Frankie Annette Reed
British High Commission (all staff resident in Suva), Tel: +679 322100, fax: +679 3229132, e-mail: consularsuva.fco.gov.uk, URL: http://ukinfiji.fco.gov.uk/en
High Commissioner: Steven Chandler

At present Kiribati does not have a permanent mission at the United Nations.

LEGAL SYSTEM

Judges are appointed by the President. The judicial system consists of magistrates' courts, the High Court and the Court of Appeal.

The government generally respects the human rights of its citizens, and the judiciary is largely effective in dealing with instances of abuse. The death penalty was abolished in 1979.

LOCAL GOVERNMENT

For administrative purposes Kiribati is divided into three units, Gilbert Islands, Line Islands and Phoenix Islands, and six districts, Banaba, Central Gilberts, Line Islands, Northern Gilberts, South Gilberts and Tarawa. In addition there are 21 Island Councils, one for each inhabited island. These are: Abaiang, Abemama, Aranuka, Arorae, Banaba, Beru, Butaritari, Kanton, Kiritimati, Kuria, Maiana, Makin, Marakei, Nikunau, Nonouti, Onotoa, Tabiteuea, Tabuaeran, Tamana, Tarawa, Teraina. The next council elections will be in 2012.

AREA AND POPULATION

Area
Kiribati comprises 33 islands which straddle the equator in the Pacific Ocean: the Gilbert Islands Group, (which includes Banaba Ocean Island), the Line Islands and the Phoenix Islands. The aggregate land area of Kiribati is estimated to be around 800 sq. km.

In 1995, Kiribati proclaimed that all of its territory lies in the same time zone as its Gilbert Islands group even though the Phoenix Islands and the Line Islands are on the other side of the International Date Line. In 1999, the government renamed Caroline Island as Millennium Island.

To view a map of the islands, please consult http://www.lib.utexas.edu/maps/cia08/kiribati_sm_2008.gif

The climate is tropical - hot and humid but moderated by trade winds.

Population
Estimates for 2010 put the population at around 99,000 with an average annual growth rate of 1.7 per cent for the period 2000-10. Approximately 44 per cent live in urban areas, but the overall population density is 131 people per km.sq. Fears of rises in sea levels, together with overcrowding in the capital city of Tarawara (now 30,000) led the government to start a migration programme in 1989 to move 5,000 people from islands that are expected to disappear. Approximately 30 per cent of Kiribatians are 14 years or younger, 53 per cent are aged 15-64 years and 7 per cent are over 65 years. (Source: http://www.who.int, World Health Statistics 2012)

The languages of Kiribati are Gilbertan and English. The people are predominantly Micronesian; collectively, they are called I-Kiribati

Births, Marriages, Deaths
According to estimates, the crude birth rate for 2010 was 23 per 1,000 inhabitants and the crude death rate was 6.9 per 1,000 inhabitants. Life expectancy in 2009 was 68 years (65 for men and 70 for women). The fertility rate is estimated to be 3 children per woman. (Source: http://www.who.int, World Health Statistics 2012)

Public Holidays 2014
1 January: New Year's Day
18 April: Good Friday
21 April: Easter Monday
18 April: National Health Day
12 July: Independence Day
7 August: National Youth Day
25 December: Christmas Day
26 December: Boxing Day

EMPLOYMENT

The latest available figures from the Asian Development Bank indicate that Kiribati had a workforce of 36,970 in 2005, (down from 40,550 in 2000). 34,720 were employed and 2,250 were unemployed, equating to 6.1 per cent of the workforce. Most of the formal jobs are on the island of Tarawa; lack of employment on the other islands has led to many people moving to Tarawa, increasing pressure on the environment and urban infrastructure of the island.

Whilst public sector employment accounts for almost 80 per cent of all formal employment, most of the population is engaged in subsistence agriculture and fishing. Many Kiribatian seafarers work on international ships.

BANKING AND FINANCE

Currency
One Australian dollar ($A) = 100 cents

GDP/GNP, Inflation, National Debt
In the past, Kiribati had a thriving phosphates industry, contributing some 80 per cent of total export earnings. However, this industry dried up in 1979, when deposits became exhausted, and Kiribati is now considered one of the poorest countries of the world. The economy is hindered by a poor infrastrucutre, its location and a shortage of skilled workforce. It depends on foreign financial aid and remittances from abroad.

The services sector heads the economy, accounting for some 66 per cent of GDP in 2008. Industry contributed 7.5 per cent in the same year, and agriculture accounted for 26 per cent. Tourism accounts for approximately 25 per cent.

Remittances from international ships' crews, together with earnings from the Revenue Equalization Reserve Fund (an offshore investment fund set up with royalties from the defunct phosphate mine) and foreign fees for fishing licenses contributed around 45 per cent of GDP. GDP has fallen in recent years, to -2.4 per cent in 2008, -2.3 per cent in 2009, and -0.4 per cent in 2010.

GDP per economic activity (figures in AUD$000)

Sector	2008	2009	2010
Agriculture	38,257	36,884	36,022
Mining	44	49	46
Manufacturing	8,623	7,973	7,906
Electricity, gas and water	1,860	1,765	1,469
Construction	2,197	2,445	2,276

- continued			
Trade	10,210	8,719	10,741
Transport and communications	15,607	16,797	16,619
Finance	11,172	11,896	9,817
Public administration	27,697	25,423	25,047
Others	38,697	39,207	38,208
Total	**156,572**	**154,238**	**154,382**

Source: Asian Development Bank

Based on the consumer price index for the capital city Tarawa, there was negative inflation of -0.9 per cent in 2004, -0.4 per cent in 2005 and -1.5 per cent in 2006. External debt rose from US$7.6 million in 2000 to US$9.5 million in 2002 and to US$15.7 million in 2003. In 2007, the government increased its withdrawals from the Revenue Equalization Reserve Fund to help fund general expenses and to repay Bank of Kiribati loans; this could undermine the fund's purpose as a permanent source of budget support. Weaker global equity market returns will require lower withdrawals, hence more careful government spending, in 2008 and 2009.

Balance of Payments / Imports and Exports
Main exports were copra, seaweed, shark fins and fish. Copra's share of export revenue dropped from over 60 per cent in 2001 to under 50 per cent in 2002. Licensing fees from deep-sea commercial fishing are a major source of revenue. Imported goods include foodstuffs, manufactured goods, fuel, machinery and equipment. Almost all essential foodstuffs have to be imported.

External Trade, A$000

	2008	2009	2010
Exports	10,310	8,084	5,666
Imports	88,076	86,113	79,886
Trade balance	-77,767	-74,220	-85,263

Source: Asian Development Bank

As of 2010, main export destinations were Thailand, Ecuador, Japan, the Republic of Korea and the US. Main importers were Japan, Fiji and Australia.

Kiribati is dependent on foreign aid. Largest donors are Japan, UK, Australia and New Zealand. Remittances from Kiribati workers abroad contribute more than US$7 million per annum.

Development Bank
Development Bank of Kiribati, PO Box 33, Bairiki Tarawa, Kiribati. Tel: +686 21345 / 21916, fax: +686 21297

MANUFACTURING, MINING AND SERVICES

Primary and Extractive Industries
Phosphate deposits ran out in 1979. They had provided over 60 per cent of export earnings and 50 per cent of government revenue. There is still a fund from revenues from sales of phosphate deposits. In 2003, the fund stood at US$400 million. Extraction of deep sea minerals such as manganese is planned. Sand gravel is quarried on South Tarawa, the aggregate contains sand, gravel, pebbles and stones, this method of quarrying was due to end in 1012 and switch to lagoon dredging.

Energy
Kiribati produces all its own electricity. In 2010 it produced an estimated 30 million kWh and consumed 20 million kWh.

Tourism
This sector is still relatively small. Between three and four million people visit each year and contribute between US$5-10 million. Attractions include eco-tourist sites, game fishing and Christmas Island.

Agriculture
The soil in Kiribati is generally not suitable for the cultivation of large-scale crops. Coconut palms and fish provide the staple foods for the large proportion of the population who live on subsistence farming and small-scale fishing. Vegetables, breadfruit and sweet potatoes are also grown. Almost all essential foodstuffs are imported. Copra is exported but production is declining due to ageing of coconut trees; in 2004, 12,334 metric tons of copra were produced, but by the following year, production had fallen to 6,194 metric tons. There are plans to build a processing plant at Tarawa.

Agricultural Production in 2010

Produce	Int. $'000*	Tonnes
Coconuts	18,106	163,750
Bananas	2,309	8,200
Roots and tubers, nes	1,410	8,500
Indigenous pigmeat	1,365	888
Vegetables fresh nes	1,206	6,400
Indigenous chicken meat	1,053	740
Fruit, tropical fresh nes	490	1,200
Nuts, nes	468	255
Taro (cocoyam)	391	1,900
Hen eggs, in shell	265	320
* unofficial figures		

Source: http://faostat.fao.org/site/339/default.aspx Food and Agriculture Organization of the United Nations, Food and Agricultural commodities production

Fishing

In 2004, Kiribati received an income of AUD$24.5 million from fishing licenses bought mainly by fleets from South Korea, Japan, China, Taiwan and the US. This represented a considerable drop in revenues from the same source in 2001 (AUD$46.6 million). Fish harvests in 2005 were below usual levels in some pacific countries, especially the Cook Islands, Kiribati and Tuvalu, raising fears of low fish stocks.

Following the establishment of the Phoenix Island Protected Area in 2006, an endowment fund is planned, to compensate the government of Kiribati for revenue it could have got from the issuing of commercial fishing licenses, and also to finance professional management of the wildlife. It is hoped that by protecting coral ecosystems, the long-term future for small-scale fishing can be secured, as the reefs provide important spawning grounds.

COMMUNICATIONS AND TRANSPORT

Travel Requirements

Citizens of the USA, Canada, Australia and the EU require a passport valid for six months and a visa, apart from UK citizens for stays of up to 30 days. Most transit passengers continuing their journey by the same or first connecting aircraft, provided holding onward or return documentation and not leaving the airport, do not require a visa. Other nationals should contact the embassy to check visa requirements.

International Airports

The airports on Tarawa and Christmas Island are served by international flights. In total there are 20 airports of which 4 have paved runways. Flights between the islands are operated by Air Kiribati and Air Nauru.

Roads

There are 650km of paved roads. Vehicles are driven on the left.

Ports and Harbours

The principal port is Betio in Tarawa. There are also harbours at Banaba and Kanton. There are 5 km of canals on the Line Islands. Ferries run between the islands.

HEALTH

In 2009, Kiribati spent approximately 13.0 per cent of its total budget on healthcare (up from 8.7 per cent in 2000), accounting for 84.7 per cent of all healthcare spending. Total expenditure on healthcare equated to 13.0 per cent of the country's GDP. Per capita expenditure on health was US$159 in 2009. There is one General Hospital at Tarawa and health centres in the more populated islands.

Figures for 2005-10 show that there are 41 physicians (3.8 per 10,000 population), 404 nurses (37.1 per 10,000 population) and 18 dentists. There are 14 hospital beds per 10,000 population. Approximately 85 per cent of births were attended by someone skilled in childbirth.

According to the latest WHO figures, in 2006 approximately 77 per cent of the urban population and 53 per cent of the rural population had access to improved drinking water. In the same year, 46 per cent of the urban population and 20 per cent of the rural population had access to improved sanitation. Diarrhoea accounts for 9 per cent of childhood deaths. In 2009, the infant mortality rate (likelihood of dying by age one) was 39 per 1,000 live births. The child mortality rate (likelihood of dying by age five) was 49 per 1,000 live births. Pneumonia accounts for 20 per cent of childhood deaths and prematurity 23 per cent.

Diseases that affect the population include cholera, typhoid and dengue fever. There are occasional cases of leprosy. HIV/AIDS is increasing significantly and diabetes is widespread. Excessive alcohol consumption is becoming a severe social and health problem. In 2012, there were 182 reported cases of leprosy and 296 of TB. There were no reported cases of cholera. (Source: http://www.who.int, World Health Statistics 2012)

EDUCATION

The education system includes 100 registered primary schools, one government school and four church secondary schools. Between the ages of 6 and 14 education is provided free and is compulsory. A government teacher training college trains primary teachers and the Tarawa Technical Institute provides commercial and technical courses. There is also a Marine Training School and Kiribati maintains links with the University of the South Pacific in Fiji.

In 2004, 68 per cent of young children were enrolled in a nursery school. Gross enrolment (including pupils of different ages) at primary school reached 115 per cent, and net enrolment (those pupils of the correct age) in secondary schools reached 70 per cent. In 2005, the pupil/teacher ratio at primary level was 24.7:1, and at secondary level it was 17:1. 16 per cent of GDP was spent on education. (Source: UNESCO, UIS, June 2006)

According to most recent estimates (1987-90) the adult literacy rate is 90.1 per cent.

RELIGION

The majority of the population is Christian, belonging either to the Roman Catholic Church (55 per cent of the population) or the Kiribati Protestant Church (36 per cent of the population), around 2.2 per cent of the population are Baha'is.

Kiribati has a religious tolerance rating of 10 on a scale of 1 to 10 (10 is most freedom). (Source: World Religion Database)

COMMUNICATIONS AND MEDIA

Freedom of expression is generally respected.

Newspapers

There are two main newspapers: the Te Ukera, the state-owned weekly, and Kiribati New Star, e-mail: newstar@skl.net.ki.

Broadcasting

Radio Kiribati is state-run. There is a very limited domestic TV service and some access to Australian and US stations.

Telecommunications

In 2008 there were 4,000 mainline telephones in use and an estimated 1,000 mobile phones. Some 2,000 people were regular internet users by 2006.

ENVIRONMENT

Kiribati is one of the countries most vulnerable to the effects of climate change, climate variability, and sea-level rise. As much of Kiribati is low lying coral atolls, global warming and rising sea levels are of great concern. Twenty of the atolls are inhabited. In 1999 two uninhabited reefs disappeared and there are predictions that Kiribati could disappear totally in the 21st century. Sea pollution is also a major problem.

In March 2006, Kiribati created the world's third-largest marine reserve, and banned fishing in the Phoenix Islands Protected Area, in an attempt to protect hundreds of species of fish and coral. The protected area covers an area twice the size of Portugal. The eight coral atolls are nearly uninhabited, and have an extraordinary variety of unique wildlife including 120 species of coral and more than 500 fish. The area is also a stopping point for migrating birds and sea turtles.

Kiribati is party to the following treaties: Biodiversity, Climate Change, Climate Change-Kyoto Protocol, Desertification, Hazardous Wastes, Law of the Sea, Marine Dumping, Ozone Layer Protection, and Whaling.

According to the EIA, in 2010, Kiribati's emissions from the consumption of fossil fuels totalled 0.04 million metric tons of carbon dioxide, the lowest in Asia and Oceania.

DEMOCRATIC PEOPLE'S REPUBLIC OF KOREA

North Korea

Chosun Minchu-Chui Inmin Konghwa-Guk

Capital: Pyongyang (Population estimate, 2010: 3,250,000)

Head of State: Kim Jong-un (The Great Successor) (page 1456)

Eternal President: the late Kim Il Sung

President of the Presidium of the Supreme People's Assembly: Kim Yong Nam (page 1456)

National Flag: Broad red horizontal band bordered by white lines bearing a five-point red star on a white disk in centre; blue horizontal bands at top and bottom

CONSTITUTION AND GOVERNMENT

Constitution

Following the Second World War North Korea was occupied by the Soviet army. North Korea was established as an independent communist state in 1948 and the Soviet troops withdrew. Two years later South Korea which, following the war, had been occupied by the US army, declared independence leading to an invasion by North Korean Troops. In 1953 an armistice was declared, although officially the war has never ended, and North and South Korea became divided.

According to the North Korea 1972 Constitution, the highest power is vested in the Supreme People's Assembly (SPA) which is composed of deputies elected every four years on the principle of universal suffrage. The President of the DPRK is head of state and is elected by the SPA for a term of four years. The President is Chairman of the Defence Commission, ratifies or abrogates treaties concluded with foreign countries, and is also Supreme Commander of the Armed Forces of the DPRK. Following the appointment of Kim Jong Il, President Kim's son and heir designate, as Armed Forces Supreme Commander in December 1991, the SPA revised the constitution in April 1992 to provide for this nomination. Kim Il Sung died in 1994 and in 1997 the constitution was amended and approved by the legislature. It named the late Kim Il Sung as eternal president, and designated the chairmanship of the National Defence Commission (held by Kim Jong Il) as the highest post of the state. It also provided that the chairman of the Presidium of the Supreme People's Assembly would represent the state on formal occasions.

In accordance with the constitution, the SPA elects a Central People's Committee (CPC), which is the highest leadership organ of state power in the DPRK. The CPC is headed by the head of state and is responsible to the SPA. The actual administrative and executive body of the country is the Administration Council (AC) or Cabinet. It works under the President and the CPC. The AC is composed of the Premier (elected by the SPA on the recommendation of the Head of State, Deputy Premiers, Ministers and other members as deemed necessary.

International Relations

Up until the end of the cold war North Korea enjoyed close relations with Russia and China but since then the country has become increasingly isolated. Relations with South Korea have improved in recent years; a summit between President King Jong Il and the then president of South Korea Kim Dae-jung took place in 1998, and since then several meetings and conferences have taken place between high ranking officials. However, relations remain tense.

Officially North Korea and the USA are still at war and as a result have no diplomatic relations with each other. In 2002 US President Bush referred to North Korea as being a member of the 'axis of evil'.

Recent Events

In June 2000 a summit was held in Pyongyang, between South Korea's President Kim Dae-jung and the North Korean leader Kim Jong Il. Amongst subjects discussed were a loose federation and possible reunification in the future, economic co-operation, and re-joining of families separated by the divide. In August 2000, 100 families from each side were reunited on a four day visit.

In July 2000 a meeting took place between the North Korean Minister of Foreign Affairs, Paek Nam Sun, and US Secretary of State, Madeleine Albright. The highest level meeting between the US and North Korea for 50 years, it was mainly concerned with the two countries' respective missile programmes.

October 2002 saw international tensions mounting with regard to North Korea's nuclear programme. In December reports were received regarding the reactivation of the Yongbyon nuclear reactor, and international inspectors were asked to leave. In February and March 2003 non-ballistic missiles were fired into the sea between North Korea and Japan. Talks over the nuclear programme took place in 2004, but were suspended in February 2005 by the North Koreans who pulled out of the talks claiming that the US Administration were trying to antagonise them. In July 2005 six nation talks resumed in Beijing. In September, it was announced that North Korea had agreed to rejoin the nuclear non-proliferation treaty which would mean giving up all nuclear activities; in return the US pledged aid and electricity, and stated that it would not invade North Korea. A day after the announcement, North Korea stated that it would not scrap its nuclear programme until it receives a civilian, light water nuclear reactor.

On the 27 and 28 July 2004 more than 450 refugees from North Korea arrived in South Korea after having passed through China and an unnamed third country.

In July 2006, North Korea conducted test-fires of long-range and medium range missiles. The long range missiles which had been reported of having the capability of reaching the US crashed shortly after take off. The test firing led to an international outcry. In the following October North Korea carried an underground nuclear weapon test. The test was universally condemned and China delivered a message to North Korea asking it not to go ahead with a second nuclear weapons test.

In February 2007, six-nation talks on North Korea's nuclear programme resumed in China; North Korea agreed to close its main nuclear reactor, the Yongbyon reactor, and to disable all nuclear facilities in exchange for fuel aid. However, in March, progress was halted when North Korea reported that its funds in a Macau bank had been frozen. These were finally released in June, and IAEA nuclear inspectors arrived to oversee the disabling of North Korea's nuclear facilities. In October North Korea said it would disable three nuclear facilities and declare all of its nuclear programmes by the end of the year.

In May 2007 May, passenger trains crossed the North-South border for the first time in 56 years.

In August 2007, more than 220 people were killed and 80 were missing after severe flooding in North Korea. The province of Kangwon suffered the highest losses, with 181 confirmed deaths. Heavy flooding left as many as 300,000 people without homes and destroyed a tenth of the country's farmland.

In October President Kim Jong-il of North Korea and President Roh Moo-hyun of South Korea agreed at a summit in Pyongyang to hold talks regarding formally ending the Korean war. The following month the Prime Ministers of each country met, the first such meeting for 15 years.

In August and September 2008, President Kim Jong-il failed to appear at several important events in August and September 2008, including a parade to celebrate 60 years since the country was founded. His absence fuelled speculation that he was too ill to attend, but these claims were dismissed by government spokesmen.

In October 2008, the USA removed North Korea from the list of states which sponsor terrorism. In return North Korea agreed to let observers have full access to its nuclear sites.

In January 2009 North Korea announced it was tearing up all military and political agreements with South Korea and accused South Korea of having hostile intent. In March it was reported that a possible long range missile had been set up on a launch pad. North Korea had said that it would be launching a satellite into orbit in April and would be using a long range missile to do this but several countries including Japan and the US were concerned that this was in fact a test launch for the missile. Japan responded by launching its missile defence shield. Pyongyang claimed a successful satellite launch had taken place in April. In May 2009 North Korea carried out an underground nuclear test which was condemned by the UN.

In June 2009 it was reported that Kim Jong-il had named his youngest son Kim Jong-un as his successor.

In October 2009 North Korea indicated it was ready to resume talks about its nuclear programme and in December US envoy Stephen Bosworth visited the country. In January 2010 North Korea called for an end to hostile relations with the US and said it would work towards making the Korean peninsula nuclear-free.

In January 2010 North Korea fired artillary into the sea near the disputed maritime border with South Korea it said it was part of a military drill. The following month North Korea announced that areas near the disputed maritime border were now naval firing zones. In March 2010 a South Korean warship the Cheonan sank near the maritime border. Investigations into why the ship sank by South Korea found that it had been sunk by a North Korean torpedo. North Korea denied the accusations and cut diplomatic relations with Seoul. In July 2010 the USA announced new sanctions against North Korea in response to the Cheonan sinking.

North Korean parliament met for a special session in June 2010 to approve a leadership reshuffle. Choe Yong-rim replaced Kim Yong-il as prime minister and economy chief. Kim Jong-il's brother-in-law Chang Song-taek was appointed vice-chair of the National Defence Commission.

In July 2010, the US announced it was increasing sanctions against North Korea in response to the sinking of the Cheonan warship.

In October 2010 a rare meeting of the party conference took place. At the meeting Kim Jong-un, the youngest son of Kim Jong-il, was made a four star general and was then made Vice Chairman of the Workers' Party Central Military Commission as well as a member of the party's Central Committee. This was seen as an indication by the international community that Kim Jong-un is being groomed as his father's successor. Little is known about Kim Jong-un; at the time of the meeting he was believed to be around 27 or 28 and was educated in Switzerland.

In November 2010 a visiting nuclear scientist from the USA was shown a secretly built facility for enriching uranium, the revelations caused international alarm. Also that month a disputed maritime border clash with South Korea resulted in the death of two South Korean marines on Yeonpyeong island. North Korea's military blamed South Korea for instigating the incident, a claim South Korea denies. Both sides fired several dozen shells.

In February 2011, North Korea suffered an outbreak of foot and mouth disease, it was feared this would increase food shortages.

In March 2012, North Korea announced that it would launch a "rocket-mounted satellite" to mark the birthday of state founder Kim Il-Sung despite having agreed to suspend long-range missile tests earlier in the year in return for US food aid. Foreign joumalists were invited to see the preparations for the launch. North Korean scienctists said that the rocket was to launch a satellite in space but many feared it would have military capabilities. In the event although the rocket launched it then broke up and crashed into the sea.

In July 2012, Kim Jong-un replaced his army chief, Ri Yong-ho with a little known general, Hyon Yong-chol.

On December 12 2012, North Korea successfully launched a satellite into space, using a three-stage rocket. This action was condemned by the US amongst others as it was a banned test of long-range missile technology. The following January the UN Security Council passed a resolution condemning the launch and expanded sanctions against the country. At the end of January, North Korea said it would proceed with a high-level nuclear test, and in February the state run news agency reported that an underground nuclear test had been successfully staged. On March 7, the UN approved fresh sanctions against North Korea. North Korea announced it had the right to a pre-emptive strike on the US. On March 11, the US began its annual joint military drills with South Korea. North Korea announced it had scrapped the Korean War armistice, the UN responded by saying this is a pact which cannot be unilaterally scrapped. North Korea then accused the US and its allies of attacking its internet servers saying that some of its official websites had become inaccessible. During March, North Korea continued to make threats against the US and South Korea, the US flew a B-52 bomber over the Korean peninsula. On March 27, North Korea cut a key military hotline between North and South Korea, this was the last official link between the two countries, three days later North Korea announced it was entering a State of War with South Korea, and at the beginning of April said it would restart its main Yongbyon nuclear complex which had been inactive since 2007. The UN Security Council approved fresh sanctions following the nuclear test, these sanctions targeted cash transfers and travel for diplomats. In a further move, North Korea annouced that it was suspending access to South Koreans to the Kaesong Industrial Complex. The complex is situated in in North Korea just outside the demilitarized zone and

DEMOCRATIC PEOPLE'S REPUBLIC OF KOREA

is a joint industrial park mainly financed by South Korea. In April 2013, North Korea warned foreigners to leave the peninsula in order to avoid the threat of war, it later offered to attend talks aimed at reducing the tension if the UN lifted the sanctions and the US and South Korea stopped military drills. South Korea rejected the approach saying the proposals were 'incomprehensible'. In May, North Korea tested four short range missiles and also sentenced US tour operator Kenneth Bae to hard labour for what it called 'anti-government crimes'. In June 2013, North and South Korea agreed to meet for talks aimed at the possible re-opening of the Kaesong industrial complex and the restoration of the Red Cross hotline. In July they agreed in principle to reopen the complex.

Legislature

North Korea has a unicameral legislature. The Supreme People's Assembly has 687 members elected for a five-year term. They elect the Premier.
Supreme People's Assembly, *Choe Go In Min Hoe Ui,* Mansoudong Central District, Pyongyang. North Korea. Tel: +850 (0)2 18111

Cabinet (as at June 2013)
Premier: Pak Png Ju
Deputy Premier: Jon Ha Chol
Deputy Premier: Kang Nung Su
Deputy Premier: Kim Rak Hui
Deputy Premier: Kang Sok Ju
Deputy Premier: Ri Thae Nam
Deputy Premier: Thae Jong Su
Deputy Premier, Chair of the Capital City Construction Commission: Kim In Sik
Deputy Premier, Minister of Machine Building Industry: Jo Pyong Ju
Deputy Premier, Chair of the State Planning Commission: Ro Tu Chol
Deputy Premier, Minister of Chemical Industry: Ri Mu Yong
Deputy Premier, Minister of Agriculture: Ri Chol Man
Minister of Foreign Affairs: Pak Ui Chun
Minister of the Electric Power Industry: Ho Taek
Minister of Construction and Building Materials Industries: Tong Jong Ho
Minister of the Metal Industry: Kim Thae Bong
Minister of Railways: Jon Kil Su
Minister of Land and Marine Transport: Ra Tong Hui
Minister of Light Industry: An Jong Su
Minister of Foreign Trade: Ri Ryong Nam
Minister of Forestry: Kim Kwang Yong
Minister of Urban Management: Kang Yong Su
Minister of Land and Environmental Protection: Kim Kyung Jun
Minister of Fisheries: Ri Hyuk
Minister of State Construction Control: Pae Tai Chun
Minister of Commerce: Kim Pong Chol
Minister of Procurement and Food Administration: Jo Yong Chol
Minister of Posts and Telecommunications: Ryu Yong Sop
Minister of Culture: Hong Kwang Sun
Minister of Finance: Choe Kwang Jin
Minister of Labour: Jong Yong Su
Minister of Public Health: Choe Chang Sik
Minister of Mining Industry: Kang Min Chol
Minister of Oil Industry: Pae Hak Yi
Minister of the Coal Industry: Kim Hyong-Sik
Minister of State Inspection: Kim Ui-sun
Minister of Physical Culture & Sport Commission: Ri Jong Moo
Minister of Education: Tae Hyung Chol
Minister of the People's Armed Forces: Gen. Jang Jong Nam
President of Academy of Sciences: Pyon Yong Rip
Minister of Natural Resources Decelopment: Ri Chun Sam
Minister of Public Security: Gen. Ri Myong Su
Minister of the Electronoics Industry: Kim Jae Seong
Chief Secretary of the Cabinet: Kim Yong Ho
President of the Central Bank: Paek Ryong chon
Director of Central Statistics Bureau: Kim Chang Su
Director of the Secretariat of the Cabinet: Kim Yong Ho

Political Parties

Complete political control is held by the Korean Workers' (Communist) Party (KWP) and no other political parties are allowed to operate. The KWP elects a Central Committee and a governing Politburo. Ultimate authority is exercised by the Presidium of the Politburo. Most members of the Administration Council are also members of the KWP Central Committee or the Politburo.

Elections

President Kim Il Sung was elected by the Supreme People's Assembly for a fifth four-year term of office in May 1990 but died on 8 July 1994. He was succeeded by his son Kim Jong-Il. In April 2009 parliament re-elected Kim Jong-il as chairman of the National Defence Commission.

Diplomatic Relations

British Embassy, Munsu Dong Diplomatic Compound, Pyongyang, Democratic People's Republic of Korea. Tel: +850 (0)2 381 7980, fax: +850 (0)2 381 7985, e-mail: postmaster.PYONX@fco.gov.uk, URL: https://www.gov.uk/government/world/organisations/british-embassy-pyongyang
Ambassador: Michael Gifford (page 1430)
Embassy of the Democratic People's Republic of Korea (North Korea), 73 Gunnersbury Avenue, London W5 4LP, United Kingdom, Tel: +44 (0)20 8992 4965
Ambassador: Ja Song Nam
Permanent Representative to the UN, New York: Sin Son Ho

LEGAL SYSTEM

Justice is administered by the Central Court, provincial courts, the people's courts of cities and counties and also by special courts in accordance with the Constitution. The officials of the Courts are elected to their office.

The Central Court is the final court of appeal for criminal and civil cases, and has initial jurisdiction for crimes against the state. It does not have the power of judicial review over the constitutionality of executive or legislative actions, nor does it have an activist role in protecting the constitutionally guaranteed rights of individuals against state actions. The Central Court supervises the judicial work of all courts, and is responsible to the SPA, the DPRK President and the CPC.

The President of the Central Court is elected by the Supreme People's Assembly (SPA), whilst its judges and people's assessors are elected by the Standing Committee of the SPA. The provincial courts and people's courts are staffed with a single judge, who is assisted by two "people's assessors," laymen who are temporarily selected for the judiciary. The constitution does not require legal education as a qualification for being elected as a judge or people's assessor, and political reliability remains the prime criterion for holding office. The term of judicial office is either four years or two years.

Prosecutions are conducted by the Central Prosecutor's Office, the procurator's offices of the province - City (district), county - and by the special office. The officials supervise the decisions and directives of state organs to see that they conform to the Constitution and the legal system. The President of the Central Procurator's Office is appointed or removed by the SPA. The work of this office is accountable to the SPA, the President and the CPC.

Law-abiding life guidance committees were established in 1977 at the provincial, city and county levels. These are chaired by the president of the people's committee, and ensure respect for public authority and conformity to the dictates of socialist society. They oversee state inspection agencies, the procuracy, and the police, as well as controlling organizations, workplaces, social groups, and citizens in their jurisdiction. The committees can apply strict legal sanctions to all violations short of crimes.

The regime commits serious abuses, subjecting its citizens to rigid controls over their lives. The government denies freedom of speech, press, assembly, and association, and restricts freedom of religion, movement, and worker rights. The citizens do not have the right to change their government. There are reports of extrajudicial killings, disappearances and arbitrary detention. People are imprisoned for their political beliefs. Prison conditions are life threatening; prisoners are subjected to forced hard labour, and torture is known to have occurred. The judiciary is not independent.

North Korea retains the death penalty, and continues to use it. Over 60 executions were reported to have been carried out in 2010 but human rights groups allege the true figure is much higher.

LOCAL GOVERNMENT

For administrative purposes North Korea is divided in two municipalities (Pyongyang and Nason si) and nine provinces. The provinces are Chagang-do (Chagang), Hamgyong-bukto (North Hamgyong), Hamgyong-namdo (South Hamgyong), Hwanghae-bukto (North Hwanghae), Hwanghae-namdo (South Hwanghae), Kangwon-do (Kangwon), P'yongan-bukto (North P'yongan), P'yongan-namdo (South P'yongan), Yanggang-do (Yanggang).. These nine provinces contain 25 cities, 38 districts, 147 counties and 147 labourer districts. There is also a free trade zone, Najin-Sonbong FTZ.

In North Korea candidates for local elections are nominated by the KWP from loyal Party members and only one candidate runs for each seat. Election day is declared a national holiday and the North Korea media encourage the people to cast a 'yes' vote for all the Party candidates. Those who cannot physically take part in elections through illness or other reasons are visited by officials of the Election Guidance Committee at their homes or hospital and given election ballots. These ballots are then taken to the appropriate polling station.

AREA AND POPULATION

Area

North Korea covers an area of 122,762 sq. km (about 47,399 sq. miles). To the north, the country is divided from China by the Yalu and the Tumen rivers. There is an eleven-mile border with the Russian Maritime Province along the estuary of the Tumen river in northeast Korea. The southern border of North Korea is formed by the Military Demarcation Line (MDL) or Demilitarised Zone with South Korea, established by the Korean War Armistice Agreement signed at Panmunjom on 27 July 1953. The MDL extends across central Korea from the Han river estuary in the west to south of Kosong on the Sea of Japan in the east.

The land is largely mountainous or upland with deep valleys. There are coastal plains to the west. The climate is temperate with wet summers.

To view a map, visit: http://www.un.org/Depts/Cartographic/map/profile/korean.pdf

Population

The population of North Korea was estimated at 24.346 million in 2010, approximately 3.25 million of whom live in the capital Pyongyang. Other large cities include Nampo, Kaesong, Chongjin and Hamhung. Recent figures put the population density at 186 people per sq km. The annual population growth rate was estimated to be 0.6 per cent over the period 1999-2009. Korean is the official language. There are small communities of Chinese and Japanese.

Births, Marriages, Deaths
2010 figures show the estimated birth rate to be 14.3 per 1,000 population and the death rate at 8.6 per 1,000 population. By 2009, the average life expectancy was estimated to be 67 years for males and 72 years for females. Healthy life expectancy was estimated to be 57 years and 61 years respectively. Approximately 23 per cent of the population is aged under 15 years and 14 per cent over 60 years. The median age was estimated to be 33. The total fertility rate per woman was 2.0 children. (Source: http://www.who.int, World Health Statistics 2012)

Public Holidays
1 January: New Year's Day
16 February: Kim Jong-Il's Birthday
15 April: Kim Il-Sung's Birthday
1 May: International Worker's Day
15 August: Liberation Day
9 September: Republic's Day
10 October: Foundation of the Worker's Party
27 December: Constitution Day

EMPLOYMENT

It has been estimated that the workforce is around 24.3 million, with around 36 per cent engaged in agriculture.

BANKING AND FINANCE

North Korea faces many economic challenges. For years, it maintained a centralised command economy based on Soviet models of the Stalin period. Economic decision-making, including the fixing of wages, prices, investment and resource allocation was strictly controlled by the agencies of the Korean Workers' Party and the government. A combination of factors including the break-up of the Soviet Union, difficulties in foreign trade and an agricultural crisis led to economic collapse and famine in the mid-1990s. The government requested aid from the UN in 1995. In 2006 the government said it would no longer accept humanitarian aid despite a general view that it still had extreme humanitarian needs. Agriculture accounts for some 25 per cent of economic activity. Limited privatisation measures were introduced in 2002 including a relaxation of restrictions on farmers' markets. In 2006, North Korea said it would no longer accept humanitarian aid. UNDP resumed its programme in 2010.

Currency
The basic unit of currency is the won. One won comprises 100 jon. Foreign visitors are required to use foreign currency.

GDP/GNP, Inflation, National Debt
Estimates for 2009 put the GDP at US$35 billion, giving a per capita figure of US$1,800. GDP generally consists of 25 per cent agriculture, 43 per cent industry, and 36 per cent services. Estimated figures show that 90 per cent of economic activity is generated from state-owned companies and the collective agricultural system. (Figures are estimates and may be based on incomplete data).

Balance of Payments / Imports and Exports
For many years North Korea enjoyed grants, loans and general preferential trading terms with the former Soviet Union. Since 1990 Moscow has insisted on hard currency payments calculated at current exchange rates for all goods and services exported to North Korea. The effect on the North Korean economy was shortages of goods and unemployment.

Main exports are minerals, metal products, textiles, chemicals, electronics and fishery products. Main imported goods are petroleum, coal, consumer goods and machinery, equipment animal products and grain. The main trading partners are China, Russia, South Korea, Japan and Thailand. At the start of the Korean War in 1950 the USA imposed sanctions against North Korea; in June 2000, some of the sanctions were lifted. Estimated figures for 2008 show that exports earned US$2.0 billion and imports cost US$3.5 billion.

In 1988 trade was legalised between North and South Korea; it was estimated in 2005 that this trade was now worth US$1 billion, much of it generated by out-sourcing assembly work from South Korea to North Korea. The Gaesong Industrial Zone was established as a platform for South Korean SMEs, providing employment for over 45,000 North Koreans. Diplomatic tensions continue to exist between the countries and cross-border transport is frequently disrupted and expansion is on hold. North Korea established a free trade zone at Rason in the 1990s but its success is hindered by its poor infrastructure and political situation. In 2012 it was reported to be in talks with China on joint industrial complexes on their borders.

Central Bank
Central Bank of the Democratic People's Republic of Korea, 58-1 Mansu-dong, Sungri str, Central District, Pyongyang, Korea (North). Tel: +850 2 18111 office 8148 / 2 3338196, fax: +850 2 3814624
Governor: Ri Kwang Gon

MANUFACTURING, MINING AND SERVICES

Primary and Extractive Industries
North Korea has extensive underground resources. Some 300 kinds of ores have been discovered, some 200 of which have economic value. Proven resources include deposits of gold, tungsten, molybdenum, graphite, magnesite, limestone, mica and fluorspar. In particular, there are rich deposits of iron ore, coal, lead, zinc and copper. Coal production in 2010 was estimated to be 34.7 million short tons and consumption was 30.3 million short tons. (Figures from US EIA)

Energy
North Korea has built two nuclear reactors at Yongbyon, about 80 miles north of Pyongyang. The country possesses natural uranium and has about 3,000 nuclear specialists. Although the DPRK signed the Nuclear Non-Proliferation Treaty in 1985, the country did not adhere to the Nuclear Safeguards Agreement which requires inspection by the Vienna-based International Atomic Energy Agency (IAEA). In April 1992 the North Korean Supreme People's Assembly ratified the Nuclear Safeguards Agreement with the IAEA which the DPRK had signed on 30 January 1992. It withdrew from the agreement in 1993 and refused to cooperate with the IAEA. In 1994 an agreed framework was worked out where the DPRK would stop its nuclear programme in exchange for two pressurised light-water reactors from a consortium including the US, South Korea, Japan and the EU. In 2002 there were three rounds of negotiations between US, China, South Korea, Japan and Russia and North Korea aimed at easing the tension. Talks started again in February 2005 but then North Korea withdrew claiming it had nuclear weapons. Talks resumed in July 2005. In September it was announced that North Korea had agreed to rejoin the nuclear non-proliferation treaty which would mean giving up all nuclear activities. In return the US pledged aid and electricity and stated that it would not invade North Korea. A day after the announcement, North Korea stated that it would not scrap its nuclear programme until it received a civilian, light water nuclear reactor. In October 2006 North Korea carried out an underground nuclear weapon test. The test was universally condemned. In February 2007 talks began again held in Beijing and North Korea agreed to close its main nuclear reactor in exchange for fuel aid. The following June international inspectors were allowed to see the Yongbyon nuclear complex and confirmed in July that the reactor had been shut down. North Korea also agreed to reveal all its nuclear complexes. However, in January 2008 the US said that North Korea was not honouring its commitments and tenison arose. Diplomatic efforts continued and in June 2008 North Korea made a declaration of its nuclear assets. In October 2008 the US said it would remove North Korea from its list of states who sponsor terrorism. In return North Korea said it would provide full access to its nuclear sites. In May 2009 North Korea announced it has successfully carried out an underground nuclear test. The test resulted in protests from China, Russia and the US.

Estimated figures for 2009 show that North Korea generated around 0.9 quadrillion Btus of energy, over 80 per cent of which came from coal, electricity production had relied on hydro power but droughts have led to water shortages resulting in blackouts and rationing of power.

North Korea has no oil and natural gas of its own and so imports all it needs. It is estimated that North Korea consumes 16,000 barrels of oil per day and has a crude oil distillation capacity of 71,000 barrels per day. North Korea has an estimated 661 million short tons of recoverable coal reserves and produces around 36 million short tons per year, all of which it uses.

Manufacturing
North Korea does not issue detailed statistics on industrial production. Under the Third Seven Year Plan (1987-93), however, ten strategic sectors in particular were targeted for development. Designated targets were not reached, while coal and electricity production have only registered one-third of their targets. The rigidities of North Korea's economic system mean that investment is concentrated on inefficient heavy industry, while investment in new technology, light industry and infrastructure is neglected. High military expenditure also diverts scarce resources away from the industrial sector. The cutbacks in Russian oil imports since 1990 have also had a detrimental effect on North Korea's industrial output.

Traditionally the North Korean manufacturing industry was dominated by heavy industries particularly, steel, machinery manufacture and cement, but recently light industries particularly textile production have become increasingly important, North Korea is also believed to be looking toward IT development.

Agriculture
Originally the chief cereal for Koreans was rice. But as the terrain and climate of North Korea is often unfavourable for large-scale rice production, the North Korean authorities began to cultivate grain crops, particularly maize, in the 1960s. Maize has now become the staple food for most North Koreans. However, grain production has never been successful in meeting the demand and the shortfall continues to rise. There were large-scale wheat imports from Canada, Australia, the EU, and even the US. These imports are partly paid for by exporting high-grade North Korean rice to South-East Asia. Floods and droughts have caused problems for several years. In June 2001 North Korea was hit by severe flooding, and the United Nations provided food aid. Aid agencies believe up to 2 million people may have died through famine. Floods hit again in July and August 2006, prompting South Korea to donate around 100,000 tons of food aid. Some agencies estimated that the floods led to the destruction of 70,000 hectares of land and around 60,000 people being left homeless. The World Food Programme (WFP) has provided assistance since 1995 but in 2006 North Korea announced that it no longer wanted to receive humanitarian aid and assistance by the WFP was cut back. However, in 2008 the WFP felt that the food situation was getting worse and North Korea would need further aid if a humanitarian disaster was to be avoided.

Much of central North Korea and the northeast of the country is forested, often with conifers, and timber production is increasingly developed. North Korea uses fishing grounds in both the Yellow Sea and the Sea of Japan. Nampo, south of Pyongyang on the Taedong estuary, is the chief fishing port for the west coast. Wonsan is the leading fishing port on the east coast of North Korea. Other east coast fishing ports are Hungnam, Chongjin, and Najin.

Figures from 2003 show that over 24 per cent of the land is used for agriculture, around 50 per cent of which is irrigated; in 2005 1,296,000 hectares were under cereal production.

Agricultural Production in 2010

Produce	Int. $'000*	Tonnes
Rice, paddy	597,308	2,426,000
Vegetables fresh nes	384,175	2,038,700
Apples	318,158	752,300

DEMOCRATIC PEOPLE'S REPUBLIC OF KOREA

- continued

Indigenous rabbit meat	248,780	133,900
Maize	226,010	1,686,000
Potatoes	224,847	1,708,000
Fruit fresh nes	191,306	548,100
Indigenous pigmeat	169,097	110,000
Hen eggs, in shell	128,555	155,000
Tobacco, unmanufactured	125,032	78,500
Beans, dry	123,211	224,300
Soybeans	89,420	350,000

* unofficial figures

Source: http://faostat.fao.org/site/339/default.aspx Food and Agriculture Organization of the United Nations, Food and Agricultural commodities production

COMMUNICATIONS AND TRANSPORT

Travel Requirements
Citizens of the USA, Canada, Australia and the EU require a passport valid for six months and a visa. Other nationals should contact the embassy to check visa requirements.

Tourism in North Korea is currently permitted only through officially recognised travel companies . Visas can be obtained through these travel companies or the North Korean Embassy. People who have recently visited areas infected by the Avian Influenza may be denied entry, and visitors entering Korea through China are advised to obtain a double-entry visa for China, as a valid Chinese visa is essential for departing North Korea at the end of a visit or in an emergency. It is not possible to enter North Korea from the Republic of Korea.

National Airlines
Air Koryo, Sunnan District, Pyongyan, North Korea. Tel: +850 2 32143, fax: +850 2 814625, URL: http://www.korea-dpr.com/airkoryo.htm
There are direct air links between Pyongyang and Beijing, Moscow, Vladivostok, Macau, Berlin and Bangkok.

Railways
The total length of the North Korean Railway system in 1997 was 5,200 km. A western rail network connects Kaesong via Pyongyang with Sinuiju on the Yalu river border with China. The eastern rail network links Wonsan with Hungnam, Chongjin and Hoeryong in north-eastern Korea. There is a lateral east-west railway connecting Wonsan with Pyongyang. In 2000 two electrified rail links were opened, one between Ganggy and Nangrim in the Jagang Province, and the other in the North Hamgyong Province linking Hamhung and Seoho. A train runs once a week from Moscow via China to Pyongyang.

In the June 2000 Summit between North and South Korea it was agreed that South Korea will fund the restoration and development of the transport infrastructure. A rail link between Seoul and the Kaesong Industrial Zone situated just north of the Demilitarised Zone has been built and cargo trains were due to start using the coonnection in December 2007.

Pyongyang has a small subway system.

Roads
The length of the road network is about 30,000 km. The North Korean terrain means that roads, like rail links, are concentrated along the east and west coasts of the country. Vehicles are driven on the right.

Ports and Harbours
North Korea has 12 main ports. One of the largest, Kamchaek in the North Hamgyong Province, was expanded in 2000. It is to be used primarily as a port for exports.

HEALTH

The state provides free medical care. In 2006, the DPR of Korea spent approximately 6 per cent of its total budget on healthcare, accounting for 85.6 per cent of all healthcare spending. Total expenditure on health care equated to 3.5 per cent of the country's GDP. Per capita spending on health care was US$16 in 2000. Figures for 2000-10 show that there are 74,597 physicians (33 per 10,000 population), 93,414 nurses (41 per 10,000 population) and 8,315 dentists. There are 132 hospital beds per 10,000 population.

In 2009 the infant mortality rate (probability of dying by first birthday) was estimated to be 26 per 1,000 live births. The under-fives mortality rate was estimated to be 33 per 1,000 live births. The most common causes of death in this age group are pneumonia (15 per cent),
prematurity (25 per cent) and diarrhoea (5 per cent). An estimated 32.4 per cent of children aged under 5 were stunted in the period 2005-11 and 18.8 per cent were classified as underweight.

An estimated 98 per cent of the population to improved drinking water and 80 per cent had access to improved sanitation. (Source: http://www.who.int, World Health Statistics 2012. NB Statistics are based on scant data).

EDUCATION

Primary and secondary education is free and compulsory. All levels of the North Korean educational system, including higher education, emphasise the teachings of President Kim Il Sung's *Juche* or self-reliance ideology. This is termed a creative adaptation of Marxism-Leninism to Korean conditions. Primary level education lasts for four years, and secondary level lasts for six years. Recent figures show around 533 university level institutions. The adult literacy rate is put at 99 per cent.

RELIGION

Buddhism is traditionally the predominant religion of Korea. Beginning in 1945, the Communist authorities in North Korea suppressed all Buddhist temples as well as Christian churches. North Korea has now set up nominal bodies known as the Buddhist League and the Christian League as part of a policy of emphasising that there is freedom of religion in North Korea. Chondo, a syncretic Korean religion is also recognised.

North Korea has a religious tolerance rating of 2 on a scale of 1 to 10 (10 is most freedom). (Source: World Religion Database)

COMMUNICATIONS AND MEDIA

There is no press freedom in North Korea. All press and broadcasters are under direct state control. Propaganda is constantly broadcast and difficulties within the country not published. Listening to foreign broadcasts risks severe punishemnt. Online access is exceeding rare and user activity monitored.

Newspapers
The leading North Korean newspaper is Rodong Shinmun (Worker's Daily), published in Pyongyang. The journal is the official newspaper of the Korean Workers' Party.

Broadcasting
The chief domestic radio and television outlet is the (North) Korean Central Broadcasting Station (KCBS) in Pyongyang. Radio Pyongyang is directed to Koreans living in Japan and China. Broadcasting is under central control.

Telecommunications
It was estimated in 2008 that 1.1 million telephone main lines were in use. Mobile phone services are reported to be available around Pyongyang.

ENVIRONMENT

Main environmental concerns for North Korea include deforestation, which has led to problems with flooding, soil erosion and water pollution. North Korea is a party to the following international agreements: Antarctic Treaty, Biodiversity, Climate Change, Climate Change-Kyoto Protocol, Desertification, Environmental Modification, Hazardous Wastes, Ozone Layer Protection and Ship Pollution. It has signed, but not ratified, the Law of the Sea.

According to figures from the EIA, in 2010, North Korea's emissions from the consumption of fossil fuels totalled 63.69 million metric tons of carbon dioxide.

SPACE PROGRAMME

The Korean Committee of Space Technology is believed to have been founded in the 1980s and is responsible for space exploration and construction of satellites. North Korea signed the Outer Space Treaty and the Registration Convention in 2009. There are believed to be two launch sites. The government has said it launched two satellites, one in 1998 and the second in 2009 although it has been alleged these may have been military launches. An launch of a observation satellite launch failed in April 2012.

REPUBLIC OF KOREA
South Korea
Taehan Min'guk

Capital: Seoul (Population estimate, 2012: 10,500,000)

Head of State: Park Geun-hye (page 1492) (President)

National Flag: A white field bearing a disk (the *Taegukki*) or yin-yang symbol, red over blue; on the white field corners, parallel black bars broken and whole, to symbolise natural opposites.

CONSTITUTION AND GOVERNMENT

Constitution
In 1945, following the Second World War, the Japanese occupation of Korea ended when Soviet troops occupied the north of the country (above the 38th parallel) and US forces occupied the south. In 1948 the Republic of Korea was proclaimed, whilst, in the north, following the withdrawal of Soviet troops, a Soviet-backed leadership was installed and the Democratic People's Republic of Korea was proclaimed. When, in 1950, the Republic of Korea declared independence, North Korea invaded, sparking the Korean War. In 1953 an armistice was declared, although officially the war has never ended, and North and South Korea remain divided.

The first representative government of Korea was formed in August 1948 and was based on a presidential system similar to that of the United States. After the April Revolution (1960), the constitution was amended giving greater power to the legislature. In May 1961, with the emergence of the military government, the National Assembly was dissolved.

On 17 December 1962 a national referendum was conducted over a proposed constitutional amendment designed to restore a presidential system. The new constitution came into force on 17 December 1963. As a result, the short-lived parliamentary system was abolished, and the presidential system re-established. On 17 October 1972 an Emergency Presidential Decree was promulgated. After a national referendum a new constitution was adopted on 21 November 1972. On 15 December 1972, under the terms of the new constitution, 2,359 deputies to the National Conference for Unification were elected. These deputies in turn re-elected Park Chung Hee for a six-year presidential term.

On 6 July 1978 President Park Chung Hee was elected to serve another six-year term by a clear majority of 2,585 members of the National Conference for Unification.

The assassination of President Park on 26 October 1979 brought about the disintegration of the *Yushin* system and the end of a political era. The transition period under martial law was headed by President Choi Kyu-hah who had been prime minister under President Park. The Choi administration established the Special Committee for National Security Measures to act in liaison with the martial law authorities and to effect reforms to solve the root causes of the social unrest, economic decline, increasing student demonstrations, and labour disputes following the assassination of President Park.

President Choi resigned on 16 August 1980 to make way for the election of a new president. Chun Doo Hwan was then elected president by the National Conference for Unification on 27 August. Korea's Fifth Republic formally came into being on 3 March 1981 with the inauguration of Chun Doo-Hwan as the 12th President. While the new constitution guaranteed the peaceful transfer of power by limiting the presidency to a single seven-year term, it still provided for the presidential election through an indirect electoral college system.

Following President Chun's declaration on 13 April 1987 to postpone the revision of the constitution until after the 1988 Seoul Olympics, harsh protest erupted across the country. On 29 June, Roh Tae-Woo, the chairman of the ruling Democratic Justice Party, made a surprise announcement that accommodated the demands of the opposition camp. The eight-point formula featured the revision of the constitution for a direct presidential election, amnesty and restoration of civil rights for opposition leader Kim Dae-Joong and the release of detained political prisoners. President Chun endorsed Roh's formula on 1 July in a special announcement and the ruling and opposition parties began negotiating to draft a revision bill for the constitution based on partisan compromise.

After a month of negotiations, the ruling and opposition parties reached a final agreement on the bill for revision on 1 September 1987. The new constitution was endorsed with the overwhelming support of the people in a national referendum. The constitution included direct presidential elections, a five-year presidential term with no re-election, and improved civil rights. Roh Tae-Woo became the 13th President of Korea on 16 December 1987 when he won the country's first direct presidential election in 16 years. Roh received 36.6 per cent of the vote and defeated rival opposition candidates Kim Young-sam and Kim Dae-joong, who split the opposition vote.

To consult the constitution, please visit: http://korea.assembly.go.kr/res/low_01_read.jsp?boardid=1000000035

International Relations
Following the end of hostilities in the Korean War, South Korea was closely allied with the west particularly the USA. The Republic of Korea became a member of the United Nations in 1991 and the OECD in 1997 it became a member of the OECD Development Assistance Committee (DAC) in November 2009. In recent years South Korea has actively sought links with former communist bloc countries and has established diplomatic links. Forces from the Republic of Korea have served recently in Iraq and Afghanistan as well as operations in East Timor, Lebanon and Nepal.

Recent Events
After a quarter of a century of hostilities, talks began between the North and South, the last political meeting between the South and North Co-ordinating Committees having been held at Panmun Jom on 12 October 1972. Since 4 September 1990, the South-North meetings have been held, alternatively, in Seoul and Pyongyang. These are headed by the prime ministers from both sides. Four-way talks between South Korea, North Korea, China and the US were held in October 1998.

In June 2000 a summit was held in Pyongyang, the North Korean capital, between South Korea's president Kim Dae-jung, and the North Korean leader Kim Jong Il. Amongst subjects discussed were the setting up of a loose federation, economic co-operation, and families separated by the divide. In August 2000, 100 relatives from each side made a four day visit to separated families.

In June 2002 North and South Korean warships clashed in the Yellow Sea resulting in deaths on both sides. The South Korean defence minister Dong-shin Kim came under criticism for what was seen as a slow reaction to the skirmish, and on 11 July 2002 he lost his post following a cabinet reshuffle.

As a result of the July 2002 cabinet reshuffle, Chang Sang was given the post of prime minister, becoming the first female to hold the post in this traditionally male-dominated country. However, parliament vetoed the appointment and Chang Dae-whan, a newspaper owner, was given the post instead.

Presidential elections were held in December 2002 and were won by Roh Moo-hyun. He was sworn in to office in February 2003 and subsequently appointed Goh Kun as Prime Minister, a post Goh Kun had previously held in 1997-98. A new cabinet was also appointed in February 2003. Goh Kun resigned as prime minister in May 2004 and was replaced by Lee Hae-chan.

In September 2002 a mine clearing exercise was carried out in the demilitarised zone by North and South Korea. During the 2003 presidential inauguration ceremony North Korea test fired a missile into the sea.

In 2004 it was announced that Sejong City, 120 km (75 miles) from Seoul was to become the new capital city by 2030. The move was announced as the existing capital Seoul has become overcrowded; around 40 per cent of the population live there and it dominates the economy. The decision was challenged by the courts who said that a referendum should be held. The new city was inaugurated in July 2012 and it was expected that some ministries would move there but the main government offices would remain in Seoul.

Since the 2002 elections Roh Moo-hyun had faced difficulties in implementing his proposed reforms because of divisions within his Uri Party and allegations of corruption. In 2004 he was out of office for two months following moves to impeach him over election law infractions and incompetence. The impeachment was overturned by the Constitutional Court.

In March 2006 Prime Minister Lee Hae-chan, resigned following criticism that he was playing golf when he was expected to oversee government response to a railway strike. Han Myung-sook was nominated by the president to take over the role of Prime Minister, making her the first woman in the job; she resigned in March 2007, to become a candidate for President in the December 2007 elections.

In October 2006 former foreign minister Ban Ki-moon was appointed secretary-general of the United Nations. The head of the largest South Korean car maker, Hyundai, was jailed for three years for embezzlement in February 2007. In April of that year, South Korea and the US signed a free-trade agreement, and in May, passenger trains crossed the North-South border for the first time in 56 years.

In October 2007 the presidents of North and South Korea agreed to hold a summit to holds talks to formally end the Korean War. The following month, the Prime Ministers of both countries met the first time in 15 years.

In April 2008 South Korea agreed to resume beef imports from the USA; imports had been suspended since 2003 following the discovery of a case of BSE in the US. The announcement of the proposed imports led to street protests as people were concerned about the safety of US beef. In July in response to ongoing protests about the lifting of the ban, president Lee Myung-bak sacked his education, health and agriculture ministers hoping that this would restore confidence in the government.

In 2008 relations between North and South Korea again became tense. In February President Lee Myung-bak announced that continuing aid to North Korea was conditional on nuclear disarmament and human rights progress. In March South Korean managers from a joint industrial plant were expelled by North Korea and test firing of short range missiles were undertaken by North Korea who accused South Korea of sending a warship into its waters. In November North Korea accused the South of adopting a confrontational policy and said it would stop overland travel between the two countries.

REPUBLIC OF KOREA

In May 2009, former President, Roh Moo-hyun committed suicide; he and his family were under investigation for alleged corruption.

Also in May 2009 South Korea announced that it would join the US led Proliferation Security Initiative (PSI), which aims to stop any vessels suspected of carrying nuclear, chemical and biological weapons and materials. North Korea objected to South Korea joining the PSI and said it would view it as an act of aggression and would respond militarily if any attempt were made to intercept its ships and would no longer be bound by the 1953 Korean War Armistice Agreement.

In August 2009 there were signs of a thawing in the relationship between North and South Korea when North Korea sent a delegation to pay its respects following the death of former South Korean president Kim Dae-jung. Later that month North Korea announced it would ease restrictions on cross border traffic and resume talks on family reunions which has been suspended in 2008.

In November 2010 there was a disputed maritime border clash with North Korea which resulted in the death of two South Korean marines on Yeonpyeong Island and two civilians. North Korea's military blamed South Korea for instigating the incident by carrying out military exercises. Both sides fired several dozen shells. Many international observers think that North Korea is concerned about South Korea's increasing prominence on the international stage such as hosting the G20 summit. South Korea said it would continue with its planned military exercises.

In July 2011 the two Koreas held nuclear talks.

The US approved a free trade agreement with South Korea in October 2011. The agreement came into force in March 2012 and is expected to increase exports by up to $10 billion.

In March 2012, South Korea played host to a global conference on nuclear security, Iran and North Korea did not attend.

In July 2012, most of the government ministries began to move to the new mini capital, Sejong City, although most of the key ministries remain in Seoul. Sejong City is around 120 km south of Seoul.

Following North Korea's testing of a long range rocket earlier in the year, in October South Korea agreed a deal with the USA to almost triple the range of its ballistic missile system to 800km.

In January 2013, South Korea successfuly launched a satellite into orbit. The launch comes weeks after a North Korean rocket placed a satellite in orbit.

In February and March 2013, relations between North Korea and the rest of the world became strained and particularly with South Korea. North Korea cut off a hotline and said it would end non-aggression pacts with South Korea. North Korea told South Korean workers based in the Kaesong Industrial Complex to leave. Kaesong is a joint run industrial park, more than 100 South Korean companies operate there and they employ over 52,000 North Koreans. In April the North Koreans did not turn up to work. In June talks between the two countries took place and in July an agreement was signed which would allow in principle for the reopening of the complex.

Legislature
South Korea's unicameral legislature is known as the National Assembly (*Kuk Hoe*) and consists of 299 members, 243 are directly elected and 56 are election on a proportional representation basis of the number of total popular votes each party earned in the general elections. Members serve a four year term. The president appoints the Prime Minister.

The National Assembly was originally formed following an election on 27 February 1973. Of the 219 seats originally in the National Assembly, 73 seats were elected by the National Conference for Unification.

Kuk Hoe (National Assembly), 1 Yeouido-dong, Yeongdeungpo-gu, 150701 Seoul, Republic of Korea. Tel: +82 2 788 2786, fax: +82 2 788 3375, URL: http://www.assembly.go.kr
Speaker: Kang Chang-hee

Cabinet (as at June 2013)
Prime Minister: Chung Hong-won (page 1405)
Deputy Prime Minister, Minister for Strategy and Finance: Hyun Oh-seok (page 1446)
Minister of Education: Seo Nam-soo (page 1512)
Minister of Unification: Ryoo Kihl-jae (page 1507)
Minister of Foreign Affairs and Trade: Yun Byung-se (page 1542)
Minister of Justice: Hwang Kyo-ahn (page 1446)
Minister of Public Administration and Security: Yoo Jeong-bok (page 1541)
Minister of Culture, Sports and Tourism: Yoo Jin-ryong (page 1541)
Minister of Food, Agriculture, Fisheries and Forestry: Lee Dong-phil (page 1461)
Minister of Health and Welfare: Chin Young (page 1404)
Minister of Environment: Yoon Seong-kyu (page 1541)
Minister of Employment: Phang Ha-nam (page 1495)
Minister of Gender Equality and Family: Cho Yoon-seon (page 1404)
Minister of Land and Transport: Suh Seoung-hwan (page 1521)
Minister of Maritime Affairs: Yoon Jin-Sook
Minister of Future Planning, ICT and Science: Prof. Choi Mun-kee
Minister of Industry, Trade and Resources: Yoon Sang-jick (page 1541)
Minister of Defence: Kim Kwan-jin

Ministries
Most ministries are to be moved to Sejong City, south of Seoul. Key ministries will remain in Seoul. The first ministries moved in 2013.
Prime Minister's Office, 77 Sejongno, Jongno-gu, Seoul. Tel: +82 2 737 0094, fax: +82 2737 0109, URL: http://www.korea.net/Government/

Ministry of Finance and Economy, 1 Jungang-dong, Gwacheon, Gyeonggi Prov., South Korea. Tel: +82 2 503 9032, fax: +82 2 502 9033, URL: http://english.mofe.go.kr/main.php
Ministry of Unification, 77-6 Sejongno, Jongno-gu, Seoul, South Korea. Tel: +82 2 3703 2423, fax: +82 2 720 2432, URL: http://www.unikorea.go.kr
Ministry of Foreign Affairs and Trade, 77-6 Sejongno, Jongno-gu, Seoul, South Korea. Tel: +82 2 3703 2198, fax: +82 2 738 9047, URL: http://www.mofat.go.kr/en/index.mof
Ministry of Justice, Building #5, Gwacheon Government Complex, Jungang-dong1, Gwacheon-si, Kyunggi-do, South Korea. Tel: +82 2 503 7023, fax: +82 2 504 3337, URL: http://www.moj.go.kr
Ministry of National Defence, 3-1 Yong San-dong, Yongsan-gu, 140 701 Seoul, South Korea. Tel: +82 2 795 0071, fax: +82 2 703 31099, e-mail: cyber@mnd.go.kr, URL: http://www.mnd.go.kr
Ministry of Science and Technology, 2 Jungang-dong, Gwacheon, Gyeonggi Prov., South Korea. Tel: +82 2 503 7619, fax: +82 2 503 7673, URL: http://www.most.go.kr/most/english/index.jsp
Ministry of Culture, Sport and Tourism, 215 Changgyeonggung-ro, Jongno-gu, Seoul, South Korea. Tel: +82 2 3704 9114, fax: +82 2 3704 9119, URL: http://www.mcst.go.kr/english/index.jsp
Ministry of Agriculture, Food and Rural Affairs, Government Complex Sejong, Da-som 2 ro 94 Euh-jin Dong, Sejong-si 339-012, South Korea. Tel: +82 2 1577 1020, fax: +82 44 868 0846, URL: http://english.mifaff.go.kr/main.jsp
Ministry of Education, 77-6 Sejong-no, Jongno-gu, 110 760 Seoul, South Korea. Tel: +82 2 2100 6060, fax: +82 2 7 2100 6579, URL: http://english.mest.go.kr/
Ministry of Trade, Industry and Energy, 47 Gwanmooro, Gwacheon-si, Gyeong gi-do, South Korea. Tel: +82 2 2110 5061, fax: +82 2 503 9496, http://www.mke.go.kr/language/eng/index.jsp
Ministry of Health and Welfare, 75 Yulfon-ro, Jongno-gu, Seoul 110-793, South Korea.Tel: +82 2 503 7215, fax: +82 2 503 7568, URL: http://www.mohw.go.kr/index.jsp
Ministry of Environment, Government Complex Sejong, qq Doume-Ro, Sejong City, 339-012, South Korea.Tel: +82 044 201 6568, URL: http://eng.me.go.kr/index.jsp
Ministry of Employment and Labour, Complex II, 47 Gwanmun-ro, Gwacheon-si, Gyeonggi-do, South Korea. Tel: +82 2 503 9723, fax: +82 2 503 9772, URL: http://www.moel.go.kr/english/main.jsp
Ministry of Gender Equality, Cheonggyechonno 8, Jung-Gu, Seoul, South Korea. Tel: +82 2 2106 5000, fax: +82 2 2106 5145, URL: http://english.mogef.go.kr/index.jsp
Ministry of Land, Infrastructure and Transport, Government Complex Sejong, A-Dong, 11, Doum6-Ro Sejong-City, 339-012, South Korea. Tel: +82 44 1599 0001, fax: +82 44 201 4672, URL: http://english.mltm.go.kr/intro.do
Ministry of Maritime Affairs and Fisheries, 139, 3-ga, Chungjeong-ro, Seodaemun-gu, Seoul, South Korea. Tel: +82 2 3148 6040, fax: +82 2 3148 6044, URL: http://www.momaf.go.kr/eng/index.asp
Ministry of Government Policy Coordination 77-6 Sejong-ro, Jongno-gu, Seoul, South Korea. Tel: +82 2 723 7777, fax: +82 720 5579,
Ministry of Planning and Budget 520-3 Banpo-dong, Socho-gu, Seoul, South Korea. Tel: +82 2 3480 7716, fax: +82 2 7480 7600, URL: http://www.mpb.go.kr/index_eng.html
Ministry of Legislation, Government Complex Building, Sejongno 77, Jongno-gu, Seoul 110-760, Republic of Korea. Tel: +82 2 3703 2114, e-mail: lawinfo@moleg.go.kr, URL: http://www.moleg.go.kr/english

Political Parties
Unified Progressive party (merger of Democratic Labor Party (DLP), URL: http://www.kdlp.org/; People's Participation Party and part of the New Progressive Party), URL: http://www.goupp.org/election/main/main.php; Democratic Party (DP), formerly the United Democratic Party; Alliance; Creative Korea Party (CKP); Grand National Party (GNP); Liberty Forward (LF).

Elections
The most recent legislative elections were held in 11 April 2012. The New Frontier Party (formerly the Grand National Party) retained a majority winning 152 seats. The UDP won 127, the United Progressive Party 13 seats, the LF five seats and independents three seats.

Presidential elections held in December 2002 were won by the Millennium Democratic Party's Roh Moo-hyun, who won 49 per cent of the vote, beating the Grand National Party's Lee Hoi Chang, who received 46.5 per cent. In March 2004 President Roo Moo-hyun was suspended following a parliament vote to impeach him over allegations of incompetence and breaking election rules. The impeachment was overruled by the Constitutional Court and the president was reinstated in May. The most recent presidential elections took place in December 2007. Myung-bak Lee of the Grand National Party won with over 48 per cent of the vote. The most recent presidential election was held in December 2012. Park Geun-hye was elected the Republic of Korea's female president after defeating her main rival, Moon Jae-in.

Diplomatic Representation
British Embassy, Taepyeongno 40, 4 Jeong-dong, Jung-gu, Seoul 100-120, South Korea. Tel: +82 2 3210 5500, fax: +82 2 725 1738, e-mail: bembassy@britain.or.kr, URL: https://www.gov.uk/government/world/organisations/british-embassy-seoul
Ambassador: Andrew Wightman (page 1536)
Embassy of the United States of America, 82, Sejong-no, Chongno-ku, Seoul, South Korea. Tel: +82 2 397 4114, fax: +82 2 725 6843, URL: http://seoul.usembassy.gov
Ambassador: Sung Kim (page 1456)
Embassy of the Republic of Korea, 60 Buckingham Gate, London, SW1E 6AJ, United Kingdom. Tel: +44 (0)20 7227 5500, fax: +44 (0)20 7227 5503, URL: http://gbr.mofat.go.kr/eng/eu/gbr/main/index.jsp
Ambassador: Park Suk-hwan (page 1492)
Embassy of the Republic of Korea, 2450 Massachusetts Ave, NW, Washington, DC 20008, USA. Tel: +1 202 939 5600, fax: +1 202 797 0595, e-mail: consular_usa@mofat.go.kr, economic_usa@mofat.go.kr, URL: http://www.koreaembassyusa.org/
Ambassador: Y.J. Choi

Permanent Mission to the UN, 335 E. 45th Street, New York, New York 10017, USA. Tel: +1 212 439 4000, fax: +1 212 986 1083, e-mail: korea@un.int, URL: http://www.un.int/korea/index.asp
Ambassador: Kim Sook

LEGAL SYSTEM

South Korea has a civil law system based on the Constitution. The civil code is based upon the Japanese civil code. Criminal law is outlined in the Korean Penal Code. Judicial Power is vested in courts composed of Judges, and all questions of law and fact are decided by judges. However, a limited system of juries was adopted for criminal cases and environmental cases in 2008.

There are three types of courts: the Supreme Court, six Courts of Appeal (located in Seoul, Busan, Daegu, Daejon, and Gwangju), 13 District Courts and Magistrats courts. The district courts located outside Seoul act as Administrative Courts within their districts. There is also a Constitutional Court which upholds the constitution and constitutionality of laws.

The chief justice of the Supreme Court is appointed by the president with the consent of the National Assembly. The 13 other Supreme Court Justices are appointed by the president on the recommendation of the chief justice and with the consent of the National Assembly. Judges other than the chief justice and the Supreme Court justices are appointed by the chief justice with the consent of the Supreme Court Justices Council.

The government respects the human rights of its citizens. However, the National Security Act limits "anti-government activities." In particular, the Act criminalizes activities such as promoting anti-government ideologies (especially communism) or joining anti-government organizations. Whilst South Korea retains the death penalty, there has been an unofficial moratorium on executions since 1998 when President Kim Dae-jung, who had been sentenced to death himself in 1980, took office.

Supreme Court of Korea, URL: http://eng.scourt.go.kr/eng/main/Main.work
Chief Justice of the Supreme Court: Yang Sung Tae

National Human Rights Commission, URL: http://www.humanrights.go.kr/

LOCAL GOVERNMENT

The nation's administrative map comprises seven metropolitan cities and nine provinces. The administrative responsibilities of the metropolitan cities, provinces, cities and '*gun*' (counties) rest with local governments formed in the 1995 local elections.

The seven metropolitan cities - Seoul, Busan, Daegu, Incheon, Gwangju, Daejeon and Ulsan - are accorded the same status in the administrative ladder as that of provinces, which are geographically larger because of their sizable populations. A metropolitan city is divided into several '*gu*' (ward), which are further subdivided into several '*dong*', the lowest administrative unit. Sejong, the site of the mini capital which will be home to some of South Korea's government ministries has become a special self-governing city.

The nine provinces are Gyeonggi, Gangwon, North Chungcheong, South Chungcheong, North Jeolla, South Jeolla, North Gyeongsang, South Gyeongsang and Jeju. A province is divided into cities and '*gun*'. There are currently 72 cities, 91 gun and 69 gu.

AREA AND POPULATION

Area
The Korean Peninsula, located in Northeast Asia, is bordered on the north by China and the Russian Federation and juts towards Japan to the southeast. Since 1948, the 222,154 sq km which make up the entire Peninsula have been divided, roughly along the 38th parallel, into the Republic of Korea in the south and the Democratic People's Republic of Korea in the north. The Republic of Korea covers 99,392 sq km. The Republic of Korea (South Korea) and the Democratic People's Republic of Korea, (North Korea) are separated by a 250 mile long strip of land, know as the demilitarised zone. The terrain of South Korea is mainly hilly or mountainous with wide coastal plains in the south and west. The climate is temperate with more rain than North Korea.

To view a map of South Korea, please consult:
http://www.lib.utexas.edu/maps/cia08/korea_south_sm_2008.gif

Population
Estimates for 2010 put the population at 48.184 million. The average annual population growth rate was 0.5 per cent in the period 2000-10. South Korea has the third highest population density in the world, only Bangladesh and Taiwan are higher. Population density in mid-2009 was 488 persons per sq. km, whilst the capital, Seoul, had a 2002 population density of 16,978 persons per sq. km. The population of the capital Seoul in 2012 was 10.575 million or one in four of the population.

The Korean language is spoken by some 60 million people living on the Peninsula and its outlying islands as well as some 1.5 million Koreans living in other parts of the world. Korean belongs to the Ural-Altaic language group. It is quite similar to Japanese in grammar and sentence structure, with part of its vocabulary borrowed from Chinese.

Births, Marriages, Deaths
Changes in attitudes towards the family have led to a declining birth rate, whilst medical advances have increased life expectancy and consequently the proportion of elderly people. Marriages in the same year numbered 306,573 (6.4 per 1,000 persons), whilst divorces numbered 145,324 (3.0 per 1,000 persons). According to the WHO, the crude birth rate was 9.9 per 1,000 population and the crude death rate was 5.3 per 1,000 population.

According to the WHO, by 2009, the average life expectancy was 77 years for males and 83 years for females. Healthy life expectancy was 68 years and 74 years respectively. Approximately 16 per cent of the population is aged under 15 years and 16 per cent over 60 years. The median age was 38. The total fertility rate per woman was 1.3 children. (Source: http://www.who.int, World Health Statistics 2012)

Public Holidays 2014
1 January: New Year's Day
4 February: Lunar New Year Holiday
1 March: Independence Movement Day
1 May: Labour Day
6 May: Bhuddah's Birthday
6 June: Memorial Day
17 July: Constitution Day (Memorial Day)
15 August: Liberation Day
September: Ch'usok, Harvest Moon Festival (14-16 days after 8th lunar moon)
3 October: National Foundation Day
25 December: Christmas Day

Note: Holidays falling on a Sunday are not observed on the following Monday. Some national holiday are dependent on the lunar calendar and therefore vary each year, among these are Buddha's Birthday which normally occurs in May and the Harvest Moon Festival (Ch'usok) which lasts for three days and usually occurs in September.

EMPLOYMENT

The Asian financial crisis badly affected employment. In February 1999 unemployment reached nearly 2 million people, nearly 9 per cent of the working population, before falling by the end of the year.

The following table sets out the employment figures for recent years:

Labour Force '000s	2005	2006	2007	2008	2009
Labour force	23,743	23,978	24,216	24,347	24,394
Employed	22,856	23,151	23,433	23,577	23,506
Unemployed	887	827	783	769	889
Unemployment rate %	3.7	3.5	3.2	3.2	3.6

Total Employment by Economic Activity

Occupation	2008
Agriculture, hunting & forestry	1,686,000
Fishing	na
Mining & quarrying	23,000
Manufacturing	3,963,000
Electricity, gas & water supply	90,000
Construction	1,812,000
Wholesale & retail trade, repairs	3,631,000
Hotels & restaurants	2,044,000
Transport, storage & communications	1,875,000
Financial intermediation	821,000
Real estate, renting & business activities	2,219,000
Public admin. & defence; compulsory social security	840,000
Education	1,784,000
Health & social work	842,000
Other community, social & personal service activities	1,782,000
Households with employed persons	150,000
Extra-territorial organisations & bodies	16,000

Source: Copyright © International Labour Organization (ILO Dept. of Statistics, http://laborsta.ilo.org)

BANKING AND FINANCE

Currency
1 won (W) = 10 hwan or 100 chun

GDP/GNP, Inflation, National Debt
South Korea has transformed itself over the last forty years from a poor country to an industrialised giant. It has the fourth largest economy in Asia and one of the largest in the world. The government implemented numerous economic reforms following the Asian financial crisis of 1997-98 which hit the country hard and exposed its economic weaknesses. Although also adversely affected by the global economic crisis, the South Korean economy has begun to recover due to export growth, low interest rates and the government 's development policies. Weakness in its economic model remain, including an over reliance on exports and an aging population. In order to maintain economic growth the Republic of Korea has been actively pursuing Free Trade Agreements and has entered into such agreements with Chile, Singapore and the European Free Trade Association. Negotiations are ongoing for others and a US-South Korea agreement came into effect in 2012.

REPUBLIC OF KOREA

Following the global financial downturn growth figures had to be revised; growth in 2008 was estimated to be 3.0 per cent. The banking sector became particularly vulnerable to the global credit crisis; banks had taken on high levels of foreign debt and in October 2008 the government announced a rescue package worth US$130 billion to help shore up the banking system. The economy returned to growth in 2009 recording growth of 0.2 per cent for the year, this was mainly due to a still buoyant housing market. Growth rebounded to over 6 per cent in 2010. Per capita GDP was 23.9 million Won in 2010. In 2011, GDP was estimated to be US$1.5 trillion with a growth rate of 3.5 per cent. Growth in Q1 and Q2 of 2013 was estimated to be 0.8 per cent.

GDP by industrial origin at current market prices (billion Won)

Industry	2008	2009	2010
GDP	1,026,452	1,065,037	1,172,803
Agriculture	24,686	26,615	27,019
Mining	2,336	2,221	2,237
Manufacturing	256,209	266,578	323,050
Electricity, gas & water	12,299	17,258	21,045
Construction	64,612	66,577	68,801
Trade	100,419	103,995	114,245
Transport & communications	81,280	81,388	86,069
Finance	186,924	190,399	201,206
Public administration	59,397	63,707	66,031
Others	131,526	140,100	147,308

Source: Asian Development Bank

The Government provided a bail-out package of over US$2 billion to help its indebted banks, with a specially created company, Korean Asset Management, to oversee it. 500 billion won is to be provided by banks and three trillion won raised by bond issues. Korea's agreement with the IMF means that in return for US$58 billion (to be paid in stages) the country must liberalise several sectors in order to increase efficiency and promote foreign investment.

Official KNSO figures show that the Consumer Price Index (CPI) (all items) has risen steadily from 104.1 in 2001 to 117.8 in 2005 (2000 = 100.0). Inflation was estimated to be 3 per cent in 2010 and 4.5 per cent in 2011.

Figures from 2009 put total external debt at US$401 billion in 2009, rising to US$445 billion by 2011.

Foreign Investment
The Korean Government is pursuing the liberalisation of foreign exchange transactions and capital markets. Foreign exchange controls have also been liberalised to a great extent. Korea is increasing the opportunities for foreign investment, with the manufacturing sector open to foreign investors and the service sector following suit.

Total direct foreign investment was estimated to be US$130 billion in 2011.

Balance of Payments / Imports and Exports
South Korea's major exports are electronics, ships, vehicles, computers, steel, footwear and textiles.

Having no oil or gas reserves of its own, the country has to import all of its requirements. Other major imports include food, metals, chemicals and machinery.

External Trade in Million US$

Year	Exports, fob	Imports, cif	Trade balance
1995	125,058	135,119	-10,061
2000	172,268	160,481	11,786
2005	284,419	261,238	23,180
2006	325,465	309,383	16,082
2007	371,489	356,846	14,643
2008	422,007	435,275	-13,267
2009	363,534	323,085	40,449
2010	466,384	425,212	41,172

Source: Asian Development Bank

The following tables show details of import and exports in recent years.

Exports by Principal Commodity (figures in mil. US$)

Product	2006	2007
Telecoms. & sound recording & reproducing equipment	46,018	50,656
Machinery & precision equipment	28,985	36,164
Chemicals & chemical products	31,325	36,823
Iron & steel products	27,172	31,594
Ships & boats not inc. warships	21,662	26,855

Exports by SITC section in mil. US$

Product	2005	2006
Food & live animals	2,468	2,354
Beverage & tobacco	521	606
Crude materials excl. fuels	2,839	3,314
Mineral fuels etc.	15,709	20,920
Animal, vegetable oil & fats	19	24
Chemicals	27,745	31,806
Basic manufactures	41,023	46,559
Machines, transport equipment	173,492	192,360

- continued		
Miscellaneous manufactured goods	20,292	26,630
Unclassified goods	310	891

Imports by SITC section in mil. US$

Product	2006	2007
Food & live animals	11,358	13,630
Beverage & tobacco	589	756
Crude materials excl. fuels	19,665	24,072
Mineral fuels etc.	86,707	96,504
Animal, vegetable oil & fats	629	750
Chemicals	27,573	32,433
Basic manufactures	42,314	51,933
Machines, transport equipment	92,718	107,499
Miscellaneous manufactured goods	26,684	27,572
Unclassified goods	1,146	1,697

Source: Asian Development Bank

The countries which take the majority of South Korean exports are China, USA, Japan, Hong Kong and Taiwan. The main countries that South Korea imports from are Japan, China, USA, Saudi Arabia and Australia.

Exports to Main Trading Partners, figures in US$ million

Country	2008	2009	2010
Total	426,763	373,207	442,236
China, People's Republic of	91,389	86,703	125,476
United States	45,501	37,803	45,993
Japan	28,253	21,771	26,044
Hong Kong, China	19,772	19,661	15,650
Singapore	16,293	13,617	16,391
Germany	10,523	8,821	11,678
India	9,090	8,013	8,685
Mexico	8,977	7,133	7,329
Vietnam	9,748	7,149	7,347
Indonesia	7,934	6,000	7,003

Source: Asian Development Bank

Imports to Main Trading Partners, figures in US$ million

Country	2008	2009	2010
Total	435,272	323,124	415,138
China	76,930	54,246	75,692
Japan	60,956	49,428	68,497
United States	38,556	29,161	42,728
Saudi Arabia	33,782	19,737	21,154
Australia	18,000	14,756	20,717
Germany	14,769	12,299	12,205
UAE	19,249	9,310	9,979
Indonesia	11,320	9,264	13,832
Qatar	14,375	8,386	8,989
Kuwait	12,129	7,992	8,565

Source: Asian Development Bank

Central Bank
Bank of Korea, 110, 3-KA, Namdaemun-Ro, Chung-ku, Seoul 100-794, Republic of Korea. Tel: +82 2 759 4114, fax: +82 2 759 4060, e-mail: bokdplp@bok.or.kr, URL: http://www.bok.or.kr
Governor: Choongsoo Kim

Chambers of Commerce and Trade Organisations
Korea's Importers Association, URL: http://www.aftak.or.kr
Korea Exchange, URL: http://www.krx.co.kr/index.html
Korea Chamber of Commerce and Industry, URL: http://english.korcham.net

MANUFACTURING, MINING AND SERVICES

Primary and Extractive Industries
Despite it being the tenth-largest oil consumer in the world in 2011, South Korea has no domestic oil reserves of its own and imports 100 per cent of its requirements. It is now the fifth-largest net importer of oil in the world. Approximately 2.1 billion barrels per day were consumed in 2010 all of which were imported, making South Korea the world's fifth-largest importer of crude oil. Saudi Arabia is the main supplier. South Korea had a January 2011 crude oil refining capacity of 2.7 million barrels per day from six facilities. To offset the country's total reliance on imported oil, the state-run Korea National Oil Corporation (KNOC) is involved in many exploration and production projects abroad - including a new find at Vung Tau, offshore of Vietnam. Total oil production in 2011 was 59,700 bbl/d.

South Korea also needs to import nearly all its liquified natural gas (LNG). Approximately 1,654 billion cubic feet of LNG were imported in 2011, making South Korea the world's second largest LNG importer. In 2009 most LNG imports come from Qatar (27 per cent) and Malaysia (23 per cent). The Korea Gas Corporation (Kogas) dominates the sector. The state retains a 27 per cent share in the company. South Korea produces a small amount of natural gas from its one offshore field. Natural gas consumption was 1,621 billion cubic feet in 2011.

South Korea has estimated coal reserves of 139 million short tons, but produced just 2.29 million short tons in 2010. Consumption of coal was 125 million short tons in 2010, requiring imports mainly from Australia, China, and the US as the native coal is of a low quality. South Korea is the world's third largest coal importer. (Source: EIA)

South Korea has deposits of iron ore which are mined. Figures for 2006 show that 408,000 metric tons were produced.

Energy
Total energy consumption was 9.853quadrillion Btu in 2009. Fuel share of energy consumption in 2008 has been estimated as follows: oil, 45 per cent; coal, 26 per cent; natural gas, 14 per cent, nuclear, 14 per cent and hydroelectricity, one per cent.

Recent figures show that South Korea had an electric generation capacity of 84.66 gigawatts in January 2010. Figures for 2010 show that the Republic produced 467.55 billion kWh of electricity and consumed 449.51 billion kWh. Electricity is generated by thermal, nuclear and hydroelectric means. More than 33 per cent of South Korea's electricity is produced by its four nuclear power stations with 20 individual reactors. Fourteen additional reactors are scheduled to be completed by 2024 with the aim of generating 50 per cent of the power supply.

As of 2012, two per cent of energy should be produced by renewable sources, with limited hydro sources. The Korean government has plans to invest $8.2 billion into offshore wind farms . Current wind capacity is 0.3 BKW; this should raise it to 2.5 BKW. (Source: EIA)

Manufacturing
Manufacturing centres around electronics, telecommunications, automobile production, chemicals and steel. Manufacturing exports drive the economy. Estimated figures for 2006 show that trade exports earned US$360.0 billion f.o.b. main products being cellular phones and equipment, vehicles, machinery, steel, ships, petrochemicals semi-conductors and computers. Manufacturing was reported to be at three-year low in 2012 with the global economic crisis and weak domestic demand as the main factors. Early indications for 2013 were that the manufacturing sector had begun to expand slightly.

Service Industries
In 2005 there were 6.0 million visitors to the Republic of Korea, bringing in a total of US$8.1 million. Recent figures show that there are a total number of 441 tourist hotels in the country, with a combined total of 45,140 rooms. In 2010, medical tourism was a growing trend.

South Korea and Japan were joint hosts of the 2002 FIFA World Cup. This generated a two trillion won investment in building new stadiums and it was expected that 100,000 hotel rooms per day would be required by visitors.
Korea Tourist Association, URL: http://english.visitkorea.or.kr/enu/index.kto

Agriculture
At the end of 1999, the farming population stood at 4.2 million, a drop for the sixth year in a row. The number of farming households also declined by over 37,000 in 1999. The number of people farming has been dropping steadily over the years; in 1985, 20.9 per cent of the population were employed in agriculture.

Main Crop Production in 2010

Crop	Int $1000*	Tonnes
Indigenous pigmeat	1,706,614	1,110,180
Rice, paddy	1,697,625	6,136,300
Indigenous Chicken meat	836,945	587,474
Indigenous cattle meat	667,113	246,953
Cow milk, whole, fresh	646,903	2,073,000
Vegetables fresh nes	568,150	305,000
Hen eggs, in shell	473,084	570,400
Strawberries	314,621	231,803
Cabbages and other brassicas	304,626	2,035,700
Onions, dry	296,493	1,411,650
Apples	194,661	460,285
Grapes	174,643	305,524

*unofficial figures
Source: http://faostat.fao.org/site/339/default.aspx Food and Agriculture Organization of the United Nations, Food and Agricultural commodities production

Recent figures show that approximately 1.7 million tonnes of seafood (including seaweed) are produced per year. However, the number of fishermen is declining.

Recent figures show that woodlands and mountain areas amounted to 6,422,000 hectares or 66 per cent of the total national land. Tree-growing land accounted for 97 per cent of the total. A nationwide reforestation programme has also been in force since the 1970s and tree cutting is now strictly controlled.

COMMUNICATIONS AND TRANSPORT

Travel Requirements
Citizens of the USA, Canada, Australia and the EU require a passport valid for three months, but do not require a visa for periods of up to 30 days. Australian and EU citizens can stay for up to 90 days without a visa (except Italians and Portuguese who may stay for up to 60 days, and citizens of Cyprus who may stay for up to 30 days). Canadians can stay for up to six months without a visa. Other nationals should contact the embassy to check visa requirements.

National Airlines
Korean Air (KAL) was government-owned until 1969, when it was taken over by the Han Jin Group. Asiana Airlines (AAR), the country's second private airline (owned by the Kumho Group), was established in 1988.
Korean Air (KAL), URL: http://www.koreanair.com
Asiana Airlines(AAR), URL: http://flyasiana.com/english/
Seoul's importance in international air traffic has grown as result of the holding of the 1988 Olympics and the World Cup tournament in 2002, Korea's geographic location and expanding relationships in the fields of diplomacy, trade and culture. Many foreign airlines have been attracted by the proximity to important markets and have opened regular services to and from Korea.

International Airports
There are four international airports in Korea: Gimpo in Seoul (URL: http://gimpo.airport.co.kr/), Kimhae which serves the big southern port of Busan, and Cheju Airport on the island off the southern tip of the peninsula. Incheon International Airport (URL: http://www.airport.kr/eng) opened in March 2001 and is situated on an island 32 miles west of Seoul. It is now the primary airport for Seoul. Domestic airports include those at Kwangju, Taegu, Ulsan, Pohang, Sachon, Yechon, Mokpo, Yosu, Kangnung and Sokcho. The construction of the New Seoul Metropolitan Airport started on November 1992 and is due to be completed by 2020 at a cost of approximately 10 trillion won. It will have four parallel runways and will be capable of handling 100 million passengers annually.

Railways
Railways are the major method of long-distance transportation. The railway network comprises 3,800km. Recent figures show that the country's railways carry a total of 820 million passengers and 53.5 million tons of freight per year.
Korean National Railroad, URL: http://app.korail.go.kr/ROOT/main-top.top?lang=eng

South Korea also has subway systems at six cities including Seoul with 197 stations, Daegu, Gwangju, Taegu, Busan and Incheon.

Roads
Recent figures show there are approximately 103,000 km of roads in the Republic of Korea, of which 3,600 km are express highways. An estimated 80km of roads are paved. Vehicles are driven on the right.

Shipping
Recent figures show that 701.1 million tons of freight were handled through the ports. Major ports include Pusan, Inchon, Donghae, Masan, Yeosu, Gunsan, Mokpo, Pohang, Ulsan, Cheju, and Kwangyang.

HEALTH

Demand for medical treatment has steadily increased since medical insurance was expanded to cover the entire population in 1989 (as of 2000 medical insurance premiums are based on income). The government created or expanded 91 public health centres in rural areas and has supported around 30 financially hard-pressed private hospitals. The government offered 100 billion won in loans to help finance the creation of 15,000 hospital beds. Since 1992 over US$60 million of medical equipment has been bought with public credits from the World Bank for 49 private hospitals. To treat cancer, the most frequent cause of death in Korea, the government opened a National Cancer Centre with 500 beds.

In 2009, the government spent approximately 12.2 per cent of its total budget on healthcare (up from 9.7 per cent in 2000), accounting for 58.2 per cent of all healthcare spending. Social security funding accounted for 76.9 per cent of health expenditure. Total expenditure on healthcare equated to 6.9 per cent of the country's GDP. Per capita expenditure on health was approximately US$1,184, compared with US$508 in 2000.

Recent figures show that there were 40,247 medical facilities, including 19,303 hospitals and clinics, 18,507 clinics, and 130 midwifery centres. According to the latest WHO figures, in the period 2000-10 there are 98,293 physicians (20.2 per 10,000 population), 255,402 nurses and midwives (52.9 per 10,000 population), 58,363 pharmaceutical personnel and 23,912 dentistry personnel (5 per 10,000 population). There are 103 hospital beds and 19.1 psychiatric beds per 10,000 population.

In 2010, the infant mortality rate (probability of dying by age one) was 4 per 1,000 live births and the child (under-five) mortality rate was also 5 per 1,000 live births. The main causes of death in children under-five years old were prematurity (24 per cent) and congenital anomalies (19 per cent).

In 2010, 98 per cent of the population had access to improved drinking water. One hundred percent of the population had access to improved sanitation. (Source: http://www.who.int, World Health Statistics 2012)

EDUCATION

Primary/Secondary Education
Primary school attendance is compulsory, with the enrolment of 99 per cent of the relevant school-age population. Korea has a 6-3-3-4 ladder system of education: six years for primary school, three years for middle school, three years for high school and four or six years for college or university. Roughly 90 per cent of pupils graduate from high school. According to UNESCO figures, 99.5 per cent of primary school age children and 95.5 per cent of secondary school age children attend school. The primary school pupil: teacher ratio was 22:1 in 2009.

Higher Education

There has been significant expansion of higher education since the late 1970s when an estimated 5 per cent of the tertiary age population went to university. As of 2012, that percentage was over 80 per cent. There were approximately 40 universities and 400 other higher education institutions. Over the coming years the sector is expected to contract with falling enrolment rates and the merging or closing of many institutions.

Figures from UNESCO show that in 2008, 15.8 per cent of total government expenditure went on education, 31 per cent of which went on primary education, 40 per cent on secondary education and 14 per cent on tertiary education. The literacy rate is over 94.5 per cent (98.8 per cent for young people).

RELIGION

Shamanism had been the sole and indigenous religion of Korean ancestors until Buddhism was introduced from China in 372 A.D. Buddhism dominated religious life until the end of the Koryo Dynasty, and in the early days of the Yi Dynasty many Korean people adopted the tenets of Confucianism. In 1784 and in 1884, Catholicism and Protestantism were introduced and began to spread during the latter half of the 19th century. Buddhism is now followed by around 15 per cent of the population, although Christianity is the most dynamic religion and is followed by almost 42 per cent of the Korean population. Some 15 per cent of the population are Ethnoreligionists, that is they follow traditional or animist religions and 10 per cent of the population are Confucianists.

The Republic of Korea has a religious liberty rating of 10 on a scale of 1 to 10 (10 is most freedom). (Source: World Religion Database)

COMMUNICATIONS AND MEDIA

Newspapers

There are more than 100 national and local daily newspapers. Newspaper readership is high. There is criticism of government in the papers.

Chosun Ilbo, URL: http://english.chosun.com
Dong-a Ilbo, URL: http://english.donga.com
Hankook Ilbo, URL: http://www.hankooki.com
Hangyore Sinmun, URL: http://english.hani.co.kr
JoongAng Ilbo, URL: http://joongangdaily.joins.com
Korea Economic Daily, URL: http://www.kdaily.com
Korea Herald, URL: http://www.koreaherald.co.kr
Korea Daily News, URL: http://www.kdaily.com
Munhwa Ilbo, URL: http://www.munhwa.com
Segye Times, URL: http://www.segye.com/Articles/Main.asp
Korea Times, URL: http://www.koreatimes.co.kr/www/index.asp

Broadcasting

There are over 100 radio stations in the Republic of Korea. The largest station, the Korean Broadcasting Company (KBS) with 20 local stations has recently taken over two of Seoul's four major private broadcasting companies. KBS also runs an overseas broadcasting network. Television broadcasting began in 1956 and there are multiple stations in Korea. Cable and satellite TV is very popular. Main TV broadcasters include:

Korea Broadcasting System (KBS) - public, operates two networks, URL: http://www.kbs.co.kr
Munhwa Broadcasting Corporation, URL: http://www.imbc.com/
Jeonju Television Corporation (JTV), commercial station bsed in Jeonju, URL: http://www.jtv.co.kr
SkyLife, digital satellite operator, URL: http://www.skylife.co.kr/eng/index.jsp

Telecommunications

In Korea, the telephone service began in 1897 with a tie up between the royal palaces in Seoul. Since then the telephone service has continually expanded. Figures for 2011 show that there were an estimated 52 million mobile phones in use and 29.5 million landlines.

By 2010, over 39 million South Korean were regular internet users and in 2009 it was estimated that almost every household had a high speed internet connection.

ENVIRONMENT

Six Northeast Asian countries agreed to form a consultative body on the environment at a symposium in Seoul in September 1992 for coping with air and sea pollution. The World Health Organization announced that Seoul was 19th among the 20 most polluted cities in the world, provoking calls for the government to clean up the air. As a developing nation, South Korea was exempt from the same requirements that developed nations must meet to reduce carbon emissions. Nevertheless, the country signed the Kyoto Environmental Protocol in September 1998 and undertook to regulate its greenhouse gas emissions from 2000 onwards.

Energy related carbon emissions in 2001 were 120.8 million metric tons, equivalent to 1.8 per cent of world carbon emissions. Per capita carbon emissions in the same year were 2.6 metric tons, compared with 5.5 metric tons in the US. Fuel share of carbon emissions in 2001 were as follows: oil, 55.3 per cent; coal, 34.9 per cent; natural gas, 9.9 per cent. By 2009 South Korea had become one of the world's largest carbon emitters. It set a target of reducing its emissions by 30 per cent. Emissions increased to approximately 640 million metric tons in 2011. (Source: EIA)

South Korea is also a party to the following environmental agreements: Antarctic-Environmental Protocol, Antarctic-Marine Living Resources, Antarctic Treaty, Biodiversity, Climate Change, Climate Change-Kyoto Protocol, Desertification, Endangered Species, Environmental Modification, Hazardous Wastes, Law of the Sea, Marine Dumping, Ozone Layer Protection, Ship Pollution, Tropical Timber 83, Tropical Timber 94, Wetlands, and Whaling.

SPACE PROGRAMME

South Korea signed a space technology accord with Russia in 2004. It launched its first space rocket in 2009. The rocket was built with the assistance of Russia. It has also produced several satellites and aims to build a rocket on its own by 2018 and a probe that can orbit the moon by 2025. The Korea Aerospace Research Institute (URL: http://www.kari.re.kr) organises the space program. The Naro Space Center was completed in 2008.

KUWAIT

State of Kuwait

Dawlat al Kuwayt

Capital: Kuwait City (Population estimate, 2010: 2.2 million)

Head of State: Sheikh Sabah al-Ahmed al-Jaber al-Sabah (Emir) (page 1376)

Heir Apparent (Crown Prince): Sheikh Nawaf al-Ahmed al-Jaber al-Sabah (page 1376)

National Flag: A fesswise tricolour of green, white and red, with a black trapezoid at the hoist

CONSTITUTION AND GOVERNMENT

Constitution

Kuwait has been ruled by the Al Sabah family since the middle of the eighteenth century and has maintained her independence apart from a period from 1899 when she entered into a Special Treaty of Friendship with Britain. This treaty ended in 1961 when Kuwait again took full control of her affairs.

The constitution was introduced in 1963 under which terms a 50 member National Assembly is elected every four years. The Assembly passes all laws and approves the heir apparent who is nominated by the Emir. The Emir appoints the Prime Minister, who appoints his Ministers. Kuwait is the only Arab country in the Gulf region with a directly elected parliament. Suffrage is extended only to literate males over the age of 21 who have held Kuwaiti citizenship for more than 20 years.

The National Assembly was dissolved by the Emir in 1986 following a disagreement about its right to scrutinise ministers. During his exile, following the Iraqi occupation of Kuwait, the Emir reinstated the Assembly in return for the support of opposition leaders.

To consult the constitution, please visit: http://www.pm.gov.kw/ConstitutionEnglish.pdf.

International Relations

In August 1990 Iraqi forces invaded Kuwait, occupying it for seven months, following a unilateral Iraqi decision to annex the country. The action was condemned by the United Nations and the Islamic Conference Organization, and in January 1991 allied forces began Operation Desert Storm aimed at the withdrawal of Iraqi forces. In February 1991 Iraqi forces left Kuwait and in November 1994 Iraq officially recognised Kuwait's borders, sovereignty, and political independence. In 2003 Kuwait allowed US led coalition forces to be based there ready for the campaign to oust Saddam Hussein from Iraq. Since Saddam Hussein was deposed, Kuwait has contributed both humanitarian aid and to the reconstruction effort.

Recent History

In December 1999, the all-male parliament narrowly rejected a Bill to give women the vote, with a result of 32-30. It was widely believed that women would win their right to vote from 2003, but two MPs who had backed their campaign abstained and one voted against.

In March 2005 the parliament agreed to speed up plans to pass a law to grant women the same political rights as men. In May of that year a law was passed giving women the right to vote, and in June Massouma al-Mubarak was appointed Minister for Planning and Administration, the first female minister in Kuwait.

The Emir of Kuwait Sheikh Jabie Al-Ahmed Al-Jabir Al-Sabah died on January 15 2006. He was succeeded by Crown Prince Sheikh Saad Al-Abdullah Al-Salim Al-Sabah, who ruled for just nine days before being replaced due to ill health. Sheikh Sabah al-Ahmed al-Jaber al-Sabah was voted to replace him in the post of Emir, having previously been in the post of Prime Minister.

In March 2007, the government resigned following a no-confidence motion against the health minister. A new cabinet was appointed, which included two women. In June 2007 the Minister for Oil Sheikh Ali resigned.

In March 2008 the parliament was dissolved, following disputes between the ministers and MPs. The cabinet resigned en masse, and elections were held in May. Following pressure from the National Assembly the entire cabinet offered their resignation on 25 November 2008 this was accepted and Shaikh Nasser was asked to form a new cabinet. This was appointed in January 2009, and was largely unchanged.

The prime minister offered the resignation of his government in March 2009 and an election was called for May.

In October 2009 the Constitutional court ruled that women can now obtain passports without the consent of their husband. A further ruling declared that women MPs do not have to wear Islamic head cover.

Anti government demonstrations were held in December 2010 with protestors opposing alleged government plans to amend the constitutional. The prime minister of Kuwait, Sheikh Nasser, survived a vote of no-confidence in parliament in January 2011; it was the second such vote in a year. As in many parts of the Arab world, political pro-reform demonstrations took place in 2011.

The prime minister, Sheikh Nasser al-Mohammad al-Sabah, resigned on 28 November along with his government over corruption allegations. Sheikh Nasser will remain in charge until a new government is appointed. The Emir of Kuwait dissolved parliament on 6 December. Elections must be held within 60 days. They took place in February; the Sunni Islamist opponents of the Emir became the largest group in the Majlis.

In May 2012 the Emir blocked a proposal by the government to make all legislation comply with Islamic law, and in June a Constitutional Court ruling in effect dissolved the Islamist dominated parliament. In September the Constitutional Court rejected a bill to make changes to constituencies ahead of the election, opposition to the bill said that the changes would give an advantage to official candidates.

Legislature

Kuwait has a unicameral legislature, the National Assembly or *Majlis al-Umma*, is made up of 50 elected members, two from each constituency elected for a four-year term. The Council of Ministers or Cabinet is appointed by the Emir and is led by the Prime Minister. Other members are appointed from the National Assembly and the Al Sabah family. A vote by the National Assembly has been held which (from 2011) will reduce the number of constituencies to five, each one being represented by 10 members.

Majlis al-Umma, P.O. Box 716, 13008, Safat, Kuwait. Tel: +965 245 5423, fax: +965 242 6190, e-mail: webadmin@alommah.gov.kw, URL: http://www.e.gov.kw/sites/KGOEnglish/Portal/Pages/KGD.aspx

Cabinet (as at June 2013)

Prime Minister: Sheikh Jaber Mubarak al-Hamad al-Sabah (page 1374)
First Deputy Prime Minister and Minister of the Interior: Sheikh Ahmad Hamoud al-Jaber al-Sabah
Deputy Prime Minister and Minister of Foreign Affairs, Minister of State for Cabinet Affairs: Sheikh Sabah Khaled al-Hamad al-Sabah
Deputy Prime Minister and Minister for Defence: Sheikh Ahmad Khalid al-Hamad al-Sabah
Deputy Prime Minister for Finance, Minister of Oil (acting): Mustafa Al-Shamali
Minister of Trade and Industry: Dr Anas Khalid Al-Saleh
Minister of Plannung and Development, Minister of State for National Assembly Affairs: Dr Rola Abdullah Dashti
Minister of Education and Higher Education: Dr Nayef Falal Al-Hajraf
Minister of Electricity and Water, Minister of State for Municipal Affairs: Abdulaziz Abdulatif Al-Ibrahim
Minister of Health: Dr Mohammad Barrak Al-Haifi
Minister of Awqaf and Islamic Affairs, Minister of Justice: Sharida Al-Meosharji
Minister of Social Affairs and Labour: Thekra Al-Rasheedi
State Minister for Cabinet Affairs and Municipalities: Sheikh Mohammad Abdullah Al-Mubarak Al-Sabah
Minister of Information, State Minister for Youth Affairs: Sheikh Salman Sabah Al-Sabah

Ministries

Office of the Amir, URL: http://www.da.gov.kw/
Office of the Prime Minister, PO Box 4, 13001 Safat, Kuwait City, Kuwait. Tel: +965 539 1111, fax: +965 539 0430, e-mail: info@dpm.gov.kw, URL: http://www.pm.gov.kw
The Council of Ministers, PO Box 1397, Safat 13014, Kuwait. Tel: +965 245 5333 / 487 7422, fax: +965 481 8028 /4 87 6656
Ministry of State for National Assembly, PO Box 1397, Safat 13014, Kuwait. Tel: +965 467 7422/245 5333, fax: +965 486 4319
Ministry of Foreign Affairs, PO Box 3, Safat 13001, Kuwait. Tel: +965 242 5141 / 9, fax: +965 241 2169, e-mail: info@mofa.org, URL: http://www.mofa.gov.kw
Ministry of Defence, PO Box 1170, Safat 13012, Kuwait. Tel: +965 484 8300 / 481 9623, fax: +965 483 7244 / 484 6059, e-mail: modkw@ncc.moc.kw, URL: http://www.mod.gov.kw
Ministry of Interior, PO Box 12500, Shamiya 71655, Kuwait. Tel: +965 243 3804 / 243 3806 / 243 3840 / 252 4199 / 252 33091, fax: +965 256 1268 / 252 3228 / 243 6570, URL: http://www.moi.gov.kw

Ministry of Communications, PO Box 318, Safat 11111, Kuwait. Tel: +965 481 9033 / 481 3777, fax: +965 481 8696 / 484 7058, URL: http://www.mockw.net
Ministry of Information, PO Box 193, Safat 13002, Kuwait. Tel: +965 241 5301 / 241 5302 / 242 7151 / 242 7141, fax: +965 241 9642 / 244 4715, e-mail: info@moinfo.gov.kwja, URL: http://www.moinfo.gov.kw/
Ministry of Justice, PO Box 6, Safat 13001, Kuwait. Tel: +965 248 0000 / 246 5600 / 246 7300, fax: +965 243 3750 / 246 6957, URL: http://www.moj.gov.kw
Ministry of Awqaf and Islamic Affairs, PO Box 13, Safat 13001, Kuwait. Tel: +965 246 6300, fax: +965 244 9943, e-mail: info@awkaf.net, URL: http://eng.islam.gov.kw/
Ministry of Commerce and Industry, PO Box 2944, Safat 13030, Kuwait. Tel: +965 246 3600, fax: +965 242 4411 / 241 1089
Ministry of Electricity and Water, PO Box 12, Safat 13001, Kuwait. Tel: +965 489 6000, fax: +965 489 7484, URL: http://www.energy.gov.kw/
Ministry of Social Affairs and Labour, PO Box 563, Safat 13006, Kuwait. Tel: +965 246 4500 / 248 0000, fax: +965 241 9877
Ministry of Oil, PO Box 5077, Safat 13051, Kuwait. Tel: +965 241 5201, fax: +965 241 7088
Ministry of Public Works, PO Box 8, Safat 13001, Kuwait. Tel: +965 244 9300/ 244 9301, fax: +965 242 4335 / 242 8362, e-mail: mciinfo@qualitynet.net, URL: http://www.mpw.gov.kw
Ministry of Public Health, PO Box 5, Safat 13001, Kuwait. Tel: +965 246 2900 / 484 2795, fax: +965 243 2288 / 484 0056, URL: http://www.moh.gov.kw
Ministry of Education & Higher Education, PO Box 7, Safat 13001, Kuwait. Tel: +965 483 6800 / 245 5454, fax: +965 483 7829 / 242 3676, e-mail: minister@moe.edu.kw, URL: http://www.moe.edu.kw
Ministry of Finance, PO Box 9, Safat 13001, Kuwait. Tel: +965 246 8200 / 246 7300, fax: +965 240 4025, e-mail: sbader@mof.gov.kw, URL: http://www.mof.gov.kw
Ministry of Planning, PO Box 15, Safat 13001, Kuwait. Tel: +965 242 8100 / 242 8200, fax: +965 241 4734 / 240 7326, URL: http://www.mop.gov.kw

Elections

In the 2006 elections, for the first time women were allowed to stand for election and vote in a national election, but no women were elected. Opposition candidates (reformists, liberals and Islamists) won almost two-thirds of the seats. Another election was held in May 2008. Again no women were elected, and radical Islamists won more than half the seats. Sheikh Nasser al-Mohammad al-Ahmad al-Sabah was re-appointed prime minister.

The emir called another election in 2009, just one year after the last election after the prime minister offered his government's resignation on 29 March. Sunni Islamists remained the largest group in parliament. Independents won 21 out of the 50 seats. Four women were elected.

The emir of Kuwait dissolved parliament again on 6 December, in accordance with protocol the entire cabinet then resigned their posts, but then Sheikh Jaber Mubarak al-Hamad al-Sabah was immediatly re-appointed to the post of prime minister. The elections had to be held with 60 days and the election was held in February 2012 the Sunni Islamist opponents of the Emir became the largest group in the Majlis. In October 2012 the Emir dissolved parliament and called snap elections for the beginning of December, the elections were boycotted by the opposition in protests over changes to the electoral law.

Diplomatic Representation

US Embassy, Area 14, Al-Masjed Al-Aqsa Street, PO Box 77 Safat, 13001 Safat, Kuwait City, Kuwait. Tel: +965 539 5307 / 5308, fax: +965 538 0282, e-mail: usisirc@qualitynet.net, URL: http://kuwait.usembassy.gov
Ambassador: Matthew H. Tueller
British Embassy, Arabian Gulf Street, PO Box 2, 13001 Safat, Kuwait City, Kuwait. Tel: +965 240 3334, fax: +965 240 7395, e-mail: general@britishembassy-kuwait.org, URL: http://ukinkuwait.fco.gov.uk
Ambassador: Frank Baker (page 1382)
Embassy of Kuwait, 2940 Tilden Street, NW, Washington, DC 20008, USA. Tel: +1 202 966 0702, fax: +1 202 966 0517, URL: http://www.kuwaitembassy.us
Ambassador: Sheikh Salem Abdullah Al Jaber Al Sabah (page 1376)
Embassy of Kuwait, 2 Albert Gate, Knightsbridge, London, SW1X 7JU, United Kingdom. Tel: +44 (0)20 7590 3400, fax: +44 (0)20 7823 1712, e-mail: kuwait@dircon.co.uk, URL: http://www.kuwaitinfo.org.uk
Ambassador: Khaled Al-Duwaisan (page 1374)
Permanent Mission of Kuwait to the United Nations, 321 East 44th Street, New York, NY 10017, USA. Tel: +1 212 973 4300, fax: +1 212 370 1733, e-mail: kuwaitmission@msn.com, URL: http://www.kuwaitmission.com/
Permanent Representative: Mansour al-Otaibi

LEGAL SYSTEM

In 1959, the Shari'ah system of Muslim law was augmented by the establishment of courts of law based on modern legal codes. The Emir has the constitutional authority to pardon and commute sentences.

There is a summary court in each district, presided over by a judge. The summary courts deal with civil and commercial cases. Tribunals of first instance hear issues involving personal status, civil and commercial cases, and criminal cases (except those of a religious nature). The High Court of Appeals is divided into two chambers, one with jurisdiction over appeals involving personal status and civil cases, the other over appeals involving commercial and criminal cases. The five-member Superior Constitutional Court is the highest level of the Kuwaiti judiciary; it interprets the constitution and deals with disputes related to the constitutionality of laws, statutes and by-laws. A military court handles offenses committed by members of the security forces.

KUWAIT

Religious courts, Sunni and Shi'a, hear family law matters, and there is a separate domestic court for non-Muslims. There is no Shi'a appellate court. Shi'a cases on appeal are adjudicated by Sunni courts of appeals.

The government respects the human rights of its citizens. However, there have been recent reports of abuse of prisoners by security forces. There is some degree of government corruption, and there are limitations on freedom of speech, press, religion, and movement. Kuwait retains the death penalty.

In June 2008, Kuwait's supreme court upheld the death sentence against Talal Nasser al Sabah, a member of the royal family, who had been found guilty of drug trafficking. The case is widely seen as a test case for the impartiality of the law. The sheikh is one of hundreds of members of the huge ruling family. He has appealed to the Emir to grant a pardon, but such a pardon could upset Kuwaiti politicians who have some oversight powers to hold the ruling family accountable. Carrying out the death sentence would cause consternation in the other family-ruled countries of the region.

Three people were executed in January 2013, the first executions since 2007.

LOCAL GOVERNMENT

An Emiri decree was issued in 1960 ordering that the country be divided into governates or 'Towns' for administrative purposes. The number of governates increased to six in December 1999. They are: Capital Town, Hawalli Town, Ahmadi Town, Jahra Town (1979), Farwaniya Town (1988), and Mubarak Al-Kabir Town (1999). The councils of these Towns meet once every two months and at national level there is a "Towns' Affairs Council" chaired by the Prime Minister. The most recent municipal council elections were held in June 2009.

AREA AND POPULATION

Area
Kuwait lies in the north-west of the Persian Gulf, bordering Iraq and Saudi Arabia. It has a total area of 17,818 sq. km. Most of the country consists of desert, which gradually slopes towards sea level in the east. The Kuwaiti mainland has no mountains or rivers.

The weather is characterised by long, hot and dry summers, short warm and sometimes rainy winters. Humidity increases in the summer and there are occasional dusty winds. The temperature ranges from an average of 45°C in summer to an average of 8°C in winter.

To view a map, visit: http://www.un.org/Depts/Cartographic/map/profile/kuwait.pdf

The official language is Arabic, although English is widely spoken and is now the official second language.

Population
The estimated population in 2010 was 2.737 million with an annual growth rate of 3.4 per cent for the period 2000-10. Ethnicity is divided as follows: Kuwaiti (38 per cent), other Arab (22 per cent), non Arab and predominantly South Asian (36 per cent). A number of stateless people (Bidoon), mainly of Iraqi and Iranian descent, live in Kuwait and in May 2000 the government extended citizenship to those who could prove they had a Kuwaiti mother or had been in residence since 1965.

Kuwait City has a population of around 2.2 million; more than 90 per cent of the population lives in the city or in a 500 sq km area around the city and harbour. Overall, 98 per cent of the population lives in urban areas.

Births, Marriages, Deaths
Estimated figures for 2010 put the birth rate at 18.2 births per 1,000 population, and the death rate at 2.2 per 1,000 population. The infant mortality rate as at 2009 was 11 per 1,000 live births. The total fertility rate was 2.2. per woman. Life expectancy from birth is 78 years for males and 79 years for females. In 2010 the median age was 28 years. An estimated 27 per cent of the population were aged less than 15 years and 4 per cent over 60 years. (Source: http://www.who.int, World Health Statistics 2012)

Public Holidays 2014
1 January: New Year's Holiday
14 January: Birth of the Prophet (Mawlid al-Nabi)*
25 February: Independence Day
26 February: Liberation Day
27 May: Al-Esra Wa al-Meraj (Prophet's Ascension into Heaven)*
29 June: Ramadan begins *
29 July: Eid al-Fitr (Ramadan ends)
5 October: Eid al-Adha (Festival of Sacrifice)*
25 October: Al Hijira (Islamic New Year)*
*Dates of Muslim holidays depend on the sighting of the moon and so vary

EMPLOYMENT

Estimated figures for 2010 put the labour force at 2.1 million. Figures from the end of 2006 show that the workforce numbered 1.9 million, 17 per cent of whom were Kuwaiti nationals. An estimated 1,197,887 were employed and 9,305 were unemployed. With around 65 per cent of the population under the age of 25 and over 90 per cent of employees in the private sector currently non-Kuwaiti nationals, the government is under pressure to create jobs for its young population. The government is also formulating plans to move some 95 per cent of Kuwaitis who are employed in the state sector to the private sector.

Employment by Economic Activity

Sector	2005
Agriculutre, hunting & fishing	29,290
Fishing	940
Mining & quarrying	21,372
Manufacturing	49,823
Electricity, gas & water supply	59
Construction	160,189
Wholesale & retail trade & repairs	157,916
Hotels & restaurants	32,482
Transport, storage & communications	43,337
Financial intermediation	13,665
Real estate, renting & business activities	62,982
Public administation & defence, compulsory social security	166,094
Education	58,834
Health & social work	26,977
Other community, social & personal service activities	47,080
Households with employed persons	246,137
Extra-territorial organisations & bodies	1,220
Other	7,466

Source: Copyright © International Labour Organization (ILO Dept. of Statistics, http://laborsta.ilo.org)

BANKING AND FINANCE

The financial centre is Kuwait City

Currency
1000 fils = 1 Kuwait Dinar (KD)

GDP/GNP, Inflation, National Debt
Kuwait is a rich country with some 10 per cent of the world's known oil reserves. Its economy suffered with the 1999 Iraqi invasion. The invasion, the allied operation Desert Storm and the ensuing recovery are all estimated to have cost Kuwait more than US$120 billion. After the Iraqi occupation of Kuwait, huge amounts of money had to be spent repairing the infrastructure of the country including 56 million dinar on repairing the desalination plants and 100 million dinar on repairing the ports. The United Nations Compensation Commission oversees compensation payments made from Iraq's oil revenue to Kuwait as a result of the occupation. The economy has recovered from the invasion and the costs of its contribution to the 2003 invasion of Iraq. The government is looking at some economic reform, including shifting employment more to the private sector. It is trying to promote itself as a base for foreign investors in Iraq. Kuwait is a an aid donor. A privatization law was passed in 2010. In 2011, the government announced it was to spend over US$130 billion in diversifiying the economy.

Estimated GDP for 2010 was US$150 billion with a growth rate of 3.6 per cent. Per capita GDP was estimated at US$34,700 in 2010. The service sector contributes around 51 per cent of GDP, industry around 48 per cent and agriculture less that one per cent. The government has committed itself to increased oil production and the economy was expected to grow by 5 per cent in 2012. Consumer price inflation was estimated at 4.5 per cent in 2011.

Kuwait earns most of its money from oil which accounts for around 91 per cent of its exports. Kuwait has set up a Future Generations Fund and around 10 per cent of oil earnings are paid into this fund to insure against the time when the oil runs out. Recent figures show the fund stands at US$50 billion.

External debt was estimated at US$30 billion in 2011.

Balance of Payments / Imports and Exports
In 2011, export earnings reached an estimated US$100 billion compared with US$65 billion in 2010. Imports cost an estimated US$21 billion in 2011 compared to US$19 billion. Kuwait's main export product is petroleum which accounts for 95 per cent of export earnings and prices of which have risen steadily in recent years, whilst its major imported products are industrial goods, consumer goods, machinery, transport equipment and food. Main trading partners are the United States, Japan, Singapore, South Korea, China and Europe. Due to the budget surplus generated from the sale of oil, Kuwait has weathered the global economic crisis which began in 2008.

Central Bank
Central Bank of Kuwait, URL: http://www.cbk.gov.kw
Governor: Dr Mohammad Y. Al-Hashel

Chambers of Commerce and Trade Organisations
Kuwait Chamber of Commerce and Industry, URL: http://www.kcci.org.kw

MANUFACTURING, MINING AND SERVICES

Primary and Extractive Industries
Over 9 per cent of the world's oil reserves are found in Kuwait; proven reserves stood at 104.0 billion barrels in 2008. Along with Saudi Arabia and the United Arab Emirates, Kuwait remains one of the few oil producing countries with significant excess oil production capacity. As one of the world's leading oil producing states, Kuwait's economy is heavily dependent on oil revenues.

In 2011 Kuwait was producing around 2.7 million barrels of oil a day, some of which came from the Divided Zone (a designated area between Kuwait and Saudi Arabia, formerly the Neutral Zone). Upstream and downstream expansion cost an estimated US$15,000 million between 1995 and 2005. Oil consumption in 2011 was an estimated 339,000 barrels per day.

Production in the onshore Divided Zone is a joint operation between the Getty Oil Co. and the Kuwait Oil Co. This area is 6,200 square miles and is shared equally between Kuwait and Saudi Arabia. It contains an estimated 5,000 million barrels of oil and 8,000 billion cubic feet of natural gas. Exploration and production of oil outside Kuwait is handled by the Kuwaiti Company for Overseas Petroleum Exploration. Exploration is ongoing; in 2001 Kuwait announced a discovery which could be as high as one billion barrels at the Kara al-Marou field and in 2003 another discovery was made at Sabriya.

Kuwait exports 60 per cent of its oil to Asian countries, particularly Japan, and it also exports to Europe and the US.

Under the current constitution, foreign ownership of Kuwait's oil is forbidden. However, there are controversial plans to allow limited foreign investment in upstream oil development.

In 1980 the Government founded the Kuwait Petroleum Corporation (KPC) which is responsible for developing, marketing, refining and integrating the country's oil operations. Kuwait's three major refineries are Shuaiba (with an estimated capacity of 190,000 barrels per day), Mina Al-Ahmadi (426,500 barrels per day) and Mina Abdullah (247,000 barrels per day).

The Ratqa oilfield, situated near the border with Iraq was originally thought to be independent but it was later discovered to be an extension of Iraq's large Rumaila oilfield. Prior to its invasion of Kuwait in 1990, Iraq had accused Kuwait of stealing from the Rumaila field. However, following the Gulf War and a United Nations survey, the border between Iraq and Kuwait was more clearly defined, placing 11 of the Ratqa wells within Kuwait's borders. Following the Gulf War, the Kuwait Petroleum Company submitted a claim to the UN compensation commission for lost oil production amounting to nearly US$16 billion. In September 2000 the UN Security Council approved the claim against Iraq. The retreating Iraqi occupation force fired 727 oil wells and it took eight months for all the fires to be capped.

Another souce of oil production could come from the clean-up of the large pools of crude that have remained since the retreat of the Iraqi army. Plans were annouced to put recovery of these pools out to tender for soil remediation, It is estimated that the projects could cost around US$3.5 billion, paid for by the UN reparations fund, and would take several years to complete.

Kuwait Petroleum Corporation (KPC), URL: http://www.kpc.com.kw

Kuwait appreciates that the bulk of its economy rests on its oil wealth and so a Future Generations Fund has been set up. 10 per cent of oil revenues are invested in this every year to insure against the time when the oil runs out. Present estimates put the fund at US$50 billion.

Kuwait has a relatively small natural gas industry. According to January 2011 figures natural gas reserves are 64.0 trillion cubic feet. Production in 2011 was estimated at 478 billion cubic feet. Kuwait has plans to use increased amounts of its natural gas particularly in production of electricity.

Energy
Nearly all the electricity in Kuwait is generated by hydropower and is closely linked to the desalination process. Electricity is also generated from the by-products of gas and oil. As of January 2010, Kuwait had an electrical generation capacity of 53.6 billion Kwh. The Ministry of Electricity and Water (MEW) projects that electricity demand is growing 7 per cent annually. In order to accommodate this increase, Kuwait has planned to extend its national power grid and has agreed in principle to link its power grid with those of other GCC countries.

Energy Production and Consumption Estimates 2006

Resource	Quantity
Proven Oil Reserves	104.000 billion barrels
OPEC Crude Oil Production Quota	2.207 million (bbl/d)
Oil Production	2.6 million bbl/d
Oil Consumption	334.68 bbl/d
Oil Refining Capacity	889 bbl/d
Natural Gas Reserves	55,500 Tcf
Natural Gas Production	434 billion cf
Natural Gas Consumption	434 billion cf
Electricity Production	41.11 kilowatthours
Total Energy Consumption	1.164 quadrillion Btu

Source: Energy Information Administration

Nuclear Power
In 2009 Kuwait began to set up a nuclear commission and in 2010 the National Nuclear Energy Committee announced a 20 year cooperative deal with the the French Atomic Energy Commission to develop nuclear power in Kuwait. Under the development plans Kuwait would have four nuclear power plants, to become operational in 2022.

Manufacturing
Kuwait is developing the non-oil-based sectors of its economy. There are several industrial areas, the largest of which is the Shuaiba Industrial Area. Manufacturing sectors there include car manufacture, paper processing, sea water treatment units, packing and plastic products and silicone products, cement plants and the manufacture of bricks. In order to encourage new industry the Government has set up a system of loans and infrastructure facilities.

Service Industries
Kuwait has started a program to privatise state-owned businesses outside the oil sector as a way of reducing subsidies. The Kuwaiti Government has begun privatising health care, electricity and telecommunications assets. Privatisation is complicated by the need to protect the jobs of Kuwaiti citizens, who have traditionally been employed mostly (93 per cent) by state-owned enterprises and the Government. Figures for 2006 show that Kuwait had 91,000 visitors.

Agriculture
As there are no rivers and only one underground water source in Kuwait, all its water comes from desalination plants, which have a total daily capacity of 254 million gallons. Despite this, Kuwait produces a good variety of crops which provide for much of the country's requirements and are also exported to neighbouring countries. Only 100 productive farms were left after the Gulf War, but their numbers are slowly increasing again. Plans to revitalise the agriculture sector included a pledge of 70,000 dinar to promote the growing of wheat and, in order to encourage farmers, the government announced that all home grown wheat would be bought at twice the market price. Figures for 2003 show that Kuwait produced 3,000 tonnes of cereals, 78,000 tonnes of meat, 196,000 tonnes of fruits and vegetables and 33,000 tonnes of roots and tubers (Figures from the FAO, UN).

Agricultural Production in 2010

Produce	Int. $'000*	Tonnes
Indigenous chicken meat	57,971	40,698
Indigenous sheep meat	30,297	11,127
Tomatoes	20,696	56,000
Hen eggs, in shell	18,661	22,500
Cow milk, whole, fresh	16,165	51,800
Cucumbers and gherkins	10,185	51,300
Dates	8,529	16,700
Vegetables fresh nes	8,499	45,100
Indigenous cattle meat	6,559	2,428
Eggplants (aubergines)	4,597	21,500
Potatoes	4,324	26,500
Chillies and peppers, green	4,190	8,900

* unofficial figures

Source: http://faostat.fao.org/site/339/default.aspx Food and Agriculture Organization of the United Nations, Food and Agricultural commodities production

Fishing, particularly of shrimp, is important both as a food source and to the economy. The total catch in 2010 was 4,000 tonnes.

COMMUNICATIONS AND TRANSPORT

Travel Requirements
Citizens of the USA, Canada, Australia and the EU require a passport valid for six months beyond the length of stay and a visa. However, visitors may be refused entry in to Kuwait if they have an Israeli visa or border stamp in their passport, or if they have they have an Egyptian or Jordanian border stamp in their passport, issued by an office bordering with Israel. Nationals of Australia, Canada, the USA and the EU (except nationals of Bulgaria, Cyprus, Czech Republic, Estonia, Hungary, Latvia, Lithuania, Malta, Poland, Romania, Slovak Republic and Slovenia), can now obtain a 90-day visa on arrival for business or tourism purposes.

Other nationals should contact the embassy to check visa requirements.

Customs Restrictions
The bringing of weapons, drugs, pork or alcohol into Kuwait is forbidden. There are no restrictions on currency being brought in or out of the country.

National Airlines
Kuwait Airways Corporation suffered losses during the Iraqi invasion estimated at KD 383 million. URL: http://www.kuwait-airways.com

International Airports
Kuwait International Airport, Safat, Kuwait. Figures for 2000 for Safat Airport show it handled 3,869,582 passengers. Kuwait has eight airports, four with paved runways, and one Heliport.
URL: http://www.kuwait-airport.com

Roads
Paved roads amount to 3,800 km, of which 160 km are motorways. Vehicles are driven on the right.

Shipping
Kuwait has three commercial ports: Shuwaikh, Shuaiba and Doha. Shuwaikh is the oldest port, established in 1960. It has 21 berths with a total length of 4 kilometres. Shuaiba was built in 1967. It is 54 kilometres south of Kuwait City. It has a new terminal for handling containers and serves the Shuaiba Industrial Area and the oil refiners. Doha was commissioned in 1981 for smaller coastal ships carrying light goods. A ferry service runs between Ash Shuwayk, Kuwait to Bushehr, Iran.

The Kuwait Oil Tankers Company operates 35 carriers.

KUWAIT

HEALTH

The healthcare system was badly damaged during the Kuwait-Iraq was in 1990. It has subsequently rebuilt and is composed of both public and privately run healthcare. All citizens have access to free healthcare in public hospitals. A mandatory expatriate insurance law was introduced in April 2000. There are more than 70 public health centres.

According to WHO figures, there were 5,340 physicians (17.9 per 10,000 population), 13,554 nursing and midwives (45.5 per 10,000 population), 1,054 dentistry personnel and 88 pharmaceutical personnel.

In 2009, Kuwait spent approximately 5.6 per cent of its total budget on healthcare, accounting for 85.4 per cent of all healthcare spending. Total expenditure on healthcare equated to 3.8 per cent of the country's GDP. Per capita expenditure on health was approximately US$1,579, compared with US$488 in 2000.

In 2009, the infant mortality rate (probability of dying by age one) was 10 per 1,000 live births and the under-five mortality rate was 11 per 1,000 live births. The most common causes of death in the under-fives are prematurity 27 per cent, congenital anomalies 43 per cent, pneumonia 6 per cent, injuries 10 per cent, diarrhoea 1 per cent, and birth asphyxia 7 per cent.

Approximately 99 per cent of the population has access to improved drinking-water and 100 per cent to improved sanitation. (Source: http://www.who.int, World Health Statistics 2012)

EDUCATION

State education is free for all Kuwaitis and attendance is compulsory between the ages of six and 14, in the primary and intermediate stages.

There is a private education sector originally set up for foreign nationals living in Kuwait who want their children educated in their mother tongue.

After the Gulf war, the Ministry of Awqaf and Islamic Affairs reopened the 14 Holy Qur'an Centres (eight for women and six for men) as well as introducing the Institutes for Islamic Studies (one for each gender) which at the moment cater for nearly 2,000 people. The Ministry also introduced 77 learning circles for the Qur'an, in which 1,232 women and 685 men are studying. There are also 128 illiteracy eradication centres.

Figures from UNESCO for 2007 show that 77 per cent of young children were enrolled in pre-primary education, 87 per cent of girls and 89 per cent of boys were enrolled in primary school, and 80 per cent of girls and 80 per cent of boys were enrolled in secondary school.

Higher Education
Kuwait University opened in 1966. It originally had 418 students and 31 teaching staff members. Recent figures show it has 17,419 students, 890 staff members and a budget of 58,280,000 KD. (Sources: Ministry of Planning/ Kuwait Facts and Figures, State of Kuwait).

The adult literacy rate is 95.2 per cent for males and 93.1 for females. For the age group 15-24 years the rate is 98.4 per cent for males and 98.5 per cent for females. In 2006 12.9 per cent of government spending went on education. (Source: UNESCO, August 2009)

RELIGION

The State Religion of Kuwait is Islam. There are over 700 mosques and a Ministry of Awqaf and Islamic Affairs to oversee the preservation of the Islamic heritage and the maintenance of Islamic aspects of daily life.

The majority of Kuwaiti Muslims are Sunni Muslims (45 per cent). 40 per cent are Shi'a Muslims. Other religions represented include Christian, Hindu, and Parsi.

Kuwait has a religious liberty rating of 3 on a scale of 1 to 10 (10 is most freedom). (Source: World Religion Database)

COMMUNICATIONS AND MEDIA

Kuwait enjoys relative press freedom compared to the other Gulf states but criticism of the emir, the constitution, religion and the judiciary is prohibited.

Newspapers
The publishers of Kuwaiti newspapers must obtain a licence from the Ministry of Information. Any publication regarded by the government as morally offensive is subject to censorship. Al Anba, Safat; Arab Times, Dubai, http://www.arabtimesonline.com/arabtimes; Kuwait Times, Safat, URL: http://www.kuwaittimes.net; Al Rai Al-Aam, Shuwaikh, http://www.alraialaam.com; Al Watan, URL: http://www.alwatan.com.kw

Broadcasting
Television transmission is the responsibility of the Ministry of Information. Private broadcasters operate alongside state-owned TV and radio. Pan-Arab satellite programes are also available. The government exercises some control over the content of television programmes, ensuring that material is not contrary to the principles of Islam. Kuwaiti TV, the state-run broadcaster, operates four networks and a satellite channel. Radio Kuwait is a public broadcasting station controlled by the Ministry of Information.
Kuwaiti TV, URL: http://www.media.gov.kw/
Al-Rai, private, URL: http://www.alrai.tv/Templates/home.aspx

Telecommunications
The telephone system is generally excellent with new telephone exchanges providing a large capacity. Mobile cellular system operates throught the state. In 2008, there were an estimated 540,000 main lines in use and an estimated 2.9 million mobile phones. Recent figures indicate that over 1 million Kuwaitis are regular internet users.

ENVIRONMENT

The country's major environmental issues include limited natural fresh water resources, air and water pollution and desertification. A Ministerial Committee headed by the Chairman of the Agriculture Affairs and Fish Resources Authority was set up in 1986 with the task of landscaping over 30,000 hectares of land with agricultural, forestation and parkland projects.

Carbon dioxide emissions were estimated at 76.69 million metric tons in 2005, up from 55.83 million metric tons in 2002. Per capita carbon dioxide emissions were estimated in the same year to be 32.85 metric tons, compared with the US figure of 20.14 metric tons. Of the country's energy related carbon emissions, 58 per cent were produced by oil and 42 per cent by natural gas. In 2006, Kuwait's total emissions from the consumption and flaring of fossil fuels were 74.79 million metric tons of carbon dioxide this figure had risen to 81.3 million metric tons in 2010. (Source: EIA)

Following the Gulf War more than 700 oil wells burned for over 250 days. The environmental impact of the pollution this caused is still not clear, although it is known that there have been increased cases of bronchial and chest infections amongst the population.

Kuwait is a party to conventions on: Biodiversity, Climate Change, Climate Change-Kyoto Protocol, Desertification, Endangered Species, Environmental Modification, Hazardous Wastes, Law of the Sea, and Ozone Layer Protection. Kuwait has signed, but not ratified, the convention on Marine Dumping.

KYRGYZSTAN

Kyrgyz Republic

Kyrgyz Respublikasy

Capital: Bishkek (Population estimate, 2010: 760,000)

Head of State: Almazbek Atambayev (President) (page 1380)

National Flag: A stylised yurt roof and sun all in gold centred on a red background. The sun has 40 rays representing the 40 Kyrgyz tribes.

CONSTITUTION AND GOVERNMENT

Constitution

In December 1990, the Supreme Soviet voted to change the republic's name to the Republic of Kyrgyzstan, and in 1991, the name of the capital, Frunze, was changed back to its prerevolutionary name of Bishkek. However, in a referendum on the preservation of the Soviet Union in March 1991, over 88 per cent of voters wanted to retain the Soviet Union as a 'renewed federation'. Following an attempted coup against President Gorbachev in August 1991, the Kyrgyz Communist Party politburo and Secretariat were dissolved. President Askar Akayev resigned, and his cabinet and secretariat followed suit. The Supreme Soviet declared independence from the Soviet Union on 31st August 1991.

President Akayev was re-elected on 12 October and a republican nationalist guard was set up in December 1991. On 21 December 1991 the Republic became a member of the Commonwealth of Independent States. A new constitution was adopted in December 1992, and the Supreme Soviet was renamed *Jogorku Kenesh*. President Askar Akayev was re-elected in December 1995 and again in 2000.

Amendments were made to the constitution in February 2003 and were approved by referendum.In November 2006, the Supreme Council approved a new constitution which would reduce some of the president's powers. This constitution was replaced on December 30 following the resignation of the government. In January a new constitution was agreed which returned some powers to the president. The constitution was further amended in October 2007 to allow for the establishment of a multi party parliamentary system.

In June 2010 a referendum approved further changes to the constitution. Amendments included a reduction of presidential powers and the limiting of the presidential term to a single term. To consult the constitution, please visit: http://www.venice.coe.int/docs/2010/CDL-AD(2010)015-e.asp.

Recent Events

Legislative elections in February 2005 were marred by protests after several opposition candidates were prevented from standing. In March, during the second round of elections, protests escalated; demonstrators occupied some official buildings and there were calls for the resignation of President Akayev. Akayev left for Russia and the election results were annulled by the Supreme Court. It was announced that parliament had appointed Kurmanbek Bakiev acting president and prime minister. The upper and lower houses also agreed to dissolve and reform as a unicameral legislature. Later that month opposition leader Feliks Kulov was released from prison where he had been serving a 10 sentence for abuse of office; charges against him were dropped. In April, Askar Akayev formally resigned as president. Presidential elections were held in July and Bakiev won a landslide victory, mainly because the popular opposition leader, Kulov, had agreed not to stand against him. In return Bakiev agreed to appoint him as prime minister. Kurmanbek Bakiev was inaugurated as president on August 14. Parliament rejected several proposed ministers.

The speaker of parliament, Omurbek Tekebayev, resigned in February 2006 after disagreements with the president. This was followed in April by the resignation of the industry minister, Almazbek Atambayev. There were several demonstrations protesting against the levels of lawlessness in the country and demanding constitutional reform. In November 2006, following civic protests, the President signed a new constitution which limited presidential powers. In December, the government resigned, in anticipation of early parliamentary elections, and President Bakiyev revised the November Constitution, reinstating some of his powers. He tried to reinstate Felix Kulov as Prime Minister, but parliament rejected him twice. In February, there were calls for the President's resignation, and in March the government resigned when faced with the prospect of demonstrations scheduled by the opposition for April.

In October 2007 constitutional changes were approved in a referendum but observers criticised the vote. Elections took place in December 2007 but were denounced by the opposition who failed to win a single seat.

There is currently uncertainty over the future of a US air base at Manas used to supply Western troops in Afghanistan. President Bakiyev announced the closure of the base. The US reported that talks were on-going.

There were a series of cabinet resignations in 2009. The entire government resigned in October 2009 but remained as the caretaker government. A new prime minister was appointed on 21 October. A new cabinet was subsequently appointed under a revised structure.

On April 6 2010 protests began in the city of Talas after an opposition member was arrested. Demonstrators stormed the town's government buildings demanding their own 'People's Governor' and calling for the resignation of President Bakiyev. In Bishkek, demonstrators marched on the main government building and were met by troops firing stun grenades and live rounds, many were killed. The protestors took control of the national TV and radio stations and the main police headquarters and President Bayiyev was swept from power. Opposition leaders who had been arrested were released and they set up an interim government led by Roza Otunbayeva. In June 2010 Edil Baisalov, Roza Otunbayeva's chief of staff, resigned as he had some doubts over the direction the interim government was going in. Mr Baisalov said he will form a new party to contest parliamentary elections which are due to take place in October. In July Roza Otunbayeva was formally sworn in as interim president to serve until the end of 2011.

Inter-ethnic clashes were reported in southern Kyrgyzstan in June 2010.

Legislative elections took place on 10 October 2010. Following discussion between the parties it was announced on 30 November that a three-party coalition would be formed, led by the SDPK and including Respublika and Ata-Meken. The cabinet was approved on 16 December 2010.

In November 2010, the trial started of the former president Kurmanbek Bakiyev for the shooting of protesters in April. Mr Bakiyev is currently in exile and is accordingly being tried in absentia.

Presidential elections were held in October 2011 and were won by the prime minister, Almazbek Atambayev.

In September 2012, the political parties Ar-Namys and Ata-Meken withdrew from the coalition government, leaving the government without a majority. Prime Minister Babanov resigned and Zhantoro Satybaldiyev of the SDPK was elected prime minister.

International Relations

Kyrgyzstan maintains strong relations with Russia. Relations became strained with the US culminating in the expulsion of two US diplomats in August 2006. Kyrgyzstan is aiming to develop its relationship with China. Relations with Uzbekistan have been difficult and Uzbekistan has often interrupted gas supplies to press for debt repayments. Kyrgyzstan has also had longstanding negotiations with Tajikistan concerning the demarcation of the common border.

Kyrgyzstan is a keen member of regional organisations including the Commonwealth of Independent States (CIS), the Shanghai Cooperation Organisation (SCO), and the Eurasian Economic Community (EAEC).

Legislature

The President determines the structure of the Government and appoints the Prime Minister with the consent of the Assembly of People's Representatives. The Government is the highest executive body and decides all issues of state governance except those powers given to the President and the Parliament (Jogorku Kenesh). The Parliament consisted of two houses: the Legislative Assembly of 60 members elected for a term of five years which sits continuously and is elected by the population; and the Assembly of People's Representatives which has 45 members, also elected for a term of five years and is elected on a territorial basis. In March 2005, the two houses dissolved and agreed to reform as a unicameral legislature.

Supreme Council, *Jogorku Kenesh*, 207-209 Abdymomunov St, 720003 Bishkek, Kyrgyzstan. Tel: +996 312 270896, fax: +996 312 226035, e-mail: snurjan@freenet.kg, URL: http://www.kenesh.kg

---

Cabinet (as at March 2013)
Prime Minister: Zhantoro Satybaldiyev (page 1509)
First Vice Prime Minister: Joomart Otorbaev
Vice Prime Minister, Minister for Social Affairs: Kamila Talieva
Vice Prime Minister, Minister for Economy and Investment: Tayirbek Sarpashev
Vice Prime Minister for Security, Law and Order and Borders Issues: Shamil Atakhanov
Minister of Finance: Olga Lavrova
Minister of Defence: Maj.-Gen. Taalaybek Omuraliyev
Minister of Economic and Antimonopoly: Temir Sariev
Minister of Education and Science: Kanatbek Sadykov
Minister of Energy and Industry: Avtandil Kalmambetov
Minister of Health Care: Dinara Sagimbaeva
Minister of Internal Affairs: Col.-Maj. of Police Suranchiyev
Minister of Foreign Affairs: Erlan Abdyldayev
Minister of Transport and Communications: Kalykbek Sultanov
Minister of Culture and Tourism: Kozhogeldi Kuluev
Minister of Youth, Migration and Labour: Aliyasbek Alymkulov
Minister of Emergency Situations: Kubatbek Boronov
Minister of Justice: Almambet Shykmamatov
Minister of Agriculture: Chyngzbek Uzakbaev
Minister of Social Development: Kylychbek Sultanov
Head of the Government Office: Nurhanbek Momunaliev
Chairman of the State Committee for National Security: Beyshenbay Zhunusov

---

Ministries
Presidential office, URL: http://www.president.kg

KYRGYZSTAN

Office of the Prime Minister, Dom Pravitelstva, 720003, Bishkek, Kyrgyzstan. Tel: +996 312 222757, URL: http://www.government.gov.kg

Ministry of Industry and Foreign Trade, 106 Chui Avenue, 720002, Bishkek, Kyrgyzstan. Tel: +996 312 223866, fax: +996 312 663498, e-mail: postmaster@mvtp.bishkek.gov.kg, URL: http://mvtp.bishkek.gov.kg/

Ministry of Foreign Affairs, 59 Razzakov Street, 720040, Bishkek, Kyrgyzstan. Tel: +996 312 220545 / 660501, fax: +996 312 663974 / 660501, e-mail: gendep@mfa.gov.kg, URL: http://www.mfa.kg

Ministry of Finance, 58 Erkindik Boulevard, 720040, Bishkek, Kyrgyzstan. Tel: +996 312 228922 / 660504, fax: +996 312 621645, e-mail: minfin@sti.gov.kg, URL: http://www.minfin.kg/

Ministry of Economic Regulations, URL: http://www.mvtp.kg/

Ministry of Labour and Social Welfare, 215 Tynystanova str., 720041, Bishkek, Kyrgyzstan. Tel: +996 312 663400, fax: +996 312 221837, e-mail: mail@mlsp.kg, URL: http://www.gks.gov.kg/www/index.html

Ministry of Agriculture and Water Resources, 96A Kievskaya Street, 720040, Bishkek, Kyrgyzstan. Tel: +996 312 221435 / 220496, fax: +996 312 226784, e-mail: mail@minagro.bishkek.gov.kg

Ministry of Emergency Situations and Environmental Protection, 2/1 Dushanbinskaya str., 720055, Bishkek, Kyrgyzstan. Tel: +996 312 541180 / 222227, fax: +996 312 427280, e-mail: mecd@bishkek.gov.kg, URL: http://www.mecd.gov.kg/

Ministry of the Interior, 469 Frunze Street, 720040, Bishkek, Kyrgyzstan. Tel: +996 312 662450, fax: +996 312 288788, e-mail: mail@mvd.bishkek.gov.kg

Ministry of Defence, 26 Logvinenko Street, 720001, Bishkek, Kyrgyzstan. Tel: +996 312 222763, fax: +996 312 228648 / 662803, e-mail: ud@bishkek.gov.kg

Ministry of Health, 148 Moskovskaya Street, 720040, Bishkek, Kyrgyzstan. Tel: +996 312 228697, fax: +996 312 660493, URL: http://www.med.kg/

Ministry of Justice, 37 Orozbekov Street, 720040, Bishkek, Kyrgyzstan. Tel: +996 312 228489, fax: +996 312 663044 / 663505, e-mail: minjust@bishkek.gov.kg, URL: http://www.minjust.gov.kg/minjust/index.php

Ministry of Communications and Transport, 42 Isanova Street, 720017, Bishkek, Kyrgyzstan. Tel: +996 312 216672, fax: +996 312 213667, e-mail: di@mtk.bishkek.gov.kg, URL: http://www.mtk.gov.kg/

Ministry of Education, Science and Culture, 257 Tynystanova Street, 720040, Bishkek, Kyrgyzstan. Tel: +996 312 66-24-42, fax: +996 312 228604, e-mail: postmaster@monk.bishkek.gov.kg

Minister of Decentralization and Regional Development, 44 Orozbekova str., 720033, Bishkek, Kyrgyzstan. Tel: +996 312 222872, fax: +996 312 665149, e-mail: gosreg@bishkek.gov.kg

State Securities Commission, 114 ave. Chui, Bishkek 720040, Kyrgyzstan. Tel: +996 312 225540, fax: +996 312 662653

Political Parties

Ar-Namys ("Dignity"); Ata-Meken ("Homeland"); Ata-Zhurt ("Fatherland"); Respublika ("Republic"); Social Democratic Party of Kyrgyzstan (SDPK), Ak Jol .

Elections

The most recent presidential election was held in October 2011 and was won by the prime minister, Mr Almazbek Atambayev, with over 60 per cent of the vote. His two main rivals each polled under 15 per cent. Both have alleged fraud. Turnout was estimated to be 60 per cent. The the previous president, Kurmanbek Bakiyev, was ousted in a violent uprising in April 2010. The interim leader, Roza Otunbayevam, did not contest the poll.

Parliamentary elections took place on December 16 2007 and were won by the President's Ak Zhol party. The opposition failed to win a single seat. Observers criticised the polls. The next election was held in October 2010. No one party gained a clear majority (Ata-Zhurt 28 seats; SDPK 26 seats; Ar-Namys 25 seats; Respublika 23 seats; Ata-Meken 18 seats) and coalition negotiations were then held. Following discussion between the parties it was announced on 30 November that a three-party coalition would be formed, led by the SDPK and including Respublika and Ata-Meken.

Diplomatic Representation

US Embassy, 171 Prospect Mira, Bishkek 720016, Kyrgyzstan. Tel: +996 312 551241, fax: +996 312 551264, URL: http://bishkek.usembassy.gov/
Ambassador: Pamela L. Spratlen

British Consulate, (All staff resident in Astana, Kazakhstan), URL: http://ukinkz.fco.uk/en
Ambassador: Judith Farnworth

Embassy of Kyrgyzstan, 1732 Wiconsin Avenue, NW, Washington, DC 20007, USA. Tel: +1 202 338 5141, e-mail: embassy@kyrgyzstan.org, URL: http://www.kgembassy.org/
Ambassador: Muktar Djumaliev

Embassy of Kyrgyzstan, Ascot House, 119 Crawford Street, London, W1H 1AF, United Kingdom. Tel: +44 (0)20 7935 1462, fax: +44 (0)20 7935 7449, e-mail: embassy@kyrgyz-embassy.org.uk, URL: http://www.kyrgyz-embassy.org.uk/
Ambassador: Aibek Tilebaliev

Permanent Representative of Kyrgyz Republic to the United Nations, 866 United Nations Plaza, Suite 477, New York, NY 10017, USA. Tel: +1 212 486 4214 / 4654, fax: +1 212 486 5259, URL: http://www.un.int/wcm/content/site/kyrgyzstan
Permanent Representative: Amb. Extraordinary and Plenipotentiary: Talaibek Kydyrov

LEGAL SYSTEM

The legal system continues to operate largely under the supervision of the Ministry of Justice, guided by Soviet-era laws and procedures. The judiciary consists of the Constitutional Court, the Supreme Court, the Higher Arbitration Court, provincial and local courts. The Constitutional Court ensures that laws and international treaties conform to the constitution. The Supreme Court is the highest judicial body in the areas of civil, criminal and administrative proceedings, and supervises the operation of the local courts. The Higher Arbitration Court, regional arbitration courts and the arbitration court of the City of Bishkek form a system of arbitration courts that resolve economic and property disputes. Traditional elders' courts may handle petty crimes in rural areas.

In 1996, the constitutional court ruled that only the defense has the right of appeal. However, the law allows judges to remand a case to the prosecutor for further investigation, rather than to declare the defendant guilty or innocent.

Constitutional court judges are appointed to fifteen-year terms, supreme court judges to ten-year terms, and local court judges to three-year terms by recommendation of the president.

There are still various human rights problems, including torture and abuse by law enforcement officials. Prison conditions are poor, and detention can be arbitrary. Corruption is widespread, though the government has recently taken steps to tackle it in the public sector and has arrested several government officials on charges of corruption. Kyrgyzstan is a signatory to UN Conventions including the International Covenant on Civil and Political Rights, the Convention against Torture and the Convention on the Rights of the Child. The death penalty was abolished in 2007.

Office of the Ombudsman of the Kyrgyz Republic, URL: http://www.ombudsman.kg/en.html

LOCAL GOVERNMENT

There are 7 administrative regions or *Oblasts*:
Chui region, population 763,400, administrative centre, Bishkek;
Issyk-Kul region, population 427,000, administrative centre, Kara-Kul;
Jalal-Abad region, population 842,000, administrative centre, Jalal-Abad;
Naryn region, population 263,000, administrative centre, Naryn;
Osh region, population 1,415,000, administrative centre, Osh;
Talas region, population 210,000, administrative centre, Talas.
Batlen, population 380,000, administrative centre, Batken.
The regions are administered by governors. Each provinces comprises a number of districts. The capital Bishkek and the second largest city, Osh, are independent cities with a status equal to a province.

AREA AND POPULATION

Area

The country lies in the north-east of Central Asia, mainly on the Tien Shan and the Pamir Alai ranges and is land locked. It borders China to the east and Kazakhstan, Uzbekistan and Tajikistan to the north, west and south. Its area is 199,900 sq. km. Around 75 per cent of the land area is mountainous. The highest peak, Jengish Chokusu (7,439 metres). A large salt lake, Issyk Kul, occupies a highland basin in the north-east. The climate varies according to region: temperate in the north, subtropical in the south west and dry continental/polar in the Tien Shan area.

To view a map, visit http://www.un.org/Depts/Cartographic/map/profile/kyrgysta.pdf

Population

Figures for 2010 put the population at approximately 5.334 million with a population density of 26 people per sq km. The annual growth rate is estimated at 0.7 per cent over the period 2000-10. The capital Bishkek has a population of about 640,000, and there are 18 towns, including Bishkek, with populations over 100,000. Around 35 per cent of the population live in urban areas. The average age of the population was 24 years. An estimated 7 per cent of the population is aged 60 years or more and 30 per cent aged less than 15 years.

The major ethnic groups are Kyrgyz 66.0 per cent, Russian 11.0 per cent, Uzbek 14.0 per cent. The other 9.0 per cent includes Dungan, German, Kazakh, Korean, Tajik, Tatar & Uighur. The Uzbek population is mainly located around the city of Osh, and this has given rise to some ethnic tension, mainly centred around control of land.

Kyrgyz and Russian are the two official languages.

Births, Marriages, Deaths

Recent figures put the birth rate at 22.8 births per 1,000 population and death rate at 7.9 per 1,000 population. The infant mortality rate was 33.0 per 1,000 live births in 2010. In 2005 the maternal mortality rate was 150 per 100,000 births. The total fertility rate per female was estimated at 2.5 in 2009. In 2009 life expectancy at birth was 66 years (63 years for males and 70 years for females) and healthy life expectancy was 57 years (55 and 59 years respectively). (Source: http://www.who.int, World Health Statistics 2012)

Public Holidays 2014
1/2 January: New Year
7 January: Christmas (Orthodox Church)
14 January: Birth of the Prophet*
1 May: International Labour Day
5 May: Constitutional Day
9 May: Victory Day
29 June: June begins*
29 July: Eid al-Fitr (end of Ramadan)*
31 August: Independence Day
5 October: Feast of the Sacrifice*
25 October: Islamic New Year*
* Islamic holidays rely on the sighting of the moon and so can vary

EMPLOYMENT

In 2006 the labour force was estimated at 2,285,000 of whom 2,096,000 were employed. Around 760,000 of the working population were employed in the agriculture sector and 407,000 were employed in manufacturing. In 2006 the unemployment rate was estimated to be around 8.3 per cent (7.7 per cent males and 9.0 per cent females). (Source: Asian Development Bank)

Total Employment by Economic Activity

Occupation	2008
Agriculture, hunting & forestry	742,900
Fishing	100
Mining & quarrying	13,300
Manufacturing	178,000
Electricity, gas & water supply	37,800
Construction	221,900
Wholesale & retail trade, repairs	319,400
Hotels & restaurants	66,200
Transport, storage & communications	133,800
Financial intermediation	12,200
Real estate, renting & business activities	49,700
Public admin. & defence; compulsory social security	101,700
Education	156,100
Health & social work	86,200
Other community, social & personal service activities	49,400
Households with employed persons	15,400
Extra-territorial organisations & bodies	300

Source: Copyright © International Labour Organization (ILO Dept. of Statistics, http://laborsta.ilo.org)

BANKING AND FINANCE

Currency
The currency of Kyrgyzstan is the Som.

GDP/GNP, Inflation, National Debt
Kyrgyzstan is one of the poorest countries of the former Soviet Union and since independence it has faced major economic difficulties. The government put into place a series of plans to bring down inflation, and boost industrial production. Agriculture is one of its most important economic sectors. The economy depends on gold exports. The economy has been hindered in recent years by political instability, civil fighting and damage to the infrastructure.

The following table shows the make up of GDP by industrial origin (figures are at current factor cost in million Soms):

Industry	2008	2009	2010
Total	187,991.9	201,222.9	212,177.4
Agriculture	44,145.7	37,743.9	39,327.8
Mining	1,001.7	1,072.3	1,451.0
Manufacturing	24,850.7	28,630.5	33,830.7
Utilities	2,672.0	4,369.1	5,811.6
Construction	9,880.3	13,488.6	11,998.9
Trade	30,712.6	33,865.4	34,206.7
Transport & Communications	14,825.1	17,670.8	19,385.9
Finance	6,939.0	8,023.4	8,680.7
Public admin.	8,660.1	10,757.7	11,974.5
Other	24,985.2	30,095.4	30,472.2

Source: ADB

Per capita GDP was estimated at 39,212 soms in 2010.

GDP growth was estimated at -0.5 per cent in 2010, rising to 5.5 per cent in 2011. GDP was estimated at US$13 billion in 2011.

Inflation fell from 770 per cent in 1993 to 5.4 per cent in 2003. Average inflation at the end of 2008 was put at 24.3 per cent, falling to 8 per cent in 2010. GDP was estimated to be over 15 per cent in 2011. Figures for 2011 put total external debt at US$3.5 billion.

Direct foreign investment was estimated to be US$1.35 billion in 2011.

Balance of Payments / Imports and Exports
Following a large depreciation of the Som in 1999 foreign exports grew. The following tables show the trade balance in recent years, and main imported and exported goods. Figures are in million US dollars:

Foreign Trade	2008	2009	2010
Exports, fob	1,642.1	1,673,0	1,812.4
Imports, cif	4,072.4	3,040.2	3,235.6
Trade balance	-2,430.3	-1,367.2	-1,423.2

Source: ADB

External Trade by HSC, 2007

HSC	Export	Import
Animal & animal products	31.0	40.7
Vegetable products	80.3	119.1
Animal or vegetable fats	9.2	30.6
Prepared foodstuffs	37.3	185.6

- continued

Mineral products	330.0	781.4
Chemical products	24.4	222.7
Plastics and rubber	18.7	104.8
Hides and skins	16.0	2.8
Wood and wood products; wood pulp products	5.6	96.2
Textiles and textile articles; footwear, headware	124.2	56.6
Stone articles, plaster, cement etc	54.8	35.9
Pearls, precious / semi-precious stones, metals	228.5	1.5
Base metals	52.9	177.7
Machinery, mechanical appliances and electrical equipment.	69.9	343.7
Transportation equipment	42.3	144.2
Instruments, measuring	3.7	34.0
Misc. manufactured articles	5.3	39.4

Source: ADB

The main export markets for Kyrgyzstan are Russia (US$340.3 million), Uzbekistan (US$208.7 million) and Kazakhstan (US$165.6 million). The largest import markets are China (US$4,509.5 million), Russia (US$1,027.3 million) and Kazakhstan (US$338.6 million).

Central Bank
National Bank of the Kyrgyz Republic, 101 Umetaliev St, 720040 Bishkek, Kyrgyzstan. Tel: +996 312 669011 / 312 669012, fax: +996 312 610730, e-mail: mail@nbkr.kg, URL: http://www.nbkr.kg
Chairman of the Board: Zina Asankojoeva

MANUFACTURING, MINING AND SERVICES

Primary and Extractive Industries
Kyrgyzstan is mineral rich and has deposits of gold, mercury, antimony and uranium. The country wants to attract foreign investment to the mineral extraction and processing sector.

Unlike its Central Asian neighbours, however, it has insignificant reserves of petroleum and natural gas and it is forced to import vast amounts of these fuels in order to meet its domestic energy requirements. The government would like to increase coal production and decrease its dependence on other nations. In 2009 production was 0.664 million short tons per annum and consumption was 1.098 million short tons.

There are seven developed oil fields and two oil/gas fields. Due to difficult geological structures and water encroachment, recovery rates are low. The country's first refinery was built in 1997 in Jalalabad, figre for 2012 show that Kyrgyzstan refines just 10,000 barrels per day. Kyrgyzstan has estimated oil reserves of 40 million barrels and in 2011 produced 950 barrels per day while consuming 17,000 barrels per day. Recent exploration has found supplies in the Fergana Valley (700 million barrels) and possibly deposits in Chuy, Alay and Issyk-Kul (1.5 billion barrels). (Source: EIA)

Although Kyrgyzstan has estimated natural gas reserves of 200 billion cubic feet, it imports almost all the gas it needs from neighbouring Turkmenistan and Uzbekistan. Inability to meet charges has meant a disrupted supply from Uzbekistan. In 2010 a total 16 billion cubic feet of gas were consumed.

Energy
The most viable option for the future, however, lies not with coal but with Kyrgyzstan's hydroelectric potential, which at present generates nearly 90 per cent of electricity produced. The total hydroelectric potential of the country is estimated to be 14 billion kWh per year. Kyrgyzstan produces more electricity than it needs and so exports to Kazakhstan and Uzbekistan. In 2010, 111.19 billion kWh of electricty were produced and 7.33 billion kWh exported. (Source: EIA) In 2012 work began on the first of twelve hydroelectric plants planned along the Naryn River, the project is going ahead with aid and expertise from Russia.

Manufacturing
In the industrial sector the most developed areas are electrical production and mining. The mining and metallurgy industries provide 10 per cent of industrial production and employ 11 per cent of the industrial labour force. As the agriculture sector is the largest contributor to GDP manufacturing is based around this, including wool, cotton, leather and silk production. Cement, glass and slate are also produced as are shoes and furniture.

Agriculture
An estimated 1.3 million hectares of land are used for arable farming and 55,000 hectares for permanent crops. An estimated 77 per cent of the land is irrigated. The main products are tobacco, wood, cotton, leather, silk, fruit and vegetables. Kyrgyzstan produces 55,000 tonnes of tobacco per annum. 60 per cent of its grain requirement is imported. The rearing of livestock is the largest sector of agricultural activity. An estimated 9.3 million hectares are used for pasture. In 2004, there were 1.003 million cattle and buffaloes and 3.7 million sheep and goats. (Source: FAO)

Agricultural Production in 2010

Produce	Int. $'000*	Tonnes
Cow milk, whole, fresh	390,792	1,317,300
Indigenous cattle meat	269,863	99,898
Potatoes	123,572	1,339,400
Indigenous sheep meat	112,304	41,246
Tomatoes	70,956	192,000
Apples	60,054	142,000
Wheat	51,371	813,300
Beans, dry	42,940	71,400
Carrots and turnips	41,167	165,000

KYRGYZSTAN

- continued

Cotton lint	34,873	24,400
Indigenous horse meat	33,815	21,709
Onions, dry	28,355	135,000

* unofficial figures

Source: http://faostat.fao.org/site/339/default.aspx Food and Agriculture Organization of the United Nations, Food and Agricultural commodities production

The government started a land privatisation programme in 1992 and has dissolved some collective farms. There are about 17,000 private farmers in Kyrgyzstan. The country is the third largest wool producer in the former Soviet Union. It has 12 million sheep and a wool production of 40,000 tonnes per annum.

COMMUNICATIONS AND TRANSPORT

Travel Requirements
Citizens of the USA, Canada, Australia and most of the EU require a passport valid for six months from date of entry and a visa. Nationals of Bulgaria, Czech Republic, Hungary, Poland, Romania, Slovak Republic and Slovenia travelling as tourists do not require a visa. All nationals (except UK citizens) must register with the department for visas and registration within three days of arrivals; hotels normally carry out this service.

Other nationals should contact the embassy to check visa requirements.

National Airlines
Kyrgyzstan Aba Joldoru, Manus Airport, Bishkek 720062, Kyrgyzstan. Tel: +996 3312 696600, fax: +996 3312 257755. This airline relies on Aeroflot for codesharing and marketing.

International Airports
Airports are located in Osh, Przhevalsk and the capital Bishkek. Regulatory bodies include: **Department of Air Transport - Kyrgyzstan**, Isanova Str. 42, Bishkek 720017, Kyrgyzstan. Tel: +996 3312 216672

Railways
The total length of the railway system is approximately 470 km, the line runs from Bishkek to Balikchi in the south. Plans have been drawn up for another north-south route. There are lines for industrial use. It is possible to travel from Bishkek to Moscow by train, the journey takes three days.

Roads
The total length of the roads is approximately 30,000 km, of which 22,500 are hard surfaced. Vehicles are driven on the right. Bishkek has a tram system.

HEALTH

In 2009, Kyrgyzstan spent approximately 11.7 per cent of its total budget on healthcare, accounting for 53.0 per cent of all healthcare spending. Total expenditure on healthcare equated to 6.4 per cent of the country's GDP. Per capita expenditure on health was approximately US$57, compared with US$13 in 2000. Out-of-pocket private expenditure accounts for 88.5 per cent of private expenditure on health. According to WHO estimates, in 2005-10 there were 12,395 doctors (23 per 10,000 population), 30,495 nurses and midwives (57 per 10,000 population), 1,021 dentistry personnel (2 per 10,000 population) and 86 pharmaceutical personnel (0.03 per 1,000 population).

In 2010, 90 per cent of the population had access to an improved water source (99 per cent urban, 85 per cent rural) compared to 76 per cent in 2002. In the same year 93 per cent of the population had access to improved sanitation, compared to 60 per cent of the population in 2002. In 2010 diarrhoea accounted for 6 per cent of deaths among children aged less than five.

In 2009, the infant mortality rate was estimated to be 33 per 1,000 live births and the under-five mortality rate was 38 per 1,000 live births. An estimated 2.7 per cent of children aged under five years of age are considered underweight for age and 18.1 per cent stunted. (Source: http://www.who.int, World Health Statistics 2012)

EDUCATION

Education in Kyrgyzstan is compulsory for ten years, for primary and lower secondary levels. Public expenditure on education was estimated at 19.2 per cent of total government expenditure in 2007 (5.3 per cent of GDP). Primary school starts at age seven and secondary at age eleven. Pupil enrolment in primary school was estimated at 86 per cent in 2006. An estimated 99 per cent of children enroled in primary education complete the course. In 2006, the pupil to teacher ratio was 24:1. An estimated 80.5 per cent of pupils are in secondary school. Most primary and secondary education is taught in the Kyrgyz language, but the language of instruction in the higher education institutions is Russian.

An estimated 99.5 per cent of males and 99 per cent of females are literate. (Source: UNESCO)

RELIGION

74 per cent of the population are Muslim, (mainly Sunni Muslims). The other major religion is Russian Orthodox (7.5 per cent of the population).

Kyrgyzstan has a religious liberty rating of 4 on a scale of 1 to 10 (10 is most freedom). (Source: World Religion Database)

COMMUNICATIONS AND MEDIA

Traditionally Kyrgystan has enjoyed greater press freedom than its neighbours but during recent ethnic unrest some television stations were closed.

Newspapers
Recent information shows there are over 120 different newspapers published in Kyrgyzstan, 41 of which are in Kyrgyz.
Slovo Kyrgyzstana, URL: http://www.sk.kg/ is owned by the government and is published three times a week.
ResPublica (URL: http://gazeta.respublica.kg/) and **Vecherniy Bishkek** (URL: http://www.vb.kg/) are privately owned and are published daily.

Broadcasting
Television is the most popular medium. The state-run television broadcaster, **Kyrgyz State National Television and Radio Broadcasting Corporation** (URL: http://www.ktr.kg/tv/ru/), operates two nationwide networks and six regional stations. There are pproximately 20 private TV stations including Piramida, Kyrgyz Public Educational TV (URL: http://www.koort.kg/) and Ecological Youth TV (URL: http://www.issyk-kul.kg/TV/). Not all the country is covered, some parts of the south receive no broadcasts at all.

The state-run news agency is **Kabar** (http://www.kabar.kg/).

Telecommunications
The telecommunications infrastructure is being upgraded. but penetration of landlines remains low and concentrated around Bishket. In 2008 there were an estimated 500,000 landlines and an estimated 3 million mobile phones in use. In 2009 there were estimated to 850,000 internet users, again mainly in urban areas.

ENVIRONMENT

Main environmental concerns include a lack of access to clean water and many people get their water directly from contaminated streams and wells. Water-borne diseases are common as a result of this. Increasing soil salinity from faulty irrigation practices is also a problem.

Kyrgyzstan is party to the international agreements: Air Pollution, Biodiversity, Climate Change, Climate Change-Kyoto Protocol, Desertification, Hazardous Wastes, Ozone Layer Protection, and Wetlands.

In 2010, Kyrgyzstan's emissions from the consumption of fossil fuels totalled 4.13 million metric tons of carbon dioxide, down from 4.94 million metric tons in 2009. (Source: EIA)

LAOS
Lao People's Democratic Republic
Sathalanalat Paxathipatai Paxaxon Lao

Capital: Vientiane (Population estimate, 2011: 725,000)

Head of State: Lt. Gen. Choummaly Sayasone (page 1509)

Vice-President: Bounnhang Vorachit (page 1532)

National Flag: Horizontal stripes red blue red with a white circle in the centre, the central blue stripe is double the width of the red

CONSTITUTION AND GOVERNMENT

Constitution
Laos, originally a Protectorate of French Indo-China, is bounded on the west by Thailand and Myanmar, on the north by China, on the east by Vietnam and on the south by Cambodia. The country became a French Protectorate in 1893. On 9 March 1945 the Japanese took control of the country and abolished the French Protectorate. The independence of Laos was proclaimed on 15 April 1945 and a Laotian Government under Japanese protection was installed. After the Japanese capitulation on 15 August the French authorities regained control, but Chinese troops who had been allotted the task of disarming the Japanese to the north of the 16th parallel gradually occupied the greater part of the country. A rebel Laotian government, the Lao Issara (Free Laos), was formed acting in collaboration with the Viet Minh. Early in 1946 the French progressively reoccupied Laos and most of the country was under their control by the middle of the year, while the Lao Issara formed a government in exile in Bangkok. A *modus vivendi* was signed on 27 August between France and the King of Laos. It confirmed the unity and partial independence of Laos and foreshadowed a new democratic political structure. Deputies were elected to a National Constituent Assembly in January 1947 and on 11 May 1947 the new constitution was proclaimed by the king. Laos was declared a parliamentary, constitutional monarchy, the king ruling through ministers responsible to a National Assembly elected for five years.

In 1949, the Lao Issara split. One group led by Prince Souvanna Phouma returned to Laos and accepted limited independence under the French. By a treaty signed in Paris in July and ratified on 2 February 1950, Laos became, like Cambodia, an Associated State within the French Union. Meanwhile the other faction of the Lao Issara organised a resistance movement called the Pathet Lao (Land of the Lao) in northern Laos. By 1953, Pathet Lao and Viet Minh forces had control of the north eastern provinces in which a Pathet Lao administration was established.

Full independence from French rule was established in 1953, and in 1954, when the Geneva Agreements ended the first Indochina war, Laos was recognised as a neutral state. Under the leadership of the Lao People's Revolutionary Party the country became fully independent, the king abdicated his powers, and the communist state of the Lao People's Democratic Republic (Lao PDR) was founded on 2 December 1975.

The current constitution dates from 1991. Head of state is the president, elected by the National Assembly for a five-year term. He appoints a Council of Ministers. The executive branch also includes a nine-member polit bureau, and a 49-member central committee. The prime minister is also appointed for a five-year term - subject to the approval of the National Assembly. Seats in the National Assembly are by popular vote and are for five years.

To consult the constitution, please visit: http://www.un.int/lao/constitution.htm

International relations
Laos is closely linked culturally to Thailand but politically as part of French Indochina she was linked with Vietnam and Cambodia. However, in recent years with improvements in foreign relations Laos has branched out and joined ASEAN in 1997 and the Asia-Europe Meeting (ASEM) in 2004 and is currently working towards membership of the World Trade Organisation.

Recent Events
In 2004 there were some armed attacks on buses and bombing incidents in and around the capital Vientiane. No one claimed responsibility for the attacks, but many believe that this is a sign of growing opposition to the ruling party.

The plight of the ethnic minority, the Hmong, has come to the fore in recent years. The Hmong were allies of the USA during the Vietnam war, and many fled to neighbouring Thailand at the end of the war. In 2004 the US agreed to resettle 14,000 refugees in the US and since then many more refugees have left Laos in the hope of getting to America but were stranded in Thailand. In December 2006, over 400 Hmong surrendered to the authorities; they were among several groups of Hmong who have been living in the jungle as fugitives since their defeat by the communists in 1975.

In March 2009 a rail connection opened across the Mekong river, linking Thailand and Laos.

In January 2011, a stock market opened in the capital Vientiane; this has been seen as an experiment with capitalism.

In November 2012, plans were approved to build a massive dam at Xayaburi on the Mekong river to generate hydroelectricity. Opposition to the plan has been rasied by environmentalists and neighbouring Cambodia and Vietnam.

Legislature
Laos has a unicameral legislature, made up of 132 directly elected members who serve a five year term. The number of seats is to increased from 115 to 132 for the 2011 election because of the growing population.

National Assemby, (PO Box 332), 1 That-Luang Square, Vientiane, Laos. e-mail: nalib@pan-laos.net.la, URL: http://www.national-assembly.la
President of the National Assembly: Samane Vignaket

Cabinet (as at June 2013)
Prime Minister: Thongsing Thammavong (page 1524)
Deputy Prime Minister: Major Gen. Asang Laoly (page 1460)
Deputy Prime Minister, Minister of Foreign Affairs: Thongloun Sisoulit (page 1515)
Deputy Prime Minister, Standing Government Member: Somsavat Lengsavad (page 1462)
Deputy Prime Minister, Minister of National Defence: Maj.-Gen. Douangchay Phichit (page 1495)
Minister of Agriculture and Forestry: Vilayvanh Phomkhe
Minister of Public Works and Transport: Sommath Pholsena
Minister of Information, Tourism and Culture: Dr Bosengkham Vongdara
Minister of Labour and Social Welfare: Onechanh Thammawong
Minister of Industry and Commerce: Dr Nam Vignaket
Minister of Justice: Dr Chaleuan Yapaoher
Minister of Finance: Phouphet Khamphouvong
Minister of Education and Sports: Phankham Viphavanh
Minister of Public Health: Dr Eksavang Vongvichit
Minister of Public Security: Thongbanh Sengaphone
Minister of Energy and Mining: Soulivong Daravong
Minister of Planning and Investment: Somdy Douangdy
Minister of the Interior: Khampane Philavong
Minister of Science and Technology: Dr Boviengkham Vongdara
Minister of Natural Resources and Environment: Noulin Sinbandith
Minister of Post, Communications and Telecommunication: Hiem Phommachanh
Minister and Head of the Government Office: Sinavong Khoutphaytoune
Minister in the Government Office: Dr Bountiem Phissamay
Minister in the Government Office: Dr Douangsavat Souphanouvong
Minister in the Government Office: Khempheng Pholsena
Minister in the Government Office: Bounheuang Duangphachanh
Minister in the Government Office: Bounpheng Munphosay
Governor of the Bank of Lao People's Democratic Republic: Sompao Phaysith
President of the Government Inspection Authority, Head of the Anti-Corruption Agency: Bounthong Chitmany

---

Members of the Political Bureau
Khamtay Siphandone (Chairman), Gen. Choumaly Sayasone, Thongsing Thammavong, Gen. Osakan Thammatheva, Boungnang Vorachith, Gen. Sisavat Keobounphanh, Gen. Asang Laoly, Bouasone Bouphavanh, Thongloun Sisoulith, Maj.-Gen. Douangchay Phichit

Ministries
Office of the President, Sethathirath Road, Vientiane, Laos. Tel: +856 21 214210, fax: +856 21 214208
Office of the Prime Minister, Lane Xang Avenue, Vientiane, Laos. Tel: +856 21 213652, fax: +856 21 213560
Ministry of Finance, That Luang Road, Vientiane, Laos. Tel: +856 21 412401
Ministry of Foreign Affairs, 23 Singha Road, Vientiane, Laos. Tel: +856 21 413148, fax: +856 21 414009, e-mail: ict@mofa.gov.la, URL: http://www.mofa.gov.la
Ministry of Agriculture and Forestry, Lane Xang Avenue, Vientiane, Laos. Tel: +856 21 412340, URL: http://www.maf.gov.la
Ministry of Communications, Transport, Posts and Construction, Lane Xang Avenue, Vientiane, Laos. Tel: +856 21 412255
Ministry of Education and Sports, Lane Xang Avenue, Vientiane, Laos. Tel: +856 21 216004, URL: http://www.moe.gov.la
Ministry of Energy and Mining, PO Box 4708, Nong Bone Roa, Vientiane, Laos. Tel: +856 21 413012, fax: +856 21 413013, URL: http://www.laoenergy.gov.la
Ministry of Industry and Handicrafts, Phon Xay Road, PO Box 4107, Vientiane, Laos. Tel: +856 21 911342, fax: +856 21 412434, e-mail: moicpsi@yahoo.com, URL: http://www.moc.gov.la
Ministry of Information, Culture and Tourism, Thanon Setthathirat, Ban Xiengyeun Tha, Muang Chanthaburi, PO Box 122, Vientiane, Laos. Tel: +856 21 212406, fax: +856 21 212401, e-mail: email@mic.gov.la, URL: http://www.mic.gov.la
Ministry of the Interior, Nongbone Road, Vientiane, Laos. Tel: +856 21 414107
Ministry of Justice, Lane Xang Avenue, Vientiane, Laos. Tel: +856 21 414103
Ministry of Labour and Social Welfare, PO Box 7798, Samsenthai Road, Ban Anou, Chanthabouly District, Vientiane, Laos. Tel: +856 21 241280, fax: +856 21 241279, e-mail: ssowebmail@ssolao.gov.la, URL: http://www.ssolao.gov.la
Ministry of National Defence, Phone Kheng Road, Vientiane, Laos. Tel: +856 21 412801

LAOS

Ministry of Public Health, Simuong Road, Vientiane, Laos. Tel: +856 21 214000, e-mail: cabinet.fr@moh.gov.la, URL: http://www.moh.gov.la
Ministry of Trade, Phone Xay Road, Vientiane, Laos. Tel: +856 21 412000, URL: http://www.mot.gov.la
Ministry of Natural Resources and Environment, PO Box: 7864, Nahaidyo Road, Vientiane, Laos. Tel: +856 21 263799, e-mail: wrea@wrea.gov.la, URL: http://www.monre.gov.la/wrea
Ministry of Science and Technology, PO Box 2279, Vientiane, Laos. Tel: +856 21 213470, fax: +856 21 213472, e-mail: stea@stea.gov.la, URL: http://www.stea.gov.la
Ministry of Education and Sports, Lane Xang Avenue, Vientiane, Laos. Tel: +856 21 216004, URL: http://www.moe.gov.la
Ministry of Science and Technology, PO Box 2279, Vientiane, Laos. Tel: +856 21 213470, fax: +856 21 213472, e-mail: stea@stea.gov.la, URL: http://www.stea.gov.la

Political PartyPhak Pasason Pativat Lao (Lao People's Revolutionary Party)
Chairman of the Central Committee: Khamtay Siphandone
Chairman of Party and State Control Committee: Vonphet Xaykeuyachongtoua

Elections
The only legal political party is the Lao People's Revolutionary Party (LPRP), formerly the People's Party. Non-communist political groups are also banned. The age of suffrage is 18.

The most recent legislative elections were held in April 2011 and presidential in June 2011. Lt. Gen. Choummaly Sayasone was re-elected president. The LPRP won 128 seats in the legislative elections and independents four.

Diplomatic Representation
American Embassy, Box 114, Rue Bartholonie, Vientiane, Laos PDR. Tel: +856 21 212581, fax: +856 21 212584, URL: http://laos.usembassy.gov
Ambassador: Karen B. Stewart (page 1520)
British Embassy (all staff reside in Bangkok), PO Box 6626, Vientiante, Las, PDR.Tel: +856 21 413606, fax: +856 21 413607, URL: http://ukinthailand.fco.gov.uk/en
Ambassador: Asif Ahmad (page 1373)
Embassy of Laos, 2222 S Street NW, Washington, DC 20008, USA. Tel: +1 202 332 6416, fax: +1 202 332 4923, URL: http://www.laoembassy.com
Ambassador: Seng Soukhathivong
Permanent Mission of the Lao PDR, 317 East 51st Street, New York, NY 10022, USA. Tel: +1 212 832 2734, fax: +1 212 750 0039, URL: http://www.un.int/lao
Ambassador: Kanika Phommachanh

LEGAL SYSTEM

The legal system is based on traditional customs, French legal norms and procedures, and socialist practice. The constitution was designed to guarantee the independence of judges and prosecutors, but in practice the courts are subject to influence of government agencies. There are district courts, which hear original civil and criminal cases. Provincial courts are the first appellate courts, and the supreme court in Vientiane is the final court of appeal. Judges are appointed by the National Assembly Standing Committee.

Rising crime rates have overburdened Laos's under-funded and understaffed legal system. There is widespread corruption in the police force and in the judiciary. Prison conditions are harsh. The 1991 constitution provides for freedom of speech, assembly, and religion, although, in practice, organized political speech and activities are severely restricted, and religious freedom is also limited. The government does not respect respect the right to freedom of speech, the press, assembly, or privacy. Laos retains the death penalty. In 2001 parliament introduced the death penalty for possessing more than 500 grammes of heroin. However, there have been no executions since 1989.

LOCAL GOVERNMENT

Laos is divided into one municipality, Vientiane, and 16 provinces, Attapu, Bokeo, Bolikhamxai, Champasak, Houaphan, Khammouan, Louangnamtha, Louangphrabang, Oudomxai, Phongsali, Salavan, Savannakhet, Viangchan, Xaignabouli, Xekong, and Xiangkhoang.

AREA AND POPULATION

Area
The People's Democratic Republic of Laos is located in the north of Indochina with China and Vietnam at its northern and eastern borders, Cambodia in the south, and Myanmar and Thailand in the west. Its area is 236,800 sq. km stretching more than 1,700 km from north to south and between 100 km and 400 km east to west.

Although there is no direct access to the sea, there are many rivers, including a 1,865 km stretch of the Mekong defining its border with Myanmar and a major part of the border with Thailand. The two countries are connected by a bridge, the Friendship Bridge opened in 1994. Principal access to the sea is via Thailand. Stretches of the Mekong are navigable and provide alluvial deposits for some of the fertile plains. In all, water covers 6,000 sq. km of the country. About two-thirds of the country is mountainous with ranges from 200 to 2,820 metres high.

To view a map, consult http://www.un.org/Depts/Cartographic/map/profile/laos.pdf

The climate is tropical with a rainy season from May to November and a dry season from December to April.

Population
Laos's ethnically diverse population is divided between the lowland Lao ethnic group living in the Mekong flood plain (roughly 60 per cent), the closely related tribal Lao Tai inhabiting upland river valleys, the semi-nomadic mountain dwelling Lao Theung (mainly of Mon Khmer descent), and the Lao Sung in the high northern mountains who were nineteenth-century migrants from China, Burma and Tibet and whose principal sub-groups are the Hmong and the Yao. In the towns there are sizeable Vietnamese and Chinese communities.

Lao is the official language but minor ethnic languages are also spoken along with some French. French usage is declining and English is becoming more widespread.

The population in 2010 was estimated at 6.201 million, compared with 4.9 million in 1998. The annual growth rate for the period 2000-10 was 1.5 per cent. The population density is 26 persons per sq. km. An estimated 67 per cent of the population is rural. The largest towns and their estimated populations are: Vientiane, 725,000; Savannakhet, 120,000; Pakse, 65,000; Luang Prabang, 50,000.

Births, Marriages and Deaths
The estimated birth rate in 2010 was 22.8 live births per 1,000 population and 7.9 deaths per 1,000 population. The infant mortality rate is estimated to be 42 per 1,000 live births in 2010. Average life expectancy is 63 years (males 62 years, females 64 years). Healthy life expectancy was 53 years and 54 years respectively. The population is young: 35 per cent are aged 14 and under and 6 per cent of the population is aged over 60 years. The median age is 21 years. The total fertility rate is 2.7 children per woman. (Source: http://www.who.int, World Health Statistics 2012)

National Day
2 December: Proclamation of the Republic Day

EMPLOYMENT

The labour force was estimated to be around 3.7 million people in 2010. Most employment is in agriculture (mainly subsistence farming), 19 per cent of the workforce is employed in the industry and services sectors. In 2009 the estimated unemployment rate was 2.5 per cent.

BANKING AND FINANCE

Currency
The unit of currency is the new kip.

GDP / GNP, Inflation, National Debt
Laos is a poor country with an inferior infrastructure. The economy is dominated by subsistence agriculture and Laos relies on foreign assistance. When the communist government came into power in 1975 it imposed a Soviet-style system, re-installing state enterprises instead of the private sector. The economy faltered and reforms began to be put in place in the late 1980s. Growth has continued with support from the IMF. Tourism is a growing industry and the government is investing in infrastructure development. In order to raise the money needed to help the country develop both socially and economically, the government introduced VAT in 2007. A stock market opened in Ventiane in 2011. Laos has begun the accession process to the World Trade Organization; its membership has been accepted and ratification is expected to take place in 2013. The country remains dependent on both foreign aid and its agricultural sector.

The following table shows the make up of GDP in recent years. Figures are in million kips and are at 1990 market prices:

Sector	2008	2009	2010
Agriculture	13,572.3	14,355.2	15,669.9
Mining	4,507.6	3,616.1	4,027.1
Manufacturing	3,848.9	4,624.6	5,132.0
Electricity, water & gas	1,141.7	1,253.7	1,999.6
Construction	2,148.1	2,245.8	2,751.3
Trade	8,435.8	9,185.4	10,947.2
Transport & Communications	2,020.9	2,262.2	2,751.3
Finance	1,394.2	1,585.8	1,935.1
Public administration	1,995.3	2,159.9	2,438.3
Others	2,236.8	2,942.1	3,241.7
Total GDP	**44,777.8**	**47,225.3**	**54,282.6**

Source: Asian Development Bank

GDP grew at 7.6 per cent in 2009 and 7.9 per cent in 2010. Per capita GDP was 8,713,000 Kips in 2010. GDP was estimated to be US$8 billion in 2011.

Development in Laos depends on international aid. Prior to 1991 most foreign aid came from the Soviet Union and Eastern Europe. Since then, major aid has been supplied by the World Bank, the ADB, Australia and the EU. In the period 2006-10, foreign aid amounted to US$2.4 billion. It is hoping for US$3.9 billion for 2011-15. Laos's foreign debt in 2011 was an estimated US$5.5 billion.

Balance of Payments / Imports and Exports
The following table shows the value of imports and exports in recent years. Exports grew by 17.6 per cent in 2008 and imports 22.3 per cent. Exports fell by -3.6 per cent in 2009 but rose by 65.9 per cent in 2010. Import costs rose by 4.1 per cent in 2009 and by 41 per cent in 2010. Figures are in US$ million.

External Trade	2008	2009	2010
Exports, fob	1,085	1,053	1,746
Imports, cif	1,303	1,461	2,060
Trade balance	-218	-408	-314

Source: Asian Development Bank

Principal exports include wood products, coffee, garments and electricity. Principal imports include fuel, food, machinery and equipment and vehicles. Earnings in recent years from the principal exports are shown in the following table:

Exports in US$ million

Commodity	2005	2006	2007
Wood products	78.0	97.8	89.5
Garments	111.0	127.5	126.3
Electricity	99.0	101.2	84.3
Coffee	7.0	9.8	28.9

Source: Asian Development Bank

Major export partners (2010) are Thailand (US$689.7 million), China (US$510.9 million), and Vietnam (US$232.1 million). Major import partners are Thailand (US$2,348.4 million), China (US$524 million) and Vietnam (US$191 million).

Central Bank
Banque de la République Democratique Populaire Lao (Bank of the Lao PDR), PO Box 19, Rue Yonnet, Vientiane, Laos. Tel: +856 21 213109 / 21 213110, fax: +856 21 213108, e-mail: BOL@pan-laos.net.la
Governor: Phouphet Khamphouvong

MANUFACTURING, MINING AND SERVICES

Primary and Extractive Industries
Sizeable deposits of gemstones such as sapphire, zircon and amethyst are present. Other minerals are gold, iron ore, tin potash, limestone, silver, lead, zinc, copper, bauxite, coal and lignite. Use of these resources is dependent on infrastructure development and investment attraction, so at present these resources are under-exploited. Plans are underway to expand the mining of gold and copper. Figures for 2010 show that Laos produced 688,000 short tons of coal, consumed 442,000 short tons and exported 246,000 short tons.

Laos has no natural deposts of oil or gas and so imports what it needs. Figures for 2011 show that Laos imported 3,000 barrels of oil per day

Energy
Laos's chief industrial product is hydroelectricity from the Nam Ngum hydro power station 45 miles north of Vientiane, and the Xeset River dam in southern Laos. Laos's electricity generation in 2010 was 3.63 billion kWh and is one of the major industries. Annual electricity consumption in 2010 was 2.35 billion kWh. Laos exports elecricity primarily to Thailand. Electricity is available in urban areas but 80 per cent of domestic energy consumption is based on fuel wood. An estimated 300,000 ha of forest are lost annually, largely due to shifting cultivation and logging.

A new dam called Nam Theun 2 on the Nam Theun river came online in 2010. The dam was built with assistance from the Asian Development Bank (ADB) and the World BAnk, under the agreement with the two banks revenues from the sale of electricity from the dam must be spent on education, healthcare and infrastructure. Power generated by the dam would benefit Laos and Thailand. It is estimated that sales of electricity to Thailand would earn around US$2 billion a year for Laos. Around 6,000 people were displaced by the building of the resevoir for the dam and provision for re-settling them was also part of the deal.

Manufacturing
The manufacturing industry is minimal and is concentrated around Vientiane. It includes rice and saw mills and small factories producing textiles, agricultural tools, chemicals and animal feed, building materials, wood processing, detergent, garments, beer, soft drinks and cigarettes. Estimated figures for 2008 show that industry made up 34 per cent of GDP. The current state policy is for privatisation or joint ventures with private investors.

Tourism
Tourism is a big income earner for Laos. In 1997 Laos had 115,000 visitors. This number rose to 270,000 in 1999.

Agriculture
Laos has less than two million hectares of cultivatable land, of which an average of 1,250 sq. km are irrigated (2,169 sq. km in the rainy season, falling to 750 sq. km in the dry season). Most farming is subsistence rice cultivation. Subsidiary food crops include maize, cassava and sweet potatoes. The main cash crops are coffee, sugar, tobacco, cotton, groundnuts, fruit and vegetables. Opium production, long an important crop in the mountains, was legalised under state control in 1975 for sale to the pharmaceutical industry.

Agricultural Production in 2010

Produce	Int. $'000*	Tonnes
Rice, paddy	735,872	3,070,640
Vegetables fresh nes	165,225	876,800
Maize	104,354	1,020,880
Indigenous pigmeat	87,140	56,686
Indigenous buffalo meat	52,408	19,470
Coffee, green	50,710	47,200
Cassava	47,017	500,090

- continued		
Tobacco, unmanufactured	46,349	29,100
Indigenous cattle meat	40,239	14,896
Indigenous chicken meat	27,428	19,256
Groundnuts, with shell	21,920	50,945
Sugar can	21,506	818,675

* unofficial figures
Source: http://faostat.fao.org/site/339/default.aspx Food and Agriculture Organization of the United Nations, Food and Agricultural commodities production

Recent figures show that Laos had an estimated 1 million buffaloes, 850,000 cattle, 1.3 million pigs and 8 million poultry.

Forests cover about 54 per cent of the country and comprise a wide variety of commercial species suitable for production of sawed timber, plywood, parquet and furniture. Laos has a great variety of hardwoods, including teak and rosewood.

River fish are an important source of nutrition. Fish farming has been developed since the 1980s and the reservoir formed behind the Nam Ngum dam has become an important new fishery. Total catch is an estimated 31,000 tonnes a year.

COMMUNICATIONS AND TRANSPORT

Travel Requirements
Citizens of the USA, Canada, Australia and the EU require a passport valid for six months and a visa. Other nationals should contact the embassy to check visa requirements. A 15-day, non extendible visa is now available for nationals arriving at Vientiane airport, Luang Prabang airport and Friendship Bridge. Other visas should be applied for through the embassy.

National Airlines
Lao Aviation International, URL: http://www.lao-aviation.com

Railways
In January 1996 work began on a 30 km railway line between Vientiane and the town of Nong Khai on the Thai border. This was due to be completed in 1998 but was postponed in February 1998 because of a severe downfall in the Thai economy. The development of a comprehensive railway network was also announced by the Government in 1997 and a contract awarded to a Thai company, in March 2009 the first stage of the rail link opened over the Mekong river connecting Laos and Thailand.

Roads
There are some 17,000 miles roads, of which some 6,000 miles are paved. However, they are often impassable during the rainy season from May to September. Vehicles are driven on the right.

Waterways
Laos is a landlocked country. The Mekong River and its tributaries provide some 2,800 miles of navigable waterways. Ferry services run on the river.

HEALTH

In 2008, Laos spent approximately 3.7 per cent of its total budget on healthcare (down from 5.1 per cent in 2000), accounting for 17.6 per cent of all healthcare spending. Total expenditure on healthcare equated to 4.0 per cent of the country's GDP. Per capita expenditure on health was approximately US$34, compared with US$10 in 2000. External resources provide 16.1 per cent of the total expenditure and private (mostly out-of-pocket) expenditure 82.4 per cent.

Figures for 2000-10 show that there are 1,614 physicians (2.7 per 10,000 population) and 5,724 nurses and midwives (9.7 per 10,000 population). There are 12 hospital beds per 10,000 population.

Life expectancy averaged 63 years in 2009. The infant mortality rate in 2008 was 48 per 1,000 live births. The child mortality rate (under 5 years) was 61 per 1,000 live births. The main causes of childhood mortality are: neonatal causes (30.9 per cent), diarrhoea (16.9 per cent), pneumonia (17.6 per cent), measles (10.9 per cent), malaria (0.2 per cent) and HIV/AIDs (0.1 per cent). Vaccination rates are low: in 2007 only 40 per cent of children were immunized against measles.

According to the latest WHO figures, in 2008 approximately 72 per cent of the urban population and 51 per cent of the rural population had access to improved drinking water. In the same year, 86 per cent of the urban population and 38 per cent of the rural population had access to improved sanitation. (Source: WHO)

EDUCATION

Education is compulsory between the ages of 7 and 15. In 2007 13 per cent of young children were enrolled in pre-school education, 84 per cent of girls and 88 per cent of boys were enrolled in primary school. The same year 33 per cent of girls and 38 per cent of boys were enrolled in secondary school and 12 per cent of the population of age were in tertiary education. In 2005 the literacy rate was estimated to be 72.7 per cent. By gender this was 82.5 per cent for males, 63.2 per cent for females.

Figures for 2007 show that 15.8 per cent of government spending or 3.2 per cent of GDP went on education. (source: UNESCO)

LATVIA

RELIGION

The 1991 constitution of the Lao PDR explicitly protects the freedom to practice any and all religions. 60 per cent of the population is Buddhist, some 30 per cent of the population follow animist religions and Christians make up around 1.5 per cent.

Laos has a religious tolerance rating of 5 on a scale of 1 to 10 (10 is most freedom). (Source: World Religion Database)

COMMUNICATIONS AND MEDIA

The government exercises strict control over the media and all media is government owned. Distorting party policies and spreading false rumours are criminal offences.

Newspapers
Pasaxon, (The People) party newspaper, URL: http://www.pasaxon.org.la
Aloun Mai (New Dawn) party theoretical journal
Kong Thap Pot Poi Pasason Lao, (Lao People's Liberation Army) army newspaper
Vientiane Times English language, URL: http://www.vientianetimes.org.la/
Vientiane Mai (New Vientiane) daily for Vientiane city and province, URL: http://www.vientianemai.net
Le Renovateur, French state paper, URL: http://www.lerenovateur.org.la
Khaosan Pathet Lao, News agency producing daily bulletins in Lao, French and English, URL: http://www.kpl.net.la/

Broadcasting
All media, both print and broadcast are government owned. In addition to the state national channels, some 15 regional stations exist. Laos Television 3 is a joint venture with a Thai company.

Lao National Radio, URL: http://www.lnr.org.la

Telecommunications
In 2008 there were an estimated 97,000 main telephone lines in use. The network applies mainly to urban areas but access is improving. Radiotelephones are needed to communicate with remote regions. In 2008 there were an estimated 2 million cellular telephones.

Recent figures show that Laos has around 130,000 internet users.

ENVIRONMENT

Deforestation is a major problem. In September 2000 there were also major floods in the Mekong River basin. The majority of the population does not have access to potable water.

Laos is a party to the following international agreements: Biodiversity, Climate Change, Climate Change-Kyoto Protocol, Desertification, Endangered Species, Environmental Modification, Law of the Sea, and Ozone Layer Protection.

According to the EIA, in 2010, Laos's emissions from the consumption of fossil fuels totalled 1.09 million metric tons of carbon dioxide, down from 1.24 million metric tons in 2009.

SPACE PROGRAMME

In 2009, China announced it was to build a communications satellite for Laos and a satellite control centre.

LATVIA
Republic of Latvia
Latvijas Republika

Capital: Riga (Population estimate, 2010: 706,500)

Head of State: Andris Berzins (President) (page 1388)

National Flag: Three horizontal bands fesswise, maroon, white, (half width) and maroon.

CONSTITUTION AND GOVERNMENT

Constitution
The country became independent after the First World War and was recognised by the Soviet government. However, in 1940, as a result of the secret pact between Hitler and Stalin, it was occupied and subsequently annexed by the Soviet Union. With the advent of *glasnost* Latvia, like that of the other Baltic states, began to receive international attention, and in May 1989 the country's Supreme Soviet declared the republic sovereign with the right to veto USSR law.

In October 1989 the Latvian Popular Front endorsed a radical programme, including a commitment to complete independence from the Soviet Union, the establishment of a multi-party democracy and a market economy. In January 1990 the Latvian Supreme Soviet abolished the clauses in Article 6 of its constitution guaranteeing the leading role of the Communist Party. The flag, state emblem, and national anthem of independent Latvia were restored to official use in February 1990. The Latvian Popular Front won a majority position in multiparty local and republican elections in December 1989 and March 1990 respectively. In April 1990 the Latvian Communist Party split into Pro-Moscow and independent parties. Latvia's Supreme Soviet declared Latvia independent from the Soviet Union on 4 May 1990, allowing for a transition period for negotiations.

Latvia's 1922 legislation was reinstated, as was the name Republic of Latvia. Full independence was renewed on 21 August 1991 and the authority of the Satversme was proclaimed. The Satversme was fully re-instituted as of 6 July 1993, when the 5th Saeima was elected. The Latvian head of state is elected by the Saeima for a period of three years. H.E. Guntis Ulmanis was elected president of the Republic of Latvia on 7 July 1993 and re-elected for a second term on 18 June 1996. H.E. Mrs Vaira Vike-Freiberga was elected president on 17 June 1999. Latvia applied to become a member of the European Union and NATO.

The present Constitution is based on that of 1922. Government consists of two tiers: the Supreme Council or Parliament and the Council of Ministers. Executive authority is vested in the Prime Minister and Council of Ministers. The Supreme Council (a unicameral parliament or *saeima* comprising 100 seats) is elected by direct proportional elections by citizens of 18 years and over. It appoints the President of State who in turn appoints the Prime Minister. The Council of Ministers (the executive body) is selected by the Prime Minister and approved by the Supreme Council. Legislation is usually initiated by parliamentary deputies.

To consult the constitution, please visit: http://www.satv.tiesa.gov.lv/?lang=2&mid=8.

International Relations
The relationship between Latvia and Russia has been troubled in recent years. During the Soviet years, many Russians moved to Latvia and Latvian speakers made up just 59 per cent of the population. Latvia brought in a citizenship law in 1998 whereby anyone applying for citizenship has to pay a fee and take a Latvian language and history exam; by 2005, 100,000 non-citizens had been naturalised. Russia accused Latvia of human rights violations against the ethnic Russian population, a charge Latvia denied. In 2007 an outstanding border agreement was signed between Latvia and Russia, and it was hoped that relations would improve.

Latvia enjoys a close relationship with her Nordic neighbours as well as with neighbouring Estonia and Lithuania.

In November 2002, Latvia was formally invited to join NATO, and became a member in March 2004. In December 2002 Latvia was formally invited to join the EU; a referendum was held in September 2003 and 67 per cent voted in favour. Latvia became a member on 1 May 2004. In June 2005, the parliament ratified the draft EU constitution.

Recent Events
In December 2007 the increasingly unpopular prime minister, Aigars Kalvitis, announced his resignation and that of his entire cabinet. The interior minister, Ivars Godmanis, was nominated as prime minister on 14 December. He was sworn into office with a reshuffled cabinet on 20 December.

In February 2009, Prime Minister Ivars Godmanis resigned after the leaders of the TP and the ZZS withdrew their support. Valdis Dombrovskis of the New Era party (JL) was named as prime minister and named a coalition government on 5 March.

In June 2009, as a consequence of the global banking crisis, Latvia's central bank had to spend approximately €1 billion to support the lat currency and prevent devaluation.

The government of Valdis Dombrovskis lost its majority in March 2010 when the coalition split following disagreements over tough austerity measures. Elections were held in October 2010.

In a surprise result, Andris Berzins was elected president by parliament in June 2010, defeating the incumbent President Zatlers by 53 votes to 47. President Zatlers had been expected to win the vote but recently accused parliamentarians of not being hard enough on corruption and called for a referendum on the dissolution of parliament. Parliament had blocked the search of a politician's home by the anti-corruption task force. A snap general election was held in September 2011, less than a year after the previous election. The pro-Russian SC party won most votes but did not form a government. A coalition was formed led by Valdis Dombrovskis of the Unity party.

In February 2012 a referendum was held on giving Russian joint official language status, it was rejected.

In January 2013 legislation was passed finalising Latvia's bid to become a member of the Eurozone as of 1 January 2014. The European Commission approved its membership in June 2013 as did the European Central Bank, although the ECB warned that high foreign deposits in banks could be a risk to future financial stability. The European Parliament also backed the membership bid.

Legislature

Latvia has a unicameral legislature, the Saeima, which has 100 directly elected members who serve a four year term.

Saeima, Parliament of Latvia, 11 Jekaba Stree, LV 1811, Riga, Latvia. E-mail: saeima@saeima.lv, URL: http://www.saeima.lv

Speaker: Gundars Daudze
Deputy Speaker: Vineta Muizniece
Deputy Speaker: Karina Petersone

Cabinet (as at June 2013)

Prime Minister: Valdis Dombrovskis (page 1416)
Deputy Prime Minister, Minister of Defence: Artis Pabriks (page 1491)
Minister for Foreign Affairs: Edgars Rinkēvičs (page 1503)
Minister of Transport: Alvis Ronis (page 1505)
Minister of Finance: Andris Vilks (page 1531)
Minister of Education and Science: Roberts Kilis
Minister of Economics: Daniels Pavluts (page 1493)
Minister of Environment and Regional Development: Edmund Sprudzs
Minister of Agriculture: Laimdota Straujuma
Minister of Welfare: Ilze Vinkele
Minister of Justice: vacant
Minister of Transport: Aivis Ronis (page 1505)
Minister of Culture: Zaneta Jaunzeme-Grende
Minister of Health: Ingrida Circene
Minister of the Interior: Rihards Kozlovskis (page 1458)

Ministries

Office of the President, Pils laukums 3, Riga LV-1900, Latvia. Tel: +371 6709 2106, fax: +371 6709 2157, e-mail: chancery@president.lv, URL: http://www.president.lv
Office of the Prime Minister, Brivibas bulv. 36, Riga LV-1520, Latvia. Tel: +371 6708 2934, fax: +371 6728 0469, e-mail: vk@mk.gov.lv, URL: http://www.mk.gov.lv
Ministry of Finance, Smilsu iela 1, Riga LV-1919, Latvia. Tel: +371 6709 5405, fax: +371 6709 5503, e-mail: info@fm.gov.lv, URL: http://www.fm.gov.lv
Ministry of Foreign Affairs, K.Valdemāra iela 3, Riga LV-1395, Latvia. Tel: +371 6701 6201, fax: +371 6782 8121, e-mail: mfa.cha@mfa.gov.lv, URL: http://www.am.gov.lv
Ministry of Agriculture, Republikas laukums 2, Riga LV-1981, Latvia. Tel: +371 6702 7010, fax: +371 6702 7250, e-mail: webmaster@zm.gov.lv, URL: http://www.zm.gov.lv
Ministry of Children and Family Affairs, Basteja bulv. 14, Riga LV-1050, Latvia. Tel: +371 6735 6497, fax: +371 6735 6464, e-mail: pasts@bm.gov.lv, URL: http://www.bm.gov.lv
Ministry of Culture, K Valdemāra iela 11A, Riga LV-1364, Latvia. Tel: +371 6722 4772, fax: +371 6722 7916, e-mail: culture@com.latnet.lv, URL: http://www.culture.lv
Ministry of Defence, K Valdemāra iela 10, Riga LV-1473, Latvia. Tel: +371 6721 0124, fax: +371 6783 0236, Latvia. e-mail: kanceleja@mod.lv, URL: http://www.mod.lv
Ministry of the Economy, Brivibas bulv. 55, Riga LV-1519, Latvia. Tel: +371 6701 3101, fax: +371 6728 0882, e-mail: em@lem.gov.lv, URL: http://www.lem.gov.lv
Ministry of Education and Science, Valnu iela 2, Riga LV-1050, Latvia. Tel: +371 6722 6209, fax: +371 6722 1195, e-mail: izm@izm.gov.lv, URL: http://www.izm.gov.lv/en/default.htm
Ministry of Electronic Government Affairs, K Valdemāra iela 33, Riga LV-1010, Latvia. Tel: +371 6711 4730, fax: +371 6711 4727, e-mail: pasts@eps.gov.lv, URL: http://www.eps.gov.lv
Ministry of the Environment, Peldu iela 25, Riga LV-1494, Latvia. Tel: +371 6702 6533, fax: +371 6782 0442, e-mail: pasts@varam.gov.lv, URL: http://www.varam.gov.lv
Ministry of Health, Brivibas bulv. 72, Riga LV-1011, Latvia. Tel: +371 6787 6000, fax: +371 6787 6002, e-mail: vm@vm.gov.lv, URL: http://www.vm.gov.lv
Ministry of the Interior, Raina bulv. 6, Riga LV-1533, Latvia. Tel: +371 6721 9210, fax: +371 6721 2255, e-mail: pc@iem.gov.lv, URL: http://www.iem.gov.lv
Ministry of Justice, Brivibas bulv. 34, Riga LV-1536, Latvia. Tel: +371 6728 2607, fax: +371 6733 1920, e-mail: justice@latnet.lv, URL: http://www.jm.gov.lv
Ministry of Regional Development and Local Governments, Lacplesa iela 27, Riga LV-1010, Latvia. Tel: +371 6777 0401, e-mail: maris.kucinskis@raplm.gov.lv, URL: http://www.raplm.gov.lv
Ministry of Society Integration Affairs, Elizabetes iela 20, 2nd Floor, Riga LV-1050, Latvia. Tel: +371 6736 5332, fax: +371 6736 5335, e-mail: iumsils@integracija.gov.lv, URL: http://www.integracija.gov.lv
Ministry of Transport, Gogola iela 2, Riga LV-1743, Latvia. Tel: +371 6722 6922, fax: +371 6721 7180, e-mail: satmin@sam.gov.lv, URL: http://www.sam.gov.lv
Ministry of Welfare, Skolas iela 28, Riga LV-1331, Latvia. Tel: +371 6702 1600, fax: +371 6727 6445, e-mail: lm@lm.gov.lv, URL: http://www.lm.gov.lv

Political Parties

Tautas partija (TP, People's Party),URL: http://www.tautapartija.lv
Zalo un Zemnieku savieniba (Green and Farmers Union), e-mail: info@zp.lv, URL: http://www.zp.lv
Jaunais Laiks (New Era), URL: http://www.jaunaislaiks.lv/
Latvijas cels (LC, Latvia's Way), URL: http://www.lc.lv
Tevzemei un brivibai (TB/LNNK For Fatherland and Freedom), URL: http://www.tb-lnnk.lv
Latvijas socialdemokratu apvieniba (LSD, Latvian Social Democratic Alliance)
Par Cilveka tiesibam vienotal Latvija (For Human Rights in a United Latvia)
Latvijas Pirma Partija, (Latvia's First Party), URL: http://www.lpp.lv
Visu Latvijai (VL, All for Latvia), URL: http://www.visulatvijai.lv;
Saskanas Centrs (SC, Harmony Centre), URL: http://www.saskanascentrs.lv

Elections

Parliamentary elections took place on 2 October 2010. The coalition block Unity (made up of the New Era Party, the Civic Union and the Society for Other Politics) was the largest grouping. Unity and its former coalition partner, the Greens and Farmers Union, had a small overall majority in parliament. The leader of the New Era Party and the Unity grouping, Vlaldis Dombrovskis, formed a government which was approved by parliament on 3 November. Following a political crisis, a snap election was called in September 2011. The pro-Russian SC won most votes, the ZRP came second. The centre-right Unity party led by the Prime Minister Valdis Dombrovskis did poorly.

The most recent presidential election was held in June 2011. Andris Berzins was elected president by parliament in the second round of voting, defeating the incumbent President Zatlers by 53 votes to 47. He took office in July 2011.

Latvia uses proportional representation as its electoral system. Suffrage is universal for citizens over 18 years. The president is elected by the Saeima.

Diplomatic Representation

American Embassy, Raina Boulevard 7, LV-1510 Riga, Latvia. Tel: +371 703 6200, fax: +371 782 0047, URL: http://riga.usembassy.gov
Ambassador: Mark A. Pekala
British Embassy, 5 J. Alunana Street, Riga, Latvia. Tel: +371 733 8126, fax: +371 733 8132, e-mail: british.embassy@apollo.lv, URL: http://www.ukinlatvia.fco.gov.uk
Ambassador: Sarah Cowley (page 1410)
Embassy of the Republic of Latvia, 2306 Massachusetts Ave., NW, Washington DC 20008, USA. Tel: +1 (202) 328-2840, fax: +1 (202) 328-2860, e-mail: embassy.usa@mfa.gov.lv, URL: http://www.latvia-usa.org
Ambassador: Andris Razans
Embassy of the Republic of Latvia, 45 Nottingham Place, London, W1M 3FE, United Kingdom. Tel: +44 (0)20 7312 0040, fax: +44 (0)20 7312 0042, e-mail: latemb@dircon.co.uk, URL: http://www.mfa.gov.lv/en/london/embassy
Ambassador: Andris Teikmanis (page 1524)
Permanent Mission of the Republic of Latvia to the United Nations, 333 East 50th Street, New York, NY 10022-7901, USA. Tel: +1 212 838 8877, fax +1 212 838 8920, URL: http://www.un.int/wcm/content/site/latvia
Ambassador Extraordinary and Plenipotentiary: H.E. Normans Penke

LEGAL SYSTEM

There are 34 district and city courts in Latvia; most civil cases are heard by one judge, whilst criminal cases and certain civil cases are heard by a panel of one professional judge and two lay judges. There are five regional courts in Latvia which hear civil and criminal cases and hear appellate cases that have been adjudicated by district (city) courts as the courts of first instance. A sixth regional court covers administrative cases for all five regions.

The Supreme Court is the highest appellate court and its judgments are final. The Supreme Court is comprised of a senate and two chambers, civil and criminal. Three departments compose the senate: civil, criminal and administrative. Judges to the Supreme Court are appointed at the recommendation of the Chairman of the Supreme Court whereas all other judges are appointed by the Saeima at the recommendation of the Minister of Justice.

The Constitutional Court exists as a separate court in Latvia, and reviews the compliance of laws to the Constitution, as well as other matters under its jurisdiction. The Constitutional Court can declare laws or other acts invalid. The Constitutional Court is independent in functional and organizational aspects. It has seven judges, approved by the Saeima.

The government respects the human rights of its citizens, but there have been instances of serious police abuse of detainees, and judicial corruption. Prison conditions are poor, and there are some limits on freedom of speech.

Latvia is the only country in the EU that retains the death penalty though only for murder committed during wartime. The last executions took place in 1996, though death sentences continued to be handed down until 1998. In 1999, the death penalty in time of peace was abolished through ratification of Protocol No. 6 to the European Convention on Human Rights. In 2002 Latvia signed Protocol No. 13 to ECHR, concerning the abolition of the death penalty under all circumstances. It was finally abolished for all circumstances in 2012.

Supreme Court of the Republic of Latvia, URL: http://www.at.gov.lv/index.php
Chief Justice: Ivars Bickovics
Latvian Human Rights Centre, URL: http://www.humanrights.org.lv/html/

LOCAL GOVERNMENT

There are two tiers of local authorities: regional, which are appointed, and county, which are elected for four-year terms. To stand for local elections, you must be 21 years old and have resided in a locality for 12 months. Each city has its own local government. Latvia is divided into 26 districts (rajons) and seven republican municipalities. The rajons are: Aizkraukles Rajons, Aluksnes Rajons, Balvu Rajons, Bauskas Rajons, Cesu Rajons, Daugavpils Rajons, Dobeles Rajons, Gulbenes Rajons, Jekabpils Rajons, Jelgavas Rajons, Kraslavas Rajons, Kuldigas Rajons, Liepajas Rajons, Limbazu Rajons, Ludzas Rajons, Madonas Rajons, Ogres Rajons, Preilu Rajons, Rezeknes Rajons, Rigas Rajons, Saldus Rajons, Talsu Rajons, Tukuma Rajons, Valkas Rajons, Valmieras Rajons and Ventspils Rajons. The city muncipalities are: Daugavpils, Jelgava, Jurmala, Liepaja, Rezekne, Riga and Ventspils. On the other level there are 486 rural municipalities, 70 town municipalities and 7 city municpalities.The most recent municipal elections were held in 2009.

LATVIA

AREA AND POPULATION

Area
Latvia lies at the eastern end of the Baltic on the Gulf of Riga. It has borders with Estonia, Lithuania, the Republic of Belarus, and the Russian Federation. The country covers an area of 64,600 sq. km. The country is flat and forested, with many lakes in the south. The River Daugava (1030 km) enters the Baltic Sea in Riga Bay. The climate is maritime with wet winters.

To view a map, consult http://www.un.org/Depts/Cartographic/map/profile/latvia.pdf

Population
Latvia had an estimated population in 2011 of 2,070,371. The population is in decline: average annual growth for the period 2000-10 was -0.6 per cent. The median age of the population is 40 years. Approximately 14 per cent of the population is aged under 15 years and 23 per cent over the age of 60. It is estimated that 68 per cent of the population lives in urban areas. The largest towns and their approximate populations (2011) are: Riga, 747,000; Daugavpils, 101,100; Liepaja, 87,000; Jelgava, 64,500; Jurmala, 56,000; Ventspils, 38,100 and Rezekne, 44,000.

Latvia is made up of various ethnic groups - Latvians, 59 per cent; Russians, 29 per cent; Belarusians, 3.8 per cent; 2.6 per cent Ukrainians; 2.45 Poles; other 3.7 per cent. During the Soviet period, many Latvians were deported and Russians were brought in. This has led to a low percentage of ethnic Latvians and has contributed to some ethnic unrest. Latvia has a high proportion of residents who do not have citizenship, mainly Russians who came to Latvia during the Soviet era. They have the right to apply for citizenship but must pass a Latvian language and history exam.

The official language is Latvian, which, apart from Lithuanian, is the only Baltic language still to be spoken but it is the first language of only 57 per cent of the population. Russian is widely spoken. In 2002 parliament voted to change an election law that required prospective parliamentary candidates to be Latvian speakers. Legislation was brought in 2004 to reduce the use of Russian in education and during the final three years of schooling, all classes must be taught in Latvian.

Births, Marriages, Deaths
Since 1991 the annual death rate has exceeded the annual birth rate. Estimated figures for 2010 put the birth rate at 10.7 births per thousand population and the death rate at 14.6 deaths per thousand population. The total fertility rate for women was 1.5 in 2010. Infant mortality was 8 per 1,000 population. The adult death rate was 300 per 1,000 for males and 115 per 1,000 for females. Average life expectancy at birth in 2009 was 67 years for males and 77 years for females. Healthy life expectancy was 59 years for males and 68 years for females. (Source: http://www.who.int, World Health Statistics 2012)

Public Holidays 2014
1 January: New Year's Day
18 April: Good Friday
21 April: Easter Monday
1 May: Labour Day
4 May: Declaration of Independence Day
23-24 June: Midsummer Festival (Ligo and Jā)
18 November: Independence Day
25 December: Christmas Day
26 December: St Stephen's Day
31 December: New Year's Eve

EMPLOYMENT

In 2010, the workforce was estimated to be 1,180.000 people of whom 18.4 per cent were unemployed. Figures for 2011 put the work force at 1,006,700 with 166,200 unemployed.

In 2006, Latvia refused to introduce a law banning discrimination at work on sexual orientation grounds, even though agreeing to introduce the law on employment discrimination was a condition for Latvia's accession to the European Union in 2004.

Total Employment by Economic Activity

Occupation	2008
Agriculture, hunting & forestry	87,300
Fishing	1,800
Mining & quarrying	2,800
Manufacturing	171,000
Electricity, gas & water supply	21,300
Construction	125,500
Wholesale & retail trade, repairs	186,600
Hotels & restaurants	30,400
Transport, storage & communications	105,800
Financial intermediation	19,600
Real estate, renting & business activities	78,100
Public admin. & defence; compulsory social security	56,600
Education	90,400
Health & social work	54,700
Other community, social & personal service activities	57,400
Households with employed persons	4,400
Total	1,124,100

Source: Copyright © International Labour Organization (ILO Dept. of Statistics, http://laborsta.ilo.org)

BANKING AND FINANCE

Currency
The unit of currency is the Lats of 100 santims. The financial centre is Riga.

Latvia wishes to adopt the Euro as its national currency but this is unlikely to happen before 2014.

GDP/GNP, Inflation, National Debt
Figures for 2006 put GDP at 11,171,693 thousand Lats giving a per capita figure of L4,883. GDP rose to 13,957,410 thousand Lats in 2007 giving a per capita figure of L6,132. The annual growth rate was estimated at -4.6 per cent in 2008, this fell to -18 per cent in 2009. GDP was estimated at US$20 billion in 2010, with a growth rate of -0.3 per cent, Growth returned in 2011: GDP was estimated at $27 billion in 2011 with a growth rate of over 5 per cent. Per capita income was estimated to be US$10,500 in 2010.

The share in GDP of the service and manufacturing sectors is increasing with the agricultural sector decreasing. Recent figures show that the services sector contributes over 70 per cent of GDP (of which retail and wholesale trade was 17 per cent), industry 14 per cent, and agriculture 3 per cent.

Inflation was judged to have risen to 15 per cent in 2008 before falling to around 4 per cent in 2009 due to falling demand for goods. It was estimated to be 2.5 per cent in 2010.

In 2005 the national debt was estimated at just over 12 per cent of GDP - one of the lowest in the EU. In recent years the Latvian economy in common with many countries has been suffering the consequences of the global economic downturn. As a result in December 2008 Latvia signed a 27 month Stand by Arrangement with the IMF, the EC amongst others for an assistance package of around €.5 billion. The package was designed to restore competitiveness through economic adjustment and fiscal prudence. In June 2009 the central bank spent nearly €1 billion to support the lat currency, the following August the government, trade union and employers agreed to a tranche of cuts in public spending to avoid bankruptcy the IMF released further monies of the rescue loans. In October the government agreed to cut the budget deficit in 2010 so that it could meet targets imposed by the EU for the rescue loans.

Foreign Investment
In order to promote foreign trade Latvia has set up special economic zones. Ventspils is a Free Port, and Liepaja and Rezekne are Special Economic Zones. Foreign investment continues to be hindered by corruption. Foreign direct investment was estimated to be US$12 billion in 2011.
Latvian Development Agency, URL: http://www.liaa.gov.lv

Balance of Payments / Imports and Exports
In 2010 exports were worth US$8.7 billion. Main exports were: wood/wood products 19 per cent; metals 14 per cent; textiles 7 per cent; machines 11 per cent; food and food products 7.0 per cent. Imports cost US$11.5 billion. Main imports were machinery 16.5 per cent; vehicles, 7 per cent; mineral products, 15 per cent; chemicals, 11.0 per cent; food and food products 16.3 per cent. Main trading partners in 2010 were Estonia, Lithuania, Russia, Germany, Poland, Sweden and Finland.

Latvia became a member of the World Trade Organisation in 1999 and the EU in 2004.

Central Bank
Bank of Latvia (Latvijas Banka), 2A Kr Valdemara iela, LV-1050 Riga, Latvia. Tel: +371 7022300, fax: +371 7022420, e-mail: info@bank.lv, URL: http://www.bank.lv
Governor: Ilmars Rimsevics (page 1503)

Chamber of Commerce
Latvian Chamber of Commerce and Industry, e-mail: chamber@sun.lcc.org.lv, URL: http://www.chamber.lv/pub/

MANUFACTURING, MINING AND SERVICES

Primary and Extractive Industries
Peat is the only combustible material found in Latvia. 450-550 thousand tons of peat are produced a year. Deposits of dolomite, limestone, gypsum, clay, gravel and sand are used for the production of building materials.

Energy
Towards the end of 2000 Latvia announced that it would sell licences for exploration and development for any offshore oil reserves. In 2011, the government was looking into the possibilities of exploring for shale gas. Territorial waters are thought to contain up to 300 million barrels of oil. A small amount of coal is imported from Poland, (140,000 short tons in 2010). Due to public demand in August 2000 the Latvian government withdrew plans to privatise the state electricity company, Latvenergo (URL: http://www.latvenergo.lv).

In 2011, Latvia consumed an estimated 44,000 barrels per day of oil, all imported. Also in 2011, 56 billion cubic feet of natural gas was consumed, all imported. In 2010, 6.41 billion kWh of electricty was produced and 6.56 billion kWh was consumed. Total installed capacity was 2.17 GWe.

Total primary energy production was 0.034 quadrillion Btu in 2009 and consumption was 0.178 quadrillion Btu. (Source: EIA)

In February 2006 Latvia, Lithuania and Estonia signed an agreement to build a nuclear power station in Lithuania, however a referendum held in 2012 made the proposed project uncertain. Their respective state-owned power companies would have equal shares. The Baltic states want to avoid too much reliance on Russia for their energy supplies.

Manufacturing

Latvia's industry produces a comparatively limited range of items. Local natural resources provide the raw materials for only 40 per cent of industrial output. About 25 per cent of products required in the country are imported, and the same proportion of output is exported. The manufacture of food and beverages is the largest manufacturing sector followed by the manufacture of wooden products. Other large products of manufacturing are machinery and electronics, textiles, metal and paper. Figures for 2006 put manufacturing earnings at 1,159.5 million lats and 1,331.0 million lats in 2007. Despite the global economic crisis, manufacturing in Latvia showed relatively strong growth in 2011, with the chemical, pharmaceutical and non-mineral minerals and fabricated metal products doing well. The following table shows provisional figures for the production value of selected manufactured goods in 2011.

Production Value of Selected Manufactured Goods

Goods	Thousand LVL
Food products	926,711
Wood & cork products excl. furniture	1,142,706
Basic metals	369,413
Non-Metallic mineral products	269,802
Beverages	195,462
Chemicals and chemical products	146,703
Rubber and plastic products	114,227
Furniture	112,584
Machinery & equipment n.e.c.	100,919

Source: Central Statistical Bureau, Latvia

Service Industries

Tourism is an expanding area. In 2011, there were approximate 1 overseas million visitors to Latvia. Most visitors were from Russia, Germany and Lithuania.

Agriculture

In the early 1990s Latvia began a programme of privatising farm collectives. Climatic conditions and the soil mean Latvia is suitable for cattle breeding and dairy farming but this potential has not been exploited. Cattle herds have substantially decreased - from 537,000 in 1995 to 381,000 in 2011. There were 375,000 pigs, 4,418,000 poultry, 80,000 sheep and 13,000 goats in 2011. In 1997 Latvian meat production only covered 48 per cent of consumption with pig breeding being the largest sector in meat production. Beef and poultry production continues to decline. Milk production covers 97 per cent of domestic demand but Latvian milk processors cannot compete with neighbouring countries in terms of cost or technology. Twelve per cent of Latvia's water consumption is for agricultural use.

Agricultural Production in 2010

Produce	Int. $'000*	Tonnes
Cow milk, whole, fresh	227,779	830,918
Wheat	138,122	1,035,400
Indigenous pigmeat	76,098	49,503
Indigenous cattle meat	68,352	25,303
Rapeseed	48,981	226,300
Potatoes	46,246	484,000
Hen eggs, in shell	37,314	44,990
Indigenous chicken meat	31,479	22,100
Barley	12,779	228,400
Cabbages and other brassicas	8,982	63,023
Carrots and turnips	8,560	34,307
Rye	4,393	70,200

* unofficial figures

Source: http://faostat.fao.org/site/339/default.aspx Food and Agriculture Organization of the United Nations, Food and Agricultural commodities production

In 2011 the total catch was 155,900 tonnes. Almost 20 per cent of the Latvian catch comes from the Baltic where in 2002, 208 vessels operate, while another 91 vessels fish in other waters. On-board processing takes place on 31 vessels. In addition, there are 13 fish processing plants on land. Around 70 per cent of the catch is exported.

Forestry

Forests cover 42 per cent of the total land area of Latvia. It is permitted to harvest 8.3 million m³ of timber per year although this figure has not been reached yet so there is room for investment and development. The timber industry is very important and contributed 29.7 per cent of exports in 1997. Most of Latvia's exported timber is destined for the UK.

COMMUNICATIONS AND TRANSPORT

Travel Requirements

Citizens of the USA, Canada, Australia and the EU require a passport valid for three months beyond the length of stay but do not need a visa for stays of up to 90 days. EU subjects holding a national Identity Card do not require a passport. Other nationals should contact the embassy to check visa requirements. All travelers must have a valid insurance policy, covering medical expenses while in Latvia. Repatriation costs, including funeral and disposition of remains costs, have to be covered by the policy. In addition, upon entering or exiting the country, travellers must declare cash in excess of 10,000 euros to Latvian customs.

Latvia is a signatory to the Schengen Agreement; with a Schengen visa, a visitor can travel freely throughout the Schengen zone, and there are few border stops and checks. See http://www.eurovisa.info/SchengenCountries.htm for details.

National Airlines
Air Baltic (ABC), URL: http://www.airbaltic.com

International Airports
The main international airport, Riga, handled over 5 million passengers in 2011.
Riga International Airport, URL: http://www.riga-airport.com

Railways

There are 2,331 km of track which carry around 45 per cent of goods transported within Latvia. The capital Riga is connected by the rail system to all the larger towns in Latvia. The use of the railway for cargo, especially through the ports, is growing although passenger carriage is declining. Cargo carried by rail was 49 million tonnes in 2000. Passenger traffic declined from 42.3 million journeys in 1995 to 18.2 million in 2000. Rail links run between Latvia and Moscow and Saint Petersburg, Russia. Latvia and Minsk, Belarus and Latvia and Vilnius, Lithuania. International passenger traffic was approximately 365,000. The infrastructure is currently being modernised.

Roads

Latvia has a dense road network with over 73,000 km of roads. Approximately 40 per cent of goods are transported on the country's 1,500 km of main highways. Vehicles are driven on the right. Riga has a tram system.

Ports and Harbours

The main ports are Riga, Ventspils and Liepaja. Russia oil exports via Ventspils(http:http://www.portofventspils.lv/) ceased in 2002. Ferries run between Riga and Stockholm, Sweden; Ventspils and Karlshamn, Sweden; Riga and Lübeck, Germany.

HEALTH

In 2009, Latvia spent approximately 9.2 per cent of its total budget on healthcare (up from 8.7 per cent in 2000), accounting for 61.6 per cent of all healthcare spending. Private expenditure accounts for the rest, almost all of which is out-of-pocket expenditure. Total expenditure on healthcare equated to 6.6 per cent of the country's GDP. Per capita expenditure on health was approximately US$756, compared with US$197 in 2000.

Figures for 2005-10 show that there are 6,753 physicians (30 per 10,000 population), 10,929 nurses and midwives (48.4 per 10,000 population) and 1,510 dentistry personnel. There are 64 hospital beds per 10,000 population.

The infant mortality rate in 2010 was 8 per 1,000 live births. The child mortality rate (under 5 years) was 10 per 1,000 live births. The main causes of deaths in the under-fives were birth asphyxia 17 per cent, congenital anomalies 35 per cent, pneumonia 9 per cent, prematurity 5 per cent, and injuries 7 per cent. Average life expectancy was 66 years.

According to the latest WHO figures, in 2009 approximately 99 per cent of the population had access to improved drinking water. In 2008, 82 per cent of the urban population and 71 per cent of the rural population had access to improved sanitation. (Source: http://www.who.int, World Health Statistics 2012)

EDUCATION

Schooling for the first nine years of education is compulsory and is provided free by the state, although private schools and universities exist. The primary enrolment rate in 2003 was 86 per cent for males and 85 per cent for females. Figures for the academic year 2011-12 show that a total of 440,980 pupils were enrolled in education, 90,859 at preschool establishments, 218,442 at general schools, 34,638 at vocational schools and 97,041 in higher education institutions and colleges. There are 2,610 institutions engaged in research and development. The study of Latvian is compulsory but there are schools where pupils are taught in Russian and schools for other ethnic minorities. (source: Central Statistical Bureau, Latvia)

In 2006 13.4 per cent of government spending or 5.1 per cent of GDP went on education. The adult literacy rate is 99.7 per cent. (Source: UNESCO)

RELIGION

The main religions in Latvia are Evangelic Lutheran, Roman Catholic and Russian Orthodox Christian churches, but many other beliefs are also represented including small Muslim, Jewish and Hindu communities.

Latvia has a religious liberty rating of 7 on a scale of 1 to 10 (10 is most freedom). (Source: World Religion Database)

COMMUNICATIONS AND MEDIA

There is general freedom of expression. Libel may lead to prison terms.

Newspapers
Approximately 140 titles are published including:
Diena, URL: http://www.diena.lv
Neatkariga Rita Avize, URL: http://www.nra.lv
Vesti Segodnja, Riga. (Russian) URL: http://www.delfi.lv/
Telegraf (Russian language) URL: http://www.telegraf.lv
Latvijas Avize, (daily tabloid), URL: http://www.la.lv

Broadcasting
Latvian State Television broadcasts on two channels. (LTV1 and LTV7). There are several independent TV stations, cable and satellite is also available with domestic and foreign broadcasts available. Latvian State radio broadcasts, in Latvian and in Russian, on four networks and there are also numerous private radio stations.
Latvian Television(LTV), URL: http://www.itv.lv/lat

Latvian Independent Television (LNT), URL: http://www.lnt.lv
Latvian Radio, URL: http://www.radio.org.lv

Telecommunications
The telecommunications sector has been open to competition since 2003. Landlines are decreasing in number whereas mobile subscribership has increased and now stands at more than 100 phones per 100 population. In 2011 there were an estimated 550,000 mainline telephones in use and 2.3 mobile telephones.

In 2011 there were an estimated 1.5 million internet users.

ENVIRONMENT

Latvia is a party to the following international environment agreements: Air Pollution, Air Pollution-Persistent Organic Pollutants, Biodiversity, Climate Change, Climate Change-Kyoto Protocol, Desertification, Endangered Species, Hazardous Wastes, Law of the Sea, Ozone Layer Protection, Ship Pollution and Wetlands.

In 2009, Latvia's emissions from the consumption of fossil fuels totalled 8.70 million metric tons of carbon dioxide, this had risen to 9.07 million metric tons by 2010. (Source: EIA)

SPACE PROGRAMME

Latvia was expected to launch its first satellite, the Venta-1, in 2012.

LEBANON
Lebanese Republic
Al Jumhuriyah al Lubnaniyah

Capital: Beirut (Population estimate, 2010: 1,900,000)

Head of State: General Michel Suleiman (page 1521)

National Flag: Fesswise stripes. Red, white, red. Each red stripe half the width of the white, which bears a cedar tree in the centre

CONSTITUTION AND GOVERNMENT

Constitution
Lebanon declared independence in November 1941 and full autonomy was granted in 1944. A series of constitutional amendments were introduced in 1990 when the civil war came to an end. A government of National Reconciliation came into being in December 1990, which dissolved all militias in April 1991. Elections were held in 1992. Israeli troops had occupied South Lebanon since 14 March 1978, but left on 24 May 2000 after 22 years of occupation.

The incorporation of the 1990 Taif Agreement into the Lebanese constitution effectively transferred executive power from the President to the Council of Ministers. The President, in consultation with members of parliament, appoints the Prime Minister and is responsible for the promulgation and execution of laws enacted by the National Assembly. The position of Speaker was also strengthened when the term of office was lengthened from one to four years.

According to a National Covenant, the President must be a Maronite Christian, the Prime Minister a Sunni Muslim and the Speaker of the House, a Shi'a Muslim. All other ministers' religions should parallel their level of representation in the National Assembly. The current President, Emile Lahoud, was elected in October 1998 for a six-year term. Veteran politician Selim El-Hoss was named President of the Council of Ministers on 2 December 1998.

The Constitution gives legislative power to the single-chamber, the 128-seat National Assembly. The Assembly is composed of an equal number of Christians and Muslims. Their terms of office are four years. The presidential term was six years, non-renewable, until 2004 when the assembly approved an increase allowing Emile Lahoud to stand for a further three years.

To consult the constitution, please visit: http://www.lp.gov.lb/SecondaryAr.Aspx?id=12

International Relations
Diplomatic relations were established with Syria for the first time in October 2008. Syria and Lebanon stated that they would respect each other's sovereignty and independence. Relations between the two countries had been strained since the 2005 assassination of former Lebanese PM Rafik Hariri, which many Lebanese blamed on Syria.

Recent Events
In February 2005 the former prime minister, Rafik Hariri, was murdered. Several governments alleged Syrian involvement in the murder. His death sparked wide-spread anti-government and Syrian protests and led to several cabinet resignations including that of prime minister designate, Omar Karami. Mr Karami was reappointed prime minister on 10 March, but the opposition rejected his call to join his government. He resigned again in April and the moderate, pro-Syrian Najib Mikata was named his successor. Syria claimed to have withdrawn all its troops by the end of April. Legislative elections were held in June. The anti-Syrian alliance won control of parliament and nominated Hariri Ali Fouad Siniora as Prime Minister. In September 2005 four generals were charged in connection with the assassination of Rafik Hariri. In June 2006 the UN investigation into the murder was extended for another twelve months. Serge Brammertz, the UN investigator leading the probe, linked the assassination of Mr Hariri with 14 other attacks on anti-Syrian figures.

On 12th July 2006, the Lebanon-based Hezbollah group captured two Israeli soldiers, and demanded the release of prisoners in exchange. The Israelis, holding the Lebanese government responsible for the capture of the soldiers, imposed a sea blockade on Lebanon and launched jet strikes on the airport, a TV station and some forty other Hezbollah targets. Hezbollah responded with rocket fire at the Israeli town of Nahariya. Israel urged the Security Council to enforce resolutions calling for the Lebanese government to disarm militias. Air and sea attacks continued for several days with high civilian casualties. The UN's emergency relief co-ordinator stated that the large scale destruction of southern Beirut and its indiscriminate nature made it a violation of humanitarian law. On Sunday 30th July, 54 Lebanese, including 30 children, were killed when the Israeli's bombed the village of Qana. The Israelis agreed to a 48 hour ceasefire to allow for an investigation and an evacuation by civilians. On the night of the 1st August, Israeli soldiers attacked the town of Baalbek, sixty miles inside the Lebanese border, capturing five Hezbollah militants and killing ten people. Hezbollah rockets were reported to have reached 70 km inside Israel. The Israeli Prime Minister said that there would be no ceasefire until an international force of peacekeepers were deployed in Southern Lebanon.

A ceasefire came into force on the 14th August. During the conflict, around 1,109 Lebanese civilians died, together with 28 Lebanese soldiers. Figures for Hezbollah fatalities differ widely. 43 Israeli civilians were killed and 116 soldiers, according to official sources. Many were also displaced. By the beginning of October, some 5,000 UN forces were deployed in southern Lebanon, together with 10,000 Lebanese soldiers. Hezbollah continued to hold the two captured soldiers.

The Shi'a and pro-Lahoud ministers resigned between 11 and 13 November 2006, after the failure of talks to form a national unity government, in which Hezbollah had been demanding more seats. In December, thousands of opposition supporters demonstrated in Beirut to demand the resignation of the government, and the following month Hezbollah-led opposition increased pressure on the government by calling a general strike. In May 2007, the Lebanese army began the siege of the Nahr al-Bared refugee camp near Tripoli following clashes with militants there; 40,000 people left before the army took over the camp in early September, and over 300 people were killed.

Antoine Ghanim, an anti-Syrian Lebanese MP, was killed in a car bomb attack in a suburb of Beirut on 19th September 2007, less than a week before MPs were due to elect a new President. Five other well-known anti-Syrian Lebanese people have been killed since the assassination of the former Prime Minister, Rafik Hariri, in 2005. The Syrian government denied involvement in the killings. In December, Gen Francois al-Hajj, the army's head of operations, was assassinated.

On 15 January 2008, a bomb blast targeted a US embassy vehicle in a northern suburb of Beirut. Four people were killed, and several others injured. The attack came at a time of political crisis in Lebanon with rival pro-Syrian and pro-Western parties deadlocked over efforts to elect a president. The power struggle continued through the spring.

On the 9th May, Hezbollah militants seized most of western Beirut in a third day of fighting between opposition and government supporters, and at least 11 people were killed. Lebanon's governing coalition said it was a coup aimed at restoring the influence of Syria and Iran. The following day, Hezbollah agreed to withdraw its gunmen from Beirut after the Lebanese army revoked two key government measures, but vowed to continue civil disobedience until its demands were met. Over the week of fighting, 65 people were killed. At peace talks in Doha, Qatar, the rival Lebanese leaders agreed on steps to end the political deadlock; the Hezbollah-led opposition, backed by Syria and Iran, will have the power of veto in a new cabinet of national unity. Under the terms of the Doha Agreement, the Western-backed ruling majority has16 cabinet seats and chooses the prime minister; the Syrian-backed opposition has 11 cabinet seats and the power of veto, and three cabinet seats are nominated by the President. The use of weapons in internal conflicts is to be banned and opposition protest camps in Beirut are to be removed.

On the 24th May, following 19 failed attempts to elect a head of state, Lebanon's parliament elected army commander General Michel Suleiman as president. President Suleiman appointed the pro-Western incumbent Fouad Siniora to lead a new unity government, but the opposition were not happy with this choice and said that it was against the spirit of the Doha accord. A new cabinet was approved by parliament on 13th August.

Following talks in Paris in July 2008, Syria and Lebanon agreed to re-open embassies. The two countries had not had diplomatic relations at ambassadorial level since they became independent in the 1940s, and relations had worsened following the forced withdrawal of Syrian troops from Lebanon in mid-2005 after Rafik Hariri's assassination.

In July 2008, the bodies of the two Israeli soldiers, whose capture sparked the 2006 war with Lebanon, were returned to Israel, in exchange for five Hezbollah militants and the bodies of 200 Lebanese and Palestinian fighters. A senior Hezbollah official said that the soldiers had been captured alive, but were injured in the cross-border attack and subsequently died. One of the returned militants was Samir Qantar, jailed in 1979 for killing a four-year-old Israeli girl, her father and a policeman.

Parliamentary elections took place on the 8th June 2009. The pro-Western coalition held on to its majority, winning 71 of the 128 seats. Hezbollah won 58 seats, and accepted the result. Saad Hariri, son of assassinated former Prime Minister Rafik Hariri, was nominated as premier after elections. After ten weeks of wrangling, he presented his proposed national unity cabinet unilaterally on the 7th September, having failed to agree the line-up with the opposition bloc. The leader of Hezbollah criticised the move, and Saad Hariri stepped aside, but was later re-appointed by the President. A unity government was finally appointed on 9 November.

In January 2011, ministers from Hezbollah and its allies the Amal Movement and the Change and Reform party resigned from the government causing it to collapse. Najib Mikati was appointed prime minister and charged with forming a new government. This took several months leaving Lebanon in a power vacuum. A new government was eventually announced in June. The new government is made up of two groups of ministers: 18 were nominated by Hezbollah and its allies (Amal Movement, Syrian Social Nationalist Party, Free Patriotic Movement, Marada Movement and the Tashnag Party), and 11 were nominated by either the president, the prime minister or the Druze leader Walid Jumblatt.

In June 2011, the UN-backed Special Tribunal of Lebanon issued four arrest warrants over the murder in 2005 of the former prime minister Rafik Hariri. The Hezbollah leader Hassan Nasrallh rejected the indictments for four of its members.

In May 2012, two anti-Syrian clerics were shot dead. At least two people were killed and others injured in subsequent clashes between pro- and anti-Syrian groups.

In October 2012 a car bomb killed Wissam al-Hassan, the head of the intelligence branch of the Internal Security Forces. Demonstrations were held following his funeral calling for the resignation of Prime Minister Mikati. Figures from the opposition blamed Syria for the attack.

In October 2012, street fighting broke out between supporters and opponents of the Syrian president. Around 160,000 Syrian refugees had fled to Lebanon.

In March 2013, Syria fired rockets from helicopters into Northern Lebanon. Syria accuses militants of crossing the border between the two countries.

Also in March 2013 Prime Minister Najib Mikati announced his and his government's resignation after it was unable to agree the procedure for forthcoming elections (due in June) as well as trying to overcome tensions created by violence and economic problems resulting from the conflict in neighbouring Syria. On April 6 Sunni politician Tamam Salam was nominated as the new Prime Minister.

Legislature
The legislature is unicameral. The National Assembly is made up of 128 directly elected members who serve a four year term. Half the members are Christian and half Muslim.
National Assembly, (Majlis al-Nawab), Place de l'Etoile, Beirut, Lebanon. Tel: +961 (0)1 982140, URL: http://www.lp.gov.lb

Cabinet (as at June 2013)
Prime Minister-designate: Tamam Salam (page 1507)
Caretaker Council of Ministers
Prime Minister (resigned): Mohammad Mikati (page 1477)
Deputy Prime Minister: Samir Mokel
Minister of State: Karwan Kheireddine
Minister of State for Parliamentary Affairs: Nicolas Fattoush
Minister of State: Ali Kanso
Minister of Public Health: Ali Hassan Khalil
Minister of Public Works and Transport: Gharzi Aridi
Minister of Finance: Mohammad Safadi
Minister of State for Administrative Development: Mohammad Fneish
Minister of Social Affairs: Wael Abu Faour
Minister of Energy and Water: Gebran Bassil
Minister of Agriculture: Hussein Hajj Hassan
Minister of Labour: Salim Jreissati
Minister of Tourism: Fadi Abboud
Minister of State: Salim Karam
Minister of Displaced Persons: Alaa El-Din Terro
Minister of State: Ahmad Karami
Minister of Environment: Nazem Khoury
Minister of Defence: Fayez Ghosn
Minister of Justice: Shakib Cortbawi
Minister of Foreign Affairs and Immigrants: Adnan Mansour
Minister of Economy and Trade: Nicolas Nahhas
Minister of Industry: Warij Sabonjian
Minister of the Interior and Municipal Affairs: Marwen Charbel
Minister of Information: Walid Daouk
Minister of State: Panos Manjian
Miinister of Education: Hassan Diab
Minister of Culture: Gaby Layyoun
Minister of Telecommunications: Nicolas Sehnawi
Minister of Sports and Youth: Faysal Karami

Ministries
Prime Minister's Office, Council of Ministers, Al-Kasr Al-Houkoumi, Al-Sanayeh, Beirut, Lebanon. Tel: +961 1 814777 / 862006

Ministry of Finance, MOF Building, Riad Solh Square, Rue des Banques, Beirut, Lebanon. Tel: +961 1 642758/9 / 642720-1, fax: +961 1 642762 / 397789, e-mail: infocenter@finance.gov.lb, URL: http://www.finance.gov.lb
Ministry of Foreign Affairs and Immigrants, Palais Bustors, Ashrafieh, Beirut, Lebanon.Tel: +961 1 334400, fax: +961 1 321845, e-mail: ministry@foreign.gov.lb, URL: http://www.emigrants.gov.lb/
Ministry of Interior and Municipal Affairs, Pres de l'ancienne Serial, Beirut, Lebanon. Tel: +961 1 754200, fax: +961 1 751622, fax: +961 1 751622, e-mail: ministry@interior.gov.lb, URL:http://www.interior.gov.lb
Ministry of Economy and Trade, The Ministry of Economy & Trade Bldg. Artois Street, Hamra, Beirut, Lebanon. Tel: +961 1 340503-5, fax: +961 1 354640, URL: http://www.economy.gov.lb
Ministry of Public Health, Al Zarif, Kireidieh Building, Beirut, Lebanon. Tel: +961 1 625701, fax: +961 1 615712, URL: http://www.public-health.gov.lb
Ministry of National Defence, Al Yarzeh, Beirut, Lebanon. Tel: +961 1 429963, fax: +961 5 457920
Ministry of Water and Energy, Immeuble Electricité du Liban, Rue du Fleuve, Beirut, Lebanon. Tel: +961 1 444700-1 / 490007 / 425134 / 580647
Ministry of Environment, Independent Treasury for Allocation, 6th Floor, Al Adlieh, Beirut, Lebanon. Tel: +961 4 522222 / 525888, fax: +961 4 525444 / 418910, URL: http://www.moe.gov.lb
Ministry of Tourism, Al Hamra Street, Face de la Banque Centrale, Beirut, Lebanon. Tel: +961 1 344290 / 350901, fax: +961 1 738590 / 340945, e-mail: mot@lebanon-tourism.gov.lb, URL: http://www.lebanon-tourism.gov.lb
Ministry of Industry, Sami Soleh Av. , Facing Adlieh, Badaro, Beirut, Lebanon. Tel: +961 1 423338 / 427006 / 427046, fax: +961 1 427112, URL: http://www.industry.gov.lb/
Ministry of Agriculture, Le Plant Vert Building, Beirut, Lebanon. Tel: +961 5 455613, fax: +961 5 455475, e-mail: ministry@agriculture.gov.lb, URL: http://www.agriculture.gov.lb
Ministry of Justice, Palais de la Justice, Rue de la Musée, Al Mathaf, Beirut, Lebanon. Tel: +961 1 422956, fax: +961 1 611142, e-mail: info@justice.gov.lb, URL: http://www.justice.gov.lb
Ministry of Information, Al Hamra Street, Face Banque Centrale, Beirut, Lebanon. Tel: +961 1 343459, fax: +961 1 744311, URL:http://www.mna-leb.gov.lb
Ministry of Public Works and Transport, Al-Fayadieh, near Defence School, Beirut, Lebanon. Tel+ 961 5 456481 / 371640, fax: +961 5 458434, URL:http://www.public-works.gov.lb
Ministry of Displaced People, Damour, Beirut, Lebanon. Tel: +961 1 366129 / 366110, Fax: +961 1 366213, URL: http://www.ministryofdisplaced/gov.lb
Ministry of National Education, UNESCO, Beirut, Lebanon. Tel: +961 1 790537, fax: +961 1 790551, URL: http://www.higher-edu.gov.lb
Ministry of Professional and Technical Affairs, Al-Mazraa Street, Freiha Building, Barbour Area, Beirut, Lebanon. Tel: +961 1 864689 / 371447-8 / 371408 / 867175
Ministry of Housing and Co-operatives, Bir Hassan, Raoucheh Shopping Centre, Beirut, Lebanon. Tel: +961 1 645940 / 200280-1 / 200277
Ministry of Employment, Ghobeiry-Mocharafieh, Beirut, Lebanon. Tel: +961 1 556811, fax: +961 1 556832
Ministry of Post and Telecommunications, Sami-el-Solh Street, Beirut, Lebanon. Tel: +961 1 826001-2 / 867696-7, fax: +961 1 888310, e-mail: webmaster@mpt.gov.lb, URL: http://www.mpt.gov.lb

Political Parties
Amal Movement (AM); Change and Reform (CR); Future Movement (FM); Hezbollah; Lebanese Forces (LF); National Struggle Front (NSF; formerly the Progressive Socialist Party - PSP).

Elections
In the September 2000 general election Prime Minister Selim El-Hoss was beaten by Rafik al-Hariri, who was previously prime minister in 1991. Rafik al-Hariri was a political opponent of the president, Emile Lahoud. In April 2003 Mr al-Hariri resigned with his council of ministers. He was re-appointed with a reshuffled cabinet later in the month but resigned again in October 2004. His murder in 2005 sparked widespread protests.

Parliamentary elections took place in May/June 2005, when an anti-Syrian alliance took control of parliament, choosing Hariri Ali Fouad Siniora as Prime Minister Designate. The presidential election was due in October 2004, but following changes to the constitution was rescheduled for September 2007. The President is elected by MPs rather than by popular vote. On 25 May 2008 parliament finally elected General Michel Suleiman as president who then appointed Fouad Siniora to the post of prime minister.

The most recent parliamentary elections took place on 8th June 2009. The pro-Western coalition held on to its majority, winning 71 of the 128 seats. Hezbollah won 58 seats, and accepted the result. The main coalition parties are: Future (Sunni); Progressive Socialists (Druze); Lebanese Forces (Maronite); Phalange (Maronite).

Diplomatic Representation
British Embassy, Embassies Complex Army Street, Zkak Al-Blat, Serail Hill PO Box 11-471 Beirut, Lebanon. Tel: +961 4 417007 / 405070, fax: +961 1 990420 , e-mail: britemb@cyberia.net.lb, URL: http://ukinlebanon.fco.gov.uk
Ambassador: Tom Fletcher CMG (page 1425)
US Embassy, P.O. Box 70-840, Antelias, Beirut, Lebanon. Tel: +961 4 543600 / 542600, fax: +961 544136, e-mail: www@usembassy.com.lb, URL: http://lebanon.usembassy.gov
Ambassador: Maura Connelly
Lebanese Embassy, 21 Kensington Palace Gardens, London W8 4QM, United Kingdom. Tel: +44 (0)20 7229 7265, fax: +44 (0)20 7243 1699, e-mail: emb.leb@btinternet.com; http://www.lebaneseembassy.org.uk
Ambassador: Inaam Osseiran (page 1490)
Lebanese Embassy, 2560, 28th Street NW, Washington, DC 20008, USA. Tel: +1 202 939 6320, fax: +1 202 939 6324, email: info@lebanonembassyus.org, URL: http://www.lebanonembassy.org
Ambassador: Antoine Chedid (page 1403)

LEBANON

Permanent Mission of Lebanon to the UN, 866 UN Plaza, Suite 355-5460, New York, NY 10017, USA.URL: http://www.un.int/wcm/content/site/lebanon
Permanent Representative: Dr Nawaf Salam

LEGAL SYSTEM

The judicial system, largely modelled after the French judicial system, is based on Lebanon's 1926 constitution (with amendments incorporated in 1990), and incorporates a mixture of Ottoman law, Canon law, Napoleonic code and civil laws.

There are four main court systems: the Judicial court system (kadaa'dli), the administrative court systems (Majlis al-Shura), the military court system and the religious court system.

There are three court levels of general jurisdiction in the judicial court system: Courts of First Instance, Courts of Appeal, and the Cassation Court. Each court is also divided into chambers. Both the courts of appeal and the cassation court are divided into chambers of one presiding and two associate judges.

The administrative court system is made up of administrative tribunals and the State Consultative Council (Majlis Shura al-Dawla). Their jurisdiction covers matters arising from administrative decisions issued by the state or state insitutions. Decisions may be appealed to the State Consultative Council which acts as a Cassation level court.

The military court system is composed of a permanent military court and a military court of cassation, both presided over by sole judges. Their jurisdiction is limited to arms and amunitions, crimes against national security, crimes involving either the military or a military facility.

The religious court system is made up of the court systems of recognised denominations relating to Christianity, Islam and Judaism. Jurisdiction is limited to personal status and family law matters.

There are also specialized tribunals including the Arbitral Labour Council and the the Judicial Council.

The human rights situation continues to be poor in Lebanon. Hezbollah hold sway over parts of the country, and militants carry out unlawful killings. Arrests by security forces can be arbitrary, and there have been cases of torture. There are long delays in the court system, and prison conditions are harsh. The government violates citizens' privacy rights, and there have been recent restrictions on freedoms of speech and press. There is official corruption. Freedom of movement for unregistered refugees is limited and there is widespread discrimination against Palestinian refugees. Lebanon retains the death penalty; after a five year moratorium Lebanon resumed capital punishment by executing three convicted murderers in 2004. A death sentence has to be approved by the president, prime minister and justice minister.

LOCAL GOVERNMENT

Lebanon is divided for administrative purposes into six areas of Beirut, South Lebanon, North Lebanon, Bekaa, Nabatiyah and Mount Lebanon. Each area has its own administrative government headed by a governor. Two new governorates (Aakar and Baalbek-Hermel) have been legislated for but are not yet created. In September 2001 South Lebanon held its first municipal elections for nearly 40 years. The most recent municipal elections were held in 2010.

AREA AND POPULATION

Area
Lebanon is situated in the Middle East, bounded by the Mediterranean to the west, Israel to the south, and Syria to the east and north. The total area of the country is 10,450 square km (4,500 square miles). The terrain is varied. There are two mountain ranges, the Mount Lebanon and the Anti Lebanon which run parallel to each other the length of the country. The Mount Lebanon range runs along the coast line and reaches an elevation of 3,000 metres. The Bekaa valley runs behind the mountain range. This fertile plateau is the northern end of the Great Rift Valley.

Along the coast the climate is mild with hot, dry summers and wet winters. There is often snow on the mountains.

To view a map, visit http://www.lib.utexas.edu/maps/cia08/lebanon_sm_2008.gif

Population
The estimated total population was 4.228 million in 2010 with an estimated annual growth rate of 1.2 per cent for the period 2000-10. This figure includes around 300,000 Palestinian refugees. Approximately 30 per cent of the population live in Beirut. Other major towns include Tripoli, with a population of 160,000, Zahle and Sidon. Some 87 per cent of the population is urban. Population density per sq. km. is 306.

The majority of the population is Arab. Approximately 4 per cent is Armenian and other nationalities make up 1 per cent. The official language is Arabic. French, Armenian and English are also spoken.

Births, Marriages, Deaths
The crude birth rate was estimated at 15.4 per 1,000 in 2010 and the death rate at 6.1 per 1,000. The average life expectancy at birth in 2009 was 71 years for males and 77 years for females. Health life expectancy was 60 years and 64 years respectively. Approximately 25

per cent of the population was aged under 15 years and 10 per cent over 60 years. The median age was 29. The total fertility rate in 2010 was 1.8 per woman. (Source: http://www.who.int, World Health Statistics 2012)

Public Holidays 2014
1 January: New Year's Day
14 January: Mawlid al-Nabi (Birthday of the Prophet)*
9 February: Feast of St. Maroun
18 April: Good Friday
21 April: Easter Monday
1 May: Labour Day
6 May: Martyr Day
29 July: Eid al-Fitr (End of Ramadan)*
15 August: Assumption Day
1 November: All Saints
5 October: Eid Al Adha (Feast of the Sacrifice)*
25 October: Muharram (Islamic New Year)*
22 November: Independence Day
13 December: Ashura
25 December: Christmas Day
*Muslim holidays follow the Islamic Lunary Calendar and take place some 10-11 days earlier each year on the Christian calendar.

EMPLOYMENT

Trade, restaurants and hotels form the country's largest employment sector accounting for over 60 per cent of employment. The industrial sector accounts for around 30 per cent of employment and agriculture, forestry and fishing accounts for around 8 per cent. Figures for 2010 put the workforce at 1,480,000, the unemployment rate in 2007 was put at 9.0 per cent.

BANKING AND FINANCE

Currency
Currency is issued by the Banque du Liban, the Lebanese central bank which commenced operations on 1 April 1964. The unit is the Lebanese pound (LL) which contains 100 piastres, it is currently pegged to the US dollar at a rate of around LL1500 = US$1.00

GDP/GNP, Inflation, National Debt
Lebanon's economy has recovered from the 1975-90 civil war which damaged Lebanon's economic infrastructure and output. Lebanon's economy is now largely free-market. Its growth sectors include banking, health and tourism. The economy has again suffered in recent years because of political uncertainty. Current instability in Lebanon and its neighbours adversely affected the economy in 2011.

Estimated figures for 2009 put GDP at US$32.0 billion a per capita figure of US$12,900. Growth for 2009 was estimated to be 7.0 per cent. In 2010, GDP was estimated at US$39 billion with a growth rate of 7.5 per cent. Per capita GDP was estimated to be US$10,000. Growth was estimated to have fallen to 1.5 per cent in 2011.

Inflation was estimated at 5 per cent in 2011.

Figures for 2010 estimated the total debt burden to be US$52 billion.

Balance of Payments / Imports and Exports
Figures for 2010 show that exports earned US$4 billion and imports cost US$17 billion.

The major export markets are Switzerland, the UAE and France. Main products for export are jewellry, metals and metal products, prepared foodstuffs, vegetable products, wood pulp and recycled paper, chemical products, mechanical and electrical appliances and textiles. 51 per cent of Lebanon's imports come from the European Union and 12 per cent from Arab countries. Main imported goods are machinery, mineral products, metallic equipment, electrical equipment, raw material, chemical products, prepared foodstuffs, vehicle and transport equipment.

Central Bank
Banque du Liban, PO Box 11-5544, Masraf Lubnan Street, Lebanon. Tel: +961 1 341230, fax: +961 1 747600, e-mail: bdlit@bdl.gov.lb, URL: http://www.bdl.gov.lb
Governor: Riad Salamé (page 1507)

Chambers of Commerce and Trade Organisations
Trade Information Centre, URL: http://www.economy.gov.lb
The Federation of the Chambers of Commerce, Industry and Agriculture in Lebanon, URL: http://www.ccib.org.lb

MANUFACTURING, MINING AND SERVICES

Primary and Extractive Industries
Lebanon has few natural resources. There are deposits of iron ore, coal, lignite, phosphates, asphalt and salt, all of which are mined for domestic use only.

Lebanon currently imports all of its oil requirements, amounting to an estimated 88,000 barrels per day in 2011. The Kuwait Petroleum Corporation is a key supplier. In 2006, Lebanon and Qatar Petroleum International looked at the possibility of building a refinery in Lebanon, with a capacity of up to 200,000 barrels per day; this was postponed due to renewed tensions with Israel.

Lebanon has no known gas reserves of its own. In February 2006, Syria agreed to supply 1.5 million cubic feet per day from late 2007, but her own growing requirements and limited production have led Lebanon to seek supplementary supplies from Egypt. Lebanon announced plans to construct a second pipeline from Syria to the Zahrani power station in the south of Lebanon in April 2006. These plans were put on hold following the 2006 conflict with Israel. Figures for 2010 show that Lebannon imports five billion cubic feet.

Figures for 2009 show that Lebannon imported 323,000 short tons of coal.

Energy
Lebanon's state-owned power utility is Electricité du Liban (EdL), and operates under the Ministry of Energy and Water Resources and the Ministry of Finance. EdL is in charge of the majority of power generation, transmission, and distribution, and generates over 90 per cent of Lebanon's electricity. Electricité du Liban is contributing to the public deficit, and its reform is being debated in parliament. Figures for 2010 show that Lebanon generated 14.81 billion kWh of electricity and consumed 14.19 billion kWh.

Manufacturing
Lebanon's industrial base has traditionally been small-scale. Prior to the civil war, the largest industrial employer was the food processing industry, followed by the well-developed textile industry. These combined to account for 44 per cent of industrial output, with furniture and wood-working factories accounting for 29 per cent, and mechanical industries accounting for 7 per cent. The remainder of industrial output was produced by the cement, ceramics, pharmaceutical and plastic industries. The civil war inflicted severe damage on the industrial sector in terms of human and capital resources. By 1985, one-quarter of the country's productive capacity had been destroyed, with 600-700 factories closed. Those that remained functioning did so at only a quarter of pre-war capacity.

In the past, this sector has performed well. According to the General Directorate for Industry, 459 new enterprises were established in 1996, up from 408 in 1994, employing around 3,400 people and requiring the approximate investment of LL101 billion ($65 million). The industrial sector reported a 3.7 per cent increase for new factories in 1998 compared with the same period in 1996. By 2001 industries performing well included cement, textiles and food processing as before, and also oil refining, wood and furniture manufacture, metal fabrication and mineral and chemical products.

Services Industries
In the years following the end of the civil war, most of the visitors to Lebanon were expatriates visiting their families. The thousands of Lebanese expatriates who return each summer give an important boost to the local economy. However the government is still working to attract visitors from the rich Gulf Arab states and the West. Figures for 1997 show that there were 558,000 visitors to Lebanon. This figure had risen to 673,000 in 1999 and 742,000 in 2000.

Prior to the civil war, the country was one of the most popular tourist destinations in the Arab world, and the sector contributed over 15 per cent to Lebanon's national income. Prior to the Israeli campaign to oust Hezbollah from Lebanon in 2006, the tourism industry had begun to re-develop but since then visitor numbers have fallen. The hotel industry in Lebanon had embarked upon a restoration project valued at $500 million, aiming to construct 18,000 rooms by the end of 2002 and to restore Beirut's hotels to their former state.

Agriculture
About one-third of the country's land area, approximately 240,000 hectares, is cultivated. The primary agricultural areas are along the Mediterranean coast and the Bekaa Valley. Most of the farmland is rain fed. However, several irrigation schemes, including dams, are planned. These are expected to increase the total area of cultivated land by 60,000 hectares. With the completion of these dams, irrigated areas will total 125,000 hectares. Development of water resources is carried out by the National Office of the Litani River.

For many years, Lebanon has been an exporter of fruit and vegetables to other Arab states such as Syria, Saudi Arabia, Jordan, Kuwait and Iraq. The principal crops are grapes, oranges, and tomatoes. Other prominent crops include olives, cane and beet sugar, potatoes, wheat, tobacco and barley. Principal livestock are goats and sheep, whilst principal livestock products are cow's milk, poultry eggs and poultry meat.

Agricultural Production in 2010

Produce	Int. $'000*	Tonnes
Indigenous chicken meat	197,609	138,731
Tomatoes	102,739	278,000
Potatoes	92,880	574,100
Almonds, with shell	84,103	28,500
Cow milk, whole, fresh	78,171	250,500
Olives	78,149	97,600
Grapes	69,509	121,600
Apples	56,417	136,400
Cherries	49,198	38,700
Oranges	46,595	241,100
Lemons and limes	44,842	113,100
Hen eggs, in shell	38,981	47,000

* unofficial figures

Source: http://faostat.fao.org/site/339/default.aspx Food and Agriculture Organization of the United Nations, Food and Agricultural commodities production

The civil war disrupted agricultural production, and the Israeli invasions had a devastating effect on cultivation, particularly in the south and the Bekaa Valley. In 1996, over production of tobacco flooded the market and pushed prices down. The Government subsequently placed restrictions on its production. In recent years the agricultural export sector has performed well due to the depreciation of the Lebanese pound, and has accounted for approximately

20 per cent of total exports. Around 39 per cent of land is under arable use, including nine per cent under permanent crops, one per cent under permanent pasture and eight per cent forest and woodland.

COMMUNICATIONS AND TRANSPORT

Travel Requirements
Citizens of the USA, Canada, Australia and the EU require a passport valid for six months and a visa. Most can obtain a visa on arrival in the Lebanon; citizens of Bulgaria, Estonia, Hungary, Latvia, Lithuania, Poland, the Slovak Republic and Slovenia must obtain a visa prior to arrival. Travelers whose passports contain Israeli stamps or visas and who also hold an "Arab nationality" may be subject to arrest and imprisonment. Transit passengers continuing their journey by the same or first connecting aircraft, holding onward or return documentation and not spending the night at, or leaving, the airport do not require a visa.

Other nationals should contact the embassy to check visa requirements.

National Airlines
Middle East Airlines / Air Liban, Airport Boulevard, PO Box 206, Beirut, Lebanon. Tel: +961 1 629125 / 629250, fax: +961 1 629260, URL: http://www.mea.com.lb

International Airports
Lebanon possesses one international airport, Beirut International Airport, the airport has been renovated and a 2.1 mile runway extends in to the sea. Figures for 2003 show that over 2.3 million passengers passed through the airport. There also two military airfields, one in the Bekaa Valley and the other in the north of the country, near Tripoli and six other airports.

Railways
The total length of railway line in Lebanon is estimated at 254 miles, of which 203 are standard gauge and 51 narrow gauge. A narrow-gauge line runs from Beirut to Rayak (in the Bekaa) and then to Damascus. A standard-gauge line runs from Beirut to Tripoli and on to Aleppo. A line exists from Beirut southwards to the Israel frontier, but this line is in use only as far as Sidon.

Roads
Lebanon has in the region of 7,300 km of roads, 6,200 of which are paved, 2,170 km are highways, and 1,370 km of which are secondary roads. Substantial rebuilding of the road system has taken place since the war. Vehicles are driven on the right.

Shipping
The chief ports are Beirut and Tripoli, the latter being used mainly by tankers for Iraqi oil. Other harbours exist at Antilyas, Chekka, El Mina, Sidon, Tyre, Naqoura, Batroun, Ez Zahrani, Jbail and Jounie. A rehabilitation project of the Port of Beirut in currently underway. Ferries operate along the coast.

HEALTH

The government recently announced that investment in health care was a priority. In 2009, Lebanon spent approximately 9.5 per cent of its total budget on healthcare (up from 7.9 per cent in 2000), accounting for 41.9 per cent of all healthcare spending. Total expenditure on healthcare equated to 7.4 per cent of the country's GDP. Per capita expenditure on health was approximately US$617.

Figures for 2005-10 show that there are 13,214 physicians (35.4 per 10,000 population), 8,324 nurses and midwives (22.3 per 10,000 population) and 4,964 dentistry personnel. There are 35 hospital beds per 10,000 population. Recent figures show that there are 160 hospitals in Lebanon.

According to the latest WHO figures, in 2010, 100 per cent of the urban population had access to improved drinking water and to improved sanitation.

Average life expectancy is 74 years. The infant mortality rate in 2009 was 19 per 1,000 live births. The child mortality rate (under 5 years) was 22 per 1,000 live births. The main causes of death in the under-fives were prematurity 29 per cent, congenital anomalies 12 per cent, pneumonia 8 per cent, diarrhoea 4 per cent and HIV/AIDS 1 per cent. (Source: http://www.who.int, World Health Statistics 2012)

EDUCATION

The overall literacy rate in 2007 was 89.6 per cent. For males this is 93.4 per cent, and for females, 86.0 per cent. Students work towards the Lebanese Baccalaureate in High School. In the education year 1998-99 there were 2,719 schools.

Higher Education
There are 13 universities in Beirut, namely the American University of Beirut, (the largest one outside the USA), the Saint Joseph University, the Lebanese University run by the Ministry of National Education, the Arab University of Beirut, Beirut University College, Université de Saint-Esprit - Kaslik, The Lebanese Academy of Arts, Notre Dame University, Haygazian College University, Al Jinan University, The Centre of Higher Studies of Makassed, University of Balamand and Superior Institute of La Sagesse.

In 2007, 9.6 per cent of government spending (2.7 per cent of GDP) was spent on education. (Source: UNESCO)

LESOTHO

RELIGION

The chief religions of Lebanon are Christianity and Islam. About half the population are Christian, and Lebanon is reputed to have the oldest Christian communities in the world. Lebanon has a religious liberty rating of 5 on a scale of 1 to 10 (10 is most freedom). (Source: World Religion Database)

Major denominations

Maronites	424,000
Greek Orthodox	150,000
Armenian Orthodox	69,000
Greek Catholics	91,000
Protestants	14,000
Armenian Catholics	14,500
Sunni Muslims	286,000
Shia Muslims	250,000
Druze	88,000
Jews	6,600

COMMUNICATIONS AND MEDIA

The media is fairly free for the region, however the government controls who may operate stations and whether they may broadcast news. Political ownership of stations is common. Defamation of the president is forbidden.

Newspapers
There are numerous newspapers and periodicals.
Ad Diyar, URL: http://www.journaladdiyar.com
Al-Anwar, URL: http://www.alanwar.com/ar

An Nahar, URL: http://www.annahar.com
As-Safir, URL: http://www.assafir.com/
L'Orient-Le Jour, URL: http://www.lorient-lejour.com.lb/
Daily Star, URL: http://www.dailystar.com.lb/

Broadcasting
Broadcasting is the responsibility of the Ministry of Information. There are a number of commercial television companies, the Lebanese Television Company (LBC) (URL: http://www.lbcgroup.tv/lbc/en/home), opened in 1959 and the Television Company of Lebanon and the Near East (Tele-Orient) opened in 1962. There are numerous private stations including the Lebanese Broadcasting Corporations, Murr Television and Al-Manar TV. At least two international stations are available through partnerships.

Telecommunication Systems
The telephone service in Lebanon is state-owned and controlled by governmental departments. The telecommunicastion ssystem has been repaired following the civil war. The mobile-cellular network is good and 1.4 million mobile phones were in use, compared to 700,000 landlines. It was estimated that by 2008, nearly 1,000,000 Lebanese were regular internet users.

ENVIRONMENT

The main environmental concerns of Lebanon include sea pollution by raw sewage and oil spills, soil erosion and desertification.

Lebanon is a party to the following international agreements: Biodiversity, Climate Change, Climate Change-Kyoto Protocol, Desertification, Hazardous Wastes, Law of the Sea, Ozone Layer Protection, Ship Pollution and Wetlands. It has signed, but not ratified the agreements, Environmental Modification and Marine Life Conservation.

In 2010, Lebanon's emissions from the consumption of fossil fuels totalled 15.24 million metric tons of carbon dioxide. (Source: EIA)

LESOTHO
Kingdom of Lesotho

Capital: Maseru (Population estimate: 432,000)

Head of State: His Majesty King Letsie III (Sovereign) (page 1463)

National Flag: Lesotho adopted a new flag in October 2006, commemorating forty years of independence. The flag is a horizontal blue, white, and green tricolour with a black mokorotlo (a Basotho hat) in the centre.

CONSTITUTION AND GOVERNMENT

Constitution
Basutoland first became a British Protectorate in January 1868 after an appeal by the Basotho, who were at war with the Boers. The country remained in an unsettled condition until it was annexed to the Cape Colony in 1871. In 1884 the Territory was separated from the Cape Colony, and Government was carried on under the direct control of the Imperial Government.

Until 1959 the Territory was governed by a Resident Commissioner under the direction of the High Commissioner for Basutoland, the Bechuanaland Protectorate and Swaziland. Until 1959, there was an annual session of the Basutoland Council which consisted of 99 members, all Africans, 36 being elected (four each from nine District Councils). Six represented various associations, five were nominated by the Government, and the rest represented the Chieftainship.

In 1959 Basutoland was granted a Constitution under an Order-in-Council made by Her Majesty the Queen. The Legislative Council, known as the Basutoland National Council, consisted of 80 members divided equally between elected and non-elected members. The Council received wide legislative powers, and acted as a consultative body on such legislative matters as were reserved under the constitution to the High Commissioner. In May 1965, a pre-independence constitution was introduced, under which the powers of the Paramount Chief were those of a constitutional monarch, exercised on behalf of the Queen and in her name.

In June 1966 it was agreed that Basutoland should become independent under the name of Lesotho on 4 October 1966. The independence constitution followed in most respects the constitution of 1965. The principal changes arose from the establishment of the Paramount Chief as King, and the transfer of the remaining powers and responsibilities exercised by the British Government representative to the Lesotho Government.

Following the constitutional changes of 1970, the Lesotho Interim Parliament of National reconciliation consisted of the king and 93 parliamentarians nominated by the king on the advice of the Prime Minister. The 22 Principal chiefs were included in the 93 member Assembly.

The current constitution dates from 1993 when the country returned to civilian rule after a coup in 1986. The Constitution allows for a hereditary monarch (although the position is mostly ceremonial) who is seen as a "living symbol of national unity". It also allows for a bicameral parliament. The National Assembly is made up of 80 members directly elected for

a five year term. Since 2002, a further 40 seats are for members elected by proportional representation. The Senate has 33 members: 22 principal chieftains and 11 other members appointed by the monarch.

King Letsie was crowned King in October 1997. He had previously reigned from 1990 - 1995 when he replaced his deposed father, King Moshoeshoe. He abdicated in 1995 to allow the return to the throne of this father, who subsequently died in 1996.

To consult the constitution, please visit: http://www.wipo.int/wipolex/en/details.jsp?id=9016.

Recent Events
Following differences within the Basotho Congress Party, the party split in 1997. The Lesotho Congress for Democracy party was formed, whose members included the prime minister and the cabinet. They continued in power whilst the Basoto Congress Party formed the opposition. In the 1998 general election, the Lesotho Congress for Democracy won 79 of the 80 seats. International observers declared the election to be fair, but civil disorder broke out when opposition parties claimed fraud. Many people were killed, and Prime Minister Misisili called on the Southern African Development Community to help. A peace keeping force was sent in. In 2001 political differences within the Lesotho Congress for Democracy surfaced and the deputy prime minister formed a new party, the Lesotho People's Congress. In May 2002, a new electoral system was introduced: 80 seats continue to be elected constituency seats but a further 40 seats are now allocated by proportional representation.

In late 2005 the Government launched an HIV testing programme, available to all its citizens. Some 30 per cent of inhabitants were believed to be infected with HIV. The former communications minister Thomas Thabane and 17 other MPs formed the opposition All Basotho Convention (ABC) in October 2006.

In October 2006, the world's largest diamond reported to have been found this century went on sale in Antwerp; the 603 carat white diamond was found in a mine in Lesotho two months earlier, and named 'Lesotho's Promise'.

Five people were charged with high treason in October 2008 after attacks on the homes of opposition leaders and cabinet members. In October 2009 the prime minister Pakalitha Mosisili survived an alleged assassination attempt.

In April 2009, Prime Minister Mosisli survived what was suspected to be an assassination attempt.

Legislature
The legislature, is bicameral. The lower house, the National Assembly, has 120 members, elected for a five-year term. The upper house, the Senate, has 33 members, consisting of 22 principal chiefs and 11 members nominated by the king.

Upper House
The Senate, P.O. Box 553, Maseru 100, Lesotho. Tel: +266 2231 5338,fax: +266 2231 0023, e-mail: senate@lesotho.co.za

Lower House
National Assembly, P.O. Box 190, Maseru 100, Lesotho. Tel: +266 2232 3035, fax: +266 2231 0438, e-mail: natasse@adelfang.co.za

Cabinet (as at March 2013)

Prime Minister and Minister of Defence, Police and National Security: Rt. Hon. Thomas Motoahae Thabane (page 1524)

Deputy Prime Minister, Minister of Local Government and Chieftainship Affairs: Hon. Mothejoa Metsing

Minister of Gender, Youth, Sports and Recreation: Hon. Thesele Maseribane

Minister of Development Planning: Hon. Prof. Maboee Moletsane

Minister of Public Service: Hon. Dr Motloheloa Phooko (page 1495)

Minister of Energy, Meteorology and Water Affairs: Hon. Dr Thahane Timothy Thahane (page 1524)

Minister of Finance: Dr Leketekete Victor Ketso (page 1456)

Minister of Tourism, Environment and Culture: Hon. Mamahele Radebe

Minister of Public Works and Transport: Hon. Keketso Rant'so

Minister of Justice, Human Rights, Correctional Services, Law, and Constitutional Affairs: Hon. Haae Edward Phoofolo

Minister of Communications, Science and Technology: Hon. Ts'eliso Mokhosi

Minister of Forestry and Land Reclamation: Hon. Khotso Matia

Minister of Trade and Industry, Cooperatives and Marketing: Hon. Temeki Phoenix Ts'olo

Minister of Mining: Hon. Tlali Khasu

Minister of Agriculture and Food Security: Hon. Lits'oane Simon Lits'oane

Minister of Education and Training: Makabelo Priscilla Mosothoane

Minister of Social Development: Hon. Matebatso Doti

Minister of Employment and Labour: Hon. Lebesa Maloi

Minister in the Prime Minister's Office: Hon. Molobeli Soulu

Minister in the Prime Minister's Office: Hon. Mophato Moshoete Monyake

Ministries

Office of HM the King, The Royal Palace, PO Box 524, Maseru 100, Lesotho. Tel: +266 2232 2170, fax +266 2231 0083, e-mail: sps@palace.org.ls, URL: http://www.lesotho.gov.ls/ministers/mnking.htm

Government Portal: URL: http://www.gov.ls

Prime Minister's Office, P.O. Box 527, Maseru 100, Lesotho. Tel: +266 2231 1000, Fax: +266 2231 0444, URL: http://www.lesotho.gov.ls/ministers/mndefence.htm

Ministry of Foreign Affairs, P.O. Box: 1387, Maseru 100, Lesotho. Tel: +266 2231 1150, fax: +266 2231 0178. URL: http://www.foreign.gov.ls

Ministry of Defence, Private Bag A166, Maseru 100, Lesotho. Tel: +266 2231 6570, fax: +266 2231 0518, URL: http://www.lesotho.gov.ls/mndefence.htm

Ministry of Home Affairs, P.O. Box 174, Maseru 100, Lesotho. Tel: +266 2232 3771, fax: +266 2231 0587, URL: http://www.lesotho.gov.ls/mnhome.htm

Ministry of Trade, Industry, Co-operatives and Marketing, PO Box 747, Maseru 100, Lesotho. Tel: +266 2231 2938, fax: +266 2231 0644, URL: http://www.lesotho.gov.ls/mntrade.htm

Ministry of Local Government, P.O. Box 174, Maseru 100, Lesotho. Tel: +226 2232 5331, fax: +266 2231 1269, URL: http://www.lesotho.gov.ls/mnlocal.htm

Ministry of Agriculture, Co-operatives and Land Reclamation, P.O. Box 24, Maseru 100, Lesotho. Tel: +266 2231 6407, fax: +266 2231 0186, URL: http://www.lesotho.gov.ls/mnagric.htm

Ministry of Justice, PO Box 402, Maseru 100, Lesotho. Tel: +266 2231 1160, fax: +266 2231 0365, URL: http://www.lesotho.gov.ls/mnlaw.htm

Ministry of Finance and Development Planning, PO Box 395, Maseru 100, Lesotho. Tel: +266 2231 0826, fax: +266 2231 0157, URL: http://www.lesotho.gov.ls/mnfinance.htm

Ministry of Education and Manpower Development, P.O. Box 47, Maseru 100, Lesotho. Tel: +266 2232 0995, fax: +266 22310562, URL: http://www.education.gov.ls

Ministry of Health and Social Welfare, P.O. Box 514, Maseru 100, Lesotho. Tel: +266 2231 4404, fax: +266 2231 0467, URL: http://www.health.gov.ls

Ministry of Energy, Meteorology and Water Affairs, PO Box 772, Maseru 100, Lesotho. Tel: +266 2232 3163, fax: +266 2231 0520, URL: http://www.lesotho.gov.ls/mnnatural.htm

Ministry of Communications, Science and Technology, PO Box 36, Maseru 100, Lesotho. Tel: +266 2232 3864, fax: +266 2231 0003, e-mail: editor@lesotho.gov.ls, URL: http://www.lesotho.gov.ls/mninfor.htm

Ministry of Public Works and Transport, P.O. Box 20, Maseru 100, Lesotho. Tel: +266 2231 1362, fax: +266 22310125, URL: http://www.lesotho.gov.ls/mnworks.htm

Ministry of Labour and Employment, Private Bag A1164, Maseru 100, Lesotho. Tel: +266 2232 2602, fax: +266 2231 0374, URL: http://www.lesotho.gov.ls/mnemploy.htm

Ministry of Tourism, Culture and Environment, PO Box 52, Maseru 100, Lesotho. Tel: +266 2231 3034, fax: +266 2231 0194, URL: http://www.lesotho.gov.ls/mnenviron.htm

Ministry of Gender, Youth and Sports, PO Box 721, Maseru 100, Lesotho. Tel: +266 2231 4763, fax: +266 2231 0506, URL: http://www.lesotho.gov.ls/sports.htm

Ministry of Foreign Affairs and International Relations, PO Box 1387, Maseru 100, Lesotho. Tel: +266 2231 1150, fax: +266 2231 0178, URL: http://www.lesotho.gov.ls/mnforeign.htm

Ministry of Defence and National Security, PO Box 527, Maseru 100, Lesotho. Tel: +266 2231 1000, fax: +266 2231 0319, URL: http://www.lesotho.gov.ls/mndefence.htm

Ministry of Forestry and Land Reclamation, PO Box 92, Maseru 100, Lesotho. Tel: +266 2231 3057, fax: +266 2231 0515, URL: http://www.lesotho.gov.ls/forestry

Ministry of Home Affairs and Public Safety, PO Box 174, Maseru 100, Lesotho. Tel: +266 2232 3771, fax: +266 2231 0587, URL: http://www.lesotho.gov.ls/mnhome.htm

Political Parties
Lesotho Congress for Democracy (LCD), Lesotho People's Congress (LPC), Basotho Congress Party (BCP), Basotho National Party (BNP), Basotho African Congress (BAC), All Basotho Convention (ABC), Basotho Democratic National Party (BNDP), Lesotho Workers' Party (LWP); National Independent Party (NIP).

Elections
The most recent parliamentary elections were held in may 2012. The All Basotho Convention led by Thomas Thabane teamed up with the Lesotho Congress for Democracy party and the Basotho National Party to form a coalition government. Outgoing prime minister Bethuel Mosisili's Democratic Congress party won the most seats, but not enough to win a majority.

Diplomatic Representation
Embassy of the Kingdom of Lesotho, 2511 Massachusetts Ave., NW Washington, DC 20008, USA. Tel: +1 202 797 5533 fax: +1 202 234 6815, URL: http://www.lesothoemb-usa.gov.ls
Ambassador: Prof. Eliachim Molapi Sebatane
US Embassy, P.O. Box 333, Maseru 100, Lesotho. Tel: +266 312666 fax: +266 310116, e-mail: amles@lesoff.co.za, URL: http://maseru.usembassy.gov
Ambassador: Michele Bond
High Commission of the Kingdom of Lesotho, 7 Chesham Place, Belgravia, London, SW1 8AN, United Kingdom. Tel: +44 (0)20 7235 5686 fax: +44 171 235 5023, URL: http://www.lesotholondon.org.uk
High Commissioner: vacant
British High Commission, Staff in South Africa, URL: http://ukinsouthafrica.fco.gov.uk/en/
High Commissioner: Dame Nicola Brewer
Permanent Representative to the UN, New York, URL: http://www.un.int/lesotho/
Permanent Representative: Ambassador Motlatsi Ramafole

LEGAL SYSTEM

The legal system is based on English common law and Roman-Dutch law. The head of the Judiciary is the Chief Justice, appointed by the King, on the advice of the Prime Minister and Council of Ministers.

The judicial system consists of the High Court, the Court of Appeal, subordinate courts, and the Judicial Service Commission (JSC). The members of the High Court are the chief justice and an unspecified number of puisne judges appointed by the chief of state, acting on the advice of the JSC. The Court of Appeal is headed by a president, appointed by the chief of state, and includes an unspecified number of justices of appeal, also appointed by the chief of state, acting on the advice of the JSC. The High Court has unlimited original jurisdiction over civil and criminal matters, as well as appellate jurisdiction from subordinate courts. It also reviews legislature, with the Court of Appeal.

Subordinate courts, comprising resident magistrate's courts, judicial commissioner's courts, and central and local courts, administer statute laws, while village chiefs administer customary and tribal laws. Military courts have jurisdiction over military cases.

The government generally respects the human rights of its citizens, but there have been recent reports of police brutality. There are long trial delays, and prison conditions are poor. Lesotho retains the death penalty, although the last reported execution was in 1995.

LOCAL GOVERNMENT

For administrative purposes Lesotho is divided into 10 districts: Berea, Butha-Buthe, Keribe, Mafeteng, Maseru, Mohales Hoek, Mokhotlong, Qacha's Nek, Quthing and Thaba-Tseka. The first local elections since independence in 1966 took place in April 2005. Members of 129 local councils were elected. Opposition parties boycotted the elections. The next local elections are due in September 2011.

AREA AND POPULATION

Area
Lesotho (formerly Basutoland) is surrounded by South Africa, bounded on the west and north by the Free State, on the east by Kwa-Zulu Natal, and on the south by the Cape Province. The area of the territory is 11,716 sq. miles. A belt between 20 and 40 miles in width, lying along the western and southern boundaries and comprising about one-third of the total, is classed as 'Lowland', ie. between 5,000 and 6,000 feet above sea level. The remaining two-thirds are classed as 'Foothills' and 'Highlands', mostly at altitudes of 7,000 to 9,000 feet but rising in the east to the high peaks (10,500 to 11,425 feet) of the Drakensburg range, which forms the boundary with Kwa-Zulu Natal. Lesotho has five main rivers running through it, the Makhaleng, Malibamat'so, Orange, Senqu and the Senqunyane.

To view a map, visit http://www.lib.utexas.edu/maps/cia08/lesotho_sm_2008.gif

Summers are hot and wet, winters are colder and drier.

Population
Lesotho has an estimated population in 2010 of 2,171,000, growing 1.0 per cent on average per year over the period 2000-10. In the lowlands the population density varies between 100 and 300 persons per sq. mile. Approximately 27 per cent of the population lives in urban areas. The principal town is Maseru, with an estimated population of 432,000. The term Basotho as applied to the inhabitants of Lesotho has primarily a political rather than an ethnic significance. It applies specifically to those groups of various tribal origin which now acknowledge the authority of the King of Lesotho. Languages spoken are Sesotho and English.

Births, Marriages, Deaths
In 2010 the crude birth rate per 1,000 was estimated to be 27.8 and the crude death rate per 1,000 was 15.4. In 1997 figures put the average life expectancy at 59 years but by 2004 the average life expectancy had fallen to 36 years. This reflects the fact that Lesotho has one of the world's highest rates of HIV/AIDS infection. In 2007 it was estimated that 23.2 per cent of the population aged between 15 and 49 was infected with the HIV virus. By 2009, the average life expectancy had risen to 46 years for males and 50 years for females reflecting

LESOTHO

increased coverage of antiretroviral therapy. Healthy life expectancy was estimated to be 40 years. Approximately 37 per cent of the population is aged under 15 years and 6 per cent over 60 years. The median age was 20. The total fertility rate per woman was 3.2 children. (Source: http://www.who.int, World Health Statistics 2012)

Public Holidays 2014

1 January: New Year's Day
11 March: Moshoeshoe's Day
18 April: Good Friday
21 April: Easter Monday
1 May: Workers' Day
25 May: Heroes' Day
29 May: Ascension Day
17 July: King's Birthday
4 October: Independence Day
25 December: Christmas Day
26 December: Boxing Day

EMPLOYMENT

Figures for 2007 put the workforce at 850,000. More than 85 per cent of the population live in rural areas and are mainly employed in agriculture, which contributes nearly 14 per cent of the GDP. This is an additional source of income, as about half of the rural households have a family member working in South Africa, mainly in the mining industry. Earnings from these migrant workers account for about 30 per cent of the GNP.

The textile industry is the largest employer followed by the shoe-making and electronics industries. Recently the garment industry has begun to decline, mainly due to the lifting of worldwide textile quotas on January 1 2005. It has been estimated that as many as 50,000 people could lose their jobs as factories begin to close. Before the lifting of the quota system, sub-Saharan countries had preferential access to the markets of North America for apparel and textile goods.

Recent figures show that around 40 per cent of the Lesotho labour force is unemployed or under-employed.

BANKING AND FINANCE

Currency
The unit of currency is the Loti (the plural of which is Maloti), divided into 100 Lisente. The financial centre is Maseru.

GDP/GNP, Inflation, National Debt
The economy of Lesotho is tightly bound to that of South Africa, the country that surrounds it. A large contributor of the economy is the export of water and electricity to South Africa as well as manufactured goods and to a lesser extent earnings sent back by labourers employed in South Africa. The government is currently investigating various avenues to improve the economic situation; reforms to the fiscal system are being formulated and involve registration of taxpayers, taxpayer identification, computerisation of the system, training of tax officials and the introduction of a VAT system. A diamond mine which was closed in 1982 has recently been reopened. Experts believe it could contribute 20 per cent of GDP. The global economic problems have resulted in a temporary decline in the diamond market. The tourism industry has the potential to boost the economy.

Estimated figures for 2010 put GDP at US$2 billion with a growth rate of 2.4 per cent. Around 7 per cent of GDP comes from the agricultural sector, 35 per cent from industry, (20 per cent of which is from manufacturing) and 58 per cent from the service sector. Per capita income was an estimated US$1,080 in 2010.

Inflation was estimated to be 4 per cent in 2010, rising to 5 per cent in 2011.

Total external debt was put at US$633.44 million in 2006. (Source: ADB)

Foreign Investment
Measures are being taken to encourage foreign investment which include the reform of public utilities and the simplification of the procedures to obtain work permits. In 2008, Lesotho received around US$300 million in economic aid mainly from the US, the World Bank, UK, UN and EU.

Balance of Payments / Imports and Exports
Lesotho's main trading partners are South Africa, Swaziland, Namibia, US and EU as well as some Asian nations. The main exports being water, wool, clothing furniture and footwear. Main imported goods are corn, medicines, petroleum products, vehicles, corn and machinery.

External Trade, US$ million

	2005	2006	2007
Trade balance	-656.62	-667.38	-732.39
Exports	650.71	699.49	742.40
Imports	1,307.32	1,366.87	1,474.78

Source: African Development Bank

Exports amounted to an estimated US$995 million in 2011 and imports cost US$2.1 billion.

Central Bank
Central Bank of Lesotho, PO Box 1184, Moshoeshoe Road, Maseru 100, Lesotho. Tel: +266 314281, fax: +266 310051, e-mail: cbl@pixie.co.za URL: http://www.centralbank.org.ls Governor & Chairman: Dr A.R. Matianyane

MANUFACTURING, MINING AND SERVICES

Primary and Extractive Industries
Geological surveys of Lesotho have been discouraging about the mineral resources of the country with the exception of diamonds. The first diamond mine has begun operations after successful prospecting by De Beers/Anglo-American Corporation group. In 2006, a 603 carat white diamond, the Lesotho Promise, was mined and in 2008 a 478 carat diamond from which the largest ever cut round diamond of 150 carats is expected to be cut was found. The diamond mines were closed in 2008 as the global economic downturn meant the demand for diamonds fell dramatically. The closure is expected to be temporary. The main natural resource of Lesotho is water. Lesotho has no reserves of oil and imports 2,000 barrels a day to meet its needs.

Energy
The Lesotho Highlands Water Project is designed to generate 274 MW of hydroelectric power. The first phase came into operation in 1999 with a generation capacity of 80 MW. In 2004 the government announced plans to sell up to 70 per cent of the state owned electric company, the Lesotho Electricity Company. Lesotho is now self sufficient in electricity production for most of the year, electricity has to be imported from South Africa during the winter. Figures for 2010 show that 0.20 billion kWh of electricity were produced and consumption was 0.31 billion kWh.

Manufacturing
Industrial development is steadily growing. A new candle factory is now in production and two well-established printing enterprises, a tyre company and a factory making building materials are situated at Maseru. A wheat milling plant has been established in Maseru, and there are two canning industries at Masianokeng, one for beans and another for asparagus, mainly for export to a European market. Textiles is an important area; however, the garment industry has begun to decline, mainly due to the lifting of worldwide textile quotas on January 1 2005. It is estimated that 20 per cent of the workforce from the textile sector lost their jobs in the first half of 2005. Before the lifting of the quota system, sub-Saharan countries had preferential access to the markets of North America for apparel and textile goods. Other industrial areas include construction materials, ceramics, engineering products and food production.

Service Industries
Another major source of income is the rapid growth of the tourist trade which started from an inflow of 4,000 tourists in the late 1960s and has now reached over 340,000 per annum. **Lesotho Tourist Board**, PO Box 1378, Maseru 100, Lesotho. Tel: +226 312896/313760, fax: +226 310108

Agriculture
The agricultural sector employs more than 85 per cent of the population. Agriculture and animal husbandry constitute Lesotho's sole major industry. Production on arable land consists of crops of maize, sorghum and beans in summer, and wheat, peas, barley and oats in winter. The fertility of the soil in the lowland arable region is very low and yields are poor. In the mixed farming areas of the foothills soil fertility is much greater. Under conditions of normal seasonal rainfall, while much of the yield is used for subsistence, there are exportable surpluses of most crops, although large quantities of maize are imported annually. In periods of short rainfall and drought substantial imports of foodstuffs are necessary. The chief source of wealth lies in the keeping of livestock. Sheep, angora goats and, to a lesser extent, cattle are of major economic importance, wool and mohair being Lesotho's principal exports. Recent figures show that Lesotho had 1.5 million sheep and goats and 540,000 cattle.

Policy reforms are currently being implemented for the agricultural sector which include steps to discontinue the announcement of producer prices of maize and wheat, cease the issuing of import permits for grain and remove the ban on importing flour. These steps are predicted to increase competition in these markets. Further incentives are being provided to producers of high value export crops such as asparagus and fruits.

In February 2004 a state of emergency was declared and Lesotho appealed for food aid. This was a result of the third year of drought. Another state of emergency was declared in October 2007 when the country experienced another drought.

Agricultural Production in 2010

Produce	Int. $'000*	Tonnes
Indigenous cattle meat	28,094	10,400
Maize	17,133	128,213
Potatoes	16,574	98,200
Game meat	11,097	5,100
Cow milk,whole, fresh	10,517	33,700
Indigenous sheep meat	8,713	3,200
Wool, greasy	7,079	3,700
Indigenous pigmeat	6,099	3,968
Vegetables fresh nes	5,804	30,800
Indigenous goat meat	5,758	2,403
Fruit fresh nes	5,131	14,700
Beans, dry	5,123	8,899

* unofficial figures
Source: http://faostat.fao.org/site/339/default.aspx Food and Agriculture Organization of the United Nations, Food and Agricultural commodities production

COMMUNICATIONS AND TRANSPORT

Travel Requirements
Citizens of the USA, Canada, Australia and the EU require a passport valid for at least six months beyond the length of stay but do not need a visa for stays of up to 14 days. The passport should have at least two spare pages to allow the immigration authorities to affix

visa stamps. Citizens of Bulgaria, Czech Republic, Estonia, Hungary, Latvia, Lithuania, Poland, Romania, Slovak Republic and Slovenia do need a visa. All nationals should contact the embassy to check precise visa requirements.

Vaccination for yellow fever is a common requirement and travelers should carry their international vaccination cards with them.

International Airports
There are international flights from Moshoeshoe I airport in Maseru. Lesotho also has another 27 airports of varying grades.

Railways
There are no railways in Lesotho with the exception of two miles of the South African Railways, which enters Lesotho at Maseru from the Free State.

Roads
A good main road runs from Butha Buthe in Northern Lesotho to Quthing in the south east (ie past Mohale's Hoek) in the south. It connects all the Government Stations. Qacha's Nek is accessible by road from Matatiele in East Griqualand and a jeep service up the Sani Pass to Mokhotlong is in operation. The total road network covers 5,000 km. Vehicles are driven on the left.

Ports and Harbours
Lesotho is landlocked so exports go through the South African port of Durban.

HEALTH

The health system works at three levels. There are over 5,000 volunteer health workers. They are unpaid individuals with basic medical training who have an advisory role within their own communities. 157 health centres offer basic medical services although like the hospitals they suffer from a shortage of nurses. There are 18 general hospitals in Lesotho. To curb the emigration of qualified doctors, nurses and skilled technical support, the government is improving financial remuneration and offering incentives to these employees.

In 2009, Lesotho spent approximately 10.3 per cent of its total budget on healthcare (up from 6.5 per cent in 2000), accounting for 74.3 per cent of all healthcare spending. Total expenditure on healthcare equated to 9.4 per cent of the country's GDP. Per capita expenditure on health was approximately US$75, compared with US$27 in 2000. Figures for 2000-10 show that there are 89 physicians (1 per 10,000 population), 1,123 nurses and midwives (6 per 10,000 population) 16 dentists, 62 pharmaceutical personnel and 55 environment and public health workers.. There are an estimated 13 hospital beds per 10,000 population.

Currently the Lesotho government is devising an information system to assess the incidence of diseases, especially AIDS. It is also improving the primary health care system. Lesotho has one of the highest rates of HIV/AIDS infection in the world with an estimated 29 per cent of 15 to 49 year olds infected. In 2005 the government introduced a programme whereby HIV/AIDS tests were available to all. The incidence of HIV/AIDS in children has fallen and now accounts for 18 per cent of childhood deaths.

In 2009, life expectancy for males was 46 years and for females, 50 years. The infant mortality rate in 2009 was 65 per 1,000 live births. The child mortality rate (under 5 years) was 85 per 1,000 live births. The main causes of childhood mortality are: HIV/AIDs (18 per cent, down from 38 per cent in 2000), prematurity (18 per cent), birth asphyxia (11 per cent), diarrhoea (7 per cent), and pneumonia (12 per cent).

According to the latest WHO figures, in 2010 approximately 78 per cent of the population had access to improved drinking water. In the same year, 26 per cent of the population had access to improved sanitation. (Source: http://www.who.int, World Health Statistics 2012)

EDUCATION

Though school attendance is not free or compulsory, about three-quarters of Basotho children attend school for some period between the ages of five and 20. The ownership and operation of schools is mainly in the hands of the Church of Lesotho, Roman Catholic and English Church Missions, each of which receives a grant-in-aid from the Government to meet the cost of teachers' salaries in aided schools.

There are 1,234 primary schools and 193 secondary institutions. Primary enrolment was 75 per cent for males and 81 per cent for females in 2002, 17 per cent of males and 26 per cent of females were enrolled in secondary school. The Government is introducing a programme of free primary education and it is hoped that all children of primary school age will have access to education by 2006. Higher education is provided by the National University of Lesotho in Roma.

Figures for 2003 put adult literacy at 85 per cent.

RELIGION

The main religion in Lesotho is Christianity with around 44 per cent of the population belonging to the Catholic Church and 48 cent belonging to Protestant Churches. Lesotho has a religious tolerance rating of 4 on a scale of 10 to 10 (10 is most freedom). (Source: World Religion Database)

COMMUNICATIONS AND MEDIA

The government controls most of the media.

Newspapers
The Mirror, published weekly in English; Makatolle, published weekly in Sesotho; MoAfrica, published weekly in Sesotho; Mopheme, The Survivor, published weekly in Sesotho and English.

Broadcasting
There is one state-owned television station and two state-owned radio stations. A satellite TV subscription is also available.

Telecommunications
Telecom Lesotho was privatised in 2001. The telecommunicaitons systems is fairly basic but both the landline system and the mobile-cellular system are expanding. According to 2008 figures there are 65,000 landline ohones in operation and over 550,00 mobile phones. There are approximately 73,000 internet users.

ENVIRONMENT

Main environmental concerns of Lesotho include overgrazing, soil erosion and soil exhaustion.

Lesotho is a party to the following international agreements: Biodiversity, Climate Change, Climate Change-Kyoto Protocol, Desertification, Endangered Species, Hazardous Wastes, Law of the Sea, Marine Life Conservation, Ozone Layer Protection and Wetlands.

According to the EIA, in 2010, Lesotho's emissions from the consumption of fossil fuels totalled 0.28 million metric tons of carbon dioxide.

LIBERIA
Republic of Liberia

Capital: Monrovia (Population estimate: 1,100,000)

Head of State: Ellen Johnson Sirleaf (President) (page 1450)

Vice President: Joseph Boakai (page 1390)

National Flag: Eleven stripes, alternate red and white, six red and five white displayed horizontally. In the upper left corner, near the staff is a blue field, five stripes deep from the top. In the centre of the blue is a five-pointed white star

CONSTITUTION AND GOVERNMENT

Constitution
The Republic of Liberia was founded by The American Colonization Society as a home for freed American slaves in 1882.

After a civil war lasting a number of years a peace agreement between the various factions was signed and a new Council of State was announced in 1994. The Government of Liberia is patterned closely after that of the United States, having its authority divided into three separate and distinct branches - the Legislative, the Executive and the Judiciary. The House of Representatives has 64 elected members who serve a six year term. The Senate has 26 elected members who serve a nine year term.

Four proposed amendments to the constitution were rejected by referendum in August 2011. The rejected amendments included proposals to reduce the residency requirements for presidential candidates from 10 years to five years prior to the election, to increase the mandatory retirement age for all judges from 70 to 75 years, and the introduction of single round first-past-the-post voting for all legislative and municipal elections.

For information on the constitution, please visit:
http://www.wipo.int/wipolex/en/details.jsp?id=8556

International Relations
Liberia is a member of the United Nations and its specialized agencies and is a member of the African Union (AU), the Economic Community of West African States (ECOWAS), the African Development Bank (ADB), the Mano River Union (MRU), and the Non-Aligned Movement. Difficulties between the three countries of the MRU (Liberia, Guinea and Sierra Leone) meant that the MRU didn't come to anything. It was relaunched in 2004. Liberia's civil war has at times spilled over into conflict with its neighbours. The UN imposed sanctions against Liberia in 2001 over President Taylor's support for the Revolutionary United Front (RUF) in Sierra Leone.

LIBERIA

Recent Events

In 1980 Sergeant Samuel Doe staged a military coup and overthrew William Tolbert. After reinstating political parties Doe was elected president in 1985. Four years later the National Patriotic Front of Liberia (NPFL), led by Charles Taylor, began an anti-government uprising, and a breakaway faction of the NPFL executed Doe in 1990. A West African peacekeeping force was sent in, but it was not until 1995 that a peace agreement was signed. In 1997 Charles Taylor was elected president. In 1999 Liberia was accused of supporting Revolutionary United Front rebels in Sierra Leone and fighting broke out. Rebel groups were determined to oust President Taylor, accusing him of causing hardship by backing rebel forces in Sierra Leone, Côte d'Ivoire and Guinea. In summer 2003 the fighting had reached the outskirts of Monrovia. In June 2003 a ceasefire was negotiated in Ghana between the government and rebel forces. However fighting broke out just days later. The Economic Community of West African States sent in peace keeping troops in August 2003. President Taylor resigned in August and left for exile in Nigeria. His vice president, Moses Zeh Blah, became interim president and a transitional government was announced in October 2003. Under the terms of the Ghana ceasefire a 76-member National Transitional Legislative Assembly was also inaugurated.

In February 2005 it was announced that presidential and legislative elections would be held in October. The presidential election was won by Ellen Johnson-Sirleaf. She has said the fight against corruption is her top priority but does not command a majority.

Following the signing of the CPA, over 100,000 combatants were disarmed in 2005, although reintegration programmes have had only patchy success. UNMIL are deployed over the entire territory to provide security.

In April 2007 the UN lifted its ban on the export of Liberian diamonds; the ban was originally imposed to stop diamonds being sold to fund the civil war.

The UN indicted the former president, Charles Taylor, on 12 counts including crimes against humanity, slavery and sexual mutilation relating to his time in office as president. He was arrested in April 2006 after the new president, Ellen Sirleaf Johnson, asked Nigeria to hand him over. He first appeared in court in the UN-backed court in Sierra Leone in April 2006. In June 2006 the International Criminal Court at The Hague agreed to host the trial, and the trial began the following June. Mr Taylor boycotted the opening, protesting he did not believe he would receive a fair trial. If found guilty, Mr. Taylor will serve his term in the United Kingdom. In May 2009 the war crimes tribunal rejected a request to acquit the former president of the charge of crimes against humanity.

The UN extended embargoes on arms and travel after a period of increased violence in December 2007.

A state of emergency was declared in February 2009 following a plague of crop-destroying insects.

There have been several recent changes to the cabinet. The minister of finance and the minister for planning and economic development resigned to take up positions at the World Bank in July 2009. The minister of information, culture and tourism was suspended in October following allegations of corruption.

In September 2009, the UN Security Council voted to extend the mandate of UN forces in Liberia (UNMIL) into 2010 to assist with the 2011 elections.

The IMF and the World Bank proposed a plan to relieve Liberia of its debt burden. In September 2010 the Paris Club of creditor countries agreed to remove US$1.2 bn worth of Liberia's debt.

The cabinet was first dismissed and then reshuffled in November 2010 with several members reinstated to their seats.

In October 2011, President Ellen Johnson Sirleaf and fellow Liberian Leymah Gbowee won the Nobel Peace Prize together with the Yemeni human rights activist Tawakul Karman.

In April 2012, former president Charles Taylor was found guilty of war crimes and was sentenced to 50 years in prison.

In June 2012, Liberia closed its border with the Ivory Coast after seven UN peacekeepers are killed on the Ivorian side, the attackers were allegedly based in Liberia.

Legislature

The Legislature is bicameral. The lower chamber, the House of Representatives, has 64 members, who are directly elected for a six year term. The upper chamber, the Senate, has 30 members, two from each of the 15 counties, members of the senate serve a nine year term.

House of Representatives, Capitol Building, Monrovia, Liberia. Tel: +231 226584

Cabinet (as at June 2013)
Minister of Foreign Affairs: Dr Augustine Ngafuan (page 1486)
Minister of Finance: Amara Konneh (page 1458)
Minister of Internal Affairs: Morris Dukuly
Minister of Justice and Attorney General: Christiana Tah
Minister of Education: Etmonia Tarpeh
Minister of Land, Mines and Energy: Patrick Sendolo
Minister of Agriculture: Dr Florence Chenoweth
Minister of Health and Social Welfare: Dr Walter Gweningale
Minister of Public Works: vacant
Minister of Gender and Development: Julia Duncan Cassell
Minister of Commerce, Trade and Industry: Axel Addy
Minister of Transport: Tornorlah Varpilah
Minister of Post and Telecommunications: Frederick Norkeh

Minister of Youth and Sports: Lenn Eugene Nagbe
Minister of Information, Culture and Tourism: Lewis Brown
Minister of National Defence: Brownie J. Samukai
Minister of State for Presidential Affairs: Edward McClain
Minister of Labour: Juah Lawson
Director General, Civil Service Agency: George Werner
Director General, General Services Agency: Pearine Davis-Parkinson
Chairman, National Investment Commission: Natty B. Davies
President and CEO, National Oil Company of Liberia: Christopher Neyor

Ministries

Office of the President, Executive Mansion, PO Box 9001, Capitol Hill, Monrovia, Liberia. e-mail: emansion@liberia.net; URL: http://www.emansion.gov.lr/

Ministry of Foreign Affairs, Capitol Hill, Tubman Boulevard, Monrovia, Liberia. Tel: +231 226763, URL: http://www.mofa.gov.lr

Ministry of Justice, Ashmun Street, PO Box 9006, Monrovia, Liberia. Tel: +231 227872

Ministry of Internal Affairs, Camp Johnson Road, Capitol Hill, Monrovia, Liberia. Tel: +231 226346

Ministry of Information, Culture and Tourism, 110 United Nations Drive, PO Box 9021, Monrovia, Liberia. Tel: +231 226269, fax: +231 226269, e-mail: webmaster@micat.gov.lr, URL: http://www.micat.gov.lr

Ministry of National Defence, Barclay Training Center, UN Drive, Monrovia, Liberia. Tel: +231 226077

Ministry of Agriculture, Tubman Blvd., PO Box 9010, Monrovia, Liberia. Tel: +231 226399, URL: http://www.moa.gov.lr/

Ministry of Commerce, Trade and Industry, Ashmun Street, PO Box 9014, Monrovia, Liberia. Tel: +231 226283, URL: http://www.moci.gov.lr/

Ministry of Finance, Broad Street, PO Box 10-9013, 1000 Monrovia 10, Liberia. Tel: +231 226863, URL: http://www.mofliberia.org/

Ministry of Lands, Mines and Energy, Tubman Boulevard, Sinkor, Monrovia, Liberia. Tel: +231 226281, URL: http://http://www.molme.gov.lr/

Ministry of Labour: Mechlin Street, PO Box 9040, Monrovia. Tel: +231 226291

Ministry of Health and Social Welfare, Bassa Community, Monrovia, Liberia. Tel: +231 226317, e-mail: appointments@moh.gov.lr, URL: http://liberiamohsw.org

Ministry of Internal Affairs, Camp Johnson Road, Capitol Hill, Monrovia, Liberia. Tel: +231 226346

Ministry of Gender and Development, Capitol Hill, PO Box 9001, Monrovia, Liberia. Tel: +231 463544, URL: http://www.mogd.gov.lr

Ministry of Education, Broad Street, PO Box 1545, Monrovia, Liberia. Tel: +231 226216, fax: +231 226216

Ministry of Post and Telecommunication, Episcopal Building, Randell Street, Monrovia, Liberia. Tel: +231 226079

Ministry of Public Works, Lynch Street, PO Box 9011, Monrovia, Liberia. Tel: +231 227972, URL: http://http://www.mpw.gov.lr

Ministry of Rural Development, 17th Street, Sinkor, Monrovia, Liberia. Tel: +231 227938

Ministry of Transport, Gurley Street, Monrovia, Liberia.

Ministry of Youth and Sports, Newport Street, Monrovia, Liberia. URL: http://www.moys.gov.lr

Political Parties

Alliance for Peace and Democracy (APD); Coalition for the Transformation of Liberia (COTOL); Congress for Democratic Change (CDC); Liberty Party (LP); National Patriotic Party (NPP); Unity Party (UP), New Deal Movement, (NDM); National Reformation Party, (NRP); Liberia Destiny Party, (LDP); National Democratic Party of Liberia, (NDPL)..

Elections

Parliamentary (both House of Representatives and Senate) took place 11 October 2005 and were won by the Congress of Democratic Change although the party was short of an overall majority . The first round of presidential elections took place on 11 October. The second round of presidential elections took place on 8 November when Ellen Johnson Sirleaf won with over 90 per cent of the vote. Her opponent, George Weah, the former international footballer, denounced the result. She then dismissed the transitional government which had been in place since 2003 following the Accra Agreement. The new cabinet was sworn in on 16 January 2006.

Presidential elections took place in October 2011. Ellen Jphnson-Sirleaf, won the second round with 90 per cent of the vote.

Legislative elections took place on October 11 2011, in the House of Representatives the Unity Party won 24 seats, the Congress for Democratic Change won 11 seats, the Liberty Party, seven seats, the National Union for Democratic , five seats, the National Democratic Coalition, five seats, other parties wond 11 seats between them and nine independents were elected.

Diplomatic Representation

British Embassy, Staff resident in Freetown, Sierra Leone, URL: http://www.britishhighcommission.gov.uk/ In 2012 plans were announced to re-open the British Embassy in Liberia
Ambassador: vacant

US Embassy, 111 United Nations Drive, PO Box 10-0098, Mamba Point, Monrovia, Liberia. Tel: +231 226370, fax: +231 226148, e-mail: montgomeryrs@state.gov, URL: http://monrovia.usembassy.gov
Ambassador: Deborah Ruth Malac

Liberian Embassy, 23 Fitzroy Square, London W1 6EW, United Kingdom. Tel: +44 (0)20 7221 1036, URL: http://www.embassyofliberia.org.uk/
Ambassador: Wesley Momo Johnson (page 1479)

Embassy of the Republic of Liberia, 5201 16th Street NW, Washington D.C. 20011, USA. Tel: +1 202 723 0437, fax: +1 202 723 0436
Ambassador: Jeremiah Sulunteh

Permanent Mission of Liberia to the United Nations, 820 Second Avenue, 13th Floor, New York, NY 10017, USA. Tel: +1 212 687 1033/1034, fax: +1 212 687 1035
Permanent Representative: vacant

LEGAL SYSTEM

The Liberian legal system is mix of statutory law based on English and American common law and traditional tribal law.

There are 15 Judicial Circuits, whose Courts have civil, criminal, equity, admiralty and probate jurisdictions. Cases travel juridically from Magistrates Court or a Court of Petty Session to the Circuit Courts and, from the latter, an appeal may be taken to the People's Supreme Court for final adjudication. The Supreme Court also has original jurisdiction over constitutional questions. It consists of the Chief Justice and four Associate Justices, who are nominated by the President and confirmed by the Senate. Traditional courts are presided over by tribal chiefs. A labor court was created in 1986.

The Truth and Reconciliation Commission of Liberia was set up to investigate the causes of the conflict, bring the truth to light and ultimately foster forgiveness and unite the nation. It presented its final report at the beginning of July 2009. URL: http://www.trcofliberia.org/

The human rights situation remains precarious. Security forces abuse and intimidate detainees and citizens. There have been cases of arbitrary arrest and detention, and prison conditions are harsh. Some incidents of trial-by-ordeal have been reported in recent years. Government corruption and impunity is pervasive. The death penalty was abolished in 2005 but was reinstated in 2008 and death sentences began to be imposed in 2009. There are believed to be 16 individuals currently sentenced to death. The last known execution was in 2000.

Chief Justice, Supreme Court: Francis Korkpor

LOCAL GOVERNMENT

The country is divided into 15 administrative divisions; Bomi, Bong, Gbarpolu, Grand Bassa, Grand Cape Mount, Grand Gedeh, Grand Kru, Lofa, Margibi, Maryland, Montserrado, Nimba, River Cess, River Gee and Sinoe. These are headed by district commissioners, clan and paramount chiefs. The main cities have an elected mayor.

In January 2008 the Supreme Court ruled that the president could appoint local mayors because the government couldn't afford to hold municipal elections. Local elections have not been held since 1985 because of either war or lack of finance.

AREA AND POPULATION

Area
Liberia is situated on the coast of West Africa between Sierra Leone and the Côte d'Ivoire, bordering Guinea to the north. It stretches inland for about 200 miles. The total area is about 111,370 sq. km. The interior is dense tropical forests, Liberia has 40 per cent of Africa's rain forest, the coastal areas are home to mangrove swamps, centrally Liberia has wooded hills and shrublands.

The climate is tropical and it is one of the wettest countries in the world. Average rainfall is approximately 500 cm.

To view a map of Liberia, please consult
http://www.un.org/Depts/Cartographic/map/profile/liberia.pdf

Population
The total population was estimated to be 3.95 million in 2010. An estimated 48 per cent of the population lives in urban areas. Monrovia, the capital, has an estimated population of 1,100,000.

The official language is English. Indigenous languages are also spoken, including Mandingo, Bandi, Bassa, Gola, Kissi, Krahn, Sapo, Vai, Dei and Grebo. Liberians who are descended from immigrants from the USA who had been slaves, make up around 4.0 per cent of the population.

Births, Marriages, Deaths
In 2010 the birth rate was estimated at 39.1 per 1,000 population and the death rate at 11.2 per 1,000 population. Total fertility rate was 5.2 children per woman. Life expectancy at birth in 2009 was estimated at 54 years for males and 57 years for females. Healthy life expectancy was 47 years for males and 49 years for females. The median age is 18 years old. (Source: http://www.who.int, World Health Statistics 2012)

Public Holidays 2014
1 January: New Year's Day
11 February: Armed Forces Day
12 March: Decoration Day
15 March: J.J. Roberts Birthday
28 March: Fast and Prayer Day
20 April: Easter Sunday
14 May: National Unification Day
24 August: National Flag Day
26 August: Independence Day
6 November: Thanksgiving Day
29 November: W.V.S. Tubman's Birthday
25 December: Christmas Day

EMPLOYMENT

Liberia's labour force in 2007 numbered 1.3 million. Agriculture employs around 71 per cent, services 10.8 per cent, industry and commerce 4.5 per cent, other 14.2 per cent. Liberia's unemployment has been estimated as high as 80 per cent.

BANKING AND FINANCE

Years of civil conflict and financial mismanagement have destroyed Liberia's economy and made it one of the poorest countries. Even in the capital many are without water and electricity, although street lighting was restored to Monrovia in 2007. Corruption is widespread. The state, its institutions, heath services, education and defence services have all had to be rebuilt. President Johnson Sirleaf has taken measures to reduce corruption and to encourage foreign investment. An estimated US$97 million of new investment was received in 2007 and the government hopes to achieve a target of US$100 million per year. Main investment opportunities are in the mining, rubber, and agro-forestry sectors.

Currency
1 Liberian Dollar = 100 cents. The US dollar is widely used.

GDP/GNP, Inflation, National Debt
Most of the population is occupied with agriculture. Agriculture is the largest contributor to GDP (77 per cent), services (18 per cent) and industry (5.5 per cent). In order to boost foreign exchange earnings and service its large national debt, Liberia relies heavily on the sale of maritime registrations.

GDP

	2005	2006	2007
GDP, US$ million	530.17	614.00	715.80
GDP growth, %	5.3	7.8	8.0
GNI per capita	120	140	..

Source: African Development Bank

Estimated figures for 2010 put GDP at US$975 million with a growth rate that year of 5.1 per cent. GDP was an estimated UD$1.5 billion in 2011, with a growth rate of 8 per cent. GDP per capita in 2011 was put at US$600.

Inflation in 2007 was 8.00 per cent and rose to 11 per cent in 2008 before falling to 7.3 per cent in 2009. Inflation was estimated to be over 7 per cent in both 2010 and 2011.

In 2006, total external debt was recorded at US$1,116.31 million. Liberia is party to several debt relief agreements. In 2010, Liberia attained its Heavily Indebted Poor Countries completion and approximately US$4.75 billion of international debt was removed. In September 2010 the Paris Club of creditor countries pardoned US$1.2 billion of Liberia's debt. The African Development Bank approved a loan of nearly US$50 million to help Liberia's economy. Total external debt was estimated to be £275 million in 2011.

Balance of Payments / Imports and Exports
In 2001 the UN imposed sanctions on Liberia including on the trade of diamonds and timber. These restrictions were lifted on timber in 2006 and diamonds in 2007. Principal exports are diamonds, iron ore, rubber, coffee, cocoa and timber. In 2006 an estimated 90 per cent of export income came from exports of rubber. Principal imports are fuel, transport equipment, machinery, rice, manufactured goods and foodstuff. Main trading partners include India, Japan, Singapore, USA and Poland.

External Trade, US$ million

	2005	2006	2007
Trade balance	-188.90	-243.06	-264.20
Exports	113.80	157.83	187.86
Imports	302.71	400.90	452.06

Source: AFDB

Exports were estimated to be US$207 million in 2010 and imports cost US$550 million.

Central Bank
Central Bank of Liberia, PO Box 2048, Warren and Carey Streets, Monrovia, Liberia. Tel: +231 227928, fax: +231 226144, URL: http://www.cbl.org.lr/
Governor: Joseph Mills Jones

MANUFACTURING, MINING AND SERVICES

Primary and Extractive Industries
Liberia's export earnings are heavily dependent on primary commodities such as iron ore and rubber. Diamond and gold exports are also important. Rough diamonds could not exported under the terms of the UN sanctions imposed in 2001, these sanctions were lifted in April 2007.

In 2012, energy companies annouced that they had found oil off the coast of Liberia. Exploration is ongoing.

Energy
Figures for 2010 show that Liberia had a net electricity generation of 0.34 billion kilowatthours, all of which was consumed domestically.

LIBERIA

Manufacturing

Since the end of the civil war manufacturing has remained on a relatively small scale. Principal commodities are iron ore production, beverages, rubber processing, palm oil processing, chemicals and tobacco.

Agriculture

A wide variety of crops are grown profitably the most important of which is rubber, others are oil palms, coconut palms, citrus fruits, rubber, pineapples, tomatoes, okra, beans, soya beans, corn, rice, banana, cassava, coffee, cocoa, sugar cane, eddoes, cucumber, and ginger. Land use is as follows: forest and woodland one per cent, permanent crops three per cent, meadows and pastures two per cent, arable land one per cent and other uses, 55 per cent. A trade embargo on Liberian timber imposed by the UN was lifted in June 2006.

Agricultural Production in 2010

Produce	Int. $'000*	Tonnes
Rice, paddy	79,008	296,090
Natural rubber	71,032	62,100
Cassava	51,500	493,000
Bananas	35,063	124,500
Palm oil	18,272	42,000
Game meat	16,319	7,500
Vegetables fresh nes	15,546	82,500
Indigenous chicken meat	15,488	1,874
Indigenous pigmeat	13,866	9,020
Plantains	9,394	45,500
Maize, green	9,270	22,400
Sugar cane	8,441	265,000

* unofficial figures

Source: http://faostat.fao.org/site/339/default.aspx Food and Agriculture Organization of the United Nations, Food and Agricultural commodities production

COMMUNICATIONS AND TRANSPORT

Travel Requirements

Citizens of the USA, Canada, Australia and the EU require a passport valid for at least six months beyond the length of stay, evidence of sufficient funds and a visa. Evidence of a yellow fever vaccination and a physician's letter attesting to absence of communicable diseases may also be required. Visa applicants may also be asked to provide evidence of health insurance.Other nationals should contact the embassy to check visa requirements.

Transit passengers continuing their journey by the same or first connecting aircraft within 48 hours, holding onward or return documentation and not leaving the airport do not require a visa. All visitors holding a visa issued abroad and intending to stay in Liberia for more than 15 days must report within 48 hours of their arrival to the Immigration Office, Monrovia.

International Airports

There are international airfields at Robertsfield (Monrovia International Airport) and James Spriggs Payne.

Railways

There is a railway transporting iron ore from the Mano River and Bomi Hills mines to the Free Port of Monrovia for shipment. Other railways link the iron-ore mines at Nimba with the port of Buchanan 175 miles away and iron-ore in the Bong Hills to the port of Monrovia. Much of the railway system was closed after iron ore production was stopped at some mines or dismantled during the civil war.

Roads

The road system connects with those in Guinea and Sierra Leone. There are over 1,000 miles of state roads suitable for motor traffic as well as roads on private plantations. Roads outside of the capital Monrovia are in a bad state of repair. Vehicles are driven on the right.

Shipping

There is a harbour constructed by the US Government at Monrovia, which is a Free Port. Another port at Buchanan handles iron ore from the Nimba Mountains. There are also ports at Greenville and Harper. Liberia is the world's second largest maritime licenser. Recent figures show around 1,800 vessels are registered under her flag. In 2004 Liberia earned around US$15 million from its maritime licencing programme. Some ferry services operate along the coast.

HEALTH

Health and sanitation are the responsibility of the National Public Health Service which is assisted by USAID (successor to the US International Co-operation Administration) and the World Health Organization. There are a number of government hospitals and clinics, as well as those run by missionaries and by large concessionary companies.

According to WHO figures for 2009, total spending on health care was the equivalent of 12.2 per cent of GDP. General government expenditure on health accounted for 34.5 per cent of total expenditure on health. External resources make up 47 per cent of total expenditure. In 2000-10, there were an estimated 51 doctors, 978 nurses and midwives (3 per 10,000 population), 4 dentists, 269 pharmacists and 40 environment and public health workers.. In 2010, 73 per cent of the urban population had sustainable access to improved water source. Approximately 18 per cent of the population had sustainable access to improved sanitation.

The infant mortality rate in 2010 was 74 per 1,000 live births. The child mortality rate (under 5 years) was 103 per 1,000 live births. The main causes of childhood mortality are: prematurity causes (12 per cent), birth asphyxia (9 per cent), diarrhoea (9 per cent), malaria (18 per cent), pneumonia (14 per cent), measles (10 per cent) and HIV/AIDs (2 per cent). The immunization rate for measles has risen from 52 per cent in 2000 to 64 per cent in 2010. Approximately 39.4 per cent of children were classified as underweight in 2000-09 and 20.4 per cent as underweight. (Source: http://www.who.int, World Health Statistics 2012)

EDUCATION

Education is under the supervision of the Ministry of Education. Education is compulsory and lasts for 10 years, six at primary level. During the civil war which lasted between 1989 and 2003, the education system was severely disrupted.

The University of Liberia was established in 1950, absorbing the Liberia College. The University is assisted by UNESCO and FAO teaching staff as well as those supported by the British, German and US governments. Other institutions of higher education include the African Methodist Episcopal University, the Don Bosco Technical College, the United Methodist University, Monrovia College, the African Methodist Episcopal Zion University, Cuttington University College and William V. S. Tubman College of Technology.

Recent UNESCO figures put adult literacy at 55.5 per cent and youth literacy at 71.8 per cent.

RELIGION

Around 42 per cent of the population profess Christianity, 40 per cent ethnoreligions, and 16 per cent are Muslim. Liberia has a religious tolerance rating of 7 on a scale of 1 to 10 (10 is most freedom). (Source: World Religion Database)

COMMUNICATIONS AND MEDIA

Years of fighting have seriously damaged the country's communications and broadcasting infrastructure. China has helped to repair the broadcasting infrastructure.

Newspapers

Newspapers are published privately and include, The Inquirer (URL: http://www.theinquirer.com.lr/); The News (URL: http://www.thenews.com.lr/); The Analyst (URL: http://www.analystliberia.com).

Broadcasting

Liberia has internal radio links. The state run broadcaster (Liberian Broadcasting System, URL: http://www.liberiabroadcastingsystem.com/) only broadcasts on radio. There are several private radio stations in existence. There are three private television stations and satellite television is available.

Telecommunications

The telephone system exists mainly in the capital, Monrovia. There are an estimated 2,000 telephone mainlines and over 700,000 mobile phones. Recent figures show that Liberia has around 20,000 regular internet users.

ENVIRONMENT

A particular environmental concern is the deforestation of the Liberian rain forest. Liberia is a party to the following international agreements: Biodiversity, Climate Change, Climate Change-Kyoto Protocol, Desertification, Endangered Species, Hazardous Wastes, Law of the Sea, Ozone Layer Protection, Ship Pollution, Tropical Timber 83, Tropical Timber 94 and Wetlands. It has signed but not ratified the agreements on Environmental Modification and Marine Life Conservation.

In 2010, Liberia's emissions from the consumption of fossil fuels totalled 0.74 million metric tons of carbon dioxide. (Source: EIA)

LIBYA
State of Libya
Dawlat Libya

Capital: Tripoli (Population estimate: 2,000,000)

Head of State: Giuma Attaiga (Chair of the National Transitional Council, acting)

Vice Chair of the National Transitional Council: vacant

National Flag: The flag under Colonel Gaddafi was plain green. The NTC used the previous flag of Libya and this was re-adopted in 2011. The flag is a horizontal tricolour of red, black and green with a white crescent and star centered on the black stripe.

CONSTITUTION AND GOVERNMENT

Constitution

After the expulsion of the Italians and Germans in 1943, Libya was placed under military administration. According to the Peace Treaty signed in February 1947, Italy renounced all claims to its former possessions in Africa. The fate of the territories was to be settled by the Governments of the United States, Britain, France and the USSR, but the four Great Powers were unable to reach agreement and the case was submitted to the General Assembly of the United Nations. After some controversy, the General Assembly, on 21 November 1949, resolved that Libya should become an independent sovereign state by the beginning of 1952, and Libya became the first country to achieve its independence through the UN. The National Assembly of Libya, consisting of 60 delegates, held its inaugural session at Tripoli on 25 November 1950 in preparation for the unification and independence of the country by 1 January 1952. It adopted the resolution of 3 December 1950 by which it formally proclaimed Muhammad Idris al-Sanussi, the Amir of Cyrenaica, as King of Libya. The Constituent Assembly prepared a constitution, which came into force with the formal declaration of independence on 24 December 1951.

In September 1969 the monarchy was overthrown in a revolution. A Revolutionary Command Council (RCC) consisting of 12 military officers and headed by Col. Mu'amar al-Qadhafi took power, and the state was named the Libyan Arab Republic. The second phase of the revolution began in April 1973, when al-Qadhafi announced a programme intended to involve the Libyan people more closely with the running of the state. This developed into a system of popular congresses and committees, formulated in the 'Green Book', which began to appear in 1975. The third phase of the revolution was marked by the 'Declaration of the establishment of the authority of the people' on 2 March 1977. The state was renamed the Socialist People's Libyan Arab Jamahiriya ('state of the masses'). The RCC was officially disbanded, and power exercised by the people through a system of People's Committees and Congresses. The head of government was the Chairman of the General People's Committee. This formed the Libyan cabinet and was established by the General People's Congress. The General People's Congress had 750 members appointed for a three-year term.

In August 2011, the National Transitional Council (NTC) announced its own draft constitution.

Recent Events

Libya was isolated internationally following the bombing of a Pan Am flight over Lockerbie, Scotland. The UN sanctions ended when Libya agreed to hand over two men suspected of planting the bomb but US sanctions remained. In December 2003 Libya announced it was scrapping its weapons programme and, in March 2004, it handed a full report of its chemical weapons programme to the UN. In response the US lifted its travel ban. The EU lifted its embargo on the sale of arms in September 2004. The US also lifted its trade embargo in 2004 and in May 2006 announced that it would be restoring diplomatic relations with Libya.

In January 2008 Libya held the one-month rotating presidency of the UN Security Council. In February 2009 President Gaddafi was elected chairman of the African Union. In January 2010 a deal was agreed between Russia and Libya with Libya buying weapons and defence systems worth $1.8 billion.

In February 2011 Libya became the scene of street demonstrations as protests that had been sweeping through the Middle East continued. A human rights campaigner was arrested in Benghazi and this acted as the catalyst for protests which spread to other major cities. Colonel Gaddafi insisted that the protests were the work of foreign agitators; the Libyan people were loyal to him and ignored calls for his resignation.

However, several rebel groups across the country remained active. Initially, rebels took control of several towns including important oil towns such as Ras Lanuf. Air strikes were carried out against the rebels, and as the Libyan army mobilised its forces the rebels had to retreat. In March the G8 nations met to discuss the imposing of a no fly zone over Libya to protect civilians. The UN Security Council authorised the no fly zone and NATO assumed command. Following NATO air raids rebels captured some territory but were later forced back by pro-Gaddafi forces. In March 2011 opposition groups came together to form the Transistional National council of the Libyan Republic.

In March the European Union and Arab League called for Colonel Gaddafi to quit. Several ministers either resigned or were reported to have fled the country.

Fighting by pro-Gaddafi troops and the rebels continued as the Gaddafi regime proved more resilient than predicted and the rebels less effective. The country's coastal cities were roughly split between the pro-Gaddafi forces who also controlled Tripoli and the rebels who also

controlled Benghazi, but following fierce fighting the rebels began to take control of areas in the west including the town of Zintan. By May the rebels declared they had liberated the western port city of Misrata. On June 27 the International Criminal Court issued arrest warrants for Colonel Gaddafi, his son Saif al-Islam and the chief of intelligence Brigadier General Abdullah al-Sanussi, for crimes against humanity following systematic attacks on civilians. In August 2011 the rebels took over Gaddafi's compound in Tripoli but Colonel Gaddaffi's whereabouts remained unknown. Pockets of pro-Gadafi resistance remained and running battles in Tripoli and Sirte continued.

Opposition groups within Libya formed an interim national council and said it would hold free and fair elections and draft a national constitution. France was the first country to recognise the Council as official and it was joined by several other countries including Italy, Turkey and Qatar. The UK Foreign Secretary William Hague met Mr Mahmoud Jabril, President of the Libyan Interim Transitional Council in March 2011. Mr Jabril continued to work for diplomatic recognition of the Interim Transitional Council and in May he met senior US officials and members of Congress. The NTC said it was seeking £1.5 billion in immediate aid. Some was to come from frozen assets although there was some oppostion to this from various countries including South Africa which said it would wait for guidance from the African Union which at that stage had not recognised the validity of the rebel leadership. The leader of the NTC, Mustafa Abdul Jalil, delivered his first speech in Tripoli on 13 September. He outlined plans to create a modern democratic state based on moderate Islam. He said a government should be in place by the end of September. In late September both the AU and South Africa recognised the validity of the National Transitional Council. As of September 2011, the National Transitional Council was composed of several disparate groups including opposition figures and former Gaddafi allies.

A mass grave containing at least 1,200 bodies was found in Tripoli in September. The grave is believed to contain the bodies of inmates killed by security forces in 1996 in the Abu Salim prison.

In September 2011, forces loyal to the transitional authorities were reported to have taken the airport in the Gaddafi stronghold of Sirte. Fighting for Sirte continued throughout the month and into October. Forces loyal to the interim authorities entered Bani Walid, one of the last towns still loyal to Col. Gaddafi.

On October 20 Colonel Gaddafi was found in Sirte. A convoy was bombed by NATO forces and Colonel Gaddafi was found hiding in a storm drain by fighters loyal to the NTC and was reported to have died from bullet wounds trying to evade capture. NATO forces signaled that the death of Gaddafi would mean an end to their involvement in the country. After several days of discussion, Gaddafi's body was buried in a secret location in the desert.

On October 23 the National Transitional Council (NTC) declared Libya to be officially liberated.

In November Gaddafi's son Saif al-Islam, was captured and the NTC said they would put him on trial.

In January 2012 clashes were reported between former rebel forces in Benghazi who felt that the pace of change under the NTC was too slow.

Local elections were held for the first time in fifty years in Benghazi in May 2012.

In May 2012 the death was announced of Abdelbaset a-Megrahi, the only man to be convicted of the 1988 Lockerbie bombing in which 270 people were killed. He was freed from Scottish prison in 2009 on compassionate grounds due to poor health.

Elections took place in July 2012. Early results suggest that secular parties will have control of the Assembly.

On July 18, a suicide bomber attacked the security headquarters in Damascus. The defence minister Gen. Daoud Rajiha was killed along with his deputy, President Assad's brother in law Assef Shawkat. The national security chief and interior minister were also badly hurt. The rebel Free Syrian Army (FSA) and a jihadist group called Lord of the Martyrs Brigade both said they were responsible for the bombing.

In September 2012, violent protests took place in several Middle East countries following the release of an amateur anti-Islam video made in the USA. In Libya a mob attacked the US consulate in Benghazi and killed the Ambassador, Chris Stevens and three other embassy staff.

In early October 2012, Prime Minister Mustafa Abu Shagur was dismissed from his post after failing to form a government following elections held in July. On October 14 2012, former diplomat Ali Zidan was elelcted to the post of prime minister by the National Congress.

In December 2012, the former Prime Minister al-Baghdadi al-Mahmoudi was put on trial for 'acts that led to the unjust killing of Libyans'. He was also accused of siphoning off around US$25 million of public money to help forces loyal to Colonel Gaddafi.

In January 2013, Britain, Germany and the Netherlands urged their citizens to leave the country's second city, Benghazi. The following May the British Foreign Office withdrew some embassy staff in response to concerns over the security situation.

LIBYA

Also in January, the name of the country was officially changed from The Great Socialist People's Libyan Arab Jamahiriya to the State of Libya.

In May 2013, parliament passed a law that any person who had worked for the government of Colonel Gaddafi would be banned from public office.

Legislature

The legislature of Libya is unicameral, and is called the General People's Congress, *Mu'tamar al-Sha'ab al-'Am*, 750 members are appointed by locally based Basic People's Congresses and serve a term of three years.

General People's Congress, PO Box 2554, Tripoli, Libya. Tel: +218 21 606700

Cabinet (as at June 2013)
President: Giuma Attaiga
Prime Minister: Ali Zidan (page 1543)
First Deputy Prime Minister: Sadiq Abdulkarim Abdulrahman Karim
Second Deputy Prime Minister: Awad Al-Barasi
Third Deputy Prime Minister: Abdussalam Al-Mehdi Al-Qadi
Minister of Foreign Affairs and International Co-operation: Mohamed Imhamid Abdulaziz
Minister of Defence: Mohammed Mahmoud Al-Barghati
Minister of Internal Affairs: Col. Mihammed Khalifa Al-Sheikh
Minister of Finance: Alkilani Abdul Kareem Al-Jazi
Minister of Justice: Salah Bashir Abaj Margani
Minister of the Economy: Mustafa Mohammed Abufunas
Minister of Oil and Gas: Abdulbari Ali Al Hadi Al-Arusi
Minister of Industry: Sulaiman Ali Al-Lteef Al-Fituri
Minister of Education: Mohammed Hassan Abubaker
Minister of Health: Nurideen Abdulhamid Dagman
Minister of Local Government: Abubaker Al-Hadi Mohammed
Minister of Social Affairs: Kamila Khamis Al-Mazini
Minister of Agriculture: Ahmed Ali Al-Orfi
Minister of Labour and Retraining: Mohamed Fitouri Abmed Sualim
Minister of Transport: Abdul Qadir Al-Ayib
Minister of Communications: osama Abdurauf Siala
Minister of Culture: Habib Mohammed Al-Sharif
Minister of Religious Affairs: Abdulsalam Mohammed Abusaad
Minister of Planning: Mahdi Ataher Genia
Minister of Housing and Public Services: Ali Hussein Al-Sharif
Minister of Electricity and Renewable Energy: Ali Mohammed Mihirig
Minister of Higher Education: Ali Muftah Obaid
Minister of Sport and Youth: Abdulsalam Guaila
Minister for Support for Families of Martyrs and the Disappeared: Ali Gadour
Miinister of State for the Wounded: Ramadan Ali Zarmuh
Minister of Water Resources: Alhadi Suleiman Hinshir
Minister of Tourism: Ikram Abdulsalam Imam

Ministries

Secretariat for Foreign Liaison and International Co-operation, Ras Lanouf, Libya. Tel: +218 21 340 0461, fax: +218 21 340 2921, URL: http://www.foreign.gov.ly
Secretariat for Health and Environment, Omar Mukhtar Street, Sirte, Libya. Tel: +218 21 333 9369, fax: +218 21 333 2951, URL: http://www.health.gov.ly
Secretariat for the Industry, Economy and Trade, Sarraj, Tripoli, Libya. Tel: +218 21 480 9361, fax: +218 21 80 9361, URL: http://www.ect.gov.ly
Secretariat for Justice and Public Security, Sirte, Libya. Tel: +218 21 480 4632, fax: +218 21 480 4630, e-mail: info@aladel.gov.ly, URL: http://www.aladel.gov.ly
Secretariat for Planning and Finance, Sirtem Libya. Tel: +218 21 360 20136, fax: +218 21 360 20138, URL: http://www.mof.gov.ly
Secretariat for Public Utilities, Sirte, Libya. Tel: +218 21 362 0106, fax: +218 21 219 9757, URL: http://www.smpt.gov.ly
Secretariat for Tourism, Sirte, Libya. Tel: +218 21 333 0913, fax: +218 21 360 3145, URL: http://www.libyan-tourism.org

Elections

The transitional council announced that elections would be held in July 2012. A constitutional referendum is hoped to be held following the election. Abdurrahim Al-Keib was made interim Prime Minister on November 22 and named his interim government. The first election in Libya for 42 years was held on July 7 2012; 2,639 candidates contested 120 seats in 69 constituencies. At the time of going to press, full results were not known. Early results suggested that secular parties had done well. The National Forces Alliance, led by former interim prime mininster, Mahmoud, Jibril won 39 out of 80 seats reserved for political parties. The Muslim Bortherhood party took 17 seats. The 200-member assembly will also include independent candidates. One of the first tasks of the newly elected parliament will be to draft a new constitution.

Political Parties

Arab Socialist Union (ASU)

Diplomatic Representation

British Embassy, PO Box 4206, Tripoli, Libya. Tel: +218 (21) 340 3644/5, fax: +218 (21) 340 3648, e-mail: britcom@lttnet.net, URL: http://ukinlibya.fco.gov.uk/en (Britain resumed diplomatic relations with Libya in 1999)
Ambassador: Michael Aron
Embassy of the United States, Corinthia Bab Africa Hotel, Souq At-Tlat Al-Qadim, Tripoli, Libya. Tel: +218 21 335 1848, e-mail: tripoliirm@state.gov, URL: http://libya.usembassy.gov/
Ambassador: Deborah Kay Jones
The People's Bureau of the Great Socialist People's Libyan Arab Jamahiriya, 15 Knightsbridge, London SW1X 7LY, UK. Tel: +44 (0)20 7201 8280, URL: hppt://libyanembassy.org

Ambassador: Mahmud Nacau
Libyan Embassy, 2600 Virginia Avenue NW, Suite 705, Washington DC 20037, USA. Tel: +1 202 944 9601, fax: +1 202 944 9060
Ambassador: vacant
Permanent Representative of the Socialist People's Libyan Arab Jamahiriya to the United Nations, 309-315 East 48th Street, New York, NY 10017, Tel: +1 212 752 5775, fax: +1 212 593 4787, e-mail: info@libya-un.org, URL: http://www.libya-un.org
Ambassador: Ab al-Rahman Muhammad Shalgham

LEGAL SYSTEM

The Libyan judicial system formerly comprised separate Sharia'a and secular courts. In 1971, Colonel Qadhafi replaced this system with a single judiciary, integrating Islamic and secular principles. The legal system of Libya under Qadhafir was based on a combination of Italian Civil Law and Islamic legal principles. The formal sources of the law included legislative provisions, Islamic principles, custom, and principles of natural law and rules of equity. In addition, judicial decisions and the thoughts and doctrines of eminent jurists guide judicial decision-making.

The judicial system was four-tiered. Summary Courts, located in small towns, heard minor cases. Courts of First Instance, located in Libya's former governorates adjudicated in all civil, criminal, and commercial cases. Jurors applied Sharia'a principles in cases involving personal status. Cases from the Courts of First Instance could be appealed to the three Courts of Appeal, located in Tripoli, Benghazi, and Sabha. Each Court of Appeal had a panel of three judges. A separate body called the Sharia'a Court of Appeals heard cases appealed from the lower court involving Sharia'a. The final court of Appeal was the Supreme Court of Libya, in Tripoli. The Court was presided over by a president, elected by the General People's Congress. The Supreme Council for Judicial Authority was the administrative authority of the judiciary, handling matters of appointment, transfer and discipline.

The Government's human rights record remained poor under Colonel Qadhafi, and it restricted freedom of speech, press, assembly, association, and religion. It also repressed certain minorities and tribal groups. Traditional attitudes continue to repress women.

Libya retains the death penalty. Capital crimes include high treason and premeditated murder. In May 2004, five Bulgarian nurses and a Palestinian doctor were sentenced to death for allegedly infecting 426 children with the HIV virus on purpose. The Supreme Court overturned the death sentences in December 2005. All six defendants later testified to having been tortured. At least 18 people were reported to have been executed in 2010.

Following the revolution and overthrow of Colonel Qadhafi, the legal system is in a state of change. The process of drafting a new constitution has begun but is in the very early stages. As of January 2013, discussions were ongoing on the composition of the Constitutional Commission. Many former deputies under Col. Qadafi's regime are being held in special prisons and are believed to have no access to legal counsel. Thousands of other lower-ranking suspected war criminals are believed to be held in militia-run dentention centres awaiting referal to the court system.

LOCAL GOVERNMENT

Libya's system of government takes the form of a *jamahiriya* (state of the masses) which is controlled by the people by way of local councils. There are 22 administrative regions or *Sha'abiyat*, and delegates from these attend General People's Congress. The Sha'abiyat are Al Butnan, Al Jabal al Akhdar, Al Jabal Al Gharbi, Al Jafarah, Al Jafrah, Al Kafrah, Al Maraj, Al Marqab, Al Murzuq, Al Wahat, An Nuqat al Khams, Az Zawiyah, Banghazi, Darnah, Ghat, Misratah, Nalut, Sibha, Surt, Tarabulus, Wadi al Hayat and Wadi ash Shati.

Local elections took place in Benghazi in May 2012. These were the first local elections in Benghazi since the 1960s. The mandate of local councils is currently unclear.

AREA AND POPULATION

Area

Libya is situated on the north coast of Africa between Egypt in the east and Tunisia and Algeria in the west. It borders Niger, Chad and Sudan to the south. The area of the country is about 1,759,540 sq. km. making it the fourth largest African country. Much of the country is covered by desert.

To view a map, please visit http://www.un.org/Depts/Cartographic/map/profile/libya.pdf

Along the coast the climate is Mediterranean but in the centre there are severe desert conditions.

Population

In 2010, the population was estimated to be 6.35 million, with an estimated annual growth rate of 1.9 per cent over the period 2000-10. Around 90 per cent of the population live in 10 per cent of the land, mostly in the coastal strip. Approximately 97 per cent of the population are Arab. Arabic is the official language and English has largely replaced Italian as the second language. Many foreign nationals left during the conflict.

Births, Marriages, Deaths

A 2010 estimate put the birth rate at 23.1 births per 1,000 of the population. The death rate was estimated at 11.2 deaths per 1,000. The infant mortality rate is in the region of 13 deaths per 1,000 live births. By 2009, the average life expectancy was 70 years for males and 75 years for females. Healthy life expectancy was 63 years and 66 years respectively.

Approximately 30 per cent of the population is aged under 15 years and 6 per cent over 60 years. The median age was 26. The total fertility rate per woman was 2.6 children. (Source: http://www.who.int, World Health Statistics 2012)

Public Holidays 2014
2 March: Jamahiriya Day
14 January: Birth of the Prophet
28 March: British Evacuation Day
11 June: Evacuation Day
27 May: Ascension of the Prophet
23 July: Revolution Day
1 September: National Day
7 September: Italian Evacuation Day
8 August: Eid al-Fitr (End of Ramadan)
5 October: Eid al-Adha (Feast of Sacrifice)
25 October: Islamic New Year
3 November: Ashura

EMPLOYMENT

Recent estimates put the work force at 1.6 million. The work force can be divided as follows: industry 31 per cent, services 27 per cent, government 24 per cent and agriculture 18 per cent. In 2004 the unemployment rate was estimated to be 30 per cent.

In January 2007 the government announced plans for mass redundancies in the public sector affecting 400,000 government workers (more than 30 per cent of the total government workforce) in an attempt to lessen public spending and stimulate the private sector.

BANKING AND FINANCE

Currency
The unit of currency is the Libyan dinar of 1,000 dirhams.

GDP/GNP, Inflation, National Debt
The mainstay of the Libyan economy is oil, accounting for some 95 per cent of export earnings and over 70 per cent of GDP. Efforts are being made both to reform the economy and to restore international relations and re-establish international trading links. Sanctions were ended. Planning for some privatisation of state companies began before the revolution and some subsidies reduced. Libya has also applied for WTO membership. Libya had also been trying to attract foreign investment but this is unlikely to progress until a stable government is in place.

Real GDP was an estimated US$37 million in 2011.

Industry is the largest contributor to GDP, responsible for nearly 50 per cent. The service sector contributes over 42 per cent and agriculture makes up just over 7 per cent.

Inflation was high in the early 1990s: 20 per cent in 1993, 30 per cent in 1994, 20 per cent in 1995 before falling to single-digit inflation (4 per cent in 1996). It remained low for a decade, even going into negative figures in the years 2000-2004. In 2005 it rose to 2 per cent, rising further to 3.5 per cent in 2006 and 7.00 per cent in 2007. It was estimated to be over 14 per cent in 2011.

Total external debt (non-military) was estimated in 1995 at US$5,600 million. By 1998 it had increased to US$3.8 billion.

Balance of Payments / Imports and Exports
Libya's major trading partners are Italy, Germany, Spain, UK, France, Turkey, Tunisia and China. The main export products are crude oil, refined petroleum products and natural gas while the main import products are machinery, transport equipment, food and manufactured goods. In 2004, an estimated 1.3 million barrels of oil were exported per day and net export revenue for oil was around US$18.0 billion.

Exports were estimated to be worth US$34 billion in 2009 and imports cost US$22 billion. Following the conflict, exports fell to an estimated US$15 billion in 2011, down over 50 per cent from 2010. Imports amounted to an estimated US$10 million, down 50 per cent from 2010.

External Trade, US$ million

	2005	2006	2007
Trade balance	20,073.00	25,906.00	21,198.85
Exports	30,948.00	38,831.00	33,298.24
Imports	10,875.00	12,925.00	12,099.39

Source: African Development Bank

In January 2002, 50 per cent was cut from customs duty rates on most imports to counter effects of the currency devaluation which took place at the same time. This was done to encourage competitiveness and foreign investment.

Trade or Currency Restrictions
The sanctions imposed on Libya from 1992-1999 by the UN, as a result of the bombing of a Pan Am flight over Lockerbie, Scotland, severely affected the economy. The UN sanctions ended when Libya agreed to hand over two men suspected of planting the bomb. In January 2001, one of the defendants was found guilty, the other cleared. The EU lifted its embargo on the sale of arms in September 2004. The US also lifted its trade embargo in 2004.

Revenue from oil exports account for nearly 95 per cent of hard currency earnings and it is estimated that US$5 billion in revenue was lost due to sanctions on oil exports and a reduction in oil prices.

Central Bank
Central Bank of Libya, PO Box 1103, Tripoli, Libya. Tel: +218 21 3333591-9 / 4441481-3, fax: +218 21 4441488, e-mail: Info@cbl-ly.com, URL: http://www.cbl.gov.ly/eg/
Governor & Chairman: Saddek Omar Ali Elkaber

MANUFACTURING, MINING AND SERVICES

Primary and Extractive Industries
Libya has deposits of iron ore, limestone and clay but by far the most important sector of the economy is the petroleum industry. Despite the UN sanctions imposed between 1992-1999 in response to Libya's refusal to extradite two nationals suspected of involvement in the 1988 Lockerbie bombing, oil revenues contributed virtually all export earnings and about a third of GDP. UN sanctions were lifted in 1999.

Libya's first commercial oilfield was discovered in 1956 and this was put into production in 1961. In 1973 the Government nationalised in full or in part most of the foreign oil companies in Libya. Some foreign companies continue to operate there, alongside Libya's National Oil Company, including Italy's Agip, Germany's Veba, Austria's OeMV, Spain's Repsol, and France's Total. These companies have effectively replaced those US companies operating in Libya prior to sanctions. During the years of UN and US imposed sanctions oil production declined; Libya tried to maintain prices in an over-supplied market, and because it wished to conserve reserves.

During the unrest in 2011, Libyan oil and natural gas exports suffered almost total shutdown, what small oil production that did go ahead was mostly used domestically. In September 2011 following the end of Colonel Qadhafi's regime, oil prouduction resumed and by mid 2012 was producing around 1.4 bbl/d.

In 2010 Libya consumed just 314,000 barrels per day leaving 187,000 barrels per day available for export. Libya exports most of its oil to Italy; it also sells to Germany, Spain and Greece. Figures for January 2012 estimated Libya's total oil reserves to be 47.1 billion barrels. In order to expand its oil industry Libya requires foreign investment.

Libya has large reserves of natural gas currently estimated to be around 55 trillion cubic feet. Production in 2010 was around 277 billion cubic feet and consumption 242 billion feet. Libya is looking for foreign investment to help exploit its gas reserves and wishes to export to Europe. At present, it exports to Spain and Italy.

Energy
Because of Libya's desire to replace domestic oil consumption with gas consumption, expansion of the gas industry is an important part of the country's energy strategy. Such a strategy would also allow more oil to be exported, and increase gas exports. In 1998 oil was accountable for 67.6 per cent of energy consumption and natural gas for 32.4 per cent.

Recent estimates put electricity generation capacity at 6.7 gigawatts. The demand for electricity in Libya has grown rapidly in recent years, leading in 2004 to power cuts when generation could not keep up with demand. Libya's state-owned General Electric Company pledged to build eight combined cycle and steam power plants. Figures for 2010 showed that Libya generated 29.72 billion kWh of electricity and consumed 25.24 billion kWh.

Manufacturing
The main industries include food processing, paper, textiles and cement.

Agriculture
Most of Libya's vast land area is desert and completely unproductive. Only about 9 per cent of the country's area is under cultivation which means that 75 per cent of food is imported. Poultry is Libya's major livestock product, yielding some 17 million head according to recent FAO estimates.

It is hoped that following completion of the Great Man Made River, a project to transport water from underground aquifers in the Sahara to the coast, water shortages will be reduced and so aid agricultural expansion as Libya currently relies heavily on imported food goods.

Agricultural Production in 2010

Produce	Int. $'000*	Tonnes
Indegenous chicken meat	183,321	128,700
Olives	144,127	180,000
Almonds, with shell	87,054	29,500
Tomatoes	85,000	230,000
Indigenous sheep meat	77,935	28,623
Dates	56,688	161,000
Hen eggs, in shell	51,837	62,500
Potatoes	46,415	290,000
Cow milk, whole, fresh	44,001	141,000
Onions, dry	40,956	195,000
Indigenous goat meat	31,089	12,975
Watermelons	27,910	245,000

* unofficial figures
Source: http://faostat.fao.org/site/339/default.aspx Food and Agriculture Organization of the United Nations, Food and Agricultural commodities production

LIBYA

COMMUNICATIONS AND TRANSPORT

Travel Requirements
Citizens of the USA, Canada, Australia and the EU require a passport valid for six months. Holders of passports containing a valid or expired visa for Israel will be refused entry or transit. All visitors entering Libya must have a minimum of foreign currency equivalent to LD500 on arrival, unless travelling in a tourist group where expenses have been covered prior to arrival. An Arabic transcript of passport's details page is also required (contact the nearest Libyan embassy or consulate for information on how to obtain an acceptable translation). A visa is required to visit Libya, but all apart from transit passengers continuing their journey by the same or first connecting aircraft within 24 hours, holding valid onward or return documentation and not leaving the airport.

Visitors must register with the immigration office within one week of arrival. Those visiting with an organised tour will usually have this done for them; some hotels also provide this service.

All visitors should contact the embassy prior to travelling, to check precise visa requirements.

National Airlines
Jamahiriya Libyan Arab Airlines, P.O. Box 2555, Haiti Street, Tripoli, Libya. Tel: +218 21 602083, fax: +218 21 602085

International Airports
Tripoli International airport is open and, since December 2011, commercial carriers have resumed flights to and from Europe. Commercial international flights also operate from Benghazi airport. The UN Security Council lifted the No Fly Zon over Libya in October 2011.

Railways
No railways have been in operation since 1965 but there are plans for the construction of new lines, including one running the length of Libya's coast linking Egypt in the east with Tunisia in the west, and one running north to south linking Libya with Chad and Niger.

Roads
The road network is over 80,000 km in length of which more than half are paved. Libya's major route is the 1,822 km national coast road linking the Tunisian and Egyptian borders, and passing through Tripoli and Benghazi. Bus services run to Tunisia and Egypt. Vehicles are driven on the right.

Ports and Harbours
The main ports are at Al Khums, Banghazi, Darnah, Marsa al Burayqah, Misratah, Ra's Lanuf, Tobruk, Tripoli and Zuwarah. Ferry services run from Tripoli to Malta and Sfax, Tunisia.

HEALTH

Libya's health centre was badly damaged during the recent conflict. It has less than 1,500 oprimary health care facilities such as local clincics and district hospitals. Many foreign health workers, who formed a significant part of the total health personnel, fled the country during the 2011 conflict and many have not returned resulting in severe staff shortages. Because of a lack of domestic health services, thousands of Libyans receive health care abroad which is costly to the government. The Libyan government asked the World Health Organisation for help in rebuilding its health care system. Action will be focused on six areas: increased primary health care; improvement of signification aspects of health service organisation; improving laboratory services; improving radiology services; better drug supply management; increasing the numbers of trained nurses.

In 2008, Libya spent approximately 5.5 per cent of its total budget on healthcare (down from 6.0 per cent in 2000), aaccounting for 66.6 per cent of all healthcare spending. Total expenditure on healthcare equated to 3.9 per cent of the country's GDP. Per capita expenditure on health was approximately US$427, compared with US$216 in 2000.

Figures for 2005-10 show that there were 12,009 physicians (19 per 10,000 population), 42,982 nurses and midwives (68 per 10,000 population) and 3,792 dentists. There were 37 hospital beds per 10,000 population.

According to WHO figures, in 2008 approximately 72 per cent of the urban population and 51 per cent of the rural population had access to improved drinking water. In the same year, 25 per cent of the urban population and 17 per cent of the rural population had access to improved sanitation.

Life expectancy at birth in 2009 was 73 years. In 2010, the infant mortality rate (probability of dying by age 1) was 13 per 1,000 live births and the under-five mortality rate was 17 per 1,000 live births. (Source: http://www.who.int, World Health Statistics 2012)

EDUCATION

Since the early 1970s education has expanded rapidly and primary education is now compulsory and free for both girls and boys between the ages of six and 15, which is reflected in the 1996 primary school enrolment rate of 112 per cent. Recent figures show that there are over 4,000 primary schools with 1.4 million primary pupils and 104,000 primary teachers. Secondary school pupils number nearly 311,000, with teachers in the region of 18,000. Higher education is provided by the Al Fatah (Tripoli) and Ghar Yunis (Benghazi) Universities. UNESCO estimates put the rate of illiteracy of over-15s at 23.8 per cent.

RELIGION

The religion of Libya is Islam and 97 per cent of the people are Sunni Muslims, around 2.6 per cent of the population are Christian.

Libya has a religious liberty rating of 5 on a scale of 1 to 10 (10 is most freedom). (Source: World Religion Database)

COMMUNICATIONS AND MEDIA

There is very little press freedom in Libya with strict government control and self-censorship is common.

Newspapers
The main newspapers are government controlled. International publications are routinely censored.
Al Fajr al Jadid, URL: http://www.alfajraljadeed.com
The Tripoli Post, English language, URL: http://www.tripolipost.com/

Broadcasting
The state controls the broadcast media. In addition to the state-owned terrestial TV stations and some state-owned satellite stations, there are local TV regional stations and pan-Arab satellite TV stations are also available. The Voice of Africa can also be heard.
Great Jamahiriyah TV and Radio, state-run, URL: http://www.ljbc.net/home.php

Telecommunications
There is a modern telecommunications system and there are an estimated 1 million landlines and over 4 million mobile telephones in operation. Over 300,000 of the population have regular access to the internet.

ENVIRONMENT

Libya's main environmental problems stem from desertification and sparse water resources. A major project arising from the resulting water shortage and dependence on imports of food is the US$25,000 million-Great Man Made River scheme to transport water from the Sahara to the Mediterranean coast along underground aquifers.

In 2006 Libya's emissions from the consumption of fossil fuels totalled 60.60 million metric tons of carbon dioxide in 2010. (Source: EIA)

On an international level Libya is a party to the following international agreements: Biodiversity, Climate Change, Climate Change-Kyoto Protocol, Desertification, Endangered Species, Hazardous Wastes, Marine Dumping, Ozone Layer Protection, Ship Pollution and Wetlands. signed, but not ratified: Law of the Sea. Libya has signed, but not ratified the agreements on Environmental Modification or the Law of the Sea.

LIECHTENSTEIN

Principality of Liechtenstein

Fürstentum Liechtenstein

Capital: Vaduz (Population estimate: 5,000)

Head of State: HSH Prince Hans-Adam II von und zu Liechtenstein (Sovereign) (page 1437)

Crown Prince: Alois von und zu Liechtenstein (page 1464)

National Flag: Divided fesswise, royal blue and red, the blue charged with a princely crown near the hoist.

CONSTITUTION AND GOVERNMENT

Constitution

Liechtenstein is an independent principality. Power rests with the monarch and the people. The Constitution of 5 October 1921 provides for a *Landtag* of 25 members elected from two constituencies for four years by direct vote, the lowland constituency elected 10 members and the highland constituency 15, according to a system of proportional representation. Liechtenstein citizens over the age of 20 are entitled to vote. Women did not get the vote until 1984, and then they were still not allowed to vote on communal affairs in three of Liechtenstein's 11 communes. Full voting rights were accorded in 1986.

In 2001 Prince Hans-Adam II proposed some constitutional changes which would lessen the power of the parliament. Under the proposed changes the Prince would be able to appoint judges and appeal more directly to the people and would allow the Royal family to veto laws and dismiss parliament. The changes were discussed by parliament and when approved went to a referendum of the people. The referendum was held in March 2003 with the people voting in favour of the proposed changes.

To consult the constitution, please visit: http://www.llv.li/verfassung-e-01-02-09.doc.pdf/

International Relations

Liechtenstein has very close political ties with her neighbour Switzerland. Switzerland represents Liechtenstein in all overseas countries apart from Switzerland, Austria, Germany and the USA. Liechtenstein has no army of its own and so Switzerland has responsibility for its defence. Liechtenstein is a member of the UN, the European Economic Area, the Council of Europe and the OSCE.

Recent Events

In August 2003 Prince Hans-Adam II announced that on 15 August 2004 he would hand over political control to his son Prince Alois while he remains as head of state. The transfer duly took place and Prince Alois is now responsible for the day to day running of the principality.

After long-standing concerns over its status as a tax haven, Liechtenstein agreed to co-operate more fully with the OECD on tax matters. In April 2009 it signed various agreements over sharing financial data. In May 2009, OECD removed it from its list of uncooperative countries.

Legislature

The parliament or *Landtag*, is unicameral and consists of 25 directly elected members who serve a four year term. The Government, which is organised on a collegiate basis, is comprised of five members.

Landtag, Kirchstrasse 10, 9490 Vaduz, Liechtenstein. Tel: +423 236 6570, fax: +423 236 6580, URL: http://www.landtag.li

---

Cabinet (as at June 2013)
Prime Minister, Minister of General Government Affairs, Minister of Finance: Adrian Hasler (page 1439)
Deputy Prime Minister, Minister of Economic Affairs, Minister of Justice, Minister of Economic Affairs: Dr Thomas Zwiefelhofer (page 1543)
Minister of Infrastructure, Minister of Environment, Minister of Sport: Marlies Amann-Marxer
Minister of Social Affairs: Dr Mauro Pedrazzini
Minister of Foreign Affairs, Minister of Education, Minister of Culture: Dr Aurelia Frick (page 1427)

Government Offices, Regierungsgebäude, 9490 Vaduz, Liechtenstein. Tel: +423 236 6111 (most ministries are based at this address)
Government Portal: URL: http://www.liechtenstein.li/
Ministry of Foreign Affairs, Heiligkreuz 14, Postfach 684, 9490 Vaduz, Liechtenstein. Tel: +423 2366057, fax: +423 2366059, e-mail: info@aaa.llv.li
Ministry of Finance, Haus Risch, Aeulestrasse 51. 9490 Vaduz, Liechtenstein. Tel: +423 2366221, fax: +423 2366224, e-mail: info@afdl.llv.li
Ministry of Environmental Affairs, Land Use, Planning, Agriculture and Forestry, Postfach 684, 9490 Vaduz, Liechtenstein. Tel: +423 2366191, fax: +423 2366199
Ministry of Transport, Postfach 684, 9490 Vaduz, Liechtenstein. Tel: +423 2366488, fax: +423 2366489

Political Parties

Fortschrittliche Burgerpartei (FBP, Progressive Citizens' Party), Feldkircherstr. 5, 9494 Schaan, Liechtenstein. Tel: +423 233 3531, fax: +423 232 2912, URL: http://www.fbp.li/

Leader: Ernst Walch
Freie Liste (FL, Free Voters' List), Postfach 177, 9494 Schaan, Liechtenstein. URL: http://www.freieliste.li/
Leader: Claudia Heeb-Fleck
Vaterländische Union (VU, Patriotic Union), Furst-Franz-Josef Str. 13, 9490 Vaduz, Liechtenstein. Tel: +423 236 1616, fax: +423 236 1617, URL: http://www.vu-online.li/
Leader: Adolf Heeb

Elections

The most recent parliamentary election was held in February 2013. The opposition Progressive Citizens Party became the largest party with 10 seats. The Patriotic Union who had previously been in power with a majority government came second with eight seats. The Independents won four seats and the green Free List, party won three seats.

Diplomatic Representation

According to an arrangement concluded in 1919, Switzerland represents Liechtenstein's interests in countries where she has diplomatic missions. Switzerland always acts only on the basis of mandates of a general or specific nature, which she may either accept or refuse, while Liechtenstein is free to enter into direct relations with foreign states or to set up her own additional diplomatic missions.

Permanent Representative of the Principality of Liechtenstein to the United Nations, 633 Third Avenue, 27th Floor, New York, NY 10017, USA. Tel: +1 212 599 0220, fax: +1 212 599 0064, e-mail: liechtenstein@un.int, URL: http://www.newyork.liechtenstein.li
Ambassador: Christian Wenaweser (page 1535)

LEGAL SYSTEM

In matters of civil law, jurisdiction is exercised in first instance by the Lower Court, in second instance by the High Court, and in third instance by the Supreme Court of Justice. The High Court and the Supreme Court of Justice each consist of five judges. These bodies contain lay as well as professional judges. In criminal cases, jurisdiction is exercised in the first instance by the Lower Court (petty offences), the Assize court (misdemeanours), the Criminal Court (felonies), and the Juvenile Court. The Assize Court and the Juvenile Court consist of three judges each and the Criminal Court of five. In criminal cases the High Court and the Supreme Court of Justice function as second and third instances.

Appeal can be made against Government decisions and orders before the Administrative Tribunal (five judges), and, in certain cases, before the State Tribunal (five judges). Members of the Administrative Tribunal and the State Tribunal enjoy judicial independence. The State Tribunal also functions as a Constitutional Court, and can decide on complaints about violation of citizens' rights as guaranteed in the Constitution.

The government respects the human rights of its citizens, and the law provides effective means of addressing instances of abuse. Capital punishment was finally abolished in 1987. The last execution took place in the 18th century.

LOCAL GOVERNMENT

Liechtenstein consists of 11 municipalities or communes which have some powers of local government. Women gained the right to vote in local elections in 1986. The following table shows the municipalities, their area and their populations in December 2011.

Municipality/District	Area sq. km.	Resident population
Vaduz	17.3	5,236
Triesen	26.4	4,834
Balzars	19.6	4,526
Triesenberg	29.8	2,611
Schaan	26.8	5,853
Planken	5.3	423
Eschen	10.3	4,249
Mauren	7.5	4,012
Gamprin	6.1	1,641
Ruggell	7.4	2,057
Schellenberg	3.5	1,033

Source: Liechtenstein in Figures

Municipality of Ruggell, URL: http://www.ruggell.li
Municipality of Schellenberg, URL: http://www.schellenberg.li
Municipality of Gamprin, URL: http://www.gamprin.li
Municipality of Eschen, URL: http://www.eschen.li
Municipality of Mauren, URL: http://www.mauren.li
Municipality of Schaan, URL: http://www.schaan.li
Municipality of Planken, URL: http://www.planken.li
Municipality of Vaduz, URL: http://www.vaduz.li
Municipality of Triesenberg, URL: http://www.triesenberg.li
Municipality of Triesen, URL: http://www.triesen.li

LIECHTENSTEIN

Municipality of Balzers, URL: http://www.balzers.li

AREA AND POPULATION

Area
Liechtenstein is situated on the eastern bank of the Rhine, between the Swiss cantons of St. Gallen and Graubunden and the Austrian province of Vorarlberg. The country comprises the former counties of Vaduz and Schellenberg. The plain in the Rhine Valley occupies about one-third of the country which constitutes the agricultural land of the Principality. The rest of the country is mountainous in character. The mountain ranges that cross the land in a south-north direction are foot-hills of the Rhätikon massif. In an isolated position in the valley stands the Eschnerberg (730 metres high), while the mountainous part of the east of the country is composed of three high-level valleys. The total area is 160 sq. km. The country is landlocked.

The climate is continental with cold, cloudy winters with frequent precipitation, and cool to warm, humid summers.

To view a map, please consult:
http://www.lib.utexas.edu/maps/cia08/liechtenstein_sm_2008.gif

Population
At the end of 2011 the population was put at 36,475 of which 24,331 are Liechtensteiners. The population growth rate is estimated at 2.1 per cent. The majority of foreign nationals living in Liechtenstein come from Switzerland, Austria, Germany and Italy. The official language is German. A colloquial dialect called Alemannic is also spoken.

Births, Marriages, Deaths
In 2008 the birth rate was estimated at 9.8 births per 1,000 population with an estimated fertility rate of 1.5 children born per woman. The infant mortality rate was estimated at 4.5 deaths per 1,000 live births. Approximately 17 per cent of the population is aged under 15 years, 70 per cent aged 15-64 years and 13 per cent aged over 65 years. The median age is 40.5 years. The death rate in 2008 was estimated at 7.4 per 1,000 population. Estimated figures for 2011 show that there were 400 births and 250 deaths.

Life expectancy at birth in 2008 was estimated at 79.9 years (76.4 years for males and 83.5 years for females).

Public Holidays 2014
1 January: New Year's Day
6 January: Epiphany
2 February: Candlemas
4 March: Shrove Tuesday
19 March: St Joseph's Day
18 April: Good Friday
21 April: Easter Monday
5 May: Labour Day
29 May: Ascension Day
8 June: Whit Sunday
9 June: Whit Monday
19 June: Corpus Christi
15 August: Assumption / National Day
8 September: Birth of Mary
1 November: All Saints' Day
8 December: Immaculate Conception
25 December: Christmas Day
26 December: St Stephen's Day

EMPLOYMENT

Figures for the end of 2011 show that 18,924 of the workforce were resident in Liechtenstein and 18,279 commuted in, mainly from Switzerland and Austria. In 2007 the unemployment rate was 2.7 per cent, (472 people), this rose to 3.0 per cent, (545 people) in 2009 before falling to 2.2 per cent (401 people) in 2010. Figures for the end of 2011 put the unemployment rate at 2.5 per cent or 463 people. The following table shows the number of people employed in selected industries for 2011.

Industry	No. employed
Agriculture	277
Mining & quarrying	48
Manufacturing	10,950
Energy & water supply	348
Construction trades	2,570
Wholesale & retail trade, retail, repairs	1,548
Transportation & communication	1,042
Accommodation & food service activities	986
Information and communication	758
Financial & insurance activities	3,223
Real estate activities	101
Legal & accounting activities	2,579
Activities of head offices; management consultancy activities	509
Architectural & engineering	840
Scientific research & development	306
Administrative & support service activities	1,749
Public administration	1,788
Education	1,215
Human health & social work activities	2,013

- continued

Arts, entertainment, recreation	327
Other service activities	658
Households as employers	373
Activities of extraterritorial organisations	64

Source: Liechtenstein in Figures

BANKING AND FINANCE

Liechtenstein and Switzerland signed a customs treaty in 2004 to form one economic area with open borders between the two countries. Liechtenstein is now highly industrialised with a liberal economy and tax system. It has reformed its tax system in order to make its banking and tax systems more transparent.

Currency
Since 1924 the Swiss Franc (CHF) of 100 rappen has been in use in Liechtenstein.

GDP/GNP, Inflation, National Debt
Estimated figures for 2010put GDP at CSF 5,329 million, GNI that year was put at 4,500 million. Industry in 2010 contributed some 39 per cent of gross value added, general services 27 per cent, financial services 27 per cent and agriculture 7 per cent.

Inflation for 2010 was an estimated 0.7 per cent and 0.2 per cent in 2011.

In 2000 Liechtenstein's banking system was criticised for allowing accounts to be used anonymously and therefore potentially for illegal money laundering. Changes were made to the law and now customers can no longer remain anonymous. In 2008, after long-standing complaints from the EU, it pledged that it would co-operate more on tax matters. In April 2009 Liechtenstein signed agreements at the G20 summit to share financial information. The following month the OECD removed Liechtenstein from its blacklist of uncooperative countries.

Balance of Payments / Imports and Exports
In 2010, exports were an estimated CHF 3,325 million rising slightly to CHF 3,329 million in 2011. Import costs in 2010 were CHF 1,882 million, rising to CHF 1,965 million in 2011. Main export products include speciality machinery, stamps, ceramics and dental products. Main imported goods include textiles, foodstuffs, machinery and vehicles.

Trade Commissions
Liechtenstein has signed several treaties with Switzerland, namely the Customs Treaty (1923), the Postal Treaty (1978), the Currency Treaty (1980) and the Patent Protection Agreement (1978). Liechtenstein is a member of the CEPT, the Council of Europe, EBRD, ECE, EEA, EFTA, SPO, EUTELSAT, IAEA, ICJ, ITU, INTELSAT, OSCE, the Social Development Fund of the Council of Europe, UNCTAD, the United Nations, UPU, WIPO, WTO.

Central Bank
The Currency Treaty of 1980 stipulated that the Swiss National Bank take over the functions of a Central Bank for Liechtenstein.
Banque Nationale Suisse, PO Box 4388, Börsenstrasse 15, CH-8022 Zürich, Switzerland. Tel: +41 (0)1 631 3111, fax: +41 (0)1 631 3911, e-mail: snb@snb.ch URL: http://www.snb.ch Liechtenstein's national bank is:
Liechtensteinische Landesbank AG, PO Box 384, Städtle 44, FL-9490 Vaduz, Liechtenstein. Tel: +423 236 8811, fax: +423 236 8822, e-mail: llb@llb.li URL: http://www.llb.li

MANUFACTURING, MINING AND SERVICES

Energy
Energy consumption/imports 2011

Type	GWh
Electricity	398.2
Firewood	57.2
Coal	0.0
Fuel oil	168.2
Diesel oil	137.6
Petrol	160.4
Liquid gas	1.2
Natural gas	295.2
Solar panel	9.0
Long distance-heating	87.4
Total	1,314.5
Self supply	128.9

Source: Liechtenstein in Figures

Manufacturing
The main industries are metal manufacturing, electrical machinery, mechanical engineering, textiles, ceramics, dental technology, vehicle components, chemicals, pharmaceuticals and food. Industry and manufacturing contribute around 39 per cent of GDP. Industrial exports earned CHF 5,100 million in 2004. In 2011, 10,950 people were employed in the production sector.

Service Industries
The banking and finance sector is important to the economy and the number of banks in Liechtenstein has doubled in the last decade. Figures for 2011 showed that the nominal balance of banks in Liechtenstein was CHF 54,643 million with a net profit of CHF 163 million. The banking sector employs approximately 3,223 people.

Tourism is increasingly important with 55,869 people visiting Liechtenstein during 2011 and stayed a total of 117,384 nights. Figures for 2010 show that there were 51,815 visitors staying a total of 115,051 nights. Most visitors come from Europe.

Agriculture

Farmland accounts for 22 per cent of Lichtenstein's 16,500 ha. Less than 1 per cent of the workforce are employed in agriculture and 0.8 per cent are employed in forestry. Two thirds of agricultural production comes from the dairy industry and Liechtenstein produces enough for its own needs and more in dairy products. Fodder-growing is another major area with 2,400 ha of land used for cattle and other fodder animals and 2,000 ha of mountain pasture. About 1,100 ha are used for arable farming, vegetables, fruit and wine production (60,000-100,000 litres per year).

Livestock and milk production

	2000	2009	2010
Cattle	5,054	6,078	5,993
of which cows	2,562	2,993	2,807
Horses	379	495	489
Pigs	2,013	1,811	1,690
Sheep	3,319	3,963	3,656
Goats	239	452	416
Poultry	na	12,003	12,629
Bee colonies	953	1,068	1,173
Milk production (1,000 kg)	12,968	13,308	13,493

Source: Liechtenstein in Figures

COMMUNICATIONS AND TRANSPORT

Travel Requirements

Citizens of the USA, Canada and Australia require a passport valid for three months beyond the length of stay but do not need a visa for stays of up to 90 days. Liechtenstein joined the Schengen area in 2011 permitting passport free travel across 26 European countries.

Other nationals should contact the embassy to check visa requirements.

National Airlines

There is no national airline.

International Airports

The nearest international airport to Liechtenstein is Zurich.

Railways

The closest railway station is Buchs, in Switzerland. There are nine km of railway track in Liechtenstein which are electrified and administered by Austrian Federal Railways. The line has four stops.

Roads

There is motorway connection to all major cities. A tunnel 740 metres in length connects the Rhine and Samina valleys. In 2012 there were 36,915 motor vehicles (1,012 per 1,000 inhabitants) of which 28,004 were cars (768 per 1,000 inhabitants). Vehicles are driven on the right.

HEALTH

The Liechtenstein health service is funded through government finances, municipal authorities, compulsory health insurance and voluntary insurance, and private expenditure. Universal healthcare is available to all.

In 2009, the infant mortality rate was estimated to be 2 per 1,000 live births. The under-fives mortality rate was also 2 per 1,000 live births. The most common causes of death were diseases of the circulation and cancer.

EDUCATION

Kindergarten schools exist for children aged five to seven. Attendance is voluntary and free of charge but once enrolled, attendance must be regular. The age when a child enters the kindergarten system is flexible. However, children who do not speak German must attend the second year of kindergarten to receive German language lessons.

Primary schools are also free but are compulsory and last for five years. Children who have had their sixth birthday by the end of June, enter primary school the same year. Maths, German, Social Studies, Art, Music, Sports, Textiles and Technical Design, Religion and English (third grade) are taught in primary school. In the fifth year, based on general assessment, the school recommends a type of secondary school appropriate to each child. A pupil may take an entrance examination if they wish to attend a different school. At the end of the fifth year, pupils move onto secondary school.

There are three types of secondary school: Oberschule (Upper School), Real Schule (Upper School) and Gumnasium (High School). The Oberschule provides general education and vocational training and lasts for four years (grades six to nine). Pupils may transfer to the Real Schule if their work reaches and appropriate standard. The Real Sschule is more academic and prepares students for either professional apprenticeships or further schooling including the upper levels of the Gymnasium or academies. It is possible to transfer at the end of each year to the Gymnasium. The Gymnasium schools lead to the high school degree after seven years of studying and prepares students for university. Liechtenstein does not have its own university and students who wish to study at university study abroad especially in Germany, Austria, and Switzerland. Students from Lichtenstein with a high school degree may enter universities in Switzerland and Austria without taking entrance exams.

Literacy is estimated at 100 per cent.

RELIGION

Liechtenstein is a Roman Catholic country and forms the Archdiocese of Vaduz. There are two Protestant Churches in the Principality. An estimated 76 per cent of the population are Roman Catholics, 7.1 per cent are Protestant and 6 per cent are from other religions including a Muslim population of around 2,300.

Liechtenstein has a religious liberty rating of 10 on a scale of 1 to 10 (10 is most freedom). (Source: World Religion Database)

COMMUNICATIONS AND MEDIA

Newspapers

Newspaper circulations are low.
Liechtensteiner Vaterland, Vaduz, URL: http://www.vaterland.li
Liechtensteiner Volksblatt, Schaan. URL: http://www.volksblatt.li

Broadcasting

Most television is supplied by foreign and satellite broadcasters. A local television station was established in 2008. Radio broadcasts are made by Radio Liechtenstein, URL: http://www.radiol.li. In

Telecommunications

Telecommunications was a state monopoly until 1997. It was privatised in 1998. In 2011 there were 19,600 landline telephone subscribers and 37,000 mobile phone subscribers.

Figures for 2009 show that Liechtenstein had around 23,000 internet users.

ENVIRONMENT

Liechtenstein is a party to the following international agreements: Air Pollution, Air Pollution-Nitrogen Oxides, Air Pollution-Persistent Organic Pollutants, Air Pollution-Sulfur 85, Air Pollution-Sulfur 94, Air Pollution-Volatile Organic Compounds, Biodiversity, Climate Change, Climate Change-Kyoto Protocol, Desertification, Endangered Species, Hazardous Wastes, Ozone Layer Protection and Wetlands. It has signed but not ratified the Law of the Sea.

LITHUANIA
Republic of Lithuania
Lietuvos Respublika

Capital: Vilnius (Population estimate, 2011: 555,000)

Head of State: Dalia Grybauskaite (page 1434)

National Flag: A tricolour, fesswise, yellow, dark green and red

CONSTITUTION AND GOVERNMENT

Constitution

Lithuanian independence was recognized by the Treaty of Versailles in 1919. During the period 1920-1940, the Republic of Lithuania regained international recognition. From 1940 onwards, Lithuania became a republic of the former USSR. 1988 saw the birth of *Sajudis*, the Lithuanian Reform Movement, which demanded democratic and national rights, and later, the restoration of the Lithuanian statehood. In 1989-90 the Lithuanian Communist Party agreed to a multi-party system and as a result new parties were formed. In 1990 Sajudis-backed candidates won the elections to the Supreme Council of Lithuania. By an Act of March 11 1990 the new Supreme Council, declared the restoration of the independence of Lithuania, formed a new Cabinet of Ministers and adopted the Provisional Basic Law (Constitution) and a number of other acts. In a referendum, in February 1991, over 90 per cent of Lithuanians voted for independence. On 25 October 1992, a new constitution was adopted by referendum and the *Seimas*, a new 141-member legislative body, was elected. The election, held on a partly proportional, partly constituency system, was won by the Lithuanian Labour Democratic Party (LDLP).

Lithuania is an independent and democratic state. Sovereign power vested in the people of Lithuania and is exercised by the *Seimas*, the President of the Republic, the Government and the Judiciary. The constitution bans alignment of Lithuania with post-Soviet Eastern alliances.

For further information on the constitution, please visit: http://www.lrkt.lt/Documents2_e.html.

International Relations

In November 2002 Lithuania was formally invited to join NATO and became a member in March 2004. In May 2003 a referendum was held asking if Lithuanians wanted to join the EU. An estimated 63 per cent of eligible voters turned out and 91 per cent of those voted to join the EU. Lithuania became a member state on May 1 2004.

Recent Events

In April 2004 President Rolandas Paksas was impeached and dismissed from office for leaking information and unlawfully granting citizenship to a Russian businessman who had funded his election campaign. Arturas Paulauskas the Parliamentary Speaker became acting president until elections in June, when Valdas Adamkus was elected. In May 2006, Prime Minister Algirdas Brazauskas resigned after the Labour Party withdrew from the ruling coalition. Gediminas Kirkilas was approved by parliament for the post.

In June 2008, parliament banned the display of Soviet and Nazi symbols. Many Baltic states feel that they were illegally occupied by the former Soviet Union following liberation from the Nazis.

In May 2009, Dalia Grybauskaite, the EU Budget Commissioner, was elected president of Latvia with nearly 70 per cent of the vote. She stood as an independent.

In December 2009, in line with Lithuania's EU entry requirements the second reactor at the Ignalina nuclear power plant was shut down.

Legislature

Lithuania has a unicameral legislature, the parliament has 141 directly elected members who serve a four year term.
Seimas, (Parliament), 53 Gedimino Avenue, Vilnius 2002, Lithuania. Tel: +370 523 96008, URL: http://www.lrs.lt

---

Cabinet (as at June 2013)
Prime Minister: Algirdas Butkevicius (LSDP) (page 1398)
Minister of Foreign Affairs: Linas Antanas Linkevicius (page 1465)
Minister of National Defence: Juozas Olekas (page 1489)
Minister of Finance: Rimantas Sadzius
Minister of the Economy: Birute Vesaite
Minister of Culture: Sarunas Birutis (page 1389)
Minister of Justice: Juozas Bernatonis (page 1388)
Minister of Transport and Communication: Rimantas Sinkevicius
Minister of Social Security and Labour: Algimanta Pabedinskiene
Minister of Health: Yvtenis Povilas Andriukaitis
Minister of the Interior: Dailis Alfonsas Barakauskas (page 1383)
Minister of Education and Science: Dainius Pavalkis
Minister of Agriculture: Vigilijus Jukna
Minister of Environment: Valentinas Mazuronis
Minister of Energy: Jaroslav Neverovic

Ministries

Office of the President, Simono Daukanto a. 3, Vilnius 01021, Lithuania. Tel: +370 5 266 4154, fax: +370 5 216 4145, e-mail: info@president.lt, URL: http://www.president.lt
Office of the Prime Minister, Gedimino pr. 11, 2039 Vilnius, Lithuania. Tel: +370 5 266 3711, URL: http://www.lrvk.lt
Ministry of National Economy, Gedimino pr. 38/2, 2600 Vilnius, Lithuania. Tel: +370 5 262 3863, URL: http://www.ukmin.lt
Ministry of Finance, Sermuksniu 6, 2695 Vilnius, Lithuania. Tel: +370 5 239 0005, URL: http://www.finmin.lt
Ministry of Justice, Gedimino pr. 30/1, 2600 Vilnius, Lithuania. Tel: +370 5 266 2980, URL: http://www.tm.lt
Ministry of Interior, Sventaragio 2, 2754 Vilnius, Lithuania. Tel: +370 5 271 7130, URL: http://www.vrm.lt
Ministry of Foreign Affairs, J. Tumo-Vaizganto g. 2, 2600 Vilnius, Lithuania. Tel: +370 5 236 2444, e-mail: urm@urm.lt, URL: http://www.urm.lt
Ministry of Defence, Totoriu 25/3, 2001 Vilnius, Lithuania. Tel: +370 5 273 5519, URL: http://www.kam.lt
Ministry of Environment, A. Juozapaviciaus 9, 2600 Vilnius, Lithuania. Tel: +370 5 266 3659, URL: http://www.am.lt
Ministry of Social Welfare and Labour, A. Vivulskio 11, 2693 Vilnius, Lithuania. Tel: +370 5 266 4201, URL: http://www.socmin.lt
Ministry of Health, Gedimino pr. 27, 2682 Vilnius, Lithuania. Tel: +370 5 268 5110, URL: http://www.sam.lt
Ministry of Culture, J. Basanaviciaus g. 5, 2683 Vilnius, Lithuania. Tel: +370 5 261 9486, URL: http://www.lrkm.lt
Ministry of Education and Science, A. Volano 2/7, 2600 Vilnius, Lithuania. Tel: +370 5 274 3080, URL: http://www.smm.lt
Ministry of Agriculture, Gedimino pr. 19, 2025 Vilnius, Lithuania. Tel: +370 5 239 1001, e-mail: zum@zum.lt, URL: http://www.zum.lt
Ministry of Transport and Communications, Gedimino pr. 17, 2679 Vilnius, Lithuania. Tel: +370 5 239 3845, URL: http://www.transp.lt
Ministry of Energy, Gedimino pr. 38/2, Vilnius 01104, Lithuania. Tel: +370 5 262 5515, fax: +370 5 262 3974, e-mail: kanc@ukmin.lt, URL: http://www.ukmin.lt
Ministry of Economy, Gedimino pr. 38/2, Vilnius 01104, Lithuania. Tel: +370 5 262 3863, fax: +370 5 262 3974, e-mail: kanc@ukmin.lt, URL: http://www.ukmin.lt

Political Parties

The main political parties in Lithuania are:
Lietuvos demokratine darbo partija (LDLP, Lithuanian Democratic Labour Party), URL: http://www.lddp.lt/
Tevynes sajunga - Lietuvos krikscionys demokratai (TS, Homeland Union - Lithuanian Christian Democrats), URL: http://www.tsajunga.lt
Pilieciu chartija (Citizen's Charter); Lietuvos socialdemokratu partija (Lithuanian Social Democratic Party), URL: http://www.lsdp.lt/
Lietuvos Respublikos Liberalu Sajudis, (Liberals' Movement of the Republic of Lithuania LRLS), URL: http://www.liberalusajudis.lt
Lietuvos Socialdemokratu Partija, (Lithuanian Social Democratic Party LSDP), URL: http://www.lsdp.lt
Lietuvos lenku sajunga (Lithuanian Poles' Union), URL: http://www.awpl.lt
Tvarka ir teisingumas, (Party "Order and Justice"), URL: http://www.ldp.lt
Rising Nation Party (TPP); The Coalition Labour Party & Youth (KDP&J); Lietuvos tautininku sajunga (Lithuanian Nationalist Union); Krikscioniu demokratu sajunga (Christian Democratic Union); Lietuvos liberalu sajunga (Lithuanian Liberal Union).

Elections

In January 1998, Valdas Adamkus was elected president, replacing Algirdas Brazauskas, chairman of the LDLP who had ruled since February 1993. Presidential elections next took place in January 2003 and were won by Rolandas Paksas. In accordance with the constitution, the prime minister and cabinet resigned. Prime Minister Brazauskas was reappointed by President Paksas and a new cabinet was approved by parliament in March 2003. Following the impeachment of President Paksas, Valdas Adamkus was re-elected president in June 2004. Presidential elections were next held in May 2009; the former European Commissioner Dalia Grybauskaitė was elected with 69 per cent of the vote and was due to take office on 12 July. She will be the country's first female president.

Elections took place in October 2008; the Homeland Union party, led by Andrius Kubilius, became the largest party in parliament but did not win enough seats for a majority. Negotiations began to form a new coalition, and in the meantime the government led by Gediminas Kirkilas remained in office. Agreement was reached at the beginning of December and the coalition consisted of Homeland Union-Lithuanian Christian Democrats (TS-LKD), the Rising Nation Party (TPP), the Liberal Movement of the Republic of Lithuania (LRLS) and the Liberal and Center Union (LCS).

The most recent parliamentary elections took place in October 2012. The Social Democrats became the biggest party after campaigning against the austerity measures of the prime minister, Andrius Kubilius.

Diplomatic Representation

British Embassy, 2 Antakalnio, 2055 Vilnius, Lithuania. Tel: +370 5 246 2900, fax: +370 5 246 2901, URL: http://ukinlithuania.fco.gov.uk

Ambassador: David Hunt (page 1445)
US Embassy, Akmenu 6, 2600 Vilnius, Lithuania. Tel: +370 2 665500, fax: +370 2 665530, URL: http://vilnius.usembassy.gov
Ambassador: Deborah A. McCarthy
Lithuanian Embassy, 84 Gloucester Place, London, W1H 3HN, United Kingdom. Tel: +44 (0)20 7486 6401, fax: +44 (0)20 7486 6403, URL: http://www.lithuanianembassy.co.uk
Ambassador: Asta Skaisgirytè Liauškienè
Lithuanian Embassy, 2622 16th Street, NW, Washington DC 20009, USA. Tel: +1 202 234 5860, fax: +1 202 328 0466, URL: http://www.ltembassyus.org
Ambassador: Zygimantas Pavilionis
Permanent Representative of the Republic of Lithuania to the United Nations, 420 Fifth Avenue, 3rd Floor, New York, N.Y. 10018, USA. Tel: +1 212 983 9474, URL: http://www.un.int/lithuania/lithuania.html
Ambassador: Dalius Čekuolis

LEGAL SYSTEM

The Lithuanian legal system is based largely on the legal traditions of continental Europe. During Soviet occupation, the system was altered to conform to that of the USSR, but since then new Codes have come into effect, and laws have been harmonised with those of the EU.

The court system consists of courts of general jurisdiction, dealing with civil and criminal matters: the Supreme Court, the Court of Appeals, and district and local courts. In addition, there are specialised administrative courts which hear administrative cases. Judges of the Supreme Court are appointed by the Seimas, while judges of the Court of Appeals are appointed by the President upon approval by the Seimas. Judges of the district and local courts are appointed by the President. The Constitutional Court is a separate independent judicial body which determines whether the laws adopted by the Seimas conform with the Constitution.

The government respects the human rights of its citizens, but there is some degree of government corruption, and prison conditions are poor. The death penalty was abolished in 1998.

Supreme Court of Lithuania: http://www.lat.lt/?item=home&lang=3

Seimas Ombudsmen's Office of Lithuania, URL: http://www.lrski.lt/

LOCAL GOVERNMENT

Local government is organised on a territorial basis. 10 counties (apskritys) with the administrative centres based in the major towns (Alytus, Kaunas, Klaipeda, Marijampole, Panevežys, Šiauliai, Taurage, Telšiai, Utena and Vilnius) are the largest local administrative units. These are divided into 60 local government municipalities. The smaller units are represented by municipal councils which are elected for a period of two years.

County	Area sq. km.	2007
Alytaus	5,425	178,955
Kuano	8,060	677,284
Klapedos	5,209	379,472
Marljampoles	4,463	182,587
Panevežio	7,881	287,119
Šiauliu	8,540	353,713
Tuarages	4,411	128,679
Telšlu	4,350	174,573
Utenos	7,201	174,743
Vilniaus	9,760	847,754

Source: Statistics Lithuania

AREA AND POPULATION

Area
Lithuania lies on the eastern coast of the Baltic Sea and is the largest of the three Baltic States, it borders Latvia, Belarus, Poland, and the Kaliningrad region (formerly East Prussia) of the Russian Federation. The area of Lithuania is 65,300 sq. km. Lithuania contains over 2,800 lakes and 750 rivers. The main rivers in terms of length are the Nemunas, Neris, Šešupė, Šventoji, Venta and the Nevėžis. The terrain is low-lying and fertile.

The climate is continental/maritime. Summers are warm. Winters are colder, sometimes severe. Rivers often freeze although the coastline is generally ice-free. Most rain falls in mid-summer.

To view a map, visit http://www.un.org/Depts/Cartographic/map/profile/lithuani.pdf

Population
The population in 2010 was estimated to be 3,324,000. The population has been falling each year since 1992 when it was 3,706,300. Lithuania had an average negative population annual growth rate of -0.5 per cent over the period 2000-10. Approximately 67 per cent live in urban areas.

The ethnic composition of the population is as follows: Lithuanian, 84 per cent; Russian, 6.0 per cent; Polish, 7.0 per cent; Belorussian, 1.5 per cent. The official language spoken is Lithuanian although a minority speak Russian and Polish

Births, Marriages, Deaths
The average life expectancy for men is 68 and for women is 79. Healthy life expectancy is respectively 58 and 68 years. In 2010 the median age was put at 39 years. Approximately 15 per cent of the population was aged under 15 years and 21 per cent over 60. The fertility rate in 2010 was 1.5 per female. (Source: http://www.who.int, World Health Statistics 2012) Provisional figures for 2007 show that there were 32,154 live births while deaths numbered 45,589. That year 23,073 marriages took place and 11,284 divorces.

Public Holidays 2014
1 January: New Year
16 February: Independence Day
11 March: Restoration of Lithuania's Statehood
18-21 April: Easter
1 May: Labour Day
24 June: Midsummer Festival
6 July: State Day (Crowning of Lithuanian King Mindaugas)
15 August: Assumption Day
1 November: All Saints Day
25-26 December: Christmas

EMPLOYMENT

The following table shows employment sector figures in 2008.

Employment Sector	No. of Persons Employed
Agriculture, hunting, forestry	116,600
Fishing	4,100
Mining & quarrying	4,000
Manufacturing	266,000
Electricity, gas & water	27,600
Construction	165,700
Wholesale & retail trade	274,900
Hotels & restaurants	38,900
Transport, storage & communication	104,500
Financial intermediation	20,300
Real estate, renting & business activities	101,300
Public administration & defence	83,300
Education	148,500
Health & social work	95,700
Other community, social & personal services	64,800

Source: Copyright © International Labour Organization (ILO Dept. of Statistics, http://laborsta.ilo.org)

Figures for 2007 show that the unemployment rate was 4.3 per cent down from 5.6 per cent in 2006 and 8.3 per cent in 2005.

BANKING AND FINANCE

Currency
In July 1993, Lithuania introduced its own currency, the Litas (1 Litas=100 centas), which replaced the provisional monetary unit, talonas. Since Lithuania's departure from the rouble, the authorities have pursued an independent monetary policy. In February 2002 the litas was pegged to the euro at L3.45 = €1.

GDP/GNP, Inflation, National Debt
After independence, Lithuania began to transform its economy to a free market one. Lithuania's economy is the largest of the Baltic States but most of Lithuania remains poor. EU funding has yet to make much of an impact. The economy has recovered from 1998 when the Russian crisis resulted in Lithuania losing 20 per cent of its eport market. The economy has recovered due to increases in domestic demand and exports to other countries and growth has been strong. Lithuania was, however, unable to join the euro in 2008 because of high inflation.

Until the current global economic crisis, GDP had shown consistent growth in recent years. However, growth fell in 2008 and 2009. The government implemented austerity measures including rising taxes and cuts in spending.

GDP, at current prices

	LTL million	€ million	% change compared to previous period
2006	82,792.8	71,779.9	7.8
2007	98,138.7	78,186.0	8.9
2008	111,498.7	80,544.6	3.0
2009	91,525.9	69,187.9	-14.8

Source: Statistics Lithuania

GDP was estimated to be US$36 billion in 2010 with a growth rate of 1.3 per cent, rising to an estimated US$40 billion in 2011.

The following table shows GDP at current prices by kind of economic activity. Figures are in million Litas.

Economic Activity	2008	2009
Agriculture, hunting, forestry & fishing	3,713.4	2,769.8
Industry	21,568.0	16,934.4

LITHUANIA

- continued

Construction	9,988.4	5,279.5
Trade, hotels & restaurants, transport, storage & communications	30,562.2	26,424.0
Financial intermediation, real estate, renting & business	16,648.1	13,618.0
Public administration, services	17,424.2	17,402.1
Gross value added	99,904.5	82,428.1
Taxes on products	12,800.7	10,370.9
Subsidies on products (minus)	1,222.6	1,273.2
Gross domestic product	111,482.6	91,525.9

Source: Statistics Lithuania

Inflation was estimated at 2.6 per cent for 2008 and 4.5 per cent in 2011.

Foreign Investment
Lithuania became a full member of the World Trade Organisation in 2001.

Free Economic Zones have been established at Klapeda, Šiauliai, and Kaunas. The main foreign investors are Denmark, Sweden, Estonia, Germany and the USA. The manufacturing sector attracts most investment. Direct foreign investment was estimated to be US$2 billion in 2011.

Balance of Payments / Imports and Exports
Earnings from exports now account for around 50 per cent of GDP. Exports amounted to 55,511.0 LTL million in 2008. Import costs were 73,006.3 LTL million resulting in a trade balance of -17,495.3 million LTL. External trade 2009 showed that exports earned 40,732.0 LTL million and imports cost 45,311.0 LTL million. The trade balance was -4,579.0 LTL million.

The following table shows import and export figures in thousand Litas, for selected trading commodities in 2009.

Commodity Group	Exports	Imports
Live animals	320,975.1	62,943.1
Vegetables and fruit	1,243,840.0	1,584,989.3
Diary products and bird's eggs	1,188,984.6	290,143.9
Cereals & cereal preparations	1,087,604.0	266,752.6
Petroleum, petroleum products & related materials	8,122,878.7	10,319,610.1
Gas, natural & manufactured	152,721.4	2,066,930.6
Organic chemicals	188,152.0	1,445,878.4
Inorganic chemicals	108,069.5	281,679.8
Medical & pharmaceutical products	663,511.1	1,849,160.3
Plastics in primary form	1,376,549.4	654,682.5
Iron & steel	509,852.8	1,022,587.6

Source: Statistics Lithuania

Trade with EU countries is increasing although raw materials are still mainly imported from CIS countries.

Key foreign trade partners, January-August 2009

Exports	LTL million	% share	% change
Total	*25,587.3*	*100*	*-32.3*
EU	16,598.6	64.9	-28.2
CIS	5,805.4	22.7	-36.6
Russia	3,283.7	12.8	-42.9
Latvia	2,605.4	10.2	-38.9
Germany	2,467.9	9.6	-9.3
Estonia	1,843.5	7.2	-14.9
Poland	1,758.6	6.9	-21.7
Imports			
Total	*28,914.5*	*100*	*-42.7*
EU	16,768.2	58.0	-41.9
CIS	9,836.9	34.0	-43.4
Russia	9,030.6	31.2	-41.8
Germany	3,223.2	11.1	-45.3
Poland	2,887.5	10.0	-41.9
Latvia	1,804.3	6.2	-29.3
Netherlands	1,226.5	4.2	-32.2

Source: Statistics Lithuania

Exports were estimated to be US$28 billion in 2011 and imports cost US$30 billion.

Central Bank
Bank of Lithuania (Lietuvos Bankas), 6 Gedimino Ave, 2001 Vilnius, Lithuania. Tel: +370 2 680029, fax: +370 2 628124, e-mail: Bank_of_Lithuania@lbank.lt, URL: http://www.lbank.lt
Governor: Vitas Vasiliauskas

Chambers of Commerce and Trade Organisations
Association of Lithuanian Chambers of Commerce, Industry and Crafts, URL: http://www.chambers.lt/en/index.php
America-Lithuania Chamber of Commerce, URL: http://www.amcham.lt/
Lithuania Chamber of Commerce in the UK, URL: http://www.lithuanianchamber.co.uk/_join-lcc-uk

MANUFACTURING, MINING AND SERVICES

Primary and Extractive Industries
Lithuania is not rich in natural resources. However, it does have iron ore deposits and granite in the south-east, limestone and clay, quartz sand and dolomite, gypsum and chalk and amber in various parts of the country, all of which are used as raw materials, and for the building industry. Lithuania has peat deposits of about 934 million tons. Figures for 2001 show that 273,000 tons were extracted of which 36,000 tons were used for fuel. Western regions and the Baltic sea shelf have oil deposits of an estimated 400 million barrels, onshore deposits are an estimated 330 million barrels. The state owned oil company Mezeikiu Naftu was partially privatised in 1999. This caused some political upheaval as a 33 per cent share was sold to Williams, an American company, rather than Lukoil, the Russian company.

Lithuania has proven oil reserves of 12 million barrels, and in 2010 produced an estimated 5,700 barrels per day and consumed 81,000 barrels per day. Lithuania has the only refinery in the Baltics at Mazeikiai, which has a refining capacity of 190,000 barrels per day. Lithuania has no natural gas reserves and imports all it needs, this amounted to 120,000 billion cubic feet in 2011.

Energy
In 1998, 70 per cent of the country's electricity was supplied by its Ignalina nuclear power station. It is of the same design as the Chernobyl nuclear plant in the Ukraine and closure of the Ignalina site was a pre-requisite of Lithuania joining the EU. The EU in 1999 provided €10 million to help with its closure and development of new power sources and agreed to provide €20 million per year until 2006. The Lithuanian government agreed to close one reactor by 2005 and the other by 2009; the last was closed on December 31 2009. Fossil fuel-fired units and hydroelectric stations made up the rest of Lithuania's electricity supply. Figures for 2010 show that Lithuania imported 337,000 short tons of coal.

Main Fuel & Energy Final Consumption

Fuel	2006
Hard coal, thous.t	384
Peat, thous.t	14
Peat blocks, thous.t	28
Firewood & wood waste, thous.m3	2,852
Natural gas, mill.m3	712
Fuel oil, thous.t	35
Transport diesel oil, thous.t	887
Motor gasoline, thous.t	363
Aviation fuel, thous.t	55
Liquefied petroleum gases, thous.t	270
Electricity, GWh	8,431
Heat, GWh	10,979

Source: Statistics Lithuania

Manufacturing
After 1945 the engineering industry was geared to meet the industrial needs of the Soviet Union, turning out products which required highly skilled labour but little metal and power. At present, the chemical industry produces mineral fertilisers (nitric and phosphorous), sulphuric, nitric and phosphoric acids, methanol, man-made fibres, synthetic resins, synthetic detergents, varnishes, dyes and paints, household chemicals and other products. Lithuania has its own oil refinery, located in Mazeikiai. Facilities for intensive timber processing and recycling of industrial waste are being expanded. At present, the industry of building materials uses predominantly local resources, such as clay, building and quartz sand, gravel, and dolomite. Large quarries are located near Vilnius, Petrasiunai, Kalnenai, and Rizgonys. Textiles and knitwear are the main branches of light industry. Linen, cotton, silk fabrics, carpets, hosiery and underwear are produced. The food industry is dominated by the meat, dairy and fishing industries.

Service Industries
In 1997 there were 288,000 million visitors to Lithuania who spent a total of US$360 million (4.2 per cent of GDP). Most visitors were from Russia, Germany, Poland and Scandinavian countries. By 2006, the number of visitors to Lithuania had increased to 2,000,000 generating US$1,077 million.

Agriculture
The former state controlled farming system is rapidly transforming into private farming. The purpose of agrarian reform is to restore the rights of the former owners to their heirs and to privatise property which belonged to the state.

Agricultural Production in 2010

Produce	Int. $'000*	Tonnes
Cow milk, whole, fresh	540,649	1,732,510
Wheat	212,974	1,708,200
Indigenous cattle meat	180,314	66,749
Indigenous pigmeat	161,601	105,124
Indigenous chicken meat	107,557	75,510
Rapeseed	69,111	416,700
Hen eggs, in shell	38,484	46,400
Potatoes	31,174	474,700
Sugar beet	27,921	722,500
Mushrooms and truffles	18,826	10,434
Other bird eggs, in shell	13,844	4,800
Apples	13,542	34,020

* unofficial figures
Source: http://faostat.fao.org/site/339/default.aspx Food and Agriculture Organization of the United Nations, Food and Agricultural commodities production

Number of livestock in thousand heads

Livestock	2005	2006	2008
Cattle	792,0	838,8	787.9
of which cows	433,9	399,0	404.5
Pigs	1073,3	1127,1	923.2
Sheep & goats	49,0	57,4	63.0
Horses	63,6	60,9	55.9
Poultry	8419.4	9439.9	9874.8

Source: Statistics Lithuania

Over 28 per cent of Lithuania's land area is covered by forest. It supports some of Lithuania's principal industries by providing pulp, paper, chemical timber, furniture, wood fibre and wood-chipboard.

COMMUNICATIONS AND TRANSPORT

Travel Requirements
Citizens of the USA, Canada and Australia require a passport valid for three months beyond the length of stay but do not need a visa for tourism stays of up to 90 days. EU subjects holding a valid national Identity Card do not require a passport or a visa for the purposes of tourism. Other nationals should contact the embassy to check visa requirements.

Lithuania is a signatory to the Schengen Agreement; with a Schengen visa, a visitor can travel freely throughout the Schengen zone, and there are few border stops and checks. See http://www.eurovisa.info/SchengenCountries.htm for details.

National Airlines
Lietuvos Avialinijos (Lithuanian Airlines, LAL), URL: http://www.flylal.com
Lietuva (Air Lithuania), Švitrigailos 26/40,Vilnius, Lithuania. Tel: +370 2 231322, fax: +370 2 231566

International Airports
The country's main airport is Vilnius Airport (VNO). There are also airports at Kaunas, Palanga (serving Klaipeda and the rest of the Lithuanian Baltic coast) and Siauliai. Aviation is regulated by the following body:
Ministry of Transport, Gedemina Prospect 17, 2679 Vilnius, Lithuania.
Kaunas State Company Airport, Karmelava, 4301 Kaunas Region, Lithuania. Tel: +370 7 541741

Railways
There are 2,200 km of railway track in Lithuania. About 72 per cent of freight is carried by rail. A number of railway lines cross the country, establishing links with neighbouring countries. In 1992 a direct railroad line between Sestokai (south Lithuania) and Poland connected Lithuania's railroad with the European railroad system. There are also plans to build a high-speed passenger railway, conforming to international standards, linking Warsaw, Bialostok (Poland), Kaunas, Šiauliai (Lithuania), Riga (Latvia) and Tallinn (Estonia). Another line is planned from Warsaw to St. Petersburg (Russia) via Vilnius and Daugavpils (Latvia). Figures for 2000 show that there were 8.9 million passenger journeys.
Lithuanian Railways, URL: http://www.litrail.lt

Roads
Roads in Lithuania are state property. All economic entities pay a monthly 0.1-1 per cent road tax levied on their sales income. Lithuania's road network consists of 79,331 km of roads of which 417 km are motorways. The close road network carries over 27 per cent of total freight and 55.8 per cent of passenger transport. The highway "Via Baltica" will stretch from Helsinki, through the Baltic states to Warsaw, Poland and will join the European highway network. Vehicles are driven on the right.

Waterways
Lithuania has 425 km of navigable waterways, which in 2000 carried over 850,000 tonnes of goods. Ferry services operate from Klaipeda to Sweden, Germany and Denmark.

Ports and Harbours
The main ice-free port, Klaipeda, links Lithuania with over 200 foreign ports. There are two ferry lines to Germany (Kiel and Mukran) and one to Sweden (Ahus). A 1,028 hectare site located near the port has been set aside as a Free Economic Zone to encourage investors. The port has a cargo capacity of 20m tons and the cargo turnover in 1997 was 16m tons. A modernisation programme will increase the capacity to 30m tons.

HEALTH

Lithuania has a state run social security system. This is state funded and provides social insurance for all persons living in Lithuania and social assistance. State social insurance covers pensions; sickness allowances; maternity, child-birth and child-care benefits, and unemployment benefits. Contributions to the Lithuanian Social Insurance Fund are fully tax deductible.

In 2009, Lithuania spent approximately 12.6 per cent of its total budget on healthcare (up from 11.6 per cent in 2000), accounting for 73.4 per cent of all healthcare spending. Total expenditure on healthcare equated to 7.5 per cent of the country's GDP. Per capita expenditure on health was approximately US$836, compared with US$212 in 2000.

Figures for 2005-10 show that there are 12,191 physicians (36.1 per 10,000 population), 24,174 nurses and midwives (71.7 per 10,000 population) and 2,347 dentists. There are 68 hospital beds per 10,000 population.

The infant mortality rate in 2010 was 5 per 1,000 live births. The child mortality rate (under 5 years) was 7 per 1,000 live births. The main causes of childhood mortality are: congenital anomalies (30 per cent), prematurity (9 per cent), diarrhoea (1 per cent), pneumonia (9 per cent), and injuries (16 per cent). (Source: http://www.who.int, World Health Statistics)

EDUCATION

During the last few years the Lithuanian education system has undergone radical transformation. New forms of education were introduced, which permitted religious education once again. Education is compulsory from the age of 6. Most educational institutions are run by the state though recently several private establishments have been set up. The following table shows the number and type of education establishments and the number of students in attendance.
Figures for Academic Year 2004/05

School	Number	Students
General schools	1,634	563,000
Vocational school	73	46,000
Professional colleges	11	5,000
Colleges	27	52,000
Universities	21	139,000

Source: Statistics Lithuania

Figures for 2007 showed that 69 per cent of young children were enrolled in pre-primary school, 90 per cent of girls and 91 per cent of boys were enrolled in primary school, 92 per cent of girls and 90 per cent of boys were enrolled in secondary school and 76 per cent of tertiary age students were enrolled in tertiary education. Adult literacy that year was recorded at 99.7 per cent for both males and females the youth literacy rate (age 15 to 24) was slightly higher at 99.8 per cent for both males and females.

In 2006 14.4 per cent of government spending or 4.9 per cent of GDP went to education. (Source: UNESCO)

RELIGION

Lithuania is predominantly a Catholic country, (79 per cent of the population). Catholicism appeared in Lithuania at the end of the 12th century. However it was the last of all European states to accept Christianity (1387-1413). The Catholic church came under attack with the occupation of Lithuania in 1940 by the Soviet Union. Many churches and all Catholic monasteries were closed down and the teaching of Catechism to children was prohibited. The religious revival started in 1989. Besides Roman Catholics, Lithuania has Russian Orthodox, Evangelical Lutheran, Evangelical Reformist, Baptist, Muslim, Judaic and some other religious communities. Islam is followed by 0.22 per cent of the population.

Lithuania has a religious tolerance rating of 8 a scale of 1 to 10 (10 is most freedom). (Source: World Religion Database)

COMMUNICATIONS AND MEDIA

The media is free.

Newspapers
There are no government-owned newspapers.
Lietuvos Aidas, URL: http://www/lrytas.lt
Lietuvos Rytas, URL: http://www.lrytas.lt
Respublika, URL: http://www.respublika.lt/

Broadcasting
The state broadcaster operates three channels. Various private commercial TV broadcasters (national and regional) also operate. Cable and satellite are also available.

Radio Lithuania broadcasts two national programmes on medium wave and VHF. There are also several independent radio stations. Lithuanian TV broadcasts two national programmes, as well as Polish and Russian programmes.
Lithuanian Radio and TV, public, URL: http://www.lrt.lt

Telecommunications
The telecommunications system is being modernised with improved capability. The number of fixed-line connections has declined (785,000) whereas the mobile-cellular services have increased recently. Figures for 2008 show that approximately 5.0 million mobile phones are in use.

Figures for 2008 show that over 1.7 million Lithuanians are regular internet users.

ENVIRONMENT

Lithuania is a party to the following international agreements: Air Pollution, Air Pollution-Nitrogen Oxides, Air Pollution-Persistent Organic Pollutants, Air Pollution-Sulphur 85, Air Pollution-Sulphur 94, Air Pollution-Volatile Organic Compounds, Biodiversity, Climate Change, Climate Change-Kyoto Protocol, Desertification, Endangered Species, Environmental Modification, Hazardous Wastes, Law of the Sea, Ozone Layer Protection, Ship Pollution and Wetlands.

In 2010, Lithuania's emissions from the consumption of fossil fuels totalled 15.98 million metric tons of carbon dioxide. (Source: EIA)

LUXEMBOURG

Grand Duchy of Luxembourg
Grand Duché de Luxembourg

Capital: Luxembourg (Population estimate: 81,800)

Head of State: His Royal Highness Grand Duke Henri (Sovereign) (page 1441)

National Flag: A horizontal tricolour - red, white and blue.

CONSTITUTION AND GOVERNMENT

Constitution

The Grand Duchy of Luxembourg is a representative democracy in the form of a constitutional monarchy. The Grand Duke has some executive power and is assisted by his Government, the Council of State. The Council consists of 21 councillors appointed by the Grand Duke. Eleven of the councillors must hold a law degree. Although the Council's opinions have no binding effect, it advises the Chamber of Deputies in the drafting of legislation.
Council of State, 5 rue Sigefroi, L 2536, Luxembourg. Tel: +352 47 30 71, URL: http://www.etat.lu/CE

To consult the constitution, please visit:
www.legilux.public.lu/leg/textescoordonnes/recueils/constitution_droits_de_lhomme/CONST1.pdf.

International Relations

Luxembourg sees itself very much as a country integrated with Europe as shown by the result of the referendum held in July 2005, when the electorate backed a proposed EU constitution, which had been rejected earlier in the year by French and Dutch voters. Luxembourg is a member of NATO. Being a small nation Luxembourg does not maintain an embassy in all nations; in countries where they do not have diplomatic representation, the Netherlands looks after its political interests and Belgium its economic interests.

Recent Events

In November 2008 Grand Duke Henri refused to sign into the law a bill approving euthanasia, he said that his conscience would not allow it. His refusal led to a constitutional reform which removed the need for laws to be approved by the monarch thus reducing the role to a more ceremonial one.

In April 2009, the G20 added Luxembourg to its grey list of countries regarding questionable banking arrangements. The following July the OECD commended Luxembourg for improving the transparency of it financial arrangements.

In October 2012 Crown Prince Guillaume married Belgian Countess Stephanie de Lannoy.

Legislature

The Grand Duke shared legislative power with the Chamber of Deputies. Legislature is unicameral and the Chamber of Deputies has 60 members, directly elected for a five-year term.
Chambre des Députés, 19 rue du Marché-aux-Herbes, L 1728, Luxembourg. Tel: +352 466 9661, URL: http://www.chd.lu
President: Lucien Weiler

Cabinet (as at July 2013)
Prime Minister, Minister of State and Minister of Finance: Jean-Claude Juncker (CSV) (page 1452)
Deputy Prime Minister, Minister of Foreign Affairs: Jean Asselbourn (LSAP) (page 1380)
Minister of the Family Affairs and Integration, Co-operation and Humanitarian Action: Marie-Josée Jacobs (CSV) (page 1448)
Minister of National Education and Vocational Training: Mady Delvaux-Stehres (LSAP) (page 1414)
Minister of Finance: Luc Frieden (CSV) (page 1427)
Minister of Justice, Civil Service and Administrative Reform, Higher Education and Research, Communication and Media: François Biltgen (CSV) (page 1389)
Minister of Economy and Foreign Trade: Jeannot Krecké (page 1458)
Minister of Health and Social Security: Mars di Bartolomeo (LSAP) (page 1415)
Minister of Home Affairs and Defence: Jean-Marie Halsdorf (page 1437)
Minister of Sustainable Development and Infrastructure: Claude Wiseler (CSV) (page 1538)
Minister of Work, Employment and Immigration: Nicolas Schmit (LSAP) (page 1509)
Minister of Culture, Relations with Parliament & Administrative Reform: Octavie Modert (CSV) (page 1478)
Minister of Housing: Marco Schank
Minister of the Middle Classes and Tourism, Minister of Equal Opportunities: Françoise Hetto-Gaasch
Minister of Agriculture, Viticulture and Rural Development, Sport: Romain Schneider

Ministries

Office of the Prime Minister and Ministry of State, Hôtel de Bourgogne, 4 rue de la Congrégation, L-1352 Luxembourg. Tel: +352 478 2100, fax: +352 461720, URL: http://www.gouvernement.lu/ministeres/mini_etat
Ministry of Agriculture, Viticulture and Rural Development, 1 rue de la Congrégation, L-1352 Luxembourg. Tel: +352 478 2500, fax: +352 464027, URL: http://www.gouvernement.lu/ministeres/minist_agriculture

Ministry of Cultural Affairs, Higher Education and Research, 20 Montée de la Pétrusse, L-2273 Luxembourg. Tel: +352 478 6619, fax: +352 402427, URL: http://www.gouvernement.lu/ministeres/mini_culture
Ministry of the Economy and Foreign Trade, 6 boulevard Royal, L-2449 Luxembourg. Tel: +352 478 4137, fax: +352 460448, URL: http://www.gouvernement.lu/ministeres/meco
Ministry of Education and Professional Training, 29 rue Aldringen, L-1118 Luxembourg. Tel: +352 478 5151, fax: +352 478 5110, URL: http://www.gouvernement.lu/ministeres/mini_educ.html
Ministry of the Environment, 18 montée de la Pétrusse, L-2918 Luxembourg. Tel: +352 478 6824, fax: +352 400410, URL: http://www.emwelt.lu
Ministry for Equal Opportunities,12-14, avenue E. Reuter, L-2420 Luxembourg. Tél: +352 478 5814, fax: +352 24 1886, URL: http://www.mega.public.lu
Ministry of the Family, Social Cohesion and Youth, 12-14 avenue Emile Reuter, L-2420 Luxembourg. Tel: +352 478 6500, fax: +352 478 6571, URL: http://www.gouvernement.lu/ministeres/minis_fam_int.html
Ministry of Finance, 3 rue de la Congrégation, L-1352 Luxembourg. Tel: +352 478 2635, fax: 352 475241, URL: http://www.etat.lu/FI
Ministry of Foreign Affairs and Immigration, 5 rue Notre-Dame, L-2240 Luxembourg. Tel: +352 478 2300, fax: +352 223144, URL: http://www.gouvernement.lu/ministeres/mae
Ministry of Health, Allée Marconi, Villa Louvigny, L-2120 Luxembourg. Tél: +352 478 5500, fax: +352 46 7963, URL: http://www.etat.lu/MS
Ministry of the Interior and Land Use, 19 rue Beaumont, L-1219 Luxembourg. Tel: +352 478 4626, fax: +352 221125, URL: http://www.etat.lu/MI
Ministry of Justice, 13 rue Erasme, batiment Pierre Werner, L-1468 Luxembourg. Tel: +352 478 4537, fax: +352 227661, URL: http//www.mj.public.lu
Ministry of Labour and Employment, 26 rue Zithe, L-2763 Luxembourg. Tel: +352 478 6118, fax: 352 478 6325, URL: http://www.etat.lu/MT
Ministry of Middle Classes, Tourism and Housing, 6 Avenue Emile Reuter, L-2420 Luxembourg. Tel: +352 478 4700, fax: +352 461 1187, URL: http://www.gouvernement.lu/ministeres/mcmt
Ministry of Public Administration and Reform, 63 avenue de la Liberté, L-1931, Luxembourg. Tel: +352 478 3130, fax: +352 478 3122, URL: http://www.mfpra.public.lu
Ministry of Public Works, 4 boulevard F.D. Roosevelt, L-2450 Luxembourg. Tel: +352 478 3300, fax: +352 223160, URL: http://www.etat.lu/MTP
Ministry of Social Security, 26 rue Zithe, L-2763 Luxembourg. Tel: +352 478 6100, fax: +352 478 6140, URL: http://www.etat.lu/MSS
Ministry of Transport, 11, rue Notre Dame, L-2240 Luxembourg. Tél: +352 478 4400, fax: +352 24 18 17, URL: http://www.gouvernement.lu/ministeres/mini_transports

Political Parties

Déi Gréng (The Greens), BP 454, L-2014 Luxembourg. Tel: +352 463740, fax: +352 463743, e-mail: greng@greng.lu, URL: http://www.greng.lu/cms/
Leaders: Sam Ranson and Christian Goebel
Parti Chrétien Social (Christian Social People's Party), 4 rue de l'Eau, L-1449 Luxembourg. Tel: +352 2257311, fax: +352 472716, URL: http://www.csv.lu
Leader: Michel Wolter
Parti Communiste Luxembourgeois (Communist Party), 8 rue Nôtre Dame, L2240 Luxembourg. Tel: +352 2620 2072, fax: 6352 2620 2073, e-mail: sekretariat@dei.lenk.lu, URL: http://www.dei-lenk.lu
Parti Démocratique Luxembourgeois (Democratic Party), Residence de Beauvoir, 51 rue de Strasbourg, L-2561 Luxembourg. Tel: +352 221021, fax: +352 211013, e-mail: secretariat@dp.lu, URL: http://www.dp.lu/
President: Claude Meisch
Parti Ouvrier Socialiste Luxembourgeois (POSL, Socialist Workers' Party), 37, rue du St. Esprit, L-1475 Luxembourg. Tel: +352 456573, fax: +352 456575, URL: http://www.lsap.lu
President: Jean Asselborn
Déi Lénk (The Left), URL: http://dei-lenk.lu
Leader: Collective
Parti réformiste d'alternative démocratique, (ADR, Alternative Democratic Reform Party), 9, rue de la Loge, Luxembourg. URL: http://www.adr.lu
Leader: Robert Mehlen

Elections

Elections are held every five years. Voting is by compulsory universal suffrage. Luxembourg has six seats in the European Parliament.

The most recent parliamentary election was held in June 2009. The Christian Social Party won 26 seats, the Socialist Workers Party won 13 seats, and the Democratic Party won 9 seats, The Green Party won 7 seats, The Alternative Democratic Reform Party won 4 seats and The Left won 1 seat. Mr Juncker remained as prime minister and continued his coalition of the CSP and the Socialist Workers parties.

In a referendum held in July 2005, voters backed a proposed EU constitution, rejected earlier in the year by French and Dutch voters.

Diplomatic Representation

British Embassy, 5, Boulevard Joseph II, L-1840 Luxembourg. Tel: +352 229864, fax: +352 229867, e-mail: britemb@pt.lu, URL: http://ukinluxembourg.fco.gov.uk/en
Ambassador: Hon. Alice Walpole (page 1533)

Luxembourg Embassy, 2200 Massachusetts Avenue, NW Washington 20008, United States of America. Tel: +1 202 265 4171, fax: +1 202 328 8270, URL: http://washington.mae.lu/en
Ambassador: Jean-Louis Wolzfeld (page 1539)
Luxembourg Embassy, 27 Wilton Crescent, London, SW1X 8SD. Tel: +44 (0)20 7235 6961, fax: +44 (0)20 7235 9734, URL: http://londres.mae.lu/en
Chargé d'affaires: Béatrice Kirsch
Embassy of the United States of America, 22 Blvd. Emmanuel-Servais, 2535 Luxembourg. Tel: +352 460123, fax: +352 461401, URL: http://luxembourg.usembassy.gov
Ambassador: Robert A. Mandell
Permanent Mission of the Grand Duchy of Luxembourg to the United Nations, 17 Beekman Place, New York, NY 10022, USA. Tel: +1 212 935 3589, fax: +1 212 935 5896, e-mail: luxun@undp.org, URL: http://www.un.int/luxembourg
Ambassador: Sylvie Lucas

LEGAL SYSTEM

The legal system is largely based on the French Napoleonic Code.

Minor cases are dealt with by one of the three justices of the peace. The two district courts, one in the city of Luxembourg and the other in Diekirch, hear more important civil and criminal cases. The Court of Appeal consists of nine benches of three judges each, hearing civil, commercial, and criminal cases, and the Court of Cassation (five judges) hears appeals from the benches of the Court of Appeal. The prosecutor as well as the defendant may appeal verdicts in criminal cases.

Members of the High Court of Justice, Justices of the Peace, presidents and vice-presidents of the district courts and judges of local law courts are all directly appointed by the Grand Duke. Judges are appointed for life terms. The constitution was amended in 1996 to make provision for a Constitutional Court.

The government respects the human rights of its citizens, and the law provides effective means of dealing with any instances of abuse. The death penalty was abolished in 1979.

The European Court of Justice is based in Luxembourg.

High Court of Justice, URL: http://www.justice.public.lu/fr
Constitutional Court,
URL: http://www.justice.public.lu/fr/organisation-justice/cour-constitutionnelle/index.html
Consultative Commission of Human Rights,
URL: http://www.gouvernement.lu/dossiers/justice/

LOCAL GOVERNMENT

For administrative purposes the Grand Duchy is divided into three districts; Luxembourg, Diekirch and Grevenmacher and 12 cantons - Luxembourg, Esch, Remich, Grevenmacher, Echternach, Mersch, Diekirch, Vianden, Clervaux, Wiltz, Redange and Capellen - which in turn are divided into 116 municipalities (communes). Each municipality forms an electoral district although they may be further divided into several electoral districts.

Each of these electoral districts has a council directly elected by the local people every six years. Communes with more than 3,500 inhabitants elect their council by proportional representation. In communes with less than 3,500 inhabitants an absolute majority system is used.

The following table shows the most populated municipalities as 2012:

Municipalities	Population*
Luxembourg-City	99.900
Esch sur Alzette	30,900
Differdange	22,300
Dudelange	18,800
Petange	16,400
Sanem	14,600
Hesperange	13,600
Bettembourg	9,800
Schifflange	8,900
Kayl	7,900
Mersh	8,200
Ettelbruck	8,200

* estimated figures
Source: STATEC

AREA AND POPULATION

Area
Luxembourg is bordered by Belgium to the west, Germany to the east and France to the south. It covers a total area of 2,586 sq. km. It is 82 km from north to south and 57 km east to west. Luxembourg is mountainous and forested in the north, with more rolling countryside in the south. The climate is continental.

To view a map of Luxembourg, please consult:
http://www.lib.utexas.edu/maps/cia08/luxembourg_sm_2008.gif

Population
The total population on January 1 2012 was estimated to be 524,900 (up from 444,100 in 2002), an estimated 229,900 of whom were foreigners. The following table shows the provisional number of people by origin living in Luxembourg in 2012:

Country of Origin	Number of Persons
Luxembourg	295,000
Portugal	85,300
Italy	18,100
France	31,100
Belgium	17,200
Germany	12,300
Britain	5,600
Netherlands	3,900
Other EU	23,200
Other	31,200

Source: STATEC

Major towns and their approximate populations (2009 figures) include Luxembourg (population: 88,600), Esch-sur-Alzette (29,900), Differdange (21,000), and Dudelange (18,300), Pétange (15,400), and Sanem (14,300).

The national language is Lëtzebuergesch or Luxembourgish, although French and German are the official languages and English is widely spoken.

Births, Marriages, Deaths
In 2011 there were approximately 5,639 live births and 3,819 deaths. That year there were 1,714 marriages and 1,275 divorces. In 2009, 68.1 per cent of the population was between 15 to 64 years old, with 18.0 per cent aged below 15 and 14 per cent aged 65 and over. The total fertility rate was 1.7 per woman in 2005. (Source: STATEC)

Average life expectancy in 2009 for males was 78 years for males and 83 years for females. In 2007, healthy life expectancy was 71 years for males and 75 years for females. The infant mortality rate and the neo-natal morality rate were both an estimated 1.0 per 1,000 births in 2009. The maternal mortality rate was an estimated 17 per 100,000 live births in 2009. The total fertility rate was 1.4 births per female. (Source: WHO)

Public Holidays 2014
1 January: New Year's Day
5-6 March: Carnival
18 April: Good Friday
21 April: Easter Monday
1 May: Labour Day
29 May: Ascension Day
9 May: Whit Monday
23 June: Grand Duke's Birthday
15 August: Assumption Day
1 September: Luxembourg City Fête
1 November: All Saint's Day
25 December: Christmas Day
26 December: St. Stephen's Day

Public holidays falling on a Sunday are usually observed on the following Monday - decreed on 1 December of the previous year to the maximum of two per year.

EMPLOYMENT

More than 30 per cent of the labour force are cross border workers, and the economy relies heavily on them. Figures for 2011 show that 776,300 cross border workers came from France, 38,900 from Belgium and 38,900 from Germany. In 2011, domestic employment was estimated to be 368,400 people. The following table shows how the domestic population was employed in 2008:

Total Employment by Economic Activity (estimated)

Occupation	2008
Agriculture, hunting, forestry & fishing	5,000
Mining & quarrying, manufacturing, electricity, gas & water supply	37,700
Construction	38,400
Wholesale & retail trade, repairs,, hotels & restaurants, Transport & communications	89,600
Financial intermediation	41,300
Real estate, renting & business activities	59,500
Public admin. & defence; compulsory social security, education, health & social work, other community activities, household with employed persons	77,100
Total	348,700

Source: Copyright © International Labour Organization (ILO Dept. of Statistics, http://laborsta.ilo.org)

Unemployment rose from 2.5 per cent in September 2000 to 3.9 per cent in 2004 and to 4.2 per cent in 2005. It rose further to 12.9 per cent in 2009 and 13.5 per cent in 2010 remaining the same in 2011.

Luxembourg's labour relations have encouraged foreign companies to operate in the country.

Industrial and Trade Associations
Confédération du Commerce Luxembourgeoise, URL: http://www.clc.lu

LUXEMBOURG

Fédération des Artisans du Grand-Duché de Luxembourg, URL: http://www.federation-des-artisans.lu
Fédération des Industriels Luxembourgeoise, URL: http://www.fedil.lu

BANKING AND FINANCE

Currency
On 1 January 2002 the European currency, the euro, became legal tender.
1 euro (€) = 100 cents
€ = 40.3399 Luxembourg Francs (European Central Bank irrevocable conversion rate)
Up until then the currency had been the Luxembourg Franc (LUF) = 100 centimes. Bank notes are in denominations of 5, 10, 20, 50, 100, 200 and 500 euro. Coins are in denominations of 1, 2, 5, 10, 20 and 50 cents and 1 and 2 euro.

GDP/GNP, Inflation, National Debt
Luxembourg enjoys a stable economy, with low unemployment, low inflation and high income. The banking and financial services sector is the dominant force in the economy. This is followed by the industrial sector, where diversification to rubber and chemical industries has helped to offset the decline in the steel industry. Farming is often a family business in Luxembourg, and is not a major contributor to the economy (just 0.4 per cent of GNP in 2008).

GDP has continued to grow in recent years as the following table shows:

Year	Billion Euro
2000	22.0
2007	37.5
2008	39.3
2009	37.4
2010	40.3
2011	42.8

Source: STATEC

Real growth was forecast to be 3.0 per cent in 2010 falling to 1.1 per cent in 2012. The following table shows the makeup of GDP in recent years.

Structure of Gross Value Added at Basic Prices (in %)

Sector	2010	2011
Agriculture	0.3	0.3
Iron, steel & metal processing	2.5	2.0
Other manufacturing industry	4.4	4.9
Energy & water	1.2	0.8
Construction	4.9	5.6
Distributive trades, lodging & catering, transport & communication	22.1	19.8
Financial activities	27.5	26.6
Estate activities, rent services & services to companies	20.8	23.0
General government services	5.2	5.3
Education, health & social protection	8.7	9.3
Other public & private services	2.3	2.3

Source: STATEC

Inflation was around 2.7 per cent in 2006, compared to 2.4 per cent in 2005. It rose to 2.7 per cent in 2006, before falling to 2.3 per cent in 2007. In 2008, it rose to 3.4 per cent.

In 2011 the national debt stood at €7785.9 million, of which €6,811.3 million came from central government, €150.6 million came from foreign debt. A further €974.6 million came from local government. This compares to 2000, when total public debt was €1,356.4 million (central government €901.8 million, of which foreign debt €423.7 million).

Balance of Payments / Imports and Exports
Luxembourg's trade account has been in deficit over the last decade.

Value of Foreign Trade Millions of Euro in 2010/11

Goods	Exports 10	Exports 11	Imports 10	Imports 11
Food & live animals	671.6	717.4	1,341.5	1,387.9
Beverages and tobacco	192.5	214.5	434.7	444.9
Crude materials, oils, fats & waxes	386.7	507.5	1,456.7	1,820.3
Mineral fuels, lubricants	99.3	95.7	2,042.6	2,382.6
Chemicals & related products	856.6	907.8	1,607.0	1,822.4
Manufactured metal goods	3152,5	3,461.0	1,465.0	1,631.1
Other manufactured goods classified by material	1,760.7	1,962.1	1,197.7	1,426.5
Machinery	1,765.6	1,868.2	2,236.7	2,369.2
Transport equipment	792.7	1,082.8	2,484.0	3,034.4
Other manufactured goods	1,107.3	1,211.8	2,186.1	2,279.3
Total	10,785.4	12,028.8	16,421.9	18,598.6

Source: STATEC

Most significant foreign trade partners in recent years.

Foreign Trade Partners in Millions of Euro in 2010/11

Country	Exports 10	Exports 11	Imports 10	Imports 11
Germany	3,085.9	3,373.6	4,733.5	5,396.6
Belgium	1,383.0	1,495.3	5,728.5	6,307.4
Spain	204.2	219.3	118.8	131.7
France	1,768.7	1,911.4	2,176.4	2,227.2
Italy	526.2	517.7	386.1	439.0
Netherlands	554.0	618.5	1,113.2	1,178.2
United Kingdom	465.5	462.1	234.9	369.4
Poland	213.3	250.9	108.3	174.3
Switzerland	200.2	339.3	432.8	334.4
USA	284.4	413.1	347.2	844.8
China	133.1	172.8	88.9	104.9

Source: STATEC

Central Bank
Banque Centrale du Luxembourg, 2 boulevard Royal, L-2983, Luxembourg. URL: http://www.bcl.lu
Governor: Gaston Reinesch (page 1502)

Chambers of Commerce and Trade Organisations
Chamber of Commerce, URL: http://www.cc.lu
Bourse de Luxembourg, URL: http://www.bourse.lu
Luxembourg Confederation of Commerce, URL: http://www.clc.lu
Association des Banques et Banquiers Luxembourg (ABBL), URL: http://www.abbl.lu
Société Nationale de Crédit et d'Investissement (SNCI), URL: http://www.snci.lu

MANUFACTURING, MINING AND SERVICES

Energy
In 2011, Luxembourg consumed 61,000 barrels of oil per day, all imported. In the same year Luxembourg consumed 48 billion cubic feet of natural gas, again all imported. In 2010 Luxembourg generated 2.5 billion kWh of electricity and consumed 6.4 billion kWh.

Service de l'Energie de l'Etat, URL: http://www.see.lu
SUDGAZ SA, URL: http://www.sudgaz.lu

Manufacturing
The manufacturing focus in Luxembourg is on rolled steel products, which typically represent one quarter of Luxembourg's total export revenues.

Steel Production in '000 tons

Product	1990	2000	2010	2011
Iron Ore Import	6,173	2,571	-	-
Steel	3,560	2,571	2,548	2,521
Rolled Steel Products	3,199	3,360	2,506	2,412
- Finished Rolled Products of which	2,773	2,918	2,276	2,219
- Shapes (joists, etc.)	1,192	1,058	1,272	1,325
- Merchants' Products	750	174	427	320
- Sheets and Coils	632	1,033	577	574
- Hot-Rolled Hoops and Strips	278	-	-	-
- Cold-Rolled Hoops and Strips	28	77	-	-

Source STATEC

Aluminium, glass, cement, tyres, magnetic tape and computer manufacturers have all established plants in Luxembourg.

Service Industries
The financial services sector has shown the greatest growth rate in Luxembourg. Figures for 2011 indicate that there were 1,948 Unit Trusts, together with 142 banks and 335 insurance firms and reinsurance companies. Luxembourg is second only to Germany in terms of the number of banks within its borders. Figures for 2002 show that the sector contributed 35 per cent of GDP. Net profit has grown from €2.5 billion in 2000 to €2.9 billion in 2003. The banks employed around 22,500 people.

Luxembourg diversified into banking following the decline of its industry sector particularly the steel manufacturing. The country had strict banking secrecy laws and this led to a system that was open to exploitation for tax evasion and fraud. This led the G20 to adding Luxembourg to a grey list. Luxembourg responded by improving its system to be more transparant and by 2009 had signed agreements on the exchange of tax information resulting in a commendation by the OECD.

In 2011, there were 383 hotels, with 8,588 rooms, and 136 camp sites, with capacity for over 48,902 people. Around 934,000 tourists visited Luxembourg in 2011, a rise on the previous year.
Office National du Tourisme, URL: http://www.ont.lu

Agriculture
Luxembourg is not rich in land naturally suited to crop-growing, hence the predominance of livestock production in this sector; STATEC estimates that roughly 80 per cent of the gross revenue from agriculture comes from livestock. Farms in Luxembourg tend to be small and family run. The Moselle Valley region is home to vineyards which produced in the year 2004-05, 155,800 hectolitres of wine, mainly for local consumption. Figures for the year 2011/12 show that Luxembourg produced 132,000 hectolitres of wine.

The following table shows recent figures for the agricultural sector:

	1990	2000	2010*
Total Number of Farms	3,803	2,728	2,201
Average Area of Each Farm (hectares)	38.37	53.22	66.1
Crop Area (hectares)	126,298	127,643	131,106
Crop Production (tons)			
- Grassland and Pasturage (dry matter)	322,040	391,170	363,218
- Maize	71,770	113,760	169,786
- Forage Crops (dry matter)	125,550	97,048	79,874
- Bread Crops	45,880	64,790	81,029
- Potatoes	24,870	23,430	19,679
- Other	102,050	88,040	109,135
- Colza		15,895	15,574
Livestock			
- Cattle	217,451	205,072	198,830
- Pigs	75,463	80,141	83,774
- Sheep	7,281	7,971	9,084
- Horses	1,722	3,154	4,601
Meat Production ('000 tons)	22.5	28.7	33.6
Milk Production ('000 tons)	290.3	264.6	292.2

Source: STATEC

Luxembourg's agricultural sector provides employment for less than 1.3 per cent of the work force.

COMMUNICATIONS AND TRANSPORT

Travel Requirements
Citizens of the USA, Canada and Australia require a passport valid for three months beyond the length of stay but do not need a visa for stays of up to 90 days. EU nationals holding a valid national Identity Card do not require a passport or a visa for up to 90 days. Other nationals should contact the embassy to check visa requirements.

Luxembourg is a signatory to the Schengen Agreement. With a Schengen visa, a visitor can travel freely throughout the Schengen zone, and there are few border stops and checks. See http://www.eurovisa.info/SchengenCountries.htm for details.

National Airlines
Luxair is Luxembourg's national airline:
Luxair, URL: http://www.luxair.lu
Cargolux Airlines International SA, URL: http://www.cargolux.com

International Airports
Approximately 1,791,000 passengers and 705,370 tons of freight passed through Luxembourg airport in 2011.
Luxembourg Airport, URL: http://www.aeroport.public.lu/fr/

Railways
The rail network consists of five main lines that converge on the city of Luxembourg and serve most urbanised areas; there is around 275 km of line. In 2006, approximately 705 370 tonnes of freight was transported, and there were approximately 1,791,000passenger journeys.
Chemins de Fer Luxembourgeois, URL: http://www.cfl.lu

Roads
As of 2011 the national network of roads stood at 2,899 km, of which 152 km was motorway. That year there were 415,943 vehicles on the road, of which 15,753 were motorcycles, 337,239 passenger cars, and 30,158 lorries (source: STATEC). Vehicles are driven on the right.

Waterways
The most important rivers in Luxembourg are the Moselle, the Our, the Alzette and the Sûre.

Ports and Harbours
In 2011 the river port of Metert loaded around 124,000 tons of cargo (down from 263,000 tons in 2005) and unloaded 660,000 tons (compared to 1,032,000 tons in 2005).

HEALTH

In 2009, Luxembourg spent approximately 12.6 per cent of its total budget on healthcare (up from 11.6 per cent in 2000), accounting for 73.4 per cent of all healthcare spending. Total expenditure on healthcare equated to 7.5 per cent of the country's GDP. Per capita expenditure on health was approximately US$8,262, compared with US$3,474 in 2000.

Figures from the WHO for 2005-10 show that there are 1,350 physicians (27.7 per 10,000 population), and 404 dentistry personnel. There are 68 hospital beds per 10,000 population.

The infant mortality rate in 2010 was 2 per 1,000 live births. The child mortality rate (under 5 years) was 3 per 1,000 live births. (Source: http://www.who.int, World Health Statistics 2012)

EDUCATION

Primary education is free and compulsory. There are also free vocational training courses, secondary education and some higher education courses.

The following tables show pupil and teacher numbers by level of education:

Number of Pupils

Level of Education	2008/09	2009/10
Nursery Education	9,966	10,026
Primary Education	32,496	32,312
Technical Secondary Education	24,323	25,184
Secondary Education	12,469	12,757
University of Luxembourg	4,517	4,934
Students at Foreign Universities	7,410	6,992

Source: STATEC

Number of Teachers

Level of Education	2008/09	2009/10
Nursery Education	864	946
Primary Education	3,359	3,498
Secondary Education	4,054	4,096

Source: STATEC

According to UNESCO figures for 2007, 87 per cent of young children were enrolled in pre-primary school, where the pupil / teacher ratio was 11 / 1. 98 per cent of girls and 97 per cent of boys were enrolled in primary school and 86 per cent of girls and 83 per cent of boys were enrolled in secondary school.

Luxembourg has several institutes of higher education but just one university, the University of Luxembourg was founded in 2003.

RELIGION

The proportion of Roman Catholics has gradually declined over the years, from 95 per cent of the population in the 1950s, to 86.6 per cent in 2003. There are now 255 priests in the country (down from 283 in 2000). Luxembourg has small Jewish and Muslim communities. Luxembourg has a religious liberty rating of 10 on a scale of 1 to 10 (10 is most freedom). (Source: World Religion Database)

Archbishop of Luxembourg, 4 rue Génistre, BP 419, L-2014 Luxembourg. Tel: +352 462023, fax: +352 475381
Most Rev. Jean-Claude Hollerich

Protestant Church
The Evangelical Church in the Grand Duchy of Luxembourg, URL: http://webplaza.pt.lu/public/kiirch/index.html

COMMUNICATIONS AND MEDIA

The constitution guarantees freedom of speech and freedom of the press. Diverse views are reflected in the press.

Newspapers
The printed press is privately owned. Titles include:
Luxemburger Wort, URL: http://www.wort.lu
Tageblatt (journal pour le Luxembourg),URL: http://www.tageblatt.lu
Letzeburger Journal, URL: http://www.journal.lu
D'Letzeburger Land, URL: http://www.land.lu/index2.html

Business Journals
Official Journal of the European Communities, URL: http://www.ojec.com

Broadcasting
The television company *Compagnie Luxembourgeoise de Télédiffusion* is the oldest commercial broadcaster in Europe (60 years old).
Luxembourg's satellite company, *Société Européenne des Satellites* operates the Astra satellite system, and Europe Online, an internet provider. The first SES "ASTRA" satellite, a 16-channel RCA 4000, was launched by Ariane rocket in December 1988. SES presently operates 12 satellites. The RTL group is a major player in Luxembourg, operating alongside other private TV and radio stations. Satellite and cable TV services are available.
Rtl Group, URL: http://rtl.lu/home.rtl
Société Européene des Satellites (SES), URL: http://www.ses-astra.com

Telecommunications
In 2010 an estimated 272,400 land line telephones and an estimated 727,000 mobile phones were in use. An estimated 424,500 people were internet users.
Entreprise des Postes et Télécommunications (P&T), URL: http://www.ept.lu

ENVIRONMENT

Luxembourg has recognised environmental concerns in its planning laws. It also has a licensing system for industrial activity which could pollute the landscape. Pollution levels throughout Luxembourg are low and are well within EC acceptable limits. Luxembourg is a party to the following international agreements, party to: Air Pollution, Air Pollution-Nitrogen Oxides, Air Pollution-Persistent Organic Pollutants, Air Pollution-Sulfur 85, Air Pollution-Sulfur 94, Air Pollution-Volatile Organic Compounds, Biodiversity, Climate Change, Climate Change-Kyoto Protocol, Desertification, Endangered Species, Hazardous Wastes, Law of the Sea, Marine Dumping, Ozone Layer Protection, Ship Pollution, Tropical Timber 83, Tropical Timber 94 and Wetlands.

MACEDONIA

In 2010, Luxembourg's emissions from the consumption of fossil fuels totalled 10.80 million metric tons of carbon dioxide, down from 12.47 million metric tons in 2008. (Source: EIA)

SPACE PROGRAMME

Société Européenne des Satellites (URL: http://www.ses-astra.com) is Europe's biggest satellite operator and is based in Luxembourg. It became the 17th member of the European Space Agency in 2005.

MACEDONIA

Republic of Macedonia

Republika Makedonija

Capital: Skopje (Population estimate, 2010: 506,500)

Head of State: Giorge Ivanov (President) (page 1447)

National Flag: A yellow sunburst across a red background

CONSTITUTION AND GOVERNMENT

Constitution

In 1991 Macedonia adopted its new constitution, the basic provisions of which include that the citizens of Macedonia are equal in their freedom and rights, irrespective of sex, race, colour, national and social origin, political and religious beliefs or property or social status. Everyone is equal before the law. The Republic of Macedonia is a sovereign, independent, democratic and social state. The power of the state is divided into legislative, executive and judicial. The constitution was amended in 2001 in order to reduce the tensions between ethnic Macedonians and ethnic Albanians.

Macedonia was admitted to the United Nations as a sovereign country on 7 April 1993. The President of Macedonia is elected for a period of five years and a maximum of two terms. The president conducts international negotiations, appoints ambassadors and gives the mandate to the nominated candidate to form a government.

To consult the constitution, please visit: www.minelres.lv/NationalLegislation/Macedonia/Macedonia_Const2001_excerpts_English.htm

Former Yugoslav Republic of Macedonia

Under the constitution the name of the country is the Republic of Macedonia. However, Greece has objections to the name as it may cause confusion with or raise implied territorial ambitions over the Greek region of Macedonia. The name Former Yugoslav Republic of Macedonia was adopted until a solution could be found, talks under the UN are still ongoing. In 2004 the USA recognised the Republic of Macedonia as the constitutional name.

Recent Events

Early in 2001 violence broke out between ethnic Albanian insurgents and the security forces, initially the trouble were confined to areas near the Kosovo border, which the Macedonian forces managed to keep under control against the National Liberation Army, who were demanding equal rights for ethnic Albanians. The troubles escalated in April and the NLA gained control of several villages in the north. Many ethnic Albanian refugees fled to Kosovo and Serbia while ethnic Macedonians fled to other parts of the country. In June NATO negotiated a ceasefire, which then extended to peace talks. The NLA was given amnesty in return for giving up their weapons and it was agreed that reforms for ethnic Albanians would be discussed, this agreement became known as the Ohrid agreement and was signed on August 13 2001. In June 2002 a law was passed recognising Albanian as an official language.

On 26 February 2004 President Boris Trajkovski was killed when a plane taking him to an international investment conference in Mostar, Bosnia, crashed in a mountainous area of southern Bosnia in bad weather. In April 2004, Branko Crvenkovski was elected president. Hari Kostov resigned as prime minister in November 2004, and was replaced by the new leader of the Social Democratic Union, Vlado Buckovski, who formed a new government.

In November 2005 the European Union recommended that Macedonia become a candidate country for membership. In November 2006 NATO announced that Macedonia may be invited to join the organisation in 2008. In April 2008 Greece blocked the bid for membership over a dispute over the name of the country, and in January 2009 Macedonia applied to the International Court of Justice for a ruling on the dispute with Greece over the country's name.

In December 2009 under the EU Schengen treaty, Macedonian citizens could travel within the zone without needing a visa.

Hearings began in March 2011 at the International Court of Justice in The Hague into the dispute over Macedonia's name. In December 2011 the court ruled that Greece was wrong to block Macedonia's bid to join NATO in 2008 because of the dispute over its name.

Legislature

Macedonia has a unicameral legislature the Assembly or Sobranie. The Assembly is composed of 120 representatives, elected for a period of four years. Of this number 85 are elected by majority in 85 constituencies and 35 are elected by a proportional system where the whole country represents one constituency.
Assembly (Sobranie), URL: http://www.sobranie.mk

Cabinet (as at March 2013)
Prime Minister: Nikola Gruevski (VMRO-DPMNE) (page 1434)

Deputy Prime Minister with responsibility for the Economy: Vladimir Pestevski (page 1494)
Deputy Prime Minister with responsibility for Implemention of the Ohrid Framework Agreement: Musa Xhaferi (BDI)
Deputy Prime Minister and Minister of Finance: Zoran Stavrevski (VMRO-DPMNE) (page 1519)
Deputy Prime Minister with responsibility for European Affairs: Teuta Arifi (BDI)
Minister of Foreign Affairs: Nikola Poposki (VMRO-DPMNE) (page 1497)
Minister of Internal Affairs: Gordana Jankulovska (VMRO-DPMNE)
Minister of Local Self-Government: Nevzat Bejta (BDI)
Minister of Health: Nikola Todorov (VMRO-DPMNE)
Minister of Defence: Fatmir Besimi (BDI)
Minister of Labour and Social Policy: Spiro Risteski (VMRO-DPMNE)
Minister of Justice: Blerim Bexheti (BDI)
Minister of the Economy: Valon Sarcini (BDI)
Minister of Culture: Elizabeta Kanceska Milevska (VMRO-DPMNE)
Minister of the Environment and Urban Planning: Abdilaqim Ademi (BDI)
Minister of Agriculture, Forestry and Water Resources: Ljupcho Dimovski (SPM)
Minister of Education and Science: Pance Kralev (VMRO-DPMNE)
Minister of Transport and Communications: Mile Janakieski (VMRO-DPMNE)
Minister of Information Society and Administration: Ivo Ivanovski (Ind.)
Minister without portfolio: Hadi Neziri (PDTM)
Minister without portfolio: Vele Samak (Ind)
Minister without portfolio: Nezdet Mustafa (OPRM)

Ministries

Government of the Republic of Macedonia, Blvd. Ilinden bb, 1000 Skopje, Macedonia. Tel: +389 2 3118 022 / 3115 455, fax: +389 2 3112 561 / 3115 285, URL: http://www.vlada.mk/
Ministry of Labour and Social Welfare, Dame Gruev br. 14, 1000 Skopje, Macedonia. Tel: +389 2 3117 787, fax: +389 2 3118 242, URL: http://www.mtsp.gov.mk
Ministry of Defence, Orce Nikolov bb, 91000 Skopje, Macedonia. Tel: +389 2 3119 577, fax: +389 2 3227 835 / 3230 928, e-mail: info@morm.gov.mk, URL: http://www.morm.gov.mk
Ministry of Foreign Affairs, Dame Gruev br. 6, 1000 Skopje, Macedonia. Tel: +389 2 3110 330, fax: +389 2 3115 790, e-mail: mnr@mnr.gov.mk, URL: http://www.mfa.gov.mk
Ministry of Justice, Dimitrie Cupovski br. 9, 1000 Skopje, Macedonia. Tel: +389 2 3117 277, fax: +389 2 3226 975, URL: http://www.covekovi-prava.gov.mk
Ministry of Finance, Dame Gruev 14, 1000 Skopje, Macedonia. Tel: +389 2 3117 288 / 3116 012, fax: +389 2 3117 280, e-mail: finance@finance.gov.mk, URL: http://www.finance.gov.mk
Ministry of Economy, Jurij Gagarin 15, 1000 Skopje, Macedonia. Tel: +398 2 3084 470 / 471, fax: +398 2 3084 472, e-mail: ms@mt.net.mk, URL: http://www.economy.gov.mk
Ministry of Interior Affairs, Dimce Mircev bb, 1000 Skopje, Macedonia. Tel: +389 2 3117 222 / 3221 972, fax: +389 2 3112 468, URL: http://www.mvr.gov.mk
Ministry of Transport and Communications, plostad Crvena skopska opstina br. 4, 1000 Skopje, Macedonia. Tel: +389 2 3126 228 / 3123 292, fax: +389 2 3126 228, URL: http://www.mtc.gov.mk
Ministry of Agriculture, Forestry and Waters, Leninova br. 2, 1000 Skopje, Macedonia. Tel: +389 2 3134 477, fax: +389 2 3239 429, e-mail: mgjorcev@mia.com.mk, URL: http://www.mzsv.gov.mk/
Ministry of Education and Science, Dimitrie Cupovski 9, 1000 Skopje, Macedonia. Tel: +389 2 3117 277 / 896 fax: +389 2 3118 414, URL: http://www.mon.gov.mk/
Ministry of Local Self-Government, Dame Gruev 14, 1000 Skopje, Macedonia. Tel: +389 2 3106 302, fax: +389 2 3106 303, URL: http://www.mls.gov.mk
Ministry of Culture, Blvd. Ilinden bb, 1000 Skopje, Macedonia. Tel: +389 2 3118 022, fax: +389 2 3127 112 / 3124 233, e-mail: vrteva@lotus.mpt.com.mk, URL: http://www.kultura.gov.mk
Ministry of Health, Vodnjanska bb, 1000 Skopje, Macedonia. Tel: +389 2 3147 147, fax: +389 2 3113 014, URL: http://www.zdravstvo.com.mk
Ministry of Environment and Land Planning, Drezdenska br 52, 1000 Skopje, Macedonia. Tel: +389 2 366 930, fax: +389 2 366 931, e-mail: infoeko@moe.gov.mk, URL: http://www.moe.gov.mk

Political Parties

VMRO-DPMNE (Internal Macedonian Revolutionary Organisation), URL: http://www.vmro-dpmne.org.mk
Social Democrat Party of Macedonia, URL: http://www.sdsm.org.mk
SKM (Communists' League of Macedonia); PDP (Party for Democratic Prosperity); NSDP (New Social Democratic Party); PDSh (Democratic Party of Albanians); Reformist Forces League in Macedonia; Socialist Party of Macedonia; Party of Yugoslavs in Republic of Macedonia; National Democratic Party in Macedonia; PCER (Party for Complete Emancipation of the Gypsies); Albanian Democratic League; Democratic Party; Macedonian National Party;

Macedonian National Front; Workers' Party; Civil Liberty Party; Democratic Alternative; Party for Democratic Action - Civil League; Party for Democratic Action - Islamic Way; SDA (Party for Democratic Action of Macedonia)

Elections

The most recent parliamentary elections took place in June 2011; the Better Macedonia alliance led by the VMRO-DPMNE won 56 seats. the Coalition for Europe won 15 seats. Although Prime Minister Gruevski's party won, it was not enough to secure a majority.

The incumbent president Branko Crvenkovski did not stand for re-election in the presidential election of March 2009. Gjorgje Ivanov of the centre-right VMRO-DPMNE party won in a run-off election against Ljubomir Frčkoski.

Diplomatic Representation

British Embassy, Dimitrija Chupovski 26, 4th Floor, Skopje 1000, Macedonia. Tel: +389 2329 9299, fax: +389 2311 7555, beskopje@mt.net.mk, URL: http://ukinmacedonia.fco.gov.uk/en
Ambassador: Christopher Yvon (page 1542)
American Embassy, Blvd. Ilinden, 1000 Skopje, Macedonia. Tel: +389 2 3116 180, fax: +389 2 3117 103, e-mail: irc@usembassy.mpt.com.mk, URL: http://skopje.usembassy.gov
Ambassador: Paul D. Wohlers
Macedonian Embassy, 2129 Wyoming Avenue N.W. 20008, Washington D.C., USA. Tel: +1 202 337 3063, fax: +1 202 337 3093, URL: http://www.macedonianembassy.org
Ambassador: Zoran Jolevski
Macedonian Embassy, Suites 2.1-2.2, Buckingham Court, 75/83 Buckingham Gate, London SW1E 6PE, United Kingdom. Tel: +44 (0)20 7976 0535; e-mail: info@macedonianembassy.org.uk URL: http://www.macedonianembassy.org.uk
Ambassador: Marija Efremova (page 1419)
Permanent Mission of the Republic of Macedonia to the UN, 866 United Nations Plaza, Suite 517, New York, NY 10017, USA. Tel: +1 212 308 8504, fax: +1 212 308 8724
Permanent Representative: Pajo Avirovik

LEGAL SYSTEM

Macedonia has 27 Courts of First Instance, three Courts of Appeal and a Supreme Court. Judges are proposed by the Judicial Council but are elected for life by the Parliament. The Judicial Council is composed of seven members elected by the Parliament for six years. The Supreme Court is the highest court and guarantees equal administration of the law by all the courts. The Constitutional Court is responsible for protecting constitutional and legal rights. It is composed of nine judges elected by the Parliament for nine years.

The government respects the human rights of its citizens, but political pressure and intimidation has occasionally limited the power of the judiciary.

The death penalty was abolished under the constitution in 1991.

Supreme Court, URL: http://www.sud.mk/VSUD/WWWVsud.nsf?OpenDatabase

Ombudsman for the Republic of Macedonia, URL: http://www.ombudsman.mk/default.aspx?Lan=EN

LOCAL GOVERNMENT

For administrative purposes the Republic of Macedonia is divided into 84 municipalities, 10 of which form the capital Skopje, the municipalities have responsibility over such areas as urban planning, basic health care, communal activities, child care, pre-school and primary school education and social security. The municipalities or *Opstina* are, Aracinovo, Berovo, Bitola, Bogdanci, Bogovinje, Bosilovo, Brvenica, Caska, Centar Zupa, Cesinovo, Cucer Sandevo, Debar, Debarca, Delcevo, Demir Hisar, Demir Kapija, Dojran, Dolneni, Drugovo, Gevgelija, Gostivar, Gradsko, Ilinden, Jegunovce, Karbinci, Kavadarci, Kicevo, Kocani, Konce, Kratovo, Kriva Palanka, Krivogastani, Krusevo, Kumanovo, Lipkovo, Lozovo, Makedonska Kamenica, Makedonski Brod, Mavrovo i Rostusa, Mogila, Negotino, Novaci, Novo Selo, Ohrid, Oslomej, Pehcevo, Petrovec, Plasnica, Prilep, Probistip, Radovis, Rankovce, Resen, Rosoman, Sopiste, Staro Nagoricane, Stip, Struga, Strumica, Studenicani, Sveti Nikole, Tearce, Tetovo, Valandovo, Vasilevo, Veles, Vevcani, Vinica, Vranestica, Vrapciste, Zajas, Zelenikovo, Zelino, Zrnovci. As well as the capital Skopje the municipalities that go towards making up the municipality of Skopje are, Aerodrom, Butel, Cair, Centar, Gazi Baba, Gjorce Petrov, Karpos, Kisela Voda, Saraj, Suto Orizari.

Local elections took place most recently in 2011.

AREA AND POPULATION

Area

The Republic of Macedonia is situated in the southern part of the Balkan Peninsula. It is landlocked, bordered by Serbia to the north, Albania to the west, Greece to the south, and Bulgaria to the east. It has an area of 25,713 sq. km. The country has three large lakes all of which are on borders, the lakes are Ohrid, Prespa and Doiran, the river Vardar flows through the country. The terrain is mountainous with deep valleys and basins.

To view a map, visit http://www.un.org/Depts/Cartographic/map/profile/macedonia.pdf

Summer and autumn are dry and warm. Winters are colder with heavy snowfalls.

Population

In 2010 the population was estimated to be 2.061 million. The annual growth rate was an estimated 0.3 per cent over the period 2000-10. Net migration was estimated to be -0.48 migrants per 1,000 population. The ethnic composition was as follows: Macedonians 64 per cent, Albanians 25 per cent, Turks 4 per cent, Romanies 3.0 per cent, Vlachs 0.5 per cent, Serbs 2.0 per cent, Bosniaks, 0.5 per cent and others 1 per cent. Macedonian written in the Cyrillic alphabet and Albanian are the official languages, Turkish and Serbian are also spoken.

Conflict exists between the Macedonians and the ethnic Albanians who want Albanian recognised as an official language and greater control of police forces in areas where Albanians make up the majority of residents. Peace talks were held in July 2001 and a peace pact was signed in August which set out some recognition of the ethnic Albanians wishes including a larger proportion of ethnic Albanians in the police force and use of the Albanian language allowed in official institutions and in areas where ethnic Albanians make up at least 20 per cent of the population. In December 2005, parliament passed a law allowing the flying of the Albanian flag in those areas where Albanians make up the major part of the population. Approximately 67 per cent of the population lives in urban areas.

Births, Marriages, Deaths

In 2010 the estimated birth rate per 1,000 inhabitants was 10.8, the death rate was 10.1, and the infant mortality rate 10.0 per live births. The average life expectancy for males is 72 years and 77 for females. The median age is 36 years. The total fertility rate in 2010 was 1.4 per female. (Source: http://www.who.int, World Health Statistics 2012)

Public Holidays 2014

1-2 January: New Year's Day
6-7 January: Orthodox Christmas
21 April: Orthodox Easter Monday
1 May: Labour Day
24 May: Saints Cyrilus and Methodius Day
2 August: Ilinden (Uprising Day)
8 September: Independence Day
29 July: End of Ramadan
11 October: Uprising against Fascist Occupation

EMPLOYMENT

The following table shows employment sector figures in 2008.

Employment Sector	No. of Persons Employed
Agriculture, hunting, forestry	119,500
Fishing	300
Mining & quarrying	6,700
Manufacturing	129,000
Electricity, gas & water	15,500
Construction	39,400
Wholesale & retail trade	86,600
Hotels & restaurants	19,100
Transport, storage & communication	37,700
Financial intermediation	7,700
Real estate, renting & business activities	16,300
Public administration & defence	42,200
Education	33,600
Health & social work	32,900
Other community, social & personal services	21,000
Households with employed persons	700
Extra-territorial organisations and bodies	800

Source: Copyright © International Labour Organization (ILO Dept. of Statistics, http://laborsta.ilo.org)

BANKING AND FINANCE

Currency

The currency is the Macedonian Denar of 100 deni.

GDP/GNP, Inflation, National Debt

Post-independence in 1991, Macedonia's economy had a period of difficult economic growth. Various outside factors include sanctions on Serbia, a Greek trade embargo and its political situation. The situation stabilised in 2004. The government has subsequently made increasing foreign investment a priority. The 2008-09 global economic crisis has affected Macedonia, with high inflation, a large increase in the current account deficit, reduced foreign currency reserves and rising unemployment. Its strong trade links with Europe mean its economy is being affected by the economic crisis.

GDP was estimated at €6.506 billion in 2008 with an annual growth rate of approximately 5 per cent. Per capita GDP was €8,200 in 2008. Estimated figures for 2009 put GDP at US$9.5 billion, a growth rate of -1.5 per cent. Estimated figures for 2011 put GDP at US$9.8 billion with a growth rate of 3.5 per cent. Per capita GDP was US$9,400 in 2010.

Inflation was estimated at 8.3 per cent in 2008 and had dipped into the negative in 2009 at -0.8 per cent. Inflation was estimated to be 1.5 per cent in 2010, rising to 3.9 per cent in 2011. It was estimated at 3.4 per cent in 2012 and is forecast to remain at that rate in 2013.

Total external debt was estimated at over US$6 billion in 2011.

Foreign direct investment was estimated at US$4 billion in 2011.

MACEDONIA

Balance of Payments / Imports and Exports

Figures for 2011 show that exports (f.o.b.) totalled an estimated US$4.1 billion and imports (f.o.b.) totalled US$6 billion. Exported goods include food, tobacco, iron and steel, and imported goods include machinery and equipment, fuels, chemicals and food. Main trading partners are Germany, Greece, Italy, Slovenia, Ukraine, Serbia and Montenegro.

Central Bank

National Bank of the Republic of Macedonia, PO Box 401, Kompleks banki bb, 1000 Skopje, Macedonia. Tel: +389 2 108108, fax: +389 2 108357, e-mail: governorsoffice@nbrm.gov.mk, URL: http://www.nbrm.mk/default-en.asp
Governor: Petar Gosev

Chambers of Commerce and Trade Organisations

Economic Chamber of Macedonia, e-mail: ic@ic.mchamber.org.mk, URL: http://www.mchamber.org.mk
American Chamber of Commerce in Macedonia, URL: http://www.amcham.com.mk

MANUFACTURING, MINING AND SERVICES

Primary and Extractive Industries

There are mineral resources of iron, coal, zinc, lead, copper, gold and chromium. The total coal production in 2010 was 7.4 million short tons all of which was used for domestic use plus 227,000 short tons that was imported.

Energy

The hydro-power plants in Struga, Debar, Gostivar and the thermal plants in Bitola, Kichevo and Negotino produce a total of 5.5 billion kWh of electricity per year. In 2010 Macedonia had an electricity installed capacity of 1.60 gigawatts. That year electricity production was 6.94 billion kWh and consumption was 7.09 billion kWh. The Republic of Macedonia has no oil reserves of its own and so has to import all that it uses. This amounted to an estimated 19,000 barrels per day in 2011. It has one oil refinery near Skopje. Natural gas also has to be imported (via a pipeline from Bulgaria) and this amounted to four billion cubic feet in 2010.

Manufacturing

Main industrial products are lead and zinc ore, sinc concentrates, lead concentrates, refrigerators, detergents, stone and marble sheets, cement, flour beer, fermented tobacco, cigarettes, non-alcoholic beverages.

Service Industries

Macedonia has about 600,000 foreign visitors per year, mainly from Austria, France, Netherlands, Germany, Switzerland, the United Kingdom and Italy.

Agriculture

The main crops are wheat, rye and corn, sesame, vegetables, tobacco and grapes.

Agricultural Production in 2010

Produce	Int. $'000*	Tonnes
Grapes	144,832	253,372
Cow milk, whole, fresh	98,956	347,103
Chillies and peppers, green	79,158	168,150
Tomatoes	62,090	168,010
Apples	51,335	121,383
Tobacco, unmanufactured	48,229	30,280
Wheat	32,588	243,137
Potatoes	24,528	202,325
Plums and sloes	22,934	38,431
Cabbages and other brassicas	22,320	149,157
Indigenous cattle meat	22,191	8,215
Hen eggs, in shell	15,609	18,820

* unofficial figures
Source: http://faostat.fao.org/site/339/default.aspx Food and Agriculture Organization of the United Nations, Food and Agricultural commodities production

COMMUNICATIONS AND TRANSPORT

Travel Requirements

Citizens of the USA and the EU require a passport but do not need a visa for stays of up to three months. Australians and Canadians need a passport of between three and six months validity following departure, and a visa. Other nationals should contact the embassy to check visa requirements

Visitors staying in a hotel are required to register within 24 hours of arrival; this is normally carried out by the hotel at check-in. Nationals staying in a private residence are required to register within three days of arrival.

National Airlines

Macedonian Airlines, Bulevar Partizansky, Opodredi 17A, Skopje, 91000, Macedonia. Tel: +389 (91) 116333/134 456, fax: +389 (91) 229 576/227 254
Macedonian Airlines in a subsidiary of Olympic Airways

International Airports

Ohrid Airport, URL: http://www.airports.com.mk
Skopje Airport, URL: http://www.airports.com.mk

Railways

The railway network is 920 km in length. A rail link to Bulgaria is currently under construction. Rail links run between the Republic of Macedonia to Greece and Serbia.
Macedonian Railways, URL: http://www.mz.com.mk

Roads

The main thoroughfare is E-75 from Tabanovtse to Bogoroditsa. It is part of a larger European motorway and all other Macedonian roads are connected to it. Bus services run from Skopje to Serbia, Kosovo, Bulgaria, Slovenia, Croatia and Turkey. Total road length is in the region of 8,600 km. Vehicles are driven on the right.

HEALTH

Health care is provided by the state. In 2009, the government spent approximately 12.5 per cent of its total budget on healthcare, accounting for 66.5 per cent of all healthcare spending. Total expenditure on healthcare equated to 6.9 per cent of the country's GDP. Per capita expenditure on health was approximately US$311, compared with US$157 in 2000. Figures for 2005-10 estimate that there are 5,364 physicians (26.3 per 10,000 population), 1,250 nurses and midwives (6.1 per 10,000 population), 1,381 dentists (6.8 per 10,000 population) and 1,022 pharmaceutical personnel. There were approximately 45 hospital beds per 10,000 population.

In 2010 the infant mortality rate (probability of dying before first birthday) was 10 per 1,000 live births and the child (under-five years old) mortality rate was 10 per 1,000 live births. The main causes of death in the under-fives are: prematurity (38 per cent), pneumonia (5 per cent), congenital anomalies (22 per cent), birth asphyxia (9 per cent) and diarrhoea (3 per cent). In the period 2000-09 an estimated 11.5 per cent of children (under five-years-old) were classified as stunted and 1.8 per cent as underweight. Approximately 16 per cent were classified as overweight.

According to the latest WHO figures, in 2010 approximately 100 per cent of the population had access to improved drinking water. In the same year, 88 per cent of the population had access to improved sanitation. (Source: http://www.who.int, World Health Statistics 2012)

EDUCATION

The education system consists of eight years of primary education, three or four years of secondary education and three or four years of higher education. Education for children ages seven to fifteen is free and compulsory. The 1,048 primary schools have 258,761 pupils, the 89 secondary schools have 72,248 pupils, the five further education colleges have 2,098 students and the 27 faculties of the universities have 26,959 students. There are two universities - St. Cyril and St. Methodius University in Skopje and St. Clement of Ohrid University in Bitola. In 1994 ethnic Albanians established an Albanian speaking university in Tetovo. This was declared by the Government to be illegal and in 2000 it was officially given the status of a private institution. The university was legally recognised in 2005.

Figures from UNESCO for 2007 show that 89 per cent of girls and 89 per cent of boys were enrolled in primary school and 94 per cent of primary ages children completed the primary course of education.

RELIGION

The majority of the population are Christian Orthodox (59 per cent). There is also a large Muslim community (25 per cent).

Macedonia has a religious liberty rating of 6 on a scale of 1 to 10 (10 is most freedom). (Source: World Religion Database)

COMMUNICATIONS AND MEDIA

The constitution guarantees freedom of speech.

Newspapers

The total number of newspapers is approximately 300 including 7dailies, 40 weeklies, 50 published twice a month and 134 monthlies. The remaining papers are in a variety of ethnic and foreign languages. The dailies include:
Nova Makedonija, URL: http://www.novamakedonija.com.mk
Vecer, URL: http://www.vecer.com.mk
Dnevnik, URL: http://www.dnevnik.com.mk

Broadcasting

Macedonian Radio and Television (MTV) is the national state-run radio and television company and operates three national channels and a satellite network. There are also over 200 private radio and television stations.
MTV, URL: http://www.mrt.com.mk

Telecommunications

Mobile phone subscriptions outnumber fixed line telephone subscriptions (2.5 million compared to 500,000). There were estimated to be around 900,000 internet users in 2008.

ENVIRONMENT

Macedonia is a party to the following international agreements: Air Pollution, Biodiversity, Climate Change, Climate Change-Kyoto Protocol, Desertification, Endangered Species,

Hazardous Wastes, Law of the Sea, Ozone Layer Protection, and Wetlands.

In 2010, Macedonia's emissions from the consumption of fossil fuels totalled 8.23 million metric tons of carbon dioxide. (Source: EIA)

MADAGASCAR
Republic of Madagascar
Repoblikan'i Madagasikara

Capital: Antananarivo (Population estimate: 1.59 million)

Head of State: Andry Rajoelina (Interim President)

Co-President: Emmanuel Rakotovahiny

Co-President: Fetison Rakoto Andrianirina

Vice President: Rajemison Rakotomaharo

National Flag: White, red and green tricolour with three rectangles of equal size: the first is vertical and white in colour and appears on the hoist, the two others are horizontal, the higher one red and the lower one green

CONSTITUTION AND GOVERNMENT

Constitution
The Republic was proclaimed on 14 October 1958 and independence was declared on 26 June 1960. On 31 December 1975, following a referendum, the Democratic Republic of Madagascar was formed. In August 1992 the Constitution of the Third Republic was agreed through a referendum.

In March 1998 a further referendum approved changes to the constitution, including increasing the power of the presidency and the autonomy of the provinces, and creating a new upper chamber of Parliament.

According to the 1992 constitution, the head of state is the president, who is directly elected by universal adult suffrage for a five-year term. The president appoints the prime minister. Under the terms of the 1998 constitutional amendment, the prime minister may be chosen from the minority party in the National Assembly. The prime minister is the head of government and appoints the Council of Ministers. In April 2007, voters in a referendum endorsed constitutional reforms to increase presidential powers and make English an official language.

Following the 2009 coup, in May 2010 discussions began on drafting a new constitution and changes were approved in November 2010.

To consult the constitution, please visit: http://www.madagascar-presidency.gov.mg/actualite/index.php?shw=histoireconstitution.

Recent Events
In October 2004 the World Bank and the IMF wrote off almost half of Madagascar's debt, amounting to around $2 billion. In March the following year, the country received aid from the US, under the United States' scheme to reward those countries it deems to be promoting democracy.

In May 2006 several opposition groups boycotted talks aimed at easing tension ahead of presidential elections in December 2006. The elections were won by the incumbent president, Marc Ravalomanana. A referendum was held in April 2007 and voters voted in favour of increased presidential powers and an end to autonomy in the provinces. The referendum was also in favour of English as an official language. President Ravalomanana subsequently dissolved parliament in July 2007 and elections were held in September.

In January 2009 opposition television and radio stations were closed down which led to violent protests in the capital Antananarivo. Opposition leader and mayor Andry Rafoelina demanded that President Ravalomanana resign. The following month the government sacked Mr Rajoelina from his post as mayor, and police opened fire on protesters. In March a group of military officers mutinied and gave their support to Andry Rojoelina. President Ravalomanana resigned, handing power to the military. The military then handed power over to Andry Rajoelina and this move was backed by the courts although constitutionally, at 34, Andry Rajoelina was too young to be president. Rajoelina suspended parliament and set up two transitional bodies to run the island, promising elections and constitutional reforms within two years. President Rajoelina was sworn in on March 21 but several foreign ambassadors and African leaders boycotted the ceremony and he has yet to be recognised as President internationally. The US suspended non-humanitarian aid to Madagascar and the African Union suspended its membership.

At the end of April 2009 supporters of ousted president Marc Ravalomanana announced a rival government with Manandafy Rakotonirina as the alternative prime minister. Talks in Mozambique in August led to an agreement on a power-sharing government; there will be a 15 month transitional period of 15 months, during which legislative and presidential elections will be held. The ousted President Marc Ravalomanana said he would not personally take part in the process; he will be granted an amnesty from a conviction for abuse of power.

The transitional government was appointed on 8 September but the situation remains difficult. In October, Mr Ravalomanana refused to sign the agreement unless Rajoelina did not stand in the forthcoming elections. Monja Roindefo refused to stand down as the prime minister as had been agreed. The decree appointing Eugue Mangalaza as consensus prime minister was finally confirmed on 22 October. However, as he was not in Madagascar, the deputy prime minister, Cecile Manorohanta, took over as acting prime minister. In December 2009 Andry Rajoelina announced that Mangalaza was no longer prime minister. In February 2010 Mr Rajoelina postpones parliamentary elections to May, these were again postponed. A constitutional referendum was also announced.

In August 2010 the former president Marc Ravalomanana was sentenced in absentia to life in prison on charges of killing opposition supporters.

In the November 2010 referendum on constitutional reform the people voted in favour of the proposed constitution which would allow Mr Rajoelina to run for president.

The entire cabinet resigned in March 2011. A new transitional unity government was named in March 2011. Elections were scheduled for September 2011 however that month eight of the political parties came to an agreement which would allow the return of Marc Ravalomanana, and the scheduling of elections in early 2012. Mr Rajoelina agreed to remain in charge of the transitional authority. Omer Beriziky of the Leader Fanilo party was named as prime minister on 28 October and a new cabinet appointed in November 2011. The former president Didier Ratsirka returned to Madgascar after nine years in exile. Elections were then expected to take place in November 2012 but were again postponed.

The former president Marc Ravalomanana was refused entry into the country in January 2012.

In July 2012, the army was reported to have quelled a mutiny at a military baracks near Madagascar's main airport.

In January 2013 the interim president, Andry Rajoelina and ex-president Marc Ravalomananana, agreed not to contest elections in 2013, as per the SADC mediation plan. However in May, Mr Rajoelina anouunced he would be standing following rumours that Mr Ravalomanana would also be contesting the election.

Legislature
The Constitution was amended in 1998 to provide for a bicameral legislature with the addition of an upper house. The current legislature consists of the Senate and National Assembly.

Upper House
The Senate (*Antenimierampirenena*) has 90 members elected for a five-year term, one third presidential nominees and two thirds elected by an electoral college.

Lower House
The National Assembly (*Antenimieramdoholana*) consists of 127 members who are all directly elected for a five-year term.
National Assembly, BP 704, Palais de Tsimbazaza, 101 Antananarivo, Madagascar. Tel: +261 20 222 4527, fax: +261 20 226 3235, e-mail: poste@assemblee-nationale.mg, URL: http://www.assemblee-nationale.mg/
Assembly President: Rakotoarivelo Mamy

Cabinet (as of June 2013)
Prime Minister: J. Omer Beriziky
Deputy Prime Minister with responsibility for Development and Land Management: Hajo Hrivelona Andrianainarivelo
Deputy Prime Minister with responsibility for the Economy and Industry: Pierrot Botozaza
Minister for Foreign Affairs: Pierrot Rajaonarivelo
Minister of Agriculture: Rolland Ravatomanga
Minister of Trade: Olga Ramalason
Minister of Communication: Harry Laurent Rahajason
Minister of Culture and Arts: Elia Ravelomanantsoa
Minister of Decentralisation: vacant
Minister of Water: Julien Reboza
Minister of National Education: Régis Manoro
Minister of Energy: Nestor Razafindroriaka
Minister of Higher Education: Etienne Razafindehibe
Minister of Technical Education and Professional Training: Jean André Ndremanjary
Minister of Environment and Forests: Joseph Randriamiarisoa
Minister of Finance and Budget: Hery Rajaonarimampianina
Minister of Civil Service: Tabera Randriamanantsoa
Minister of Armed Forces: Gen. André Lucien Rakotoarimasy

MADAGASCAR

Minister of Fossil Fuels: Bernard Marcel
Minister of the Interior: Florent Rakotoarisoa
Minister of Youth and Leisure: Jacques Ulrich Andriantiana
Keeper of the Seals and Minister of Justice: Christine Razanamahasoa
Minister of Mines: Daniella Randrianefo
Minister of Fishing and Marine Resources: Sylvain Manoriky
Minister of the Population and Social Affairs: Olga Vaomalala
Minister of the Postal Service, Telecommunications and New Technologies: Ny Hasina Andriamanjato
Minister of Handicrafts: Alibena Elisa Razafitombo
Minister of Institutional Relations: Victor Manantsoa
Minister of Public Health: Johanita Ndahimananjara
Minister of Livestock: Ihanta Randriamandranto
Minister of Interior Security: Arsène Rakotondrazaka
Minister of Sports: Gérard Botralahy
Minister of Tourism: Jean Max Rakotomamonjy
Minister of Transport: Benjamina Ramanantsoa
Minister of Public Works: Col. Botomanovatsara
Secretary of State with responsibility for the Police: Gen. Thierry Randrianazary

Ministries

Office of the Prime Minister, Mahazoarivo, BP 241, Antananarivo, Madagascar. Tel: +261 20 223 3113, URL: http://www.primature.gov.mg
Ministry of Agriculture, BP 301, Ampandrianomby, 101 Antananarivo, Madagascar. Tel: +261 20 222 7227, fax: +261 20 222 6561, e-mail: nfo@maep.gov.mg, URL: http://www.agriculture.gov.mg
Ministry of Finance and Budget, BP 61, Antaninarenina, 101 Antananarivo, Madagascar. Tel: +261 20 223 0173, fax: +261 20 226 4680, URL: http://www.mefb.gov.mg
Ministry of Defence, BP 8, Ampahibe, 101 Antananarivo, Madagascar. Tel: +261 20 22 27395 / 22211, fax: +261 20 22 35420 / 60473, URL: http://www.defense.gov.mg/
Ministry of Economy & Industry, BP 527, Immeuble ARO, Ampefiloha, 101 Antananarivo, Madagascar. Tel: +261 20 22 32251, fax: +261 20 22 28024, e-mail: celenv-mind@dts.mg, URL: http://www.meci.gov.mg/
Ministry of Foreign Affairs, BP 836 Anosy, 101 Antananarivo, Madagascar. Tel: +261 20 22 20781 / 21198, fax: +261 20 22 34484, URL: http://www.madagascar-diplomatie.net/news.php
Ministry of Labour and Social Legislation, Immeuble FOP - 67 Ha, 101 Antananarivo, Madagascar. Tel: +261 20 33859 / 21309, URL: http://www.mfptls.gov.mg/
Ministry of Energy and Mines, BP 527, Ampandrianomby, 101 Antananarivo, Madagascar. Tel: +261 20 22 28928, fax: +261 20 22 32554, URL: http://www.mem.gov.mg/
Ministry of Decentralisation and Planning, BP 24, Bis, 101 Antananarivo, Madagascar. Tel: +261 20 22 35881 / 37516, fax: +261 20 22 37516, URL: http://www.matd.gov.mg
Ministry of Environment and Forests, BP 651, Ampandrianomby, Antananarivo, Madagascar. Tel: +261 22 40908, fax: +261 20 22 41919, URL: http://www.meeft.gov.mg/
Ministry of Interior and Administrative Reforms, BP 833 , 101 Antananarivo, Madagascar. Tel: +261 20 22 23084, fax: +261 20 22 27777 / 22 31115, URL: http://www.mid.gov.mg/
Ministry of Health, BP 88 Ambohijatovo, 101 Antananarivo, Madagascar. URL: http://www.sante.gov.mg
Ministry of National Education, Tsimbazaza, 101 Antananarivo, Madagascar. Tel: +261 20 222 9423, fax: +261 20 2234508, URL: http://www.education.gov.mg
Ministry of Higher Education and Scientific Research, BP 4163 Fiadanana, 101 Antanarivo, Madagascar. Tel: +261 20 22 29423, fax: +261 20 22 34508, e-mail: spensup@syfed.refer.mg, URL: http://www.education.gov.mg
Ministry of Technical Education and Professional Training, Tsimbazaza, 101 Antananarivo, Madagascar. Tel: +261 20 222 9423, fax: +261 20 223 4508, URL: http://www.metfp.gov.mg
Ministry of Internal Security, BP 3200, 101 Antananarivo, Madagascar. Tel: +261 20 223 1861, URL: http://www.policenationale.gov.mg
Ministry of Justice, BP 231, Rue Joel Rakotomalala, Faravohitra, 101 Antananarivo, Madagascar. Tel: +261 20 22 37684, fax: +261 20 22 64458, e-mail: pgjustic@wanadoo.mg, URL: http://www.justice.gov.mg/
Ministry of Telecommunications, Post and Communication, Antaninarenina, 101 Antananarivo, Madagascar. Tel: +261 20 22 23267, fax: +261 20 22 35894, URL: http://www.mtpc.gov.mg
Ministry of Public Works and Meteorology, BP 4139, 101 Antananarivo, Madagascar. Tel: +261 20 222 3215, fax: +261 20 222 0890, e-mail: viceprimature@mttpat.gov.mg, URL: http://www.mtpm.gov.mg
Ministry of Youth, Sports and Leisure, BP 681, Place Goulette, Ambohijatovo, 101 Antananarivo, Madagascar. Tel: +261 20 22 27780, fax: 261 20 22 34275, URL: http://www.mscl.gov.mg/
Ministry of Transport, Anosy, 101 Antananarivo, Madagascar. Tel: +261 20 22 35612, fax: +261 20 22 24001, URL: http://www.transport.gov.mg
Ministry of Water, BP 571, rue Farafaty, 101 Antananarivo, Madagascar. Tel: +261 20 224 0908, fax: +261 20 224 1919, URL: http://www.mineau.gov.mg
Ministry of Tourism and Handicrafts, BP 305, Antaninarenina, 101 Antananarivo, Madagascar. Tel: +261 20 222 7477, fax: +261 20 222 9848, e-mail: publicrelation@mtoura.gov.mg, URL: http://www.mtoura.gov.mg
Ministry of Population, BP 88, Ambohidahy, 101 Antananarivo, Madagascar. Tel: +261 20 226 3121, fax: +261 20 226 4228, e-mail: cabminsan@dts.mg, URL: http://www.population.gov.mg

Political Parties

Tiako I Madagasikara (TIM, I Love Madagascar), URL: http://www.tim-madagascar.org/ Andry sy Riana Enti-Manavotra an'i Madagasikara, (AREMA, The Vanguard of the Malagasy Revolution); Rénaissance du Parti Social-Démocratique (RPSD, Rebirth of the Social-Democratic Party); Toamasina Tonga Saina (TTS); Forces for Change (FC)

Elections

A presidential election took place on 16 December 2001 when Marc Ravalomanana won 51.5 per cent of the vote and former president Didier Ratsiraka won 35.9 per cent. However, in early January 2002, the opposition accused the President of vote-rigging; a run-off on 25 January 2002 was inconclusive, and by the end of February, after Ravalomanana declared himself president, violent protests had taken place in the capital. The two rivals signed a peace agreement in Senegal on 18 April, and Ravalomanana was sworn in as president on 16 May 2002. Presidential elections took place in December 2006 and Marc Ravalomanana was re-elected. In April 2007 a referendum was called and voters approved changes to the constitution to increase presidential power. The next presidential election is now scheduled to take place on 30 November 2012.

The last parliamentary election took place on the 23rd September 2007. The I Love Madagascar party (TIM), which supports President Marc Ravalomanana, won a large majority in the National Assembly and in the Senate.

Elections are currently due to take place on 23 August 2013 although they have been postponed several times.

Diplomatic Representation

Embassy of the Republic of Madagascar, 2374 Massachusetts Ave, NW, Washington, DC 20008, USA. Tel: +1 202 265 5525, fax: +1 202 483 3034, e-mail: malagasy@embassy.org, URL: http://www.madagascar-embassy.org/embassy/index.html
Chargé d'Affaires: Velotiana Rakotoanosy Raobelina
British Embassy, Tour Zital, Ankorondrano, Ravoninhitriniarivo Street, Antananarivo 101, Madagascar. URL: http://ukinmadagascar.fco.gov.uk
Ambassador: Timothy Smart
US Embassy, 14 rue Rainitovo, Antsahavola, Antananarivo 101, Madagascar. Tel: +261 20 22 21257, fax: +261 20 22 34539, URL: http://www.antananarivo.usembassy.gov/
Charge d'Affaires: Eric Wong
Embassy of Madagascar, UK. The embassy closed in Feburary 2011. For visas, please contact the Madagascan Embassy in France.
Embassy of Madagascar, 4 avenue Raphael, 75016 Paris, France. +33 (0)1 45 04 62 11, +33 (0)1 45 03 58 70, e-mail: info@ambassade-madagascar.fr
Permanent Mission of Madagascar at the United Nations, 820 Second Avenue, Suite 800, New York, NY 10017, USA. Tel: +1 212 986 9491 / 9492, fax: +1 212 986 6271, e-mail: madagascar@un.int, URL: http://www.un.int/wcm/content/site/madagascar/
Ambassador: Zina Andrianarivelo-Razafy

LEGAL SYSTEM

Madagascar's legal system is based on the French civil law system and traditional Madagasy law. It consists of the Constitutional High Court, the Supreme Court, the Court of Appeal, as well as courts of first instance for civil and criminal cases, ordinary and special criminal courts, and military courts, which also hear cases involving national security when presided over by civilian magistrates. There is also a High Court of Justice to try high officials.

The traditional courts handle some civil disputes and have been used in criminal cases due to the inadequacy of the formal court system. Decisions by these courts are not subject to the formal procedural protections of the formal court system, and punishments can be severe. Traditional courts can hand down capital punishment.

The human rights situation in Madagascar is poor, and there have been recent abuses of power by security forces, including unlawful killings. Arrests can be arbitrary, and prison conditions are life-threatening. There is widespread official corruption and impunity. Madagascar retains the death penalty, but the last executions were carried out under colonial rule in 1958. In December 2008, Madagascar voted in favour of the Resolution on a Moratorium on the Use of the Death Penalty at the UN General Assembly.

National Human Rights Commission, Lot II N 184 EB, Analamahitsy Antananarivo 101, Madagascar. Tel: +261 32 049 2903

LOCAL GOVERNMENT

The country is divided into six autonomous, 'federal' *faritany* (provinces): Antananarivo, Antsiranana, Fianarantsoa, Mahajanga, Toamasina and Toliary. The provinces are subdivided into regions, which are further divided into communes. Each province is headed by a governor and up to 12 commissioners, as well as a provincial council.

AREA AND POPULATION

Area

Madagascar is situated in the Indian Ocean, 240 miles off the east coast of Africa, and is the fourth largest island in the world. The surface area of the island is 592,800 sq. km (228,880 sq. miles), with a length of 1,590 km and a width of 600 km. There is 4,828 km of coastline. The coastal plain is narrow, with a high plateau behind and mountains in the centre.

To view a map of Madagascar, please consult http://www.lib.utexas.edu/maps/cia08/madagascar_sm_2008.gif

The climate is sub-tropical. The south is the driest part of the country with sometimes inadequate rainfall. Cyclones are common, sometimes causing flooding.

Population
The population in 2010 was estimated at 20.7 million, with an annual growth rate of 3.0 per cent per annum. The majority of the population is aged between 15 and 60 years, with 43 per cent aged up to 14 years, and 5 per cent aged 60 or over. Around 70 per cent of the population lives in rural areas. The major towns are Antananarivo (1.4 million), Toamasina, Fianarantsoa, Mahajanga, Toliary and Antseranana.

The population consists of 18 tribes of Malayo-Polynesian origin with African, Arab and European elements. Languages spoken are French, Malagasy and local dialects. In April 2007 following a referendum English became an official language.

Births, Marriages, Deaths
The estimated birth rate in 2010 was 35.3 births per 1,000 population, and the death rate was 7.0 deaths per 1,000 population. According to WHO, in 2010 the infant mortality rate is an estimated 43 deaths per 1,000 live births. The fertility rate is 4.7 children born per woman. The maternal mortality rate was 240 per 100,000 live births. Life expectancy at birth was 65 years in 2009 (63 years for males, 67 years for females). Healthy life expectancy was 52 years. (Source: http://www.who.int, World Health Statistics 2012)

Public Holidays 2014
1 January: New Year's Day
29 March: Memorial Day/Martyrs' Day for 1947 Rebellion
18 April: Good Friday
21 April: Easter Monday
6 May: Labour Day
26 June: Independence Day
15 August: Assumption Day
1 November: All Saints' Day
25 December: Christmas Day
30 December: Anniversary of the Democratic Republic of Madagascar

EMPLOYMENT

Subsistence agriculture is a mainstay of the economy, employing 80 per cent of the population. Industry employs about 7 per cent. An estimated 50 per cent of the population live below the poverty line.

The following table shows employment sector figures in 2005.

Employment Sector	No. of Persons Employed
Agriculture, hunting, forestry	7,745,300
Fishing	99,000
Mining & quarrying	18,800
Manufacturing	367,500
Electricity, gas & water	27,500
Construction	13,000
Wholesale & retail trade	470,500
Hotels & restaurants	63,900
Transport, storage & communication	86,300
Financial intermediation	4,100
Public administration & defence	202,400
Education	44,500
Health & social work	9,900
Other community, social & personal services	517,700
Total	9,570,400

Source: Copyright © International Labour Organization (ILO Dept. of Statistics, http://laborsta.ilo.org)

BANKING AND FINANCE

Currency
The unit of currency is the Malagasy franc (FMG / MGF).

GDP/GNP, Inflation, National Debt
Despite being rich in mineral resources such as sapphires, emeralds and gold, Madagascar's economy is dominated by agriculture, forestry and fishing. Economic growth has been very low for the last thirty years, but in recent years this has improved with some economic liberalisation. The on-going political crisis has, however, had an adverse effect on the economy. Tourism has been particulary hard hit with revenues falling by 50 per cent. Foreign investment is also difficult to attract.

In 2007, GDP was estimated at US$7,313.64 million with a growth rate of 6.3 per cent. Figures for 2009 put GDP at US$9,584 million with a growth rate of 0.6 per cent. GDP was estimated at US$9.5 billion in 2011.

Agriculture, forestry and fishing, together contribute approximately 30 per cent of GDP and 70 per cent of export earnings. The services sector contributes the greatest proportion of GDP (55 per cent in 2011), followed by agriculture (27 per cent), and industry (16 per cent).

The inflation rate was 9.0 per cent in 2009 down from 9.8 per cent in 2007, compared to 10.6 per cent in 2006 and 18.4 per cent in 2005. GDP was estimated to be 9.5 per cent in 2011.

Total external debt was US$2.2 billion in 2011.

Foreign Investment
As a result of its eligibility under the Heavily Indebted Poor Countries (HIPC) Initiative, Madagascar was granted US$103 million by the IMF for 2001-03 under the Poverty Reduction and Growth Facility (PRGR). The funds were channelled towards the development of education, health, infrastructure, and water systems. In March 2001 the Paris Club approved a debt cancellation of $161 million, whilst the African Development Bank (ADB) cancelled debts of nearly US$71.5 million and granted an additional credit for the fight against poverty and AIDS. In October 2004, the World Bank and IMF wrote off nearly half of Madagascar's debt, approximately $2 billion, and in March 2005, Madagascar became the first state to receive development aid from the US under the scheme to reward nations that the US considers are promoting democracy and instigating market reforms. EU decided to suspend development aid after elections failed to take place.

Balance of Payments / Imports and Exports
Major export trading partners are France, the US, Germany, Italy and Japan. Export commodities include coffee, vanilla, shellfish, cloves, graphite and chromite, cotton cloth and gemstones. Major import trading partners are France, Hong Kong, China, Belgium and the United States. Import commodities include petroleum products, consumer goods, vehicles, electronics and foodstuffs.

External Trade, US$ million

	2005	2006	2007
Trade balance	-590.59	-546.67	-854.30
Exports	835.78	974.09	1,051.39
Imports	1,426.37	1,520.74	1,905.69

Source: African Development Bank

Exports were estimated to be US$1.2 billion in 2011 and imports US$3.3 billion.

Along with Angola, Comoros, DRC, Malawi, Mauritius, Namibia, Seychelles, Swaziland, Zambia and Zimbabwe, Madagascar is a member of the Common Market for Eastern and Southern Africa (COMESA).

Central Bank
Banque Centrale de Madagascar, PO Box 550, Rue Revolisiona Sosialista Malagasy, Antananarivo 101, Madagascar. Tel: +261 20 22 21751, fax: +261 20 22 27596, URL: http://www.banque-centrale.mg
Interim Governor: Guy Ratovondrahona

Chambers of Commerce and Trade Organisations
Madagascar Chamber of Commerce and Industry, URL: http://www.indomadagascar.com/home.html

MANUFACTURING, MINING AND SERVICES

Primary and Extractive Industries
Sapphires, emeralds and semi-precious stones are found in Madagascar, as well as gold, chrome, graphite, bauxite and ilmenite. Two kimberlites which may contain diamonds have recently been discovered. In 2007, a nickel cobalt mining project opened in Tamatave. The mine is one of the largest of its kind in the world.

Despite an oil refining capacity of 15,000 barrels per day as at the beginning of 2005, there is as yet no significant oil production in Madagascar. Imports and consumption of oil totalled an estimated 24,000 barrels per day in 2011, most of which was crude oil. In 2006, oil reserves were discovered in the seas off Madagascar; official estimates were as high as five billion barrels of oil. Initial projections were that Madagascar could produce 60,000 barrels per day in three to four years, which would make the oil industry the main contributor to the country's gross domestic product (GDP). In 2008 the first barrels of oil were produced and 19 licenses to search for offshore oil were granted.

Madagascar imported 11,000 short tons of coal for consumption in 2010 (up from 9,000 short tons in 2000), all of it hard coal.

Energy
Electricity generation in 2010 reached 1.21 billion kilowatthours (kWh) and Madagascar consumed 1.13 billion kWh. The country neither imports nor exports electricity.

Manufacturing
Major industries include food processing, garment production and textiles, tanning, soap manufacture, sugar refining, mining construction and paper products.

Agriculture
The economy of Madagascar is predominantly agricultural. The majority (88 per cent) of the working population is engaged in agricultural pursuits, and 30 per cent of GDP is agricultural revenue. The most important crops produced are rice, coffee, sugar cane, corn, butter beans, sisal, peanuts, cloves, tobacco and vanilla. An estimated 2.9 million hectares of land is used for arable farming, of which 600,000 hectares are used for permanent crops. An estimated 31,000 per cent of the arable land is irrigated.

Livestock is predominantly cattle, pigs and goats. In 2004, there were 10.5 million cattle and buffloes, and 1.85 million sheep and goats. An estimated 24 million hectares are used for pasture. Fishing is becoming an increasingly important part of the economy. In 2004, an estimated 12,000 tonnes of pelagic fish were caught and 33,000 tonnes of freshwater.

Agricultural Production in 2008

Produce	Int. $'000*	Tonnes
Rice, paddy	592,679	3,000,000

MADAGASCAR

- continued

Indigenous cattle meat	311,172	150,450
Cassava	172,944	2,400,000
Cow milk, whole, fresh	140,948	530,000
Sweet potatoes	62,605	890,000
Vegetables fresh nes	58,171	310,000
Indigenous pigmeat	55,290	54,600
Coffee, green	54,776	67,000
Mangoes, mangosteens, guavas	53,567	220,000
Sugar cane	51,841	2,600,000
Bananas	46,315	325,000
Indigenous chicken meat	42,604	36,525

* unofficial figures
Source: http://faostat.fao.org/site/339/default.aspx FAOSTAT, Statistics Division, Food and Agriculture Organization of the UN

Forestry
Latest figures from the FAO (2004) show forestry production as: industrial roundwood 183,000 tonnes; wood fuel 10,770 tonnes; wood charcoal 872,000 tonnes; and sawn wood 893,000 tonnes.

COMMUNICATIONS AND TRANSPORT

Travel Requirements
Citizens of the USA, Canada, Australia and the EU require a passport valid for six months after the date of entry, a return or onward ticket and a visa. Other nationals should contact the embassy to check visa requirements. Transit passengers continuing their journey by the same or first connecting aircraft within 24 hours provided holding onward or return documentation and not leaving the airport. Since April 2009 tourists of any nationality can enter without a visa if they are staying less than one month.

National Airlines
Air Madagascar, URL: http://www.airmadagascar.com
Tiko Air, Antananarivo, Madagascar. Est. 2000, Owner: Marc Ravalomanana

International Airports
There are five international airports: Ivato (15km from Antananarivo) (URL: http://www.adema.mg/), Nosy Be, Toamasina, Taolagnaro and Mahajanga. Ivato International Airport is undergoing expansion and the main runway is due to be extended by 2011.

Railways
Built at the beginning of the century, the railway network consists of two independent systems: the Northern Network and the Southern Network. The Northern Network consists of the TCE (Tananarive-East Coast) linking the capital to the East coast, 372 km; MLA (Moramanga-Lake Alaotra) providing a service between Moramanga and Lake Alaotra, 167 km; and TA (Tananarive-Antsirabe) linking the capital and town of Antsirabe, 154 km. The Southern Network consists of the FCE (Fianarantoa-East Coast), providing a service between Fianarantsoa and the port of Manakara, 163 km.

Roads
There are 40,000 km of roads of which 4,694 km are paved. Some roads are impassable during the rainy season, November to March. Vehicles are driven on the right.

Ports and Harbours
The main ports are Toamasina, Antsiranana, Mahajanga, Taolagnaro, Morondava and Toliara. Ferry services travel between Toamasina and Mauritius via Reunion.

Rivers
The Pangalanes channel is a popular form of transport for passengers and goods along the East coast.

HEALTH

In 2009, Madagascar spent approximately 14.7 per cent of its total budget on healthcare (down from 15.5 per cent in 2000), accounting for 64.5 per cent of all healthcare spending. Total expenditure on healthcare equated to 4.2 per cent of the country's GDP. Per capita expenditure on health was approximately US$18, compared with US$9 in 2000. In 2005-10, there were an estimated 3,150 doctors (1.6 per 10,000 population) and 57 dentists. Latest WHO figures estimated there were 5,661 nurses and midwives (3 per 100,000 population). There were 2 hospital beds per 10,000 population.

The infant mortality rate was 43 per 1,000 live births in 2008 and the child mortality rate (under fives) was 62 per 1,000 live births. According to the World Health Organization, just 51 per cent of births in 2003 were attended by a person skilled in midwifery. The most common causes of deaths for children under 5 years old are: prematurity 16 per cent; pneumonia 18 per cent; malaria 6 per cent; diarrhoeal diseases 10 per cent.

Over 1.7 per cent of the population is affected by HIV/AIDS and over half of those affected are women. 70 per cent of people live below the poverty line. In 2010 an estimated 15 per cent of the population had sustainable access to improved sanitation. In the same year 46 per cent of the population had sustainable access to improved drinking water. (Source: http://www.who.int, World Health Statistics 2012)

EDUCATION

Primary/Secondary Education
In Madagascar, compulsory education lasts from the age of six to 13. Primary education lasts from six to 10 years. Secondary education begins at 11 and ends at 17. Enrolment in primary school is high, (98 per cent in 2007 - up from 69 per cent in 2002); however, in 2004 only 45 per cent of pupils completed the six year course. An estimated 55 per cent of children go on to secondary school but enrolment rates in secondary schools are low: 21 per cent of girls and 21 per cent of boys attend secondary schools.

The pupil/teacher ratio in primary school was 48 to one in 2006. Some 20 per cent of pupils repeat years in primary schools.

In addition to a large number of elementary and secondary schools, there is one vocational school, seven training centres, 101 district workshops, and one school of medicine and pharmacy. The University of Tananarive has about 3,000 students. An estimated three per cent of the population attend higher education.

Public expenditure on education, as a percentage of total government spending, was 16.4 per cent in 2007 (3.4 per cent of GDP).

The adult literacy rate was estimated to be 76.5 per cent of adult men and 65.3 per cent of adult women. The youth literacy rate (ages 15-24) was estimated at 72.7 for males and 68.2 for females. (Source: UNESCO Institute for Statistics, August 2009)

RELIGION

Almost half the population practises traditional native beliefs. The remainder are predominantly Christian (53 per cent) and Muslim (around 2 per cent). Some customs from traditional beliefs are incorporated into Christian practises.

Madagascar has a religious liberty rating of 9 on a scale of 1 to 10 (10 is most freedom). (Source: World Religion Database)

COMMUNICATIONS AND MEDIA

Newspapers
Daily: The Madagascar Tribune (URL: http://www.madagascar-tribune.com/), the Midi Madagasikara (URL: http://www.midi-madagasikara.mg/) and L'Express (URL http://www.lexpressmada.com/) and La Gazette de la Grande Ile (URL: http://www.lagazette-dgi.com/)
Weekly: Lakroan'i M/Kara; Dans les Media Demain (URL: http://www.dmd.mg/); Feon'ny Merina

Broadcasting
The Malagasy National Radio (RNM) is the only station which is broadcast throughout Madagascar and can be picked up on both medium wave and FM. There are some 20 private radio stations which broadcast in English, French and Malagasy. Reception for the state-owned Television Malagasy is accessible in several cities in Madagascar. MBS TV (URL: http://www.mbs.mg/) is a commercial station that is owned by President Ravalomanana. There are two other privately-owned stations.

Telecommunications
There is a cellular network in a few of the larger cities, supported by companies such as Telecel, Madacom, Antaris and Sacel. There has been much recent development of the landline system. There are about 120,000 telephone main lines in Madagascar and two million mobile phones.

According to UNESCO, around 70,500 people are internet users, and there are 773 internet hosts.

ENVIRONMENT

Because of its isolation, Madagascar has unique flora and fauna. Most of its mammals, half of its birds and the majority of its plants exist only in Madagascar.

Major environmental problems affecting Madagascar include desertification, soil erosion from deforestation, and polluted surface water. Madagascar experiences occasional cyclones and droughts.

In 2010, Madagascar's emissions from the consumption of fossil fuels totalled 3.38 million metric tons of carbon dioxide. (Source: EIA)

Madagascar is a party to the following international environmental agreements: Biodiversity, Climate Change, Climate Change-Kyoto Protocol, Desertification, Endangered Species, Hazardous Wastes, Law of the Sea, Marine Life Conservation, Ozone Layer Protection, Ship Pollution and Wetlands.

MALAWI
Republic of Malawi
Dziko la Malawi

Capital: Lilongwe (Population estimate: 886,000)

Head of State: Joyce Banda (President) (page 1383)

Vice-President: Khumbo Hastings Kachali (page 1452)

National Flag: In August 2010 a new flag was adopted amid some controversy. The new flag had three equal horizontal stripes of red, black and green with a full white sun in the middle. This replaced the flag of three equal horizontal stripes of black, red and green with a red rising sun superimposed in the centre of the black stripe. However in May 2012 the parliament voted to restore the old rising sun flag. The move was supported by all the opposition parties with the exception of the DPP. President Banda is expected to sign the bill to make the change lawful.

CONSTITUTION AND GOVERNMENT

Constitution
Formerly known as the British Central African Protectorate, the territory was renamed Nyasaland in 1907. It joined Northern and Southern Rhodesia in 1953 to become the Federation of Rhodesia and Nyasaland. On 6 July 1964 Nyasaland became independent from Rhodesia and was named Malawi.

Following the country's independence from Britain, the title of Commissioner and Consul-General was changed to that of Governor, and the first Legislative Council was inaugurated. The Council consisted of the governor as president and six other members all nominated by the governor, a pattern which was followed closely for the next 50 years. The first two African members were appointed in 1948, and a third in 1953. In July 1961 the Lancaster House Conference was held in London. This led to the introduction of an entirely new constitution, providing for the direct election of Africans to the Legislative Council. The constitution introduced higher and lower qualitative franchise. With the Malawi Congress Party's overwhelming victory in the General Election of August 1961, elected Africans were in a majority.

At the same time a ministerial system was introduced, and Dr Banda and four of his leading followers became ministers, together with three *ex-officio* and two nominated ministers. In February 1963 Dr Banda became prime minister and the Legislative Council was re-titled the Legislative Assembly. On 6 July 1966, two years after the attainment of independence, Malawi became a republic, and the number of nominated members (nominated by the President to represent interests of the minority) was increased to five. In 1971 Dr Banda was made Life President.

Until 1993 all Malawian citizens were obliged to be members of the Malawi Congress Party. Political opposition was not accepted and only president-approved candidates could contest elections to the National Assembly. In June 1993, however, the people voted in a referendum on the future of the single-party constitution. A year later, in May 1994, the first multi-party legislative and presidential elections were held. By an overwhelming majority, the leader of the United Democratic Front, Bakili Muluzi, was voted the Republic's new president.

Government changes in September 1994 included the appointment of a second vice president. This provoked severe criticism from the Malawi Congress Party as it entailed a constitutional change. The change was approved and the constitution took effect in May 1995. The president is elected by universal suffrage for a period of five years renewable only once.

Suffrage is universal at 18.

To consult the constitution, please visit: http://www.sdnp.org.mw/constitut/brfindx.html.

Recent Events
In January 2005 three members of the ruling United Democratic Party (UDF) were charged with treason after taking guns to a meeting with the president. President Mutharika later pardoned the men. In February 2005 President Mutharika resigned from the UDF alleging resistance to his anti-corruption plans. He formed the Democratic Progressive Party (DPP). In June 2005 he survived an impeachment motion backed by the UDF. The speaker of Parliament collapsed and died during the angry exchanges in parliament. In April 2006 Vice-President Chilumpha was charged with treason.

In January 2008 Malawi ended its diplomatic ties with Taiwan and reinstated ties with China.

In May 2008 there was further political instability when several opposition figures were arrested, accused of plotting to depose President Mutharika.

In May 2010, Malawi came in for international criticism when a gay couple were convicted of breaching anti-homosexuality laws. The couple received a presidential pardon and were released.

President Mutharika controversially introduced a new national flag in August 2010.

There was diplomatic tension between Malawi and Mozambique in October 2010 over a new waterway connecting the two countries.

President Bingu wa Mutharika died of a heart attack in April 2012. The vice president, Joyce Banda, became president, as prescribed by the constitution. She is the first female president in southern Africa.

Panic buying of basic commodities was seen in the shops and markets of Malawi in May 2012 when the currency was devalued by 33 per cent. The devaluation was a move to restore donor funding.

In October 2012, Malawi asked the African Union to help resolve a border-dispute with Tanzania over Lake Malawi. Tanzania claims half the lake which is potenially rich in oil and gas.

In November 2012, laws criminalising homosexual relationships were suspended.

The cabinet was reshuffled in December.

Legislature
Malawi's unicameral legislature consists of the National Assembly, whose 193 members are elected by universal adult suffrage for five-year terms. Plans for a second chamber of parliament were also endorsed to take place in 1999; however, to date the legislature remains unicameral.

Malawi National Assembly, Parliament Building, Private Bag B362, Lilongwe 3, Malawi. Tel: +265 1 773566 / 773208, fax: +265 1 774196 / 771340

Cabinet (as at March 2013)

Interim President; Commander-in-Chief of the Armed Forces; Chief of the Police Service; Disaster Management; Nutrition, HIV and AIDS Management: Joyce Banda (page 1383)
Minister of Finance: Dr Ken Lipenga (page 1465)
Minister of Foreign Affairs: Ephraim Mganda Chiume (page 1404)
Minister of Education, Science & Technology: Eunice Kazembe
Minister of Mining: John Bande
Minister of Energy: Ibrahim Matola
Minister of Gender, Children and Social Welfare: Anita Kalinde
Minister of Economic Planning and Development: Goodall Gondwe
Minister of Justice, Attorney General: Ralph Kasambara
Attorney General: Anthony Kamanga
Minister of Agriculture & Food Security: Peter Mwanza
Minister of Water Development and Irrigation: Ritchie Muheya
Minister of Information: Moses Kalonga Shawa Kunkuyu
Minister of Transport & Public Works: Muhamed Sidik Mia
Minister of Local Government: Grace Maseko
Minister of Health: Catharine Harai
Minister of Industry and Trade: Sosten Gwengwe
Minister of Lands, Housing and Urban Development: Henry Phoya
Minister of Home Affairs: Uladi Mussa
Minister of Defence: Ken E. Kandodo (page 1453)
Minister of Tourism and Culture: Rachel Zulu
Minister of Labour: Eunice Makangala
Minister of the Environment and Climate Change: Jeniffer Chilunga
Minister of Youth and Sports: Enoch Chakufwa
Minister of Disability and Senior Citizens: Renee Kachere

Ministries
Government Portal: http://www.malawi.gov.mw
Office of the President and Cabinet, Private Bag 301, Lilongwe 3, Malawi. Tel: +265 1 789311, fax: +265 1 788456, e-mail: opc@malawi.gov.mw, URL: http://www.malawi.gov.mw/
Ministry of Information and Civic Education, Private Bag 310, Capital City, Lilongwe 3, Malawi. Tel: +265 1 783 233, fax: +265 1 784 568, URL: http://www.sdnp.org.mw/min-information/
Ministry of Finance, P.O. Box 30049, Lilongwe 3, Malwi. Tel: +265 789355, fax: +265 789173, e-mail: finance@malawi.gov.mw, URL: http://www.finance.malawi.gov.mw/
Ministry of Defence, Private Bag 339, Lilongwe 3, Malawi. Tel: +265 1 789600, fax: +265 1 789176, e-mail: defence@defence.gov.mw, URL: http://www.malawi.gov.mw
Ministry of Justice and Constitutional Affairs, Private Bag 333, Lilongwe 3, Malawi. Tel: +265 1 788411, fax: +265 1 788 332 / 788841, e-mail: justice@malawi.gov.mw URL: http://www.malawi.gov.mw/mojca/mojca.htm
Ministry of Foreign Affairs & International Cooperation, P.O. Box 30315, Lilongwe 3, Malawi. Tel: +265 1 788020 / 789088, fax: +265 1 788482 / 788516, e-mail: foreign@malawi.gov.mw
Ministry of Lands, Physical Planning & Surveys, P.O. Box 30548, Lilongwe 3, Malawi. Tel: +265 774766, fax: +265 1 773990; URL: http://www.malawi.gov.mw/lands/lands.htm
Economic Planning and Development, P.O. Box 30136, Lilongwe 3, Malawi. Tel: +265 788390, fax: +265 788131, e-mail: nec@malawi.gov.mw
Ministry of Education, Science & Technology, Private Bag 328, Lilongwe 3, Malawi. Tel: +265 1 789382, fax: +265 1 788064 / 788184, e-mail: education@malawi.gov.mw, URL: http://www.malawi.gov.mw/educ/educ.htm

MALAWI

Ministry of Health and Population, P.O. Box 30377, Capital City, Lilongwe 3, Malawi. Tel: +265 1 789400, fax: +265 1 789431, e-mail: health@malawi.gov.mw, URL: http://www.malawi.gov.mw/health/health.htm

Ministry of Gender, Youth & Community Services, Private Bag 330, Lilongwe 3, Malawi. Tel: +265 1 770411, fax: +265 1 770806, e-mail: gender@malawi.gov.mw, URL: http://www.malawi.gov.mw/gender/gender.htm

Ministry of Natural Resources, Energy and Environment, Private Bag 350, Lilongwe 3, Malawi. Tel: +265 1 789 488, fax: +265 1 773 379, e-mail: naturalres@malawi.gov.mw, URL: http://www.malawi.gov.mw/natres/natres.htm

Ministry of Youth, Sports and Culture, Lingadzi House, Private Bag 384, Lilongwe 3, Malawi. Tel:+265 1 774999 / 771319, fax:+265 1 771018, e-mail: sports@malawi.gov.mw, URL: http://www.malawi.gov.mw/sports/sports.htm

Ministry of Agriculture, Irrigation and Water Development, PO Box 30134, Capital City, Lilongwe 3, Malawi. Tel: +265 1 789 033, fax: +265 1 789 218, e-mail: agriculture@malawi.gov.mw, URL: http://www.malawi.gov.mw/agric/agric.htm

Ministry of Industry and Trade, PO Box 30366, Lilongwe 3, Malawi. Tel:+265 1 770 244, fax: +265 1 770 680, e-mail: commerce@malawi.gov.mw, URL: http://www.malawi.gov.mw/commerce/commerce.htm

Ministry of Tourism, National Parks & Wildlife, Private Bag 326, Capital City, Lilongwe 3, Malawi. Tel: +265 1 770 650 / 771295 / 771073, fax: +265 1 770 65033, e-mail: tourism@malawi.net, URL: http://www.malawi.gov.mw/tourism/tourism.htm

Ministry of Transport and Public Infrastructure, Private Bag 322, Capital City, Lilongwe 3, Malawi. Tel: +265 1 789 377, fax: +265 1 789 328, e-mail: transport@malawi.gov.mw, URL: http://www.malawi.gov.mw/transport/transhq.htm

Ministry of Local Government and Rural Development, PO Box 30312, Lilongwe 3, Malawi. Tel: +265 1 789 388, fax: +265 1 788 083, e-mail: local@malawi.gov.mw, URL: http://www.malawi.gov.mw/local_gov/local_gov.htm

Ministry of Statutory Corporations, PO Box 30061, Lilongwe 3, Malawi. Tel: +265 1 774 266, fax: +265 1 774 110, e-mail: statutory@malawi.gov.mw, URL: http://www.malawi.gov.mw/StatCoorp/statco.htm

National Research Council of Malawi, Lingadzi House, P.O. Box 30745, Lilongwe 3, Malawi. Tel: +265 1 771550, fax: +265 1 771487 / 772431, e-mail: nrcm@sdnp.org.mw

Elections
The penultimate presidential election took place in May 2004 when the UDF's Bingu wa Mutharika was elected with 36 per cent of the vote. The MCP's John Tembo won 27 per cent. The next presidential election was held in May 2009 and President Mutharika won a resounding victory.

The last parliamentary election was also held in May 2009 when the Democratic Progessive Party won 114 of the National Assembly's 192 seats. The MCP won 26 seats, and the UDF 17 seats.

Political Parties
The main political parties are:
United Democratic Front (UDF). URL: http://www.udfparty.com, Leader: Joyce Banda; Malawi Congress Party (MCP). Pres.: John Tembo; Democratic Progressive Party (DPP); Alliance for Democracy (AFORD)

Diplomatic Representation
British High Commission, PO Box 30042, Lilongwe 3, Malawi. Tel: +265 772 400, fax: +265 772 657, e-mail: bhclilongwe@fco.gov.uk, URL: http://ukinmalawi.fco.gov.uk/en
High Commissioner: Michael Nevin (page 1485)
US Embassy, PO Box 30016, Lilongwe 3, Malawi. Tel: +265 773166, fax: +265 770471, e-mail: ngwirasx@state.gov, URL: http://lilongwe.usembassy.gov/
Ambassador: Jeanine Jackson (page 1448)
High Commission of Malawi, 36 John Street, London, WC1N 2AT, United Kingdom. Tel: +44 (0)20 8455 5624, E-mail: malawihghcommission@btconnect.com
URL: http://www.malawihighcommission.co.uk
High Commissioner: Bernard Sande
Malawi Embassy, US, 2408 Massachusetts Avenue NW, Washington DC 20008, USA. Tel: +1 202 721 0270, fax: +1 202 721 0288
Ambassador: Hawa Ndilowe
Malawi Mission to the United Nations, 600 Third Avenue, 21st Floor, New York, NY 10016, USA. Tel: +1 212 949 0180, fax: +1 212 599 5021, e-mail: malawi@un.int, URL: http://www.un.int/
Ambassador: H.E. Mr Charles Msosa

LEGAL SYSTEM

The legal system is based on the English system. There are local and appeal courts in each district, as well as a Supreme Court of Appeal and a High Court. The High Court consists of a chief Justice and four puisne judges. The High Court has unlimited jurisdiction in criminal and civil matters. The Chief Justice is appointed by the President, but puisne Judges are appointed on the advice of the Judicial Service Commission.

In 1969 the president to authorized traditional African courts to try all types of criminal cases and to impose the death penalty; the president was also permitted to deny the right of appeal to the High Court against sentences passed by the traditional courts. Traditional court justices are all appointed by the president. Appeals from traditional courts go to the district traditional appeals courts and then to the National Traditional Appeal Court. In 1993, the attorney general suspended the operation of regional and national level traditional courts. Since then, serious criminal and political cases have been heard in the modern courts.

The government respects the human rights of its citizens,but there have been cases of brutality, and even unlawful killings, by security forces. The government succeeded in prosecuting some abusers. There is some official corruption, and arbitrary arrest and detention are not unusual. The government restricts freedom of assembly and, at times, limits freedom of speech and the press. Malawi retains the death penalty, but there are signs that this may change; in 2007 the Constitutional Court declared that mandatory death sentences were unconstitutional, inhumane and a degradation to human dignity.

High Court of Malawi, URL: http://www.judiciary.mw

LOCAL GOVERNMENT

For local government purposes Malawi is divided into three administrative regions: Northern, Central, and Southern Malawi. The regions are subdivided into 28 districts: Balaka, Blantyre, Chikwawa, Chiradzulu, Chitipa, Dedza, Dowa, Karonga, Kasunga, Likoma, Lilongwe, Machinga (Kasupe), Mangochi, Mchinji, Mulanje, Mwanza, Mzimba, Neno, Ntcheu, Nkhata Bay, Nkhotakota, Nsanje, Ntchisi, Phalombe, Rumphi, Salima, Thyolo, Zomba. The regions are administered by regional administrators and district governors approved by central government.

Local elections were held in 2000 when the ruling UDF gained 70 per cent of seats. Elections scheduled for 2005 but were postponed due to a severe drought. Local elections were resheduled for August 2010 but were postponed to April 2011 and then again to 2014.

AREA AND POPULATION

Area
Malawi is a land-locked country bounded on the south-east and south-west by Mozambique, on the north-east by Tanzania and on the north-west by Zambia. A strip of land some 520 miles long, varying in width from 50 to 100 miles, the total area is 45,748 sq. miles. Over 20 per cent of the country comprises Lake Malawi. The Great Rift Valley crosses the country from north to south.

The main towns are Blantyre (population, 2010 (E): 751,500); Lilongwe (817,500); Mzuzu (168,900); and Zomba (108,000).

The climate is sub-tropical with a rainy season from November to May and a dry season which lasts from May to November.

To view a map, visit http://www.un.org/Depts/Cartographic/map/profile/malawi.pdf

Population
The population in 2010 was estimated at 14.9 million, with an annual growth rate of 2.8 per cent over the period 2000-10. This varies according to region: northern, 2.7 per cent; central, 2.4 per cent; and southern, 1.4 per cent. The population is expected to double by 2028. The average population density in 1998 was 10.5 persons per square km, although there were strong regional variations. In the northern region the population density was 46 persons per square km, in the central region 114 persons per square km, and in the southern region 146 persons. An estimated 20 per cent the population lives in urban areas.

In 2010, the median age was 17 years old. An estimated 5 per cent of the population is over 60 years old and 46 per cent under 15 years.

The languages spoken are English and Chichewa. Other Bantu languages are also spoken.

Births, Marriages, Deaths
The estimated birth rate in 2010 was 44.3 births per 1,000 people. The fertility rates have fallen slightly in recent years. Rural areas have higher fertility rates. The median age of women at their first childbirth is 19.1; approximately 50 per cent of women have had a child by the age of 20. In 2010 the average fertility rate was 6.0 children per woman. In 2009 the maternal mortality rate was an estimated 510 deaths per 100,000 births. Childhood mortality rates are high but improving. In 2009 the child mortality rate was estimated to be 110 per 1,000 children compared to 188.6 in 2000. There is a higher mortality rate in rural areas. Poor water quality, malaria and AIDS are all factors. In 2010 the estimated death rate was 16.0 per 1,000 population.

In 2009, the estimated average life expectancy of males was 44 years and of females was 51 years. (Source: http://www.who.int, World Health Statistics 2012)

Public Holidays 2014
1 January: New Year's Day
15 January: John Chilembwe Day
3 March: Martyr's Day
18 April: Good Friday
20 April: Easter Sunday
5 May: Labour Day
14 June: Freedom Day
6 July: Independence Day
25 December: Christmas Day
26 December: Boxing Day

EMPLOYMENT

In 2007 the workforce was estimated to be 5.7 million. Less than 25 per cent of women are part of the workforce, compared to 50 per cent of males. Nearly 90 per cent of the population is involved in subsistence farming and 55 per cent are below the poverty line. The development of the sector is hindered by its vulnerability to climatic conditions, high transport costs, poor road conditions, poor national electrical and water services.

BANKING AND FINANCE

Currency
The unit of currency is the *Kwacha* (K). One hundred *tambala(s)* are equal to 1 *Kwacha* (K 1.00).

GDP/GNP, Inflation, National Debt
Malawi's economy is very dependent on agriculture and the country has few mineral resources. High transport costs and a poor infrastructure have hindered economic development. The agricultural sector is under pressure with poor farming methods and increasing populations. Economic reforms are ongoing and in 2005 President Mutharika launched anti-corruption initiatives. Improvements in the economic situation have largely been due to an increase in agricultural production, an increase in exports, deregulation of markets, liberalisation of prices, and a reduction in public expenditure. Foreign aid contributes approximately 40 per cent of the budget. The economy was boosted in 2009 when uranium deposits began to be exported. An estimated 1,500 tonnes will be exported each year for the next 10 years generating an annual income of around US$100 million. Approximatelyu 50 per cent of the population lives below the poverty line.

Figures for 2009 put GDP at US$4.2 billion, a growth figure for that year of 7.6 per cent and giving a per capita figure of US$328. GDP was estimated to be US$5.2 billion in 2011. GDP (2011) was made up of agriculture (29 per cent), services (55 per cent) and industry (17 per cent).

Average national price inflation rates have fallen rapidly in recent years. The inflation rate was estimated to be 8.3 per cent in early 2010 compared to 13.9 per cent in 2006. This represents a substantial fall from 44.9 per cent in 1999 and 29.5 per cent in 1998.

In 2006, external debt was estimated to be US$766 million.

Foreign Investment
The Investment Promotion Act of 1991 created the Malawi Investment Promotion Agency (MIPA). Government-established industrial estates have also been established to attract foreign investment.

Foreign Aid
Malawi is heavily dependent on economic aid. Major aid donors include the US, Canada, Denmark, Germany, Iceland, Japan, the Netherlands, Norway, Sweden, the UK, Taiwan, the EU and the World Bank. In 2006, the World Bank and IMF agreed that Malawi qualified for full debt relief, reducing the debt from US$3 billion to US$400 million. In 2011, major aid donors suspended contributions worth over US$1 billion due to corruption concerns and reports of human rights abuses.

Balance of Payments / Imports and Exports
Through the Lomé Convention, agricultural products and virtually all manufactured goods have preferential access to all member states of the EU. Malawi is also a member of the PTA (Preferential Trade Area for Eastern and Southern Africa), SADC (Southern Africa Development Community) and GATT (General Agreement on Tariffs and Trade). In addition, the country has bilateral trade agreements with South Africa and Zimbabwe. In order to encourage the import and export markets the government plans to reduce average tariff rates, and remove export taxes as well as export and import licensing requirements.

Tobacco is responsible for around 60 per cent of export earnings, sugar, tea and coffee contribute around five per cent each.

External Trade, US$ million

	2005	2006	2007
Trade balance	-565.20	-426.14	-319.45
Exports	504.59	463.25	408.84
Imports	1,069.78	889.39	728.29
Source: African Development Bank			

Exports were estimated to be worth US$912 million in 2009 and imports cost US1.5 billion in 2009. Imexports amounted to an estimated UD$950 million in 2011 and imports cost US$1.68 billion.

Central Bank
Reserve Bank of Malawi, PO Box 30063, Convention Drive, Lilongwe 3, Malawi. Tel: +265 770600, fax: +265 772752 / 774289, URL: http://www.rbm.mw/
Governor: Charles Chuka

Chambers of Commerce and Trade Organisations
Malawi Confederation of Chambers of Commerce and Industry, Masauko Chipembere Highway, Post Box 258, Blantyre, Malawi. Tel: +265 671988, fax: +265 671147, URL: http://www.mccci.org

MANUFACTURING, MINING AND SERVICES

Primary and Extractive Industries
Natural resources include limestone, uranium, coal, bauxite, phosphates, graphite, granite, black granite, vermilite, aquamarine, tourmaline, rubies and sapphires. Malawi has reserves of limestone in Changalume in the southern part of the country and Kasagu in the central part. Recoverable coal reserves have been estimated at 2.3 million short tons with exploration of the Shire River valley area ongoing. However in 2007 no coal was produced. 20,000 tons were imported and consumed. Known reserves of uranium have been explored at Kayerekera, near the Tanzanian border. Malawi consumes 9,000 barrels per day of oil, according to 2011 estimates, all of which is imported. Most fuel imports are supplied via South African and Tanzanian ports.

Energy
Malawi had an installed electricity capacity of 0.29 Gwe, according to 2010 estimates. Total electricity generation in 2010 was an estimated 1.97 billion kWh, whilst consumption stood at 1.83 billion kWh. There are four hydroelectric plants on the Shire River and most of the electrical ouput is hydro-electric. Work is ongoing with the Kapichira hydroelectric power scheme, with phase 1 opening in 2000.

Manufacturing
The principal manufacturing industries are naturally associated with the existing agricultural economy. Wherever possible indigenous raw materials are used, but since the home market is as yet relatively undeveloped, imported raw materials are also frequently required. Products already manufactured in Malawi include oils and fat products, textile products, tobaccos, mineral waters, rope twines and yarns, and a wide range of metal products. Other industries include brewing and distilling; the spinning, weaving and dyeing of cotton textiles (with locally grown cotton); the production and milling of sugar; and radio assembly and printing.

Industrial output has been growing steadily from 1995 due to the removal of export licensing requirements and levies, reduction in import tariffs, liberalisation of investment regulations and simplifying of the procedure for the registration of companies or businesses.

Agriculture
Arable land covers 34 per cent of the country and, of this, 86 per cent is cultivated. Four crops, namely tobacco, tea, sugar and groundnuts, account for almost 90 per cent of agricultural exports. Dairy farms are maintained on estates near towns, and ghee is produced in the Central and Northern Regions. Smallholder production increased by 34 per cent in 1995 and 40 per cent in 1996 due to the liberalisation of prices, the lifting of export licensing requirements for beans and groundnuts, the removal of restrictions on trade in fertilisers, the removal of restrictions on crops only previously produced by estates and the removal of monopoly rights of the Agricultural Development and Marketing Corporation. Further, the construction of dams and reservoirs has assisted the agricultural sector to survive drought conditions although only 1 per cent of the land is irrigated. However, in February 2002, President Muluzi warned that Malawi was facing a humanitarian disaster because of widespread famine, due largely to climatic conditions. In 2002 the IMF halted its aid programme because of allegations of government corruption and mismanagement. The crops also failed in 2005.

Agricultural Production in 2010

Produce	Int. $'000*	Tonnes
Potatoes	546,943	3,673,540
Cassava	417,955	4,000,990
Maize	412,876	3,419,410
Tobacco, unmanufactured	350,723	220,198
Groundnuts, with shell	123,554	297,487
Bananas	117,722	418,000
Indigenous cattle meat	87,052	32,225
Sugar cane	82,093	2,500,000
Pigeon peas	74,348	193,005
Indegenous pigmeat	68,786	44,746
Beans, dry	68,686	152,300
Plantains	67,078	324,900

* unofficial figures
Source: http://faostat.fao.org/site/339/default.aspx Food and Agriculture Organization of the United Nations, Food and Agricultural commodities production

In 2003 there were 750,000 cattle and buffalo, 1,815,000 sheep and goats. Twenty per cent of the land is used for pasture. Forests cover 68,200 hectares of the land area of Malawi of which half the total area is state-controlled forest reserve. However, there is very little natural forest with timber suitable for general construction or joinery work. The only suitable indigenous tree is the Mulanje cedar, which grows on Mulanje mountain above an altitude of 4,500 feet. The country's planting programme did not start in earnest until the early 1950s and it is only now that supplies of local softwood are produced in reasonable quantities. A major planting programme of 15,000 acres of timber per annum, adding to the 70,000 acres already established in 1975, is being carried out on the Vipya and its foothills to supply a bleached kraft pulp mill at Chintheche.

Fish is a vital part of the population's diet and considerable attention is being given to the development of the fisheries on Lakes Malawi, Malombe, Chirwa, and Shire River. In 2002 the Shire River became infested with a water weed which threatens to choke it. In 2010 the total catch of fish was put at 98,000 tonnes.

COMMUNICATIONS AND TRANSPORT

Travel Requirements
Citizens of the USA, Canada, Australia and the EU require a passport valid for at least six months beyond the length of stay, and a return air ticket (except in special circumstances). They do not need a visa for stays of up to 90 days, apart from subjects of Austria, Bulgaria,Czech Republic, Estonia, Greece, Hungary, Latvia, Lithuania, Poland, Romania, Slovak Republic and Slovenia, who do need a visa. Other nationals should contact the embassy to check visa requirements.

International Airports
The country's main international airport is near Lilongwe. In total there are six airports with paved runways.

National Airlines
Air Malawi, URL: http://www.africaonline.co.ke/airmalawi

MALAWI

Railways
Malawi's railway lines run over a total of 790 km. A railway line runs from Salima through Lilongwe to Mchinji.

Roads
Malawi has a total of 28,500 km of roads, 5,250 km of which are paved and 23,150 km of which are unpaved. Vehicles are driven on the left.

Ports and Harbours
Major ports and harbours include Monkey Bay, Chipoka, Nkhotakota, Nkhata Bay, and Chilumba. There are 144 km of water ways including Lake Nyasa (Lake Malawi).

HEALTH

In 2008, the government spent approximately 14.2 per cent of its total budget on healthcare (up from 9.0 per cent in 2000), accounting for 65.2 per cent of all healthcare spending. Total expenditure on healthcare equated to 6.7 per cent of the country's GDP. Per capita expenditure on health was approximately US$25, compared with US$9 in 2000. According to latest WHO figures in 2005-10 there were 257 doctors (less than1 per 10,000 population), 3,896 nurses and midwives (3 per 10,000 population), 318 environment and public health workers, 211 dentists and 10,055 community health workers (7 per 10,000 population). In 2005-11 there were an estimated 13 hospital beds per 10,000 population.

The government is presently concentrating on the purchase and distribution of drugs and vaccines, and in directing expenditure to rural health facilities where health conditions of the population are relatively poor. In 2009 the infant mortality rate (probability of dying by age one) was 58 per 1,000 live births. The under-five mortality rate was 92 per 1,000 live births (compared to 167 in 2000). In 2007, 86 per cent of babies were estimated to have the neonatal tetanus immunization, 83 per cent MCV, and an estimated 80 per cent had measles immunization. The main causes of death of children aged under five are: pneumonia 14 per cent, prematurity 13 per cent, diarrhoea 7 per cent, HIV/AIDS 13 per cent, malaria 13 per cent and measles 2 per cent. In 2009, the vaccination rates were 93 per cent for measles, hepatitus and diptheria. In 2005-09, an estimated 25 per cent of young children slept under insecticide-treated nets.

Malnutrition is a major problem in rural areas: In the period 2005-11 an estimated 13.8 per cent of children under five were either moderately or severely underweight, and 47.7 per cent of children under five had stunted growth. Over 40 per cent of the population lives below the poverty line. The UN also warned that poverty would be increased because of the number of people suffering from HIV and AIDS. According to 2003 estimates 15 per cent of the adult population had HIV/AIDS. In 2005 there were an estimated 605 deaths due to HIV/AIDS per 100,000 population.

In 2009, there were 5,751 reported cases of cholera, 759 of leprosy, 5,455,423 of malaria, 21 of measles, 53 of rubella, and 22,674 of tuberculosis.

In 2008 approximately 83 per cent of the population had a safe water supply. In the same year, 51 per cent of people had sustainable access to improved sanitation. (Source: http://www.who.int, World Health Statistics 2012)

EDUCATION

In 2003 the government spent an estimated 4.2 per cent of GDP on education.

Primary/Secondary Education
Malawi's primary (compulsory) education system lasts eight years. The Government introduced free primary education in 1994. The primary school-age population rose from 2,064,000 in 1990 to 2,162,000 in 1996. By 2007 the enrolment rate was estimated to be 90 per cent for girls and 84 per cent for boys. An estimated 55 per cent of the children complete their primary education with 21 per cent repeating some of the grades.

Malawi's secondary education system lasts for four years. Enrolment was estimated in 2007 at 23 per cent for girls and 25 per cent for boys.

Higher Education
According to 1996 statistics there were 58 tertiary students per 100,000 inhabitants. The tertiary student gross enrolment ratio was 0.6 per cent in 1996, no change from the 1990 ratio. There are seven teacher training colleges offering two-year courses. The University of Malawi has approximately 1,200 students. The government is presently focusing on the poor attendance of females in post-primary schooling and encouraging them to enroll.

Literacy Rate
The adult literacy rate in 2006 was estimated at 70.9 per cent for adults and 82 per cent for youths. (Source: UNESCO)

RELIGION

Around 65 per cent of the population are Christian with around 43 per cent belonging to Protestant Churches and 23 per cent to the Cathaolic church. 13 per cent of the population are Muslim with the majority being Sunnis. Approximately 3 per cent of the population hold indigenous beliefs.

Malawi has a religious liberty rating of 9 on a scale of 1 to 10 (10 is most freedom). (Source: World Religion Database)

COMMUNICATIONS AND MEDIA

There is some freedom of expression in the media. Criticism of the government does appear but the government has used libel laws against journalists.

Newspapers
The Nation, (daily, URL: http://www.nationmalawi.com
The Daily Times, (opposition newspaper), URL: http://www.dailytimes.bppmw.com/
Malawi News, (weekly), URL: http://www.malawinews.bppmw.com/

Broadcasting
Radio is the main source of information for many Malawians. Radio Malawi was established in 1963, when the Protectorate Government assumed responsibility for broadcasting. The service, now known as the Malawi Broadcasting Corporation, provides programmes in English and Chichewa. In 1997 there were estimated to be 2.6 million radios in use. Other stations include Capital Radio (URL: http://www.capitalradiomalawi.com), MIJ FM, Radio Maria (http://www.radiomaria.mw). In 2010 there was one television broadcast network - the state-run Television Malawi. Relays of international broadcasters are available.
Malawi Broadcasting Corporation, URL: http://www.mbcradios.com

Telecommunications
The service was privatised in 2006 and has been undergoing some improvements. In 2008 there were approximately 230,000 telephone lines and 1.7 million cellular phones. The cellular network is concentrated in urban areas.

In 2004 there was one internet server and just 3 in every 1,000 people had access to the internet. By 2008 an estimated 1 per cent of the population used the internet. The Malawi internet country code is .mw.

ENVIRONMENT

Malawi's main environmental problems are land degradation, deforestation, water pollution from agriculture and industry, and the siltation of rivers which threatens fish populations. However the latest figures for deforestation put it at 1.6 per cent compared to reforestation at 10 per cent.

The country is a party to the following international environmental agreements: Biodiversity, Climate Change, Climate Change-Kyoto Protocol, Desertification, Endangered Species, Environmental Modification, Hazardous Wastes, Marine Life Conservation, Ozone Layer Protection, Ship Pollution and Wetlands. Malawi has signed but not ratified the Law of the Sea.

According to the EIA, in 2010, Malawi's emissions from the consumption and flaring of fossil fuels totalled 1.36 million metric tons of carbon dioxide.

MALAYSIA

Capital: Kuala Lumpur (Population estimate, 2011: 1.7 million)

Administrative Centre: Putrajaya

Head of State: Tuanku Abdul Halim (Paramount Ruler) (page 1371)

Deputy Head of State: H.M. Sultan Muhammad V

National Flag: On a field of fourteen stripes fesse-wise and countercharged red and white, a blue canton charged with a yellow crescent and star with fourteen points.

CONSTITUTION AND GOVERNMENT

Constitution
On 31 August 1957, Malaya became an independent sovereign nation within the Commonwealth of Nations. On 16 September 1963 a larger federation came into being whereby the Federation of Malaya, the State of Singapore (internally self-governing since 1959) and the former territories of British North Borneo (Sabah) and Sarawak were federated under the title of Malaysia. The federation then consisted of 14 states. To the nine Malay States (Sultanates) and the two former settlements (now States) Malacca and Penang, were added the State of Singapore and the former territories of Sabah and Sarawak.

The general scheme of government is founded upon that of the former Federation of Malaya which adopted a constitution recommended by the Reid Commission in 1957. This provides for a Senate (Dewan Negara) and a House of Representatives (Dewan Rakyat).

Governmentally, the autonomy of the States within the federation is represented by the provision of constitutions for all the component States. Each State has a sovereign Ruler or Yang di-Pertuan Negri (Governor). Whilst the constituent States form a strong central government, the constitutional rights of each individual State are preserved.

In August 1965, Singapore left Malaysia and has since been an independent republic within the Commonwealth. The territory of the former Federation of Malaya is known as Peninsular Malaysia and the States of Sabah and Sarawak.

The head of state (paramount rule) is rotated every five years among the sultans of the nine Malay kingdoms.

To consult the constitution, please visit: http://www.jac.gov.my/jac/images/stories/akta/federalconstitution.pdf.

International Relations
Malaysia has strong ties with other ASEAN member countries. As a UN member, Malaysia has sent peace keeping forces to Bosnia, Liberia, East Timor, Kuwait, Western Sahara and Angola in recent years. Malaysia and her neighbour Singapore have been in dispute over land and water claims, this appeared to be resolved and the two countries agreed to build a connecting bridge and tunnel but further disputes about air space have hindered the plans.

Recent Events
Prime Minister Dato' Seri Dr. Mahathir bin Mohamad resigned late in 2003, after being in power for 22 years. Deputy Prime Minister Dato' Seri Abdullah bin Haji Ahmad Badawi took over the post in October 2003.

In December 2004, Malaysia was one of the Asian countries hit by the devastating tsunami triggered by a large underwater earthquake off the Indonesian coat of Sumatra. Around 68 people were thought to have died.

Deputy Prime Minister Anwar Ibrahim was arrested in 1998 in charges of sexual misconduct, and was sentenced to nine years imprisonment, in 2000 he received an additional six year sentence for corruption. In 2004 he was released after the convictions for sexual misconduct were overturned. As leader of the opposition Ibrahim won a by election in August 2008 and returned to parliament as an MP. Anwar then announced to supporters that he had enough defecting MPs to force a change in power.

In 2001 Malaysia and Singapore resolved disputed claims over land and water, and agreed to build a bridge and tunnel connecting the two countries. The bridge was to replace a causeway which becomes congested. The bridge would be big enough to allow ships to pass underneath, but in April 2006 Malaysia threatened to abandon its building programme as other disputed claims between Malaysia and Singapore, such as use of air space, remained unresolved.

In December 2006 and January 2007, Malaysia was hit by severe flooding; more than 120,000 people had to be evacuated.

In October 2008, following disastrous election results, Prime Minister Abdallah Ahmad Badawi announced that he would resign in March 2009. The king accepted his resignation in early April and deputy prime minister Najib Razak took over as Prime Minister.

Malaysia has been adversely affected by the global financial crisis as its economy is heavily dependent on manufacturing. In an effort to protect jobs, Malaysia banned the recruitment of foreign workers in February 2009. In March 2009, the Malaysian government unveiled a $16 billion economic stimulus plan to boost the economy. As part of the package over 160,000 new jobs were to be created.

In January 2010, religious tensions increased after a court decision was made to allow non-Muslims to use the word Allah to refer to God.

In February 2010 Islamic punishment was used against women for the first time when three Malay women were flogged for extra-marital sex.

Political protests spread to Malaysia and police used tear gas to disperse protestors calling for political reform at a rally in Kuala Lumpur. The following month the prime minister announced a parliamentary committee on electoral reform was to be set up.

Tuanku Abdul Halim was appointed the 14th paramount ruler in December 2011. He is the first Malaysian king to take the throne twice, having already served as king from 1970 to 1975.

In January 2012, the High Court acquitted the opposition leader Anwar Ibrahim of charge of sodomy.

The ruling National Front coalition retained power in the May 2013 general election.

Upper House
The Senate comprises two Senators elected by the Legislative Assemblies of each of the 13 States and 44 nominated by His Majesty the Yang di-Pertuan Agong, making 70 in all. The Senate is presided over by a President and members serve a six year term.
Dewan Negara (Senate), Jalan Parlimen, 50680 Kuala Lumpur, Malaysia. Tel: +60 3 2072 1955, e-mail: info@parlimen.gov.my, URL: http://www.parlimen.gov.my/

Lower House
The House of Representatives (Dewan Rakyat) is elected in single-member constituencies by citizens of 21 years and above. The House consists of 219 elected members who serve a five year term and are presided over by a Speaker.
Dewan Rakyat (House of Representatives), Balgunan Parlimen, 20680, Kuala Lumpur, Malaysia. Tel: +60 3 2072 1955, e-mail: info@parlimen.gov.my, URL: http://www.parlimen.gov.my/

Cabinet (as at June 2013)
Prime Minister, Minister of Finance: Najib Tun Abdul Razak (page 1528)
Deputy Prime Minister, Minister of Education: Muhyiddin bin Mohd. Yassin (page 1541)
Second Minister for Finance: Ahmad Husni Bin Mohamad Hanadzlah (page 1446)
Minister for Education and Higher Learning: Idris Jusoh
Minister for Defence: Hishammuddin bin Tun Hussein (page 1528)
Minister of Communication and Multimedia: Ahmad Shabery Cheek (page 1403)
Minister of Rural and Regional Development: Shafie Bin Haji Apdal (page 1379)
Minister of Youth & Sports: Khairy Jamaluddin Abu Bakar
Minister of International Trade and Industry: Mustapa bin Mohamed (page 1389)
Minister of Energy, Green Technology and Water: Maximus Johnity Ongkili (page 1490)
Minister of Tourism & Culture: Mohamed Nazri Abdul Aziz
Minister of Agriculture: Ismail Sabri Bin Yaakob (page 1540)
Minister of Science, Technology & Innovation: Dr Ewon Ebin
Minister of Agricultural Development and Commodities: Douglas Embas
Minister of Home Affairs and Internal Security: Dr Ahmad Zahid Bin Hamidi (page 1542)
Minister of Works: Fadillah Yusof
Minister of Human Resources: Richard Riot
Minister of Health: Dr S. Subramaniam (page 1521)
Minister of Domestic Trade and Consumer Affairs: Hasan Malek
Minister of Housing and Local Government: Abdul Rahman Dahalan
Minister of Foreign Affairs: Datuk Anifah bin HJ. Aman (page 1378)
Minister of Federal Territories: Tengku Adnan Tengku Mansor
Minister of Natural Resources and Environment: G. Palanivel
Minister of Women, Family & Community Development: Rohani Abudl Karim
Ministers in the Office of the Prime Minister
Minister in the Prime Minister's Department for Islamic Affairs: Major Jamil Khir bin Baharomn
Minister in the Prime Minister's Department: Idris Jala
Minister in the Prime Minister's Department without portfolio: Abdul Wahid Omar
Minister without portfolio: Joseph Kurup
Minister without portfolio: Shadian Kassim
Minister without portfolio: Joseph Belaun
Minister without portfolio: Nancy Shukri
Minister without portfolio: Paul Low Seng Kuan

Ministries
Government portal, URL: http://www.malaysia.gov.my
Prime Minister's Department, Blok Utama, Bangunan Perdan Putra, Pusat Pentadbiran Kerajaan Persekutuan, 62502 Putrajaya, Malaysia. Tel: +60 (0)3 8888 1957/8888 8000, fax: +60 (0)3 8888 3424, URL: http://www.pmo.gov.my
Ministry of Home Affairs, Blok D1 & D2, Parcel D, Pusat Pentadbiran Kerajaan Persekutuan, 62546 Putrajaya, Malaysia. Tel: +60 (0)3 8886 8000, fax: +60 (0)3 8889,1763, URL: http://www.kdn.gov.my
Ministry of Federal Territories, Level G-7, Block 2, Menara Seri Wilayah, Precint 2, Federal Government Administrative Centre, 62100 Putrajaya, Malaysia. Tel: +60 (0)3 8889 7888, fax: +60 (0)3 8888 0375, URL: http://www.kwpkb.gov.my
Ministry of Foreign Affairs, 1 Jalan Wisma Putra, Presint 2, 62603 Putrajaya, Malaysia. Tel: +60 (0)3 8887 4000, fax: +60 (0)3 8889 1717, URL: http://www.kln.gov.my
Ministry of Information, Communication & Culture, Angkasapuri, 50610 Kuala Lumpur, Malaysia. Tel: +60 3(0) 2282 4297, URL: http://www.kempen.gov.my

MALAYSIA

Ministry of Education, Complex Kerajaan Persekutuan Parcel E, pusat Pentadbiran Kerajaan Persekutuan, 62604 Putrajaya, Malaysia. Tel: +60 (0)3 8884 6000,URL: http://www.moe.gov.my

Ministry of Finance, Kompleks Kementerian Kewangan, Pusat Pentadbiran Kerajaan Persekutuan, 62592 Putra Jaya, Malaysia. Tel: +60 (0)3 8882 3000, fax: +60 (0)3 8882 3892/8882 3894, URL: http://www.treasury.gov.my

Ministry of International Trade & Industry, Blok 10, Kompleks Pejabat Kerajaan, Jalan Duta, 50622 Kuala Lumpur. URL: http://www.miti.gov.my

Ministry of Transport, Aras 5,6,& 7, Blok D5, Pusat Pentadbiran Kerajaan Persekutuan, Malaysia. Tel: +60 (0)3 8886 6000, fax: +60 (0)3 8889 1569, URL: http://www.mot.gov.my

Ministry of Defence, Wisma Pertahanan, Jalan Padang Tembak, 50634 Kuala Lumpur, Malaysia. Tel: +60 (0)3 292 1333 / 230 1033, fax: +60 (0)3 298 4662, URL: http://www.mod.gov.my

Ministry of Works , Tingkat 5, Block B, Kompleks Kerja Raya, Jalan Sultan Salahuddin, 50580 Kuala Lumpur, Malaysia. Tel: +60 (0)3 2711 1100, fax: +60 (0)3 2711 6612, URL: http://www.kkr.gov.my

Ministry of Agriculture, Wisma Tani, 28 Persiaran Perdana, Precint 4, 62624 Putrajaya, Malaysia. Tel: +60 (0)3 8870 1000, URL: http://www.moa.my

Ministry of Entrepreneur Development, Presint 2, Pusat Pentadbiran Kerajaan Persekutan, 62100 Putrajaya, Malaysia. Tel: +60 (0)3 8880 5000, URL: http://www.malaysia.gov.my

Ministry of Energy, Green Technology and Water, Blok E4/5 Kompleks Kerajaan, Pusat Pentadbiran Kerajaan, 62668 Putrajaya, Malaysia. Tel: +60 (0)3 8883 6000, URL: http://www.ktak.gov.my

Ministry of Youth & Sports, Menara KBS Lot 3, Precint 4 Pusat Pentadbiran, Kerajaan persekutuan, 62570 Putrajaya, Malaysia. Tel: +60 (0)3 8871 3333, fax: +60 (0)3 8888 8767, URL: http://www.kbs.gov.my

Ministry of Science, Technology & Environment, Blok C5, Parcel 5, 62662 Putrajaya, Malaysia. Tel: +60 (0)3 885 8300, URL: http://www.mastic.gov.my

Ministry of Tourism, Peti Surat 5-7, Pusat Dagangan Dunia Putra, 45 Jalan Tun Ismail, 50480 Kuala Lumpur, Malaysia. Tel: +60 (0)3 2693 7111, fax: +60 (0)3 2694 1146, URL: http://www.motour.gov.my

Ministry of Human Resources, Blok D3, Aras 1-9 & D4, Pusat Pentadbiran Kerajaan Persekutuan, Putrajaya, Malaysia. Tel: +60 (0)3 8886 5116, fax: +60 (0)2 8889 2381, http://www.jaring.my/ksm

Ministry of Rural Development, Aras 5-9, Blok D9, Pusat Pentadbiran Kerajaan Persekutuan, 50606 Putrajaya, Malaysia. Tel: +60 (0)3 8886 3700, fax: +60 (0)3 8886 3500, e-mail: info@kplb.gov.my, URL: http://www.kplb.gov.my

Ministry of Housing and Local Government, Level 4 & 5, Blok K, Pusata Bandar Damansara, Peti Surat 12579, 50782 Kuala Lumpur, Malaysia. Tel: +60 (0)3 254 7033, fax: +60 (0)3 254 9720, e-mail: admin@kptk.gov.my, URL: http://www.kptk.gov.my

Ministry of Domestic Trade & Consumer Affairs, Lot 2G3, Precesint 2, Pusat pentadbiran Kerajaan Persekutuan, 62623 Putrajaya, Malaysia. Tel: +60 (0)3 8882 5500, URL: http://www.kpdnhep.gov.my

Ministry of Health, Ibu Pejabat KKM Blok E1, Parcel E, Pusat Pentadbiran Kerajaan Persekutuan, 62590 Putrajaya, Malaysia. Tel: +60 (0)3 8883 3888, URL: http://www.moh.gov.my

Ministry of Women, Family & Community Development, Blok E, Kompleks Pejabat Kerajaan Bukit Perdana, Jalan Dato'Onn, 50515 Kuala Lumpur, Malaysia. Tel: +60 (0)3 2693 0095, fax: +60 (0)3 2693 4982, URL: http://www.kpwkm.gov.my/

Political Parties

Barisan Nasional (National Front), (Pejabat Timbalan Perdana Menteri, Jabatan Perdanan Menteri, Jalan Dato' Onn, 50502 Kuala Lumpur, Malaysia. Tel: +60 (0)3 984895, URL: http://www.bn.org.my

Parti Tindakan Demokratik, (DAP Democratic Action Party), No 24, Jalan 20/9, Paramount Garden, 46300, Petaling Jaya, Selangor, Malaysia.URL: http://dapmalaysia.org/newenglish

Parti Keadilan Rakyat, (People's Justice Party), URL: http://www.keadilanrakyat.org
Parti Islam Se-Malaysia, (Pan-Malaysian Islamic Party, PAS), URL: http://www.pas.org.my

The Barisan Nasional party is a coalition of several parties, including the United Malays National Organisation, the Malaysian Chinese Association, and the Malaysian Indian Congress.

Elections

The Supreme Head of State, *Yang di-Pertuan Agong* (He Who is Made Lord), or King is elected every five years by the nine hereditary Malay rulers from amongst their own number. In February 1999 Salehuddin Abdul Aziz, Sultan of Selangor, was elected, and was sworn in in April. He died in November 2001 following heart surgery, and the Raja of Perlis, Tuanku Syed Sirajudddin, was elected King. In December 2006 following the end of King Tuanku Syed Sirajuddin's five year term, Sultan Mizan Zainal Abidin of Terengganu was elected to the post of King. In December 2011 H.M. Tuanku Abdul Halim was elected head of state.

Since independence from Britain in 1957, Malaysia has been ruled by the Barisan Nasional, (National Front) a coalition, of which the dominant party is the United Malays National Organisation, (UMNO). Other parties in the coalition are, Malaysian Chinese Association (MCA), Malaysian Indian Congress (MIC), Malaysian People's Movement Party (PGRM), People's Progressive Party (PPP), Parti Pesaka Bumiputera Bersatu Sarawak (PBB), Sarawak United People's Party (SUPP), Sarawak National Party (SNAP), Parti Bangsa Dayak Sarawak (PBDS)

At the March 2008 elections, the Barisan Nasional recorded its worst result in years winning only 140 seats, and Prime Minister Ahmad Badawi resigned in 2009 and was replaced by his deputy, Najib Abdul Razak. The most recent election took place in May 2013. The ruling National Front coalition retained power.

Diplomatic Representation

Embassy of the United States of America, 376 Jalan Tun Razak, POB 10035, 50700 Kuala Lumpur, Malaysia. Tel: +60 (0)3 2168 5000, fax: +60 (0)3 2168 4961, URL: http://malaysia.usembassy.gov
Ambassador: Paul W. Jones (page 1451)

British High Commission, 185 Jalan Ampang, 50450 Kuala Lumpur, Malaysia. Tel: +60 (0)3 2148 2122, fax: +60 (0)3 2144 7766, e-mail: political.kualalumpur@fco.gov.uk, URL: http://ukinmalaysia.fco.gov.uk/en
High Commissioner: Simon Featherstone (page 1423)

Embassy of Malaysia, 3516 International Court, NW, Washington, DC 20008, USA. Tel: +1 202 572 9700, fax: +1 202 572 9882, e-mail: embmaldc@erols.com, URL: http://www.kln.gov.my/
Ambassador: Hashim Othman

High Commission of Malaysia, 45 Belgrave Square, London, SW1X 8QT, United Kingdom. Tel: +44 (0)20 7235 8033, fax: +44 (0)20 7235 5161, URL: http://www.jimlondon.net/
High Commissioner: Datuk Zakaria bin Sulong

Permanent Mission to the UN, 313 East 43rd Street, New York, USA. Tel: +1 212 986 6310, e-mail: malnyun@kln.gov.my, URL: http://www.un.int/malaysia
Permanent Representative to the UN: H.E. Ambassador Haniff Hussein

LEGAL SYSTEM

As a result of British colonisation up until the 1960s, Malaysian law is largely based on the common law legal system, The Constitution sets out the legal framework and rights of Malaysian citizens. Whilst Federal laws apply throughout the country, there are also state laws enacted by the individual State Legislative Assemblies. The constitution of Malaysia provides for a dual justice system, encompassing both secular laws (criminal and civil) and shari'a laws. The shari'a laws are only applicable to Muslims, and normally address personal law matters, though in some states there are shari'a criminal laws. The states of Sabah and Sarawak joined Malaya in 1963, and there are special laws applicable only to these two states.

The judicial structure comprises a Federal Court, a Court of Appeal and two High Courts (one in mainland Malaysia and the other in Sarawak), as well as Sessions Courts, Magistrates' Courts and the Penghulu's Courts (where cases are heard by a headman appointed by a state government).

The Federal Court of Malaysia is the Supreme Court and highest judicial authority in the country as well as the final court of appeal in Malaysia. It reviews decisions referred from the Court of Appeal and has original jurisdiction in constitutional matters and in disputes between states or between the federal government and a state. The criminal jurisdiction of a Penghulu's Court is limited to the trial of offences of a minor nature which can be adequately punished by a fine not exceeding RM25.00. There is also a Juvenile Court for offenders below the age of 18.

Although the government largely respects the rights of its citizens, there are areas of concern. Deaths have occurred during arrests and detention, and arrests can be arbitrary. There have been many reports of abuses by the People's Volunteer Corps (RELA), including rape, beatings, extortion and theft. The impartiality and independence of the judiciary has been questioned. The government has arrested opposition leaders and journalists for political reasons. The civil courts have allowed Shari'a courts to exercise jurisdiction in cases involving families that included non-Muslims. The government restricts freedom of press, association, assembly, speech, and religion.

Malaysia retains the death penalty, which can be handed down in cases of murder, drug trafficking, treason, waging war against the ruler, and acts of terrorism (including aiding terrorism). Over 300 people are thought to have been handed down death sentences in the last five years. At least one person was reported to have been executed in 2010 and in 2011. No executions were reported in 2012.

Federal Court of Malaysia, URL: http://www.kehakiman.gov.my

Human Rights Commission of Malaysia, URL: http://www.suhakam.org.my/home

LOCAL GOVERNMENT

Malaysia is divided into 13 states, and three federal territories, Kuala Lumpur, Labuan Island, and Putrajaya federal administrative territory. Each of the states has its own assembly and government headed by a chief minister, and nine have hereditary rulers (generally titled "sultans") from among whom the head of state is elected every five years. The remaining four states have appointed governors in counterpart positions. In 1957 the Federation of Malaya (mainland Peninsular states) gained independence from Britain and in 1963 the Federation of Malaysia was formed, comprising the Federation of Malaya, Singapore, Sabah and Sarawak, and three federal territories (Kuala Lumpur, Labuan Island, Putrajaya federal administrative territory). Singapore left the Federation in 1965.

Each state has its own unicameral legislature, a State Assembly called Dewan Undangan Negeri, and each state sends two representatives to the Senate House of the federal parliament.

Johore

Johore is the southernmost of the states which lie between the Straits of Malacca and the South China Sea. To the south of it are the Straits of Johore and the Causeway linking the state with the independent Republic of Singapore. Johore covers an area of 18,987 square kilometres. The capital is Johore Bahru. The state came under British protection by a treaty signed in 1885 and is headed by a sultan.
Ruler: Sultan Ibrahim Ismail

Kedah

Extending along the north-western coast of the Malay Peninsula, Kedah has an area of 9,425 square kilometres and a population of 1,649,756, giving a density of 175 people per sq. km. The state includes the sparsely populated Langkawi Islands and is headed by a sultan. Its capital is Alor Star. In 1511, Kedah came under the suzerainty of its neighbour, Siam, and remained thus until 1909, when the signing of an Anglo-Siamese treaty transferred suzerainty to Britain until independence in 1957.
Ruler: Sultan Abdul Halim

Kelantan

One of the northern states of Malaysia, Kelantan has as its neighbours Perak, Pahang and Trengganu. It has a relatively short seaboard and only one port. Tumpat Malaysian Airline System serves the towns of Kota Bharu, Kuala Trengganu and Kuantan. Its area comprises 915,024 square kilometres. Much of the southern part of the state is still jungle and it also contains Gunong Tahan (7,186 ft.). The capital of Kelantan is Kota Bharu and it is headed by a sultan. The state was under Siamese protection until 1909, when a treaty was concluded with Great Britain.
Ruler: Sultan Muhammad V

Malacca

This historic state lies on the western side of the peninsula bordering the Straits and with Negri Sembilan to the north and Johore to the south. Covering an area of 1,652 square kilometres, the land is largely devoted to the production of paddy and rubber. Its capital is the ancient port of Malacca, an international trading port since the 15th century. Malacca's history was eventful; first the Portuguese and then the Dutch seized the port, followed by the British, during the Napoleonic wars. In 1818, however, it was returned to the Dutch but by treaty of 1824 returned once again to the British until independence.
Ruler: Sultan Mahmud Shah

Negri Sembilan

The state is bordered by Selangor, Pahang, Malacca and Johore, and has a seaboard of about 30 miles, on the Malacca Strait. Its area is 6,644 square kilometres. The capital is Seremban. Negri Sembilan means Nine States, the name deriving from its nine districts, parts of which have since been incorporated in adjacent states. Although so named, the present state of Negri Sembilan now consists of six political units and was formed in 1895. Although from 1844 onwards Britain's influence had been exercised in the state, in an advisory capacity to the chiefs, active intervention came only in the latter part of the century, and was due to the growing importance of tin, one of Malaysia's foremost products, in the world economy.
Ruler: Duli Yang Maha Mulia Yang di-Pertua Besar Negri Sembilan

Pahang

The largest state in Peninsular Malaysia, Pahang covers an area of 13,820 square miles, much of which is still unexplored jungle. Its coastline of 130 miles borders the South China Sea. Kuantan is the capital. In 1887 Pahang concluded its first treaty with Britain; a second one in the following year placed the state under British protection until independence.
Ruler: Ahmad Shah

Penang

This state consists of the Island of Penang, a number of smaller islands and the mainland of Province Wellesley. Its total area is 35,965 square kilometres. Penang Island, which lies at the northern extremity of the Straits of Malacca, is about 15 miles long and nine miles broad. The mainland, facing it, is about eight miles wide and 45 miles long. The capital is George Town. In the late eighteenth century the Island of Penang was ceded to the East India Company. The mainland strip was ceded to Britain in 1880.
Governor: Tun Dato'Seri Haji Abdul Rahman bin Haji Abbas

Perak

This state, which extends northwards to the border of Thailand and on its western side skirts the Straits of Malacca, contains some of the country's most productive tin mines within its 21,005 square kilometres. On the eastern side of the state, adjoining Kelantan and Pahang, lies the main mountain range. Perak is headed by a Sultan. Ipoh is the state capital. Early in the seventeenth century the Dutch built up powerful trading connections with Perak and their influence predominated until 1818, in which year Britain secured a treaty that gave her subjects the right to free trade in the state. In 1874 the Perak chiefs accepted a British Resident.
Sultan: Azlan Shah

Perlis

The smallest of the Malay States, Perlis lies between two provinces of Thailand and the Malay state of Kedah, and was in fact a part of the latter until the Siamese occupation in 1721. Perlis came under British suzerainty as the result of an Anglo-Siamese Treaty, and the state concluded a treaty with Britain in 1930. The capital is Kangar. The state covers an area of 795 square kilometres and is headed by a Raja.
Raja: Tuanku Syed Sirajuddin ibni Almarhum Tuanku Syed Putra Jamallullail

Sabah

Sabah covers an area of 29,388 sq. miles with a coast-line of about 900 miles washed by the South China Sea on the west and north, and the Sulu and Celebes Seas on the east. Sabah is a mountainous country of dense tropical forests, with mountain ranges rising to 6,000 ft. Rising to a height of 13,455 ft., Mount Kinabalu is the highest mountain in Malaysia and South East Asia. On 31 August 1963, the country gained self-government and on 16 September 1963, Sabah joined the Federation of Malaysia as an independent state. The capital is Kota Kinabalu. Only 5 to 6 per cent of Sabah is cultivated as agriculture is restricted by poor communications and a relatively small population. Sabah has a good timber industry which plays an important part in the economy of the State.
Crown Prince: Tuanku Syed Sirajuddin ibni Tuanu Syed Putra Jamallullail

Sarawak

Sarawak in Borneo covers an area of 124,450 square kilometres on the northwest coast of the island. The country is low-lying along the coast but inland there is a tangled mass of hills, its dominant feature being the multitude of rivers. Sarawak's economy depends on agriculture, rubber being its chief product. There are about 6,000 sq. miles of swamp forest and they produce most of Sarawak's commercial timber. Sarawak's chief exports are petroleum, bauxite, rubber, pepper, timber and sago. The capital of Sarawak is Kuching.
Chief Minister: Abdul Taib Mahmud

Selangor

Selangor lies to the south of Perak and has an extensive seaboard on the Straits of Malacca. On that part of the northern border joining Pahang the country is mountainous. Selangor covers an area of 7,960 square kilometres. The capital is Shah Alam. In 1818 Britain concluded a commercial treaty with Selangor and subsequently an agreement of peace and friendship with Sultan Ibrahim Shah. His successor had difficulty in controlling his chiefs, however, and anarchy prevailed until the state came under British protection in 1874.
Ruler: Sultan Tengku Idris Shah

Terengganu

Terengganu is one of the eastern states of the peninsula, its long coastline bordering the South China Sea. Its neighbouring states are Kelantan and Pahang. A good deal of the interior is mountainous, thickly forested and uninhabited. The state covers an area of 12,955 square kilometres. The capital is Kuala Terengganu. British political influence began in 1909, with a treaty concluded with Siam, to which the state paid tribute. A second treaty in the following year brought Terengganu under British protection, until independence. Terengganu is headed by a sultan.
Ruler: Sultan Mizan Zainal Abidin

AREA AND POPULATION

Area

Malaysia, in the heart of Southeast Asia, occupies two distinct regions: the Malay Peninsular extending south to southeast from the Thai border, and the northwestern coastal area of the island of Borneo, consisting of Sabah (North Borneo) and Sarawak. It has land frontiers with the Republic of Indonesia (about 900 miles) in the island of Borneo. Singapore is located on the southern tip of the Malay Peninsular. Coastal plains extend to hills and mountains with a high point of 4,100 metres. The climate is tropical with two monsoon seasons.

To view a map, consult http://www.lib.utexas.edu/maps/cia08/malaysia_sm_2008.gif

Population

The population in 2010 was put at 28.4 million giving a population density of 86 people per sq km. The growth rate for 2000-10 was estimated to be 1.9 per cent per year. Approximately 72 per cent of the population lives in urban areas.

Malays, Chinese, Indians, Ibans, Kadazans and other races make up the varied population of Malaysia. Malays and other indigenous people account for some 60 per cent of the population, Chinese 25 per cent, Indians 7 per cent and other races 8 per cent. The national language is Bahasa Malaysia but English is widely used in commerce and industry. Chinese and Tamil are also widely spoken. Chinese dialects used are Cantonese, Mandarin, Hokkien, Hakka, Hainan, and Foochow. Telugu, Malayalam, and Panjabi are used and in East Malaysia several indigenous languages are spoken, the largest are Iban and Kadazan. Traditionally those of Malay descent dominate politics while those of Chinese descent hold economic power.

Births, Marriages, Deaths

Estimated figures for 2010 show that the crude birth rate was 20.3 births per 1,000 population and the crude death rate was 4.8 deaths per 1,000 population. Life expectancy from birth in 2009 was 71 years for males and 76 years for females. Healthy life expectancy was 64 years. Approximately 30 per cent of the population was aged 14 or under and 8 per cent over 60. The median age was 26. The total fertility rate was 2.6 per female. (Source: http://www.who.int, World Health Statistics 2012)

Public Holidays 2014

1 January: New Year's Day
14 January: Prophet's Birthday*
31 January: Chinese New Year
1 May: Labour Day
14 May: Wesak Day (Birth of Buddha)
3 June: King's Birthday
29 July: End of Ramadam*
31 August: National Day
5 October: Hari Raya Haji (Feast of the Sacrifice)*
23 October: Diwali
25 October: Islamic New Year*
25 December: Christmas Day
The birthday of each Sultan in his province is a holiday. * Islamic holidays depend on the sighting of the moon so dates can vary.

EMPLOYMENT

Figures for 2012 put the labour force at approximately12.7 million of whom 12.3 million were employed and 402,000 were unemployed giving an unemployment rate of 3.2 per cent. Unemployment was estimated to be 3.2 per cent in February 2012, up from 2.9 per cent in February 2011. In 2008, 1,472,000 of the workforce were employed in the agriculture sector, 1,807,000 in the manufacturing sector, 63,000 in mining and 7,557,000 in other sectors including services.

MALAYSIA

Although foreign nationals from Indonesia, India, the Philippines and Sri Lanka are allowed into the country to work, the country has been cracking down on illegal workers. Malaysia announced in 2002 that it would introduce tough laws on illegal immigrants and encouraged illegal immigrants to leave Malaysia before the introduction of punishments including imprisonment and whippings in 2005. Most of the illegal immigrants are workers from Indonesia. There were an estimated 7 million foreign nationals working in Malaysia in 2012.

Total Employment by Economic Activity

Occupation	2008
Agriculture, hunting & forestry	1,365,600
Fishing	122,100
Mining & quarrying	54,500
Manufacturing	1,944,700
Electricity, gas & water supply	60,500
Construction	998,000
Wholesale & retail trade, repairs	1,729,400
Hotels & restaurants	783,600
Transport, storage & communications	583,400
Financial intermediation	276,000
Real estate, renting & business activities	553,200
Public admin. & defence; compulsory social security	751,100
Education	656,500
Health & social work	252,600
Other community, social & personal service activities	274,200
Households with employed persons	253,000
Extra-territorial organisations & bodies	1,100

Source: Copyright © International Labour Organization (ILO Dept. of Statistics, http://laborsta.ilo.org)

BANKING AND FINANCE

Currency
One Malaysian Ringgit (RM) = 100 Sen

GDP / GNP, Inflation, National Debt
Malaysia is trying to diversify its economy away from production of raw materials and dependence on oil exports and is looking to attract investment in finance, high technology biotechnology and services. The oil and gas sector contributes more than 40 per cent of government revenue.

GDP in 2000 grew for the third year running since the Asian financial crisis of 1997-98, showing a growth of 8.2 per cent, mainly as a result of growing demand for manufactured goods. A government economic plan was introduced in 2001; the National Vision Policy is designed to guide economic development between 2001 and 2010, including increased spending on education and focusing on the production of high technology products. The service sector has become increasing important, making up 54 per cent of GDP in 2007.

Since the Asian financial crisis, Malaysia has gone some way to reform its banking and financial system. Local banks have been consolidated and there is now greater competition. Malaysia has established its Islamic Finance capability and has become a major hub in the Asia Pacific region. The economy still faces some challenges particularly improving the performance of Government Linked Companies and the rise of the Chinese economy. GDP growth in 2005 was recorded at 5.3 per cent, down from 7.0 per cent in 2004; this was mainly due to a slowdown in the export market for Malaysia's electronic items. In 2005 the government removed the peg linking the ringgit's values to the US dollar; the exchange peg had been in place for seven years and was replaced by a managed float against a basket of currencies.

Growth of GDP in 2006 has been put at 5.8 per cent. By 2007, GDP growth was 6.5 per cent. In line with the global downturn in economic growth, GDP growth in 2008 fell to 4.8 per cent and -1.6 per cent in 2009. In March 2009, the government announced a US$16 million economic stimulus plan. Economic growth grew by over 7.0 per cent in 2010. Per capita GDP was estimated to be 27,114 ringgit in 2010. In 2011, GDP was estimated at US$280 billion, a growth rate of 5 per cent.

The following table shows the make up of GDP in recent years. Figures are in million ringgit and are at current market prices:

Sector	2008	2009	2010
Agriculture	75,611	64,724	81,400
Mining	123,978	84,102	96,131
Manufacturing	194,324	173,558	200,028
Utilities	16,950	17,803	19,213
Construction	20,605	22,436	24,773
Trade	100,926	100,518	111,037
Transport & communications	46,205	46,649	50,802
Finance	89,469	93,455	100,754
Public administration	53,237	55,096	58,488
Others	33,223	35,367	37,421
GDP	742,470	679,938	765,965

* Provisional figures
Source: Asian Development Bank

In 2008, inflation was put at 5.4 per cent, falling to an estimated 2.0 per cent in 2009, and 1.7 per cent in 2010. It rose to an estimated 3 per cent in 2011. External debt was estimated to be US$85.1 million in 2011.

Foreign Investment
Sarawak has been cultivated as a major foreign investment centre with a number of tax incentives for foreign companies. The state has tax exemptions of 85 per cent, 15 per cent higher than in the other Malaysian states. The Kuala Lumpur Commodity Exchange (KLCE) is promoting more trading and higher liquidity in its futures contract market. Forums and workshops have been held to stimulate the interest and knowledge of domestic and foreign players.

Balance of Payments / Imports and Exports
Malaysia's major primary export commodities are: natural rubber, palm oil, petroleum crude, crude and refined oil, sawlogs and sawn timber, pepper, cocoa, tin and liquid nitrogen gas (LNG). Manufactured export products include textiles, clothing and footwear; chemicals and petroleum; electrical and electronic machinery and appliances; iron, steel and metals. In order to encourage exports there are 14 Free Industrial Zones throughout the country.

Trade Balance, figures in million Ringgit

Year	Exports, fob	Imports, cif	Trade Balance
2007	604,300	502,045	102,255
2008	663,494	521,611	141,883
2009	552,518	434,670	117,848
2010	639,428	529,195	110,234

Source: Asian Development Bank

Exports increased by 15.7 per cent in 2010 and imports by 21.7 per cent. This compares to falls of over 16 per cent in external trade the previous year.

Principal Exports in Million Ringgit

Commodity	2006	2007
Thermionic valves, tubes, photocells etc.	93,505	96,471
Parts & accessories for office machines	41,875	36,746
Telecommunications equipment	33,621	28,828
Petroleum, crude & partly refined	31,967	32,863
Palm oil	22,117	32,643
Liquefied natural gas	23,285	26,157
Clothing & clothing accessories	5,036	4,972
Saw logs and sawn timber	7,666	5,292
Sound recorders & reproducers, inc. tv images	5,797	5,292
Rubber	8,235	7,335

Source: Asian Development Bank

Malaysia's main trading partners are the US, Singapore, Japan, China and Hong Kong, the Netherlands, Thailand, Republic of Korea, Germany and the UK. The value of imports and exports by main trading partners is shown in the following tables.

Exports by Main Trading Partners in US$ million

Country	2008	2009	2010
Total	199,510	157,427	231,122
Singapore	29,416	21,974	33,053
US	24,936	17,255	24,208
China	19,049	19,157	45,796
Japan	21,466	15,473	20,650
Thailand	9,571	8,499	9,852
Hong Kong	8,530	8,209	9,921
Netherlands	7,031	5,248	7,483
Korea, Republic of	7,800	5,995	6,161
Australia	7,345	5,692	8,329
Indonesia	6,243	4,921	7,862

Source: Asian Development Bank

Imports by Main Trading Partners in US$ million

Country	2008	2009	2010
Total	156,932	123,835	185,256
Singapore	17,293	13,713	46,104
China	20,084	17,277	26,199
Japan	19,592	15,456	19,401
US	16,969	13,844	15,380
Thailand	8,802	7,490	11,626
Indonesia	7,269	6,558	10,299
Korea, Rep. of	7,292	5,732	5,890
Germany	6,745	5,241	5,949
Hong Kong	4,116	3,076	3,652
Australia	3,527	2,696	3,680

Source: Asian Development Bank

Central Bank
Bank Negara Malaysia (Central Bank of Malaysia) , Jalan Dato Onn, 50480 Kuala Lumpur, Wilayah Persekutan, Malaysia. Tel: +60 3 2698 8044, fax: +60 3 2691 2990, e-mail: info@bnm.gov.my, URL: http://www.bnm.gov.my
Governor: Tan Sri Dato Dr Zeti Akhtar Aziz (page 1373)

Chambers of Commerce and Trade Organisations
Malaysian International Chamber of Commerce & Industry, URL: http://www.micci.com

Associated Chinese Chambers of Commerce and Industry of Malaysia, URL: http://www.acccim.org.my

Malaysia External Trade Development Corporation, URL: http://www.matrade.gov.my

MANUFACTURING, MINING AND SERVICES

Primary and Extractive Industries

Malaysia has extensive resources of petroleum oil and natural gas. As of January 1 2012, Malaysia had oil reserves of 4.0 billion barrels. Estimated production in 2011 was 616,000 bbl/d, of which 83 per cent was crude oil. In 2011 Malaysia consumed 547,000 barrels per day. As Malaysia's oil reserves began to decline the state oil company Petronas has began to explore and also produce oil abroad mainly from Syria, Turkmenistan, Iran, Pakistan, China, Vietnam, Burma, Algeria, Libya, Tunisia, Sudan, and Angola. In 2009 Petronas announced that seven new Malaysian oil fields had come online in 2008, making a total of 68 producing oil fields. An oil recovery project at the offshore Tapis field is due for completion in 2013. Petronas and ExxonMobil have agreed to the development of seven mature fields including Tapis. Malaysia exported 69,000 bbl/d of crude oil in 2011.

Malaysia had natural gas reserves of 83 trillion cubic feet (Tcf) as of January 1 2011. Figures for 2010 show that Malaysia produced 2.7 Tcf and consumed 1.1 Tcf. Malaysia exports natural gas mainly to Japan, South Korea, and Taiwan. The world's largest liquid natural gas (LNG) plant was completed in 2003 in Bintulu, Sarawak. Exports of LNG go mainly to South Korea, Japan and Taiwan. Malaysia has one of the most extensive natural gas pipeline networks in the world.

In May 2011 Petronas announced plans to a build a US$20 billion factory complex which would produce chemicals and refine crude oil. The factory was expected to be commissioned by 2016.

Construction began on Petronas' Sabah Oil and Gas Terminal in Sabah 2011 and is expected to be completed by the end of 2013. Its handling capacity will be 1.3 Bcf/d of natural gas and it will supply gas for domestic use in Sabah. A reported 500,000 cubic feet per day will be piped to the Bintul complex to be as exported as LNG. The Sabah-Sarawak Gas Pipline project is part of this development.

In 2010, Malaysia produced 2.64 million short tons of coal. It consumed 21.3 million short tons. (Source: EIA)

Energy

Government approval was given in 1994 for the construction of a hydroelectric project with a maximum capacity of 2.4 gigawatts in Bakun, Sarawak. Completion was scheduled for 2002 but in 1997 rising costs and the economic crisis in Asia meant that the project was postponed. In 2001 the government announced that work on the project would resume. Around 70 per cent of output will go to Kuala Lumpur via specially constructed overhead lines.

Total energy produced amounted to 3.70 quadrillion Btu in 2009. It consumed 2.69 quadrillion Btu in the same year.

Most of Malaysia's electricity is generated by thermal means (87 per cent) and 13 per cent is hydroelectric. Figures for 2010 show that Malaysia generated 118 billion kWh of electricity of which 110 billion kWh were consumed. Its installed capacity was 25.3 billion kWh. (Source: EIA)

Manufacturing

The manufacture of electrical and electronic goods, chemicals and chemical products, wood products and textiles are a significant part of Malaysia's industry. Due to the world wide slump in demand for electronic goods, manufacturing output fell by 5.0 per cent in 2001, but has risen steadily since.

Manufacturing Production in Thousand Metric Tons

Product	2006	2007
Cement	19,456	22,021
Diesel oil	9,052	8,805
Kerosene	3,419	3,306
Iron & steel bars & rods	3,021	2,756
Prepared animal feeds	2,238	2,234
Liquefied petroleum gas	3,437	3,798
Fuel oil	1,794	1,597
Refined sugar	1,460	1,574
Wheat flour	839	889

Source: Asian Development Bank

Service Industries

In 2010 tourist arrivals were estimated at 24.6 million, up from 22 million in 2008 and 16.4 million in 2005. Tourism receipts were approximately RM 56 billion. The service sector contributes over 40 per cent of GDP and accounts for over 20 per cent of employment.

Agriculture

The mainstay of the Malaysian economy along with manufacturing is still agriculture. Output is dominated by the production of tree crops, namely rubber and palm oil, which account for 48.3 per cent of the total production in the sector. The export of palm oil and related products alone account for RM22,700 million. The current efforts to revitalise the sector as envisaged in the National Agricultural Policy 1992-2010 (NAP) will emphasize the maximization of farm income through raising the productivity of traditional export crops and development of new crops as well as the production of food and industrial crops.

The production of saw logs is, however, expected to decline in anticipation of the policy of sustainable forest management.

Main Crop Production in 2010

Crop	Int $1000	Tonnes
Palm oil	7,392,924	16,993,000
Indigenous chicken meat	1,965,810	1,380,090
Palm kernels	1,107,847	4,292,000
Natural rubber	982,440	858,900
Rice, paddy	683,280	2,548,000
Hen eggs, in shell	448,202	540,400
Indigenous pigmeat	362,185	235,607
Indigenous duck meat	191,464	116,210
Pineapples	118,599	416,070
Bananas	82,949	294,530
Fruit, tropical fresh nes	82,674	294,530
Pepper (Piper spp.)	61,904	29,700

*unofficial figures

Source: http://faostat.fao.org/site/339/default.aspx Food and Agriculture Organization of the United Nations, Food and Agricultural commodities production

COMMUNICATIONS AND TRANSPORT

Travel Requirements

Citizens of the USA, Canada, Australia and the EU require a passport valid for six months but do not need a visa for stays of up to three months (one month in the case of Bulgarians). Passes are issued on arrival. Other nationals should contact the embassy to check visa requirements. All visitors must have proof of adequate funds and an onward ticket.

Malaysian immigration authorities conduct regular sweeps and routinely detain foreigners who overstay their social visit passes. Visitors should carry their passports (containing the Malaysian entry stamp) with them at all times.

National Airlines

All parts of Malaysia are linked by air services provided by the Malaysian Airline System (MAS), which also operates international air services.

Malaysia Airlines (MAS), URL: http://www.malaysiaairlines.com

International Airports

The principal airports are Subang, 23 km from Kuala Lumpur, Penang, Bayan Lepas, Penang, Labuan, Kota Kinabalu, Sandakan, Tawau, Kuching, Sibu, Miri, Senai and Kuantan. There are many others suitable for small aircraft.

Kuala Lumpur International Airport (KLIA) opened in July 1998, and can handle 25 million passengers and a million tonnes of cargo annually. URL: http://www.klia.com.my

Railways

The railway system of 2,680 km is due to be improved by investments in rolling stock and other facilities, thereby moving some of the passenger and freight transport from the roads to the railways. Plans are underway for a rail link between Kuala Lumpur and Bangkok (Asean Rail Express), which would then further expand to become a Trans-Asian Rail Link, including Singapore, Vietnam, Cambodia, Laos, Myanmar and Kunming in China. A rail link between central Kuala Lumpur and the new Kuala Lumpur International Airport has been opened. Kuala Lumpur has a Light Rail Transit system.

Roads

There are over 28,700 km of metalled roads in the Malaysian Peninsula. Due to the increasing volume of traffic, 650 km of rural roads and 14,600 km of village roads are scheduled to be improved and upgraded during the next five years. Vehicles drive on the left.

Shipping

The principal shipping ports in Peninsular Malaysia are Port Kelang, Johor Port, Kuantan Port and Kemaman Port, which can all handle containerised cargo, and Bintulu Port in Sarawak which mainly handles goods for the liquified natural gas industry. Work has commenced on the extension to existing port facilities at Kota Kinabalu and Sandakan through general cargo berths. In Sarawak a new port is planned at Kuching and the expansion of port facilities at Sibu has been completed. Port of Tanjung Pelepas (PTP) (URL: http://www.ptp.com.my/) opened officially in 2000. Its total cargo tonnage is estimated to be over 125 million tonnes. Over 95 per cent of Malaysia's trade passes through its ports.

Ferries run between Penang and Butterworth; Port Kelang, Kuantan, Sarawak and Sabah; Kuala Perlis, Kuala Kedah, Penang, Satun and Langkawi.

HEALTH

In 2009, Malaysia spent approximately 8.4 per cent of its total budget on healthcare (up from 8.0 per cent in 2000), accounting for 55.7 per cent of all healthcare spending. Total expenditure on healthcare equated to 4.6 per cent of the country's GDP. Per capita expenditure on health was approximately US$316, compared with US$125 in 2000. Figures for 2005-10 show that there are 25,102 physicians (9.4 per 10,000 population), 72,847 nurses and midwives (27.3 per 10,000 population), 4,571 pharmaceutical personnel and 3,640 dentistry personnel. There are 18 hospital beds per 10,000 population.

According to the latest WHO figures, in 2010 approximately 100 per cent of the population had access to improved drinking water. In the same year, 96 per cent of the population had access to improved sanitation. Diarrhoea accounts for 2 per cent of childhood deaths.

MALAYSIA

The infant mortality rate in 2010 was 5 per 1,000 live births. The child mortality rate (under 5 years) was 6 per 1,000 live births. The main causes of childhood mortality are: prematurity (24 per cent), congenital anomalies (31 per cent), birth asphyxia (8 per cent), pneumonia (6 per cent). (Source: http://www.who.int, World Health Statistics 2012)

EDUCATION

Pre-school Education
Under the 1996 Education Bill, pre-school education is now part of the formal education system. Prior to this education was carried out by government agencies, private, social or voluntary organisations.

Primary/Secondary Education
The Education Ordinance, 1957, and the Education Act 1961, have the basic aim of providing six years of free primary education to every child. In addition, national schools are given financial assistance (those using Bahasa Malaysia, English, Chinese and Tamil as media of instruction). In fact, the national education system is designed to promote national integration and unity. It therefore provides for an educational system in which Bahasa Malaysia will ultimately become the main medium of instruction and English a second language in all schools.

Malaysia now provides six years of free primary education and since 1964 an additional three years of lower secondary education. Promotion into upper secondary levels depends on the pupils' performance in the Lower Certificate of Education examination. They are then streamed into arts, science, technical or vocational courses. After two years the pupils will sit for either the Malaysian Certificate of Education or the Vocational Certificate of Education. If they do well, they have another two years before sitting their Higher School Certificate. This qualification entitles the pupil to go to a university.

Recent figures for primary school enrolment show that 97.9 per cent of the relevant population attend and 78 per cent attend secondary school.

Higher Education
Post-secondary institutions of learning include: the MARA Institute of Technology and the Tunku Abdul Rahman College in Kuala Lumpur, the Ungku Omar Polytechnic in Ipon, the Kuantan Polytechnic, Kuantan and the Agriculture University. The other universities are the University of Malaya, established in Kuala Lumpur in 1959, the University of Penang (now named Universiti Sains Malaysia - Science University of Malaysia) (established in 1969) and the Universiti Kebangsaan (National University) established in 1970. Other colleges include the University of Technology, the Northern University of Malaysia and the International Islamic University. Degree courses are also available from institutions set up by corporations, including Telekom Malaysia Berhad and Petronas. There are also technical schools and industrial training institutes to equip students for industry.

According to the most recent UNESCO statistics, the adult literacy rate in 2009 was 94.2 for adults (96.7 per cent for males, and 91.6 for females), rising to over 98 per cent for young people (aged 15-24). In 2009, 18.9 per cent of total government spending went on education, 46 per cent of which went on secondary education, 18 per cent on tertiary and 35 per cent on primary education.

RELIGION

Islam is the official religion of Malaysia with 57.0 per cent of the population adherants. Buddhism, Hinduism, Christianity and other religions are practiced freely.

In December 2009 courts in Malaysia ruled that Christians have a constitutional right to use the word Allah to refer to God. The court found that a government ban on non-Muslims using the word 'Allah' was unconstitutional.

Malaysia has a religious liberty rating of 4 on a scale of 1 to 10 (10 is most freedom). (Source: World Religion Database)

COMMUNICATIONS AND MEDIA

There are strict censorship laws in place to protect both national security and religious and cultural sensitivities. Publishing licences are issued annually and the government has the authority to revoke or suspend.

Newspapers
Business Times, URL: http://www.btimes.com.my
The Star, URL: http://thestar.com.my
Malay Mail, URL: http://www.mmail.com.my
New Straits Times, URL: http://www.nst.com.my

Broadcasting
Radio Malaysia broadcasts in Malay, English, Chinese and Tamil on several networks. In addition to the national programmes, a number of local stations broadcast in a variety of languages. Television programmes are broadcast to the whole of Malaysia. Both commercial and pay-TV stations exist. The leading terrestial broadcaster is TV3.

Radio Malaysia, Radio Television Malaysia, URL: http://www.rtm.net.my
TV 3 (Sistem Televisyen Malaysia Bhd), URL: http://www.tv3.com.my
Radio Television Malaysia (RTM), URL: http://www.rtm.net.my/

Telecommunications
There are over 4 million telephone land lines in use. As part of the continuing development programme, new switchgear and exchanges have been installed for international traffic and the network is being extended in rural areas. The international service is now excellent. Figures for 2010 show that over 34 million mobile phones are in use. Estimates for 2010 indicated that almost 15 million Malaysians were regular internet users. In 2009 the government abandoned plans to introduce filters to censor online sites and said it would instead use existing laws.

ENVIRONMENT

Environmental concerns include air pollution from industry and vehicles and water pollution. Deforestation is also a major concern. In February 2007, Malaysia, Indonesia and Brunei Darussalam signed an agreement to protect 200,000 square kilometres of rainforest on the island of Borneo.

Malaysia is a party to the following international agreements: Biodiversity, Climate Change, Climate Change-Kyoto Protocol, Desertification, Endangered Species, Hazardous Wastes, Law of the Sea, Marine Life Conservation, Ozone Layer Protection, Ship Pollution, Tropical Timber 83, Tropical Timber 94, and Wetlands.

In 2010, carbon dioxide emissions amounted to 181.93 million metric tons. (Source: EIA)

SPACE PROGRAMME

Sheikh Muszaphar Shukor became the first Malaysian astronaut when he joined the crew of a Russian spacecraft heading to the International Space Station (ISS). Mr Shukor was also the first Muslim in space during the holy month of Ramadan; Muslim clerics prepared special guidelines for him on observing religious rules while on the ISS.

The Malaysian National Space Agency (URL: http://www.angkasa.gov.my/) was set up in 2002. It is responsible for leading the development of space technology in Malaysia.

MALDIVES
Republic of the Maldives
Dhivehi Raajjeyge Jumhooriyyaa

Capital: Malé (Population estimate, 2011: 103,700)

Head of State: Dr Mohamed Waheed Hassan Manik (President) (page 1533)

Vice President: Mohamed Waheed Deen (page 1414)

National Flag: Green, red-bordered and charged with a white crescent

CONSTITUTION AND GOVERNMENT

Constitution
Maldives became a British protectorate of a special nature in 1887 under an agreement between the Sultan of the Maldives and the Governor in Ceylon, Sri Lanka. The special nature of the protectorate was that Britain did not rule the country or dispatch any representative to reside in the country, but that all external relations of the Maldives were to be conducted through the British Government.

When Ceylon gained independence in 1947, an agreement was signed in 1948 between the Governments of Maldives and Britain reaffirming protectorate status. The first Republic, established in 1953, was under the same status of a protectorate but was short-lived. In September 1953 the country reverted to a Sultanate. On 26 July 1965 the British Government and the Maldives Government signed an agreement which ended Britain's control over the Maldives, and accepted the independence and full sovereignty of the Maldives. The independent Maldives reverted from a Sultanate to a Republic on 11 November 1968.

In 1998, a new constitution replaced that of 1968 and allowed for more than one candidate to stand for the presidency. In June 2005, constitutional reforms were approved by parliament, allowing for the legalisation of political parties. A referendum was held in August 2007 and voters backed plans for a Presidential system of government. The country's first multi-party elections were held in 2008.

To consult the constitution, please visit: http://www.maldivesinfo.gov.mv/home/upload/downloads/Compilation.pdf.

Recent Events
On 26 December 2004, the Maldives were hit by the devastating tsunami in the Indian Ocean. 80 people are believed to have died and 12,000 displaced. The World Bank estimated that about US$304 million would be needed for reconstruction. The Maldives preliminary impact and recovery assessment estimated damage at about US$470 million dollars, the equivalent to almost two-thirds of the country's annual domestic economic output.

The opposition leader Mohamed Nasheed was charged with terrorism in August 2005 after the government accused him of criticising the president and inciting violence.

President Gayoooom survived an assassination attempt in January 2008.

In August 2008, a new constitution was ratified paving the way for the first multi-party presidential elections to be held in October. Mohamed Nasheed known as Anni was elected president ending the 30 year presidency of President Gayoom. Legislative elections took place in May 2009.

On February 7 2012, President Mohamed Nasheed resigned from his post, following protests and a mutiny by the police force. Vice-President Muhammad Waheed Hassan was sworn in as his replacement. Mr Nasheed later claimed he was forced out in a coup but a subsequent investigation decided this was not the case. In October, an arrest warrant was issued for Mr Nasheed for ignoring a court summons and travel ban. He was also accused of illegally arresting a judge, a claim Mr Nasheed says is politically motivated . If convicted he would not be able to stand in future presidential elections. Mr Nasheed was arrested in March 2013 after he failed to attend a hearing. He had ignored two earlier arrest warrants.

Legislature
There is a People's Majlis (Parliament). This is made up of 50 members, eight of those nominated by the President, and 42 directly elected for a term of 5 years: two from Malé and two from each of the 20 administrative districts, all members serve a five year term. The President is elected by the People's Majlis and then by national referendum.
People's Assembly, Medhuziyaaraiy Magu, Malé 20080, Maldives. Tel: +960 322617, fax: +960 324104, e-mail: admin@majlis.gov.mv, URL: http://www.majlis.gov.mv

Cabinet (as at March 2013)
President, C-in-Chief of the Armed Forces and Police: Dr Mohamed Waheed Hassan Manik (page 1533)
Vice-President: Mohamed Waheed Deen (page 1414)
Minister of Defence and National Security: Col. (Ret'd) Mohamed Nazim
Minister of Finance and Treasury: Abdulla Jihad (page 1449)
Minister of Home Affairs: Dr Mohamed Jameel Ahmed
Minister of Economic Development: Ahmed Mohamed
Minister of Foreign Affairs: Abdul Samad Abdulla (page 1507)
Minister of Transport & Communications: Ahmed Shamheed
Minister of Human Resources, Youth and Sports: Mohamed Hussein Shareef

Minister of Fisheries and Agriculture: Ahmed Shafeeu
Minister of Health: Dr Ahmed Jamsheed
Attorney General: Aishath Azima Shakoor
Minister of Housing and Infrastructure: Mohamed Muizzu
Minister of the Environment and Energy, Acting Minister of Gender, Family and Human Rights: Dr Mariyam Shakeela
Minister of Tourism, Arts and Culture: Ahmed Adheeb Ghafoor
Minister of Islamic Affairs: Sheikh Mohamed Shaheem Ali Saeed
Minister of Education: Dr Asim Mohamed

Ministries
Office of the President, Medhuziyaaraiy Magu, Malé 20113, Maldives. Tel: +960 332 3701, fax: +960 332 5500, e-mail: info@po.gov.mv, URL: http://www.presidencymaldives.gov.mv
Attorney General's Office, Huravee Building, Ameer Ahmed Magu, Malé 20114, Maldives. Tel: +960 332 3809, fax: +960 331 4109, e-mail: attorney@dhivehinet.net.mv, URL: http://www.justice.gov.mv
Ministry of Defence and National Security, Ameer Ahmed Magu, Malé 20114, Maldives. Tel: +960 332 2607, fax: +960 332 5525, e-mail: defence@dhivehinet.net.mv, URL: http://www.defence.gov.mv
Ministry of Economic Development, Ghazee Building, Ameer Ahmed Magu, Malé 20125, Maldives. Tel: +960 332 3668, fax: +960 332 3840, e-mail: contact@tradmin.gov.mv, URL: http://www.trademin.gov.mv
Ministry of Education, Ghazee Building, Ameer Ahmed Magu, Malé 20125, Maldives. Tel: +960 332 3261, fax: +960 332 1201, e-mail: education@dhivehinet.net.mv, URL: http://www.moe.gov.mv
Ministry of Finance and Treasury, Ameeni Magu, Malé 20121, Maldives. Tel: +960 332 2343, fax: +960 332 4432, e-mail: minfin@dhivehinet.net.mv, URL: http://www.finance.gov.mv
Ministry of Fisheries and Agriculture, Ghazee Building, Ameer Ahmed Magu, Malé 20125, Maldives. Tel: +960 332 2625, fax: +960 332 6558, e-mail: fishagri@dhivehinet.net.mv, URL: http://www.fishagri.gov.mv
Ministry of Foreign Affairs, Boduthakurufaanu Magu, Malé 20077, Maldives. Tel: +960 332 3400, fax: +960 332 3841, e-mail: admin@foreigngov.mv, URL: http://www.foreign.gov.mv
Ministry of Health and Family, Ameeni Magu, Malé 20121, Maldives. Tel: +960 332 8887, fax: +960 332 8889, e-mail: health@dhivehinet.net.mv, URL: http://www.health.gov.mv
Ministry of Home Affairs, Huravee Building, Ameer Ahmed Magu, Malé 20114, Maldives. Tel: +960 332 3820, fax: +960 332 4739, e-mail: minhah@dhivehinet.net.mv, URL: http://www.homeaffairs.gov.mv
Ministry of Housing and Environment, 3rd Flr Fen Building, Ameer Ahmed Magu, Malé, Maldives. Tel: +960 332 4861, fax: +960 332 2286, e-mail: secretariat@environment.gov.mv, URL: http://www.environment.gov.mv
Ministry of Human Resources, Youth and Sports, Ghazee Building, Ameer Ahmed Magu, Malé 20125, Maldives. Tel: +960 333 1579, fax: +960 333 1578, e-mail: info@employment.gov.mv, URL: http://www.employment.gov.mv
Ministry of Islamic Affairs, Al Masjid Muhammad Thakurufán, Malé 20103, Maldives. Tel: +960 335 2671, fax: +960 332 3103
Ministry of Tourism, Arts and Culture, Ghazee Building, Ameer Ahmed Magu, Malé 20125, Maldives. Tel: +960 332 3224, fax: +960 332 2512, e-mail: info@vistmaldives.com, URL: http://www.visitmaldives.com
Ministry of Transport and Communication, Huravee Building, Ameer Ahmed Magu, Malé 20114, Maldives. Tel: +960 332 3993, fax: +960 332 3994, e-mail: transport@gov.mv, URL: http://www.transport.gov.mv

Elections
The President is elected by popular vote every five years. In October 2008 the first multi-party presidential elections were held. Six candidates stood and, although President Gayoom won most votes, he failed to win outright. A second round was held between President Gayoom and Mohamed Nasheed. Nasheed won, bringing to an end 30 years of rule by Gayoom. The next presidential election is due to take place in 2013.

Parliamentary elections were held on 22 January 2005. As no political parties were allowed at the time, all candidates for the 42 elected seats ran officially as independents. However the Maldivian Democratic Party (MDP), operating in exile in Sri Lanka, supported several of them. In June 2005, political parties were legalised and four parties were registered by December 2005, the first being the MDP.

The most recent parliamentary election took place in May 2009. The DRP have now 28 seats, the MDP 25 seats, the PA 7 seats, the DQP 2 seats, the AP 1 seat. Independents took 13 seats. One seat was left unfilled. The next leigslative elections are due to be held in 2014.

Political Parties
Maldivian People's Party (DRP), URL: http://www.drp.org.mv. Chairman: President Moumoon Abdul Gayoom
Islamic Democratic Party (IDP), URL: http://www.idp.org.mv. Founder Member: Umar Naseer
Justice Party (AP), URL: http://www.adhaalath.org.mv, Leader: Hussain Rasheed Ahmed
Maldivian Democratic Party (MDP), URL: http://mdp.org.mv, Leader: Ibrahim Didi

MALDIVES

Diplomatic Representation

High Commission of the Republic of Maldives, 22 Nottingham Place, London, W1M 3FB, UK. Tel:+44 (0)20 7224 2135, fax: +44 (0)20 7224 2157, e-mail: maldives.high.commission@virgin.net, URL: http://www.maldiveshighcommission.org
High Commissioner: Her Excellency Dr Farahanaz Faizal
British High Commission, Staff resident in Colombo, Sri Lanka. URL: http://ukinsrilanka.fco.gov.uk/en/
High Commissioner: John Rankin (page 1500)
US Embassy, all staff based in Colombo, Sri Lanka. URL: http://maldives.usvpp.gov/
Ambassador: Patricia A. Butenis
Permanent Mission of the Republic of the Maldives to the United Nations, 800 Second Ave., Suite 400E, New York, N.Y. 10017, USA. Tel: +212 599 6194/6195, fax: +212 661 6405, e-mail: maldives@un.int, URL: http://www.un.int/maldives
Permanent Representative to the UN & Ambassador to the US: Ahmed Sareer

LEGAL SYSTEM

The administration of justice is carried out in accordance with Islamic (Shari'ah) law, through the High Court on Malé and lower courts, which handle specific areas such as theft, property or family law. Judges must be Muslim, and are appointed by the President. Civil law is also applied but it is subordinate to Shari'ah.

There is a five-member advisory council appointed by the president to review High Court decisions. The president can affirm judgments, order a second hearing, or to overturn the court's decision. He can also grant pardons and amnesties. There are some 204 general lower courts situated on each of the other inhabited islands.

The government's human rights record is good, though security forces occasionally abuse detainees. The death penalty has not been implemented in the Maldives since the 1950s, though it continues to exist under the country's legal system. Murderers may be sentenced to death, but have traditionally seen their sentences commuted to life in jail by the President.

High Court of the Maldives, URL: http://www.highcourt.gov.mv

Human Rights Commission of the Maldives, URL: http://www.hrcm.org.mv/

LOCAL GOVERNMENT

A new local government system was created in 2010. It has two spheres of government: national and local. The main acts of for local government are the Decentralisation Act 2010 and the Local Council Election Act 2010. There are two tiers for local government: island councils and city councils. There are 20 atoll councils, two city councils (Malé and Addu) and 66 island councils. City councils must have a population of at least 25,000. The first local council elections took place in 2011. The next are due in 2014.

AREA AND POPULATION

Area
Maldives lies about 420 miles south-west of Sri Lanka and comprises over 1,190 low lying coral islands, grouped into 26 atolls. 199 of the islands are inhabited and 87 of these are designated tourist islands, another 20 islands are designated industry islands. At their highest point the islands are just 2.4 metres above sea level. The total area including land and sea is 90,000 sq. km.

To view a map, consult http://www.lib.utexas.edu/maps/cia08/maldives_sm_2008.gif

The climate is tropical, hot and humid. There are two monsoon seasons: dry (November-March), and rainy (June to August).

Population
The results of the 2000 census put the population at 270,101 (137,200 males and 132,901 females). By 2010 it was estimated to be 316,000. Approximately 40 per cent live in urban areas. The annual population growth rate was estimated to be 1.5 per cent over the period 2000-10. The population density is 1,016 persons per sq km.

The official language of the Maldives is Dhivehi. English is widely spoken.

Births, Marriages, Deaths
Life expectancy in 2009 was 74 years for males and 76 years for females. Healthy life expectancy was 64 years. The median age was 25 years. Approximately 27 per cent of the population was aged under 15 years and 7 per cent over 60 years. In 2010 the infant mortality rate was 14 per 1,000 live births. The maternal mortality rate was an estimated 37 per 100,000 live births. The total fertility rate per women in 2010 was 1.8. (Source: http://www.who.int, World Health Statistics 2012)

Public Holidays 2014
1 January: New Year's Day
14 January: Birth of the Prophet
29 June: Ramadan begins
26 July: Independence Day (National Day)
27 July: Independence Day Celebrations
29 July: Eid al-Fitr (End of Ramadan)
3 November: Victory Day
11 November: Republic Day
12 November: Republic Day Celebrations
25 October: Al-Hijira (Islamic New Year)

Maldives is a Muslim country and Islamic holidays are observed. As they are based on the sighting of the moon dates are variable.

EMPLOYMENT

The government is a major employer. The following table shows how the working population were employed in 2006:

Employment Sector	No. of Persons Employed
Agriculture, hunting, forestry	4,236
Fishing	8,388
Mining & quarrying	339
Manufacturing	19,259
Electricity, gas & water	1,229
Construction	5,930
Wholesale & retail trade	11,711
Hotels & restaurants	12,090
Transport, storage & communication	7,098
Financial intermediation	582
Real estate, renting & business activities	1,156
Public administration & defence	15,949
Education	9,872
Health & social work	4,182
Other community, social & personal services	3,248
Extra-territorial organisations & bodies	216
Other	3,248
Total	110,231

Source: Copyright © International Labour Organization (ILO Dept. of Statistics, http://laborsta.ilo.org)

BANKING AND FINANCE

Currency
One Rufiyaa = 100 Laari

GDP/GNP, Inflation, National Debt
Tourism is the largest contributor to GDP, accounting for almost 30 per cent of it. In December 2004 the Maldives was hit by the Asian Tsunami, and economic growth was adversely affected. By 2006, the country had recovered to some extent. The government economy came under severe strain in 2009 and the IMF confirmed a US$79 million agreement. However the IMF withheld some disbursements due to concerns over the government's budget deficit. A new tourism tax was introduced in 2011 and a business profit tax in 2012. These taxes should increase government revenue by up to 25 per cent. The government is also undertaking some privatisation. It is also promoting the tourism industry including expansion of existing resorts and construction of new resorts. There are worries that the Maldives is relying too heavily on its tourism industry and that it must find was to diversify.

The following table shows the contribution to GDP by industrial origin in recent years. Figures are in million Rufiyaa at current market prices:

Sector	2008	2009	2010
Agriculture	1,327.1	1,354.2	1,364.7
Manufacturing	1,346.8	1,227.9	1,276.1
Utilities	347.3	335.0	373.5
Construction	2,287.7	1,188.9	1,374.3
Trade	1,258.2	965.2	1,021.3
Transport & communications	2,369.9	2,187.1	2,343.3
Public administration	3,116.0	4,178.6	4,146.1
Finance	1,426.7	1,331.3	1,451.7
Others	10,494.0	10,466.5	12,167.4
GDP at 1995 market prices	22,909.0	22,294.0	24,428.0

Source: Asian Development Bank

GDP contracted by an estimated at 4.6 per cent following the tsunami, but grew by 21.4 per cent in 2006, by 12.1 per cent in 2007 and 12 per cent in 2008. The growth rate was put at -6.5 per cent in 2009 but recovered to 9.9 per cent in 2010. Per capita GDP was 62,067 Rufiyaa in 2010.

Inflation ran at 0.9 per cent in 2002, -2.9 per cent in 2003, 6.4 per cent in 2004 and 3.3 per cent in 2005. Inflation was estimated to have risen to 6 per cent in 2011.

Total external debt was estimated at US$935 million in 2011.

Balance of Payments / Imports and Exports
Foreign trade in recent years is shown in the following table. Figures are in US$ million.

Foreign Trade	2008	2009	2010
Exports, fob	331.1	169.0	199.9
Imports, cif	1,387.5	967.3	1,095.1
Trade balance	-1,056.4	-798.3	-895.2

Source: Asian Development Bank

Exports grew by 18.3 per cent in 2010 and imports grew by 13.2 per cent.

Main export trading partners in 2010 were Thailand (US$18.9 million), UK (US$12.8 million), Sri Lanka (US$14.4 million) and France (US$15.1million). The Maldives' main exports goods are fresh tuna fish, dry fish and dry, salted fish. Main import trading partners in 2010 were Singapore (US$306 million), the UAE (US$196 million), India (US$90 million), and Malaysia (US$81 million). Imports from China (a growth area) amounted to US$69 million.

Central Bank
Maldives Monetary Authority, 3rd Floor, Umar Shopping Arcade, Chandhanee Magu, Male 20-01, Maldives. Tel: +960 323763 / 322292, fax: +960 323862, e-mail: mma@dhivehinet.net.mv, URL: http://www.mma.gov.mv
Governor: Fazeel Najeeb

MANUFACTURING, MINING AND SERVICES

Primary and Extractive Industries
Maldives has no oil reserves of its own and so imports all it needs, figures for 2010 showed that this amounted to 7,000 barrels per day.

Energy
In 2010, 30 billion kWh of electricity was produced and 28 billion kWh consumed. (Source: EIA) In 2009, President Nasheed said that the country would change to using only renewable energy sources with the aim of being carbon neutral by 2020. The Maldives are very low-lying and are threatened by any rise in sea levels.

Manufacturing
The Maldivian economy is principally based on fishing, tourism and shipping. Modern industries include fish canning, manufacture of garments, production of PVC pipes, boat building, bottling of aerated water and construction of fibre-glass boats. Estimated figures for 2007 showed that manufacturing contributed 7 per cent of GDP.

Tourism
Tourism is the major foreign currency earner and accounts for over 30 per cent of GDP. There are 87 tourist islands with a total of 208 tourist establishments offering almost 19,000 beds. There were approximately 560,000 tourists in 2004 with an annual growth rate of approximately 8 per cent. Over 50 per cent of tourists come from Europe.

Agriculture
There are no mineral resources and, apart from coconut palms (Maldivians cultivated approximately 17.77 million kg of coconuts in 2005), vegetation is sparse and cultivation virtually non-existent. All food requirements other than fish have to be imported.

Agricultural Production in 2010

Produce	Int. $'000*	Tonnes
Nuts, nes	4,033	2,200
Bananas	1,831	6,500
Meat nes	1,110	840
Fruit fresh nes	827	2,369
Vegetables fresh nes	399	2,115
Roots and tubers, nes	342	2,000
Papayas	309	1,089
Chillies and peppers. green	101	214
Tomatoes	56	151
Pulses, nes	37	70
Coconuts	35	320
Mangoes, mangosteens, guavas	32	53

* unofficial figures
Source: http://faostat.fao.org/site/339/default.aspx Food and Agriculture Organization of the United Nations, Food and Agricultural commodities production

Fishing
Principal exports are canned, frozen, dried and salted varieties of tuna and other fish. Japan is a major importer of Maldivian fish. The use of nets and trawling is prohibited and all fishing is done by pole and line. In 2010 the total catch was 95,000 tonnes.

COMMUNICATIONS AND TRANSPORT

Travel Requirements
Citizens of the USA, Canada, Australia and the EU require a valid passport and return or onward tickets. They also require a minimum of US$100, and US$50 per person per day, or a confirmed hotel reservation for the duration of their stay. Tourist visas are issued on arrival and are valid for 30 days. Travellers need a yellow fever immunisation if they are arriving from an infected area.

Repairing the damage to the transport infrastructure following the December 2004 tsunami will cost an estimated US$68 million. Many jetties and harbours were damaged or destroyed.

National Airlines
Island Aviation Services Ltd., operates domestic flights. URL: http://www.island.com.mv

Malé International Airport handles international air traffic, and in 2001 handled 49,049 aircraft, 1,629,091 passengers, 90,689 kg of mail, and 19,135,694 kg of airfreight.
There are direct flights from Colombo, Trivandrum, Dubai, Karachi, Singapore, Frankfurt, Munich, Dusseldorf, Zurich, Bucharest, Bombay, Rome, London, Narita, Doha, Vienna, Madrid, Moscow, Sharjah, Kualalumpur, Bahrain, Gatwick, Manchester and Paris.

Roads
In 2001 there were 1,937 registered cars, 12,647 motor/auto cycles, 688 lorries/trucks, 1,212 jeep landrovers, 573 taxis (used in Malé) and 573 other vehicles.

Shipping
The common mode of inter-island transport is by locally built boats known as *Dhoni*. In 2001 there were 244 registered yacht dhoni, 848 launches and 319 boats. No regular ferry service between the islands exists but crossings by *Dhoni* are frequent.

HEALTH

There are two hospitals on the main island Malé and six regional hospitals serving all the remaining islands. There are 45 smaller scale health centres and 36 health posts serving the islands. Reconstructing the health system is one of the government's priorities following the 26 December 2004 tsunami. The hospital on the island of Muli was destroyed.

In 2008, the Maldives spent approximately 13.8 per cent of its total budget on healthcare (down from 11.1 per cent in 2000), accounting for 61.2 per cent of all healthcare spending. Total expenditure on healthcare equated to 13.7 per cent of the country's GDP. Per capita expenditure on health was approximately US$566, compared with US$200 in 2000.

Figures for 2000-10 show that there are 552 physicians (16 per 10,000 population), 1,539 nurses and midwives (44.5 per 10,000 population), 285 pharmaceutical personnel and 4 dentistry personnel. There are 26 hospital beds per 10,000 population.

According to the latest WHO figures, in 2008 approximately 99 per cent of the urban population and 86 per cent of the rural population had access to improved drinking water. In the same year, 100 per cent of the urban population and 96 per cent of the rural population had access to improved sanitation. Sanitation has improved in recent years and diarrhoea now accounts for 7 per cent of childhood deaths, down from 15 per cent in 2006.

Life expectancy at birth was 75 years in 2009. The infant mortality rate in 2009 was 11 per 1,000 live births. The child mortality rate (under 5 years) was 13 per 1,000 live births. The main causes of childhood mortality are: prematurity (27 per cent), congenital abnormalities (9 per cent), birth asphyxia (12 per cent), diarrhoea (7 per cent), pneumonia (14 per cent), and malaria (3 per cent). (Source: WHO, 2011)

EDUCATION

Education is not compulsory. There are three types of formal education:
- *Kiyavaage* or *Edhuruge*, where children are taught to read the Qur'an, to read and write Dhivehi, and basic arithmetic;
- *Makthab* or *Madhurasaa*, further teaching of the Qur'an, reading and writing, arithmetic and additional subjects.
- English middle schools, primary and secondary. These schools are equipped to teach a standard curriculum. In 1984, a national curriculum was introduced in all schools. Primary education is from age six and secondary from age eleven.

Although not compulsory around 99 per cent of children of primary age attend school. There are 337 schools (many with under 100 pupils), and approximately 5,230 teachers (of whom an estimated 20 per cent are untrained). The pupil: teacher ratio is approximately 1:20. An estimated 68 per cent of pupils go onto secondary education.

The adult literacy rate is almost 100 per cent, one of the highest literacy rates in South Asia. Figures for 2006 show that 11 per cent of total government spending (7.9 per cent of GDP) went on education.

RELIGION

Over 98 per cent of the population are Muslims the majority being Sunni Muslims. There are small Christian, Hindu and Buddhist communities.

The Maldives has a religious liberty rating of 3 on a scale of 1 to 10 (10 is most freedom). (Source: World Religion Database)

COMMUNICATIONS AND MEDIA

In 2009 President Nasheed announced that the government would deregulate the state-controlled media and guarantee a free and competitive media. There is some freedom of media expression; newspapers do carry criticism of the government, but self-censorship is common and the government does have the power to close media operations.

Newspapers
Haveeru Daily Online, URL: http://www.haveeru.com.mv/
Aafathis News, URL: http://www.aafathisnews.com.mv/di/news/
Miadhu News, http://www.miadhu.com/

Broadcasting
Voice of Maldives (URL: http://www.vom.gov.mv/) and Television Maldives are government controlled. Radio licenses are very expensive. The first private radio station opened in 2007. A small number of private television stations also exist including a cable channel.

Telecommunications
The Satellite Earth Station in Villingili provides direct dialling telephones, telex as well as facsimile services to any part of the world. Telephone and facsimile service is available in all the islands. In 2009 there were estimated to be 50,000 mainline telephones and 450,000 mobile phones. In 2008 there were an estimated 70,000 internet users.

STATES OF THE WORLD

761

MALI

ENVIRONMENT

As an environmental measure, inshore coral mining has been banned. This is to guard against encroachment by the sea and land erosion.

Global warming and its relation to rising sea levels is a particular concern to the Maldives as its highest point above sea level is less than three metres. In 1987 Maldives experienced high tides which swept over the islands; much of Malé and nearby islands were underwater. On 26 December 2004 they were hit by the Indian Ocean tsunami but escaped relatively lightly: 80 people died, and 12,000 were displaced.

According to figures from the EIA, in 2010 the Maldives' emissions from the consumption of fossil fuels totalled 0.92 million metric tons of carbon dioxide, the same as the previous year. In March 2009, President Nasheed announced that the Maldives will become carbon-neutral within a decade by switching completely to renewable energy sources.

The Maldives is a party to the following international agreements: Biodiversity, Climate Change, Climate Change-Kyoto Protocol, Desertification, Hazardous Wastes, Law of the Sea, Ozone Layer Protection, and Ship Pollution.

MALI
Republic of Mali
République de Mali

Capital: Bamako (Population estimate, 2011: 1.8 million)

Head of State: Dioncounda Traore (Interim Leader) (page 1527)

National Flag: A tricolour pale-wise, green, yellow, red

CONSTITUTION AND GOVERNMENT

Constitution
The Republic of Mali, formerly the territory of French Sudan, became independent on 22 September 1960. A new government was formed in February 1994. As a result of discussions between the presidents of Ghana, Guinea and Mali at the end of 1960, the Union of African States was formed in July 1961. The Charter of the Union is designed to strengthen friendship and co-operation between the member states and to guarantee, collectively, territorial integrity and co-operation in defence.

A new constitution was approved in 1974 which created a one-party state. Single party legislative and presidential elections were held in 1979 and won by Gen. Moussa Traoré. A period of instability followed in the early 1980s, including several coup attempts. In 1990, the Tuaregs in the north of the country, clashed with the military over demands for greater autonomy. Following the overthrow of President Moussa Traoré in March 1991, the Constitution was suspended. A civilian-led government was installed. A new Constitution was approved in a national referendum on 12 January 1992. This allowed for political parties. In April 1992 a peace agreement was signed between the government and most opposing factions. Parliamentary and presidential elections were held. Alpha Oumar Konare of the Association for Democracy in Mali won the presidential election.

The Constitution of the Third Republic of Mali upholds the principles of national sovereignty and the rule of law in a secular, multi-party state. It provides for the separation of the powers of the executive, legislative and judicial organs of state.

Executive power is vested in the President of the Republic, who is elected for five years by universal suffrage. The President appoints the Prime Minister, who appoints the Council of Ministers.

To consult the constitution, please visit: http://www.wipo.int/wipolex/en/details.jsp?id=7446.

International Relations
As a former part of the French Empire in Africa, Mali has strong links with France and is a member of the West African Franc Zone organisation UEMOA. Mali is a member of several international organisations including the African Development Bank (AFDB), the Economic Community of West African States (ECOWAS), the Organisation of the Islamic Conference (OIC), and the West African Economic and Monetary Union (UEMOA).

In 1985 there was a brief border war with Burkina Faso, and relations between the two countries are still uneasy.

Recent Events
In 2002, France cancelled 40 per cent of debt owed to it by Mali, amounting to around US$79 million. In September 2004, parts of west Africa were hit by a locust plague; it was estimated that Mali lost around 45 per cent of its cereal crop.

Mali has been hit by sporadic rebellions by the Tuareg in the north of the country; the Tuareg want a greater level of regional autonomy. In June 2006 a peace deal brokered by Algerian mediators was signed by the Mali government and Tuareg rebels. However there have since been outbreaks of violence; in August 2007 Tuareg rebels were believed to behind the abduction of government soldiers and in May 2008 rebels killed 17 soldiers despite a ceasefire agreement a few weeks earlier.

In April 2007 President Toure won his second presidential election. In July the ruling coalition, the Alliance for Democracy and Progress, increased its majority in parliamentary elections.

In recent years there have been various incidents of rebel activity. In August 2007 Tuareg rebels kidnapped Malian soldiers near the Niger and Algerian borders. A ceasefire between the Tuareg rebels and the government was signed in April 2008 but did not last. In May 2008 the rebels killed 17 soldiers in an attack on an army base in the north of Mali. In December

of the same year the rebels attacked another army base resulting in 20 fatalities. The government responded and in February 2009 had gained control of all the major rebel bases. An estimated 700 rebels surrenderd and returned to the peace process.

Prime Minister Modibo Sidibe resigned along with his entire cabinet on 30 March 2011. Mr Sidibe is expected to run in next year's presidential election. The new prime minister is Cisse Mariam Kaidama Sidibe who is Mali's first female prime minister. She took office on 4 April 2011 and her new council of ministers was named shortly afterwards.

In January 2012, a Tuareg rebellion was feared following attacks in the north leading many civilians to flee to Mauritania.

In March 2012, military officers announcd on television that they had seized control of the country. The leader of the coup, Captain Amadou Sanogo, said that he had seized control to restore security and that he would restore control to an elected government once the Tuareg rebellion had been put down. Following the coup, Mali was suspended from the regional bloc, Ecowas The rebels seized the whole of the north, including the city of Timbuktu. On April 6, Tuareg rebels declared independence for the north. This has not been internationally recognised. Hundreds of people have been displaced, and this combined with a drought, are leading to fears of a humanitarian disaster. The country's first female prime minister, Cissé Mariam Kaidama Sidibé, was placed under house arrest after the March 2012 coup. Mr Toure and his family fled to Senegal. On 12 April the speaker of parliament, Dioncounda Traore, was sworn in as intermin leader. In a deal with Ecowas, it was agreed that he would remain as interim leader for one year. The day after the deal, Mr Traore was beaten unconscious by protesters.

In May 2012, the two rebel groups controlling northern Mali, announced they were to merge and turn their territory into an Islamist state. The two groups, the secular Tuareg MNLA and the Islamist Ansar Dine seized the land following the March coup. Ansar Dine has already started to impose Islamic law on towns such as Timbuktu.

In July 2012, a meeting of Western African leaders called for a national unity government to be formed and so bring to an end to the political crisis.

Also in July, Ansar Dine and its Al-Qaeda ally turned against the MNLA and took control of the cities of Timbuktu, Kidal and Gao. They destroyed many Muslim shrines that they said offended their puritan views. Later that month at the request of the Malian government, the International Criminal Court began a preliminary inquiry into alleged atrocities committed in rebel-held northern areas.

Interim president Dioncounda Traoré announced a government of national unity on 20 August 2012. Several ministers from the previous government left their posts. The cabinet has increased to 31 members (of which four are women). Virtually all the major political parties are represented.

In September it was reported that Islamist rebels had captured the central town of Douentza.

In December 2012, Prime Minister Diarra resigned from his post, after being arrested by soldiers. The rest of the government also stood down. President Traore appointed a presidential official, Django Sissoko, to succeed him. The UN and US threatened to impose sanctions.

In January 2013, Islamist fighters moved south and captured the central town of Konna. President Traore then asked France for help. France responded by sending troops and carrying out air strikes on rebel bases. At the end of January French led troops took control of Timbuktu airport. Following apparent weakening of the Islamist position, France announced it would scale down its military intervention in April 2013.

In June 2013 the government signed a peace deal with Tuareg nationalist rebels. The rebels agreed to hand over the town of Kidal.

The president reshuffled the cabinet in June 2013, just ahead of elections scheduled for July.

The state of emergency, in place since January 2013, was lifted in July 2013.

Legislature

The legislative body is the unicameral National Assembly, which is elected for five years by universal suffrage. The chamber has 147 deputies, of whom 13 are elected to represent the interests of Malians living abroad.

National Assembly, (*Assemblée Nationale*), BP 284, Bamako, Mali. Tel: +223 221 5724, fax: +223 221 0374, e-mail: madou@blonba.malinet.ml. URL: http://www.blonba.malinet.ml

Council of Ministers (as at June 2013)

Prime Minister: Django Sissoko (page 1515)
Minister of Economy and Humanitarian Work: Mamadou Namory Traore:
Minister of Defence and Veterans: Gen. Yamoussa Camara
Minister of Foreign Affairs and International Co-operation: Tieman Coulibaly
Minister of Territorial Administration, Decentralisation and Land Management: Col. Moussa Sinko Coulibaly
Minister of Finance: Abdel Karim Konate
Minister of Trade & Industry: Tièna Coulibaly
Minister of Mines: Dr Amadou Baba Sy
Minister of Education, Literacy and Promotion of National Languages: Bocar Moussa Diarra
Minister of Higher Education and Scientific Research: Messa Ould Mohamed Lady
Minister of Work, Civil Service and Relations with Institutions: Me Demba Traore
Minister for Internal Security and Civil Protection: Gen. Tiefing Konaté
Minister of Agriculture: Baba Berthé
Minister of Justice and Keeper of the Seals: Malick Coulibaly
Minister of Transport and Equipment: Col. Abdoulaye Koumare
Minister of Health: Soumana Makadji
Minister of Handicrafts and Tourism: Yaya Ag Mohamed Ali
Minister of Town Planning & Housing: David Sagara
Minister of Employment and Professional Training: Dr Diallo Kattra
Minister of Post and New Technolgies: Bréhima Tolo
Minister for Women, the Family and Children: Mme Alwata Sahi
Minister for Energy & Water: Makan Tounkara
Minister of Environment and Sanitation: Ousmane Ag Rhissa
Minister of Youth & Sport: Hamèye Mahalmadane
Minister of Social Development, Solidarity and Senior Citizens: Dr Mamadou Sidibé
Minister of Livestock and Fishing: Diané Mariam Koné
Minister of Religious Affairs and Worship: Dr Yacouba Traoré
Minister of Communication, Government Spokesperson: Manga Dembelé
Minister of Culture: Bruno Maiga
Minister of Malians Abroad and African Integration: Marimpa Samoura

Ministries

Office of the Prime Minister, BP 97, quartier du Fleuve, Bamako, Mali. Tel: +223 2022 5534, fax: +223 2029 9403
Ministry of Culture, BP 4075, Korofina, Bamako, Mali. Tel: +223 2024 6663, , fax: +223 2023 2646, e-mail: info@culture.gov.ml, URL: http://www.culture.gov.ml
Ministry of Justice, Keeper of the Seals, BP 97, quartier du Fleuve, Koulouba, Bamako, Mali. Tel: +223 2022 2651, e-mail: ucprodej@afribone.net.ml, URL: http://www.justicemali.org
Ministry for the Promotion of Women, Children and Family Affairs, Rue 305, Porte 160, Torokorobougou, BP 2688, Bamako, Mali. Tel: +223 2022 7442, e-mail: mpfef@fib.com, URL: http://www.fib.com/minifef
Ministry of Handicrafts and Tourism, Badalabougou Semagesco, BP E-2211, Bamako, Mali. Tel: +223 2023 8201, fax: +223 2023 8201, e-mail: malitourisme@afribone.net.ml, URL: http://www.malitourisme.com
Ministry of Foreign Affairs and International Co-operation, Cité du Niger, Route de l'Hotel Mandé, Bamako, Mali. Tel: +223 2022 5092 , fax: +223 2022 5954, e-mail: info@maliensdelexterieur.gov.ml, URL: http://www.maliensdelexterieur.gov.ml
Ministry of Education, Bamako, Mali. Tel: +223 2022 2450 / 2125 / 2126, fax: +223 2022 7767, URL: http://www.education.gov.ml
Ministry of Health, BP 232, Koulouba, Bamako, Mali. Tel: +223 2022 5302, fax: +223 2023 0203
Ministry of Economy, Industry and Trade, BP 234, Koulouba, Bamako, Mali. Tel: +223 2022 0903, fax: +223 2022 0269, URL: http://www.meic.gov.ml
Ministry of Housing and Town Planning, Bamako, Mali. Tel: +223 2022 0548
Ministry of Agriculture, Livestock and Fishing, BP 1676, Bamako, Mali. Tel: +223 2022 2785
Ministry of Equipment and Transport, BP 78, Bamako, Mali. Tel: +223 2022 2901
Ministry of Defence and Veterans, BP 2083, route de Koulouba, Bamako, Mali. Tel: +223 2022 5021, fax: +223 2022 0605
Ministry of Territorial Administration and Local Communities, BP 215, Bamako, Mali. Tel: +223 2022 4212, e-mail: matcl@matcl.gov.ml, URL: http://www.matcl.gov.ml
Ministry of Mines, Energy and Water Resources, BP 238, Bamako, Mali. Tel: +223 2022 3547
Ministry of the Environment, BP 1676, Bamako, Mali. Tel: +223 2023 1939
Ministry of Security and Civil Protection, Bamako, Mali. Tel: +223 2022 3431
Ministry of Communications and Information Technology, Bamako, Mali. Tel: +223 2022 2647, fax: +223 2022 8319, URL: http://www.mcnt.gov.ml
Ministry of Social Development, Solidarity and the Elderly, Bamako, Mali. Tel: +223 2023 1475 / 1345, fax: +223 2023 7834
Ministry of Civil Service, Reform and Relations with the State, BP 80, route de Koulouba, Bamako, Mali. Tel: +223 2022 3431, fax: +223 2022 3431
Ministry of Youth and Sports, BP 91, route de Koulouba, Bamako, Mali. Tel: +223 2022 3153, fax: +223 2022 1087, URL: http://www.undp.org/fomlil
Ministry of Fisheries, URL: http://www.mep.gov.ml
Ministry of Malians Abroad and African Integration, Tel: +223 2021 8149, fax: +223 2022 0757
Ministry of Economy and Finance, BP 234. Koulouba, Bamako, Mali. Tel: +223 2022 5687, fax: +223 2022 8853

Ministry of Employment and Professional Training, BP 80, route de Koulouba, Bamako, Mali. Tel: +223 2022 3431, fax: +223 2022 3431
Ministry of Foreign Affairs and International Co-operation, Koulouba, Bamako, Mali. Tel: +223 2022 2150, fax: +223 2022 5226, e-mail: info@maliensdelexterieur.gov.ml, URL: http://maliensdelexterieur.gov.ml
Ministry of Education, BP 71, Bamako, Mali. Tel: +223 2022 5780, fax: +223 2022 2126, e-mail: info@education.gov.ml, URL: http://www.education.gov.ml
Ministry of Agriculture, BP 1676, Bamako, Mali. Tel: +223 2022 2785
Ministry of Communications and New Technology, BP 116, Bamako, Mali. Tel: +223 2022 2647, fax: +223 2022 8319
Ministry of Justice and Keeper of the Seals, BP 97, quartier du Fleuve, Koulouba, Bamako, Mali. Tel: +223 2022 2651, fax: +223 2023 0063, e-mail: ucprodej@malinet.net.ml, URL: http://www.justicemali.org

Political Parties

Alliance for Democracy in Mali (ADEMA); Front for Democracy and the Republic (FDR); Party for African Solidarity, Democracy, and Integration (SADI).

Elections

Elections were held in April 1997 but were annulled by the courts. The re-run held in July 1997 was boycotted by some parties, and ADEMA (the Alliance for Democracy in Mali) won over 80 per cent of the National Assembly seats. Preliminary results of elections in July 2002 indicated a victory for ADEMA , but this result was overturned by the constitutional court in August 2002. The most recent legislative elections took place in July 2007; ADEMA , which has dominated government coalitions since 1992, increased its representation in the National Assembly, and the Alliance for Democracy and Progress (ADP) coalition, comprising ADEMA, the Union for the Republic and Democracy (URD) and the National Rally for Democracy (RND), retained its overall majority.

Presidential elections were held in 2007 when Amadou Toumani Toure was elected for a second term in office. He reappointed the cabinet. The age of suffrage is 18.

Before the 2012 coup, the next presidential election was due in April and May 2012. It is scheduled for 7 July 2013.

Legislative elections were due to take place July 2012 but were again delayed. They are currently scheduled for 21 July 2013. The results were not known at the time of going to press.

Diplomatic Representation

British Embassy Liaison Office (The British Embassy closed in 2003, all staff reside in Dakar, Senegal), URL: http://ukinsenegal.fco.gov.uk/en/
Embassy of Mali, 2130 R Street NW, Washington D.C. 20009, USA. Tel: +1 202 332 2249, fax: +1 202 332 6603, e-mail: info@maliembassy-us.org, URL: http://www.maliembassy.us/
Ambassador: H.E. Al Maamoun Baba Lamine Keita
US Embassy, Rue Rochester NY and rue Mohamed V, B.P. 34, Bamako, Mali. +223 222 5663, fax: +223 222 7112, e-mail: ipc@usa.org.ml, URL: http://mali.usembassy.gov/
Ambassador: Mary Beth Leonard
Mali Permanent Mission to the United Nations, 111 East 69th Street, New York, NY 10021, USA. Tel: +1 212 737 4100/6788, fax: +1 212 472 3778, URL: http://www.un.int/wcm/content/site/mali/
Ambassador & Permanent Representative: currently vacant

LEGAL SYSTEM

The legal system is based on French civil law and customary law. The Constitution guarantees the independence of the judiciary.

There is a Supreme Court and a Court of Appeal in Bamako, as well as Sectional Courts at Kayes, Segou and Skiasso with circuits. The Constitutional Court has final jurisdiction in constitutional matters, and a High Court of Justices has the authority to try senior government officials accused of treason. There are also two magistrate courts of first instance, courts for labor disputes, and a special court of state security. The president heads the Superior Judicial, which supervises judicial activity, and the Ministry of Justice appoints judges and oversees law enforcement.

The Supreme Court is made up of 19 members, nominated for five years, and has both judicial and administrative powers. The judicial section has three civil chambers and one criminal chamber. The administrative section deals with appeals and rulings.

Constitutional provisions for freedom of speech, press, assembly, association, and religion are generally respected. However, the government has considerable influence over the judiciary. There have been recent instances of police abuses of civilians, prison conditions are poor, and there can be long delays before cases come to trial. President Amadou Toumani Touré introduced a bill to abolish the death penalty in 2007 but protests from religious groups put the bill on hold. Though the death penalty has not been enforced in Mali since 1979, banning it would go against Islamic principles.

In August 2009, President Toumani Touré bowed to pressure by Muslim groups and reluctantly announced that he would not sign a new family law, and returned it to parliament for review. The law would have given greater rights to women; women would no longer be required to obey their husbands and would have gained greater inheritance rights. Muslim leaders called also objected to the fact that marriage is defined as a secular institution.

Commission nationale consultative des droits de l'homme, BP E 2556, Bamako, Mali. Tel: +223 239908, fax: +223 238954

MALI

LOCAL GOVERNMENT

The country is divided into eight regions: Kayes, Segou, Mopti, Koulikoro, Kidal, Gao, Sikassao and Timbukto, and the capital district of Bamako. Each has an appointed governor. The regions are made up of administrative districts (*cercles*) administered by a commandant. Plans were drawn up for further decentralisation of municipal councils, elected mayors, and elected local officials. This process is underway there are so far 702 elected municipal councils headed by mayors.

AREA AND POPULATION

Area
The Republic of Mali is situated in west Africa and is landlocked. It borders Algeria to the north, Mauritania to the west, and Niger to the east. In the south it borders Senegal, Guinea, Cote d'Ivoire and Burkina Faso. Its area is 1,240,190 sq km. The climate is equatorial, mainly hot and dry. Around 60 per cent of the land is covered by the Sahara desert. The Niger river basin in the south and east of the country provides fertile growing areas. The Bafing and Bakoy rivers known respectively as the black and white rivers flow through Mali as do the Bani, Falémé, Karakoro and Sankarani rivers.

To view a map, consult http://www.un.org/Depts/Cartographic/map/profile/mali.pdf

Population
In 2010, the population was approximately 15.37 million. The average annual growth rate was 3.1 per cent for the period 2000-10. The population is expected to double by 2020. In 2003, population density was 10 people per km. sq. Around 10 per cent of the population is nomadic.

The population is ethnically diverse including the Manding, Fulani, Songhai, Tuareg and Mianka. Women make up 51.7 per cent of the population.

Major towns are: Bamako (population approx. 1.8 million); Segou (110,000), Sikasso (120,000), Mopti (90,000), Gao (65,000), Kayes (65,000), and Timbukto (38,000). There is increasing migration to urban areas (5.4 per cent in 1995). By 2010, an estimated 36 per cent of the population lived in urban areas.

The official language is French. Other national languages are: Bambara, which is spoken by around 80 per cent of the population, Dogoso, Fulfulde, Koyracini, Mandinka, Berber and Arabic.

Births, Marriages, Deaths
In 2009, estimated average life expectancy was 50 years for males and 56 years for females. Healthy life expectancy was 49 years. In 2010, some 47 per cent of the population was aged under 15 and 4 per cent was over 60. The median age was 16 years. Average fertility was 5.4 children per woman. The crude birth rate in 2010 was 46.4 per 1,000 population and the crude death rate was 13.5 per 1,000 population. (Source: http://www.who.int, World Health Statistics 2012)

Public Holidays 2014
1 January: New Year
20 January: Memorial Day
14 January: Mawlid al-Nabi (Birthday of the Prophet)*
26 March: Day of the Martyrs
1 May: Labour Day
25 May: African Unity Day
29 June: 1st Day of Ramadan*
29 July: End of Ramadan (Eid-El-Fitr)*
22 September: Independence Day
5 October: Feast of the Sacrifice*
25 December: Christmas
*Islamic holidays are dependent on the sighting of the moon and so dates can vary.

EMPLOYMENT

In 2008 the estimated labour force was 4.0 million. Some 70 per cent of the population is engaged in the agricultural and fishing sectors. 15 per cent work in services, and 15 per cent in industry and commerce.

BANKING AND FINANCE

Currency
The monetary unit is the Mali CFA franc.

GDP/GNP, Inflation, National Debt
Mali is among the poorest nations of the world and in 2000-09, approximately 50 per cent of the population were living below the national poverty line. Since the 1980s, the government has implemented many economic reforms including abolishing price controls and import quotas, and revising investment codes. Many public sector industries have been privatised or partially privatised. The country is dependent on foreign aid from multi-lateral organisations, western countries and China. In 2011, Mali received a US$46 million but it was cancelled in March 2012 after a coup toppled the president and Islamic rebels seized control of several northern cities. The EU and the US suspended aid. In November 2012 the IMF agreed a Rapid Credit Facility US$18 million loan. There is expected to be a budget shortfall of US$110 million in 2013. The government has said it will freeze spending if it does not fund the gap with aid.

GDP has grown steadily in recent years. In 2009, GDP was US$9 billion with a growth rate of 4.5 per cent. GDP was put at US$8,800.0 million in 2008 up from US$7,113.00 million in 2007 with a growth rate of 4.2 per cent. GDP was estimated to be US$10.1 billion in 2011 with a growth rate of 2.7 per cent. The service sector contributes around 45 per cent of GDP, agriculture, 40 per cent and industry 22 per cent. Per capita income was US$1,000 in 2011.

In 2011, inflation was 2.75 per cent, up from 1.2 per cent in 2010. External debt was estimated to be US$2.2 billion in 2011.

Balance of Payments / Imports and Exports
Major trade partners are: Côte d'Ivoire, France, Senegal, China, the Netherlands, Spain, United Kingdom, the USA, Germany, Thailand, Japan, Italy and Switzerland. Main export commodities are cotton, livestock, fish, leather, groundnuts, diamonds and gold. Agriculture accounts for over 80 per cent of the exports. Major imported commodities include machinery, vehicles, chemical, textiles, petroleum, and food.

External Trade, US$ million

	2005	2006	2007
Trade balance	-803.18	199.58	136.91
Exports	625.14	1,366.57	1,329.67
Imports	1,498.32	1,166.99	1,192.76

Source: African Development Bank

Exports amounted to US$2.2 billion in 2010 and imports cost US$2.95 billion.

Central Bank
Banque Centrale des Etats de l'Afrique de l'Ouest, PO Box 3108, Avenue Abdoulaye Fadiga, Dakar, Senegal. Tel: +221 8 390500, fax: +221 8 239335, e-mail: webmaster@bceao.int, URL: http://www.bceao.int
Governor: Tiémoko Meyliet Kone

MANUFACTURING, MINING AND SERVICES

Primary and Extractive Industries
According to geographical surveys there is a rich supply of iron, bauxite, lithium, manganese, phosphate and salt, but at present only three of these are mined, namely phosphates at Bourem, gold at Kalana and marble at Selinkeni. The following table shows estimated reserves of mineable products:

Estimated Reserves

Product	Tonnes	Area
Gold	800	Kalana
Phosphate	20 million	Tilemsi
Limestone	40 million	Bafoulabe, Hombori
Rock salt	53 million	Taoudenit
Bauxite	1.2 billion	Kayes
Iron	2 billion	Kayes
Manganese	10 million	Ansongo
Bituminous-shale	10 billion	
Marble	60 million	Selinkeni
Crypse	405,000	
Oil Shale	na	Gao region

Gold mining is now the largest mining activity and is the country's third largest export after cotton and livestock. Recent figures show that gold makes up 60 per cent of Mali's export earnings and cotton, 24 per cent.

Mali has no oil reserves and so imports all it needs, figures for 2011 put this at 6,000 barrels per day.

Energy
Figures for 2010 show that Mali generated 0.52 billion kWh of electricity and consumed 0.48 billion kWh.

Manufacturing
This is focused on agricultural products and makes up some 8 per cent of GDP. Main industries are food and fish processing and beverage bottling. Textiles, cigarettes and plastics also contribute to the GDP.

Tourism
Tourism is becoming increasingly important to Mali's economy. 1995 saw 42,000 visitors to Mali, generating receipts of US$26 million; this rose to 153,000 visitors in 2006 earning some US$167 millions.

Agriculture
Mali has a substantial agricultural sector. 1.4 million hectares are cultivable. Most farming is either small scale or subsistence. Over 80 per cent of the population works in agriculture. It was badly hit by severe droughts in the 1970s and government restraints on production. Agricultural reforms started in the late 1980s and have helped the country produce surplus crops. Reforms include improved government management, open markets and fewer price controls. Cotton is a major export commodity, and tea, sugar cane, and tobacco are also exported. The most fertile farming area is by the Niger river, which is used for irrigating some 60,000 hectares of rice and sugar cane cultivation. In 2004 Mali lost an estimated 50 per cent of its cereal crop to a locust plague. This was compounded the following year when the rains failed.

There are estimated to be 800,000 sq km. of forest. About 1,195,440 hectares of the area is reserved for hunting, mainly elephants.

In the 1970s, 40 per cent of the country's livestock was lost due to drought. However, animal husbandry is well-developed. In 2003 the number of cattle, sheep and goats increased to 56 million. There were over 1 million donkeys, horses, camels and pigs. Bee-keeping is another industry and 4,000 tonnes of honey and some 200 tonnes of beeswax are produced annually. On average, animal produce makes up 20 per cent of GNP.

Agricultural Production in 2010

Produce	Int. $'000*	Tonnes
Rice, paddy	630,064	2,308,230
Indigenous cattle meat	420,747	155,753
Goat milk, whole, fresh	231,293	689,234
Millet	216,309	1,373,340
Sorghum	168,345	1,256,810
Indigenous goat meat	166,297	69,404
Maize	156,199	1,403,580
Indigenous sheep meat	133,264	48,944
Groundnuts, with shell	131,224	314,458
Cashewapple	114,184	121,000
Cotton ;omt	111,478	78,000
Camel milk, whole, fresh	102,945	301,916

* unofficial figures
Source: http://faostat.fao.org/site/339/default.aspx Food and Agriculture Organization of the United Nations, Food and Agricultural commodities production

Fishing employs around 300,000 people and Mali exports fish to Côte d'Ivoire and Ghana. The total catch in 2010 was estimated at 100,000 tonnes. Fishing has declined in recent years, in part because of droughts and diversion of rivers for irrigation.

COMMUNICATIONS AND TRANSPORT

Travel Requirements
Citizens of the USA, Canada, Australia and the EU require a passport valid for six months, a return or onward ticket and a visa. Citizens of ECOWAS (Economic Community of West African States) may enter Mali without a visa. Other nationals should contact the embassy to check visa requirements. Transit passengers continuing their journey within 24 hours, with onward documentation and not leaving the airport do not require a visa.

Travellers must have international vaccination cards with a current yellow fever immunisation.

National Airlines
Several international airline companies link Mali with other countries. Internal connections are provided by the national airline company MALITAS.

Railways
There is a rail link from Bamako - Dakar, Senegal (1,250 km), the journey takes around 50 hours, the service was suspended in 2009.

Roads
In all, Mali has 4,000 km of tarred roads and 10,500 km of tracks. There are a number of main roads to the coast, Bamako - Abidjan (1,115 km), Bamako - Conakry (1,100 km) and Bamako - Lome (1,400 km). Vehicles are driven on the right.

Shipping
During the high season (approximately 6 months) the river Niger is navigable from Koulikoro, the main administrative region to Gao via Segou and Mopti.

HEALTH

The government has committed to increase its spending on health, and a programme to increase the number of children being immunised is underway. In 2009, the government spent approximately 10.0 per cent of its total budget on healthcare (up from 8.9 per cent in 2000), accounting for 47.2 per cent of all healthcare spending. External resources account for 26.3 per cent of expenditure on health. All private expenditure is out-of-pocket expenditure. Total expenditure on healthcare equated to 5.5 per cent of the country's GDP. Per capita expenditure on health was approximately US$33, compared with US$15 in 2000. Figures for 2005-10 show that there are an estimated 729 physicians (0.5 per 10,000 population), 4,383 nurses and midwives (3 per 10,000 population) and 12 dentistry personnel. There is estimated to be one hospital bed per 10,000 population. Emigration of healthcare personnel is a problem.

Poor living conditions contribute to the high child mortality rates and the generally low life expectancy (53 years). One in four children does not reach their fifth birthday. The infant mortality rate (likelihood of dying before first birthday) is estimated to be 99 per 1,000 live births. An estimated 38.5 per cent of children are classed as stunted and 27.9 as underweight (2005-11). Poverty and hard geographical and geophysical conditions, including droughts, are contributing factors. In 2010, 64 per cent of the population had regular access to drinking water. In the same year 22 per cent of the population had access to improved sanitation.

In 1997 official figures indicated that 2 per cent of the population between the ages of 15 and 49 had AIDS; this figure was put at 1.7 per cent in 2003, over 59 per cent of whom were women. The rate was estimated to have fallen to 1 per cent in 2009. Average life expectancy in 2009 was 53 years. The child mortality rate (likelihood of dying before fifth birthday) is estimated to be 178 per 1,000 live births. The main causes of childhood mortality are: prematurity causes (11 per cent), diarrhoea (14 per cent), pneumonia (20 per cent), malaria (16 per cent) and measles (3 per cent). Immunization rates against major diseases have risen for infants: in 2010 63 per cent of children received the measles vaccinations. Rates for the DTP3, HepB3 and Hib3 vaccinations were all over 75 per cent. Just 27 per cent of children sleep under insecticide-treated nets. Approximately 32 per cent received some anti-malarial treatment. (Source: http://www.who.int, World Health Statistics 2012)

EDUCATION

In 2007 primary school enrolment was 63 per cent. Secondary education enrolment in 2002 was under 20 per cent and just two per cent were engaged in higher education. General enrolment is much higher in urban areas. Enrolment by gender is 65 per cent boys, 35 per cent girls. Adult literacy was 26.2 per cent in 2006. The government is committed to increased spending on education and health, and aims to have increased enrolment to 50 per cent by 2001 and by 90 per cent in 2020. Figures for 2007 showed that 16.8 per cent of government spending went on education, 60 per cent of which went on primary education.

RELIGION

87 per cent of the population are Muslim, 10 per cent hold traditional African beliefs, and 3.0 per cent are Christian.

Mali has a religious liberty rating of 10 on a scale of 1 to 10 (10 is most freedom). (Source: World Religion Database)

COMMUNICATIONS AND MEDIA

The media is relatively free.

Newspapers
Mali has a relatively free press producing more that 40 independent newspapers including the state-owned L'Essor (URL: http://www.essor.gov.ml), Le Republicain (URL: http://www.lerepublicain.net.ml), and L'Aurore.

Broadcasting
Television broadcasts are provided by Office de la Radiodiffusion Television du Mali (ORTM) in French and other local languages. There are also two private broadcasters. Radio is also provided by ORTM which provides national and regional stations.
URL: http://ww.ortm.net

Telecommunications
The system is improving nationally with increasing rural coverage. The country has an estimated 80,000 telephone landlines, over 3 million mobile phones are in use. The internet is also available, but just 200,000 people have regular access.

ENVIRONMENT

The expansion of the Sahara desert is a big environmental problem for Mali; it covers around 60 per cent of the land and grows each year covering previously fertile land. The scarcity of potable water is a huge concern.

Mali is party to the following international agreements: Biodiversity, Climate Change, Climate Change-Kyoto Protocol, Desertification, Endangered Species, Hazardous Wastes, Law of the Sea, Ozone Layer Protection, and Wetlands.

According to the figures from the EIA, in 2010 Mali's emissions from the consumption of fossil fuels totalled 0.89 million metric tons of carbon dioxide, up from 0.74 million metric tons in 2009.

MALTA
Republic of Malta
Repubblika ta' Malta

Capital: Valletta (Population estimate: 7,000)

Head of State: George Abela (President) (page 1371)

National Flag: Two equal vertical stripes, white at the hoist and red at the fly. A representation of the George Cross, awarded to Malta by His Majesty King George VI on 15 April 1942, is carried, edged with red, in the canton of the white stripe.

CONSTITUTION AND GOVERNMENT

Constitution
In 1814 Malta became a crown colony of the British Empire, and in 1942 Malta was awarded the George Cross, the highest civilian decoration, for heroism in defending the islands during the second world war. Malta became an independent state on 21 September 1964. Malta was, until 1974, a Constitutional Monarchy with Queen Elizabeth II as Queen of Malta and a Governor-General representing her in Valletta. In December 1974 the Constitution was modified to make Malta a Republic. The Head of State was henceforth the President. Under the Constitution the Office of the President becomes vacant after five years from the date of appointment. He appoints the Prime Minister on whose advice he appoints the other Ministers, the Chief Justice, the Judges and the Attorney General. Executive power lies with the Prime Minister and Cabinet, on the Westminster Model.

Following the 1981 general election when the Christian Democrat Nationalist Party won an absolute majority of votes but was prevented from winning a majority of seats in parliament, the Constitution was amended to provide that any political party winning more than 50 per cent of all valid votes (but less than 50 per cent of elected members) should have the number of its Members of Parliament increased in order to have a majority in the House of Representatives.

To consult the constitution, please visit: http://president.gov.mt/constitution_malta?l=1.

International Relations
Malta is a strong and active member of the Commonwealth and has strong ties with the UK. Malta is also a member of the UN, the Council of Europe, and the Organisation for Co-operation and Security in Europe.

Geographically Malta is close to North Africa, particularly Libya (which is just 180 miles away); Malta has close economic ties in the region and is a supporter of Libya's entry to the EuroMed Partnership should Libya apply to join.

Recent Events
In July 1990, Malta submitted an application to become a member of the European Union; the application was suspended in November 1996, and a request to re-activate the application was made in September 1998. In 2002 at the EU summit held in Copenhagen, Malta was formally invited to join the EU. A referendum was held in Malta in March 2003 and 54 per cent of those who voted said yes to EU membership. Malta became a member on May 1 2004 and ratified the proposed EU constitution in July 2005.

Malta adopted the Euro as its legal currency as of January 1 2008.

In May 2011 a referendum was hell, the question being, should divorce be made legal in Malta if the married couple has been separated or living apart for at least four years; that there is no reasonable hope for reconciliation; that adequate maintenance is guaranteed; that children are protected. The yes camp won the vote and so the matter subsequently went before parliament which passed the law.

In January 2012, the IMF warned that Malta's economy was threatened by the global economic crisis. Its credit rating was downgraded by Standard & Poor's rating agency.

Legislature
The legislature of Malta is unicameral, 65 directly elected members sit in the *Il-Kamra Tad-Deputati*, House of Representatives. The life of the House of Representatives, unless dissolved sooner, is five years, after which a general election is held.
Il-Kamra Tad-Deputati, The Palace, CMR 02, Valletta, Malta. Tel: +356 21 222294, fax: +356 21 242552, URL: http://www.parliament.gov.mt

Cabinet (as at June 2013)
Prime Minister: Dr Joseph Muscat (page 1483)
Minister for European Affairs and Implementation of the Election Manifesto: Louis Grech (page 1433)
Minister for Foreign Affairs: George Vella (page 1531)
Minister for Tourism: Karmenu Vella
Minister for the Economy, Investment and Small Business: Christian Cardona (page 1400)
Minister for Gozo: Anton Refalo
Minister for Infrastructure, & Transport and Communications: Joe Mizzi
Minister for Sustainable Development, the Environment and Climate Change: Leo Brincat
Minister for Education and the Employment: Evarist Bartolo

Minister for Social Dialogue and Civil Liberties: Helena Dalli
Minister of Finance: Edward Scicluna
Minister of Health: Godfrey Farrugia
Minister for Energy and Water Conservation: Konrad Mizzi
Minister of Home Affairs and National Security: Dr Emanuel Mallia
Minister for the Family: Marie-Louise Coleiro Preca

Ministries
Office of the Prime Minister, Auberge de Castille, Valletta VLT 2000, Malta. Tel: +356 2200 1852, fax: +356 2200 1851. e-mail: customercare.opm@gov.mt, URL: http://opm.gov.mt/
Ministry for Justice and Home Affairs, Auberge d' Aragon, Independence Square, Valletta VLT 2000, Malta. Tel: +356 2295 7000, fax: +356 2295 7348, e-mail: mjha@gov.mt, URL: http://www.mjha.gov.mt/
Ministry for Social Policy, Palazzo Ferreria, 310 Republic Street, Valletta CMR02, Malta. URL: http://www.msp.gov.mt
Ministry for Resources and Rural Affairs, Baarriera Wharf, Valletta VLT 1970, Malta. Tel: +356 2295 2000, fax: +356 2295 2212, e-mail: info.mrra@gov.mt, URL: http://www.mrra.gov.mt
Ministry of Education, Employment and the Family, Casa Leon, Sta Venera, Malta. Tel: +356 2598 2404, fax: +356 2598 2120, e-mail: communications.moed@gov.mt, URL: http://www.education.gov.mt
Ministry for Gozo, St Francis Square, Victoria, Gozo. Tel: +356 2156 1482, fax: +356 2155 9360, e-mail: fo.mog@gov.mt, URL: http://www.gozo.gov.mt/
Ministry of Finance, the Economy and Investment, Maison Demandols, South Street, Valletta VLT 2000, Malta. Tel: +356 2124 9640, fax: +356 2599 8244, e-mail: info.mfin@gov.mt, URL: http://www.mfin.gov.mt
Ministry of Health, the Elderly and Community Care, Palazzo Ferreria, 310 Republic Street, Valletta VLT 2000, Malta. Tel: +356 2590 3100, fax: +356 2590 3216, e-mail: info.mfss@gov.mt, URL: http://www.mfss.gov.mt/
Ministry for Infrastructure, Transport and Communications, 168 Triq id-Dejqa, Valletta VLT 1433, Malta. Tel: +356 2122 6808, fax: +356 2125 0685, e-mail: mitc@gov.mt, URL: http://www.mitc.gov.mt/
Ministry of Foreign Affairs, Palazzo Parisio, Merchant's Street, Valletta VLT 1171, Malta. Tel: +356 2204 2340, fax: +356 2124 2853, e-mail: info.mfa@gov.mt, URL: http://www.foreign.gov.mt/
Ministry for Resources and the Rural Affairs, Baarriera Wharf, Valletta VLT 1970, Malta. Tel: +356 2295 2000, fax: +356 2295 2212, e-mail: info.mrra@gov.mt, URL: http://www.mrra.gov.mt/

Elections
The country is divided into 13 electoral divisions, each division returning five members. Election is by universal adult suffrage on the principle of proportional representation using the Single Transferable Vote system. The voting age is eighteen.

In March 2003 Malta held a referendum on whether they should join the EU and 54 per cent of voters voted to join. Malta became a member of the EU on May 1 2004.

In March 2004, Prime Minister Edward Fenech Adami resigned and former Speaker Lawrence Gonzi was sworn into the post. Six days later Mr Adami was elected president. George Abela was elected president on 12 January 2009. The next presidential election is due to take place in 2014.

The most recent parliamentary elections were held on 9 March 2013. The Labour Party won with 38 seats and the Nationalist Party won 29 seats.

Political Parties
Partit Tal-Haddiema (Malta Labour Party), National Labour Centre, Milend Street, Hamrun HMR 02, Malta. Tel: +356 249900, fax: +356 244204, URL: http://www.partitlaburista.org/home
Leader: Joseph Muscat
Partit Nazzjonalista (Nationalist Party), Dar Centrali PN, Pieta, Malta. Tel: +356 243641, fax: +356 243640, URL: http://www.pn.org.mt
Leader: Lawrence Gonzi
Alternattiva Demokratika, 149 Archbishop Street, Valletta, Malta. Tel: +356 240334, fax: +356 224745, URL: http://www.alternattiva.org.mt
Secretary General: Michael Brigulio

Diplomatic Representation
Embassy of the Republic of Malta, 2017 Connecticut Avenue, N.W, Washington, DC 20008, USA Tel: +1 202 462 3611/2, fax: +1 202 387 5470, URL: http://www.mfa.gov.mt/Default.aspx?MDIS=504
Ambassador: Joseph Cole
Embassy of the Republic of Malta, 36-38 Piccadilly, London W1V OPQ, United Kingdom. Tel: +44 (0)20 7292 4800 / 734 1821, fax: +44 (0)20 7734 1831/2, e-mail: maltahighcommission.london@gov.mt, URL: http://www.foreign.gov.mt/london
High Commissioner: Joseph Zammit Tabona
American Embassy, 3rd Floor, Development House, St. Anne Street, Floriana, Malta, PO Box 535, Valletta, Malta. Tel: +356 235960, fax: +356 223322, e-mail: usembassy@kemmunet.net.mt, URL: http://malta.usembassy.gov/
Ambassador: Gina Abercrombie-Winstanley

British High Commission, Whitehall Mansions, Ta'Xbiex Seafront, Ta'Xbiex MSD 11, Malta GC. Tel: +356 2323 0000, Fax: +356 2323 2216, e-mail: bhc@vol.net.mt, URL: http://www.ukinmalta.fco.gov.uk
High Commissioner: Louise Stanton
Permanent Mission of Malta to the United Nations, 249 East 35th Street, New York, NY 10016, USA. Tel: +1 212 7252345/9, fax: +1 212 779 7097, e-mail: malta-un.newyork@gov.mt
Ambassador and Permanent Representative: Christopher Grima

LEGAL SYSTEM

The legal system consists of enactments of the Parliament of Malta and those of the British Parliament not repealed or replaced by enactments of the Maltese legislature. Maltese Civil Law derives largely from Roman Law, while British Law has had great influence on public law.

The Courts of Civil Jurisdiction are divided into two separate tiers, the Superior Courts made up of the Constitutional Court, the Court of Appeal, the Criminal Court, the Civil Court and the Commercial Court and the Inferior Courts made up of the Court of Magistrates, Juvenile Court and the Small Claims Tribunal. Gozo has its own Court of Magistrates.

In 1987, Malta adopted the European Convention on Human Rights as part of its laws and Maltese citizens have the right to appeal to the European Court of Human Rights. Judges and Magistrates are appointed by the President of Malta acting on the advice of the Prime Minister and they are independent of the Executive.

Capital punishment for civilians was abolished in 1971 and totally abolished in 2000.

Chief Justice: His Hon. Silvio Camilleri, M.O.M., LL.D.
Attorney-General: Peter Grech
Judiciary, URL: http://judiciarymalta.gov.mt/

LOCAL GOVERNMENT

In 1993, local government was re-introduced to Malta. The Local Council Act regulates the Councils which handle basic services within all local communities. Malta and Gozo have 68 local councils, 54 in Malta, and 14 in Gozo. For the purposes of general elections, Malta is divided into 13 constituencies.

AREA AND POPULATION

Area
Located in the Mediterranean Sea, just south of Sicily, the Maltese archipelago consists of six islands the largest of which are Malta, Gozo and Comino. The total area of the Maltese Islands is 316 sq. km. Malta, the largest island, covers an area of 246 sq. km. Gozo and Comino have an area of 67 sq. km and 3 sq. km respectively. Malta is 27 km long at its longest point and 14.5 km wide at its widest point. The corresponding figures for Gozo are 14.5 km and 7.2 km. The distance between Malta and the nearest point in Sicily is 93 km. The distance from the nearest point on the North African mainland (Tunisia) is 288 km. Gibraltar is 1,826 km to the west and Alexandria is 1,510 km to the east.

The terrain is mainly low and flat. The climate is Mediterranean with mild wet winters and hot dry summers.

To view a map, please consult http://www.lib.utexas.edu/maps/cia08/malta_sm_2008.gif

Population
The population in 2010 was estimated at 417,000, an annual increase of 0.5 per cent for the period 2000-10. An estimated 95 per cent of people live in urban areas.

The Maltese people come from a number of different mixed origins, with predominant Phoenician, Arab, Italian and English strains. Maltese, the official language along with English, is believed to derive from the Carthaginian and Phoenician languages. In recent years Malta has seen an influx of emigrants coming from Africa, seeking asylum, entry into Europe and work; in 2005 1,800 arrived and 1,700 arrived during the first nine months of 2006. Malta has asked the EU for help patrolling its waters.

Births, Marriages, Deaths
For the year 2010 the crude birth rate was 9.2 births per 1,000 population and the crude death rate at 7.4 deaths per 1,000 population. The total fertility rate was 1.3 children per woman in 2010. The maternal mortality rate was 8.0 per 100,000 live births in 2009. An estimated 21 per cent of the population are aged over 60 years and 16 per cent are aged under 15 years old. The median age was 39 years. Life expectancy was estimated at 80 years (female 82 years, male 78 years) in 2009. Healthy life expectancy was estimated at 72 years in 2008. (Source: http://www.who.int, World Health Statistics 2012)

Figures for 2006 show that 2,536 marriages took place. In May 2011, the people voted yes in a non-binding referendum on legalizing divorce. Malta is one of two countries in the world where divorce is not allowed. Parliament will need to uphold the result for the law to change which would leave only the Philippines as a divorce-free country. Currently the options for the Maltese are: a legal separation in the courts, a church annulment (a lengthy process), or to get divorced outside the country.

Public Holidays 2014
1 January: New Year's Day
10 February: St Paul's Shipwreck
19 March: St Joseph

18 March: Good Friday
20 March: Easter Sunday
31 March: Freedom Day
1 May: St Joseph the Worker
7 June: Memorial of 1919 Riot
29 June: St Peter and St Paul
15 August: Assumption Day
8 September: Our Lady of Victories
21 September: Independence Day
8 December: Immaculate Conception
13 December: Republic Day
25 December: Christmas Day
Although not an official holiday, carnivals take place in February

EMPLOYMENT

Labour force figures for 2007 show that 142,836 people were full-time gainfully employed of whom 16,806 were full-time self-employed. There were 6,172 people registered unemployed at the end of 2007. The following table shows the total employed persons classified by economic activity in 2008.

Occupation	2008
Agriculture, hunting & forestry	2,800
Fishing	400
Mining & quarrying	600
Manufacturing	24,300
Electricity, gas & water supply	3,700
Construction	12,400
Wholesale & retail trade, repairs	25,000
Hotels & restaurants	13,300
Transport, storage & communication	13,000
Financial intermediation	6,100
Real estate, renting & business activities	11,500
Public admin. & defence; compulsory social security	14,300
Education	13,500
Health & social work	12,200
Other community, social & personal service activities	7,500
Private households with employed persons	100
Extra-territorial organizations & bodies	300

Source: Copyright © International Labour Organization (ILO Dept. of Statistics, http://laborsta.ilo.org)

The average unemployment rate for 2007 was 4.5 per cent, down from 5 per cent the previous year. Average unemployment in 2008 was 6.1 per cent. In February 2012 the rate was estimated at 6.8 per cent.

BANKING AND FINANCE

Currency
Malta adopted the Euro as the official currency on January 1 2008. Prior to that the currency was the Maltese Lira (Lm) = 100 cents.

GDP/GNP, Inflation, National Debt
Malta's economy is based on tourism and exports. It has few raw materials and a small domestic market.

GDP (at market prices) was €5,749.7 million in 2009 and €5,014,906,000 in 2008, compared to €4,741,701,00 in 2007. The growth rate was 5.2 per cent in 2008, compared to 7.0 per cent in 2007. GDP was estimated at €6,393 million in 2011. GDP growth was estimated at 3.7 per cent in 2010 and 2.5 per cent in 2011. In 2012, the IMF warned that the global economic crisis was in danger of spreading to Malta.

GDP (ESA) 1995, Production Approach, €000s

	2007p	2008p	2009p
Output of goods and services	10,346,981	10,768,206	10,440,724
Intermediate consumption	5,604,725	5,767,227	5,468,511
Gross value added	4,742,256	5,000,979	4,972,213
Consumption of fixed capital	744,370	781,151	808,736
Value added, net	3,997,886	4,219,828	4,163,477

Source: Malta Statistics Office

Per capita GDP was estimated at $25,500 in 2011 (PPP).

The following table shows the percentage contribution to Gross Value Added by industry.

Industry	2007p	2008p	2009p
Agriculture, hunting & fishing	1.70	1.60	1.78
Fishing	0.76	0.27	0.06
Mining & quarrying	0.28	0.32	0.33
Manufacturing	16.29	16.39	13.58
Electricity, gas & water supply	1.69	1.30	2.07
Construction	3.63	3.56	3.42
Wholesale & retail trade, repairs	11.83	11.4	10.53
Hotels & restaurants	5.09	5.08	4.41

MALTA

- continued

Transport, storage & communication	9.45	9.24	8.31
Financial intermediation	4.23	4.30	5.84
Real estate, renting & business activities	16.92	17.46	18.47
Public admin. & defence, compulsory social security	6.66	6.69	7.07
Education	5.71	5.70	5.94
Health & social work	6.02	6.34	6.83
Other community, social & personal service activities	9.43	10.02	11.03
Private households with employed persons	0.31	0.32	0.33

Source: National Statistics Office, Malta (prov. figs)

Inflation is relatively low. In 2007 it was 1.25 per cent, a fall from 2.77 in 2006 and 3.01 in 2005. Inflation was 2.4 per cent in February 2012, a fall of 0.3 per cent on the same month in 2011.

Malta's national debt was €3.9 billion in 2010, approximately 69 per cent of GDP.

Balance of Payments / Imports and Exports

Figures for imports and exports of goods and services are shown the following table. Figures are in €000.

Year	Exports	Imports
2005	1,959,075	3,117,192
2006	2,256,703	3,487,943
2007	2,287,339	3,579,495
2008	2,030,748	3,404,040
2009	1,646,635	3,066,183

Source: National Statistics Office, Malta

Imports were estimated to be €5.2 million in 2011 and exports €3.7 million.

The European Union is Malta's leading trading partner. In 2008, from a total of €2,030.7 million worth of exports, Europe took €960.2 million (EU €920.3 million). Approximately €671.3 million went to Asia and €222.9 million to the USA. Of a total of €3,404 million imports in 2008, €2,600 million came from Europe (of which the EU accounted for €2,379 million). Approximately €596.3 million imports were of Asia origin and €121 million came from the USA

The sectoral analysis of import and exports is shown in the following tables. Figures given are in Lm '000:

Imports by Sector

Commodity	2008	2009
Food and live animals	435,276	381,423
Beverages and tobacco	61,604	59,079
Crude materials, inedible, except fuels	25,552	30,281
Mineral fuels, lubricants & related materials	515,970	305,778
Animal and vegetable oils and fats	9,047	6,901
Chemicals & related products	341,156	309,619
Manufactured goods classified by material	353,669	287,445
Machinery and transport equipment	1,430,446	1,310,007
Misc. manufactured goods	423,013	353,365
Commodities and transactions n.e.c.	25,652	22,284
Total	3,621,387	3,066,183

Source: Central Office of Statistics Malta

Exports by Sector, €000s

Commodity	2008	2009
Food and live animals	161,277	69,575
Beverages and tobacco	15,843	17,666
Crude materials, inedible, except fuels	12,517	9,602
Mineral fuels, lubricants & related materials	49,389	26,623
Animal & vegetable oils, fats & waxwa	524	39
Chemicals & related products	221,825	196,081
Manufactured goods classified by material	112,884	88,993
Machinery & transport equipment	1,173,488	939,012
Misc. manufactured goods	335,035	307,148
Commodities and transactions	7,120	1,895
Total	2,089,701	1,656,635

Source: Central Office of Statistics Malta

Central Bank
Central Bank of Malta, PO Box 378, Castille Place, CMR Valletta 01, Malta. Tel: +356 21247480, fax: +356 243051, e-mail: info@centralbankmalta.com, URL: http://www.centralbankmalta.com
Governor: Prof. Josef Bonnici (page 1391)

Chamber of Commerce
Malta Chamber of Commerce and Enterprise, Exchange Building, Republic Street, Valletta, VLT 05, Malta. Tel: +356 247211/233873, fax: +356 245223, e-mail: admin@chamber.org.mt, URL: http://www.chamber.org.mt/

MANUFACTURING, MINING AND SERVICES

Energy
Malta's oil consumption was an estimated 20,000 barrels per day in 2011. All of which is imported. Coal is also imported. In 2010, Malta generated 1.99 billion kWh of electricity and consumed 1.6 million kWh. It had an installed capacity of 0.57 GWe in 2010.

Manufacturing
Manufactured goods include electrical machinery, plastic and rubber products, tobacco, chemical and leather products. The following table shows the total sales value of manufactured goods in recent years. Figures are in € '000.

Manufacturing Sales

Product	2006	2007	2008
Food & beverages & tobacco products	319,286	262,023	287,003
Textiles & textile products	44,788	44,526	42,822
Wearing apparel & clothes	52,479	38,275	31,164
Leather & leather products	6,620	5,012	2,222
Wood & wood products	1,620	1,620	3,018
Paper & paper products	17,004	15,640	16,055
Printing & publishing	121,783	139,798	147,440
Chemicals & chemical products	163,737	215,411	219,706
Rubber & plastic products	92,745	98,632	94,833
Other non-metallic mineral products	50,432	49,192	62,531
Fabricated metal products	43,691	47,157	54,565
Machinery & equipment n.e.c.	33,272	32,915	33,032
Electrical machinery & apparatus	114,110	142,580	132,453
Radio, TV & communication equipment	1,181,299	1,105,235	908,157
Medical, precision & optical instruments	49,612	45,526	46,738
Motor vehicles, trailers & semi-trailers	1,301	1,017	535
Other transport equipment	30,314	28,084	28,025
Furniture & manufacturing n.e.c.	111,722	113,920	97,363
Totals	2,435,813	2,386,592	2,207,662

Source: National Statistics Office, Malta

Service Industries
Tourism is the major foreign currency earner. Figures for 2011 showed 1.4 million tourist arrivals, up 6 per cent from 2011. A Lm 10m cruise terminal has been constructed at Valletta, and the number of cruise passengers has been growing steadily, and has increased from 170,782 in 2000 to 555,840 in 2008. Tourists stayed for a total number of 10,890,217 nights. Tourist spending amounted to over €1.2 billion in 2011.

Agriculture
New potatoes are Malta's main agricultural export and the main cash crop. In 2008, Malta exported 2,700 tonnes of potatoes. Malta is self-sufficient in milk, pork, poultry and eggs. Rabbit is Malta's national dish and with an estimated consumption of 3,500 tonnes, Malta has the highest per capita consumption in the world. There are 2,906 full-time and 21,418 part-time farmers.

Agricultural Production

Product	2007	2008
Beef (tonnes)	1,386	1,480
Pork (tonnes)	8,018	8,503
Broilers	4,567	4,979
Milk producer sales ('000 litres)	39,410	38,863
Estimated egg production ('000 eggs)	123,200	128,800
Vegetables ('000 tonnes)	44.6	44.2
Potato exports ('000 tonnes)	2.6	2.7
Fruit ('000 tonnes)	2.2	3.1
Swordfish	213	261
Dorado	264	245
Blue-fin Tuna	124	142
Other	247	269

Source: Central Office of Statistics, Malta

In December 1997 the fishing industry had 1,699 power-propelled and nine other fishing boats and employed 374 full-time and 1,442 part-time fishermen. The catch for 1997 was 887 tonnes, valued at Lm 1,549,693. Production from fish farms in 1997 was 1,800 tonnes. It is estimated that during 1998 the local aquaculture industry produced 2,000 tonnes of sea bass and sea bream valued at Lm 4.4 m. 95 per cent of the local production is for export, mainly to Italy. It is estimated that the aquaculture industry employs 120 people full-time and 60 part-time.

COMMUNICATIONS AND TRANSPORT

Travel Requirements
Citizens of the USA, Canada and Australia require a passport valid for three months beyond the length of stay but do not need a visa for stays of up to three months. EU visitors do not require a passport if they carry a valid national Identity Card; nor do they require a visa. Other nationals should contact the embassy to check visa requirements.

Malta is a signatory to the Schengen Agreement; with a Schengen visa, a visitor can travel freely throughout the Schengen zone with few border stops and checks. See http://www.eurovisa.info/SchengenCountries.htm for details.

National Airlines
Air Malta plc, URL: http://www.airmalta.com

Air Malta operates passenger and cargo scheduled services to many destinations throughout Europe, the Middle East and North Africa. Air Malta also operates extensive charter services throughout Europe. Its subsidiary Malta Air Charter operates a seasonal Malta-Gozo helicopter airlink and sightseeing flights.

International Airports
Malta International Airport, URL:http://www.maltairport.com. The international airport handled an estimated 3.1 million passengers in 2008.

Roads
In 1997 there were 1,961 km of roads including 157 km of arterial roads, 1,167 km of urban roads and 647 km of non-urban roads. About 94 per cent of roads are paved. In March 2000 registered motor vehicles included agricultural vehicles, 953; coach, 156; commercial vehicle, 42,791; garage hire, 980; mini-bus, 389; motor-cycle, 11,795; private cars, 177,714; route bus, 571; self-drive, 4978; self-drive motor-cycle, 209; taxi, 245. Vehicles are driven on the left.

Ports and Harbours
The principal port of Malta is the Grand Harbour in Valletta. It is a deep-water harbour and has adequate shore facilities for handling import, export and transhipment of cargoes and cereals especially since the construction of the Kordin Grain Terminal. The Grand Harbour is being developed into a hub for cruise liners. At the end of 1998 the number of vessels registered in Malta was 3,120. Ships entering harbour, excluding yachts and fishing vessels, during 1998, totalled 5,034. 212 cruise vessels put in during 1998. Malta Freeport has three main activities which are container handling, oil products handling and storage and industrial warehousing. The strategic position on the Mediterranean between Gibraltar and the Suez Canal means the Freeport provides facilities for linking markets across continents.

A ferry service runs from Malta to Gozo. It carried 3,068,516 passengers in 2000. There are also ferry services from Valetta to Catania and Pozzallo, Sicily.

HEALTH

The Health Division of the Ministry of Health provides comprehensive hospital services, community care services, public health services and pharmaceutical services to all citizens. Every resident is entitled to free hospital care, free community care services (including general practitioner service), free public health services, free pharmaceuticals (subject to means test) and other forms of personal medical assistance. Besides the services provided by the Government there is also a well developed private health sector, both in primary and hospital care.
There are currently eight hospitals, three of which are privately run, with a total of 2,110 beds. In addition there is a Government residence for the elderly with 1,054 beds (approximately 78 beds per 10,000 population). The Government also operates eight Health centres which provide general practitioner, nursing services and specialised primary care services.
In 2009, the government spent approximately 12.7 per cent of its total budget on healthcare (up from 12.1 per cent in 2000), accounting for 64.8 per cent of all healthcare spending. Total expenditure on healthcare equated to 8.5 per cent of the country's GDP. Per capita expenditure on health was approximately US$1,668, compared with US$643 in 2000. Figures for 2005-10 show that there are 1,259 physicians (31.1 per 10,000 population), 2,838 nurses and midwives (69.1 per 10,000 population), 301 pharmaceutical personnel and 184 dentistry personnel. There are 45 hospital beds per 10,000 population.
In 2010, the infant mortality rate (probability of dying by age 1) was 5 per 1,000 live births. The under-fives mortality rate was 6 per 1,000 live births. The most common causes of deaths in children aged under five are: prematurity 17 per cent and congenital anomalies 48 per cent. Vaccination rates for measles, DTP3, HebB and Hib3 are respectively 73 per cent, 76 per cent, 86 per cent and 76 per cent. (Source: http://www.who.int, World Health Statistics 2012)

EDUCATION

In 2008, public expenditure on education amounted to 5.8 per cent of GDP and 13.3. per cent of total government expenditure. Approximately 6 per cent went on pre-primary education, 23 per cent on primary, 53 per cent on secondary and 18 per cent on tertiary education. (Source: UNESCO)

Primary/Secondary Education
Education is compulsory between the ages of five and 16 and is available free of charge in state schools from kindergarten to university. About 30 per cent of the student population attend non-state schools. Under an agreement between the Government and the Church, the Government subsidises church schools and students attending them do not pay any fees.

Kindergarten education is provided for three and four year old children. UNESCO estimates that 100 per cent of children are enrolled in kindergarten. An estimated 95 per cent of children are enrolled in primary education. The pupil/teacher ratio was 9:1 in 2009. An estimated 99 per cent of children complete their primary education and 99 per cent go onto secondary education.

Secondary education is provided in secondary schools, junior lyceums and trade schools. At the end of their primary education, pupils sit for the 11+ examination. Pupils who qualify are admitted into the junior lyceums while the others attend the secondary schools. Secondary schools and junior lyceums offer a five year course leading to the Secondary Education Certificate and the General Certificate of Education, Ordinary Level. Junior lyceums offer a more challenging curriculum. At the end of their third year of secondary education, students may opt for a course with a technology bias in a trade school, where the full course lasts six years. Trade school students generally come from the Secondary schools. Courses run by trade schools lead to a Journeyman's Certificate and or a City and Guilds of London certificate.

Higher Education
At the end of their five year secondary education course, students may opt to follow a higher academic or technological or vocational course. The duration of these courses ranges from one to four years. An estimated 33 per cent of people of tertiary age are in tertiary education. The academic courses generally lead to Intermediate and Advanced Level Matriculation examinations set by the University of Malta or to Advanced Level examinations set by British universities. The Junior College, administrated by the University, prepares students specifically for a university course. The Matriculation Certificate, which qualifies students for admission into the university, is a broad-based qualification. About 4,500 students (2,150 females) attend State higher secondary educational institutions, while 2,200 students (1,300 females) attend the Junior College. The University of Malta is one of the oldest universities in the Commonwealth. It has approximately 7,500 students including 500 from overseas.

RELIGION

The Roman Catholic religion is established by law as the religion of the country, but full liberty of conscience and freedom of worship are guaranteed. The majority of the population (98 per cent) belong to the Roman Catholic Church. There are small communities of Muslims and Baha'is.

Malta has a religious liberty rating of 10 on a scale of 1 to 10 (10 is most freedom). (Source: World Religion Database)

COMMUNICATIONS AND MEDIA

Media laws are based on European law. There are several newspapers, both in English or Maltese. Many have strong political affiliations.

Newspapers
In-Nazzjon, (Maltese), URL: http://www.mument.com.mt/ (Owned by the Nationalist Party)
L-Orizzont, URL: http://www.l-orizzont.com (Maltese)
The Times, URL: http://www.timesofmalta.com/ (English)
Malta Independent, URL: http://www.independent.com.mt/ (English)
Il Torca, URL: http://www.it-torca.com/ (Maltese, owned by the General Workers' Union)

Broadcasting
The Broadcasting Act 1991 liberalised the media. There are two publicly owned television stations, Television Malta, and an educational station. There are several national stations and cable and satellite channels are also available. The publicly owned radio station operates one station. Approximately 50 commercial radio stations also exist.
Public Broadcasting Services Ltd, URL: http://www.pbs.com.mt
Super One TV and Radio, URL: http://www.super1.com/ (owned by Malta Labour Party)
Net TV, URL: http://www.nettv.com.mt/ (owned by Nationalist Party)

Telecommunications
The telecommunications infrastructure is fully digitised. In 2010 there were an estimated 245,000 landlines in use and 455,000 mobile phones.

In 2010 Malta had around 240,000 internet users.

ENVIRONMENT

Malta's main environmental issue is its limited natural fresh water resources. It is increasingly reliant on desalination.

Malta is a party to the following international environment agreements: Air Pollution, Biodiversity; Climate Change, Climate Change-Kyoto Protocol, Desertification, Endangered Species, Hazardous Wastes, Law of the Sea, Marine Dumping, Ozone Layer Protection, Ship Pollution, and Wetlands.

According to figures from the EIA, in 2010 Malta's emissions from the consumption of fossil fuels totalled 3.1 million metric tons of carbon dioxide.

SPACE PROGRAMME

In February 2012, Malta signed an agreement with the European Space Agency getting observer status on the ESA Council and related committees.

MARSHALL ISLANDS
Republic of the Marshall Islands

Capital: Majuro Island (Population estimate, 2005: 25,000)

Head of State: Christopher J. Loeak (President) (page 1466)

National Flag: Twenty-four pointed star with two diagonal rays on a blue background, the top ray is orange the lower, white

CONSTITUTION AND GOVERNMENT

Constitution
Named after the English explorer John Marshall who visited in 1799, the Marshall Islands were claimed by Spain in 1874 and became a German protectorate in 1885. During the war they came under Japanese control until the US took control in 1944. The US conducted nuclear weapons tests in the Marshall Islands between 1946-58. In 1954 the most powerful hydrogen bomb ever tested by the US was detonated at Bikini Atoll. Islanders were allowed to return to the atoll in 1970 but were evacuated after many developed health problems. In 1980 people were allowed to return to Enewetak Atoll after top soil had been removed. The constitution was adopted in 1979. The islands were officially renamed the Republic of the Marshall Islands in 1982. The Marshall Islands were granted independence from the US in 1986 but in return for American aid the US maintain a military base at Kwajalein. In 1988 a tribunal was set up to establish compensation claims. However, by 2001 it was found there was not enough money to honour the awards made.

To consult the constitution, please visit: http://www.rmiembassyus.org/Constitution.htm

Recent Events
The Marshall Islands were admitted to the UN in 1991.

In 2003 the USA signed a new Compact of Free Association, the agreement is worth US$3.5 billion of aid to be paid over 20 years to the Marshall Islands and the Federated States of Micronesia.

A state of emergency was declared in December 2008 after waves flooded the urban centres of Majuro and Ebeye.

In 2009 President Litokwa Tomeing was ousted in a vote of no confidence. In October 2009, Jurelang Zedkaia was elected president by a margin of 17 votes to 15.

Christopher Loeak became president in January 2012.

Legislature
The Marshall Islands have a legislature of 33 members known as the *Nitijela* who are elected for a four year term. A 12 member Council of Chiefs (*Iroij*) has a consultative function on matters relating to land and custom. The president also has his own cabinet of ministers whom he appoints personally.
Parliament, Parliament Building, PO Box 24, 96960 Majuro, Marshall Islands. Tel: +692 625 8678, URL: http://www.rmiembassyus.org/government/nitijela.htm

---

Cabinet (as at March 2013)
President & Head of Government: Christopher Loeak (page 1466)
Assistant to the President: Anton 'Tony' Debrum
Minister of Education: Hilda Heine
Minister of Finance: Dennis Momotaro
Minister of Foreign Affairs & Trade: Phillip H. Muller
Minister of Health: David Kabua
Minister of Internal Affairs: Wilbur Heine
Minister of Justice: Thomas Heine
Minister of Public Works: Hiroshi Yamamura
Minister of Resources and Development: Michael Konelios
Minister of Transportation and Communications: Rien Morris

Ministries
Government portal, URL: http://www.rmigovernment.org/index.jsp / http://www.rmi-op.net
Office of the President, PO Box 2, MH 96960, Majuro, Marshall Islands. Tel: +692 625 3213, fax: +692 625 4021, e-mail: presoff@ntamar.com
Ministry of Finance, PO Box D, Cabinet Building 96960, Majuro, Marshall Islands. Tel: +692 625 8320, fax: +692 625 3607, e-mail: minfin@ntamar.com
Ministry of Foreign Affairs, PO Box 2, Cabinet Building 96960, Majuro, Marshall Islands. Tel: +692 625 3181, fax: +692 625 4979, e-mail: mofatadm@ntamar.com
Ministry of Education, PO Box 3, Majuro, Marshall Islands. Tel: +692 625 5262, fax: +692 625 3861, e-mail: secmoe@ntamar.com
Ministry of Internal Affairs, Cabinet Building 96960, Majuro, Marshall Islands. Tel: +692 625 3842, fax: +692 625 5353, e-mail: rmihpo@ntamar.com
Ministry of Resources and Development, PO Box 326, Cabinet Building 96960, Majuro, Marshall Islands. Tel: +692 625 3206, fax: +692 625 5447, e-mail: rndsec@ntamar.com
Ministry of Health and Environment, Cabinet Building 96960, Majuro, Marshall Islands. Tel: +692 625 3355, fax: +692 625 3432, e-mail: mipamohe@ntamar.com

Political Parties
Aelon Kein Ad (Our Islands) coalition (AKA); United People's Party (UPP, part of the AKA coalition); United Democratic Party (UDP).

Elections
The Nitijela is elected every four years. The last parliamentary elections were held in November 2007 and the last presidential in January 2008. The Aelon Kein Ad (Our Islands - AKA) coalition won the largest number of seats in the elections, although formally all candidates took part as independents. The coalition supported Litokwa Tomeing of the United People's Party in the presidential election, and he won the presidency.

However, in 2009, Litokwa Tomeing lost a vote of no confidence. In October 2009 the parliamentary speaker, Jurelang Zedkaia, was elected president, beating the only other candidate, former president Kessai Note, by 17 votes to 15.

The most recent presidential election took place on 4 January 2012; Christopher Loeak, an independent, won with 21 votes against the incumbent Jureland Zedkaia who got 11 votes. President Loeak appointed a new cabinet on 21 January 2011.

Diplomatic Representation
High Commission (in Suva, Fiji), URL: http://ukinfiji.fco.gov.uk
Acting High Commissioner: Steven Chandler
US Embassy, URL: http://majuro.usembassy.gov/
Ambassador: Charles Paul
Permanent Mission of the Republic of the Marshall Islands to the UN, URL: http://www.un.int/wcm/content/site/marshallislands
Ambassador: Amatlain Kabua

LEGAL SYSTEM

The Marshalls have a Supreme Court, a High Court, a district court, community courts and a traditional rights court.

The Supreme Court consists of three judges. The district court is composed of one Presiding Judge and one Associate Judge who have been appointed for 10-year terms. The district court is limited to offences for which the maximum penalty is less than three years confinement. It may hear appeals from the community courts, of which there are around 20. Judges in community courts are appointed on the basis of local government recommendations for up to four years. Kwajalein Community Court Judges are appointed for one year terms.

The Traditional Rights court holds hearings and determines opinions on questions relating to titles, land rights or other items of traditional practice or customary law referred to it by trial judges from all courts except the Supreme Court.

Legal services in the Republic are provided by the Public Defender and the Micronesian Legal Services Corporation. The latter is a Micronesia-wide organisation, with a central administrative office in Saipan.

The government respects the human rights of its citizens, though prison conditions are poor, and there is some degree of government corruption. The death penalty was abolished in 1986.

LOCAL GOVERNMENT

There are no provinces or states in the Marshalls but each of the 24 inhabited atolls has a local government.

AREA AND POPULATION

Area
The Marshall Islands consist of a double chain of 29 coral atolls comprised of 1,225 islands and reefs lying in the Pacific Ocean. The total land area is 181 sq. km. The ocean area is over 1.2 million sq. km. The islands are situated mid way between Hawaii and Australia.

Kwajalein is the largest of its many atolls, made up of about 90 islets around a lagoon 120 km long and 24 km. wide. Other significant atolls include Rongelap (land area 4.9 sq. km) and Maloclap (land area 6.1 sq. km, lagoon area 604.3 sq. km). Lib, Jabwot, Kili, Mejit and Jemo are low coral islands without lagoons. Most of them are low coral islands without lagoons. Most of them are less than one sq. km in area. The distance from Taongi in the north of the group to Ebon in the south is about 1,300 km. The highest point in the entire group is on Likiep, 10 metres above sea level. The most famous atoll is probably Bikini Atoll, used by the US for nuclear tests in the 1950s. The climate is tropical with a wet season running from May to November. Typhoons also occur.

A UN report has warned that because of rising sea levels the islands may be submerged by 2030.

To view a map, consult http://www.lib.utexas.edu/maps/cia08/marshall_islands_sm_2008.gif

Population
The population of the islands was estimated at 54,000 in 2010, with an annual growth rate of 0.4 per cent. Figures for 2006 show a population density of 317 people per square km. In 2010, 72 per cent of the population was living in urban areas.

Marshall Islanders are categorised as Micronesians. English is the official language, two Marshallese dialects are widely spoken and Japanese is also spoken by some.

Births, Marriages, Deaths
Life expectancy is 58 years for males and 60 years for females (2009). An estimated 30 per cent of the population is aged under 15 years old and 7 per cent over 60 years. The infant mortality rate was 22 per 1,000 live births in 2010. The average fertility rate was an estimated 3.6 children per female. (Source: http://www.who.int, World Health Statistics 2012)

Public Holidays 2014
1 January: New Year's Day
1 March: Nuclear Survivor's Day
1 May: Constitution Day
4 July: Fisherman's Day (first Friday in July)
5 September: Rijerbal Day (Worker's Day) (first Friday in September)
26 September: Manit Day (Customs Day) (last Friday in September)
20 November: Kamolol Day (Thanksgiving Day) (third Thursday in November)
17 November: President's Day
5 December: Gospel Day (first Friday in December)
25 December: Christmas Day

EMPLOYMENT

Figures for 2006 put the workforce at 25,700. The service sector is the largest employer, accounting for around 60 per cent of the working population, 18 per cent of people were employed in the agriculture and fishing sector, and 18 per cent in the construction sector. The unemployment rate for 2006 was put as high as 60 per cent.

BANKING AND FINANCE

Currency
US dollars.

GDP/GNP, Inflation, National Debt
Nearly three-quarters of the Marshall Islands GDP is made up from US grants and payments amounting to some US$65 million per year. GDP at constant prices was estimated at US$134.7 million in 2008, compared to US$133.1 million in 2007. Per capita GDP in 2008 was estimated at US$2,371.

The following table shows GDP at current market prices. Figures are in thousand US$.

Year	GDP
2000	107,413
2001	110,851
2002	116,088
2003	119,789
2004	126,909
2005	129,075
2006	130,133
2007	133,086
2008	134,731

Source: Asian Develpment Bank

GDP growth was estimated at 0.8 per cent in 2006, 2.3 per cent in 2007 and -0.5 per cent in 2008.

Inflation was estimated at 12 per cent in 2008.

Total external debt was estimated at US$85 million.

Foreign Investment
The Marshall Islands receive an annual grant and federal categorical grants from the United States of America. The islands have also been awarded a nuclear compensation fund of US$150m, and a US$10m development fund has been created to offset cuts in federal programmes.

Balance of Payments / Imports and Exports
Imports amounted to US$75 million in 2008 and exports to US$19.5 million in 2008.

The main exported goods included coconut oil, copra cake which make up around 90 per cent of exports, fish and handicrafts. Main imported goods were fuels, machinery and transport equipment, food and animals and crude materials. The main trading partners of the Marshall Islands are the US, Australia, Japan, New Zealand, Hong Kong and Taipei, Philippines, Singapore and the Fiji Islands.

Bank of the Marshall Islands, URL: http://www.bomi.biz/

MANUFACTURING, MINING AND SERVICES

Primary and Extractive Industries
Preliminary seabed surveys indicate significant deposits of manganese, phosphate, high grade cobalt and polymetallic modules which could potentially be extracted.

Manufacturing
Small factories exist producing drinking water and beer, and processing of breadfruit and taro.

Agriculture
Copra production in 2006 amounted to 4,646 short tons. The atoll of Arno in the Ratak chain is the greatest producer, averaging 901 tonnes per year. Figures for 2010 show that 42,500 metric tonnes of coconuts were produced.

A coconut replanting scheme was reported at the South Pacific Forum of 1991.

In 1985 an estimated US$33,000 worth of cash crops - including banana, papaya, pandanus and bread-fruit - was sold in markets in Majuro and Ebeye. A farm operated by the Taiwanese Agriculture and Trade Mission at Laura on Majuro atoll produced 6,000 kilos of assorted vegetables in the same year.

Fishing
In 2010 the total fish catch was estimated at around 60,00 tonnes. Japanese fishing fleets are also active in the area. Trochus shell processing and black pearl culture are becoming more widespread as are oyster and clam farming.

The government is encouraging the use of the Marshalls as a tuna processing and transshipment centre for the US tuna fleet in view of its location between the fishing grounds of Melanesia and Kiribati and the mainland. The sale of fishing licences and supplying fishing vessels is a lucrative business.

COMMUNICATIONS AND TRANSPORT

Travel Requirements
Citizens of the USA, Canada, Australia and the EU require a passport valid for at least one year from date of arrival, proof of adequate funds and onward tickets. Tourist visas are issued on arrival, and are required by Canadians and EU subjects, but not by USA and Australian citizens, citizens of countries in the Pacific Islands Forum, the Federated States of Micronesia, and Palau. Other nationals should contact the embassy to check visa requirements.

National Airlines
Airline of the Marshall Islands is the national airline. URL: http://www.airmarshallislands.com

International Airports
There are international airports on Kwajalein and Majuro.

Roads
There are 152 km of primary (paved) roads in the islands, mostly on Majuro and Ebeye.

Shipping
Domestic shipping is a government responsibility with four ships providing cargo and passenger services throughout the islands. Sea transport within each island group is by private speed boat, copra boats or lagoon boats operated by the local governments.

Nauru Pacific Line operates regular cargo services from Melbourne to Nauru, Majuro and Tarawa (Kiribati). NYK (Japan) Shipping Line operates monthly between Japanese and Micronesian ports. PM & O lines operate monthly between the US west coast and Pacific island ports.

Ports and Harbours
There are 12 deepwater docks on the islands. The ports of Majuro and Ebeye provide full service facilities, containerised cargo handling, bulk storage and transshipment operations.

HEALTH

In 2009, the government spent approximately 19.5 per cent of its total budget on healthcare (down from 21.1 per cent in 2000), accounting for 84.0 per cent of all healthcare spending. Total expenditure on healthcare equated to 18.9 per cent of the country's GDP. Per capita expenditure on health was approximately US$540. According to latest WHO estimates (2005-10), there were 32 physicians (4.4 per 10,000 population), 127 nurses (17.4 per 10,000 population), 11 dentistry personnel and 10 pharmaceutical personnel.

According to the latest WHO figures, in 2010 approximately 94 per cent of the population had access to improved drinking water. In the same year, 75 per cent of the population had access to improved sanitation. Diarrhoea accounts for 6 per cent of childhood deaths (children under five years old). Other main causes of childhood deaths include pneumonia (19 per cent) and prematurity (20 per cent). The infant mortality rate (probability of dying by age one) was 22 per 1,000 live births. The child mortality rate (probability of dying by age five) was 26 per 1,000 live births. (Source: http://www.who.int, World Health Statistics 2012)

EDUCATION

Education for children aged six to 14 is compulsory. Enrolment in primary schools is estimated at over 90 per cent, in secondary schools at approximately 70 per cent and in tertiary schools at 21 per cent. The primary school ratio of pupils to teacher is 17:1.

In addition a number of private schools operate in the Marshall Islands under charters granted by the Minister of Education. Most private schools are church affiliated. Secondary education is not universal in the Marshall Islands and admission to public high schools is selective. There are two institutions of tertiary education in the Marshall Islands, The College of the Marshall Islands and The University of the South Pacific.

MAURITANIA

RELIGION

Over 95 per cent of the population are Christian. Approximately 2.7 per cent are Baha'is and 1.4 per cent agnostic. The Marshall Islands have a religious liberty rating of 10 on a scale of 1 to 10 (10 is most freedom). (Source: World Religion Database)

COMMUNICATIONS AND MEDIA

There is freedom of speech although the press does practise some self-censorship on some political issues.

Newspapers
Marshall Islands Journal (weekly). (URL: http://www.majurochamber.net). The Marshall Islands Gazette is a monthly government publication.

Broadcasting
The government-owned radio station, WSZO, broadcasts in both Marshallese and English. There is also a commercial station, Micronesia Heatwave, a religious broadcaster V7AA and the AFN (Central Pacific Network) which is run by the US military. URL: http://abs-afn.army.mil/Kwajalein/

The Marshalls Broadcasting Company operates a subscriber funded TV station.

Telecommunications
In 2008 it was estimated there were 4,500 telephone lines in use and 1,000 mobile phones. Internet access is limited by high costs and a slow serice. In 2008, there were an estimated 2,200 internet users.

ENVIRONMENT

In 1946 and 1958 the US used the atolls of Enewetak and Bikini for nuclear testing, Enewetak has been partly decontaminated. Islanders were allowed to return in 1980 after topsoil was removed. In 1996 the levels of radiation on Bikini Atoll were considered low enough for tourists to visit the island.

A 1989 UN report said that if sea levels rise as expected with climate change, then the islands may be submerged by 2030.

MAURITANIA

Islamic Republic of Mauritania

Al Jumhuriyah al Islamiyah al Muritaniyah

Capital: Nouakchott (Population estimate: 635,000)

Head of State: Gen. Mohamed Ould Abdelaziz (page 1491) (President)

National Flag: A gold five-pointed star and crescent, in the centre of a green background

CONSTITUTION AND GOVERNMENT

Constitution
Formerly part of French West Africa, Mauritania gained independence in 1960 with Moktar Ould Daddah as Head of State. After independence all political parties were merged, and in 1964 Mauritania was declared a one-party state. Mauritania established its own currency (the ougiya) and joined the Arab League.

A military coup of 1978 replaced the ruling party and dissolved the National Assembly. The 1961 constitution was also abandoned. Frequent changes of leadership since then have involved periods of instability. Internal relations have been strained between the Moorish majority and black southern minority and externally with Morocco, Libya, Tunisia and Algeria, over the conflicting Arabicisation and Islamicisation policies of successive governments.

Municipal elections, the first since independence, were held in December 1986, paving the way for parliamentary elections. A new constitution came into effect in 1991 which provided for a multiparty system. In June 2006 a referendum vote approved constitutional changes limiting the length of a presidency to two five-year terms.

To consult the constitution, please visit: http://www.mauritania.mr/fr/index.php.

Recent Events
In June 2003 an attempted coup was staged and was only suppressed after heavy fighting. At the time it was not clear what the aim of the coup was but it was suspected that it had been staged by dissatisfied army officers and hardline Islamists protesting at the rule of President Taya (who came to power himself during a coup in 1984), and his support of Israel and the West.

In August 2005, while President Taya was in Saudi Arabia attending the funeral of King Fahd, troops took control of key government buildings and a group of army officers announced that they had overthrown the president. The group established a military council, the Military Council for Justice and Democracy, led by Colonel Ely Ould Mohammed Vall, who had been the director of national security since 1987. Colonel Vall announced that free and fair presidential elections would be held within two years and that leaders of the coup would not stand for election. One of the Council's first acts was to appoint an interim government with Sidy Mohamed Ould Boubacar as prime minister. Presidential elections took place in March 2007, and were won by a former cabinet minister, Sidi Ould Cheikh Abdallahi.

In April 2007 the African Union agreed to the readmission of Mauritania; it had been suspended following the 2005 coup.

In August 2007, parliament passed legislation that would outlaw slavery. The practise was still going on despite a ban in 1981.

On 6 August 2008, troops staged a coup and formed a state council to run the country. President Sidi Ould Cheikh Abdallahi had tried to dismiss four senior army officers, including the head of the presidential guard, Gen Mohamed Ould Abdelaziz, who responded by launching the coup. The President and the Prime Minister were arrested. The African Union (AU) condemned the coup. Later that week the AU suspended Mauritania's membership of the group and the US suspended all non-humanitarian aid. The military government has since promised to hold a constitutional referendum and elections.

In April 2009 the military coup leader, Gen. Mohamed Ould Abdelaziz (page 1491), resigned as chair of the High Council of State so that he could stand in the forthcoming presidential elections, scheduled for mid-July 2009. The leader of the Senate, Ba Mamadou M'Baré, became the interim president. Following the elections, which Gen. Mohamed Ould Abdelazis won, there were allegations of vote rigging, and the electoral commission resigned.

In April 2010 Mauritania, Mali, Niger and Algeria formed a joint anti-terrorism command. Mauritania has recently suffered a spate of attacks and kidnapping of tourists thought to have been carried out by al-Qaeda. In August 2010 new laws came into force aimed at fighting al-Qaeda. In August two aid workers kidnapped several months previously were released in Mali. Mauritania later carried out an air strike on suspected al-Qaeda sites in Mali.

In April 2011, protesters against the government took to the streets, the police responded with tear gas. In September 2011, a dialogue started on reform.

Further protests organised by the opposition took place in May 2012 calling for President Abdelaziz to stand down.

President Abdelaziz was flown to Paris in October 2012 for medical treatment after the convoy he was travelling in was shot at by a military patrol. The shooting was later described by officials as accidental.

Legislature
The Parliament of Mauritania is bicameral. The National Assembly or Al Jamiya-al-Wataniya has 81 directly elected members who serve for a five year term. The Senate or Majilis al-Chouyoukh has 56 indirectly elected members who serve a six year term. Three of the Senate members represent Mauritanian nationals living abroad.

Upper House
Senate, (Majlis al-Chouyoukh), B.P. 5838, Avenue de l'Indépendance, Nouakchott, Mauritania. Tel: +222 5256 877, fax: +222 5257 373, e-mail: aldedew@mauritel.mr, URL: http://www.senat.mr

Lower House
National Assembly, (Jamiya-al-Wataniya), B.P. 185, Avenue de l'Indépendance, Nouakchott, Mauritania. Tel: +222 5251 130, fax: +222 5257 078

Cabinet (as at June 2013)
Prime Minister: Moulaye ould Mohamed Laqhdaf (page 1461)
Secretary-General to the President: Adama Sy
Minister of Foreign Affairs and Co-operation: Hamadi ould Baba ould Hamadi
Minister of Economy and Development: Sidi Ould Tah
Minister of Interior and Decentralisation: Mohamed Ould Boilil
Minister of Industry and Mines: Mohamed Abdallahi ould Oudaa
Minister of Finance: Amedi Camara
Minister of Fisheries and Maritime Economy: Ghdafna ould Eyih
Minister of Oil & Energy: Wane Ibrahima Lamine
Minister of Equipment and Transport: Yahya Hademine
Minister of Health: Cheikh el Moctor ould Horma ould Babana
Minister of Culture, Youth and Sport: Cissé mint Cheikh Ould Boyde
Minister of Justice: Abidine ould el Khaire
Minister of Water Resources and Sanitation: Mohamed Lemine ould Aboye

---

Minister of Defence: Ahmedou ould Idey ould Mohamed Radhi
Minister of Islamic Affairs and Religious Education: Ahmed ould Neini
Minister of State, Minister of Secondary and Higher Education: Ahmed ould Baya
Minister of Trade, Tourism and Handicrafts: Bamba ould Dermane
Minister of Housing, and Town and Country Planning: Ismail ould Bedde ould Cheikh Sidiya
Minister of Rural Development: Ould M'Bareck ould Mohamed el Moctar
Minister of Relations with Parliament and Communications: Hamdy ould Mahjoub
Minister of Social Affairs, Childhood and Family: Moulaty mint el Moctar
Minister of the Civil Service & Administrative Reform: Maty mint Hamedi

Ministries

Office of the Prime Minister, Immeuble du Gouvernement, B.P. 184, Nouakchott, Mauritania. Tel: +222 529 3743, e-mail: mobaba@mauritania.mr, URL: http://www.mauritania.mr/
Ministry of Economic Affairs and Development, B.P. 238, Nouakchott, Mauritania. Tel: +222 525 1612, fax: +222 525 5110, e-mail: webmaster@maed.gov.mr, URL: http://www.maed.gov.mr
Ministry of Foreign Affairs, BP 230, Nouakchott, Mauritania. Tel: +222 525 2682
Ministry of Fishing and Maritime Economy, B.P. 137, Nouakchott, Mauritania. Tel: +222 525 4607, fax: +222 525 3146, e-mail: ministre@mpem.mr, URL: http://www.mpem.mr/
Ministry of Finance, BP 238, Nouakchott, Mauritania. Tel: +222 525 1612, fax: +222 525 5110, e-mail: webmaster@maed.gov.mr, URL: http://www.finances.gov.mr
Ministry of Oil and Energy, BP 366, Nouakchott, Mauritania. Tel: +222 5251 500, fax: +222 5257 475, URL: http://www.toptechnology.mr/sisaar
Ministry of the Interior and Decentralization, BP 195, Nouakchott, Mauritania. Tel: +222 5252 020, e-mail: webmaster@mipt.mr, URL: http://www.interieur.gov.mr
Ministry of Rural Development, Water Power and Environment, B.P. 366, Nouakchott, Mauritania. Tel: +222 525 1500, fax: +222 525 7475, URL: http://www.agriculture.gov.mr/mdrhe/home
Ministry of Health, BP 177, Nouakchott, Mauritania. Tel: +222 5252 052, fax: +222 5252 268, URL: http://www.sante.gov.mr
Ministry of National Education, BP 387, Nouakchott, Mauritania. Tel: +222 525 1237, fax: +222 525 1222
Ministry of Mines and Industry, BP 356, Nouakchott, Mauritania. Tel: +222 5252 688, fax: +222 5252 699, e-mail: mmi@mauritania.mr
Ministry of Justice, BP 350, Nouakchott, Mauritania. Tel: +222 525 1083, URL: http://www.mjustice.mr
Ministry of Trade, Handicrafts and Tourism, BP 183, Nouakchott, Mauritania. Tel: +222 5253 337, fax: +222 5253 582, e-mail: mmi@mauritania.mr
Ministry of Civil Service and Modernization of the Administration, BP 193, Nouakchott, Mauritania. Tel: +222 5290 863, URL:http://www.fonctionpublique.gov.mr
Ministry of Communications and Relations with Parliament, BP 223, Nouakchott, Mauritania. Tel: +222 525 3337
Ministry of Culture, Youth and Sport, BP 223, Nouakchott, Mauritania. Tel: +222 525 1130
Ministry of Defence, BP 184, Nouakchott, Mauritania. Tel: +222 525 2020
Ministry of Employment, Professional Training, and New Technology, BP 193, Nouakchott, Mauritania. Tel: +222 525 8410, fax: +222 525 8410
Ministry of Housing and Town and Country Planning, BP 237, Nouakchott, Mauritania. Tel: +222 525 3337
Ministry of the Interior and Decentralization, BP 195, Nouakchott, Mauritania. Tel: +222 525 2020, e-mail: webmaster@mipt.mr, URL: http://www.interieur.gov.mr
Ministry of Islamic Affairs and Religious Education, Nouakchott, Mauritania. URL: http://www.affairesislamiques.gov.mr
Ministry of Social Affairs, Childhood and Families, Nouakchott, Mauritania. URL: http://www.promotionfeminine.gov.mr/
Ministry of Trade, Handicrafts and Tourism, BP 183, Nouakchott, Mauritania. Tel: +222 525 3337, fax: +222 5253 582, e-mail: mmi@mauritania.mr

Political Parties

Regroupement des Forces Démocratiques, (RFD, Rally of Forces for Democracy); Parti Républicain Démocratique et Renouvellement, PRDRRepublican Party for Democracy and Renewal; Union pour la république, (UPR, Union for the Republic); Union des Forces du Progrès, (UFP, Union of Forces of Progress).

Elections

In August 2005, a group of army officers overthrew the President and established a military council, the Military Council for Justice and Democracy, led by Colonel Ely Ould Mohammed Vall, former director of national security. As promised, presidential elections took place within two years, in March 2007; Sidi Ould Cheikh Abdallahi won 53 per cent of the votes. The opposition leader, Ahmed Ould Daddah, won 47 per cent of the ballot. The elections were considered free and fair, and indicated the restoration of civilian rule after the 2005 coup.

Presidential elections took place on the 18th July 2009; the electoral commission proclaimed Gen. Mohamed Ould Abdelaziz (page 1491) the winner with 52 per cent of the vote, though there were allegations of vote rigging. International observers said the vote had been largely free and fair.

The most recent elections to the National Assembly were held in November 2006 and elections to the Senate took place the following January. Yahya ould Ahmed el Waghf, leader of the pro-presidential PNDD-ADIL (National Pact for Development and Democracy) party, was appointed Prime Minister by the President in May 2008. However, in response to a threatened no-confidence vote, el Waghf resigned with his entire Council of Ministers on 3 July. He was immediately reappointed, and his new government, entirely composed of members of the PNDD-ADIL, was appointed on 15 July 2008. On the 6th August, troops overthrew the government and formed a state council to rule the country.

Diplomatic Representation

Embassy of Mauritania, 2129 Leroy Place, NW, Washington, DC 20008, USA. Tel: +1 202 232 5700, fax: +1 202 319 2623, URL: http://www.mauritaniaembassy-usa.org
Ambassador: Mohamed Lemine El Haycen
Embassy of Mauritania, 8 Carlos Place, Mayfair, London W1K 3AS, United Kingdom. Rel: +44 (0)20 7478 9323
Ambassador: Mohamed Yahya Ould Sidi Haiba
British Embassy (All Staff resident in Rabat, Morocco), URL: http://ukinmorocco.fco.gov.uk/en/
Ambassador: Clive Alderton
US Embassy, Rue Abdallaye, Nouakchott, BP 222, Tel: +222 525 2660, fax: +222 525 1592, e-mail: aemnouak@opt.mr, URL: http://mauritania.usembassy.gov/
Ambassador: Jo Ellen Powell
Permanent Representative of the Islamic Republic of Mauritania to the United Nations, 116 East 38th Street, New York, NY 10016, USA. Tel: +1 212 252 0113 / 0141, fax: +1 212 252 0175, URL: http://www.un.int/wcm/content/site/mauritania/
Representative: Ambassador Abderahim Ould Hadrami

LEGAL SYSTEM

Nominally independent but in effect controlled by the government, the judiciary consists of a Supreme Court, three Courts of Appeal and over 50 Departmental Courts. Decisions are rendered mainly on the basis of Shari'a (Islamic law) for social and family matters. In commercial and some criminal cases, western style legal codes are applied.

The human rights situation deteriorated following the coup in August 2008. There were arbitrary arrests, and prison conditions continue to be harsh. Abuse and torture of detainees and prisoners has been reported. Limits on freedom of the press and assembly continue, and slavery and slavery-like practices persist. There is widespread corruption. Mauritania retains the death penalty for high treason, premeditated murder and torture. With the introduction of Islamic law in 1980, the death penalty can also be handed down for apostasy, homosexuality and rape. However, the last execution was carried out in 1987.

Commissariat aux Droits de l'Homme à la Lutte contre la Pauvreté et l'Insertion, BP 6808 Nouakchott, Mauritania. Tel: +222 529 1195, fax: +222 529 0960

LOCAL GOVERNMENT

For administrative purposes Mauritania is divided into 12 regions, plus the capital district Nouakchott. The regions are, Adrar, Assaba, Brakna, Dakhlet Nouadhibou, Gorgol, Guidimaka, Hodh Ech Chargui, Hodh El Gharbi, Inchiri, Tagant, Tiris Zemmour, Trarza.

AREA AND POPULATION

Area
The Islamic Republic of Mauritania is bounded by Senegal and Mali to the south and east, Algeria and the Western Sahara to the north, and the Atlantic Ocean to the west. The total area of the country is 1,030,000 sq. km. and the principal towns are Nouakchott with a population of 708,000; Nouadhibou, 72,000; Kaedi, 34,000; Atar, 24,000; Rosso, 50,000. Around 60 per cent of the country is desert. The climate is desert: very hot and dry.

To view a map, visit http://www.lib.utexas.edu/maps/cia08/mauritania_sm_2008.gif

Population
In 2010 the population stood at an estimated 3.46 million. Approximately 41 per cent of the population lives in urban areas. The majority of the population live in or near the capital Nouakchott and along the Senegal river.

The official language is Arabic, but French, Poular, Wolof and Solinke are also spoken.

Births, Marriages, Deaths
Estimated figures for 2010 put the birth rate at 33.8 births per 1,000 population and the death rate at 9.6 per 1,000 population. The total fertility rate in 2010 was 4.5 per female. The average life expectancy in 2009 was 57 years for males and 60 years for females. Healthy life expectancy was 49 years for males and 52 years for females. The median age is 20 years. Figures for 2009 show that 40 per cent of the population in aged 14 or under and 4 per cent over 60 years. (Source: http://www.who.int, World Health Statistics)

National Day
28 November: Independence Day

EMPLOYMENT

Figures for 2007 put the labour force at 1.3 million. Recent figures show that over 50 per cent of the labour force is engaged in the agricultural sector, 20 per cent government employees, 20 per cent work in the service sector and 10 per cent in industry. Estimated figures for 2008 put unemployment at 30 per cent.

BANKING AND FINANCE

Currency
1 Ouguiya = 5 khoums

MAURITANIA

GDP/GNP, Inflation, National Debt
Most of the population are still dependent on agriculture for a living and are subsistence farmers. The country has mineral resources but exploitation is limited by poor infrastructure. There is a small oil industry but it has not developed thus far as quickly as hoped.

Offshore oil extraction began in 2006 and contributed to GDP growth of 11.7 per cent. Growth fell in 2007 to 2.0 per cent and -0.9 per cent. In 2007 GDP was made up by 13 per cent from the agriculture sector, 47 per cent from industry and 41 per cent from the service sector. GDP was estimated to be US$3.8 billion in 2010 with a growth rate of 4.7 per cent. Per capita GDP was estimated to be US$2,100. GDP was estimated to be US$4 billion in 2011 with a growth rate of 3.75 per cent.

In 2004, inflation was recorded at 10.4 per cent. This rise was mainly due to rising prices following food shortages. It rose further to 12.1 per cent in 2005, before falling to 6.2 per cent in 2006, rising again to 7.6 per cent in 2007. It was estimated to be 7.5 per cent in 2011.

As part of the Heavily Indebted Poor Countries initiative, the Paris Club agreed in 2002 to write off some of Mauritania's debt. This was in response to Mauritania implementing economic reforms. In June 2006 Mauritania's had its multi-lateral debt cancelled under the G8 Multilateral Debt Relief Intiative. Total external public debt was US$2.75 billion in 2011.

Balance of Payments / Imports and Exports
Mauritania's main trading partners are Japan, France, China, Italy, Germany, Spain, Belgium, the US, Russia and the UK. Main exported goods are iron ore, fish, and gold. Imports include machinery, petroleum products and foodstuffs.

External Trade, US$ million

	2005	2006	2007
Trade balance	-803.18	199.58	136.91
Exports	625.14	1,366.57	1,329.67
Imports	1,428.32	1,166.99	1,192.76

Source: African Development Bank

Exports were estimated to be US$1.37 billion in 2009 and import costs were US$1.5 billion.

Central Bank
Banque Centrale de Mauritanie, PO Box 623, Avenue de l'Indépendance, Nouakchott, Mauritania. Tel: +222 252206 / 252888, fax: +222 252759, URL: http://www.bcm.mr Governor: Sid'Ahmed Ould Raiss

Chambers of Commerce and Trade Organisations
Mauritania Chamber of Commerce and Industry, PO Box 215, Avenue de la Republique, Nouakchott, Mauritania. Tel: +222 252214, fax: +222 253895, URL: http://www.mcci.org

MANUFACTURING, MINING AND SERVICES

Primary and Extractive Industries
Mining of lower grade ores in the Guelbs region began at El Rhein in 1984, and mining of high grade iron ore is carried out at Kedia near Zouérate. In 1985 iron ore exports were worth US$155.1 million, just over 40 per cent of total exports, and were the second largest source of foreign exchange. Iron ore mining is being restructured with the backing of the World Bank and other donors. Gold and diamonds have been found but exploitation is limited. In 2003, 68 per cent of Mauritania's exports were of metal and ore origin. Deposits of blue granite were discovered recently in the North.

Copper mining at Akjoujt was suspended in 1978. In 2006 copper cencentrate was mined for the first time from the Guelb Moghrein copper-gold mine, that year from the same mine, 322 kg of gold was produced. A US$10 million gypsum mining and processing project was inaugurated near Nouakchott in 1984. Phosphate reserves estimated at 95 million tons remain unexploited because of transport problems and current low world prices. In 2006 several licences for exploration and prospecting for uranium were issued.

Exploration is under way offshore, seismic surveys having suggested high potential oil and gas reserves. In 2001 a significant oil discovery was made off the country's southwest coast. Production started from the Chinguettil oilfield in 2006 at a rate of 15,000 barrels per day. It was hoped that this would be increased to a rate of 75,000 barrels per day by the end of that year. The Tiof oilfield was discovered in 2005 and was scheduled to come online in 2007. Mauritania had proven reserves of 200 million barrels in 2012 and that year produced 17.700 barrels per day all of which were crude. Mauritania has proven reserves of natural gas of one trillion cubic feet, although at present none of this is exploited.

Energy
Electricity generation has expanded rapidly with the growth of the mining industry. In 2010 electric generating capacity was 0.26 gigawatts. The main power station near Nouakchott is being rehabilitated and electricity supply improved with the help of funds from OPEC. As one of the members of the Organisation pour la Mise en Valeur du Fleuve Senegal (OMVS), Mauritania should benefit from hydro-electricity generated from the Manantali and Diama dams in neighbouring Mali and Senegal. At present over 80 per cent of electricity is generated from fossil fuels. In 2010, 0.70 kilowatthours (kWh) of electricity were generated and 0.65 billion kWh were consumed. Before the coup in 2005 plans were underway to privatise the state power company.

Manufacturing
There is a very small manufacturing industry. A petroleum refinery with capacity for 1 million tons of Algerian oil a year began operating in 1978 near Nouadhibou. It was shut down in 1983, but was reopened in April 1987 with Algerian help. A sugar refinery was reopened in 1982.

In 1986 the World Bank provided a US$20 million loan towards mining and industry as part of a programme to diversify Mauritania's economy. A steel rolling mill has recently been renovated. There is also small scale manufactuing of food processing, chemicals, plastics, building materials, and paper and packaging materials.

Agriculture
Agriculture remains the main occupation of the majority of the population. However, Mauritania suffers from the effect of drought and pests, and in recent years has been heavily dependent on foreign aid. Mauritania meets less than half of its food needs and in recent years 20,000 tonnes of grain have been imported. With the help of foreign aid, a major irrigation scheme is being developed in the Gorgol Valley. Main crops include millet, rice, sorghum and pulses.

Aid has been given by the FAO, the International Development Association (IDA), the African Development Fund, the International Fund for Agricultural Development (IFAD), and the OPEC Fund for International Development as well as France, Germany, Japan and Arab countries. In January 2002 torrential rains hit Mauritania and crops and grazing land were severely damaged. In 2004 much of northern Africa was hit by an invasion of locusts. Mauritania was the worst hit country and crops were wiped out. As a result of this in 2005 the UN called for food aid to be sent.

Agricultural Production in 2010

Produce	Int. $'000*	Tonnes
Indigenous sheep meat	92,711	34,050
Indigenous cattle meat	71,031	26,295
Indigenous camel meat	52,184	24,900
Sheep milk, whole, fresh	44,977	115,500
Goat milk, whole, fresh	41,534	123,768
Indigenous goat meat	39,715	16,575
Cow milk, whole, fresh	39,320	126,000
Rice, paddy	36,892	134,447
Sorghum	15,327	114,249
Pulses, nes	10,369	20,700
Dates	10,163	19,900
Camel milk, whole, fresh	8,951	26,250

* unofficial figures

Source: http://faostat.fao.org/site/339/default.aspx Food and Agriculture Organization of the United Nations, Food and Agricultural commodities production

Fishing
Mauritania's rich fishing grounds were largely exploited by foreign companies until 1980 when the government declared a 200-mile economic exclusion zone along the coastline. With tighter controls on the industry, fishing receipts greatly increased and boosted the fish processing and freezing industry at Nouadhibou.

Conservation measures were introduced in July 1987 to try to prevent over-fishing. Figures for 2010 put the total catch at 276,000 tonnes.

Port and landing facilities are to be improved and small-scale fishing encouraged. The World Bank is funding a study of the fisheries sector with a view to formulating a long-term strategy for the industry. In 2001 an agreement was reached with the EU that would allow European trawlers to fish in Mauritanian waters for four years.

COMMUNICATIONS AND TRANSPORT

Travel Requirements
Citizens of the USA, Canada, Australia and the EU require a valid passport and a visa, unless in transit within 24 hours, with onward documentation and not leaving the airport. Other nationals should contact the embassy to check visa requirements.

Evidence a yellow fever vaccination is also required.

The transport system is geared to the mining industry.

National Airlines
Air Mauritania which was privatised in 1999.

International Airports
There are international airports at Nouakchott and Nouadhibou. There are also four domestic airports.

Railways
The iron ore mines are linked to the port of Nouadhibou by a 704 km railway line. Although operated by mining companies the service is open to both people and vehicles and runs between Nouadhibou and Atar.

Roads
At the end of 1999 there were about 7,660 km of roads, of which 900 km were paved. Border crossings for cars exist with Western Sahara, Mali and Senegal. Vehicles are driven on the right.

Shipping
Nouakchott's deepwater harbour, built with Chinese aid and completed in 1985, can handle 400,000 tons. It became operational in 1986. There are also harbours at Bogue, Nouadhibou, Rosso and Kaedi.

HEALTH

In 2009, the government spent approximately 7.3 per cent of its total budget on healthcare (down from 12.8 per cent in 2000), accounting for 52.8 per cent of all healthcare spending. Total expenditure on healthcare equated to 4.2 per cent of the country's GDP. Per capita expenditure on health was approximately US$38, compared with US$24 in 2000. In 2005-10, there were 445 doctors (1.3 per 10,000 population), 2,303 nurses and midwives (6.7 per 10,000 population), and 93 dentists.

In 2010, 50 per cent of the population had sustainable access to an improved water source. In the same year, 26 per cent of the population had sustainable access to improved sanitation. Diarrhoea accounts for 11 per cent of deaths of children aged less than five. Other major causes of childhood mortality are: measles 7 per cent, malaria 6 per cent, pneumonia 17 per cent and prematurity 14 per cent. In 2009 life expectancy was put at 58 years. The infant mortality rate (probability of dying by age one) was 75 per 1,000 live births. The child mortality rate (probability of dying by age five) was 111 per 1,000 live births. Immunization rates for major diseases are just over 60 per cent. (Source: http://www.who.int, World Health Statistics 2012)

EDUCATION

Education has expanded considerably since 1960, but illiteracy among the population over six years old is still high. A major literacy programme was launched in 1986. Education is now compulsory between the ages of six and fourteen. Although state education is free parents are expected to pay for books which can inhibit poorer families, also many children in rural areas suffer from the poor infrastructure in some areas which means it is difficult to travel to the nearest school.

Primary education starts at age six and lasts for six years. Figures for 2007 show that 66 per cent of girls and 67 per cent of boys were enrolled in primary school. Approximately 43 per cent complete primary education. The pupil:teacher ratio was 45:1 in 2004. Secondary education starts at age 12 and lasts for six years, three at lower level and three at upper level. Figures for the same year show that 47 per cent of girls and 43 per cent of boys were enrolled in secondary school. Three per cent of the population of tertiary age is in tertiary education. (Source: WHO and UNESCO)

Adult literacy in 2007 was 52 per cent.

RELIGION

Islam is the official and predominant religion of the Islamic Republic of Mauritania with 99 per cent of the population adherants. There is a very small community of Christians (0.24 per cent). Mauritania has a religious tolerance rating of 4 on a scale of 1 to 10 (10 is most freedom). (Source: World Religion Database)

COMMUNICATIONS AND MEDIA

Mauritanian main television and radio networks are state owned. Freedom of the press has improved in recent years and newspapers no longer need to seek pre-approval to publish. In 2010 the government passed a law to liberalise broadcasting and in November 2011, the government approved new radio and television stations.

Newspapers
Chaab, URL: http://www.ami.mr/chaab/index.htm
Horizon, URL: http://www.ami.mr/horizons/index.htm
Akhbar Nouakchott, http://www.akhbarnouakchott.com/

Broadcasting
The state-run channel is the Television de Mauritanie (TVM), URL: http://www.tvm.mr/. It also operates regional stations. Broadcasts are in Arabic and French.

Telecommunications
The system is limited. According to 2008 estimates, there an estimated 75,000 mainlines and 2 million mobile phones. Mobile phone services are expanding rapidly. There were an estimated 150,000 internet users in 2012.

ENVIRONMENT

One of the main environmental concerns for Mauritania is desertification brought about by overgrazing and deforestation and made worse by drought.

Mauritania is a party to the following international agreements: Biodiversity, Climate Change, Climate Change-Kyoto Protocol, Desertification, Endangered Species, Hazardous Wastes, Law of the Sea, Ozone Layer Protection, Ship Pollution, Wetlands, and Whaling.

According to the EIA, in 2010 Mauritania's emissions from the consumption of fossil fuels totalled 2.89 million metric tons of carbon dioxide.

MAURITIUS
Republic of Mauritius

Capital: Port Louis (Population estimate: 145,000)

Head of State: Rajkeswur Kailash Purryag (page 1498)

Vice-President: Monique Ohsan Bellepeau (page 1489)

National Flag: Four horizontal stripes of red, blue, yellow and green

CONSTITUTION AND GOVERNMENT

Constitution
After various steps of constitutional development, Mauritius became an independent state within the Commonwealth on 12 March 1968.

The executive authority was vested in the Queen with a Governor-General, the local representative of the Queen, who was the Head of State. The Constitution, as amended in 1992, provides for an elected president who serves a five year term. The cabinet consists of the Prime Minister and 24 ministers.

To consult the constitution, please visit: http://www.gov.mu/portal/site/AssemblySite

International Relations
Mauritius has friendly relations with other African states in the region, particularly South Africa, its largest continental trading partner. The country is a member of several regional organisations such as the Southern Africa Development Community (SADC), the Indian Ocean Commission, Community of Eastern and South African States (COMESA), and the recently formed Indian Ocean Rim Association. Mauritius coordinates much of its foreign policy with the Southern Africa Development Community and the African Union.

Mauritius has strong relations with the West and with India due to historical and commercial links. It is a member of the World Trade Organization (WTO) and the Commonwealth.

In June 2010, France and Mauritius agreed to manage the Indian Ocean of Tromelin.

President Sir Anerood Jugnauth resigned in March 2012 . The vice-president, Monique Ohsan-Bellepeau, took over as acting president until the presidential election in July when Rajkeswur Purryag was elected president by parliament on 20 July 2012.

Legislature
The Constitution also provides for a Legislative Assembly, consisting of a Speaker, elected from its own members, 62 elected members (three each for the 20 constituencies of Mauritius and two for the island of Rodrigues), and eight additional seats in order to ensure a fair and adequate representation of each community in the Assembly without disturbing the political equilibrium established by the election results.
National Assembly, Port Louis, The Maldives. Tel: +230 201 1414, URL: http://www.mauritiusassembly.gov.mu

Cabinet (as at March 2013)
Prime Minister, Minister of Defence and Home Affairs, Minister of External Relations: Hon. Dr. Navinchandra Ramgoolam (page 1500)
Deputy Prime Minister, Minister of Energy and Utilities: Hon. Dr Ahmed Rashid Beebeejuan (page 1386)
Vice Prime Minister, Public Infrastructure, National Development Unit, Land Transport and Shipping: Anil Kumar Bachoo
Vice Prime Minister, Minister of Finance and Economy: Hon. Charles Gaëtan Xavier-Luc Duval (page 1418)
Minister of Agro-Industries, Production and Food Security: Hon. Satya Faugoo
Ministry of Labour, Industrial Relations and Employment: Hon. Shakeel Ahmed Yousuf Abdul Razack Mohamed
Minister of Foreign Affairs, Regional Cooperation and International Trade: Hon. Dr Arvin Boolell (page 1391)
Minister of Education and Human Resources: Hon. Dr Vasant Kumar Bunwaree
Attorney General: Hon. Yatindra Nath Varma (page 1531)
Minister of Social Security, National Solidarity and Senior Citizens Welfare and Reform Institutions: Hon. Sheilabai Bappoo (page 1383)
Minister of Public Infrastructure, Transport and Shipping: Hon. Anil Kumar Bachoo (page 1381)
Minister of Health and Quality of Life: Hon. Lormus Bundhoo
Minister of Industry, Trade and Consumer Protection: Hon. Sayyad Abd-al-Cader Sayed-Hossen
Minister of Housing and Lands: Hon. Dr Abu Twalib Kasenally
Minister of Information Technology and Telecommunications: Hon. Tassarajen Pillay Chedumbrum
Minister of Youth and Sports: Satyaprakash Ritoo
Minister of the Environment and Sustainable Development: Devanand Virahsawmy
Minister of Further Education, Science, Research and Technology: Rajeshwar Jeetah
Minister of Tourism and Leisure: John Tzoun Sao Yeung Sik Yuen
Minister of Fisheries: Louis Joseph Von-Mally

MAURITIUS

Minister of Social Integration and Economic Empowerment: Surendra Dayal
Minister of Local Government and Outer Islands: Louis Hervé Aimée
Minister of Arts and Culture: Mookesswur Choonee
Minister of Business, Enterprise and Co-operatives: Jangbahadoorsing Iswurdeo Mola Roopchand Seetaram
Minister of Gender Equality, Child Development and Family Welfare: Sheilabi Bappoo
Minister of Civil Service and Administrative Reforms: Sutaydeo Moutia

Ministries

Office of the President, State House, Port Louis, Mauritius. Tel: +230 454 3021, fax: +230 464 5370, e-mail: president@mail.gov.mu, URL: http://ncb.intnet.mu/presid/
Office of the Prime Minister, New Treasury Building, Port Louis, Mauritius. Tel: +230 201 2850, fax: +230 208 6642, e-mail: saujeet@mail.gov.mu, URL: http://primeminister.gov.mu
Ministry of Finance, Ground Floor, Government House, Port Louis, Mauritius. Tel: +230 201 1146, fax: +230 211 0096, e-mail: finance@mof.intnet.mu, URL: http://mof.gov.mu/
Ministry of Agri-Industries and Food Security, Levels 8 & 9 Renganaden Seeneevassen Building, Cnr Jules Koenig & Maillard Streets, Port Louis, Mauritius. Tel: +230 212 2335, fax: +230 212 4427, e-mail: moamic@intnet.mu, URL: http://agriculture.gov.mu
Ministry of Social Security, National Solidarity and Senior Citizen Welfare, 13th Floor, R. Seeneevassen Building, C/r Jules Koenig & Maillard Streets, Port Louis, Mauritius. Tel: +230 212 3001-6, fax: +230 212 8190, e-mail: mss@mail.gov.mu, URL: http://socialsecurity.gov.mu
Ministry of Public Utilities, Level 10, Air Mauritius Centre, John Kennedy Street, Port-Louis, Mauritius. Tel: +230 210 1816, fax: 208 6497, e-mail: mpu@mail.gov.mu, URL: http://www.gov.mu
Ministry of Tourism, Level 12, Air Mauritius Centre, John Kennedy Street, Port Louis, Mauritius. Tel: +230 210 1329, fax: +230 208 6776, e-mail: mot@intnet.mu, URL: http://tourism.gov.mu
Ministry of Environment, Ken Lee Tower, Cnr Barracks & St Georges Streets, Port-Louis, Mauritius. Tel: +230 212 3363, fax: +230 211 9524 / 212 8324, e-mail: admenv@intnet.mu, URL: http://environment.gov.mu/
Ministry of Public Infrastructure, Land Transport and Shipping, Public Infrastructure Division Moorgate House, Sir William Newton Street, Port Louis, Mauritius. Tel: +230 208 0281, fax: +230 208 7149, e-mail: webmaster-mpi@mail.gov.mu, URL: http://publicinfrastructure.gov.mu/
Ministry of Civil Service Affairs and Administrative Reforms, 7th Floor, New Government Centre, Port Louis, Mauritius. Tel: +230 201 2886/8, fax: +230 212 9528, e-mail: civser@mail.gov.mu, URL: http://civilservice.gov.mu
Ministry of Labour and Industrial Relations, Victoria House, Cnr Barracks-St-Louis, Port Louis, Mauritius. Tel: +230 212 3049, fax: +230 212 3070, e-mail: mol@mail.gov.mu, URL: http://labour.gov.mu/
Ministry of Women, Family Welfare & Child Development, C.S.K Building, Corner Remy Ollier/Emmanuel, Anquetil Streets, Port Louis, Mauritius. Tel: +230 240 1377, fax: +230 240 7717, e-mail : mwfwcd@mail.gov.mu, URL: http://women.gov.mu/
Ministry of Foreign Affairs and Regional Cooperation, 5th floor, New Government Centre, Port Louis, Mauritius. Fax: +230 208 8087 / 212 6764, e-mail: mfa@mail.gov.mu, URL: http://foreign.gov.mu
Ministry of Education and Scientific Research, IVTB House, Pont Fer, Phoenix, Port Louis, Mauritius. Tel: +230 698 0464 / 1084, fax: +230 698 2550, e-mail: moeps@mail.gov.mu, URL: http://ministry-education.gov.mu/
Ministry of Health & Quality of Life, 5th floor, Emmanuel Anquetil Building, Port Louis, Mauritius. Tel: +230 201 2175, fax: +230 208 7222, e-mail: moh@mail.gov.mu, URL: http://health.gov.mu/
Ministry of Commerce & Co-operatives, 3rd Floor, LICI Building, John Kennedy Street, Port Louis, Mauritius. Tel: +230 208 4812, fax: +230 208 9263, e-mail: pscoop@intnet.mu, URL: http://cooperatives.gov.mu/
Ministry of Housing and Lands, SILWF Building, Edith Cavell Street, Port Louis, Mauritius. Tel: 230 208 2831, fax: +230 212 9369, e-mail: mhou@mail.gov.mu, URL: http://housing.gov.mu/
Ministry of Information Technology & Telecommunications, Level 9 Air Mauritius Centre, President John Kennedy Street, Port-Louis, Mauritius. Tel: +230 210 0201, fax: +230 212 1673, e-mail: mtel@mail.gov.mu, URL: http://telecomit.gov.mu
Attorney General & Ministry of Justice & Human Rights, 2nd Floor, R. Seeneevassen Building, Port Louis, Mauritius. Tel: +230 212 2139 / 0544, fax: +230 212 6742, e-mail: sgo@mail.gov.mu, URL: http://attorneygeneral.gov.mu
Ministry of Youth and Sports, 3rd floor, Emmanuel Anquetil Bldg, Port Louis, Mauritius. Tel: +230 211 2543, fax: +230 211 2986, e-mail: mys@mail.gov.mu, URL: http://youthsport.gov.mu/

Political Parties
Parti Travailliste, (Labour Party, PTr), URL: http://www.labourparty.mu
Leader: Navin Ramgoolam
Parti Mauricien Social-Démocrate, (Mauritian Social Democrat Party, PMSD), URL: http://www.pmsd.mu
Leader: Xavier Luc Duval
Mouvement Socialiste Mauricien, (Mauritian Socialist Movement, MSM), URL: http://www.msmparty.org
Leader: Pravind Jugnauth
Mouvement Militant Socialiste Mauricien, (Militant Mauritian Movement, MMM)
Mouvement Rodriguais, (Rodrigues Movement, MR)
National Union (UN)

Elections
General elections are held every five years on the basis of universal adult suffrage. The voting age is from 18.

An early election was called in September 2000, by Prime Minister Dr Ramgoolam following accusations of corruption against some ministers. It resulted in a coalition government formed by the Mouvement Socialiste Militant (MSM) and the Mouvement Militant Mauricien (MMM). Prime Minister Sir Agnerood Jugnauth served for the first three years of the five year term and in 2003 became president. Deputy Prime Minister Paul Raymond Bérenger took over as prime minister, but was ousted following National Assembly elections in July 2005 when Navim Ramgoolam's opposition Social Alliance party won 38 of the 62 seats. The most recent parliamentary election took play in May 2010; a coalition called The Alliance of the Future won an overall majority. It is made up of the Mauritius Labour Party (MPT) led by Prime Minister Navin Ramgoolam; the Militant Socialist Movement (MSM) and the Mauritian Social Democrat Party (PMSD).

President Cassam Uteem resigned in February 2002 in protest at a controversial anti-terrorism bill. His replacement, Angidi Chettiar, resigned three days after taking office, also in protest at the anti-terrorism legislation. Karl Offman was elected president on 25 February 2002 and retired in October 2003, at which point Prime Minister Sir Anerood Jugnauth became president. In September 2008 he was re-elected unanimously. He resigned in March 2012 over disagreements with the prime minister. Rajkeswur Purryag (PTr) was elected president by parliament on 20 July 2012.

The next parliamentary election is due in 2015 and the next presidential election in 2013.

Diplomatic Representation
British High Commission, Les Cascades Building, Edith Cavell Street, Port Louis, PO Box 1063, Mauritius. Tel: +230 202 9400 fax: +230 202 9408, e-mail: bhc@intnet.mu, URL: http://ukinmauritius.fco.gov.uk/en
High Commissioner: Nick Leake (page 1461)
US Embassy, Rogers House 4th Floor, John Kennedy Avenue, Port Louis, Mauritius. Tel: +230 202 4400, fax: +230 208 9534, e-mail: usembass@intnet.mu, URL: http://mauritius.usembassy.gov/
Ambassador: Shari Villarosa
Mauritius High Commission, 32/33 Elvaston Place, London, SW7 5NW, United Kingdom. Tel: +44 (0)20 7581 0294, e-mail: londonmhc@btinternet.com
High Commissioner: Abhimanu Mahendra Kundasamy
Mauritius Embassy, 4301 Connecticut Avenue, Suite 441, Washington, D.C. 20008, USA. Tel: +1 202 244 1491/2, fax: +1 202 966 0983, e-mail: Mauritius.embassy@prodigy.net, URL: http://www.maurinet.com/embasydc.html
Interim Chargé d'Affaires: Joyker Nayeck
Mauritius Mission to the United Nations, 211 East 43rd Street, 15th Floor, New York, NY 10017, USA. Tel: +1 212 949 0190/91, fax:+1 212 697 3829, e-mail:mauritius@un.int, URL: http://www.gov.mu/portal/sites/mfamission/newyork/index.htm
Ambassador and Permanent Representative: H.E. Jaya Nyamrajsingh Meetarbhan

LEGAL SYSTEM

The laws of Mauritius are mainly based on the old French Codes, the Civil Code, the Penal Code, the Code of Commerce and the Code of Civil Procedure, although a number of amendments have been made. The Bankruptcy Law, the Law of Evidence and the Law of Criminal Procedure and Labour Laws are to a great extent based on English Law.

The Courts exercising jurisdiction in Mauritius are the Supreme Court, the Intermediate Court, the District Courts and the Industrial Court. A Family Court became operational in January 2008, to reduce the caseload on the Supreme Court. The Supreme Court has a chief justice (nominated by the President) and six other judges who also serve on the Court of Criminal Appeal, the Court of Civil Appeal, the Intermediate Court, the Industrial Court, and 10 district courts. Final appeal can be made to the UK Privy Council.

The government respects the human rights of its citizens. However, there have been recent instances of torture and abuse of suspects and detainees by security forces. Prison conditions are poor, and there is some degree of official corruption. The death penalty was abolished in 1995, the last execution having been carried out in 1987.

Attorney General: Rama Valayden
URL: http://attorneygeneral.gov.mu/English/Pages/default.aspx
Supreme Court, URL: http://www1.gov.mu/scourt/pubjudgment/pubViewP.do
Chief Justice: Hon. Y.K.J. Yeung sik Yuen

National Human Rights Commission, URL: http://www.gov.mu/portal/site/nhrcsite

LOCAL GOVERNMENT

Mauritius has two tiers of local government. The first comprises urban councils (municipalities) and rural authorities (district councils). The second tier relates to district councils which oversee 124 village councils. The municipalities are: Port Louis, Plaines Vilhems, Beau Bassin - Rose Hill, Quatre Bonnes, Vacoas-Phoenix, and Curepipe. The districts are: Pamplemousses-Riviere du Rempart, Moka-Flacq, Black River, Grand Port-Savanne.

The district councils are made up of representatives from the village councils. The village council is the smallest unit of local government and has its own constitution and powers. Local authority representatives are democratically elected every five years.

Mauritius also has three dependencies: the Agalega Islands, Saint Brandon (Cargados Carajos Shoals), and the island of Rodrigues. The first Rodrigues Regional Assembly opened on 15 October 2002.

AREA AND POPULATION

Area
Mauritius consists of a number of volcanic islands surrounded by coral reefs in the Indian Ocean about 500 miles off the east coast of Madagascar.

The main island, named Mauritius, has an area of approximately 720 square miles. It is 36 miles long and 29 miles wide. The great increase in population during the last century has made Mauritius one of the most densely populated regions of the world, at 622 people per km. sq.

The other major island is Rodrigues. This lies about 350 miles (560 km) east of Mauritius. It has an area of 105 sq. km and at 1 July 2000 its population was 35,663 with a density of 343 people per sq. km. The population of the outlying islands of Agalega and Saint Brandon (Cardagos Carajos Shoals) was estimated at 170.

The terrain is mountainous. Mauritius has a number of micro-climates and weather conditions vary across the island, though the temperature range is moderate, from 16°C in the winter, to 35°C in summer. The islands are in the Indian Ocean cyclone belt and there is occasionally extensive damage during the November to April cyclone season.

To view a map of Mauritius, please consult http://www.lib.utexas.edu/maps/cia08/mauritius_sm_2008.gif

Population
Figures for 2010 estimated the total population at 1,299,000. Annual population growth over the period 2000-10 was around 0.8 per cent. Approximately 42 per cent of the population live in urban areas. The capital Port Louis has an estimated population of 145,000, whilst the town of Plaine Wilhems has the largest population at around 359,500, followed by Flacq with 156,000 inhabitants.

The official language is English but a number of other languages are spoken, namely French, Creole, Hindi, Urdu, Hakka, Chinese and Arabic.

Births, Marriages, Deaths
In 2010, the crude birth rate was 12.8 births per 1,000 inhabitants and the crude death rate was 7.0 per 1,000 inhabitants. The provisional fertility rate for the year 2010 was 1.6 children per woman. The infant mortality rate was 13 per 1,000. Life expectancy at birth was 69 years for men and 76 years for women. Healthy life expectancy was 63 years. (Source: http://www.who.int, World Health Statistics 2012)

Public Holidays 2014
1 January: New Year
31 January: Chinese New Year
28 February: Shivaratri
12 March: Independence Day
18 April: Good Friday
5 May: Labour Day
15 August: Assumption
9 September: Father Leval Day
29 July: Eid al-Fitr (end of Ramadan)*
1 November: All Saints Day
25 December: Christmas

* Islamic holidays are calculated by sighting of the moon.
Hindu festivals are also celebrated including Thaipoosam Cavadee, Maha Shivaratree, Ougadi, Ganesh Chaturti and Divali

EMPLOYMENT

Traditionally sugar production was the main employer in Mauritius, but in the 1980s the government introduced an Export Processing Zone (EPZ) - a policy encouraging manufacturing, particularly textiles and clothing (about 90 per cent). The EPZ is made up of enterprises operating mainly for export which benefit from incentives (particularly tax). This was set up with IMF support and has resulted in a high rate of economic growth.

Continuing with its programme of diversification, Mauritius became a provider of offshore banking and investment services in the 1990s and, in 2002, the country began building the infrastructure to create a 'cyber city', offering amongst other services, a secure back-up facility for international data systems.

Provisional figures for 2005 indicate that of the 542,500-strong labour force, 490,400 were in employment. 329,100 were men and 161,300 were women. In general, almost 20 per cent of people were employed in manufacturing, nearly 10 per cent in construction, 22 per cent in trade and tourism, 16.5 per cent in government services, and almost ten per cent in agriculture and fishing.

The unemployment figures decreased from 14.8 per cent in 1985 to 1.6 per cent in 1994 but from then until 2004, they gradually increased. In 2005, unemployment stood at 9.6 per cent of the workforce.

Total Employment by Economic Activity

Activity	2008
Agriculture, hunting & forestry	40,800
Fishing	5,300
Mining & quarrying	500
Manufacturing	102,200
Electricity, gas & water supply	3,700

- continued

Construction	57,700
Wholesale & retail trade, repairs	71,600
Hotels & restaurants	37,100
Transport, storage & communications	38,300
Financial intermediation	13,400
Real estate, renting & business activities	26,400
Public administration and defence	34,000
Education	30,100
Health & social work	16,600
Other community, social and personal service activities	19,800
Private households with employed persons	19,100
Extra-territorial organisations & bodies	300
Other	2,100
Total	519,000

Source: Copyright © International Labour Organization (ILO Dept. of Statistics, http://laborsta.ilo.org)

BANKING AND FINANCE

Currency
The currency of the island is the rupee (Rs). The rupee is linked to a basket of foreign currencies.

Mauritius has few natural resources, yet the country has developed one of the most successful and competitive economies in Africa. The economy is based on tourism, textiles, sugar, and financial services. Information and communication technology (ICT) is a growing sector, with the creation of *cyber cities*, as is the seafood industry and off shore banking. There have been recent government economic reforms aimed at global competitiveness through stronger fiscal regulation and an improved investment climate for foreign investors, as well as the use external expertise.

GDP/GNP, Inflation, National Debt
Over the past twenty years, real output growth has averaged almost 6 per cent per annum. In 2009, Gross Domestic Product reached US$9.1 billion, indicating growth of 4.6 per cent over the previous year. GDP growth in 2009 was estimated to be 2.1 per cent. GDP was estimated to be US$9.5 billion with a growth rate of 4.2 per cent. Per capita GDP was US$13,600 (ppp) in 2010. GDP was estimated to be US$11.3 billion in 2012 with a growth rate of 4.1 per cent. The agricultural sector contributed an estimated 4.5 per cent towards GDP in 2011, whilst the industry sector accounted for 25 per cent, and the services sector 70 per cent.

The following table shows the growth of GDP at current prices in (figures are in million rupees):

Sector	2000	2007*	2008*
Agriculture, hunting, forestry & fishing	7,491	9,930	10,155
Mining & quarrying	163	96	10,054
Manufacturing	24,701	41,075	46,888
Electricity, gas & water	1,820	3,668	4,759
Construction	5,899	13,145	16,216
Wholesale & retail trade, repairs & household goods	12,810	25,598	28,840
Hotels & restaurants	6,872	19,517	20,048
Transport, storage, communication	13,663	24,727	26,056
Financing intermediation	10,156	21,607	25,410
Real estate renting & business activities	9,341	22,615	26,886
Public admin. & defence; compulsory social security	7,043	12,674	14,618
Education	4,761	9,110	10,443
Health & social work	3,106	6,824	7,909
Other services	3,498	7,981	9,425
FISM	-5,955	-11,528	-14,000
GDP at basic prices	**105,206**	**206,943**	**233,653**
Taxes on products (net of subsidies)	15,085	28,549	31,201
GDP at market prices	**120,291**	**235,492**	**264,854**

*revised estimates
Source: Central Statistics Office, Mauritius

Inflation was estimated to have fallen below 3 per cent in 2010, rising to over 6 per cent in 2011 and 2012.

Foreign direct investment rose by 15.5 per cent in 2012Q1 to 1.598 billion rupees ($53 million). Most investment was directed towards the real estate sector followed by construction. South Africa is the main investor (511 million rupees) followed by France (341 million rupees).

Balance of Payments, Imports & Exports
Figures for 2011 show that total exports for that year earned some US$2.5 million and imports cost the islands some US$4.9 million.

Textiles and clothing, sugar, canned tuna, watches and clocks, jewelry, optical goods, toys and games, and flowers were the main items exported. The main export markets were Europe (67.9 per cent) and the USA. Some 22 per cent of goods go to the United Kingdom. The other main markets are France, the USA, Italy and Madagascar.

MAURITIUS

Mineral fuels and lubricants accounted for over 20 per cent of imports, manufactured goods 19 per cent and food and live animals 18 per cent. Raw materials for the textile industry were also imported. Asia supplied 54 per cent of imports and Europe 24.8 per cent. The main source of imports was India (23.9 per cent), followed by China (11.5 per cent) and South Africa (8.1 per cent). Imports from India rose by 23. per cent following an increase in the imports of petroleum products.

The following table gives a comparison of external trade in recent years (figures are in million rupees):

Commodity	2007*	2008**
Total	64,265	59,455
Food & live animals	19,666	18,548
Beverages & tobacco	467	600
Crude material, inedible except fuels	857	977
Mineral fuels, lubricants & related materials	91	19
Animals and vegetable oils, fats & waxes	52	49
Chemicals & related products	1,310	1,834
Manufactured goods	5,675	5,283
Machinery and transport equipment	4,078	3,789
Misc. manufactured articles	31,972	28,337
Other commodities	97	69
Imports c.i.f.		
Total	121,037	132,564
Food & live animals	20,032	23,872
Beverages & tobacco	1,545	2,126
Crude materials, inedible except fuels	3,369	3,821
Mineral fuels, lubricants etc.	22,180	28,352
Animal & vegetable oil & fats	1,147	1,579
Chemicals & related products	9,414	10,415
Manufactured goods	24,733	25,035
Machinery & transport equipment	28,529	26,272
Miscellaneous manufactured goods	9,583	10,807
Other	505	285

* revised, ** provisional
Source: Central Statistics Office, Mauritius

Central Bank
Bank of Mauritius, PO Box 29, Sir William Newton Street, Port Louis, Mauritius. Tel: +230 208 4164, fax: +230 208 9204, e-mail: bomrd@bow.intnet.mu, URL: http://bom.intnet.mu
Governor: Rundheersingh Bheenick

Chambers of Commerce and Trade Organisations
Mauritius Chamber of Commerce and Industry, URL: http://www.mcci.org

MANUFACTURING, MINING AND SERVICES

Energy
Mauritius has no natural energy resources. In 2011, imports of oil were estimated to reach 24,000 barrels per day. Iin 2010 Mauritius imported 540, 000 short tons of coal. 2.54 billion kWh of electricity was generated in 2010 and 2.36 billion kWh consumed.

The government encourages sugar refineries to use bagasse, the fibrous residue remaining after the extraction of the juices from sugar cane, as an alternative to coal for the generation of electricity. In 2005, bagasse contributed around 28 per cent of the electrical energy in Mauritius. Coal accounted for 34.7 per cent of electricity generation, whilst fuel oil contributed 34.2 per cent.

Manufacturing
Manufacturing, including export processing zone, accounted for 20 per cent of GDP in 2007. Textile yarn and fabrics, garments, leather products and footwear, processed diamonds and synthetic stones, optical goods, watches and clocks, electric and electronic products, jewellery and related articles, toys, carnival articles and other manufactured goods are now exported in appreciable quantities. The EPZ is dominated by the clothing and textile industry which provides 89 per cent of the EPZ jobs and 83 per cent of exports.

Product in '000 tonnes	2005
Sugar	519.8
Molasses	145.9
Tea	1.4
Iron bars & steel tubes	60.6
Fertilizers	85.0
Product in '000 H. Litres	
Denatured spirit	5.3
Beer & stout	339.0
Wine (country liquor)	52.8
Electricity generated (Gwh)	2,242.2

Source: Central Statistics Office, Mauritius

Service Industries
After sugar and EPZ, tourism is the third largest foreign exchange earner, generating an estimated 8.5 per cent of GDP in 2007. In 2005, there were 761,100 tourists, the largest numbers coming from France (220,000), Reunion, South Africa and western European countries. By 2005 there were 99 hotels in operation.

The financial services sector accounted for 10.3 per cent of GDP in 2007.

Agriculture
The agricultural sector accounts for a declining share of the country's GDP. In 2011 it accounted for 4.5 per cent of GDP down from 5.8 per cent in 2005. The fertile, volcanic soils of Mauritius support extensive sugar plantations which cover 89 per cent of the total area of cultivated land. Sugar accounts for about 67 per cent of the domestic exports and approximately 6 per cent of the GDP. Besides sugar and its by-products, Mauritius exports molasses, tea, flowers, canned fish and a number of other commodities.

The agricultural sector provides employment for around 49,300 people.

Agricultural Production in 2010

Produce	Int. $'000*	Tonnes
Sugar cane	143,361	4,365,830
Indigenous chicken meat	33,264	46,521
Hen eggs, in shell	8,294	10,000
Tomatoes	4,560	12,338
Potatoes	3,369	21,709
Bananas	3,362	11,936
Pumpkins, squash and gourds	3,254	18,557
Cucumbers and gherkins	2,239	11,277
Pineapples	1,861	6,529
Tea	1,560	1,467
Game meat	1,360	625
Carrots and turbips	1,357	5,439

* unofficial figures
Source: http://faostat.fao.org/site/339/default.aspx Food and Agriculture Organization of the United Nations, Food and Agricultural commodities production

Large scale planting of sugar has reduced to some extent the native flora but there are at present some 65,400 ha. under forest, scrub areas, grasslands, and grazing lands. Timber such as pine and eucalyptus and other woods are available for local consumption.

COMMUNICATIONS AND TRANSPORT

Travel Requirements
Citizens of the USA, Canada, Australia and the EU require a passport valid for six months from date of entry, an onward ticket and adequate funds for the visit. US, Canadian, Australian and most EU subjects do not need a visa for stays of up to 90 days, but Bulgarians and Romanians must obtain a visa on arrival. Other nationals should contact the embassy to check visa requirements

Travelers coming from yellow fever-infected areas may be asked to present a yellow fever vaccination certificate.

International Airports
Mauritius is served by the Sir Seewoosagur Ramgoolam International Airport situated at Plaisance, at the South East of the Island. It is managed and operated by the Department of Civil Aviation of the Mauritius Government.

There is one other airport with a paved runway and three unpaved airfields.

Air Mauritius, P.O. Box 441, Air Mauritius Centre, President John Kennedy Street, Port Louis, Mauritius. Tel: +230 208 7700, fax: +230 208 8331

Roads
There are 9.5 miles of motorway, 351 miles of main roads, 369 miles of urban roads and 380 miles of rural roads. All the main roads and 656 miles of urban and rural roads have a bitumen surface. Figures for 2004 showed that Mauritius had 291,600 registered vehicles on the road. Vehicles are driven on the left.

The Ministry of Works is responsible for the care of the motorway and of the main roads, the Municipalities for the urban roads and the District Councils for the rural roads.

Shipping
Port Louis is the only port of the island. It comprises a main basin with a water spread area of 129.5 ha and two adjacent basins with water areas of 8.9 ha and 7.3 ha. A modern Bulk Sugar Terminal complex has been in operation since 1980. Its storage sheds can store a total of 350,000 tonnes of raw sugar. Mauritius has a small merchant and fishing fleet of 30 vessels, although the government is supporting the development of the merchant fleet by providing training for cadets at the Sea Training School.

HEALTH

The health care system has two levels of care. In 2005, the peripheral sector consisted of 27 Area Health Centres and 125 Community Health Centres, providing primary health care and referring patients to district or regional hospitals. The specialised level consisted of 14 public hospitals, which provide specialised treatment. The private sector consists of 12 private clinics and several nursing homes. The public hospitals had 3,724 beds in 2005.

In 2009, the government spent approximately 8.3 per cent of its total budget on healthcare (up from 8.7 per cent in 2000), accounting for 37.1 per cent of all healthcare spending. Total expenditure on healthcare equated to 5.6 per cent of the country's GDP. Per capita expenditure on health was approximately US$382, compared with US$145 in 2000. Figures for 2000-10 show that there are 1,303 physicians (11 per 10,000 population), 4,604 nurses and midwives (37 per 10,000 population) and 233 dentistry personnel. There are 34 hospital beds per 10,000 population.

According to the latest WHO figures, in 2008 an estimated 99 per cent of the population had access to improved drinking water. In the same year, 89 per cent of the population had access to improved sanitation.

The infant mortality rate in 2010 was 13 per 1,000 live births. The child mortality rate (under 5 years) was 15 per 1,000 live births. The main causes of childhood mortality are: prematurity (27 per cent), birth asphyxia (9 per cent), congenital anomalies (26 per cent), pneumonia (9 per cent), injuries (7 per cent) and HIV/AIDS (1 per cent). (Source: http://www.who.int, World Health Statistics 2012)

EDUCATION

Primary/Secondary Education
The number of schools in 2004 is shown in the following table:

School Type	Number
Pre-primary	1,070
Primary	291
Secondary	134
Technical/vocational	12

Primary school consists of six grades, each taking a year, followed by either three years secondary schooling or vocational training. In 2006, 96 per cent of girls and 94 per cent of boys were enrolled in a primary school. In 2005, 92 per cent of children completed the primary course, and 71 per cent of children went on to secondary schooling. Both primary and secondary education is free. 17 per cent of the population of tertiary age went on to tertiary education in 2006. In the same year, 12.7 per cent of total government spending went on education.

It is estimated that 87 per cent of the adult population is literate, this figure rising to 96.1 per cent among the 15-24 years age-group. Both figures are well above the sub-saharan regional averages. (Source: UNESCO, UIS, November 2008)

RELIGION

Recent figures show that around 43 per cent of the population are Hindu, 34 per cent are Christian, 17 per cent are Muslim and 2.0 per cent Bah'ai.

Mauritius has a religious liberty rating of 8 on a scale of 1 to 10 (10 is most freedom). (Source: World Religion Database)

COMMUNICATIONS AND MEDIA

Freedom of expression is guaranteed by the constitution. Political criticism does appears.

Newspapers
There are seven dailies, five appearing in French with occasional articles in English, and two in Chinese. The main papers are: L'Express, Le Mauricien and Le Matinal. There are also 13 weeklies and a certain number of periodicals.

Broadcasting
The Mauritius Broadcasting Corporation (MBC) was founded in 1964 and is funded by a licence fee and advertising. RPRivate radio stations have been available since 2002. Television is the most-popular medium. Multichannel TV is available in the capital.

Telecommunications
Telecommunications services were liberalized in 2003. Mauritius has a well-developed digital infrastructure. Fixed-line usage was approximately 30 per cent (365,000 people) in 2008 whilst over 75 per cent of people (1 million) had a mobile phone. Figures for 2008 indicate that there were 380,000 internet subscribers.

ENVIRONMENT

Currently the major environmental issues concerning Mauritius are the quality of water, inadequate sewerage systems, run-off from intensive agriculture and coastal degradation from the mining of coral sand. The government has taken several measures to address these problems including the establishment of the Ministry of Environment and Quality of Life, the introduction of the Environment Protection Act, and the formulation of an Environmental Action Plan and Environmental Investment Programme. The Environmental Impact Assessment became compulsory for all major investment projects in 1991.

Mauritius is a party to the following international agreements: Antarctic-Marine Living Resources, Biodiversity, Climate Change, Climate Change-Kyoto Protocol, Desertification, Endangered Species, Environmental Modification, Hazardous Wastes, Law of the Sea, Marine Life Conservation, Ozone Layer Protection, Ship Pollution, and Wetlands.

In 2010, emissions from the consumption of fossil fuels by Mauritius totalled 4.55 million metric tons of carbon dioxide. (Source: EIA)

MEXICO
United States of Mexico
Estados Unidos Mexicanos

Capital: Mexico City (Population estimate, 2011: 22.1 million, metro area)

Head of State: Enrique Pena Nieto (page 1486)(President)

National Flag: A pale-wise tricolour of green, white and red. The white is charged with the national badge: an eagle on a cactus devouring a snake

CONSTITUTION AND GOVERNMENT

Constitution
Mexico is a Federal Republic, gaining independence from Spain on 16 September 1810. The current Constitution dates from 5 February 1917 but has been frequently amended since that date. The main concepts of the original constitution included separation of powers, a bill of rights, and federalism. The National Legislature consists of the Congress of the Union (Congreso de la Union) which is made up of the Senate (Camara de Senadores) and the Chamber of Deputies (Camara de Diputados).

To consult the constitution, please visit: http://www.juridicas.unam.mx/infjur/leg/constmex/pdf/consting.pdf.

Upper House
The Senate is the upper chamber with 128 members (two for each State, including the Federal District), elected for a period of six years. Half are elected every three years. Election is a mixture of direct election and proportional representation.

Lower House
The Chamber of Deputies, the lower chamber, has 500 members elected for a three-year term. Three hundred are elected by a majority and 200 by proportional representation.

There is one member for every 250,000 inhabitants or faction exceeding 125,000. Members of both Houses of Congress cannot be re-elected until a further six-year period has elapsed. The President appoints the Governor of the Federal District and the Ministers who form part of the President's Cabinet. The President is elected for a six-year term and presidential candidates must not have held public office in the six months prior to the election.

International Relations
Mexico is becoming more active in international affairs, participating in discussions on climate change, human rights and regional issues. Mexico is developing relations with its Central American neighbours, and is a member of the Plan Puebla Panama. Mexico enjoys good relations with the US and Canada, and is a partner in the North American Free Trade Agreement. The US has extensive commercial, cultural, and educational ties with Mexico. There are almost one million legal border crossings a day; over 500,000 American citizens live in Mexico, and more than 2,600 U.S. companies have operations there. The problem of illegal immigration of Mexicans to the USA has given rise to some tension between Mexico and North America in recent years; however, the two countries are united in their anti-drug efforts.

Mexico is a member of the UN, the World Trade Organisation and the OECD.

Recent Events
In November 2001 President Fox appointed a prosecutor to investigate the disappearance of many left-wing activists in the 1970s and 1980s. In 2002 secret security files were released revealing details of torture and in July 2002 the former president Luis Echeverria was questioned over student massacres.

In May 2006 President Fox voiced concerns over President Bush's plans to use the National Guard to patrol the Mexico-US border. President Bush insisted that the patrols did not mean a militarisation of the border but were an attempt to reduce illegal immigration. There are estimated to be over 6 million Mexicans living illegally in the US. In October 2006, President Bush signed legislation to build 700 miles of fencing along the US-Mexico border. Mexico condemned the plans.

Following the close result of the July 2006 presidential election, between 500,000 and two million people rallied in support of the left-wing candidate Andres Manuel Lopez Obrador. Sr. Obrador claimed that the vote count was rigged at around half the country's polling stations and sought a recount. EU observers found no irregularities, and the winning candidate, Sr. Calderon, rejected calls for a recount. Over August, the protesters camped out in the city centre, but in September, the Federal Electoral Tribunal confirmed that Mr Calderon had won.

MEXICO

At the end of October 2007, massive floods swamped about 70 per cent of the south-eastern state of Tabasco where rivers burst their banks after heavy rain. 500,000 people were forced to evacuate and some 300,000 were trapped in their houses for days. The floods were triggered by storms which also cost the lives of 21 people when an oil platform collided with another rig in the Gulf of Mexico; three of Mexico's oil ports were closed, halting a fifth of the country's oil production.

On the 8th May 2008, Edgar Millan Gomez, a senior police officer was shot dead in Mexico City; he was in charge of co-ordinating national police operations against drugs traffickers. The head of Mexico City's anti-kidnap unit was killed the following day, and on the 10th May, the deputy police chief of the border city of Ciudad Juarez was shot dead. Mexico has seen a surge in drug-related killings recently. Over 2007, some 2,500 people were killed. President Felipe Calderon has committed thousands of soldiers and federal police to fight the powerful drug cartels since he took office in 2006. The drugs cartels have fought back by attacking security forces.

On the 4th November, a Learjet plane, owned by the Interior Ministry, crashed in central Mexico City; Interior Minister Juan Camilo Mourino died along with other 12 people. Mr Mourino had been in charge of security during the government's battle with Mexico's powerful drug cartels. In mid-November, the former head of Mexico's anti-organised crime agency, Ramirez Mandujano, was arrested as part of a probe into links to drug cartels. The attorney general alleged that Mr Ramirez accepted $450,000 from cartels and was offered a monthly fee for information. Mr Ramirez is the highest-ranking law official yet detained in Operation Clean-up, which was launched to try to curb corruption linked to drug smuggling. Five senior officials and two federal agents have been held in the campaign., and the arrests include the head of Mexico's Interpol office. Dozens of officials have been sacked.

In December 2008, nine decapitated bodies were discovered in the southern state of Guerrero; the victims were a policeman and eight soldiers. This brought the the total number of drugs-related killings to almost 5,700 over 2008. President Calderon has deployed about 40,000 troops and police since December 2006 against the drugs cartels.

In January 2009, Congress agreed to debate the issue of reinstating capital punishment for some crimes, in response to a surge in murders and kidnappings, many linked to drug cartels and organised crime. The campaign to reinstate judicial executions has been led by Mexico's Green Party; polls suggest that around 70 per cent of the population are in favour of reinstating the death penalty, which was abolished in 2005 (the last execution was carried out in 1961). The government, church and human rights groups all strongly oppose reinstatement.

In January, thousands of people attended a rally in Mexico City to protest at the economic policies of the government. Most of the protesters were from rural areas and were angry that the government had frozen the price of petrol but not diesel, and therefore the cost of running farm machinery had become prohibitive.

On the 10th February, Mexican troops arrested the police chief and 36 other officers in the resort of Cancun, in connection with the murder of ex-army general, Mauro Enrique Tello, who had just taken command of a squad to tackle crime in Cancun. The following day, gun battles between suspected drug gang members and troops left 21 people dead in northern Mexico. On the 4th March 2009, Mexican troops entered Ciudad Juarez to try to regain control of the city in which more than 2,000 people had been murdered over twelve months. The city is a key entry point for drug smuggling into the USA.

Over March and April 2009, an epidemic of swine flu hit the country, killing an estimated 100 people mainly in and around Mexico City. Over 1,500 people were thought to have been infected. Mexican authorities closed public buildings, suspended public events and launched a vaccination campaign. By the beginning of May, the authorities announced that the peak of infections had passed.

Mid-term elections took place on the 5th July 2009. The opposition centrist Institutional Revolutionary Party won approximately 40 per cent of the vote, whilst the president's National Action Party (PAN) won approximately 29 per cent.

It was estimated that during 2009, approximately 6,500 people died in drug-related killings. Although President Calderon has insisted his anti-drugs policies are working, in August 2010 he called for a debate on the legalisation of drugs. In the same month, President Obama signed into law a $600 million bill to increase security on the Mexico-US border to stop the flow of illegal immigrants.

Throughout 2011 thousands of people protested against drug-related violence which has spread from the northern border regions to the Nuevo Leon and Tamaulipus states. There was a series of mass killings in the Veracruz area. In January 2012 the government issued figures which showed that over 12,000 people had been killed in violence blamed on drug-related crime in the period January to September 2011. Over 45,500 people have died in drug-related violence in the five years of Mr Calderon's presidency. In May 2012 a drug cartel leader was arrested over the mass killing of 50 people whose mutilated bodies were dumped on a road.

Cabinet (as at March 2013)
Secretary of Foreign Affairs: José Antonio Meade Kuribrena (page 1475)
Secretary of the Interior: Miguel Angel Osorio (page 1490)
Secretary of Finance: Luis Videgaray Caso (page 1531)
Secretary of the Economy: Ildefonso Guajardo Villarreal (page 1434)
Secretary of National Defence: Salvador Cienfuegos Zepeda
Secretary of the Navy: Admiral Vidal Soberon
Attorney General: Jesus Murillo Karam (page 1482)
Secretary of Public Education: Emilio Chuayffet
Secretary of Agriculture, Livestock, Rural Development and Fisheries: Enrique Martiniez
Secretary of Energy: Pedro Joaquin Coldwell
Secretary of the Environment: Juan José Guerra

Secretary of Social Development: Rosario Robles
Secretary of Communications and Transport: Gerado Ruiz Esparza
Secretary of Health: Mercedes Juan Lopez
Secretary of Agrarian Reform: Jorge Carlos Ramirez
Secretary of Tourism: Claudia Ruiz

Ministries
Office of the President, Los Pinos, Puerta 1, Col. San Miguel Chapultepec, 11850 Mexico, DF. Tel: +52 55 5277 7455, fax: +52 55 5510 3717, URL: http://www.presidencia.gob.mx
Secretariat of Agrarian Reform, Poniente 81 No 37, Col. Cove, Del. Álvaro Obregón 01120, Mexico DF. Tel: +52 55 5632 3676, fax: +52 55 5650 6100, URL: http://www.sra.gob.mx
Secretariat of Agriculture, Livestock, Rural Development, Fisheries and Food, Ave. Insurgentes Sur 476, Col. Roma Sur, Deleg. Cuauhtémoc 06760, Mexico DF, Tel: +52 55 5584 8000, fax: +52 55 5584 0268, e-mail: c.informacion@sagar.gov.mx, URL: http://www.sagar.gob.mx
Secretariat of State for the Interior, Bucareli 99, Col. Juárez, 06600 Mexico, DF. Tel: +52 55 5566 8188, fax: +52 55 5703 2171, URL: http://www.gobernacion.gob.mx/
Secretariat of State for Foreign Affairs, Plaza Juarez 20, piso 22, Col. Centro. Del. Cuahutémoc, C.P. 06010, Mexico, Df. Tel: +52 55 36866036, fax: +52 55 36866042, e-mail: comment@sre.gob.mx, URL: http://www.sre.gob.mx/
Secretariat of State for National Defense, Blvd Manuel Avila Camacho y Avda Industria Militar, Col. Lomas de Sotelo, 11640 Mexico, DF. Tel: +52 55 5395 6766, fax: +52 55 5557 1370, URL: http://www.sedena.gob.mx
Secretariat of the Civil Service, Insurgentes Sur 1735 No 10. Col. Guadalupe Inn 01020, Mexico DF. Tel: +52 55 3003 4090, fax: +52 55 5662 4763, e-mail: ltacher@secodam.gob.mx, URL: http://secodam.gob.mx
Secretariat of Communications and Transport, Avda Universidad esq. Xola, Edif C, Col. Narvarte, Deleg. Benito Juarez, 03028 Mexico DF. Tel: +52 55 5519 7456, fax: +52 55 5519 0692, URL: http://www.sct.gob.mx
Secretariat of State for Naval Affairs, Eje 2 Oriente 861, Tramo H. Escuela Naval Militar, Col. Los Cipreses, Coyocán, 04830 Mexico, DF. Tel: +52 55 5624 6500, fax: +52 55 5624 6500, URL: http://www.semar.gob.mx/i
Secretariat of State for Finance and Public Credit, Palacio National Primer Patio Mariano, 3 Fl. Of. 3045., Col. Centro, Cuauhtemoc 06000, Mexico DF. Tel: +52 55 5542 2213, fax: +52 55 5228 1142, e-mail: webmaster@shcp.gob.mx, URL: http://www.shcp.gob.mx/
Secretariat of State for Environment and Natural Resources, Periférico Sur 4209, 5 Piso, Col. Jardines en la Montaña, 14210, Mexico DF. Tel: +52 55 5628 0891, fax: 52 55 5628 0778, e-mail: web@semarnat.gob.mx , URL: http://www.semarnap.gob.mx/
Secretariat of State for Energy, Insurgentes Sur 890, Col. Del Valle, 03100 Mexico, DF. Tel: +52 55 5584 9744, fax: +52 55 5574 3396, e-mail: felipech@energia.gob.mx, URL: http://www.energia.gob.mx/
Secretariat of State for Agriculture, Livestock, Rural Development, Fisheries and Food, Insurgentes Sur 476, Col. Roma Sur, 06760 Mexico, DF. Tel: +52 55 5584 8000, fax: +52 55 5584 0268, e-mail: contacto@sagarpa.gob.mx, URL: http://www.sagar.gob.mx
Secretariat of State for Transport and Communications, Avda Universidad y Xola, Edif. C, Col. Narvarte, 03028 Mexico, DF. Tel: +52 55 55319 7456, fax: +52 55 5519 0692, URL: http://www.sct.gob.mx
Secretariat of State for Public Education, Republica de Argentina 28, Col. Centro, 06029 Mexico, DF. Tel: +52 55 5329 6827, fax: +52 55 5329 6822, e-mail: educa@sep.gob.mx, URL: http://www.sep.gob.mx
Secretariat of State for Labour and Social Welfare, Edif. A, Periferico Sur 4271, Col. Fuentes del Pedregal, 14149 Mexico, DF. Tel: +52 55 5645 3715, URL: http://www.stps.gob.mx
Secretariat of State for Agrarian Reform, Poniente 81, 37, Col.Cove, Alvaro Obregon, 01120 Mexico, DF. Tel: +52 55 5632 3676, fax: +52 55 5650 6100, URL:http://www.sra.gob.mx
Secretariat of State for Tourism, Presidente Masarik 172, 10, Col. Bosques de Chapultepec, 11587 Mexico, DF. Tel: +52 55 5250 8604, fax: +52 55 5254 0014, URL: http://www.mexico-travel.com
Secretariat of State for Economy, Alfonso Reyes 30, Col. Hipodromo Condesa, Cuauhtemoc, 06179 Mexico, D.F. Tel: +52 55 5729 9100, fax: +52 55 5286 1543, URL: http://www.economia.gob.mx/
Secretariat of State for Health, Lieja 8, Col. Juárez, 06600 Mexico, D.F. Tel: +52 55 5553 8019, fax: +52 55 5286 5497, URL: http://www.ssa.gob.mx/
Secretariat of State for Social Development, Avda. Constituyentes, 947, Edif.B, 01110, México, D.F. Tel: +52 55 5515 4508, fax: +52 55 5272 0118, URL: http://www.sedesol.gob.mx
Secretariat of Public Safety, Londres 102 No. 7, Col. Juárez, Deleg. Cuauhtémoc, 06600 Mexico DF. e-mail: ssp@snsp.gob.mx, URL: http://www.ssp.gob.mx
Office of the Attorney General, Reforma No 211, 2 piso, Col. Guerrero, Deleg. Cuauhtémoc 06300, Mexico DF. Tel: +52 55 5346 2600, fax: +52 55 5346 2760, URL: http://www.pgr.gob.mx

Political Parties
Partido Acción Nacional (PAN, National Action Party), 1546 Avenida Coyocan, Mexico City 03100. URL: http://www.pan.org.mx
President: Gustavo Madero Muñoz
Partido de la Revolución Democrática (PRD, Party of the Democratic Revolution), 84 Benjamin Franklin, Mexico City, Mexico. URL: http://www.prd.org.mx
President: Jesus Zambrano
Partido del Trabajo (PT, Labour Party), URL: http://www.partidodeltrabajo.org.mx
Leader: Alberto Anaya
Convergencia (Convergence), URL: http//www.convergenciamexico.org.mx
Leader: Luis Maldonado Venegas
Partido Revolucionario Institucional (PRI), URL: www.pri.org.mx
President: Humberto Moreira
Partido Verde Ecologista de México (PVEM, Green Ecologist Party of Mexico), URL: http://www.pvem.org.mx

President: Jorge Emilio González Torres
Partido Nueva Alianza (PNA, New Alliance Party), URL: http://www.nueva-alianza.org.mx
President: Jorge Kahwagi
Social Democratic & Peasant Alternative Party, URL: http://www.alternative.org.mx
President: Alberto Begné Guerra

Elections

Presidential elections took place on 2nd July 2006. President Vicente Fox of the National Action Party was not eligible to stand. The result was so close that there were calls for a recount. Sr. Felipe Calderón (National Action Party) won 36.38 per cent of the vote, whilst Sr. Andrés Manuel López Obrador of the Alliance for the Good of All won 35.34 per cent. Supporters of Sr. López staged a camp-out and demonstrations in the centre of Mexico City, which lasted some 33 days, protesting that the electoral count was fraudulent. The electoral court called for a partial recount, before naming Sr. Calderón President-elect.

The most recent presidential and legislative elections took place July 2012. The Institutional Revolutionary Party candidate Enrique Pena Nieto won the election, defeating veteran left wing candidate Andres Manuel Lopez Obrador and bringing to an end 12 years of right wing rule by the National Action Party (PAN). Mr Obrador contested the results but the results were officially upheld in August 2012. Pena named his cabinet on 30 November and was sworn in as president on 1 December 2012.

Diplomatic Representation

British Embassy, Rio Lerma 71, Col Cuauhètmoc, 06500 Mexico City, Mexico. Tel: +52 55 5242 8500, fax: +52 55 5242 8517, e-mail: commsec@embajadabritanica.com.mx, URL: http://ukinmexico.fco.gov.uk/en
Ambassador: Judith Macgregor (page 1468)
US Embassy, Paseo de la Reforma 305, 06500 Mexico City, Mexico. Tel: +52 55 5080 2000, fax: +52 55 5080 2005, URL: http://www.mexico.usembassy.gov
Ambassador: Earl Anthony Wayne
Embassy of Mexico, 16 St. George Street, London W1S 1LX, United Kingdom. Tel: +44 (0)20 7499 8586, fax: +44 (020) 7495 4035, e-mail: embgbretana@sre.gob.mx, URL: http://www.sre.gob.mx/reinounido/
Ambassador: Eduardo Medina-Mora
Embassy of Mexico, 1911 Pennsylvania Avenue, NW, Washington DC 20006, USA. Tel: +1 202 728 1600, fax: +1 202 728 1698, URL: http://www.embassyofmexico.org
Ambassador: Eduardo Medina-Mora Icaza (page 1476)
Permanent Mission of Mexico to the UN, Two United Nations Plaza 28th floor, New York, NY 10017, USA. Tel: +1 212 752.0220, fax +212 688.8862, URL: http://www.un.int/mexico
Permanent Representative: Luis Alfonso de Alba Gongora

LEGAL SYSTEM

The legal system in Mexico provides for both Federal Laws and State laws. It is based largely on the French or Napoleonic Code. There is a Supreme Court of Justice, circuit courts and district courts. For most criminal cases the defendant is tried by judge only, not by a jury.

The government respects human rights at the national level. However there have been unlawful killings and abuse by security forces. Arrests can be arbitrary, and the judiciary is inefficient. There is corruption in all levels of government. Mexico abolished the death penalty in 2005.

Supreme Court, URL: http://www.scjn.gob.mx
Minister President: Juan Silva Meza

National Commission for Human Rights, Periferico Sur 3469, Col. San Jeronimo Lidice, Delagacion Magdalena Contreras, CP 10200, MExico DF. Tel: +55 5681 8125, URL: http://www.cndh.org.mx/

LOCAL GOVERNMENT

Mexico is divided into 31 states and one federal district (Mexico City and environs). Each has the right to manage its own affairs and, besides the federal legislation, each has its own constitution, government and laws. The states levy their own taxes, but inter-state customs duties do not exist.

Each state has its own governor, legislature and judiciary, elected by popular vote. State governors are elected for six years. The President appoints the governors of the territories and of the federal district. In the Federal District the office of Governor is discharged by a Chief of the Central Department which forms part of the Presidential Cabinet. Each state has its own Chamber of Deputies elected for a three-year term.

The following table shows the states and their capitals.

State	Capital
Aguascalientes	Aguascalientes
Baja California	Mexicali
Baja California Sur	La Paz
Campeche	Campeche
Coahuila de Zaragoza	Saltillo
Colima	Colima
Chiapas	Tuxla Gutierrez
Chihuahua	Chihuahua
Distrito Federal	Mexico City
Durango	Victoria de Durango
Guanajuato	Guanajuato

- continued

Guerrero	Chilpancingo
Hidalgo	Pachuca de Soto
Jalisco	Guadalajara
Mexico	Toluca de Lerdo
Michoacan de Ocampo	Morelia
Morelos	Cuernavaca
Nayarit	Tepic
Nuevo Leon	Monterrey
Oaxaca	Oaxaca de Juarez
Puebla	Puebla de Zaragoza
Queretaro de Arteaga	Queretaro
Quintana Roo	Chetumal
San Luis Potosi	San Luis Potosi
Sinaloa	Culiacan Rosales
Sonora	Hermosillo
Tabasco	Villahermosa
Tamaulipas	Ciudad Victoria
Tlaxcala	Tlaxcala
Veracruz-Llave	Jalapa Enriquez
Yucatan	Merida
Zacatecas	Zacatecas

Source: National Institute of Statistics, Geography and Information, Mexico

AREA AND POPULATION

Area

Mexico is situated in the south of the North American continent. It is bordered by the USA to the North, the Pacific Ocean to the west, Belize and Guatemala and the Gulf of Mexico to the east. The area covers 1,972,500 sq. km. About 75 per cent of the country's area is mountainous and 64 per cent receives very little rain. Northern Mexico has dry, desert conditions whereas the south is mountainous jungle.

To view a map, consult http://www.lib.utexas.edu/maps/cia08/mexico_sm_2008.gif

Population

The population in 2010 was estimated at 113,423 million, assuming a annual growth rate of 1.3 per cent per annum for the period 2000-10. It is the most populous Spanish-speaking country in the world. Some 78 per cent of the population lives in urban areas with around 21 million living in and around the capital Mexico City, making this the largest concentration of people in the Western Hemisphere. Cities on the border with the US (such as Cuidad Juarez and Tijuana) have recently experienced sharp population rises.

Most of the population speaks Spanish, but native American languages including Náhuati, Maya and Zapoteco are also spoken. Ethnic groups in Mexico are as follows: Mestizo (Indian-Spanish) 60 per cent, Amerindian 30 per cent, Caucasian 9 per cent and other 1 per cent. There is widespread poverty with 40 million people living on less than 60 pence a day. The social divisions are amongst the worst in the world.

Births, Marriages, Deaths

The estimated number of births per 1,000 inhabitants in 2010 was 19.5, continuing a downward trend. The fertility rate was around 2.3 children per woman in 2009. The number of deaths was 5.0 per 1,000 inhabitants. Life expectancy in 2009 was approximately 73 for men and 78 for women. Healthy life expectancy was 67 years. The median age was 27 years. Approximately 29 per cent of the population is aged under 15 years and 9 per cent over 60. The infant mortality rate (children under 1 years old) stood at approximately 14 deaths per 1,000 children. (Source: http://www.who.int, World Health Statistics 2012)

Public Holidays 2014

1 January: New Year's Day
5 February: Constitution Day
21 March: Birthday of Benito Juarez
17 April: Maundy Thursday
18 April: Good Friday
21 April: Easter Monday
1 May: Labour Day
5 May: Anniversary of the Battle of Puebla
16 September: Independence Day
14 October: Discovery of America
1 November: Dia de los Muertos (Day of the Dead)
20 November: Anniversary of the Revolution
12 December: Day of Our Lady of Guadalupe
25 December: Christmas
31 December: New Year's Eve

EMPLOYMENT

Figures for 2008 estimated the workforce to be 45,322,000 of which over 15 per cent were employed in agriculture, nearly 26 per cent in industry and nearly 60 per cent in services, unemployment in 2008 was put at 4 per cent. Figures for 2006 indicate that Mexico had a workforce of 43.2 million people over the age of 15, constituting 59.8 per cent of the total population over 15 years old. The following table shows employment by economic sector, in 2008:

Employment Sector	No. Employed
Agriculture, hunting and forestry	5,628,900
Fishing	129,600
Mining and quarrying	183,200

MEXICO

- continued

Manufacturing	7,228,100
Electricity, gas and water supply	206,200
Construction	3,641,200
Wholesale and retail trade; Repair of motor vehicles and Personal Goods	9,974,400
Hotels and Restaurants	2,836,700
Transport, Storage & communications	2,034,400
Financial Services	405,800
Real Estate, renting and business activities	2,189,200
Public Administration and defence; Compulsory Social Security	2,172,000
Education	2,326,000
Health and Social Work	1,252,800
Other community, social and personal services	1,469,400
Private households with employed persons	1,851,800
Extra-territorial organizations and bodies	3,800
Not classifiable by economic activity	333,000
Total	**43,866,700**

Source: Copyright © International Labour Organization (ILO Dept. of Statistics, http://laborsta.ilo.org)

BANKING AND FINANCE

Currency
1 peso = 100 centavos
The financial centre is Mexico City.

GDP/GNP, Inflation, National Debt
Mexico has one of the world's largest economies (equalling Spain and Brazil). However, wealth is unevenly distributed and around half the population lives in poverty. Living standards are higher in the north than in the rural south.

The Mexican economy follows the fortunes of the US economy, and is therefore suffering the effects of the global economic downturn; under the North American Free Trade Agreement, some 85 per cent of Mexico's exports go to the US market, which makes the country vulnerable to falling US demand. With the global economic slowdown, demand from the US fell in 2009. Remittances from Mexicans living in the USA are the country's second largest source of foreign income, and represents almost 3 per cent of Mexico's GDP; these remittances have recently fallen for the first time since 1995.

Average annual GDP growth over the period 2000-05 was 3.2 per cent. GDP growth was 4.8 per cent in 2006, falling to 3.3 per cent in 2007 and 1.4 per cent in 2008. Growth in 2009 was put at -6.5 per cent in response to the global economic downturn. GDP in 2009 was put at US$875 billion and US$1.0 trillion in 2010. Growth in 2010 was estimated at 5.4 per cent. Per capita GDP was US$9,395 in 2010. GDP was estimated to be US$1.14 trillion in 2011 with a growth rate of 3.75 per cent.

In 2011, the services sector contributed 62 per cent of GDP, industry was the second largest earning sector, contributing 34 per cent of GDP, and the agricultural sector accounted for 3.7 per cent.

The inflation rate (based on consumer prices) was an estimated 6.3 per cent in 2008, 3.5 per cent in 2009 and 4.5 per cent in 2010. GDP was estimated to be 3.5 per cent in 2011. Estimated total external debt in 2011 was estimated to be US$205 billion.

Mexico is one of the world's top five oil producers, and oil contributes around 3 per cent of GDP. Over 11 million Mexicans live and work in the US, many of them illegally. Each year, Mexicans living abroad send around US$20 billion to their families in Mexico, making this the second largest source of revenue for the Mexican economy. Tourism has grown rapidly over recent years, and is now the fourth largest contributor to GDP. The 'maquiladora' industry is another important part of the Mexican economy; this consists of manufacturing plants near the US border which import raw materials from the US, and then re-export the finished products duty free to the US.

Balance of Payments / Imports and Exports
Mexico is highly dependent on trade with the United States, which accounted for some 86 per cent of its total export revenue and was the source of 53 per cent of imports in 2005. Canada, Japan, Germany and the UK are also importers of Mexican merchandise, which include crude oil and products, coffee, silver, engines, motor vehicles, cotton and consumer electronics. Mexico's main imports include metal-working machines, steel mill products, agricultural machinery, electrical equipment, aircraft and motor vehicle and aircraft parts. Apart from the US, the EU, Japan, Canada and China are other significant suppliers of goods.

Mexico exported an estimated US$298 billion worth of goods in 2010, and imported US$301 billion worth of goods. The US is the major trade partner. Some US$230 billion of exports (80 per cent of total) go to the US, and some 50 per cent of imports are supplied by the US.

The United States is Mexico's primary source of foreign direct investment, helped by the North American Free Trade Agreement (NAFTA). Implemented in January 1994, NAFTA has liberalised Mexico's trade with the US and Canada, and future trends point to even closer ties between the US and Mexico, in terms of economic integration, immigration and energy. Mexico is also a major recipient of remittances, most of which come from Mexicans working in the United States. Recent estimates put remittances at around US$21 billion per year.

Mexico has signed Free Trade Agreements (FTAs) with 44 countries, including with the EU and with Japan.

Central Bank
Banco de Mexico, Avenida 5 de Mayo 2, Col Centro, Del Cuauhtemnoc, 06059 México City D.F., Distrito Federal, Mexico. E-mail: comsoc@banxico.org.mx, URL: http://www.banxico.org.mx
Governor: Augustin Carstens Carstens

MANUFACTURING, MINING AND SERVICES

Primary and Extractive Industries
In 2011 Mexico was the eighth largest oil producer in the world. The oil sector is a crucial component of Mexico's economy generating over 10 per cent of the country's export earnings and around 33 per cent of total Government revenue. However production has declined in recent years.

The country has vast oil fields in the Gulf of Mexico and smaller oil wells in coastal towns. With estimated proven reserves of 10.1 billion barrels in January 2012, Mexico has the third largest crude oil reserves in the Western Hemisphere after Venezuela and the USA. Reserves are, however, declining. Production at the Cantarell oil field, one of the largest oil fields in the world, is in long-term decline.

Figures for 2011 put production at 2.9 million barrels per day, nearly all of which was crude. In the same year, oil consumption stood at 2.1 million barrels per day. An estimated 825,000 bbl/d were exported, mostly to the United States. Mexico has six refineries and a fifty per cent share in a USA based refinery. Total capacity is 1.54 million barrels per day. Despite being one of the world's largest crude oil exporters, Mexico is a net importer of refined petroleum products; rapid economic growth is one cause for the increase in imports. Pemex, the state oil company, has increased capacity following a series of refinery upgrades.

Pemex is the world's sixth largest oil company. However, some 60 per cent of revenues are given to the Government, and 8 per cent are used to cover pension liabilities. These commitments prohibit increased spending on exploration and production. The Government has proposed changes in the way the company is taxed, in order to release more money for reinvestment in the industry. However, there is little support for change within Congress. The President has suggested that the company be more open to foreign partnerships, to assist in oil exploration, particularly in the deepwater areas of the Gulf. Capital spending reached $10.3 billion in 2003 and $12 billion in 2004.

January 2011 figures put natural gas reserves at 12 trillion cubic feet. In the same year, production stood at to 1,761 Bcf, whilst demand was 2,364 Bcf. Mexico imported 502 billion cubic feet per day of natural gas in 2011.

In 2007, total recoverable coal reserves were estimated to be 1.3 billion short tons, and production in 2010 reached 10.9 million short tons with consumption of 19.8 million short tons. Mexico imported the shortfall from the United States, Canada, Colombia, and Australia. Electricity generation and the steel industry account for most coal consumption; however, the government is gradually replacing coal powered electricity generation by natural gas powered stations. (Source: EIA)

Energy
Demand for electricity continues to increase; some 95 per cent of the population now has access to the grid, and growth in demand is anticipated to be 5-6 per cent over the next decade. In 2009, Mexico used a total of 6.99 quadrillion Btu of energy and produced 8.6 quadrillion Btu.

In 2010, installed generating capacity stood at 62.0 GWe, and Mexico generated around 257.2 billion kilowatthours (Bkwh). The country consumed 212.3 billion kWh. Of the total generated, 56 per cent came from petroleum, 29 per cent came from natural gas, five per cent from coal, four per cent from hydroelectric sources, five per cent can from non-dydro renewables and one per cent from nuclear power.

Mexico has one nuclear power plant, the 1,640-MW Laguna Verde nuclear reactor in Veracruz. In November 2006, Mexico's Energy Ministry recommended the building of a second nuclear power plant in order to diversify the country's electricity mix. The largest hydroelectric plant in the country is the 2,400-MW Manuel Moreno Torres in Chiapas. Construction on the 750 MW hydroelectric El Cajon dam was completed in 2007.

Manufacturing
Manufacturing and industry currently accounts for 34 per cent of GDP. Industrial development along the border with the United States has benefited from the NAFTA trade agreement. Manufactured goods such as cars and glass are produced in the north, whilst in the south the textile and crafts industry are predominant. So-called maquiladora plants which assemble imported products for export now form an important part of the manufacturing industry, the main areas being electric and electronic products, transportation equipment and textiles and garments. On the down side, Mexico has to import a large proportion of the raw materials and components used in its exported manufactures. Other manufactured products include food and beverages, tobacco, iron and steel, and chemicals.

Service Industries
The services sector is the largest contributor to GDP, accounting for around 63 per cent. The main contributors in 2005 were commerce and tourism (21 per cent), the financial services sector (13 per cent) and transport and communications (11 per cent).

Tourism is now the fourth largest source of currency income for Mexico, following a period of rapid development. There were over 20 million visitors to Mexico in 2000, but this figure dropped gradually over the following years to 18.7 million in 2003. However, whilst numbers had fallen, the revenue from tourism rose over the same period from US$8.3 million to US$9.5 million. Most visitors come from USA and Canada. Resorts on the Caribbean coast of the Yucatan peninsula (Cancun, Playa del Carmen and Cozumel) have grown very quickly and the Pacific coast resorts of Puerto Vallarta, Huatulca and Los Cabos have also increased in popularity. Figures for 2006 show that tourist arrivals had risen to 21.3 million generating earnings of US$13.3 million.

Fondo Nacional de Fomento al Turismo, URL: http://www.fonatur.gob.mx

Agriculture

Over 16 per cent of the population are currently employed in agriculture, which produces just four per cent of GDP. 78 per cent of the land is used for agriculture and hunting; 42 per cent of this is pasture and 14 per cent is arable. In 2003, agricultural exports earned $7,894 million, whilst exports of fish products earned $602 million and the forestry sector earned export revenues of $198 million.

The sector suffers from poor investment, as agricultural loans to the many small farms are seen as risky by banks. There are signs that farmers are selling up or diversifying their activities. The government attempted to raise productivity by allowing for the transfer of communal land to the farmers who cultivated it. The land could then be rented or sold, thus creating larger farms. However, there is general opposition to the selling of communal land.

Main products include, corn, coffee and beans. Sisal is largely grown in the southern state of Yucatán and is a chief source of wealth in the region. Mexico is a large grower of vegetable fibres for rope-making, cords, and string, and produces about half the world's supply of fibres for harvester twine.

Agricultural Production in 2010

Produce	Int. $'000*	Tonnes
Indigenous cattle meat	5,278,516	1,954,010
Indigenous chicken meat	3,811,428	26,775,800
Cow milk, whole, fresh	3,331,782	10,676,700
Hen eggs, in shell	1,975,090	2,381,380
Maize	1,936,384	23,301,900
Indigenous pigmeat	1,804,229	1,173,680
Sugar cane	1,655,694	50,421,600
Tomatoes	1,107,820	2,997,640
Chillies and peppers, green	1,099,484	2,335,560
Mangoes, mangosteens, guavas	978,230	1,632,650
Oranges	783,010	4,051,630
Avocados	767,204	1,107,140

* unofficial figures

Source: http://faostat.fao.org/site/339/default.aspx Food and Agriculture Organization of the United Nations, Food and Agricultural commodities production

The fishing industry produced 1,524,000 tonnes of fish in 2010. In 2004, the forestry sector produced 38.2 million cubic metres of wood fuel, 6.9 million cubic metres of industrial roundwood and 4.3 million cubic metres of paper and paper board.

COMMUNICATIONS AND TRANSPORT

Travel Requirements

Citizens of the USA, Canada, Australia and the EU require a passport valid for at least six months beyond the entry date, an onward/return ticket and proof of financial means. A visa is not required by those who have a Blue Tourist Card, with is valid for 180 days for all the citizens above apart from nationals of Australia, Cyprus, Czech Republic, Estonia, France, Greece, Latvia, Lithuania, Malta, Poland, Portugal, Slovak Republic and Slovenia who can stay for up to 90 days. Tourist Cards must be kept by the visitor during the entire length of stay as they will have to be presented and stamped on leaving. Business visitors should check with the consulate regarding visa requirements. Other nationals should contact the embassy to check visa requirements.

National Airlines

The national airlines is Aerovías de México, established in 1934. Corporación Mexicana de Aviación was sold to a private investor in 2005.

Aerovias de Mexico, (operating as Aeroméxico) URL: http://www.aeromexico.com

International Airports

There are over 1,800 airports in Mexico, of which 250 have paved runways, and 12 have runways of over 3,047 metres. A further 30 have runways of between 2,438 and 2,047 metres. There is also a heliport.

Railways

The rail network consists of 17,166 km of track.

Roads

Road and highway infrastructure in Mexico exceeds 360,000 km. Vehicles are driven on the right.

Shipping

Shipping is vital to Mexico's foreign trade; in 2003, Mexican ports moved around 1.7 million containers. Work is in progress on updating port facilities. The main ports on the Gulf Coast are Cayo Arcos, Dos Bocas, Pajaritos, Tuxpan and Ciudad Madero. Salina Cruz and Rosarito are the main ports on the Pacific Coast. Ferry services are in operation.

There are also 2,900 km of navigable rivers and coastal canals.

HEALTH

In 2009, expenditure on health equated to 6.5 per cent of Mexican GDP, equating to US$525 per capita. An estimated 48.3 per cent was government expenditure and 51.6 per cent was private expenditure (approximately 92.3 per cent of which was out-of-pocket costs). Expenditure on health accounts for 11.9 per cent of total government expenditure.

In the period 2005-10 there were 219,560 physicians (19.6 per 10,000 population). According to WHO figures for 2000-10 there were an estimated 417,665 nurses and midwives (40 per 10,000 population), 148,456 dentists and 79,925 pharmaceutical personnel. There are 16 hospital beds per 10,000 population. In 2010 the infant mortality rate (probability of dying by age one) was 14 deaths per 1,000 live births and the child (under-five) mortality rate was 17 per 1,000 live births. The main causes of death in the under-fives are: congenital anomalies 23 per cent, prematurity 17 per cent, pneumonia 12 per cent and diarrhoea 4 per cent. An estimated 0.3 per cent of 15-49 year olds had HIV. (Source: http://www.who.int, World Health Statistics 2012)

In April 2007, Mexico City's legislative assembly voted to legalise abortion in the city, the capital of the world's second-largest Roman Catholic country. Mexico City previously allowed abortion only in cases of rape, if the woman's life was at risk or if there were signs of severe defects in the foetus. An estimated 200,000 illegal abortions are performed in Mexico each year and some 1,500 women die during operations. The Mexico City Legislative Assembly is currently considering legalising euthanasia. Active euthanasia is illegal but as of 2008 passive euthanasia (allowing the terminally ill to refuse treatment to extend life) is permitted.

EDUCATION

Education is compulsory from six to 18, but standards are considered to be low. In an effort to improve standards, funding has been increased by some 25 per cent over the past ten years, and education has been decentralised to improve accountability. In 2004, one year of compulsory pre-school education was introduced. 99 per cent of children attended in 2007.

Enrolment figures have risen since education was prioritised; in 2005, enrolment in primary schools was 98 per cent, and in secondary schools, 65 per cent of the relevant age group were enrolled. 24 per cent of students went into higher education.

In 2006, 12.7 per cent of government expenditure went spent on education, of which 28 per cent went on primary education and 47 per cent on secondary education. In 2007 the adult literacy rate was estimated to be around 87.4 per cent, rising to 96.2 per cent among the 15-24 age group. (Source: UNESCO, UIS)

RELIGION

82 per cent of the population is Roman Catholic, but no state religion exists and freedom of worship for all denominations is guaranteed. Seven per cent are Protestant.

Mexico has a religious liberty rating of 5 on a scale of 1 to 10 (10 is most freedom). (Source: World Religion Database)

COMMUNICATIONS AND MEDIA

A variety of views are expressed in the media. Traditionally dominated by the Telesisa corporation, the sector has seen greater competition in recent years. There have been reports of attacks on journalists.

Newspapers

Excélsior, URL: http://www.exonline.com.mx/home
El Universal, URL: http://www.eluniversal.com.mx
La Jornada, URL: http://www.jornada.unam.mx/2007/10/30/index.php
El Sol de Mexico, URL: http://www.oem.com.mx/elsoldemexico/

Broadcasting

The main broadcaster is Televisa which operates four networks. As part of the programme of privatisation, Azteca were given the concession to operate the two previously state-owned television channels. Cable television has flourished in major cities, and television and radio are the main entertainment sources in Mexico. The state-run radio broadcaster is the Instituto Mexicano de la Radio. There are over 1,400 local and regional radio stations.

Televisa: URL: http://www.esmas.com/televisa.home
TV Azteca: URL: http://www.tvazteca.com.mx
IMER: URL: http://www.imer.com.mx

Telecommunications

The system has improved in recent years. Approximately 20 million households have a telephone, but there are more cellular phones in use, with over 85 million customers in 2010. Over 30 million Mexicans have access to the internet.

ENVIRONMENT

The National Program for Ecological Protection which began in 1990 is a formal recognition of the government's commitment to balance economic development with environmental improvement.

MICRONESIA

Natural fresh water resources are scarce and polluted in the north, and inaccessible and of poor quality in the centre and extreme south east. Raw sewage and industrial effluents pollute rivers in urban areas. Other major environmental issues are deforestation, widespread erosion, desertification and serious air pollution in Mexico City and urban centres along the US-Mexico border.

Energy-related carbon-dioxide emissions fell from 389.43 million metric tons in 2003 to 381.85 million metric tons in 2004, before rising to 398.25 in 2005. Per capita emissions rose from 3.64 metric tons in 2004 to 3.75 metric tons in 2005. In 2009, Mexico's emissions from the consumption of fossil fuels totalled 443.6 million metric tons of carbon dioxide. (Source: EIA)

Mexico is party to the following international agreements: Biodiversity, Climate Change, Climate Change-Kyoto Protocol, Desertification, Endangered Species, Hazardous Wastes, Law of the Sea, Marine Dumping, Marine Life Conservation, Ozone Layer Protection, Ship Pollution, Wetlands, and Whaling.

SPACE PROGRAMME

In 2008, the Mexican parliament approved the creation of a Mexican space Agency. The inital cost of the project was estimated at US$80 million.
Mexico Space Agency, URL: http://www.aem.gob.mx/

MICRONESIA
Federated States of Micronesia

Capital: Palikir (Population estimate: 7,000)

Head of State: Emmanuel 'Manny' Mori (President) (page 1480)

Vice-President: Alik L. Alik (page 1374)

National Flag: Four white stars (for the four states) on a pale blue background

CONSTITUTION AND GOVERNMENT

Constitution
Micronesia is headed by a President elected from the fourteen member National Congress of the Federated States of Micronesia. A vice-president is similarly elected, but cannot be from the same state. The capital of the congress is Pohnpei, but each of the four states (Pohnpei, Yap, Chuuk and Kosrae) elects its own legislature and governor and has executive, legislative and judicial branches. A national judicial branch is headed by a Chief Justice of the Supreme Court, and the national executive branch is composed of various departments headed by secretaries.

To consult the constitution, please visit: http://www.fsmlaw.org/fsm/constitution

Recent Events
Like the other components of the Trust Territory, Micronesia came into existence only after a protracted series of negotiations on political status with various US administrations which began in 1969. Almost 20 years later, the negotiations were finalised and in late 1986 the Compact of Free Association, defining the political status of Micronesia and its relationship with the USA, was implemented and the Trusteeship terminated by the UN Council. Under the terms of the Compact of Free Association the USA would defend Micronesia and if necessary establish military bases there in return for aid and free entry into the USA. The agreement ran out in 2001 and a new agreement was signed in 2003 worth US$3.5 billion to Micronesia and the Marshall Islands.

Legislature
All states have unicameral legislatures except for Chuuk which has two houses. The State governments are responsible for most major governmental functions, although the National Government is responsible for such areas as foreign affairs and defence. The National Government or Congress has 14 members who are elected to serve a two year term, there are also four senators, each representing one of the four states who are elected for a four year term. The president and vice president are then chosen from among the four senators. **Congress**, PO Box PS3, Palikir 96941, Pohnpei, Federated States of Micronesia. URL: http://www.fsmgov.org/congress

> **Cabinet (as at June 2013)**
> *Secretary of Foreign Affairs:* Lorin Robert
> *Secretary of Resource and Development:* Marion Henry
> *Secretary of Transport, Communications and Infrastructure:* Francis Itimai
> *Secretary of Finance and Administration:* Finley Perman
> *Secretary of Health and Social Affairs:* Dr Vita Akapito Skilling
> *Secretary of Justice, Attorney General:* Hon. Maketo Robert
> *Secretary of Education:* Dr Rufino Mauricio
> *Public Defender:* Julius J. Sapelalutt

Ministries
Office of the President, PS53, Palikir, Pohnpei State, 96941, Federated States of Micronesia. Tel: +691 320 2228, fax: +691 320 2785, URL: http://www.fsmgov.org/bio/falcam.html
Department of Foreign Affairs, PS123, Palikir, Pohnpei State, 96941 Federated States of Micronesia. Tel: +691 320 2641, fax: +691 320 2933, e-mail: foreignaffairs@mail.fm, URL: http://www.fsmgov.org/ovmis.html
Department of Economic Affairs, PS12 Palikir, Pohnpei State, 96941, Federated States of Micronesia. Tel: +691 320 2646, fax: +691 320 5854, e-mail: fsmdea@mail.fm, URL: http://www.visit-fsm.org
Department of Transportation, Communication and Infrastructure, PS2, Palikir, Pohnpei State, 69641, Federated States of Micronesia. Tel: +691 320 2865, fax: +691 320 5853, URL: http://www.fsmgov.org/ngovt.html
Department of Finance and Administration, PS158, Palikir, Pohnpei State, 96941, Federated States of Micronesia. Tel: +691 320 2640, fax: +691 320 2380, URL: http://www.fsmgov.org/ngovt.html

Department of Health, Education and Social Services, PS70, Palikir, Pohnpei State, 96941, Federated States of Micronesia. Tel: +691 320 2872, fax: +691 320 5263, URL: http://www.fsmgov.org/ngov0.html
Department of Justice, PS105, Palikir, Pohnpei State, 96941, Federated States of Micronesia. Tel: +691 320 2644, fax: +691 320 2234, URL: http://www.fsmgov.org/ngovt.html
Office of Public Defender, PS174, Palikir, Pohnpei State, Federated States of Micronesia. Tel: +691 320 2648, fax: +691 320 5775, e-mail: fsmpio@mail.fm, URL: http://www.fm/fsmpio
Ministry of Education, 87 Palikir, 96941 FM, Pohnpei, Federataed States of Micronesia. Tel: +691 320 2643, fax: +691 320 5500, URL: http://www.fsmgov.org
Ministry of Resources and Development, PS12 Palikir, 96941 FM, Pohnpei, Federated States of Micronesia. Tel: +691 320 2646, fax: +691 320 5854, e-mail: fsmrd@dea.fm, URL: http://www.fsmgov.org/

> **State Governments (as at June 2013)**
> **Chuuk State**, URL: http://www.fsmgov.org/sgovt.html
> Governor: Hon. Johnson Wesley Simina
> **Kosrae State**, URL: http://www.fsmgov.org/sgovt.html
> Governor: Robert Weilbacher
> **Pohnpei State**, URL: http://www.fsmgov.org/sgovt.html
> Governor: John Ehsa
> **Yap State**, URL: http://www.fsmgov.org/sgovt.html
> Governor: Sebastian Anefal

Elections
The most recent presidential elections took place on 11 May 2011. The incumbent, Emmanuel Mori, was re-elected for his second term as president.

The most recent legislative elections were held 8 March 2011. Special FSM congress elections for the states of Chuuk and Kosrae are scheduled to take place on 1 July 2011. Micronesia has no established political parties and senators are elected to Congress as independents.

Diplomatic Representation
Micronesian Embassy, US, 1725 N Street, NW, Washington DC, 20036, USA. Tel: +1 202 223 4383, fax: +1 202 223 4391, e-mail: admin@fsmembassydc.org, URL: http://www.fsmembassydc.org/
Ambassador: Asterio Takesy
Embassy of the US, PO Box 1286, Pohnpei, 96941, Federated States of Micronesia. Tel: +691 320 2187, fax: +691 320 2186, URL: http://kolonia.usembassy.gov/
Ambassador: Dorothea-Maria Rosen
British Embassy, URL: http://ukinthephilippines.fco.gov.uk/en
Ambassador: Stephen Lillie
Permanent Mission of Micronesia to the UN: URL: http://www.fsmgov.org/fsmun/
Ambassador Extraordinary & Plenipotentiary: Ms. Jane Jimmy Chigiyal

LEGAL SYSTEM

The Supreme Court of Micronesia is the highest court in the land, and consists of a trial and appellate division, with two judges permanently assigned to the Court. The Chief Justice handles trials in Pohnpei and Kosrae and an Associate Judge handles trials in Chuuk and Yap. When a decision is appealed, whichever judge did not hear the trial sits with two designated judges on the appellate panel. The Supreme Court has original and exclusive jurisdiction in cases involving disputes between states, foreign officials, admiralty and maritime cases, the Constitution, national laws and other domestic laws.

All four states have their own state supreme court. Justice Ombudsmen carry out traditional court functions as probation officers and keep the Supreme Court in touch with the local communities. The office of the Attorney-General provides legal services to the President and the executive branch of the national government.

The government respects the human rights of its citizens. There is some government corruption, and court cases can be delayed. No execution has been carried out since independence was declared on November 3, 1986. In December 2007, Micronesia voted in favour of the UN "Moratorium on the use of the death penalty".

Chief Justice: Hon. Andon L. Amaraich

LOCAL GOVERNMENT

For administrative purposes the states of Micronesia are divided into municipalities, governed by elected councils and villages organized on traditional lines.

Governor of Chuuk State: Wesley Simina
Governor of Kosrae State: Robert J. Weilbacher
Governor of Pohnpei State: John Ehsa
Governor of Yap State: Sebastian Anefal

AREA AND POPULATION

Area

The Federated States of Micronesia (FSM) consists of 607 islands and atolls in the western Pacific Ocean, though only about 40 are of significant size and even several of these are unpopulated. The total land area of Micronesia is about 702 sq. km or 271 sq. miles, although the scattered islands cover a total area of the Pacific Ocean of 2,978,000 sq km. The highest point is just under 800 metres. The climate is tropical with all-year round heavy rainfall. Micronesia is at the edge the typhoon belt.

To view a map, please consult http://www.lib.utexas.edu/maps/cia08/micronesia_sm_2008.gif

Population

The estimated population in 2010 was 111,000 with the annual growth rate of 0.4 per cent for the period 2000-10. The average population density is 152 per square kilometre.

In 2000 the area and population distributed was as follows: Pohnpei, 345.4 sq. km, 33,692 people; Kosrae, 109.6 sq. km, 7,317 people; Yap, 121.2 sq. km, 11,178 people; Chuuk, 118 sq. km, 53,319 people. After these, the land area of individual islands rapidly decreases although population densities are high in many cases. Approximately 23 per cent of the population lives in urban areas.

English is the official language although there are eight officially recognized indigenous languages: Trukese, Pohnpeian, Yapese, Kosrean, Ulithian, Woleaian, Nukuoro, Kapingamarangi. Several dialects are also spoken.

Births, Marriages, Deaths

Estimated figures for 2010 put the birth rate at 24.7 per thousand. The death rate was 5.9 per thousand and the infant mortality rate was 34 per thousand live deaths. The total fertility rate per female was 3.5 births. The average life expectancy is 69 years with 68 years for males and 70 years for females. Healthy life expectancy was 61 years for males and 62 years for females. The median age is 21 years. Approximately 37 per cent of the population is under 15 years old and 6 per cent aged over 60 years. (Source: http://www.who.int, World Health Statistics 2012) About 54 per cent of the population is married and the average age of first marriage is 25.4 years.

Public Holidays 2014

1 January: New Year's Day
10 May: Proclamation of the Federated States of Micronesia
18 April: Good Friday
25 December: Christmas Day
Each state celebrates its own holiday, dates of these vary.

EMPLOYMENT

For years Micronesians were employed in subsistence farming. This has changed in recent years with more businesses opening in the private sector, including construction companies, road maintenance companies, auto repair companies, and concrete companies and three air conditioning companies. Around half of the working population are employed by the government. Figures for 2000 put the workforce at 37,400, with an unemployment rate of 22 per cent.

BANKING AND FINANCE

Currency

Official currency is the US dollar.

GDP/GNP, Inflation, National Debt

The following table shows GDP at constant 1998 prices and growth rate in recent years.

Year	GDP US$ mil.	Growth Rate %
2000	208.9	4.7
2001	209.1	0.1
2002	211.0	0.9
2003	217.0	2.9
2004	209.9	-3.3
2005	208.7	-0.6
2006	203.9	-2.3
2007	197.5*	-3.2*
2008	195.5*	-1.0*

Source: Asian Development Bank
*provisional figures

Per capita GDP was estimated at US$2,271 in 2008. The service sector contributes around 22 per cent of GDP, agriculture 19 per cent and industry 4 per cent. Figures for 2011 put the inflation rate at 3.5 per cent.

International reserves stood at an estimated US$40 million in 2007. External debt was estimated at US$67.2 million in 2007 (28.6 per cent of GDP). Total debt service payments were US$2.9 million.

Foreign Investment

Funding for government operational support and capital improvement programmes in the Federated States of Micronesia was derived from three major sources:
1) An annual grant provided from funding appropriated to the Secretary of the Interior of the US.
2) Federal categorical grants provided on a matching or outright grant basis. In effect the Trust Territory was treated as a state of the US for participation in federal programmes.
3) Tax revenues levied by the government of the Federated States of Micronesia.

The termination of the Trusteeship and the implementation of the Compact of Free Association resulted in more than US$1.4 billion in US assistance to the Federated States of Micronesia over a 15 year period (ending in 2001). Under the terms of the renegotiated Compact of Free Association with the US in 2003, Micronesia and the Marshall Islands will receive US$3.5 billion over the next 20 years.

Chairman Pohnpei Foreign Investment Board, URL: http://www.pohnpeimet.fm/pohnpei_fib.htm

Balance of Payments / Imports and Exports

The following table shows external trade in recent years (figures are in thousand US dollars):

Trade	2005	2006	2007
Exports, fob	12,984	8,922	16,190
Imports, cif	130,214	137,993	142,659
Trade balance	-117,230	-129,071	-126,469

Source: Asian Development Bank

The main exported goods are garments, betel nuts, kava, copra and crab and lobsters. Main imports are foodstuffs, mineral products, chemicals products animals and animal products wood and wood products and textiles. Micronesia's main trading partners are Japan, the USA, Australia, the Marshall Islands, Northern Mariana Islands, Australia and China. The top export destinations is the US (2007, US$6.47 million) followed by the Northern Mariana Islands (US$693,000) and Japan (US$660,000). The top importers are the US (2007, US$79.3 million), Singapore (US$12,413) and Japan (US$12.01 million).

In recent years, the annual issuing of licences to foreign vessels for tuna fishing has secured around US$20 million for Micronesia.

MANUFACTURING, MINING AND SERVICES

Energy

Most electricity in the islands is generated by diesel generators. Kosrae and Pohnpei have some hydro electricity and solar power is beginning to be introduced.

Manufacturing

Such activity as there is tends to be very small scale, concentrating on those which utilize natural and human resources. These include fish processing, coconut oil extraction, garment manufacture and soap making and handicrafts using wood, shells and pearls. Recently charcoal has been produced from coconut shell as a bi-product of the coconut oil industry, and brooms, brushes, ropes and mats are being produced from processed fibre from the coconut husks. There are plans for small canneries in at least one state. It is hoped that foreign investment will be able to boost the very limited manufacturing sector.

Service Industries

Tourism is a fast growing industry. Micronesia has good scuba diving facilities. Americans account for 60 per cent of arrivals and Japanese 25 per cent. Infrastructure improvement is needed for expansion.

Agriculture

The agricultural sector provides over 60 per cent of food supplies and employs almost 50 per cent of the workforce. There is only one agricultural commodity of any export consequence - copra, which is exported to Japan - although at various times bananas, black pepper, betelnut and trochus shell have been exports. The copra industry is regulated by the Coconut Development Authority, which is also seeking ways to manufacture other products from the coconut tree. Figures for 2004 show that exports of copra earned US$174,000 Main agricultural products are coconuts, bananas, betel nuts, cassava, and sweet potatoes.

Agricultural Production in 2010

Produce	Int. $'000*	Tonnes
Coconuts	5,529	50,000
Indigenous pigmeat	1,347	876
Cassava	1,055	10,100
Bananas	845	3,000
Indigenous cattle meat	698	258
Vegetables fresh nes	641	3,400
Sweet potatoes	242	3,200
Indigenous chicken meat	199	140
Fruit fresh nes	192	550
Hen eggs, in shell	172	207
Plantains	58	280
Cocoa beans	42	40

* unofficial figures
Source: http://faostat.fao.org/site/339/default.aspx Food and Agriculture Organization of the United Nations, Food and Agricultural commodities production

MICRONESIA

Livestock comprises mainly chickens and pigs, although goats are becoming more numerous. There are about 120 head of cattle and 70 buffalo in Pohnpei.

Fishing
Management of the 200-mile marine economic zone is undertaken by the Micronesian Maritime Authority (MMA). Fisheries in the Federated States of Micronesia are said to be in a state of flux due to a decrease in tuna prices and a general stagnation of worldwide markets. However, the MMA has concluded fishing agreements with Japan, Taiwan, Korea, Mexico and the US.

In 1985 Japanese fishing fleets maintained 85 pole and line vessels and 43 purse seiners. In 2005 exports of fish from Micronesia were worth US$12.1 million. Estimated figures for 2010 put the total catch at 31,000 tonnes.

Timber is used for the construction of rural homesteads and firewood while Mangrove timber is used for handicrafts and furniture making.

Coconut Development Authority, PO Box 297, Kolonia, Pohnpei, 96941, Federated States of Micronesia. Tel: +691 320 2892, fax: +691 320 5383
National Fisheries Corporation, Nox R, Kolonia, Pohnpei, 96941, Federated States of Micronesia. Tel: +691 320 2529, fax: +691 320 2239

COMMUNICATIONS AND TRANSPORT

Travel Requirements
Citizens of Canada, Australia and the EU require a passport valid for 120 days beyond the date of entry but do not need a visa for tourism stays of up to 30 days. USA citizens do not require a passport if they carry acceptable documentation. All visitors must provide proof of adequate funds and return/onward tickets. An entry permit is required for non-tourism stays, and for visits of over 30 days; US tourists can stay for one year without an entry permit. Other nationals should contact the embassy to check visa requirements.

National Airlines
International and interstate air services are provided to and from the FSM by Continental Air Micronesia and Air Nauru, while domestic air service is provided by the Pacific Missionary Aviation in Yap State and Pohnpei State. There are six airports of which five have paved runways and four are capable of receiving international flights. An island hopper service run by Continental Airlines runs between Honolulu, Majuro, Kwajalein, Kosrae, Pohnpei, Chuuk and Guam.

Roads
Road conditions are generally poor in the FSM, although improvements are constantly being made. There are approximately 240 km of roads, of which 42 km are paved and 198 km are unpaved. The first five-year plan acknowledged the need for infrastructural development and is devoting an average of over 50 per cent of plan funding in each of the four states to that purpose.

Shipping
International sea transport services in the FSM have stabilized with an average frequency of every 30 days from East Asia, the US West Coast and the South Pacific to the major ports of Colonis, Kolonia, Lele and Moen. Each port is able to provide handling of containerised cargo, warehousing and transshipment facilities. Carriers include Tokyo Senpaku Kaisha, Saipan Shipping Company, Palau Shipping Company, Orient Navigation Company and Naura Pacific Lines.

HEALTH

The US Public Health Service provides the four state hospitals with doctors. Volunteer physicians often visit to perform specialized treatment. In 2009, Micronesia spent approximately 18.9 per cent of its total budget on healthcare (up from 10.9 per cent in 2000), accounting for 90.7 per cent of all healthcare spending. Total expenditure on healthcare equated to 13.4 per cent of the country's GDP. Per capita expenditure on health was approximately US$336, compared with US$170 in 2000. Figures for 2005-10 show that there are 20 physicians (1.8 per 10,000 population), 375 nurses and midwives (33.2 per 10,000 population), 40 dentistry personnel, 16 pharmaceutical personnel, 40 environmental and public health workers and 31 community health workers. There are 32 hospital beds per 10,000 population.

According to the latest WHO figures, in 2006 approximately 95 per cent of the urban population and 94 per cent of the rural population had access to improved drinking water. In the same year, 61 per cent of the urban population and 14 per cent of the rural population had access to improved sanitation. Diarrhoea accounts for 6 per cent of childhood deaths.

The infant mortality rate in 2010 was 34 per 1,000 live births. The child mortality rate (under 5 years) was 42 per 1,000 live births. (Source: http://www.who.int, World Health Statistics 2012)

EDUCATION

The administrative responsibilities for education in the Federated States of Micronesia are based on the constitution, which provides for concurrent power between national and state governments. State governments are responsible for the actual provision of education, instruction at primary and secondary levels, planning and development and teacher training. The responsibility of the national government is essentially that of supporting and co-ordinating educational services throughout the nation.

Previously, only small numbers of high school graduates from the Federated States of Micronesia went on to post-secondary education with scholarships. Since 1972 when Micronesia became eligible for US federal grants for post-secondary education in the US, the number of Micronesian students enrolled in colleges and universities has risen sharply and now totals 1,500. Annual current level of US support for students in post-secondary education on Guam, Hawaii or mainland US is estimated to be between four and eight million dollars.

The College of Micronesia, established in 1972, maintains a Community College on Pohnpei, currently with 170 full-time students. In addition, there are numbers of part-time students in the four states. Courses in general business, education, liberal arts, home economics and marine science are offered. Private educational facilities are also available, namely the Pohnpei Agricultural and Trade School and the Xavier High School.

The literacy rate is approximately 89 per cent.

RELIGION

The people of Micronesia are overwhelmingly Christian, with Protestant and Catholic faiths in rough equilibrium, although Kosrae is over 98 per cent Protestant (Congregationalist). The Church of Jesus Christ of the Latter-day Saints is also represented, but in a small minority, as are Seventh Day Adventists, Jehovah's Witnesses and the Assembly of God. Despite outward appearances, traditional religious beliefs are still quite strong in some areas. The United Church Board of World Ministries maintains regional headquarters on Pohnpei, while the Catholic Vicariate of the Marshall and Caroline Islands is headquartered on Chuuk.

Micronesia has a religious liberty rating of 10 on a scale of 1 to 10 (10 is most freedom). (Source: World Religion Database)

COMMUNICATIONS AND MEDIA

The constitution provides for freedom of expression.

Newspapers
National Union, (English) published fortnightly; Micronesian Weekly. Each of the state governments provide a newsletter.

Broadcasting
Each state has a multi-channel TV cable service. Nearly all the programming is imported. Approximately six radio stations are in operation.

Telecommunications
Many of the population still live without electricity and the infrastructure system is limited. The islands are connected by shortwave radiotelephones, satellite ground stations and some coaxial cable links. As of 2008 there were estimated to be 8,700 telephone subscribers in Micronesia and 34,000 mobile phone subscription. In 2008 an estimated 18,000 people were regular internet users.

ENVIRONMENT

Micronesia is a party to the following international agreements: Biodiversity, Climate Change, Climate Change-Kyoto Protocol, Desertification, Hazardous Wastes, Law of the Sea, and Ozone Layer Protection.

Micronesia was badly hit by the typhoon Sudel in April 2004. Yap was seriously damaged with most of the infrastructure destroyed. A state of emergency was declared.

A UN backed environmental package has been launched to help marine conservation in Micronesia, its aim is to establish protection for 30 per cent of inshore marine life and 20 per cent of land ecosystems.

MOLDOVA
Republic of Moldova
Republica Moldova

Capital: Chisinau (Population estimate, 2011: 794,500)

Head of State: Nicolae Timofti (President) (page 1525)

National Flag: A tricolour, pale-wise, blue, orange and red, with the arms of the state in the centre

CONSTITUTION AND GOVERNMENT

Constitution
In August 1989 a process of liberalisation started in Moldova; the Romanian language became the state language and a new Parliament adopted new symbols of state (the tricolour flag, the emblem, the hymn).

In August 1991 the Republic of Moldova proclaimed its independence from the USSR. A referendum was held on 6 March 1994 in which continuing Moldovan independence, rather than union with Russia or Romania, was strongly endorsed. The Constitution of 27 August 1997 declares Moldova to be a democratic presidential republic.

Recent constitutional amendments have abolished direct presidential elections, and the president is currently elected by the legislature. The President serves for a term of four years and nominates a Prime Minister-designate and a government. Executive power is vested in the Government of 20 ministries and 11 state departments.

To consult the constitution, please visit:
http://www.president.md/const.php?lang=eng.

International Relations
Relations with Russia have deteriorated since 2003. Russia has weapons and munitions of the Operational Group of Russian Forces (formerly the Russian 14th Army) stationed in Trans-Dniestria, although it promised to remove them. There has been no progress on Russian withdrawals since early 2004.

The Trans-Dniester region of eastern Moldova is the subject of a claim for independence by the majority Slavic population led by supporters of the 1991 Moscow coup attempt. A cease-fire was agreed in 1992 between the Moldovan government and the so-called Trans-Dniestrian Republic. In June 2005, the government approved a Ukrainian plan giving Trans-Dniester autonomy within Moldova. In March 2006, a customs agreement between the two countries was implemented; this effectively meant that Trans-Dniestrian companies who wanted to trade across the border had to register in the capital. In September 2006, a referendum held in Dniester backed independence from Moldova and a plan eventually to become part of Russia; however, this was not recognised by Chisinau and the international community.

In 2005, the Government agreed a European Union (EU)-Moldova Action Plan, with the EU. This comprised a set of reforms to strengthen the democratic and economic situation of the country and facilitate integration. Moldova was a founding member of GUAM, a regional cooperative agreement made up of Georgia, Ukraine, Azerbaijan, and Moldova and is a member of the Commonwealth of Independent States (CIS).

Moldova has enjoyed cordial relations with its neighbour Romania, but Romania's accession to the EU in 2007 meant that Moldovans had to obtain a visa to travel or to transit through the country, accession also brought to an an end of the Free Trade Agreement between the two countries.

Recent Events
In 2006, Gazprom, a major Russian gas supplier, cut supply when Moldova refused to pay twice the previous price. A temporary arrangement was reached, and a new price was agreed July 2006. The Moldovan Government had further problems when the Russians suspended the import of Moldovan wine on health grounds; the Moldovans believe that the suspension was politically motivated. In January 2009, gas supplies were again cut off for several weeks, this time as a result of a dispute over prices between supplier Russia and transit country Ukraine.

On the 7th April, demonstrators attacked parliament, smashing windows and setting light to furniture, in protest at the victory of the governing Communist Party in general elections. President Vladimir Voronin urged an end to "destabilisation", but opposition leaders backed the protests, claiming the election result was fraudulent. The Organisation for Security and Co-operation in Europe gave a positive assessment of the poll but noted some flaws, and some observers thought that there had been manipulation. Moldova's president, and the Russians, accused neighbouring Romania of stoking the protests. The cabinet resigned on 4th May, but was reappointed as a caretaker government in early June. Repeat elections were held on the 29th July 2009, and the Communist Party lost its majority. The four main opposition parties won over 50 per cent of the poll, and formed a coalition government. However it was announced in April that parliament was to be dissolved in June and early elections held.

Presidential elections held in May, then June failed to achieve a result. The cabinet was sworn in on 25 September 2009. The next presidential poll held on 10 November also failed to produce a result. In December, the opposition Communist MPs refused to back a coalition candidate, Marian Lupu, for the presidency. As the constitution states that parliament may not be dissolved twice within 12 months, parliament could not be dissolved immediately.

Parliamentary elections took place at the end of November 2010; no party won enough seats to form a government. The PCRM remained the largest party. A rival alliance, the Alliance for European Integration (AEI), held a narrow majority of seats in Parliament but not enough to elect a president. Marian Lupu was elected as speaker of parliament and therefore became acting president. He confirmed Vlad Filat as prime minister and a new coalition government was named on 14 January 2011, made up of members from the PLDM, the PDM, the PL and one independent.

Nicolae Timofti, a senior judge with no political experience, was elected president in a parliamentary vote in March 2012. The country had been without a president since 2009.

Prime Minister Vlad Filat lost a no-confidence vote in March 2013. Deputy Prime Minister Iurie Leanca took office as interim prime minister on 25 April and was approved by parliament on 20 May. His new cabinet, still a coalition of the PLDM, the PDM and the PL, was sworn in on 31 May.

Legislature
Moldova's unicameral Parliament (*Parlamentul*) is the supreme legislative body and, according to a constitutional amendment of 2000, is now responsible for electing the President. The Parliament, which originally consisted of 370 deputies, dissolved itself in autumn 1993 and a new proportional system of voting was introduced which resulted in the election of 101 deputies in the 1998 elections for a four-year term.
Parliament, 105 Stefan cel Mare Blvd., Chisinau 2073, Moldova. Tel: +373 22 237403, e-mail: info@parlament.md, URL: http://www.parlament.md
Speaker: Marian Lupu

Cabinet (as at June 2013)
Prime Minister: Iurie Leanca (PLDM) (page 1461)
Deputy Prime Minister, Minister of Economy: Valeriu Lazar (PDM) (page 1461)
Deputy Prime Minister, Minister of Foreign Affairs and EU Integration: Natalia Gherman (PLDM)
Deputy Prime Minister: Eugen Carpov
Deputy Prime Minister: Tatiana Poting
Minister of Agriculture and Food Industry: Vasile Bumacov
Minister of Defence: Vitale Marinuta
Minister of Interior: Dorin Recean
Minister of Finance: Vaceslav Negruta (PLDM) (page 1485)
Minister of Youth and Sport: Octavian Bodisteanu (PL)
Minister of Justice: Oleg Efrim
Minister of Culture: Monica Babuc
Minister of Health: Andrei Usatii (PLDM)
Minister of Construction: Marcel Raducan (PDM)
Minister of Environment and Natural Resources: Gheorghe Salaru (PL)
Minister of Labour, Social Protection, Family and Children: Valentina Buliga (PDM)
Minister of Education: Maia Sandu
Minister of IT and Telecommunications: Pavel Filip (PDM)
Minister of Transport & Road Infrastructure: Vasile Botnari

Ministries
Office of the President, Stefan cel Mare 154, Chisinau, Moldova. Tel: +373 22 504244, fax: +373 22 245089, URL: http://www.president.md
Office of the Prime Minister, Piata Marii Adunari Nationale 1, MD2033, Chisinau, Moldova. Tel: +373 22 233092, fax: +373 22 242696, URL: http://gov.md
Ministry of the Economy, Piata Marii Adunari Nationale 1, MD2033, Chisinau, Moldova. Tel: +373 22 237448, fax: +373 22 234064, e-mail: minecon@moldova.md, URL: http://www.mec.gov.md
Ministry of External Affairs and European Integration, 31 August 80, MD2012, Chisinau, Moldova. Tel: +373 22 578207, fax: +373 22 232302, e-mail: secdep@mfa.un.md, URL: http://www.mfa.md
Ministry of Foreign Affairs and European Integration, Str. 31 August 1989, 80, MD2012, Chisinau, Moldova. Tel: +373 22 578 207, fax: +373 22 232 302, e-mail: secdep@mfa.un.md, URL: http://www.mfa.gov.md/start-page-en
Ministry of Finance, Cosmonautilor 7, MD2005, Chisinau, Moldova. Tel: +373 22 233575, fax: +373 22 228610, e-mail: cancelaria@minfin.moldova.md, URL: http://www.mf.gov.md
Ministry of Agriculture and the Food Industry, Stefan cel Mare 162, MD2001, Chisinau, Moldova. Tel: +373 22 233536, fax: +373 22 232368, e-mail: adm_maia@moldova.md, URL: http://www.maia.gov.md
Ministry of Construction and Regional Development, Cosmonautilor 9, MD2005, Chisinau, Moldova. Tel: +373 22 204569, fax: +373 22 220748, e-mail: mii.gov@mail.md, URL: http://www.mcdr.gov.md
Ministry of Culture, Piata Marii Adunari Nationale 1, MD2033, Chisinau, Moldova. Tel: +373 22 227620, fax: +373 22 232388, e-mail: office@mc.gov.md, URL: http://www.mc.gov.md

MOLDOVA

Ministry of Defence, Hincesti 84, MD2048, Chisinau, Moldova. Tel: +373 22 232631, fax: +373 22 233507, URL: http://www.army.gov.md

Ministry of Education, Piata Marii Adunari Nationale 1, MD2033, Chisinau, Moldova. Tel: +373 22 233515, fax: +373 22 233474, e-mail: viceministra@edu.md, URL: http://www.edu.gov.md

Ministry of Environment and Natural Resources, Cosmonautilor 9, MD2005, Chisinau, Moldova. Tel: +373 22 221668, fax: +373 22 220748, e-mail: capcelea@moldova.md, URL: http://www.mediu.gov.md/

Ministry of Health, Vasile Alexandri 1, MD2009, Chisinau, Moldova. Tel: +373 22 729860, fax: +373 22 738781, e-mail: msps@mednet.md, URL: http://www.ms.gov.md

Ministry of Information Technology and Telecommunications, Stefan cel Mare 134, MD2012, Chisinau, Moldova. Tel: +373 22 251102, fax: +373 22 251164, e-mail: mtic@mtic.gov.md, URL: http://www.mtic.gov.md

Ministry of Internal Affairs, Stefan cel Mare 75, MD2001, Chisinau, Moldova. Tel: +373 22 233569, fax: +373 22 222723, e-mail: mai@mai.md, URL: http://www.mai.gov.md/

Ministry of Justice, 31 August 82, MD2012, Chisinau, Moldova. Tel: +373 22 222525, fax: +373 22 234797, e-mail: dagri@cni.md, URL: http://www.justice.gov.md

Ministry of Labour, Social Protection, Family and Children, Vasile Alexandri 1, MD2009, Chisinau, Moldova. Tel: +373 22 269 301, fax: +373 22 269 310, e-mail: secretariat@mpsfc.gov.md, URL: http://www.mmpsf.gov.md

Ministry of Transport and Road Infrastructure, Stefan cel Mare 162, MD2004, Chisinau, Moldova. Tel: +373 22 820702, fax: +373 22 546564, URL: http://www.mtid.gov.md

Ministry of Youth and Sports, Stefan cel Mare 162, MD2004, Chisinau, Moldova. Tel: +373 22 820861, dfx: +373 22 820861, e-mail: ministru@mts.gov.md, URL: http://mts.gov.md

Major Political Parties
Partidul Comunistilor din Republica Moldova (PCRM, Communist Party of the Republic of Moldova), URL: http://www.ournet.md/pcrm/
Alianța Moldova Noastră (Party Alliance Our Moldova), URL: http://www.amn.md
Partidul Democrat din Moldova (PDM, Social Democratic Party of Moldova), URL: http://www.pdm.md
Partidul Popular Crestin Democrat (PPCD, Christian Democratic People's Party), URL: http://www.ppcd.md
Partidul Liberal Democrat din Moldova, (PLDM, Liberal Democratic Party of Moldova), URL: http://www.pldm.md
Partidul Liberal, (PL, Liberal Party), URL: http://www.pl.md

Elections
Presidential elections took place on 20 May but failed to achieve a result, as did a poll on 3 June 2009. A further round on 10 November also failed to produce a result. In December 2010 the Communists refused to back a coalition candidate. Nicolae Timofti, an independent, was finally elected president by parliamentary vote in March 2012.

Parliamentary elections were held on the 5th April 2009. The Communist Party won 50 per cent of the votes, whilst the Liberal Party won almost 13 per cent, the Liberal Democratic Party won12 per cent, and Our Moldova Alliance won almost 10 per cent. The Communists need 61 seats in the 101-seat parliament to elect Mr Voronin's successor unopposed. On the 12th April, a poll recount was ordered following days of anti-government protests in which one person died. Opposition groups claimed that election infringements included the insertion of the names of long-dead residents on electoral lists. They demanded a fresh election, which was held on the 29th July. The Communists lost their majority, and the four main opposition pro-Western parties (The Liberal Democratic Party of Moldova, the Liberal Party, the Democratic Party of Moldova, and the Party Alliance Our Moldova) formed a new coalition (The Alliance for European Integration) government.

Parliament was dissolved on 16 June, less than one year into its term, and early elections were held in November 2010. Again, no single party won an overall majority. The Alliance for European Integration won most seats but even as a coalition were short of the 61 seats needed to elect the president.

Diplomatic Representation
US Embassy, 103 Mateevici Street, Chisinau MD 2009, Moldova. Tel: +373 22 404300, fax: +373 22 233044, e-mail: chisinau@amemb.mldnet.com, URL: http://moldova.usembassy.gov/
Ambassador: William H. Moser
British Embassy, 18 Nicolae Iorga str., Chisinau, MD-2012, Moldova. Tel: +373 22 225902, URL: http://ukinmoldova.fco.gov.uk
Ambassador: Keith Shannon
Embassy of the Republic of Moldova, 2101 S Street, NW, Washington, DC 20008, USA. Tel: +1 202 667 1130, fax: +1 202 667 1204, e-mail: washington@mfa.md, URL: http://www.sua.mfa.md/about-embassy-en/
Ambassador: Igor Munteanu (page 1482)
Embassy of the Republic of Moldova, 5 Dolphin Square, Edensor Road, London W4 2ST, UK. Tel +44 (0)208 995 6818, fax: +44 (0)208 995 6927, URL: http://www.britania.mfa.gov.md/
Chargé d'Affaires: Mihaela Manoli
Permanent Mission of the Republic of Moldova to the United Nations, 35 East 29th Street, New York, NY 10016, USA. Tel: +1 212 447 1867, fax: +1 212 447 4067, e-mail: moldova@un.int, URL: http://www.un.int/moldova
Ambassador: Vladimir Lupan

LEGAL SYSTEM

The judiciary is composed of ordinary courts, Courts of Appeal and the Supreme Court. There is also a Constitutional Court whose six judges decide constitutional cases, as well as special courts for economic, military and other specialised matters. The seven judges of the Audit Court control the ways of creating, administering and utilizing public financial resources.

In general the government respects the human rights of its citizens. There have been instances of brutality on detainees by security forces, and prison conditions are harsh. There have been reports of judicial and police corruption. The government has attempted to intimidate journalists and restricts freedom of assembly. Moldova abolished the death penalty in 1995.

Supreme Court of Justice, URL: http://www.csj.md/index.php?lang=4

Centre for Human Rights of Moldova, URL: http://www.ombudsman.md/en/general/

LOCAL GOVERNMENT

Moldova is divided administratively into 32 districts and three municipalities, Balti, Bender and Chisinau. There are 60 towns (including the 5 municipalities) and 917 villages.

There is one autonomous territorial unit, Gagauzia, and one territorial unit, Stinga Nistrului.

AREA AND POPULATION

Area
The Republic of Moldova is landlocked, situated between Ukraine and Romania. It is the second smallest country of the former Soviet Union, its total area being 33,800 sq. km. The terrain consists of rolling steppe. Rich soils make it very good agricultural land. The weather is cold to moderate in the winter and warm in the summer.

To view a map of Moldova, please visit http://www.un.org/Depts/Cartographic/map/profile/moldova.pdf

Population
The total population at 2010 was estimated at 3.573 million, with an annual average growth of -1.4 per cent over the period 2000-10. Population density is around 118 people per square kilometre. The majority of the population (71.8 per cent) is aged between 15 and 64, with 17 per cent aged up to 15 years, and 16 per cent aged 60 or over. The median age is 35 years. An estimated 51.8 per cent of the population are women.

In 2006, around 6,685 people emigrated, most going to Russia and the Ukraine. Many went to Italy and Spain. In the same year, 1,968 people immigrated to Moldova, mainly from Russia and the Ukraine.

At the beginning of 2007, some 2.1 million Moldovans lived in rural areas, whilst 1.4 million lived in urban areas. The capital, Chisinau, has a population of 717,900. Other significant towns are Balti, Ribnita, Tignina and Tiraspol. The ethnic composition of Moldova is Moldavian/Romanian 64.5 per cent, Ukrainian 13 per cent, Russian 3.5 per cent, Gagauz 2 per cent, Bulgarian 2 per cent and Jewish and others 1.7 per cent. The Russian and Ukrainian minorities are predominant in the Dniester region and the Gagauzi in the south. Moldavian is the official language, which is virtually the same as the Romanian language. Less widely spoken languages are Russian and Gagauz (a Turkish dialect).

Births, Marriages, Deaths
According to 2010 estimates, the crude birth rate is 12.3 per 1,000 of the population, whilst the crude death rate is 12.9 per 1,000 population. Average life expectancy at birth in 2009 was 69 years (65 years for men and 73 years for women). Healthy life expectancy was 61 years. The infant mortality rate is 16 deaths per 1,000 live births. The fertility rate is 1.5 children born per woman. (Source: http://www.who.int, World Health Statistics 2012) In 2005, there were 27,128 marriages and 12,594 divorces.

Public Holidays 2014
1 January: New Year's Day
6-7 January: Orthodox Christmas
8 March: International Women's Day
21 April: Easter Monday (Orthodox)
1 May: Labour Day
9 May: Victory Day
28 July: National Day of Remembrance
27 August: Independence Day
31 August: National Language Day

EMPLOYMENT

Moldova's total labour force of people over the age of 15 numbered about 1.36 million in 2006. 1,257,300 people were employed and 99,900 were unemployed. The average unemployment rate during 2006 was 7.4 per cent. (Source: International Labour Organisation)

Recent figures estimate that around 600,000 people have left Moldova to search for work. Many are working illegally in EU countries.

Employment by economic sector, 2008

Economic activity	No. of Employees
Agriculture, hunting and forestry	387,400
Fishing, fish farming	1,200
Mining and quarrying	3,800
Manufacturing industry	136,200
Electricity and heat, gas and water	23,300
Construction	82,800
Wholesale and retail trade	187,600
Hotels and restaurants	21,200
Transport and communications	70,800

- continued

Financial intermediation	17,000
Real estate, renting and business services	30,400
Public administration & Defence, Compulsory Social Security	68,100
Education	112,000
Health and social work	68,100
Other community, social and personal service activities	35,700
Households with employees	4,500
Extra-territorial organisations and bodies	900
Total	**1,251,000**

Source: Copyright © International Labour Organization (ILO Dept. of Statistics, http://laborsta.ilo.org)

BANKING AND FINANCE

Currency
The currency is the Moldovan leu (MDL), and replaced the rouble in 1993.

GDP/GNP, Inflation, National Debt
Moldova is the poorest country in Europe, but economic growth has been steady since 2000. Although the services sector is Moldova's greatest contributor to GDP, Moldova's economy is primarily based on agriculture, particularly vegetables, fruits, wine and tobacco. Agriculture contributes around a third of Moldova's GDP. With Russia as its leading trade partner, Moldova has been adversely affected by its neighbour's economic problems but growth was steady in the period 2000-06. It then faltered due to a steep rise in gas prices, a drought and export difficulties with Russia. However, growth was again strong in 2008. The government has initiated reforms with integration into the EU as its goal. The economy faltered in 2009 as remittances from abroad fell. The economy suffered as a result of the global economic crisis and in 2009 the IMF allocated approximately US$185 million for its immediate needs and then in 2010, an US$575 million agreement was reached.

GDP fell by 8.6 per cent in 1998 and by 4.4 per cent in 1999. However, with improvements in industrial and agricultural output, Moldova's GDP rose by 1.9 per cent in 2000, 6.1 per cent in 2001 and 7.0 per cent in 2002. GDP grew by 6.5 per cent in 2004, and by 8.6 per cent in 2005. In 2006, GDP reached US$3.35 billion (up from US$2.9 billion in 2005, indicating growth of 5 per cent. GDP was US4.4 billion in 2007, with a growth rate of 4 per cent. Figures for 2009 put GDP at US$5,400 billion, with a growth rate that year of -6.5 per cent in response to the global economic downturn. GDP was estimated to be US$5.8 billion in 2010 with a growth rate of over 6 per cent. Per capita GDP was US$1,600. GDP was estimated to have risen to US$6.5 billion in 2011.

Over a million Moldovans are estimated to be working abroad, (a quarter of the country's population), making Moldova the world's most remittance-dependent economy. The money they send back home makes up more than a third of the country's gross domestic product and amounts to around $1.2 billion a year.

Inflation fell from 105 per cent in 1994 to a low of 4.4 per cent in 2002 before rising again to 11.6 per cent in 2003, 12.4 per cent in 2004, and 11.9 per cent in 2005. In 2006, inflation reached 12.7 per cent. It was estimated to have remained at this rate in 2007. In 2013, inflation stood at 3.7 per cent against a traget of 5 per cent. External debt stood at an estimated US$4.7 billion in 2011.

Foreign Investment
Ineffective law enforcement and economic and political uncertainty have had a negative effect on foreign investment in the country. The communist administration has negotiated with the IMF and World Bank, but in 2003, the IMF withdrew its financial package in view of the government's failure to meet requirements. In the spring of 2006, the IMF agreed to a Poverty Reduction and Growth Facility for Moldova, designed to bolster foreign reserves against external shocks. A three-year, $175 million program was put in place.

In 2007, Parliament introduced new approaches to privatizing and managing state-owned assets, giving priority to economic efficiency. With the EU expansion to Moldova's border, 2006 saw high foreign direct investment. However, cumulative FDI since independence falls well below the country's requirements.

Balance of Payments / Imports and Exports
In 2006, Moldova's trade deficit worsened due to a two-fold increase in the cost of gas and the Russian ban on imports of Moldovan wine and other agricultural products; Moldova traditionally exported between 70-80 per cent of its wine production to Russia. Although Russian President Putin announced an end to the wine ban in November 2006, Russia had still not resumed importing Moldovan wine as of September 2007. In January 2006, the Russian energy giant Gazprom temporarily cut off natural gas deliveries to Moldova and then doubled the price of gas.

Export revenue in 2010 was put at US$1.5 billion, rising to US$2 billion in 2011. The main export commodity is food, followed by wine and tobacco, textiles and footwear, and machinery. Some 52 per cent of exports go to the EU and an estimated 20 per cent to Russia.

Imports cost the country some US$3.8 billion in 2010, rising to US$5 billion in 2011. Major imported goods include fuel and mineral products, machinery and equipment, vehicles, textiles and chemicals. 60 per cent of goods come from countries other than the former Soviet Union countries, though the main suppliers are Ukraine, Russia and Romania.

Central Bank
National Bank of Moldova (Banca Nationala a Moldovei), 7 Renasterii Avenue, MD-2006 Chisinau, Moldova. Tel: +373 2 221679, fax: +373 2 220591, e-mail: official@bnm.org, URL: http://www.bnm.org
Governor: Dorin Drăguțanu

MANUFACTURING, MINING AND SERVICES

Primary and Extractive Industries
Moldova has minimal reserves of oil, natural gas and coal. These reserves are not currently being exploited although exploration is underway. In 2011, Moldova imported and consumed an estimated 22,000 bbl/d of oil, and 75, billion cubic feet of gas.

Plans are underway to develop the Valenskoye field in the south of the country, which could yield up to 2,000 barrels per day. There are also plans to build a refinery linked to the Ukraine's Brody-Odessa oil pipeline, allowing Moldova to import crude oil and process it domestically. The Giurgiulesti oil terminal on the Danube River is also due to be developed.

Moldova has no natural gas resources and is dependent on Russia to meet its requirements. Moldova no longer has coal reserves and imports all its requirements. (Source: EIA)

Energy
Moldova generates and consumes little electricity. Total primary energy consumption was an estimated 0.131 quadrillion Btu in 2009. Electricity generation capacity in 2010 was 0.55 GWe, production was an estimated 3.34 billion kilowatthours (kWh), and consumption was 3.53 billion kWh.

Construction of a gas-fired power plant in Burlaceni, to help decrease Moldovan reliance on imports of electricity, began in 2010. The plant will have a capacity of 450 MW. (Source: EIA)

Manufacturing
The food processing industry is of prime importance for Moldova. It includes wine-making, fruit and vegetable canning, and the production of vegetable and essential oils and sugar. In addition, tobacco is processed, and machinery for the agricultural sector is produced.

The wine industry is of major importance to the economy, and can contribute up to 50 per cent of total export revenues in a good year. Some 130,000 acres are dedicated to vineyards. Moldova produces 200-300 million bottles of still wine per annum, as well as 20 million bottles of sparkling wines. Brandy and vermouth are also produced. Ninety per cent of wines are exported, mainly to Russia, and give a revenue of around US$150 million per annum.

The fruit and vegetable processing sector is also a major industrial sector, comprising seven large, 15 medium and over 100 small companies. Tomato and apple processing are the main areas and represent about 80 per cent of the total output of food preservation. The other 20 per cent of products are canned plums, dry fruit, baby food and jams. Crops are still mainly harvested by hand.

The tobacco industry consists of eight companies and about 40,000 employees. It requires reorganisation and investment.

The sugar industry is based on raw material grown on approximately 80,000 ha, employing 30,000 people with 10 factories. Annual processing capacity is 3 million tons of sweet roots. Every year 1.8 million tons of sugar beet is processed and 0.22 million tons of granulated sugar produced.

Service Industries
The privatisation process in Moldova began in 1993 when the Government took a strategic decision to launch a mass privatisation program. As a result, by the end of 1996, more than 3 million Moldovan citizens became shareholders and more than 2,000 state enterprises were privatised. The process has continued, companies being sold to both local and foreign investors. Nearly all of Moldova's agricultural land has now moved from state to private ownership.

Tourism is a small sector and figures for 2010 show that there were an estimated 9,000 foreign visitors.

Agriculture
The land is suitable for cultivation as the climate is temperate and the soils fertile. Although just 19 per cent of the working population are officially employed in this sector, up to 50 per cent of the population are involved in subsistence agriculture. In January 2005, around 85 per cent of the land was arable and 14 per cent was used for perennial plantations, mainly orchards and vineyards. The total area of land under cultivation in 2005 was 2.138 million hectares.

Moldova held second place in the former USSR for gross yield of grapes and third place for fruit and berries. There are plantations of roses, clary sage, mint, lavender and geraniums. The Republic grows winter wheat, maize, sunflowers, sugar beet and tobacco. Vegetables are grown in all parts of the Republic. Animal husbandry comprises cattle, pigs and sheep. Poultry farming is well developed.

A severe drought during much of 2007 caused major losses in the agriculture sector, and there were concerns about food availability.

Agricultural Production in 2010

Produce	Int. $'000*	Tonnes
Grapes	275,302	481,620
Cow milk, whole, fresh	154,360	544,136
Wheat	97,066	744,160
Apples	87,925	207,903
Indigenous pigmeat	79,728	51,864
Sunflower seed	65,805	382,316
Indigenous chicken meat	47,924	33,645
Indigenous cattle meat	33,936	12,563
Hen eggs, in shell	33,341	40,200

MOLDOVA

- continued

Sugar beet	32,806	837,624
Potatoes	32,164	279,650
Plums and sloes	32,116	53,816

* unofficial figures

Source: http://faostat.fao.org/site/339/default.aspx Food and Agriculture Organization of the United Nations, Food and Agricultural commodities production

Livestock and poultry, 2003-04 (thousand head)

	2003	2004
Cattle	373	331
- of which, cows	256	231
Pigs	446	398
Sheep	817	823
Goats	121	121
Horses	78	73
Poultry	15,756	17,522

Source: National Bureau of Statistics

COMMUNICATIONS AND TRANSPORT

Travel Requirements
Citizens of the USA, Canada, Australia and the EU require a passport valid for at least six months but do not need a visa for stays of up to 90 days - apart from Australians who do need a visa. All foreign visitors must register with the police within three days of arrival. Other nationals should contact the embassy to check visa requirements.

National Airlines
Air Moldova International, URL: http://www.ami.md
Moldavian Airlines, URL: http://www.mdv.md

International Airports
An estimated 1 million passengers passed through Chisinau Airport in 2010.
Chisinau Airport, URL: http://www.airport.md/homepage-ro/

Railways
The railway accounts for the transportation of 95 per cent of external cargo and extends to 1,190 km. It is linked to the CIS countries and there are regular services to Sofia, Istanbul, Kiev and Moscow. In 2004, some 13.3 million tonnes of goods were transported by rail, and 5.1 million passenger travelled by rail.
Railway of Moldova: URL: http://www.railway.md

Roads
The public roads network is administered by the Ministry of Transport and Communications. The national road network covers 10,000 km. 21.3 million tonnes of goods were transported by road in 2004, and 98.3 million people travelled by bus. Vehicles are driven on the right.

Shipping
River transport is used for merchant shipping on the Nistru, as well as for the transportation of tourists and local cargo. Total length of the interior navigable ways is 1,356 km, including the River Prut (716 km) and the River Nistru (640 km). Length of the interior navigable ways with guaranteed depth are 85 km, of the River Prut and 324 km of the River Nistru. In 2004, 119.7 million tonnes of goods were transported by river, and 100,000 million passengers travelled by river boat.

HEALTH

In 2009, the Moldovan government spent approximately 13.4 per cent of its total budget on healthcare (up from 9.5 per cent in 2000), accounting for 49.5 per cent of all healthcare spending. Total expenditure on healthcare equated to 12.5 per cent of the country's GDP. Per capita expenditure on health was approximately US$191, compared with US$24 in 2000. Figures for 2005-10 show that there are 11,161 physicians (26.8 per 10,000 population), 27,536 nurses and midwives (66.1 per 10,000 population), 2,862 pharmaceutical personnel and 1,622 dentists. There are an estimated 62 hospital beds per 10,000 population.

According to the latest WHO figures, in 2010 approximately 96 per cent of the population had access to improved drinking water. In the same year, 85 per cent of the population had access to improved sanitation.

Those living with HIV/AIDS numbered around 5,500. Approximately 300 have died of the disease. In 2009, the infant mortality rate (probability of dying before first birthday) was estimated to be 16 per 1,000 live births and the under-five mortality was estimated to be 19 per 1,000 live births. The most common causes of death in the under-fives are: prematurity 7 per cent, congenital anomalies 29 per cent, pneumonia 21 per cent, and injuries 13 per cent. Approximately 11.3 per cent of children aged less than 5 years were classified as stunted in the period 2005-11 and 3.2 per cent as underweight. (Source: http://www.who.int, World Health Statistics 2012)

EDUCATION

Primary/Secondary Education
Moldova's compulsory education system lasts for 11 years. Primary education lasts for four years and secondary education for seven years. Whilst there is private sector education, this is small in comparison to the public sector. Expenditure on education rose from 16.8 per cent of total budget expenditure in 2000 to 19.8 per cent in 2007.

Figures for 2004 indicate that there were 1,269 pre-school institutions, with 109,692 children enrolled. Primary schools numbered 1,570, with 546,615 pupils enrolled, and secondary vocational education institutes numbered 81, with 22,696 pupils. There were 56 colleges and 35 Institutes of Higher Education, with enrolment numbers of 23,618 and 114,552 respectively. (Source: National Bureau of Statistics)

The adult literacy rate is estimated to be around 99 per cent.

RELIGION

Approximately 96 per cent of the population is Christian. Approximately 87 per cent of the population belongs to the Christian Orthodox church. The rest are Baptist, Adventist, Roman Catholic, Muslim (0.42 per cent), or Jewish (0.76 per cent). Moldova has a religious tolerance rating of 6 on a scale of 1 to 10 (10 is most freedom). (Source: World Religion Database)

COMMUNICATIONS AND MEDIA

Freedom of the press is written into the constitution but defamation and insulting the state are prohibited. Political pressure on the media was reported following the post-election protests in 2009.

Newspapers
Over 200 newspapers are published in Moldova, approximately 90 in Romanian. The media tends to divide along political lines.The main papers published in Moldovan are Timpul (URL: http://www.timpul.mdl.net) and Flux (URL: http://www.flux.md). Kommersant Moldoviy (URL: http://www.km.press.md) and Komsomolskaya Pravda (URL: http://www.kp.md) are published in Russian. Circulation figures are low.

Broadcasting
Television is the most popular medium. In 2009 there were 37 terrestial television stations, many rebroadcasting from Russian and Romanian stations. Moldova One (URL: http://trm.md) and Radio Moldova (URL: http://www.trm.md/) are state-owned.

Telecommunications
The system is generally poor, but with ongoing improvements especially around the cabinet. In 2010, there were an estimated 1.1 million mainline telephones and 3 million mobile phones in use. In 2009, there were an estimated 1 million internet users.

ENVIRONMENT

Major environmental problems in Moldova include soil erosion and the contamination of soil by pesticides.

Carbon dioxide emissions in Moldova increased from 6.61 million metric tons in 2004 to 7.16 million metric tons in 2005. This equated to 1.65 metric tons per capita, well below the average for the region. In 2010 Moldova's emissions from the consumption of fossil fuels totalled 7.38 million metric tons of carbon dioxide. (Source: EIA)

Moldova is a party to the following international environmental agreements: Air Pollution, Air Pollution-Persistent Organic Pollutants, Biodiversity, Climate Change, Climate Change-Kyoto Protocol, Desertification, Endangered Species, Hazardous Wastes, Ozone Layer Protection, Ship Pollution, and Wetlands.

MONACO
Principality of Monaco
Principauté de Monaco

Capital: Monaco-Ville (Population estimate: 1,500)

Head of State: HSH Prince Albert II (Sovereign) (page 1373)

National Flag: Divided fesswise, red and white.

CONSTITUTION AND GOVERNMENT

Constitution
The Principality of Monaco is a hereditary and constitutional monarchy which guarantees separation of power between the executive, legislative and judicial branches of government. The present constitution was promulgated on 17 December 1962. Executive power is vested in the Sovereign and exercised by a Council of Government consisting of five members presided over by a Minister of State, who is chosen by the Sovereign from a panel put forward by the President of France. The Sovereign is advised by his Government and has an absolute power of veto.

The government is advised by three councils: the Crown Council, the State Council and the Social and Economic Council.

The Crown Council consists of seven members, nominated by the Prince, who serve a renewable three-year term, and advises the Prince on constitutional matters such as the signing and ratifying of treaties, and the dissolution of the National Council. The President and three of the Council members are appointed by the Prince. The remaining three members are chosen by the prince after being approved by the National Council and they may not be Assembly members.

The State Council comprises 12 members recommended by the Minister of State and nominated by the Prince, and is responsible for advising the Prince on questions of law and order.

The Social and Economic Council is a committee consisting of 30 members nominated by the Prince and serving a three-year term. Ten members are recommended by the Government, 10 are chosen from a list draw up by the Unions, and 10 are chosen from a list drawn up by the Mongasque Employers' Federation.

A series of constitutional amendments were approved by the *Conseil National* (National Council) in April 2002, including the enlargement of the *Conseil National* from 18 to 24 members following the 2003 elections; the transfer of a number of executive powers from the Prince to the *Conseil National*; the law on succession modified to allow succession through the female line; and the age of majority reduced from 21 years to 18 years.

To consult the constitution, please visit http://www.monaco.gouv.mc

Legislature
Legislative power is held by the National Council (*Conseil National*) of 24 members, elected by universal adult suffrage every five years. The National Council convenes twice a year, each session lasting for a maximum of two months. The *Union pour Monaco* (Union for Monaco) holds the majority of seats.

National Council (Conseil National), 12 rue Colonel Bellando de Castro, MC 98000 Monaco. Tel: +377 93 30 41 15, URL: http://www.conseil-national.mc
President: Jean-François Robillon, Vice President: Fabrice Notari

Recent Events
Prince Rainier, Head of State of Monaco for 56 years, died in April 2005 and was succeeded by his son, Prince Albert.

In 2008 Monaco abandoned plans to expand into the sea through a large land reclamation project. Environmental concerns and the international financial crisis were given as reasons.

In July 2011, Prince Albert married South African Olympic swimmer, Charlene Wittstock.

Council of Government (as at June 2013)
Minister of State: Michel Roger (page 1504)
Minister for the Interior: Paul Masseron (page 1472)
Minister for Equipment, Environment and Town Planning: Marie-Pierre Gramaglia
Minister of Social Affairs and Health: Stéphane Valeri
Minister for Finance and the Economy: Jean Castellini
Minister for Foreign Affairs and International Economic Affairs: José Badia
---

Ministries
Government portal: http://www.gouv.mc/
Office of the Prince, Palais de Monaco, Place du Palais, BP 518, 98015 Monaco. Tel: +377 93 25 18 31, fax: +377 93 30 26 26, e-mail: centre-info@gouv.mc, URL: http://www.gouv.mc
Ministry of State, BP 522, place de la Visitation, 98015 Monaco. Tel: +377 93 15 80 00, fax: +377 93 15 82 17, e-mail: centre-info@gouv.mc, URL: http://www.gouv.mc/

Department of Facilities, Urban Planning and Environment, BP 522, 98015 Monaco. Tel: +377 93 15 80 00, fax: +377 93 15 82 17, e-mail: centre-info@gouv.mc, URL: http://www.gouv.mc/
Department of Health and Social Services, BP 522, 98015 Monaco. Tel: +377 93 15 80 00, fax: +377 93 15 82 17, e-mail: centre-info@gouv.mc, URL: http://www.gouv.mc
Department of the Interior, Place de la Visitation, BP 522, 98015 Monaco. Tel: +377 93 15 80 00, fax: +377 93 50 82 45, e-mail: centre-info@gouv.mc, URL: http://www.gouv.mc
Department of Finance and Economy, Place de la Visitation, BP 522, 98015 Monaco. Tel: +377 93 15 80 00, e-mail: centre-info@gouv.mc, URL: http://www.gouv.mc
Department of Foreign Affairs, BP 522, 98015 Monaco. Tel: +377 93 15 80 00, fax: +377 93 15 82 17, e-mail: centre-info@gouv.mc, URL: http://www.gouv.mc

Political Parties
Union pour Monaco (UPM, Union for Monaco), URL: http://www.unionpourmonaco.com. Leader: Stéphane Valeri. Includes:
- Union pour la Principauté (Union for the Principality)
- Union Nationale pour l'Avenir de Monaco (National Union for the Future of Monaco), URL: http://www.unam-monaco.com/
- Rassemblement pour la famille monégasque (Rally for the Monegasque Family)
Rassemblement et Enjeux pour Monaco, URL: URL: http://www.rassemblement-enjeux.org/index2.php

Elections
Legislative elections for the Conseil National last took place on 3 February 2008; the Union pour la Monaco coalition (UPM) was re-elected with 21 of the Council's 24 seats. The Rassemblement et Enjeux pour Monaco won 41 per cent and 3 seats.

Diplomatic Representation
British Embassy, URL: http://ukinfrance.fco.gov.uk/
Ambassador (resident in Paris): Sir Peter Ricketts GCMG (page 1503)
Embassy of Monaco, 7 Upper Grosvenor Street, London SW1K 2LY, UK. Tel: +44 (0)20 7823 1771, fax:: +44 (0)20 7823 1089, e-mail: embassy.uk@gouv.mc, URL: http://www.monaco-consulate-uk.gouv.mc/
Ambassador: S.E. Mrs Evelyne Genta
US Embassy, (The US does not have a diplomatic mission in Monaco. The US Embassy in France is accredited to Monaco. URL: http://france.usembassy.gov
Ambassador: Charles H. Rivkin (page 1503)
Embassy in the US, URL: http://www.monaco-usa.org
Ambassador to the US: Gilles Noghès
Permanent Representative of the Principality of Monaco to the United Nations, 866 United Nations Plaza, Suite 520, New York, NY 10017, USA. Tel: +1 212 832 0721, fax: +1 212 832 5358, e-mail: monaco@un.int, URL: http://www.monaco-un.org/
Ambassador: H.E. Mme Isabelle Picco

LEGAL SYSTEM

The law is largely based on the French Code Civil. Though judicial authority is vested in the Prince, he delegates it to the Courts and Tribunals, which dispense justice in his name but completely independently (there is no Minister of Justice in the Principality).

A justice of the peace tries petty cases. Other courts are the court of first instance, the court of appeal, the court of revision, and the criminal court. The highest judicial authority is vested in the Supreme Court, which interprets the constitution and sits as the highest court of appeals. It has five full members and two assistant members, named by the prince.

A Supreme Tribunal may be called by the Prince for constitutional, administrative or jurisdictional matters.

The government respects the human rights of its citizens. However, citizens do not have the right to change their government. The death penalty was abolished in 1962.

Supreme Court, URL: http://www.gouv.mc/
President: Hubert Charles

LOCAL GOVERNMENT

The Principality is divided into four quarters: Monaco-Ville, La Condamine, Monte Carlo, and Fontvieille. They are administered by a Communal Council (*Conseil Communal*) comprising 15 members elected by direct universal suffrage for a four-year term. The council is headed by a Mayor and comprises nine Deputies appointed by the Council from among its own members, four Councillors, and a Secretary-General. The last Communal Council elections took place in March 2011.

MONACO

AREA AND POPULATION

Area
The Principality of Monaco covers an area of approximately three quarters of a sq. mile (1.95 sq. km) and is the second-smallest independent state in the world (after the Holy See). Monaco lies in the south-east corner of France on the Mediterranean coast. The coastline is about 4.1 km in length. Monaco is situated about 20 km east of Nice and 10 km west of Menton which is itself adjacent to the Italian frontier. The climate is Mediterranean, with hot, dry summers and mild, wet winters.

To view a map, please consult http://www.lib.utexas.edu/maps/cia08/monaco_sm_2008.gif

Population
With an estimated population of 35,000 in 2010 and an area of three-quarters of a sq. mile, Monaco is the world's most densely populated state. However, population growth is relatively low at 0.1 per cent, according to 2010 estimates. The majority of the population (59 per cent) is aged between 15 and 60 years, with 23 per cent aged over 60 years, and just over 18 per cent aged up to 15 years.

Only about 15 per cent of the population is Monégasque, almost half being French, about 17 per cent Italian and around 5 per cent British. Most European nationalities are well represented, as are many Americans, Canadians, Australians and South Africans and nationals of Middle Eastern countries.

French is the official language but Italian, English and Monegasque are widely spoken and understood.

Births, Marriages, Deaths
According to 2010 estimates the birth rate is 7.0 births per 1,000 inhabitants, whilst the death rate is 8.1 deaths per 1,000 people. Average life expectancy at birth was 78 years for men and 85 years for women for 2009. Healthy life expectancy at birth is 71 years and 76 years respectively. Infant mortality is 3 deaths per 1,000 live births, and the fertility rate is 1.5 children born per woman. (Source: http://www.who.int, World Health Statistics 2012)

Public Holidays 2014
1 January: New Year's Day
27 January: Feast of Sainte Dévote (Monaco's Patron Saint)
21 April: Easter Monday
5 May: Labour Day
29 May: Ascension
9 June: Whit Monday
19 June: Corpus Christi
15 August: Assumption
1 November: All Saints' Day
19 November: National Day
8 December: Immaculate Conception
25 December: Christmas Day

EMPLOYMENT

An estimated 91.5 per cent of employees (43,164) worked in the private sector in 2007, and of these, 83.08 per cent worked in the services sector, 16.85 per cent worked in industry and 0.07 per cent were employed in agriculture. The public sector employs 8.48 per cent of the total population.

People of Monégasque nationality made up just 2.19 per cent of those employed in the Principality, the majority of employees being French (67.23 per cent). Within the private sector, 6,558 employees (16.28 per cent) were resident in Monaco in 2005. 10,667 workers (26.48 per cent) came from the Communes Limitrophes (Beausoleil, Cap d'Ail, La Turbie and Roquebrune-Cap-Martin). 19,393 (48.13 per cent) employees travelled in from France (mainly from Nice and Menton), and 3,578 (8.88 per cent) commuted from Italy. (Source: Service de l'Emploi, Government of Monaco)

BANKING AND FINANCE

Currency
One euro (€) = 100 cents
The official currency is the euro (with effect from 1 January 2002). Euro banknotes come in denominations of 5, 10, 20, 50, 100, 200, and 500. Euro coins come in denominations of 2 and 1 euro, 50, 20, 10, 5, 2, and 1 cents. Euro minted in Monaco have special Monegasque features on one side of the coin.

Monaco is a fully integrated part of the French monetary system and has therefore, along with France, abolished exchange control in line with EU policy.

GDP/GNP, Inflation, National Debt
Monaco's economy is largely based on finance, commerce, and tourism. Because of its low taxes, it is a popular base for foreign companies. GDP (current prices) was estimated at €3,441,691,000 in 2005, rising to €3,717,458,000 in 2006. Figures for 2008 put GDP at €4.4 billion, growth rate that year was put at 0.40 per cent. GDP was €4.002 billion in 2010 (-10.9 per cent on the previous year). Per capita GDP was estimated to be €54,464 in 2009.

Balance of Payments / Imports and Exports
Export revenue rose from €763,263,907 in 2006 to €834,108,693 in 2007. Import costs, over the same period, rose from €821,623,547 to €850,202,845, giving a 2007 negative trade balance of -€16,094,152. An estimated 54.7 per cent of exports went to Europe, 19.14 per cent to Asia, 13.73 per cent to Africa, 10.51 per cent to the Americas and 1.91 to Oceania.

Principal destinations by country: Germany (€89,014,321, 10.67 per cent), Italy (€69,920,084, 8.38 per cent), Spain (€65,632,922, 7.87 per cent), UK (€55,121,105, 6.61 per cent), and Lithuania (€43,564,304, 5.22 per cent). Exports were estimated to be US$710 million in 2010.

In 2007, imports by region were as follows: Asia, 45.34 per cent, Europe 44.63 per cent, Africa 5.0 per cent, the Americas 4.10 per cent and Oceania 0.93 per cent. Germany imported 18 per cent, Italy 10.8 per cent, the UK imported 8.4 per cent and Japan imported 2.9 per cent. China became Monaco's largest supplier of goods in 2007, at €296,595,773 or 34.89 per cent (compared to 17.4 per cent in 2005). Other main suppliers of goods include: Italy (€157,727,571, 18.55 per cent), Japan (€72,312,680, 8.51 per cent), UK (€60,065, 879, 7.06 per cent), and Belgium (€45,312,801, 5.33 per cent). (Source: Monaco en Chiffres). Imports were estimated to cost US$875 million in 2010.

Monaco and France are united in a single customs union and so Monaco applies French customs regulations as well as French import and export codes.

Trade or Currency Restrictions
The only form of direct tax is that on firms generating at least 25 per cent of their profits outside Monaco. Residents of the Principality are exempt from income tax except for French nationals. France and Monaco form a single customs union so French regulations and import and export codes apply.

Central Bank
Association Monégasque des Banques, URL: http://www.monaco-privatebanking.com/en/banking-sector.html

Business Addresses
Chamber of Economic Development, URL: http://www.cde.mc/

MANUFACTURING, MINING AND SERVICES

The economy is broadly based, with tourism, property development and commerce providing major sources of revenue. By virtue of its customs union with France, Monaco has benefited from the single European market since 1992, even though not itself a member state of the European Union.

Manufacturing
Types of industry in Monaco include construction, chemicals, food products, plastics, precision instruments, ceramics and cosmetics. As of 2007 there were 104 establishments, employing nearly 3,500 people.

Services
As of 2007 there were more than 80 banking establishments, finance and management companies with assets amounting to over €78 billion. Financial services are controlled by SICCFIN (Financial Network Information and Monitoring Services). The services sector (including IT, telecommunications, transportation, banking, insurance) employs nearly 17,000. The retail sector generates some €1.6 billion.

Tourism
Since its casino was established in 1856 Monaco has been a popular destination for tourists. In 2007 there were 327,000 arrivals and the number of overnight stays reached 943,000. Most visitors were from neighbouring France and Italy, but large numbers also came from the UK and from the USA. Tourism has been helped by the development of Port Hercule. Full-size cruise liners may now be accommodated. Monaco has long been a meeting ground for businesses, and following a slump in recent years, the number of conventions organised in the Principality grew to 637 in 2007. (Source: Monaco en Chiffres, 2008)
Monaco Tourist Authority, URL: http://www.gouv.mc/357/wwwDtc.nsf/fr_home.htm

Agriculture
Monaco produces no agricultural products.

COMMUNICATIONS AND TRANSPORT

Travel Requirements
Citizens of the USA, Canada , Australia and the EU require a passport valid for three months beyond the length of stay. A visa is not required for visits of up to 90 days. Monaco is not a member of the EU, and visitors should contact the embassy or French Consular Authority to check visa requirements.

International Airports
Air services are provided by the international airport at Nice which is 20 km away and has direct flights to all major European centres. There is a helicopter service.

Railways
The French railway system runs train services through Monaco connecting with neighbouring towns. A journey from the Monaco-Monte Carlo railway station to Paris takes around six hours. Trains also run to Ventimiglia in Italy.

Ports and Harbours
There are two ports: the port of Monaco and the port of Fontvieille. A new sea wall was constructed in 2002 and since then traffic has increased. An estimated 200,000 passengers visit Monaco.

HEALTH

According to the most recent WHO statistics, there are an estimated 186 doctors (58 per 10,000 population), 34 dentists, 464 nursing and midwifery personnel (145 per 10,000 population), 61 pharmacists (19 per 10,000 population). In 2009, Monaco spent approximately 18.5 per cent of its total budget on healthcare (down from 17 per cent in 2000), accounting for 88.0 per cent of all healthcare spending. Total expenditure on healthcare equated to 4.2 per cent of the country's GDP. Per capita expenditure on health was approximately US$5,932, compared with US$2,435 in 2000.

General life expectancy at birth in 2009 was 89 years. In 2010 the infant mortality rate was 3 per 1,000 live births and the under-fives-child mortality rate was 4 per 1,000 live births. The main causes of childhood mortality are prematurity (25 per cent), pneumonia (4 per cent), congenital anomalies (22 per cent), birth asphyxia (7 per cent) and injuries (7 per cent). (Source: http://www.who, World Health Statistics 2012)

EDUCATION

Monaco's compulsory education system lasts for 10 years, of which five are primary education. Secondary education lasts for seven years (four for the lower school and three for the upper school). The education system conforms to the standards of the French national system. In addition the following are studied: religious instruction, Monegasque language, and the history of Monaco. In 2004 the pupil/teacher ratio in primary schools was 14 to 1. Enrolment in primary school is estimated at 95 per cent and secondary enrolment is estimated at 90.5 per cent.

In 2006, 5.1 per cent of total government expenditure went towards education. This expenditure breaks down thus: 5 per cent tertiary, 46 per cent secondary, 17 per cent primary, 4 per cent pre-primary and 28 per cent other.

Literacy is estimated at 99.5 per cent. (Source: UNESCO)

RELIGION

Religious freedom is guaranteed by the Constitution. The State religion is Catholicism, practised by about 87 per cent of the population. An estimated 1.7 per cent of the population is Jewish and 0.46 per cent Muslim. Monaco has a religious tolerance rating of 7 on a scale of 1 to 10 (10 is most freedom). (Source: World Religion Database)

COMMUNICATIONS AND MEDIA

Newspapers
No daily newspapers are published in Monaco; however, French newspapers cover events in the principality.
Journal de Monaco, http://www.gouv.mc/Dataweb/jourmon.nsf (government weekly)
Monaco Hebdo, URL: http://monacohebdo.free.fr/ (weekly)

Broadcasting
The Principality is cabled for the reception of many international TV stations by satellite. Local radio stations exist which relay such programmes as the BBC World Service from London. A service for the Arab World, Monte-Carlo Doualiya is now operated by Radio France Internationale.
Radio Monte-Carlo, URL: http://www.rmc.fr/
Télé Monte-Carlo, URL: http://www.tmc.tv/
Monte-Carlo Doualiya, URL: http://www.rmc-mo.com/
Radio Monaco was set up in 2007. URL: http://www.radio-monaco.com/

Telecommunications
There are about 35,000 telephone main lines in use in Monaco, with approximately 22,000 mobile phones. Monaco is connected to the French communications systems. There are an estimated 22,000 internet users.

ENVIRONMENT

Monaco is a party to the following international environmental agreements: Air Pollution, Air Pollution-Sulfur 94, Air Pollution-Volatile Organic Compounds, Biodiversity, Climate Change, Climate Change-Kyoto Protocol, Desertification, Endangered Species, Hazardous Wastes, Law of the Sea, Marine Dumping, Ozone Layer Protection, Ship Pollution, Wetlands, Whaling.

Monaco is almost totally urban.

MONGOLIA
Mongol Uls

Capital: Ulaanbaatar (Ulaan Bataar) (Population estimate, 2010: 1.3 million)

Head of State: Tsakhiagiin Elbegdor (page 1420)

National Flag: A tricolour pale-wise, red, blue, red, with the red nearest the hoist charged with a mystical symbol (*soyombo*) all gold

CONSTITUTION AND GOVERNMENT

Constitution
In October 1949 the People's Republic of China recognised Mongolia's independence and agreed to set up diplomatic relations. Mongolia was admitted to the United Nations in October 1961.

According to the 1960 Constitution, the supreme organ of state power was the People's Great Hural (*Ardyn Ih Hural*) or National Assembly, elected by universal direct suffrage. The number of deputies gradually increased until 1981, when it was fixed at 370, whose term was five years. Between sessions, the functions of the People's Great Hural passed to its Presidium. From 1974 the MPRP's General Secretary was concurrently the Chairman of the Presidium (head of state). The supreme executive authority was the Council of Ministers, the Chairman (premier) and Deputy Chairmen being MPRP Politburo members.

In 1990, the new-born democratic movement forced the resignation of the MPRP Politburo, and subsequently the Presidium and Council of Ministers as well, and the Constitution was amended to remove the reference to the MPRP's 'leading role' in Mongolian society. In the same year, new political parties were legalised and the Constitution was amended in preparation for multiparty elections. Any party which has 800 members or the same number of the name list registered in the Supreme Court can be considered as a legitimate party in Mongolia.

The number of deputies in the People's Great Hural was increased to 420, while an indirectly-elected Little Hural (*Baga Hural*) of 50 members formed the country's standing legislature. The offices of Prime Minister and President were inaugurated. The Chairman of the Little Hural became *ex officio* the country's Vice President.

Current Constitution
Mongolia's current (fourth) Constitution was adopted in January 1992, following debate in the Little Hural. The words 'People's Republic' were dropped from the country's official name; a new national emblem was adopted comprising the traditional *soyombo*, a flying horse and Buddhist symbols; and the five-pointed star was removed from the national flag.

The President is the Head of State and the embodiment of the unity of the people, and has the right to veto the laws and resolutions of the Parliament and render support to various organisations exercising legislative, executive and judicial powers in co-operation with each other. Any indigenous citizen of at least 45 years of age who has permanently resided in Mongolia for the last five years is eligible for election to the post of President for a term of four years. Political parties that have obtained seats in the State Great Hural nominate Presidential candidates individually or collectively, one candidate per party or coalition of parties. The elected President appoints a Chairman and advisers, and is head of the National Security Council and Commander-in-Chief of the Armed Forces.

To consult the full constitution, please visit: http://www.mfat.gov.mn/index.php?option=com_content&view=category&id=34&Itemid=53&lang=en.

International Relations
Mongolia was closely allied to the Soviet Union over the 20th century, and remains closely linked; Mongolia receives oil and energy from Russia. Over the last ten years, relations with China have improved, with regular high-level visits and growing trade links; Mongolia imports food from China, and exports copper and cashmere to the Chinese. Ties with Japan and South Korea are particularly strong. Japan is the largest bilateral aid donor to Mongolia, and South Korea has a Mongolian population of around 20,000-30,000 people. Mongolia also has diplomatic relations with North Korea.

Mongolia is an active participant in UN sponsored peacekeeping activities; as at June 2008, there were 250 Mongolian soldiers in Sierra Leone, and small contingents in Kosovo and Afghanistan. Mongolia also contributes troops to operations in Iraq. Mongolia became a full participant in the ASEAN Regional Forum (ARF) in July 1998 and a full member of the Pacific Economic Cooperation Council in April 2000. Mongolia is currently seeking to join the Asia-Pacific Economic Cooperation forum (APEC).

Recent Events
In January 2006, the coalition government collapsed after the MPRP pulled out of it in protest over slow economic growth. Miyeegombo Ehkhbold became the new Prime Minister. On November 5 2007 Prime Minister Enkhbold resigned from his post after he was ousted as leader of the MPRP; Sanj Bayer became party leader and was elected to the post of prime minister later that month.

The governing Mongolian People's Revolutionary Party (MPRP) won a clear victory in parliamentary elections at the end of June 2008, but the opposition Democrats alleged fraud, and there was rioting in Ulan Bator, which left five dead and hundreds injured. Rioters set fire to the headquarters of the MPRP and the Cultural Palace, home to a theatre, museum

MONGOLIA

and national art gallery. The president declared a four-day state of emergency. On 14 July the General Election Committee (GEC) formally announced that the MPRP had won 39 seats and the DP 25. The Foreign Minister's Civil Will Party and the Civil Coalition won one each.

In February 2010, Mongolia was hit by such cold temperatures that it lost much of its livestock; the UN had to launch a programme to pay animal herders to clean and collect the carcuses. It has been estimated that between 2.7 and 3.0 million animals died.

Parliamentary elections took place in June 2012. The Democratic Party won most votes but failed to win an overall majority.

The former president Nambaryn Enkhbayar was sentenced to four years in jail for corruption in August 2012.

Legislature

In June 1992 the People's Great Hural and Little Hural were replaced by a new directly-elected unicameral parliament, the Mongolian Great Hural (*Mongol Ulsyn Ih Hural*), which approves the Prime Minister and Cabinet members. Its 76 members are elected for a four-year term in single-seat constituencies by a simple majority amounting to at least 25 per cent of the votes cast. The Great Hural is currently composed of a coalition government of the Democratic Union of the Mongolian National Democratic Party and the Mongolian Social Democratic Party.

Ulsyn Ih Hural, Government House, Ulaanbaatar 12, Mongolia. Tel: +976 11 322150, fax: +976 11 322866, e-mail: egi@mail.parl.gov.mn, URL: http://www.parl.gov.mn/

Cabinet (as at June 2013)
Prime Minister: Norov Altankhuyag (DP) (page 1377)
Deputy Prime Minister: Dendev Terbishdagva (MPRP)
Minister of Economic Development: Nyamjav Batbayar
Minister of Finance: Chultem Ulaan (page 1405)
Minister of Foreign Affairs: Luvsanvandan Bold (page 1391)
Minister of Justice and Home Affairs: Khishsigdemberel Temuujin
Minister of Construction and Urban Development: Tsevelmaa Bayarsaikhan
Minister of Education and Science: Luvsannyam Gantumur
Minister of Energy: Mishig Sonompil
Minister of Roads and Transport: Amarjargal Gansukh
Minister of Culture, Sport and Tourism: Tsedevdamba Oyungerel
Minister of Mining: Davaajav Gankhuyag
Minister of Labour: Yadamsuren Sanjmyatav
Minister of Defence: Dashdemberel Bat-Erdene
Minister of Population Development and Welfare: Sodnomzundui Erdene
Minister of Industry and Agriculture: Khaltmaa Battulga
Minister of Health: Natsag Udval
Minister of Nature and Environment: Sambuu Oyun
Head of Government Office: Chimed Saikhanbileg

Ministries

Office of the President, State Palace, Sukhbaatar Square 1, Ulaan Baatar 12, Mongolia. Tel: +976 11 323 240, fax: +976 11 329 281, e-mail: webmaster@presi.pmis.gov.mn, URL: http://gate1.pmis.gov.mn/president

Office of the Prime Minister, Government of Mongolia, Government House, Ulaanbaatar-12, Mongolia. Tel: +976 1 323673, fax: +976 1 328329, e-mail: erdenebaatar@pmis.gov.mn, URL: http://pmis.gov.mn/primeminister/

Ministry of Foreign Affairs, Peace Avenue 7A, Ulaanbaatar 210648, Mongolia. Tel: +976 1 311311, fax: +976 1 322127, e-mail: merinfo@magicnet.mn, mongmer@magicnet.mn, URL: http://www.extmin.mn

Ministry of Health, Government Building no 8, Olympic Street 2, Sukhbaatar District, Ulaan Baatar, Mongolia. Tel: +976 11 323381, fax: +976 11 320916, e-mail: moh@moh.mng.net, URL: http://www.pmis.gov.mn/health

Ministry of Finance, Government Building no 2, United Nations Street 5/1, Chingeltei District, Ulaan Baatar 210646, Mongolia. Tel: +976 11 322712, fax: +976 11 320247, URL: http://www.mof.pmis.gov.mn

Ministry of Justice and Home Affairs, Government Building no 5, Commercial Street 6/1, Chingeltei District, Ulaan Baatar 210646, Mongolia. Tel: +976 11 322383, fax: +976 11 325225, e-mail: moj@moj.pmis.gov.mn , URL: http://www.monjus.url.mn

Ministry of Food and Agriculture and Light Industry, Government Building no 9, Peace Avenue 16a, Bayanzurkh District, Ulaan Baatar 210349, Mongolia. Tel: +976 11 450258, fax: +976 11 452554, e-mail: mofa@mofa.pmis.gov.mn, URL: http://www.gate1.pmis.gov.mn/mofa

Ministry of Environment and Tourism, Government Building no 5, Baga Toiruu 44, Sukhbaatar District, Ulaan Baatar 210620a, Mongolia. Tel: +976 11 320943, fax: +976 11 321401, e-mail: mtt@magicnet.mn, URL: http://www.pmis.gov.mn/men

Ministry of Infrastructure, Fax: +976 11 310612, URL: http://www.mid.pmis.gov.mn

Ministry of Labour and Social Welfare, Government Building no 2, United Nations Street 5/1, Chingeltei District, Ulaan Baatar 210646, Mongolia. Tel: +976 11 328559, fax: +976 11 328634, e-mail: mswl@mongolnet.mn, URL: http://mswl.gov.mn

Ministry of Defence, Dandar Street, Bayanzurkh District, Ulaan Baatar 61, Mongolia. Tel: +976 11 458495, fax: +976 11 451727, e-mail: mdef@mongonet.mn, URL: http://www.pmis.gov.mn/mdef/mongolian

Ministry of Education, Culture and Science, Government Building no 5, Baga Toiruu 44, Sukhbaatar District, Ulaan Baatar 210620a, Mongolia. Tel: +976 11 321401, e-mail: mtt@magicnet.mn, URL: http://www.pmis.gov.mn/men

Ministry of City Planning and Transport, Government Building no 2, United Nations Street 5/1, Chingeltei District, Ulaan Baatar 210646, Mongolia. URL: http://www.pmis.gov.mn/men

Ministry of Foreign Affairs, Peace Avenue 7a, Sukhbaatar District, Ulaan Baatar 210648, Mongolia. Tel: +976 11 311311, fax: +976 11 322127, e-mail: mongmer@magicnet.mn, URL: http://www.mongolia-foreign-policy.mn

Ministry of Minerals and Energy, Government Building no 2, United Nations Street 5/1, Chingeltei District. Ulaan Baatar 210646, Mongolia. Tel: +976 11 326222, fax: +976 11 310612, e-mail: webmaster@mfe.pmis.gov.mn, URL: http://www.mfe.pmis.gov.mn

Political Parties

Thirteen political parties took part in the 2008 elections, three of which formed a coalition. However, political power is concentrated in only the Mongolian People's Party (formerly the Mongolian People's Revolutionary Party (MPP) and the Democratic Party (DP). A new breakaway Mongolian People's Revolutionary Party (MPRP) has recently formed.

Mongol Ardiin Nam, (Mongolian People's Party), URL: http://www.mpp.mn
Leader: Sükhbaataryn Batbold
Ardchilsan Nam, (Democratic Party), URL: http://www.demparty.mn
Leader: Norovyn Altankhuyag
Irgeni Zorig Nam (CWP, Civil Will Party), URL: http://www.izn.mn
Leader: Oyun Sanjaasuren

Elections

The most recent presidential election took place on 26 June 2013. Tsakhiagiin Elbegdorj (DP) was re-elected for a second term with 50 per cent of the vote, defeating Badmaanyambuugiin Bat-Erdene (MPP)took 42 per cent.

A parliamentary election was held on 29 June 2008. Around 74 per cent of registered voters voted. The Mongolian People's Revolutionary Party MPRP won 43 of the State Great Assembly's 76 seats. The opposition Democrats alleged fraud, and rioting ensued. The most recent parliamentary election was held on 28 June 2012. Recounts had to be ordered after discrepancies were found in the electronic and manual votes. The DP won most seats but was short of an overall majority. It agreed to form a coalition with the MPRP.

Diplomatic Representation

American Embassy, Micro Region 11, Big Ring Road, CPO1021, Ulaanbaatar 13, Mongolia, Tel: +976 11 329095, fax: +976 11 320776, URL: http://mongolia.usembassy.gov/
Ambassador: Jonathan Addleton
British Embassy, 30 Enkh Taivny Gudamzh (PO Box 703), Ulaanbaatar 13, Mongolia. Tel: +976 11 458133, fax: +976 11 458036, email: britemb@magicnet.mn, URL: http://ukinmongolia.fco.gov.uk/en/
Ambassador: Christopher Stuart
Embassy of Mongolia, 2833 M Street NW, Suite 570, Washington, DC 20007, USA. Tel: +1 202 333 7117, fax: +1 202 298 9227, e-mail: esyam@mongolianembassy.us, URL: http://www.mongolianembassy.us/
Ambasador: Khasbazar Bekhbat
Embassy of Mongolia, 7 Kensington Court, London, W8 5DL. Tel: +44 (0)20 7937 0150, fax: +44 (0)20 7937 1117, e-mail: office@embassyofmongolia.co.uk, URL: http://www.embassyofmongolia.co.uk/index.php?lang=en
Ambassador: H.E. Bulgaa Altangerel
Permanent Representative of Mongolia to the United Nations, 6 East 77th Street, New York, NY 10021, USA. Tel: +1 212 861 9460 / 472 6517, fax: +1 212 861 9464, e-mail: mongolia@un.int, URL: http://www.un.int/mongolia/
Representative: Od Och

LEGAL SYSTEM

Civil, criminal and administrative cases are handled by Ulan Bator City and urban district courts, the 18 *aymag* (provincial) courts and *sum* (rural district) courts.

The Supreme Court is the court of highest instance; it can review all lower court decisions upon appeal and provide official interpretations on all laws except the constitution. Justices are nominated by the General Council of Courts (GCC) and confirmed by the SGH and president. The independence of the judiciary is protected by the GCC, of which the Chief Justice (Chairman of the Supreme Court), the Chairman of the Constitutional Court, Procurator General and Minister of Law are members. The Administrative Cases Court was established in 2004.

The Constitutional Court consists of nine members, whose jurisdiction extends solely over the interpretation of the constitution.

The government respects the human rights of its citizens. However, there have been instances of alleged police involvement in the deaths and injuries of citizens during the 2008 post-election protests. There have been cases of arbitrary arrest, and corruption and official impunity within the judiciary. Conditions in detention centres are poor. Mongolia retains the death penalty but in January 2010 Mongolia announced a moratorium on capital punishment.

Supreme Court of Mongolia, URL: http://www.supremecourt.mn/english/index.php
Chief Justice: Tsevegmid Zorig

National Human Rights Commission of Mongolia, URL: http://www.mn-nhrc.org/

LOCAL GOVERNMENT

For administrative purposes Mongolia is divided into one municipality, Ulaan Baatar, and 21 provinces: (*aymag*) Arhangay, Bayanhongor, Bayan-Olgiy, Bulgan, Darhan Uul, Dornod, Dornogovi, Dundgovi, Dzavhan, Govi-Altay, Govi-Sumber, Hentiy, Hovd, Hovsgol, Omnogovi, Orhon, Ovorhangay, Selenge, Suhbaatar, Tov, and Uvs. Governors for each province are assisted by elected local assemblies or *hurals*.

AREA AND POPULATION

Area

Mongolia is a landlocked country in central Asia with an area of 1,564,660 sq. km. The Russian Federation is located to the north of Mongolia, and the People's Republic of China to the south, east and west. It is one of the highest countries in the world, with an average elevation of 1580m. It has six differing geographical zones: high mountains, steppe, forest steppe, dessert steppe, taiga and desert. The southern third of Mongolia is dominated by the seven Gobi Deserts, where temperatures range from -40°C in winter to +40°C in summer.

To view a map of Mongolia, please visit http://www.un.org/Depts/Cartographic/map/profile/mongolia.pdf

Population

2009 estimates put the population at about 2.756 million, with an annual growth rate of 1.3 per cent for the period 2000-10 and a population density of two people per sq. km. Projections of population trends show a steady rise to a figure of between 4 million and 4.8 million in 2025. The majority of the population (68 per cent) are aged between 15 and 64 years, with 28 per cent aged under 14 years, and 6 per cent aged 60 years and over. About two-thirds of the total population is under age 30. The median age is 25 years.

Approximately one million people live in Ulaan Baatar. Mongolia's towns now contain over 57 per cent of the total population, with a further 22 per cent in rural areas, and the remainder living a nomadic lifestyle. Semi-nomadic life still predominates in the countryside, but settled agricultural communities are becoming more common. Ethnically, Mongolia is divided in the following way: Mongol (mainly Khalkha) 86 per cent, Turkic (largely Kazakh) 6 per cent, Tungusic 4.6 per cent, Chinese and Russian 3.4 per cent.

Khalkha Mongol is the official language, spoken by about 90 per cent of the population. Kasak is spoken in the province of Bayan-Ölgiy. Turkic (7 per cent of the people) and Russian are also spoken. About four million Mongols live outside Mongolia; about 3.4 million live in China, mainly in the Inner Mongolia Autonomous Region, and some 500,000 live in Russia, primarily in Buryatia and Kalmykia.

Births, Marriages, Deaths

According to 2010 estimates, the birth rate is 23.5 births per 1,000 inhabitants, whilst the death rate is 5.9 deaths per 1,000 population. Average life expectancy at birth is 69 years (65 years for men and 74 years for women). The infant mortality rate is 26 deaths per 1,000 live births, whilst the total fertility rate is 2.5 children per woman. (Source: http://www.who.int, World Health Statistics 2012)

Public Holidays 2014

1 January: New Year
2 March: Tsgaaan Sar - 3 days (Lunar New Year)*
1 June: Mother and Child Day
11-13 July: National Days
26 November: Independence Day
*Precise date depends on sighting of the moon.

EMPLOYMENT

In 2008, of an estimated population of 2.6 million, some 1, 071,600 million were economically active. Figures for 2009 put the unemployment rate at 11.3 per cent.

Total Employment by Economic Activity

Occupation	2008
Agriculture, hunting, forestry & fishing	377,600
Mining & quarrying	46,500
Manufacturing	47,500
Electricity, gas & water supply	30,100
Construction	66,800
Wholesale & retail trade, repairs	169,700
Hotels & restaurants	34,500
Transport, storage & communications	46,300
Financial intermediation	19,800
Real estate, renting & business activities	12,000
Public admin. & defence; compulsory social security	50,900
Education	66,200
Health & social work	42,300
Other community, social & personal service activities	19,700
Households with employed persons	11,800

Source: Copyright © International Labour Organization (ILO Dept. of Statistics, http://llaborsta.ilo.org)

BANKING AND FINANCE

Currency

The national unit of currency is the Tugrik (MNT) which is divided into 100 möngö.

Mongolia's financial centre is Ulaan Baatar.

GDP/GNP, Inflation, National Debt

With the dismantling of the USSR, which contributed up to one third of GDP and 80 per cent of its trade, Mongolia's economy suffered a decade of deep recession in the 1990s. Following the election of the Democratic Coalition government, Mongolia began the development of a free-market economy through privatisation, the relaxation of price controls, the restructure of the banking system, and the liberalisation of trade. However, the liberalisation process was initially opposed by the Mongolian People's Revolutionary Party (MPRP), thereby prolonging the recession. However, the MPRP, when returned to government, continued with economic reform.

After slowing in 1996, as a result of a number of natural disasters and a decline in world copper and cashmere prices, Mongolia's economy began to grow in 1997-99. However, following bad weather and natural disasters in 2000 resulting in the loss of 2.4 million livestock, Mongolia's GDP fell from 3.2 per cent in 1999 to 1.1 per cent in 2000 to 1.0 per cent in 2001. In 2002, the economy began to grow, influenced by high copper prices and gold production; growth in 2003 was 5 per cent and in 2004 it was 10.6 per cent. In 2005, GDP grew by an estimated 7.3 per cent, to 2,779.6 billion tugriks, in 2006 it grew by 8.6 per cent to reach 3,715 billion tugriks, and in 2007 it grew by 9.9 per cent to 4,557 billion tugriks. In response to the global economic downturn GDP growth in 2009 was put at -1.5 per cent. GDP grew by 6.1 per cent in 2010. The economy is expected to grow significantly in 2013 based on development of the Oyu Tolgoi copper and gold mine.

In the past, Mongolia's economy was largely based on the agriculture and livestock industry, and the sector continues to contribute significantly to the economy; 16 per cent of GDP, and employing some 40 per cent of the Mongolian workforce. The livestock herd - predominantly sheep, cattle and goats - grew to 40 million in response to higher cashmere prices, increased demand for meat and other animal products. Industry contributed 32.4 per cent of GDP in 2010, agriculture 15.9 per cent and the services industry for around 51 per cent of GDP. (Source: Asian Development Bank)

GDP by industrial origin, current market prices, billion Tuhtiks

	2008	2009	2010
GDP	6,555.6	6,590.6	8,255.1
Agriculture	1,259.7	1,177.4	1,312.4
Mining	1,324.2	1,285.9	1,800.8
Manufacturing	430.2	425.0	532.9
Electricity, gas and water	146.0	183.8	231.3
Construction	122.1	86.2	107.0
Trade	472.2	432.6	595.3
Transport and communications	640.7	762.2	933.7
Finance	236.3	212.7	158.1
Public Administration	247.7	267.2	301.2
Others	1,676.5	1,757.5	2,282.3

Source: Asian Development Bank, 2011

Inflation peaked in 1992 at 325 per cent, but had fallen to 7.5 per cent by 1999. Inflation grew in 2007, to 15.1 per cent, driven by increases in the world price of oil and wheat, and by wage inflation and an increase in the minimum wage. It was estimated to be 10 per cent in 2010 and 9.5 per cent in 2011. External debt at the end of 2011 was an estimated US$1.8 million.

Foreign Investment

In October 2001 the IMF approved a total of US$40 million in low-interest loans to be paid over the following three years to assist economic growth and help tackle poverty. Over 2,399 foreign businesses from over 70 countries invested a total of US$660.5 million in Mongolia over the period 1990 to 2002.

Between 1990-2008, Mongolia received US$3.6 billion in official development assistance from donors.

Balance of Payments / Imports and Exports

Main export trading partners in 2010 were China (US$2,288.3 million), Canada (US$225.4 million) and Russia (US$70 million). Export commodities include copper, livestock, cashmere, wool, and fluorspar. Import commodities include equipment and machinery, fuel, food, chemicals, and industrial goods. Main import trading partners in 2010 were China (US$1,594.2 million), Russia (US$794.1 million) and Japan (US$177.1 million).

External Trade, US$ million

	2008	2009	2010
Exports	2,534.5	1,885.4	2,908.5
Imports	3,244.5	2,137.7	3,200.1
Trade balance	-710.0	-252.3	-291.6

Source: Asian Development Bank

China is a main source of the 'grey' economy, which could be about half the size of the official economy (US$1.4 billion in 2005), though it is impossible to calculate as the money does not pass through official sources. Remittances from Mongolians working abroad contribute to the 'grey' economy, and money laundering is of growing concern.

Mongolia joined the World Trade Organization (WTO) in 1997.

Central Bank

Bank of Mongolia, Baga Toiruu 3, 15160, Ulaanbaatar 46, Töv, Mongolia. Tel: +976 11 322166, fax: +976 11 311471, URL: http://www.mongolbank.mn
Governor: N. Zoljargal

Chambers of Commerce and Business Addresses

Mongolian Chamber of Commerce and Industry, URL: http://www.mongolchamber.mn/
Foreign Investment and Foreign Trade Agency, URL: http://www.mol.mn

MONGOLIA

MANUFACTURING, MINING AND SERVICES

Primary and Extractive Industries

Mongolia is rich in natural resources, principally gold, copper (the country's gold and copper reserves are amongst the highest in the world), coal, molybdenum, iron, phosphates, tin, nickel, zinc, wolfram, flourspar, uranium, and petroleum. However, the country relies entirely on imports to satisfy its oil requirements. The mining sector accounts for about 20 per cent of Mongolian GDP and half the country's exports, and attracts most foreign investment.

However, growth in the mining sector has slowed recently due to government interventions; in 2006, extensive legislative changes were made, including a new Minerals Law, a 68 per cent windfall tax on gold and copper and a requirement for State equity participation in mineral deposits of strategic importance to Mongolia. The future of Mongolia's mineral reserves has become an increasingly sensitive issue, with concern that foreign investors are making huge profits with little benefit to the people of Mongolia.

Coal production in 2010 was 27.831 million short tons up from 15.921 million short tons in 2009. In 2010 Mongolia consumed 9.495 million short tons.

According to 2011 EIA figures, Mongolia produced nearly 7,000 barrels per day all of which was crude and consumed 19,000 barrels per day and so imported around 12,000 barrels per day, (up from 9.86 thousand barrels per day in 2001), most of which was gasoline and distillate.

Energy

Coal-fuelled thermal power stations provide the principal source of energy.

Mongolia had a 2010 installed capacity of 0.83 GWe, with generation at 4.21 billion kilowatthours (kWh) (up from 2.6 billion kWh in 1999). Consumption was 3.95 billion kWh in the same year.

Manufacturing

In 1991 the new multiparty administration adopted a policy of privatisation of state-owned enterprises and developed a market economy. This brought about the abandonment of the traditional pattern of five-year plans which had dominated the country's political and economic life since the 1960s. Vouchers were issued to give the population a stake in both 'little' privatisation - small shops and service enterprises - and 'big' privatisation - large state-owned industries, excluding gold mines, oil and the vodka distillery in which the government decided to retain a monopoly holding. A stock exchange was opened in Ulaanbatar, although its transactions were mostly on paper and in the country's own currency.

In 2007, industry (comprising mining, manufacturing, utilities and construction) accounted for 38.4 per cent of GDP. Main industrial areas were minerals (mainly copper and gold), animal-derived products, building materials and foods and drink.

Agriculture

Agriculture accounted for an estimated 16 per cent of GDP and 34 per cent of employment in 2011. Principal agricultural products are livestock (sheep, goats, cattle, camels, and horses) and byproducts, hay fodder and vegetables (especially potatoes). The agricultural industry can be severely affected by bad weather and natural disasters.

Agricultural Production in 2010

Produce	Int. $'000*	Tonnes
Indigenous sheep meat	210,856	77,441
Indigenous cattle meat	128,430	47,542
Indigenous goat meat	117,592	49,077
Cow milk, whole, fresh	70,155	242,812
Wheat	44,662	345,458
Wool, greasy	42,663	22,300
Indigenous horse meat	37,905	24,335
Potatoes	19,599	167,956
Nuts, nes	12,283	6,700
Indigenous camel meat	12,062	5,756
Goat milk, whole, fresh	10,608	37,188
Sheep milk, whole, fresh	7,410	22,385

* unofficial figures

Source: http://faostat.fao.org/site/339/default.aspx Food and Agriculture Organization of the United Nations, Food and Agricultural commodities production

COMMUNICATIONS AND TRANSPORT

Travel Requirements

Citizens of the USA, Canada, Australia and the EU require a passport valid for six months, and a visa, apart from US tourists staying up to 90 days. Visitors intending to stay for longer than 30 days should register with the police within ten days of arrival. All travellers to Mongolia should contact the embassy to check visa requirements.

National Airlines

External air services operate to Moscow, Irkoutsk, Ulaan-Ude and Beijing, Huhehoto. Internal services link Ulaan Baatar with all *aimag* (province) centres and there are also internal *aimag* services.

Mongolian International Air Transport: URL: http//:www.miat.com

Railways

Mongolia has 1,815 km of railway lines. Ulaan Baatar is connected by rail with the TransSiberian system via Sukhebaatar, Naushki and Ulaan-Ude and with the Chinese railways via Zamyn-Uud and Erlian. Chiobalsan is connected by a branch line to the main railway system and branches have been built to Erdenet, Baganuur and Bor Undor.

Roads

Mongolia has a total of 3,387 km of roads, of which 1,563 km are paved and 1,824 km are unpaved. Almost all passenger transport is by motor vehicle, bus routes connect Erlian with Beijing. Vehicles are driven on the right.

Waterways

There are 400 km of waterways in Mongolia.

HEALTH

In 2009, the Mongolian government spent approximately 8.8 per cent of its total budget on healthcare (down from 10.7 per cent in 2000), accounting for 54.8 per cent of all healthcare spending. Private expenditure accounted for 45.2 per cent of total expenditure and external resources 4 per cent. Total expenditure on healthcare equated to 5.7 per cent of the country's GDP. Per capita expenditure on health was approximately US$97, compared with US$22 in 2000. Figures for 2005-10 show that there are 7,584 physicians (27.6 per 10,000 population), 9,605 nurses and midwives (35 per 10,000 population), 1,088 pharmaceutical personnel, 85 environment and public health workers, and 513 dentistry personnel. There are 59 hospital beds per 10,000 population.

According to the latest WHO figures, in 2008 approximately 97 per cent of the urban population and 49 per cent of the rural population had access to improved drinking water. In the same year, 64 per cent of the urban population and 32 per cent of the rural population had access to improved sanitation. Diarrhoea accounts for 7 per cent of childhood deaths.

The infant mortality rate (probability of dying before first birthday) in 2009 was 24 per 1,000 live births. The child mortality rate (under 5 years) was 29 per 1,000 live births. The most common causes of death in children aged under five are: pneumonia 15 per cent, prematurity 16 per cent, congenital anomalies 13 per cent, birth asphyxia 8 per cent, injuries 9 per cent and diarrhoea 7 per cent. In the period 2000-09 an estimated 27.5 children aged under 5 were classified as stunted and 5.3 per cent as underweight. (Source: http://www.who.int, World Health Statistics 2012)

EDUCATION

Education is compulsory from six to 16 years. Higher education encompasses vocational, technical schools which are attended from 16-18 years. There are nine universities in Mongolia and it is not uncommon for Mongolian students to attend technical schools and universities in the Russian Federation or Germany.

Figures for 2007 show that 54 per cent of young children were enrolled in pre-school, 89 per cent were enrolled in primary education and 81 per cent were enrolled in secondary education. In 2007, Mongolia had a 97.3 per cent adult literacy rate. Tertiary level enrolment was estimated at 48 per cent. (Source: UNESCO Institute of Statistics)

RELIGION

Freedom of religion is guaranteed by the constitution, and the traditional Lamaism (Mahayana Buddhism) is gaining new strength, following suppression under the communist regime. Lamas trained at the Mongolian Buddhist Centre, Gandantegchinlen monastery in Ulan Bator (*hamba lama* or abbots, Dembereliyn Choyjamts) are moving out into the countryside to establish new communities and restore old monasteries damaged or destroyed in the years of religious oppression.

Recent figures show there are more than 140 working monasteries and 2,700 people working in them, of which 2,000 are monks. The Sunni Muslim Kazakhs of western Mongolia have also begun the renewal of their religious life, and Christian missionary activity has also increased. The Presidential Council for Religious Affairs was established in 1991. Under the new freedom of belief, many other religions are practised, including more than 40 mostly Christian churches and cults. Another popular religion is Islam, practised by a 60,000 strong Kazakh minority in the Bayan Ulgii province.

Mongolia has a religious liberty rating of 7 on a scale of 1 to 10 (10 is most freedom). (Source: World Religion Database)

COMMUNICATIONS AND MEDIA

The media is generally free and criticism of the government does appear.

Newspapers

Since the adoption of democracy, many new newspapers and magazines have been published, some of them independent and others affiliated to new political parties, although not all have survived. The cost of newsprint has curtailed circulations and reduced many otherwise daily papers to thrice-weekly or even less regular appearance.

Daily newspapers include: *Odriyn Sonin* (Daily News) (URL: http://www.dailynews.mn); the government (MPRP) *Unen* (Truth) (URL: http://www.unen.mn/), founded in 1920 and Mongolia's oldest newspaper; and the independent *Onoodor*. (URL: http://www.mongolnews.mn) The Mongol Messenger is an English language weekly.

Broadcasting

The state-run radio and TV provider became a public service provider in 2005 (Mongolian National Broadcaster, MNV). Private radio and TV broadcasters also operate. Statellite and cable TV is also available. More than 100 radio stations are in operation.

Telecommunications
The network has improved in recent years and in ternational direct dialling is avlalble. A fiber optic network has been installed in many major urban centres. Telephone lines numbered 165,000 in 2008, with mobile phones numbering 1.7 million. Nearly 330,000 of Mongolians were regular internet users in 2008.

ENVIRONMENT

Mongolia's current environmental problems include the effects of rapid industrial and urban growth, air pollution from coal-fired power plants (Mongolia's entire power industry is reliant on fossil fuels), deforestation, over-grazing of land, soil erosion, desertification, and mining. Over the last few years, there has been an increase in the number of gold miners, who use mercury illegally; it is feared that this may lead to an epidemic of mercury poisoning.

Mongolia is a party to the following environmental agreements: Biodiversity, Climate Change (Kyoto Protocol), Desertification, Endangered Species, Environmental Modification, Hazardous Wastes, Nuclear Test Ban, and Ozone Layer Protection.

In 2010, Mongolia's emissions from the consumption of fossil fuels totalled 9.44 million metric tons of carbon dioxide. (Source: EIA)

SPACE PROGRAMME

Mongolia hopes to launch its first space satellite with help from Japan in 2015.

MONTENEGRO
Crna Gora

Capital: Podgorica (Population estimate, 2011: 151,000)

Head of State: Filip Vujanovic (President) (page 1532)

Flag: Red with a golden coat of arms depicting a two-headed eagle below a royal crown and carrying a shield on which a lion is engraved

CONSTITUTION AND GOVERNMENT

Constitution
The breakup of the Yugoslav federation after 1989 left Montenegro in a precarious position. The first multi-party elections in 1990 showed much public support for the League of Communists, confirming Montenegrin support for the federation. Montenegro joined Serbian efforts to preserve the federation in the form of a 'Third Yugoslavia' in 1992. In January 1998, Milo Djukanovic became Montenegro's President following bitterly contested elections in November 1997.

On 31 May 2002 the Yugoslav parliament voted to end the Yugoslav Federation and replace it with a more flexible union between its remaining members Serbia and Montenegro. The new state, known as Serbia and Montenegro, was formed in March 2003, with a constitution based on that drawn up by the European Union in March 2002. In May 2002 the Yugoslav parliament's upper house approved the plan by 23 votes to six, whilst the lower house agreed it by 74 votes to 23. The Montenegrin and Serbian parliaments agreed the plan in March 2002. Under the terms of the agreement there is a joint parliamentary chamber in addition to Serb and Montenegrin parliaments. The new union has a single army and a rotating seat at the UN and other international organisations. However, after a three-year period, both Serbia and Montenegro would be allowed to secede from the union.

The President of Serbia and Montenegro was elected by the Serbia-Montenegro union parliament. The union government consisted of the Council of Ministers, comprising three Serb and two Montenegrin ministers, with the president the ex-officio chair. As individual republics Serbia and Montenegro still retained their own governments, each of which was headed by a prime minister.

In a referendum on independence for Montenegro held on 21 May 2006 a majority voted to split from Serbia. On 4th June, Montenegro formally declared its independence from Serbia in a special session of parliament.

In June 2011, the Montenegrin Government proposed a set of amendments to the Constitution aimed at limiting political influence over key judicial appointments, which is one of the EU's key recommendations for the national judicial reform.

To consult the constitution, please visit: http://www.wipo.int/wipolex/en/details.jsp?id=6920.

International Relations
Montenegro became a member of the UN on 29 June 2006. In December 2006 Montenegro joined the NATO Partnership for Peace programme, on its way to becoming a member and in January 2007, Montenegro joined the IMF and World Bank. In October 2007 the EU and Montenegro signed The Stabilisation and Association Agreement (SAA) which will open up trade between the EU and Montenegro, and brings Montenegro a step closer to becoming an official candidate for membership of the EU.

Recent Events
In April 2002 Prime Minister Filip Vujanovic resigned over the EU-brokered agreement with Serbia. In 2003 he was elected president.

In July 2004 Montenegro's parliament voted to adopt a new flag, a new national anthem and a new national day. This was part of a push for independence from Serbia. The new national day of 13 July marks the date in 1878 when the Berlin Congress recognised Montenegro as an independent state, and later, in 1948, it was the day Montenegrins staged an uprising against Nazi Occupiers. In February 2005 Serbia rejected a Montenegrin plan on independence, calling it a breach of the 2003 Belgrade agreement. However, in May 2006 a referendum was held, and the majority of Montenegrins voted in favour of independence. On 4th June, Montenegro formally declared its independence from Serbia in a special session of parliament.

In October 2006, Prime Minister Milo Djukanovic, having led Montenegro to independence, stepped down and was succeeded in November by Zeljko Sturanovic. In February 2008 Prime Minister Sturanovic resigned on the grounds of ill health, Milo Djukanovic became Montenegro's prime minister for a fifth time.

In December 2009, under the terms of the EU's Schengen zone agreement Montenegian citizens can now travel without the need for visas. In November 2010, the European Commission recommended that Montenegro be named as a candidate to join the EU/

In December 2010, the prime minister Milo Djukanovic resigned and was replaced by Igor Luksic. The government was automatically dissolved and a new coalition government was sworn in.

Montenegro agreed terms that should allow it to join the World Trade Organisation in 2012.

Elections took place in October 2012 and Milo Djukanovic was nominated as prime minister. A coalition was formed in December 2012.

Legislature
Montenegro has a unicameral legislature, the Assembly of the Republic of Montenegro (Skupstina Republike Crne Gore). It has 81 members who are elected to serve a four year term. Five of those elected must come from the ethnic Albanian community.
Assembly of the Republic of Montenegro (Skupstina Republike Crne Gore), Bulevar Svetog Petra Cetinjskog 10, 81000 Podgorica, Montenegro. Tel: +381 81 241083, fax: +381 81 242192, URL: http://www.skupstina.mn.yu

Cabinet (as at March 2013)
Prime Minister: Milo Djukanovic (DPS) (page 1416)
Deputy Prime Minister for European Integration and Foreign Affairs: Dr Igor Lukšić (page 1467)
Deputy Prime Minister, Minister for Political System, Minister of Justice: Dusko Markovic (page 1471)
Deputy Prime Minister and Minister for Economic Policy, Information Society and Telecommunications: Vujica Lazovic
Minister of the Interior: Rasko Husovic
Minister of Finance: Radoje Zugic
Minister of Education and Sport: Slavoljub Stijepovic (page 1520)
Minister of Culture: Branislav Micunovic
Minister of Economy: Vladimir Kavaric
Minister of Agriculture: Peter Ivanovic
Minister of Tourism and Sustainable Development: Branimir Gvozdenovic
Minister of Health: Miodrag Bobo Radunovic
Minister of Human and Minority Rights: Suad Numanovic (page 1488)
Minister of Maritime Affairs & Transport: Ivan Brajovic
Minister of Employment and Social Welfare: Predag Boskovic
Minister of Defence: Milica Pejanovic Djurisic
Minister for Science: Sanja Vlahovic
Minister without portfolio: Marija Vucinovic

Ministries
Office of the President, Bulevar Blaza Jovanovica 2, 81000 Podgorica, Montenegro. Tel: +382 20 242 382, URL: http://www. predsjednik.me
Office of the Prime Minister, Jovana Tomasevica bb, 81000 Podgorica, Montenegro. Tel: +382 20 242 530, fax: +382 20 242 329, e-mail: kabinet.premijera@gov.me, URL: http://www.vlada.me
Ministry of Finance, Stanka Dragojevića br. 2, 81000 Podgorica, Montenegro. Tel: +382 20 242 835, fax: +382 20 224 450, e-mail: mf@mif.gov.me, URL: http://www.mif.gov.me
Ministry of Foreign Affairs and European Integration, Stanka Dragojevica br.2, 81000 Podgorica, Montenegro. Tel: +382 20 246 357, fax: +382 20 224 670, e-mail: mip.ministar@gov.me, URL: http://www.mip.gov.me
Ministry of Interior, Bulevar Svetog Petra Cetinjskog 22, 81000 Podgorica, Montenegro. Tel: +382 20 241 252, fax: +382 20 246 779, e-mail: mup.kabinet@t-com.me, URL: http://www.mup.gov.me
Ministry of Economics, Rimski trg 46, 81000 Podgorica, Montenegro. Tel: +382 20 234 012, fax: +382 20 242 028, e-mail: kabinet@gov.me, URL: http://www.mek.gov.me

MONTENEGRO

Ministry of Labour and Social Welfare, Rimski trg 46, 81000 Podgorica, Montenegro. Tel: +382 20 242 276, fax: +382 20 242 762, e-mail: ministar.mrss@mrss.gov.me, URL: http://www.mrs.gov.me
Ministry of Agriculture, Forestry and Water Management, Poslovni centar "Vektra", Cetinjski put bb, 81000 Podgorica, Montenegro. Tel: +382 20 482 109, fax: +382 20 234 306, e-mail: kabinet.mpsv@gov.me, URL: http://www.mpr.gov.me
Ministry of Defence, Jovana Tomasevica br. 29, 81000 Podgorica, Montenegro. Tel: +382 20 224 042, fax: +382 20 224 702, e-mail: kabinet@mod.me, URL: http://www.mod.gov.me
Ministry of Justice, Vuka Karadzica 3, 81000 Podgorica, Montenegro. Tel: +382 20 231 552, fax: +382 20 407 515, e-mail: minpravde@gov.me, URL: http://www.pravda.gov.me
Ministry of Health, Rimski trg 46, 81000 Podgorica, Montenegro. Tel: +382 20 242 276, fax: +382 20 242 762, e-mail: mzdravlja@gov.me, URL: http://www.mzd.gov.me
Ministry of Education and Sports, Vaka Durovica bb, 81000 Podgorica, Montenegro. Tel: +382 20 410 100, fax: +382 20 410 101, e-mail: mps@mps.gov.me, URL: http://www.mps.gov.me
Ministry of Maritime Affairs and Transport, trg Vektre bb, 81000 Podgorica, Montenegro. Tel: +382 20 482 156, fax: +382 20 234 342, e-mail: jelena.raspopovic@msp.gov.me, URL: http://www.msp.gov.me/
Ministry for Human and Minority Protection, Cetinjski put bb, 81000 Podgorica, Montenegro. Tel: +382 20 482 126, fax: +382 20 234 198, e-mail: min.manj@t-com.me, URL: http://www.mmp.gov.me/
Ministry of Culture, Vuka Karadzica br.3, 81000 Podgorica, Montenegro. Tel: +382 20 248 273, fax: +382 20 224 164, e-mail: kabinet.kultura@gov.me, URL: http://www.mku.gov.me
Ministry of Information Society and Telecommunications, Karadordeva bb, 81000 Podgorica, Montenegro. Tel: +382 20 241 412, fax: +382 20 241 790, e-mail: mid@gov.me, URL: http://www.potpredsjednikekon.gov.me
Ministry of Science, Rimski trg 46, 81000 Podgorica, Montenegro. Tel: +382 20 482 145, fax: +382 20 234 168, e-mail: kabinet@mna.gov.me, URL: http://www.mna.gov.me
Ministry of Sustainable Development and Tourism, Kancelarija br. 8, Rimski trg 46, 81000 Podgorica, Montenegro. Tel: +382 20 482 329, fax: +382 20 234 168, e-mail: mt@gov.me, URL: http://www.mrt.gov.me

Political Parties

Democratic Party of Socialists (DPS), Social Democratic Party (SDP), Movement for Change (PZP), Socialist People's Party (SNP), People's Socialist Party (NSS), People's Party (NS), Democratic Serb Party (DSS), Serb Radical Party (SRS), Serb People's Party (SNS), Liberal Party (LP), Party of Democratic Prosperity (PDP), Croatian Civic Initiative (HGI), Bosniak Party (BS), Democratic Party of Unity (DSJ), Democratic Union of Albanians (DUA), Democratic Alliance of Albanians (DSA), Albanian Alternative; New Serb Democracy (NOVA).

Elections

Presidential elections took place in December 2002, February 2003 and May 2003 when Filip Vujanovic, the former prime minister of Montenegro, won over 63 per cent of the vote (unofficial results). However, because less than half the electorate voted, the results were cancelled. Following an amendment of Montenegro's electoral law, the results were determined by a majority of votes cast. The most recent presidential election took place in April 2008, and Filip Vujanovic was re-elected.

Parliamentary elections took place on 20 October 2002, and was won by the Social Democratic Party and Democratic Party of Socialists coalition. Following the result, Milo Djukanovic resigned as President in order to take up the post of Prime Minister.

In May 2006, 55.4 per cent of Montenegrins voted in favour of Montenegrin independence. The turnout was 86.3 per cent, with thousands of ex-patriate Montenegrins returning home to vote. Montenegro's union with Serbia was established in 2003, through the Belgrade agreement, when both sides were given the option of leaving after three years. The last time Montenegro was independent was nearly 90 years ago at the end of World War I, when it was absorbed into the newly-formed Yugoslavia.

The penultimate parliamentary election (and the first since independence) took place on 10 September 2006. The ruling coalition the Democratic Party of Socialists, led by Milo Djukanovic won. Milo Djukanovic resigned as Prime Minister the following October citing personal reasons and Zeljko Sturanovic took over the post. At the March 2009 elections. Milo Djukanovic was returned to the office of prime minister and appointed a cabinet, based on the a coalition of the DPS, the SDP, the DUA and the Bosniak Party (BS).

The most recent election was held on 14 October 2012. The ruling coalition led by Milo Djukanovic had been returned to power. It lost its overall majority and formed another coalition government. The results were as follows: For a European Montenegro (DPS, SDP and other allies) 39 seats; Democratic Front 20 seats; SNP 9 seats; Positive Montenegro 7 seats; Bosniak Party 3 seats.

Diplomatic Representation

Embassy of the Republic of Montenegro, 18 Callcott Street, London W8 7SU, Unted Kingdom. Tel: +44 (0)20 7727 6007, fax: +44 (0)20 7243 9358, URL: http://www.visit-montenegro.com
Ambassador: Ljubisa Stankovic
British Embassy, Ulcinjska 8, Gorica C, 81000 Podgorica, Montenegro. Tel: +382 81 205 460, e-mail: podgorica@britishembassy.cg.yu, URL: http://ukinmontenegro.fco.gov.uk/en/
Ambassador: Catherine Knight-Sands (page 1457)
Embassy of the United States, URL: http://podgorica.usembassy.gov/
Ambassador: Sue Brown
Permanent Mission in the UN, 801 Second Avenue, 7th Floor, New York, NY 10017, USA. Tel: +1 212 661 3700, URL: http://www.mip.gov.me/en/index.php/
Permanent Representative: Milorad Scepanovic
Ambassador to the US: Srdan Darmanovic

LEGAL SYSTEM

Montenegro has made reforms to its legal system in recent years both to meet EU requirements and to attract more foreign investment. Many recent legislative acts include laws governing business and corporate government. A new consitution was adopted in October 2007 and meets European standards especially in the areas of human rights and the judiciary. As part of its recent judicial reform, the Law on Judicial Council was adopted in 2008, which gives the right to elect and dismiss judges on the Judicial Council.

The Supreme Court is the highest court and final resort for all types of cases. There are also two Superior Courts that mainly hear appeal cases. The first level of courts is made of up of 15 general courts dealing with civil and criminal cases. There are also specialised courts that deal with commercial matters and administrative courts. The country is in the process of strengthening the independence and efficiency of its judiciary, and harmonising its legislation with that of the EU and international standards. There are plans to establish a High Commerical Court or a Chamber in the Supreme Court dedicated to commercial cases.

The Consitutional Court is composed of five justices nominated by the President and appointed by parliament. The Constitutional Courts assess the constitutionality and legality of legislative acts, any alleged violations of the Constitution by the president and any other complaints of violations of the consitutition.

The government respects the human rights of its citizens in general. However, the police have been known to mistreat suspects, prison conditions are poor and the judiciary is slow and inefficent. There is widespread perception of corruption in law enforcement agencies, and arrests can be arbitrary. The death penalty was abolished in 2002.

Courts of Montenegro, URL: http://en.sudovi.me/
Supreme Court, President: Vesna Medenica

LOCAL GOVERNMENT

Montenegro is divided into 21 communes or municipalities, *opstini,* which are then divided into 1,256 localities, and 40 urban localities. The municipalities are Andrijevia, Bar, Berane, Bijelo Polje, Budva, Cetinje, Danilovgrad, Herceg Novi, Kolasin, Kotor, Mojkovac, Niksic, Plav, Pluzine, Pljevlja, Podgornica, Rozaje, Savnik, Tivat, Ulcinj, and Zabljak. The most recent municipal elections were held in 2010.

AREA AND POPULATION

Area

The Republic of Montenegro covers an area of 13,398 sq. km. It is bordered by the Adriatic coast in the west, Bosnia-Herzegovina in the northwest, Serbia in the northeast, and Albania in the southeast. The country is heavily forested and is home to the Tara River canyon, the longest and deepest in Europe. The coastal plain is narrow and is flanked by limestone mountains and plateaus. The climate is Mediterranean with hot dry summers and autumns and colder winters with heavy snowfalls in the interior.

To view a map, visit http://www.un.org/Depts/Cartographic/map/profile/montenegro.pdf

Population

The population was estimated to be 631,000 in 2010 with an annual growth rate of 0.0 per cent for the period 2000-10. The immigration rate in 1999 was 2,525 per 1,000 population, whilst the emigration rate was 3,375 per 1,000 population. The majority of the population consists of Montenegrins, with minority communities of Muslims, Serbs, Albanians, and Croats, amongst others. The main towns are the capital Podgorica (2000 population of 117,875), Niksic (56,141), Plejevlja (20,187), Cetinje (15,946), and Kotor (5,620). (Source: Federal Statistics Office).

Births, Marriages, Deaths

In 2005, 3,291 marriages took place and 499 divorces were granted. (Source: Statistical Office of Montenegro) According to the WHO, the average life expectancy was 72 years for males and 77 years for females in 2009. Healthy life expectancy was 65 years. The median age is 36 years. The crude birth rate was recorded in 2010 at 12.3 per 1,000 population and the crude death rate was 5.3 per 1,000 population. (Source: http://www.who.int, World Health Statistics)

Public Holidays 2014

1-2 January: New Year
7-8 January: Orthodox Christmas
18 April: Orthodox Good Friday
21 April: Orthodox Easter Monday
27 April: Statehood Day
1-2 May: Labour Days
9 May: Victory Day
29-30 November: Republic Day

EMPLOYMENT

Employment by Sector, 2006

Sector	No. employed
Agriculture, forestry & water-power economy	2,607
Fishing	115
Mining & quarrying	4,159
Manufacture	26,065
Production and supply of electricity, gas & water	5,627

- continued

Construction	6,853
Wholesale & retail trade, repair of vehicles, personal & household	29,602
Hotels & restaurants	10,928
Transport, storage & communication	12,133
Financial intermediation	3,114
Real estate, renting & business activities	5,905
Public administration & compulsory social security	10,345
Education	12,846
Health & social work	12,012
Other community, social & personal service activities	8,489
Total	150,800

Source: Statistical Office of Montenegro

BANKING AND FINANCE

Currency
On 1 January 2002 the euro became the official currency of Montenegro. Until January 2002 the official currency was the Deutschmark.

GDP/GNP, Inflation, National Debt
Prior to independence from Serbia, the Republic of Montenegro had set up a central bank and managed its own budget. In response to rising inflation, they adoped the euro in 2002. Reforms of the financial sector have helped strengthen the economy. Tourism is a developing industry. The recent global financial crisis has adversely affected Montenegro's economy, especially a decline in aluminium exports and a decline in real estate. In 2011 Montenegro approached the World Bank for an US$85 million loan.

Figures for 2009 put GDP at US$3.7 billion that year the growth rate was -7 per cent. In 2010, GDP was estimated at US$4 billion with a growth rate of 0.5 per cent. In 2009 the tourism sector contributed 21 per cent to GDP, industry, 19 per cent, agriculture, 8 per cent and the service sector, 50 per cent. GDP was estimated to be US$4.2 billion in 2011.

The following table gives details of GDP in recent years:

GDP, €000	2005	2006	2007
GDP at current prices	1,815	2,148.9	2,807.9
GDP per capita	2,912	3,443	4,484
GDP growth rate at constant prices (%)	4.2	8.6	10.7

Source: Statistical Office of Montenegro

Inflation in 2005 was estimated to be 1.8 per cent. In 2007 it had risen to 6.2 per cent and 8.4 per cent in 2008. It was estimated to have fallen below 1 per cent in 2010 before rising to 2.9 per cent in 2011.

External debt was estimated to be US$1 billion in 2011.

Balance of Payments / Imports and Exports
Estimated figures for 2011 put export earnings at €635 million with Serbia, Italy, Greece, Slovenia and Bosnia and Herzegovina the largest markets. That year imports cost an estimated $US2.2 billion, the main markets being Serbia, Germany, Italy and Greece.

Export and Import by SITC, €000

	Exports 2006	Exports 2007	Imports 2006	Imports 2007
Total	627,460	600,799	1,482,689	2,317,758
Food and live animals	30,887	10,445	174,207	216,596
Beverages and tobacco	38,504	54,982	41,201	60,223
Crude materials except fuels	41,605	38,123	33,070	39,412
Mineral fuels and lubricants	40,371	7,612	236,739	275,869
Animal and vegetable fats	376	74	9,484	9,698
Chemical products	13,327	12,544	122,146	145,978
Manufactured goods	390,504	431,060	225,062	317,187
Machinery and transport equip.	40,237	19,392	304,125	485,310
Misc. manuf. goods	9,967	12,256	159,248	493,459
Commodities, n.e.c.	21,682	14,310	177,407	274,028

Source: SY MNE 2008

Foreign Investment
In June 2001, the former Yugoslavia received pledges of aid from international governments and organisations offering nearly US$1.3 billion to help rebuild the economy and infrastructure. At the Brussels meeting, which took place just after the extradition of Slobodan Milosevic to the Hague, the European Union pledged US$450 million, the US offered almost US$200 million, and the World Bank US$600 million.

There are many opportunities for foreign investment, largely due to the effects of the 1999 conflict and subsequent sanctions, but also due to Serbia and Montenegro's geographical position and its abundance of natural resources.

In 2008, net foreign direct investment reached US$1.223 billion much of which was destined for the growing tourism industry.

Central Bank
Central Bank of Montenegro, URL: http://www.cb-mn.org

MANUFACTURING, MINING AND SERVICES

Primary and Extractive Industries
Montenegro has substantial deposits of bauxite, lead, zinc and coal. Pljevlja is one of five regions in which large coal deposits are found (18,200 million short tons in total). Almost all of the coal in this region is lignite, accessible by surface mining. Figures from the EIA show that in 2010 Montenegro produced 1.631 million short tons of coal all of which was used domestically.

Montenegro has no reserves of oil and in 2011 imported around 4,000 barrels per day.

Manufacturing
Until the end of the Second World War Montenegro's economy was based on agriculture. Industrialisation put the main emphasis on basic industrial sectors and the infrastructure. A giant overhaul of the country's water supply is currently in progress to bring the hydro-industry in line with that of the states of western Europe. Today, a number of projects in the sectors of ferrous and non-ferrous metallurgy, power generation, metal working, electrical engineering, textile, timber and clothing are in operation. There is also a growing tourist industry.

Montenegro's electricity production, transmission, and distribution is the responsibility of the state-run Elektroprivreda of Montenegro (EPCG). EPCG has been earmarked for privatisation in the near future. Hydropower plants are located on the Moraca, Piva, and Zeta rivers.

Service Industries
Montenegro is hoping to expand its tourist industry especially along the Adriatic coast. Total arrivals of visitors rose from 820,457 in 2004 to 953,928 in 2005.

Agriculture
Among principal agricultural products grown are tobacco, citrus fruit, olives, grapes and other types of fruit. Livestock farming has been developed in recent years. Large parts of the country are covered by woodland, predominantly beech and conifers.

Agricultural Production in 2010

Produce	Int. $'000*	Tonnes
Cow milk, whole, fresh	53,313	170,840
Potatoes	24,845	149,252
Grapes	23,324	40,804
Indigenous cattle meat	15,668	5,800
Chillies and peppers, green	8,580	18,226
Cabbages and other brassicas	8,314	55,557
Tomatoes	8,289	22,430
Watermelons	4,863	42,687
Plums and sloes	4,130	6,921
Hen eggs, in shell	3,152	3,800
Sheep milk, whole, fresh	3,143	8,070
Indigenous chicken meat	2,977	2,090

* unofficial figures

Source: http://faostat.fao.org/site/339/default.aspx Food and Agriculture Organization of the United Nations, Food and Agricultural commodities production

Figures for January 2005 show that the numbers of livestock are as follows: Cattle, 117,842; Sheep, 544,898; Pigs, 10,697; Poultry, 462,149; Horses, 7,119; Beehives, 42,613. The total fish catch for 2010 was put at 1,140 tonnes.

COMMUNICATIONS AND TRANSPORT

Travel Requirements
Citizens of the USA, Canada and Australia require a valid passport; EU subjects who hold a valid national Identity Card do not need a passport. US, Canadian, Australian and EU subjects do not need a visa for tourist stays of up to 90 days. All nationals should contact the embassy to check visa requirements.

Visitors must declare currency in excess of 2,000 Euros upon entry, and obtain from customs officials a declaration form that must be presented at departure. Visitors staying in private accommodation must register with the local police within 24 hours of arrival; those who fail to register may face difficulties in departing the country.

International Airports
Podgorica airport is situated 12 km outside the city.
Tivat airport is situated near the city of Tivat.

National Airlines
Montenegro Airlines, Beogradska 10, Podgorica, 81304, Montenegro. Tel: + 381 (81) 405 501, e-mail: contact@mgx.cg.yu, URL: http://www.montenegro-airlines.cg.yu

Railways
Recent figures show that there are 250 km of track in Montenegro. Figures for 2006 show that 1,067,000 passenger journeys were made that year and 2,494,000 tonnes of freight were carried.

Roads
Recent figures show that road network in Montenegro is approximately 7 368 km. In order to remain the best (and shortest) link between Western Europe and the Middle East, Serbia and Montenegro was planning to build 1,700 km of motorways by 2010, many of which would be toll roads. Vehicles are driven on the right.

STATES OF THE WORLD

MOROCCO

Ports and Harbours
Montenegro has ports at Bar, Herceg Novi, and Zelenika.

HEALTH

In 2009, the Montenegrin government spent approximately 13.6 per cent of its total budget on healthcare, accounting for 71.3 per cent of all healthcare spending. Total expenditure on healthcare equated to 9.4 per cent of the country's GDP. Per capita expenditure on health was approximately US$621 in 2009, compared with US$112 in 2000. Figures for 2005-10 show that there are 1,310 physicians (21 per 10,000 population), 3,480 nurses and midwives (55.8 per 10,000 population), 36 dentistry personnel and 92 pharmaceutical personnel. There are 39 hospital beds per 10,000 population.

The infant mortality rate (probability of dying before age one) was 7 per 1,000 in 2010. In the same year the under-five mortality rate was 8 per 1,000. The main causes of death among children aged under 5 years are: prematurity 45 per cent & birth asphyxia 39 per cent. Approximately 7.9 per cent of children aged less than five are classified as stunted (2005-11).

According to the latest WHO figures, in 2010 approximately 98 per cent of the population had access to improved drinking water. In the same year, 90 per cent of the population had access to improved sanitation. (Source: http://www.who.int, World Health Statistics 2012)

EDUCATION

The following table shows the number of schools and pupils in the academic year 2006/07:

Education Statistics

School	Number	Students
Kindergarten	88	10,511
Primary schools	455	75,179
Secondary schools	47	31,627

Source: Statistical Office of Montenegro

The language of instruction in schools has been Montenegrin and Albanian where a high proportion of students are Albanian, but in 2008 the government announced that as from 2009 all school text books including dictionaries would only be printed in Montenegrin.

Primary or elementary education in Montenegro is compulsory and free for students aged between 6 and 14. After that students go on onto one of the three tiers of secondary education. A Gymnasium is seen as providing an education which will lead to college or university and lasts for four years. Professional schools specialise in certain fields and last for three of four year and vocational schools offer a three year education which does not lead onto further education.

RELIGION

Recent figures show around 79 per cent of the population are Christian, predominantly members of the Orthodox Church. Some 16 per cent are Muslim. Montenegro has a religious liberty rating of 7 on a scale of 1 to 10 (10 is most freedom). (Source: World Religion Database)

COMMUNICATIONS AND MEDIA

Press freedom is guaranteed by the constitution. There are some reports of political influence over the media.

Newspapers
Vijesti, URL: http://www.vijesti.cg.yu
Pobjeda, URL: http://www.pobjeda.co.yu/naslovna.phtml
Dan, URL: http://www.dan.cg.yu
Republika, URL: http://www.republika.cg.yu/naslovna.phtml

Broadcasting
TV Montenegro and Radio Montenegro (URL: http://www.rtcg.me/) are state funded, there are several private broadcasters including TV In and ntv montena.

Telecommunications
The system is modern with expanding mobile phone coverage. Figures for 2008 show that Montenegro has 350,00 land lines in use and 750,000 mobile phones. Approximately 295,000 of the population subscribe to the internet.

ENVIRONMENT

Montenegro is a party to the following international agreements: Air Pollution, Biodiversity, Climate Change, Climate Change-Kyoto Protocol, Desertification, Hazardous Wastes, Law of the Sea, Marine Dumping, Marine Life Conservation, Ozone Layer Protection, and Ship Pollution.

MOROCCO

Al Mamlaka al Maghribiyah

Kingdom of Morocco

Capital: Rabat (Population estimate: 1.6 million)

Head of State: HM Mohammed VI (King) (page 1479)

National Flag: Red, charged with a green five-pointed star composed of interlaced triangles

CONSTITUTION AND GOVERNMENT

Constitution
Morocco is an independent Arab Kingdom. Previously a French and Spanish Protectorate, it gained its independence in March 1956. Tangier lost its status as a free money market and free trade zone in 1960.

A Constitutional Council of 78 members was appointed towards the end of 1960 and a Basic Law was enacted in June 1961. A permanent Constitution was promulgated on 14 December 1962. The Constitutional Council is composed of six members appointed by the King for a nine-year term, and oversees legislative elections and referendums.

On 8 June 1965, the King proclaimed a state of emergency and appointed himself head of a new cabinet. In 1970, and again in 1971, the King modified the constitution and the changes were approved via referendum. In 1970 a single chamber composed of 240 deputies was created. Of these deputies, 150 were elected by indirect vote through an electoral college. These represented the town councils, the regional assemblies, the chambers of commerce, industry and agriculture and the trade unions. Further revisions were made in 1992 and 1996 again approved by referendum. The 1992 Constitution confirmed the law of primogeniture.

The 1992 Constitution was amended in September 1996 and set up a bicameral parliament (*Barlaman*) consisting of the Chamber of Representatives (*Majlis an-Nuwab*) and the Chamber of Councillors (*Majlis al-Mustashareen*).

Morocco is a constitutional and democratic monarchy in which sovereignty belongs to the nation. The King promulgates legislation and appoints the prime minister. The prime minister appoints the ministers of the Cabinet.

In September 2000 King Mohammed reduced the number of ministers from 41 to 33 and in 2002 he lowered the voting age from 20 to 18.

In July 2011 a referendum backed King Mohammed's constitutional reform proposals. The amendments include increased powers for the prime minister and for parliament.

To consult the full constitution, please visit:
http://www.justice.gov.ma/an/legislation/legislation.aspx?ty=1

International Relations
Morocco maintains close relations with Europe and the United States. It is a member of the UN, the Arab Maghreb Union, the Organization of the Islamic Conference and the Non-Aligned Movement. Morocco regularly contributes to UN peacekeeping efforts in Africa. Morocco maintains diplomatic contact with Israel, and also has close relations with Saudi Arabia and the Gulf States. Following the 2001 September 11 terrorist attacks on the USA, Morocco declared solidarity with the war against terror, and has suffered attacks in Casablanca.

Morocco claims the territory of Western Sahara, which has caused strained relations with Algeria (supporters of the Polisario Liberation Front) in the past. The dispute remains the primary impediment to regional integration and development goals. Some differences were overcome when, in August 2004, the Polisario released 404 Moroccan prisoners of war. Morocco presented a proposal for autonomy for Western Sahara within Morocco to the UN Secretary-General on 11 April 2007. Four rounds of negotiations under the auspices of the UN were held in New York, in late 2007 and early 2008.

Approximately 90,000 Sahrawi refugees live in camps around Tindouf, Algeria. Several thousand Sahrawis also live in the Moroccan-controlled area of Western Sahara among a large number of Moroccan settlers.

Recent Events
A referendum on the future of the Western Sahara, a former Spanish colony, was scheduled for January 1992 under UN auspices but has yet to be held. A ceasefire and settlement plan went into effect in 1991. There is interest in oil exploration in areas offshore of the Western Sahara, but the validity of exploration contracts remains questionable whilst the status of the territory is unsettled.

In February 2003, the Moroccan government jailed three Saudi members of al-Qaeda for plotting to attack US and British warships in the Straits of Gibraltar. On May 16, 2003, Moroccan suicide bombers simultaneously attacked five sites in Casablanca, killing more than 40 people and wounding over 100. More than a million people subsequently demonstrated to condemn the attacks.

A Free Trade Agreement with the U.S. came into effect in July 2004; the United States government considers the Moroccans to be non-Nato allies.

An earthquake at Al Hoceima in the north of the country killed over 500 people early in 2004.

In September 2005, hundreds of African migrants tried to cross the borders of the Spanish territories of Melilla and Ceuta, in an attempt to claim European asylum. Morocco deported hundreds of illegal immigrants thereafter. In January 2006, Jose Luis Rodriguez Zapatero became the first Spanish PM to visit the territories in 25 years.

In April 2007, a series of suicide bomb attacks occurred in central Casablanca, one taking place near the U.S. consulate general and one near the American Language Center. In the same month, police raided a militant hideout in Casablanca, setting off gunfights and suicide bombings that left at least five men dead. Three of the suspected militants blew themselves up during the police manhunt, and one was shot dead. A police officer died in one of the suicide blasts. The authorities claimed to have foiled a plot to target foreign and strategic interests by suicide bombers. The militants were believed to belong to al-Qaeda Organisation in the Islamic Maghreb, a group recruited, trained and financed in Algeria.

In June 2007, Morocco and the Polisario Front held talks in New York but failed to come to any agreement over the future of Western Sahara.

In April 2008, nine people convicted of involvement in the Casablanca suicide bombings escaped from a Moroccan prison by tunneling their way out. The 2003 attacks left 45 people dead, including 12 bombers. A further 40 people were found guilty in October 2008. Two Moroccan men were found guilty of involvement in the 2004 Madrid train bombings and were sentenced in December 2008.

In February 2011 there were widespread protests in the capital calling for constitutional reform. Some government buildings and banks were reported to have been attacked and there were reports of casualties. There were also reports of unrest in Tangiers. In March 2011, the king promised constitutional reforms including a restriction of his own powers. He said parliament should choose the prime minister. A referendum was held at the beginning of July to vote on the king's proposed changes, these changes would mean that the king would remain the head of state, the military, and the Islamic faith in Morocco, but a prime minister would be chosen from the largest party elected to parliament and he would become the head of the government. The judiciary would be more independent and corruption would be tackled, also there would be guaranteed freedom of expression and gender rights and the Berber language would become an official language, alongside Arabic. The reported result of the referendum was a landslide in support of King Mohammed's proposed changes; 98 per cent of voters approved the reforms. Some opposition campaigners said the figure was unbelievable and took to the streets to protest.

Parliamentary elections took place on 25 November. The moderate Islamist Justice and Development Party (PJD) won 107 out of the 395 seats. The nationalist and ruling Istiqlal party came second with 60 seats. Abdelilah Benkirane of the Justice and Development Party (PJD) was appointed prime minister on 29 November and started talks on forming a coalition government. The new government took office in January 2012.

Mass anti-government demonstrations took place in May 2012, with people protesting against an alleged failure by the government to deliver promised reforms.

Upper House
The 270 members of the Chamber of Councillors are elected for nine years, renewable in thirds every three years. Two-thirds of the Chamber of Councillors are elected by electoral colleges composed of members of local assemblies and councils, whilst the remaining one-third are elected by professional organisations and representatives of trade unions.
Chamber of Councillors, BP 432, Rabat, Morocco. Tel: +212 37 762707, fax: +2112 37 767726. URL: http://www.parlement.ma

Lower House
The 325 members of the Chamber of Representatives are elected for five years by direct universal suffrage.
House of Representatives, BP 431, Rabat, Morocco. Tel: +212 37 762620, fax: +212 37 767726, URL: http://www.majiliss-annouwab.ma

Cabinet (as at June 2013)
Prime Minister: Abdelilah Benkirane (page 1386)
Minister of State: Abdellah Baha (page 1381)
Minister of the Interior: Mohand Laenser (page 1459)
Minister of Foreign Affairs and Co-operation: Saad-Eddine El Othmani (page 1491)
Minister of Habous and Islamic Affairs: Ahmed Toufiq
Minister for Energy, Mines, Water and Environment: Fouad Douiri
Minister of Economy and Finance: Nizar Baraka (page 1383)
Secretary General of Government: Dr Driss Dahak
Minister of Agriculture and Marine Fisheries: Aziz Akhenouch
Minister of Housing and Town Planning: Nabil Benabdellah
Minister of Employment and Vocational Training: Abdelouahed Souhail
Minister of National Education: Mohamed El Ouafa
Minister of Tourism: Lahcen Haddad
Minister of Equipment and Transport: Aziz Rabbah
Minister of Culture: Mohamed Amine Sbihi
Minister of Justice and Liberties: Mustafa Ramid
Minister for Relations with Parliament: Lahbib Choubani

Minister of Youth and Sport: Mohamed Ouzzine
Minister of Communications, Government Spokesman: Mustapha El Khalfi
Minister of Health: El Hossein El Ouardi
Minister of Solidarity, Women, Family and Social Development: Bassima Hakkaoui
Minister of Industry, Trade and New Technologies: Abdelkader Aamara
Minister of Higher Education, Scientific Research and Professional Training: Lahcen Daoudi
Minister of Handicrafts: Abdessamad Qaiouh

Ministries
Government portal, URL: http://www.pm.gov.ma/
Prime Minister's Office, URL: http://www.pm.gov.ma/ar/index.aspx
Ministry of Commerce and Industry and Telecommunications, rue Maa al-Aynayn, Rabat, Morocco. URL: http://www.mcinet.gov.ma/Pages/default.aspx
Ministry of Economy and Finance, Avenue Muhammad V, Rabat-Maroc, Morocco. Tel: +212 537 763171, URL: http://www.finances.gov.ma/
Ministry of Foreign Affairs and Co-operation, Avenue Franklin Roosevelt, Rabat, Morocco. Tel: +212 537 761763, fax: 212 537 764679, e-mail: ministere@maec.gov.ma, URL: http://www.maec.gov.ma/
Ministry of Habous and Islamic Affairs, Mechouar, Rabat, Morocco. Tel: +212 537 76 68 01 / 76 60 70, e-mail: Webmaster@habous.gov.ma, URL: http://www.habous.gov.ma/ministere/ar/index.htm
Ministry of the Interior, Quartier Administratif, Rabat, Morocco. Tel: +212 537 765660 / 760526, fax : +212 537 762056
Ministry of Justice, rue Beyrout, Rabat, Morocco. Tel: +212 537 21589, URL: http://www.justice.gov.ma/
Ministry of Equipment and Transport, Avenue Mohammed V, Quartier administratif, Rabat Chellah, Rabat, Morocco. Tel: +212 537 68 41 51, URL: http://www.mtpnet.gov.ma/
Ministry of Agriculture & Fisheries, Quartier Administratif. Place Abdellah Chefchaouni, B.P. 607, Rabat, Morocco. Tel: +212 537 760933, e-mail: webmaster@madrpm.gov.ma, URL: http://www.madrpm.gov.ma/
Ministry of Communications, URL: http://www.mincom.gov.ma/mincom/AR
Ministry of Employment & Training, Rabat, Morocco. Tel: +212 537 760318 / 761855, fax: +212 537 768881, URL: http://www.emploi.gov.ma
Ministry of National Education and Youth, Bab Rouah, Rabat, Morocco. Tel: +212 537 772048 / 774839, URL: http://www.men.gov.ma/
Ministry of Higher Education and Scientific Research, BP 4500, Rabat, Morocco. URL: http://www.enssup.gov.ma/
Ministry of Culture, Rue Ghandi, Rabat, Morocco. Tel: +212 537 209427, fax: +212 537 708814, URL: http://www.minculture.gov.ma
Ministry of Tourism, Quartier Administratif, Chellah, Rabat, Morocco. Tel: +212 537 761701, fax: +212 537 761336, URL: http://www.tourisme-marocain.com
Ministry of Health, Rabat, Morocco. Tel: +212 537 760037 / 660885, fax: +212 537 768401, URL: http://www.sante.gov.ma/
Ministry of Energy, Mining, Water & Environment, URL: http://www.mem.gov.ma/

Political Parties
Union constitutionnelle (UC, Constitutional Union), URL: http://www.unionconstitutionnelle.org/
Secretary General: Mohammed Abied
Rassemblement national des indépandants (RNI, National Union of Independents)
Mouvement populaire (MP, Popular Movement)
Mouvement démocratique et social (MDS, Democratic and Social Movement)
Mouvement national populaire (MNP, National Popular Movement)
Parti national démocrate (PND, National Democratic Party)
Istiqlal (Independence) Party (PI)
Parti de la Justice et du Développement, (Justice and Development Party, PJD), URL: http://www.pjd.ma
Leader: Abdelilah Benkirane
Rassemblement National des Indépendants, (National Rally of Independents, RNI), URL: http://www.rni.ma
Leader: Salaheddine Mezouar
Union Socialiste des Forces Populaires, (Socialist Union of Popular Forces,USFP), URL: www.usfp.ma
Leader: Abdelwahed Radi

Elections
Parliamentary elections took place on 25 November 2011. The moderate Islamist Justice and Development Party (PJD) won 107 out of the 395 seats. The nationalist and ruling Istiqlal party came second with 60 seats and the two are likely to form a coalition. Under the recent constitutional reform King Mohamed must appoint the prime minister from the party which wins the most seats. The group February 20 had called for a boycott of the vote in protest at some of the constitutional reforms and claimed this was reflected in the low turnout of approximately 45 per cent.

A partial election for the Chamber of Councillors was held on 2 October 2009 for one third of the Councillors.

Diplomatic Representation
US Embassy, 2 Avenue de Mohamed El Fassi, Rabat, Morocco. Tel: +212 37 762265, fax: +212 37 765661, URL: http://morocco.usembassy.gov
Chargé d'Affaires: Patricia Newton Moller
Embassy of the Kingdom of Morocco, 1601 21st Street, N.W., Washington, DC 20009, USA. Tel: +1 202 462 7979, URL: http://www.embassyofmorocco.us/
Ambassador: H.E. Mohamed Rachad Bouhlal
British Embassy, 28 avenue S.A.R. Sidi Mohammed, Souissi, Rabat, Morocco. Tel: +212 (0) 37 63 33 33, fax: +212 (0) 37 758709, URL: http://ukinmorocco.fco.gov.uk/en
Ambassador: Timothy Morris

MOROCCO

Embassy of the Kingdom of Morocco, 49 Queen's Gate Gardens, London SW7 5NE, United Kingdom. Tel: +44 (0)20 7581 5001/4, fax: +44 (0)20 7225 3862, e-mail: ambalondres@maec.gov.ma, URL: http://www.moroccanembassylondon.org.uk
Ambassador: Princess Lalla Joumala Alaoui
Permanent Representative of the Kingdom of Morocco to the United Nations,
866 Second Avenue, 6th and 7th Floors, New York, NY 10017, USA. Tel: +1 212 421 1580, fax: +1 212 980 1512, e-mail: morocco@un.int, URL: http://www.morocco-un.org
Ambassador: Mohamed Loulichki

LEGAL SYSTEM

Morocco's legal system consists of secular courts based on French legal tradition, and courts based on Jewish and Islamic traditions. The Supreme Council of the Judiciary regulates the judiciary and is presided over by the king. Judges are appointed on the advice of the council. Judges in the secular system are university-trained.

Courts of the First Instance handle appeals, civil affairs, disputes related to personal and successional statutes and commercial, administrative and social cases. Regional and District courts deal with all affairs related with personal and property actions brought against persons living in the same district of their jurisdiction. Appeal Courts hear appeals from first instance courts and orders rendered by their presidents. The Supreme Court (*Majlis el Aala*) is responsible for the interpretation of the law and regulates the jurisprudence of the courts and tribunals of the kingdom. It sits at Rabat and is divided into five chambers. The Special Court was created in 1965 in order to deal with corruption among public officials. There is also a military court for cases involving military personnel and occasionally matters pertaining to state security.

There are 27 Sadad courts, which are courts of first instance for Muslim and Jewish personal law. Criminal and civil cases are heard, and cases with penalties exceeding a certain monetary amount may be appealed to regional courts. The Sadad courts are divided into Shari'ah; Rabbinical; Civil, Commercial, and Administrative sections; and a criminal section.

On 25 January 2004, the government adopted a new Family Law which granted women new rights e.g. equal divorce rights; right to be joint head of household.

Reform of the legal system is under discussion.

Human rights are limited in Morocco. Citizens do not have the right to change the constitutional provisions establishing the monarchy or the practice of Islam. There have been recent reports of torture and other abuses by the security forces. Arrests can be arbitrary, and the judiciary is not viewed as independent. Prison conditions are poor. Freedom of speech and the press is limited, and corruption is widespread.

Human Rights Advisory Council, URL: http://www.ccdh.org.ma/

LOCAL GOVERNMENT

Morocco is divided into 15 administrative regions, which are further divided into 43 provinces, 9 wilayas and 22 prefectures, which in turn are split into 1,547 urban and rural communes. The regions are Grand Casablanca, Chaouia-Ouardigha, Doukkala-Abda, Fes-Boulemane, Gharb-Chrarda-Beni Hssen, Guelmim-Es Smara, Laayoune-Boujdour-Sakia El Hamra, Marrakech-Tensift-Al Haouz, Meknes-Tafilalet, Oriental, Rabat-Sale-Zemmour-Zaer, Souss-Massa-Draa, Tadla-Azilal, Tanger-Tetouan and Taza-Al Hoceima-Taounate. The regions are administered by Walis (governors) appointed by the King. The most recent municipal elections took place in 2009.

AREA AND POPULATION

Area
Morocco is situated in the north-west of Africa. It is bordered in the north by the Strait of Gibraltar and the Mediterranean sea, to the south by Mauritania and Western Sahara, to the east by Algeria, and to the west the Atlantic Ocean. Its area is 446,550 sq. km, not counting the area of Western Sahara which covers a further 267,028 km sq. Morocco's coastal plains are rich and fertile. The northern coast and interior are mountainous with high plateaus. The highest point is Jebel Toubkal at 4,165 metres. The climate is Mediterranean, but more severe in the interior.

The Atlas Mountains separate the west of the country from the Sahara Desert. Rabat is the seat of government, but Casablanca is the commercial and industrial centre. Marrakech is a major tourist centre.

To the south of Morocco is the disputed region of Western Sahara. Still occupied by Morocco but regarded as an independent state by the Polisario Liberation Front, the territory is likely to be the subject of a referendum overseen by the United Nations.

To view a map of Morocco, please visit http://www.un.org/Depts/Cartographic/map/profile/morocco.pdf

Population
The population in 2010 was estimated at 31.951 million, with an average annual growth rate of 1.0 per cent over the period 2000-10. Approximately 350,000 people live in the disputed Western Sahara. The 2000 population density was almost 40.5 people per sq. km. The majority of the population (64 per cent) is aged between 15 and 60, with around 28 per cent aged under 15, and about 8 per cent aged 60 or over. Rabat, the capital, has a population of about 1,220,000. Around 58 per cent of the population lives in urban areas.

Arabic is the official language but French, Spanish and various Berber dialects are also spoken.

Births, Marriages, Deaths
The birth rate in 2010 was around 19.5 births per 1,000 people, whilst the death rate was 5.3 deaths per 1,000 people. According to World Health Organization statistics, average life expectancy rose from the age of 65 in 1997 to 73 in 2009 (71 for men and 75 for women). Healthy life expectancy was 62 years. The median age was 26 years. The child mortality rate in 2010 was an estimated 30 deaths per 1,000 children who survived beyond five years. The total fertility rate was 2.3 children born per woman. (Source: http://www.who.int, World Health Statistics 2012)

Public Holidays 2014
1 January: New Year
11 January: Independence Manifesto Day
14 January: Birth of the Prophet*
1 May: Labour Day
23 May: National Day
30 July: Festival of the Throne Day
14 August: Oued ed-Dahab Day
29 June: Ramadan begins
29 July: Eid Al Fitr (end of Ramadan)*
5 October: Eid Al Adha (Feast of Sacrifice)*
25 October: Al-Hijira (Islamic New Year)*
6 November: Anniversary of the Green March
18 November: Independence Day
* Islamic holiday: exact date depends upon sighting of the moon

EMPLOYMENT

Morocco's labour force (15+) numbered 11.14 million in 2006, equivalent to around 51.2 per cent of the total population. 9.9 million people were employed, 7.2 million of whom were men and 2.7 million were women. The national unemployment rate in 2005 was estimated to be 11 per cent, affecting 1.2 million people, but unemployment in urban areas is estimated to be as high as 33 per cent among the young. Slightly under half the workforce is based in urban areas. Figures for 2007 put the unemployment rate at 9.6 per cent, 9.4 per cent in 2008 and 9.1 per cent in 2009.

Total Employment by Economic Activity

Occupation	2007
Agriculture, hunting, forestry & fishing	4,235,100
Mining & quarrying	48,400
Manufacturing	1,191,300
Electricity, gas & water supply	39,400
Construction	838,900
Wholesale & retail trade, repairs, hotels & restaurants	1,637,000
Transport, storage & communications	401,900
Financial intermediation, real estate, renting & business activities	171,900
Public admin. & defence; compulsory social security, education, health & social work and & service activities	1,478,700
Other	13,700

Source: Copyright © International Labour Organization (ILO Dept. of Statistics, http://laborsta.ilo.org)

BANKING AND FINANCE

Currency
The Moroccan unit of currency is the dirham (DH), created on 1 July 1959 and composed of 100 Moroccan centimes. The financial centre is Casablanca.

GDP/GNP, Inflation, National Debt
Morocco's economy relies largely on the performance of its agricultural sector. The industry is prey to natural forces; three years of drought culminating in 2000 had a major impact on agriculture, and severe flooding following the three years of drought caused serious damage to the infrastructure in 2002. The government is modernising and diversifying its economy, with the development of tourism and manufacturing. The economy has been aided by the construction of a new port and a free trade zone near Tangier. The service sector is the largest contributor to GDP, at 55.5 per cent, followed by the industrial sector, which contributes some 29 per cent. Although 50 per cent of the workforce are employed in agriculture, its contribution to GDP has declined and in 2008 contributed an estimated 12 per cent.

In 2008, GDP was estimated at US$88.3 billion with a growth rate of 5.8 per cent, GDP growth fell in 2009 to 5.1 per cent and 4.4 per cent in 2010. GDP was estimated at US$91 billion in 2009. Per capita GDP was US$4,500 in 2009. GDP was estimated to be US$95 billion in 2011.

The inflation rate stayed low between 1999 and 2004, not exceeding 1.5 per cent. In 2005, it was further reduced, to 1 per cent. In 2011, it was still just under one per cent. Morocco's external debt was around US$38 billion in 2011.

Morocco has adopted tighter monetary and fiscal policies, liberalised foreign trade, deregulated sectors of the economy and privatised state enterprises. Between 1993 and 2005, approximately 66 Moroccan state-owned enterprises were privatised. The rules for oil and gas exploration have been liberalised and concessions for public services in major cities have been granted.

Foreign Investment

Direct foreign investment (FDI) has been authorised in practically all sectors of the economy since 1990, but still represents only a small percentage of GDP. In January 2002 King Mohammed VI announced a series of measures aimed at encouraging foreign investment. The European Free Trade Association (EFTA) came into operation on 4 December 1999 and, in January 2006, the bilateral Free Trade Agreement (FTA) between the United States and Morocco went into effect, the first such agreement in Africa. The US-Morocco FTA eliminates tariffs on 95 per cent of bilateral trade in consumer and industrial products with all remaining tariffs to be eliminated within nine years.

Balance of Payments / Imports and Exports

Export revenues have been rising steadily since 2000, and rose from US$9.78 billion in 2004 to an estimated US$11.72 billion in 2006. Estimates for 2009 put exports at US$13.8 billion, rising to US$17 billion in 2010. Morocco's main export markets were in the EU (over 70 per cent), and India (5.3 per cent). Exports to France represented 25 per cent of the total.

Import costs rose slightly from US$17.5 billion in 2004 to an estimated US$21.22 billion in 2006. In 2009, they cost US$32 billion, rising to US$32 billion in 3020. Main import products include semi-processed goods, machinery and equipment, food and beverages, consumer goods, and fuel. Morocco's main suppliers are the EU (52 per cent), Saudi Arabia (4.4 per cent), China (7.8 per cent) and US (7.1 per cent).

As most of its trade is carried out with EU countries, Morocco has made a bid for EU membership. In 2008, it was granted an Advance Status agreement with the EU.

Central Bank

Bank Al-Maghrib, PO Box 445, 277 Avenue Mohammed V Rabat, Morocco. Tel: +212 37 702626, fax: +212 37 706677 , e-mail: dai@bkam.gov.ma, URL: http://www.bkam.ma Governor: Abdellatif Jouahri

Chambers of Commerce and Trade Organisations

Casablanca Chamber of Commerce, URL: http://www.ccisc.gov.ma
American Chamber of Commerce in Morocco,
URL: http://www.amcham-morocco.com/

MANUFACTURING, MINING AND SERVICES

Primary and Extractive Industries

Phosphates are the most important of the minerals produced in Morocco and 75 per cent of the world's known phosphate reserves originate there. Phosphates play an important role in the production of fertilizers and phosphoric acid. Manganese, lead, silver, and copper are mined in Morocco.

Morocco had proven oil reserves of 1.00 million barrels at the beginning of 2008. However, the country relies heavily on imports, largely from Saudi Arabia, Iran, Iraq, and Nigeria. Oil production in 2011 was an estimated 3,940 bbl/d per day. The kingdom has a crude oil refining capacity of 155,000 barrels per day (January 2011). The Moroccan Office of Hydrocarbons and Mining (ONHYM) is optimistic about finding offshore oil reserves, following discoveries in neighbouring Mauritania.

The state oil company is the Office National de Recherches et d'Exploitation Petrolieres (ONAREP). In March 2000, Morocco modified its hydrocarbons law, offering a 10-year tax break to offshore production firms and reducing the government's stake in future oil concessions to a maximum of 25 per cent. There is progressive liberalization of the energy sector.

At 58 billion cubic feet, Morocco's natural gas reserves are relatively small. Most reserves are located in the Essaouira Basin, with smaller reserves in the Rharb and Pre-Rif basins. Natural gas production in 2011 was estimated at 2 billion cubic feet and and consumption at 7 billion cubic feet meaning Morocco imports around 5 billion cubic feet per year. (Source: Energy Information Administration, EIA)

Energy

Morocco is self-sufficient in electricity, some 75 per cent of which is supplied by thermal generators driven by coal, whilst 25 per cent is generated by hydroelectric plants. According to 2010 estimates, Morocco has an electricity generation capacity of 6.62 GWe, 70 per cent of which is thermal and 30 per cent of which is hydroelectric. Electricity generation rose to 21.13 billion kWh in 2010. Despite Morocco's current self-sufficiency in electricity there is a need to build additional power plants. There has been a successful rural electrification programme and demand is expected to grow. The government has embarked on a electricity generation capacity-build proframm and hopes to double capacity by 2020. Renewables should contribute over 40 per cent by 2020.

Morocco is gradually integrating its electrical grid with those of its neighbors in Africa and Europe. In December 2005, Tunisia, Algeria, and Morocco signed a funding agreement with the EU which will pay for a study on North African-European electricity market integration.

In November 2011 it was announced that Morocco had been chosen as the first location for a €400 bn project to construct a network of solar and windfarms across North Africa and the Middle East. The vast network should supply 15 per cent of Europe's electricity supply by 2050. The Desertec Industrial Initiative (DII) said the first phase of the construction of a 500 MW solar farm is scheduled to start in 2012. The solar far is expected to be sited near Ouarzazate and will use parabolic mirrors to generate heat for conventional steam turbines. DII is a coalition of companies includuding E.ON, Siemens, Munich Re and Deutsche Bank.

In 2009, total energy consumption in Morocco was estimated at 0.609 quadrillion Btu. (Source: EIA)

Manufacturing

Manufacturing is a growing sector of the Moroccan economy. In 2006, industry, including phosphate mining and the energy sector, contributed some 31.2 per cent of GDP. The most important sector is the food products industry. Other significant industries are the textile and paper industries, assembly plants for cars, lorries and tractors, and a number of light consumer goods industries.

The Government is keen to diversify from the traditional agricultural economy and is providing significant incentives to attract foreign investment that will enable Morocco to meet its domestic requirements and create significant export potential, including agricultural equipment and machinery, diesel engines, transport equipment, construction machinery and mining. Morocco has a highly-valued textile industry.

Service Industries

The tourist industry is of growing importance. Morocco's four major cities, Rabat, Meknes, Fes and Marrakesh, are rich in cultural attractions. Long-term plans include the construction of major winter resort areas in the mountains near Marrakesh, seaside resorts and marinas. There are also plans to construct more hotels aimed at business travellers as well as tourists and to increase recreational facilities such as golf courses and casinos.

The tourism industry was adversely affected by the terrorist attacks in the USA in September 2001 and the suicide bombings in Casablanca in May 2003. However, figures for 2004 indicated a recovery in visitor numbers, and in 2006 there were 6.56 million visitors, up 12 per cent on the previous year. The number of hotel beds has increased over the past three years, and occupancy rates have risen by 10 per cent over the same period. Despite the global economic crisis, the tourism industry remains strong. According to latest figures, 8.3 million tourists visited the country in 2009, up by 6 per cent on the previous year.
National Office of Tourism, URL: http://www.tourisme-marocain.com

Agriculture

Morocco has traditionally relied on agriculture, despite insufficient rain. The sector accounts for between 12 and 20 per cent of the economy (depending on weather factors) and employs up to 50 per cent of the workforce. Produce is varied due to an almost European climate in the north, a very dry interior and almost tropical conditions in the south.

There is a lot of subsistence farming, but large mechanised farms are becoming more commonplace. Crops include wheat, barley, oats, maize, peas, lentils, potatoes, and other vegetables as well as cotton, flax and hemp. Morocco also produces essential oils, medicinal plants and forage for animals. In 2004, there were 22.4 million goats and sheep, and 2.7 million cattle. There were six tractors per 1000 hectares in 2003, and no harvesters or threshers.

Agricultural Production in 2010

Produce	Int. $'000*	Tonnes
Olives	1,187,851	1,483,510
Indigenous chicken meat	795,933	558,782
Wheat	700,694	4,876,140
Indigenous cattle meat	507,475	187,858
Tomatoes	472,210	1,277,750
Cow milk, whole, fresh	444,673	1,900,000
Indigenous sheep meat	378,475	139,002
Almonds, with shell	301,501	102,170
Potatoes	251,214	1,604,620
Barley	245,447	2,466,450
Onions, dry	237,615	1,131,320
Apples	213,843	505,641

* unofficial figures

Source: http://faostat.fao.org/site/339/default.aspx Food and Agriculture Organization of the United Nations, Food and Agricultural commodities production

Morocco's coast runs for some 3,500 km. It is the world's leading producer of sardines and its rich coastal waters also produce enormous quantities and varieties of other seafood, including lobster, swordfish and cephalopods. Figures for 2010 put the total catch at 1,136,000 tonnes.

COMMUNICATIONS AND TRANSPORT

Travel Requirements

Citizens of the USA, Canada, Australia and the EU require a passport valid for at least six months from date of entry but do not need a visa for stays of up to 90 days. Other nationals should contact the embassy to check visa requirements.

National Airlines

Morocco is served by a number of foreign airlines as well as Royal Air Maroc.
Royal Air Maroc, URL: http://www.royalairmaroc.com

International Airports

There are 25 air terminals including 10 international airports (Agadir, Al-Hoceima, Casablanca-Mohamed V, Fes-Saiss, Marrakech, Rabat-Sale, Tangiers, Oujda, Laayoune, Dakhla).

Railways

Morocco has 1,907 kilometres of normal track with lines from Casablanca to Algeria via Meknes and Oujda, Casablanca-Marrakech, Casablanca-Tangier-Oujda-Colomb Bechar and Casablanca-Oued-Zem. There are also branch lines to the phosphate and coal mines. In October 2011 construction started on a TGV high-speed rail link connecting Casblanca with Rabat and Tangiers. Trains are due to start running by 2015. The budget for the 219 mile (350 km) rail link is an estimated US$4billion.

MOROCCO

Roads
There are over 57,500 km of roads, 32,000 paved. The border crossing with Algeria is currently closed. Vehicles are driven on the right.

Shipping
There are 21 ports including nine major ones (Casablanca, Tangiers, Kenitra, Safi, Mohamedia, Agadir, Nador, Jorf-Lasfar and Tan-Tan.) Ferries run from Morocco to Morocco, mainly from Spain. Algeciras in Spain, the enclave of Ceuta and Tangier.

HEALTH

In 2008, Morocco spent approximately 7.2 per cent of its total budget on healthcare (up from 4.0 per cent in 2000), accounting for 38.8 per cent of all healthcare spending. Total expenditure on healthcare equated to 5.2 per cent of the country's GDP. Per capita expenditure on health was approximately US$152, compared with US$54 in 2000. Figures for 2005-10 show that there are 20,682 physicians (6.2 per 10,000 population), 29,689 nurses and midwives (8.9 per 10,000 population), 2,668 dentistry personnel, 9,006 pharmaceutical personnel (2.7 per 10,000 population) and 737 environment and public health workers. There are 11 hospital beds per 10,000 population.

According to the latest WHO figures, in 2010, 83 per cent of the population had access to improved drinking water. In the same year, 70 per cent of the population had access to improved sanitation. Diarrhoea accounts for 6 per cent of childhood deaths.

The infant mortality rate (probability of dying by first birthday) was estimated at 33 per 1,000 live births in 2009. The under-fives mortality rate was 38 per 1,000 live births. The main causes of death in children aged under 5 were: prematurity 28 per cent, pneumonia 15 per cent, birth asphyxia 13 per cent, neonatal sepsis 3 per cent, congenital anomalies 12 per cent, and diarrhoea 6 per cent. In 2000-09 approximately 23.1 per cent of children aged less than 5 years were classified as stunted and 9.9 per cent were classified as underweight. Life expectancy at birth in 2009 was 71 years for men and 75 years for women. As at 2009, there was a relatively low prevalence of HIV/AIDS in the country, at 0.1 per cent. (Source: http://www.who.int, World Health Statistics 2012)

EDUCATION

Primary/Secondary Education
Education is free and compulsory through primary school, though many do not attend, particularly girls in rural areas.

Education is divided into three cycles: a primary (compulsory) cycle lasting six years (children aged 6-12 years), a lower secondary cycle lasting three years, and an upper secondary education period of three years. Secondary education is the final cycle before the baccalauréat is obtained. Three different styles of education, the Modern track, which is the continuation of the French system, the Original track, which specialises in Qur'anic teachings and the Technical track, which is vocational.

Figures for 2006 show that 60 per cent of nursery-school aged children attended a pre-primary school. Figures for 2007 show that 86 per cent of girls and 91 per cent of boys were enrolled in primary school, and a gross figure of 56 per cent of children attended secondary school (below the regional average of 66 per cent). Eleven per cent of students went into tertiary education. (Source: UNESCO, UIS, August 2009)

Morocco has 14 public universities: Mohammed V University in Rabat has faculties of law, sciences, liberal arts, and medicine; Karaouine University in Fes, is a longstanding center for Islamic studies and is the oldest university in the Maghreb.

The overall adult literacy rate has remained at around 50 per cent for some years. It is estimated that, whilst the women's literacy rate nationwide is around 39 per cent, in rural areas it drops to only 10 per cent. The regional literacy average is 68.6 per cent. In 2006, just over 26 per cent of government expenditure was spent on education.

RELIGION

The majority of the population are Muslim (99.9 per cent). There are around Jewish inhabitants, and less than 1,000 Christians.

Morocco has a religious liberty rating of 3 on a scale of 1 to 10 (10 is most freedom). (Source: World Religion Database)

COMMUNICATIONS AND MEDIA

The media tend to reflect the official line. Topics such as the monarchy and religion cannot be questioned in the media. Under the Press Law, prison terms may be imposed on transgressors.

Newspapers
Daily newspapers include the Arabic Al-Anbaa, the French language Le Matin (http://www.lematin.ma), and the Arabic Al Massae (URL: http://www.almassae.press.ma/) (http://www.assabah.press.ma). Morocco's official press agency is Maghreb Arab Presse (URL: http://www.map.ma/eng)

Broadcasting
Morocco's state television station is Radio-Television Marocaine (RTM) (http://www.rtm.ma/). In addition, there is the French Medi-1 (URL: http://www.medi1.com/) which also provides radio broadcasts. Satellite telivison is widely available.

Telecommunications
Morocco has a good telephone system which is nearly totally digitalised. The internet is available but expensive. In 2009, there were an estimated 3.5 million mainline telephones in use, and over 30 million mobile phones. Around 13 million Moroccans are connected to the internet according to 2009 figures.

ENVIRONMENT

Carbon dioxide emissions were 38.89 million metric tons in 2005, equivalent to 1.19 metric tons per capita. Both figures show an increase on the previous year. In 2006, Morocco's emissions from the consumption of fossil fuels totalled 34.53 million metric tons of carbon dioxide and in 2010, they equalled 35.66 million metric tons. (Source: EIA)

The major environmental issues affecting Morocco at the moment are desertification due to soil erosion from overgrazing and destruction of vegetation, water supplies contaminated by raw sewerage, the silting of reservoirs and oil pollution of coastal waters.

On an international level Morocco has been involved in conventions on Biodiversity, Climate Change, Climate Change-Kyoto Protocol, Desertification, Endangered Species, Hazardous Wastes, Law of the Sea, Marine Dumping, Ozone Layer Protection, Ship Pollution, Wetlands and Whaling. It has signed but not ratified Environmental Modification.

WESTERN SAHARA
The Sahrawi Arab Democratic Republic
As-Sahrā' al-Ġarbiyyah

Main City: El Aalun (Laayoune) (Population, unofficial estimate: 20,000)

Head of State: Mohamed Abdelaziz (page 1371)

CONSTITUTION AND GOVERNMENT

The area called Western Sahara came under Spanish rule in 1884, and was administered by Spain as a Spanish province until 1976. Both Morocco and Mauritania laid claim to the area. When the Spanish left, Morocco moved into the northern two-thirds of Western Sahara and called it its Southern Provinces. Mauritania laid claim to the southern third and called it Tiris al-Gharbiyya. Following pressure from Polisario, Mauritania withdrew in 1979, and Morocco moved in. The northern two-thirds are now administered by Morocco and the southern third is under control of the The Sahrawi Arab Democratic Republic.

Polisario
In 1973 independence group Frente Popular para la Liberción de Saguia y Rio de Oro (Polisario) was established, with the aim of gaining independence for the Saharan people. In February 1976 Polisario proclaimed the Western Sahara to be the independent state of The Sahrawi Arab Democratic Republic. Since then it has been recognised by over 70 countries including South Africa in 2004.

Madrid Agreement
The International Court of Justice in October 1975 rejected the claims of Morocco and Mauritania over the Western Sahara and recognised the right of the Saharawis to self-determination, and it was agreed that Spain would organise a referendum. The following month King Hassan II of Morocco ordered more than 300,000 Moroccan nationals into the area and this became known as the Green March. Following this the Spanish backed down from organising the referendum and instead agreed a settlement with Morocco and Mauritania in what came to be known as the Madrid Agreement. Spain would agree to end colonial rule and the northern two-thirds of the territory would be partitioned to Morocco and the southern third to Mauritania. The agreement was signed on 14 November 1975.

MINURSO
Between 1976 and 1991 a guerilla war went on between Polisario and Morocco. In April 1991 the UN established MINURSO the United Nations Mission for a Referendum in Western Sahara. The first thing MINURSO did was to establish a ceasefire to come into effect on September 6 1991. Then its brief was to establish who was eligible to vote in a referendum on whether the people of the Western Sahara wanted independence or integration with Morocco. Identification of who was eligible to vote became a key sticking point; Polisario did not want any Moroccans who had settled in the territory following the Green March in 1975 to have a vote and Morocco was worried that its best interests would not be served.

In May 1996 the identification process was suspended. In 1997 talks were held between MINURSO, Morocco and Polisario and the identification process was resumed in December of that year. In October 1998 MINURSO announced it had completed identifying eligible voters apart from three tribal groupings. In 1999 Polisario and Morocco accepted the findings of MINURSO and an appeals process was put into place concerning members of the three tribal groupings and others who felt they were eligible. The appeals process has still to be finished as both sides differ on agreeing all the terms of the appeals including the repatriation of refugees. The Security Council has repeatedly voted for extensions of the mandate of MINURSO.

The Baker Plan

Between 1997 and 2000 UN special envoy James Baker acted as mediator in talks between Polisario and Morocco. Although the two parties agreed to the release of Prisoners of War they still could not reach an agreement about the eligibility of voters for the referendum on independence or integration. In an effort to break the deadlock James Baker introduced a strategy called The Third Way, whereby Saharawis would be autonomous under Moroccan sovereignty with a referendum being held after four years. This plan was rejected by Polisario. A new plan was announced in July 2003 whereby Western Sahara would become a semi-autonomous region of Morocco for a period of five years after which a referendum would be held on independence, integration or semi-autonomy. Morocco rejected this plan and in 2004 James Baker resigned his post. The issue of a referendum is yet to be resolved.

Direct talks between the Polisario Front and the Moroccan government began in June 2007 in the United States; a fourth round took place in December 2010. Talks took place most recently in 2011.

Legislature

The government of The Sahrawi Arab Democratic Republic is in exile in the town of Tindouf, Algeria. The National Parliament, Majlis al-Watani is unicameral and is made up of 51 elected members

Cabinet (as at June 2013)

Prime Minister: Abdelkader Taleb Oumar
Minister for the Occupied Territories and Emigration: Mohammed Lwali Akaik
Minister of Foreign Affairs: Mohamed Salem Ould Salek
Minister of Development: Nema Said Youmani
Minister of the Interior: Hamada Selma Adaf
Minister of Commerce: Abah Sheikh
Minister of Justice and Religious Affairs: Abba Dih Sheikh
Minister of Construction and Reconstruction of Liberated Territories: Bellahi Mohammed Fadl
Minister of Health: Mohammad Lamine Daddy
Minister of Equipment: Sid Ahmed Batal
Minister of National Defence: vacant
Minister of Education: Mariem Salek H'Mada
Minister of Information: Mohamed el Mami Tamek
Minister of Culture: Khadija Hamdi
Minister of Transport: Babiya Chiia
Minister of Co-operation: Hadj Ahmed Barek Allah
Minister of State for Security: Brahim Mohamed Mahmoud
Minister of Youth and Sports: Mohamed Molud Mohamed Fadl
Minister of Social Care and Promotion of Women: Mahfuda Mohamed Rahal
Minister of Training, Human Resources & the Public Sector: Khira Bullahi Abad
Minister of Water and Environment: Hamdi Mayara
Minister of State, Counsellor of the Presidency: Bashir Mostafa El-Sayed
Minister and Adviser to the Prime Minister: Salik Bobih

AREA AND POPULATION

Area

The Western Sahara is in North Africa it borders Morocco to the north, Algeria to the north east, Mauritania to the east and south, and its west coast borders the Atlantic Ocean. It covers an area of 266,000 sq. km. and the terrain is mostly desert flatlands, with mountains to the south and northeast. The climate is hot, dry desert.

To view a map of Western Sahara, please consult http://www.un.org/Depts/Cartographic/map/profile/wsahara.pdf

Population

The population has been estimated at 273,000 (not including around 160,000 Moroccan military). An estimated 165,000 Saharawi refugees are based in camps in Tindouf, Algeria. The main ethnic group is the Saharawis, a nomadic tribespeople. The official language is Arabic, Spanish is widely spoken.

BANKING AND FINANCE

Currency

Moroccan Dirham

The economy is based on nomadic herding, fishing and some phosphate mining.

MANUFACTURING, MINING AND SERVICES

Primary and Extractive Industries

Phosphate mining is carried out in parts of the country and there may be offshore oil deposits.

Agriculture
Agricultural Production in 2010

Produce	Int. $'000*	Tonnes
Indigenous camel meat	3,144	1,500
Goat milk, whole, fresh	2,433	7,251
Indigenous goat meat	1,342	560
Barley	238	2,000
Indigenous sheep meat	191	70
* unofficial figures		

Source: http://faostat.fao.org/site/339/default.aspx Food and Agriculture Organization of the United Nations, Food and Agricultural commodities production

COMMUNICATIONS AND TRANSPORT

Airports

There is an international airport at El Aaiun, there are also airports at Dakhla and Smara.

Shipping

A ferry runs between Wester nSahara and Las Palmas de Gran Canaria.

RELIGION

Islam is the main religion of the Western Sahara.

COMMUNICATIONS AND MEDIA

The Moroccan state-owned broadcaster, Radio Television Marocaine (URL: http://www.snrt.ma/) operates a radio service from Laayoune and relays a televison service. The telecommunication system is limited.

STATES OF THE WORLD

805

MOZAMBIQUE
Republic of Mozambique
República de Moçambique

Capital: Maputo (Population estimate, 2011: 1.4 million)

Head of State: Armando Emilio Guebuza (President and Commander in Chief of the Armed Forces) (page 1434)

National Flag: Three equal horizontal bands of green (top), black, edged in white, and yellow with a red isosceles triangle based on the hoist side. Centred in the triangle is a yellow five-pointed star bearing a crossed rifle and hoe in black superimposed on an open white book.

CONSTITUTION AND GOVERNMENT

Constitution
Following the Lusaka Agreement between the Portuguese government and the Mozambique Liberation Front (FRELIMO), signed on 7 September 1974, power was exercised by a Transitional Government. The new constitution was drawn up by FRELIMO and approved by its Central Committee on 20 June 1975, five days before independence.

The first revision of this Constitution took place in 1977, and enshrined elected people's power within a system of Assemblies, from the national legislative People's Assembly to Assemblies at a local level, the country's smallest administrative unit.

The second constitutional revision took place in July 1986. The national People's Assembly session that approved it also elected a national committee for revising the Constitution, and presented a preliminary draft to the Assembly at the end of 1987. At the beginning of 1990 the Frelimo Party approved a new draft revision of the Constitution, which was widely debated throughout the country in the following months.

The ratification of this constitution by the Mozambican Parliament was the outcome of a long process in the full tradition of Mozambique's participatory democracy. It was also the culmination of a period of transformation underway since 1986, characterised by the introduction of an economic restructuring which gave a greater role to private enterprise and ended the single-party system. In the new constitution and multi-party system there is a distinction between the Party and government. Further modifications were made in 2004. The president serves a five-year term, renewable only once.

The president heads the executive branch of government, and is elected by the people. The president is the head of state and head of the government, as well as commander-in-chief of the armed forces. The president appoints the prime minister and the Council of Ministers.

To consult the full constitution, please visit: http://www.mozambique.mz/pdf/constituicao.pdf

Recent Events
Mozambique has been hit by devastating floods in 2000, 2001 and again in 2007.

In 2005 work began on the Unity Bridge. The bridge will connect Mozambique and Tanzania across the Ruvuma river. The bridge will be 720 metres long and carry two lanes of traffic. It is expected to be completed in 2008 at a cost of US$33 million.

In July 2006 the World Bank agreed to a proposal put forward by the G8 nations to cancel the majority of Mozambique's debt.

In October 2009 Mozambique secured a $500 million loan from the EU, the Danish and Dutch governments. The loan was to construct a railway line linking the northern Moatize coal mines with the port of Nacala, the project is scheduled to be completed in 2015.

President Guebuza was re-elected in the 2009 elections. There were allegations of fraud.

In February 2010 a former minister, Antonio Munguambe, was found guilty of corruption and embezzlement and sentenced to 20 years in prison.

In September 2010 several people were killed when the police opened fire on people protesting about the cost of food.

Diplomatic tensions arose with Malawi in 2010 over a new waterway connecting the two countries. Mozambique impounded the first barge to use the new route.

In October 2011, a giant offshore gas discovery was reported.

In April 2012, a dispute with Portugal ended when Portugal finally agreed to give up its stake in the Cahora Bassa hydro-electric scheme.

Legislature
Mozambique's unicameral legislature is known as the Assembly of the Republic (*Assembléia da Republica*), whose 250 members are directly elected for a five-year term.
Assembly of the Republic, Allembleia da Republica, C.P. 1516, Maputo, Mozambique. Tel: +258 1 400826, URL: http://www.mozambique.mz/parlamen

Cabinet (as at June 2013)
Prime Minister: Alberto Vaquina
Minister of Foreign Affairs and Co-operation: Hon. Oldemiro Balói (page 1382)
Minister of Defence: Hon. Filipe Nyusi
Minister of the Interior: Hon. Ricardo Mondlane
Minister of Finance: Hon. Manuel Chang
Minister of Development and Planning: Hon. Aiuba Cuereneia
Minister of Mineral Resources: Hon. Esperanca Bias
Minister for Environment: Hon. Alcinda Abreu
Minister of Education: Augusto Jone
Minister of Culture: Armando Artur Joao
Minister of Science and Technology: Luis Pelembre
Minister of Industry and Trade: Hon. Armando Inrogo
Minister of Tourism: Carvalho Muaria
Minister of Justice: Hon. Maria Benvinda Levy
Minister of Youth and Sport: Fernando Sumbana Junior
Minister of Public Service: Vitoria Dias Diogo
Minister for Women and Social Affairs: Hon. Iolanda Cintura
Minister of Public Works and Housing: Hon. Cadmiel Muthemba
Minister of Fisheries: Hon. Victor Manuel Borges
Minister of Energy: Hon. Salvador Namburete
Minister of Health: Hon. Alexandre Jaime Manguele
Minister of Labour: Hon. Maria Helena Taipo
Minister of Transport and Communications: Hon. Paulo Zucula
Minister for State Administration: Hon. Carmelita Namashalua
Minister of Agriculture: Hon. Jose Pacheco Condungua
Minister of Veterans' Affairs: Hon. Mateus Oscar Kida
Minister in the Presidency for Social Affairs: Feliciano Gundana
Minister for the Office of the President: Antonio Sumbana
Minister of Parliamentary Affairs in the Office of the President: Adelaide Amurane

Ministries
Office of the President, Avenida Julius Nyerere 2000, Maputo, Republic of Mozambique. Tel: +258 21 4911121, fax: +258 21 492068, URL: http://www.presidencia.gov.mz/
Office of the Prime Minister, Praca da Marinha Popular 4, Maputo, Republic of Mozambique. Tel: +258 21 426861, fax: +258 21 426881
Ministry of Foreign Affairs and Co-operation, Avenida 10 de Novembro 620-40, Maputo, Republic of Mozambique. Tel: +258 21 327000, fax: +258 21 327020, e-mail: minec@minec.gov.mz, URL: http://www.minec.gov.mz
Ministry for State Administration, Rua da Radio Mozambique 112, Maputo, Republic of Mozambique. Tel: +258 21 426666, fax: +258 21 428565, URL: http://www.mae.gov.mz
Ministry of Agriculture and Rural Development, C.P. 1406, Praca dos Herois Mocambicanos, Maputo, Republic of Mozambique. Tel: +258 1 460011 / 460105, fax: +258 1 460055 / 460187 / 460676, e-mail: cda@map.gov.mz, URL: http://www.map.gov.mz
Ministry for Defence and Security in the President's Office, Avenida Julius Nyerere 1780, Maputo, Republic of Mozambique. Tel: +258 1 491121, fax: +258 1 492087/492068
Minister in the Presidency for Parliamentary, Municipal & Provincial Assembly Affairs, Avenida Julius Nyerere 1780, Maputo, Republique of Mozambique. Tel: +258 21 491121, fax: +258 21 492065
Ministry of the Environment, C.P. 2020, Avenida Acordos e Lusaka 2115, Maputo, Republic of Mozambique. Tel: +258 1 465843, fax: +258 1 465849, e-mail: jwkacha@virconn.com
Ministry of National Defence, Avenida Mártires de Mueda 280 & 373, Maputo, Republic of Mozambique. Tel: +258 21 492081, fax: +258 21 491619
Ministry of Education and Culture, C.P. 34, Avenida 24 de Julho 167, Maputo, Republic of Mozambique. URL: http://www.mec.gov.mz/
Ministry of Higher Education, Science and Technology, 1586 Julius Nyerere Ave., Maputo, Republic of Mozambique. Tel: +258 1 499491, fax: +258 1 490446, URL: http://www.mct.gov.mz/
Ministry of Industry and Trade, Praça 25 de Junho 300, Maputo, Republic of Mozambique. Tel: +258 21 426093, fax: +258 21 421301, e-mail: infomic@mic.gov.mz, URL: http://www.mic.gov.mz
Ministry of Tourism, C.P. 4101, 300, Av. 25 de Setembro 1018, Maputo, Republic of Mozambique. Tel: +258 1 306210, fax: +258 306212, URL: http://www.moztourism.gov.mz/
Ministry of Justice, Avenida Julius Nyerere 33, Maputo, Republic of Mozambique. Tel: +258 21 491613, fax: +258 21 494264
Ministry of Youth and Sport, Avenida 10 de Novembro 1196, Maputo, Republic of Mozambique. Tel: +258 21 312172, fax: +258 21 308844, e-mail: addamvalia@mijude.gov.mz, URL: http://www.mjd.gov.mz
Ministry for Women and Social Action, Rua da Tchamba 86, Maputo, Republic of Mozambique. Tel: +258 21 497901, fax: +258 21 492757, URL: http://www.mmas.gov.mz/
Ministry of Public Works and Housing, Avenida Karl Marx 606, Maputo, Republic of Mozambique. Tel: +258 21 430028, fax: +258 21 421369, URL: http://www.dnep.gov.mz
Ministry of Finance, C.P. 272, Rua Dr. Egas Moniz, Praca da Marinha, Maputo, Republic of Mozambique. Tel: +258 1 306808 / 420648 / 420328, fax: +258 1 306261 / 420137 / 428170, e-mail: dnpo@dnpo.uem.mz, URL: http://www.mozambique.mz/governo/mpf/dnpo
Ministry of Mineral Resources, Avenida Fernão Magalhães 34, Maputo, Republic of Mozambique. Tel: +258 21 314843

Ministry of Labour, C.P. 258, Praca 24 de Junho, 2351, Maputo, Republic of Mozambique. Tel: +258 1 428527 / 424071 / 427051, fax: +258 1 421881, URL: http://www.mitrab.gov.mz
Ministry of Transport and Communications, Avenida Martires de Inhaminga 336, Maputo, Republic of Mozambique. Tel: +258 21 320223, fax: +252 21 359816, e-mail: celular@zebra.uem.mz, URL: http://www.mtc.gov.mz
Ministry of Fisheries, Rua Marquês 285, Maputo, Republic of Mozambique. Tel: +258 21 357100, fax: +258 21 302528, http://www.mozpesca.gov.mz
Ministry of the Interior, Avenida Olof Palme 46/48, Maputo, Republic of Mozambique. Tel: +258 21 303510, fax: +258 21 420084
Ministry of Health, Avenida Eduardo Mondlane 1008, Maputo, Republic of Mozambique. Tel: +258 21 427131, fax: +258 21 427133, http:// www.misau.gov.mz
Ministry of Energy, Avenida 25 de Setembro 1218-3, Maputo, Republic of Mozambique. Tel: +258 21 303265, fax: +258 21 313971
Ministry of Planning and Development, Avenida Ahmed Sekou Touré 21, Maputo, Republique of Mozambique. Tel; +258 21 490006, e-mail: dgi@mpd.gov.mz, URL: http://www.mpd.gov.mz
Ministry of Science and Technology, Avenida Patrice Lumumba 770, Maputo, Republique of Mozambique. Tel: +258 21 352800, URL: http://www.mct.gov.mz
Ministry of Tourism, Avenida 10 de Novembro 1196-40, Maputo, Republique of Mozambique. Tel: +258 21 303650, fax: +258 21 306212
Ministry of Veterans, Rua General Pereira d'Eça 35, Maputo, Republique of Mazambique. Tel: +258 21 494912

Political Parties
Democratic Movement of Mozambique (MDM); Front for the Liberation of Mozambique (Frelimo); Mozambique National Resistance (Renamo).

Elections
The country's first democratic elections took place in 1994 and Joaquim Chissano was elected president. He was re-elected in 1999 with 52 per cent of the vote, whilst his party Frelimo won a majority of 133 of the Assembléia da Republica's 250 seats. Results of both elections were disputed by the opposition Mozambique National Resistance (Renamo) alliance which was leading the legislative polls in the initial results, but polled only 39 per cent in the final results.

The elections were held on 1-2 December 2004. Under the terms of the constitution Joaquim Chissano was unable to stand for re-election as president. Frelimo, now led by Armando Guebuza, retained both the presidency and its majority in the Assembly. Results were contested by the opposition. Mr Guebuza was inaugurated as president in February 2005.

On October 28, 2009 Mozambique held presidential, legislative, and provincial assembly elections. Mr Guebuza won with approximately 75 per cent of the presidential vote. His Frelimo party won 192 of the 248 parliamentary seats, Renamo 48, and MDM 8.

Diplomatic Representation
US Embassy, Avenida Kenneth Kuanda 193, (PO Box 783) Maputo, Republic of Mozambique. Tel: +258 1 492797, fax: +258 1 490114, e-mail: library@mail.tropical.co.mz, URL: http://maputo.usembassy.gov
Ambassador: Leslie Rowe
British High Commission, Av. Vladimir I Lenine 310, Caixa Postal 55, Maputo, Republic of Mozambique. Tel: +258 1 320111/2/5/6/7, fax: +258 1 321666, e-mail: bhc@virconn.com, URL: http://ukinmozambique.fco.gov.uk/en/
High Commissioner: Shaun Cleary
Republic of Mozambique Embassy, 1990 M Street, NW, Suite 570, Washington, DC 20036, USA. Tel: +1 202 293 7146 fax: +1 202 835 0245, e-mail: embamoc@aol.com, URL: http://www.embamoc-usa.org/
Ambassador: Amelia Sumbana
Republic of Mozambique High Commission, 21 Fitzroy Square, London, W1T 6EL, United Kingdom. Tel: +44 (0)20 7383 3800, fax: +44 (0)20 7383 3801, URL: http://www.mozambiquehighcommission.org.uk
High Commissioner: Carlos dos Santos
Permanent Mission of Mozambique to the United Nations, 420 East 50th Street New York, NY 10022, USA. Tel: +1 212 644 5965, fax: +1 212 644 5972, e-mail: mozambique@un.int, URL: http://www.un.int/mozambique/
Ambassador: H.E. Antonio Gumende

LEGAL SYSTEM

The legal system is based on Portuguese civil law and traditional customs. There is a Supreme Court, provincial, district and municipal courts. The 1990 constitution established an independent judiciary, with judges nominated by other jurists instead of designated by administrative appointment. However, the president continues to appoint the justices of the Supreme Court. In 2012, President Guebuza appointed seven more judges to the Supreme Court, bringing the number in total to 16. The new judges include Attorney General Augusto Paulino who will transfer to the Supreme Court when his term as Attorney-General ends in 2017.

The civil and criminal justice system is run by the Ministry of Justice, whilst the military justice system is under the joint supervision of the Ministries of Defense and Justice. The Supreme Court hears appeals from both systems. Provincial and district courts are below the Supreme Court, and there are special courts such as administrative courts, customs courts, fiscal courts, maritime, and labor courts. Local customary courts handle property, divorce, and other social and family issues.

There have been recent incidents of serious human rights abuses in Mozambique, including unlawful killings by security forces (the government prosecuted the perpetrators). Prison conditions are life threatening, and there have been several deaths. Arrests can be arbitrary. The judiciary suffers from a lack of qualified personnel and financial resources, and is influenced by the ruling party.

The death penalty was abolished in 1990, the most recent execution was carried out in 1986.

Attorney General: Augusto Paulino

LOCAL GOVERNMENT

Mozambique is divided into 11 provinces, including Maputo City which has the status of a province. The provinces (and their capitals) are: Cabo Delgado (Pemba), Niassa (Lichinga), Nampula (Nampula), Tete (Tete), Zambezia (Quelimane), Manica (Chimoio), Sofala (Beira), Inhambane (Inhambane), Gaza (Xai-Xai), and Maputo (Maputo). Each province is headed by a Governor who is appointed by the president.

AREA AND POPULATION

Area
Mozambique is situated in south-east Africa. It stretches along 2,570 km of coast between the Rovuma River in the north and the Maputo River in the south. The landward border is 2,470 km. long. To the north is Tanzania and to the south, South Africa. On the west, Mozambique has borders with Malawi, Zambia, Zimbabwe, Swaziland and South Africa. Mozambique covers a total area of 801,590 sq. km. The terrain is mostly coastal plains, rising to uplands in the centre of the country and plateaus in the north-west, and a mountainous region in the west.

The climate is tropical to sub-tropical.

In early 2000 Mozambique was hit by floods following heavy rainfall. At one point the Limpopo River was over ten miles wide. Nearly 700 people died and millions were made homeless. The full effect on the economy was severe. Mozambique was again hit by severe flooding the following year, this time in the Zambezi Valley.

To view a map, visit http://www.un.org/Depts/Cartographic/map/profile/mozambiq.pdf

Population
Mozambique's population according to 2010 estimates was 23.391 million. The majority of the population (51 per cent) is aged between 15 and 60 years, with 44 per cent aged under 15 years. The median age is 18 years. Approximately 38 per cent of the population lives in urban areas.

The official language is Portuguese. Bantu languages are widely spoken.

Births, Marriages, Deaths
According to 2010 estimates, the birth rate is 37.7 births per 1,000 population, whilst the death rate is 15.3 deaths per 1,000 people. Average life expectancy at birth is 47 years for males and 51 years for females. Healthy life expectancy is 43 years. The infant mortality rate is an estimated 92 deaths per 1,000 live births. The average fertility rate is 4.9 children per female. (Source: http://www.who.int, World Health Statistics 2012)

Public Holidays 2014
1 January: New Year's Day
3 February: Heroes Day
8 March: Women's Day
1 May: Labour Day
25 June: Independence Day
7 September: Lusaka Agreement Day
25 September: Armed Forces Day
4 October: Peace Day
25 December: Family Day

EMPLOYMENT

Despite the fact that Mozambique's economy has been growing steadily over the past few years, a skills shortage is hindering further development. The main stumbling block is low adult literacy, at just 45 per cent, and one of the world's lowest school enrolment ratios, at just 25 per cent.

Mozambique's labour force was estimated to be 9.85 million in 2010 and is primarily engaged in agricultural work (over 80 per cent), with services (12 per cent) and industry (6 per cent) making up the balance.

It has been estimated that for every 100 persons of working age there are 110 dependants.

Recent estimates indicate that there are 8 million women in Mozambique, but whilst overall participation rate of the labour force (15-64 years) is 53.3 per cent, that of women is 50.4 per cent. It is estimated that female participation in leadership posts in the civil service in 1993 did not exceed 10 per cent. An analysis of incomes by source indicates that most women derive their income from the traditional agricultural sector.

BANKING AND FINANCE

The financial centre is Maputo.

Currency
The unit of currency is the meticales (MT) = 100 centavos.

MOZAMBIQUE

GDP/GNP, Inflation, National Debt
Mozambique's economy has been badly affected by years of conflict. It has transformed itself from the world's poorest country at the beginning of the 1990s to Africa's second-fastest growing economy, with average GDP growth of nearly 8 per cent per year since 1990, helped by aluminium mining. Poverty levels are now below 55 per cent compared to 70 per cent in 1996. Despite the strong economic growth it remains one of the poorest countries in the region and per capita income is below the regional average. Problems with governance remain. The government has been carrying out extensive reforms to the economy including the privatization of many state owned enterprises. The economy has been transformed again by the discovery of off-shore gas reserves. Coal reserves have also been discovered. The rising cost of living caused riots in 2010 and the government put in subsidies and other fiscal measures to try to reduce the cost of living.

GNP was put at US$7,662.9 million in 2007, with a growth rate of 7.2 per cent. GDP for 2006 was put at US$6,833.0 million and US$6,678.51 million in 2005. The respective growth rates were 8.0 per cent and 8.4 per cent. Figures for 2009 show that GDP grow 4.5 per cent and 6.5 per cent in 2010. GDP was estimated to be US$9.5 billion in 2010, rising to US$11.5 billion in 2011. Per capita income in 2010 was put at US$415. Mozambique's main GDP-contributing sectors are services (40 per cent), agriculture (21 per cent), and industry (31 per cent).

Inflation was 12.7 per cent in 2006. It fell to an estimated 8 per cent in 2007. It was estimated to be 3 per cent in 2009, rising to 13 per cent in 2010. It fell to an estimated 10.2 per cent in 2011.

Total external debt was recorded at US$4,930 million in 2003. In 2005, the British Chancellor Gordon Brown announced that Britain was to cancel Mozambique's total debt to Britain of £80 million; in addition Britain would pay 10 per cent of the country's debt owed to international lenders such as the IMF and the World Bank. Heavily indebted countries benefiting from this scheme must use the money saved for health, education and poverty programmes. In July 2006, under a plan set out by the G8 nations, the World Bank cancelled most of Mozambique's debt. External debt was estimated to be US$4.5 billion in 2011.

Foreign Investment
Gross investment in GDP rose from 45.9 per cent in 1990 to an estimated 55.3 per cent in 1995. This relatively high rate of investment is mainly due to the high level of foreign assistance in support of the government's policy reform and reconstruction programmes. Mozambique relies heavily on external assistance which in recent years has accounted for over 50 per cent of GDP and provided over 63 per cent of the government's budget. Foreign direct investment was estimated to be US$800 million in 2010.

Balance of Payments / Imports and Exports
Mozambique's main export trading partners are the EU, South Africa, Zimbabwe, India, the US and Japan. Major import trading partners are South Africa, the EU, the US, Japan, Pakistan and India. Major exports are aluminium, prawns, cashews, sugar, cotton, citrus and timber. Major imports are machinery and equipment, mineral products, metals, chemicals, food and textiles. Exports have increased dramatically within the last ten years: in 1997 they were worth US$230 million in 1997. They virtually doubled to US$703 million in 2001 to over US$925 million by 2004 and have continued to increase, largely due to aluminium exports.

External Trade, US$ million

	2005	2006	2007
Trade balance	-721.3	-632.94	-1,025.58
Exports	1,745.30	2,381.06	3,709.85
Imports	2,466.60	2,914.00	4,735.43

Source: African Development Bank

Exports were estimated to be US$2.3 billion in 2010 and imports US$3.8 billion.

Mozambique is one of 14 sub-Saharan countries that constitute the Southern African Development Community (SADC).

Central Bank
Banco de Moçambique, PO Box 423, Av. 25 de Setembro 1679, Maputo, Mozambique. Tel: +258 1 428150/9, fax: +258 1 429721, e-mail: info@bancomoc.uem.mz, URL: http://www.bancomoc.mz
Governor: Ernesto Gove

MANUFACTURING, MINING AND SERVICES

Primary and Extractive Industries
Mozambique has natural resources of coal, gold, marble, bauxite, bentonite, turmalines, quartz, aquamarines and garnet.

Energy
Mozambique has plentiful hydropower, coal, gas and forestry reserves. More than 100 sites have been identified for possible hydropower generation with a combined average energy output of 75,000 gWh/year and potential installed capacity of about 12,000 MW. So far only 2,200 MW capacity has been installed. Coal deposits exist extensively throughout central and western Mozambique. Proven reserves are estimated at about 87 million tons; however, the estimates of the reserves exceed 3 billion tons. Mozambique exports a samll amount of coal . Some 800 km north of Maputo, the Pande gas field has been discovered with proven reserves of 60 billion cubic metres and 70 per cent of its gas recoverable. A large natural off-shore gas field was discovered in October 2011. The field is estimated to contain upto 425 billion cubic metres of gas. The field is approximately 40 km off the coast. Figures for 2011 put total reserves of natural gas at 5 trillion cubic feet.

In 2011, Mozambique consumed an estimated 22,000 barrels of oil per day. In 2011 Mozambique produced 135 billion cubic feet of natural gas and consumed 18 billion cubic feet meaning it exported 117 billion cubic feet. In 2007 it produced 0.03 million short tons of coal and consumed 0.01 million tons. In 2010 Mozambique produced 16 billion kWh of electricity, consuming 10 billion kWh.

Manufacturing
The industrial sector accounted for about 31 per cent of GDP in 2007. The sector's production is centred around the processing of agricultural exports (tea, sugar, cashew nuts) and use of imported raw materials to produce commodities for local consumption (soap, shoe manufacturing, grain milling, oil, etc). Production also takes place of titanium ore, aliminium, textiles, cement, asbestos, tobacco and glass.

Mozal has invested significantly in Mozambique with a giant smelting plant. It produces 500,000 tonnes of aluminium a year and employs over 1,000 workers.

Service Industries
Following peace after the civil war, there has been substantial investment in the tourism sector by the private sector, both local and foreign. It is estimated that tourism has a potential to contribute US$80 million to the country's export earnings, or 10 per cent of the current levels of exports. Figures for 2006 show that Mozambique received 578,000 tourists, generating tourism receipts of US$145 millions.

Agriculture
Mozambique is chiefly an agricultural country and agricultural products still account for a large proportion of output. The agricultural sector contributed nearly 35 per cent of Mozambique's GDP in 1998, although the sector was badly affected by the devastating floods in early 2000. Mozambique also suffered a drought in 2002 which affected many areas including those previously flooded. Figures for 2006 estimated the agricultural contribution to GDP at 22 per cent.

Major food crops include rice, maize, beans, vegetables, cassava and citrus. The main export crops are cashew nuts, tea, cotton, sugar and copra. In 2001 an estimated 40,000 jobs were lost in Mozambique's cashew nut industry as a result of a World Bank decision to end state tariffs, which allowed local processors to purchase Mozambican nuts more cheaply than other countries.

Agricultural Production in 2010

Produce	Int. $'000*	Tonnes
Cassava	595,439	5,700,000
Maize	233,257	1,878,000
Indigenous pigmeat	149,415	97,197
Tobacco, unmanufactured	136,978	86,000
Pulses, nes	106,941	205,000
Sugar cane	91,944	2,800,000
Cotton lint	82,894	58,000
Sweet potatoes	69,486	920,000
Cashew nuts, with shell	58,821	67,200
Sorghum	57,492	395,000
Indigenous goat meat	56,356	23,520
Indigenous cattle meat	50,476	18,685

* unofficial figures
Source: http://faostat.fao.org/site/339/default.aspx Food and Agriculture Organization of the United Nations, Food and Agricultural commodities production

It is estimated that of the total land area of 78.6 million ha, about 46.0 per cent is considered suitable for arable use. However, only some 3.4 million ha, or about 10 per cent of the arable land, is estimated to be cultivated. About 90 per cent of the area under production in the last few years is thought to have been cultivated by the family sector. In 1991, the private sector was estimated to have accounted for 86 per cent of the marketed output of food crops and 71 per cent of export crops.

Mozambique has about 19 million ha of productive woodland ranging from eucalyptus and pine to rare hardwoods which were a major export in colonial times. The role of the private sector is rising, notably from South African private interests in the rehabilitation of saw mills and in reforestation.

The sustainable fishing catch of Mozambique is estimated at 500,000 tons of fish and 14,000 tons of prawns. Since independence, prawns and shrimps have become major exports and total annual fish catches have shown an overall increase. Figures for 2010 put the total fishing catch at 150,000.

COMMUNICATIONS AND TRANSPORT

The transport and communications sector in Mozambique accounts for 10.4 per cent of GDP and about one quarter of the country's export earnings. The country's ports and transport corridors serve Zimbabwe, South Africa, Swaziland, Botswana, Malawi, Zambia and the Democratic Republic of Congo.

Travel Requirements
Citizens of the USA, Canada, Australia and the EU require a passport valid for six months beyond the length of stay, a return/onward ticket and a visa, apart from Portuguese nationals who do not need a visa. Other nationals should contact the embassy to check visa requirements.

National Airline
The national airline is *Linhas Aereas de Mozambique (LAM)*. URL: http://www.lam.co.mz

International Airports
There is a good internal air service, as well as a regular service to Durban and to South Africa (Johannesburg). There are also flights to Lisbon, Paris, Sofia, Maseru (Lesotho), Harare, Rio de Janeiro, Dar es Salaam, Lusaka, Luanda, Berlin, Tananarive (Malagasy Republic) and Manzini (Swaziland).

Railways
3,288 km total; 3,140 km 1.067-meter gauge; 148 km 0.762-metre narrow gauge;

Roads
Total 26,498 km; 4,593 km paved; 829 km unpaved gravel, crushed stone, stabilised earth; 21,076 km unimproved earth. Vehicles are driven on the left.

Shipping
The principal ports are Maputo in the south, Beira in the centre and Nacala in the north. The three ports have good road and rail links to South Africa, Zimbabwe, Zambia, Malawi and Swaziland.

HEALTH

Health services seriously declined over the five-year period 1985-89. The combined destruction, attrition and inaccessibility due to the war led to a virtual standstill in programmes for the expansion of the health system. According to WHO estimates, in 2000-10 there were 548 physicians (less than 1 per 10,000 population), 6,214 nurses and midwives (3 per 10,000 population), 817 pharmaceutical personnel and 159 dentistry personnel. In the same period there were an estimated 8 hospital beds per 10,000 population.

In 2008, Mozambique spent approximately 12.6 per cent of its total budget on healthcare, accounting for 75.2 per cent of all healthcare spending. Total expenditure on healthcare equated to 4.7 per cent of the country's GDP. Per capita expenditure on health was approximately US$21, compared with US$14 in 2000.

The average daily calorie intake is estimated at 77 per cent of the minimum daily requirement, compared with 93 per cent for sub-Saharan Africa. Approximately 47 per cent of children aged less than 5 were classified as stunted and 21.2 per cent as overweight.

Recent figures suggest that only 420,000 of Maputo's 1.4 million city residents had a water supply to their home, and most of them only for certain hours. In 2008, an estimated 77 per cent of the urban population and 28 per cent of the rural population had access to an improved water source. In the same period, 38 per cent of the urban population and 17 per cent of the rural population had sustainable access to improved sanitation. In the past several years of drought and poor rainfall, water supply contracted substantially, particularly in the rural areas, creating conditions where diseases such as cholera thrive.

AIDS continues to present a major problem in Mozambique, with the more than one million adults, over 60 per cent of them women, suffering from HIV/AIDS. The HIV/AIDS prevalence rate was estimated to be 11.9 per cent in 2009. TB, malaria and cholera have also afflicted the population of Mozambique in recent years. In 2007, there were 2,622 reported cases of cholera and 6.3 million cases of malaria. An estimated 7 per cent of the population (2000-07) sleep under insecticide-treated nets. Approximately 23 per cent of those with fever received anti-malarial treatment. The current TB rate is just over 104 notified cases per 100,000 of the population, according to the World Health Organization.

Average life expectancy was 51 years in 2008. The infant mortality rate (probability of dying by age 1) in 2009 was 96 per 1,000 live births. The child mortality rate (under 5 years) was 142 per 1,000 live births. The main causes of childhood mortality are: prematurity causes (10 per cent), diarrhoea (12 per cent), pneumonia (18 per cent), HIV/AIDs (14 per cent) and malaria (12 per cent). (Source: WHO)

EDUCATION

Education services and establishments were adversely affected by civil war. From 1983 to 1992, 3,995 rural primary schools, comprising 68 per cent of the primary school network, were destroyed or closed, affecting 1.2 million pupils. Consequently, by 1992, only 60 per cent of the school age population had access to primary school education.

The rate of school enrolment is 64 per cent for children aged 11 to 12, and 52 per cent for children aged 13 to 15. The rate of primary school enrolment was estimated at 62 per cent in 1996.

It is estimated that over 85 per cent of the employees in the civil service have only completed primary school levels, which is a serious constraint to sustainable economic growth. Figures for 2007 show that just 3 per cent of boys and 2 per cent of girls were enrolled in secondary school. The total number of university graduates in 1995 was estimated at about 3,000.

The government has embarked on a programme to improve education in Mozambique and in 2005 it announced that there were some 9,000 operational primary schools. Most of the schools are heavily over subscribed and there are still not enough teachers. In 2005 the pupil:teacher ratio in primary schools was 65 to 1. Illiteracy is estimated at 67 per cent, compared with 45 per cent for sub-Saharan Africa. In 2006 the literacy rate was estimated at 43.8 per cent for adults (57.0 males and 32.0 per cent females). An estimated 52.3 per cent of young people (15-24) were literate (58.3 males, 46.3 females). (Source: UNESCO)

RELIGION

Although more than 150 religious groups are registered in Mozambique, many have no more than a few hundred followers. Recent census figures show that 36 per cent of the population were Roman Catholics, 29 per cent described themselves as belonging to other Christian groups and 18 per cent were Muslims. This last figure was less than was expected.

Mozambique has a religious liberty rating of 9 on a scale of 1 to 10 (10 is most freedom). (Source: World Religion Database)

COMMUNICATIONS AND MEDIA

Freedom of expression is the media is included in the constitution but criminal libel laws exist. The state media is accused of not allowing full expression of opposition views. The print media's influence is limited by low circulation figures and high hevels of illiteracy.

Newspapers
Noticias; Diaro de Mocambique; Domingo; Demos; Savana; Zambeze.

Broadcasting
Televisao de Mozambique (URL: http://www.tvm.co.mz/) and Radio Mozambique are state run. Radio Mozambique broadcasts in Portuguese, English and several indigenous languages. Radio coverage reaches virtually all parts of the country. There are some private radio broadcasters in operation.

Telecommunications
Telephone lines extend over 47,312 km. Inter-continental telecommunications traffic is handled through an earth station near Maputo, while there are regional links with neighbouring countries. The domestic telephone service satisfies about 60 per cent of expressed demand with nearly 75,000 telephone lines in use. Figures for 2008 estimated that around 4 million mobile phones were in use. Internet access is available, and figures for 2008 show that over 350,000 people were regular internet users.

ENVIRONMENT

Civil strife and drought in the hinterland have led to increased migration to urban and coastal areas with adverse environmental consequences. The already inadequate public services and utilities have been stretched beyond capacity and coastal mangrove forests have been decimated for fuelwood and building materials.

Deforestation is a major concern. It has been estimated that 40 per cent of the wooded areas have been degraded to scrubland and that 70 per cent of the mangrove forests along the coastal strip have been lost over the last two decades. The mangroves constitute the breeding grounds for shrimp and protect the fragile region from coastal erosion. Traditional slash and burn techniques have led to soil degradation and erosion. It is estimated that about 120,000 ha of forest is lost annually due to shifting agriculture and bush-fires.

Rivers have been polluted by industrial and domestic effluent which is discharged directly into the river without primary treatment.

Mozambique is a party to the following international environmental agreements: Biodiversity, Climate Change, Climate Change-Kyoto Protocol, Desertification, Endangered Species, Hazardous Wastes, Law of the Sea, Ozone Layer Protection, Ship Pollution, and Wetlands.

According to figures from the EIA, in 2010 Mozambique's emissions from the consumption of fossil fuels totalled 1.73 million metric tons of carbon dioxide.

STATES OF THE WORLD

MYANMAR

Myanmar Naingngandaw

Capital: Yangon, formerly Rangoon. (Population estimate, 2007: 5.8 million). In November 2005, the administrative capital was moved to Nay Pyi Taw, in central Myanmar (population estimate: 200,000).

Head of State: Lt. Gen. Thein Sein (page 1511)

First Vice President: Nyan Tun

Second Vice President: Dr Sai Mauk Kham

National Flag: A horizontal tricolour flag of yellow, green and red with a five-pointed white star in the middle.

CONSTITUTION AND GOVERNMENT

Constitution

Formerly a member of the British Commonwealth, Burma achieved independence and status as a republic in 1948 and existed as a parliamentary democracy for the next 14 years. In March 1962, however, the army took control and, abolishing all state institutions, established a socialist state. The military regime changed the name of the Union of Burma to the Union of Myanmar in June 1989. However, the leaders of Burma's democracy movement who won the 1990 elections were not in favour of the change of name.

Up to 1998 the Pyithu Hluttaw (People's Assembly) was the Highest Organ of state power. It elected the Council of State and delegated the executive and judicial powers of the State to central and local organs of state power. The Council of State was composed of 29 members. Fourteen represented the 14 states and divisional territorial units, while 14 represented the Pyithu Hluttaw as a whole. The Prime Minister was the 29th member. The Council of Ministers was the highest executive organ of the State. The Council of People's Justices was the highest judicial organ of the State. The Council of People's Attorneys protected and safeguarded the Socialist system as well as the rights and privileges of the working people. The Council of People's Inspectors was the highest organ of inspection of public undertakings. The People's Councils at state, division, township, ward and village-tract level were the Local Organs of State Power.

In September 1988, however, the armed forces leader, General Saw Maung, took over power and abolished the People's Assembly, the Council of State and the Council of Ministers, replacing them with the State Law and Order Restoration Council (SLORC). A number of National League for Democracy (NLD) members fled to neighbouring Thailand and set up a government in exile there. In April 1992 the government began discussions with the NLD and set up a Constitutional Convention to consider a future constitution. However, whilst discussions have continued ever since, little progress has been made.

In November 1997 the Junta changed its name from the State Law and Order Restoration Council (SLORC) to the State Peace and Development Council (SPDC) and purged some senior generals. The SPDC currently consists of a chairman, vice chairman, one secretary, and 14 members. There were originally three secretaries of the SPDC, but following the November 2001 cabinet re-shuffle it was announced that the second and third secretaries would not be replaced.

In 2003 Khin Nyunt became Prime Minister and announced that he would hold a convention charged with drafting a new constitution. In May the National Convention got underway despite the fact that the NLD boycotted it. In September 2007, the Military government declared the constitutional talks complete and closed the National Convention, which lays down the basic principles for the new constitution. In April 2008 the proposed constitution was published and a referendum for its adoption was set for May. The proposals were overwhelmingly endorsed and came into force after the 2010 elections. The SDC was dissolved in March 2011 when the post-election cabinet was sworn in.

Under the 2010 Constitution, the head of state is a president, elected by an electoral college composed of members from both houses of the People's Assembly. The presidential term is five years, renewable only once. The military members of the People's Assembly chose the first vice president. Under the 2010 Constitution, the president is also the head of government, and appoints the members of the Union Government, subject to approval by the People's Assembly. The president also chairs the National Defence and Security Council.

To consult the constitution, please visit: http://www.wipo.int/wipolex/en/details.jsp?id=6187.

International Relations

Myanmar is a member of ASEAN and other member nations form Myanmar's main trading partners. In September ASEAN Foreign Ministers voiced their disappointment when Aung San Suu Kyi's house arrest was extended and urged Myanmar to work closely with the UN to achieve a peaceful transition to becoming a democratic nation.

Since 1996, the EU has had a Common Position on Myanmar which implements restrictive measures designed to disrupt those working against reform and progress. In October 2007 EU Ministers agreed additional restrictive measures targeted at those sectors which provide a source of revenue to the regime, specifically timber, metals and gems. The EU has also pledged to provide humanitarian and development assistance to the people of Myanmar and will help to assist the process of transition. Following local elections in April 2012 when Aung San Suu Kyi stood and won her seat, the EU announced it would be suspending sanctions against the country. Sanctions concerning arms would remain in place.

Recent Events

In 1990 elections were held and the National League for Democracy (NLD) won over 80 per cent of the vote which the military then refused to recognise. The opposition leader Aung San Suu Kyi was released from six years of house arrest in 1995. In September 2000, she was prevented from leaving the capital, Rangoon, and was under virtual house arrest until May 2002. Since January 2001, the military regime has held talks with Aung San Suu Kyi, released more than 270 political prisoners and re-opened over 50 NLD offices. A year after her release from house arrest, and following a clash between NLD and government supporters, she was detained again. In September 2003 she underwent a major operation and, following her release from hospital, was once more detained at her home. In November 2004 the government freed thousands of political prisoners, including Min Ko Naing, leader of the 1988 pro-democracy student demonstrations. In May 2007 it was announced that Aung San Suu Kyi's house arrest was to be extended for a further year.

In November 2005 it was announced that the capital city would move to Nay Pyi Taw an area near the remote town of Pyinmana in central Myanmar. The move was completed in March 2006.

The summer of 2007 saw a series of protests and dissent following an increase of fifty per cent on fuel prices, which led to hikes in the cost of staple commodities such as rice and oil. Most of the protests were led by activists and members of the main opposition party - the National League for Democracy; then they were joined by Buddhist monks in protests in the central town of Pakokku. The army arrested some of the monks, which led to a further 400 monks demanding an apology for the treatment of their colleagues, and threatening to withhold religious duties from anyone connected to the army (being shunned by the monks is the highest form of punishment for a Buddhist). On September 23 an estimated 20,000 monks and nuns took to the streets to protest; the Alliance of All Burmese Buddhist Monks called Burma's military rulers "the enemy of the people" and pledged to continue peaceful demonstrations. In September Aung San Suu Kyi was allowed to leave her house to greet monks; it was her first appearance in public since 2003. The military then began to crack down on the protesters; by October the streets were quiet but there was a heavy military presence. It was estimated that 31 people were killed during the protests.

Senior General Than Shwe appeared in public in March 2008 to celebrate Armed Forces Day. During his speech he indicated that power would be handed over to a civilian government following polling in 2010.

On May 3 2008 the low-lying Irrawaddy delta area of Myanmar was hit by Cyclone Nargis. Initially up to 15,000 people were believed to have been killed with many more reported missing. The military announced that they would be willing to accept help from outside agencies and also said they would postpone the referendum on the new constitution in the worst affected areas from 10 May to 24 May. In the days following the cyclone it became apparent that the death toll was much higher than originally thought, with up to 100,000 people dead and more than two million homeless. The military restricted foreign aid coming in and neighbouring countries, members of ASEAN, began talks to reach a compromise with the military regime. By the end of May the death toll was put at 134,000 and the military was still restricting foreign aid workers from getting to the Irrawaddy delta area. The planned constitution referendum went ahead, and the government announced that 92 per cent had voted in favour of the draft constitution.

Also in May the military junta extended Aung San Suu Kyi's house arrest. In November 2008 the UN declared that the government was violating its own countries laws by detaining Aung San Suu Kyi and called for immediate release. In May 2009 it was announced that Aung San Suu Kyi would stand trial for a violation of her house arrest. An American citizen swam across the lake bordering her garden and entered her house he was also arrested. Her defence team maintain that she did not know or invite the man and is not responsible for his actions. Many feel that her arrest is a pretext for keeping her under house arrest until the elections due in 2010 have taken place. In October 2009 Aung San Suu Kyi was allowed to begin talks with military leaders and was allowed to meet with Western diplomats. During a meeting in November with the Asean group US President Obama called for her release. In February 2010 Tin Oo, Aung San Suu Kyi's deputy was freed; he had spent over 10 years either in prison or under house arrest.

In May 2009 Myanmar was hit by Cyclone Nargis. The worst affected area was the Irrawaddy Delta where the UN said thousands of people needed help.

In September 2008 over 9,000 prisoners were granted amnesties; among them were just a few political prisoners.

In October 2010 a new flag was officially introduced, previously the flag had been red with a canton blue charged with ears of rice and a cog wheel and surrounded by fourteen white stars. The new flag is a horizontal tricolour flag of yellow, green and red with a five-pointed white star in the middle.

The main military-backed party, the Union Solidarity and Development Party (USDP), won elections held in November 2010, the first elections to be held for 20 years. Two weeks after the election Aung San Suu Kyi who had been prevented from taking part in the elections was released from house arrest. On January 2011, the government authorized internet connection for Aung San Suu Kyi.

Transfer of power to the new government was completed in March 2011. A human rights commission was established six months later. In October more than 200 political prisoners were freed and new labour laws permitting unions were passed. In November 2011 the NLD party said it was to re-register as a political party. It had been banned for 20 years and had boycotted the 2010 election because of laws preventing Aung San Suu Kyui from standing in the election. These laws have now been changed.

Following local elections in April 2012 when Aung San Suu Kyi stood and won her seat, the EU announced it would be suspending sanctions against the country in recognition of the historic changes which had been made. Sanctions concerning arms would remain in place. The following month the Indian prime minister, Manmohan Singh, paid the first official visit by an Indian prime minister since 1987. He signed 12 agreements to strengthen trade and diplomatic ties.

A state of emergency was declared in the Rakhine State on the Bangladeshi border in June 2012 after violence broke out between Rakhine Buddhists and the Muslim Rohingya minority.

In July 2012, 20 political prisoners were released as part of a presidential amnesty. Opposition leader Aung San Suu Kyi called for all political prisoners to be freed; a further 330 remained in jail.

In August 2012, the government announced it was to end media censorship.

The European Commission offered Myanmar more than $100 million in development aid in Novermber 2012. The US president, Barack Obama, visited the country and urged more reforms.

In January and February 2013 the army launched an attack on Laiza, the largest town under Kacin rebel control. Political talks began.

In May 2013, President Thein Sein visited the US.

Legislature

The People's Assembly (Pyidaungsu Hluttaw) is bicameral. The lower chamber, the House of Representatives (Pyithu Hluttaw) has 440 members. The upper chamber, the House of Nationalities (Amyotha Hluttaw) has 224 members. The military has 25 per cent of the seats in each house; the remainder of the seats are directly elected. Both houses serve a five-year term.

Cabinet (as at June 2013)

Minister of Agriculture and Irrigation: U Myint Hlaing
Minister of Foreign Affairs: Wunna Maung Lwin
Minister of National Planning and Economic Development: Dr Kan Zaw
Minister of Finance and Revenue: U Win Shein
Minister of Transport: Col (ret'd) Nyan Tun Aung
Minister of Co-operatives: Brig.-Gen (ret'd) Kyaw Hsan
Minister of Rail Transportation: Maj.-Gen. Zayar Aung
Minister of Energy: Brig.-Gen. (ret'd) Than Htay
Minister of Education: U Mya Aye
Minister of Labour, Employment and Social Security: U Maung Myint
Minister of Health: U Pe Thet Khin
Minister of Commerce: U Win Myint
Minister of Telecommunications: Thura Thien Tin
Minister of Religious Affairs: Brig.-Gen. Thura Myint Maung
Minister of Science and Technology: Dr Ko Ko Oo
Minister of Culture: U Aye Myint Kyu
Minister of Information: U Aung Kyi
Minister of Electric Power: U Khin Maung Soe
Minister of Construction: U Kyaw Lwin
Minister of Sports: U Tint Hsan
Minister of Environment Conservation and Forestry: U Win Tun
Minister of Home Affairs: Lt. Gen. Ko Ko
Minister of Mines: Dr Myint Aung
Minister of Hotels and Tourism: U Htay Aung
Minister of Defence: Vice Senior General Wai Lwin
Minister of Border Affairs: Maj.-Gen. (ret'd) Thein Htay
Minister in the Office of the President: Col. Thein Nyunt
Minister in the Office of the President: Maj.-Gen. (ret'd) Soe Maung
Minister in the Office of the President, Finance: Gen. (ret'd) Hla Htun
Minister in the Office of the President, Economic Planning: Brig.-Gen. (ret'd) Tin Naing Thein
Minister in the Office of the President, National Reconciliation: Gen. (ret'd) Aung Min
Minister in the Office of the President, Industry: Lt.-Gen. (ret'd) Soe Thein
Minister of Livestock and Fisheries: Brig. (ret'd) Ohn Myint
Minister of Relief and Resettlement: Dr Myat Myat Ohn Khin
Minister of Industry: Brig.-Gen. (ret'd) Aye Myint
Auditor General: Lt.-Gen. (ret'd) Thein Htalk
Attorney General: U Tun Shin

Ministries

Ministry of Agriculture and Irrigation, Thirimingala Lane, Kaba Aye Pagoda Road, Yankin Township, Yangon, Myanmar. Tel: +95 1 663270, fax: +95 1 663984, URL: http://www.myanmar.com/Ministry/agriculture/default.html
Ministry of Commerce, 228/240 Strand Road, Yangon, Myanmar. Tel : +95 1 287034 / 256163, fax : +95 1 289578, URL: http://www.myanmar.com/commerce/index.html
Ministry of Communications, Posts and Telegraphs, 80 Corner of Merchant Street and Theinbyu Street, Botataung Township, Yangon, Myanmar. Tel: +95 1 293112, fax: +95 1 292977, URL: http://www.mcpt.gov.mm/
Ministry of Defence, Alanpya Paya Road, Yangon, Myanmar. Tel: +95 1 281611
Ministry of Finance and Revenue, 26A Set Hmu Road, Yankin Township, Yangon, Myanmar. Tel: +95 1 543745, fax: +95 1 543621, URL: http://www.myanmar.com/Ministry/finance/

Ministry of Foreign Affairs, Pyay Road, Dagon Township, Yangon, Myanmar. Tel: +95 1 221544, fax: +95 1 222950, e-mail: mofa.aung@mptmail.net.mm, URL: http://www.mofa.gov.mm/
Ministry of Health, 27 Pyidaungsu Yeiktha Road, Dagon Township, Yangon, Myanmar. Tel: +95 1 533170, URL: http://www.myanmar.com/Ministry/health/
Ministry of Home Affairs, Corner of Saya San Road and No.1 Industrial Road, Yankin Township, Yangon, Myanmar. Tel: +95 1 549208, fax: +95 1 549663, URL: http://www.myanmar.com/Ministry/Moha/default.htm
Ministry of Industry, 56 Kaba Aye Pagoda Road, Yankin Township, Yangon, Myanmar. Tel: +95 1 666134, fax: +95 1 666135
Ministry of Information, 365-367 Bo Aung Gyaw Street, Kyauktada Township, Yangon, Myanmar. Tel: +95 1 245642, fax: +95 1 289274
Ministry of Military Affairs, Alanpya Paya Road, Yangon Myanmar.
Ministry of Rail Transportation, 88 Theinbyu Street, Brotataung Township, Yangon, Myanmar. Tel: +95 1 292769, fax: +95 1 292769 / 282267
Ministry of Religious Affairs, Kaba Aye Pagoda Road, Mayangon Township, Yangon, Myanmar. Tel: +95 1 665621, fax: +95 1 665728, URL: http://www.myanmar.com/Ministry/religious/
Ministry of Science and Technology, 6 Kaba Aye Pagoda Road, Mayangon Township, Yangon, Myanmar. Tel: +95 1 667246, fax: +95 1 667423
Ministry of Social Welfare, Relief and Resettlement, Theinbyu Street, Brotataung Township, Yangon, Myanmar. Tel: +95 1 276697, URL: http://www.myanmar.com/Ministry/social-welfare/
Ministry of Sport, Thuwunna National Stadium, Thingangyun Township, Yangon, Myanmar. Tel: +95 1 577381, URL: http://www.myanmar.com/Ministry/sport/default.htm
Ministry of Transport, 80 Theinbyu Street, Botataung Township, Yangon, Myanmar. Tel: +95 1 296816, fax: +95 1 296824, URL: http://www.myanmar.com/Ministry/Transport/

Political Parties

The main opposition party:
National League for Democracy (NLD), URL: http://www.angelfire.com/ok/NLD
General Secretary: Aung San Suu Kyi
Other parties include:
Union Solidarity and Development Party (USDP); National Unity Party (NUP); Shan Nationalities League for Democracy (SNLD).

Elections

Myanmar (formerly Burma) was under military rule from 1962-2011. In 1990 elections were held and the National League for Democracy (NLD) won over 80 per cent of the vote, which the military then refused to recognise. Myanmar brought in new election laws and elections took place in November 2010. The NLD refused to take part, they felt the elections would be biased in view of the fact that 110 seats were reserved for the military. The main military-backed party, the Union Solidarity and Development Party (USDP), won 259 seats in the lower house and 129 seats in the upper house but opposition groups alleged widespread fraud.

The newly elected legislature elected former prime minister Thein Sein as president in February 2011. Thein Sein gained 405 votes. Tin Aung Myint Oo won 171 votes and became first vice president and Sai mauk Kham won 75 votes and became second vice president.

In April 2012 by elections were held for 46 seats. For the first time since 1990 the NLD was able to stand in elections and won 43 out of the 46 seats. Aung San Suu Kyi stood as one of the candidates and won her seat.

Diplomatic Representation

Embassy of Myanmar, 19a Charles Street, Berkeley Square, London, W1J 5DX, United Kingdom. Tel: +44 (0)20 7499 4340, fax: +44 (0)20 7409 7043, URL: http://www.myanmarembassyuk.co.uk/
Ambassador: Kyaw Myo Htut
Embassy of Myanmar, USA, 2300 South Street, NW, Washington, DC 20008, USA. Tel: +1 202 332 9044, fax: +1 202 332 9046, e-mail: info@mewashingtondc.com, URL: http://www.mewashingtondc.com/
Ambassador: Than Swe
British Embassy, 80 Strand Road, POB 638, Rangoon, Myanmar. Tel: +95 1 370863, fax: +95 1 370866, e-mail: BE.Rangoon@fco.gov.uk, URL: http://ukinburma.fco.gov.uk
Ambassador: Andrew Heyn
US Embassy, 581 Merchant Street, POB 521, Yangon, Myanmar. Tel: +95 1 379880 / 379881, fax: +95 1 256018, e-mail: info.rangoon@state.gov, URL: http://rangoon.usembassy.gov
Ambassador: Derek J. Mitchell
Permanent Representative of the Union of Myanmar to the United Nations, 10 East 77th Street, New York, NY 10021, USA. Tel: +1 212 535 1310 / 1311, fax: +1 212 737 2421, e-mail: myanmar@un.int
Permanent Representative: Tin Kyaw

LEGAL SYSTEM

The judiciary is not independent of the executive branch, and there is no guarantee of a public trial, despite the fact that ex-colonial British laws and legal systems remain intact. Burma does not accept compulsory International Court of Justice jurisdiction. The highest court in the land is the Supreme Court - the High Court. There are also divisional courts and township courts. There are Martial Law Courts, staffed by military officers, in operation in various parts of the country.

Reform of the constitution is currently been discussed ahead of elections in 2015. Campaigners are hoping for that the constitution will provide for less executive control over the judiciary and greater judicial independence.

MYANMAR

The regime continues to commit severe human rights abuses. Security forces allow custodial deaths to occur and have been associated with other extrajudicial killings, disappearances, rape, and torture. The government has detained civic activists indefinitely and without charges. The army has targeted ethnic minority villagers, whilst the government routinely infringes on citizens' privacy and restricts freedom of speech, press, religion, and movement. The government does not allow domestic human rights non-governmental organizations (NGOs) to function independently. Workers' rights remain restricted. The government does not prosecute or punish those responsible for human rights abuses. Aung San Suu Kyi, general secretary of the National League for Democracy (NLD), was finally released from house arrest in 2010.

Martial law is applied on fairly regular intervals; in 2013 the government imposed it on four townships following ethnic clashes.

Myanmar retains the death penalty, though no executions have taken place since 1988. In 2008, Myanmar voted against the Resolution on a Moratorium on the Use of the Death Penalty at the UN General Assembly.

Chief Justice of the Supreme Court: Tun Tun Oo

LOCAL GOVERNMENT

For administrative purposes Myanmar is divided into seven divisions (Ayeyarwady, Bago, Magway, Mandalay, Sagaing, Tanintharyi, and Yangon) and seven states (Chin State, Kachin State, Kayin State, Kayah State, Mon State, Rakhine State, and Shan State).

AREA AND POPULATION

Area
Situated in the western part of Indo-China, Myanmar has borders with China in the north and east, Bangladesh in the north-west, Laos in the east, Thailand in the east and south, and the Bay of Bengal in the south and west. The total area of the Union is 676,552 sq. km (261,218 sq. miles). Mountains enclose the land in the north, east and west and surround a central valley along the Irrawaddy River. Most of the population is concentrated in this area. Rainforests extend over most of the land area. The climate is tropical with monsoon rains.

To view a map, visit http://www.un.org/Depts/Cartographic/map/profile/myanmar.pdf

Population
Estimates for 2010 put the population at 47.963 million with an annual population growth rate of 0.6 per cent for the period 2000-10. Figures for 2005 put the population density is around 84 people per sq km. Just over 64 per cent of the population is aged between 15 and 60, with some 26 per cent aged up to 15 years, and 8 per cent aged over 60. The median age is 28 years.

Nearly 27 per cent of the population live in urban areas. Myanmar's chief towns are: Rangoon, with 3,598,980 inhabitants; Mandalay, 417,000; Moulmein, 202,000; Bassein, 336,000; Akyab, 143,000; and Taunggyi, 149,000.

Just over two-thirds of the total population are Burmese. Other ethnic groups have survived in the country (the Kayan, Kashin, and others) and minority groups of Indians, Tamils and Chinese also exist. Burmese is the official language.

Births, Marriages, Deaths
According to 2010 estimates the birth rate is 17.3 births per 1,000 of the population, whilst the death rate is 8.9 deaths per 1,000 population. Average life expectancy at birth in 2008 is 61 years for men and 67 years for women. Healthy life expectancy is put at 50 years. The infant mortality rate is 50 deaths per 1,000 live births, whilst the total fertility rate is 2.3 children born per woman. It is estimated that a total of 330,000 people were living with HIV/AIDS in 2003, with 20,000 deaths in that year. (Source: http://www.who.int, World Health Statistics 2012)

Public Holidays 2014
4 January: Independence Day
12 February: Union Day
2 March: Peasants' Day
16 March: Full Moon of Tabaung*
27 March: Tatmadaw Day (Armed Forces Day)
12 April: Thingyan (Water Festival)
16 April: Myanmar New Year *
1 May: May Day (Workers' Day)
5 May: Full Moon of Kason*
11 July: Full Moon of Wason (Beginning of Buddhist Lent)*
18 July: Martyrs' Day
8 October: Full Moon of Thadingyut (End of Buddhist Lent)*
22 November: Tazaungdaing (Festival of Lights)*
8 December: National Day*
25 December: Christmas Day
* The date varies according to the Myanmar calendar year.

EMPLOYMENT

Of a total labour force estimated at 31.6 million in 2010, Myanmar had an estimated unemployment rate of nearly 6.0 per cent. The majority of the labour force is employed in agriculture (70 per cent), with 23 per cent in the services sector, and 7 per cent in industry.

A new law was signed by the president in October 2011 permitting trade unions and also giving workers the right to strike. Unions have not been allowed to operate since 1962.

BANKING AND FINANCE

Currency
The unit of currency is the kyat (MMK) of 100 pya.

GDP/GNP, Inflation, National Debt
Despite good natural resources, Myanmar is a poor country. Economic mismanagement and high inflation continue. Myanmar's economy is based on: (private sector) agriculture, light industry, and transport; and (state sector) heavy industry, energy, and rice. Myanmar is also one of the largest producers of illicit opium in the world, and a major supplier of methamphetamines. Agriculture still contributes the greatest proportion towards GDP, 54 per cent coming from agriculture, livestock, fisheries and forestry in 2004. An increase in gas exports have meant that in recent years the economy has been growing. Figures for 2009 put GDP at US$27.5 billion.

Official figures put GDP growth at 13.6 per cent in 2006, while unofficial estimates put it at -0.5 per cent. According to the Asian Development Bank Myanmar has had 10 per cent growth in the last few years. The following table shows the makeup of GDP in recent years. Figures are in million Kyats at current market prices:

Sector	2008	2009	2010
Agriculture	11,773,735	12,916,382	14,729,014
Mining	254,409	331,351	367,042
Manufacturing	4,917,322	6,136,416	7,905,155
Electricity, gas & water	218,167	337,675	418,532
Construction	1,236,065	1,518,309	1,839,335
Trade	6,175,062	6,890,046	8,037,819
Transport & communications	3,731,536	4,586,601	5,577,546
Finance	20,938	27,392	31,417
Public administration	399,679	551,654	866,630
Others	506,375	609,840	735,452
Net factor income from abroad	349	222	314
GDP by Industrial origin	29,233,288	33,905,666	40,507,942
Source: Asian Development Bank

In 2010, agriculture contributed 36.4 per cent of agriculture, industry 26 per cent and services 37.6 per cent.

Inflation remains high, at nearly 39 per cent, according to 2007 estimates, in 2010 inflation had fallen to 10 per cent. External debt was an estimated US$6,011 million in 2004.

Foreign Investment
Foreign investment, which was on the increase in the early to mid-1990s, declined sharply from 1999 as a result of political pressure from the West and an increasingly hostile business environment. Wide-ranging economic sanctions have been imposed on Myanmar by the US, the European Union, Canada, Australia, Japan, and Korea in response to alleged human rights abuses, drug trafficking and repression of the opposition party, the NLD. Prior to sanctions, Myanmar received foreign direct investment in 1998-99 totalling nearly US$879 million. Most came from the UK (US$289 million) and Singapore (US$279 million). The oil and gas industry received the greatest proportion of foreign investment (32 per cent at the end of the first quarter 2001), followed by manufacturing (21 per cent), and hotels and tourism (14 per cent).

Balance of Payments / Imports and Exports
Major export products include raw rubber, base metals and ores, foodstuffs (particularly pulses, beans and rice), fish (including prawns), and teak. Major import products include transport equipment, machinery, food, textiles, petroleum products, and construction equipment. Main export trading partners are Thailand (31 per cent in 2003), the US (10 per cent), India, China, and Japan. Main import trading partners are China (31 per cent in 2003), Singapore (22 per cent), Thailand, South Korea, Malaysia, and Japan.

The following table shows the trade balance in recent years; figures are in million Kyats. Source: Asian Development Bank.

External Trade	2008	2009	2010
Exports, fob	37,028	41,289	49,107
Imports, cif	24,874	22,837	35,508
Trade balance	12,154	18,452	13,598

Exports grew by 4.9 per cent in 2008, 11.5 per cent in 2009 and by 18.9 per cent in 2010. Imports grew by 35 per cent in 2008, -8.2 per cent in 2009 and by 55.5 per cent in 2010. Main trading partners in 2010 were Thailand (US$2,590 million), India (US$1,198 million) and China (US$873 million). Main import trading partners were China (US$3,828 million), Thailand (US$2,280 million) and Singapore (US$1,271 million).

Exports by Principal Commodity, million Kyats

Commodity	2003	2004
Teak & other hardwood	2,049	2,242
Pulses & beans	1,731	1,283
Rice & rice products	131	180
Base metals & ores	340	547
Raw rubber	99	87
Source: Asian Development Bank

Central Bank

Central Bank of Myanmar, PO Box 184, 26A Settmu Road, Yankin T/S, Yangon, Myanmar. Tel: +95 1 543511 , fax: +95 1 543621

Chambers of Commerce and Trade Organisations

Burma Chinese Chamber of Commerce, 312/314 Strand Road, Yangon, Myanmar.
The Union of Myanmar Chamber of Commerce and Industry, 74/86 Bo Sun Pet Street, Yangon, Myanmar. Tel: +95 1 77103

MANUFACTURING, MINING AND SERVICES

Primary and Extractive Industries

Myanmar is well endowed with mineral resources. The main minerals produced are lead, silver, zinc, copper, tin and gold. Rubies, sapphires, diamonds and jade are mined, as are coal, gypsum, baryte, limestone, dolomite, bentonite, chromite, fireclay, fluoride and granite.

The exploration, development, production and transportation of crude oil and natural gas in Myanmar are the responsibility of Myanmar Oil and Gas Enterprise (MOGE). MOGE operates 14 oil and gas fields in onshore areas for the production of oil and gas.

Total oil production in 2011 was 20.79 thousand barrels per day (up from 9.70 thousand barrels per day in 1999), of which 2011.0 thousand barrels per day was crude oil. Refined oil in 2001 was 57 thousand barrels per day , most of which was distillate, gasoline, and residual. Myanmar imported 24,000 barrels of oil per day in 2011 (down from 29.71 thousand barrels per day of oil in 1999), most of which was crude oil and distillate. Oil exports fell from 1.40 thousand barrels per day in 1999 to zero in 2001 and since then oil has been imported to meet demand. Consumption in 2011 was estimated at 20,000 barrels per day.

Gross production of natural gas was 421 billion cubic feet in 2011 and consumption that year was 118 billion cubic feet, the increase in gas exports had led to a growth in the economy. Figures for 2011 show that 303 billion cubic metres of gas were exported.

Coal production totaled 1.483 million short tons in 2010. Coal consumption in the same year was 1.116 million short tons .

Energy

Myanmar Electric Power Enterprise (MEPE) is responsible for planning, design, construction, maintenance and operation of electricity supplies. Over 60 per cent of Myanmar's electricity is produced from fossil fuel, whilst the balance is produced by hydro-power.

Total 2010 electricity installed capacity was 1.71 GWe, of which 77 per cent was thermal and 23 per cent hydroelectric. Generation in the same year was 7.35 billion kilowatthours (kWh). Consumption in 2010 was 6.09 billion kWh.

Construction of the controversial Myitsone hydro-electric dam was halted in 2011. The Chinese-backed dam is at the head of the Irrawaddy river in the northern Kachin state. It was due to be completed in 2019 and was to be 500ft high, creating a reservoir of some 300 sq miles, displacing thousands of ethnic Kachin villagers.

Manufacturing

Industry contributes about 13 per cent of Myanmar's GDP annually, according to 2002 estimates. The major manufacturing industries are textiles and footwear, cement, paper, cotton, wood products, pharmaceuticals, fertilizer and construction materials.

The following table shows manufacturing production in recent years. Figures are in thousand metric tons:

Manufactured goods	2003	2004	2005
Cement	592.3	542.0	551.8
Fertilizer, compound	142.3	95.3	100.1
Bricks & tiles (mil. pcs.)	82.6	77.7	72.3
Salt	78.8	77.1	113.1
Sugar	54.9	53.8	38.7
Paper	18.1	16.7	19.3
Cotton yarn	3.5	4.1	4.1

Source: Asian Development Bank

Service Industries

The services industry accounted for about 33 per cent of annual GDP in 2004 and employed 25 per cent of the workforce. In the 1990s there was a construction boom in the country linked to the drive to increase tourism.

Agriculture

Agriculture contributes about 55 per cent towards Myanmar's GDP, according to 2004 estimates.

Agricultural Production in 2010

Produce	Int. $'000*	Tonnes
Rice, paddy	8,109,981	33,204,500
Indigenous chicken meat	1,176,445	825,919
Beans, dry	1,155,280	3,029,800
Indigenous pigmeat	704,810	458,490
Vegetables fresh nes	700,869	3,719,300
Sesame seed	587,328	880,000
Groundnuts, with shell	538,809	1,341,000
Fruit fresh nes	471,196	1,350,000
Indigenous cattle meat	405,363	150,058
Pigeon peas	377,089	724,200

- continued		
Cow milk, whole, fresh	355,313	1,138,600
Sugar cane	305,384	9,700,000

* unofficial figures

Source: http://faostat.fao.org/site/339/default.aspx Food and Agriculture Organization of the United Nations, Food and Agricultural commodities production

Myanmar has a long coastline of 2,832 km. The total catch for 2010 was estimated at 3,060,000 tonnes.

Myanmar is rich in forest resources, with forests covering about 50.87 per cent of the total land area. There are over 8,570 different plant species, including 2,300 tree species, 850 kinds of orchids, 97 varieties of bamboo and 32 different types of cane. Reserved forest area is 101,425 sq. km. Myanmar has the largest share of the worldwide teak market and produces about 0.6 million cubic metres per year.

COMMUNICATIONS AND TRANSPORT

Travel Requirements

Citizens of the USA, Canada, Australia and the EU require a passport valid for six months beyond the length of stay and a visa, apart from transit passengers continuing their journey by the same or first connecting aircraft, provided holding valid onward or return documentation and not leaving the airport. Other nationals should contact the embassy to check visa requirements. Tourist visas are only valid for two months.

The Government of Myanmar strictly controls travel to, from, and within the country. The authorities rarely issues visas to persons with occupations they deem "sensitive," including journalists. Visitors should have sufficient cash to cover expenses for the duration of their visit; travellers cheques and credit cards are not accepted anywhere.

National Airlines

Myanmar Airways International, URL: http://www.maiair.com

Railways

All major urban centres are connected by rail. The total railway network runs for 3,990 km. The journey time from Yangon to Mandalay is around 13 hours.

Roads

Myanmar has a total road network of 28,000 km, of which nearly 3,500 km is paved and 24,500 km is unpaved. New roads and bridges have been constructed in the Ayeyarwardy Division to lessen the dependency on waterways transportation. Some roads can become impassable during the rainy season which is May to October. Vehicles are driven on the right.

Ports and Harbours

Myanmar has waterways running for nearly 13,000 km, almost a quarter of which is navigable by large vessels. The Main international port of Myanmar is Yangon which handles over 90 per cent of the sea-borne trade of the country. Myanma Five Strae Line (MFSL) is the State-owned shipping line which operates coastal and transport services with a fleet of twenty one vessels.

Waterways

Myanmar has an extensive system of river ferries most of which are government run.

HEALTH

In 2006, Myanmar spent an estimated 1.0 per cent of its total budget on healthcare, accounting for 11.3 per cent of all healthcare spending. Total expenditure on healthcare equated to 2.1 per cent of the country's GDP. Out-of-pocket expenditure accounted for almost all private expenditure on health. External resources accounted for 9.5 per cent. Per capita expenditure on health was approximately US$145, compared with US$3 in 2000. Figures for 2005-10 show that there are an estimated 23,709 physicians (4.6 per 10,000 population), 41,424 nurses and midwives (8 per 10,000 population) and 2,549 dentistry personnel. There are 6 hospital beds per 10,000 population.

According to the latest WHO figures, in 2010 approximately 83 per cent of the population had access to improved drinking water. In the same year, 76 per cent of the population had access to improved sanitation.

The infant mortality rate in 2009 was 50 per 1,000 live births. The child mortality rate (under 5 years) was 66 per 1,000 live births. The main causes of childhood mortality are: prematurity (14 per cent), birth asphyxia (10 per cent), diarrhoea (8 per cent), pneumonia (17 per cent), malaria (1 per cent) and HIV/AIDs (1 per cent). (Source: http://www.who.int, World Health Statistics 2012)

EDUCATION

A unified system of education has been introduced since 1948. Education is free and there are plans to make it compulsory. There are now three grades of schools, Primary, Middle and High. Burmese has replaced English as the language of instruction, and English as a compulsory second language is introduced from the fifth grade. The Social Welfare Directorate is endeavouring to impart social education along with the eradication of illiteracy. There are also special schools for the deaf, dumb and blind.

Primary education is officially compulsory. There are 37,008 primary schools, 2,058 middle schools and 858 high schools. There are 45 universities and colleges. The state budget for education was US$96 million in 2001.

NAMIBIA

RELIGION

The main religion of the country is Buddhism (74 per cent), followed by Christianity (7.9 per cent), Islam (3.8 per cent), Hinduism (1.7 per cent), and Animists make up 10.3 per cent.

Myanmar has a religious liberty rating of 2 on a scale of 1 to 10 (10 is most freedom). (Source: World Religion Database)

COMMUNICATIONS AND MEDIA

The media has been strictly controlled at all levels, and all news from politics to sports news has been heavily censored. However in August 2012, the government announced that reporters would no longer have to submit their work to state censors before publication. A new media law to abolish political censorship was also announced and access to news sites unblocked. For the first time users should have unrestricted access to political content. The government also pledged to support the private media.

Newspapers
The military government maintained strict control of Myanmar's media until August 2012 when an end to pre-publication censorship was announced. Daily newspapers include: Botahtaung, Guardian, and Kyehmon. In addition, the State Peace and Development Council (SPDC) (now dissolved) disseminated information through Myanmar Alin and the English-language New Light of Myanmar.

In April 2013, four private newspapers appeared for the first time.

Broadcasting
Estimates put the number of television receivers at 250,000. Broadcasting is state run and two stations are operated, TV Myanmar and MRTV-3, another television station is run by the army. Estimates put the number of radio receivers at just over 4 million. Apart from the state run Radio Myanmar, a station broadcast by the opposition is based in Norway called Democratic Voice of Burma, and broadcasts via shortwave.

Telecommunications
Telecommunications are poor and further hindered by an unreliable power supply. According to 2012 estimates there were 500, 000 internet users. Until August 2012 access was tightly controlled.

ENVIRONMENT

Myanmar is a party to the following international environmental agreements: Biodiversity, Climate Change, Climate Change-Kyoto Protocol, Desertification, Endangered Species, Law of the Sea, Ozone Layer Protection, Ship Pollution, Tropical Timber 83, and Tropical Timber 94.

Major environmental issues include inadequate sanitation of the water system, deforestation, and industrial pollution.

In 2010, Myanmar's emissions from the consumption of fossil fuels totalled 12.80 million metric tons of carbon dioxide. (Source: EIA)

NAMIBIA
Republic of Namibia

Capital: Windhoek (Population estimate, 2011: 320,000)

Head of State: H.E. President Hifikepunye Pohamba (page 1496)

National Flag: Diagonal stripes across a rectangular flag, the top left hand corner blue, the centre red and the bottom right hand corner green. The colours are separated by narrower bands of white. In the blue area is a golden sun with twelve triangular rays.

CONSTITUTION AND GOVERNMENT

Constitution
Formerly administered by the Republic of South Africa, Namibia made a peaceful transition to independence on 21 March 1990, aided by the International Court in The Hague and UN Resolution 435.

In November 1989 a Constituent Assembly was elected, and after independence this became the National Assembly.

Under the constitution adopted by the Constituent Assembly in February 1990 Namibia is a multi-party state, headed by an executive president who is directly elected by universal adult suffrage for a maximum of two successive five-year terms. Subsequent re-election is unconstitutional. However, Parliament passed a bill in November 1998 to amend the constitution allowing the first president of Namibia to stand for a third term at the 1999 elections. The president appoints the prime minister and the 16 ministers of the Cabinet.

Following years of apartheid, Namibia's constitution aims at national reconciliation. There is complete freedom of press, freedom of movement, and recognition of human rights. The death penalty was abolished. Namibia's revised constitution allowed for gender equality, affirmative action and led to the establishing of the Department of Women Affairs, which deals with all aspects pertaining to a women's role in the community and development of the country.

Namibia joined the United Nations on 23 April 1990 as its 160th member, and joined the British Commonwealth as its 50th member.

To consult the constitution, please visit: http://www.superiorcourts.org.na/supreme/nam_constitution.html

Recent Events
In November 2005, two mass graves were found near a former South African military base in the north of Namibia. They were thought to date back to the independence struggle. In July 2007, a local rights group asked the International Criminal Court to investigate ex-president Sam Nujoma with regard to the deaths of thousand of people during the struggle for independence. In September 2008, graves on both sides of the border with Angola were discovered, containing the remains of up to 1,600 civilians who disappeared between 1994 and 2003. International experts were called upon to investigate the sites.

The government announced in July 2011 that it had found an estimated 11 billion barrels of offshore oil reserves.

International Relations
Namibia maintains good relations with its neighbours, apart from the occasional friction with Botswana over disputed boundaries. Relations with the Angolan government are especially close due to Angolan support during the struggle for independence; the government also supports the Mugabe regime in Zimbabwe, possibly due to feelings of liberation struggle solidarity.

Namibia is a member of the UN, the Commonwealth, the Southern African Development Community (SADC) and the African Union (AU) and other African organisations.

Legislature
The bicameral legislature consists of a National Council and a National Assembly.

Upper House
The 26-member National Council consists of two members from each geographical region as defined by an Act of Parliament (National Assembly). Members of the National Council are elected by, and from, members of the various Regional Councils and serve terms of six years. The National Council reviews bills passed by the National Assembly and recommends legislation on matters of regional concern.
National Council, Parliament Buildings, Private Bag 13371, Windhoek, Namibia. Tel: +264 61 280 3111, URL: http://www.parliament.gov.na/

Lower House
The National Assembly enacts legislation and consists of 78 members. Seventy-two are elected by proportional representation for a five-year term, and six non-voting members are appointed by the president.
National Assembly, Parliament Buildings, Private Bag 13323, Windhoek, Namibia. Tel: +264 61 288 9111, URL: http://www.parliament.gov.na/

Cabinet (as at March 2013)
Prime Minister: Dr Hage Geingob (page 1429)
Deputy Prime Minister: Hon. Marco Hausiku (page 1439)
Minister for Foreign Affairs: Hon. Netumbo Nandi-Ndaitwah (page 1484)
Minister for Health and Social Services: Hon. Richard Kamwi
Minister for Trade and Industry: Hon. Calle Schlettwein
Minister for Education: Dr David Namwandi
Minister for Justice: Hon Utoni Nujoma (page 1488)
Minister for Agriculture, Water and Forestry: Hon. John Mutorwa (page 1483)
Minister for Environment and Tourism: Hon. Uahekkua Herunga
Minister for Regional and Local Government, Housing and Rural Development: Major-Gen. (rtd.) Charles Namoloh
Minister for Home Affairs and Immigration: Hon. Pendukeni Ivula-Ithana
Minister of Lands, Resettlement and Rehabilitation: Alpheus Naruseb
Minister for Finance: Hon. Saarah Kuugongelwa-Amadhila (page 1459)
Minister of Mines and Energy: Isak Katali
Minister of Gender Equality and Child Welfare: Hon. Rosalia Nghidinwa
Minister for Youth, National Service, Sport and Culture: Jerry Ekandjo (page 1419)
Minister for Defence: Hon. Nahas Angula
Minister for Fisheries and Marine Resources: Bernhard Esau
Minister for Works and Transport: Hon. Errki Nghimtina (page 1486)
Minister of Labour and Social Welfare: Doreen Sioka
Minister of Veterans Affairs: Hon. Dr. Nickey Iyambo
Minister of Information and Communications: Hon. Joel Kaapanda
Minister for Presidential Affairs; Attorney General: Hon. Dr. Albert Kawana (page 1454)

Minister of Safety and Security and Prisons: Hon. Immanuel Ngatizeko
Director-General of the National Planning Commission: Tom Alweendo
Director-General of the Namibian Central Intelligence: Lt-Gen. (retd.) Peter Lucas Hangula

Ministries

Office of the President, State House, Private Bag 13339, Windhoek, Namibia. Tel: +264 61 220010, URL: http://www.op.gov.na

Office of the Prime Minister, Private Bag 13338, Windheok, Namibia. Tel: +264 61 287 9111, fax: +264 61 226189, e-mail: jnel@opm.gov.na, URL: http://www.opm.gov.na

Office of the Attorney General, Government Buildings, 6th Floor West Wing, Private Bag 13345, Windhoek, Namibia. Tel: +264 61 282 9111, fax: +264 61 223937, e-mail: initialsurname@moj.gov.na, URL: http://www.moj.gov.na/

Ministry of Foreign Affairs, Government Buildings, 4th Floor, East Wing, Private Bag 13347, Windhoek, Namibia. Tel: + 264 61 282 9111, fax: + 264 61 223937, e-mail : headquarters@mfa.gov.na, URL: http://www.mfa.gov.na

Ministry of Health and Social Services, Old State Hospital, Nightingale Street, Private Bag 13198, Windhoek, Namibia. Tel: +264 61 221332, e-mail: initialsurname@mhss.gov.na, URL: http://www.op.gov.na/Decade_peace/health.htm

Ministry of Information and Communication Technology, Private Bag 13344, Windhoek, Namibia. Tel: +264 61 223 9111, fax: +264 61 222343, e-mail: namines@iwwn.com.na, URL: http://www.op.gov.na/Decade_peace/info.htm

Ministry of Mines and Energy, Trust Centre Building, Independence Ave, Private Bag 13297, Windhoek, Namibia. Tel: +264 61 284 8111, fax: +264 61 238643, E-mail: initialsurname@mme.gov.na, URL: http://www.mme.gov.na/

Ministry of Environment and Tourism, Government Buildings, 5th Floor, Private Bag 13346, Windhoek, Namibia. Tel: +264 61 284 2111, fax: +264 61 229 936, e-mail: initialsurname@met.gov.na, URL: http://www.met.gov.na

Ministry of Trade and Industry, Government Buildings, Private Bag 13340, Windhoek, Namibia. Tel: +264 61 283 7111, fax: +264 61 220148, e-mail: initialsurname@mti.gov.na, URL: http://www.mti.gov.na

Ministry of Fisheries and Marine Resources, Private Bag 13355, Windhoek, Namibia. Tel: +264 61 205 3911, fax: +264 61 233286, URL: http://www.mfmr.gov.na

Ministry of Defence, Private Bag 13307, Windhoek, Namibia. Tel: +264 61 204 9111, fax: +264 61 204 2092, e-mail: initialsurname@mod.gov.na, URL: http://www.mod.gov.na

Ministry of Agriculture, Water and Rural Development, Private Bag 13184, Windhoek, Namibia. Tel: +264 61 208 7111, fax: +264 61 229 961, e-mail: initialsurname@mawrd.gov.na, URL: http://www.op.gov.na/Decade_peace/agri.htm

Ministry of Finance, Fiscus Building, John Meinert St, Private Bag 13295, Windhoek, Namibia. Tel: +264 61 209 9111, fax: +264 61 230179, e-mail: initialsurname@mof.gov.na, URL: http://www.op.gov.na/Decade_peace/mof.htm

Ministry of Home Affairs, Cohen Building, Kasino Street, Private Bag 13200, Windhoek, Namibia. Tel: +264 61 292 2111, fax: +264 61 292 2185, e-mail: initialsurname@mha.gov.na, URL: http://www.nampol.gov.na/

Ministry of Education, Winco Building, Stuebel Street, Private Bag 13391, Windhoek, Namibia. Tel: +264 61 270 6111, fax: +264 61 253 671, e-mail: initialsurname@mhev.gov.na, URL: http://www.op.gov.na/Decade_peace/h_edu.htm

Ministry of Lands, Resettlement and Rehabilitation, Private Bag 13343, Windhoek, Namibia. Tel: +264 61 285 2111, fax: +264 61 228 240, URL: http://www.op.gov.na/Decade_peace/lands.htm

Ministry of Regional, Local Government and Housing, Windhoek, Namibia. Tel: +264 61 2975213, fax: +264 81 124 2816, e-mail: jvanhorsten@mrlgh.gov.na, URL: http://www.mrlgh.gov.na

Ministry of Works and Transport, Private Bag 13341, Windhoek, Namibia. Tel: +264 61 208 9111, fax: +264 61 228 560, e-mail: initialsurname@mwtc.gov.na, URL: http://www.op.gov.na/Decade_peace/works.htm

Political Parties

Democratic Turnhalle Alliance (DTA); National Unity Democratic Organization (NUDO); Rally for Democracy and Progress (RDP); South West Africa People's Organization (SWAPO); United Democratic Front (UDF).

Elections

Elections were held in November 2004. President Nujoma did not stand for re-election. The SWAPO candidate, Hifikepunye Pohamba, won the presidency with 76.4 per cent of the vote. In the legislative elections to the National Assembly, also held in November 2004, SWAPO retained its overall majority, winning 55 seats. The opposition is divided by ethnic rivalries; SWAPO's continued electoral success can be ascribed in part to the support of the Ovambo tribes, which represent over half the Namibian population.

The most recent presidential and parliamentary elections were held on 27 and 28 of November 2009. President Hifikepunye Pohamba and his ruling South West African People's Organization retained power.

Diplomatic Representation

British High Commission, PO Box 22202, 116 Robert Mugabe Avenue, Windhoek, Namibia. Tel: +264 61 274800, fax: +264 61 228895, e-mail: windhoek.general@fco.gov.uk, URL: http://ukinnamibia.fco.gov.uk/en/
High Commissioner: Marianne Young (page 1542)

Embassy of Namibia, 1605 New Hampshire Avenue, NW, Washington, DC 20009, USA. Tel: +1 202 986 0540, fax: +1 202 986 0443, URL: http://www.namibianembassyusa.org/
Ambassador: H.E . Mr. Martin Andjaba

US Embassy, 14 Lossen Street, Private Bag 12029, Windhoek, Namibia. Tel: +264 61 221601, fax: +264 61 229 792, e-mail: kopfgb@state.gov, URL: http://windhoek.usembassy.gov
Ambassador: Wanda Nesbitt (page 1485)

High Commission of the Republic of Namibia, 6 Chandos Street, London, W1M 0LQ, United Kingdom. Tel: +44 (0)20 7636 6244, fax: +44 (0)20 7637 5694, URL: http://www.namibiahc.org.uk/
High Commissioner: George Mbanga Liswaniso

Permanent Mission to the United Nations, 135 East 36th Street, New York, NY 10016, USA. Tel: +1 212 685 2003, fax: +1 212 685 1561, e-mail: namibia@un.int, URL: http://www.un.int/namibia
Ambassador and Permanent Representative: H.E. Wilfried Emvula

LEGAL SYSTEM

The common law of Namibia is Roman-Dutch Law, inherited from South Africa, along with elements of the traditional court system.

The judiciary is independent and the law courts of Namibia are structured as follows: the Supreme Court, the highest appeals court in Namibia, which also exercises constitutional review of legislation; High Court of Namibia and 29 lower courts made up of Regional and Magistrate's Courts; Traditional Courts (where traditional leaders hear matters ranging from cattle theft to adultery). Fines are usually in the form of animals or money. Judges are appointed by the President on the recommendation of the Judicial Service Commission.

The constitution calls for an extensive bill of rights protecting freedom of speech, press, assembly, association, and religion and a guarantee of redress for those whose fundamental rights have been violated.

Whilst the government respects the human rights of its citizens, some abuses continue. Police use of excessive force, and there are arbitrary arrests. Conditions in prisons are poor, and there are long delays in trials due to a shortage of trained magistrates. Some SWAPO supporters have been known to intimidate opposition members, and there is official corruption. The death penalty was abolished in Namibia in 1990, the last execution having taken place in 1988.

Supreme Court of Namibia, URL: http://www.superiorcourts.org.na/supreme/
Chief Justice: Peter Shivute (page 1514)

Office of the Ombudsman, URL: http://www.ombudsman.org.na

LOCAL GOVERNMENT

The Delimitation Commission divided Namibia into 13 regions in March 1992: Omusati, Oshana, Ohangwena, Oshikoto, Kunene, Okavango, Caprivi, Erongo, Otjozondjupa, Omaheke, Khomas, Hardap, and Karas.

Regional and local governments are elected every five years. The regional councils have various functions ranging from drawing up their own budget to the planning and development of physical facilities and land use. Two members from each regional council are elected to represent their region in the upper house of the Parliament. The most recent elections took place in 2010.

AREA AND POPULATION

Area

Namibia borders Angola to the north, Botswana to the east, and the Cape province of South Africa to the south. The northeastern Caprivi Strip also connects it to Zambia and Zimbabwe. Its area is 825,418 sq. km, with a coastline of 1,572 km. In August 1993 the South African government conceded Walvis Bay to Namibia after negotiations on the territory's future.

Namibia's climate is semi-arid and subtropical. The hottest months are January and February, with an average high of 30°C and a low of 17°C. The coldest months are June and July, with average temperatures ranging from 6°C to 20°C. There are frequent prolonged periods of drought; the driest month is July, with an average of 1 mm of rainfall, whilst the wettest month is January, with an average of 350 mm of rainfall. Due to the Benguela Current from the Antarctic, the coastline is cooler than the rest of the country.

To view a map, consult http://www.lib.utexas.edu/maps/cia08/namibia_sm_2008.gif

Population

The estimated population in 2010 was 2.283 million, with an annual average population growth rate of 1.9 per cent for the period 2000-10. The growth rate has slowed due to a high incidence of HIV/AIDS. Population density is approximately 1.7 people per sq. km. The median age of Namibians is 21 years. Although about 63 per cent of the population resides in rural areas the growth rate in urban areas is rapidly increasing. The largest town is the capital, Windhoek, with 321,000 inhabitants. Other major towns are: Ondangwa, with 65,000 inhabitants; Oshakati, 54,000; Walvis Bay, 45,000; and Swakopmund, 28,000.

Namibians are predominantly African (87.5 per cent), with 6 per cent of European descent (mainly British and German), and 6.5 per cent mixed. Over half the population belongs to nine associated Ovambo tribes. The Ovambo, Kavango, and East Caprivian peoples, who occupy the relatively well-watered and wooded northern part of the country, are settled farmers, but many have settled throughout the country in recent decades as a result of urbanisation, industrialisation, and the demand for labour.

The official language is English, although Afrikaans is spoken by about 60 per cent of the white population, and German by about 32 per cent. Other languages spoken include Oshivambo, Nama/Damara, Herero, Lozi, Kwangali, and Tswana.

Births, Marriages, Deaths

According to 2010 estimates, the birth rate is 26.3 births per 1,000 people, whilst the death rate is 10.7 deaths per 1,000. Average life expectancy at birth in 2009 was 57 years (53 years for men and 62 years for women). Healthy life expectancy was 52 years. The total fertility rate is 3.2 children per woman. (Source: http://www.who.int, World Health Statistics 2012)

STATES OF THE WORLD

NAMIBIA

EMPLOYMENT

According to recent figures the labour force is estimated at about 678,600 (2008). The unemployment rate in the same year was estimated to be between 30 and 40 per cent of the workforce, though unofficial figures put this figure higher; unemployment, combined with underemployment, is thought to affect over fifty per cent of the workforce. Many Namibians lack the skills and training required for jobs in the formal sector. The government is addressing this problem through education reform. Of those employed, 47 per cent are employed in the agricultural sector, three per cent in mining, 17 per cent in industry and about 33 per cent in the services sector.

The largest labour organisation, the National Union of Namibian Workers (NUNW), comprises seven affiliated trade unions and is closely linked with the ruling SWAPO party. The revised Namibian constitution made provision for gender equality in the workplace. In 2007, Namibia passed a new labour act, which contains controversial new provisions, such as leave time and the banning of labour hire companies.

Total Employment by Economic Activity

Occupation	2004
Agriculture, hunting & forestry	102,636
Fishing	12,720
Mining & quarrying	7,562
Manufacturing	23,755
Electricity, gas & water supply	6,151
Construction	19,605
Wholesale & retail trade, repairs	53,895
Hotels & restaurants	13,132
Transport, storage & communications	15,861
Financial intermediation	7,582
Real estate, renting & business activities	9,375
Public admin. & defence; compulsory social security	30,685
Education	31,168
Health & social work	14,010
Other community, social & personal service activities	12,632
Households with employed persons	24,081
Other	407

Source: Copyright © International Labour Organization (ILO Dept. of Statistics, http://laborsta.ilo.org)

BANKING AND FINANCE

Currency
The unit of currency is the Namibian Dollar (N$) which is pegged to the South African Rand (R).

GDP/GNP, Inflation, National Debt
The Namibian economy is closely linked with that of South Africa; approximately 80 per cent of its trade goes through this neighbouring state. The economy is largely based on the mining industry, particularly the extraction and processing of diamonds, uranium and zinc. Mining contributes over 8 per cent of Namibia's GDP and provides over half the country's exports. Tourism, fisheries and manufacturing are potential areas for economic diversification.

It was estimated to be US$13 billion in 2010 with a growth rate of 6 per cent, rising to UD$14 billion in 2011. The services sector contributed 60 per cent towards GDP, the industry sector 35 per cent, and agriculture 8 per cent.

Average per capita GDP (purchasing power parity) was US$7,300 in 2011. Namibia's per capita GDP illustrates the country's economic and social differences; per capita GDP is as low as US$85 per year for subsistence farmers (55 per cent of the population), but rises to US$16,500 for the richest (mainly white) population (5 per cent).

There are around 5,000 commercial farmers in Namibia. From the beginning of independence, the government purchased farms on the 'willing-buyer willing-seller' principle, and redistributed the land to landless families. In recent years, however, supporters of land reform have become more vocal, and the expropriation of white-owned farms began in 2005; the government aims to resettle many thousands of landless citizens.

The 2011 inflation rate was estimated at 5 per cent. External debt was an estimated US$3 billion in 2011.

Foreign Investment
The government is encouraging foreign investment to develop diversity in the economy and to alleviate unemployment and rural poverty.

The Namibian government has taken several measures to encourage foreign investment including: the Foreign Investment Act (1990) which guarantees compensation against expropriation and allows the retention of foreign exchange profits from exports; the Export Processing Zone Act (1995), which offers relief to investors from import tariffs imposed by the South African Customs Union; full exemption from import duties on inputs and 80 per cent income tax exemption on all profits gained from the exporting of manufactured goods; and an Investment Centre established by the Ministry of Trade and Industry to offer assistance to all prospective investors.

The European Union is the largest aid contributor. Namibia belongs to the Southern African Common Monetary Area, the International Monetary Fund, and the World Bank.

Balance of Payments / Imports and Exports
Over 80 per cent of Namibia's imports originate in South Africa, and many Namibian exports are destined for the South African market or transit that country. Outside of South Africa, the EU (primarily the U.K.) is the chief market for Namibian exports. Namibia is seeking to diversify its trading relationships away from its heavy dependence on South African goods and services. Europe has become a leading market for Namibian fish and meat, and the mining industry has purchased heavy equipment and machinery from Europe, the United States, and Canada.

External Trade, US$ million

	2005	2006	2007
Exports	2,067.67	2,650.65	2,830.64
Imports	2,333.11	2,666.84	2,846.72
Trade balance	-265.44	94.81	-16.09

Source: African Development Bank

Exports were estimated to be US$4.6 billion in 2010 and imports US$6 billion.

Namibia's major export trading partners are the UK (43 per cent), South Africa, Spain, France, and Japan. Main import trading partners are South Africa (81 per cent), the US and Germany. Namibia also trades with members of the Southern Africa Custom Union (SACU) and the Southern Africa Development Community (SADC).

Main export industries are mining (diamonds, gold, copper, zinc, uranium, lead) and agriculture (cattle, fish, and karakul skins). Main imports are food, petroleum products, chemicals, and machinery and equipment.

Namibia is a member of the Southern African Development Community (SADC) and the Southern African Customs Union (SACU) with South Africa, Botswana, Lesotho, and Swaziland. Namibia became a signatory of the GATT (General Agreements on Tariffs and Trade) agreement in 1993. In December 2007 Namibia signed an interim Economic Partnership Agreement (EPA) with the European Union, which provides duty- and limited quota-free access to European markets for Namibian exports.

Central Bank
Bank of Namibia, PO Box 2882, 71 Robert Mugabe Avenue, Windhoek, Namibia. Tel: +264 61 2835111, fax: +264 61 283 5067, e-mail: governor.office@bon.com.na, URL: http://www.bon.com.na/
Governor: I.W. Shiimi

Business Addresses
Namibia Chamber of Commerce and Industry (NCCI), URL: http://www.ncci.org.na/

MANUFACTURING, MINING AND SERVICES

Primary and Extractive Industries
Namibia's mining industry is a mainstay of the economy, contributing over 8 per cent of GDP, and over half the country's exports. Mineral extraction and processing are key sectors. Namibia is the fourth largest African exporter of non-fuel minerals and the world's fifth largest uranium producer.

The country has rich mineral deposits, which fall into five groups: uranium, diamonds, base metals (copper, zinc, lead, tin), precious metals (gold, silver), and other minerals including granite, marble, pyrite, lithium, salt, cadmium, arsenic, and semi-precious stones. Namibia's production of uranium, gem quality diamonds, and arsenic places the country in the world league. In an African context, Namibia is also a major producer of copper, lead, zinc, cadmium, antimony, lithium, tin, silver, fluorspar, and sulphur. All mineral rights are vested in the State, but exploration and mining is undertaken exclusively by the private sector.

Namibia produces 8 per cent of the world's diamonds. The country produced two million carats in 2006 (5 per cent of GDP), and generated over US$700 million in export earnings.

Of Namibia's 40 mines currently operating, only eight employ more than 200 people and generate gross annual revenue in excess of R10 million. All eight are owned by foreign companies, the government only having a minor equity share in Rössing. Some 98 per cent of mineral earnings come from these mines, representing between 60 and 85 per cent of Namibia's foreign exchange earnings. Due to a decline in world demand for uranium and the implementation of the general quota on the production of diamonds by the Diamond Central Selling Organization, Namibia has experienced a decline in earnings from the mining industry.

Oil
Namibia has no proven oil reserves and relies on imports for its consumption requirements. The country consumed an estimated 26,000 barrels of oil per day in 2011 (up from 8,000 barrels per day in 2000), all of which was imported. Most of the oil was distillate and gasoline.

Foreign oil companies have signed Memorandums of Understanding with Namibia's Ministry for Mines and Energy, allowing them exploration rights for a period of two years. In 2011, the government announced that 11 billion barrels of offshore oil reserves had been discovered.

Natural Gas

Reserves of natural gas, estimated at 2 trillion cubic feet, have been discovered in Namibia. Tullow Oil (U.K.) is developing the offshore Kudu natural gas field which has estimated proven reserves of 1.3 Tcf. Tullow operates Kudu with 90 per cent of the shares, whilst the National Petroleum Corporation of Namibia owns 10 per cent of the shares. No natural gas is produced from these fields as yet.

Energy

Total energy consumption in 2009 was 0.072 quadrillion Btu. Installed capacity was 0.3 gigawatts in 2010, and the country consumed 3.3 billion kilowatthours over the year.

Around half of Namibia's electricity is generated domestically, mainly from the 240 MW Ruacana hydropower plant. However, the level of production is cyclical, necessitating periodic imports from South Africa. South Africa's excess capacity is declining, so the Namibian government is considering the development of other sources of energy, such as a natural gas-fired power plant, a wind-powered plant and further hydroelectric supplies. Namibia's Nam Power continues to support a project to construct a 20 MW hydroelectric plant at Popa Falls on the Okavango River, but the project remains in limbo due to environmental concerns. It is anticipated that power rationing will become a reality in Namibia in the near future.

Manufacturing

The manufacturing sector's contribution to GDP was around 12.6 per cent in 2006. Fifty per cent of employees in the industrial sector are employed in the food and beverages sector, followed by the metal and wood industries at 14 per cent and 10 per cent respectively. The sector has been limited by a small domestic market, lack of local capital, a small skilled labour force and high relative wage rates, and subsidised competition from South Africa.

In 2004, under the US African Growth and Opportunity Act, nearly US$300 million was invested in the manufacturing sector creating more than 9,000 jobs in the textile industry.

Tourism

Namibia's 19 parks and reserves cover approximately 15 per cent of the land area. Tourism is a rapidly growing sector which accounts for 6 per cent of the GDP and an estimated 11 per cent of foreign exchange earnings, making it the third largest industry (after mining and fishing). In 2002, the government declared the Caprivi Strip, scene of secessionist troubles in the 1990s, safe for tourists. Figures for 2003 show that Namibia had over 695,000 visitors, slightly down of the previous year when there were over 752,000. Most tourists arriving by air come from South Africa (46,700 in 2004), Germany (45,000) and the United Kingdom (10,000) (Source: Namibia Ministry of Environment and Tourism). Figures from 2006 show that Namibia had 833,000 visitors generating earnings of US$473 million.
Ministry of Tourism, e-mail: tourism@iwwn.com.na, URL: http://www.met.gov.na

Agriculture

The livelihood of about 70 per cent of the population depends directly or indirectly on agriculture and forestry, though the sector accounted for only 6 per cent of GDP and around 5 per cent of total exports in 2006. The infrastructure is under-developed. In particular, permanent water supplies, technical expertise, and markets for surplus products of small farmers need to be improved.

In 1994 the government introduced land reform legislation. As part of the reforms white owned farms could change hands under a 'willing-seller, willing-buyer' scheme but by 2004 it was felt that this was not progressing fast enough; almost half of the land was owned by 4,000 farmers, most of whom are white, and an estimated 200,000 of the poor black population still needed land. Expropriation of white-owned farms began in 2005.

Crop and irrigation farming are at present mostly limited to the northern regions and the Hardap and Orange River irrigation schemes, where maize, millet, sorghum, wheat, lucerne, and grapes are being grown. There are also developments for the production of tomatoes and other vegetables, and sugar. One per cent of the land is irrigated.

Beef production is the largest contributor to the agricultural GDP. Commercial cattle farms are situated in northern areas. At present dairy products play a relatively unimportant role, with local producers supplying local needs, while cheese and butter are imported on a large scale. Karakul sheep flourish in the arid southern and western parts of Namibia. They provide meat, wool and pelts. A local industry for the processing of pelts into garments has recently been established.

Agricultural Production in 2010

Produce	Int. $'000*	Tonnes
Indigenous cattle meat	149,308	55,271
Roots & tubers, nes	56,434	330,000
Indigenous sheep meat	40,556	14,895
Cow milk, whole, fresh	35,762	114,600
Indigenous goat meat	15,196	6,342
Game meat	13,926	6,400
Grapes	12,290	21,500
Indigenous bird meat, nes	11,136	3,800
Pulses, nes	9,735	19,000
Indigenous chicken meat	9,686	6,800
Maize	7,650	58,000
Indigenous pigmeat	6,764	4,400

* unofficial figures
Source: http://faostat.fao.org/site/339/default.aspx Food and Agriculture Organization of the United Nations, Food and Agricultural commodities production

Forestry

It is estimated that 20 per cent of the total land area is covered by woodland and 64 per cent by savannah. The local timber industry is small and is controlled by planned logging. It is estimated that only 9,400 cubic metres are cut annually.

Fishing

Namibia has a coastline of 1600 km. The Atlantic Ocean off this coast is exceptionally rich in nutrients, with pilchard, mackerel and anchovy close to shore, and hake, sole, and sardines, as well as squid, deep sea crab and rock lobster further out to sea. In 1990, Namibia proclaimed a 2,000 mile Exclusive Economic Zone. With potential sustainable fishing yields of up to 1.5 million metric tons per year, Namibian commercial fishing and fish processing is the fastest growing sector of the economy in terms of export earnings, contribution to GDP, and employment.

However, Namibia's own fishing fleet is relatively small, consisting of less than 60 vessels, and can use only about 15 per cent of fishing resources. The fishing industry, employing about 6,000 people, mostly supplies South Africa. In 2002 fish exports amounted to US$369 million.

The Namibian government now pursues a conservative resource management policy. Namibia is a signatory to the Convention on Conservation and Management of Fisheries Resources in the South-East Atlantic (Seafo Convention). The country is also part of the Benguela Current Large Marine Ecosystem (BCLME) program, designed to help the Governments of Namibia, Angola, and South Africa manage their shared marine resources in a sustainable way.

COMMUNICATIONS AND TRANSPORT

Namibia's transport system was devised to meet the requirements of moving people and goods to and from South Africa. Consequently, the main network extends in a north-southerly direction, linking the central mining districts, while the infrastructure in the rural areas, especially in the north, where more than 60 per cent of the population lives, is underdeveloped.

Travel Requirements

Citizens of the USA, Canada, Australia and the EU require a passport valid for six months beyond the length of stay but do not need a visa for tourism stays of up to 90 days, apart from nationals of Bulgaria, Cyprus, Czech Republic, Estonia, Greece, Hungary, Latvia, Lithuania, Malta, Poland, Romania, Slovak Republic and Slovenia who do require a visa. Other nationals should contact the embassy to check visa requirements.

Travellers coming for work or study, whether paid or voluntary, must obtain a work or study permit prior to entering Namibia. All visitors travelling via South Africa are advised to have several unstamped visa pages in their passports; South Africa requires two unstamped visa pages, and Namibia usually also requires an unstamped page to stamp a visa upon arrival.

National Airlines

The national airline, Air Namibia, operates domestic flights between Windhoek and a number of centres as well as regular international flights to South Africa, Botswana, Zambia, Zimbabwe and European destinations.
Air Namibia, URL: http://www.airnamibia.com.na

International Airports

In addition to its modern international airport at Windhoek, the Hosea Kutako International Airport, Namibia has a large number of airfields of varying quality, including Eros Airport also situated at Windhoek which caters for domestic and regional flights. Eight of Namibia's airports and aerodromes, including Hosea Kutako, are the responsibility of the Namibia Airports Company (NAC). Only 16 of Namibia's 300 airfields are licensed.

Railways

Namibia's 2,382 km railway system of 1,067 metre narrow gauge railway is managed by NamRail. The Namibian system connects with the main system of the South African railways at Ariamsvlei and includes stops at Windhoek, Okahandja, Swakopmund, and Walvis Bay. The northern service connects with Omaruru, Otjiwarongo, Otavi, Tsumeb, and Grootfontein. In addition, the Desert Express service, which began in 1998, travels overnight from Windhoek to Swakopmund.

Roads

Namibia's total national road network is some 42,450 km, approximately 5,450 km of which is tarred. Vehicles are driven on the left. The TransKalahari highway links Namibia and Botswana, whilst the TransCaprivi highway links the Namibia with Zambia. In 1996 the government introduced road user charges to assist with the funding of the highway network.

In May 2004 a bridge was opened across the River Zambezi, connecting Namibia and Zambia. It is hoped that the new bridge will open up trade to the port at Walvis Bay. There are border crossings with Angola at Oshikango and Ruacana and South Africa at Araimsvlei, Verloorsdrift, Noordoewer and Oranjemund.

Ports and Harbours

Namibia's two main harbours are Walvis Bay and Luderitz, both operated by NamPort. Most direct imports into the country are landed at Walvis Bay, an eight-berth, deep-sea harbour servicing southern, west and central Africa, as well as Europe. The smaller harbour at Luderitz, in turn, accommodates small ships.

HEALTH

Although advanced health care institutions exist where the population is concentrated, primary and preventive health care, especially in rural areas, is underdeveloped and fragmented. Windhoek has two private and two state hospitals, each of which has extensive facilities including intensive care units. Smaller hospitals are available in most major towns, with clinics and healthcare centres in smaller towns, villages, and rural. In 2009, the government spent approximately 12.1 per cent of its total budget on healthcare (down from 13.1 per cent in 2000), accounting for 55.0 per cent of all healthcare spending. Total expenditure on healthcare equated to 7.2 per cent of the country's GDP. Per capita expenditure on health was approximately US$297, compared with US$126 in 2000. Figures for 2005-10 show that there are 774 physicians (3.7 per 10,000 population), 5,750 nurses and midwives (27.9 per 10,000 population) 90 dentistry personnel, 376 pharmaceutical personnel and 198 environment and public health workers. There are an estimated 27 hospital beds per 10,000 population.

Namibia has one of the highest rates of HIV infection in the world although the rate has now fallen to 17.5 per cent of the population; it is the single biggest cause of death in the country. 150,000 adults currently live with HIV/AIDS, 85,000 of whom are women. Over 50 per cent of deaths of children under 5 were due to HIV/AIDS in 2003, and 16,000 deaths per 100,000 deaths were due to HIV/AIDS. The infant mortality (likelihood of dying by age 1) rate in 2009 was 29 per 1,000 live births. The child mortality rate (under 5 years) was 40 per 1,000 live births. The main causes of childhood mortality are: HIV/AIDS (14 per cent), prematurity (14 per cent), diarrhoea (5 per cent), congenital anomalies (9 per cent), and pneumonia (12 per cent). An estimated 29.6 per cent of children under five years old were considered stunted in the period 2005-11.

In 2008, total access to improved water was 93 per cent. In the same year, 32 per cent of population had access to improved sanitation. (Source: http://www.who.int, World Health Statistics 2012)

EDUCATION

With the introduction of apartheid, government policy formalised a history of racial division in education by introducing different syllabi for the black and the white populations. Up to independence education was fragmented countrywide, with each of the 11 ethnic groups having its own department of education. It is the aim of present educational policy to enhance the cultural rights of the individual as well as to ensure a broad based national curriculum with an effective administrative structure. In practice, this incorporates the concept of non-formal education, combining aspects of health care, hygiene, practical agriculture, and basic economics. Education is compulsory between the ages of 6 and 16 and primary education is free although fees are payable for uniforms, books and hostels for those in rural areas.

In 2007, it was estimated that 87 per cent of the relevant age-group attended primary school, and 50 per cent of the relevant age-group were enrolled in secondary education (44 per cent of boys, 55 per cent of girls). Six per cent of young adults go on to study at tertiary level. In 2006, 21 per cent of total government spending, and 6.9 per cent of GDP, went on education.

Namibia still has an inadequate supply of qualified teachers. The adult literacy rate is currently 88.6 per cent for males and 87.4 per cent for females. For the age group 15-24 years the literacy rates are 90.9 per cent for males and 94.4 per cent for females. These figures are considerably higher than the average literacy levels for the region. (Source: UNESCO, UIS, August 2009)

RELIGION

The Constitution states that, 'all persons shall have the right of freedom to practice any religion and to manifest such practice' and Namibia has a religious liberty rating of 10 on a scale of 1 to 10 (10 is most freedom). (Source: World Religion Database). About 91 per cent of the population is Christian. During the movement towards independence, the various Christian churches united in the Council of Churches in Namibia. Its members are: the African Methodist Episcopal Church; the Anglican Diocese of Namibia; the Evangelical Lutheran Church in SWA (ELC); Evangelical Lutheran Church in Namibia (ELCiN); Roman Catholic Church; Evangelical Reformed Church in Africa; Methodist Church in Southern Africa; and the United Congregational Church in Southern Africa. Around six per cent of the population follow traditional beliefs.

COMMUNICATIONS AND MEDIA

The constitution provides for press freedom and this is generally respected by the government. Criticism of the government does appear in the media.

Newspapers
Namibia's newspaper industry includes: Namibia Economist (URL: http://www.economist.com.na), The Namibian (URL: http://www.namibian.com.na/), Namibia News, and Allgemeine Zeitung (URL: http://www.azcom.na). Die Republikein is an Africaans newspaper (URL: http://www.republikein.com.na).
The Namibian, URL: http://www.namibian.com.na/

Broadcasting
The state-owned Namibian Broadcasting Corporation (NBC) (URL: http://www.nbc.com.na) operates eight radio stations and one television channel. The Windhoek service broadcasts in six languages, whilst the northern transmitters broadcast in three indigenous languages. In addition to the state-run service there is are one private television channel and some private radio stations in operation. International stations such as the BBC, CNN, and South Africa's M-Net can be received via satellite. Namibian's cable/satellite network is Multichoice Namibia. Private radio stations include Radio Antenna, Radio 99, Radio Wave 96.7, and Katutura Community Radio.

Telecommunications
Namibia has a good telecommunications system with a combined fixed-line and mobile-cellular usage of about 45 per 100 persons. In 2007, there were 140,000 fixed line telephones in use, and 1 million mobile phones. According to 2009 estimates, 101,000 people are internet users.

ENVIRONMENT

Since independence, the government has taken several steps to preserve and improve the environment. In 1992 the following environmental policies were introduced: Sustainable Development Policy, Environmental Assessment Policy, Park Management Policy and Desertification Policy. The government took steps to restock its marine resources by introducing a 200 nautical mile exclusive economic zone, fixing the annual quotas of total allowable catches, granting of fishing rights, and strengthened fisheries research and surveillance capacities. The Namib Desert coastal strip is protected by the constitution.

Current environmental issues include limited fresh water resources, wildlife poaching, land degradation, and desertification.

Namibia is a party to the following international environmental agreements: Antarctic-Marine Living Resources, Biodiversity, Climate Change, Climate Change-Kyoto Protocol, Desertification, Endangered Species, Hazardous Wastes, Law of the Sea, Ozone Layer Protection, and Wetlands.

According to figures from the EIA, carbon dioxide emissions totalled 2.67 million metric tons in 2005, up from 0.32 million metric tons in 2000. This is equivalent to 1.32 metric tons per capita, slightly higher than the African average per capita emissions of 1.17 metric tons, but well below the US per capita emissions of 20.14 metric tons. In 2010, Namibia's emissions from the consumption of fossil fuels totalled 3.81 million metric tons of carbon dioxide.

SPACE PROGRAMME

A Chinese tracking station is based in Swakopmund, Namibia. The station opened in 2011 and tracks the re-entry of Chinese manned space vehicles. In March 2012 it was announced it had participated in six launches.

NAURU
Republic of Nauru

Capital: Yaren (Population estimate: 14,000)

Head of State: Baron Waqa (page 1534)

National Flag: A Royal Blue background, symbolising the Pacific Ocean, divided by a narrow horizontal gold band, signifying the equator, with a twelve pointed white star at the lower left representing the island's geographical position, with the points symbolising the original twelve tribes of Nauru.

CONSTITUTION AND GOVERNMENT

Constitution
A former British mandated territory with joint trusteeship granted to Britain, Australia and New Zealand under the League of Nations, Nauru achieved full independence in 1968 when its people, under the leadership of Head Chief Hammer DeRoburt, established the island as a republic. Nauru became a member of the United Nations in 1999 and a member of the Commonwealth in 2000.

The 1968 Constitution provides for a parliamentary democracy with an English system of government. The President is elected by Parliament for a three-year term. It is mandatory for a general election to be held not less than once every three years. On election the President shall appoint four or five Members of Parliament to be Ministers of the Cabinet, in which the executive authority of Nauru is vested and over which the President presides. To qualify as an elected President a person must be a Member of Parliament.

To consult the constitution, please visit: http://www.naurugov.nr/parliament/constitution.html

International Relations
Nauru is a full member of the Commonwealth, and was admitted as a member of the UN in 1999. Nauru is a member of the Pacific Islands Forum and the Secretariat of the Pacific Community (SPC). The country maintains close links with Australia and New Zealand, and also with Kiribati where many of its workforce come from.

Recent Events
In 2001, Australia paid Nauru $30 million to hold asylum seekers who were trying to enter Australia illegally. They were supposed to be gone by the following year, but a detention centre has now been established and the immigrants are obliged to stay there until their applications have been processed. In September 2006, Australia sent Burmese asylum seekers to Nauru, and these were followed, in March 2007, by Sri Lankan asylum seekers.

In April 2004, Nauru defaulted on loan payments and its assets were placed in receivership in Australia. President Rene Harris resigned in June, and was succeeded by Ludwig Scotty, who sacked the parliament in September for failing to pass a reform budget. Mr. Scotty was re-elected unopposed in October 2004.

Nauru re-established diplomatic ties with Taiwan in May 2005, angering China. In October of the same year, Nauru was removed from a list of 'uncooperative' countries by the Financial Action Task Force which was set up to combat money-laundering. In December, Air Nauru's only aircraft was repossessed by a US bank after the country failed to make debt repayments. It was resurrected late in 2006 and renamed Our Airline.

In December 2007, President Scotty was ousted in a no-confidence vote. Marcus Stephens chosen as President. On 31 March 2008, the Parliamentary Speaker, Opposition MP David Adeang, claimed that the President (who is also the Police Minister) had tried to assume authority over him when the Police Commissioner rejected his orders to remove two Ministers from the House. The previous week, the speaker had pushed through changes to the Citizenship Act, barring MPs from holding dual citizenship. This Act would rule out two cabinet members. The Government maintained the amendment had no validity, because there was no quorum. Snap elections were held towards the end of April 2008. Legislative elections were held in in April 2010, which failed to end the political stalemate Marcus Stephens remained as caretaker president. He called a state of emergency in an attempt to end the deadlock and called another election in June 2010. Although one opposition seat was lost, the political stalemate continued.

President Stephen resigned over corruption allegations in November 2011. He was succeeded by Frederick Pitcher, a minister in the cabinet, who, however lasted only five days before a vote of no-confidence. Sprent Dabwido, who had been the minister for transport and communications under Mr Stephen's administration, was elected president on 15 November 2011. President Dabwido sacked his cabinet in June 2012.

Parliament was dissolved in March 2013 by the speaker of Parliament, Ludwig Scotty, citing persistent 'unruly' behaviour of MPs. The move followed the resignation of three cabinet members in February 2013. In March 2013, Nauru's Supreme Court declared that the dissolution of parliament was null and void and cancelled the election planned for 6 April.

Parliament was dissolved in May and an election called for June 22. However President Dabwido then declared a state of emergency and brought forward the date of the election to 8 June.

Legislature
Nauru's unicameral legislature, the Parliament, consists of 18 members elected for a term of three years by Nauruan citizens who have attained the age of 20 years.

Speaker: Ludwig Scotty

Cabinet (as at June 2013)
President, Cabinet Chairman, Minister of Public Service; Police and Emergency Services; Foreign Affairs and Trade; Climate Change: Baron Waqa (page 1534)
Minister of Commerce, Industry & Environment; Nauru Phosphate; Nauru Rehabilitation Corp.: Aaron Cook
Minister of Telecommunications; Nauru Utilities Corporation; Phosphate Royalties Trust: Shadloq Bernicke
Minister of Education & Youth; Land Management; Home Affairs: Charmaine Scotty
Minister assisting the President; Finance; Sustainable Development: David Adeang

Ministries
Government portal, URL: http://www.naurugov.nr/
Parliament of Nauru, Parliament House, Nauru Island, Central Pacific.
Office of the President, Government Offices, Yaren, Nauru. Tel: +674 444 3100, fax: +674 444 3199, e-mail: presidential.counsel@naurugov.nr, URL: http://www.naurugov.nr
Ministry of Finance, Government Offices, Yaren, Nauru. Tel: +674 444 3100/444 3284, fax: +674 444 3215, e-mail: minister.finance@naurugov.nr, URL: http://www.naurugov.nr
Nauru Phosphate Royalties Trust, Government Offices, Yaren, Nauru, e-mail: minister.nprt@naurugov.nr, URL: http://www.naurugov.nr
Ministry of Foreign Affairs, Government Offices, Yaren, Nauru. Tel: +674 444 3191, fax: +674 444 3105, e-mail: minister.foreignaffairs@naurugov.nr, URL: http://www.naurugov.nr
Ministry of Education, Government Offices, Yaren, Nauru. Tel: +674 444 3122, fax: +674 444 3157, e-mail: minister.education@naurugov.nr, URL: http://www.naurugov.nr/
Ministry of Commerce, Industry and Resources, Government Offices, Yaren, Nauru, Tel: +674 444 3181, fax: +674 444 3791, e-mail: minister.cir@naurugov.nr, URL: http://www.naurugov.nr
Ministry of Health, Government Offices, Yaren, Nauru. Tel: +674 444 3166, fax: +674 444 3136, e-mail: minister.health@naurugov.nr, URL: http://www.naurugov.nr
Ministry of Internal Affairs, Government Offices, Yaren, Nauru. Tel: 674 444 3134, fax: +674 3110, e-mail: minister.homeaffairs@naurugov.nr, URL: http://www.naurugov.nr
Ministry of Island Development and Industry, Government Offices, Yaren, Nauru. Tel: +674 444 3181, fax: +674 444 3791
Ministry of Justice, Government Offices, Yaren, Nauru. Tel: +674 444 3155, fax: +674 444 3158, e-mail: minister.justice@naurugov.nr, URL: http://www.naurugov.nr
Ministry of Public Service, Government Offices, Yaren, Nauru. Tel: +674 444 3134, fax: +674 444 3110, e-mail: minister.publicservice@naurugov.nr, URL: http://www.naurugov.nr/
Ministry of Works and Community Services, Government Offices, Yaren, Nauru. Tel: +674 444 3703, fax: +674 444 3107
Ministry of Fisheries, Government Offices, Yaren, Nauru. e-mail: minister.fisheries@naurugov.nr, URL: http://www.naurugov.nr
Ministry of Police, Government Offices, Yaren, Nauru. e-mail: minister.police@naurugov.nr, URL: http://www.naurugov.nr
Ministry of Sports, Government Offices, Yaren. Nauru. e-mail: minister.sport@naurugov.nr, URL: http://www.naurugov.nr
Ministry of Telecommunications, Government Offices, Yaren, Nauru. e-mail: minister.telecommunications@naurugov.nr, URL: http://www.naurugov.nr
Ministry of Trade, Government Offices, Yaren, Nauru. e-mail: minister.trade@naurugov.nr, URL: http://www.naurugov.nr
Ministry of Transport, Government Offices, Yaren, Nauru. e-mail: minister.transport@naurugov.nr, URL: http://www.naurugov.nr/
Ministry of Utilities, Government Offices, Yaren, Nauru. Tel: +674 444 3703, fax: +674 444 3806, e-mail: minister.utilities@naurugov.nr, URL: http://www.naurugov.nr
Ministry of Youth, Government Offices, Yaren, Nauru. e-mail: minister.youthaffairs@naurugov.nr, URL: http://www.naurugov.nr/

Elections
Rene Harris became president following a parliamentary vote in March 2001. He resigned following a vote of no confidence in January 2003 and Ludwig Scotty was elected president by MPs in May 2003. In August 2003, Ludwig Scotty lost a vote of no confidence and Rene Harris again became president until he too lost a no confidence vote in June 2004 in the midst of a financial crisis. MPs then re-elected Ludwig Scotty to the post of president. The next presidential election was due in December 2010.

A snap election took place on 26 April 2010, a year ahead of schedule in an attempt to end ongoing political deadlock; however all 18 MPs retained their seats, thus both parties in parliament have nine seats. Neither side could agree on the election of speaker without which the government cannot officially be formed. Mr Stephen's administration accordingly continued to act in a caretaker capacity while negotiations continued. President Marcus Stephen, needing to pass the budget, declared a state of emergency in June and called a second election. The election took place on 20 June 2010 and the opposition group lost one of its nine seats. However, political stalemate continued. President Stephen Stephen announced he would not call a third ballot and suggested that the constitution should be changed to give the Parliament a 19th seat. However former President Ludwig Scotty accepted the position of speaker, giving the government a majority in the deadlocked house. The government then used the slim majority to re-elect Mr Stephen as president. He was forced to resign over corruption allegations in 2011. His successor Frederick Pitcher lasted only five days before losing a confidence vote. Sprent Dabwido was elected president on 15 November 2011.

NAURU

Elections called for April 2013 were declared unconstitutional. Amidst great political uncertainty parliament was dissolved in May 2013. A election date of 22 June 2013 was set. However President Dabwido called a state of emergency and brought forward the presidential election to 11 June 2013 and legislative elections to 8 June 2013. The newly elected parliament voted in Baron Waqa as its new president in June 2013 and he was sworn in immediately.

Diplomatic Representation

British High Commission, (staff are resident at Suva) Victoria House, 47 Gladstone Road (PO Box 1355), Suva, Fiji. Tel: +679 322 9100, fax: +679 322 9132, URL: http://ukinfiji.fco.gov.uk/en/
Acting High Commissioner: Martin Fidler
US Embassy, (in Fiji) 31 Loftus Street, Suva, Fiji. Tel: +679 331 4466, e-mail: usembsuva@gmail.com, URL: http://suva.usembassy.gov/
Ambassador: Frankie Annette Reed
Embassy of Fiji to the USA, 4290 Suva Place, Washington DC 20521-4290, USA. Tel: +1 679 3314 466, e-mail: usembsuva@gmail.com, URL: http://suva.usembassy.gov/
Ambassador: H.E. Ms Marlene Moses
Embassy to the USA and Permanent Representative of the Republic of Nauru to the United Nations, 800 Second Avenue, Suite 400D, New York, NY 10017, USA. Tel: +1 212 937 0074, fax: +1 212 937 0079, e-mail: nauru@un.int, URL: http://www.un.int/nauru/nauru_un.html
Ambassador: H.E. Ms Marlene Moses

LEGAL SYSTEM

Nauru's law is based on Acts of the Nauru Parliament and British common law.

The Supreme Court, headed by the Chief Justice, exercises both original and appellate jurisdiction, and is paramount on constitutional issues. Other cases can be appealed to the two-judge Appellate Court, whose rulings can be appealed to the High Court of Australia, though in practice this rarely happens. Lower courts consist of the District Court and the Family Court, both of which are headed by a Resident Magistrate. There also are two quasi-courts: the Public Service Appeal Board and the Police Appeal Board, both presided over by the Chief Justice.

The government respects the human rights of its citizens. Nauru has, de facto, abolished the death penalty, the last execution having been carried out in 1968.

LOCAL GOVERNMENT

The Nauru Local Government Council administers Nauru's 14 districts and consists of nine elected members from such districts. Its Head Chief comes from, and is elected by, the Council itself. The 14 districts are: Aiwo, Anabar, Anetan, Anibare, Baiti, Boe, Buada, Denigomodu, Ewa, Ijuw, Meneng, Nibok, Uaboe, and Yaren.

AREA AND POPULATION

Area

Nauru consists of a single island, 8 sq. miles in area (21.2 sq. km), situated in the Western Pacific Ocean to the North East of the Solomons and some 26 miles south of the Equator at 166.55° East. Its nearest neighbour is Ocean Island (Banaba), approximately 160 miles to the east. Nauru is 2,500 miles from Sydney, 2,600 miles from Honolulu and 3,000 miles from Tokyo.

To view a map, consult http://www.lib.utexas.edu/maps/cia08/nauru_sm_2008.gif

The mainland of Nauru merges directly with a fringing reef and, as a consequence, has no natural harbours. It is oval in shape and 12 miles in circumference, with a fertile coastal belt between 100 and 300 yards wide, rising inland to a plateau, the highest point of which is 213 feet above sea level.

The climate is tropical, tempered by sea breezes, with variable rainfall which reaches its height during the monsoon season from November to February.

Population

The population, which is mainly of Polynesian origin, is concentrated around the coastal belt. The population according to a census taken in 2002 is 10,131, with an average annual growth rate of just over 2 per cent. The indigenous population numbers approximately 6,830. The population was estimated at 10,000 in 2009 with an annual growth rate of 0.2 per cent for the period 2000-10. Nauru has its own distinct Pacific island language, but English is used for government and commercial purposes.

Between 2001 and 2008, Nauru accommodated asylum seekers on the island in a detention centre. Australia ended its policy of sending asylum seekers in February 2008, and the last refugees left Nauru.

Births, Marriages, Deaths

The birth rate was estimated at 28 per 1,000 people in 2010, whilst the death rate was an estimated at 10.8 per 1,000 people. According to World Health Organization figures for 2010, the infant mortality rate was 32 deaths per 1,000 infants. The average life expectancy was estimated at 56 years for men and 65 years for women in 2009. Healthy life expectancy was 53 years for males and 57 years for females. The median age is 21 years. An estimated 30 per cent of the population is under 15 years and 7 per cent over 60 years. The fertility rate was an estimated 3.1 children per woman in 2010. (Source: http://www.who.int, World Health Statistics 2012)

Public Holidays
31 January: Independence Day
17 May: Constitution Day
26 October: Angam Day (Homecoming Day)

EMPLOYMENT

The total workforce was 3,182, according to the 1992 census, but this figure had grown to around 4,500 in 2005. Employment in phosphate mining has dwindled. Main areas of employment are now public administration, transport and education. Unemployment is currently estimated to be very high, at approximately 50 per cent, (1,588 people in 2006).

BANKING AND FINANCE

Currency
Australian dollar (A$)

GDP/GNP, Inflation, National Debt

In the past, Nauru's economy depended on the phosphate industry, which provided the population with a relatively high per capita income. Phosphate resources have now been exhausted from a largescale commercial point of view, although smallscale mining continues. The government placed a large percentage of earnings from phosphate mining into the Nauru Phosphate Royalties Trust (NPRT) to generate income once mining ceased. However, a combination of excessive consumption, poor investment advice, and mismanagement led to the asset portfolio of the NPRT being placed into receivership in 2004. The economy is now reliant on revenues from issuing deepwater fishing licenses for Nauru's exclusive economic zone (EEZ), and foreign aid.

In an effort to diversify its economic base, Nauru has tried to establish itself as an offshore banking centre. This ran into difficulties over allegations of money-laundering, in 2003. In 2005, Nauru was taken off the list of 'uncooperative' countries by the Task Force established to fight money-laundering.

The Government recently signed two contracts with Australian and New Zealand private companies to recommence mining, which may yield medium term economic growth. Aid-funded rehabilitation of the mined land could also generate economic activity.

The services sector contributed around 63.7 per cent in 2005, with agriculture accounting for 7 per cent and industry contributing 10.8 per cent.

GDP by industrial origin, at current market prices (figures in AUD$ million)

Economic sector	2007	2008	2009
Agriculture	2.6	2.6	2.6
Mining	1.9	6.4	10.2
Manufacturing	0.2	7.1	17.3
Electricity, gas and water	1.5	3.1	5.8
Construction	1.3	2.2	2.3
Trade	6.0	6.6	6.7
Transport and communications	-0.4	6.1	6.4
Finance	1.8	2.0	2.9
Public Administration	4.1	4.1	4.9
Others	8.6	9.3	10.3
Total	27.6	49.5	69.5

Source: Asian Development Bank

GDP was estimated to be US$69 million in 2010, and US$69.5 million. Per capita GDP was estimated to be US$6,925 in 2010.

In 2009, agriculture contributed 51 per cent of GDP, services 45 per cent and agriculture 4 per cent.

Inflation was estimated at 2.2 per cent in 2009.

Foreign Investment

Although Nauru does not offer incentives for foreign investors, it does have a financial centre which allows international companies to register there for tax planning purposes. Nauru receives development aid from the UN, New Zealand, Australia, European Union, Japan and Taiwan. Australia is the greatest contributor, providing over AUD$25 million per annum.

The deterioration in Nauru's financial situation has led to a worsening of the country's infrastructure. In 2006, in an effort to help the country address its problems, Pacific Island leaders approved the 'Pacific Regional Assistance to Nauru' (PRAN) programme which covered aspects of governance, economy and finances, social development and environment and population.

Balance of Payments / Imports and Exports

Phosphates are the sole export of Nauru. Exports have declined significantly in recent years. Estimated figures for 2010 put exports at US$42.5 million and imports at US$96 million. India is the main destination (38 oer cent), followed by Australia (12 per cent). Imports include almost necessities, especially fuels, manufactured goods and food, Only tobacco and alcoholic beverages are liable for import duties. The main supplier is Russia (80 per cent), followed by Australia.

Central Bank

Bank of Nauru, PO Box 289, Civic Centre, Nauru, Nauru. Tel: +674 4443238, fax: +674 4443203. The bank is currently insolvent.

MANUFACTURING, MINING AND SERVICES

Primary and Extractive Industries
Before the Asian financial crisis, Nauru had one of the world's most valuable deposits of phosphates. Phosphate was primarily exported to Australia and New Zealand. Out of the profits received from the sale of phosphate, royalties were paid to land owners, whilst other royalties were paid to Trust Funds such as the L.T.I.F., set up to provide for the economic needs of Nauru when phosphate deposits are exhausted. As a result substantial sums were invested overseas through the Nauru Phosphate Royalties Trust. However, by 2004 it was clear that the fund was severely depleted with large sums unaccounted for.

Nauru received a settlement in the action taken against Australia at the International Court of Justice to recover losses sustained through devastation to its land mined under the Australian administration, prior to independence. Australia agreed to pay Nauru a total of A$107 million in present day values in staggered payments to contribute to the rehabilitation of the destroyed land. Phosphate mining continues in Nauru but on a much reduced scale.

Energy
Electricity generation in the year 2010 was 40 million kilowatthours (kWh), all of which was thermally produced. Consumption was 30million kWh.

According to recent EIA statistics, Nauru imported just over one thousand barrels per day of oil in 2011 (residual, gasoline, jet fuel, and distillate).

Service Industries
Nauru does not have any manufacturing industries apart form some handicrafts. Income comes predominately from phosphate mining and banking and insurance. Internet-based banking is emerging as a potentially lucrative sector.

Tourism is small mainly because of the distances needed to be travelled to the island, currently there are just two hotels but the government has pledged to expand the sector.

Agriculture
Arable land is confined to an area of 100-300 metres of the coastal strip. Cultivation is restricted and local vegetation is chiefly confined to coconut palms, pandanus trees and some indigenous hardwoods. The main crops are coconut (1,600 metric tons per year), pineapples and bananas. All food supplies other than fish (which is caught locally), chickens and pigs are imported. The total catch for 2010 was estimated at 200 tonnes.

Agricultural Production in 2010

Produce	Int. $'000*	Tonnes
Coconuts	332	3,000
Fruit tropical fresh nes	139	340
Indigenous pigmeat	111	72
Vegetables fresh nes	89	470
Hen eggs, in shell	13	16
Indigenous chicken meat	6	4

* unofficial figures
Source: http://faostat.fao.org/site/339/default.aspx Food and Agriculture Organization of the United Nations, Food and Agricultural commodities production

COMMUNICATIONS AND TRANSPORT

Travel Requirements
Citizens of the USA, Canada, Australia and the EU require a passport valid for six months from the date of entry, return or onward travel documents and a visa. A 30 day tourist visa can be obtained on arrival by citizens of Australia, Canada, Ireland, the UK and the USA. Other nationals should contact the embassy to check visa requirements. Business visitors must have a visa and a local sponsor.

A visa is not required by transit passengers continuing their journey by the same or first connecting aircraft, provided they hold onward or return documentation and do not leave the airport.

National Airlines
Air Nauru was grounded on several occasions in recent years due to problems paying for the maintenance of its one aircraft; this was repossessed in December 2005 due to non-payment of debts to an American bank. The aircraft was resurrected late in 2006, and renamed Our Airline.
Air Nauru, e-mail: write2us@airnauru.com.au, URL: http://www.airnauru.com.au/

Railways
There are 5.23 kilometres (3.258 miles) for the exclusive service of the phosphate works.

Roads
Total road length is 30 km, of which 24 km is paved and 6 km is unpaved. A main road of 19.3 km circles the island and all residential areas are linked by surfaced roads. Vehicles drive on the left.

Shipping
The island has its own cargo shipping line which serves the island as well as other countries in the region.

Ports and Harbours
Nauru has one port.

HEALTH

The health service is free on Nauru. Yellow fever vaccinations are mandatory if arriving from an infected area. There are two hospitals, the Nauru Government Hospital and the Nauru Phosphate Corporation Hospital, both situated in the Denig District.

In 2009, the government spent approximately 9.2 per cent of its total budget on healthcare (up from 11.2 per cent in 2000), accounting for 68.5 per cent of all healthcare spending. External resources accounted for 39.2 per cent of total expenditure. Total expenditure on healthcare equated to 11.2 per cent of the country's GDP. Per capita expenditure on health was approximately US$595, compared with US$333 in 2000. Figures for 2005-10 show that there are 10 physicians (7.1 per 10,000 population), 99 nurses and midwives (70.7 per 10,000 population), 7 dentists and 10 pharmaceutical personnel. There are 50 hospital beds per 10,000 population.

Nauru has one of the world's highest level of diabetes, affecting over a fifth of the population. There are occasional outbreaks of typhoid. The infant mortality rate in 2009 was 32 per 1,000 live births. The child mortality rate (under 5 years) was 40 per 1,000 live births. The main causes of childhood mortality are: diarrhoea (7 per cent), pneumonia (17 per cent), and prematurity (24 per cent). The measles vaccination rate has increased from 8 per cent in 2000 to 99 per cent in 2007. (Source: http://www.who.int, World Health Statistics 2012)

EDUCATION

Education is free and compulsory between the ages of six and 16. There are four pre-primary schools, seven primary schools, two general secondary schools and a technical school. Scholarships are available for higher education overseas.

An estimated 97 per cent of the population is literate.

RELIGION

The majority of the popuation are Christian around 75 per cent of the population. The main denominations comprise the Congregational Protestant church, the Roman Catholic church and the Independent church. Some 10 per cent of the population are Chinese folk religionists and 10 per cent are Baha'is.

Nauru has a religious liberty rating of 6 on a scale of 1 to 10 (10 is most freedom). (Source: World Religion Database)

COMMUNICATIONS AND MEDIA

Newspapers
Nauru has no daily newspaper. The Bulletin is published weekly, and the Central Star News is printed fortnightly.

Broadcasting
The radio service is the state-owned Radio Nauru, which broadcasts world and local news. Nauru Television, NTV, is also state-owned and broadcasts programmes from New Zealand.

Telecommunications
There is a satellite earth station on the island and the domestic and international phone system is adequate. There are an estimated 1,800 mainline telephones and 1,500 mobile phones. An estimated 4,000 people are internet users.

ENVIRONMENT

Phosphate mining on Nauru has been environmentally devastating. Four-fifths of the island was predicted to be rendered barren by the end of the twentieth century as a result of phosphate mining. Nauru has planned rehabilitation of these mined areas, which will take an estimated twenty years to complete. Other environmental problems include limited fresh water.

Nauru has signed (but not ratified) the following international environmental agreements: Biodiversity, Climate Change, Desertification, Law of the Sea, and Marine Dumping.

Nauru's emissions from the consumption of fossil fuels totalled 0.22 million metric tons of carbon dioxide in 2010. (Source: EIA)

NEPAL

Federal Democratic Republic of Nepal

Sanghiya Loktantrik Ganatantra Nepāl

Capital: Kathmandu (Population estimate, 2011: 1.7 million)

Head of State: Ram Baran Yadav (President) (page 1540)

Vice President: Parmananda Jha (page 1449)

National Flag: Two right-angled triangles overlapping, crimson bordered blue, the upper bearing a white stylised moon crescent and the lower a white sun in splendour

CONSTITUTION AND GOVERNMENT

Constitution

Nepal is an independent kingdom, ruled from 1846 until 1951 by a succession of hereditary Prime Ministers from the Rana family, the reigning family playing little part in the conduct of the State. In 1951, King Tribhuban re-assumed the powers of a constitutional monarch, assisted by a Cabinet, and was succeeded by a number of other governments nominated from leading politicians, but it was not until 1959 that a general election was held.

In this 1959 election the Nepali Congress Party won a large majority and a Government under Mr. B. P. Koirala as prime minister was appointed. In December 1960, King Mahendra, who had succeeded his father in 1955, again assumed full powers of government and proscribed all political parties. Two years later he introduced a new Constitution embodying a tiered, party less system of panchayat (council) democracy, under which there were elected councils at village level which in turn elected members to district and zonal councils. In 1975, King Birendra set up a Commission to consider constitutional reforms. As a result, a number of changes were introduced, but they did not affect the essentials of the party less panchayat system. In May 1979 student disturbances prompted wider expressions of discontent; a referendum was held.

The May 1980 referendum resulted in the King introducing the Third Amendment to the Constitution. This provided for direct elections in 75 districts to the National Panchayat, to whose members the Cabinet would be responsible. The Assembly of 140 members, 28 nominated by the King, would elect a prime minister. After elections in May 1981, Surya Bahadur Thapa was elected prime minister by the National Panchayat. The Assembly passed a vote of no confidence in July 1983 and elected Lokendra Bahadur Chand.

Elections were held in May 1986 and Marich Man Singh Shrestha was appointed prime minister, serving until April 1990. Following the sometimes violent movement for the Restoration of Democracy, the King lifted the ban on political parties in Nepal on 8 April 1990. Marich Man Singh was replaced by Lokendra Bahadur Chand, who in turn made way 13 days later for an interim Coalition Government headed by the Acting President of Nepali Congress, Krishna Prasad Bhattarai. A new Constitution establishing a multi-party democracy and a constitutional monarchy was promulgated on 9 November 1990. Elections were held in May 1991. The Nepali Congress won the majority and Girija Prasad Koirala was elected prime minister.

In March 1997, the coalition government, led by Lokendra Bahadur Chand came to power, promising to continue the process of privatisation, raise national revenue and introduce a value added tax.

In February 2005 King Gyanendra sacked the government and assumed power, saying he was responding to the increase in Maoist rebel attacks. Following protests and strikes, the King recalled parliament in April 2006 and in June parliament voted to amend the constitution limiting the King's political powers.

An interim Constitution was approved by parliament in 2007. This allows for a 330 member Interim Legislature Parliament with 330 members, made of members of the Sansad, 73 Maoists and 48 members nominated to represent civil society and ethnic minorities. Originally a deadline of May 2010 was set for the writing of a new constitution but the deadline passed without agreement being reached. The interim constitution has been repeatedly extended.

To consult the full constitution, please visit:
http://www.supremecourt.gov.np/main.php?d=lawmaterial&f=constitution

Maoist Rebels

The Maoist fight to overthrow the constitutional monarchy began in 1996. In September 2005 the Maoists called for a unilateral three month ceasefire. The following November they announced a 12 point plan of understanding aimed at ending direct rule by the King. In December the Maoists announced their intention of extending the ceasefire but the government which had been appointed by the King failed to reciprocate and attacks began again. The attacks were aimed primarily at disrupting planned municipal elections. Following the attacks and the increased demonstrations by the population, King Gyanendra reinstated parliament in April 2006. In May peace talks began between the Maoist rebels and the government, resulting in a ceasefire and plans for elections to a Constituent Assembly. In June 2006 talks were held between the rebel leader Prachanda and the Prime Minister Koirala; it was agreed that the Maoists would form part of an interim government.

Recent Events

On 1 June 2001, a shooting incident at the royal palace resulted in the deaths of nine members of the Royal family including King Birendra, Queen Aishwarya and Prince Nirajan. Crown Prince Dipendra was also wounded and in a coma after the incident but was declared king. He died of his injuries on June 4 and the late King Birendra's brother Gyanendra was crowned king. After his coronation King Gyanendra commissioned an inquiry into the killings, the conclusion of which was that Crown Prince Dipendra had been responsible.

In July 2001 Girija Prasad Koirala stepped down as prime minister following criticism of his handling of the ongoing Maoist revolt. Sher Bahadur Deuba was elected leader of the Nepali Congress Party and became prime minister. Fresh elections were called in May 2002. A state of emergency was called over increased tensions with Maoist rebels. In October Prime Minister Deuba asked for the elections to be postponed, King Gyanendra sacked Deuba and appointed Lokendra Bahadur Chand as interim prime minister. In May 2003 Prime Minister Chand resigned in the hope that political parties would co-operate better without him. After the failure of Nepal's political parties to agree on a candidate, King Gyanendra appointed Surya Bahadur Thapa as prime minister. Following protests from opposition groups and renewed violence from Maoist rebels Thapa resigned. Sher Bahadur Deuba was reappointed in June 2004. Violence continued and rebels blockaded the capital in August and December 2004. On 1 February 2005 King Gyanendra sacked the government and declared a state of emergency and assumed direct power, in the name of defeating the Maoist rebels. He lifted the state of emergency in April 2005. In May 2005 seven opposition parties demanded a return to democracy.

King Gyanendra reinstated parliament in April 2006 in the face of increased opposition, protests and strikes. In May peace talks began between the Maoist rebels and the government, resulting in a ceasefire and plans for elections to a Constituent Assembly. In June they agreed to form an interim government which would include Maoists, and that the House of Representatives and the Maoist governments would be dissolved. A peace agreement was signed in November 2006 between the Maoists and the government, bringing to an end 10 years of insurgency. In April 2007 former Maoist rebels formally joined the interim government.

In May 2012, the prime minister called new elections as parliament failed again to meet a deadline to agree a new constitution. The election was scheduled to take place on 22 November but was again postponed. There were clashes in the capital between the police and rival groups as the most recent deadline to create a new constitution passed.

A Nepalese Supreme Court judge, Bahadur Bam, was shot dead in May 2012. Mr Bam was under investigation for corruption.

In February 2013, the four main parties agreed on Chief Justice Khil Raj Regmi as interim prime minister. The Supreme Court approved the appointment and he was sworn into office in March. The government must organise new elections but these are not expected until late 2013.

Republic

Elections were held in April 2008 for the new Constituent Assembly. Former Maoist rebels won most of the seats and the Maoist leader Prachanda announced that the first meeting of the assembly would abolish Nepal's monarchy.

On May 28 2008 the Constituent Assembly voted to abolish the Monarchy and for Nepal to become a republic. The vote was successful by 560 votes to 4. The resolution stated that Nepal would become 'an independent, indivisible, sovereign, secular and inclusive republic nation'. The Assembly now has two years to draw up a new constitution. This has since been repeatedly extended.

The CPN-UML resigned from the coalition in 2009, following the prime minister's decision to dismiss the chief of army staff because of his refusal to integrate former Maoist fighters into the army as had been specified in the 2006 peace accord. Dahal resigned as prime minister the following day. Madhav Kumar Nepal of the CPN-UML was elected prime minister on 23 May, and appointed a new cabinet.

In June 2010 the prime minister Madhav Kumar Nepal resigned following pressure from the Maoists. Jhalnath Khanal was appointed prime minister seven months later.

The UN peace monitoring mission ended in January 2011.

In August 2011, the prime minister resigned after the government failed to reach agreement with opposition parties on the new constitution and the fate of former Maoist fighters. Baburam Bhattari of the Maoist Party was elected by parliament as prime minister. He vowed to find concensus on the new constitution and to resolve the Maoist fighters issue.

In November 2011 the main political parties agreed on the final part of a peace deal: some 6,000 former Maoist fighters will be integrated into the security forces and the remaining 12,000 will be paid off. Weapons must be handed into the state and a peace and reconciliation commission will be formed within a month. Some land seizures will also be reversed.

Legislature

The 1990 constitution provided for a bicameral legislature but an interim constitution in 2007 established a unicameral legislature. This was to be called the Interim Legislature-Parliament and to consist of 330 members made up of 83 Maoists, 48 members nominated as representatives of ethnic minorities and the civil society. The remaining members were to come from those remaining members of the parliament dissolved in 2002. This interim Parliament was to be dissolved following the appointment of a new Constituent Assembly which would take as one of its first actions, the debate of a new constitution. On April 11 2011, Prime Minister Jhalanath Khanal announced he was expanding the cabinet by adding 12 new ministers, they would come from his own Communist Party of Nepal-Unified Marxist-Leninist (CPN-UML).

House of Representatives (currently dissolved), Pratinidhi Sabha, Parliament House, Singh Durbar, Kathmandu, Nepal. Tel: +977 1 4227 480, e-mail: nparl@ntc.net.np

Interim Cabinet (as at June 2013)
Prime Minister, Minister of Defence: H.E. Chief Justice Khil Raj Regmi (page 1501)
Minister of Foreign Affairs & Home Affairs: Madhav Prasad Ghimire (page 1430)
Minister for Law and Justice; Labour & Employment: Hari Prasad Neupane
Minister of Finance and Industry: Shankar Koirala
Minister of Education, Information and Communication: Madhav Paudel
Minister of Energy, Environment, Irrigation, Science & Technology: Uma Kanta Jha
Minister of Infrastructure & Transport; Urban Development: Chabi RajPanta
Minister of Federal Affairs and Local Development: Biddhyadhar Mallik
Minister of Agriculture and Forest and Soil Conservation: Tek Bahadur Thapa Gharti
Minister of Youth & Sports; Peace and Reconstruction; Tourism: Ram Kumar Shrestha
Minister of Women, Family and Social Welfare; Minister of Land Reform: Riddhi Baba Pradhane

Ministries
Office of the Council of Ministers, Central Secretariat, Singha Durbar, Kathmandu, Nepal. Tel: +977 1 422 8555, fax: +977 1 422 7286, e-mail: info@pmo.gov.np, URL: http://www.opmcm.gov.np/
Ministry of Home Affairs, Singha Durbar, Kathmandu, Nepal. Tel: Tel: +977 1 422 8801, fax: +977 1 422 7186, e-mail: homegon@wlink.com.np, URL: http://www.moha.gov.np
Ministry of Environment, Singha Durbar, Kathmandu, Nepal. Tel: +977 1 421 1661, fax: +977 1 421 1754, e-mail: info@moenv.gov.np, URL: http://www.moenv.gov.np
Ministry of Finance, Singha Durbar, Kathmandu, Nepal. Tel: Tel: +977 1 421 1412, e-mail: admindivision@mof.gov.np, URL: http://www.mof.gov.np/
Ministry of Commerce and Supplies, Singha Durbar, Kathmandu, Nepal. Tel: +977 1 423 0967, fax: +977 1 422 0319, e-mail: moc@wlink.com.np, URL: http://www.moics.gov.np
Ministry of Water Resources, Department of Irrigation, Jawalakhel, Lalitpur, Nepal. Tel: +977 1 421 1426, fax: +977 1 420 0026, e-mail: info@moir.gov.np, URL: http://www.moir.gov.np
Ministry of Science and Technology, Singha Durbar, Kathmandu, Nepal. Tel: +977 1 421 1661, fax: +977 1 421 1754, e-mail: info@most.gov.np, URL: http://www.most.gov.np
Ministry of Defence, Singha Durbar, Kathmandu, Nepal. Tel: +977 1 422 8089, fax: +977 1 422 8204, e-mail: mod@mos.com.np, URL: http://www.mod.gov.np/
Ministry of Education and Sports, Keshar Mahal, Kathmandu, Nepal. Tel: +977 1 421 1661, fax: +977 1 421 1754, e-mail: info@moenv.gov.np, URL: http://www.moenv.gov.np/
Ministry of Foreign Affairs, Maharajgunj, Kathmandu, Nepal. Tel: +977 1 441 6011, fax: +977 1 441 6016, e-mail: mofa@mos.com.np, URL: http://www.mofa.gov.np/
Ministry of Forests and Soil Conservation, Singh Durbar, Kathmandu, Nepal. Tel: +977 1 224892, fax: +977 1 230862, e-mail: nbu@biodiv-nepal.gov.np, URL: http://www.biodiv-nepal.gov.np
Ministry of General Administration, Singha Durbar, Kathmandu, Nepal. Tel: +977 1 424 5367, fax: +977 1 424 2138, e-mail: mog@ntc.net.np, URL: http://www.moga.gov.np
Ministry of Health and Population, Ramshah Path, Kathmandu, Nepal. Tel: +977 1 4262587, fax: +977 1 426 2587, e-mail: info@moh.gov.np, URL: http://www.moh.gov.np
Ministry of Information and Communications, Singh Durbar, Kathmandu, Nepal. Tel: +977 1 422 0150, fax: 977 1 422 7310, e-mail: moichmg@ntc.net.np, URL: http://www.moic.gov.np
Ministry of Labour and Transport, Singha Durbar, Kathmandu, Nepal. Tel: +977 1 424 7842, fax: +977 1 425 6877, e-mail: ddt@dotm.gov.np, URL: http://www.moltm.gov.np
Ministry of Land Reform and Management, Singha Durbar, Kathmandu, Nepal. Tel: +977 1 424 8797, fax: +977 1 422 0108, e-mail: lrm@most.gov.np, URL: http://www.molrm.gov.np
Ministry of Law and Justice, Singha Durbar, Kathmandu, Nepal. Tel: +977 1 422 3727, fax: +977 1 422 0684, e-mail: molaw@wlink.com.np, URL: http://www.moljpa.gov.np
Ministry of Physical Planning and Works, Singhadurbar, Kathmandu. Tel: +977 1 4228420, fax: +977 1 412199, URL: http://www.moppw.gov.np/
Ministry of Women, Children and Social Welfare, Singha Durbar, Kathmandu, Nepal. Tel: +977 1 424 1728, fax: +977 1 424 1516, e-mail: mwcsm@ntc.net.np, URL: http://www.mowcsw.gov.np
Ministry of Tourism and Civil Aviation, Singha Durbar, Kathmandu, Nepal. Tel: +977 1 423 2411, fax: +977 1 422 7758, e-mail: motca@ntc.net.np, URL: http://www.tourism.gov.np
Ministry of Physical Planning and Works, Singha Durbar, Kathmandu, Nepal. Tel: +977 1 422 7280, fax: +977 1 422 8420, e-mail: moppwnp@ntc.net.np, URL: http://www.moppw.gov.np
Ministry of Peace and Reconstruction, Singha Durbar, Kathmandu, Nepal. Tel: +977 1 421 1189, fax: +977 1 421 1173, e-mail: info@peace.gov.np, URL: http://www.peace.gov.np
Ministry of Local Development, Sri Mahal. Pulchowk, Lalitpur, Patan District. Nepal. Tel: +977 1 552 1727, fax: +977 1 552 2045, e-mail: info@mld.gov.np, URL: http://www.mld.gov.np

Political Parties
Communist Party of Nepal - Marxist-Leninist-Socialist (CPN ML-Socialist); Communist Party of Nepal - Unified Marxist-Leninist (CPN-UML); Communist Party of Nepal (CPN (United)); Madhesi People's Rights Forum (MPRF); Nepali Congress (NC); Unified Communist Party of Nepal - Maoist (UCPN-M).

Elections
Elections to the new Constituent Parliament were due to take place in November 2007, but were eventually held in April 2008. The former Maoist rebels won the most seats in the new constituent assembly. In June 2010 Prime Minister Madhav Kumar resigned following pressure from Maoists. There followed a period of a caretaker government until Jhalnath Khanal was elected to the post in February 2011.

Following parliament's failure to agree a new constitution, the prime minister called for early elections for 22 November 2012. These were again postponed and are expected to place during 2013.

Nepal's first presidential elections were held on the 19th and 21st July 2008. Ram Baran Yadav of the Nepali Congress party won 308 of the 590 votes cast in the second round, defeating Ram Raja Prasad Singh of the Communist Party of Nepal. Ram Baran Yadav assumed office on 23rd July.

Diplomatic Representation
American Embassy, Pani Pokhari, Kathmandu, Nepal. Tel: +977 1 4411179; fax: +977 1 4419963, URL: http://nepal.usembassy.gov
Ambassador: Peter W. Bodde
British Embassy, PO Box 106, Lainchaur, Kathmandu PO Box 106, Nepal. Tel: +977 1 410583, fax: +977 1 411789, e-mail: bekathmandu@fco.gov.uk, URL: http://ukinnepal.fco.gov.uk/en/
Ambassador: Andrew Sparkes CMG (page 1518)
Royal Nepalese Embassy, 12A Kensington Palace Gardens, London, W8 4QU, United Kingdom. Tel: +44(0) 20 7229 1594/6231, fax: +44 (0) 20 7792 9861, e-mail: info@nepembassy.org.uk, URL: http://www.nepembassy.org.uk
Ambassador: Dr Suresh Chandra Chalise
Royal Nepalese Embassy, 2131 Leroy Place NW, Washington, DC 20008, USA. Tel: +1 202 667 4550, fax: +1 202 667 5534, e-mail: info@nepalembassyusa.org, URL: http://www.nepalembassyusa.org
Ambassador: Shankar Prasad Sharma
Permanent Mission of the Kingdom of Nepal to the UN, 820 Second Avenue, Suite 17B, New York, NY 10017, USA. Tel+1 212 370 3988, fax: +1 212 953 2038, e-mail: nepal@un.int, URL: http://www.un.int/nepal
Ambassador: Gyan Chandra Acharya

LEGAL SYSTEM

The Interim Constitution of Nepal, 2007, provides for three tiers of Court, which include the Supreme Court of the Kingdom of Nepal, the Court of Appeal and the District Courts. The Supreme Court is the highest court. All courts and judicial instituions except the constitutional assembly court, are under the supreme court. The Distirict Court is the Court of First Instance. There is provision to establish special types of court or tribunaks.

The judicial council, established under the Interim constitution of Nepal 2007, recommends the appointment, transfer, disciplinary action and dismissal of judges.

During and following the recent political upheavals in Nepal, there have been many instances when the security forces have acted independently of government, at times committing serious human rights abuses, as did the Maoists and the Young Communist League (YCL). The Nepal Army (NA) were confined to barracks in accordance with the Comprehensive Peace Agreement (CPA) of 2006, whilst the police force occasionally used excessive force to dispel demonstrations. Violence and intimidation continue, and there is impunity for human rights violators. The independence of the judiciary has been compromised.

The death penalty was abolished in 1997.

Supreme Court of Nepal, URL: http://www.supremecourt.gov.np/
Chief Justice: Rt. Hon'ble Mr. Min Bahadur Rayamajhee

National Human Rights Commission, Harihar Bhawan, Pulchowk, Lalitpur, Nepal. Tel: +977 (0)1 501 0015, e-mail: nhrc@nhrcnepal.org, URL: http://www.nhrcnepal.org/

LOCAL GOVERNMENT

The country is divided for administrative purposes into 14 zones, Bagmati, Bheri, Dhawalagiri, Gandaki, Janakpur, Karnali, Kosi, Lumbini, Mahakali, Mechi, Narayani, Rapti, Sagarmatha and Seti. There are also 75 districts and for development purposes five regions, the Eastern, Central, Western, Midwestern and Far Western Development Regions. There are elected Development Committees at village, district and national level, so there are 75 district development committees, 3,913 village development committees and 36,023 ward committees.

AREA AND POPULATION

Area
Nepal is a landlocked country situated in the central Himalayas between India and the Tibet Autonomous Region, in the People's Republic of China. It has an area of 54,362 sq. miles. Its highest point is Mount Everest at 8,848 metres. The climate varies according to the region, with sub-tropical summers and mild winters in the south and cool summers and harsh winters in the north.

To view a map, consult http://www.un.org/Depts/Cartographic/map/profile/nepal.pdf

NEPAL

Population

Estimated figures for 2010 put the population at 29.259 million. Approximately 19 per cent of the population lives in urban areas. The capital, Kathmandu, has an estimated population of 1.7 million. Other important towns are Lalitpur (466,000) and Bhaktapur (225,000). The figures for these three towns include some outlying villages and rural areas. On average the population is growing by 2.1 per cent annually.

The Nepalese people descend from Mongolian, Indian and Tibetan ancestors. Over 50 per cent of the population are Nepalese the next largest ethnic group are Bihari which make up around 19 per cent. Nepali is the official language but is spoken by only half the population. Newari is also spoken although mainly in Kathmandu, Tibetan languages are common and some Indian languages are also spoken. Numerous other languages are spoken according to the cultural community.

Births, Marriages, Deaths

Figures from 2010 show that the birth rate is around 24.1 per 1,000 population and the death rate 6.2 per 1,000 population. Life expectancy from birth was an average of 65 years for males and 69 years in 2009. Healthy life expectancy is estimated at 55 years. Approximately 36 per cent of the population is under 15 years old and 6 per cent over 60 years. The median age is 21 years. The total fertility rate is estimated as 2.7 children per female. (Source: http://www.who.int, World Health Statistics 2012)

Public Holidays 2014

11 April: Nepali New Year
8 October: Ghatasthapana
3 October: Bijaya Dashami
23 October: Lakshmi Puja
25 October: Bhai Tika

EMPLOYMENT

75 per cent of the population are employed in agriculture, 18 per cent in services and only around 7 per cent are employed in industry. In 2008 the unemployment rate was estimated at 45 per cent. As agriculture forms the basis of the economy the majority of those unemployed live in urban areas.

Bonded labour was abolished in July 2000 freeing up an estimated 38,000 people.

BANKING AND FINANCE

Currency

1 Nepalese Rupee = 100 paisa.

GDP/GNP, Inflation, National Debt

Nepal is the poorest country in Asia. The economy is largely based on agriculture with a developing tourism industry. Remittances from abroad contribute a significant amount (US$2 billion). The infrastructure is weak, with regular power shortages. Per capita GDP was 30,272 rupees in 2008. Approximately 30 per cent of the population live below the poverty line. Figures for 2009 put GDP at US$12.5 billion giving a growth rate that year of 4.7 per cent. Growth in 2010 was estimated at 4.5 per cent and forecast to be 4.0 per cent in 2011. In 2010, agriculture made up 35 per cent of GDP, 15 per cent of industry and services 50 per cent.

The following table shows the industrial origin of GDP in recent years at current prices (million Rupees).

Sector	2008	2009	2010
Agriculture	247,191	309,553	383,094
Mining	4,375	5,084	5,782
Manufacturing	57,185	65,447	70,490
Electricity, water & gas	15,219	14,629	16,526
Construction	54,134	63,521	71,082
Trade	116,808	138,064	163,684
Transport & communications	76,818	92,618	95,239
Finance	107,174	120,725	137,460
Public administration & others	100,537	129,031	152,680
Total	815,658	988,053	1,170,993
Source: Asian Development Bank			

Inflation in 2010 was estimated at 10 per cent and 9.5 per cent in 2011. Total external debt was an estimated US$3.7 billion in 2011.

Balance of Payments / Imports and Exports

In April 2004 Nepal joined the World Trade Organisation.

The following table shows the value of external trade in recent years. Figures are in million rupees, and for financial years ending July 15.

Foreign Trade

Trade	2008	2009	2010
Exports, fob	59,267	67,698	60,824
Imports, cif	221,938	284,470	374,335
Trade balance	-162,671	-216,772	-313,511
Source: Asian Development Bank			

In 2009 the principal exports were garments, carpets, jute goods and pulses. Main imported goods are fuels, basic manufactured goods, machinery including vehicles and chemicals. Nepal's main trading partners are India, China, the EU, and the USA.

Central Bank

Nepal Rastra Bank, Central Office, Baluwatar, Kathmandu, Nepal. Tel: +977 1 419804, fax: +977 1 414553, e-mail: nrb@mos.com.np, URL: http://www.nrb.org.np
Governor: Dr. Yuba Raj Khatiwada

Chambers of Commerce and Trade Organisations

Nepal Britain Chamber of Commerce and Industry, URL: http://www.nbcci.org
Nepal Chamber of Commerce, URL: http://www.nepalchamber.org
Pokhara Chamber of Commerce and Industry, URL: http://www.pokharachamber.org.np

MANUFACTURING, MINING AND SERVICES

Primary and Extractive Industries

Nepal has small deposits of quartz, lignite, copper and iron ore.

Energy

Marsyangdi, Kulekhani and Devighat electricity generating schemes provide 60 mW and 14.1 mW for the national grid respectively. Other schemes are in various stages of development including the Pancheshwore Multipurpose Project in the Mahakali River, the Australian West Seti project and the Arun 3 project in eastern Nepal. Over 80 per cent of electricity is generated from hydroelectric sources. Electricity is seen as an export of the future. At present a programme for rural electrification is under way. Figures from the EIA show in 2010 Nepal generated 3.17 billion kilowatthours and consumed 2.74 billion kilowatthours. Nepal has no oil resources of its own and used an estimated 19,000 barrels per day in 2011.

Manufacturing

The Government's stated policy is to encourage domestic and overseas investment in small industries. Nepal exports products such as handicrafts, skins and hides, garments, jute and tea and imports machinery, construction materials, transport equipment and medicines. Main export products are carpets, clothing, jute goods, leather and grain. Main imported goods are petroleum products, machinery and fertilizer. The following table shows manufacturing output in recent years. Figures are in thousand metric tons:

Manufacturing Production

Product	2004	2005
Cement	279.4	277.7
Iron goods	140.0 (2002)	155.0 (2003)
Sugar	96.2	97.8
Soap	53.8	55.1
Jute goods	35.7	36.1
Tea	11.4	12.5
Source: Asian Development Bank		

Tourism

Figures for 2006 show that there were 375,000 tourist arrivals, down from 385,000 visitors in 2004.

Agriculture

The agricultural sector accounts for around 80 per cent of employment and contributes 40 per cent of GDP. The main crops grown are rice, sugarcane, maize, wheat, potatoes and pulses. The following table shows agricultural production in recent years.

Agricultural Production in 2010

Produce	Int. $'000*	Tonnes
Rice, paddy	1,040,201	4,023,820
Vegetables fresh nes	566,043	3,003,820
Indigenous buffalo meat	444,193	165,021
Buffalo milk, whole, fresh	425,544	1,066,870
Potatoes	387,808	2,517,700
Fruit fresh nes	246,757	706,972
Wheat	226,392	1,556,540
Maize	217,400	1,855,180
Ginger	142,754	210,790
Indigenous cattle meat	134,941	49,953
Cow milk, whole, fresh	133,884	429,030
Indigenous goat meat	112,208	46,830

* unofficial figures
Source: http://faostat.fao.org/site/339/default.aspx Food and Agriculture Organization of the United Nations, Food and Agricultural commodities production

Fishing

The total catch for 2010 was estimated at 21,500 tonnes.

COMMUNICATIONS AND TRANSPORT

Travel Requirements

Citizens of the USA, Canada, Australia and the EU require a valid passport and a visa, which can be obtained on arrival at the airport. Business can be conducted on a Tourist visa for up to 30 days. Other nationals should contact the embassy to check visa requirements.

Transit passengers not leaving the airport and continuing their journey on the same day as arrival do not require a visa.

National Airlines
The national carrier of Nepal is, **Royal Nepal Airlines** URL: http://www.royalnepal-airlines.com
Services are international, regional and domestic passenger. The airline employs approximately 2,200 and has a fleet of approximately 15.

International Airports
Nepal has one international airport and around 40 domestic airfields. Many international carriers now fly to Nepal including Thai Airways, Dragon Air/Cathay Pacific and ArkeFly.

Railways
There is around 100 km of rail track close to the Indian border.

Roads
Recent estimates put total road length at around 17,000 km. Vehicles are driven on the left. Bridge work on the East/West Highway to Butwal is now complete, as is the Dharan/Dhankuta Road. Recent figures show there are around 100,000 vehicles on the roads.

HEALTH

Recent figures show that Nepal has approximately 89 hospitals with nearly 7,000 beds. There is also a system of health centres, health posts and sub health posts. In 2009, the government spent approximately 7.7 per cent of its total budget on healthcare (up from 6.5 per cent in 2000), accounting for 32.0 per cent of all healthcare spending. External resources accounted for 16.4 per cent of total expenditure. Total expenditure on healthcare equated to 5.5 per cent of the country's GDP. Per capita expenditure on health was approximately US$24, compared with US$12 in 2000. Figures for 2000-10 show that there are 5,384 physicians (2 per 10,000 population), 11,825 nurses and midwives (5 per 10,000 population), 358 pharmaceutical personnel and 359 dentists. There are 50 hospital beds per 10,000 population.

According to the latest WHO figures, in 2010 approximately 89 per cent of the population had access to improved drinking water. In the same year, 31 per cent of the population had access to improved sanitation. Diarrhoea accounts for 15 per cent of childhood deaths.

The infant mortality rate (probability of dying before age 1) in 2009 was 39 per 1,000 live births. The child mortality rate (under 5 years) was 48 per 1,000 live births. In 2008, the most common causes of death in children aged under five were: prematurity 32 per cent, birth asphyxia 12 per cent, neonatalsepsis 8 per cent, pneumonia 16 per cent, and diarrhoea 6 per cent. In the period 2005-11, approximately 49.3 per cent of children aged under 5 years old were classified as stunted and 38.8 per cent were classified as underweight. (Source: http://www.who.int, World Health Statistics 2012)

EDUCATION

Compulsory, free, government-run education is available from six to 11 years. Secondary education lasts from 11-16 years, divided into two stages of two and three years.

There are two state universities: the Tribhuvan University, Kathmandu and the Mahendra Sanskrit Viswavidyalaya in Beljhundi Dang.

Figures for 2007 show that primary school enrolment was put at 76 per cent, 78 per cent for males and 74 per cent for females, secondary school enrolment that year was 42 per cent, 44 per cent for males and 40 per cent for females. Adult illiteracy rates are high. Recent statistics from UNESCO estimated the average rate of literacy in 2007 to be 56.5 per cent, amongst the younger population, 15-24 years olds, the average literacy rate was 79.3 per cent the rate is considerably higher in men than women.

RELIGION

The official religion is Hinduism followed by some 69 per cent of the population. Buddhism is also practiced (9.0 per cent). There are also small numbers of Muslims (4.0 per cent) and Christians (3.0 per cent)

Nepal has a religious liberty rating of 3 on a scale of 1 to 10 (10 is most freedom). (Source: World Religion Database)

COMMUNICATIONS AND MEDIA

During the 10-year Maoist rebellion both sides perpetrated attacks on the media.

Newspapers
Nepal's main newspapers are:
Gorkhapatra, URL: http://www.gorkhapatra.org.np; Nepali Hindi Daily; The Rising Nepal, (English), URL: http://www.gorkhapatra.org.np; Motherland, (English); The Commoner, (English); The Independent; Kantipur, URL: http://www.kantipuronline.com

Broadcasting
Private TV and radio stations operate alongside state run services. The state-run Nepal Television Corporation also runs the NTV Metro Channels.

Telecommunications
The telephone system is generally poor. An estimated 800,000 landlines are in operation and 4.2 million mobiles. Approximately 500,000 Nepalese have regular access to the internet.

ENVIRONMENT

Nepal is a party to the following international agreements: Biodiversity, Climate Change, Climate Change-Kyoto Protocol, Desertification, Endangered Species, Hazardous Wastes, Law of the Sea, Ozone Layer Protection, Tropical Timber 83, Tropical Timber 94, and Wetlands.

In 2010 Nepal's emissions from the consumption of fossil fuels totalled 3.36 million metric tons of carbon dioxide.

NETHERLANDS
Kingdom of the Netherlands
Koninkrijk der Nederlanden

Capital: Amsterdam (Population estimate, 2011: 780,000)

Seat of Government: The Hague (Population estimate, 2011: 500,000)

Head of State: King Willem-Alexander (page 1537)

National Flag: Three horizontal stripes coloured red, white then blue

CONSTITUTION AND GOVERNMENT

Constitution
The foundation of the Dutch Republic was laid in 1579. Provision was made for a democratic form of government, with the leadership entrusted to the House of Orange. The republic became a kingdom under the House of Orange in 1815 after the defeat of Napoleon, and the first constitution of this kingdom was approved in that year. In 1848 the constitution was revised and the Netherlands became a Constitutional Monarchy. The Monarch is the head of state for the Netherlands and also for Aruba, Curaçao, Sint Maarten, Bonaire, Sint Eustatius and Saba, although the monarchy is represented by a Governor in each of these.

The Constitution of the Netherlands guarantees fundamental democratic rights, including freedom of the press, religion and speech, the right of association, assembly and petition and, since its revision in 1983, a number of social rights, including the proviso that it shall be the concern of the authorities to promote the provision of sufficient employment and to secure the means of subsistence of the population. It declares that the ministers shall be responsible to Parliament for acts of government. The cabinet discusses and agrees government policy. It is responsible collectively to both houses of parliament. The Cabinet must resign if it loses the confidence of Parliament.

To consult the full constitution, please visit: http://english.minbzk.nl/subjects/constitution-and.

International Relations
The Netherlands enjoys close relations with its Benelux partner countries, Belgium and Luxembourg and was a founding member of the European Communities, now known as the EU, as well as being a founding member of the International Monetary Fund (IMF), the World Bank, the UN, the Western European Union (WEU), and NATO.

Recent Events
On June 1 2005, the Netherlands held a referendum on whether to ratify the proposed European Union Constitution. Turnout for the vote was nearly 63 per cent and the Constitution was rejected by nearly 62 per cent of those that voted. It was felt that among the reasons for the no vote was anxiety about the rapid enlargement of the EU, disillusionment with the Euro and defence of the Netherlands traditionally liberal policies.

Following the 2003 election a coalition government was formed made up of the Christian Democrats, the People's Party for Freedom and Democracy and the Democrats-66 Party. In June 2006 the coalition fell apart when the Democrats-66 withdrew. This was due to disagreements within the coalition on the immigration policy. Prime Minister Balkenende announced a temporary cabinet which would serve until an early election called for 22 November 2006.

NETHERLANDS

In November 2006 the government backed a proposal which would ban Muslim women from wearing the burqa in public. The ban was thought to affect a very small minority of women and was aimed at promoting social cohesion.

During celebrations for Queen's Day in April 2009, a man deliberately drove his car through crowds watching the Royal family passing in an open topped bus. Six members of the crowd were killed but the Royal Family were unharmed

In February 2010 the coalition government collapsed following disagreements about Dutch troops deployed in Afghanistan. Originally Dutch troops should have left Afghanistan in 2008 but at the request of NATO they were to stay until August 2010. NATO then made a further request for Dutch troops to stay on past the August deadline. The Labour Party, the second largest party in the coalition, could not agree to the troops staying and left the coalition leading to the collapse of the government. Prime Minister Balkenende offered his resignation and was then re-appointed on February 23 to lead a caretaker government until elections could be held on June 9. The People's Party for Freedom and Democracy (VVD) became the largest party in the parliament, just ahead of the Labour Party (PvdA). Negotiations then began to form a new coalition. In August 2010 the Netherlands withdrew its 1,900 soldiers from Afghanistan. The same month the Liberal Party began talks with the Christian Democrats and Geert Wilders' Freedom Party over the forming of a coalition government, in September the talks collapsed after Geert Wilders walked out of the talks following objections from the Christian Democrats over his anti-Islamic and anti-immigration opinions.

In October 2010 the anti-Islam MP Geert Wilders went on trial in Amsterdam accused of inciting hatred against Muslims.

On October 10 2010 the dependency known as the Netherlands Antilles ceased to exist and the five islands assumed their new constitutional status. Curacao and St Maarten became autonomous countries within the Kingdom of the Netherlands, joining Aruba, which gained the status in 1986. Bonaire, St Eustatius and Saba are now autonomous special municipalities of the kingdom. Under the new arrangement, the Dutch government remains responsible for defence and foreign policy and in the case of Curacao will initially oversee the island's finances under a debt relief agreement.

A new government was finally sworn in on 14 October 2010. The new government is formed of a coalition between the Christian Democratic Alliance (CDA) and the People's Party for Freedom and Democracy (VVD). It will receive parliamentary support from the Freedom Party (PVV). The number of government members has been reduced from 27 to 20. The CDA and the VVD each have six ministers and four state secretaries. The number of ministries has also been reduced from 13 to 11. The Ministry of Economic Affairs and the Ministry of Agriculture, Nature and Food Quality are being merged into the new Ministry of Economic Affairs, Agriculture and Innovation. The Ministry of Transport, Public Works and Water Management and the Ministry of Housing, Spatial Planning and the Environment are being merged into the new Ministry of Infrastructure and the Environment.

In July 2011, a Dutch appeals court ruled that the Dutch state was responsible for three men who died in the Srebrenica massacre. The ruling was unexpected and may mark the start of more compensation claims. The case focused on three Bosnian Muslims who were working for the Dutch force, Dutchbat, during the 1992-95 Bosnia war and who were among thousands who took shelter in the UN compound as Serb forces overran Srebrenica on 11 July 1005. On 13 July Dutch peacekeepers began to expel the refugees from their base, as demanded by the Bosnia Serb troops. Approximately 8,000 men and boys were killed in the massacre. The Dutch have argued they were let down by the UN and that its troops did not have adequate support. Gen. Mladic, who was in charge of the Bosnian Serb forces, is currently on trial in The Hague on charges including genocide.

In February 2012, Prince Friso was buried in an avalanche whilst skiing. Although rescued he suffered massive brain damage and has remained in a coma.

In April 2012 following the government's proposed austerity budget, the Freedom Party withdrew its support and refused to back the budget. Prime Minister Mark Rutte tendered the resignation of his cabinet. Mark Rutte will stay in the role of caretaker until new elections can be organised. Elections took place on 12 September 2012. Prime Minister Mark Rutte claimed victory for his liberal VVD party which won 41 seats. Labour came a close second and coalition talks began. The anti-immigrant Freedom Party sustained losses.

The new Rutte-Asscher coalition government was sworn in on 5 November 2012. The coalition comprises the People's Party for Freedom and Democracy (VVD) and the Labour Party (PvdA), with seven ministers and three state secretaries from the VVD and six ministers and four state secretaries from the PvdA. Two new ministerial posts have been formed: Minister for Foreign Trade and Development Co-operation and Minister for Housing and the Central Government Sector. The position of Minister for Immigration, Integration and Asylum Policy no longer exists; immigration and asylum policy is now the responsibility of the Ministry of Security and Justice and Integration is now the responsibility of the Ministry of Social Affairs and Employment. The government has warned that tough austerity measures lie ahead.

In January 2013, Queen Beatrix announced that she would abdicate in favour of her son Prince Willem-Alexander. She formally abdicated on 30 April 2013 and her son became King Willem-Alexander.

Legislature
Parliament, which is called the States-General or *Staten-Generaal*, consists of two chambers, the Upper House and the Lower House.

Upper House
The Senate (*Eerste Kamer*) has 75 members indirectly elected for a term of four years by members of the 12 Provincial Councils (the electorate vote in members of the Provincial Councils). The functions of the Senate are restricted to approving or rejecting bills passed by the Second Chamber, without the power of inserting amendments.

Eerste Kamer der Stanen-General, Binnenhof 22, Postbus 20017, 2500 EA The Hague, Netherlands. Tel: +31 (0)70 312 9200, fax: +31 (0)70 365 3868, e-mail: griffie@eerstekamer.nl, URL: http://www.eerstekamer.nl
President: G.J. (Fred) de Graaf

Lower House
The Lower House, or *Tweede Kamer*, has 150 members who are voted for by universal suffrage, under the system of proportional representation for a term of four years. The Lower House has to approve new legislation proposed by the government. Members of parliament may also put forward bills.

Tweede Kamer der Staten-General, Lange Poten 4, Postbus 20018, 2500 EA The Hague, Netherlands. Tel: +31 70 318 2211, fax: +31 70 318 3441, URL: http://www.tweedekamer.nl
President: Anouchka van Miltenburg

Cabinet (as at June 2013)
Prime Minister, Minister for General Affairs: H.E Dr Mark Rutte (VVD) (page 1506)
Deputy Prime Minister, Minister of Social Affairs and Employment: Lodewijk Asscher (page 1380)
Minister of Foreign Affairs: Frans Timmermans (page 1525)
Minister of Security and Justice: Ivo Opstelten (VVD) (page 1490)
Minister of the Interior and Kingdom Relations: Ronald Plasterk (page 1496)
Minister of Education, Culture and Science: Jet Bussemaker (page 1397)
Minister of Finance: Jeroen Dijsselbloem (page 1415)
Minister of Defence: Jeanine Hennis-Plasschaert (page 1440)
Minister of Infrastructure and the Environment: Melanie Schultz Van Haegen-Maas Geesteranus (VVD) (page 1510)
Minister of Economic Affairs: Henk Kamp (VVD) (page 1453)
Minister of Health, Welfare and Sport: Edith Schippers (CDA) (page 1509)
Minister for Foreign Trade and Development Co-operation: Lilianne Ploumen (page 1496)
Minister for Housing and the Central Government Sector: Stef Blok (page 1390)
State Secretary for Security and Justice and Minister for Migration: Fred Teeven (VVD) (page 1524)
State Secretary for Education, Culture and Science: Sander Dekker (page 1414)
State Secretary for Finance: Frans Weekers (VVD) (page 1535)
Minister for the Environment: Wilma Mansveld (page 1470)
Minister for Agriculture: Sharon Dijksma (page 1415)
State Secretary for Social Affairs and Employment: Jetta Klijnsma (page 1457)
State Secretary for Health, Welfare and Sport: Martin van Rijn (page 1530)

Ministries
Government portal: URL: http://www.rijksoverheid.nl/international / http://www.government.nl/
Prime Minister's Office and Ministry of General Affairs, Binnenhof 19, Postbus 20001, 2500 EA, The Hague, Netherlands. Tel: +31 (0)70 356 4100, fax: +31 (0)70 356 4683, URL: http://www.government.nl/ministries/az; http://www.postbus51.nl/
Ministry of Defence, Plein 4, Postbus 20701, 2500 ES The Hague, Netherlands. Tel: +31 (0)70 318 8188, fax: +31 (0)70 318 7888, URL: http://www.mindef.nl
Ministry for Foreign Affairs, Bezuidenhoutseweg 67, The Hague (Postbus 20061, 2500 EB The Hague), Netherlands. Tel: +31 (0)70 348 6486, fax: +31 (0)70 348 4848, URL: http://www.minbuza.nl/en
Ministry of the Interior and Kingdom Relations, Schedeldoekshaven 200, 2511 EZ The Hague, Netherlands. (Correspondence: Postbus 20011, 2500 EA The Hague, The Netherlands) Tel: +31 (0)70 426 6302, fax: +31 (0)70 363 9153, e-mail: info@minbzk.nl, URL: http://www.minbzk.nl
Ministry of Security and Justice, Schedeldoekshaven 100, 2511 EX The Hague (Postbus 20301, 2500 EH The Hague), Netherlands. Tel: +31 (0)70 370 6850, fax: +31 (0)70 370 7594, URL: http://www.government.nl/ministries/venj
Ministry of Education, Culture and Science, Europaweg 4, Postbus 25000, 2700 LZ Zoetermeer, Netherlands. Tel: +31 (0)79 323 2323, fax: +31 (0)70 323 2320, URL: http://www.government.nl/ministries/ocw
Ministry of Finance, Korte Voorhout 7, Postbus 20201, 2500 EE The Hague, Netherlands. Tel: +31 (0)70 342 7540, fax: +31 (0)70 342 7900, URL: http://www.minfin.nl
Ministry for Social Affairs and Employment, Anna van Hannoverstraat 4, Postbus 90801, 2509 LV The Hague, Netherlands. Tel: +31 (0)70 333 4444, fax: +31 (0)70 333 4040, URL: http://www.government.nl/ministries/szw
Ministry of Health, Welfare and Sport, Parnassusplein 5, 2511 VX The Hague (Postbus 20350, 2500 EJ The Hague), Netherlands. Tel: +31 (0)70 340 7911, fax: +31 (0)70 340 7834, URL: http://www.government.nl/ministries/vws
Minister of Infrastructure and the Environment, Plesmanweg 1-6, 2597 JG The Hague, Netherlands. Tel: +31 (0)70 351 6171, fax: +31 (0)70 351 7895, URL: http://www.government.nl/ministries/ienm
Ministry of Economic Affairs, Agriculture and Innovation, PO Box 20401, 2500 EK The Hague, Netherlands. Tel: +31 77 465 6767, URL: http://www.government.nl/ministries/eleni
Office of the Queen of the Netherlands, Paleis Noordeinde, PO Box 30412, 2500 GK, The Hague, Netherlands. URL: http://www.koninklijkhuis.nl/

Political Parties
Christen Democratisch Appel (CDA, Christian Democrat Appeal, Dr. Kuyperstraat 5, POB 30453, 2500 GL The Hague, Netherlands. Tel: +31 (0)70 342 4888, fax: (0)70 364 3417, e-mail: cda@bureau.cda.nl, URL: http://www.cda.nl/
President: Sybrand van Haersma Buma
Democraten 66 (D66, Democrats 1966) Noordwal 10, 2513 EA The Hague, Netherlands. Tel: +31 (0)70 356 6066, fax: +31 (0)70 364 1917, URL: http://www.d66.nl
Party Leader: Alexander Pechtold
Partij van de Arbeid (PvdA, Labour Party) Herengracht 54, 1015 BN Amsterdam (Postbus 1310, 1000 BH Amsterdam), Netherlands. Tel: +31 (0)20 551 2155, fax: +31 (0)20 551 2250, e-mail: pvda@pvda.nl, URL: http://pvda.nl

Political Leader: Diederik Samsom

Volkspartij voor Vrijheid en Democratie (VVD, People's Party for Freedom and Democracy) Laan Copes van Cattenburch 52, 2585 GV The Hague (POB 30836, 2500 GV The Hague), Netherlands. Tel: +31 (0)70 361 3006, fax: +31 (0)70 360 8276, e-mail: int.sec@vvd.nl, URL: http://www.vvd.nl

Party Leader: Mark Rutte

GroenLinks (The Green Left) Oudegracht 312, POB 8008, 3503 RA Utrecht, Netherlands. Tel: +31 (0)30 239 9900, fax: +31 (0)30 230 0342, e-mail: info@groenlinks.nl, URL: http://www.groenlinks.nl

Leader: Jolande Sap

ChristenUnie (Christian Union), Puntenburgalaar 91, 3812 CC Amersfoort, Netherlands. Tel: +31 (0)334 226969 fax: +31 (0)334 226968, e-mail: bureau@christenunie.nl, URL: http://www.christenunie.nl

Political Leader: Arie Slob

Socialistische Partij (SP, Socialist Party) Vijverhofstraat 65, 3032 SC, Rotterdam. Tel: +31 (0)10 243 5555, fax: +31 (0)10 243 5566, e-mail: sp@sp.nl, URL: http://www.sp.nl

Leader: Emile Roemer

Partij voor de Dieren, (PvdD Party for Animals), URL: http://www.partijvoordedieren.nl

Leader: Marianne Thieme

Staatskundig Gereformeerde Partij, (SGP, Political Reformed Party), URL: http://www.sgp.nl

Leader: Kees van der Staaij

Partij voor de Vrijheid, (PVV, Party for Freedom), URL: http://www.pvv.nl

Leader: Geert Wilders (page 1537)

Onafhankelijke Senaatsfractie (OSF, Independents Senate Fraction), URL: http://www.osf.nl

Leader: Kees de Lange

50 Plus, URL: http://www.50pluspartij.nl

Leader: Henk Krol

Elections

The age of voting in the Netherlands is 18, and voting for the members of the Lower House takes place every four years.

In April 2002 the government, headed by Wim Kok of the Labour Party, resigned following a report which held them politically responsible over the failure by Dutch peacekeepers to prevent the massacre of thousands of Muslims by Bosnian Serb forces at Srebrenica in 1995. As a consequence a general election was held in May 2002.

Pim Fortuyn, leader of the anti-immigration List Pim Fortuyn Party (now dissolved), formed three months earlier, was killed by a gunman in the same month as the election. Following the election his party came second with 26 seats, with the Christian Democrats winning an overall majority with 46 seats. In July 2002 Jan Peter Balkenende, leader of the Christian Democrats, became prime minister leading a coalition government composed of the Christian Democrats, the List Pim Fortuyn Party and the People's Party for Freedom and Democracy.

The following October the government collapsed following infighting within the List Pim Fortuyn Party. A general election was held on 22 January 2003 resulting in a narrow win for the Christian Democrats. A coalition government was formed headed by the Christian Democrats the People's Party for Freedom, Democracy (VVD) and Democrats-66. In June 2006 the coalition fell apart when the Democrats-66 withdrew. This was due to disagreements within the coalition on the immigration policy. Prime Minister Balkenende announced a temporary cabinet which would serve until an early election called for 22 November 2006. Although the election took place in November the cabinet was not sworn in until the following February due to protracted coalition negotiations. The coalition was again headed by the Christian Democrats and also included the Labour Party and the Christian Union.

Election was held on June 9 2010. The People's Party for Freedom and Democracy (VVD) became the largest party in the parliament with 31 seats, just ahead of the Labour Party (PvdA) with 30 seats. The Freedom Party an anti-Islamic party led by Geert Wilders increased its number of seats to 9 to 24. The breakdown of the rest of the seats is as follows: the CDA 21 seats, the SP 15 seats, the D66 10 seats; GL 10 seats; others 9 seats. Negotiations then began on the formation of a new coalition. A caretaker government remained in place until a coalition was agreed. On 5 October 2010 the VVD agreed to form a minority government with the CDA. As their combined number of seats amounts to 52 members it means the coalition depends on the Freedom Party to pass legislation. The new government took office on 14 October.

Following the resignation of the government in April, elections were held in September 2012. Prime Minister Mark Rutte claimed victory for his liberal VVD party. Centre-left Labour came a close second. Coalition talks took place and in November a coalition was formed by the Liberals and Labour.

Election results September 2012

Party	Seats	Change
VVD	41	+10
PvdA	38	+8
Freedom Party	15	-9
Socialist	15	0
Christian Democrat Appeal	13	-8
Democrats 66	12	+2
Christian Union	5	0
Green Left	4	-6
Reformed Political Party	3	+1
50 plus	2	+2
Party for the Animals	2	0

The most recent elections for the Senate took place on 23 May 2011. The results were as follows: VVD 16 seats; PvdA 14 seats; CDA 11 seats; PVV 10 seats; SP 8 seats; D66 5 seats; GL 5 seats; others 6 seats.

Diplomatic Representation

American Embassy, Lange Voorhout 102, 2514 EJ The Hague, Netherlands. Tel: +31 (0)70 310 9209, fax: +31 (0)70 361 4688, URL: http://netherlands.usembassy.gov
Chargé d'Affaires ad interim: Edwin Nolan
British Embassy, Lange Voorhout 10, 2514 ED The Hague, Netherlands. Tel: +31 (0)70 427 0427, fax: +31 (0)70 427 0345, e-mail: library@fco.gov.uk, URL: http://ukinnl.fco.gov.uk/en
Ambassador: Paul Arkwright (page 1379)
Royal Netherlands Embassy 4200 Linnean Avenue NW, Washington, DC 20008, USA. Tel: +1 202 244 5300, fax: +1 202 362 3430, e-mail: was-az@minbuza.nl, URL: http://dc.the-netherlands.org
Ambassador: Rudolf Bekink
Royal Netherlands Embassy 38 Hyde Park Gate, London SW7 5DP, United Kingdom. Tel: +44 (0)20 7590 3200, fax: +44 (0)20 225 0947, e-mail: london@netherlands-embassy.org.uk, URL: http://www.netherlands-embassy.org.uk
Ambassador: Laetitia van den Assum (page 1530)
Netherlands Mission to the UN 235 East 45th Street, 16th Floor, New York, NY 10017, USA. Tel: +1 212 697 5547, fax: +1 212 370 1954, e-mail: netherlands@un.int, URL: http://www.netherlandsmission.org/homepage.asp
Permanent Representative: H.E. Herman Schaper

Reigning Royal Family

This is the younger branch of the house of Nassau (see also Luxembourg) descended from Otto, Count of Nassau-Siegen, who died in the late 13th Century. Succession has been in the male and female lines since 29 March 1814. The sons of the Queen bear the title Prince of the Netherlands, Prince of Orange-Nassau, Jonkheer van Amsberg.

H.M. Beatrix Wilhelmina Armgard, Queen of the Netherlands, succeeded her mother, Juliana, following her abdication on 30 April 1980. The Queen was married to Claus George Willem Otto Frederik Geert von Amsberg, created H.R.H. Prince of the Netherlands, Jonkheer van Amsberg by Royal Decree (6 February 1966). They had three sons: King Willem-Alexander (page 1537), Prince Johan Friso and Prince Constantin. On 2 February 2002, Crown Prince Willem-Alexander married Ms Maxima Zorreguieta, now Queen Maxima. They have three daughters, Catharina-Amalia, Princess of Orange, Princess Alexia and Princess Ariane. On April 30 2013, Queen Beatrix formally abdicated and her eldest son became King.

LEGAL SYSTEM

The law is based on civil law system incorporating French penal theory. The judiciary is independent. Changes to the judiciary in the 1990s included the abolition of military courts and administrative courts, resulting in the following levels of court:

(i) Sub-District Court (*Kantongerecht*) is the lowest level of court. There are 62 of these courts, one in each Canton. Two-thirds of the Cantons have one Sub-District Court Judge; the remaining third have more than one. Assessors assist the judge in trying cases concerning leases. The court deals with minor criminal cases (mostly traffic offences), civil cases, small claims, and disputes such as landlord and tenant or labour. In order to make justice easily accessible people can, if they wish, represent themselves in a Sub-District Court.

(ii) District Court (*Arrondissementsrechtbank*) is the second step in The Netherlands' judicial system. There are 19 District Courts, each varying greatly in size. Each court covers three or four Cantons, and the number of judges at a court varies from 12 to 50, according to the district and inhabitants covered. In total there are 1,097 District Court judges. District Courts try criminal cases, civil cases not covered by the Sub-District Courts, and appeals from Sub-District Courts, as well as family law and commercial law cases.

(iii) Court of Appeal (*Gerechtshof*) deals with appeals from the District Courts. There are five such courts in the Netherlands, each covering three to four Districts or *ressorts*. Courts of Appeal justices number 259.

(iv) Supreme Court (*Hoge Raad der Nederlanden*) deals with the small number of appeals already dealt with by a Court of Appeal by considering whether the law has previously been correctly applied to the case. The Supreme Court's Attorney-General is the highest representative. The Supreme Court is also able to pass judgement on cases that have been heard in Aruba and the Netherlands Antilles. There are a total of 79 Supreme Court justices.

A Public Prosecutor's Office is attached to each court, and comprises a Chief Public Prosecutor, some Public Prosecutors and sometimes Traffic Commissioners. The head of the Public Prosecutions Department is the Minister of Justice, who may give instructions to a Public Prosecutor to prosecute or not.

Judges are appointed for life and there is no trial by jury.

The Council for the Judiciary advises on new legislation which has implications for the administration of justice and acts as a spokesperson for the judiciary on both national and international levels. It is also responsible for allocation of budgets, supervision of financial management and personnel policy amongst other areas.

The government respects the rights of its citizens. The Netherlands was one of the earliest states to abolish the death penalty, in 1870.

Supreme Court, URL: http://www.rechtspraak.nl/information+in+english

NETHERLANDS

Dutch Equal Treatment Commission, Commissie Gelijke Behandeling, Postbus 16001, 3500 DA Utrecht, The Netherlands. Tel: +31 (0)30 888 3888, fax: +31 (0)30 888 3883, URL: http://www.cgb.nl/

LOCAL GOVERNMENT

The Netherlands is divided for administrative purposes into 12 provinces. Each province has its representative council, elected by residents of that state. A Provincial Executive is then appointed from amongst those elected which is responsible for the administration of the province, including spatial planning, environmental issues, energy and social work, sport and culture. A Queen's Commissioner (see below) is appointed by the Queen and government ministers for six years (can be extended to a second term) and he/she chairs the Provincial Council and the Provincial Executive. The number of members of each council varies with the size of the population in the province they represent. The most densely populated province is Zuid Holland (83 members), while the least populated is Flevoland (43 members). Council members are elected for four years by universal suffrage.

As of 2012 there were 415 municipalities, reduced from 548 following the merger of some of the smaller municipalities. The municipalities are governed by municipal councils elected by universal suffrage, and their areas of responsibility include water supply, public schools, health care, social services and traffic. The number of members varies with the size of the population. The municipal councils are presided over by a burgomaster, who is appointed by the Government for six years. In each municipality there is a committee of the burgomaster and two to six aldermen charged with executive powers.

In an effort to reduce the gap between central government and its citizens, some central government powers are being devolved to provincial and municipality level. Municipalities can now set up a city district with its own council if it has a resident population of more than 100,000. Amsterdam and Rotterdam now have their own district councils.

The provinces and their capital cities are shown in the following table:

Province	Capital
Groningen	Groningen
Friesland	Leeuwarden
Drenthe	Assen
Overijssel	Zwolle
Gelderland	Arnhem
Utrecht	Utrecht
North Holland	Haarlem
South Holland	The Hague
Zeeland	Middelburg
North Brabant	Des Hertogenbosch
Limburg	Maastricht
Flevoland	Lelystad

AREA AND POPULATION

Area
The Netherlands, also known as Holland, is situated in northern Europe, bordering Germany to the east and Belgium to the south. It has a surface area of 41,526 sq. km, of which 8,000 sq. km. is water. Almost a quarter of the country is below sea level. The country's lowest point, at 6.7 metres below sea level, is near Rotterdam. The highest point, the Vaalserberg, is 321 metres high, and lies in the southeast, near the border with Germany and Belgium. The Netherlands is, of course, famous for its windmills, which were originally used to drain the land, although pumping stations are now used. The Netherlands has an extensive range of seawalls and coastal dunes which protect it from the sea which together with a system on levees and dikes inland along the rivers protects the country from flooding. The Netherlands has 451 km of coastline. Main rivers running through the Netherlands include the Rhine, the Scheldt and the Meuse.

To view a map of the Netherlands, please consult:
http://www.lib.utexas.edu/maps/cia08/netherlands_sm_2008.gif

The climate is moderate with an average summer temperature of 17°C and an average winter temperature of 2°C. Annual rainfall is approximately 750 mm.

Population
The total estimated population was 16,730,000 in January 2012 (up from 16,305,526 in 2005). The largest age group, according to January 2012 figures, is 40-65 years (5,977,000), followed by 20-40 years (4,142,000), 0-20 years (3,895,000), 65-80 years (2,030,000), and 80 years and over (686,000). The Netherlands is one of the most densely populated countries in the world. Population density for the whole country rose from 472 inhabitants per sq. km in 2001 to 482 inhabitants per sq. km in 2004. The number of people living in an urban area rose from almost 6.3 million in 1998 to more than 6.8 million (41.7 per cent of last year's population) in 2005.

Of the 2010 population of 16,575,000, a total of 7,777,000 live in West Netherlands; 3,567,000 live in South Netherlands; 3,517,000 in East Netherlands; and 1,714,000 (per cent) in North Netherlands. The capital city is Amsterdam and in March 2005 it had a population of 739,000. The Hague (Den Haag), is the seat of government and had a population of 468,000.

Total number of immigrants in 2010 was 154,000 up from the 2009 figure of 146,000, whilst emigrants numbered 91,000 in 2010 up from 85,000 in 2009. Figures for 2008 show that the Netherlands had 13.4 thousand first requests for asylum, up from 7.4 thousand in 2007. (Source: Statistics Netherlands).

The official languages of the Netherlands are Dutch and Frisian.

Births, Marriages, Deaths
The number of births fell to 179,000 in 2011 from 184,000 in 2010. The number of deaths in 2011 stayed the same as the previous year at 136,000. Infant mortality rose from 1,088 in 2001 to 1,104 in 2002 (equivalent to 5.0 infant deaths per 1,000 live births). Provisional figures for 2011 show that the number of immigrants arriving in the Netherlands was 160,000 and the number of people emigrating was 134,000.

Marriages numbered 75,400 in 2010 (down from 88,100 in 2000). In 2005 the number of divorces had risen to 33,000. At the end of 2000 legislation was passed that allowed same-sex marriages to take place. The number of recorded marriages between men fell from 1,339 in 2001 to 935 in 2002, whilst the number of marriages between women fell from 1,075 in 2001 to 903 in 2002. In January 2005 nearly 750,000 unmarried couples were living together. In 2005 3.3 million people aged 18-62 lived without a partner (single people, 1.6 million; children living at home, 1.1 million; single parents, 394,000; other members of multi-person households, 178,000). (Source: Statistics Netherlands, Voorburg/Heerlen 2007)

Public Holidays 2014
1 January: New Year's Day
18 April: Good Friday (Banking Sector only)
21 April: Easter Monday
30 April: King's Birthday (Koninginnedag)
5 May: Liberation Day (public holiday for Civil Service only)
29 May: Ascension Day
9 June: Whit Monday
25 December: Christmas Day
26 December: Boxing Day

EMPLOYMENT

Unemployment rose to a ten-year high in 1994 when it was recorded at 547,000 (8.0 per cent). Since then, however, the figure has fallen steadily until 2002, when it began to rise again. Former prime minister Wim Kok introduced an economic system call the Polder Model, where policy was agreed by government, unions and employers; as a result of this collaborative system, wages were kept low, and towards the mid 1990s the Netherlands experienced a strong economy and very low unemployment. Towards the end of the 1990s, wages began to rise and this, coupled with the downturn in the global economy, adversely affected the Dutch economy resulting in low economic growth and higher unemployment.

In common with many countries the Netherlands has been hit by the global economic downturn and credit crisis but unemployment has not risen as drastically. In January 2009 the unemployment rate was put at the relatively low figure of 2.7 per cent. It rose to 4.4 per cent by March and was predicted to rise to 5.5 per cent in 2010. The actual figure was slightly lower than expected at 5.34 per cent and it stayed at this rate for 2011. The government has introduced a scheme of target benefits which are designed to keep people in their jobs. If a company is in a position where its orders are falling, it can apply for 'wage top ups' from the government whereby if employees are put on reduced hours the government will make up the shortfall in their wages for a short period of time. Figures for July 2012 put the unemployment rate at 6.8 per cent. This rose to 6.9 per cent in December, 7.7 per cent in January 2013 and 8.2 in April 2013.

Working population, '000s

Labour Market	2005	2009	2010	2011
Labour force	7,455	7,846	7,817	7,811
Employed labour force	6,973	7,469	7,391	7,392
Unemployed labour force	482	377	426	419

Source: Statistics Netherlands, Voorburg/Heerlen 2012

Employment by Economic Activity

Sector	2010*	2011*
Agriculture, hunting, forestry & fishing	109,000	109,000
Manufacturing and energy	884,000	876,000
Construction	381000	372,000
Trade, transport, hotels & restaurants	1,988,000	2,019,000
Information & communication	240,000	242,000
Financial institutions	264,000	259,000
Renting, buying, selling real estate	71,000	70,000
Business services	1,300,000	1,315,000
Public administration & services	535,000	523,000
Education	513,000	512,000
Health & social work	1,311,000	1,341,000
Culture, recreation, other services	274,000	270,000
Total	7,870,000	7,910,000
Men	4,218,000	4,227,000
Women	3,652,000	3,683,000

* Provisional figures
Source: Statistical Yearbook Netherlands 2012

Federatie Nederlandse Vakbeweging (FNV) (Netherlands Trade Union Confederation), URL: http://www.fnv.nl/

BANKING AND FINANCE

Currency

On 1 January 2002 the euro became legal tender. Prior to that the currency was the Guilder (Gld), or Dutch florin (dfl) = 100 cents

1 euro (€) = 100 cents

€ = 2.20371 Dutch guilders (European Central Bank irrevocable conversion rate)

Bank notes are in denominations of 5, 10, 20, 50, 100, 200 and 500 euro. Coins are in denominations of 1, 2, 5, 10, 20 and 50 cents and 1 and 2 euro.

GDP/GNP, Inflation, National Debt

The Netherlands' export-based economy was hit by the global recession at the turn of the century, and experienced slow growth over the years 2001 to 2004. The Dutch economy is heavily dependent on its exports of goods and services and therefore any global downturn will affect growth. High wage increases since the 1990s has also made some goods less competitive in the international market.

Economic growth was recorded at 3.9 per cent in 1999, falling to 3.3 per cent in 2000, 1.3 per cent in 2001, 0.2 per cent in 2002, -0.8 per cent in 2003 and one per cent in 2004. GDP grew by 1.5 per cent in 2005, an estimated 3.0 per cent in 2006 and 3.7 per cent in 2007. Forecast figures for 2008 put GDP growth at 2.1 per cent and 2 per cent in 2009. Following the global economic slowdown and credit crisis, these figures were revised with growth in 2008 being put at 2.2 per cent and forecast to be -0.75 per cent in 2009 before rising to 1.75 per cent in 2010 (mainly due to a stronger export market). The government introduced a stimulus package to boost spending for the year 2009-10 and then a package of austerity measures will introduced when the economy begins to recover. Figures for 2011 put the average economic growth rate at 1.2 per cent even though the country went into recession in the second half of the year. The economy was forecast to contract in the first half of 2012 with a modest recovery of 1 per cent in 2013.

GDP and GNI in €million

Year	GDP (gross, market prices)	GNI (net, market prices)
2005	513,407	440,176
2010*	588,414	493,924
2011*	602,105	517,032

* provisional

Source: Statistics Netherlands, Statistical Yearbook 2012

Gross Value Added by Industry at basic prices, € million

Economic Sector	2008*	2009*
Agriculture, forestry and fishing	9,414	7,886
Mining and quarrying	21,579	15,095
Manufacturing	71,767	63,770
Electricity, gas and water	10,779	12,136
Construction	30,570	30,409
Trade, hotels, restaurants and repair	75,857	70,661
Transport, storage and communication	35,007	31,926
Financial and business activities	149,658	144,812
General government	58,675	61,349
Care and other service activities	35,692	70,027
Total	528,998	508,071

* Provisional figures

Source: Statistics Netherlands, Yearbook 2010

Inflation in 2010 averaged 1.3 per cent, 2.3 per cent in 2011 and 2.7 per cent in 2012.

Foreign Investment

Over 50 per cent of Dutch foreign investment is destined for EU member countries.

Balance of Payments / Imports and Exports
Imports & Exports of Goods, Totals, Billion €

Trade	2010	2011*
Imports total	332	364
of which European Union	177	194
Other countries	155	170
Exports total	372	405
of which European Union	276	302
Other countries	96	103
Balance of trade total	40	41
of which European Union	99	108
Other countries	-59	-67

*provisional

Source: Statistics Netherlands, Yearbook 2012

Trading patterns have changed in recent years. In 2005, the value of imports and exports with non-EU countries increased, up 15 per cent from 2004. In 2005, total imports from non-EU countries reached €11649 million, up 8 per cent from 2004. Exports to non-EU countries were worth €65,122 million. Imports from EU countries reached €138,195 million in 2005, whilst exports to EU countries reached €216,179 million, up 8 per cent from 2004. Russia and China are key import partners. The Netherlands now imports goods worth €31 billion from China.

Trade according to SITC classification is shown on the following table:

Foreign Trade by Product Group in 2011* (€ billion)

Goods	Imports	Exports
Food and live animals	32	48
Beverages and tobacco	4	7
Inedible raw materials except fuel	16	21
Mineral fuels	79	65
Animal & vegetable oils and fats	4	4
Chemical products	47	71
Manufactured goods	39	37
Machines & transport equipment	103	112
Miscellaneous articles n.e.c.	41	40
Total	364	405

*Provisional figures

Source: Statistical Yearbook 2012

Central Bank

De Nederlandsche Bank NV, PO Box 98, Westeinde 1, 1000 AB Amsterdam, Netherlands. Tel: +31 (0)20 524 9111, fax: +31 (0)20 524 2500, e-mail: info@dnb.nl, URL: http://www.dnb.nl
President: Prof. Klas Knot (page 1457)

Major Banks

ABN AMRO Bank NV, (now owned by RBS, Santander and the Dutch government), URL: http://www.abnamro.com
ING Bank NV (Internationale Nederlanden Bank NV), URL: http://www.ingbank.com, http://www.inggroup.com
Rabobank Nederland, URL: http://www.rabobank.nl
Bank Nederlandse Gemeenten NV, URL: http://www.bng.nl, http://www.bng.com
SNS bank Nederland NV, URL: http://www.sns.nl
NIBC NV, URL: http://www.nibcapital.com
F van Lanschot Bankiers NV, URL: http://www.vanlanschot.com
Friesland Bank NV, URL: http://www.frieslandbank.nl

Bankers' Associations

Nederlandse Bankiersvereniging (Netherlands Bankers' Association), URL: http://www.ncb.nl

Government Agencies

Netherlands Foreign Investment Agency, Bezuidenhoutseweg 2, 2594 AV The Hague, Postbus 20101, 2500 EC The Hague, Netherlands. Tel: +31 (0)70 379 8818, fax: +31 (0)70 379 6322, URL: http://www.nfia.nl
Sociaal-Economische Raad (Socio-Economic Council), Bezuidenhoutseweg 60, 2594 AW The Hague, Postbus 90405, 2509 LK The Hague, Netherlands. Tel: +31 (0)70 349 9499, fax: +31 (0)70 383 2535, URL: http://www.ser.nl

Chambers of Commerce and Trade Organisations

Amsterdam Chamber of Commerce, URL: http://www.kck.nl
Rotterdam and Lower Maas Chamber of Commerce, URL: http://rotterdam.kvk.nl
Delft The Hague Chamber of Commerce, URL: http://www.kvk.nl
Nederlands Centrum voor Handelsbevordering (Netherlands Council for Trade Promotion), URL: http://www.handelsbevording.nl
Amsterdam Exchanges NV (AEX), URL: http://www.euronext.nl
World Trade Center Rotterdam NV, URL: http://www.wtcrotterdam.nl

MANUFACTURING, MINING AND SERVICES

Primary and Extractive Industries

Over 175 oil and natural gas fields are exploited in the Dutch areas of the North Sea. As of 1 January 2012 the Netherlands had proven oil reserves of 0.29 billion barrels and proven reserves of natural gas of 49 trillion cubic feet. The government has decided to reduce production of natural gas to maintain reserves. 50 per cent of natural gas comes from the Groningen gas field. The largest offshore field is K15. Both are operated by Nederlandse Aarodolie Maatschappj (a consortium of ExxonMobil and Royal Dutch Shell).

The following tables show the energy balance for coal, oil and gas:

Coal Balance Sheet, figures in mln kg.

	2008	2009*
Imports	19,128	19,924
Exports (-)	6,510,	4,732
Net change in stocks	178	-3,320
Total supply	12,796	11,872
Total use	12,796	11,872
-Electricity plants	8,233	8,404
-Coking factories	3,063	2,464
-Iron and steel industry	1,438	938
-Other uses	62	66

* Provisional

Source: Statistics Netherlands, Yearbook 2010

Petroleum Balance Sheet, figures in mln kg.

Domestic Transfers	2008	2009*
Total supply	60,418	59,139
extraction	2,163	1,704
production of fossil additives	357	434
supply of biological additives	589	513

NETHERLANDS

- continued

imports	61,267	60,879
exports (-)	4,176	3,702
Total use	60,418	59,139
Stocks		
initial stock	4,042	3,826
final stock (-)	3,826	4,514

Source: Statistics Netherlands

Natural Gas Balance Sheet in mln m³

	2008	2009*
Total supply	45,935	46,301
extraction	79,325	74,659
imports	25,081	24,323
exports (-)	58,504	52,717
net change in stock	33	36
Total use	45,935	46,301
via national supply network	23,192	23,913
electricity plants	8,618	9,133
other uses	14,574	14,780
via regional supply networks	22,124	21,707
for own production process	619	681

* provisional figures
Source: Statistics Netherlands Yearbook 2010

Energy

Total primary energy production was 2.720 quadrillion Btu in 2009, down from 2.881 quadrillion Btu in 2008. Total consumption was 4,050 quadrillion Btu in 2009, down from 4,136 quadrillion Btu in 2008.

In 2009, net electricity from renewable sources represented almost 9 per cent of net electricity consumption, up from 7.5 per cent in 2008 (wind energy 4 per cent and bio mass 4.7 per cent). The Netherlands aims to have 40 per cent of its electricity derived from sustainable sources by 2050. The remaining 60 per cent will come from gas, nuclear fuel and modern coal-powered plants using carbon capture and storage (CSS) technology. By 2020, the aim is to have increased sustainable energy use by 20 per cent. To that aim, the government has pledged to invest €7.5 billion in the sector. The Netherlands aiming to achieve 6,000 MW of wind power and is also developing energy from waves, and other sources such as biomass.

Nuclear power supplies approximately 4 per cent of the Netherlands' electricity output. The Borssele plant has been in operation since 1973. Its capacity is 485 MW and it is currently expected to operate until 2033. A plan to build a new plant at Borssele was put on hold in 2012 due to economic uncertainties.

Electricity Balance Sheet (mln kWh)

Electricity	2010	2011*
Total supply	120.9	121.8
production	118.2	112.7
central	75.8	70.5
local	42.3	40.2
imports	15.6	20.6
exports (-)	12.8	11.5
Electricity consumption	120.9	121.8
via public network	103.8	105.0
via self-generation networks	13.4	13.1
for production process	3.8	3.7
Net losses	4.5	4.6

* provisional figures
Source: Statistics Netherlands Yearbook 2012

The following table shows the percentage of electricity consumed by renewable sources:

Source	2010	2011*
Domestic production	9.69	9.61
-Hydro power	0.08	0.08
-Wind energy	3.72	3.86
-Solar power	0.05	na
-Biomass	5.84	5.61
Imports	13.67	21.45
-Hydro power	13.1	18.6
-Wind energy	0.38	1.93
-Solar power	-	-
-Biomass	0.18	0.86
Exports	0.36	2.77

*Provisional figures
Source: Source: Statistics Netherlands Yearbook 2012

Manufacturing

The three main areas of manufacturing are food processing, chemicals and the metal, mechanical and electrical engineering (MME) industry. The Dutch chemical industry has the ninth highest turnover in the world. It consists primarily of the production of artificial resins, pharmaceuticals, artificial fertiliser, paint and chemicals for plastics industries. Recently areas of growth have included the transport, storage and communications sector. Following the global financial crisis in 2008, demand for manufactured products has fallen. Figures for the first six months of 2009 show that Dutch manufacturing fell by around 25 per cent, turnover in the export market was particularly badly hit. Production across the board was cut at the beginning of 2009 but showed the beginnings of recovering towards the end of the year although in 2011 manufacturing had still not regained its pre-2009 levels.

The following table shows manufacturing turnover and production per sector, in recent years (2005=100):

Turnover	2010	2011*
Turnover	118.2	134.7
Domestic sales	119.4	132.1
Exports	117.2	136.6
Sector		
Food industry	116.5	127.0
Textiles, clothing & leather	90.4	94.3
Wood, construction materials	94.9	102.3
Paper & publishing	94.0	97.3
Oil, chemicals, rubber & synthetics	134.0	160.9
Basic metal & metal products	106.6	121.4
Electrical engineering	114.5	131.9
Transport equipment	113.5	130.5
Furniture	84.9	81.8
Production	102.1	105.3
Sector		
Food industry	103.6	105.1
Textiles, clothing & leather	99.6	102.3
Wood, construction materials & other manufacturing	79.7	84.6
Paper & publishing	99.3	100.0
Oil, Chemicals, rubber & synthetics	105	104.7
Basic metal and metal products	95.5	99.2
Electrical engineering	106.5	113.0
Transport equipment	91.8	111.7
Furniture	79.5	78.8

* provisional figures
Source: Statistics Netherlands Yearbook 2012

In 2009 the production value of manufactured goods was €247.1 billion, 31 per cent of which came from oil, chemicals, rubber and synthetics; 10 per cent came from basic metal and metal products; 22 per cent came from the food industry; 15 per cent came from electrical engineering and machinery; 16 per cent from textiles, paper, wood, furniture and other manufacturing; 1 per cent came from transport equipment. Employment figures for 2009 show that 909,000 full-time employees were engaged in the manufacturing sector. In 2009, 45,565 companies involved in manufacturing were operating, 50 per cent of which were engaged in textiles, paper, wood, furniture and other manufacturing and 20 per cent in basic metal and metal products.

Agriculture

With its high yield per hectare, the Netherlands is the world's third largest exporter of agricultural products. The country is a large producer of fresh fruit, vegetables, and flowers, as well as being the world's largest exporter of potatoes, cocoa and dairy products. Agriculture employs around five per cent of the workforce. The number of regular workers engaged in the agriculture and horticulture sector numbered 209,000 in 2011, down from the 2005 figure of 236,000.

According to Statistics Netherlands the number of agricultural holdings in the Netherlands has fallen from 120,100 in 1992 to 72,000 in 2010. The most dramatic fall came in the period 2000-03 when on average 80 farmers a week were giving up their farms. The main reason behind this was the government buying up land. Figures for 2011 show that the area of cultivated land stood at 1.9 million hectares.

In 2009 there were an estimated 73,008 agricultural holdings including 10,923 arable holdings, 7,966 horticultural holdings, 4,257 permanent crops holdings, 38,299 grazing livestock farms, 1,320 combined crop holdings. In 2004 six per cent more land in the Netherlands was used for organic farming than in 2003, bringing the total area of organically farmed land to nearly 40 thousand hectares. The number of organic farms also rose slightly, from 1,185 in 2003 to 1,201 in 2004.

According to Statistics Netherlands the 2005 arable output was substantially smaller than in 2004. This is almost entirely due to a smaller yield per hectare and a decrease of arable land. Onion and potato crops in particular were considerably smaller. In 2005, nearly 7 billion kilos of potatoes were harvested; a reduction by more than 9 per cent on 2004. The potato crop of 2005 was considerably smaller than the average potato crop over the period 2000-2004. Table and seed potato crops were down 13 per cent. Total harvest of seed onions was 20 percent smaller than in 2004, mainly caused by a reduction in area but the overall production of 1 billion kg was quite high.

Spring barley and rape had high yields in 2005. Compared to 2004, the area of spring barley increased by 7 per cent; the yield per hectare was stable. The area where rape was grown, increased by almost one third from 1,600 hectares in 2004 to 2,100 hectares in 2005. Yet, the yield per hectare was 20 per cent below the level of 2004, when production was high. Sugar beets account for almost 5 per cent of the total agricultural area in the Netherlands and for 2 per cent of total agricultural output. In 2004 the sugar beet harvest amounted to more than 6 million tons. The annual output of an average farm (covering 6 ha of sugar beets) is 360 tons. Figures for 2008 show that the pear crop fell. This was mainly due to cold weather during the flowering period.

The following table shows recent figures for selected crop yields:

Selected Crop Yield in mln kg.

Crop	2010	2011
Potatoes, ware	3,546	3,857
Potatoes, seed	1,452	1,313
Sugar beet	5,280	5,858

- continued

Sowing onions	1,252	1,582
Barley	204	205
Oats	8	8
Rye	10	6
Triticale	14	10
Wheat	1,370	1,175
Apples	338	418
Pears	274	336
Strawberries	43	47
Cucumbers	435	430
Mushrooms	235	250
Sweet peppers	365	365
Tomatoes	815	815
Cauliflower	42	39
White cabbage	132	137
Winter carrots	362	357

*provisional
Source: Statistical Yearbook 2012

Beef cattle farmers suffered a setback due to the BSC, mad cow disease scare, when large numbers of imported calves had to be slaughtered. The livestock sector was hit again in spring 2001 with the outbreak of foot and mouth disease, originating from the UK. There were 13 reported cases and 115,000 animals had to be destroyed.

The following table shows recent figures for livestock:

Livestock

Livestock ('000s)	2005	2010	2011*
Cattle	3,797	3,975	3,885
Pigs	11,312	12,255	12,429
Sheep	1,361	1,130	1,088
Chickens	92,914	101,248	96,919

*provisional
Source: Statistics Netherlands, Yearbook 2012

Meat, Dairy & Egg Production (mln kg)

Product	2010	2011*
Meat production (inc. bones & fat)		
- calves	222	219
- mature cattle	166	163
- meat chickens	751	809
- pigs	1,288	1,347
- sheep & goats	15	15
Unprocessed cow's milk delivered to dairy factories	11,626	11,627
Milk processed to		
- butter	133	125
- condensed milk	347	356
- milk powder	199	189
- processed cheese	753	746
Chicken's eggs	631	657

* provisional
Source: Statistical Yearbook 2012

Horticulture, both in the open and under glass, contributes a large amount to the agricultural production. The Netherlands is world famous for its tulips.

Fishing

The Netherlands has a fishing fleet of over 400 ships including cutters, trawlers and mussel dredgers.

Fish Landed in Dutch Harbours (1.000 kg)

Fresh	2007	2008
Flounder	3,234	2,385
Shrimp	8,717	10,857
Brill	939	696
Cod	3,023	2,125
Langoust	2,059	1,295
Mussel	43,731	36,082
Gurnard	2,128	1,506
Dab	8,121	6,687
Turbot	2,644	2,073
Sole	11,583	10,424
Bass	327	296
Frozen		
Whiting	268,758	115,355
Herring	289,564	173,267
Horse mackerel	90,637	90,726
Mackerel	103,416	92,426

Source: Statistical Yearbook 2010

Tourism

In 2010, 17.7 million holidays were taken in the Netherlands with tourists spending €3.0 billion. Over 80 per cent of the Dutch population go on holiday at least once a year and over 53 per cent take their holiday in the Netherlands.

Nederlands Bureau voor Toerisme (Netherlands Board of Tourism), URL: http://www.holland.com

COMMUNICATIONS AND TRANSPORT

Travel Requirements

Citizens of the USA, Canada and Australia require a passport valid for three months beyond the length of stay, and return/onward ticket and sufficient funds for the intended stay. EU nationals holding a valid national ID card do not require a passport. Citizens of the aforementioned countries do not require a visa. Australian subjects may be asked for evidence of health insurance. Other nationals should contact the embassy to check visa requirements.

The Netherlands is a signatory to the Schengen Agreement; with a Schengen visa, a visitor can travel freely throughout the Schengen zone, with few border stops and checks. See http://www.eurovisa.info/SchengenCountries.htm for details.

National Airlines

KLM Royal Dutch Airlines, URL: http://www.klm.nl
Services are international and regional, scheduled passenger and cargo to 149 cities in 83 countries. It has a fleet of around 100, and employs approximately 30,000 people. Total operating income achieved in March-December 2011 was €6.985 million. 25 million passengers and 485,000 tons of cargo were transported in that period.
Martinair Holland, URL: http://www.martinair.nl
Services are international scheduled and charter passenger and cargo. It employs 2,050 and has a fleet of approximately 21.
Transavia Airlines, URL: http://www.transavia.com

International Airports

There are a total of 29 airports in the Netherlands, the largest being:
Amsterdam Schiphol Airport, URL: http://www.schiphol.nl
Passengers in 2011: 53 million, Cargo: 1.5 million tonnes, Aircraft movements: 450,000

Railways

Dutch Rail provides an InterCity service between main cities. Local lines provide services to smaller towns. In 2004 over 14,000 million passenger km were travelled. Approximately 26 million tonnes of freight is transported by rail every year. In 2005 there was an investment of €371 million in services, trains and stations. An infrastructure levy of €146 million was paid in the Netherlands. In 2011 the Netherlands had a total of 3,013 km of rail track. Amsterdam has a subway system and a tram network. Rotterdam has a small subway system and a tram network. The Hague has a tram network.
NV Nederlandse Spoorwegen, URL: http://www.ns.nl

Roads

The number of cars in use has increased dramatically over recent years, rising by almost one million during the last decade. The total length of the Dutch road network in 2011 was 137,692 kilometres. Vehicles are driven on the right. There are 19,100 km of cycle lanes. Over 50 per cent of car travel is work related and 60 per cent of commuters travel by car. Owing to the flat terrain of the Netherlands the bicycle is a popular and practical mode of transport. Figures for 2002 show that there were 13.1 million bikes on the road compared to 6.7 million cars. In 2003 cyclists covered 13.9 billion km (up 7 per cent from 2003). Bicycles are used mainly for recreational purposes although 25 per cent of people commute to work by bike. In 2011 there were over 636,000 motorcycles and 7.7 million cars on the roads. (Source: Statistics Netherlands)

Waterways

The national waterway network covered approximately 6,219 kilometres in 2011, of which 2,689 kilometres were canals. Nearly 50 per cent of the waterways can be used by boats of at least 1,000 metric tons capacity.

Shipping

Figures for 2009 showed that over 85,200 ships entered and left Dutch ports, with German and British vessels being the most common overseas vessels. Rotterdam is the world's busiest port with 48,700 arrivals and departures, followed by Amsterdam with 8,700 shipping movements. (Source: Statistics Netherlands)

Principal Companies

Hudig & Veder's Stoomvaart Maatschappij BV, URL: http://www.hudig-veder.nl
Stena Line, URL: http://www.stenaline.com
Koninklijke Nederlands Redersvereniging (Royal Netherlands Shipowners' Association), URL: http://www.kvnr.nl/cms/showpage.aspx

Ports and Harbours

The main Dutch ports are Amsterdam, Rotterdam, Ijmuiden, Zaanstad, Vlaardingen, Hook of Holland, Dordrecht, Scheveningen, Delfzijl en Eemshaven, Harlingen, Flushing and Terneuzen. Rotterdam has been the largest port in the world for over 30 years, and in 2004 approximately 353 million tonnes of goods passed through it. Dutch ports as a whole unloaded approximately 325 million tonnes of goods and loaded just under 100 million tonnes in 2000. Seventy-five per cent of goods which arrive or leave the Netherlands are loaded or unloaded in the port of Rotterdam, 10 per cent through Amsterdam and 5 per cent through Ijmuiden. Crude petroleum accounts for approximately 30 per cent of unloaded goods. The sea ports have over 40 per cent of the market between northern Germany and southern Spain. (Source: Statistics Netherlands)

HEALTH

Health care is available to all and is financed through a system of national insurance and government contributions.

NETHERLANDS

Key figures for care expenditure in €bln.

	2009	2010*
Total	84,053	87,106
- policy and management	3,001	2,998
- mental health care	5,273	5,435
- care for the disabled	7,802	7,902
- medicines an aids	8,874	9,120
- care for the elderly	15,211	15,974
- medical/paramedical practices	6,748	7,008
- hospital/specialist practices	21,629	22,390
- other	15,515	16,279
Spending		
Euro per capita	5,085	5,243
% of GDP	14.7	14.8

*provisional figures
Statistics Netherlands, Yearbook 2012

Expenditure by Care Providers in million €

Type of health care	2008	2009
Hospitals/specialist care	20,003	21,445
Mental health care	4,899	5,273
Medical & paramedical practices	6,335	6,879
Medicines & aids	9,027	8,902
Care for the elderly	14,775	15,216
Care for the disabled	7,138	7,787
Policy & management	2,992	2,991
Other	14,120	15,074

Source: Statistics Netherlands

Recent figures show that the country has 129 general hospitals, with approximately 3.3 beds per 1,000 inhabitants; There are roughly 142 ambulance services. In 2000-10, there were approximately 64,417 doctors, and 2,444 nurses and midwives, 8,390 dentists, and 2,871 pharmacists. (Source: WHO)

The main cause of death for males is cancer, followed by cardiovascular diseases. For women, the main cause of death is cardiovascular diseases followed by cancer. In 2004 there were 85 deaths attributed to AIDS compared to 444 in 1994. The decline is due to better treatment rather than lower infection rates. An estimated 16,000 people in the Netherlands are estimated to have HIV/AIDS.

In 2001, the Netherlands became the first country to legalise euthanasia.

EDUCATION

The Netherlands has a central educational policy and schools are run on a day-to-day level by local authorities. Educational policy stipulates the amount of hours pupils must attend school, what lessons must be taught and what educational achievements are required.

Primary/Secondary Education
Compulsory education begins at the age of five although primary school education usually begins at age four. Most schools request financial contributions from parents for extra-curricular activities. Primary education hands over to secondary school at the age of 12. Exams are taken to establish which type of school will suit the pupil. Parents may choose schools, and schools decide whether or not to accept a child, taking into account exam results and school recommendations.

There are various types of secondary schools available: junior general secondary education (MAVO), senior general secondary education (HAVO), pre-university education (VWO), preparatory vocational education (VBO), and individualised preparatory vocational education (IVBO). The first, MAVO, lasts four years, when the pupil chooses a minimum of six subjects for examination. HAVO lasts five years and prepares students for higher professional education. After three years at a HAVO school, examinations are taken in six subjects of the student's choice, with one of these subjects being the Dutch language, and another being a foreign language. VWO, or pre-university education takes six years. After four years examinations are taken in seven selected subjects, including Dutch and a foreign language. VBO lasts four years and is preparation for a vocational school. IVBO also lasts four years and is for students with learning difficulties who intend to go on to vocational schools.

Compulsory education ends at age 18 although from the age of sixteen there is a partial compulsory education (partiële leerplicht), meaning a pupil must attend some form of education for at least two days a week

Higher Education
Hogescholen differ from universities as they provide skills and knowledge geared towards professional practice. Diplomas from a HAVO, VWO or MBO secondary education school allow entrance to Hogescholen. University admittance is by VWO diploma.

Vocational Education
The Netherlands has an apprenticeship system where a student works for a company and attends school for one or two days a week. Students holding a diploma from a VBO, MAVO or HAVO school can attend senior secondary vocational education (MBO), whose courses usually last three or four years. As of the 1997-98 academic year there were 68 vocational schools in the Netherlands.

Enrolment figures in government funded schools/institutions in 2010/11*

Type of Education	No. of Regular Schools/Insts.	Enrolled Pupils/students
Primary education	6,849	1,534,000
Special needs primary education	308	43,000
Special schools	324	69,000
Secondary education	659	940,000
Senior vocational education	71	358,000
General secondary education for adults	37	16,000
Higher professional education	51	384,000
University education	13	242,000

*provisional figures
Source: Statistics Netherlands

Provisional figures for 2010 show that, €38,917 million was spent on education.

RELIGION

Freedom of religion is guaranteed by the constitution. Recent figures show that 25 per cent of Dutch people profess to have no religion. Roman Catholicism is the most popular religion (32 per cent), Protestantism (21 per cent) other religions (7 per cent) including Islam (6.4 per cent). There are approximately 400 mosques and prayer centers in Holland (245 Turkish, 130 Moroccan and 25 Surinamese). Approximately 0.69 per cent of the population follows Hinduism. There are an estimated 25,100 Jews (0.15 per cent). The Netherlands has a religious tolerance rating of 8 on a scale of 1 to 10 (10 is most freedom). (Source: World Religion Database)

Raad van Kerken in Nederland (Council of Churches in the Netherlands), URL: http://www.raadvankerken.nl
Bishops' Conference URL: http://www.katholieknederland.nl
Archbishop of Utrecht: The Most Reverend Willem Jacobus Eijk

COMMUNICATIONS AND MEDIA

Freedom of speech and freedom of the press are guaranteed by the constitution.

Newspapers
The major Dutch daily newspapers are:
De Telegraaf, URL: http://www.telegraaf.nl
Algemeen Dagblad, URL: http://www.ad.nl
De Volkskrant, URL: http://www.volkskrant.nl
NRC Handelsblad, URL: http://www.nrc.nl
Trouw, URL: http://www.trouw.nl
Het Parool, URL: http://www.parool.nl

Business Journals
Het Financieele Dagblad (Financial Daily Newspaper), URL: http://www.fd.nl/home/
FEM Business, URL: http://www.fembusiness.nl/fembusiness/

Broadcasting
Dutch television national broadcasters: Nederland 1 broadcasts programmes by KRO, NCRV, EO and AVRO; Nederland 2 (the "popular" channel) shows programmes from the companies of TROS, Veronica, VARA and VPRO; and Nederland 3 is used by the NOS and those broadcasting companies with no members, showing, for example, educational programmes. Each of the provinces has at least one public broadcasting station. Cable and satellite television also operate. Companies must obtain a licence to broadcast as a cable operator. The majority of homes have access to cable television.
NOS, Oversees the three national stations, URL: http://www.omroep.nl
BVN TV, public, for Dutch speakers overseas, URL: http://www.bvn-tv.nl
RTL, commercial, RTL4 and RTL5, URL: http://www.rtl.nl
SBS, commercial, operates SBS6, Net5, Veronica, URL: http://www.sbs6.sbs.nl

Dutch radio has five stations: Radio 1 (news and current affairs), Radio 2 (various lighter programmes), Radio 3 (pop music), Radio 4 (classical and arts), and Radio 5 (information and courses for target groups). There is also the Netherlands World Broadcasting Organization (Stichting 'Radio Nederland Wereldomroep') at Hilversum, which broadcasts in seven foreign languages, particularly to the English-speaking world, the Middle East, Indonesia and South America.
NOS, oversees public radio stations, URL: http://www.omreop.nl
Radio Netherlands, URL: http://www.radionetherlands.nl

Broadcasting policy is determined by the Media Authority, the Media Council, the Dutch Cultural Broadcasting Productions Promotion Fund and the Netherlands Broadcasting Services Corporation (NOB).

Regulatory Authorities
Nederlandse Omroepprogramma Stichting (NOS) Netherlands Broadcasting Authority, URL: http://www.nob.nl
Nederlandse Programma Stichting (NPS), URL: http://www.omroep.nl/nps

Postal Service
The state telecommunications and postal service corporation, the PTT, was privatised in 1989. Mail, express and logistics company TPG was to operate globally under the brand TNT for all its activities from 2006. In May 2011 it changed its name to PostNL and split into two companies, Post NL and TNT Express.
PostNL, URL: http://www.postnl.nl/voorthuis/

Telecommunications

Figures for 2011 show that around 7.1 million land lines and 19.8 mobile phones are in use. There are approximately 15 million internet users in the Netherlands. More than 100,000 households in the Netherlands have fibre-optic cables.

The state telecommunications and postal service corporation, KPN Telecom (formerly PTT Telecom), was privatised in 1989. KPN Telecom is now the leading telecommunications and ICT service provider in The Netherlands and employs over 30,500 people.

KPN Telecom, URL: http://www.kpn.com
OPTA (Independent Post and Telecommunications Authority), URL: http://www.opta.nl/en/

ENVIRONMENT

The Dutch government has a national environment plan (NEPP) which, amongst other aims, has set targets for reductions in carbon emissions as well as energy consumption. The NEPP also supports the development of wind energy and encouraged initiatives for recycling cars.

The emission of greenhouse gases in the Netherlands increased marginally from 214 billion kilograms of carbon dioxide equivalents in 2003 to 217 billion kilograms in 2004. The emission of greenhouse gases in 2004 was 2 per cent up on 1990. In the period 2008-2012 the Kyoto Protocol commits the Netherlands to reduce its greenhouse gas emissions by 6 per cent compared to 1990. Between 1990-2004 emissions of carbon dioxide increased by more than 13 per cent to reach 179 billion kilograms, but the amount of methane, dinitrogen oxide and fluoride gases reduced by 30 percent (CO_2 equivalents). This largely compensates for the increase in CO_2 emissions. The emissions of methane and dinitrogen oxide were brought down as a result of the reduction of the number of cattle. The decrease in the emissions of fluoride gases are the result of restrictive measures.

Air pollution, actual emissions by all sources (million kg)

Greenhouse gases (IPCC norm)	2005	2006
Dinitrogen oxide	55	55

- continued		
Carbon dioxide	175,800	172,000
Methane	802	775
Acidifying & large scale air pollution (NEC norm)		
Ammonia	133	130
Fine particulate matter	38	38
Nitrogen organic compounds	173	168
Sulphur dioxide	65	65

Source: Statistics Netherlands

In 2010 total municipal waste was 10.063 million kg.

The Netherlands is a party to the following international agreements: Air Pollution, Air Pollution-Nitrogen Oxides, Air Pollution-Persistent Organic Pollutants, Air Pollution-Sulfur 85, Air Pollution-Sulfur 94, Air Pollution-Volatile Organic Compounds, Antarctic-Environmental Protocol, Antarctic-Marine Living Resources, Antarctic Treaty, Biodiversity, Climate Change, Climate Change-Kyoto Protocol, Desertification, Endangered Species, Environmental Modification, Hazardous Wastes, Kyoto Protocol, Law of the Sea, Marine Dumping, Marine Life Conservation, Ozone Layer Protection, Ship Pollution, Tropical Timber 83, Tropical Timber 94, Wetlands and Whaling.

SPACE PROGRAMME

The Netherlands is a member of the European Space Agency (ESA). One of ESA's four main sites is at Noordwijk in the Netherlands. The European Space Research and Technology Centre (ESTEC) is based in Noordwijk and employs 1,100 staff. ESTEC is responsible for preparing space missions, satellites testing and developing new space technology. ESTEC has the largest spacecraft test facilities in Europe.
ESTEC, URL: http://www.esa.int

OVERSEAS NETHERLANDS

The former Netherlands Colonies, Surinam and the Netherlands Antilles, acquired a new status set out in a Decree proclaimed on 29 December 1954. The Charter of the Kingdom provides that the Overseas Territories of the Netherlands Antilles shall have what is essentially a commonwealth standing with independent governments and ministries but with a constitution within the framework of that of the Netherlands. They owe allegiance to the Netherlands Crown, and the Government and ministry are invested with the same responsibilities as those of the Netherlands itself. In both States the Crown is represented by a Governor. Each member of the Kingdom is independently administered but matters of mutual concern in the field of foreign policy and of defence, etc., are acted upon after consultation between the partners.

The Overseas Territory of Surinam became an independent Country on 25 November 1975. Aruba, one of the Netherlands Antilles, was granted separate status in 1986. Plans for Aruba to become fully independent were cancelled in 1994, but this has not been ruled out completely.

In early 2005 a series of referenda were held in the Antilles to determine future of the islands. Voters opted to dismantle the Netherlands Antilles and create new structures between the various islands and the Kingdom. St. Maarten and Curacao opted for an autonomous country status within the Kingdom similar to Aruba's status. Saba, Sint Eustatius, and Bonaire opted for closer ties to the Kingdom.

The Netherlands Antilles were scheduled to be dissolved in October 2010 as a unifed political entity and each would assume new constitutional status with the Kingdom of the Netherlands. The change officially came into effect on October 10 when the dependency known as the Netherlands Antilles ceased to exist and the five islands assumed their new constitutional status. Curacao and St Maarten are now autonomous countries within the Kingdom of the Netherlands, joining Aruba, which gained the status in 1986. Bonaire, St Eustatius and Saba have now become autonomous special municipalities of the kingdom.

ARUBA

Capital: Oranjestad

Head of State: King Willem-Alexander (page 1537)

Governor: Fredis Refunjol

National Flag: Light blue background with two narrow yellow horizontal stripes in the bottom third and a four-pointed white-edged star in the canton.

CONSTITUTION AND GOVERNMENT

Constitution
Aruba was part of the Netherlands Antilles until 1986 when it obtained separate status within the Kingdom of the Netherlands. Plans for full independence were put on hold indefinitely at a meeting in The Hague in 1994. The Dutch government controls defence and foreign affairs and the island's government handles local matters.

The Netherlands are represented in Aruba by the governor who is appointed for a six-year term by the monarch.

Recent Events
In early 2005 a series of referenda were held in the Antilles to determine the future of the islands. Voters opted to dismantle the Netherlands Antilles and create new structures between the various islands and the Kingdom. St. Maarten and Curacao opted for an autonomous country status within the Kingdom similar to Aruba's status. Saba, Sint Eustatius, and Bonaire opted for closer ties to the Kingdom. The Netherlands Antilles was formally dissolved in October 2010.

Legislature
Parliament or Staten is made up of 21 directly elected members who serve a four-year term. The Prime Minister and Deputy Prime Minister are elected by parliament.

Cabinet (as at March 2013)
Prime Minister, Minister of General Affairs: Michiel Eman (page 1421)
Minister of Finance, Communication and Utilities: Mike Eric de Meza
Minister of Tourism, Transportation and Labour: Otmar E. Oduber
Minister of Integration, Ingrastructure and Environment: Osin Benito Sevinger
Minister of Justice and Education: Arthur Dowers
Minister of Economic Affairs, Social Affairs and Culture: Michelle Janice Hooyboer-Winklaar
Minister of Public Health and Sport: Dr Richard Wayne Milton Visser
Secretary of the Council of Ministers: Edwin Bibiano Abath
Minister Plenipotentiary of Aruba in the Netherlands: Edwin Bibiano Abath

---

Political Parties
Aruba Solidarity Movement, MAS; Aruban Democratic Alliance; Aruban Democratic Party, PDA; Aruban Liberal Party, OLA; Aruban Patriotic Party, PPA; Aruban People's Party, AVP; Concentration for the Liberation of Aruba, CLA; People's Electoral Movement Party, MEP; For a Restructured Aruba Now, PARA; National Democratic Action, ADN.

Elections
The most recent election was held in September 2009, The Aruban People's Party (AVP) won 12 seats, the People's Electoral Movement won eight seats and the Real Democracy Party won one seat.

NETHERLANDS

LEGAL SYSTEM

Aruba has a legal system based on the Dutch system and consits of three courts, the *Gerecht in Eerste Aanleg,* Court of First Instance; a *Gemeenschappelijk Hof van Justitie voor de Nederlandse Antillen en Aruba,* Common Court of Justice of the Netherlands Antilles and Aruba; and the *Hoge Raad der Nederlanden,* Supreme Court of Justice of the Netherlands.

LOCAL GOVERNMENT

For administrative purposes Aruba is divided into eight regions: Noord Tank Leendert, Oranjestad (west), Oranjestad (east), Paradera, Santa Cruz, Savaneta, Sint Nicolaas (north), and Sint Nicolaas (south).

AREA AND POPULATION

Area
Aruba has an area of 193 sq km (75 sq miles) and is generally flat with no rivers. It is located in the Leeward Antilles island arc of the Lesser Antilles in the Caribbean Sea. To the east of Aruba lie the islands of Bonaire and Curaçao, and the three islands are often known collectively as the ABC islands. The coast of the south and west of the island have sandy beaches. The island's considerable tourist industry is based here. The north and eastern coasts are less protected and as a result are hardly developed.

Population
Recent figures put the population at 101,500 in 2010.

Dutch is the official language but Papiamento, Spanish, and English also are spoken.

EMPLOYMENT

Recent figures estimated the workforce to be in the region of 51,600. The largest sectors of employment were the wholesale and retail trade, hotels and restaurants, and oil refining. In 2005, the unemployment rate was put at 6.9 per cent.

Total Employment by Economic Activity

Occupation	2007
Agriculture, hunting, forestry	352
Mining & quarrying	17
Manufacturing	3,246
Electricity, gas & water supply	699
Construction	6,500
Wholesale & retail trade, repairs	7,283
Hotels & restaurants	8,712
Transport, storage & communications	2.832
Financial intermediation	1,905
Real estate, renting & business activities	6,811
Public admin. & defence; compulsory social security	3,983
Education	1,589
Health & social work	3,177
Other community, social & personal service activities	3,218
Households with employed persons	1,163
Extra-Territorial organisations & bodies	33
Other	87
Total	51,607

Source: Copyright © International Labour Organization (ILO Dept. of Statistics, http://laborsta.ilo.org)

BANKING AND FINANCE

Currency
The unit of currency is the Aruban Guilder of 100 cents

GDP/GNP, Inflation, National Debt
The economy is dominated by tourism and offshore banking. The government is seeking to diversify the economy including the sectors of sustainable agriculture and renewable energy. The economy dipped in 2010, following the economic crisis of 2008/9 but returned to growth in 2011. Lact of demand for oil in 2008/09 meant that oil production temporarily halted in 2009 and 2010.

Figures for 2007 put GDP at US$ 2.61 billion with a growth rate of 2.1 per cent. The main contributors of GDP are tourism, oil refinery & offshore banking. GDP was estimated at Afl 4.35 million in 2010, rising to Afl 4.87 million in 2011. Growth was estimated to be 2.4 per cent in 2011.

Balance of Payments / Imports and Exports
Figures for 2010 put the value of trade exports at Afl2.700 million, rising to Afl3.385 million, the main products being oil products, live animals and animal products and machinery and electrical equipment. Imported goods in 2010 cost an estimated Afl3.3 billion, and Afl3.97 in 2011. Main imports being crude petroleum, food and manufactured goods. Main trading partners include Panama, Colombia, the Netherlands Antilles, the USA, Venezuela and the The Netherlands.

MANUFACTURING, MINING AND SERVICES

Primary and Extractive Industries
Oil processing is the main industry in Aruba

Service Industries
Tourism is an important part of the Aruban economy. Around 1.25 million tourists per year visit Aruba, 75 per cent of whom are from the United States.

Off shore banking is also large sector but, in 2000, Aruba was named as one of 35 "non-co-operative tax havens" by the Organisation for Economic Cooperation and Development (OECD). Having agreed to more openness in its dealings, Aruba was later removed from the list. In 2003 an agreement to exchange tax data was agreed with the USA in an effort to combat money laundering.

COMMUNICATIONS AND TRANSPORT

International Airport
Reina Beatrix International Airport is used by many international carriers including KLM, First Choice Airways, American Airlines, United, and Delta.

EDUCATION

The education system is based on the Dutch model and education is paid for by the government. Recent figures show that Aruba had 68 primary schools, 12 secondary schools and five universities. In 2007, there were 22,930 full-time students.

RELIGION

The predominant religion is Christianity, the professed religion of 96 per cent of the population. Aruba has a religious liberty rating of 10 on a scale of 1 to 10 (10 is most freedom). (Source: World Religion Database)

COMMUNICATIONS AND MEDIA

Aruba has two newspapers, Diario Aruba, URL: http://www.diario.aw, and Bon Dia, URL: http://www.bondia.com.

There are two commercial television stations, ATV and Tele Aruba, URL: http://www.telearuba.aw/. Cable is also available. Some 20 commercial radio stations also operate.

The telecommunications system is fully automatic. As of 2008, an estimated 38,000 main lines were in use and 127,000 mobile cellular phones. Internet users were estimated to be 24,000.

ENVIRONMENT

In 2006 Aruba's emissions from the consumption of fossil fuels totalled 0.93 million metric tons of carbon dioxide.

CURAÇAO
Autonomous Country within the Kingdom of the Netherlands
Land Curaçao / Pais Kòrsou

Capital: Willemstad

Head of State: King Willem-Alexander (page 1537)

Governor: Adele can der Pluijm-Vrede (acting)

CONSTITUTION AND GOVERNMENT

Constitution
On October 10, 2010 Curaçao become an autonomous country within the Kingdom of the Netherlands. Up until that date it had been part of the Dutch Caribbean dependency, the Netherlands Antilles, along with Sint Maarten, Sint Eustatius, Bonaire and Saba.

Under the new arrangement, the Dutch government will remain responsible for defence and foreign policy in the new countries, and will initially oversee Curaçao's finances under a debt relief agreement.

Legislature
Curaçao's legislature is unicameral. The *Estates of Curaçao* will be made up of 21 members elected for a four-year-term by proportional representation. Following the dissolution of the Netherlands Antilles, a new Curaçao prime minister and council of ministers was sworn in.

Recent Events
A no-confidence vote was passed on the government of Prime Minstter Gerrit Schotte. The acting governor of Curaçao accepted the resignation of Schotte's government and swore in an interim government headed by Stanley Betrian. Daniel Hodge later became prime minister on a provisional basis in 2012.

Helmin Wiels, the leader of Curaçao's largest political party, the Pueblo Soberano Party, was murdered in May 2013. Ivar Asjes wwas sworn in as prime minister in June 2013, succeeding Daniel Hodge. Mr Asjes' coalition government includes Pueblo Soberano, PAIS, PNP and one independent.

Cabinet (as at June 2013)
Prime Minister: Ivar Asjes (PS) (page 1380)
Minister of Health, Environment and Nature: Ben Whiteman (PS)
Minister of Education, Science, Culture & Sports: Rubina Bitorina (PS)
Minister of Finance: José Jardim (PNP)
Minister of Economic Development: Stanley Palm (PAIS)
Minister of Justice: Nelson Navarro (PAIS)
Minister of Administration, Planning & Service: Etienne van der Horst (PAIS)
Minister of Traffic, Transport & Spatial Planning: Earl Balboarda
Minister of Social Development, Labour & Wellbeing: Jeanne Marie Francisca
Minister Plenipotentiary in the Hague: Marvelyne Wiels (PS)

Office of the Governor, URL: http://kabinetvandegouverneur.org/

Political Parties
Democratic Party (Democratische Partij); Forsa Kòrsou; Labour Party People's Crusade (Partido Laboral Krusada Popular); LPNA (Lista Niun Paso Atras); National People's Party (Partido Nashonal di Pueblo); New Antilles Movement (Movishon Antia Nobo); Party for the Restructured Antilles (Partido Antiá Restrukturá); Party Workers' Liberation Front 30th of May (Frente Obrero Liberashon 30 Di Mei 1969); Sovereign People (Pueblo Soberano); C93

Elections
Elections were held on 27 August 2010. The Movementu Futuro Korsou (MFK) became the second largest party and formed a coalition with the Sovereign People's party and the National People's Party. The coalition became the first government of Curaçao after the dissolution of the Netherlands Antilles.

The most recent election took place on 19 October 2012. The Sovereign People Party lead by Helmin Wiels took 5 seats as did the Movement for the Future of Curaçao led by Gerrit Schotte. The Party for the Restrucutred Antilles took 4 as did the Partido pa Adelanto I Inovashon Soshal. Party Man took two seats and the National People's Party one.

LEGAL SYSTEM

St. Maarten and Curaçao share a supreme court. Curaçao has a civil law system largely based on the Dutch civil law system with some English common law influence.

AREA AND POPULATION

Area
Curaçao is an island in the southern Caribbean Sea, off the Venezuelan coast and covers an area of 444 sq km (171.4 sq miles), and includes the uninhabited island of Little Curaçao, Klein Curaçao.

Population
Figures from the 2009 census put the population at 141,766.

The population of Curaçao is diverse; the majority are of Afro-Caribbean and European descent, along with large minorities of Dutch, Latin American, French, South Asian, East Asian and Portuguese descent. Sephardic Jews arrived from the Netherlands and then Dutch Brazil in the 17th century. The 19th century saw an influx of Portuguese and Lebanese migrants. Following World War II Ashkenazi Jews settled in the country. In more recent years Curaçao has had migrants from neighbouring countries such as the Dominican Republic, Haiti, the Anglophone Caribbean and Colombia. Curaçao has also become a popular place for Dutch pensioners to retire to and who are known locally as pensionados.

The official languages of Curaçao are Dutch and Papiamaento.

BANKING AND FINANCE

Currency
Netherlands Antillean Guilder of 100 cents.

GDP/GNP, Inflation, National Debt.
The government is attempting to diversity its industry and trade. The infrastructure is relatively good. Agriculture is hindered by poor soils and inadequate water supplies. GDP was estimated at US$2.8 billlion (ppp) in 2008 with a growth rate of 3.5 per cent. Growth was estimated to be just over 1 per cent in 2009 and 0.5 per cent in 2010. Curaçao has a relatively high standard of living and estimated figures for 2009 put GDP per capita at US$20,500.

Following the dissolution of the Netherlands Antilles, Curaçao and St. Maarten have the power to use of their own tax revenues. The Dutch government agreed to initially oversee Curaçao's finances under a debt relief agreement. Together the islands that made up the Netherlands Antilles had amassed a debt of around €2 billion (£1.75bn), most of which is owed to the Netherlands. The smaller islands of St. Maarten, Bonaire, St. Eustatius and Saba claim that the majority of the debt was run up by Curaçao, whereas Curaçao claims that as the largest island and de facto capital of the former Netherlands Antilles, it carried the financial burden for the smaller islands.

Curaçao does business with the United States, Venezuela and the European Union. It has an Association Agreement with the European Union which allows companies to export products to the European markets, without paying import duties and quotas. Curaçao is also a participant in the US Caribbean Basin Initiative which allows it preferential access to the US market.

Balance of Payments / Imports and Exports
The main export commodity is petroleum products. Exports were estimated to be US$1.3 billion in 2011 and imports US$2.5 billion.

MANUFACTURING, MINING AND SERVICES

Primary and Extractive Industries
Oil has been an important factor in the Netherlands Antilles economies. The Shell refineries were established on Curaçao in 1918. The oil industry caused many workers to leave the other less remunerative sectors, so that agriculture and fishing went into decline. After the oil crisis in 1973 Shell's sales in the United States fell by 40 per cent and the problems were felt in the Antilles. However, Shell believed that they could find new markets. The Lago Company was the first to recognize that, as the ports on the eastern side of the United States were too shallow to receive large tankers, there were many possibilities for transhipment in the islands. In 1975 the first pier was completed to serve mammoth tankers, and a number of bays were also adapted for transhipment purposes. However, because of the overproduction of refined oil in this region during the 1980s Shell had to lease its refinery to the Venezuelan oil company PDSVA.

Phosphate is mined near Tafelberg on Curaçao. The phosphate on Curaçao is highly suitable for processing into animal feed because of its low fluorine content. Limestone is a by-product.

Energy
Electricity is a by-product of water distilleries, which is supplied to electricity companies on the islands. Each island has its own power station and Curaçao has three. As the grids of the individual islands cannot be linked because of the large distances electricity is relatively expensive to produce. Propane gas in cylinders is available.

Tourism
Tourism is seen as an important growth industry. Figures for 1999 show that there were 972,000 visitors to the Antilles. This figure includes stop-overs by cruise ships.

NETHERLANDS

Agriculture

Arable farming is of little significance and is still declining due to the uncontrolled felling of timber in earlier years. Natural factors have also contributed. The most important products are maize, dividivi pods, aloes and laraha fruit, peanuts and sorghum are also grown. As with arable farming stock breeding is of little importance. However, goat breeding is widespread and flocks roam freely over the islands. Pig-breeding is also relatively successful.

COMMUNICATIONS AND TRANSPORT

International Airport

Curaçao has an international airpot and the Dutch airline KLM flys daily to Curaçao. The airport also provides flights to the USA.

Roads

Curaçao has an extensive road system.

Ports and Harbours

Curaçao has a large natural harbour with a capacity of 150,000 tonnes. This gives it the largest commercial docks in South America.

HEALTH

Health care in the Antilles has been supervised by the Department of Public Health which is based on Curaçao. The largest hospital in the islands is St. Elisabeth, on Curaçao.

EDUCATION

In the Netherlands Antilles the education system is similar to that in the Netherlands. Education is not compulsory, but there is very little illiteracy in the islands. Many of the schools are denominational. Figures for 2002 from UNESCO show that 96 per cent of primary aged children were enrolled at school and 81 per cent of secondary school age children attended school. As the population on the islands is small it is not possible to provide every branch of education locally. It is often necessary to go abroad for further education. Teacher training courses have recently been introduced on Curaçao to qualify the teachers to take the lower class of senior general secondary and pre-university schools. There is one university on Curaçao: the University Institute of the Netherlands Antilles.

Until recently the language of instruction was Dutch, instruction is now bilingual at primary level in Papiamentu and Dutch. is also available. Curaçao also has private and parochial schools and The International School of Curaçao and C.A.P.S. (Curaçao American Preparatory School) provide education for the children of English-speaking immigrants.

RELIGION

The majority of the islanders are Roman Catholic (85%), other Christian denominations exist on Curaçao, particularly Seventh-day Adventists and the Methodist Church. Some African religions such as Montamentu are practiced. There are small Muslim and Hindu communities and as a result of immigration a Jewish community. Curaçao is home to the oldest active Jewish congregation in the Americas, which dates from 1651.

COMMUNICATIONS AND MEDIA

Newspapers

Two daily newpapers are published on Curacao, La Prensa, URL: http://news.laprensacur.com and Amigoe, URL: http://www.amigoe.com. Four international press agencies have representatives on Curaçao: ANP, AP, UPI and Reuters.

Broadcasting

A government-run television on Curacao (Telecuracao, URL: http://www.telecuracao.com/web/homepage.aspx) broadcasts to Bonaire and Saba. Satellite and cable is also available from the US and Venezuela. The main radio stations broadcasting in Curacao are, Radio Hoyer, URL: http://www.radiohoyer.com; -Easy FM, URL: http://www.easyfm.com, Dolfijn FM, URL: http://www.dolfijnfm.com.

Telecommunications

Figures for 2008 showed that the Antilles had an estimated 75,000 internet users.

ENVIRONMENT

Tourism is a large contributor to the economy and the island is a popular destination for divers. Unfortunately some of the coral reefs have been damaged and research is ongoing into preserving the reef system.

SPACE PROGRAMME

In October 2010 a signing of a Memorandum of Understanding was signed between Space Experience Curacao (SXC) and XCOR Aerospace, Inc. The agreement paves the way for space travel to take off from the island and it is hoped that such a service will start in 2014. It is currently hoped that the service will be available for space tourists as well as scientists engaged in research and companies wishing to take small satellites into orbit.

SINT MAARTEN

Autonomous Country within the Kingdom of the Netherlands

Capital: Philipsburg

Head of State: King Willem-Alexander (page 1537)

Governor: Eugene Holiday (page 1443)

CONSTITUTION AND GOVERNMENT

Constitution

On October 10, 2010 Sint Maarten become an autonomous country within the Kingdom of the Netherlands. Until that date it had been part of the Dutch Caribbean dependency, the Netherlands Antilles, along with Curaçao, Sint Eustatius, Bonaire and Saba. Under the new arrangement, the Dutch government will remain responsible for defence and foreign policy in the new countries. The Queen of the Netherlands is Head of State and is rpesented by the Governor. As of October 2010, St Maarten is now governed by its own Constitution and the following institutions of government: Governor as Head of State, Parliament, and the Council of Ministers headed by the prime minister.

To consult the constitution, please visit:
http://www.sxmparliament.org/about-parliament/the-constitution.html.

Legislature

Sint Maarten's legislature is unicameral. The Estates of Sint Maarten is made up of 15 members, elected for a four-year-term. The parliament elects a president and a deputy president from its own numbers. Following the dissolution of the Netherlands Antilles, a new prime minister and council of ministers was sworn in.
Parliament, URL: http://www.sxmparliament.org/

Recent Events

Four cabinet ministers resigned in April 2012 leading to the resignation of the whole cabinet in May 2012. The resignations marked the end of the United People and the Democratic Party coalition. The UP party lost its majority support in parliament when the UP fraction leader MP Romain Laville resigned from the party. A new cabinet was sworn in that month made up of a coalition of NA & DP members and three independent MPs.

Council of Ministers (as at June 2013)
Prime Minister, Minister of General Affairs & Minister of Tourism, Economic Affairs, Transport and Telecommunication: Sarah Wescot-Williams (page 1535)
Deputy Prime Minister and Minister of Justice: Dennis L. Richardson
Minister of Finance: Martinus Hassink
Minister of Housing & Spatial Planning, Environment & Infrastructure: Maurice Lake
Minister of Education, Culture, Youth and Sports Affairs: Patricia Lourens-Philip Jacobs
Minister of Health Care, Social Development and Labour: Cornelius De Weever

Political Parties

Democratic Party (DP); National Alliance (NA); United People (UP); Concordia Political Alliance (CPA).

Ministries

Office of the Governor, URL: http://www.kabgsxm.com/default.aspx?language=EN
Government portal, URL:http://www.sintmaartengov.org/

Elections

Elections were held in September 2010. The Democratic Party won two seats; the National Alliance, won seven seats; the United People's party won six seats; the Concordia Political Alliance failed to win any seats. A coalition government was formed between the Democratic Party and the United People's party. Although the Democratic Party won only two seats their leader Sarah Wescot-Williams was elected to the post of prime minister leading the first government of Sint Maarten after the dissolution of the Netherlands Antilles.

LEGAL SYSTEM

St. Maarten has a civil law system based on Dutch law. St Maarten has a Court of the First Instance and a Court of Appeal. The Supreme Court is the Supreme Court in the Hague.

AREA AND POPULATION

Area
Sint Maarten comprises the southern half of the island of Saint Martin (the north of the island is the French territory of Saint-Martin) situated in the northeast Caribbean, the Leeward Islands, 300 km (186 miles) east of Puerto Rico. It covers an area of 34 sq km, about 40 per cent of the total island.

Population
Figures from the 2009 census put the population at 40,917. Although the capital is Philipsburg the largest town by population is Lower Prince's Quarter.

The official languages are Dutch and English.

BANKING AND FINANCE

Currency
Netherlands Antillean Guilder of 100 cents.

GDP/GNP, Inflation, National Debt
Estimates put GDP at US$795 million in 2008, a per capita figure of US$15,000. The growth rate was estimated to be 1.6 per cent. Services contribute over 80 per cent of GDP, industry 15 per cent and agriculture just 1 per cent. The main industries are tourism and manufacturing. Sugar is the main export commodity. Inflation was estimated to be under 1 per cent in 2009.

MANUFACTURING, MINING AND SERVICES

Energy
Electricity is a by-product of water distilleries, which is supplied to the electricity company. Sint Maarten has its own power station.

Tourism
The tourism sector is a large contributor to the economy.

Agriculture
Arable farming is of little significance. The most important products are maize, dividivi pods, aloes and laraha fruit, peanuts and sorghum. Fishing is mainly organised on a commercial basis on St. Maarten where, since 1963, a Japanese fishing fleet has been taking a catch of 6,000 tonnes each year.

COMMUNICATIONS AND TRANSPORT

International Airports
St. Maarten has an international airport, the Princess Juliana International Airport (URL: http://www.pjiae.com/)

Ports and Harbours
Phillipsburg has a harbour mainly used by tourist ships.

EDUCATION

The education system is similar to that in the Netherlands. Education is not compulsory, but there is very little illiteracy in the islands. Many of the schools are denominational.

In 1995 the American University of the Caribbean School of Medicine (AUC), founded in 1978, relocated to Sint Maarten from the island of Montserrat following the devastating volcanic eruption there that year. The University of St. Martin (USM) in based in Philipsburg.

COMMUNICATIONS AND MEDIA

Newspapers
The Daily Herald is published in Sint Maarten, URL: http://www.thedailyherald.com

Broadcasting
The Leeward Broadcasting Corporation is based in Sint Maarten. A radio station called the Voice of St Maarten broadcasts from the island.

Telecommunications
Figures for 2008 showed that the Antilles had an estimated 75.000 internet users.

BONAIRE

Autonomous Special Municipality of the Kingdom of the Netherlands

Capital: Kralendijk

Head of State: King Willem-Alexander (page 1537)

Lieutenant-Governor of Bonaire: Lydia Emerencia (page 1421)

CONSTITUTION AND GOVERNMENT

Recent Events
Up until October 10, 2010 Bonaire had been part of the Dutch Caribbean dependency, the Netherlands Antilles, along with Curaçao, Sint Maarten, Sint Eustatius and Saba. Under the new arrangement, the Dutch government will remain responsible for defence and foreign policy in the new countries.

Cabinet (as at June 2013)
Lieutenant-Governor: Lydia Emerencia (page 1421)
Minister of Environment, Sport, Land Management, Agriculture and Transport: P.J. Kroon
Minister of Health, Culture, Education, Labour, Welfare and Housing: I.S. Serfilia
Minister of the Economy, Legal And General Affairs, ICT, Telecommunications, Government Companies, Finance and Tourism: E.F el Hage

Ministries
Government portal: URL: http://www.bonairegov.an/
Department of Economic & Labour Affairs, URL: http://www.bonaireeconomy.org/

AREA AND POPULATION

Area
Bonaire is situated in the Caribbean in the chain of the Leeward Islands, it consists of the island of Bonaire and the uninhabited islet of Klein Bonaire. It covers an area of 294 sq. km. or 113 sq. miles.

Population
Bonaire's earliest known inhabitants were the Caquetios Indians, who arrived from Venezuela. The Spanish arrived in 1499 and the Dutch took control of the island from the Spanish in 1636. During the Napoleonic Wars, the Dutch lost control of Bonaire to the British, Bonaire was then returned to Dutch control under the terms of the Anglo-Dutch Treaty of 1814.

According to figures from the 2006 census the population is 14,006, estimated figures for 2010 put the population at 15,700. The official languages are Dutch, Papiamento and English

BANKING AND FINANCE

Currency
Netherlands Antillean Guilder of 100 cents although US$ are accepted by most shops and restaurants.

MANUFACTURING, MINING AND SERVICES

Primary and Extractive Industries
The Netherlands Antilles exports salt and phosphate. The salt is mainly produced on Bonaire by evaporation in salt pans. The average production of unrefined salt per annum is 400,000 tonnes.

Energy
Bonaire has its own power station and propane gas in cylinders is available.

Tourism
Bonaire's economy is mainly based on tourism. The island is an attractive destination for scuba divers, snorkelers and wind surfers.

COMMUNICATIONS AND TRANSPORT

Airports
The airport at Bonaire is Flamingo International Airport (URL: http://www.flamingoairport.com/). Flights go to Aruba, Venezuela and Curaçao.

EDUCATION

The language of instruction at primary level is Papiamentu, Dutch is then gradually introduced.

The US offshore Saint James School of Medicine is based on Bonaire.

COMMUNICATIONS AND MEDIA

Newspapers
Bonaire publishes the weekly newspaper, The Bonaire Reporter.

NETHERLANDS

Broadcasting
There is one radio station broadcasting on Bonaire, Voz di Bonaire, URL: http://www.vozdibonaire.com

ENVIRONMENT

The entire coastline of Bonaire has been declared a marine sanctuary so as to preserve local fish life. Bonaire is also home to a large flamingo population.

Located on the north side of the island is the Washington Slagbaai National Park, an ecological preserve.

An area of environmental concern is the unregulated and illegal dumping of raw sewage and chemical pollutants which leach through the permeable limestone of the island and threaten the quality of groundwater from the island's landfill site.

SINT EUSTATIUS

Autonomous Special Municipality of the Kingdom of the Netherlands

Statia

Capital: Oranjestad

Head of State: King Willem-Alexander (page 1537)

Lieutenant Governor: Gerald Berkel (page 1387)

CONSTITUTION AND GOVERNMENT

Constitution
Up until October 10, 2010 Sint Eustatius had been part of the Dutch Caribbean dependency, the Netherlands Antilles, along with Curaçao, Sint Maarten, Bonaire and Saba. In a referendum held in April 2005 on becoming independent of the Netherlands, 77 per cent of Statians voted to remain within the Netherlands Antilles, compared to 21 per cent who voted for closer ties with the Netherlands. Since the other islands of the Antilles had voted to leave, the Netherlands Antilles would become defunct, the island council of Sint Eustatius opted to become a special municipality of the Netherlands like Saba and Bonaire.

The Island Council consists of five members and is chaired by the Island Governor. The Island Council appoints two commissioners who along with the governor form the Executive Council. The Executive Council is made up of commissioners elected for four-year-terms.

Under the new arrangement, the Dutch government will remain responsible for defence and foreign policy in the new countries.

Island Council (as at June 2013)
Chair: Gerald Berkel (page 1387)
Island Council Members: M. Lijfrock-Marsdin, F. Brown, R. Zaandam, R. Merkman, F. Spanner

---

The most recent executive council was appointed in February 2012.

Executive Council (as at June 2013)
Lieutenant Governor, Good Governance, Census, Civil Registry, Elections, Education, Disaster Management, Public Order: Gerald Berkel (page 1387)
Commissioner for Finance, Economic Affairs, Taxation, Information & Autonomy, Energy, Water, Tourism, Constitutional Affairs; Planning; Research; Government Buildings; Airport; Harbour; Information: Nicolaas Sneek
Commissioner for Public Works, Spatial Planning, Traffic and Communication, Housing, Waste Management, Environment, Agriculture, Airport, Social Affairs, Culture & Sport, Labour, Women/Gender Affairs, Senior Citizens, Youth: C. Tearr

---

Government portal, URL: http://www.statiagovernment.com
Lieutenant Governor, e-mail: lt.governor@statiagovernment.com
Island Council, e-mail: island.council@statiagov.com

LEGAL SYSTEM

St Eustatius has a civil law system. The main body of civil law is the Civil Code.

AREA AND POPULATION

Area
Sint Eustatius is situated in the northern Leeward Islands of the West Indies, southeast of the Virgin Islands and northwest of Saint Kitts and Nevis. The island covers an area of 21 sq. km. (8.1 sq. miles).

Population
Figures from the 2006 census put the population at 3,100. As of 2011, the population was estimated at 3,800.

The official languages are Dutch and English.

BANKING AND FINANCE

Currency
Netherlands Antillean Guilder of 100 cents. The US$ is widely accepted in shops and restaurants.

Economy
The economy is based on tourism.

Foreign Investment
There are some exchange control and currency regulations but generally there are no specific restrictions or authorizations required for foreign investment. Authorization may be necessary in certain areas including banking and financial services. The government is seeking investors in tourism, service sectors, infrastrucutre and industry.

MANUFACTURING, MINING AND SERVICES

Energy
Sint Eustatius has its own power station

Tourism
The tourist sector is a main contributor to the island's economy.

COMMUNICATIONS AND TRANSPORT

International Airports
The airport at St. Eustatius is called the F. D. Roosevelt Airport. WINAIR is the only scheduled carrier and runs a regular air service to the island.

Ports and Harbours
Although St. Eustatius is regularly visited by cruise ships the harbour is not large or deep enough for them to anchor so passengers are brought to the island by tender.

EDUCATION

The language of instruction is Dutch and English, Spanish is also taught at schools.

The University of Sint Eustatius, School of Medicine is located on the island, the majority of the students come from the United States and Canada.

COMMUNICATIONS AND MEDIA

Broadcasting
Radio Statia broadcasts on the island.

SABA

Autonomous Special Municipality of the Kingdom of the Netherlands

Capital: The Bottom

Head of State: King Willem-Alexander (page 1537)

Flag: The top of the flag is divided into two equal red triangles, the bottom is divided into two equal blue triangles. The centre of the flag is a white diamond with a golden five pointed star in the centre.

CONSTITUTION AND GOVERNMENT

Recent Events
Up until October 10, 2010 Saba had been part of the Dutch Caribbean dependency, the Netherlands Antilles, along with Curaçao, Sint Maarten, Sint Eustatius and Bonaire. Under the new arrangement, the Dutch government will remain responsible for defence and foreign policy in the new countries.

Executive Council (as at June 2013)
Island Governor: Jonathan Johnson
Minister of Finance, Health, Sports and Culture: Bruce Zagers
Minister of Constitutional Affairs, Public Works and Education: Chris Johnson

LEGAL SYSTEM

The civil law system based on Dutch law. The judicial system also originates directly from Dutch law.

AREA AND POPULATION

Area
Saba covers an area of 13 sq. km. or 5 sq. miles. It is situated in the Caribbean to the southwest of Sint Maarten and Saint Bartélémy.

Population
The most recent population figures put the population at 1, 424. Dutch is the official language although English is spoken by almost everyone.

Public Holidays 2014
21 March: Easter Monday
30 April: King's Birthday
5 May: Labour Day
29 May: Ascension Day
21 October: Antillian Day
25 December: Christmas Day
26 December: Boxing Day

BANKING AND FINANCE

Currency
The Netherlands Antilles Guilder of 100 cents.

Economy
Tourism and eco-tourism are growth markets. The economy also depends on agriculture including livestock and vegetable cultivation.

MANUFACTURING, MINING AND SERVICES

Tourism
The main contributor to economy is the tourism sector especially ecotourism. The island is also a popular destination for divers. Approximately 25,000 people visit the island each year.

COMMUNICATIONS AND TRANSPORT

Airport
The Sabu airport is called Juancho E. Yrausquin Airport and flights connect the island with Sint Maarten and Sint Eustatius

Roads
Sabu has one road called "The Road". It connects Fort Bay, The Bottom, Windwardside and St. Johns.

Ports and Harbours
A pier is located at Fort Bay. A ferry service runs from Saba and Sint Maarten.

HEALTH

Saba has one hospital, the A.M. Edwards Medical Center.

EDUCATION

Saba has one primary school, Sacred Heart Primary School, where the language of instruction is English. There is a Comprehensive school at St. Johns.

American expatriates in coordination with the Netherlands government founded the SABA University School of Medicine.

ENVIRONMENT

In 1987 the waters around Saba were designated as the Saba National Marine Park and are subject to government regulation to preserve the coral reefs and marine life.

NEW ZEALAND

Capital: Wellington (Population estimate: 386,000)

Head of State: Her Majesty Queen Elizabeth II (Sovereign) (page 1420)

Governor-General: Rt Hon. Lt.-Gen. Sir Jerry Mateparae (page 1472)

National Flag: The Blue Ensign, charged in the fly with four stars five-pointed red and bordered white, to represent the Southern Cross, with the Union Flag (Jack) in the upper left quarter.

CONSTITUTION AND GOVERNMENT

Constitution
New Zealand has no written constitution. Executive power is held by the British Sovereign and exercised by the Governor-General. The Sovereign elects the Governor-General as her personal representative on the recommendation of the Prime Minister, normally for a term of five years. The British Sovereign, Queen Elizabeth II, who has the title 'Queen of New Zealand, and of Her other Realms and Territories, head of the Commonwealth, Defender of the Faith'. The Governor-General executes power on the advice of the Executive Council.

The Cabinet and Executive Council are set up by the party with the confidence of the House of Representatives. All ministers are members of the Executive Council, which advises the Governor-General on the basis of decisions made by the Cabinet.

Treaty of Waitangi
New Zealand was first settled by the Maori, descended from Polynesians, during the tenth century. In 1769 James Cook sighted the North Island and returned several times in the following years to chart and explore the islands. Encouraged by his reports, settlers came from Europe and Australia. As a result the Maori were in danger of becoming a dispossessed people.

In an effort to preserve their lands and way of life, over 500 Maori chiefs agreed to cede sovereignty to the British Crown in return for exclusive undisturbed possession of their lands, estates, forests and fisheries, and the rights and privileges of British subjects. This agreement was formalised in the Treaty of Waitangi, which was signed on 6 February 1840. Due to differences in translation in the treaty, and therefore its interpretation, acceptance was reached by the government that differences existed between the two texts. This led to the 1975 Treaty of Waitangi Act, which established the Waitangi Tribunal (set up to consider grievances caused by breaches of the Treaty), and directs the Tribunal to have regard to the two texts.

For further details on the constitution, please visit:
http://www.gov-gen.govt.nz/role/constofnz.htm

International Relations
Through its membership of the UN New Zealand contributes to the reconstruction efforts in Afghanistan and Iraq. New Zealand is also a member of the Antarctic Treaty system and the New Agenda Coalition on nuclear disarmament issues.

NEW ZEALAND

New Zealand has jurisdiction over Tokelau and the Ross Dependency and is in free association with the Cook Islands and Niue. New Zealand enjoys close relations with other Pacific nations. New Zealand has signed a Closer Economic Partnership agreement with Thailand and a Free Trade Agreement (FTA) with Singapore, Chile, and Brunei. A FTA was signed with China in 2008 and discussions for a FTA with India are underway.

Recent Events

In August 2006, the Queen of the Maoris died. Te Arikinui Dame Te Atairangikaahu had reigned for 40 years.

In February 2009 the government agreed to pay a compensation package of NZ$300 million to eight Maori tribes. The compensation was for illegal land seizures and breaches of the Treaty of Waitangi. Some of the grievances went back 150 years.

In November 2009 Fiji expelled New Zealand's top diplomat in retaliation for New Zealand banning travel by members of Fiji's military-led government. New Zealand retaliated by expelling Fijian diplomats. New Zealand and Fiji then re-appointed senior staff following negotiations in January 2010.

New Zealand was hit by an earthquake measuring 5.4 on the Richter scale in September 2010. Approximately two thirds of homes in Christchurch were damaged & the country's infrastructure also suffered with damage to roads and water supplies. Central government is expected to bear most of the costs. A state of emergency was declared.

In November 2010 a series of explosions at the Pike River mine, near Greymouth on South Island killed 29 miners.

Christchurch was hit by an earthquake in February 2011 which caused major damage. At least 160 people were killed. It is estimated that up to a third of the city's buildings have been or will have to be demolished and rebuilding costs are expected to be in the billions of dollars.

A stricken cargo ship leaked at least 350 tonnes of heavy fuel oil into the waters off the northern coast in October. More than 1,000 birds have died and environmentalists have warned off disastrous consequences if all 1,700 tonnes of oil and 2000 tonnes of diesel leak. The accident happened in good weather on a well-marked reef.

A general election took place on 26 November 2011. John Key, leader of the National Party, swept to victory taking 60 of the 121 seats, the largest share of seats since New Zealand opted for proportional representation in 1996. In December 2011, the National Party agreed a coalition deal with the ACT party and the United Future party, which both have one seat in parliament. The opposition leader Phil Goff resigned following a poor showing for the Labour Party.

In February 2012, amidst a row about foreign ownership of agricultural land, the New Zealand High Court blocked the sale of dairy farms to a Chinese consortium.

Legislature

New Zealand's unicameral legislature is known as the House of Representatives, and is made up of 120 Members of Parliament: 61 from the Electorate, 53 from the Member of Parliament list, and seven from Maori constituencies. All are elected for three-year terms by universal adult suffrage.

House of Representatives, Parliament Buildings, Wellington, New Zealand. Tel: +64 4 471 9999, fax: + 64 4 473 2439, e-mail: parlinfo@parliament.govt.nz, URL: http://www.parliament.nz
Speaker of the House: Rt Hon David Carter (page 1401)

Cabinet (as at July 2013)
Prime Minister and Minister of Tourism: Rt. Hon. John Key (page 1456)
Deputy Prime Minister, Minister of Finance: Bill English (page 1421)
Leader of the House, Minister for the Canterbury Earthquake, Minister of Transport: Gerry Brownlee
Minister of Economic Development, Science and Innovation, Tertiary Education, Skills and Employment: Steven Joyce (page 1452)
Minister of Justice, Minister of Accident Compensation Corporation, Minister of Ethnic Affairs: Judith Collins (page 1407)
Minister of Health, for State Owned Enterprises: Tony Ryall (page 1506)
Minister of Education, Minister of Pacific Island Affairs: Hekia Parata
Attorney General, Minister for Treaty of Waitangi Negotiations, Minister for Arts, Culture and Heritage: Christopher Finlayson (page 1424)
Minister of Social Development: Paula Bennett
Minister of Defence, Minister of State Services: Dr Jonathan Coleman (page 1407)
Minister of Foreign Affairs, Minister for Sport and Recreation: Murray McCully (page 1474)
Minister of Police, Corrections, Deputy Leader of the House: Anne Tolley (page 1526)
Minister of Conservation, Minister of Housing: Dr Nick Smith (page 1517)
Minister of Trade, Minister for Climate Change Issues: Tim Grosner (page 1434)
Minister of Primary Industries, Minister of Racing: Nathan Guy
Minister of Commerce, Minister of Consumer Affairs, Minister of Broadcasting: Craig Foss
Minister of Internal Affairs, Minister of Local Government: Chris Tremain
Minister of Energy and Resources; Labour: Simon Bridges
Minister for Food Safety; Civil Defence; Youth Affairs: Nikki Kaye
Ministers outside Cabinet
Minister for Building and Construction, Minister of Customs, Minister of Land Information, Minister for Statistics: Maurice Williamson (page 1537)
Minister for the Community and Voluntary Sector; Senior Citizens; Women's Affairs: Jo Goodhew
Minister for Courts: Chester Borrows
Minister of Immigration; Veterans' Affairs: Michael Woodhouse

Minister of Revenue: Todd McClay

Support Party Ministers (as at July 2013)
Minister of Regulatory Reform and Small Business: John Banks
Minister of Maori Affairs: Dr Pita Sharples
Minister of Whanau Ora; Disability Issues: Tariana Turia (page 1528)

Ministries
Department of the Prime Minister and Cabinet, Level 5, Reserve Bank Building, 2 The Terrace, New Zealand. Tel: +64 (0)4 471 9074, fax: +64 (0)4 473 3181, e-mail: information.dpmc@parliament.govt.nz, URL: http://www.dpmc.govt.nz
The Treasury, 1 The Terrace (PO Box 3724), Wellington, New Zealand. Tel: +64 (0)4 472 2733, fax: +64 (0)4 473 0982, e-mail: information@treasury.govt.nz, URL: http://www.treasury.govt.nz
Ministry of Agriculture and Forestry, 101-103 The Terrace (PO Box 2526), Wellington, New Zealand. Tel: +64 (0)4 474 4100, fax: +64 (0)4 474 4244, e-mail: hayesj@maf.govt.nz, URL: http://www.maf.govt.nz
Ministry of Civil Defence and Emergency Management, 33 Bowen Street (PO Box 5010), Wellington, New Zealand. Tel: +64 (0)4 473 7363, fax: +64 (0)4 473 7369, e-mail: emergency.management@dia.govt.nz, URL: http://www.civildefence.govt.nz
Ministry of Consumer Affairs, 8th Floor, Ministry of Commerce Building, 33 Bowen Street (PO Box 1473), Wellington, New Zealand. Tel: +64 (0)4 474 2750, fax: +64 (0)4 473 9400, e-mail: mcainfo@mca.govt.nz, URL: http://www.consumer-ministry.govt.nz
Ministry for Culture and Heritage, Level 5, Radio New Zealand House, 155 The Terrace (PO Box 5364), Wellington, New Zealand. Tel: +64 (0)4 499 4229, fax: +64 (0)4 499 4490, e-mail: info@mch.govt.nz, URL: http://www.mch.govt.nz
Ministry of Defence, 3rd Floor, Defence House, 15 - 21 Stout Street (PO Box 5347), Wellington, New Zealand. Tel: +64 (0)4 496 0270, fax: +64 4 496 0290, e-mail: pauline.medhurst@nzdf.mil.nz, URL: http://www.defence.govt.nz
Ministry of Economic Development, 33 Bowen Street (PO Box 1473), Wellington, New Zealand. Tel: +64 (0)4 472 0030, fax: +64 (0)4 473 4638, e-mail: info@med.govt.nz, URL: http://www.med.govt.nz
Ministry of Education, 45-47 Pipitea Street, Thorndon (Private Box 1666), Wellington, New Zealand. Tel: +64 (0)4 463 8000, fax: +64 (0)4 463 8001, e-mail: communications@minedu.govt.nz, URL: http://www.minedu.govt.nz
Ministry for the Environment, 84 Boulcott Street (PO Box 10 362), Wellington, New Zealand. Tel: +64 (0)4 917 7400, fax: +64 (0)4 917 7523, e-mail: library@mfe.govt.nz, URL: http://www.mfe.govt.nz
Ministry of Fisheries, 101-103 The Terrace (PO Box 1020), Wellington, New Zealand. Tel: +64 (0)4 470 2600, fax: +64 (0)4 470 2601, e-mail: info@fish.govt.nz, URL: http://www.fish.govt.nz
Ministry of Foreign Affairs and Trade, Stafford House, 40 The Terrace (Private Bag 18 901), Wellington, New Zealand. Tel: +64 (0)4 494 8500, fax: +64 (0)4 494 8512, e-mail: enquiries@mft.govt.nz, URL: http://www.mft.govt.nz
Ministry of Health, 133 Molesworth Street (PO Box 5013), Wellington, New Zealand. Tel: +64 (0)4 496 2000, fax: +64 (0)4 496 2340, e-mail: peter_abernethy@moh.govt.nz, URL: http://www.moh.govt.nz
Ministry of Housing, Level 12, Vogel Building, Aitken Street (PO Box 10729), Wellington, New Zealand. Tel: +64 (0)4 472 2753, fax: +64 (0)4 499 4744, e-mail: info@minhousing.govt.nz, URL: http://www.minhousing.govt.nz
Ministry of Justice, 10th Floor, Charles Fergusson Building, Bowen Street (PO Box 180), Wellington, New Zealand. Tel: +64 (0)4 494 9700, fax: +64 (0)4 494 9701, e-mail: reception@justice.govt.nz, URL: http://www.justice.govt.nz
Department of Labour, Unisys House, 56 The Terrace (PO Box 3705), Wellington, New Zealand. Tel: +64 (0)4 915 4000, fax: +64 (0)4 915 4015, e-mail: info@dol.govt.nz, URL: http://www.dol.govt.nz
Ministry of Pacific Island Affairs, Level 1, Charles Fergusson Building, Ballantrae Place (PO Box 833), Wellington, New Zealand. Tel: +64 (0)4 473 3493, fax: +64 (0)4 473 4301, e-mail: contact@minpac.govt.nz, URL: http://www.minpac.govt.nz
Ministry of Research, Science and Technology, Level 10, 2 The Terrace (PO Box 5336), Wellington, New Zealand. Tel: +64 (0)4 472 6400, fax: +64 (0)4 471 1284, e-mail: talk2us@morst.govt.nz, URL: http://www.morst.govt.nz
Ministry of Social Development, Charles Fergusson Building, Bowen Street (Private Bag 39993), Wellington, New Zealand. Tel: +64 (0)4 916 3860, fax: +64 (0)4 916 3918, e-mail: information@msd.govt.nz, URL: http://www.msd.govt.nz
Ministry of Transport, 38-42 Waring Taylor Street (PO Box 3175), Wellington, New Zealand. Tel: +64 (0)4 472 1253, fax: +64 (0)4 473 3697, e-mail: reception@transport.govt.nz, URL: http://www.transport.govt.nz
Ministry of Women's Affairs, 48 Mulgrave Street, Wellington (PO Box 10 049), Wellington, New Zealand. Tel: +64 (0)4 473 4112, fax: +64 (0)4 472 0961, e-mail: mwa@mwa.govt.nz, URL: http://www.mwa.govt.nz
Ministry of Youth Affairs, 48 Mulgrave Street (PO Box 10 300), Wellington, New Zealand. Tel: +64 (0)4 471 2158, fax: +64 (0)4 471 2233, e-mail: info@youthaffairs.govt.nz, URL: http://www.youthaffairs.govt.nz

Political Parties
ACT New Zealand, ACT Parliamentary Office, Parliament Buildings, New Zealand. Tel: +64 4 470 6624, fax: +64 4 473 3532, e-mail: act@parliament.govt.nz, URL: http://www.act.org.nz
ACT National Office: Level 1, Block B, Old Mercury Building, Nuffield St (Opposite Balm St), PO Box 99651, Newmarket, Auckland 1031, New Zealand. Tel: +64 (0)9 523 0470, fax: +64 (0)9 523 0472, e-mail: info@voteact.org.nz
Leader: John Banks
The Green Party of Aotearoa New Zealand, PO Box 11-652, Wellington, New Zealand. Tel: +64 (0)4 801 5102, fax: +64 (0)4 801 5104, e-mail: greenparty@greens.org.nz, URL: http://www.greens.org.nz
Leaders: Metiria Turei, Russel Norman
New Zealand Labour Party, 1st Floor, Fraser House, 160-162 Willis Street, P.O. Box 784, Wellington, New Zealand. Tel: +64 (0)4 384 7649, fax: +64 (0)4 384 8060, e-mail: labour.party@parliament.govt.nz, URL: http://www.labour.org.nz

Outgoing Leader: David Shearer

New Zealand National Party, P O Box 1155, 14th Floor Willibank House, 57 Willis Street, Wellington, New Zealand. Tel: +64 (0)4 472 5211, fax: +64 (0)4 478 1622, URL: http://www.national.org.nz

Leader: John Key

Maori Party, PO Box 50-271, Porirua, New Zealand. Tel: +64 (0)7 471 9900, e-mail: hekeretari2@maoriparty.com, URL: http://www.maoriparty.com

Leaders: Tariana Turia, Dr Pita Sharples

United Future New Zealand, PO Box 18-020, Wellington, New Zealand. Tel: +64 (0)9 486 2421, fax: +64 (0)9 486 0005, URL: http://www.unitedfuture.org.nz

Leader: Peter Dunne

New Zealand First Party, Parliament Buildings, Wellington, New Zealand. Tel: +64 (0)4 471 9292, fax: +64 (0)4 472 7751, URL: http://www.nzfirst.org.nz

Leader: Winston Peters (page 1495)

Mana Party, URL: http://mana.net.nz

Leader: Hone Harawira

Elections

A general election was held on 17 September 2005. Helen Clark's Labour Party won 50 seats, down from 52 seats in the 2002 election. In a controversial move, Winston Peters, leader of the anti immigration New Zealand First Party, was appointed to the out of cabinet post of Foreign Minister.

The current system of voting is called Mixed Member Proportional (MMP) and came into effect after a 1993 referendum. Each individual has two votes, a Party Vote for the party they would like to be in power and an Electorate Vote for their own Member of Parliament. A party must win at least 5 per cent of all the party votes or win at least one electorate seat through the electorate vote to receive a proportional allocation of seats in Parliament.

The House of Representatives is elected by universal suffrage. Although voting is not compulsory, enrolment to vote is mandatory for all citizens over the age of 18. Maori and persons of Maori descent may enrol for either a Maori or general electorate. Electoral district boundaries are reviewed every five years.

The most recent election took place on 27 November 2011. Preliminary results were as follows:

Preliminary Results, 2011 General Election

Party	Votes	Electorate Seats	List Seats	Total Seats
National Party	957,769	41	19	60
Labour Party	541,499	22	12	34
Green Party	211,931	0	13	13
New Zealand First Party	135,865	0	8	8
Maori Party	26,887	3	0	3
ACT New Zealand	21,446	1	0	1
Mana	19,898	1	0	1
United Future	12,159	1	0	1
Conservative Party	55,070	0	0	0

Source: Elections New Zealand

The Conservative Party, the Aotearoa Legalise Cannabis Party, Democrats for Social Credit, Libertarianz, and Alliance gained no seats. Voter turnout was estimated to be 74 per cent.

A referendum on whether to retain the current Mixed Member Proportional (MMP) voting system was also held with approximately 54 per cent

Diplomatic Representation

British High Commission, 44 Hill Street, Wellington 1, New Zealand, Wellington, New Zealand. (Mailing address: PO Box 1812, Wellington, New Zealand.) Tel: +64 (0)4 924 2888, fax: +64 (0)4 473 4982, e-mail: PPA.Mailbox@fco.gov.uk, URL: http://ukinnewzealand.fco.gov.uk/en/

High Commissioner: Vicki Treadell (page 1527)

Embassy of the United States of America, 29 Fitzherbert Terrace, Thorndon, Wellington, New Zealand. (Mailing address: PO Box 1190, Wellington, New Zealand.) Tel: +64 (0)4 462 6000, fax: +64 (0)4 499 0490, URL: http://newzealand.usembassy.gov/.

Ambassador: David Huebner (page 1445)

New Zealand High Commission, New Zealand House, 80 The Haymarket, London SW1Y 4TQ, United Kingdom. Tel: +44 (020) 7930 8422, e-mail: newzealandhc@newzealandhc.org.uk, URL: http://www.nzembassy.com/united-kingdom

Acting High Commissioner: Rob Taylor

Embassy of New Zealand, 37 Observatory Circle, Washington DC 20008, USA. Tel: +1 202 328 4800, fax: +1 202 667 5227, e-mail: nz@nzemb.org, URL: http://www.nzembassy.com/usa

Ambassador: Rt. Hon. Michael Moore (page 1479)

New Zealand Permanent Mission to the United Nations, One United Nations Plaza, 25th floor, New York, NY 10017, United States of America. Tel: +1 212 826 1960, fax: +1 212 758 0827, e-mail: nzmissionny@earthlink.net, URL: http://www.nzembassy.com/home.cfm?c=51

Permanent Representative: James McLay

LEGAL SYSTEM

The court system is structured thus: Supreme Court, Court of Appeal, the High Court and the district courts. These are courts of general jurisdiction. Their jurisdiction is defined by statute. In addition, the court system allows for specialist courts: Employment Court, Family Court, Youth Court, Environment Court, Māori Land Court and Māori Appellate Court, as well as over 100 tribunals.

The District Courts carry out the functions of both High Courts and District Courts. Legislation was passed in 1998 to allow the appointment of community magistrates, who would take on some of the workload of district judges and provide a closer link between the community and the justice system. As part of a pilot scheme four new courts at Hamilton, Huntly, Tauranga and Whakatane were set up in 1999, with 16 community magistrates. There are also two small courts where the local police officer acts as the court registrar. The District Court includes Disputes Tribunals, Family Courts and the Youth Court. The District Court hears and decides the following: criminal cases; civil cases up to $200,000; disputes up to $3,000 (or $5,000 if both parties agree) through the Disputes Tribunal; family and marriage disputes and complaints concerning care, custody and control of children, through the Family Court; and charges against young people through the Youth Court. It also regulates business activities. There are a number of specialised tribunals, committees and boards which act either as licensing or reviewing boards or as dispute and appeal authorities. They monitor, regulate and enforce certain legislation, for example: Planning Tribunal; Motor Vehicle Disputes Tribunal. The Waitangi Tribunal is a special tribunal established to hear claims related to the Treaty of Waitangi.

There are currently 133 District court judges, 52 Disputes Tribunal Referees and approximately 400 Justices of the Peace.

The High Court hears and decides the most serious criminal charges as well as large or important civil cases, some matrimonial property cases and some appeals from the District Court.

The Court of Appeal in Wellington hears and decides appeals from the High Court and appeals after jury trials in the District Court. New Zealanders also have access to the Privy Council in England which can review special civil and criminal cases on appeal from the Court of Appeal. The Court consists of a president and eight judges.

The Supreme Court is the final appellate court. It hears only a small proportion of cases as the Court of Appeal is generally the last court for an appeal for most cases in the legal system. Cases may only go to the Supreme Court if the court grants leave to appeal. The criteria for granting 'leave to appeal' are set out in s13 Supreme Court Act 2003. A decision by a higher court is binding on lower courts and decisions of the Supreme Court, as the final court of appeal, are binding on all other courts.

The death penalty was abolished in 1989. The Cook Islands was the last of New Zealand's overseas territories to abolish capital punishment in 2007.

Courts of New Zealand, URL: http://www.courtsofnz.govt.nz/
Supreme Court, PO Box 61, Wellington, New Zealand. Tel: +64 4 918 8222, fax: +64 4 914 3560, e-mail: supreme court@justice.govt.nz
Chief Justice of High Court and Court of Appeal: Rt. Hon. Dame Sian Elias, GNZM (page 1420)
Court of Appeal of New Zealand, Cnr Molesworth & Aitken Streets (PO Box 1606 Wellington), New Zealand. Tel: +64 4 914 3540, fax: +64 4 914 3570
President of the Court of Appeal: Justice Mark O'Regan

Wellington High Court, 2 Molesworth Street, (PO Box 1091, Wellington), New Zealand. Tel: +64 4 914 3600, fax: +64 4 914 3603, URL: http://www.justice.govt.nz/

Human Rights Commission, PO Box 6751, Level 10, Tower Centre, Wellesley Street, Auckland 1030, New Zealand. Tel: +64 9 309 0874, e-mail: hrc@hrc.co.nz, URL: http://www.hrc.co.nz

LOCAL GOVERNMENT

The structure of local government was re-organised in 1989. As of 2011 there were 11 regional councils (Auckland; Bay of Plenty; Canterbury; Gisborne-Hawke's Bay; Manawatu-Wanganui; Nelson-Marlborough; Northland; Otago; Southland; Taranaki; Waikato; Wellington; West Coast), 12 city councils, 54 district councils (including the Chatham Islands and four unitary councils which have regional functions); and one Auckland Council (which amalgamated eight former councils on 1 November 2010). Auckland Council as well as the city and district councils are collectively refered to as territorial authorities of which there are 67 in total. Six of the territorial authorities (including Auckland) have the powers of a regional council and are sometimes referred to as unitary authorities. New Zealand has 108 regional councillors, 716 territorial councillors, 149 Auckland local board members and 67 mayors, local government employs nearly 23,000 staff.

The functions of regional councils include resource management, plant and pest control, river management and flood control, erosion, regional land transport planning, civil defence. City and district council responsibilities include the well being of the community, environmental health and safety, infrastructure, recreation and culture and resource management including land use planning. In 2010, local authorities contributed 4 per cent of total GDP.

AREA AND POPULATION

Area
New Zealand is situated in the South Pacific Ocean, 1,600 km to the east of Australia. Its total area is 266,171 sq. km. It comprises two main islands, the North Island and South Island, and several smaller islands (some uninhabited), including Stewart Island and the Chatham Islands which lie about 850 km eastwards. Over half of New Zealand is pasture and arable land and a quarter forest, including 1.3 million hectares of exotic plantation forest. Much of the land is mountainous and hilly. New Zealand is home to several active but quiet volcanoes, hot springs mudpools and geysers situated in Rotorua on the North Island. The capital, Wellington, is situated at the southern end of the North Island.

The climate is temperate.

NEW ZEALAND

To view a map of New Zealand, please consult
http://www.lib.utexas.edu/maps/australia/new_zealand_pol_2006.jpg

Population

New Zealand's estimated resident population was 4,840,000 at the middle of 2012, up from the 2002 figure of 3,948,500. It is projected to rise to 4,840,000 by 2022. The population change is partly due to a natural population increase and partly due to net permanent and long term migration. In 2011 the natural increase of the population was 33,500, including 3,900 through net migration. Population density in 1999 was an estimated 14 people per sq. km. Of a 2001 Census population of 3,792,654, a total of 2,849,721 lived on the North Island, whilst 942,213 lived on the South Island.

In 2012 an estimated 892,300 inhabitants were under 15 years, 1,497,000 inhabitants were aged 15-39 years, 1,432,300 were aged 40-64, and 611,400 were aged 65+ years.

Provisional figures for 2010 show that the main urban areas are Auckland (1,354,900 inhabitants), Wellington, (389,700), Christchurch, (390,300), Hamilton, (203,400), Napier-Hastings, (124,400), and Dunedin (116,600). The majority of the population, over 80 per cent live in urban areas.

New Zealand's main ethnic groups are European/Pākehā (79.6 per cent), New Zealand Māori (14.5 per cent), Pacific Islands (5.6 per cent), Chinese (2.2 per cent), and Indian (1.2 per cent). English and Maori are both official languages.

Births, Marriages, Deaths

As at year ending December 2012 figures put the number of live births at 61,178. The fertility rate was 2.0 births per woman in 2012 (compared to 4.3 births per woman in 1961). Figures for 2011 show that 20,231 marriages took place and 8,551 divorces were granted. The Civil Union Act came into force in 2005. This is a new legal relationship which can apply to same or opposite sex couples. In 2006 there were 430 civil unions (348 same-sex and 82 opposite sex). Total number of civil unions at the end of December 2006 was 708.

Figures for 2012 put the number of deaths at 30,099. The average age of death in 2006 was 76.3 years for males and 82.3 years for females. In 2012 there were 256 registered infant deaths. Life expectancy of girls born in 2006 is an estimated 81.1 years and boys 76.3 years. Life expectancy at birth for the Maori ethnic group is 69 years for males and 73.2 years for females. The components of population change for the five years ending 30 June 2012 was live births 314,920, deaths 145,664, giving a natural increase of 163,256. Migration figures for that period showed 424,213 arrivals and 389,786 departures resulting in net migration of 34,427. (Source: Statistics New Zealand)

Public Holidays 2014

1-2 January: New Year
6 February: Waitangi Day
18 April: Good Friday
21 April: Easter Monday
25 April: ANZAC Day
2 June: Queen's Birthday (1st Monday in June)
27 October: Labour Day (4th Monday in October)
25 December: Christmas Day
26 December: Boxing Day

Each region also celebrates an anniversary day:*
17 January: Southland
22 January: Wellington
29 January: Auckland, Northland
1 February: Nelson
23 March: Otago
31 March: Taranaki
1 November: Hawkes Bay, Marlborough
30 November: Chatham Islands
1 December: Westland
16 December: Canterbury
*The actual days taken as holiday occur on the first weekday following the anniversary day.

EMPLOYMENT

The unemployment rate in December 2007 was 3.4 per cent, down by 0.4 per cent from December 2006. There were 2,173,000 employed people (up 2.5 per cent from December 2006) and 77,000 people were registered unemployed (down 7.4 per cent from December 2006). An estimated 1,022,000 people were not in the labour force. Figures for September 2008 show that 2,172,000 were employed, 94,000 were unemployed and 1,034,000 were not in the labour force. The unemployment rate was 4.2 per cent. By June 2009 the economy had shrunk for the fifth consecutive quarter making it the worst recession New Zealand has experienced, this was reflected in the unemployment figures which rose to a nine year high of 6.5 per cent in the third quarter of 2009. Figures for the third quarter of 2010 showed that the unemployment rate had risen to 6.8 per cent but had fallen slightly in the fourth quarter to 6.4 per cent. The unemployment rate for the end of 2011 was 6.3 per cent, (150,000 people). Figures for the fourth quarter of 2012 show that the total number of people employed was 2,357,000. The unemployment rate in December 2012 was registered at 6.9 per cent.

The unadjusted unemployment rates by ethnic group for the December 2007 quarter were: 7.3 per cent for Maori, 5.4 per cent for the 'Other' ethnic group, 4.7 per cent for Pacific peoples and 2.3 per cent for European.

Employment by Economic Activity

Sector	2007	2008
Agriculture, hunting & forestry	153,000	149,400

- continued

Fishing	2,400	2,600
Mining & quarrying	5,200	4,000
Manufacturing	279,200	278,000
Electricity, gas & water supply	8,800	12,000
Construction	185,300	179,200
Wholesale & retail trade & repairs	377,700	387,100
Hotels & restaurants	108,200	101,000
Transport, storage & communications	118,100	123,100
Financial intermediation	70,800	68,100
Real estate, renting & business activities	248,700	254,000
Public administration & defence, compulsory social security	138,100	132,700
Education	169,600	175,400
Health & social work	203,500	207,800
Other community, social & personal service activities	91,100	99,900
Households with employed persons	3,700	2,200
Other	10,700	11,800

Source: Copyright © International Labour Organization (ILO Dept. of Statistics, http://laborsta.ilo.org)

BANKING AND FINANCE

Currency

One New Zealand Dollar = 100 cents

GDP/GNP, Inflation, National Debt

Gross Domestic Product (GDP) was $131,449 million in 2007 up from $111,886 million in 2002. This was made up of primary industries $9,362 million (compared to $8,661 million in 2002), goods producing industries $27,237 million ($23,822 million in 2002), service industries $89,790 million ($75,361 million in 2002). Economic growth was estimated at 1.9 per cent in 2006. In 2008, New Zealand began, along with other economies worldwide, to experience a downturn in economic growth. In September 2008 GDP decreased by 0.4 per cent, the third successive quarterly decline. By June 2009 the economy had shrunk for the fifth consecutive quarter, making it the worst recession New Zealand has experienced. In the fourth quarter of 2010, the economy showed a positive growth of 0.2 per cent. Figures for the year ending September 2011 showed that had grow by 1.3 per cent. (Source: Statistics New Zealand)

The following table shows annual GDP in recent years. Figures are in NZ$ million and at 1995-96 prices:

Industry	2011	2012
Agriculture	4,739	6,153
Forestry & logging	1,421	1,468
Fishing, aquaculture & agriculture support	913	924
Mining	1,374	1,174
Food, beverage & tobacco	6,300	6,580
Textile, leather, clothing and footwear	651	594
Wood & paper products	2,303	2,304
Printing	514	509
Petroleum, chemical, polymer & rubber product	2,954	2,951
Non-metallic product	711	695
Metal product	1,877	1,893
Transport equipment, machinery & equipment	2,430	2,595
Furniture & other manufacturing	375	355
Manufacturing	18,131	18,529
Electricity, gas, water & waste services	3,217	3,169
Construction	6,601	6,058
Wholesale trade	7,735	7,973
Retail trade	7,022	7,355
Accommodation & food services	2,119	2,188
Transport postal & warehousing	7,415	7,478
Information media & telecommunications	9,036	8,860
Financial & insurance services	6,743	6,931
Rental, hiring & real estate services	7,896	8,047
Ownership of owner occupied dwellings	9,802	9,885
Professional, scientific & technical services	8,665	9,137
Administrative & support services	2,318	2,435
Local government admin.	760	735
Central government admin. defence & public safety	5,265	5,245
Education & training	4,612	4,658
Health care & social assistance	7,751	7,579
Arts & recreation services	1,743	1,677
Other services	2,789	2,809
Unallocated industries	11,018	11,180
GDP	140,096	142,820

Source: Statistics New Zealand

Annual GDP (Chain-volume expressed in 1995/96 prices)

Year	NZ$ million
2004	124,592
2005	129,117
2006	133,530
2007	137,389
2008	141,358
2009	138,636

- continued

2010	138,034
2011	140,096
2012	142,820

Source: New Zealand Statistics

GDP per capita was US$14,900 in 2002. New Zealand's total public debt rose from NZ$23,498 million in 2002 (year ending 30 June) to NZ$24,380 million in 2003. Per capita GDP in 2009 was put at US$28,100.

The Consumer Price Index was 3.4 per cent in December 2007.

Foreign Investment

Total foreign investment in New Zealand was NZ$254.1 billion at 31 March 2007, an increase of $19.4 billion from 31 March 2006. Investment comes mainly from Australia ($79.0 billion) and Canada, and from the OECD and APEC. New Zealand investment abroad was $11.0 billion at 31 March 2007, an increase of $6.4 billion from the previous year.

Balance of Payments / Imports and Exports

The following table shows international trade according to the top countries for imports and exports:

Figures in NZ$ Mil.

Country	2012
Exports	
Australia	10,460
People's Republic of China	6,106
USA	4,083
Japan	3,387
Republic of Korea	1,556
United Kingdom	1,443
Total all countries	46,688
Imports	
People's Republic of China	7,658
Australia	7,240
USA	4,695
Japan	3,229
Singapore	2,283
Germany	2,076
Total all countries	47,451

Source: Statistics New Zealand

Principal exports are milk powder, butter and cheese; meat and edible offal; logs, wood and wood articles; fish, crustaceans and molluscs; mechanical machinery and equipment. Principal imports are mechanical machinery and equipment; vehicles, parts and accessories; petroleum and products; electrical machinery and equipment; and textiles.

The following tables show the value of exports of main commodities.

Exports of Main Commodities in NZ$ million

Commodity	2006	2011
Milk powder, butter & cheese	5,762	11,334
Meat & edible offal	4,500	5,398
Logs, wood & wood articles	1,960	3,200
Crude oil	513	1,997
Mechanical machinery & equipment	1,791	1,733
Fruit	1,161	1,487
Fish, crustaceans & molluscs	1,146	1,382
Aluminium and aluminium articles	1,261	1,260
Total all commodities	32,430	46,072

Source: Statistics New Zealand

Oil is New Zealand's largest import. The following table shows major import commodities.

Imports of Main Commodities in NZ$ million

Commodity	2006	2011
Petroleum & products	5,240	7,236
Mechanical machinery & equipment	5,150	5,487
Electrical machinery & equipment	3,340	3,890
Vehicles, parts & accessories	5,006	4,270
Textiles & textile articles	1,768	2,077
Plastics & plastic articles	1,432	1,645
Aircraft & parts	1,889	1,439
Optical, medical & measuring equipment	1,159	1,373
Total all commodities	39,040	45,073

Source: Statistics New Zealand

Central Bank

Reserve Bank of New Zealand, 2 The Terrace, PO Box 2498, Wellington 6011, New Zealand. URL: http://www.rbnz.govt.nz
Governor: Graeme Wheeler (page 1536)

Trade Organisations and Chambers of Commerce

New Zealand Chambers of Commerce, URL: http://www.nzchamber.co.nz/
Auckland Chamber of Commerce and Industry, URL: http://www.chamber.co.nz
Wellington Regional Chamber of Commerce, URL: http://www.wgtn-chamber.co.nz
Chamber of Commerce Tauranga Region, URL: http://www.tauranga.org.nz

Waikato Chamber of Commerce and Industry, URL: www.mngt.waikato.ac.nz/chamber

MANUFACTURING, MINING AND SERVICES

Primary and Extractive Industries

Oil is the primary fuel source in New Zealand, however New Zealand has limited reserves of 0.10 billion barrels and consumption outstrips domestic production. According to 2011 EIA statistics, New Zealand produced a total of 52.03 thousand barrels of oil per day in that year (up from 51.04 thousand barrels of oil per day in 1999). Most of it (46.32 thousand barrels per day) was crude oil. Oil consumption in 2011 was 148.92 thousand barrels per day (up from 133.15 thousand barrels per day in 1999). Consequently, imports totalled 96.88 thousand barrels per day. New Zealand's refinery capacity was 107,00 bbld.

Natural gas in New Zealand is also a premium energy resource. The principal gas source is the Taranaki Maui field. The two largest uses of natural gas are in electricity generation (30 per cent) and in the synfuels industry (30 per cent), which produces methanol and gasoline. Gross natural gas production in 2011 was 154 billion cubic feet with consumption at 151 billion cubic feet.

Coal represents New Zealand's largest indigenous fossil fuel resource. Most coal is found in the south of the South Island. Recoverable coal totals 117,620 petajoules. Production in 2010 totalled 5,876,000 tons (up from 4,084,000 tons in 1999). Consumption in 2010 was 3,514,000 tons. Exports in 2000 were 1,685,000 tons (up from 1,469,000 tons in 1999). New Zealand does not import any quantities of coal.

New Zealand's largest source of potential iron ore is the black sands of the west coast beaches, from Westport South in the South Island and from Wanganui to Muriwai in the North Island. The beach sands of North Island have been estimated to contain 800 million tonnes of titanomagnetite and 8.6 million tonnes of ilmenite. The South Island sands contain some 43 million tonnes of ilmenite. Gold occurs in New Zealand in alluvial, lode and disseminated form. The hard rock forms of gold can be mined by underground as well as opencast methods. Most present day New Zealand gold mining is for alluvial gold.

Beaches south of Greymouth contain rich mineral reserves and are currently subject to prospecting and development proposals. The main interest is in ilmenite as a source of titanium dioxide, used as a pigment in paint, paper, plastics and rubber, but there has recently been an increased interest in zircon and other heavy minerals.

There are small deposits of manganese in many localities. Uranium occurs in Westland. Some areas of Northland, Coromandel, Nelson, and Westland have potential for base metals (copper, lead and zinc). Iron ore, antimony, arsenic, chromium, monazite, nickel and rutile have been mined in the past and some are presently being investigated. Tin is known on Stewart Island. The aluminium ore, bauxite, is found in Northland where reserves of 20 million tonnes have been indicated by the DSIR. Molybdenite occurs in north west Nelson. Cinnabar, the principal ore of mercury, is widely distributed in New Zealand and was produced in limited quantities from sinter deposits in the Northland. Some prospecting of platinum also occurs.

Energy

In 2010 an estimated 43.80 billion kWh of electricity was generated and 40.76 was consumed. New Zealand has an installed capacity of 9.68 GWe.

Total primary energy produced in 2009 was 0.698 quadrillion Btu and 0.850 Quadrillion Btu was consumed. (Source: EIA)

Manufacturing

Manufacturing is New Zealand's second largest contributor to GDP. Over the last 20 years manufacturing activity as a proportion of GDP has remained relatively constant, contributing on average approximately 15 per cent of GDP at 1995/96 prices.

The following table shows total income from manufacturing industries for the 2010 financial year:

Manufacturing industries sales in 2010 in NZ$ million (unadjusted)

Sector	Q1	Q2	Q3	Q4
Structural, sheet & fabricated metal product	1,098	1,203	1,187	1,241
All manufacturing excluding meat & dairy	14,187	14,776	14,911	15,773
Meat & dairy product	6,614	6,843	4,996	6,861
Fruit, oil cereal & other food manufacturing	1,654	1,735	1,694	1,763
Beverage & tobacco manufacturing	1,001	963	954	1,321
Textile & apparel manufacturing	542	505	537	501
Wood & paper product manufacturing	1,745	1,939	1,964	1,879
Printing manufacturing	413	423	433	452
Petroleum & coal manufacturing	1,636	1,596	1,671	1,706
Chemical, polymer & rubber product manufacturing	1,589	1,713	1,577	2,001
Non-metallic mineral product manufacturing	619	626	617	616
Metal product manufacturing	2,055	2,271	2,333	2,317
Transport equipment, machinery & equipment manufacturing	2,089	2,129	2,253	2,281
Furniture & other manufacturing	390	395	419	441

NEW ZEALAND

- continued

All manufacturing	20,801	21,907	19,907	22,634

Source: Statistics New Zealand

In 2008, a total of 278,000 people were employed in the manufacturing industry. Figures for 2011 show that New Zealand had 20,938 manufacturing enterprises, down from 22,538 in 2006.

New Zealand's largest manufacturing industry is fabricated metal products, machinery and equipment. Aluminium is manufactured and exported to Japan and other Asian countries. Aluminium fabrication and foil manufacture for products widely used in the building and packaging industries is also carried out in New Zealand.

The food and beverage sector of the manufacturing industry is one of the longest established and collectively employs more people than any other type of manufacturing. Along with the dairy and meat industries, food processing also produces significant export products. The New Zealand Dairy Board is the country's biggest export earner.

The motor industry relies on the assembly of imported built-up and completely-knocked-down (ckd) vehicles although certain components and accessories are produced domestically. Recent figures show that around 40 manufacturers, employing 4,000 people, are involved in the automotive components business, accounting for NZ$400 million annually with the exports around NZ$180 million.

New Zealand has a long-established footwear manufacturing industry.

Business NZ, URL: http://www.businessnz.org.nz

Service Industries
New Zealand's services industry is the largest contributor to GDP, accounting for NZ$26,774 million of the 2002 GDP (up from NZ$25,869 million in 2001).

Tourism
Tourism plays an increasingly important part in the country's economy. Figures for 2009 show that there were 2.4 million tourist arrivals up from 1.7 million in 2000. In 2007 the top five visitor source countries were Australia, UK, USA, Japan, and China. (Source: Statistics New Zealand)
Tourism New Zealand, URL: http://www.tourisminfo.govt.nz

Agriculture
In 2010, 14.58 million hectares of land were used for agriculture, of which 11.30 million hectares were used for grazing, arable, fodder and fallow land, 1.60 million hectares for planted production forest, 127,000 hectares for horticultural land. Agriculture contributed NZ$5,823 million towards GDP in 2002 (1995/96 prices), up from NZ$5,693 million in 2001. The fishing, forestry and mining industry accounted for NZ$3,034 million of New Zealand's 2002 GDP (1995/96 prices), up from the 2001 figure of NZ$3,001 million.

Total income from the agriculture, forestry and fishing industry in the 2000 financial year is shown on the following table:

Income from agriculture, 2000

Sector	Income ($m)
Horticulture and fruit growing	2,271
Livestock and cropping farming	5,425
Dairy cattle farming	4,893
Other farming	1,380
Services to agriculture	1,340
Forestry and logging	2,429
Fishing	944

Source: Statistics New Zealand

Exports of agricultural products particularly the dairy sector is the largest export earning sector for New Zealand, as shown in the following tables:

Main agricultural exports year ending June 2003

Product	NZ$ million
Dairy products	4,679
Meat & meat products	4,171
Pastoral based products	1,279
Casein	959
Wool	936
Other	427

Source: Statistics New Zealand

Dairy exports year ending June 2003

Product	NZ$ million
Wholemilk powder	1,770
Cheese	1,001
Butter	922
Skim & buttermilk powder	866
Dairy products	119

Source: Statistics New Zealand

New Zealand is famous for having far more sheep than people.

Livestock Figures in Recent Years (Year Ending June 30)

Livestock	2007	2012
Sheep	38,500,000	31,200,000
Dairy cattle	5,300,000	6,500,000
Beef cattle	4,400,000	3,700,000
Total deer	1,400,000	1,000,000

Source: Statistics New Zealand

Around 80 per cent of meat produced goes for export and makes up 18 per cent of merchandise exports. Major export markets being the UK, Germany, France, the US, Canada, South Korea and Saudi Arabia.

The wool produced in New Zealand is crossbred (strong) wool and is mainly used in carpets, clothing and upholstery. In the year 1997-98 exports of wool products earned NZ$25.2 million, main export markets being China and Hong Kong. UK, India, Germany, and Australia.

The following table shows crop production in recent years, the year refered to end on June 30.

Crop Production in Tons

Crop	2009	2010
Wheat	403,500	466,700
Barley	435,300	314,200
Oats	33,700	48,900
Maize	237,800	202,600
Other	na	13,100

Source: New Zealand Statistics

Forestry
More than 65 per cent of wood from planted production forests is eventually exported. In 2007 43,000 hectares of forest were harvested. An estimated 34,1000 hectares were replanted and a further 2,600 hectares of new area were planted. In 2005 an forest production included an estimated 19,3 million m³ of roundwood, 4.4 million m³ o f sawn timber, 1.6 million tonnes of pulp, 920,00 tonnes of paper and paperboard, 850,000 m³ of fibreboard and 694,000 m³ of veneer. The largest markets for forestry exports are Australia, Japan, China and Korea. Forest exports amounted to nearly NZ$3 million in 2007.

Planted production forests produce 97 per cent of the country's wood. Radiata pine makes up 90 per cent of the plantation estate. Major private sector forestry companies include Carter Holt Harvey Limited, Kaingaroa Timberlands, Matariki Forests and the Hancock Natural Resource Group.

Fishing
New Zealand's principal species of fish are the prime demersal inshore finfish, pelagic finfish, rock lobster and dredge oysters. Deep-water species now account for about 80 per cent of the total catch. Trawling is the principal method of deep-water fishing. Pelagic fish are caught mainly by purse-seining. The remaining finfish are caught by various line methods and set nets. Nearly 80 per cent of landings are consigned overseas. The main export markets are Japan, the USA, and Australia. New Zealand has an Exclusive Economic Zone (EEZ) of 3.1 million nautical sq. km.

COMMUNICATIONS AND TRANSPORT

Travel Requirements
Citizens of the USA, Canada, Australia and the EU require a passport valid for at least a month beyond the length of stay. UK citizens can stay in New Zealand without a visa for up to six months, and Australians can stay indefinitely without a visa. EU and USA nationals can stay for up to three months without a visa. A return ticket is required by USA, Canadian, UK and EU subjects. Other nationals should contact the embassy to check visa requirements.

National Airlines
New Zealand's national airline is:
Air New Zealand (NZ), URL: http://www.airnz.com

International Airports
There are international airports at Christchurch, Wellington and Auckland.
Auckland International Airport, URL: http://www.auckland-airport.co.nz
Christchurch International Airport, URL: http://www.christchurch-airport.co.nz

Railways
A railway network extending nearly 4,300 km links almost all the principal centres of population. There are also a number of short private railways mainly serving collieries and other industrial undertakings. Rail services are operated by Tranz Rail. Wellington has a tram system.

Roads
There are 74 national and provincial state highways in New Zealand, comprising 11,523 km of road. Vehicles drive on the left. This network includes major routes that carry the greatest volume of traffic between residential communities, commercial and industrial areas. In addition, there are 14,251 km of urban roads and 67,200 km of rural roads, making a total of 92,974 km of developed road, which includes 15,800 bridges. Figures for 2007 show that there were 2,300,000 cars on the road and 66,000 motorcycles.

Shipping
Approximately 90 per cent of New Zealand exports and imports by value, and almost 99 per cent by volume, are carried by sea. Regular ferries cross the Cook Strait between Wellington and Picton carrying cars, passengers and freight operated by Tranz Rail.

Ports and Harbours

The main container ports are at Auckland, Tauranga, Wellington, Christchurch and Dunedin. Figures for 2007 show that the weight of import cargo was 18.5 million tonnes. Its value was NZ$39 billion, up 6.8 per cent on the previous year. In the same period, the weight of export cargo was 23.0 million tonnes, with a value of NZ$35.7 billion, up 8.6 on the previous year. (Source: Statistics New Zealand)

HEALTH

Health care in New Zealand is made up of public, private and voluntary sectors. According to the latest WHO figures (2005-10), there were 11,452 doctors (27.4 per 10,000 population), 44,424 nurses and midwives (108.7 per 10,000 population), 1,877 dentists (4.6 per 10,000 population), 2,889 pharmacists (7.1 per 10,000 population) and 5,259 community health workers (14 per 10,000 population). In 2000-09 there were an estimated 23 hospital beds per 10,000 population.

Total expenditure on health as a percentage of GDP was an estimated 10.0 per cent in 2009. Private expenditure accounted for approximately 17.0 per cent of total expenditure. General government expenditure on health accounts for 83.0 per cent of total expenditure on health (of which 11.7 per cent was social security). The government spent 19.8 per cent of its budget on health care. Per capita expenditure amounted to US$2,702.

In 2010, the infant mortality rate (likelihood of dying by age one) was 5 per 1,000 live births and for children aged under 5 it was 6 per 1,000 live births. The most common causes of death for the under-fives are: prematurity 20 per cent, congenital anomalies 24 per cent, birth asphyxia 6 per cent, pneumonia 8 per cent, and injuries (17 per cent).

In 2009, the prevalence of HIV/AIDs was 58 per 100,000 population. (Source: http://www.who.int, World Health Statistics 2012)

EDUCATION

Education is available on a free and secular basis in state primary and secondary schools. There are also private schools which usually have a religious affiliation. Education is compulsory between the ages of six and 16. In 2006, 482,769 children were enrolled in primary education, 277,992 in secondary education, and 491,018 in further education.

Pre-school Education

Kindergartens usually cater for three and four year olds. There are also Maori early childhood centres, *Kohanga reo* (language nests), which encourage children to use the Maori language.

Primary/Secondary Education

Primary education is compulsory from the age of six. It consists of levels called Standards One to Four and Forms One to Seven. There are about 2,300 primary schools in New Zealand. All state owned primary schools are co-educational. Children spend about two years in the infant classes and then progress through Standards One to Four. There are also 38 state funded *kura kaupapa Maori* teaching all subjects in Maori.

Some children attend an intermediate school (ages 11 to 13). Here, they go through Forms One and Two. If there are no intermediate schools in the area, children complete these stages at primary school.

Colleges, or high schools are for children of the age of 13 upwards. There are about 350 secondary schools in the country. These can be co-educational or single-sex. After three years of secondary education, most children take the School Certificate consisting of up to six subjects. In Form Seven, or their fifth year in secondary education, students may take the University Bursaries and Entrance Scholarship Examination in order to attain supplementary awards with which to enter university.

Higher Education

There are seven universities, Auckland, Waikato, Massey, Wellington, Canterbury, Otago and Lincoln (a university college of agriculture) and about 200,000 students. There are several private colleges and two Maori colleges in receipt of state funding, *Te Wananga O Raukawa* in Otaki and *Te Wananga O Aotearoa* in Awamutu, both of which offer degree and diploma programmes in Maori studies as well as other subjects.

There are 25 polytechnics and five teacher training colleges in New Zealand.

The literacy rate is estimated at 99 per cent.

RELIGION

There is no state religion in New Zealand. Around 70 per cent of the population are Christian, the main denominations are Anglican, Methodist, Presbyterian and Roman Catholic. The are also Hindu and Buddhist communities.

New Zealand has a religious liberty rating of 10 on a scale of 1 to 10 (10 is most freedom). (Source: World Religion Database)

COMMUNICATIONS AND MEDIA

Newspapers
The New Zealand Herald, URL: http://www.nzherald.co.nz
The Press, URL: http://www.press.co.nz
Manawatu Standard, URL: http://www.manawatustandard.co.nz
The Dominion Post, http://www.dompost.co.nz

Business Journals
National Business Review, URL: http://www.nbr.co.nz
Management (New Zealand), URL: http://www.management.co.nz
NZ Business, URL: http://www.nzbusiness.co.nz

Broadcasting
Television New Zealand operates two channels, TV ONE and TV2. It has an audience of almost 100 per cent of the population. TV3 is a private national network with transmission to approximately 98 per cent of the population. Since 1990, SKY also broadcasts satellite television in New Zealand. There are also regional television services and cable television. Maori Television is a public broadcaster.
Television New Zealand, URL: http://tvnz.co.nz
TV3, URL: http://www.tv3.co.nz
Maori Television, URL: http://www.maoritelevision.com/
Radio New Zealand Limited is the predominant radio broadcaster. URL: http://www.tvnz.co.nz
Ruia Mai, URL: http://www.ruiamai.co.nz/ (Maori-owned radio broadcaster)
Prime TV (Private Network). URL: http://www.primetv.co.nz

Postal Services
New Zealand Post Limited is a state-owned organisation and has the monopoly on postal services. There are almost 1,000 retail outlets (postshops and post centres). Nearly 1 billion items of mail are delivered per annum. (URL: http://www.nzpost.co.nz)

Telecommunications
Telecom Corporation of New Zealand Limited had a monopoly on telecommunications until deregulation in 1987, when competition such as CLEAR Communications Limited (leased line services) and BellSouth Limited (GSM cellular service) entered the market. In 2011 there were an estimated 1.8 million main telephone lines and an estimated 4.8 million mobile phones. An estimated 3.4 million people were internet users in 2009.

ENVIRONMENT

The New Zealand government has a 2010 Strategy on the Environment, a statement of broad strategic environmental direction to be read alongside other strategic documents such as Path to 2010 and Investing in our Future. National Parks cover 12 per cent of New Zealand. The 1991 Resource Management Act is an important and comprehensive law designed to promote sustainable growth in a maintainable environment. New Zealand is a member of various institutions which promote environmental issues including: the United Nations Environmental Programme, the Commission on Sustainable Development, the Global Environment Facility, the Framework Convention on Climate Change, the Vienna Convention, the Montreal Protocol, the Convention on Biological Diversity, the International Whaling Commission and the South Pacific Regional Environmental Programme.

New Zealand is party to the following international treaties: Antarctic-Environmental Protocol, Antarctic-Marine Living Resources, Antarctic Treaty, Biodiversity, Climate Change, Climate Change-Kyoto Protocol, Desertification, Endangered Species, Environmental Modification, Hazardous Wastes, Law of the Sea, Marine Dumping, Ozone Layer Protection, Ship Pollution, Tropical Timber 83, Tropical Timber 94, Wetlands, Whaling. New Zealand has signed, but not ratified: Antarctic Seals, Marine Life Conservation.

According to figures from the EIA, in 2010 New Zealand's emissions from the consumption of fossil fuels totaled 39.58 million metric tons of carbon dioxide.

Office of the Parliamentary Commissioner for the Environment, URL: http://www.pce.govt.nz/

COOK ISLANDS

Capital: Avarua (Population estimate: 13,000)

Head of State: Her Majesty Queen Elizabeth II (Sovereign) (page 1420)

Queen's Representative: Sir Frederick Goodwin KBE

National Flag: A Royal blue ensign, in the upper left quarter of which is the Union Jack, and on the fly are 15 white stars in a symmetrical circle.

CONSTITUTION AND GOVERNMENT

Constitution
The Cook Islands, named after Captain Cook who discovered them, were a British protectorate from 1888. Administrative control was transferred to New Zealand in 1990.

In 1965 the population of the islands opted for self-government in free association with New Zealand. The British Queen, represented in the Cook Islands by the Queen's Representative, is Head of State, whilst the Chief Minister is the head of government. The Cook Islands are now fully responsible for both internal and external affairs, though defence remains the responsibility of New Zealand. In recent times, the Cook Islands have adopted an increasingly independent foreign policy; as of 2005, they have diplomatic relations in its own name with 18 countries. Executive power is exercised by the government. Legislative power is vested in both the government and the Parliament of the Cook Islands.

The Cook Islands are not United Nations full members but participate in WHO and UNESCO, and are an associate member of the Economic and Social Commission for Asia and the Pacific (UNESCAP).

Legislature
The Cook Islands' parliament is composed of 25 members elected by universal adult suffrage for five-year terms. One of its members is elected by overseas voters.

The House of Ariki, composed of 15 hereditary chiefs, plays an advisory role to government but has no powers to legislate.

> **Cabinet (as at June 2013)**
> *Prime Minister, Attorney General, Minister of Justice, Police, Parliamentary Services, Energy and Emergency Management:* Hon. Henry Puna
> *Deputy Prime Minister, Minister for Foreign Affairs, Immigration, Transport, Ministerial and Natural Resources :* Tom Marsters
> *Minister of Education, Marine Resources, Tourism and National Human Resource Development:* Teina Bishop
> *Minister for Finance and Economic Management, Business and Trade, Internal Affairs:* Mark Brown
> *Minister of Infrastructure and Planning, Cultural Development, House of Ariki:* Teariki Heather
> *Minister Agriculture, Minister of Health:* Nandi Glassie

Ministries
Prime Minister's Office, Private Bag, Rarotonga, Cook Islands. Tel: 682 25494, fax: 682 20856, e-mail: coso@pmoffice.gov.ck, URL: http://www.cook-islands.gov.ck
Ministry of Finance and Economic Management, PO Box 120, Rarotonga, Cook Islands. Tel: 682 22878, fax: 682 23877, e-mail: finsec@oyster.net.ck; URL: http://www.mfem.gov.ck
Ministry of Foreign Affairs and Immigration, PO Box 105, Rarotonga, Cook Islands. Tel: 682 29347, fax: 682 21247, e-mail: secfa@mfai.gov.ck
Ministry of Justice, PO Box 111, Rarotonga, Cook Islands. Tel: 682 29410, fax: 682 29610, e-mail: secretry@oyster.net.ck

Elections
The most recent election was held in November 2010. The Cook Islands Party won 16 seats and the Democratic Party eight seats.

Diplomatic Representation
Cook Islands High Commission, New Zealand: Tel: (04) 472 5126 / 7, e-mail: cookhcnz@clear.net.nz,
New Zealand High Commission, Rarotonga, Cook Islands: Tel: (+682) 22 201, e-mail: nzhcraro@oyster.net.ck

LEGAL SYSTEM

The law is based on the Constitution, and incorporates English common law, certain British and New Zealand statutes and customary laws.

There are two types of High Court: those overseen by Justices of the Peace who are appointed by the Queen's Representative, and those where a the Chief Justice and another judge, appointed by the Queen's Representative sit. The Court of Appeal consists of three judges: the Chief Justice and puisne judges of the High Court. Appeals from the Court of Appeal can be referred to the UK Privy Council in certain circumstances.

In 2007 the Cook Islands became the last of New Zealand's overseas territories to abolish capital punishment.

Chief Justice: Justice Thomas Crowley Weston

AREA AND POPULATION

Area
The Cook Islands consist of 13 inhabited and two uninhabited islands located in the South Pacific between American Samoa and French Polynesia. The islands form two main groups: the Northern Cooks and the Southern Cooks. The total area of the Cook Islands is 2 million sq. km. The capital, Avarua, is located on Roratonga.

The Cook Islands are made up of volcanic, hilly islands in the south with low coral islands in the north. There is a dry season from April to November and a more humid season which lasts from December to March.

To view a map, consult http://www.lib.utexas.edu/maps/cia08/cook_islands_sm_2008.gif

Population
Large numbers of Cook Islanders have migrated to New Zealand, Australia and elsewhere over the years, mostly to seek better employment opportunities. More than 58,000 Cook Islanders live in New Zealand and an estimated 15,000 in Australia. The government has placed high priority on educating and training Cook Islands workers in an effort to stem emigration and there was a population increase of 10.3 per cent in 2004, and of 6.9 per cent in 2006. The population rose from 18,400 inhabitants in 2003 to 21,600 in 2006. In 2006, 14,153 people lived on Rarotonga island. The population trend is expected to be downwards. In 2010, the WHO estimated the population to have fallen to 20,000.

In 2009, the average life expectancy for men was 72 years, and 80 years for women. Healthy life expectancy was estimated at 63 years for males and 66 years for females. The infant mortality rate was 8.0 per 1,000 live births in 2010. (Source: http://www.who.int, World Health Statistics 2012)

Three main languages are spoken: Maori, English, and Pukapukan.
Public Holidays 2014
1-2 Jan.: New Year's Day plus the following day
18 April: Good Friday
21 April: Easter Monday
25 April: Anzac Day
2 June: Queen's Birthday (first Monday in June)
July: Rarotonga Gospel Day
4 August: Constitution Day
26 October: Gospel Day
25 December: Christmas
26 December: Boxing Day

EMPLOYMENT

Recent figures show around 55 per cent of the working population are engaged in the service sector, 30 per cent in agriculture and 15 per cent in manufacturing. Recent estimated figures put the labour force at 6,900 with unemployment at 13 per cent.

BANKING AND FINANCE

Currency
The currency on the Cook Islands is the New Zealand dollar.

GDP/GNP, Inflation, National Debt
The Cook Islands' economy is largely based on tourism. The government is developing an offshore banking industry, and there is a growing fishing industry. Black pearls continue to be an important source of revenue.

According to figures from the Asian Development Bank, in 2009 GDP was around NZ$330 million (at current market prices), reflecting a very slight increase of 0.1 per cent on the previous year. The service sector contributed 85.2 per cent, whilst agriculture accounted for 4.8 per cent and industry contributed 10.0 per cent.

GDP by industrial origin and current market prices, NZ$'000s

Sector	2007	2008	2009
GDP	310,146	332,119	330,486
-Agriculture	18,249	16,931	16,858
-Mining and manufacturing	10,766	11,845	12,556
-Electricity, gas and water	6,120	7,350	7,425
-Construction	11,049	11,984	14,667
-Trade	116,664	133,531	118,806
-Transport and communications	50,263	52,210	59,034
-Finance	32,165	35,208	41,586
-Public administration	28,962	29,188	28,841
-Others	46,365	47,032	48,163
-Less Financial intermediation services	10,458	13,161	17,451

Source: ADB

Per capita GDP in 2008 was NZ$13,909 and NZ$14,623 in 2009. GDP was estimated at US$240 million in 2010.

Inflation was estimated at 1.8 per cent in 2010.

Total external debt was estimated at US$68 million in 2005.

Balance of Payments / Imports and Exports

Export commodities are black pearls (earning NZ$2,044,000 in 2006), fish (NZ$1,066,000), copra and citrus fruit, coffee, and clothing. Imports include food, textiles, fuels, and timber. The Cook Islands' major trading partner is New Zealand, with exports also going to Japan and Hong Kong, and imports coming from Australia and Italy. Imports from New Zealand amounted to an estimated NZ$142.17 million in 2008 and exports NZ$738,000. The main export destination in 2008 was Japan (NZ$2.856 million).

Trade Balance (NZ$ 000s)

	2007	2008	2009
Exports f.o.b.	7,052	5,895	4,396
Imports c.i.f.	144,746	212,962*	290,228*
Balance	-137,694	-207,067*	-285,832*

Source: Asian Development Bank
provisional figures

New Zealand is the largest bilateral donor to the Cook Islands. Further assistance is given by the Australian Agency for International Development, the Asian Development Bank, Canada Fund, the South Pacific Regional Environmental Programme, the United Nations Environmental Programme and the Food and Agriculture Organisation. The European Union started contributing financial and technical assistance in 2000.

MANUFACTURING, MINING AND SERVICES

Tourism

This sector now contributes about 80 per cent of GDP and is the leading economic sector. The industry has grown massively since 1971 when only a few hundred tourists ventured to the Cook Islands. In the year 2000 a record 75,000 people visited the country, bringing huge economic benefits and major developments in tourist infrastructure.

Tourism was affected by the terrorist attacks in September 2001 but, by the end of 2002, it was well on the way to recovery. In 2006, some 92,000 people visited the Islands. Most tourists come from New Zealand (51,000), Australia (11,000), Europe, the United States and Canada, and most stay on Rarotonga, though Aitutaki has developed into an important secondary resort.

Cook Islands Tourism Corporation: URL: http://www.cook-islands.com

Agriculture

About 70 per cent of all households in the Cook Islands are engaged in some form of agricultural activity. Most farming is concentrated in the Southern group of islands where commercial crops include fruit, vegetables, taro and bananas.

The Ministry of Agriculture has an ongoing research programme focused on finding new varieties of fruit and vegetables that will grow in the Cook Islands. At present there are projects aimed at reviving the citrus, banana and pineapple-growing industries.

Agriculture, together with fishing, contributes around 12.8 per cent of the country's GDP.

Agricultural Production in 2010

Produce	Int. $'000*	Tonnes
Indigenous pigmeat	852	554
Vegetables fresh nes	283	1,500
Roots & tubers, nes	262	1,700
Coconuts	204	1,900
Papayas	167	590
Fruit fresh nes	161	460
Mangoes, mangosteens, guavas	138	230
Tomatoes	107	290
Cassava	96	1,120
Sweet potatoes	50	700
Hen eggs, in shell	30	36
Bananas	25	90

* unofficial figures
Source: http://faostat.fao.org/site/339/default.aspx Food and Agriculture Organization of the United Nations, Food and Agricultural commodities production

Fishing

Commercial fishing is a relatively new industry to the islands, and experienced rapid growth to the beginning of 2003 when around 20 tonnes of fish were being exported to Japan and the USA each week. Total export revenue from fresh and chilled fish has since slumped, from a high of NZ$8,258,000 in 2003 to NZ$3,381,000 in 2005 and NZ$1,066,000 in 2006.

Most of the catch is flown to New Zealand for shipment to overseas markets, mainly in the US and Japan. The catch from Northern fishing sectors is transported to Pagopago in American Samoa, for processing in their canneries. The main catch is tuna (albacore, yellowfin, bluefin and bigeye), striped marlin and broadbill.

The Cook Islands receives about $1 million a year from a fishing treaty which allows a certain number of US tuna fishing boats to operate in the country's waters. The Government has a policy of ensuring local involvement in the fishing industry, but allows some joint ventures with foreign companies. The Government is also encouraging the industry with tax concessions

and providing training, as well as processing and storage facilities. Ministry of Marine Resources officials estimate that about 100 tonnes a year are caught by foreign fishing boats operating illegally in the area.

In August 2012, The Cook Islands announced the creation of the world's largest marine reserve which amounts to a one million-sq-km (411,000-sq-mile) area of the Pacific Ocean.

Pearls

Black pearls are the Cook Islands' leading export, ranking second only to tourism in their importance to the nation's economy. Cultivated mainly on Manihiki and Penrhyn islands, the largest market is Japan which buys about 50 percent of Cook Islands production. Europe, Australia, Hawaii are also significant buyers.

The black pearl industry is an important employer, and, on Manihiki island, it has stimulated the telecommunications, transport and social sectors.

COMMUNICATIONS AND TRANSPORT

Airlines

Air Rarotonga (URL: http://www.airraro.com/) provides passenger and cargo flights connecting the islands.

Air New Zealand runs flights between Rarotonga and Auckland as well as to Fiji, Tahiti and Los Angeles, USA.

Ports and Harbours

Ports are located at Rarotonga, Aitutaki and Atiu in the Southern group, and Penrhyn and Pukapuka in the Northern group.

HEALTH

In 2009, the government spent approximately 11.6 per cent of its total budget on healthcare (up from 9.9 per cent in 2000), accounting for 93.8 per cent of all healthcare spending. Total expenditure on healthcare equated to 4.3 per cent of the country's GDP. Per capita expenditure on health was approximately US$435, compared with US$175 in 2000. Figures for 2005-10 show that there are 52 physicians (28.9 per 10,000 population), 116 nurses and midwives (64.4 per 10,000 population) and 19 dentists. There are 63 hospital beds per 10,000 population.

The infant mortality rate (likelihood of dying by age one) was 8 per 1,000 live births and the child mortality rate (likelihood of dying before 5th birthday) was 9 per 1,000 live births. Approximately 97 per cent of the population had access to improved drinking-water sources and 95 per cent with improved sanitation. (Source: http://www.who.int, World Health Statistics 2012)

EDUCATION

The Cook Islands follow the same curriculum as New Zealand. Education is compulsory for children aged five to 15. The government provides free education at both primary and secondary school levels and provides some financial assistance for independent schools. The country also has a Teachers Training College, a Trade Training Centre, Hospitality and Tourism Training Centre and Nursing School. The University of the South Pacific, based in Fiji, maintains a centre in Rarotonga and provides vocational and degree courses.

RELIGION

The state is secular but the majority of the population (98 per cent) are Christian.

The Cook Islands has a religious tolerance rating of 10 on a scale of 1 to 10 (10 is most freedom). (Source: World Religion Database)

COMMUNICATIONS AND MEDIA

Newspapers
Cook Islands News, URL: http://www.cinews.co.ck/
Cook Islands Herald, URL: http://www.ciherald.co.ck/ (weekly)

The privately owned Elijah Communications operates the main radio and television stations: Cook Islands Television and Radio Cook Islands (URL: http://www.radio.co.ck/). Radio Cook Islands was originally state-owned.

As of 2009, there were an estimated 7,200 mainline telephones and 7,8700 mobile phones. There are an estimated 6,000 internet users.

ENVIRONMENT

The Cook Islands are prone to tropical storms from November to March. They were badly hit by Hurricane Martin in 1997. In the spring of 2005, the islands were hit by four cyclones, which caused widespread damage.

In 2010, the Cook Islands' emissions from the consumption of fossil fuels totalled 0.30 million metric tons of carbon dioxide.

The Islands are party to the following agreements: Biodiversity, Climate Change, Climate Change-Kyoto Protocol, Desertification, Hazardous Wastes, Law of the Sea and Ozone Layer Protection.

KERMADEC ISLANDS, TOKELAU AND ROSS DEPENDENCY

Kermadec Islands

Administered by the New Zealand Department of Conservation, this is a group of five islands located about 930 kilometres north-east of Auckland, on the edge of an ocean trench. They are prone to occasional earthquakes and volcanic eruptions. The main island is Raoul (Sunday) island; Herald, Macaulay, Curtis and L'Esperance Islands are smaller. They are volcanic with a mild equable climate and plentiful but not excessive rainfall. Most of the land in the Kermadec Islands serves as a nature reserve and provides a habitat for marine animals and sea birds. Their total area is 33 sq. km. The small resident population includes scientists, weather station personnel and rangers. Visits to the islands are restricted to protect the environment.

The Kermadec Marine Reserve was created in November 1990. It extends 12 nautical miles from the cliffs and boulder beaches of the various Kermadec Islands and rocks, out to the edge of the territorial sea. The marine reserve is large by world standards, and covers 7,450 square kilometres.

Tokelau

A territory under New Zealand's administration, Tokelau is a scattered group of three atolls in the South Pacific - Atafu, Nukunonu and Fakaofo - with a total land area of about 12 sq. km and a population in 2008 of around 1,433. Sovereignty was transferred from Britain, and Tokelau was included within the boundaries of New Zealand, in 1948. A referendum on self-determination was held in Tokelau on 22-24 October 2007; a majority of two-thirds of voters was necessary for the referendum to be accepted. Whilst 64.4 per cent of the people voted in favour of the change, 35.6 per cent were against it, and therefore the proposal failed.

To view a map of Tokelau, please consult http://www.lib.utexas.edu/maps/cia08/tokelau_sm_2008.gif

Tokelau lies between Micronesia and Polynesia, but its inhabitants are Polynesian. They retain linguistic, family and cultural links with Western Samoa, although the culture of Tokelau is shaped by its atoll environment, Tokelauan is spoken, with English as a second language.

Administrative responsibility for Tokelau lies with the Administrator, who is appointed by the New Zealand Minister of Foreign Affairs. Many of the Administrator's powers are delegated to the Official Secretary who heads the Office for Tokelau Affairs, based in Apia by agreement with Western Samoa. The Administrator reports annually to the New Zealand Parliament.

Government portal, URL: http://www.mfat.govt.nz/Countries/Pacific/Tokelau.php

Tokelau has a separate legal system, though the Supreme Court in New Zealand exercises civil and criminal jurisdiction. Local government is conducted through representative institutions. The *Faipule* (usually the magistrate) and *Pulenuku* (mayor) are elected every three years by adult suffrage. The *General Fono*, or territorial assembly, is composed of 20 members who serve for a three-year term, and meets two or three times a year. Members are elected on the basis of proportional representation from the three islands: Atafu and Fakaofo have seven seats each, whilst Nukunonu has six seats. Local government is administered through *taupulegas* island councils.

Tokelau's economy is based on fishing, crops and livestock, although the soil is barren and resists fertilisation. Local industries include small-scale enterprises for copra production, wood work, plaited craft goods, stamps, coins, and fishing. Agriculture and livestock produces coconuts, copra, breadfruit, papayas, and bananas, pigs, poultry, and goats. The isolation and lack of resources limits economic development and agriculture remains at subsistence levels. Limited natural resources contribute to emigration to New Zealand, resulting in a population decline of about 0.9 per cent per year.

Tokelau has annual revenues of less than US$500,000 but has outgoings of around US$2.8 million. The deficit is made up by aid from New Zealand. Exports of stamps, copra and handicrafts, woven and carved artifacts earn around US$100,000 and imports of foodstuffs, building materials and fuel cost around US$300,000. Tokelau has recently added 10 per cent to its GDP through registrations of domain names under its top-level domain, .tk.

In 2005, around 80 per cent of the national budget was funded by New Zealand Agency for International Development (NZAID). The New Zealand government pays directly for the cost of medical and education services. Tokelau also receives considerable assistance from various international agencies, the UN Development Programme being the largest donor. Western Samoa gives medical assistance. The Tokelau International Trust Fund was established in 2004, with $5 million, and by 2006 it had $26 million invested.

Each atoll has a small general hospital and a school. Some patients are referred for treatment to New Zealand. Public health education programmes have been strengthened over recent years, particularly those relating to diet and lifestyle diseases. Primary education is compulsory and available to everyone on the atolls. Schooling goes up to Form Five level. Thereafter, distance learning is provided by the University of the South Pacific, and scholarships are available to students who go on to tertiary education.

Regular sea links exist between the atolls and Samoa, and there is also a monthly service to Fiji. There is no airstrip or road system.

Administrator: Jonathan Kings

(Ulu-o-Tokelau) Titular Head of Tokelau: Aliki Faipule Foua Toloa (Fakaofo)

Council for the Ongoing Government of Tokelau (as at June 2013)
Nukunonu
Minister for Support Services, Minister for Health: Aliki Faipule Salesio
Mayor: Pulenuku Lino Isaia

Atafu
Minister for Education, Minister for the Economic Development and the Environment: Aliki Faipule Kelisiano Kalolo
Mayor: Pulenuku Nouata Tufoua

Fakaofo
Titular Head of Tokelau, Minister of Foreign Affairs, Finance, Transport and Power: Aliki Faipule Foua Toloa
Mayor: Pulenuku Otinielu Tuumuli

Ross Dependency

The Ross Dependency consists of the land, permanent ice-shelf and islands of Antarctica between 160° east and 150° west. The land is almost all covered by ice, and is uninhabited except for people working on scientific research programmes. It has a total area of 750,300 sq. km, of which 413,550 sq. km is land and 336,750 sq. km is ice. New Zealand has exercised jurisdiction over the territory since 1923, has maintained an Antarctic scientific research programme since 1957 and operates Scott Base on Ross Island as a permanent base, with a seasonal base at Lake Vanda in the Dry Valleys region. Recent work undertaken includes the monitoring of the hole in the ozone layer. New Zealand is an original party to the Antarctic Treaty, which requires Antarctica to be used for peaceful purposes only and promotes international co-operation, freedom of scientific investigation, and exchange of information and scientific personnel. The 43 parties to the treaty meet regularly to consider questions within its framework.

MANUFACTURING, MINING AND SERVICES

Agriculture
Agricultural Production in Tokelau in 2007

Produce	Int. $'000	Tonnes
Coconuts	271	3,000
Roots & tubers	35	300
Indigenous pigmeat	19	19
Hen eggs, in shell	6	8
Fruit, tropical fresh	5	46
Indigenous chicken meat	5	4
Bananas	2	15

Source: FAOSTAT, Statistics Division, Food and Agriculture Organization of the UN

NIUE

Capital: Alofi (Population estimate: 700)

Head of State: Her Majesty Queen Elizabeth II (Sovereign) (page 1420)

Represented by: Governor General of New Zealand: Jeremiah Mateparae (page 1472)

National Flag: A yellow background, in the upper hoist corner of which appears the Union Jack, with each arm of the cross of St. George bearing a yellow five-pointed star and in the centre of the cross a larger yellow five-pointed star on a blue circle

CONSTITUTION AND GOVERNMENT

Constitution
Originally named Savage Island by Captain Cook, who was refused entry by Niuean warriors, Niue became a British Protectorate in 1900. In 1901 it was annexed to New Zealand, and in 1974 it gained independence in 'free association' with the country. Niue is the smallest self-governing state in the world. Its government is democratically elected by its 1,600 inhabitants. The Legislative Assembly elects the Premier for a term of three years. The current Prime Minister was elected for a second term in 2005. The Cabinet comprises the Premier and three ministers.

To consult the constitution, please visit: http://www.gov.nu/wb/media/Volume%201.pdf

Legislature
Niue's parliament is the unicameral Legislative Assembly and consists of 20 members (14 village representatives and six elected from a common roll), all serving three-year terms. Elections were last held on 7 May 2011. The incumbent premier Toke Talagi was re-elected with 12 out of the 20 votes. The Speaker of the Assembly, Atapana Siakimotu, announced his retirement. Ahohiva Levi was elected in his place. For the first time a woman has been included in the cabinet.

Cabinet (as of June 2013)
Premier & Chairman of Cabinet (With responsibility for Legislative Affairs, Cabinet Services, Corporate Services, Crown Law Office, External Affairs, Private Sector, Trade, Finance, Transport, Police and National Security, Immigration and Population, Civil Aviation, Tourism, Post and Telecommunications, Niue Development Bank): Hon. Toke Tufukia Talagi
Minister for the Education Dept., the Agriculture, Forestry and Fishery Dept., & Administrative Services: Hon Pokotoa Sipel
Minister for the Public Works Department; Niue Power Corporation; Justice, Lands & Survey; Bulk Fuel: Hon Halene Kupa Magatogia
Minister for the Health Department, the Community Affairs Department and the Niue Broadcasting Coporation: Hon. Joan Tahafa Viliamu

Government portal, URL: http://www.gov.nu/

LEGAL SYSTEM

Since 1974 the legal system is derived from the Constitution, statues of the Niue Legislative Assembly, statutes of New Zealand, and English civil law. The Constitution provides a provision where title to land may be determined according to Niuean custom.

The highest court of Niue is the Court of Appeal (constituted in 1992). Prior to that appeals were held in the Court of Appeal of New Zealand. It has jurisdiction to hear an appeal from a decision of the High Court as of right. Its decisions are final except where the Queen grants permission to appeal to the Privy Council. There are three judges; the Chief Justice and two puisne judges.

The High Court has unlimited first instance jurisdiction in civil and criminal matters. It is divided into civil, criminal and law divisions. Jurisdiction can be exercised by a single judge. Commissions of the of the High Court may be appointed by Cabinet. The Cabinet may also appoint justices of the peace and any two justices acting together may fulfill the role of a commissioner.

AREA AND POPULATION

Area
Niue is located 2,400 km north-east of New Zealand, between the Cook Islands, Tonga, and Samoa. Known as the 'Rock of Polynesia', the island is 260 sq. km in area and is formed by a raised coral atoll. At no point does it exceed 69 metres above sea level.

The climate is tropical. Typhoons are a natural hazard. In January 2004 Niue was hit by Cyclone Heta, resulting in one death and around 200 people being made homeless. Many of those chose not to rebuild their homes, but to move to New Zealand.

To view a map, consult http://www.lib.utexas.edu/maps/cia08/niue_sm_2008.gif

Population
The population of the island had dropped from a peak of 5,200 in 1966 to an estimated 1,400 in 2011. There are concerns about migration to New Zealand, and the government is trying to coax ex-patriate Niueans back to the island. On his re-election in 2005, Mr. Young emphasized the climate, lifestyle and the ready availability of land. The annual growth rate was estimated to be -2.6per cent in 2000-10.

In 2004, there was a drop of 45 per cent in the birth rate, and natural increase in population stood at zero per cent. (Source: Economic Planning Development and Statistics, Government of Niue) Life expectancy is around 66 years for males and 80 years for females. (Source: http://www.who.int, World Health Statistics 2012)

Islanders speak Niuean and English and, in free association with New Zealand, have dual citizenship.

Public Holidays 2014
1 January: New Year's Day
18 April: Good Friday
21 April: Easter Monday
25 April: ANZAC Day
2 June: Queen's Birthday
24: Peniamina Gospel Day (4th Friday in October)
19 October: Constitution Day
25 December: Christmas Day
26 December: Boxing Day

EMPLOYMENT

Due to high unemployment (10.59 per cent in 2002) more Niueans live and work in New Zealand than live on the island. Those in Niue work on family plantations and a small number in government service or industry.

BANKING AND FINANCE

GDP/GNP, Inflation, National Debt
Niue's economy is largely dependent on agricultural produce and the sale of postage stamps to collectors. Industry comprises factories to process passion fruit, lime oil, honey, and coconut cream. The Niue government is also developing the tourism and financial services industries. However, the economy suffers from geographic isolation, few resources, and a small population. Government expenditure regularly exceeds revenue, and the shortfall is made up by grants from New Zealand. GDP was an estimated US$15.9 million in 2010. Per capita GDP was an estimated US$10,500 in 2009.

Inflation was estimated to be 11.5 per cent in 2009 and 5.4 per cent in 2010.

Balance of Payments / Imports and Exports
Export revenue was around NZ$264,000 whilst import costs exceeded NZ$11,898,000 in 2004. Main export trading partners are New Zealand, Australia, Fiji, and the Cook Islands. Major import trading partners are New Zealand, Fiji, Japan, Australia, and the US. Niue exports mainly fruit, as well as stamps and footballs. Imports are mainly food, live animals, manufactured goods, fuels, lubricants, machinery, and chemicals.

MANUFACTURING, MINING AND SERVICES

Primary and Extractive Industries
Niue has neither oil nor gas resources, and has to import all its requirements. An Australian mining company began prospecting for uranium beneath the island in 2005.

Tourism
Tourism is a growth industry on the island. The government is promoting sustainable eco-tourism, marketing to whale and dolphin watchers, divers and yachting enthusiasts. Hotels and restaurants have contributed steadily growing revenues to GDP. The number of visitors grew from around 1,650 in 2000 to 2,550 in 2004, and to 3,008 in 2006. Over 60 per cent of visitors came from New Zealand. Australians and people from the South Pacific also visited in significant numbers.
Niue Tourism, URL: http://www.niueisland.com

Agriculture
The mainstay of the economy, the government is encouraging the production of high added-value crops, such as vanilla and nonu, for export. Taro, tapioca, yams, kumaras, bananas, copra, limes and passionfruit are also grown. Commercial fishing is also a growth industry. The total catch for 2010 was estimated to be 113 tonnes.

Agricultural Production in 2010

Produce	Int. $'000*	Tonnes
Taro (cocoyam)	592	3,100
Coconuts	398	3,600
Fruit fresh nes	293	840
Indigenous pigmeat	92	60
Fruit, tropical fresh nes	53	130
Yams	38	150
Lemons and limes	36	90
Bananas	31	110
Indigenous chicken meat	26	18
Vegetables fresh nes	25	130
Cow milk, whole, fresh	19	60
Sweet potatoes	16	260

NICARAGUA

- *continued*
* unofficial figures
Source: http://faostat.fao.org/site/339/default.aspx Food and Agriculture Organization of the United Nations, Food and Agricultural commodities production

COMMUNICATIONS AND TRANSPORT

Airports
Hanan International Airport is the only airport and is about two km from Alofi.

Roads
There are 234 km. of roads, but most are unpaved.

Ports and Harbours
There are no ports, and anchorage is offshore.

HEALTH

In 2008, the government spent approximately 12.6 per cent of its total budget on healthcare (up from 6.3 per cent in 2000), accounting for 98.6 per cent of all healthcare spending. Total expenditure on healthcare equated to 13.5 per cent of the country's GDP. Per capita expenditure on health was approximately US$1,348, compared with US$323 in 2000. Figures for 2000-10 show that there are 4 physicians (40 per 10,000 population), 15 nurses and midwives (150 per 10,000 population) and 3 dentists. There are 52 hospital beds per 10,000 population. All the population have access to improved drinking water and improved sanitation. In 2009, the infant mortality rate was 15 per 1,000 live births and the under-five mortality rate was 17 per 1,000 live births. The most common causes of childhood mortality were prematurity (20 per cent) and pneumonia (23 per cent). (Source: WHO, 2011)

EDUCATION

Education is free and compulsory for children between the ages of four and sixteen. There is one primary school on the island and one secondary school. Figures for 2005 record 190 students at primary level and 206 at secondary (both figures down on the previous year).

There were 24 teachers at primary level and 26 at secondary level. Tertiary education is provided at the University of the South Pacific or St. Clemens University. (Source: Economic Planning Development and Statistics, Government of Niue). Recent figures show that just over 10.0 per cent of government spending goes on education.

RELIGION

The majority of the population some 97 per cent are Christian. Niue has a religious liberty rating of 10 on a scale of 1 to 10 (10 is most freedom). (Source: World Religion Database)

COMMUNICATIONS AND MEDIA

Newspapers
The Niue Star is the island's weekly paper.

Broadcasting
Radio Sunshine and Television Niue are both operated by the Niue Broadcasting Corporation.

Telecommunications
In June 2003 Niue became the world's first country to have a wireless internet system. The population of the island is able to use the internet at any location using a laptop and an aerial. Investment in the latest communications technology has been funded by the sale of rights to Niue's .nu internet domain name. There are an estimated 1,000 main telephone lines and 600 mobile phones. An estimated 1,000 people are internet users.

ENVIRONMENT

In 2010, Niue's emissions from the consumption of fossil fuels totalled 0.010 million metric tons of carbon dioxide.

NICARAGUA

Republic of Nicaragua

República de Nicaragua

Capital: Capiyal-Managua (Population estimate, 2011: 1.5 million)

Head of State: Daniel Ortega (page 1490) (President)

Vice President: Jaime Morales Carazo (page 1480)

National Flag: A tricolour fesswise, blue, white, blue, the white charged with the national badge: five mountains and a cap of liberty on a triangle encircled in gold with 'Republica de Nicaragua-America Central'.

CONSTITUTION AND GOVERNMENT

Constitution
Nicaragua gained independence from Spain in 1821. After the civil war at the end of the 1970s, a Joint National Directorate of nine FSLN commanders vested power in a five-member Junta, representing the left-wing Sandinistas and civilian political groups. On 4 November 1984, elections were held for president, vice-president and a 90-seat National Assembly, which had the task of drawing up a new constitution. The Sandinistas won 69 per cent. The USA denounced the elections as unrepresentative because a right-wing group, the Nicaraguan Democratic Coordinating Committee (CDN), led by Dr Arturo Cruz, refused to participate. The CDN was invited to contribute to a national dialogue on the new constitution after the elections. The region became politically unstable. Free elections were held in 1990 and the ruling Sandinista government lost.

According to the 1987 constitution, the head of state is the President, directly elected by universal adult suffrage for a five-year term. The President may not serve two successive terms but may stand for re-election at a later date. The Constitutional Court lifted this ban in 2009. The President appoints the Cabinet.

The 1987 constitution was changed in 1995 to provide for a more even distribution of power among the four branches of government. In 2000, further amendments were made, affecting the Supreme Court and allowing for a president to be elected with 35 per cent of the popular vote so long as is at least a five percentage point difference between the first and second place candidates.

To view the constitution (in Spanish), please visit: http://www.cse.gob.ni/index.php?s=8&ley=3

International Relations
Nicaragua pursues an independent foreign policy and encourages regional demilitarization and peaceful settlement of disputes within states in the region. Nicaragua has one outstanding territorial dispute, with Colombia, which has been submitted to the International Court at

The Hague for resolution. There is also a disagreement over navigation rights on the San Juan River, in the Nicaragua-Costa Rica border area and this too has been sent for resolution to the International Court of Justice.

Nicaragua belongs to the United Nations and several specialized and related agencies. It is also a member of the Organization of American States (OAS) and the Central American Bank for Economic Integration (CABEI).

Recent Events
In September 2002 former president Arnoldo Aleman was dismissed as chairman of the National Assembly following accusations of the theft of over US$100 million of public funds. In December 2003 Sr. Aleman was sentenced to 20 years in prison for corruption.

In January 2004 the World Bank announced that it was wiping 80 per cent of Nicaragua's debt from its books, whilst in July of that year Russia wrote off Nicaragua's multi-million dollar debt from the Soviet era. However, rises in fuel prices and the cost of living resulted in street protests in April 2005 and political crises in June. In October 2005, the Government approved the Central American Free Trade Agreement (Cafta), which came into effect in April 2006.

In October 2006, President Bolaños unveiled plans to build a ship canal linking the Atlantic and Pacific Oceans, and in the same month, a new bill was passed banning all abortions, regardless of maternal health issues. Presidential elections were held in November 2006, and the former Sandinista president, Daniel Ortega, was returned to office.

The International Court of Justice in the Hague settled a long-running territorial dispute between Honduras and Nicaragua, in October 2007.

In November 2008, two people were killed during post municipal election violence. With the majority of votes counted in 146 municipalities, the Sandinistas led in most of the major races. However, the opposition and monitors alleged voting irregularities. President Ortega, a critic of US foreign policy, had refused to accredit election observers, claiming that they were financed by outside powers.

In 2009, President Ortega announced plans to change the constitution to allow him to stand for another term in office. In October the same year, the Constitutional Court lifted a ban preventing presidents from seeking re-election.

In November 2011, President Ortega won a landslide victory in presidential elections.

In September 2012, thousands of people had to be evacuated when the San Cristobal volcano erupted.

In June 2013, the Nicaraguan Congress approved plans to have a canal built linking the Pacific and Atlantic Oceans.

Legislature

Nicaragua's unicameral legislature is known as the National Assembly (Asamblea Nacional) and is composed of 90 members directly elected through a proportional representation system for a period of five years. Additionally, any presidential or vice presidential candidate who is not successfully elected, and who receives as many votes nationally as the average of the winning percentages in each regional electoral district, becomes a member of the National Assembly.

National Assembly, Asamblea Nacional de la República de Nicaragua, Apto. 4650, Avenida Bolivar, Contiguo a la Presidencia de la República, Managua, Nicaragua. E-mail: webmaster@correo.asamblea.gob.ni, URL: http://www.asamblea.gob.ni/

Cabinet (as of June 2013)
Minister of Agriculture and Forests: Ariel Bucardo Rocha
Secretary General of Defence: Ruth Tapia Roa (page 1503)
Minister of Development, Industry and Commerce: Orlando Solorzano Delgadillo
Minister of Education, Culture and Sports: Miriam Raudez
Minister of the Environment and Natural Resources: Juana Argenal Sandoval
Minister of Finance and Public Credit: Alberto Guevara Obregon
Minister of Foreign Affairs: Samuel Santos Lopez (page 1508)
Minister of Health: Sonia Castro Gonzalez
Minister of Labour: Jeannette Chaves Gomez
Minister of Transport and Infrastructure: Pablo Fernando Martinez
Minister of Energy and Hydrocarbons: Emilio Rapacciolli
Minister of the Interior: Ana Isabel Marales Mazun
Minister of Family, Youth and Children: Marcia Ramirez Mercado
Minister of Tourism: Mayra Salinas
Private Secretary to the President: Dr Paul Oquist Kelley

Ministries

Office of the President, URL: http://www.presidencia.gob.ni
Ministry of Agriculture and Forestry, Km 8 1/2 Carretera a Masaya. Managua, Nicaragua. Tel: +505 276 0200, URL: http://www.magfor.gob.ni/
Ministry of Defence, Del Hotel Intercontinental 2 c. al Sur, 1 c. Oeste. Managua, Nicaragua. Tel: +505 266 3580, URL: http://www.midef.gob.ni/
Ministry of Development, Trade and Industry, Km. 6 Carretera a Masaya, Frente a Camino de Oriente, Apartado Postal No. 8, Managua, Nicaragua. Tel: +505 278 8712, URL: http://www.mific.gob.ni/
Ministry of Education, Culture and Sport, Centro Cívico 'Camilo Ortega Saavedra', Apartado Postal 108, Managua, Nicaragua. Tel: +505 265 0342, fax: +505 265 1595, URL: http://www.mecd.gob.ni/
Ministry of the Environment and Natural Resources, Km. 12 1/2 Carretera Norte, Managua, Nicaragua. Tel: +505 233 1111, URL: http://www.marena.gob.ni/
Ministry of Energy and Hydrocarbon, Hospital Bautista 1C al Oeste, 1C al Norte, Managua, Nicaragua. Tel: +505 2280 9500, fax: +505 2280 9516, e-mail: informacion@mem.gob.ni, URL: http://www.mem.gob.ni/
Ministry of Finance and Public Credit, Frente a la Asamblea Nacional, Managua, Nicaragua. Tel: +505 222 7231, URL: http://www.hacienda.gob.ni
Ministry of Foreign Affairs, Kilometro 3 1/2, carretera sur, Managua, Nicaragua. Tel: +505 266 6187, fax: +505 266 2572 / 266 6079, URL: http://www.cancilleria.gob.ni/
Ministry of Health, Complejo Nacional de Salud 'Dra. Concepción Palacios', Managua, Nicaragua (Semáforos de Rubenia, 500 mts. al Este, 2 c. al Sur). Tel: +505 289 3482, URL: http://www.minsa.gob.ni/
Ministry of Transport & Infrastructure, Frente al Estadio Nacional, Managua, Nicaragua. Tel: +505 222 5111, URL: http://www.mti.gob.ni/
Ministry of Family, Youth and Children, Altamira de Este Vicky, 2c. al O. Managua, Nicaragua. Tel: +505 2277 5942, fax: +505 2277 5984, URL: http://www.mifamilia.gob.ni
Home Office, Edificio Silvio Mayorga, Managua, Nicaragua. Tel: +505 222 7538, URL: http://www.migob.gob.ni
Ministry of Tourism, Hotel Intercontinental, 1c Sur, 1c. Oeste, Managua, Nicaragua. Tel: +505 2222 3333, fax: +505 2222 6610, URL: http://www.intur.gob.ni
Ministry of Transport and Infrastructure, Frente al Estadio Nacional, Managua, Nicaragua. Tel: +505 2222 5111, fax: +505 2228 2060, e-mail: webmaster@mti.gob.ni, URL: http://www.mti.gob.ni

Major Political Parties
Alianza Liberal Nicaraguense ALN-PC, (Nicaraguan Liberal Alliance)
Frente Sandinista de Liberacion Nacional (FSLN), (Sandinista National Liberation Front), URL: http://www.fsln-nicaragua.com/
Movimiento de Renovacion Sandinista (MRS) (Sandinista National Liberation Front), URL: http://www.partidomrs.com/
Partido Liberal Constitucionalista (PLC) (Liberal Constitutionalist Party), URL: http://www.PLC.org.ni

Elections
Suffrage is universal for adults over 16.

The most recent presidential election took place on 6 November 2011 and was won by the incumbent president Daniel Ortega. He polled over 60 per cent of the vote. His nearest rival, Fabio Gadea of the PLI won just over 30 per cent of the vote. Legislative elections took place on the same day and were won by the Sandinista National Liberation Front (FSLN). The composition of the Assembly is now FSLN 63, PLI 27 and the PLC 2 seats.

Diplomatic Representation
British Embassy, (The ambassador for Nicaragua is based in Costa Rica) Apartado 815-1007, Edificio Centro Colón, (Piso/floor 11), San José, Costa Rica. Tel: +506 2258 2025, fax: +506 2233 9938, URL: http://ukincostarica.fco.gov.uk/en/
Ambassadors: Chris and Sharon Campbell
US Embassy, Km. 4 1/2 Carretera Sur, Managua, Nicaragua. Tel: +505 266 6010, fax: +505 266 9074, e-mail: usbusiness@amemb.org.ni, URL: http://nicaragua.usembassy.gov/
Ambassador: Phyliss Powers
Embassy of Nicaragua, Suite 31, Vicarage House, 58-60 Kensington Church Street, London W8 4DB, United Kingdom. Tel: +44 (0)20 7938 2373, fax: +44 (0)20 7937 0952, URL: http://www.cancilleria.gob.ni
Ambassador: Carlos Arguello-Gomez
Nicaraguan Embassy, 1627 New Hampshire Avenue, NW, Washington, DC 20009, USA. Tel: +1 202 939 6570, fax: +1 202 939 6545, URL: http://consuladodenicaragua.com/
General Consul: Francisco Obadiah Campbell
Permanent Representative of Nicaragua to the United Nations, 820 Second Avenue, 8th Floor, New York, NY 10017, USA. Tel: +1 212 490 7997, fax: +1 212 286 0815, e-mail: nicaragua@un.int, URL: http://www.un.int/nicaragua/
Ambassador: H.E. Mrs. Maria Rubiales de Chamorro

LEGAL SYSTEM

The Organic Law of the Judiciary establishes a two-tier legal system, consisting of local judges, district judges, Court of Appeals and the Supreme Court of Justice. Local and district judges usually specialise in either civil, labour, family or criminal cases, though in small towns one judge could be competent in all four areas. The monetary amount of the lawsuit will sometimes determine which kind of judge will hear a case. Courts of Appeal, consisting of no less than five magistrates, hear cases referred from the district judges. The Supreme Court, based in Managua, consists of sixteen justices elected by the National Assembly for a term of five years. The highest court in the Republic, it is divided in four chambers: civil, criminal, constitutional and contentious-administrative.

There are serious violations of human rights in Nicaragua. There are instances of brutality and unlawful killings by the security forces. Corruption is widespread, and there is a general lack of respect for the rule of law. The prisons are overcrowded, and pretrial detention is often lengthy. Freedom of speech and of the press is limited, and government officials have been known to intimidate journalists. There is government interference with the operation of political parties, and government harassment of nongovernmental organizations (NGOs).

The death penalty was abolished in 1979.

Supreme Court of Justice, URL: http://www.csj.gob.ni/

Office of the Ombudsman, URL: http://www.pddh.gob.ni/nosotros.asp

LOCAL GOVERNMENT

For administrative purposes Nicaragua is divided into 15 departments, Boaco, Carazo, Chinandega, Chontales, Esteli, Granada, Jinotega, Leon, Madriz, Managua, Masaya, Matagalpa, Nueva Segovia, Rio San Juan and Rivas. Nicaragua also has two autonomous regions, Atlantico Norte and Atlantico Sur. There are also 153 municipalities. Elections for 146 of the municipalities were held in 2008 f

AREA AND POPULATION

Area
With an area of 130,688 sq. km (50,446 sq. miles), Nicaragua is the largest republic in Central America. It borders Honduras to the north, Costa Rica to the south, the Atlantic to the east, and the Pacific to the west. Nicaragua has a coastline of about 524 km on the Atlantic and 410 km on the Pacific. The country has 25 volcanoes, five of which are active. It also has the largest freshwater lake in the Central American region. There is a mountain range in the central interior of the country. Most Nicaraguans live in the Pacific lowlands and the adjacent interior highlands. The climate is tropical on the coast and lowlands, and cooler in the highlands.

To view a map of Nicaragua, please visit http://www.un.org/Depts/Cartographic/map/profile/nicaragu.pdf

Population
The population was estimated at 5.788 million in 2010, with an average annual population growth rate of 1.3 per cent over the period 2000-10. Population density is around 42 people per sq. km., though 57 per cent now live in urban areas. The majority of the population (58 per cent) is aged between 15 and 60 years, with 34 per cent aged under 15, and 6 per cent aged 60 years or over. The median age is 22 years.

The population is mostly (69 per cent) of mixed Indian and Spanish (mestizo) descent, with 17 per cent white, 9 per cent black, and 5 per cent indigenous Amerindian.

Spanish is the official and predominant language, although English and indigenous languages are spoken on the Atlantic coast.

Births, Marriages, Deaths
According to 2010 estimates the birth rate is 23.8 births per 1,000 of the population, whilst the death rate is 4.4 deaths per 1,000 population. Figures for 2012 published by the World Health Organization indicate that average life expectancy at birth is 74 years (71 years for

NICARAGUA

men and 77 years for women). Healthy life expectancy is estimated to be 64 years old. The infant mortality rate is 23 deaths per 1,000 children, whilst the fertility rate is 2.6 children born per woman. (Source: http://www.who.int, World Health Statistics 2012)

Public Holidays 2014
1 January: New Year's Day
17 April: Maundy Thursday
18 April: Good Friday
5 May: Labour Day
19 July: Liberation Day
14 September: Battle for San Jacinto Day
15 September: Independence Day
1 November: All Souls Day
8 December: Immaculate Conception
25 December: Christmas Day

EMPLOYMENT

The workforce was estimated at 2.2 million in 2006; 2.08 million were employed, and 114,500 were unemployed. The official rate of unemployment stood at 5.2 per cent in 2006. However, approximately 60 per cent of the workforce is employed in the 'informal' sector, where underemployment is high and the data is not clear. Figures for 2007 put the unemployment rate at 4.9 per cent. Estimated figures for 2010 put the workforce at 2.8 million with an unemployment rate at 7.7 per cent.

All public and private sector workers, except the military and the police, are entitled to form and join unions, and they exercise this right extensively; almost half of Nicaragua's workforce, including agricultural workers, is unionised. Workers have the right to strike.

Total Employment by Economic Activity

Occupation	2006
Agriculture, hunting & forestry	593,600
Fishing	15,500
Mining & quarrying	6,700
Manufacturing	289,200
Electricity, gas & water supply	6,500
Construction	100,800
Wholesale & retail trade, repairs	409,100
Hotels & restaurants	72,000
Transport, storage & communications	89,000
Financial intermediation	15,900
Real estate, renting & business activities	54,000
Public admin. & defence; compulsory social security	73,700
Education	94,500
Health & social work	54,300
Other community, social & personal service activities	89,200
Households with employed persons	117,400
Extra-territorial organisations & bodies	8,100

Source: Copyright © International Labour Organization (ILO Dept. of Statistics, http://laborsta.ilo.org)

BANKING AND FINANCE

Currency
The unit of currency is the *córdoba* of 100 *centavos*.

GDP/GNP, Inflation, National Debt
Nicaragua is the second-poorest country in the Western Hemisphere. However, a degree of economic stability has been attained since the introduction of free market reforms following the Sandinista regime; inflation came down from 33,500 per cent in 1988 to 9.45 per cent in 2006, and external debt as a percentage of GDP has been reduced from over 400 per cent in 1990 to 59.1 per cent in 2007. This has been achieved through the Heavily Indebted Poor Countries Initiative, the Multilateral Debt Reduction Initiative, and a $1 billion commercial debt buyback led by the World Bank. Real economic growth averaged 4 per cent per annum between 1995 and 2005. Rising wages, food prices and energy costs have slowed economic grow over the last two years, and inflation is rising once again, to 16.9 per cent in 2007. It fell to an estimated 13.8 per cent in 2008 and fell dramatically in 2009 to 1 per cent. Economic growth was estimated at 3.2 per cent in 2008 but fell in 2009 to -1.5 per cent due to a fall in demand for Nicaraguan goods. It grew by 4.5 per cent in 2010.

Nicaragua's economy was traditionally based on agriculture, but light industry, tourism, banking, mining, fisheries, and general commerce are expanding sectors. The service industry has replaced agriculture as the largest contributor to GDP. According to 2009 estimates, the real estate sector accounted for about 7.5 per cent of GDP, with agriculture, fishing and agricultural processing accounting the 17 per cent, manufacturing contributed around 18 per cent of GDP, retail, hotels and restaurants, 14 per cent, government, 12.5 per cent, personal services 6.5 per cent, communications and transportation, 5.5 per cent and financial services, 5.1 per cent.

GDP was estimated at US$6.5 billion in 2010, rising to US$7 billion in 2011, with a growth rate of 4.5 per cent. In 2007, Nicaraguans received $740 million in remittances from abroad, the majority of which came from the United States. This equates to almost 13 per cent of GDP.

Inflation was estimated to be 6.5 per cent in 2012.

Foreign Investment
Foreign investment inflows totalled $337 million in 2007; over 100 US companies are involved in Nicaraguan organisations, mainly within the energy, financial services, apparel, manufacturing, and fisheries sectors. Despite investment protections written into CAFTA-DR, the investment climate has worsened since Sandinista President Ortega took office; poor enforcement of property rights deters both foreign and domestic investment, especially in real estate development and tourism. The lack of transparency surrounding Venezuelan bilateral assistance, channelled through state-run enterprises, has become a serious issue for the IMF and international donors.

In 2007 Nicaragua signed a three year Poverty Reduction and Growth Facility (PRGF) with the International Monetary Fund (IMF), as part of the agreement the government agreed to implement free market policies. The agreement was extended for a futher year in 2010.

Nicaragua is a member of the World Bank, the Inter-American Development Bank (IDB), the Central American Bank for Economic Integration (CABEI), and the International Monetary Fund (IMF).

Balance of Payments / Imports and Exports
Normal merchandise export revenues (from the sale of coffee, beef, sugar, seafood, bananas, gold and industrial goods) rose from an estimated US$1.202 billion in 2007 and US$1.489 billion in 2008. Exports from the free trade zone (such as textiles, apparel, automobile wring harnesses) earned a further $1.088 billion. Exports for 2010 amounted to US$3.1 billion(free trade zone US$970 million). Nicaragua's major export partners are her Central American neighbours, the USA, the European Union, Mexico and Japan.

In 2010, imports cost Nicaragua US$4.7 billion (free trade zone imports US$830 million). The US is the source of nearly a quarter of Nicaragua's imports, and the Central American Common Market members are major import partners. The EU and China also supply goods.

Nicaragua is a member of the Central American Common Market (CACM), the Caribbean Basin Free Trade Initiative, and the World Trade Organization (WTO). On April 1, 2006, CAFTA-DR entered into force for Nicaragua, and Nicaraguan exports to the USA rose by over 36 per cent from 2005 to 2007 (approximately 55 per cent of Nicaragua's total exports). Over the same period, US exports to Nicaragua rose 43.6 per cent.

Trade or Currency Restrictions
A Free Zone Law was passed in November 1991 which created the Corporation of Free Zones. Las Mercedes Industrial Free Zone is an industrial park with the lowest leases in Central America. Five new private free zones have recently started operations. The Law allows total tax exemption from income tax, general sales tax, export tax, municipal tax and import tax.

Central Bank
Banco Central de Nicaragua, Carretera Sur Km 7, Managua, Nicaragua. Tel: +505 2255 7171, fax: +505 2265 0495, e-mail: bcn@bcn.gob.ni, URL: http://www.bcn.gob.ni
President: Alberto José Guevara Obregón

MANUFACTURING, MINING AND SERVICES

Primary and Extractive Industries
Nicaragua has gold, silver and industrial minerals such as gypsum. There are eight gold and silver mines in the country, only two of which are in production. Gold exports earned Nicaragua around US$48 million in 2004 (up from US$35 million in 2003). Since 1979 all mineral exploration and production has been controlled by INMINE, the Instituto Nicaraguense de la Mineria. All natural resources are state property and exploitation rights are leased on a long-term basis.

Nicaragua has no oil reserves and has to import all of its requirements. Imports rose from 23.58 thousand barrels per day in 1999 to 32.00 thousand barrels per day in 2011, originating mainly from Mexico and Venezuela. These two countries offer preferential terms and pricing through the San Jose pact. Nicaragua has a refining capacity of 20,000 barrels of oil per day.

In July 2002 President Bolaños announced new legislation allowing foreign oil companies to begin exploration. Onshore concessions are to be granted to foreign investors, as well as offshore fields in the Pacific and Atlantic Oceans. Nicaragua has a long-running dispute with Colombia over the ownership of areas in the Caribbean Sea, and issued a formal complaint in 2005 following Colombia's granting of exploration concessions in the areas concerned.

The Nicaraguan Canal Project, linking the Atlantic and Pacific Oceans, has recently been revived. The canal would be around 170 miles long, and would be designed to accommodate ships that are too large to navigate the Panama Canal. The Nicaraguan government and a company run by a Chinese businessman signed a memorandum of understanding that commits Hong Kong-based HK Nicaragua Canal Development Investment Co. Ltd. to financing and building the canal.

Nicaragua neither produces nor consumes natural gas.

Energy
Total energy consumption was 0.071 quadrillion Btu in 2006, slightly up on previous years. Petroleum contributes around 88 per cent, geothermal, waste and wood nine per cent, and hydroelectric around 3 per cent. Nicaragua generates and consumes the least amount of electricity in the Central American region, at under three billion kWh.

Bidding started in 2005 for the construction of the Sistema de Interconexion Electrica de los Paises America Central (SIEPAC), a 1,100-mile transmission line linking Panama, Costa Rica, Honduras, Nicaragua, and El Salvador. An independent company, Empresa Propietaria de la Red (EPR) has been created to achieve this goal.

In is estimated that population increase and a growth in economic activities will lead to an increase in demand of 10 per cent per annum for the next 14 years. Electrification of rural areas remains a major initiative of the Nicaraguan government. The country's National Rural Electrification Program aimed to bring power to 90 per cent of the country's rural areas by 2012.

Manufacturing
The manufacturing sector grew by 6.5 per cent over 2005, and by 5.3 per cent the following year, accounting for 16.2 per cent of the national GDP. The construction industry experienced strong growth of 7 per cent in 2005, but this fell by 8 per cent in 2006, contributing 5.6 per cent of GDP. Main areas of production include food processing, machinery and metal products, petroleum refining and distribution, chemicals, textiles, clothing, beverages, footwear and wood.

Services
This is the largest sector in the Nicaraguan economy, accounting for some 51 per cent of GDP in 2007. In 2006, the banking and insurance sector showed the greatest growth, at 10.3 per cent, followed by government services at 6.3 per cent.

Tourism
This sector continues to expand and is the third largest source of foreign income. In 2007, there were over 978,000 visitors to Nicaragua (up from 890,000 in 2006); of these, 799,000 stayed overnight, and 178,000 were day trippers. Most (514,500) were from other parts of Central America, and around 200,000 were from North America. Approximately 51,000 came from Europe. The number of hotels and rooms increased to 406 and 6,233 respectively. **Nicaraguan Institute of Tourism**, Instituto Nicaraguense de Turismo, URL: http://www.intur.gob.ni

Agriculture
In the 1980s, the Sandinista government made many administrative changes in this sector, which have had a long term effect; a government role in production through farms in the People's Property Area (APP); strict control of agricultural activities through the Ministry of Agricultural Development; and a monopoly of the external marketing of coffee, cotton, sugar and bananas. The nationalisation of some banana operations in Nicaragua meant low exports for some years. The US trade embargo in 1985 compounded the decline in the sector.

In recent years, however, there has been a revival of the sector; agriculture, fishing and forestry accounted for around 21 per cent of GDP in 2004 before dropping to 17 per cent in 2006. In combination with agro-processing, the sector accounted for 33 per cent of GDP in 2007. The sector also contributes a large proportion of export revenues. Over the year 2005-06, growth in agricultural earnings was 6.8 per cent and in livestock the growth rate was 2.5 per cent. Livestock and dairy production have seen steady growth over the past decade and have taken the greatest advantage of free trade agreements.

Agricultural Production in 2010

Produce	Int. $'000*	Tonnes
Indigenous cattle meat	341,200	126,306
Cow milk, whole, fresh	229,796	753,281
Sugar cane	160,702	4,893,930
Rice, paddy	125,952	453,990
Indigenous chicken meat	125,681	88,234
Coffee, green	84,565	78,712
Groundnuts, with shell	80,364	180,250
Beans, dry	78,575	138,448
Maize	56,903	456,974
Hen eggs, in shell	20,317	24,496
Oranges	13,026	67,400
Indigenous pigmeat	11,814	7,684

* unofficial figures
Source: http://faostat.fao.org/site/339/default.aspx Food and Agriculture Organization of the United Nations, Food and Agricultural commodities production

The seafood industry is significant in Nicaragua as the country has access to both the Atlantic and the Pacific coasts. The continental shelf of the Pacific Coast is one of the largest tropical sources of lobster, shrimp and scalefish in the world. Both bodies of water have huge, under-fished reserves of grouper, tuna, clams and mackerel. Commercial shrimp farming is being encouraged. Estimated figures for 2010 put the total catch at 37,500 tonnes.

Nicaragua has 65 varieties of forest species identified as profitably exploitable. There are more than 6 million acres of rain forest and more than 1 million acres of dry forest available for sustainable projects. The government has created two large natural reserves: BOSAWAS on the border with Honduras and Si-A-Paz that borders Costa Rica. Exploitation of the forests has declined in recent years.

COMMUNICATIONS AND TRANSPORT

Travel Requirements
Citizens of Canada, Australia and the EU require a passport valid for at least six months from the date of arrival, but do not need a visa. US citizens need a valid passport, but no visa. All visitors must have an onward/return ticket and evidence of sufficient funds for their stay, and they must purchase a Tourist Card on arrival in Nicaragua; these are usually issued for between 30 and 90 days. Other nationals should contact the embassy to check visa requirements.

Nicaragua is party to the Central America Border Control Agreement (CA-4). Under the terms of this agreement, tourists may travel within any of the CA-4 countries (El Salvador, Guatemala, Honduras and Nicaragua) for a period of up to 90 days, without completing entry and exit formalities at border immigration checkpoints. This period begins at the first point of entry into any of the CA-4 countries.

National Airlines
TACA (Transportes Aeros Centro-Americano), connects Managua with other capitals of Central America, Mexico, New Orleans and Miami. COPA (Compañia Panameña de Aviación) connects Managua with other capitals of Central America. Aeronica is the State airline.

International Airport
There is one international airport in Nicaragua, the Augusto C. Sandino International Airport, Managua, which handles an average of 15,000 passengers a month. Forty weekly international flights arrive in Managua, Bluefields, Corn Island and Puerto Cabezas.

Roads
There are a total of 16,382 km of roads of which 1,800 are paved. The Inter-American highway runs for 385 km from Honduras through Managua to Costa Rica. International bus routes connect Nicaragua with Costa Rica, San Salvador, El Salvador, Honduras, Panama City and Guatemala City. Vehicles are driven on the right.

Railways
The State-owned Pacific Railway has a total length of 331 km. It links the capital with Granada, on Lake Nicaragua, where it connects with boat services to other towns. Northwest from the capital the line runs to León, Chinandega and Corinto.

Shipping
The chief seaports are Corinto, Puerto Somoza and San Juan del Sur on the Pacific, and Puerto Cabezas, Bluefields and San Juan del Norte on the Atlantic. Corinto handles about 47 per cent of the seaborne trade of the country. Nanica is the state-owned shipping company. There are 2,220 km of waterways.

Ports and Harbours
Key seaports are: Corinto in Chinandega; Puerto Sandino in Leon; El Bluff on the Atlantic coast; Puerto Cabezas and San Juan del Sur.

HEALTH

In Nicaragua, adequate health care is available at a price. Health services are not easily accessible to the majority of the population. In the more isolated regions of Nicaragua, there are almost no doctors, and clinics often lack personnel, equipment and medicines. However, in recent years, the country has successfully controlled the spread of many diseases by reaching and maintaining a vaccination coverage level of 98-99 per cent, and by introducing new vaccines. The infant mortality rate dropped from 112 deaths per 1,000 live births in 1990 to 23 deaths per 1,000 live births in 2010 and the child mortality rate was 27 per 1,000 live births. The main causes of deaths in children aged under five are: prematurity 19 per cent, pneumonia 14 per cent, congenital abnormalities 18 per cent, diarrhoea 9 per cent, and birth asphyxia 7 per cent.

In 2009, the prevalence rate of HIV/AIDS was 121 per 100,000 population.

In 2009, the government spent approximately 18.1 per cent of its total budget on healthcare (up from 13.1 per cent in 2000), accounting for 54.8 per cent of all healthcare spending. Total expenditure on healthcare equated to 9.6 per cent of the country's GDP. Per capita expenditure on health was approximately US$104 in 2009, compared with US$54 in 2000. Figures for 2000-10 show that there are 2,045 physicians (4 per 10,000 population), 5,862 nurses and midwives (11 per 10,000 population) and 243 dentists. There are 9 hospital beds per 10,000 population.

According to the latest WHO figures, in 2010 approximately 85 per cent of the population had access to improved drinking water. In the same year, 52 per cent of the population had access to improved sanitation. Diarrhoea accounts for 9 per cent of childhood deaths. (Source: http://www.who.int, World Health Statistics 2012)

EDUCATION

Elementary education in Nicaragua is free and compulsory.

In 2006, an estimated 52 per cent of young children attended a pre-primary school. In 2007, 96 per cent of the relevant age-group attended primary school, 46 per cent of the relevant age-group attended secondary school - 42 per cent of boys and 49 per cent of girls. (Source: UNESCO, August 2009)

There are 14 universities in Nicaragua including the Central American Institute for Business Management (INCAE), which is affiliated with Harvard Business School; Central American University (UCA), affiliated with Georgetown University; the University of Mobile, affiliated with Mobile College, Alabama; Nicaraguan Catholic University (UNICA) and the National Engineering University (UNI).

In 2006, it was estimated that 80.1 per cent of Nicaraguan adults was literate. In the 15-24 year banding, the percentage rises to 88.4 per cent. UNESCO figures for 2002 show that 15.2 per cent of total government expenditure went on education.

NIGER

RELIGION

Roman Catholicism is the predominant religion, practised by over 55 per cent of the population. There is an archbishopric at Managua and seven bishoprics. There are strong Anglican and Moravian communities on the Caribbean coast, and Evangelical Protestantism is growing.

Nicaragua has a religious liberty rating of 8 on a scale of 1 to 10 (10 is most freedom). (Source: World Religion Database)

COMMUNICATIONS AND MEDIA

A wide variety of opinions appear in the media. The printed media are often partisan.

Newspapers
La Prensa, URL: http://www.laprensa.com
Nuevo Diario, URL: http://www.elnuevodiario.com.ni/

Broadcasting
There are currently three commercial television channels providing national coverage, as well as the state-owned Canal 6. Radio Nicaragua (URL: http://www.radionicaragua.com.ni/) is the state radio station. Cable television is available in urban areas. There are more than 100 radio stations.

Canal 10, URL: http://www.canal10nicaragua.com/
Televicentro Canal 2, URL: http://www.canal2tv.com/

Telecommunications
The telecommunications systems are currently being upgraded, with the help of foreign investment. Digital technology is now being widely used. Telephone main lines numbered 310,000 in 2008, with 3 million mobile phones in use. In 2008, some 600,000 Nicaraguans had access to the internet.

ENVIRONMENT

Major national concerns are: deforestation, water pollution, and soil erosion.

Nicaragua is a party to the following international environmental agreements: Biodiversity, Climate Change, Climate Change-Kyoto Protocol, Desertification, Endangered Species, Hazardous Wastes, Law of the Sea, Ozone Layer Protection, Ship Pollution, and Wetlands. Nicaragua has signed but not ratified the Environmental Modification agreement.

According to figures from the EIA, total carbon dioxide emissions rose to 4.3 million metric tons in 2005, whilst per capita emissions rose to 0.79 metric tons, well below the Central and South American average of 2.45 metric tons per capita. In 2010, Nicaragua's emissions from the consumption of fossil fuels totalled 4.82 million metric tons of carbon dioxide.

NIGER

Republic of Niger

République du Niger

Capital: Niamey (Population estimate, 2011: 755,000)

Head of State: Mahamadou Issoufou (page 1447)

National Flag: Three horizontal stripes, orange, white and green. The white charged with an orange disc.

CONSTITUTION AND GOVERNMENT

Constitution
Formerly part of French West Africa, Niger became independent in 1960 under President Hamani Diori and his Parti Progressiste Nigérien. Niger then became a member of the Conseil d'Entente, a grouping of ex-French colonies dependent on the Ivory Coast. Close administrative, commercial and military links with France were nevertheless maintained.

Diori ruled the country with a council of thirteen ministers. Growing opposition to the government came to a head over the distribution of food aid during the drought of the early 1970s and in April 1974 Diori was overthrown in a coup. The coup was led by the army chief of staff Lt-Col Seyni Kountché, who established the Conseil Militaire Supreme (CMS) as the ruling body. After initial liberalisation opposition was once more suppressed and political parties were banned. Kountché ruled until his death in 1987.

In 1991 the Constitution was suspended and a national conference on political rule was held. A new constitution was inaugurated on 26 November 1992. The constitution stipulated multiparty elections and a new president, Mahamane Ousmane, was elected in 1993. President Ousmane designated Mahamadou Issoufou as prime minister and a new government was formed in April 1993.

In 1996 Ibrahim Bare Mainassara staged a coup and ousted the country's first democratically elected government. He cited the Ousmane regime's failure to rectify Niger's economic and political problems as the reason for the coup. In 1999 he annulled regional elections. In April 1999 President Mainassara was assassinated by members of his own personal security guard. The commander of Niger's presidential guard, Daouda Mallam Wanke, was named as the country's new head of state until elections took place at the end of 1999, which resulted in the election of Mamadou Tandja. The country has since been relatively stable.

President Tandja has tried to change the constitution to allow to him stand for a third term. When the Constitutional Court ruled against the president and insisted that any amendment be approved by parliament, President Tandja disbanded both the court and the parliament and assumed emergency powers. A referendum was held on both allowing a third term and extending the current term in August 2009 and President Tandja received overwhelming support, although concerns were raised over the vote. President Tandja was ousted in a coup in February 2010 and Col. Salou Djibo was named head of a military government. Col. Djibo promised to return Niger to democracy and appointed a transitional government headed by a civilian prime minister.

A new constitution aimed at restoring civilian rule was approved overwhelmingly by referendum in October 2010. Under the terms of the new constitution, the presidential mandate is limited to fixed terms of five years renewable only once. It also provides an amnesty for the instigators of the coup d'état of February 18.

To consult the constitution, please visit: http://cour-constitutionnelle-niger.org/constitution.php

Recent Events
There were street protests in May 2005 over a food crisis. Up to 3 million people were believed to be desperately short of food following drought and an infestation of locusts. In June 2006 the Unions called a national strike, protesting against the high cost of living. The health and education ministers were sacked in June 2006 following allegations of corruption. Prime Minister Hama Amadou resigned in May 2007 after losing a vote of no confidence following allegations of corruption. He was arrested in June 2008 on charges of embezzlement of state funds.

In August 2007 the government gave the army greater powers to fight the Tuareg rebels in the north of the country. In April 2009 rebels from the Movement of Niger People for Justice and the government agreed to end hostilities.

In February 2010 President Tandja was deposed in a coup in protest as his attempts to change the constitution. The leader of the coup Colonel Salou Djibo became president and said he would restore democracy. The military junta under Coloner Djibo appointed a transitional government with Mahamadou Danda as Prime Minister. The junta which called itself the Supreme Council for the Restoration of Democracy, said none of its members would be in the transitional government or stand in elections. Following the coup the African Union expelled Niger from its membership.

In May 2010 there were warnings that food shortages were affecting up to 7 million people.

Following approval of the new constitution in 2010, legislative elections took place in January 2011 and presidential elections in March 2011 which were won by the veteran opposition leader Mahamadou Issoufou.

Former president Mamadou Tandja, ousted in the 2009 coup, was released from prison after corruption charges were dropped. In July 2011 five soldiers were reported to have been arrested after an alleged attempted coup.

In February 2012, thousands of people were reported to have crossed into Niger to escape fighting in Mali.

In May 2013, several suicide bomb attacks took place on a military barracks and a French-run uranium mining site. The government said that al-Qaeda militants were believed to have carried out the attacks.

International Relations
Niger maintains good relations with its seven neighbours although it does have a border dispute with Benin. It continues to have a strong relationship with France, its former colonial power. Niger is a member of many international and regional organisations such as GATT and the Economic Community of West African States.

Legislature
The National Assembly, *Assemblée Nationale*, is the sole chamber of government and is made up of 113 elected members who serve a five year term.
National Assembly, B.P. 12234, Place de la Concertation, Niamey, Niger. Tel: +227 20 722738, fax: +227 20 724308, e-mail: an@assemblee.ne, URL: http://www.assemblee.ne

> **Cabinet (as at June 2013)**
> *Prime Minister:* Brigi Rafini (page 1499)
> *Minister of State and Minister for the Interior, Public Security and Decentralization & Religious Affairs:* Abdou Labo

Minister of State and Minister of Foreign Affairs & Co-operation: Mohamed Bazoum (page 1385)
Minister of State, and Minister of Planning, Land Management, and Community Development: Amadou Boubacar Cissé
Minister of State in charge of Mines and Industrial Development: Omar Hamidou Tchiana
Minister of Health: Soumana Sanda
Minister of Energy and Oil: Pierre Foumakoye Gado
Minister of Justice, Keeper of the Seals and Government Spokesperson: Marou Amadou (page 1377)
Minister of Town Planning, Lodging and Sanitation: Moussa Bako Abdoulkarim
Minister of Trade and Promotion of the Private Sector: Saley Seybou
Minister of Communication & New Technology: Salifou Labo Bouché
Minister of the Population, Promotion of Women and Protection of Children: Mme Maikibi Kadidia Dandobi
Minister of National Defence: Karidjo Majhamadou
Minister of Finance: Jules Bayé
Minister of Professional Training and Employment: Mme N'Gadé Nana Hadiza Noma Kaka
Minister of Higher Education and Scientific Research: Mahamadou Youba Diallo
Minister of National Education, Literacy and Promotuion of National Languages: Mme Ali Mariama Elhadj Ibrahim
Minister of Agriculture: Ouha Seydou
Minister of Hydraulics & the Environment: Issoufou Issaka
Minister of Livestock: Mahammane Elhadj Ousmane
Minister of Transport & Civil Aviation: Ibrahim Yacouba
Minister of Youth, Sport & Culture: Kounou Hassane
Minister of Industrial Development and Tourism: Mme Yahaya Baré Haoua Abdou
Minister of Civil Service: Mme Sabo Fatouma Zara Boubacar

Ministries
Government portal: URL: http://www.gouv.ne/
Office of the President, BP 550, Niamey, Niger. Tel: +227 20 722380, fax: +227 20 723396, URL: http://www.presidence.ne
Office of the Prime Minister, BP 893, Niamey, Niger. Tel: +227 20 72269, fax: +227 20 723859, URL: http://www.gouv.ne/
Ministry of Commerce and Promotion of the Private Sector, BP 480, Niamey, Niger. Tel: +227 723467, fax: +227 732150
Ministry of Tourism and Handicrafts, BP 12130, Niamey, Niger. Tel: +227 20 722907, fax: +227 20 733685
Ministry of Basic Education, Literacy & Promotion of National Languages, BP 557, Niamey, Niger. Tel: +227 20 722833, fax: +227 722105
Ministry of Finance, BP 389, Niamey, Niger. Tel: +227 20 722374, fax: +227 20 735934
Ministry of National Defence, BP 626, Niamey, Niger. Tel: +227 20 722076, fax: +227 20 724078
Ministry of Foreign Affairs, Nationals living abroad & African Integration, BP 396, Niamey, Niger. Tel: +227 20 722907, fax: +227 20 735231
Ministry of Justice & Keeper of the Seals, BP 466, Niamey, Niger. Tel: +227 20 723131, fax: +227 20 723577, URL: http://www.justice.gouv.ne/
Ministry of Secondary Education, Research and Technology, BP 628, Niamey, Niger. Tel: +227 20 722620, fax: +227 20 724040
Ministry of Social Development, Population, Promotion of Women and Protection of Children, BP 11286, Niamey, Niger. Tel: +227 20 722330, fax: +227 20 736165
Ministry of Interior and Decentralisation, BP 622, Niamey, Niger. Tel: +227 20 723262, fax: +227 20 722176
Ministry of Public Health, BP 623, Niamey, Niger. Tel: +227 20 722808, fax: +227 20 733570
Ministry of Transport and Civil Aviation, BP 403, Niamey, Niger. Tel: +227 20 735357, fax: +227 20 722171
Ministry of Equipment, Housing and Territorial Development, BP 403, Niamey, Niger. Tel: +227 20 735357, fax: +227 20 722171
Ministry of Agriculture, BP 10427, Niamey, Niger. Tel: +227 20 733155
Ministry of Oil and Energy, BP 11700, Niamey, Niger. Tel: +227 20 734582, fax: +227 20 732812
Ministry of Youth and Sport, BP 12501, Niamey, Niger. Tel: +227 20 736988, fax: +227 20 733593
Ministry of Culture and Arts, BP 452, Niamey, Niger. Tel: +227 20 722874, fax: +227 733685

Political Parties
National Movement for the Development of Society (MNSD-Nassara); Nigerien Alliance for Democracy and Progress (ANDP-Zaman Lahiya); Nigerien Democratic Movement for an African Federation (Moden FA-Lumana); Nigerien Party for Democracy and Socialism (PNDS-Tarayya); Rally for Democracy and Progress (RDP-Jama'a).

Elections
The most recent presidential election took place on 31 January 2011, with a second round of voting on 12 March 2011. Veteran opposition leader Mahamadou Issoufou of the PNDS-Tarayya took 58 per cent of the vote in the second round, with Seyni Oumarou of the MNSD 42 per cent.

The most recent parliamentary elections took place on 31 January 2011. The PNDS-Tarayya party gained most seats but was short of an overall majority. Breakdown of seats is as follows: PNDS-Tarayya 39 seats; MNSD-Nassara 26 seats; Moden FA-Lumana 24 seats; ANDP-Zaman Lahiya 8 seats; RDP-Jama'a 7 seats; others 9 seats.

Diplomatic Representation
Embassy of Republic of Niger, 2204 R Street, NW, Washington, DC 20008, USA. Tel.: +1 202 483 4224, fax, +1 202 483 3169, URL: http://www.embassyofniger.org/

Ambassador: Maman Sidikou
Embassy of the Republic of Niger, 154 rue de Longchamp, 75116 Paris, France. Tel: +33 (0)1 45 04 80 60, URL: http://www.nigeriafrance.com/
Ambassador: Akin Fayomi
British Embassy, All staff resident in Ghana. URL: http://ukinghana.fco.gov.uk/en/
High Commissioner: Peter Jones (page 1451)
US Embassy, Rue Des Ambassades, B.P. 11201, Niamey, Niger. Tel: +227 20 722661, fax: 227 20 733167, e-mail: usemb@intnet.ne, URL: http://niamey.usembassy.gov/
Ambassador: Bisa Williams
Permanent Representative of the Niger to the United Nations, 417 East 50th Street, New York, NY 10022, USA. Tel: +1 212 42 3260 / 3261 / 3286, fax: +1 212 753 6931, URL: http://www.un.int/niger
Ambassador: H.E.M. Ousmane Moutari

LEGAL SYSTEM

The legal system is based on the French civil law system and customary law. Niger has not accepted compulsory ICJ jurisdiction.

Rulings from lower courts can be appealed first to the Court of Appeals and then to the Supreme Court. The seven members of the Constitutional Court have jurisdiction over constitutional and electoral matters. The High Court of Justice can try the president and members of the government for crimes or offenses committed in performance of their official duties. This court is appointed by the National Assembly from among its own members.

Traditional and customary courts hear cases involving divorce or inheritance. Traditional courts are held within local communities and presided over by tribal chiefs. Located in larger towns and cities, customary courts are presided over by a legal practitioner with basic legal training who may advised about local tradition by a local assessor. Appeals can be taken from both customary and traditional courts to the formal court system.

There is also a Court of State Security to try crimes against the state.

Human rights abuses include extrajudicial killings and brutality by security forces. Arrests and detentions can be arbitrary, and prison conditions are poor. There is widespread official corruption, and government interference in the judiciary. Freedom of the press and freedom of movement are restricted. Niger has, de facto, abolished the death penalty; the last execution took place in 1976. However, the National Assembly adopted a new criminal code in May 2003, which introduced punishments of death for infringement of international humanitarian laws such as crimes against humanity, slavery, summary executions, deportation and torture.

LOCAL GOVERNMENT

Niger is divided into eight departments, Agadez, Diffa, Dosso, Maradi, Niamey, Tahoua, Tillaberi and Zinder. Each is administered by a prefect and each is sub-divided into districts, of which there are 36, headed by a sub-prefect, and 265 communes. Niame is the capital district.

The cities of Niger are Niamey, Maradi, Tahoua, and Zinder, each headed by a mayor. The mayors of the cities come under the aegis of the prefects, while mayors of communes are under the authority of the sub-prefects.

In 2004, local elections were held for the first time. Parties that supported President Tandja won the majority of seats. Municipal elections took place in 2009 but opposition parties called for a boycott.

AREA AND POPULATION

Area
Niger is a large landlocked republic, bounded by Algeria and Libya to the north, Mali and Burkina Faso to the west, Chad to the east, and Nigeria and Benin to the south. The country is a vast undulating plain at an average altitude of 300 meters above sea level. There are, however, a number of extensive depressions, usually filled with sand, the tops of the ridges sometimes formed of volcanic structures. The highest of these is Mount Greboun (2,310 metres) in the Air Massif. Crop farming is possible in the Niger Valley. The total area of Niger is 1,267,000 sq. km.

Along the river border between Niger and Benin are some islands whose ownership has been disputed by both countries. In 2005 the International Court of Justice ruled that the most of the islands belonged to Niger.

Niger has a mainly dry climate with considerable temperature ranges. It is one of the hottest countries in the world. Potential evaporation is from two to three metres per annum, while rainfall in no place exceeds 800 mm and even falls to below 100 mm in over almost half the country. Almost two thirds of the country is covered by desert which is gradually encroaching on land used for agriculture.

To view a map, visit http://www.un.org/Depts/Cartographic/map/profile/niger.pdf

Population
The population of the country was an estimated 15.5 million in 2010 with an annual growth rate of 3.5 per cent. An estimated 17 per cent of the population lives in urban areas. There are several large towns including Zinder, Maradi, Tahoua, Dosso, Agadez, Diffa, and Arlit.

NIGER

Niger has a young population: 50 per cent of its people are less than 15 years old. An estimated 4 per cent are over 60 years old. The median age is 15. The principal ethnic groups are the Hausa, Djerma-Songhai, Fulani, Tuareg and Beriberi-Manga. There is a large nomadic population.

French is the official language but Hausa is spoken by about 70 per cent of the population. Arabic, Djerma, Fula and Tamashek are also spoken.

Births, Marriages, Deaths
Estimates for 2009 put average life expectancy at 57 years for males and 58 years for females. Healthy life expectancy in 2007 was estimated at 44 years for males and 45 for females. The crude birth rate was estimated to be 48.5 per 1,000 births and the crude death rate was estimated to be 11.5 per cent. The fertility rate was 7.1 per women. The infant mortality rate is around 73 per 1,000 live births. The maternal mortality rate in 2009 was an estimated 850 per 100,000 live births. (Source: http://www.who.int, World Health Statistics)

Public Holidays 2014
1 January: New Year's Day
14 January: Mawlid al-Nabi (Prophet's birthday)*
21 April: Easter Monday
24 April: Concord Day
1 May: Labour Day
3 August: Independence Day
29 July: Eid al-Fitr (end of Ramadan)*
5 October: Eid al-Adha (Festival of Sacrifice)*
18 December: Republic Day
25 December: Christmas Day
*Islamic holidays based on lunar observation so dates vary

EMPLOYMENT

Estimated figures for 2007 put the labour force at 4.6 million. Around 90 per cent of the population are involved in agriculture and six per cent in industry.

BANKING AND FINANCE

The financial centre is Niamey.

Currency
The unit of currency is the CFA franc linked to the French franc.

GDP/GNP, Inflation, National Debt
Niger is one of the poorest nations in the world. Its most important export is uranium, the value of which fluctuates. The value has increased since 2004 which has aided the economy. Oil was discovered in 2005. Other than that, its economy is based on agriculture and livestock, which is prone to disruption by the harsh climate. In recent years there have been droughts and locust plagues. Niger is one of the countries in the Enhanced Highly Indebted Poor Countries initiative, which will result in around US$500 million of debt relief when it reaches completion of the initiative. To work its way toward completion, Niger has implemented a Poverty Reduction Strategy Paper, the aims of which include economic growth, structural reforms in the finance sector and the privatisation of utilities. The government has had to implement reform measures to stabilise the economy including raising taxes on some goods by as much as 20 per cent. This has led to widespread protests. Some privatisation has taken place.

GDP was estimated to be US$5 billion on 2009. The growth rate was estimated to be 10 per cent in 2010. GDP was estimated to be US$5.9 billion in 2011. Per capita GDP was US$700.

Inflation was put at 0.7 per cent in 2007. This compares to 0.1 per cent in 2006, and 7.8 per cent in 2005. In 2010 it was estimated to be 2 per cent, rising to 2.9 per cent in 2011.

Total external debt was estimated at US$1.2 billion in 2011. Total debt service was US$89 million.

Balance of Payments / Imports and Exports
Principal exports are uranium ore, livestock products, and some agricultural produce. The price of uranium has increased since 2004. Niger licensed three Chinese companies to search for further uranium in 2006. Signficiant export partners include France (45 per cent), Japan (15 per cent), the US (13 per cent) and Nigeria (8 per cent). Main imports are petroleum, consumer goods, foodstuffs, machinery, vehicles and parts. Main import trading partners are China (over 40 per cent), France, the US and the UK.

Foreign Trade, US$ million

	2005	2006	2007
Balance of payments	-293.72	-265.48	-217.38
Exports	454.48	494.00	688.89
Imports	748.21	759.47	906.27
Source: African Development Bank			

Exports were estimated to be worth US$480 million in 2010 and imports cost US$1.6 billion.

Foreign Aid
Niger receives aid from various organisations including the World Bank, the IMF and several UN agencies France is the major state donor. Other donors include the EU, the US, Belgium, Germany, Switzerland, Japan, China, Italy, Canada and Saudi Arabia. Foreign aid represents 8.3 per cent of its GDP and over 40 per cent of government revenue. Niger qualified for enhanced debt relief under the IMF programme for Highly Indebted Poor Countries in 2000.

This relief significantly reduced Niger's debt service obligations, providing it with approximately US$40 million to spend on basic health care, education infrastructure and poverty reduction programes. Debt service will account for approximately 4.5 per cent of government revenue in the period 2010-2019 (compared to 44 per cent in 1999 and 10.9 per cent in 2003). In 2005, the IMF cancelled all of Niger's debts to it (US$111 million). In 2006, the African Development Fund cancelled approximately US$190 million of debt. The World Bank also reported that US$745 million of debt relief would be phased in until 2040.

In 2012, a the IMF approved a new three-year US$120 million loan arrangement to Niger.

Central Bank
Banque Centrale des Etats de l'Afrique de l'Ouest, PO Box 3108, Avenue Abdoulaye Fadiga, Dakar, Senegal. Tel: +221 8 390500, fax: +221 8 239335, e-mail: webmaster@bceao.int, URL: http://www.bceao.int
Governor: Tiémoko Meyliet Kone

Chambers of Commerce and Trade Organisations
Chamber of Commerce, Agriculture, Industry and Handicrafts, URL: http://www.ccaian.org/

MANUFACTURING, MINING AND SERVICES

Primary and Extractive Industries
Mining became very important to Niger's economy in the 1970s. Uranium is mined at Arlit and Akoutaand and accounts for over 55 per cent of the country's export earnings thanks to recent global rise in prices. In 1992 Niger was the fourth largest producer in the world, behind Canada, Australia, and the USA. In 2006 the government licenced three Chinese companies to prospect for more uranium. Other mineral resources include cassiterie (tin), iron, phosphate, salt, coal, gold, silver, platinum, nickel, cobalt, chrome, titanium, vanadium, copper, and lithium. A functioning gold mine has recently started operations and Niger began exports in 2005. Niger has been hoping to discover oil deposits and in January 2005 the Malaysian company Petronas discovered oil in Agadem. Figures for 2011 show that 6,710 barrels per day were produced, 6,000 barrels pwe day were consumed the rest going for export. In 2010, Niger produced 198,000 short tons of coal, all consumed domestically.

Work began on an uranium mine in May 2009. The mine, which will be the world's second largest uranium mine, should yield 5,000 tonnes of uranium per annum. The French company Areva is building the mine and will be a majority shareholder.

Energy
Uranium companies consume much of Niger's electricity output, the generation of which was expanded rapidly in the 1970s. About half the requirements are generated within the country and the rest imported from Nigeria, but major steps are being taken to develop domestic generation with the construction of a number of thermal power stations. All electricity produced is generated from fossil fuels. An estimated 0.25 billion kWh of electricity were generated in 2010 and 0.83 billion kWh consumed. (Source: EIA)

Manufacturing
In the past few years considerable efforts to industrialise have been made. Manufacturing is limited to agricultural processing (extraction of groundnut oil, cotton ginning, rice and flour milling, tanning) and import substitution (production of textiles, cement, beverages, packaged food and agricultural implements). Industry accounted for 11 per cent of GDP in 2006.

Agriculture
Agriculture, animal husbandry and mining are the mainstays of the economy. Farming and livestock rearing account for nearly half of GDP and employ 90 per cent of the population.

The droughts of the early 1970s and 1980s hit farming severely, and much food aid had to be supplied from abroad. In other years food production has expanded considerably, keeping pace with population growth. Niger has received much foreign aid in recent years to develop agriculture and combat the drought. Amongst others, the IDA, the OPEC countries, the EU and FAO have financed irrigation schemes, soil conservation and anti-desertification measures, livestock and rice production projects.

About 12 per cent of the country is suitable for crop-growing. The main crops are millet, sorghum, groundnuts, rice, maize, potatoes, cotton, cassava cowpeas, peanuts and sugar cane. The 1984 drought cut production by 40 per cent, but food output has since recovered, thanks to better rains. Crops were badly affected by a plague of pests which swept the Sahel region in the second half of 1986, despite a spraying campaign. The improvement in food production was nevertheless sustained, and Niger was able to meet most of its food needs in 1986 and by 2001 agriculture accounted for 40 per cent of GDP and 30 per cent of GDP in 2006.

Agricultural Production in 2010

Produce	Int. $'000*	Tonnes
Millet	593,006	3,843,350
Indigenous cattle meat	580,769	214,990
Cow peas, dry	461,423	1,774,460
Indigenous sheep meat	193,054	70,903
Sorghum	169,983	1,304,830
Groundnuts, with shell	161,734	406,245
Indigenous goat meat	161,252	67,298
Cow milk, whole, fresh	151,649	485,958
Mangoes, mangosteens, guavas	104,854	175,000
Fruit fresh nes	101,070	289,570
Goat milk, whole, fresh	96,357	287,135
Onions, dry	77,049	366,840

- continued
* unofficial figures
Source: http://faostat.fao.org/site/339/default.aspx Food and Agriculture
Organization of the United Nations, Food and Agricultural commodities production

Animal husbandry (livestock, meat, hides and skins) is second only to uranium in export figures. Cattle breeding is the most important activity of the nomadic population. The main livestock are cattle (2 million), sheep (8 million), goats (5 million) and dromedaries (350,000).

COMMUNICATIONS AND TRANSPORT

Travel Requirements
Citizens of the USA, Canada, Australia and most of the EU require a passport valid for six months and a visa. Citizens of Denmark and Finland do not require a visa; nor do most transit passengers continuing their journey within 24 hours and who do not leave the airport. An exit permit must be obtained from the Immigration Department in Niamey before departure (except for nationals who do not require an entry visa). Proof of yellow fever inoculation may be required. All foreigners travelling to Niger should contact the embassy to check precise visa requirements.

Passports must be presented to the police in each town where an overnight stay is intended. Passports are stamped at each town, so blank pages are required.

International Airports
There are two international airports at Niamey and Agadez. There are also some 27 small airports around the country. In total nine have paved runways.

Roads
Niger has one of the best macadamised road networks in sub-Saharan Africa. All-weather roads, the most important of those between Niamey and Zinder and Arlit and Tahoma, have been developed with finance from the World Bank, the European Development Fund and Saudi Arabia. The road network is some 14,500 km long. Vehicles are driven on the right.

Waterways
Although Niger has no ports or harbours, the river Niger is navigable from Niamey to the Benin border from December to March.

HEALTH

Recent figures show that Niger has three national hospitals, five smaller hospitals and a system of maternity units and dispensaries. In 2009, the government spent approximately 11.1 per cent of its total budget on healthcare (up from 10.3 per cent in 2000), accounting for 50.3 per cent of all healthcare spending. External resources amounted to 19.9 per cent of total expenditure. Total expenditure on healthcare equated to 5.4 per cent of the country's GDP. Per capita expenditure on health was approximately US$19. According to WHO estimates in 2005-10 there were: 288 doctors (less than 1 per 10,000 population), 2,115 nurses and midwives (1 per 10,000 population), 16 dentists, 21 pharmacists 137 environment and public health workers. There were an estimated 3 hospital beds per 10,000 population.

Vaccination programmes for children have increased in recent years but poor health and nutrition rates mean that child mortality rates are still very high. The infant mortality rate in 2010 was 73 per 1,000 live births. The child mortality rate (under 5 years) was 143 per 1,000 live births. The main causes of childhood mortality are: prematurity (12 per cent), birth asphyxia (7 per cent), diarrhoea (14 per cent), pneumonia (22 per cent) and malaria (15 per cent) and HIV/AIDS (1 per cent). An estimated 7 per cent of children now sleep under insecticide-treated nets.

Approximately 54.8 per cent of children aged less than 5 were classified as stunted and 39.9 per cent as underweight. The maternal mortality rate was an estimated 820 per 100,000 births in 2008. It was estimated that in 2009 the HIV/AIDS prevalence was estimated to be 400 per 100,000 adult population.

In 2008, 96 per cent of the urban population and 39 per cent of the rural population had sustainable access to an improved water source. In the same year, 34 per cent of the urban population and 4 per cent of the rural population had sustainable access to improved sanitation. (Source: http://www.who.int, World Health Statistics 2012)

EDUCATION

Niger has eight years of compulsory education, six of which are primary school years. Many children work on the land during planting and harvesting seasons and in the north of the country nomadic families do not often have regular access to schools. Enrolment rates are low but have improved in recent years. In 2007, 38 per cent of girls and 45 per cent of boys were enrolled in primary education. The pupil / teacher ratio in primary education was 40:1. Just 7 per cent of girls and 11 per cent of boys were enrolled in secondary education.

There are about 50 secondary schools, 10 high schools and two universities. A programme to develop primary education was launched in late 1986 with assistance from the World Bank, Norway and Germany.

In 2005 the literacy rates for people aged 15 years and above were 42.9 years for males and approximately 15.1 per cent for females. For the age group 15-24 years, the literacy rates were 52.4 per cent for males and 23.2 per cent for females.

In 2006, of total government expenditure 17.6 per cent went on education of which 64 per cent went on primary education.(Source: UNESCO)

RELIGION

About 92 per cent of the population is Muslim with a small number of Christians (0.33 per cent) and those following traditional beliefs (7 per cent). Niger has a religious tolerance rating of 7 on a scale of 1 to 10 (10 is most freedom). (Source: World Religion Database)

COMMUNICATIONS AND MEDIA

Much of the nation's broadcasting is state-owned although private radio stations have increased recently. Radio is the most important form of broadcast communication. The import of the press is limited by high levels of illiteracy.

Newspapers
Le Sahel, (state-run), URL: http://www.lesahel.org/
Le Republicain, (weekly), URL: http://www.republicain-niger.com/

Broadcasting
Tele-Sahel (URL: http://www.ortn-niger.com/) is a government-owned television broadcasting station. Radio is the most significant news source due to the low literacy rate. La Voix du Sahel is a state owned radio station broadcasting in several languages. Niger also has some independent stations, mainly broadcasting in French. Other private stations include Anfani FM, R& M, Horixon and Africa No1, a pan-African station.

Telecommunication Systems
The telecommunications system is generally inadequate. In 2008 an estimated 24,000 people had access to a main telephone line. There were an estimated 1.6 million mobile phone subscribers in the same year. In 2008, there were an estimated 80,000 internet users.

ENVIRONMENT

In 2001 Niger banned hunting in an attempt to save its wildlife population which is threatened because of poaching and declining habitat. Recurring droughts are a problem. Other environmental concerns include soil erosion, deforestation and desertification.

Niger is party to the following international agreements: Biodiversity, Climate Change, Climate Change-Kyoto Protocol, Desertification, Endangered Species, Environmental Modification, Hazardous Wastes, Ozone Layer Protection, Wetlands. It has signed, but not ratified the Law of the Sea.

According to figures from the EIA, in 2006 Niger's emissions from the consumption of fossil fuels totalled 1.26 million metric tons of carbon dioxide. This figure rose to 1.80 million metric tons in 2010.

NIGERIA
Federal Republic of Nigeria

Capital: Abuja (Population estimate, 2011: 6 million)

Head of State: H.E. Dr Goodluck Jonathan (President) (page 1451)

Vice-President: Namadi Sambo (page 1507)

National Flag: A pale-wise tricolour: green, white, green

CONSTITUTION AND GOVERNMENT

Constitution
A former British colony, Nigeria became independent on 30 September 1960 and a republic on 1 October 1963. Mounting political disturbance followed and in 1966 the Nigerian armed forces took control, suspending the constitution bequeathed by the British. Since then, successive changes of military leadership and political disturbances have taken place, as well as a civil war lasting from 1967-70 when eastern states tried to set up an independent state of Biafra.

The 1970s saw a gradual return to civil rule and a new constitution was introduced in 1978. Nigeria moved away from the Westminster parliamentary model to a presidential system with a clear separation of powers and with an executive governor in each state. The twelve-year ban on political parties was lifted and five parties eventually emerged to contest the election in July-August 1979.

The National Party of Nigeria (NPN) emerged the winner and its leader Alhaji Shehu Shagari narrowly won the presidential election. He was sworn in as the country's first executive president in October 1979.

A military coup in December 1983 created the Supreme Military Council (SMC) led by Major-General Muhammadu Buhari. The SMC suspended the constitution and banned political parties.

In August 1985 the regime was reconstituted and a 28-member Armed Forces Revolutionary Council (AFRC) was set up. Elections held in 1993 were annulled. In 1994 the government re-addressed their earlier promise to hand over to civilian rule in announcing a two-stage transition to civilian government.

Following the death of General Sani Abacha in June 1998, General Abdulsalam Abubakar was elected president, and promised a return to democracy and the return to power of a civilian president following the 1999 elections. President Abubakar sacked his cabinet on 7 July following the death of Moshood Abiola, who was being held as a political prisoner. Chief Abiola was widely believed to have won the 1993 election. Although the cabinet was sacked, the Provisional Ruling Council, a military body and main organ of state power, remained intact.

In March 1999 Olusegun Obasanjo, the former military ruler, became the first elected civilian leader since the 1970s. In May 1999 Nigeria adopted a new constitution which allows for a President who is the Head of State, to serve a term of four years, renewable only once. The President can then nominate a Vice-President and Cabinet with approval of the Senate. The legislative power of the country rests with the National Assembly.

In July 2011 President Jonathan said he wished to amend the constitution leading to a single, longer presidential term.

To consult the constitution, please visit: http://www.nigeria-law.org/ConstitutionOfTheFederalRepublicOfNigeria.htm

Recent Events
Following an ongoing dispute about ownership of the oil rich Bakassi peninsula, the International Court of Justice awarded the area to Cameroon despite Nigeria's assertion that the area belonged to it. In 2004 the UN brokered a deal whereby both countries would patrol the border, and in August 2006 Nigeria agreed to hand over control of the peninsula to Cameroon. In June 2006, the Nigerian Government agreed to abide by a 2002 World court ruling and transfer jurisdiction of the Bakassi peninsular to Cameroon. The final handover took place in August 2008. A new ministry of the Niger Delta region was created in September 2008. Nigeria and Cameroon has pledged to work together to explore the area.

The first half of 2006 saw an increase in violence in the Niger Delta region. Despite being an oil rich area, some 75 per cent of young people are unemployed and many live in poverty. Activists seeking greater local control over the region's oil wealth, have cost the country millions of dollars in lost oil revenues.

In April 2007, Umaru Yar'Adua, of the ruling People's Democratic Party, won the presidential election, with 70 per cent of the vote. EU observers said that the elections were a charade. The two main opposition candidates accused the PDP of election rigging and called for a re-run. At least 200 people were killed during the campaign. The opposition parties appealed in an attempt to annul the election but the ruling went against them.

In September 2007, militants from Nigeria's oil-rich Delta called off the voluntary ceasefire that followed the inauguration of President Umaru Yar'Adua; the Movement for the Emancipation of the Niger Delta (Mend - formed in 2006) promised a campaign of violence and kidnappings of oil workers. The militants demand that the Delta region control its oil resources and pay tax to the federal government.

Former ministers were among twelve top officials charged with embezzling $4 million dollars of public health funds in April 2008.

In November 2008 approximately 200 people were reported to have been killed during riots between Christians and Muslims following a state election in Plateau state. The election was won by the ruling Christian party, the People's Democratic Party. Most of the fatalities occured in the mainly Muslim capital, Jos.

In March 2009, 19 opposition parties announced they were to unite to compete against the ruling People's Democratic Party in the 2011 parliamentary elections.

President Umaru Yar'Adua announced that he would consider granting amnesty to violent groups in the Niger Delta; in recent years, attacks and kidnappings of foreign oil workers in the Delta area have increased. The militant group Mend rejected the offer in May 2009 and declared an offensive on the military. In October Mend said that it would honour a ceasefire but wanted Nigerians to be given a greater share in profits from oil resources and land. In January 2010 Mend announced it was abandoning the ceasefire and oil companies should be prepared for an all-out onslaught against both installations and personnel.

In February 2010 Vice President Goodluck Jonathan became acting president in place of President Umaru Yar'Adua, who underwent medical treatment in Saudi Arabia the previous November, President Yar'Adua died in May 2010 and President Jonathan subsequently succeeded to the post.

A presidential election took place on 16 April 2011 and was won by the incumbent Goodluck Jonathan with 59 per cent of the vote. Parliamentary elections took place on 9 and 26 April 2011. The PDP won most seats in both the House of Representatives and the Senate. The outgoing Speaker of the House of Representatives, Dimeji Bankole, was arrested on corruption charges in June 2011. He is accused of misappropriating millions of dollars of government funds.

At least 10 people were killed in explosions near military barracks in Bauchi on 29 May. In August 2011, a reported 23 people were killed and over 80 injured in a bomb attack on the UN headquarters in Nigeria. It is thought the Islamist group Boko Haram which has links to al-Qaeda was behind the attack.

The former leader of the breakaway state of Biafra, Chujweumeka Ojukwu, died aged 78. Col. Ojukwu's declaration of independence for the state in 1967 sparked a civil war in which more than 1 million people are thought to have died.

In November 2011 President Jonathan sacked the head of his anti-corruption agency.

The Boko Haram group claimed responsibilty for a gun and bomb attack in the eastern town of Damaturu in November 2011 in which over 60 people were killed. In further violence, an estimated 70 people were killed in December in fighting between security forces and Boko Haram militants. Boko Haram also claimed responsibility for a bomb on Christmas Day which killed an estimated 40 people. The president declared a state of emergency in an attempt to halt the violence. However in January 2012 more than one hundred people were killed in a day of bombings and shootings. President Idriss of Chad warned that the violence might spread to neighbouring countries. In June 2012 Boko Harma attacked two churches, killing one person and injuring others. Six Muslims were killed in retaliation. In August the army was reported to have killed 20 Boko Haram fighters in the north east. In October Boko Haram attacked army bases in Maidufguri.

In November 2012, at least 100 people are charged with treason after a march supporting independence for the Biafra region. A Boko Haram leader was reported to have been killed by the army.

In December 2012, some 20 Christians were killed by suspected Islamist militants.

In May 2013, a state of emergency was declared in the states of Yobe, Borno & Adamawa. Government troops were sent to the region.

In July 2013, schools across the state of Yobe were ordered to close after suspected Islamist extremists killed 22 students.

Legislature
Nigeria's legislature, the bicameral National Assembly, is composed of the Senate (upper house) and House of Representatives (lower house).

Upper House
The Senate has 109 members who are elected for terms of four years. Each state elects three members and one from the federal capital territory.
The Senate, Private Bag 141, Abuja, Nigeria. Tel: +234 9 234 0630, fax: +234 9 234 2157, URL: http://www.nigerianassembly.org

Lower House

Members of the 360 seat House of Representatives are also elected for four-year terms.
House of Representatives, Private Bag 141, Abuja, Nigeria. Tel: +234 9 234 0303, fax: +234 9 234 0393, e-mail: office@ngspeaker.org, URL: http://www.ngspeaker.org

Cabinet (as at June 2013)

President, Minister of Power: Dr Goodluck Jonathan (page 1451)
Vice-President: Namadi Sambo (page 1507)
Minister of Foreign Affairs: Olugbenga Ashiru (page 1379)
Minister for Agriculture & Natural Resources: Dr Akinwunmi Ayo Adesina
Minister of Trade and Investment: Olusegun Olutoyin Aganga (page 1372)
Minister of Culture and Tourism: Edem Duke
Minister of Defence: vacant
Minister for Education: Prof. Rugayyatu A Rufa'i
Minister for the Environment: Hadiza Ibrahim Mailafa
Minister of the Federal Capital Territory: Sen. Bala Muhammed
Coordinating Minister of the Economy and Minister of Finance: Ngozi Okonjo-Iweala (page 1489)
Minister of Health: Prof. Christian Otu Onyebuchi
Minister of Information and Communications: Labaran Maku
Minister of Communication Technology: Omobola Johnson Olubusola
Minister of Justice and Attorney General: Justice Mohammed Bello Adoke (page 1372)
Minister of the Interior: Abba Moro
Minister of Labour and Productivity: Chukwuemeka Ngozichineke Wogu
Minister of Mines and Steel Development: Musa Mohammed Sada
Minister of Niger Delta Affairs: Peter Godsay Orubebe
Minister of Police Affairs: Caleb Olubolade
Minister for Petroleum: Diezani Alison-Madueke (page 1374)
Minister of Science and Technology: Ita Okon Bassey Ewa
Minister for Transport: Idris Umar
Minister for Women's Affairs: Zainab Maina
Minister of Lands & Housing: Ama Pepple
Minister of Aviation: Stella Oduah-Goiemwonyi
Minister for the National Planning Commission: Dr Shamsudeen Usman
Minister of Power: Chinedu Nebo
Minister of Works: Michael Onolememen
Minister of Youth Development: Inuwa Abdulkadir
Minister of Sport: Bolaji Abdullahi
Minister for Water Resources: Sarah Ochekpe
Minister in the Presidency: Kabiru Saminu Turaki

Ministries

Government portal: http://www.nigeria.gov.ng
Office of the President, Federal Secretariat PhaseII, Shehu Shagari Way, Abuja, NIgeria. Tel: +234 9 234 9909 / 523 4150
Ministry of Agriculture and Water Resources, FCT Secretariat, Area 1, Garki, Abuja, Nigeria. Tel: +234 9 234 314 1185 / 234 2331, email: agricminister.rosecom.net, URL: http://www.nigeria.gov.ng
Minister sof Aviation, New Federal Secretariat, Shehu Shagari Way, Nigeria. Tel: +234 9 523 2112
Ministry of Commerce and Industry, Old Federal Secretariat Complex, Are 1, P.M.B. 88, Garki, Abuja, Nigeria. Tel: +234 9 234 1884 / 234 1661, e-mail: info@commerce.gov.ng, URL: http://www.commerce.gov.ng
Ministry of Communications, Federal Secretariat Complex, Shehu Shagari Way, Maitama, P.M.B. 12578, Garki, Abuja, Nigeria. Tel: +234 9 523 7183 / 523 7135 / 523 7250, URL: http://www.nigeria.gov.ng
Ministry of Co-operation and Integration in Africa, The Presidency, Plot 496, Central Business District, IPCR Building, Airport Road, Wuse, Abuja, Nigeria. Tel: +234 9 523 9624
Ministry of Culture and Tourism,Federal Secretariat, Phase II. Bulet Building, Abuja, Nigeria.
Ministry of Tourism, Old Federal Secretariat, Area 1, Garki, Abuja, Nigeria. Tel: +234 9 234 2727 / 234 1687
Ministry of Defence, Ship House, Olusegun Obasanjo Way, Central Business District, P.M.B 196, Garki, Abuja, Nigeria. Tel: +234 9 523 0549 / 234 0534, URL: http://www.nigeria.gov.ng
Ministry of Education, Federal Secretariat Complex, Shehu Shagari Way, Maitama, P.M.B 146, Garki, Abuja, Nigeria. Tel: +234 9 523 2800, URL: http://www.fme.gov.ng
Ministry of Environment, Federal Secretariat Complex, (Floors 7 & 9), Shehu Shagari Way, Maitama, P.M.B 468, Garki, Abuja, Nigeria. Tel: +234 9 523 4931
Ministry of the Federal Capital Territory, FCT Secretariat Complex, Area 11, P.M.B. 24/25, Garki, Abuja, Nigeria. +234 9 523 4014 / 234 1295
Ministry of Finance, Federal Ministry of Finance Building, Ahmadu Bello Way, Central Business District, P.M.B 14, Garki, Abuja, Nigeria. Tel: +234 9 234 6932 / 234 6928
Ministry of Foreign Affairs, Maputo Street, WuseZone 3 , P.M.B 130, Garki, Abuja, Nigeria. Tel: +234 9 523 0491 / 234 4686
Ministry of Health, Federal Secretariat Complex, Shehu Shagari Way, Maitama, P.M.B 83, Garki, Abuja, Nigeria. Tel: +234 9 523 6228 / 523 0576
Ministry of Industry, Old Federal Secretariat, Area 1, P.M.B. 85, Garki, Abuja, Nigeria. Tel: +234 9 234 1690 / 523 0576
Ministry of Information and National Orientation, Radio House, Herbert Macauley Way (south), P.M.B 247, Garki, Abuja, Nigeria. Tel: +234 9 234 5793 / 234 6350, fax: +234 9 234 4106 / 234 3508, URL: http://www.nigeria.gov.ng/ministryinformation/Information.htm
Ministry of Internal Affairs, Old Federal Secretariat Complex, Area 1, P.M.B 7007, Garki, Abuja, Nigeria. Tel: +234 9 234 1934 / 234 6884
Ministry of Justice, Federal Secretariat Complex, Shehu Shagari Way, Maitama, P.M.B 192, Garki, Abuja, Nigeria. Tel: +234 9 523 5208 / 523 5194
Ministry of Labour and Productivity, Federal Secretariat Complex, Shehu Shagari Way, Maitama, Abuja, Nigeria. Tel: +234 9 523 5980 / 523 5988

Ministry of Planning, Federal Secretariat Complex, Shehu Shagari Way, Maitama, P.M.B 230, Garki, Abuja, Nigeria. Tel: +234 9 523 6628, fax: +234 9 523 6625
Ministry of Petroleum Resources, Federal Secretariat Complex, Shehu Shagari Way, Maitama, P.M.B 449, Garki, Abuja, Nigeria. Tel: +234 1 261 4123, fax: +234 9 523 7332, e-mail: publicaffairs@dprnigeria.com, URL: http://www.dprnigeria.com
Ministry of Police Affairs, Federal Secretariat Complex, Shehu Shagari Way, Maitama, P.M.B 140, Garki, Abuja, Nigeria. Rel: +234 9 523 6064 / 523 0549
Ministry of Power and Steel, Federal Secretariat Complex, Shehu Shagari Way, Maitama, P.M.B 278, Garki, Abuja, Nigeria. Tel: +234 9 523 7064 / 523 7066
Ministry of Science and Technology, Federal Secretariat Complex, Shehu Shagari Way, Maitama, P.M.B 331, Garki, Abuja, Nigeria. Tel: +234 9 523 3397, e-mail: 180m@ax.com, URL: http://www.fmst.gov.ng
Ministry of Solid Minerals, Federal Secretariat Complec, Shehu Shagari Way, Maitama, P.M.B 107, Garki, Abuja, Nigeria. Tel: +234 9 523 5830 / 523 6517
Ministry of Sports and Social Development, Federal Secretariat Complex, Shehu Shagari Way, Maitama, Abuja, Nigeria. +234 9 523 5907 / 523 5905
Ministry of Transport, National Maritime Agency Building, Central Area, Abuja, Nigeria. Tel: +234 9 523 7050 / 523 7053
Ministry of Water Resources, Old Federal Secretariat, Area 1, P.M.B 150, Garki, Abuja, Nigeria. Tel: +234 9 234 2376 / 234 2372
Ministry of Women's and Youth Development, Federal Secretariat Complex, Shehu Shagari Way, Maitama, P.M.B 229, Garki, Abuja, Nigeria. Tel: +234 9 523 7115 / 523 7051
Ministry of Works and Housing, Mabuchi Shehu Musa Yar' Adua Way, Utako District, Abuja, Nigeria. Tel: +234 9 523 9623 / 521 1622

Political Parties

People's Democratic Party (PDP), Leader: Dr. Okwesilieze Nwodo
Alliance for Democracy (AD), Chmn: Mojisoluwa Akinfewa
All Nigeria People's Party (ANPP), Chmn: Chief Okey Nwosu
Action Congress of Nigeria (ACN), Chmn: Usman Bugaje;
Congress for Progressive Change (CPC), Chmn: Tony Momoh

Elections

A presidential election took place on 16 April 2011 and was won by the incumbent Goodluck Jonathan with 59 per cent of the vote. Parliamentary elections took place on 9 and 26 April 2011. The PDP retained its majority in both the House of Representatives and the Senate.

Diplomatic Representation

Nigerian High Commission, Nigeria House, 9 Northumberland Avenue, London WC2N 5BX, United Kingdom. Tel: +44 (0)20 7839 1244, fax: +44 (0)20 7839 8746, URL: http://www.nigeriahc.org.uk
High Commissioner: Dr Dalhatu Sarki Tafida
Nigerian Embassy, 3519 International Court, NW, Washington DC 20008, USA. Tel: +1 202 986 8400, fax: +1 202 775 1385, URL: http://www.nigeriaembassyusa.org
Chief of Mission: Amb. Adebowale Ibidaop Adefuye
British High Commission, Aguiyi Ironsi Street, Abuja, Nigeria. Tel: +234 9 413 2010, fax: +234 9 413 3552, URL: http://ukinnigeria.fco.gov.uk/en
High Commissioner: Andrew Lloyd CMG MBE
US Embassy, Diplomatic Drive, Central District, Abuja, Nigeria, Tel: +234 09 523 0916, fax: +234 09 523 2083, e-mail: uslagos@stat.gov, URL: http://nigeria.usembassy.gov
Ambassador: Terence McCulley
Permanent Representative of Nigeria to the United Nations, 828 Second Avenue, New York, N.Y. 10017, USA. Tel: +1 212 953 9130, fax: +1 212 697 1970, e-mail: ngaun@undp.org, URL: http://www.un.int/nigeria/
Ambassador: H.E. Joy Ogwu

LEGAL SYSTEM

The Nigerian legal system is based on English common law, modified by statutes to meet local demands and conditions. The constitution of Nigeria is the supreme law of the land, and all laws enacted by the country's legislatures conform to its provisions.

The regular court system comprises federal and state trial courts, state appeals courts, the Federal Court of Appeal, the Federal Supreme Court, and Shari'ah (Islamic) and customary (traditional) courts of appeal for each state and for the federal capital territory of Abuja. Courts of the first instance include magistrate or district courts, customary or traditional courts, Shari'ah courts, and for some specified cases, the state high courts.

The Federal Supreme Court is the highest court. It consists of the Chief Justice of the Federation and Justices as prescribed by the National Assembly. The Justices must be qualified to practice in Nigeria and have practiced for 15 years. The Court of Appeal consists of the President and the Justices of the Court of Appeal. At least three must be qualified in Islamic Law and three in Customary Law. The Constitutional Court consists of a president and justices.

By 2012, twelve states had adopted Shari'ah law, and some of these states had issued sentences of public caning for consumption of alcohol, amputations for stealing, and death by stoning for committing adultery. In principle, customary and Shari'ah courts have jurisdiction only if both plaintiff and defendant agree, but fear of legal costs, delays, and distance to alternative venues encourage many litigants to choose these courts.

The government's human rights record is poor. There is excessive brutality by security forces, sometimes leading to unlawful killings, and widespread impunity for these abuses. Detainees and suspects are subjected to torture, rape, and other degrading treatment, and conditions in prisons are life-threatening. Arrests can be arbitrary and pretrial detention prolonged. There is judicial corruption and undue government influence on the judiciary. Freedom of speech, press, assembly, religion, and movement are all restricted. Nigeria retains the death penalty.

NIGERIA

A new Freedom of Information law came into effect in June 2011 which should provide access to public records and should make the government more accountable. It is now a criminal offence to destroy public records.

Supreme Court of Nigeria,
URL: http://www.nigeria-law.org/Supreme%20Court%20of%20Nigeria.htm
Chief Justice of Nigeria : Hon. Justice Dahiru Musdapher

Nigerian Human Rights Commission, URL: http://www.nigeriarights.gov.ng/

LOCAL GOVERNMENT

Nigeria now comprises one territory, Abuja Federal Capital Territory, and 36 states. Each state is headed by a governor who is elected for four years. The 36 states are divided into over 774 local government areas.

The states are as follows: Abia (Capital: Umahia), Adamawa (Yola), Ananbra (Awka), Akwalbom (Uyo), Bauchi (Bauchi), Bayelsa, Benue (Makurdi), Borno (Majduguri), Cross River (Calabar), Delta (Asaba), Ebonyi, Edo (Benin City), Ekiti, Enugu (Enugu), Gombe, Imo (Owerri), Jigawa (Dutse), Kaduna (Kaduna), Kano (Kano), Katsina (Katsina), Kebbi (Birnin Kebbi), Kogi (Lokoja), Kwara (Ilorin), Lagos (Ikeja), Nassarawa, Niger (Minna), Ogun (Abeokuta), Ondo (Akure), Osun (Osogbo), Oyo (Ibadan), Plateau (Jos), Rivers (Port Harcourt), Sokoto (Sokoto), Taraba (Jalingo), Yobe (Damaturu), Zamfara.

Local elections took place most recently in 2011.

AREA AND POPULATION

Area
The Federal Republic of Nigeria is the largest single geographic unit along the west coast of Africa and occupies a position where the western and equatorial parts of the continent of Africa meet. Nigeria is bounded in the west by the Republic of Benin, in the north by the Niger Republic, in the North East by Lake Chad and in the east by the Republic of Cameroon and in the south by the Atlantic Ocean.

The area of Nigeria is 923,772 sq. km. Its greatest length from east to west is over 1,120 miles and from north to south about 1,040 miles. The Atlantic coast line is about 500 miles long. The terrain in the southern half of the country includes tropical forest and swamps on the coast, in the north of the country there is savannah and semi-desert conditions. The rivers Niger and Benue run through Nigeria.

The climate is equatorial in the south, tropical in the centre and arid in the north.

To view a map, visit http://www.un.org/Depts/Cartographic/map/profile/nigeria.pdf

Population
Nigeria's population in 2010 was estimated at 158.423 million with an annual growth rate of 2.5 per cent for the period 2000-10. Population density is about 95.8 per sq. km. Approximately 43 per cent of the population is aged under 15 years old. Approximately 5 per cent of the population was aged over 60 years. The median age is 18. There are over 250 different ethnic groups, 10 of which account for over 80 per cent of the population: the Hausa-Fulani, Yoruba, Ibo, Tiv, Nupe, Kanuri, Ibibio, Ijaw and Edo.

Approximately 50 per cent of the population lives in urban areas. There are eight cities with populations over 1,000,000 and many more towns with more than 100,000 inhabitants. Abuja, the new federal capital, lies in the Federal Capital Territory in the centre of the country, and has an estimated population of 6,000,000. Lagos the former capital has an estimated population of 15,000,000.

English and French are the official languages, although Hausa, Igbo and Yoruba are widely spoken.

Births, Marriages, Deaths
In 2010 there were an estimated 39.9 births and 13 deaths per 1,000 of the population. The total fertility rate per woman was estimated in 2010 at 5.5. The maternal mortality rate was estimated at 840 per 100,000 live births in 2008. HIV/AIDS is a serious problem in Nigeria and it is estimated that there are 3,547 cases of HIV/AIDS per 100,000 population. Life expectancy is low; in 2009 life expectancy at birth was estimated at 53.5 years. Healthy life expectancy was estimated at 42 years. (Source: http://www.who.int, World Health Statistics 2012)

Public Holidays 2014
1 January: New Year's Day
14 January: Mawlid al-Nabi (Birthday of the Prophet)*
18 April: Good Friday
21 April: Easter Monday
1 May: Labour Day
29 May: Democracy Day
29 July: Eid al-Fitr (end of Ramadan)*
1 October: Independence Day
5 October: Eid al-Adha, (Festival of the Sacrifice)*
25 October: Muharram (Islamic New Year)*
25 December: Christmas Day
*Islamic calendar based on lunar observation, so dates can vary

EMPLOYMENT

The workforce was estimated at 51.0 million in 2008 with an unemployment rate of 5 per cent. 70 per cent of the working population is engaged in agriculture (mainly subsistence), whilst the service sector employs around 20 per cent of the workforce, and industry employs around 10 per cent. An estimated 70 per cent of the population live below the poverty line.

Total Employment by Economic Activity

Occupation	2007
Agriculture, hunting, forestry	19,236,350
Fishing	482,270
Mining & quarrying	193,160
Manufacturing	2,282,920
Electricity, gas & water supply	301,660
Construction	658,190
Wholesale & retail trade, repairs	8,834,090
Hotels & restaurants	217,120
Transport, storage & communications	1,404,550
Financial intermediation	126,430
Real estate, renting & business activities	414,250
Public admin. & defence; compulsory social security	1,829,620
Education	1,909,150
Health & social work	575,333
Other community, social & personal service activities	1,839,600
Households with employed persons	197,940
Extra-Territorial organisations & bodies	66,350
Total	40,567,980

Source: Copyright © International Labour Organization (ILO Dept. of Statistics, http://laborsta.ilo.org)

BANKING AND FINANCE

The financial centre is Lagos.

Currency
The unit of currency is the naira (N) which is divided into 100 kobo.

GDP/GNP, Inflation, National Debt
Nigeria's economy is heavily dependent on the oil sector, which accounts for around 95 per cent of exports. It is the world's 11th largest producer of oil with an output of 2.2 million bbl/d. There is the capacity to produce more but the industry is hindered by the security situation in the Nigeria delta. The economy is also hindered by a poor infrastructure, widespread corruption and mismanagement. The financial sector has been adversely affected by the global economic crisis and reforms have been implemented. The government is making efforts to diversify the economy and to tackle corruption. Despite the strong growth of recent years there is still much social inequality; an estimated 60 per cent of the population lives below the poverty line.

Nigeria's oil accounts for almost 50 per cent of its GDP. In 2009, GDP was estimated at over US$330 billion with a per capita figure of US$2,300. Growth for that year was put at 6.0 per cent. Growth has continued, boosted by strong oil prices. Growth was estimated to be US$10.8 per cent in 2011. GDP was estimated to be US$225 billion in 2011, rising to US$239 billion in 2012. Per capita GDP was estimated to be US$1,490.

Inflation was estimated to be over 8 per cent in 2007 and 11.5 per cent in 2009. It rose to 11.8 per cent in 2010.

In January 1999 Nigeria entered into an agreement with the IMF to reschedule the country's debt and resume World Bank funding. In August 2001 the World Bank agreed credit of US$300 million. This was to help Nigeria's privatisation programme and to help in the fight against HIV and Aids. Although national debt is high and poverty is widespread (it has been estimated that up to 70 per cent of the population lives on less than one dollar a day), Nigeria does not qualify for the Heavily Indebted Poor Countries initiative because of her oil industry. Most of Nigeria's debt is owed to the Paris Club and after several years of lobbying it was agreed that the Paris Club would cancel 60 per cent of the debt in return for the balance being paid immediately. Total external debt was estimated to be US$9.5 billion in 2011. Domestic debt was estimated to be US$39 billion.

Balance of Payments / Imports and Exports
Nigeria's principal exports are crude oil, natural gas, cocoa, manufactured goods, rubber and timber. Its principal imports are food, machinery and equipment, petroleum goods, and manufactured goods. Major trading partners are the US, the EU, Brazil, China, Japan and India. Oil accounts for 90 per cent of Nigeria's total export revenues.

External Trade, US$ million

	2005	2006	2007
Trade balance	27,700.00	31,600.00	25,476.20
Exports	63,100.00	62,600.00	61,110.32
Imports	26,400.00	30,900.00	36,634.13

Source: African Development Bank

Exports were estimated to be US$75 billion in 2010, rising to an estimated US$90 billion in 2011. Imports cost an estimated US$45 billion in 2010, rising to almost US$60 billion in 2011.

Central Bank
Central Bank of Nigeria, PMB 0187, Zaria Street, Garki, Abuja, Nassarawa State, Nigeria. Tel: +234 9 234 3191, fax: +234 9 234 3137, e-mail: info@cenbank.org, URL: http://www.cenbank.org
Governor: Sanusi Lamido Sanusi

Business Addresses
National Council on Privatisation / Bureau of Public Enterprise: URL: http://www.bpeng.org
Nigeria Stock Exchange: URL: http://www.nse.com.ng

Chambers of Commerce and Trade Organisations
The Lagos Chamber of Commerce and Industry, URL: http://www.lagoschamber.com/

MANUFACTURING, MINING AND SERVICES

Primary and Extractive IndustriesOil
The petroleum industry accounts for almost 50 per cent of GDP and about 95 per cent of foreign exchange earnings. Nigeria is an OPEC member with a Crude Production Quota of 1.67 million barrels per day (2010). Proven oil reserves in 2012 were estimated to be 37.2 billion barrels, including recent new deepwater discoveries. Most reserves are located in the Niger delta. Oil production was estimated in 2011 at 2,528 thousand barrels per day, of which 98 per cent was crude oil. National consumption that year was put at 286,000 barrels per day leaving 2,242,000 barrels per day for export. Nigeria exports her oil to the US, Western Europe and Asia. Nigeria has four refineries, but from a joint capacity of 445,000 billion barrels per day they are running at only about 38 per cent capacity. Despite its reserves Nigeria is forced to import oil because of insufficient refinery capacity. In July 2010, it was announced that China is to build an US$8 billion oil refinery in Lagos. It will be the first of three refineries between the state oil company NNPC and the China State Construction Engineering Corporation. In July 2012 it was announced that a preliminary deals had been sighed between Nigeria and the US based Vulcan Petroleum to build six oil refineries.

Production from joint ventures accounts for 95 per cent of crude oil production of which 50 per cent is with Shell. Insufficient government funding has hindered some joint ventures. Political and ethnic strife in the Delta region continues to disrupt oil production. There are also environmental protests over the plight of the Ogoni people. Nigeria offered offshore sites for licensing in 2005. Despite the situation Shell started producing oil from the Bonga deepwater field in 2005 and the Agbami offshore field became operational in 2008. There is a Joint Development Zone shared by Nigeria and Sao Tome and Principe which contains 23 exploration blocks and is estimated to hold 14 billion barrels of oil reserves. Block one is currently undergoing development.

In October 2002 the International Court of Justice ruled that the Bakassi peninsula belonged to Cameroon not Nigeria. The area is believed to have substantial oil reserves.

In 2006 the president vowed to crack down on the increasing number of kidnappings of foreign and Nigerian oil workers. Security patrols were to be increased and foreign oil companies were warned not to pay the kidnappers.

Gas
Nigeria is estimated to have the largest natural gas reserves in Africa, most of which are located in the Niger delta. Natural gas reserves were 187 trillion cubic feet in 2011 with production in that year put at 1,107 billion cubic feet. Natural gas consumption was estimated in 2011 at 191 billion cubic feet. Net natural gas exports amounted to an estimated 917 billion cubic feet in 2011. In 1999 a LNG facility was completed on Bonny Island and a significant proportion of Nigeria's natural gas is processed. Capacity at the Bonny island plant stands at 22 million tons per year. The Nigerian government has awarded several contracts to foreign companies including Shell in the UK and French based Technip and Chevron.

There is also ongoing construction of new pipelines. Nigeria began exporting natural gas via the West African Gas Pipeline in 2010. The pipeline may possibly be expanded further west to Cote d'Ivoire. The West African Gas Pipeline carries natural gas from Nigeria to Ghana, Togo and Benin. (Source: US Energy Information Administration)

Mining
Coal, iron ore, tin and columbite are mined in Nigeria, although output has declined in recent years. In 2010 Nigeria produced an estimated 0.009 million short tons of coal all of which was consumed domestically. Coal reserves were estimated to be 209 million short tons. Steel complexes have been established in Ajaokuta and Aladja and rolling mills in Oshogbo, Katsina and Jos.

Electricity
Nigeria has an electricity generating capacity of 5.9 GW. The government of Nigeria is encouraging further foreign investment in the country's electricity industry and negotiations are currently underway between NEPA and Mobil to build a 350 MW gas-fired power plant in southern Nigeria. Electricity production in 2010 was estimated at 24.8 billion kWh and consumption was estimated at 20.3 billion kWh. In 2009 approximately 50 per cent of the population had access to electricity. The government has announced intentions to increase capacity but this will depend on its ability to use flared natural gas.

Energy
Total energy consumption was estimated to be 0.77 quadrillion Btus in 2009. In 2010 total energy consuption was made up from, oil 13 per cent, natural gas 4 per cent, hydroelectricity 1 nadn traditional biomiass and waste, 82 per cent. Total per capita energy was estimated at 8.1 million Btus in 2007.

Manufacturing
This sector principally encompasses food-processing, brewing, petroleum-refining, iron and steel, motor vehicles, cigarettes, textiles, footwear, pharmaceuticals, cement, wood and paper pulp. Manufacturing contributed nearly 10 per cent of GDP in 2008 up from 5 per cent in 1997.

A large cement factory was opened in the central Jogi state in 2012. The Obajana plant is expected to produce an estimated 10 million tonnes of cement per year and is the largest cement factory in sub-Saharan Africa.

Agriculture
Nigeria is traditionally an agricultural country, and agriculture accounts for about 70 per cent of total employment. It contributed around 40 per cent of GDP in 2003. The major cash crops include cocoa, rubber, ground nuts, cotton, and palm nuts, while staple crops comprise rice, wheat, yams, cassava, cocoyams, sweet potatoes, sorghum, and millet. Recent figures show that the main cash crop, cocoa, is suffering from a migration of agricultural workers to the oil sector and poor weather. A governent plan (1999-2003) was designed to improve overall agricultural production.

Agricultural Production in 2010

Produce	Int. $'000*	Tonnes
Yams	5,947,259	29,148,200
Cassava	3,917,791	37,504,100
Citrus fruit, nes	1,576,945	3,488,400
Vegetables fresh nes	1,120,395	5,945,600
Groundnuts, with shell	1,106,055	2,636,230
Rice, paddy	872,025	3,218,760
Maize	816,120	7,305,530
Millet	700,088	4,124,560
Indigenous goat meat	696,924	290,859
Tomatoes	687,611	1,860,600
Sorghum	684,353	4,784,100
Indigenous cattle meat	656,705	243,100

* unofficial figures
Source: http://faostat.fao.org/site/339/default.aspx Food and Agriculture Organization of the United Nations, Food and Agricultural commodities production

Fisheries
In 2010 the estimated total catch for Nigeria according to FAOSTAT figures was 617,000 tonnes.

COMMUNICATIONS AND TRANSPORT

Travel Requirements
Citizens of the USA, Canada, Australia and the EU require a passport valid for at least six months beyond the length of stay, and a visa. Most transit passengers continuing their journey by the same or first connecting aircraft, provided holding valid onward or return documentation and not leaving the airport do not require a visa, but USA transit passengers do. Other nationals should contact the embassy to check visa requirements.

International Airports
Murtala Muhammed Airport at Ikeja is located 22 miles north-west of central Lagos. Over 5 million passengers used the airport in 2009. Other international airports are at Kano, Port Harcourt, Calabar and Abuja.

Railways
The network covers 3,500 km and consists of two main routes, Lagos-Kano and Port Harcourt-Enugu-Kaduna. The Nigerian Railway Corporation is based in Lagos, the railway is mainly used for the transportation of freight.

Roads
Roads are the key to interstate commerce. The roads cover over 193,000 km. About 15 per cent of the roads are hard-surfaced. The Nigerian Road Federation is based in Lagos. Vehicles are driven on the right.

Shipping
The main ports are Lagos-Apapa, Lagos-Tin Can Island, Port Harcourt, Warri and Calabar. The petroleum ports are Bonny and Burutu. The Nigerian National Shipping Line and Nigerian Green Lines handle shipping and foreign shipping lines.

Ferries operate along the south coast, there are also river ferries along the Niger and Benue rivers
Nigeria Ports Authority: http://www.nigeria-ports.com

HEALTH

Nigeria introduced the Basic Health Service in 1977 with a view to providing some level of health care for the population. In 2000-10 there were an estimated 55,376 doctors (4 per 10,000 population), 224,943 nurses and midwives (16 per 10,000 population), 3,781 dentistry personnel, 19,268 community health workers (1 per 10,000 population) and 18,682 pharmaceutical personnel . Total healthcare expenditure in Nigeria was the equivalent of 6.1 per cent of GDP in 2009. General government expenditure on health accounts for 5.9 per cent of total government expenditure and 35.1 per cent of total expenditure on health. Private expenditure on health was 64.9 per cent of health expenditure, almost all of it out-of-pocket expenditure. External resource accounted for 5.9 per cent.

Nigeria has the third most HIV infections (after India and South Africa), with some 4 million cases, and fighting the disease has become a priority. In May 2006, the government pledged to provide all anti-retroviral drugs free of charge. Funding is from a grant of $250 million from the Global Fund to fight AIDS, tuberculosis and malaria, and from money released after the cancellation of Nigeria's international debts. In 2009, the HIV/AIDS prevalence rate was 2,104 per 100,000 population.

In 2010, an estimated 58 per cent of the population (42 per cent rural, 75 per cent urban) had sustainable access to improved drinking water sources. In the same year, 30 per cent of the population (28 per cent rural, 36 per cent urban) had sustainable access to improved sanitation.

The infant mortality rate (probability of dying before first birthday) was 88 per 1,000 live births was in 2010 and the child mortality rate was 1,438 per 1,000 live births. The most common causes of deaths of children under 5 years old are: prematurity (12 per cent), malaria (20 per cent), pneumonia (17 per cent), diarrhoeal diseases (11 per cent), and HIV/AIDS (4 per cent). Immunization rates have risen in recent years and the vaccination rate for measles now stands at over 70 per cent. In 2005-11 just over 6 per cent of children slept under treated nets. An estimated 26.7 per cent of children under five years of age are classified as underweight and 41 per cent stunted. (Source: http://www.who.int, World Health Statistics 2012)

EDUCATION

Primary/Secondary Education
Free compulsory education is provided for six to 15 year olds. Primary education begins at six years old and ends at 11. Primary education includes instruction in either Hausa, Yoruba, or Ibo as well as English, French is taught in some private schools. Secondary education begins at 12 and ends at 18. Figures for 2006 show that 14 per cent of children were enrolled at pre-school and 67 per cent of girls and 73 per cent of boys were enrolled in primary school. Also that year 23 per cent of girls and 27 per cent of boys were enrolled at secondary school. The school life expectancy is estimated at 8.4 years. An estimated 3 per cent of children repeat primary education. The primary school pupil to teacher ratio was estimated at 37:1. (Source: UNESCO Institute for Statistics (UIS)

Higher Education
Some 0.38 million students enroll annually in higher education, either in one of the 30 universities or in a non-university establishment, comprising various specialised types of college, e.g. technology, paramedical, teacher training.

Vocational Education
Some types of secondary school are specifically vocational or technical. In addition, arrangements are made, outside the Education Ministry, for workers to continue their education. Those leaving at 14 can enter a four-year apprenticeship, with day release, leading to a professional certificate.

The literacy rate is estimated at 62.1 per cent for adults (71.0 for males, and 53.7 per cent for females). The youth literacy rate was estimated at 71.8 per cent (76.8 per cent for males and 67.1 per cent for females).

RELIGION

Around 45 per cent of the population are Muslims, 45 per cent are Christian and around 10 per cent hold traditional beliefs. Tensions rose between the Muslim and Christian communities at the beginning of 2000 following the imposition of Muslim Sharia law in 12 northern states.

Nigeria has a religious liberty rating of 4 on a scale of 1 to 10 (10 is most freedom). (Source: World Religion Database)

COMMUNICATIONS AND MEDIA

Although some restrictive laws exist, press freedom has improved and the media is generally in good condition. Criticism of the government appears. There are some reports of attacks on journalists.

Newspapers
There are more than 100 national and regional newspapers. Several newspapers are available online at http://www.nigeriatoday.com.
The Guardian, URL: http://www.ngrguardiannews.com
The Champion, URL: http://www.champion-newspapers.com/
The Punch, URL: http://www.punchng.com/
Daily Trust, URL: http://www.dailytrust.com/
The Vanguard, URL: http://www.vanguardngr.com/

Broadcasting
The Nigerian Television Authority, (NTA), which is government controlled, operates some 70 stations. There are several commercially run TV stations. Cable and satellite TV subscription services are available.

The government-controlled Federal Radio Corporation of Nigeria (FRCN) (URL: http://ww2.radionigeria.gov.ng/home2.php, broadcasts external services in English, French, Hausa, Arabic, German and Kiswahili and domestic services in English, Igbo, Izon; Efik, Tiv, Yoruba, Edo, Urhobo, Igala, Hausa, Kanuri, Fulfulde and Nupe.

The national regulatory authority is the Nigerian Communications Commission, URL: http://www.ncc.gov.ng

Telecommunications
The main line telephone network needs modernising and expansion. There are an estimated 1 million land lines in use and a further 85 million mobile telephones. According to 2009 estimates there are over 40 million internet users.

ENVIRONMENT

Nigeria's major environmental problems are deforestation, water pollution, droughts, soil degradation and increasing urbanisation. Nigeria suffers from occasional droughts and flooding. Its renewable water resources have been estimated at 286.2 cu km.

Nigeria is a party to the following international agreements: Biodiversity, Climate Change, Climate Change-Kyoto Protocol, Desertification, Endangered Species, Hazardous Wastes, Law of the Sea, Marine Dumping, Marine Life Conservation, Ozone Layer Protection, Ship Pollution, Wetlands.

Nigeria's emissions from the consumption of fossil fuels fell to 80 million metric tons of carbon dioxide in 2010, down from 100 million metric tons in 2008. (Source: EIA)

SPACE PROGRAMME

Nigeria's space agency was established in 1999 has an annual budget of US$50 million. In September 2003, Nigeria's first satellite, NigeriaSat-1, was launched from Plesetsk in Russia.
National Space Agency, URL: http://www.nasrda.gov.ng/

NORWAY

Kingdom of Norway

Kongeriket Norge

Capital: Oslo (Population estimate, 2011: 600,000)

Head of State King Harald V (Sovereign) (page 1438)

National Flag: Red, charged with a white cross bearing a cross of blue, the uprights slightly towards the hoist.

CONSTITUTION AND GOVERNMENT

Constitution
The present Norwegian Constitution was drafted by a National Assembly at Eidsvoll and proclaimed on 17 May 1814. The most recent amendment was passed in 23 July 1995. There are 112 articles. It lays down that the Kingdom of Norway is a free, independent, indivisible and inalienable Kingdom. Its form of government is a limited and hereditary monarchy. Executive power is vested in the King and legislation in the Parliament, the *Storting*. On 29 May 1990 a constitutional amendment was passed which gave both men and women equal rights to the throne. This new law will not affect the present male line of succession, but only those born after 1990. H.M. King Harald V succeeded to the throne on 17 January 1991.

The people's legislative power is exercised through the Storting which has two departments, the *Lagting* and the *Odelsting*. The Storting is composed of 169 members from 19 multi-member constituencies. The first meeting of the Storting elects from among its members 41 to constitute the Lagting, while the rest form the Odelsting. This division is of importance only with regard to proposals of laws which must be discussed separately in the Odelsting and the Lagting. All other decisions are made by the united Storting. The Storting may require modifications to be made in treaties with foreign powers and it is its prerogative, when and where necessary, to elect the heir to the throne, the King and the Regency. The King exercises his executive authority through the cabinet, called the *Statsråd*, composed of the prime minister and at least seven ministers. The Ministers are entitled to be present during sittings of the Storting and to take part in discussions but not to vote.

Parliamentary elections take place every four years. There are no by-elections. There is no constitutional provision to dissolve the Storting between elections.

In February 2007 the Constitution was amended to abolish the bicameral division of the Storting parliament after the 2009 elections.

To consult the constitution, please visit: http://www.stortinget.no/en/In-English/About-the-Storting/The-Constitution/The-Constitution/

Recent Events

Following two ministerial resignations, Jens Stoltenberg reshuffled his cabinet. The cabinet was appointed by King Harald V on 17 October 2005. It is a majority government representing the Labour Party, the Socialist Left Party and the Centre Party. The minister for trade and industry and the minister for petroleum and oil resigned in September 2007 and the cabinet was reshuffled. Elections took place in September 2009 and were won by the Labour Party.

On July 22 2011, 32 year old Anders Behring Breivik, carried out the worst peace time atrocity in Norway; he made and planted a bomb outside government buildings in central Oslo and then carried out a massacre of teenagers at an Labour Party island youth camp. There were 77 fatalities and 151 people were injured. Breivik has admitted that he carried out the attacks in Oslo and on Utoeya Island, but he has pleaded not guilty to terror charges, saying that the attacks were necessary in his fight to defend Europe from a Muslim invasion, which he felt that Labour Party and European Union policies were enabling. Breivik was due to stand trial in April 2012 but in November 2011 he was judged by two psychiatrists to be insane. This was later withdrawn and the trial began in April as planned and he was subsequently found guilty and sentenced to a minimum of 21 years.

In November 2011 in order to ensure Norway's preparedness to handle challenges caused by risks and threats, the role of the Ministry of Justice and the Police for security and preparedness was strengthened and clarified. Extra resources were allocated and its name changed to the Ministry of Justice and Public Security from 1 January 2012. Grete Faremo was appointed Minister of Justice and Public Security.

In June 2012, Norway's oil and gas production was under threat of being completely shut-down when an offshore workers strike began following plans by employers to increase the retirement age from 62 to 67. The Government had to intervene to stop the strike.

International Relations

Norway is not a member of the European Union; referendums on the EU were held in 1972 and 1994, and the no vote won on both occasions. Norway contributes to international peacekeeping operations and currently has troops in Afghanistan. Until 2004, Norway had troops on the ground in Bosnia-Herzegovina, and Norwegian troops were deployed in Iraq but they have now been withdrawn.

Norway asserts a territorial claim in Antarctica (Queen Maud Land and its continental shelf). Russia and Norway continue to dispute their maritime limits in the Barents Sea.

Legislature

The Norwegian electoral system is based on the principle of direct election and proportional representation. Voting is by secret ballot. The ballot is a vote for a list of representatives from a political party and the names on the party list are candidates representing that particular party. These candidates have been chosen on the nomination conventions of each party.

There are 19 counties in Norway which constitute the constituencies. The 19 constituencies have different numbers of seats in the Storting according to their size and population. Each constituency has a seat reserved as an "additional seat". The additional seats are assigned to even out discrepancies between the number of votes received and the number of seats in the Storting. The total number of seats is 169.

All men and women who are entitled to vote and who have resided in Norway for at least ten years are eligible for election to the Storting. The electoral period is four years and the Storting cannot be dissolved during an electoral period. All Norwegian subjects have the right to vote, provided that they have attained the age of 18 years at the latest in the year of the election and have not had their right to vote suspended.

The Parliament is now unicameral. On 20 February 2007, Article 76 in the Constitution was amended to abolish the Odelstinget (Lower Chamber) and the Lagtinget (Upper Chamber). These changes came into effect following the September 2009 elections and as of 1 October 2009 they ceased to exist.

Storting, Karl Johansgate 22, 0026 Oslo, Norway. Tel: + 47 23 31 30 50, fax: +47 23 31 38 50, e-mail: stortinget.postmottak@stortinget.no, URL: http://www.stortinget.no
President of the Storting: Dag Terje Andersen (Labour Party)

Cabinet (as at June 2013)

Prime Minister: Jens Stoltenberg (Lab.) (page 1520)
Minister of the Environment: Bård Vegar Solhjell (Socialist Left Party) (page 1517)
Minister of Local Government and Regional Development: Liv Signe Navarsete (Cent.)
Minister of Foreign Affairs: Espen Barth Eide (page 1419) (Lab.)
Minister of Justice and Public Security: Grete Faremo (page 1423) (Lab.)
Minister of Finance: Sigbjorn Johnsen (Lab.) (page 1450)
Minister of Trade and Industry: Tronde Giske (Ap) (page 1431)
Minister of Defence: Anne-Grete Strom-Erichsen (Lab.)
Minister of Health and Care Services: Jonas Gahr Støre (page 1427) (Lab.)
Minister of Education and Research: Kristin Halvorsen (Soc.)
Minister & Chief of Staff, Office of the Prime Minister: Karl Eirik Schjott-Pedersen (Lab.)
Minister of Labour: Anniken Huitfeldt (page 1445) (Lab.)
Minister of Government Administration, Reform and Church Affairs, Minister for Nordic co-operation: Rigmor Aasrud (Lab.)
Minister of Fisheries and Coastal Affairs: Lisbeth Berg-Hansen (Lab.)
Minister of Transport and Communications: Marit Arnstad (Cent.)
Minister of Petroleum and Energy: Ola Borten Moe (Cent.)
Minister of International Development: Heikki Hollmas
Minister of Children, Equality and Social Inclusion: Inge Marte Thorkildsen
Minister of Agriculture and Food: Trgve Slagsvold Vedum (Cent)
Minister of Culture: Hadia Tajik

Secretaries of State (as of June 2013)
To the Prime Minister
Rita Skjaervik (Lab.)
Tor Brostigen (Soc.)
Erik Lahnstein (Cent.)
Hans Kristain Amundsen
Snorre Wikstrøm (Lab.)
Inger-Anne Ravlum
Mette Nord (Lab.)
Ministry of Finance
Hilde Singsaas
Kjetil Lund
Roger Schjerva (Soc.)
Morten Søberg
Ministry of Local Government and Regional Development
Anne Beathe Kristiansen (Cent.)
Eli Blakstad (Centre)
Erlend Fuglum (Centre)
Ministry of Foreign Affairs
Gry Larsen (Lab.)
Torgeir Larsen
Ministry of Defence
Eirik Øwre Thorshaug
Ministry of the Environment
Henriette Killi Westhrin (SV)
Ketil Raknes
Ministry of Petroleum and Energy
Ane Hansdatter Kismul
Ministry of Education and Research
Elisabet Dahle (Socialist Left)
Katrine Gramnaes (Socialist Left)
Ministry of Justice and the Police
Kristin Bergersen (Lab.)
Pal Lønseth (Lab.)
Ministry of Health and Care Services
Robin Martin Kass
Kjell Erik Øie
Ministry of Transport and Communications
Lars Erik Bartnes (Cent.)
Geir Pollestad
Ministry of Agriculture and Food
Erlend Grimstad
Ministry of Culture
Mina Gerhardsen
Kjersti Stenseng
Ministry of Trade and Industry
Jeaneete Iren Moen
Ministry of Government Administration, Reform and Church Affairs
Tone Toften (Lab.)
Ragnhild Vassvik Kalstad (Lab.)
Ministry of International Development
Torgeir Larsen
Ministry of Children and Social Inclusion
Ahmad Ghanizadeh

Sami Parliament, Sametinget, Ávjovárgeaidnu 50, NO-9730 Karasjok/Kárá.ajjohka, Norway. E-mail: samediggi@samediggi.no, URL: http://samediggi.no/

The Sámediggi is elected every fourth year by the Sámi people. The elections are held concurrently with general parliamentary elections. Prior to the election in 2009, the number of constituencies was reduced from 13 to 7, and the number of members of parliament was cut from 43 to 39.

Elections are due to take place on 9 September 2013. Results were not known at the time of going to press.

Sami Parliament Council (as of June 2013)
Sami Parliament: President: Egil Olli (AP)
Vice President: Odd Iver Sara (Arja)
Council member: Vibeke Larson (AP)
Council member: Marianne Balto (AP)
Council member: Ellinor Marita Jåma (Aarjel-Saemiej Geith)

Ministries
Office of the King, Det Kongelige Slott, 0010 Oslo, Norway. Tel: +47 2204 8700, URL: http://www.kongehuset.no/
Office of the Prime Minister, Akersgaten 42, PB 8001 Dep, 0030 Oslo, Norway. Tel: +47 2224 9090, fax: +47 2224 9500, e-mail: postmottak@smk.dep.no, URL: http://www.odin.dep.no/smk
Ministry of Agriculture and Food, Akersgaten 59, PB 8007 Dep, 0030 Oslo, Norway. Tel: +47 2224 9090, fax: +47 2224 9555, e-mail: postmottak@lmd.dep.no, URL: http://www.odin.dep.no/lmd
Ministry of Children, Equality and Social Inclusion, Akersgaten 59, PB 8036 Dep, 0030 Oslo, Norway. Tel: +47 2224 9090, fax: +47 2224 9515, e-mail: postmottak@bfd.dep.no. URL: http://odin.dep.no/bld
Ministry of Culture, Akersgaten 59, PB 8030 Dep, 0030 Oslo, Norway. Tel: +47 2224 7839, fax: +47 2224 9550, e-mail: postmottak@kkd.dep.no, URL: http://www.odin.dep.no/kkd
Ministry of Defence, Myntgaten 1, PB 8126 Dep, 0032 Oslo, Norway. Tel: +47 2309 8000, fax: +47 2309 6075, e-mail: postmottak@fd.dep.no, URL: http://www.odin.dep.no/fd

NORWAY

Ministry of Education and Research, Akersgaten 44 , PB 8119 Dep, 0032 Oslo, Norway. Tel: +47 2224 9090, e-mail: eg@kd.dep.no, URL: http://www.odin.dep.no/ufd

Ministry of the Environment and International Development, Myntgaten 2, PB 8013 Dep, 0030 Oslo, Norway. Tel: +47 2224 9090, fax: +47 2224 9560, e-mail: postmottak@md.dep.no, URL: http://www.odin.dep.no/md

Ministry of Finance, Akersgaten 42, PB 8008 Dep, 0030 Oslo, Norway. Tel: +47 2224 9090, fax: +47 2224 9505, URL: http://www.odin.dep.no/fin

Ministry of Fisheries and Coastal Affairs, Grubbegaten 8, PB 8118 Dep, 0032 Oslo, Norway. Tel: +47 2224 6400, fax: +47 2224 9585, e-mail: postmottak@fkd.dep.no, URL: http://www.odin.dep.no/fkd/

Ministry of Foreign Affairs, 7 juni plassen 1, PB 8114 Dep, 0032 Oslo, Norway. Tel: +47 2224 3600, fax: +47 2224 9580, e-mail: post@mfa.no, URL: http://www.odin.dep.no/ud/

Ministry of Government Administration, Reform and Church Affairs, Akersgaten 59, PO Box 8004 Dep, 0030 Oslo, Norway. Tel: +47 2224 9090, URL: http://www.odin.dep.no/fad

Ministry of Health and Care Services, PB 8011 Dep, 0030 Oslo, Norway. Tel: +47 2224 9090, fax: +47 2224 9575, URL: http://www.odin.dep.no/hod

Ministry of Justice and Public Security, Akersgaten 42, PB 8005 Dep, 0030 Oslo, Norway. Tel: +47 2224 9090, fax: +47 2224 9530, URL: http://www.odin.dep.no/jd/

Ministry of Labour, PB 8019, Dep. 0030 Norway. Tel: +47 2224 9090, fax: +47 2224 9575, URL: http://www.odin.dep.no/aid

Ministry of Local Government and Regional Development, Akersgaten 59, PO Box 8112 Dep, 0032 Oslo, Norway. Tel:+47 2224 9090, fax: +47 2224 9545, URL: http://www.odin.dep.no/krd/

Ministry of Petroleum and Energy, PB 8148 Dep, 0033, Oslo, Norway. Tel: +47 2224 9090, fax: +47 2224 9565, e-mail: postmottak@oed.dep.no, URL: http://www.odin.dep.no/oed

Ministry of Trade and Industry, PO Box 8014 Dep, 0030 Oslo, Norway. Tel: +47 2224 9090, e-mail: postmottak@nhd.dep.no, URL: http://www.odin.dep.no/nhd

Ministry of Transport and Communications, Akersgaten 59, PO Box 8010 Dep, 0030 Oslo, Norway. Tel:+47 2224 9090, fax: +47 2224 9570, e-mail: postmottak@sd.dep.no, URL: http://www.odin.dep.no/sd

Political Parties

Det Norske Arbeiderparti (DNA, Norwegian Labour Party), PO Box 8743, Youngstorget, 0184 Oslo 1, Norway. Tel: +47 2414 4000, fax: +47 2414 4001, e-mail: dna@dna.no, URL: http://www.dna.no
Leader: Jens Stoltenberg (page 1520)

Fremskrittspartiet (FP, Progress Party), PO Box 8903, Youngstorget, 0028 Oslo 1, Norway. Tel: +47 2241 0769, fax, +47 2242 3255, e-mail: frp@frp.no, URL: http://www.frp.no
Chairman: Siv Jensen (page 1449)

Høyres Hovedorganisasjion (H, Conservative), PO Box 1536, Vika, 0117 Oslo, Norway. Tel: +47 2282 9000, fax: +47 2282 9080, e-mail: politikk@hoyre.no, URL: http://www.hoyre.no
Chair: Erna Solberg

Kristelig Folkeparti (KRK, Christian Democratic Party), Ovre Slottsgt. 18-20, PO Box 478 Sentrum, 0105 Oslo, Norway. Tel: +47 2310 2800, fax: +47 2310 2810, e-mail: krf@krf.no, URL: http://www.krf.no
President: Knut Arild Hareide

Senterpartiet (SP, Centre Party), Kristian Augustsgt. 7B, 0130 Oslo 1, Norway. Tel: +47 2298 9600, fax: +47 2298 9610, e-mail: post@senterpartiet.no, URL: http://www.senterpartiet.no
Leader: Liv Signe Navarsete

Sosialistisk Venstreparti (SV, Socialist Left Party), Storgt. 45, 0182 Oslo 1, Norway. Tel: +47 2193 3300, fax: +47 2193 3301, e-mail: post@sv.no, URL: http://www.sv.no
Leader: Kristian Halvorsen

Venstre (V, Liberal), Møllergt. 16, 0179 Oslo, Norway. Tel: +47 2240 4350, fax: +47 2242 4351, e-mail: venstre@venstre.no, URL: http://www.venstre.no
Leader: Trine Skei Grande

Kystpartiet (Coastal People's Party), e-mail: post@kystpartiet.no, URL: http://www.kystpartiet.no
Leader: Kjell Ivar Vestå

Norges Kommunistiske Parti (Communist Party), Postboks 9288, Grønland, 0134 Oslo, Norway. Tel: +47 2271 6044, e-mail: nkp@nkp.no, URL: http://www.nkp.no
Leader: Zafer Gözet

Elections
Seats Won

Party	2005 Election	2009 Election
Labour Party	61	64
Progress Party	38	41
Conservative Party	23	30
Centre Party	11	11
Socialist Left	15	11
Liberals	10	2
Christian Democrats	11	10

The Labour government resigned in October 1997 paving the way for a three-party coalition of the Christian, Liberal and Centre parties headed by Kjell Magne Bondevik, the Christian Party leader. Bondevik resigned on 9 March 2000 following a vote of no confidence over a dispute about energy generation and carbon dioxide emissions and Jens Stoltenberg of the DNA (Labour Party) became Prime Minister.

At the election held in September 2001 the Labour Party had its worst result for some years and won only 43 seats. In October this Labour minority government resigned and was replaced by a coalition of the Christian Democrats, the Conservatives and the Liberals, with support from the Progress Party. The coalition was led by Christian Democrat, Kjell Magne Bondevik.

The legislative elections took place on 12 September 2005. It was won by a coalition led by Jens Stoltenberg's Labour Party (AP), together with the Socialist Left (SV) and Centre (SP) parties. Jens Stoltenberg, leader of the AP, was sworn in as prime minister on 17 October 2005 at the head of a coalition government made up of the three parties.

Elections to the Norwegian parliament, the Sami Assembly and State church local and dioceses councils took place on 14 September 2009. Prime Minister Jens Stoltenberg's Labour Party remained in power.

Diplomatic Representation

British Embassy, Thomas Heftyesgate 8, 0244 Oslo, Norway. Tel: +47 23 132700, fax: 47 23 132741, e-mail: britemb@online.no, URL: http://ukinnorway.fco.gov.uk/en
Ambassador: Jane Owen (page 1491)

US Embassy, Drammensveien 18, 0244 Oslo, Norway. Tel: +47 2244 8550, fax: +47 2243 8377, e-mail: irc@usa.no, URL: http://norway.usembassy.gov/
Ambassador: Barry White (page 1536)

Norwegian Embassy, 25 Belgrave Square, London, SW1X 8QD, United Kingdom. Tel: +44 (0)20 7591 5500, fax: +44 (0)20 7245 6993, e-mail: emb.london@mfa.no, URL: http://www.norway.org.uk
Ambassador: Kim Traavik (page 1527)

Norwegian Embassy, 2720 34th Street NW, Washington, USA. Tel: +1 202 333 6000, fax: +1 202 337 0870, e-mail: emb.washington@mfa.no, URL: http://www.norway.org
Ambassador: Wegger Christian Strommen

Permanent Mission of Norway to the United Nations
825 Third Avenue, 39th Floor, New York, NY 10022, USA. Tel: +1 212 421 0280, fax: +1 212 688 0554, e-mail: delan@mfa.no, URL: http://www.norway-un.org
Ambassador to the UN: Ambassador Geir O. Pedersen

The Foreign Service, Postal address: Postboks 8114 Dep, 0032 Oslo, Norway. Tel: +47 2224 3600, fax: +47 2224 9580. Visiting address: 7 juni plass/1 Victoria Terrasse 7, Oslo, Norway

The Royal Family
The Royal Family consists of HM King Harald V, HM Queen Sonja, HRH Crown Prince Haakon, HRH Crown Princess Mette-Marit and Princess Märtha Louise. HRH Crown Prince Haakon and HRH Crown Princess Mette-Marit have one daugher, HRH Princess Ingrid Alexandra, born January 2004 and one son HRH Prince Sverre Magnus, born 2005. Princess Märtha Louise and her husband, Ari Behn, have one daughter, Maud Angelica Behn, who is fourth in line to the throne.

LEGAL SYSTEM

Norwegian law is based on customary law, a civil law system, and common law traditions.

The courts of general jurisdiction are the District (also known as Rural and Urban Municipal Courts) and City courts. The judicial system is organised so that there are three levels of court for criminal cases and four levels for civil cases. In the District Court most civil cases are decided by a single professional judge. Most criminal cases are decided by a professional judge assisted by two lay judges. In special criminal cases, the court may be fortified with one extra professional judge and one extra lay judge. Some criminal cases can be decided by a single professional judge, but only if the defendant admits his offence. Before a civil case reaches the District Court it has, as a rule, to be subjected to mediation by a conciliation council (one for each municipality) consisting of laymen who try to help the parties come to an agreement. A conciliation council has jurisdiction to decide cases of minor importance and is considered the lowest court instance in civil cases. There are currently 65 District Courts.

There are six High Courts/Courts of Appeal (*Lagmannsrett*). They are: the Borgarting Court of Appeal, Oslo; the Eidsivating Court of Appeal, Hamar; the Agder Court of Appeal, Skien; the Gulating Court of Appeal, Bergen; the Frostating Court of Appeal, Trondheim; the Halogaland Court of Appeal, Tromso. In the Courts of Appeal a civil case is decided by three professional judges; lay judges may participate at the request of either party, each court is led by a chief court of appeals judge. Due to a criminal procedure reform in 1995, all criminal cases are now heard in the first instance by the District Courts. Prior to this reform more serious criminal cases were started in the Courts of Appeal. All demands of review of decisions by the District Courts are now referred to the Court of Appeal. In more serious criminal appeals the issue of guilt is decided by a jury of 10 laymen, four of whom are chosen by lot to assess, with the professional judges, any punishment. The maximum sentence is 21 years.

The Supreme Court *Høyesterett* consists of 18 permanent judges under the presidency of the Chief Justice. During a regular session of the court a case is decided by five judges; in special cases the Supreme Court may sit in plenum. The Appeals Selection Committee of the Supreme Court is classed as a separate court and consists of three judges. All judges serve both the Supreme Court and on the Committee. As well as adjudicating on interlocutory appeals, the Committee also functions as a filter for appeals in both civil and criminal cases. No appeal may be brought before the Supreme Court without the consent of the Committee. Decisions made by the Supreme Court are final and may not be appealed.

There are a few special courts in Norway, the most important of which is the Labour Disputes Court. All judges are appointed by the King-in-Council, on the advice of the Ministry of Justice.

In general, the government respects the rights of its citizens. The death penalty was abolished in 1905.

Norwegian Centre for Human Rights, URL: http://www.jus.uio.no/smr/english/

The Supreme Court of Norway, URL: http://www.domstol.no/
Chief Justice of the Supreme Court of Norway: Tore Schei

Justices of the Supreme Court of Norway: Karin M. Bruzelius, Kirsti Coward, Hans Flock, Liv Gjølstad, Karenanne Gussgard, Magnus Matningsdal, Jens Edvin A. Skoghøy, Ingse-Else Stabel, Ole Bjørn Støle, Steinar Tjomsland, Karl Arne Utgård, Toril M. Øie, Bård Tønder, Clemet Endresen, Hilde Indreberg, Arnfinn Bårdsen, Erik Møse, Bergljot Webster, Wilhelm Matheson. (Source: The Supreme Court.)

LOCAL GOVERNMENT

The current local government system is based on the Local Government Act of 1847, substantially revised in 1993. Norway is divided into 430 municipalities and 19 counties. The capital, Oslo, is classed as both a municipality and a county. Both municipalities and counties have extensive local self-government and can undertake any task except those explicitly prohibited by law. However local self-government is not in the constitution and the Local Government Act can be changed by a majority in the Storting.

The municipalities' most important tasks concern primary schools, primary health care, public relief, water supply, sanitation, electricity distribution, building and maintenance of local roads. The counties' main concerns are hospitals, secondary education and local communication. Both the municipalities and the counties have taxation rights, but their expenditures are also covered by grants from central government. Municipal and county councils are elected by proportional representation for a term of four years. Each county has a Governor and five cities (Olso, Bergen, Stravanger, Trondheim and Tromso) have mayors.

The most recent local elections were held in 12 September 2011. All 430 municipalities and 20 county councils (incl. Svalbard) were up for re-election. Each municipality's local legislature is elected through proportional representation, and in most cases and in the largest cities the mayor is not elected directly. There are 727 county councillors overall. In the municipal elections the Labour Party (Ap) won 3,381 seats (31.7 per cent of the vote), the Conservative Party 2,352 seats (28 per cent), Progress Party 1,141 seats (11.4 per cent), Center Party 1,419 seats (6.8 per cent), Liberal Party 639 seats (6.3 per cent), Christian People's Party 652 seats (5.6 per cent), Socialist Left 361 seats (4.1 per cent), Red, 57 seats (1.7 per cent), Others 3.6 per cent (13 seats).

In the County Council elections the Labour Party won 33.2 per cent and the Conservative Party 37.6 per cent.

The following table lists the 19 counties and their populations:

County	Pop. 1 Jan. 2012	Area
Østfold	278,352	3,922
Akershus	556,254	4,620
Olso	613,285	427
Hedmark	192,791	26,244
Oppland	187,147	23,878
Buskerud	265,164	13,870
Vestfold	236,424	2,157
Telemark	170,023	13,894
Aust-Agder	111,495	8,353
Vest-Agder	174,324	6,706
Rogalund	443,115	8,605
Hordaland	490,570	14,554
Sogn og Fjordane	108,201	17,709
Møre og Romsdal	256,628	14,614
Sør-Trøndelag	297,950	17,909
Nord-Trøndelag	133,390	20,881
Nordland	238,320	36,194
Troms Romsa	158,650	24,950
Finnmark Finnmárku	73,787	45,984
Source: Statistics Norway		

Governor of Svalbard: Per Sefland, URL: http://www.sysselmannen.no/

Mayor of Oslo: Fabian Stang, URL: http://www.oslo.kommune.no/
Mayor of Bergen: Trude H. Drevland, URL: http://www.bergen.kommune.no/
Mayor of Stavanger: Leif J. Sevland, URL: http://www.stavanger.kommune.no/
Mayor of Trondheim: Rita Ottervik, URL: http://www.trondheim.kommune.no/
Mayor of Tromsø: Jens Johan Hjort, URL: http://www.tromso.kommune.no/

AREA AND POPULATION

Area
Norway's total area (including Svalbard and Jan Mayen) is 385,155 sq. km and it shares borders with Sweden (1,619 km), Finland (727 km), and the Russian Federation (196 km). About half the country lies inside the Arctic Circle. Three-quarters of the country's area is mountainous and the distance from the northernmost to the southernmost point is 1,752 km. It has a coastline, including fjords and inlets, of 21,347 km. Land use breaks down thus: 50 per cent of the area is mountains, plateaus and moors, 23 per cent is productive forest, 15 per cent is unproductive forest, 12 per cent is wild landscape, 5 per cent is fresh water, 3 per cent is agricultural, and 1 per cent is built upland.

Norway has three dependencies in the Antarctic: Queen Maud's Land (on the mainland), Peter I Island and Bouvet Island.

There are strong regional climatic variations. It is generally warmer and wetter than other countries at similar latitudes. The northernmost part has a maritime sub-arctic climate. The southern and western parts experience more precipitation with milder winters. The lowlands around Oslo have warm, sunny summers and cold winters. Because of its high latitude there are seasonal variations in daylight. From late May to late July the sun never completely descends beneath the horizon in areas north of the Arctic Circle while the rest of the country experiences up to 20 hours of daylight a day. However from late November to late January the sun does not rise above the horizon in the north and the rest of the country experiences short daylight hours.

To view a map, consult http://www.lib.utexas.edu/maps/cia08/norway_sm_2008.gif

Population
In January 2012, the total population was estimated to be 4,985,870. The annual increase in 2011 was 52,724. The population growth is mainly due to immigration and is concentrated in urban areas. Of the total population, 415,300 were foreign citizens (8.3 per cent of total population). Most immigrants in 2010-11 came from Poland. The number of immigrants was recorded at 666,961 in 2008, compared to 223,615 emigrants.

The Sami are an indigenous people of the far north of Norway and are approximately 30,000 in number.

Norway's population is expected to continue to rise. By 2020 it is expected to reach 4,975,000 (PGR, 0.53 per cent); and by 2050 it is expected to reach 5,591,000 (PGR, 0.28 per cent).

Total average population density is 16 per km^2. However, 80 per cent of people live in urban areas and average population density in urban areas is 1,580 residents per km^2. In 2007, Norway had 917 urban settlements of which 19 had a population of more than 20,000. Four settlements had a population of more than 100,000. Oslo is the city with the greatest population, (Urban area) 906,681 as of January 1 2011, followed by Bergen, 235,046, Stavanger, 197,852, Trondheim, 164,953, Fredrikstad, 104,382, Drammen, 100,303, Porsgrunn, 88,335, Kristiansand, 69,380, and Tromsø, 56,466.

In 2007, 19 per cent of the population were aged 0-14 years old, 12.8 per cent 15-24 years, 34.8 per cent 25-49 years, 18.7 per cent 50-64 years, 10.1 per cent 65-79 years and 4.6 per cent were over 80 years old. The median age in 2008 was 39 years. Average life expectancy in 2008 was 78 years for males, and 83 years for women. By 2050 this is expected to rise to 81.6 for males and 81.9 for females.

The Norwegians have two official written languages, standard Norwegian and New Norwegian, which has been developed over the last 100 years.

Births, Marriages, Deaths
In 2009 there were 61,807 live births (31,833 boys and 29,974 girls). An estimated 34,038 births occurred outside of marriage. There were 117 stillbirths. Figures for 2011 show that there were 60,220 births.

In 2008, the average fertility rate was 1.96 per woman, up from the 2007 rate of 1.9 which represented the highest rate since 1991. The increase is attributed to births due to immigrants. In 2007, 46 per cent of children were born to married parents, and 42 per cent had cohabiting parents. An estimated 11 per cent were born to a single mother. Infant mortality was 3.2 per 1,000 live births for boys and 2.9 per 1,000 live births for girls in 2007.

Figures for 2007 show that 23,471 marriages took place, 1,750 more than the previous year. In 2006, 227 registered partnerships were contracted. There were 10,280 divorces in 2007. Over 50 per cent of marriages currently end in divorce. In 2005, 62 registered partnerships were ended by divorce.

In 2011 there were an estimated 41,393 deaths. (Source: Statistics Norway, http://www.ssb.no)

Public Holidays 2014
1 January: New Year's Day
13 April: Palm Sunday
17 April: Maundy Thursday
18 April: Good Friday
20 April: Easter Sunday
21 April: Easter Monday
5 May: Public Holiday
29 May: Ascension Day
17 May: Constitution Day
9 June: Whit Monday
25 December: Christmas Day
26 December: Boxing Day

EMPLOYMENT

Employment is relatively high in Norway; in 2011 the labour force was 2,629,000 people (1,387,000 males and 1,243,000 females). An average of 86,000 people were unemployed in 2011 (compared with 94,000 people in 2010). Figures for January 1 2011 put the unemployment rate at 3.3 per cent.

Employment persons by major industry division.

Industry	2011
Agriculture and forestry	54,700
Fishing and aquaculture	15,100
Mining & quarrying	5,200
Oil and gas extraction inc services	54,000
Manufacturing	245,400
Electricity, gas and steam	13,100
Water supply, sewerage, waste	14,100
Construction	196,100
Wholesale and retail trade, repair of motor vehicles	369,600
Transport via pipelines	400

NORWAY

- continued

Ocean transport	44,000
Other transport activities	110,700
Postal and courier activities	19,800
Transport and storage	140,000
Accommodation and food services	79,400
Information and communication	87,500
Finance & insurance	53,700
Real estate activities	25,500
Professional, scientific and technical activities	121,300
Admin. & support services	111,200
Public admin. & defence	157,000
Education	199,000
Health & social work	542,600
Arts, entertainment and other services	89,100

Source: Statistics Norway, http://www.ssb.no/english/yearbook/tab/tab-209.html

BANKING AND FINANCE

Currency
One Kroner (NOK) = 100 öre

GDP/GNP, Inflation, National Debt
Statistics Norway estimated GDP for 2009 at 2.400 billion NOK, compared to 2.271 billion in 2007. The total GDP for 2006 was put at 2,155,780 million NOK compared to 1,939,217 million NOK in 2005 and NOK 1,710,402 million in 2004. GDP per capita was NOK 483,550 in 2007 and NOK 516 076 on January 1 2011. The following table shows value added by kind of activity at basic values in million kroner.

Gross Domestic Product by Activity, Million NOK

Activity	2000	2009	2011*
GDP	1,481,242	2,356,599	2,720,499
Agriculture, hunting & forestry	15,679	14,692	15,775
Fishing and fish farming	11,634	14,391	19,528
Oil and gas extraction	325,659	537,301	614,836
Mining and quarrying	2,575	4,089	5,011
Manufacturing	138,231	170,973	187,659
Electricity, gas & steam supply	24,533	50,309	59,593
Water supply	1,891	12,522	15,319
Construction	53,633	121,389	142,893
Wholesale & retail trade	166,171	171,069	180,727
Hotels & restaurants	18,832	28,789	31,529
Transport via pipelines	14,981	18,348	13,996
Ocean transport	26,708	25,100	6,641
Other transport activities	45,422	62,706	59,183
Post	8,581	10,810	10,420
Communications	46,921	81,875	86,724
Financial intermediation, insurance	39,602	97,194	106,366
Residential services	64,179	93,942	103,623
Business services	26,601	56,782	69,363
Professional, scientific and technical services	39,999	92,086	102,157
Real estate activities	29,081	62,992	71,989
Public admin. & defence	72,075	119,083	131,441
Education	56,332	98,090	108,387
Health & social work	102,979	209,623	238,340
Art, entertainment and other service activities	28,747	41,161	46,095

*Provisional figures
Source: Statistics Norway

GNI was 1,939,217 million NOK in 2005.

Inflation has been low in Norway for several years. It is currently estimated at 2.6 per cent. Gross external debt was estimated at 3.388 billion NOK in Q3, 2009.

Norway has also been hit by the global economic downturn. In December 2008 the Central Bank announced that the risk of a significant downturn to the economy had increased. It warned that GDP was likely to contract in the last quarter of 2008 and the first of 2009, despite a forecast of continued growth made in the third quarter of 2008. Its sovereign wealth lost over 70 billion euros. Money from oil and gas sales is used to buy international stocks and bonds as a fund for future generations when the oil runs out. These funds have been severely affected by the global crisis.

Foreign Investment
Norway is heavily dependent on foreign trade. Recent figures show that total exports and imports account for over 70 per cent of GDP. Norway participates in the major international economic and trade organisations such as EFTA, OECD, the IMF and the WTO. Although an agreement was negotiated for EU membership, a national referendum in 1994 rejected joining the EU with 52.2 per cent of the vote. Norway had previously rejected joining the EEC in 1972.

At the end of 2005, total foreign direct investment was an estimated NOK 325,221 million. Almost 60 per cent of total outward direct investment was in EU countries.

Balance of Payments, NOK million

	2000	2007	2011*
Exports, total	689,316	1,039,693	1,145,179
Imports, total	435,895	691,404	769,750
Balance of goods/services	253,421	348,289	375,429
Balance of income & current transfers	-31,043	-27,786	18,512
Current account balance	222,378	320,503	393,941
Net lending	221,513	319,532	392,442

*provisional figures
Source: Statistics Norway, http://www.ssb.no/english/yearbook/tab/tab-304.html

Norway's imports and exports reached an all-time high in 2004. Preliminary figures show imports of NOK 320.3 bn and exports of NOK 548.6 bn. The trade surplus for external trade in goods, excluding ships and oil platforms, reached NOK 228.3 bn. The high trade surplus is due largely to the high price of crude oil. Export prices continued to increase in 2005 to 865,267 million NOK. Import costs were 546,340 million NOK.

The following table shows imports of traditional commodities for 2007 and 2010. The figures exclude ships and oil platforms. Figures are in NOK million.

Imports

Commodity	2009	2011*
Total	660,408	769,750
Crude oil & natural gas	13,633	14,739
Ships, oil platforms, aircraft	31,649	36,124
Other goods	398,761	470,105
Agriculture, forestry & fishing	11,971	14,396
Mining and quarrying	4,446	6,209
Manufacturing products	380,559	444,419
Food products, beverages & tobacco	23,798	28,224
Textiles, wearing apparel. leather & leather products	23,291	26,946
Wood products	8,313	10,104
Pulp, paper & paper products	7,778	8,085
Printing & publishing	69	60
Refined petroleum products	19,722	28,861
Basic chemicals, chemical & mineral products	60,887	69,479
Basic metals	52,588	69,846
Machinery & other equipment	139,929	147,360
Furniture and other manufacturing products	21,115	22,628
Transport equipment non-competitive imports	19,186	29,119
Electricity	1,785	5,081
Other goods excl. refined petroleum goods	379,039	441,244
Services	216,365	248,782

*Provisional figures
Source: http://www.ssb.no/english/yearbook/tab/tab-300.html

The following table shows exports of commodities. Figures are in NOK million.

Exports

Commodity	2009	2011*
Total	929,116	1,145,179
Crude oil & natural gas	416,054	562,366
Ships, oil platforms, aircraft	11,878	13,653
Other goods	277,181	316,420
Agriculture, forestry & fishing	21,211	25,954
Mining & quarrying	4,119	5,543
Manufacturing products	247,444	280,644
Food products, beverages & tobacco	27,900	32,696
Textiles, wearing apparel, leather	1,944	2,074
Wood products	2,055	2,253
Pulp, paper & paper products	9,190	9,539
Printing & publishing	24	15
Refined petroleum products	21,402	38,341
Basic chemicals, chemical & mineral products	41,062	49,691
Basic metals	56,980	70,817
Machinery & other equipment n.e.c	82,067	69,923
Furniture & other manufacturing products	4,552	5,063
Transport equipment, non-competitive imports	268	232
Electricity	4,407	4,279
Other goods excl. refined petroleum goods	255,779	278,079
Services	224,003	252,740

Source: http://www.ssb.no/english/yearbook/tab/tab-298.html

The following table shows main trading partners in traditional commodities. Imports exclude ships and oil platforms. Exports exclude ships, oil platforms, crude oil, condensates and natural gas. Figures are in NOK million and are preliminary.

Value of Imports and Exports, main trading countries, NOK million

Country	Imports 2011	Exports 2011
Sweden	68,254.7	58,150.3
Germany	60,984.4	95,004.8
United Kingdom	28,518.1	249,791.7
Denmark	32,357.2	32,372.7
China	46,196.8	16,230.0
USA	27,242.0	49,858.5

- continued

Canada	20,635.0	14,467.4
Netherlands	21,282.9	103,333.5
France	16,540.9	58,428.8
Finland	12,908.3	14,127.4
Italy	13,175.5	20,643.9
Japan	11,063.4	10,334.5

Source: http://www.ssb.no/english/yearbook/tab/tab-314.html

Central Bank

Norges Bank, PO Box 1179, Sentrum, N-0107 Oslo, Norway. Tel: +47 2231 6000, fax: +47 2241 3105, e-mail: central.bank@norges-bank.no, URL: http://www.norges-bank.no Governor: Øystein Olsen (page 1489) (term of office 2011-2016) Deputy Governor: Jan F. Qvigstad

Chambers of Commerce and Trade Organisations

Oslo Chamber of Commerce, URL: http://www.chamber.no
Bergen Chamber of Commerce and Industry, URL: http://www.bergen-chamber.no
Stavanger Chamber of Commerce, URL: http://www.stavanger-chamber.no/
Tromso Chamber of Commerce and Industry, URL: http://www.tromso-chamber.no
Trondheim Chamber of Commerce, URL: http://www.trondheim-chamber.no
Oslo Stock Exchange, URL: http://www.oslobors.no
Innovation Norway, URL: http://www.ntc.no, http://www.eksport.no

MANUFACTURING, MINING AND SERVICES

Primary and Extractive IndustriesOil and Gas

Norway's oil and gas industry accounts for approximately 21 per cent of GDP, with oil accounting for roughly 40 per cent of Norway's total export revenues. There are about 52 oil fields and 43 gas producing fields around the coast of southern Norway. In 2005 the biggest oil fields were Ekofisk, Trollvest and Grane. Two fields, Volve and Alvheim, started their production in 2008. In May 2009, the government approved a plan for the development and the operation of the Goliat oil field, the first oil field in the Barents Sea to be developed. The field is estimated to contain approximately 200 million barrels of oil reserves. Production is expected to start in 2013.

In 2009, Norway estimated it would spend 145.7 billion NOK on investments in oil and gas, including pipeline transportation. An estimated 29.1 billion is to be spent on exploration activity. In 2006 Norway increased its exploration for oil in Arctic waters and the Barents Sea despite environmentalists fears for the environment. The government has limited drilling in a 31-mile zone near the Norwegian coast to protect the environment. The protected area includes the Lofoten islands.

Norway's oil reserves stood at 5.3 billion barrels as of 2012 and are estimated to last for a further 20 years; these reserves represent the largest of any country in Europe, and 50 per cent of Western European reserves. Oil production for 2011 was estimated at 2.00 million barrels per day. In 2012 the crude oil refining capacity was 319,000 bbld. Norway uses very little of the oil it produces (255,000 bbld in 2011), and so exports most of its production. Production is expected to be maintained until 2050. Net oil exports in 2009 were estimated to be 2.12 million barrels per day; Norway is the largest European oil exporter and the largest oil exporter in the world after Saudi Arabia and Russia. In 2011, Norway exported approximately 1.7 million bbl/d. Most exports are to the UK, the Netherlands, France, Germany and the US. The state operates a petroleum fund to soak up surplus revenue from oil and gas sales; this is used to fund social welfare programmes and as of 2002 was NOK 609 bn (40 per cent of the country's GDP). The state-run oil and gas company is Statoil, although there are plans for some limited privatisation. International oil companies must work in partnership with Statoil. Overall the government has direct ownership of 40 per cent of oil production.

Gas reserves stood at 72.0 trillion cubic feet on 1 January 2011 and are estimated to last for a further 100 years. Estimated gas production in 2011 was 3.5 trillion cubic feet, most of which was exported. An estimated 146 billion cubic feet were consumed. Norwegian gas accounts for 11 per cent of European consumption and this percentage is expected to rise.

In 2012 investment in the oil and gas industries was estimated to be US$29 billion, exploration is a large area of investment. Following exploration four new fields began producing in the first half of 2012. The Johan Sverdrup oil field was the largest oil discovery in the world in 2011, with reserves estimated at between 1.7 and 3.3 billion barrels of recoverable oil. It will be developed as a stand alone projects and is hoped to come online in 2018.

Coal

Coal mining is a small and declining sector. In 2010, 2.1 million short tons were produced and 1.3 million short tons were consumed. (Source: EIA)

Energy

Norway, with its numerous waterfalls, has developed its hydropower over the last 100 years and has become the fifth largest producer of energy by this method in the world.

About 98 per cent of electricity comes from hydro-power. In 2005 there were 306 electricity plants and 681 power stations of which 651 were hydro-electric, 19 were thermal power and 12 were wind power. 137,811 GWh of electric energy were produced (hydro-electric 109,291 GWh; thermal 929 GWh; wind 252 GWh). In 2010, total electricity consumption was 120.9 billion kWh.

Total 2008 energy consumption was estimated to be 819 Pewtajoule (TWh), 17 per cent more than in 1990. Electricity forms a high share of the country's total energy consumption. Power consumption per capita is also high, approximately 10 times that of the world average.

Contributing factors include extensive power-intensive manufacturing. Electricity is also the most common source of heating. Electricity prices have increased rapidly in recent years. (Source: Statistics Norway)

Norway has opened the world's first power project that generates energy by mixing fresh water with sea water. The prototype plant has been built on the Oslo fiord. The plan is the produce enough electricity to light and heat a small town within five years.

Manufacturing

During the 1950s, the manufacturing industry accounted for 25 per cent of all value creation in Norway. By 2006, this had fallen to less than 9 per cent. The manufacturing industry today remains raw-materials based. The oil industry and supplier industry is important. The oil industry is significant for platform production and the engineering industry. There is significant international demand for industrial raw materials and engineering products. The production of food, beverages and tobacco made the largest contribution to the value creation in manufacturing and mining sector in 2006, followed by petroleum products and chemical products. Important individual goods included modules for drilling and production platforms and aluminium.

The majority of Norwegian firms are small and medium-sized; only 20 per cent of Norwegian companies have more than 20 employees. Despite this, over 40 per cent of the total output value in industry comes from SMEs. In 2006, foreign-controlled enterprises accounted for almost 39 per cent of the value creation in the industry and employed some 23 per cent of all employees in Norwegian industry.

Figures for 2009 show that 243,601 people were employed in 19,584 manufacturing companies.

Sales of manufactured goods for large enterprises, figures in NOK 1,000

Sector	2010	2011
Mining and quarrying	8,070,402	9,187,712
Manufacturing, of which	594,670,543	610,822,844
Food products, beverages & tobacco	122,965,320	130,560,212
Textiles, clothing, leather	4,338,870	4,694,047
Wood & wood products	15,948,501	17,409,863
Paper & paper products	12,800,695	12,033,099
Printing, reproduction	5,707,153	6,159,684
Refined petrol., chemicals, pharmac.	114,965,420	135,604,089
Rubber and plastic products	6,779,351	7,427,513
Other non-metallic mineral products	17,142,050	18,633,924
Basic metals	61,328,507	63,338,178
Fabricated metal products	33,570,194	31,873,512
Computer & electrical equipment	32,784,923	34,463,903
Machinery & equipment	57,244,476	49,634,330
Ships, boats & oil platforms	62,388,196	50,606,680
Transport equipment n.e.c.	6,727,939	7,054,479
Repair, installation of machinery	30,386,418	33,116,183
Furniture & manufacturing n.e.c.	9,592,530	8,213,145

Source: Norway Statistics
http://www.ssb.no/english/subjects/10/07/vti_en/tab-2012-06-29-01-en.html

Unadjusted figures show that there was a 9.5 per cent fall in Norwegian manufacturing turnover from October 2008 to October 2009. Manufacturing turnover in the Euro area dropped 16.5 per cent in the same period. Figures showed that sales of goods from manufacturing, mining and quarrying were up by 4.8 per cent from 2010 to 2011. (Source: Statistics Norway)

Service Industries

In 2008, foreign tourists made approximately 8.1 million overnight stays. German tourists accounted for 21 per cent and Danes 12 per cent. In 2008 Norwegians took 22.1 million overnight trips and 80 per cent took at least one holiday trip. Approximately 34 per cent of the trips were international and the most popular destinations were Sweden, Denmark and Spain.

Provisional figures for 2008 estimate that accommodation enterprises had a turnover of approximately 22 million and food and beverage service activities had a turnover of approximately NOK 34 billion. Norwegian and foreign tourists spent NOK 108 billion in 2008 according to preliminary figures. Total production figures in the Norwegian industry were put provisionally at NOK 181 billion in 2008, 4.4 per cent of Norway's total production and accounts for 6 per cent of total employment. In 2007, there were 14,090 local kind-of-activity units in the Norwegian tourism industry with a total turnover of NOK 85 billion. (Source: Statistics Norway)
Norwegian Tourist Board (NORTRA), URL: http://www.ntr.no

Agriculture

In 2008, 2.6 per cent of the working population were employed in agriculture compared to 20 per cent in 1950. There are 10.2 million decares of agricultural land, of which 65 per cent is meadow land and 31 per cent is used for grains and oils. Approximately 4.3 per cent of the area is used for organic farming. Traditionally most farms are small due to Norway's topography, but as the number of farmers has decreased, so the average size has increased. In 2009 there were 47,900 farm holdings (compared to 61,500 farm holdings in 2002). Of this number, 11,700 had dairy cows and 15,400 had sheep. The areas most suitable for farming are in the southeast, southwest and in Trøndelag. In 2009, agriculture made up 0.5 per cent of GDP.

Yield of agricultural crops, 2009-11 ('000 tonnes)

Crop	2009	2010	2011*
Grain	1,054.9	1,205.7	1,039.0

NORWAY

- continued
of which:

Wheat	278.0	331.4	265.0
Rye and triticale	27.4	34.2	16.0
Barley	473.0	541.2	460.0
Oats	276.5	298.9	220.0
Potatoes	332.5	333.2	297.6
Crops for green fodder & silage	216.0	198.7	155.6
Hay	2,695.3	2,392.7	2,411.9

*Provisional figures

Source: Statistics Norway http://www.ssb.no/english/yearbook/tab/tab-336.html

The grain harvest for 2008 increased by 11 per cent compared to 2007 with an average yield per decare of 440 kg. The area used for wheat increased by 2 per cent to 931,000 decares in 2008. The average decare yield of wheat was 494 kg in 2008. The area used for barley decreased by 125,000 decares to 1.28 million decares in 2008. Average yield per decare was 413 kg. Average yield per decare for barley for the whole country was 373 kilos and wheat was 459 kilos. Most grain is grown in the counties of Ostfold, Akershus and Hedmark, accounting for 57 per cent of total grain area and 61 per cent of the total grain harvest.

The following table details horticulture production.

Horticultural Production, tonnes

Crop	2008	2009	2010
Fruit, total	19,814	17,176	14,103
-incl. apple	16,717	13,581	11,484
Berries, total	13,511	13,077	11,377
-incl. strawberries	9,607	9,119	8,329
Vegetables, field grown	156,412	157,594	106,934
Incl:			
-Cauliflower	10,132	10,269	7,812
-Winter cabbage	17,624	18,662	13,273
-Swede	15,685	13,931	12,693
-Carrot	43,307	44,706	45,934
-Onion	22,711	20,552	17,625
Vegetables, greenhouse grown	28,539	30,522	31,917
-incl. Cucumber	12,843	15,821	14,051
-Tomato	14,075	12,672	12,920

Source: Statistics Norway
http://www.ssb.no/english/yearbook/tab/tab-339.html

The following table shows figures for livestock production:

Livestock production in tonnes

Commodity	2006	2007	2008*
Beef & veal	87,642	84,655	86,449
Pork	116,356	117,742	122,706
Mutton and lamb	25,278	23,544	24,246
Poultry	62,894	70,282	84,723
Horse	425	383	363
Eggs	50,545	53,187	55,869
Cow's milk (1,000 litres)	1,505,000	1,545,100	1,530,300
Goat's milk (1,000 litres)	20,500	20,300	20,000
Wool	4,901	4,490	4,466

*Source: Statistics Norway *Preliminary/provisional figures*

In 2008 the provisional figures for domestic animals indicated there were 891,414 cattle, 316,122 cows (of which 261,812 were dairy and 54,310 were beef), 1,025,144 sheep, 38,692 dairy goats, 96,985 pigs for breeding, 1,436,809 pigs for slaughter, 3,591,808 laying hens and 50,627,189 broilers. With the exception of poultry, the number of animals has declined.

Currently 2,300 farms are organic (4 per cent).

In 2008/09, 193,200 hunters bought hunting tax cards, up from 191,290 the previous season.

Forestry

70 per cent of farmers are also involved in forestry and part-time farming is common. In total 38 per cent of the land is wooded. The productive forest area of Norway is estimated at 67,000 sq. km. This area accounts for about 24 per cent of the total land area (excluding Svalbard and Jan Mayen). Approximately 80 per cent of the productive forest area is covered with coniferous trees. The best areas for forestry are inland districts of south and mid Norway. Annual commercial roundwood removal is estimated at 8.2 million m³. An estimated 2.8 million m³ is consumed for energy by households.

Sawmills and wood industries bought 54 per cent of the timber in 2005, while 34 per cent was purchased by the pulp industry. Some 6 per cent of the wood was exported.

The aggregated gross value of the roundwood sold to the industry in 2005 totalled NOK 2.6 billion, an increase of 18 per cent compared with the previous year.

261,000 decares of young forest was cultivated in 2004. Public subsidies for looking after young forests have been reintroduced. In 2004, NOK 77 million was invested in planting and interplanting in total. 116,300 decares were planted on a national basis, 4,700 more than in 2003. Government subsidies for planting forests have ceased but there is a Forest Trust Fund instead. 57,400 decares were scarificated in 2004. There was less use of eradicants in 2004: 6,700 decares were sprayed in 2004 compared to 8,400 decares in 2003 and 11,400

decares in 2001. In 2008, 141 km² of forest were planted and 311 km² were cleared. 23 million trees were planted. Total expenditure was approximately NOK 241.1 million of which approximately 52 million was public subsidy.

Fishing

Norwegians fish some of the richest fishing waters in the world - the North Sea, the Norwegian coast, the Barents Sea and the polar front. In 2010, there were an estimated 12,280 registered fishermen (compared to 20,075 in 2000 and 43,018 in 1970). The total value of the catch, including crustaceans and molluscs, reached NOK 13.2 billion in 2010. Fishing and fish farming account for 0.4 per cent of GDP.

In 2011 an estimated 2.288 million tonnes of fish were caught (up from an estimated 2.256 million tonnes in 2006). Major catches by species are as follows (2011 figures): cod catch 340,099 tonnes; herring, 633,489 tonnes; saithe, 190,295 tonnes; mackerel, 208,079 tonnes; and haddock, 159,512 tonnes. An estimated 523 tonnes of salmon and sea trout were caught at sea in 2006 and 499 tonnes in rivers.

Foreign vessels delivered 169 000 tonnes of fish and crustaceans in Norway in 2005. Total value of the foreign landings was NOK 1.6 billion.

In 2007 there were 4,337 people involved employed in fish-farming, compared to 3,000 in 2005. There were an estimated 1,509 licences. In 2006, according to preliminary figures, 629,888 tonnes of farmed salmon, 62,703,000 tonnes of farmed trout, and 11,087 tonnes of farmed cod were sold. This was worth NOK 15,600 million (salmon), NOK 1,600 million (trout), and NOK 261.4 million (cod).

In 2011, an estimated 10,334 seals were caught (all of which were harp seals) and 95 tonnes of blubber were produced. The catch was worth an estimated 1,923,000 (Source: Statistics Norway)

COMMUNICATIONS AND TRANSPORT

Travel Requirements

Citizens of the USA, Canada and Australia require a passport valid for three months beyond the length of stay but do not need a visa for stays of up to 90 days. Most EU nationals holding a valid national ID card do not require a passport, but some do, so they should contact the embassy to check. Other nationals should contact the embassy to check visa requirements.

On 25 March 2001 Norway became a signatory to the Schengen Agreement; with a Schengen visa, a visitor can travel freely throughout the Schengen zone, and there are few border stops and checks. See http://www.eurovisa.info/SchengenCountries.htm for details.

Norwegian Directorate of Immigration, URL: http://www.udi.no

National Airlines
Braathens ASA, URL: http://www.braathens.no
Widerøe Flyveselskap A/S, (a member of the SAS Group), URL: http://www.wideroe.no/

International Airports
Bergen Airport, URL: http://www.avinor.no/lufthavn/bergen
Passengers carried 2004: 4.4 million
Stavanger (Sola) Airport, e-mail: stavanger.lufthaven@avinor.no
Passengers carried 2005: 3.1 million
Oslo (Gardermoen) Airport, URL: http://www.osl.no/
Passengers carried 2006: 18 million (approx); 77,000 tonnes freight (approx)
Trondheim Airport
Passengers carried 2006: 3.2 million

Civil Aviation Administration, URL: http://www.luftfartstilsynet.no

The air transport sector had a turnover of NOK 21.5 bn in 2004 and employed 10,346 people. In 2007 there were 41.09 million domestic and international passenger flights, of which 38.7 million were scheduled flights. An estimated 132,359 tonnes of freight and mail were received and sent in 2006.

Avinor is a state-owned limited company. It owns and operates 46 airports within Norway, 14 with the military. It is also responsible for air traffic control.
URL: http://www.avinor.no

Railways
Most of the rail network in Norway is state-owned. The state railway network includes over 4,114 km. of lines, of which 2,552 km is electrically operated. In 2007, 25.1 million tons of goods, including service goods, were transported. A total of 3.46 tonnes-kilometres were transported. In 2009, 57.9 million passengers were transported by Norwegian State Railways and 7.4 million by other railways. A total of 2.9 million passenger-kilometres were travelled. Turnover was NOK 5.5 bn in 2005. The sector employed 4,877 people. Oslo has a subway system and tram network. Approximately 97 million passengers were transported in 2007 by suburban railways/trams, compared to 91 million in 2004.
Norwegian National Rail Administration, URL: http://www.jernbaneverket.no

Roads
The total length of roads was 92,869 km. in 2008, including national, county and municipal roads. Vehicles are driven on the right. As of 2007 there were more than 2.7 million private cars, 360,000 vans and 126,207 motor cycles. On average there were 500 cars registered per 1,000 population. Figures for 2010 show that there were 2.9 million vehicles registered. There were 3.6 bn passenger journeys in 2003, 81 per cent of all journeys. The average car is over 10 years old. 70 per cent of households have a car. 220,113 vehicles were registered

for goods transport in 2002 with a total carrying capacity of almost 730,000 tonnes. In 2007, 270.5 million tonnes were transported by road. In 2004, 63,912 people were employed in the land transport sector.

Shipping

The Norwegian Merchant Fleet is the fourth largest in the world. In 2007 it consisted of approximately 1,314 merchant vessels with an aggregate tonnage of over 16,782 gross tons. These figures refer only to vessels of 100 gross tons and over, and exclude fishing and catching boats, floating whaling factories, tugs, salvage vessels and ice-breakers. The fleet includes 289 tankers.

Norwegian shipping is a private industry, wholly owned and operated by private individuals and companies. About 80 per cent of the fleet transports goods exclusively between foreign ports. The fleet serving international trade is managed by about 250 shipping companies.

Ferry services operate from coastal towns.

Odfjell ASA, URL: http://www.odfjell.com/
Tschudi Schipping ASA, URL: http://www.tschudishipping.no/
Eitzen Group, URL: http://www.eitzen-group.com/
Ugland Marine Services AS, URL: http://www.jjuc.no/
Wilhelmsen ASA, URL: http://www.2wglobal.com/www/WEP/

In 2005 there were 48 million passenger water transport journeys of which 39 million were made using ferries.

Ports and Harbours

The main international ferry ports are Stavanger, Bergen, Egersund, Kristiansand, Larvik, Oslo and Moss. The major international ferry lines are Color Line, Fjord Line and Smyril line. There is an express boat service for domestic services.

In 2007 approximately 182 million tonnes of cargo were loaded and unloaded in Norwegian ports. Figures for 2010 show the sea transport division of freight business had a turnover of NOK118.7 billion.

Stavanger Port, URL: http://www.stavanger.havn.no/

HEALTH

The health services in Norway are well developed. All those resident in Norway have a right to assistance during illness and old age. Approximately 37 per cent of the state's budget is spent on health and welfare. The health and welfare system is mainly publicly financed through compulsory national insurance contributions, although much of the money comes from Norway's petroleum fund. In 1998 no individual paid more than NOK 1,290 a year for public health services (Source: Ministry of Foreign Affairs).

The health service is decentralised with five health regions, 19 counties and 436 municipalities all responsible for the health service in their area. Resources are evened out taking into account regional differences in wealth. There is a general practitioner service throughout the country. A waiting list system has been in operation since 1990 and generally the wait for treatment is no more than six months.

The latest official statistics for health care employment were updated in 4Q 2006. They showed that there were 311,493 people with health care education working in the health care industry. This included 71,402 auxiliary nurses, 80,492 nurses, 3,231 occupational therapists, 6,243 midwives and public health nurses, 9,741 physiotherapists, 2,512 radiographers, 6,124 medical laboratory technologists, 9,391 physicians, 10,921 specialised physicians, 5,221 psychologists and 3,228 pharmacists.

In 2003, there were approximately 42,000 beds for the aged and disabled. A further 46,000 people resided in specialist dwellings. 162,000 received a home-based service. As of November 2003 there were 9,227 care workers, 3,394 child-care workers, 5,653 professional health workers for the mentally retarded, 3,165 child welfare officers and 4,202 social workers.

As of 31 December 2006 there were a total of 2,986.0 total man years for public dental health care and 6,411.1 in private dental health care. In 2006 more public dental health expenditure was the highest it had ever been. Public dental health expenditure per capita was NOK 2,000.

The most common causes of death in 2005 were heart and circulatory diseases (14,537 or 35.3 per cent), followed by malignant tumours (10,564 or 25.6 per cent), and respiratory diseases (4,082 or 9.9 per cent). (Source: Statistics Norway).

In 2004, a ban on smoking in public places came into effect. An average of 26 per cent of people smoked in 2002-03, down 3 per cent from the previous year.

EDUCATION

Education is compulsory for all Norwegian children between six and 16 years of age. Education became compulsory in 1997 for children aged six. Education is free although there are a few private establishments.

Pre-school Education

In 2011, 282,737 children were in Kindergarten. In 2007, 250,000 children had places in kindergarten (approximately 84 per cent), an increase of 15,000 from the previous year. A further 7,500 children used open kindergarten programmes. 41 per cent of the kindergarten

places were in private kindergartens. An estimated 69 per cent of children aged 1-2 years attended kindergarten and 94 per cent of children aged 3-5 years. In 2007 there were 6,600 kindergartens and 76,100 employees (92 per cent female).

Primary/Secondary Education

In 2008/09 there were 1,822 primary schools, 759 combined primary and lower secondary schools and 477 lower secondary schools with a school population of 619,450. The number of schools has decreased slightly with the trend towards fewer, larger schools. There were a total of 425,732 primary school pupils and 188,065 lower secondary school pupils. An estimated 2.5 per cent of pupils were in private education. In 2011, 614,374 children attended primary and lower secondary schools and 195,418 children attended upper secondary schools.

Higher Education

The number of educational institutions has declined in recent years due to the mergers of regional colleges into state colleges in 1994. These offer more occupationally-orientated courses than the four universities, Bergen, Tromsø (which provides education in the Suomi language), Trondheim and the Norwegian University of Science and Technology (NTNU). There are six specialized colleges at university level, one each for architecture, music, veterinary science, economics and business administration and physical education and sport. The state also funds labour market courses which provide occupational qualifications and are run jointly by school authorities, labour market authorities and adult education associations.

Figures for 2005/06 state there are 70 universities and colleges (compared to 228 in 1984/85) with 211,264 pupils (compared to 92,083 in 1984/85). There were a further 30 private universities/colleges with 29,166 pupils/students (compared to 67 in 1984/85 with 15,402 pupils). In 2006/07, 34,500 pupils completed a higher education of a lower or higher degree. Figures for 2010 show that 93,263 students attended university.

An estimated 13,630 foreign students were studying in Norway in 2005/06. An estimated 8,210 Norwegian pupils were on exchange or study-abroad programmes in the same period.

Figures from UNESCO for 2006 show that 16.2 per cent of total government expenditure went on education of which 33 per cent went on tertiary education and 25 per cent on primary education.

RELIGION

The Evangelical Lutheran Church is the National Church of Norway, as laid down in section two of the Constitution. There is, however, complete freedom of religion. The Church is administered by the Ministry of Education, Research and Church Affairs. The constitutional head of the church is the king of Norway. The religious head of the state church is the Bishop of Oslo, currently Ole Christian Mælen Kvarme. In 2008, there were 11 dioceses, 103 deaneries and 1,290 parishes. There were an estimated 1,400 pastors. Municipal councils issued grants to the church worth NOK1.6 billion in 2006.

In November 2006, the Church of Norway voted to change radically the church's relations to the state. Synod delegates voted that the church should no longer be referred to in the country's constitution as a state church. Rather, the church should be founded on a separate act passed by parliament, and the general synod should take over all church authority currently held by the King and the government. Any fundamental changes would have to be approved by parliament.

The Lutheran Church of Norway and the Evangelical Lutheran Free Church of Norway moved closer to unity in 2006 with an agreement of full recognition and co-operation. The agreement must be passed by their synods.

As of 1 January 2007, the Church of Norway had 3.9 million members. This represents 83 per cent of the population. In 2008, 411,790 people were also registered as being part of a religious community or philosophical group, including approximately: 226,969 Christians, 83,684 Muslims, 1,024 Baha'ists, 11,038 Buddhists, 4,566 Hindus, 850 Jews, 2,537 Sikhs, 80,659 life stance followers. (Source: Statistics Norway).

Norway has a religious tolerance rating of 8 on a scale of 1 to 10 (10 is most freedom). (Source: World Religion Database)

National Church of Norway, URL: http://www.kirken.no

COMMUNICATIONS AND MEDIA

Newspapers

There are three major media groups in newspapers: Schribsted, which owns the tabloid Verdens Gand and the broadsheet Aftenposten; Orkla; and A-Pressen, which was formerly a newspaper co-operative for Labour. No media company is allowed to own more than 33 per cent of the total newspaper and broadcasting market.

Verdens Gang (VG), URL: http://www.vg.no
Aftenposten, URL: http://www.aftenposten.no
Dagbladet, URL: http://www.dagbladet.no
Bergens Tidende, URL: http://www.bt.no

Other daily newspapers include:
Adresseavisen, URL: http://www.adressa.no/) published Trondheim; Stavanger Aftenblad (URL: http://aftenblatet.no), Stavanger; Dagens Næringsliv, (URL: http://www.dn.no) Oslo; Drammens Tidende (URL: http://www.dt.no), Drammen; Fædrelandsvennen, (URL: http://www.fedrelandsvennen.no) Kristiansand.

NORWAY

Broadcasting

There are four national radio stations: NRK P1 (general interest, news, light entertainment); NRK P2 (cultural, music, news); NRK Petre (youth, music & talk) and P4 (commercial). There are five national television stations: NRK TV (national and regional TV stations); TV2 (commercial) and TV Norge, TV3 Norge & TV 1000 Norge which are cable/satellite stations. The market is dominated by NRK and TV2. 98 per cent of people have access to more than NRK1. 67 per cent of people have access to channels through satellite.

NRK, URL: http://www.nrk.no
TV2, URL: http://www.tv2.no
TV3, URL: http://www.tv3.no
TV Norge, URL: http://www.tvnorge.no
Radio Norge, URL: http://www.radionorge.fm (national, state)
Radio P4, URL: http://www.p4.no (national, commercial)

The Ministry of Culture and Church Affairs is responsible for media policy. The Norwegian Mass Media Authority is the overall regulatory and supervisory body for the sector.

Postal Service

In 2005 turnover in the postal services sector was 30.5 billion NOK and it employed 37,028 people. This is a decrease of 4 per cent and 11 per cent respectively from 2002.

Telecommunications

In 2007 the information sector employed 116 people with a turnover and value added of NOK 272 and 98 billion respectively.

An estimated 5.5 million mobile phones were in use in 2010.

In 2008, over 86 per cent of people had a home computer, and over 84 per cent of households had access to the internet. In 2005, on an average day, 58 per cent of people used the internet at home, compared to 84 per cent television and 59 per cent radio. By the end of the third quarter of 2008 there were 1,558,000 broadband subscriptions- up from 550,000 for the same quarter in 2004. Figures from 2010 show that an estimated 4.4 million people were internet users.

ENVIRONMENT

In 1972 Norway created an environmental protection ministry, the first one of its kind in the world. According to the Directorate for Nature Management's statistics on protected areas, in 2003 there were 21 national parks covering 1,839,455 hectares, 1,659 nature reserves covering 328,590 hectares, 135 landscape protection areas (1,228,405 hectares) and 12,406 hectares of other protected land.

Acid rain is a problem for Norway, with an area of 70,000 sq. km. too acid for fish to breed. Norway banned spray cans containing chlorofluorocarbons some ten years before it became part of an international agreement. Norway recognises ocean pollution as a very important environmental issue and wishes to ban the dumping of radioactive waste.

At the 1992 UN conference on the environment Norway was named as "the most constructive participating nation". A SO_2 agreement was signed in Oslo in 1994. Norway tries to be a leader in global environmental policies and supports the World Commission on Environment and Development.

Norway is one among 36 industrialised countries that ratified the Kyoto Protocol; emissions currently stand at 8.5 per cent higher than the 1990 Kyoto Protocol levels. In 2005, the total Norwegian emissions of greenhouse gases amounted to 54.0 million tonnes CO2 equivalents. Government projections put 2010 emissions at 59.2 million tonnes. If the emissions stabilise at this level through the whole of the Kyoto period, Norway will have to buy emission quotas in the range of 45 million tonnes for the period 2008-2012 as a whole. The projection for 2010 does not include overall emissions of up to 2 million tonnes CO2 from the power plants at Kårstø and Mongstad as these are not expected to be up and running until 2011/12 and 2014 respectively.

Greenhouse gases did reduce in 2002 due to lower industrial activity but have since increased. In 2005 total Norwegian emissions of greenhouse gases were 54 million tons CO^2 equivalent. Emissions were down slightly in 2005 and fell again in 2006 to 53.7 million tons CO^2 but are expected to increase again when the plants at Karsto and Melkoya start up. Emissions of greenhouse gases were estimated at 54 million tons CO^2 equivalent in 2007.

In 2005, 197,000 tonnes of nitrogen oxides were emitted, 1.5 per cent less than in 2004. The decline continued with an estimated 194,506 tonnes emitted in 2006. In 2008 they were estimated to be 179,000 tonnes. Under the Gothenburg protocol emissions in 2010 should not be higher than 156,000 tonnes. The required cut is approximately equal to the emissions from Norway's gas and oil industries (46,000 tonnes). There has been a significant decrease in hydrocarbons (NMVOC). In 2006 they were estimated to be 196,345 tonnes. The 2010 target is 195,000.

Manufacturing produces 29 per cent, oil and gas activities 25 per cent, and traffic 18 per cent. Agriculture accounts for 8 per cent. Emissions from road traffic continue to increase, due to greater use of diesel cars. However emissions from the aluminium industry decreased despite increased production. Emissions from gas and oil have increased by 205 per cent from 1990. Traffic emissions have increased by 27 per cent during the same period. Of the total greenhouse gas emissions, over 75 per cent comes from CO^2 and accounts for all of the 2002 increase.

From 1986-2002 sulphur (SO^2) emissions declined but rose by 3 per cent to 22,800 tonnes in 2003 (compared to 51,904 tonnes in 1990). In 2004 it had risen further to 25,191 tonnes. The rise is due to increased emissions from iron, steel and ferroalloys production. The target set by the Gothenburg protocol is 22,800 tonnes.

In 2001, Norway extracted 18,800 tonnes of methane from landfill sites (compared to 9,800 tonnes in 1988). 6,000 tonnes of methane gas was used as an energy source in 2001, compared to 1,300 in 1998. Methane emissions from landfill sites accounts for some 7 per cent of greenhouse gas emissions.

In 2007, an estimated 10.7 million tonnes of waste were produced, compared to 8.4 million tonnes in 2004 and 7.5 million in 1995. 40 per cent of the waste is from manufacturing and 18 per cent from households. 4.7 million tonnes of waste were sent for recovery in 2005. 62 per cent was recycled, while 31 per cent were energy recovered. The remaining was composted. The amount sent for recovery increased by 51 per cent in 2005 compared to 1995. In the same period, the amount sent for disposal dropped by 5 per cent, due to a 13 per cent decline in amounts being sent to landfills.

Approximately 1.1 million tonnes of hazardous waste was generated in 2007, up from 672,000 in 2000. (Source: Statistics Norway)

In 2004 the Norwegian Act on the Right to Environmental Information entered into force. All citizens now have the legal right to obtain environmental information, both from public authorities and from public and private enterprises.

In 2007 the Norwegian government published a white paper with ambitious climate targets. Its aim is that Norway will be carbon neutral by 2050 (including emission trading). It also wants to improve on Norway's commitment under the Kyoto Protocol by 10 per cent, and plan to cut global emissions of greenhouse gases by the equivalent of 30 per cent of the 1990 emissions by 2020. It aims to meet these targets both by reducing Norway's emissions and by paying for cuts in other countries. The whole of the extra 10 per cent will be accounted for by reductions outside Norway.

Research and technological development are major priority areas in the Government's climate policy. Proposed measures for reducing emissions include:
-Prohibiting landfilling of biodegradable waste from 2009.
-Prohibiting the installation of oil-fired boilers in new buildings from 2009.
-Conversion of oil-fired boilers to boilers using renewable energy.
-Development of marine wind turbines. This will intensify the efforts to develop emission-free energy systems, particularly on the Norwegian continental shelf.
-Taking targeted and coordinated measures to expand the production of bioenergy by up to 14 TWh.
-Improvement of public transport.

Norway is party to the following international agreements: Air Pollution, Air Pollution-Nitrogen Oxides, Air Pollution-Persistent Organic Pollutants, Air Pollution-Sulfur 85, Air Pollution-Sulfur 94, Air Pollution-Volatile Organic Compounds, Antarctic-Environmental Protocol, Antarctic-Marine Living Resources, Antarctic Seals, Antarctic Treaty, Biodiversity, Climate Change, Climate Change-Kyoto Protocol, Desertification, Endangered Species, Environmental Modification, Hazardous Wastes, Law of the Sea, Marine Dumping, Ozone Layer Protection, Ship Pollution, Tropical Timber 83, Tropical Timber 94, Wetlands, Whaling.

SPACE PROGRAMME

The Norwegian Space Centre is a government agency. It promotes the development of national space activities and supports Norway within the ESA. Norway has been a member of the European Space Agency since 1987. The NSC aims include the growth of the space sector, increase Norway's space research and maintain its space-related ground infrastructure.

In 2010 the total turnover within the Norwegian space sector was approximately NOK 5.7 billion of which Norwegian produced goods accounted for over €650 million. Exports account for over 70 per cent of turnover. Satellite communications is the leading sector and accounts for over 80 per cent of turnover.

In January 2008, the Galileo station was inaugurated at the Troll station on Queen Maud's Land. Another station, Trollsat, also became operational. Trollsat is closely associated with the Troll research station.

In 2010, the Norwegian company Norspace won space contracts worth 170 million kroner as part of the Galileo programme. In the same year, Japan and Norway signed an agreement on increased co-operation in space research.

Norwegian Space Centre, URL: http://www.spacecentre.no/

BOUVETOYA

The uninhabited Bouvetøya (Bouvet Island) is situated in the Southern Atlantic at 54° 25' and 3° 21' E, and covers an area of about 50 sq. km (19 sq. miles), of which 93 per cent is glacier covered. The island was discovered by the French naval officer Jean Baptiste Lozier Bouvet in 1739. In 1825 it was claimed for Great Britain by the British sealing skipper George Norris, who landed and hoisted the British flag. He had no authorization, however, and the British Government did nothing to maintain the occupation.

On 1 December 1927, on the 'Norvegia', Captain Horntvedt's expedition sent out by Lars Christensen, claimed it for Norway, and by Order in Council of 23 January 1928 it was placed under the sovereignty of Norway. A diplomatic dispute concerning the claim arose between the United Kingdom and Norway, resulting in the renouncement of the British claim in November 1928. By law of 27 February 1930, the island became a Norwegian dependency. Norway operated a manned meteorological station on the island from December 1978 to March 1979, and has had an automatic weather station in operation since February 1977. Bouvetøya has been a nature reserve since 1971.

To view a map of Bouvetøya, please consult
http://www.lib.utexas.edu/maps/cia08/bouvet_sm_2008.gif

Head of State: King Harald V (Sovereign) (page 1438)

DRONNING MAUD LAND
Queen Maud Land

Dronning Maud Land is part of Antarctica situated between 20° W and 45° E. The land is highly ice-covered, with the coast mostly surrounded by extensive ice-shelves forming a high barrier towards the sea. The territory was first explored by Norwegian, German, and American expeditions. The first wintering took place at Maudheim (about 71° 03' S and 10° 56' W) by the Norwegian-British-Swedish Antarctic Expedition over the period 1949-52.

The Norwegian Antarctic Expedition, 1956-60, had its base at Norway Station (about 70° 30' S, 2° 30' W). This station was taken over by South Africa, which closed it in 1962 and erected in the neighbourhood a new station, SANAE, which is still working. A second (small) South African station, of varying name and position, has been in operation for some years from 1969. Two Japanese stations, Syowa (69° 00' S and 39° 35' E), erected February 1957, and Mizuho (70° 42' S and 44° 20' E), established 1977, are still working. A Soviet station (Lasarev) was erected near the shore at about 12 E° in the season of 1959-60. A new Soviet station, Novolazarevskaja, which is still working, was erected about 90 km inland. The Federal Republic of Germany established a station, Georg-von-Neumayer-Station (70° 37' S, 08° 22' W) in February 1981, and India established a station, Dakshin Gangolri, (70° 05' S, 12° 00' E) in February 1984. On 14 January 1939, Dronning Maud Land was pronounced Norwegian territory by the Norwegian Government. From 1957 the land has had the status of Norwegian dependency. Other than the above-mentioned stations, the land is uninhabited.

Head of State: King Harald V (Sovereign) (page 1438)

JAN MAYEN

Jan Mayen is a mountainous island of 377 sq. km (145 sq. miles) in area, situated at about 71° 00' N and 8° 30' W (between Iceland and Svalbard) entirely of volcanic origin. Beerenberg, its highest peak, reaches 2,277 m (7,470 ft.), on the north-eastern side of which a major volcanic eruption started on 18 September 1970. A smaller eruption was observed in January 1985. The discovery of the island was claimed by several skippers at the beginning of the whaling period early in the 17th century, but it is generally assumed that Henry Hudson was the discoverer. Its present name derives from the Dutch whaling captain Jan Jacobsz May, who indisputably landed there in 1614. The island came under Norwegian sovereignty in 1929. By a law of 27 February 1930, Jan Mayen was made part of the Kingdom of Norway. It is uninhabited, save for a meteorological station (established 1921) expanded by LORAN (1959) and CONSOL (1968), navigation transmitter stations.

To view a map of Jan Mayen, please consult
http://www.lib.utexas.edu/maps/cia08/jan_mayen_sm_2008.gif

Head of State: King Harald V (Sovereign) (page 1438)

PETER I OY
Peter I Island

Peter I Øy is an almost completely ice-covered uninhabited Antarctic island of volcanic origin at 68° 48' S and 90° 35' W, with an area of 156 sq. km (69 sq. miles). It was discovered in 1821 by the Russian Admiral von Bellingshausen and is situated in the Bellingshausen Sea. On 2 February 1929, Dr. Ola Olstad, leader of the second 'Norvegia' Expedition, claimed it for Norway. On 1 May 1931, the island was placed under the sovereignty of Norway, and by Act of 24 March 1933, added to Norway as a dependency. A map of Peter I Øy to the scale of 1:50,000 was made after the visit of a Norwegian expedition to the Island in January 1987. An automatic weather station is situated on the island.

Head of State: King Harald V (Sovereign) (page 1438)

SVALBARD

Svalbard is believed to have been discovered in the late 12th century by Norsemen, but was re-discovered in 1596 by the Dutch navigator, Willem Barents. During the 17th and 18th centuries whale hunting took place by British, Dutch, Danish-Norwegian, German and other whalers, and the three nations first mentioned tried to gain sovereignty. When the whaling died out, the interest in sovereignty also faded away. Russian fur hunters regularly wintered in the islands from about 1715 to about 1820, and from the end of the 18th century Norwegian trappers and sealers wintered in Svalbard.

By the treaty of 9 February 1920, sovereignty was given to Norway, and in 1925 Svalbard was officially taken over by this country as part of the Kingdom of Norway.

Head of State: King Harald V (Sovereign) (page 1438)

AREA AND POPULATION

The archipelago of Svalbard includes all the islands situated between 10°-35°E and 74°-81°N; that is, Spitsbergen (formerly Vestspitsbergen), Nordaustlandet, Edgeøya, Barentsøya, Prins Karls Forland, Bjørnøya, Hopen, Kong Karls Land, Kvitøya, and many smaller islands. The total area is about 62,000 sq. km (24,000 sq. miles); the largest island, Spitsbergen, covers 39,400 sq. km (15,000 sq. miles).

The terrain is mountainous, with the higher elevations covered in ice all year. The west coast is clear of ice for approximately six months. The climate is arctic, moderated by the North Atlantic current which keeps the west and north coasts navigable for most of the year.

To view a map of Svalbard, please consult
http://www.lib.utexas.edu/maps/cia08/svalbard_sm_2008.gif

The total population as of 1 January 1991 was 3,309, of which 1,148 were Norwegians. By 2000 this had fallen because of the decline in mining. It was estimated to be just over 2,000. In 2011, it was estimated to be 2,700. Five Norwegian meteorological stations are in operation in Svalbard: Bjørnøya (since 1920), Hopen (since 1945), Ny-Ålesund (since 1961), Svalbard Lufthavn (since 1975), and Sveagruva (since 1978). A Norwegian research station at Ny-Ålesund, administered by Norsk Polarinstitutt, was established in 1968, and since then geophysical observations and varied research work have been carried out there.

MANUFACTURING, MINING AND SERVICES

Coal has been known in Spitsbergen for a long time, but it was not until about 1900 that the coalfields aroused economic interest, and the first mining started a few years afterwards. Coalmining is now the principal industry in Svalbard. Coal used to be mined in two Norwegian

OMAN

communities (Longyearbyen, Sveagruva) and in two Soviet communities (Barentsburg, Pyramiden). In 1988, 251,180 metric tons of coal were exported from the Norwegian mines and 502,525 metric tons from the Soviet mines, although in 2000 the Russian mine at Pyramiden was no longer in operation and only one Norwegian mine was still working. In 2002 plans to increase production were discussed. Coal is mined by the company, Store Norske Kulkompani (SNSK).

COMMUNICATIONS AND MEDIA

Svalbard produces its own newspaper called Svaldbarposten (URL: http://www.svalbardposten.no/) The Norwegian Broadcasting Corporation (URL: http://www.nrk.no) transmits to Svalbard via satellite.

OMAN

Sultanate of Oman

Saltanat Uman

Capital: Muscat (Population estimate: 750,000)

Head of State: HM Sultan Qaboos Bin Said Al Said (Sovereign) (page 1376)

National Flag: Three horizontal bands of white, red, and green of equal width with a broad, vertical, red band on the hoist side. The national emblem (a khanjar dagger in its sheath superimposed on two crossed swords in scabbards) in white is centred near the top hoist side.

CONSTITUTION AND GOVERNMENT

Constitution

The independent Sultanate of Oman was known until 1970 as the Sultanate of Muscat and Oman. Sultan Qaboos bin Said Al Said, who was born in 1940, succeeded his father Said bin Taimur on 23 July 1970, following a bloodless coup. The Sultan is directly descended from the Arab Al Bu Said dynasty which rose to power in the middle of the 18th century. Another branch of the same family ruled in the island of Zanzibar until 1964. The Sultan has treaties of friendship and commerce with Britain, the United States, France, the Netherlands and India.

The Sultan is declared by Oman's November 1996 first Constitution to be the state's absolute monarch. He is responsible for, inter alia, presiding over the Council of Ministers, appointing and dismissing Ministers and Deputy Ministers, presiding over Specialised Councils, appointing their Chairmen, and appointing and dismissing senior judges. The Sultan is advised by the Consultative Council and the Cabinet.

The administrative system of the State consists of the Diwan of Royal Court, the Ministry of the Palace Office, the Cabinet of Ministers and Secretariat of the Cabinet, the Specialised Councils, the Governorate of Muscat, the Governorate of Dhofar and the Council of Oman (Majlis Oman). The Cabinet of Ministers is the highest executive authority and is collectively responsible to His Majesty the Sultan. It is currently composed of 23 members.

There are no political parties.

To consult the constitution, please visit: http://www.wipo.int/wipolex/en/details.jsp?id=6118

Recent Events

Oman became a member of the World Trade Organization in October 2000.

The death of Saif bin Hamad al-Busaidi resulted in a minor cabinet reshuffle in November 2001. A further reshuffle took place in February 2002. In March 2004 the minister for higher education was replaced by Rawya bint Saud al-Bussaidi the first female cabinet minister.

In January 2005, 100 people were arrested for allegedly plotting to overthrow the government. Thirty-one were subsequently convicted. They were pardoned by the Sultan in June of the same year.

In July 2006 Oman and the USA signed a Free Trade Agreement.

Cyclone Gonu struck Oman in June 2007, killing over 50 people and disrupting oil production. Over the same summer, Oman's Arabian Oryx sanctuary (established in 1994) became the first UNESCO World Heritage site to be removed from the list; the government had cut the park size by 90 per cent in order to allow oil prospecting, and numbers of the rare species had fallen from 450 in 1996 to 65 in 2007.

In February 2011, protesters held demonstrations, calling for political reform and jobs. One protestor was shot dead. In response, Sultan Qaboos promised jobs and benefits.

Elections took place in October 2011 to the Consultative Council. Sultan Qaboos has promised that it will have greater powers.

Legislature

The Council of Oman consists of the Consultative Council (Majlis al-Shoura) and the Council of State (Majlis ad-Dawlah). The Consultative Council (Majlis al-Shoura) was set up by Sultan Qaboos in 1991 to further involve the population of Oman in the reconstruction and development of the country. Its 82 members are elected from Oman's wilayats, and there are also two vice-presidents who are elected by the Council itself. Members serve single terms of three years. The Council has no legislative power and is simply an advisory body. The main functions of the Majlis al-Shura are to review draft economic and social legislation; to put forward proposals for the upgrading of social and economic laws; to discuss public

policy issues proposed by the government; and to prepare and monitor Oman's development plans. A recent Royal Directive has increased the participation of women in the Majlis al-Shoura to 30 per cent. The Council of State (Majlis ad-Dawlah) comprises 59 members appointed by the Sultan, and is intended to operate between government and the people.

Consultative Council, (Majlis al-Shoura), PO Box 2361, Muscat 112, Oman. Tel: +968 24 510444, fax: +968 24 510666

The Cabinet of Ministers is the highest executive authority and is collectively responsible to His Majesty the Sultan. It is currently composed of 23 members.

Cabinet (as at June 2013)

Sultan of Oman, Prime Minister, Commander of Armed Forces: H.M. Qaboos Bin Said Al Said (page 1376)
Deputy Prime Minister: Fahd bin Mamud al-Said
Minister of the Diwan of the Royal Court: Khalid bin Hilal al-Busaidi
Minister of Defence: Badr bin Saud bin Hareb Al-Busaidi
Minister of Foreign Affairs: Yusuf bin Alawi bin Abdullah (page 1371)
Minister of the Interior: Hamud bin Faisal bin Said al-Busaidi
Minister of Finance: Darwish Bin Isma'eel bin Ali Bl-Balushi
Minister of Oil and Gas: H.E. Dr Mohammed bin Hamad bin Saif al-Romhi
Minister of Commerce & Industry: Ali bin Mohammed bin Said bin Saif al-Kalbani
Minister of Justice: Abulmalik bin Abdullah bin Ali Al-Khalili
Minister of Awqaf (Religious Endowments) and Religious Affairs: H.E. Shaikh Abdullah bin Mohammed al-Salimi
Minister of Higher Education: Rawya bint Saud al-Bussaidiyah
Minister of Information: Dr Abdulmunen bin Mansour bin Said al-Hasani
Minister of Housing: Shaikh Saif al-Shabibi
Minister of Agriculture & Fisheries: Fuad bin Jafar bin Muhammad al-Sajwani
Minister of Transport and Communications: Ahmad bin Muhammad bin Salim al-Futaisi
Minister of Health: Dr Ahmed bin Mohammed bin Obaid Al-Sa'eedi
Minister of Regional Municipalities and Water Resources: Ahmad bin Abdallah bin Muhammad al-Shuhi
Minister of the Environment and Climate Affairs: Mohammed bin Salim bin Said al-Toobi
Minister of Manpower: Abdallah bin Nasser bin Abdallahal-Bakri
Minister of Social Development: Muhammad bin Said bin Said al-Kalbani
Minister of the Civil Service: Khalid bin Umar bin Said al-Marhun
Minister of Education: Madiha bint Ahmad bin Nasir al-Shibyaniyan
Minister of National Heritage and Culture: Haytham bin Tareq al-Said
Minister of Tourism: Ahmed bin Nasser bin Hamad al-Mehrzi
Minister for Legal Affairs: Dr Abdullah bin Mohammed bin Said Al-Saeedi
Minister of Royal Office Affairs: Gen. Sultan bin Muhammad al-Numani
Minister of Sports Affairs: Sa'ad bin Mohammed bin Said al Mardhouf al-Sa'adi
Minister of State and Governor of Muscat: Sayyid Saud bin Hilal bin Hamad al-Busaidi
Minister of State and Governor of Dhofar: Sheikh Mohammed bin Sultan bin Hamoud al-Busaidi
Secretary-Gen. of the Council of Ministers: Shaykh al-Fadhl bin Muhammad bin Ahmad al-Harthi

---

Ministries

Office of the Sultan, URL: http://www.diwan.gov.om
Ministry of Agriculture and Fisheries, PO Box 467, Muscat 113, Sultanate of Oman. Tel: +968 24 696300, URL: http://www.maf.gov.om/
Ministry of Civil Services, PO Box 3994, Ruwi 112, Sultanate of Oman. Tel: +968 24 696000 / 696300, fax: +968 24 601371URL: http://www.omanmocs.com/
Ministry of Commerce and Industry, PO Box 550, Muscat 113, Sultanate of Oman. Tel: +968 24 813500, fax: +968 24 817239e-mail: minister@mocioman.gov.om, URL: http://www.mocioman.gov.om/
Ministry of Education, PO Box 3, Muscat 113, Sultanate of Oman. Tel: +968 24 775209, fax: +968 24 708485e-mail: moe@moe.gov.om, URL: http://www.edu.gov.om/moe/
Ministry of Finance and National Economy, PO Box 506, Muscat 113, Sultanate of Oman. Tel: +968 24 738201, fax: +968 24 738140 e-mail: info@mof.gov.om, URL: http://www.mof.gov.om/
Ministry of Foreign Affairs, PO Box 252, Muscat 113, Sultanate of Oman. Tel: +968 24 699500, fax: +968 24 696141
Ministry of Health, PO Box 393, Muscat 113, Sultanate of Oman. Tel: +968 24 602177, fax: +968 24 601430, e-mail: moh@moh.gov.om, URL: http://www.moh.gov.om/
Ministry of Higher Education, PO Box 82, Ruwi 112, Sultanate of Oman. Tel: +968 24 693148, URL: http://www.mohe.gov.om/
Ministry of Housing, PO Box 173, Muscat 113, Sultanate of Oman. Tel: +968 24 693333

Ministry of Information, PO Box 600, Muscat 113, Sultanate of Oman. Tel: +968 24 603222, fax: +968 24 693770, e-mail: webmaster@omanet.com, URL: http://www.omanet.om/
Ministry of the Interior, PO Box 127, Ruwi, Sultanate of Oman. Tel: +968 24 602244, fax: +968 24 660644, URL: http://www.moi.gov.om/
Ministry of Justice, PO Box 354, Ruwi 112, Sultanate of Oman. Tel: +968 24 697699, URL: http://www.moj.gov.om/
Ministry of Legal Affairs, PO Box 578, Ruwi 113, Sultanate of Oman. Tel: +968 24 605802, URL: http://www.mola.gov.om/
Ministry of National Economy, PO Box 506, Muscat, 113, Sultanate of Oman. Tel: +968 24 738201, fax: +968 24 698467, e-mail: mone@omantel.net.om, URL: http://www.moneoman.gov.om/
Ministry of National Heritage and Culture, PO Box 668, Muscat 113, Sultanate of Oman. Tel: +968 24 602555, fax:+968 24 602735, URL: http://www.mnhc.gov.om/
Ministry of Petroleum & Gas, PO Box 551, Muscat 113, Sultanate of Oman. Tel: +968 24 603333 / 702233, fax: +968 24 696972, URL: http://www.mog.gov.om/
Ministry of Transport and Communications, PO Box 338, Ruwi 112, Sultanate of Oman. Tel: +968 24 697888, URL: http://www.comm.gov.om/
Ministry of Regional Municipalities and Water Resources, PO Box 323, Muscat 113, Sultanate of Oman. Tel: +968 24 692550 / 696444, URL: http://www.mrmwr.gov.om/
Ministry of Defence, PO Box 113, Muscat 113, Sultanate of Oman. Tel:+968 24 312605, fax: +968 24 702521
Ministry of Awqaf & Religious Affairs, Muscat, Sultanate of Oman. Tel: +968 24 696870, e-mail: admin@mara.gov.om, URL: http://www.mara.gov.om/
Ministry of Social Development, PO Box 560, Muscat 113, Sultanate of Oman. Tel: +968 24 602444, URL: http://www.mosd.gov.om/

Elections
In 1997 women were allowed to vote and stand for election for the first time.

Parliamentary elections were on 27 October 2007 for the mainly advisory Consultative Assembly of Oman. All the candidates were independents. About 390,000 people were eligible to vote for the 631 candidates (among them 21 women) standing for 84 mandates. For the first time, all women and men over the age of 21 were enfranchised. The two seats won by women in the previous election were lost to men in 2007.

The most recent elections were held on 15 October 2011.

Diplomatic Representation
US Embassy, PO Box 202, 115 Madinat Al Sultan Qaboos, Muscat, Sultanate of Oman. Tel: +968 24 698989, fax: +968 24 699779, e-mail: aemctgnr@omantel.net.om, URL: http://oman.usembassy.gov
Ambassador: Richard J Schmierer
British Embassy, PO Box 185, Mina Al Fahal 116, Sultanate of Oman. Tel: +968 24 609000, fax: +968 24 609010, e-mail: enquiries.Muscat@fco.gov.uk, URL: http://ukinoman.fco.gov.uk/en
Ambassador: Jamie Bowden
Embassy of the Sultanate of Oman, 2535 Belmont Road, NW, Washington, DC 20008. Tel: +1 202 387 1980, fax: +1 202 745 4933, URL: http://www.omani.info
Ambassador: H.E. Hunnaina Sultan Ahmed Al Mughairi
Embassy of the Sultanate of Oman, 167 Queen's Gate, London SW7 5HE, United Kingdom. Tel: +44 (0)20 7225 0001, fax: +44 (0)20 7584 6435 (Cultural Section), +44 (0)20 7589 2505 (Commercial Section), e-mail: theembassy@omanembassy.org.uk, URL: http://www.omanembassy.org.uk
Ambassador: H.E. Abdul Aziz Al Hinai
Permanent Representative of the Sultanate of Oman to the United Nations, 866 United Nations Plaza, Suite 540, New York, NY 10017, USA. Tel: +1 212 355 3505 / 3506 / 3507, fax: +1 212 644 0070, e-mail: oman@un.int, URL: http://www.un.int/wcm/content/site/oman
Ambassador: Lyutha bint Sultan bin Ahmad al-Mughairi

LEGAL SYSTEM

The principles taken from Sharia law are the basis for all laws in Oman, including family law. However, in recent years, separate bodies have been set up to deal with matters like arbitration in civil and commercial disputes to which Sharia law cannot always be applied.

The highest court in Oman is the Supreme Court located in Muscat. Appeals can be made to the sultan, who exercises powers of clemency. Below the Supreme Court are six Courts of Appeal, located at Muscat, Ibra, Ibri, Nizwa, Salalah and Sohar. The Courts of Appeal hear cases from the 40 Courts of the First Instance based in 40 wilayats or districts. These courts along with an Administrative Court came into existence following a judicial review in 2001. The Ministry of Legal Affairs is responsible for the preparation of Royal Decrees and for reviewing all draft laws, regulations and Ministerial decisions before they are published in its Official Gazette.

There is also a security court, rarely used, which handles internal security cases. A commercial dispute may be resolved at the Authority for Settlement of Commercial Disputes.

Citizens do not have the right to change their government, and the government restricts freedoms of privacy, speech, press, assembly, association, and religion. In 2008, the government established an independent human rights commission with membership from both the public and private sectors. It also passed a comprehensive law to combat trafficking in persons. Oman is party to the UN convention on the Rights of the Child and the International Convention on the Elimination of Raical Discrimination. The death penalty has not be been used since 2001 although it remains in force. A death sentence cannot be carried out before ratification by the Sultan.

LOCAL GOVERNMENT

There are five regions and four governorates* (Al Dakhiliyah, Al Batinah, Al-Buraymi*, Al Wusta, Al Sharqiyah, Az Zahirah, Dhofar*, Masqat*, Musandam* and Al Batinah) are subdivided into 61 wilayats, or districts. Each wilayat is governed by a Wali who is responsible to the Ministry of the Interior.

AREA AND POPULATION

Area
The area of the Sultanate, situated on the easterly corner of Arabia, is approximately 309,500 sq. km. Except for an area between Dibba and Kalba, on the east coast of the Musandam peninsula belonging to Sharjah and Fujairah of the United Arab Emirates, the coast line of the Sultanate extends from just south of Tibat on the west coast of Arabia about half-way to Aden and includes the Sultan's southern province of Dhofar. Inland, the Sultanate border meets the desert sands of the Rub-al-Khali. Several islands are located in Oman's waters, the largest of which is Masirah in the south-east.

The Sultanate consists of three geographical divisions: a coastal plain, a range of hills and a plateau. The coastal plain varies in width from ten miles near Suwaigto to practically nothing in the vicinity of Matrah and Muscat, where the hills descend abruptly into the sea. The mountain range runs generally from west to south-west. The hills are for the most part barren, but in the high area around Jabal Akhdar there is considerable cultivation. The plateau has an average height of 1,000 feet. North-west of Muscat the coastal plain is known as the Batinah, which is fertile and relatively prosperous. The coastline between Muscat and the fertile province of Dhofar is barren. Along the littoral rainfall is low and Muscat itself is judged to be one of the hottest harbours in the world. Special permission is required from the Ministry of the Interior for travel outside the Capital Area. Over 80 per cent of the land area of Oman is desert.

To view a map, please visit http://www.un.org/Depts/Cartographic/map/profile/oman.pdf

Population
The population of Oman in 2010 was 2.782 million, of whom approximately 660,000 people were non-nationals. The average annual population growth rate was estimated at 1.9 per cent for the period 2000-10. Population density is 6.5 inhabitants per sq. km. The majority of Omanis (69 per cent) are aged between 15 and 60, with 27 per cent aged 14 years or younger, and approximately 4 per cent aged 60 years or over. The median age of the population is 25 years.

In the coastal towns of Muscat and Matrah the population includes Baluchis, Indians, Pakistanis and Zanzibaris.

Arabic is the official language, with Farsi, Baluchi and Urdu also being used. English is widely used in Oman.

Births, Marriages, Deaths
H.M. the Sultan has advised the people of Oman to limit the number of children per family and advice is given to mothers in all health clinics on how to limit the number of pregnancies. The fertility rate has subsequently dropped from 6 children born per mother in 2003 to an average of 3.0 children per mother in 2009. The crude birth rate, according to 2010 figures was 17.9 births per 1,000 people and the crude death rate was 3.3 per 1,000 births. The infant mortality rate in 2010 was 8 deaths per 1,000 live births.

Average life expectancy at birth in 2009 was 74 years (72 years for men, 77 years for women). Healthy life expectancy was 64 years for males and 67 years for females (2007). (Source: http://www.who.int, World Health Statistics 2012)

Public Holidays 2014
14 January: Birth of the Prophet (Mouloud)*
27 May: Ascension of the Prophet (Leilat al-Meiraj)*
23 July: Renaissance Day (beginning of the reign of Sultan Qaboos)
29 July: End of Ramadan (Eid Al Fitr)*
18 November: National Day and Birthday of Sultan Qaboos
5 October: Feast of the Sacrifice (Eid Al Adha)*
25 October: Islamic New Year*
* Islamic holiday: precise date depends upon sighting of the moon.

EMPLOYMENT

According to 2007 estimates, Oman has a labour force of about 959,000. In 1998 the Public Authority for Social Insurance (PASI) registered 46,171 Omanis seeking employment, and in 1999 the figure rose to 50,660. Currently there are 119,849 expatriate workers in construction, 56,748 in agriculture and fisheries and 52,189 in domestic services. The majority foreign workers come from South Asia, Egypt, Jordan, and the Philippines.

One of the government's highest priorities is 'Omanisation', by which Omanis are encouraged to take jobs currently performed by expatriates. The Ministry of Labour has insisted that there is a fixed Omanisation ratio in six areas of the private sector. Transport, storage and communications are to have 60 per cent; finance, insurance and real estate, 45 per cent; industry, 35 per cent; hotels and restaurants, 30 per cent; wholesale or retail industry, 20 per cent; and contracting, 15 per cent. In 1998 the Ministry issued a decision that 50 per cent of employees in the service stations of fuel marketing companies must be Omanis. The government issues a 'Green Card' to those companies who have successfully met its Omanisation plans.

The unemployment rate was estimated at 15 per cent in 2004.

OMAN

BANKING AND FINANCE

Currency
1 Omani Rial = 1,000 Baisa.
Oman's financial centre is Ruwi. Omani Rial are available in denominations of 50, 20, 10, 5 and 1; Biasa in denominations of 500, 200 and 100.

GDP/GNP, Inflation, National Debt
Oman has an oil-based economy which accounts for about 80 per cent of export earnings and 40 per cent of GDP. The economy is therefore greatly affected by changes in the world's oil markets.

Oman's Sixth Five Year Plan (2001-2005) was a development of previous economic strategies with the aim of sustainable financial policies, the enhancement of Omanisation, the further development of the private sector, and the encouragement of foreign investment. It also concentrated on the development of gas-related industries, tourism, agriculture, fisheries, and financial services. The Seventh Five Year Plan (2006-2010), is viewed as a continuation of the Sixth Year Plan, with emphasis on boosting the private sector, a commitment to diversify the economy away from its dwindling oil reserves, and targeting GDP growth at 3 per cent per annum. The government is also trying to replace migrant-workers with Omani nationals to combat rising unemployment in young Omanis.

In 2007, GDP was estimated at US$40.52 billion and US$59.9 billion in 2008 reflecting a growth rate that year of 7.8 per cent. GDP per head was estimated at US$21,600 in 2008. GDP was estimated at US$70 billion in 2011 with a growth rate of 5.1 per cent.

Inflation was estimated at 4 per cent in 2007. It was estimated to be just over 3 per cent in 2010, rising to 4 per cent in 2011.

Oman's total external debt was US$9 billion in 2011.

Foreign Investment
In order to encourage foreign investment - particularly power generation, light industry, and tourism - the Foreign Investment Law was introduced and major amendments were made to the Commercial Law, the Agency Law and the Corporate Income Tax Law. These amendments allow foreign investors to own up to 65 per cent of stock in public infrastructure, to own up to 49 per cent in trust accounts and, under certain circumstances, to be exempted from corporate tax during the first five years of establishment. Further, incentives include no personal income tax and foreign exchange controls, tax and import duty exemptions, interest free long term loans for industrial and tourism projects and protection of investment guaranteed by law.

Balance of Payments / Imports and Exports
Oman's major export products are oil, fish, processed copper, and textiles. Major import products are machinery, transport equipment, manufactured goods, food, livestock, and lubricants. Major export trading partners are China (30 per cent), Thailand, South Korea, the United Arab Emirates, and the United States. Major import trading partners are the United Arab Emirates (27.5 per cent), Japan, the US and China.

Export figures for 2011 were estimated at US$45 billion. Imports cost an estimated US$20 billion.

In October 2000, Oman joined the World Trade Organisation (WTO).

Central Bank
Central Bank of Oman, PO Box 1161, Central Business District, 44 Muttrah Commercial Centre St, Ruwi 112, Oman. Tel: +968 24 777 777, URL: http://www.cbo-oman.org/
Governor: Hamood al Zadjali

Chambers of Commerce and Trade Organisations
Oman Chamber of Commerce and Industry, URL: http://chamberoman.com/

MANUFACTURING, MINING AND SERVICES

Primary and Extractive Industries
Oil was first discovered in commercial quantities in 1962 but its fields are more scattered and generally less productive than others in the Persian Gulf. Current oil reserves as at January 1 2012 are estimated to be 5.5 billion barrels. There has been a downward trend in production although estimated figures for 2008 show a rise in production from the previous year. Estimated figures for 2008 put oil production at 757,300 barrels per day, of which 91 per cent was crude, production figures for 2011 were 888,910 barrels per day. Oil production was expected to increase by 30,000 bbl/d in 2012 when the Harweel Enhanced Oil Recovery project began.

Oil consumption rose from 53,000 bb/d in 2000 to 98,000 bb/d in 2008. Exports of oil go mainly to the Far East: China, Japan, South Korea, Thailand, Singapore, Taiwan, and India. Net oil exports fell from an estimated 844,730 barrels per day in 2002 to 790,000 in 2011.

PDO (Petroleum Development Oman) controls more than 90 per cent of Oman's oil reserves and 94 per cent of production. Oman's second largest employer, PDO is a consortium of the Oman government (60 per cent), Shell (34 per cent), Total (4 per cent), and Partex (2 per cent). Most of Oman's oil fields are operated by Shell; however, PDO plans to increase its oil production by 34 per cent. Recently, two major oilfields were discovered in southern Oman at Al-Noor and Al-Shomou. Estimates put reserves from both at 340 million barrels, rising to 2.7 billion barrels by 2011. Oman's largest oilfield is Yibal; discovered in 1962, Yibal supplies a quarter of PDO's total production, currently at around 180,000 barrels per day.

The government is to increase its investment in upstream oil and natural gas projects including enhanced oil recovery. Exploration will also increase (both oil and natural gas).

Natural Gas
Oman's government has committed itself to becoming a major natural gas user and exporter. Natural gas production has risen sharply in recent years, from 197,000 million cubic feet in 1999 to 851,000 million cubic feet in 2007 and 937,000 million cubic feet in 2011. Consumption has also risen, from an estimated 181 billion cubic feet in 1999 to to 388 billion cubic feet in 2007 and 619 billion cubic feet in 2011.

Oman began exporting liquefied natural gas (LPG) in 2000, and completed a 6.6-million-ton-per-year liquefaction plant at Qalhat near Sur. The project was developed by Oman Liquefied Natural Gas Company (OLNGC), a consortium of the Omani government (51 per cent), Shell (30 per cent), Total (5.54 per cent), Korea LNG (5 per cent), Mitsubishi (2.77 per cent), Partex (2 per cent), and Itochu (0.92 per cent). In 2004 some 66 per cent of LNG exports went to South Korea. Oman also exported LNG to Japan, Taiwan, Spain, France and the USA.

Copper is mined in Wadi Jizzi near Sohar. However, the level of deposits are beginning to decrease and the smelter there was threatened with closure in 1994. An additional 8.4 million tonnes of mineable copper ore was found at Hayl Al Safil. There is an estimated 36 million tonnes of coal in the Sur region and other minerals mined include silica sand, quartzite, gypsum and marble.

Energy
Oman's total energy consumption in 2009 was estimated at 0.7 quadrillion Btu, less than 0.1 per cent of world energy consumption. Per capita energy consumption in 2004 was an estimated 128.7 million Btu, compared with 339.1 million Btu in the US. Natural gas forms the greatest proportion of energy consumption (67.6 per cent in 2000), followed by oil (36.7 per cent).

Oman had a 2010 electric generation capacity estimated at 4.2 gigawatts. Production fell from 8,600 million kilowatthours (kWh) in 1999 to 8,100 million kWh in 2000 but rose again to 18.6 billion kWh in 2010. There is an increasing demand for electricity in Oman which recent estimates put at about 5 per cent per year. Consequently, the government is involving the private sector by selling off a number of power plants. All state-owned companies should be privatised by the end of 2009. In addition, it is constructing several new ones, including the 90-megawatt al-Manah plant, the 280-megawatt Al-Kamil plant (being built by International Power plc and Arab International Contractor of Egypt), and the 430-megawatt Barka power plant (being built by AES). The Ministry of Electricity and Water is also considering constructing two gas-fired power plants in Dhahirah and Sharqiya, at least one of which would have a 300 MW capacity. Currently the electricity system consists of 31 power stations, 220 main sub-stations and 11,000 distribution transformers. The power stations are fuelled by gas (69.3 per cent), diesel (24.3 per cent) and steam (6.4 per cent).

Manufacturing
Industrial production grew at four per cent in 2000. Medium and light industry is rapidly expanding, with a recently-constructed flour mill in Muttrah, the first textile mill in Oman and three industrial estates at Rusayl, Sohar and Raysut, there is also a copper mining and refining plant at Sohar. There are currently approximately 200 industrial establishments employing over 29,000 workers. More than half of these industries are involved in the production of cement and metals, and more than half of the work force is involved in either cement production or garment making. Oman's industrial sector contributes about 40 per cent towards GDP.

Service Industries
The services industry is Oman's major contributor to GDP - an estimated 65 per cent in 2008. The tourism sector forms a growing part of the services industry. Revenue from tourism is currently about 1 per cent; however, the government aims to increase that proportion to 3 per cent by 2020. The majority of tourists visiting Oman come from Germany, Switzerland, Austria and Great Britain. During 1997 the 52 hotels in Oman received 463,150 guests, and it is estimated that the hotel trade generated RO42 million. The ports of Mina Sultan Qaboos and Mina Raysut also received some 600 tourists from cruise liners who were taken on sightseeing excursions. A programme of hotel building is underway in Oman. As at the end of 1999 more than 100 hotels, with more than 7,570 beds, had been opened. Figures for 2003 show that Oman had 817,000 visitors rising to 1,306,000 in 2006.

Agriculture
An area of 100,000 hectares is suitable for agriculture and 60,000 hectares of this is presently being cultivated. Over half of the population is employed in agriculture and fishing. The Sultanate of Oman had aimed for agricultural self-sufficiency by the year 2000.

Dates are a major agricultural product, with some 20,000 hectares being used for their production, 40 per cent of which is consumed by growers, 25 per cent by livestock and 30 per cent sold within Oman and abroad. Limes are also a valuable agricultural export. They are grown along the Batinah Coast, along with mangos, tobacco, tomatoes, onions, aubergines, peppers and others. Tropical fruit, including coconuts, bananas and pawpaws, are grown in Dhofar in the south because of its frequent monsoons.

Agricultural Production in 2010

Produce	Int. $'000*	Tonnes
Dates	136,869	276,400
Indigenous goat meat	47,922	20,000
Goat milk, whole, fresh	33,747	100,562
Tomatoes	30,083	81,400
Vegetables fresh nes	26,947	143,000
Cow milk, whole, fresh	21,719	69,600
Indigenous sheep meat	17,190	6,313
Bananas	15,969	56,700
Indigenous camel meat	15,966	7,618
Chillies and peppers, green	10,649	22,620
Sorghum	8,198	53,300

- continued

Hen eggs, in shell	7,672	9,250

* unofficial figures

Source: http://faostat.fao.org/site/339/default.aspx Food and Agriculture Organization of the United Nations, Food and Agricultural commodities production

The mountains behind the coastal plain are important for cattle-breeding and the Jebali tribesmen are the only cattle-breeders in the Sultanate. Until recently these tribesmen only reared cattle for their milk.

There are an estimated 240,260 sheep, 854,060 goats, 213,120 cattle and 98,550 camels in Oman, making it the leading producer of livestock in the Arabian peninsula. Although Oman produces approximately 2,757 tonnes of beef and 3,086 tonnes of mutton annually, it is not sufficient to meet the needs of the country. The government is currently implementing projects to increase poultry and dairy production by offering financial assistance to dairy farmers and building small egg and poultry farms.

Fishing

The Sultanate of Oman has 2,600 km of coastline and more than 150 species of fish. Over the last 20 years the Government has sought to develop the fishing industry. The quantity of fish caught has steadily risen to 164,000 metric tons. However, there has been a decline in the stock of some important fish species, for example, lobsters, abalone and kingfish.

COMMUNICATIONS AND TRANSPORT

Travel Requirements

Citizens of the USA, Canada, Australia and the EU require a passport valid for six months, and a visa. A visa is obtainable on arrival at Oman Seeb Airport. Visitors are not allowed to enter Oman by road unless their visa states such validity and a designated point of entry. Foreign travellers to Oman should contact the embassy to check precise visa requirements prior to travelling.

National Airlines

Oman Aviation Services provides international and domestic scheduled and charter passenger services, and employs nearly 2,500.
Oman Aviation Services, URL: http://www.omanair.aero

International Airports

Oman has six airports at Muscat, Salalah, Sur, Masirah, Khasab and Diba. Muscat, the country's largest airport, deals with more than four million passenger arrivals, departures and transits annually. Sur and Diba are used by light aircraft only. Muscat International Airport is currently undergoing exapnsion and by 2011 capacity should be 12 million passengers per annum. Further expansion is also envisaged with a capacity of 48 million passengers by 2050.
Airport: URL: http://www.omanairports.com

Roads

In the 1970s Oman's road network was very limited. A major programme of road construction was undertaken and the coastal strip of north Oman was concentrated on first because of its high population. By the end of 1986 there were 3,906 km of asphalt roads and 18,790 km of gravelled roads linking the coast with the interior and beyond to the towns of the United Arab Emirates. This rose in 1995 to 6,213 km of asphalt roads and 24,276 of graded roads. The towns of Muscat and Matrah are linked by a tarmac road to Sohar in the north. This road provides access to the International Airport at Seeb. Good roads exist between Nizwa and Sib, Gbri and Buraimi and Sohar and Buraimi. A 780 km highway links Muscat and Salalah. A bus service runs between Muscat and Dubai (UAE). Vehicles are driven on the right.

Ports and Harbours

The port Mina Sultan Qaboos at Muttrah was completed in 1974 and was designed to handle some two million tonnes of cargo per annum. There is also a port in Khasab and plans for the construction of another port in Sohar which will be built to serve the industrial sector in Sohar. The port of Mina Raysut is to be developed as a container port and free trade zone, upon completion of the renovations the port should be one of the largest and most sophisticated in the world. The country has a rocky coastline and cruising its waters is dangerous.

HEALTH

Oman's free National Health Service provides 57 hospitals and 118 health centres, with a total of just over 4,700 beds. Doctors are trained at the Faculty of Medicine at the Sultan Qaboos University and there are eleven institutes affording training to nurses. According to latest WHO figures (2005-10), there were 5,194 doctors (19 per 10,000 population), 11,233 nurses and midwifery personnel (41 per 10,000 population), 208 environmental and public health workers (1 per 10,000 population), 2,222 pharmacists (8 per 10,000 population) and 557 dentists (2 per 10,000 population).

The infant mortality rate (probability of dying before first birthday) according to 2010 figures was 8 deaths per 1,000 live births and the child (under-five) mortality rate was 9 deaths per 1,000 live births. The most common causes of death for infants (under 5 years old) are: prematurity (29 per cent), congenital anomalies (12 per cent), pneumonia (5 per cent), injuries (8 per cent) and diarrhoea (1 per cent). An intensive immunisation program has been carried out and to date 98 per cent of children have been immunised against killer childhood diseases.

In 2009 total expenditure on health amounted to 3.0 per cent of GDP on health. General government expenditure on heath as a total government expenditure was 5.8 per cent. Government expenditure accounts for 79.8 per cent of total health expenditure. Private expenditure accounts for the remainder. Per capita expenditure was US$520 in 2009.

In 2008 an estimated 89 per cent of the population had sustainable access to improved drinking water sources. In the same year an estimated 99 per cent of the population had sustainable access to improved sanitation. (Source: http://www.who.int, World Health Statistics 2012)

EDUCATION

In 2006, 4 per cent of GDP went on education or 31.1 per cent of total government expenditure, of which 50 per cent went on primary education and 41 per cent on secondary education. Approximately 8 per cent went on tertiary education. (Source: UNESCO)

Primary/Secondary Education

Education has seen enormous progress in the years since Qaboos became Sultan. In the academic year 2004-05, there were 1,240 schools in Oman, including primary, preparatory, and secondary. According to 2007 UNESCO figures 74 per cent of girls and 72 per cent of boys are enrolled in primary school and 94 per cent complete the course. The pupil: teacher ratio is 13:1. In 2007 it was estimated that 79 per cent of children are enroled in secondary school.

There have been recent improvements in the literacy rates. Oman has introduced a programme of adult education to help combat adult illiteracy even though the adult literacy rates are higher than the regional average. Figures for 2007 put adult literacy rate at 84.4 per cent, 89.4 per cent for males and 77.5 per cent for females, this figure rises for youth literacy (ages 15-24) to a rate of 98.4 per cent, 98.8 for males and 97.9 for females.

Higher Education

As well as institutes of health sciences and banking, there were eight teacher-training colleges and five technical institutes. There is at present one university, the Sultan Qaboos University, which opened in 1986. University students number some 4,300. Tertiary enrolment is estimated at 25 per cent of the tertiary age population.

Vocational Training

In 1997 about 4,000 students received vocational training at government centres and 16 private institutions. The private sector is being encouraged to take responsibility for vocational training.

RELIGION

Islam is the official religion of Oman, the Ibhadi being the main sect (75 per cent of the population). There is also a large South Asian Hindu community (7.0 per cent) and some Christians (3.0 per cent).

Oman has a religious liberty rating of 5 on a scale of 1 to 10 (10 is most freedom). (Source: World Religion Database)

COMMUNICATIONS AND MEDIA

Oman's main broadcasters are state-run. The government is allowed to censor publications on political or cultural grounds.

Newspapers

There are more than 20 newspapers. The government also publishes the Official Gazette which contains all Royal Decrees and Ministerial Decisions.
Al Watan (Oman), URL: http://www.alwatan.com/
Oman, URL: http://www.omandaily.com/
Oman Daily Observer, URL: http://www.omanobserver.com/
Times of Oman, URL: http://www.timesofoman.com/

Oman News Agency, URL: http://www.omannews.com/

Broadcasting

The official radio broadcaster in Oman is Radio Oman. A private radio station began operating in 2007.

Television transmissions commenced in 1974. In addition to the state-run Oman TV, stations also transmit from Saudi Arabia, the UAE and Yemen.
Oman TV and Radio, URL: http://www.oman-tv.gov.om/ (Arabic and English networks)
Halafm, URL: http://www.halafm.com/ (private Arabic station)

Telecommunications

The telecommunication system is modern and is the landline network is being expanded to remote villages using wireless loop systems. Estimates for 2008 put the number of landlines at approximately 275,000 and mobile phone subscribers at over 3 million.

Oman provided internet access at the beginning of 1997 through the government-run General Telecommunications Organisation (GTO). Figures for 2008 indicate that 450,000 Omanis have regular access to the internet.

ENVIRONMENT

Oman's major environmental problems include the scarcity of fresh water, oil pollution of beaches, soil salinity and oil pollution. There are periodic droughts. Oman is a signatory to the following international environmental agreements: Biodiversity, Climate Change, Climate Change-Kyoto Protocol, Desertification, Hazardous Wastes, Law of the Sea, Marine Dumping, Ozone Layer Protection, Ship Pollution, and Whaling.

Recent EIA estimates put the country's energy-related carbon emissions at 23.3 million metric tons in 2004. Per capita carbon emissions in the same year were estimated at 8.0 metric tons. Most of Oman's carbon emissions are generated by the industry sector (41.7 per cent in 1998), while the balance comes from the transport (27.4 per cent), residential (19.6 per cent), and commercial (11.6 per cent) sectors. In 2006, Oman's emissions from the consumption and flaring of fossil fuels totalled 34.73 million metric tons of carbon dioxide.

In 2007, UNESCO removed Oman's Arabian Oryx sanctuary from its World Heritage list after the numbers of the Arabian oryx declined and the government cut the park size and opened virtually the whole area to oil exploration.

SPACE PROGRAMME

Oman was one of the first Gulf states to make use of satellite for domestic transmissions and has recently signed an agreement with the Egyptian Satellite Company for the allocation of a transmission channel and four audio channels on the Nilesat system.

PAKISTAN

Islamic Republic of Pakistan

Islami Jamhuriya e Pakistan

Capital: Islamabad (Population estimate, 2010: 1.7 million)

President: Asif Ali Zardari (page 1543)

National Flag: Green, charged at the centre with a crescent and star five-pointed white; a white stripe pale-wise at the hoist to one-quarter width of the flag.

CONSTITUTION AND GOVERNMENT

Constitution
Pakistan, comprising the two provinces of East Pakistan and West Pakistan, became an independent sovereign state as a result of the partition of India on 14 August 1947, and became a republic within the Commonwealth on 23 March 1956. The province of East Pakistan seceded from Pakistan in 1971 and became the independent state of Bangladesh.

According to the 1973 constitution the head of state is the president, elected by parliament for a five-year term. The head of government is the prime minister, who is responsible to parliament and appoints the cabinet.

In April 2010, President Asif Ali Zardari submitted to parliament a set of constitutional reforms which were aimed at reducing the powers of the presidency. The measures were approved in the same month.

To consult the full constitution, please visit: http://www.mofa.gov.pk/Publications/constitution.pdf

1999 Military Coup
In October 1999 the prime minister, Mohammad Nawaz Sharif, was deposed in a military coup by the army chief General Pervez Musharraf who suspended the Constitution and declared a state of emergency. An eight-member National Security Council, led by General Musharraf, took executive control of the country, promising a return to democracy within three years. On 20 June 2001, General Pervez Musharraf was sworn in as president. An official announcement confirmed that General Musharraf would continue as chief executive and leader of Pakistan's armed forces, and that the national and provincial assemblies would be dissolved.

The former prime minister, Mohammad Nawaz Sharif, was sentenced to life imprisonment on charges of hijacking and terrorism and, in July 2000, convictions of corruption added a further 14 years imprisonment to his sentence. Mr Sharif went into exile in Saudi Arabia.

Following a referendum on 30 April 2002, General Musharraf's presidency was extended for a further five years. On 21 August 2002 General Musharraf changed the Constitution by way of a Legal Framework Order (LFO) allowing the president to dismiss an elected parliament and government, and increasing the number of members of parliament.

The LFO met with resistance from the opposition which resulted in an impasse lasting over a year. In December 2003, the government reached an agreement with the opposition and obtained the two-thirds majority required to pass the 17th Constitutional Amendment Bill. Under the deal, President Musharraf agreed to consult the prime minister on the appointment of armed forces chiefs, and to step down as Chief of Army Staff by December 2004. However, following the passing of legislation which allowed the President to hold both offices until 2007, President Musharraf announced to the nation in December 2004 that he would retain both roles.

In April 2004 Parliament approved the creation of a National Security Council, led by the military, which would institutionalise the role of the armed forces in civilian affairs. In September 2006, ahead of the 2007 elections, the two main opposition parties agreed on a 'charter of democracy' committed to removing the military from politics; a group of retired generals, politicians and academics urged the President to end the military's role in politics by separating the two offices of state.

International Relations
Pakistan has long had strong ties with China. Following a period of strain in the aftermath of the Iranian Revolution, and during the Afghan conflict, the country's relations with Iran have now improved. During the Soviet invasion of Afghanistan, the Pakistan government supported the resistance movement, and provided a haven for refugees; it was one of three countries to recognise the Taliban government after the Soviet withdrawal. However, following

the terrorist attacks on the USA in September 2001, the Pakistani government allied itself to the USA in the fight against terror, and pledged to eliminate terrorist training camps from its territories.

Having been suspended from the Councils of the Commonwealth following the coup in 1999, Pakistan was reinstated in 2004. It was again suspended in 2007 and reinstated in 2008 following local elections and after President Mubsharraf stepped down as Chief of Army staff. Relations with the EU were also suspended in the wake of the coup, and were reinstated in 2001. The EU is Pakistan's largest trading partner.

Pakistan and Kashmir
The border with India in the Kashmir area is currently under dispute between the two nations. Following Independence in 1947, Kashmir was free to join India or Pakistan. Hari Singh, the Maharaja, at first wanted to be independent but ceded Kashmir to India in exchange for military aid. Pakistan has long argued that, since the majority of Kashmir's population are Muslim, the territory should be a part of Pakistan. Following the first Kashmiri war in 1947-48, a demarcation line was established. War broke out again in 1965 which resulted in the Simla Agreement in 1972 under with the Line of Control was established, dividing Kashmir into Indian-administered Jammu and Kashmir, and Pakistan-administered Kashmir.

Violence has continued to break out sporadically although casualties have fallen in recent years. Tensions came to a head in 2002 when India successfully test fired a ballistic missile. Pakistan then tested missiles capable of carrying nuclear warheads. By the middle of 2002 diplomatic moves were being made to avert full scale war and in October India announced it was withdrawing its troops from the border. Early 2003 saw relations failing again when tit-for-tat expulsions of diplomats began. In November, Pakistan declared a Kashmir ceasefire, which was reciprocated by India. In December, and Pakistan and India agreed to resume direct air links from the beginning of 2004 after a two-year ban and in 2005 India and Pakistan agreed to a landmark bus service over the ceasefire line. Following the earthquake of 2005, further cooperation between the two countries included the notification of missile testing, the creation of new bank branches and an increase in the number of airline destinations in both counties. The leaders of both countries met in Cuba in 2006, and agreed to seek a peaceful, negotiated settlement to the Kashmir issue.

Recent Events
Following the 11 September 2001 attacks on the USA, Pakistan ceased supporting the Taliban and became a US ally. However, the move was not universally popular within Pakistan and the number of suicide bomb attacks increased, often with heavy casualties. The US carried out targeted air strikes, sometimes with civilian casualties.

On 8th October 2005, an earthquake measuring 7.6 on the Richter scale struck the regional capital of Muzaffarabad, in Pakistan-administered Kashmir. In total 15,000 villages were devastated. The number of those killed in the devastation was estimated to be over 73,000; some 69,000 were known to be injured and three million were left homeless.

In August 2006, the Pakistani authorities reported that Sardar Akbar Bugti, a tribal rebel leader in Balochistan, had been killed in a bombing raid. For decades, Baloch nationalists have been critical of the central government in Islamabad, accusing it of exploiting the province's massive natural gas and other resources, and giving very little in return. Over the past two years, they have targeted power facilities, railway tracks and other key installations. The government has responded with helicopter attacks and rocket raids.

On 21 February 2007, India and Pakistan signed an agreement aimed at reducing the risk of accidental nuclear war in the region.

In March, lawyers boycotted courts across Pakistan in protest at President Musharraf's suspension of Chief Justice Iftikhar Mohammed Chaudhry, for alleged misuse of office. The judge was noted for his firm line on government misdeeds and human rights abuses. On 20th July 2007, the Supreme Court judges ruled to quash all charges against Mr Chaudhry.

In an effort to curtail an increasingly aggressive campaign by clerics to enforce strict Sharia law in Islamabad, Pakistani troops first laid siege to the Red Mosque and its Islamic school, and then stormed it on the 10th July. Some 1,100 people left the mosque during the week-long siege; more than 100 people, including militants and troops, died in the raid.

In the run-up to the Presidential elections in October 2007, the election commission controversially decided that President Musharraf could run for president whilst still the army chief; he stated that he would stand down as army chief if elected for another presidential term. On 3rd October, President Musharraf named his successor as army chief; the nominee, Lt. Gen. Ashfaq Pervez Kiani, was a former head of intelligence. Scores of opposition MPs resigned from the national parliament and provincial assemblies in protest at President Musharraf's eligibility to stand. President Musharraf reached an agreement with the former PM, Benazir Bhutto, two days before the election; corruption charges against Ms. Bhutto were dropped, and her party did not join the opposition boycott, but abstained from voting. As expected, Gen Musharraf won the 6th October election by a landslide. Opposition MPs abstained or boycotted the vote, calling it unconstitutional.

On 19th October, former PM Benazir Bhutto returned to Pakistan after eight years of self-imposed exile. Her return to Karachi, celebrated by some 200,000 supporters, was marred when two bombs exploded close to her convoy, killing 130 people.

In late October 2007, fighting broke out in the north-western Swat Valley. A ceasefire was reached on 29th October. On 3 November 2007, the as yet unconfirmed President Musharraf called a state of emergency and suspended the constitution. On 16 November a caretaker cabinet was appointed. On 22 November, the Supreme Court dismissed the last of the objections to President Musharraf's eligibility to run for office whilst still the army chief; the President had appointed loyal judges to the bench. Pakistan was suspended from the Commonwealth because of its imposition of emergency rule.

On 25th November, former Prime Minister Nawaz Sharif returned to Pakistan after seven years in exile, intending to contest the parliamentary elections. President Musharraf handed over command of the army to General Ashfaq Pervez Kayani in advance of being sworn in as a civilian President on the 29th November. He lifted the state of emergency on the 15th December. On December 27th, Benazir Bhutto was assassinated by a suicide bomber; the Pakistan authorities said that they had proof that al-Qaeda had carried out the assassination, which killed a further 20 people. There was rioting across the country in the days following the assassination. Benazir Bhutto's son, Bilawal Bhutto, though legally too young to stand for parliament, was chosen to head the Pakistan People's Party. The parliamentary elections were postponed until February 2008.

Violence, including several suicide bombings, continued in the run-up to the parliamentary elections in February. On the 18th of February, the Pakistanis went to the polls; the Pakistan People's Party (PPP) won the largest number of votes, but not enough for an outright victory. On 9th March, an agreement on a coalition government was signed.

The new government adopted a policy of dialogue with Islamic militants. On 12th May, the PML-N announced that it was pulling out of the government, because of differences over the reinstatement of judges sacked by President Pervez Musharraf.

On the 21st May, the provincial government in north-west Pakistan agreed to pull troops out of the Swat valley, and to allow the imposition of some elements of Sharia law in the area, in return for the promise by pro-Taliban militants to close training camps, hand over foreign militants and end attacks on security forces.

On the 11th June, the US used artillery and air strikes at a border post between Afghanistan and Pakistan after coming under fire from "anti-Afghan" forces. Eleven Pakistani soldiers were killed, along with eight Taliban militants. There was increasing anger in Pakistan at US strikes on its territory.

On the 18th August 2008, President Musharraf announced his resignation. He was facing impeachment by the coalition government, on charges of violation of the constitution and gross misconduct. The Speaker of the Senate, Muhammad Mian Sumroo, took over as caretaker president. Asif Ali Zardari, leader of the Pakistan People's Party, won the presidential election on 6 September 2008.

However, bomb attacks continued, many on soft targets with heavy civilian losses. On the 20th September, a massive bomb blast hit the Marriott Hotel in Islamabad, killing at least 53 people including the Czech Ambassador. Over 266 people were injured in the attack. A few days later, a Pakistani militant group, Fidayeen-e-Islam, claimed to have carried out the attack, to halt American interference in Pakistan.

The US continued its targeted attacks on key areas. The Pakistani army denounced the raids, fearing that the emerging anti-Taliban sentiment could turn into an anti-American one. At least 60 militants were killed after the Pakistani army launched air strikes on two Taliban training camps in north-west Swat Valley on the 17 October. On the 26th October, a suspected US missile strike on Mandatta village, South Waziristan, killed 20 people, including top Taliban commander Mohammad Omar.

An earthquake of 6.4 magnitude on the 28th October left at least 215 people dead and up to 50,000 homeless near Quetta, Balochistan province.

At the beginning of November, President Asif Ali Zardari sought assistance from Saudi Arabia to help alleviate Pakistan's severe economic problems. Pakistan needed over $5bn urgently to meet its international obligations, and to tide over trade and budget deficits. The government borrowed billions of dollars from the International Monetary Fund to overcome its spiralling debt crisis.

On the 7th December, Pakistani security forces attacked a camp in Pakistani-administered Kashmir used by a militant group that India had linked to the Mumbai attacks the previous week which left 170 people dead. The Lashkar-e-Taiba group's operational chief, Zaki-ur-Rehman Lakhvi, who is said by Delhi to have ordered the attacks, was seized with up to four other people.

On the 26th December, a Taliban commander in the Swat valley ordered parents to stop sending their daughters to school by 15 January, and threatened to blow up schools which enrolled female students. During 2008, Taliban militants destroyed over 130 schools in the

Swat valley, depriving more than 17,000 students of an education. The militants also threatened to destroy private schools, since these are not Islamic religious institutions and the students are taught courses based on the government syllabus.

The violence continued. The banned Lashkar-e-Jhangvi, one of Pakistan's most ruthless militant groups, is blamed for most of the violence.

On the 14th February, 27 militants were killed in a suspected US missile attack in South Waziristan. Pakistani leaders had hoped that the administration of Barack Obama would halt the controversial maneuvers, but President Obama said there was no doubt militants were operating in safe havens in Pakistan's tribal belt, and that the US would make sure Pakistan was a strong ally in fighting that threat.

On the 15th February, Taliban fighters in the Swat valley announced a 10-day ceasefire after local officials signed a deal with a militant leader to enforce Sharia law in the district. Pakistani President Asif Zardari warned that the entire country is fighting for its survival against the Taliban.

Pakistan's Supreme Court upheld bans on former prime minister Nawaz Sharif and his brother, Shahbaz, from elected office. Shahbaz Sharif had to step down from his position as chief minister in Punjab.

On the 3rd March, 12 gunmen attacked a convoy carrying the visiting Sri Lankan cricket team in Lahore. Officials said the incident bore similarities to the November attacks in Mumbai, which were blamed on Pakistan-based Islamic militants.

On the 27th April, Taliban talks with the government in the north-west were suspended when troops and Taleban militants clashed in Lower Dir in North West Frontier Province (NWFP), forcing hundreds of civilians to flee. The Taliban warned of militant attacks in all parts of Malakand division - the group of six districts where the new Sharia law has been enforced - if the military operation in Dir was not halted. The government and the military insist that the Taliban should fulfill their part of the deal - to disarm and to concede administrative power to government departments.

On the 9th May, the army began operations to retake the main towns in the Swat Valley from the Taliban. By the 25th May, some order had been restored. The fighting displaced some 2.4 million people from the Swat valley.

Further atrocities included a suicide bomb attack on a mosque in Hayagai Sharki village, Upper Dir. 38 people were killed and many more injured. In response, hundreds of tribesmen began an offensive against Taliban militants, attacking militant strongholds in the area. On the 10th June, a suicide bomb attack on the Pearl Continental Hotel in Peshawar left 15 people dead and 60 injured. In early August, the Taliban leader in Pakistan, Baitullah Mehsud, was killed in a US drone attack.

On the 14th August, President Zardari announced reforms to integrate the country's war-torn Federally Administered Tribal Areas (Fata) into mainstream Pakistan. The new laws will allow political parties to operate in the seven semi-autonomous regions which have not been politically and administratively integrated into the rest of the country since the British left in 1947. The Fata have been ruled by government-appointed agents in concert with tribal leaders, who have had the power to hold tribesmen in custody for three years without trial and to confiscate or destroy property.

On 29 November, President Asif Ali Zardari handed control of Pakistan's nuclear arsenal to his prime minister. Mr Zardari is currently very unpopular: an amnesty protecting him from possible prosecution has just expired and critics believe his actions are aimed at placating his political critics.

In December 2009, President Obama called for greater co-operation from Pakistan in the fight against terror. Pakistan rejected a charge that Osama bin Laden is in Pakistan. In the same week, bomb attacks in Lahore killed at least 48 people and injured many more. In the same month, the Supreme Court ruled that an amnesty decree protecting President Zardari against corruption charges was illegal.

Sporadic violence continued and in January 2010 a suicide attack on a volleyball match in the north-west of the country resulted in over 100 people being killed.

In April 2010, President Asif Ali Zardari proposed wide-ranging constitutional reforms aimed at reducing the powers of the presidency.

In August 2010 the monsoon triggered devastating floods, the worst in 80 years, affecting more than 20 million people. International aid was sent in but the effects are predicted to have long term consequences with crops washed away, millions homeless and a severely damaged infrastructure.

In January 2011 the governor of Punjab province, Salman Taseer was assassinated in the street by a member of his own security. It was believed he was attacked because of his campaign for the release of a Christian woman who faced the death penalty under the country's strict blasphemy laws.

Shahbaz Bhatti, the Minister for Minorities, was assassinated in March 2011. Mr Bhatti was the only Christian member of the government and had faced death threats after calling for the blasphemy laws to be reformed. The Pakistan People's Party abandoned plans to amend the blasphemy laws were in February 2011.

On May 2nd 2011 US President Barack Obama announced that Al Qaeda's leader Osama Bin Laden had been found and killed by the US military. He had been found living in a compound in the town of Abbottabad, he was shot during the raid and his body was buried at sea later that day. The Pakistan Government denied any knowledge that Bin Laden was living in Pakistan.

Sectarian attacks continued to occur. In September 2011 the group Lashkar-e-Jhangvi was responsible for attacks in which 26 Shia pilgrims were killed in the Balochistan province.

In November 2011, more than 24 Pakistan troops were killed in a Nato air strike on the Afghan border. Pakistan responded by closing the border crossing to American supply lines. The crossing was opened again in July 2012 in an effort to improve relations between the two countries.

In January 2012, tension rose between army chiefs and the government after the prime minister criticised army leaders and sacked a senior defence official.

In May 2012, the US cut its aid to Pakistan by $33 million after Pakistan jailed Dr Shakil Afridi on treason charges. Mr Afridi had helped the CIA find Osama Bin Laden.

In June 2012, the Supreme Court ruled that Prime Minister Gilani was disqualified from holding office after he refused to investigate corruption charges. The Minister of Water and Power, Raja Pervez Ashraf, was appointed by parliament as his successor. Mr Ashraf is also under under investigation for alleged corruption over the leases of power plants.

In July 2012, the US apologized to Pakistan for the deaths of 24 soldiers the previous year. Pakistan agreed to reopen Nato supply routes to Afghanistan.

In October 2012, Malala Yousafzai, a 14 year old girl who had written an online diary about life under the Taliban and spoke out for the right for girls to be educated, was targeted and shot at by the Taliban. Malala was seriously injured and following initial treatment in Rawalpindi was flown to the UK to receive more specialist care.

In November 2012, during the Shia holy month of Muharram, there were several suicide bomb attacks. Over 20 people were killed at a Shia procession in Rawalpindi.

In January 2013, the Supreme Court ordered the arrest of the prime minister Raja Pervez Ashraf over corruption allegations dating back to 2010. Mr Ashraf denies the charges. In the same month the chief minister of Balochistan was sacked over bomb blasts in the provinical cpaital Quetta in which over 90 Shia Muslims were killed.

In January 2013, the anti corruption campaigner T. Qadri led a march on Islamabad calling for the resignation of the government. After several days of protests the government agreed to dissolve parliament early and to consult Mr Qadri over the formation of a caretaker government.

In Aptil 2013, former president, Pervez Musharrf was remanded in custody over claims that in 2007 he had illegally detained several judges.

Legislature
A bicameral parliament (*Majlis as-Shoora*) was introduced under the constitution of 12 April 1973 and comprises an upper house (the Senate) and a lower house (the National Assembly). Parliament was suspended after the 1999 coup and was dissolved on 20 June 2001. Elections for the upper house next took place in February 2003, and elections for the lower house next took place on 10 October 2002.

Upper House
Following the August 2002 Legal Framework Order (LFO), the number of Senate members was increased from 87 to 100, of which 66 are elected from the provincial assemblies, eight from the Federally Administered Tribal Areas, and two from the federal capital. 17 seats are reserved for women and 17 seats are reserved for Islamic lawyers, technocrats and other professionals. The numbers increased to 104 in 2012. Members serve a four-year term.
Senate, Parliament House, Constitution Avenue, 44000, Islamabad, Pakistan. Tel: +92 51 922 3475-76 (Chairman), fax: +92 51 922 3477 (Chairman), e-mail: info@Senate.gov.pk, URL: http://www.senate.gov.pk/
Chairman: Syed Nayyer Hussain Bokhari (PPP-P)

Lower House
The National Assembly is elected for a five year term on the basis of universal adult suffrage. It has 342 members, increased from 237 by the LFO. Seats are reserved for 10 non-Muslim members and 60 women members.
National Assembly, Parliament House, Constitution Avenue, 44000, Islamabad, Pakistan. E-mail: assembly@isb.paknet.com.pk, URL: http://www.na.gov.pk/
Speaker: Dr Fehmida Mirza

Pakistan National Security Council
The Council has thirteen members. Besides the President, the other members of the Council are the Prime Minister, the Chairman of the Senate, the Speaker of the National Assembly, the Leader of the Opposition in the National Assembly, the Chief Ministers of the Provinces, the Chairman of the Joint Chiefs of Staff Committee (CJCSC) and the Chiefs of Staff of the Pakistan Army, Pakistan Navy and Pakistan Air Force.

Chiefs of Staff (as of June 2013)
Chair of the Joint Chiefs of Staff Committee: Lt.General Khalid Shamim Wyne
Chief of Naval Staff: Admiral Mohammad Asif Sandila
Chief of Air Staff: Air Marshal Tahir Rafique Butt
Chief of Army Staff: Gen.Ashfaq Pervez Kayani

Cabinet (as at June 2013)
Prime Minister and Minister of Defence: Mian Muhammad Nawaz Sharif (page 1513)
Minister of Finance and Economic Affairs: Mohammad Ishaq Dar (page 1412)
Minister of Planning and Development: Ahsan Iqbal (page 1447)
Minister of Defence Production: Rana Tanveer Hussain
Minister of Information and Broadcasting: Pervez Rashid
Minister of the Interior & Narcotics Control: Nisar Ali Khan (page 1456)
Minister of Kashmir Affairs and Gilgit-Baltistan: Muhammad Barjees Tahir

Minister of Law, Justice and Human Rights: Zahid Hamid
Minister of National Food Security: Sikandar Hayat Bosan
Minister of Overseas Pakistanis and Human Resources: Khaqan Abbasi
Minister of Industry & Production: Ghulam Murtaza Jatoi
Minister of Ports and Shipping: Sen. Kamran Micheal
Minister of Railways: Khwaja Saad Rafiq
Minister of Religious Affairs: Sardar Muhammad Yusuf
Minister of States and Frontier Regions: Gen. Abdul Qadir Baloch
Minister of Water and Power: Mohammad Asif
Minister of Petroleum and Natural Resources: Khaqan Abbasi

Ministries
Government portal, URL: http://www.pakistan.gov.pk
Office of the President, Aiwan-e-Sadr, Islamabad, Pakistan. Tel: +92 (0)51 820606, fax: +92 51 921 1018, URL: http://www.pakistan.gov.pk/
Office of the Prime Minister, F6/5 Cabinet Division, Cabinet Block, Constitution Avenue, Islamabad, Pakistan. Tel: +92 (0)51 816 1111, URL: http://www.pakistan.gov.pk/
Ministry of Climate Change, URL: http://moenv.gov.pk
Ministry of Commerce, Pakistan Secretariat, Islamabad, Pakistan. Tel: +92 (0)51 214936, URL: http://www.commerce.gov.pk
Ministry of Communications, Block D, Pakistan Secretariat, Islamabad, Pakistan. URL: http://www.communication.gov.pk
Ministry of Defence, No 11, Pakistan Secretariat, Islamabad, Pakistan. Tel: +92 51 927 1107, URL: http://www.mod.gov.pk
Ministry of Foreign Affairs, Constitution Avenue, Islamabad, Pakistan. Tel: +92 (0)51 920 1297, fax: +92 (0)51 920 2518 / 922 4205, URL: http://www.mofa.gov.pk
Ministry of Finance, Revenue and Planning, Pakistan Secretariat, Islamabad, Pakistan. Tel: +92 (0)51 820928, URL: http://www.finance.gov.pk/
Ministry of Health, URL: http://www.health.gov.pk
Ministry of Information & Broadcasting, 4th Floor, Cabinet Block, Pakistan Secretariat, Islamabad, Pakistan. URL: http://www.infopak.gov.pk
Ministry of Information Technology, Agha Khan Road, F-5/1 Islamabad, Pakistan. URL: http://www.moitt.gov.pk/
Ministry of the Interior, 4th Floor, Block R, Pakistan Secretariat, Islamabad, Pakistan. URL: http://www.interior.gov.pk/
Ministry of Parliamentary Affairs, Law & Justice, Block R, Pakistan Secretariat, Islamabad, Pakistan. URL: http://mopa.gov.pk
Inter Provincial Coordination Division, Cabinet Block, Constitution Avenue, Islamabad, Pakistan. URL: http://www.ipc.gov.pk
Ministry of Petroleum and Natural Resources, 3rd Floor, A Block, Pak Secratariat, Islamabad, Pakistan. Tel: +92 (0)51 920 8233, fax: +92 (0)51 920 5437, e-mail: info@mpnr.gov.pk, URL: http://www.mpnr.gov.pk/
Pakistan Post Office Department, URL: http://www.pakpost.gov.pk/
Ministry of Privatisation, EAC Building, Constitution Avenue, Islamabad, Pakistan. URL: http://www.privatisation.gov.pk/
Ministry of Professional Training, Education and Standards in Higher Education, URL: http://moptt.gov.pk/

Political Parties
Pakistan Muslim League-Q (PML-Q), URL: http://www.pml.org.pk/
President: Chaudhry Shujaat Hussain
Pakistan People's Party (PPP), House 8, Street 19, Sector F-8/2, Islamabad, Pakistan. E-mail: ppp@comsats.net.pk, URL: http://www.ppp.org.pk/
Chairperson: Bilawal Bhutto / Asif Ali Zardari
Pakistan Muslim League-N (PML-N), House No. 20, H. Streets 10, Sector F-8/3 Islamabad, Pakistan. Tel: +92 (0)51 285 2662, URL: http://www.pmln.org.pk
Leader: Nawaz Sharif
Muttahhida Majlis-e-Amal Pakistan, (MMA, United Assembly of Action), coalition between religious-political parties. URL: http://www.mma.org.pk
Muttahida Qaumi Movement (MQM), Nine Zero, 494/8 Azizabad, Federal B. Area Karachi, Pakistan. Tel: +92 (0)21 631 3690, 632 9131, 632 9900, fax: +92 (0)21 632 9955, URL: http://www.mqm.com/
Leader: Altaf Hussain

Elections
The Constitution requires that the president be Muslim and over 45 years of age. The president is elected for a term of five years by a secret ballot through an Electoral College comprising the Members of the Senate, National Assembly and the Provincial Assemblies. The winner needs simple majority of votes.

President Muhammad Rafiq Tarar was deposed in the October 1999 coup led by General Musharraf, who assumed the role of president and chief executive. Presidential elections took place on 6th October 2007, but were boycotted by opposition parties; President Musharraf won a further term in office, though his eligibility to stand as a candidate was questioned and opposition MPs called the election unconstitutional. He announced his resignation on the 18th August 2008 when the newly elected government decided to impeach him on charges of violation of the constitution and gross misconduct.

National Assembly elections were due to take place in November 2007, but were delayed until the 18th of February 2008 due to the assassination of Benazir Bhutto. The Pakistan People's Party (PPP) won the largest number of votes, but not enough for an outright victory. The PML-N, or Pakistani Muslim League-Nawaz, came in second place. The Pakistan Muslim League's pro-Musharraf wing, the PML-Q suffered heavy defeats. Neither Mr. Zardari of the PPP nor Mr. Sharif of the PML-N were eligible to become Prime Minister. A coalition government was agreed between the two major parties, but the PML-N withdrew when Asif Ali Zardari announced that he intended to run for President following the resignation of President Musharraf in August. Mr. Zardari won the presidential election on the 6th September, winning 481 of the total 702 votes.

The most recent National Assembly election took place in May 2013, the branch of the Pakistan Muslim League led by Nawaz Sharif, won 126 seats but was still 11 seats short of a majority.

National Assembly, May 2013

Party	No. of Seats
Pakistan Muslim League (Nawaz)	126
Pakistan People's Party	31
Pakistan Movement for Justice	29
Muttahhida Qaumi Movement	18
Jamiat Ulama-e-Islam	11
Others	28
Independents	29
Reserved seats (women)	60
Reserved seats (minorities)	10

The partial Senate elections were held on 4th March 2009. The Pakistan People's Party won most seats (27 of the 100 seats) whilst the President's PML-Q won 21 seats. The PML-N came fourth, with seven seats. Partial elections were held most recently on 2 March 2012 for 54 of the now 104 seats.

Diplomatic Representation

Embassy of Pakistan, 3517 International Court, NW, Washington DC, 20008, USA. Tel: +1 202 243 6500, fax: +1 202 686 1534, e-mail: info@embassyofpakistan.org, URL: http://www.embassyofpakistanusa.org/
Ambassador: Sherry Rehman (page 1501)
High Commission for Pakistan, 35-36 Lowndes Square, London, SW1X 9JN, United Kingdom. Tel: +44 (0)20 7664 9200, fax: +44 (0)20 7664 9224, e-mail: hoc@phclondon.org, URL: http://www.phclondon.org/HC/index.asp
High Commissioner: H.E. Mr Wajid Shamsul Hasan
British High Commission, Diplomatic Enclave, Ramna 5, PO Box 1122, Islamabad, Pakistan. Tel: +92 51 201 2000, fax: +92 51 282 3439, e-mail: visqry.islamabad@fco.gov.uk (Visa), Cons.Islamabad@fco.gov.uk (Consular), bhc-ukti@dsl.net.pk (Trade and Investment), bhcmedia@dsl.net.pk (Media & Public Affairs), URL: http://ukinpakistan.fco.gov.uk/en/
High Commissioner: Adam Thomson CMG
US Embassy, Diplomatic Enclave, Ramna 5, Islamabad, Pakistan. Tel: +92 51 2080 0000, fax: +92 51 227 6427, e-mail: webmasterisb@state.gov, URL: http://islamabad.usembassy.gov/
Ambassador: Richard Olson
Permanent Mission of Pakistan to the United Nations, 8 East 65 Street, New York, NY 10021, USA. Tel: +1 212 879 8600, fax: +1 212 744 7348, e-mail: pakistan@un.int, URL: http://www.pakun.org/
Ambassador: Masood Khan

LEGAL SYSTEM

The Supreme Court of Pakistan is the highest Court of Appeal in the country. It can accept appeal against any judgement, decree, order or sentence of a High Court, and it exercises original jurisdiction regarding disputes between the Federal Government and a Provincial Government, or between two or more Provincial Governments. The Court may sit *en bloc* or in panels. The Supreme Court consists of the Chief Justice and 13 other judges. The Chief Justice is appointed by the President whilst the judges are appointed by the President and the Chief Judge. Both Chief Justice and judges can hold office until the age of 65.

There are four High Courts in Pakistan, one for each Province. Under the High Courts, there are courts of District and Sessions, Civil Judge and Magistrates which are courts of general jurisdiction. There are special courts and tribunals of which Family Courts, Labour Courts and Civil Services Tribunals are the most important. At present there is one High Court Judge for each province as well as 50 judges in the Lahore High Court of the Punjab, 28 judges in the High Court of Sindh, 15 in the Peshawar High Court of NWFP, and six in High Court of Balochistan. High Court judges are appointed by the President and the Chief Justice of Pakistan, the Governor of the Province and the Chief Justice of the High Court in which the appointment is made.

A Federal Sharia Court was introduced in 1980. It is based principally in Islamabad with circuits in Lahore, Karachi, Peshawar and Quetta. The Court consists of not more than eight Muslim Judges including the Chief Justice. Of the Judges, four should be Judges or ex-Judges of the High Court and not more than three should be well-versed in Islamic law. The Court can examine whether or not any law is repugnant to the Injunctions of Islam. The Court's decisions can be appealed before the Supreme Court.

In July 2008, Taliban militants in Pakistan's north-western Mohmand tribal area announced that they had set up permanent Islamic courts. The districts have been divided into four judicial zones, each having two judges and a permanent court address. The permanent courts show the diminishing authority of the central and local governments. In July, two Afghan nationals accused of spying for the US were publicly killed on the orders of a Taliban court in Bajaur, and in June, a court in Orakzai ordered the public killing of half a dozen alleged bandits. In March, the Taliban killed a couple after they were allegedly found guilty of adultery by a court in Mohmand.

Against a background of ongoing battles with militants in the northwest, and natural disasters, which together have led to hundreds of thousands of people being displaced, the human rights situation in Pakistan is poor. Local police act independently of government authority. Collective punishment is a problem in the Federally Administered Tribal Areas (FATA). There is a general failure to prosecute people responsible for abuses. There is a lack of judicial independence, and corruption within government and security forces is widespread. Prison conditions are life-threatening.

Pakistan retains the death penalty. While under military rule Pakistan had one of the highest execution rates in the world but there was a short-lived unofficial moratorium on the death penalty following the departure of General Musharaff; this ended in 2012 with the execution of a soldier. Despite this, the ruling PPP party has repeatedly said it is against the death penalty. In 2007, 309 prisoners were sentenced to death and 134 were hanged. In 2010, 365 people were sentenced to death and 313 in 2011. More than 7,000 prisoners are believed to be on death row.

Supreme Court of Pakistan, URL: http://www.supremecourt.gov.pk/
Chief Justice: Mr. Justice Iftikhar Muhammad Chaudhry
Lahore High Court, URL: http://www.lhc.gov.pk/
Chief Justice: Mr. Justice Umar Ata Bandial
Federal Shari'at Court, URL: http://www.federalshariatcourt.gov.pk/
Chief Justice: Agha Rafiq Ahmed Khan

LOCAL GOVERNMENT

Pakistan is divided into four provinces (Balochistan, Kyber-Pakhtunkhwa, Punjab and Sindh), two centrally administered areas (Azad Kashmir and Gilgit Baltistan), one territory (Federally Administered Tribal Areas) and one capital territory (Islamabad).

Provincial Governors (June 2013)
Balochistan: Muhammad Khan Achakzai
Khyber-Pakhtunkhwa: Khan Shaukatullah
Punjab: Ahmad Mahmood
Sindh: Dr Ishrat ul-Ibad Khan
Gilgit-Baltistan: Pir Karam Ali Shah

Chief Ministers of Provincial Governments (June 2013)
Balochistan: Dr Abdul Malik Baloch
Khyber-Pakhtunkhwa: Pervez Khan Khattak
Punjab: Shahbaz Sharif
Sindh: Syed Qaim Ali Shah (PPP)
Gilgit-Baltistan: Syed Mehdi Shah (PPP)

City of Islamabad, URL: http://www.islamabad.gov.pk/islamabad/default.asp

The province of the Punjab extends over an area of 205,344 sq. km. It comprises 36 districts and 106 tehsils and two provincially administered tribal areas. About 72 per cent of the population lives in rural areas. Area-wise, Bahawalpur Division is the largest (45,589 sq. km.), followed by D.G. Khan (38,778 sq. km.). Lahore is the smallest district (16,105 sq. km.) in which the largest share of the population live (18.3 per cent), while D.G. Khan has the lowest share (7.9 cent).
Punjab Government, URL: http://pportal.punjab.gov.pk/portal/

Sindh comprises four divisions (Karachi, Hyderabad, Larkana and Sukkur), 18 districts and 80 talukas. Larkana was created after 1981 census. The talukas are divided into supervisory tapedar circles and tapedar circles. Each division is headed by a Commissioner and the district by a Deputy Commissioner. They are responsible for general administration, law and order, internal security and revenue collection.
Government of Sindh, URL: http://www.sindh.gov.pk/

There are seven divisions, 20 districts and 46 tehsils (settled and unsettled) in Khyber-Pakhtunkhwa Province. Peshawar division has three districts, Hazara division has two districts, Malakand division has five districts, Mardan division has two districts, Kohat division has two districts, Bannu division has two districts, and D.I. Khan division has two districts. After the census of 1981 the provincial government created three divisions, eight districts and eight tehsils in the province in order to provide people better access to administration. The Tribal Agencies of Bajaur, Mohmand, Khyber, Kurram, North Waziristan, South Waziristan and Orak-Zai are administered by the Federal Government through the Governor of NWFP. He exercises the powers delegated to him by the President of Pakistan.
Government of Khyber-Pakhtunkhwa, URL: http://www.khyberpakhtunkhwa.gov.pk/

With its capital at Quetta, the province of Balochistan comprises 30 districts, 54 tehsils and 55 sub-tehsils. The main reason for creating new districts and tehsils is the pressing demand of the people living in far-flung areas. The districts in Balochistan are Awaran, Barkhan, Chagai, Dera Buti, Gwadar, Harnai, Jaffarabad, Jhall Magsi, Kachhi, Kalat, Kech Kharan, Khuzdar, Killa Abdullah, Killa Saifulllah, Kohlu, Lasbela, Loralai, Mastung, Musakhail, Nasirabad, Nushki, Panjgur, Pishin, Quetta, Sheerani, Sibi, Washuk, Zhob, and Ziarat.
Government of Baluchistan, URL: http://www.balochistan.gov.pk/

Gilgit-Baltistan is the northernmost part of the country, it borders Pakistan's Khyber Pukhtunkhwa province to the west, Afghanistan's Wakhan Corridor to the north, China to the northeast, Azad Kashmir to the south, and Jammu and Kashmir , India to the southeast. Gilgit-Baltistan covers an area of 72,971 sq km and has a population in the region of one million people. Its administrative center is Gilgit. Originally the territory became a single administrative entity in unit 1970 and was known as the Northern Areas. Its districts are: Gilgit, Skardu, Diamir, Ghizer, Astor, Hunza Nagar.
Government of Gilgit-Baltistan, URL: http://www.gilgitbaltistan.gov.pk/

Federally Administered Tribal Areas
Under the Constitution, FATA is included among the "territories" of Pakistan. It is represented in the National Assembly and the Senate but remains under the direct executive authority of the President. Today, FATA is administered by Governor of the NWFP in his capacity as an agent to the President of Pakistan, under the overall supervision of the Ministry of States and Frontier Regions in Islamabad. FATA is divided into two administrative categories: 'protected' areas (regions under the direct control of the government), and 'non-protected' areas (administered indirectly through local tribes). The area can be divided into the northern, central and southern regions. The northern zone consists of the Bajaur and Mohmand

PAKISTAN

agencies. The central region covers the Khyber, Kurram and Orakzai agencies, and the FRs of Kohat and Peshawar. The southern region comprises the North Waziristan and South Waziristan agencies, and the FRs of Bannu, Dera Ismail Khan, Lakki Marwat and Tank.
Federally Administered Tribal Areas, URL: http://www.fata.gov.pk/

AREA AND POPULATION

Area
Pakistan lies in the northwest of India and has borders with China to the north, and Iran and Afghanistan to the west. It has an Arabian Sea coastline of 1,064 km. The total area of Pakistan, excluding the territories of Azad Jammu and Kashmir (AJK), Junagadh and Manavadar, is 796,095 sq. km. Pakistan's terrain is diverse: flat in part (Indus plain to the east, Balochistan plateau to the west) and elsewhere mountainous (north and north-west). The highest point is the K2 mountain (Mt. Godwin-Austen) at 8,611 metres.

The climate is mainly hot with desert conditions, more temperate in the north-west, and arctic to the north.

To view a map, visit http://www.un.org/Depts/Cartographic/map/profile/pakistan.pdf

Population
Pakistan had an estimated population of 173.5 million people in 2010, though accurate figures are difficult to acquire. The average annual growth rate is estimated to be 1.8 per cent over the period 2000-10. The declining population growth rate is the result of a fall in the birth rate, female education and government extended programmes of family planning. Population density averages 200 inhabitants per sq. km, though 37 per cent of the population lives in urban areas, where the growth rate is higher than in the rural areas. The population of Islamabad has surged over the last 10 years to 1.7 million.

The following table shows the population according to province:

2003 Population according to province

Province	Population
Punjab	79,429,701
Sindh	30,439,893
North West Frontier Province	19,343,242
Balochistan	7,167,554
Federally Administered Tribal Areas	3,341,070
Islamabad Capital Territory	955,629

The main ethnic groups are the Punjabi, Sindhi, Pashtun (Pathan), Baloch, and Muhajir.

Urdu and English are the official languages, with several other languages and dialects spoken, including Punjabi, Sindhi, Siraiki, Pashtu, and Balochi.

Births, Marriages, Deaths
In 2010, the crude birth rate was 27.3 births per 1,000 population, while the death rate was 8.4 deaths per 1,000 population. Life expectancy at birth in 2009 was 62 years for men and 64 years for women. Healthy life expectancy is 55 years. The median age is 22 years and approximately 35 per cent of the population is aged under 15 years. Just 6 per cent is aged over 60 years. The infant mortality rate is 70 infant deaths per 1,000 live births, whilst the total fertility rate is 3.4 children born per woman, above the target of 2 children per couple. The maternal mortality rate was estimated at 260 per 100,000 live births for the period 2000-09. (Source: http://www.who.int, World Health Statistics 2012)

Public Holidays 2014
14 January: Eid-i-Milad-un-Nabi (Birth of the Prophet)**
23 March: Pakistan Day
18 April: Good Friday*
21 April: Easter Monday*
5 May: Labour Day
29 June: Beginning of Ramadan**
29 July: Eid al-Fitr (End of Ramadan)**
14 August: Independence Day
6 September: Defence of Pakistan Day
11 September: Anniversary of the Death of Quaid-i-Azam
5 October: Eid al-Adha (Feast of the Sacrifice)**
25 October: Al-Hijira (Islamic New Year)
9 November: Birthday of Allama Iqbal (National Poet)
3 November: Ashura**
25 December: Birthday of Quaid-i-Azam; Christmas Day*
26 December: Boxing Day*
* For the Christian minority only
** Islamic holiday: precise date depends on appearance of the moon

EMPLOYMENT

Pakistan had a civilian labour force of 50.8 million in June 2007, up 0.6 per cent on the figure for 2006. Those in employment numbered 48.1 million in 2007, up from 47.37 million the previous June. The unemployed numbered 2.7 million in 2007, down from 3.1 million, and the unemployment rate fell from 6.2 per cent in 2006 to 5.3 per cent in 2007. The labour force participation rate varies widely between men (70.1 per cent) and women (19 per cent), with an overall participation rate of 45.2 per cent. (Source: Asian Development Bank)

Total Employment by Economic Activity

Occupation	2008
Agriculture, hunting, forestry & fishing	21,919,000
Mining & quarrying	57,000
Manufacturing	6,377,000
Electricity, gas & water supply	343,000
Construction	3,088,000
Wholesale & retail trade, repairs, hotels & restaurants	7,178,000
Transport, storage & communications	2,681,000
Financing, insurance, real estate & business services	692,000
Community, social & personal service activities	6,706,000
Others	49,000
Total	49,090,000

Source: Copyright © International Labour Organization (ILO Dept. of Statistics, http://laborsta.ilo.org)

BANKING AND FINANCE

Currency
One Pakistan Rupee = 100 paisa

GDP/GNP, Inflation, National Debt
Pakistan remains a low-income country although the economy is improving following the lifting of US sanctions (imposed in response to Pakistan's testing of nuclear weapons). The International Monetary Fund praised the country for meeting its obligations for an IMF Poverty Reduction and Growth Facility loan, which it completed early, in 2004. High population growth and low levels of social service spending mean that many Pakistanis live in poverty, especially in rural areas. The government is committed to using international aid in the education and health sectors.

An earthquake struck in October 2005; whilst killing 73,000 people and damaging the country's infrastructure, it had little impact on the economy; indeed, international aid arriving in the aftermath helped strengthen the economy. Relief agencies estimated that the country would need billions of dollars and up to ten years to fully rebuild.

Real gross domestic product (GDP) grew by 7 per cent in 2007, a slow down following growth rates of 7.5 and 9.0 in 2004 and 2005 respectively, but above the 2006 rate of 6.6 per cent. GDP growth was 4.1 per cent in 2008. Growth of 6.6 per cent was seen in the services sector over the year, whilst growth in industry was recorded at 1.7 per cent in 2008. The agriculture sector grew by 1.1 per cent. The services sector is Pakistan's largest contributor to GDP, accounting for an estimated 53.0 per cent in 2008, followed by industry (26.8 per cent) and agriculture (20.2 per cent). GDP per capita was estimated to have reached 63,890 rupees in 2008, up from 48,876 rupees the previous year. GDP was an estimated US$176.8 billion in 2010 in current prices. GDP growth was an estimated 3 per cent in the period 2010-11. It was an estimated 3.2 per cent in Q1 2012 and growth for the year has been revised down from the predicted 4 per cent. The economy has been hit by energy shortages, floods and militant attacks.

The following table shows GDP by industrial origin, at current factor cost:

GDP by industrial origin (Rupees billion)

Sector	2007	2008
Agriculture	1,685.2	2,016.5
Mining and quarrying	252.5	301.5
Manufacturing	1,567.3	1,949.9
Electricity, gas, water	169.5	149.7
Construction	225.2	264.8
Trade	1,441.8	1,829.2
Transport and communications	1,012.2	1,178.9
Finance and insurance	653.5	804.7
Public administration	467.7	530.1
Others	760.1	936.9
Taxes less subsidies	437.9	322.1
Total GDP	8,235.0	9,962.2

Source: Asian Development Bank

Consumer price inflation fell from a high of 9.3 per cent in 2005 (attributable to high oil prices and housing costs) to 7.9 per cent over 2006 and 7.8 per cent in 2007. Inflation was an estimated 10 per cent in 2011.

With external debt equivalent to about half of government spending in 2002, the government made debt reduction a key element of its fiscal policy. In April 2003 the US provided aid in the form of US$1,000 million in debt forgiveness and cancelled a further US$495 million in government-to-government debt. In 2006, the World Bank approved loans of $185 million for various reform and infrastructure projects, in addition to the nearly $850 million loaned to the country in 2005. Total external debt was around US$33,675 million in 2005, down from US$35,741 million in 2003. By 2007, it had risen to US$40,679.8 million. According to the Asian Development Bank, external debt as a percentage of GNI was 46.2 per cent in 2002; by 2006, it had fallen to 27.8 per cent. In 2011, external debt was estimated to be US$57 billion.

Foreign Investment
Direct investment in Pakistan rose from US$485 million in 2001-02 to US$798 million in 2002-03. In 2004-07, the World Bank pledged over $500 million in investment projects. The main areas of investment are chemicals, pharmaceuticals and fertilisers; financial business; and food, beverages and tobacco. At present, concern over the security situation and regional political violence deters foreign investment.

Pakistan has received significant assistance from international financial institutions and bilateral donors, particularly after it began using its military resources in the war on terror. The USA pledged $3 billion for the period 2005-09 in economic and military aid to Pakistan. The IMF and World Bank have pledged $1 billion in loans to Pakistan.

Balance of Payments / Imports and Exports
Pakistan has a high and growing trade deficit due to weak world demand for its exports. Her exports continue to be dominated by cotton textiles and apparel, despite government diversification efforts. Exports were an estimated US$17.8 billion in 2009 and imports US$28.3 billion. In 2010, they were estimated to be US$21 billion, rising to US$26 billion in 2011. Imports cost US$33 billion in 2010, rising to US$39 billion in 2011.

Top five import and export trading partners are shown on the following table:

Imports/Exports by Trading Partner (US$m)

Exports/Imports	2006	2007	2008
Exports			
United States	3,604.0	3,482.4	3,480.3
United Arab Emirates	1,550.8	2,018.8	2,537.7
Afghanistan	1,316.3	1,571.2	1,865.0
United Kingdom	874.5	928.6	968.6
Germany	639.1	729.1	826.3
China	915.6	1,004.8	958.5
Imports			
China	4,664.8	6,363.4	7,097.2
Saudi Arabia	3,544.6	4,276.1	5,620.7
United Arab Emirates	3,293.8	3,973.6	5,223.1
United States	2,188.5	2,238.6	2,192.4
Japan	1,936.1	1,715.7	1,599.4
Kuwait	1,588.9	1,916.8	2,519.5

Source: Asian Development Bank

The three major export groups are primary commodities (rice, raw cotton, fish and fish preparations, and leather); textile manufactures (cotton yarn, cotton fabrics, knitwear, bed linen, readymade garments, and synthetic textiles); and other manufactures (carpets, sports goods, leather manufactures, and surgical instruments).

The following table show exports by major commodity group (million Rupees):

Exports

Commodity Group	2006	2007
Food and live animals	113,760	115,759
Beverages and tobacco	1,713	1,421
Crude materials, excluding fuels	18,249	20,313
Mineral fuels	49,593	52,094
Animal, vegetable oil, and fats	6,362	5,374
Chemicals	25,916	23,742
Basic manufactures	475,679	507,733
Machines, transport equipment	13,106	14,399
Miscellaneous manufactured goods	280,041	288,202
Unclassified goods	422	273
Re-exports	7,717	9,726

Source: Asian Development Bank

Imports

Commodity sector	2006	2007
Food and live animals	103,890	82,331
Beverage and tobacco	769	1,126
Crude materials, excluding fuels	113,152	141,345
Mineral fuels, etc.	414,114	469,509
Animal, vegetable oil, and fats	50,332	63,857
Chemicals	250,350	266,954
Basic manufactures	200,619	206,482
Machines, transport equipment	498,388	546,736
Miscellaneous manufactured goods	4,2258	58,917
Unclassified goods	37,286	14,547
Re-imports	614	232

Source: Asian Development Bank

Central Bank
State Bank of Pakistan, PO Box 4456, I.I. Chundrigar Road, Karachi, Sindh, Pakistan. Tel: +92 (0)21 2445 0298, fax: +92 (0)21 921 2433, e-mail: sbp.prd@cyber.net.pk; URL: http://www.sbp.org.pk
Governor: Yaseen Anwar

Chambers of Commerce and Trade Organisations
Karachi Stock Exchange, URL: http://www.kse.com.pk/
Federation of Pakistan Chambers of Commerce and Industry, URL: http://www.fpcci.com.pk
Employers' Federation of Pakistan, , URL: http://www.efp.org.pk

MANUFACTURING, MINING AND SERVICES

Primary and Extractive Industries
Pakistan has substantial reserves of a large variety of minerals. The following minerals are found in the country in commercial quantities: rock salt, coal, iron ore, limestone, chromite, gypsum, marble, copper, and uranium, magnesium, sulphur, barites, china clay, bauxite, antimony ore, bentonite, celestite, dolomite, fireclay, fluorite, fuller's earth, phosphate rock, silica sand, soapstone, gemstone, and molybdenum.

The following table shows mining production for selected minerals (tonnes):

Mining Production (tonnes)

Mineral	2002-03	2005-06
Aragonit/Marble	1,142,113	1,828,513
Limestone	11,880,275	18,391,364
Rock Salt	1,412,102	1,858,931
Gypsum	424,107	601,027
Sulphur	19,402	24,695

Source: Federal Bureau of Statistics

A major project to mine the copper and gold deposits at Saindak in Western Balochistan is in progress. In Sindh, coal mines are being developed for a 150 MW fluidised bed power generation plant.

Proven oil reserves were 0.28 billion barrels in January 2012, according to recent EIA statistics. Oil production in 2011 was an estimated 62,090 barrels per day, 97 per cent of which was crude oil. Consumption fell from an estimated 383,000 barrels per day in 2008 to 397,000 bbl/d in 2009 and 371,000 bbl/d in 2011. Because Pakistan's production falls far short of its consumption requirements, it relies heavily on imports (338,000 barrels per day) from Middle Eastern countries. These are projected to rise substantially as demand increasingly exceeds production. Pakistan has a crude oil refining capacity of around 308,000 barrels per day (2011).

The state-owned company is Oil and Gas Development Corporation (OGDCL). Foreign oil companies operating in Pakistan include Total, ExxonMobil, Monument Oil and Gas, and Royal Dutch Shell. Pakistan's oil reserves are located mainly in the Potwar Plateau in Punjab and lower Sindh province.

Natural gas reserves were an estimated 30 billion cubic feet at the beginning of 2011. Production in 2011 was an estimated 1,383 billion cubic feet, all of which was used domestically, and, if production does not increase, Pakistan will become a natural gas importer. Natural gas accounts for the largest share of Pakistan's energy use, amounting to about 50 percent of total energy consumption. Pakistan ranks third in the world for use of natural gas as a motor fuel (behind Brazil and Argentina), and the country hopes to use gas in future electric power generation projects. The government is planning to build a pipeline that stretches from Iran to India crossing Pakistani territory.

The largest productive gas fields are Sui, Adhi and Kandkhot, Mari, and Kandanwari. The state-owned gas companies are Pakistan Petroleum Ltd (PPL) and Oil and Gas Development Corporation (OGDCL), with foreign companies including BP, Eni, OMV, and BHP also operating.

Pakistan's recoverable coal reserves are estimated at 3,362 million short tons. Production in 2010 was an estimated 3.7 million short tons (down from 3.8 million short tons the previous year), while consumption was 11.5 million short tons (up from 9 million short tons in 2005). At present, coal is used in just 1 per cent of electric power generation. (Source: Energy Information Administration, EIA)

Energy
Pakistan's primary energy consumption rose from 1.978 quadrillion Btu in 2003, to 2.252 quadrillion Btu in 2005. It increased to 2.5 quadrillion Btu in 2009.

Pakistan has 22.2 gigawatts (GW) of electric generating capacity. Thermal plants using oil, natural gas, and coal account for about 70 per cent of this capacity, with hydroelectricity contributing 28 per cent and nuclear 2.5 per cent. Total electricity generation in 2010 reached 89.60 billion kWh, whilst net consumption, according to EIA estimates, was 74 billion kWh.

Over the past decade, annual growth in demand has grown by some seven per cent. Whilst per capita energy consumption in Pakistan is low, the large and growing population means that requirements are high. Pakistan's total power generating capacity has increased rapidly in recent years, due largely to foreign investment; however, much of Pakistan's rural areas do not have access to electric power and about half the population is not connected to the national grid. Transmission losses run at 30 per cent, due to poor infrastructure and a significant amount of theft. Droughts affect the availability of hydropower. Pakistan's rural population relies on firewood and agricultural residues for its energy requirements (Source: EIA)

Manufacturing
Pakistan's manufacturing sector accounts for around 26.8 per cent of GDP. Cotton textile production and apparel manufacturing are Pakistan's largest industries, accounting for about 70 per cent of total exports and employing around 45 per cent of the workforce. Other major industries include food processing, beverages, construction materials, clothing, and paper products. As technology improves in the industrial sector, it continues to grow. In 2006/2007, the sector grew by 6.8 per cent. Despite government efforts to privatize large-scale parastatal units, the public sector continues to account for a significant proportion of industry.

The following table shows manufacturing production:

PAKISTAN

Production of selected manufacturing items, ('000 metric tonnes)

Product	2006	2007
Cement	20,284	24,725
Cycle tubes (rubber) '000 units	10,360	10,220
Urea	4,806	4,759
Sugar	3,058	3,678
Cotton yarn, Mn. kg.	2,695	2,909
Pig iron	9,951	1,002
Vegetable products	1,160	1,255
Cotton cloth, Mn. sq. m.	966	986

Source: Asian Development Bank

Service Industries

The services sector is the largest contributor to GDP at 53.7 per cent. It grew by 8 per cent in 2007. Recent figures estimate that Pakistan earns US$126 million per annum from tourism, with an estimated 379,000 foreign tourists visiting the country every year.
Pakistan Tourism Development Corporation (PTDC), URL: http://www.tourism.gov.pk/Index.html

Agriculture

Around 22.14 million hectares of land (28 per cent of Pakistan's total land area) is cultivated and is watered by one of the largest irrigation systems in the world. The agricultural sector employs around 45 per cent of the work force and accounted for 21.0 per cent of GDP in 2011. The most important crops are cotton, wheat, rice, sugarcane, fruits, and vegetables. Pakistan remains a net food importer, though it exports rice, fish, fruits, and vegetables and imports vegetable oil, wheat, cotton (net importer), pulses, and consumer foods.

The country suffers from sporadic droughts and, in 2005, flash floods and avalanches.

Agricultural Production in 2010

Produce	Int. $'000*	Tonnes
Buffalo milk, whole, fresh	8,442,125	22,279,000
Cow milk, whole, fresh	3,687,048	12,437,000
Wheat	3,401,059	23,310,800
Cotton lint	2,784,375	1,948,200
Indigenous buffalo meat	2,046,347	760,233
Indigenous cattle meat	1,997,362	739,387
Rice, paddy	1,952,838	7,235,000
Sugar cane	1,459,132	49,372,900
Mangoes, mangosteens, guavas	1,105,763	1,845,500
Indigenous chicken meat	1,002,778	703,997
Cottonseed	875,914	3,700,000
Indigenous goat meat	660,599	275,699

*unofficial figures

Source: http://faostat.fao.org/site/339/default.aspx Food and Agriculture Organization of the United Nations, Food and Agricultural commodities production

Fishing

The total catch for 2010 was put at 453,000 tonnes.

COMMUNICATIONS AND TRANSPORT

Travel Requirements

Citizens of the USA, Canada, Australia and the EU require a passport valid for six months beyond the length of stay, a return/onward ticket and a visa. Transit passengers continuing their journey within 24 hours by the same or first connecting aircraft, provided they are holding onward or return documentation and not leaving the airport do not need a visa, and nor do holders of a UN laissez-passer. Visitors should contact the embassy to check precise visa requirements.

National Airlines

Pakistan International Airlines, URL: http://www.piac.com.pk
Shaheen Air International, URL: http://www.shaheenair.com

International Airports

Karachi, Islamabad, Lahore, Peshawar, Quetta and Gwadar have international airports.
Jinnah International, Karachi, URL: http://www.karachiairport.com.pk/

Railways

The railway network comprises 7,790 km of track. Pakistan has a history of deadly accidents on its ageing railway system. Signalling faults and poorly maintained tracks are often the cause of the accidents.
Pakistan Railways, URL: http:// www.pakrail.com

Roads

There are around 260,500 km of roads in Pakistan, 190,000 km of which are of a high standard. Traffic in Pakistan drives on the left and the minimum driving age is 18.

Ports and Harbours

The main ports are Karachi (URL: http://www.kpt.gov.pk) and Port Muhammad Bin Qasim (URL: http://www.pqa.gov.pk/). The port of Karachi is the largest port and handles approximately 60 per cent of Pakistan's sea trade which amounts to 25 million tons of cargo per year. Port Qasim handles approximately 40 per cent.

HEALTH

Around 80 per cent of the population has access to local health services in rural areas and 100 per cent in cities; however, there are regional variations. According to 2004 figures published by Pakistan's Federal Bureau of Statistics, there are 916 hospitals in the country, together with 5,201 sub heath centres, 906 maternity and child health centres, 552 rural health centres and 289 TB centres. There were a total of approximately 99,900 hospital beds, equating to one bed per 1,540 people.

Figures for 2005-10 show that there are 139,555 physicians (8.1 per 10,000 population), 95,538 nurses and midwives (5.6 per 10,000 population), 9,822 dentists. 8,102 pharmaceutical personnel, 106 environment and public health workers, and 10,731 community health workers. There are 6 hospital beds per 10,000 population.

Although public sector expenditure on health as part of overall public expenditure has increased recently, in general, health investment is low. In 2009, the government spent approximately 3.3 per cent of its total budget on healthcare, accounting for 34.8 per cent of all healthcare spending. Total expenditure on healthcare equated to 2.2 per cent of the country's GDP. Per capita expenditure on health was approximately US$20, compared with US$15 in 2000. More than 65 per cent of health financing is private, over 80 per cent of which is out-of-pocket. External resources account for 4.4 per cent of total expenditure.

According to WHO figures, in 2010 the HIV/AIDS prevalence rate was 54 per 100,000 population and the TB prevalence rate was 364 per 100,000 population.

According to the latest WHO figures, in 2010 approximately 92 per cent of the population had access to improved drinking water. In the same year, 48 per cent of the population had access to improved sanitation.

The infant mortality rate in 2010 was 70 per 1,000 live births. The child mortality rate (under-five-years) was 87 per 1,000 live births. The main causes of childhood mortality are: diarrhoea (11 per cent), pneumonia (19 per cent), prematurity (20 per cent), birth asphyxia (13 per cent) and congential anomalies (5 per cent). Vaccination rates amongst young children have risen to nearly 100 per cent for major diseases.

In 2009 there were 240,5912 reported cases of malaria, 261,199 of TB, 816 of tetanus, 4,321 of measles, 396 of leprosy, 164 of cholera and 192 reported cases of polio.(Source: http://www.who.int, World Health Statistics 2012)

EDUCATION

Education in Pakistan begins at the age of five. The government promotes technical and vocational education as well as a literacy programme with the aim of providing universal primary education. There is also a traditional religious education based on the Qur'an, some of these Madrassa or religious schools particularly those in the north of the country have been criticised by other countries for fostering intolerance and encouraging Jihad or holy war. The following table shows figures for educational institutions and enrolments:

School and Enrolment numbers, 2003-04

Institution	No. of Institutions	Enrolment
Primary total:	164,970	19,795,356
- Public	133,952	13,681,625
- Private	17,621	5,828,336
- Other	3,397	285,395
Middle School total:	28,728	4,318,721
- Public	13,668	3,075,678
- Private	15,000	1,171,475
- Other public	60	71,568
Secondary and High total:	9,819	1,988,587
- Public		1,497,496
- Private		491,091

Source: Federal Bureau of Statistics

According to 2003-04 figures, there were a total of 218,275 university students, 83,127 of whom were women. There were 29 universities staffed by 11,400 lecturers. There were also some 382 professional colleges.

Fewer girls than boys attend school and this is reflected in the adult literacy rate, in 2006 was estimated to be 54.2 per cent, 67.7 per cent for males and 39.6 per cent for females, these figures rose slightly for the youth literacy rate (age 15-24) where the literacy rate was 69.2 per cent, 79.1 per cent for males and 58.4 per cent for females, but these figures were still well below the regional average. In rural areas, literacy rates are lower. (Source: UNESCO, UIS, August 2009)

RELIGION

Census data indicates that over 97 per cent of the population are Muslims. Nearly 75 per cent of Pakistani Muslims are Sunni Muslims and 20 per cent are Shi'a Muslims. 1.5 per cent of the population are Christians (2.8 million people), and 1.4 per cent are Hindu. There are also Buddhists, Sikhs, and Parsis.

Pakistan has a religious liberty rating of 1 on a scale of 1 to 10 (10 is most freedom). (Source: World Religion Database)

COMMUNICATIONS AND MEDIA

Press freedom is limited by legal and constitutional laws. Private TV stations have occasionally been closed under states of emergency. Private FM radio statios are not permitted to broadcast their own news programmes.

Newspapers
The impact of the press is limited by the low literacy rate in Pakistan. Titles include:
Mashriq, URL: http://dailymashriq.com.pk/
Dawn, URL: http://www.dawn.com
The Pakistan Times, URL: http://www.pakistantimes.net/
Daily Jang (Urdu), URL: http://jang.com.pk
The News, URL: http://thenews.jang.com.pk/

Broadcasting
Television is the dominant media. The state-run Pakistan Television Corporation operates six channels. There are approximately 50 private television channels available through satellite. The Pakistan Broadcasting Corporation has around 40 radio stations and the home services broadcast in 20 languages. External services cover 70 countries in 15 languages.
Pakistan Television Corporation Ltd, URL: http://ptv.com.pk/index.asp
Geo TV, leading private company, URL: http://www.geo.tv/

Telecommunications
The telecommunications infrastructure has improved recently but is still limited in rural areas. Mobile phone coverage has increased dramatically; more than 90 per cent of Pakistanis now live in areas with coverage. In 2010 there were approximately 3.5 million mainline telephones in use and in 2011 an estimated 110 million mobile phones were in use. An estimated 20 million Pakistanis were regular internet users in 2011.

ENVIRONMENT

Environmental problems in Pakistan include deforestation and desertification, whilst some of the country's limited water resources have been polluted by industrial waste, agricultural run-off and raw sewage.

Use of hazardous chemicals, vehicle emissions, and industrial activity has contributed to environmental and health hazards. There is a shortage of drinking water due to industrial waste and agricultural run-off that contaminates supplies. High population growth and lack of resources are major contributory factors in the environmental problems.

Pakistan's energy related carbon emissions (2005) were estimated at 121.49 million metric tons, whilst per capita carbon emissions were an estimated 0.77 metric tons of carbon, compared with 0.67 metric tons in 2004. The industrial sector generates the largest proportion of carbon emissions, according to recent estimates, at 44.9 per cent, followed by the transport (27.2 per cent), residential (22.2 per cent), and commercial (5.7 per cent) sectors. In 2010, Pakistan's emissions from the consumption of fossil fuels totalled 151 million metric tons of carbon dioxide. (Source: EIA)

Whilst Pakistan is not a signatory to the Kyoto Protocol, it is a party to Conventions on Biodiversity, Climate Change, Climate Change-Kyoto Protocol, Desertification, Endangered Species, Environmental Modification, Hazardous Wastes, Law of the Sea, Marine Dumping, Ozone Layer Protection, Ship Pollution, and Wetlands. It has signed but not ratified Marine Life Conservation.

SPACE PROGRAMME

The Pakistan Space and Upper Atmosphere Research Commission (SUPARCO) was established in 1961. It is the state national space agency and works on development of space technology. It was one of the first countries to launch a rocket for upper atmosphere research. It launched its first indigenously developed satellite in 1990. It developed a communications satellite in cooperation with China; this was successfully launched in 2011. It is now aiming to develop a remote sensing satellite.
SUPARCO, URL: http://www.suparco.gov.pk

PALAU
Republic of Palau
Beluu er a Belau

Capital: Melekeok - in 2006 the capital was relocated to Melekeok on the island of Babeldaon; up until then the capital was Koror, (Population estimate: 500)

Head of State: Tommy Remengesau Jr. (President) (page 1502)

Vice-President: Tony Bells

National Flag: A large gold disc slightly to the hoist side on a light blue background

CONSTITUTION AND GOVERNMENT

Constitution
After the Second World War Palau was administered by the US as part of the UN-created Trust Territory of the Pacific Islands. Palau became independent on 1 October 1994 but has a Compact of Free Association with the US. The Compact calls for the two governments to review its terms on its15th, 30th, and 40th anniversaries. The first of these anniversaries is in October 2009. The current terms of the Compact means that the US is responsible for the defence of Palau for 50 years. Palau receives financial assistance from the US for the initial period of 15 years, and the US is permitted to use the islands as a military base during that period.

According to the current constitution, which came into effect on 1 January 1981, the President is head of state and, along with the Vice-President, is elected by popular vote every four years. They are advised on traditional matters by a Council of Chiefs composed of one traditional leader from each of the Republic's states. The President appoints the Cabinet. A referendum on the constitution, held in November 2004, has opened the way to dual citizenship, and limited to three terms the length of time that a person can be in Congress. It also allows for the election of President and Vice-President as a team.

To consult the full constitution, please visit: http://www.wipo.int/wipolex/en/details.jsp?id=8110

Recent Events
In 2006 government departments began moving to the new capital Melekeok on the island of Babeldaon, previously the capital had been Koror.

In January 2010 the US agreed an aid payment of US$250 million to Palau.

Parliamentary and presidential elections took place in November 2012.

Legislature
The bicameral legislature, the Palau National Congress (*Olbiil Era Kelulau - House of Whispered Decisions*), consists of an upper chamber, the Senate, and a lower chamber, the House of Delegates directly elected for four year term. The Senate has 9 members, who are directly elected. The House of Delegates has 16 members, one member from each of Palau's 16 states. Members of both houses are elected as Independents.
House of Delegates, Olbiil era Kelulau, PO Box 8, Koror 96940, Palau. Tel: +680 488 2507, URL: http://www.palaugov.net/

Cabinet (as at June 2013)
Minister of Finance: Elbuchel Sadang (page 1507)
Minister of Health: Gregorio Ngirman
Minister of Public Infrastructure, Industries and Commerce: Charles Obichang
Minister of Community and Cultural Affairs: Baklai Temengil
Minister of Education: currently vacant
Minister of Natural Resources, Environment and Tourism: Flemming Sengebau
Minister of Justice: Tony Bells
Chief Negotiator with the USA: Billy Kuartei

Ministries
Government portal, URL: http://www.palaugov.net/
Office of the President, PO Box 100, 96940 Koror, Palau. Tel: +680 488 2702, fax: +680 488 1725, e-mail: roppresoffice@palaunet.com, URL: http://www.palaugov.net
Ministry of Community and Cultural Affairs, PO Box 100, 96940 Koror, Palau. Tel: +680 488 1126, fax: +680 488 3354, e-mail: mcca@palaunet.com, URL: http://www.palaugov.net/mincommunity/mocommunity.html
Ministry of Education, PO Box 189, 96940 Koror, Palau. Tel: +680 488 1464, fax: +680 488 1465, e-mail: moe@palaumoe.net, URL: http://www.palaugov.net/mineducation/moeducation.html
Ministry of Finance, PO Box 6011, 96940 Koror, Palau. Tel: +680 488 2561, fax: +680 488 2168, e-mail: esadang@palaugov.net, URL: http://www.palaugov.net/minfinance/mofinance.html
Ministry of Health, PO Box 100, 96940 Koror, Palau. Tel: +680 488 2552, fax: +680 488 1211, e-mail: healthminister@palaunet.com, URL: http://www.palaugov.net/minhealth/publichealth/index.htm
Ministry of Justice, PO Box 100, 96940 Koror, Palau. Tel: +680 488 2702, fax: +680 488 4567, e-mail: justice@palaunet.com, URL: http://www.palaugov.net/minjustice/mojustice.html
Ministry of Natural Resources, Environment and Tourism, PO Box 100, 96940 Koror, Palau. Tel: +680 488 2701, fax: +680 488 3380, e-mail: mrd@palaunet.com, URL: http://www.palaugov.net/minresources/moresources.html
Ministry of Public Infrastructure, Industries and Commerce, PO Box 1471, 96940 Koror, Palau. Tel: +680 488 2111, fax: +680 488 3207, e-mail: mincat@palaunet.com, URL: http://www.palaugov.net/mincommerce/mocommtrade.html

PALAU

Ministry of State, PO Box 100, 96940 Koror, Palau. Tel: +680 488 2509, fax: +680 488 2443, e-mail: ministryofstate@bdarop.com, URL: http://www.palaugov.net/minstate/mostate.html

Elections

The most recent presidential election took place on 6 November 2012. Tommy Remengesau, the former president, was eligible to run again. He beat the incumbent president Johnson Toribiong by 49 per cent to 33 per cent.

The most recent parliamentary election was also held on 6 November 2012. Candidates are elected as independents.

Diplomatic Representation
British Embassy, (The British Ambassador lives at Manila, Philippines), URL: http://ukinthephilippines.fco.gov.uk
Ambassador: Stephen Lillie
US Embassy, Taoch ra Mechang, Ngermid Hamlet, Koror, Palau 96940 (POB 6028), Tel: +680 488 2920, fax: +680 488 2911, e-mail: usembassykoror@palaunet.com, URL: http://palau.usembassy.gov
Ambassador: Helen Reed-Rowe
Embassy of Palau,1700 Pennsylvania Avenue NW, Washington, DC 20006, USA. Tel: +1 202 452 6814, fax: +1 202 452 6281, URL: http://www.palauembassy.com
Ambassador: Hersey Kyota
Palau Permanent Mission to the UN, URL: http://www.palauun.org/
Permanent Representative: Stuart Beck

LEGAL SYSTEM

There is a Supreme Court, a National Court, a lower Court of Common Pleas, and a Land Court. The Supreme Court includes Trial and Appellate Divisions.

The government respects the human rights of its citizens, though there have been cases of government corruption, and discrimination against foreign workers. Palau abolished the death penalty in 1994.

Palau Courts, URL: http://www.palausupremecourt.net/
Chief Justice: Arthur Ngiraklsong

LOCAL GOVERNMENT

For administrative purposes Palau is divided into municipalities and villages. The municipalities are administered by elected Magistrates and Councils. Palau's 16 states are as follows: Aimeliik, Airai, Angaur, Hatobohei, Kayangel, Koror, Melekeok, Ngaraard, Ngarchelong, Ngardmau, Ngatpang, Ngchesar, Ngeremlengui, Ngiwal, Peleliu and Sonsoral.

AREA AND POPULATION

Area
The Republic of Palau is about 500 miles equidistant from the Philippines to the west and from Papua New Guinea to the south. Palau covers an area of 458 sq. km. and consists of more than 340 islands, of which only 9 are inhabited. The islands vary geologically from the high, mountainous main island of Babelthuap to low, coral islands fringed by large barrier reefs. Most of the islands are of volcanic origin, and others are of raised limestone. Babeldaob makes up 80 per cent of the total land area. The climate is tropical, with a wet season from May to November.

To view a map of Palau, please consult http://www.lib.utexas.edu/maps/cia08/palau_sm_2008.gif

Population
The population was estimated at 20,000 in 2010, with an average annual growth rate of 0.7 per cent per annum for the period 2000-10. Population density is 46 people per sq. km., though around 83 per cent of the population live in urban areas. The majority of the population is aged between 15 and 60 years (63 per cent), and the median age is estimated to be 32 years. English is the official language but Palauan is also spoken.

Births, Marriages, Deaths
Estimates for 2010 estimated the crude birth rate was 11 per 1,000 people) the crude death rate was 5.0 per 1,000 people. The infant mortality rate was an estimated 15 per 1,000 live births. Average life expectancy is 68 years for men and 77 for women. Healthy life expectancy is 64 years old. The fertility rate is an estimated 1.7 children per woman. (Source: http://www.who.int, World Health Statistics 2012)

Public Holidays 2014
1 January: New Year's Day
15 March: Youth Day
5 May Senior Citizens' Day
1 June: President's Day
9 July: Constitution Day
3 September: Labour Day
1 October: Independence Day
24 October: United Nations Day
27 November: Thanksgiving Day
25 December: Christmas Day

EMPLOYMENT

In 2005, the labour force numbered around 10,203 people, 9,777 of whom were employed. 8,757 people were employed in the service industry, 761 were agricultural workers and 259 worked in the manufacturing sector. The unemployment rate was 4.2 per cent, affecting 426 people. (Source: Asian Development Bank, ADB)

Total Employment by Economic Activity

Occupation	2008
Agriculture, hunting & forestry	100
Fishing	100
Manufacturing	400
Construction	1,000
Wholesale & retail trade, repairs, hotels & restaurants	1,800
Hotels & restaurants	1,700
Transport, storage & communications	900
Financial Intermediation	100
Real estate, renting and business activities	700
Public administration & defence, compulsory social security	3,000
Education	600
Health & social work	100
Other community, social & personal service activities	300
Households with employed persons	800
Total	11,700

Source: Copyright © International Labour Organization (ILO Dept. of Statistics, http://laborsta.ilo.org)

BANKING AND FINANCE

Currency
The unit of currency is the US dollar.

GDP/GNP, Inflation, National Debt
Following the Asian financial crisis of the late 1990s, Palau's economy grew by 3.3 per cent in 2000 and by 3.1 per cent in 2001. Since 2004, annual growth has averaged 5.4 per cent, and in the year to the end of September 2006, the economy grew by 5.7 per cent. The growth was due largely to expansion of the tourism sector, and was assisted by foreign-funded infrastructure projects.

GDP reached an estimated US$164.289 million in 2007, up from US$156.614 million the previous year. In 2008, GDP was estimated at US$180.716 million, giving a per capita figure of US$8,940. The services sector accounted for 76 per cent of GDP, the manufacturing sector contributed 21 per cent and agriculture for 3.5 per cent in 2007.

The inflation rate, as measured by consumer prices, averaged 3.3 per cent over 2007, though food costs rose by 5.3 per cent over the year.

The 1994 Compact of Association with the US granted Palau $447 million in grants over the period 1994 to 2009. A further $70 million was set aside in a trust fund for use after the end of the Compact grants; by 2007, the fund had increased to $175 million. The total U.S. grant income in 2006 was $23.7 million. In January 2010 the US agreed to an additional US$250 million in aid.

Balance of Payments / Imports and Exports
Major export commodities are fish and handicrafts sold to markets in Japan and Korea. Commodities, imported mainly from Japan and the Philippines, include fuels, food and drinks, and manufactured goods.

Trade Balance (US$ millions)

	2005	2006	2007
Exports	13.4	13.6	10.081
Imports	105.2	115.3	91.287
Balance	-91.8	-101.69	-81.206

Source: Asian Development Bank

External debt fell from US$20 billion in 2002, to US$17.5 billion in 2006, before rising to 22.9 billion in 2007.

MANUFACTURING, MINING AND SERVICES

Manufacturing
Construction is an important industrial activity, contributing over 15 per cent of GDP. There have been several large infrastructure projects recently, including the Compact Road, relocation of the new capital to Babeldaob, and new hotels. The main manufacturing product are garments, units producing furniture and handicrafts exist but are geared towards the domestic market only.

Service Industries
The service sector contributed over 70 per cent of GDP in 2007, and employs over half of the work force. The government alone employs nearly 25 per cent of workers and accounts for 23 per cent of the GDP.

Tourism
Tourism is now the main industry in Palau. New air services and the construction of more hotels have helped to expand the sector. The government aims at low volume, high spending luxury tourism. The industry focuses on the rich marine life, attracting scuba divers and

snorkellers. In 2006, 86,400 tourists visited the islands, an increase of two per cent over the previous year. Most tourists are from Japan, Taiwan and the USA. Revenue from tourism (estimated at $62 million in 2006) accounts for around 45 per cent of national GDP.

Agriculture
This sector employs just 3 per cent of the workforce and is mainly on a subsistence level. Palau produces coconuts, copra, cassava, sweet potatoes and bananas. Fishing is a potential source of revenue, though it has not yet been exploited to any commercial degree. The islands exports of fish earned US$967,000.

COMMUNICATIONS AND TRANSPORT

Travel Requirements
Citizens of the Canada, Australia and the EU require a passport valid for a month beyond the length of stay. They do not require a visa for stays of up to 30 days; an entry permit is issued on arrival. US citizens holding proof of citizenship and other photo ID documentation do not need a passport and can stay for up to one year without a visa. For longer stays, permission must be sought from the chief of immigration.

Other nationals should contact the embassy to check visa requirements.

Roads
Of a total of 61 km of roads, 36 km are paved and 25 km are unpaved.

Ports and Harbours
Koror is Palau's major port.

International Airports
There are three airports on the islands, just one with a paved runway.

HEALTH

In 2009, the government spent approximately 14.3 per cent of its total budget on healthcare, accounting for 74.8 per cent of all healthcare spending. Total expenditure on healthcare equated to 10.6 per cent of the country's GDP. External resources accounted for 39 per cent of total expenditure. Per capita expenditure on health was approximately US$854. In 2000-10, there were 26 doctors, 5 dentistry personnel and 118 nurses and midwives. There were 49 hospital beds per 100,000 population.

Life expectancy for men is 68 years and for women it is 77 years. In 2010, the infant mortality rate was estimated at 15 per 1,000 live births and the child mortality rate (less than five years) 119 per 1,000 live births. The vaccination rates against major diseases (infants) are estimated to be over 75 per cent for measles, 49 per cent against diptheria and 80 per cent for hepatitis.

According to the latest WHO figures, in 2006 approximately 79 per cent of the urban population and 94 per cent of the rural population had access to improved drinking water. In the same year, 96 per cent of the urban population and 52 per cent of the rural population had access to improved sanitation. Diarrhoea accounts for 7.9 per cent of childhood deaths. (Source: http://www.who, World Health Statistics 2012)

EDUCATION

Most Palauan children attend free public schools. The only post-secondary education is provided by the Palau Community College. UNESCO figures for 2002 show that the equivalent of 10.3 per cent of GDP was spent on education. The literacy rate is around 92 per cent.

RELIGION

The majority of people are Christian (95 per cent) and there is an indigenous religion called Modekngei. Palau has a religious liberty rating of 9 on a scale of 1 to 10 (10 is most freedom). (Source: World Religion Database)

COMMUNICATIONS AND MEDIA

The constitution provides for press freedom.

Broadcasting
Palau has approximately 5 radio stations including the state-run T8AA Eco Paradise. There are no television stations based in Palau but cable television is widely available.

Telecommunications
According to 2008 statistics there are 7,500 telephone main lines in Palau, and 12,000 mobiles. High costs have hindered the domestic expansion of internet access but it is available in schools, businesses and internet cafes.

ENVIRONMENT

Palau is a party to the following international environmental agreements: Biodiversity, Climate Change, Climate Change-Kyoto Protocol, Desertification, and Law of the Sea.

Current environmental problems include sand and coral dredging, over-fishing, illegal fishing, and inadequate facilities for solid waste disposal.

PANAMA
Republic of Panama
República de Panamá

Capital: Panama City (Population estimate, 2011: 430,000)

Head of State: Ricardo Martinelli (page 1471) (President)

Vice-President: Juan Carlos Varela Rodriguez (page 1531)

National Flag: Quartered, first and fourth white, second, red, third, blue; the first quarter charged with a five-pointed blue star and the fourth with a like red star.

CONSTITUTION AND GOVERNMENT

Constitution
Panama was ruled by Spain from the 16th century until 1821 when it became part of Colombia. After a revolt in 1903 Panama declared its independence from Colombia and became a separate state. It also signed an agreement with the USA to allow construction of the Panama Canal and gave the US sovereignty of the land either side of the canal.

The National Guard led by Gen. Torrijos deposed President Arnulfo Arias Madrid in 1967 and dissolved the National Assembly (Asamblea Nacional). Political parties were banned a year later. A new legislative body, the 505-member National Assembly of Community Representatives (Asamblea Nacional de Corregidores), was created in 1972 when elections were held. In April 1983 a number of constitutional amendments were agreed by referendum, including restricting the power of the National Guard. However, military power was increased following a decision to bring the country's armed forces into one security organisation: the National Defence Forces. A new 67-seat Legislative Assembly (Asamblea Legislativa) was created in 1984.

In 1988, President Devalle failed in his bid to remove Gen. Noriega as Commander of the Defence Force and was ousted by the latter. Noriega annulled the results of presidential elections the following year, and assumed power as head of state in December 1989. The US invaded the same month and installed G. Endara, the likely winner of the election, as president. In 1992, Noriega was tried in the US for drugs offences, and jailed for forty years.

In December 1991 the Legislative Assembly approved the abolition of the armed forces and the constitution was changed. Under the present constitution, the President holds Executive power and is directly elected for a non-renewable five-year term. The President, who is responsible to the Legislative Assembly, is assisted by two Vice Presidents and the appointed Cabinet. The President appoints the Cabinet. The age of suffrage is 18, and voting is compulsory.

To view the Panamanian Constitution (in Spanish), please follow the site map at: http://www.asamblea.gob.pa/asamblea/constitucion/index.htm

International Relations
Relations with neighbouring Colombia are strained occasionally by the presence on Panamanian territory of Colombian paramilitaries and guerrilla groups. Panama has a very close relationship with the US; the 1977 Torrijos - Carter treaties returned sovereignty of the Panama Canal to Panama on 31 December 1999, and the US withdrew all troops. The Neutrality Treaty of 1977 calls for the US and Panama to defend the Canal from any threats, and grants expeditious passage to US warships.

Panama has Free Trade Agreements with Taiwan and Singapore, as well as the USA and El Salvador. It is negotiating FTAs with other Central American states, and the EU.

Recent Events
On 31 December 1999, under the terms of the Panama Canal Treaty, Panama took on sovereignty of the Panama Canal. In November 2004 November, the government announced that the Panama Canal had earned record revenues of $1 billion for the financial year.

PANAMA

In September 2003 there were strikes over the management of the social security fund, bringing social services to a standstill. On his election victory in 2004, President Torrijos pledged to sort out the under-funded social security system. However, plans to raise the minimum age of retirement and to increase pension contributions met with more protests and strikes in May 2005.

In April 2006, plans were announced to widen the 50 mile long Canal so that it can handle the new giant container ships. The Canal links the Pacific and Atlantic Oceans, and around 40 ships a day pass through it. The project, which will cost US$5.3 billion, was given the go-ahead by a national referendum in October 2006.

Elections were held in May 2009. The right-wing coalition Alliance for Change won the majority in the Assembly, whilst their leader, supermarket magnate Ricardo Martinelli, won the presidential poll.

In July 2010, a French court convicted the former military leader, Manuel Noriega, on charges of laundering drug money and sentenced him to seven years in jail. In April 2010 Noriega was extradited from the US where he had spent twenty years in prison for drug trafficking. He was finally imprisoned in December 2011.

Three ministers (Housing, Micro, SME Business, and Foreign Affairs) resigned early in 2013 in order to contest the 2014 presidential election.

Legislature

Legislative power is held by the unicameral Legislative Assembly (*Asamblea Legislativa*) which replaced the National Assembly of Community Representatives (*Asamblea Nacional de Corregidores*). The Legislative Assembly has 71 members elected for five years by universal and compulsory adult suffrage. All legislators must be at least 21 years old and citizens of Panama.

Legislative Assembly, Palacio Justo Arosemana, Apartado Postal 3346, Zona 4, Panama City, Panama. Tel: +507 2 62 6091, URL: http://www.asamblea.gob.pa/

Cabinet (as at June 2013)
Minister of Foreign Affairs: Fernando Nunez Fabrega (page 1488)
Minister of Economy and Finance: Frank De Lima
Minister of Public Safety: José Raul Mulino
Minister of Trade and Industry: Ricardo Quijano
Minister of the Presidency: Roberto Henriquez
Minister of Agricultural Development: Oscar Osario
Minister of Health: Javier Diaz
Minister of Labour: Alma Cortes Aguilar
Minister of Education: Lucinda Molinar
Minister of Public Security: José Raul Mulino
Minister of Public Works: Jaime Ford
Minister of Canal Affairs: Roberto Roy
Minister of Social Development: Guillermo Ferrufino
Minister of Micro, Small and Medium Business: vacant
Minister of Housing: Jasmina Pimentel
Minister of the Interior: Jorge Ricardo Fabrega (page 1422)
Administrator, Panamanian Tourist Authority: Salomon Shamah

Ministries

Office of the President, Presidential Palace, San Felipe, Republic of Panama. Tel: +507 227 4158, fax: +507 227 0076, e-mail: ofasin@presidencia.gob.pa, URL: http://www.presidencia.gob.pa

Ministry of Commerce and Industry, Piso 3, Edificio Plaza Edison, Avenida Ricardo J Alfaro, Panamá, Republic of Panama. Tel: +507 560 0656, fax: +507 360 0663, e-mail: uti@mici.gob.pa, URL: http://www.mici.gob.pa

Ministry of Agriculture, Edificio No. 576, Altos de Curundu, Avenida Frangipany, Panama, Republic of Panama. Tel: +507 232 5042, fax: +507 232 5044, e-mail: infomida@mida.gob.pa, URL: http://www.mida.gob.pa/

Ministry of Health, Hospital Gorgas, Edificio 237-265, Ancón, Panamá, Republic of Panama. Tel: +507 512 9400, fax: +507 227 5276, e-mail: daimimsa@yahoo.com, URL: http://www.minsa.gob.pa

Ministry of Labour and Social Welfare, Piso 5, Edificio Plaza Edison, Avenida Ricardo J Alfaro, Panamá, Republic of Panama. Tel: +507 560 1100, fax: +507 260 44669, e-mail: mitrabs2@sinfo.net, URL: http://www.mitradel.gob.pa

Ministry of Housing, Piso 4, Edificio Plaza Edison, Avenida Ricardo J Alfaro, Panamá, Republic of Panama. Tel: +507 579 9200, fax: +507 321 0028, URL: http://www.mivi.gob.pa

Ministry of Education, PO Box 2440 Panama 3, Republic of Panama. Tel: +507 511 4400, fax: +507 232 7786, URL: http://www.meduca.gob.pa

Ministry of Government and Justice, PO Box 1628, Panama 1, Republic of Panama. Tel: +507 262 1702/2993, fax: +507 262 7877, URL: http://www.gobiernoyjusticia.gob.pa

Ministry of Public Works, PO Box 1632, Panama 1, Republic of Panama. Tel: +507 232 5572/5505, fax: +507 232 5776, URL: http://www.mop.gob.pa/

Ministry of Foreign Affairs, Altos del Cerro Ancón, Panama 4, Republic of Panama. Tel: +507 221 4100, fax: +507 211 0491, URL: http://www.mire.gob.pa/

Ministry of Economy and Finance, PO Box 2694 Panama 3, Republic of Panama. Tel: +507 507 7000, fax: +507 264 7755, e-mail: webmaster@mef.gob.pa, URL: http://www.mef.gob.pa

Political Parties

Partido Revolucionario Democrático (PRD), URL: http://www.prd.org.pa/

Partido Panamenista (formerly named Partido Arnulfista), URL: http://partidopanamenista.com

Movimiento Liberal Republicano Nacionalista (MOLIRENA), Leader: Arturo Vallarino

Cambio Democrático, URL: http://www.cambiodemocratico.org/, Leader: Ricardo Martinelli

Elections

The most recent presidential election was held in May 2009. The right-wing coalition Alliance for Change won the majority in the Assembly, with preliminary results indicating that it had won 37 seats in the 71-seat National Assembly. Leader of the Alliance for Change - supermarket millionaire Ricardo Martinelli - won the presidential poll; preliminary results showed him ahead of governing party candidate Balbina Herrera, with 61 per cent of the vote. Former President Guillermo Endara was a distant third. Panamanians also elected a vice president, mayors and other local officials.

The next presidential election is due in 2014.

The most recent legislative elections took place on 3 May 2009 and were won by the Alliance for Change group.

Diplomatic Representation

US Embassy, Avenida Balboa y Calle 38, Panama City, Rep de Panama. Tel: +507 207 7000, fax: +507 227 1964, e-mail: sispan@pty.com, URL: http://panama.usembassy.gov/
Ambassador: Phyllis Powers

British Embassy, MMG Tower, Calle 53, (Apartado 889), Zona 1, Panama City, Panama. Tel: +507 269 0866, fax: +507 263 5138, e-mail: britemb@cwpanama.net, URL: http://ukinpanama.fco.gov.uk/en
Ambassador: Michael Holloway (page 1443)

Embassy of the Republic of Panama, UK, 40 Hertford Street, London W1Y 7TG, United Kingdom. Tel: +44 (0)20 7493 4646, fax: +44 (0)20 7493 4333, URL: http://www.panamaconsul.co.uk/
Ambassador: Ana Irene Delgado

Embassy of the Republic of Panama, US, 2862 McGill Terrace, NW, Washington DC 20008, USA. Tel: +1 202 483 1407, fax: +1 202 483 8413, URL: http://www.embassyofpanama.org/cms/index3.php
Ambassador: Mario E. Jaramillo

Permanent Representative of Panama to the United Nations, 866 United Nations Plaza, Suite 4030, New York, NY 10017, USA. Tel: +1 212 421 5420 / 5421, fax: +1 212 421 2694, e-mail: panama@un.int, URL: http://www.panama-un.org/en.html
Ambassador: H.E. Pablo Antonio Thalassinos

LEGAL SYSTEM

The legal system is based on the civil law system.

Panama's highest court is the Supreme Court of Justice, and consists of nine magistrates and nine alternates, appointed by the president for 10-year terms. The Supreme Court magistrates appoint judges of the superior courts who in turn appoint circuit court judges in their respective jurisdictions. There are four superior courts, 18 circuit courts (one civil and one criminal court for each province), and at least one municipal court in each district. At the local level, judges similar to Justices of the Peace hear minor civil and criminal cases involving sentences under one year. They are not subject to the Code of Criminal Procedure and defendants lack the safeguards afforded in the regular courts.

The 1996 amendment to the constitution abolished the army, and contains a provision for the temporary formation of a "special police force" to protect the borders.

The government respects the human rights of its citizens. However, there have been instances of abuse by prison guards, and prison conditions are harsh. There is some degree of corruption, and judicial inefficiency, leading to prolonged pretrial detention. Panama abolished the death penalty on gaining its independence. The last execution was carried out in 1903. In 2008, Panama co-sponsored the Resolution on a Moratorium on the Use of the Death Penalty at the UN General Assembly.

Supreme Court of Justice, URL: http://www.organojudicial.gob.pa
President: Alejandro Moncado Luna

Defensoria del Pueblo, URL: http://www.defensoriadelpueblo.gob.pa/

LOCAL GOVERNMENT

Administratively, Panama is divided into three indigenous territories (Embera-Wounaan, Ngobe-Bugle, Los Santos) and nine provinces (Bocas del Toro, Chiriqui, Cocle, Colon, Darien, Herrera, Kuna Yala, Panama, Veraguas). There are 75 districts.

AREA AND POPULATION

Area
Panama has an area of 75,517 sq. km. It is located in Central America, bordered by the Caribbean Sea in the north, the Pacific Ocean in the south, Costa Rica to the west, and Colombia to the south-east. The land is mountainous; the highest peak, at Cerro Volcan, is at 3,475 metres. The climate is tropical. The country is traversed by the 50-mile long Panama Canal, built by the USA between 1904 and 1914, and controlled by the USA until 1999.

To view a map, consult http://www.lib.utexas.edu/maps/cia08/panama_sm_2008.gif

Population
The estimated total population in 2010 was 3.517 million, with an average annual growth rate of 1.7 per cent. The majority of Panamanians are aged between 15 and 64 years, with 29 per cent aged under 15 years, and 10 per cent aged over 60. The median age is 27 years. Around 74 per cent of the population lives in urban areas. Panama City has a population of around 800,500.

Most of the population (70 per cent) are mestizo (mixed Amerindian and white), with 14 per cent Amerindian and mixed, 10 per cent white, and 6 per cent Amerindian.

Spanish is the official language, whilst English is spoken by about 14 per cent of the population.

Births, Marriages, Deaths
According to 2010 estimates the birth rate is 19.9 births per 1,000 inhabitants, whilst the death rate is 4.6 deaths per 1,000 people. Infant mortality is relatively high at 17 deaths per 1,000 live births. The fertility rate was 2.5 children per woman in 2010. Average life expectancy is 74 years for males and 79 years for females. Healthy life expectancy was put at 67 years. (Source: http://www.who.int, World Health Statistics 2012)

Public Holidays 2014
1 January: New Year's Day
9 January: National Martyrs' Day
5 March: Carnival
18 April: Good Friday
5 May: Labour Day
15 August: Foundation of Panama City (Panama City only)
4 November: Flag Day
3 November: Independence Day (from Colombia, 1903)
10 November: Uprising of Los Santos
28 November: Independence from Spain
8 December: Immaculate Conception/Mothers' Day
25 December: Christmas Day

EMPLOYMENT

In 2010, Panama had an estimated labour force of 1.4 million. Unemployment stood at 9.1 per cent, in 2006 down from 10.3 per cent the previous year, and the lowest for a decade. Unemployment rates have continued to fall to 6.8 per cent in 2007, 5.8 per cent in 2008 and 4.3 per cent in 2010.

Total Employment by Economic Activity

Occupation	2008
Agriculture, hunting & forestry	176,500
Fishing	9,100
Mining & quarrying	3,300
Manufacturing	114,100
Electricity, gas & water supply	6,900
Construction	136,700
Wholesale & retail trade, repairs	258,600
Hotels & restaurants	70,800
Transport, storage & communications	100,900
Financial intermediation	28,400
Real estate, renting & business activities	71,700
Public admin. & defence; compulsory social security	78,700
Education	74,600
Health & social work	55,100
Other community, social & personal service activities	70,000
Households with employed persons	77,400
Extra-territorial organisations & bodies	900

Source: Copyright © International Labour Organization (ILO Dept. of Statistics, http://laborsta.ilo.org)

During the peak construction period of the widening of the Panama Canal in 2009-2011, it is anticipated that between 7000 and 9,000 new jobs will be created.

BANKING AND FINANCE

Currency
One Balboa (Ba, PAB) = 100 Centésimos
The official currency is the Balboa which only circulates in coins. Panama does not issue paper currency. The US dollar is accepted as legal tender and is circulated freely.

GDP/GNP, Inflation, National Debt
Panama's economy is one of the most stable in Latin America. It is reliant largely on the service sector, which contributed about 80 per cent of GDP in 2006. Service industries include offshore finance, insurance, canal-related businesses including a shipping registry, and the Colon free trade zone, the second largest in the world and home to around 2,000 companies. The economy has been boosted by development of the infrastructure including the expansion of the Panama Canal. The expansion is due to be completed in 2014 and should double its capacity. The distribution of wealth is an issue in Panama; although the country has the highest GDP per capita in Central America at $14,000 (2011), around 40 per cent of its population lives in poverty.

GDP reached US$15 billion in 2006, with a growth rate of 8.7 per cent, up from 6.9 per cent in 2005. The economy grew by 12.0 per cent in 2007, 11.0 per cent in 2008 and fell to 2.5 per cent in 2009 and rose again to 5.5 per cent in 2010. GDP was estimated to be US$20.8 billion. GDP was estimated to be US$27 billion in 2011. Per capita GDP was estimated at US$14,000.

Bananas are the main cash crop, but the trade has been hit by disease and is vulnerable to tariff changes in the European export. Industry contributes 14 per cent of GDP, with sectors such as food and drink processing, metalwork, petroleum products and refining, paper and paper products, chemicals, printing and mining. The agriculture sector contributes about 6 per cent of GDP.

Inflation was 8.7 per cent in 2008. Panama's foreign debt was estimated at US$12 billion in 2011.

Foreign Investment
Panama has recently signed the Bilateral Investment Treaty Amendment and an agreement with the Overseas Private Investment Corporation (OPIC). Panama has Free Trade Agreements with Taiwan and Singapore, as well as the USA and El Salvador. It is negotiating FTAs with other Central American states, and the EU.

Balance of Payments / Imports and Exports
Exports in 2010 were estimated at US$725 million, and consisted mainly of tuna, beef, watermelon, shrimp, and pineapples. In 2009, the United States (29 per cent), Canada (10 per cent), China (5 per cent), Taiwan, the Netherlands and Costa Rica were the main export markets.

Imports in 2010 reached an estimated US$9 billion and were largely made up of capital goods, crude oil, food, chemicals, and other intermediate and consumer goods. Panama's main import trading partners are the USA (27 per cent), China, Japan, Costa Rica and Mexico.

Colón Free Zone
The Colón Free Zone is located 50 miles north-west of Panama City and is the largest and oldest free zone in the western hemisphere. Goods may be imported, stored, modified, processed, assembled, repacked, and then re-exported without any custom formalities. There is a tax on net income from sales in the Colón Free Zone. Additionally, export-orientated businesses receive substantial tax benefits.
Colón Free Zone, URL: http://www.colonfreezone.com

Central Bank
Banco Nacional de Panama, PO Box 5220, Banconal Tower, Via Espana, Panamá City 5, Panama. Tel: +507 2635151, fax: +507 2690091 / 2692573, e-mail: bnpvalores@cwp.net.pa, URL: http://www.banconal.com.pa

Chambers of Commerce and Trade Organisations
Panama Chamber of Commerce, Industry and Agriculture, e-mail: infocciab@panacamara.com, URL: http://www.panacamara.com/
National Banking Association (Asociación Bancaria Nacional), URL: http://www.asociacionbancaria.com

MANUFACTURING, MINING AND SERVICES

Primary and Extractive Industries
In the central provinces of the country there are vast amounts of mineral resources. There is the potential for exploiting gold, silver, copper, zinc, lead and molybdenum. Fiscal incentives and long term concessions are being offered for mining exploration. No government restrictions exist for foreign companies to participate in mining operations.

Panama has almost no hydrocarbon resources but is the highest energy consumer in the region. In 2008 Panama produced no oil but consumed an estimated 94,000 barrels per day (up from 58,000 bbld in 2001). Panama consumed an estimated 70,000 short tons of coal in 2002, all of which was imported. The major domestic energy resource is hydroelectricity, which fulfils some 11 per cent of the country's requirements. Other renewable resources make up the remaining 1 per cent of energy needed.

In 2005, approximately 27.7 million tons of crude oil and petroleum products passed through the Panama Canal. About 70 percent of petroleum shipments go from the Atlantic to Pacific Ocean. The relevance of the Panama Canal to global trade, especially petroleum, is currently threatened by the increasing size of modern shipping vessels; petroleum shipments represented 15 per cent of total canal traffic in 2005, up from 12 percent in 2004. Some oil tankers, such as ultra-large crude carriers (ULCC), can be nearly five times larger than the maximum capacity of the Panama Canal. The Panama Canal Authority (ACP) has addressed this problem with a plan to widen the Canal, which was approved by a referendum in October 2006.

The currently under-used Trans-Panama Pipeline (TPP) is the subject of talks with the Venezuelan President, Hugo Chavez; he wants to reverse the current directional flow of the pipeline to east to west, enabling Venezuelan crude oil exports to China via the pipeline by 2007. (Source: Energy Information Administration, EIA)

Energy
Panama's total energy consumption was estimated at 0.226 quadrillion Btu in 2006, up from 0.197 quadrillion Btu in 2003.

Total electricity generation capacity was 1.5 gigawatts in 2006, over 50 per cent of which was hydroelectric. Electricity generation in 2006 was around six billion kilowatthours (kWh) and electricity consumption in the same year was 4.7 billion kWh. Panama exports electricity to neighbouring countries.

There are eight electricity generating companies and three distributors operating in Panama. The US, Canada and Spain are all have electricity companies in Panama. A regulatory body, Ente Regulador, oversees the electric, water, and telecommunications industries.

The Plan Puebla-Panama is a project to integrate the electricity markets and transmission grids of the seven Central American states. The first phase of the project is the construction of the Sistema de Interconexion Electrica de los Paises America Central (SIEPAC), an 1,100-mile

PANAMA

transmission line linking Panama, Costa Rica, Honduras, Nicaragua, and El Salvador. Construction work has begun in Guatemala and Panama, and the first phase should be completed by the end of 2008. Funding is by the Inter-American Development Bank ($170 million) and Spain ($70 million).

Manufacturing

Manufacturing accounts for around 16 per cent of GDP. The main areas of industry are food and drink processing, petroleum products, chemicals, paper and paper products, printing, mining, refined sugar, clothing, furniture and construction. Manufacturing has been helped by the Caribbean Basin Initiative, a preferential import scheme for Caribbean products extended by the USA.

Service Industries

The services sector is the largest contributor to Panama's GDP; around 80 per cent according to recent figures. The banking, commerce and tourism industries are key sectors. The Colon Free Zone is one of the world's largest free trade zones and the income generated by the Panama Canal contributes a significant amount to GDP.

Tourism is a growing sector; in 2000, 395,551 people visited Panama (through Tocumen international airport); by 2003, this figure had risen to 454,396 visitors. The largest number came from the United states (119,024 in 2003), whilst 90,000 came from Colombia and 23,000 from Chile. Figures for 2006 show that Panama had 843,000 visitors.

Agriculture

Agriculture currently contributes about seven per cent of Panama's GDP. The Government is using price controls and lifting trade restrictions in order to increase productivity. Only a small proportion of the total land area is cultivated, although there are large fertile areas suitable for agriculture. Panama's chief crop, bananas, is exported to the United States and accounts for about half of total exports.

Sugar, coffee and rice are grown for local consumption. Cattle are reared in the Savannah Country and in most cases are slaughtered for consumption within the country and the hides exported. In 2004, there were 1.55 million head of cattle and 6,000 sheep and goats.

There are large areas of forest, containing many valuable hard woods, especially mahogany, but their potential has not yet been fully exploited. Other forest products include sarsaparilla and ipecacuanha.

Agricultural Production in 2010

Produce	Int. $'000*	Tonnes
Indigenous cattle meat	214,092	79,253
Indigenous chicken meat	175,721	123,364
Bananas	91,702	338,280
Rice, paddy	75,274	274,021
Sugar cane	66,234	2,095,010
Cow milk, whole, fresh	61,778	197,966
Indigenous pigmeat	45,396	29,531
Pineapples	27,624	96,909
Hen eggs, in shell	20,430	24,632
Plantains	17,403	95,194
Coffee, green	13,397	12,470
Oranges	9,802	50,722

* unofficial figures
Source: http://faostat.fao.org/site/339/default.aspx Food and Agriculture Organization of the United Nations, Food and Agricultural commodities production

COMMUNICATIONS AND TRANSPORT

Travel Requirements

Citizens of the USA, Canada and Australia require a passport valid for six months and can be issued a tourist card in lieu of a visa for stays of up to 30 days. Most EU subjects do not require a visa for stays of up to 90 days, but Bulgarians and Romanians do require a visa. However, it should be noted that passport and visa regulations are liable to change at short notice in Panama, so visitors are strongly advised to contact the embassy to check precise entry requirements before travelling.

National Airlines

International airlines connect Panama with the United States, Cuba and other southern and central American states. The Compañia Panameña de Aviación provides an internal service.

The main airport is Tocumen International Airport which serves both domestic and international airlines. Panama also has six domestic airports.

Railways

The principal railway runs between Panama City and Colón, for the greater part of its length through the Canal Zone territory. There is also a narrow-gauge railway with a terminus at Puerto Armuelles on the Pacific Coast, connecting Concepción, Pedregal and David. The United Fruit Company now operates about 55 miles of lines among the banana plantations of Bocas del Toro Province. The total railway network consists of 222 miles of track.
Panama Canal Railway Company, URL: http://www.panarail.com

The railroad system is one of the latest to be privatised. It was awarded to the US company, Kansas City Southern Rail.

Roads

Panama's roads total 7,036 miles, of which 66 per cent are unpaved. Vehicles drive on the right. The Darien Gap, an almost impenetrable jungle, lies between Panama and Colombia; it creates a break in the Pan-American Highway, which otherwise forms a complete road from Alaska to Chile.

The Panama Canal

The Panama Canal is a lock-type canal, extending approximately 50 miles from Panama City on the Pacific Ocean to Colon on the Caribbean Sea. The canal can accommodate 50 ships a day. From Alaska to the US Gulf Coast via the canal takes 16 days. If re-routed around Cape Horn, the journey would take 40 days.

The Panama Canal Treaty, signed in 1903, allowed the USA to build and operate a canal to connect the Pacific Ocean and the Caribbean Sea through the Isthmus of Panama. The treaty also bestowed full sovereign rights on the Canal Zone. In return, the independence of Panama was guaranteed, and Panama received $10 million, as well as an annuity of $250,000, which each year increased at a rate far beyond inflation. A new Panama Canal Treaty was signed on 7 September 1977 by President Torrijos of Panama and President Carter of USA, which declared that full responsibility for the canal would return to Panama at noon on 31 December 1999. It also guarantees permanent neutrality of the Canal and allows America to intervene to preserve the Canal's neutrality. The transition to Panamanian control was smooth, though since then there has been concern regarding toll charge increases, and some operators are considering the alternative Suez Canal as a route through from the Americas to Asia.

In 2005 a total of 14,000 ships traversed the canal, shipping 200 million tonnes of cargo. Petroleum represented approximately 11 per cent of total shipped commodities; in 2001, 613,000 barrels of oil per day and more than six million tons of coal were shipped through the canal. Most trade is for the US Gulf/East Coast-Asia route, but North-South trade is expected to increase as Latin America increases her trading relations with the US.

In April 2006 the Panama Canal Authority unveiled its plans for the enlargement of the canal, to accommodate the new giant container ships and remain a key East/West route. The project would cost around US$5.3 billion, and create several thousand jobs. The proposal to expand the Canal was approved by a national referendum by around 80 per cent, in October 2006. The project will provide 7,000-9,000 direct new jobs during the peak construction period of 2009-2011 and is expected to be financed through a combination of increased tolls and debt. The project is due to be completed in 2014.

The following table shows the principal commodities shipped through the Panama Canal in 2001 (thousands of long tons):

Commodity	Atlantic to Pacific	Pacific to Atlantic
Petroleum/Petroleum Products	19,143	10,886
Ores and Metals	3,041	9,164
Nitrates, Phosphates, Potash	10,044	1,553
Chemicals	7,108	2,830
Iron and Steel Manufactures	3,611	5,148
Timber	4,488	3,455
Foods	1,496	6,323
Minerals	80	7,135
Coal	922	4,920
Other Agricultural Commodities	547	3,616
Coke	21	2,179
TOTAL	109,180	83,960

Other Shipping

Major harbours include: Balboa, Cristobal, Coco Solo, Manzanillo, and Vacamonte. In addition to the Panama Canal there are 500 miles of waterways.

HEALTH

In 2009, the government spent approximately 14.7 per cent of its total budget on healthcare (down from 21.3 per cent in 2000), accounting for 74.8 per cent of all healthcare spending. Total expenditure on healthcare equated to 8.1 per cent of the country's GDP. Per capita expenditure on health was approximately US$564. Figures for 2000-10 showed that there were 4,431 physicians (15 per 10,000 population), 8,158 nurses and midwives (28 per 10,000 population), 2,231 dentists, 2,526 pharmaceutical personnel and 948 environmental and public health workers. There were 22 hospital beds per 10,000 population.

Around 40 per cent of the population lives below the poverty line, despite the country having one of the highest per capita GDPs in Central America. The indigenous people are most affected by poverty and more than half of indigenous children under five suffer from malnutrition. The Government has adopted a Social Protection policy; food bonuses and cash for extremely poor families, who live mostly in areas with a predominantly indigenous population are available on condition that parents register themselves and their children in the National Registry, have their children vaccinated and ensure they attend school. In 2000-09 approximately 19.1 per cent of children aged under 5 were classified as stunted and 3.9 per cent as underweight. The infant mortality rate (probability of dying before the age of 1) was 17 per 1,000 live births and the child (under-five) mortality rate was 20 per 1,000 live births. The most common causes of death in children under five are: prematurity 14 per cent, congenital anomalies 24 per cent, pneumonia 9 per cent, diarrhoea 11 per cent and neonatal sepsis 7 per cent. The HIV/AIDS prevalence rate was 585 per 100,000 population in 2009.

According to the latest WHO figures, in 2008 approximately 97 per cent of the urban population and 83 per cent of the rural population had access to improved drinking water. In the same year, 75 per cent of the urban population and 51 per cent of the rural population had access to improved sanitation. Diarrhoea accounts for 11 per cent of deaths of children aged less than five years old. (Source: http://www.who.int, World Health Statistics 2012)

EDUCATION

Primary/Secondary Education
State education is free at all pre-university levels. The first six years are compulsory. Whilst attendance is estimated to be 99 per cent in primary education, it drops to 64 per cent at secondary level. Approximately 97 per cent of children complete primary school education, and around 65 progress to secondary level education. 44 per cent of students go on to study at tertiary level, well above the regional average of 29.5 per cent. In 2005, 8.9 per cent of government expenditure went on education.

Overall adult literacy rate is around 93.4 per cent (above the regional average) and rises to 96.3 per cent in the 15-24 age group. (Source: UNESCO, UIS, August 2009)

RELIGION

There is complete freedom of worship. Nearly 80 per cent of the population is Roman Catholic.

Panama has a religious liberty rating of 9 on a scale of 1 to 10 (10 is most freedom). (Source: World Religion Database)

COMMUNICATIONS AND MEDIA

There is freedom of expression in the media.

Newspapers
La Estrella de Panama, URL: http://www.estrelladepanama.com
Critica Libre, URL: http://www.critica.com.pa
La Prensa, URL: http://www.prensa.com
Critica Libre, URL: http://www.critica.com.pa/

Broadcasting
There are several privately-owned television networks and a government-owned educational TV station. Cable and satelite TV subscription services are also available. More than 100 commercial radio stations also operate.
Telemetro, commercial, URL: http://www.telemetro.com/
FETV, URL: http://www.fetv.org/ (educational)

Telecommunications
Domestic and international telecommunications are well-developed. The average number of telephones per person is the highest in Latin America. In 2008 there were an estimate 525,000 mainline telephones in use and around 3.5 million mobile phones.

In 2009, nearly 1 million people in Panama were regular internet users (approx. 30 per cent of the population).

ENVIRONMENT

Panama's major environment issues include water pollution to fishery resources caused by agricultural runoff, deforestation of the tropical rainforest, and land degradation.

The Meteorology and Hydrology Branch of Panama's National Institute of Natural Renewable Resources (INRENARE), the Smithsonian Tropical Research Institute and several non-governmental agencies, have, over the past decade, increased awareness and lowered the rate of deforestation in the Panama Canal watershed. Deforestation and misuse of the watershed could cause serious sedimentation problems that could affect the Canal's future.

Panama is a party to the following international environmental agreements: Biodiversity, Climate Change, Climate Change-Kyoto Protocol, Desertification, Endangered Species, Hazardous Wastes, Law of the Sea, Marine Dumping, Nuclear Test Ban, Ozone Layer Protection, Ship Pollution, Tropical Timber 83, Tropical Timber 94, Wetlands, and Whaling.

According to figures from the EIA, energy related carbon emissions were estimated at 14.33 million metric tons in 2005, up from 12.56 mmt in 2002. Per capita carbon emissions were an estimated 4.56 metric tons in the same year, compared to the regional average of 2.45 metric tons. In 2006 Panama's emissions from the consumption of fossil fuels totalled 14.43 million metric tons of carbon dioxide.

PAPUA NEW GUINEA
Independent State of Papua New Guinea

Capital: Port Moresby (Population estimate, 2011: 950,000)

Head of State: Her Majesty Queen Elizabeth II (Sovereign) (page 1420)

Governor-General: Sir Michael Ogio (page 1489)

National Flag: A rectangle divided diagonally from the top of the hoist to the bottom of the fly, with the upper segment scarlet and containing a soaring yellow Bird of Paradise. The lower segment is black charged with five pointed stars representing the Southern Cross.

CONSTITUTION AND GOVERNMENT

Constitution
Papua New Guinea attained full independence on 16 September 1975 when the Constitution came into effect, establishing a parliamentary democracy based on the Westminster model but excluding an upper chamber. The Government comprises the National Parliament (109 members), the National Executive and the National Judicial System. The constitution was amended in 1998 to allow for the island of Bougainville to move towards autonomy. Universal suffrage exists with the minimum voting age of 18.

To consult the constitution, please visit: http://www.igr.gov.pg/constitution.pdf

Bougainville
The island of Bougainville is part of Papua New Guinea and is rich in copper. Bougainvillians, angry that they were not benefiting from the profits of copper mining, began calling for independence. An armed struggle began in 1989 and after several truces and cease fires the Bougainville Peace Agreement was signed in 2001. In 2005 the islanders voted for the first time to elect an autonomous government and president; Jospeh Kabui was duly elected as president in June. Although Bougainville is autonomous, the Papua New Guinea government is responsible for defence and the economy.

Recent Events
In August 2009, Papual New Guinea suffered its first ever outbreak of cholera, it was centred in the northern province of Morobe and 40 people lost their lives.

In December 2009, an agreement was signed to export liquified natural gas to China.

On 10 December 2010 the Supreme Court ruled that the re-election of Sir Paulius Matane as governor-general in June 2010 was invalid. Parliament must be recalled to re-elect his successor by the end of January 2011. The cabinet was also reshuffled in December 2010. Prime Minister Somare appointed his ally Sam Abal as deputy prime minister. Mr Abal took over as prime minister when Mr Somare stood down to face charges of financial irregularities.

Mr Somare returned to his position as prime minister in January 2011 but took indefinite medical leave later in the year, with the deputy prime minister, Mr Abal as acting prime minister. However, in August 2011, following a report on the health of Mr Somare, parliament declared that Mr Somare must step down permanently and elected the minister for works and transport, Peter O'Neill, as prime minister. He subsequently appointed his cabinet.

In October 2011 fighting broke out between the Agarabi and Kamano tribes; at least 15 people were reported to have been killed.

In December the supreme court ruled that Sir Michael should be reinstated as prime minister. Somare announced a cabinet the next day which included most of those from his cabinet dimissed in August. The cabinet was sworn in on 14 December by the governor general, Michael Ogio, but O'Neill refused to step down. His supporters in parliament then voted to suspend Ogio and replace him with Jeffery Nape, the Speaker of Parliament. Nape then swore in O'Neill as the prime minister on 15 December. Somare however refused to step down. The Supreme Court ruled in May 2012 that the government of Sir Michael Somare was legitimate. However, later in the month, the deputy speaker of parliament contended that as Sir Michael Somare had missed three consecutive sittings of parliament he was now disqualified. Peter O'Neill was again elected prime minister by parliament and sworn into office. Legislative elections took place in July 2012. The PNC won most seats although it remained short of an overall majority. Peter O'Neill announced his new government the same month with the support of Sir Michael Somare who resigned as leader of the NAP party following its poor performance.

National Executive
The National Executive comprises the Head of State and the National Executive Council (consisting of all ministers including the Prime Minister) and is responsible for the executive Government of Papua New Guinea.

National Parliament
The National Parliament is a single chamber legislature of 109 members elected from single member open provincial electorates by universal adult suffrage. The normal term of office is five years.
National Parliament, Parliament House, Post Office, Waigini, Port Moresby, NCD, Papua New Guinea. Tel: +675 327 7406, fax: +675 327 7404, URL: http://www.parliament.gov.pg

Cabinet (as at March 2013)
Prime Minister: Peter O'Neill (PNC)
Deputy Prime Minister & Minister for Intergovernmental Relations: Leo Dion
Minister of Treasury: Don Poyle (page 1497)
Minister of Public Enterprise: Ben Micah
Minister of Climate Change and Forestry: Patrick Pruaitch
Minister of Transport: Ano Pala

PAPUA NEW GUINEA

Minister of Agriculture and Livestock: Assik Tommy Tomscoll
Minister of Foreign Affairs: Rimbink Pato (page 1492)
Minister of Education: Paru Aihi
Minister of Finance: James Marape
Minister of Health and HIV/AIDS: Michael Malabag
Minister of Police: Nixon Philip Duban
Minister of Correctional Services: Jim Simatab
Minister of Defence: Dokta Fabian Pok
Minister of Labour: Mark Maipakai
Minister of Commerce & Industry: Richard Maru
Minister of Sports: Justin Tkatchenko
Minister of Public Service: Sir Puka Temu
Minister of Youth and Community Development, Minister of Religion: Loujaya Toni
Minister of Housing & Urban Development: Paul Isikiel
Minister of Petroleum and Energy: William Duma
Minister of Fisheries and Marine Resources: Mao Zeming
Minister of Higher Education, Research and Science: David Arore
Minister of Environment & Conservation: John Pundari
Minister of Culture and Tourism: Boka Kondra
Minister of Communications and Information Technology: Jim Miringtoro
Minister of Mining: Byron Chan
Minister of Civil Aviation: Davies Steven
Minister of Justice, Attorney General: Kerenga Kua
Minister of National Planning: Charles Abel
Minister of Autonomous Affairs: Steven Pirika Kama
Minister of Works: Francis Awesa
Minister for Lands: Benny Allan

Ministries

Department of the Prime Minister and NEC, 5th Floor, Morauta Haus, PO Box 639, Waigani, NCD, Papua New Guinea. Tel: +675 327 6713 / 6733 / 6715, fax: +675 323 3903, URL: http://www.pm.gov.pg/pmsoffice/PMsoffice.nsf

Department of Agriculture and Livestock, PO Box 417, Konedobu, NCD, Papua New Guinea. Tel: +675 321 3302 / 321 3308, fax: +675 321 1387, URL: http://www.agriculture.gov.pg/

Department of Defence, Free Mail Bag Services, Boroko, NCD, Papua New Guinea. Tel: +675 324 2358 / 324 2270 / 323 1854, fax: +675 325 2689, URL: http://www.defence.gov.pg/

Department of Education, PSA Haus, PO Box 446, Waigani, NCD, Papua New Guinea. Tel: +675 301 3446 / 301 3447, fax: +675 323 1031, URL: http://www.education.gov.pg/

Department of Higher Education, Research, Science and Technology, 2nd Floor Mutual Rumana Building, PO Box 5117, Boroko NCD, Papua New Guinea. Tel: +675 327 7528, fax: +675 327 7480, URL: http://www.education.gov.pg/

Department of Foreign Affairs, Trade & Immigration, 2nd Floor Somare Foundation Building, Independence Drive, PO Box 422, Waigani NCD, Papua New Guinea. Tel: +675 301 4158, f,Fax: +675 327 7480

Department of Health and HIV/AIDS, 5th Floor Aopi Centre, PO Box 807, Waigani NCD, Papua New Guinea. Tel: +675 301 3605, fax: +675 301 3604, URL: http://www.health.gov.pg

Department of Justice and Attorney General, 11th Floor Sir Buri Kidu Building, PO Box 591, Waigani NCD, Papua New Guinea. Tel: +675 323 0628, fax: +675 323 0241, URL: http://www.justice.gov.pg

Department of Labour and Industrial Relations, PO Parliament House, Waigani NCD, Papua New Guinea. Tel: +675 327 7582, fax: +675 327 7480

Department of Mining, Private Mail Bag, Port Moresby NCD 121, Papua New Guinea. Tel: +675 322 7670, fax: +675 321 3958, URL: http://www.mineral.gov.pg/

Department of InterGovernment Relations, 11th Floor Somare Foundation Building, Independence Drive, PO Box 1287, Waigani NCD, Papua New Guinea. Tel: +675 325 0251, fax: +675 321 7462, e-mail: igr@global.net.pg, URL: http://www.igr.gov.pg

Department of Petroleum and Energy, 2nd Floor AON Building, PO Box 1993, Port Moresby NCD, Papua New Guinea. Tel: +675 327 7680, fax: +675 321 5251, e-mail: firstname_surname@petroleum.gov.pg, URL: http://www.petroleum.gov.pg

Department of Trade and Industry, 2nd Floor Moale Haus, PO Box 375, Waigani NCD, Papua New Guinea. Tel: +675 327 7346, fax: +675 301 3205

Department of Works, Transport and Civil Aviation, PO Box 1489, Port Moresby, NCD, Papua New Guinea. Tel: +675 300 2301 / 300 2302, fax: +675 300 2304, URL: http://www.works.gov.pg/

Department of Treasury and Finance, Vulupindi Haus, PO Box 710, Waigani, NCD, Papua New Guinea. Tel: +675 328 8452 / 328 8455, fax: +675 328 8431 / 328 8425, URL: http://www.treasury.gov.pg

Department of Information and Communication, 8th Floor Somare Foundation Building, Independence Drive, PO Box 1122, Waigani NCD, Papua New Guinea. Tel: +675 325 0148, fax: +675 325 0412, e-mail: hiduhu@datec.com.pg, URL: http://www.communication.gov.pg

Department of Housing and Urban Development, 2nd Floor Mutual Rumana Building, PO Box 1550, Boroko NCD, Papua New Guinea. Tel: +675 325 9344, fax: +675 325 9918

Department of the Environment and Conservation, 7th Floor Somare Foundation Building, Independence Drive, PO Box 6601, Boroko NCD, Papua New Guinea. Tel: +675 325 0174, fax: +675 325 0182

Department of Fisheries and Marine Resources, 2nd Floor First Heritage Centre, PO Box 2016, Port Moresby NCD, Papua New Guinea. Tel: +675 327 7346, fax: +675 327 7480, URL: http://www.fisheries.gov.pg

Department of Forests, PO Box 5055, Boroko NCD, Papua New Guinea. Tel: +675 327 7800, Fax: +675 325 4433

Department of Community Development, Women and Religion, Sambra Investment House, Waigani, PO Box 7354, Boroko NCD, Papua New Guinea. Tel: +675 325 0120, fax: +675 325 0118

Department of Culture and Tourism, Level 2, Era Rumana Building, PO Box 1291, Port Moresby NCD, Papua New Guinea. Tel: +675 320 0275, fax: +675 320 0302

Department of Public Services, 2nd Floor Morauta Haus, PO Box 519, Waigani NCD, Papua New Guinea. Tel: +675 327 6418, fax: +675 325 0835, URL: http://www.dpm.gov.pg

Department of State Enterprises, 4th Floor Pacific Place, PO Box 320, Port Moresby NCD, Papua New Guinea. Tel: +675 321 2977, fax: +675 321 0192

Department of Transport and Works, Wnga Haus 1 & 2, 7-Mile, PO Box 1489, Port Moresby NCD, Papua New Guinea. Tel: +675 323 6460, fax: +675 325 4436, URL: http://www.works.gov.pg

Department of Treasury and Finance, 4th Floor Vulupindi Haus, PO Box 710, Waigani NCD, Papua New Guinea. Tel: +675 312 8870, fax: +675 323 2239, URL: http://www.treasury.gov.pg/treasury/treasury.nsf

Political Parties

National Alliance Party; Pangu Pati (PP); People's Action Party (PAP); Melanesian Alliance (MA); National Party (NP); League for National Advancement (LNA); People's National Congress (PNC); United Resources Party (URP); PNG Party (PNG).

Elections

Elections are held every five years. Voters must be over the age of 18 years.

The most recent parliamentary elections were held in July 2007. The ruling coalition headed by the National Alliance Party remained the largest party in parliament, although as in the 2002 elections, most seats were won by independent MPs. Sir Michael Somare, the incumbent prime minister, was re-elected to the post by parliament on 13 August 2007. He formed a new coalition made up of seven parties: the National Alliance Party, the People's Action Party, the PNC, the URP, the Pangu party, the Melanesian Alliance and the United party. The new cabinet was sworn in on 29 August. Dispute over the legitmacy of the government continued. The Supreme Court starting hearing the case in April 2012, eventually ruling in favour of Sir Michael Somare. However, the Deputy Speaker of Parliament ruled that as Sir Michael had missed several sittings of parliament he was disqualified. Parliament duly elected Mr O'Neill as prime minister in May 2012.

The most recent legislative elections took place between 27 June and 13 July 2012. The PNC of Mr O'Neill won 27 seats; independents 16, THEP 12, PNGP 8; URP 7; NAP 7; PPP 6; PP 6.

Diplomatic Representation

Papua New Guinea High Commission, 3rd Floor, 14 Waterloo Place, London, SW1Y 4AR, UK. Tel: +44 (0)20 7930 0922/7, fax: +44 (0)20 7930 0828, URL: http://www.pnghighcomm.org.uk
High Commissioner: Winnie Anna Kiap
Embassy of Papua New Guinea, 1779 Massachusetts Avenue NW, Suite 805, Washington, DC 20036, USA. Tel: +1 202 745 3680, fax: +1 202 745 3679, e-mail: Kunduwash@aol.com, URL: http://www.pngembassy.org
Interim chargé d'affaires: Elias Wohengu
US Embassy, Douglas Street, PO Box 1492, Port Moresby, Papua New Guinea. Tel: +675 321 1455, fax: +675 321 3423, URL: http://portmoresby.usembassy.gov/
Ambassador: Teddy Taylor
British High Commission: URL: http://ukinpng.fco.gov.uk
High Commissioner: Jackie Barson (page 1384)
Permanent Representative of Papua New Guinea to the United Nations, 201 East 42nd Street, Suite 405, New York, NY 10017, USA. Tel: +1 212 557 5001, fax: +1 212 557 5009, e-mail: png@un.int
Permanent Representative: Robert Aisi

LEGAL SYSTEM

The laws of Papua New Guinea are based on English and Australian common law. The judicial system comprises the Supreme Court, National Court, District Courts, Local Courts and Village Courts.

The Supreme Court is the final Court of Appeal and consists of the Chief Justice, Deputy Chief Justice and no fewer than four or more than six other judges. The Chief Justice is appointed or dismissed by the Head of State on the proposal of the National Executive Council. The Deputy Chief Justice and other judges are appointed by the Judicial and Legal Service Commission. Many local matters are settled by village courts and local village administrators.

The government respects the rights of its citizens, but there have been recent instances of unlawful killings and brutality by police. The police force is perceived to be corrupt, and officers are not punished for their misdeeds. Prison conditions are poor, and pretrial detention can be lengthy. There is corruption in government corruption, intertribal violence and ineffective enforcement of labor laws.

The death penalty is part of the criminal code but the last execution was carried out in 1959. However, murder, treason and piracy are capital crimes and as of 2012 there were 10 people on death row. The current attorney general is considering reactivating the death penalty.

In 2012, the Chief Justice Sir Salomo was arrested and charged with sedition ater calling for Sir Michael Somare to be reinstated as prime minister.

Supreme Court, URL: http://www.pngjudiciary.gov.pg/home/index.php

LOCAL GOVERNMENT

For the purpose of administration Papua New Guinea is divided into 18 Provinces, one autonomous region, Bougainville and one district, National Capital, each with an Administrative Secretary to represent the Central Government. Each Province has a Provincial Government and a Premier. The National Capital District is administered by an Interim Commission under an Act of Parliament.

Each Province has concurrent power with the national government in areas such as agriculture, business development, town planning, forestry, and natural resources. In the event of conflict between local and national government, national government laws take precedence.

The provinces are: Central; Chimbu; Eastern Highlands; East New Britain; East Sepik; Enga; Gulf; Madang; Manus; Milne Bay; Morobe; New Ireland; Northern; Sandaun; Southern Highlands; Western; Western Highlands; West New Britain.

AREA AND POPULATION

Area
Papua New Guinea lies completely within the southern tropics and north of Australia. Total area (including 600 other islands): 460,000 sq. km (46,410,000 hectares). Papua New Guinea is the Eastern half of the island of New Guinea, Irian Jaya (an Indonesian province) being the Western half. The geography of Papua New Guinea is diverse. Mountains reaching a height of 2,800 metres run the length of the island. Along the coastal plains there are many coral reefs. Almost 50 per cent of the land is mountainous and some 20 per cent either permanently or seasonally flooded.

The climate is tropical. There are two monsoon seasons: the northwest monsoon takes place from December to March, and one from the southeast from May to October.

To view a map of Papua New Guinea, please visit http://www.un.org/Depts/Cartographic/map/profile/papua.pdf

On 19 July 1998 a 30 foot tidal wave hit Papua New Guinea's remote north coast. More than 1,000 people died and a further 6,000 were left homeless. An undersea earthquake which measured seven on the Richter scale occurred 18 miles from the northwest coast. The country is situated in an area of frequent natural disaster and is part of the volcano belt known as the Ring of Fire. Volcanoes stretch along its entire northern coastline.

In November 2007, Cyclone Guba caused flooding and the deaths of 163 people. Over 13,000 people were displaced in the provinces of Oro and Milne.

Population
According to estimated figures, Papua New Guinea's population in 2010 was 6.858 million, an increase on the 1995 estimate of 4.25 million. The average annual change was 2.4 per cent for the period 2000-10. Population density is 13 people per sq. km. The National Capital District (NCD) is the most densely populated of Papua New Guinea's provinces, with a 1990 figure of 815 people per sq. km. The Western Highlands has 40 people per sq. km., whilst Chimbu has 30 per sq. km. The area with the lowest population density is Western province, with 1 person per sq. km. Only 12 per cent of the population live in major urban areas. Since the 1990s there has been a trend for people to move to urban areas particularly Port Moresby; this has led to increased unemployment, ethnic tensions and crime. The population of Port Moresby is expected to reach 1 million soon.

The following table shows the area and population in 2000 according to province:

Province	Capital	Area (sq. km)	Population
Central	Port Moresby	29,500	176,772
Eastern Highlands	Goroka	11,200	357,629
East New Britain	Rabaul	15,500	237,080
East Sepik	Wewak	42,800	326,027
Enga	Webag	12,800	282,519
Gulf	Kerema	34,500	86,800
Madang	Madang	29,000	350,939
Manus	Lorengau	2,100	42,459
Milne Bay	Alotau	14,000	204,510
Morobe	Lae	34,500	503,605
National Capital District	Port Moresby	240	275,681
New Ireland	Kavieng	9,600	118,211
North Solomons (Bougainville)	Arawa	9,300	204,111
Oro (Northern)	Popondetta	22,800	112,985
Sandaun (West Sepik)	Vanimo	36,300	160,349
Simbu (Chimbu)	Kundiawa	6,100	205,190
Southern Highlands	Mendi	23,800	390,240
Western	Daru	99,300	143,652
Western Highlands	Mount Hagen	8,500	429,916
West New Britain	Kimbe	21,000	199,057
Source: Embassy of Papua New Guinea

English is the official language though there are over 700 interrelated indigenous languages spoken. Pidgin and Motu are important local languages, with Pidgin being understood by the majority of the population. The inhabitants are mostly Melanesian (95 per cent) with small Micronesian and Polynesian groups and a minority of Europeans.

Births, Marriages, Deaths
According to 2010 estimates, the birth rate is 30.2 per 1,000 population, whilst the death rate is 7.2 per 1,000. Average life expectancy at birth in 2009 was 62 years for men and 65 years for women. Healthy life expectancy was 55 years for males and 57 years for females. The median age is 20 years. An estimated 39 per cent of the population are aged under 15 years and 5 per cent over 60 (2010). The infant mortality rate was 47 deaths per 1,000 live births. The total fertility rate was 4.0 children per female. (Source: http://www.who.int, World Health Statistics 2012)

Public Holidays 2014
1 January: New Year's Day
18 April: Good Friday
20 April: Easter Sunday
21 April: Easter Monday
18 July: Provincial Government Day
23 July: Remembrance Day
16 September: Independence Day and Constitution Day
25 December: Christmas Day
26 December: Boxing Day

EMPLOYMENT

Papua New Guinea's labour force is about 3.8 million. Subsistence agriculture employs about 85 per cent of Papua New Guinea's population. Despite government measures to increase employment, such as reducing the minimum wage and improving higher education, the unemployment rate has been rising. The unemployment rate in 2005 was estimated at 70 per cent. The government is by far the largest employer. About 10 per cent of the labour force is made up of expatriates. Employment trends are influenced by the seasonal aspect of agriculture.

BANKING AND FINANCE

Currency
100 toea = One Kina. Its exchange rate is a floating rate.

Financial Centre: Port Moresby

GDP/GNP, Inflation, National Debt
Because of its rich natural resources, Papua New Guinea's economy is primarily based on agriculture and mining. Agriculture employs about 85 per cent of the workforce, whilst mineral deposits account for over 70 per cent of export earnings. In 2007, parliament passed a law to allow casinos and online gambling in the hope that these activities would boost the economy. The services sector contributes around 20 per cent towards annual GDP, with agriculture accounting for 35.6 per cent and industry 44 per cent. A liquefied natural gas production facility is under construction by a US-led consortium. It should transform the economy and is scheduled to open in 2014. The government created a Sovereign Wealth Fund in 2012 to manage surpluses from oil and gas projects.

GDP growth was slow during the 1990s, due in part to the 1998 tidal wave disaster, as well as the Asian economic crisis and low oil and mineral prices. GDP growth was an estimated 7.2 per cent in 2008, compared to an estimated 4.1 per cent in 2007, 2.3 per cent in 2006, and 3.9 per cent in 2005. Figures for 2009 put GDP growth at 4.5 per cent, 5.5 per cent in 2010 and 7.5 per cent in 2011. Per capita GDP was 3,338 kina in 2008. The global economic crisis has not affected Papua New Guinea.

The following table shows GDP by industrial origin in recent years (current market prices). Figures are in million Kina.

Sector	2008	2009	2010
GDP	21,601.3	22,207.0	25,837.2
Agriculture	6,916.7	7,207.9	8,056.0
Mining	5,894.9	4,714.9	5,801.2
Manufacturing	1,247.6	1,328.8	1,500.1
Utilities	404.1	461.7	534.5
Construction	2,226.2	2,844.2	3,453.2
Trade	1,393.3	159.9	1,872.6
Transport & communications	440.3	603.7	749.0
Finance	760.0	929.0	1,083.4
Public administration	1,818.8	2,010.1	2,211.4
Source: Asian Development Bank

Inflation was put at 7.6 per cent in 2009, 6.1 per cent in 2010 and 8 per cent in 2011.

External debt was an estimated US$5 billion in 2011. Corruption is rife. In 2004, the Australian Strategic Policy Institute issued a report warning that Papua New Guinea was heading towards economic and social collapse and suggested that Australia should take over some aspects of government. Foreign Minister Sir Rabbie Namaliu dismissed the report as inaccurate.

Foreign Investment
There are several bilateral development programmes with support from Australia, Japan, the People's Republic of China, Germany, the Republic of Korea, New Zealand, and the USA.

Balance of Payments / Imports and Exports
Most imports come from Australia, Singapore, Japan, the USA, New Zealand, and Malaysia. Papua New Guinea exports to Australia, Japan, Germany, South Korea, the Philippines, and the UK. External trade in recent years is shown in the following tables. Figures are in million Kina.

Year	Exports fob	Imports cif	Trade Balance
2008	15,655	8,459	7,196
2009	12,081	7,889	4,192
2010	15,257	9,344	5,913

Exports by Principal Commodity

Commodity	2004	2005	2006
Gold	2,780	2,834	3,069
Crude petroleum	1,652	2,283	2,967
Copper	1,544	2,498	4,330
Forest products	460	476	520
Coffee beans	284	471	337

PAPUA NEW GUINEA

- continued

Palm oil	439	391	428
Cocoa	218	199	204

Source: Asian Development Bank

Main export trading partners are Australia (US$2,778 million), Japan (US$906 million), China (US$709 million), Germany and the Philippines. Main import trading partners are Australia (US$2,067 million), Singapore (US$646 million), China (US$388 million), Japan, Malaysia, and the US.

Central Bank
Bank of Papua New Guinea, PO Box 121, Douglas Street, Port Moresby, Papua New Guinea. Tel: +675 3227200, fax: +675 3211617, e-mail: bpng@datee.com.pg, URL: http://www.bankpng.gov.pg
Governor: Loi Bakani

Chambers of Commerce and Trade Organisations
Papua New Guinea Chamber of Commerce & Industry, URL: http://www.pngcci.org.pg

MANUFACTURING, MINING AND SERVICES

Primary and Extractive Industries
Papua New Guinea is rich in mineral resources. It receives its single largest revenue from copper mining, and the Porgera gold mine is one of the largest in the world. Other major mines include the Ok Tedi mine in the Western Province, the Lihir project in the New Ireland Province, and the Misima mine in the Milne Bay province. The mining industry suffered a setback at the end of the 1980s with the closure of the world's largest copper mine, situated on Papua New Guinea's Bougainville Island. The Ok Tedi mine has recently undergone some investment which is hoped will extend the life of the mine to 2025.

Papua New Guinea produced 30.22 thousand barrels per day of oil in 2011, all of which was crude oil. Consumption the same year was 45.0 thousand barrels per day, meaning 14.7 thousand barrels per day had to be imported..

The Kutubu Oil Refinery, in the Southern Highlands, began production in 1992 and currently produces 33,000 barrels of crude oil a day. Recoverable assets have been estimated at 240 million barrels. The Globe Oil Project, located in the Gulf and Southern Highlands Provinces, began production in late 1997 and early 1998 at a rate of 50,000 barrels per day.

Natural gas production in 2011 was 4 billion cubic feet, all of which was consumed domestically. In 2009, China signed a deal to import liquified natural gas from Papua New Guinea.

Energy
In 2010, Papua New Guinea produced 3.35 billion kW, of electricity, both from thermal and hydroelectric sources. It consumed nearly all the electricity it produced.

Manufacturing
Recent government plans have focused on the need to diversify the economy and reduce reliance on the minerals industry. Hence the establishment of new industrial endeavours, wood products, a cement factory, fish canneries and oil refineries, food processing, beverage production and processing of tobacco. The larger industries are usually part or totally owned by overseas organisations. National investment in business is not significant and restricted mainly to the agricultural sector.

Agriculture
Subsistence agriculture is the principal economic activity for most Papua New Guineans. Papua New Guinea's most important crops are coffee, oil palm, coconut, rubber and tea - together these constitute over 94 per cent of the total agricultural export value. Other important crops are yams, taros, potatoes and sweet potatoes. Eighty per cent of all households grow their own food and 40 per cent grow coffee. Forest products have become a major export commodity. There are 36 million hectares of enclosed forest including 15 million hectares of high quality hardwoods.

Agricultural Production in 2010

Produce	Int. $'000*	Tonnes
Game meat	772,434	355,000
Fruit fresh nes	330,814	947,800
Bananas	266,141	1,050,000
Berries nes	224,406	128,800
Palm oil	217,529	500,000
Coconuts	132,245	1,196,000
Indigenous pigmeat	105,147	68,400
Maize, green	95,220	230,100
Yams	93,015	364,700
Coffee, green	72,197	67,200
Taro (cocoyam)	57,497	271,100
Roots and tubers, nes	54,467	318,500

* unofficial figures

Source: http://faostat.fao.org/site/339/default.aspx Food and Agriculture Organization of the United Nations, Food and Agricultural commodities production

Fishing
The total catch for 2010 was put at 225,000 tonnes.

COMMUNICATIONS AND TRANSPORT

Travel Requirements
Citizens of the USA, Canada, Australia and the EU require a passport valid for at least one year after entry, an onward/return ticket, evidence of sufficient funds and a visa. Citizens of Australia, Austria, Belgium, Canada, Cyprus, Denmark, France, Germany, The Netherlands, Portugal, Sweden, the UK and the USA may all apply for a 60-day tourist visa on arrival in the country. Other nationals should contact the embassy to check visa requirements.

International Airline
Air Niugini, URL: http://www.airniugini.com.pg

International Airports
Jackson International Airport at Port Moresby. There are 457 aerodromes in Papua New Guinea, most of them being the responsibility of the Ministry of Tourism and Civil Aviation. **Office of Civil Aviation**, Jacksons' Airport, PO Box 684, Boroko, Papua New Guinea. Tel: +675 324 440, fax: +675 3251919

Roads
There are 25,000 km of roads, of which only one fifth are sealed. Vehicles are driven on the left.

Shipping
Papua New Guinea Shipping Corporation Pty. Ltd., PO Box 643, Port Moresby.

HEALTH

In 2009, the government spent approximately 8.5 per cent of its total budget on healthcare, accounting for 70.6 per cent of all healthcare spending. Total expenditure on healthcare equated to 3.7 per cent of the country's GDP. Per capita expenditure on health was approximately US$44. In 2005-10, there were an estimated 333 doctors (0.05 per 10,000 population), 2,844 nurses (4.5 per 10,000 population), 46 dentists (0.1 per 10,000 population) and 3,883 community health workers.

Life expectancy at birth in Papua New Guinea is 62 years for men and 65 years for women. Healthy life expectancy in 2007 was 55 and 57 years respectively. The biggest killers in Papua New Guinea are malaria, pneumonia, tuberculosis, meningitis, heart disease and peri natal deaths. HIV/AIDS is on the increase especially in the Port Moresby area. In 2010, the infant mortality rate was 47 per 1,000 live births and the under-fives mortality rate was 61 per 1,000 population. Main causes of childhood mortality include: pneumonia (17 per cent), prematurity (18 per cent), malaria (10 per cent), diarrhoea (8 per cent) and HIV/AIDS (2 per cent).

In 2010 , 40 per cent of the population (87 per cent of the urban population and 33 per cent of the rural population) had sustainable access to an improved water source. In the same year, 45 per cent of the population had sustainable access to improved sanitation. (Source: http://www.who.int, World Health Statistics 2012)

EDUCATION

Children begin their education at the age of five, although primary education begins at the age of seven and lasts until the age of 12. Secondary education begins at 13 and ends at 16. Education is compulsory between the ages of 7 and 16. Enrolment in community schools is poor and a large number of school-leavers have not completed their primary education. International schools are available for both expatriate and national children. Papua New Guinea does have six universities. Recent figures show that 17.5 per cent of total government expenditure (2.3 per cent of GDP) went on education.

UNESCO estimated the adult literacy rate to be 57.8 per cent in 2007, youth literacy (age 15-24) that year was put at 64.1. per cent.

RELIGION

97 per cent of the population are followers of the Christian faith. Only 2.6 per cent are declared atheists. Latest figures show that 30 per cent are Roman Catholic, 23 per cent Evangelical Lutheran, 13 per cent United Churches, 9 per cent Evangelical Alliances, 8 per cent Seventh Day Adventists and 7 per cent Pentecostalists. Pantheistic beliefs are widespread and an important part of Papuan culture.

Papua New Guinea has a religious liberty rating of 9 on a scale of 1 to 10 (10 is most freedom). (Source: World Religion Database)

COMMUNICATIONS AND MEDIA

Radio is the most important national medium. News coverage is reported to be balanced.

Newspapers
The newspapers are published in a variety of languages, including English, Motu and Pidgin.
Post Courier, URL: http://www.postcourier.com.pg/
The National, URL: http://www.thenational.com.pg/

Broadcasting
Television broadcasting is mainly limited to Port Moresby and the provincial capitals. A commercial television has been in operation for over 20 years and a state-run station launched in 2008. Satellite and cable TV is also available. Several radio stations (branches of NBC) also broadcast in different vernacular languages.

National Broadcasting Commission, Broadcasting in Melanesian Pidgin, English and Motu, URL: http://www.nbc.com.pg/

Telecommunications

The service is rudimentary and there is not wide spread access. In 2009 there were estimated to be 60,000 landlines and over 500,000 mobile phones. By 2009, approximately 120,000 people had regular access to the internet.

ENVIRONMENT

Papua New Guinea is one of the most bio-diverse nations on earth, harbouring 5 per cent of the world's species in 1 per cent of the world's land area. Of the world's 43 species of birds of paradise, 33 are native to Papua New Guinea. It is estimated that 21 per cent of Papua New Guinea's 400,000 sq. km forests have already been logged.

Papua New Guinea is a party to the following international environmental agreements: Antarctic Treaty, Biodiversity, Climate Change, Desertification, Endangered Species, Environmental Modification, Hazardous Wastes, Law of the Sea, Marine Dumping, Nuclear Test Ban, Ozone Layer Protection, Ship Pollution, Tropical Timber 83, Tropical Timber 94, and Wetlands.

In 2010, Papua New Guinea's emissions from the consumption of fossil fuels totalled 5.31 million metric tons of carbon dioxide. (Source: EIA)

PARAGUAY
Republic of Paraguay
República del Paraguay

Capital: Asunción (Population estimate, 2011: 750,000)

Outgoing Head of State: Federico Franco (President)

Outgoing Vice-President: Oscar Denis

Incoming Head of State: Horacio Cartes (President-Elect) (page 1401)

National Flag: Horizontal tricolour, red, white and blue with a centre-piece on the front formed by the national emblem of a yellow star surrounded by a wreath of palm and olive leaves. The centre-piece on the reverse side is the Treasury seal formed by a lion, with the words 'Paz y Justicia' above it. The Paraguayan flag is unique among national flags in having different emblems on its obverse and reverse sides

CONSTITUTION AND GOVERNMENT

Constitution

Paraguay, which had been a Spanish colony since 1535, gained its independence in 1811.

Constitutions were passed in 1940 and 1967 before the most recent constitution was signed into law by a Constituent Convention elected by popular vote on 20 June 1992. It is based on the principle of the separation of powers and provides for a President, a two-chamber Congress and an independent Judiciary.

As head of state, the President is elected by universal adult suffrage for a single five-year term of office and is responsible for appointing the Council of Ministers.

The Constitution was amended in 2011 to give the vote to citizens living abroad.

To consult the constitution, please visit: http://www.wipo.int/wipolex/en/text.jsp?file_id=224932

International Relations

Paraguay has friendly relations with all its neighbouring countries. Its economy is strongly dependent on those of Brazil and Argentina. Paraguay's geographical position and lack of radar cover mean that it has been used as a transit country for cocaine-trafficking, and there may be the beginnings of marijuana cultivation. The National Anti-Drugs Secretariat (SENAD) and the Paraguayan Narcotics Police (DINAR) were established in 1991 to combat these problems.

Paraguay is a founding member of Mercosur (the Southern Cone Common Market), whose other members are Argentina, Brazil and Uruguay. It is also a founding member of Banco de Sur, a new regional development bank. Within the UN, Paraguayan forces have participated in UN peacekeeping missions in Cyprus and DR Congo. Paraguay is the only country in South America that recognizes Taiwan and not the People's Republic of China.

Recent Events

In April 2002 President Macchi was formally charged with corruption following the illegal investment of US$16 million of state funds in US bank accounts. President Macchi declared a state of emergency in July 2002 following violent anti-government protests which left two people dead and dozens injured.

Nicanor Duarte Frutos was elected President in April 2003, and his Colorado Party remained in power following the April legislative elections. From April 2004, peasants demanded a redistribution of agricultural land in a series of protests and land occupancies. Land rights are of great importance to Paraguayans, many of whom live by subsistence farming.

In the spring of 2005, President Duarte promised to tackle organised crime following the kidnapping and murder of the daughter of former president Raul Cubas. In June 2005, former president Luis Macchi was sentenced to six years in jail over illegal bank transfers, and in August Alfredo Stroessner, the military ruler of Paraguay from 1954-89, died in Brazil.

At the beginning of March 2007, the government declared a state of emergency following the deaths of 10 people from dengue fever. Officials said that 14,654 people had been diagnosed with dengue, but doctors believed the figure to be ten times higher, and were worried about a new more virulent variant of the disease. Brazil and Bolivia have also seen a rise in cases of dengue, which is spread by mosquitoes. Experts blamed the unusually rapid spread of the disease on a higher rainfall and uncommonly warm weather, which boosted the population of the mosquito species.

On 20 April 2008, the people of Paraguay went to the polls in elections that ended 61 years of domination by the Colorado Party (the longest serving party in continuous rule in the world). Sr. Fernando Lugo, a former Roman Catholic bishop, won the presidential election. In April 2009, Mr Lugo admitted that he was the father of a two-year old child. There have been further allegations that he may have fathered more children and in June 2012 Mr Lugo admitted he was the father of a second child. Mr Lugo had resigned as a bishop in 2004, and declared his intention to leave the priesthood altogether in 2006 but Pope Benedict XVI did not accept his resignation until shortly before he became president. Since becoming president, Mr Lugo has also had to battle cancer. Mr Lugo was controversially impeached in June 2012 after clashes over land evictions left 11 people dead. He was replaced by his vice-president Federico Franco.

Mercosur suspended Paraguay's membership in July 2012 in protest at the ousting of President Lugo.

In December 2012, Vidal Vega, leader of landless peasants, was shot dead.

In February 2013, a presidential candidate, Lino Oviedo, died in a helicopter crash. Mr Oviedo had helped overthrow the Stroessner dictatorship in 1989.

Legislature

Paraguay's bicameral legislature, the Congress (*Congreso*), consists of the Senate (*Camara de Senadores*) and the Chamber of Deputies (*Camara de Diputados*). The two chambers are elected simultaneously every five years by universal suffrage (voting is compulsory for all citizens over 18).

Upper House

The 45 Senators serve terms of five years. Members of the Chamber of Senators are elected on a directly proportional basis over the whole of the country.
Senate, Palacio Legislativo, Avda Republica y Chile, Asunción, Paraguay. Tel: +595 21 414 5000, URL: http://www.senado.gov.py/

Lower House

The 80 Deputies also serve terms of five years. According to the new constitution, the members of the Chamber of Deputies are elected on a geographical basis by the number of votes obtained by their party in each department.
Chamber of Deputies, Palacio Legislativo, 14 de Mayo y 15 de Agosto, Asunción, Paraguay. Tel: +595 21 414 4000, URL: http://www.camdip.gov.py/

> **Outgoing cabinet (as at June 2013)**
> *Cabinet Chief:* Martin Burt
> *Minister of Foreign Affairs:* Jose Felix Fernandez
> *Minister of Finance and Economy:* Manuel Ferreira
> *Minister of Justice and Labour:* Maria Segovia
> *Minister of Industry and Trade:* Francisco Rivas Almada
> *Minister of Public Works and Communications:* Enrique Buzarquis
> *Minister of Agriculture and Livestock:* Enzo Cardozo
> *Minister of Education and Culture:* Horacio Galeano
> *Minister of the Interior:* Carmelo Caballero
> *Minister of National Defence:* Maria Garcia de Arnold
> *Minister of Public Health and Social Welfare:* Dr Antonio Arbo

Ministries

Office of the President, Palacio de Lopez, Asunción, Paraguay. URL: http://www.presidencia.gov.py/

PARAGUAY

Ministry of the Interior, Chile y Manduvira, Asunción, Paraguay. Tel: +595 21 493661 / 446433 / 446743, fax: +595 21 448446, URL: http://www2.paraguaygobierno.gov.py/mininterior/
Ministry of Foreign Affairs, O'Leary y Pte. Franco, Asunción, Paraguay. Tel: +595 21 494593, fax: +493910, URL: http://www.mre.gov.py/
Ministry of Finance & Economy, Chile y Pte. Franco, Asunción, Paraguay. Tel: +595 21 440 010 / +595 21 440017, fax: +595 448283, URL: http://www.hacienda.gov.py/
Ministry of Education and Culture, Chile y Humanitá, Asunción, Paraguay. Tel: +595 21 443078, fax: +595 21 443919, URL: http://www.mec.gov.py/cms
Ministry of Agriculture, Edificio Ayer 1er. Piso Pte. Franco y Ayolas, Asunción, Paraguay. URL: http://www.mag.gov.py/
Ministry of Public Works and Communications, Oliva y Alberai, Asunción, Paraguay. Tel: +595 21 448079, fax: +595 21 449792, URL: http://www.mopc.gov.py/
Ministry of Defence, Mcal. Lopez y Vice Pte. Sánchez, Asunción, Paraguay. Tel: +595 21 214477, fax: +595 21 211583. URL: http://www.mdn.gov.py/
Ministry of Public Health and Social Welfare, Avenida Pettirossi y Brasil, Asunción, Paraguay. Tel: +595 21 214741 / 206266, fax: +595 21 207328, URL: http://www.mspbs.gov.py/
Ministry of Justice and Labour, Gaspar Rodríguez de Francia y EEUU, Asunción, Paraguay. Tel: +595 21 491555, fax: +595 21 208469, URL: http://www.mjt.gov.py/
Ministry of Industry and Commerce, Avenida España 323, Asunción, Paraguay. Tel: +595 21 204638, fax: +595 21 213529, URL: http://www.mic.gov.py/v1/index.php
Secretariat of Culture, URL: http://www.cultura.gov.py/
Secretariat for Sport, URL: http://snd.gov.py/

Political Parties

Authentic Radical Liberal Party (PLRA), URL: http://www.pira.org.py; National Republican Association-Colorado Party (ANR-PC), URL: http://www.anr.org.py; National Union of Ethical Citizens (UNACE), URL: http://www.unace.org; Forward Country (Avanza pais)

Elections

Presidential and parliamentary elections took place on 21 April 2013.

The out-going president, Fernarndo Lugo, won the 2008 presidential election, ending 19 years of ANR-PC rule. He was impeached in June 2012 and removed from office. He was replaced by the vice-president, Federico Franco. In the 2013 elections, the ANR-PC returned to power when their candidate Horacio Cartes took 49 per cent of the vote. Efrain Alegre of took 39 per cent. He is due to take office on 15 August 2013.

Following the April 2013 elections, the ANR-PC remained the largest party in both houses of Congress.. In the lower house the results were as followed: ANR-PC 44 seats; PLRA 27 seats; others 9 seats. In the Senate the ANR-PC took 19 seats, the PLRA 12 seats ; FG 5 seats; others 9 seats.

Diplomatic Representation

Embassy of Paraguay, 2400 Massachusetts Avenue, NW, Washington, DC 20008, USA. Tel: +1 202 483 6960, fax: +1 202 234 4508, URL: http://www.embaparusa.gov.py
Ambassador: Fernando Pfanni Caballero
Embassy of Paraguay, 344 High Street Kensington, 3rd Floor, London W14 8NS, United Kingdom. Tel: +44 (0)20 7610 4180, fax: +44 (0)20 7371 4297, e-mail: embapar@btconnect.com, URL: http://www.paraguayembassy.co.uk
Ambassador: Miguel Angel Solano Lopez Casco
British Embassy, The British Government is now represented through its Embassy in Buenos Aires. URL: http://ukinargentina.fco.gov.uk/en/
Ambassador: Shan Morgan
US Embassy, 1776 Mariscal Lopez Ave, Casilla Postal 402, Asunción, Republica del Paraguay. Tel: +595 (21) 213715, fax: +595 (21) 213728, URL: http://paraguay.usembassy.gov/
Ambassador: James Thessin (page 1525)
Permanent Representative of Paraguay to the United Nations, 211 East 43rd Street, Suite 400, New York, NY 10017, USA. Tel: +1 212 687 3490 / 3491, fax: +1 212 818 1282, e-mail: paraguay@un.int; http://www.un.int/paraguay/
Ambassador: Jose Antonio Dos Santos

LEGAL SYSTEM

The Supreme Court of Justice, composed of nine judges, sits in the capital, Asunción. The Supreme Court supervises all other sectors of the judiciary. These include appellate courts with three members each in the areas of criminal, civil, administrative, and commercial jurisdiction; courts of first instance in these same four areas; justices of the peace dealing with more minor issues; and military courts.

The Supreme Court hears disputes concerning jurisdiction and competence, and has the power to declare unconstitutional any law or presidential act. Supreme Court justices serve five-year terms of office concurrent with the president and the National Congress and may be reappointed. They must be Paraguayan, possess a Doctor of Law degree and have recognized experience in legal matters.

There have been serious human rights abuses in recent years, including instances of killings by police who were rarely prosecuted. There have been allegations of torture in prisons, as well as of judicial corruption and inefficiency. Pretrial detentions are common, and prisons are overcrowded. Government corruption is widespread. Paraguay abolished the death penalty in 1992; the last execution was carried out in 1928. In 2008 Paraguay co-sponsored the Resolution on a Moratorium on the Use of the Death Penalty at the UN General Assembly.

Supreme Court of Justice, URL: http://www.pj.gov.py/
Defensoria del Pueblo, URL: http://www.defensoriadelpueblo.gov.py/

LOCAL GOVERNMENT

The country is divided into the capital district of Asunción and 17 departments: Alto Paraguay, Alto Parana, Amambay, Boqueron, Caaguazu, Caazapa, Canindeyu, Central, Concepcion, Cordillera, Guaira, Itapua, Misiones, Neembucu, Paraguari, Presidente Hayes and San Pedro. Administration of each is carried out by elected governors. Fourteen departments are located in eastern Paraguay and four in western Paraguay, the large tract of sparsely populated land known as the Chaco. Municipal elections took place in 2010.

AREA AND POPULATION

Area

Landlocked Paraguay is situated almost in the centre of South America, bounded on the east by Brazil, on the south and west by Argentina and on the north and west by Bolivia. The country's total area is 406,752 sq. km with Eastern Paraguay covering 159,827 sq. km. and Western Paraguay 246,925 sq. km. A total of 397,300 sq. km is land, whilst 9,450 sq. km is water. Geographically, the country is divided into two parts - Eastern and Western Paraguay - by the river Paraguay which flows from north to south. The Gran Chaco (Western Paraguay) is an alluvial plain that extends from Paraguay into Bolivia (west), Argentina (south) and Brazil (east). It has a semi-arid climate and consists mainly of grassy plains, swamps and scrub forest. The Chaco accounts for about 60 per cent of the land but, apart from a few Mennonite colonies, it is almost unpopulated. The eastern region consists mainly of the southern extension of the Parana plateau, which has a grassy and fertile soil. Around 95 per cent of the population lives in Eastern Paraguay.

The climate is subtropical, with heavy rainfall in summer. Average temperatures range from about 17°C in July to over 40°C in January. Annual rainfall is in the region of 1,600 mm.

To view a map, visit http://www.un.org/Depts/Cartographic/map/profile/paraguay.pdf

Population

The population in 2010 was estimated at 6.455 million with an average annual growth rate of 1.9 per cent. The majority of the population (58 per cent) is aged between 15 and 64, with 34 per cent aged up to 14 years, and around 8 per cent aged 60 years and over. Population density is one of the lowest of the continent at 13.5 people per square kilometre.

The official language of Paraguay is Spanish, but Guaraní, the language of the original Indian inhabitants, is also widely spoken. Ethnically, Paraguay has one of the most homogeneous populations in South America. Most of the people are of mixed Spanish and Guarani Indian descent. Brazilians, Argentines, Germans, Arabs, Koreans, Chinese, and Japanese have settled in Paraguay. Some 200,000 Japanese migrated to Paraguay following the Second World War.

A relatively high population growth rate has contributed to greater urbanisation of the population, and the growth of shanty towns. Approximately 61 per cent of the population lives in urban areas. Poverty currently affects some 60 per cent of the population.

Births, Marriages, Deaths

The birth rate, according to 2010 estimates, is 24.2 births per 1,000 people, whilst the death rate is 4.6 deaths per 1,000 people. The infant mortality rate is estimated at 21 deaths per 1,000 children who live beyond five years. Average life expectancy at birth is 74 years, 72 years for men and 77 years for women. (Source: http://www.who.int, World Health Statistics 2012)

The fertility rate in indigenous populations is over twice the national rate, at 6.3 children per woman (3 in urban areas and 6.5 in rural ones). There are enormous differences among ethnic groups: from 3.4 and 3.5 children per woman among the Enhlet Norte and Toba respectively, to 8.8 and 8.9 children per woman in the Guanás and Manajui, respectively.

Public Holidays 2014

1 January: New Year
3 February: San Blás (Patron Saint of Paraguay)
1 March: Heroes' Day
18 April: Good Friday
21 April: Easter Monday
1 May: Labour Day
15 May: National Independence Day
29 May: Ascension Day
12 June: Peace of El Chaco
19 June: Corpus Christi
15 August: Founding of Asunción
29 September: Battle of Boqueron Day
1 November: All Saints Day
8 December: Virgin of Caacupe celebration/Immaculate Conception
25 December: Christmas Day

EMPLOYMENT

Total Employment by Economic Activity

Occupation	2008
Agriculture, hunting, forestry & fishing	745,200
Mining & quarrying	6,600
Manufacturing	340,200
Electricity, gas & water supply	10,800
Construction	174,100
Wholesale & retail trade, repairs, hotels & restaurants	673,800
Transport, storage & communications	118,400

- continued

Financial intermediation, real estate, renting & business activities	120,800
Public admin. & defence, compulsory social security, education, health & social work, other community, social & personal services	620,000
Other	300
Total	2,810,500

Source: Copyright © International Labour Organization (ILO Dept. of Statistics, http://laborsta.ilo.org)

There is considerable urban unemployment and underemployment.

BANKING AND FINANCE

Currency
The unit of currency is the Guaraní (Gs), made up of 100 céntimos.

GDP/GNP, Inflation, National Debt
The economy of Paraguay is predominantly agricultural, and is largely dependent on exports of its produce. It is, therefore, vulnerable to weather conditions and to the fortunes of the Argentine and Brazilian economies. At the beginning of the millennium, recessions in Brazil and Argentina, together with political instability, led to a recession in Paraguay. By 2006, the economy was benefitting from a significant increase in agriculture exports and exports of electricity from the country's hydroelectric dams.

Following recession in the early years of the millennium, the economy began to pick up in 2004, with growth of 3.9 per cent, and in 2005, with growth of 2.9 per cent. The economy grew strongly over the next two years, recording an estimated GDP of US$12.8 billion in 2007 (up from US$$9.8 billion in 2006), with a growth rate of 6.4 per cent. In 2008, real GDP reached $16.1 billion, an increase of 26 per cent on 2007. Per capita GDP rose to $2,593 (current dollars), up from $1,928 the previous year. Figures for 2010 put GDP at US$17 billion reflecting a growth rate of 9.0 per cent for that year, GDP per capita that year was put at US$2,700. GDP was estimated at US$21 billion in 2011, with a growth rate of 5.5 per cent in 2011.

The greatest contributors to Paraguay's GDP are the services sector (over 45 per cent of GDP) and hydroelectric power generation. Paraguay's economy is predominantly agricultural, this sector contributed around 20 per cent of GDP in 2008. Manufacturing and construction together accounted for around 17 per cent of GDP.

Official external debt was estimated to be $5 billion in 2011.

Inflation averaged 8.1 per cent over 2011, up from 4.5 per cent in 2010. Inflation was estimated to be 3.1 per cent in 2012 and is forecast to rise to over 4.5 per cent in 2013.

Paraguay has a large 'informal' economy, for which accurate measures are difficult to obtain, though it is thought that it equals the official economy in size. An industry has grown up around the import of goods from Asia and the United States for re-export to neighbouring countries; the recorded figures of this sector have declined recently, due to tighter controls on imports and contraband by the Brazilian authorities. The Paraguay government has implemented a programme to increase revenue through new tax systems and this has led to improved public finances.

Balance of Payments / Imports and Exports
Exports earned Paraguay some US$3.1 billion in 2009. Exports rose to US$4.5 billion to 2010. Major export products include hydroelectricity, soybeans and soybean flour, cotton, sugar, timber, vegetable oils, apparel, tobacco and meat products. Most exports were destined for Brazil (15 per cent), Uruguay (22 per cent), Argentina (12 per cent), and Chile (12 per cent). Exports are forecast to rise to an estimated US$6.8 billion in 2013.

Import costs rose to an estimated US$6.5 billion in 2009. They rose to US$9.4 billion in 2010. Major import products are fuels, machinery, plastics and articles thereof, vehicles, consumer goods and industrial chemicals and fertilizers. China is the main supplier of goods (32 per cent), followed by Brazil (24 per cent), Argentina (16 per cent), the US (5 per cent) and Japan (5.0 per cent). Imports are forecast to rise steeply to US$11 billion in 2013.

MERCOSUR (The Southern Cone Common Market)
In 1991 the Asunción Treaty was signed. This provided for the economic integration process between the Republics of Argentina, Brazil, Paraguay and Uruguay.

Central Bank
Banco Central del Paraguay, PO Box 861, Avenida Federación Rusa y Sargento Marecos, Barrio Santo Domingo, Asunción, Paraguay. Tel: +595 21 608011, e-mail: ccs@bcp.gov.py, URL: http://www.bcp.gov.py/
Governor: Jorge Corvalan

MANUFACTURING, MINING AND SERVICES

Primary and Extractive Industries
Oil has not yet been discovered in Paraguay although exploration is currently being carried out in the Chaco region. There are no known natural gas reserves in the country, although a pipeline is planned to transport natural gas from Bolivia to Brazil, with Paraguay as a transit point. There are known deposits of manganese, kaolin, iron, talc, marble and granite.

Paraguay relies entirely on imports of oil to meet its consumption requirements. Oil consumption rose to around 28,000 barrels per day in 2011. Paraguay's crude oil refining capacity was 8,000 barrels per day in 2011. Almost all of Paraguay's oil imports come from Argentina's Palmar Largo field in Formosa Province. The government is considering deregulating the state's monopoly on the country's domestic oil market. (Source: EIA)

Energy
Paraguay's total energy consumption was estimated at 0.437 quadrillion Btu in 2009, up from 0.415 quadrillion Btu in 2004.

Paraguay is a major producer of electricity, the fourth largest in South America, with a generating capacity of 7.4 gigawatts, 99.5 per cent of which is hydroelectric. In 2010, Paraguay generated 53.5 billion kilowatthours (kWh), and used just 6.7 billion kWh. The country exports some 45.0 billion kilowatthours of its generated energy.

Paraguay's state-owned utility, Administracion Nacional de Electricidad (ANDE), controls the country's entire electricity market - generation, distribution and transmission. Paraguay's electricity is generated through the Itaipu and Yacyreta hydroelectric power plants. Itaipu is one of the world's largest hydroelectric dams, built jointly by the governments of Brazil and Paraguay. It has an output of 12.6 gigawatts. The Yacyretá dam, which was constructed with Argentina, has an output of 3.5 gigawatts. (Source: EIA)

Manufacturing
The most important industries are the production of beef, vegetable oils, textiles, beverages and processed goods derived from timber and leather. The state owns the cement plant, the steel works and the public utilities such as the Electricity, Communications and Water Authorities. There are about 10 cotton ginning plants, two breweries, two multinational soft drink bottlers, a match factory, eight sugar mills, two medium sized textile mills, flour mills, saw mills, cigar and cigarette factories.

Tourism
The number of visitors to Paraguay increased by nearly nine per cent in the first six months of 2005 (compared to the same period of 2004). There were 1.2 million visitors, who generated revenue of some US$35.5 million. Most visitors were from the region - Argentina, Brazil, Chile and Uruguay. Around 3 per cent were from the US, and small percentages came from Germany and Spain.
National Secretariat of Tourism, URL: http://www.senatur.gov.py

Agriculture
This is the dominant sector of the economy of Paraguay, contributing almost 26 per cent of GDP in 2008, and employing around a quarter of the workforce. More than 250,000 families depend on subsistence farming activities and maintain marginal ties to the larger productive sector of the economy.

Over 9.5 per cent of the country's territory is devoted to agriculture and the sector produces nearly all the country's food requirements. Principal agricultural products are corn, cotton, sugar cane, cassava, soy, maize, rice, manioc and wheat. Coffee is becoming a valuable export. A wide variety of fruits are also grown. Meat from cattle-raising and large numbers of the cattle on the hoof are exported to Brazil every year. Forestry is an important part of the economy, products including timber, tannin and petitgrain oil, which is used as a perfume base.

Soybean production has increased enormously in response to Chinese demand and a decline in US production of the crop. Soy now accounts for more than 50 per cent of the country's exports, and the acreage dedicated to this crop has increased five-fold over seven years. This is a matter of concern: the soy farms are highly mechanised, and have taken over from the labour-intensive cotton farming that is traditional in the area, and there has been large-scale deforestation due to land clearance for soy crop production.

Agricultural Production in 2010

Produce	Int. $'000*	Tonnes
Soybeans	1,951,898	7,460,440
Indigenous cattle meat	1,039,716	384,884
Maize	430,575	3,108,820
Wheat	190,915	1,401,990
Indigenous pigmeat	184,443	119,983
Cassava	132,919	2,624,080
Cow milk, whole, fresh	123,670	396,300
Hen eggs, in shell	106,162	128,000
Sugar cane	105,569	5,130,940
Rice, paddy	86,926	315,213
Sunflower seed	71,863	262,293
Oranges	44,430	229,898

* unofficial figures
Source: http://faostat.fao.org/site/339/default.aspx Food and Agriculture Organization of the United Nations, Food and Agricultural commodities production

COMMUNICATIONS AND TRANSPORT

Travel Requirements
Citizens of the USA, Canada, Australia and the EU require a passport valid for six months beyond the length of stay and a visa, apart from nationals of Austria, Belgium, Czech Republic, Denmark, Estonia, France, Finland, Germany, Greece, Hungary, Ireland, Italy, Latvia, Luxembourg, Malta, The Netherlands, Poland, Portugal, Slovak Republic, Slovenia, Spain, Sweden and the UK, for stays of up to 90 days. Transit passengers do not need a visa if leaving within six hours and not leaving the airport. Other nationals should contact the embassy to check visa requirements.

STATES OF THE WORLD

PARAGUAY

National Airlines
TAM Airlines, also known as Transportes Aéreos del Mercosur S.A., formerly known as TAM Mercosur and LAP (Líneas Aéreas Paraguayas), is based at Silvio Pettirossi International Airport, in Asuncion, Paraguay. In 2008, the TAM Mercosur name was dropped and the airline was named TAM Airlines, becoming a part of Brazilian TAM Airlines instead of a different airline.
TAM Airlines, URL: http://www.tam.com.br/

International Airports
There are international airports in Asunción and Ciudad del Este.

Railways
The principal railway, Ferrocarril Carlos Antonio Lopez, used to link the capital with Encarnación in the south-east of the country whilst, from Posadas on the opposite side of the River Paraná, there was a connection with the Argentine railway system but this has been discontinued. Encarnación and Posadas were to be connected via a bridge over the river Paraná, and Asunción was linked to Buenos Aires.

Roads
There are 2,000 km of asphalted road in the country and 20,000 km of earth roads. Vehicles are driven on the right. Asphalt roads link Asunción to Sao Paulo and Rio de Janeiro and connect by ferry to Pilcomayo and the road to Buenos Aires in Argentina. International bus routes connect Paraguay with Santiago, Chile; Sao Paulo, Brazil; Buenos Aires and Cordoba, Argentina; Santa Cruz, Bolivia; Montevideo, Uruguay; Rio de Janeiro, Brazil.

Ports and Harbours
River transport plays an important role in the economy of Paraguay, a landlocked country. The Paraguay-Paraná river system connects the country with the Atlantic. The capital, Asunción, is the chief river port. From Asunción the river flows southward for about 150 miles until, just above the Argentine city of Corrientes, it joins the Paraná, which continues for another 800 miles through Argentina to the River Plate and Buenos Aires. There are no regular passenger services on the river.

HEALTH

A Social Security Service exists which provides insured workers with benefits for illness, maternity, disability, old age, professional risks and death. Dental care and necessary medicines are also covered. Public and private school teachers and domestic servants have compulsory coverage. In 2009, the government spent approximately 10.4 per cent of its total budget on healthcare (down from 17.7 per cent in 2000, accounting for 39.0 per cent of all healthcare spending. Private expenditure accounted for 61 per cent, of which over 99 per cent was out-of-pocket. Total expenditure on healthcare equated to 6.6 per cent of the country's GDP. Per capita expenditure on health was approximately US$147, compared with US$124 in 2000. Figures for 2000-10 show that there are 6,355 physicians (11 per 10,000 population), 10,261 nurses and midwives (18 per 10,000 population) and 3,182 dentists. There are 13 hospital beds per 10,000 population.

According to the latest WHO figures, in 2010 approximately 86 per cent of the population had access to improved drinking water. In the same year, 71 per cent of the population had access to improved sanitation. Diarrhoea accounts for 9 per cent of childhood deaths.

The infant mortality rate (probability of dying before age one) in 2010 was 21 per 1,000 live births. The child mortality rate (under 5 years) was 25 per 1,000 live births. An estimated 17.5 per cent of children under one are classified as stunted (2005-11). (Source: http://www.who.int, World Health Statistics 2012)

EDUCATION

Education in Paraguay is free and compulsory, and begins at the age of six and lasts until the age of 11. In the year 2002-03, 92 per cent of primary school aged children were enrolled in a school. Secondary education begins at 12 and ends at 17. In 2002-03, around 50 per cent of secondary school aged children were enrolled in a school. 30 per cent of students go on to study at tertiary level.

In 2006, 10 per cent of government spending went on education, 46 per cent went on primary education and 30 per cent on secondary education. The overall adult literacy rate is estimated at 94.6 per cent, although this rises to 98.8 per cent among the 15-24 year old group. However, among indigenous peoples, schooling averages 2.2 years, and the illiteracy rate is as high as 51 per cent (Source: WHO, September 2009)

RELIGION

There is freedom of worship in Paraguay. Approximately 95 per cent of the population follow Christianity. The predominant religion is the Catholic Roman Apostolic Church followed by around 88 per cent of the population. Paraguay has a religious tolerance rating of 9 on a scale of 1 to 10 (10 is most freedom). (Source: World Religion Database)

COMMUNICATIONS AND MEDIA

The media is free to express a variety of views but there are reports of intimidation against reporters exposing alleged corruption and civil discontent.

Newspapers
There are over 40 daily newspapers in Paraguay. Those with the greatest circulation are ABC Color, URL: http://www.abc.com.py; La Nacion, URL: http://www.lanacion.com.py; Ultima Hora, URL: http://www.ultimahora.com

Broadcasting
There are approximately 75 commercial and community radio stations and five television stations (two commercial, three cable TV) in Paraguay. The state-run broadcaster is Radio Nacional del Paraguay.

Telecommunications
The state still has a monopoly on fixed-lines; service is poor. Mobile phone services have expanded rapidly under numerous providers. In 2008, there were some 490,000 mainline telephones in use and 5.8 million mobile telephones. In 2008, approximately 900,000 people had access to the internet.

ENVIRONMENT

Paraguay's main environmental problems are deforestation, water pollution, and inadequate waste disposal facilities.

Total energy-related carbon emissions were estimated at 3.85 million metric tons in 2005, up from 3.72 million metric tons the previous year. Per capita carbon emissions in the same year were an estimated 4.56 metric tons, compared with the regional average of 2.45 metric tons in the US. In 2010, Paraguay's emissions from the consumption of fossil fuels totalled 4.39 million metric tons of carbon dioxide. (Source: EIA)

Paraguay is a party to the following international environmental agreements: Biodiversity, Climate Change, Kyoto Protocol, Desertification, Endangered Species, Hazardous Wastes, Law of the Sea, Ozone Layer Protection and Wetlands.

PERU

Republic of Peru
República del Perú

Capital: Lima (Population estimate, 2012: 8.4 million)

Head of State: Ollanta Humala Tasso (President) (page 1445)

First Vice President: Marisol Espinoza (page 1421)

Second Vice President: vacant

National Flag: A tricolour, pale-wise, red, white, red, the white charged with the national coat of arms: a vicuna pink on blue, a tree green on white, and a horn-of-plenty yellow on red.

CONSTITUTION AND GOVERNMENT

Constitution
Peru, originally the largest and most important of the Spanish Vice-Royalties in South America, became an independent state on 28 July 1821. Peru's governmental structure is established by the Constitution, which took effect in 1993. Under the new charter, human and civil rights are guaranteed. Executive, legislative and judicial functions are divided. The President, two Vice-Presidents and members of the Congress are elected by direct popular vote. The relationship between the executive and legislative branches contains elements of both the presidential and parliamentary systems.

The President of the Republic is Chief of State and head of the executive branch of the government. Through the Consejo de Ministros (Cabinet), the President directs the overall policy of the government. Under the new Constitution the powers of the President have been significantly strengthened in order to provide for more effective policy formulation and execution. The Ministers are entrusted with the conduct and administration of the State. They form the Council of Ministers, which is presided over by the President of the Council of Ministers. The President of the Republic is empowered to appoint and remove ministers. The presidential term is five years, renewable once.

To consult the constitution, please visit: http://www2.congreso.gob.pe/sicr/RelatAgenda/constitucion.nsf/$$ViewTemplate%20for%20constitucion?OpenForm

International Relations
Peru's relations with Ecuador have improved following the formal demarcation of the Peru-Ecuador border in 1999, and relations with Chile are also improving despite a dispute over their shared maritime border; several programmes are in place to strengthen political and economic links.

Peru joined the UN in 1949 and the Peruvian Javier Perez de Cuellar served as Secretary General from 1981-1991. Peru is also an active member of the Andean Community, APEC and the WTO.

Recent Events
In April 1999 the Peruvian cabinet resigned amid a rift over corruption allegations. President Fujimori was elected for a third term in office in May 2000, despite Article 135 of the new constitution which limits presidents to two consecutive terms of office. In November 2000 President Fujimori was sacked by congress for being 'morally unfit', following political and financial scandals. He went into exile in Japan. Alejandro Toledo, a centre-left economist, was elected president and took office in July 2001.

On 25 June 2003 the cabinet resigned en masse in protest over President Toledo's new tax plans. Former congresswoman Beatriz Merino Lucero was sworn in as Peru's first woman prime minister on 29 June 2003 but resigned six months later following disagreements with the President over cabinet appointments. The post was then held by Carlos Ferrero.

In January 2005 there was an armed uprising in which six people died. The Minister of the Interior, Javier Reategui, resigned. President Toledo was found guilty of election fraud in May 2005; signatures in the 2000 presidential poll were discovered to be forged. In October 2006, the former Shining Path rebel leader, Abimael Guzman, was sentenced to life in prison.

In April 2007, Parliament granted emergency powers to President Garcia, allowing him to rule by decree on issues related to organised crime and drug trafficking.

A devastating earthquake hit Pisco and other towns south-west of Lima on 15th August 2007, leaving 500 people dead and many more injured. Power and communications lines came down and some 80 per cent of houses in some areas were destroyed. The 8.0-magnitude earthquake struck off the coast of Peru, and severe aftershocks followed, the strongest of which measured 6.3. Two tectonic plates clash at this region, the Nazca plate and the South American plate.

The former President, Alberto Fujimori, was extradited back to Peru on 22 September 2007, facing charges of human rights abuse and corruption. The human rights charges date back to the early 1990s, when his government was allegedly responsible for killing civilians in the fight against Shining Path Maoist guerrillas. The corruption charges include embezzling $15 million and payoffs to congress members.

On the 19th August 2008, Peru declared a state of emergency in jungle areas where indigenous groups were blocking oil and gas installations in protest at a new land sale law. The Amazon tribes had been demonstrating for over a week at hydro-electric dams and oil and gas installations in three different parts of Peru's Amazon basin; they claimed the law would make it easier for energy companies to buy up their land. Indigenous communities complained that some 70 per cent of Peruvian Amazon territory had been leased for oil and gas exploration, putting at risk their own lives and the biodiversity of the Amazon. On the 24th of August, Peru's Congress voted to repeal two land laws.

PM Jorge Del Castillo and his cabinet resigned in October 2008, amidst a government corruption scandal involving oil kickbacks. President Garcia named Regional Governor of Lambayeque Yehude Simon Munaro as his new Prime Minister.

In November, Prime Minister Simon declared a state of emergency in the southern Tacna region after reports that three people had been killed during violent protests against a new law approved by Congress. The controversial bill will cut the amount of mining tax revenues given to Tacna, in favour of the neighbouring region of Moquegua. Peru's mining sector is enjoying high metals prices, driven by demand from China and India, but the export-based economy largely benefits the main cities on the coast while in the Andean and Amazon interior many people still live in poverty.

In April 2009, following a 15 month trial, former President Alberto Fujimori was sentenced to 25 years in jail for ordering killings and kidnappings by security forces. He was found guilty of two death-squad killings of 25 people during the conflict with guerrillas in the 1990s. Mr Fujimori, who is already serving a six-year term on separate charges of abuse of power, said he would appeal against the verdict. In January 2010 Peru's Supreme Court upheld the sentence.

On the 12th April, Shining Path rebels killed 13 soldiers in two ambushes in the south-east of the country, in one of the deadliest operations in the past decade. Both attacks occurred in the Ayacucho region, 550km south-east of the capital, Lima. The Shining Path group is believed to be a fraction of its former size, now numbering a few hundred guerrillas, and is split between two cocaine-producing zones of Peru.

In June 2009, 38 police officers defending a petrol facility were captured by Amazonian indigenous protesters. Of these, nine were killed during a rescue operation, and a further seven went missing. Protesters were angry at plans to drill for oil and gas on their ancestral land. The government imposed a curfew, but thousands of Indians with wooden spears said they would keep up blocking roads if government forces did not halt efforts to break up their demonstrations. The dispute led to a diplomatic row between Peru and neighbours Venezuela and Bolivia. After weeks of strikes in which 34 people died, the land laws were revoked. The entire Council of Ministers resigned on 19 June. Mr Javier Velasquez was appointed as the president of the council of ministers in July and a reshuffled council was appointed. Several ministerial resignations occured in the following months.

An indigenous leader, Alberto Pizango, was detained and then freed on bail following his return from exile. He is accused of inciting protests against gas and oil exploration in the rainforest.

Mr Velasquez resigned as the president of the Council of Ministers in September 2010. The Minister of Education, José Antonio Chang Escobedo was appointed in his place and a new Council of Ministers sworn in.

Parliamentary elections took place on 10 April 2011 and the Peru Wins alliance took most seats but did not gain a majority. Presidential elections took place on 10 April 2011 with a second round on 5 June 2011. Mr Ollanta Humala Tasso of the PNP won in the second round and took office on 28 July 2011. A new Council of Ministers was also sworn in.

In October 2011, in an attempt to reform the police service and tackle alleged corruption President Humala sacked two thirds of Peru's senior police officers. Thirty police generals have been retired including the overall head and the head of the anti-drugs force.

It was announced on 14 November that vice-president Omar Chehade had left the executive over corruption allegations. The cabinet was reshuffled extensively in December 2011.

A state of emergency was declared in the south after violence erupted at anti-mining protests. A state of emergency was also declared in the north following further anti-mining protests at the Conga mining project. Five protesters died leading to the resignation of Prime Minister Oscar Valdes. He was replaced by Juan Jiminez Mayor. The state of emergency was lifted in September 2012.

Legislature
Peru's unicameral legislature is known as the Congress of the Republic (*Congreso de la República del Peru*), and consists of 120 members elected by popular vote for five-year terms.

Congress of the Republic, (Congreso de la República), Palacio Legislativo, Plaza Bolivar, Av. Abancay s/n, Lima 1, Peru. Tel: +51 (0)1 311 7700, e-mail: oficialmayor@congreso.gob.pe, URL: http://www.congreso.gob.pe

PERU

Cabinet (as at March 2013)
President of the Council of Ministers: Juan Jimenez Mayor (page 1449)
Minister of Foreign Affairs: Rafael Roncagliolo (page 1505)
Minister of Defence: Pedro Cateriano (page 1401)
Minister of Economy & Finance: Luis Miguel Castilla Rubio (page 1401)
Minister of the Interior: Wilfredo Pedraza (page 1493)
Minister of Health: Midori de Habich
Minister of Agriculture: Milton von Hesse
Minister of Labour and Employment Promotion: Teresa Laos Caceres
Minister of Foreign Trade and Tourism: José Luis Silva Martinot
Minister of Energy and Mines: Jorge Humberto Merino Tafur
Minister of Transportation and Communications: Carlos Paredes Rodriguez
Minister of Production: Gladys Trevino
Minister of Housing and Construction: René Cornejo Diaz
Minister of Education: Patricia Salas O'Brien
Minister for the Advancement of Women: Ana Jara
Minister of Social Development: Carolina Trivelli
Minister of the Environment: Manuel Gerardo Pedro Pulgar-Vidal
Minister of Culture: Luis Alberto Peirano Falconi
Minister of Justice: Eda Rivas

Ministries

Office of the President, Jirón de la Union, s/n 1ra cuadra, Lima 1, Peru. Tel: +51 1 311 3900, fax: +51 1 426 6770, e-mail: webmaster@presidencia.gob.pe, URL: http://www.presidencia.gob.pe
Office of the President of the Council of Ministers, URL: http://www.pcm.gob.pe/
Ministry of Agriculture, Avenida Salaverry S/N, Jesús Maria, Lima 11, Peru. Tel: +51 (0)1 433 3034 / 2951 / 2271, fax: +51 (0)1 432 9098, URL: http://www.minag.gob.pe
Ministry of Defense, Avenida Arequipa 291, Lince, Lima 14, Peru. Tel: +51 (0)1 433 5150 / 435 9567, fax: +51 (0)1 433 5150, URL: http://www.mindef.gob.pe/
Ministry of Economy and Finance, Jr. Junin 339 4th Floor, Lima 1, Peru. Tel: +51 (0)1 427 3930, fax: +51 (0)1 431 7836, URL: http://www.mef.gob.pe
Ministry of Education, Avenida San Develde No. 160, San Borja, Lima 41, Peru. Tel: +51 (0)1 436 / 5906 / 1240, fax: +51 (0)1 433 0230, URL: http://www.minedu.gob.pe
Ministry of Energy and Mines, Avenida Las Artes S/N, San Borja, Lima 41, Peru. Tel: +51 (0)1 475 0206 / 475 0278 / 475 0212, fax: +51 (0)1 475 0689, URL: http://www.mem.gob.pe
Ministry of Fisheries, Calle Uno Oeste S/N, Urbanizacion Corpac, San Isidro, Lima 27. Tel: +51 (0)1 224 3336 / 3332 / 3333, fax: +51 (0)1 224 3233, URL: http://www.minpes.gob.pe
Ministry of Foreign Affairs, Palacio de Torre Tagle, Jr. Ucayali 363, Lima 1. Tel: +51 (0)1 427 3860 / 1992, fax: +51 (0)1 426 3266, URL: http://www.rree.gob.pe
Ministry of Health, Avenida Salaverry Cdra. 8, Jesús María, Lima 11, Peru. Tel: +51 (0)1 432 3535 / 3505, fax: +51 (0)1 431 3671, URL: http://www.minsa.gob.pe
Ministry of Tourism and International Trade, Calle Uno Oeste S/N, Corpac, San Isidro, Lima 27, Peru. Tel: +51 (0)1 224 3347; fax: +51 (0)1 224 3347 / 3362, fax: +51 (0)1 224 3264 / 3144, URL: http://www.mitinci.gob.pe
Ministry of Interior, Plaza 30 de Agosto No. 150, San Isidro, Lima 27. Tel: +51 (0)1 475 2995 / 225 0202 / 225 0402, fax: +51 (0)1 441 5128, URL: http://www.mininter.gob.pe
Ministry of Justice, Scipion Llona No. 350, Miraflores, Lima 18, Peru. Tel: +51 (0)1 441 7320 / 440 4310, fax: +51 (0)1 440 4407, URL: http://www.minjus.gob.pe
Ministry of Labour and Social Promotion, Avenida Salaverry 655, Jesús María , Lima 11, Peru. Tel: +51 (0)1 433 2512 / 424 1744, fax: +51 (0)1 433 8126, URL: http://www.mtps.gob.pe
Ministry of Transportation, Communication, Housing & Construction, Avenida 28 de Julio No. 800, Lima 1, Peru. Tel: +51 (0)1 433 1212 / 7800, fax: +51 (0)1 433 9378, URL: http://www.mtc.gob.pe
Ministry of the Presidency, Avenida Paseo de la Republica No. 4297, Lima 1, Peru. Tel: +51 (0)1 222 3666 / 446 5886, fax: +51 (0)1 447 0379
Ministry for the Advancement of Women & Human Development, Avenida Emancipación 235 o Esquina Jr. Camaná 616, Lima 1, Peru. Tel: +51 (0)1 426 4336, URL: http://www.promudeh.gob.pe

Political Parties

Alliance for Progress (APP); American Popular Revolutionary Alliance (APRA); Force 2011; National Solidarity (SN); Peru Possible (PP); Peruvian Nationalist Party (PNP).

Elections

Elections are by universal suffrage over the age of 18. Until the age of 70 it is compulsory to vote.

President Fujimore stood for a controversial third term in the elections of 2000. He was elected but was forced to flee the country because of the ensuing political and economic turmoil. In April 2001 Alejandro Toledo became the first indigenous Peruvian to hold the presidential office. He was defeated in the 2006 presidential elections by Alan Garcia of the Aprista Party. President Garcia lost the 2011 presidential election in the second round to Ollanta Humala Tasso of the PNP party who won over 51 per cent of the vote. Mr Humala took office on 28 July 2011.

The most recent parliamentary elections were held on 10 April 2011. They were won by the Peru Wins alliance. Breakdown of seats was as follows: Peru Wins alliance, 47 seats; Force 2011 alliance 37 seats; PP alliance 21 seats; Alliance for Great Change, 12 seats; National Solidarity Alliance, 9 seats; APRA 4 seats.

Diplomatic Representation

Embassy of Peru, UK, 52 Sloane Street, London, SW1X 9SP, England. Tel: +44 (0)20 7235 1917, fax: +44 (0)20 7235 4463, URL: http://www.peruembassy-uk.com
Ambassador: Julio Munoz-Deacon
US Embassy, Avenida Encalada, Cuadra 17, Monterrico, Lima, PO Box 1995, Lima 1, Peru or American Embassy (Lima), APO AA 34031-5000; Tel: +51 (0)1 434 3000; fax: +51 (0)1 434 3037, URL: http://lima.usembassy.gov/

Ambassador: Rose Likins (page 1464)
British Embassy, Torre Parque Mar (Piso 22), Avenida Jose Larco 1301, Miraflores, Lima, Peru. Tel +51 (0)1 617 3000; fax +51 (0)1 617 3100, e-mail: belima@fco.gov.uk, URL: http://www.ukinperu.fco.gov.uk
Ambassador: James Dauris (page 1412)
Embassy of Peru, US, 1700 Massachusetts Avenue, NW, Washington, DC 20036, USA. Tel: +1 202 833 9860, fax: +1 202 659 8124, URL: http://www.peruvianembassy.us
Ambassador: Harold W. Forsyth Melia
Permanent Mission to the United Nations, URL: http://www.un.int/wcm/content/site/peru
Permanent Representative: Enrique Armando Roman-Moray

LEGAL SYSTEM

The legal system is largely based on the Napoleonic Code, and the independence of the judiciary is guaranteed in the 1993 Constitution.

The judiciary comprises a Supreme Court, which has jurisdiction over the whole nation, and Superior Courts which sit in the 28 departmental capital cities and hear appeals from the provincial Courts of the First Instance (trial courts). These are divided into civil, penal and special chambers. Justices of the peace hear minor civil cases. The nine-member Court of Constitutional Guarantees has jurisdiction in human rights cases.

The National Judiciary Council proposes the judges of the Supreme and Superior Courts, who are later appointed by the President and ratified by the Senate. Judges service until the age of 70 years. The Supreme Court consists of a president and 16 members. The President is elected by secret ballot in December every two years.

In general, the government respects the human rights of its citizens. However, in 2008, there were reports of unlawful killings by government forces as well as harsh prison conditions and long trial delays. There were also attacks on the media, instances of corruption and discrimination against indigenous communities, ethnic minorities, and gay and lesbian persons.

Peruvian law provides for the use of the death penalty only for exceptional crimes - such as crimes committed under military law or in exceptional circumstances.

Supreme Court, URL: http://www.pj.gob.pe/
Ombudsman of Peru, URL: http://www.defensoria.gob.pe/

LOCAL GOVERNMENT

The Republic of Peru is divided into 25 departments, and one constitutional province (Lima): Amazonas; Ancash; Apurimac; Arequipa; Ayacucho; Cajamarca; Callao; Cusco; Huancavelica; Huanuco; Ica; Junin; La Libertad; Lambayeque; Lima; Loreto; Madre de Dios; Moquegua; Pasco; Piura; Puno; San Loreto; Madre de Dios; Moquegua; Pasco; Piura; Puna; San Martin; Tacna; Tumbes and Ucayali. All are governed by Prefects. Peru has 164 provinces and 1,707 districts, which are governed by Mayors and Aldermen. Local authorities are elected by direct popular voting every three years.

AREA AND POPULATION

Area

The Republic of Peru is the third largest country in South America. Its area is 496,225 sq. miles. It shares its borders with Ecuador and Colombia to the north; Brazil and Bolivia to the east; Chile to the south; and is bordered on the west by a 1,450 mile-long Pacific Ocean coastline.

The country is divided into three distinct topographic and climatic regions: a narrow coastal area, the Costa; a mountainous central zone, the Sierra; and the upper Amazon basin, the Selva. The narrow Costa accounts for only 10 per cent of Peru's land area, but supports over 50 per cent of the population. The climate in the Costa is dry, desert. The Sierra consists of the Andean mountains, high plateaux and valleys that cover 27 per cent of the land area. It is inhabited by 47 per cent of the population. The climate varies from temperate to cold in this region. The Selva is the largest of the regions and extends from the eastern slopes of the Andes to the lowlands of the Amazon basin. Much of it consists of tropical rain forests and the population is sparse. The climate is tropical.

To view a map of Peru, please visit http://www.un.org/Depts/Cartographic/map/profile/peru.pdf

Population

Peru is the fifth most populous country in Latin America (after Brazil, Mexico, Colombia and Argentina). The population reached an estimated 29.077 million in 2010, with an average annual growth rate of 1.2 per cent over the period 2000-10. The overall population density is 21.2 people per km. sq. Rural migration has increased the urban population to an estimated 77 per cent in 2010. Twenty-one cities have a population of 100,000 or more, and the province of Lima has over 8.4 million inhabitants. Approximately 45 per cent of the population is native Indian, 37 per cent is mestizo (persons of mixed white, mainly Spanish and Indian, background), 15 per cent is European and the remaining 3 per cent is of African, Japanese, Chinese and other origins.

The official languages are Spanish and Quecha. In other geographic areas Aymara is spoken. There are many other dialects spoken in the aboriginal communities of the desert.

Births, Marriages, Deaths

In 2010, the crude birth rate was 20.4 per 1,000 population and the crude death rate was 4.7 per 1,000 population. The fertility rate of women of childbearing age is 2.3 in urban areas and 4.3 in rural areas. Life expectancy from birth in 2009 was 74 years for men and 77 years for women. Healthy life expectancy was 67 years. In 2009, the median age was 25 years. An estimated 30 per cent of the population are aged less than 15 years and 9 per cent over 60 years. (Source: http://www.who.int, World Health Statistics 2012)

Public Holidays 2014

1 January: New Year's Day
17 April: Maundy Thursday
18 April: Good Friday
5 May: Labour Day
29 June: St. Peter and St. Paul Day
28-29 July: Independence Day
30 August: St. Rose of Lima Day
8 October: Battle of Angamos Day
1 November: All Saints Day
8 December: Feast of the Immaculate Conception
25 December: Christmas Day

EMPLOYMENT

The work force in 2010 was estimated to number 10,580,000. It is estimated that 49 per cent of the working population is underemployed. Estimated figures for 2010 put the unemployment rate at 8.0 per cent. Below is a table showing employment by economic activity:

Number of Employees by economic activity

Sector	2007	2008
Agriculture, hunting and forestry	41,800	33,700
Fishing	6,700	4,300
Mining and quarrying	22,300	21,300
Manufacturing	728,000	725,300
Electricity, gas and water	9,000	8,600
Construction	245,900	251,700
Wholesale and retail trade; repair of motor vehicles, motorcycles and personal goods	901,300	932,100
Hotels and restaurants	271,700	300,300
Transport, storage and communications	404,100	449,700
Financial services	40,100	62,200
Real Estate, renting and business activities	306,300	289,700
Public administration and defence; compulsory Social Security	205,700	167,400
Education	250,200	258,900
Health and social work	131,100	145,600
Other community, social and personal services	309,100	321,700
Private household employees	289,100	271,500
Total	4,163,700	4,246,300

Source: Copyright © International Labour Organization (ILO Dept. of Statistics, http://laborsta.ilo.org)

BANKING AND FINANCE

Currency

The unit of currency is the Nuevo Sol. There are 100 centimos in a Nuevo Sol. The financial centre is Lima.

GDP/GNP, Inflation, National Debt

After President Fujimori's election in 1990, the government adopted more free-market orientated economic policies, hyperinflation was reduced and government price subsidies were abolished. Following a lull in growth between 1998 and 2001, Peru's economy once again expanded. The economic expansion has been driven by the construction and mining sectors, as well as an increase in exports, domestic consumption and private investment. The economy is hindered by a poor infrastructure, especially in coastal areas. Social inequality still exists. The current administration is trying to develop free trade and attract foreign investment.

In 2007, GDP grew by 7.7 per cent, and in 2008, it grew by around 9.8 per cent, reaching US$127.8 billion. The global financial crisis was expected to impact on the Peruvian economy in 2009, with GDP growth to dropping to 0.9 per cent with a figure of US$127.1 billion. GDP was estimated to be US$153 billion in 2010, with a growth rate of 8.8 per cent. GDP was estimated at US$170 billion in 2011. The services sector is the main contributor to GDP (over 55 per cent in 2010); agriculture accounts for 7.5 per cent, mining 5 per cent, construction 7 per cent and fisheries 0.3 per cent.

The inflation rate, which peaked at 7,646 per cent in 1990, has remained below 6.5 per cent since 1997; in 2010, it stood at an estimated 1.5 per cent, rising to over 3 per cent in 2011, largely due to hikes in global foods and oil prices.

External debt dropped to $19.2 billion in 2008.

Gross Domestic Product by Activity, 2007

Sector	% of total GDP	New Sol., 1,000 (current value)
Agriculture	5.4	18,220,344
Fishing	0.7	2,182,904
Mining	11.4	38,413,493
Electricity & Water	1.8	6,010,516
Manufacturing	14.5	48,810,671
Construction	6.1	20,395,026
Commerce	12.6	42,200,070
Transport and Communications	8.5	28,622,330
Restaurants and Hotels	3.5	11,659,037
Government Services	6.6	22,193,747
Other Services	20.5	68,694,913
Aggregate value	**91.6**	**307,403,051**
Import taxes	0.7	2,198,028
Product taxes	7.8	26,128,502
Total GDP	**100.00**	**335,729,581**

Source: Instituto Nacional de Estadística e Información (INEI), Peru

Foreign Investment

Peru's constitution guarantees the non-discriminatory treatment of foreign investors, no prior registration or approval, investors may invest in any economic sector and there is unrestricted transfer of all capital, dividends and royalties. Peru currently has foreign direct investments to the value of US$15.4 billion, the main investors being Spain, the UK and the US. Most foreign investment is directed towards telecommunications, mining, manufacturing, finance and electricity.

Peru is a member of the Andean Community and the Asia Pacific Economic Cooperation forum. It has signed several trade agreements including South Korea, Mexico and Japan.

Balance of Payments / Imports and Exports

Foreign trade plays a central role in Peru's economic development. Exports have become increasingly diversified in recent years, reducing the country's vulnerability to changes in world demand for any specific product. Leading exports are copper and other minerals, petroleum, and non-traditional products including manufactured goods, processed food and frozen and canned fish. Of lesser importance are traditional agricultural exports of sugar, coffee, cotton and wool. Peru exports mainly to the USA (16 per cent in 2010), China (15.5 per cent), Switzerland (11 per cent), Canada (9.5 per cent) and Japan (5 per cent). Major imports are raw materials for agriculture and industry, and capital goods, for industry. Peru imports mainly from the United States (19.5 per cent), China (17 per cent), Brazil (8 per cent) and Ecuador (5 per cent).

Peru's new free trade agreement with the USA came into force in January 2009. The EU and the Andean Community (including Peru) began talks on an Association Agreement in January 2009. Figures for 2009 put exports at US$27.0 billion and imports cost US$20.3 billion. In 2010, exports were estimated to be worth US$35 billion and imports US$28 billion.

Central Bank

Banco Central de Reserva del Peru
Jirón Miró Quesada 441, 445 Lima 1, Peru. Tel: +51 (0)1 427 6250, fax: +51 (0)1 427 5888 / 5889, URL: http://www.bcrp.gob.pe
President: Julio Velarde Flores

MANUFACTURING, MINING AND SERVICES

Primary and Extractive Industries

Peru is endowed with large deposits of many mineral resources and rates among the six major mining countries in the world. It has been estimated that some 13 metals and 25 non-metallic minerals are mined or quarried and that only five per cent of total reserves are presently being developed. Copper is the leading mineral export, followed by zinc, lead and refined silver, iron ore and phosphate. Coal is also mined.

Among world producers, Peru ranks second in bismuth production, third in silver, fifth in zinc and lead, and seventh in copper. With the exception of the copper and iron deposits on the southern coast, the developed mineral resources are concentrated almost entirely in the Sierra.

Oil production in Peru is run by foreign consortia, with the National Agency of Hydrocarbons (Perupetro) overseeing all exploration and production activities. The Ministry of Energy and Mines also has a hand in developing planning.. According to Perupetro, 75 per cent of Peru's crude oil output in 2011 was produced by three companies: Argentina's Pluspetrol, Brazil's Petrobras, and Peru's Savia. It is estiamted that over 50 foreign oil companies are currently engaged in oil exploration in Peru.

There were proven oil reserves of 582 million barrels in January 2012, production in 2011 stood at 153,700 barrels per day, 67 per cent of which was crude. Meanwhile, oil consumption rose slightly to 161,000 barrels per day; Peru imported the balance of 7,200 barrels per day from Ecuador, Colombia and Venezuela. Peru has six major oil refineries, with total capacity of 199,000 barrels per day.

In 2011, Peru had proven Natural Gas reserves of 12 trillion cubic feet. Production in 2011 was an estimated 401 billion cubic feet of natural gas, up from 255 billion cubic feet in 2010, due to increasing production at the Camisea project.

PERU

The Camisea natural gas fields in the Ucayali basin in southeastern Peru are thought to have between nine and thirteen trillion cubic feet of natural gas, and it is anticipated that production will exceed domestic demand for some time. South America's first liquefied natural gas (LNG) plant is based south of Lima, and has a capacity of around 4.2 million tons per year. (Source: Energy Information Administration, EIA)

Petroperu, URL: http://www.petroperu.com

Energy

In 2009, Peru's total energy consumption reached 0.777 quadrillion Btu, up from 0.727 quadrillion Btu in 2008. Oil represented approximately 56 per cent of energy consumption in 2004, and hydroelectricity accounted for 33 per cent. Coal contributed six per cent to the energy mix in 2004, and natural gas accounted for five per cent. The Peruvian government hopes to lessen the reliance on oil and hydroelectricity with the advent of natural gas from the Camisea project, and is encouraging investment in gas-fired power plants.

In 2010, Peru had an estimated 8.61GWe installed generating capacity, and generated 33.3 billion kilowatthours of electricity. Electricity consumption reached 29.58 billion kilowatthours. Even though installed capacity is evenly divided between hydroelectricity and conventional thermal, 80 percent of Peru's total electricity comes from hydroelectric facilities: conventional thermal plants operate only during peak load periods or when weather factors dampen hydroelectric output.

As part of the Andean Community's efforts to create a common electricity market, Peru is in the process of integrating its grid with those of Bolivia, Ecuador and Chile.

The government has the power to block any acquisition giving a private company more than a five per cent market share in more than one electric power sector and to veto any acquisition considered contrary to the national interest. (Source: EIA)

Manufacturing

Industry currently employs 16.6 per cent of the labour force, and in 2008 it accounted for 15.5 per cent of GDP. Over the past decade, manufacturing has become increasingly diversified with a rapid expansion in capacity. Although most production was consumed by the local market in the past, recent economic policies have fostered export growth. In the past few years, manufactured goods exports have become an important source of foreign exchange earnings and contributed to greater export diversification. Principal industries include metalworking, textiles, chemical, steel, automotive, cement, and pulp and paper. The majority of manufacturing establishments are small although production in most industrial sectors is dominated by a few large firms.

Service Industries

Since 1990 Peru has once again become a popular tourist market with the stabilising of the economy and political situation. Visitors to Peru numbered almost 650,000 in 1997, rising to over 830,000 in 2001. In 2005 Peru submitted a US$130 million plan to UNESCO on how to preserve the Inca city of Machu Picchu. UNESCO has threatened to remove its world heritage status if action is not taken.

Agriculture

The agricultural sector accounted for 8.0 per cent of GDP in 2011. A modern subsector produces Peru's primary agricultural exports of sugar, cotton and coffee, whilst the traditional subsector produces the bulk of domestic crop consumption and employs three-quarters of the agricultural workforce. Cooperatives own approximately 60 per cent of agricultural land and produce approximately 40 per cent of agricultural output. Among crops suitable for large scale production in new areas are sugar, cacao, coffee, tropical fruits, rice, peanuts, oil seeds and African palm. Peru is the world's largest producer of quinoa, and has the world's largest number of llamas. Potential for increased livestock raising includes beef and dairy cattle in the lower regions as well as sheep in the highlands.

Agricultural Production in 2010

Produce	Int. $'000*	Tonnes
Indigenous chicken meat	1,454,362	1,021,030
Rice, paddy	779,237	2,831,370
Potatoes	539,149	3,814,370
Cow milk, whole, fresh	520,633	1,678,370
Indigenous cattle meat	464,191	171,835
Plantains	414,419	2,007,280
Sugar cane	317,235	9,660,900
Asparagus	305,095	335,209
Coffee, green	284,281	264,605
Mangoes, mangosteens, guavas	274,283	457,774
Hen eggs, in shell	236,461	285,102
Indigenous pigmeat	179,288	116,630

* unofficial figures

Source: http://faostat.fao.org/site/339/default.aspx Food and Agriculture Organization of the United Nations, Food and Agricultural commodities production

With 209 million acres of forest containing stands of valuable hardwoods, vast quantities of raw material for pulp, and access to ocean transport through the Amazon and its tributaries, Peru has great potential for commercial development of forest products. Some 50 species with commercial potential have been identified and an additional 250 are being studied. The most important lumber centres are Pucallpa and Iquitos, which account for 36 per cent of total lumber production. Both are located in the Selva where a great part of forest resources are found.

Coca is still grown in Peru but following an active campaign to stop the production and trafficking of cocaine it is estimated that 70 per cent less is grown now than in 1995.

The catch of fish for human consumption has fallen significantly. In 2004, 9,600,000 tonnes of fish were landed. Fish canning remains an important export area. The total catch for 2010 was put at 4,260,000 tonnes.

COMMUNICATIONS AND TRANSPORT

Travel Requirements

Citizens of the USA, Canada, Australia and the EU require a valid passport valid but do not need a visa for stays of up to 90 days, apart from Latvians and Romanians, who do require a visa. Peru does not require any immunizations for entry, although it recommends vaccination against Yellow Fever. All visitors to Peru are advised to check with the Peruvian Consulate prior to departure to obtain current details of any documentation which might be required.

International Airports

Jorge Chávez International Airport is situated just outside Lima, and 236 other airports in the country. 54 airports have paved runways, and 6 have runways of 3,049 metres or more. There is one heliport.

National Airline

LAN Peru S.A. URL: http://www.lan.com

Railways

There are 19 lines in the Republic, nine of which are State owned. Most lines are of standard gauge, and one, the Central Railway, is the highest standard-gauge railway in the world, reaching an altitude of 15,801 ft.
Peru Rail, URL: http://www.perurail.com

Roads

Peru has around 78,829 km of roadways, the majority of which is unpaved. Vehicles are driven on the right. A highway connecting Brazil's Atlantic coast with the Peru's Pacific coast was opened in January 2011.

Waterways

Inland waterways include 8,800 km of navigable tributaries of the Amazon River and Lake Titicaca, the world's highest navigable lake.

Ports and Harbours

Main ports of Peru include Callao, Chimbote, Ilo, Matarani, Paita, Puerto Maldonado, Salaverry, San Martin, and Talarate. The harbours of Iquitos, Pucallpa, and Yurimaguas are located on the upper reaches of the Amazon and its tributaries.

HEALTH

In 2009, the government spent approximately 11.9 per cent of its total budget on healthcare, accounting for 57.7 per cent of all healthcare spending. Social security expenditure amounts to 44.5 per cent of general government expenditure on health. Total expenditure on healthcare equated to 5.3 per cent of the country's GDP. Per capita expenditure on health was approximately US$236, compared with US$96 in 2000. Lima and Peru's other main cities have modern hospitals and clinics with trained physicians. Figures for 2005-10 show that there are 27,272 physicians (9.2 per 10,000 population), 37,672 nurses and midwives (12.7 per 10,000 population) and 3,507 dentists. There are 15 hospital beds per 10,000 population.

Whilst wealth is concentrated in the urban areas, rural communities are suffering poverty. According to recent figures, 54 per cent of the population lives in poverty, 24 per cent in extreme poverty. Approximately a third of children are undernourished. In 2009, the infant mortality rate (probability of dying by age one) was 15 per 1,000 live births and the under-five mortality rate was 19 deaths per 1,000 live children. Immunisation programmes have enabled Peru to ensure that 97.5 per cent of all children under the age of one have been immunised. The most common causes of death in children aged less than 5 years old are: prematurity 20 per cent, congenital anomalies 20 per cent, pneumonia 10 per cent, birth asphyxia 6 per cent, diarrhoea 4 per cent and HIV/AIDS 1 per cent. (Source: http://www.who.in, World Health Statistics 2012)

EDUCATION

Primary and secondary education is compulsory and in state run schools is free. In 2001, there were 173,877 primary schools, and 137,451 secondary schools in Peru. In 2007, approximately 65 per cent of young children attended a nursery school. In the same year, 93 per cent of the relevant age-group enrolled in primary school, and 89 per cent went to secondary schools. Some 34 per cent of students continued into tertiary education. University education is free for students who can't afford the fees.

The national adult literacy rate is 91 per cent. There is a marked difference between the male literacy rate (93.7 per cent), and that of Peruvian women (82.5 per cent). Both male and female literacy rates rise in the 15-24 age group, to 97.9 per cent and 96.3 per cent respectively, above the region average.

The Ministry of Education is responsible for outlining the national curricula, regulating state and private institutions, and supervising education standards. Recent figures show that on average 16.5 per cent of government spending goes on education.

RELIGION

Peru has freedom of religion, but the Roman Catholic religion is protected by the State. Catholics represent approximately 75 per cent of the population with other Christian denominations making up around 20 per cent of the population. Ethnoreligions comprise 1.5 per cent of the population. Peru has a religious tolerance rating of 9 on a scale of 1 to 10 (10 is most freedom). (Source: World Religion Database)

COMMUNICATIONS AND MEDIA

Privately-run broadcasting dominates the media scene. There is reported to be a high level of violence against reporters.

Newspapers

El Comercio, Lima, URL: http://www.elcomercio.com.pe/online; El Callao, Callao; El Nacional, Lima; El Peruano, Lima; El Popular, Lima; Expreso, Lima; Extra, Lima; Hoy, Surquillo; La Crónica, Lima; La Republica, Lima, URL: http://www.larepublica.com.pe; Ojo, San Isidro, URL: http://www.ojo.com.pe; Página Libre, San Isidro.

Broadcasting

There are several hundred radio stations, many of which broadcast in indigenous languages. Television Nacional de Peru is the state-run station (URL: http://www.tnp.com.pe/Index.do?). There are a further five private television networks.

Telecommunications

In 2008, there were an estimated 2.8 million mainline telephones in Peru, and 20 million mobile phones in use. There are an estimated 7 million internet users.

ENVIRONMENT

Peru's oil and gas resources are predominantly located in largely virgin rainforest. Most of this is virtually inaccessible and contains rich biodiversity. The forest also houses indigenous peoples whose lives would be affected by any oil and gas development in their region. As of 2011, oil companies leased around 40 per cent of the Peruvian Amazon and this figure could rise to as much as 70 per cent.

Carbon dioxide emissions from the consumption and flaring of fossil fuels rose from 25.98 million metric tons in 2002 to 31.31 mmt in 2005. This equates to per capita emissions of 1.12 metric tons, lower than the Central and South American average of 2.45 metric tons. In 2010 Peru's emissions from the consumption of fossil fuels totalled 41.88 million metric tons of carbon dioxide. (Source: EIA)

In May 2008, Peru created its first environment ministry. A scientific study has said that Peru is one of the three nations that will be most affected by global warming. Peru's Andes mountains are home to over half the world's tropical glaciers, but its Andean peaks are already subject to accelerated glacial melt, and it is estimated that in 25 years time they will be gone. On the other side of the Andes lies the fourth largest tropical rainforest in the world (after Brazil, DR Congo and Indonesia), comprising around 70 million hectares covering nearly 60 per cent of Peru's territory.

In May 2008, an unknown group of native Amazonians were photographed near the border with Brazil, and the following month the Peruvian government took steps to protect them. Authorities in the state of Madre de Dios are now committed to stopping illegal loggers who travel deep into the forest in search of tropical hardwoods. Apart from the possibility of violent confrontations, encounters with outsiders can be fatal because the isolated people lack the antibodies to protect themselves from a common cold or the flu.

Peru is party to the following international agreements: Antarctic-Environmental Protocol, Antarctic-Marine Living Resources, Antarctic Treaty, Biodiversity, Climate Change, Climate Change-Kyoto Protocol, Desertification, Endangered Species, Hazardous Wastes, Marine Dumping, Ozone Layer Protection, Ship Pollution, Tropical Timber 83, Tropical Timber 94, Wetlands, Whaling.

SPACE PROGRAMME

Peru is aiming to launch its second satellite in 2014 for research purposes, including studying its deforestation.
Space Agency of Peru, URL: http://www.conida.gob.pe/

PHILIPPINES
Republic of the Philippines
Republika ng Pilipinas

Capital: Manila (Population estimate: 1.7 million)

President: Benigno Aquino (page 1379)

Vice-President: Jejomar Binay

National Flag: Divided fesswise, blue and red; with a white triangle, base at hoist, enclosing a yellow sun with eight three-pointed rays between three yellow five-pointed stars.

CONSTITUTION AND GOVERNMENT

Constitution

On 24 May 1898, a ranking leader of the Revolution, General Emilio Aguinaldo, announced the formation of a Filipino dictatorial Government in order to buttress the struggle against Spain. On 12 June 1898 he proclaimed Philippine Independence and, shortly after, inaugurated a revolutionary Government which took over the task of partly administering and partly restructuring the Government. But the most memorable achievement of the revolutionary Government was its promulgation of a democratic Constitution which is regarded as the most noteworthy of its kind in East Asia during this period.

Unknown to the revolutionary Government, a combination of circumstances began to conspire against the declaration of Filipino autonomy. Following US Commodore Dewey's victory over the Spanish fleet in Manila Bay on 1 May 1898, the Americans steadily brought in reinforcements to Manila. Tensions between the Americans and the Filipinos built up until hostilities erupted. Superior American arms finally won. American authority was established over the entire country and pacification took less time than would have been normally necessary because of the promise of eventual autonomy.

The Americans helped in rebuilding the shattered economy, established a nationwide educational system, brought in English as the official language and language of instruction, reorganised the Governmental system and acquainted the people with the juridical and political institutions of Anglo-Saxon democracy. Passing through phases of increasing autonomy, interrupted by three years of Japanese military occupation during the Pacific War of 1941-45, the Philippines eventually regained its independence on 4 July 1946.

Between 1946 and 17 January 1973, the Republic of the Philippines operated according to the 1935 Constitution which provided for a tripartite system: the Executive, represented by a President who was elected by direct vote of the people for a four-year term, with a right to re-election; a bicameral Congress, made up of Congressmen with four-year terms and

Senators with six-year terms; and a Judiciary, with the power of judicial review. The Constitution was nationalistic, contained a Bill of Rights, and some nationalistic provisions, and explicitly provided for a strong Chief Executive.

On 21 September 1972 the incumbent President Ferdinand E. Marcos, declared nationwide martial law. Under martial law Congress was abolished and a new Constitution which provided for the eventual adoption of a Parliamentary Government in the Philippines. The parliamentary form of government, however, was somewhat modified by a series of amendments that followed the introduction of the 1973 Constitution. It was amended in 1976, 1980, 1981 and 1984 at a frequency of more than once every two and a half years. The most controversial issue among these was Amendment No. 6 which empowered the president to issue decrees, orders, or letters of instruction.

The eventual abuse of such power, coupled with growing disenchantment over the political and economic situation, led to mounting external and internal pressures which eventually forced the then President Marcos to seek the renewal of his mandate through a snap election. This was the second election held since the adoption of 1973 charter. The first was in 1981 which saw the re-election of Marcos for another six-year term. After a peaceful 'People Power Revolution' on 25 February 1986, opposition leader Corazon C. Aquino, the wife of Benigno Aquino, assumed the presidency that had been held by Marcos for more than twenty years.

For purposes of reconstructing the economy and eradicating the inefficiency left by the previous regime, the government vested upon the head of state extraordinary powers which are deemed only temporary. In line with these initiatives a new Presidential Commission on Good Government and a Presidential Commission on Government Reorganization were created for the purpose of restructuring bureaucracy and recovering the wealth of the Marcoses and their associates.

President Aquino abolished the National Assembly (Batasang Pambansa) and formed a 50-member Constitutional Commission for the writing of a new constitution. Work of the Commission was completed 15 October 1986. The drafted Constitution was ratified by popular referendum on 2 February 1987, marking a shift from a modified parliamentary republic to a presidential form of government. A Bicameral Congress of 24 Senators elected by nationwide vote and 200 members of the House of Representatives elected by district, was voted in May and formally convened in 26 July 1987. As a result of the 1992 General Elections, President Aquino was succeeded by Fidel V. Ramos who remained as president until 1998, when elections were won by Joseph Estrada.

President Arroyo has said that she would like to amend the constitution to end the presidential system and create a parliamentary style of government.

PHILIPPINES

To consult the full constitution, please visit: http://www.philippinecountry.com/philippine_constitution/

International Relations

The Philippines enjoys close relations with its neighbour Malaysia. Malaysia has acted as a mediator in talks between the Philippine Government and the Moro Islamic Liberation Front, a Muslim separatist organisation based in Mindanao.

The Philippines is a founder member of ASEAN in 1967, recently a Code of Conduct in the South China Sea was agreed between China and ASEAN countries, it was hoped that this would relieve tensions between China and the Philippines over claims to the Spratly Islands. In June 2011, US Secretary of State Hillary Clinton committed the USA to the defence of the Philippines in reference to the tensions in the South China Sea with China over the disputed Spratly islets. Under the agreement the US would honour its defence pact and offer the Philippines affordable weapons.

Until 1991 the USA had military bases in the Philippines but the closure of these resulted in some difficulties. However, relations between the two countries have remained strong and the Philippines supported the US-led campaign in Iraq and sent army police and medical teams. These personnel were withdrawn in July 2004 following the kidnap of a Filipino lorry driver, later released.

Recent Events

In January 2001 President Joseph Estrada was forced to resign from office following mass protests and the collapse of an impeachment trial. He was arrested in April 2001 and faced charges of economic plunder, punishable by death under Philippines law. Former President Estrada's immunity from prosecution was removed by the Supreme Court. In September 2007 he was found guilty and was jailed for life, but was then granted a presidential pardon.

The Moro Liberation Front are a group fighting for an independent Moro nation and in 1996 an agreement was signed which gave the predominantly Muslim areas of Mindanao some elements of self rule as the Autonomous Region of Muslim Mindanao. A splinter group of the Moro Liberation Front is the Moro Islamic Liberation Front. Their aim is to establish an Islamic state in the southern Philippines and has as yet not reached an agreement with the government. Abu Sayyaf, another Islamic separatist group, aims to establish an independent Islamic state on the islands of Mindanao and Sulu. They are on Washington's list of terrorist organisations and are known to kidnap western nationals and demand ransoms.

In January 2005 fighting broke out between the army and the Moro Islamic Liberation Front, (MILF), breaking the 2003 ceasefire agreement. In April 2005 a breakthrough occurred during peace talks held in Malaysia between the Government and MILF over the issue of ancestral lands.

In July 2005 following the resignation of eight ministers, President Arroyo requested the resignation of the entire cabinet. At the same time calls were made to impeach President Arroyo following allegations of vote-rigging in the elections. The congress threw out the allegations against her in August.

In February 2006 President Arroyo called a week-long state of emergency after the army said it had foiled an attempted coup. In the following August the president survived efforts to impeach her following allegations of corruption and election fraud.

In April 2007 seven Christians were taken hostage by the Islamic group Aby Sayyaf. The hostages were beheaded, leading the military to increase its offensive against the group. The incident happened on the island of Jolo, and, the following August, 26 soldiers were killed during fighting on the same island.

During 2008 attempts were made to negotiate an agreement with MILF rebels on the expansion of a Muslim autonomous region in the south. However the agreement was short-lived and fighting broke out in August 2008. Peace talks with the New People's Army also broke down in December 2008. The government claimed to capture a major MILF base in 2009 and also captured one of the MILF leaders, Camarudin Hadji Ali in September 2009.

Martial law was imposed in the southern province of Maguindanao in December 2009 following the massacre of 57 people, the Ampatuan clan were believed to be responsible. A state of emergency was declared. Peace talks resumed between the government and the Moro Islamic Liberation Front in Malaysia, the first to be held since mid-2007.

Troubles continued into 2010. Abu Sayyaf rebels massacred 11 villages on vasilan island. Another one of the abu Sayyaf leaders, Mujibar Ali Amomn, was captured in the same month.

In February 2010 almost 200 people were charged with murder over the 2009 Maguindanao massacre. The accused included Andal Ampatuan, a former provincial governor and an ally of President Arroyo.

In February 2011 the government and the communist New People's Army (NPA) held peace deal talks in Oslo.

In November 2011, the former president Gloria Arroyo was arrested on vote-fraud charges over a Senate seat election in 2007. She denied the charges.

In May 2012, tension flared between the Philippines and China over ownership of the Scarborough Shoal reef in the South China Sea. Both countries claim the reef, which is thought to have reserves of oil and gas.

In October 2012, the government signed a peace plan with the Moro Islamic Liberation Front, ending a 40-year conflict in which over 120,000 people are thought to have died. Under the plan an autonomous region will be set up in the south of the country where the majority of the population are Muslim. The Abu Sayyaf group which is linked to al-Qaeda has not signed the plan.

In December 2012 the southern Philippines was hit by a typhoon, around 300 people were feared killed.

Also in December 2012 parliament voted to approve a bill to provide state funded contraception, the bill had been debated for 13 years, the bill was seen by some as defying the Catholic Church.

Executive

Executive power is vested in the President of the Philippines, who is also the Commander-in-Chief of the Armed Forces. The president may suspend the privilege of the writ of habeas corpus or place the Philippines or any part thereof under Martial Law only for a period not exceeding 60 days; the president will have to report to Congress within 48 hours from the proclamation of martial law or suspension of habeas corpus. The president, who must be at least 40 years of age, shall be elected by direct vote of the people for a term of six years and be disqualified for any re-election. The president is responsible for the appointment of the Cabinet, subject to the consent of the Commission on Appointments.

The vice-president shall have the same qualifications and terms of office and be elected with and in the same manner as the president. The vice-president may be appointed as a member of the Cabinet, and shall not serve the government for more than two successive six-year terms. Like the president, however, the vice-president shall not receive during his tenure any other emolument from the Government or any other source. In case of death, permanent disability, removal from office, or resignation of the president, the vice-president shall act as the president to serve the unexpired term. The president of the Senate or, in the event of his inability, the speaker of the House of Representatives, acts as president in case of death, permanent disability, removal from office, or resignation of both the president and vice-president. Congress is expected to convene and call for a special election to elect a president and vice-president.

Legislature

The legislative power is vested in the Congress of the Philippines which consists of a Senate and a House of Representatives. The Congress shall convene once a year on the fourth Monday of July for its regular session and continue to be in session until thirty days before the opening of its next regular session. The president, however, may call a special session at any time. The president of the Senate or, in his absence, the speaker of the House of Representatives shall act as the president and, should the incumbent president or vice-president be incapacitated, until such time as the Congress, by law, convenes and calls for a special election to elect a president and vice-president.

President Arroyo proposed plans to move towards a more parliamentary system of government.

Upper House

The Senate is composed of 24 Senators duly elected by the qualified voters in the Philippines. Senators shall have a term of six years and are not allowed to serve for more than two consecutive terms. The Senate shall elect its president, and the House of Representatives its speaker, by a majority vote of all its respective members.
Senate, GSIS Building, Financial Center, Roxas Boulevard, Pasay City, Philippines. +632 552 6601 (Public Information and Media Relations Office), e-mail address: pimro@senate.gov.ph, URL: http://www.senate.gov.ph
Senate President: Juan Ponce Enrile

Lower House

The House of Representatives is composed of not more than 250 Congressmen elected by legislative districts. A total of 204 Congressmen are directly elected, while the remaining 46 are elected from party and minority-group lists. Congressmen serve a term of three years and are not allowed to serve for more than three consecutive terms. The House of Representatives also elects its Speaker by a majority vote of all its respective members.
House of Representatives, Constitution Hills, 1126 Quezon City, Philippines. Tel: +63 2 931 5001, URL: http://www.congress.gov.ph
Speaker: Feliciano 'Sonny' Belmonte, Jr.

Cabinet (as at June 2013)
Executive Secretary: Paquito Ochoa Jr (page 1488)
Secretary of Agrarian Reform: Virgilo de Los Reyes
Secretary of Transportation and Communications: Joseph Abaya
Secretary of Agriculture: Proceso Alcala (page 1374)
Secretary of the Budget and Management: Florencio Abad (page 1371)
Secretary of Energy: Jose Rene Almendras
Secretary of Education: Bro. Armin Luistro
Secretary of the Environment and Natural Resources: Ramon Paje
Secretary of Foreign Affairs: Albert del Rosario
Secretary of Health: Enrique Ona (page 1489)
Secretary of Justice: Leila de Lima (page 1414)
Secretary of Labour and Employment: Rosalinda Baldoz (page 1382)
Secretary of National Defence: Voltaire Gazmin (page 1429)
Secretary of Public Works and Highways: Rogelio Singson
Secretary of the National Economic Development Authority: Cayetano Paderanga
Secretary of Science and Technology: Mario Montejo
Secretary of Social Welfare and Development: Corazon Soliman
Secretary of Tourism: Ramon Jiminez
Secretary of Finance: Cesar Purisima
Secretary of the Interior and Local Government: Manuel Roxas
Secretary of Trade and Industry: Gregory Domingo
Presidential Adviser on the Peace Process: Teresita Deles
Head of the Presidential Management Staff: Julia Abad
Presidential Spokesman: Edwin Lacierda
Presidential Legal Counsel: Eduardo de Mesa
Chairman of Commission on Higher Education: Patricia Liguanan
Commissioner of the Bureau of Internal Revenue: Kim Jacinto-Henares

Ministries

The Office of the President, Malacanang Palace, JP Laurel Street, San Miguel 1005, Manila, Philippines. Tel: +63 2 564 1451 to 80, fax: +63 2 742 1641, URL: http://www.op.gov.ph/

The Office of the Vice President, Executive House, P. Burgos Street, 1005 Manila, Philippines. Tel: +63 2 527 0203, fax: +63 2 741 9199, URL: http://www.ovp.gov.ph

The Office of the Executive Secretary to the Cabinet, 2F New Executive Building, JP Laurel Street, San Miguel 1005, Manila, Philippines. Tel: +63 2 735 6023 / 733 3608. fax: +63 2 742 1643

Department of Agrarian Reform, Room 209, PTA Building, Diliman 1100, Quezon City, Philippines. Tel: +63 2 928 7031, fax: +63 2 928 3968, e-mail: info@dar.gov.ph, URL: http://www.dar.gov.ph/

Department of Agriculture, D A Building, Elliptical Road, Diliman, Quezon City, Philippines. Tel: +63 2 928 8741 to 45, fax: +632 978183, URL: http://www.da.gov.ph

Department of Budget and Management, 2nd Floor, DBM Building III, General Solano Street, San Miguel, Manila, Philippines. Tel: +63 2 735 4926, fax: +63 2 742 4173, e-mail: dbmbiss@dbm.gov.ph, URL: http://www.dbm.gov.ph

Department of Education, University of Life Building, Meralco Avenue, 1600 Pasig, Metro Manila, Philippines. Tel: +63 2 632 1361 to 71, fax: +63 2 632 0805, e-mail: osec@deped.gov.ph, URL: http://www.deped.gov.ph

Department of Energy, Energy Centre, Merritt Road, Fort Bonifacio, Taguig, Makati, Metro Manila, Philippines. Tel: +63 2 840 1401, fax: +63 2 817 8603, URL: http://www.doe.gov.ph

Department of Environment and Natural Resources, DENR Building, Visayas Avenue, Diliman, 1100 Quezon City, Philippines. Tel: +63 2 929 6626, fax: +63 2 920 4352, URL: http://www.denr.gov.ph/

Department of Finance, 5/F Executive Tower Building, Bangko Sentral ng Pilipinas, Vito Cruz cor. Mabini St., Malate 1004, Manila, Philippines. Tel: +63 2 521 2948, fax: +63 2 521 9495, URL: http://www.dof.gov.ph/

Department of Foreign Affairs, DFA Building, 2330 Roxas Blvd, Pasay City, Metro Manila, Philippines. Tel: +63 2 834 4000, fax: +63 2 832 1597, URL http://www.dfa.gov.ph

Department of Health, San Lazaro Compound, Rizal Avenue, Santa Cruz, Manila, Philippines. Tel: +63 2 743 8301-23, fax: +63 2 711 6055, URL: http://www.doh.gov.ph/

Department of Interior and Local Government, PNCC Building, EDSA Corner Reliance Street, Mandaluyong, Metro Manila, Philippines. Tel: +63 2 925 0320, fax: +63 2 631 8831, URL: http://www.dilg.gov.ph/

Department of Justice, 2nd Floor, BOJ Main Building, Padre Faura Street, Ermita, Manila, Philippines. Tel: +63 2 523 8481, fax: +63 2 521 1614, URL: http://www.doj.gov.ph/

Department of Labour and Employment, Room 107, Executive Building, San Jose Street, Intramuros, Manila, Philippines. Tel: +63 2 527 3464, fax; +63 2 527 3499, URL: http://www.dole.gov.ph/

Department of National Defence, Room 301, Third Floor, DND Building, Camp Aguinaldo, Quezon City, Philippines. Tel: +63 2 911 6001, fax: +63 2 911 6213, URL: http://www.dnd.gov.ph

National Economic and Development Authority, NEDA Building, Amber Avenue, Pasig City, 1600, Philippines. Tel: +63 2 631 0945, fax: +63 2 631 3747, URL: http://www.neda.gov.ph

Department of Public Works and Highways, DPWH Building, Bonifacio Drive, Port Area 1002, Manila, Philippines. Tel: +63 2 304 3000, fax: +63 2 527 5635, e-mail: PublicInformationDivision@dpwh.gove.ph, URL: http://www.dpwh.gov.ph/

Department of Science and Technology, General Santos Avenue, Bicutan, Taguig 1604, Metro Manila, Philippines. Tel: +63 2 837 2071, fax: +63 2 837 2937, URL: http://www.dost.gov.ph/

Department of Social Welfare and Development, DSWD Building, Constitution Hills, Batasan Complex, 1100 Quezon City, Philippines. Tel: +63 2 931 8101, fax: +63 2 931 0149, URL: http://www.dswd.gov.ph/

Department of Trade and Industry, Industry and Investment Building, 385 Gil J. Puyat Avenue, Makati 1200, Philippines. Tel: +63 2 895 3640, fax: +63 2 896 1116, URL: http://www.dti.gov.ph/

Department of Tourism, DOT Building, TM Kalaw Street, Agrifina Circle, Rizal Park, Manila, Philippines. Tel: +63 2 523 8411, fax: +63 2 5217374, URL: http://www.wowphilippines.com.ph

Department of Transportation and Communications, Philcomcen Building, Ortigas Avenue, Pasig 1600, Metro Manila, Philippines. Tel: +63 2 727 1710, fax: +63 2 632 9985, URL: http://www.dotcmain.gov.ph/

Office of the Press Secretary, Malacanang Palace, J.P. Laurel Street, Manila, Philippines. Tel : +63 2 733 3605, fax: +63 2 741 6395, e-mail: opsnews@ops.gov.ph, URL: http://www.ops.gov.ph/

Office of the Head of the National Security Council, NICA Compound, V. Luna Street. Diliman, Quezon City, Philippines. Tel: +63 2 922 7320, fax: +63 2 922 7331, URL: http://www.nsc.gov.ph/

Office of the Chief Presidential Legal Counsel, Malacanang Palace, J.P. Laurel Street, Manila, Philippines. Tel: +63 2 564 1451 to 80, fax: +63 2 742 1641

Political Parties

Liberal Party, Expo Centro, Araneta Center, EDSA Cubao, Quezon City, Philippines. URL: http://www.liberalparty.org.ph/LP12011/Home/Home.html
Leader: Pres. Noynoy Aquino

Lakas-Kabalikat ng Malayang Pilipino, Christian Muslim Democrats, 7th Floor L.T.A. Building 118 Perea St. Legazpi St. Makati City, Philippines. URL: http://www.lakaskampicmd.org.ph
Leader Gloria Macapagal-Arroyo

Nationalist People's Coalition, Pasig City, Philippines. URL: http://www.npcparty.org
Leader: Eduardo Cojuangco Jr.

Nacionalista Party, 2nd Level Starmall, EDSA corner Shaw Boulevard, Mandaluyong City, Philippines. URL: http://www.nacionalistaparty.com
Leader: Manuel Villar, Jr.

Pwersa ng Masang Pilipino, (Force of the Filipino Masses), URL: http://nelson5108.tripod.com
Leader: Joseph Estrada

Laban ng Demokratikong Pilipino, (Fight of Democratic Filipinos), URL: http://www.edangara.com
Leader: Edgardo Angara

Kilusang Bagong Lipunan, New Society Movement, Laoag City, Philippines
Leader: Imelda Marcos

Partido Demokratiko Pilipino-Lakas ng Bayan, Philippine Democratic Party-People's Power, Makati City, Philippines. URL: http://www.pdplaban.org

People's Reform Party, Quezon City, Philippines. URL: http://www.miriam.com.ph

Workers and Peasants Party

Party of the Filipino Masses (PMP)

Elections

After winning the 1998 presidency with the largest majority in Philippines history, Joseph Estrada was forced from power in January 2001 following mass protests and the collapse of an impeachment trial. He was replaced by Gloria Macapagal-Arroyo, the former vice president.

Parliamentary elections and elections for half of the senate (twelve seats) took place in May 2010. LAKAS remained the largest party in parliament but did not gain an overall majority.

The most recent presidential election took place in June 2010 and was won by Benigno Aquino, son of the former president Cory Aquino and the pro-democracy hero Benigno 'Ninoy' Aquino.Mr Aquino took approximately 42 per cent of the vote.

Diplomatic Representation

Embassy of the Philippines, 1600 Massachusetts Avenue NW, Washington, DC 20036, USA. Tel: +1 202 467 9300, fax: +1 202 467 9417, URL: http://www.philippineembassy-usa.org
Ambassador: Jose Cuisia, Jr (page 1411)

Embassy of the Philippines, 9a Palace Green, Kensington, London W8 4QE, United Kingdom. Tel: +44 (0)20 7937 1600, fax: +44 (0)20 7937 2925, e-mail: embassy@philemb.co.uk, URL: http://www.philembassy-uk.org/
Ambassador: Enrique A. Manalo

Embassy of the United States of America, 1201 Roxas Boulevard, Ermita 1000, Manila, Philippines. Tel: +63 2 523 1001, fax: +63 2 522 4361, URL: http://manila.usembassy.gov
Ambassador: Harry Thomas Jr.

British Embassy, 120 Upper McKinley Road, McKinley Hill, Taguig City 1634, Metro Manila, Philippines. Tel: +63 2 858 2200 , fax: +63 2 858 2216 , URL: http://www.ukinthephilippines.fco.gov.uk/en
Ambassador: Stephen Lillie (page 1465)

Permanent Mission to the United Nations, 556 Fifth Avenue, 5th floor, New York, NY 10036, United States. Tel: +1 212 764 1300, fax: +1 212 840 8602, URL: http://www.un.int/philippines/
Permanent Representative and Ambassador: Libran N. Cabutulan

LEGAL SYSTEM

The Constitution vests judicial power in the Supreme Court and its subordinate courts. Members of the Supreme Court, composed of a Chief Justice and 14 Associate Justices, and Judges of Subordinate Courts are appointed by the President. All subordinate courts include an Intermediate Appellate Court, composed of a presiding Appellate Justice and 49 Associate Appellate Justices, who are also appointed by the President of the Philippines.

The Supreme Court has both judicial and administrative functions. Administratively, the Court supervises and controls the judiciary and its employees. The Court's judicial authority is as the last Court of Appeal. The Intermediate Appellate Court functions through ten divisions and may sit solely to exercise administrative, ceremonial or other non-adjudicatory tasks. It has original jurisdiction to issue writs of *mandamus, certiorari, habeas corpus* and *quo warranto*, and has can annul the judgments of Regional Trial Courts.

The 13 Regional Trial Courts handle prescribed civil and criminal cases in their territorial jurisdictions and appellate jurisdiction over all cases decided by Metropolitan Trial Courts, Municipal Trial Courts and Municipal Circuit Trial Courts.

Metropolitan Trial Courts exercise jurisdiction in each metropolitan area, and a Municipal Circuit Trial Court. These lower courts handle civil, criminal and certain special cases.

Special Courts

Sandiganbayan: The present anti-graft court know as Sandiganbayan has jurisdiction over criminal and civil cases involving graft and corruption practices and such other offences committed by public officers and employees, including those in government-owned or controlled corporations.

Tanodbayan: The Office of the Ombudsman, known as Tanodbayan, is an independent body created to investigate complaints regarding public offices and government-owned or controlled corporations, to make appropriate recommendations, and where appropriate, to prosecute criminal, civil or administrative cases.

The rights of the citizen's are not adequately protected. In recent years, there have been cases of extrajudicial killings by the security forces, and cases physical abuse and torture of suspects and detainees. Concerns about judicial corruption and official impunity persist. Arrests are often arbitrary, and pretrial detention and prison conditions are harsh. Trials are often delayed, and procedures are prolonged. Human rights activists are often intimidated by security forces.

The death penalty was abolished in 1987, but then re-introduced in 1993 following a spate of kidnappings in the country. The death penalty was finally re-abolished in 2006. The last execution took place in 2000.

PHILIPPINES

Supreme Court of the Philippines, URL: http://sc.judiciary.gov.ph/
Chief Justice: Maria Lourdes P.A. Sereno

Commission on Human Rights of the Philippines, URL: http://www.chr.gov.ph/

LOCAL GOVERNMENT

There are 15 regions: Ilocos Region, Cagayan Valley, Central Luzon, Calabarzon, Mimaropa, Bicol Region, Western Visayas, Central Visayas, Eastern Visayas, Zamboanga Peninsula, Northern Mindanao, Davao Region, Soccsksargen, Caraga, Autonomous Religion in Muslim Mindanao, and the Cordillera Administrative region.

The country is divided into 80 provinces, each of which is headed by a governor, as well as the national capital region. The provinces are, Abra, Agusan del Norte, Agusan del Sur, Aklan, Albay, Antique, Apayao, Aurora, Basilan, Bataan, Batanes, Batangas, Biliran, Benguet, Bohol, Bukidnon, Bulacan, Cagayan, Camarines Norte, Camarines Sur, Camiguin, Capiz, Catanduanes, Cavite, Cebu, Compostela, Davao del Norte, Davao del Sur, Davao Oriental, Eastern Samar, Guimaras, Ifugao, Ilocos Norte, Ilocos Sur, Iloilo, Isabela, Kalinga, Laguna, Lanao del Norte, Lanao del Sur, La Union, Leyte, Maguindanao, Marinduque, Masbate, Mindoro Occidental, Mindoro Oriental, Misamis Occidental, Misamis Oriental, Mountain Province, Negros Occidental, Negros Oriental, North Cotabato, Northern Samar, Nueva Ecija, Nueva Vizcaya, Palawan, Pampanga, Pangasinan, Quezon, Quirino, Rizal, Romblon, Samar, Sarangani, Siquijor, Sorsogon, South Cotabato, Southern Leyte, Sultan Kudarat, Sulu, Surigao del Norte, Surigao del Sur, Tarlac, Tawi-Tawi, Zambales, Zamboanga del Norte, Zamboanga del Sur, Zamboanga Sibugay. The provinces are further divided into 120 chartered cities, over 1,500 municipalities, and thousands of local units.

A *Sangguniang Pampook* or Regional Council exists in each autonomous region. This local body exercises legislative powers over regional affairs within the framework of national development plans, policies and goals. It is composed of 21 members, 17 of whom are representatives from the different provinces and cities of the region and a sectoral representative each from among the youth, agricultural workers and professionals of the region.

In addition, the President may appoint at least five members whenever some sectors in the region are inadequately represented. The *Lupong Tagapagpaganap ng Pook* or the Regional Executive Council also exists in each autonomous region. It implements, or where appropriate, causes and supervises the implementation of policies, programs and legislation enacted by the *Sangguniang Pampook* when the latter is not in session.

AREA AND POPULATION

Area

The Philippines is an archipelago of 7,107 islands located approximately 500 miles off the southeast coast of Asia. It has a total area of 300,000 sq. km. (115,830 sq. miles), of which 298,170 sq. km is land and 1,830 sq. km is sea. The Philippines ranks fifty-seventh among all other countries of the world in terms of land area. It is also the thirteenth largest of the 35 countries of Asia. Most of the Philippines' population inhabits 11 islands: Luzon, Mindanao, Samar, Negros, Palawan, Panay, Mindoro, Leyte, Cebu, Bohol and Masbate. The three main island groups are Luzon, Visayas and Mindanao. The terrain in two-thirds of the area is mountainous, and one third coastal plains. The climate is tropical with a typhoon season.

In March 2002, an earthquake struck the southern Philippines killing 15 and displacing tens of thousands from their homes. The earthquake, the most powerful since 1990, measured 6.8 on the Richter scale. In November 2004, hundreds were killed when strong storms and a typhoon hit, causing floods and mudslides.

To view a map, consult http://www.lib.utexas.edu/maps/cia08/philippines_sm_2008.gif

Population

Estimated figures for 2011 put the population at 93.26 million with a population density of 307 people per sq km. According to the WHO, the average annual growth rate was 1.9 per cent for the period 2000-10.

The Southern Tagalog region in Luzon remains the most populous area of the country with an estimated population of nearly 12 million. Provinces which make up the region are: Batangas, Cavite, Laguna, Marinduque, Occidental Mindoro, Oriental Mindoro, Palawan, Quezon, Rizal, Romblon and Aurora. The second most populous region is the National Capital Region, with nearly 11 million inhabitants, and includes the city of Metro Manila. The third largest region is Central Luzon, with 9.7 million people. The approximate populations of other regions are: Western Visayas, 6.8 million; Central Visayas, 6.3 million; Bicol, 5.1 million; Ilocos, 405 million; Southern Mindanao, 4.03 million; Northern Mindanao, 3.9 million; Eastern Visayas, 3.9 million.. Cagayan Valley is the least populated region with 3.0 million.

Pangasinan is the largest province with 2.64 million inhabitants, followed by Cebu with 2.43 million people, Balucan with 2.82 million, Negros Occ. with 2.37 million, Cavite with 2.85 million, Laguna with 2.47 million, Batangas with 2.24 million, Rizal with 2.28 million, Quezon with 1.64 million, and Nueva Ecija with 1.85 million.

In terms of ethnic composition, the Philippines is predominantly Christian Malay (91 per cent), with smaller numbers of Muslim Malay (4 per cent), Chinese (1.5 per cent), and others (3.5 per cent).

The official languages of the Philippines are Filipino and English. Filipino is derived from the Malay-Polynesian languages. Many other dialects are spoken regionally. Spanish, no longer an official language, is now spoken only by a tiny minority. English is used for instruction and in government.

Births, Marriages, Deaths

Estimated figures for 2010 put the annual birth rate at 25.1 births per 1,000 population and the death rate at 5.2 deaths per 1,000 population. Life expectancy at birth in 2008 was estimated at 67 for males and 74 for females. Healthy life expectancy was 59 years and 64 years respectively. The median age was 22 years in 2010. Approximately 35 per cent of the population is aged under 15 years and 6 per cent aged over 60 years. The total fertility rate was 3.1 births per female. (Source: http://www.who.int, World Health Statistics 2012)

Public Holidays 2014

1 January: New Year's Day
25 February: People's Power Day
17 April: Maundy Thursday
18 April: Good Friday
20 April: Easter Sunday
9* April: Bataan Day
1 May: Labour Day
12 June: Independence Day
29 July: Eid Ul Fitr*
10 June: Araw ng Maynila (observed Manila only)
10 August: Quezon Day (observed Quezon City only)
25 August: National Heroes' Day
1 November: All Saints' Day
30 November: Bonifacio Day
25 December: Christmas Day
30 December: Rizal Day
31 December: Last Day of the Year
* Islamic holidays depend on the sighting of the moon so dates can vary.

EMPLOYMENT

Estimated figures for 2010 put the labour force at 40,000,000 (up from 35,918,000 in 2007), of whom 92.1 per cent were employed and 7.3 per cent were unemployed, up from 6.3 per cent in 2007.

Figures for October 2009 show that Philippinos working abroad sent home remittances of US$9,973.7 million.

Total Employment by Economic Activity

Occupation	2008
Agriculture, hunting & forestry	10,604,000
Fishing	1,426,000
Mining & quarrying	158,000
Manufacturing	2,926,000
Electricity, gas & water supply	130,000
Construction	1,834,000
Wholesale & retail trade, repairs	6,446,000
Hotels & restaurants	953,000
Transport, storage & communications	2,590,000
Financial intermediation	368,000
Real estate, renting & business activities	953,000
Public admin. & defence; compulsory social security	1,676,000
Education	1,071,000
Health & social work	391,000
Other community, social & personal service activities	833,000
Households with employed persons	1,729,000
Extra-territorial organisations & bodies	2,000
Total	34,089,000

Source: Copyright © International Labour Organization (ILO Dept. of Statistics, http://laborsta.ilo.org)

BANKING AND FINANCE

Currency

One Philippine Peso (Peso, PHP) = 100 centavos

GDP/GNP, Inflation, National Debt

The Philippines has recovered from the 2008 global financial crisis. The government is hoping that recent progress in peace talks will encourage foreign investment. The Philippines economy is heavily dependent on remittances of workers based overseas. The service sector has been particularly strong with a combination of cheaper labour and English speakers and the Philippines has become a popular country for large western businesses to locate their call centres.

In response to the global financial crisis, growth in 2008 fell to 3.8 per cent and 1.1 per cent in 2009. Figures for 2010 show that the economy grew by 7.6 per cent, the largest growth rate for nearly 35 years. The large growth was attributed to optimism for a new government, election related spending and the outsourcing of some industry. Growth for 2011 was predicted to slow to around 3.5 per cent. Remittances sent home by workers overseas continued to make up a large part of the economy, contributing around 10 per cent of GDP in 2010. The Business Process Outsourcing (BPO) industry is the fastest growing sector of the Philippines economy and accounts for around 15 per cent of the global outsourcing market.

GDP and GNP at current market prices in Billion Pesos

Year	GNP	GDP
2001	3,876.6	6,631.5

- continued

2002	4,218,9	3,963.9
2003	4,591.4	4,293.0
2004	6,305.1	5,120.4
2005	7,150.3	5,677.7
2006	7,883.1	6,271.2
2007	8,634.1	6,692.7
2008	9,776.2	7,720.9
2009	10,552.5	8,026.1
2010	11,996.1	9,003.5

Source: Asian Development Bank

GDP at current market prices in Bn. Pesos

Sector	2008	2009	2010
GDP by industrial origin	7,720.9	8,026.1	9,003.5
Agriculture	1,022.5	1,049.9	1,108.7
Mining	95.4	106.4	128.7
Manufacturing	1,760.9	1,706.4	1,930.5
Utilities	262.8	271.9	321.5
Construction	419.4	460.4	551.2
Trade	1,316.1	1,359.5	1,563.8
Transport & communications	548.9	561.1	586.2
Finance	499.9	544.5	622.4
Public admin.	285.9	323.6	372.3
Others	1,509.2	1,642.4	1,817.5
Net factor income from abroad	2,055.3	2,626.3	2,992.6

Source: Asian Development Bank

Inflation was estimated at 4.7 per cent in 2011. Total external debt was estimated at US$71 billion in 2011.

Foreign Investment
Foreign direct investment was estimated at US$1.95 billion in 2009.

Balance of Payments / Imports and Exports
External Trade in Million US$

Year	Exports, fob	Imports, cif	Trade Balance
1990	8,186	13,042	-4,856
1995	17,447	28,488	-11,041
2001	32,150	34,939	-2,789
2002	35,208	41,092	-5,884
2003	36,231	42,576	-6,345
2004	39,681	46,102	-6,422
2005	41,255	49,487	-8,233
2006	47,410	54,078	-6,668
2007	50,466	57,996	-7,530
2008	49,077	62,418	-13,341
2009	38,435	45,877	-7,442
2010	51,432	58,229	-6,797

Source: Asian Development Bank

Principal Exports in Million US$

Commodity	2008	2009*
Electronic products	28,500.8	9,758.7
Articles of apparel & clothing accessories	1,948.7	764.8
Cathodes & sections of cathodes	1,309.2	365.2
Petroleum products	1,240.2	na
Woodcrafts & furniture	1,139.6	461.6
Ignition wiring sets & other wiring sets used in vehicles	901.9	266.2
Coconut oil	1,039.6	201.2
Other products manufactured from materials imported on consignment basis	656.6	309.2
Metal components	577.7	195.4
Bananas (fresh)	397.4	198.2

* Provisional figures
Source: Phillippines National Statistics Office

Principal Imports in Million US$C

Commodity	2008	2009*
Electronic products	20,026.1	7,114.0
Mineral fuels, lubricants & related materials	12,394.8	3,285.0
Transport equipment	2,718.0	1,018.6
Cereals & cereal preparations	2,599.4	1,459.2
Industrial machinery & equipment	2,297.5	776.2
Iron & steel	1,609.8	422.1
Organic & inorganic chemicals	1,258.8	559.0
Plastics in primary & non-primary forms	1,088.9	355.1
Textile yarns, fabric, made-up articles & related products	795.7	300.3
Telecommunication equipment & electrical machinery	895.7	na

*Provisional figures
Source: Phillippines National Statistics Office

The principal countries that the Philippines trade with are the United States, Japan, the Netherlands, Singapore, China and Hong Kong, Singapore, Thailand, Malaysia and the Republic of Korea.

Central Bank
Bangko Sentral ng Pilipinas, A Mabini, Corner Pablo Ocampo Sr Streets, Malate, Manila 1004, Metro Manila, Luzon, Philippines. Tel: +63 2 524 7011 / 51, fax: +63 2 536 0056/5360076, e-mail: bsp@gov.ph, URL: http://www.bsp.gov.ph
Governor: Amando M. Tetangco, Jr.

Chambers of Commerce and Trade Organisations
Philippine Chamber of Commerce and Industry, URL: http://www2.philcham.com/
European Chamber of Commerce of the Philippines, URL: http://www.eccp.com/

MANUFACTURING, MINING AND SERVICES

Primary and Extractive Industries
Natural resources of the country include petroleum, cobalt, silver, gold, nickel, copper and salt. Recent statistics show that, annually, one million troy ounces of gold was mined, 1.6 million troy ounces of silver, 214,000 metric tons of copper, 8,510 tons of nickel, and 466,500 tons of salt.

The mining industry contributed 119.2 billion pesos to the Philippines' GDP in 2009. There are currently 180 mining and quarrying establishments in operation. The mining industry employed 166,000 people in 2009 (up from 108,000 in 2000).

The Philippines production of oil increased in 2003 from an average of 1,000 barrels per day to 25,000 barrels a day; this was due to a new development of deep sea oil reserve drilling in the Malampaya field. Proven oil reserves at the beginning of January 2012 stood at 279 million barrels (down from 289 million barrels at the beginning of January 2001). Consumption in 2011 was 316,000 barrels per day (down from 377,000 barrels per day in 2000). Net imports in 2011 were an estimated 289,000 barrels per day. The Philippines had a crude oil refining capacity of 273,000 barrels per day at the beginning of January 2011. Oil production in 2008 was put at 26,810 barrels per day. Consumption that year was put at 316,000 barrels per day, resulting in net imports of 289,000 barrels per day.

Other areas being developed include the San Isidro well in the East Visayan Basin, north-west Palawan, and the Minduro-Cuyo basin. A number of foreign oil companies are involved in development of sites in the Philippines, including Caltex, Royal-Dutch Shell, the Petroleum Authority of Thailand, and TotalFinaElf. Petron is the largest oil refining company, whilst Shell and Caltex also refine significant quantities. Major oil refineries are Limay, Bataan, Tabangao, and Batangas. The state-owned company with responsibility for oil is the Philippine National Oil Company (PNOC).

Since the oil industry was deregulated in February 1998, long term investments of nearly US$250 million have been pledged and more are expected. Deregulaton has not been received well by all Filipinos, some of whom see it as the cause of the recent rise in world oil prices. However, the Supreme Court recently upheld the deregulation of the oil industry as constitutional.

The Philippines' natural gas industry is to be developed by the government both to reduce oil import expenses and for the generation of electricity. One of the major projects undertaken was the development of the Malampaya field in the South China Sea. The Malampaya offshore field has a 312 mile (504-kilometer) pipeline linking the field to three power plants in Batangas. Proven natural gas reserves stood at 3.0 trillion cubic feet at the beginning of 2011. Production in 2011 was estimated at 102 billion cubic feet and has been used particularly for electricity generation as the government endeavours to lessen the country's dependence on oil.

The largest source of fossil energy in the Philippines is coal. Philippines had coal reserves of 2.2 million short tons in 2003 but used 9.6 million short tons and so relies on imported coal mainly from China, Indonesia and Australia. A number of new mines are likely to begin production in the near future, including the Lalat mine and the Little Baguio mine in Zambouanga de Sur, and the Diplahan mine in Mindanao. Total annual production from these mines is expected to be as much as 716,000 short tons. At present, the Philippines imposes restrictions whereby coal importers must obtain a certificate of compliance before they import coal. Following World Trade Organisation requirements that import restrictions be lifted, the government is considering abandoning the regulation requiring that importers purchase domestic coal when they buy coal from abroad.

Energy
Electricity generation in 2010 was an estimated 6.64 billion kilowatthours (kWh) and consumption was 56.84 billion kWh was consumed. Demand for electric power is predicted to rise at a rate of about nine per cent a year until the end of the decade, requiring a further 10,000 megawatts of electric capacity. The Philippines currently has three major power grids - Luzon, Visayas, and Mindanao - but no unified grid linking its many islands. The government planned to provide electricity to all rural towns by 2008 in addition to linking its three main grids.

Two major electric power companies operate in the Philippines: the state-owned National Power Corporation (Napocor) and Manila Electric Company (Meralco). Legislation was passed through the Philippines Congress to sell off most of Napocor's generating plants. The Power Industry Reform Act, 2001, enabled privatised electricity generating companies to sell to private distribution companies. Napocor's assets earmarked for privatization were put into two state holding companies: the National Transmission Corporation (TransCo), which took on much of the company's transmission assets, and the Power Sector Assets and Liabilities Management (PSALM) Corporation, which assumed control of Napocor's power plants. The government was also required to sell off its equity stake in the Manila Electric Company

PHILIPPINES

(Meralco), the country's largest electricity distribution company. PSALM began selling off Napocor's power generation assets in 2004 and, as at April 2006 had only sold off 16 per cent.

Total energy consumption in the Philippines was estimated at 1.20 quadrillion Btu in 2009. Net generation was 0.451 quadrillion Btu.

Manufacturing

The principal goods produced in the Philippines are pharmaceuticals, textiles, wood products and chemicals. The principal industries are food processing, petroleum refining and electronics assembly. Manufacturing expanded by only 0.3 per cent in 1998 compared to four per cent in 1997. (Source: NEDA). Manufacturing contributed 1,556.7 billion pesos towards GDP in 2009. That year the manufacturing sector employed 2,893,000.

Service Industries

The services industry accounted for 1,533,945 million pesos of GDP at the end of the first three quarters of 2002 and is the largest of the Philippines' economic sectors. Top services sub-sectors at the time were trade (393,257 million pesos), private services (353,262 million pesos), and government services (272,528 million pesos). Recent figures register a slower growth rate for services - 5.6 per cent in recent years compared with 6.5 per cent in the first half of the decade. The only sub-sector to actually experience faster growth was communication, transport and storage. Employment in the services industry was 14.34 million, representing 47.5 per cent of the total Philippines labour force. The top employment sub-sector is wholesale and retail trade, which employed 5.77 million, or 19.1 per cent of the labour force, in April 2002. A growing service sector are call centres, with a large proportion of English speaking workers, the Philippines is an attractive destination for foreign firms looking to staff call centres and for outsourcing. Recent figures show that outsourcing to the Philippines accounts for around 15 per cent of the global outsourcing market.

Figures for 2008 show that 2.9 million foreign visitors arrived in the Philippines, the majority of visitors came from South Korea. The USA and Japan.

Agriculture

Arable farmland accounts for over 40 per cent of land use in the Philippines. Agricultural exports are a significant part of the Philippines' economy. The agriculture sector accounted for 1,138.5 billion pesos in 2009. Employment in agriculture, forestry and fisheries was 11.32 million in 2009, representing over 35 per cent of the total labour force. Principal agricultural products are rice, corn, coconut, sugar-cane and abaca. Approximately 26 per cent of land used is arable land, 11 per cent is used for crop cultivation and the remaining land is either forest and woodland, meadows and pastures or mountainous areas. The Philippines' rain forests are considered among the finest in the world and are one of the country's most valuable assets. The dipterocarp is from the family of trees which produces the main bulk of the country's timber, such as mahogany.

The country's agricultural production was badly hit by the effects of *El Niño* and the 1998 typhoons, Recent figures for food production are shown below:

Main Crop Production in 2010

Crop	Int $1000	Tonnes
Rice, paddy	4,159,474	15,771,700
Indigenous pigmeat	2,478,571	1,612,350
Bananas	2,306,898	9,101,340
Coconuts	1,695,967	15,540,000
Fruit, tropical fresh nes	1,365,618	3,341,600
Indigenous chicken meat	1,059,306	743,682
Sugar cane	950,093	743,682
Vegetables fresh nes	912,469	4,842,200
Pineapples	618,330	2,169,230
Indigenous cattle meat	504,803	186,869
Mangoes, mangosteens, guavas	494,718	825,676
Maize	3222,546	6,376,800

*unofficial figures

Source: http://faostat.fao.org/site/339/default.aspx *Food and Agriculture Organization of the United Nations, Food and Agricultural commodities production*

Fishing

Estimated figures from FAO put the total catch in 2010 at 2,612,000 tonnes.

COMMUNICATIONS AND TRANSPORT

Travel Requirements

Citizens of the USA, Canada, Australia and most of the EU require a passport valid for six months beyond the length of stay and return/onward tickets but do not need a visa for stays of up to 21 days. Estonian, Latvian, Lithuanian and Slovenian subjects do require a visa. Transit passengers continuing their journey to a third country within 72 hours and holding onward/return documentation do not require a visa. All visitors who intend to stay longer than 21 days need a visa. Other nationals should contact the embassy to check visa requirements.

National Airlines

The Bureau of Air Transportation is in charge of the technical and operational side of aviation, establishing policies, rules and regulations for the efficient operation and control of civil aviation in the Philippines

Bureau of Air Transportation, Manila International Airport, Pasay City, Metrol Manila, Philippines

Air Philippines, URL: http://www.airphils.com/

Services operated: Passenger charter flights to Dubai, Hong Kong, Iraq, Japan, Jordan, Malaysia, Qatar, and Singapore

Philippine Air Lines (PAL), URL: http://www.philipppineair.com

Services operated: Domestic and international services to Australia, Bahrain, The People's Republic of China, France, The Federal Republic of Germany, Greece, Hawaii, Hong Kong, Indonesia, Italy, Japan, Republic of Korea, Malaysia, The Netherlands, Pakistan, Papua New Guinea, Singapore, Switzerland, Taiwan, Thailand, United Kingdom, United States of America

Cebu Pacific Air, URL: http://www.cpacific.com.ph

Pacific East Asia Cargo Airlines, URL: http://www.peacairlines.com/

International Airports

There are 170 airports and airfields in the Philippines. In addition to the international airports at Manila and Mactan (Cebu), there are four alternative international airports: Laoag City, Ilocos Norte; Davao City; Puerto Princesa City; and Zamboanga City.

Railways

The Philippine National Railways and the Philippine Railway Company run the railway systems in the country with a railway network covering some 890 km. Considering the low fuel consumption of railway transportation and its importance in giving steady transport of commodities, expansion and improvement of the existing facilities are among the government priority programmes. The biggest project that has been undertaken by the PNR is the complete replacement of the existing 377.5 km Manila-Naga line with new and heavier tracks. Under the railway rehabilitation programme, the PNR also purchased 30 coaches worth USD4.74 million as part of the trade agreement between Romania and the Philippines.

The Metro Manila Commuter Service provides a commuter train service with 80 train-trips carrying some 30,000 passengers daily. The MMRC covers the existing lines from Angeles City in Pampanga in the north and covers a distance of 78 kilometres to College, Laguna in the south (67 km), extending towards the east up to Hulo and Guadalupe (13 km), and to Carmona, Cavite with 40 km.

Roads

Land transportation in the Philippines is entrusted to the Bureau of Land Transportation which among other things handles the administration and enforcement of laws connected with the registration and operation of motor vehicles and the licensing of owners, dealers, conductors, drivers and similar matters. The total length of roads in the country was 200,000km in 2003. Vehicles are driven on the right.

Shipping

Water transport has always been the most economical means of transporting people and goods in the country and it accounts for about 85 per cent of the total traffic volume with approximately 550 ships in total. Consequently, inter-island shipping constitutes a major instrument of national development. For this reason, the development of shipping ports has been an essential component of the long-term infrastructure programme and commands a priority in the government's five-year Development Plan. Figures for 2008 show that 145.90 million metric tonnes of freight was carried by ships.

Ports and Harbours

There are 23 ports in the country, the busiest being Manila NH, Manila SH, MICT and Cebu.

HEALTH

In 2009, the government spent approximately 7.1 per cent of its total budget on healthcare, accounting for 35.1 per cent of all healthcare spending. Total expenditure on healthcare equated to 3.6 per cent of the country's GDP. Per capita expenditure on health was approximately US$66, compared with US$33 in 2000. Figures for 2000-10 show that there are 93,862 physicians (11.5 per 10,000 population), 488,434 nurses and midwives (60 per 10,000 population) and 45,903 dentists. There are 5 hospital beds per 10,000 population.

According to the latest WHO figures, in 2010 approximately 92 per cent of the population had access to improved drinking water. In the same year, 74 per cent of the population had access to improved sanitation.

The infant mortality rate (probability of dying by age 1) in 2010 was 23 per 1,000 live births. The child mortality rate (under 5 years) was 29 per 1,000 live births. In the period 2005-11, 32.3 per cent of children aged less than five years were classified as stunted and 20.7 per cent were classified as underweight. The most common causes of death in children aged less than five years were: pneumonia 23 per cent, prematurity 19 per cent, birth asphyxia 7 per cent and diarrhoea 6 per cent. (Source: http://www.who.int, World Health Statistics 2012)

EDUCATION

Primary and Secondary Education

The Philippines public primary education system was first established at the beginning of the American occupation in 1898. At present, education in the Philippines is compulsory for children aged between seven and 12 and is run by the government or by private persons or corporations. Education is not free. Public elementary schools are established in almost every barangay in the country. The number of years necessary to complete the elementary and secondary levels are six and four years respectively, whilst at tertiary level at least four years are necessary to complete an academic degree. In general, children from seven to 12 attend elementary schools, 13 to 16 year-olds attend secondary level schools, and 17 year-olds and upwards, tertiary level institutions. In 2004, the Department of Education announced that instruction in the Arabic language and Islamic Values would be available to Muslim students in state schools.

Recent statistics put the number of primary schools at 37,650, the number of primary students at 11.90 million, and the number of teachers at 341,190. Secondary schools number 5,900, secondary pupils number 4.88 million, and secondary teachers number 154,700. The number of students in higher education was recorded at 2.01 million, whilst the number of lecturers was 66,880.

Figures from UNESCO for 2007 show that 92 per cent of girls and 90 per cent of boys were enrolled in primary school and 67 per cent of girls and 56 per cent of boys were enrolled in secondary school. In 2005 15.2 per cent of total government expenditure went on education, 54 per cent of which went on primary education and 29 per cent on secondary education.

The English language is spoken and understood by at least 83 per cent of the population. All officials and employees in the Government, as well as a great number of business people, speak or understand English. Although Filipino is taught in schools English is still the major language of instruction. The current literacy rate is nearly 94 per cent.

Higher Education
Over one million students attend universities and colleges in the Philippines. Major universities include: the University of the Philippines, Quezon City; Adamson University, Manila; University of the East, Manila; Far Eastern University, Manila; Feati University, Manila; University of Santo Tomas, Manila; Bicol University, Legaspi; and the University of Mindanao, Davao.

RELIGION

There are three principal religions: Roman Catholicism, which embraces about 84.9 per cent of the population; Protestantism, which accounts for 10 per cent; and Islam, 4 per cent. In 1902 the Philippine Independent Church was established by Mons. Gregorio Aglipay, a Filipino priest who seceded from the Roman Catholic Church. The new religion retains most of the beliefs and rituals of the Catholic Church. His followers are estimated to be more than 1,500,000 and are scattered throughout the country.

Protestantism came with the American occupation, and its adherents are spread throughout the islands. The Muslims, numbering some 500,000, mainly inhabit the Sulu Islands and parts of the coastal regions in Mindanao, the second largest island in the Philippines.

The Philippines has a religious liberty rating of 8 on a scale of 1 to 10 (10 is most freedom). (Source: World Religion Database)

COMMUNICATIONS AND MEDIA

The 1987 constitution guarantees press freedom. However, there are reports of threats and attacks against some media workers in some regions.

Newspapers
The Philippines has over 25 daily newspapers, including the Manila Bulletin, the Daily Inquirer, and the Manila Times, most of which are published in Manila. A large number of newspapers appear in both English and Filipino.

Manila Bulletin, URL: http://www.mb.com.ph
Philippine Star, URL: http://www.philstar.com/philstar/index20070301.htm
Philippine Daily Inquirer, URL: http://www.inq7.net
Manila Times, URL: http://www.manilatimes.net

Broadcasting
The Philippines' broadcasting system includes over nine million television receivers and nine million radio receivers. The most popular free networks are ABS-CBN and GMA. There is a well-developed cable TV system.
ABS-CBN, URL: http://www.abs-cbnnews.com/
GMA, URL: http://www.gmanews.tv/index.html
Philippine Broadcasting Service, URL: http://www.pbs.gov.ph/ (government-run)

Telecommunications
The Philippine Long Distance Telephone Company has been providing a telecommunications service since 1905. Today, the company is the largest of many companies providing telephone services in the Philippines. The PLDT serves as the principal supplier of long distance telephone services in the country. There are an estimated 6.8 million telephones in the country and more than 92 million mobile phones in use.

Recent figures show that over 8.2 million people in the Philippines have access to the internet.

ENVIRONMENT

The main threats to the environment of the Philippines are deforestation, soil erosion, and industrial air and water pollution in Manila. The deforestation rate was 2.1 per cent in the years 2001-07.

Energy related carbon emissions were estimated at 19.55 million metric tons in 2000, representing 0.3 per cent of world carbon emissions. Per capita carbon emissions in the same year were an estimated 0.3 metric tons, compared with 5.6 metric tons in the US. Industry contributes most carbon emissions (55.0 per cent in 1998), followed by the transport (22.2 per cent), residential (16.1 per cent), and commercial (6.7 per cent) sectors. According to the ADB, nitrous oxide emissions were put at 18,940 thousand metric tons CO^2 equivalent. Methane emissions were estimated at 44,860 thousand metric tons CO^2 equivalent. Consumption of ozone-depleting CFCs were 143 (OPD metric tons). Figures for 2010 show that carbon dioxide emissions amounted to 85.63 million metric tons.

The Philippines is a party to the following international environmental agreements: Biodiversity, Climate Change, Climate Change-Kyoto Protocol, Desertification, Endangered Species, Hazardous Wastes, Law of the Sea, Marine Dumping, Ozone Layer Protection, Ship Pollution, Tropical Timber 83, Tropical Timber 94, Wetlands, and Whaling . It has signed, but not ratified, the treaty on Air Pollution-Persistent Organic Pollutants.

POLAND
Republic of Poland
Rzeczpospolita Polska

Capital: Warsaw (Population estimate, 2011: 1.714 million)

Head of State: Bronislaw Komorowski (President) (page 1458)

National Flag: Divided fesswise, white and red.

CONSTITUTION AND GOVERNMENT

Constitution
Following the second world war Poland became a Communist People's Republic. In 1980 following demonstrations and strikes at the Gdansk shipyard, there emerged a trade union called Solidarity, led by Lech Walesa. Martial law was imposed in 1981 and lifted in 1983, by 1989 Solidarity had evolved to be a political force and took part in talks with the church and the Communists which led to partially free elections being held. Solidarity did well and formed part of the coalition government. The following year Lech Walesa was elected president. In 1992 Soviet troops began their withdrawal from Poland.

The present Constitution was adopted by the National Assembly on 16 January 1997, approved by referendum on 25 May 1997, and came into effect on 16 October 1997. The head of state is the President who is directly elected by universal adult suffrage for a five-year term, renewable once. The Sejm (lower chamber of parliament) appoints the Council of Ministers (cabinet). The Prime Minister is the Chairman of the Council of Ministers and is appointed by the Sejm following a presidential motion.

To consult the constitution, please visit:
http://www.sejm.gov.pl/prawo/konst/angielski/kon1.htm

International Relations
In 1999 Poland joined NATO and became a member of the European Union on May 1 2004.

Recent Events
In March 1999 Poland was one of the first three eastern European countries to be admitted to NATO. However, the new armies in the Czech Republic, Hungary and Poland are under-funded and badly equipped.

Poland was one of five countries (Poland, Germany, Czech Republic, Slovakia and Hungary) that met in Gniezno, the ancient Polish capital, on 28 April 2000, to sign 'The Gniezno Declaration' in favour of building a united Europe against nationalism, xenophobia and totalitarian ideologies.

Towards the end of April 2000, the Polish Government adopted the National Programme of Preparation to EU Membership for 2000-02. In June 2003 Poland held a referendum on the question of joining the EU. 59 per cent of the electorate turned out and over 77 per cent of them voted yes. Poland became a member of the EU on 1 May 2004.

In April 2007 charges were brought against the former communist leader General Jaruzelski over his role in the introduction of martial law in 1981 following the creation of the union Solidarity at the Gdansk shipyard. Solidarity leaders, including Lech Walesa, were imprisoned under the law. His trial finally started in September 2008.

In February 2008, the government agreed in principle to allow the siting of a US missile defence system on Polish territory; the system itself and its siting have been controversial.

On April 10 2010 a plane crashed in heavy fog coming into land at the Russian city of Smolensk. All 96 people on board were killed and amongst the dead were the Polish president Lech Kaczynski and his wife; Chief of the National Security Office, Aleksander Szczyglo; Governor of the National Bank of Poland, Slawomir Skrzypek; Deputy speaker of the parliament, Jerzy Szmajdzinski; Chief of the General Staff, General Franciszek Gagor; former President in-Exile, Ryszard Kaczorowski; Deputy Head of the Law and Justice Party, Przemyslaw Gosiewski; Deputy Foreign Minister, Andrzej Kremer; Deputy Minister of National Defence, Stanislaw Komorowski; Head of the Air Force, Andrzej Blasik; Head of the Navy, Andrzej Karweta; Commander of the Land Forces, Tadeusz Bukhead; Anna Walentynowicz, a trade union activist at the Gdansk shipyard whose dismissal in 1980 sparked the strike that led to the creation of the Solidarity movement and several MPs and historians. The delegation was

POLAND

flying to Russia to attend events marking the 70th anniversary of the Katyn massacre of thousands of Poles by Soviet secret police during WWII. The Russian Aviation Authority later blamed the crash on pilot error.

A presidential election was held on 20 June 2010. The first round of voting was inconclusive and the second round took place on 4 July. Acting president Bronislaw Komorowski (page 1458) won the election with 53 per cent of the vote, ahead of Lech Kaczynski's twin brother Jaroslaw.

The Minister of Defence, Bogdan Kilch, resigned in July 2011 following the report into the Smolensk air crash in 2010.

In December 2010, Nigerian-born John Abraham Godson became the first black member of the Polish parliament.

In July 2011, Poland took over the rotating presidency of the EU for first time.

Parliamentary elections took place in October 2011 and were won by the prime minister's Civic Platform party.

In January 2012, the former interior minister, Czeslaw Kiszczak, was sentenced in absentia for his role in the 1981 martial law crackdown. He received a two-year suspended prison sentence. The communist party leader at the time, Stanislaw Kania, was acquitted.

Legislature
Poland's bicameral legislature, the National Assembly (*Zgromadzenie Narodowe*), consists of the upper chamber, or Senate (*Senat*), and the lower chamber, or Diet (*Sejm*).

Upper House
The Constitution provides that the Senate be made up of 100 senators elected in *voivodships* (districts), two from each *voivodship* and three from the Warsaw and Katowice *voivodships*. Its term is four years, exactly as long as the Sejm term. Earlier dissolution of the Sejm is tantamount to the dissolution of the Senate.

The Senate reviews the laws adopted by the Sejm; it may proffer its comments and proposals to these laws or even propose their rejection in full. The Senate can be overridden by the Sejm by a qualified majority of two-thirds. It also reviews drafts of national socio-economic plans, annual budget and financial plans of the state. It has the right of legislative initiative. The Senate's prerogatives also include consent (in addition to the Sejm) to prolongation of a state of emergency and consent to appointment of a Civil Rights Ombudsman by the Sejm.

Senate of the Republic of Poland, ul. Wiejska 4/6, 00-902 Warsaw, Poland. Tel: +48 22 694 2410, fax: +48 22 694 2224, e-mail: senat@nw.senat.gov.pl, URL: http://www.senat.gov.pl/
Speaker: Longin Hieronim Pastusiak

Lower House
As specified in the Constitution, the Sejm is made up of 460 deputies elected by proportional representation for a four-year term. There is a 5 per cent threshold for parties and 8 per cent for coalitions, but seats are reserved for representatives of ethnic minorities even if their vote falls below 5 per cent. Sixty-nine of the Sejm seats are awarded from the national lists of parties polling more than 7 per cent of the vote. The Sejm elects the Council of State and the Council of Ministers.

The Sejm term may be cut short when it dissolves itself by its own resolution. It may also be dissolved by the President (after consulting with the Speaker of the Sejm and the Speaker of the Senate) in situations specifically outlined in the Constitution: if for three months it fails to appoint a government or adopt the national socio-economic plan or the annual budget; or if it adopts a law or resolution preventing the President from executing his constitutional prerogatives concerned with the sovereignty and security of the state, its territorial integrity, observance of alliance obligations or observance of the Constitution.

The main prerogatives of the Sejm are the adoption of laws; the adoption of national socio-economic plans and financial plans of the state as well as annual budgets, and further granting annual exoneration to the Government; appointing and recalling the Chairman of the Council of Ministers (at the motion of the President); appointing and recalling the Cabinet or its individual members; appointing the Civil Rights Ombudsman (with consent of the Senate); adopting a resolution concerning a state of war in case of an armed assault on Poland or when international agreements dictate common defence against aggression, and appointment of the Commander-in-Chief of the armed forces for the time of war; expressing consent for prolongation (at most for three months) of any state of emergency imposed by the President.

Sejm of the Republic of Poland, ul. Wiejska 4/6/8, 00-902 Warsaw, Poland. Tel: +48 22 694 2500, fax: +48 22 694 2215, URL: http://www.sejm.gov.pl

Cabinet (as at July 2013)
Prime Minister: Donald Tusk (page 1528)
Deputy Prime Minister, Minister of the Economy: Janusz Piechochinski
Deputy Prime Minister, Minister of Finance: Jan Vincent-Rostowski (page 1532)
Minister of Foreign Affairs: Radoslaw Sikorski (page 1514)
Minister of Health: Bartosz Arlukowicz
Minister of Regional Development: Elzbieta Bienkowska (page 1388)
Minister of Administration and Digitization: Michal Boni
Minister of the Treasury: Wlodzimierz Karpinski
Minister of the Interior and Control of Special and Intelligence Services: Barlomiej Sienkiewicz Cichocki
Minister of Justice: Marek Biernacki
Minister of the Environment: Marcin Korolec
Minister of Transport, Construction & Maritime Economy: Slawomir Nowak

Minister of Labour and Social Policy: Wladyslaw Kosiniak-Kamysz
Minister of Higher Education and Science: Barbara Kudrycka (page 1459)
Minister of Agriculture and Rural Development: Stanislaw Kalemba
Minister of National Defence: Tomasz Siemoniak
Minister of National Education: Krystyna Szumilas
Minister of Culture and National Heritage: Bogdan Zdrojewski (page 1543)
Minister of Tourism and Sport: Johanna Mucha
Head of the Chancellery of the Prime Minister and Chief of Permanent Committee of the Council of Ministers: Jacek Cichocki
Minister of Health: Bartosz Arlukowicz

Ministries
Chancellery of the President, ul. Wiejska 10, 00-902 Warsaw, Poland. Tel: +48 22 695 2900, URL: http://www.prezydent.pl/dflt/index.php3
Office of the Prime Minister, Aleje Ujazdowskie 1/3, 00-583 Warsaw, Poland. Tel: +48 22 841 3832 / 694 69 83, fax: +48 22 625 28 72 / 694 7265. e-mail: cirinfo@kprm.gov.pl, URL: http://www.kprm.gov.pl
Ministry of Agriculture and Rural Development, ul. Wspólna 30, 00-930 Warsaw, Poland. Tel: +48 22 623 1000, fax: +48 22 623 2750, e-mail: Rzecznik.Prasowy@minrol.gov.pl, URL: http://www.minrol.gov.pl
Ministry of Culture and National Heritage, ul. Krakowskie Przedmiescie 15/17, 00-071 Warsaw, Poland. Tel: +48 22 620 0231, fax: +48 22 826 7533, e-mail: rzecznik@mk.gov.pl, URL: http://www.mkidn.gov.pl
Ministry of Defence, ul. Klonowa 1, 00-909 Warsaw, Poland. Tel: +48 22 845 0441, fax: +48 22 645 5378, e-mail: bpmon@mon.wp.mil.pl, URL: http://www.wp.mil.pl/pl/index
Ministry of Economy, pl. Trzech Krzyzy 5, 00-507 Warsaw, Poland. Tel: +48 22 693 5000, URL: http://web.mg.gov.pl/portalout
Ministry of Education and Sport, Aleja J.Ch. Szucha 25, 00-918 Warsaw, Poland. Tel: +48 22 628 0461 / 629 7241, fax: +48 22 628 8561, e-mail: minister@menis.gov.pl, URL: http://www.men.waw.pl
Ministry of the Environmental Protection, Natural Resources and Forestry, ul. Wawelska 52-54, 00-922 Warsaw, Poland. Tel: +48 22 285 0001-9, fax: +48 22 253355, e-mail: comments@mos.gov.pl, URL: http://www.mos.gov.pl
Ministry of Finance, ul. Swietokrzyska 12, 00-916 Warsaw, Poland. Tel: +48 22 694 5555, fax: +48 22 826 5561, e-mail: info@mofnet.gov.pl, URL: http://www.mf.gov.pl
Ministry of Foreign Affairs, Aleja J.Ch. Szucha 25, 00-580 Warsaw, Poland. Tel: +48 22 623 9000, fax: +48 22 629 0287, URL: http://www.mfa.gov.pl
Ministry of Health, ul. Miodawa 15, 00-952 Warsaw, Poland. Tel: +48 22 634 9600, fax: +48 22 831 1212, e-mail: mzios001@medianet.com.pl, URL: http://www.mzios.gov.pl
Ministry of Interior and Administration, ul. Stefana Batorego 5, 02-591 Warsaw, Poland. Tel: +48 22 621 0251, fax: +48 22 849 7494, URL: http://www.mswia.gov.pl/index_s.html
Ministry of Justice, Al. Ujazdowskie 11, 00-950 Warsaw, Poland. Tel: +48 22 521 2888, fax: +48 22 621 5540, e-mail: nagorska@ms.gov.pl, URL: http://www.ms.gov.pl
Ministry of Labour and Social Policy, ul. Nowogrodzka 1/3/5, 00-513 Warsaw, Poland. Tel: +48 22 661 0100, fax: +48 22 621 4942, e-mail: BPI@mpips.gov.pl, URL: http://www.mpips.gov.pl
Ministry of Post and Telecommunications, Plac Malachowskiego 2, 00-940 Warsaw, Poland. Tel: +48 22 656 5000, fax: +48 22 2826 4840, URL: http://www.ml.gov.pl
Ministry of Transport and Maritime Economy, ul. T. Chalubinskiego 4/6, 00-928 Warsaw, Poland. Tel: +48 22 628 4000, URL: http://www.mtigm.gov.pl
Ministry of the Treasury, ul. Krucza 36, 00-522 Warsaw, Poland. Tel: +48 22 695 8000, fax: +48 22 628 4840, e-mail: minister@mst.gov.pl, URL: http://www.mst.gov.pl
Office of the Committee for European Integration, Al. Ujazdowskie 9, 00-918 Warsaw. Tel: +48 022 455 53 37, fax: +48 022 455 53 40, e-mail: info@mail.ukie.gov.pl, URL: http://www.ukie.gov.pl/index.html

Main Political Parties
Civic Platform (PO), URL: http://www.platforma.org
Leader: Donald Tusk
Law & Justice (PiS), URL: http://www.pis.org.pl
Leader: Jarosław Kaczyński
Polish People's Party (PSL), URL: http://www.psl.pl
Leader: Waldemar Pawlak
Union of Labour (UP), URL: http://www.uniapracy.org.pl
Leader: Waldemar Witkowski
Democratic Left Alliance (SLD), URL: http://www.sld.org.pl
Leader: Leszek Miller
Poland Comes First (PJN), URL: http://www.stronapjn.pl
Leader: Pawel Kowal
Social Democracy of Poland, URL: http://www.sdpl.pl
Leader: Leszek Miller
Palikot's Movement, URL: http://www.ruchpalikota.org.pl
Leader: Janusz Palikot

Elections
A presidential election took place on the 9 and 23 of October 2005 when Lech Kaczynski of the Law and Justice Party won. He took office in December 2005. The next presidential election was due in October 2010, but following the death of President Lech Kaczynski in a plane crash, elections had to be held on or before June 20 2010. The first round of voting was inconclusive and a second round was scheduled for 4 July. Acting president Bronislaw Komorowski (page 1458) won the election with 53 per cent of the vote, ahead of Lech Kaczynski's twin brother Jaroslaw.

Following the legislative elections in September 2005, Jaroslaw Kaczynski, the leader of the Law and Justice Party, announced that he would not take up the post of prime minister if his twin brother Lech Kaczynski, won the presidential election. Lech Kaczynski won the election and Kazimierz Marcinkiewicz became prime minister. However, following the resignation of Mr Marcinkiewicz in July 2006, Jaroslaw Kaczynski offered the position of prime minister to his brother, who accepted it. The governing coalition led by Prime Minister

Kacsynski collapsed in August 2007 leading to an early election in October. The elections were won by the centre-right Civic Platform; coalition talks began with the Peasants Party. Donald Tusk, leader of the Civic Platform, became prime minister. The most recent parliamentary elections were held in October 2011, Prime Minister Donald Tusk's Civic Platform won the election.

General Election Results 2011

Party	Seats
Civic Platform	207
Law and Justice	157
Palikot's Movement	40
Polish Peasant's Party	28
Democratic Left Alliance	27
German Minority	1

Diplomatic Representation

Embassy of Poland, 47 Portland Place, London W1B 1JH, United Kingdom. Tel: +44 0870 774 2700, fax: +44 (0)20 7323 4018, e-mail: london@msz.gov.pl, URL: http://london.polemb.net/
Ambassador: Witold Sobkow (page 1517)
Embassy of Poland, 2640 16th Street, NW, Washington, DC 20009, USA. Tel: +1 202 234 3800, fax: +1 202 328 6271, e-mail, washington.info@msz.gov.pl, URL: http://www.polandembassy.org
Ambassador: Ryszard Schnepf
British Embassy, Aleje Roz No 1, 00-556 Warsaw, Poland. Tel: +48 22 628 1001, fax: +48 22 621 7161, e-mail: britemb@it.com.pl, URL: http://ukinpoland.fco.gov.uk/en/
Ambassador: Robin Barnett (page 1383)
US Embassy, Aleje Ujazdowskie 29/31, 00-540 Warsaw, Poland. Tel: +48 22 628 3041, fax: +48 22 628 8298, URL: http://poland.usembassy.gov/
Ambassador: Stephen Mull
Permanent Representative of the Republic of Poland to the United Nations, 9 East 66th Street, New York, NY 10021, USA. Tel: +1 212 744 2506, fax: +1 212 517 6771, URL: http://nowyjorkonz.msz.gov.pl/en
Ambassador: H.E. Ryszard Sarkowicz

LEGAL SYSTEM

The law of Poland is enshrined in the Constitution, and is based on the Civil Code of Poland. This derives from a mix of Continental (Napoleonic) civil law and holdover Communist legal theory. Court decisions can be appealed to the European Court of Justice, and Poland accepts compulsory ICJ jurisdiction with reservations.

The court system consists of a Constitutional Tribunal, a Tribunal of State, a Supreme Court, a Supreme Administrative Court, General Courts and Court Martials. The Constitutional Tribunal rules on the constitutionality of laws and normative acts issued by the top and central state administration agencies. The State Tribunal is empowered to pass judgment on the guilt or innocence of the highest office holders accused of violating the constitution and laws. The 27 judges in the State Tribunal are independent and bound only by the law. The chairperson of the State Tribunal is the president of the Supreme Court. The Supreme Court reviews the decisions of all lower courts, hears appeals and adopts legal interpretations and clarifications. The court is organized into four chambers: criminal, civil, labor and social insurance, and military.

Judges for higher courts are appointed by the President of the Republic from candidates proposed by the National Council of the Judiciary. Judges have life tenure. The 24 member National Judicial Council oversees the judiciary, establishes professional standards and recommends judgeship candidates to the president

The government respects the rights of its citizens. However, excessive use of force by the police can be a problem. The prisons are overcrowded, and an inefficient judiciary often leads to lengthy pretrial detentions. Corruption is widespread. In 1995 the death penalty was suspended for five years; it had not been applied since 1988. A new penal code abolishing the death penalty was adopted in June 1997.

The Supreme Court, URL: http://www.sn.pl
First President: Stansilaw Dabrowski
Human Rights Defender of the Republic of Poland, URL: http://www.brpo.gov.pl/index.php?s=3

LOCAL GOVERNMENT

The network of 49 centrally administered regions in place in the Communist era has now been replaced with 16 self-governing provinces (*voivodships*) and three city governments (Warsaw, Kraków and Llódz) as of 1 January 1999. These are divided into 308 municipalities (*powiat*) and 65 cities with *powiat* status, and sub-divided into 2,489 communes (*gmina*).

Local government is carried out by councils elected every fours years at every level. Communities of fewer than 40,000 inhabitants elect councils on a first-past-the-post basis, whilst larger communities have a proportional party list system. The most recent local government elections took place in 2010.

Population of *voivodships*

Voivodship	Area (sq. km.)	Population, Dec. 2010
Dolnoslaskie	19,948	2,887,840
Kujawsko-Pomorskie	17,970	2,069,543

- continued		
Lubelskie	25,115	2,151,895
Lubuskie	13,984	1,011,024
Łódzkie	18,219	2,534,357
Mallopolskie	15,144	3,310,094
Mazowieckie	35,597	5,242,911
Opolskie	9,412	1,028,585
Podkarpackie	17,926	2,103,505
Podlaskie	20,180	1,188,329
Pomorskie	18,293	2,240,319
Slaskie	12,294	4,635,882
Swietokrzyskie	11,672	1,266,014
Warminsko-Mazurskie	29,826	1,427,241
Wielkoposkie	29,825	3,419,426
Zachodniopomorskie	22,902	1,693,072

Source: Polish Official Statistics

This system recreates the pre-Second World War local government structure and emphasises regional economic development. Each *voivodship* is headed by a locally-elected leader rather than a centrally appointed one as before. *Voivodships* are responsible for region-wide services such as higher education, specialised medical services, ambulances and road networks, as well as cultural activities.

Local government is financed partly by local taxes and partly by central government taxes. The proportion of public money being administered at a local level has increased by about 25 per cent to 40 per cent. The majority of this, however, is spent on essential services such as education where provisions are set nationally.

AREA AND POPULATION

Area
Poland lies in central Europe. It borders Lithuania, Belarus and the Ukraine to the east, the Czech Republic and Slovakia to the south, Germany to the west, and the Russian enclave of Kaliningrad and the Baltic Sea to the north. It has an area of 312,683 sq. km. making it the largest country in Central Europe. The main rivers of Poland are the Vistula and the Bug. Most of the land is less than 200 metres above seas level and is fertile, often used for arable farming, but in the south the Tatra and Carpathian mountain regions rise to a peak of 2,499 metres.

Poland experiences hot summers and cold winters, with average July temperatures in Warsaw at 18°C and average January temperatures at -4°C. In the mountainous regions of the south, home to the Tatra and Carpathian mountain ranges temperatures can fall as low as -15°C. Annual rainfall in Warsaw is in the region of 550 mm.

To view a map, consult http://www.un.org/Depts/Cartographic/map/profile/poland.pdf

Population
Poland is Europe's eighth most populous country. According to WHO estimated figures, the population was 38,277 million in 2010, with an average annual growth rate of 0.0 per cent over the period 2000-10. That year, approximately 61 per cent of the population lived in urban areas. An estimated 15 per cent of the population is under 15 years and 19 per cent over 60 years old. The median age is 38.
The official language is Polish.

Births, Marriages and Deaths
According to figures from the WHO, the total fertility rate was 1.4 children per female. The crude birth rate was 10.6 per 1,000 population and the crude death rate was 10.2 per 1,000 population. Average life expectancy in 2009 was 72 years and 80 years for females. Healthy life expectancy was 64 years for males and 70 years for females. (Source: http://www.who.int, World Health Statistics 2012)

National Holidays 2014
1 January: New Year's Day
21 April: Easter Monday
1 March May Day
3 May: Constitution Day (Passage of 3 May Constitution in 1791)
19 June: Corpus Christi
15 August: Assumption Day
1 November: All Saints Day
11 November: Independence Day
25-26 December: Christmas
Holidays that fall on a Saturday or Sunday are not observed on the following Monday

EMPLOYMENT

Employment by Economic Activity

Sector	2010
Agricultre, hunting, forestry & fishing	2,128,800
Mining & quarrying	172,700
Manufacturing	2,465,300
Electricity, gas, steam air conditioning supply	159,100
Water supply & waste management	140,300
Construction	904,700
Wholesale & retail trade & repairs	2,219,800
Hotels & restaurants	260,500
Transport & storage	696,000
Information & communication	242,800

POLAND

- continued

Finance & insurance	336,700
Real estate, renting & business activities	197,100
Professional, scientific & technical activities	506,300
Admin. & support service activities	416,500
Public admin. & defence, compulsory social security	970,100
Education	1,081,500
Health & social work	764,100
Arts, enertainment & recreation	149,600
Other service activities	209,000
Households with employed persons	19,000

Source: Polish Official Statistics

Poland's unemployment rate was just 6.5 per cent in 1990 but rose to 15.1 per cent in 2000, 17.4 per cent in 2001 and 18.1 per cent in 2002. It reached a high of 20.6 per cent in March 2003 before falling gradually to 18.7 per cent in November 2004. It fell to 17.7 per cent in 2005 and 13.8 per cent in 2006. By August 2008 the unemployment rate had fallen to 9.3 per cent. The government has pledged to cut unemployment. It has been estimated that nearly two million people left Poland between May 1, 2004 and the end of 2006 to work in other EU countries, mainly the UK, but many have since returned.

Figures from the Polish Official Statistics Office show that the number of people registered unemployed in December 2009 was 1,892,700 (926,300 men and 966,400 women). This figure rose in December 2010 to 1,954,700 unemployed (939,900 men and 1,014,800 women). The unemployment rate was estimated at 14.3 per cent in March 2013.

Trade Unions

In 1980, under the leadership of President Lech Walesa, Solidarity (URL: http://www.solidarnosc.org.pl/) was an engine of political reform. Dissolved in 1982, it was re-legalised in 1989 and successfully contested the parliamentary elections but was defeated in 1993. It had 2.3 million members in 1991; it currently represents some 722,000 people. The official union of the 1980s, OPZZ (URL: http://opzz.org.pl/), had 5 million members in 1990. There were also about 4,000 small unions not affiliated to it. At present it has 3 million members, and there are about 340 registered nation-wide unions. As 22 per cent of members of parliament belong to the two leading unions, they constitute a significant political power.

BANKING AND FINANCE

Currency
1 zloty (PLZ) = 100 groszy
(10,000 old zloty replaced with 1 new zloty on 1 January 1995). In 1998, in anticipation of joining the European Union, Poland announced that the euro would be the main reference for the exchange rate of the zloty.

GDP/GNP, Inflation, National Debt
Poland's economic policies since the latter half of the 1990s reflect the country's aim to join the European Union; membership negotiations began in July 1997 and an Accession Partnership was adopted in March 1998. In December 2002, Poland was formally invited to join the EU, and the country officially joined on May 1 2004.

Poland's economic growth showed signs of slowing at the beginning of the century; GDP growth fell from 4.0 per cent in 2000 to 1.3 per cent in 2001, whilst government revenue fell as low as 49 per cent of the target for January to July 2001. However, on the back of strong exports, the economy has recently been growing faster than any of the other ex-communist countries in Europe. Figures for 2002 estimated the GDP growth rate to be 1.5 per cent and since then economic growth has been estimated at 3.8 per cent in 2003, 5.4 per cent in 2004, 6.2 per cent in 2006 and 6.6 per cent in 2006. Forecasts of GDP growth in 2012 were between 2.5 per cent and 3.1 per cent. Growth in the economy has seen the high unemployment figures begin to fall. Poland would like to adopt the Euro in 2017.

As part of the global economic crisis, Poland's GDP fell by up to 1.4 per cent in 2009, before recovering in 2010. Although the forecast is worse than expected, Poland was the only EU state to avoid recession in 2011.

GDP at Current Prices

Year	Million PLZ
2007	1,176,737
2008	1,275,432
2009	1,343,366
2010 (E)	1,415,385

Source: Central Statistics Office

Per capita GDP was estimated at 37,065 zl in 2010.

Gross Domestic Product at Current Prices in 2010

Sector	Million PLZ
Agriculture, hunting and forestry	43,950
Industry	305,944
- Mining & quarrying	32,724
- Manufacturing	230,463
- Electricity, gas & water supply	42,757
Construction	88,351
Trade & repair	234,837
Total	1,415,385

Source: Central Statistics Office

Inflation at the end of 2011 was recorded at 3.9 per cent.

According to figures from the Polish Statistical Office, total external debt was an estimated US$352,210 million in Q3 2012.

Foreign Investment
The privatisation programme created many opportunities for foreign investment in Poland. In 2007, Poland received nearly €13 billion in Foreign Direct Investment most of which came from EU countries particularly France and Germany.
Polish Agency for Foreign Investment (PAIZ), URL: http://www.paiz.gov.pl

Balance of Payments / Imports and Exports
The following table shows imports/exports in recent years.

Trade Balance in Million zln (current prices)

Trade	2005	2010	2011
Imports	328,192	536,221	614,428
Exports	288,781	481,058	554,769
Balance	-39,411	-55,163	-59,659

Source: Central Statistics Office

Germany is Poland's main trading partner, accounting for nearly 30 per cent of Poland's foreign trade. The following tables show foreign trade by major countries in the recent years. Figures are in million zloty:

Exports

Country	2009	2010
Germany	110,680	121,882
France	29,384	32,055
United Kingdom	27,107	29,011
Italy	29,017	28,739
Czech Republic	24,707	27,976
Russia	15,531	20,152
Netherlands	17,825	19,532
Hungary	11,427	13,093
Sweden	11,335	13,401
Spain	11,083	12.524

Imports

Country	2009	2010
Germany	103,673	113,543
Russia	39,520	54,871
China	42,971	49,695
Italy	31,687	29,734
France	21,348	22,477
Czech Republic	16,727	19,004
The Netherlands	16,815	18,892
United Kingdom	13,687	14,303
United States	10,722	13,455
Belgium	10,757	12,434

Source: Central Statistical Office

Major exports are manufactured goods, machinery and transport equipment, food, and chemicals. Major imports are machinery and transport equipment, manufactured goods, chemicals, mineral fuels and lubricants.

Imports and Exports for 2010

Imports	US$ mil.
Live animals, animal products	3,847
Vegetable products	3,798
Fats & oils	652
Prepared foodstuffs	5,923
Mineral products	20,337
Products of the chemical industry	17,517
Plastics & rubber	12,660
Wood & articles of wood	1,426
Pulp of wood, paper & paperboard	4,841
Textiles & textile articles	7,812
Footwear & headgear	1,072
Articles of stone, ceramic products & glass	2,254
Base metals & articles thereof	17,876
Machinery & mechanical appliances, electrical & electrotechnical equipment	42,075
Transport equipment	17,881
Optical, photographic, measuring, checking insturments	5,514
Miscellaneous manufactured articles	2,962
Exports	
Live animals, animal products	5,881
Vegetable products	3,164
Fats & oils	429
Prepared foodstuffs	8,126
Mineral products	6,258
Products of the chemical industry	10,211
Plastics & rubber	10,097
Wood & articles of wood	3,300
Pulp of wood, paper & paperboard	4,827
Textiles & textile articles	4,956
Footwear & headgear	617

- continued

Articles of stone, ceramic products & glass	2,956
Base metals & articles thereof	17,330
Machinery & mechanical appliances, electrical & electrotechnical equipment	40,733
Transport equipment	24,941
Optical, photographic, measuring, checking insturments	1,463
Miscellaneous manufactured articles	8,712

Source: Polish Official Statistics

National Bank of Poland, (Narodwny Bank Polski), Swietokrzyska 11/21, 00-919 Warsaw, Poland. Tel: +48 (0)22 653 1000, fax: +48 (0)22 620 8518, URL: http://www.nbp.pl President: Professor Marek Belka (page 1386)

MANUFACTURING, MINING AND SERVICES

Primary and Extractive Industries
Poland is one of the world's leading producers and exporters of hard coal, sulphur and copper. There are also reserves of zinc, lead, natural gas, salt and other minerals.

Poland relies heavily on imports for its oil consumption (97 per cent in 2001), and demand is expected to increase by 50 per cent by 2020. At the beginning of January 2012 Poland had proven oil reserves of 160 million barrels, a fraction of its requirements. Oil production in 2011 was an estimated 328,300 barrels per day (up from production of 10,000 barrels per day in 2000). Domestic oil comes primarily from fields in southern and western Poland. Consumption in 2011 was estimated at 576,000 barrels per day. Net oil imports in 2011 were an estimated 548,000 barrels per day. At the beginning of January 2009 Poland had a crude oil refining capacity estimated at 493,000 barrels per day.

Natural gas reserves were estimated at the beginning of January 2011 at 6.00 trillion cubic feet. Natural gas production was an estimated 221,000 million cubic feet in 2011, with consumption an estimated 606,000 million cubic feet. Poland's gas requirements are such that 415,000 million cubit feet were imported in 2011. However, demand for natural gas in Poland remains fairly steady.

Coal represents 95 per cent of Poland's primary energy production, even though it accounts for just 2 per cent of total GDP. Poland had recoverable coal reserves of 15,432 million short tons in 2003. Production was 146 million short tons in 2010 (down from 190 million short tons in 1999). Consumption was 148.8 million short tons in 2010 (down from 164 million short tons in 1999). Net exports of coal in 2010 were an estimated 2.9 million short tons, making Poland the world's ninth largest coal exporter, with customers mainly in Europe and the former Soviet Union. Poland has been privatising and modernising its coal industry but it is a slow process.

Energy
Poland's total energy consumption in 2009 was estimated at 3.98 quadrillion Btu, equivalent to about 1.0 per cent of world energy consumption.

Installed electric capacity in 2010 was estimated at 33.36 gigawatts (an increase on the 1998 figure of 29.9 GW). Electricity generation in 2006 was an estimated 151.25 billion kilowatthours (kWh), up from 134,400 million kWh in 1999. Consumption rose from 126.24 billion kWh in 2000 to 134.84 billion kWh in 2010.

Manufacturing
The most important areas in industry are fuels and energy, iron and steel, defence, heavy chemistry, pharmaceuticals, textiles and clothing, and they have all undergone major restructuring in the past few years. There is also much foreign investment in the car industry.

Value in 2007 of sold production of goods at current prices:

Sector	Mil. zl.
Mining & quarrying	39,117
Food & beverages	153,080
Tobacco products	4,273
Textiles	11,186
Wearing apparel & fur	8,873
Leather & leather products	3,826
Wood & wood, straw & wicker	27,276
Pulp & paper	17,909
Publishing, printing & reproduction of recording equipment	22,420
Coke & refined petroleum prooducts	46,357
Chemicals & chemical products	50,328
Rubber & plastic products	44,963
Non-metallic mineral products	40,190
Basic metals	42,124
Metal products	61,857
Machinery & equipment n.e.c.	51,251
Office machinery & computers	2,175
Electrical machinery & apparatus n.e.c.	30,349
Radio, television & communication equipment & apparatus	16,819
Medical precision & optical instruments, watches & clocks	8,899
Motor vehicles, traliers & semi-trailers	80,819
Other transport equipment	13,158
Furniture, manufacturing n.e.c.	32,768
Recycling	5,593

Source: Polish Official Statistics

The modernisation of the steel industry is beset with problems of ageing technology and over employment. As financing this modernisation is difficult for Poland, investment is being encouraged.

Tourism
Annual tourism revenue exceeds US$8 billion, and the Polish government plans to spend over US$11 million on promotion. Figures for 2011 show that tourist arrivals were 10.76 million in 2011.
Polish National Tourist Office in London, URL: http://www.poland.travel/en-gb

Agriculture
Agriculture employs over 28 per cent of the working population. The main crops produced in Poland are cereals, potatoes, sugar beet and fruits and vegetables. Poland is the world's biggest exporter of apple concentrate and a leading producer of berries, cabbages and carrots. Livestock in 2011 was put at 5,762,000 head of cattle of which 2,626,000 were cows. That year there were 13,509,000 pigs and 251,000 sheep. Hens numbered 127 million.

In 2011, 9,351 thousand hectares (ha) of the area of Poland were forests and over 23.000 million cubic metres of timber were gained. The total fish catch in 2010 was put at 190,000 tonnes down from 224,000 tonnes the previous year.

In 2011 from a total land area of 31,268,000 hectares (ha), 14,139,000 hectares were agricultural land, of which 12.4 million ha were arable. In 2006 over 88 per cent of farms were in private hands. Poland is pursuing a policy of more organic farming.

It is deemed necessary for efficiency and productivity that private farms be made into bigger farming units. During the 1990s production fell by 20 per cent and demand by 25 per cent. Though the EU, through its Common Agricultural Policy, has promised financial support, the farmers have staged protests after sales in Russia and agricultural prices in general have fallen.

Agricultural Production in 2010

Produce	Int. $'000*	Tonnes
Cow milk, whole, fresh	3,706,679	12,278,700
Indigenous pigmeat	2,674,723	1,739,950
Indigenous chicken meat	1,588,385	1,115,120
Indigenous cattle meat	1,258,841	466,000
Potatoes	998,333	8,765,960
Wheat	789,825	9,487,800
Apples	796,184	1,858,970
Rapeseed	558,066	2,077,630
Hen eggs, in shell	512,144	618,496
Sugar beet	422,522	9,822,900
Mushrooms and truffles	322,060	178,500
Rye	258,007	3,270,300

*unofficial figures

Source: http://faostat.fao.org/site/339/default.aspx Food and Agriculture Organization of the United Nations, Food and Agricultural commodities production

COMMUNICATIONS AND TRANSPORT

Travel Requirements
Citizens of the USA, Canada and Australia require a passport valid for three months beyond the length of stay but do not need a visa for stays of up to 90 days. EU citizens who have a valid national ID card do not require a passport. Other nationals should contact the embassy to check visa requirements.

All visitors must possess travel or medical insurance to cover possible medical expenses for at least €30,000, as well as sufficient funds for accommodation and food.

Poland is a signatory to the Schengen Agreement; with a Schengen visa, a visitor can travel freely throughout the Schengen zone, with few border stops and checks. See http://www.eurovisa.info/SchengenCountries.htm for details.

National Airlines
Lot-Polish Airlines, URL: http://www.lot.com

International Airports
Warsaw's Chopin Airport (formerly Okecie Airport) (URL: http://www.lotnisko-chopina.pl) is the largest and most modern of Poland's airports. It currently has a capacity of around 3.5 million passengers, and a freignt capacity of 50,000 tonnes per year. The other major airport is John Paul II International Aiport Krakow-Balice (URL: http://www.krakowairport.pl.en). In 2011, 45,000 tonnes of goods were transported by air. In the same year, 6,491,000 passengers were also transported. (Source: Concise Statistical Yearbook of Poland).

Aviation Authority
General Inspectorate of Civil Aviation (Glówny Inspektorat Lotnictwa Cywilnego), URL: http://www.ulc.gov.pl

Railways
In 2011, railways comprised 20,228 km. of which 20,113 were standard guage. Some regional railways are operated by local authorities. There are tram/light rail networks in 13 cities. The busiest route, between Warsaw and Berlin, is being upgraded. Warsaw has a subway and tram network. There is a single rapid transit metro network. A second line is due to open in 2014. In 2011, 248.6 million tonnes of goods were transported by rail. In the same year, 263.5 million passengers were also transported. (Source: Concise Statistical Yearbook of Poland).
PKP Polskie Koleje Panstwowe (Polish State Railways), URL: http://www.pkp.pl

POLAND

Roads
In 2010, there were 274,000 km. of hard surfaced roads, including 857 km. of motorways. Vehicles drive on the right. In 2011, there were 18.1 million passenger cars, 3.1 million lorries, 1.6 million tractors and 100,000 buses. As of 2013, there were three toll motorways in Poland. In 2011, 1,596.2 million tonnes of goods were transported by road. (Source: Concise Statistical Yearbook of Poland).

Shipping
In 2011, 7.73 million tonnes of goods were transported by sea. In the same year, 637,000 passengers were also transported. In 2011, the maritime fleet consisted of 2,931 vessels. There were 37 ferries. (Source: Concise Statistical Yearbook of Poland).
Polish Ocean Lines, URL: http://www.pol.com.pl/

Ports and Harbours
In 2011, 57,738,000 tonnes of goods were loaded and unloaded in total. The three main Baltic ports are Szczecin, Gdynia and Gdansk. In 2011, goods loaded and unloaded transit cargo amounted to 1.963 million tonnes at Gdansk, 1.287 million tonnes at Szczecin and 2.3 million tonnes at Swinoujscie. In 2011, passenger arrivals at sea ports amounted to 781,000 and passenger departures 803,000. (Source: Concise Statistical Yearbook of Poland).

Waterways
Poland has nearly 4,000 km of navigable waterways. In 2011, 5.09 million tonnes of goods were transported by inland waterway. In the same year, 1.5 million passengers were also transported. (Source: Concise Statistical Yearbook of Poland).

HEALTH

Medical treatment is free and funded from the state budget. Medical care is also available in private clinics. Poland has around 720. Health service reform was introduced at the beginning of 1999. Where previously the health care system was administered regionally and people were treated in the area where they lived, the reform gives people the opportunity to register with a doctor of their choice. State healthcare is funded in part by the government and in part by compulsory individual contributions. Approximately 8.5 per cent of gross wages is compulsory deducted from people's income tax payments and put into 'Patients Funds' which are based in each local government provinces.

In 2009, the government spent approximately 11.9 per cent of its total budget on healthcare (up from 9.4 per cent in 2000), accounting for 72.3 per cent of all healthcare spending. Social security expenditure accounts for 83.7 per cent of total health care expenditure. Total expenditure on healthcare equated to 7.4 per cent of the country's GDP. Per capita expenditure on health was approximately US$829, compared with US$247 in 2000. Figures for 2005-11 show that there are 82,813 physicians (21.6 per 10,000 population), 222,627 nurses and midwives (58.0 per 10,000 population), 24,238 pharmaceutical personnel and 12,169 dentists. There are 67 hospital beds per 10,000 population.

The infant mortality rate in 2010 was 5 per 1,000 live births. The child mortality rate (under 5 years) was 6 per 1,000 live births. The main causes of death among children aged less than five years are: 33 per cent prematurity, congenital abnormalities 34 per cent, birth asphyxia 6 per cent and pneumonia 5 per cent. (Source: http://www.who.int, World Health Statistics 2012)

EDUCATION

Pre-school Education
There are kindergartens and pre-school sections of primary schools for children between three and six years old.

Primary/Secondary Education
Basic education from the age of seven to 16 is free and compulsory. Figures from 2007 show that 96 per cent of girls and 95 per cent of boys were enrolled in primary school. Pupils must obtain a certificate to progress to the year above and a general certificate to progress to secondary school at the age of 13. Free secondary education is then optional in general, liceum or technikum or vocational schools.

The subjects studied are diverse, and specialisation is introduced in the last year leading towards the matriculation exam. Pupils graduate at the end of secondary education with a matura examination similar to the International Baccalaureat. The language of instruction in Polish and secondary school students usually study two foreign languages, English and German being the most popular. There are also three-year basic vocational schools which are sometimes attached to factories for practical experience. In 2007 some 95 per cent of girls and 93 per cent of boys were enrolled in secondary education. Secondary and vocational school graduates account for 26 per cent and 34 per cent of the total population respectively.

Higher Education
Around 20 per cent of students in post-primary education go on to higher education. There are 178 universities, technical universities and high schools. Admission to universities is based on results in the matriculation exam and often an entrance exam. State universities offer a four to five and a half year course similar to a master's degree, whereas private universities offer three year courses which are more like bachelor's degrees. University graduates constitute over 7 per cent of the total population.

Numbers in education (2011/12)

School	Institutions	Teachers '000	Students '000
Primary schools	13,772	173,3	2,187.2
Lower secondary schools	7,331	106,8	1,210
Special upper secondary job-training	448		10.4

- continued

Basic vocational	1,754	16.5	210.9
General secondary	2,345	47.8	606.1
Specialised secondary	362	2.2	26.6
Technical secondary	2,060	44.6	528.8
Post-secondary	2,830	9.9	330.6
Tertiary	460	102.7	1,764.1

Source:
http://www.stat.gov.pl

The adult literacy rate is 99 per cent.

RELIGION

Church-State religions are regulated by laws of 1989 which guarantee religious freedom, grant the Roman Catholic Church radio and TV programmes and permit it to run schools, hospitals and old age homes. On 28 July 1993 the Government signed the Concordat with the Holy See regulating mutual relations, and after almost five years discussion this agreement was made legal by the Parliament. The Archbishop of Warsaw, currently Kazimierz Nycz, is the primate of Poland. The religious capital is Gneizno, whose Archbishop simultaneously holds a title of primate. In October 1978 Cardinal Karol Wojtyla, Archbishop of Cracow, was elected Pope as John Paul II. Over 96 per cent of the population belong to the Roman Catholic Church. An estimated 9,600 (0.03 per cent) people follow Judaism and 8,900 (0.02 per cent) are Muslim.

Poland has a religious tolerance rating of 8 on a scale of 1 to 10 (10 is most freedom). (Source: World Religion Database)

COMMUNICATIONS AND MEDIA

There is freedom of expression but laws forbidding criticism of the state still exist.

Newspapers
There are currently over 300 newspapers available, many owned by foreign groups. Circulation figures are low.
Gazeta Wyborcza, URL: http://www.gazeta.pl
Super Express, URL: http://www.se.com.pl
Rzeczpospolita, URL: http://www.rzeczpospolita.pl/index.rol
Dziennik, Warsaw, URL: http://www.dziennik.pl/
Fakt, biggest seller, URL: http://www.fakt.pl/

Broadcasting
The public *Polskie Radio i Telewizja* operates two national channels plus several regional channels and niche channels. Privately-owned networks also exist nationally and locally. Approximately 50 per cent of households have either satellite or cable TV system with access to foreign television networks. The state-run radio network operates five national networks and 17 regional radio stations. Privately owned radio networks and commercial stations also exist.
Telewizja Polska SA (Polish Television), URL: http://www.tvp.pl/
PolSat (Satellite Channel), URL: http://www.polsat.pl/
Polskie Radio SA (Polish Radio), http://www.polskieradio.pl/default.aspx

Telecommunications
The telecommunications network has been undergoing modernization in recent years. The pace has increased with greater market-based competition. The fixed line service is weaker in rural areas. Mobile cellular services have increased dramatically and coverage is generally good. There were an estimated 10 million land line telephone subscribers and 44 million mobile phone subscribers in 2006.

By 2008, nearly 18 million people were regular internet users.

ENVIRONMENT

Poland has been implementing a National Environment Policy since 1991 after being one of the most polluted countries in Europe during the 1980s. As the country is so dependent on coal there have been several projects to improve air quality, such as installing a flue-gas 'cleanup' process at Skawina Power Station, and the implementation of a programme to reduce emissions from coal-fired ovens and boilers in Krakow. At the end of March 2000, the Government accepted a new environmental protection act and made amendments to several related regulations.

Figures from 2005 show energy-related carbon emissions per annum at 289.8 million metric tons. Per capita carbon emissions in the same year were estimated at 7.87 metric tons, lower than the European per capita average of 7.99 metric tons. In 2009, Poland's emissions from the consumption of fossil fuels totalled 304.45 million metric tons of carbon dioxide. This figure fell slightly to 303.70 million metric tons in 2010. (Source: EIA)

Poland is a party to the following international environmental agreements: Air Pollution, Antarctic-Environmental Protocol, Antarctic-Marine Living Resources, Antarctic Seals, Antarctic Treaty, Biodiversity, Climate Change, Climate Change-Kyoto Protocol, Desertification, Endangered Species, Environmental Modification, Hazardous Wastes, Kyoto Protocol, Law of the Sea, Marine Dumping, Ozone Layer Protection, Ship Pollution, Wetlands. The country has signed but not ratified the following agreements: Air Pollution-Nitrogen Oxides, Air Pollution-Persistent Organic Pollutants, and Air Pollution-Sulfur 94.

SPACE PROGRAMME

Members of ESA unanimously approved Poland's accession to the ESA Convention. Poland immediately became an observer in the ESA Council and will become the 20th ESA member state following an international ratification process. Poland has been a European Cooperating State (PECS) since 2007. There are currently over 40 PECS projects ongoing in Poland with a total budget of €11 million.

PORTUGAL
Portuguese Republic
República Portuguesa

Capital: Lisbon (Population estimate, 2011: 547,650)

Head of State: Anibal Cavaco Silva (President) (page 1402)

National Flag: Divided pale-wise green and red about 2:3; at the juncture a yellow armillary sphere charged with the arms of the former monarchy; a white shield bearing five blue shields, each with five disks white, the whole bordered red with seven yellow castles.

CONSTITUTION AND GOVERNMENT

Constitution
Portugal is a parliamentary democracy. According to the 1976 Constitution (revised in 1982 and 1989), the President of the Republic is the Head of State and Commander-in-Chief of the armed forces. The Constitution came into being following the bloodless coup ending the right wing dictatorship of Antonio de Oliveira Salazar and subsequently Marcelo Caerano. The president is elected by the people for a maximum of two consecutive five-year terms. Presidential responsibility includes the appointment of the prime minister and, with the prime minister's assistance, government ministers. They form the *Conselho de Ministros*, or Council of Ministers.

To consult the constitution, please visit:
http://www.portugal.gov.pt/pt/GC17/Portugal/SistemaPolitico/Constituicao/Pages/default.aspx

Foreign Relations
Portugal has been a beneficiary of the European Union. During 2007 Portugal held the EU presidency, and focused on EU relations with North Africa and the Middle East, and a common EU approach toward migration flows.

Portugal was a founding member of NATO and is an active member, contributing proportionally large contingents in Balkans peacekeeping forces. In July 1996, Portugal and her former colonies formed the Commonwealth of Portuguese-speaking countries (CPLP) whose stated aims are to increase co-operation between the member countries and to prevent the erosion of the Portuguese language. Portugal was a strong advocate of independence for East Timor, a former colony, committing troops and money, in cooperation with the United States, Asian allies and the UN. Portugal contributed a small force to Iraq until February 2005, and has contributed funds and personnel for other training and development projects for Iraq reconstruction.

Recent Events
The Socialist party swept to victory in the general elections of February 2005, and introduced a series of social and economic reforms which provoked a series of strikes among public sector workers.

In March 2007, there were mass demonstrations against the government's economic reforms. The following month, the President backed a new law permitting abortion in the first ten weeks of pregnancy, thus aligning Portugal with most other EU countries.

In April 2008, the Assembly voted overwhelmingly in favour of ratifying EU's Lisbon treaty.

In May 2009, the Assembly voted to bring the spelling of Portuguese more in line with the Brazilian spelling; opponents said that it was a surrendering to Brazilian influence.

Parliamentary elections took place on 27 September 2009, and resulted in the formation of a minority government.

Following a Government announcement of austerity measures to reduce the country's budget deficit, tens of thousands of civil servants held a strike in March 2010. They objected to plans to freeze public sector workers' pay. Several leading credit rating agencies downgraded the government debt which further undermined confidence in the economy. In November 2010 parliament passed an austerity budget which was designed to bring down the high public debt levels, including cuts in public sector pay and an increase in sales tax of two per cent. European attention was at this time focused on the economies of Portugal, Spain, and Ireland which were all struggling.

In March 2011 Prime Minister Jose Socrates tried to bring in a further austerity budget but which included spending cuts and tax rises. All five opposition parties rejected the budget and Prime Minister Socrates felt this made his position untenable and resigned from the post. In April 2011 Portugal was forced to apply for financial assistance to help tackle its budget deficit. The bail-out was worth €78 billion ($116 billion / £70 billion), is in the form of loans from other European countries and the International Monetary Fund.

The PSD won most seats in the 5 June 2011 general election. The leader, Pedro Passos Coelho, formed a coalition government which included four independents.

In July 2011 the credit ratings agency Moody's Investors Service downgraded Portugal's debt to junk status, believing there was an increasing risk the country would need a second-bail-out. In August the government announced it was planning to cut public spending from 44.2 per cent of GDP to 43.5 per cent by 2015. Higher tax rates for the highest earners were also announced. In November, international inspectors cleared the way for Portugal to receive the next tranche of its bailout package. The prime minister visited Angola. President Eduardo Dos Santos later said Angola would help its former colonial power cope with their financial crisis. Angola has already increased its investments in Portgual in recent years from $2 million in 2002 to over $150 million in 2009.

In August 2011, the government announced plans for the biggest spending cut for 50 years, the aim was to reduce public spending by 0.7 per cent of GDP by 2015. A further package of spending cuts and tax increases were submitted to parliament the following October. In November thousands of workers went on strike prior to the government vote on the austerity package. Also that month Portugal's credit rating was downgraded to junk status by the credit ratings agency Fitch. Credit agency Standard and Poor followed suit in January 2012. In March 2012 many major cities came to halt when public-sector workers went on a 24 hour strike in protest at the austerity measures.

Further austerity measures were announced in May 2012 when the government said it was to suspend four of its 14 public holidays. Two religious festivals and two other public holidays will not be taken for five years from 2013.

In June, the government said that it had passed the fourth review of its continuing spending cuts and economic reforms, fulfilling all the bailout criteria set by the EU, the ECB and the IMF. This should enable Portugal to receive another €4 billion of funds from the EU, ECB and IMF. The government said it was also to inject more than €6 billion into three of the country's banks to improve their liquidity. Figures released in August 2012 showed that GDP had shrunk by 1.2 per cent during the second quarter of the year. The following month the EU, IMF and the European Central Bank granted Portugal a further year to reduce its deficit to below three per cent of GDP, this followed the progress that had been made in rebalancing the economy. In November 2012, another austerity budget was passed by Parliament.

In July 2013 the future of the existing government was put in doubt when Finance Minister Victor Faspar resigned over the ongoing economic pressures. Former treasury secretray Maria Luis Albuquerque was appointed to the post, Albuquerque is seen as a supporter of the austerity measures and this prompred foreign minister and junior coalition leader, Paulo Portas, to resign.

Legislature
The unicameral *Assembleia da Republica*, or Assembly of the Republic, holds legislative power, and is also responsible for assessing government legislation and ensuring compliance with the constitution. The Assembly consists of 230 members elected by the people for a single term of four years.
Assembleia da Republica, Palácio de S. Bento, 1249-068 Lisbon, Portugal. Tel.: +351 21 391 9000, fax: +351 21 391 7440, e-mail: Correio.geral@ar.parlamento.pt, URL: http://www.parlamento.pt
Speaker of the Assembly: Maria da Assunção Esteves

Cabinet (as at July 2013)
Prime Minister: Pedro Passos Coelho (PSD) (page 1492)
Minister for Finance: Maria Luis Albuquerque
Minister for Foreign Affairs: vacant
Minister for National Defence: José Pedro Aguiar Branco (PSD) (page 1373)
Minister for Internal Administration: Miguel Macedo (PSD) (page 1468)
Minister for Justice: Paula Teixeira da Cruz (PSD) (page 1524)
Assistant Minister and Minister for Parliamentary Affairs: Miguel Relvas (PSD) (page 1502)
Minister for the Economy and Employment: Alvaro Santos Pereira (Ind.) (page 1508)
Minister for Agriculture, Rural Development and Fisheries: Assunçao Cristas (CDS-PP) (page 1410)
Minister for Health: Paulo Macedo (Ind.) (page 1468)
Minister for Education & Science: Nuno Crato (Ind.) (page 1410)
Minister for Social Solidarity: Pedro Mota Soares (CDS-PP) (page 1481)

Ministries
Office of the President, Palace of Belem, Presidência da Republica, Praça Afonso Albuquerque, 1300 Lisbon, Portugal. Tel: +351 21 361 4600, fax: +351 21 361 4611, URL: http://www.presidenciarepublica.pt

PORTUGAL

Office of the Prime Minister, Presidência do Conselho de Ministros, Rua da Imprensa à Estrela 4, 1200 Lisbon, Portugal. Tel: +351 21 395 2953, fax: +351 21 395 1616, e-mail: pm@pm.gov.pt,
URL: http://www.portugal.gov.pt/pt/GC17/PrimeiroMinistro/Pages/PrimeiroMinistro.aspx
Presidency of the Council of Ministers, Rua Professor Gomes Teixeira, 1399-022 Lisbon, Portugal. Tel: +351 21 392 7600, fax: +351 21 392 7615, e-mail: relacoes.publicas@pcm.gov.pt, URL: http://www.portugal.gov.pt
Ministry of Agriculture, Rural Development and Food, Praça do Comércio, 1149-010, Lisbon, Portugal. Tel: +351 21 323 4600 fax: +351 21 323 4601, e-mail: recepcao@min-agricultur.pt, URL: http://www.min-agricultura.pt
Ministry of Culture, rua Do Francisco Manuel de Melo 15, 1070-05 Lisbon, Portugal. Tel: +351 213 848400, fax: +351 213 848439, e-mail: sgmc@mail.min-cultura.pt, URL: http://www.min-cultura.pt
Ministry of Defence, Av. Ilha De Madeira 1, 1400-204 Lisbon, Portugal. Tel: +351 213 038528, fax: +351 213 019555, e-mail: gcrp@sg.mdn.gov.pt, URL: http://www.mdn.gov.pt
Ministry of the Economy, Rua da Horta Seca 15, 1200-221 Lisbon, Portugal. Tel: +351 21 322 8600, fax: +351 21 322 8811, e-mail: secretaria.geral@sg.min-economia.pt, URL: http://www.min-economia.pt
Ministry of Education, Av. 5 de Outubro 107-13, 1069-018 Lisbon, Portugal. Tel: +351 21 793 1603, fax: +351 21 796 3119, e-mail: secsg@min-edu.pt, URL: http://www.min-edu.pt
Ministry of Employment, Praça de Londres, 2-16, 1049-009 Lisbon, Portugal. Tel: +351 21 842 4100, fax: +351 21 842 4115, URL: http://www.mts.gov.pt
Ministry of the Environment, Rua de O Século 51, 1200-433 Lisbon, Portugal. Tel: +351 21 323 1500, fax: +351 21 323 1515, URL: http://www.sg.moat.gov.pt
Ministry of Finance, rua da Alfândega 5, 1100-006 Lisbon, Portugal. Tel: +351 21 881 6800, e-mail: relacoes.piblicas@sgmf.pt, URL: http://www.min.financas.pt
Ministry of Foreign Affairs, Largo do Rilvas 1, 1399-030 Lisbon, Portugal. Tel: +351 21 394 6000, e-mail: gii@mne.gov.pt, URL: http://www.min-nestrangeiros.pt/mne
Ministry of Health, A. Joao Crisóstomo 9, 1069-062 Lisbon, Portugal. Tel: +351 21 330 5000, fax: +351 21 330 5161, e-mail: dmrs@sgeral.min-saude.pt, URL: http://www.min-saude.pt
Ministry of Home Affairs, Praça do Comércio, 1149-015 Lisbon, Portugal. Tel: +351 21 323 3000, fax: +351 21 346 8031, e-mail: dirp@sg.mai.gov.pt, URL: http://www.mai.gov.pt
Ministry of Justice, Rua do Ouro 6, 1149-019 Lisbon, Portugal. Tel: +351 21 322 2300, fax: +351 21 342 3198, e-mail: correio@sg.mj.gov.pt, URL: http://www.mj.gov.pt
Ministry for Public Works, Transport and Housing, Palácio Penafiel, Rua de S. Mamede do Caldas 21, 1149-050 Lisbon, Portugal. Tel: +351 218 815100, fax: +351 218 676131, e-mail: correio@min-equipamentosocial.pt, URL: http://www.mes.gov.pt
Ministry of Science and Higher Education, Palácio das Laranjeiras, Estrada das Laranjeiras, 1649-018 Lisbon, Portugal. Tel: +351 217 231000, fax: +351 217 231160, e-mail: gmces@mces.gov.pt, URL: http://www.mces.pt
Ministry of Social Security and Work, Praha de Londres 2, 16° Andar, 1049-056 Lisbon, Portugal. Tel: +351 21 8424100, fax: +351 218 424115, e-mail: gmsst@msst.gov.pt, URL: http://www.msst.gov.pt
Ministry of Towns, Territorial Planning and Environment, Rua de O Século 15, 1200-433 Lisbon, Portugal. Tel: +351 21 323 2500, fax: +351 21 323 1539, e-mail: sg.ambiente@se.mcota.gov.pt, URL: http://www.ambiente.gov.pt

Political Parties
The main political parties are:
Partido Comunista Português (PCP, Portuguese Communist Party), Rua Soeiro Pereira Gomes 3, 1699-196 Lisbon, Portugal. Tel: +351 21 781 3800, fax: +351 21 796 9126, e-mail: pcp@pcp.pt, URL: http://www.pcp.pt
General Secretary: Jerónimo de Sousa
Centro Democrático e Social - Partido Popular (CDS-PP, People's Party), Largo Adelino Amaro da Costa 5, 1149-63 Lisbon, Portugal. Tel: +351 21 888 3648, fax: +351 21 888 3477, URL: http://www.cdspp.pt
Leader: Paulo Portas
Partido Social Democrata (PSD, Social Democratic Party), Rua de Sao Caetano 9, 1249-087 Lisbon, Portugal. Tel: +351 21 395 2140, fax: +351 21 397 6967, e-mail: psd@psd.pt, URL: http://www.psd.pt
Leader: Pedro M. Mamede Passos Coelho
Partido Socialista (PS, Socialist Party), Largo do Rata 2, 1269-143 Lisbon, Portugal. Tel: +351 21 382 2000, fax: +351 21 382 2027, e-mail: portal@ps.pt, URL: http://www.ps.pt
Sec. Gen.: António José Seguro
Os Verdes (The Greens), Calcada Salvador Correia de Sa 4, 1 dto., 1200-399 Lisbon, Portugal. Tel: +351 21 343 3363, fax: +351 21 343 2764, URL: http://www.osverdes.pt

Elections
Presidential elections are held every five years. Presidents can serve two consecutive terms. The most recent presidential election was held on 23 January 2011 when the incumbent centre-right Anibal Cavaco Silva won 52.9 per cent of the vote.

Parliamentary elections are held every four years. Members of the Assembly of the Republic (Parliament) are elected by constituencies, the number elected by each depending upon the size of the constituency. All elections use the system of proportional representation by universal suffrage. All nationals over the age of 18 may vote. Non-residential nationals may also vote for parliamentary elections.

The most recent parliamentary election took place on 5 June 2011. The PSD won most seats but did not gain an absolute majority. The breakdown of seats was as follows: PSD 108 seats; PS 74; CDS-PP 24 seats; PCP-PEV 16 seats; BE 8 seats.

Diplomatic Representation
Portuguese Embassy, 2121 Kalorama Road, NW, Washington, DC 20008, United States of America. Tel: +1 202 328 8610, fax: +1 202 462 3726, e-mail: portugal@portugalemb.org, URL: http://www.embassyportugal-us.org
Ambassador: H.E. Nuno Filipe Alves Salvador e Brito (page 1394)
Portuguese Embassy, 11 Belgrave Square, London, SW1X 8PP, United Kingdom. Tel: +44 (0)20 7235 5331 fax: +44 (0)20 7245 1287, URL: http://portuguese-embassy.co.uk/en.html

Ambassador: João de Vallera (page 1415)
British Embassy, Rua de Sao Bernardo 33, 1249-082 Lisboa, Portugal. Tel: +351 21 392 4000, fax: +351 21 392 4185, e-mail: PPA@Lisbon.mail.fco.gov.uk, URL: http://ukinportugal.fco.gov.uk/en
Ambassador: Jill Gallard (page 1428)
Embassy of the United States, Avenida das Forças Armadas, 1600-081 Lisbon, Portugal. Tel: +351 21 727 3300, fax: +351 21 727 9109, URL: http://portugal.usembassy.gov/
Ambassador: H.E. Allan J. Katz (page 1454)
Permanent Mission of Portugal to the United Nations, 866 Second Ave, 9th floor, New York, NY 10017, USA. Tel: +1 212 759 9444, fax: +1 212 355 1124, e-mail: portugal@un.int, URL: http://www.missionofportugal.org/pmop
Ambassador: Alvaro Jose de Mendonca e Moura

LEGAL SYSTEM

The legal system is based on the civil law as outlined in the Constitution. It has been influenced by Napoleonic and German law, but latterly the major influence is EU law. The judiciary is independent.

The judiciary consists of the Supreme Court of Justice, seated in Lisbon, five courts of appeal (in Lisbon, Oporto, Coimbra, Évora and Guimarães), district courts of first instance and special courts. The autonomous regions of the Azores and Madeira come under the jurisdiction of the Judicial District of Lisbon. There is also a Constitutional Court, the Supreme Administrative Court and other Administrative and Fiscal Courts, the Court of Audits and the Military Courts.

The Supreme Court of Justice consists of a president and around 60 judges. An Ombudsman, elected by the Assembly of the Republic to a four-year term, serves as the nation's chief civil and human rights officer. The jury system was reintroduced in 1976, but it is used only when requested by either the prosecutor or the defendant.

The government respects the rights of its citizens, though prison conditions are poor, and police and prison guards have occasionally used excessive force on detainees. Portugal abolished the death penalty for civilian crimes in 1867 and in all circumstances in in 1976.

Supremo Tribunal de Justica (Supreme Court), URL: http://www.stj.pt
President: Luís António Noronha Nascimento (page 1487)
Supremo Tribunal Administrativo, URL: http://www.stadministrativo.pt
President: António Francisco de Almeida Calhau
Tribunal Constitucional, URL: http//www.tribunalconstitucional.pt
President: Joaquim de Sousa Ribeiro
Tribunal de Contas (Court of Auditors), URL: https://www.tcontas.pt/index.shtm

Office of the Ombudsman, URL: http://www.provedor-jus.pt/

LOCAL GOVERNMENT

Portugal is divided into 18 districts, Aveiro, Beja, Braga, Braganca, Castelo Branco, Coimbra, Evora, Faro, Guarda, Leiria, Lisboa, Portalegre, Porto, Santarem, Setubal, Viana do Castelo, Vila Real and Viseu, and two autonomous regions, Azores and Madeira. All of these have their own local government, appointed by the Ministers of Internal Administrations. These districts are divided into 335 municipalities (305 on the mainland, 19 in the autonomous region of Azores and 11 in the autonomous region of Madeira), administered through a *Câmara Municipal* headed by a President, elected directly by the residents. The municipalities are subdivided into parishes.

Each autonomous region has its own legislative assembly elected by universal suffrage for regional matters and a government with executive and administrative functions appointed by the Prime Minister in accordance with election results. A minister appointed by the central Government coordinates actions of the autonomous regions and of the mainland. Taxes in these regions go directly to regional budgetary expenditure.

Under the plans of the federal government to reduce spending plans have been drawn up to reform the administrative division in order the streamline and economise. The plans included reducing the number representatives and abolishing some civil parishes.

Azores Regional Assembly (Assembleia Legislativa Regional dos Azores), URL: http://www.alra.pt
President: Ana Luis
Regional Assembly of Madeira (Assembleia Legislativa Regional Autónoma da Madeira), URL: http://www.alram.pt/
President: José Miguel Jardim d'Olival Mendonça

AREA AND POPULATION

Area
Mainland Portugal lies on the western side of the Iberian Peninsula, bordering Spain and the North Atlantic Ocean. The autonomous island regions of Madeira and the Azores are also Portuguese territory and are situated in the Atlantic Ocean. The total land area is 91,982 sq. km. The terrain is mountainous in the north, with rolling plains in the south.

Portugal has a Mediterranean climate, and is warmer and drier in the south.

The Madeira archipelago lies about 360 miles from the coast of Africa and 535 miles from Lisbon. Its climate is classified as oceanic subtropical. Influenced by the Gulf Stream, the sea water temperature remains warm, from 26 °C over the summer to 17 °C in the winter.

The archipelago of the Azores lies about 950 miles from Lisbon and about 2,400 miles from the east coast of North America. The nine major Azorean islands and the eight small Formigas extend for more than 373 miles. Some of the islands have had volcanic activity as recently as 1957. The archipelago has a moderate oceanic subtropical climate.

To view a regional map, please consult
http://www.lib.utexas.edu/maps/cia08/portugal_sm_2008.gif

Population

According to the Portuguese Instituto Nacional de Estatistica, the total population of Portugal at the end of 2008 was 10,627,250, an increase of just 0.09 per cent over the 2007 population. In terms of natural growth, in 2008 the population remained the same, but immigration resulted in the overall slight population increase. Figures for 2009 showed that the population grew slightly to 10,637,713, a growth rate of 0.1 per cent. Figures from the 2011 census put the population at 10,561,614.

Population density over Portugal averages 115.4 people per km. sq.; this rises to 959 people per sq. km. in Lisbon. In 2008, there were 5,142,566 men and 5,484,684 women. 10,135,209 people lived in mainland Portugal, whilst 244,780 lived in the Azores, and 247,161 were residents of Madeira.

Portugal's major cities are Lisbon and Oporto. Over 64 per cent of the population live in urban areas.

At the end of December 2008, 436,020 foreigners had legal resident status in Portugal. The large increase in the numbers over the years 2006-08 (totalling 161,389) was due to a conversion of 'stay permits' into 'resident permits' in 2001. Most foreign residents came from other Portuguese-speaking countries such as Brazil (104,500), Cape Verde (51,000) and Angola (27,300). (Source: Instituto Nacional de Estadistica)

The official language is Portuguese.

Births, Marriages, Deaths

In 2010 the birth rate was put at 935 live births per 1,000 population one the lowest birth rates the country has ever recorded. The number of deaths recorded in 2010 was 105,954

The population of Portugal has been ageing as a result of lower fertility rates and an increase in longevity. Average life expectancy at birth was estimated at 78.48 (75.18 for men and 81.57 for women) over the period 2005-07. The 65 and over age group now accounts for 17.4 per cent of the total population, whilst those aged up to 14 years account for 15.3 per cent, and those aged 15-24 just 11.6 per cent.

The fertility rate was 1.4 children per woman in 2008. The rate has not reached the minimum 'replacement of generation' value of 2.1 children per woman for around 25 years. The average age of a woman at the birth of her first child is around 28.4 years.

The number of marriages performed in Portugal during 2010 numbered 39,993 of which 266 were same sex marriages, that year 27,556 divorces were granted. The average age for a first marriage is around 29.7 years for a man and 28.1 years for a woman.

Public Holidays 2014

1 January: New Year's Day
5 March: Mardi Gras
17 April: Holy Thursday
18 April: Good Friday
25 April: Liberty Day
1 May: Labour Day
10 June: National Day
15 August: Assumption Day
8 December: Immaculate Conception
25 December: Christmas Day

In addition, 18 May is a local holiday in Ponta Delgada, 1 June is a local holiday in the Azores, 13 June (St Anthony) is a local holiday in Lisbon, 24 June is a local holiday in Oporto, 1 July is a holiday in Madeira, 21 August is a holiday in Funchal, and Boxing Day, 26 December, is a holiday in Madeira. Any holiday falling on a Sunday is not observed on the following Monday.

In May 2012 the government announced that they would be suspending four public holidays from 2013 for five years, it was hoped that this step would boost productivity. The suspended holidays are 1 November, All Saints Day; Corpus Christi, which falls 60 days after Easter; Republic day, 5 October; 1 December, Independence Restoration Day.

EMPLOYMENT

The following table shows annual average employment figures for 2005-08:

	2005	2006	2007	2008
Total workforce	5,544,900	5,587,300	5,618,300	5,624,900
Employed	5,122,600	5,159,500	5,169,700	5,197,800
Unemployed	422,300	427,800	448,600	427,100
Unemployment rate %	7.6	7.7	8.0	7.6

Source: Instituto Nacional de Estatistica

The activity rate (for those aged 15-64) increased by one per cent in 2008, reaching 74.2 per cent of the population. The composition of the labour force has grown older as people postpone retirement, and the proportion of women continued to increase. Between 1998 and 2008, the female activity rate for the age-group rose by 6.7 per cent to 68.5 per cent, whilst the male activity rate rose by 0.7 per cent to 79.5 per cent. Unemployment among the 15-24 age group was much higher, at 16.4 per cent.

The impact of the global economic crisis has caused the unemployment to rise over 2008-10; in 2009, it rose by 23.8 per cent to 9.5 per cent, affecting some 528,600 people. In the fourth quarter of 2009, unemployment reached an all-time high of 10.1 per cent. The unemployment rate for 2010 was put at 10.8 per cent. By the beginning of March 2013 the unemployment rate was 17.6 per cent.

The proportion of the working population with tertiary education is still relatively low at 14.8 per cent. 23 per cent of people were self-employed, and 88.1 per cent of the total workforce were employed full-time.

Within the regions, the North of Portugal suffered the highest rate of unemployment in 2008, at 8.7 per cent, whilst the Centre has the lowest rate, at 5.4 per cent. Long-term unemployment (lasting one year or more) declined from 51.7 per cent of unemployed people in 2006 to 48.9 per cent in 2007.
(Source: Instituto Nacional de Estadistica)

Employment by Economic Activity

Sector	2007	2008
Agriculture, hunting & forestry	584,300	577,700
Fishing	17,100	17,900
Mining & quarrying	19,300	18,000
Manufacturing	654,000	916,900
Electricity, gas & water supply	33,700	32,400
Construction	570,800	553,600
Wholesale & retail trade & repairs	750,200	777,300
Hotels & restaurants	288,800	319,400
Transport, storage & communications	223,700	224,900
Financial intermediation	95,700	96,100
Real estate, renting & business activities	325,400	336,300
Public administration & defence, compulsory social security	327,000	341,900
Education	306,700	343,700
Health & social work	340,200	305,400
Other community, social & personal service activities	162,400	158,800
Households with employed persons	167,500	175,500
Extra-territorial organisations & bodies	2,800	2,100

Source: Copyright © International Labour Organization (ILO Dept. of Statistics, http://laborsta.ilo.org)

BANKING AND FINANCE

Currency

One euro (€) = 100 cents
€ = 200.482 escudo (European Central Bank irrevocable conversion rate)
On 1 January 2002 the euro became legal tender in Portugal and 11 other member states of the EU. Portugal's old currency, the escudo, ceased to be legal tender from 28 February 2002. Euro banknotes come in denominations of 5, 10, 20, 50, 100, 200, and 500. Euro coins come in denominations of 2 and 1 euros, 50, 20, 10, 5, 2, and 1 cents.

GDP/GNP, Inflation, National Debt

Portugal's economy is based on traditional industries such as textiles, cork products, wine, and ceramics. The motor industry has expanded, and the services sector, particularly tourism, plays an increasingly important role.

In 2001, the Portuguese budget deficit breached the euro area's stability-and-growth pact limit of three per cent of GDP, leading to cuts in public spending and tax rises. The main aims of economic policy in recent years have been to increase productivity and reduce external debt and the budget deficit, as well as reforming public administration. The three per cent target was met in 2002, but the deficit rose to four per cent of GDP in 2003, and then surged to an all-time high of six per cent in 2005. The deficit was reduced to 4.6 per cent in 2006 - mainly through revenue generating measures, and in 2007, the government reduced it to 2.6 per cent of GDP through spending cuts and structural reforms. In 2008, it was brought down still further, to 2.2 per cent (its lowest rate in 30 years); however, the budget deficit soared to 9.3 per cent of GDP following a sharp drop in tax revenues due to the global recession.

Portugal's public debt reached 66.3 per cent of GDP in 2008 and it was estimated to have reached 76.6 per cent in 2009. It was thought that it would rise to over 85 per cent of GDP in 2010.

GDP reached an estimated €144.3 billion in 2004, rising to estimated figures of €149 billion in 2005 and €155 billion in 2006. Annual growth was estimated to be 1.2 per cent in 2004 and 0.3 per cent in 2005. In 2006, GDP rose 1.3 per cent in real terms, and in 2007 it rose by 1.9 per cent, to €163,083 billion. In 2008, GDP struggled to reach €166,433 billion with the advent of the economic crisis, and the economy went into recession in 2009, when GDP contracted by 2.6 per cent over the year, back to €163 billion. Estimated figures for 2010 put GDP at €160.4 billion reflecting a growth rate of 0.3 per cent. The service sector that year contributed over 75 per cent of GDP, industry 22 per cent and agriculture just over 2.0 per cent.

Portugal has been badly affected by the global economic crisis. Low growth in its economy has meant the government has found it hard to fund its spending. By November 2010 many thought that Portugal would need to be bailed out by the EU. The budget deficit in 2009 was put at 9.3 per cent and gross debt was 76.1 per cent. The strength of the Euro was also a problem for Portugal with a reduction in the number of tourists, particularly from the UK which is one of its biggest markets, because of the poor exchange rate. The manufacturing sector has also been hit in recent years by cheap imports from Asia, particularly China.

STATES OF THE WORLD

PORTUGAL

Portugal has traditionally been a larger manufacturer of footwear and this market has been severely undercut by Asian markets. Portugal had to be bailed out in May 2011 when it was no longer able to manage its debts. It is meant to cut its budget deficit to 3 per cent of GDP by 2013. On May 3, 2011, the government reached an agreement with the European Commission, the European Central Bank, and the IMF, they agreed to provide a €78 billion bailout payable over three years on the understanding that Portugal would implement austerity measure and privatization of state-owned enterprises. The economy shrank by 1.7 per cent in 2011 and was projected to shrink again by three per cent in 2012 and one per cent in 2013.

The following table shows GDP at market prices:

Year	€ million
2000	127,317
2005	154,269
2006	160,855
2007	169,317
2008	171,983
2009	168,504
2010 (est.)	172,571

Source: Instituto Nacional de Estadistica - Portugal

Per capita GDP was €15,373 in 2007, up from €14,657 in 2006. In 2008, it stood at an estimated €15,176.

The following table shows recent Gross Value Added composition by major sectors, at basic prices (base 2006) figures are in € million:

Sector	2008	2009	2010
Agriculture, forestry, fishing	3,518	3,411,	3,398
Industry, energy	21,053	19,376	19,855
Energy, water supply & sewerage	4,845	5,325	5,292
Construction	10,888	9,964	10,059
Wholesale & retail trade, repairs, accommodation & food service	27,146	29,061	29,300
Transportation & storage information & communication	12,847	13,011	12,990
Financial, insurance, real estate activities	23,829	22,515	22,887
Other service activities	45,197	47,041	47,241

Source: Instituto Nacional de Estadistica - Portugal

In 2004, inflation stood at 2.4 per cent (as measured by the Consumer Price Index - Base 100=2002); it ran at 2.3 per cent in 2005 and 3.1 per cent in 2006. In 2006, the rise in oil prices and in raw materials in general (by some 26.5 per cent) was a major factor in the increase in CPI. Over 2007, there was a rise of 2.5 per cent in the CPI, reflecting a slowdown in price rises on imported goods. Over 2008, the CPI rose by 2.6 per cent, the largest rises being in alcoholic beverages and tobacco (7.5 per cent) and housing and utilities (3.9 per cent). (Source: Instituto Nacional de Estatistica - Portugal). Inflation in 2010 was put at 1.2 per cent, 3.6 per cent in 2011 and 2.8 per cent.

Estimated figures for 2012 put public debt at 119 per cent of GDP.

Foreign Investment
EU expansion into eastern Europe has denied Portugal her historic competitive advantage and relative low labour costs. However, the European Union continues to represent the largest investor in Portugal, the UK investing most. Other large European investors include France, Spain, Belgium and the Netherlands. The United States, Brazil and Japan also invest in Portugal. The government agency ICEP - Investimentos, Comercio e Turismo de Portugal (Investment, Trade and Tourism of Portugal) - is an arm of the Ministry of Economy and provides information and services regarding business and investment opportunities in Portugal.

Balance of Payments / Imports and Exports
Foreign trade has increased over recent years. Portugal's main exports are vehicles, aircraft, machinery and mechanical appliances, vessels and associated transport equipment, textiles, mineral products and base metals. These make up around 60 per cent of total exports. The main imported goods are mineral products, machinery and mechanical appliances, aircraft, vehicles, vessels and associated transport equipment, bases metals and chemical products, which together make up around 66 per cent of the total value of imports.

International Trade in €thousand

	2007	2008
Total		
Exports (fob)	37,588.7	37,949.4
Imports (cif)	57,055.6	61,174.4
Balance	-19,466.9	-23,225.0
European Union		
Exports (fob)	28,819.8	26,006.1
Imports (cif)	43,015.9	44,987.5
Balance	-14,196.1	-18,981.4
Non EU Countries		
Exports (fob)	8,768.9	9,943.3
Imports (cif)	14,039.7	16,186.9
Balance	-5,270.8	-6,243.6

* Estimated figures

Source: Instituto Nacional de Estadistica - Portugal

The European Community is an increasingly important market for Portugal, accounting for 77 per cent of exports in 2006, and 75 per cent of imports. Figures for 2008 are shown in the table below (figures in thousands of Euros):

Intracommunity Trade: Imports and Exports by main trading partners, 2008 (provisional figures)

	Exports	Imports
Spain	10,327,942	18,853,677
Germany	4,882,196	7,581,607
France	4,435,579	5,070,500
United Kingdom	2,080,367	1,971,452
Italy	1,432,532	3,248,526
Belgium	935,896	1,21,788
Netherlands	1,245,060	2,816,936

Source: INE, Estadisticas do Comercio Internacional

The United States is an important trading partner, importing €1.34 billion worth of Portuguese goods in 2008, and supplying €1 billion worth of goods. Brazil supplied €1.36 billion worth of goods in 2008, and China is also an important supplier, at €1.34 billion. However, Nigeria was the largest supplier, at €1.7 billion worth of goods. (Source: INE)

International trade of Goods by Broad Economic Catergories in 2010 (figures in thousand €)

Categories	Exports	Imports
Food & beverages	3,675,924	6,955,963
Industrial goods not specified elsewhere	12,342,086	15,189,695
Fuels & oils	2,284,282	8,017,667
Machines, other capital goods (except transport) & accessories	4,132,564	8,620,947
Transport material & accessories	6,495,664	8,036,237
Consumer goods not specified elsewhere	6,967,057	8,927,168
Goods not specified elsewhere	39,879	1,065,562

Source: Instituto Nacional de Estatistica - Portugal (Statistics Portugal)

Central Bank
Banco de Portugal, Rua do Ouro 27, 1100-150 Lisbon, Portugal. Tel: +351 21 321 3200, fax: +351 21 346 4843, e-mail: info@bportugal.pt, URL: http://www.bportugal.pt
Governor: Carlos da Silva Costa (page 1409)

Trade Organisations and Chambers of Commerce
British - Portuguese Chamber of Commerce, URL: http://www.bpcc.pt
Portuguese Industrial Association, URL: http://www.aip.pt
ICEP, (Portuguese Investment, Commerce & Tourism), URL: http://www.icep.pt
Lisbon Chamber of Commerce, URL: http://www.port-chambers.com
Oporto Chamber of Commerce, URL: http://www.cciporto.com
Chamber of Commerce and Industry of the Azores, URL:http://www.ccipd.pt

Stock Exchanges
Euronext Lisbon (formerly Associaçao da Bolsa de Valores de Lisboa), URL: http://www.euronext.pt

MANUFACTURING, MINING AND SERVICES

Primary and Extractive Industries
Copper and tin are mined in Portugal. Coal mining ceased in 1996; though the country used some 2.976 million short tons in 2010, all of it imported. There are no proven oil reserves and exploration for natural gas has yet to yield positive results.

Oil consumption was 300.96 barrels per day in 2007, and Portugal has a crude oil refining capacity of 304,000 barrels per day. Although Portugal has no reserves of petroleum, there are plans for exploration of the onshore Lusitanian basin area, north of Lisbon, and the offshore Galician area near the Spanish border.

Petrogal, a wholly-owned subsidiary of Galp Energia, is the largest oil company in Portugal. Galp Energia is owned by the Portuguese government (25.77 per cent) and a collection of international companies. Petrogal operates the two oil refineries, controls the retail market for refined oil products and operates the country's oil pipeline network. Petrogal also has operations in Angola and Brazil.

Portugal's natural gas industry has only just begun to explore the country's gas resources. Natural gas consumption has risen from less than 5 billion cubic feet in 1997 to an estimated 183 billion cubic feet in 2011, all of it imported. The increase in natural gas consumption can be attributed to the construction of the Sines liquefied natural gas (LNG) import terminal and the Maghreb-Europe pipeline, which connects the Iberian Peninsula to Algerian natural gas sources.

Most natural gas is used for electricity production. Investments in the gas infrastructure are partly funded by the EU. The Portuguese government plans to extend the gas network from its current 3,760 miles to 5,950 miles by 2010. Gas de Portugal (GdP), a subsidiary of Galp Energia, controls natural gas importation, transportation and supply. The company also controls distribution indirectly, through its shares in six regional distribution companies.

In October 2003, Portugal's first LNG terminal was completed in Sines, with an output capacity of 530 Mmcf per day of natural gas. The Sines terminal gives Portugal greater independence of its natural gas supply, which is dependent on Spain's natural gas network to process and transport natural gas to the country. (Source: Energy Information Administration, EIA)

Energy

Portugal's total energy consumption in 2009 was estimated at 1.176 quadrillion Btu, up from 1.117 billdion Btu in 2003.

Portugal has limited energy resources, importing over 90 per cent of its requirements. In 2010, installed capacity stood at 18.92 gigawatts, and Portugal generated 51.91 billion Kwh of electricity. Consumption in the same year was 50.26 billion Kwh. Hydropower, traditionally depended upon to provide a large share of total electricity generation, made up just 35 per cent of the energy mix in 2003. The Portuguese government now promotes thermal generating capacity (especially natural gas-fired) as an alternative to hydroelectricity, which proved unpredictable and dependent on weather conditions in the past.

Portugal has invested in combined-cycle, gas-fired turbines (CCGFTs) as an alternative to hydropower. In April 2004, EdP completed its Central Termoelectrica do Ribatejo, a 1,200-MW CCGFT, and in 2005, the Portuguese Ministry of Finance approved licenses for five new CCGFT projects, with total generating capacity of 2,870 MW.

In June 2004, Portugal's Ministry of Economy provided a reported $51.4 million grant to fund 20 wind park projects, with a combined installed capacity of 244.5 MW. Portugal has also invested into solar power; construction began in 2004 by BP Solar on a 64-MW solar power plant in Moura. Portugal has also been on the forefront of wave generation; Portugese energy group Enersis plans to install the world's first commercial wave power generators off the coast of Povoa de Varzim. Construction on the wave power generators were nearing completion at the beginning of 2013. More than half of Portugal's energy currently comes from wind, solar and hydro power.

In 2007, construction began in southern Portugal on the world's largest solar power station. The 11-megawatt solar power plant, near Serpa, produces enough electricity for 8,000 homes. It was developed by Portuguese renewable energy company Catavento, in conjunction with Powerlight and funded by General Electric Energy Financial Services. Portugal plans other solar plants to counter a rise in carbon emissions.

Portugal's 113,767 miles of electricity transmission lines are linked with Spain's power grid. The formerly state-owned EdP (Electricidad de Portugal) is responsible for the transmission and distribution of electric power in Portugal, and also generates 72 per cent of the country's electricity. In addition to an independent electricity system, Portugal also has a public system, regulated by the government to guarantee a supply. The independent system is for large consumers only, and is open to competition.

In January 2004, Spain and Portugal formally signed an agreement to create a pan-Iberian electricity market (Mibel). Despite administrative delays, the project is progressing; a new 40-kilovolt transmission line has been created between the two countries at Cartelle-Lindosa.

In 2005, a consortium of energy companies called Energia Nuclear de Portugal (Enupor) announced that it was considering the construction of Portugal's first nuclear power plant, to have a generating capacity of 1,600 MW and source its fuel from the re-opening of the Urgeirica uranium mines. (Source: Energy Information Administration, EIA)

Manufacturing

Manufacturing industry comprised some 97,958 companies in 2006, down six per cent on the previous year. 830,116 people worked in the sector, down 4.5 per cent on 2005. There was growth of around 5.2 per cent in industrial turnover. Around 95.4 per cent of all companies had fewer than ten employees, and they accounted for around 44 per cent of total employment. Larger enterprises, with 250 or more employees, whilst employing less than 20 per cent of total employed workforce, generated almost 30 per cent of total turnover.

The Gross Value Added in manufacturing enterprises totalled €18,712,922,000 in 2006. Highest GVA was in the Food and Beverages subsector (€2,695,275,000) and in Textiles (€2,203,740,000).

Service Industries

Services contributed an estimated €102,112 million towards Portugal's GDP in 2007. The services sector employed some 2,850,100 people (or 57.8 per cent of the population compared with 35 per cent in 1997).

Tourism

Tourism is an important industry in Portugal. In 2006, the country's 87,478 hotels and restaurants accounted for over eight per cent of total businesses. The sector employed some 275,980 people, and turnover reached €8,880 million.

The number of tourists staying overnight in Portugal rose from 10,901,968 in 2004 to 11,469,314 in 2005. Of these, 10,140,406 stayed on mainland Portugal, whilst 1,011,921 went to Madeira and 316,987 stayed in the Azores. The most popular destinations within mainland Portugal were Lisbon (3.2 million visitors in 2005) and the Algarve (2.6 million). Most tourists came from European countries, 10,352,738 from the EU15 states. Of this total, 5.5 million were from other parts of Portugal, 1.3 million were from the UK and 1.1 million were from Spain. (Source: INE.Tourism Statistics)

Direcçao-Geral do Turismo, URL: http://www.dgturismo.pt

Agriculture

Portugal's agriculture industry accounts for less than five per cent of the economy. In 2007, the sector earned an estimated €3.53 billion, down from €3.7 billion in 2006 partially due to heavy rainfall in the autumn which reduced wine production and sugar beet harvest in particular. The agricultural labour force numbered some 339,877 people, most of whom belonged to farming families.

Among the principal agricultural products are cereals, olives, wine, potatoes, tomatoes for industry, fresh and dried fruits and animal produce. Whilst crop production and revenues over the last few years indicate an overall decline, livestock has managed to maintain and

at times improve its levels. Revenues from crops fell from €4,081.4 million in 2001 to €3,527.6 million in 2005, whilst animal output rose from €2,418.9 million to €2,625.0 million over the same period. The following table illustrates crop production in Portugal:

Agricultural Production in 2010

Produce	Int. $'000*	Tonnes
Cow milk, whole, fresh	610,594	1,956,650
Grapes	540,407	945,400
Tomatoes	519,644	1,406,100
Indigenous pigmeat	482,093	313,609
Indigenous chicken meat	435,051	305,426
Olives	372,973	465,807
Indigenous cattle meat	250,503	92,732
Vegetables fresh nes	124,936	663,000
Hen eggs, in shell	108,650	131,000
Pears	72,322	176,900
Apples	69,654	164,700
Indigenous sheep meat	54,183	19,900

*unofficial figures

Source: http://faostat.fao.org/site/339/default.aspx Food and Agriculture Organization of the United Nations, Food and Agricultural commodities production

Livestock figures are as follows:

Livestock (head)

	2005	2007
Cattle	1,441,000	1,443,000
Sheep	3,583,000	3,356,000
Goats	551,000	509,000
Pigs	2,344,000	2,295,000

Source: INE Agricultural Statistics

Forestry covers a large area of the territory, estimated at 34 per cent. The most important species are pine, cork oak, holm oak and eucalyptus. Portugal is responsible for 60 per cent of all cork traded internationally. The Gross Value Added of the forestry industry in 2007 was €645 million, up from €642.2 million in 2006. Of this, cork production earned €275.3 million.

Portugal has a large exclusive zone for fishing due to its long coastline, and its fishing fleet amounts to some 8,637 registered vessels. Unloaded fishing amounts for the whole of Portugal were 160,834 tons in 2007, up from 141,683 tons in 2006 and equivalent to a value of €275,295,000. Sardines are the most commonly caught fish, accounting for 58,201 tons in 2007. Mackerel and tuna are also commonly landed. Crustaceans earned some €14,817,000 and molluscs earned €53,510,000. Overall, both the catch and the sector earnings were up on the previous year. (Source: Instituto Nacional de Estadistica). Estimated FAO figures for 2010 put the total catch at 223,000 tonnes.

COMMUNICATIONS AND TRANSPORT

Travel Requirements

Citizens of the USA, Canada and Australia require a passport valid for three months beyond the length of stay but do not need a visa for tourism stays of up to 90 days. EU subjects who hold a valid national ID card do not require a passport. Sufficient funds are required by all except EU nationals. Other nationals should contact the embassy to check visa requirements.

Portugal is a signatory to the Schengen Agreement; with a Schengen visa, a visitor can travel freely throughout the Schengen zone, with few border stops and checks. See http://www.eurovisa.info/SchengenCountries.htm for details.

National Airlines

The main national airlines are:
TAP Air Portugal, URL:http://www.flytap.com/UK/en/Homepage/
Portugalia, URL: http://www.pga.pt
Sata, URL: http://www.sata.pt

International Airports

The main airports in Portugal are:
Porto, URL: http://www.ana-aeroportos.pt/porto
Faro, URL: http://www.ana-aeroportos.pt/ANAIngles/Faro/
Lisbon, URL: http://www.ana-aeroportos.pt/Lisboa
Funchal, Madeira Islands. Tel: +351 291 524941 / 524965

Aviation Authority

Directorate General of Civil Aviation (Direccao-Geral de Aviacao Civil), Tel: +351 21 842 3500

During 2007, 143,225 flights landed at Portugal's airports, 105,301 of which were international. The airports handled some 135,000 tonnes of cargo during the year, as well as 18,000 tonnes of post.

Railways

There are 3,320 km of railways, and in 2005 the railway system carried over 12.6 million passengers and 791,000 tons of freight per month. The Lisbon Metropolitan system carried 15.6 million passengers and the Oporto Metropolitan system carried 2.5 passengers over December 2005.

PORTUGAL

A high-speed rail link between Lisbon and Oporto and Madrid is in planning stages. Construction is due to begin in 2008 and the lines are scheduled to be completed by 2014. It is expected to cut the rail journey time between Lisbon and Madrid from 10 hours to less than three hours.

Lisbon and Porto both have subway and tram systems.

Caminhos de Ferro Portugueses, EP (CP), URL: http://www.cp.pt

Roads
In 2012 there were 82,000 km of highways of which 2,600 km were motorways. Vehicles are driven on the right. There are 1,437 km of toll roads. In 2000 there were 350 cars per 1,000 inhabitants. Recent figures show that approximately 20.7 per cent of the population use motorbikes and 54.7 per cent use automobiles or other vehicles.

Shipping
In December 2005 there were 2.5 million passenger journeys on the River Tejo. Over 2006, some 14,886 vessels visited Portuguese ports, transporting some 685,000 passengers to and from Portugal. 19,975,226 tons of cargo were loaded for export and 46,886,245 tons were unloaded. The main ports are in Lisbon, Setubal, Leixoes (near Porto) and Sines, which between them handle over 96 per cent of all shipped goods.

The following are the principal shipping lines:
Portline, Transportes Maritimos Internacionais SA, URL: http://www.portline.pt
Transinsular, URL: http://www.transinsular.pt
Soponata, URL: http://www.soponata.pt

HEALTH

In 2007 there were 196 hospitals, down by four on the previous year. In the same year, there were 36,178 hospital beds (down from 36,563 in 2006), equating to 3.5 beds per 1,000 inhabitants. There were 781 operating theatres. There were also 377 primary health centres, with 1,874 health centre units and 668 beds.

In 2008, there were 3.7 doctors per 1,000 inhabitants and 5.3 nurses per 1,000 people. The number of specialised doctors rose by two per cent over 2006 figures. There were 4,985 general practitioners, 1,479 paediatric specialists, 1,441 obstetricians and gynaecologists and 1,430 general surgeons.

The infant mortality rate continued to decrease, reaching a low of 3.3 per one 1,000 live births in 2008. The major causes of death among the total population were circulatory system diseases and malignant tumours; however, there were decreases in the morbidity rates of both these illnesses.(Source: Instituto Nacional de Estatistica)

In February 2007, a referendum was held on legalising abortion in the first 10 weeks of pregnancy. A clear majority (59 per cent) voted in favour of the proposal. However, fewer than half the electorate voted, meaning the result is not legally binding. The governing Socialists have said that they will carry through the legislation. "No" campaigners, who cited a falling birth rate as one of the reasons to block reform, called for more generous maternity benefits to encourage women to go through with their pregnancies.

EDUCATION

The Comprehensive Law on the Education System of 14 October 1986 established the framework for the modern Portuguese education system. Education is compulsory and free.

Pre-school Education
Pre-school education is for children aged three to six. It is not mandatory. Almost 70 per cent of children of this age attend a pre-school. The population enrolled in pre-primary education increased by 53.8 per cent between the 1990/1991 and 2006-07 academic years. This was due particularly to the expansion of the pre-primary education network. The number of children enrolled at public pre-primary institutions showed an annual average growth of 3.9 per cent over the period, compared to 1.7 per cent at equivalent private institutions.

Primary/Secondary Education
Children attend *Ensino Basico*, or mandatory education, for nine years from the ages of six to fifteen. The schooling is split into three stages (called 'ciclos'); at the end of the third stage, at 15 years old, pupils receive a basic education diploma which is required prior to enrolling in 'secondary' education.

Ensino Secundario is for three years, the 10th, 11th and 12th grades, and is not mandatory. Pupils completing secondary education receive a *diploma de estudos secundários*. Those completing technological courses also receive a vocational qualification certificate, the *certificado de qualificação profissional*. Students of secondary school age can alternatively attend vocational training schools *Escolas Profissionais* whose courses generally correspond to the requirements of the economic and social regions where they are based. They can be state run or private and are often set up on a private initiative basis.

Certificates awarded at the end of secondary education are needed to enter higher education.

Since the 1990-91 academic year, enrolment numbers have been falling, reflecting the ageing demographic structure of the Portuguese population. In the case of basic and primary education, the falls have been of 25.2 per cent and 28.2 per cent respectively, but only in the public sector. Over the year 2006-07, just over 10 per cent of students that did not complete primary education.

The total number of students in secondary education fell over the period 1996-2005, but then increased by some 10,000 pupils in 2006-07.

Figures from UNESCO for 2007 show that 98 per cent of girls and 99 per cent of boys were enrolled in primary school and 92 per cent of girls and 84 per cent of boys were enrolled in secondary school. In 2006, 11.3 per cent of total government expenditure went on education, 41 per cent of which went on secondary education and 31 per cent on primary education. The adult literacy rate in 2007 was 94.9 per cent, this rose in the age group 15-24 year olds to 99.7 per cent.

Higher Education
There are four private and cooperative universities and 68 higher education establishments. Fees are paid for state-run higher education although there are some grants available. Most university courses last for four or five years and lead to *licenciado* degrees. Polytechnic courses last for three or four years and lead to *bacharel* or *licenciado* degrees respectively. Private and cooperative higher education run courses leading to three, four or five years, depending on whether they lead to *bacharel* or *licenciado* degrees.

Tertiary education expanded considerably between 1990/1991 and 2006/2007, and the number of students almost doubled, (from 187,200 to 366,700). The number of students enrolled in private tertiary education grew from 26.7 per cent in 1990/1991 to 36.2 per cent in 1995/1996, before falling to around 25 per cent in 2006-07. The numbers of students in higher education began to fall in 2003/2004, as the demographic structure began to indicate an ageing population.

Since 2001, there have been more women on higher education courses than men. In 2005, teaching staff in higher education institutions totalled 37,434.

Vocational Education
There is an Institute of Employment and Vocational Training deals with vocational education in co-ordination with the Ministry of Employment and Social Security. Vocational schools run courses equivalent to secondary education.

Apprenticeships exist for young people aged 14 to 24 who have completed at least six years of compulsory schooling. The system covers 60 occupations within 13 sectors of activity. Apprentices who succeed receive a *Certificado de Aptidão Profissional*, or certificate of vocational aptitude. There are also training schemes for the young unemployed. Vocational training programmes within the upper secondary school system saw average annual rises in the number of students of nine per cent over the period 1991-2007.

In 2006-07, the number of schools in mainland Portugal was as set out below:

Type of School	Public	Private
Pre-School	4,684	2,172
Basic School - Stages 1-3	8,392	1,090
Secondary School	546	374
Higher Education	178	141
Source: INE		

RELIGION

The predominant religion is Roman Catholicism. 84 per cent of the population is Catholic, and 1 per cent is Protestant.

Portugal has a religious liberty rating of 10 on a scale of 1 to 10 (10 is most freedom). (Source: World Religion Database)

COMMUNICATIONS AND MEDIA

Newspapers
Newspapers with the greatest circulation are:
Correio da Manha, URL: http://www.correiomanha.pt
O Publico, URL: http://www.publico.pt
Jornal de Noticias, URL: http://www.jornaldenoticias.pt
Diario de Noticias, URL: http://www.dn.pt

Business Journals
Expresso, URL: http://www.expresso.pt
Exame (Portugal), URL: http://www.exame.pt/
Semanario Economico, http://www.semanarioeconomico.com/
Diaro Economico, http://diarioeconomico.com/

Broadcasting
Major broadcasters are:
RTP - Radiotelevisao Portuguesa EP, URL: http://www.rtp.pt
RDP - Radiodifusao Portuguesa EP, URL: http://www.rdp.pt
SIC - URL: http://sic.aeiou.pt/online/homepage
TVI -Televisao Independente, SA, URL: http://www.tvi.iol.pt/

Postal Service
The use of the traditional postal service is decreasing: over the period 2003-07, there was a fall of around six per cent (or 73 million objects posted). The number of attended post offices fell from 6.638 in 1995 to 2,853 in 2007, and the number of post boxes fell from 18,141 to 17,808 over the same period. However, the turnover has increased, from €401,268,000 in 1995 to €641,071 in 2007.

Telecommunications
Portugal has a modern telecommunications system, its network benefiting from broadband and high speed capabilities. There has been a trend over recent years for the growing use of mobile phone services, to the detriment of fixed line services. The use of text messaging has also become more widespread; between 2002 and 2006, these grew by more than 500

per cent, the major share of which occurred in the most recent years (growth of around 100 per cent in 2005 and 2006). The amount of time that people spend on the phone has decreased on fixed line phones (to 7,499,930 thousand units), but increased on mobile phones (to 12,451,930 thousand units).

The three main cellular phone companies operating in Portugal: TMN (owned by Portugal Telecom), Vodaphone Telecel SA and Optimus SA. Portugal Telecom was privatized in 2000. Estimated figures for 2011 show that there were 4.5 million land lines in use and 12.3 million mobile phones.

Figures for 2012 indicate that were 5.9 million regular internet users in Portugal.

Telecom Portugal, URL: http://www.telecom.pt

ENVIRONMENT

Portugal's primary environmental issues are air pollution from vehicle and industrial emissions, soil erosion, and water pollution.

Energy related carbon emissions were estimated in 2005 at 64.97 million metric tons. Per capita carbon dioxide emissions were estimated to be 6.15 metric tons, below the European average of 7.93 metric tons. Figures for 2010 show that total carbon dioxide emissions from the consumption of fossil fuels had fallen to 51.43 million metric tons. (Source: EIA)

Portugal is a party to the following international environmental agreements: Air Pollution, Biodiversity, Climate Change, Desertification, Endangered Species, Hazardous Wastes, Law of the Sea, Marine Dumping, Marine Life Conservation, Ozone Layer Protection, Ship Pollution, Tropical Timber 83, and Wetlands. Portugal is also a signatory to the 1998 Kyoto Protocol.

SPACE PROGRAMME

Portugal became the European Space Agency's 15th member in 2000.

QATAR
State of Qatar
Dawlat Qatar

Capital: Doha (Population estimate: 1.3 million)

Head of State: H.H. Sheikh Tamim Bin Hamad Bin Khalifa Al-Thani (Sovereign) (page 1377)

National Flag: Maroon; a white stripe pale-wise at the hoist, with a serrated edge of nine and a half points.

CONSTITUTION AND GOVERNMENT

Constitution

Qatar is a fully independent sovereign Arab state on the western shore of the Arabian Gulf. Its independence was proclaimed on 3 September 1971, two days after special treaty arrangements with Britain had been abrogated. From 1916 up to the present decade, Britain's responsibility for Qatar declined until its role was limited to the exercise of purely administrative functions concerning Anglo-Qatari affairs.

The Emir of Qatar and Head of State is His Highness Sheikh Hamad bin Khalifa Al-Thani, who assumed the Emirship on 27 June 1995. According to Qatar's provisional constitution, under which it has operated since 1970, he has full legislative and executive powers, and is assisted in his duties by a 15-member Council of Ministers.

Qatar's Parliament, the 30-member Advisory Council, was appointed by the Emir for four-year terms. The power to question ministers on budgetary and administrative matters was added to the Council's constitutional rights in 1975. There are no organised political parties in Qatar.

A committee was set up in 1999 to draft a new constitution. A draft of the new constitution was presented in July 2002, and included provision for a 45 member Legislative Council, of which two thirds are to be elected and the other third appointed by the Emir. In April 2003 a referendum on the new constitution was held, and 96 per cent of voters approved it. The new constitution came into effect in June 2005. The constitution also guarantees freedom of assembly, expression and religion.

To consult the full constitution, please visit: http://english.mofa.gov.qa/details.cfm?id=80

Recent Events

In November 2002 the Emir's sister, Shaikha Hassa bint Khalifa Al-Thani was appointed to the cabinet with responsibility for family issues. She became the first woman to hold a ministerial post in Qatar.

In August 2003 The Emir of Qatar announced he was replacing his elder son, H.H. Sheikh Jassem Bin Hamad Bin Khalifa Al-Thani , with his younger son, H.H. Sheikh Tamim Bin Hamad Al-Thani as heir apparent. No reason was given at the time of the announcement.

In March 2005, Qatar suffered its first terrorist attack, a suspected suicide bomber who killed a British man and injured others. Western embassies rank the threat of terrorism high in the Gulf State.

In June 2005 Qatar's first written constitution came into effect after being approved by 96 per cent of voters at a referendum. Qatar and Dubai became the two biggest shareholders of the London Stock Exchange, the world's third largest stock exchange, in 2007.

Following the resumption of diplomatic ties, Qatar finally settled a border delineation dispute with Saudi Arabia in December 2008. In 2009, it severed diplomatic ties with Israel.

In December 2010, Qatar won the bid to host the 2022 Fifa World Cup.

In November 2011, Sheikh Hamad bin Khalifa al-Thani announced that elections for its advisory council will be held in 2013. The elections would be the state's first legislative elections. Political parties remain banned.

In June 2013, The Amir, Sheikh Hamad bin Khalifa Al Thani, announced that he was standing down in favour of his son Crown Prince, Sheikh Tamim bin Hamad Al Thani. (page 1377) Sheikh Tamim took over as emir on 25 June and announced his cabinet the following day.

Cabinet (as at June 2013)
Head of State and Minister of Defence and Commander-in-Chief of the Armed Forces: HH Sheikh Tamim bin Hamad Al Thani (page 1377)
Prime Minister and Minister of Interior: Sheikh Abdullah bin Nasser bin Khalifa Al Thani (page 1377)
Deputy Prime Minister, Minister of Cabinet Affairs: Ahmed bin Abdullah Al-Mahmoud (page 1375)
Minister of Foreign Affairs: Khalid bin Mohammad al-Attiyah (page 1373)
Minister of State for Defence: Major Gen. Khalid bin Ali Al-Attiyah
Minister of Municipal Affairs and Urban Planning: Shaikh Abdulrahman bin Khalifa bin Abdulaziz al-Thani
Minister of Energy and Industrial Affairs: Dr Mohamed bin Saleh Al-Sada
Minister of Finance: Ali Sherif Al-Emadi
Minister of Economy and Trade: Shaikh Ahmed bin Jassim bin Mohamed al-Thani
Minister of Justice: Dr Hassan Lahdan Saqr Al-Mohannadi
Minister of Culture, Arts and Heritage: Dr Hamad bin Abdulaziz Al-Kawari
Minister of Public Health: Abdullah bin Khalid Al-Kahtani
Minister of Islamic Affairs: Dr Ghaith bin Mubarak bin Imran Al-Kuwari
Minister of Administrative Development: Dr Issa Saad al-Jafali Al-Muaimi
Minister of Youth and Sports: Saleh bin Ghanem bin Nasser Al-Ali
Minister of Communication and Information Technology: Dr Hessa Sultan Al-Jaber
Minister of Education: Mohammed Abdul Wahed Ali Al-Hammadi
Minister of Development Planning and Statistics: Dr Saleh Mohamed Salem Al-Nabit
Minister of Labour and Social Affairs: Abdullah Saleh Mubarak Al-Khulaifi
Minister of Transport: Jassim Seif Ahmed Al-Sulaiti
Minister of the Environment: Ahmed Amer Mohamed Al-Humaide

Ministries
Office of H.H. the Emir, PO Box 923, Doha, Qatar. Tel: +974 446 2300, fax: +974 436 1212, e-mail: adf@diwan.gov.qa, URL: http://www.diwan.gov.qa/
Ministry of Defence, PO Box 37, Doha, Qatar. Tel: +974 4461 4111, fax: +974 432 4743
Ministry of Foreign Affairs, PO Box 250, Doha, Qatar. Tel: +974 4433 4334, fax: +974 432 4131, e-mail: webmaster@mofa.gov.qa, URL: http://www.mofa.gov.qa
Ministry of Interior, PO Box 8895, Doha, Qatar. Tel: +974 4434 2522, fax: +974 4432 3339, e-mail: info@moi.gov.qa, URL: http://www.moi.gov.qa/
Ministry of Labour and Social Affairs, PO Box 36, Barzan Tower, Doha, Qatar. Tel: +974 4484 1111, fax: +974 4484 1000, e-mail: customerservice@mol.gov.qa, URL: http://www.mol.gov.qa/
Ministry of Communications and Transport, PO Box 3416, Doha, Qatar. Tel: +974 464000, fax: +974 835888
Ministry of Energy and Industry, PO Box 2599, Doha, Qatar. Tel: +974 4484 6444, fax: +974 4483 2024, e-mail: did@mei.gov.qa, URL: http://www.mei.gov.qa
Ministry of Municipal Affairs and Urban Planning, PO Box 22332, Doha, Qatar. Tel: +974 4441 3331, fax: +974 4443 0239, e-mail: info@baladiya.gov.qa, URL: http://www.baladiya.gov.qa/
Ministry of Justice, PO Box 36, Barzan Tower, Al Corniche opposite Q-Post, Doha, Qatar. Tel: +974 4484 1111, fax: +974 4484 1000, e-mail: customerservice@mol.gov.qa, URL: http://www.mol.gov.qa/
Ministry of Education, PO Box 80, Doha, Qatar. Tel: +974 441 3444, fax: +974 431 3886, URL: http://www.moe.edu.qa/

QATAR

Supreme Education Council, PO Box 35111, Doha, Qatar. Tel: +974 4455 9555, fax: +974 4465 9444, e-mail: info@sec.gov.qa, URL: http://www.sec.gov.qa/
Supreme Council of Health, PO Box 42, Asiad Building, Medical City, Doha, Qatar. Tel: +974 4407 0000, fax: +974 4407 7778, e-mail: info@sch.gov.qa, URL: http://www.sch.gov.qa
Ministry of Endowments and Islamic Affairs, PO Box 422 Doha, Qatar. Tel: +974 4447 0777, fax: +974 4447 0700, e-mail: islam@islam.gov.qa, URL: http://www.islam.gov.qa/
Ministry of Finance and Economy, PO Box 83, Doha, Qatar. Tel: +974 4446 1177, fax: +974 4443 1177, URL: http://www.mof.gov.qa
Ministry of Business and Trade, PO Box 1968, Doha, Qatar. Tel: +974 4494 5555, fax: +974 4493 0992, e-mail: pru@mbt.gov.qa, URL: http://www.mbt.gov.qa
Ministry of Culture, Arts and Heritage, PO Box 23700, C-Ring Road, Doha, Qatar. Tel: +974 4466 8777, e-mail: qatar_culture@hotmail.com, URL: http://www.moc.gov.qa/
Ministry of Social Affairs, PO Box 36, Doha, Qatar. Tel: +974 4484 1111, fax: +974 4484 1000, e-mail: mosa@mosa.gov.qa, URL: http://www.mosa.gov.qa/

Elections
The first elections in Qatar took place in March 1999 for a new municipal council to be responsible for municipal affairs. There were 227 candidates including six women, and 22,000 votes were cast. Sheikh Hamed said the elections were the first step towards an elected national legislature.

Parliamentary elections were due to be held in 2008, but were postponed until 2010. The new electoral law, passed in May 2008, specifies that people from the age of 18 upwards will be able to vote and vote-buying is outlawed. The Consultative Assembly will have 45 members, 30 of whom will be directly elected, and 15 of whom will continue to be appointed by the Emir.

Diplomatic Representation
Qatar Embassy, 1 South Audley Street, London W1K 1NB, United Kingdom. Tel: +44 (0)20 7493 2200, fax: +44 (0)20 7493 2661, URL: http://qatar.embassyhomepage.com/
Ambassador: Khalid bin Rashid bin Salim Al-Hamoudi Al-Mansouri
US Embassy, 22 February Road, Doha, Qatar (P.O.Box 2399), Tel: +974 488 4101, fax: +974 488 4298, URL: http://qatar.usembassy.gov
Ambassador: Susan Ziadeh
British Embassy, PO Box 3, Doha, Qatar. Tel: +974 442 1991, fax: +974 443 8692, URL: http://ukinqatar.fco.gov.uk
Ambassador: Michael O'Neill (page 1489)
Qatar Embassy, 4200 Wisconsin Avenue, NW, Washington DC 20016, USA. Tel: +1 202 274 1600, fax: +1 202 237 0061, URL: http://www.qatarembassy.net/
Ambassador: Muhammad bin Abdallah bin Mitib al-Rumayhi
Permanent Mission to the United Nations, 809 United Nations Plaza, 4th Floor, New York, NY 10017, USA. Tel: +1 212 486 9335, fax: +1 212 758 4952, URL: http://www.qatarmission.org/
Ambassador: Mishal bin Hamad bin Muhammad Al Thani

LEGAL SYSTEM

The Amir heads the law system. There are three main divisions of courts, namely the Sharia courts (which have jurisdiction over personal status matters), the civil courts (which have jurisdiction over civil and criminal matters), and the Qatar Financial Center legal system. There are courts of first instance and courts of appeal, and there are plans to establish a higher appeal division similar to the courts of cassation in other Arab countries. Judges are usually appointed by the Ministry of Justice from amongst graduates of recognised law or Shariah colleges. The Qatar Financial Center legal system handles commercial cases arising out of Qatar's special econmic zone.

The government places restrictions on civil liberties, including freedoms of speech, press, assembly, and religion. Foreign laborers face restrictions on foreign travel, and worker rights are severely restricted. Qatar retains the death penalty for threats to national security, espionage and apostasy. The most recent reported execution was in 2003.

National Human Rights Committee, URL: http://www.nhrc-qa.org/

LOCAL GOVERNMENT

Qatar is divided into seven municipalities: Ad Dawhah, Al Khawr wa adh Dhakhirah, Al Wakrah, Ar Rayyan, Ash Shamal, Az Za'ayin, and Umm Salal. The first elections held in Qatar took place in March 1999 for a new municipal council to be responsible for municipal affairs, agriculture, buildings, public health, food quality and public waste. The council has 29 members. The most recent elections were held in 2007.

AREA AND POPULATION

Area
Qatar occupies a peninsula of approximately 4,000 sq. miles that projects north into the Gulf for about 100 miles and has an estimated maximum width of 55 miles. Qatar shares borders with Saudi Arabia on the west and Abu Dhabi on the east and its nearest seaward neighbour is Bahrain. The eastern Iranian shore of the Gulf is 120 miles off Qatar's rounded northern extremity. Basra, the Iraqi port at the northern head of the Gulf, is 350 miles away and the southern Strait of Hormuz, 310 miles. Qatar, therefore, occupies an important pivotal position on the Gulf. The peninsula's terrain, except for that of the Dukhan anticline in the west, is flat. Blown sand covers much of the south and sand dunes predominate in the south-east. The capital, Doha, is situated on the eastern coast.

The climate is arid with hot, humid summers, and milder winters.

A dispute with Bahrain over sovereignty of the Hawar and surrounding islands was resolved in March 2001 by the International Court of Justice who ruled the the Hawar Islands belonged to Bahrain and the islands of Zubarah and Janan belonged to Qatar.

To view a map, consult http://www.un.org/Depts/Cartographic/map/profile/qatar.pdf

Population
The total estimated population in 2010 was 1.759 million with an average annual growth rate of 10.9 per cent over the period 2000-10. The median age is 32 years. Approximately 13 per cent of the population are aged less than 15 years and 2 per cent over 60. Around 40 per cent of the population are Arabs, 18 per cent Pakistani, 18 per cent Indian, 10 per cent Iranian and 14 per cent other ethnic groups. Approximately 80 per cent of the population are foreign workers. Over 96 per cent of the population lives in urban areas. The largest concentration of people is in Doha, with an estimated 80 per cent of the population located there. Other well populated areas include Dukhan, Mesaieed, Al Wakra, Ras Laffan and Al Khor.

The official language of Qatar is Arabic, but most senior Qatari officials are fluent in English.

Births, Marriages, Deaths
Figures for 2010 put the crude birth rate at 12.7 per thousand people and the crude death rate at 1.4 per thousand people. The infant mortality rate was estimated to be 7 per thousand live births in 2007. Total fertility rate for women in 2009 was 2.4. Life expectancy at birth in 2009 was 78 years for males and 79 years for females. Healthy life expectancy was 68 years for males and 74 years for females in 2007. (Source: http://www.who.int, World Health Statistics 2012)

Public Holidays 2014
1 January: New Year's Day
4 January: Birth of the Prophet (Mouloud)*
27 May: Ascension of the Prophet (Leilat al-Meiraj)*
29 July: End of Ramadan (Eid Al Fitr)*
3 September: Independence Day
5 October: Feast of the Sacrifice (Eid Al Adha)*
25 October: Islamic New Year*
* All Islamic holidays are observed but dates vary each year as they are based on the sighting of the moon.

EMPLOYMENT

Total Employment by Economic Activity

Occupation	2007
Agriculture, hunting & forestry	15,854
Fishing	3,581
Mining & quarrying	43,650
Manufacturing	71,893
Electricity, gas & water supply	5,498
Construction	307,381
Wholesale & retail trade, repairs	101,608
Hotels & restaurants	16,209
Transport, storage & communications	35,874
Financial intermediation	9,024
Real estate, renting & business activities	28,405
Public admin. & defence; compulsory social security	52,544
Education	26,164
Health & social work	21,130
Other community, social & personal service activities	12,738
Households with employed persons	72,780
Extra-territorial organisations & bodies	1,731
Other	1,519
Total	827,583

Source: Copyright © International Labour Organization (ILO Dept. of Statistics, http://laborsta.ilo.org)

BANKING AND FINANCE

Currency
Qatar's unit of currency is the Riyal.
1 Riyal = 100 Dirhams

GDP/GNP, Inflation, National Debt
The economy is based on Qatar's earnings from oil and gas which gives it one of the highest per capita incomes in the world. Qatar's reserves of gas are expected to last for 200 years. There is currently a programme of infrastructure investment, largely funded through gas revenue. The tourism sector is being developed and ahead of the World Cup in 2022 new roads, a metro system, hotels, a new international airport, sports stadiums are all being constructed.

GDP was estimated at US$165 billion in 2011 with a real growth of 14 per cent. Per capita income in 2011 was estimated at US$95,000. Oil and gas contribute more than 50 per cent of GDP.

The inflation rate was 1.9 per cent in 2011, rising to over 2 per cent in 2012, fuelled by rising food costs.

External debt in 2012 was US$68 billion. Qatar's debt came about from financing the infrastructure for increased production of oil and gas.

Foreign Investment

In previous years, with the decline in both production of oil and oil prices, foreign finance became an important element in the financing of Qatari development projects. Provided that a Qatari partner holds 51 per cent interest in a venture, foreigners can invest in any area apart from banking, insurance, real estate and commercial agencies.

In September 2007, Qatar and Dubai became the two biggest shareholders of the London Stock Exchange, the world's third largest stock exchange.

Balance of Payments / Imports and Exports

There has been substantial growth in exports in recent years because of a large increase in exports of natural gas. Figures for 2010 estimated merchandise exports to have earned US$70 billion, of which oil made up almost 50 per cent and gas 36 per cent. Main export partners are Japan (25 per cent), South Korea (20 per cent), India and Singapore.

Merchandise imports cost an estimated US$20 billion in 2010. Main imports are consumer goods, machinery and food. The major import partners are the US, Japan, China, Germany, Saudi Arabia, UK, Italy, South Korea, and the UAE.

All imports require a licence. Licences are only issued to Qatari nationals.

Central Bank

Qatar Central Bank, PO Box 1234, Doha, Qatar. Tel: +974 4456456, fax: +974 4414190, e-mail: webmaster@qcb.gov.qa, URL: http://www.qcb.gov.qa
Governor: Abdullah Saud al-Thani

Chamber of Commerce

Qatar Chamber of Commerce and Industry, URL: http://qatarchamber.com/

MANUFACTURING, MINING AND SERVICES

Primary and Extractive Industries

Oil has been the bedrock of the economy since it was discovered more than 30 years ago. Total proven reserves in 2012 were 25.315.2 billion barrels, with an estimated production in 2011 of 1,637,540 barrels per day. Qatar consumes 183,000 barrels per day and exports 1,0454,540 barrels per day, mainly to Japan. The crude oil distillation capacity in 2006 was estimated at 200,000 bbld.

Oil is produced from several offshore fields including the offshore North Field and the onshore Dukhan field. As of 1997 Dukhan was estimated to have reserves of 2.2 billion barrels. Maximum production here was recently estimated to be about 250,000 barrels a day. All the offshore fields are within 40 km of Halul island where there is an oil terminal with a 4.5 million barrel storage capacity.

Exploration has been carried out in recent years, resulting in the discovery of the al-Rayan field which is now on-line, as well as discoveries in the upstream sector including al Khalij. Although Qatar's oil reserves are expected to last for a shorter period of time than the reserves of other countries in the Gulf, technology is being introduced in order to extend production. Reserves are expected to be depleted by 2020.

Gas

Qatar has very large natural gas reserves (896 trillion cubic feet as of January 2011) . Its offshore North Field, lying about 70 km off the northeast of the Qatari peninsula, was estimated in 1997 to hold 380 trillion cubic feet of gas, with recoverable reserves of 239 trillion cubic feet, reserves in this field have recently been estimated to be closer to the region of 900 trillion cubic feet. The field covers about 1,000 sq. miles. Qatar's total production was estimated to be 4.1 billion cubic feet in 2011, 4.0 billion cubic feet of which was exported. Consumption is an estimated at 770 billion cubic feet in 2010.

Qatar first exported liquified natural gas in 1996, and this resource has grown steadily in importance to the economy since. Qatar may join the United Arab Emirates backed Dolphin Project, an integrated gas pipeline grid joining Qatar, the UAE and Oman.

Natural gas is a highly important energy supply in Qatar, and is used as a source of energy for factories and power stations and as feedstock for the petrochemical industries producing nitrogenous fertilisers, ethylene and polyethylene. It is also used as a reducing agent in the iron and steel industry.

In 2011, the UK company Centrica signed a gas supply deal with Qatargas worth £2 billion. The deal should meet approximately 10 per cent of UK domestic consumption.

Energy

Qatar's total energy consumption in 2009 was estimated at 1.0 quadrillion Btu . Per capita energy consumption in 2004 was 812.9 million Btu. Of the total energy consumed natural gas supplied 83 per cent and oil 13 per cent. In 2000 assets owned by the Ministry of Electricity and Water were transferred to the Qatar General Electricity and Water Corporation. The government maintains a 47 per cent share.

Figures for 2010 show that Qatar generated 22.28 billion Kwh of electricity and consumed 20.51 billion Kwh.

Agriculture

Production of certain vegetables continues at a sufficiently high rate to justify the export of small surpluses and yields of fruit continue to increase, but agriculture only contributes an estimated 2 per cent to GDP. The government is actively helping farmers to improve their yield and find ways of developing water sources and reclaim arable land.

Agricultural Production in 2010

Produce	Int. $'000*	Tonnes
Dates	12,002	23,500
Indigenous chicken meat	7,335	5,149
Iindigenous goat meat	4,035	1,684
Tomatoes	3,954	10,700
Indigenous sheep meat	3,023	1,110
Vegetables fresh nes	2,789	14,800
Hen eggs, in shell	2,488	3,000
Sheep milk, whole, fresh	2,064	5,300
Goat milk, whole, fresh	2,014	6,000
Camel milk, whole, fresh	1,671	4,900
Cow milk, whole, fresh	1,654	5,300
Onions, dry	924	4,400

* unofficial figures
Source: http://faostat.fao.org/site/339/default.aspx Food and Agriculture Organization of the United Nations, Food and Agricultural commodities production

Fishing

The pearling industry was one of Qatar's major resources but the introduction of cultured pearls caused a decline in the industry. The Qatar National Fishing Co., incorporated in Doha in 1966 to fish for shrimp in territorial waters and process these catches, exports a considerable amount of head-off fish, particularly to Japan. Doha is now the headquarters of the UNDP Regional Fisheries Survey. Estimated figures from FAO for 2010 put the total fish catch at 13,760 tonnes.

COMMUNICATIONS AND TRANSPORT

Travel Requirements

Citizens of the USA, Canada, Australia and the EU require a passport valid for six months, a return/outward ticket, a hotel voucher, QAR5,000 in cash or a foreign currency equivalent (or carry an international credit card), and a visa. Transit passengers continuing their journey within eight hours. Citizens of Australia, Austria, Belgium, Canada, Denmark, Finland, France, Germany, Greece, Ireland, Italy, Luxembourg, Portugal, Spain, Sweden, the UK and the USA can obtain tourist visas upon arrival at the airport in Doha for stays of up to 21 days, or business visas for stays of up to seven days. Visa requirements are subject to change, and travellers are strongly advised to contact an embassy or consulate of Qatar for up-to-date information.

National Airlines

Qatar Airways, Almana Tower, Airport Road, PO Box 22550, Doha, Qatar. Tel: +974 430707, fax: +974 352433 URL: http://www.qatarairways.com

International Airports

Qatar's only international airport is at Doha. The first stage of the construction of a new airport to replace Doha is expected to be completed in 2008. The new airport will be able to handle 12.5 million passengers per year compared to approximately 4 million per year currently. The old airport is also being expanded so that it will be able to handle increased numbers of passengers during construction of the new airport. Completion of airport and transport including a suspended mono-rail link, is due to be completed by 2015.
Doha International Airport, URL: http://www.qatar-airport.com

Railways

Qatar has no rail system.

Roads

There are over 1,000 miles of roads, and all the major cities are now connected to each other. Vehicles are driven on the right. Qatar's only road connection to other countries is through Saudi Arabia.

Shipping

Qatar National Navigation & Transport Company Ltd, PO Box 153, Doha, Qatar.

Ports and Harbours

Qatar has two main ports; the nine-berth Umm Said for bulk shipments and the 11-berth Doha Port for general cargo. Since 1997 the port of Ras Laffan has been exclusively used for the export of liquefied natural gas.

HEALTH

The State has traditionally provided free health services to all residents of the peninsula, but the decline in oil revenues resulted in a cut back in free care, particularly for expatriates. In addition to the 20 state-owned and operated health centres, private clinics also operate. The 660-bed Hamad General Hospital operates the country's only maternity hospital, which has 300 beds. The government has recently invested millions of dollars to improve and expand the healthcare system to cope with the increased population.

In 2009, the government spent approximately 12.2 per cent of its total budget on healthcare (up from 5.0 per cent in 2000), accounting for 78.4 per cent of all healthcare spending. The remaining expenditure is made up of private expenditure, of which over 73 per cent is out-of-pocket expenditure. Total expenditure on healthcare equated to 2.6 per cent of the country's GDP. Per capita expenditure on health was approximately US$1,612, compared with US$688 in 2000. Figures for 2005-11 show that there are 2,313 physicians (27.6 per 10,000 population), 6,185 nurses and midwives (74 per 10,000 population), 1,056 pharmaceutical personnel and 486 dentists. There are 14 hospital beds per 10,000 population.

ROMANIA

The infant mortality rate (likelihood of dying by first birthday) in 2010 was 7 per 1,000 live births. The child mortality rate (under 5 years) was 8 per 1,000 live births. The most common causes of death in children aged less than five years old are: prematurity (30 per cent), congenital anomalies (25 per cent), birth asphyxia (11 per cent), pneumonia (2 per cent) and measles (1 per cent).

An estimated 100 per cent of the population have access to improved drinking water supplies and improved sanitation. (Source: http://www.who.int, World Health Statistics 2012)

EDUCATION

Education in Qatar is free, but not compulsory. It begins with pre-primary between the ages of four and six, primary school between the ages of six and twelve. Preparatory education begins at twelve and lasts for three years, whilst secondary education begins at fifteen and lasts for a period of three years. Qatar has one university, the University of Qatar, which was established in 1977, just outside Doha. Recent figures show that there were 7,800 students. Qatar has many private and international schools for the large number of expatriate families in the country.

Figures for 2007 showed that 47 per cent of young children attended kindergarten, 93 per cent of primary aged children were enrolled in primary school and 93 per cent of secondary school aged children were enrolled in secondary schools. Primary school pupil: teacher ratio was 11:1. Ninety-six per cent of pupils go onto secondary education. Approximately 20 per cent go onto tertiary education.

Recent UNESCO figures put Qatar's literacy rate at 93.8 per cent for males and 90.4 for females aged 15+. For the age group 15-24 years, the rate is 99.1 for males and 99.0 for females.

RELIGION

Islam is enshrined in the Constitution as the state religion and 86 per cent of the population is estimated to be Muslim. In March 2008 a Roman Catholic Church opened in Doha; it is estimated that many thousands of Christians live in Qatar, most being Catholics from Asian countries such as the Philippines. Around 10 per cent of the population is thought to be Christian there are also small Hindu and Buddhist communities.

Qatar has a religious liberty rating of 4 on a scale of 1 to 10 (10 is most freedom). (Source: World Religion Database)

COMMUNICATIONS AND MEDIA

Censorship officially ended in 1995 and the press is generally free. However, self-censorship is common.

Newspapers
Al-Watan, URL: http://www.al-watan.com/

Al-rayah, URL: http://www.raya.com
Gulf Times, URL: http://www.gulf-times.com
Al Sharq Newspaper, URL: http://www.al-sharq.com/
The Peninsula, URL: http://www.thepeninsulaqatar.com/
Qatar Tribune, URL: http://www.qatar-tribune.com/

Broadcasting
Television and radio media are state-controlled. Transmissions of some international broadcasters are available. 1997 saw the launch of the government-owned Al Jazeera television channel. Al Jazeera now broadcasts across the Middle East and into North Africa. The station came to be known worldwide after the terrorist attacks in USA of 11 September 2001 as it was the only station to broadcast from Afghanistan and showed footage of Osama Bin Laden. An English-language version was launched in 2006 called Al-Jazeera International. The network has an estimated audience of over 200 million households worldwide.

The state owned radio company, Qatar Broadcasting Corporation (QBS), was established in 1968 and broadcasts on FM, medium wave and short wave frequencies. FM broadcasting is mainly in English, while medium wave broadcasting is mainly in Arabic.
Qatar Broadcasting Services, URL: http://www.qatarradio.net/
Qatar Television (QTV), PO Box 1944, Doha, Qatar. Tel: +974 894444, fax: +974 438316
Al Jazeera Satellite Channel, URL: http://www.aljazeera.net / http://www.english.aljazeera.net/

Telecommunications
The telecommunications system is modern. In 2008 there were estimated to be 260,000 main telephone lines in use, and over 1.6 million mobile phones. It has recently been estimated that there are approximately 430,000 internet users in Qatar (2008).

ENVIRONMENT

Qatar's main environmental concern is fresh water supply.

In 2003, energy-related carbon dioxide emissions were estimated at 27.9 million metric tons of which natural gas makes up over 80 per cent. Per capita energy-related carbon dioxide emissions were estimated at 45.7 metric tons. In 2010, Qatar's emissions from the consumption of fossil fuels totalled 64.68 million metric tons of carbon dioxide. (Source: EIA)

Qatar is party to the following environmental agreements: Biodiversity, Climate Change, Climate Change-Kyoto Protocol, Desertification, Endangered Species, Hazardous Wastes, Law of the Sea, Ozone Layer Protection.

SPACE PROGRAMME

In January 2012, Qatar's Civil Aviation Authority announced plans to establish a $3 billion Space City to be built in the Al-Khor area of the state. The area will include the establishment of a university in cooperation with NASA. The Qatar satellite company, Es'hailSat, has chosen Arianespace to launch their first satellite Es'hail 1 during 2013. The high-capacity satellite will increase broadband capacity for the region.

ROMANIA
România

Capital: Bucharest (Population estimate, 2011: 1.937 million)

Head of State: Traian Basescu (page 1384)

National Flag: A tricolour pale - wise of blue, yellow and red.

CONSTITUTION AND GOVERNMENT

Constitution
As a consequence of the Churchill-Stalin agreement of October 1944, Romania came under the influence of the Communist Party and the then USSR. On 30 December 1947 King Mihai I was forced to abdicate and Romania was proclaimed a Popular Republic. Between 1948 and 1964, the Communist government launched a policy of industrialisation. Opposition parties and the old political class structure were swiftly abolished.

Steps towards some degree of independence from the USSR, initiated by Gh. Gheorghiu- Dej in 1964, were continued after 1965 by Nicolae Ceausescu who obtained a degree of international support. However, Ceausescu pursued a repressive régime and was overthrown and executed by a popular movement in the December Revolution of 25 December 1989. The National Salvation Front headed by Ion Iliescu, previously a senior Communist, formed the next government. Petre Roman, an engineer and also a Communist, was appointed prime minister.

In March 1990 a new electoral law was adopted proclaiming political power in Romania as the possession of the people. General elections were held in May 1990. The elections were won by the National Salvation Front, under the leadership of Ion Iliescu. Radical constitutional changes followed and a new constitution was adopted on 21 November 1991. The country ceased to be the Socialist Republic of Romania and a democratic and pluralist system of government was established and a free market economic system was adopted. The constitution was amended to include reforms necessary for EU membership and an extension to the presidential term in 2003.

To consult the constitution, please visit: http://www.cdep.ro/pls/dic/site.page?id=371

International Relations
In November 2002 Romania was formally invited to join NATO at the Prague summit, and became a member in March 2004. Romania signed an Accession Treaty to EU paving the way for it to become a member of the European Union from 1 January 2007. Parliament ratified the EU accession treaty in May 2005. As part of its preparations for entry, a new leu currency was introduced (four zeros were stripped from the old leu). Romania joined the EU on 1 January 2007.

Recent Events
In December 2005 Romania signed an agreement with the US to allow the US to use military bases in Romania. In February 2006 the former prime minister Adrian Nastase was charged with corruption. He denied the charges.

In April 2007, the parliament voted to suspend President Basescu on grounds that he was exceeding the powers of his position as set out in the constitution. A referendum held in May endorsed him as president and rejected plans by parliament to impeach him. In 2007 the European Commission called upon Romania to do more to combat corruption and the EU has threatened to withhold subsidies.

Romanian's went to the polls in November 2008. It was a tight race between the centrist Liberal Democrats and the leftist Social Democrats. Emil Boc, leader of the Liberal Democrats, was asked to form a new government.

In October 2009 the Social Democrat Party pulled out of ruling coalition, this resulted in Prime Minister Emil Boc at head of minority government which then lost a vote of no confidences a confidence vote in parliament. In November President Basescu nominated Lucian Croitoru (independent) to take over as prime minister but this was rejected by parliament. Liviu Negoita (PD-L) was also nominated and also rejected. On 17 December 2009 Emil Bloc was once again nominated as prime minister. His new government was formed of a coalition between the PD-L and the Democratic Union of Hungarians in Romania (UDMR) . Five independents are also part of the coalition. This government was approved on 23 December.

In September 2010, France and Germany prevented Romania from joining Schengen passport-free zone, saying it needed to make progress in its fight against corruption and organised crime.

Prime Minister Emil Bloc resigned from his post on February 6 2012 following continued protests at austerity measures, these included a freeze on pensions and a 25 per cent cut in public sector wages. Mihai-Razvan Ungureanu of the PDL was nominated as his replacement. A coalition cabinet was announced the following day. His government lost a vote of confidence in April 2012 and Victor Ponta of the PSD was designated prime minister. Ponta formed a new coalition government made up of the PSD, the PC, the PNL and three independents. The new government took office on 7 May.

In July 2012, parliament voted to suspend President Basescu from office for 30 days. Parliament accused him of exceeding his presidential authority. He survived an impeachment referendum as less than 50 per cent of the electorate turned out for the vote.

Legislative elections took place on 9 December 2012 and the centre-left coalition of PM Victor Ponta was returned to power; the Social Liberal Union won nearly 60 per cent of the vote.

Legislature
The President of Romania is elected by universal vote for a four year term and can only be re-elected once. The President nominates the Prime Minister and appoints the Government on the basis of votes by Parliament. The Parliament is made up of two chambers: the Chamber of Deputies has 412 members, 18 of which are from minorities, members are directly elected and serve a four year term. The Senate has 176 members who also serve a four year term. Together the two chambers of Parliament make up the Constituent Assembly whose task has been to adopt Romania's new constitution.

Chamber of Deputies, Palatul Parlamentului, St. Izvor 2-4, Sector 5 050563 Bucharest, Romania. Tel: +40 21 402 1444, fax: +40 21 402 2149, URL: http://www.cdep.ro
Senate, Piata Revolutiei 1, 010086 Bucharest, Romania. Tel: +40 21 312 3079, fax: +40 21 312 1184, URL: http://www.senat.ro

Cabinet (as at July 2013)
Prime Minister: Victor Ponta (PSD) (page 1497)
Deputy Prime Minister: Gabriel Oprea (page 1490)
Deputy Prime Minister and Minister of Administration and Regional Development: Liviu Dragnea (page 1417)
Deputy Prime Minister and Minister of Finance: Daniel Chitoiu (page 1404)
Minister of Energy: Constantin Nita
Minister of Foreign Affairs: Titus Corlatean (page 1408)
Minister of European Funds: Eugen Teodorovici
Minister of the Interior: Radu Stroe
Minister of Environment: Rovana Plumb
Ministry of Forestry and Water: Lucia Varga
Minister of Education: Remus Pricopie
Minister of Youth and Sports: Nicolae Banicioiu
Minister of SMEs, Tourism & Business Environment: Maria Grapini
Minister of Labour: Mariana Campeanu
Minister of National Defence: Mircea Dusa
Minister of Justice: Robert Cazanciuc
Minister of Agriculture and Rural Development: Daniel Constantin
Minister of Health: Dr Eugen Nicolaescu
Minister of Culture and National Heritage: Daniel Barbu
Minister of Communications and Information Technology: Dan Nica
Minister of Transport: Relu Fenechiu
Ministry of Industry: Varujan Vosganian
Minister-Delegate for the Budget: Liviu Voinea
Minister-Delegate for Relations with Parliament: Mihai Voicu
Minister-Delegate for Research: Mihnea Costoiu
Minister-Delegate for Social Dialogue: Doina Pana
Minister-Delegate for Romanians Abroad: Cristian David
Minister-Delegate for Infrastructure Projects of National Interest: Dan Sova

Ministries
Office of the President, Palatul Cotroceni, Blvd. Geniului 1, 76238 Bucharest, Romania. Tel: +40 1 410 0581, fax: +40 1 312 1247/ 312 1179, e-mail: webmaster@presidency.ro, URL: http://www.presidency.ro
Office of the Prime Minister, Piata Victoriei 1, 71201 Bucharest, Romania. Tel: +40 1 212 1660, fax: +40 1 222 5814, URL: http://www.gov.ro/
Ministry of Foreign Affairs, Aleea Alexandru nr. 31, Sector 1, Bucharest, Romania. Tel: +401 230 2071, fax: +40 1 230 7489, e-mail: mae@mae.ro, URL: http://www.mae.ro
Ministry of Economy and Trade, Calea Victoriei nr 152, sector 1, Sector 5, Bucharest, Romania. URL: http://www.minind.ro/
Ministry of Justice, Apolodor Street 17, Sector 5, Bucharest, Romania. Tel: +40 1 311 2266, fax: +40 1 315 5389, e-mail: webmaster@gov.ro, URL: http://www.just.ro
Ministry of Communications and Information Society, URL: http://www.mcsi.ro/

Ministry of National Defence, Izvor Street 13-15, Sector 5, Bucharest, Romania. Tel: +401 410 4000, fax: +40 1 312 0863, e-mail: cabinet.ministru@mapn.ro, URL: http://www.mapn.ro
Ministry of Administration and Interior, Str. Mihai Voda Street 6, Sector 5, Bucharest, Romania. Tel: +40 1 315 8616, fax: +40 1 314 6960, e-mail: infodoc@mira.ro, URL: http://www.mira.gov.ro
Ministry of Labour, the Family and Equality, Demetru I. Dobrescu Street 2-4, Sector 1, Bucharest, Romania. Tel: +40 1 222 3850 / 3860, fax: +40 1 312 2768, URL: http://www.mmuncii.ro/nou/index.php/ro/
Ministry of Industry and Resources, Calea Victoriei 152, Sector 1, Bucharest, Romania. Tel: +401 231 0262 / 313 6666, fax: +401 312 0513, e-mail: liniaintreprinzatorului@minind.ro, URL: http://www.minind.ro/
Ministry of Agriculture and Rural Development, Carol Avenue 24, Sector 3, Bucharest, Romania. Tel: +40 1 614 4020 / 615 4412, fax: +40 1 312 4410, e-mail: public@madr.ro, URL: http://www.madr.ro/
Ministry of Environment and Sustainable Development, Blvd. Libertatii 12, 76106 Bucharest, Romania. Tel: +40 1 410 0482 / 410 0568, fax: +40 1 312 1436 / 4227, URL: http://www.mmediu.ro/
Ministry of Infrastructure & Transportation, Blvd. Dinicu Golescu 38, Sector 1, Bucharest, Romania. URL: http://www.mt.ro/nou/index.php
Ministry of Culture and Religions, 1 Presei Libere Square, Sect. 1, 71341 Bucharest, Romania. Tel: +40 1 223 1516 / 222 3338 , fax: +40 1 223 4951, e-mail: mc-ministru@cultura.ro, URL: http://www.cultura.ro
Ministry of Health, Sector 1, Bucharest, Romania. Tel: +40 1 222 3850 / 3860, fax: +40 1 312 4916, URL: http://www.ms.ro/
Ministry of Education, Research, Youth & Sports, Str. Gen. Berthelot 28-30, 70749 Bucharest, Romania. Tel: +40 1 614 4588 / 2680, fax: +40 1 312 4719, URL: http://www.edu.ro/
Ministry of Environment, B-dul Libertatii nr 12, Sector 5, Bucharest, Romania. URL: http://www.nmediu.ro/

Political Parties
Partidul Social Democrat (PSD, Social Democrat Party), Sos. Kiseleff, 10, Bucharest, Romania. URL: http://www.psd.ro
Leader: Victor Ponta
Partidul National Liberal (PNL, National Liberal Party), Blvd. Nicolae Balecescu 21, 70112 Bucharest, Romania. Tel: +40 1 614 3235 / 7680, fax: +40 1 323 9508, URL: http://www.pnl.ro
Leader: Crin Antonescu
Partidul Democrat (PD, Democrat Party), Aleea Modrogan1, Bucharest, Romania. URL: http://www.pd.ro
Leader: Emil Boc
Partidul Romania Mare (PRM,Greater Romania Party), Str. G. Clemenceau 8-10, 70101 Bucharest, Romania. Tel: +40 1 613 0967 / 0023, fax: +40 1 312 6182, URL: http://www.prm.org.ro/
Democratic Alliance of Ethnic Hungarians in Romania (UDMR), Str. Herastrau 13, 71297 Bucharest, Romania. Tel/fax: +40 1 212 0569 / 1675, URL: http://www.rmdsz.ro/
Partidul Conservator (PC, Conservative Party), Calea Victoriei 118, Bucharest, Romania. URL: http://www.partidulconservator.ro/
President: Daniel Constantin

Elections
The most recent presidential election took place on 28 November 2009 but there was no clear winner between the incumbent Traian Basescu and Social Democrat Mircea Geoana. A run off election was held on December 6 and was won by Traian Basescu, backed by the Democratic Liberal Party. An attempt to impeach him in 2012 narrowly failed: Parliament voted on 6 July 2012 to suspend him for exceeding his authority. A referendum on his impeachment was called and despite a large majority voting in favour it narrowly failed after it did not reach the required 50 per cent.

Legislative elections took place on 9 December 2012 and the centre-left coalition of PM Victor Ponta was returned to power;. The Social Liberal Union won nearly 60 per cent of the vote. The Right Romania Alliance of President Traian Basescu came second with approximately 18 per cent. Mr Basescu has suggested that he might refuse to appoint Mr Ponta as prime minister. The standings in the Houses are as follows: House of Deputies: Social Liberal Union 273 seats; Right Romania Alliance 56 seats; PP-DD 47 seats; UDMR 18 seats; minority representatives 18 seats/ Senate: USL 122 seats; ARD 24 seats; PP-DD 21 seats; UDMR 9 seats.

Diplomatic Representation
British Embassy, 24 Strada Jules Michelet, 010463 Bucharest, Romania. Tel: +40 21 201 7200, fax: +40 21 201 7299, e-mail: roemb@roemb.co.uk, URL: http://ukinromania.fco.gov.uk/
Ambassador: Martin Harris
US Embassy, Strada Tudor Arghezi 7-9, Bucharest, Romania. Tel: +40 21 210 4042, fax: +40 21 210 0395, e-mail: webadmin@usembassy.ro, URL: http://bucharest.usembassy.gov
Ambassador: Mark Gitenstein
Romanian Embassy, Arundel House, 4 Palace Green, London, W8 4QD, United Kingdom. Tel: +44 (0)20 7937 9666, fax: +44 (0)20 7937 8069, URL: http://londra.mae.ro
Ambassdor: Ion Jinga
Romanian Embassy, 1607 23rd Street, NW, Washington, DC 20008, USA. Tel: +1 202 232 4846, fax: +1 202 232 4748, URL: http://www.roembus.org
Ambassador: Adrian Cosmin Vierita
Permanent Mission of Romania to the United Nations, 573-577 Third Avenue, New York, NY 10016, USA. Tel: +1 212 682 3273 / 3274, fax: +1 212 682 9746, URL: http://www.un.int/romania/
Ambassador: Simona-Mirela Miculescu

STATES OF THE WORLD

ROMANIA

LEGAL SYSTEM

The Romanian legal system is based on the Napoleonic Code.

There is a hierarchical system of courts culminating with the supreme court- The High Court of Justice and Cassation. This Court supervises the work of all the courts, passes judgement on appeals, rules on the uniform application of the law and has original jurisdiction in certain cases. The Court is divided into four areas of expertise: civil, criminal, economic and military. The president and other judges of the Supreme Court are appointed for a term of six years and may serve consecutive terms.

There are 40 county tribunals in addition to the municipal tribunal of Bucharest. In every county there are two or three law courts subordinated to the county tribunals and in Bucharest there are six sectional law courts. The county tribunals are mainly appeal tribunals. A Military Territorial Tribunal in Bucharest is used mainly as an Appeal Court and the Military Section of the Supreme Court of Justice.

The Constitutional Court judges issues of constitutionality and judges the compliance of laws or other state regulations to the Romanian Constitution. There are nine judges who serve a nine year non-renewable term. Following the 2003 revision of the Constitution, its decisions cannot be overturned by any majority of the Parliament.

Human rights abuses continue in Romania. The judiciary is not viewed as impartial, and corruption is widespread. Police harass detainees and Roma, and there are limits on religious freedom due to a discriminatory religion law; several minority religious groups complain that local authorities and Orthodox priests prevent religious activities from taking place. Property restitution following the Communist regime is slow.

Romania abolished the death penalty in 1990. The last people to be executed in Romania were the former dictator Nicolae Ceausescu and his wife, Elena, following the 1989 Revolution.

In 2011, in total there were 4,205 judges. In the same year, 2,351,000 actions were entered at Courts. There were 47,577 convictions. The crime rate (convictions) was 222 per 100,000 inhabitants. (Source: Romania in Figures, 2012)

Supreme Court of Justice, URL: http://www.scj.ro/monogr_en.asp
Constitutional Court of Romania, URL: http://www.ccr.ro/

Ombudsman of Romania, URL: http://www.avp.ro/

LOCAL GOVERNMENT

Public administration is based on the principles of local autonomy and the decentralisation of public services. In villages, towns and municipalities, local councils have responsibility for providing public services. Council members are elected as are mayors. County councils are lead by prefects, appointed by the government. Local elections take place every four years. According to the Romanian Statistics Office, the country's territory is organised into 41 counties *Judet*, 217 towns, 2,861 communes, 103 municipalities and 12,957 villages. Bucharest, the capital, is a municipality with the status of a district and is divided into six sectors. Counties have responsibility for development planning, water supply, sewage, public transport, roads, social assistance for children and education.

The 41 counties are Alba, Arad, Arges, Bacau, Bihor, Bistrita-Nasaud, Botosani, Braila, Brasov, Buzau, Calarasi, Caras-Severin, Cluj, Constanta, Covasna, Dambovita, Dolj, Galati, Gorj, Giurgiu, Harghita, Hunedoara, Ialomita, Iasi, Ilfov, Maramures, Mehedinti, Mures, Neamt, Olt, Prahova, Salaj, Satu Mare, Sibiu, Suceava, Teleorman, Timis, Tulcea, Vaslui, Valcea and Vrancea.

Municipality of Bucharest, URL: http://www.pmb.ro/
Municipality of Sibiu, URL: http://www.sibiu.ro/

AREA AND POPULATION

After the Second World War, a third of Romania's area and population were annexed by neighbouring countries. Successive political border changes over the last two centuries account for the ethnic diversity within Romania's present day boundaries as well as the 8 million Romanians who now live abroad.

The country today has an area of 238,391 sq. km and borders with the Republic of Moldova, the Ukraine, Bulgaria, Serbia and Montenegro, Hungary and the Black Sea. The main rivers of Romania are the Danube, the Mures, Prut, Olt and the Siret. The Danube flows along the southern border. The country is mainly fertile plains, hilly to the east, with mountain ranges (the Carpathians) running north and west. The highest mountain is Mt. Moldoveanu (2544m above sea level). The climate is temperate with hot, dry summers and cold winters with frequent snow especially in the mountains.

To view a map, please consult http://www.un.org/Depts/Cartographic/map/profile/romania.pdf

Population
The population has been in decline since 1997. Estimates from the WHO for 2010 put the population at 21.486 million compared to 22.49 million in 1999. The population grew at an annual average rate of -0.3 per cent over the period 2000-10. According to the Romanian Statistics Office, the population was 21.4 million in 2011. The median age is 39.8. An estimated 3.2 million are aged under 15 years old, 13.8 million aged betwee 15 and 59 years, and 4.4 million aged over 60 years. The average of the population was 39.8 years in 2011. Around 89.4 per cent of the population are Romanian, 7.1 per cent Hungarian, 1.8 per cent Romany, 0.5 German and 0.3 per cent Ukrainian. In 2009, 57 per cent of the population lived in urban areas.

Population distribution in July 2005 by municipality is shown below.

Municipality	Population	Municipality	Population
Alba	379,189	Hunedoara	480,459
Arad	459,286	Ialmita	292,666
Arges	646,320	Iasi	813,943
Bacau	723,518	Ilfov	283,409
Bihor	595,685	Maramures	515,610
Bistrita-Nasaud	317,254	Mehedinti	303,869
Botosani	459,900	Mures	583,383
Brasov	595,211	Neamt	570,682
Braila	370,428	Olt	483,674
Buzau	494,052	Prahova	827,512
Caras-Severin	331,876	Satu Mare	368,702
Calarasi	317,652	Salaj	245,638
Cluj	694,511	Sibiu	422,259
Constanta	715,148	Suceava	705,752
Covasna	223,886	Teleorman	422,314
Dambovita	537,090	Timis	658,837
Dolj	718,874	Tulcea	252,485
Galati	620,500	Vaslui	460,751
Giurgiu	286,208	Valcea	415,181
Gorj	384,852	Vrancea	393,766
Harghita	326,558		

Source: National Institute of Statistics from Romania

The towns with the most inhabitants are: Bucharest (19.37 million), Cluj-Napoca (307,136), Timisoara (306,854), Iasi (304,043) and Constanta (300385).

The official language is Romanian. Other languages spoken include English, Hungarian, German and French.

Births, Marriages, Deaths
Figures from the National Institute of Statistics from Romania for 2011 show there are 105,600 marriages and 35,800 divorces. Life expectancy in 2011 was 74 years. According to WHO estimates, healthy life expectancy was 65 years. The total fertility rate was 1.3 children per female. The crude birth rate in 2010 was 10.3 per 1,000 population and the crude death rate was 12.0 per 1,000 population. (Source: http://www.who.int, World Health Statistics 2012)

Public Holidays 2014
1-2 January: New Year's Day
6 January: Epiphany
18 April: Good Friday (Orthodox)
21 April: Easter Monday (Orthodox)
1 May: Working People's Day
1 December: National Day, marks the 1918 unification of Romania
25 December: Christmas Day
26 December: Boxing Day
Holidays falling on Sunday are not observed on the following Monday.

EMPLOYMENT

In 2011, the workforce was estimated at 9.8 million. That year the unemployment rate was put at 7.4 per cent. In 2011, of the total number of unemployed, 28.9 per cent were young people (15-24 years). (Source: Romania in Figures, 2012)

Total Employment by Economic Activity

Occupation	2008
Agriculture, hunting & forestry	2,689,900
Mining & quarrying	107,200
Manufacturing	1,929,800
Electricity, gas & water supply	161,400
Construction	746,400
Wholesale & retail trade, repairs	1,178,200
Hotels & restaurants	154,200
Transport, storage & communications	508,500
Financial intermediation	110,400
Real estate, renting & business activities	298,300
Public admin. & defence; compulsory social security	476,100
Education	396,900
Health & social work	396,000
Other community, social & personal service activities, households with employed persons, other	211,500

Source: Copyright © International Labour Organization (ILO Dept. of Statistics, http://laborsta.ilo.org)

BANKING AND FINANCE

Currency
1 Leu (plural, Lei) = 100 bani (singular ban).

On 1 July 2005, Romania reformed its currency and redenominated its currency; it switched from the old leu (ROL) to the new leu (RON). 1 RON = 10,000 ROL.

GDP/GNP, Inflation, National Debt

Since the fall of the communist markets and the end of the Ceausescu regime in 1989, Romania has been striving to build a western style economy. Consumer subsidies have been abolished, and exchange rates liberalised, a programme of privatisation has also been pursued particularly in the energy and mining sector. Emergency measures have been taken on occasion by successive Romanian governments in order to halt the 'slowdown' in the economy since the transition from a rigidly centralised command economy to a liberal market-led one began in 1990. Since 2000, a programme of privatisation has been followed and several sectors have been reformed, including mining, energy and industry. Reform in agriculture has been slow. The government has been trying to attract foreign investment.

Romania hopes to be ready to join the euro by 2015.

Until the current economic crisis, GDP had shown steady growth, rising from US$73.2 billion in 2004 to US$165 billion in 2007. The economy grew by 8.3 per cent from 2003 to 2004 and by an estimated 7.8 per cent in 2006 and 7.7 per cent in 2007. The economy initially remained relatively stable despite the 2008/09 economic crisis but growth fell sharply in 2009 to -6 per cent. The government requested assistance from the IMF and the EU and a deal worth €19.95 billion was agreed in May 2009. Significant cuts in public expenditure were implemented to bring the deficit down; the government proposed cuts of 25 per cent in public salaries and pension cuts of 15 per cent. GDP was estimated to be US$162 billion in 2010 with a growth rate of -1.3 per cent. In 2011, Romania signed a precautionary stand by agreement with the IMF, EU and World Bank worth US$4.9 billion aimed at structural reform and financial sector stability. The government hopes not to have to use the fund.Growth exceeded expectations in 2011, reaching 2.5 per cent, largely due to a good harvest. GDP was estimated to be in nominal terms, was 578551.9 million lei, 27017.7 lei per capita.In 2012, growth was estimated to be under 2 per cent, due to a fall in exports.

Agriculture, hunting, forestryand fish breeding accounts for an estimated 6.5 per cent of GDP, industry 26.3 per cent and services 45.4 per cent.

Inflation for 1999 was estimated at 44 per cent and 35 per cent in 2000. By 2004, inflation had fallen to an estimated 9 per cent. In 2009 it was 5.1 per cent. The rate for 2010 was an estimated 6.1 per cent, rising to 5.8 per cent in 2011. Inflation was estimated to be 4.5 per cent in 2012, higher than the government target. The target for 2013 is 2.5 per cent.

Figures for 2011 estimated total foreign debt was US$125 billion. Public debt was estimated to be less than 40 per cent of GDP.

Foreign Investment.

Foreign direct investment was estimated at US$1.5 billion in 2011, substantially down on the levels of financial investment prior to the global economic crisis.

Balance of Payments / Imports and Exports

Main exports include chemicals, wood products, machinery and equipment, textiles, fuels, metals and light manufactures. The main imports include, fuel, coal, iron ore, machinery and equipment, mineral products, and machinery and equipment. Romania maintains economic relations with 120 countries on all continents. The EU is the most significant partner taking over 71 per cent of exports and providing over 72 per cent of imports. Germany accounts for 18.6 per cent of exports, Italy 12.8 per cent, France 7.5 per cent and Turkey 6.2 per cent. Germany supplies 17.1 per cent of imports, Italy approximately 11.3 per cent and Hungary 8.7 per cent. China supplies 4.6 per cent of goods. International trade registerd a growth in 2011 from 2010.

International trade of goods operations

header	2009	2010*	2011**
FOB exports			
euro million	29,084	37,368	45,041
USD million	40,579	49,508	62,692
lei million	123,344	157,471	190,922
CIF imports			
euro million	38,953	46,902	54,824
USD million	54,344	62,140	76,365
lei million	165,171	197,596	232,318
Balance			
euro million	-9,869	-9,534	-9,783
USD million	-13,765	-12,632	-13,673
lei million	-41,827	-40,125	-41,396

* semi-final data, **
provisional data
Source: Romania in Figures, 2012

In order to promote foreign trade Romania has set up five Free Zones. These are located at the Sulina Free Harbour, Constanta Sud-Agigea, Giurgiu, Braila and Galati.

Central Bank

The rebuilding of the banking system started with the creation of a two-tier system with the Central Bank forming the higher level. Since November 1990 the National Bank of Romania has been fulfilling the functions of the Central Bank. The lower tier of the banking system includes commercial banks established as joint stock companies.
National Bank of Romania, 25 Lipscani St, 70421 Bucharest 3, Romania. Tel: +40 1 6130410 / 1 6152750, fax: +40 21 312 3831, e-mail: bnr@bnro.ro, URL: http://www.bnro.ro
Governor: Prof. Mugur Constantin Isarescu (page 1447)

Chambers of Commerce and Trade Organisations

Chamber of Commerce and Industry of Romania and Bucharest Municipality, URL: http://www.ccir.ro
National Register of Commerce, URL: http://www.onrc.ro/english/recom.php

MANUFACTURING, MINING AND SERVICES

Before World War II Romania was an agrarian-industrial state. After World War II a programme of economic development was applied. As a result, in a relatively short period Romania has become an industrial-agrarian state. Romania started the complex process of transition from a centrally planned economy to a free-market system in 1990, and since then the private sector has become the prime mover in economic growth.

Primary and Extractive Industries

Romania has attempted to increase its raw material and energy source. Geological research has been carried out and new reserves of coal, crude oil, natural gas as well as ferrous, non-ferrous and non-metal ores have been found. One site chosen for investigation has been the continental shelf of the Black Sea. Romania has proven oil reserves of 0.60 billion barrels. Output in 2011 estimated at 105,050 barrels per day, and consumption is around 217,000 barrels per day. Romania imports oil from Russia. Romania is the largest oil refiner in southeastern Europe and has 10 refineries, of which several have been privatised and most of which are currently working under capacity. Refining capacity in 2012 was 537,000 barrels.

Romania has proven natural gas reserves of 2.0 trillion cubic feet, with production running at 375 billion cubic feet. National gas consumption was estimated at 486 billion cubic feet.

Coal reserves have been estimated at 2.9 billion short tons and production runs at around 33.9 million short tons.

National Agency of Mineral Resources, URL: http://www.namr.ro/main_en.htm

Energy

Electric energy production amounted to 57.7 billion kWh in 2010. Nearly 60 per cent of Romania's electricity is generated from fossil fuels and just over 30 per cent from hydro power. The rest comes from nuclear facility at Cernavoda. In 2005 Romania announced that 66 per cent of its energy sector had now been privatised, as part of the EU membership requirements.

National Commision for Nuclear Activities Control, URL: http://www.cncan.ro

Manufacturing

Since the introduction of reform measures, industrial production has decreased year by year. This is partly because before 1990 the country was over-producing in regard to its actual resources. In 2007, industry contributed 37 per cent of GDP.

The following table shows the value of industrial production of selected items in 2004 at current prices.

Commodity	Million Lei
Mining & quarrying	85,580,2
Food & beverages	255,750,8
Textile products	42,482,2
Clothing articles	74,425,2
Leather goods & footwear	33,027,6
Chemical substances & products	109,903,8
Metallurgy	187,147,8
Machinery & equipment	61,177,3
Electric machinery & appliances	39,307,3
Wood & wooden products	55,437,4
Crude oil processing, coal coking & nuclear fuel treatment	174,056,9

Source: National Institute of Statistics from Romania

Service Industries

The most popular tourist destinations in Romania are Bucharest, Moldavia, southern Transylvania and the Danube delta. In 2011, the number of arrivals of foreign visitors to Romania amounted to 7,611,000 persons, up 1.5 per cent from 2010. The number of departures of Romanian visitors abroad amounted to 10,936,000 persons, up 0.3 per cent as compared to 2010. Of international visitors, most came from Hungary (1.546 million) and Moldova (1.33 million). (Source: Romania in Figures, 2012)
Romanian Tourism Promotion Office, URL: http://www.turism.ro

Agriculture

In order to encourage farming and agricultural production after the end of the communist era, the government postponed farming taxes for a number of years, allowed the buying and selling of land, initiated a programme of privatisation and restructuring and reformed the financing of the agriculture sector. As a result of the Land Fund Law application on 31 December 1991, the private sector holds almost 80 per cent of the total area of agricultural land. Agricultural land covers 14.7 million hectares (out of a total 23.9 million hectares). Of this, 9.4 million hectares are arable, 3.4 million hectares are pastures, 1.5 million are hayfields and 224,100 hectares are used for vineyards and 218,000 hectares for orchards and nurseries.

Agricultural Production in 2010

Produce	Int. $'000*	Tonnes
Cow milk, whole, fresh	1,376,451	4,410,840
Wheat	709,177	5,811,810
Indigenous pigmeat	558,312	363,191
Indigenous cattle meat	538,606	199,382
Maize	520,017	9,042,030
Grapes	423,064	740,118
Indigenous chicken meat	397,330	278,944
Potatoes	352,055	3,283,870
Sunflower seed	346,063	1,262,930
Tomatoes	284,022	768,532

ROMANIA

- continued

Rapeseed	261,575	943,033
Sheep milk, whole, fresh	253,632	651,317

*unofficial figures
Source: http://faostat.fao.org/site/339/default.aspx Food and Agriculture Organization of the United Nations, Food and Agricultural commodities production

Figures for 2011 show that Romania had 1,989,000 head of cattle, 5,346,000 pigs, 8,533,000 sheep, 1,236,000 goats, 596,000 horses and 79,842,000 poultry. There were 1,250,000 bees. (Source: Romanian in Figures, 2012)

A severe drought in 2012 damaged crops.

The winemaking industry is an important part of the agricultural sector with 1,230.4 thousand tonnes of grapes being produced in 2004.

Forestry

At the end of 2011, the forest fund covered an area of 6,519,000 hectares, more than 49,000 hectares than in 20008. In 2011, the forest area amounted to 6,232,000 hectares, with coniferous trees covering 1,947,000 hectares and decidous trees covering 4,415,000 hectares. The volume of wood harvested was 18,705,000 m³ (gross volume), of which coniferous trees amounted to 7,521,000 m³ and beech trees 6,175,000 m³. (Source: Romania in Figures, 2012)

COMMUNICATIONS AND TRANSPORT

Travel Requirements

Citizens of the USA, Canada and Australia require a passport valid for three months beyond the length of stay but do not need a visa for stays of up to 90 days. EU citizens do not require a passport if they hold a valid national Identity Card, and do not require a visa unless staying for longer than three months, when they should apply to the Romanian Authority for Aliens for a registration certificate Other nationals should contact the embassy to check visa requirements.

National Airlines

TAROM (Romanian Air Transport), URL: http://www.tarom.ro/en/

International Airports

Bucharest is served by two airports, the Henri Coanda Bucuresti Airport and the Aurel Vlaicu International Airport. The other major international aiports include Traian Vuia International Airport and the Cluj-Napoca International Airport. In 2011, 11 million passengers were transported and 27,000 tonnes were transported. (Source: Romania in Figures, 2012)
International Airport Henri Coanda Bucharest, URL: http://www.otp-airport.ro/
Baneasa Airport, URL: http://www.bucharestairports.ro/

Railways

The construction of Romanian railways started with railway lines connecting the Danube ports with the interior of the country. The railway network at the end of 2000 was 11,385 km, of which 35 per cent was electrified. The central point of the railway network is Bucharest. Upgrading of the railway is to take place so that high-speed trains can use the system. Figures for 2011 show 61 million passengers were transported on the railways per annum, covering 5,073 km-passengers. In 2011, 61 million tons of freight per annum were transported by rail. Bucharest has a subway and tram system, most large towns have a tram system.
Societatea Nationale a Cailor Ferate Române, URL: http://www.cfr.ro/

Roads

The total length of public roads is approximately 195,000 km, of which 68,000 km are paved. Vehicles drive on the right. As with the railways, the central junction is Bucharest. Main roads run to all industrial centres and to all important frontiers. Figures from 2011 show 184 million tons of freight were transported by road. In 2011, the number of registered vehicles was: 41,000 buses and microbuses, 4,335,00 passenger cars, 90,000 mopeds and motorcycles and 696,000 goods road motor vehicles. (Source: Romania in Figures, 2012)

Shipping

The Black Sea, the River Danube and the Black Sea-Danube canal make it possible to make great use of water-borne transport. 1,075 km of the river Danube flow through Romania and a great part of the commercial traffic between Central Europe is carried along it. On the Romanian portion, ships with higher register tonnage (2,000 tons) can sail. In May 1984 the Danube-Black Sea Canal between Cernavoda and Constanta was opened to traffic. It is 64.2 km in length and shortens the shipping route by approximately 400 km. The chief port is Constanta which has modern loading and unloading facilities. The Romanian marine ships serve the regular international routes. In 2011, 23 freight ships were registered and 39 million tonnes of goods were transported. (Source: Romania in Figures, 2012)

Ports and Harbours

There are several ports on the Danube such as Orsova, Turnu Magurele, Giurgiu, Calarasi, Braila, Galati and Tulcea (the last three being both river and sea ports). The largest port on the Black Sea is Constanta (capable of taking ships weighing over 150,000 dwt); the Black Sea also has the free port of Sulina.
Port of Constanta, URL: http://www.portofconstantza.com/apmc/

Inland Waterways

In 2011, 29 million tonnes of freight were transported by inland waterway.

HEALTH

Health care is generally free of charge. In 2009, the government spent approximately 10.8 per cent of its total budget on healthcare (down from 9.1 per cent in 2000), accounting for 79.0 per cent of all healthcare spending. Total expenditure on healthcare equated to 5.6 per cent of the country's GDP. Per capita expenditure on health was approximately US$432, compared with US$87 in 2000. There are 66 hospital beds per 10,000 population. According to official figures, as of 2011 there were 52,613 physicians (24.6 per 10,000 population), 13,364 dentists (6.2 per 10,000 population), pharmaceutical chemists 14,564 (6.8 per 10,000 population), ancillary medical staff (126,589 (59 per 10,000 inhabitants).(Source: Roman in Figures, 2012)

According to the latest WHO figures, in 2006 approximately 99 per cent of the urban population and 76 per cent of the rural population had access to improved drinking water. In 2008, 88 per cent of the urban population and 54 per cent of the rural population had access to improved sanitation.

The infant mortality rate in 2009 was 11 per 1,000 live births. The child mortality rate (under 5 years) was 14 per 1,000 live births. The main causes of childhood mortality are: prematurity (14 per cent), congenital anomalies (25 per cent), pneumonia (29 per cent), and injuries (7 per cent).

In 2010 there were 296 reported cases of mumps, 193 of measles, 10 of pertussis, 350 of rubella and 18,379 of TB. (Source: http://www.who.int, World Health Statistics 2012)

EDUCATION

Education is compulsory and open to all Romanian citizens. Pupils are also able to transfer from one type of school to another by passing the relevant examinations. The first private education establishments opened in 1990 after fifty years, although most schools are still run by the State and the education system is centralised. Romania is home to many ethnic groups, although the language of instruction in schools is Romanian if the local population numbers 10 per cent or more children from a different ethnic background then some classes will be taught in their native language and Romanian language classes are compulsory. Among the different languages used in the education system are Hungarian, Romani, Polish, Serbian, Slovak, Turkish, Bulgarian, German and Ukrainian. Reforms to the education system have been implemented during 2008-11. The number of education institutions decreased by 12.4 per cent (1,017 institutions) over this period to a total of 7,204 educational units. The reforms reflect a decrease in the school population.

In the academic year 2011/12 the number of students and teaching staff was as follows:

School	No. of students	Teaching staff
Pre-School	674,000	38,000
Primary & Secondary	1,629,00	121,000
High School	889,000	59,000
Vocational & apprenticeship	12,000	-
Post High School & Foreman Education	80,000	1,000
Tertiary Education	540,000	28,000

Source: http://www.insse.ro

In 2011, the enrolment rate for the school age population was 73.8 per cent in for males and 75.9 per cent for females. In 2007 the adult literacy rate was 97.6 per cent.

RELIGION

The Romanian Orthodox Church, which enjoys the support of 86.8 per cent of the population, was organized in 1925 as a patriarchy. It has five metropolitan sees, 10 archbishoprics, 9 bishoprics, 113 archpriests' offices, 12,311 parishes and as many churches and chapels. The Romanian Orthodox Church also has a number of archbishoprics and parishes abroad. Eight theological institutes and faculties and 15 high-school seminars cater for the training of its clergy. There are about 19,600 churches and chapels in Romania and a great number of monasteries with over 13,600 clergymen and 4,000 monks and nuns.

After the 1989 Revolution, the Greek Catholic Church, which was formally dissolved in 1948, recovered its full rights. Within the context of this recovery process, Pope John Paul II appointed bishops for all the five dioceses.

In addition, 5.0 per cent of the population are Catholics of the Oriental and Roman rite, 3.0 per cent are Reformed/Lutheran, and 1.0 per cent are Unitarian. There are also Neo-Protestant, Armenian, Muslim and Jewish communities.

Romania has a religious liberty rating of 3 on a scale of 1 to 10 (10 is most freedom). (Source: World Religion Database)

Romanian Orthodox Church, Leader: Daniel I, Archbishop of Bucharest

COMMUNICATIONS AND MEDIA

The constitution allows for freedom of the press but forbids 'defamation of the country'. However, following amendments to the penal code in 2007, journalists may no longer be jailed for defamation.

Newspapers

After the revolution in December 1989, Romania experienced a press boom but many titles have subsequently closed due to increased costs.
Adevarul, English language, URL: http://www.adevarul.ro
România Libera, URL: http://www.romanialibera.ro
Evenimentul Zillei, URL: http://www.expres.ro
Libertatea, URL: http://www.libertatea.ro
Jurnalul National, URL: http://www.jurnalul.ro

Nine o'Clock, URL: http://www.nineoclock.ro (English language)

Business Journals
Business Review, URL: http://www.businessromania.com
Capital, URL: http://www.capital.ro/

Broadcasting
Television is the most popular medium for news. The service is a combination of public and private TV stations. The public broadcaster operates multiple stations. Approximately 100 private national, regional and local stations are also in operation. More than 75 per cent of households have cable TV or satellite TV subscriptions. The state-owned public broadcaster operates four national networks plus regional and local stations. More than 100 private radio stations also exist.
TVR, URL: http://www.tvr.ro/ (state-owned, operates Romania 1 and TVR 2)
Antena 1, URL: http://www.antena1.ro/
Pro TV, URL: http://www.protv.ro/
Radio Romania, URL: http://www.srr.ro/ (state-owned)
Europa FM (Commercial), http://www.europafm.ro/

Telecommunications
In 1991 the Romanian government launched a 15-year plan to reorganise and improve the country's telecommunications system; the market was liberalised, private concerns were allowed to operate in a variety of telecommunication sectors (including manufacture and maintenance) and the Ministry of Communications became a strictly regulatory body. This led to rapid growth in the sector. In 2011 an estimated 4.5 million telephone main lines were in use and an estimated 23 million mobile phones.

In 2011, 47 per cent of households had internet access. There were estimated to be 7.5 million internet users in 2009.

ENVIRONMENT

Protected zones in Romania have increased in recent years. These include 13 national parks and 699 nature reserves.

Protected areas in 2011

Categories of protected areas	Number	Area (ha)
Scientific reservations	64	218,145

- continued

National parks	13	316,872
Natural monuments	206	15,406
Natural reservations	699	346,933
Natural parks	15	772,810
Biosphere reservations	3	664,446
Humid areas of international importance	8	680,859
Avifauna special protection areas	148	3,694,394
Sites of Community importance	383	4,152,153

Source: Romania in Figures, 2012

The first law relating to environmental matters was passed in 1930 - The Law on the Protection of the Monuments of Nature, and the following year the Commission for the Protection of Natural Monuments was created. The Law on Environmental Protection was passed in 1973.

Main environmental concerns are soil erosion, water pollution, air pollution, and contamination of the Danube wetlands.

Romania is party to the following agreements: Air Pollution, Air Pollution-Persistent Organic Pollutants, Antarctic-Environmental Protocol, Antarctic Treaty, Biodiversity, Climate Change, Climate Change-Kyoto Protocol, Desertification, Endangered Species, Environmental Modification, Hazardous Wastes, Law of the Sea, Ozone Layer Protection, Ship Pollution, Wetlands.

In 2010, Romania's emissions from the consumption of fossil fuels totalled 78.43 million metric tons of carbon dioxide, down from 80.81 million metric tons in 2009. (Source: EIA)

SPACE PROGRAMME

The Romanian Space Agency (ROSA) co-ordinates the national space activities, programs and technology. Its annual budget is approximately $8 million. Romania has contributed to more than 30 scientific and technological space missions. During the 1970s and 1980s Romania was an active member of the Soviet Union's Interkosmos programme. In 1992 Romania was one of the first Eastern European countries to sign a Co-operation Agremment with ESA and has participated in several ESA missions. Romania signed an Accession Agreement to the ESA Convention in January 2011 to become the 19th ESA state.
ROSA, URL: http://www.rosa.ro

RUSSIA
Russian Federation
Rossiyskaya Federatsiya

Capital: Moscow (Population estimate, 2012: 11.55 million)

Head of State: Vladimir Putin (page 1498) (President)

National Flag: Three equal-sized horizontal stripes of white, blue and red.

CONSTITUTION AND GOVERNMENT

Constitution
The Russian Federation came into being following the dissolving of the Union of Soviet Socialist Republics (USSR) on December 31 1991. Following the break-up of the former USSR new constitutional amendments were agreed by popular referendum in December 1993. The constitution allows for the separation of legislative, executive and judiciary powers. Russia is a secular state and all religions are separate from the state.

Under the terms of the 1993 constitution the head of state is the president, directly elected by universal adult suffrage for a maximum of two consecutive four-year terms. The president appoints the chairman of the Council of Ministers, subject to the approval of parliament. The president is also entitled to chair Council sessions. In November 2008 the parliament voted in favour of extending the presidential term of office from four to six years.

To consult the constitution, please visit: http://kremlin.ru/eng/articles/ConstMain.shtml

International Relations
Russia continues to have close links with many of the CIS states. Relations with the UK have became tense following the death of former Russian security services officer Aleksandr Litvinenko who was poisoned with a radioactive substance whilst in London in November 2006.

A long-standing dispute over the breakaway Georgian regions of Abkhazia and South Ossetia escalated into a two-week military conflict in August 2008.

The relationship between Russia and former Soviet republic Ukraine has been rocky in recent years and in January 2009 the Russian Prime Minister, Vladimir Putin, instructed Gazprom to cut gas supplies sent via Ukraine to Europe.

Russia formally joined the WTO in August 2012 after 18 years of negotiation.

Recent Events
Following the revolution of 1917 the Russian Soviet Federal Socialist Republic was formed. The Second World War enabled Russia to expand its sphere of influence into the east of Europe. After the war the communist rule was eased by Khruschev, Brezhnev and finally Gorbachev.

In September 1989 the CPSU plenum on nationalities proposed a new constitutional, political and economic structure for Russia, resembling more closely that of the other republics. It also proposed greater autonomy for government departments.

A Russian bureau of the CPSU Central Committee was established in December 1989 with 16 members and chaired by Michael Gorbachev. Local and republican elections were held in March 1990. Boris Yeltsin was elected President of the Republic with a platform of greater republican independence and more radical economic reform. The founding congress of the Russian Federation Communist Party took place in June 1990 and the Russian Federation declared its sovereignty in June 1990.

Following the coup against Michael Gorbachev on 19-21 August 1991, the function of several USSR ministries was transferred to Russian ministries and a decree was passed suspending the activities of the Communist Party. On 29 August 1991 the majority of the autonomous republics within the Russian Federation made joint declarations of their wish to stay in the Federation. President Yeltsin put himself forward for the post of Prime Minister and on 1 November 1991 his economic programme was approved by parliament. On 6 November 1991 a new Russian government was named with Boris Yeltsin as Prime Minister.

The Russian Supreme Soviet granted citizenship to Russians living outside the geographic borders of the Russian Federation on 28 November 1991. The liquidation of Soviet structures was generally completed in December, transferring power from the Soviet Union to Russia.

On 19 December 1991 President Yeltsin took control of the Kremlin and other key Soviet institutions and established new Russian ministries. In April 1993 Boris Yeltsin received a vote of confidence in a referendum which also approved his reform policies. Voter turnout was 64 per cent. A new constitution was approved in December 1993. This outlines the president's powers including appointments, relationship with parliament, powers of the government and the structure of parliament.

RUSSIA

On 9 August 1999 President Yeltsin sacked his prime minister Sergei Stepashin and his cabinet. Mr. Stepashin had been in the position less than three months. Four prime ministers had been sacked in the preceding 17 months. Vladimir Putin, the security chief, was approved as the new prime minister on 16 August 1999. The Duma voted by 233 to 84 to approve the position. At the end of 1999, Boris Yeltsin resigned as President.

The Russian Federation was an original signatory to the Commonwealth of Independent States agreement on 9 December 1991 and later signed the Alma-Ata declaration of 21 December 1991. The CIS was formed first by Russia, Belarus and Ukraine, followed by all the former Soviet republics except the baltic states. As of June 1997, Russia became part of the Summit of Eight (the former G7).

In May 2002 a NATO-Russia Council was agreed. This superseded the NATO-Russia Founding Act. Also during that month Russian and the USA reached an agreement on weapons reduction, both agreeing to reduce the amount of strategic nuclear weapons from 6,000 to 2,000.

In January 2006 Russia stopped supplying Ukraine with gas following rows over payment; supplies were soon restored but Ukraine said the stoppages were politically motivated. In March of that year Russia signed an economic agreement with China which included the supply of gas to China.

Early in 2007 the USA began talking about expanding its missile defences to bases in Eastern Europe. President Putin responded by talking of a renewed arms race but at the G8 summit in Germany in June, he proposed a joint system using bases in Azerbaijan.

In August 2007, government officials announced that a Russian expedition had proved that the Lomonosov Ridge (a ridge of mountains below the Arctic Ocean) is part of Russia's continental shelf. It is thought that the Arctic is rich in oil, gas and mineral reserves, which are becoming more accessible as the polar ice caps melt. Russia's claim to a vast swathe of Arctic territory has sparked rivalry with Denmark, Canada and the US, who believe they have a claim.

Mikhail Fradkov was replaced as prime minister on 13 September 2007. President Putin named Viktor Zubkov as his replacement. President Putin's second term as president ended in March 2008. He had stood for and won a seat in the Duma in the legislative election held in December 2007, and was appointed Prime Minister by the new President, Mr. Medvedev, within hours of the latter's inauguration in May 2008.

Military tension increased between Russia and Georgia in Spring 2008. Russia sent 200 troops to the breakaway province of Abkhazia in May 2008. Georgian troops mounted an attack on separatists in South Ossetia. Russia responded by what it called an attack on its citizens by sending thousands of troops to the area. After more than a week, the two sides signed a peace agreement brokered by the French. Russia withdrew most of its troops but maintained a buffer zone. President Medvedev later said that Russia would formally recognise the independence of Abkhazia and South Ossetia.

Russia has been hit by the economic crisis. In October 2008 the parliament approved a US$68 billion package aimed at rescuing banks.

Relations with the US improved following the election of Barak Obama as president. In January 2009 Russia said it would halts its short-range missile plans. A meeting with between President Medvedev and President Obama in July 2009 was also seen as very successful.

In January 2009, under orders from the Russian government, Gazprom cut off gas supplies to the Ukraine because of a row over allegedly unpaid bills and a new pricing contract. Ukraine denied siphoning off gas, and claimed that technical problems were disrupting the flow. The disruption meant that many European countries who received gas from Russia via Ukraine had their supplies disrupted.

A bomb blast was believed to be the cause of an explosion which derailed the Nevsky Express travelling between Moscow and St. Petersburg in November 2009. 26 people were killed. No group claimed responsibility.

In March 2010, 39 people were killed when two suicide bombers detonated their bombs on the Moscow Metro system. Chechen rebel leader Doku Umarov said his group was behind the attacks.

In April 2010 Russia and the USA signed a new Strategic Arms Reduction Treaty. The treaty set out plans to reduce each country's deployed nuclear arsenal to 1,550 weapons.

In January 2011 a suicide bomb exploded at Moscow's Domodedovo airport, 36 people were killed and over 100 injured. Doku Umarov, a wanted Chechen warlord, said he had ordered the attack.

In September 2011 Vladimir Putin announced he would stand for president in March 2012.

In October 2011 Russia did not put its clocks back for winter, remaining on summertime. The mornings will be darker but the afternoons will remain lighter for longer.

Legislative elections held on December 4 were followed by widespread protests and opposition rallies after Vladimir Putin's United Russia party claimed a slim majority in the Duma. Putin accused America of being behind the protests.

Presidential elections were held in March 2012 and were won by Vladimir Putin with over 60 per cent of the vote. Some allegations of fraud have been made and there were many protests against the result with hundreds arrested. Mr Putin, who previously held the position from 2000-08, took office in May 2012.

A major opposition rally took place in Russia in June 2012 despite a new law coming into force which increased fines for protesters.

In July 2012, parts of Russia were hit by flash floods, in the southern Krasnodar region 171 people were killed when the volume of rain water forced open sluice gates leading to widespread flooding.

In August 2012 Russia was criticised by the USA, EU and several human rights groups after three members of a punk band called Pussy Riot were jailed for two years after performing an anti-Putin protest in a cathedral in Moscow.

In November 2012, a new law was introduced, it redefined treason to now include citizens who provide consultancy or other assistance to a foreign state or international bodies, directed against Russia's security. Critics of the law say it aims to stop Russians from working with Western Non-Government Organisations

In December 2012, Russian-US relations took a turn for the worse when Washington passed a bill blacklisting Russian human-rights violators. Russian responded by stopping US funded NGOs from doing political work in Russia. Americans were also banned from adopting Russian children.

Legislature

The Russian Parliament, the Federal Assembly (*Federalnoy Sobraniye*), consists of two chambers: the State Duma (*Gosudarstvennaya Duma*) and the Federation Council (*Soviet Federatsii*). The first Federal Assembly sat in 1994.

Lower House

The Duma has 450 deputies directly elected on both a first-past-the-post and proportional basis for a four-year term. Under the new constitution it passes votes of confidence in the government and approves legislation. In April 2002 the State Duma voted to change the chairmanships of a third of its committees and the Communist Party subsequently lost eight top posts.

Following elections in December 2011, the Duma was composed of the following political parties:

Party	No. of seats
United Russia	238
Communist Party of Russian Federation (CPRF)	92
Liberal and Democratic Party of Russia (LDPR)	56
Fair Russia	64

State Duma of the Russian Federation, Ok hotny Ryad 1, 103265, Moscow, Russian Federation. Tel: +7 095 292 3057, fax: +7 095 292 5358, e-mail: stateduma@duma.ru, URL: http://www.duma.ru
Chairman: Gennady Seleznev

Upper House

The Federation Council has 178 representatives (two from each Federation member). This house approves Duma legislation and presidential decrees. Individual terms of members depends on the electing region.
Federation Council of the Russian Federation, 26 Bolshaya Dmitrovka, Moscow 103426, Russian Federation. Tel: +7 095 292 5969, fax: +7 095 292 5967, e-mail: post_sf@gov.ru, URL: http://www.council.gov.ru
Chairman: Ms Valentina Matviyenko

Council of Ministers (as at June 2013)
President: Vladimir Putin (page 1498)
Prime Minister, Chair of the Council of Ministers: Dmitry Medvedev (page 1476)
First Deputy Chairman: Igor Shuvalov (page 1514)
Deputy Prime Minister: Olga Golodets (page 1432)
Deputy Prime Minister: Arkady Dvorkovich
Deputy Prime Minister: Dmitry Kozak
Deputy Prime Minister: Dmitry Rogozin
Deputy Prime Minister & the President's Plenipotentiary Representative in the North Caucasus Federal District: Alexander Khloponin
Minister of Justice: Alexander Konovalov (page 1458)
Minister of Energy: Alexander Novak (page 1487)
Minister of Defence: Sergei Shoygu
Minister of Civil Defense, Emergencies and Natural Disasters: Vladimir Puchkov
Minister of Economic Development: Andrei Belousov
Minister of Finance: Anton Siluanov (page 1514)
Minister of Industry and Trade: Denis Manturov
Minister of Health: Veronika Skvortsova
Minister of the Interior: Vladimir Kolokoltsev (page 1458)
Minister of Education and Science: Dmitry Livanov
Minister of Transport: Maxim Sokolov
Minister of Culture: Vladimir Medinsky
Minister of Labour and Social Security: Maxim Topilin
Minister for Liaison with Open Government: Mikhail Abyzov
Minister of Agriculture: Nikolai Fyodorov
Minister of Communications and Mass Media: Nikolai Nikiforov
Minister of Regional Development: Igor Slyunyayev
Minister of Far East Development: Viktor Ishayev
Minister of Natural Resources and Environmental Protection: Sergei Donskoi
Minister of Sport, Youth & Tourism: Vitaly Sokolov
Minister of Foreign Affairs: Sergei Lavrov (page 1461)

Ministries

Office of the President, Staraya pl. 42, 103132 Moscow, Russian Federation. Tel: +7 495 925 3581, fax: +7 495 206 5173, e-mail: president@gov.ru, URL: http://president.kremlin.ru

Office of the Prime Minister, Krasnopresnenskaya 2, 103274 Moscow, Russian Federation. Tel: +7 495 205 5735, fax: +7 495 205 4219, URL: http://www.government.ru

Ministry of Agriculture, 107139 Moscow, Orlikov per 1/11, Russian Federation. Tel: +7 095 207 8362, fax: +7 095 207 8000, e-mail: web@gvc.aris.ru, URL: http://www.aris.ru

Ministry of Atomic Energy, 101000 Moscow, Bolshaya Ordinka Street, 24/26, Russian Federation. Tel: +7 095 239 2254, fax: +7 095 239 2535, e-mail: info@minatom.ru, URL: http://www.minatom.ru

Ministry of Defence, ul. Znamenka 19, 119160 Moscow, Russian Federation. Tel: +7 495 296 8437, fax: +7 495 296 8436, URL: http://www.mil.ru

Ministry of Economic Development and Trade, ul. Tverskaya-Yamskaya 1/3, POB A47, 103009, Moscow, Russian Federation. URL: http://www.economy.gov.ru

Ministry of Finance, ul. Ilyinka 9, 109097 Moscow, Russian Federation. Tel: +7 495 298 9101 , fax: +7 495 925 0889, URL: http://www.minfin.ru

Ministry of Foreign Affairs, 121200 Moscow, Smolenskaya-Sennaya pl. 32/34, Russian Federation. Tel: +7 095 244 4021 / 4119, fax: +7 095 924 323232/34 / 244 4112, e-mail: dip@mid.ru, URL: http://www.mid.ru

Ministry of Health and Social Development, Rakhmanovsky per. 3/25, 127994 Moscow, Russian Federation. Tel: +7 495 927 2848, fax: +7 495 928 5815, e-mail: minzdrav@cnt.ru, URL: http://www.minzdravrf.ru

Ministry of Regional Development, ul. Sadovo-Samotechnaya 10/23, 101433 Moscow, Russian Federation. Tel: +7 495 200 2565

Ministry of Industry and Energy, Kitaygorodsky Proyezd 7, 109074 Moscow, Russian Federation. Tel: +7 495 928 3872, fax: +7 495 220 5656, e-mail: abs@cdu.oilnet.ru, URL: http://www.mkmk.ru

Ministry of Internal Affairs, ul. Zhitnaya 16, 117049 Moscow, Russian Federation. Tel: +7 495 239 6971, fax: +7 095 293 5998, URL: http://www.mvd.ru

Ministry of Transport, 109012 Moscow, Russian Federation. Tel: +7 095 926 1000, fax: +7 095 926 9128, e-mail: mcc@morflot.ru, URL: http://www.mintrans.ru

Ministry of Culture and Media, Kitaygorodsky Proyezd 7, 109074 Moscow, Russian Federation. Tel: +7 495 710 5500, fax: +7 495 710 5722, URL: http://www.mte.gov.ru

Ministry of Justice, ul. Zhitnaya 14, 119991 Moscow, Russian Federation. Tel: +7 495 955 5999, fax: +7 495 916 2903, URL: http://www.minjust.ru

Ministry of Natural Resources, ul. Bolshaya Gruzinskaya 4/6, 123242 Moscow, Russian Federation. Tel: +7 495 254 4800, fax: +7 495 254 4310, URL: http://www.mnr.gov.ru

Ministry of Education and Science, ul. Tverskaya 11, 103905 Moscow, Russian Federation. Tel: +7 495 237 9763, fax: +7 495 237 8381, URL: http://www.mon.gov.ru

Ministry of Information Technology and Communications, ul. Tverskaya 7, 125375 Moscow, Russian Federation. Tel: +7 495 771 8100, fax: +7 495 771 8718, URL: http://www.minsvyaz.ru

Ministry of Emergencies, Natural Disasters and Civil Defence, Teatralny pr. 3, 109012 Moscow, Russian Federation. Tel: +7 495 926 3738, fax: +7 495 924 1946, URL: http://www.mchs.gov.ru

Elections

A presidential election took place in March 2008. Vladimir Putin was not eligible to stand for re-election, having already served two terms. Dmitry Medvedev, strongly supported by Mr. Putin, won the presidency with 70.3 per cent of the vote, and appointed Mr. Putin as Prime Minister within hours of taking office.

The presidential election took place in March 2012, Vladimir Putin won the first round with 63 per cent of the vote. Many voters protested that the election had been fixed and observers from the Organisation for Security and Cooperation in Europe reported irregularities at polling stations. Protesters took to the streets and many hundreds were arrested. Mr Putin was sworn in on 7 May 2012.

Legislative elections were held in December 2007, when President Putin's United Russia party won a landslide victory; Western critics described the elections as neither free nor democratic. The most recent parliamentary election took place in December 2011 and again there were widespread allegations of fraud. The result, which gave victory to Vladimir Putin's United Russia party, albeit with a reduced majority, was followed by widespread protests and numerous opposition rallies. Over 800 people were reported to have been arrested in the days following the elections.

The next legislative elections are due in December 2015.

Political Parties

Yedinaya Rossiya (United Russia), URL: http://www.er.ru
Leader: Vladimir Putin
Communist Party of the Russian Federation (Kommunisticheskaya Partiya Rossiiskoi Federatsii), URL: http://www.cprf.ru
Liberal Democratic Party of the Russian Federation (LDPR, Liberalno-Demokraticheskaya Partiya Rossii), URL: http://www.ldpr.ru
Fair Russia, URL: http://www.spradedlivo.ru
Democratic Party of Russia, (Demokraticheskaya Partyiya Rossii, DPR) URL: http://www.democrats.ru

Diplomatic Representation

British Embassy, Smolenskaya Naberezhnaya 10, Moscow 121099, Russian Federation. Tel: +7 095 956 7200, fax: +7 095 956 7201, e-mail: moscow@britishembassy.ru, URL: http://ukinrussia.fco.gov.uk/en/
Ambassador: Tim Barrow (page 1384)
US Embassy, Bolshoy Deviatinsky Pereulok No. 8, 121099 Moscow, Russian Federation. Tel: +7 095 728 5000, fax: +7 095 728 5090, URL: http://moscow.usembassy.gov
Ambassador: Michael McFaul (page 1474)

Embassy of the Russian Federation, 13 Kensington Palace Gardens, London W8 4QX, United Kingdom. Tel: +44 (0)20 7229 3628, fax: +44 (0)20 7727 8625, e-mail: info@rusemb.org, URL: http://www.rusemb.org.uk/
Ambassador: Alexander Yakovenko (page 1540)
Embassy of the Russian Federation, 2650 Wisconsin Avenue, NW, Washington, DC 20007, USA. Tel: +1 202 298 5700, fax: +1 202 298 5735, URL: http://www.russianembassy.org
Ambassador: Sergey Ivanovich Kislyak (page 1457)
Permanent Representative of the Russian Federation to the United Nations, 136 East 67th Street, New York, NY 10021, USA. Tel: +1 212 861 4900 / 4901, fax: +1 212 628 0252 / 517 7427, URL: http://www.un.int/russia
Ambassador: Vitaly Ivanovich Churkin

LEGAL SYSTEM

Under the 1993 Constitution the judiciary is independent and judges are appointed for life by the President. Based on civil law, Russian legal practice is restricted to applying and interpreting the law, and precedent does not serve as a legal source.

The judicial system is divided into three branches: regionally based federal courts of general jurisdiction; courts of arbitration (commercial) for the resolution of economic disputes; and the Constitutional Court. Justices of Peace resolve of small claims at the local level. Civil and criminal cases are tried in courts of primary jurisdiction (municipal and regional), followed by district courts of appeal, and then the Supreme Court, which has three divisions: civil, criminal, and military. The thirteen Justices of the Supreme Court are appointed by the Federation Council and comprise the Presidium of the Supreme Court.

Arbitration courts are organized at the level of constituent components of the Russian Federation, and their function is to adjudicate economic disputes between business entities, and to decide on complaints against organs of state whose decisions may affect business operations.

The 19 member Constitutional Court decides whether federal laws, presidential and governmental decrees, and regional constitutions and laws comply with the federal constitution. Its rulings are final, and acts which have been deemed unconstitutional, become invalid.

Administrative courts have recently been introduced to hear complaints by citizens against unlawful actions by officials at different levels and acts issued by ministries, departments, Presidential decrees, and government decisions. Administrative courts also consider cases of violations of electoral and tax laws, and disputes between different bodies of state power .Administrative courts are independent of state bodies, and their territorial structure is different from that of courts of general jurisdiction.

There have been many government human rights abuses over recent years in the face of increased oppostion from the peoples of Ingushetiya, Dagestan and Chechnya. Security forces have allegedly been involved in unlawful killings, torture, abductions and other brutal treatment. Military operations by Russian forces in Georgia in August 2008 resulted in civilian casualties. The government restrict freedom of the press through ownership of media outlets, pressure and intimidation. Local governments limit freedom of assembly and there is limited freedom of association. The activities of religious groups in some regions have been restricted. Prison conditions continue to be life threatening. There is corruption among law enforcers and undue government influence over judicial decisions.

Russia has a moratorium on the death penalty, and no executions have been carried out since 1996. However, the death penalty still remains codified.

In November 2012, a new law redefining treason came into force. Under the new law treason includes citizens who provided help to a foreign state or international organisation 'directed against Russia's security'.

Supreme Court of the Russian Federation, URL: http://www.supcourt.ru/

LOCAL GOVERNMENT

The Russian Federation is made up of 85 federal subjects, which are divided into 21 republics (respublik), nine territories (krais), 46 regions (oblasts), four autonomous regions, and the cities of Moscow and St Petersburg. There are plans to merge some of the Federal subjects in the future.

The 21 Republics are: Adygeya; Altay; Bashkortostan; Buryatiya; Chechnya; Chuvashia; Dagestan; Ingushetia; Kabardino-Balkariya; Kalmykiya; Karachayevo-Cherkesiya; Karelia; Khakasia; Komi; Mari-El; Mordovia; North Ossetia-Alania; Sakha; Tatarstan; Tuva; Udmurtia.

The 46 Regions or Oblasts are: Amur; Arkhangel'sk; Astrakhan; Belgorod; Bryansk; Chelyabinsk; Chita; Irkutsk; Ivanovo; Kaliningrad; Kaluga; Kemerovo; Kirov; Kostroma; Kurgan; Kursk; Leningrad; Lipetsk; Magadan; Moscow; Murmansk; Nizhniy Novgorod; Novgorod; Novosibirsk; Omsk; Orenburg; Orel; Penza; Pskov; Rostov; Ryazan; Sakhalin; Samara; Saratov; Smolensk; Sverdlovsk; Tambov; Tomsk; Tula; Tver; Tyumen; Ul'yanovsk; Vladimir; Volgograd; Vologda; Voronezh; Yaroslavl.

The four autonomous regions are Chukotka; Khanty-Mansi; Nenets; Yamalo-Nenets. The nine territories or krais are Altay; Kamchatka; Khabarovsk; Krasnodar; Krasnoyarsk; Perm; Primorskiy; Stavropol; Zabaykal'sk

The Republics:
Adygeya
President: Aslan Tkhakushinov, URL: http://www.adygheya.ru/

STATES OF THE WORLD

RUSSIA

Capital: Maikop
Recent figures put the population at 447,000, Adygeya covers an area of 7,600 sq km and is situated in the North Caucasus. It has reserves of natural gas which are exploited and agriculture is a large contributor to the economy with wheat, maize, fruit and flowers being grown.

Altai
President: Alexander Berdnikov, URL: http://eng.altai-republic.ru/index.php?newlang=eng
Capital: Gorno-Altaisk
Altai shares borders with Mongolia, China and Kazakhstan and covers an area of 92,902 sq km. Altai had mineral reserves of gold, silver, iron ore and lithium but agriculture is the most important sector, although tourism is growing in importance. Languages spoken are Russian and Altay.

Bashkortostan
President: Rustem Zakievich Khamitov, URL: http://www.bashkortostan.ru/en/bashkortostan/
Captial: Ufa
Recent figures put the population at 4,072,000 with over a quarter living in the capital, the main languages spoken are Russian, Tatar and Bashkir. Bashkortostan covers an area of 143,600 sq km and is situated south of the Ural mountains. Bashkortostan has over 800 lakes, which are believed to have healing properties and attract tourists. The economy is based on the extraction of mineral resources particularly oil, natural gas, coal, copper and iron. Agriculture also plays a large part, particularly livestock - cattle, pigs, sheep and chickens. Bashkortostan is also famous for its horses. As well as the lakes, Bashkortostan has over 1,000 rivers, many of which are deep enough for transport to ports on the Baltic and Black seas.

Buryatiya
President: Vyacheslav Nagovitsyn, URL: http://egov-buryatia.ru/eng/
Capital: Ulan Ude
Recent figures put the population at 972,000. Buryatiya is located in the Siberian region and shares a border with Mongolia. It covers an area of 351,300 sq km. Languages spoken are Russian and Buryat. The economy is based on agriculture particularly wheat, vegetables, potatoes and timber. Sheep, cattle and fur farming also takes place. Natural resources include gold, zinc, uranium and tungsten.

Chechnya
President: Ramzan Kadyrov, URL: http://egov-buryatia.ru/eng/
Capital: Grozny
Recent figures put the population at 1.2 million. The main languages spoken are Chechen and Russian.
Following the break up of the Soviet Union in 1991, Azhokhar Dudayev was elected president and declared independence for Chechnya. In 1994 Russia invaded the breakaway republic of Chechnya. In 1996 a peace treaty was signed. In 1999 Chechen militants invaded the Russian republic of Dagestan; Russian troops were sent into Chechnya and captured the capital, Grozny. By 2000 the government was claiming control of the situation but in 2002 the conflict had still not been resolved, with heavy casualties suffered on both sides. In October 2002 Chechen terrorists seized a Moscow theatre and took over 800 people hostage. Russian troops eventually stormed the building, killing approximately 50 terrorists and over 110 hostages. In March 2003, despite no peace agreement, a referendum was held resulting in approval for a new constitution which states that Chechnya remains part of the Russian Federation although it has some autonomy. Two days later an attempted suicide attack was made on the Moscow backed president Akhmad Kadyrov. Suicide bombings continued to claim lives and in May 2004, president Kadyrov was killed in a bomb blast in Grozny. In September 2004 a school in Beslan, North Ossetia was seized by armed gunmen; parents, children and teachers were held hostage for three days until security forces went in. 330 people, mainly children were killed. Russia blamed international terrorists linked to the Chechen separatists; separatist leader, Aslan Maskhadov, blamed madmen wanting revenge against Russia for actions against Chechnya.

In October 2004 Alu Alkhanov was sworn in as president, with the backing of Moscow. The elections were criticised in some quarters and the main opposition candidate was barred from standing on a technicality. In February 2005, Aslan Maskhadov called for a ceasefire and peace talks, but this was rejected. In March, he was killed by Russian troops.

The separatist leader Aslan Maskhadov called for a ceasefire in February 2005 and wanted peace talks, but the official leadership of Chechnya called for him to give himself up. Maskhadov was reported to have been killed by Russian forces in March. Abdul-Khalim Saidullayev became the new rebel leader.

Chuvashia
President: Mikhail Vasilyevich Ignatiev, URL: http://gov.cap.ru/hierarhy_cap.asp?page=./25505
Capital: Cheboksary
Recent figures put the population at 1,313,800 but with an area of just 18,300 sq km Chuvashia has a population density of 72 people per sq km. The main languages spoken are Russian and Chuvash. Chuvashia is situated in the Volga-Vyatka region, the European part of Russia. The economy is industry-based; goods produced include chemicals and metalwork. Chuvashia also produces electricity and power systems. Agricultural produce includes hops and the region is famous for its beer.

Dagestan
President: Ramazan Abdulatipov (acting), URL: http://www.e-dag.ru/
Capital: Makhachkala
Dagestan is located in the North Caucasus and shares borders with Chechnya, Georgia, Azerbaijan and the Caspian Sea in the east. The popluation is around 3.0 million. Russian is spoken, as are languages of the Dagestan peoples. In recent years trouble has spilled over from neighbouring Chechnya. Chechen rebels have crossed the border and many Dagestanies have been held hostage. There have also been reports of bomb explosions, some of which have been blamed on local militants who have been influenced by the rebels. Dagestan has reserves of oil and gas, and fishing is a large contributor to the economy - particularly caviar. The majority of the population are Muslim.

Ingushetiya
President: Yunus-Bek Yevkurov, URL: http://www.ingushetia.ru/
Capital: Magas

Ingusetiya is situated between Chechnya and North Ossetia and is a predominantly Muslin region. Recent figures put the population at 400,000, the main languages spoken are Ingush and Russian.

Kabardino-Balkaria
President: Arsen Kanokov, URL: http://eng.president-kbr.ru/
Capital: Nalchik
Kabardino-Balkaria covers an area of 12,500 sq km and is situated in the North Caucasus, bordering Georgia in the south west. Recent figures put the population at 850,000.

Kalmykiya
President: Alexey Orlov, URL: http://www.kalm.ru/en/
Capital: Elista
Kalmykiya covers an area of 76,150 sq km situated on the north western shore of the Caspian Sea. Recent figures put the population at 300,000. The main languages spoken are Kalmyk and Russian. Kalmykiya's economy is based on agriculture although intensive farming has reduced some of the fertile areas to desert. Main products are wool and caviar. Kalmykiya has a large Buddhist population as well as many practicing Christians.

Karachayevo-Cherkesiya
President: Rashid Temrezov, URL: http://www.kchr.info/
Capital: Cherkessk
Karachayevo-Cherkesiya covers an area of 14,300 sq km and is situated north west of the North Caucasus region and borders Georgia to the south. Recent figures put the population at 447,000. The main languages spoken are Russian, Karachay and Cherkess. Mining and agriculture are the main contributors to the economy although the republic is keen to diversify into tourism particularly the area of winter sports.

Karelia
Head of Republic: Alexander Petrovich Khudilainen, URL: http://gov.karelia.ru/gov/index_e.html
Capital: Petrozavodsk
Karelia covers an area of 172,400 sq km and is situated in the north west of the Russian Federation and shares a border with Finland. The majority of the republic is covered in forest but it also has over 50,000 lakes. Recent figures put the population at 716,300 and the official language is Russian.

Khakassia
Chairman of the Government: Viktor Mikhailovich Zimin, URL: http://www.r-19.ru/
Capital: Abakan
Recent figures put the population at 540,000 and the main languages spoken are Russian and Khakass. Khakassia has large reserves of coal. Coal and ore mining form a large part of the economy.

Komi
President: Vyacheslav Mikhailovich Gaizer, URL: http://www.rkomi.ru/en/
Capital: Syktyvkar
Recent figures put the population at 1,018,700, the main languages are Komi and Russian. Komi covers an area of 415,900 sq km and is situated in the Northwestern Federal district to the West of the Ural mountains. The economy of Komi is based around mining; Komi has natural reserves of oil, natural gas, coal gold and diamonds.

Mari-El
President: Leonid Markelov, URL: http://gov.mari.ru/
Capital: Yoshkar Ola
Mari-El is situated in the European part of Russia along the East European Plain of the Russian Federation, along the Volga River. Recent figures put the population at 700,000, the main languages are Russian and Mari.

Mordovia
President: Vladimir Volkov, URL: http://www.e-mordovia.ru/
Capital: Saransk
Mordovia covers an area of 26,200 km^2 and is located in the east European region of the Russian Federation. Recent figures put the population at 888,800 and the main languages spoken are Russian, Moksha and Erzya.

North Ossetia-Alania
President: Taymuraz Mamsurov, URL: http://rso-a.ru/
Capital: Vladikavkaz
North Ossetia has an area of 8,000 sq km and is situated in North Caucasus region, it shares a border with South Ossetia situated in Georgia.Recent figures put the population at 710,000. The main languages spoken are Ossetian and Russian. North Ossetia has reserves of oil and natural gas but at present these are not exploited.

In September 2004 an armed attack was carried out on a school in the North Ossetia town of Beslan; 330 people were killed. Russia blamed international terrorists linked to the Chechen separatists for the attack.

Sakha
President: Egor Afanasievich Borisov, URL: http://www.sakha.gov.ru/
Capital: Yakutsk
Sakha covers an area of 1,030,200 sq km, and is located in eastern Siberia. Over a third of the area is located around the Arctic circle. Recent figures put the population at 958,000. The main languages are Russian and Yakut. The economy is largely based on mining particularly diamond, gold and tin ore. Sakha has around 45 per cent of Russia's coal deposits. It also has reserves of oil, gas and silver.

Tatarstan
President: Rustam Nurgalievich Minnikhanov, URL: http://tatarstan.ru/
Capital: Kazan
Tatarstan cover an area of 67,836 sq km in the East European region of Russia. The capital Kazan is 850 km to the east of Moscow. Recent figures put the population at 4,000,000 and the main languages area Russian and Tatar. The economy is based on heavy industry and agriculture; there are also large oil reserves as well as natural gas.

Tuva
Chairman of the Government: Sholban Kara-ool, URL: http://gov.tuva.ru/news.aspx
Capital: Kyzyl

Tuva is located in Southern Siberia and covers an area of 170,500 sq km. It shares a border with Mongolia. Recent figures put the population at 307,000. The main languages are Russian and Tuvan. Tuva has reserves of gold, oil, cobalt and iron ore, which are mined.

Udmurtia
President: Aleksandr Volkov, URL: http://www.udmurt.ru/en/
Capital: Izhevsk
Udmurtia is located in the East European plain of the Russian Federation and covers an area of 42,100sq km. Recent figures put the population at 1,570,400. The main languages are Russian and Udmurt. The economy is based on the oil and gas industries.

AREA AND POPULATION

Area
The Russian Federation lies in the eastern part of Europe and the northern part of Asia and is bounded in the northwest by Norway and Finland, in the west by Poland and in the southeast by China, Mongolia and the People's Democratic Republic of Korea. It shares its eastern border with Azerbaijan, Georgia, Ukraine, Belarus, Latvia and Estonia. The Federation faces the Arctic Ocean in the north, the Pacific in the east, the Baltic Sea in the west and the Black Sea in the south west; it also borders the Caspian Sea. The region of Kaliningrad, situated some 200 miles away from the rest of Russia, is separated from Russia by Lithuania and Belarus; it was given to Russia following World War II, and provides Russia with an ice-free port on the Baltic Sea.

The Russian Federation is the largest of the former republics of the Soviet Union. It occupies over 76 per cent of the total area of the former USSR and covers 17,075,400 sq. km. Geographically, it is very diverse from mountainous terrain, to the taigra and tundra of Siberia and then the open areas of the heartlands. It spans ten time zones and areas of sub-arctic to sub-tropical conditions.

To view a map of Russia, please visit
http://www.un.org/Depts/Cartographic/map/profile/russia.pdf

Population
As of 2010 the population was estimated to be 142.958 million, down from an estimated 144 million in 2005. Population density is 8.4 persons per sq. km. The population is in decline, with an average annual growth rate of -0.3 per cent over the period 2000-10. The decline is due to a death rate greater than the birth rate. Contributing factors to the high death rate are poverty and alcohol abuse. Some forecasts have predicted that population figures will continue to fall, reaching somewhere between 80 and 100 million by 2050.

The Russian Federation enjoyed a net migration increase of 49,840 people in 2001, with 187,413 immigrants and 137,573 emigrants. Russia now receives on average 200,000 immigrants per year, the majority of whom are ethnic Russians from republics of the former Soviet Union. Russia also has many illegal immigrants drawn to the larger cities from Georgia, Armenia, Azerbaijan, Tajikistan and Ukraine.

Approximately 73 per cent of the population lived in urban areas in 2010. The major cities are Moscow (11,500,000 inhabitants in 2012), St. Petersburg (4,750,000 in 2010), Novosibirsk (1,400,000), Nizhni Novgorod (1,300,000), and Yekaterinburg (1,257,000). The cities of Samara, Omsk, Ufa, Rostov-on-Don, Volgograd, Chelyabynsk and Ekaterinburg all have populations over one million.

Over 130 nationalities live in the Federation; Russians comprise 81.5 per cent, Tartars make up 3.8 per cent and Ukrainians, 3.0 per cent. The main language is Russian.

Births, Marriages, Deaths
Estimated figures for 2010 put the birth rate at 11.8births per 1,000 population and the death rate at 14.9 deaths per 1,000 population. The marriage rate in 2001 was 6.9 per 1,000 population (up from 6.2 per 1,000 in 2000), whilst the divorce rate was 5.3 per 1,000 population (up from 4.3 per 1,000 in 2000). Average life expectancy in 2009 according to the WHO was 62 years for men and 74 years for women. Healthy life expectancy was respectively 55 years for males and 65 years for females. The total fertility rate for women was 1.5 years. (Source: http://www.who.int, World Health Statistics 2012)

Public Holidays 2014
1 & 2 January: New Year
7 January: Russian Orthodox Christmas Day
14 January: Orthodox New Year
24 February: Defence of the Motherland (previously Soviet Army Day)
8 March: International Women's Day
18 April: Orthodox Good Friday
21 April: Orthodox Easter Monday
1 May: Spring and Labour Day
9 May: Victory Day
12 June: Day of Russia
22 August: Day of the Russian Federation Flag
4 November: People's Unity Day

In December 2004 parliament voted to change some of Russia's public holidays. November 7, previously, Accord and Reconciliation Day, the anniversary of the 1917 revolution and December 12, Constitution Day have been abolished in favour of November 4, Peoples' Unity Day, celebrating the anniversary of liberation from Polish troops in 1612. A 10-day Christmas and New Year holiday has now been introduced running from the beginning of January until after the Orthodox Christmas Day.

EMPLOYMENT

The Russian Federation had an economically active population of 75,756,000 in 2008, of which 37,076,000 were female and 38,681,000 were male. In 2008, the unemployment rate was put at 6.3 per cent, up from 6.1 per cent in 2007. Estimated figures for 2010 put the unemployment rate at 7.5 per cent.

Employment by Economic Activity in '000s

Sector	2007	2008
Agriculture, hunting & forestry	6,155	5,994
Fishing	192	141
Mining & quarrying	1,324	1,350
Manufacturing	12,324	11,663
Electricity, gas & water supply	2,017	2,116
Construction	4,933	5,413
Wholesale & retail trade	11,096	10,774
Hotels & restaurants	1,344	1,4467
Transport, storage & communications	6,573	6,560
Financial intermediation	1,249	1,316
Real estate, renting & business activities	4,410	4,448
Public administration & defence	4,903	5,409
Education	6,420	6,442
Health & social work	5,177	5,243
Other community, social & personal service activities	2,439	2,580
Private households	16	43
Extra territorial organisations & bodies	-	5

Source: Copyright © International Labour Organization (ILO Dept. of Statistics, http://laborsta.ilo.org)

BANKING AND FINANCE

Currency
One rouble (also ruble) = 100 Copeks

GDP/GNP, Inflation, National Debt
Liberalisation of the economy began in 1990 when the Russian Supreme Soviet approved the implementation of the radical *Shatalin* '500 day' economic programme that liberalised prices and began a process of privatisation. However, political instability at the centre and in the regions contributed to economic stagnation. Economic growth has since been boosted by the rise in oil prices. The economy is dependent on oil and gas; the sectors account for 25 per cent of GDP and 70 per cent of exports.

Foreign assistance for development of the economy has come from Western governments and agencies such as the IMF and the World Bank. At the 2002 G8 Summit the leaders agreed a proposal to look at cancelling some of Russia's debts in exchange for safeguarding materials in Russia that could be used by terrorists.

The economy is hindered by high levels of corruption, a difficult business investment climate and a dwindling and aging population.

Russia was invited to join the WTO in 2011.

In recent years, the Russian economy has shown consistently strong growth, growing by an estimated 8.1 per cent in 2007 up from 6.8 per cent in 2006. GDP in 2007 was put at an estimated US$1.3 trillion, up from the 2006 figure of US$975 billion, making it the tenth largest world economy. In recent years the Russian economy has benefited from high oil prices: oil and gas account for over 20 per cent of GDP, 50 per cent of federal budget revenues and 70 per cent of exports. However, due to falling oil prices and the global economic crisis, Russia's economy contracted in 2008/09 and government growth forecasts had to be revised. With a recovery in oil prices, GDP grew by 4 per cent in 2010 and GDP reached US$1.47 trillion. GDP was estimated to be US$1850 billion in 2011 with a growth rate of 4.3 per cent. Per capita GDP was estimated to be US$13,000.

The agricultural sector used to be a large GDP earner contributing over 13 per cent of GDP in the early 1990s. Estimates from 2008 put its contribution at 4.7 per cent. Industrial based GDP contributions have also fallen from nearly 50 per cent to an estimated 35 per cent in 2008. In contrast the retail and service sector's contribution grew from around 34 per cent in the early 1990s to nearly 58 per cent in 2008.

Foreign debt in 2008 was estimated to be US$540 billion, of which US$500 billion was short-term debt.

At its highest point in 1992 inflation was running at over 2,300 per cent. The government had aimed to reduce it to around 5 per cent by 1998 but the financial crisis and the devaluation of the rouble in that year meant it rose to 84 per cent after being around 11 per cent in 1997. In 2000 inflation was over 20 per cent, but fell to 18.6 per cent in 2001. The 2002 budget was based on an inflation rate of 12 per cent but estimates put it at 15.8 per cent, falling to 13.7 per cent in 2003 and 11.7 per cent in 2004. Inflation was estimated at 10.1 per cent in 2005, falling to 9 per cent in 2006, rising to an estimated 11 per cent in 2007. In 2008 it was estimated to have risen to 13 per cent. It was estimated to be 8 per cent in 2011.

Total external debt was estimated to be US$595 billion in 2012.

RUSSIA

Foreign Investment
Foreign investment in Russia reached US$103 billion in 2008. The areas that have accumulated the most foreign investment are management (23.8 per cent), the fuel industry (18.8 per cent) and finance and insurance (10.4 per cent). Germany provided the greatest share of total foreign investment in 1998 (25.9 per cent), followed by the US (18.9 per cent), France (17.0 per cent) and the UK (15.7 per cent).

A variety of legislation, both at state and federal level, has recently been passed to attract foreign investment. The country is also endeavouring to make various aspects of the process, such as taxation and customs, more transparent and more favourable to foreign business. Export duties have been abolished and import regulations are in accordance with World Trade Organisation rules. Russia has spent several years trying to negotiate terms of entry into the WTO, and membership was offered in 2011. It is currently looking for membership as a customs union with Belarus and Kazakhstan.

Balance of Payments / Imports and Exports
Estimated export earnings for 2010 were US$376 billion (compared to US$355 billion in 2007) and imports cost US$192 billion (compared to US$223 billion in 2007). Metals make up over 15 per cent, machinery and equipment nearly 7 per cent and chemicals, 6 per cent. Main import goods are machinery and equipment, which account for over 27 per cent of impost costs, food and agricultural products make up around 12 per cent, chemicals 11 per cent and metals nearly 5.0 per cent.

Russia's major export trading partners are the Netherlands (12 per cent), Italy (8.6 per cent), Germany (8.4 per cent), China (5.4 per cent), the Ukraine (5.1 per cent), Turkey (4.9 per cent) and Switzerland (4.1 per cent). Major import partners are Germany (14 per cent), China (10 per cent), Japan (6 per cent), South Korea (5.1 per cent), the USA (4.8 per cent), France (3.3 per cent) and Italy (4.1 per cent). Main export products are oil, fuel and natural gas, which together make up over 60 per cent of export earnings.

Central Bank
Central Bank of the Russian Federation (Bank of Russia), URL: http://www.cbr.ru
Chairman: Sergey Mikhailovich Ignatiev

Chambers of Commerce
Chamber of Commerce and Industry of the Russian Federation, URL: http://www.tpprf.ru/en/
Moscow Chamber of Commerce and Industry, URL: http://www.mostpp.ru/eng/

MANUFACTURING, MINING AND SERVICES

Primary and Extractive Industries
The Russian Federation has the eighth largest oil reserves in the world. In 2012 proven oil reserves were estimated at 60 billion barrels. Oil is extracted principally from fields in West Siberia (6,507,000 bbl/d, 2010), the Urals-Volga region (2,101,000 bbl/d, 2010), Akhangelsk (454,000 bbl/d, 2010) and Sakhalin, (295,000 bbl/d, 2010). After a decline in oil production, in part due to old equipment and difficulties in developing existing fields, Russia increased oil production from 6.62 million barrels per day in 2000 to 10.2 million barrels per day in 2011 (of which 95 per cent was crude) as oil prices rose and 10.2 million barrels per day in 2011.. However, increased productivity has depleted reserves. At the end of 2000 an agreement was reached between Russia and the European Union that the EU would help with the development of Russian oil and gas reserves in return for an increase in energy supplies from Russia. Exploration for new reserves continues particularly in the Russian Arctic, northern Caspian Sean and Eastern Siberian regions. ExxonMobil, Shell and BP are all currently involved in projects in these areas. Of the 9.9 million barrels per day produced in 2009, 2.9 million barrels per day were consumed and the surplus was available for export. Russia has 40 oil refineries and crude oil refining capacity was 5.4 million barrels per day in 2012.

Figures for 2009 show that Russian exported around 7 million bbl/d of crude oil. Some 1.3 million bbl/d were exported to Belarus, Ukraine, Germany and Poland, Hungary, Slovakia and the Czech Republic via the via the Druzhba pipeline. Approximately 1.3 million bbl/d were exported via the port of Primorsk near St. Petersburg, and around 900,000 bbl/d were exported via the Black Sea. Russia is currently expanding its pipeline network. Current capacity of the Tengiz-Novorossisk pipeline is due to increase from 565,000 bbl/d to 1.34 million bbl/d by 2014. When completed the Eastern Siberia-Pacific Ocean pipeline will be 2,610 miles long and able to transport 1.6 million bb/ld. Stage one (1,491 bbl/d, 6000,00 bbld) was expected to be completed at the ned of 2012.

As Russia's recent economic growth has come to rely on the production of oil and gas, it has become susceptible to fluctuations in price, as well as concerns for the economy when oil and gas reserves begin to run out. In 2004 Russia started a stability fund whereby some monies from oil receipts were set aside; the fund was estimated to be worth nearly US$158 billion at the end of 2007.

Following the collapse of the Soviet Union privatisation of the oil industry began. The sector is now dominated by a few privately-owned companies. The state-run Rosneft is the largest oil producer in Russia. Foreign companies may invest in Russia, but often in partnership with a Russian company, usually Rosneft.

Natural Gas
The Russian Federation has the largest natural gas reserves in the world (an estimated 1,680 trillion cubic feet), which are mainly located in the Northern Caucasus, the Volga region, the North-West zone and West Siberia. Approximately 95 per cent of Russia's natural gas reserves are located in Siberia. Gas production was estimated at 23,686 billion cubic feet in 2011, with consumption at 17,975 billion cubic feet. Estimated net exports in that year were 6.5 billion cubic feet. Various gas pipelines including to China are under consideration.

Gazprom is Russia's state-run natural gas monopoly, and holds almost a third of the world's natural gas reserves and over 60 per cent of Russia's reserves, produces nearly 90 per cent of Russia's natural gas, and operates its natural gas pipeline grid. Although independent producers such as Novatek and LUKoil have increased their production in recent years Gazprom currently controls most of the Federation's gas production. Gaxprom holds the legal monopoly on gas exports. Reforms decreed in 1997 stated that Gazprom will lose its monopoly over the right to develop new gas deposits. There were disputes between Russia and its neighbours including Ukraine resulted in natural gas being cut off to much of Europe.

There are currently nine major pipelines in Russia, seven of which are export pipelines. There are three proposed natural gas pipelines. The NorRussia is currently building a major new pipeline which will cross the Baltic Sea and will be able to supply Western Europe without passing through Belarus, Ukraine and Poland. It was due to be completed in 2010 but completion is now expected in 2013. It will be the longest sub-sea pipline with a capacity to transport 1.9 Tcf of natural gas.

Gazprom, URL: http://www.gazprom.ru

Coal
The Russian Federation has the second largest coal reserves in the world (after the US), an estimated 173,000 million short tons. Coal is mined primarily in Kuznetsk, Pechora, Irkutsk Coal production was estimated at 357 million short tons in 2010, up from 304 million short tons in 2009. Consumption was estimated at 256.79 million short tons in 2010, up from 204 million short tons in 2009. Coal consumption is expected to rise to more than 400 million short tons by 2020. Following a joint Russian/World Bank restructuring of the coal industry between 1996 and 2001, the state monopoly RosUgol was dissolved, and now nearly 80 per cent of domestic coal production comes from independent producers.

Peat is produced in the Central, Volga-Vyatka and Urals economic zones. Iron ores are found in the Kursk Magnetic Anomaly and in iron ore deposits in the Urals, Siberia and other locations. Yakutia, in East Siberia, is rich in diamond deposits.

Russia is also one of the world's largest producers and exporters of gold, although both production and demand have declined in recent years.

Energy
The Russian Federation is the second largest energy producer in the world and the largest exporter. Since 1999, after years of decline, the production of oil, gas and coal has begun to increase. Over 50 per cent of Russia's energy consumption is natural gas. Total energy production was 49.51 quadrillion Btu in 2009, up from 45.679 quadrillion Btu on 2007.

Total energy consumption in 2008 was estimated at 30.426 quadrillion Btus, 55 per cent of which came from natural gas, 19 per cent from oil, 16 per cent from coal, 6 per cent from hydroelectric sources and 5 per cent from nuclear sources. Per capita energy consumption was 208.8 million Btu in 2007.

Electricity
Electricity is mainly generated by thermal power stations, the largest being the Konakovo Thermal Power Plant. Altogether there are 440 thermal and hydroelectric power stations. Electricity is controlled by the Unified Energy Systems of Russian (UES), headed by Anatoly Chubais. Major hydroelectric power stations include the Krasnoyarsk station and hydropower plants on the Volga and Angara. High-capacity atomic power stations have been built in St. Petersburg, Beloyarsk and other areas. Safety issues are a major concern and plans to build 15 new nuclear plants to replace old unsafe reactors had been put on hold due to the country's economic crisis. However in June 2006 the prime minister approved a US$55 billion programme to provide 10 new nuclear reactors by 2015.

In 2010, total electricity capacity was 229.1 gigawatts, of which 68 per cent was thermal, 22 per cent hydro, and 10 nuclear. Electricity generation in the same year was estimated at 983.81 billion kilowatthours (kWh), of which 861.47 billion kWh was consumed.

Manufacturing
The Federation manufactures a wide variety of products and ranks first in their output in nearly all industrial branches among the former Union Republics. All industries, except textiles are developed on the basis of local raw materials. Many sectors such as car manufacturing, oil refineries, offices and shops, airport construction, are involved in joint ventures with Western organisations and companies. Main centres for mechanical engineering are Moscow, St. Petersburg, the Urals, the Volga region and west Siberia. Timber and paper industries are based in the European North. Textiles are produced in the central zone. Ferrous metallurgy has its centres in Magnitogorsk, Chelyabinsk, Nizhny Tagil, Novokuznetsk, Lipetsk and other areas. Non-ferrous metallurgy is concentrated in Norilsk, Krasnoyarsk, Irkutsk and also in the Urals and the Northern Caucasus. The chemical and petrochemical industries specialise in the production of plastics, mineral fertilisers, man-made fibres, synthetic rubber, and sulphuric acid.

Tourism
Figures for 2010 estimate that the Russian Federation had over 20 million foreign visitors. Visitors are expected to increase in the coming years as Russia is hosting several major sporting events in the coming years including the Winter Olympics in 2014 and the football World Cup in 2018.

Agriculture
In 1998 the Russian Federation had 218.8 million hectares of farmland. Figures for 2000 show that 124 million hectares were used for arable farming, 1.8 million hectares of permanent crops and about 90 million hectares of pasture. Considerable efforts have been made in recent years to advance agriculture in the non-Black Earth zones.

Principal grain crops are wheat, rye, maize, millet, buck-wheat and rice. The government has encouraged private ownership of land in recent years, passing a law in 1991 which enabled co-operative farms to re-register as private concerns. In 2002 the Duma passed another new land code aimed at restructuring the industry and increasing new domestic investment. Recent figures estimate over 243,000 private farms in Russia, with a total land area of 15,000,000 ha. Private farms and small holdings account for over 50 per cent of agricultural production.

The Federation accounts for more than half of livestock production in the former USSR. In animal husbandry, animals are raised for milk and meat or for wool. Deer breeding is developed far in the north. Fur farming and fur hunting are widespread in taiga areas. Figures from 2004 show that there were nearly 25 million head of cattle and over 17 million sheep and goats.

Agricultural Production in 2010

Produce	Int. $'000*	Tonnes
Cow milk, whole, fresh	8,855,246	31,585,200
Indigenous cattle meat	4,647,528	1,720,430
Wheat	4,103,531	41,507,600
Indigenous chicken meat	3,630,671	2,548,900
Indigenous pigmeat	3,490,936	2,270,910
Hen eggs, in shell	1,874,917	2,260,600
Potatoes	1,563,030	21,140,500
Sunflower seed	1,360,889	5,344,820
Sugar beet	925,340	22,255,900
Tomatoes	757,473	2,0496,40
Indigenous sheep meat	445,739	163,706
Apples	416,993	986,000

*unofficial figures
Source: http://faostat.fao.org/site/339/default.aspx Food and Agriculture Organization of the United Nations, Food and Agricultural commodities production

Forestry

Nearly 40 per cent of Russia is covered by forests and it has a timber reserve of nearly 80 billion cubic metres.

Forestry Production in 2004

Produce	'000 Cubic Metres
Industrial roundwood	134,000
Wood fuel	48,000
Wood charcoal	60
Sawn wood	21,500
Wood based panels	7,159
Wood pulp	6,885
Paper, paperboard	6,789

Source: FAOSTAT, Food & Agricultural Organization of the UN

COMMUNICATIONS AND TRANSPORT

Travel Requirements

The Russian government has restrictive and complicated entry requirements for foreigners who visit or transit the Russian Federation, and visa laws change regularly, and at times with little warning or clarity. In general, entry requirements are as follows, but visitors are strongly advised to contact the embassy to check details prior to travelling.

Citizens of the USA, Canada, Australia and the EU require a passport valid for six months beyond the expiration of a visa, and at least two blank pages, but do not need a visa for stays of up to 90 days. They also require a visa. Transit passengers continuing their journey within 24 hours without leaving the transit area, do not need a visa if they arrive from their country of origin. Other nationals should contact the embassy to check visa requirements.

All visitors must have confirmed accommodation for every night of their stay in the Russian Federation and must register their visas within three working days of arrival with the local branch of the Ministry of the Interior (most major hotels do this automatically. Private visitors must register with local police on arrival). Citizens of the Schengen states, Estonia and Israel must submit travel insurance documents with their visa applications; French citizens have to submit bank statements, return ticket and insurance documents with their applications, and all nationals applying for a multiple-entry/working/student visa must also submit a HIV certificate.

National Airlines

Aeroflot - Russian International Airlines (ARIA), URL: http://www.aeroflot.org
Transaereo, URL: http://www.transaero.ru/
Vnukovo Airlines, URL: http://www.vnukovo.ru/eng/for-passengers/airline/

International Airports

In total there are nearly 600 airports with paved runways. Major international airports include: Moscow Domodedovo Airport (http://www.domodedovo.ru/en/), Moscow-Sheremetyevo International (URL: http://www.sheremetyevo-airport.ru)

Railways

Railways in the Federation account for over 48 per cent of passenger transportation and 77 per cent of freight transportation. Total length of rail track is 87,150 km of which over 39,000 is electrified. This is now expanding with the electrification of the Trans-Siberian line. Just over 47,000 km of Russian railways takes diesel locomotives. There are 6,085 stations.

There are subway systems in Moscow, St. Petersburg, Nizhni Novgorod, Samara, Yekaterinburg and Novosibirsk, and subway systems are planned for Krasnoyarsk, Ufa, Kazan and Omsk.

Roads

The total length of motor roads exceeds 980,000 km; of this 770,000 km is hard-surfaced, including 46,000 km of federal highways. Vehicles drive on the right. Roads are well-developed in the European area of the Federation and least developed in eastern Siberia and the far east.

Ports and Harbours

The main ports of the Federation are Vladivostok, Nakhodka, Vostochnyi and Magadan in the east, St. Petersburg and Kaliningrad on the Baltic Sea, the Black Sea ports of Novorossiisk, Rostov and Sochi, and the ports of Murmansk and Arkhangelsk which serve the Atlantic Ocean via the Barents Sea. The merchant marine fleet consists of over 1,140 vessels.

Waterways

The network is over 100,000 km long.

HEALTH

Healthcare funding was reformed after the end of the Societ union. Compulsory health insurance was introduced: for those in employment contributions are paid by the employer; the municipal government makes contributions for those not in employment. There is also an unofficial sector where patients make direct payments for healthcare.

In 2009, the Russian government spent approximately 8.5 per cent of its total budget on healthcare (up from 12.7 per cent in 2000), accounting for 63.4 per cent of all healthcare spending. Social security accounted for 38.7 per cent of expenditure. Total expenditure on healthcare equated to 5.6 per cent of the country's GDP. Per capita expenditure on health was approximately US$476, compared with US$96 in 2000. Figures for 2005-11 show that there are 614,183 physicians (43 per 10,000 population), 1.214.3 million nurses and midwives (85.2 per 10,000 population), 45,628 dentistry personnel, 11,521 pharmaceutical personnel and 72,515 environment and public health workers. There are 97 hospital beds per 10,000 population.

According to the latest WHO figures, in 2010 approximately 97 per cent of the population had access to improved drinking water. In the same year, 70 per cent of the population had access to improved sanitation. The infant mortality rate in 2010 was 9 per 1,000 live births. The child mortality rate (under 5 years) was 12 per 1,000 live births. The main causes of deaths among children aged less than five years old are: congenital anomalies (25 per cent), prematurity (21 per cent), injuries (7 per cent), birth asphyxia (7 per cent), pneumonia (8 per cent), HIV/AIDS (9 per cent), and diarrhoea (1 per cent).

In 2010, there were 118,641 reported cases of TB, 547 of rubella, 4,795 of pertussis, 510 of mumps, and 129 of measles. Alcoholism is a major health problem. (Source: http://www.who.int, World Health Statistics 2012)

EDUCATION

Kindergartens are organised by regional authorities and recent figures show that over 80 over cent of young children attend pre-school. In 2004 it was suggested that pre-school education should be paid for by parents but opposition to this proposal was strong and it was amended so that a local authority could only ask for a parental contribution up to 20 per cent of the cost although some groups are exempt, including families of twins, children of college students, refugees, and Chernobyl veterans.

Primary and general secondary education is compulsory and recent figures show that there are over 59,000 general secondary schools with over 21 million students, as well as general secondary schools, students of secondary school age can attend advanced learning schools which specialise in particular subjects or vocational technical school.

There are over 500 higher education institutes and 48 universities. Approximately 5 million students are enrolled in higher education. The vast majority of education is provided free by the state, although a small number of private schools and colleges have opened in recent years.

There are on-going reforms of the education system.

According to the latest UNESCO statistics, in 2009 an estimated 93 per cent of children were enrolled in primary school and 89 per cent in secondary. Enrolment in tertiary education was estimated at 76 per cent. The pupil: teacher ratio in primary school was 18:1.

RELIGION

The main religion is the Russian Orthodox Church. There is a Muslim community, most of whom are Sunnies. There is also a Jewish community and some Buddhists. In 1997 a law was passed giving accredited status to religious groups that have been existence for over 15 years.

Russia has a religious liberty rating of 4 on a scale of 1 to 10 (10 is most freedom). (Source: World Religion Database)

COMMUNICATIONS AND MEDIA

Broadcasting is dominated by channels either owned by the state or with close links to it. This has caused concern over the lack of independence of broadcasters. There are reports of harrassment of journalists, especially those investigating politicians.

Newspapers

More than 400 titles exist, most nationals are produced from Moscow.

Argumenty i Fakty, weekly, URL: http://www.aif.ru
Izvestia, run by Gazprom, URL: http://www.izvestia.ru
Komsomolskaya Pravda, controlled by YeSN, URL: http://www.kp.ru
Nezavisimaya Gazeta, private, URL: http://www.ng.ru/
Kommersant, URL: http://www.kommersant.ru
Moskovskiy Komsomolets, private, URL: http://www.mk.ru
Rossiyskaya Gazeta, government-owned, URL: http://www.rg.ru
Nevavisimaya Gazeta, private, URL: http://www.ng.ru
The Moscow Times, URL: http://www.themoscowtimes.com/indexes/01.html and **The Moscow News**, URL: http://english.mn.ru/english are both English language publications.

Broadcasting

Television is the main source of news and the broadcasting market is competitive. There are currently six national TV stations. The Russian State Television and Radio broadcasting Company (VGRTRK) runs the national networks Russia One (TV) and Radio Russia. Satellite and cableTV are available. The pay-TV market is dominated by the satellite broadcaster Tricolor. Numerous radio stations operate.
Russia One, URL: http://www.rutv.ru/?d=0
Channel 1, URL: http://www.1tv.ru/
Voice of Russia, URL: http://english.ruvr.ru/
Tricolor, URL: http://www1.tricolor.tv/DefaultEng.aspx

Telecommunications

The system has improved in recent years although the landline situation is much better in urban areas than rural arewas. Access to digital communication lines has increased in recent years, with internet and e-mail services expanding. Figures from 2010 estimate that 44 million phone land lines are in use as well as 235 million mobile phones.

According to 2010 estimates there are approximately 59 million internet users in the Russian Federation. The Russian Federation's internet country code is '.ru'. The internet is less strictly controlled than traditional media.

ENVIRONMENT

Major environmental problems include radioactive contamination of food and water supplies, industrial pollution, deforestation, greenhouse gas emission and acid rain. Russia's forests account for over 20 per cent of the world's forest cover. Russia's ability to deal with environmental problems is hampered by its economic difficulties. In 2000, President Putin dissolved the State Committee for Environmental Protection (SCEP) and State Committee on Forestry and set up a combined Ministry of Natural Resources.

An estimated 250,000 people die each year from health problems caused or aggravated by environmental conditions. There is severe urban air pollution caused by industry and vehicle emissions. The country's powerplants are old and several leaks and emissions have been reported. Lake Baikal, which contains 20 per cent of the world's fresh water, is under threat of contamination. The nuclear industry is also a concern. Many plants and reactors are old and poorly maintained and there is some radioactive contamination. The Duma recently approved a bill to allow storage of foreign nuclear waste on Russian soil. The revenue generated will be put towards an environmental fund.

Total carbon dioxide emission from the consumption of fossil fuels were put at 1,633.80 million metric tons in 2010, up from 1,448.46 million metric tons in 2009. (Source: EIA)

The Russian Federation is a party to the following international environmental agreements: Air Pollution, Air Pollution-Nitrogen Oxides, Air Pollution-Sulfur 85, Antarctic-Environmental Protocol, Antarctic-Marine Living Resources, Antarctic Seals, Antarctic Treaty, Biodiversity, Climate Change, Climate Change-Kyoto Protocol, Desertification, Endangered Species, Environmental Modification, Hazardous Wastes, Law of the Sea, Marine Dumping, Ozone Layer Protection, Ship Pollution, Tropical Timber 83, Wetlands and Whaling. Russia has signed but not ratified the Air Pollution-Sulfur 94 agreement.

SPACE PROGRAMME

The former USSR launched the first man into space, as well as the Earth's first artificial satellite. Since 1957 the country has launched more than 2,500 rockets, and over 180 Russian satellites are currently in orbit.

The Russian space agency, Roscosmos, has an annual budget of an estimated 200 billion rubles. In 2011 it published a draft strategy for space development until 2030. Plans included the launch of several long-term space missions to Mars and a manned flight around the moon. Russia currently handles approximately 40 per cent of global space launches.

Between 1995-2000, the Russian space station Mir played host to astronauts from the National Aeronautics and Space Administration (NASA) in the USA and the European Space Agency (ESA). After some difficulties, partly due to accidents and partly due to its advanced age, Mir was finally brought back to earth in 2001. A new orbital station called Alpha,was built in co-operation with NASA, ESA, Japan and Canada. A new launch facility in Vostochny, in eastern Russia, is being constructed and is due to become operational in 2015.

In April 2001 the first 'space tourist', American businessman Dennis Tito, paid to be a passenger on board a Russian rocket and visited the International Space Station.

In 2011 NASA announced that Roscosmos will be paid $753 million to ferry US astronauts to the space station between 2014-16.

Roscosmos, URL: http://www.federalspace.ru/?lang=en

RWANDA

Republic of Rwanda

Republika y'u Rwanda

Capital: Kigali (Population estimate 2009: 965,000)

Head of State: Maj.-Gen. Paul Kagame (President)

National Flag: The top half is blue with a yellow sun in the right hand corner; the bottom half is equally divided into two horizontal stripes, the top half yellow, the bottom half green

CONSTITUTION AND GOVERNMENT

Constitution

Formerly part of the United Nations Trust territory of Ruanda-Burundi, which lies east of the Congo, Rwanda became a sovereign state on 1 July 1962. It was formerly colonised by Belgium. It became a member of the UN in September of the same year. Attempts to federate the northern territory of Rwanda with its southern neighbour Burundi failed and all common organisations came to an end in 1964.

A new Constitution was introduced in 1991. A Prime Minister was appointed in 1992 and a transitional government was named to oversee the move to multi-party elections.

In April 1994 a plane carrying President Juvenal Habyarimana was shot down. The Hutu government accused Tutsi Rwandan Patriotic Front (RPF) of carrying out the attack, whilst the Tutsi's thought that the Hutus had done it as an excuse for their subsequent actions. The country descended into a brutal civil war between the Tutsi and Hutu tribes in which 800,000 people were murdered, mainly from the Tutsi minority. French and British troops were sent into Rwanda and the borders of Zaire (now the Democratic Republic of Congo) under UN auspices to protect people from groups of hostile opposing tribe members and to provide aid to the multitude of refugees.

In February 2000, following allegations of corruption, President Pasteur Bizimungu dissolved the cabinet and appointed a new government. Bernard Makuza of the MDR was appointed Prime Minister.

On 30 July 2002 a peace deal was signed between Rwanda and the Democratic Republic of Congo aimed at ending the four-year conflict, in which two million people died.

Rwanda's current constitution was approved by the Transitional National Assembly on 23 April 2003, accepted by the people in a referendum in June 2003, and signed by President Kagame on 4 June. According to the 2003 Constitution the head of state is the President, elected for a maximum of two consecutive seven-year terms. The president appoints the Council of Ministers, which is headed by the prime minister.

To access the constitution, please visit: http://www.ambarwanda.ch/spip.php?article917

International Relations

Since the genocide of 1994, Rwanda's relations with the DRC (formerly Zaire) have been strained, and at times violent. Remnants of the forces that carried out the genocide ('exFAR/I'), who fled to Zaire, have conducted raids into Rwanda. In response, in 1996 the Rwandan government sent its army into Zaire, which led to the removal of long-standing dictator Mobutu Sese Seko from power, and his replacement by Laurent Kabila. Significant numbers of exFAR/I continued to plan operations against Rwanda, and tensions between the countries led to a second Rwandan intervention in the Congo in 1998, supported by Uganda and Burundi. This triggered a conflict in the DRC that continued until 2003. The last Rwandan troops withdrew in late 2002, but relations remain difficult between the two countries.

Relations with Uganda, strained for many years due to mutual accusations of support for dissidents, are gradually improving. Rwanda plays an active role in the African Union (AU), and joined the East African Community in June 2007. The country is also a strong supporter of the New Partnership for African Development, NEPAD. Rwanda is an active member of the UN, and most of the UN development and humanitarian agencies have had a large presence in Rwanda. In addition to receiving assistance from the international community, Rwanda has also contributed to international peacekeeping missions. Currently, Rwanda Defense Forces (RDF) has deployed four battalions in support of the UNAMID Mission in Sudan. In the fall of 2006, Rwanda broke diplomatic relations with France, following a French judge's indictment of senior Rwandan officials on charges of having participated in the shooting down of the presidential jet in 1994. Rwanda rejects these charges. Relations with

Germany were strained in November 2008, when the Rwandan protocol chief Rose Kabuye was detained in Germany on a French arrest warrant; she is one of nine senior officials wanted over the shooting down of former President Juvenal Habyarimana's plane and triggering the 1994 genocide in Rwanda.

Recent Events

In June 2004 Pasteur Bizimungu, the first post-genocide president, was jailed for 15 years on charges including inciting civil disobedience; he was released in April 2007, having received a presidential pardon. In December 2004 Rwanda withdrew a threat to invade DRC and denied involvement in recent clashes. In March 2005 the former defence minister, Gen. Gatsinzi, appeared in court on charges relating to the 1994 genocide. The main ethnic Hutu rebel group, the Democratic Forces for the Liberation of Rwanda (FDLR), announced it had abandoned its armed struggle in 2005. In an attempt to create ethnically-diverse administrative areas, Rwanda's 12 provinces were replaced by a smaller number of regions in January 2006.

Rwanda broke off diplomatic ties with France in November 2006, when a French judge issued an international arrest warrant for President Kagame, alleging he was involved in bringing down Habyarimana's plane. In December, The International Criminal Tribunal sentenced Father Athanase Seromba to 15 years in prison for involvement in the 1994 genocide.

Around 8,000 prisoners accused of genocide were released in February 2007, bringing the total of freed suspects to 60,000 since 2003, to ease prison overcrowding. In October 2007, an inquiry was launched into the 1994 plane crash that killed President Habyarimana and sparked the genocide.

Rwanda signed a peace agreement with the Democratic Republic of Congo in November 2007. Under its terms, the DRC must hand over people wanted in connection with the genocide. In January, the French authorities arrested former Rwandan army officer Marcel Bivugabagabo who is on list of war criminals. In February 2008, a Spanish judge issued arrest warrants for 40 Rwandan officers whom he accused of genocide, terrorism and crimes against humanity, but President Kagame refused to hand over the officers. In May, former cabinet minister, Callixte Kalimanzira, went on trial at the International Criminal Tribunal for Rwanda, charged with taking part in the 1994 genocide. In August 2008, Rwanda accused France of being actively involved in the genocide of 1994, and named over 30 senior French officials. In November, Rose Kabuye (a senior Rwandan presidential aide) was extradited to France from Germany, accused of involvement in the shooting down of Juvenal Habyarimana's plane in 1994, which helped trigger Rwanda's genocide. She denied involvement, and her arrest led to protests in Rwanda. Ms Kabuye, a former guerrilla fighter with the Rwandan Patriotic Front (RPF), now Rwanda's ruling party, has heroic status in Rwanda; she has served as an MP and mayor of Kigali, and is one of President Paul Kagame's closest aides.

In December 2008, a draft report by the UN alleged that the Rwandan authorities have supplied Gen. Nkunda's forces in DRC with military equipment and the use of Rwandan banks; they have allowed the rebels to launch attacks from Rwandan territory on the Congolese army, and have brought recruits (including child soldiers) to the border on behalf of the rebels. The report revealed that the UN had been monitoring phone calls between the Rwandan presidency and Gen Nkunda.

In January 2009 the former minister of justice, Agnes Ntamabyariro, was jailed for life for her part in the genocide. In the same month Rwanda troops entered the DRC to attack Hutu rebels. They withdrew in February.

In November 2009, Rwanda became a member of the Commonwealth. Most Commonwealth countries were former members of the British Empire or have colonial ties to the United Kingdom. Rwanda is only the second member nation not to have had such a relationship with the UK, the other country being Mozambique.

In December 2009, it was declared that Rwanda was free of landmines.

The opposition leader and potential presidential candidate, Victoire Ingabire Umuhoza, was arrested in April 2010. The elections took place in August 2010 and were won by the incumbent President Kagame.

In June 2011, Pauline Nyiramasihuko, the former minister for family, was found guilty of genocide by an international court.

The Minister of State in charge of Community Development and Social Affairs, Christine Nyatanyi, died in September 2011.

The former civil service minister Prosper Mugiraneza and the former trade minister Justin Mugenzi were convicted in October 2011 of complicity to commit genocide and incitement to commit genocide. Two other ministers, the former health minister, Casimir Bizimungu and the former foreign affairs minister, Jerome-Clement Bicamumppaka, were acquitted of involvement in the 1994 genocide due to lack of evidence. The Hutu leader Cllixte Mbarushimana was freed after the ICC ruled there was insufficient evidence against him.

In May 2012, the UN said it had evidence that Rwanda was fuelling a rebellion in the neighbouring Democratic Republic of Congo, a claim denied by Rwanda.

The opposition leader, Victoire Ingabire, was sentenced to eight years in jail on charges of threatening state security in October 2012.

In December 2012, the International Criminal Tribunal for Rwanda (ICTR) convicted a former government minister, Augustin Ngirabatware to 35 years in prison.

The minister responsible for gender and family promotion died in December 2012. The cabinet was reshuffled in February 2013.

In March 2013, the ICTR overturned the 2011 genocide convictions of former ministers Justin Mugenzi and Prosper Mugiraneza.

Legislature

Rwanda formerly had a unicameral legislature known as the Transitional National Assembly (*Assemblée Nationale de Transition*) which had 74 members (increased from 70 members in 2000) who served a five-year term. Under the terms of the 2003 constitution the parliament became bicameral. The lower house, the Chamber of Deputies, has 80 members, of whom 53 are directly elected. Each of the 12 provinces also elects two women members, two members represent youth organisations, and one member represents organisations of disabled people. The term of office is five years. The upper house, the Senate, has 26 members indirectly elected for an eight-year term. Former heads of state can be additional members of the Senate.

Legislature: URL: http://www.rwandaparliament.gov.rw/

Cabinet (as at March 2013)

Prime Minister: Dr Pierre Habumuremyi (page 1436)
Minister of Local Government: James Musani
Minister of Infrastructure: Silas Lwakabamba (page 1467)
Minister of Foreign Affairs and Regional Co-operation: Mme Louise Mushikiwabo (page 1483)
Minister of State for Trade and Industry: François Kanimba
Minister of Agriculture and Animal Resources: Dr Agnes Kalibata
Minister of Finance and Economic Planning: Amb. Claver Gatete (page 1429)
Minister of Land, Forests, Environment and Natural Resources: Stanislas Kamanzi
Minister of Disaster Management and Refugee Affairs: Mme Serafine Mukantabana (page 1481)
Minister of Education: Dr Vincent Biruta
Minister of Health: Dr Agnes Binagwaho
Minister of Defence: Gen. James Kabarebe
Minister of Justice and Attorney General: Tharcisse Karugarama (page 1454)
Minister of Cabinet Affairs: Protais Musoni
Minister of Culture and Sports: Protais Mitali Kabanda
Minister of Information & Youth: Jean Nsengimana
Minister of Public Service and Labour: Anastase Murekezi
Minister of the Internal Security: Sheikh Mussa Fazil Harerimana
Minister in the President's Office: Mme. Venantia Tugireyezu
Minister of East African Community: Monique Mukaruliza
Minister in the Prime Minister's Office: Mme Oda Gasinzigwa (page 1429)

Ministries

Office of the President, PO Box 15, Kigali, Rwanda. Tel: +250 84085 / 84087 / 83358, fax: +250 84390, URL: http://www.presidency.gov.rw/
Office of the Prime Minister, PO Box 1334, Kigali, Rwanda. Tel: +250 85444 / 77554, fax: +250 83714 / 76969, URL: http://www.primature.gov.rw/
Ministry of Defence and National Security, PO Box 23, Kigali, Rwanda. Tel: +250 575386, fax: +250 576969, URL: http://www.minadef.gov.rw/
Ministry of Foreign Affairs, PO Box 179, Kigali, Rwanda. Tel: +250 575339, fax: +250 572904, URL: http://www.minaffet.gov.rw/
Ministry of Justice and Institutional Affairs, PO Box 160, Kigali, Rwanda. Tel: +250 86561 / 86398 / 85844, fax: +250 86509, e-mail: minijust@minijust.gov.rw, URL: http://www.minijust.gov.rw
Ministry of National Education, Kigali, Rwanda. Tel: +250 83051 / 86970, fax: +250 82162, URL: http://www.mineduc.gov.rw/
Ministry of Finance and Economic Planning, BP 158, Kigali, Rwanda. Tel: +250 55756 / 75113, fax: +250 57581 / 77581, e-mail: mfin@rwanda1.com, URL: http://www.minecofin.gov.rw/
Ministry of Trade and Industry, Kigali, Rwanda. Tel: +250 574725, fax: +250 575465, URL: http://www.minicom.gov.rw/
Ministry of Health, PO Box 84, Kigali, Rwanda. Tel: +250 577458, fax: +250 573797, e-mail: info@minaffet.gov.ru, URL: http://www.moh.gov.rw/
Ministry of Public Service and Labour, PO Box 403, Kigali, Rwanda. Tel: +250 585714, fax: +250 583621, URL: http://www.mifotra.gov.rw/
Ministry of Gender and Women in Development, PO Box 1413, Kigali, Rwanda. Tel: +250 577626 / 577203, fax: +250 577543, URL: http://www.migeprofe.gov.rw/
Ministry of Agriculture and Animal Industry, PO Box 621, Kigali, Rwanda. Tel: +250 585008, fax: +250 585057, e-mail: info@minagri.gov.rw, URL: http://www.minagri.gov.rw/
Ministry of Youth, Culture and Sports, PO Box 1044, Kigali, Rwanda. Tel: +250 83527 / 83525, fax: +250 83518, URL: http://www.mijespoc.gov.rw/
Ministry of Local Government, Information and Social Affairs, Kigali, Rwanda. Tel: +250 85406 / 83170, fax: +250 82228, e-mail: webmaster@minaloc.gov.rw, URL: http://www.minaloc.gov.rw
Ministry of Infrastructure, Tel: +250 585503, fax: +250 585755, e-mail: info@mininfra.gov.rw, URL: http://www.mininfra.gov.rw/
Ministry of Internal Security, PO Box 446, Kigali, Rwanda. URL: http://www.mininter.gov.rw/

Political Parties

Liberal Party (PL); Rwandan Patriotic Front (FPR); Social Democratic Party (PSD).

Elections

A presidential election took place on 25 August 2003; Paul Kagame won just over 95 per cent of the vote. Parliamentary elections took place on 29 and 30 September 2003 when President Kagame's Rwandan Patriotic Front (Tutsi) won 73 per cent of the vote and 40 of the parliament's 53 seats. EU observers reported irregularities. The most recent presidential election took place in August 2010 and President Kagame was re-elected.

On the 15th September 2008, Rwandans held their second parliamentary elections since the genocide of 1994. The Rwandan Patriotic Front (FPR) won 42 of the 53 directly elected seats in the Chamber of Deputies, retaining their majority. Most opposition groups were in exile

RWANDA

and did not contest the election. The governing coalition includes the Centrist Democratic Party (PDC), the Ideal (formerly Islamic) Democratic Party (PDI), the Rwandan Socialist Party (PSR) and the Democratic Union of Rwandan People (UDPR).

Diplomatic Representation

Embassy of the Republic of Rwanda, 120-122 Seymour Street, London W1H 1NR, United Kingdom. Tel: +44 (0)20 7224 9832, fax: +44 (0)20 78642, e-mail: uk@ambarwanda.org.uk, URL: http://www.ambarwanda.org.uk/
Ambassador: Ernest Rwamcuyo
British Embassy, Parcelle No 1131, Blvd de l'Umuganda, Kacyira-Sud, BP 576 Kigali, Rwanda. Tel: +250 584098, fax: +250 582044, e-mail: embassy.kigali@fco.gov.uk, URL: http://ukinrwanda.fco.gov.uk/en
Ambassador: Benedict Llewellyn-Jones OBE
US Embassy, 2657 Avenue de la Gendarmerie, Kacyiru, P.O. Box 28, Kigali, Rwanda. Tel: +250 596400, fax: +250 596591, URL: http://rwanda.usembassy.gov/
Ambassador: Donald W. Koran
Embassy of the Republic of Rwanda, 1714 New Hampshire Avenue, NW, Washington, DC 20009, USA. Tel: +1 202 232 2882, fax: +1 202 232 4544, URL: http://www.rwandaembassy.org/
Ambassador: Zac Nsenga
Permanent Representative of the Rwandese Republic to the UN, 124 East 39th Street, New York, NY 10016, USA. Tel: +1 212 679 9010 / 9023 / 9024, fax: +1 212 679 9133, e-mail: rwanda@un.int, URL: http://www.un.int/wcm/content/site/rwanda/
Ambassador: H.E. Mr. Eugène-Richard Gasana

LEGAL SYSTEM

Rwanda's legal system is based on the German and Belgian civil law systems and customary law. The constitution provides for an independent judiciary; however, provisions give the executive branch and the president authority to appoint and dismiss judges, and so, in practice, the courts are susceptible to government influence and manipulation.

Rwanda's court system consists of the Supreme Court, Constitutional Court (composed of the court of cassation and a council of state), and a Court of Appeals. There is also a court of accounts, which examines public accounts, and a court of state security for treason and national security cases.

Defendants have a right to counsel, but a shortage of trained lawyers means that many criminal defendants are unrepresented.

People involved in the orchestration of the 1994 genocide appear before the UN-mandated International Criminal Tribunal for Rwanda (ICTR) in Arusha, Tanzania. As of March 2013, the ICTR had convicted 63 people of genocide offenses (17 pending appeal), and acquitted 12 people. Two detainees were deceased before judgement, four cases transferred to national jurisdiction and two released. In December 2008, a former senior defence official, Theoneste Bagosora, was convicted of instigating the genocide and sentenced to life in prison. It was the first time the Rwanda tribunal had convicted anyone of organising the 800,000 killings. Prosecutors said Bagosora assumed control of military and political affairs in Rwanda when President Habyarimana's plane was shot down in 1994, though the indictment alleges that he began planning the massacre as far back as 1990.

Some 56,000 people have been released from overcrowded prisons to be tried by gacaca courts (traditional community courts). Approximately 12,000 gacaca courts were set up specifically to try all those involved in the genocide. Under the gacaca system, judges were elected by the local community and could impose sentences of up to life imprisonment. The Courts began a trial period of operation in 2002 and started operating fully in 2004. During their operation, approximately 2 million people were tried with a conviction rate of approximately 65 per cent. The courts ceased operating in 2012.

Human rights abuses continue, but the situations is improving in Rwanda. Arrests and detentions can be arbitrary, and pretrial detention is prolonged by an overstretched judiciary. Prison conditions remain harsh. Freedom of speech, of the press and of association are all restricted. Official corruption is widespread. Rwanda abolished the death penalty for all crimes in 2007.

Gacaca Commission, URL: http://www.inkiko-gacaca.gov.rw/
International Criminal Tribunal for Rwanda, URL: http://www.ictr.org

National Commission for Human Rights, URL:http://www.cndp.org.rw/

LOCAL GOVERNMENT

Until 2006, Rwanda consisted of 12 prefectures: Kigali City - PVK, Kigali Rural, Butare, Byumba, Cyangugu, Gikongoro, Gisenyi, Gitarama, Kibungo, Kibuye, Ruhengeri, and Umutara. The country was subdivided into 106 districts.

In January 2006, in an attempt to create ethnically-diverse administrative areas and to blur the distinction between ethnic Hutu and Tutsi areas, Rwanda's 12 provinces were replaced by five regions. These are named the North, South, East and West provinces, and Kigali, the capital. The new provinces were overseen by governors appointed by the government until elections took place. The most recent elections took place in 2011.

The capitals of the provinces are as follows: East Province (Province de l'est), capital: Rwamagana; North Province (Province du nord), capital: Byumba; South Province (Province du sud), capital: Nyanza; West Province (Province de l'ouest), capital: Kibuye. Rwanda is further divided into 30 districts, 416 sectors and 2,148 cells and 14,837 villages.

AREA AND POPULATION

Area

Rwanda is approximately 26,338 sq. km (10,100 sq. miles) in area, of which 24,948 sq. km is land and 1,390 sq. km is water. Main water bodies are: Lake Kivu, Lake Muhazi, Lake Ihema, Lake Bulera, Lake Ruhondo, Lake Mugesera. Rwanda is landlocked and borders Burundi to the south, the Democratic Republic of Congo to the west, Uganda to the north, and Tanzania to the east. Rwanda's terrain consists mostly of grassy uplands, hills and areas of rugged mountains that extend southeast from a chain of volcanoes in the northwest. Although only two degrees south of the Equator, Rwanda's high elevation makes the climate temperate. The country has two rainy seasons, from February to May, and from September to December.

To view a map, consult http://www.un.org/Depts/Cartographic/map/profile/rwanda.pdf

Population

In 2010, Rwanda's population was estimated at 10.624 million, with an annual average growth rate of 2.7 per cent over the period 2000-10. Rwanda is one of the most densely populated countries in Africa, with 322 inhabitants per square kilometre. The population is expected to reach 12 million by the year 2012, putting immense strain on meagre natural resources. Population control is therefore one of the government's top priorities.

An estimated 81 per cent of the population lives in rural areas. Approximately 53 per cent of the population is aged between 15 and 60 years, with 43 per cent aged up to 15 years, and 4 per cent aged 60 years or over. Over 1.3 million refugees returned to Rwanda in 1996 after fleeing the country's civil war; estimates put the number killed during the April-July 1994 genocide at 800,000, with two million Hutus crossing the border to neighbouring Zaire (now Democratic Republic of Congo). Over 40 per cent of Rwanda's women are widowed.

Rwanda's three ethnic groups are the Hutu (85 per cent), the Tutsi (14 per cent) and the Twa (1 per cent).

The official languages are Kinyarwanda, French and English. Swahili is also spoken.

Births, Marriages, Deaths

Estimates for 2010 put the birth rate at 41 births per 1,000 population, and the death rate at 9.8 deaths per 1,000 population. The average life expectancy is estimated at 57 years for males and 60 years for females. The fertility rate was 5.4 children per woman in 2010. (Source: http://www.who.int, World Health Statistics 2012)

Public Holidays 2014

1 January: New Year's Day
7 April: National Mourning Day
21 April: Easter Monday
5 May: Labour Day
1 July: Independence Day
15 August: Assumption
25 September: Kamarampaka Day
1 October: Armed Forces Day
1 November: All Saints' Day
25 December: Christmas

EMPLOYMENT

Of Rwanda's estimated labour force of 4.4 million, around 90 per cent work in subsistence agriculture, with 8 per cent in the commerce, services, and government sectors. The government is pursuing educational and healthcare programs that should improve the long-term quality of Rwanda's human resource skills base.

BANKING AND FINANCE

Currency

The unit of currency is the Rwanda franc (Frw). The financial centre is Kigali.

GDP/GNP, Inflation, National Debt

The Rwandan economic situation was badly hit by the civil war. Post-war, the economy strengthened, due largely to massive foreign assistance. Rwanda signed an Enhanced Structural Adjustment Facility (ESAF) with the International Monetary Fund (IMF) in 1998, and began a privatisation programme. Lack of economic diversification means that the country is vulnerable to market fluctuations. The government has adopted a fiscal policy aimed at reducing poverty by improving education, infrastructure, and foreign and domestic investment, and pursuing market-oriented reforms. However, power shortages, regional instability and an inadequate transport system limit growth. A Sepcial Economic Zone has been developed in Kigali to attract investment in all sectors.

Landlocked Rwanda has few exploitable resources and most Rwandans exist on subsistence agriculture which is periodically threatened by drought. Agriculture and agribusiness contribute about 36 per cent of the country's GDP and 60 per cent of exports. Tea and coffee are the main contributors to export earnings.

Gross Domestic Product has been rising steadily since 1994. In 1996 GDP grew at a rate of 13 per cent, mainly due to improvements in the collection of tax revenues, faster privatisation of state enterprises, and increases in export crop and food production. Real GDP growth averaged almost 8 per cent per year from 1998 to 2002. Growth has been in single digits for the last 10 years. In 2007, it was 4.9 per cent, compared to 5.3 per cent in 2006 and 6.0 per cent in 2005. GDP was US\$5.1 billlion in 2009, growth in 2010 was put at 6.4 per cent. In 2011, GDP was estimated to be US\$6 billion, with a growth rate of 8 per cent. GDP breaks down into: agriculture 34 per cent; industry 14 per cent and services 52 per cent.

Inflation has been fairly high for the last five years: 7.4 per cent in 2003, 12.0 per cent in 2004, 9.0 per cent at 2005, 8.9 per cent in 2006 and 8.9 per cent in 2007. Inflation was estimated to be 7.8 per cent in 2011.

Total external public debt was put at US$1,419.62 million in 2005. Total public debt service was US$19.41 million (22.7 per cent of exports). Total external debt was estimated to be US$900 million in 2011.

Foreign Investment
Rwanda's inadequate infrastructure and transport have limited foreign investment. Existing foreign investment is in commerce, tea, coffee, mining, and tourism.

Rwanda has made real progress in poverty reduction and, in April 2005, qualified for debt relief under the enhanced HIPC initiative. This relief will amount to some US$1.4 billion. However, Rwanda remains one of the 20 poorest countries in the world and is highly aid-dependent; some 50 per cent of revenue comes from donor support.

Balance of Payments / Imports and Exports
Rwanda's foreign trade largely consists of coffee and tea exports, as well as hides and skin, cassiterite, and pyrethrum (used in insect repellant). Rwanda's major export trading partners are China, Kenya and the Democratic Republic of Congo.

Main imports include food, machinery and equipment, petroleum products, steel, cement, and construction materials. Import trading partners include Kenya, Uganda, the UAE and Tanzania.

External Trade, US$million

	2005	2006	2007
Trade balance	-249.10	-296.40	-384.97
Exports	125.00	142.30	164.15
Imports	374.10	437.70	549.12

Source: African Development Bank

Exports were estimated to be US$295 million in 2011 and imports US$1.3 billion.

Rwanda is a member of the Common Market for East and Southern Africa (COMESA).

Central Bank
Banque Nationale du Rwanda, Avenue Paul VI, BP 531, Kigali, Rwanda. Tel: +250 574282 / 575249, fax: +250 572551, e-mail: info@bnr.rw, URL: http://www.bnr.rw
Governor: Ambassador Claver Gatete

MANUFACTURING, MINING AND SERVICES

Primary and Extractive Industries
A number of different minerals are produced in Rwanda, of which cassiterite is the most important in terms of both production and foreign exchange earnings. Other minerals mined include wolfram, colombo-tantalite (a side product of cassiterite), beryl, and methane. Minerals accounted for 35.9 per cent of export earnings in 2007.

Rwanda has no fossil fuel resources and is therefore reliant on imports to satisfy its oil requirements. In 2011, an estimated six thousand barrels per day of oil was imported (up from four thousand barrels per day in 1998), most of it distillate, gasoline, residual, and jet fuel.

Rwanda and Tanzania are the only two countries in the Great Lakes region with natural gas reserves, but it is not yet exploited in either country. Rwanda has natural gas reserves estimated at 2,000 billion cubic feet (January 2010). Methane gas has been discovered at the bottom of Lake Kivu, a huge inland lake. The reserve is estimated to be 55 billion cubic metres, and the government has signed a deal with an international consortium to start exploiting the discovery. It is hoped that Rwanda's electricity supply could double within two years, but the long term aim is to increase energy production to around 700 megawatts and for the country to become a gas exporter.

Energy
In 2009, total primary energy consumption stood at 0.012 quadrillion Btu. Per capita energy consumption fell from 1.4 million Btu to 1.3 million Btu in 2004 and remains well below the African per capita average of 16.1 million Btu.

There are four power plants: one is hydro-electric, two are thermal, while the fourth is hydro-electric and thermal combined. An agreement to build an electricity generating plant using methane gas from Lake Kivu was signed in March 2005 with a British Company, Dane Associates. In 2005 total electricity generating capacity was 31 megawatts. 98 per cent of this was hydroelectric power and 2 per cent thermal. In 2010 generation was 0.28 billion kilowatthours, and consumption 0.32 billion kilowatthours.

In May 2002 Rwanda joined the African Energy Commission (AFREC). Rwanda's national utility company is Electrogaz.

Manufacturing
Rwanda's manufacturing and industry sector contributed 14 per cent of GDP in 2008. Main manufacturing industries include cement, beverages, soap, furniture, cement, shoes, plastic goods, textiles, pharmaceuticals and cigarettes. In addition to the primary processing of coffee and tea, rice and sugar are also produced on a factory scale. Light industry includes the manufacture of footwear, radios, paint and shirts.

Service Industries
Along with agriculture, the services sector is a key aspect of Rwanda's economy, contributing about 40 per cent towards GDP annually. The tourism sector requires further development but has potential; mountain gorillas and other animal parks could become an important source of tourism revenue. There are currently around 8,000 visitors per year (2006).

Agriculture
Rwanda is predominantly an agricultural country, with a great proportion of agricultural production deriving from subsistence-type farming. Agriculture is a major part of the economy, accounting for about 33 per cent of GDP in 2010 and in 2007, 40.2 per cent of export revenues.

The principal cash crops are coffee, pyrethrum and tea, with coffee and tea accounting for more than half of the total exports. Bananas, sweet potatoes, manioc, sorghum and beans are the main crops for domestic consumption.

Despite Rwanda's fertile ecosystem, food production often does not keep pace with population growth, requiring food imports. Farm sizes are decreasing, due to population growth and the Government's resettlement of returning refugees. The land itself is suffering from soil erosion and over-use. However, the government has undertaken various agricultural reforms, aimed at improving farming methods, and increasing crop yields and national food supply.

Agricultural Production in 2010

Produce	Int. $'000*	Tonnes
Plantains	567,584	2,749,150
Potatoes	281,658	1,789,400
Cassava	248,331	2,377,210
Beans, dry	191,195	327,497
Indigenous cattle meat	100,326	37,139
Sweet potatoes	63,449	840,072
Maize	60,472	432,404
Cow milk, whole, fresh	57,326	183,700
Avocados	50,891	135,000
Tomatoes	49,891	135,000
Taro (cocoyam)	39,441	185,964
Pumpkins, squash and gourds	36,891	210,400

* unofficial figures

Source: http://faostat.fao.org/site/339/default.aspx Food and Agriculture Organization of the United Nations, Food and Agricultural commodities production

COMMUNICATIONS AND TRANSPORT

Travel Requirements
Citizens of the USA, Canada, the UK, Germany, Sweden and Australia require a passport valid for at least six months but no visa for stays of up to 30 days. Evidence of yellow fever immunisation may be required. Transit passengers continuing their journey within 24 hours by the same or first connecting aircraft, holding onward or return documentation and not leaving the airport do not require a visa. Other nationals should contact the embassy to check visa requirements.

National Airlines
Rwanda Airlines, PO Box 3246, Kigali, Rwanda. Tel: +250 77564, fax: +250 77669, URL: http://www.rwandair.com/index.php

International Airports
Rwanda's international airport is located at Kigali. There are also two commercial airports located at Kigali and Gyangugu. There are in addition landing strips in all the main provincial towns, and a regular service between Kigali and Kampala.

Railways
Improvement in the transport infrastructure remains a priority, to strengthen the country's economy. Transportation costs are high and burden import and export costs. Rwanda has no railway system for port access in Tanzania but in 2009 a plan was announced to construct a railway linking Kigali with Isaka, Tanzania.

Roads
Landlocked, Rwanda needs strong highway maintenance and good transport links to Uganda and Tanzania. There is a network of 14,000 kilometres of road (approximately 2,600 km of which is macadamized). Vehicles are driven on the right.

Waterways
Lac Kivu is navigable by shallow barges and native crafts.

Ports
The main ports are Cyangugu, Gisenyi and Kibuye.

HEALTH

In 2009, the government spent approximately 20.1 per cent of its total budget on healthcare (up from 8.2 per cent in 2000), accounting for 48.6 per cent of all healthcare spending. External resources account for over 49 per cent of total expenditure. Total expenditure on healthcare equated to 10.1 per cent of the country's GDP. Per capita expenditure on health was approximately US$52, compared to US$9 in 2000. Figures for 2005-10 show that there are 221 physicians (less than 1 per 10,000 population), 4,050 nurses and midwives (4 per 10,000 population), 35 dentistry personnel, 14 pharmaceutical personnel, 36 environment and public health workers and 12,00 community health workers.

Rwanda is facing a generalized HIV/AIDS epidemic. In 2010, the HIV/AIDS prevalence rate was 1,664 per 100,000 population (compared with 2,127 in 2000) and the HIV/AIDS incidence rate was 88 per 100,000 population (compared with 207 in 2000). Those with HIV/AIDS are susceptible to tuberculosis; in 2010 the TB prevalence rate was 128 per 100,000 population (compared with 361 in 2000) and the incidence rate was 106 per 100,000 population (compared with 266 in 2000). In 2010 there were 638,689 reported cases of malaria, 36 of leprosy, 121 of measles, 6,703 of TB, and 36 of rubella.

Life expectancy from birth rose to 59 years in 2009, compared to 45 years in 2000. The infant mortality rate (probability of dying by first birthday) was 44 deaths per 1,000 live births (compared to 109 in 2000) and the child mortality rate was 64 deaths per 1,000 live births (compared to 163 in 2000). The main causes of death in children aged five or under were pneumonia (20 per cent), prematurity (15 per cent) and diarrhoeal diseases (12 per cent). An estimated 2 per cent were due to malaria and 2 per cent due to HIV/AIDs. Approximately 24 per cent of children sleep under insecticide-treated nets and 6 per cent of those with fevers received treatment. Within the period 2005-11, an estimated 51.7 per cent of children aged less than five years were classified as stunted and 18.0 per cent as underweight.

In 2008, 65 per cent of the population had sustainable access to improved drinking water. In the same year, 55 per cent of the population had sustainable access to improved sanitation. (Source: http://www.who.int, World Health Statistics 2012)

EDUCATION

Primary/Secondary Education
Rwanda's compulsory education system lasts for six years. Its primary education system lasts for seven years.

Rebuilding the education system following the civil war was one of the government's priorities. The national university in Butare re-opened 1995, and most of the primary and secondary schools were re-opened by then. In 2008 the government announced that all education would be taught in English instead of French.

In 2007, 94 per cent of primary school aged children were enrolled in a school. The pupil/teacher ratio was 69 to one. In 2006, 14 per cent of children went to secondary school in the same year, though this figure includes pupils of other age groups. Three per cent of students of the relevant age-group enrolled in tertiary education. In 2004, some 2.8 per cent of GDP was spent on education.

64.9 per cent of adults were considered literate in 2004, rising to 77.6 per cent within the 15-24 year old group. Both these figures are above the regional averages.

RELIGION

Whilst about 93.5 per cent of the population is Christian, and 4.6 per cent is Muslim, traditional African religions are practised by most of the population.1.7 per cent of people claim to have no religious beliefs. The majority of the Christian community is Roman Catholic.

Rwanda has a religious liberty rating of 8 on a scale of 1 to 10 (10 is most freedom). (Source: World Religion Database)

COMMUNICATIONS AND MEDIA

Radio is the main source of news and the import of the written press is limited by high levels of illiteracy. Self-censorship is common. In the run-up to the 2010 elections, there were reports of government interference in broadcasting, including imprisonment of journalists.

Newspapers
Main newspapers include:
Rwanda Newsline, English language
The New Times, private, pro-government, URL: http://www.newtimes.co.rw/
Rwanda Herald, private, English language
Umeseso, Kinyarwanda language
La Nouvelle Releve, state-owned, URL: http://www.orinfor.gov.rw/DOCS/lnr.htm
Imvaho, state-owned, URL: http://www.orinfor.gov.rw/DOCS/lnr.htm

Broadcasting
There are two television stations, and eight FM radio stations. The state-owned broadcaster produces Television Rwandaise (TVR) and Radio Rwanda (URL: http://www.orinfor.gov.rw/). Radio is the most important media for news. During the 1994 genocide, Radio Tele Libre Mille Collines (RLTM) broadcast extreme anti-Tutsi propaganda. Radio Rwanda broadcasts in French, English, Kiswahili and Kinyarwanda.

Telecommunications
The telecommunications system is poor, and generally limited to urban areas and is primarily used for business and government. It is estimated that in 2008 there were 18,000 main telephone lines in use, and 1.3 million mobile phones. In the same year, around 300,000 Rwandans had access to the internet.

ENVIRONMENT

Current environmental issues include soil erosion, soil exhaustion, over grazing, deforestation, and poaching of wildlife.

Rwanda has one of the world's lowest per capita carbon dioxide emissions. In 2010, Rwanda's emissions from the consumption of fossil fuels totalled 0.87 million metric tons of carbon dioxide. (Source: EIA)

Rwanda is a party to the following international environmental agreements: Biodiversity, Climate Change, Climate Change-Kyoto Protocol, Desertification, Endangered Species, Hazardous Wastes, Ozone Layer Protection, Wetlands. Rwanda has signed, but not ratified: Law of the Sea.

SAINT KITTS AND NEVIS
Federation of Saint Christopher and Nevis

Capital: Basseterre (Population estimate, 2010: 13,000)

Head of State: Her Majesty Queen Elizabeth II (Sovereign) (page 1420)

Governor-General: H.E. Sir Cuthbert Montraville Sebastian, GCMC, OBE (page 1510)

National Flag: Two triangles, one green and one red, separated by a broad black diagonal stripe, edged in yellow, bearing two white stars with five points

CONSTITUTION AND GOVERNMENT

Constitution
Carib Amerindians were the first settlers in the islands before their sighting by Columbus in 1493 when he renamed Liamuiga St. Christopher (possibly after himself or the patron saint of travellers) and its neighbouring island Los Nieves (the snows) due to its cloud-covered peak. St. Kitts was the first British settlement in the Caribbean in 1623 and was subsequently fought over by English and French settlers before being ceded to Britain in 1783. In 1967, it became an associated state of the UK and was proclaimed independent in 1983.

Under the 1983 constitution the two islands form the Federation of St. Christopher and Nevis, with each island possessing its own Parliament. The Head of State of the Federation is the British Monarch, represented locally by a Governor-General. Executive power is vested in the Prime Minister and his Cabinet (five ministers plus the Attorney-General).

Under the constitution Nevis has the right to secede if the majority of the population vote for it at a referendum, the most recent of which took place in 1998 when the yes vote narrowly missed the two thirds majority needed. In 2003 the Nevis Island Administration proposed having another referendum in the future.

To consult the Constitution, please visit: http://welcometostkitts.com/govtcons.php

International Relations
St. Kitts and Nevis has close relations with its neighbours and shares a currency and judicial system with Anguilla, Antigua and Barbuda, British Virgin Islands, Dominica, Grenada, Montserrat, St. Lucia and St. Vincent & the Grenadines.

Recent Events
After several years of falling sugar prices, the government took the decision in 2005 to close down the island's sugar industry, resulting in the loss of 1,400 jobs.

In 2012, the Paris Club agreed to restructure the country's public debt, reducing interest payments by 90 per cent.

Legislature
The unicameral legislature is the House of Assembly, consisting of 15 seats, 11 elected and three appointed, of which two are filled on the advice of the Prime Minister and one on the advice of the opposition leader, and one ex-officio member. The House of Assembly sits for between four and five years. Nevis has a separate legislature with its own Premier, deputy Governor-General and five member assembly, and is guaranteed central representation. The full electoral term is five years.
House of Assembly, PO Box 164, Basseterre, St. Kitts. Tel: +1 869 465 2521, fax: +1 869 465 5040, URL: http://www.gov.kn
Speaker: Hon. Marcella Liburd

Cabinet (as at March 2013)
Prime Minister, Minister of Finance, Sustainable Development, Human Resources, Constituencies and Social Security: Hon. Dr. Denzil L. Douglas (page 1417)
Deputy Prime Minister, Minister of Housing, Energy, Public Works and Utilities: Dr Earl Asim Martin (page 1471)
Minister of Justice, Legal Affairs, National Security, Foreign Affairs and Labour: Patrice Nisbett (page 1487)
Minister of Health, Social Services, Community Development, Culture and Gender Affairs: Marcella Liburd

---

Minister of Sports, Youth Empowerment, IT, Telecommunications and Posts: Glen Phillip
Minister of Education, Information, Agriculture, Marine Resources, and Co-operatives: Nigel Alexis Cart
Minister of Tourism and International Transport, International Trade, Commerce, Consumer Affairs: Richard Skerrit
Attorney General: Jason Hamilton

Ministries
Government portal: URL: http://www.gov.kn
Prime Minister's Office, URL: http://www.cuopm.com/

Political Parties
People's Action Movement (PAM), URL: http://www.pamdemocrat.org, *Leader:* Lindsay Grant
Nevis Reformation Party (NRP), URL: http://nevispolitics.net, *Leader:* Joseph Parry
St. Kitts-Nevis Labour Party (SKLP), URL: http://www.sknlabourparty.org, *Leader:* Dr. Denzil Douglas.
Concerned Citizens' Movement (CCM), URL: http://www.myccmparty.com, *Leader:* Vance Amory

Elections
The most recent elections took place in January 2010. Dr Denzil Douglas and his Labour party were re-elected for a fourth term. A cabinet shuffle followed the election. Elections for the Nevis legislature took place in January 2013. The CCM now has three of the five elected seats and the NRP two.

Diplomatic Representation
High Commission for St. Christopher and Nevis, 10 Kensington Court, London, W8 5DL, United Kingdom. Tel: +44 (0)20 7937 9718, e-mail: info@sknhc.co.uk, URL: http://www.stkittsnevisuk.com/
High Commissioner: Kevin Monroe Issac
British High Commission, (staff resident in Barbados), URL: http://ukinbarbados.fco.gov.uk/en/
British High Commissioner: Paul Brummell
Embassy of St. Kitts and Nevis, 3216 New Mexico Avenue, NW, Washington, DC 20016. Tel +1 202 686 2636, URL: http://www.embassy.kn.org/
Ambassador: Jacinth Henry-Martin
US Embassy, All staff resident in Barbados, http://barbados.usembassy.gov/
Chargé d'Affaires i.a.: Larry Palmer
Permanent Mission to the UN, 414 East 75th Street, 5th Floor, New York, NY 10021, USA. Tel: +212 535 1234, URL: http://www.stkittsnevis.org/
Permanent Representative to the UN: Delano Bart

LEGAL SYSTEM

The islands' legal system is based on English common law as exercised by the Eastern Caribbean Supreme Court of Justice (based in St. Lucia). A puisne judge of the East Caribbean Supreme Court is resident on St. Christopher. Provision is made for appeal to the Privy Council in London.

Whilst the government generally respects the rights of its citizens, there have been instances of corruption and the use of excessive force by the police. St Kitts and Nevis retains the death penalty, though it seemed as though there was a moratorium on its use. The penultimate execution was carried out in 1998, but an increase in the number of murders led the government to execute a man as recently as December 2008.

Eastern Caribbean Supreme Court, URL: http://www.eccourts.org

LOCAL GOVERNMENT

St. Kitts and Nevis is divided into 14 parishes, Christ Church Nichola Town, Saint Anne Sandy Point, Saint George Basseterre, Saint George Gingerland, Saint James Windward, Saint John Capesterre, Saint John Figtree, Saint Mary Cayon, Saint Paul Capesterre, Saint Paul Charlestown, Saint Peter Basseterre, Saint Thomas Lowland, Saint Thomas Middle Island, and Trinity Palmetto Point

AREA AND POPULATION

Area
The islands of St. Christopher and Nevis form part of the Leeward Islands, 225 miles south-east of Puerto Rico, near the northern shoulder of the Caribbean chain. Nevis lies directly off the south-east tip of St. Christopher, separated by a channel less than three miles wide. St. Christopher has an area of 176 sq. km (68 sq. miles), Nevis one of 93 sq. km (36 sq. miles).

Both islands are volcanic, with forested hills at the centre, skirted by coastal plains. St. Kitts, 23 miles by 6.5 miles, rises to 3,792 ft. (1,156 m) at Mount Liamuiga. Nevis is about seven miles by six, and Nevis Peak rises to 3,732 ft. (985 m). The climate is one of low humidity and constant breezes with average temperatures at 27°C and an average rainfall of 55 inches in St. Kitts and 48 inches in Nevis.

To view a map of the islands, please consult:
http://www.lib.utexas.edu/maps/cia08/saint_kitts_and_nevis_sm_2008.gif

Population
The population was estimated at 52,000 (approximately 11,500 in Nevis) in 2010 with an average annual growth rate of 1.3 per cent over the period 2000-10. The majority of the islanders are of African descent. The official language is English.

In 2010, the crude birth rate was estimated at 14 per 1,000 population and the crude death rate was 6.5 per 1,000 population. Average life expectancy at birth in 2010 was 71 years for male and 78 years for females. Healthy life expectancy was 62 years and 67 years respectively. Approximately 24 per cent of the population were aged less than 15 years and 10 per cent were aged over 60 years. (Source: http://www.who.int, World Health Statistics 2012)

Public Holidays 2014
1 January: New Year
2 January: Carnival
18 April: Good Friday
21 April: Easter Monday
5 May: Labour Day
9 June: Whit Monday
7 August: Emancipation Day
17 September: Heroes' Day
19 September: Independence Day
25 December: Christmas Day
26 December: Boxing Day

EMPLOYMENT

After the closure of the sugar industry in 2005, tourism and services became the largest employers. The government offered re-training to the 1,400 people formerly employed in the sugar industry. Figures for 2006 put the unemployment rate at 5.1 per cent.

BANKING AND FINANCE

Currency
The unit of currency is the Eastern Caribbean Dollar of 100 cents.

GDP/GNP, Inflation, National Debt
The economy has diversified recently from being predominantly agricultural to being dependent on tourism. Following a poor sugar harvest the government closed the last remaining sugar factory. Since then the government has made efforts to diversify the economy, largely in financial services and manufacturing. Foreign investment has increased in recent years, mainly in the tourism industry. The tourism industry suffered in the global economic downturn.

Figures for 2008 estimated GDP at market prices to be US$552 million, with a growth rate in 2008 of 4.6 per cent. The service sector makes up the bulk of GDP followed by industry and agriculture. GDP was estimated at US$680 million in 2010, with a growth rate of -1.5 per cent. Per capita GDP was US$13,500 in 2010. GDP was estimated to be US$701 million in 2011.

Inflation in 2006 was 8.5 per cent. It fell to 4.3 per cent in 2007 and 3.6 per cent in 2008. Inflation was estimated at under 1 per cent in 2010.

St. Kitts and Nevis is the second most heavily indebted country in the world, but the country is able to service its debt. Figures for 2011 put public debt at 200 per cent of GDP.

Foreign Investment
The government is actively seeking foreign investment, offering a number of incentives including tax holidays of up to fifteen years, duty-free importation, duty-free concessions for hotel investors and double taxation treaties with the US, the UK and several other countries.

Balance of Payments / Imports and Exports
Estimated figures for 2011 show that merchandise exports earned US$55 million. The main exported goods are food, beverages, tobacco, electronics and machinery. Merchandise imports that year cost an estimated US$310 million. Main imported goods are manufactured goods, fuel, food and machinery. Main trading partners include CARICOM countries, Trinidad and Tobago, Japan, USA, and the EU. The trade deficit is partly offset by tourist earnings, capital inflows and remittances from islanders working overseas.

MANUFACTURING, MINING AND SERVICES

Energy
The islands have no resources of oil or gas and figures for 2012 show that St Kitts and Nevis imported 1,000 barrels of oil per day to meet its needs.

Figures for 2010 show that St. Kitts and Nevis produced 0.14 billion kWh of electricity and consumed 0.13 billion kWh.

Manufacturing
Traditional manufacturing industries included sugar refining, rum distilling, and tobacco processing. The sugar industry had been in decline for several years and was eventually closed in 2005. There has been some success in building up a light manufacturing sector, much of it labour-intensive, which exports mainly to the US market. Products include garments and shoes, electrical equipment and furniture.

SAINT KITTS AND NEVIS

Service Industries

Tourism is expanding steadily with over 100,000 visitors a year, a third of whom come from cruise ships. Earnings are about EC$100m a year. Following hurricane damage in 1998 and 1999 the tourism sector was badly hit but new investment followed, hotels and shipping berths have now been rebuilt and a large hotel and convention centre, the largest in the eastern Caribbean opened in March 2003. Tourism is now the largest foreign exchange earner, having overtaken the sugar industry. In 2007 over 117,000 tourists visited the islands plus over 251,000 cruise ship visitors, most visitors come from the USA.

Agriculture

St. Christopher and Nevis has an agricultural economy, the mainstay of which is the sugar industry, accounting for 20 per cent of GDP and occupying 90 per cent of arable land in St. Kitts. It is also the major export and largest employer. The government is now looking for ways to diversify the agricultural sector which also includes cotton, peanuts and vegetables. In 2005 the government took the decision to close the sugar industry down.

Agricultural Production in 2010

Produce	Int. $'000*	Tonnes
Fruit, tropical fresh nes	658	1,610
Indigenous cattle meat	264	98
Indigenous chicken meat	212	149
Hen eggs, in shell	200	241
Coconuts	129	1,165
Pulses, nes	112	210
Indignous pigmeat	92	60
Roots and tubers, nes	53	280
Vegetables fresh nes	53	280
Tomatoes	44	119
Pineapples	39	136
Carrots and turnips	35	140

* unofficial figures

Source: http://faostat.fao.org/site/339/default.aspx Food and Agriculture Organization of the United Nations, Food and Agricultural commodities production

COMMUNICATIONS AND TRANSPORT

Travel Requirements

Citizens of Australia and the EU require a passport valid for six months beyond the length of stay but most do not need a visa for stays of up to 90 days; the exceptions are citizens of Bulgaria, Czech Republic, Estonia, Hungary, Latvia, Lithuania, Luxembourg, Poland, Portugal, Romania and Slovak Republic who do require a visa. Nationals of Canada and the USA do not need a passport if they carry a valid photo ID, and they do not require a visa. Transit passengers do not need a visa if they are not leaving the airport. Other nationals should contact the embassy to check visa requirements.

Visitors may be asked to present an onward/return ticket and proof of sufficient funds to cover the cost of their visit.

International Airports

St. Kitts Airport, near Basseterre, is large enough to accommodate international jets. The Nevis airport is at Newcastle. The following airlines operate flight services: American Airlines, BWIA, LIAT, Air BVI, Four Islands, Winair and American Eagle.

Roads

The combined road networks of both islands amount to about 200 km. At the end of 1989, a long-awaited road was opened into the south-east peninsula of St. Kitts, making a further third of the islands' land area and beaches accessible to the public. Vehicles are driven on the left.

Ports and Harbours

Basseterre is a deep water port capable of berthing ships of up to 400 feet. It is regularly used by a variety of cruise lines. There is also a port at Charlestown in Nevis. A regular ferry service operates between St. Kitts and Nevis.

HEALTH

St. Kitts and Nevis is among five Caribbean nations that have signed the necessary documents to formally establish the Caribbean Public Health Agency (CARPHA, http://www.carpha.org). The Inter-Governmental Agreement (IGA) was also signed by Antigua and Barbuda, Belize, Grenada and St. Lucia.

The islands have four hospitals. In 2009, the government spent approximately 5.4 per cent of its total budget on healthcare, accounting for 49.0 per cent of all healthcare spending. Private expenditure amounted to 51 per cent of total expenditure, almost all of which was out-of-pocket. External resources accounted for 1.7 per cent of expenditure. Total expenditure on healthcare equated to 5.1 per cent of the country's GDP. Per capita expenditure on health was approximately US$523. According to latest figures from the WHO (2000-10), there were 46 doctors (11 per 10,000 population), 198 nurses and midwives (474 per 10,000 population), 17 dentistry personnel, 21 pharmaceutical personnel, 17 environment and public health workers and 65 community health workers. There were an estimated 60 hospital beds per 10,000 population.

In 2009, the infant mortality rate (probability of dying by first birthday) was 7 per 1,000 live births and the child mortality rate (under-five) was 8 per 1,000 live births. The main causes of death in the under-fives are prematurity (21 per cent) and birth asphyxia (31 per cent).

Approximately 90 per cent of the population had access to improved drinking water sources in 2010 and 96 per cent had access to improved sanitation. (Source: http://www.who.int, World Health Statistics 2012)

EDUCATION

Primary and secondary school education is compulsory and free. Adult literacy is around 98 per cent. Figures from UNESCO Institute for Statistics for 2007 show that 88 per cent of girls and 86 per cent of boys were enrolled in primary school and 89 per cent of girls and 80 per cent of boys were enrolled in secondary school. An average of 12.7 per cent of government spending goes on education, 58 per cent of which went on secondary education.

RELIGION

The islanders are mainly Protestant, there are minorities of Roman Catholics and Evangelical Protestants. There is a small Hindu community.

Saint Kitts has a religious liberty rating of 10 on a scale of 1 to 10 (10 is most freedom). (Source: World Religion Database)

COMMUNICATIONS AND MEDIA

Newspapers

There are a limited number of newspapers, all published in English:
Democrat (weekly), URL: http://www.pamdemocrat.org/Newspaper
The Observer (weekly), URL: http://www.stkittsnevisobserver.com
Sun St. Kitts & Nevis, (Daily) URL: http://sunstkitts.com/paper

Broadcasting

The government operates a national television service (ZIZ, URL: http://www.zizonline.com/) which broadcasts through two stations and a national radio service. Cable TV is also available including international broadcasts. Approximately 15 radio stations are in operation.

Telecommunications

The phone service is fully digital. In 2008 it was estimated there were 24,000 telephone main lines are in use and 80,000 mobile phones. Recent figures estimate the islands to have 16,000 regular internet users.

ENVIRONMENT

St Kitts and Nevis is party to the following international agreements: Biodiversity, Climate Change, Desertification, Endangered Species, Hazardous Wastes, Law of the Sea, Ozone Layer Protection, Ship Pollution and Whaling.

In 2010, Saint Kitts and Nevis' emissions from the consumption of fossil fuels totalled 0.30 million metric tons of carbon dioxide. (Source: EIA)

SAINT LUCIA

Capital: Castries (Population estimate, 2010: 65,500)

Head of State: Her Majesty Queen Elizabeth II (Sovereign) (page 1420)

Governor-General: Dame Pearlette Louisy (page 1466)

National Flag: On a plain blue field, a device consisting of a white and black triangular shape, at the base of which a golden triangle occupies a central position. The triangles which share a common base, are superimposed on one another, the black on the white, and the gold on the black.

CONSTITUTION AND GOVERNMENT

Constitution
St. Lucia is an independent member of the Commonwealth, gaining independence in 1979. The constitution dates from then. The Head of State is Queen Elizabeth II. She is represented in St. Lucia by a Governor-General.

To consult the Constitution, please visit:
http://www.stlucia.gov.lc/saint_lucia/saintluciaconstitution/the_saint_lucia_constitution.htm

Legislature
Government is based on the Westminster Parliamentary model; there are two chambers - the House of Assembly, whose 17 members are elected for a five-year term, and the Senate, whose members are nominated. The Senate has 11 seats: six of the members are appointed on the advice of the prime minister, three on the advice of the leader of the opposition, and two by the Governor General following discussions with religious, economic, and social groups. Elections to the 17-member House of Assembly are by universal adult suffrage; the Prime Minister must have majority support in the House, to which the Cabinet is responsible.
Legislature, Parliament Office, Laborie Street, Castries, St Lucia. Rel: +1 758 468 3917, fax: +1 758 452 5451, e-mail: parliament@candw.lc, URL: http://www.stlucia.gov.lc
President of the Senate, Senator Claudius Francis
Speaker of the House of Assembly: Hon. Peter Foster

Cabinet (as at May 2013)
Prime Minister, Minister of Finance & Economic Affairs: Dr Kenny Anthony (page 1378)
Minister of Infrastructure, Port Services and Transport: Philip Pierre
Minister of Education, HR Development and Labour: Dr Robert Lewis
Minister for Health, Wellness, Human Services and Gender Relations: Alvina Modesta
Minister of Agriculture, Food Production, Fisheries and Rural Development: Moses Jean Baptiste
Minister of Social Transformation, Local Government and Community Empowerment: Harold Dalson
Minister of Commerce, Business Development, Industry & Consumer Affairs: Emma Hippolyte
Minister for Legal Affairs, Home Affairs and National Security: Sen. Victor Philip LaCorbiniere
Minister for Tourism, Heritage and the Creative Industries: Lorne Theophilus
Ministry for Youth Development and Sport: Shawn Edward
Minister for Public Service, Sustainable Development, Energy, Science and Technology: Sen. Dr. James Fletcher
Minister of Physical Development, Housing and Urban Renewal: Sen. Stanley Felix
Attorney-General: Mrs Kim Rose

Ministries
Office of the Governor General, URL: http://www.stluciagovernmenthouse.com
Office of the Prime Minister, 5th Floor, Greaham Louisy Administrative Building, Waerfront, Castries, St. Lucia. Tel: +1 758 468 2111, fax: +1 758 453 7352, URL: http://www.stlucia.gov.lc/
Ministry of Tourism and Civil Aviation, NIS Building, The Waterfront, Castries, St. Lucia. Tel: +1 758 451 6849, fax: +1 758 451 6986, URL: http://www.stlucia.gov.lc
Ministry of Agriculture, Forestry and Fisheries, NIS Building, The Waterfront, Castries, St. Lucia. Tel: +1 758 452 2526, fax: +1 758 453 6314, e-mail: adminag@candw.lc, URL: http://www.maff.egov.lc/
Ministry of Health, Family Affairs, Women and Human Services, Chausee Road, Castries, St. Lucia. Tel: +1 758 452 2859, fax: +1 758 452 5655, e-mail: health@candw.lc, URL: http://www.stlucia.gov.lc
Ministry of Commerce, Business Devlopment and Consumer Affairs, 4th Floor, Block B, NIS Building, The Waterfront, Castries, St. Lucia. Tel: +1 758 453 2627, fax: +1 758 453 7347, e-mail: mitandt@candw.lc, URL: http://www.commerce.gov.lc
Ministry of Communications, Works, Transport and Public Utilities, Williams Building, Bridge Street, Castries, St. Lucia. Tel: +1 758 452 4444, fax: +1 758 453 2769, e-mail: mcwandt@candw.lc, URL: http://www.stlucia.gov.lc
Ministry of Home Affairs, Legal Affairs and National Security, Manoel Street, Castries, St. Lucia. Tel: +1 758 451 3772, fax: +1 758 453 6315, URL: http://www.stlucia.gov.lc
Ministry of External Affairs and International Trade and Civil Aviation, Greaham Louisy Administrative Building, The Waterfront, Castries, St. Lucia. Tel +1 758 452 1178, fax: +1 758 452 7427, e-mail: foreign@candw.lc, URL: http://www.stlucia.gov.lc
Ministry of Finance, Economic Affairs, Planning & Social Security, 2nd Floor, Financial Centre, Bridge Street, Castries, St. Lucia. Tel: +1 758 468 5520, fax: +1 758 451 9231, URL: http://www.finance.gov.lc
Ministry of Education, Human Resource Development and Labour, NIS Building, The Waterfront, Castries, St. Lucia. Tel: +1 758 452 2476, fax: +1 758 453 2299, e-mail: minedu@candw.lc, URL: http://www.education.gov.lc/

Ministry for Planning, Sustainable Development and the Environment, Greaham Louisy Administrative Building, The Waterfront, Castries, St. Lucia. Tel: +1 758 452 4266, fax: +1 758 452 2506, e-mail: esmpde@candw.lc
Ministry for Justice, Old Education Building, Cnr. Micoud and Laborie Streets, Castries, St. Lucia. Tel: +1 758 452 3772, fax: +1 758 453 6315, e-mail: atgen@gos.gov.lc URL: http://www.stlucia.gov.lc
Ministry of Labour, Information and Broadcasting, 5th Level, Conway Business Centre, The Waterfront, Castries, St. Lucia. Tel: +1 758 468 2701, fax: +1 758 456 0490, e-mail: agencyadmin@gosl.gov.lc, URL: http://www.stlucia.gov.lc
Ministry of Physical Development, Housing, Urban Renewal, Greaham Louisy Administrative Building, The Waterfront, Castries, St. Lucia. Tel: +1 758 453 1487, fax: +1 758 453 7921, URL: http://www.stlucia.gov.lc
Ministry of Social Transformation, Public Service, Human Resource Development, Youth and Sports, 4th Floor, Greaham Louisy Administrative Building, The Waterfront, Castries, St. Lucia. Tel: +1 758 468 5101, fax: +1 758 453 7921, URL: http://www.stlucia.gov.lc
Ministry of Tourism, Heritage and Creative Industries, 4th Floor Heraldine Rock Building, The Waterfront, Castries, St. Lucia. Tel: +1 758 468 4202, fax: +1 758 451 6986, e-mail: mitandt@candw.lc, URL: http://www.stlucia.gov.lc
Ministry of Economic Affairs, Economic Planning and National Development, 3rd Floor Greaham Louisy Administrative Building, The Waterfront, Castries, St. Lucia. Tel: +1 758 468 2202, fax: +1 758 452 2506, e-mail: econdept@candw.lc, URL: http://www.stlucia.gov.lc
Ministry of External Affairs, International Trade and Investment, Conway Business Centre, The Waterfront, Castries, St. Lucia. Tel: +1 758 468 4501, fax: +1 758 452 7427, e-mail: foreign@candw.lc, URL: http://www.stlucia.gov.lc

Political Parties
Saint Lucia Labour Party (SLP), URL: http://www.stlucialabourparty.org. Leader: Dr. Kenny D. Anthony (page 1378)
United Workers' Party (UWP), URL: http://unitedworkersparty.org. Leader: Stephenson King

Elections
Elections took place in December 2006. Sir John Compton came out of retirement to lead his United Workers Party to power, winning 11 of the 17 seats and ending the government of Kenny Anthony's St Lucia Labour Party which had been in power since 1997. Sir John Compton suffered a series of small strokes in May 2007 and Stephenson King became acting Prime Minister. After the death of Sir John in September 2007, Mr King became prime minister.

The most recent election took place in the House of Assembly on 26 November 2011 and was won by the SLP with 11 seats. The UWP won 6 seats.

Diplomatic Representation
Saint Lucian High Commission, UK, 10 Kensington Court, London, W8 5DL, UK. Tel: +44 (0)29 7937 9522, fax: +44 (0)20 7937 8704, URL: http://www.stluciahcuk.org/
High Commissioner: Eldrige Stephens
Saint Lucian Embassy, US, 3216 New Mexico Ave, NW, Washington, DC 20016, USA. Tel: +1 202 364 6792, fax: +1 202 364 6723
Ambassador: Dr Michael Louis
British High Commission, NIS Waterfont Building, 2nd Floor (PO Box 227), Castries, Saint Lucia. Tel: +1 758 452 2484, fax: +1 758 453 1543, e-mail: britishhc@candw.lc, URL: http://www.britishhighcommission.gov.uk/barbados
Resident High Commissioner: Karl Burrow
US Embassy, (Barbados) http://barbados.usembassy.gov/
Chargé d'Affaires: Brent Hardt
Permanent Mission of St. Lucia to the United Nations, 800 Second Ave., 9th Floor, New York, NY 10017, USA. URL: http://www.un.int/stlucia
Permanent Representative to the United Nations: Menissa Rambally

LEGAL SYSTEM

The judiciary is independent and based on English common law and Napoleonic code. The lowest court is the district or magistrate's court, above which is the Court of Summary Jurisdiction. Appeals can be heard by the Eastern Caribbean Supreme Court, which has jurisdiction in many Caribbean countries. It consists of the High Court, made up of a chief justice and seven puisne judges, and the Court of Appeal, made up of the chief justice and two other appellate justices.

Prior to 2003, cases could ultimately be referred to the Privy Council in London. St Lucia was one of only six countries that decided to replace the Privy Council with the Caribbean Court of Justice (CCJ) as its final court of appeal.

The government respects the rights of its citizens, though there have been instances of police abuse of suspects and prisoners. St. Lucia retains the death penalty, though the last execution took place in 1995. Murder and treason are capital crimes.

Office of the Ombudsman, URL: http://www.stlucia.gov.lc/
Eastern Caribbean Supreme Court, URL: http://www.eccourts.org/
Caribbean Court of Justice, URL: http://www.caribbeancourtofjustice.org/

SAINT LUCIA

LOCAL GOVERNMENT

Until 1990 St Lucia had an elected system of local government; this was abolished in favour of a system where serving members were nominated. In 2001 the system was again reformed to reintroduce a system of an elected local government. There are 11 administrative areas, Anse-la-Raye, Castries, Choiseul, Dauphin, Dennery, Gros-Islet, Laborie, Micoud, Praslin, Soufriere, and Vieux-Fort. The local governments have jurisdiction over local matters, including markets, minor roads and sanitation.

AREA AND POPULATION

Area
St. Lucia is part of the Windward Islands group, situated 24 miles to the south of Martinique and 26 miles to the south-east of St. Vincent. It is 27 miles in length and 14 miles in breadth and has an area of 616 sq. km. The island is mountainous (volcanic) and the highest point is Mount Gimie at 959m. St Lucia is located in the hurricane belt and has a rainy season from May to November.

To view a map, consult http://www.lib.utexas.edu/maps/cia08/saint_lucia_sm_2008.gif

Population
The estimated population in 2010 was 174,000, with an average annual growth rate of 1.0 per cent for the period 2000-10. An estimated 28 per cent of the population lives in urban areas. English is the official language, but a large part of the population also speak a French-based patois, Kweyol.

Births, Marriages, Deaths
The average life expectancy in 2009 was 71 years for males and 78 years for females. Healthy life expectancy was 64 years for males and 69 years for females. The infant mortality rate is around 14 per 1,000 live births, the crude birth rate around 17.6 per 1,000 population and the death rate 6 per 1,000 population. The median age of the population is 27 years. An estimated 26 per cent of the population is younger than 15 years and 9 per cent is over 60 years. (Source: http://www.who.int, World Health Statistics 2012)

Public Holidays 2014
1-2 January: New Year's Day
22 February: Independence Day
18 April: Good Friday
21 April: Easter Monday
5 May: Labour Day
9 June: Whit Monday
19 June: Corpus Christi
1 August: Emancipation Day
6 October: Thanksgiving Day
1 November: All Saints Day
13 December: St. Lucia Day (celebrates the discovery by Christopher Columbus)
25 December: Christmas Day
26 December: Boxing Day

EMPLOYMENT

Total Employment by Economic Activity

Occupation	2004
Agriculture, hunting & forestry	8,490
Fishing	753
Manufacturing	4,668
Electricity, gas & water supply	428
Construction	4,928
Wholesale & retail trade, repairs	9,778
Hotels & restaurants	6,760
Transport, storage & communications	3,325
Financial intermediation	1,153
Real estate, renting & business activities	2,535
Public admin. & defence; compulsory social security	8,180
Education	1,058
Health & social work	385
Other community, social & personal service activities	1,953
Households with employed persons	1,850
Other	6,025

Source: Copyright © International Labour Organization (ILO Dept. of Statistics, http://laborsta.ilo.org)

The work force was estimated to be 79,700 in 2007. The general unemployment rate was 21.0 per cent in 2004 (17.5 per cent for males, 25 per cent for females).

BANKING AND FINANCE

Currency
The unit of currency is the Eastern Caribbean Dollar of 100 Cents. The Eastern Caribbean Central Bank has kept the EC$ pegged at EC$2.7 = US$1.

GDP/GNP, Inflation, National Debt
The economy depends on banana production and tourism. The improvements to the infrastructure have helped the economy develop in recent years. The Caribbean Development Bank helped fund an airport expansion project. Although the banana industry is in decline

following the end of preferential trade tariffs, St Lucia is still the leading producer in the Caribbean. The tourism industry recovered from the effects of 11 September 2001 but the global economic downturn meant that tourism revenue fell in 2009.

GDP in 2009 was put at US$990 million, reflecting a -3.8 per cent growth for that year. The service sector is the main contributor to GDP with 70 per cent; industry accounts for around 20 per cent and agriculture, 7 per cent. GDP was estimated at US$1.2 billion in 2011.

The inflation rate was estimated at 0.7 per cent in 2009 and 0.6 in 2010. It rose to over 2 per cent in 2011.

External debt was estimated at US$460 million in 2011.

Saint Lucia benefits from the US Caribbean Basin Initiative. It is also a member of CARICOM.

Balance of Payments / Imports and Exports
Saint Lucia's major trading partners are the USA, Trinidad and Tobago, United Kingdom, Japan, Canada, Barbados, China, France, Netherlands, St. Vincent and the US Virgin Islands. St Lucia is having to diversify its agricultural production as the chief export for many years was bananas. Following the protests by the US to the World Trade Organisation that Europe was giving priority to former colonies at the expense of growers in Latin America, the market has changed and St Lucia has begun promoting the growth of mangoes and avocados. Estimated figures for 2011 put export earnings at US$199 million, with bananas still being a leading export commodity. Fruits, cocoa, vegetables, other agricultural products, oils and fats, and manufactured goods were also exported. Imports that year cost an estimated US$525 million; the main imports were fuel, manufactured goods, food, machinery, and transport equipment.

Central Bank
Eastern Caribbean Central Bank, PO Box 89, Basse Terre, St Kitts, West Indies. Tel: +1 869 465 2537, fax: +1 869 465 9562, email: info@eccb-centralbank.org, URL: http://www.eccb-centralbank.org

Business Addresses
Saint Lucia Chamber of Commerce, Industry and Agriculture, URL: http://www.stluciachamber.org/

MANUFACTURING, MINING AND SERVICES

Energy
In 2010 electricity generation was estimated to be 0.36 billion kWh, with the consumption estimated at 0.33 billion kWh. Saint Lucia has no oil reserves all oil is imported. Oil consumption was estimated at 3,000 bbl/d in 2011.

Manufacturing
Industry is based on agricultural products and some textiles. The major industrial commodities are copra, coconut oil, coconut meal, lime production,rum, clothing, beverages and tobacco, electronic components, and corrugated boxes.

Service Industries
Tourism the principal earner of foreign exchange. Saint Lucia is one of the main cruise destinations and yachting also generates a lot of income. Tourism declined in the aftermath of 11 September 2001 it recovered briefly but numbers of visitors has continued to decline from 317,939 in 2005 to 287,407 in 2007. In the face of the global economic downturn numbers of visitors are expected to continue to fall.

Agriculture
Agriculture is the main sector, with bananas and cocoa being the major crops, although production for both commodities has decreased; from 90,900 tons and 114,000 tons in 1994, respectively, to 65,100 tons and 47,800 tons in 1999. Despite the drop in production of traditional crops, the production of non-traditional crops has remained constant from 1994-99. The other major crops are citrus, nutmeg, coconuts and mace. Other crops grown for export include pumpkins, sweet potatoes, yams, plantains and hot peppers. Production of mangoes and avocados is being concentrated on for the export market.

Agricultural Production in 2010

Produce	Int. $'000*	Tonnes
Bananas	9,044	53,000
Indigenous pigmeat	2,098	1,365
Indigenous chicken meat	1,988	1,396
Fruit, tropical fresh nes	1,553	3,800
Coconuts	1,238	11,200
Indigenous cattle meat	1,229	455
Hen eggs, in shell	975	1,175
Fruit fresh nes	873	2,500
Pepper (Piper spp.)	417	200
Cow milk, whole, fresh	375	1,200
Grapefruit (inc. pomelos)	292	1,300
Indigenous sheep meat	272	100

* unofficial figures

Source: http://faostat.fao.org/site/339/default.aspx Food and Agriculture Organization of the United Nations, Food and Agricultural commodities production

Fishing is a growing industry with catches increasing from an estimated 883 tonnes in 1994 to 1,795 in 2000 and 1,845 tonnes in 2010.

COMMUNICATIONS AND TRANSPORT

Travel Requirements

Citizens of the EU require a valid passport but do not need a visa (except nationals of Austria, Belgium, Bulgaria, Cyprus, Czech Republic, Denmark, Estonia, Finland, Greece, Hungary, Latvia, Lithuania, Luxembourg, Malta, Poland, Portugal, Romania, Slovak Republic, Slovenia, Spain and Sweden who do require a visa, unless continuing their journey to next destination by the same aircraft without leaving the airport). Australians need a valid passport and a visa. US and Canadian visitors do not need a passport or visa (for up to six months) if carrying valid proof of identity and a return/onward ticket. Other nationals should contact the embassy to check visa requirements.

International Airports

Hewanorra International Airport is situated at Vieux Fort, about 40 miles south of the capital Castries. George FL Charles Airport, is situated near Castries.

Roads

There is a road network totaling about 500 miles. Vehicles are driven on the left.

Ports and Harbours

The country's main port is Castries with six berths totaling 2,470 feet. The port at Vieux Fort is suitable for deep-water anchorage and related cargo facilities. Ships entering ports increased from approximately 2,080 in 1995 to 2,250 in 1998 and the combined registered net tonnage increased from an estimated 4.7 million to 9 million.

Several ferries run from St. Lucia to neighbouring islands.

HEALTH

There are currently six hospitals and 34 health centres which provide an average of one bed per 520 people. In 2009, the government spent approximately 14.8 per cent of its total budget on healthcare, accounting for 63.0 per cent of all healthcare spending. Private expenditure accounted for 38.1 per cent of expenditure, of which over 98 per cent was out-of-pocket. External resources accounted for 1.9 per cent of expenditure. Total expenditure on healthcare equated to 8.4 per cent of the country's GDP. Per capita expenditure on health was approximately US$467. Latest figures from the WHO show that there are 70 physicians (4.7 per 10,000 population), 320 nurses and midwives (21.6 per 10,000 population) and 7 dentists.

In 2009, the infant mortality rate (probability of dying by first birthday) was 14 per 1,000 live births and the child mortality rate (under-fives) was 16 per 1,000 live births. Most common causes of death in the under-fives were prematurity (44 per cent), congenital abnormalities (12 per cent), and birth asphyxia (39 per cent). Other causes include diarrhoea (3 per cent).

In 2010, 96 per cent of the population was using improved water sources and 65 per cent were using improved sanitation. (Source: http://www.who.int, World Health Statistics 2012)

EDUCATION

Education is compulsory and free of charge between the ages of 5 and 15. Figures from UNESCO Institute for Statistics estimate that in 2006, 69 per cent of children were enrolled in pre-primary school. In 2007, 97 per cent of girls and 98 per cent of boys were enrolled in primary school, 88 per cent of girls and 76 per cent of boys were enrolled in secondary school

and 10 per cent of the population were enrolled in tertiary education. In 2006, the pupil/teacher ratio in primary school was 24:1. Public expenditure on education as a percentage of GDP was 6.6 per cent (19.1 per cent of total government expenditure of which 42 per cent went on secondary education).

In 2006, the adult (15+ years) literacy rate was estimated at 91.3 per cent (males 92.0, females 90.7). The youth (15-24 years) literacy rate was estimated at 97.0 per cent (males 96.5, females 97.4).

RELIGION

Approximately 96 per cent of the population is Christian and (80 per cent Roman Catholic). The Anglican, Methodist, Baptist, Seventh Day Adventist, Pentecostal, Bethel Tabernacle and Jehovah's Witness denominations are also represented. There are also Spiritulist, Hindu (0.89 per cent), Muslim (0.45 per cent) and Jewish minorities. Saint Lucia has a religious tolerance rating of 8 on a scale of 1 to 10 (10 is most freedom). (Source: World Religion Database)

COMMUNICATIONS AND MEDIA

In 2006, the government repealed a media law which allowed for jail terms for knowingly publishing false news harmful to public interest.

Newspapers

There are no daily newspapers.
The Voice Castries, three times a week, URL: http://www.thevoiceslu.com/
The Crusader Castries, weekly
The Star Castries, 3 times per week, URL: http://www.stluciastar.com
One Caribbean weekly
The Mirror weekly, URL: http://www.stluciamirroronline.com

Broadcasting

There are several radio stations: Radio St. Lucia (URL:http://www.rslonline.com/), Radio Caribbean International, Radio Caraibes, Radio 100-Helen FM. Television is well provided: Helen TV systems (URL:http://www.htsstlucia.com/), National Television Service of St Lucia and nine cable network channels.

Telecommunications

The system is generall adequate. There are an estimated 40,000 mainline telephones. Recent figures show that St Lucia has around 165,000 mobile phone users and 100,000 internet users.

ENVIRONMENT

Environmental concerns for Saint Lucia include deforestation and soil erosion. Saint Lucia is a party to the following international agreements: Biodiversity, Climate Change, Climate Change-Kyoto Protocol, Desertification, Endangered Species, Environmental Modification, Hazardous Wastes, Law of the Sea, Marine Dumping, Ozone Layer Protection, Ship Pollution, Wetlands and Whaling.

In 2010, Saint Lucia's emissions from the consumption of fossil fuels totalled 0.43 million metric tons of carbon dioxide. (Source: EIA)

SAINT VINCENT AND THE GRENADINES

Capital: Kingstown (Population estimate: 26,000)

Head of State: Her Majesty Queen Elizabeth II (Sovereign) (page 1420)

Governor-General: H.E. Sir Frederick Ballantyne, GCMG (page 1382)

National Flag: Three vertical stripes of blue, gold and green with three green diamond shapes arranged in the form of a 'V' in the central panel

CONSTITUTION AND GOVERNMENT

Constitution

St. Vincent and the Grenadines are an independent constitutional monarchy, with the British Monarch as Head of State. The Monarch is represented locally by the Governor-General. In January 1999 the then prime minister of St. Vincent, Sir James Mitchell, told the Organisation of Eastern Caribbean States that they should work together on constitutional reform, looking to replace the Queen as head of state with an executive president. In November 2009 a constitutional referendum was held on replacing the monarch with a republic. This was rejected by voters.

To consult the constitution, please visit: http://www.embsvg.com/Constitution_of_SVG.htm

Legislature

Parliament has legislative power and comprises the Governor-General and the House of Assembly, 15 members of which are elected by universal adult suffrage for a term of five years and six senators are appointed by the Governor General, four following advice from the Prime Minister and two on the advice of the leader of the opposition.

House of Assembly, Kingstown, St. Vincent. Tel: +1 784 457 1872, fax: +1 784 457 1825, e-mail: svgparliament@vincysurf.com, URL: http://www.gov.vc/govt/index.asp

Cabinet (as at June 2013)
Prime Minister, Minister of Finance, National Security, Grenadine Affairs and Telecommunications: Hon. Dr. Ralph E. Gonsalves (page 1432)
Deputy Prime Minister and Minister of Education: Hon. Girlyn Miguel (page 1477)
Minister of Foreign Affairs, International Trade & Consumer Affairs: Hon. Douglas Slater (page 1516)
Minister of National Reconciliation and Public Service, Minister of Information, Labour and Ecclesiatical Affairs: Maxwell Charles
Minister of Tourism, Sports & Culture: Cecil McKie
Minister of Housing, Informal Human Settlements, Lands & Surveys & Physical Planning: Hon. Montgomery Daniel
Minister of Transport and Works, Urban Development & Local Government: Hon. Julian Francis
Minister of National Mobilization, Social Development, Family, Gender Affairs and Persons with Disabilities: Frederick Stephenson
Minister of Health, Wellness & Environment: Hon. Clayton Burgin
Attorney General: Judith Jones-Morgan

Ministries

Government portal, URL: http://www.gov.vc
Prime Minister's Office, Bay Street, Kingstown, St. Vincent. Tel: +784 451 2939, fax: +784 457 2152, URL: http://www.gov.vc
Ministry of National Mobilization and Social Development, Egmont Street, Kingstown, St. Vincent. Tel: +784 456 1111, fax: +784 457 2476, URL: http://www.gov.vc/
Ministry of Agriculture, Lands and Fisheries, Government Buildings, Kingstown, St Vincent. Tel: +1 784 456 111, fax: +1 784 457 1688, URL: http://www.gov.vc/

SAINT VINCENT AND THE GRENADINES

Ministry of Education, Government Buildings, Kingstown, St. Vincent. Tel: +1 784 457 2676, fax: +1 784 457 1114, URL: http://www.gov.vc/
Ministry of Finance and Economy, Bay Street, Kingstown, St Vincent. Tel: +1 784 456 2707, fax: +1 784 457 2820, URL: http://www.gov.vc/
Ministry of Foreign Affairs, Commerce and Trade, Bay Street, Kingstown, St Vincent. Tel: +1 784 456 1721, fax: +1 784 456 2610, e-mail.minister.foreignaffairs@mail.gov.vc, URL: http://www.gov.vc/

Elections
Elections were held in March 2001 having been brought forward from 2003 following anti-government protests. The United Labour Party under Dr Ralph Gonsalves won 12 of the 15 seats ending almost 17 years of unbroken government by the New Democratic Party led by James Mitchell. The next election was held in December 2005, the United Labour Party won a second term. The most recent parliamentary elections took place on 13 December 2010. The ULP led by Ralph Gonzales won 8 seats, the NDP 7 seats.

Political Parties
New Democratic Party (NDP), URL: http://www.ivotingndp.com
United Labour Party (ULP), URL: http://voteulp.com

Diplomatic Representation
High Commission for St. Vincent and the Grenadines, 10 Kensington Court, London, W8 5DL, United Kingdom. Tel: +44 (0)20 7565 2874, fax: +44 (0)20 7937 6040, URL: http://www.svghighcom.co.uk/site/Home.html
High Commissioner: Cenio Elwin Lewis
St. Vincent and the Grenadines Embassy, US, 3216 New Mexico Avenue, NW, Washington, DC 20016, USA. Tel: +1 202 364 6730, URL: http://www.embsvg.com/
Ambassador: La Celia Prince
British High Commission, Granby Street, Kingstown, St Vincent and the Grenadines. Tel: +1 784 457 1701, fax: +1 784 456 2750, URL: http://ukinbarbados.fco.gov.uk/en/
High Commissioner for the Eastern Caribbean: Paul Brummell (page 1396)
US Embassy, staff resident in Bridgetown, Barbados, URL: http://barbados.usembassy.gov
St. Vincent & the Grenadines, Permanent Mission to the UN, URL: http://www.svg-un.org/
Permanent Representative: Ambassador Camillo Gonsalves

LEGAL SYSTEM

The legal system is based on British common law. The islands are divided into three judicial districts, each with a magistrate's court. Appeals are heard in the Eastern Caribbean supreme court which comprises a High Court and a Court of Appeals. Before 2003, appeals could be taken before the Judicial Committee of the UK Privy Council; these are now heard by the Caribbean Court of Justice (CCJ).

Whilst the government generally respects the rights of its citizens, there have been instances of police impunity when they use excessive force. The court system is overburdened and prison conditions are poor. St. Vincent retains the death penalty, though the last execution took place in 1995.

Eastern Caribbean Supreme Court, URL: http://www.eccourts.org/
Caribbean Court of Justice, URL: http://www.caribbeancourtofjustice.org/

LOCAL GOVERNMENT

There are no local government bodies. The islands have six parishes: Charlotte, Grenadines, St. Andrew, St. David, St. George and St. Patrick, which are administered by the central government.

AREA AND POPULATION

Area
St. Vincent is situated 24 miles to the south-west of St. Lucia and 100 miles west of Barbados. It is 18 miles in length and 11 miles in breadth and covers an area of 150 sq. miles. The State consists of, in addition to the main island of St. Vincent, the Grenadine group of islands to the south, which includes Bequia, Mustique, Palm Island and Union Island. Altogether there are 32 smaller islands. The terrain is volcanic and mountainous. The highest point is the volcanic peak La Soufrière (1,234 m).

The climate is tropical with a rainy season from May to November. St Vincent and the Grenadines are sometimes hit by hurricanes, 1998, 1999 and 2002 being particularly bad seasons with banana and coconut plantations being hit. It last erupted in 1979 causing damage to agricultural land but no one was killed.

To view a map, consult http://www.lib.utexas.edu/maps/cia08/saint_vincent_sm_2008.gif

Population
The population in 2008 was estimated at 109,000. The population consists of African origin 66 per cent, mixed 19 per cent, West Indian 6 per cent and Caribbean Indian 2 per cent. English is the official language although French Patois is also spoken. The emigration rate is high mainly because of high unemployment.

Births, Marriages, Deaths
The average life expectancy is about 70 years, with females at 76 years and males at 66 years. Healthy life expectancy is 63 years. The median age is 27 years. An estimated 27 per cent of the population is aged less than 15 years and 9 per cent over 60 years. Estimated figures for 2007 put the birth rate at 16 births per 1,000 population and 6 deaths per 1,000 population, migration for that year was estimated at -8.0 per 1,000 population, most of whom leave to look for work. (Source: WHO)

Public Holidays 2014
1 January: New Year's Day
18 April: Good Friday
21 April: Easter Monday
1 May: Labour Day
9 June: Whit Monday
last week of June-first week of July: Vincy Mas, Carnival
7 July: CARICOM Day
4 August: Emancipation Day
27 October: Independence Day
25 December: Christmas Day
26 December: Boxing Day

EMPLOYMENT

Recent estimates (2007) put the workforce at 57,000, of which about 25 per cent are employed in the agricultural sector and 56 per cent in the growing service sector. High unemployment and under employment are large problems in the islands. Recent figures put unemployment at around 22 per cent, leading to a high rate of emigration as workers leave the islands in search of employment. Included in the government's priorities is a programme of job creation and sustainable economic development.

BANKING AND FINANCE

Currency
The unit of currency is the Eastern Caribbean Dollar of 100 cents.

GDP/GNP, Inflation, National Debt
The economy used to be predominatly based on agriculture, especially banana production. As the sector is subject to climatic variations and also suffered with the modification of the EU protective tariffs , the government has made efforts to diversify the economy with notable success in high-end tourism. The government is also investing in some infrastructure projects including road improvements. VAT was introduced in 2007 and generated some US$40 million in 2008.

GDP grew by just 0.7 per cent in 2002. This was partly due to the devastating effects of tropical storm Lili which hit in September and wiped out large areas of crops. GDP for that year was put at US$360 million. The GDP growth rate in 2003 rose to 2.7 per cent and an estimated 2.8 per cent in 2004 and 4.9 per cent in 2005. In 2007, GDP was estimated to be US$535 million with a growth rate estimated at over 7 per cent. Per capita GDP was estimated at US$5,500 in 2007. GDP was estimated to be US$559 billion in 2011.

The service sector is the biggest contributor of GDP with over 70 per cent mainly from the tourism industry, agriculture contributes around 10 per cent of GDP, bananas being the largest crop.

Inflation was estimated to be 1.9 per cent in 2011.

External debt was estimated to be US$260 million.

Balance of Payments / Imports and Exports
The major trading partners are UK, US, CARICOM and Japan. The main export products are arrowroot starch, bananas, flowers and foliage, eddoes and dasheen. Plantains and sweet potatoes are exported mainly to Barbados and Trinidad and Tobago. The main imported products are food, chemicals, fertilizers, machinery and equipment. Estimated figures for 2011 show that exports earned US$65 million and imports cost US$345 million.

MANUFACTURING, MINING AND SERVICES

Energy
In 2010 electricity generation was estimated to be 0.14 billion kWh, with the consumption estimated at 0.13 billion kWh. Saint Vincent and the Grenadines has no oil reserves all oil is imported. Oil consumption was estimated at 2,000 bbl/d in 2011.

Manufacturing
Industries within this sector include agro-processing and milling (rice and flour), electronics, boat building, plastic products, cement, furniture, clothing and sports goods, chicken feed and polypropylene bags. There is also a brewery. The Grenadines has no industry.

Service Industries
Tourism has surpassed banana exports to become the largest earner of foreign income. St. Vincent attracts about 120,000 visitors a year. Figures for 2002 show that the islands had 251,000 visitors. The islands are also popular with the yachting community.

Agriculture
St. Vincent is the largest producer of arrowroot in the world. Other activities include cocoa, eddoes, dasheen, tannias and flour, coconuts and coconut oil, copra, sweet potatoes, nutmeg, citrus fruits, ornamental flowers and fishing. FAO figures put the total catch in 2010 at 65,000 tonnes.

Agricultural Production in 2010

Produce	Int. $'000*	Tonnes
Bananas	9,153	62,500
Roots & tubers, nes	2,193	13,500
Mangoes, mangosteens, guavas	959	1,600
Indigenous pigmeat	886	576
Apples	719	1,700
Indigenous chicken meat	667	468
Hen eggs, in shell	630	760
Vegetables fresh nes	603	3,200
Sugar cane	591	18,000
Indigenous cattle meat	562	208
Plantains	516	2,500
Coconuts	509	4,600

* unofficial figures
Source: http://faostat.fao.org/site/339/default.aspx FAOSTAT, Statistics Division, Food and Agriculture Organization of the UN

COMMUNICATIONS AND TRANSPORT

Travel Requirements
Citizens of the USA, Canada, Australia and the EU require a valid passport, a return/onward ticket, and proof of accommodation and adequate funds. They do not need a visa. Length of stay is determined by immigration authority on arrival. Other nationals should contact the embassy to check visa requirements.

International Airports
E.T. Joshua Airport is an international airport about two miles from Kingstown, while a number of smaller airstrips exist on other islands. There are flights between St. Vincent and Mustique, Canouan and Union Island.

Roads
There is a road network totalling about 1,040 km, although only about 350 km of these are all-weather roads. Vehicles are driven on the left.

Ports and Harbours
Kingstown is a natural harbour and can accommodate two ocean going ships at a time. A new cruise ship terminal is planned. Some of the Grenadine Islands have ports, which are served by cruise lines. A ferry service runs from Kingstown to Bequia.

HEALTH

Recent figures show that St. Vincent and the Grenadines has six public hospitals, three private hospitals and a network of clinics and dispensaries.

According to the latest WHO figures, in 2009, the government spent approximately 11.5 per cent of its total budget on healthcare, accounting for 84.3 per cent of all healthcare spending. Total expenditure on healthcare equated to 4.6 per cent of the country's GDP. Per capita expenditure on health was approximately US$296. Figures for 2000-10 show that there are 89 physicians (8 per 10,000 population), 447 nurses and midwives (38 per 10,000 population), 45 community health workers and 5 dentistry personnel. There are an estimated 30 hospital beds per 10,000 population.

In 2010 the infant mortality rate was estimated to be 19 per 1,000 live births and the under-fives mortality rate 21 per 1,000 live births. Prematurity accounts for 31 per cent of childhood deaths, birth asphyxia 4 per cent, neonatal sepsis 13 per cent, pneumonia 2 per cent, injuries 21 per cent.

SAINT VINCENT AND THE GRENADINES

In 2010, an estimated 96 per cent of the population had access to improved drinking-water and an estimated 98 per cent had access to improved sanitation. (Source: http://www.who.int, World Health Statistics 2012)

EDUCATION

Education is free and available at primary and secondary level. It is compulsory up to the age of 15. UNESCO figures for 2007 show that 88 per cent of girls and 94 per cent of boys were enrolled in primary school.

The literacy rate is over 95 per cent. The islands have several Polytechnics and a medical school. a campus of St. George's University, Grenada is situated near the capital. Figures from 2007 show that just over 16.o per cent of government spending goes on education.

RELIGION

Most of the population belong to the Christian faith (87 per cent), with Roman Catholics, Anglicans and Methodists forming the largest denominations. Hinduism (3.8 per cent), Spiritualism (2.0 per cent) and Islam (1.7 per cent) are also practiced. Saint Vincent has a religious tolerance rating of 9 on a scale of 1 to 10 (10 is most freedom). (Source: World Religion Database)

COMMUNICATIONS AND MEDIA

The constitution guarantees a free press and broadcasters are able to criticise the government. The prss is privately-owned.

Newspapers
The Independent; The Herald; The News; Searchlight, URL: http://www.searchlight.vc; The Westindian Crusader; The Vincentian, URL: http://www.thevincentian.com

Broadcasting
There is one government-owned radio station and several privately run stations.The Saint Vincent and the Grenandines Broadcasting Corporation operates one television station and several repeater stations. SVG also covers southern St Lucia, northern Grenada and western Barbados. Multi-channel cable TV is also available.
SVG Television, URL: http://www.svgbc.com/svgtv.htm
NBC Radio, URL: http://www.nbcsvg.com/

Telecommunications
There is a fully automatic telephone system. Figures from 2008 show the islands have around 22,500 telephone main lines in use and an estimated 130,000 mobile phone subscriptions. There are around 65,000 internet users.

ENVIRONMENT

Pollution of coastal waters, particularly from pleasure yachts, is a major concern for the islands. St. Vincent and the Grenadines are party to the following international agreements: Biodiversity, Climate Change, Climate Change-Kyoto Protocol, Desertification, Endangered Species, Environmental Modification, Hazardous Wastes, Law of the Sea, Marine Dumping, Ozone Layer Protection, Ship Pollution, and Whaling.

According to figures from the EIA, in 2010, Saint Vincent and the Grenadines' emissions from the consumption of fossil fuels totalled 0.33 million metric tons of carbon dioxide.

SAMOA
Independent State of Samoa
Malo Sa'oloto Tuto'atasi o Samoa

Capital: Apia (Population estimate: 41,000)

Head of State: Tuiatua Tupua Tamasese Efi (page 1528)

National Flag: Red with first quarter blue and bearing thereon five white regular five-rayed stars representing the Southern Cross

CONSTITUTION AND GOVERNMENT

Constitution

Western Samoa, which had been administered since 1920 by New Zealand initially under a League of Nations Mandate and later under a United Nations Trusteeship Agreement, attained full independence on the 1st January 1962. The name was shortened to Samoa following a constitutional amendment in July 1997.

The Constitution provides for a Head of State (O le Ao O le Malo) with a role not unlike a Constitutional Monarch. The previous Head of State, Malietoa Tanumafili II, held the position for life; his successors are elected by Parliament for a five-year term.

The Executive Government is carried out by a Cabinet consisting of a Prime Minister, appointed by the Head of State, who holds the confidence of a majority in the Legislative Assembly and who selects the twelve ministers of the Cabinet. Universal suffrage was introduced in 1991. However, by convention, only tribal chiefs (Matai) may stand for election.

To consult the constitution, please visit: http://www.talofa.net/GeneralInformation/Constitution/tabid/5177/language/en-US/Default.aspx

International Relations

Samoa is a member of the Pacific Islands Forum, the UN, the Commonwealth and the ACP grouping, which allows it access to European Union development funding. Samoa's international interests are mainly economic and environmental. Samoan Police have participated in UN and other international peacekeeping missions including in East Timor, Liberia and the Solomon Islands.

Recent Events

The cabinet was extensively reshuffled after the assassination of Luagalau Levaulu Kamu, the Minister for Posts and Telecommunication, in July 1999. Two of his cabinet colleagues, Leafa Vitale and Toi Aukusa, were convicted of his murder in April 2000.

The head of state, Malietoa Tanumafili II, died on 13 May 2007 at the age of 94. A traditional High Chief, he was appointed to his post in 1962, when the islands gained independence from New Zealand, and became the world's third-longest serving head of state.

On September 29 2009 an earthquake in the South Pacific triggered a devastating tsunami which hit Samoa, destroying several villages and killing an estimated 200 people.

In July 2011 the cabinet approved a bill to be forwarded to parliament to shift the international dateline west of Samoa to the east to bring their clocks closer to Australasia. The change took place on 29 December 2011.

Samoa joined the World Trade Organisation on 10 May 2012.

Legislature

The Parliament consists of a Legislative Assembly (Fono) of 49 members, 47 of whom are Matai (clan leaders) elected by territorial constituencies, and the remaining two by individual voters (i.e. non Samoans, other Pacific islanders and Europeans) by numerical suffrage. Members serve a five year term. Universal suffrage was first introduced in 1990, before which time only Matai could stand as parliamentary candidates.

Cabinet (as of June 2013)

Prime Minister & Minister in charge of Foreign Affairs, Tourism Authority and Attorney General: Tuilaepa Sailele Malielegaoi (page 1469)
Deputy Prime Minister and Minister for Trade, Commerce, Industry and Labour: Fonotoe Nuafesili Pierre Lauofo
Minister of Agriculture and Fisheries: Le Mamea Ropati
Minister of Communication & Information Technology: Tuisugaletaua Sofara Aveau
Minister of Education, Sports and Culture: Magele Mauiliu
Minister of Finance: Faumuina Tiatia Liuga
Minister of Health: Dr Tuitama Talalelei Tuitama
Minister of Justice and Courts Administration: Fiame Naomi Mata'afa
Minister of Natural Resources and the Environment: Faamoetauloa Ulaitino Faale Tu'umalli'i
Minister of Police, Prisons and Fire Services: Sala Fata Pinati
Minister of Revenue: Tuiloma Pule Lameko
Minister of Women, Community and Social Development: Tolofuaivalelei Falemoe Lei'ataua
Minister of Public Works, Transport and Infrastructure: Manu'alesagalala Enokati Posala

---

Ministries

Government portal: URL: http://www.govt.ws

Ministry of the Prime Minister and Cabinet: PO Box L 1861, Apia, Samoa. Tel: +685 22940, fax: +685 21339, URL: http://www.mpmc.gov.ws/

Department of Agriculture and Fisheries, PO Box 1874, Apia, Samoa. Tel: +685 22561, fax: +685 23426, URL: http://www.maf.gov.ws

Ministry of Foreign Affairs and Trade: Tel: +685 21171, fax: +685 21504, e-mail: mfa@mfa.gov.ws, URL: http://www.mfat.gov.ws/

Department of Natural Resources and Environment, Private Bag, Apia, Samoa. Tel: +685 22481, fax: +685 23671, URL: http://www.mnre.gov.ws/

Ministry of Finance, URL: http://www.mof.gov.ws/

Department of Commerce, Industry & Labour, PO Box 862, Apia, Samoa. Tel: +685 20472, fax: +685 21646, URL: http://www.mcil.gov.ws/

Ministry of Communications and IT, URL: http://www.mcit.gov.ws/

Ministry of Education, Sports & Culture, URL: http://www.mesc.gov.ws/

Ministry of Justice, URL: http://www.mjca.gov.ws/

Ministry of Health, URL: http://www.health.gov.ws/

Ministry of Revenue, URL: http://www.revenue.gov.ws/

Ministry of Women, Community and Social Development, URL: http://www.mwcsd.gov.ws/

Ministry of Works, Transport & Infrastructure, URL: http://www.mwti.gov.ws/

Political Parties

Human Rights Protection Party (HRPP); Tautua Samoa Party (TSP).

Elections

There are two main political parties, the governing Human Rights Protection Party (HRPP) and the opposition Samoa Democratic United Party (SDUP), plus a small number of Independent MPs. The HRPP has dominated politics over the past two decades.

Following the death of Malietoa Tanumafili II, Tupua Tamasese Tupuola Tufuga Efi was elected Head of State by the Assembly in June 2007, for a five-year term.

The last parliamentary election was held on 4 March 2011 when the Human Rights Protection Party (HRPP) won with an overall majority; the HRPP has been in power since 1981.

Diplomatic Representation

Embassy of Samoa, Ave. de l'Oree, Bte 4, Brussels, 1000, Belgium.

US Embassy, PO Box 3430, Apia, Tel: +685 21631, fax: +685 22030, URL: http://samoa.usembassy.gov/
Ambassador: David Huebner (resident Wellington, NZ)

British High Commission, Samoa served by High Commission in Wellington, NZ): Tel: +64 4 924 2888, fax: +64 4 924 2809, URL: http://ukinnewzealand.fco.gov.uk/en
Ambassador: Vicki Treadell (page 1527)

Samoan Embassy and Permanent Mission to the UN, Suite 400J, 800 Second Avenue, New York, NY 10017, USA. Tel: +1 212 599 6196, fax: +1 212 599 0797, e-mail: samoa@un.int, URL: http://www.un.int/wcm/content/site/samoa
Permanent Ambassador: H.E. Ali'ioaiga Feturi Elisaia

LEGAL SYSTEM

Samoan law is based on English common law and local customs. Samoa has a written constitution which embodies the fundamental legal rules of Government. It provides for a three-tier legal system: the supreme court has full civil and criminal jurisdiction for the administration of justice in Samoa. It is under the jurisdiction of the chief judge, who is appointed by the head of state; the court of appeal consists of three judges who may be supreme court judges; Magistrates' courts have varying degrees of authority and hear criminal cases involving short prison terms or only just fines. There is, in addition, a Land and Titles Court that deals with customary matters; for example, land and "matai" (title) disputes. Lawyers do not appear in the land and titles court; each party appoints its own leader, usually a chief or an orator. Court decisions are based largely on Samoan custom.

Some civil and criminal matters are handled by village "fonos" (traditional courts). The Village Fono Law of 1990 affords legal status to the decision of the village fono and allows appeal from fono decisions to the lands and titles court and to the supreme court.

The government respects the rights of its citizens. Samoa abolished the death penalty in 2004, the last execution having been carried out in 1952.

LOCAL GOVERNMENT

For administrative purposes Samoa is divided into 11 districts: A'ana, Aiga-i-le-Tai, Atua, Fa'asaleleaga, Gaga'emauga, Gagaifomauga, Palauli, Satupa'itea, Tuamasaga, Va'a-o-Fonoti, and Vaisigano.

Every village has its own traditional Council or 'fono' which meets weekly and lays down regulations on social and developmental projects for the village as a whole. The Council imposes penalties for transgressions of village rules. As well as the village 'fono', there is a 'pulenuu' (a government appointed agent) who ensures that Government projects affecting a particular village is well explained and accepted by the village.

AREA AND POPULATION

Area
Samoa is the larger, westerly part of the Samoan archipelago whose geographic position is some 1,900 miles north-west of New Zealand, 2,600 miles south-west of Hawaii and 800 miles east of Fiji. The Samoa group comprises the two large islands of Savai'i and Upolu together with seven other smaller islands of which only Manono and Apolima are inhabited.

The total area of the islands is 2,830.8 sq. km (1,093.0 sq. miles). Rugged high country forms the core of the main islands with mountains rising to some 3,600 feet on Upolu and 6,100 feet on Savai'i. It has a tropical climate with a rainy season from November to April.

To view a map, consult http://www.lib.utexas.edu/maps/cia08/samoa_sm_2008.gif

Population
Samoa's population was estimated at 183,000 by 2010, with a population growth rate of 0.4 per cent for the period 2000-10. The population density is 64 people per sq. km. A relatively high proportion of the people are young, some 38 per cent being under the age of 15, giving a high dependency ratio. Around 58 per cent of the population is under the age of 24. Most inhabitants (80 per cent) live in rural areas. Samoans are mostly Polynesian in origin. They speak Samoan and English.

Births, Marriages, Deaths
The birth rate was estimated at 24.6 births per 1,000 of the population in 2010, whilst the death rate was an estimated 6.4 deaths per 1,000 people. Infant (under 1) mortality was an estimated 17 deaths per 1,000 live births in 2007. The neonatal mortality rate was estimated at 12 per 1,000 live births in 2009. The fertility rate was 3.9 children per woman. Life expectancy at birth in 2009 was 68 years for males and 72 years for females. Healthy life expectancy was 61 years. The median age is 21 years. (Source: http://www.who.int, World Health Statistics 2012)

Public Holidays 2014
1-2 January: New Year's Day
6 January: Head of State's Birthday (First Monday in Jan.)
21 April Easter Monday
25 April: Anzac Day
1-2 June: Independence Day
3 November: Arbor Day (First Friday in Nov.)
25 December: Christmas Day
26 December: Boxing Day

EMPLOYMENT

Samoa's labour force was estimated at 55,000 in 2007. 54,200 people were employed and the unemployment rate was estimated at 1.3 per cent. Over 60 per cent of people are employed in informal subsistence village agriculture, whilst the service sector employs around 30 per cent, and industry, under ten per cent. Only 12 per cent of the total population in Samoa is engaged in formal paid employment.

BANKING AND FINANCE

Currency
One Western Samoan Tala (WS$) = 100 sene

GDP/GNP, Inflation, National Debt
Samoa is dependent on agriculture, fishing and family remittances from abroad. Subsistence agriculture, forestry, and fishing employ two-thirds of the labor force and around 90 per cent of total export revenues come from the sector. The manufacturing sector processes mainly agricultural products. The Samoan economy is vulnerable to external economic conditions and weather extremes, such as storms and droughts. Around three quarters of the population relies on land and coastal resources as a main or supplementary source of income and over half the inhabitants live in coastal villages. Samoa receives important financial assistance from the 100,000 Samoans who live overseas; direct remittances currently reach $90 million per year (around 25 per cent of GDP). In addition to the expatriate community, Samoa receives more than $28 million annually in official bilateral development assistance; the main donors are China, Japan, Australia, and New Zealand.

GDP in 2007 is estimated to have reached Tafa 1,372 million. Services is the greatest contributor at 61.3 per cent, greatly helped by the growing financial services and tourism industries. Industry contributed 27.2 per cent and agriculture, including fishing, accounted for 11.5 per cent. GDP grew by 6.1 per cent in 2007. The agriculture sector showed the greatest growth rate, at 11.7 per cent. The construction sector was boosted by Samoa's hosting of the South Pacific Games in 2007.

GDP by economic sector (figures in million Tala) at current market prices

Sector	2008	2009	2010
Agriculture	167.9	169.7	144.5
Manufacturing	163.5	123.1	148.3
Electricity, gas, water	67.9	72.4	76.0
Construction	181.0	177.4	193.9

- continued

Trade	330.2	337.7	353.2
Transport and communications	195.8	203.5	208.5
Finance	121.4	124.9	130.0
Public administration	124.8	135.7	144.2
Others	108.7	107.3	110.5
Total	**1,444.2**	**1,432.6**	**1,489.4**

Source: Asian Development Bank

External debt was US$245 million in 2011. Inflation rose from 3.8 per cent in 2006 to 5.5 per cent in 2007, driven largely by food cost increases of 7.7 per cent. Inflation was estimated to be 5.1 per cent in 2011.

Foreign Investment
There is a steady growth of local industry and foreign investment in the manufacturing and production sectors. Diversification both within and outside agriculture, as well as generous government incentives, encourage foreign investment. Direct foreign investment was estimated to be US$7 million in 2010.

Balance of Payments / Imports and Exports
Trade is predominantly agriculture-based, with coconut related products being the main export earner. Other export products include copra, fish, and beer.

External Trade, figures in thousand Tala

Year	Exports, fob	Imports, cif	Trade Balance
2008	26,988	659,181	-557,452
2009	29,471	558,779	-529,308
2010	29,732	694,602	-664,870

Source: Asian Development Bank

Exports by main destination countries (figures in US$ million) (E)

Destination Country	2008	2009	2010
Totals	154.1	120.3	123.7
Australia	58.0	29.3	40.9
American Samoa	55.6	48.6	50.0
United States	4.5	4.8	3.5
New Zealand	4.3	2.2	2.0
Tonga	3.0	2.6	2.7

Source: Asian Development Bank

Imports consist largely of industrial supplies, food and drinks.

Imports by main countries of origin (figures in US$ million) (E)

Country	2008	2009	2010
Totals	375.3	341.6	444.4
New Zealand	74.9	82.5	101.3
Fiji Islands	67.8	59.3	60.9
Singapore	67.5	42.9	60.1
Australia	32.4	41.0	77.1
Japan	12.5	33.7	29.1

Source: Asian Development Bank

Central Bank
The financial system consists of the Central Bank, two Commercial Banks and six Non-Bank Financial Institutions. The Central Bank is responsible for monetary policy, management of foreign exchange reserves, regulation of the commercial banks and supervision of the offshore banking centre.
Central Bank of Samoa, PO Box Private Bag, Apia, Upolu, Samoa. Tel: +685 34100 / 34237, fax: +685 20293 / 24058, e-mail: cbs@lesamoa.net, URL: http://www.cbs.gov.ws
Governor: Ms Atalina Enari

Chambers of Commerce and Trade Organisations
Samoa Chamber of Commerce and Industry, URL: http://www.samoachamber.ws/
America-Samoa Chamber of Commerce, URL: http://www.amsamoachamber.com

MANUFACTURING, MINING AND SERVICES

Primary and Extractive Industries
Samoa imports all of its oil requirements, averaging 1,000 barrels per day in 2011, most of which was distillate.

Energy
Samoa has a total electricity capacity of 0.04 GWe. In 2010, electricity generation was 0.12 billion kWh (mainly thermal) and consumption was 0.11 billion kWh.

Manufacturing
Industry contributes 27.5 per cent of Samoa's GDP, and employs just 6 per cent of the work force. Main industrial activities are food processing, construction and the production of automobile components. Manufactured goods aimed at the export market include canned coconut cream, beer and cigarettes and electrical wiring assembly.

SAMOA

Service Industries

The service sector accounts for over 61 per cent of GDP and employs around 30 per cent of the work force. Tourism is a major growth industry, visitor numbers having doubled over the past decade. It accounts for around 25 per cent of gross domestic product. Tourist arrivals increased to an estimated 101,390 in 2005. Tourism revenues grew by 4 per cent over the previous year.

Tourism Bureau, URL: http://www.visitsamoa.ws/

Agriculture

Samoa's agricultural industry contributes about 13 per cent of GDP and employs around two thirds of the labour force.

Taro used to be the main crop of the islands, but the government diversified following a taro leaf blight in 1994. Main sources of export revenue in the sector are coconut products (cream and oil), copra and fresh fish.

Agricultural Production in 2010

Produce	Int. $'000*	Tonnes
Coconuts	23,685	214,200
Bananas	7,756	32,400
Indigenous pigmeat	7,220	4,697
Taro (cocoyam)	4,231	21,000
Fruit, tropical fresh nes	3,515	8,600
Indigenous cattle meat	2,972	1,100
Mangoes, mangosteens, guavas	2,217	3,700
Pineapples	1,283	4,500
Indigenous chicken meat	892	627
Avocados	832	1,200
Papayas	795	2,800
Yams	689	3,000

* unofficial figures

Source: http://faostat.fao.org/site/339/default.aspx Food and Agriculture Organization of the United Nations, Food and Agricultural commodities production

Samoa is a party to the Fishing Treaty between the US and certain Pacific States signed in 1986, in which US fishing vessels licensed under this Treaty are allowed to fish in permitted areas of the Exclusive Economic Zones of certain Pacific States. So far there has been no recorded fishing in Samoa's EEZ. Figures for 2010 from the FAO put the total catch at 13,000 tonnes.

Control has been enforced on the cutting down of native forests. Reforestation projects are undertaken by the Department of Agriculture, financed mostly by foreign assistance from bilateral and multilateral agencies.

COMMUNICATIONS AND TRANSPORT

Travel Requirements

Citizens of the USA, Canada, Australia and the EU require a passport valid for six months beyond the length of stay, onward tickets and sufficient fund for their stay. Tourists will be issued with a free 60 day visa on arrival, apart from US citizens who should apply for a residence permit before arrival. Other nationals should contact the embassy to check visa requirements.

National Airlines

The national airline is Polynesian Airlines but other carriers such as Air New Zealand, Air Pacific, South Pacific Airways and Hawaiian Airlines operate in Samoa. There are daily inter-island air services between Updu and Savai'i operated by Polynesian Airlines.
Polynesian Airlines, URL: http://www.polynesianairlines.co.nz

International Airports

Samoa's main airport is in Faleolo.

Roads

There are 2,100 km of roads in Samoa. Vehicles were driven on the right up until September 7 2009, vehicles were then directed to drive on the left. The thinking behind this was that it would be cheaper for Samoans to buy new and used left hand drive cars from Australia, Japan and New Zealnd than right hand drive cars from the USA. It was hoped that more people in remote areas would then be able to afford vehicles to use on the land and to transport goods.

Shipping

Regular services operate to Western Europe, the US West Coast, New Zealand, Japan and other major Pacific Islands. Local shipping provides a daily frequent service between the two main islands.

HEALTH

Most healthcare is funded through public money. Samoa has two public hospitals, three district hospitals, 11 health centres and 17 health subcentres. There is one private hospital.

In 2009, the government spent approximately 16.2 per cent of its total budget on healthcare, accounting for 85.3 per cent of all healthcare spending. Total expenditure on healthcare equated to 5.4 per cent of the country's GDP. Per capita expenditure on health was approximately US$154, compared with US$79 in 2000. In 2005-10, there were estimated to be 90 physicians (4.8 per 10,000 population), 348 nurses and midwives (18.5 per 10,000 population), 63 dentistry personnel (3.4 per 10,000 population) and 59 pharmaceutical personnel.There were an estimated 10 hospital beds per 10,000 population.

In 2010, 96 per cent of the population had access to improved drinking water sources. An estimated 98 per cent of the population have sustainable access to improved sanitation.

There is high immunization coverage and most communicable diseases are now well controlled; over 96 of infants are fully immunized and the infant and under-five mortality rates have declined in recent years. However, many Samoans have an unhealthy diet, and lack physical activity. Over 57 of the population are overweight or obese, and smoking prevalence continues to increase despite anti-smoking and stop-smoking campaigns. In 2010, the infant mortality rate (probability of dying by first birthday) was 17 per 1,000 live births and the child mortality rate (under-five) was 20 per 1,000 live births. The most common causes of death in the under-fives are prematurity (17 per cent), birth asphyxia (9 per cent), neonatalsepsis (4 per cent), congenital anomalies (24 per cent), pneumonia (8 per cent). Diarrhoea accounts for 3 per cent of the deaths. (Source: http://www.who.int, World Health Statistics 2012)

EDUCATION

Primary/Secondary Education

Samoa's compulsory education lasts for eight years. Primary education begins at five and lasts until the age of 12. Secondary education begins at 13 and ends at 17. In 2004, 90 per cent of primary school aged children were enrolled in a school, and 66 per cent of secondary school aged children were registered with a school. In 2006, 13.7 per cent of government spending went on education.

According to most recent estimates, the adult literacy rate is 98.7 per cent overall, and 99.4 per cent for the 15-24 age group. This is above the regional average.

RELIGION

The Constitution provides for freedom of religion and worship. The main religious groups are the Congregational Christian Church, Catholics, Mormons and Seventh-Day Adventists.

Samoa has a religious liberty rating of 9 on a scale of 1 to 10 (10 is most freedom). (Source: World Religion Database)

COMMUNICATIONS AND MEDIA

Samoa has a generally free press.

Newspapers

There are two main newspapers: The Samoa Observer (URL: http://www.samoaobserver.ws/) and the Samoa Times which are printed daily. Le Samoa prints weekly in English and Samoan.

Broadcasting

The state-owned television station was privatised in 2008. Four privately-owned television stations boadcast and several privately-owned radio stations. Broadcasts from American Samoa are available.

Radio Polynesia Ltd, URL: http://www.fmradio.ws/

Telecommunications

The capital, Apia, has an excellent international telecommunication system. Most of the country has coverage. In 2008, there were 28,000 mainline telephones in use and in 124,000 people had a mobile telephone.

The government has adopted a national strategy for information and communications technology, and is planning to make access to the internet available to all, viewing it as essential to future economic growth. By 2009, an estimated 9,000 people had access to the internet.

ENVIRONMENT

Samoa's main environmental problem is soil erosion and the possibility of rising sea levels. Samoa is a party to the following international environmental agreements: Biodiversity, Climate Change, Desertification, Law of the Sea, Nuclear Test Ban, Ozone Layer Protection, Ship Pollution, Wetlands and Hazardous Wastes.

In 2010, Samoa's emissions from the consumption of fossil fuels totaled 0.15 million metric tons of carbon dioxide. (Source: EIA)

SAN MARINO

Republic of San Marino
Repubblica di San Marino

Capital: San Marino (Population estimate: 4,000)

Heads of State: Denis Amici and Antonella Mularoni (page 1481) (Captains Regent)

National Flag: White and blue, divided fesswise. The national arms are charged within a wreath of oak and laurel.

CONSTITUTION AND GOVERNMENT

Constitution
San Marino is possibly the world's oldest surviving republic. The state does not have a constitution; its legal framework is based principally on the Statutes of 1600 (in Latin) and the Declaration of Citizen Rights, 1974 (amended 2002). The political system is one of parliamentary democracy following the declaration of 8 July 1974. Being a representative democracy, it stands apart from other European governments.

Lower House
The Great and General Council (*Consiglio Grande e Generale*) has 60 members and is headed by the Captains Regent (*Capitani Reggenti*). It is elected every five years by direct vote of all citizens over the age of twenty-one. Every six months (in mid-March and mid-September) two members of the Council are nominated to act as Captains Regent. The Great and General Council also elects a committee of 12 members to act as a Supreme Court, known as the Council of XII, which has civil, penal and administrative functions, and is the ultimate court of appeal. The Captains Regent hold executive power and represent the Republic in its relations with other countries. Their inauguration takes place on 1 April and 1 October each year with picturesque ceremony. Captains Regents cannot be re-elected until three years have expired after their last term of office. They are personally responsible for the mandate assumed, and at the termination of their office are subject to a Syndicate to which any citizen may present his claims.

Great and General Council, Palazzo Pubblico, San Marino. Tel: +378 882319, fax: +378 882389, e-mail: seg.istituzionale@omniway.sm, URL: http://www.consigliograndeegenerale.sm/

There is a Congress of State (*Congresso di Stato*), composed of ten members chosen by the Great and General Council, which in the past had exclusively consultative functions. Now, however, this organ is invested with directive and executive powers of government and is divided into ten departments.

Congress of State, Palazzo Pubblico, San Marino. Tel: +378 882283 / 882277, fax: +378 882197, e-mail: affariinterni@omniway.sm, URL: http://www.consigliograndeegenerale.sm/on-line/Home.html

Cabinet (as at June 2013)
Secretary of State for Foreign and Political Affairs, Telecommunications and Transport: Pasquale Valentini
Secretary of State for Territory, Environment & Agriculture: Gian Carlo Venturini
Secretary of State for Internal Affairs: Valeria Ciavatta
Secretary of State for Finance & Budget: Claudio Felici
Secretary of State for Industry & Trade: Marco Arzilli
Secretary of State for Labour: Franceso Mussoni
Secretary of State for Health, Social Welfare & Social Security: Claudio Podeschi
Secretary of State for Education, Culture, University and Youth Policy: Romeo Morri
Secretary of State for Justice, Information and Research: Augusto Casali
Secretary of State for Tourism, Sport, Economic Planning: Fabio Berardi

Ministries
Office of the Captains Regent, Palazzo Pubblico, 47031 San Marino. Tel: +378 882259, URL: http://www.reggenzadellarepubblica.sm/on-line/Home.html
State Secretariat for Finance and Budget, URL: http://www.finanze.sm/on-line/Home.html
State Secretariat for Education and Culture, URL: http://www.educazione.sm/
State Secretariat for Foreign Affairs, URL: http://www.esteri.sm/
State Secretariat for Health, Social Welfare and Social Security, URL: http://www.sanita.segreteria.sm/
State Secretariat for Industry, Handicrafts, Trade and Research, URL: http://www.industria.segreteria.sm/
State Secretariat for Internal Affairs, URL: http://www.interni.segreteria.sm/
State Secretariat for Justice, URL: http://www.giustizia.sm/on-line/Home.html
State Secretariat for Labour and Cooperation, URL: http://www.lavoro.segreteria.sm/
State Secretariat for Tourism, Sport, Telecommunications and Post, URL: http://www.visitsanmarino.com/
State Secretariat for Environment, Territory and Agriculture, URL: http://www.segreteriaterritorio.sm/on-line/Home.html

Political Parties
Christian Democratic Party, URL: http://www.pdcs.sm/
Popular Alliance, URL: http://www.alleanzapopolare.net
United Left (Sinistra Unita), URL: http://www.sxun.org/
Centre Democrats (DdC), URL: www.democraticidicentro.sm

Freedom List (LdL), URL: http://www.listadellaliberta.com
San Marino Christian Democratic Party (PDCS), URL: www.socialistiedemocratici.sm
San Marino Union of Moderates (USdM), URL: www.alleanzanazionalersm.sm
United Left (SU)
We Sammarinese (NS), URL: http://www.noisammarinesi.com

Elections
Women voted for the first time in the 1964 elections.

A parliamentary election was held on 9 November 2008. It was contested by two major coalitions: centre-right Patto per San Marino, and centre-left Riforme e Libertà. The Patto per San Marino won with 54.22 per cent of the votes, and 35 of the 60 seats. 68.48 per cent of eligible voters turned out.

Elections for the Captains-Regent are held in March and September every year by the Great and General Council. Oscar Mina of the Christian Democrat Party and Massimo Cenci of the New Socialist Party were elected in March 2009.

Diplomatic Representation
British Consulate General, Via XX Settembre 80/A, 00187 Rome.
Ambassador: Christopher Prentice CMG (page 1498)
US Embassy,URL: http://sanmarino.usvpp.gov/ http://italy.usembassy.gov/
Ambassador to Italy and San Marino: David Thorne
Consulate General in Washington, 888 17th Street NW, Suite 900, Washington, DC 20006, USA.
Ambassador: Paolo Rondelli
Permanent Representative of the Republic of San Marino to the United Nations, 327 East 50th Street, New York, NY 10022, USA. Tel: +1 212 751 1234, fax: +1 212 751 1436, e-mail: sanmarino@un.int
Permanent Representative: Daniele Bodini

LEGAL SYSTEM

The legal system is based on the civil law system with some Italian influences. It is composed of the following: a Conciliatory Judge who has the power to judge civil cases up to a maximum of 10,000 lire; a Judge of First Hearing, called Commissioner of the Law (who has power to judge all civil and penal cases where the maximum penalty does not exceed six months); a Penal Judge (for penal cases which are beyond the competence of the Judge of First Hearing); a Judge for civil and penal appeals; and the Council of XII, whose members constitute the tribunal for third hearing, and who are presided over by the Captains Regent.

Some reforms were made recently to the legal system. Since 2004 the final court of review is the judge of the last appeal. A constitutional court was established in 2005. Its functions include verifying that laws conform to the constitution; assessing the admissibility of referenda; ruling on conflicts between constitutional bodies. The consitutitional court is made up of three standing and three alternate judges, selected by the Great and General Council for four-year terms.

The government respects the rights of its citizens. Capital punishment was abolished for civil crimes in 1848 and was completely abolished for all crimes in 1865.

LOCAL GOVERNMENT

San Marino is divided into nine administrative districts called *Castelli* (townships). The administrative districts are: Acquaviva, Borgo Maggiore, Chiesanuova, Domagnano, Faetano, Fiorentino, Montegiardino, San Marino Citta and Serravalle. For each township a council is elected every five years by direct suffrage. Each council is chaired by a captain and its functions include the control and management of local services.

AREA AND POPULATION

Area
The Republic of San Marino is located in central Italy, between the cities of Pesaro and Forlì, 24 km from the seaside resort of Rimini. Its territory covers an area of 61.19 sq. km and is mainly mountainous. San Marino is landlocked. The climate is Mediterranean with mild winters and warm sunny summers.

To view a map, consult http://www.lib.utexas.edu/maps/cia08/san_marino_sm_2008.gif

Population
The estimated population in 2010 was 32,000, with an average annual growth rate of 1.6 per cent. An estimated 14 per cent of the population is aged 15 or less and 27 per cent is over 60. An estimated 94 per cent of people live in urban areas. The capital, San Marino, has a population of about 4,335 people. About 12,500 Sammarinese live abroad, whilst 3,000 foreign citizens live in San Marino. The official language is Italian.

SAN MARINO

Births, Marriages, Deaths

The estimated birth rate in 2010 was 9 per 1,000 people. The estimated death rate was 8.8 per 1,000 people. According to World Health Organization statistics for 2010, infant mortality was just 1 death per 1,000 births (one of the lowest in Europe). Average life expectancy at birth in 2009 was 82 years for males and 85 years for females. Healthy life expectancy was 74 years and 76 years respectively in 2007. The fertility rate was an estimated 1.5 children per woman in 2010. (Source: http://www.who.int, World Health Statistics 2012)

Public Holidays 2014

1 January: New Year's Day
6 January: Epiphany
5 February: Liberation Day
25 March: Anniversary of the Arengo
18 April: Good Friday
21 April: Easter Monday
1 April and 1 October: Ceremony of the investiture of the Captains Regent
5 May: Labour Day
19 June: Corpus Christi
28 July: The fall of fascism
15 August: Assumption Day
3 September: Foundation of the Republic
1 October: Regency Exchange
1 November: All Saints Day
2 November: All Souls Day
25 December: Christmas Day

EMPLOYMENT

20,695 people were in employment in 2006 and just 595 were unemployed. The unemployment rate was estimated at 2.8 per cent in 2004, the lowest rate in Europe and down from 3.1 per cent in 2003. Figures for 2008 show that 21,995 people were employed and 713 unemployed. Estimated figures for 2010 put the workforce at 22,900 with an unemployment rate of 3.7 per cent.

Total Employment by Economic Activity

Occupation	2008
Agriculture, hunting & forestry	76
Manufacturing	6,398
Construction	1,716
Wholesale & retail trade, repairs	3,513
Hotels & restaurants	218
Transport, storage & communications	615
Financial intermediation	1,017
Real estate, renting & business activities	3,047
Public admin. & defence; compulsory social security	4,030
Education	42
Health & social work	191
Other community, social & personal service activities	1,115
Other	17

Source: Copyright © International Labour Organization (ILO Dept. of Statistics, http://laborsta.ilo.org)

BANKING AND FINANCE

Currency

One euro (€) = 100 cents
€ = 1,936.27 lire (European Central Bank irrevocable conversion rate)
On 1 January 2002 the euro became legal tender in Italy and San Marino. Italy's old currency, the lire, ceased to be legal tender from 28 February 2002.

GDP/GNP, Inflation, National Debt

San Marino's economy is allied to that of Italy. Its stability is due to diversity; the main source of revenue is currently tourism, but quarrying continues to be a significant contributor, and light industry is coming to the fore.

Annual GDP growth has averaged over 5.5 per cent over the past decade, due largely to the banking sector, foreign investment and trade with Italy and other economies. GDP growth was put at 2.1 per cent per annum in 2008 and GDP was estimated to be €1.8 billion in 2008. GDP was estimated to have fallen to €1.1 billion with a growth rate of -12 per cent. Per capita GDP was estimated at €25,000 in the same year. Inflation was 2.8 per cent in 2010. San Marino has no national debt, and the standard of living is on a par with that of Italy.

Tourism contributes over half of San Marino's GDP. Other sources of revenue are taxes from non-residents, banking and an annual sum paid by the Italian government in return for various economic concessions. Sales of San Marino postage stamps to collectors provide around 10 per cent of the government's income, and San Marino mints its own coins, which are also sought after by collectors.

Balance of Payments / Imports and Exports

San Marino is a tax haven and, as such, attracts a large amount of cash from non-residents. There are no customs barriers between San Marino and Italy.

Exports earned the country €2.80 billion in 2008. The main trading partner is Italy (90 per cent) and commodities include building stone, ceramics, clothing, spirits and wines.

Imports cost the country an estimated €2.60 million in 2008. Main products were manufactured goods and food. Italy, Europe, South America, China and Taiwan all supplied goods.

Central Bank

Banca Centrale della Repubblica di San Marino, URL: http://www.bcsm.sm

MANUFACTURING, MINING AND SERVICES

Manufacturing

Light industrial production includes textiles and cement. Small quantities of paper, leather, soap, paint, wine, cheese and furniture are produced in the Republic. San Marino's ceramic work dates from the 16th century, and is a considerable industry. It employs more than 400 skilled workers in ten workshops. Electronics is a newer industry and the minting of coins and medals and the printing of stamps also add to the economy.

Service Industries

Tourism is the primary industry, contributing half of San Marino's GDP. On average, the country plays host to over 2 million tourists per year.

Agriculture

San Marino is rich in agricultural resources. There are 3,940 ha of arable land. Animal husbandry has moved from the traditional sheep farming to rearing cattle and swine and production of hides. Wheat, fruit and vines are the main crops.

COMMUNICATIONS AND TRANSPORT

Travel Requirements

All visitors enter San Marino through Italy. Since there are no border formalities, any person visiting San Marino must comply with Italian passport/visa regulations.

International Airports

The nearest international airport is Rimini in Italy and a helicopter service operates from the airport.

Railways

There is no rail service between San Marino and Italy, but the capital is linked with Rimini and the Italian *autostrade* network by a modern highway. There is a funicular service from the city of San Marino to Borgo Maggiore. The nearest railway station is Rimini in Italy.

Roads

The network of roads in the Republic has a total length of 220 kilometres. A regular bus service runs between San Marino and Rimini.

HEALTH

In 2009, the government spent approximately 13.6 per cent of its total budget on healthcare (down from 20.4 per cent in 2000), accounting for 85.2 per cent of all healthcare spending. Total expenditure on healthcare equated to 7.1 per cent of the country's GDP. Per capita expenditure on health was approximately US$3,864, compared with US$2,154 in 2000. In 2004, for every 100,000 people, there were 251 doctors and 505 nurses. In 2010, the infant mortality rate was 2 per 1,000 live births as was the child mortality rate. (Source: http://www.who.int, World Health Statistics 2012)

EDUCATION

Primary/Secondary Education

Education is compulsory between the ages of six and 14. Primary education lasts for eight years, from the age of six to 10. Primary school enrolment for primary school age children is estimated at 95 per cent. The pupil: teacher ratio was estimated at 6:1. Secondary education lasts for a total of eight years (three at lower school and five at upper school), starting at 11 and concluding at 18. Secondary school enrolment is estimated at 91 per cent.

Language teaching begins at elementary school where all students study English. French is taught at secondary school.

The literacy rate is over 99 per cent. (Source: UNESCO)

Higher Education

The University was opened in 1988 and has departments of history, semiotics, technology and teacher training. An estimated 70 per cent of children go onto higher education.

Vocational Training

Courses are organised by the Ministry of Labour at the State Training Centre.

RELIGION

The population is predominantly Roman Catholic.

COMMUNICATIONS AND MEDIA

Newspapers

La Tribuna Sammarinese, URL: http://www.latribunasammarinese.net
San Marino Oggi, URL: http://www.omniway.sm

Broadcasting
San Marino RTV (URL: http://www.sanmarinortv.sm/) broadcasting company was established in 1993. It includes one television station and two radio stations.

Telecommunications
The San Marino phone system is integrated in the Italian phone network. The number of mainline telephones in use in 2008 is estimated at 21,300. Mobile phones numbered approximately 17,500 in the same year. There were over 17,000 internet users in San Marino in 2008.

ENVIRONMENT

San Marino is a party to the following international environmental agreements: Biodiversity, Climate Change, Desertification, and Whaling. It has signed but not ratified the agreement on Air Pollution.

In 2008, the UN added San Marino's historic centre and Mount Titano to the World Heritage list of protected sites.

SÃO TOMÉ AND PRÍNCIPE
Democratic Republic of Sao Tome and Principe
República Democrática de São Tomé e Príncipe

Capital: São Tomé (Population estimate: 57,000)

Head of State: Manuel Pinto da Costa (President) (page 1496)

National Flag: Three horizontal stripes of green, yellow, green with a red triangle on the left side and two five-pointed black stars on the central stripe

CONSTITUTION AND GOVERNMENT

Constitution
São Tomé and Príncipe became independent from Portugal on 12 July 1975. A new Constitution was approved by 72 per cent of votes at a referendum in August 1990. Under the terms of the Constitution the head of state is the President, directly elected by universal adult suffrage for a maximum of two successive five-year terms. Candidates are chosen at their party's national conference or individuals may run independently. A presidential candidate must obtain an outright majority of the popular vote in either a first or second round of voting in order to be elected president. The prime minister is named by the president but must be ratified by the majority party and thus normally comes from a list of its choosing. The prime minister, in turn, names the 14 members of the Cabinet.

To consult the constitution, please visit: http://www.tribunalconstitucional.st/tc/constituicao.htm

International Relations
Following independence, São Tomé forged close ties with the Russian bloc countries and Cuba. Angola was a strong ally. More recently, the country has increased relations with Portugal and other Portuguese-speaking African countries, and is expanding its partnerships with Western institutions as part of its economic reform programme. São Tomé's relationship with Nigeria has grown due to their mutual oil interests; the Nigerian president personally intervened to prevent a military coup in 2003. In 2007, Nigeria and São Tomé agreed to establish a joint military commission to protect their common oil interests in the Gulf of Guinea. São Tomé is a signatory to the African Union treaty.

Recent Events
In July 2003 the government was overthrown by a military coup while President De Menezes was in Nigeria. The coup leaders accused the government of corruption and mismanagement of public money. On the president's return, an agreement with the coup leaders gave them amnesty from prosecution, and democratic rule was re-established.

Hundreds of millions of dollars in license money for São Tomé was generated in October 2003 when oil companies were allowed to bid for offshore oil blocs controlled by the country.

In September 2004, the president sacked the prime minister and government after a series of corruption scandals. In June 2005, the prime minister, Vaz de Almeida, and his government resigned over disagreements with the president over offshore oil drilling contracts and a civil service strike for more pay. Parliamentary elections were held in March 2006 but protests took place in several constituencies over poor living conditions, and the results were delayed. The president's Democratic Movement of Forces for Change (MDFC) won 23 of the 55 seats in parliament.

In March 2007, the IMF wrote off $360 million in debt owed by São Tomé, equivalent to around 90 per cent of the country's foreign debt.

The opposition leader Patrice Trovoada became prime minister in February 2008, but was dismissed in May when parliament passed a vote of no confidence against the coalition government. Rafael Branco, head of São Tomé's second largest party, became prime minister in June. An alleged coup plot was foiled in December 2010.

An opposition leader, Arlecio Costa, was freed from prison in January 2010 where he been imprisoned for an alleged coup plot.

Presidential elections took place and were won by the independence era leader Manual Pinto da Costs. President Pinto da Costa dismissed the prime minister Patrice Trovoada, after a no-confidence vote in parliament.

Legislature
The unicameral legislature is known as the Assembléia Nacional (National Assembly) which has 55 members and is elected every four years. Since April 1995 Príncipe has enjoyed internal self-government, with an eight-member regional government and an elected assembly.
National Assemby, C.P. 181, Palácio dos Congressos, São Tomé. Tel: +239 222 986, fax: +239 222 835, e-mail: sganstp@cstome.net, URL: http://www.parlamento.st

Cabinet (as at March 2013)
Prime Minister: Gabriel Arcanjo Ferreira da Costa (page 1424)
Minister of Foreign Affairs, Co-operation & Communities: Natalie Pedro Da Costa Umbelina Neto (page 1529)
Minister of Interior and Civilian Protection: Raul Antonio Da Costa Cravid
Minister of Labour, Solidarity, Women and Family Affairs: Maria Tome De Araujo
Minister of Defence and Security: Lt. Col. Oscar Aguiar Sacremento E Sousa
Minister of Public Works & Infrastructure, Urban Development, Natural Resources & Environment: Benjamin Cruz
Minister of Health & Social Affairs: Leonel Pinto D'Assuncao Pontes
Minister of Agriculture, Rural Development & Fisheries: Antonio Alvaro Da Graca Dias
Minister of Commerce, Industry & Tourism: Demostenes Vasconelos Pires Dos Santos
Minister of Justice, State Reform & Parliamentary Affairs: Edite Ramos Da Costa Ten Jua
Minister of Planning and Finance: Helio Silva Vaz d'Almeida
Minister of Education & Culture: Jorge Lopes Bom Jesus

Ministries
Office of the President: Palácio dos Congressos, C.P., 181, Sao Tomé. Tel: +239 222986-22, fax: +239 222835, URL: http://www.presidencia.st/
Office of the Prime Minister: Palácio dos Congressos, C.P., 181, Sao Tomé. Tel: +239 222 986-22, fax: +239 222 835, URL: http://www.gov.st
Ministry of Foreign Affairs, Avenida 12 de Julho, 101/201 Sao Tomé. Tel: +239 222309, fax: +239 223237, URL: http://www.mnecc.gov.st/

Political Parties
Movimento de Libertaçao de São Tomé et Príncipe - Partido Social Democrata (MLSTP - PSD, Liberation Movement of São Tomé **and Príncipe). URL: http://www.mlstp.st/, Leader: Joaquim Rafael Branco**
Acçao Democrática Independente (ADI, Independent Democratic Action), URL: http://www.adidigital.com/, Leader: Patrice Emery Trovoada
Partido de Convergência Democrática - Grupo de Reflexao (PCD, Democratic Convergence Party - Reflection Group). Leader: Leonel Mário d'Alva
Movimento Democrático das Forças da Mudança-Partido Liberal (Force for Change Democratic Movement). Sec. Gen.: Tomé Vera Cruz

Elections
Presidential elections took place on 17 July 2011. Manuel Pinto da Costa, won as an independent candidate in the 2011 presidential election, defeating the ADI candidate in the second round; he took office on 3 September. Mr da Costa was the country's first post-independence president and leader of the Marxist MLSTP from 1975 to 1990.

Legislative elections took place in March 2006. The coalition of the Force for Change Democratic Movement and the Democratic Convergence Party became the largest party in parliament, winning 23 seats. In anticipation of a parliamentary defeat over the budget, Prime Minister Vera Cruz resigned in February 2008, and Patrice Trovoada, leader of the opposition ADI and son of former president Miguel Trovoada, was named as prime minister. However, on 20 May Trovoada's government lost a vote of confidence. Joaquim Rafael Branco became prime minister on 21 June and his cabinet included members of previous administrations from the MDFM, the PCD and the Movement for the Liberation of Sao Tome and Principe-Social Democratic Party (MLSTP-PSD).

The most recent parliamentary elections took place in August 2010, the Independent Democratic Alliance (ADI) became the largest party but did not win a majority. A cabinet was formed of members of the ADI and independents.

Diplomatic Representation
British Embassy, (all Staff Resident in Luanda, Angola) Rua Diogo Cao 4, Caixa Postal 1244, Luanda, Angola. Tel: +244 2 334582, fax: +244 2 333331, URL: http://ukinangola.fco.gov.uk/en/
Ambassador to Angola and São Tomé and Príncipe: Richard Wildash (page 1537)

SÃO TOMÉ AND PRÍNCIPE

US Embassy, URL: http://libreville.usembassy.gov/
Ambassador: Eric Benjaminson (page 1386)
Permanent Representative of São Tomé and Príncipe to the United Nations, 400 Park Avenue, 7th Floor, New York, NY 10022, USA. Tel: +1 212 317 0533, fax: +1 212 317 0580, e-mail: stp@un.int, URL: http://www.unohrlls.org/en/orphan/294/
Permanent Representative & Ambassador to the US: H.E. Ovidio Manuel Barbosa do Nascimento Pequeno

LEGAL SYSTEM

The legal system is based on the Portuguese system and customary law. The judiciary is independent under the current constitution. Justice is administered at the highest level by the Supreme Court, whose members are appointed by the National Assembly. Sao Tomé has not accepted compulsory ICJ jurisdiction

The government respects the rights of its citizens. However, problems of official corruption and impunity, prolonged pretrial detention and harsh prison conditions persist. The death penalty was abolished in 1990.

LOCAL GOVERNMENT

The country is divided into two provinces: São Tomé and Principe. The provinces comprise seven counties, six on Sao Tome and one on Principe. In 1994, the National Assembly granted political and administrative autonomy to the island of Príncipe. It has a Regional Assembly which is accountable to Sao Tome. Governing councils in each district have limited autonomous decision-making powers, and are re-elected every 5 years. Local elections took place in 2010.

AREA AND POPULATION

Area
The islands of São Tomé and Príncipe are situated off the west coast of Africa in the Gulf of Guinea. They form the smallest state in Africa, with a total area of 1,001 sq. km. The republic, which lies 200 km off the west coast of Gabon comprises the main islands of São Tomé and Príncipe and several smaller islets including Pedras, Tinhosas and Rolas. The islands are part of an extinct volcanic mountain range, and its rugged terrain renders much of the land inaccessible. The climate is tropical at sea level, but cooler at higher altitudes.

To view a map of the islands, please consult:
http://www.lib.utexas.edu/maps/cia08/sao_tome_principe_sm_2008.gif

Population
The estimated population in 2010 was 165,000, with an annual growth rate of around 1.6 per cent. Most people inhabit Sao Tomé, and there are around 6,000 inhabitants on Principé. The majority of Sao Tomeans (55 per cent) are aged between 15 and 64 years, with 40 per cent aged under 15 years, and 5 per cent aged 65 years and over. The people are of mixed origins: Mestico (descendants of African slaves brought to the islands during the early years of settlement from Benin, Gabon, and Congo); Angolares (possible descendants of Angolan slaves who survived a 1540 shipwreck); Forros (descendants of freed slaves); Servicais (contract laborers living on the islands temporarily); Tongas (children of servicais born on the islands) and Europeans, (mainly Portuguese).

The official language is Portuguese. Lungwa São Tomé - a Portuguese Creole - and Fang - a Bantu language - are also spoken.

Births, Marriages, Deaths
According to 2010 estimates, the birth rate is 31.2 births per 1,000 population, and the death rate is 6.5 deaths per 1,000 population. Average life expectancy at birth in 2009 was 68 years (66 years for men and 70 years for women). Healthy life expectancy was 53 years. The infant mortality rate was 53 infant deaths per 1,000 live births, whilst the fertility rate is 3.7 children born per woman. (Source: http://www.who.int, World Health Statistics 2012)

Public Holidays 2014
1 January: New Year's Day
3 February: Heroes' Day
18 April: Good Friday
21 April: Easter Monday
1 May: Labour Day
12 July: Independence Day
6 September: Armed Forces Day
30 September: Agricultural Reform Day
26 November: Argel Accord Day
21 December: São Tomé Day (Catholic)
25 December: Christmas Day

EMPLOYMENT

Around 15 per cent of the workforce is employed in agriculture; trade, industry and services employ around 36 per cent of people, and over 11 per cent are employed by the government. Most people are involved in subsistence agriculture and fishing. Recent figures put the workforce at 52,500.

BANKING AND FINANCE

Currency
One Dobra = 100 cêntimos

GDP/GNP, Inflation, National Debt
Sao Tome remains highly dependent on donor assistance; around 70 per cent of its budget is externally supported, and the country receives one of the highest per capita amounts of development assistance in the world. The Paris Club forgave Sao Tome and Principe $24.5 million of debt in May 2007. This was additional to previous substantial debt write-offs by the World Bank and African Development Fund. Some 54 per cent of the population continues to live below the poverty line.

The mainstay of Sao Tomé and Principé's economy is its agricultural sector. Cocoa production accounts for around 95 per cent of export revenues; other crops are coffee, copra and palm kernels. Fishing is an important economic activity, and there is a small industrial sector engaged in processing local agricultural produce.

The country is poised to benefit from oil revenues: following prolonged licensing rounds, exploratory drilling started in January 2006. The government adopted an Oil Revenue Management Law in 2004 to ensure that oil revenue is managed transparently and efficiently. The Law also provides for a government Trust Fund. In 2011 the government said it had found commercially viable oil in offshore fields that it had jointly explored with Nigeria. Production could start by 2014.

Following two decades of stagnation, the economy of Sao Tomé and Principé is showing signs of growth. In 2003, GDP grew by an estimated 5 per cent, and in 2005, it grew by 6 per cent, reaching US$ 72.48 million. Growth has continued: in 2006 growth was estimated at 8.0 per cent with GDP at US$79.12 million, and in 2007 growth was put at 7.0 per cent with GDP reaching US$90.04 million. Figures for 2009 put GDP at US$190 million, reflecting a growth rate that year of 4.0 per cent. The service industry contributes the largest proportion of GDP, nearly 71 per cent GDP was estimated at US$245 million in 2011.

The inflation rate (consumer prices) fell from a 1997 high of 71.3 per cent to 8.9 per cent in 2002. Inflation was estimated to be 11 per cent in 2011, rising to 12.1 per cent the following year.

External debt was estimated at US$336.41 million in 2006, up from US$323 million in 2005. Total debt service amounted to US$8.73 million, approximately 47 per cent of export revenue.

Balance of Payments / Imports and Exports
The main export products were cocoa (95 per cent), copra, coffee, and palm kernels. Major export partners are the Portugal, Netherlands, Spain, Germany, and China. Main import suppliers were Portugal (43 per cent), France (16 per cent) and the UK (14 per cent). Major import commodities are electrical equipment and machinery, petroleum products, and foodstuffs.

External Trade, US$ million

	2005	2006	2007
Trade balance	-38.23	-68.66	-66.60
Exports	3.37	3.82	4.46
Imports	41.60	70.47	71.06

Source: African Development Bank

Exports were estimated to be US$14 million in 2009 and imports cost US$93 million.

Central Bank
Banco Central de São Tomé e Príncipe, CP 13, Praça da Independencia, São Tomé, São Tomé & Príncipe. Tel: +239 12 21966, fax: +239 12 22501 / 12 22777, e-mail: bcentral@sol.stome.telepac.net, URL: http://www.bcstp.st/
Governor: Maria do Carmo Silveira

MANUFACTURING, MINING AND SERVICES

Primary and Extractive Industries
São Tomé and Príncipe neither produces nor consumes natural gas or coal, and imports all of its oil requirements. In 2006 imports were 660 barrels per day, most of which was distillate.

The country hoped to become an oil producer from 2010. Oil fields lying between Sao Tome and Nigeria will be developed jointly with Nigeria in a Joint Development Zone (JDZ). Under the agreement, Nigeria will take 60 per cent of the profits and Sao Tome 40 per cent. Several Blocs have been awarded. The government passed an Oil Revenue Management Law in 2004 to ensure that oil revenue is managed transparently and efficiently. In 2011, the government said it had discovered commercially viable offshore oil fields. Production could begin by 2014.

Energy
São Tomé had a total electricity capacity of 9 million kWh in 2006, most of which was hydroelectric power. In the same year it generated 20 million kWh of electricity, all of which was used internally.

Manufacturing
Industry is concentrated mainly around agriculture and timber processing although there are factories manufacturing bricks, ceramics, textiles, palm oil, beer and soap. Industry accounted for nearly 15.3 per cent of GDP in 2005.

Service Industries
The services industry contributes around 64 per cent of GDP annually. The tourist industry is expanding; visitors are attracted by big game fishing in the islands' coastal waters, exclusive beach resorts and the unspoilt scenery and bird life of the island's volcanic mountains.

Agriculture

The agricultural sector accounts for around 15 per cent of GDP. The main products of the state are cocoa, coconuts, copra, palm oil and coffee. Other products are cinnamon, pepper, bananas, beans and poultry. The country is not self-sufficient in food, and has to import foodstuffs. The government aims to expand food production. The plantations, nationalised at independence, have since been re-privatised as part of the economic reforms introduced in the late 1980s. Working conditions on many of the cocoa plantations, the main wage employment sector, are harsh, although land reform has given peasant farmers plots for subsistence.

Around 484 km. sq. of the land is cultivated; 60 per cent of the land is covered by forest.

Agricultural Production in 2010

Produce	Int. $'000*	Tonnes
Bananas	9,407	33,400
Taro (cocoyam)	5,249	27,500
Coconuts	2,919	26,400
Cocoa beans	2,077	2,000
Vegetables fresh nes	1,696	9,000
Palm oil	1,436	3,300
Fruit fresh nes	1,257	3,600
Indigenous chicken meat	1,007	707
Cassava	836	8,000
Yams	485	1,900
Hen eggs, in shell	482	581
Roots and tubers nes	479	2,800

* unofficial figures

Source: http://faostat.fao.org/site/339/default.aspx Food and Agriculture Organization of the United Nations, Food and Agricultural commodities production

Fishing

Estimated figures from the FAO put the total catch in 2010 at 4,650 tonnes.

COMMUNICATIONS AND TRANSPORT

Travel Requirements

Citizens of the USA, Canada, Australia and the EU require a valid passport, a return/onward ticket and a visa. Evidence of yellow fever vaccination may also be required. Transit passengers continuing their journey to another country by the same or first connecting aircraft within 24 hours, holding valid onward or return documentation and not leaving the airport do not require a visa. Other nationals should contact the embassy to check visa requirements.

National Airlines

Air São Tomé e Principe, CP 45, Avenida 12 de Julho, São Tomé, 45, São Tomé e Principe. Tel: +239 12 21976, fax: +239 12 21375

International Airports

There is an international airport in São Tomé.

Roads

There are 380 km of roads, of which 250 km are asphalt. Vehicles are driven on the right.

Ports and Harbours

The main port is at São Tomé but does not have a deep water harbour. The main fishing port is at Neves which also deals with oil imports. A ferry service operates between São Tomé and Principe.

HEALTH

In 2009, the government spent approximately 13.2 per cent of its total budget on healthcare (up from 9 per cent in 2000), accounting for 40.1 per cent of all healthcare spending. Total expenditure on healthcare equated to 7.2 per cent of the country's GDP. Per capita expenditure on health was approximately US$93, compared with US$52 in 2000. Figures for 2000-10

show that there are 81 physicians (5 per 10,000 population), 308 nurses and midwives (19 per 10,000 population), 11 dentistry personnel, 24 pharmaceutical personnel, 19 environment and public health workers and 150 community workers. There are an estimated 32 hospital beds per 10,000 population.

In 2010, life expectancy was 68 per cent. Healthy life expectancy in Sao Tomé is 61 years. The infant mortality rate in 2010 was 53 per 1,000 live births. The child mortality rate (under 5 years) was 80 per 1,000 live births. The main causes of childhood mortality are: diarrhoea (11 per cent), prematurity (15 per cent), pneumonia (18 per cent), measles (1 per cent) and malaria (4 per cent).

In 2010 approximately 89 per cent of the population had access to improved drinking water. In the same year, 26 per cent of the urban population had access to improved sanitation. (Source: http://www.who.int, World Health Statistics 2012)

EDUCATION

Education is free and compulsory. The compulsory education system lasts for four years. Primary education lasts for four years, whilst secondary education lasts for seven years (five years at lower school and two years at upper school).

In 2007, 34 per cent of young children were enrolled in pre-primary school, 98 per cent of girls and 97 per cent of boys were at primary school and 40 per cent of girls and 36 per cent of boys were enrolled in secondary school. Figures were above the regional average.

The adult literacy rate in 2007 was estimated at 87.9 per cent (93.4 per cent of men and 82.7 per cent among women). The figure rises and is more evenly balanced in the 15-24 year olds age group, at 95.2 per cent overall. (Source: UNESCO, UIS Statistics, August 2009)

RELIGION

Almost 70 per cent of the population are Roman Catholic with the remainder of the population being Protestant and various other Christian religions. Close ties with churches in Portugal have been maintained. There is a small Bahai community.

The islands have a religious liberty rating of 10 on a scale of 1 to 10 (10 is most freedom). (Source: World Religion Database)

COMMUNICATIONS AND MEDIA

Freedom of expression is guaranteed by the constitution and is generally respected.

Newspapers

There are four weekly newspapers including Tela Non Diario de Sao Tome, URL: http://www.telanon.info/

Broadcasting

Televisao Saotomense (TVS) is the state-run television broadcaster, and Radio Nacional de Sao Tome e Principe is the main state-run radio station. There are currently no private broadcasters.

Telecommunications

According to 2008 estimates São Tomé and Principe has about 7,700 mainline telephones in use and 50,000 mobile telephones. Internet users numbered some 25,000 in 2009.

ENVIRONMENT

Current environmental problems include deforestation and soil erosion. São Tomé and Príncipe is a party to the following international environmental agreements: Biodiversity, Climate Change, Desertification, Environmental Modification, Law of the Sea, and Ship Pollution.

In 2006, São Tomé and Príncipe's emissions from the consumption of fossil fuels totalled 0.10 million metric tons of carbon dioxide.

SAUDI ARABIA
Kingdom of Saudi Arabia
Al Mamlakah al Arabiyah as Suudiyah

Capital: Riyadh (Seat of government. Population estimate (including expatriates), 2012: 4,500,000)

Religious Capital: Mecca

Head of State: HRH King Abdullah Bin Abdul Aziz Al-Saud (page 1376)

Crown Prince: Prince Salman bin Abdul Aziz al-Saud (page 1376)

National Flag: Green, bearing in white the Arabic inscription 'La ilaha illa Allah Muhammad rasul Allah' (There is no God but God, and Mohammed is his Prophet) over a white sword.

CONSTITUTION AND GOVERNMENT

Constitution
Saudi Arabia is a monarchy with executive and legislative authority exercised by the King and the Council of Ministers within the framework of Islamic law. The Kingdom's ministries and all other government agencies are ultimately responsible to the King. The name Saudi Arabia was given to it by Ibn Saud in 1932, when he proposed to form a constitution covering the whole area. The only constitution as yet in force, however, is that issued for the Hejaz in 1926. In its present form it provides for a Central Council of Ministers, a consultative Legislative Assembly for Mecca, municipal councils for Mecca, Jeddah and Medina, and tribal councils elsewhere. Ministers and council members are appointed by the King, who is also the religious leader of the people.

A translation of the constitution can be found at:
http://www.the-saudi.net/saudi-arabia/saudi-constitution.htm

Saudi Arabia plays a important role in the search for peace in the Middle East. Saudi Arabia is a member of many international organisations including Gulf Cooperation Council, the Arab League, the Organisation of Petroleum Exporting Countries, the Organisation of Islamic Countries, the UN and the World Trade Organisation.

Recent Events
Saudi Arabia stripped Osama Bin Laden, leader al al-Qaeda, of his Saudi nationality in 1994. Suicide bomb attacks have been carried out in recent years in Saudi Arabia; many suspect that the bombers have links with al-Qaeda.

In September 2003 a petition was signed by more than 300 prominent intellectuals who want political reform. The following month, a rally was held, again calling for political reforms. In November of that year King Fahd granted powers to the Consultative Council which meant that it could propose legislation without seeking his permission. February 2005 saw the first municipal elections take place but women were not able to vote.

In August 2005 King Fahd died. He was succeeded by the Crown Prince, Abdullah Bin Abdul Aziz Al-Saud.

172 terror suspects were arrested in April 2007, some of whom may have trained as pilots for suicide missions. In July, religious police were banned from detaining suspects following accusations of over-zealous behaviour after some deaths in custody.

A long-standing border dispute between Saudi Arabia and Qatar was settled in December 2008.

There was a rare government reshuffle in February 2009. King Abdullah sacked the head of the religious police, most senior judges and the head of the central bank. He also appointed Saudi Arabia's first female minister.

Following demonstrations and protests in January 2011 President Zine al-Abidine Ben Ali of Tunisia took sanctuary in Saudi Arabia. In the face of continuing demonstrations for reform in the Arab world, King Abdullah announced that there would be increased spending on welfare. In March public protests were outlawed and police fired on crowds defying the ban. The protests were mainly in Shia areas in the east of the country. King Abdullah warned that any threat to the nation's stability would not be tolerated.

In September 2011 King Abdullah announced that women were to be given the right to vote and to run in future municipal elections. They would also have the right to be appointed to the Shura Council. The changes will take place after the September municipal elections.

Crown Prince Sultan Bin Abdul Aziz Al-Saud died on 22 October 2011. His brother Prince Naif bin Abdul Aziz al-Saud, formerly the second deputy prime minister, was appointed as crown prince and deputy prime minister. Changes to the cabinet were made in November and December 2011.

Legislature
Under a royal decree of 20 August 1993 the term of the office of the 120 members of the Council or Majlis Al-Shura was fixed at four years. In November 2003 King Fahd issued a decree extending the powers of the Council of Ministers. The Council is now able to propose a new law without asking the King's permission first. This has been welcomed in the light of protests held in October 2003 calling for political and economic reforms.

In 2005 the number of seats in the Shura was increased from 120 to 150. There are no political parties in the country. In February 2005, the first elections were held in the country. Half the seats in Municipal Governments are now won through election. In the first of these elections, there were 650 candidates for the seven seats available in Riyadh. Women have not been banned from voting; nor have they been given the ID cards required to register.

In 2006, King Abdallah created the Allegiance Commission. The function of the Commission is to select crown princes upon the death or incapacitation of the king. The current members of the Commission are descendents of the founder of Saudi Arabia, King Abdul Aziz. Only direct male descendents are eligible to become the crown prince or king.

In June 2012 Crown Prince Nayef bin Abdul Aziz al-Saud died in Switzerland while undergoing medical treatment. Prince Salman bin Abdul Aziz al-Saud was named as the new Crown Prince.

In the summer of 2012, female athletes were able to compete in the Olympic games. There had been some speculation that if women were not allowed to take part the whole of the Saudi team would be disqualified on the grounds of gender discrimination.

In February 2013, 30 women were sworn in to the previously all male Shura consultative council. It was a ground breaking move as it was the first time women have been able to hold a political office.

The Consultative Council, (Majlis al-Shura)
Al-Yamamh Palace, 11212 Riyadh, Saudi Arabia. Tel: +966 1 482 1666, URL: http://www.shura.gov.sa

Cabinet (as at July 2013)
King, Custodian of the Two Holy Mosques, Prime Minister: HRH King Abdullah Bin Abdul Aziz Al-Saud (page 1376)
Crown Prince, Deputy Prime Minister, and Minister of Defence: HRH Prince Salman bin Abdul Aziz al-Saud (page 1376)
Second Deputy Prime Minister: HRH Prince Mugrin bin Abdul Aziz al-Saud
Minister of the Interior: HRH Prince Mohamed bin Nayef bin Abdul Aziz al-Saud
Minister of Municipal and Rural Affairs: HRH Prince Mansour Met'eb Bin Abdul Aziz Al-Saud (page 1376)
Minister of Foreign Affairs: HRH Prince Saud Al-Faisal Bin Abdul Aziz Al-Saud (page 1376)
Minister of Agriculture: Fahd bin Abd-al-Rahman bin Sulayman Balghunaym
Minister of Civil Service: Dr Abdulrahman bin Abdullah bin Abdul Aziz Albarak
Minister of Commerce and Industry: Tafeeq bin Fozan bin Mohammed Al-Rabee'a
Minister of Education: HRH Prince Faisal Bin Abdullah Muhammad Al-Saud
Minister of Finance: Dr. Ibrahim Bin Abdul Aziz Al-Assaf (page 1373)
Minister of Health: Abdullah bin Abdulaziz Al-Rabiah
Minister of Housing: Dr Shuwaish bin Saudi bin Duwaihi Al-Duwaihi
Minister of Higher Education: Dr. Khalid Bin Muhammed Al-Ankary (page 1373)
Minister of Water Resources and Electricity: Abdullah bin Abd-al-Rahman Al-Hosain
Minister of Islamic Affairs and Endowments: Shaikh Salah bin Abdel Aziz al-Shaikh
Minister of Justice: Shaykh Muhammed bin Abdulkarim bin Abdulaziz Al-Issa
Minister of Social Affairs: Dr Yusif bin Ahmad al-Uthaymin
Minister of Labour: Adil bin Mohammed bin Abdulqader Faqiyah
Minister of Petroleum and Mineral Resources: Ali Bin Ibrahim Al-Naimi (page 1376)
Minister of Hajj (Pilgrimage): Dr Bandar bin Mohammed bin Hamza Assad Hajjar
Minister of Communications and Information Technology: Muhammad bin Jamil bin Ahmad Mulla
Minister of Transport: Jubarah bin Ayd al-Suravsiri
Minister of Culture and Information: Abd al-Aziz bin Muhaydin al-Khoja
Minister of Economy and Planning: Dr Mohammed bin Sulaiman bin Mohammed Al-Jasser
Minister of the National Guard: HRH Prince Muitaib bin Abdullah
Minister of State: HRH Prince Abdulaziz Bin Fahd Bin Abdul Aziz
Minister of State: Dr. Abdul Aziz Bin Abdullah Al-Khuweiter
Minister of State: Dr. Muttlab Bin Abdullah Al-Nafissa
Minister of State: Dr. Musaid Bin Muhammad Al-Eiban
Minister of State: Dr Abdulaziz bin Abdullah Al-Khuweiter
Minister of State for Shoura Council Affairs: Saud bin Saeed Almathami
Minister of State for Foreign Affairs: Dr Nizar bin Ubayd Madani
Secretary General of the Supreme Commission for Tourism and Antiquities: Prince Sultan bin Salman bin Abdul Aziz

Ministries
Office of the King and Prime Minister, Royal Diwan, Riyadh, Saudi Arabia. Tel: +966 (0)1 401 4576, e-mail: kfb@saudinf.com, URL: http://www.saudinf.com
Office of the Council of Ministers, PO Box 21433, Riyadh 11475, Saudi Arabia. Tel: +966 (0)1 488 2555

Ministry of Agriculture and Water, PO Box 2639, Riyadh 11195, Saudi Arabia. Tel: +966 (0)1 401 6666, fax: +966 (0)1 403 1415, email: infodc@agrwat.gov.sa, URL: http://www.agrwat.gov.sa
Ministry of Civil Service, Washem Street, PO Box 18367, Riyadh 11114, Saudi Arabia. Tel: +966 (0)1 402 6900, fax: +966 (0)1 403 4998, URL: http://www.mcs.gov.sa
Ministry of Commerce, P.O. Box 1774, Airport Road, Riyadh 11162, Saudi Arabia. Tel: +966 (0)1 401 2220, fax: +966 (0)1 403 8421, URL: http://www.commerce.gov.sa
Ministry of Communications, Airport Road, Riyadh 11178, Saudi Arabia. Tel: +966 (0)1 404 2928/ 3000, fax: +966 (0)1 403 1401
Ministry of Defence and Aviation, PO Box 26731, Airport Road, Riyadh 11165, Saudi Arabia. Tel: +966 (0)1 478 5900 / 477 7313, fax: +966 (0)1 401 1336, URL: http://www.pca.gov.sa
Ministry of Education, PO Box 3734, Riyadh 11481, Saudi Arabia. Tel: +966 (0)1 404 2888/2952, fax: +986 (0)1 401 2365, URL: http://www.moe.gov.sa
Ministry of Economy and Planning, PO Box 1358, University Street, Riyadh 11183, Saudi Arabia. Tel: +966 (0)1 401 3333, fax: +966 (0)1 402 9300, e-mail: info@planning.gov.sa, URL: http://www.planning.gov.sa
Ministry of Finance, Airport Road, Riyadh 11177, Saudi Arabia. Tel: +966 (0)1 405 0000, fax: +966 (0)1 405 9202, URL: http://www.mof.gov.sa
Ministry of Foreign Affairs, Nasseriya Street, Riyadh 11124, Saudi Arabia. Tel: +966 (0)1 406 7777, fax: +966 (0)1 403 0159, URL: http://www.mofa.gov.sa
Ministry of Health, Airport Road, Riyadh 11176, Saudi Arabia. Tel: +966 (0)1 401 2220/2392, fax: +966 (0)1 402 9876, URL: http://www.moh.gov.sa
Ministry of Higher Education, King Faisal Hospital Street, Riyadh 11153, Saudi Arabia. Tel: +966 (0)1 464 4444, fax: +966 (0)1 441 9004, URL: http://www.mohe.gov/sa
Ministry of Information, Nasseriya Street, Riyadh 11161, Saudi Arabia. Tel: +966 (0)1 401 4440/401 3440, fax: +966 (0)1 402 3570, email: sair@saudinf.com, URL: http://www.saudinf.com
Ministry of the Interior, P.O. Box 2933 Riyadh 11134, Saudi Arabia. Tel: +966 (0)1 401 1944, fax: +966 (0)1 403 1185
Ministry of Islamic, Endowments, Call and Guidance Affairs, King Abdul Aziz Street, Riyadh 11232, Saudi Arabia. Tel: +966 (0)1 473 0401, URL: http://www.islam.org.sa
Ministry of Justice, University Street, Riyadh 11137, Saudi Arabia. Tel: +966 (0)1 405 7777/405 5399, URL: http://www.moj.gov.sa
Ministry of Labour and Social Affairs, Omar Ibn Al-Khatab Street, Riyadh 11157, Saudi Arabia, Tel: +966 (0)1 477 1480/478 7166, fax: +966 (0)1 477 7336, URL: http://www.mol.gov.sa
Ministry of Municipal and Rural Affairs, Nasseriya Street, Riyadh 11136, Saudi Arabia. Tel: +966 (0)1 441 5434, e-mail: info@momra.gov.sa, URL: http://www.momra.gov.sa
Ministry of Petroleum and Mineral Resources, PO Box 757, Airport Road, Riyadh 11189, Saudi Arabia. Tel: +966 (0)1 478 1661/478 1133, fax: +966 (0)1 479 3596, email: karasham@aramco.com.sa, URL: http://www.mopm.gov.sa
Ministry of Pilgrimage, Omar Ibn Al-Khatab Street, Riyadh 11183, Saudi Arabia. Tel: +966 (0)1 402 2200, fax: +966 (0)1 402 2555, URL: http://www.hajinformation.com
Ministry of Water and Electricity, PO Box 5729, Omar bin al-Khatab Street, Riyadh 11127, Saudi Arabia. Tel: +966 (0)1 205 2981, fax: +966 (0)1 205 0557, URL: http://www.mow.gov.sa
Ministry of Culture and Information, PO Box 570, Nasseriya Street, Riyadh 11161, Saudi Arabia. Tel: +966 (0)1 401 4440, fax: +966 (0)1 402 3570, URL: http://www.saudinf.com
Ministry of Social Affairs, Omar bin al-Khatab Street, Riyadh 11157, Saudi Arabia. Tel: +966 (0)1 477 1480, fax: +966 (0)1 477 7336
Ministry of Transport, Airport Road, Riyadh 11178, Saudi Arabia. Tel: +966 (0)1 404 2928, fax: +966 (0)1 403 1401

Elections
Municipal elections were held on 29 September 2011. The municipal polls are the only public elections to take place in Saudi Arabia. More than 5,000 men are expected to compete in the elections to fill half the seats in local councils. The other half are appointed by the government. The next elections should take place in 2015 and King Abdullah has promised that women will have the right to vote and to run for office by that stage. They will be able to stand for election in the municipal elections as well as having the right to be appointed to the consultative Shura Council.

Diplomatic Representation
Royal Embassy of Saudi Arabia, 30 Charles Street, London W1X 8LP, United Kingdom. Tel: +44 (0)20 7917 3000, fax: +44 (0)20 7917 3330, URL: http://www.saudiembassy.org.uk
Ambassador: HRH Prince Mohammed bin Nawaf Al-Saud (page 1376)
Royal Embassy of Saudi Arabia, 601 New Hampshire Avenue, NW, Washington DC 20037, USA. Tel: +1 202 342 3800, fax: +1 202 944 5983, URL: http://www.saudiembassy.net
Ambassador: Adel A. Al-Jubeir (page 1375)
British Embassy, PO Box 94351, Riyadh 11693, Saudi Arabia. Tel: +966 (0)1 488 0077, fax: +966 (0)1 488 2373, URL: http://ukinsaudiarabia.fco.gov.uk
Ambassador: Sir John Jenkins (page 1449)
Embassy of the USA, Collector Road M, Riyadh Diplomatic Quarter or American Embassy, Unit 61307, Riyadh 11693, Saudi Arabia. Tel: +966 (0)1 488 3800, fax: +966 (0)1 488 7360, URL: http://riyadh.usembassy.gov
Ambassador: James B. Smith (page 1516)
Permanent Mission of Kingdom of Saudi Arabia To the United Nations, 809 UN Plaza 10th floor, New York, New York 10017, USA. Tel: +1 212 697-4830, URL: http://www.saudimission.org/
Ambassador: Abdallah bin Yahya al-Mouallimi

LEGAL SYSTEM

The law of the country is based on the religious law of Islam, and sentences are based on the Qur'an and the Sunnat of the Prophet Muhammed.

The Saudi court system is made up of three main parts. The Shaari'ah Courts hear most cases. These courts are organized into several categories: Courts of the First Instance (Summary and General Courts), Courts of Cassation; and the Supreme Judicial Council. In addition to the Shari'ah courts is the Board of Grievances whch hears cases that involve the government. The third part consists of various committees within government ministries that address specific disputes. Decisions can be appealed to the Office of the King or Crown Prince who acts as the final court of appeal and whose decision is final.

In October 2007, King Abdullah announced a series of reforms to its legal system, which will include the replacement of the Supreme Judicial Council with the creation of a supreme court, an appeals court and new general courts. Islamic law will remain at the heart of the system and the king will appoint the head of the Supreme Court. Reformers say the reforms will improve human rights, help modernise the country and limit the powers of the conservative clerics who lead the judiciary. As of 2013, not all the reforms have been implemented. In 2013 the King appointed a new head of the Supreme Court and named nine new judges. Reformers are hoping these moves will reinvigorate the reform process.

The rights of the citizens are limited. Saudis have no right to change their government. Corporal punishment is judicially sanctioned, and there is a lack of due process in the judicial system. Trials are not held in public. There are severe restrictions on religious freedom, as well as limitations on freedoms of speech, assembly and movement. The sponsorship system limits the rights of foreign workers. Saudi Arabia follows a strict interpretation of Islamic sharia law, which provides for the death penalty for murder, apostasy, rape, highway robbery, sabotage and armed robbery, as well as drug trafficking. Twenty-seven people were reported to have been executed in 2010 and over 80 in 2011.

Head of the Supreme Court: Sheikh Ghaihab al-Ghaihab
Secretary General, Supreme Judicial Council: Sheikh Salman bin Nashwan

LOCAL GOVERNMENT

There are 210 members in Provincial Councils of the 13 regions of Saudi Arabia. A Regional Governor, appointed by the King and a Vice-Governor act as chairman and vice-chairman of their Regional Council. Every council has a minimum of 10 private citizens and a committee system to deal with various local issues. Reports are submitted to the Ministry of the Interior and then passed to the appropriate government body.

Elections to half the 178 municipal councils were held for the first time in 2005, further municipal elections are yet to be held.

The 13 regions and the cities in which the council sits:
Riyadh Region: capital: Riyadh City
Makkah Region: capital: Holy City of Mecca
Madinah Region: capital: Holy City of Madinah
Qasim Region: capital: Buraidah City
Eastern Region: capital: Dammam City
Asir Region: capital: Abha City
Tabouk Region: capital: Tabouk City
Hail Region: capital: Hail City
Northern Border Region: capital: Ar'ar City
Jizan Region: capital: Jizan City
Najran Region: capital: Najran City
Al-Baha Region: capital: Al-Baha City
Al-Jouf Region: capital: Sikaka City

AREA AND POPULATION

Area
Saudi Arabia occupies most of the Arabian Peninsula. It borders Yemen, Oman, Qatar, and the UAE to the south, and Jordan, Iraq and Kuwait to the north. The Red Sea borders its west coast and the Persian Gulf its east coast. The total area of the country is about 2,253,000 sq. km or 865,000 sq. miles. The Kingdom is a plateau sloping eastward from a mountain range extending along its western edge.

The country is generally arid and barren. The only area with significant regular rainfall is the high mountain area in the south-west. The rest of the country is desert with areas of numerous but widely scattered oases in dry stream beds that flood on a few occasions every year. There are no rivers, no forests and only a few permanent pools or small lakes.

It is extremely hot in the summers, but can be cold at night in the desert. Nearer the coast temperatures are more moderate with high humidity.

To view a map, visit: http://www.un.org/Depts/Cartographic/map/profile/westasia.pdf

Population
The population in 2009 was estimated to be 27.45 million, up from the 2000 estimation of 22.1 million. This figure includes around 6 million non-nationals who are living in Saudi Arabia. Approximately 30 per cent of the population are under 15 years of age; the majority (approximately 66 per cent) of the population are between 15 and 60 years; only 4 per cent of the population are above 60. The median age was 26 years. The population average annual growth rate was estimated as 3.1 per cent over the period 2000-10. Net migration in Saudi Arabia is approximately -3.8 / 1,000.

Major cities are Riyadh, Jeddah, Mecca, Medina, Dammam, Jubayl, and Buraydah. Nomadic life is now the exception rather than the rule. The population of Riyadh is currently 4.5 million. This is expected to double by 2020. As of 2009, 82 per cent of the population lived in urban areas.

SAUDI ARABIA

The official language is Arabic, although English is widely spoken in the business world.

Births, Marriages and Deaths
The birth rate in the 2010 was 21.6 births per 1,000 of the population; the death rate was 4.4 deaths per 1,000 population. The total fertility rate in 2009 was 2.8 per female. Average life expectancy was 69 years for males and 75 years for females. Healthy life expectancy was 62 years. (Source: http://www.who.int, World Health Statistics 2012)

Public Holidays
September 23: Saudi National Day

There are two official holidays in the Islamic calendar.
Eid Al-Fitr: 25th day of Ramadan which lasts until the 5th day of the following month (starts 9 August 2013 / 29 July 2014)
Eid Al-Adha: the end of the Hajj (pilgrimage) which runs from the fifth to the fifteenth of the month Zul Hijjah. (15 October 2013 / 5 October 2014)

EMPLOYMENT

Recent figures show that less than half of the workforce are Saudi nationals. Approximately 12 per cent of people are employed by the government and over 70 per cent of these are Saudi nationals. Saudi Arabia has launched a privatisation plan to increase job opportunities for its growing young population and at the end of 2000 plans were announced for a training institute to be set up, which would provide vocational courses for the unemployed. Estimated figures for 2010 put the unemployment rate at 10.5 per cent.

Total Employment by Economic Activity

Occupation	2008
Agriculture, hunting, forestry & fishing	382,400
Mining & quarrying	107,688
Manufacturing	508,844
Electricity, gas & water supply	66,902
Construction	745,774
Wholesale & retail trade, repairs	1,257,941
Hotels & restaurants	279,128
Transport, storage & communications	361,909
Financial intermediation	86,003
Real estate, renting & business activities	313,469
Public admin. & defence; compulsory social security	1,502,913
Education	932,507
Health & social work	365,459
Other community, social & personal service activities	163,050
Households with employed persons	876,596
Extra-territorial organisations & bodies	6,277

Source: Copyright © International Labour Organization (ILO Dept. of Statistics, http://laborsta.ilo.org)

Due to population growth many young people entering the job market cannot find employment and recent unemployment figures have been put at 9 per cent although some unofficial estimates give a higher figure of 25 per cent. To combat this, companies employing more than 20 people must include a percentage of Saudi nationals. Culturally women are not encouraged to work and it is estimated that only five per cent of female graduates are in employment.

BANKING AND FINANCE

Currency
One Riyal: 100 halalahs

GDP/GNP, Inflation, National Debt
Saudi Arabia has the largest proven oil reserves in the world and is the largest exporter, It is the dominant member of OPEC. Large earnings from the oil industry over the last thirty years have enabled the government to spend heavily and build its infrastructure. The economy is heavily dependent on oil earnings and growth has recently been driven by high oil prices. A varied private sector has developed but remains susceptible to fluctuations in the oil prices. Saudi Arabia has continued to make economic reforms and some foreign investment, although not in the oil industry, is now permitted. Economic policy is based on a series of five yearly development plans, and is predicated on the drive to escape dependence on oil revenue as the main state income via the diversification of the non-industrial base.

Saudi Arabia has been hit by the global economic crisis. Falling demand for oil and lower oil prices mean that Saudi Arabia's economy will be adversely affected. Oil accounts for 75 per cent of government revenue, 45 per cent of GDP and 90 per cent of exports.

GDP was estimated to be US$585 billion in 2011 with a growth rate of 7 per cent. Per capita GDP was estimated tobe US$24,000. GDP was estimated to have grown by 6.8 per cent in 2012.

Inflation has been very low in recent years. In 2011, however it rose to over 5 per cent. It is forecast to fall slightly to 4.8 per cent in 2012 and 4.5 per cent in 2013.

Foreign Investment
The Saudi economy is currently undergoing some reforms including the opening up of some areas of investment to foreign companies, although not the oil industry. Saudi Arabia became a member of the World Trade Organisation in 2005.

Balance of Payments, Imports/Exports
As the Kingdom is so heavily dependent on oil for its revenues, its balance of payments is closely linked to fluctuations in the price of oil, hence the balance may vary considerably from year to year.

Crude oil and petroleum products remain the Kingdom's major exports. Main export partners are Asian countries, mainly Japan, and also the USA and the EU. Plastics are the second largest export commodity. Major imports include food, industrial goods, transportation equipment, textiles and metal. Major trading partners are Japan, the USA, the European Union, South Korea and Singapore.

Estimated figures for 2008 put earnings from merchandise exports at US$364 billion and merchandise imports at US$103 billion. Exports were estimated to be US$235 billion in 2010 and imports US$90 billion.

Central Bank
Saudi Arabian Monetary Agency, PO Box 2992, Riyadh 11169, Saudi Arabia. Tel: +966 1 4633000, fax: +966 1 4662936 / 1 4662966, URL: http://www.sama.gov.sa/sites/SAMAEN/Pages/Home.aspx
Governor: Dr. Fahad Al Mubarak

Chambers of Commerce
Council of Saudi Chambers of Commerce and Industry, URL: http://www.csc.org.sa/arabic/Pages/home.aspx/index.htm
Riyadh Chamber of Commerce and Industry, URL: http://www.riyadhchamber.com
Jeddah Chamber of Commerce and Industry, URL: http://www.jcci.org.sa

MANUFACTURING, MINING AND SERVICES

Primary and Extractive Industries
Saudi Arabia has the largest reserves of oil, and is the largest producer and exporter of oil in the world. The oil wells are situated on the Persian Gulf, and are worked mainly by Saudi Aramco, formerly the Arabian-American Oil Company, and the General Petroleum and Minerals Organization (Petromin). In recent years, Saudi Arabia has directed its energies away from the production of medium and heavy crudes in favour of lighter crudes such as Arab Super Light and Extra Light.

Proven oil reserves, as at 1 January 2012, were 267 billion barrels (25 per cent of the world's total). In 2011, including the Saudi-Kuwaiti Neutral Zone, the Kingdom produced approximately 11.1 million barrels of oil per day (of which 9.4 million barrels per day was crude oil) and exported 8.1 million barrels per day. As of 1 January 2012, the country had a crude oil refining capacity of 2.1 million barrels per day. Consumption was estimated at 2,986 thousand bbl/d.

There are also large reserves of natural gas; 276 trillion cubic feet in 2011. In 2011 Saudi Arabia produced 3,258 billion cubic feet and consumed 3,504 billion cubic feet were consumed. In 2001, Saudi Aramco discovered reserves of gas in the Almazaleej area, north of Riyadh. The new well produced 21.9 million cubic feet of gas per day. (Source: EIA)

Figures for 2009 showed that 57 per cent of crude oil exports went to the Far East, 14 per cent went to the USA, five per cent to the Mediterranean and four per cent to Europe That year 50 per cent of refined producrts went to the Far East, nine per cent to Europe and three per cent to the USA.

Mining is an important part of the diversification of the economy. Gold is being mined and other minerals have been found such as phosphates, iron ore, copper, lead, tin, bauxite and various other precious and non-precious metals. To improve their mining capability and so lessen economic dependence on oil, Saudi Arabia offers such incentives as 30 year extraction concessions and 5-10 year tax holidays for foreign investors in this field.

Saudi Arabian Oil Company (Saudi Aramco), URL: http://www.saudiaramco.com
Arab Petroleum Investments Corporation, URL: http://www.apicorp-arabia.com/html/cms

Energy
As of 2010, the country had an estimated electric generating capacity of 49 gigawatts, and produced 212 billion kWh per annum. It is estimated that domestic electricity demands have increased by 4 per cent every year. In 2006, consumption was 156 billion kWh. The electricity sector is controlled by four state-owned companies: Saudi Consolidated Company (SCECO) South, West, East and Central, the last of which has invited bids (as of July 1997) for the expansion by 300 MW of the 450 MW Al-Quassim power plant. In 2000 the possibility of privatising the electricity sector was under consideration. The government wants to double its capacity by 2020 to meet the needs of a growing population and increased industry. All electricity production in Saudi Arabia is thermal.

Manufacturing
In order to develop a non-oil industrial sector the government has concentrated on establishing industries which use petroleum and minerals. Cement and fertilizer are both produced Eight industrial cities have been built, such as Jubail (15 major plants and 30,000 workers), and Yanbu, although there are no Free Trade Zones. Products are sold on the international market or used to produce consumer goods. Recent figures show that Saudi Arabia has over 3,500 factories operating.

Tourism
Figures for 2006 show that Saudi Arabia had 8.6 million visitors; a large number of these were pilgrims to Mecca. The proposed railway line linking Mecca with the pilgrim destinations of Mina, Arafat and Muzdalifah should further increase tourist numbers.

Agriculture

Due to the desert nature of the country, there is not a great deal of agriculture in Saudi Arabia; wheat and barley are grown in the Nejd (central plateau), and there is some export of dates. In recent years Saudi Arabia has been able to export some of its wheat crop to more needy countries. The main agricultural occupation is raising and exporting camels, horses and sheep, as well as exporting hides and wool. Honey, clarified butter and fruit are also produced. Agricultural production has greatly increased in recent years with the demand for previously imported products, such as eggs and dairy products, being met locally. The infrastructure of roads, storage facilities and irrigation networks has been improved which had meant a large improvement in the agriculture sector. Estimated figures for 2011 showed that agriculture made up just two per cent of GDP and employed just over six per cent of the population.

Agricultural Production in 2010

Produce	Int. $'000*	Tonnes
Indigenous chicken meat	821,625	576,819
Dates	550,692	1,078,300
Cow milk, whole, fresh	521,142	1,670,000
Wheat	201,961	1,300,000
Tomatoes	181,012	489,800
Hen eggs, in shell	160,072	193,000
Indigenous sheep meat	127,972	47,000
Fruit fresh nes	125,652	360,000
Indigenous cattle meat	107,786	39,900
Vegetables fresh nes	95,200	505,200
Grapes	92,773	162,300
Indigenous camel meat	76,903	36,695

* unofficial figures

Source: http://faostat.fao.org/site/339/default.aspx Food and Agriculture Organization of the United Nations, Food and Agricultural commodities production

COMMUNICATIONS AND TRANSPORT

Travel Requirements

Citizens of the USA, Canada, Australia and the EU require a passport valid for six months at the time of entry, an onward/return ticket and a visa. Muslim pilgrims holding a Pilgrim Pass and entering the country via Jeddah or Medina do not require a passport. Transit passengers continuing their journey within 18 hours, holding valid onward or return documentation, not leaving the airport and making no further landing in Saudi Arabia do not require a visa. Other nationals should contact the embassy to check visa requirements.

Holders of passports with Israeli stamps in them may not be allowed to enter Saudi Arabia. Women and under-aged children should be accompanied by a close male family member. Unaccompanied women must be met at the airport by their husband or sponsor (there are restrictions on women travelling by car with men who are not related by blood or marriage, though it is acceptable for women visiting for business purposes to be accompanied and met at the airport by male business partner). An Exit Permit is required for most nationals; travellers should enquire at the nearest embassy for further information.

Visitors to Saudi Arabia should generally obtain a meningitis vaccination prior to arrival. As of June 2007, all travelers to and from the Kingdom carrying cash amounts, transferable monetary instruments, or precious metals exceeding 60,000 Saudi Riyals (or $16,000) are required to declare them to Saudi Customs.

National Airlines

Saudi Arabian Airlines, URL: http://www.saudiairlines.com
There are over 20 million passengers each year.

International Airports

Saudi Arabia has three International airports, King Khalid International Airport at Riyadh, King Abdul Aziz International Airport, which has a terminal specifically for pilgrims visiting Mecca and King Fahd International Airport. The King Khalid International Airport has a capacity of 15 million passengers per year and the King Fahd International Airport, 7 million. There are also 22 regional and local airports.
Presidency of Civil Aviation, off Palestine Road East, PO Box 887, Jeddah 21421, Saudi Arabia. Tel: +966 (0)2 667 9000

Railways

There is only one railway line, between Riyadh and the port of Dammam, and this is being extended to the industrial city of Jubail. In 2000 plans were announced to further extend the railway from the ports of Jeddah and Dammam via Riyadh, from Riyadh to Qasim, and from linking ports of Damman and Jubail. The possibility of privatising the railway system is also to be discussed. Development of the railway to link to Jordan and Syria is also under consideration. In 2009 a deal with China was announced to expand the railway network: the new railway will connect Mecca with various pilgrim destinations. A high speed link between Mecca and Medina is also planned. The link would cut travel time to 30 minutes compared to a four-hour road journey.

Recent figures show that 500,000 passengers use the existing railway annually and over 1.5 million tons of goods are carried.
Saudi Government Railway Organization, URL: http://www.saudirailways.org

Roads

Recent figures show that there are 47,000 km of primary roads and 108,000 km of secondary roads, all of which are the responsibility of the Saudi Arabian Public Transport Company. In recent years there has been much investment in the road system so that it reaches even isolated villages. Vehicles are driven on the right, women are not permitted to drive.

Saudi Arabian Public Transport Company, PO Box 10667, Riyadh 11443, Saudi Arabia. Tel: +966 (0)1 454 5000, fax: +966 (0)1 454 0086 / 2100

Ports and Harbours

The Jeddah Islamic Port is the main commercial port and the main entry point for pilgrims to Mecca and Madinah. In 2000 it handled 18,120,000 tons of cargo. The King Abdul Aziz Port handled 11,379,000 tons of cargo in 2000.
Saudi Ports Authority, URL: http://www.ports.gov.sa

The other main ports are Jizan, which handled 1,192,000 tons of cargo in 2000; Jubail, which handled 1,595,000 tons of cargo in 2000; and Yanbu, which handled 1,970,000 tons of cargo in 2000. The newest port is Dhiba situated at the north end of the Red Sea and is the country's nearest port to the Suez Canal. In 2000 it handled 521,000 tons of cargo.

HEALTH

During the last two decades the Kingdom of Saudi Arabia has made great progress in the national health care sector. Hospitals have been greatly expanded in various cities and other locations, either by the Ministry of Health or by other official departments such as the Armed Forces, National Guard, Internal Security Forces, the universities, the Ministry of Education and the General Presidency for Youth Welfare. Most of the hospitals and primary health care centres provide free medical treatment. The Ministry of Health provides more than 60 per cent of health services and the private sector approximately 30 per cent. Medication is subsidised by the government. Saudi Arabia also conducts advanced medical research.

In 2009, the government spent approximately 6.4 per cent of its total budget on healthcare (down from 9.2 per cent in 2000), accounting for 62.4 per cent of all healthcare spending. Private expenditure accounted for 37.6 per cent of total health care expenditure. Total expenditure on healthcare equated to 4.4 per cent of the country's GDP. Per capita expenditure on health was approximately US$608, compared with US$400 in 2000. According to the latest WHO figures in the period 2005-10 there are 24,802 doctors (9.4 per 10,000 population), 55,429 nurses and midwives, 1,529 pharmacists (0.6 per 10,000 population), and 6,049 dentists (2 per 10,000 population). There are over 3,500 medical centres. Saudi Arabia is a member of the Red Crescent Society.

The infant mortality rate (probability of dying by age 1) in 2010 was 15 per 1,000 live births and the under-five mortality rate was 18 per 1,000 live births. The main causes of death were 30 per cent prematurity, congenital anomalies 23 per cent, pneumonia 7 per cent, and diarrhoea 2 per cent. (Source: http://www.who.int, World Health Statistics 2012)

EDUCATION

Education is free and available to all, although it is not compulsory. There are eight universities, 94 colleges and 22,000 schools. General education consists of kindergarten, six years at primary school and three years at both intermediate and high school. Pupils may attend high school or vocational schools. Figures from 2007, 11 per cent of young children were enrolled in pre-primary school, 84 per cent of girls and 85 per cent of boys were enrolled in primary school and 76 per cent of girls and 70 per cent of boys were enrolled in secondary school.

Degree courses are available in most fields and there were approximately 200,000 students in 1996 compared with 7,000 in 1970.

The Kingdom has recognised the importance of vocational training to aid plans for economic and social development. The General Organisation for Technical Education and Vocational Training operate training programmes in health care, agriculture and teaching all over the country.

In 2004, 27.6 per cent of government spending went on education.US$13.17 billion was allocated in the 2000 budget for development of education including vocational training.

In 2004 the Ministry of Education announced the Ministry of Education Ten Year Plan, which was set to run from 2004-2014, included in the plan was a review of the education for female students and the development of special needs education.

RELIGION

Islam is the official and virtually single religion. Mecca (*Makkah*), a city in the west, is the spiritual centre of the Islamic world. One of the five pillars of Islam is that Muslims must, if possible, make a pilgrimage to Mecca. The pilgrimage is called the Hajj. On average around 2 million pilgrims travel to Saudi Arabia for the Hajj each year.

Saudi Arabia has a religious liberty rating of 1 on a scale of 1 to 10 (10 is most freedom). (Source: World Religion Database)

The principles and social customs of Islam are strictly observed and influence all aspects of life.

Custodian of the Two Holy Mosques: HRH King Abdullah Bin Abdul Aziz Al-Saud (page 1376)

COMMUNICATIONS AND MEDIA

The media is very strictly controlled by the government and criticism of the government and the royal family, and questioning of religious principles is not tolerated. However in recent years some reporting has been more open with coverage of militant attacks. New restrictive media laws, covering print and online media, were introduced in April 2011.

Newspapers

Newspapers are created by royal decree. There are numerous dailies and magazines. Many are subject to censorship. The government blocks access to websites it considers offensive.
Al-Riyadh, URL: http://www.alriyadh.com
Al-Watan, URL: http://www.alwatan.com.sa/
Al-Jazirah, URL: http://www.al-jazirah.com/
Arab News, URL: http://www.arabnews.com (English language)
Saudi Gazette, URL: http://www.saudigazette.com.sa (English language)

Broadcasting

The Broadcasting Service of the Kingdom of Saudi Arabia (BSKSA), Mecca, is responsbile for all broadcasting. It operates four TV networks, several medium and short-wave stations and broadcasts programmes in Arabic, English, French, Urdu, Indonesian, and Swahili languages. There are six television stations located at Jeddah, Riyadh, Medina, Kassim, Dammam and Abha. Private TV stations cannot operate in Saudi Arabia but there are several pan-Arab statellite and pay-TV broadcasters. In the eastern part of the country, viewers can pick up television stations from neighbouring countries.
Broadcasting Service of the Kingdom of Saudi Arabia (BSKSA), URL: http://www.saudinf.com

Telecommunications

Recent figures show that there are some 4 million telephone lines. Figures for 2007 estimated that over 36 million mobile phones were in use.

The internet became available in Saudi Arabia in 1999. The government has a security system in place which prevents access to websites which it considers offensive. Figures from 2009 estimate that over 9 million people are regular internet users, of whom over 66 per cent were believed to be women.

ENVIRONMENT

Environmental concerns include desertification and limited water supply.

Urban, industrial and agricultural growth in recent years has put a greater strain on the already limited water supply. The National Water Plan co-ordinates supply and distribution, and includes desalination projects, the use of wells and reservoirs. Urban water is treated and recycled, and targets are set to limit total consumption. Desalination projects are co-ordinated by the General Organisation of Sea Water Desalination. Saudi Arabia is now able to produce enough potable water to meet the needs of people on the east and west coasts, and can now cover inland areas including Riyadh and Madinah, enabling subterranean water supplies to be used for agriculture. In the last 25 years, over 160 dams have been built. The most significant are: Wadi Najran with a storage of 85 million cubic metres; Wadi Jizan with a capacity of 75 million cubic metres; and Wadi Fatima with a storage of 20 million cubic metres.

Saudi Arabia is a party to the following international agreements: Biodiversity, Climate Change, Climate Change-Kyoto Protocol, Desertification, Endangered Species, Hazardous Wastes, Law of the Sea, Marine Dumping, Ozone Layer Protection, and Ship Pollution.

According to figures from the EIA, in 2010 Saudi Arabia's emissions from the consumption and flaring of fossil fuels totalled 478.41 million metric tons of carbon dioxide.

SPACE PROGRAMME

In September 2000 a Russian rocket launched from Kazakhstan put Saudi Arabia's first two satellites into orbit. Twelve satellites have been launched to date.
National Space Research Institute, URL: http://www.kacst.edu.sa

SENEGAL

Republic of Senegal

République du Sénégal

Capital: Dakar (Population estimate, 2011: 2.77 million)

Head of State: Macky Sall (President) (page 1507)

National Flag: On pale-wise tricolour of, green, yellow and red. A five-pointed green star is centred on the yellow

CONSTITUTION AND GOVERNMENT

Constitution

After three centuries of French colonial rule, Sénégal became an independent republic in 1960 and Léopold Senghor was elected the country's first president.

Senghor's steadily increased political power allowed him in 1962 to remove the prime minister, Mamadou Dia, and revise the constitution. His party, the Union Progressiste Sénégalese (UPS) won the 1963 National Assembly elections and by 1966 Senegal was effectively a one-party state.

There were some constitutional changes in 1968, and in 1970 Abdou Diouf was appointed to the revived post of prime minister. A gradual return to a multi-party system was reversed when, in the 1978 elections, Senghor returned as president and his renamed party, the Parti Socialiste (PS), returned to power.

Sénégal is a presidential republic, with an elected National Assembly. The Senate was abolished in 2001, but reintroduced in 2007 before being abolished again in 2012. The President is permitted to stand for two terms of 5 years, although President Wade did one term of 7 years from 2000 to 2007, in line with constitutional provision in 2000. A referendum was held in 2001 to change the constitution, to increase the powers of the prime minister, reduce the presidency from seven years to five years and to limit the presidency to two five-year terms. However, amendments in 2008 increased once more the presidential term to seven years.

To consult the constitution, please visit: http://www.gouv.sn/spip.php?rubrique17.

International Relations

Senegal pursues an active foreign policy and aims to represent Africa on the UN Security Council. France is its main European ally. Senegal also cultivates closer links with the US.

Senegal has a prominent role in Africa. President Wade played an important role in creating and promoting the NEPAD regeneration plan adopted by the African Union in 2001. Although he has criticised it for not doing enough, he remains a key supporter of the project. Senegal has contributed troops to international peacekeeping operations, including in Liberia, DR Congo, Darfur and Cote d'Ivoire.

There have been disputes with Gambia over cross-border access. A meeting took place between the two heads of state in 2003 aimed at resolving some of these issues. Relations with Guinea-Bissau have improved since the death of the Casamance leader Ansumane Mane in 1999.

Recent Events

In October 2003, Jean-Marie Francois Biagui, Secretary General of the MFDC, announced that the 21-year-old secession war in Casamance was at an end. The conflict caused hundreds of deaths and thousands of refugees. An amnesty for political prisoners was announced in June 2004.

In 2006, Sénégal and Spain agreed to jointly patrol the Senegalese coast to curb the exodus of illegal migrants heading for Europe, and in December the two countries agreed a series of measures to curb illegal migration to the Canary Islands. Spain agreed to give 4,000 Senegalese temporary work permits over two years. In September 2007, the Spanish authorities launched a television campaign in Sénégal to discourage illegal migration.

In November 2007, the enforcement of a new policy to clear vendors off the streets of Dakar led to a riot and around 200 arrests; thousands of people earn a living from peddling goods. Dakar officials quickly offered concessions to the vendors, including the provision of market areas and reopening some streets for roadside sales.

The Senegalese army launched an offensive against rebels in the southern Casamance region in 2008, when 16 villagers had their left ears cut off; the MFDC rebel group, waging a renewed separatist campaign in the region, denied carrying out the mutilations. The cashew-nut harvest time has regularly seen an upsurge in violence and armed attacks; cashew nuts are one of the area's main cash crops.

In 2009 the National Assembly amended the constitution to allow the trial of the former president, Hissene Habre, for human rights abuses committed during his term of office. The ICC later started proceedings to try to bring him to trial.

In September 2012, MPs voted to abolish the Senate and the post of vice president in an effort to save money for flood relief.

In April 2013, Karim Wade, the son of the former president Abdoulae Wade, was charged with corruption over his time as a minister during his father's rule.

Casamance Separatism

Opposition to the government erupted in the southern province of Casamance, where a separatist movement was involved in serious clashes with police in 1982 and 1983. In 1992 a commission was established to try to resolve the situation but the armed Mouvement des Forces Démocratiques de la Casamance (MFDC) continued to disrupt the region and many people fled across the border to Guinea-Bissau. Much of the apparently rebel activity is little more than banditry. A framework peace agreement was signed in December 2004, but its implementation has not been complete due to splits within the MFDC. One faction opposed to the agreement was involved in 2006 in armed clashes with the Senegalese army. On 14

January 2007 the historic leader of the MFDC Fr Augustin Diamacoune Senghor died in a hospital in Paris. Low-level rebellion continues to simmer in Casamance; the region's people claim that they are still marginalised by the Wolof, Senegal's main ethnic group.

Legislature

Under the constitution changes in 2001 the legislature became unicameral following the abolition of the Senate. The National Assembly has 150 members directly elected for a five year term, of whom 90 members are directly elected and 60 by proportional representation.
National Assembly, Assemblée Nationale, B.P. 86, Dakar, Senegal. Tel: +2218231 099, fax: +221 8239 402, URL: http://www.assemblee-nationale.sn/

Cabinet (as at June 2013)

Prime Minister: Abdoul Mbaye (page 1473)
Minister for Foreign Affairs and Senegalese Abroad: Mankeur Ndiaye (page 1485)
Minister for Interior: Pathé Seck
Minister for Economy and Finance: Amadou Kane (page 1453)
Minister for Justice and Keeper of the Seals: Aminata Touré (page 1527)
Minister for Environment and Sustainable Development: Haidar Ali
Minister of Tourism and Leisure: Youssou Ndour
Minister of Culture: Abdou Aziz Mbaye
Minister for Energy and Mines: Aly Ngouille Ndiaye (page 1484)
Minister of Livestock: Aminata Mbenque Ndiaye
Minister of Water and Sanitation: Oumar Gueye
Minister of Agriculture and Rural Equipment: Abdoulaye Baldé
Minister of Education: Serigne Mbaye Thiam
Minister of Health and Social Action: Eva Marie Coll Seck
Minister of Fisheries and Maritime Affairs: Pape Diouf
Minister of Infrastructure and Transport: Thierno Alassane Sall
Minister of the Armed Forces: Augustin Tine (page 1526)
Minister of Women, Children and Women Entrepreneurs: Mariama Sarr
Minister of Land Management and Local Government: Mme Arame Ndoye
Minister of Commerce, Industry and Handicrafts: Alioune Sarr
Minister of Promotion of Good Governance, Government Spokesperson: Abdou Latif Coulibaly
Minister of Higher Education and Research: Mary Teuw Niane
Minister of Youth, Employment & Civic Values: Benoit Sambou
Minister of Urban Development and Housing: Khoudia Mbaye
Minister of Communication and Information Technologies: Mamadou Abiboulaye Dieye
Minister of Public Service, Labour and Relations with Institutions: Mansour Sy
Minister of Sport: Mbagnick Ndiaye
Minister of Professional Trainin &, Apprenticeships: Mamadou Talla
Minister of Restructuring: Khadim Diop
Minister Delegate for the Budget: Abdoulaye Diallo Daouda
Minister Delegate for Senegalese Abroad: Mme Seynabou Gaye Toure

Ministries

Government portal: http://www.gouv.sn
Office of the President, Immeuble Administratif, ave Léopold Sédar Senghor, BP 168, Dakar, Senegal. Tel: +221 33 823 1088, fax: +221 33 821 8660, URL: http://www.gouv.sn/institutions/president.html.
Office of the Prime Minister, Immeuble Administratif, ave Léopold Sédar Senghor, BP 4029, Dakar, Senegal. Tel: +221 33 823 1088, fax: +221 33 822 5578, URL: http://www.primature.sn
Ministry of Agriculture, Immeuble Administratif, 3e étage, BP 4005, Dakar, Senegal. Tel: +221 33 849 7312, fax: +221 33 823 32 68, e-mail: agric@agric.gouv.sn, URL: http://www.agriculture.gouv.sn
Ministry of the Armed Forces, Immeuble Administratif, 8e étage, BP 4041, Dakar, Senegal. Tel: +221 33 849 7612, fax: +221 33 823 6338, URL: http://www.forcesarmees.gouv.sn
Ministry of the Civil Service and Employment, Immeuble Administratif, 1er étage, BP 4007, Dakar, Senegal. Tel: +221 33 849 7000, fax: +221 33 823 7429, URL: http://www.fonctionpublique.gouv.sn
Ministry of Commerce, Immeuble Administratif, 5e étage, Dakar, Senegal. Tel: +221 33 822 9542, fax: +221 33 822 4669, URL: http://www.commerce.gouv.sn
Ministry of Communication and Telecommunications, 58 Bd de la République, BP 4027, Dakar, Senegal. Tel: +221 33 823 1065, fax: +221 33 821 4504, URL: http://www.information.gouv.sn
Ministr**y of Culture and Leisure,** Immeuble Administratif, 3e étage, BP 4001, Dakar, Senegal. Tel: +221 33 849 7311, fax: +221 33 822 16 38, URL: http://www.culture.gouv.sn
Ministry of Fisheries and Maritime Affairs, Immeuble Administratif, Dakar, Senegal. Tel: +33 889 1721, URL: http://www.gouv.sn
Ministry of the Environment & Protection of Nature, Immeuble Administratif, 2e étage, BP 4055, Dakar, Senegal. Tel: +221 33 889 0234, fax: +221 33 822 2180, URL: http://www.environnement.gouv.sn
Ministry of Women's, Children & Women Entrepreneurship, Immeuble Administratif, 6e étage, BP 4050, Dakar, Senegal. Tel: +221 33 849 7061, fax: +221 33 822 9490, URL: http://www.famille.gouv.sn
Ministry of Finance and Economy, rue René Ndiaye, BP 4017, Dakar, Senegal. Tel: +221 33 889 2100, fax: +221 33 822 41 95, e-mail: i_diouf@minfinance.sn, URL: http://www.finances.gouv.sn
Ministr**y of Foreign Affairs,** 1 place de l'Indépendance, BP 4044, Dakar, Senegal. Tel: +221 33 889 1300, fax: +221 33 823 54 96, URL: http://www.diplomatie.gouv.sn
Ministry of Health, Fann Résidence, Rue Aimé Césaire, BP 4024, Dakar, Senegal. Tel: +221 33 869 7701, fax: +221 33 869 7717, URL: http://www.sante.gouv.sn
Ministry of Water & Sanitation, Blvd Dail Diop, BP 2372, Dakar, Senegal. Tel: +221 33 823 9127, fax: +221 33 823 6245, URL: http://www.habitat.gouv.sn
Ministry of Information Technology and Communication, 58 Boulevard de la Republique, BP 4027, Dakar, Senegal. Tel: +221 33 823 1065, fax: +221 33 821 4504, URL: http://www.gouv.sn

Ministry of the Interior, Place Washington, Blvd. de la République, BP 4002, Dakar, Senegal. Tel: +221 33 889 9100, fax:+221 33 821 0542, URL: http://www.interieur.gouv.sn
Ministry of Justice, Immeuble Administratif, 7e étage, BP 4030, Dakar, Senegal. Tel: +221 33 823 5024, fax: +221 33 823 2727, e-mail: justice@justice.gouv.sn, URL: http://www.justice.gouv.sn
Ministry of Public Service, Labour and Professional Organizations, Building LAM Yoro, 60 Avenue Georges Pompidou, Dakar, Senegal. URL: http://www.fonctionpublique.gouv.sn/
Ministry of Livestock, VDN, Bd du Kuwait, PO Box 45 677, Dakar Fann, Senegal. Tel: +221 33 849 5073, fax: +221 33 864 6311, URL: http://www.gouv.sn
Ministry of Energy & Mines, avenue André Peytavin 122 bis, BP 4037, Dakar, Senegal. Tel: +221 33 889 5757, fax: +221 33 822 554, URL: http://www.industrie.gouv.sn
Ministry of Education, 56 Avenue Lamine Gueye, BP 4025, Dakar, Senegal. Tel: +221 33 849 5402, fax: +221 33 821 8930, URL: http://www.education.gouv.sn
Ministry of Public Health and Local Environment, Place de l'Independence, rue Amadou Assane Ndoye X Ferraud Beranger, 5th Floor, Dakar, Senegal. Tel: +221 33 889 1724, URL: fttp://www.gouv.sn
Ministry of Relations with Institutions, Blvd de la République 58, BP 4027, Dakar, Senegal. Tel: +221 33 823 1065, fax: +221 33 821 4504, URL: http://www.information.gouv.sn
Ministry of Infrastructure and Transport, Administrative Building, 6th Floor, Dakar, Senegal. Tel: +221 33 849 7000, fax: +221 33 842 0292, URL: http://www.gouv.sn
Ministry of Scientific Research, Higher Education and Universities, Administrative Building, 5th Floor Aile droite, PO Box 36005, Dakar, Senegal. Tel: +221 33 849 7552, fax: +221 33 822 4563, URL: http://www.gouv.sn
Ministry of Senegalese Abroad, Administrative Building, 7e étage, Dakar, Senegal. Tel: +221 33 849 7688, fax: +221 33 821 8060, URL: http://www.senex.gouv.sn
Ministry of Social Action and National Solidarity, Immeuble Administratif, Dakar, Senegal. Tel: +221 33 889 5208, URL: http://www.gouv.sn
Ministry of Sport, Immeuble Administratif, Point E, Dakar, Senegal. Tel: +221 33 869 1601, fax: +221 33 822 9764, URL: http://www.sports.gouv.sn
Ministry of Technical and Professional Education, bloc 23 rue Calmette 23, Dakar, Senegal. Tel: +221 33 822 6099, fax: +221 33 821 7196, URL: http://www.education.gouv.sn
Ministry of Urban Development and Housing, 54 Avenue Georges Pompidou X Raffenel, Plaza Building 1st floor, Dakar, Senegal. Tel: +221 33 849 0730, URL: http://www.gouv.sn
Ministry of Youth, URL: http://www.jeunesse.gouv.sn/

Elections

Senegal went to the polls on 25 March 2007 to elect a president. The incumbent President Abdoulaye Wade won re-election for a second term, winning 55.86 per cent of the votes. The former Prime Minister, Idrissa Seck, polled 14.93 per cent and Socialist Party leader Ousmane Tanor Dieng won 13.57 per cent of the vote. Opposition parties said they had evidence of fraud but observers from the Economic Community of West African States said the voting was free and fair.

The most recent presidential election took place on 26 February 2012. The incumbent president, Abdoulaye Wade, took 35 per cent of the vote and faced the former prime minister Macky Sall in the second round of the election on 18 March. Mr Sall defeated Mr Wade in the second round. Mr Sall was a former associate of President Wade who broke away to form his own opposition party.

Elections to the National Assembly, postponed since February 2007, were held on 3 June 2007. The Sopi coalition, led by the PDS, retained its majority. Macky Sall, prime minister since 2004, resigned after the elections and was replaced by Cheikh Hadjibou Soumare at the head of a reshuffled and restructured government. Elections to the newly established Senate took place on 19th August 2007; the PDS won all but one seat.

The most recent parliamentary elections took place on 1 July 2012; President Sall's United in Hope party won a landslide victory winning 119 of the 150 seats. Following a change to the law regarding gender equality, 64 of the new MPs are women.

Political Parties

Sénégal has over 60 political parties, the main ones being:
Parti Socialiste du Sénégal (PS), URL: http://www.ps-senegal.com/
Alliance for the Republic, UTL: http://www.apr.sn
Democratic Party of Senegal (PDS), URL: http://www.pds.sn/
Alliance des Forces de Progrès (AFP), URL: http://www.afp-senegal.org/
Bes du Nakk; Bokk Gis Gis; United to Boost Senegal

Diplomatic Representation

US Embassy, B.P.49, Avenue Jean XXIII, Dakar (PO Box 49), Senegal. Tel: +221 823 4296 fax: +221 822 2991, URL: http://dakar.usembassy.gov/
Ambassador: Lewis Lukens
Embassy of Senegal 2112 Wyoming Avenue, NW. Washington DC, 20008 USA. Tel:+1 202 234 0540, fax: +1 202 332 6315, URL: http://www.ambasenegal-us.org
Ambassador: H.E. Cheikh Niang
Embassy of Senegal 39 Marloes Road, London W8 6LA. UK. Tel: +44 (0)20 7937 7237 fax: +44 (0)20 7938 2546, e-mail: mail@senegalembassy.co.uk, URL: http://www.senegalembassy.com
Ambassador: Mr Abdou Sourang
British Embassy, 20 rue du Docteur Guillet, BP 6025, Dakar, Senegal. +221 33 823 7392, URL: http://ukinsenegal.fco.gov.uk/en/
Ambassador: Robert Marshall
Permanent Representative of the Republic of Senegal to the United Nations, 238 East 68th Street, New York, NY 10021, USA. Tel: +1 212 517 9030 / 9031 / 9032, fax: +1 212 517 3032, e-mail: senegal.mission@yahoo.fr, URL: http://www.un.int/wcm/content/site/senegal
Ambassador: Mr Abdou Salem Diallo

SENEGAL

LEGAL SYSTEM

The constitution declares the independence of the judiciary. The legal system of Senegal is based on the French Civil Law System. Judges are appointed by the president.

The highest court is the 'Cour de Cassation' (Court of Final Appeal). Petty offenses are dealt with by justices of the peace in each department; ranked next in the judicial system are courts of first instance in each region. There are assize courts in Dakar, Kaolack, Saint-Louis, and Ziguinchor and a Court of Appeal in Dakar.

There is also a Constitutional Court and Council of State Court for Administrative Questions. A 16-member High Court of Justice, elected by the National Assembly from among its own members, presides over impeachment proceedings, and a Court of State Security deals with political offenses. There is also a military court system and a special court for the repression of the unlawful accumulation of wealth. Muslims have the right to choose customary law or civil law for cases involving family inheritance.

The government respects the rights of its citizens, but problems such as overcrowded prisons, prolonged pretrial detention and mistreatment of detainees persist. Corruption and official impunity continue, and there are limits on freedoms of speech, press, and assembly. Senegal abolished the death penalty for all crimes in 2004.

A joint session of the National Assembly and the Senate voted in July 2008 to approve a bill empowering Senegalese courts to try people for crimes committed in other countries and for crimes that were committed more than ten years beforehand; this made it constitutionally possible to try Chad's ex-leader Hissene Habré, who is accused of ordering 40,000 political killings in the eight years he was in power. Habré has been in exile for 22 years in Senegal. A special court, the Extraordinary African Chambers, was inaugurated in February 2013 for the case. The pre-trial phase is expected to last for over a year, followed potentially by a trial in 2014.

Senegalese Committee for Human Rights, URL: http://www.csdh.sn/

LOCAL GOVERNMENT

For local administration the country is divided into 14 regions: Dakar, Diourbel, Fatick, Kaffrine, Kaolack, Kedougou, Kolda, Louga, Matam, Saint-Louis, Sedhiou, Tambacounda, Thies and Ziguinchor. The regions are then divided into 34 departments and 94 districts. Each of the regions is headed by a regional councillor.

Local elections took place most recently in March 2009. Opposition parties gained control of several major cities including Dakar.

AREA AND POPULATION

Area
Senegal is situated on the West African coast, surrounded by Guinea-Bissau and Guinea to the south, Mali to the east and Mauritania to the north. Apart from a small stretch of the Atlantic coast, Senegalese territory completely surrounds the neighbouring state of the Gambia. The area below the Gambia is known as Casamance, until recently the site of violent struggle.

The area of the country is 197,161 square km. Senegal's principal towns are Dakar, Thies, Kaolack, Saint Louis, Ziguinchor, Diourbel and Tambacounda. The River Senegal (1,750 km) is the longest river followed by the River Gambia (750 km) and Casamance River (350 km). The north of the country is dry and suffers from increasing desertification. The Casamance region has a rainy season that lasts around 4-5 months.

To view a map, visit http://www.un.org/Depts/Cartographic/map/profile/senegal.pdf

Population
The population in 2010 was estimated at 12.434 million. The capital, Dakar, has a population of around 2.7 million. The average annual population growth rate was 2.7 per cent for the period 2000-10. Forty-two per cent of the population lives in urban areas. The Senagalese are made up of various ethnic groups, the main ones being Wolof 35 per cent, Fulani nearly 18 per cent, Serer 16 per cent and others including Mandingo, Jola and Sarakole. The official language is French, though local languages including Wolof, Mandinka and Pular are also spoken.

Births, Marriages, Deaths
Figures for 2010 put the birth rate at 37.4 per thousand inhabitants and the death rate at 7.7 per thousand people. Life expectancy at birth in 2009 was 60 years for men and 63 years for women. Healthy life expectancy was 51 years. The median age was 18 years. Approximately 44 per cent of the population was under 15 years old and 4 per cent over 60 years. The total fertility rate in 2010 was 4.8 children per woman. The infant mortality rate in 2010 was 50 deaths per 1,000 live births. (Source: http://www.who.int, World Health Statistics 2012)

Public Holidays 2014
1 January: New Year's Day
14 January: Birth of the Prophet
4 April: Independence Day
21 March: Easter Monday
5 May: May Day
29 May: Ascension
9 July: Beginning of Ramadan
29 July: Eid al Fitr
5 October: Eid ad-Adha
25 October: Islamic New Year
3 November: Ashura
25 December: Christmas Day

EMPLOYMENT

The workforce was estimated to number 4.9 million in 2008. Agriculture is the largest employer accounting for around 77 per cent, largely subsistence farming or cash crops. 200,000 people are employed in the fishing industry. Over half the population lives below the poverty line. Figures for 2007 estimated the unemployment rate to be as high as 48 per cent.

Total Employment by Economic Activity

Occupation	2006
Agriculture, hunting & forestry	986,937
Fishing	76,872
Mining & quarrying	14,142
Manufacturing	245,374
Electricity, gas & water supply	21,807
Construction	186,590
Wholesale & retail trade, repairs	785,886
Hotels & restaurants	28,580
Transport, storage & communications	141,702
Financial intermediation	16,700
Real estate, renting & business activities, public admin. & defence; compulsory social security, education, health & social work	157,720
Extra-territorial organisations & bodies	7,049
Other	483,985
Total	3,152,937

Source: Copyright © International Labour Organization (ILO Dept. of Statistics, http://laborsta.ilo.org)

BANKING AND FINANCE

Currency
The unit of currency is the CFA franc.

GDP/GNP, Inflation, National Debt
The economy of Senegal is predominantly rural, and as such is vulnerable to changes in weather conditions and fluctuations in commodity prices; a good rainy season in 2005 helped the agricultural sector recover from a locust invasion the previous year. Several key sectors, such as groundnut oil and fertilizer production suffer from management problems and stiff competition from imports. There has recently been much investment in the infrastructure including the development of a second international airport (currently due to open in 2014) and in roads. A bridge between Senegal and Gambia is also planned. Tourism and remittances from abroad make a significant contribution to the economy. Remittances in 2010 amounted to US$1.4 billion. Senegal depends heavily on foreign assistance; in 2007, foreign aid amounted to 23 per cent of government spending.

The economy has had a period of growth. Figures for 2009 put GDP at US$12.5 billion. In 2010 the growth rate was recorded at 3.8 per cent and per capita GDP was put at US$1,900 in 2010. GDP was estimated to be US$14.5 billion in 2012. The service sector contributes around 64 per cent of GDP. Industry contributes almost 20 per cent and agriculture 17 per cent. Inflation was estimated to be 1.5 per cent in 2011.

2011 figures put Senegal's external debt at US$4 billion.

Foreign Investment
The government is trying to increase foreign investment in the country. There are no restrictions on the repatriation or transfer of capital or income earned.

Foreign aid of some US$700 million per annum comes mainly from France, the EU, Germany, US, Japan, China and the Middle East. In 2006 Senegal received US$86 million in debt relief from Heavily Indebted Poor Countries initiatives, but in the same year, Senegal's IMF negotiated Poverty Reduction and Growth facility loan package expired. Senegal has now negotiated a financial monitoring arrangement with the IMF which provides technical support for its domestic poverty reduction programme.

Balance of Payments / Imports and Exports
Senegal's major trading partners are France, Italy, the Netherlands, Germany, Spain, Côte d'Ivoire, Mali, Benin, Nigeria, Cameroon, Congo, USA, India, Japan and the UK. Imports cost the country US$5 billion in 2011, the main imported goods being food, consumer products, machinery, petroleum and transport equipment. Export revenues reached US$2.4 billion and the main export commodities were fish, peanut and phosphate products.

Central Bank
Banque Centrale des États de l'Afrique de l'Ouest, PO Box 3108, Avenue Abdoulaye Fadiga, Dakar, Senegal. Tel: +221 8 390500, fax: +221 8 239335, e-mail: webmaster@bceao.int, URL: http://www.bceao.int
Governor: Tiémoko Meyliet Kone

Chambers of Commerce and Trade Organisations
Chambre de Commerce, d'Industrie et d'Agriculture de Dakar, URL: http://www.cciad.sn/

MANUFACTURING, MINING AND SERVICES

Primary and Extractive Industries

Phosphates are mined near Thiès and at one time phosphates were the third main export earner and employed over 2,000 people. There are plans to exploit deposits of iron ore at Falémé. Petroleum and natural gas have been discovered offshore. Wells have been drilled in the offshore Dome Flore block estimated to contain 800 million barrels of heavy oil.

In 2011, oil production had not yet started, and oil consumption stood at an estimated 43,000 barrels per day. Senegal has the capacity to refine 25,000 bbl/d of crude oil per day.

In 2011, 1 billion cubic feet of natural gas were produced and consumed, and in 2010 345,000 short tons of coal were imported and consumed.

Recently gold has begun to be mined at the Sabodala mine, which has proven gold reserves of over 2.5 million tons of ore. There are also deposits of titanium.

Energy

Electricity production is fairly well-developed in response to industrial demand. Present capacity is about 300 MW, all thermally generated. Thermal generation is being expanded with the aid of French and World Bank funds. In 2009, total energy consumption was 0.091 quadrillion Btu and production was 0.004 quadrilliom Btu. An estimated 80 per cent of the rural population and 20 per cent of the urban population used solid fuels.

Recent fuel shortages have led to blackouts in capital, Dakar. In April 2006, Morocco's Samir oil refinery agreed to ship fuel to Senegal's power company, the Societe Nationale d'Electricite (SENELEC) in order to return electricity generation to normal in the country. In June 2005, the African Development Bank (ADB) approved a $10 million loan to finance the development of the Kounoune 67.5 MW heavy diesel-fuel plant. It is hoped that the project will help meet the county's growing demand for electricity. As continuing power outages have begun to effect production and manufacturing Senegal has begun to invest in coal technology and the development of biofuel technology.

Manufacturing

This sector is well-developed and includes fish and agricultural processing including oil mills, sugar refineries, fish canneries, flour mills, bakeries, beverage and dairy processing, groundnut-processing and textiles. Oil refining, chemicals, engineering, construction and fertilizer manufacture are all carried out. Industry and mining represent almost 20 per cent of GDP.

Service Industries

The services sector accounts for around 64 per cent of GDP. Within the sector, trade contributes over 20 per cent of GDP, and services represent almost 40 per cent.

Senegal's tourist industry has greatly expanded and is now a major source of foreign exchange and contributes about 3 per cent of GDP. In 2006, there were 769,000 tourist arrivals. Around half of all foreign travellers are French.

Agriculture

In 2011, this sector accounted for around 15 per cent of GDP and employed over 75 per cent of the workforce, mainly in subsistence farming. The principal crops are peanuts, millet, sorghum, manioc, rice, cotton, vegetables and flowers, and fruit. Until recently, the groundnut (peanut) industry was the mainstay of the economy, accounting for about one third of export earnings and occupying around 40 per cent of Senegal's cultivated area. However, production is now in decline. The parastatal (Sonacos) which dealt with groundnuts and groundnut production was privatised in 2005. Fish has overtaken peanuts as the main agricultural export earner. Droughts have hit food production and the country has had to import grain. It has also received large quantities of food aid. Senegal is one of the world's largest rice importers.

There were 576 mm of rain in 2002. 2003 saw an increase in rainfall and Senegal was set to produce a bumper crop as a result. However, large parts of West Africa, including part of Senegal, were hit by swarms of locusts in 2004. Over 90 per cent of water use is agricultural. Five per cent of the land is irrigated.

The country's livestock includes 3,018,000 cattle, 8,582,000 sheep and goats and 5,619,000 poultry. 565,000 hectares are used as pasture land.

Agricultural Production in 2010

Produce	Int. $'000*	Tonnes
Groundnuts, with shell	553,489	1,286,860
Rice, paddy	165,451	604,043
Indigenous cattle meat	142,607	52,790
Millet	139,407	813,295
Indigenous chicken meat	69,966	49,119
Tomatoes	60,978	165,000
Mangoes, mangosteens, guavas	59,917	100,000
Indigenous sheep meat	49,191	18,066
Cow milk, whole, fresh	44,663	143,124
Onions, dry	33,605	160,000
Indigenous goat meat	31,951	13,335
Sugar cane	27,912	850,000

* unofficial figures

Source: http://faostat.fao.org/site/339/default.aspx Food and Agriculture Organization of the United Nations, Food and Agricultural commodities production

Forestry

In 2004, 794,000 cubic meters of industrial roundwood, 5,243,000 cubic meters of wood fuel, 110,000 tonnes of wood charcoal and 23,000 cubic metres of sawn wood were produced.

Fishing

Fish production is expanding. The total catch in 2010 was put at 409,578 tonnes by the FAO, this figure was down on the 2009 figure of 442,295 tonnes.

COMMUNICATIONS AND TRANSPORT

Travel Requirements

Citizens of the USA, Canada, Australia and the EU require a passport valid for at least six months after the date of entry, but most do not need a visa for stays of up to 90 days. The exceptions are nationals of Australia, Bulgaria, Cyprus, Czech Republic, Estonia, Hungary, Latvia, Lithuania, Malta, Poland, Romania and Slovak Republic who do need a visa. Transit passengers not leaving the airport do not require a visa. Other nationals should contact the embassy to check visa requirements.

A WHO vaccination card, with current yellow fever, cholera and meningitis vaccinations, may be required if travelling from an endemic area. Travelers unable to provide proof of vaccinations may be required to pay for and receive vaccinations at the Dakar airport.

International Airports

The international airport at Dakar, Léopold Senghor, (previously known as Dakar-Yoff) is served by the large airline companies, and Senegal participates in Air Afrique with twelve other African states and France. Another international airport (Blaise Diagre Airport) is under construction and is currently due to open in 2014. Internal services operate between 15 domestic airports.

Dakar Léopold Senghor Airport, URL: http://www.aeroportdedakar.fr.st
The national airline was Air Senegal, but this was wound up 2009, a new airline, Senegal Airlines was due to start operating in 2010.

Railways

There are 1,180 km of track linking the country with Niger, Mali, Guinea and Mauritania. Rail transport is particularly important in the movement of phosphates. Rolling stock has been replaced under a three-year rehabilitation programme part-financed by Canada, France and Denmark.

Roads

Senegal has one of the best road networks in West Africa, totalling 9,320 miles. Vehicles are driven on the right. Nearly half can be used throughout the year and nearly a quarter are tarred. A programme of maintenance and feeder road construction has been embarked upon with financial help from the World Bank. The road between Dakar and Bamako has been improved.

Shipping

The port at Dakar (URL: http://www.portfocus.com/senegal/dakar) is the second largest in West Africa and has stimulated industrial development in Senegal. It has 43 docks, a large container terminal and covered storage space of 77,000 square metres. There are also ports at Podor, Kaolack, Matam, Saint-Louis and Ziguinchor. The rivers Senegal and Saloum are navigable by boat.

A ferry service runs from Dakar to Ziguinchor and from Dakar harbour to the Île de Gorée. A service also links Banjul, Dakar and Ziguinchor.

HEALTH

In 2009, the government spent approximately 11.6 per cent of its total budget on healthcare (up from 8.5 per cent in 2000), accounting for 54.5 per cent of all healthcare spending. External resources contributed 14.5 per cent. Total expenditure on healthcare equated to 5.7 per cent of the country's GDP. Per capita expenditure on health was approximately US$60, compared with US$21 in 2000.

Recent figures show that Senegal has 16 hospitals and around 110 clinics. Life expectancy averages 62 years. According to the latest WHO figures (2005-10), there are 741 doctors (0.6 per 10,000 population), 5,254 nurses and midwives (4.2 per 10,000 population), 127 pharmacists, 105 dentists, and 1,212 environment and public health workers. There are an estimated 3 hospital beds per 10,000 population.

There have been outbreaks on cholera and yellow fever over the past few years. The The major causes of death in children under five are: malaria (14 per cent), pneumonia (16 per cent), prematurity (15 per cent), diarrhoreal diseases (9 per cent) and HIV/AIDS 1 per cent. In 2000-09 it was estimated that 20 per cent of children under five years of age were stunted for their age and 14.5 per cent were underweight. An estimated 31 per cent of children sleep under insecticide-treated nets. The infant mortality rate (likelihood of dying by first birthday) was 50 per 1,000 population and the childhood mortality rate (likelihood of dying by fifth birthday) was 75 per 1,000 population.

In 2010, an estimated 72 per cent of the population had access to improved water. Approximately 52 per cent of the population had access to improved sanitation. (Source: http://www.who.int, World Health Statistics 2012)

EDUCATION

Primary/Secondary Education

Under the constitution education is compulsory and free for all students up to the age of 16, However, there are insufficient places in schools for all those of school age, more schools are located in urban rather than rural areas and so many children in rural areas only have access to an Islamic education. Figures for 2007 show that 72 per cent of girls and 72 pr cent of boys were enrolled in primary school. Secondary education is also available and, in 2006, 20 per cent of the relevant age were registered in secondary education.

SERBIA

Five per cent of GDP public expenditure went on education in 2006, which was 26.3 per cent of total government expenditure. Most (46 per cent) was spent on primary education. The pupil/teacher ratio is 39:1 in primary education. (Source: UNESCO)

Tertiary/Higher

There are two universities, one in Saint Louis and one in Dakar. In 2006, 24 per cent of the education budget was spent on higher education.

In 2006 the adult literacy rate was 52.7 per cent for men and 31 per cent for women. For the age group 15 -24 years the literacy rate was 58.5 per cent for men and 43.2 per cent for women. (Source: UNESCO, UIS)

RELIGION

The main religions are Islam (88 per cent), Christianity (5 per cent) and traditional (6 per cent).

Senegal has a religious liberty rating of 10 on a scale of 1 to 10 (10 is most freedom). (Source: World Religion Database)

COMMUNICATIONS AND MEDIA

The constitution guarantees media freedom. However, there are laws in place which prohibit reports that discredit the state or spread 'false news'. Self-censorship is common but criticism of the government does however still appear. There are reports of threats and violence against journalists.

Newspapers

There are some 20 newspapers in circulation. The foreign press is also available.

Le Soleil, Dakar, (state-owned daily) URL: http://www.lesoleil.sn/
Sud Quotidien, URL: http://www.sudonline.sn
Wal Fadjri L'Aurore, URL: http://www.walf.sn

Broadcasting

Television broadcasting is provided by the state run Radiodiffusion Television Senegalese (http://www.rts.sn). Private TV subscription channels rebroadcast foreign channels.RTS also provides radio broadcasts and there are several privately owned radio stations.

Telecommunications

Loans from the World Bank and France helped improve the telecommunications system. Coverage in rural areas still needs improvement. In 2008, there were an estimated 240,000 main line telephones and 5.3 million mobile phones in use. By 2008, there were an estimated 1 million regular internet users.

ENVIRONMENT

Principal environmental concerns for Senegal are deforestation, overgrazing and soil erosion resulting in desertification. Wildlife is under threat from poachers.

In 2005, Senegal's carbon dioxide emissions reached 5.49 million metric tons, up from 4.43 mmt in 2002. This was equivalent to 0.46 metric tons per capita, below the African average of 1.17 metric tons. In 2010, Senegal's emissions from the consumption and flaring of fossil fuels totalled 6.68 million metric tons of carbon dioxide. (Source: EIA)

Senegal is party to the following international agreements: Biodiversity, Climate Change, Climate Change-Kyoto Protocol, Desertification, Endangered Species, Hazardous Wastes, Law of the Sea, Marine Life Conservation, Ozone Layer Protection, Ship Pollution, Wetlands, Whaling.

SERBIA
Republic of Serbia
Republika Srbija

Capital: Belgrade (Population estimate, 2011: 1.7 million)

Head of State: Tomislav Nikolic (President) (page 1487)

Flag: A horizontal tricolour red, blue then white with the coat of arms centred and slightly to the hoist.

CONSTITUTION AND GOVERNMENT

Constitution

The four original constituent Yugoslav republics of Bosnia-Herzegovina, Croatia, Macedonia and Slovenia declared their independence during 1991. With the exception of Macedonia, all were recognised internationally between January and April 1992. The remaining two republics, Serbia and Montenegro, formed a new republic, the Federal Republic of Yugoslavia, which comprised about 40 per cent of the area and 44 per cent of the former state.

A Constitution for the Federal Republic was promulgated on 27 April 1992. Under its terms each of the member republics maintained relations with foreign states, could join international organisations and conclude international agreements as long as these were not to the detriment of the Federal Republic of Yugoslavia. Authority in the Federal Republic was based on the principle of separation of powers between legislature, executive and judiciary.

On October 1 2003 a new constitution was approved with Kosovo acknowledged as an integral part of Serbia. The constitution was narrowly approved by a referendum in October, and was ratified in November.

In 2006 Montenegro voted to separate from Serbia. The Serbian parliament acknowledged the separation and declared itself the successor state to Serbia and Montenegro, thereby allowing Serbia to remain party to all the international agreements which had been signed as Serbia and Montenegro.

Serbia and Montenegro

On 31 May 2002 the Yugoslav parliament voted to end the Yugoslav Federation and replace it with a more flexible union between its remaining members Serbia and Montenegro. The new state, known as Serbia and Montenegro, was formed in March 2003, with a constitution based on that drawn up by the European Union in March 2002. Under the new constitution each state would share defence and foreign policy but would retain their own currencies, economies and customs services. In May 2002 the Yugoslav parliament's upper house approved the plan by 23 votes to six, whilst the lower house agreed it by 74 votes to 23. The Montenegrin and Serbian parliaments agreed the plan in March 2002. Under the terms of the agreement there was a joint parliamentary chamber in addition to Serb and Montenegrin parliaments. The new union had a single army and a rotating seat at the UN and other international organisations. However, after a three-year period, both Serbia and Montenegro would be allowed to secede from the union. In February 2005, Montenegrin leaders floated the proposal for an early end to the union and the establishment of two republics; the Serbian Prime Minister Volislav Kostunica rejected the idea. However, on 26th May 2006, a referendum was held and 55 per cent of the population voted in favour of Montenegro becoming an

independent state with full international and legal subjectivity. Montenegro formally declared its independence from Serbia in a special session of the parliament on 4th June 2006. Serbia subsequently declared itself to be the successor state to Serbia and Montenegro.

The President of Serbia and Montenegro was elected by the Serbia-Montenegro union parliament. The union government consisted of the Council of Ministers, comprising three Serb and two Montenegrin ministers, with the president the ex-officio chair. As individual republics Serbia and Montenegro retain their own governments, each of which is headed by a prime minister.

To consult the constitution, please visit: http://www.srbija.gov.rs/cinjenice_o_srbiji/ustav.php?change_lang=en

Recent Events

In July 2000 both houses of parliament approved changes to the constitution that would have allowed the President to run for a further two terms of office. The legislation put forward by the ruling coalition would have meant that when Slobodan Milosevic's four-year presidential term expired in July 2001 he could have remained in office for a further eight years. The move was opposed by Montenegro who believed that it threatened their own constitutional rights.

Following the September 2000 presidential election, in which Slobodan Milosevic banned international observers from monitoring proceedings, hundreds of thousands of opposition supporters took to the streets in protest against the President. Protesters occupied the parliament building and state television station, and held a general strike. In April 2001 former president Milosevic was placed under house arrest, and at the end of June he was extradited to the international war crimes tribunal in The Hague. Milosevic appeared briefly at the tribunal at the beginning of July to face charges of crimes against humanity. On 12 February 2002 the trial of former president Slobodan Milosevic began at The Hague. Milosevic was charged with genocide in Bosnia and war crimes in Croatia and Kosovo. Milosevic died in March 2006 before the end of the trial.

At the beginning of October 2000 Russia formally recognised Vojislav Kostunica as Yugoslavia's new president. Since then, the country has rejoined the UN and the OSCE, and sought closer links with Europe and the EU.

In June 2001, Yugoslavia received pledges of aid from international governments and organisations representing nearly US$1.3 billion to help rebuild the economy and infrastructure. At the Brussels meeting, which took place just after the extradition of Slobodan Milosevic to The Hague, the European Union pledged US$450 million, whilst the US offered almost US$200 million, and the World Bank US$600 million.

A general election was held in Kosova in November 2007; Hashim Thaci of the Democratic Party of Kosova won and announced he would declare Kosova as independent. On February 17 2008 the Kosovan parliament formally endorsed a declaration of independence from Serbia. The announcement was condemned by Serbia, but some EU member countries recognised Kosova's independence, and this led to a crisis in the Serbian coalition which collapsed in March 2008. President Boris Tadic dissolved parliament, and snap elections were called. On the 11 May, no party gained enough seats to form a government on its own, but the coalition lead by the DS won most seats in the National Assembly. President Tadic on 28 June nominated Mirko Cvetkovic of the DS as prime minister and he formed a coalition Council of Ministers.

Radovan Karadzic was arrested in Belgrade in July 2008 by Serbian security forces and extradited to The Hague.

In March 2010 Serbia withdrew from EU enlargrment talks being held in Slovenia over objections that Kosovo was included at the talks on an equal footing. Serbia had wanted Kosovo to attend as a UN protectorate rather than a nation.

In June 2010 EU Foreign Ministers decided to ratify a long-delayed trade agreement with Serbia, seen as a further step towards EU integration. The progress came after the UN war crimes tribunal said that Serbia had co-operated with its inquiries.

In May 2011 it was announced that former Bosnian Serb military commander General Ratko Mladic had been found and arrested. He will be transferred to the UN war crimes tribunal to face genocide charges. He is accused of committing war crimes during the Bosnian war, including the 1995 Srebrenica massacre when 7,500 Muslim men and boys were killed.

The European Union recommended Serbia for EU candidate status but said that it must normalise its ties with Kosovo. It granted Serbia candidate member status in May 2012.

Tomislav Nikolic was elected president in May 2012, defeating the incumbent Boris Tadic. His parliamentary party, the Progress Party, won most seats in the parliamentary elections. A coalition between two nationalist parties, the Progress Party and the Socialist Party was formed in July 2012.

In July 2012, the Socialist Party formed a coalition government with the nationalist Progressive Party of President Nikolic.

In January 2013, the parliament approved support for minority Serb rights within Kosovo. EU-mediated talks resumed between Kosovo and Serbia. After a landmark agreement was signed between the two, the EC gave the go-ahead to open Serbia's EU membership talks.

Montenegro
On 21st May 2006, 55.5 per cent of the Montenegran population voted in favour of Montenegro becoming an independent state with full international and legal subjectivity. Montenegro formally declared its independence from Serbia on 4th June 2006. The following day the Serbian parliament voted to acknowledge the independence of Montenegro. Prime Minister Kostunica announced that the ministries of foreign affairs, defence and human rights which had previously been ministries in the federal government of Serbia and Montenegro held by Serb ministers would now be included in the Serbian Cabinet.

Kosovo
On February 17 2008 the Kosovan parliament formally endorsed a declaration of independence from Serbia. The announcement was condemned by Serbia. An emergency session of the UN Security Council was convened, as Russia condemned the announcement stating that the 1999 UN resolution to administer Kosovo was still in force. On June 15 2008 Kosovo's new constitution came into force formally ending nine years of UN control. Serbia still does not recognise Kosovo's independence. In response the Kosovon Serbs set up their own assembly based in Mitrovica.

In March 2011 direct talks on ending the dispute between Kosovo and Serbia began. In January 2013, the parliament approved support for minority Serb rights within Kosovo, indicating recognition of Kosovar sovereignty. EU-mediated talks resumed between Kosovo and Serbia and a landmark agreement was signed between the two.

Legislature
Legislative power is the responsibility of the unicameral National Assembly of Serbia, composed of 250 deputies elected for four-year terms. Parties must pass a five per cent threshold of votes in order to take seats in the parliament. In 2004 a new electoral law came into force whereby parties of ethnic minorities do not have to meet the threshold; as a result, Albanian, Hungarian, Bosniak and Roma minorities had representation for the first time following the 2007 election. The Assembly convenes twice a year, the first session beginning in March and the second in October. Sessions do not last longer than 90 days.
National Assembly of the Republic of Serbia, *(Narodna Skupstina Republike Srbije)*, Kralja Milana 14, 11000 Belgrade, Republic of Serbia. Tel: +381 11 322 2001
Chairman of the Serbian Assembly: Predrag Markovic

Cabinet (as at June 2013)
Prime Minister: Ivica Dacic (page 1411)
First Deputy Prime Minister, Minister of Defence, Security and Anti-Corruption: Aleksandar Vucic (page 1532)
Deputy Prime Minister for EU Integration: Suzana Grubjesic (page 1434)
Deputy Prime Minister, Minister of Labour: Jovan Krkobabic
Deputy Prime Minister, Minister of Trade, Minister of Telcommunications: Rasim Ljajic
Minister of Foreign Affairs: Ivan Mrkic (page 1481)
Minister for Finance and Economy: Mladan Dinkic (page 1415)
Minister of Energy, Environment and Development: Zorana Mihajlovic
Minister of Agriculture: Goran Knezevic
Minister of Justice: Nikola Selakovic (page 1511)
Minister of Regional Development, State Administration and Local Services: Verica Kalanovic
Minister of Town Planning: Velimir Ilic
Minister of Education & Science: Dr Zarko Obradovic
Minister of Mining, Natural Resources & Spatial Planning: Dr Milan Bacevic

---

Minister of Culture & Media: Bratislav Petkovic
Minister of Health: Prof. Slavica Dukic-Dejanovic
Minister of Transport: Milutin Mrkonjic
Minister of Sports: Alisa Maric
Minister without Portfolio: Sulejman Ugljanin

Ministries
Office of the President, URL: http://www.predsednik.rs/
Prime Minister's Office, 11 Nemanjina Street, Belgrade, Republic of Serbia. Tel: +381 11 361 7719, fax: +381 11 361 7609, URL: http://www.srbija.gov.rs/
Office of the Deputy Prime Minister, http://www.srbija.gov.rs/
Ministry of Agriculture, Trade, Forestry and Water Management, 22-26 Nemanjina Street, Belgrade, Republic of Serbia. Tel: +381 11 361 6271, fax: +381 11 361 6272, URL: http://www.mpt.gov.rs/
Ministry of Culture, Media and Information Society, Vlajkoviceva 3, Belgrade, Republic of Serbia. URL: http://www.kultura.gov.rs/
Ministry of Defence, 5 Bricaninova Street, Belgrade, Serbia. E-mail: info@mod.gov.rs, URL: http://www.mod.gov.rs/
Ministry of Economy and Regional Development,Blvd. Kralja Aleksandra 15, Belgrade 11000, Republic of Serbia. URL: http://www.merr.gov.rs/
Ministry of Education and Science, 22-26 Nemanjina Street, Belgrade, Republic of Serbia. Tel: +381 11 361 6489, fax: +381 11 361 6491, e-mail: min.edu.sr@YUBC.net, URL: http://www.min.edu.yu
Ministry of Finance, Kneza Milosa Street 20 Street, Belgrade, Republic of Serbia. URL: http://www.mfin.gov.rs/
Ministry of Environment, Mining and Spatial Planning, Omladinskih brigada 1, 11000 Belgrade, Republic of Serbia. Tel: +381 11 361 7717, fax: +381 11 13617 722, URL: http://www.ekoplan.gov.rs/en/index.php
Ministry of Foreign Affairs, 24-26 Kneza Milosa St., 11000 Belgrade, Serbia. Tel: +381 11 3616-333, fax: +381 11 3618-366, URL: http://www.mfa.gov.rs/
Ministry of Health, Nemanjina 22 - 26, 11000 Belgrade, Serbia. Tel: +381 11 3613734, fax: +381 11 2656548, URL: http://www.zdravlje.gov.rs/index.php?
Ministry of Human Rights, URL: http://www.drzavnauprava.gov.rs/
Ministry of Infrastructure and Energy, Kralja Milana 36, 11000 Belgrade, Serbia. Tel: +381 11 334 6755, fax: +381 11 361 6603, URL: http://www.mem.gov.rs/
Ministry of the Interior, Bulevar Mihajla Pupina 2, Belgrade, Republic of Serbia. Tel: +381 11 361 2589, fax: +381 11 361 7814, e-mail: muprs@mup.sr.gov.yu, URL: http://www.mup.gov.rs/
Ministry of Justice, 22-26 Nemanjina Street, Belgrade, Republic of Serbia. Tel: +381 11 361 6548, fax: +381 11 361 6419, e-mail: kabinet@mpravde.gov.rs, URL: http://www.mpravde.gov.rs/
Ministry of Kosovo-Metohija, Mihailo Pupin Boulevard 2, Belgrade, Serbia. Tel: +381 11 3111 425, URL: http://www.kim.gov.rs/cms/view.php
Ministry of Labour and Social Policy, 22-24 Nemanjina Street, Belgrade, Republic of Serbia. Tel: +381 11 363 1402, fax: +381 11 361 6498, URL: http://www.minrzs.gov.rs/cms/en/home
Ministry of Religion, 4 Nusiceva Street, Belgrade, Republic of Serbia. Tel: +381 11 334 6649, URL:http://www.mv.gov.rs/cir/
Ministry of Youth and Sports, URL: http://www.mos.gov.rs/

Political Parties
Democratic Party (DS), URL: http://www.ds.org.rs/en/; Democratic Party of Serbia - New Serbia (DSS-NS), URL: http://dss.rs/; Liberal Democratic Party (LDP), URL: http://istina.ldp.rs/Liberalno-demokratska-partija/1/Naslovna.shtml; Party of United Pensioners of Serbia (PUPS), URL: http://www.pups.org.rs/; Serbian Radical Party (SRS), URL: http://www.srpskaradikalnastranka.org.rs/; Socialist Party of Serbia (SPS), URL: http://sps.org.rs/en/; United Serbia (JS), URL: http://www.jedinstvenasrbija.org.rs/.

Elections
The most recent presidential elections were held on 6 and 20 May 2012. The incumbent Boris Tadic came second to Tomislav Nikolic of the SNS. In the second round Nikolic narrowly defeated Tadic and was sworn in as president in June 2012.

Following the declaration of independence by Kosovo, Prime Minister Vojislav Kostunica and his government resigned. Parliamentary elections took place on 11 May 2008, and the coalition group led by the Democratic Party won most seats. President Tadic nominated Mirko Cvetkovic of the Democratic Party as prime minister, who formed a coalition government.

The most recent legislative elections took place on 6 May 2012. The SNS won 73 seats, the DS 67. A coalition made up of the SPS, PUPS and JS took 44 seats, the DSS 21 seats, Turnover 19 seats, United Regions of Serbia 16 and others 10.

Diplomatic Representation
British Embassy, Resavska 46, 11000 Belgrade, Serbia. Tel: +381 11 2645 055, fax: +381 11 2659 651, e-mail: belgrade.man@fco.gov.uk, URL: http://ukinserbia.fco.gov.uk/en/
Ambassador: Michael Davenport
US Embassy, Kneza Milosa 50, 11 000 Belgrade, Republic of Serbia. Tel: +381 11 361 9344, URL: http://belgrade.usebassy.gov
Ambassador: Michael Kirby
Embassy of the Republic of Serbia, 28 Belgrave Square, London SW1X 8QB, United Kingdom. Tel: +44 (0)20 7235 9049, URL: http://www.serbianembassy.org.uk/
Ambassador: Dr Dejan Popovic
Embassy of the Republic of Serbia, 2134 Kalorama Road, NW, Washington, DC 20008, USA. Tel: +1 202 332 0333, URL: http://www.serbiaembusa.org/
Ambassador: H.E. Vladimir Petrovic
Permanent Mission of the Republic of Serbia to the United Nations, URL: http://www.un.int/serbia/
Permanent Representative: H.E. Feodor Starcevic

STATES OF THE WORLD

SERBIA

LEGAL SYSTEM

The constitution provides for an independent judiciary. The courts in Serbia are divided into regular courts (municipal courts, 30 district courts and the Supreme Court of Serbia) and special courts (commercial courts, High Commercial Court). The Supreme Court is divided into four branches: civil, criminal, administrative and case law. Judges are appointed by the National Parliament upon proposal of the High Judicial Council.

Since the partition of Serbia and Montenegro, the legal framework has been undergoing some changes; the Supreme Court is to become a Court of Cassation under the new constitution.

There is also a Constitutional Court which has the power to invalidate laws and other regulations of the institutions of Serbia that are found to be contrary to the Constitutional Charter and the laws of Serbia.

In the main, the government respects the rights of its citizens. However, police brutality and harassment of those critical of the government continues. There are limitations on freedom of speech and religion, and corruption is widespread in the police and the judiciary. Serbia abolished the death penalty for all crimes in 2002, and in 2008 Serbia co-sponsored the Resolution on a Moratorium on the Use of the Death Penalty at the UN General Assembly.

Constitutional Court of Serbia,
URL: http://www.ustavni.sud.rs/page/home/en-GB

LOCAL GOVERNMENT

The administration of Serbia is regulated by the Law on Territorial Organization adopted in 2007. The units are: municipalities, cities and autonomous provinces.The Republic of Serbia is also divided into 29 districts: Borski, Branicevski, Jablanicki, Backa South, South Banat, Kolubarski, Kosovski, Kosovsko-Mitrovacki, Kosovsko-Pomoravski, Macvanski, Moravicki, Nisavski, Pcinjski, Pecki, Pirotski, Podunavski, Pomoravski, Prizrenski, Rasinski, Raski, Backa North, North Banat, Banat Central, Sremski, Sumadijski, Toplicki, Zajecarski, Backa West and Zlatiborski. Serbia is further divided into 167 municipalities, 211 communes, 6,168 settlements, and 207 urban localities.

Serbia has two autonomous provinces: Vojvodina in the north (39 municipalities and 6 cities) and Kosovo and Metohija in the south (28 municipalities and one city). The most recent municipal elections were held in May 2010.

AREA AND POPULATION

Area
The Republic of Serbia covers an area of 88,361 sq. km, of which 55,968 sq. km is Serbia, while the autonomous provinces of Vojvodina and Kosovo are 21,506 sq. km and 10,887 sq. km respectively. Serbia is entirely landlocked, bordered by Hungary in the north, Romania in the north-east, Bulgaria in the east, Macedonia in the south, Albania in the south-west, Montenegro in the south-west, and Bosnia-Herzegovina and Croatia in the west. The capital and largest city is Belgrade. The terrain varies from flat, fertile plains in the north rising to hilly and mountainous regions in the south and southeast. The north has a more continental climate with cold winters and hot summers, with some rainfall. Elsewhere the summers are hot and drier, with cold winters with some heavy snowfalls.

To view a map, consult
http://www.un.org/Depts/Cartographic/map/profile/serbia.pdf

Kosovo
Kosovo is situated in the bottom south west corner of Serbia and as well as Serbia has borders with Macedonia, Albania and Montenegro. It had an estimated population of 1.794 million in 2011, the capital city, Pristina has an estimated population of 500,000.

Population
Serbia's total population was estimated to be 9.856 million in 2010. Vojvodina's population has been estimated at around 1.95 million. Serbia's average annual population growth rate was -0.3 per cent in the period 2000-10. The population density is approximately 111 inhabitants per sq. km. An estimated 56 per cent of the population live in urban areas. The majority of the population are Serbs (66 per cent) with another 37 nationalities also living on its territory: Albanians 17 per cent, Hungarians 3.5 per cent, followed by Romanians, Romanies, Slovaks, Croats, Bulgarians, Turks and others.

The official language is Serbian and the alphabet in official use is Cyrillic, as well as Latin. In areas dominated by non-Serbs, the language and alphabet of the minority group is in use.

Births, Marriages, Deaths
Figures for Serbia in 2010 show that the crude birth rate was 11.3 per 1,000 population and the crude death rate was 14.7 per 1,000 population. In 2009, the total fertility rate was 1.6 per female. Life expectancy was 71 years for males and 76 for females in 2009. Healthy life expectancy was 65 years in 2007. The median age was 37 years in 2009. Approximately 18 per cent of the population is 14 years or less and 20 per cent over 60 years. (Source: http://www.who.int, World Health Statistics 2012)

Public Holidays 2014
1-2 January: New Year
7 January: Christmas (Orthodox)
27 January: St. Sava's Day*
15 February: Constitution Day
18-20 May: Orthodox Easter
1-2 May: Labour Days

9 May: Victory Day*
28 June: St. Vitus Day*
* Working festival days

EMPLOYMENT

Figures for 2008 show that 3,267,100 people were economically active, 2,821,700 were employed and the unemployed numbered 445,400 giving an unemployment rate of 13.6 per cent. Estimated figures for 2010 put the labour force at 3.3 million with an unemployment rate of 17.1 per cent.

Employment Figures for 2008

Sector	Number Employed
Agriculture, hunting & forestry	707,300
Fishing	1,500
Mining & quarrying	32,400
Manufacturing	484,300
Electricity, gas & water supply	45,000
Construction	177,500
Wholesale & retail trade, repairs	418,100
Hotels & restaurants	83,900
Transport, storage & communications	157,200
Financial mediation	56,600
Real estate transactions, renting	91,800
Public admin. & social insurance	135,700
Education	122,500
Health care & social work	176,300
Other public utility, social & individual services	123,900
Households with employed persons	6,600
Extra-territorial organisations & bodies	1,200
Total	2,821,700

Source: Copyright © International Labour Organization (ILO Dept. of Statistics, http://laborsta.ilo.org)

BANKING AND FINANCE

Currency
One Serbian Dinar (din) = 100 para

GDP/GNP, Inflation, National Debt
Following the 1999 NATO air strikes on Yugoslavia, Serb military operations, and trade sanctions imposed on the country by the EU, the country's infrastructure was left severely damaged and the economy badly affected. Some 120,000 buildings were damaged in the conflict and total damage was estimated at over US$4 billion. The international community pledged over US$3 billion in aid for reconstruction.

In order to start re-building the economy a series of reforms were introduced which included streamlining the tax system, introduction of VAT, liberalising price controls and enacting laws on privatisation and inward foreign investment. These reforms have led to debt settlements with both the Paris and London clubs of creditors, and the successful completion of an IMF three year standby programme. There has been some privatisation but many large enterprises including utilities and telecommunications are still under state control. Serbia is also working towards membership of the WTO and EU. The global economic crisis has adversely affected the economy and in 2011 Serbia agreed a US$1.3 billion stand by arrangement with the IMF. The government is committed to expanding the economy through increased exports.

The following table shows GDP in recent years:

GDP in Recent Years

Year	US$ Million	US$ Per Capita
2001	11,484.7	1530.6
2002	15,102.6	2,013.7
2003	19,550.8	2,.613.5
2004	23,649.9	3,168.9
2005	25,234.4	3,391.4
2006	29,221.1	3,942.6
2007	39,385.4	5,335.6
2008	48,856.6	6,647.0
2009*	41,628.7	5,690.5

*=estimated
Source: Statistical Office of the Republic of Serbia

GDP was estimated to be US$40.3 billion in 2010, rising to US$42.5 billion in 2011. Growth was 1.6 per cent in 2011. Per capita GDP was estimated to be US$5,400.

The following table shows 2004 Gross Domestic Product by activity at basic prices:

Sector	GDP (million dinars)
Agriculture, hunting, forestry & waterworks supply	164,438.6
Fisheries	363.9
Mining and quarrying	23,085.5
Manufacturing	206,330.0
Utilities	53,016.6
Construction	57,047.9

- *continued*

Wholesale and retail trade, repairs	115,989.6
Hotels and restaurants	13,315.3
Transport and communications	94,817.1
Financial intermediation	48,594.1
Real estate & renting activities	188,064.6
Public admin. & defence, compulsory social security	84,041.3
Education	50,998.5
Health and social work	69,234.1
Other community, social & personal services	30,489.2
Private households with employed persons	1,326.8
Total	1,201,150.1

Source: Statistical Office of the Republic of Serbia

Inflation was estimated to be over 10 per cent in 2010.

Foreign Investment

In June 2001, the former Yugoslavia received pledges of aid from international governments and organisations offering nearly US$1.3 billion to help rebuild the economy and infrastructure. At the Brussels meeting, which took place just after the extradition of Slobodan Milosevic to the Hague, the European Union pledged US$450 million, the US offered almost US$200 million, and the World Bank US$600 million.

There are many opportunities for foreign investment, largely due to the effects of the 1999 conflict and subsequent sanctions, but also due to Serbia and Montenegro's geographical position and its abundance of natural resources. The UK Department of Trade and Industry (DTI) has identified the following sectors that are attracting foreign capital from private investors and IFIs: the proposed high-speed trans-Serbia Railway to link Western and Central Europe with Greece and Turkey (the DTI estimates that this will require over US$3.5 billion of investment, half of which is expected to come from abroad); power generation (the DTI estimates that new plants planned between will almost certainly require over US$900 million in investment); and road-building (the government is offering concessions to foreign consortia to help create new roads). The DTI also identifies agriculture and food, medical equipment and supplies, machinery and equipment as being good opportunities for business.

Balance of Payments / Imports and Exports

After a decade of war, and following the recent lifting of sanctions, Serbia's export revenue has begun to rise.

Balance of Payments million US$

Sector	2004	2005	2006
Current account	-2,869	-2,224	-3,656
Goods	-6,469	-5,290	-6,230
Exports f.o.b.	4,082	4,970	6,486
Imports f.o.b.	-10,551	-10,260	-12,716
Services	175	-6	-62
Export services	1,477	1,636	2,107
Import services	-1,302	-1,642	-2,169
Income	-216	-324	-395
Receipts	80	98	194
Payments	-296	-422	-589
Current transfers	3,166	3,067	2,803
Receipts	3,766	3,902	4,355
Payments	-600	-826	-1,552
Officials transfers (grants)	475	329	228

Source: Statistical Yearbook of Serbia 2007

Exports amounted to US$9.8 billion in 2010. The major markets are Bosnia and Herzegovina, Montenegro, Germany and Italy. Imports amounted to US$16 billion. The major trade partners are Russia, Germany, Italy and China.

Central Bank

Narodna Banka Srbije (National Bank of Serbia), Kralja Petra 12, 11000 Belgrade, Serbia. Tel: +381 11 3027-100, e-mail: informativni.centar@nbs.rs, URL: http://www.nbs.rs/internet/english/
Governor: Jorgovanka Tabakovic

MANUFACTURING, MINING AND SERVICES

Primary and Extractive Industries

Serbia has modest mineral and energy reserves. The reserves of ferrous and non-ferrous metals and reserves of coal are somewhat more abundant (the largest in the region), while the reserves of oil and natural gas are very small. Employment in the mining and quarrying industry fell from 53,000 in 1998 to 32,400 in 2008.

The former Yugoslavia's petroleum industry capability was severely compromised by NATO air strikes, the oil embargo and sanctions. Most of Serbia's oil refineries oil storage depots were destroyed during the air strikes, whilst the railway line between Serbia and the Montenegrin ports was cut following the destruction of railway bridges. In addition, ports and bridges on the Danube River were destroyed, preventing the transport of petroleum products into Serbia by barge. As well as the NATO oil embargo and EU sanctions, Croatia stopped shipments of crude oil through the Adria pipeline.

Figures for the beginning of January 2006 show that the then Serbia and Montenegro had proven crude oil reserves of 77.5 million barrels, with a crude oil refining capacity estimated at 158,000 barrels per day (compared with 158,250 barrels per day in 2001). Serbian production of crude oil was 16,000 barrels per day in 2000, mainly from the Vojvodina province in the north. This provides just over a quarter of domestic oil consumption. Figures

for 2011 show that Serbia had proven oil reserves of 0.08 billion barrels, with production that year of 19.89 thousand barrales per day, consumption that year was 81.00 thousand barrels per day meant that 61.1 thousand barrels per day had to be imported.

The state-run oil and gas company is Nafta Industrija Srbije (NIS) Jugpetrol which is currently in the process of being privatised. NIS took over control of oil imports in March 2001.

Natural gas reserves at the beginning of 2006 were estimated at 1,700 billion cubic feet. Production/consumption was 20.0 billion cubic feet in 2003. 75 per cent of natural gas is imported from Russia. Natural gas is used by power plants for district heating and to make fertilizer and synthetic rubber. Although most gas is imported from Russia, negotiations were underway between Serbia and Russia's Gazprom following the collapse of credit arrangements with the company. In 2012 a new agreement was reached with Gazprom insuring supplies to Serbia until 2021.

Serbia is the only Balkan country with large coal deposits. Recoverable coal reserves were estimated in January 2001 at 17,919 million short tons, most of it lignite. Small amounts of bituminous hard coal are also extracted. Reserves originate from five basins: Kostolac, Kolubara, Kosovo, Metohija, and Pljevlja. Coal production was 41.169 million short tons in 2010 and consuptiono was 42.085. Imports in 2010 were 916,000 tons.

Manufacturing

Serbia's industry is well developed, with a number of industries having been set up on the basis of the country's raw materials. it contributes around 18 per cent of GDP. Main products are chemicals, including pharmaceuticals and man-made fibres, metallurgical and metal products, a wide range of engineering products, including motor vehicles and machine tools, as well as electric and electronic products. In 2008, the Serbian Government signed an agreement with the car maker Fiat to purchase and invest in Serbia's state owned car manufacturer, Zastava.

Energy

Energy is provided by the hydro-electric power stations on the Danube and a number of thermo-electric plants. Electricity in Serbia is provided by Elektroprivreda of Serbia (EPS). Figures for 2006 10,964 GWh of electricity were produced by hydro power plants and 25,378 GWh by thermal power plants.

Agriculture

Most of the land is privately owned. About 1.7 million farmers hold 82 per cent of the arable land. Agriculture is of great importance to the economy of Serbia, employing about 21 per cent of the active population, and contributes over 11 per cent of GDP. Main products are wheat, maize, sugar beet, plums and grapes. Animal husbandry is well developed, as is the production of related products.

Agricultural Production in 2010

Produce	Int. $'000*	Tonnes
Cow milk, whole, fresh	463,286	1,484,600
Indigenous pigmeat	414,682	269,757
Maize	338,710	7,207,190
Indigenous cattle meat	288,677	106,863
Plums and sloes	254,728	426,846
Grapes	188,674	330,070
Wheat	173,809	1,630,400
Raspberries	162,288	83,870
Sugar beet	143,015	3,324,850
Soybeans	134,365	540,859
Indigenous chicken meat	121,652	85,405
Sunflower seed	103,621	378,409

* unofficial figures
Source: http://faostat.fao.org/site/339/default.aspx Food and Agriculture Organization of the United Nations, Food and Agricultural commodities production

COMMUNICATIONS AND TRANSPORT

Travel Requirements

Citizens of the USA, Canada, Australia and most of the EU require a valid passport but do not need a visa for tourism stays of up to 90 days. Bulgarians can stay for tourism purposes for up to 30 days without a visa, but Hungarians and Romanians do require a visa. Other nationals should contact the embassy to check visa requirements. Visitors not staying at hotels must register with the police within 24 hours from arrival. All nationals staying longer than three days must register with the police.

International Airports

International airports are situated at Belgrade (Belgrade Nikola Tesla Airport), Podgorica, Nis and Tivat.

Railways

Recent figures show that there are 3,959 km of track in Serbia and Montenegro. Of this approximately 277 km is double track and 1,342 km is electrified track. Belgrade has a tram network. Some international trains run from Belgrade to Budapest, Vienna, Munich and Zurich.
Serbian Railways, URL: http://www.serbianrailways.com

Roads

Recent figures show that road network in Serbia and Montenegro was approximately 45,000 km. Vehicles are driven on the right. In order to remain the best (and shortest) link between Western Europe and the Middle East, Serbia and Montenegro was planning to build 1,700 km of motorways by 2010, many of which will be toll roads.

SERBIA

HEALTH

In 2008, the government spent approximately 14.1 per cent of its total budget on healthcare, accounting for 62.5 per cent of all healthcare spending. Total expenditure on healthcare equated to 10 per cent of the country's GDP. Per capita expenditure on health was approximately US$499, compared with US$44 in 2000. Figures for 2005-10 show that there are 20,806 physicians (21.1 per 10,000 population), 44,807 nurses and midwives (45.5 per 10,000 population) and 2,282 dentistry personnel and 2,042 pharmaceutical personnel. There are an estimated 54 hospital beds per 10,000 population.

The infant mortality rate in 2010 was 6 per 1,000 live births. The child mortality rate (under 5 years) was 7 per 1,000 live births. The main causes of death in the under-fives are prematurity (41 per cent) and congenital anomalies (22 per cent). In 2005-11 approximately 9.1 per cent of the children aged under 5 years were classified as stunted and 1.8 per cent as underweight. Some 19 per cent were classified as overweight.

According to the latest WHO figures, in 2010, 99 per cent of the population had access to improved drinking-water sources. Approximately 92 per cent of the population used improved sanitation. (Source: http://www.who.int, World Health Statistics 2012)

EDUCATION

Serbia's education system starts at age six. Figures for 2007 show that 95 per cent of girls and 95 per cent of boys were enrolled in primary school. Secondary schools in 2004 numbered 480 with total secondary pupils at 297,708, English is a compulsory subject at secondary level. Secondary school education is based on the American system and schools are either Grammar schools, which offer a broad education, professional schools which specialise in certain areas as well as offering all round subjects or vocational schools which specialise but students attending them don't have the option of going on to university. In 2004, there were 218,508 students studying at universities or other institutions of higher education.

RELIGION

The main religion is Christian Orthodox followed by around 80 per cent of the population. Beside the Christian Orthodox population, there are Islamic (7.0 per cent), Roman Catholic, Protestant, Jewish (0.4 per cent) and other religious communities within the country. Approximately 12 per cent of the population does not have religious beliefs. Serbia has a religious liberty rating of 7 on a scale of 1 to 10 (10 is most freedom). (Source: World Religion Database)

COMMUNICATIONS AND MEDIA

Newspapers
There were over 80 newspapers in Serbia and Montenegro, published in a variety of languages such as Albanian, Bulgarian, Hungarian, Romanian, Romany, Ruthann, Slovak and Turkish. The main newspapers published now in the Republic of Serbia include: Politika (URL: http://www.politika.rs/), daily; Blic (URL: http://www.blic.rs/), daily; Danas, URL: http://www.danas.rs/danasrs/naslovna.1.html,daily; Glas Javnosti, daily, URL: http://www.glas-javnosti.rs/.

Broadcasting
The national government funded TV and radio broadcaster is RTS. It aims to be come a public service. There are numerous private TV and radio stations. Five national radio and television licences have been granted. A UN-backed service, Blue Sky Radio, broadcasts impartial news. RTS, URL: http://www.rts.rs/

Telecommunications
Much of the telecommunications system was damaged during the 1999 war. The sytem has now been upgraded, more than 95 per cent digitalized. In 2008 it was estimated there were 3 million landlines and approximately 9.5 million mobile phones. By 2009 just some 2.5 million people had access to the internet.

ENVIRONMENT

Air pollution in Belgrade, despite having fallen from 522 micrograms per sq. metre in 1998 to 223 micrograms per sq. metre in 2000, is still above 1996 levels of 204 micrograms per sq. metre.

KOSOVO

Republic of Kosovo

Republika e Kosovës

Capital: Pristina (Population estimate: 600,000)

Head of State: Atifete Jahjaga (page 1448)

Flag: Blue background with a gold silhouette of Kosovo centred, six white stars are in an arc above the silhouette.

CONSTITUTION AND GOVERNMENT

Constitution
On February 17 2008 the Kosovan parliament formally endorsed a declaration of independence from Serbia. The announcement was condemned by Serbia. An emergency session of the UN Security Council was convened, as Russia condemned the announcement stating that the 1999 UN resolution to administer Kosovo was still in force. Since the declaration around 40 countries have recognised the new state including most European countries, the United States, Australia and Japan.

After declaring independence from Serbia, Kosovo adopted a new constitution in April 2008. The constitution promises to protect minorities and to establish good relations with all neighbours. The new constitution came into force on June 15 2008, the date that the UN completed its handover to the new state. The UN Mission in Kosovo (UNMIK), has been in place since the end of the 1998-99 conflict.

To consult the constitution, please visit: http://www.kushtetutakosoves.info/?cid=2,302

Recent Events
Since the eighth century Slavic and Albanian people have lived in the Kosovo region and over the centuries the ethnic balance of power had grown in favour of the Albanians. Following the defeat of Serbia at the Battle of Kosovo in 1389 the area came under the rule of the Ottoman empire and Serbia did not regain control of the area until 1913 when the region became part of Yugoslavia. There was an uneasy peace between the Serbs and the ethnic Albanians. In 1974 the Yugoslav Constitution named Kosovo as an autonomous province, but following the death of Yugoslav President Tito in 1980, Kosovo began pressure to become independent. In 1989 Slobodan Milosevic became president and stripped Kosovo of its autonomy, and ethnic Albanians found themselves excluded from employment, education and the healthcare system. In response to this Kosovo Albanians set up parallel institutions which in 1991 voted for independence. Following a secret election in 1992 Ibrahim Rugova was appointed president.

Between 1993 and 1997 ethnic tensions between Serbs and Ethnic Albanians escalated and in 1998 they boiled over into open conflict between the Serb police and the Kosovo Liberation Army. Many civilians were forced to leave their homes. The UN intervened and in June 1999 the Serbian Parliament voted to accept the NATO peace proposal for Kosovo. Under international rule since June 1999, Kosovo was then governed by an interim administration council. The council, set up by Bernard Kouchner of the UN's Interim Administration Mission in Kosovo (UNMIK), consisted of four UN and four local representatives. Hans Haekkerup was the Secretary-General's Special Representative in Kosovo from January to December 2001. He was replaced by Michael Steiner in February 2002. Although one of the local representatives was required to be Serbian, the Serbs boycotted the council until April 2000 when they agreed to the status of observers for a trial period of three months.

Assembly elections were held in October 2004. The Government was formed of a coalition of the Democratic League of Kosovo and the Alliance for the Future of Kosovo with the support of some smaller parties. Ibrahim Rugova was re-elected to the post of President in the following December and he nominated Ramush Haradinaj as prime minister. In January 2006 President Rugova died of lung cancer and was succeeded by Fatmir Sajdiu.

UN-sponsored talks on the future status of Kosovo began in February 2006 and in July talks began between the ethnic Serbian and Albanian leaders in Vienna. In October a referendum was held in Serbia to approve a new constitution which would declare Kosovo to be an integral part of Serbia. Kosovo Albanians boycotted the vote. UN brokered talks continued and in February 2007 UN envoy Martti Ahtisaari unveiled a plan to take Kosovo forward to independence, the proposal was rejected by Serbia. In July 2007 the UN resolution had to be re-drafted to drop the promise of independence for Kosovo on the insistence of Russia, the promise was replaced by a pledge to review the situation if there is no agreement following further talks.

A general election was held in November 2007 and Kosovo declared independence in February 2008 which was immediately declared illegal by Serbia but several major European nations and the USA recognized the independence of Kosovo.

On June 15 2008 Kosovo's new constitution came into force formally ending nine years of UN control. Serbia still does not recognise Kosovo's independence. In response the Kosovon Serbs set up their own assembly based in Mitrovica. The UN General Assembly voted to refer Kosovo's independence declaration to the International Court of Justice.

In December 2008, a European Union mission (Eulex) took over responsibility for police, justice and customs services from UN. Serbia accepted the EU mission. The following month a new multi-ethnic Kosovo Security Force was launched under NATO supervision.

Kosovo and Serbia held their first talks in March 2011 since Kosovo broke away from Serbia.

In October 2012, Kosovan prime minister Hashim Thaci, and Ivica Dacic from Serbia met in Brussels for the first talks between the two nations since Kosovo proclaimed independence.

In January 2013 the EU mediated talks between Kosovo and Serbia after the parliament in Belgrade approved support for the minority Serb rights within Kosovo. In April, Kosovo and Serbia reached an agreement on normalising their relations. Under the terms of the deal both sides agree not to block each other's efforts to try for EU membership.

Legislature

The Kosovo Assembly is made up of 120 seats; 100 are directly voted for, 20 are reserved for non Albanian minorities, 10 for Kosovo Serbs and the remaining ten are divided between representatives of the Roma, Ashkali, Egyptian, Bosniak, Turk and Goran minorities. All members are elected for a term of four years.

Assembly of the Republic of Kosovo, (Republika e Kosovës Kuvendi), Rruga Nëna Tereze p.n.10 000 Pristina, Republic of Kosovo. Tel: +381 (0)38 211 186, e-mail: mail@ks-gov.net, URL: http://www.kuvendikosoves.org; http://www.ks-gov.net/portal/eng.htm

Cabinet (as at June 2013)

Prime Minister: Hashim Thaci (page 1524)
First Deputy Prime Minister, Minister of Foreign Policy and Foreign Investments: Behgjet Pacolli
Deputy Prime Minister, Minister for Foreign Policy and National Security: Edita Tahiri
Deputy Prime Minister, Minister of Public Governance: Slobodan Petrovic
Deputy Prime Minister, Minister for Economic Development: Bujar Bukoshi
Deputy Prime Minister, Minister of Justice: vacant
Deputy Prime Minister, Minister of Trade and Industry: Mimoza Kusari-Lila
Minister of Finance: Bedri Hamza
Minister of Education, Science and Technology: Rame Buja
Minister of Internal Affairs: Bajram Rexhepi
Minister of Health: Ferid Agani
Minister of Infrastructure: Fehmi Mujota
Minister of Kosovo Security Force: Agim Ceku
Minister of Public Administration: Mahir Yagcilar
Minister of Agriculture, Forestry and Rural Development: Blerand Stavileci
Minister of Returns and Communities: Radojica Tomic
Minister of Foreign Affairs: Enver Hoxhaj
Minister of the Environment and Spatial Planning: Dardan Gashi
Minister of Labour and Social Welfare: Nenad Rasic
Minister of Culture, Youth and Sport: Memli Krasniqi
Minister of Integration with the EU: Vlora Citaku
Minister of Economic Development and Energy: Besim Beqaj
Minister of Culture, Youth and Sport: Memli Krasniqi
Minister of Kosovans Abroad: Ibrahim Malolli

Ministries

Office of the President, Mother Theresa Street, 10 000 Prishtina, Kosovo. URL: http://www.president-ksgov.net/
Office of Prime Minister, URL: http://www.kryeministri-ks.net/
Minister of Culture, Youth and Sport, Tel: +381 38 211 637, fax: +381 38 211 440, e-mail: info@mkrs-ks.org, URL: http://www.mkrs-ks.org/
Ministry of Defence, Emshiri - 1, 10 000 Prishtina, Kosovo. URL: http://mksf-ks.org/
Ministry of Economics and Finance, Sheshi Nënë Tereza, Ndërtesa Qeveritare, Prishtina 10000, Kosovo. URL: http://www.mef-rks.org/
Ministry of Infrastructure, Ndertesa e Kuvendit të Kosovës, Aneksi i Ri, 10000, Prishtina, Kosovo. E-mail: info@mtpt.org, URL: http://www.mtpt.org/
Ministry of Internal Affairs, Luan Haradinaj p.n., 10000 Prishtina, Kosovo. URL: http://www.mpb.org/
Ministry of Justice, Tel: +381/38/200-18-001, URL: http://www.md-ks.org/
Ministry of Trade and Industry, URL: http://www.mti-ks.org/

Political Parties

The main political parties are Democratic Party of Kosovo (PDK); Democratic League of Kosovo (LDK); New Kosovo Alliance (AKR); Democratic League of Dardania (LDD); Alliance for the Future of Kosovo (AAK); Serbian Liberal Party (SLS).

Elections

The new Kosovo government replaced the United Nations' Mission in Kosovo (UNMIK), set up to bring about 'substantial autonomy' for the province as set out in UN Resolution 1244. At the beginning of March 2002 the 120-member Kosovo Assembly elected Ibrahim Rugova President of Kosovo and Bajram Rexhepi Prime Minister. The Assembly also agreed the appointment of a 10-member cabinet, with four ministries going to the Democratic Alliance of Kosovo, two to the Democratic Party of Kosovo, two to the Alliance for the Future of Kosovo, and one each for Serbs and Bosniaks. The Assembly has a term of three years beginning on the date of the inaugural session thirty days after election results are formally announced. Ten seats are reserved for Serbs, and 10 for other ethnic minorities such as Roma, Turks and Bosniaks. Its Presidency consists of seven Assembly members, including one Serb community member. The Assembly was composed of the following political parties: Democratic League of Kosovo (45.6 per cent), Democratic Party of Kosovo (25.7 per cent), Povratak Coalition (11.3 per cent), Alliance for Kosovo Future (7.8 per cent), and others (9.5 per cent). The Assembly is responsible for the adoption of laws and resolutions, as well as the election of the President of Kosovo. However, it does not have the power to decide on Kosovo's political status. Meetings of the Assembly are conducted in the Albanian and Serbian languages, and official documents are printed in Albanian and Serbian.

Assembly elections were held in October 2004. The Democratic League of Kosovo (DLK) won 47 seats, the Democratic Party of Kosova won 30 seats and the Alliance for the Future of Kosovo won nine seats. The Government is a coalition of the Democratic League of Kosova and the Alliance for the Future of Kosova with the support of some smaller parties. Ibrahim

Rugova leader of the DLK was re-elected to the post of President the following December and he nominated Ramush Haradinaj prime minister. In March 2005 Prime Minister Haradinah resigned following charges of war crimes brought by the UN tribunal at The Hague. Bajram Kosumi was named as the new prime minister. UN sponsored talks began in November 2005 with the aim of paving the way to establishing a democratic government. On January 22 2006, President Rugova died and Fatmir Sejdiu was elected by the parliament to the post. Prime Minister Kosumi offered his resignation in March and Lt.-Gen. Agim Ceku was appointed to the post.

The next election was held in November 2007 but was boycotted by the Serb minority. The Democratic Party of Kosovo (PDK) led by Hashim Thaci claimed victory and Mr Thaci announced that he would declare independence on 10 December, the deadline for talks on Kosovo's future at the UN. Independence was declared on February 17 2008.

The most recent legislative elections were held on 12 December 2010 and 9 January 2011. The results were as follows: PDK 34 seats; LV 14 seats; AAK 12 seats; New Kosovo Coalition (led by the AKR) 8 seats; SLS 8 seats; others 17 seats. An agreement on a coalition government was reached in February .

A presidential election was held on 22 February 2011. Behgjet Pacolli's was the only candidate in the election and took office in February. However the constitutional court ruled on 28 March that the election was unconstitutional because after a boycott by opposition deputies not enough members of parliament were present for the vote. The speaker of parliament, Jakup Krasniqi, became acting president. President Behget Pacolli formally resigned on 30 March and was invited to become first deputy prime minister. On 7 April Atifete Jahjaga, a non-party candidate, was elected president and took office immediately.

Local elections took place in November 2009.

Diplomatic Representation

US Embassy, Arberia/Dragodan, Nazim Hikmet 30, Pristina, Kosovo. Tel: +381 38 59 59 3000, fax: +381 38 549 890, e-mail: PaPristina@state.gov, URL: http://pristina.usembassy.gov
Ambassador: Tracey Ann Jacobson (page 1448)
British Embassy, Ismail Qemali 6, Arberi-Dragodan, Pristina, 10000, Kosovo. Tel:+381 (0)38 254 700, fax:+381 (0)38 249 799, e-mail: britishembassy.pristina@fco.gov.uk, URL: http://ukinkosovo.fco.gov.uk
Ambassador: Ian Cameron Cliff, OBE (page 1406)
Kosovan Embassy, 100 Pall Mall, London SW1Y 5NQ, UK. Tel: +44 (0)20 7659 6140, fax: +44 (0)20 7659 6137, e-mail: embassy.uk@ks-gov.net, URL: http://www.ambasada-ks.net/gb/?page=2,1
Ambassador: Lirim Greiçevci
Kosovan Embassy, Suite 400, 900 19th Street, Presidential Plaza, NW, Washington DC 20006, USA. Tel: +1 202 380 3581, fax: +1 202 380 3628, e-mail: embassy.usa@ks-gov.net, URL: http://ambasada-ks.net/us
Ambassador: Akan Ismaili

LEGAL SYSTEM

The Kosovo judicial system has recently been reformed, with reforms to court structure.

The Supreme Court is the highest judicial authority and is located in Prishtina.

The Constitutional Court was set up in 2009 and is the supreme authority on interpretations of the constitution. The court has nine judges, overseen by a president. The Court of Appeals is the court of second instance. The Basic Courts are the courts of first instance. A new prosecutorial system has been developed headed by the Chief State Prosecutor.

The **Kosovo Judicial Council** was set up to ensure the independence and impartiality of the judicial system. URL: http://kgjk-ks.org/

The **Kosovo Prosecutorial Council** is also an independent institution which acts to ensure an independent and impartial prosecution system.

Capital punishment is prohibited under the 2008 constitution.

Office of the Ombudsman in Kosovo,
URL: http://www.ombudspersonkosovo.org/?id=3,e,1

LOCAL GOVERNMENT

Kosovo is divided into 38 municipalities: Decan (Decani), Dragash (Dragas), Ferizaj (Urosevac), Fushe Kosove (Kosovo Polje), Gjakove (Dakovica), Gjilan (Gnjilane), Gllogovc/Drenas (Glogovac), Istog (Istok), Kacanik, Kamenice/Dardana (Kamenica), Kline (Klina), Leposaviq (Leposavic), Lipjan (Lipljan), Malisheve (Malisevo), Mitrovice (Mitrovica), Novoberde (Novo Brdo), Obiliq (Obilic), Peje (Pec), Podujeve (Podujevo), Prishtine (Pristina), Prizren, Rahovec (Orahovac), Shterpce (Strpce), Shtime (Stimlje), Skenderaj (Srbica), Suhareke (Suva Reka), Viti (Vitina), Vushtrri (Vucitrn), Zubin Potok, Zvecan, Gracanice (Gracanica), Hani i Elezit (Dzeneral Jankovic), Junik, Kllokot-Verboc (Klokot-Vrbovac), Mamushe (Mamusa), Partes, and Ranillug (Ranilug). It has been proposed that the existing Mitrovice (Mitrovica) municipality will be divided into Mitrovice (Mitrovica) North and Mitrovice (Mitrovica) South. Further municipalities are expected to be created. Municipal elections took place most recently in 2009.

SERBIA

AREA AND POPULATION

Area
Kosovo is a landlocked country covering an area of 10,887 sq km. It is situated in the south western corner of Serbia and has borders with Montenegro, Former Yugoslav Republic of Macedonia and Albania. Some of the land is a flat fluvial basin, rising to high mountain ranges, rising over 2,500 metres. With some regional variations, winters are cold with heavy snowfall and summers are hot and dry.

To view a map, consult http://www.lib.utexas.edu/maps/cia08/kosovo_sm_2008.gif

Population
2011 figures estimate the population to be 1.85 million. Albanians make up about 88 per cent of the population with Serbs making up six per cent, Bosniaks three per cent, Roma three per cent and Turks, one per cent. Main languages spoken are Albanian, Serbian, Bosniak and Turkish.

Public Holidays 2014
1-2 January: New Year's Day
7 January: Orthodox Christmas Day
17 February: Independence Day
18-21 April: Catholic Easter, Orthodox Easter
9 April: Kosovo Constitution Day
1-3 May: Labour Day
11 May: Europe Holiday
8 August: Eid al-Fitr*
5 October: Festival of the Sacrifice Eid al-Adha*
25 December: Catholic Christmas
*Islamic holidays are based on the sighting of the moon so dates may vary.

EMPLOYMENT

Kosovo suffers from high unemployment which will initially effect the growth of the economy. Estimated figures for 2009 put the labour force at 310,000 with an unemployment rate of 45 per cent.

BANKING AND FINANCE

The economy is driven by the government sector. Although the economy has progressed since the 1990s it is still dependent on the international community for financial assistance and remittances from abroad. Unemployment is high and per capita income is the lowest in Europe. Kosovo is trying to develop its market-orientated economy.

Currency
One Euro (€) = 100 cents

GDP/GNP, Inflation, National Debt
GDP was estimated to be US$6.2 billion in 2010 with a per capita GDP of US$2,750. The growth rate was estimated to be 4 per cent. GDP was estimated to be US$6.4 billion in 2011. Inflation was estimated to be 8 per cent in 2011. GDP by sector was approximately: Agriculture 13 per cent, industry 22 per cent and services 65 per cent.

Kosovo joined the IMF and the World Bank in 2009.

External debt was estimated to be US$325 million in 2011.

Balance of Payments / Imports and Exports
Figures for 2010 estimated Kosovo's export earnings to be US$400 million and the cost of imports to be US$3 billion.

Kosovo's main trading partner is the former Yugoslav republic of Macedonia, followed by Serbia, Germany, China and Turkey.

MANUFACTURING, MINING AND SERVICES

Primary and Extractive Industries
Kosovo has deposits of coal, lead, zinc, nickel, magnesium, bauxite, chromium, silver and halloysite.

Agriculture
The agriculture sector is the largest employer and contributes around 30 per cent of GDP. Main crops grown include wheat, corn, and potatoes, fruits including apples, pears and plums and vegetables including tomatoes and peppers.

COMMUNICATIONS AND TRANSPORT

Travel Requirements
Citizens of the USA, Canada, Australia and most of the EU require a valid passport but do not need a visa for tourism stays of up to 90 days. Hungarians and Romanians do require a visa to enter the country, and Bulgarians need a visa for stays of up to 30 days for tourism purposes. Other nationals and people wishing to visit for reasons other than tourism should contact the embassy to check visa requirements.

All foreigners arriving in Kosovo must present documentation supporting their reason for entry to the border police at their point of entry. Visitors not staying at hotels must register with the police within 24 hours from arrival. All nationals staying longer than three days must register with the police.

Railways
Kosovo Railways runs services to Pistina, Peja, Fushë Kosovë, Gracanica, Han I Elezit and Mitrovica. There is a rail link to Skopje in Macedonia but there is currently no link to Belgrade in Serbia.
Kosovo Railways: URL: http://www.kosovorailway.com

Roads
Kosovo has nearly 2,000 km of road system, Vehicles are driven on the right.

HEALTH

Major investment in the quality of basic health is need to improve health. There are five regional hospitals. In 2006 there were an estimated 7 maternal deaths per 100,000 live births. The perinatal mortality rate was 23 per 1,000 live births. The life expectancy at birth is 69 years. In 2006, an estimated 78 per cent of the rural population had access to safe water.

RELIGION

The majority of the population are Muslim but there are Eastern Orthodox Christian and Roman Catholic minorities.

COMMUNICATIONS AND MEDIA

A UN-backed commission created a code of conduct for journalists aimed at preventing incitement to hatred. Most of the media use Albanian as their language.

Newspapers
The market is fairly limited. Titles include:
Koha Ditore (The Daily Times), biggest circulation, daily, URL: http://www.koha.net/index.php
Bota Sot (The World Today), daily, and Kosova Sot (Kosovo Today).

Broadcasting
Most Kosovans use the television as their news source. The public broadcaster Kosovo Radio Television (RTK) was set up to be editorially independence. It operates Radio Kosova and the former UN station Radio Blue Sky. There are nearly 100 licensed radio stations.
RTK, URL: http://www.rtklive.com/

Telecommunications
In 2006/07 there were estimated to be approximately 105,000 main lines in use and 550,00 mobile phones.

SEYCHELLES
Republic of Seychelles

Capital: Victoria (Population estimate: 25,000)

Head of State: James Michel (President) (page 1477)

Vice-President: Danny Fauré (page 1423)

National Flag: Five oblique bands of blue, yellow, red, white and green, the bands originating in the bottom left fanning out to fill up the fly

CONSTITUTION AND GOVERNMENT

Constitution
The Seychelles, a former Crown Colony, has been an independent Republic within the Commonwealth since June 1976. The constitution dates from June 1993 when a referendum approved the constitution drafted by the Constitutional Commission, an elected body. Executive power lies with the president, who is elected by universal adult suffrage for a maximum of three successive five-year terms. As the head of government, the president appoints the Council of Ministers.

To consult the constitution, please visit: http://www.ecs.sc/pages/legislations/constitution.aspx.

International Relations
The Seychelles Government supports the 'Indian Ocean zone of peace' concept, and wants an end to the US presence on Diego Garcia. The country aims to promote its reputation as a safe and secure tourist destination, and a leader in environmental and conservationist matters.

The Seychelles is a member of the Nonaligned Movement (NAM), the African Union, Commonwealth, International Monetary Fund (IMF), Indian Ocean Commission (IOC), La Francophonie, and the UN and some of its specialised and related agencies.

Recent Events
Although located more than 7,000 km from the epicentre of the earthquake that triggered the tsunami on 26 December 2004, the Seychelles suffered severe flooding and widespread damage to roads, fishing infrastructure and tourism facilities. Government estimates of the cost of the tsunami and subsequent heavy rains that lashed the islands amounted to $30 million, though other estimates for repairing the damage were more conservative.

The Seychelles has been affected by the global economic downturn. In 2008 the IMF agreed a US$26-million rescue package. In January 2009 the Seychelles asked creditors to cancel some 50 per cent of its US$800 million foreign debt. Later that year the World Bank approved a US$9 million loan to help to restore the country's economic stability.

The Seychelles became a signatory to the International Criminal Court in August 2010.

Legislature
Legislative power rests with the unicameral National Assembly, which consists of 34 members, 23 of whom are directly elected for a five-year term, and 11 of whom are appointed by proportional representation. All serve terms of five years.
National Assembly, PO Box 734, Victoria, Mahé, Republic of Seychelles. Tel: +248 321333, e-mail: parlsg@seychelles.net, URL: http://www.nationalassembly.gov.sc/

Cabinet (as of March 2013)
Minister of Defence; Legal Affairs, Information, Youth and Hydrocarbons: President James Michel (page 1477)
Minister of Information Technology, Communication & Public Administration: Vice President Danny Fauré (page 1423)
Minister of Foreign Affairs: Jean-Paul Adam (page 1372)
Minister of Finance & Trade: Pierre Laporte (page 1460)
Minister of Internal Affairs & Transport: Joel Morgan
Minister of Education: MacSuzy Mondon
Minister of Community Development & Social Affairs: Vincent Meriton
Minister of Tourism and Culture: Alain St Ange
Minister of Health: Mitcy Larue
Minister of Employment & Human Resources: Idith Alexander
Minister of Lands and Housing: Christian Lionnet
Minister of Environment & Energy: Rolph Payet
Minister of Natural Resources & Industry: Peter Sinon
Secretary of State in the Office of the President: Barry Faure

---

Ministries
Office of the President, PO Box 55, State House, Victoria, Mahé, Republic of Seychelles. Tel: +248 224155, fax: +248 225255, e-mail: state@seychelles.net, URL: http://www.virtualseychelles.sc
Attorney General's Chambers, P.O. Box 58, National House, Victoria, Mahé, Republic of Seychelles. Tel: +248 383000, fax: +248 225063, e-mail: agdepart@Seychelles.net
Ministry of Foreign Affairs, P.O. Box 656, "Maison Quéau de Quinssy", Mont Fleuri, Mahé, Republic of Seychelles. Tel: +248 283500, fax: +248 224845, URL: http://www.virtualseychelles.sc/
Ministry of Internal Affairs & Transport, Victoria, Mahé, Seychelles. URL: http://www.virtualseychelles.sc

Ministry of Finance, Liberty House, PO Box 113, Central Bank Building, Victoria, Mahé, Republic of Seychelles. Tel: +248 382000, fax: +248 225265, e-mail: ps-finance@finance.gov.sc, URL: http://www.finance.gov.sc
Ministry of Information Technology and Communication, 3rd Floor Caravelle House, Manglier Street, PO Box 737, Victoria, Mahé, Republic of Seychelles. Tel: +248 286600, fax: +248 323720, e-mail: psoffice@ict.gov.sc, URL: http://www.ict.gov.sc
Ministry of Land Use and Habitat, Independence House, PO Box 119, Victoria, Mahé, Republic of Seychelles. Tel: +248 284444, fax: +248 225014, URL: http://www.virtualseychelles.sc
Ministry of Social Affairs, Community Development and Sports, National Library, Victoria, Mahé, Republic of Seychelles. URL: http://www.virtualseychelles.sc
Ministry of Health and Social Services, P.O. Box 52, Victoria, Mahé, Republic of Seychelles. Tel: +248 388016, fax: +248 224792, e-mail: mohps@seychelles.net, URL: http://www.moh.sc
Ministry of Education, PO Box 48, Mont Fleuri, Mahé, Republic of Seychelles. Tel: +248 283283, fax: +248 224859, e-mail: ps@eduhq.edu.sc, URL: http://www.virtualseychelles.sc
Ministry of Environment & Energy, P.O Box 445, Botanical Gardens, Victoria, Mahé, Republic of Seychelles. Tel: +248 224644, fax: +248 224500, URL: http://www.env.gov.sc/
Ministry of Employment & HR, Independence House, PO Box 1097, Victoria, Mahé, Republic of Seychelles. Tel: +248 676250, fax: +248 610795, e-mail: psemploy@seychelles.net, URL: http://www.virtualseychelles.sc

Elections
In April 2004, President René stepped down and was succeeded by the former vice-president, James Michel. In the July 2006 elections, Mr. Michel won nearly 54 per cent of the vote whilst his rival, the Anglican priest Wavel Ramkalawan, won 46 per cent. The win extended the 30-year rule of the People's Progressive Front SPPF) for another five years. The most recent presidential elections took place on 19-21 May 2011 and were won again by Mr Michel with over 55 per cent of the vote.

The last parliamentary election was held in May 2007, following a six-month boycott in the National Assembly by the SNP opposition party. The SPPF party was re-elected, retaining its 23 seats; the SNP (in alliance with the DP) retained 11 seats. The electoral process for the 2007 National Assembly elections was determined to be credible by international observers. The next parliamentary election is due in May 2012.

Political Parties
Front Progressiste du Peuple Seychellois (SPPF). URL: http://www.sppf.sc/
Leader: France Albert René
Seychelles National Party (SNP), PO Box 81, Arpent Vert, Mont Fleuri, Mahé, Seychelles. Tel: +248 224124, fax: +248 225151, e-mail: snp2003@hotmail.com, URL: http://www.seychelles.net/snp/
Party Leader: Wavel Ramkalawan

Diplomatic Representation
British High Commission, 3rd Floor, Oliaji Trade Centre, Francis Rachel Street, PO Box 161, Victoria, Mahé, Republic of Seychelles. Tel: +248 283666, fax: +248 283657, e-mail: bhcvictoria@fco.gov.uk, URL: http://ukinseychelles.fco.gov.uk/en
High Commissioner: Matthew Forbes
US Embassy, (The Port Louis embassy is also responsible for the Seychelles) 4th Floor, Rogers House, John Kennedy Avenue, Port Louis, Mauritius. Tel: +230 202 4400, fax: +230 208 9534, e-mail: usembass@intnet.mu, URL: http://seychelles.usvpp.gov
Chargé d'Affaires: Troy Fitrell
Embassy of the Seychelles, 800 Second Avenue, Suite 400, New York NY 10017, USA. Tel: +1 212 687 9766, fax: +1 212 972 1786
Ambassador: Ronald Jean Jumeau (page 1452)
Seychelles High Commission, (The Seychelles is not represented in the UK. The nearest diplomatic mission is located in Paris.) 51 Avenue Mozart, 75016 Paris, France. Tel: +33 (0)1 42 30 57 47, fax: +33 (0)1 42 30 57 40, e-mail: seyhclon@aol.com
High Commissioner: Patrick Pillay
Permanent Representative of the Republic of Seychelles to the United Nations, 800 Second Avenue, Suite 400C, New York, NY 10017, USA. Tel: +1 212 972 1785, fax: +1 212 972 1786,
URL: http://www.un.int/wcm/content/site/seychelles/cache/offonce/pid/3805
Ambassador: Ronald Jean Jumeau (page 1452)

LEGAL SYSTEM

The legal system is similar to the English system except that civil law is based the French Napoleonic Code, not common law.

The highest court in Seychelles is the Court of Appeal, headed by the President who sits with two other Justices of Appeal when hearing cases. Next is the Supreme Court which is headed by the Chief Justice. The Supreme Court is the trial court for complex and 'high-value' civil matters and tries serious criminal offences. It is also has appellate jurisdiction. It is the appeal court for all the lower courts and tribunals. There are five Magistrate's Courts, which handle less serious criminal offences and civil matters where a low monetary value is in dispute. Magistrates are fully qualified lawyers. The administrative head of these courts is the Registrar of the Supreme Court.

SEYCHELLES

There are also Family Tribunals, Employment Tribunals and a Constitutional Court. The latter is presided over by any three of the five Supreme Court Judges who hear petitions regarding breaches of the Constitution. Decisions of the Constitutional Court can be appealed in the Court of Appeal.

The government respects the rights of its citizens. However, there have been instances of arbitrary arrest and prolonged pretrial detention, as well as reports of abuse of detainees. Official corruption persists, and there are restrictions on speech, press, and assembly. There have also been recent violations of labor rights; and discrimination against foreign workers. Seychelles abolished the death penalty for all crimes in 1993.

President, Court of Appeal: Francis MacGregor

LOCAL GOVERNMENT

The Seychelles is divided into 23 administrative districts: Anse aux Pins, Anse Boileau, Anse Etoile, Anse Louis, Anse Royale, Baie Lazare, Baie Sainte Anne, Beau Vallon, Bel Air, Bel Ombre, Cascade, Glacis, Grand' Anse (Mahe), Grand' Anse (Praslin), La Digue, La Riviere Anglaise, Mont Buxton, Mont Fleuri, Plaisance, Pointe La Rue, Port Glaud, Saint Louis, and Takamaka.

AREA AND POPULATION

Area
The Seychelles is a group of 115 islands and atolls, situated in the Indian Ocean to the northwest of Madagascar and east of Kenya. Their total land area is 455 sq. km. This figure includes the former British Indian Ocean Territories (Aldabra, Farquhar, Desroches) that were returned to the Seychelles on 29 June 1976. The Mahe group of islands has a rocky, hilly terrain, whilst the other islands are flat coral reefs. The climate is tropical marine, with a cooler season during the south-east monsoon, May to September, and a warmer season during the north-west monsoon, March to May. Aldabra, with its unique ecology, has been designated a World Heritage site and the Vallée de Mai, on Praslin, is also a World Heritage site.

To view a map, please see
http://www.lib.utexas.edu/maps/cia08/seychelles_sm_2008.gif

Population
The estimated total population of the Seychelles in 2010 was estimated at 87,000 with an average annual population growth of 0.9 per cent over the period 2000-10. The majority of Seychellois (76 per cent) are aged between 15 and 64, with 23 per cent aged up to 14 years, and 11 per cent 60 years and over. Most of the Seychellois live on Mahe Island. Around 10 per cent live on Praslin and La Digue, and the remaining smaller islands are either sparsely populated or uninhabited.

Most Seychellois are descendants of French settlers and the African slaves freed them from slave ships on the East African coast. Indians and Chinese account for just over one per cent of the population, and there is a small Arab community. Creole is the native language of 94 per cent of the people, but English is used in government and business, and French is also widely used.

Births, Marriages, Deaths
According to 2010 estimates the crude birth rate is 16 births per 1,000 people, whilst the death rate is 8.2 deaths per 1,000 people. Infant mortality is 12 deaths per 1,000 live births, whilst the total fertility rate is an estimated 1.9 children born per woman. Average life expectancy was 73 years (69 years for men and 77 years for women) in 2009. Healthy life expectancy was 60 years and 65 years respectively. (Source: http://www.who.int, World Health Statistics 2012)

Public Holidays 2014
1-2 January: New Year
18 April: Good Friday
21 April: Easter Monday
5 May: Labour Day
5 June: Liberation Day
19 June: Corpus Christi
18 June: National Day
29 June: Independence Day
15 August: Assumption
1 November: All Saints' Day
8 December: Immaculate Conception
25 December: Christmas Day

EMPLOYMENT

In 2004, the Seychelles had an estimated 32,780 people in paid work (i.e. excluding self-employed, domestic servants and family workers). Estimated figures for 2006 put the workforce at 39,560 with an unemployment rate of 2 per cent.

Total Employment by Economic Activity

Occupation	2008
Agriculture, hunting & forestry	619
Fishing	334
Mining & quarrying	18
Manufacturing	4,170
Electricity, gas & water supply	1,013
Construction	5,726

- continued

Wholesale & retail trade, repairs	2,778
Hotels & restaurants	6,030
Transport, storage & communications	4,242
Financial intermediation	865
Real estate, renting & business activities	1,987
Public admin. & defence; compulsory social security	6,039
Education	2,694
Health & social work	1,690
Other community, social & personal service activities	3,137
Total	41,342

Source: Copyright © International Labour Organization (ILO Dept. of Statistics, http://laborsta.ilo.org)

BANKING AND FINANCE

The financial centre is Victoria.

Currency
The monetary unit is the Seychelles rupee (SCR).

GDP/GNP, Inflation, National Debt
The economy is primarily based on fishing and tourism; employment, foreign revenue, construction and banking are largely dependent on these two industries. The tourist sector employs approximately 30 per cent of the workforce, but is subject to the changes in the global economy and as a result in the last few years, the fishing industry has become the largest foreign exchange earner with tuna canning and exports accounting for over 50 per cent of GDP. However, these industries face increasing regional competition. Also, the tourism industry has been severely affected by the global economic downturn. In January 2009, the Seychelles asked creditors to cancel some 50 per cent of its US$800 million foreign debt. In November 2009 the World Bank approved a US$9 million loan to help the country restore economic stability.

The services sector as a whole accounts for around 70 per cent of GDP, whilst manufacturing industry contributes between 15 and 20 per cent (depending on output from the Indian Ocean Tuna cannery), and agriculture accounts for just under 3 per cent. GDP was an estimated US$710 million in 2007, with growth of around 5.3 per cent. Figures for 2009 put GDP at US$655 million reflecting a growth rate that year of -8.6 per cent, per capita GDP that year was put at US$19,400. Estimates for 2010 put GDP at US$750 million with a growth rate of over 6 per cent. It was estimated to be US$1 billon in 2011.

Inflation has been brought under control from its high of 32 per cent in 2009. Estimates put 2011 inflation at 2.5 per cent. Total external debt in 2011 was US$1.4 billion.

The main feature of the economy has been a shortage of foreign exchange over recent years. The International Monetary Fund (IMF) has urged devaluation of the Rupee and is concerned at the fiscal and balance of payments deficits that have been financed by accumulating large external debt arrears. In October 2006, the Minister of Finance announced measures to start the process of a gradual liberalization of foreign exchange transactions.

Foreign Investment
In order to remain competitive in the tourism sector, the Seychelles government has sought to encourage foreign investment in hotels and services so that these can be upgraded. Direct foreign investment was estimated to be US$365 million.

Balance of Payments / Imports and Exports
The foreign sector of the Seychelles is characterised by a small volume of exports and by large imports of food commodities, fuel and manufactured products. This significant commercial deficit is compensated by the surplus generated by the service sector. The Seychelles' major export commodities include canned tuna, frozen fish, copra, cinnamon bark and petroleum products. Import commodities include food, petroleum products, machinery and equipment and chemicals.

In 2009, exports earned the country some $360 million, rising to US$405 million in 2010. Principal exports were canned tuna, frozen/fresh fish, frozen prawns and cinnamon bark. Export trading partners are the United Kingdom, France, Italy, and Germany. Imports cost the Seychelles around $657 million. Import trading partners are Saudi Arabia, South Africa, Spain, France, Italy, Singapore, and the UK. Imports cost an estimated US$900 million in 2010.

The Seychelles used to belong to the Southern African Development Community (SADC) whose aims included the development of sustainable trade, including an 85 per cent reduction of internal trade barriers by 2008. The Seychelles left SADC in 2004.

Central Bank
Central Bank of Seychelles, PO Box 701, Victoria, Mahé, Seychelles. Tel: +248 428 2000, fax: +248 422 6104, e-mail: enquiries@cbs.sc, URL: http://www.cbs.sc/
Governor: Caroline Abel

Chambers of Commerce and Trade Organisations
Seychelles Chambers of Commerce and Industry, URL: http://www.scci-sey.org/
Seychelles International Business Authority, URL: http://www.siba.net/

MANUFACTURING, MINING AND SERVICES

Energy
The Seychelles has no reserves of oil, natural gas or coal, and relies on imports. In 2011, a total of 9,000 barrels of oil was imported, mainly distillate, as well as jet fuel, gasoline, residual, and kerosene.

Electricity is produced entirely from imported oil. The cost of energy is a major problem. Installed electrical capacity was 0.09 gigawatts in 2010. Total electrical generation was 0.28 billion kilowatthours (kWh) in the same year, all of which was thermally produced. Electricity consumption was 0.26 billion kWh.

Total energy consumption was 0.015 quadrillion Btu in 2009.

Manufacturing
The Seychelles has little manufacturing capacity and is almost totally reliant on imports of basic commodities, from fuel to rice and vegetable oil. The current government has directed reform towards privatisation and greater market liberalisation. Industrial activities are limited to small scale manufacturing, particularly agro-processing. Despite attempts to improve its agricultural base and emphasize locally manufactured products and indigenous materials, the Seychelles continues to import 90 per cent of its requirements. Imports are controlled by the Seychelles Marketing Board (SMB), a government organisation which operates all the major supermarkets and is the distributor of most imports.

Service Industries
The service industries sector is the largest contributor to the Seychelles' economy, contributing nearly 71 per cent of GDP and employing over 70 per cent of the workforce.

Tourism
Together with the fishing industry, tourism is a pillar of the economy in the Seychelles, employing about 30 per cent of the labour force in 2003 and contributing some 26 per cent of GDP in the same year. In 2003, tourism earned $681.3 million. About 122,000 tourists visited Seychelles that year, 81.7 per cent of them from Europe (UK, Italy, France, Germany, Switzerland). By 2005, these figures had fallen to 17 per cent of the workforce and 10-15 per cent of GDP. In the past, the industry sought to attract the luxury end of the market; however, following the downturn in visitor numbers, there is a move to expand into offering more family-oriented holidays. Some argue for a devaluation of the Seychelles rupee against major currencies, to stimulate further tourism. However, the industry has been badly affected by the 2008/09 global economic crisis.

Visitors are charged approximately £60 to visit the islands. Some of the revenue is to fund conservation and the charge also includes entry to some of the top tourist sites, including coral reefs.

Agriculture
Once a major contributor to the economy, agriculture now provides less than 3 per cent of the Seychelles' GDP and employs three per cent of the workforce. Main agricultural industries include the cultivation of copra, cinnamon and tea for export, fruit and vegetables for local consumption, forestry and livestock. However, the Seychelles traditional plantation economy has faltered, with traditional export crops such as cinnamon barks and copra falling to negligible amounts by the beginning of the 1990s. Priority has always been given to activities which reduce imports. Much of the state holdings in the agricultural sector have been privatized, and the government's role is now limited to conducting research and providing infrastructure. Land has been redistributed and farmers are given greater freedom to market their products.

Agricultural Production in 2010

Produce	Int. $'000*	Tonnes
Hen eggs, in shell	1,037	1,250
Indigenous chicken meat	937	658
Indigenous pigmeat	469	305
Vegetables fresh nes	415	2,200
Bananas	394	1,400
Coconuts	188	1,700
Fruit, tropical fresh nes	82	200
Tomatoes	74	200
Cinnamon (canella)	68	49
Tea	52	49
Indigenous goat meat	50	21
Cow milk, whole, fresh	50	160

* unofficial figures
Source: http://faostat.fao.org/site/339/default.aspx Food and Agriculture Organization of the United Nations, Food and Agricultural commodities production

Fishing
Whilst agriculture's contribution to GDP has declined in recent years, the fishing industry, including industrial fishing, has developed and now accounts for around 40 per cent of the country's income. Earnings are growing annually from licensing fees paid by foreign trawlers fishing in Seychelles' territorial waters. Fishing also provides food, employment and local revenue. The sector employs around 10 per cent of the active population and fishing exports represent about 88 per cent of total exports. Fishing is carried out as a cottage industry as well as in semi-industrial and industrial forms. Annually, around 350 boats land between 3,000 and 4,000 mt of marine life, using mainly hook and line, beach seine nets and bamboo fish traps. The total catch for 2010 was put at 87,108 tonnes.

COMMUNICATIONS AND TRANSPORT

Travel Requirements
Citizens of the USA, Canada, Australia and the EU require a passport valid for the length of stay, an onward/return ticket, sufficient funds (US$100-150 per day) and proof of organised accommodation for the duration of the stay. If they fulfill the above criteria, they do not need a visa, but will be issued with a visitor's permit, valid for up to three months. Other nationals should contact the embassy to check visa requirements.

National Airlines
Air Seychelles, URL: http://www.airseychelles.net

International Airports
Air travel in the Seychelles has developed considerably since the construction of the international airport in 1971.

Roads
There is a total of 331 km of roads, of which 252 km are surfaced. Vehicles are driven on the left.

Ports and Harbours
The Seychelles are situated on the major commercial shipping routes of the Indian Ocean. Port Victoria is the only deep water port in the country, capable of dealing with commercial cargo such as large quantities of oil, and imports of cement and containers. In 1994 the Government took steps to make Port Victoria the principal shipping port of the west Indian Ocean, and the number of ships docking at Port Victoria rose from 358 in 1970 to 764 in 1994. In recent years, some port operations have been privatized, transshipment fees have been cut and there has been an overall increase in efficiency. This has sparked a recovery in port services.

HEALTH

The Seychelles have a vast infrastructure of integrated healthcare which includes community clinics in each district and health centres which are found throughout the country. Practically all the population has access to primary health care. Health care is essentially financed by social security tax. In 2009, the government spent approximately 9.0 per cent of its total budget on healthcare, accounting for 92.7 per cent of all healthcare spending. Total expenditure on healthcare equated to 3.3 per cent of the country's GDP. Per capita expenditure on health was approximately US$301, compared with US$377 in 2000.

According to 2000-10 WHO figures, there are 121 doctors (15 per 10,000 population), 634 nurses and midwives (79 per 10,000 inhabitants), 94 dentistry personnel, 61 pharmaceutical personnel, and 77 environment and public health workers. There are an estimated 39 hospital beds per 10,000 population.

All the urban population have access to improved drinking water and an estimated 97 per cent have sustained access to improved sanitation.

The infant mortality rate was estimated to be 12 per 1,000 live births in 2010 and the under-five mortality rate was 14 per 10,000 live births. An estimated 30 per cent of deaths in the under-fives were due to prematurity, 8 per cent to birth asphyxia, 25 per cent to congenital anomalies and 7 per cent to pneumonia. (Source: http://www.who.int, World Health Statistics 2012)

EDUCATION

Primary/Secondary Education
In 2006, 96 per cent of the relevant age group attended primary school, and 100 per cent of children were enrolled in secondary school. In primary schools, the pupil/teacher ratio was 12 to one.

Tertiary Education
Vocational, Technical and Advanced Level academic education are provided free of charge at the Seychelles Polytechnic founded in 1983.

In 2007, 12.6 per cent of government expenditure was spent on education, of which 42 per cent went on secondary education and 31 per cent on primary education. In 2004, it was estimated that 91.8 per cent of the adult population was literate, well above the regional average of 62.5 per cent. The literacy rate of school-aged children is around 99 per cent.

RELIGION

The Seychellois are predominantly Roman Catholic (82 per cent), with Anglicans, Seventh Day Adventists, Hindus and Muslims making up the balance.

The Seychelles has a religious liberty rating of 10 on a scale of 1 to 10 (10 is most freedom). (Source: World Religion Database)

COMMUNICATIONS AND MEDIA

Much of the media including the only daily paper is government controlled. There are tough libel laws. However freedom of expression has improved since the one-party rule was abolished in 1993.

Newspapers
The Nation, daily, URL: http://www.nation.sc/

SIERRA LEONE

The People, URL: http://www.thepeople.sc/
Le Nouveau Seychelles Weekly, URL: http://www.seychellesweekly.com/

Broadcasting
SBC TV(URL: http://www.sbc.sc/) is the state-run television and radio broadcaster. Satellite and cable television is widely available.

Telecommunications
The Seychelles has around 22,700 main line telephones in use (2007), and around 83,000 mobile phones. In 2008, there were approximately 32,000 internet users.

ENVIRONMENT

The Seychelles are a party to the following international environmental agreements: Biodiversity, Climate Change, Climate Change-Kyoto Protocol, Desertification, Endangered Species, Hazardous Wastes, Law of the Sea, Marine Dumping, Ozone Layer Protection, and Ship Pollution.

The Seychelles is vulnerable to climate change, and the government is therefore aware of the need for environment protection and natural disaster prevention. The country is linked to the Indian Ocean Tsunami Warning and Mitigation System (IOTWS). Other environment issues include periodic droughts and a water supply dependent on catchments to collect rainwater.

In 2010, the Seychelles' emissions from the consumption and flaring of fossil fuels totalled 1.25 million metric tons of carbon dioxide. (Source: EIA)

SIERRA LEONE
Republic of Sierra Leone

Capital: Freetown (Population estimate: 1.5 million)

Head of State: Ernest Bai Koroma (page 1458)

Vice President: Samuel Sam-Sumana

National Flag: A tricolour, fesswise, green, white and blue

CONSTITUTION AND GOVERNMENT

Constitution
Formerly a British Protectorate, Sierra Leone was governed under the provisions of the 1956 Constitution by an Executive Council over which the Governor presided. Under the Constitution of 14 August 1958, a House of Representatives was established comprising 15 elected and two nominated members. Fourteen elected members were from the Colony, 24 from the Protectorate and one from the Bo region.

Under the interim constitution of 1960 the Executive Council became the cabinet, over which the prime minister presided. On 27 April 1961 Sierra Leone became an independent sovereign state taking its place as a member of the British Commonwealth of Nations.

A military coup in March 1967 led to the formation of the National Reformation Council which suspended parliament and the offices of governor-general and prime minister.

Full civilian rule was restored in April 1968. In April 1971 the country attained Republic status, and Dr. Siaka Stevens was appointed executive president, a position he held for two terms. A multi-party system of government was provided under the constitution adopted in 1991. Under the Constitution the President heads the executive branch of government and is directly elected by universal adult suffrage for a maximum of two five-year terms. The President appoints the Cabinet subject to the approval of the Parliament.

To consult the 1991 Constitution, please visit:
http://www.sierra-leone.org/Laws/constitution1991.pdf

International Relations
Sierra Leone has good relations with its neighbours although there is an ongoing border dispute with Guinea. In the past, Sierra Leone had poor relations with Liberia. Sierra Leone's membership of international organisations includes: United Nations (UN), African Union (AU), Organisation of Islamic Conference (OIC), Commonwealth, Economic Community of West African States (ECOWAS), African Development Bank (AFDB), Mano River Union.

The UN has maintained a presence in Sierra Leone since 1999.

Recent Events
In May 1997 the elected president, Ahmad Kabbah, was ousted by a military junta led by Col. Johnny Koroma, and exiled to Guinea. Early in 1998 the Junta collapsed as Nigerian forces, led by Maj.-Gen. Timothy Shelpidi, captured most of the capital, and Kabbah was restored to power.

A peace agreement was negotiated between the Sierra Leone government and Foday Sankoh's rebels in July 1999, in which the rebels were given government posts and immunity from prosecution for war crimes. However, in November 1999 UN troops were mobilized to police the peace agreement. Rebel atrocities continued and up to 300 UN troops were taken captive by rebel soldiers. They were released following the capture of Foday Sankoh in May 2000. Negotiations between the Revolutionary United Front (RUF) and the government took place in May 2001 and a ceasefire was agreed. Foday Sankoh died on 30 July 2003 whilst awaiting trial for war crimes. Over 50,000 people are believed to have been killed in the 10-year civil war, and many thousands more mutilated.

The disarmament and rehabilitation of more than 70,000 civil war combatants was officially completed in February 2004 and trials for war crimes began in June 2004. The UN handed over control of security in the capital to local forces in September.

In December 2004, 10 men were sentenced to death for their part in attempting a coup in 2003. Six of the men belonged to the Armed Forces Revolutionary Council who ruled Sierra Leone following the 1997 coup. In March 2005 the trials opened of Alex Tamba Brima, Brima Bassy Kamara and Santigie Borbor Kanu for war crimes including charges of murder, rape, sexual slavery and recruitment of child soldiers. The alleged ringleaders of the violence are yet to be brought to justice. Johnny Paul Koroma, the former leader of the AFRC, who seized power from Ahmad Tejan Kabbah in 1997, is missing. The former Liberian leader, Charles Taylor, accused of arming and training the RUF, was in exile in Nigeria but in April 2006 he faced charges of war crimes in a UN backed court in Sierra Leone. In June 2007 his trial started in The Hague in The Netherlands.

In February 2009, the UN-backed Special Court for Sierra Leone found Issa Sesay, Morris Kallon and Augustine Gbao, of the Revolutionary United Front rebel group, guilty of most of 18 counts of war crimes and crimes against humanity carried out during the country's brutal civil war. The war killed over 120,000 people and left tens of thousands maimed after their arms, legs, noses or ears were cut off by RUF rebels, who were financed using Sierra Leone's diamonds. The UN-backed Special Court closed after seven years in October 2009. The remaining case of Charles Taylor continues to take place in The Hague.

The UN Security Council lifted its final sanctions against Sierra Leone in September 2010.

The cabinet was reshuffled in December 2010.

In April 2012, the UN-backed Sierra Leone war crimes court in The Hague convicted the former leader of Liberia Charles Taylor of aiding and abetting war crimes in the Sierra Leone civil war. He was sentenced to 50 years. Mr Taylor has since said he is to appeal.

Presidential and parliamentary elections took place in November 2012. President Koroma was returned to power. Although the opposition alleged voting fraud international observes passed the election.

The defence minister, Major Paolo Conteh, was reported to have been attacked by ex-soldiers, protesting over their retirement benefits.

Legislature
Sierra Leone's unicameral legislature, the Parliament, consists of 112 members directly elected to represent 14 constituencies, and 12 indirectly elected from the 12 provincial districts. Deputies all serve a five-year term.
Parliament, Parliament Building, OUA Drive, Tower Hill, Freetown, Sierra Leone. Tel: +232 22 223140, fax: +232 22 222483

Cabinet (as at June 2013)

Minister of Defence and National Security: Major (retd.) Paolo Conteh (page 1408)
Minister of Foreign Affairs and International Co-operation: Samura Kamara (page 1453)
Minister of Finance and Development: Dr Kaifala Marah
Minister of Health and Sanitation: Miatta Kargbo
Minister of Internal Affairs: Joseph Dauda
Minister of Local Government and Rural Development: Fina Konomanyi
Minister of Education, Science and Technology: Minkailu Bah
Minister of Employment and Social Security: Matthew Teambo
Minister of Trade and Industry: Osman Boie Kamara
Minister of Transport and Aviation: Leonard Balogun Koroma
Minister of Sports: Paul Kamara
Minister of Mineral Resources: Alhaji Minkailu Mansaray (page 1470)
Minister of Marine Resources: Capt. Alieu Mohamed Pat-Sowea
Minister of Tourism and Culture: Peter Bayuku Konte
Minister of Works, Housing and Infrastructure: Alimany Koroma
Minister of Social Welfare, Gender and Children: Emmanuel Kaikai
Minister of Justice and Attorney General: Frank Karbgo
Minister of Political and Public Affairs: Ibrahim Sesay
Minister of Energy: Oluniyi Robbin-Coker
Minister of Agriculture and Food Security: Sam Sesay
Minister of Lands, Planning and the Environment: Musa Tarawally
Minister of Youth Affairs: Alimany Kamara
Minister of Water Resources: Momodu Maligi

Resident Minister for the East: William Juana Smith
Resident Minister for the South: Muctarr Conteh
Resident Minister for the North: Alie Kamara

Ministries

Office of the President, Freetown, Sierra Leone. Tel: 232 22 232101, fax: 232 22 231404, e-mail: info@statehouse-sl.org, URL: http://www.statehouse-sl.org/

Ministry of Finance, Ministerial Building, George Street, Freetown, Sierra Leone. Tel: +232 22 225612, fax: +232 22 228472, e-mail: info@statehouse-sl.org, URL: http://www.statehouse-sl.org/ministryfinance.htm

Ministry of Foreign Affairs & International Cooperation, Gloucester Street, Freetown, Sierra Leone. Tel: +232 22 224778, fax: +232 22 225615, e-mail: info@statehouse-sl.org, URL: http://www.statehouse-sl.org/ministryforeignaffairs.htm

Ministry of Development & Economic Planning, 6th Floor, Youyi Building, Freetown, Sierra Leone. Tel: +232 22 225236, fax: +232 22 241599, e-mail: info@statehouse-sl.org, URL: http://www.statehouse-sl.org/ministrydevelopment.htm

Ministry of Justice, Guma Building, Lamina Sankoh Street, Freetown, Sierra Leone. Tel: +232 22 227444, fax: +232 22 229366, e-mail: info@statehouse-sl.org, URL: http://www.statehouse-sl.org/ministryjustice.htm

Ministry of Education, Science & Technology, New England, Freetown, Sierra Leone. Tel: +232 22 240881, fax: +232 22 240137, e-mail: info@statehouse-sl.org, URL: http://www.statehouse-sl.org/ministryeducation.htm

Ministry of Youth & Sports, New England, Freetown, Sierra Leone. Tel: +232 22 240881, fax: +232 22 240137, e-mail: info@statehouse-sl.org, URL: http://www.statehouse-sl.org/ministryyouths.htm

Ministry of Social Welfare, Gender & Children's Affairs, New England, Freetown, Sierra Leone. Tel: +232 22 241256, fax: +232 22 242076, e-mail: info@statehouse-sl.org, URL: http://www.statehouse-sl.org/ministrysocialwelfare.htm

Ministry of Mineral Resources, 5th Floor, Youyi Building, Brookfields, Freetown, Sierra Leone. Tel: +232 22 240142, fax: +232 22 242107, e-mail: info@statehouse-sl.org, URL: http://www.statehouse-sl.org/ministrymines.htm

Ministry of Information & Broadcasting, 8th Floor, Youyi Building, Brookfields, Freetown, Sierra Leone. Tel: +232 22 240339, fax: +232 22 241757, e-mail: info@statehouse-sl.org, URL: http://www.statehouse-sl.org/ministryinformation.htm

Ministry of Trade & Industry, Ministerial Building, George Street, Freetown, Sierra Leone. Tel: +232 22 222755, e-mail: info@statehouse-sl.org, URL: http://www.statehouse-sl.org/ministrytrade.htm

Ministry of Transport & Communication, Ministerial Building, George Street, Freetown, Sierra Leone. Tel: +232 22 22758, fax: +232 22 227337, e-mail: info@statehouse-sl.org, URL: http://www.statehouse-sl.org/ministrytransport.htm

Ministry of Health & Sanitations, 6th Floor, Youyi Building, Brookfields, Freetown, Sierra Leone. Tel: +232 22 240427, fax: +232 22 241283, e-mail: info@statehouse-sl.org, URL: http://www.statehouse-sl.org/ministryhealth.htm

Ministry of Agriculture, Forestry and Food Security, 3rd Floor, Youyi Building, Brookfields, Freetown, Sierra Leone. Tel: +232 22 222242, fax: +232 22 241613, e-mail: info@statehouse-sl.org, URL: http://www.statehouse-sl.org/ministryagriculture.htm

Ministry of Marine Resources, Marine House, 11 Old Railway Line, Brookfields, Freetown, Sierra Leone. Tel: +232 22 242117, e-mail: info@statehouse-sl.org, URL: http://www.statehouse-sl.org/ministrymarine.htm

Ministry of Works, Housing & Technical Maintenance, New England, Freetown, Sierra Leone. Tel: +232 22 240937, fax: +232 22 240018, e-mail: info@statehouse-sl.org, URL: http://www.statehouse-sl.org/ministryworks.htm

Ministry of Energy & Power, Electricity House, Siaka Stevens Street, Freetown, Sierra Leone. Tel: +232 22 226566, fax: +232 22 228199, e-mail: info@statehouse-sl.org, URL: http://www.statehouse-sl.org/ministryenergy.htm

Ministry of Labour, Industrial Relations & Social Security, New England, Freetown, Sierra Leone. Tel: +232 22 241947, e-mail: info@statehouse-sl.org, URL: http://www.statehouse-sl.org/ministrylabour.htm

Ministry of Tourism & Culture, Ministerial Building, George Street, Freetown, Sierra Leone. Tel: +232 22 222588, e-mail: info@statehouse-sl.org, URL: http://www.statehouse-sl.org/ministrytourism.htm

Ministry of Lands, Country Planning & the Environment, 4th Floor, Youyi Building, Brookfields, Freetown, Sierra Leone. Tel: +232 22 242013, e-mail: info@statehouse-sl.org, URL: http://www.statehouse-sl.org/ministrylands.htm

Ministry of Defence, State Avenue, Freetown, Sierra Leone. Tel: +232 22 227369, fax: +232 22 229380, e-mail: info@statehouse-sl.org

Ministry of Internal Affairs, Liverpool Street, Freetown, Sierra Leone. Tel: +232 22 226979, fax: +232 22 227727, e-mail: info@statehouse-sl.org, URL: http://www.statehouse-sl.org/ministryinternalaffairs.htm

Ministry of Political & Parliamentary Affairs, State House, State Avenue, Freetown, Sierra Leone. Tel: +232 22 228698, fax: +232 22 222781, e-mail: info@statehouse-sl.org, URL: http://www.statehouse-sl.org/ministryparliamentry.htm

Ministry of Local Government & Community Development, New England, Freetown, Sierra Leone. Tel: +232 22 226589, fax: +232 22 222409, e-mail: info@statehouse-sl.org, URL: http://www.statehouse-sl.org/ministrylocalgovernment.htm

Ministry of Presidential Affairs, State House, Freetown, Sierra Leone. Tel: +232 22 229728, fax: +232 22 229799, e-mail: info@statehouse-sl.org, URL: http://www.statehouse-sl.org/ministrypresidential.html

Elections

The last presidential election took place on 17 November 2012. The incumbent candidate Ernest Bai Koroma won after the first round of voting. He took approximately 59 per cent of the vote. His closest rival, Julius Maada Bio of the SLPP took approximately 37.5 per cent of the vote. There were seven other candidates.

The last parliamentary election was also held on 17 November 2012; the All People's Congress party won 67 out of 124 seats in Parliament, while the Sierra Leone People's Party won 42 seats. Twelve indirectly elected members of parliament are chosen by the traditional chiefs. A further 3 seats were undecided. The APC improved its position on the previous election in 2007 where it fell just short of an overall majority.

Political Parties

There are currently eight registered political parties including:
Sierra Leone People's Party (SLPP), 29 Rawdon Street, Freetown, Sierra Leone, West Africa. Tel: +232 22 228222, fax: +232 22 228222, e-mail: slpp@sierratel.sl, URL: http://www.slpp.ws
All People's Congress (APC), URL: http://www.new-apc.org/
People's Movement for Democratic Change (PMDC)

Diplomatic Representation

British High Commission, Spur Road, Freetown, Sierra Leone. Tel: +232 22 232961 / 22 232362, fax: +232 22 228169 / 22 232070, e-mail: bhc@sierratel.sl, URL: http://ukinsierraleone.fco.gov.uk/en/
High Commissioner: Peter West
Sierra Leone High Commission, 41 Eagle Street, Holborn, London WC1R 4TL, United Kingdom. Tel: +44 (0)20 7404 0140, fax: +44 (0)20 7734 3822, e-mail: info@slhc-uk.org.uk, URL: http://www.slhc-uk.org.uk
High Commissioner: Edward Turay
US Embassy, corner of Walpole and Siaka Stevens Streets, Freetown, Sierra Leone. Tel: +232 22 226481, fax: +232 22 225471, URL: http://freetown.usembassy.gov/
Ambassador: Michael Owen
Embassy of Sierra Leone, 1701 19th Street, NW, Washington DC 20009, USA. Tel: +1 202 939 9261, fax: +1 202 483 1793, URL: http://www.embassyofsierraleone.org/
Ambassador: Bockari K. Stevens
Permanent Representative of the Republic of Sierra Leone to the United Nations, 245 East 49th Street, New York, NY 10017, USA. Tel: +1 212 688 1656 / 4985, fax: +1 212 688 4924, e-mail: sierraleone@un.int, URL: http://www.un.int/sierraleone
Ambassador: Shekou Momodou Touray

LEGAL SYSTEM

A decade of war destroyed much of the human and physical infrastructure of Sierra Leone's judiciary. The law is based on the English code.

Elected indigenous leaders preside over the local courts which apply traditional law. There are Magistrates courts in the various districts and in Freetown, and appeals from these courts are heard by the High Court, which also has unlimited original civil and criminal jurisdiction. Appeals from High Court decisions may be made to the Court of Appeal and finally to the Supreme Court. The Supreme Court, the final court of appeal for civil and criminal cases, comprises a Chief Justice and two associate Justices. There is also a military court system, based on British military codes and common law.

The government respects the rights of its citizens, but problems of brutality, theft and extortion on the part of security forces continue. Arrests can be arbitrary, there is insufficient legal representation, leading to prolonged pretrial detention, and conditions in prisons are harsh. Official corruption and impunity are widespread. There are restrictions on freedom of speech and press.

Sierra Leone has, de facto, abolished the death penalty. though murder, aggravated robbery and treason are capital crimes. The last executions took place in 1998.

LOCAL GOVERNMENT

Administratively, Sierra Leone is divided into three provinces - the Northern, Eastern, and Southern - and one area - the Western Area. They are further divided into 12 districts, which are themselves divided into 147 chiefdoms. Each chiefdom is governed by a chief assisted by a Council of Elders. The towns of Freetown, Bo, Kenema and Makeni have elected councils and a mayor.

Local elections took place in 2009 but were marred by violence.

AREA AND POPULATION

Area

Sierra Leone is situated on the west coast of Africa. It borders Guinea to the north and west, and Liberia to the east, and covers an area of 71,740 sq. km. The terrain consists of a coastal belt of mangrove swamps, wooded hills, an upland plateau, and mountains to the east. The climate is tropical, with a summer rainy season (May to December) and a winter dry season (December to April).

To view a map, consult http://www.un.org/Depts/Cartographic/map/profile/sierrale.pdf

Population

Total population in 2010 was estimated at 5.868 million with an average annual population growth rate of 3.5 per cent over the period 2000-10. The majority of the population (53 per cent) is aged between 15 and 60 years, with 43 per cent aged up to 14 years, and about 4 per cent aged 60 or over. The median age is 18 years old. Approximately 38 per cent of Sierra Leone's population lives in urban areas.

Ethnically, Sierra Leoneans are predominantly from one of 20 native African tribes (including Temne and Mende), whilst 10 per cent are Creole, and small numbers of Europeans, Lebanese, Pakistanis and Indians.

English is the official language, whilst native languages include Mende, Temne and Krio.

SIERRA LEONE

Births, Marriages, Deaths
According to 2010 estimates the birth rate is 38.6 births per 1,000 of the population, and the death rate is 14.7 deaths per 1,000 people. The fertility rate is 5.0 children born per woman. In 2009 the average life expectancy at birth was 48 years for men and 50 years for women. In 2008 healthy life expectancy was 34 years for males and 37 years for females. (Source: http://www.who.int, World Health Statistics 2012)

Public Holidays 2014
1 January: New Year's Day
14 January: Birth of the Prophet (Mouloud)*
18 April: Good Friday
21 April: Easter Monday
27 April: Independence Day
29 June: Beginning of Ramadan*
29 July: Id al-Fitr (end of Ramadan)*
5 October: Eid al-Adha (Festival of the Sacrifice)*
25 December: Christmas Day
26 December: Boxing Day
*Islamic holiday: the precise date will depend on the observance of the moon

EMPLOYMENT

Sierra Leone's active labour force in 2007 numbered 2.2 million. The agriculture sector employs over 50 per cent of the population, whilst 30 per cent of the work force are employed in industry and 17 per cent in services.

Poverty is high: over 57 per cent live on less than a dollar a day and almost 75 per cent live on less than US$2 a day.

Total Employment by Economic Activity

Occupation	2004
Agriculture, hunting & forestry	1,272,234
Fishing	51,139
Mining & quarrying	68,974
Manufacturing	9,412
Electricity, gas & water supply	8,347
Construction	39,068
Wholesale & retail trade, repairs	269,495
Hotels & restaurants	4,931
Transport, storage & communications	15,682
Financial intermediation	6,934
Real estate, renting & business activities	10,785
Public admin. & defence; compulsory social security	25,979
Education	34,580
Health & social work	19,828
Other community, social & personal service activities	83,486
Households with employed persons	8,289
Extra-territorial organisations & bodies	3,846
Total	1,933,009

Source: Copyright © International Labour Organization (ILO Dept. of Statistics, http://laborsta.ilo.org)

BANKING AND FINANCE

The financial centre is Freetown.

Currency
The currency is the Leone.

GDP/GNP, Inflation, National Debt
Sierra Leone is rated by the UN as the second poorest country in the world. Almost 60 per cent live on less than US$1 a day and almost 75 per cent live on under US$2 a day. Sierra Leone's economy was largely destroyed by the civil war of the 1990s. Massive outside assistance since the end of hostilities has put the country on the road to recovery, though it is likely that restoration of the economy to pre-civil war levels will take years. It is thought that official corruption was a significant factor in the decline towards civil war in the 1980s and this is an area that will have to be tackled. An anti-corruption Commission was established in 2002.

The government has been successful in attracting some foreign investment, particularly in the mining and agri-business sectors. Approximately one million hectares of arable land have been leased or are under negotiotiaton for leasing by foreign investors, attracted by the deals offered by the government. The new wealth is at present not distributed through society. Although many workers now receive wages there have been some protests over loss of land and livelihoods.

The diamond industry is of major importance to the economy and Sierra Leone's principal export earner. However, whilst annual production is estimated to reach between $250 and $300 million, a relatively small amount passes through official channels, ($127 million in 2003). The rest is smuggled out of the country. Iron-ore mining has developed in recent years. China has taken a share in an iron-ore mine and has rebuilt a port and railway line. Projected earnings from the mine for Sierra Leone are estimated to be in the region of US$1.5 billion per annum. Offshore oil reserves were discovered in 2010 but are as yet undeveloped. Tourism is seen as a future significant industry with construction of a new highway from Freetown to the country's beaches.

Estimated Gross Domestic Product was estimated at US$1.97 million in 2008. Figures for 2009 put GDP at US$2.0 billion reflecting a growth rate of 1.0 per cent.By 2011, it had risen to US$2.2 million. Around two thirds of the population relies on subsistence farming, but agriculture accounts for just 43 per cent of GDP. Industry contributes some 31 per cent of GDP, whilst services contribute around 26 per cent.

Inflation was estimated at 11 per cent in 2008, before falling to 9.2 per cent in 2009. It rose again to over 15 per cent in 2010 and to over 16 per cent in 2011.

External debt was estimated at US$765 million in 2010. Sierra Leone is dependent on foreign aid, mainly from multi-lateral donors. In 2010, the IMF approved a new three-year program worth US$45 million.

Balance of Payments / Imports and Exports
Estimated export (f.o.b.) revenue rose from US$65 million in 2000, US$158 million in 2005 and US$206 million in 2006. Exports were estimated to amount to US$340 billion. Major export commodities include diamonds, rutile, cocoa, fish and coffee. Sierra Leone's main export trading partners are Greece, Belgium, the US and the UK.

Import costs (f.o.b.) rose from US$145 million in 2000, US$330 million in 2005 and US$372 million in 2006. Imports amounted to US$750 million in 2010. Major import commodities include food, machinery and equipment, chemicals, lubricants and fuels. Main import trading partners are the UK (25 per cent), US, China, Cote d'Ivoire (fuel) and Germany.

The large number of Sierra Leoneans living abroad send significant remittances back home.

Central Bank
Bank of Sierra Leone, PO Box 30, Siaka Stevens Street, Freetown, Sierra Leone. Tel: +232 22 226501, fax: +232 22 224764, URL: http://www.bsl.gov.sl/
Governor: Shehu Sambadeen Sesay

Chambers of Commerce and Trade Organisations
Sierra Leone Chamber of Commerce, Industry and Agriculture, Freetown, Sierra Leone. Tel: +234 1 7741 4509, fax: +234 1 496 2571, e-mail: sicc@sl.baobab.com, URL: http://www.chamberofcommerce.sl/default.asp?iId=HILHG

MANUFACTURING, MINING AND SERVICES

Primary and Extractive Industries
Diamond mining is a significant source of hard currency; however, many diamonds mined in Sierra Leone are smuggled to other countries. Whilst annual production is estimated between US$250-300 million, official export figures show considerably less. In 2000, a certification system for diamond exports was initiated, which resulted in a large increase in legal exports, and 2001 saw the creation of a mining community development fund, raising local communities' stake in legal diamond trading. In 2009 diamond exports reached an estimated 400,500 carats of diamonds, both industrial and gem.

Sierra Leone has large deposits of the mineral rutile (used in paint pigment and welding rod coatings). Mining was suspended during the civil war, but is gradually resuming. Gold is also found in Sierra Leonne and new modernised gold mines are hoped to be in production by 2015..

In 2011, 0.03 thousand barrels per day of oil were produced and an estimated 10,000 were consumed. In 2012, energy companies reported the discovery of oil off the coast of Sierra Leone. Exploration is ongoing.

Energy
Sierra Leone's electricity industry uses mainly thermal means for generation. Electricity capacity in 2001 was 0.128 gigawatts (97 per cent thermal, and 3 per cent hydroelectric). Generation in 2010 was an estimated 0.15 billion kilowatthours (kWh), and consumption was an estimated 0.15 billion kWh. No electricity is imported or exported.

Manufacturing
Sierra Leone's industrial sector contributes just over a quarter of the annual GDP and is mainly geared to the domestic rather than export market. Main manufacturing industries include beverages, textiles, cigarettes, paint, soap and cosmetics and footwear.

Agriculture
Agriculture provides 51 per cent of Sierra Leone's GDP. Around 30 per cent of the land is potentially arable, though only eight per cent is currently cultivated. Some two thirds of the population is involved in subsistence farming.

In the Western Area farming is largely confined to the production of cassava and garden crops, such as maize and vegetables for local consumption. In the Provincial Area the principal agricultural products include rice, which is the staple food of the country, and export crops such as palm kernels, sorghum, peanuts, beans, cocoa beans, coffee and kola nuts. Livestock, such as poultry, cattle, sheep and pigs, are also reared.

Agricultural Production in 2010

Produce	Int. $'000*	Tonnes
Rice, paddy	270,793	1,026,670
Vegetables fresh nes	57,606	305,700
Citrus fruit, nes	49,003	108,400
Pulses, nes	42,614	80,400
Groundnuts, with shell	38,938	94,366
Cassava	37,743	361,300
Fruit fresh nes	29,249	83,800
Palm oil	22,623	52,000

- continued		
Indigenous chicken meat	16,948	11,898
Coffee, green	14,719	13,700
Cocoa beans	14,539	14,000
Indigenous rabbit meat	13,935	7,500

* unofficial figures

Source: http://faostat.fao.org/site/339/default.aspx Food and Agriculture Organization of the United Nations, Food and Agricultural commodities production

COMMUNICATIONS AND TRANSPORT

Travel Requirements
Citizens of the USA, Canada, Australia and the EU require a passport valid for at least six months beyond the length of stay and a visa. Transit passengers continuing their journey within 24 hours, holding onward or return documentation and not leaving the airport do not require a visa. Other nationals should contact the embassy to check visa requirements.

Visitors to Sierra Leone are required to show International Certificates of Vaccination (yellow card) upon arrival at the airport with a record of vaccination against yellow fever.

International Airlines
A number of international airlines operate through Freetown International Airport. These include Air Mali, Ghana Airways, KLM Royal Dutch Airlines, and Nigeria Airways.

Airports
Sierra Leone has 10 airports of which one has a paved runway.

Roads
There are 11,300 km of roads of which approximately 1,000 km are paved. Vehicles are driven on the right.

Waterways
There are 800 km of waterways.

Shipping
Main ports are Freetown, Pepel and Sherbro Islands. Ports are connected by ferry services.

HEALTH

In 2009, the government spent approximately 4.2 per cent of its total budget on healthcare, accounting for 6.5 per cent of all healthcare spending. External resources amounted to 17 per cent of total expenditure. Total expenditure on healthcare equated to 13.3 per cent of the country's GDP. Per capita expenditure on health was approximately US$47, compared with US$22 in 2000. In 2000-10 there were an estimated 95 doctors (0.2 per 10,000 population), 911 nurses and midwives (1.7 per 10,000 population), 24 dentistry personnel, 192 pharmaceutical personnel, 135 public and environmental health workers and 132 community workers. In 2000-09 there were an estimated 4 hospital beds per 10,000 population.

In 2010 there were 934,028 reported cases of malaria, 382 of leprosy, 1,089 of measles and 11,859 of tuberculosis. The HIV/AIDS prevalence rate among adults was estimated to be 960 per 100,000 population and the TB prevalence rate was 1,282 per 100,000 population. Almost 38 per cent of children under five years of age are stunted for their age and 21 per cent underweight. The infant mortality rate in 2010 was 114 per 1,000 live births. The child mortality rate (under 5 years) was 174 per 1,000 live births. The main causes of childhood mortality are: diarrhoea (12 per cent), pneumonia (15 per cent), malaria (23 per cent), and HIV/AIDs (1 per cent). The measles immunization rate rose from 37 per cent in 2000 to over 80 per cent in 2010. Approximately 26 per cent of children sleep under insecticide-treated nets.

In 2010, an estimated 55 per cent of the population had sustainable access to improved drinking water sources. In the same year, an estimated 13 per cent of the population had sustainable access to improved sanitation. (Source: http://www.who.int, World Health Statistics 2012)

EDUCATION

Primary/Secondary Education
Education in Sierra Leone for primary school and the first three years of secondary school known as primary and junior secondary education is officially compulsory, but a shortage of schools, teachers and poor infrastructure makes this impossible. Figures form 2005 put spending on education at the equivalent 3.7 per cent of GDP. Primary education lasts for six years. According to recent UNESCO figures, the primary school-age population is 761,000 representing 50 per cent of primary school-age children. However, the percentage of children attending schools varies considerably in different parts of the country. The pupil: teacher ratio in 2007 was 44:1.

Secondary education lasts for seven years, ages 12 to 15 attend junior secondary school and ages 15-18 attend senior secondary school. Enrolment in secondary schools in 2007 was put at 27 per cent for males and 19 per cent of females. (UNESCO).

Tertiary/Higher
Fourah Bay College and Njala University College are the constituent colleges of the University of Sierra Leone. Just 2.2 per cent college aged students are currently enrolled in tertiary education.

Just 36 per cent of the population was considered literate in 2004 (46.9 per cent for males and 24.4 per cent for females). The previously impressive education tradition of Sierra Leone has been eroded by the civil war. In the age group 15-24 years, the rates are slightly higher (59.1 per cent for males and 37.2 per cent for females).

RELIGION

Sierra Leone is predominantly Muslim (47 per cent of the population). Around 13 per cent of the population follow Christianity and 38 per cent traditional beliefs.

Sierra Leone has a religious liberty rating of 10 on a scale of 1 to 10 (10 is most freedom). (Source: World Religion Database)

COMMUNICATIONS AND MEDIA

Media freedom is sometimes limited with the authorities allegedly using courts and libel laws to target critics. Broadcasting is also hindered by poor electricity supplies.

Newspapers
There are dozens of newspapers, many privately run, despite low literacy levels. Private newspapers are often critical of government policies. The most circulated are Awoko (URL: http://www.awoko.org/), the Democrate, Concord Times (URL: http://www.concordtimessl.com/) and the Standard Times (URL: http://standardtimespress.net/cgi-bin/artman/publish/index.shtml).

Broadcasting
The government-run SLBS is to be transformed into the Sierra Leone Broadcasting Corporation (SLBC). In addition the government-owned TV station, one private TV station and a pay-per-view TV service is in operation. In addition to the government-owned national radio broadcast station over 20 private radio stations exist. Transmission of several international broadcasters are available.

Telecommunications
The telecommunications infrastructure is poor. The mobile-cellular service is expanding rapidly and coverage is limited. According to 2008 estimates, there are 31,00 mainline telephones and 1 million mobile phones. In 2009 an estimated 13,500 people had access to the internet.

ENVIRONMENT

Major environmental problems include rapid population growth, the effect on natural resources caused by the civil war, deforestation and soil.

In 2010, Sierra Leone's emissions from the consumption and flaring of fossil fuels totalled 1.33 million metric tons of carbon dioxide. (Source: EIA)

Sierra Leone is a party to: Biodiversity, Climate Change, Climate Change-Kyoto Protocol, Desertification, Endangered Species, Law of the Sea, Marine Life Conservation, Ozone Layer Protection, Ship Pollution, Wetlands, It has signed, but not ratified: Environmental Modification

STATES OF THE WORLD

SINGAPORE
Republic of Singapore

Head of State: Tony Tan (President) (page 1523)

National Flag: Two equal horizontal bands, red over white, at the top of the hoist a white crescent moon sided by five stars in a circle.

CONSTITUTION AND GOVERNMENT

Constitution
Singapore was founded by Sir Stamford Raffles in 1819. In 1826, Singapore together with Malacca and Penang formed the Straits Settlements, with the Governor of Penang in overall responsibility of the administration. In 1832, Singapore became the administrative centre of the Straits Settlements which remained under the control of the British East Indian Company until 1867, when Singapore became a British colony. After the Japanese occupation from 1942-45, Singapore moved gradually to self-government, which it achieved in 1959. In 1963, it became a state within the Federation of Malaysia. On 9 August 1965, Singapore ceased to be a part of Malaysia and became an independent nation and a member of the Commonwealth on 15 October 1965. In 1991 the constitution was amended to allow for the election of a president and to change the role from ceremonial to one with more responsibility. The Head of State is the President, directly elected and serves for a term of five years.

To consult the 1991 Constitution, please visit: http://statutes.agc.gov.sg/

International Relations
Singapore is a member of the UN, the WTO, the Non-Aligned Movement and the Commonwealth. The country plays an active role in ASEAN and the Asia Pacific Economic Cooperation forum, supporting the idea of Southeast Asian regionalism.

Recent Events
In April 2005, the government approved a plan to legalise casino gambling. Almost 30,000 people petitioned against the idea, but the Prime Minister argued that the country risked becoming a backwater, and the two planned casinos would help to double the number of tourists to 17 million per year.

In September of the same year, President Nathan won a second, six-year term in office; his rivals were disqualified from the election.

In May 2006, Lee Hsien Loong's ruling People's Action Party (PAP) won the general election. PAP has been the ruling party in Singapore since independence in 1965. The poll was the first electoral test for Prime Minister Lee Hsien Loong since his appointment in August 2004. For the first time, the opposition parties contested more than half the seats.

In October 2007, Parliament voted against a proposal to decriminalise sex between men.

In February 2008, the suspected leader of the Islamist militant group Jemaah Islamia, escaped from jail; security forces mounted the largest manhunt ever launched in Singapore, for Mas Selamat Kastari. He was suspected of plotting to bomb Singapore Changi Airport in 2002, but has never been formally charged with any terrorism-related offences; instead he was detained under the Internal Security Act, which allows indefinite detention without trial. He remained at large until May 2009, when he was captured in Malaysia.

Like many countries around the world Singapore was hit by the global economic downturn and in 2008 was officially declared to be in recession following two quarters of negative growth. In April 2009 recorded figures showed the economy had shrunk by 19.7 per cent in the first quarter of 2009 compared to the previous quarter; it was the biggest fall ever recorded by the Singaporean economy. However, in July 2009 Singapore emerged from recession with growth at an annualised rate of over 20 per cent.

Legislative elections took place on 7 May 2011 and presidential elections on 27 August 2011. The PAP won the legislative elections. The presidential election was won by Tony Tan, formerly of the PAP.

Legislature
The Singapore Parliament is unicameral. MPs serve a five year term. There is provision to appoint up to three Non-Constituency Members of Parliament (NCMPs) from the opposition political parties, to ensure a minimum number of opposition representatives and that views other than the Government's can be expressed in Parliament. Up to nine Nominated Members of Parliament (NMPs) can be appointed by the President of Singapore for a term of two and a half years. NMPs are not members of any political party.

The present Eleventh Parliament has 94 MPs consisting of 84 elected MPs, one NCMP and nine NMPs.
Parliament, Parliament House, 1 Parliament Place, Singapore 178880. Tel: +65 6332 6666, fax: +65 6332 5528, e-mail: parl@parl.gov.sg, URL: http://www.parliament.gov.sg

Cabinet (as at June 2013)
Prime Minister: Lee Hsien Loong (page 1461)
Deputy Prime Minister, Co-ordinating Minister for National Security & Minister for Home Affairs: Rear Adml. Teo Chee Hean (page 1524)
Deputy Prime Minister and Minister of Finance: Tharman Shanmugaratnam (page 1524)
Minister for Trade and Industry: Lim Hng Kiang (page 1465)
Minister for Information and Communication; Muslim Affairs: Dr Yaacob Ibrahim (page 1540)

Minister for National Development: Khaw Boon Wan (page 1456)
Minister for Defence: Dr Ng Eng Hen (page 1486)
Minister for the Environment and Water Resources: Dr Vivian Balakrishnan (page 1382)
Minister for Foreign Affairs; Law: K. Shanmugam
Minister for Health: Gan Kim Yong
Minister for Transport: Lui Tuck Yew
Minister for Education: Heng Swee Keat
Minister, Prime Minister's Office: Grace Fu Hai Yien
Minister, Prime Minister's Office: Lim Swee Say (page 1522)
Acting Minister for Social and Family Development: Maj.-Gen.Chan Chun Sing
Acting Minister for Manpower: Tan Chuan-Jin
Acting Minister for Culture, Community and Youth and Senior Minister of State for Communication and Information: Lawrence Wong

Ministries
Office of the President, Istana Singapore, Orchard Road, Singapore 238823. Tel: +65 6737 5522, fax: +65 6735 3135, e-mail: istana_general_office@istana.gov.sg, URL: http://www.istana.gov.sg
Prime Minister's Office, Orchard Road, Istana Office Wing, Singapore 238823. Tel: +65 6737 5133, fax: +65 6835 6261, URL: http://www.pmo.gov.sg
Ministry of Community Development, Youth and Sports, 512 Thomson Road, MCYS Building, Singapore 298136. Tel: +65 6354 8309 fax: +65 6837 9480, URL: http://www.mcys.gov.sg
Ministry of Defence, MINDEF Building, Gombak Drive, Off Upper Bukit Timah Road, Singapore 669645. Tel: +65 6760 8844, fax: +65 6233 6667, e-mail: imindef@starnet.gov.sg, URL: http://www.mindef.gov.sg
Ministry of Education,1 North Buona Vista Drive, Singapore 139675. Tel: +65 6872 2220, fax: +65 6775 5826, e-mail: contact@moe.edu.sg, URL: http://www.moe.edu.sg
Ministry of the Environment, 40 Scotts Road, Environment Building, Singapore 228231. Tel: +65 6732 7733, fax: +65 6731 9456, e-mail: MEWR Feedback@env.gov.sg, URL: http://www.app.mewr.gov.sg
Ministry of Finance, Treasury Building, 100 High Street, Singapore 179434. Tel: +65 6225 9911, fax: +65 6332 7435, URL: http://www.mof.gov.sg
Ministry of Foreign Affairs, Tanglin, Singapore 248163. Tel: +65 6379 8000, fax: +65 6474 7885, e-mail: mfa@mfa.gov.sg, URL: http://www.mfa.gov.sg
Ministry of Health, 16 College Road, College of Medicine Building, Singapore 169854. Tel: +65 6325 9220,fax: +65 6224 1677, URL: http://www.moh.gov.sg
Ministry of Home Affairs, New Phoenix Park, 28 Irrawaddy Road, Singapore 329560. Tel: +65 6235 9111, fax: +65 6254 6250, URL: http://www.mha.gov.sg
Ministry of Information, Communications and the Arts, 140 Hill Street 02-02, MICA Building, Singapore 179369. Tel: +65 6270 7988, fax: +65 6837 9480, e-mail: mita duty officer@mica.gov.sg, URL: http://www.mica.gov.sg
Ministry of Manpower, 18 Havelock Road, 07-01 Singapore 059764. Tel: +65 6438 5122, fax: +65 6534 4840, e-mail: mom hq@mom.gov.sg, URL: http//www.mom.gov.sg
Ministry of National Development, 5 Maxwell Road, 21/22-00, Tower Block, MND Complex, Singapore 069110. Tel: +65 6222 1211, fax: +65 6325 7254, URL: http://www.mnd.gov.sg
Ministry of Law, 08-02 The Treasury, 100 High Street, Singapore 179434. Tel: +65 6332 8840, fax: +65 6332 8842, e-mail: contact@mlaw.gov.sg, URL: http://www.minlaw.gov.sg
Ministry of Trade and Industry, 100 High Street, 09-01 The Treasury, Singapore 179434. Tel: +65 6225 9911, fax: +65 6332 7260, URL: http://www.mti.gov.sg
Ministry of Transport, 460 Alexandra Road 39-00, PSA Building, Singapore 119963. Tel: +65 6270 7988, fax: +65 6375 7734, e-mail: mot@mot.gov.sg, URL: http://www.mot.gov.sg

Political Parties
People's Action Party, Block 57B New Upper Changi Road, 01-1402 PCF Building, Singapore 463057. Tel: +65 6244 4600, fax: +65 6243 0114, e-mail: paphq@pap.org.sg, URL: http://www.pap.org.sg
Secretary General: Lee Hsien Loong (page 1461)
Singapore Democrats, 1357-A Serangoon Road, Singapore 328240. Fax: +65 6398 1675, URL: http://yoursdp.org/
Secretary General: Dr. Chee Soon Juan
The Workers' Party, 216 Syed Alwi Road, 02-03, Singapore 207799. Tel: +65 6298 4765, fax: +65 6454404, e-mail: wp@wp.sg, URL: http://wp.sg
Chair: Sylvia Lim Swee Lian

Elections
The most recent legislative election was held on May 7 2011; the People's Action Party (PAP), won 81 of the 87 seats available. However the election was seen as significant as the Workers Party made gains including winning the seat held by the country's foreign minister.

The most recent presidential election took place on 27 August 2011. Tony Tan, an independent candidate formerly leader of the PAP, won with 35.2 per cent of the vote, narrowly defeating Tan Cheng Bock, also an independent candidate and formerly of the PAP, who gained 34.8 per cent. Mr Tan took office on 1 September.

Voting in elections is compulsory. Suffrage is universal from the age of 21.

Diplomatic Representation
Embassy of the United States of America, 27 Napier Road, Singapore 258508. Tel: +65 6476 9100 fax: +65 6476 9340, URL: http://singapore.usembassy.gov
Ambassador: David Adelman

British High Commission, 100 Tanglin Road, Singapore 247919. Tel: +65 6424 4200, fax: +65 6424 4218 e-mail: commercial.singapore@fco.gov.uk, URL: http://ukinsingapore.fco.gov.uk/en/
High Commissioner: H.E. Antony Phillipson
Embassy of Singapore, 3501 International Place NW, Washington, DC 20008, USA. Tel: +1 202 537 3100, fax: +1 202 537 0876, URL: http://www.mfa.gov.sg/washington
Ambassador: Ashok Kumar Mirpuri
Singapore High Commission, 9 Wilton Crescent, London, SW1X 8SP, United Kingdom. Tel: +44 (0)20 7235 8315, fax: +44 (0)20 7245 6583, URL: http://www.mfa.gov.sg/london
High Commissioner: T. Jasudasen
United Nations, 231, East 51st Street, New York, NY 10022, USA. Tel: +1 212 826 0840, fax: +1 212 826 2964, e-mail: sgun@prodigy.net, URL: http://www.mfa.gov.sg/newyork
Permanent Representative: Albert Chua

LEGAL SYSTEM

The judicial power in Singapore follows a three tier system and is based on the English system. The Judiciary administers the law independently of the Executive, and this independence is safeguarded by the Constitution of the Republic of Singapore. The Court of Appeal is the final appellate court and has a Chief Justice and two appeal judges. The middle tier consists of The Supreme Court, also in the administration of the Chief Justice and the High Court. The Chief Justice and the other judges of the Supreme Court are appointed by the president, acting on the advice of the prime minister. There are 14 judges in the Supreme Court. The Subordinate Courts consist of District Courts, Juvenile Courts, Magistrates' Courts, Coroners' Courts and a Small Claims Tribunal.

The government limits citizens' rights, and there are restrictions on freedom of speech and of the press. There have been recent instances of preventive detention, and infringement of privacy rights. Caning is the punishment given for many offenses, and Singapore retains the death penalty. The state is believed to have the highest per capita execution rate in the world and has executed more than 400 people since 1991, mostly for drug offences. Under the Misuse of Drugs Act (MDA), judges are obliged to hand down the death penalty to anyone trafficking more than 15 grams of heroin, 30 grams of cocaine or 500 grams of cannabis - no mitigating factors are taken into account. There has been a progressive reduction of the death penalty with more than 70 people executed per year in the mid-90s compared to less than 10 per year since 2004. Eight people were reported to have been handed death sentences in 2010 and five in 2011. There were no reported executions for 2010, but four were reported for 2011.

Supreme Court, URL: http://app.supremecourt.gov.sg/default.aspx?pgID=40
Chief Justice: Chan Sek Keong (page 1402)

AREA AND POPULATION

Area
The main island of Singapore and the 63 outlying small islands together cover an area of 682.7 sq. km, with Indonesia to the south, Borneo to the south-east, East Malaysia to the east and Peninsula Malaysia to the north. Singapore is linked to Malaysia by two bridges. The terrain is generally low and either flat or undulating. The highest hill (Bukit Timah) is 165 metres above sea level and the longest river (Sungei Seletar) is about 15 km long.

The climate is tropical: humid, hot and rainy. There are two monsoon seasons: the southwestern monsoon from June to September and the Northeastern from December to March.

To view a map, consult http://www.lib.utexas.edu/maps/cia08/singapore_sm_2008.gif

Population
The population of Singapore was estimated to be 5.086 million as at 2010, indicating an annual average growth of 2.6 per cent over the period 2000-10. These figures include permanent foreign residents and workers. The population density (one of the highest in the world) was 7,022 per square km. in 2009. The median age was 38 years in 2010. An estimated 17 per cent of the population is aged under 15 years and 14 per cent over 60 years. Approximately 76.8 per cent of the population is Chinese, 13.9 per cent Malay and 7.9 per cent Indian, with 1.4 per cent made up from other ethnic groups. Malay, Mandarin, Tamil and English are all official languages; Malay is the national language and English is the language of administration. Indian languages and other Chinese dialects are also spoken.

Births, Marriages, Deaths
In 2010, the crude birth rate was estimated at 9.1 per 1,000 people, whilst the crude death rate was 4.3 per 1,000 inhabitants. The fertility rate was 1.3 children per woman in 2010. The infant mortality rate was 2 deaths per 1,000 live births in 2010. Life expectancy at birth is now 79 years for men and 84 years for women. (Source: http://www.who.int, World Health Statistics 2012)

Figures for 2006 show that there were a total of 19,761 marriages. There were 5,117 divorces in the same year.

Public Holidays 2014
1 January: New Year's Day
31 January: Chinese New Year
18 April: Good Friday
14 May: Vesak Day (Birth of the Buddha)
1 May: Labour Day
29 July: End of Ramadan
9 August: National Day
5 October: Hari Raya Haji (Feast of the Sacrifice)
23 October: Diwali

25 December: Christmas Day

Muslim festivals are timed according to local sightings of various phases of the moon and the dates given above are approximations. Hindu festivals are declared according to local astronomical observations and it is only possible to forecast the month of their occurrence.

EMPLOYMENT

In 2009, the total labour force numbered 3,030,000, up from 2,940,000 the previous year. The labour force participation rate in 2009 was 65.4 per cent (76.3 per cent for men and 55.2 per cent for women). 2,906,000 people were employed (up from 2,506,000 in 2006) and 124,000 were unemployed, an unemployment rate of 4.1 per cent, up from the 2008 figure of 2.8 per cent. The number of people employed rose to 3.228 million in 2011, of which 70 per cent were employed in services, 16 per cent manufacturing and 12.5 per cent in construction

The overall unemployment rate in 2007 was 2.9 per cent, the lowest since before 2002, though still higher than its maintained level of around 2 per cent before the year 2000. This is due to the impact of globalisation and China's low-wage manufacturing economy. The unemployment rate in 2008 stayed around the same but rose in 2009 in response to the global economic downturn. In December 2011 it was reported to be 2 per cent.

Employment by Economic Activity

Sector	2008
Agriculture, hunting, forestry, fishing, mining & quarrying, utilities	22,700
Manufacturing	311,900
Construction	105,500
Wholesale & retail trade & repairs	269,500
Hotels & restaurants	120,000
Transport & storage	182,400
Information & communication	87,000
Finance and insurance	123,600
Real estate, renting & business activities	43,000
Professional, scientific and technical activities	109,600
Admin. & support service activities	84,900
Education, other community, social & personal service activities	228,500
Health & social work	74,300
Other	89,100

Source: Copyright © International Labour Organization (ILO Dept. of Statistics, http://laborsta.ilo.org)

BANKING AND FINANCE

Currency
1 Singapore dollar = 100 cents

GDP/GNP, Inflation, National Debt
In 2000, the Singaporean economy was recovering from the Southeast Asian economic crisis, expanding at 9.9 per cent that year. However, in 2001 the economy slowed, with GDP falling by 2 per cent, mainly due to a slowdown in the export market which was reacting to a global economic slowdown. The economy picked up again in 2002 but was hit in early 2003 by the loss of confidence and output in Asian economies following the outbreak of the SARS (Severe Acute Respiratory Syndrome) virus. In 2004, the economy bounced back with 9 per cent growth, benefiting from growth in world oil and technology industries and Singapore enjoyed four years of strong economic growth.

GDP grew by 7.3 per cent in 2005, by 8.2 per cent in 2006 and in 2007, GDP grew by 7.7 per cent; whilst output in the agriculture sector collapsed from 15.5 per cent in 2006 to 0.2 per cent in 2007, industry and services grew by 7.3 per cent and 7.8 per cent respectively.

The services sector accounted for some 70.5 per cent of GDP in 2007 (up from 68.6 per cent the previous year). Industry contributed 29.4 per cent and agriculture just 0.1 per cent. (Source: Asian Development Bank)

In November 2008 the Singapore government confirmed that the country had entered a recession after two consecutive quarters of negative growth. Economic growth was put at just 1.1 per cent in 2008 and fell to -1.3 per cent. In response to the global economic downturn and competition from neighbouring countries Singapore is actively seeking to strengthen its services sector in particular the tourism industry. The economy grew by over 10 per cent in 2010 to S$3109 billion. The weak external environment adversely affected growth in 2011 with GDP growth falling to an average of 4.9 per cent in 2011. GDP was estimated to be S$327 billion. Growth is expected to be around 2 per cent in 2012. Manufacturing is forecast to remain weak but the services sector is expected to grow.

The following tables show national income and economic growth rates in recent years:

Major Indicators of National Accounts at current market prices (million Singapore $)

Year	Gross Domestic Product	Gross National Income
1990	66,778.1	68,602.1
1995	123,399.8	124,165.9
2000	162,584.1	161,232.6

SINGAPORE

- continued

2005	208,763.7	194,250.0
2006	230,509.2	219,382.7
2007	266,405.1	256,117.2
2008	273,537.2	271,562.3
2009	265,057.9	260,605.2

Source: Asian Development Bank

The following table shows GDP per sector (Mn. Singapore dollars):

GDP by Industry at Current Prices (million Singapore $)

Industry	2008	2009
Agriculture and Mining	109.6	107.6
Manufacturing	52,473.7	48,910.2
Electricity, gas and water	3557.8	3537.8
Construction	11,642.4	13,585.0
Wholesale & retail trade	54,819.6	49,907.7
Transport & communications	35,019.2	31,953.4
Finance	66,198.3	66,011.8
Public administration and others	35,784.8	37,135.4

Source: Asian Development Bank

Per capita GDP rose from an estimated Singapore $49,301 in 2006 to Singapore $54,834 in 2007 before falling to $53,192 in 2008. It was estimated to be S$46,000 in 2011.

The consumer price index fell by 0.4 per cent in 2002, then rose by 0.5 per cent in 2003. In 2004 and in 2005, it rose again by 1.7 per cent and 0.4 per cent respectively, and in 2006, it grew by 1 per cent. Over 2007, inflation accelerated, reflecting domestic cost pressures and escalating international prices; the consumer price index grew by 2.1 per cent; the Food Price Index grew by 3 per cent in the same year. Inflation was estimated to be 5.2 per cent in 2011.

Sovereign debt was estimated to be 95 per cent of GDP in 2011.

Foreign Investment
Foreign investment comes mainly from South-East Asia and the US. Total direct foreign investment was estimated to be over $618 billion in 2010, of which over 40 per cent was in the finance and services sector. Overseas investments totalled S$802,600 million by the end of 2010 (of which China over $70,500 million)

Balance of Payments / Imports and Exports
The following table shows the value of imports and exports in recent years (figures in mn. Sing. dollars):

Current Account Balance	2007	2008	2009
Trade Balance	54,648	25,869	34,819
- Exports fob	450,628	476,762	391,118
- Imports cif	395,980	450,893	256,299
Trade Balance % change			
- Exports of Goods	4.4	5.8	-18.0
- Imports of Goods	4.5	13.9	-21.0

Source: Asian Development Bank

Total exports were estimated to amount to S$514.7 billion in 2011 and imports cost S$459.7 billion.

Major exports include chemicals, telecommunications equipment, computer equipment, petroleum and related products, rubber, food and livestock, tobacco and clothing. Major imports include machinery, crude materials, transport equipment, textiles, iron and steel. Singapore's most important trading partners are Japan, Malaysia, Hong Kong, China and the US. The following tables show imports and exports of specific commodities. Figures are in million Singaporean dollars:

Imports

Commodity	2007
Animal and animal products	3,316
Vegetable products	2,153
Animal or vegetable fats	700
Prepared foodstuffs	5,412
Mineral products	84,466
Chemical products	20,639
Plastics and rubber	8,101
Hides and skins	970
Wood and wood products	677
Wood pulp products	2,621
Textiles and textile articles	5,375
Footwear and headgear	694
Articles of stone, plaster, cement, asbestos	1,758
Pearls, precious or semi-precious stones, metals	6,695
Base metals and articles thereof	21,669
Machinery, mechanical appliances and electrical equipment	189,394
Transportation equipment	19,771
Instruments-measuring, musical	13,229
Arms and ammunition	23
Miscell. manufactured articles	2,824
Works of art	440

Source: Asian Development Bank

Exports

Commodity	2007
Animal and animal products	1, 078
Vegetable products	809
Animal or vegetable fats	630
Prepared foodstuffs	5,439
Mineral products	62,475
Chemical products	45,205
Plastics and rubber	14,436
Hides and shins	675
Wood and wood products	310
Wood pulp products	3,034
Textiles and textile articles	4,202
Footwear and headgear	330
Articles of stone, plaster, cement, asbestos	793
Pearls, precious or semi-precious stones, metals	4,978
Base metals and articles thereof	16,832
Machinery, mechanical appliances and electrical equipment	241,864
Transportation equipment	11,614
Instruments-measuring, musical	12,107
Arms and ammunition	34
Miscell. manufactured articles	1,735
Works of art	218

Source: Asian Development Bank

The next table shows the value in 2009 of imports and exports with major trading partners. Figures are in Singaporean dollars:

Country	Imports $ mil	Exports $ mil
Malaysia	28,554	30,972
USA	29,217	17,747
Hong Kong	-	31,253
Indonesia	14,258	26,111
People's Rep. of China	25,964	26,357
Japan	18,758	12,305
Thailand	8,223	10,094
Australia	-	10,582
Korea, Republic of	14,061	12,570
Saudi Arabia	8,099	-
Germany	7,884	-
France	8,375	-
India	-	9,253

Source: Asian Development Bank

Central Bank
Monetary Authority of Singapore, MAS Building, 10 Shenton Way, Singapore 079117, Singapore Tel: +65 6225 5577, fax: +65 6229 9491, e-mail: webmaster@mas.gov.sg, URL: http://www.mas.gov.sg/index.html
Chairman: Tharman Shanmugaratnam

Chambers of Commerce and Trade Organisations
Singapore Business Federation, URL: http://www.sbf.org.sg/
Singapore Chinese Chamber of Commerce and Industry, URL: http://www.sccci.org.sg
Singapore International Chamber of Commerce, URL: http://www.sicc.com.sg/

Stock Exchange
Stock Exchange of Singapore, URL: http://www.ses.com.sg

MANUFACTURING, MINING AND SERVICES

Primary and Extractive Industries
Singapore has established itself as one of the world's top three global oil trading centres, as well as one of the top three refining centres, helped by its location in the Strait of Malacca, and a skilled workforce.

Singapore has a total crude oil refining capacity of approximately 1.357 million barrels per day (bbl/d) from its three main refineries: ExxonMobil's 605,000-bbl/d refinery; Royal Dutch/Shell's 458,000-bbl/d refinery on Pulau Bukom island; and the Singapore Refining Corporation's (SRC) 273,000-bbl/d refinery. In 2011, Singapore produced an estimated 10,910,000 barrels per day, up from 9,840,000 in 2006. The market for Singaporean refined petroleum has begun to face competition from refineries in India and Malaysia, and Thailand has signalled its intent to join the competition.

In 2011, Singapore used an estimated 896,000 thousand barrels of oil per day. Net imports reached 916,000 thousand barrels per day. Singapore National Oil Company and Singapore Petroleum Company are both state-run although the three major oil refineries are run by Esso, Mobil and Shell Eastern.

Singapore has a large petrochemical industry mainly based as the Jurong Island complex. Seven islands have been reclaimed in order to extend this complex to support the growth in petrochemicals and chemical production. The project links Jurong to Singapore Island by a 1.62-mile causeway. Singapore's petrochemical industry benefits from its proximity to major markets such as China.

All of the country's natural gas is imported, as is all of its coal: roughly 297 billion cubic feet per day of the former and 39,000 short tons per year of the latter. The state-run Singapore Power (http://www.singaporepower.com.sg/irj/portal/spservices) oversees natural gas and power management, while gas is distributed by its subsidiary PowerGas. In 2002, the government set a target of 60 per cent of the country's electricity to be generated from natural gas by 2012; this goal had been met by 2003, and around 80 per cent of electricity demand is now fulfilled using natural gas. Two power cuts led to a review of gas suppliers, and the government decided to diversify its sources away from total reliance on Indonesia. Singapore is developing its own liquid natural gas (LNG) import terminal at Tuas View. It is scheduled to go live in 2013.

Energy

The people of Singapore consumed 2.260 quadrillion Btu of energy in 2009, down from 2.544 quadrillion Btu in 2008. Per capita energy consumption reached 457.1 million Btu in 2005, the second highest rate in the Asia and Oceania region (behind Brunei), and well above the regional average of 41 million Btu.

Electricity is generated at four power stations. In 2010, production reached an estimated 343.80 billion kWh, whilst consumption reached 40.60 billion kWh. Installed generation capacity stood at 10.25 GW in 2010, an increase of 50 per cent since 2004. (Source: EIA)

Manufacturing

Manufacturing contributed some 29 per cent of GDP in 2007. Singapore manufactures electronic and electrical products and components, petroleum products, machinery and metal products, chemical and pharmaceutical products and transport equipment (mainly aircraft repairs/maintenance, shipbuilding/repair and oil rigs). It also produces food and beverages, printing and publishing, optical and photographic equipment, plastic products/modules and instrumentation equipment. The sector grew by 15 per cent in 2000, but this was followed by a contraction of 11.6 per cent in 2001. In 2002, 13.9 per cent growth was recorded. The sector grew by 8.4 per cent and three per cent over the following two years. In 2004, manufacturing grew by almost 14 per cent, and in 2005, it grew by 9.5 per cent. Over 2007, manufacturing growth slipped to 5.8 per cent from 11.9 per cent in 2006, due to poor performances by the pharmaceutical and electronics sectors. Transportation engineering grew by 23.5 per cent boosted by global demand for shipbuilding, ship repairs, and oil-rig building. The construction industry had a strong year, as the property market grew. (Source: ADB)

Tourism

There were around 11.6 million international visitors to Singapore in 2010, up 8.9 per cent on the previous year, and the highest number of tourists yet. Most visitors were from China (1.8 million), Australia, India, Japan, the UK and the USA.
Singapore Tourism Board, URL: http://www.stb.com.sg

Agriculture

The main crops are orchids, ornamental plants, vegetables and fruit. There are 103 orchid/ornamental plant farms and 71 vegetable/fruit farms occupying 371 and 128 hectares respectively. Approximately S$46.6 million worth of orchids and other plants are exported. The livestock population was recently put at 2.1 million poultry, 504,000 cattle, and 221,120 ducks. Figures for 2010 estimated the total fish catch at 1,730 tonnes.

Main Production in 2010

Crop	Int $1000*	Tonnes
Hen eggs, in shell	16,903	20,380
Other bird eggs, in shell	4,903	1,700
Vegetables fresh nes	3,123	16,572
Spinach	441	1,883
Mushrooms and truffles	211	117
Lettuce and chicory	171	366
Indigenous cattle meat	122	45
Cabbages and other brassicas	82	546
Coconuts	19	170
Fruit fresh nes	4	10
Indigenous chicken meat	3	2
Tomatoes	2	6

* unofficial figures
Source: http://faostat.fao.org/site/339/default.aspx Food and Agriculture Organization of the United Nations, Food and Agricultural commodities production

COMMUNICATIONS AND TRANSPORT

Travel Requirements

Citizens of the USA, Canada, Australia and the EU require a passport valid for at least six months beyond the length of stay but do not need a visa; a Social Visit Pass is issued on arrival, provided the traveller has a valid passport, sufficient funds, a confirmed onward/return ticket and entry documentation for further destinations. For British and Irish passport holders can stay for 30 days on a Social Visit Pass; for other nationals the maximum length of stay is 14 days. Extensions of up to 90 days can be applied for. Other nationals should contact the embassy to check visa requirements.

National Airlines

Singapore Airlines (SIA), URL: http://www.singaporeair.com

International Airports

Singapore Changi Airport (http://www.changiairport.com/) is operated by the Changi Airport Group. It serves more than 100 international airlines flying to approximately 60 countries . The airport handled more than 46 million passengers in 2011.

There are a further seven airports in Singapore.

Railways

Singapore had a rail network of 138.2 km by the beginning of 2007. The 83 km Mass Rapid Transit (MRT) System consists of three lines running north-south, east-west (NSWEL) and the Circle Line (CCL). The NSEWL is 93 km long with 53 stations and the CCL extends 35 km wth 31 stations. More than 1.5 million passengers use the lines daily. The North-East Line (NEL) is a fully-automated underground heavy rail system. It extends 20 km long and runs from Punggol to Harbour Front. It is used by an average 375,000 passensgers in 2010. The Light Rapid Transit (LRT) opened in 1999 linking Bukit Panjang to the MRT at Choa Chu Kang station. Sengkand LRT was opened in 2003, and the Punggol system opened in January 2005.
Land Transport Authority, URL: http://www.lta.gov.sg

Roads

Singapore has 3,262 km of public roads, which includes 150 km of expressways. Vehicles drive on the right. In 2007 there were a total of 851,336 motor vehicles on the roads in Singapore, of which 514,685 were private cars. In 1998 Singapore introduced the Electronic Road Pricing Scheme (ERP). Vehicles are fitted with an in-vehicle unit, and each time the vehicle passes an ERP gantry, the motorist is charged. Charges change according to the time of day and size of vehicle.

Singapore has recently converted buses to run on compressed natural gas.

Causeway

Singapore is connected to Malaysia via a causeway that runs across the straits of Johor. The link is 1.2 km long and carries road and rail links as well as a water pipeline. 1998 saw the opening of a bridge across the straits.

Ports and Harbours

Its location in the Straits of Malacca ensure that Singapore is one of the busiest ports in the world. It has however declined in recent years. At any one time there are more than 1,000 ships in port and Singapore attracts some 130,000 vessels annually (down from 145,000 in 2000). In 2010, over 500 million tonnes of cargo was handled at the port.

The port of Singapore is managed by the Port of Singapore Authority (PSA). Ferry services run to Singapore's islands, Sentosa, Malaysia and the Indonesian Riau islands.
Port of Singapore Authority, URL: http://www.mpa.gov.sg

HEALTH

Healthcare financing is based on individual responsibility coupled with help from the government. As of 2011, four schemes operate through which Singaporeans finance their healthcare: Medisave, Medishield, Medifund and Eldershield. Private practitioners provide 80 per cent of primary healthcare services and government polyclinics the remaining 20 per cent. Public hospitals provide 80 per cent of the more costly hospital care. The island network includes 18 outpatient polyclinics and approximately 2,000 private medical practitioner's clinics. There are seven public hospitals including five general hospitals, a women's and children's hospital and a psychiatry hospital. Approximately 75 per cent of public hospital beds are subsidised. There are also six national speciality centres for cancer, cardiac, eye, skin, neuroscience and dental care.

In 2008, 3.3 per cent of GDP was spent on healthcare; the government contributed 34.1 per cent of the total finances for healthcare. The private sector contributed the remaining 65.9 per cent of health expenditure, 94.3 per cent of it in the form of out-of-pocket finances. Total government expenditure accounted for 7.8 per cent of its total expenditure. Per capita total expenditure on health equated to US$1,404, compared to US$648 in 2000.

In 2000-10, there were 8,323 doctors (18 per 10,000 population), 26,792 nurses and midwives (59 per 10,000 population), 1,463 dentists and 1,658 pharmacists. There were also around 1,450 acupuncturists and 1,460 TCMs (Traditional Chinese Medicine practitioners). There are an estimated 31 hospital beds per 10,000 population.

In 2009, the estimated infant mortality rate (probability of dying before age one) was 2 per 1,000 live births and the child (under-five) mortality rate was 3 per 1,000 live births. The most common causes of death in the under-fives were prematurity (19 per cent), congenital abnormalities (34 per cent) and pneumonia (12 per cent). In the period 2000-09, approximately 4.4 per cent of children aged less than five years were classified as stunted and 3.3. per cent as underweight. Approximately 2.6 per cent were classified as overweight.

All the population have access to improved drinking water and improved sanitation. (Source: World Heath Organization)

EDUCATION

Primary education in Singapore became compulsory in January 2003. Children complete an average of ten years of formal education, starting at the age of six. At the end of six years, Primary School Leaving Examinations complete primary education. The primary school curriculum covers English; mother tongue; mathematics; science; moral education, physical education and social studies. Although education in Singapore is not free, the school fees in public schools are heavily subsidised so no child is left out.

Secondary education, lasting four to five years, ends in GCE O-levels and the curriculum covers English; mother tongue; mathematics; humanities; science; home economics, or design and technology; art; civic and moral education and music. Students can then continue with pre-university studies leading to GCE A levels in preparation for tertiary education. The curriculum here covers a maximum of four A level subjects from the humanities or sciences.

As of 2002, there were 175 primary schools, with 305,992 registered pupils, 162 secondary schools, with 176,132 registered pupils, 16 junior colleges (JC) and two centralised pre-university institutes. Institutes of higher education include: Nanyang Polytechnic, Ngee

SLOVAKIA

Ann Polytechnic, Singapore Polytechnic, Temasek Polytechnic, Nanyang Technological University and the National University of Singapore. In 2005, an estimated 43,663 students were registered at Singapore's Universities and a further 58,880 students were enrolled at the polytechnics. Due to the large amount of ex-patriot communities in Singapore there are several international and private schools catering to these groups.

In 2007, the adult literacy rate of Singapore was estimated to be 94.4 per cent, this figures rose to 99.7 per cent among the 15-24 age group.

Figures from UNESCO show that in 2009 11.6 per cent of total government expenditure went on education.

RELIGION

There is freedom of worship in Singapore. The main religions are Chinese folk religions (39 per cent), Muslims (18.6 per cent), Christians (16.6 per cent), Buddhists (14 per cent) and Hindus (4.9 per cent). Singapore has a religious liberty rating of 6 on a scale of 1 to 10 (10 is most freedom). (Source: World Religion Database)

COMMUNICATIONS AND MEDIA

The media is regulated and censorship is common. May journalist praactice self censorship and the government punishes the press for perceived attacks on officials. Private ownership of satellite dishes is not allowed. Internet access is regulated. Social media is available.

Newspapers
English:
The Straits Times, URL: http://www.straitstimes.asia1.com.sg.
The New Paper, URL: http://www.newpaper.asia1.com.sg.
The Business Times, URL: http://www.business-times.asia1.com.
Chinese:
Lianhe Zaobao, URL: http://www.zaobao.com.
Lianhe Wanbao, URL: http://www.sph.com.sg/newspapers/wanbao.html
Shin Min Daily News, URL: http://www.sph.com.sg/newspapers/shinmin.html
Malay: **Berita Harian**, URL: http://cyberita.asia1.com.sg.

Business Journals
Singapore Business, URL: http://www.businesstimes.com.sg/

Broadcasting
The Radio Corporation of Singapore Pte Ltd (URL: http://www.mediacorpradio.sg/) operates the nation's largest radio network comprising 12 local and three international radio stations. Five local radio stations broadcast in English, Gold, Symphony, NewsRadio, Class and Perfect. Three broadcast in Mandarin, YES, Capital Radio and Love; two in Malay, Warna and Ria; and Oli broadcasts to the Indian Population. There is also a private radio station called Radio Heart.

Media Corp TV (formerly Television Corporation of Singapore) operates Channels 5 and 8 which are broadcast in English and Mandarin respectively. Singapore CableVision offers three subscription channels. Singapore Television Twelve operates two channels, Prime 12 broadcasts programmes in Malay, Hindi and Indian dialects. Premier 12 broadcasts in English. **Media Corp**, URL: http://www.mediacorp.sg/index.php

Telecommunications
Singapore Telecom operates a modern telecommunications system; in 2010 there were some 1.9 million mainline telephones in use, and around 7 million mobile phones.

As of 2010, Singapore had approximately 3.7 million internet users, and there are over 992,000 hosts. Infocomm Development Agency of Singapore (IDA) was established for policy formulation and regulation in this field.

ENVIRONMENT

Major environmental issues include waste management and air and water pollution.

In April 2006, Singapore ratified the Kyoto Protocol to help tackle global greenhouse gas (GHG) emissions. However, Singapore is a non-Annex I party to the agreement and is not legally bound to a specific emissions target. Singapore has established its own targets as part of its National Climate Change Strategy (NCCS), aiming to reduce its carbon intensity by 25 per cent compared to 1990 levels. In 2005, carbon dioxide emissions were estimated to be around 133.88 million metric tons, whilst per capita emissions were around 30.25 metric tons in the same year, the highest in the Asia and Oceania region and higher than the rate in the US, of 20.14 metric tons. By 2010, carbon dioxide emissions had risen to 172 million metric tons, ranking Singapore 32nd in the world. (Source: EIA)

Of growing environmental concern is the state of repair of some tankers using regional waters, especially ageing Russian and Eastern European ships crossing the waters of East Asia. In 2002, the Singaporean government created a ten-year environmental initiative known as the Singapore Green Plan 2012. Among other targets, the government set out to generate 60 per cent of the country's electricity from natural gas. It achieved this target by 2003.

Singapore is party to the following environmental agreements: Biodiversity, Climate Change, Climate Change-Kyoto Protocol, Desertification, Endangered Species, Hazardous Wastes, Law of the Sea, Ozone Layer Protection, Ship Pollution.

SPACE PROGRAMME

Singapore's first satellite was launched in 2011 from India. Singapore is hoping to develop itself as a space industry centre. Several satellite companies including Astrium Satellite Services and DigitalGlobe, have their headquarters there.
Singapore Space and Technology Association (SSTA), URL: http://www.space.org.sg/

SLOVAKIA
Slovak Republic
Slovenská Republika

Capital: Bratislava (Population estimate: 450,000)

Head of State: Ivan Gasparovic (President) (page 1429)

National Flag: Three horizontal stripes of white, blue and red, with the national emblem left of centre. The national emblem is a red early Gothic shield with a silver double cross, mounted on the central peak of the blue three hill group

CONSTITUTION AND GOVERNMENT

Constitution
From 1918 onwards the former state of Slovakia became part of the Czech and Slovak Federal Republic. A communist government ruled from 1948. After forty years of dictatorship Czechoslovakia's 1989 Velvet Revolution opened the way for democracy and independence. Subsequently, in June 1992, Vladimir Meciar's movement for a democratic Slovakia party received a clear mandate from voters, winning 74 of the 150 seats in Slovakia's parliament. Slovakia declared itself a sovereign republic in July and adopted its own constitution in September. The Slovak Republic came into being on 1 January 1993 and the first president, Michal Kovac, was elected on 15 February.

The constitution was amended in 1998 to allow the speaker to assume powers to appoint a cabinet in the event that the country has no president. The constitution was also amended in January 1999 to allow for the president to be elected by popular vote for a maximum period of two successive five-year terms. The president appoints the prime minister, who is the head of government, and, on the advice of the prime minister, the cabinet. The highest executive body is the government of the Slovak Republic, consisting of the prime minister, deputy prime ministers and department ministers.

To consult the constitution, please visit: http://www.concourt.sk/en/A_ustava/ustava_a.pdf

International Relations
In January 2002, following amendments to the constitution, eight new regional parliaments were created, one of the requirements for entry to the EU. On 16-17 May 2003 a referendum was held approving the Slovak Republic's accession to the EU and on 1 May 2004 the Slovak Republic was one of ten countries to join the EU. In March 2004 Slovakia became a member of NATO. In November 2005 Slovakia joined the European Exchange Rate Mechanism.

Recent Events
Following membership of the EU in 2004, the Euro became the official currency on January 1 2009. Ivan Gasparovic was re-elected president in April 2009.

In March 2010, President Gasparovic vetoed a controversial patriotism law that had recently been passed by parliament. Amongst the laws requirements, schools would have to play the national anthem every Monday.

In September 2010, a referendum of reducing the size of parliament and restricting privileges for parliament failed as not enough people voted.

The coalition government effectively collapsed in October 2011 after a member of the coalition abstained in a vote against the eurozone expansion of the European Financial Stability Facility. The Freedom and Solidarity party said it was opposed to the taxpayers of Slovakia paying for the debts of richer countries. The government agreed to hold an early election in March 2012 and parliament later ratitified the eurozone bailout plan.

The opposition party Smer, led by former prime minister Robert Fico, won a landslide victory in the general election in March 2012.

Legislature

The Slovak Republic's unicameral parliament is the National Council (*Narodna Rada Slovenskej*) and is the country's supreme legislative body. It considers and approves the Constitution, Constitutional statutes and other laws. It consists of 150 members who are elected by proportional representation for a four-year term. The National Council is responsible for the election of the country's judges, and the president and vice president of the Supreme Court. The National Council also submits the nominees for the office of judge of the Constitutional Court to the president of the Republic.

National Council of the Slovak Republic, Mudronova 1, 812 80 Bratislava, Slovak Republic. Tel: +421 2 5934 1111 / 421 2 5441 2500, e-mail: odkazy@mail.nrsr.sk, URL: http://www.nrsr.sk
Speaker: Pavol Paska

Cabinet (as at June 2013)

Prime Minister: Robert Fico (page 1424)
Minister of the Interior: Robert Kalinak (page 1453)
Minister of Finance: Peter Kazimir (page 1454)
Minister of Foreign Affairs: Miroslav Lajcak (page 1459)
Minister of the Economy and Construction: Tomas Malatinsky
Minister of Transport, Posts and Telecommunications: Jan Pociatek
Minister of Agriculture and Rural Development: Lubomir Jahnatek (page 1448)
Minister of Defence: Martin Glvac
Minister of Justice: Tomas Borec
Minister of Labour and Social Affairs: Jan Richter
Minister of the Environment: Peter Ziga
Minister of Education, Research and Sport: Dusan Caplovic
Minister of Culture and Tourism: Marek Madaric
Minister of Health: Zuzana Zvolenska

Ministries

Office of the President, Stefanovikova 2, PO Box 128, 810 00 Bratislava, Slovak Republic. Tel: +421 2 5441 6624, e-mail: tlac@prezident.sk, URL: http://www.prezident.sk/
Government portal, URL: http://www.government.gov.sk/
Ministry of Foreign Affairs, Hlboká cesta 2, 833 36 Bratislava, Slovak Republic. Tel: +421 2 5978 1111, e-mail: infopublic@foreign.gov.sk, URL: http://www.foreign.gov.sk/
Ministry of Economy, Mierová 19, 827 15 Bratislava 212, Slovak Republic. Tel: +421 2 4854 1111, fax: +421 2 4333 7827, e-mail: info@economy.gov.sk, URL: http://www.economy.gov.sk/
Ministry of Defence, Kituzovova 8, 832 47 Bratislava, Slovak Republic. Tel: +421 2 4425 0320, URL: http://www.mod.gov.sk/
Ministry of the Interior, Pribinova 2, 812 72 Bratislava, Slovak Republic. Tel: +421 2 5094 1111, URL: http://www.minv.sk/
Ministry of Finance, Stefanovicova 5, PO Box 82, 817 82 Bratislava, Slovak Republic. Tel: +421 2 5958 1111, fax: +421 2 5249 8042, e-mail: info@mfsr.sk, URL: http://www.finance.gov.sk/
Ministry of Health, Límbova 2, PO Box 52, 837 52 Bratislava 3, Slovak Republic. Tel: +421 2 5937 3111, URL: http://www.health.gov.sk/
Ministry of Education, Stromová 1, 813 30 Bratislava, Slovak Republic. Tel: +421 2 5937 4111, http://www.education.gov.sk/
Ministry of Justice, Zupné nám. 13, 813 11 Bratislava 1, Slovak Republic. Tel: +421 2 5441 5952, http://www.justice.gov.sk/
Ministry of Labour, Social Affairs and Family, Spitáliska 4, 816 43 Bratislava 1, Slovak Republic. Tel: +421 2 5975 1111, http://www.employment.gov.sk/
Ministry of the Environment, Nám. L'Stura 1, 812 35 Bratislava, Slovak Republic. Tel: +421 2 5956 1111, fax: +421 2 5956 2031, http://www.lifeenv.gov.sk/
Ministry of Transport, Post and Telecommunications, Nám. slobody 6, 810 05 Bratislava 1, Slovak Republic. Tel: +421 2 5949 4111, fax: +421 2 5249 4794, URL: http://www.telecom.gov.sk/
Ministry of Construction and Public Works, Spitálska 8, 816 44 Bratislava, Slovak Republic. Tel: +421 2 5975 1111, fax: +421 2 5293 1203, URL: http://www.build.gov.sk/
Ministry of Agriculture, Dobrovicova 12, 812 66 Bratislava, Slovak Republic. Tel: +421 2 5926 6111, URL: http//www.mpsr.sk/

Political Parties

Smer - Sociálna Demokracia (Smer, The Direction - Social Democracy Party), Sumracná 27, 821 02 Bratislava, Slovakia. Tel / fax: +421 2 4342 6297, URL: http://www.strana-smer.sk
Leader: Robert Fico
Slovenská Národná Strana, (SNS, Slovak National Party), URL: http://www.sns.sk
Slovenská Demokratická a Kresťanská únia - Demokratická Strana, (SDKÚ-DS Slovak Democratic and Christian Union - Democratic Party), Ruzinovská 28, 821 03 Bratislava, Slovak Republic. Tel: +421 2 4341 4102 - 05, fax: +421 2 4341 4106, e-mail: sdku@sdkuonline.sk, URL: http://www.sdkuonline.sk
Ľudová Strana, Hnutie za Demokratické Slovensko (LS- HZDS, People's Party - Movement for a Democratic Slovakia), Tomasikova 32/A, 830 00 Bratislava, Slovak Republic. Tel: +421 2 48 220104 (Department of Foreign Relations), URL: http://www.hzds.sk
Leader: Vladimír Mečiar
Strana madarskej koalície - Magyar Koalíció Pártja (SMK, Party of the Hungarian Coalition), Cajakova 8, 811 05 Bratislava, Slovak Republic. Tel: +421 2 5249 7684, fax: +421 2 5249 5791, e-mail: smk@smk.sk, URL: http://www.mkp.sk
Leader: Pál Csáky
Krest'ansko-demokratické hnutie (KDH, Christian Democratic Movement), Zabotova 2, 811 04 Bratislava, Slovak Republic. Tel: +421 2 5249 2541- 6, e-mail: kdhba@isternet.sk, URL: http://www.kdh.sk
Leader: Pavol Hrušovský
Aliancia Nového Obcana (ANO, New Civic Alliance), Drobného 27, 841 01 Bratislava, Slovak Republic. Tel: +421 2 6920 2919, fax: +421 2 6920 2920, e-mail: ano@ano-aliancia.sk, URL: http://www.ano-aliancia.sk

Leader: Pavol Rusko
Komunistická strana Slovenska (KSS, Slovak Communist Party), Hattalova 12 A, 831 03 Bratislava, Slovak Republic. Tel: +421 2 5477 4102, fax.: +421 2 4437 2540, URL: http://www.kss.sk/

Elections

The last presidential elections took place in April 2009. In the second round of voting the incumbent candidate Ivan Gasparovic beat the centre-right candidate Iveta Radicova.

The most recent parliamentary election took place on 10 March 2012. The Smer-DS increased its share of the vote to gain an overall majority. Results were as follows: Smer-SD 83 seats; KDH 16 seats; OLaNO 16 seats; MH 13 seats; SDKU-DS 11 seats; SaS 11 seats.

Diplomatic Representation

British Embassy, Panska 16, 811 01 Bratislava, Slovak Republic. Tel: + 421 (2) 5998 2000, fax: + 421 (2) 5998 2237, e-mail: bebra@internet.sk, URL: http://ukinslovakia.fco.gov.uk
Ambassador: Susannah Montgomery
US Embassy, Hviezdoslavovo Namestie 4, 81102 Bratislava, Slovak Republic. (Mailing address: PO Box 309, 814 99 Bratislava, Slovak Republic.) Tel: +421 7 5443 3338, fax: +421 7 5443 0096, URL: http://slovakia.usembassy.gov
Ambassador: Theodore Sedgwick
Embassy of the Slovak Republic, 25 Kensington Palace Gardens, London, W8 4QY, United Kingdom. Tel: +44 (0)20 7243 0803, fax: +44 (0)20 7727 5824, e-mail: mail@slovakembassy.co.uk, URL: http://www.slovakembassy.co.uk
Ambassadors: Miroslav Wlachovsky
Embassy of the Slovak Republic, 3523 International Court, NW, Washington, DC 20008, USA. Tel: +1 202 237 1054, fax: +1 202 237 6438, e-mail: emb.washington@mzv.sk URL: http://www.mzv.sk/washington
Ambassador: Peter Kmec
Permanent Mission of the Slovak Republic to the UN, 801 Second Ave., New York, NY 10017, USA. Tel: +1 212 286 8880, fax: +1 212 286 8419, URL: http://www.unnewyork.mfa.sk/App/WCM/ZU/NewYorkOSN/main.nsf?Open
Ambassador: Frantisek Ruzicka

LEGAL SYSTEM

The Slovak Republic has a two-level court system. District courts try proceedings at first instance, whilst regional courts hear cases on appeal. The Supreme Court is an appellate review court, and never acts as a first instance court. There are also military courts.

The Constitutional Court is an independent judicial body which protects the Slovak Republic's constitution. There are 13 Constitutional Court judges, each serving terms of 12 years. They are appointed by the president.

The death penalty was abolished in 1990 when Slovakia was still part of Czechoslovakia.

Constitutional Court, URL: http://www.concourt.sk

Slovak National Centre for Human Rights, URL: http://www.snslp.sk/

LOCAL GOVERNMENT

The Slovak Republic is divided into administrative territorial units of 8 regions and 79 districts. The Slovak Republic's 2,891 municipalities make independent decisions on issues connected with their own administration and are governed by municipal councils and mayors. 138 of the municipalities have a town statute.

The Slovak Republic's eight regions are: Bratislava, Trnava, Trencin, Nitra, Zilina, Banska, Presov, and Kosice. Each has a regional parliament.

AREA AND POPULATION

Area

The Slovak Republic is a land locked country located in the centre of Europe and borders Poland and the Czech Republic to the north, Austria to the west, Hungary to the south, and Ukraine to the east. The river Danube forms the border with Hungary and Austria. The northern and central part of the country is mountainous. The highest peak is the Gerlachovsky Stit (2,655m). It has an area of 49,035 sq. km.

The climate is temperate with cold, cloudy winters and cool summers.

To view a map, consult http://www.un.org/Depts/Cartographic/map/profile/slovakia.pdf

Population

Estimated WHO figures for 2010 put the population at 5,462,000. An estimated 15 per cent of the population is aged less than 15 years and 17 per cent over 60 years. The median age is 37 years. Figures from the Statistical Office of the Slovak Republic show that the population at the end of 2005 was 5,389,180 (up from 5 384 822 in 2004), of which 2,773,308 were female and 2,615,872 were male. The population density in 2003 was recorded at 110 people per sq. km. Bratislava's population is estimated at 450,000. Other major cities include Kosice (250,000), Presov (95,000), Nitra (85,000), Zilina (85,000), and Banská Bystrica (84,000). Approximately 56 per cent of the population lives in urban areas.

The population according to region is shown on the following table. Figures are from the 2001 Housing Census.

SLOVAKIA

Population by Region, 2001 Housing Census

Region	Population
Bratislava	599,015
Trnava	551,003
Trencin	605,582
Nitra	713,422
Zilina	692,332
Banska	662,121
Presov	789,968
Kosice	766,012

Source: Statistical Office of the Slovak Republic

The official language is Slovak and 85.8 per cent of the population are Slovakian. The largest ethnic minority is Hungarian which accounts for 9.7 per cent of the total population. Others include Gypsy or Roma of whom there are estimated to be 400,000, Czech, Ruthenian and Ukrainian. The constitution grants and guarantees members of national minorities the right to receive and impart information in their mother tongue.

Births, Marriages, Deaths
In 2005 marriages numbered 26,149, divorces numbered 11,553. (Source: Statistical Office of the Slovak Republic). According to latest figures from the WHO, the crude birth rate was 10.4 per 1,000 population and the crude death rate was 9.8 per 1,000 population. The total fertility rate for women was estimated to be 1.3 in 2010. Average life expectancy for males was estimated to be 71 years in 2009 and 79 years for females. Healthy life expectancy was 67 years in 2007. (Source: http://www.who.int, World Health Statistics 2012)

Public Holidays 2014
1 January: New Year's Day / Independence Day: Origin of the Slovak Republic
6 January: Epiphany
18 April: Good Friday
21 April: Easter Monday
5 May: May Day
8 May: Victory Day
5 July: St. Cyril and St. Methodius Holiday
29 August: Revolution Day (Slovak National Uprising, 1944)
1 September: Constitution Day
15 September: Our Lady of Seven Sorrows
1 November: All Saints' Day
17 November: Fight for Freedom and Democracy Day
24 December: Christmas Eve
25 December: Christmas Day
26 December: St. Stephen's Day

EMPLOYMENT

Total annual employment in 2005 was 2,216,200 compared to 2,170,400 in 2004. Registered unemployment fell from 407,637 in September 2003 (481,033 in September 2002) to 407,074 in October 2003 (478,631 in October 2002). The unemployment rate fell from 13.9 per cent in September 2003 (16.6 per cent in September 2002) to 13.8 per cent in October 2003 (16.4 per cent in October 2002). Unemployment in June 2004 was put at 18.5 per cent. Average unemployment in 2005 was 16 per cent and 12 per cent in 2006 and an estimated 10.5 per cent in 2008.

Employment by sector

Sector	2008
Agriculture, hunting, forestry & fishing	98,000
Mining & quarrying	14,200
Manufacturing	647,600
Electricity, water & gas	42,100
Construction	256,700
Wholesale & retail trade, repairs	298,900
Hotels & restaurants	107,600
Transport, storage, post, telecommunications	177,700
Financial, intermediation	55,200
Real estate, renting & business activities	157,900
Public admin. and defence, compulsory social security	167,100
Education	163,800
Health & social care	154,100
Other community, social, personal activities	86,400
Households with employed persons	5,700
Extra-territorial organisations	700
Not identified	300
Total	2,433,800

Source: Copyright © International Labour Organization (ILO Dept. of Statistics, http://laborsta.ilo.org)

BANKING AND FINANCE

Currency
The currency was the Slovenská Koruna (SKK) of 100 hellers. The Euro was adopted as the official currency on January 1 2009.

GDP/GNP, Inflation, National Debt
The Slovak Republic initially found the transition from a Communist state to a market economy more difficult than the Czech Republic. However, revenue from privatised steel, energy, telecoms, and financial institutions helped reduce the 2001 budget deficit of 3.7 per cent.

In 2004 the Slovak Republic was singled out by a World Bank report for becoming one of the 20 easiest countries for doing business. Recent economic policies continue to promote strong growth and lowering inflation. However, the economy contracted in 2009.

The country adopted the Euro as its currency in 2009.

Estimated figures for 2006 put GDP at US$55.1 billion with a growth rate for that year of 8.2 per cent, and US$107.6 billion in 2007. Figures for 2008 estimated GDP to have risen to US$96 billion with a growth rate of 6.4 per cent.

Slovakia had to revise downwards its growth forecasts for 2009 and the economy contracted sharply, due to both the global economic crisis and a dispute with Russia which led to disruption of Slovakia's natural gas supply. GDP growth was an estimated 2 per cent in 2010, and 3.2 per cent in 2011. GDP was estimated at €69 billion in 2011. Growth was revised downwards to a projected 1.2 per cent in 2012. Per capita GDP was estimated at €23,000 in 2011.

Inflation was estimated at 4 per cent in 2011. It had fallen to 3.74 per cent by March 2012.

Direct foreign investment was estimated at US$50 billion in 2011.

National debt amounted to 42 per cent of GDP in 2010.

Balance of Payments / Imports and Exports
Exports were estimated at US$64.5 billion and imports US$63 billion in 2010. Main exports are machinery and energy equipment, audio equipment, vehicles, mineral products, plastics and rubber, iron and steel and plastics. The main export partners are Germany (20 per cent), the Czech Republic (14 per cent) and France (7 per cent), Poland (7.3 per cent) and Hungary (6.5 per cent). Major imports are machinery, vehicles, electrical equipment, fuels and base metals. Germany is the main trading partner again (16 per cent), followed by the Czech Republic (10 per cent) and the Russian Federation (9.8 per cent). Exports were estimated at US$76 billion in 2011 and imports were estimated at US$75 billion.

Central Bank
Národná banka Slovenska (National Bank of Slovakia), Imricha Karvasa 1, 813 25 Bratislava, Slovakia. URL: http://www.nbs.sk
Governor: Jozef Makúch (page 1469)

Chambers of Commerce and Trade Organisations
Slovak Chamber of Commerce and Industry, URL: http://www.scci.sk/

MANUFACTURING, MINING AND SERVICES

Primary and Extractive Industries
Reserves of coal, natural gas and crude oil are all exploited. In January 2012 the Slovak Republic had reserves of crude oil amounting to 10 million barrels, and a crude oil refining capacity of 115,000 barrels per day. Oil production in 2011 was 9,860 barrels per day, of which 0.2 thousand barrels per day) were crude oil. Oil imports in 2011 were 74,000 barrels per day.

Slovakia had estimated reserves of natural gas totalling 1 trillion cubic feet in 2011. Gross production of natural gas in 2011 was 4.0 billion cubic feet. Net imports in 2011 were 208 billion cubic feet, whilst consumption was 199 billion cubic feet.

Coal production in 2010 was estimated at 2.6 million short tons. Imports totalled 4.78 million tons in 2000, down from 7,468 thousand tons in 1999. Consumption was an estimated 7.7 million tons in 2010.

Among the raw materials also available in the Slovak Republic are the following resources: copper, antimony, iron ore, lead, zinc, mercury, precious metals, magnesite, limestone, dolomite, gravel, ceramic materials, mineral salt. (Source: EIA)

Energy
Total energy consumption was 0.722 quadrillion Btu in 2009 (up from 0.787 quadrillion Btu in 2007). Total energy production in the same period was 0.266 quadrillion Btu.

Over 50 per cent of electricity production is generated by nuclear power plants. Total installed electricity generating capacity was 7.16 million kilowatts in 2008. Electricity is produced by means of coal, natural gas, hydro and nuclear power, with nuclear power set to take over as Slovakia's primary source of electricity generation. Electricity generation fell from 29.73 billion kWh in 2006 to 24.64 billion kWh in 2009. Consumption rose from 25,413 million kWh in 1998 to 26.00 billion kWh in 2006. In 2009 it was estimated to be 25.17 billion kWh. (Source: EIA)

Manufacturing
The major industries of the Slovak Republic include, production of metal and metal products, earthenware and ceramics, food and beverages, chemicals, manmade fibres, vehicles, textiles, paper and rubber goods. Figures for 2005 show that turnover of the industrial sector was SKK 1,597,651 million, the largest contributer being the manufacture of basic metals and metal products (SKK 251,921 million); manufacture of transport equipment (SKK 218,498 million); food, beverages and tobacco (SKK 119,024 million); manufacture of machinery and equipment, (SKK89,513 million).

Service Industries
In 2003, 1,387,000 people visited the Slovak Republic and 408,000 Slovaks travelled abroad. Czechs, Germans, Poles and Hungarians were the most common visitors and the industry earned US$879 million in tourism receipts. Figures for 2006 show that the Slovak Republic had 1,612,000 visitors generating receipts of US$1,513 million

Agriculture

In 2001, there were 7,189 farms in the Slovak Republic, 2,527 specialising in crop production, 713 in animal production and 3,949 with combined production. 87,639 ha of land was classed as agricultural land of which 55,273 was arable. A further 6,500 ha of agricultural land was rented out to others.

Agricultural Production in 2010

Produce	Int. $'000*	Tonnes
Cow milk, whole	286,487	918,047
Indigenous pigmeat	132,679	86,310
Wheat	126,545	1,227,800
Indigenous chicken meat	120,837	84,833
Maize	102,013	952,300
Indigenous cattle meat	94,279	34,900
Rapeseed	89,944	322,452
Hen eggs, in shell	61,911	74,646
Sugar beet	42,055	977,694
Sunflower seed	40,677	150,326
Barley	17,896	361,400
Other bird eggs, in shell	15,286	5,300

*unofficial figures
Source: http://faostat.fao.org/site/339/default.aspx Food and Agriculture Organization of the United Nations, Food and Agricultural commodities production

Forestry

Figures for 2002 show that the Slovak Republic had 2,003,000 ha of forest and 6,248,000 square metres of wood was produced.

Fishing

Figures for 2010 from the FAO put the total catch at 1,608 tonnes.

COMMUNICATIONS AND TRANSPORT

Travel Requirements

Citizens of the USA, Canada and Australia require a passport valid for three months beyond the length of stay and funds to the sum of US$50 per day, but do not need a visa for tourism stays of up to 90 days. USA citizens staying overnight in Slovakia must register with local border and aliens police within three working days of arrival; nationals staying at hotels are registered automatically. EU citizens do not need a passport if they carry a valid national Identity Card. Full British passport holders do not need visas for business, tourist or transit purposes for an indefinite period. Other nationals should contact the embassy to check visa requirements.

The Slovak Republic is a signatory to the Schengen Agreement; with a Schengen visa, a visitor can travel freely throughout the Schengen zone, with few border stops and checks. See http://www.eurovisa.info/SchengenCountries.htm for details.

National Airlines

Air Slovakia (SVK), URL: http://www.airslovakia.sk/en/ (Est. 1995)

In 2003 goods to the value of SKK 1,524 million were transported by air.

International Airports

Besides Ivanka/M.R. Stefanik International Airport in the capital Bratislava, there are international airports in Kosice, Poprad, Sliac and Piestany. There are also several regional airports running internal scheduled flights.
Bratislava/Stefanik Ivanka Airport, URL: http://www.airportbratislava.sk/cestujuci/
Civil Aviation Authority, URL: http://www.caa.sk/

Roads

Slovakia has a well developed road network covering 17,734 km, of which 295 km is motorway and 3,220 km is trunk road. Vehicles drive on the right. Roads connecting directly with those of surrounding countries are used as long haulage routes. The maximum speed limit on a motorway is 130 km/h, outside a village is 90 km/h, and in a village is 60 km/h. The use of seatbelts is compulsory whilst the consumption of alcohol before driving is prohibited.

Railways

Railway routes run west to east. A number of industrial complexes have their own lines. There was a total of 3,665 km of railway line in 1999, of which 1,020 km was double-tracked, and 1,535 km electrified. In 2003 goods to the value of 28,251 million SKK were transported on railways. Bratislava has a tram network.
Slovak Railways: URL: http://www.zsr.sk

Shipping

The Slovak Republic has a total of 172 navigable water courses which run for a total of 2,379 km. Slovakia is connected to the Western European waterway system through to Rotterdam as well as to the Black Sea through the Danube. Bulk freight is transported from Bratislava and Kománo, the largest Slovak docks.

HEALTH

In 2009, the government spent approximately 14.5 per cent of its total budget on healthcare (up from 9.4 per cent in 2000), accounting for 65.7 per cent of all healthcare spending. Total expenditure on healthcare equated to 9.1 per cent of the country's GDP. Per capita expenditure

on health was approximately US$1,474. Figures for 2005-10 show that there are 16,201 physicians (30 per 10,000 population), 2,517 pharmaceutical personnel, and 2,697 dentistry personnel. There are 66 hospital beds per 10,000 population.

The infant mortality rate was 7 per 1,000 live births in 2010 and the child mortality rate (aged less than 5) was 8 per 1,000 live births. The major causes of childhood deaths were: prematurity 29 per cent, congenital anomalies 32 per cent, pneumonia 8 per cent and injuries 7 per cent.

In 2010 there were 386 reported cases of TB and 1,379 of pertussis.

All of the population has access to improved sanitation and improved drinking water. (Source: http://www.who.int, World Health Statistics 2012)

EDUCATION

Since 1990 the education system has changed substantially. Foreign language teaching has been included on the curriculum, and numerous church-affiliated and private schools have come into being. A New Education Act came into existence in 2008 which dictated changes to the curricula that were to be implemented gradually.

Pre-school Education

Pre-primary education caters for children from three to six years of age. Attendance is not compulsory. The gross enrolment ratio was 85.9 per cent in 2010. Public-sector institutions charge partial feels.

Primary/Secondary Education

Compulsory schooling takes place from age 6 to 16 and is free. Primary education takes nine years and consists of primary education (grades 1-4) and lower secondary education (Grades 5-9). According to UNESCO figures, more than 97 per cent of all students continue their education to high school level. The pupil/teacher ratio in primary schools is approximately 16: 1.

There are three types of high school in Slovakia: general high schools (gymnasium), technical high schools (SOS), and technical educational establishments (SOU). General high schools usually teach four-year courses, concentrating on preparing students for university. Technical high schools prepare students to work in industry and after passing the final exams students may go onto university or into a career. The Technical education establishments train students for apprentice occupations. In addition to vocational education there are also artistic schools which allow students with a particular talent to develop it further. Currently there are artistic elementary schools, technical secondary schools of applied arts, musical secondary schools (conservatoires), technical secondary schools for artistic disciplines, and universities with an artistic bias.

Higher Education

Education at public and state universities is currently free of charge. Private universities may charge. A bachelor's degree course lasts for three to four years, whilst a master's, medicine or veterinary degree lasts for four to six years. A doctoral degree usually takes between two and four years to complete.

Figures from UNESCO show that in 2008, 10.3 per cent of total government expenditure went on education, 18 per cent of which was spent on primary education, 46 per cent on secondary and 20 per cent on tertiary.

RELIGION

The Constitution of the Slovak Republic proclaims its state to be secular, non-denominational, a lay state, ideologically and religiously neutral. However, the Ministry of Culture lists a total of 48 religious orders and congregations in the Slovak Republic with their legal dependency deriving from the Roman Catholic and Greek Catholic church. Approximately 85 per cent of the population are Christians. 11 per cent are Protestant and around one per cent Orthodox, there is a small Jewish community (0.5 per cent) and Muslim community (0.1 per cent). Some 23 per cent have no religious affiliation.

Slovakia has a religious tolerance rating of 7 on a scale of 1 to 10 (10 is most freedom). (Source: World Religion Database)

COMMUNICATIONS AND MEDIA

The constitution guarantees freedom of the press. A controversial new press act came into force in 2008 regarding alleged defamation.

Newspapers

All of the major daily newspapers are privately owned.
NovýCas, URL: http://www.novycas.sk
Pravda, URL: http://www.pravda.sk
SME, URL: http://www.sme.sk

Broadcasting

Slovak Television (STV) and Slovak Radio are public services. There are many privately owned TV and radio stations such as Markiza TV, which broadcasts nationwide and currently has the highest viewer rating. Cable and satellite TV are popular.
Slovak Television, URL: http://www.stv.sk
Markiza TV, URL: http://www.markiza.sk/uvod

STATES OF THE WORLD

SLOVENIA

Telecommunications

The telecommunications system has expanded especially in the mobile phone sector. In 2010 there were an estimated 1.1 million telephone land lines in use and 5.9 million mobile phones. Figures for 2010 show an estimated 4 million people were regular internet users.

ENVIRONMENT

The Slovak Republic is the only post-communist country to have pledged itself to the reduction of Carbon Dioxide emissions by 20 per cent by the year 2005. It has also joined the UN General Convention on Climate Changes. Energy-related carbon dioxide emissions in 2005 were 39.8 million metric tons, equivalent to 7.01 metric tons per capita, which is lower than the European average of 7.99 metric tons per capita. In 2010, Slovakia's emissions from the consumption of fossil fuels totalled 34.54 million metric tons of carbon dioxide. (Source: EIA)

Forests cover approximately 40 per cent of Slovakia and four per cent of them are heavily damaged or dying. Acid rain and dust falling from emissions from local sources are the main factors affecting the quality of agricultural and forest soil.

The Slovak Republic is a party to the following international agreements: Air Pollution, Air Pollution-Nitrogen Oxides, Air Pollution-Persistent Organic Pollutants, Air Pollution-Sulfur 85, Air Pollution-Sulfur 94, Air Pollution-Volatile Organic Compounds, Antarctic Treaty, Biodiversity, Climate Change, Climate Change-Kyoto Protocol, Desertification, Endangered Species, Environmental Modification, Hazardous Wastes, Law of the Sea, Ozone Layer Protection, Ship Pollution, Wetlands, and Whaling.

SPACE PROGRAMME

Slovakia took the first step towards membership of the European Space Agency in 2010 when it signed an official co-operation agreement.

SLOVENIA

Republic of Slovenia

Republika Slovenija

Capital: Ljubljana (Population estimate, 2011: 280,200)

Head of State: Borut Pahor (President) (page 1491)

National Flag: Horizontal tricolour flag in white, blue and red bearing the national coat of arms in the top left hand corner.

CONSTITUTION AND GOVERNMENT

Constitution

Slovenia gained independence from the Federal Republic of Yugoslavia on 25 June 1991 after becoming a part of the Yugoslav state in 1945. In the referendum held in April 1990, 88 per cent of the electorate voted for independence.

Under the current constitution, adopted on 23 December 1991, Slovenia is a democratic republic governed by the law. The state's authority is based on the principle of the division of power into legislative, executive and judicial branches, with a parliamentary system of government. Power is held by the people and is exercised directly through referendums and elections.

The head of state is the president of the Republic, who is directly elected by universal adult suffrage for a maximum of two consecutive five-year terms. The president is also supreme commander of the armed forces. The president calls elections to the National Assembly, proclaims laws adopted by the National Assembly, proposes a candidate for prime minister to the National Assembly, and ratifies international treaties. Executive power is vested in the prime minister who, as head of government, appoints the cabinet of 20 members. The cabinet must be approved by the National Assembly.

To consult the constitution, please visit: http://www.us-rs.si/en/about-the-court/legal-basis/

International Relations

Slovenia joined the United Nations in 1992. Following referendums in March 2003, Slovenia became a member of NATO in March 2004 and the EU on 1 May 2004. Parliament ratified the draft EU Constitution in February 2005. Slovenia was accepted into the Eurozone, adopting the Euro, in January 2007.

Slovenia has an ongoing dispute with Croatia over sea and land borders, which dates back to the break up of Yugoslavia. In March 2009 Slovenia, set aside this dispute with Croatia over the maritime border at Piran Bay, and ratified Croatia's membership in NATO. In June 2010, Slovenia backed the idea of international arbitration on the border issue in a referendum.

Recent events

In March 2004, Slovenia became a member of NATO, and in May of the same year, the country joined the EU, along with ten other new states.

Slovenia ratified the EU constitution in February 2005. In October, Parliament declared the Slovenian coast to be an ecological zone, with the rights to protect and use the sea bed.

In January 2007, Slovenia was the first former communist state to adopt the single European currency, the euro. Slovenia was the first former communist state to assume the EU presidency, from 1st January to 30th June in 2008.

Leftist former diplomat Danilo Turk was elected president in November 2007. Parliamentary elections in September 2008 were inconclusive and the Social Democratic leader Borut Pahor formed a government with three other parties. In June 2011 the Zares party withdrew from the coalition and a cabinet reshuffle took place.

In June 2011 voters rejected the government's planned reforms to public television. In September the government of Prime Minister Borut Pahor resigned after losing a confidence vote in parliament. The government remained as caretaker government until parliamentary elections.

Early elections were held in December 2011 for the National Assembly. Positive Slovenia (PS) won most seats, but not enough for an overall majority. Coalition negotiations began. However, parliament rejected the candidate chosen for prime minister by Jorank Jankovic, leader of the LZJ-PS. Janez Jansa of the SDA was named as prime minister in January to lead a coalition. He named his cabinet on 3 February 2012.

Strikes were held in April 2012 over austerity measures. Protests continued over the year.

The government lost its majority in parliament when the DLGV left the coalition in January 2013. A vote of no-confidence followed and Mr Jansa's government was duly ousted. The PS party leader, Alenka Bratusek, was nominated as interim prime minister. She presented a cabinet made up of the PS, the DLGV, the DeSUS and the SD for approval by parliament in March 2013. One minister resigned by the end of the month and was replaced in April 2013.

Legislature

Legislative authority is exercised by the unicameral National Assembly (*Drzavni Zbor Republike Slovenije*) which has exclusive jurisdiction over the passing of laws. The legislative powers of the National Assembly are not stipulated in detail, meaning that the National Assembly itself decides upon which matters must be regulated by statute. The National Assembly passes amendments to the constitution and decides on the declaration of a state of war or emergency and the use of defence forces. The National Assembly is composed of 90 members directly elected for a four-year term. Italian and Hungarian ethnic minorities are guaranteed a seat each in the National Assembly.

The National Council (*Drzavni Svet*) is a mainly advisory body composed of representatives of social, economic, professional and local interests. It may propose laws to the National Assembly and at the latter's request gives opinion on specific issues. It may demand that the National Assembly reviews a law and may require the calling of a referendum or parliamentary inquiry. The National Council has 40 members (known as councillors) indirectly elected for five years, who represent social, economic, professional and local interests.

Drzavni Zbor (National Assembly), Šubiceva 4, 1000 Ljubljana, Slovenia. Tel: +386 1 478 9400, fax: +386 1 478 9845, URL: http://www.dz-rs.si/
President: Dr. Pavel Gantar

Drzavni Svet (National Council), Šubiceva 4, 1000 Ljubljana, Slovenia. Tel: +386 1 478 9802, fax: +386 1 478 9851, URL: http://www.ds-rs.si/
President: Blaž Kavčič

Cabinet (as at June 2013)
Prime Minister: Alenka Bratusek (PS) (page 1393)
Minister of Finance: Dr Uros Cufer (page 1411)
Minister of Economic Development: Stanko Stepisnik (page 1520)
Minister of Defence: Roman Jakic
Minister of Labour, Family, Social Matters and Equality: Dr Anja Mrak
Minister of Foreign Affairs: Karl Erjavec (page 1421)
Minister without Portfolio: Tina Komel
Minister of the Interior: Dr Gregor Virant (page 1532)
Minister of Justice: Dr Senko Plicanic (page 1496)
Minister of Education, Science and Sport: Jernej Pikalo
Minister of Agriculture and the Environment: Dejan Zidan
Minister of Health: Tomaz Gantar
Minister of Infrastructure: Samo Omerzel
Minister of Culture: Uros Grilic

Ministries

Office of the President, URL: http://www.up-rs.si/
Office of the Prime Minister, Gregorciceva 20, 1000 Ljubljana, Slovenia. Tel: +386 1 478 1000, URL: http://www.kpv.gov.si/
Ministry of Finance, Županciceva 3, 1502 Ljubljana, Slovenia. Tel: +386 1 369 6610, fax: +386 1 369 6619, URL: http://www.mf.gov.si/
Ministry of the Interior, Štefanova 2, 1000 Ljubljana, Slovenia. Tel: +386 1 472 5125, URL: http://www.mnz.si/
Ministry of Foreign Affairs, Presernova 25, SI-1000 Ljubljana, Slovenia. Tel: +386 1 478 2340 , fax: +386 1 478 2340, +386 1 478 2341, e-mail: info.mzz@gov.si, URL: http://www.mzz.gov.si/
Ministry of Justice, Županciceva 3, 1000 Ljubljana, Slovenia. Tel: +386 1 369 5783, fax: +386 1 369 5519, URL: http://www.mp.gov.si/
Ministry of Defence, Kardeljeva ploščad 25, 1000 Ljubljana, Slovenia. Tel: +386 1 471 2211, e-mail: info@pub.mo-rs.si, URL: http://www.mo.gov.si/
Ministry of Labour, Family and Social Affairs, Kotnikova 5, 1000 Ljubljana, Slovenia. Tel: +386 1 478 3330 / 478 3331, fax: +386 1 478 3344, URL: http://www.mddz.gov.si/
Ministry of Economic Development and Technology, Kotnikova 5, 1000 Ljubljana, Slovenia. Tel: +386 1 478 3311, fax: +386 1 433 1031, URL: http://www.mgrt.gov.si/
Ministry of Agriculture & the Environment, Dunajska 56-58, 1000 Ljubljana, Slovenia. Tel: +386 1 478 9000, URL: http://www.mkgp.gov.si/
Ministry of Education, Science, Culutre and Sport, Masarykova 16, 1000 Ljubljana, Slovenia. URL: http://www.mszs.gov.si
Ministry of Health, Štefanova 5, 1000 Ljubljana, Slovenia. Tel: +386 1 478 4329, fax: +386 1 478 6058, URL: http://www.mz.gov.si/
Ministry of Public Administration, Trzaska cesta 21, 1001 Ljubljana, Slovenia. Tel: +386 1 478 8330, fax: +386 1 478 8331, URL: http://www.mju.gov.si
Ministry of Higher Education, Science and Technology, Trg OF 13, 1000 Ljubljana, Slovenia. Tel: +386 1 478 4000, fax: +386 1 478 4719, URL: http://www.mvzt.gov.si

Political Parties

Socialnih Demokratov (SD, Social Democrats), Levstikova 15, 1000 Ljubljana, Slovenia. Tel: +386 1 244 4100, fax: +386 1 244 4123, URL: http://www.socialnidemokrati.si
President: Borut Pahor (page 1491)
Liberalna Demokraticna Slovenije (LDS, Liberal Democracy of Slovenia), Slovenska cesta 27, 1000 Ljubljana, Slovenia. Tel: +386 1 200 0310, fax: +386 1 200 0311, URL: http://www.lds.si/
President: Katarina Kresal
Slovenska Nacionalna Stranka (SNS, Slovene National Party), Tivolska 13, 1000 Ljubljana, Slovenia. Tel: +386 1 132 5207, fax: +386 1 132 5207, URL: http://www.sns.si/
President: Zmago Jelincic
Social Demokratska Stranka Slovenije (SDS, Social Democratic Party of Slovenia), Komenskega 11, 1000 Ljubljana, Slovenia. Tel: +386 1 434 5450, URL: http://www.sds.si
President: Janez Janša
Slovenska Ljudska Stranka (SLS, Slovenian People's Party), Beethovnova ulica 4, 1000 Ljubljana, Slovenia. Tel: +386 1 241 8820, fax: +386 1 251 1741, URL: http://www.sls.si/
President: Bojan Šrot
Democratic Party of Pensioners of Slovenia (DESUS), Kersnikova 6, 1000 Ljubljana, Slovenia. Tel: +386 1 439 7350, fax: +386 1 431 4113, URL: http://www.desus.si
President: Karl Erjavec
Nova Slovenija - Krščanska ljudska stranka (New Slovenia - Christian People's Party). URL: http://nsi.si/
Leader: Ljudmila Novak
Zares (For Real - New Politics), URL: http://www.zares.si, Leader: Gregor Golobič

Elections

The most recent presidential election was held on 11 November 2012; Borut Pahor (SD) won 39 per cent of the vote, the incumbent Danilo Türk won 36 per cent of the vote and Milan Zver (SDS) 24 per cent. A second round of voting took place on 2 December 2012 and Bortut Bahor defeated Mr Turk. He took office on 22 December.

Parliamentary elections were held on 21st September 2008. The SD, led by Borut Pahor, won the largest number of seats in the National Assembly, but by a very narrow margin. The Slovenian Democratic Party (SDS), previously the largest party in the National Assembly, won one seat less. Mr. Pahor was nominated Prime Minister and named a coalition cabinet in November. The cabinet comprised the SD, the DeSUS, the LDS, For Real - New Politics (Zares), and several independents.

The next parliamentary election was due in October 2012 but was held early on 4 December 2011. The results were Zoran Jankovic List-Positive Slovenia 28 seats; SDS 26 seats; SD 10 seats; DLGV 8 seats; DeSus 6 seats; SLS 6 seats; NSi 4 seats; and minority parties 2 seats. The final coalition was made up of the SDS, the SLS, the NSi, the DLGV and the DeSUS and was led by Janez Jansa of the SDS.

Diplomatic Representation

British Embassy, 4th Floor Trg Republike 3, 1000 Ljubljana, Slovenia. Tel: +386 1 200 3910, fax: +386 1 425 0174, e-mail: info@british-embassy.si, URL: http://www.ukinslovenia.foc.gov.uk
Ambassador: H.E. Andrew Page (page 1491)
Embassy of the Republic of Slovenia, 10 Little College Street, London SW1P 3SH, United Kingdom. Tel: +44 (0) 20 7222 5400, fax: +44 (0)20 7222 5277, e-mail: Vlo@mzz-dkp.gov.si, URL: http://slovenia.embassy-uk.co.uk/
Ambassador: H.E. Mr Iztok Jarc
US Embassy, Presernova 31, 1000 Ljubljana, Slovenia. Tel: +386 1 200 5500, fax: +386 1 200 5555, e-mail: USEmbassyLjubljana@state.gov, URL: http://slovenia.usembassy.gov/
Ambassador: Joseph Mussomeli

Embassy of the Republic of Slovenia, 2410 California Street, NW, Washington, DC 20008, USA. Tel: +1 202 386 6601, fax: +1 202 286 6633, URL: http://washington.embassy.si/en
Ambassador: H.E. Roman Kirn
Permanent Mission of the Republic of Slovenia to UN, 600 Third Avenue, 24th Floor, New York, NY 10016, USA. Tel: +1 212 370 3007, fax: +1 212 370 1824, e-mail: slovenia@un.int, URL: http://newyork.predstavnistvo.si/en
Ambassador: currently vacant

LEGAL SYSTEM

The court system consists of a Supreme Court, which is the highest court in Slovenia; four High Courts, which serve as appeal courts; and 11 circuit courts and 44 district courts, which serve as courts of first instance. Labour courts decide labour disputes while social courts have jurisdiction in disputes over pensions, disability insurance, health insurance and disputes over family and social benefits. Judges are nominated by the Court Council, and are appointed for life by the National Assembly.

The Constitutional Court determines the compliance of legislation with the Constitution, international law and international agreements. The Court may annul unconstitutional laws. It decides on jurisdictional disputes between the Parliament, President and the Government and makes rulings in disputes between the state and individual municipalities. The Court is composed of nine judges who are elected for nine years.

The highest statute is the Constitution which is adopted and amended by the Parliament in a special procedure (a two-thirds majority is needed). Other legal acts in hierarchical order are: laws passed by the Parliament, decrees issued by the Government for the implementation of laws, regulations, guidelines and orders issued by ministries for the implementation of laws and Government decrees; regulations which local Government bodies have passed in order to regulate affairs under their jurisdiction.

The government respects the rights of its citizens. Slovenia abolished the death penalty for all crimes in 1989, and co-sponsored the Resolution on a Moratorium on the Use of the Death Penalty at the UN General Assembly in 2008.

Constitutional Court of the Republic of Slovenia, URL: http://www.us-rs.si/en/
President: Ernest Petrič
Supreme Court of the Republic of Slovenia, URL: http://www.sodisce.si/
President: Branko Maleša

Human Rights Ombudsman for the Republic of Slovenia, URL: http://www.varuh-rs.si/index.php?id=1&L=6

LOCAL GOVERNMENT

Slovenia has a single level system of local government where the municipality regulates local affairs. Accoring to the Local Self-Government Act a municipality must have at least 5,000 inhabitants, and an urban municipality at least 20,000. There are 210 municipalities of which 11 are urban municipalities: Celje, Koper, Kranj, Ljubljana, Maribor, Murska Sobota, Nova Gorica, Novo mesto, Ptuj, Slovenj Gradec, Velenje. They are financed by their own levied taxes and duties; only economically underdeveloped municipalities receive additional finance from the state. The municipalities are led by a Mayor and Municipal Council. The Mayor is directly elected.

In addition to the municipalities there are 2,830 cadastral communities, 5,996 settlements, 8,262 statistical districts, and 16,563 census districts.

AREA AND POPULATION

Area

The Republic of Slovenia is situated in south-east Europe. It has borders with Croatia to the east and south-east, Hungary to the north-west, Austria to the north, and Italy and the Adriatic Sea to the west. Slovenia's total area is 20,273 sq. km, of which 122 sq. km is water, with approximately 50 kms. of coastline on the Adriatic Sea. Its geography is predominantly mountainous, with over half the country covered by forest.

The climate varies from a Mediterranean climate on the coast, to hot summers and cold winters on the plateaus and in the valleys to the east.

To view a map, consult http://www.un.org/Depts/Cartographic/map/profile/slovenia.pdf

Population

The population of Slovenia was estimated at 2.03 million in 2010, representing an average annual natural growth rate of 0.2 per cent over the period 2000-10. (Source: WHO) A net migration rate of 12.6 per cent gave an overall population increase of 13.5 per cent over 2008. (Source: EU, 27.1.2009)

Population density in mid-2004 was 98.5 people per sq. km. Approximately 48 per cent of the population lives in urban areas. The capital city, Ljubljana, has a population of around 280,200. Other major towns include Marlbor, with over 115,500 people; Kranj, 52,000; and Novo Mesto, 41,000.

Slovenes make up nearly 88 per cent of the population. Italians (0.15 per cent) and Hungarians (0.43 per cent) are considered indigenous minorities in Slovenia, with rights protected under the constitution. Other ethnic groups (11.5 per cent), which mostly arrived in Slovenia after WWII as economic immigrants, are Croats, Serbs, Muslims, Yugoslavs, Macedonians, Montenegrins and Albanians.

SLOVENIA

The official language is Slovene, and most Slovenes speak English, Italian or German.

Births, Marriages, Deaths
In 2010, the birth rate was estimated at 10 per 1,000 inhabitants, and the death rate was estimated at 9.4 per 1,000 people.

Average life expectancy at birth was around 76 years for men and 82 years for women in 2009. The median age in 2010 was 42 years. Approximately 14 per cent of the inhabitants are aged under 15, and a high proportion (22 per cent) are aged over 60. The infant mortality rate was estimated to be 2 per l,000 live births, and the fertility rate was 1.4 children per woman. (Source: http://www.who.int, World Health Statistics 2012)

Public Holidays 2014
1-2 January: New Year
8 February: Prešeren Day (Culture Day)
18 April: Good Friday
21 April: Easter Monday
27 April: National Resistance Day (WWII)
5 May: Labour Day
25 June: National Day
15 August: Assumption Day
31 October: Reformation Day
2 November: All Souls' Day
25 December: Christmas Day
26 December: Independence Day

EMPLOYMENT

The labour force in 2007 was 1,033,000 (up from 1,004,000 in 2005), which represented 51.0 per cent of the total population over the age of 15. Those employed in 2006 numbered 969,000 (15+), of whom 521,000 were men and 448,000 were women. The number of registered unemployed fell from 95,993 in 2003 to 58,000 in 2005, before rising to 61,000 in 2006. The unemployment rate rose by 0.1 per cent to stand at 5.9 per cent in 2006. (Source: International Labour Organisation, ILO). Estimated figures for 2010 put the labour force at 935,000 with an unemployment rate of 10.6 per cent.

Total Employment by Economic Activity

Occupation	2007
Agriculture, hunting & forestry	101,000
Mining & quarrying	4,000
Manufacturing	266,000
Electricity, gas & water supply	9,000
Construction	61,000
Wholesale & retail trade, repairs	119,000
Hotels & restaurants	37,000
Transport, storage & communications	60,000
Financial intermediation	23,000
Real estate, renting & business activities	66,000
Public admin. & defence; compulsory social security	59,000
Education	78,000
Health & social work	57,000
Other community, social & personal service activities	44,000
Households with employed persons	1,000
Other	10,000

Source: Copyright © International Labour Organization (ILO Dept. of Statistics, http://laborsta.ilo.org)

Slovenia's labour market suffers from rigid employment legislation and high social taxes. Labour costs are competitive when compared with old EU countries, but not when compared with the other former communist EU members.

BANKING AND FINANCE

Currency
Slovenia adopted the Euro on 1 January 2007, with an exchange rate of 239.64 Slovene tolars to the Euro.

GDP/GNP, Inflation, National Debt
One of the more prosperous of the ten new EU member states, Slovenia enjoys economic stability and a good economic record, and benefits from a well-educated and productive work force. The Government is set on a programme of reform, aiming for strong economic growth and a free market. Slovenia joined the Exchange Rate Mechanism (ERM II) in 2004. Slovenia met eurozone criteria for public debt, budget deficit, interest rates and inflation levels in 2006, and was the first former communist state to be accepted into the 12-member eurozone in January 2007.

The Government adopted a Development Strategy in 2005, based on a market economy, the aim of which was for Slovenia to exceed the average development of the EU by 2015. A new Government Office for Growth was created to monitor its implementation.

Slovakia became a member of the OECD in 2010.

Slovenia enjoyed steady economic growth over the eight years to 2006, with GDP increasing by an average rate of 4 per cent per annum. Slovenia's GDP rose from US$34 billion in 2005 to an estimated US$51.99 million at the end of 2007 with a growth rate of 6.1 per cent. In 2008, it was estimated at £54 billion with a growth rate of 3.5 per cent. Per capita GDP was

an estimated €25,755 in 2007. Slovenia's economy is highly dependent on foreign trade, and around two-thirds of that trade is with the EU. The economy has been adversely affected by the economic crisis in the Eurozone.

The Slovenian economy went into recession in 2009, following two consecutive quarters of negative growth. Growth in 2009 was estimated to be -8.0 per cent. Although it recovered to 1.4 per cent in 2010, it fell back to -0.2 per cent in 2011, and remained negative in 2012. Growth is expected to remain weak but is forecast to rise above 1 per cent in 2013.

The largest contributor to GDP in 2008 was the services sector at 63.5 per cent. Industry accounted for 34.4 per cent (of which, the construction industry comprises 6 per cent), and agriculture, forestry and fishing accounted for just 2 per cent.

The authorities succeeded in bringing down inflation from more than 200 per cent in 1992 to just 2.5 per cent in 2006. Inflation remained at this level over 2007. Controlling inflation remains a top government priority but inflation has begun to rise: 3.6 per cent in 2007 and to 6.7 per cent in 2008. It is projected to fall in 2009 to under 1 per cent. In 2012, inflation had risen to over 2 per cent. It is forecast to fall slightly in 2013.

In 2012, the new government pledged to cut spending by 800 million euros to try and reduce the size of its national debt which has more than doubled since 2007.

Gross foreign debt was an estimated €42 million in 2012.

Foreign Investment
Foreign investment to Slovenia almost tripled between 2001 and 2002, before falling sharply, reflecting the lack of major privatisations and foreign acquisitions. Some barriers to foreign investment have since been removed, and, along with membership of the EU, there has been more investor interest in the country. Privatisation has been slow and foreign investment remains low. It was estimated to be US$999 million in 2012.

Slovenia became a member of the International Monetary Fund (IMF) and World Bank in 1993, graduating in 2004 to be a donor rather than a recipient country. It is a member of the World Trade Organization, Central European Free Trade Association (CEFTA) and OECD.

Balance of Payments / Imports and Exports
Slovenia's economy is highly dependent on foreign trade, around two-thirds of which is with the European Union. Integration in the EU is expected to lead to an increase in trade within the market. The country has also penetrated the south and east European markets successfully, including the former Soviet Union region.

In 2008 exports totalled an estimated €25 billion. The main goods exported were machinery, transportation equipment, electrical and optical equipment, basic metals and fabricated products. In the same year, imports cost the country around €26 billion. The main trading partners were Germany, Italy, France, Austria, Russia and Croatia. Exports fell sharply in 2009 by an estimated 17 per cents and imports by over 19 per cent. Exports rose by an estimated 9.5 per cent in 2010 and by 8 per cent in 2011. Imports rose by 7 per cent in 2010 and almost 5 oer cent in 2011. Exports were expected to weaken in 2012.

Central Bank
Banka Slovenije (Bank of Slovenia), Slovenska 35, 1505 Ljubljana, Slovenia. Tel: +386 1 471 9000, fax: +386 1 251 5516, e-mail: bsl@bsi.si, URL: http://www.bsi.si
Governor: Bostjan Jazbec

Chambers of Commerce and Trade Organisations
Slovenian Chamber of Commerce and Industry, URL: http://www.gzs.si/eng

MANUFACTURING, MINING AND SERVICES

Mining
Slovenia's raw material basis includes mineral and thermal springs, stone, and some coal deposits. In 2010, the country produced 4.8 million short tons of coal, which fell short of domestic consumption of 5.6 million short tons over the year. The country imported 0.6 million short tons.

Slovenia has no proven oil deposits. Consumption stood at some 55,000 barrels per day in 2011, up from 52,000 barrels per day in 2003. Similarly, there are no gas reserves. Consumption was an estimated 37 billion cubic feet in 2011. (Source: EIA)

Energy
In 2009, Slovenia's total energy consumption reached 0.327 quadrillion Btu, up from 0.314 quadrillion Btu in 2007. With installed electricity capacity of 3.1 GWe, Slovenia produced 15.67 billion kWh of electricity in 2010, and consumed 12.60 billion kWh.

Manufacturing
This sector accounts for the largest number of jobs in Slovenia and, together with the construction industry, contributes around 34 per cent of GDP. Foreign capital has been invested in the electronics industry which employs more than 46,000 people. Slovenia exports digital telephone exchanges, electro-optical products and electronics components. The metallurgy industry is being modernised and the textile, leather and footwear industries have developed their own trademarks. Other industries include the manufacture of chemical products and transport equipment.

Service Industries
This sector is the largest part of the economy, contributing over 63 per cent of GDP in 2006. The main areas are communications, real estate, the retail sector, transportation and business activities.

Slovenia caters for many different kinds of tourism: coastal, alpine, farm, winter, hunting and health spa. The country has a number of sports facilities and conference centres, especially in Ljubljana, Portoroz, Rogaska Slatina, and Radenci. In 2006, there were 2.48 million arrivals, up from 2.39 million the previous year. 1.6 million visitors were foreigners.
Slovenian Tourist Board, URL: http://www.slovenia-tourism.si/

Agriculture
Around 10 per cent of Slovenian land is used for crop growing, and 16 per cent is used for pasture. In 2011, the agriculture sector contributed around 2.5 per cent of national GDP. Main products include wheat, corn, pork, poultry, milk, potatoes, orchard fruits and wine.

Slovenia ranks among the most densely forested countries in Europe, forests covering some 54 per cent of the land. There is ample scope for fishing in Slovenia's lakes, rivers and creeks, and in the sea. Permits are required which can be obtained from local fishing clubs. Figures from the FAO put the total catch at 932 tonnes.

Agricultural Production in 2010

Produce	Int. $'000*	Tonnes
Cow milk, whole	195,201	625,521
Indigenous cattle meat	117,022	43,319
Indigenous chicken meat	65,338	45,870
Indigenous pigmeat	63,044	108,541
Grapes	62,044	180,541
Apples	49,722	117,569
Wheat	19,363	153,481
Hen eggs, in shell	17,930	21,618
Maize	16,358	311,117
Potatoes	15,690	101,208
Hops	7,052	2,073
Honey, natural	4,793	1,910

*unofficial figures
Source: http://faostat.fao.org/site/339/default.aspx Food and Agriculture Organization of the United Nations, Food and Agricultural commodities production

COMMUNICATIONS AND TRANSPORT

Travel Requirements
Citizens of the USA, Canada and Australia require a passport valid for three months beyond the length of stay but do not need a visa for stays of up to three months. EU nationals who have a valid national Identity Card do not require a passport or a visa for stays of up to three months. Other nationals should contact the embassy to check visa requirements.

All non-EU citizens staying longer than 3 days in Slovenia must register with the local police within 3 days of arrival and inform the office about any change in their address. Registration of foreign visitors staying in hotels or accommodations rented through an accommodation company is done automatically by the hotelier or accommodation company.

Slovenia joined the Schengen Agreement on 21 December 2007 for overland entry points and seaports, and on 29 March 2008 for airports. With a Schengen visa, a visitor can travel freely throughout the Schengen zone, with few border stops and checks. See http://www.eurovisa.info/SchengenCountries.htm.

National Airlines
Adria Airways is the national airline, linking Ljubljana with some 40 destinations, mainly in Europe. The company owns 13 aircraft, and operates 140 scheduled flights per week. In 2011, the airline carried over 1.1 million passengers and transported approximately 1,940 tonnes of cargo.
Adria Airways, URL: http://www.adria.si

International Airports
The country has three international airports at Ljubljana (URL: http://www.lju-airport.si/eng), Maribor (URL: http://www.maribor-airport.si/Default.aspx?tabid=97), and Portorož (URL: http://www.portoroz-airport.si/). There are a further 16 airports, 7 of which have paved runways.

Railways
The length of the Slovenian railway network is 1,229 km, of which 504 km is electrified.
Slovenia Railways: URL: http://www.slo-zeleznice.si

Roads
Slovenia has a well developed road network covering 38,451 km, including 483 km of motorways. Vehicles drive on the right. Due to its central position, road transport runs over 91 border crossings.

Shipping
Seaborne transport in Slovenia passes through three ports: Koper, Izola and Piran. Slovenia has its own shipping company, Splosna plovba Piran.

HEALTH

In 2009, the government spent approximately 13.8 per cent of its total budget on healthcare (up from 13.1 per cent in 2000), accounting for 73.4 per cent of all healthcare spending. Out of pocket expenditure accounts for 48.8 per cent of total private expenditure on health. Total expenditure on healthcare equaled to 9.3 per cent of the country's GDP. Per capita expenditure on health was approximately US$2,231, compared with US$829 in 2000.

Figures for 2000-10 show that there are 4,915 physicians (25.1 per 10,000 population), 16,460 nurses and midwives (83.9 per 10,000 population), 1,236 dentistry personnel and 1,066 pharmaceutical personnel. There are 46 hospital beds per 10,000 population.

In 2010, the infant mortality rate was estimated to be 2 per 1,000 live births in 2009 and the child (aged less than 5 year) mortality rate was 3 per cent. The major causes of childhood deaths were: prematurity 21 per cent, congenital abnormalities 25 per cent, neonatal sepsis 9 per cent, birth asphyxia 13 per cent.

In 2010, there were 169 reported cases of TB and 610 of pertussis.

In 2010, an estimated 100 per cent of the population had sustained access to improved drinking water and to improved sanitation. (Source: http://www.who.int, World Health Statistics 2012)

EDUCATION

In 2007, 81 per cent of young children attended a pre-primary school. 96 per cent of children were registered in a primary school, and 89 per cent attended secondary school. These figures are comfortably above the regional averages. 86 per cent of students went on to higher education at university or college, well above the regional average of 60 per cent.

In 2006, 12.9 per cent of government spending went on education (5.8 per cent of GDP), some 49 per cent of which was spent on secondary education. Primary education received 20 per cent of government education funding, whilst tertiary education received 23 per cent.

The adult literacy rate was estimated to be 99.7 per cent in 2007, rising to 99.8 per cent among 15-24 year olds.

National Education Institute of the Republic of Slovenia, (Zavod Republike Slovenije za Šolstvo - ZRSŠ), URL: http://www.zrss.si/default_ang.asp

RELIGION

The religion of many of the population is Roman Catholicism (46 per cent). There are also small communities of other Christian denominations, in particular Protestants in the eastern parts of the country, as well as Muslims and Jews.

Slovenia has a religious liberty rating of 8 on a scale of 1 to 10 (10 is most freedom). (Source: World Religion Database)

COMMUNICATIONS AND MEDIA

The constitution provides for freedom of expression. In December 2010, the government held a referendum on plans to reform public TV. The plans were rejected.

Newspapers
The main newspapers are privately owned.
Slovene Press Agency (STA), URL: http://www.sta.si/
Delo, URL: http://www.delo.si/
Vecer, URL: http://www.vecer.si/
Dnevnik, URL: http://www.dnevnik.si/
Finance, URL: http://www.finance.si/

Broadcasting
There are over 35 television stations in Slovenia; the public sector RTV Slovenia broadcasts national and regional TV channels. The main private stations are Pop TV and Kanal A. Around two out of three households are connected to cable or satellite. There are many commercial and public radio stations. RTV Slovenia runs three national radio stations and four regional.
RTV Slovenija - Televizija Slovenija, URL: http://www.rtvslo.si/

Telecommunications
Fixed telephone subscribers numbered approximately 900,000 in 2010 whilst the number of mobile phone subscribers increased to 2.2 million. According to 2010 statistics, there were 1.3 million regular internet users.

ENVIRONMENT

Slovenia is party to the following international environmental agreements: Air Pollution, Air Pollution-Nitrogen Oxides, Air Pollution-Persistent Organic Pollutants, Air Pollution-Sulfur 94, Biodiversity, Climate Change, Climate Change-Kyoto Protocol, Desertification, Endangered Species, Environmental Modification, Hazardous Wastes, Law of the Sea, Marine Dumping, Ozone Layer Protection, Ship Pollution, Wetlands, Whaling.

In 2010, Slovenia's emissions from the consumption of fossil fuels totalled 17.4 million metric tons of carbon dioxide. (Source: EIA)

The main areas of environmental concern are pollution of rivers due to domestic and industrial waste, and the pollution of coastal waters with heavy metals and toxic chemicals. Of particular concern is damage to forests near Koper caused by acid rain originating from metallurgical and chemical plants.

SOLOMON ISLANDS

SPACE PROGRAMME

Slovenia joined the European Space Agency in 2010. It has not developed a space programme or established a national space agency. However a consortium of Slovenian companies and academic institutes working in the field of space technology has been established. The Centre of Excellence Space-Si (CE-Space-Si) is working to develop Slovenia's space research and technical expertise.

Centre of Excellence Space-Si (CE-Space-Si), http://www.space.si/en/about/centre-of-excellence-space-si/

SOLOMON ISLANDS

Capital: Honiara (situated on the island of Guadalcanal) (Population estimate: 65,000)

Head of State: Her Majesty Queen Elizabeth II (Sovereign) (page 1420)

Governor-General: Sir Frank Kabui (page 1452)

National Flag: The flag is divided diagonally from the bottom corner of the staff to the opposite top corner by a thin yellow line. The bottom half is green and the top half is blue containing five stars

CONSTITUTION AND GOVERNMENT

Constitution
The Solomon Islands was a British Protectorate between 1893 and 1978. There was rapid constitutional development after World War II, particularly from 1974, leading to full independence within the Commonwealth on 7 July 1978.

The country is a Constitutional Monarchy. HM Queen Elizabeth II is the Head of State and is represented by the Governor General, appointed by the Queen on the recommendation of the National Parliament for a term of five years. A Governor General may only serve for up to two consecutive terms.

To consult the constitution, please visit: http://www.parliament.gov.sb/files/business&procedure/constitution.htm

Recent Events
After months of ethnic unrest the Malaita Eagle Force staged a coup in June 2000. The prime minister, Bartholomew Ulufa'alu, later resigned in an effort to bring about conciliation. Elections were held at the end of June and a new prime minister was elected. In October 2000 a peace treaty was signed ending nearly two years of civil war between natives of the main island Guadalcanal and nearby Malaita island.

Trouble erupted again in March 2002 after the social and economic situation deteriorated and a government minister was shot. After Prime Minister Kemakeza asked for help, an Australian-led peace keeping force arrived in the Solomon Islands in August 2003. Harold Keke, a rebel leader, surrendered to the peace-keeping force. In 2005 he was jailed for life for the murder of a Catholic priest. Corruption is rife and several ministers have been arrested on charges including corruption and extortion. There have been several cabinet reshuffles.

The prime minister, Manasseh Sogavare, was ousted in December 2007 after a vote of no confidence. His successor, Derek Sikua, reshuffled the cabinet.

After the 2010 general election and several weeks of negotiation, Danny Philips was sworn in as prime minister. Several ministers resigned in November 2011 following Mr Philip's dismissal of Gordon Darcy Lilo as finance minister. Mr Philip subsequently resigned and Mr Lilo was himself elected by parliament to be prime minister. He then reshuffled the cabinet.

There were several changes to the cabinet throughout 2012 and more in October 2012 ahead of a vote of no-confidence by parliament. The government survived after the opposition abstained.

International Relations
The Solomon Islands has followed a policy of non-alignment since independence. It is an active supporter of the South Pacific Nuclear Free Zone Treaty and has completed a Nuclear Proliferation Treaty safeguards agreement with the IAEA. Relations were strained with Papua New Guinea until the 2004 Bougainville Peace Accord. Relations are currently strained with Australia.

The Solomon Islands is a member of several international organisations including the Commonwealth, South Pacific Forum, the United Nations (UN), the World Trade Organisation (WTO), the International Monetary Fund (IMF), and the World Bank

Legislature
There is a unicameral legislature of 50 seats, called the National Parliament. Suffrage is universal for qualified citizens of 18 years of age and over. The party system is not strong and politics are fluid. The government is formed by the election of a Prime Minister by secret ballot by the Members of Parliament.

The elected Prime Minister is appointed by the Governor General and recommends his Ministers for appointment by the Governor General. Ministers can be removed from office or moved between offices on the recommendation of the Prime Minister, but the Prime Minister can only be removed by a vote of 'no confidence' in Parliament. In such a case the process of secret election and appointments is repeated. Parliament runs for four years and can only be dissolved earlier by a resolution of Parliament.

National Parliament, PO Box G19, Honiara, The Solomon Islands. Tel: +677 22732, fax: +677 23866, URL: http://www.parliament.gov.sb/

Cabinet (as at June 2013)
Prime Minister: Gordon Darcy Lilo (page 1465)
Deputy Prime Minister and Minister of Home Affairs: Manasseh Maelanga (page 1469)
Minister of Finance and Treasury: Rick Houenipwela
Minister of Foreign Affairs and Trade Relations: Clay Forau Soalaoi
Minister of Development Planning & Aid Co-operation: Connelly Sandakabatu
Minister of Police & National Security: Christopher Laore
Minister of Agriculture & Livestock: David Tome
Minister of Mines, Energy and Rural Electrification: Moses Garu
Minister of Commerce, Industry, Employment and Immigration: Elijah Doro Muala
Minister of Education: Dick Ha'amori
Minister of Justice and Legal Affairs: Commins Aston Mewa
Minister of Infrastructure Development: Seth Gukuna
Minister of Lands and Housing: Joseph Onika
Minister of Communications & Aviation: Walter Folotalu
Minister of Forestry: Dickson Mua
Minister of Provincial Government: Silas Tausinga
Minister of National Unity & Reconciliation: Hypolite Taremae
Minister of Culture and Tourism: Samuel Manetoali
Minister of Health and Medical Services: Charles Sigoto
Minister of Rural Development and Indigenous Affairs: Lionel Alex
Minister of the Environment and Conservation: Bradley Tovosia
Minister of Fisheries and Marine Resources: Alfred Ghiro
Minister of Public Service: Stanley Sofu
Minister of Women, Youth and Children's Affairs: Peter Tom
Attorney General: Billy Titiulu

Ministries
Prime Minister's Office, URL: http://www.pmc.gov.sb
Ministry of Commerce, Industries and Employment, URL: http://www.commerce.gov.sb/

Elections
Elections took place in April 2006. Snyder Rini was originally chosen to be prime minister but his appointment led to riots and Manesseh Sogavare, leader of the Social Credit Party was elected to the post. The most recent parliamentary election took place in August 2010. The Solomon Islands Democratic Party became the largest party in the legislature with 11 seats, independents won 28 seats.

Political Parties
Direct Development Party (DDP); Ownership, Unity, and Responsibility (OUR); Solomon Islands Democratic Party (SIDP); Solomon Islands Party for Rural Advancement (SIPRA).

Diplomatic Representation
British High Commission, Telekom House, Mendana Avenue, Honiara, Solomon Islands. Tel: +677 21705, fax: +677 21549, URL: http://ukinsolomonislands.fco.gov.uk/
High Commissioner: H.E. Dominic Meiklejohn
US Embassy to the Solomon Islands, URL: http://portmoresby.usembassy.gov/
US Ambassador: Teddy Taylor (resident in Papua New Guinea)
Solomon Islands Mission to the United Nations, 800 Second Avenue, Suite 400L, New York, NY 10017, USA. Tel: +1 212 599 6192, fax: +1 212 661 8925, URL: http://www.un.int/wcm/content/site/solomonislands
Ambassador to the US and Permanent Representative to the UN: Collin Beck

LEGAL SYSTEM

English Common Law and UK Statutes of General Application up to 1961 apply. There is a body of Statute Law which is administered through the system of courts, namely the High Court of Solomon Islands, the Magistrate Courts and a Court of Appeal. The Principal Magistrates are generally qualified lawyers, while the lower courts are often staffed by lay magistrates appointed by the Chief Justice.

Local Courts are made up of local Elders and administer customs and local by-laws. The Customary Land Appeal Courts hear land appeals from local courts. An Ombudsman hears complaints against central and local government departments and agencies.

The government respects the rights of its citizens, but there is some degree of government corruption and pretrial detention can be lengthy.

The death penalty was abolished in 1978.

A national truth and reconciliation commission, based in Honiara, was set up in 2009. The panel was set up to investigate the 1997-2003 conflict between rival ethnic militias in which more than 100 people died and 20,000 were displaced on the island of Guadalcanal.

LOCAL GOVERNMENT

The Solomon Islands are divided into nine Provinces and the Honiara Municipal Authority. The provinces are Central; Choiseul; Guadalcanal; Isabel; Makira; Malaita; Rennell and Bellona; Temotu; Western Bellona. Provincial Assemblies are elected by voters within the Provinces and the Provincial President and the Council are selected and appointed in a way similar to the National Government, except that the appointing authority is the Minister for Home Affairs. The Honiara Municipal Authority is an administratively appointed body at present.

AREA AND POPULATION

Area

The Solomon Islands consist of a double row of mountainous islands extending from Bougainville Straits to Mitre Island in the Santa Cruz Group for a distance of 900 miles, and north and south from the Ontong Java group to Rennell Island for a distance of 430 miles. The total land area of the territory is about 11,500 sq. miles (28,900 sq. km). There are six main islands: Choiseul, New Georgia, Santa Isabel, Guadalcanal, Malaita and Makira and 986 smaller islands. The land is a mixture of volcanic mountains and coral reefs. The climate is tropical monsoon.

To view a map of the Solomon Islands, please consult
http://www.lib.utexas.edu/maps/cia08/solomon_islands_sm_2008.gif

Population

The population was an estimated 538,000 in 2010, with an annual growth rate of approximately 2.8 per cent over the period 2000-10. The population comprises about 93 per cent Melanesian, 4 per cent Polynesian, 2 per cent Micronesian and 1 per cent other. The population density is roughly 16 people per sq. km, and some 19 per cent of the population live in urban areas. The population is young with an estimated 40 per cent being aged 18 or under and just 5 per cent over 60 years old. Approximately 65,000 people live in the capital Honiara which is situated on the island of Guadalcanal. Other main towns include Gizo, Auki and Kirakira. The official language is English although Solomon Islands pidgin is also spoken.

Births, Marriages, Deaths

Figures for 2010 show that the birth rate was 31.9 per 1,000 population and the death rate was 4.6 per 1,000 population. Life expectancy from birth in 2009 was 69 for males and 72 for females. Healthy life expectancy was 59 years for males and 60 years for females. The total fertility rate for women was 4.2 in 2010. (Source: http://www.who.int, World Health Statistics 2012)

Public Holidays 2014

1 January: New Year's Day
18 April: Good Friday
20 April: Easter Sunday
21 April: Easter Monday
9 June: Queen's Official Birthday (second Monday in June)
9 June: Whit Monday
7 July: Independence Day
25 December: Christmas Day
26 December: Boxing Day

EMPLOYMENT

In 2007 the workforce was estimated to be 202,500, of whom 76 per cent were involved in agriculture, 6 per cent in industry and commerce, and 18 per cent in services.

BANKING AND FINANCE

Currency

The Solomon Islands introduced its own currency in 1977: the Solomon Islands Dollar of 100 cents. The financial centre is Honiara.

GDP/GNP, Inflation, National Debt

The Solomon Islands is one of the poorest countries in the Pacific region. The economy is hindered by political instability, weak governance and a poor infrastructure. It is dependent on foreign aid and has low levels of foreign investment. The country experienced good economic growth in 2011 although this was expected to weaken due to the global economic crisis.

GDP was estimated to be SI$4,092 million in 2008 (compared to SI$3,278 million in 2007) with an annual growth rate of 6.7 per cent. Per capita income was SI$7809 in 2008. Growth for 2009 and 2010 was put at -2.2 per cent. Around 50 per cent of GDP is made up from the agriculture sector; industry contributes just under 4 per cent. GDP was estimated to be SBD$5,575million in 2011 with a growth rate of 4.4 per cent. Per capita GDP was US$1480 in 2011.

Inflation was estimated at 1.3 per cent in 2009/10, rising to 7.4 per cent in 2011. Inflation was 4.7 per cent in Q3 2012. Total debt was put at US$185.7 million in 2003.

Balance of Payments / Imports and Exports

Total exports amounted to Solomon Islands SBD$3,150 million in 2011. The major export markets are China (60 per cent), the Republic of Korea and Thailand. The main export products are logs, fish, timber, cocoa, copra, palm oil and kernels. Imports cost Solomon Islands SBD$3,180 million in 2011. The major import suppliers are Australia (29 per cent), Singapore (21 per cent), China and New Zealand. The main import products are fuel, food, beverages, machinery and transport equipment. The trade balance was Solomon Islands $-1,151 million.

Central Bank

Central Bank of Solomon Islands, PO Box 634, Honiara, Solomon Islands. Tel: +677 21791, fax: +677 23513, e-mail: info@cbsi.com.sb, URL: http://www.cbsi.com.sb/
Governor: Denton Rarawa

Development Bank

Development Bank of Solomon Islands, PO Box 911, Honiara, Solomon Islands. Tel: +677 21595 / 21596, fax: +677 23715

MANUFACTURING, MINING AND SERVICES

Primary and Extractive Industries

The Solomon Islands has no oil or gas reserves of its own and in 2011 imported 2,000 barrels oer day to meet its needs.

Gold has been mined at Gold Ridge on Guadalcanal since 1998. The mine was closed in 2000 due to civil unrest. It was opened again in 2010, having been bought and modernised by Allied Gold, the mine is currently operated by St Barbara Ltd an Australian company. Recent figures show proceeds from the mine contributed around 20 per cent of GDP. Extraction of nickel ore has recently begun on the Islands of San Jorge and Isobel.

Energy

In 2010, 0.08 billion kWh of electricity were produced and consumed.

Manufacturing

Local industries include palm oil milling, mineral water, nails, rice milling, boats, fish canning, fibreglass products, beer, wooden and rattan furniture and saw milling. The closure of the Solomon Islands Plantation Limited, due to unrest between the Guadalcanal islanders and Malaitans, had an adverse effect on the economy as SIP Ltd was responsible for 20 per cent of national export earnings from palm oil.

Service Industries

Diving is an important tourist attraction but the industry is hampered by a lack of infrastructure and limited transportation. In 1999, the Solomon Islands had 13,000 visitors, generating US$13 million. As the Islands' economy needs to diversify, tourism has been seen as an area that could be exploited and ecotourism in particular has great possibilities.

Agriculture

Most farming is on a subsistence level. Commercial crops include copra. Crops grown on the island are Oil palm, yams, taro, beans, rice, vegetables, bananas, pineapples and cocoa. Spices are grown on a small scale. Livestock industries are currently expanding, with efforts being made to improve production of chickens and pigs.

Most of the timber is exported as logs. Timber working is done by about 10-12 private companies. A reduction in demand for tropical timber has severely affected the market and is estimated to have reduced the GDP by up to 20 per cent. Some 50 per cent of the jobs in the industry were lost as a result.

There are two fishing bases in the islands: Tulagi and Noro. The only fishing cannery is foreign operated. However, fish products are a valuable export commodity. FAO figures for 2010 put the total catch at 35,179 tonnes.

Agricultural Production in 2010

Produce	Int. $'000*	Tonnes
Coconuts	42,460	384,000
Palm oil	18,272	42,000
Fruit fresh nes	10,192	29,200
Taro (cocoyams)	9,756	46,000
Yams	9,590	37,600
Sweet potatoes	6,548	86,700
Cocoa beans	5,405	5,205
Indigenous pigmeat	3,689	2,400
Palm kernels	2,839	11,000
Pulses, nes	2,506	4,700
Indigenous cattle meat	1,999	740
Vegetables fresh nes	1,244	6,600

*unofficial figures
* unofficial figures
Source: http://faostat.fao.org/site/339/default.aspx FAOSTAT, Statistics Division, Food and Agriculture Organization of the UN

COMMUNICATIONS AND TRANSPORT

Travel Requirements

Citizens of the USA, Canada, Australia and the EU require a passport valid for six months and a return/onward ticket, but not a visa, as a Visitor's Permit for up to three months is issued to most travellers. Citizens of Cyprus, Estonia, Latvia and Lithuania need clearance in advance from the immigration department of the Solomon Islands. Other nationals should contact the embassy to check visa requirements.

National Airlines

It was the government's intention to build ten grass airfields by the end of 2000 to allow access to the remote islands.
Solomon Airlines, URL: http://www.solomonairlines.com.au

Railways

There are 100 km of private railway on one plantation.

SOMALIA

Roads
There are 2,100 km of main roads. Vehicles are driven on the left.

Ports and Harbours
The main ports are Honiara, Noro and Yandina.

HEALTH

Central Hospital acts as a national hospital. It provides supportive services such as laboratory, pharmacy, X-rays, physiotherapy, and dental therapy. There are five provincial hospitals. General health provision is provided through health centres, clinics, aid posts and clinics operated by the government. The most recent figures from the WHO show that in the period 2005-10 there were 118 physicians (2.2 per 10,000 population), 1,080 nurses and midwives (20.5 per 10,000 population), 52 dentistry personnel and 53 pharmaceutical personnel. In 2003, there were 22 beds per 10,000 population. In 2010, general government expenditure on health accounted for 23.7 per cent of total government expenditure. General government expenditure accounted for 93.5 per cent of total health expenditure. External resources for health amounted to 29.4 per cent of total health expenditure. Total expenditure on health as a percentage of GDP in 2009 was 8.7 per cent. Per capita expenditure on health amounted to US$102 in 2009.

Malaria is a major health threat in the Solomon Islands, although attempts are made to control it. Drugs have enabled leprosy to be brought under control. The infant mortality rate was 23 per 1,000 live births in 2009 and the child mortality rate was 27 per 1,000 live births. The neonatal mortality rate was 12 per 1,000 live births. In 2008, some 19 per cent of deaths among children under five years of age are due to prematurity, 10 per cent due to malaria (compared to 29 per cent in 2000), 5 per cent are due to diarrhoeal diseases, and 16 per cent due to pneumonia. An estimated 32.8 per cent of children were considered stunted in the period 2005-11 and 11.5 per cent underweight.

In 2004, 94 per cent of the urban population and 65 per cent of the rural population had sustainable access to improved drinking water supplies. In 2004, 98 per cent of the urban population and 18 per cent of the rural population had sustainable access to improved sanitation. (Source: http://www.who.int, World Health Statistics 2012)

EDUCATION

The central government finances the national system of education. Education in the Solomon Islands is not compulsory, although figures for 2003 show that 85 per cent of primary school aged children were enrolled at school. Secondary school figures for the same year show that 14 per cent were enrolled at school. There are 388 primary schools. There are two types of secondary schools, national and provincial, with a total enrolment of 6,175 and 1,223, respectively. Pupils can now take the Solomon Islands School Certificate examination.

Primary and secondary school teachers are trained at the Solomon Islands College of Higher Education. Two government-aided schools can prepare students for university study abroad. Adult literacy is an estimated 64 per cent.

RELIGION

The population of the Solomon Islands is mainly Christian (45 per cent Anglican, 18 per cent Roman Catholic, 12 per cent Methodist-Presbyterian, 9 per cent Baptist, 7 per cent Seventh Day Adventist). Minority local religions are also practiced.

The Solomon Islands has a religious liberty rating of 9 on a scale of 1 to 10 (10 is most freedom). (Source: World Religion Database)

COMMUNICATIONS AND MEDIA

Newspapers
There is freedom of the press. Newspapers include:
Solomon Star, daily, (URL: http://www.solomonstarnews.com/); The Solomon Voice, weekly; Solomon Times (URL: http://www.solomontimes.com/), weekly; Agrikalsa Nius, weekly

Broadcasting
The Solomon Islands Broadcasting Corporation (URL: http://www.sibconline.com.sb/) was established in 1977. The mult-channel pay-TV is available. SIBC also operates two national radio stations and two regional stations. Local commerical radio satios also operate.

Telecommunications
In 2008, there were an estimated 8,000 main telephone line and 14,000 mobile phones. Four per cent of the population had a computer. There were an estimated 10,000 internet users.

ENVIRONMENT

Major environmental concerns for the Solomon Islands are deforestation and soil erosion. The islands have surrounding coral reefs which are either dead or dying.

The Solomon Islands are a party to the following international agreements: Biodiversity, Climate Change, Climate Change-Kyoto Protocol, Desertification, Environmental Modification, Law of the Sea, Marine Dumping, Marine Life Conservation, Ozone Layer Protection, and Whaling.

According to figures from the EIA, in 2010 the Solomon Islands emissions from the consumption of fossil fuels totalled 0.36 million metric tons of carbon dioxide.

SOMALIA
Somali Republic
Jamhuuriyada Soomaaliya

Capital: Mogadishu (Population estimate: 1.5-2 million)

Head of State: H.E. Mr Hassan Sheikh Mohamud (page 1479)

National Flag: Blue; a star five-pointed centred white

CONSTITUTION AND GOVERNMENT

Constitution
Somalia was formed in 1960 by the merger of the former British Somaliland and the Italian Somaliland. On 1 July 1976 the newly formed Somali Socialist Revolutionary Party had taken over the responsibilities of the country from the Supreme Revolutionary Council which came into power through a bloodless military takeover on 21 October 1969. At the same time the previous constitution was abolished and the multi-party system banned. The new constitution, adopted in 1969, decreed that the sole legal party was the Somali Revolutionary Socialist Party. At the same time, General Mohammed Siad Barre was confirmed as President.

Barre was overthrown by guerrillas led by the United Somali Congress early in 1991 and the country subsequently experienced a fierce civil war as Barre attempted to regain power and hostile tribes fought each other for supremacy. The United Somali Congress reinstated the constitution, abolished in 1969, and appointed an interim government in 1991. Barre and his remaining forces fled to Kenya at the end of 1991 as the two main warring factions of Aideed and Ali Mahdi continued to dispute claims to the presidency. The last general elections in Somalia were held in 1986. The Constitution is no longer in force; a Transitional Federal Charter was established in 2004.

The constituent assembly approved a new constitution, based on a federal system, on 1 August 2012.

The north-west area of Somalia, formerly under British Protectorate, declared independence as the "Republic of Somaliland" in 1991, a claim as yet unrecognised in official terms. In contrast to the rest of the country, relative stability prevails in the north-west, and following

a conference in Borama in May 1993, agreement was reached on the formation of a new inter-clan government of "Somaliland". Former Somali Prime Minister Mohammed Ibrahim Egal was elected President by the clan representatives. In August 2000 President Egal called for the Republic of Somaliland to be given special status by the UN. Somaliland has a population of around 3.5 million; its capital city is Hargeisa.

In 1998, Puntland in the north-east of the country also declared itself to be an autonomous region with its own president.

Recent Events
The country remained divided into warring clan fiefdoms over the decade. In May 1993 the UN took control of foreign forces in Somalia from UNITAF (United Task Force, a US-led coalition of forces). As well as administering humanitarian aid, the UN attempted to broker political reconciliation in the volatile area of Somalia with a view to re-installing government institutions. A political meeting between Somali factions was convened by the UN in Addis Ababa in January 1993 and culminated in agreements over a cease-fire and a national reconciliation conference held in March 1993. Little progress was subsequently made with the cease-fire, and unrest continued. The UN peacekeeping troops withdrew in 1995.

After nearly 10 years without a central government, and following months of negotiations between traditional elders and clan leaders, a 245-member transitional assembly was finally set up in 2000, in exile in Djibouti due to security concerns within Somalia itself. The first President of Somalia since 1991, Abdulkassim Salat Hassan, was elected and was sworn in, in August 2000. Among the intentions of the Transitional National Government was the creation a new constitution and the holding of elections within three years. In October Hassan returned to Mogadishu with Prime Minister Galayadh who announced an interim government. Some Somali warlords were still opposed to the agreement and announced in March 2001 that Hussein Aydid was to head a rival council. In October 2001 Prime Minister Galayadh lost a vote of no confidence, following which he resigned. Hasan Abshir Farah was appointed Prime Minister in November of that year.

In May 2002, Dahir Riyale Kahin became the new president of the breakaway territory of Somaliland following the death of Mohamed Ibrahim Egal. Presidential elections followed in April and Kahin was elected to the post. It was the first presidential election to take place in Somaliland.

In July 2003 peace talks were held in Kenya between warlords and government and, at further talks held the following January, agreement was reached to set up a new parliament. Following an upsurge in violence in June 2004, the new transitional parliament was inaugurated at a ceremony in Kenya in August. In October, the transitional parliament appointed Abdullahi Yusuf as president, and in December 2004 Ali Mohammed Ghedi was approved as prime minister. Further government appointments were made in April 2005. The government continues to operate from Kenya because of the Somali security situation. In March 2005 the government voted to return to the country but not to Mogadishu. However several ministers and warlords boycotted the vote and in May 2005 at least ten people were killed and 28 wounded when a bomb exploded at a political rally in Mogadishu where the prime minister, Ali Muhammad Ghedi, was speaking during his first visit to the capital since taking office. The President and Prime Minister are currently based in Jowhar, north of Mogadishu, until a permanent site for the government can be agreed upon. The cabinet began returning from exile in Kenya in June 2005. The prime minister survived an assassination attempt in November 2005.

The transitional government met for the first time in Somalia in February 2006. They met at the central town of Badoia. However violence continued with fierce fighting between rival militias in Mogadishu. In June 2006 militias loyal to the Union of Islamic Courts took control of the capital and other parts of the south. The network of eleven Islamic courts was initially set up to restore a system of Sharia law in the capital and to end the violence on the streets; however, there is an element pushing for an Islamic state. The transitional government accused Eritrea of arming the Union of Islamic Courts. In July 2006 the prime minister, Ali Mohamed Gehdi, survived a vote of confidence after 18 of his ministers resigned apparently in protest at his refusal to sign an agreement with the Union of Islamic Courts. A further 11 ministers resigned on 2 August 2006 in protest at the prime minister's decision to postpone talks with the Union of Islamic Courts. A new, smaller, cabinet was announced 21 August, and the transitional government and the Union of Islamic Courts began peace talks in the Sudanese capital, Khartoum at the beginning of September.

In December 2006, the UN security council said it supported the placement of African peacekeepers to support the interim government; however, Islamist leaders said they would view any outside forces as hostile. Following skirmishes with government and Ethiopian forces, Islamists relinquished the port of Kismay, their last stronghold, in January 2007. President Abdullahi Yusuf entered Mogadishu for the first time. In March 2007 fighting broke out in Mogadishu between government and Ethiopian troops and insurgents, leading to thousands of civilians fleeing the area. On October 29 2007, Prime Minister Ali Mohamed Ghedi resigned his post having been blamed for failing to end the fighting and bringing in Ethiopian troops whom many native Somalis distrust. He had refused to negotiate with armed Islamists and other opposition groups. Nur Hassan Hussein (also known as Nur Adde) was named prime minister in November.

By November 2007, it was estimated that there were one million Somali refugees. The Islamist-led insurgency continued to spread through the Spring of 2008, and in April, a US air strike killed Aden Hashi Ayro, a leader of the Al-Shabaab insurgent group. There were a series of hijackings and attacks on vessels off the Somali coast, prompting calls for international efforts to tackle piracy. In May the UN Security Council voted to allow foreign warships in the Somalia's territorial waters.

June 2008 saw the government sign a three-month ceasefire pact with the Alliance for Re-Liberation of Somalia. The pact was rejected by Islamist leader Hassan Dahir Aweys, who said that the Union of Islamic Courts would not cease fighting until all foreign troops had left the country. Under the terms of the agreement Ethiopian troops would have stayed in Somalia for a period of time not exceeding 120 days. In July 2008, gunmen in Mogadishu killed Osman Ali Ahmed, head of the UN Development Programme in Somalia.

On December 14th 2008, President Abdullahi Yusuf sacked Prime Minister Nur Hassan Hussein because he had failed to end years of conflict in Somalia. The following day, Somalia's parliament declared the sacking illegal and passed a confidence vote in the Prime Minister, who is thought to be the only government member with international support. Somalia's two leaders had clashed over attempts to deal with the Islamist-led opposition, and the rift spread to parliament.

In January 2009 during meeting in Djibouti the Somalian parliament swore in 149 new members from the opposition party Alliance for the Re-Liberation of Somali. Sheikj Sharif Sheikh Ahmad was elected president he is widely thought of as a moderate. It was agreed that the interim government should go on for another two years. In February President Ahmad selected former diplomat Omar Abdirashid Ali Sharmarke as prime minister.

Several ministers resigned or were killed in 2009-10 including the internal security minister who was killed in a suicide bomb attack in June 2009.

In February 2010 Islamist militants were reported to be stopping convoys of food reaching more than 360,000 displaced people. Militants said that accepting foreign aid was damaging the Somalian farming sector and the economy. The UN's World Food Programme (WFP) had already had to pull out of parts of southern Somalia because of threats from rebel groups. Also that month the radical Islamist al-Shabab militia group formally declared an alliance with al-Qaeda; it was believed it was planning a major offensive to capture the capital.

In July 2010 Al-Shabab said it was responsible for the bomb blasts in Uganda which killed over 70 people watching the football world cup on television.

The prime minister, Omar Abdirashid Ali Sharmarke, resigned in September 2010. He was replaced by Mohamed Abdullahi Mohamed who was sworn into office on 1 November 2010 and the cabinet was reshuffled.

In February 2011, Parliament voted to extend its mandate for another three years.

The interior minister was assassinated in June 2011. The prime minister, Mohamed Abdullahi Mohamed resigned in June 2011 as part of a UN-backed deal to extend the mandates of the curent president and parliament for a further year until August 2012, at which point elections should take place.

In July 2011 Somalia and other horn of Africa countries began to feel the effects of the region's worst drought for 60 years. Thousands of animals have died and crops have withered in fields. The crisis has been further fuelled by food shortages following a drought in 2009. Western aid agencies are fearful that the drought will escalate into a full blown famine. Somalian refugees have been leaving for Ethiopia and Kenya in the hope of finding relief. The militant Islamist group al-Shabab lifted its ban on foreign aid agencies so relief could be brought into the country. They had previously banned aid agencies, accusing them of being anti-Muslim. However, in November 2011, despite the severe drought being experienced, al-Shabab closed down several aid agencies including some from the UN.

In December 2011 new clashes were reported in Mogadishu between Islamist al-Shabab militants and government forces, supported by African Union troops. Al-Shabab announced earlier this week it is to change its name to Imaarah Islamiya. In January 2012, al-Shabab banned the Red Cross from providing famine relief in areas under their control. The Red Cross is one of the few aid agencies still operating in southern and central Somalia. The following month al-Shabab lost control of the town of Baidoa and announced its merger with al-Qaeda. In another success for the Somali government, its forces, with the help of African Union troops, captured the town of Afgoye in the south of Mogadishu.

In August 2012 the country's first formal parliament for more than 20 years was sworn in, ending an eight-year transitional period. In the same month pro-government forces captured the port of Merca, south of Mogadishu, from al-Shahab.

In September 2012, clan elders chose sufficient members of parliament for the presidential election to take place. This was duly won by challenger Hassan Sheikh Mohamud. The following day four security officers were killed in a suicide bomb attack on the president's hotel. In the same month, newly elected MP Mustafa Haji Maalim was shot in an attack as he left a Mosque.

In October 2012, President Mohamud appointed businessman Abdi Farah Shirdon Saaid as prime minister.

Also in October 2012, government forces and the African Union took back the last major city held by al-Shabab. They also retook the town of Wanla Weyn.

In January 2013, two people died in a suicide attack at the presidential compound in Mogadishu. Both the president and prime minister were unharmed.

In March 2013, the UN Security Council voted for a partial embargo on selling arms to Somalia for a year.

Somaliland

The former British protectorate of Somaliland in the north of the country declared unilateral independence, calling itself the Somaliland Republic on 18 May 1991. Mohammed Ibrahim Egal was elected president and was re-elected in 1997. The government approved a system of multiparty politics in 1999. On 31 May 2001 a referendum was held on the future constitution of Somaliland, the result was a landslide for independence. President Egal died in May 2002 and was succeeded by the Vice President Dahir Riyale Kahin who was elected to the post on 14 April 2003. Legislative elections were held on 29 September 2005. The president's term of office was extended for a further year in May 2008, and again for a further six months in April 2009.

As well as its established system of government, Somaliland has its own government institutions, police force, currency (the Somaliland Shilling) and government-run TV station called Somaliland TV. Somaliland like Somalia is very poor and the economy depends heavily on remittances sent home by family members living broad. Income also comes from duties paid for the use of the port at Berbera, particularly used by landlocked Ethiopia. Livestock exports were an important source of revenue, though, following an outbreak of Rift Valley Fever in 2000, several Arab nations put an embargo on imports of livestock from Somalia and Somaliland.

Captial City: Hargeisa
The population is estimated to be between 2 and 3 million.
Major languages spoken: Somali, Arabic, and English

Puntland

Puntland is in the North East of Somalia and declared itself an autonomous region in 1998, although unlike Somaliland it does not want independence from Somalia. Garowe is the administrative capital and Puntland has a population estimated to be 2.5 million. The government is made up of a 66-member House of Representatives as well as a traditional council of elders. In January 2005 presidential elections were held and General Mohamud Muse Hersi (Adde) was elected to the post. In January 2009, parliament elected Abdirahman Mohamed Farole to the 'presidency' of Puntland.

Capital City: Capital: Garowe (administrative), Bosasso (commercial)
The Population is estimated to be around 2.4 million.
Major languages spoken: Somali, Arabic
Currency: Somali shilling

Cabinet (as at June 2013)

Prime Minister: Dr Abdi Farah Shirdon (page 1507)
Deputy Prime Minister, Minister of Foreign Affairs: Fawziyo Yussuf Haji Aadan (page 1372)

SOMALIA

Minister of Defence: Abdihakim Mohamoud Haji Fiqi
Minister of Trade and Industry: Mohamud Ahmed Hassan
Minister of Finance and Planning: Mohamud Hassan Suleiman
Minister of Interior and National Security: Abdikarim Husein Guled
Minister of Public Works and Reconstruction: Muhayadin Mohamed Kalmoi
Minister of Information and Telecommunications: Abdullahi Alimoge Hersi
Minister of Justice, Endowments & Religious Affairs: Abdullahi Abyan Nur
Minister of Natural Resources: Abdirizak Omar Mohamed
Minister of Social Development: Maryam Qasim

Ministries

Office of the President, People's Palace, Mogadishu, Somalia. Tel: +252 1 723, e-mail: president@somaligovernment.org

Office of the Prime Minister, Mogadishu, Somalia.

Ministry of Agriculture and Livestock, Mogadishu, Somalia. e-mail: ministryofagriculture@somaligovernment.org

Ministry of Commerce and Industry, PO Box 928, Mogadishu, Somalia. Tel: +252 1 21453, e-mail: ministryofcommerce@somaligovernment.org

Ministry of Constitution and Federal Affairs, Mogadishu, Somalia

Ministry of Defence, Mogadishu, Somalia. Tel: +252 1 710, e-mail: ministryofdefense@somaligovernment.org

Ministry of Education, Higher Education and Culture, PO Box 1182, Mogadishu, Somalia. Tel: +252 1 35042, e-mail: ministryofeducationandsports@somaligovernment.org

Ministry of Finance and Treasury, Mogadishu, Somalia. Tel: +252 1 33090, e-mail: ministryoffinance@somaligovernment.org

Ministry of Fisheries, Marine Resources and Environment, Mogadishu, Somalia.

Ministry of Foreign Affairs, Mogadishu, Somalia. Tel: +252 1 721, e-mail: ministryofforeignaffairs@somaligovernment.org

Ministry of Health, Mogadishu, Somalia. Tel: +252 1 31055, e-mail: ministryofhealth@somaligovernment.org

Ministry of Information, Post and Telecommunication, PO Box 1748, Mogadishu, Somalia. Tel: +252 1 999621, e-mail: ministryofinformation@somaligovernment.org

Ministry of the Interior and National Security, Mogadishu, Somalia. e-mail: ministryofinterior@somaligovernment.org

Ministry of Justice, Religious Affairs and Endowment, Mogadishu, Somalia. Tel: +252 1 36062, e-mail: ministryofjustice@somaligovernment.org

Ministry of Land, Air, and Sea Transport, Mogadishu, Somalia. Tel: +252 1 23025, e-mail: ministryoftransportation@somaligovernment.org

Ministry of Planning and International Co-operation, PO Box 1742, Mogadishu, Somalia. Tel: +252 1 80384

Ministry of Public Works and Reconstruction, Mogadishu, Somalia. Tel: +252 1 21051, e-mail: ministryofpublicwork@somaligovernment.org

Ministry of Water and Mineral Resources, Mogadishu, Somalia. e-mail: ministryofenergy@somaligovernment.org

Ministry of Women and Family Affairs, Mogadishu, Somalia.

Ministry of Youth, Sports, Labour, Social and Workforce Development, Mogadishu, Somalia. Tel: +252 1 33086

Elections

Following an extension to its mandate, parliamentary elections took place on 12 August 2012. Clan elders choose the members of the parliament, who will then elect the president. The process of choosing the MPs took until September 2012. Enough MPs had been chosen for the presidential election to take place.

Presidential elections took place on 10 September 2012. Twenty-two candidates took part. Hassan Sheikh Mohamud gained 190 votes and the incumbent president of the transitional regime, Sharif Sheikh Ahmed, obtained 79 votes. In the second round, Hassan Sheikh Mohamud gained an overall majority. He was inaugurated on 16 September.

Diplomatic Representation

British Embassy, Mogadhishu International Airport, Somalia.
Ambassador: John Baugh
United States Virtual Presence Post, Somalia, URL: http://somalia.usvpp.gov/
Permanent Representative to the UN, New York: Elmi Ahmed Duale

LEGAL SYSTEM

The judiciary of Somalia began to be formed in early 2007 when the first judges were sworn in by the Transitional Federal Government (TFG). The national religion is Islam, and Sharia law is the basis of national legislation.

The court system consists of a Transitional Supreme Court located in Mogadishu, a Transitional Appeals Court, and other courts. However, at present, many decisions continue to be made by local tribal meetings.

A Judicial Service Council administers the judiciary and advises on judicial appointment; this Council consists of the President of the Supreme Court, the Attorney General, three Supreme Court Judges and four lawyers. Judges and the Attorney General are appointed by the President.

Whilst human rights awareness is becoming more widespread, the overall situation for Somali citizens continues to deteriorate in the absence of effective governance institutions and ongoing conflict. Human rights abuses include unlawful killings, kidnapping, torture, and rape. Arrest and detention can be arbitrary, prison conditions are life-threatening, and official impunity is widespread. There are restrictions on freedoms of speech, press, assembly, association, religion, and movement.

Somalia retains the death penalty, and there have been reports of child executions in areas controlled by the Islamic Courts Union. Ten executions were reported to have been carried out in 2011.

In 2013, the government announced plans to reform the judicial system. Recommendations include the formation of a constitutional court, an independent committee for the protection of human rights, an anti-graft committee and select judges to serve under national federal courts. Other recommendations included the establishment of a National Judical Training Institute, the rebuilding of court buildings destroyed by the civil war and better funding for the judiciary. A period of consultation should now take place.

LOCAL GOVERNMENT

For administrative purposes Somalia has 18 regions or *gobolka*: Awdal; Bakool; Banaadir; Bari; Bay; Galguduud; Gedo; Hiiraan; Jubbada Dhexe; Jubbada Hoose; Mudug; Nugaal; Sanaag; Shabeellaha Dhexe; Shabeellaha Hoose; Sool; Togdheer; Woqooyi Galbeed.

AREA AND POPULATION

Area

Somalia is situated on the horn of Africa. It is bordered by Djibouti, Ethiopia and Kenya to the west. Somalia has a longer coastline than any African country, extending over 3,000 km along the Gulf of Aden and the Indian Ocean. It has an area of about 246,201 sq. miles (637,657 sq. km). The land is mainly flat or plateau, rising to mountains. About one-eighth of this area is suitable for cultivation. Only 5 per cent of these eight million hectares of arable land is estimated to be under the plough, and this has been badly affected by years of drought.

The climate is predominantly desert with more moderate temperatures in the mountains. There are two rainy seasons, and two dry. The two rainy seasons are from April to June and then October to November. Most of the country receives less than 500 mm of rain per year and much of the northern part of the country less that 50 mm per year.

On 26 December 2004 Somalia was hit by the tsunami which started in the Indian Ocean. Approximately 200 people were believed to have died, and as many as 30,000 displaced.

To view a map, consult http://www.un.org/Depts/Cartographic/map/profile/somalia.pdf

Population

The population of Somalia in 2010 was estimated to be 9.331 million. The chief towns are Mogadishu (1.5 - 2 million), Hargeisa (40,200), and Kismayo (17,800). Many people have begun to return to Mogadishu and some estimates put the population as high as 3 million in 2011. Other major cities are Berbers and Merca. Around 60 per cent of the population live a nomadic or semi nomadic lifestyle.

Languages spoken are Somali and Arabic. Italian and English are also used in some areas.

Births, Marriages, Deaths

Estimated figures for 2010 put the birth rate at around 43.5 per 1,000 population and the death rate at 15 per 1,000 population. Infant mortality was put at 109 deaths per 1,000 live births. Life expectancy from birth in 2009 was 51 years. Healthy life expectancy was 45 years. The median age was 18 years. Approximately 45 per cent of the population is aged under 15 years and 4 per cent over 60. The total fertility rate per woman was 6.3 in 2010. (Source: http://www.who.int, World Health Statistics 2012)

Public Holidays

26 June: Independence Day in Somaliland
1 July: Independence Day

EMPLOYMENT

Recent estimates (2007) put the workforce at 3.4 million, around 70 per cent of whom are employed in agriculture. Around 25 per cent of the population work established farms, the majority of agricultural workers are nomadic or semi-nomadic.

BANKING AND FINANCE

Currency

The unit of currency is the Somali shilling, divided into 100 cents. Other currencies are in use including the Somaliland shilling. The financial centre is Mogadishu.

GDP/GNP, Inflation, National Debt

Without a central government, the Somali economy operates without any economic policies and does not have the usual financial institutions and infrastructure which means it is unable to receive funds from the IMF. The economy benefits from remittances sent home by Somalis living abroad, estimated at US$2 billion in 2008. 60 per cent of the population lives below the US$1 per day poverty line. The economy is largely agriculture-based. Drought has adversely affected agricultural and livestock production. The economy is further hampered by a poor infrastructure. There is a small fishing industry. There are some natural resources but they are generally unexploited. The petroleum industry has ceased because of the political instability.

Estimates in 2010 put GDP at US$5.9 billion (compared to US$5.7 billion in 2008), with growth estimated at 2.6 per cent. Per capita GDP was estimated at US$600. Estimates in 2001 put the inflation rate at 6.0 per cent; since then figures have not been available. Total debt was put at US$2,836 million in 2006.

Foreign Investment

The UN has provided much monetary aid to Somalia and runs humanitarian and development programmes from Nairobi, Kenya. The estimated cost of the first six months of the UN's direction of defence forces in Somalia in 1993 was $856 million. In 2002 an estimated US$ 271.6 million of aid was distributed in Somalia; main international donors included the US, European Union, Australia, Canada, Finland, Italy, Japan, UK, Norway, Netherlands, Egypt, Sweden and Germany.

The UK is one of the main contributors of humanitarian aid in Somalia. In the year 2004-05 it sent £8 million, and this figure was expected to rise to £13 million in 2005-06. Half the budget of the International Committee of the Red Cross is spent in Somalia.

Balance of Payments / Imports and Exports

In 2010, exports were estimated at US$300 million. Most of Somalia's exports go to Italy and the Arab States; Saudi Arabia was a major trading partner until imposing a ban on livestock imports from Somalia after an outbreak of Rift Valley Fever in 2000. Imports mainly come from Djibouti, Kenya, India, Saudi Arabia, Italy, Japan, UK and China. In 2006 they were estimated to cost US$750 million.

Central Bank

Central Bank of Somalia, PO Box 11, Corso Somalia 55, Mogadishu, Somalia. Tel: +252 1 657733

MANUFACTURING, MINING AND SERVICES

Primary and Extractive Industries

Mineral and ground water surveys in Somalia have been carried out since 1963 by the United Nations Special Fund with the cooperation of the Somali Government. One of the first major achievements of this project was the discovery of more than 50 million tons of iron ore near Baidoa (about 200 miles from the capital). The survey has also uncovered a large quantity of uranium deposits in extended areas.

Deposits in the area of Burn Galan have also been studied by the survey team. The reserves are estimated to be in excess of 100 million tons. Recently, another reserve deposit of more than seven million cubic metres of sepiolite were discovered in this area. There are other varieties of mineral deposits of commercial value in Somalia. They include the following: tin, gypsum, limestone, sandstone, titanium, salt, anhydrite, feldspar, lead, platinum, mica, beryl, columbite, tantalite, copper, galena, talc, emery, asbestos, coal, lignite, kaolin, graphite, rutile, vermiculite, manganese and petroleum. Encouraging signs of oil deposits have also been established by some of the international oil companies who have obtained Somali government concessions. Figures of 2011 show that Somalia produced 0.11 thousand barrels of oil per day and consumed 5.00 thousand barrels per day meaning the shortfall had to be imported.

Energy

In 2010, Somalia generated 0.231 billion kWh of electricity and consumed 0.29 billion kWh.

Manufacturing

Some of the most important manufacturing plants include sugar factories, textile mills, meat packing factories, fish-processing plants, fruit canneries and construction material manufacturing plants.

Agriculture

Somalia's two main export commodities are bananas and livestock, which account for about 80 per cent of total exports. The government is giving the highest priority to developing and diversifying agricultural resources and to improving, through better grazing and veterinary services, the standard of the Somali livestock.

Agricultural Production in 2010

Produce	Int. $'000*	Tonnes
Camel milk, whole, fresh	434,806	1,275,200
Sheep milk, whole, fresh	229,910	590,400
Cow milk, whole, fresh	178,873	573,200
Indigenous cattle meat	171,785	63,592
Goat milk whole, fresh	167,991	500,600
Indigenous sheep meat	152,985	56,187
Indigenous goat meat	119,672	49,945
Indigenous camel meat	117,960	56,285
Sesame seed	47,224	70,500
Fruit fresh nes	42,792	122,600
Maize	16,146	120,000
Sorghum	14,246	100,400

* unofficial figures

Source: http://faostat.fao.org/site/339/default.aspx FAOSTAT, Statistics Division, Food and Agriculture Organization of the UN

Forests cover an estimated 14 per cent of the total area. They consist mainly of bush, shrubs and thorn trees. Actual forests with acacias, euphorbias and other trees are situated along the two main rivers. Incense, myrrh and arabic gum are collected from free-growing trees in the North-Eastern part of the country.

At present there are four fish processing plants along the Northern Coast (Alula, Candala, Habo and Laskore) and a lobster canning factory at Kismaio. FAO figures for 2010 estimate the total catch at 30,000 tonnes.

Somalia's territory can be divided as follows:

Territory	Million Hectares	% of total
Area suitable for cultivation	8.0	12.5
Area suitable for livestock raising	35.0	54.9
Forest	8.8	13.8
Others	12.0	18.8
Total	63.8	100.0

COMMUNICATIONS AND TRANSPORT

Travel Requirements

Citizens of the USA, Canada, Australia and the EU require a valid passport, a return/onward ticket and a visa, unless in transit with an onward ticket and not leaving the airport. Other nationals should contact the embassy to check visa requirements. Upon arrival, visitors must exchange US$100 or equivalent into local currency. Visitors to Somaliland should register with their embassy or high commission in Addis Ababa, Ethiopia, and to other parts of Somalia with their embassy or high commission in Nairobi, Kenya. Please note that the exact amount to be exchanged may vary according to region.

A passport is required for travel to Somaliland and Puntland. Both regions require a visa and issue their own. For travel to other parts of Somalia, a passport is required; however, there is no established governing authority capable of issuing a universally recognised visa.

National Airlines

Somali Airlines, P.O. Box 726, Via Medina, Mogadishu, Somalia. Tel: +252 1 81533, fax: +252 1 80489, URL: http://www.somaliairlines.com

Airports

Aaden Cabdulle Cismaan International Airport is situated just outside Mogadishu, it is estimated that Somalia has around 60 airports. Daallo Airlines and Jubba Airways both fly to Somalia. Turkish Airlines became the first major carrier from ouside East Africa to land in Mogdishu in more than 20 years when it started a twice-weekly service to Mogadishu in 2012.

Roads

Somalia has a road network of around 22,000 km. Vehicles are driven on the right.

Ports and Harbours

Somalia has several ports including Mogadishu, Berbera, Merca and Chisimayu. At the end of 2000 the government announced it was to re-open the port at Mogadishu. It finally opened in August 2006 as did the airports.

HEALTH

In the absence of government, the country's infrastructure has collapsed. There are five hospitals in Mogadishu. The most recent estimates from the WHO show that in the period 2005-10 there are 300 doctors and an estimated 965 nurses and midwives, 50 pharmaceutical personnel and 41 environment and public healthworkers. According to the latest WHO figures, in 2010 approximately 29 per cent of the population had access to improved drinking water. In the same year, 23 per cent of the population had access to improved sanitation. In 2010, the infant mortality rate was 108 per 1,000 live births and the under-five mortality rate was 180 per 1,000 live births. Diarrhoea accounts for 16 per cent of childhood deaths. Other main causes are pneumonia (25 per cent), prematurity (12 per cent), and malaria (7 per cent). Approximately 1 per cent were due to HIV/AIDS In the period 2005-11, an estimated 42.1 per cent of children aged under five were classified as stunted and 32.8 per cent underweight. The HIV/AIDS prevalence rate was estimated to be 373 per 100,000 population in 2009 and the TB rate 513 per 100,000 population. (Source: http://www.who.int, World Health Statistics 2012)

EDUCATION

Education is free. Primary education is in theory compulsory and lasts for eight years; secondary education lasts for four years. Recent figures estimate that only 14 per cent of school age children attend school. There are several privately run universities.

RELIGION

The majority of the population are Muslim (98 per cent) most of whom are Sunni Muslims. There is a small Christian community.

Somalia has a religious liberty rating of 2 on a scale of 1 to 10 (10 is most freedom). (Source: World Religion Database)

COMMUNICATIONS AND MEDIA

The media is often partisan. Violence and threats against journalists are common.

Newspapers

Most newspapers are affiliated to a political faction. The sector is relatively weak.

Broadcasting

Radio is the most important medium. There are around 20 radito stations but no domestic national broadcaster. Radio Mogadishu (URL:http://radiomuqdisho.net/), Voice of the Republic of Somali, is run by the transitional government. The most popular private radio station is Radio HornAfrik (URL: http://www.hornafrik.com/).

Telecommunications
The telecommunications network was almost totally destroyed by the civil war. In 2008 it was estimated that there were 100,000 landlines in operation and over 600,000 mobile phones. Somalia's three telecommunication companies, Telecom Somali, Hormuud and Nationlink, co-operated together to set up an internet company, the Global Internet Company. Approximately 100,000 Somalians have access to the internet.

ENVIRONMENT

Main environmental concerns for Somalia include deforestation, overgrazing and soil erosion leading to increased desertification. Somalia is also prone to droughts.

In 2010, Somalia's emissions from the consumption of fossil fuels totalled 0.90 million metric tons of carbon dioxide. (Source: EIA)

SOUTH AFRICA
Republic of South Africa

Seat of Administration: Pretoria (Population estimate, 2011: 1.5 million)

President: Jacob Zuma (page 1543)

Deputy President: Kgalema Motlanthe

National Flag: A green Y shape divides the flag horizontally with the open end of the Y against the staff. The area above the Y is red and the area below is blue. The outer edge of the Y has a white border and the inner edge a gold border. The triangle of the Y is black.

CONSTITUTION AND GOVERNMENT

Constitution
South Africa became an independent republic in 1961, and until the early 1990s its social and political structure was based on a racial segregation policy called apartheid. This led to great social unrest in the 1960s, early 1970s and more recently in the 1980s. The African National Congress (ANC) was banned and a state of emergency was declared. However, due to mounting international pressure, the pace of reform quickened from the late 1980s. Nelson Mandela, an ANC leader, imprisoned since 1962, was released in 1990. In 1992 a referendum for the white population approved continued negotiations and reforms. Agreement was eventually reached on a multi-racial election. This was held in May 1994. The result was victory for the ANC and Nelson Mandela, who was sworn in as President.

Under the terms of the present 1997 Constitution, the President is head of government and serves a maximum of two five-year terms of office. The members of the National Assembly choose the president. The president is responsible to Parliament, and appoints the Cabinet.

To consult the constitution, please visit:
http://www.constitutionalcourt.org.za/site/theconstitution/thetext.htm

International Relations
South Africa was readmitted to the Commonwealth in 1994 and is a member of the Southern African Development Community (SADC). South Africa provides peace keeping operations for Burundi, Darfur and the Democratic Republic of Congo and is involved through membership in the African Union in the conflict in Cote d'Ivoire.

Recent Events
In June 2005 President Mbeki sacked his Vice President, Jacob Zuma, following allegations of corruption. Phumzile Mlambo-Ngcuka, previously the minister for minerals and energy, was appointed to the post. In May 2006 Jacob Zuma was acquitted of the rape charge against him and he resumed his post as deputy leader of the ANC. In November 2007 the court of appeal allowed corruption charges to be brought against him after the seizure of documents from his home and office was deemed to be legal. In December 2007 elections were held for the leadership of the ANC party; President Mbeki was defeated by Jacob Zuma, placing the latter in a strong position to become the next President. In September 2008 the corruption case against Jacob Zuma came to court and the charges were dropped.

In December 2006, South Africa became the first African country to allow same sex marriages.

In June 2007 South Africa was disrupted by four weeks of strikes by public-sector workers.

In September 2008 President Mbeki was sacked by the ANC prompting him to resign from the post of president. Although under Mbeki the economy has grown, the ANC disagreed in principle with some of the measures taken to achieve growth - in particular Growth, Employment and Redistribution, or Gear, which was introduced in 1999. Deputy leader of the ANC Kgalema Motlanthe was appointed interim president. Eleven cabinet ministers resigned together with the executive deputy president.

In December 2008 a new political party was launched. The Congress of the People (COPE) was expected to present a challenge to the ANC at the elections in April 2009. The party is made up of several defectors from the ANC and is led by former defence minister Mosiuoa Lekota. The elections were won by the ANC and Jacob Zuma was then elected president by parliament.

In May 2009 the World Bank agreed an assistance payment of US$22 million, the first such payment since 2000. Zimbabwe had hoped to receive a much larger sum to help towards rebuilding the economy but this payment was seen by many as a first step to assistance by the World Bank.

In April 2010 Eugene Terreblanche, leader of the white supremist Afrikaner Resistance Movement, was killed on his farm. Initial reports said he had been killed by two farm workers following a dispute over unpaid wages. It was feared that the death could incite racial violence and President Zuma appealed for calm.

South Africa hosted the World Cup in June 2010.

The 2011 UN Conference on Climate Change took place in Durban in November 2011.

In August 2012 a strike over pay at the at the Marikana platinum mine resulted in the deaths of over 30 protesters. Police were sent in to break up the protest held by around 3,000 miners some of whom were armed with clubs. The circumstances which led the police to open fire on the miners is presently unclear. The company has since said that the miners will be sacked if they do not return to work. President Zuma declared a week of national mourning. In October platinum mine owners, Amplats sacked 12,000 striking miners.

In December 2012, President Zuma was re-elected.

In February 2013 Olympic paralympian Oscar Pistorius was arrested for killing his girlfriend. He maintains that he shot her in error after mistaking her for an intruder.

In May 2013, the University of KwaZulu-Natal announced that as of the next academic year, Zulu language classes would be compulsory for all first year students.

The health of former president Nelson Mandela (page 1470) declined and as of July 2013 he was critical but stable in hospital.

Legislature
South Africa's bicameral legislature consists of the National Council of Provinces and the National Assembly.
Parliament of South Africa, Parliament Building, Parliament Street, Cape Town, South Africa. Tel: +27 (0) 21 403 2911, fax: +27 (0)21 461 5372, URL: http://www.parliament.gov.za

Upper House
In 1997 the current Constitution replaced the Senate with the National Council of Provinces (NCOP), *Nationale Raad van Provinses*, which is composed of 90 members, indirectly elected for a term of five years. Each of South Africa's nine provinces is represented by ten NCOP members.
National Council of Provinces, NCOP Building, Cape Town, South Africa. URL: http://www.parliament.gov.za/ncop

Lower House
The National Assembly, *Volksraad*, has 400 Members of Parliament (MPs), directly elected for a term of five years. The Assembly is presided over by a Speaker and a Deputy Speaker.
National Assembly, Parliament Building, Parliament Street, Cape Town, South Africa. URL: http://www.parliament.gov.za
Speaker: M V Sisulus Baleka Mbete
Deputy Speaker: Ms N C Mfeketo

Cabinet (as at June 2013)
Minister in the Presidency, Chair of the National Planning Commission: Trevor Manuel (page 1470)
Minister in the Presidency, Performance Monitoring and Evaluation and Administration in the Presidency: Collins Chabane
Minister of Economic Development: Ebrahim Patel
Minister of Co-operative Government and Traditional Affairs: Richard Baloyi
Minister of Correctional Services: Joel Sbusiso Ndebele (page 1484)
Minister of Agriculture, Forestry and Fisheries: Tina Joemat-Pettersson
Minister of Public Service and Administration: Lindiwe Nonceba Sisulu (page 1515)
Minister of Arts and Culture: Paul Mashatile
Minister of Defence & War Veterans: Nosiviwe Mapisa-Nakula
Minister of Justice and Constitutional Development: Jeff Radebe (page 1499)
Minister of Science and Technology: Derek Hanekom
Minister of Finance: Pravin Gordhan (page 1432)
Minister of Home Affairs: Grace Naledi Pandor (page 1492)
Minister of Communications: Dina Pule
Minister of Labour: Mildred Oliphant
Minister of Energy: Elizabeth Dipuo Peters (page 1494)
Minister of Trade and Industry: Rob Davies
Minister of State Security: Siyabonga Cwele
Minister of Basic Education: Angie Motshekga
Minister of Transport: Ben Martins
Minister of Public Works: Thembelani Nxesi

Minister of Housing: Tokyo Sexwale
Minister of Social Development: Bathabile Dlamini
Minister of Water and Environment Affairs: Edna Molewa (page 1479)
Minister of Sport and Recreation: Fikile Mbalula
Minister of Health: Aaron Motsoaledi
Minister of Tourism: Marthinus van Schalkwyk (page 1530)
Minister of Mining: Susan Shabangu
Minister of Public Enterprises: Malusi Gigaba
Minister of Police: Nathi Mthethwa
Minister of Women, Youth, Children and People with Disabilities: Lulu Xingwana
Minister of High Education and Training: Blade Nzimande
Minister of International Relations and Co-operation: Maite Nkoana-Mashabane
Minister of Rural Development and Land Reform: Gugile Nkwint

Ministries

Parliament, PO Box 15, Cape Town 8000, South Africa. Tel: +27 (0)21 403 2911, fax: +27 (0)21 461 4331, URL: http://www.parliament.gov.za

Office of the Speaker of the National Assembly, Parliament Building, Room E125, Parliament Street, Cape Town 8001, South Africa. Tel: +27 (0)21 403 2595, fax: +27 (0)21 461 9462

Office of the President, Union Buildings, West Wing, Government Avenue, Pretoria 0002, South Africa or Private Bag X 1000, Pretoria 0001, South Africa. Tel: +27 (0)21 319 1500, fax: +27 (0)21 323 2573, e-mail:communications@po.gov.za, URL: http://www.info.gov.za/leaders/president/index.htm

Office of the Executive Deputy President, Union Buildings, West Wing, 2nd Floor, Government Avenue, Pretoria 0002, South Africa. Tel: +27 (0)12 323 2502, fax: +27 (0)12 323 2573, URL: http://www.gcis.gov.za/level3/ministry.htm

Ministry of Agriculture, Agriculture Building, Block DA, corner of Beatrix Street and Soutpansberg Road, Arcadia, Pretoria, South Africa. Tel: +27 (0)12 319 6000 / 7219, fax: +27 (0)12 325 3618, e-mail: segoatim@nda.agric.za, URL: http://www.nda.agric.za

Ministry of Arts, Culture, Science and Technology, Oranje Nassau Building, Room 7077, 188 Schoeman Street, Pretoria 0002, South Africa. Tel: +27 (0)12 337 8000, fax +27 (0)12 323 2720, URL: http://www.dac.gov.za

Ministry of Communications, Iparioli Office Park, 399 Duncan Street, Hatfield, Pretoria, South Africa. Tel: +27 (0)12 427 8000, fax: +27 (0)12 427 8026, e-mail: joseph@doc.gov.za, URL: http://docweb.pwv.gov.za

Ministry of Correctional Services, Poyntons Building, West Block, corner Church and Schubart Streets, Pretoria, South Africa. Tel: +27 (0)12 307 2000, fax: +27 (0)12 328 6149, e-mail: charmaineg@dcsmail.pwv.gov.za, URL: http://www.dcs.gov.za/

Ministry of Defence, Armscor Building, Block 5, Level 4, Nossob Street, Erasmusrand, Pretoria 0181, South Africa. Tel: +27 (0)12 355 6101, fax: +27 (0)12 347 0118, URL: http://www.mil.za

Ministry of Education, Magister Building, Room 910, 123 Schoeman Street, Pretoria 0002, South Africa. Tel: +27 (0)12 326 0126, fax: +27 (0)12 323 5989, URL: http://www.doe.gov.za

Ministry of Environmental Affairs and Tourism, Fedsure Forum Building, North Tower, cor Van der Walt and Pretorius Streets, Pretoria 0001, South Africa. Tel: +27 (012) 310 3911, fax: +27 (012) 322 2682, URL: http://www.environment.gov.za

Ministry of Finance, 240 Vermeulen Street, 26th Floor, corner Andries and Vermeulen Streets, Pretoria 0002, South Africa. Tel: +27 (0)12 323 8911, fax: +27 (0)12 323 3262, URL: http://www.finance.gov.za/

Ministry of Foreign Affairs, Union Buildings, East Wing, Government Avenue, Pretoria 0002, South Africa. Tel: +27 (0)12 351 1000, fax: +27 (0)12 351 0257, URL: http://www.dfa.gov.za

Ministry of Health, Civitas Building, Room 2027, corner Andries and Struben Streets, Pretoria 0002, South Africa. Tel:+27 012) 312 0000, fax: +27 (012) 325 5706, e-mail:joanvs@health.gov.za, URL: http://www.doh.gov.za

Ministry of Home Affairs, Civitas Building, 10th Floor, corner Andries and Struben Streets, Pretoria 0002, South Africa. Tel: +27 (0)12 326 8081, fax: +27 (0)12 321 6491, URL: http://www.home-affairs.gov.za

Ministry of Housing, 240 Walker Street, Sunnyside, Pretoria 0002, South Africa. Tel: +27 (012) 421 1311, fax: +27 (012) 341 2998 e-mail:gege@housepta.pwv.gov.za, URL: http://www.housing.gov.za

Ministry of Justice and Constitutional Development, (Private Bag X81, Pretoria, 0001) Presidia Building, corner Paul Kruger and Pretorius Streets, Pretoria 0001, South Africa. Tel: +27 (0)12 315 1111, fax: +27 (0)12 323 1846,e-mail: elsa@justice1.pwv.gov.za, URL: http://www.doj.gov.za

Ministry of Labour, Laboria Building, corner Schoeman and Paul Kruger Streets, Pretoria 0002, South Africa. Tel: +27 (012) 309 4000, fax: +27 (012) 320 1942, e-mail: jerry@labourhq.pwv.org.za, URL: http://www.labour.gov.za

Ministry of Land Affairs, Old Building, 184 Jacob Marè Street, Pretoria, South Africa. Tel: +27 (0)12 312 8911, fax: +27 (0)12 323 7124, e-mail: slebethe@sghq.pwv.gov.za, URL: http://land.pwv.gov.za

Ministry of Minerals and Energy, Mineralia Centre, 228 Visagie Street, Pretoria 0001, South Africa. Tel: +27 (012) 317 9000, fax: +27 (012) 322 3416 e-mail: esther@mepta.pwv.gov.za, URL: http://www.dme.gov.za

Ministry of Public Enterprises, Infotech Building, Suite 401, 1090 Arcadia Street, Hatfield, Pretoria 0028, South Africa. Tel: +27 (0)12 342 7111, fax: +27 (0)12 342 7224, e-mail:goudens@ope.pwv.gov.za, URL: http://www.dpe.gov.za

Ministry of Public Service and Administration, Transvaal House, 22nb Floor, corner Vermeulen and van der Walt Streets, Pretoria 0002, South Africa. Tel: +27 (012) 314 7911, fax: +27 (012) 323 2386 e-mail:info@dpsa.pwv.gov.za, URL: http://www.dpsa.gov.za

Ministry of Public Works, Central Government Building, corner Bosman and Vermeulen Streets, Pretoria 0002, South Africa. Tel: +27 (012) 337 2000, fax: +27 (012) 323 2856, URL: http://www.publicworks.gov.za

Ministry of Science and Technology, Oranje Nassau Building, 188 Schoeman Street, Pretoria, South Africa. Tel: +27 (012) 324 4096, fax: +27 (012) 324 2687, URL: http://www.dst.gov.za

Ministry of Sport and Recreation, 188 Oranje Nassau Building, 3rd Floor, Schoeman Street, Pretoria 0002, South Africa. Tel: +27 (012) 334 3100, fax: +27 (012) 321 6187 e-mail:Rita@sport1.pwv.gov.za, URL: http://www.srsa.gov.za

Ministry of Trade and Industry, House of Trade and Industry, 11th Floor, Prinsloo Street, Pretoria 0002, South Africa. Tel: +27 (012) 310 9791, fax: +27 (012) 322 2701, URL: http://www.dti.gov.za

Ministry of Transport, Forum Building, Room 4111, corner Struben and Bosman Streets, Pretoria 0002, South Africa. Tel: +27 (012) 309 3000, fax: +27 (012) 324 3486, URL: http://www.transport.gov.za

Ministry of Water Affairs and Forestry, Sedibeng Building, 185 Schoeman Street, PRETORIA 0002, South Africa. Tel: +27 (012) 338 7500, fax: +27 (012) 326 2715 e-mail:webmaster@dwaf.gov.za, URL: http://www-dwaf.gov.za

Political Parties

African National Congress (ANC), 54 Sauer Street, Johannesburg 2001, South Africa. Mailing address: PO Box 61884, Marshalltown 2107, South Africa. Tel: +27 (0)11 376 1000, fax: +27 (0)11 376 1134, e-mail: anchq@anc.org.za, URL: http://www.anc.org.za
President: Jacob Zuma (page 1543)

African Christian Democratic Party (ACDP), URL: http://www.acdp.org.za. Leader: Kenneth Meshoe

Freedom Front/Vryheidsfront (FF/VF), URL: http://www.vryheidsfront.co.za. Leader: Pieter Mulder

Inkatha Freedom Party (IFP), Good Hope Building, Cape Town (PO Box 15, Cape Town, 8000), South Africa. URL: http://www.ifp.org.za
President: Dr Mangosuthu.G. Buthelezi (page 1398)

Pan Africanist Congress of Azania (PAC), URL: http://www.pac.org.za. Leader: Letlapa Mphahlele

United Democratic Party, URL: http://www.udm.org.za. Leader: Bantu Holomisa

Independent Democrats, URL: http://www.id.org.za. Leader: Patricia de Lille

Minority Front, URL: http://www.mf.org.za. Leader: Shameen Thakur Rajbansi

South African Communist Party (SACP), URL: http://www.sacp.org.za. Leader: Blade Nzimande

Azanian People's Organisation, (AZAPO), URL: http://www.azapo.org.za. Leader: Jacob Dikobo

Congress of the People (COPE), URL: http://www.cope.za.org. Keader: Mosiuoa Lekota

Democratic Alliance (DA), URL: http://www.da.org.za. Leader: Helen Zille

Elections
The most recent parliamentary election was held on 22 April 2009. The ANC won with a large majority. Parliamentary (National Assembly) seats break down as: ANC 264, DA 57, COPE 30, IFP 18; others 21 seats. In the Upper House: ANC 35 seats, DA 10; COPE 7; others 2; special delegates 36 seats.

The most recent presidential election was held in December 2012, Jacob Zuma was re-elected to the post.

Diplomatic Representation

South African High Commission, South Africa House, Trafalgar Square, London WC2N 5DP, UK. Tel: +44 (0)20 7451 7299, fax: +44 (0)20 7451 7284, e-mail: general@southafricahouse.com, URL: http://southafricahouseuk.com
High Commissioner: Zola Themba Skweyiya

South African Embassy, 3051 Massachusetts Avenue, NW, Washington, DC 20008, USA. Tel: +1 202 232 4400, fax: +1 202 265 1607, e-mail: info@saembassy.org, URL: http://www.saembassy.org
Ambassador: Ebrahim Rasool

British High Commission, 255 Hill Street, Arcadia 0002, South Africa. Tel: +27 12 483 1402 (Visas), +27 12 483 1401 (Passports), fax: +27 12 483 1302, URL: http://ukinsouthafrica.fco.gov.uk/en/
High Commissioner: Dame Nicola Brewer

Embassy of the United States of America, 877 Pretorius Street, Pretoria (PO Box 9536, Pretoria 0001), South Africa. Tel: +27 12 342 1048, fax: +27 12 342 2244, e-mail: embassy@pd.state.gov, URL: http://southafrica.usembassy.gov
Ambassador: vacant

South African Mission to the United Nations, 333 East 38th Street, 9th Floor, New York, NY 10016, USA. Tel: +1 212 213 5583, fax: +1 212 692 2498, e-mail: southafrica@un.int, URL: http://www.southafrica-newyork.net/pmun/index.htm
Permanent Representative: vacant

LEGAL SYSTEM

South African law is based on Common Law, Statute Law and Case Law. Principles of English law were introduced in the areas of civil and criminal procedure, evidence and mercantile matters, whilst Roman-Dutch law prevails in all other areas. Since the establishment of the Republic in 1961, the influence of English law has been significantly diminished.

The Constitutional Court is the highest court in matters regarding the protection, interpretation and enforcement of the constitution. It comprises of a President, a deputy President and nine judges.

The Supreme Court of Appeal is the highest court in all matters that do not pertain to the constitution and deals with appeals on decisions made by the High Courts. It consists of the Chief Justice (appointed by the President), Deputy Chief Justice and a number of judges. It is situated in Bloemfontein. The High Court deals with cases of a serious nature and has unlimited authority when imposing sentences. The High Court is divided into ten provincial and three local divisions. The provincial divisions are: Western Cape (with its seat at Cape Town); Free State (Bloemfontein); Eastern Cape (Grahamstown); Northern Cape (Kimberley); Kwazulu-Natal (Pietermaritzburg); Gauteng (Pretoria); Transkei (Umtata); Ciskei (Bisho),

SOUTH AFRICA

Venda (Sibasa) and Bophutswana (Mmabatho). These divisions are presided over by a Judge President, and may include one or more deputy judge presidents and any number of puisne judges.

The three local divisions are the Witwatersrand Local Division (Johannesburg), the Durban and Coast Local Division (Durban); and the South-East Cape Local Division (Port Elizabeth). These divisions are presided over by judges from the provincial division in the area where they are located.

Judges are normally appointed by the State President-in-Council, although acting appointments or ones of short duration may be made by the Minister of Justice. Judges are normally appointed from the Bar, and may only be removed on direction of the State President. Special superior courts may be set up at the discretion of the State President in consultation with the Minister of Justice, in cases directly relating to the security of the state or the maintenance of public order.

Regional courts preside over magisterial districts which are determined by the Minister of Justice. Regional courts do not have the same authority as the High Courts and are bound by legislation when sentencing. The lower courts are primarily Magistrates' Courts. Magistrates are appointed by the Minister of Justice and have jurisdiction over all offences except treason, rape and murder. Although the Regional courts have a higher penal jurisdiction they cannot hear appeals from the Magistrates courts.

The small claims court deals with civil claims of less than R3,000. Cases are heard by a commissioner, whose decision is final and neither party may have counsel or a representative. There is currently no appeal system for decisions made at a small claims court.

Chief's courts are available to hear cases which deal with disputes according to ethnic law and custom. These courts are overseen by an authorised headman or chief.

In general, the government respects the rights of its citizens. However, there have been recent instances of excessive force used by the police, sometimes resulting in deaths and serious injury. Prisons are overcrowded, and there have been cases of prisoner abuse. Delays in the judicial system can lead to prolonged pretrial detention. South Africa abolished the death penalty in 1995, a year after the end of apartheid, but in the face of some 18,000 murders a year, there have been calls to reinstate it.

Constitutional Court of South Africa, URL: http://www.constitutionalcourt.org.za/site/home.htm
Chief Justice of the Constitutional Court: Chief Justice Mogoeng Mogoeng
Supreme Court of Appeal, URL: http://www.justice.gov.za/sca/
President: L. Mpati
South African Human Rights Commission (SAHRC), URL: http://www.sahrc.org.za

LOCAL GOVERNMENT

South Africa is divided into nine provinces: the Free State (formerly the Orange Free State); the Eastern Cape; the Northern Cape; the Western Cape (also known as the Cape of Good Hope); Kwazulu-Natal; Mpumalanga (formerly the Eastern Transvaal), the North West Province; Gauteng (formerly Pretoria-Witwatersrand-Vereeniging); and Limpopo Province (formerly the Northern Province).

These provinces have their own governments, and are themselves divided into local authorities and districts. Local authorities are financially independent of both central and provincial governments, but some aspects of their loan and revenue sources are subject to approval by the Treasury and the provincial administrations.

For further details on each province please see their separate entries following this country entry.

AREA AND POPULATION

Area
South Africa borders Namibia, Botswana, Zimbabwe, Mozambique, and Swaziland to the north. In the south-east, the Kingdom of Lesotho is enclosed by South African territory. The total area of the Republic of South Africa is 1,228,376 sq. km, with a coastline of 2,954 km.

A mountain range runs down the east coast and the area enjoys a sub-tropical climate. The north of the country is characterised by savannah-type vegetation, whilst in the south there is a Mediterranean-type climate.

To view a map, visit http://www.un.org/Depts/Cartographic/map/profile/southafr.pdf

South Africa's ANC-controlled city councils are currently embarking on a programme of re-naming those areas with colonial names. Amongst areas already re-named, Pretoria will become the City of Tshwane, and will incorporate the townships of Mamelodi and Atteridgeville, whilst Port Elizabeth will become part of a larger metropolitan area to be called Nelson Mandela Metropole. Durban, currently named after a colonial governor, is holding a competition for a new title. Johannesburg and Soweto will become part of a larger metropolitan area whose new name is currently being debated. Cape Town will retain its name in view of its international recognition.

Population
South Africa's total population in 2011 was put at 51,770,560.

South Africa's constitution recognises 11 official languages: Afrikaans, English, isiNdebele, isiXhosa, isiZulu, Sepedi, Sesotho, Setswana, siSwati, Tshivenda, and Xitsonga.

The following tables show population statistics for the nine provinces.

Populations of the nine provinces, 2011

Province	Population
Eastern Cape	6,562,053
Mpumalanga	4,039,939
KwaZulu-Natal	10,267,300
North West	3,509,953
Northern Cape	1,145,861
Limpopo Province	5,404,868
Free State	2,745,590
Gauteng	12,272,263
Western Cape	5,822,734
Total	**51,770,560**

Source: Statistics South Africa

Overall approximately 54 per cent of the population lives in urban areas and 46 per cent in rural areas.

Births, Marriages, Deaths
Estimated figures for 2011 show that 1,059,417 live births were recorded and 591,366 deaths. The crude birth rate in 2011 was estimated to be 21.0 with a total fertility rate of 2.35. The crude death rate was estimated to be 11.7. The high death rate takes into consideration that an estimated 16.6 per cent of adults have AIDS or are HIV positive. In 2011 around 257,910 deaths were from AIDS. Average life expectancy was estimated in 2011 at 54.9 years for males and 59.1 years for females. Approximately 31.3 per cent of the population is aged less than 14 years and approximately 7.7 per cent aged over 60 years.

Marriages in 2010 numbered an estimated 170,826, whilst divorces in 2006 numbered 31,270. In 1998 the Recognition of Customary Marriage Act was passed, giving recognition of marriages entered into in accordance with traditional and customary laws. The act introduces measures which protect the women and children in these marriages by bringing customary law in line with the constitution and international obligations.

The infant mortality rate was estimated at 37.9 per 1,000 live births in 2011, and the under-five mortality rate at 54.3 per 1,000 live births. The 2009 fertility rate was 2.38 children per female. (Source: Statistics South Africa)

Public Holidays 2014
1 January: New Year's Day
21 March: Human Rights Day
18 April: Good Friday
20 April: Easter Sunday
21 April: Family Day (usually the Monday after Easter Sunday)
27 April: Freedom Day
1 May: Workers' Day
2 May: Workers Day additional holiday
16 June: Youth Day
9 August: National Women's Day
24 September: Heritage Day
16 December: Day of Reconciliation
25 December: Christmas Day
26 December: Day of Goodwill
When a public holiday falls on a Sunday it is celebrated on the following Monday.

EMPLOYMENT

In 1998 the Employment Equity Act was introduced. This Act makes certain employment policies and practices, which do not discriminate on the basis of race, sex, disability, marital status, sexual orientation, religion and culture, compulsory. Companies who do comply with the Act may tender for government contracts, whilst those who do not face heavy fines.

The total population of working age in 2011 was 32,555,000. The labour force was estimated at 17,761,000 and the number of employed was 13,318,000. Estimated figures for 2011 put the unemployment rate at 25.0 per cent. The total population of working age in March 2012 was estimated at 32,786,000. The labour force was estimated at 17,948,000 and the number of employed was 13,422,000. Estimated figures for March 2012 put the unemployment rate at 25.2 per cent. (Source: Statistics South Africa)

The following table shows employment in recent years according to selected industry:

Total Employment by Economic Activity

Occupation	2008
Agriculture, hunting, forestry & fishing	776,000
Mining & quarrying	328,000
Manufacturing	1,961,000
Electricity, gas & water supply	94,000
Construction	1,141,000
Wholesale & retail trade, repairs, hotels & restaurants	3,141,000
Transport, storage & communications	767,000
Financial intermediation, real estate, renting & business activities	1,646,000
Public admin. & defence; compulsory social security, education, health & social work, other community service activities	2,624,000

- continued

Households with employed persons	1,232,000
Other	3,000

Source: Copyright © International Labour Organization (ILO Dept. of Statistics, http://laborsta.ilo.org)

BANKING AND FINANCE

Following the transition to a democratic, non-racial government in 1990, the government looked to achieve sustained economic growth whilst also addressing the economic imbalances caused by apartheid. A Reconstruction and Development Program (RDP) was set up with this aim and is still supported by various ministries. The government has faced enormous economic challenges. In 2001 the Black Economic Empowerment Commission was started in an effort to redress the imbalance in the distribution of wealth and company ownership. A strategy dubbed Gear (after Growth, Employment and Redistribution) was introduced for the period 1996-2000 which would start a programme of privatisation and commitments to open markets. Privatisation has proved unpopular with the unions and large demonstrations and strikes were held in 2006 in protest against the restructuring of the state owned transport system, many felt that privatisation would lead to more companies being transferred into the control of whites and the 'black-elite'.

The Gear strategy has had mixed results. The economy is still suffering the after-effects of the apartheid era and poverty and a lack of economic empowerment remain. The economy is also hampered by poor infrastructure. An estimated 50 per cent of the population are still believed to be below the poverty line. However, growth was relatively strong between 2004 and 2008, but suffered in 2009 because of the global economic crisis. The government has said that it was facing its worst recession for 17 years. In the first quarter of 2009 the economy contracted by 6.4 per cent and by 3 per cent in the second quarter. However, growth returned in 2010, 2011 and 2012.

South Africa is a member of the BRICS club (Brazil, Russia, India, China and South Africa) of emerging world economic powerhouses.

Currency
One Rand (R) = 100 cents

GDP/GNP, Inflation, National Debt
Economic indicators have persuaded the World Bank, among a number of international financial institutions, to praise the South African economy. The country received investor-grade status from Standard and Poor's and Moody's Investor Service in 2000.

Real GDP at market prices increased by 2.9 per cent in 2010, by 3.5 per cent in 2011 and 2.5 per cent in 2012. Nominal GDP in 2012 was R238 billion up on the 2011 figure of R3 trillion which was up by R303 billion from 2010. The structure of GDP in 2012 was as follows: finance, real estate and business services 21.5 per cent; general government 16.6 per cent; wholesale, retail and motro trade, catering and accommodation 16.0 per cent; and the manufacturing industry 12.4 per cent.

The following table shows GDP according to industry in recent years at constant 2005 prices in R millions:

Industry	2010	2011
Agriculture, forestry, fishing	41,701	41,553
Mining and quarrying	99,223	99,415
Manufacturing	282,215	289,015
Electricity, gas and water	34,287	34,749
Construction	57,781	58,241
Wholesale, retail & motor trade, catering & accommodation	224,653	234,630
Transport, storage and communications	167,283	172,733
Finance, real estate, business	386,745	400,382
General Gov. services	248,817	258,405
Personal services	101,127	103,601
TOTAL GDP (Market Prices)	1,838,264	1,895,668

* sum of four quarters
Source: Statistics South Africa

Inflation in 2010 was recorded at 4.3 per cent and 5.0 per cent in 2011. It was estimated at 6.1 per cent in February 2012.

The public sector's borrowing requirement was reduced from 10.4 per cent of GDP in 1993 to 3.3 per cent in 1998. General government revenue amounted to 32 per cent of GDP in 1998 and was predicted to fall to 30.7 per cent of GDP in 2001. Further government expenditure fell from 38.1 per cent in 1996 to 36.1 per cent in 1998. South Africa's total debt in 1999 amounted to R364 billion which is 55 per cent of GDP. Figures for 2008 show that total debt had fallen and was 28 per cent of GNI.

Balance of Payments / Imports and Exports
As from January 1999 VAT became payable on all goods imported from neighbouring countries which secured an additional R2.6 million in revenue on imports. Other economic reforms include reducing the role of the government in the economy, encouraging investment, reduction of tariffs and export subsidies. A new competition law was passed in 1999.

Exports were estimated at US$85.8 billion in 2010 and imports were estimated at US$81.8 billion. South Africa's major trading partners are Japan, Germany, Italy, the United Kingdom, and the United States, China, East Asian and Sub Saharan countries.

South Africa's major export is gold, followed by coal and then other metals and minerals. Although South Africa still relies heavily on the export of primary and intermediate products, manufactured goods still account for 70 per cent of exports. Main imported goods include transport equipment, petroleum products, machinery and chemicals.

Central Bank
South African Reserve Bank, PO Box 427, Pretoria 0002, South Africa. E-mail: info@resbank.co.za, URL: http://www.resbank.co.za
Governor: Ms Gill Marcus (page 1471)

Chambers of Commerce and Trade Organisations
Cape Chamber of Commerce and Industry, URL: http://www.ccci.co.za
Durban Chamber of Commerce, URL: http://www.durbanchamber.co.za/site/home
Johannesburg Chamber of Commerce and Industry, URL: http://www.jcci.co.za/
South African Chamber of Business (SACOB), URL: http://www.sacob.co.za

MANUFACTURING, MINING AND SERVICES

Primary and Extractive Industries
South Africa is a worldwide leader in the production and supply of a wide range of minerals, such as gold, coal, the platinum-group metals (PGM), diamonds, iron ore, copper, manganese ore, titanium, zirconium, asbestos, chrome ore and vanadium. The country also has substantial reserves of other industrially important metals and minerals and the mining sector is its largest foreign exchange earner. There are over 700 mines employing over 466,000 people. Total income from the mining industry in 2009 was R437,200 million. The largest contribution came from the mining of coal and lignite (R123,975 million, 28 per cent), followed by mining of platinum group metal ore (R106,362 million , 24 per cent) and mining of gold and uranium ore (R53,552 million, 12 per cent). Total value of mineral sales in 2011 including gold (actual indices) was R370,573 million, up from R300,686 million in 2010.

The country has recoverable coal reserves estimated at 33 billion short tons in 2008. Total coal production in 2010 was 280 million short tons consumption was 206 million short tons. . Major coal fields are located in Waterberg, Witbank and Highveld.

South African proven oil reserves were estimated at 0.02 billion barrels in 2012. Total oil production in 2011 was estimated at 183,140 barrels per day, of which crude 4,000 bbl/d. Oil consumption in 2010 was an estimated 610,000 barrels per day, with net oil imports at 426,860 barrels per day (mainly from Saudi Arabia and Iran) to make up the shortfall between production and consumption. South Africa has a crude oil refining capacity of 485,000 barrels per day.

Natural gas production amounted to 45,000 billion cubic feet in 2011. Consumption was estimated to be 162,000 billion cubic feet. Imports amounted to 117,000 billion cubic feet.

Energy
South Africa had a 2010 electricity generation capacity estimated at 241 billion kWh. Electricity consumption in 2010 was an estimated 214 billion kWh. South Africa has a nationwide electrification rate of 75 per cent (88 per cent in urban areas). The country suffers from a poor energy infrastructure. The government's 2010 electricity strategy plans reforms of the distribution structure and investment in new power projects to increase capacity by over 40,000 MW by 2030. In the short term three coal-fired power stations have been recommissioned, there are plans for a new coal-fired plant and a 3,500 MW nuclear power station. The state electricity company is Eskom (URL: http://www.eskom.co.za/live/index.ph).

South Africa's nuclear power programme is aimed at self-sufficiency; it has 14 per cent of the western world's uranium reserves and ranks second in such reserves after Australia. It is also the largest producer in the West. In 2008, nuclear energy accounted for 2.5 per cent of South Africa's energy.

An estimated 0.1 per cent of South Africa's energy comes from hydro sources and 10.4 per cent from combustible, renewables and waste. (Source: EIA)

Industry consumes nearly 50 per cent of the country's energy followed by households and transportation which almost consume the remaining 50 per cent.

The South African government is incestigating green energy initiatives. Under the Integrated Resource Plan 2010, there is a 20 year projection on electricity demand and production and that about 42 per cent of electricity generated must come from renewable resources.

Manufacturing
Manufacturing is South Africa's largest contributor to its Gross State Product. The following table shows the value of sales by manufacturing divisions. Figures are in R millions:

Division	2010	2011
Food & beverages	248,529	270,534
Textiles, clothing, leather & footwear	39,304	39,157
Wood & wood products, paper & printing	106,469	111,054
Petroleum, chemical products, rubber & plastic goods	280,738	327,052
Glass & non-metallic mineral products	40,233	42,524
Basic iron & steel, metal products & machinery	283,445	306,476
Electrical machinery	39,094	41,524
Radio, TV & communication apparatus	13,829	15,336
Motor vehicles, parts & other transport equipment	161,651	173,977
Other manufacturing divisions	54,874	59,138

SOUTH AFRICA

- continued

Total	1,268,166	1,386,772

Source: Statistics South Africa

Tourism

Recent figures show that over 11.5 million foreign visitors arrived in South Africa in 2010. Tourism makes up 4.6 per cent of GDP and approximately 550,000 people are employed in the industry. Total income from the industry was R20,123.8 million (E) in 2010.

Ecotourism is the fastest growing area of tourism in South Africa.

South African Tourism Board (SATOUR), URL: http://www.southafrica.net

Agriculture

Agriculture contributes 4.1 per cent to the country's GDP. Thirteen per cent of the employed population work in agriculture. Figures for 2002 show that South Africa had 45,818 farming units.

South Africa has introduced the The Land and Agrarian Reform Project (LARP), among the projects aims are speeding up agricultural reform; redistributing five million hectares of previously white owned agricultural land to new producers, and increasing the level of agricultural support. Land had changed hands on a 'willing buyer, willing seller' basis, but officals have indicated that large scale expropriations may be the way forward. The government aims to transfer 30 per cent of farmland to black South Africans by 2014.

Agricultural Production in 2010

Produce	Int. $'000*	Tonnes
Indigenous cattle meat	2,176,836	805,825
Indigenous chicken meat	2,098,679	1,473,370
Maize	1,203,858	12,815,000
Cow milk, whole, fresh	908,548	3,233,000
Grapes	720,986	1,261,310
Sugar cane	525,904	16,015,600
Indigenous pigmeat	519,588	338,000
Hen eggs, in shell	392,301	473,000
Indigenous sheep meat	361,885	132,909
Apples	306,288	724,232
Potatoes	304,911	2,090,210
Oranges	273,381	1,414,590

* unofficial figures

Source: http://faostat.fao.org/site/339/default.aspx FAOSTAT, Statistics Division, Food and Agriculture Organization of the UN

Gross Value of Horticulture Production in 2007

Produce	R'000
Viticulture	2,907,086
Citrus fruit	5,013,038
Subtropical fruit	1,689,069
Deciduous & other fruit	5,755,887
Vegetables	5,476,294
Potatoes	3,405,277
Other	1,437,148
Total	25,683,799

Source: Pocket Guide to South Africa

Gross Value of Animal Products in 2007

Produce	R'000
Wool	1,312,768
Poultry & poultry prodcuts	20,409,362
Cattle & cattle products	12,689,536
Sheep & goats slaughtered	2,296,452
Pigs slaughtered	2,247,136
Milk	7,565,475
Other	2,446,444
Total	48,967,173

Source: Pocket Guide to South Africa

South Africa is virtually self-sufficient in its timber needs and has one of the world's largest man-made forestry resources. It has been a net exporter of forest products since 1985 and net exports were valued at R1.6 billion (6.7 per cent of overall exports) in 1997. The annual turnover of in 1997 was R13 billion. Of the 1,518,138 ha of plantations, 53 per cent were pine, 39 per cent eucalyptus, 7 per cent wattle and 1 per cent various other species. Imports now consist mainly of specialised timber products such as hardwood sleepers, certain types of high-quality paper, and hardwood furniture wood and accessories.

In 1997 the private sector owned 70 per cent of the total plantation area, with 1,800 private timber growers and more than 11,000 unregistered growers. There are 148 primary wood processing plants of which the private sector own 136. Wood is the primary source of fuel for about 12 million rural and urban dwellers.

COMMUNICATIONS AND TRANSPORT

Travel Requirements

Citizens of the USA, Canada, Australia and the EU require a passport valid for thirty days beyond the date of departure, with at least two blank pages (not including endorsement pages) for entry stamps. A visa is not needed by most of the above-mentioned citizens for stays of up to 90 days, the exceptions being nationals of Cyprus, Hungary, Poland and Slovak Republic who may stay for up to 30 days without a visa, and nationals of Bulgaria, Estonia, Latvia, Lithuania, Romania and Slovenia who do require a visa. Transit passengers holding onward documentation and not leaving the airport do not need a visa.

Visitors from countries where yellow fever is endemic are often required to present their yellow World Health Organization (WHO) vaccination record or other proof of inoculation. If they are unable to do so, they must be inoculated at the airport.

Transport System

The public company Transnet was founded in April 1990 and is a rail, port and pipeline company. Its transport businesses include: Transnet freight rail (formerly Spoornet), Transnet pipelines (formerly Petronet), Transnet national port authority and Transport port terminals. SAA left the Transnet group in 2006.
Transnet, URL: http://www.transnet.net

National Airlines

South African Airways (SAA), the national carrier, is a member of the International Air Transport Association (IATA) and operates a comprehensive network of services. It flies to over 30 international destinations. Flights began to Beijing in January 2012.
South African Airways, URL: http://www.flysaa.com/gb/en/

International Airports

Currently there are over 30 airports dealing with international flights but the intention is to reduce the number to eight to assist with the control of imports and exports. Major airports include Or Tambo (formerly Johannesburg), Durban and Cape Town. Or Tambo International is the country's busiest airports and deals with over 13 million passengers per year.
Airports Company South Africa, URL: http://www.acsa.co.za/index.asp

Railways

Recent figures show that there are over 31,700 km of railway lines, 3,500 locomotives and 124,000 trucks and carriages in South Africa. The rail service is utilised mainly for the transport of goods and containers. General freight accounts for 70 per cent of Spoornet's turnover. Figures for 2011 show that 691 million tons of freight was carried by rail in 2011.

Spoornet operates one of the most luxurious passenger trains, called the Blue Train, which operates between Pretoria and Cape Town, Pretoria and Victoria Falls (Zimbabawe), and Cape Town and Port Elizabeth. There are also several other passenger trains which operate between the main centres, namely: Trans Karoo, Algoa, Amatola, Bosvelder, Bulwayo, Diamond Express and Komati.
Spoornet, URL: http://www.spoornet.co.za

Roads

Currently there are 7,000 km of national roads of which 1,440 km are dual carriage highway, 290 km single carriage highway and 4,400 km single carriage main roads. Vehicles drive on the left. National roads are maintained and built by the government while the building and maintenance of provincial bridges and roads is the responsibility of the provincial governments. Municipal roads, those within the municipal boundaries of towns and cities, are maintained by the municipality concerned.

Toll roads cover about 1,000 km and the toll fees are collected by 21 toll-plazas. Private investors are being encouraged to play an active role in the financing, building, operating and maintaining of toll roads through the Build, Operate and Transfer (BOT) mechanism. The BOT scheme does have a concession period of 30 years after which the facility must be transferred back to the state at no cost.

Shipping

The Transnet national ports authority manages South Africa's eight commercial harbours. As harbour authority, it endeavours to promote national and international trade by providing the necessary port infrastructure. The ports include: Richards Bay, which is the largest, has the world's biggest bulk coal terminal and handles 53 per cent of South Africa's total tonnage of cargo; Durban, which has the largest capacity in Africa and deals with more than 70 per cent of the country's container traffic; East London, which is the only river port; Ngqura, Port Elizabeth; Mossel Bay; Cape Town and Saldanha, which is the largest port on the west coast of Africa. Durban, Port Elizabeth and Cape Town have large container terminals for deep-sea and coastal container traffic.

HEALTH

Forty per cent of South Africa's population live in poverty. Of these, 75 per cent have not got access to health services.

Several policies have already been implemented to restructure and develop the health service including free health care to children under the age of six, and pregnant mothers. Primary health services are now free at the point of delivery and offer immunisation, communicable and endemic disease prevention, maternity care, screening of children and family planning. Services have been decentralised and a drug policy has been introduced to improve access and the quality and affordability of services.

There are about 6,676 foreign doctors working in South Africa to try and relieve the shortage of skilled doctors. Further, all newly qualified interns are required to do a year's compulsory community service in a state hospital and only upon completion of the year will they be granted permission to register with the Health Professions Council of South Africa (HPCSA). Latest figures from the World Health Organisation show that in 2000-10, South Africa has 34,829 physicians, 184,459 nurses and midwives, 5,995 dentists, 12,521 pharmacists, and 2,529 environment and public health workers. In 2009, the government spent 11.9 per cent of its total budget on health expenditure, accounting for 51 per cent of total expenditure. Private expenditure accounts for 41 per cent of total health care expenditure. Total expenditure amounted to 7.5 per cent of GDP. Per capita expenditure amounted to US$521.

HIV/AIDS and TB are South Africa's biggest killers. In November 2003, the Government approved a programme of education about HIV/AIDS a topic that has been taboo in South Africa. In 2008 there were 138,803 reported cases of TB. In 2007, over 3.2 million people were infected with HIV/AIDS, with an estimated 1,500 new infections every day of which over 50 per cent are amongst the age group 15 to 24. Current official estimates suggest that 21 per cent of people aged under 20 are HIV+, 26 per cent of those aged 25-29, 19 per cent of those aged 30-34, 13 per cent of those aged 35-39, 10 per cent of those aged 40-44, and 10 per cent of those aged 45-49. It's estimated that by 2010 over 5 million people will have died from AIDS. In 2011, the number of new HIV infections among the population aged 15 years and older was estimated at 316,900. An estimated 63,600 new HIV infections will be among children aged 0-14 years. Approximately 20 per cent of women of reproductive age are estimated to be HIV positive. In 2011 an estimated 1,058,399 people aged 15 and over were receiving ART (Anti retroviral Therapy) that year an estimated 150,123 children were receiving ART. (Source: Statistics South Africa).

According to the latest WHO figures, in 2010 approximately 91 per cent of the population had access to improved drinking water. In the same year, 79 per cent of the population had access to improved sanitation.

The infant mortality rate (probability of dying before first birthday) in 20109 was 41 per 1,000 live births. The child mortality rate (under 5 years) was 57 per 1,000 live births. The main causes of childhood mortality are: HIV/AIDs (28 per cent), prematurity (163 per cent), diarrhoea (5 per cent), and pneumonia (11 per cent). (Source: http://www.who.int, World Health Statistics 2012)

EDUCATION

According to the constitution, all South Africans have the right to a basic education, including adult basic education and further education. Decisions on all aspects of education are taken by the Ministry of Education which was established in May 1994, while overall responsibility is vested in the Department of Education, which acts through several departments. School attendance is compulsory for all children between the ages of seven and fifteen years. The majority of pre-schools are privately funded and are required to register with their local authority.

The government's latest strategy (Action Plan to 2014: Towards the Realisation of Schooling 2025) aims to improve learning and the work of teachers. A new curriculum with a focus on literacy and numeracy has been developed. The new curriculum has specific guidelines on what is to be taught in schools, aiming to close the gap between well-resourced and poor schools. Other reforms include standardised assessments of certain grades, an emphasis on early child development, improvements to the school infrastructure and better school management. The education of the poorest remains a priority. No-fee schools have been identified and the state should provide complete funding so that no fees charged. Additionally a National Schools Nutrition Programme should provide more than 7 million school children with a cooked meal five days a week.

Figures from Statistics South Africa show that in 2010 there were 12.64 million pupils and students enrolled in all sectors of the education system, attending 30,586 educational institutions. There were 439,394 teachers and lectureres. According to the figures there were 25,850 ordinary schools and 4,736 other education institutions (early childhood development centres and special schools). Over 93 per cent of enrolled learners were in public schools. Of the 25,850 ordinary schools there were 14,456 primary schools with 5.99 million pupils and 187,520 teachers. There were 6,231 secondary schools with 3.8 million pupils and 142,181 teachers and 5,163 combined and intermediate schools, with 2,445,473 puils and 88,408 teachers. The average pupil to teacher ration is 29.3 to one.

Higher Education
There are 23 state-funded tertiary institutions including 11 universities, six technology universities and six comprehensive institutions. There are also new institutes of higher education, the Northern Cape National Institute for Higher Education and the Mpumalanga National Institute for Higher Education. Approximately 893,000 pupils were enrolled in higher education in 2010. There were also 88 private registered institutions.

According to latest UNESCO figures, 88.0 per cent of adults are literate (88.9 per cent of males and 87.2 per cent of females). For young people (age 15-24) this rises to 95.4 per cent (94.6 per cent for males and 96.3 per cent for females).

RELIGION

There is no State Church in South Africa. In terms of religious affiliation South Africa is a plural community. It is estimated that about 80 per cent of the population follow a Christian denomination, with Muslims, Hindus and Jews making up the rest of the population. The African Independent Churches is the largest group of Christian churches, with over 4,000 independent churches and ten million members. The Dutch Reformed churches have a following of about 3.5 million and about 1,200 congregations country wide, making it the second largest church group in South Africa. The Roman Catholic Church has grown in numbers over the past few years and is working closely with many other churches. Other established churches are the Methodist, Anglican, Lutheran, Presbyterian, Congregational, Baptist, Apostolic Faith Mission, Assemblies of God and Full Gospel Church. Approximately eight million people are African traditionalists.

Archbishop Emeritus: Most Revd Desmond Mpilo Tutu (page 1528)

South Africa has a religious liberty rating of 8 on a scale of 1 to 10 (10 is most freedom). (Source: World Religion Database)

COMMUNICATIONS AND MEDIA

The constitution provides for freedom of expression and this is generally respected by the authorities. The media carries criticism of the government.

Newspapers
In addition to the main national newspapers: the Sunday Times, Rapport and The Sunday Independent there are several weekly and regional papers. The majority of newspapers are published in English and Afrikaans. It is estimated that 4.6 million adults read daily newspapers, 8.6 million weekly newspapers and 8.8 million magazines. (Source: CSS)
Times / Sunday Times, http://www.thetimes.co.za/home.aspx
Beeld, URL: http://www.news24.com/Beeld/Home
Sowetan, URL: http://www.sowetan.co.za
The Star, URL: http://www.thestar.co.za

Broadcasting
Commercial TV networks broadcast alongside state-run networks. Satellite and cable pay-TV services have hundreds of thousands of subscribers. The South African Broadcasting Corporation (SABC) has financial difficulties. It currently operates four TV stations (thre free to air). The private E-tv station broadcast to at least 50 per cent of the country. Community radio stations are becoming increasingly popular and there are currently about 100 stations.
South African Broadcasting Corporation (SABC), URL: http://www.sabc.co.za/
E-tv, URL: http://www.etv.co.za/
M-Net, URL: http://beta.mnet.co.za/ (pay TV)

Telecommunications
The telecommunications system is the most developed in the region. There are currently an estimated 4 million installed telephones and 4.3 million exchange lines and 45 million mobile phones. In 2010, there were over 4 million internet users.

ENVIRONMENT

Environmental programmes form a substantial part of the Reconstruction and Development Programme (RDP).

South Africa is semi-arid and water is in short supply. Average annual rainfall is a little less than 500mm, in comparison to the world's average of approximately 860mm. The problem is intensified as water usage is increasing. Deforestation is also a major problem because the most widely used renewable source of energy is wood and there is evidence of desertification and acid rain.

Formally protected areas of land account for 5.5 per cent of the surface area of the country. There are 422 terrains within which fauna and flora are conserved, ecologically degraded areas are restored and water catchment areas are protected. If rock art or other historic buildings are sited in the terrains these are also preserved.

Carbon emissions for 2000 were estimated to be 2.4 metric tons per capita. Since 1996 the price of unleaded fuel has been cut, and all new cars must now run on unleaded petrol. In 2000 almost three-quarters of total energy consumption was coal. In 2010, South Africa's emissions from the consumption of fossil fuels totalled 465.10 million metric tons of carbon dioxide.

South Africa is a party to the following international agreements: Antarctic-Environmental Protocol, Antarctic-Marine Living Resources, Antarctic Seals, Antarctic Treaty, Biodiversity, Climate Change, Climate Change-Kyoto Protocol, Desertification, Endangered Species, Hazardous Wastes, Law of the Sea, Marine Dumping, Marine Life Conservation, Ozone Layer Protection, Ship Pollution, Wetlands, Whaling.

SPACE PROGRAMME

The Council for Scientific and Industrial Research (CSIR) is one on the leading scientific and research organisations in Africa. Its satellite applications centre is based in Pretoria. The establishment of the country's first space agency - with responsibility for coordinating the use of space technology and local space science research was approved in 2006.
CSIR, URL: http://www.csir.co.za/SAC/index.html

STATES OF THE WORLD

SOUTH AFRICA

EASTERN CAPE

Capital: Bisho

CONSTITUTION AND GOVERNMENT

The legislature consists of 63 members.
Eastern Cape Provincial Legislature, URL: http://www.eclegislature.gov.za/

Executive Council (as at June 2013)
Premier: Noxolo Kiviet
MEC for Economic Development and Environmental Affairs: Mcebisi Jonas
MEC for Finance & Provincial Planning: Phumulo Masualle
MEC for Health: Sicelo Gqobana
MEC for Human Settlements, Safety and Liaison: Helen August-Sauls
MEC for Local Government & Traditional Affairs: Milbo Qhoboshiane
MEC for Rural Development and Agrarian Reform: Zoleka Capa
MEC for Public Works, Roads & Transport: Thandiswa Lynette Marawu
MEC for Education & Training: Mandla Makupula
MEC for Social Development, Women, Children & People with Disabilities: Pemmy Majodina
MEC for Sport, Recreation, Arts & Culture: Xoliswa Tom

Speaker: Fikile Xasa

Ministries
Government portal: http://www.ecprov.gov.za/
Office of the Premier, Independence Avenue, Legislative Building, First Floor, Bisho (Private Bag X0047 Bisho 5605), Eastern Cape, South Africa. Tel: +27 (40) 609 2207, fax: +27 (40) 635 1166,
URL: http://www.ecprov.gov.za/premier/index.html
Department of Economic Affairs, Environment and Tourism, Private Bag X0029, Bisho 5605, Eastern Cape, South Africa. Tel: +27 40 609 4889/90, URL: http://gis.ecprov.gov.za/Environmental_Affairs/default.aspx
Department of Finance, Private Bag X0029, Bisho 5605, Eastern Cape, South Africa. Tel: +27 (40) 609 4889/90, URL: http://www.ectreasury.gov.za/
Department of Health, Private Bag X0038, Bisho 5605, Eastern Cape, South Africa. Tel: +27 (40) 609 3700, URL: http://www.ecdoh.gov.za/
Department of Sport, Recreation, Arts and Culture, Private Bag X0020, Bisho 5605, Eastern Cape, South Africa. Tel: +27 (40) 609 5879/5833
Department of Roads and Public Works, Private Bag X0022, Bisho 5605, Eastern Cape, South Africa. Tel: +27 (40) 636 4327
Department of Agrarian Reform, URL:http://www.agr.ecprov.gov.za/
Department of Education, Private Bag X0032, Bisho 5605, Eastern Cape, South Africa. Tel: +27 (40) 608 4202, URL: http://www.ecdoe.gov.za/
Department of Transport, Private Bag X0023, Bisho 5605, Eastern Cape, South Africa. Tel: +27 (40) 609 2136, URL: http://www.ectransport.gov.za/
Department of Social Development, Private Bag X0038, Bisho 5605, Eastern Cape, South Africa. Tel: +27 (40) 609 3939/635 2935, URL: http://www.socdev.ecprov.gov.za/Pages/socialdevelopment.aspx
Department of Local Government and Housing, Private Bag X0026, Bisho 5605, Eastern Cape, South Africa. Tel: +27 (40) 639 4331

Elections
The most recent elections were held on 22 April 2009. The African National Congress Party (ANC) won 44 seats, the Democratic Alliance (DA) 6 seats, the Congress of the People nine seats, the United Democratic Movement three seats, and the African Independent Congress one seat. Municipal by-elections took place in March 2012. Full provincial elections are due in 2014.

AREA AND POPULATION

Area
The Eastern Cape is the second largest of the nine provinces, covering about 169,580 square km, or 13.9 per cent of South Africa's total area. The Eastern Cape borders with Kwa-Zulu Natal and Free State to the north, Northern Cape to the north-west, and Western Cape to the west. The Indian Ocean runs along its eastern border.

The Eastern Cape's climate can vary from arid conditions in the west to sub-tropical humid conditions in the east. Topographically, the province consists of 53 per cent sloping plateaux, 31 per cent mountains, 16 per cent irregular plains, and 5 per cent river valleys.

To view a map of the province, please consult http://www.un.org/Depts/Cartographic/map/profile/southafr.pdf

Population
According to recent Statistics South Africa estimates, the population of the Eastern Cape in 2011 was 6,652,052, (3,089,701 males, 3,472,353 females). Most of the population live in settlements within the former homelands of the Ciskei and Transkei. Population density varies from 99 people per sq. km to under three people per sq. km. Net migration for the period 2006-2011 has been estimated at -273,600.

IsiXhosa is spoken by 83.8 per cent of the population, Afrikaans 9.6 per cent, English 3.7 per cent, and SeSotho 2.2 per cent.

Births, Marriages, Deaths
In 2010 a total of 106,431 live births were recorded and 82,132 deaths in 2009. The total fertility rate for the period 2001-06 was put at 3.27, and projected to be 2.83 for the period 2006-11. The number of marriages recorded in 2010 was 22,329. The number of divorces in 2006 was 2,765. Life expectancy at birth is estimated at 50.3 years for males (53.5 years in South Africa as a whole) and 55 years for females (57.2 years in South Africa). (Source: Statistics South Africa)

EMPLOYMENT

Figures for the fourth quarter of 2012 show that the Eastern Cape had a labour force of 1,797,000 of which 1,261,000 were employed and 536,000 were unemployed giving an unemployment rate of 29.8 per cent. The following table shows recent employment figures:

Occupation	March 2011	March 2012
Agriculture	64,000	47,000
Mining & quarrying	-	-
Manufacturing	183,000	158,000
Utilities	-	-
Construction	120,000	108,000
Wholesale & retail trade	295,000	327,000
Transport, storage & communication	57,000	75,000
Finance	125,000	126,000
Community & social services	333,000	336,000
Private households	139,000	94,000
Total	1,325,000	1,279,000

Source: Statistics South Africa

Top international employers include Volkswagen, General Motors, DaimlerChrysler, Nestlé, Goodyear Tyres, and Cadbury's.

BANKING AND FINANCE

GDP/GNP, Inflation, National Debt
GDP in 2004 was R112,908 million compared to R45,333 million in 1995. Over the years 1995-2004, Eastern Cape contributed 8.1 per cent of South Africa's total GDP. Economic growth in Eastern Cape was put at 4.2 per cent in 2004 and 4.8 per cent in 2005.

GDP at current prices by contribution, 2004

Sector	%
Agriculture, forestry and fishing	1.9
Mining and quarrying	0.2
Manufacturing	16.5
Electricity, gas and water	1.1
Construction	1.7
Wholesale and retail trade; hotels and restaurants	13.1
Transport, storage and communication	7.9
Finance, real estate and business	19.4
Personal services	8.9
General government services	18.7

Source: Statistics South Africa

In the period 1995-2004, the construction industry sector had the highest growth rate (8.8 per cent), followed by finance, real estate and business industry (8.3 per cent) and utilities (8.1 per cent).

MANUFACTURING, MINING AND SERVICES

Energy
At present, electricity is supplied to 42 per cent of the Eastern Cape's properties, some 700,000 households. Targets for the year 2000 were the supply of electricity to 2.5 million households, as well as all schools and clinics. Figures for 2011 show that Eastern Cape consumed 9,710 gigawatt hours of electricity.

Manufacturing
The motor manufacturing industry is the Eastern Cape's largest industry. There are currently major American and German plants established in Port Elizabeth and East London, including Mercedes-Benz, Volkswagen, Ford and Delta. The main agro-industry is textiles, particularly wool.

Service Industries
The Eastern Cape's varied geography offers a range of tourist activities, including snow-skiing, water sports, and hiking. The Eastern Cape's many sandy beaches and lagoons are also a popular tourist attraction.

Agriculture
Fruits are predominantly grown in the Langkloof Valley. Chicory, coffee, tea, maize and sorghum are grown in the Eastern Cape and an olive nursery has recently been established. The cultivation of canola has also begun to develop biofuels. Cattle and sheep farming produce wool and dairy products and ostrich farms exist in parts of the province.

There are also extensive exotic forestry plantations which provide employment for a large number of the population. The main timber harvests include yellowwood and stinkwood, and are located in the province's mountain areas.

The fishing industry generates about R200 million a year while the squid industry generates an estimated R150 million annually and employs approximately 3,000 people.

COMMUNICATIONS AND TRANSPORT

Airports
There are four airports, at Port Elizabeth, East London, Umtata and Bulembu.

Ports and Harbours
There are two ports - Port Elizabeth and South Africa's only river port, East London - both of which have good harbour facilities.

Roads
Recent figures show that Eastern Cape has 6,930 km of paved roads and 42,439 km of gravel roads.

HEALTH

In 2004, there were 1,008 health facilities in Eastern Cape of which 683 were clinics. There were 63 district hospitals, 11 regional hospitals and 12 specialised hospitals. Other facilities include 27 community healthcare centres, 143 mobile services, 35 satellite clinics and 32 community health services. In 2004 approximately 26,000 people were employed in the health sector. Of the 6,505,000 population in Eastern Cape only 606,000 had medical aid in 2004.

According to official figures, in 2002 the HIV prevalence rate was 23.6 per cent. An estimated 23.6 per cent of pregnant women were infected by HIV. The HIV prevalence rate in the 20-24 age group was estimated at 33.1 per cent, and 31.8 per cent in the 25-29 age group. An estimated 12.4 per cent of the population aged less than 20 were infected with HIV. There was a cholera outbreak in 2002 resulting in 45 deaths. This fell to 38 reported deaths in 2003 and seven in 2004. (Source: Statistics South Africa)

EDUCATION

There are five universities, three technikons and 20 technical colleges. Figures for 2001 show the number of full-time students at primary schools at 627,602, secondary schools at 397,614 and combined schools at 1,002,575. Approximately 20.9 per cent of adults over the age of 20 have received no formal education and 4.7 per cent have completed a higher level education. State schools or public schools are government funded and there are some private schools.

COMMUNICATIONS AND MEDIA

Telecommunications
According to 1997 statistics, the Eastern Cape had 26,000 telephone lines. However, many areas have fewer than four telephones per 1,000 people. Some R400 million was invested in the Eastern Cape's telecommunications system in fiscal year 1997-98.

ENVIRONMENT

Nearly half of the Eastern Cape's population do not have access to basic potable water supplies; just over 80 per cent do not have access to the World Health Organisation's (WHO) minimum requirement of seven litres of potable water per day; and 87 per cent do not have basic sanitation. However, R550 million has been allocated towards nearly 330 projects which are aimed at providing the province with adequate potable water supplies. Some 1.9 million people in nearly 2,000 villages and 77 districts will benefit.

FREE STATE

Capital: Bloemfontein (Population estimate: 584,000)

CONSTITUTION AND GOVERNMENT

Executive Council (as at June 2013)
Premier: Ace Magashule
MEC for Economic Development, Tourism and Environmental Affairs: Mamiki Qabathe
MEC for Education: P.H.I. Makgoe
MEC for the Treasury: Seeiso Mohai
MEC for Public Works: E.S. Mabe
MEC for Co-operative Governance, Traditional Leadership and Human Settlements: Olly Mlamleli
MEC for Police, Roads and Transport: Thabo Manyoni
MEC for Health: Dr. Benjamin Malakoane
MEC for Sports, Arts, Culture & Recreation: D.A.M. Khothule
MEC for Social Development: Sefora Sisi Ntombela
MEC for Agriculture and Rural Development: M.J. Zwane

Ministries
Government portal, URL: http://www.fsl.gov.za
Department of Health Services, PO Box 264, Bloemfontein, 9300, South Africa. Tel: +27 (0)51 405 5703
Department of Social Development, PO Box 264, Bloemfontein, 9300, South Africa. Tel: +27 (0)51 405 5000
Department of Local Government and Housing, PO Box 264, Bloemfontein, 9300, South Africa. Tel: +27 (0)51 405 5304/5730
Department of Sport, Arts, Culture, Science and Technology, PO Box 264, Bloemfontein, 9300, South Africa. Tel: +27 (0)51 403 3080
Department of Agriculture, Private Bag X02, Bloemfontein, 9300, South Africa. Tel: +27 (0)51 448 3011
Department of Public Safety, Security and Liaison, PO Box 119, Bloemfontein, 9300, South Africa. Tel: +27 (0)51 409 8849
Department of Tourism, Environmental and Economic Affairs, Private Bag X20801, Bloemfontein, 9300, South Africa. Tel: +27 (0)51 400 4904
Department of Transport, Roads and Public Works, PO Box 264, Bloemfontein, 9300, South Africa. Tel: +27 (0)51 405 5298
Department of Finance, Private Bag X20537, Bloemfontein, 9300, South Africa. Tel: +27 (0)51 405 4141/5737
Department of Education, PO Box 264, Bloemfontein, 9300, South Africa. Tel: +27 (0)51 404 8411

Elections
The most recent elections were held in April 2009. The African National Congress Party won 22 seats, the Democratic Alliance Party won three seats, the Congress of the People won 4 seats and the Vryheidsfront Plus Party won one seat.

AREA AND POPULATION

Area
The Free State (formerly the Orange Free State) borders six of the nine South African provinces in the heart of the country. Northern Cape and North West are to the west, Eastern Cape to the south, Kwa-Zulu Natal to the west, and Mpumalanga and Gauteng to the north. The Free State is the third largest province, covering an area of 129,480 square km or 10.6 per cent of the total land area in South Africa.

To view a map of the province, please consult http://www.un.org/Depts/Cartographic/map/profile/southafr.pdf

Population
Although the third largest province in South Africa, the Free State has the second lowest population with 2,745,590 inhabitants in 2011. The province's capital, Bloemfontein, has an estimated 583,900 inhabitants. The main language is Sesotho (spoken by 62.1 per cent of the population) followed by Afrikaans (14.5 per cent) and Isi Xhosa (9.4 per cent).

Births, Marriages, Deaths
Figures for 2010 show that 50,678 live births were recorded, 47,265 deaths were recorded in 2009. Life expectancy at birth is estimated at 48.5 years for males (the second lowest of all the South African provinces) and 52 years for females (the lowest of all the South African provinces), compared with the national average of 53.5 years for males and 57.2 years for females. Infant mortality, according to recent statistics, is 45 deaths per 1,000 live births. In 2010 there were 11,905 marriages and 1,711 divorces in 2006. The total fertility rate was estimated at 2.76 in the period 2001-06, and forecast to be 2.51 in the period 2006-2011. (Source: Statistics South Africa)

EMPLOYMENT

Figures for the fourth quarter of 2012 show that Free State had a labour force of 1,096,000 of which 732,000 were employed and 363,000 were unemployed giving an unemployment rate of 33.2 per cent. The following table shows recent employment figures:

Occupation	March 2011	March 2012
Agriculture	62,000	72,000
Mining & quarrying	21,000	28,000
Manufacturing	63,000	54,000
Utilities	-	-
Construction	56,000	47,000
Wholesale & retail trade	167,000	160,000
Transport, storage & communications	36,000	27,000
Finance	80,000	70,000
Community & social services	199,000	181,000
Private households	90,000	92,000
Total	780,000	737,000
Source: Statistics South Africa

SOUTH AFRICA

BANKING AND FINANCE

GDP/GNP, Inflation, National Debt

Free State contributed 5.5 per cent to the South African economy in 2004. The average annual economic growth rate was 2.0 per cent. In 2004, the growth rate was 3.9 per cent in 2004, largely due to the growth in contributions by mining and quarrying (20.9 per cent).

Breakdown of GDP by sector, 2004

Sector	%	R Million
Agriculture	4.6	2,133
Mining and quarrying	10.9	5,426
Manufacturing	12.6	6,139
Electricity	2.8	1,652
Construction	1.2	880
Trade	10.3	6,395
Transport	7.5	4,831
Financial	15.8	8,845
Comm/soc./ personal services	10.3	5,804
General Gov. services	13.6	7,111

Source: Statistics South Africa

The Consumer Price Index (CPI) rose by 4.2 per cent over the period 2001-02, and by 1.2 per cent over the period December 2001 to January 2002. Source: Statistics South Africa)

MANUFACTURING, MINING AND SERVICES

Primary and Extractive Industries

The mining industry is the biggest employer. It is accountable for 22.6 per cent of the province's GDP and contributes about 16.5 per cent towards South Africa's total mineral output. The Free State Consolidated Goldfields are the largest gold mining fields, producing 82 per cent of the province's mineral production value and 30 per cent of South Africa's total gold production. Silver, uranium, diamonds and coal are also mined in the Free State.

Bituminous coal and diamonds are also mined in the province.

Energy

Figures for 2011 show that Free State consumed 8,804 gigawatt hours of electricity.

Manufacturing

Chemical production at the Sasol plant is the largest industry followed by the many industries which have developed around the production of chemicals from coal. Two of the largest asparagus canning factories are in the Free State. 14 per cent of the state's manufacturing is classed as high-technology industry.

Agriculture

Field crops constitute 60 per cent of the Free State's gross agricultural income and animal products around 30 per cent. Free State is known as the Granary of the Country. The main crops are soya, sorghum, sunflowers, asparagus and wheat. Approximately 40 per cent of the country's potato production and 90 per cent of the cherry production come from the Free State. Many of the farmers specialise in seed production. The Free State's cultivated land covers some 3.2 million ha, whilst natural veld and grazing cover 8.7 million ha.

COMMUNICATIONS AND TRANSPORT

Roads

The Free State's road network density is the third highest in South Africa. The major highway linking Gauteng and the Western and Eastern Cape passes through the Free State.

HEALTH

In 2003, there were 31 public hospitals in Free State. By type, the figures are as follows: 24 district hospitals with 2,072 beds; 5 regional/general hospitals with 1,930 beds; and one central hospital with 647 beds. There is also one psychiatric hospital with 864 beds. Primary healthcare facilities include 212 clinics, five community health centres, 78 mobile facilities, and three visiting points. An estimated 15 per cent of people are believed to be covered by medical aid.

Free State figures for child mortality rates are worse than the national rate. The infant mortality rate in 2002 was 53 per 1,000 compared to 45.0 per 1,000 for South Africa. An estimated 39.8 per cent of children aged 2 or under were stunted and 3.2 per cent were wasted.

According to a recent survey, HIV and AIDS prevalence was estimated at around 25 per cent in 2001, higher than the national average. The rate fell slightly in 2002. (Source: Statistics South Africa)

EDUCATION

Government expenditure on education in financial year 1997-98 was R2,758.84 million.

Figures for 2001 show that Free State had 344,787 students at primary school, 208,292 students at secondary school, 43,396 students at combined schools and 107,646 students at intermediate and middle schools. There is one university and a number of training institutes.

Over 16 per cent of people over the age of 20 have not received any formal education. The adult literacy rate is 62 per cent, according to recent figures.

GAUTENG

Capital: Johannesburg (Population estimate: 4,074,600)

Administrative Capital: Pretoria

CONSTITUTION AND GOVERNMENT

Executive Council (as at June 2013)
Premier: Ms Nomvula Paula Mokonyane
MEC for Finance: Mandla Gladstone Nkomfe
MEC for Economic Development: Nkosiphendule Kolisile
MEC for Education: Barbara Creecy
MEC for Health and Social Development: Anthony Hope
MEC for Community Safety: Nonhianhia Faith Mazibuko
MEC for Agriculture and Social Development: Nandi Mayathula-Khoza
MEC for Infrastructure Development: Qedani Mahlangu
MEC for Roads and Transport: Ismail Vadi
MEC for Sport, Recreation, Arts and Culture: Lebogang Maile
MEC for Local Government and Housing: Ntombi Mekgwe

Speaker: Lindiwe Maseko
Ministries
Government portal, URL: http://www.gautengonline.gov.za/Pages/default.aspx
Department of Agriculture & Rural Development, URL: http://www.gdard.gpg.gov.za
Department of Infrastructure Development, URL: http://www.did.gpg.gov.za
Department of Education, PO Box 7710, Johannesburg 2000, South Africa. Tel: +27 (0)11 355 0524, URL: http://www.finance.gpg.gov.za
Department of Economic Development, URL: http://www.ecodev.gpg.gov.za
Department of Housing & Local Government, URL: http://www.dlgh.gpg.gov.za
Department of Community Safety, PO Box 62440, Marshalltown, 2107, South Africa. Tel: +27 (0)11 355 1868, URL: http://www.gautsafety.gpg.gov.za
Department of Sports, Arts, Culture and Recreation, Private Bag X33, Johannesburg, 2000, South Africa. Tel: +27 (0)11 355 2504, URL: http://www.sacr.gpg.gov.za
Department of Roads & Transport, Private Bag X83, Marshalltown, 2107, South Africa. URL: http://www.roadsandtransport.gpg.gov.za
Department of Finance, URL: http://www.finance.gpg.gov.za
Department of Health, URL: http://www.healthandsocdev.gpg.gov.za

Elections

The most recent elections were held in April 2009. The African National Congress Party, (ANC) won 47 seats, the Democratic Alliance (DA) 16 seats, Congress of the People six seats, the Inkatha Freedom Party (IFP) one seat, the African Christian Democratic Party one seat, and the Vryheidsfront Plus one seat.

AREA AND POPULATION

Area

Gauteng (formerly Pretoria-Witwatersrand-Vereeniging) is South Africa's smallest province, bordering the Free State to the south, Mpumalanga to the east, North West to the west and the Northern Province to the north. It covers an area of 17,010 square km and makes up 1.4 per cent of South Africa's total land area.

To view a map of the province, please consult http://www.un.org/Depts/Cartographic/map/profile/southafr.pdf

Population

Gauteng is the most densely populated province in South Africa. The 2011 population was estimated at 12,272,263, of whom 6,189,875 were male and 6,082,388 were female. The population estimate takes into account additional deaths due to HIV/AIDS. Johannesburg has an estimated population of 4.07 million. Pretoria has a population estimated at 1.41 million. The main languages spoken are IsiZulu, Afrikaans and English. Approximately 97 per cent of the population lives in urban areas.

Births, Marriages, Deaths

Recorded live births in 2010 numbered 179,210, the number of deaths in 2009 was recorded at 114,729. Life expectancy at birth is 57.3 years for males (compared with the South African average of 53.5 years) and 60.8 for females (57.2 years for South Africa). The number of marriages in 2010 was 41,396, whilst divorces numbered 10,544 in 2006. The total fertility rate was estimated at 2.06 in the period 2001-06, and forecast to be 2.01 in the period 2006-2011. (Source: Statistics Africa)

EMPLOYMENT

Figures for the fourth quarter of 2012 show that Gauteng had a labour force of 5,477,000 of which 4,079,000 were employed and 1,062,000 were unemployed giving an unemployment rate of 20.7 per cent. The following table shows recent employment figures:

Occupation	March 2011	March 2012
Agriculture	34,000	62,000
Mining & quarrying	22,000	28,000
Manufacturing	663,000	608,000
Utilities	25,000	26,000
Construction	284,000	265,000
Wholesale & retail trade	930,000	944,000
Transport, storage & communication	244,000	263,000
Finance	705,000	761,000
Community & social services	760,000	824,000
Private households	332,000	359,000
Total	3,999,000	4,140,000

Source: Statistics South Africa

A higher percentage of the workforce is involved in professional, technical, managerial and executive positions than any other province. Consequently, there is a great attraction for migrant workers from poorer provinces.

BANKING AND FINANCE

GDP/GNP, Inflation, National Debt
In 2004, Gauteng made the highest regional contribution to South Africa's economy (33.3 per cent), with the highest annual growth rate of 3.3 per cent. Finance, real estate and business services was the leading contributor (21.4 per cent) to the state's GDP, followed by manufacturing (20.5 per cent). Agriculture, forestry and fishing industry had the lowest contribution (0.5 per cent).

Contribution of major industries to GDP, 2004

Industry	R (million)	%
Primary industries	**10,514**	**2.3**
Agriculture, forestry and fishing	2,441	0.5
Mining and quarrying	8,073	1.7
Secondary industries	**115,706**	**25.0**
Manufacturing	94,934	20.5
Electricity, gas and water	9,162	2.0
Construction	11,610	2.5
Tertiary industries	**287,883**	**62.3**
Wholesale & retail trade; hotels and restaurants	61,823	13.4
Transport, storage and communications	37,913	8.2
Finance, real estate and business	98,885	21.4
Personal services	18,290	4.0
General government services	70,972	15.4
All industries at basic prices	414,103	89.6
Taxes less subsidies on products	47,941	10.4
GDPR at market prices	**462,044**	**100.0**

Source: Statistics South Africa

Gauteng's Consumer Price Index (CPI) rose by 4.7 per cent over the period 2001-02, and 1.8 per cent over the period December 2001 and January 2002. The Pretoria/Centurion/Akasia urban area CPI rose by 6.0 per cent over 2001-02, whilst the Witwatersrand urban area rose by 4.5 per cent.

MANUFACTURING, MINING AND SERVICES

Primary and Extractive Industries
Gauteng has large deposits of gold and recent figures show the mining industry employed 159,000 people.

Energy
Figures for 2011 show that Gauteng consumed 61,256 gigawatt hours of electricity.

Manufacturing
The major industrial areas are the Vaal Triangle, the East, West and Central Rand and Pretoria. The main pruducts produced in Gauteng include basic iron, steel and aluminium, fabricated and metal products; food; machinery, electrical machinery, appliances and electrical supplies, chemical products and vehicle parts and accessories. The Ford Motor Company has am assembly plant in Gauteng.

In order to encourage technology based companies an Innovation Hub is located in Pretoria

Service Industries
Gauteng is the financial services capital of South Africa, over 70 foreign banks have head offices in the state and many South African banks and insurance companies have their bases there.

Tourism is a growing sector in Gauteng.

Agriculture
The main crops are maize, groundnuts, sunflowers, cotton and sorghum, although much of the agricultural sector concentrates on supplying dairy products, vegetables, fruit, meat, eggs and flowers to the cities daily.

COMMUNICATIONS AND TRANSPORT

International Airports
Johannesburg International Airport receives the majority of arrivals of foreign visitors.
Johannesburg International Airport, Johannesburg, South Africa. Tel: +27 (0)11 921 6911, fax: +27 (0)11 395 1736

Roads
Recent figures show that Gauteng has 2,950 km of paved roads and 1,300 km of gravel roads.

HEALTH

In 2004, there were 281 public hospitals and 5 special hospitals in Gauteng with a total of 15,871 beds (13,704 in public hospitals and 2,167 in private hospitals). In 2004, health personnel in the state amounted to 43,152 of which 43.1 per cent were administration and support staff posts. There were an estimated 1,520 medical officers, 344 medical interns, 1,830 medical specialists, 226 dentists, 8,250 professional nurses, 2,476 staff nurses, 5,378 nursing assistants, 2,094 student nurses, 1,865 professional and technical staff and 286 pharmacists.

In 2004, HIV prevalence among pregnant women was estimated at 29.5 per cent, compared to 27.9 per cent in 2003. (Source: Statistics South Africa)

EDUCATION

In the 1997-98 financial year, of total appropriations of R95,031.12 million, a total of R5,934.36 million was allocated to education.

Figures for 2001 show that Gauteng had 858,482 students at primary school, 488,218 students at secondary school and 98,161 students at combined schools.

The University of Pretoria is the largest residential university in South Africa and the University of South Africa (UNISA) is believed to be the largest correspondence university in the world. Pretoria has numerous scientific institutions, including the Council for Scientific and Industrial Research (CSIR), Onderstepoort Veterinary Institute and the South African Bureau of Standards (SABS). Johannesburg has two residential universities: the Rand Afrikaans University and the Witwatersrand. There are also several teacher training colleges, technical colleges and technikons.

About 9.5 per cent of adults have received no formal education.

KWAZULU-NATAL

Capital: Pietermaritzburg (Population estimate: 400,000)

Head of State: King Goodwill Zwelithini

CONSTITUTION AND GOVERNMENT

Constitution
KwaZulu-Natal is the only province whose constitution provides for a monarchy.

Executive Council (as at June 2013)
Premier: Dr Zweli Lawrence Mkhize
MEC for Agriculture, Environmental Affairs and Rural Development: Dr Bonginkosi Meshack Radebe
MEC for Education: Edward Senzo Mchunu
MEC for Finance: Catharina Magdalena Cronje
MEC for Health: Dr. (Brig. Gen.) Sibongiseni Maxwell Dhlomo
MEC for Human Settlement and Public Works: Ravi Pillay
MEC for Cooperative Governance and Traditional Affairs: Nomusa Dube
MEC for Transport, Community Safety and Liaison: Thembinkosi W. Mchunu
MEC for Social Development: Weziwe Gcotyewa Thusi
MEC for Economic Development and Tourism: Michael Mabuyakhulu
MEC for Arts, Culture, Sports and Recreation: Ntombikayise Sibhidla-Saphetha

---

Ministries
Government portal, URL: http://www.kwazulunatal.gov.za/
Department of Agriculture and Environmental Affairs, URL: www.kznded.gov.za
Department of Economic Development and Tourism, URL: www.kznded.gov.za
Department of Finance, URL: http://www.kzntreasury.gov.za
Department of Traditional Affairs, Local Government and Housing, URL: http://www.kzncogta.gov.za
Department of Transport and Safety and Security, URL: www.kzntransport.gov.za / http://www.kzncomsafety.gov.za
Department of Education, URL: http://www.kzneducation.gov.za
Department of Public Works, URL: http://www.kznworks.gov.za
Department of Arts, Culture, Sport and Recreation, URL: http://www.kzndac.gov.za
Department of Health, URL: http://www.kznhealth.gov.za

Elections
The most recent election was held in April 2009. Out of the 80 seats available the African National Congress Party (ANC) won 51 seats, and the Inkatha Freedom Party (IFP) won 18 seats. The Democratic Alliance (DA) won seven seats, the Congress of the People won one seat, the African Christian Democratic Party one seat and the Minority Front two seats.

AREA AND POPULATION

Area
KwaZulu-Natal borders the Free State and Lesotho to the west, Eastern Cape to the south, and Mpumalanga to the north, covering an area of 92,100 square km or 7.6 per cent of the country's total land area. The Indian Ocean runs along the coastline to the east.

To view a map of the province, please consult http://www.un.org/Depts/Cartographic/map/profile/southafr.pdf

Population
KwaZulu-Natal's population of 10,267,300, represents 21.0 per cent of the total South African population. The population figure takes into account additional deaths due to HIV/AIDS. IsiZulu is spoken by 80 per cent of the population, English by 16 per cent, and Afrikaans by 2 per cent.

Births, Marriages, Deaths
The number of live births in 2010 was recorded as 184,471, compared with 889,691 in the whole of South Africa. The number of recorded deaths in 2009 was 127,369 compared to 572,673 in South Africa as a whole. Life expectancy at birth is 47.3 years for males (the lowest of South Africa's provinces) and 51 years for females, compared with the national average of 53.5 years for males and 57.2 years for females. Marriages in 2010 numbered 25,862, whilst divorces in 2006 numbered 4,092. The total fertility rate was estimated at 2.76 in the period 2001-06, and forecast to be 2.6 in the period 2006-2011. (Source: Statistics South Africa)

EMPLOYMENT

Figures for the fourth quarter of 2012 show that KwaZulu-Natal had a labour force of 3,215,000 of which 2,493,000 were employed and 722,000 were unemployed giving an unemployment rate of 22.5 per cent. The following table shows recent employment figures:

Occupation	March 2011	March 2012
Agriculture	108,000	91,000
Mining & quarrying	14,000	18,000
Manufacturing	389,000	386,000
Utilities	19,000	na
Construction	226000	210,000
Wholesale & retail trade	536,000	570,000
Transport, storage & communication	174,000	180,000

- continued

Finance	259,000	276,000
Community & social services	487,000	540,000
Private households	188,000	239,000
Total	2,429,000	2,519,000

Source: Statistics South Africa

BANKING AND FINANCE

GDP/GNP, Inflation, National Debt
In 2004, KwaZulu-Natal contributed approximately 16.7 per cent to South Africa's economy. Its average annual economic growth rate was approximately 3.1 per cent. The growth rate in 2004 was 4.9 per cent, compared to the South African growth rate of 4.5 per cent. During the period 1995-2004 the manufacturing sector was the highest contributor (21.8 per cent).

GDPR and value added estimates per industry at current prices, 2004

Industry	Rand million
Agriculture, forestry and fishing	10,014
Mining and quarrying	3,695
Manufacturing	50,448
Electricity, gas and water	5,319
Construction	4,958
Wholesale and retail trade; hotels and restaurants	29,448
Transport, storage and communication	26,755
Finance, real estate and business services	36,798
Personal services	12,774
General government services	27,501
Taxes less subsidies on products	23,905
GDPR at market prices	**231,616**

Source: Statistics South Africa

The Consumer Price Index (CPI) for KwaZulu-Natal rose by 5.1 per cent over the period 2001-02 and 1.5 per cent over the period December 2001 to January 2002.

MANUFACTURING, MINING AND SERVICES

Primary and Extractive Industries
KwaZulu-Natal does not have large mineral resources, although coal is mined in the northern regions. A large sand-mining and mineral processing plant is located at Richards Bay. Recent figures show around 12,000 people employed in the mining industry.

Energy
Figures for 2011 show that KwaZulu-Natal consumed 41,923 gigawatt hours of electricity.

Manufacturing
The main industries of KwaZulu Natal include steel production, meat production, aluminium and motor vehicle-manufacturing.

Tourism
There are many coastal and mountain resorts that attract tourists to the province.

Agriculture
The coastal belt is a large producer of sugar cane and sub tropical fruit, while the midlands concentrate mainly on vegetable, dairy and stock farming. Forestry is also a major source of income in KwaZulu-Natal. The following table shows the value of selected agricultural produce in 2002:

Produce	R'000
Sugar Cane	2,276,804
Dairy Cattle	55,653
Milk & cream	537,985
Beef cattle	1,016,063
Cabbage & red cabbage	34,788
Potatoes	137,435
Carrots	12,212
Mushrooms	21,576

Source: Statistics South Africa

COMMUNICATIONS AND TRANSPORT

Ports and Harbours
Durban harbour is one of the ten largest ports in the world and the busiest in South Africa. The Richards Bay harbour deals mainly with the exporting of coal.

HEALTH

In KwaZulu Natal in 2001 there were 59 public hospitals with 23,705 beds. There were a further 27 private hospitals with 3,471 beds and 14 semi-private hospitals with 4,090 beds. Primary healthcare facilities included 365 clinics, 10 community health centres, 166 mobile facilities and 97 visiting points. The total number of health care posts in KwaZulu Natal was

60,183 (of which approximately 20 per cent were vacant. In 2001 per 10,000 population there were 4.8 doctors (public sector 2.6); 64.0 nurses (35.9 per public sector); 2.5 pharmacists (1.7 public sector); dentists 1.8 (1.2 public sector).

KwaZulu Natal has the highest rate of HIV prevalence in South Africa. In 2000 the HIV prevalence among pregnant women was 36.32 per cent, falling to 33.5 per cent in 2001.

Approximately 11 per cent of the population is covered by medical aid. (Source: Statistics South Africa)

EDUCATION

Figures for 2001 show that KwaZulu-Natal has 1,663,697 students at primary school, 851,723 students at secondary schools and 146,088 students at combined schools. There are several universities, technikons and various other educational institutions although almost 23 per cent of adults have not received any formal education. The adult literacy rate is 60 per cent, according to recent figures, compared with 63 per cent for the whole of South Africa.

Government expenditure on education for the financial year 1997-98 was R7,331.20 million.

LIMPOPO PROVINCE

Capital: Polokwane (formerly Pietersburg) (Population estimate: 500,000)

CONSTITUTION AND GOVERNMENT

Constitution
The Northern Province, formerly known as Northern Transvaal, was re-named Limpopo Province at the beginning of 2002. At a speech on 14 February 2002, the Premier, Ngoako Ramatlhodi, announced that section 103 (1)(g) of the Constitution of the Republic of South Africa would be amended to re-name the state.

Executive Council (as at June 2013)
Premier: Cassel Mathale
MEC for Agriculture: Jacob Marule
MEC for Education: Namane Dickson Masemola
MEC for the Provincial Treasury: David Masondo
MEC for Economic Development, Environment and Tourism: Pinkie Kekana
MEC for Health and Social Development: Dr Norman Mabasa
MEC for Local Government and Housing: Clifford Motsepe
MEC for Public Works: Thabitha Mohlala
MEC for Safety, Security and Liaison: Florence Dzhombere
MEC for Sports, Arts and Culture: Dipuo Letsatsi-Duba
MEC for Roads and Transport: Pitsi Moloto

Speaker: Rudolph Phala

Ministries
Government Portal: URL: http://www.limpopo.gov.za
Office of the Premier, 26 Bodenstein Street, Pietersburg (Private Bag X9483, Pietersburg 0700), South Africa. Tel: +27 (0)15 291 2136, fax: +27 (0)15 295 3427
Department of Economic Development, Tourism and Environmental Affairs, URL: http://www.ledet.gov.za/
Department of Education, Corner 113 Biccard and 24 Excelsior Street, Pietersburg (Private Bag X9489, Polokwane 0700), South Africa. Tel: +27 (0)15 290 7600, URL: http://www.edu.limpopo.gov.za/
Department of Finance and Economic Development, Private Bag X9486 Polokwane, 0700, South Africa. URL: http://www.ledet.gov.za/
Department of Health and Welfare, Private Bag X9302, Polokwane 0700, South Africa. Tel: +27 (0)15 293 6000, URL: http://www.dhsd.limpopo.gov.za/
Department of Transport, Private Bag X9491, Polokwane 0700, South Africa. Tel: +27 (0)15 295 1000
Department of Public Works, Private Bag X9490, Polokwane 0700, South Africa. Tel: +27 (0)15 293 1913
Department of Provincial Safety, Security and Liaison, Private Bag X9492, Polokwane, 0700, South Africa. Tel: +27 (0)15 295 8977/8
Department of Sport, Recreation, Arts and Culture, Private Bag X9549, Polokwane, 0700, South Africa. Tel: +27 (0)15 295 7414/5/9
Department of Local Government and Housing, Private Bag X9485, Polokwane, 0700, South Africa. Tel: +27 (0)15 295 6851
Department of Agriculture, URL: http://www.lda.gov.za/

Elections
The most recent election was held in April 2009. The African National Congress Party (ANC) won 43 seats, the Congress of the People four seats and the Democratic Alliance (DA) won two seats.

The cabinet was reshuffled in March 2012.

AREA AND POPULATION

Area
Limpopo Province is located in the north eastern corner of South Africa and shares its borders with Mozambique, Zimbabwe and Botswana and the provinces of Mpumalanga and the North West to the south. It covers an area of 123,910 sq. km, 10.2 per cent of South Africa's total land area. The terrain ranges from Bushveld to mountains, forests to plantations, wilderness to farming land. Major towns include Warmbaths (a mineral spa), Nylstroom (grape industry), Potgietersrus, Pietersburg, Louis Trichardt, Messina, Phalaborwa and Thabazimbi (mining), and tzaneen (tea, forest products and tropical fruit).

In January 2002 the Department of Local Government and Housing announced changes to the names of the following municipalities: Pietersburg, Louis Trichard, Potgietersrus, Duiwelskloof, Tzaneen, Naboomspuit, Nylstroom, Warmbaths, Ellisrus Bochum, Dendron,

Hoedspruit, Ellisras, Messina, and Soekmekaar. Public hearings have been set up to receive the views of stakeholders and the new names will be published in the Provincial Gazette. Ultimately, the names of streets, rivers, and dams will also be changed.

To view a map of the province, please consult http://www.un.org/Depts/Cartographic/map/profile/southafr.pdf

Population
2011 estimates put the population at 5,524,136, of which 2,524,136 were male and 2,880,732 were female. The figure takes into account additional deaths due to HIV/AIDS. The population of Limpopo Province represents 10.60 per cent of the total South Africa population. (Source: Statistics South Africa) The annual population growth rate was 2.3 per cent in 2000, compared with the national average of 2.1 per cent. The main language spoken is Sepedi (52.7 per cent), followed by Xitsonga (23 per cent), Tshivenda (15.5 per cent) and Afrikaans.

Births, Marriages, Deaths
There were a total of 109,128 recorded live births in 2010, and in 2009 there were 52,907 recorded deaths. Life expectancy at birth is 52.6 years for males (compared with 53.5 years across the whole of South Africa) and 55.8 years for females (57.2 in South Africa). Infant mortality is 55 deaths per 1,000 live births, the second highest in South Africa. Marriages in 2010 numbered 9,699, whilst divorces numbered 949 in 2006. The total fertility rate was estimated at 3.25 in the period 2001-06, and forecast to be 2.67 in the period 2006-2011. (Source: Statistics South Africa)

EMPLOYMENT

Figures for the fourth quarter of 2012 show that Limpopo State had a labour force of 1,358,000 of which 1,092,000 were employed and 266,000 were unemployed giving an unemployment rate of 19.6 per cent. The following table shows recent employment figures:

Occupation	March 2011	March 2012
Agriculture	52,000	88,000
Mining & quarrying	57,000	70000
Manufacturing	62,000	69,000
Utilities	-	-
Construction	93,000	92,000
Wholesale & retail trade	243,000	246,000
Transport, storage & communications	33,000	55,000
Finance	64,000	58,000
Community & social services	227,000	234,000
Private households	101,000	76,000
Total	940,000	996,000

Source: Statistics South Africa

BANKING AND FINANCE

GDP/GNP
In 2004, Limpopo contributed 6.7 per cent to South Africa's total GDP. Limpopo had a real economic growth rate of 2.7 per cent, the lowest of the provinces. Mining and quarrying was the highest contributor to the economy (21.7 per cent) followed by general government services (17.3 per cent).

GDPR and value added estimates per industry at current prices, 2004

Industry	Rand million
Agriculture, forestry and fishing	2,881
Mining and quarrying	20,202
Manufacturing	3,242
Electricity, gas and water	2,580
Construction	1,288
Wholesale and retail trade; hotels and restaurants	10,696
Transport, storage and communication	7,761
Finance, real estate and business services	14,523
Personal services	4,165
General government services	16,159
Taxes less subsidies on product	9,691
GDPR at market prices	**93,188**

Source: Statistics South Africa

SOUTH AFRICA

The Consumer Price Index (CPI) for Limpopo Province rose by 4.7 per cent over the period 2001-02 and by 1.5 per cent over the period December 2001 to January 2002. The Polokwane (Pietersburg) urban area CPI rose by 2.3 per cent from 2001-02 and by 1.4 per cent from December 2001 to January 2002.

MANUFACTURING, MINING AND SERVICES

Primary and Extractive Industries
Limpopo Province is rich in minerals such as copper, asbestos, coal, iron ore, platinum, chrome, diamonds, nickel, cobalt, vanadium, tin, and phosphates. Minerals including gold, emeralds, scheelite, magnetite, vermiculite, silicon and mica are also found. The mining industry accounts for over 20 per cent of GDP. Recent figures show 70,000 workers are employed in the mining sector.

Energy
Figures for 2011 show that Limpopo used 12,129 gigawatt hours of electricity.

Agriculture
The main crops are sunflowers, cotton, maize, peanuts, coffee, tea and citrus fruits. Many tropical fruits are also grown such as bananas, lychees, pineapples, mangoes and pawpaws. The largest tomato farm in South Africa is situated in Limpopo Province.

Limpopo Province supplies 75 per cent of South Africa's mangoes, 75 per cent of its tomatoes, 65 per cent of its papaya, 60 per cent of its avocados, 36 per cent of its tea, and 25 per cent of its bananas, citrus and lychees. Grapes are also grown.

There are cattle ranches located in the bushveld area.

There are extensive plantations of hard woods which are suitable for furniture manufacturing.

The following table shows the value of selected agricultural products in 2002:

Produce	R '000
Sunflower seed	111,527
Ground nuts	12,816
Soya beans	27,953
Cotton	81,663
Tobacco	200,212

Source: Statistics South Africa

COMMUNICATIONS AND TRANSPORT

International Airports
The Gateway International Airport is situated in Polokwane and opened in 1996. It provides services mainly to sub-Saharan Africa, processing nearly 40,000 passengers and almost two million kilograms of freight annually.

Roads
Limpopo Province's major highway, the Great North Road, runs through the centre of the province. A major new road project, the Maputo Corridor, will connect Limpopo Province with the port at Mozambique.

HEALTH

In 2004, there were a total of 43 public hospitals with a total of 7,630 hospital beds. The HIV prevalence rate in the province was 13.2 per cent in 2000, 14.5 per cent in 2001 and 15.6 per cent in 2002. (Source: Statistics South Africa)

EDUCATION

Figures for 2001 show that Limpopo Province has 1,136,515 students attending primary school, 639,300 students at secondary school and 17,973 students attending combined schools.

MPUMALANGA

Capital: Nelspruit (Population estimate: 221,500)

CONSTITUTION AND GOVERNMENT

Executive Council (as at June 2013)
Premier: David Dabede Mabuza
MEC for Health and Social Development: Ms Candith Mashego-Dlamini
MEC for Culture, Sport and Recreation: Ms Sbongile Manana
MEC for Human Settlement: Andries Gamede
MEC for Agriculture, Rural Development and Land Administration: Ms Violet Siwela
MEC for Co-operative Governance and Traditional Affairs: Sikhosana Sbd

Speaker: Hon. Sipho William Lubisi

Ministries
Government portal: URL: http://www.mpumalanga.gov.za
Department of Finance, P/Bag X11205, Nelspruit, 1200, South Africa. Tel: +27 (0)13 766 4554, URL: http://finance.mpu.gov.za/
Department of Health and Social Services, P/Bag X11213, Nelspruit, 1200, South Africa. Tel: +27 (0)13 766 3098
Department of Economic Development and Planning, P/Bag X11205, Nelspruit, 1200, South Africa. Tel: +27 (0)13 766 4554
Department of Roads and Transport, P/Bag X11310, Nelspruit, 1200, South Africa. Tel: +27 (0)13 766 6607
Department of Local Government and Housing, P/Bag X11304, Nelspruit, 1200, South Africa. Tel: +27 (0)13 766 6607/6978
Department of Education, PO Box 3011, Nelspruit, 1200, South Africa. Tel: +27 (0)13 766 5555
Department of Public Works, P/Bag X11302, Nelspruit, 1200, South Africa. Tel: +27 (0)13 766 6695
Department of Cultural Affairs, Sports and Recreation, P/BagX11341, Nelspruit, 1200, South Africa. Tel: +27 (0)13 766 5297
Department of Agriculture, Conservation, Environment and Land Administration, P/Bag X11269, Nelspruit, 1200, South Africa. Tel: +27 (0)13 766 6074
Department of Safety and Security, P/Bag X11269, Nelspruit, 1200, South Africa. Tel: +27 (0)13 766 4088

Elections
The most recent elections were held in April 2009. The African National Congress Party (ANC) won 27 seats, the Democratic Alliance (DA) two seats, and the Congress of the People one seat.

AREA AND POPULATION

Area
Mpumalanga (formerly Eastern Transvaal) borders with KwaZulu-Natal and Free State to the south, Gauteng to the west, Northern Province to the north, and Mozambique to the east. It covers an area of 79,490 square km, 6.5 per cent of South Africa's total land area.

To view a map of the province, please consult http://www.un.org/Depts/Cartographic/map/profile/southafr.pdf

Population
Estimates for 2011 put the population at 4,039,939 inhabitants of Mpumalanga (1,974,055 males, 2,065,883 females), representing 7.3 per cent of the total South African population. The principal languages are SiSwati (30 per cent), IsiZulu (25.4 per cent) and IsiNdebele (12.5 per cent).

Births, Marriages, Deaths
The number of recorded live births in 2010 was 70,011, the number of deaths recorded in 2009 was 45,709. The average life expectancy at birth is 48.8 years for males and 52.20 years for females, compared with the national average of 53.5 years for males and 57.2 years for females. The infant mortality rate, per 1,000 live births, is 40, according to recent statistics. The number of marriages in 2010 was 8,809, whilst the number of divorces was 1,263 in 2006. The total fertility rate was estimated at 3.0 in the period 2001-06, and forecast to be 2.57 in the period 2006-2011. (Source: Statistics South Africa)

EMPLOYMENT

Figures for the fourth quarter of 2012 show that Mpumalanga had a labour force of 1,357,000 of which 959,000 were employed and 399,000 were unemployed giving an unemployment rate of 29.4 per cent. The following table shows recent employment figures:

Occupation	March 2011	March 2012
Agriculture	71,000	83,000
Mining & quarrying	52,000	64,000
Manufacturing	77,000	81,000
Utilities	22,000	24,000
Construction	69,000	64,000
Wholesale & retail trade	218,000	228,000
Transport, storage & communications	34,000	48,000
Finance	82,000	79,000
Community & social services	172,000	149,000
Private households	81,000	94,000
Total	877,000	913,000

Source: Statistics South Africa

BANKING AND FINANCE

GDP/GNP
Mpumalanga contributed 6.8 per cent to South Africa's economy. It had the fifth highest economic growth rate (3.0 per cent) in the period 1996-2004. The mining and quarrying industry and manufacturing were the highest contributors. The real economic growth rate in 2004 was 4.2 per cent, below the national average growth rate of 4.5 per cent.

GDP, value added per industry at current prices, 2004

Industry	Rand million
Agriculture, forestry and fishing	3,577
Mining and quarrying	16,939
Manufacturing	17,586
Electricity, gas and water	4,206
Construction	1,284
Wholesale & retail trade; hotels and restaurants	9,613
Transport, storage and communication	7,551
Finance, real estate and business services	10,789
Personal services	4,604
General government services	8,500
Taxes less subsidies on product	9,802
GDPR at market prices	**94,450**

Source: Statistics South Africa

The Consumer Price Index (CPI) for Mpumalanga rose by 6.2 per cent over the period 2001-02 and 2.0 per cent over the period December 2001 to January 2002. For the Nelspruit/Witbank urban area, the CPI rose by 6.5 per cent from 2001-02 and 1.6 per cent from December 2001 to January 2002.

MANUFACTURING, MINING AND SERVICES

Primary and Extractive Industries
Mpumalanga has large coal reserves and Witbank is the biggest coal producer in Africa. Recent figures show that Mpumalanga had 71,585 people employed in the mining sector.

Energy
The largest power stations in South Africa are situated in Mpumalanga, three of which are the biggest in the southern hemisphere. The coal to petroleum installation, Secunda, is also located in Mpumalanga.

Figures for 2011 show that Mpumalanga consumed 35,152 gigawatt hours of electricity.

Manufacturing
The largest industries are steel and vanadium producers and paper mills.

Agriculture
The main agricultural crops grown are cotton, tobacco, wheat, potatoes, sunflower seeds, maize, peanuts and vegetables. There is an abundance of citrus fruit and subtropical fruits such as mangoes, avocados, bananas, pawpaws, litchis, grenadillas and guavas. Nelspruit is the second largest producer of citrus fruits in South Africa and produces one third of the country's orange exports.

The Sabie area is the biggest single region of forestry plantations in South Africa with exotic trees including pine, gum and Australian wattle.

Sheep also provide an important source of revenue in Mpumalanga.

The following table shows the value of sales of selected agricultural produce in 2002:

Produce	R '000
Sheep	45,075
Wool	41,248
Chickens	553,502
Sunflower seeds	42,173
Soya beans	89,572
Maize for grain	1,490,707
Wheat	106,647
Sugar cane	337,416
Cotton	72,576
Tobacco	246,212
Potatoes	177,249
Tomatoes	32,901

Source: Statistics South Africa

HEALTH

The province had 26 public hospitals in 2004. In 2001, there were also 221 clinics, 28 community health care centres, 91 mobile facilities and 46 visiting points. An estimated 13 per cent of the population were covered by medical aid.

In 2004, there were 306 medical practitioners, 8 specialists, 45 dental practitioners, 2,220 professional nurses, 967 staff nurses and student nurses, 1,723 nursing assistants, 447 student nurses, 78 pharmacists, 1,387 allied health professionals and technical staff, and 4,027 managers, administrators and logistical staff.

An estimated 29 per cent of pregnant women were estimated to be HIV positive in 2001. Of South Africa's 8,016 malaria cases in 2003, 2,909 were from Mpumalanga. (Source: Statistics South Africa)

EDUCATION

Figures for 2001 show that 494,754 students attended primary school, 286,682 students attended secondary schools and 112,848 students attended combined schools. (Figures from Statistics South Africa).

Almost 29 per cent of adults over the age of 20 have not received any formal education. The adult literacy rate is 57 per cent, according to recent statistics.

The province's government spent R2,509.73 million on education in the financial year 1997-98.

ENVIRONMENT

Three of Mpumalanga's power stations are also the largest in the southern hemisphere, making the province's carbon emissions the highest in South Africa.

NORTHERN CAPE

Capital: Kimberley (Population estimate: 211,000)

CONSTITUTION AND GOVERNMENT

The Provincial Administration of the Northern Cape is headed by the Premier and the Director-General. The Chief Executive Officer of the Provincial Administration is the Director-General, who is responsible for decisions taken by the Executive Committee and for those laws passed by the House. The Executive Committee consists of the Premier (the Executive Authority), and seven members (each heading one of the Province's government departments). The Executive Committee develops policies, implements laws and ensures the correct running of government departments.

In November 2012, corruption charges were brought against several people including the finance MEC John Block and the social development MEC Alvin Botes.

Executive Council (as at June 2013)
Premier: Sylvia Lucas (page 1467)
MEC for Agriculture and Land Reform: Norman Shushu
MEC for Economic Affairs, Finance and Tourism: John Block
MEC for Education: Grizelda Cjikela
MEC for Health: Mxolisi Sokatsha
MEC for Environmental Affairs & Nature Conservation: Patrick Mabilo
MEC for Transport, Safety and Liaison: Mac Jack
MEC for Social Development & Population Development: Chukelwa Chotelo
MEC for Corporate & Governance, Human Settlement and Traditional Affairs: Alvin Botes
MEC for Sports, Arts and Culture: Pauline Williams
MEC for Roads and Public Works: Dawid Rooi

Speaker: Kenny Mmoiemang

Ministries
Government portal: URL: http://www.northern-cape.gov.za
Office of the Premier, Kimberley, Northern Cape, South Africa. Tel: +27 531 830 9555, URL: http://www.northern-cape.gov.za
Department of Agriculture and Land Reform, Private Bag X5018, Kimberley, 8300, South Africa. Tel: +27 (0)53 831 4049
Department of Tourism, Environment and Conservation, Private Bag X5054, Kimberley, 8300, South Africa. Tel: +27 (0)53 832 7834
Department of Education, Private Bag X5023, Kimberley, 8300, South Africa. Tel: +27 (0)53 874 4297
Department of Sport, Arts and Culture, Private Bag X6091, Kimberley, 8300, South Africa. Tel: +27 (0)53 831 4152
Department of Finance and Economic Affairs, Private Bag X6108, Kimberley, 8300, South Africa. Tel: +27 (0)53 839 4026
Department of Health, Private Bag X5049, Kimberley, 8300, South Africa. Tel: +27 (0)53 2000
Department of Transport, Roads and Public Works, Private Bag X5065, Kimberley, South Africa. Tel: +27 (0)53 831 4934/5
Department of Social Development, Private Bag X6110, Kimberley, 8300, South Africa. Tel: +27 (0)53 832 7834/5/9
Department of Local Government and Housing, Private Bag X5005, Kimberley, 8300, South Africa. Tel: (0)53 830 9422/3/4
Department of Safety and Liaison, Private Bag X1368, Kimberley, 8300, South Africa. Tel: +27 (0)53 839 1719/1700/1701-3

Elections
The most recent election was held in April 2009. The African National Congress Party won 19 seats, the Congress of the People five seats, the Democratic Alliance four seats, and the Independent Democrats two seats.

SOUTH AFRICA

AREA AND POPULATION

Area
Northern Cape borders with Western Cape and Eastern Cape to the south and Free State and the North West province to the east. The Atlantic Ocean flanks its western border. Northern Cape is the largest province, covering an area of 361,830, which is 29.7 per cent of the country's total land area.

To view a map of the province, please consult
http://www.un.org/Depts/Cartographic/map/profile/southafr.pdf

Population
Despite being the largest province, the Northern Cape has the least number of inhabitants. 2011 estimates put the population at 1,145,861, (564,972 male and 580,889 female). The main language is Afrikaans (69.3 per cent) followed by Setswana (19.9 per cent) and IsiXhosa (6.3 per cent).

Births, Marriages, Deaths
The number of recorded live births in 2010 was 69,706, the number of recorded deaths in 2009 was 40,372. Life expectancy at birth is 56.3 years for males and 59.7 years for females, compared with the national average of 53.5 years for males and 57.2 years for females. Marriages in 2010 numbered 13,193, whilst divorces numbered 1,777 in 2006. The total fertility rate was estimated at 3.03 in the period 2001-06, and forecast to be 2.58 in the period 2006-2011. (Source: Statistics South Africa)

EMPLOYMENT

Figures for the fourth quarter of 2012 show that the Northern Cape had a labour force of 408,000 of which 292,000 were employed and 116,000 were unemployed giving an unemployment rate of 28.4 per cent. The following table shows recent employment figures:

Occupation	March 2011	March 2012
Agriculture	53,000	47,000
Mining & quarrying	11,000	16,000
Manufacturing	14,000	16,000
Utilities	-	-
Construction	14,000	19,000
Wholesale & retail trade	35,000	41,000
Transport, storagae & communications	14,000	na
Finance	15,000	24,000
Community & social services	79,000	83,000
Private households	25,000	25,000
Total	261,000	286,000

Source: Statistics South Africa

BANKING AND FINANCE

The Northern Cape receives 97 per cent of its budget from central government and raises the balance by way of hospital and vehicle licensing fees.

GDP/GNP, Inflation, National Debt
Northern Cape contributed 2.2 per cent to the economy of South Africa in the period 1996-2004, with a growth rate of 2.2 per cent in the same period. The growth rate was 3.0 per cent in 2004, compared to the national average of 4.5 per cent.

GDP at current prices, 2004

Industry	2004
Agriculture, forestry and fishing	2,412
Mining and quarrying	7,773
Manufacturing	1,037
Electricity, gas and water	650
Construction	352
Wholesale and retail trade; hotels and restaurants	2,902
Transport, storage and communication	2,475
Finance, real estate and business services	3,586
Personal services	2,458
General government services	3,315
Taxes less subsidies on products	3,127
GDPR at market prices	**30,087**

Source: Statistics South Africa

The Consumer Price Index (CPI) for the Northern Cape rose by 6.1 per cent over the period 2001-02 and by 1.7 per cent over the period December 2001 to January 2002. The Kimberley urban area CPI rose by 8.3 per cent from 2001-02 and by December 2001 to January 2002.

MANUFACTURING, MINING AND SERVICES

Primary and Extractive Industries
Northern Cape has extensive mineral resources. The country's main diamond mines are found in Kimberley. Alluvial diamonds are also extracted from the beaches and sea between Port Nolloth and Alexander Bay. De Beers is currently working on a R600 million treatment plant which will process material from old mines and mine dumps. De Beers believe that the plant will extend the life of mines for almost ten years and, in the process, save hundreds of jobs.

Copper is mined at Springbok, Okiep and Aggeneys. Iron ore is mined at the Sishen Mine. Other mineral resources in the province are asbestos, manganese, fluorspar, semi-precious stones and marble.

Energy
Figures for 2011 show that Northern Cape consumed 4,985 gigawatt hours of electricity.

Manufacturing
The largest industries are wine making, dried fruit and karakul pelts.

Service Industries
The Northern Cape's major tourist attraction is the Kimberley 'Big Hole', the results of the 19th century mining industry. There are also several national parks and conservation areas, including the Kgalagadi Transfrontier Park which covers an area of over two million hectares. The spring flowers and San rock engravings are also popular tourist attractions.

The government had identified out-sourcing as a potential growth area and the province's first call centre was established in February 2008.

Agriculture
Fruit, grapes, wheat, peanuts, maize and cotton are grown in the Northern Cape. A large portion of the economy relies on sheep and karakul farming.

COMMUNICATIONS AND TRANSPORT

Airports
There are airports at Kimberley and Upington.

Railways
Kimberley's railway station is located in Florence Street, from which the Blue Train connects Pretoria with Cape Town via Johannesburg and Kimberley.

Roads
Bus services operate from Kimberley (Intercape, Greyhound, Translux, Big Sky Coaches), Springbok (Carstens Bus Service, Intercape, Van Wyk's Bus Service), and Upington (Intercape).

HEALTH

Northern Cape had 27 hospitals in 2003. There were a further 16 community health centres, 82 clinics, 47 mobile and 58 satellite facilities. In 2003 there were 1,880 nurses, 247 doctors, 54 pharmacists, 363 professionals, and 1,668 support staff. Leading causes of death were tuberculosis, influenza and pneumonia. Approximately 85 per cent of people in the province weren't covered by medical aid in 2004. (Source: Statistics South Africa)

EDUCATION

Figures for 2001 show that 96,817 students attended primary schools, 45,523 students attended secondary schools, 22,949 students attended combined schools and 29,088 students attended intermediate and middle schools. (Figures from Statistics South Africa)

According to 1999 statistics, enrolments at Northern Cape tertiary institutions numbered just under 500. Universities enrolled 270, technicons 210, and colleges 15. Just over two-thirds of university students and about three-quarters of technicon students are female. In the Northern Cape's colleges, however, about half the student population is male.

Government expenditure on education for financial year 1997-98 was R845,908,000.

ENVIRONMENT

Northern Cape Nature Conservation Service, 224 Du Toitspan Road, Private Bag X6102, Kimberley 8300, Northern Cape, South Africa. Tel: +27 531 832 2143, fax no: +27 531 831 3530, e-mail: miggie@natuur.ncape.gov.za

NORTH WEST

Capital: Mafeking

CONSTITUTION AND GOVERNMENT

> **Executive Council (as at June 2013)**
> *Premier:* Thandi Modise
> *Minister of Economic Development, Environment and Tourism:* Motlalepula Rosho
> *Minister of Local Government and Traditional Affairs:* China Dodovu
> *Minister of Finance:* Paul Sebegoe
> *Minister of Agriculture and Rural Development:* Desbo Mohono
> *Minister of Health:* Dr Magome Masike
> *Minister of Public Works, Roads and Transport:* Raymond Elisha
> *Minister of Education:* Morukgomo L. Mabe
> *Minister of Human Settlement, Safety and Liaison:* Nono Maloi
> *Minister of Sport, Arts and Culture:* Tebogo Modise
> *Minister of Social Development, Women, Children and Persons with Disability:* Mosetsanagape Mokomela-Mothibi

Government portal: URL: http://www.nwpg.gov.za/

North West Provincial Legislature, URL: http://www.nwpl.gov.za/public/index.php
Speaker: S. Mahumapelo

Elections
The most recent election was held in April 2009. The African National Congress Party won 25 seats, the Democratic Alliance three seats, the Congress of the People three seats and the United Christian Democrat Party two seats.

AREA AND POPULATION

Area
The North West province borders the Free State to the south, Western Cape to the west, Gauteng to the south and Botswana to the north. It covers an area of 116,320 sq. km, 9.5 per cent of South Africa's total land area. Temperatures range from 22°C to 34°C in the summer and 2°C to 18 °C in the winter.

To view a map of the province, please consult
http://www.un.org/Depts/Cartographic/map/profile/southafr.pdf

Population
According to Statistics South Africa 2011 estimates, put the population at 3,509,953, of which 1,779,903 were male and 1,730,049 were female. The population of the North West Province represents 7 per cent of the total South African population. Annual average population growth was 2 per cent in 2000, compared with the national growth rate of 2.1 per cent in 2000. Setswana is spoken by 67.2 per cent of the population followed by Afrikaans (7.5 per cent) and IsiXhosa (5.4 per cent).

Important towns include Klerksdorp, Orkney, and Stilfontein, three key centres of uranium and gold production.

Births, Marriages, Deaths
The number of recorded live births in 2010 was 22,538, the number of deaths in 2009 was 15,082. Average life expectancy at birth is 56.3 years for males and 59.7 years for females, compared with the national average of 53.5 years for males and 57.2 years for females. Marriages in 2010 numbered 4,552, whilst divorces numbered 618 in 2006. The total fertility rate was estimated at 3.03 in the period 2001-06, and forecast to be 2.58 in the period 2006-2011. (Source: Statistics South Africa)

EMPLOYMENT

Figures for the fourth quarter of 2012 show that North West had a labour force of 973,000 of which 747,000 were employed and 227,000 were unemployed giving an unemployment rate of 23.3 per cent. The following table shows recent employment figures:

Occupation	March 2011	March 2012
Agriculture	37,000	38,000
Mining & quarrying	131,000	109,000
Manufacturing	62,000	56,000
Utilities	-	-
Construction	45,000	46,000
Wholesale & retail trade	150,000	152,000
Transport, sotrage & communication	21,000	26,000
Finance	61,000	52,000
Community & social services	152,000	161,000
Private households	61,000	60,000
Total	722,000	704,000
Source: Statistics South Africa		

BANKING AND FINANCE

GDP/GNP, Inflation, National Debt
The NorthWest province contributed 6.3 per cent to the province's economy in 2004, the third lowest contribution. GDP real annual economic growth was estimated at 4.9 per cent in 2004, higher than the national average of 4.5 per cent. The top performing sectors were mining and quarrying; finance, real estate and business; and general government services.

GDP, value added per industry at current prices, 2004

Industry	Rand million
Agriculture, forestry and fishing	2,239
Mining and quarrying	21,692
Manufacturing	6,067
Electricity, gas and water	879
Construction	1,429
Wholesale & retail trade; hotels and restaurants	9,543
Transport, storage and communication	7,086
Finance, real estate and business services	11,839
Personal services	6,746
General government services	10,548
Taxes less subsidies on products	9,058
GDPR at market prices	**87,127**
Source: Statistics South Africa	

The Consumer Price Index (CPI) for the North West Province rose by 4.7 per cent over the period 2001-02 and by 1.1 per cent from December 2001 to January 2002.

MANUFACTURING, MINING AND SERVICES

Primary and Extractive Industries
The mining industry employs a quarter of the workforce and contributes to about 55 per cent of the province's GDP. Diamonds, gold, uranium, marble, platinum and fluorspar are mined, with the Rustenburg and Brits area being the largest single platinum producing area in the world.

Energy
Figures for 2011 show that North West consumed 25,972 gigawatt-hours of electricity.

Manufacturing
The majority of industries revolve around the mining and agricultural industries, with some construction industries. The main industrial towns are Brits (manufacturing and construction), Klerksdorp (mining), Vryburg (agriculture), and Rustenburn (agriculture). The main products are metals, non-metallic metals and food processing.

Tourism
The biggest tourist attractions are the Pilanesberg National Park, Madikwe Game Reserve and the Sun City and Lost City holiday resorts.

Agriculture
The main crops are maize, sunflowers, groundnuts, tobacco, citrus, paprika, wheat, peppers and cotton. Some of the largest herds of cattle in the world can be found on farms in the North West.

The following table shows the sales value of selected produce in 2002:

Produce	R '000
Beef cattle	1,078,882
Dairy Cattle	36,450
Milk & cream	215,840
Chickens	481,022
Maize for grain	1,755,904
Wheat	127,001
Sunflower seed	291,871
Ground nuts	66,694
Tobacco	65,368
Source: Statistics South Africa	

COMMUNICATIONS AND TRANSPORT

Mmabatho International Airport Tel: +27 18 385 1166

HEALTH

There were 32 public hospitals in North West in 2004. Of these, two were community health centre, 24 district hospitals, four provincial hospitals and two specialised hospitals. There were a total of 3,757 beds. Health personnel included 3,001 professional nurses, 337 medical officers, 60 medical specialists, 75 pharmacists and 46 dentists. An estimated 463,000 people in the province had medical aid cover. An estimated 25.2 per cent of the population were HIV positive in 2001.

SOUTH AFRICA

EDUCATION

Figures from 2001 show that 494,991 students attended primary schools, 235,855 students attended secondary schools, 13,028 students attended combined schools and 139,693 students attended intermediate and middle schools. There are two universities: the University of the North West and Potchefstroom University.

About 22.7 per cent of the adult population have received no formal education. The adult literacy rate is 57 per cent, the second lowest in South Africa, according to recent figures. (Source: Statistics South Africa)

WESTERN CAPE

Capital: Cape Town (Population estimate: 2,522,500)

CONSTITUTION AND GOVERNMENT

Legislature
Western Cape's legislature is known as the Western Cape Provincial Parliament (*Ipalamente Yentshona Koloni / Wes-Kaapse Provinsiale Parlement*) and consists of 42 members elected for a term of five years.
Western Cape Provincial Parliament, PO Box 648, Cape Town, 8000, USA. Tel: +27 (0)21 487 1698, fax: +27 (0)21 487 1697, URL: http://www.wcpp.gov.za/public/Main/Home.aspx
Speaker of the Western Cape Provincial Parliament: Hon. Richard Majola

---

Executive Council (as at June 2013)
Premier: Helen Zille (page 1543)
Minister of Agriculture & Rural Development: Gerrit van Rensburg
Minister of Community Safety: Dan Plato
Minister of Education: Donald Grant
Minister of Housing: Bonginkosi Madikizela
Minister of Health: Theuns Botha
Minister of Local Government, Environmental Affairs and Development Planning: Anton Bredell
Minister of Social Development: Albert Fritz
Minister of Cultural Affairs and Sport: Dr Ivan Meyer
Minister of Finance, Economic Development and Tourism: Alan Winde
Minister of Transport and Public Works: Robin Carlisle
Speaker: Richard Majola

Ministries
Western Cape Government portal: URL: http://www.westerncape.gov.za
Department of the Premier, Tel: +27 (0)21 483 4705, fax: +27 (0)21 483 3421, e-mail: premier.westerncape@pgwc.gov.za
Department of Community Safety, PO Box 5346, Cape Town, 8000, South Africa. Tel: +27 (0)21 481 69,49, fax: +27 (0)21 483 6591, e-mail: fatima.samuels@pgwc.gov.za
Department of Human Settlements, Tel: +27 (0)21 483 2342, fax: +27 (0)21 483 2589, e-mail: pmadanjith@pgwc.gov.za
Department of Social Development, Tel: +27 (0)21 483 5045, fax: +27 (0)21 483 3855
Department of Economic Development and Tourism, PO Box 648, Cape Town, South Africa. Tel: +27 (0)21 483 5065, fax: +27 (0)21 483 3409, e-mail: ecohead@pgwc.gov.za
Department of Agriculture, Private Bag X9179, Cape Town, 8000, South Africa. Tel: +27 (0) 483 4700, e-mail: info@elsenburg.com
Department of Education, Private Bag X9161, Cape Town, 8000, South Africa. Tel: +27 (0)21 467 2000, fax: +27 (0)21 467 2996, e-mail: media1@pgwc.gov.za
Department of Environmental Affairs and Development Planning, Private Bag X9179, Cape Town, 8000, South Africa. Tel: +27 (0)21 483 4091, fax: +27 (0)21 483 3016, e-mail: enquiries.eadp@pgwc.gov.za
Department of Health, PO Box 2060, Cape Town, 8000, South Africa. Tel: +27 (0)21 483 2145, fax:+27 (0)21 483 6169, e-mail: angelique.jordan@pgwc.gov.za
Department of Local Government, Private Bag X9180, Cape Town, 8000, South Africa. Tel: +27 (0)21 483 2661, fax: +27 (0)21 483 5592, e-mail: pdikilili@pgwc.gov.za
Department of Transport and Public Works, PO Box 2603, Cape Town, 8000, South Africa. Tel: +27 (0)21 483 4391, fax: +27 (0)21 483 8755, e-mail: internal.communications@pgwc.gov.za
Department of Sport and Cultural Affairs, PO Box 15653, Cape Town, 8000, South Africa. Tel: +27 (0)21 483 9503, fax: +27 (0)483 9504, e-mail: dcas.com@pgwc.gov.za
Provincial Treasury, Tel: +27 (0)21 483 4709, fax: +27 (0)21 483 3855, e-mail: westerncape.treasury@pgwc.gov.za

Elections
The most recent elections were held in April 2009. The Democratic Alliance Party (DA) won 22 seats, the African National Congress Party won 14 seats, the Congress of the People (COPE) three seats, the Independent Democrats two seats and the African Christian Democratic Party one seat.

LOCAL GOVERNMENT

With effect from 6 December 2000, six metropolitan local councils (MLCs) merged to form the new City of Cape Town. The six MLCs were: Blaauwberg Municipality, City of Cape Town, City of Tygerberg, Helderberg Municipality, Oostenberg Municipality, South Peninsula Municipality and the Cape Metropolitan Council.

AREA AND POPULATION

Area
The Western Cape is on the south-western tip of Africa with the Atlantic Ocean on the west coast and the Indian Ocean on the south coast. It borders with Eastern Cape to the East and Northern Cape to the north. It has an area of 129,370 square km.

To view a map of the province, please consult http://www.un.org/Depts/Cartographic/map/profile/southafr.pdf

Population
2011 estimates put the population at 5,822,734, of which 2,858,506 were male and 2,964,228 were female. The figure took into account additional deaths due to HIV/AIDS. The population constitutes 10.9 per cent of South Africa's total population and is growing at just over 2 per cent per year. The Cape Town district has an estimated 2.52 million inhabitants. Most of the Western Cape's population (2.2 million) are Afrikaans-speaking native South Africans, with IsiXhosa-speaking Africans making up a quarter. Afrikaans is the predominant language (60 per cent), although English (20 per cent) and IsiXhosa (20 per cent) are also spoken.

Births, Marriages, Deaths
The number of recorded births in 2003 was 95,000, the number of recorded deaths in 2002 was 43,667 according to latest Statistics South Africa figures. Life expectancy at birth is 61.6 years for males (53.5 years for South Africa as a whole) and 67.9 years for females (57.2 years for South Africa). Marriages in 2010 numbered 26,855, whilst divorces numbered 4,699 in 2006. The total fertility rate was estimated at 2.19 in the period 2001-06, and forecast to be 2.11 in the period 2006-2011. (Source: Statistics South Africa)

EMPLOYMENT

Figures for the fourth quarter of 2012 show that the Western Cape had a labour force of 2,396,000 of which 1,824,000 were employed and 573,000 were unemployed giving an unemployment rate of 23.9 per cent. The following table shows recent employment figures:

Occupation	March 2011	March 2012
Agriculture	121,000	127,000
Mining & quarrying	-	-
Manufacturing	290,000	294,000
Utilities	11,000	na
Construction	124,000	135,000
Wholesale & retail trade	388,000	391,000
Transport, storage & communication	112,000	100,000
Finance	239,000	293,000
Community & social services	390,000	382,000
Private households	115,000	134,000
Total	1,784,000	1,847,000

Source: Statistics South Africa

BANKING AND FINANCE

The provincial budget for 2003/04 was R16.4 billion.

GDP/GNP, Inflation, National Debt
The Western Cape's total Gross Regional Product (GRP) rose from R115 billion in 1999 to R126 billion in 2000. In 2004, the Western Cape contributed 199,412 million rand to GDP (14.4 per cent). Major contributors to GDP include government, community and social services; manufacturing; finance and business services; and trade. In 2003, real growth in the province was estimated at 5.3 per cent, above the national average of 4.5 per cent.

Balance of Payments / Imports and Exports
Main export products include agricultural products (including fruits and wine), fish, textiles and clothing, industrial products, and mineral products.

Chambers of Commerce and Trade Organisations
Cape Chamber of Commerce and Industry, URL: http://www.capechamber.co.za/
Western Cape Investment and Trade Promotion Agency, URL: http://www.wesgro.co.za/

MANUFACTURING, MINING AND SERVICES

Primary and Extractive Industries
One of the Western Cape's main exports is processed mineral products. Mining and quarrying contributes just over 6 per cent of Gross Regional Product and employs about 2,999 people.

Energy
Figures for 2011 show that Western Cape consumed 22,779 gigawatt-hours of electricity.

Manufacturing

The clothing and textile industry is the largest employer in Western Cape. Most of South Africa's printing and publishing industries are situated in Cape Town.

Service Industries

Tourism is an important source of revenue, contributing over 9 per cent of the Western Cape's Gross State Product in 2000. The tourism sector is the fourth largest employer, providing work for over 160,000 people in 2000.

The captial, Cape Town is home to many large banks and insurance companies.

Agriculture

The Western Cape agriculture, forestry and fishing industry employs almost 165,000 people and contributes nearly 6 per cent of Gross Regional Product. The sector grew by over 9 per cent in 1998.

The Western Cape is renowned for its fruit and vegetable produce. Fruits such as apples, table grapes, olives, peaches and oranges grow well in the sheltered valleys. Viticulture plays an important role and Cape wines are internationally recognised. Wheat also provides an important source of revenue.

Ostrich farming provides ostrich leather, feathers and meat for export. Sheep farming is popular in the Karoo region, producing both wool and mutton. Chickens, eggs, dairy products, beef and pork are also important products of livestock in the region.

The fishing sector supplies jobs for over 28,000 people who are directly dependent on the industry. These are some of the richest fishing waters in the world and are protected by commercial fishing zones and a quota system.

The Knysna-Tsitskamma region has the largest indigenous forests in the country and produce yellowwood, stinkwood and white pear.

COMMUNICATIONS AND TRANSPORT

International Airports

Cape Town International Airport is the only international airport in the Western Cape.

HEALTH

Western Cape had 55 public hospitals in 2003. Of these, 21 were districts, 9 were regional, 3 were academic, and 13 were provincial aided. There were 14,326 authorised beds. In 2002 there were 1,529 medical practitioners and 9,767 nurses. The prevalence of HIV was estimated at 15.4 per cent in 2002. The leading cause of death in 2002 was tuberculosis followed by ischaemic heart disease. (Source: South Africa Statistics)

EDUCATION

Figures from 2002 show that 504,465 students attended primary schools, 285,538 students attended secondary schools, 21,601 students attended combined schools and 77,284 students attended intermediate and middle schools. (Figures from Statistics South Africa)

There are three universities (Cape Town, Stellenbosch and Western Cape), two technikons and many other higher educational institutes. Only 6.7 per cent of the population over the age of 20 have not received formal education.

SOUTH SUDAN
Republic of Southern Sudan

Capital: Juba (Population estimate, 2011: 1 million)

Head of State: Salva Kiir Mayardit (President) (page 1456)

Vice President: Dr Riek Machar Teny

National Flag: Three horizontal stripes of black, red and green, the red having white edging. A blue triangle is positioned at the hoist charged with a five-pointed gold star.

CONSTITUTION AND GOVERNMENT

Constitution

South Sudan gained its independence on 9 July 2011. A new Transitional Constitution was approved by the Southern Sudan legislative assembly on 8 July. It allows for a four-year transitional period during which time a new permanent constitution will be drafted. The Transitional Constitution is built on the Interim Constitution of Southern Sudan, in force since 5 December 2005.

Under the Transitional Constitution the head of state is a president, directly elected by universal adult suffrage. The current president was elected President of the Government of Southern Sudan during the Interim Period, and in October 2010 all parties agreed that on independence he should become President of South Sudan for the transitional period. His term of office as four years from the date of independence. The president is also the head of government. The president appoints the National Council of Ministers.

Under the Transitional Constitution, the legislature, the National Legislature, is bicameral. The term of office of both chambers is for the remainder of the four-year transitional period.

To consult the draft constitution, please visit: http://www.sudantribune.com/Draft-constitution-of-the-Republic,38679

Independence

Under the Machakos Protocol signed in 2002, Southern Sudan was able to seek self determination, and in September 2005 a new government was announced which included many leading figures from the Sudanese People's Liberation Movement (SPLM). The government was responsible for the internal affairs of the area. Foreign policy, defence and energy remained the responsibility of the government in Khartoum. Following the formation of a mainly autonomous administration in the south in October 2005, it was announced a referendum would be held in 2011 regarding the question of independence. The terms of the referendum were agreed in December 2009 and in January 2010 President Bashir said he would accept the result of the referendum even if meant independence for the South. In December 2010 the SPLM publicly supported independence for the south. The referendum took place on 9 January 2011 and the result was overwhelming: 98.83 per cent were in favour of full independence from the north. The south declared formal independence on 9 July. South Sudan became a member of the United Nations on 14 July 2011.

Recent Events

In November 2011 there were reports of aerial bombardments near the border with Sudan and trouble along the border. South Sudan has accused the Sudanese military of involvement. The new border is still not officially demarcated and the region of Abyei has still not held a referendum on which Sudan to join. Sharing of oil revenues is also still to be clarified.

A disaster area was declared in the Jonglei State after clashes between rival ethnic groups in January 2012.

In February 2012 Sudan and South Sudan signed a non-aggression pact. However, Sudan then closed down the South's oil export pipelines in a dispute over fees. South Sudan subsequently dramatically cut public spending as its export revenues fell. Trouble between the two countries continued with border fighting. South Sudan troops pushed into the oil field and town of Heglig before being driven back. Sudanese warplanes attacked the Bentiu area in South Sudan. Peace talks resumed in May 2012 and Sudan pledged to withdraw its troops out of the disputed border region of Abyei.

In June 2012, the parliament voted to suspend at least 75 senior officials accused of corruption. Allegedly $4 billion is missing, and some $60 million has been recovered.

An estimated 200,000 refugees fled into South Sudan to escape fighting in the border states of Sudan in August 2012.

In September 2012, the presidents of South Sudan and Sudan held talks in Ethioipia. Trade, security and oil deals were agreed. A demilitarised buffer zone is to be set up. The disputed Abyei territory issue was not resolved. In March 2013, the two countries ageed to withdraw troops from the buffer zone. They also agreed to resume pumping oil.

Legislature

Under the Transitional Constitution, the legislature, the National Legislature, is bicameral. The former unicameral Southern Sudan Legislative Assembly was replaced on 1 August 2011 by a National Legislative Assembly with 332 members. For this transitional period the Assembly is composed thus: 170 members from the former chamber as directly elected in April 2010, plus the 96 former Southern members of the National Assembly of the Republic of Sudan, also directly elected in April 2010, and 66 new members appointed by the president. A new 50-seat upper house, the Council of States, was created, comprising the 20 former Southern members of the Council of States of the Republic of Sudan (two per state) and 30 new members appointed by the president. The term of office of both chambers is for the remainder of the four-year transitional period.

```
Cabinet (as at June 2013)
Minister of Cabinet Affairs: Deng Alor Kuol
Minister of Defence and Veteran Affairs: Gen. John Kong Nyuon
Minister of Foreign Affairs and International Co-operation: Gen. Nhial Deng Nhial
(page 1486)
Minister in the Office of the President: Emmanuel Lowilla
Minister of National Security: Gen. Oyay Deng Ajak
Minister of Petroleum and Mining: Stephen Dhieu Dau (page 1415)
Minister of Internal Affairs: General Alison Manani Magaya
Minister of Labour and Public Service: currently vacant
Minister of Parliamentary Affairs: Michael Makuei Lueth
Minister of Finance and Economic Planning: Kosti Manibe Ngai
Minister of Justice: John Luk Jok (page 1451)
Minister of Agriculture & Forestry: Dr Betty Achan Ogwaro
Minister of Animal Resources and Fisheries: Martin Elia Lomuro
Minister of Transport: Agnes Poni Lokudu
Minister of Roads and Bridges: Maj.-Gen. Gier Chuang Aluong
Minister of Commerce and Industry: Garang Diing Akuong
```

SOUTH SUDAN

STATES OF THE WORLD

1011

SOUTH SUDAN

Minister of Electricity and Dams: David Deng Athorbei
Minister of Water Resources and Irrigation: Paul Mayom Akec
Minister of Housing and Physical Planning: Jemma Nunu Kumba
Minister of Education: Joseph Ukel Abango
Minister of Health: Dr. Michael Milli Hussein
Minister of Information and Broadcasting: Dr. Barnaba Marial Benjamin
Minister of Communications and Postal Services: Maj. Gen. Madut Biar Yel
Minister of Gender, Social Welfare and Religious Affairs: Agnes Kwaje Lasuba
Minister of Wildlife Conservation and Tourism: Gabriel Changson Chang
Minister of Environment: Alfred Lado Gore
Minister of Higher Education, Research, Science and Technology: Dr Peter Adwok Nyaba
Minister of Culture, Youth, and Sports: Dr Cirino Hitend Ofuho
Minister of Humanitarian Affairs and Disaster Management: Joseph Lual Acuil

Ministries
Government Portal: URL: http://www.goss.org

Political Parties
Sudan People's Liberation Movement (SPLM); National Congress (NCP); Union of Sudan African Parties 1 (USAP 1); Union of Sudan African Parties 2 (USAP 2); United Democratic Sudan Forum (UDSF); South Sudan Democratic Forum (SSDF); United Democratic Front (UDF); Sudan African National Union (SANU); South Sudan Defense Force (SSDF); SPLM-Democratic Change.

Diplomatic Representation
Mission of the South Sudan in the UK, 28-32 Wellington Road, London, NW8 9SF, United Kingdom. Tel: +44 (0)20 7483 9260
Ambassador: H.E. Sabit Abbe Alley
British Embassy in the South Sudan, EU Compound, Thom ping, Juba, South Sudan. Tel: +249 955 584193, e-mail: ukinsouthsudan@dfid.gov.uk, URL: http://ukinsouthsudan.fco.gov.uk/en/
Ambassador: Ian Hughes
Embassy of the Republic of South Sudan, 1233 20th Street NW Suite 602, Washington DC 20036, USA. Tel: +1 202 293 7940, fax: +1 202 293 7941, URL: http://www.gossmission.org/goss/
Head of Mission: Ajec Khoc Aciew Khoc
US Mission in South Sudan, E-mail: usembassyjuba@state.gov, URL: http://southsudan.usembassy.gov/
Ambassador: Susan Page
Permanent Mission of South Sudan to the United Nations. Permanent Representative to the UN: Francis Mading Deng

LEGAL SYSTEM

Under the terms of the 2005 constitution the Judiciary of Southern Sudan is an independent decentralized institution. The highest court is the Supreme Court of Southern Sudan. There are also Courts of Appeal, High Courts, County Courts and provision has been made to set up other courts and tribunals should it be deemed necessary.

President of Supreme Court: Justice John Wol Makec

LOCAL GOVERNMENT

Southern Sudan consists of ten states: Central Equatoria; Eastern Equatoria; Western Equatoria; Northern Bahr el Ghazal; Western Bahr el Ghazal; Lakes; Warrap; Jonglei; Unity; Upper Nile. The ten states are further subdivided into 86 counties.

AREA AND POPULATION

Area
Southern Sudan used to be part of Sudan; it is bordered to the east by Ethiopia, to the south by Kenya, Uganda, and the Democratic Republic of the Congo, and to the west the Central African Republic. Its northern border is with Sudan.

It covers an area of 239,285 sq miles or 619,745 sq km. and includes the swamp region of the Sudd which is formed by the White Nile, high-altitude plateaux and escarpments, wooded and grassy savannahs, floodplains, and wetlands.

To view a map, consult
http://www.lib.utexas.edu/maps/africa/txu-oclc-219400066-sudan_pol_2007.jpg. The area of Southern Sudan is shown on the map by a thick red border.

Population
Southern Sudan is inhabited by a number of tribes, sometimes in very small units, speaking a large number of separate languages and dialects. These tribes can be classified as follows: (a) the various Sudanic tribal groups west of the Nile, including the Azande and Moru-Madi tribes; (b) the Nilotic peoples, the Dinka, Nuer and Shilluk-Acoli tribes; (c) the Nilo-Hamitic peoples of the southern Nile valley, for example the Bari and Latuka. Many of Sudan's tribes have links with those in Abyssinia, Kenya, Uganda or the Congo.

A census was taken in 2008 and 2009 ahead of the referendum on independence; on each occasion the results were disputed. The population is estimated to be somewhere between 6 and 10 million.

Arabic is the official language but English is the language of education and government business and is also widely spoken. There are a number of indigenous Southern Sudanese languages.

Public Holidays
1 January: Independence Day
9 January: Peace Agreement Day
16 May: SPLA Day
30 July: Martyrs Day
25 December: Christmas Day
26 December: Boxing Day

BANKING AND FINANCE

Currency
Sudanese Pound

Economy
South Sudan has signficant oil reserves and almost all budget revenues stem from oil. Its total output is nearly 500,000 bbl/d. South Sudan's other resources include fertile agricultural land, gold, diamonds, limestone, iron ore, tungsten and silver. The economy is primarily subsistence farming. An estimated 50 per cent of the population lives below the poverty line. The major trading partner is currently Sudan, and the country depends on Sudan for imports. The country receives foreign aid, mainly from the US, UK, Norway and the Netherlands. Development of the economy is hindered by its poor infrastructure, poor living standards and high level of illiteracy.

The economy is driven by oil production but in January 2012 the government shut down its oil fields as part of its post-independence dispute with Sudan. The government has implemented budget cuts. After an agreement between the governments of Sudan and South Sudan was reached is hoped that oil production will resume in early 2013. GDP was estimated to be US$13 billion in 2010 and per capita GDP was estimated to be US$1,550.

Inflation has been high since independence, reaching 80 per cent in 2011, driven by high food prices.

Central Bank
Bank of Southern Sudan. Tel: +249 811-820218, e-mail: info@bankofsouthernsudan.org, URL: http://www.bankofsouthernsudan.org

MANUFACTURING, MINING AND SERVICES

Primary and Extractive Industries
Southern Sudan has large mineral resources including petroleum, iron ore, copper, chromium ore, zinc, tungsten, mica, silver and gold.

Oil
Southern Sudan has several oil fields including in the disputed area of Abyei. It has been estimated that Southern Sudan produced around 85 per cent of Sudan's total oil output. Several foreign companies are involved in oil production in the south including France, China, UAE, Malaysia and India.

In April 2013, South Sudan resumed oil production, Althou South Sudan has large oil reserves, being landlocked has menat it has been reliant on Sudan to export the oil. Production was halted in 2011 as the two countries negotiated over costs of exporting oil through Sudan. Initial figures show that output would initially be in the region of 150,000 to 200,000 barrels per day eventually rising to pre shutdown figures of 350,000 barrels per day.

Manufacturing
The industrial sector is small and is centered around handicrafts, the building and construction industries and mining.

Tourism
The government of Southern Sudan is committed to developing the tourism sector focusing primarily on the natural resources of wildlife, promoting safari style holidays.

Agriculture
Agriculture forms the mainstay of the economy and most people are employed in the sector. Main agricultural products include cotton, peanuts, sorghum, millet, wheat, gum arabic, sugarcane, cassava , mangos, papaya, bananas, sweet potatoes, and sesame. Animal products including camels, goats and sheep are exported to Egypt and the Middle-East.

RELIGION

The majority of southern Sudanese follow traditional beliefs. Although there is believed to be a sizeable Christian minority, estimated figures vary greatly.

SPAIN
Kingdom of Spain
Reino de España

Capital: Madrid (City population estimate, 2009: 3,255,944)

Sovereign: HM King Juan Carlos I de Borbón y Borbón (page 1452)

National Flag: A tricolour fesswise, red, yellow, red, the yellow in width equal to the two red stripes combined, the flag charged with the national arms, flanked by the Pillars of Hercules.

CONSTITUTION AND GOVERNMENT

Constitution
Following the death in 1975 of General Franco, Spain returned to being a democracy with a parliamentary monarchy. The 1978 constitution established Spain as a constitutional monarchy. The king is the head of state and appoints the president of the government (prime minister) and the Council of Ministers.

To consult the constitution, please visit: http://www.senado.es/constitu_i/index.html

Recent Events
In March 2004, 191 people were killed in explosions on rush-hour trains in Madrid in pre-election attacks by an Islamic group with links to al-Qaeda. Over 1,800 people were injured in the attacks. The Socialists under Jose Luis Rodriguez Zapatero won the ensuing general election, and withdrew all Spanish troops from Iraq within two months of taking office.

In June 2005 the Spanish Parliament legalised gay marriage and gave homosexual couples the same adoption and inheritance rights as heterosexual ones, angering the Roman Catholic Church.

In March 2006 the Basque terrorist group ETA declared a permanent ceasefire after nearly forty years of carrying out guerrilla attacks in Spain. Reaction to the announcement varied from hope for the future of the region to disbelief. In October, ETA announced that it would not give up its weapons until the Basque region was granted its independence from Spain; the government ruled out Basque independence. In December 2006, Prime Minister Zapatero suspended moves to seek dialogue with ETA following a car bomb attack at a Madrid airport. In June 2007 ETA called off the ceasefire.

In October 2007, a leader of the Basque group, Batasuna (part of the terrorist ETA group) said that the arrest of 23 of its key members was a "declaration of war" by the Spanish government and hundreds of people protested in Basque towns and cities against the arrests. The group was banned in 2003 for failing to condemn violence and cut links to ETA. Before its ban, Batasuna represented around 15 per cent of the Basque people in regional government.

At the end of October 2007, 21 of the 28 people on trial for the Madrid terrorist attack in 2004 were convicted of murder. Moroccans Jamal Zougam and Otman el Ghanoui and Spaniard Emilio Trashorras were sentenced to thousands of years in jail but the suspected mastermind, Rabei Osman, was acquitted. Of the 27 men and one woman defendants, 19 were mostly Moroccan Arabs and nine were Spaniards, and they faced charges including murder, forgery and conspiracy to commit a terrorist attack. Six of the nine Spaniards were acquitted. Seven suspected ringleaders died in a suicide blast in a Madrid apartment three weeks after the attacks. It is believed that the group were part of a local Islamist militant group with no direct links to Al-Queda.

In December 2007, 47 people were sentenced to prison terms of between two and 20 years over their links to the terrorist group, ETA. In January 2008, raids in Barcelona, in which bomb-related material was found, led to the arrest of 14 people suspected of links with an Islamist terror network; the Spanish intelligence agency had warned France, the UK and Portugal that a terror cell was preparing an imminent attack.

In February 2008, Spanish police arrested 14 suspected members of Batasuna, the party banned for its links to the terrorist group ETA. Spain's government, which in the past tried to negotiate with ETA, now demands that the separatists unconditionally lay down their arms.

Eight suspected members of ETA were arrested on 22nd July 2008, near the city of Bilbao. The arrests followed four bombs explosions in beach resorts on the country's northern coastline. One of those arrested was Arkaitz Goikoetxea, allegedly the leader of the cell blamed for nearly a dozen attacks. On the 4th October, a bomb exploded outside a court in Spain's north-eastern Basque region, and on the 30th October, following the arrest of four ETA suspects, a car bomb exploded in a car park at the University of Navarra, Pamplona.

At the beginning of November, the government announced that the descendants of people who fled Spain during the civil war are to be allowed to apply for citizenship, allowing an estimated 500,000 children and grandchildren of civil war exiles to return. Descendants of Spaniards who left the country for fear of political persecution or economic hardship between 1936 and 1955 can apply for Spanish nationality before 2011.

In November 2008, the military head of ETA, Mikel Aspiazu Rubina ('Txeroki') was arrested and, following the murder of a businessman in the Basque region in early December, a man suspected of being his replacement, Aitzol Irionda, was arrested in France. Once a safe haven for Basque militants, France began arresting ETA suspects after the group called off a 15-month-old ceasefire in June 2007. France and Spain signed a special accord in January 2008 which allowed Spanish agents to operate in south-western France. Since then, at least 36 ETA members or people linked to the group have been arrested.

Figures released by the central bank in January 2009 indicated that Spain's economy was in recession for the first time since 1993. The government forecast that GDP would shrink by 1.6 per cent during 2009, following declines of 1.1 per cent and 0.2 per cent in the previous two quarters. By March 2009, the unemployment rate had reached 17.4 per cent and over 4 million people were out of work.

At the end of July 2009, there were two bombings in Spain; the first was a car bomb attack on a police barracks in Burgos which injured 46 people, and the second, a detonated bomb under a patrol car, killed two Civil Guard officers in Mallorca. The government blamed both on Basque separatist group ETA. The attacks heralded the 50th anniversary of ETA's founding, on 31st July. At the beginning of March, 2010, Judge Eloy Velasco accused the Venezuelan government of assisting ETA.

In April 2009, Prime Minister Zapatero reshuffled his cabinet, ousting his fiscally conservative finance minister in a bid to restore political confidence in the face of the economic crisis. Tensions had risen between Mr. Zapatero and Minister Solbes on public sector spending, which had soared as the government announced stimulus plans of about €50 billion.

It was announced that the economy had contracted by 3.6 per cent over 2009. The government announced a 50 billion euro austerity package, including a civil service hiring freeze, at the beginning of January 2010. Over the first quarter of 2010, the economy grew by 0.1 per cent, ending six successive quarters of contraction; however, Spain continues to have the highest rate of unemployment in the eurozone, reaching 20 per cent in May 2010. In early June, Spain's two main trade unions called a strike across the public sector to protest against an average 5 per cent cut in pay, part of a 15 billion euro austerity package introduced in May in an attempt to cut the budget deficit. The cut in public sector pay represented a U-turn in policy for the governing Socialists.

ETA announced a ceasefire in September 2010. The move was dismissed by the government which said that ETA must disarm and fully renounce violence.

In May 2011 the town of Lorca is south eastern Spain was hit by two earthquakes of 4.4 and 5.2 magnitude, nine people were killed and approximately 3,000 made homeless.

Troubles with the economy deepened in 2011. In September, parliament approved constitutional amendments to set a legally binding cap on public sector borrowing.

The opposition Popular Party (PP) won the November 2011 parliamentary election. It announced further austerity measures for a rapid reduction of the public deficit. In January 2012 the unemployment rate rose to almost 23 per cent, the highest rate in the eurozone.

Worries about the strength of the banking sector continued in 2012. The credit ratings agency Moody's cut its rating for 16 Spanish banks over fears that property loans would not be repaid. Borrowing costs have risen and the government confirmed that Spain was in recession again in Q1 2012.

Trading in shares in Spain's Bankia were suspended in May 2012. The bank, which was recently part-nationalised, requested a government bailout of €19 billion. The autonomous region of Catalonia appealed for financial aid. Catalonia is Spain's richest region and represents one-fifth of the Spanish economy. It has taken out €13 billion of loans this year. Spain was given €100 billion in emergency loans in June 2012 to help its banking sector which is struggling following the collapse of the Spanish property market. Despite the bailout, the credit agency Moody's downgraded the economy to one above junk status. Spanish borrowing costs reached their highest level since it joined the euro in 1999; lenders are demanding an interest rate of 7 per cent for 10 year bonds, leading to fears that Spain may require a full international bailout.

In September 2012 large demonstrations took place particularly in Madrid against the continuing economic crisis. In September, the government created a bank in which to off-load toxic property assets. This is one of the requirements of any Eurozone bail-out loans. The EC approved the government's plan to restructure several ailing banks which were nationalised after experiencing heavy losses on mortgages.

In November 2012, regional elections took place in Catalonia. In January 2013 Catalonia went to the central government for a €9.0 billion financial bailout, this was further to the €5.0 billion bailout it received in August 2012.

In November 2012, the terrorist group Eta announced that was ready to disarm and enter talks with the French and Spanish governments.

SPAIN

King Juan Carlos's son-in-law, Inaki Urdangarin, (the Duke of Palma), was suspended from official royal engagements in December 2012, this followed allegations of involvement in a corruption scandal. The Duke denied the allegations.

In March 2013 the European Court of Justice ruled that Spanish law doesn't do enough to protect homeowners who default on their mortgages from being evicted. It was estimated that around 350,000 families have been evicted since the 2008 property crash.

In April 2013, Spain's unemployment reached a record 27.2 per cent, over six million people.

Legislature

Parliament, or the *Cortes Generales*, has legislative power and comprises two elected chambers: the Congress of Deputies and the Senate. Each House elects its own president and governing body and makes its own rules. The *Cortes* sits twice a year: for one four month session and one five month session. No person may be a member of both chambers simultaneously or be a representative in the Assembly of an Autonomous Community if he is a member of either chamber.

Upper House

The Senate (Senado) comprises 259 members, 208 directly elected and 48 indirectly elected by the autonomous regions. All serve a four-year term. Each of the 50 provinces elects four Senators to the Senate, by universal suffrage. Each of the 17 Autonomous Communities also elects a further Senator each and another for each million inhabitants.
Senate, Palacio del Senado, Plaza de la Marina Española, no. 8, 28071 Madrid, Spain. Tel: +34 91 538 1000, fax: +34 91 538 1003, e-mail: informacion@senado.es, URL: http://www.senado.es
Senate Speaker: Pio Garcia-Escudero

Lower House

The Congress of Deputies (Congreso do los Diputados) consists of 350 members directly elected for a four-year term. The number of Deputies elected to the Congress by each province is determined by population. Deputies are elected by universal suffrage. The Congress has supreme legislative power.
Congress of Deputies, Palacio del Congreso de los Diputados, Calle Floridanlanca 1, 28014 Madrid, Spain. Tel: +34 91 390 6000, fax: +34 91 429 9627, URL: http://www.congreso.es/
Speaker of the Congress: Jesus Maria Posada Moreno

Cabinet (as at June 2013)
Prime Minister (President of the Government): Mariano Rajoy (page 1499)
First Vice President of the Government, Minister of the Presidency, Government Spokesman: Soraya Saenz de Santamaria Anton
Minister of Finance and Public Administration: Cristobal Montoro Romero (page 1479)
Minister of Economy and Competitiveness: Luis de Guindos Jurado
Minister of the Interior: Jorge Fernandez Diaz
Minister of Foreign Affairs and Co-operation: Jose Manuel Garcia Margallo (page 1428)
Minister of Labour and Social Security: Maria Fatima Banez Garcia
Minister of Justice: Alberto Ruiz Gallardon (page 1428)
Minister of Defence: Pedro Morenes Eulate
Minister of Education, Culture and Sport: Jose Ignacio Wert Ortega
Minister of Industry, Energy and Tourism: Jose Manuel Soria (page 1518)
Minister of Development: Ana Pastor Julian
Minister of Agriculture, Livestock and the Environment: Miguel Arias Cañete
Minister of Health, Social Services and the Equality: Ana Mato Adrover (page 1472)

Ministries

Prime Minister's Chancellery, Complejo de la Moncloa, Edif. INIA, Avda. de Puerta de hierro s/n, 28071 Madrid, Spain. Tel: +34 91 335 3535, fax: +34 91 390 0700, e-mail: portal.presidencia@mp.boe.es, URL: http://www.la-moncloa.es
Ministry of Agriculture, Fisheries and Food, Paseo Infanta Isabel 1, 28071 Madrid, Spain. Tel: +34 91 347 5141, fax: +34 91 347 5142, URL: http://www.mapya.es
Ministry of Defence, Paseo de la Castellana 109, 28071 Madrid, Spain. Tel: +34 91 395 5000, fax: +34 91 556 3958, e-mail: infodefensa@mde.es, URL: http://www.mde.es
Ministry of Development, Paseo de la Castellana 67, 28071 Madrid, Spain. Tel: +34 91 597 7000, fax: +34 91 597 8502, URL: http://www.mfom.es
The Treasury, Calle Alcala 9, 2Planta Baja, 28071 Madrid, Spain. Tel: +34 91 595 8348, fax: +34 91 595 8869, e-mail: información.alcala@minhac.es, URL: http://www.minhac.es
Ministry of Economy and Finance, Paseo de la Castellana 162, 28071 Madrid, Spain. Tel: +91 583 8348, e-mail: informacion.alcala@meh.es, URL: http://www.minhac.es
Ministry of Education, Calle Alcalá 36, 28071 Madrid, Spain. Tel: +34 91 701 8500, fax: +34 91 701 8648, URL: http://www.mec.es
Ministry of the Environment, Rural Affairs and Fisheries, Plaza San Juan de la Cruz s/n, 28071 Madrid, Spain. Tel: +34 91 597 6000, fax: +34 91 597 6349, URL: http://www.mma.es
Ministry of Foreign Affairs, Plaza de la Provincia 1, 28071 Madrid, Spain. Tel: +34 91 379 9700, fax: +34 91 366 5000, URL: http//www.mae.es
Ministry of Health and Consumer Affairs, Paseo del Prado 18-20, 28014 Madrid, Spain. Tel: +34 901 400100, fax: +34 91 596 4480, e-mail: informacion@msc.es, URL: http://www.msc.es
Ministry of the Interior, Calle Rafael Calvo 33, 28071 Madrid, Spain. Tel: +34 91 537 1111, fax: +34 91 537 1003, URL: http://www.mir.es/
Ministry of Industry, Commerce and Tourism: Po de la Castellana 160, 28071 Madrid, Spain. Tel: +34 91 244 6006, URL:http://www.min.es/
Ministry of Justice, C/ San Bernardo, 45, 28015 Madrid, Spain. Tel: +34 91 390 4500 , URL: http://www.mju.es
Ministry of Labour, Social Affairs and Immigration, Agustín de Betancourt 11, 28071 Madrid, Spain. Tel: +34 91 553 6000, fax: +34 91 553 4033, URL: http://www.mtas.es
Ministry of Territories, Paseo de la Castellana 3, 28071 Madrid, Spain. Tel: +34 91 586 1139, fax: +34 91 319 2448, URL: http://www.mpt.es

Ministry of Culture, Plaza del Rey 1, 28004 Madrid, Spain. Tel: +34 91 701 7000, URL: http://www.mcu.es
Ministry of Housing, Paseo de la Castellana 112, 28071 Madrid, Spain. Tel: +34 91 728 4004, URL: http://www.mviv.es
Ministry of Science and Innovation, C/ Albacete 5, 28027 Madrid, Spain. Tel: +34 90 221 8600, e-ail: juanj.gomez@micinn.es, URL: http://www.micinn.es
Ministry of Territorial Policy and Public Administration, Paseo de la Castellana 3, 28071 Madrid, Spain. Tel: +34 91 273 9000, fax: +34 91 586 1012, e-mail: cia.difusion@igsap.map.es, URL: http://www9.mpt.es

Political Parties

The main Spanish political parties are:
Convergencia Democratica de Catalunya (CDC, Democratic Convergence of Calalunya), Còrsega, 331-333, 08037 Barcelona, Spain. Tel: +34 93 236 3100, fax: +34 93 236 3115, e-mail: cdc@convergencia.org, URL: http://convergencia.org/
President: Jordi Pujol i Soley
Secretary General: Artur Mas i Gavarro
Izquierda-Unida (IU, United Left), IU-Federal, Olimpo 35, 28043 Madrid, Spain. Tel: +34 91 722 7500, fax: +34 91 388 0405, e-mail: org.federal@izquierda-unida.es, URL: http://www.izquierda-unida.es/
General Coordinator: Cayo Lara
Partido Nacionaliste Vasco (EAJ-PNV, Basque Nationalist Party), Ibanez de Bilbao 16, 48001 Bilbao, Spain. Tel: +34 94 403 9400, fax: +34 94 403 9413, URL: http://www.eaj-pnv.com/
President of National Executive: Iñigo Urkullu Rentería
Partido Comunista de España (PCE, Communist Party of Spain), Olimpo 35, 28043 Madrid, Spain. Tel: +34 91 300 4969, fax: +34 91 300 4744, e-mail: webmasterpce@pce.es, URL: http//www.pce.es
General Secretary: José Luis Centella
Partido Popular (PP, Popular Party), Génova 13, 28004 Madrid, Spain. Tel: +34 91 557 7300, fax: +34 91 319 2322, URL: http://www.pp.es
President: Mariano Rajoy Brey (page 1499)
Partido Socialista Obrero Español (PSOE, Socialist Workers' Party of Spain), Ferraz 70, 28008 Madrid, Spain. Tel: +34 91 582 0444, fax: +34 91 582 0422, e-mail: administrador-web@psoe.es, URL: http://www.psoe.es
Secretary General: José Luis Rodríguez Zapatero
Unión Valenciana (UV, Valencian Union), Avda de César Giorgeta 16, 2A, 46007 Valencia, Spain. Tel: +34 96 380 6267, fax: +34 96 380 2308, URL: http://www.uniovalenciana.org
President: José Manuel Miralles i Piqueres
Canarian Coalition (CC), URL: http://www.coalicioncanaria.org. Leader: Claudina Morales
Convergence and Union (CiU), URL: http://www.ciu.cat. Leader: Artur Mas
Republican Left of Catalonia (ERC), URL: http://www.esquerra.cat. Leader: Oriol Junqueras i Vies

Elections

The most recent general elections to the Cortes and the Senado took place on 9th March 2008. Jose Luis Rodriguez Zapatero's ruling Socialist Party (PSOE) won 169 seats, short of the 176 needed for a majority in the Cortes, and 89 seats in the Senate. The conservative Popular Party (PP) won 153 seats (up from 148 in the 2004 election) in the Cortes, and 101 seats in the Senate. Over 75 per cent of the electorate voted. The new cabinet contained more women than men for the first time.

A general election was held in March 2004, in the wake of the 11 March Madrid bombings, when the Socialist Workers' Party's Jose Luis Rodriguez Zapatero beat the Popular Party's Jose Maria Aznar.

The most recent general election was held on 20 November 2011, the Popular Party defeated the ruling Socialist Party. The Popular Party won 186 seats the PSOE won 110 seats and the United Left 11 seats.

In regional elections in March 2009, the Nationalists, who have governed the Basque Country for 29 years, again won the most votes in the region, but fell short of a majority. In Galicia, the governing Socialists lost to the conservative opposition.

Diplomatic Representation

British Embassy, Calle de Fernando el Santo 16, 28010 Madrid, Spain. Tel: +34 91 700 8200, fax: +34 91 700 8210, e-mail: enquiries.madrid@fco.gov.uk, URL: https://www.gov.uk/government/world/spain
Ambassador: Giles Paxman (page 1493)
Spanish Embassy, 2375 Pennsylvania Avenue, NW, Washington, DC 20037, United States of America. Tel: +1 202 452 0100, fax: +1 202 833 5670, e-mail: espan@spainemb.org, URL: http://www.maec.es/subwebs/Embajadas/Washington/es/home/Paginas/Home.aspx
Ambassador: Ramon Gil-Casares Satrustegui
Spanish Embassy, 39 Chesham Place, London, SW1X 8SB. Tel: +44 (0)20 7235 5555, fax: +44 (0)20 7259 5392, URL: http://www.maec.es/subwebs/Embajadas/Londres
Ambassador: D. Federico Trillo-Figueroa Martinez-Conde
Embassy of the United States of America, Serrano 75, 28006 Madrid, Spain. Tel: +34 91 587 2200, fax: +34 91 587 2303, URL: http://madrid.usembassy.gov
Ambassador: Alan D. Solomont (page 1517)
Permanent Mission of Spain to the United Nations, 823 UN Plaza, 9th Floor, New York, NY 10017, USA. Tel: +1 212 661 1050, fax.- +1 212 949 7247, e-mail: general@spainun.org, URL: http://www.spainun.org
Ambassador: Fernando Arias Gonzalez

LEGAL SYSTEM

Spanish law is based on comprehensive legal codes and laws rooted in Roman law.

The *Tribunal Supremo* (Supreme High Court) is situated in Madrid and is composed of six courts: the court of cassation for civil and commercial actions, the court of criminal appeal, the court of appeal in social matters, and three courts dealing with contentious administrative matters. The president of the Supreme Court is appointed by the king on the recommendation of the General Council of the Judiciary.

There are 22 *Audiencias Territoriales* (Territorial High Courts), most of them covering several provinces, which decide in the second instance on sentences passed in civil matters. The *Audiencia Provincial* (Provincial High Court) deals with criminal cases for each of the 50 provinces.

There are 467 *Juzgados de Primera Instancia* (Court of First Instance) for each *partido* (division), 256 *Juzgados Municipales* (Municipal Courts), 443 *Juzgados Comarcales* (District Courts) and 7,680 *Juzgados de Paz* (Courts of Peace). There are 301 Judicial Districts.

The Constitutional Court does not form part of the legal system of Spain but exists purely to interpret the constitution. The court has 12 members, eight of which are proposed by parliament, two by the government, and two by the general judiciary board. Each member serves a nine-year term and cannot be re-appointed.

The governing body of the judiciary is the General Council of the Judiciary. Composed of the president of the Supreme Court and 20 members appointed by the king for a five-year period, the General Council oversees the setting up, operation and control of Spain's courts and tribunals. Its members are nominated by the Congress of Deputies and the Senate, four members from lawyers and six members from judges and magistrates.

The government respects the rights of its citizens. However, in recent years there have been alleged cases of suspect abuse by security forces. Spain abolished the death penalty for peacetime cases in 1978 and it was totally abolished in 1995.

Tribunal Supremo, URL: http://www.poderjudicial.es.
President: D. Carlos Divar Blanco

Ombudsman for Spain, Zurbano 42, Spain. Tel: +34 91 432 7900, fax: +34 91 308 1158, e-mail: registro@defensordelpueblo.es, URL: http://www.defensordelpueblo.es/#

LOCAL GOVERNMENT

Spain is divided into 17 Autonomous Communities or *autonomías* with their own elected governments which are headed by a President. Ceuta and Melilla, situated on the North coast of Africa, are Autonomous Cities.

The following table shows the Autonomous Communities, and their areas:

Autonomous Community	Area in sq. km.	President
Andalucia	87,599	José Antonio Grinan
Aragon	47,720	Luisa Rudi
Cantabria	5,321	Ignacio Diego
Castilla-La Mancha	79,461	Maria Dolores de Cospedal
Castilla y León	94,224	Juan Vincente Herrera Campo
Cataluña	32,113	Artur Mas i Gavarró
Extremadura	41,634	José Antonio Monago
Galicia	29,575	Alberto Nunez Feijóo
las Islas Baleares	4,992	José Ramón Bauza
las Islas Canarias	7,447	Paulino Rivero Baute
Madrid	8,028	Esperanza Aguirre
País Vasco	7,234	Patxi López
la Rioja	5,045	Pedro Maria Sanz Alonso
Valencia	23,255	Alberto Fabra
Foral de Navarra	10,391	Yolanda Barcina
Asturias	10,604	Javier Fernandez
Murcia	11,314	Ramón Luis Valcarcel Siso
Ceuta	20	Juan J. Vivas Lara
Melilla	12	Juan José Imbroda Ortiz

The country is divided into 50 provinces, including the Balearic Islands and the Canaries. Each province has a *Diputación Provincial* (Provincial Council). This Council has one deputy for each *partido* (legal division) in the province. Spain also has over 8,000 townships.

Each township has its own *Ayuntamiento* (Town Council) headed by an *Alcalde* (Mayor) who is nominated by the government in the provincial capitals and by the Civil Governor in the other towns. The other councillors are elected, and their number varies with the size of the population. A third of the councillors are elected by heads of households, a third by the syndical organisations, the rest being co-opted by the first two groups from among the

leading citizens of the municipality. Both the Provincial and the Town Councils have their own budgets and a large measure of autonomy in expenditure and the means of covering it.

The Balearic Islands have the same administration as the mainland, but the two groups of the Canary Islands and Las Palmas and Santa Cruz de Tenerife are each governed by a *Cabildo* (Chapter).

AREA AND POPULATION

Area
Spain consists of the mainland, the Balearic Isles, the Canary Islands and Ceuta and Melilla on the north coast of Africa. It covers an area of 505,925 sq. km. The mainland is bordered by France to the north and Portugal to the west. Mainland Spain is dominated by high plateaus and mountain ranges: the Sierra Nevada in the south and the Pyrenees in the north. Along the coast there are several alluvial plains. Significant rivers include the Tagus, the Ebro, the Duero, the Guadiana and Guadalquivir.

The climate is very diverse. Most of the interior has a continental Mediterranean climate, with hot summers and cold winters. The southeast is semi-arid. The coastal strip near the Bay of Biscay has a more oceanic climate. The coast is generally cooler.

To view a map, please consult http://www.lib.utexas.edu/maps/cia08/spain_sm_2008.gif

The Balearic Islands are situated in the Mediterranean, off the east coast of Spain, opposite Valencia. They consist of four large and seven small islands. The four large islands are Mallorca, Menorca, Ibiza and Formentera. Their combined area is 5,014 sq. km.

The Canary Islands are situated off the north-west coast of Africa, to the south of Casablanca. They are divided into two groups, each considered a province of Spain and each named after their respective capitals: Las Palmas de Gran Canaria and Santa Cruz de Tenerife. The first group contains Gran Canaria, Fuerteventura, Lanzarote and six islets; the second group consists of Tenerife, Palma, Gomera and Hierro. They cover a total area of 7,273 sq. km.

Gibraltar adjoins Spanish territory on the south coast by a sandy isthmus about 1.7 km. long and 0.8 km. wide. Talks were held between Britain and Spain on the possible joint sovereignty of Gibraltar, in 2001 and 2002 but no agreement was reached. In December 2004 agreement was reached for the establishment of a trilateral dialogue independent of the sovereignty question. Meetings have since been held by the three sides to discuss such subjects as the expanded use of Gibraltar's airfield, pensions for Spanish workers formally employed in Gibraltar and telephone communications between Gibraltar and Spain. Bilateral talks between the UK government and a cross-section of Gibraltar residents began in 2005 aimed at modernising Gibraltar's Constitution; Gibraltar would remain British but in a non-colonial capacity. On 30 November 2006, a referendum was held on whether to accept the new Gibraltar constitution; 60.4 per cent of voters went to the polls, and 60.24 per cent of those voted to approve the constitution.

A £2 billion project to develop luxury hotels and a marina in waters off the Rock infuriated Spanish MPs in January 2009, who accused the Gibraltar authorities of an "illegal incursion" into Spanish waters. Although Gibraltar claims three miles into the Mediterranean as its own, the Treaty of Utrecht did not give it territorial waters.

Population
According to estimated figures, the resident population on 1 January 2012 was 46,818,200, up from 45,888,956 at the beginning of April 2009. An estimated 23.100,100 of the population were male, whilst 23,300,000 were women. Andalucía is the largest Autonomous community, with a 2011 population of approximately 8,424,102, followed by Catalonia, with 7,539,618 people, and the Community of Madrid with 6,489,680 people. The population of Spain's five largest cities in 2009 was as follows: Madrid, 3,255,944; Barcelona, 1,621,537; Valencia, 814,208; Seville, 703,206; and Zaragoza, 674,317. (Source: Instituto Nacional de Estadistica)

In 2011, some 5.7 million residents of Spain (around 12.2 per cent) were not Spanish. Of all the EU countries, Spain has the largest net immigrant population. The majority came from Latin America (1.78 million), Europe (1.7 million) and Africa (767,000). In 2011, Romanians comprised the largest foreign community (865,707 registered inhabitants), followed by Moroccans (773,995); Britons (391,194), and Ecuadorians (360,710). 1,162,391 Spaniards were living abroad at the beginning of 2007, most in European Union countries or the Americas. The countries that registered the highest number of Spanish nationals were France, Venezuela, Germany, Mexico, and the United States. (Source: INE).

The official language of Spain is Castilian, but all other languages included in the Statutes of the Autonomous Communities - for example Basque, Catalan, Valencian and Galician - are also recognised.

Births, Marriages, Deaths
Figures for 2008 indicate that the birth rate was 11.4 per 1,000 inhabitants and there were an average of 1.38 children per woman. The number of births rose from under 380,000 in the mid -to-late 1990s to around 519,000 births in 2008. Births to foreign mothers increased to108,195 over the year. The number of births to unmarried mothers increased by 6.7 per cent in 2007, and represented 30.24 per cent of the total births. Figures for 2011 show that the number of births was 470,553 down from the 2010 figure of 485,252 and the 2009 figure of 493,717.

The crude death rate in 2008 was estimated to be 8.47 deaths per 1,000 population, down from 8.59 in 2007. In 2008, there were 386,324 deaths. Infant mortality rate fell from 3.46 deaths per 1,000 live births in 2007 to 3.35 deaths per 1,000 births in 2008. The rate of natural population increase over 2008 was 2.93 per 1,000 inhabitants. The average age at which a woman had her first child was 29.3 years, and the fertility rate was 1.38 children per woman. Figures for 2011 show the number of deaths that year was 84,536.

SPAIN

Average life expectancy at birth in 2009 was 80 years for men and 85 years for women. In 2007 the marriage rate fell to 4.49 marriages per 1,000 people. The age at which people marry fell slightly for the first time since the 1980s; the average age for a first marriage was 34.09 years for men and 31.09 years for women. Over 2007 there were 137.510 marriage endings, down 5,8 on 2006; 91.5 per cent of these marriages ended in divorce, and 8.4 per cent ended in separation.

National Holidays 2014
1 January: New Year
6 January: Epiphany
17 April: Maundy Thursday
18 April: Good Friday
21 April: Easter Monday
1 May: Labour Day
15 August: Assumption Day
12 October: Spanish National Day
1 November: All Saints Day
6 December: Constitution Day
8 December: Immaculate Conception
25 December: Christmas Day

When a national day falls on a Sunday, each Autonomous region has the choice of celebrating the holiday on either the following Monday or changing it for a regional festivity.

EMPLOYMENT

Spain's workforce numbered around 23,006,900 in March 2010, equivalent to 59.8 per cent of the population. An estimated 18,394,200 people were employed, down 3.65 per cent over the same quarter in 2009, and 4,612,700 people were unemployed. The unemployment rate, which had fallen from a high of around 16 per cent in 2003 to 8.26 per cent in 2007, grew sharply to 11.3 per cent through 2008, in the wake of the global economic downturn. By March 2010 an estimated 20.05 per cent of the population were unemployed. Construction workers were the hardest hit, due to the collapse of mortgage markets and its impact on the building industry. Figures for February 2011 put the unemployment rate at 20.5 per cent; the average unemployment rate for EU countries at that time was 9.9 per cent. It rose further over the year: official figures for February 2012 put the unemployment rate at 22.8 per cent, the highest rate in the eurozone. Almost 50 per cent of 16-24-year-olds are out of work. Figures for February 2013 put the unemployment rate at 26.3 per cent, Youth unemployment was particularly high, registering 55.7 per cent. By April 2013, unemployment had reached a record 27.2 per cent (6.2 million people).

Employment according to economic sector over the period 2008-10 is shown in the table below:

Sector	2008	2009	2010
Agriculture	951,200	979,300	1,011,900
Industry	3,410,500	3,138,700	2,872,200
Construction	2,877,800	2,558,800	2,158,200
Services	14,741,400	14,871,500	14,838,000
Other	867,300	1,489,200	2,208,600
Total employment	22,848,200	23,037,500	23,088,900

Unemployment affected more women than men, at all ages. Employment by gender is shown in the table below:

Employment status	2010
MEN	
Workforce	12,819,200
- Employed	10,289,200
- Unemployed	2,529,300
WOMEN	
Workforce	10,269,700
- Employed	8,166,600
- Unemployed	2,103,100

Source: Instituto Nacional de Estadistica

In almost all the regions of Spain, the average salary of women is between 25 per cent and 35 per cent lower than that of men.

Highest rates of employment are found in the cities of Madrid, Bilbao and Barcelona as well as along the east coast and on the Balearics. The areas of highest unemployment are found in Andalucia (17.8 per cent in 2008) and the Canaries (17.4 per cent), though unemployment in Ceuta and Melilla was higher still at 18.9 in 2008. The lowest rates of unemployment were in the Basque Country, at 6.5 per cent, and the Community of Navarra (6.7 per cent).

BANKING AND FINANCE

Currency
On 1 January 1999 Spain became one of the first 11 European Union countries to adopt the single European currency, the euro. On 1 January 2002 the euro became legal tender. Prior to that the currency was the Peseta (1 Peseta = 100 céntimos).

1 euro (€) = 100 cents
€= 166.386 Spanish pesetas (European Central Bank irrevocable conversion rate)
Bank notes are in denominations of 5, 10, 20, 50, 100, 200 and 500 euro. Coins are in denominations of 1, 2, 5, 10, 20 and 50 cents and 1 and 2 euro.

GDP/GNP, Inflation, National Debt
Following a decade of rapid economic expansion, the millennium got off to a slow economic start in Spain, with growth in GDP of 1.9 per cent in 2002, 2.2 per cent in 2003 and 2.7 per cent in 2004. However, the economy grew by 3.4 per cent in 2005, 3.9 per cent in 2006, and 3.8 per cent in 2007, to €1,049,848 million at current market prices. Spain's economic growth continued to exceed the average EU-27 growth of 2.9 per cent. However the global economic crisis hit Spain in the autumn of 2008.

Financial Crisis
Until the financial crisis of 2008 the government's borrowing was zero and its debt ratio had been falling. However public borrowing increased, mainly on mortgages fuelled by a housing boom; house prices rose by nearly 50 per cent between 2004-08. The economy's reliance on the construction sector led to recession following the collapse of the real estate bubble; house prices have fallen by 25 per cent and mortgage lending declined by 51 per cent in November 2008. In 2009, Spain's economy entered a recession for the first time since 1993, shrinking by 3.6 per cent over the year. It has been falling by approximately 1 per cent a year since then. The government has had to increase its borrowings to make up the shortfall of decreased tax revenues and increased unemployment benefits.

In January 2010, the government announced a €50 billion cuts austerity budget. The economy struggled out of recession over the first quarter of the year, with growth of 0.1 per cent. However, unemployment continued to rise, reaching 20.15 per cent in May 2010 (double the rate of 2008), and making reduction of the government deficit more difficult. GDP growth for 2010 as a whole was put at 0.1 per cent.

Spain's budget deficit has been growing since the government introduced high spending on public works and unemployment benefits to combat the recession. Austerity reforms were introduced in May 2010 which were designed to reduce the deficit. The deficit reached 8.5 per cent of economic output in 2011. The government said it would miss its 2012 deficit target (set by the EC) of 4.4 per cent. A revised target of 5.3 per cent was agreed.

Following the November 2011 election, the new prime minister, Mariano Rajoy, committed himself to reducing the deficit. In January 2012 he announced €8.9 billion ($11.8 billion, £7.4 billion) in new budget cuts plus tax increases worth €6.3 billion. Other cuts including reducing maximum severance pay, a freeze on public sector worker salaries and department budgets reduced by almost 17 per cent. The measures have been deeply unpopular.

GDP
Over 2009, there was negative GDP growth in all the Autonomous Communities and autonomous cities; the largest recessions were in Aragón (-4.4 per cent), Comunitat Valenciana (-4.3 per cent) and Canaries (-4.2 per cent), whilst Melilla and Ceuta suffered the least, with falls of 1.4 per cent and 1.7 per cent respectively. Figures for early 2011 showed that unemployment was still very high around 1 in 5 adults were unemployed, this put a huge strain on the welfare sector which was already struggling under austerity measures.

The northeastern territory, together with Comunidad de Madrid, continued to register the highest per capita GDP. The Basque Country continued to contribute the highest per capita GDP, at €30,703, some 34.2 per cent higher than the national average. Comunidad de Madrid followed, with €30,02, and Comunidad Foral de Navarra was next, with €29,598. In comparison, per capita GDP in the poorest region of Extremadura was €16,301, (28.8 per cent below the national average) and that of Castilla-La Mancha stood at €17,208. The EU average per capita GDP was €23,600 in 2009.

GDP was expected to fall by 1.7 per cent in 2012 before rising to 0.2 per cent in 2013.

GDP at market prices

Industrial Sector	2010*	2011**
Agriculture and Fishing	24,554	24,383
Industry	154,770	165,051
Construction	104,762	98,546
Wholesale & retail trade, transportation & storage, accommodation & food service activities	233,814	242,066
Information & communication	41,310	42,280
Financial & insurance activities	44,003	40,650
Real estate activities	70,346	75,637
Professional, scientific & technical activities, admin. & support services	71,206	73,755
Public admin. & defence; compulsory social security; education human health & social work activities	177,667	178,184
Arts, entertainment & recreation, repair of household goods& other services	35,339	35,759
Taxes less subsidies on products	91,112	87,044
GDP at market prices	1,048,883	1,063,355

* Provisional ** Estimated
Source: Instituto Nacional de Estadistica

In 2008, the construction sector contributed 10.6 per cent of total GDP (market prices), down from 11 per cent in 2007. The service sector had increased from 60.4 per cent of GDP to 62.6 per cent over the same period.

In 2008, Spain's current account deficit fell slightly (by 1.2 per cent) to €104,664 million, mainly due to a decrease in the trade deficit of (€84,980 million). Gross debt was forecast to be over 66 per cent of GDP in 2010 (compared with 36 per cent in 2007).

Provisional figures indicate that the annual average Consumer Price Index (CPI) (all items) rose 4.1 per cent over 2008, to 107.0 in 2008 (base 2006 = 100). The largest cost increases were in housing (up 6.6 per cent over the year), food and non-alcoholic beverages (up 5.9 per cent) and transport (up 5.8 per cent). All sectors apart from recreation and culture (down 0.1 per cent) saw rising prices.

In 2012, the inflation rate was an estimated 3.1 per cent.

Foreign Investment

Investment comes primarily from the European Union, which Spain joined in 1984. Foreign investment in Spain fell sharply from around €245 billion in 2007 to around €165 billion in 2008; Spanish investments abroad also fell, to around €70 billion, almost €50 billion of which was in the form of direct investment.

Balance of Payments / Imports and Exports
Foreign Trade in Millions of Euros

Trade	2009	2010*	2011**
Imports of Goods & Services	270,189	308,109	330,251
Exports of Goods & Services	250,667	285,110	321,819

* provisional **estimated
Source: Instituto Nacional de Estadistica

Exports amounted to an estimated $25.7 billion in 2011 and imports $31 billion.

Imports and exports by commodity, 2008 (€ millions)

Commodity	Imports (cif)	Exports (fob)	Balance
Consumer Goods:	**71,271.2**	**69,476.5**	**-1,794.7**
- Food, drink and tobacco	15,983.9	22,512.6	6,528.8
- Cars	15,033.8	20,558.7	5,534.9
- Energy products	240.4	1,816.3	1,576.8
- Other consumer goods	40,013.1	24,577.9	-15,435.2
Intermediate Goods	**186,705.7**	**102,176.4**	**-84,529.4**
- Agricultural products	5,928.3	1,194.8	-4,733.5
- Energy products	56,737.5	9,916.4	-46,821.2
- Industrial products	124,039.9	91,065.2	-32,974.7
Capital Goods	**24,274.3**	**16,531.4**	**-7,742.9**
- Machinery and other equipment	16,825.1	8,618.3	-8,206.9
- Transport equipment	3,815.4	6,794.6	2,979.2
- Other capital goods	3,633.8	1,118.5	-2,515.3
TOTAL	**282,251.3**	**188,184.3**	**-94,067.0**

Source: Instituto Nacional de Estadistica

In 2010, Spanish wine exports increased by over 15.5 per cent in volume and 10 per cent in values to €1.9 billion. Top markets for wine are Germany, the UK and the US. Sales are growing in China.

The EU remains the country's main trading partner (primarily Germany, France, Italy, Portugal and the UK). Around 69 per cent of Spain's exports go to EU27 countries, and Spain imported 59.1 per cent of its goods from EU27 countries in 2007. The US is another important market for Spanish goods. Main import and export trading partners are shown on the following table:

Main trading areas (€ thousands) in 2008

Trading partner	CIF Imports	FOB Exports
Europe	170,702,666.8	137,613,231.1
China	20,492,570.0	2,152,730.86.3
All of Asia	56,460,598.7	15,518,074.6
United States	11,283,154.4	7,544,367.8
All of America	27,123,241.2	17,000,392.8
Africa	26,526,969.3	10,154,027.5
Oceania	2,572,773.8	2,038,961.6

Source: Instituto Nacional de Estadistica

Principal trading partners are shown below (approximate figures in € billion):

Principal Trading partners, 2011

Country	Imports	Exports
Germany	31	23
France	28	37
Italy	17	16
United Kingdom	10	16
China	18	3
Portugal	10	13

Central Bank

Banco de España, Alcalá, 50, 28014 Madrid, Spain. Tel: +34 91 338 5000, fax: +34 91 338 6088, e-mail: bde@bde.es URL: http://www.bde.es
Governor: Luis Linde (page 1465)
Deputy Governor: Fernando Restoy

Trade Organisations and Chambers of Commerce

Spanish Chamber of Commerce, URL: http://www.spanishchamber.co.uk/
Madrid Chamber of Commerce and Industry, URL: http://camaramadrid.es/
High Council of the Chamber sof Commerce, Industry and Navigation of Spain, URL: http://www.camaras.org/publicado/
Madrid Stock Exchange, URL: http//www.bolsamadrid.es

MANUFACTURING, MINING AND SERVICES

Primary and Extractive Industries

Spain has rich deposits of coal and mercury (from the Asturias region), lead, uranium and copper (from the Andalusia region), and potash (from the Catalonia region), as well as iron, pyrites, tin, wolfram, quartz, fluorspar, glauberite, sea and rock salt. Recent figures show that there are around 3,700 mines in Spain employing 85,000 people.

Oil

EIA estimates for January 2012 show that the Iberian peninsular had proven oil reserves of 150 million barrels. Spain has seven active oil fields: Alga, Ayoluengo, Barracuda, Boqueron, Casablanca, Chipiron, and Rodaballo. Exploration for new reserves is currently underway in the Malaga area of the southern Mediterranean. In comparison with its oil reserves, Spain's total oil production is relatively small, an estimated 37.38 thousand barrels per day in 2011. Total consumption in 2011 was an estimated 1.38 million barrels per day. Spain depends upon imports, the largest suppliers being Russia, Libya and Saudi Arabia. Spain had a crude oil refining capacity of 1.3 million barrels per day in 2012.

The largest oil company in Spain is Repsol (URL: http://www.repsol.com/es_en/), created in 1999 through the merger of the former, state-owned oil company and Yacimientos Petroliferos Fiscales (YPF), formerly owned by the Argentine government. The group is one of the world's largest oil operators, with activities in over 28 countries. Cepsa is the second-largest oil company in Spain (URL: http://www.cepsa.com/).

Natural Gas

Spain has limited natural gas reserves, estimated at 90 billion cubic feet in January 2011. Most of Spain's natural gas production (totalling two billion cubic feet in 2011) comes from the offshore Poseidón field. In 2010, Spain consumed 1,265 billion cubic feet of natural gas. Natural gas consumption has risen dramatically in recent years; over the decade to 2004, consumption tripled, mainly due to the introduction of gas-fired power plants and, more recently, the construction of the Sines liquefied natural gas (LNG) import terminal and the Maghreb-Europe pipeline, connecting the Iberian Peninsula to Algerian natural gas sources. A further pipeline, the Medgaz line, linking Beni Saf, Algeria to Almeria, Spain, (with an eventual extension to France) was due to be completed in 2008, but initial construction on the project was delayed, and in 2007, a dispute between the Algerian state energy company and the Spanish government threatened to derail the project. In 2011, the pipeline started to be filled to begin testing with gas at the terminal in Almeria.

Spain is one of Europe's largest LNG importers. The company Enagas's facilities include 10,000 km of pipeline, two underground natural gas storages and three regasification plants.

Coal

Coal is Spain's most plentiful energy source. Coal reserves were estimated at 584 million short tons in 2003, most of which was lignite and sub-bituminous. Production has fallen in recent years, a trend that is expected to continue as EU regulations on environmental standards are met. Coal production was around 9.24 million short tons in 2010, down from 25.8 million short tons in 2005. Consumption fell to 18.5 million short tons in 2010 from 52.6 million short tons in 2005. EU regulations require that Spain reduce coal production by 65 per cent over the period 2002-2012. (Source: Energy Information Administration, EIA)

Energy

Spain has the fifth largest electricity market in Europe (after Germany, France, the UK, and Italy). Both generation and consumption have grown at almost double the rate of Western Europe, straining the country's electricity infrastructure. In 2005, net consumption rose to 243.03 billion kilowatthours, and Spain produced 270.33 billion kWh. In 2010 net generation was 286.58 billion kWh and net consumption 267.04 billion kWh.

The largest source of energy is from conventional thermal sources which provides over half the country's total power; oil provided 51 per cent, natural gas, 17 per cent and coal, 14 per cent. The emphasis is moving away from coal towards natural gas power stations. Nuclear power generated 10 per cent of the country's needs in 2004. Spain now has eight operating nuclear plants, having closed two. The government has announced a moratorium on the construction of new nuclear power plants.

Hydroelectricity was the source of five per cent of power in 2004, whilst solar, wind and other renewable sources accounted for three per cent of power generation. Spain is the world's second largest producer of wind power, and in 2002 the country ranked ninth in the EU in terms of consumption of energy from renewable resources. In 2008 the Spanish government committed to achieving a target of 12 per cent of primary energy from renewable energy by 2010 and expected to have an installed solar generating capacity of 10,000 MW by 2020. Total solar power in Spain was 3.859 GW by the end of 2010 and solar energy produced 6.9 TW-h. Europe's first solar power tower plant was opened in Seville in 2007. The Andasol 1 solar power station situated in Andalusia is Europe's first parabolic trough commercial power plant (50 MWe)and went online in November 2008. Following the 2008 financial crisis the government announced it was to cut subsidies within the solar industry.

Endesa (URL: http://www.endesa.com) is the largest electric utility company in Spain, controlling 45 per cent of the regulated market and 36 per cent of the liberalized market. Other important companies in the sector are Iberdrola (the second largest power utility), Union Fenosa, HCEnergia and Gas Natural. Red Electricia de Espana (REE) is part-owned by the government and operates Spain's electricity grid. In 2004, Spain and Portugal signed an agreement to create a single Iberian electricity market called Mibel. (Source: EIA)

Manufacturing

In 2007, Spain had the fifth highest industrial turnover in the EU, and contributed 7.7 per cent of EU total turnover.

Industry is Spain's second largest sector in terms of the country's GDP, contributing 115.7 per cent in 2007 (including energy production but not the construction sector which accounted for a further 11 per cent of GDP). In 2007, net manufacturing turnover was €625,889 million,

SPAIN

up by 6.4 per cent on the previous year, but indicating a slowing of growth. Around 2.6 million people were employed in the sector in 2007, down by 1.7 per cent on 2006. Figures for 2010 show that net turnover had fallen to €520,864 million

The following table shows figures for Spain's manufacturing sector in 2010:

Percentage of Turnover per Industrial Activity

Activity	% of Total	Inter-annual variation %
Mining & quarrying, energy, water & waste industries	21.7	5.2
Food, beverages & tobacco	18.2	2.3
Transport material	12.2	8.1
Metallurgy & manufacture of metallic products	11.9	13.4
Chemical & pharmaceutical industry	9.6	12.2
Wood, cork, paper & graphic arts	5.0	1.6
Electrical, electronic & optical material & equipment	4.5	3.6
Various non-metallic ore products	4.0	-13.1
Rubber & plastic products	3.5	9.4
Various manufacturing industries, repair & installation of machinery & equipment	3.3	1.4
Mechanical machinery & equipment	3.2	-4.3
Textile, clothing, leather & footwear industry	2.9	1.0
TOTAL	**100.00**	**5.0**

Source: Instituto Nacional de Estadistica

In 2010, nearly hallf of total manufacturing revenue emanated from four Autonomous Communities: Catalonia (24.0 per cent), Comunidad de Madrid (9.8 per cent), the Comunidad Valenciana (9.8 per cent), and Andalucia (11.2 per cent).

Around 77 per cent of manufactured goods are sold within Spain, and 18 per cent of goods are exported to the EU.

Spain headed the EU in terms of construction in 2006, with a turnover of €294,594 million. However the real estate market collapsed. There was a significant decrease in residential construction over 2007, and the number of licences granted for the construction of residential new buildings fell by 20.3 per cent. House sales fell by 28.6 per cent over 2008 and house prices fell by 25 per cent.

Services

In 2007, the service sector accounted for over 60 per cent of GDP, 47 per cent of which comes from the private sector. Turnover in private sector services reached €1,200,295 million, an increase of eight per cent on the previous year. Spain had the fifth largest service sector turnover in Europe.

There were 2.1 million service sector businesses in 2006, an increase of 3.6 per cent on 2004. The services sector employed some 8.9 million people in 2006, up 4.8 per cent on the previous year. Around 38 per cent of the sector's employees are employed in trade, whilst around 19 per cent work in business services. The tourist industry employs some 13.9 per cent. Around a quarter of those employed in the services sector are 'self-employed' and not salaried employees. Companies of less than 20 employees accounted for 98 per cent of the total number of service sector companies, and almost 55 per cent of companies have fewer than two employees. Figures for 2010 showed that there were 1.2 million companies operating in the service sector employing 5.2 million people (a decrease of 4.6 per cent on the previous year).

Within the service sector, trade accounted for 60.2 per cent of total turnover. The largest percentage increases were seen in services to businesses (13.2 per cent), and transport (11.2 per cent).

The following table shows volume of business in the services sector:

Turnover and Employment in 2009 (%)

Sector	Turnover	Employed Personnel
Transport & storage	23.5	17.9
Information & communications	20.3	8.1
Professional, scientific & technical activities	19.5	19.2
Administrative & support services activities	14.7	23.4
Accommodation	14.4	23.5
Real estate activities	5.0	4.0
Sporting activities, recreational & entertainment activities	2.0	3.0
Repair of computers, personal effects & household items	0.5	0.9

Source: Instituto Nacional de Estadistica

26.6 per cent of the service sector turnover was generated in Madrid. Catalonia contributed 19.4 per cent in 2006.

Tourism

Tourism is one of the most important sectors of the Spanish economy, accounting for some 10.8 per cent of GDP. In 2007, Spain earned the second largest tourism revenues in the world at US$51.1 billion (behind the USA with $85.7 billion).

In 2011, there were 389.5 million overnight stays, over 70 per cent of which were in hotels. There were 1.3 million hotel places, as well as a further one million places in campsites, apartments and rural accommodation. The average hotel occupancy rate was 53.6 per cent. Most foreign tourists came from the United Kingdom, Germany and France, and most foreign tourists visited the Canaries (31.4 per cent) and the Balearics (24.2 per cent) in 2007.

In 2001 some of the largest tourist areas introduced a tourist tax with the aim of protecting the environment and repairing damage created by the large number of visitors.
Turespaña (Spanish Institute of Tourism), URL: http://www.spain.info

Agriculture

The farming, forestry and fishing sector contributed an estimated 2.6 per cent of total GDP in 2007. In 2006, the sector earned around €37,176 million (down from €37,599 million in 2005). The sector employed around 3,210,900 people in 2004, up from 3,200,800 the previous year.

In 2010, Spain ranked second to France within the 15 countries of the EU in terms of land used for farming; some 2,4,892,520 hectares were farmed, on 1,043,910 farms. Almost two-thirds of farmland was used for cultivated crops, whilst the remaining third was used as permanent pasture. In 2007, there was a 3.6 per cent increase (to 2.2 million hectares) in the surface area of cultivated lands dedicated to olive groves.

The following shows cultivated land by crop in 2009:

Produce	Percentage of Land
Herbaceous & fallow lands	73.4
Fruit trees	6.8
Olive trees	14.0
Vineyards	5.5
Woody crops	0.3

The average area per farm grew from 23.4 hectares in 2005 to 24.2 hectares in 2007. However, over 54 per cent of farming occurs on plots of land of less than 5 hectares, whilst less than nine per cent of farms exceed 50 hectares. Over 50 per cent of those in charge of agricultural operations are over the age of 55 years.

The most commonly grown cereal is wheat. 4.4 million tons were harvested in 2003, over 3.5 million tons in Andalucia. 836,902 tons of olive oil were produced in the same year. Spain is ranked third in the world league for wine production after France and Italy; and it produced 34.5 million hl of wine in 2002, around a half of which came from the Castille/La Mancha region. Oranges and lemons are grown in Valencia and Murcia, and bananas in the Canary Islands. Tomatoes (3.8 million tons in 2003) are the major vegetable produce, followed by potatoes (2.7 million tons) and melons (1 million tons). The olive is one of the major Spanish crops; over the 2002-03 season, some 4.4 million tons were grown, of which 3.5 million were harvested in Andalusia. 836,902 tons of olive oil were produced in the same year.

Agricultural Production in 2010

Produce	Int. $'000*	Tonnes
Olives	6,416,834	8,014,000
Indigenous pigmeat	5,377,331	3,498,040
Grapes	3,490,979	6,107,200
Cow milk, whole, fresh	1,910,481	6,357,140
Tomatoes	1,538,384	4,312,700
Indigenous chicken meat	1,462,838	1,026,980
Indigenous cattle meat	1,271,997	470,870
Hen eggs, in shell	696,687	840,000
Almonds, with shell	652,164	221,000
Peaches and nectarines	617,775	1,134,750
Oranges	602,965	3,120,000
Tangerines, mandarins, clem.	421,963	1,708,200

* unofficial figures
Source: http://faostat.fao.org/site/339/default.aspx Food and Agriculture Organization of the United Nations, Food and Agricultural commodities production

Maize and rice are grown along the Valencian coast and in the north, where potatoes and vegetables are also grown. Industrial crops grown include sunflower, sugar beet and cotton.

Fishing

Figures for 2010 indicate that the Spanish fishing industry had the largest catch in Europe, at over a million tonnes. Aquaculture has recovered over the past few years, with an 32.7 per cent over 2005 figures.

In 2006, Spain harvested around 210,000 tonnes of molluscs, most of which were reared off the coast of Galicia. Large quantities of mussels, oysters and clams were produced.

COMMUNICATIONS AND TRANSPORT

Travel Requirements

Citizens of the USA, Canada and Australia require a passport valid for three months beyond the length of stay but do not need a visa for stays of up to 90 days. EU citizens do not require a passport if they are carrying a valid national Identity Card, and do not require a visa, regardless of purpose and/or length of stay. Other nationals should contact the embassy to check visa requirements.

Spain is a signatory of the Schengen Agreement; with a Schengen visa, a visitor can travel freely throughout the Schengen zone, with few border stops and checks. See http://www.eurovisa.info/SchengenCountries.htm for details.

National Airlines
The largest airlines in Spain are:
Iberia, URL: http://www.iberia.com
Air Europa, URL: http://www.aireurope.es

Iberia and British Airways merged in 2010, creating one of the world's largest airline groups with 408 aircraft flying to 200 destinations and carrying over 58 million passengers per year. Whilst both airlines will retain their current operations and operate under their individual names, the merger will create a new holding company called International Consolidated Airlines Group SA, which will be known as International Airlines Group.

In 2011, more than 127 million air passengers passed through Spain's airports and in 2009, 565,000 tonnes of freight.

International Airports
Major international airports are:
Barcelona, URL: http://www.aena-aeropuertos.es/csee/Satellite/Aeropuerto-Barcelona/en/ (30 million passengers, 2010)
Gran Canaria, http://www.aena-aeropuertos.es/csee/Satellite/Aeropuerto-Gran-Canaria/en/ (10 million passengers per annum)
Málaga, URL: http://www.malagaairport.eu/. A third terminal opened in 2010, and a second runway opened in 2012. Approximately 12 million passengers used the airport in 2010.
Madrid, URL: http://www.madrid-airport.info/ (Approx. 50 million passengers per annum)

Aviation Authorities
Directorate General of Civil Aviation (Dirección General de Aviatión Civil), URL: http://www.fomento.es/
AENA - Management of Air Navigation Services and Airports (Aeropuertas Españolas y Navegación Aérea), URL: http://www.aena.es/csee/Satellite/Home

Railways
Recent figures show that Spain has a total of 14,343km of railway. All regions are covered by the state-run company, the Red Nacional de Ferrocarriles Espanoles, or RENFE. Spain is expanding its high-speed rail links (AVE - `Alta Velocidad España). Lines include Seville and Madrid (opened 1992), Barcelona and Madrid (opened 2008), Madrid-Malaga, Barcelona-Malaga, Mardir - Toledo, and Madrid-Valladolid.The trains can reach speeds of 300km/h (186mph); the Madrid to Barcelona journey of 550 km (342 miles) takes 155 minutes and the 240 mile Madrid-Valenica journey takes 98 minutes. By 2020, it is planned that routes to Cadiz, Alicante and Bilbao will be opened.
Red Nacional de los Ferrocarriles Espanoles, URL: http//www.renfe.es

Roads
In 2007 there were 166,011 km of roads in Spain, 14,689 km of which were dual carriageway or motorways. According to the INE, there were 30.3 million vehicles on the roads in 2007, 21 million of which were passenger cars, and there were 1,146,826 driving licence holders. Over 2006, there were 99,797 road accidents where someone was injured (up 9.4 per cent on 2005); 3,119 people were killed in road accidents. (Source: INE). Vehicles are driven on the right.

Shipping
Links with the Balearic Isles, the Canary Islands and North Africa are provided by:
Transmediterranea, URL: http://www.transmediterranea.es

Ports and Harbours
Ports handling the greatest amount of commercial traffic are Bilbao (38 million tonnes of cargo, 2011), Algeciras-La Linea, Tarragona and Barcelona (handles over 20 per cent of Spanish trade). Barcelona is also an important port for passenger lines 2.4 million passengers per year), as are Valencia, Palma de Mallorca, Malaga, Santander, Cadiz, Las Palmas and Tenerife.
Port of Bilbao, URL: http://www.bilbaoport.es/aPBW/web/en/index.jsp
Barcelona Port, URL: http://www.portdebarcelona.es/
Tarragona Port, URL: http://www.porttarragona.cat/

HEALTH

Health care is the responsibility of the autonomous regions. Funding for the health service comes mainly from the General State Budget, and all employed people pay into a national insurance scheme.

According to the WHO, in 2009, total expenditure on health equated to 9.6 per cent of GDP. General government expenditure on health equated to 73.6 per cent of total expenditure on health. and private expenditure 26.4 per cent. Private prepaid plans account for just over 20 per cent of private expenditure Expenditure on health accounts for 15.2 per cent of Spain's total government expenditure. Per capita total expenditure was $3,032 in 2009, compared to $1,040 in 2000. (Source: WHO)

Figures for 2006 indicate that Spain had 746 hospitals, with 96,108 beds in public hospitals and 50,094 beds in private hospitals. Around two thirds of hospitals were general hospitals, whilst 14 per cent were geriatric or long stay hospitals and around 12 per cent were psychiatric hospitals.

Figures for 2005-10 show that around 174,100 doctors were employed in the health sector, equating to an average of 39.6 doctors for every 10,000 inhabitants over Spain as a whole. In regions such as Madrid and Bilbao, there were over 525 doctors per 100,000 people, whereas areas such as the plateau to the south of Madrid had less than 375 doctors per 100,000 inhabitants. There were 224,900 nurses and midwives (51.1 per 10,000 population), 26,725 dentists (6.1 per 10,000 population), and 37,000 in 2005-10. (Source: WHO, 2012)

In 2004 there were 1,494 organ donors, an increase of 3.5 per cent on the previous year when there were 34 donors per million inhabitants. Spain leads Europe in terms of organ donation, well ahead of the United Kingdom where there were just 12.7 donations per one million inhabitants.

Cardiovascular disease is the main cause of death among Spaniards (32.2 per cent of deaths in 2007), followed by cancers (26.8 per cent of deaths). Deaths due to traffic accidents continued in a downward trend, the figures falling by eight per cent in 2007. AIDS and HIV now cause less than 0.5 per cent of deaths. According to the Instituto Nacional de Estadistica figures for 2007, over 27 per cent of the 2-17 year olds is overweight or obese. Over 26 per cent of Spaniards over 16 years old smoke regularly and 37.8 per cent are overweight (15.6 per cent is obese). On the positive side, the weekly diet of most Spaniards includes plenty of fruit, fish, vegetables, salad and dairy products.

EDUCATION

Although education is provided free by the state, the autonomous regions are responsible for overseeing education up to university level. In 1990 an education law, la Ley Orgánica de Ordenacion General del Sistema Educativo (LOGSE), was introduced laying down minimum requirements for educational standards, with implementation over a 10 year period (age 6-16). In 1995 a further education law, of Participation, Evaluation and Governing of Education Institution (LOPEG), came into force. There were further reforms in 2001 and 2002, targeting vocational education and ensuring quality education for all. In 2006 the Ley Organica de Educacacion LOE, Education Act) and the Ley Organica de Modification de le LOU (LOMLOU) have also introduced further reforms. The LOMLOU encourages university autonomy. Reforms to the curriuculum are being developed. In response to the economic crisis, government funding to education is being cut.

Pre-school Education
Infant education is divided into two programmes: for children up to three years old, and for three to six year olds. Introduced in the 1991-92 academic year, it is both voluntary and free. In the 2011-12 academic year, some 1.93 million children attended, an increase of 3.1 per cent on the previous year.

Primary/Secondary Education
Primary education is for six to 10 year olds. It is compulsory and free and is divided into three programmes over a period of two years. Its subject areas include Castilian/Spanish language and literature, and its objectives include introduction to a foreign language. Provisional figures for 2008-09 indicate that 2.66 million pupils were enrolled at primary schools.

Secondary education is also compulsory and free and is for children up to the age of 16. There are two stages to the programme: the Educacion General Basica and Educacion Secundario Obligatoria. The curriculum covers Spanish language and literature, foreign languages, mathematics, social sciences, geography and history, physical education, natural sciences, plastic and visual arts, technology, music and religious studies. On completion of secondary education a student becomes a High School Graduate. Provisional figures for 2011-12 indicate that there were 1.79 million students in secondary education (including the Bachillerato), over 70 per cent within the state system. A further 610,860 undertook vocational courses. (Source: Espana en Cifras, 2009, INE)

There is a two year Baccalaureate (Bachillerato) course for 16 to 18 year olds. This comprises four branches: health and natural sciences, humanities and social sciences, technology, and fine arts. These include electives and basic subjects, physical education, philosophy, one foreign language, Spanish language and literature (and language and literature of the various Autonomous Communities) and Spanish history. Students can then go on to university or to vocational education. (Source: Espana en cifras, 2008, INE)

In 2004-05, there were 571,780 teachers within the elementary and secondary systems, and the pupil/teacher ratio was 12.2 to one.

Over the decade from 1994 to 2004, there was an overall fall of 11.4 per cent in the numbers of pupils in Spanish schools. The only regions where there were increased numbers were in Melilla (11 per cent) and the Balearics (3 per cent), where a 10.1 per cent increase in the number of foreign students has augmented the figures. All other regions of Spain show falls in student numbers of up to 32 per cent in Asturias and 25 per cent in Galicia.

Higher Education
In 2008-09, there was a 1.6 per cent decrease in the number of university students, to 1.41 million. This follows a downward trend in numbers which began in 1999-2000 when student numbers exceeded 1.57 million. The most popular courses in 2008 were within the Technical Sciences (36.8 per cent of male students), Health Sciences (29.7 per cent of women and 20.4 per cent of men), and the Social Sciences (36.1 per cent of women and 28.2 per cent of men). (Source: Espana en cifras, 2009, INE)

The literacy rate among adults is estimated to be 97.9 per cent, rising to 99 per cent among the 15-24 years age group.

RELIGION

Although Spain has no official religion around 90 per cent of the population are Christian, most of whom are Catholic. There are nine Archbishoprics: Toledo, Seville, Tarragona, Santiago, Valencia, Zaragoza, Granada, Burgos and Valladolid. The Anglican, Muslim and Jewish faiths are also represented.
Bishop's Conference, URL: http//www.conferenciaepiscopal.es
President: Emmo. y Rvmo. Sr. D. Antonio Mª Rouco Varela, Cardinal Archbishop of Madrid

Spain has a religious liberty rating of 8 on a scale of 1 to 10 (10 is most freedom). (Source: World Religion Database)

SRI LANKA

COMMUNICATIONS AND MEDIA

Newspapers
Newspapers with the greatest circulation are:
El País, URL: http//www.elpais.es
ABC, URL: http/ww.abc.es
El Mundo, URL: http//www.elmundo.es
La Vanguardia, URL: http//www.lavanguardia.es
El Periódico de Catalunya, URL: http://www.elperiodico.com/

Business Journals
El Mundo Financiero, URL: http://www.elmundofinanciero.com/

Broadcasting
Stations include TVE 1, which commands the greatest audience, Antena 3 TV, Tele 5, 24 horas, LA 2, TV3, Canal Sur, Canal Plus, Telemadrid, Canal 9, Canal 33, TVG, ETB 2 and ETB1. TVE and 24 Horas are state owned companies. Spain completed the switchover to digital in 2010.
Radiotelevision Española, URL: http://www.rtve.es/
Cuatro, http://www.cuatro.com
Tele Cinco, http://www.telecinco.es
Antena3. http://www.antena3.com

The main public network is *Radio Nacional de España*, with five different stations which is owned by the state. The SER network, *Sociedad Española de Radiodifusión* has the greatest number of listeners. Cadena COPE is a radio station controlled by the church.
Radio Nacional de España, URL: http://www.rtve.es/radio/

Telecommunications
There are an estimated 19 million landlines and 51 million mobile phones (2010). In 2009, there were an estimated 298 million internet users.

ENVIRONMENT

Spain has over 1,600 protected areas and 14 National Parks. The Law of Conservation of Protected Natural Areas and of Wild Flora and Fauna regulates control over these parks. Spain is the most bio-diverse country in Europe; it is home to 10,000 different species of plant, 20,000 species of fungus, litchen and moss, approximately 9,0000 species of vascular plants and 68,000 animal species.

Environmental concerns include periodic droughts, desertification, pollution of the Mediterranean Sea, and air pollution. Its biodiversity is also threatened: approximately 25 per cent of its vertebrates are considered endangered, vulnerable or rare. Spain has been criticised for inadequate protection of the environment.

In November 2002 the oil tanker Prestige sank off the north western coast of Spain releasing 50,000 tons of oil into the seas bordering the Spanish, Portuguese and French coasts. The Spanish fishing industry was severely affected, with fishermen relying on state handouts for several months after the disaster. The effects of the spill were felt as far away as Scotland, where the Royal Society for the Protection of Birds reported the deaths of 300,000 British seabirds, including Scottish Puffins, guillemots and razorbills. In September 2003 the EU banned single-hulled tankers carrying heavy fuel oil from its ports.

In February 2007, the Spanish navy advised ships in the Strait of Gibraltar to slow down to avoid hitting whales. The speed limit has been set at 13 knots (15mph; 24km/h). Dozens of sperm whales flock to the strait to eat squid, and it is also the habitat of about 260 pilot whales. Every year several whales are hit by ships that do not see them or fail to change course. Six pilot whales were found on Andalucian beaches over the previous three months, having seemingly died of pollution.

According to the Energy Information Administration (EIA), total carbon dioxide emissions from consumption of energy in Spain decreased from 360.13 million metric tons in 2008 to 329.86 million metric tons in 2009 and fell again in 2010 to 316.43 million memtric tons. Per capita carbon dioxide emissions fell from 9.6 metric tons in 2005 to 8.86 metric tons in 2008. This was above the European average of 7.805 metric tons but below the USA per capita emissions of 19.183 metric tons in 2008.

Spain is party to the following international agreements: Air Pollution, Air Pollution-Nitrogen Oxides, Air Pollution-Sulfur 94, Air Pollution-Volatile Organic Compounds, Antarctic-Environmental Protocol, Antarctic-Marine Living Resources, Antarctic Treaty, Biodiversity, Climate Change, Climate Change-Kyoto Protocol, Desertification, Endangered Species, Environmental Modification, Hazardous Wastes, Law of the Sea, Marine Dumping, Marine Life Conservation, Ozone Layer Protection, Ship Pollution, Tropical Timber 83, Tropical Timber 94, Wetlands, Whaling. It has signed but not ratified Air Pollution-Persistent Organic Pollutants.

SPACE PROGRAMME

Spain is one of the founding members of the European Space Agency. The national space agency, the National Instiute of Aerospace Technology (INTA, Instituto Nacional de Técnica Aeroespacial), was founded in 1942. It specialises in aerospace research and technology development. Its annual budget is over €100 million.
INTA, URL: http://www.inta.es/

SRI LANKA
Democratic Socialist Republic of Sri Lanka
Sri Lanka Prajatantrika Samajaya di Janarajaya

Capital: Colombo (Population estimate, 2012: 2.3 million)

Head of State: Mahinda Rajapakse (President) (page 1499)

National Flag: A yellow field bearing two panels; in the hoist two vertical strips of green and orange in the fly dark red with a gold lion holding a sword and in each corner a gold 'bo' leaf

CONSTITUTION AND GOVERNMENT

Constitution
The Democratic Socialist Republic of Sri Lanka, formerly Ceylon, was frequently invaded throughout its history by a succession of Chinese, Indians, Arabs and Europeans. In 1796 the island came under the control of the British East India Company and in 1802 was made a Crown Colony. Independence was reached peaceably in 1948 and in 1972 Ceylon was named the Republic of Sri Lanka.

Under the present Constitution, promulgated on 7 September 1978, Sri Lanka is a free, sovereign, independent and democratic socialist republic. A unitary state, sovereignty rests with the people and is inalienable. Sovereignty includes the powers of government (legislative, executive and judicial power), fundamental rights and the franchise. The territory of the Republic of Sri Lanka consists of 25 administrative districts and the territorial waters.

The president, who is the Head of State, Head of the Executive and of Government (Cabinet of Ministers) and the Commander-in-Chief of the Armed Forces, is directly elected by the people. His term of office is six years and shall not exceed two consecutive terms. The Prime Minister and other ministers, who must be Members of Parliament, are appointed by the president. The president has, by virtue of his office, the right to at any time attend, address and send messages to parliament. In the exercise of this right the president is entitled to all the privileges, immunities and powers, other than the right to vote, of a Member of Parliament and is not liable for any breach of the privileges of parliament or of its members. The president may also choose to hold any position within the cabinet.

Under a state of emergency the president has the power to introduce legislation directly.

In September 2010, parliament approved a constitutional change removing the two-term presidential limit which allows President Rajapaksa to seek an unlimited number of terms.

To consult the constitution, please visit:
http://www.priu.gov.lk/Cons/1978Constitution/Introduction.htm

International Relations
Sri Lanka is a member of the UN, the Commonwealth, the South Asian Association for Regional Cooperation (SAARC), the World Bank, International Monetary Fund, Asian Development Bank, and the Colombo Plan.

Recent Events
Sri Lanka gained its independence in 1948. The country was initially ruled by the United National Party (UNP) which aimed to protect the rights of the minority Hindu Tamil population in the north of the main island. In 1951 the socialist Sri Lanka Freedom Party (SLFP) was formed, advocating the recognition of Sinhala as the official language and Buddhism as the main religion.

The SLFP won the 1956 elections and remained in power until 1965. The founder of the SLFP, Solomon Bandaranaike, was assassinated in 1959 and his widow, Sirimavo Bandaranaike, became the world's first female Prime Minister.

The Tamil United Liberation Front (TULF), whose aims was a separate Tamil state (Eelam) in the northern and eastern parts of the country, was formed of various Tamil groups in 1976, but by 1986 the Liberation Tigers of Tamil Eelam (LTTE) had emerged as the principal separatist group. They increased the violence against civilians and rejected the government call for a ceasefire.

In the 1990s, President Kumaratunga attempted to reform the constitution to allow limited autonomy for Tamil-majority areas, but was unable to secure enough support to push the measures through. The ethnic issue was at the fore in the parliamentary elections of October 2000 with growing national unrest at the government handling of the crisis. The president dissolved parliament early and elections were held on 5 December 2001. The new prime minister, Ranil Wickeremesinghe, pledged to restart talks with the Tamil Tigers. In January 2002 the government eased some fishing restrictions and lifted an economic embargo on Tamil-held areas in the north of the country. Elections held in April 2004 resulted in a minority government formed by the newly created United People's Freedom Alliance (UPFA).

The tsunami that devastated many coastlines and islands of the Indian Ocean, hit the north and eastern coasts of Sri Lanka on 26 December 2004, destroying homes, crops and fishing boats. It is estimated that at least 31,000 Sri Lankans perished and over 4,000 remain missing. Approximately 800,000-1 million Sri Lankans were left homeless. Over $1.5 billion of aid was committed to the island but distribution of the aid was delayed by the conflict between the government and the Tamil Tigers. In June 2005 the government controversially agreed to let the LTTE have a say in the distribution of the aid.

In 2005 a deal was reached between the government and the Tamil Tigers on sharing the US$3 billion worth of aid that the country received after the 2004 tsunami. Peace negotiations took place in Geneva in February 2006 in an attempt to halt escalating violence, but fighting broke out again in April. The violence continued over the rest of the year.

By the end of March 2007, around one million people had left their homes, and an estimated 65,000 people had been killed since the beginning of the conflict, despite a ceasefire being in place. At the end of April, Tamil Tiger rebels carried out an air raid on targets in and around Sri Lanka's capital, Colombo. Later, the Air Force bombed areas held by the rebels in an effort to destroy their aircraft. Airlines stopped flights to Sri Lanka. In July, the government claimed to have driven rebels from their last jungle stronghold in the east, Thoppigala, and in October 2007 the navy claimed to have destroyed the last seaworthy Tamil Tiger ship. On 2nd January 2008, the Sri Lankan government formally withdrew from the ceasefire agreement brokered by the Norwegians in 2002. In March 2008, the International Committee of the Red Cross (ICRC) accused Sri Lanka's government of manipulating confidential information to defend its human rights record. There had been allegations of extra-judicial killings and abductions as the island slipped back into civil war. Sri Lanka's government rejected calls for a UN human rights monitoring mission.

In April 2008, a suicide bombing near Colombo killed at least 14 people, including a senior government minister, Jeyaraj Fernandopulle. On the 23rd April, at least 52 Tamil Tiger rebels and 38 soldiers were killed in fighting in the Jaffna peninsula in the far north of the country. On the 26th August 2008, Tamil Tiger rebels dropped two bombs on a naval base at Trincomalee on the east of the island. In mid September, a new military offensive began as troops tried to take the Tamil Tigers' political centre of Kilinochchi. On 20th November, the Sri Lankan army claimed to have captured the first line of defence of Tamil Tiger rebels on the northern Jaffna peninsula.

On the 14th January, the army took control of the last remaining strip of rebel-held land on the northern Jaffna peninsula, and ten days later, troops captured the last Tamil Tiger rebel stronghold of Mullaitivu. In March 2009, the UN estimated that thousands of civilians had been killed and wounded in the conflict in the north-east of Sri Lanka, and said that people were being killed in the no-fire area which has been hit by artillery attacks. Following battles over the first weekend in April, Sri Lanka's army claimed that it had taken all rebel-held territory in the north-east. On the 12th April, the government declared a temporary halt to the offensive to allow civilians leave the conflict zone safely. On the 26th April, the rebels declared a unilateral ceasefire, but government officials insisted that they surrender. On the 17th May, the rebels declared a ceasefire, and on the following day, the army announced that the Tamil Tiger leader, Velupillai Prabhakaran, had been killed whilst trying to flee the last rebel-held area of jungle. On the 19th May 2009, Sri Lankan leader Mahinda Rajapaksa declared the country "liberated" after the 26-year war.

The government promised to resettle most of the 280,000 displaced Tamils within six months, but said that pockets of rebels still needed to be captured and the infrastructure rebuilt before the civilians could return home.

On the 24th May, the Sri Lanka government announced local elections to be held by the end of August in Jaffna and Vavuniya; many Tamil civilians, displaced by the war, are housed in camps nearby, but are not included in the voting area. The government promised to devolve as many powers as possible to the provinces as part of a programme to meet more of the aspirations of the Tamil minority.

The justice minister, Amarasiri Dodangoda, died in July 2009. There was a subsequent minor cabinet reshuffle. In October, the government announced early presidential and parliamentary elections. The former prime minister, Ranil Wickeremesinghe, formed a new alliance including Muslim and Tamil parties. The incumbent president, Mahinda Rajapaksa, won January 2010's presidential election. Parliamentary elections were held in April 2010 and were won by the government.

In January 2011, the Minority Rights Group International released a report that minorities still faced repression and marginalisation. In April the UN reported its findings that both sides committed atrocities during the civil war.

State of emergency laws which had been in place for most of the last four decades were lifted in August 2011. New legislation was put in place allowing the detention of people suspected of terror offences without charge.

In March 2012, the UN Human Rights Council adopted a resolution urging Sri Lanka to investigate war crimes allegedly committed during the final stages of the conflict with the Tamil Tigers.

The former presidential candidate Sarath Fonseka was released from jail in May 2012 after two years of imprisonment. Gen. Fonseka led the campaign in 2009 as army chief.

In October 2012, the government announced that the most senior surviving Tamil tiger leader, Selvvarasa Pathnabathan, was now would not face any charges.

In January 2013, parliament passed an impeachment motion against Chief Justice Shirani Bandaranayake. President Rajapaksa subsequently dismissed her and she was succeeded by Mohan Peiris, the government's senior legal adviser.

The cabinet was expanded in January 2013.

Legislature
Parliament consists of one Chamber, composed of 225 members under the Proportional Representation System (196 elected and 29 from the national list). The term of parliament is six years. The Cabinet of Ministers including the president is collectively responsible and answerable to parliament.
Parliament House, Sri Jayewardenepura Kotte, Colombo, Sri Lanka. Tel: +94 11 277 7288, fax: +94 11 277 7275, e-mail: secretary-general@parliament.lk, URL: http://www.parliament.lk

Cabinet (as at March 2013)
President and Minister of Defence, Minister of Finance, Minister of Highways: Mahinda Rajapaksa (page 1499)
Prime Minister and Minister of Religious Affairs: Dissanayake Mudiyanselage Jayaratne (page 1449)
Minister of Foreign Affairs: G.L. Peiris (page 1493)
Minister of Education: Bandula Gunawardena
Minister of Education Services: Duminda Dissanayake
Minister of Public Administration and Home Affairs: John Seneviratne
Minister of Justice: Rauff Hakeen (page 1436)
Minister of Agriculture: Mahinda Yapa Abeywardena
Minister of Buddha Sasana & Religious Affairs: Dissanayake Mudiyanselage Jayaratne
Minister of Women's Empowerment and Child Development: Tissa Karaliyadde
Minister of Construction, Engineering, Housing & Amenities: Wimal Weerawansa
Minister of Health: Maithripala Sirisena
Minister of Petroleum and Petroleum Resources: Anura Priyadharshana Yapa
Minister of National Heritage: Jagath Balasuriya
Minister of Food and Nutrition: P. Dayaratne
Minister of Internal Trade and Co-operatives: Johnston Fernando
Minister of Traditional Industries and Small Enterprise Development: Douglas Devananda
Minister of Power and Energy: Pavithra Wanniarachchi
Minister of Social Services: Felix Perera
Minister of Mass Media and Communication: Keheliya Rambukwelle
Minister of Fisheries and Aquatic Resources: Rajitha Senaratne
Minister of Good Governance and Infrastructure: Ratnasiri Wickramanayake
Minister of Indigenous Medicine: Salinda Amunugama
Minister of Rehabilitation and Prison Reform: Chandrasiri Gajadeera
Minister of Plantation Industries: Mahinda Samarasinghe
Minister of Youth Affairs & Skills Development: Dullas Alahaperuma
Minister of Resettlement: Gunaratne Weerakoon
Minister of Industry and Commerce: Rishad Bathiyutheen
Minister of Disaster Management: Mahinda Amaraweera
Minister of Environment and Renewable Energy: Susil Premajayantha
Minister of Land and Land Development: Janaka Bandara Tennekoon
Minister of Irrigation and Water Resources: Nimal Siripala de Silva (page 1415)
Minister of Sports: Mahindananda Aluthgamage
Minister of Post and Telecommunications: Jeewan Kumaranatunga
Minister of Economic Development: Basil Rajapaksa
Minister of Livestock and Rural Community Development: Arumugam Thondaman (page 1525)
Minister of Higher Education: S.B. Dissanayake
Minister of Labour Relations and Productivity Improvement: Gamini Lokuge
Minister of Transport: Kumara Welgama
Minister for Local Government and Provincial Councils: A.L.M. Athaullah
Minister of National Languages and Social Integration: Vasudeva Nanayakkara
Minister of Technology and Research: Patali Ranawaka
Minister of Private Transport Services: C.B. Rathnayake
Minister of Small Export Crops Promotion: Reginold Cooray
Minister of Foreign Employment Promotion and Welfare: Dilan Perera
Minister of Coconut Development and State Plantations Development: Jagath Pushpakumara
Minister of Consumer Affairs: S.B. Navinne
Minister of Culture and Aesthetic Affairs: T.B. Ekanayake
Minister of Agrarian Services and Wildlife: S.M.Chandrasena
Minister of Botanical Gardens & Public Parks: Jayarathne Herath
Minister of Civil Aviation: Priyankara Jayaratna
Minister of Human Resources: D. Gunasekera
Ministerof International Monetary Co-operation: Sarath Amunugama
Minister of Investment Promotion: Lakshman Yapa Abeywardena
Minister of National Assets: Piyasena Gamage
Minister of Public Co-ordination and Public Affairs: Mervin Silva
Minister of State Resources and Enterprise Development: Dayasritha Tissera
Minister of Telecommunication and Information Technology: Ranith Siyambalapitiya
Minister of State Management Reforms: Navin Dissanayake
Minister of Parliamentary Affairs: Sumedha Jayasena

Ministries
Office of the President, Republic Square, Colombo 01, Sri Lanka. Tel: +94 11 2248 010, URL: http://www.priu.gov.lk
Office of the Prime Minister, 58 Sir Ernest de Silva Mawatha, Colombo 7, Sri Lanka. URL: http://www.gov.lk
Ministry of Agriculture, 80/5 Govijana Mandiraya, Rajamalwatta Road, Battaramulla.URL: http://www.agrimin.gov.lk

SRI LANKA

Ministry of Buddha Sasana, 135 Anagarika Dharmapala Mawatha, Colombo 7, Sri Lanka.Tel: +94 11 2326125-7, fax: +94 11 2437997, URL: http://www.gov.lk/

Ministry of Child Development and Women's Affairs, 177, Nawala Road, Narahenpita, Colombo 05, Sri Lanka. Tel: +94 11 2505584-5, fax: +94 11 2503766, URL: http://www.childwomenmin.gov.lk/

Ministry of Coconut Production and Janatha Estate Development, URL: http://www.cdjedmin.gov.lk/

Ministry of Construction, Engineering & Housing, 2nd Floor, Sri Jayawardanapura Kotte, Battaramulla, Sri Lanka. Tel: +94 11 288 2412, e-mail: info@houseconmin.gov.lk, URL: http://www.houseconmin.gov.lk/

Ministry of Co-operatives & Internal Trade, Galle Road, Colombo 3, Sri Lanka. Tel: +94 11 2385367, fax: +94 11 2385383, e-mail: secretary@trade.gov.lk, URL: http://www.trade.gov.lk/

Ministry of Culture & the Arts, URL: http://www.cultural.gov.lk/

Ministry of Defence, 15/5 Baladaksha Mawatha, Colombo 3, Sri Lanka. Tel: +94 11 2430860-9, fax: +94 11 2446300, e-mail: modadm@sltnet.lk, URL: http://www.mod.gov.lk

Ministry of Disaster Management, Vidya Mawatha, Colombo 7, Sri Lanka. Tel: +94 112 665185, URL: http://www.disastermin.gov.lk/

Ministry of Education, "Isurupaya", Sri Jayawardenapura Kotte, Sri Lanka. Tel: +94 11 2784141, fax: +94 11 2784325, URL: http://www.moe.gov.lk

Ministry of the Environment, 82 Sampathpaya, Rajamalwatte Road, Battaramulla, Sri Lanka. Tel: +94 11 286 5452, URL: http://www.environmentmin.gov.lk/

Ministry of Finance, Secretariat Building, Colombo 1, Sri Lanka. Tel: 94 11 2484500, fax: +94 11 2489893, URL: http://www.treasury.gov.lk

Ministry of Fisheries and Ocean Resources, Maligawatte, Colombo 10. Sri Lanka. Tel: +94 11 2446183-5, fax: +94 11 2541184, e-mail: secmof@sltnet.lk, URL: http://www.fisheries.gov.lk

Ministry of Foreign Affairs, Republic Building, Colombo 1, Sri Lanka. Tel: +94 11 2325371, fax: +94 11 2446091, e-mail: minister@formin.gov.lk, URL: http://www.gov.lk

Ministry of Health, "Suwasiripaya", 385 Deans Road, Colombo 10, Sri Lanka. Tel: +94 11 2698471, fax: +94 11 2690198 URL: http://www.health.gov.lk

Ministry of Higher Education, URL: http://www.hohe.gov.lk

Ministry of Indigenous Medicines, URL: http://www.indigenousmedimini.gov.lk

Ministry of Justice, PO Box 555, Superior Courts Complex, Colombo 12, Sri Lanka. Tel: +94 11 2323022, fax: +94 11 2320785, URL: http://www.justiceministry.gov.lk

Ministry of Labour Relations, Labour Secretariat, Kirula Road, Narahenpita, Colombo 5, Sri Lanka. Tel: +94 11 2368064, fax: +94 11 2582938, URL: http://www.labourmin.gov.lk/

Ministry of Livestock and Rural Communities, 45 St Michael's Road, Colombo 03, Sri Lanka. Tel: +94 11 254 1369, URL: http://www.livestock.gov.lk/

Ministry of Local Government & Provincial Councils, 330 Union Place, Colombo 2, Sri Lanka. Tel: +94 11 2326732, fax: +94 11 2347529, URL: http://www.pclg.gov.lk/

Ministry of Mass Media & Information, URL: http://www.media.gov.lk

Ministry of Parliamentary Affairs, 464B Pannipitiya Road, Pelewattha, Battaramulla, Colombo, Sri lanka. Tel: +94 11 278 6988, URL: http://www.minparliament.gov.lk/

Ministry of Plantation Industries, URL: http://www.plantationindustries.gov.lk/

Ministry of Ports & Highways, URL: http://www.mohsl.gov.lk/

Ministry of Posts & Telecommunications, 310 D.R. Wijewardana, Mawatha, COlombo 10, Sri Lanka. E-mail: info@telepost.gov.lk, URL: http://www.telepost.gov.lk/

Ministry of Power & Energy, 80, Sir Ernest de Silva Mawatha, Colombo 07, Sri Lanka. Tel: +94 11 2564363, fax: +94 11 2564474, URL: http://www.powermin.gov.lk

Ministry of Public Administration and Home Affairs, Independence Square, Colombo 7, Sri Lanka. Tel: +94 11 2696211-3, fax: +94 11 2695279, e-mail: info@pubad.gov.lk, URL: http://www.pubad.gov.lk

Ministry of Resettlement, 146 Galle Road, Colombo 03, Sri Lanka. URL: http://www.resettlementmin.gov.lk/

Ministry of Social Services, URL: http://www.socialwelfare.gov.lk

Ministry of Sports, 100/7, Independence Avenue, Colombo 7, Sri Lanka. URL: http://www.sportsmin.gov.lk/main/index.php?lang=en

Ministry of Technology and Research, URL: http://www.most.gov.lk

Ministry of Traditional Industries and SMEs, URL: http://www.tisedmin.gov.lk/

Ministry of Transport, 1 D R Wijewardena Mawatha., Colombo 10, Sri Lanka. Tel: +94 11 2687105, fax: +94 11 2694547, URL: http://www.transport.gov.lk

Ministry of Youth Affairs & Skills Development, URL: http://www.youthskillsmin.gov.lk/

Official Government Website: http://www.gov.lk

Elections

The most recent presidential election took place in January 2010 and Nahinda Rajapakse was re-elected. Parliamentary elections were held in April 2010. The ruling United People's Freedom Alliance (UPFA), led by the Sri Lanka Freedom Party (SLFP), increased its majority.

Political Parties

The United People's Freedom Alliance is made up of some seven political parties and is dominated by the SNP (Sri Lanka Freedom Party), whose leader is President Rajapaksa. The other parties represented in parliament are the United National Party (UNP) - the main opposition party, People's Liberation Front (Janatha Vimukthi Peramuna), The Tamil National Alliance (a coalition of Tamil parties), the Sri Lanka Muslim Congress (SLMC), Tamil United Liberation Front (TULF) (member of the TNA), the Eelam People's Democratic Party (EPDP) and the Ceylon Workers Congress (CWC)

Diplomatic Representation

American Embassy, 210 Galle Road, Kollupitiya, (PO Box 106), Colombo 3, Sri Lanka. Tel: +94 1 448007, fax: +94 1 437345, URL: http://colombo.usembassy.gov
Ambassador: Michele J. Sison (page 1515)

British High Commission, 389 Bauddhaloka Mawatha, Colombo 7 (PO Box 1433), Sri Lanka. Tel: +94 11 539 0639, fax: +94 11 539 0694, e-mail: bhctrade@slt.lk, URL: http://ukinsrilanka.fco.gov.uk/en
High Commissioner: John Rankin (page 1500)

High Commission of the Democratic Socialist Republic of Sri Lanka, 13 Hyde Park Gardens, London, W2 2LU. Tel: +44 (0)20 7262 1841, fax: +44 (0)20 7262 7970, e-mail: mail@slhc-london.co.uk, URL: http://www.srilankahighcommission.co.uk/
High Commissioner: Chris Nonis (page 1487)

Embassy of the Democratic Socialist Republic of Sri Lanka, 2148 Wyoming Avenue NW, Washington DC 20008, USA, Tel: +1 202 483 4025, fax: +1 202 232 7181, e-mail: slembassy@slembassyusa.org, URL: http://www.slembassyusa.org/
Ambassador: Jaliya Chitran Wickramasuriya

Permanent Mission of the Democratic Socialist Republic of Sri Lanka to the UN, 823 United Nations Plaza, 345 East 46th Street, 9th Floor, New York, NY 10017, USA. Tel: +1 212 661 1050, fax: +1 212 949 7247, URL: http://www.slmission.com/contact-us.html
Permanent Representative: Palitha Kohona

LEGAL SYSTEM

The systems of law in operation in Sri Lanka are Roman-Dutch Law, English Law, Tesawalamai Law, Muslim Law and Kandyan Law.

The Constitution of 1978 established two superior courts: the Supreme Court and the Court of Appeal. The Supreme Court is the highest and final superior court of record, and exercises jurisdiction in constitutional matters, the protection of fundamental rights, final appellates, consultative matters, election petitioning and breaches of parliamentary privileges. The Court of Appeal exercises appellate jurisdiction to correct all errors committed by any court, tribunal or institution. It may also try the election petitions of MPs.

The courts of central jurisdiction are the High Court, Provincial Courts, District Courts, Magistrates' Courts and Primary Courts. The High Court tries major crimes and exercises admiralty jurisdiction. Provincial High Courts exercise criminal jurisdiction on behalf of the High Court for offences committed within their province and appellate. They are also charged with exercising revisionary jurisdiction in the case of appeals from the Magistrates' and Primary Courts within the province. The District Court has unlimited civil jurisdiction in civil, revenue, trust, insolvency and testamentary matters over persons and the estates of persons of unsound mind and over wards. The Magistrates' Courts exercise criminal jurisdiction with the power to impose terms of imprisonment not exceeding two years and fines not exceeding Rs1,500.

Kandyan Law applies to the Kandyan Sinhalese in all matters relating to inheritance, matrimonial rights and donations. Tesawalamai Law is applied to all inhabitants of Jaffna in all matters relating to inheritance, marriages, gifts, donations, purchases and sales of land. Muslim Law serves all Muslims in matters of succession, donations, marriage, divorce and maintenance. These customary and religious laws have been modified in many respects by local enactments.

The government's respect for the rights of Sri Lankan citizens has been coloured by the conflict with the Liberation Tigers of Tamil Eelam (LTTE). There have been reports of unlawful killings and politically motivated killings; progovernment paramilitary groups have allegedly participated in attacks on civilians, torture, kidnapping and extortion with impunity. Arrests and detention can be arbitrary, and prison conditions are harsh. The government is deemed to be corrupt. There are limitations on the freedom of movement, and discrimination against minorities.

Capital punishment was reinstated in 2004 for cases of rape, drug trafficking and murder. The most recent execution took place in 1976 since when a moratorium has been in place.

Supreme Court, URL: http://www.supremecourt.lk/
Chief Justice, 2013: Mohan Peiris
Court of Appeal, URL: http://www.courtofappeal.lk/

Human Rights Commission of Sri Lanka, URL: http://www.hrcsl.lk/

LOCAL GOVERNMENT

there are three levels of government: central, provincial and local. Local government is detailed in the 13th amendment to the constitution. The second-tier provincial councils are governed by the Provincial Councils Act 1987. Provincial councils are directly elected for 5-year terms. The leader of the council majority serves as the province's Chief Minister with a board of ministers; a provincial governor is appointed by the president. There are now nine provinces; Central, Eastern, North Central, Northern, North Western, Sabaragamuwa, Southern, Uva and Western. The provinces are divided for administrative purposes into 25 districts and 335 divisional secretariats. There are 330 third tier local authorities (18 municipal councils, 42 urban councils and 270 rural pradeshiya sabhas). Municipal councils are headed by a mayor who serves a four-year term.

Elections for local government authorities were held in March 2011. Elections for municipal councils and some urban councils were postponed unitl 2012.

AREA AND POPULATION

Area

The Republic of Sri Lanka (formerly known as Ceylon) is located in the Indian Ocean separated from the southern tip of India by the Palk Strait. It consists of one main island and several small islands and has a total area of 65,610 sq. km (25,332 sq. miles). The land rises to a central massive over 1,500 metres high. The climate is tropical with temperatures ranging from 24°C to 30°C and humidity levels of up to 75 per cent. Two monsoons pass through the islands (May to September and November to March) providing the country with most of its rainfall.

To view a map, consult
http://www.un.org/Depts/Cartographic/map/profile/srilanka.pdf

Sri Lanka was severely affected by the tsunami on 26 December 2004; some 40,000 people were killed and up to 500,000 people were left homeless. Half the fishing fleet was destroyed, and a quarter of hotels in the affected areas sustained serious damage.

Population
The latest census figures indicate a population of 20.860 million in 2010 and an average annual growth rate of 1.1 per cent for the period 2000-10. Average population density was 314 people per sq. km. in 2005. Density is highest in the southwest where Colombo, the country's main port and industrial centre, is located. Approximately 15 per cent of the population lives in urban areas. The most populated towns are Colombo (2,305,000 in 2012) and Gampaha (2,294,000 in 2012).

During the conflict between the government and Tamil separatists, several hundred thousand Tamil civilians sought refuge abroad, around 200,000 in the West. (2007) Approximately 74 per cent of the population are Sinhalese and 18 per cent Tamils. The official languages are Sinhala and Tamil. English is the link language.

Births, Marriages, Deaths
According to provisional figures, the birth rate was 18.2 per 1,000 population in 2010, whilst the death rate stood at 8.6 per 1,000 people in the same year. The infant mortality rate was 14 per 1,000 live births in 2010. In 2009, life expectancy was estimated to be 65 for males and 77 for females. Healthy life expectancy was 61 years and 65 years respectively. The total fertility rate was around 2.3 per woman in 2010. (Source: http://www.who.int, World Health Statistics 2012)

Public Holidays
Poya Days. Every full moon day is a public holiday
4 February: Independence Day

EMPLOYMENT

In 2005, the work force of Sri Lanka numbered 8.14 million. Of these, 7.52 million people were employed. The unemployment rate has declined in recent years, to 7.7 per cent in 2005 when it affected 623,000 people. The rate of unemployment among women (13 per cent), however, is considerably higher than for men (6 per cent). Whilst literacy rates are high, the IT industry and certain manufacturing sectors report a shortfall in skilled workers. There is a tendency among the more highly skilled people to leave the country, resulting in one of the highest 'brain drain' ratios of the world. The unemployment rate in 2006 was 6.5 per cent falling to 6.0 per cent in 2007 and 5.2 per cent in 2008. Estimated figures for 2010 put the unemployment rate at 5.7 per cent.

More than 20 per cent of the work force are members of a union and there are more than 1,650 registered trade unions and 19 federations. Many unions have political affiliations. The Ceylon Workers Congress (CWC) and Lanka Jathika estate workers union are the two largest unions, representing workers in the plantation sector.

Total Employment by Economic Activity

Occupation	2008
Agriculture, hunting, fishing & forestry	2,344,400
Mining & quarrying, electricity, gas & water supply	533,100
Manufacturing	1,354,900
Wholesale & retail trade, repairs	924,500
Hotels & restaurants	103,800
Transport, storage & communications	426,000
Financial intermediation, real estate, renting & business activities	236,000
Public admin. & defence; compulsory social security	426,600
Education	298,800
Health & social work	110,900
Other community, social & personal service activities	128,800
Households with employed persons	84,100
Other	166,700

Source: Copyright © International Labour Organization (ILO Dept. of Statistics, http://laborsta.ilo.org)

BANKING AND FINANCE

Currency
The Central Bank of Ceylon is the sole currency-issuing authority and issues both notes and coins. The standard unit of monetary value is the Sri Lanka Rupee divided into 100 cents. The financial centre is Colombo.

GDP/GNP, Inflation, National Debt
Sri Lanka is a middle-income economy but about 10 per cent of the population lives in poverty. Despite civil war from 1983 to 2008, economic growth over the decade to 2001 averaged 4.5 per cent. The 2001 ceasefire together with economic reform led to annual growth rates of 6 per cent and 5.4 per cent over the following two years. Despite the devastation caused by the tsunami in December 2004, the economy grew by 6 per cent in 2005; the reconstruction effort offset the estimated $1 billion cost in damage. Sri Lanka's economy downturned in 2009. The future growth of the economy depends on political stability, reforms, and the global situation.

In 2006, the economy grew by 7.2 per cent; the services sector grew by 7.7 per cent, and, aided by a strong recovery of the fishing industry after the tsunami, the agricultural sector grew by 5.9 per cent. The south and west of the country accounted for all but 9 per cent of GDP, the north and eastern provinces being severely hampered by the conflict. Growth was estimated at 6 per cent in 2008, 3.5 per cent in 2009, 8 per cent in 2010 and estimated to be 8 per cent in 2011 and 6.6 per cent in 2012. GDP was estimated to be US$59 billion in 2011, rising to US$64 billion in 2012.

The service sector continues to be the largest component of GDP at 58 per cent. Agriculture accounts for 13 per cent of GDP, and the manufacturing industry contributes 30 per cent.

GDP by Industry sectors, Mn Rupees, Current Market Prices

	2008	2009	2010 (E)
GDP	4,410,682	4,835,293	5,602,321
-Agriculture	590,114	613,694	716,892
-Mining	71,768	79,204	89,100
-Manufacturing	791,898	875,563	1,009,003
-Electricty, gas & water	104,666	113,687	127,625
-Construction	327,138	366,248	423,414
-Trade	949,372	948,425	1,096,323
-Transport & Communications	530,980	599,934	709,400
-Finance	413,322	499,304	597,540
-Public Administration	380,765	445,543	500,547
-Others	250,660	293,692	332,477
Net factor income from abroad	-105,032	-55,795	-71,858
GNI at current market prices	4,305,651	4,779,498	5,530,464

Source: Asian Development Bank

Inflation was estimated at 23.0 per cent in 2008, 3.5 per cent in 2009, 6.5 per cent in 2010 and 7.0 per cent in 2011.

Sri Lanka is highly dependent on foreign aid, receiving around $1.2 billion every year. Donors pledged around US$500 million for post-tsunami reconstruction. An IMF loan of US$2.6 million was approved in 2009.

At the end of 2007, external debt amounted to US$14,020.4 million.

Balance of Payments / Imports and Exports
External Trade, million Rupees

header	2008	2009	2010 (E)
Exports, fob	878,499	813,911	937,737
Imports, cif	1,525,705	1,172,618	1,526,604
Trade balance	-647,206	-358,707	-588,867

Source: ADB

The top export trading partners in 2010 were the United States (US$1,664.7 million); United Kingdom (US$884.4 million) and India (US$363.2 million). Top import partners were India (US$2,452 million), China, People's Rep. of (US$2,194 million), and Singapore (US$1,319 million).

Trade or Currency Restrictions
Foreign direct investment is encouraged. 100 per cent foreign investment is permitted in most sectors.

Central Bank
Central Bank of Sri Lanka, PO Box 590, 30 Janadhipathi Mawatha, Colombo 1, Colombo, Sri Lanka. Tel: +94 1 477168, fax: +94 1 477712, e-mail: cbslglen@sri.lanka.net, URL: http://www.cbsl.gov.lk
Governor: Ajith Nivard Cabraal

Chambers of Commerce and Trade Organisations
National Chamber Of Commerce of Sri Lanka, URL: http://www.nccsl.lk/
Ceylon Chamber of Commerce, URL: http://www.chamber.lk/

MANUFACTURING, MINING AND SERVICES

Mining
In 2008 the government signed an agreement with the company Cairn Inida Ltd to explore for oil and gas off the north-western coast. In October 2011, the government announced that an off-shore gas field had been found in the Mannar basin. Further exploration is needed to discover the commercial viability of the field which is at a depth of 4,300 metres. At present, Sri Lanka relies on imports for all its petroleum needs, 97,000barrels per day in 2011.

Energy
The electric power grid extends to all parts of the country. Total energy consumption reached 0.220 quadrillion Btu in 2009 up from 0.213 quadrillion Btu in 2005.

In 2010, Sri Lanka produced 10.40 billion kWh of electricity, and consumed 8.92 billion kWh. The Mahaweli Development Project is the country's largest hydro-electric power plant. Electricity prices in Sri Lanka are among the highest in the region but there is a rising power demand which is putting increased pressure on the transmission and distribution system.

SRI LANKA

Manufacturing

Industry accounted for 28 per cent of GDP in 2008, the largest sector being garments, textiles and leather products which accounted for over 40 per cent of export revenue. However, growth in this subsector has slowed to 5 per cent, due to the end of the quota system on 1 January 2005, lack of workers and strong competition from Bangladesh, China and Vietnam. Food, beverages and tobacco, and chemicals, petroleum, rubber and plastics continue to be strong subsectors. Following the 2004 tsunami, there has been strong growth in construction now making up 7 per cent of GDP, further boosted by a surge in property prices and demand for high-quality housing by Sri Lankan expatriates, and by returnees to the country. The electronics industry continues to grow and there are now over 600 light engineering and metal working companies on the island.

Service Industries

The service sector was the largest contributor to GDP in 2006, accounting for 55.7 per cent. The telecoms industry has grown dramatically over recent years, with some companies reporting growth in earnings of over 40 per cent in the first half of 2006. Growth in international trade has boosted port services and warehousing.

Following the signing of a cease-fire agreement between the government and the Tamil Tigers in 2002, tourism grew strongly. However, in the wake of the 2004 tsunami, the sector suffered, and, although many beach resorts have been reconstructed, the tourists have not yet returned in appreciable numbers. More recently, they have been discouraged by heightened hostilities between government forces and the LTTE, and travel warnings from key European markets. Occupancy rates are thought to have dropped from around 90 per cent in pre-tsunami January to between 30 and 50 per cent in January 2007. Around 120,000 people are directly and indirectly employed in the industry. In 2003, there were 500,642 visitors, most coming from Britain (93,278), followed by India (90,603), Germany (58,908), France (28,585) and Australia (19,958).

Sri Lanka Tourist Board, URL: http://www.lanka.net/ctb

Agriculture

Traditionally the mainstay of the Sri Lankan economy, the agricultural sector now accounts for 13 per cent of GDP and employs around 33 per cent of the work force. Principal products are tea and rubber and subsidiary products coffee and spices, rice, coconuts, grain, pulses, tobacco, pepper and cocoa. Sri Lanka is the largest exporter of black tea, accounting for almost 25 per cent of the total world tea exports, and one of the top ten exporters of rubber. More than 100,000 tons of rubber are produced annually. In 2006, there was sharp growth of 55 per cent in the fishing sector, as the industry returned to its pre-tsunami state. FAO figures put the total catch in 2010 at 436,355 tonnes.

Agricultural Production in 2010

Produce	Int. $'000*	Tonnes
Rice, paddy	1,167,992	4,300,620
Tea	300,220	282,300
Coconuts	194,794	1,761,680
Natural rubber	159,336	139,300
Indigenous chicken meat	140,505	98,641
Plantains	118,181	572,420
Indigenous cattle meat	63,465	23,494
Pepper (piper spp.)	55,484	26,620
Hen eggs, in shell	53,603	64,630
Arecanuts	52,210	29,880
Mangoes, mangosteens, guavas	51,876	86,580
Cow milk, whole, fresh	50,582	162,090

* unofficial figures
Source: http://faostat.fao.org/site/339/default.aspx Food and Agriculture Organization of the United Nations, Food and Agricultural commodities production

COMMUNICATIONS AND TRANSPORT

Travel Requirements

Citizens of the USA, Canada, Australia and the EU require a passport valid for six months from date of entry and a visa; a no-cost visitor visa, valid for 30 days, is granted to tourists at the time of entry, apart from Maltese tourists who require a visa in advance. Business travellers should obtain a visa prior to arrival, as should people arriving for purposes other than tourism (i.e. volunteering or working).Visitors staying more than 30 days for any purpose must pay residency visa fees. Foreign guests in private households should register in person at the nearest local police station.

Visitors from countries not mentioned above should contact the embassy to check visa requirements. Travellers need yellow fever and cholera immunisations if coming from an infected area.

National Airlines

Sri Lankan Airlines, URL: http://www.srilankan.aero

Sri Lanka's domestic airline, Lionair, has had the exclusive rights to maintain domestic services between Palaly and Ratmalana since 1995. In February 1998, a second domestic airline, Monara, was launched to run weekly services to Jaffna from Colombo.

International Airports

Bandaranaike International Airport, Colombo has daily connections to Europe, the USA, the Middle East and Asia. Cargo facilities were being expanded with the aim of being able to handle some 100,000 tons of air freight per year by 2000.

Railways

The railways are owned and operated by the government, and are 1,460 km in length. Recently services to Jaffna, Batticaloa and Talaimannar have been disrupted.
Railway Tourist Office, Fort Railway Station, Colombo 1, Sri Lanka. Tel: +94 1 435838

Roads

Sri Lanka has over 15,660 miles of roads. Vehicles are driven on the left.

Ports and Harbours

The port of Colombo is the country's leading commercial port. There are also ports at Jaffna, Galle and Trincomalee.

HEALTH

Health care is provided free of charge. In 2009, the government spent approximately 5.9 per cent of its total budget on healthcare (down from 6.9 per cent in 2000), accounting for 46.2 per cent of all healthcare spending. Total expenditure on healthcare equated to 3.2 per cent of the country's GDP. Per capita expenditure on health was approximately US$65, compared with US$32 in 2000. Figures for 2005-10 show that there are 10,279 physicians (4.9 per 10,000 population), 40,678 nurses and midwives (19.3 per 10,000 population), 1,743 dentistry personnel, 886 pharmaceutical personnel and 2,411 environment and public health workers. There are 31 hospital beds per 10,000 population.

In 2010, the infant mortality rate (probability of dying before first birthday) was 14 per 1,000 live births and the child (under-five years old) mortality rate was 17 per 1,000 live births. The main causes of death in the under-fives are: prematurity (11 per cent), pneumonia (7 per cent), congenital abnormalities (30 per cent), birth asphyxia (27 per cent), diarrhoea (3 per cent). In the period 2000-09 an estimated 17.3 per cent of children (under five-years-old) were classified as stunted and 21.1 per cent as underweight.

According to the latest WHO figures, in 20108 approximately 91 per cent of the population had access to improved drinking water. In the same year, 92 per cent of the population had access to improved sanitation. (Source: http://www.who.int, World Health Statistics 2012)

EDUCATION

Education is compulsory from age 5-14 and free. In 2003, there were 10,475 primary and secondary schools in Sri Lanka, 9,790 of which were government-run. There are 13 universities on the island. In the same year, there were 194,931 teachers and 4,096,886 pupils. The teacher/pupil ratio stood at one teacher to 21 pupils.

Figures for 2004 indicate that 97 per cent of the relevant age group were enrolled in primary school. Five per cent of those repeated a year in primary school. 83 per cent of children go on to study at secondary school.

The quality of schooling differs considerably between rural and urban regions, as well between provinces. Those children in the western and southern provinces do noticeably better than those in the North and East of the country.

The adult literacy rate was around 90.7 per cent in 2004, well above the regional average of 61.8 per cent. Among the 15-24 years age group, the figure reached 95.6 per cent, again above the regional average of 75.8 per cent. (Source: UNESCO, UIS, June 2006). However, the IT and certain manufacturing sectors report a shortage of skilled labour.

RELIGION

Nearly seventy per cent of the population follow Buddhism, 13 per cent Hinduism, 10 per cent Islam and 9 per cent Christianity.

Sri Lanka has a religious liberty rating of 3 on a scale of 1 to 10 (10 is most freedom). (Source: World Religion Database)

COMMUNICATIONS AND MEDIA

There are reports of media pressure by the authorities. At the end of the civil war the government promised to protect freedom of expression and journalists.

Newspapers

Sri Lanka's major newspapers include:
The Daily News, state-owned, URL: http://www.dailynews.lk
Lankadeepa, daily, Singhalese URL: http://www.lankadeepa.lk
Lakbima, daily, Singhalese, URL: http://www.laknima.lk
The Island, URL: http://www.island.lk
Daily Mirror, URL: http://www.dailymirror.lk
Uthayan, Tamil, URL: http://www.uthayan.com

Broadcasting

The Sri Lanka Broadcasting Corporation broadcasts in Sinhala, Tamil and English. The government operates two television channels and a radio network. Private television and radio stations also exist. Satellite and cable TV subscription services are available.

Telecommunications

Some 3.4 million landlines are in operation and 11 million mobile phones. Just over 1.1 million Sri Lankans have access to the internet.

ENVIRONMENT

Sri Lanka is a party to the following international agreements: Biodiversity, Climate Change, Climate Change-Kyoto Protocol, Desertification, Endangered Species, Environmental Modification, Hazardous Wastes, Law of the Sea, Ozone Layer Protection, Ship Pollution and Wetlands. It has signed, but not ratified, the agreement on Marine Life Conservation.

All new industrial ventures must apply to the Central Environment Authority (CEA) for a license before they start production.

According to figures from the EIA, in 2005, total carbon emissions for the country reached 12.38 million metric tons, slightly up on the previous year. Per capita carbon emissions were 0.60 metric tons in the same year, compared to 20.14 metric tons per capita in the USA. In 2010, Sri Lanka's emissions from the consumption of fossil fuels totalled 14.09 million metric tons of carbon dioxide.

SPACE PROGRAMME

Following an agreement with China, Sri Lanka said it was to launch its first telecommunications satellite in 2015. SupremeSAT said it had signed the agreement with the China Great Wall Industry Corp. which is the only commercial organization authorised by the Chinese government to provide satellites, commercial launch services and to carry out international space cooperation.

SUDAN
Republic of the Sudan
Jumhuryat es-Sudan

Capital: Khartoum (over 5 million)

Head of State: Field Marshal Omar Hassan Ahmed el-Bashir (President) (page 1373)

First Vice-President: Ali Osman Mohammad Taha (page 1523)

Vice President: Dr Al-Haj Adam Youssef (page 1542)

National Flag: Fesswise, black, white and red. Green triangle on the hoist side

CONSTITUTION AND GOVERNMENT

Constitution

Sudan, jointly governed by the British and Egyptians since 1899, declared its independence on 1 January 1956. The two main political parties, UMMA and the National Unionist Party (NUP), broke up into conflicting splinter groups, forming an unstable base for parliamentary government. Governments changed but cabinets were slow to form, and when constituted they were unwieldy coalitions. A military coup occurred in November 1958. General Aboud's regime continued in power until 1964 when civilian rule was restored after a popular uprising. Following a coup d'état in May 1969 General Gaafar al-Nimeiry gained power, dissolving parliament and establishing a single political party system with the Sudanese Socialist Union (SSU). Nimeiry was re-elected as president for a third term in 1983. However, two years later he was ousted.

Under this constitution the President was nominated by the SSU and approved by popular referendum for a term of six years. The President exercises the executive powers of government and is supreme commander of the armed forces. Ministers are appointed by him and are responsible to him. A Prime Minister is authorised by the Constitution of 1973.

Legislative power is formally vested in a 250 member People's Assembly, 25 of whom are appointed by the President, 125 directly elected from geographical constituencies, 70 selected by functional and occupational associations, and 30 selected by Provincial People's Councils. All candidates must be approved by the SSU. Major legislative proposals are initiated by the President after having been approved by the Political Bureau of the SSU and are referred to functional committees before consideration by the full Assembly. Legislation may be enacted over a Presidential veto by a two-thirds majority of the Assembly.

Though the government had hitherto been highly centralised in Khartoum, under the provisions of the People's Local Government Act of 1971 Government operations in all fields other than foreign affairs, national defence and justice are to be decentralised to the 18 provinces. Among the delegated functions are education, public health, agriculture, community development, livestock, minor public works, housing, and social welfare. It is intended that a substantial number of officials now serving in Khartoum will gradually be assigned to the Provincial Governments while Ministry headquarters will retain control over policy, national priorities, standards of administration, review of performance, the execution of large development projects, and the management of public corporations.

A Provincial Commissioner, appointed by the President, is responsible for planning, integrating and directing the public services which are being devolved to the provinces. Civil servants from the national Ministries are seconded to the provinces and are administratively responsible to the Provincial Commissioner. In each province there is a People's Executive Council composed of representatives selected by local councils and occupational groups and of senior civil servants in the provincial government. The Council has a broad range of legislative powers over provincial and local administration. It reviews the consolidated provincial budget before it is submitted to Khartoum and approves the budgets of local authorities. It is empowered to propose major development projects and to recommend national policies to the President, the relevant Ministries and the People's Assembly.

The People's Executive Council in each province is enjoined to delegate powers over local social and economic services and to authorise taxing powers to People's Local Councils in towns, rural areas and villages. Members of the People's Local Councils, a quarter of whom must be women, are chosen by popular election. Civil servants have been posted in growing numbers by the Provincial Commissioners to serve the local councils.

The parallel structures of the SSU and the Government are intended to ensure a close and continuous link between politics and administration. The Party is subordinate to Government. Major policies of Government are shaped by the SSU which is also responsible for guiding the administration at all levels in the execution of these policies. Civil servants are required to demonstrate a positive commitment to the objectives and policies of the SSU. At the local level, SSU cadres and members are expected to counteract the influence of traditional sectarian, ethnic and political groups, where these are disinclined to support the political and administrative authorities.

Elections held 6-17 March 1996 resulted in Lt. General Omar Hassan Ahmed Al-Bashir being re-elected with 75.7 per cent of the vote. Of the National Assembly's 400 members, 125 had previously been chosen by a national conference in February. 900 candidates stood for the remaining 275 seats, of those 51 were uncontested. Due to the civil war in the southern part of the country, no voting took place in 11 districts. After the elections the President declared that Sudan would continue to be guided by Islamic orientation, with no return to party politics, during his new five-year term.

A new constitution was put before the people of Sudan in a referendum, and was passed, coming into effect on 1 January 1999. Sudanese citizens can now join political associations, but they would come under Islamic Shari'ah Law (political parties were banned in 1990). This constitution was superceded by a constitution signed in 2005, this constitution formally ended the civil war and set out a power sharing structure for the north and south of the country. The new constitution also made provision for a transitional bicameral legislature replacing the unicameral system. The power-sharing arrangements of the 2005 constitution were superseded by the south's vote in a referendum on 9-15 January 2011 for full independence, which took place on 9 July 2011.

To consult the Constitution in English, please visit: http://www.sudanjudiciary.org/newse/news.php?id=10

International Relations

Sudan's international relations are very poor. The USA has frequently expressed concern about Sudan's connection with Iran. Its alleged involvement with terrorism has resulted in the detention of five Sudanese suspected of plotting to blow up buildings and road tunnels in New York. They were also believed to be plotting the assassination of President Mubarak of Egypt on a visit to the USA. Sudan is presently on the USA's list of countries sponsoring terrorism. Increased isolation has been threatened if Sudan does not improve its human rights record. Along with atrocities in connection with fighting in the South, other denials of human rights include the right of freedom of speech, and freedom to conduct political activities.

Recent Events

In December 1999 a three month state of emergency was declared by Omar Al-Bashir due to a power struggle between Omar Al-Bashir and Hassan el-Tourabi, leader of the National Islamic Front and Secretary of the National Congress. Mr Bashir advised that the state of emergency was to be implemented to allow for the dissolution of parliament and for new elections to be held. In December the National Assembly and some of the articles in the new constitution were suspended, although government and state governors remained.

In July 2002, following talks held in Kenya, the Sudan People's Liberation Army (SPLA) and the government signed the Machakos Protocol to end the civil war that had been raging for 19 years. Under the agreement the government recognised that the south of Sudan has the right to seek self determination following a six year interim period, and the rebels from the south recognise that the north has the right to implement Shari'ah law. Peace talks continued throughout 2003.

Darfur

In January 2004 an uprising began in the Darfur region and refugees from the fighting began leaving Sudan for Chad. Pro-government Arab militias are accused of killing African villagers in Darfur. The militias, the Janjaweed, have been accused of carrying out a campaign of ethnic cleansing against non Arab civilians. Various army officers and opposition politicians were arrested over an alleged coup plot. Progress was made in peace talks in May 2004 when the government and southern rebels agreed on some power-sharing protocols. In July 2004 UN Secretary General Kofi Annan called on the international community for aid to help

SUDAN

with the increasing humanitarian crisis. A peace deal was signed in January 2005. Its terms included a permanent ceasefire and accords on power sharing, including a referendum on autonomy after a six-year period. In March 2005 the UN Security Council authorised sanctions against those who violated the ceasefire in Darfur but stopped short of calling the violence genocide. In May 2006 a peace accord was signed between the Khartoum government and the Sudan Liberation Movement, but other rebel groups would not sign the agreement and the violence continued. The following August Sudan rejected a UN peacekeeping force in the area as they claimed it would compromise sovereignty. In April 2007 as the violence continued and international pressure increased the government agreed to a partial UN peace keeping force to compliment the African Union peacekeepers already on the ground. In May 2007 President Bush of the USA announced new sanctions against Sudan. In September 2007 talks with the UN regarding the make up of a Dafur peacekeeping force broke up without agreement.

In June 2005 the government and the exiled NDA party signed a power-sharing reconciliation deal and the former rebel leader John Garang was appointed vice-president in July. He was killed on 1 August 2005 when his helicopter crashed. Riots followed the announcement of his death. The following month saw the formation of a power sharing government and in October an autonomous government was formed in the south of the country in line with the January agreement. In May 2006 the Khartoum government signed a peace agreement with the main rebel group in Dafur. The following August the government declined a UN Peacekeeping force in the Dafur region saying it would compromise sovereignty. In November the African Union increased its time in the area for peacekeeping duties and in April 2007 Sudan agreed to accept a small UN peacekeeping unit to bolster the African Union troops. In January 2008 the UN took over the peacekeeping mission. In March 2008 leaders from Sudan and Chad signed a peacekeeping agreement aimed at ending hostilities, but relations became strained the following May when Darfur rebel groups raided Omdurman, the twin city of Khartoum across the Nile. Diplomatic relations were broken off.

The International Criminal Court in The Hague issued an arrest warrant in March 2009 for President Omar al-Bashir on charges of war crimes and crimes against humanity in Dafur.

In February 2010 Sudan announced it was ready to adopt normal relations with neighbouring Chad, it was hoped that this would bring to an end the conflict in Darfur where both countries had accused each other of sponsoring rebels.

In March 2010 the main Darfur rebel group, the Justice and Equality Movement (Jem) signed a peace accord with the government. President Bashir declared the Darfur war over, but clashes with other groups have continued and the specifics of the deal are not clear.

In June 2010 two rebel leaders wanted on charges of war crimes surrendered to the ICC in The Hague. Abdallah Banda Abakaer Nourain and Saleh Mohammed Jerbo Jamus are wanted in connection with the deaths of 12 African Union peacekeepers in 2007. In July 2010 the ICC issued a second arrest warrant for President al-Bashir on charges of genocide.

In November 2011 a Kenyan court issued an arrest for President Omar al-Bashir over alleged war crimes. The ruling came after Kenya allowed Mr Bashir to visit. The court said Mr Bashir would be arrested if he returned to Kenya.

Southern Sudan

Under the Machakos Protocol signed in 2002, southern Sudan was able to seek self determination, and in September 2005 a new government was announced which included many leading figures from the SPLM. The government has between 17 and 19 ministers as well as seven presidential advisers. The government was responsible for the internal affairs of the area. Foreign policy, defence and energy remained the responsibility of the government in Khartoum. Following the formation of a mainly autonomous administration in the south in October 2005, it was announced a referendum would be held in 2011 regarding the question of independence. Terms of the referendum were agreed in December 2009 and in January 2010 President Bashir said he would accept the result of the referendum even if meant independence for the South. In December 2010 the SPLM publicly supported independence for the south.

The referendum took place on 9 January 2011. The result was overwhelming: 98.83 per cent in favour of full independence from the north and the south declared formal independence on 9 July 2011.

In November attacks and bombardments were reported around the border with Southern Sudan. South Sudan has accused President Bashir of supporting the rebels. The new border has still not been officially agreed and the status of the disputed territory of Abyei remains unresolved. The area still has not held a referendum on whether to join Sudan or South Sudan.

In December 2011 the ICC requested an arrest warrant for the defence minister, Abdelrahim Mohamed Hussein, for alleged war crimes relating to Darfur. In the same month the government killed one of the Darfur rebel leaders, Khalil Ibrahim.

In February 2012, Sudan and South Sudan signed a non-agression pact. Talks continued on outstanding secession issues including oil export fees. In April 2012 following weekes of fighting on the border, the South Sudan troops temporarily occupied the border town of Heglig which is home to an oil field. UN Secretary General condemned the bombing of the border by Sudan. South Sudan's President Salva Kiir said Sudan had 'declared war' on his country. Sudan pledged to pull its troops out in May 2012. The UN reported that some 655,000 people had been displaced or badly affected by the fighting in the region. In August the two countries managed to reach a deal on the South's export of oil through Sudan's pipelines.

Other Recent Events

In August 2012 a plane crashed killing all 32 people on board including two state ministers, the leader of a national political party and the minister for religion, Ghazi al-Sadiq Abdel Rahim.

In August 2012, Sudan and South Sudan agreed a deal on the export of South Sudan's oil via Sudan's pipelines. The following month the Presidents of Sudan and South Sudan attended talks in Ethiopia and agreed trade, oil and security deals. Border issues including the disputed Abyel Territory were not resolved. A demilitarized zone was agreed on. In March 2013, Sudan and South Sudan agreed to resume pumping oil and also agreed to withdraw troops from the border area.

More than 60 people were reported killed in ethnic clashes in the Darfur region over land producing gum arabic. Gum arabic is one of Sudan's most important export products.

Legislature

Following the signing of the 2005 Constitution a transitional bicameral legislature was established, replacing the previous unicameral legislature. The National Assembly *Majlis Watani*, has 400 members and is made up according to the peace agreement by 234 members from the National Congress party, 126 members from the Sudan People's Liberation Movement, 63 members from opposition groups from the north and 27 members from opposition groups from the south.

The Council of States has 52 members, made up of two representatives from each state.

National Assembly, People's Hall, CP 14416, Omdurman, Sudan. Tel: +249 1 8755 7918, e-mail: info@sudan-parliament.org, URL: http://www.sudan-parliament.org

Cabinet (as at June 2013)

Minister at the Presidency: Maj. Gen. Bakri Hassan Salih (NCP) (page 1507)
Minister of Cabinet Affairs: Ahmed Saad Omar Khadr
Minister of Foreign Affairs: Ali Ahmed Karti (NCP) (page 1454)
Minister of Defence: Gen. Abdel-Rahim Hussein (NCP)
Minister of Interior: Ibrahim Mahmud Hamad (NCP)
Minister of Finance and National Economy: Ali Mahmood Abdel-Rasool (NCP) (page 1371)
Minister of Justice and Prosecutor General: Mohammed Bushara Dousa
Minister of Agriculture: Abdul Halim Isma'il al-Muta'afi
Minister of Industry: Abdel Wahab Mohammed Osman
Minister of Trade: Osman Omar Al-Sharef
Minister of Livestock and Fisheries: Faisal Hasan Ibrahim (NCP)
Minister of Higher Education: Dr Khames Kundah
Minister of Education: Suad Abdel Raziq
Minister of Transport, Roads and Bridges: Ahmed Babikrt Nahar
Minister of Electricity and Water Resources: Osama Abdalla Al-Hassan
Minister of Labour: Farah Mustafa Abdullah
Minister of Health: Bahr Idris Abu Garda
Minister of Antiquities, Tourism and Wildlife: Mohamed Abdel Karim al-Had
Minister of Environment, Forestry and Planning: Hassan Abdel Qader Hilal
Minister of Religious Guidance and Endowments: vacant
Minister of Youth and Sports: Abduallah Al-Fatih Taj al-Sir
Minister of Science and Technology: Essa Bushra Mohamed (NCP)
Minister of Human Resources Development: Abdeen Mohammed Sharif
Minister of Minerals: Kamal Abdel Latif
Minister of Petroleum: Awad Ahmed al Jaz
Minister of Culture: Ahmed Bilal Osman
Minister of Welfare and Social Security: Mashir Mohamed Al-Amin
Minister of Communications: Mohamed Abdul Karim al-Had

Ministries

Office of the President, People's Palace, PO Box 281, Khartoum, Sudan. Tel: +249 1 8377 8426
Office of the Prime Minister, Khartoum, Sudan. Tel: +249 1 8377 0726
Ministry of Foreign Affairs, P.O. Box 873, Khartoum, Sudan. URL: http://www.sudanmfa.com
Ministry of Interior, P.O. Box 281, Khartoum, Sudan. Tel: +249 11 779 990, fax: +249 11 776 554
Ministry of Finance and National Economy, Nile Street, P.O. Box 700, Khartoum, Sudan. Tel: +249 11 775969, fax: +249 11 775630
Ministry of Commerce and Co-operation, PO Box 194, Khartoum, Sudan. Tel: +249 1 8377 9157
Ministry of Energy and Mining, PO Box 2087, Khartoum, Sudan. Tel: +249 11 77 3472, fax: +249 11 77 7554
Ministry of National Industry and Investments, PO Box 2184, Khartoum, Sudan. Tel: +249 1 8377 7830
Ministry of Science and Technological Research, Khartoum, Sudan. e-mail: wazir@sudan-most.net, URL: http://www.sudan-most.net
Ministry of Transport, Gaba Street, Khartoum, Sudan. Tel: +249 1 8377 9700
Ministry of Health, PO Box 303, Khartoum, Sudan. Tel: +249 1 8377 3000
Ministry of Irrigation and Water Resources, PO Box 878, Khartoum, Sudan. Tel: +249 1 8377 7533
Ministry of Agriculture and Forestry, PO Box 285, al Gamaa Avenue, Khartoum, Sudan. Tel: +249 1 8378 0951, e-mail: moafcc@sudanmail.net
Ministry of Education, PO Box 284, Khartoum, Sudan. Tel: +249 1 8377 0016, e-mail: info@moe-sd.net
Ministry of Justice an Office of the Attorney-General, PO Box 302, an Nil Avenue, Khartoum, Sudan. Tel: +249 1 8377 4842

Elections

The most recent presidential and legislative elections were held in December 2000. Lt. General Omar Hassan Ahmed Al-Bashir was re-elected; some opposition parties boycotted the elections. Turnout was recorded as being low. The National Congress party (previously the National Islamic Front) won by a large majority. Elections were due to be held in 2004 but were postponed. They were expected to be held in April 2010, but international observers had suggested that they be delayed because of security risks, however President Omar al-Bashir reacted strongly against the observers saying they should not try and interfere in Sudan's affairs. Until the new elections were held a Transitional National Assembly sat. The cabinet was made up of NCP and SPLM members and included ministers from north and south opposition parties.

The elections went ahead on 11-15 April 2010, the first multi-party election for 24 years, initially there were complaints that there were delays getting ballot papers out and names were missing from the electoral roll, the election was to be held over three days but this was later extended to five days because of the delays. Some opposition parties had boycotted the elections saying they would not be fair. President Bashir won a new term in the presidential elections the first contested presidential election since 1986. President Bashir's National Congress Party (NCP), won an overall majority.

Voters in Dafur were able to vote but there were many logistical problems as so many people are in refugee camps. In Southern Sudan the election is a pre-cursor to a referendum scheduled for January 2011 on possible independence. The referendum went ahead and the South voted overwhelmingly in favour of independence. Turnout was more than 60 per cent.

Suffrage is universal from the age of 17, but not compulsory.

Political Parties
Umma Party, The Democratic Unionist Party, (DUP); National Congress Party, (NCP), formerly National Islamic Front; Sudanese People's Liberation Movement, (SPLM); The Republican Brothers, Sudanese Communist Party, The Baath Party.

Diplomatic Representation
US Embassy, Sharia Ali Abdul Latif, PO Box 699, APO AE 09289, Khartoum, Sudan. Tel: +249 11 774611, fax: +249 11 774137, URL: http://sudan.usembassy.gov/
Charge Ambassador: Mary Yates
Embassy of Sudan, US, 2210 Massachusetts Ave, NW, Washington, DC 20008, USA. Tel: +1 202 338 8565, fax: +1 202 667 2406, URL: http://www.sudanembassy.org/
Chargé d'Affaires: Ali Mohamed Fatahelraman
Embassy of Sudan, UK, 3 Cleveland Row, St James's, London, SW1A 1DD, England. Tel: +44 (0)20 7839 8080, fax: +44(0)20 7839 7560, e-mail: admin@sudanembassy.co.uk, URL: http://www.sudan-embassy.co.uk
Ambassador: Abdullah Hamad Ali Al-Azraq
British Embassy, off Sharia Al Baladia, Khartoum East (PO Box 801), Sudan. Tel: +249 (11) 777105, fax: +249 (11) 776457, e-mail: information.khartoum@fco.gov.uk, URL: http://ukinsudan.fco.gov.uk/en/
Ambassador: Peter Tibber
Permanent Representative of the Republic of the Sudan to the United Nations, 655 Third Avenue, Suite 500-510, New York, NY 10017, USA. Tel: +1 212 573 6033, fax: +1 212 573 6160, URL: http://www.un.int/sudan
Ambassador: Daffa Alla Al-Haj Ali Osman

LEGAL SYSTEM

Legal system based on English common law and Islamic law.

Under the Self-Government Statute the Judiciary has become an independent state department directly and solely responsible to the Supreme Council of the Armed Forces. Civil justice is administered by the Chief Justice and judges of the High Court, who are also members of the Court of Appeal, and by subordinate district judges. The religious law of Islam is administered by the Law Courts in matters of inheritance, marriage, divorce and family relations amongst the Muslim population and non Muslims in the northern states. There are District and Provincial courts and a High Court at Khartoum presided over by the Grand Kadi.

Serious crimes are tried by major courts constituted under the code of Criminal Procedure and composed of a President and two members. In the provinces in which circuits of the High Court extend, major courts are, as a rule, presided over by a judge of the High Court. In the other provinces a provincial judge presides. Decisions of a major court require confirmation by the Chief Justice, to whom there is a right of appeal. Lesser crimes are tried by minor courts with three magistrates, and by Magistrates' Courts consisting of a single magistrate or a bench of lay magistrates.

There are also Courts of Sheikhs or Chiefs with varying powers of limited jurisdiction throughout the country. They administer civil and criminal justice in accordance with native custom and deal with offences against specific ordinances under the general supervision of the Sudan Government Authorities.

The government's human rights record is poor. There have been unlawful killings by government forces throughout the country, as well as torture, beatings, and other inhumane treatment or punishment by security forces. Arrests can be arbitrary, and pretrial detention can be prolonged. Prison conditions are harsh. The government interfers in the workings of the judiciary and obstructs the delivery of humanitarian assistance. There are restrictions on privacy, freedom of speech and of the press, assembly, association, religion, and movement.

Sudan retains the death penalty and it is used in cases of apostasy, homosexuality, waging war against the state, prostitution; treason; acts that may endanger the independence or unity of the state; murder; armed robbery; weapons possession and smuggling. At least 19 executions were reported to have been carried out in 2012.

LOCAL GOVERNMENT

Until recently the country was divided into nine Provinces and two Commissionerships. In each Province there is a Provincial Council of some 12-20 members representing local authorities in the Province. The Provinces were sub-divided into a total of 46 districts, each under a district Commissioner.

The Sudan is now divided into 25 states, each one headed by a governor (appointed by the President), assisted by five or six state ministers. This is known as the Federal Rule System. The states are: A'ali an Nil (Upper Nile), Al Bahr al Ahmar (Red Sea), Al Buhayrat (Lakes), Al Jazira (Gezira), Al Khartoum (Khartoum), Al Qadarif (Gedaref), Al Wahda (Unity), An Nil al Abyad (White Nile), An Nil al Azraq (Blue Nile), Ash Shimaliyya (Northern), Bahr al Jabal (Central Equatoria), Gharb al Istiwa'iyya (Western Equatoria), Gharb Bahr al Ghazal (Western Bahr el Ghazal), Gharb Darfur (Western Darfur), Janub Darfur (Southern Darfur), Janub Kurdufan (Southern Kordofan), Junqoley (Jonglei), Kassala (Kassala), Nahr an Nil (River Nile), Shimal Bahr al Ghazal (Northern Bahr el Ghazal), Shimal Darfur (Northern Darfur), Shimal Kurdufan (Northern Kordofan), Sharq al Istiwa'iyya (Eastern Equatoria), Sinnar (Sinnar) and Warab (Warab).

AREA AND POPULATION

Area
Sudan is the largest of the African countries. Prior to the split with Southern Sudan its approximate area was 2.5 million sq. km. With the split is approximate area has been reduced to 1.8 million sq. km. It shares borders with Egypt, Libyan Jamahiria, Chad, the Central African Republic, Southern Sudan, Ethiopia and Eritrea. Saudi Arabia is located just across the Red Sea. While the north of Sudan is desert land, the south is rainforest. The rivers of the White Nile and Blue Nile join at Khartoum before continuing as the Nile to Egypt.

To view a map, consult http://www.lib.utexas.edu/maps/africa/txu-oclc-219400066-sudan_pol_2007.jpg. The area of Southern Sudan is shown on the map by a thick red border.

Population
Ethnic groups: Indigenous, 52 per cent; Arab, 39 per cent; Beja, 6 per cent; foreigners, 2 per cent; and other, 1 per cent.

Figures from 2010 estimated the population at 43.5 million with an average annual growth rate of 2.4 per cent for the period 2000-10. The area of metropolitan Khartoum, which includes Khartoum, Omduran (site of the national government) and Khartoum north has a population estimated to be between six and seven million.

Arabic is the official and principal language of Sudan; however, there are a further 100 local languages. There is a programme of Arabization in progress. The people of Northern Sudan are predominantly Arab and Muslim and number around 22 million. The main tribal divisions comprise: (a) the Hadendoa, Bisharin and Bani 'Amer of the Red Sea Hills speaking their own Hamitic and Semitic languages; (b) the Berbinne (Nubian) tribes of the northern Nile valley, with remnants of their old languages; (c) Arab tribes occupying the whole central belt of the Sudan, e.g. Kababish, Kawahla, Ja'alin and the various Baggara (cattle owning) tribes; (d) descendants of earlier peoples such as the Nuba, Fur and Ingessana peoples. These tribes have their own languages for the most part; however, Arabic is also spoken.

Southern Sudan is inhabited by a number of tribes, sometimes in very small units, speaking a large number of separate languages and dialects. These tribes can be classified as follows: (a) the various Sudanic tribal groups west of the Nile, including the Azande and Moru-Madi tribes; (b) the Nilotic peoples, the Dinka, Nuer and Shilluk-Acoli tribes; (c) the Nilo-Hamitic peoples of the southern Nile valley, for example the Bari and Latuka. Many of Sudan's tribes have links with those in Abyssinia, Kenya, Uganda or the Congo. Recent estimates put the population of southern Sudan at around six million.

A civil war between Arab-Muslims of the North and the Christians and Animists of the south lasted for twenty years. Recent estimates say that over 1.5 million people have been killed. In January 2004 an uprising began in the Darfur region and refugees from the fighting began leaving Sudan for Chad. Pro-government Arab militias, the Janjaweed, have been accused of carrying out a campaign of ethnic cleansing against non Arab civilians. A power-sharing reconciliation deal was signed in June 2005.

Births, Marriages, Deaths
In 2010 the birth rate was estimated at 32.8 births per 1,000 people and the death rate was put at 10.00 deaths per 1,000 people. In 2009 the average life expectancy at birth was 59 years. Healthy life expectancy was 50 years. The median age is 20 years. Approximately 40 per cent is aged under 15 years and 6 per cent over 60 years. The average fertility rate was 4.4 children per female in 2010. Sudan has suffered from drought and famine, as well as civil war and economic crisis. The problem has been augmented by the huge number of refugees in the southern provinces, mainly from Chad and Ethiopia. Figures compiled by Africa Watch revealed that in four years 500,000 civilians had been killed by the war and man-made famine.

National Day
1 January: Independence Day

EMPLOYMENT

Estimated figures for 2007 put the work force at 11.9 million. Agriculture employs 80 per cent of the working population, although only about 5 per cent of the country's land is arable. Industry and commerce employ 7 per cent and government 13 per cent. The unemployment rate is around 10 per cent.

BANKING AND FINANCE

Currency
Following the secession of South Sudan, the Sudanese government introduced a new currency, still called the Sudanese pound.

SUDAN

GDP/GNP, Inflation, National Debt

The economy has been severely undermined by the 21-year civil war and the country's poor infrastructure. There are some moves to develop a more market economy but the state is heavily involved. The economy has been largely dependent on oil prodution; approximately 75 per cent of oil production occurs in the what is now South Sudan. Since secession, the economy has accordingly dipped and Sudan is attempting to diversify its economy whilst implementing austerity measures. A large percentage of the population is expected to remain below the poverty line for years to come.

Estimates for 2008 put GPD at US$88 billion (compared to an estimated US$12.5 billion in 2001). This rise was attributable to Sudan beginning to export its oil, an end to the civil war and the introduction of macroeconomic policies. GDP grew by an estimated 6.5 per cent in 2004 and 7.0 per cent in 2005. Growth was put at 5.3 per cent in 2008. Estimated figures for 2009 put GDP at US$93.0 billion refecting a growth rate of 3.7 per cent. Per capita GDP was estimated at US$2,000 in 2008. GDP was estimated at US$90 billion in 2010 with a growth rate of 3.8 per cent.

The average annual inflation rate between 1990-96 was over 86 per cent, reaching a high of 163 per cent in 1996 but decreasing in 1997 to 46.7 per cent and 9.0 per cent in 2004. It was estimated at over 15 per cent in 2008, falling to 12 per cent in 2009.

The chief sources of revenue are indirect taxation from customs duties on imported goods and royalties on products exported, profit on trading concerns (Sudan Railways, shares of cotton scheme profits, sugar monopoly, etc.) and direct taxation.

Sudan has a large foreign debt with huge arrears. In 1990 the International Monetary Fund (IMF) took the unusual step of declaring Sudan non-cooperative due to its non-payment of arrears to the fund after Sudan went back on promised reforms in 1992-93. The IMF threatened to expel Sudan from the Fund. To avoid this Khartoum agreed to make payments on its arrears, liberalize exchange rates and reduce subsidies; measures it has partially implemented. This is not helped by the severe shortage of foreign exchange, as imports exceed exports by more that two to one. In 2010, its foreign debt was estimated to be US$37 billion in 2010, of which an estimated US$30 billion was in arrears. Sudan's foreign debt is expected to reach US$46 billion in 2013.

Imports and Exports

According to estimated 2009 figures total value of exports was US$8.5 billion, with the main commodities being oil and petroleum, cotton, gold, sorghum, sesame, peanuts, sugar, livestock/meat and gum arabic. Total value of imports in 2009 was estimated at US$6.8 billion. Imported goods included foodstuffs, petroleum products, pumping and refining equipment, manufactured goods, machinery and equipment, textiles, foodstuffs, medicines and chemicals. Sudan's main trade partners are the EU, Saudi Arabia, Malaysia, China, India and Egypt.

External Trade, US$ million

	2005	2006	2007
Trade balance	-1,068.45	-1,291.27	49.37
Exports	4,877.54	5,813.36	7,587.35
Imports	5,945.99	7,104.63	7,517.98

Source: African Development Bank

Foreign Investment

Foreign investors are wary due to the political instability and Sudan's poor relations with international bodies.

Central Bank

Bank of Sudan, PO Box 313, Khartoum, Sudan. Tel: +249 11 774419, fax: +249 11 780273 / 11 778547, e-mail: cbank@sudanet.net, URL: http://www.bankofsudan.org

Sudan is a member of the African Development Bank, the Arab Bank for Economic Development in Africa, the Arab Fund for Economic and Social Development, the Islamic Development Bank, the Arab Monetary Fund and the Council for Arab Economic Unity.

MANUFACTURING, MINING AND SERVICES

Primary and Extractive Industries

The country has huge mineral resources which have yet to be fully exploited. They include gold, marble, granite, silica and manganese. Small amounts of chromium, manganese, and mica are produced, as are gold, magnesite and salt. There are also significant oil reserves that Sudan began to export in 1999. Sudan had proven oil reserves of 5 billion barrels and at the beginning of 2008 and that year producing 477,800 barrels per day, of which 395,000 barrels per day were being exported. Sudan has three oil refineries at El Gily, Khartoum and Port Sudan with a combined capacity of 122,000 barrels per day. Sudan also has deposits of natural gas of an estimated three trillion cubic feet, but these are not currently being exploited.

Energy

In the early 1990s Sudan produced 905 million kWh of electricity per year. Supplies of hydroelectricity are from the large installations at Khashm al Qirbah and Sannar. These are supplemented by thermal electricity produced by burning refined petroleum. Sudan signed an agreement with Russia in 1995 to build a dam in the province of Shamalia on the Nile River. It will have the capacity to produce 300,000 kW of electricity. In 2006, an estimated 4.04 billion kWh of electricity were generated and 3.40 billion kWh were consumed. At present, around 50 per cent of electricity produced comes from hydro power. (Source: EIA)

Manufacturing

Paper and textile mills, sugar and petroleum refineries and factories producing gum arabic have been established, and some factories produce consumer goods such as cigarettes, beverages, and shoes, tannery and leather production. However, manufacturing in Sudan is in its early stages of development and is mainly concentrated on the processing of agricultural produce, poor infrastructure is also a hindrance to industrial expansion

Agriculture

The annual rainfall in the Sudan ranges from less than 100 mm on the Egyptian border to over 1,200 mm in the south. Irrigation is essential to crop production in areas which receive less than 400 mm of rain. The chief irrigated area is in the Gezira Scheme which, with the Managil Extension, has an area of 1.8 million acres. These are cropped annually in a canalised area of over one million acres, fed by gravity irrigation from the Sennar Dam. In addition the Sudan has some 400,000 acres watered by pump irrigation and an average of 170,000 acres cultivated by flood irrigation annually. The implementation of new irrigation plans has been postponed due to civil war.

Sudan's chief export is cotton, mainly in the form of lint averaging 73,000 tons and of seed averaging 140,000 tons. The staple food crop is millet, grown on both rain assisted and irrigated land. Sesame and groundnuts grown in the rainy areas of central and southern Sudan are important as a food source and for their oil. Surplus production is exported. Dates, citrus fruits and mangoes are grown. The Sudan produces 75 per cent of the world's gum arabic needs.

Figures for the early 1990s put the livestock population at 21.6 million cattle, 22.6 million sheep, 18.7 million goats, 2.8 million camels, and 35 million poultry. Most camels and sheep are owned by nomad tribes in the vast grazing areas of the Sudan and an accurate census is not possible.

Much of the Sudan is covered by acacia, gum arabic is made from its resin. Timber is cut from the tropical forests of the south, and further north an extensive system of reservation and afforestation ensures supplies of building material, railway sleepers and basic fuel. There are four sawmills - in the Blue Nile province, Wau, Loka and Katire, with a total annual output of 1,000,000 cubic feet. There are 2,664,546 acres of forest reserves. Forestry, however, accounts for only 2 per cent of the National Income. In the early 1990s, about 829 million cubic feet of timber was produced, of which more than 90 per cent was utilised for fuel.

The following table shows agricultural production for the former Sudan in 2010.

Agricultural Production in 2010

Produce	Int. $'000*	Tonnes
Indigenous cattle meat	3,372,128	1,248,060
Cow milk, whole, fresh	1,733,343	5,554,500
Indigenous sheep meat	1,013,113	372,085
Goat milk, whole, fresh	521,439	1,601,900
Mangoes, mangosteens, guavas	374,240	624,600
Sorghum	370,558	2,630,000
Tea nes	340,176	213,000
Groundnuts, with shell	338,801	762,500
Indigenous goat meat	299,616	125,044
Onions, dry	234,397	1,116,000
Sugar cane	220,927	6,728,000
Dates	220,113	431,000

* unofficial figures

Source: http://faostat.fao.org/site/339/default.aspx Food and Agriculture Organization of the United Nations, Food and Agricultural commodities production

COMMUNICATIONS AND TRANSPORT

Travel Requirements

Citizens of the USA, Canada, Australia and the EU require a passport valid for six months beyond the length of stay and a visa (apart from transit passengers leaving within six hours with confirmed onward tickets). Other nationals should contact the embassy to check visa requirements.

It should be noted that the government routinely denies visas to travellers whose passports contain visas issued by the Government of Israel or other evidence of travel to Israel such as exit or entry stamps. Special permits, obtainable from the Passport and Immigration Office, are required for all travel outside Khartoum. Visitors staying in Sudan for longer than three days must report to the police within 24 hours of arrival.

There are restrictions on what can be brought into the country, some devices (such as video cameras, satellite phones, facsimile machines, televisions, and telephones) not being permitted. Travellers who wish to take any photographs must obtain a photography permit from the Government of Sudan, Ministry of Interior, Department of Aliens. Visitors are not allowed to take out ivory, some other animal products, or large quantities of gold, and must obtain an exit visa before departure from Sudan as well as pay any airport departure tax due.

National Airlines

Sudan Airways, SDC Building, Street 15, New Extension, PO Box 253, Khartoum, Sudan. Tel: +249 11 775803, fax: +249 11 47978, URL: http://www.sudanair.com/destinations.htm This is a government owned airline. It operates scheduled international flights, as well as regular services throughout the country.

In 2006 it was estimated that there were 85 airports in Sudan, 15 with paved runways. Two heliports are in existence.

Railways
The Sudan railway system, consisting of approximately 6,000 km of rail-road, owned and operated by the government, extends from Wadi Halfa in the north to Wau in the south and from Port Sudan in the east, through Atbara, Khartoum and Sennar to Nyala in the west. The rail network includes the Sennar-Haiya loop line, branch lines to Karima, El Obeid, and Roseires and an eastern rail line to the coast from Sennar via Haiya.

Waterways
Over 4,000 km of the Blue and White Nile rivers are in use all year round.

Ports and Harbours
Steamers are used for the transportation of goods and passengers. Services cover an area of 2,500 miles and operate on most of Sudan's waters. Port Sudan is administered by Sudan Railways. There are also ports at Khartoum, Kusti, Sawaking, Juba, Nimule and Malakal. A ferry runs fom Wadi Halfa to Aswan in Egypt.

Roads
In 1999, 36 per cent of Sudan's roads were paved. Rural roads in Northern Sudan are unpaved and almost impassable after rainfall. Improvements to the roads in Southern Sudan have been impossible because of the conflict. Vehicles are driven on the right.

HEALTH

Recent figures show that Sudan has 159 hospitals as well as dispensaries, health centres, dressing stations and health care units.

In 2009, the government spent approximately 9.9 per cent of its total budget on healthcare (up from 8.3 per cent in 2000), accounting for 81 per cent of all healthcare spending. Total expenditure on healthcare equated to 7.3 per cent of the country's GDP. Per capita expenditure on health was approximately US$94.

Figures for 2005-10 show that there are 10,813 physicians (3 per 10,000 population), 32,489 nurses and midwives (8.4 per 10,000 population), 772 dentistry personnel, 386 pharmaceutical personnel, 2,897 environment and public health workers, and 4,716 community health workers. There are 7 hospital beds per 10,000 population. The infant mortality rate was 69 per 1,000 live births in 2009 and the under-five mortality rate was 108 per 1,000 live births.

According to the latest WHO figures, in 2010 approximately 58 per cent of the population had access to improved drinking water. In the same year, 26 per cent of the population had access to improved sanitation. Diarrhoea accounts for 12 per cent of childhood deaths. (Source: http://www.who.int, World Health Statistics 2012)

EDUCATION

Primary/Secondary Education
Elementary schooling in Sudan lasts for eight years and is free and compulsory. 20 per cent of its pupils go on to study at intermediate level for a further four years. In 2004 the elementary school enrolment rate was 60 per cent. The pupil:teacher ratio was 29:1. Secondary education up to school certificate standard is provided by the government at Wadi Seidna (Khartoum Province), Hantoub (Blue Nile Province), Khor Taggat (Kordofan Province), Rumbek (Bahr-el-Ghazal Province) where there are full boarding facilities, and at Khartoum and Atbara day secondary schools. There are also three non-government secondary schools in Omdurman, one in Port Sudan and three community and denominational schools in Khartoum. A commercial secondary school is run under government auspices in Omdurman. The secondary school enrolment rate was estimated at 66 per cent in 2004. Traditionally girls have not had the same access to education as boys but this has begun to change slowly.

Vocational Education
Technical education is provided for at intermediate technical schools at Omdurman, El Obeid, Wad Medani and Atbara, Port Sudan, Kosti and Nyala. The Khartoum Technical Institute gives a four-year course in technical education. There are a number of teacher training institutions, namely Bakht-er-Ruda, Shendi, Dilling and Meridi. Bakht-er-Ruda is the parent institution which not only trains teachers up to the intermediate level but also prepares syllabuses and is the centre of the subject inspectorate.

Higher Education
University College of Khartoum. The enrolment rate for tertiary education is 21 per cent. (Source: UNESCO)

In 2007 the adult illiteracy rate was estimated to be 52 per cent.

RELIGION

Recent figures show that 70 per cent of the population are Sunni Muslims (predominantly those living in Northern Sudan); 11 per cent (mostly those living in Southern Sudan) follow traditional indigenous beliefs; whilst 16 per cent are Christian.

Sudan has a religious liberty rating of 2 on a scale of 1 to 10 (10 is most freedom). (Source: World Religion Database)

COMMUNICATIONS AND MEDIA

The government imposes restrictions on broadcasting. The news reflects official views and government policy. The press has slightly more freedom than the broadcast media. Pre-publication censorship of the press was officially lifted in 20009 but it is still alleged to happen.

Newspapers
Government daily newspapers includes the Al-Anba. Private papers include the al-Ray'u al-Amm (URL: http://www.rayaam.net/).

Broadcasting
Sudan National Broadcasting Corporation (URL: http://www.srtc.gov.sd) is government-run and operates two stations. Broadcasting is restricted with censorship. State-run broadcasters reflect government policy. There are no privately owned television stations although one cable service is jointly owned by the government and private investors.

The Sudan National Radio Corporation, is government controlled, and broadcasts in Arabic, English and several southern Sudanese languages. Miraya FM, URL: http://www.mirayafm.org is run by the UN. Radio is the most popular medium in the south.

Telecommunications
The system has improved in recent years and most cities have now good coverage. According to estimates in 2008, there were 356,100 mainline telephones and 11 million mobiles.

Whilst the internet is accessible in the Sudan, usage is low. An estimated 4 million people use the internet. Six per cent of the population have personal computers. The government filters the internet. Source: WHO.

ENVIRONMENT

In 2006, Sudan's emissions from the consumption of fossil fuels totalled 12.26 million metric tons of carbon dioxide.

SURINAME
Republic of Suriname
Republiek Suriname

Capital: Paramaribo (Population estimate: 250,000)

Head of State: Dési Bouterse (page 1392)

Vice-President, Chair of the Council of Ministers: Robert Ameerali

National Flag: A central, horizontal red stripe with a yellow five-pointed star with white and green stripes above and below

CONSTITUTION AND GOVERNMENT

Constitution
The first large scale colonisation of Suriname was made by Francis Willoughby, the 5th Baron Willoughby, the English Governor of Barbados. He sent an expedition to Suriname under Anthony Rowse, who became its first governor.

At the peace of Breda in 1667, between England and the United Netherlands, Suriname was assigned to the Netherlands in exchange for the Colony of New Netherland in North America, and this was confirmed by the Treaty of Westminster of February 1674. Since then Suriname has been twice in the possession of England, from 1799 until 1802 when it was restored at the Peace of Amiens, and from 1804 to 1816 when it was returned according to the Convention of London of 31 August 1814. This was confirmed at the Treaty of Vienna in 1815 with the return of all other Dutch colonies, except Berbice, Demerara, Essequibo and the Cape of Good Hope.

A new legal order was enacted by the Netherlands Suriname and the Netherlands Antilles, which took effect on 29 December 1954 and was embodied in the Charter for the Kingdom of the Netherlands. By this, these countries were given management of their own affairs and are united with the Netherlands on a footing of equality for the protection of their common interests and the granting of mutual assistance. On 25 November 1975 Suriname became an independent democratic republic.

SURINAME

There have been two military coups since 1975. In February 1980 the government was toppled in a coup led by military leaders. A second coup occurred in August of the same year which restored the former president, Henck Chin-A-Sen. Parliament was dissolved and replaced by a National Military Council. The Council nominated a 31 member National Assembly, a Topberaad or supreme decision-making body, and a 14 member Cabinet.

In 1986 a new cabinet was installed. It consisted of representatives from labour, business and members of the three major political parties. Although a transition to civilian life had been underway since 1985, an attempt to overthrow Colonel Bouterse's regime by a guerrilla group led by former soldier Ronny Brunswijk complicated the process.

On 24 December 1990 the country was again taken over by the military. On 25 May 1991 new general, free and secret elections were held and another democratic government was established. Ronald Venetiaan, who had served as education minister in the civilian government, was elected president.

To consult the constitution, please visit: http://www.wipo.int/wipolex/en/text.jsp?file_id=209753

International Relations
The Dutch relationship continues to be an important factor in the economy; with the Dutch insisting that Suriname undertake economic reforms and produce specific plans for projects on which aid funds could be spent.

Longstanding border disputes with Guyana and French Guiana remain unresolved. In 2004 Guyana brought a complaint against Suriname under the United Nations Convention on the Law of the Sea (UNCLOS) regarding their maritime border dispute. In 2007, the UN International Tribunal on the Law of the Sea (ITLOS) ruled that both Suriname and Guyana are entitled to their share of the disputed offshore basin which is believed to be rich in oil and gas deposits. Using the equidistance line, the tribunal awarded Suriname 6,900 sq. miles and Guyana 12,800 sq. miles of this basin.

Suriname is a member of the United Nations, the OAS, the Organization of the Islamic Conference, and the Non-Aligned Movement, as well as the Caribbean Community and Common Market and the Association of Caribbean States. It is associated with the European Union through the Lome Convention. Suriname participates in the Amazonian Pact, a grouping of the countries of the Amazon Basin that focuses on protection of the Amazon region's natural resources from environmental degradation. The country also belongs to the Economic Commission for Latin America, the Inter-American Development Bank, the Islamic Development Bank, the International Finance Corporation, the World Bank, and the International Monetary Fund. In 2008, Suriname signed the Rome Statute of the International Criminal Court.

Recent Events
In September 2007, a UN tribunal ruled on the Guyana-Suriname dispute over maritime territory; it gave both countries a share of a potentially oil-rich offshore basin.

Legal proceedings began in November 2007 against 25 defendants accused of participating in the December 8, 1982 murders of 15 political opponents of the former military-dominated government. The court martial tribunal convened on November 30, 2007, with a series of preliminary motions. The trial itself, with judges hearing witness testimonies, started on July 4, 2008.

Legislature
Under a Constitution approved in 1987 the National Assembly is the highest and therefore the most powerful institution in the country. The members of the 51 member Assembly are elected by the people for a term of five years. The President and the Vice-President appoint the Council of Ministers.
National Assembly, 10 Onafhankelijkheidsplein, Paramaribo, Suriname. Tel: +597 475180, fax: +597 410364

Council of Ministers (as of June 2013)
Minister of Defence: Lamure Latour
Minister of Foreign Affairs: Winston Lacin
Minister of Justice and Police: Edward Belfort
Minister of Finance: Adelin Wijnerman (page 1536)
Minister of Home Affairs: Soewarto Moestadja
Minister of Agriculture, Animal Husbandry and Fisheries: Hendrik Setrowidjojo
Minister of Labour, Technological Development and Environment: Michael Miskin
Minister of Education & Community Development: Shirley Sitaldien
Minister of Physical Planning, Land & Forestry Management: Ginmardo Kromosoeto
Minister of Trade and Industry: Raymond Sapoen
Minister of Regional Development: Stanley Betterson
Minister of Transport, Communication and Tourism: Falisi Pinas
Minister of Natural Resources: Jim Hok
Minister of Regional Development: Linus Diko
Minister of Social Affairs and Housing: Alice Amafo
Minister of Public Health: Michael Blokland
Minister of Public Works: Ramon Abrahams
Minister of Sport and Youth Affairs: Ismanto Adna

Ministries
Office of the President, Kleine Combe Road #1, Paramaribo, Suriname. Tel: +597 472841, fax: +597 475266, e-mail: kabpressur@sr.net, URL: http://www.kabinet.sr.org/
Office of the Vice President, Dr S Redmond Street #118, Paramaribo, Suriname. Tel: +597 474805, fax: +597 472917
Ministry of Foreign Affairs, Lim A Po Street #25, Paramaribo, Suriname. Tel: +597 471209, fax: +597 410411
Ministry of Defence, Kwaitta Road #29, Paramaribo, Suriname. Tel: +597 474244, fax: +597 420055

Ministry of Transport, Communication and Tourism, Prins Hendrik Street #24-26, Paramaribo, Suriname. Tel: +597 420422 / 411951, fax: +597 420425, e-mail: mintct@sr.net, URL: http://www.mintct.sr/
Ministry of Planning and Development Co-operation, Dr S. Redmond Street #118, Paramaribo, Suriname. Tel: +597 421085 / 473628, fax: +597 421056, e-mail: plos@sr.net, URL: http://www.plos.sr/
Ministry of Home Affairs, Wilhelmina Street #3, Paramaribo, Suriname. Tel: +597 476461, fax: +597 421056
Ministry of Trade and Industry, Haven Lane North, Paramaribo, Suriname. Tel: +597 402886 / 402080, fax: +597 402602
Ministry of Public Works, Coppenames Street #167, Paramaribo, Suriname. Tel: +597 462500, fax: +597 464901
Ministry of Education and Community Development, Dr S Kafiluddis Street #117-123, Paramaribo, Suriname. Tel: +597 498383, fax: +597 495083
Ministry of Labour, Wagenweg Street #13, Paramaribo, Suriname. Tel: +597 477045, fax: +597 410465
Ministry of Social Affairs and Housing, Waterkant #30-32, Paramaribo, Suriname. Tel: +597 472340, fax: +597 470516
Ministry of Health, Graven Street #64, Paramaribo, Suriname. Tel: +597 474941, fax: +597 410702
Ministry of Regional Development, Van Roseveltkade #2, Paramaribo, Suriname. Tel: +597 471574, fax: +597 424517
Ministry of Justice and Police, Graven Street #1, Paramaribo, Suriname. Tel: +597 475805, fax: +597 412109, e-mail: ipoffsur@sr.net
Ministry of Agriculture, Animal, Husbandry and Fisheries, Letitia Vriesde Lane, Paramaribo, Suriname. Tel: +597 403209 / 477698, fax: +597 404407 / 470301, e-mail: veeteelt@cq-link.sr, URL: http://www.cq-link.sr/bedrijven/nonprofit_veeteelt/
Ministry of Finance, Onafhankelukheidsplein #3, Paramaribo, Suriname. Tel: +597 472610, fax: +597 472911

Elections
The most recent legislative elections took place on 25 May 2010. The Mega Combination Coalition became the largest group in the National Assembly, winning 23 out of 51 seats. The new cabinet took office in August 2010.

Presidential elections were held after the inauguration of the new legislature in July 2005. However, by the end of July, MPs had failed to choose a president at its second attempt so the regional assemblies decided the outcome in August, which saw the re-election of Ronald Venetiaan, who had previously won the election in 1991 and 2000. The most recent presidential election took place in July 2010; Dési Bouterse was elected to the post.

Prior to entering politics Dési Bouterse was a military leader during the 1980s and early 1990s. He was accused of murdering political opponents during military rule, something that he has always denied. In 1999 he was convicted in absentia by a Netherlands court of drug trafficking which he has also denied. In April 2012, the parliament passed a law under which the president has immunity for alleged violations commited under this military rule. Mr Bouterse is currently one of several people on trial for the murder of 15 political opponents but has so far refused to attend the court. It is currently unclear if the trial will continue.

Political Parties
The coalition government (the New Front for Democracy and Development) is made of the National Party of Suriname (NPS), Progressive Reform Party (VHP), Pertjajah Luhur and the Suriname Workers Party (NPS). National Democratic Party, the People's Alliance for Progress coalition of three parties, the A-Com coalition of three parties and the A1 coalition of four parties; Party for Democracy and Development through Unity (DOE); People's Alliance for Progress (VVV).

Diplomatic Representation
Embassy of the Republic of Suriname, 4301 Connecticut Avenue, NW, Suite 460, Washington, DC 20008, USA. Tel: +1 202 244 7488, fax: +1 202 244 5878, URL: http://surinameembassy.org
Ambassador: Subhas Mungra
US Embassy, Dr. Sophie Redmonstraat 129, PO Box 1821, Paramaribo, Suriname. Tel: +597 472900, 477881, 476459, fax: : +597 479829 / 420800, URL: http://suriname.usembassy.gov/
Ambassador: Jay Anania
British High Commission, (staff resident in Guyana), URL: http://ukinguyana.fco.gov.uk
High Commissioner: Andrew Ayre
Acting **Permanent Representative of the Republic of Suriname at the United Nations**, 866 United Nations Plaza, Suite 320, New York, 10017, USA. Tel: +1 212 826 0660, fax: +1 212 980 7029, URL: http://www.un.int/wcm/content/site/suriname/cache/offonce/pid/6819
Ambassador: H.E. Henry L. MacDonald

LEGAL SYSTEM

The legal system is based on the constitution which came into effect in September 1987. The Supreme Court sits at Paramaribo and controls the magistrate courts. Members are elected for life by the president, upon approval from the National Assembly. There are three Cantonal Courts.

Suriname has signed on to use the new Caribbean Court of Justice (CCJ) (URL: http://www.caribbeancourtofjustice.org/)

The government generally respects the rights of its citizens but there have been instances of police and guard mistreatment of detainees and prisoners. Prisons are overcrowded and an overwhelmed judiciary has led to lengthy pretrial detentions. There is official corruption. The death penalty has been retained in Suriname for aggravated or premeditated murder and treason, though no execution has taken place since 1982.

LOCAL GOVERNMENT

The Constitution makes provision for regional development. There are ten administrative districts each with a district commissioner elected by the president. The members of the district councils are elected by the electorate in every area by direct vote. The districts are Brokopondo, Commewijne, Coronie, Marowijne, Nickerie, Para, Paramaribo, Saramacca, Sipaliwini and Wanica.

AREA AND POPULATION

Area

Suriname is situated on the north coast of South America, between French Guiana and Guyana, and bounded in the south by Brazil. Suriname has a total area of 163,270 sq. km. The country has large areas of tropical rainforest, as well as savannah and hills. There is a narrow coastal plain with swamp areas, which is liable to flood. The climate is tropical, but moderated by trade winds. Temperatures range from 21°C-32°C.

To view a map, consult
http://www.lib.utexas.edu/maps/cia08/suriname_sm_2008.gif

Population

Suriname had an estimated population of 525,000 in 2010. The annual rate of growth stood at approximately 1.2 per cent for the period 2000-10. Population density is 6.5 per sq. mile. The population is one of the most ethnically diverse in the world; the major ethnic groups being Creole (34 per cent), Indian (34 per cent), Indonesian (15 per cent), Bush Negro (10 per cent), American Indian (3 per cent), Chinese (2 per cent), European and others (2 per cent). Dutch is the official language, although Sranang Tongo, Hindustani, Javanese, Sarnami, Chinese and English are also spoken, as are different tribal languages spoken by Amer-Indian and Bush Negro tribes. The majority of the population lives on the coastal plain, and 69 per cent of the population live in urban areas.

Births, Marriages, Deaths

Average life expectancy is 68 years for men and 75 years for women. Healthy life expectancy is respectively 58 years and 64 years. The child mortality rate (children dying before their fifth birthday) was 24 per 1,000 in 2009. Approximately 29 per cent of the population is aged less than 15 years and 9 per cent over 60 years. The median age was 27 years in 2010. The total fertility rate was 2.3 children per female in 2010. (Source: http://www.who.int, World Health Statistics 2012)

Public Holidays 2014

1 January: New Year's Day
17 March: Phagwa
18 April: Good Friday
21 April: Easter Monday
5 May: Labour Day
1 July: Emancipation Day
29 July: Eid-ul-Fitr*
25 November: Independence Day
25 December: Christmas Day
26 December: Boxing Day
31 December: New Year's Eve
* date depends on the sighting of the moon so can vary.

EMPLOYMENT

The labour force was estimated to be 165,500 persons in 2007, with unemployment running at around 9.5 per cent, a drop on previous years. Around 14 per cent of the working population is engaged in industry and eight per cent in agriculture. The remaining 78 per cent works in the services industry.

BANKING AND FINANCE

Currency

The unit of currency was the Surinamese guilder (Sf). In January 2004 this was replaced by the Surinamese dollar in an effort to promote confidence in the economy. The financial centre is Paramaribo.

GDP/GNP, Inflation, National Debt

Suriname's exchange rate stabilised following the introduction of an austerity program, tax rises and spending controls. The economy is dominated by the bauxite industry, which accounts for more than 15 per cent of GDP and 70 per cent of export earnings. In 2008, the IMF estimated GDP to be around US$2.81 billion. Annual growth in 2007 was 5.5 per cent due to strong mining, oil and the informal sectors. Suriname's economy is expected to continue with strong growth primarily due to strong commodity prices and improvements in policies. The services sector is the largest contributor to GDP, followed by the industrial sector and agriculture. In 2010, GDP was estimated to be US$3 billion with an annual growth rate of 3 per cent.

Annual inflation fell from 138 per cent in 1998 to 75 per cent in 2000 and to 7 per cent in 2007. However, inflation is likely to be volatile and on an upward trend due to significant increases in the price of local food after heavy rainfall in April and May. Figures for 2010 put inflation at 10 per cent; it rose to over 15 per cent in 2011.

External debt was estimated to be US$645 million in 2010 approximately 20 per cent of GDP.

Balance of Payments / Imports and Exports

Suriname's principal exports are alumina, aluminium, bauxite, crude oil, wood and wood products, shrimp, fish and fish products, rice, bananas and vegetables. The economy is dominated by the exports of alumina, oil, and gold; in 2007, gold, alumina, and oil accounted for 31.7 per cent, 41.9 per cent, and seven per cent respectively of Suriname's exports. Its principal export trading partners are Canada (23 per cent), Norway (14.4 per cent), USA (12.1 per cent) and Trinidad (7.2 per cent). According to the IMF, in 2007 the country exported an estimated $1.542 billion worth of goods, f.o.b. In the same year, Suriname spent an estimated $1.242 billion f.o.b. on imports. Main imports were capital equipment, petrol, foods, cotton and consumer goods, and most originated from the US (31.7 per cent), the Netherlands (20.4 per cent), Trinidad and Tobago (17.9 per cent), and China (5.5 per cent). In 2011, exports were estimated to be worth US$2.2 billion and imports cost an estimated 1.7 billion.

Economic arrangements are being established between Suriname and Brazil, Colombia and Venezuela. Suriname is also a beneficiary under Lomé 4, with privileged access to European Union markets. It is also part of the US Caribbean Basin Initiative (CBI).

Central Bank

Centrale Bank van Suriname, Waterkant 16-20, Paramaribo, Suriname. Tel: +597 473741 / 477645, 411183, fax: +597 476444, e-mail: info@cbvs.sr, URL: http://www.cbvs.sr/

Chambers of Commerce and Trade Organisations

Suriname Association of Trade and Industry, Prins Hendrikstraat, Paramaribo, Suriname. Tel: +597 4 75286, fax: +597 4 72287

MANUFACTURING, MINING AND SERVICES

Primary and Extractive Industries

Suriname is one of the world's largest producers of bauxite, alumina and aluminium. There are also gold deposits. Gold reserves at the Gross Rosebel mine have been estimated in excess of two million ounces. Bauxite is among the country's main exports, along with alumina, aluminium, crude petrol and crude oil. The mining company BHG Billiton announced it was to cease operations in Suriname by 2010 in a dispute over a new bauxite mine.

The gold mining sector constitutes an important part of the informal economy and is estimated to earn as much as 100 per cent of GDP. However, it is largely unregulated and untaxed.

The oil sector is expected to expand rapidly in the near future expansion. It is estimated that there are up to15 billion barrels of oil in the Guyana Plateau. The state-owned oil company, Staatsolie, is the only company with the right to operate; other companies can access the market through production sharing agreements. In 2011, Suriname produced an estimated 15,420 barrels of oil per day, and consumed 15,000 barrels per day. The country had proved reserves of 0.07 billion barrels in 2012. Suriname has no natural gas resources.

Energy

The state-owned electricity company, EBS, is the primary utility responsible for the generation, transmission and distribution of energy in Suriname. There is a severe shortage of affordable energy sources which limits Suriname's industrial expansion. To alleviate the shortages, the state-owned oil company, Staatsolie, built a 14 megawatt (MW) diesel-generated energy plant in 2006, and plans to expand its capacity to 18 MW. Suriname and France recently signed an agreement that would connect the power grids of Suriname and French Guiana.

Hydroelectric power plays a large role in the supply of electricity and its main supply is from the dam in Afobaka. In 2006, 1.60 billion kWh of electricity were generated and 1.46 billion kWh were consumed.

Total primary energy production was 0.046 quadrillion Btu. in 2009, and total energy consumption was 0.036 Btu.

Service Industries

The estimated number of visitors to Suriname in 2004 was 145,000. Ecotourism is a growth area, though at present the industry infrastructure is limited.

Agriculture

Agriculture is carried on along the coastal belt and the rivers. Like the Dutch polders, in the coastal belt the soil is in many places muddy and is kept in condition by a system of ditches and dykes. The main agricultural products are rice, bananas, palm kernels, coconuts, plantains and peanuts. Beef and chicken are reared, and shrimp are farmed. Timber is a main export commodity.

Agriculture is a major employer, and therefore important to the economy. The banana industry, recently strengthened following restructuring, faces uncertainty due to the EU banana regime. The rice industry suffers from high costs and is threatened by a phasing out of EU trade preferences. A palm oil plantation, funded by China, may provide employment opportunities and improve the sector's long-term outlook.

Agricultural Production in 2010

Produce	Int. $'000*	Tonnes
Rice, paddy	46,867	226,686
Bananas	24,310	94,272
Indigenous chicken meat	16,006	11,237
Indigenous cattle meat	5,075	1,879
Indigenous pigmeat	2,937	1,911
Oranges	2,926	15,138
Sugar cane	2,653	120,000
Plantains	2,164	12,330
Cow milk, whole, fresh	1,977	6,500
Hen eggs, in shell	1,906	2,298
Vegetables fresh nes	1,328	8,637

SURINAME

- continued

Citrus fruit, nes	1,127	2,494

* unofficial figures

Source: http://faostat.fao.org/site/339/default.aspx Food and Agriculture Organization of the United Nations, Food and Agricultural commodities production

There is international interest in extensive development of a tropical hardwoods industry, but proposals for exploitation of the country's tropical forests and undeveloped regions of the interior traditionally inhabited by indigenous and Maroon communities have raised the concerns of environmentalists and human rights activists.

Fishing
FAO figures for 2010 put the total fishing catch at 34,402 tonnes.

COMMUNICATIONS AND TRANSPORT

Travel Requirements
Citizens of the USA, Canada, Australia and the EU require a passport valid for six months from arrival and a visa (unless in transit, leaving within 24 hours, with onward documentation and not leaving the airport). Other nationals should contact the embassy to check visa requirements.

Visitors must report to the immigration service within eight days at Police Precinct Nieuwe Haven, Van't Hogerhuysstraat, Paramaribo. Travellers arriving from areas where yellow fever is endemic may be required to show proof of a yellow fever vaccination.

National Airlines
Suriname Airways (SLM) Coppenamestraat 136, Paramaribo, Suriname. Tel: +597 465700, fax: +597 491213, URL: http://www.slm.nl

International Airports
Johan Adolph Pengel International Airport, Zanderij.

Railways
The total length of railroad in Suriname is 224 km (140 miles). There are two short railways which are both used for the transportation of logs and quarry products.

Roads
Suriname has a road network of over 4,300 km. Vehicles are driven on the left.

Ports and Harbours
The major seaport is Paramaribo with others at Paranam, Moengo, Albina and New Nickerie. The main shipping lines in operation in Suriname are Bernuth Lines, CGM, Europe West Indies Lines (EWL), Nedloyd Lines, Schhepvart Maatschappij Suriname N.V., Seafreight Line, Sea-Land Service, Tecmarine Lines and Ten Shipping. Over 1,000 km of rivers and waterways are navigable.

Ferries run between Albina, Suriname and Saint Laurent , French Guiana, and a river ferry connects Suriname with Guyana.

HEALTH

In 2009, the government spent approximately 11.9 per cent of its total budget on healthcare (down from 9.7 per cent in 2000), accounting for 51.0 per cent of all healthcare spending. Total expenditure on healthcare equated to 7.5 per cent of the country's GDP. Per capita expenditure on health was approximately US$467. Figures for 2000-10 show that there are 191 physicians (5 per 10,000 population), 688 nurses and midwives (16 per 10,000 population) and 4 dentists. There are 31 hospital beds per 10,000 population.

According to the latest WHO figures, in 2010 approximately 92 per cent of the population had access to improved drinking water. In the same year, 83 per cent of the population had access to improved sanitation. Diarrhoea accounts for 34 per cent of childhood deaths.

The infant mortality rate in 2010 was 27 per 1,000 live births. The child mortality rate (under 5 years) was 31 per 1,000 live births. HIV/AIDS accounts for 2 per cent of early childhood deaths. (Source: http://www.who.int, World Health Statistics 2012)

EDUCATION

Primary/Secondary Education
Primary education is free and compulsory up to the age of 12. Primary education takes place between the ages of six and 12. The junior level of secondary school education serves to either prepare for pre-university courses at the next level or for vocational courses. There are also self-contained vocational courses for those students not progressing beyond this level. The senior level of secondary education consists of broad-based courses preparing students for higher education and vocational courses.

In 2006, some 84 per cent of young children attended a pre-primary school. In 2007, 95 per cent of girls and 93 per cent of boys were enrolled at primary school. Around 77 per cent of children went on to secondary school, with a larger proportion of girls attending than boys.

Higher Education
There are five teacher training colleges, five technical schools, an Academy of Fine Arts and Communication and a university. In 2002, just 12 per cent of the relevant age group attended higher education, with more women attending than men.

Adult literacy according to UNESCO figures in 2007 was 92.7 per cent for males and 88.1 per cent for females, this figure rose to 95.7 per cent for males and 94.6 per cent for females for youth literacy (ages 15-24).

RELIGION

The majority of the population (51 per cent) are Christian, some 21 per cent of the population are Hindu and 16 per cent Muslim.

Suriname has a religious liberty rating of 10 on a scale of 1 to 10 (10 is most freedom). (Source: World Religion Database)

COMMUNICATIONS AND MEDIA

Freedom of expression in the media is generally respected.

Newspapers
There are two daily newspapers, both of which are privately owned:
De Ware Tijd/ Kompas, URL: http://www.dwtonline.com/
De West, RL: http://www.dewestonline.cq-link.sr/

Broadcasting
There are two television stations, both state-run: Surinaamse Televisie Stichting (STVS) and Algemene Televisie Verzorging (ATV).
ATV, URL: http://www.atv.sr/
There are several radio stations, amongst which are:
Radio Apintie, URL: http://www.apintie.sr/
ABC, URL: http://www.abcsuriname.com/cms/

Telecommunications
TELESUR (the Telecommunications Corporation Suriname) is the state-owned monopoly responsible for local and long-distance telecommunications services. In 2006, there were some 81,500 main line telephones and 320,000 cellular phones in use. By 2007, there were 44,000 internet users and 28 internet hosts in Suriname.

Telecommunications legislation introduced in April 2007, goes some way to liberalising the market.

ENVIRONMENT

Suriname is densely forested, and the country's tropical rain forest is one of the most diverse ecosystems in the world. Increased interest in large-scale commercial logging and mining in the interior have raised environmental concerns. On December 1, 2000, UNESCO designated the 1.6-million hectare Central Suriname Nature Reserve a World Heritage site. Another environmental concern is the pollution of inland waterways, mainly by mining activities.

Suriname plays an active role in the Amazonian Pact, and is party to the international environmental agreements on Biodiversity, Climate Change, Desertification, Endangered Species, Law of the Sea, Marine Dumping, Nuclear Test Ban, Ozone Layer Protection, Ship Pollution, Tropical Timber 94 and Wetlands.

According to figures from the EIA, in 2010, Suriname's total emissions from the consumption of fossil fuels totalled 2.34 million metric tons of carbon dioxide.

SWAZILAND

Kingdom of Swaziland

Umbuso weSwatini

Capital: Mbabane (Population estimate: 95,500)

Head of State: His Majesty King Mswati III, Ngwenyama of Swaziland (Sovereign) (page 1481)

National Flag: Five unequal horizontal stripes of blue, yellow, crimson, yellow, blue. A black and white Swazi shield is positioned in the centre of the crimson stripe and behind that are set horizontally two assegais and a staff.

CONSTITUTION AND GOVERNMENT

Constitution

A constitution for Swaziland was established by the Swaziland Order in Council 1963. It made provision for an Executive Council of eight members (four official and four unofficial) and a Legislative Council of four members, 24 elected members and up to three members nominated by Her Majesty's Commissioner. In August 1965 the number of unofficial members in the Executive Council was increased from four to six, and in October 1966 it was increased to seven. Her Majesty's Commissioner, a post equivalent to the status of Governor, assented to legislation and was directly responsible to the Secretary of State.

On 25 April 1967 the Kingdom of Swaziland came into being under a new internal self-government constitution, which took effect on that day. Sobhuza II was recognised as King and Head of State, and the constitution established a Parliament partly elected by the people and partly appointed by the King. Under a special treaty, the Protected State Agreement, which also came into force 25 April 1967, Britain was responsible for defence, external affairs, internal security, the civil service and certain aspects of finance until Swaziland became fully independent on 6 September 1968 under a constitution which varied only slightly from the 1967 constitution.

Revisions of the constitution in 1992 formally included the Tinkhundla Centres, 'local institutions for government and national business', thus involving ordinary people in the political process. In 1997 a Constitutional Review Commission was set up. It eventually presented its findings in 2001 saying that the majority of people wished for wider ranging powers for the king. This conclusion met with some opposition. In May 2003 the constitution was released for comment and in November 2004 went before parliament. In August 2005 the king signed the new constitution; it allows for equality before the law, freedom of religion and equality for women but political parties were still banned. The continuation of the ban on political parties led to protests and arrests. The constitution came into effect in 2006 but political parties remain banned. In February 2008 opposition groups decided to boycott the forthcoming elections to protest against the lack of multi-party elections.

To consult the constitution, please visit: URL: http://www.gov.sz

Recent Events

Mario Masukp, of the opposition group Pudemo, was detained under anti-terrorism laws over an alleged bomb attempt on the presidential palace in November 2008. He was freed in 2009. In April 2011, the police cracked down on opposition supports ahead of planned demonstrations.

Swaziland is currently experiencing a financial crisis caused in part because of the global economic cris and new trade rules in the region. The government is also accused of overspending. In August 2011 South Africa agreed to a US$355m / £218m loan. Civil servants went on strike in August over unpaid salaries and there are warnings that the country is running out of money to fund its health care programmes.Swaziland has the world's highest AIDS/HIV infection rate. Schools and the country's university failed to open in September because of lack of state finance.

In November 2012, the Anglican Church of Southern Africa ordained the first woman bishop in Africa. Ellinah Wamukoya was ordained as the bishop of Swaziland.

Senate

Parliament consists of a Senate and a House of Assembly. The Senate has 30 members - 10 elected by the House of Assembly and 20 appointed by the King, senators serve a five year term.
Senate, Houses of Parliament, P.O. Box 37, Lobamba, Swaziland. Tel: +268 41 62407, fax: +268 41 61603, e-mail: clerk@parliament.gov.sz

House of Assembly

The National Assembly (previously the House of Assembly) has 65 members, 55 representing each constituency, or *Inkhundla*, and 10 appointed by the King. The Attorney-General is also a member but has no vote. Elections to the House of Assembly were last held in October 2003. Members serve a five-year term.
House of Assembly, Houses of Parliament, PO Box 37, Lobamba, Swaziland. +268 41 62407, fax: +268 41 61603, e-mail: clerk@parliament.gov.sz, URL: http://www.gov.sz

Cabinet (as at June 2013)
Prime Minister: Barbabas S. Dlamini (page 1416)
Deputy Prime Minister: Themba Masuku
Minister of Natural Resources and Energy: Princess Tsandzile

Minister of Foreign Affairs: Mtiti Fakudze
Minister of Finance: Hon. Majozi V. Sithole (page 1515)
Minister of Public Service: Patrick Mamba
Minister of Economic Planning and Development: Prince Hlangusemphi
Minister of Home Affairs: Prince Gcokoma
Minister of Justice and Constitutional Affairs: Chief Mqwaqwa Gamedze
Minister of Housing and Local Government: Pastor Lindiwe Gwebu
Minister of Public Works and Transport: Ntuthuko Dlamini
Minister of Education and Training: Wilson Ntjangase
Minister of Health: Benedict Xaba
Minister of Agriculture and Co-operatives: Clement Dlamini
Minister of Labour and Social Security: Lutfo Dlamini
Minister of Commerce, Industry and Trade: Jabulile Mashwama
Minister of Sports, Culture and Youth Affairs: Hlobsile Ndlovu
Minister of Information, Communications and Technology: Winnie Magagula

Ministries

Government Portal: URL: http://www.gov.sz
Prime Minister's Office, P.O. Box 395, Mbabane, Swaziland. Tel: +268 4042251, fax: +268 4043943
Deputy Prime Minister's Office, P.O. Box A33, Swazi Plaza, Mbabane, Swaziland. Tel: +268 4045980/4042723, fax: +268 4040084
Ministry of Foreign Affairs and Trade, P.O. Box 518, Mbabane, Swaziland. Tel: +268 4042661, fax: +268 4042669
Ministry of Finance, P.O. Box 433, Mbabane, Swaziland. Tel: +268 4042142/4042145, fax: +268 4043187
Ministry of Economic Planning, P.O. Box 602, Mbabane, Swaziland. Tel: +268 4043765, fax: +268 4042157
Ministry of Home Affairs, P.O. Box 432, Mbabane, Swaziland. Tel: +268 4042941, fax: +268 4044303
Ministry of Tourism, Environment and Communication, P.O. Box 2652, Mbabane, Swaziland. Tel: +268 4046421, fax: 4046438
Ministry of Housing and Urban Development, P.O. Box 798, Mbabane, Swaziland. Tel: +268 4046035, fax: +268 4045224
Ministry of Public Works and Transport, P.O. Box 58, Mbabane, Swaziland. Tel: +268 4042321, fax: +268 4042364
Ministry of Education, P.O. Box 39, Mbabane, Swaziland. Tel: +268 4042491, fax: +268 4043880
Ministry of Justice and Constitutional Affairs, P.O. Box 924, Mbabane, Swaziland. Tel: +268 4046010, fax: +268 4043533
Ministry of Health, P.O. Box 5, Mbabane, Swaziland. Tel: +268 4042431, fax: +268 4042092
Ministry of Enterprise and Employment, P.O. Box 451, Mbabane, Swaziland. Tel: +268 4043201, fax: +268 4044711
Ministry of Agriculture, P.O. Box 162, Mbabane, Swaziland. Tel: +268 4042731, fax: +268 4044700
Ministry of Public Service and Information, P.O. Box 170, Mbabane, Swaziland. Tel: +268 4043521, fax: +268 4045379
Ministry of Natural Resources and Energy, P.O. Box 57, Mbabane, Swaziland. Tel: +268 4046244, fax: +268 4042436

Political Parties

There are no political parties in Swaziland.

Elections

On September 19 2008 Swaziland held its first parliamentary elections since adopting its new constitution in 2006. Political parties are still banned. Elections were for 55 unaffiliated members to sit in the National Assembly. Indirect elections to the senate also took place.

Diplomatic Representation

British High Commission, URL: http://ukinsouthafrica.fco.gov.uk/en (staff resident in South Africa)
High Commissioner: Dame Nicola Brewer
US Embassy, 7th Floor, Central Bank Building, Warner Street, Mbabane, PO Box 199, Swaziland. Tel: +268 404 6441, fax: +268 404 5959, e-mail: usembswd@realnet.co.sz, URL: http://swaziland.usembassy.gov/
Ambassador: Makila James
High Commission of Swaziland, 20 Buckingham Gate, London, SW1E 6LB, United Kingdom. Tel: +44 (0)171 630 6611, fax: +44 (0)171 630 6564, e-mail: swaziland@swaziland.btinternet.com
High Commissioner: Dumisle Sukati
Embassy of Swaziland, 1712 New Hampshire Avenue, NW, Washington DC 20009, USA. Tel: +1 202 234 5002, fax: +1 202 234 8254
Ambassador: Mary Madzandza Kanya
Permanent Representative of the Kingdom of Swaziland to the United Nations, 408 East 50th Street, New York, N.Y. 10022, USA. Tel: +1 212 371 8910, fax: +1 212 754 2755, URL: http://www.un.int/wcm/content/site/swaziland
Permanent Representative: H.E. Zwelethu Mnisi

SWAZILAND

LEGAL SYSTEM

The law is based on Roman-Dutch law in the statutory courts, whilst Swazi traditional law is used in traditional courts.

The constitution provides for a Court of Appeal consisting of a President and two Judges. The High Court of Swaziland has civil and criminal jurisdiction, as well as the power to review the proceedings of all subordinate courts and hear appeals. Judges in the High Court and Courts of Appeals are appointed by the King. There are subordinate courts of the First, Second and Third classes presided over by professional magistrates and District Officers.

There are 14 Swazi Courts, two Courts of Appeal and a Higher Swazi Court of Appeal. Swazi Courts have civil and criminal jurisdiction where the parties are Africans. Appeal in criminal cases lies from the courts of first instance to a Swazi Appeal Court, to the Higher Swazi Court of Appeal, to the Judicial Commissioner and thence, in certain cases, to the High Court of Swaziland. Appeals in certain civil cases may go direct from the Higher Swazi Appeal Court to the High Court.

Human rights abuses include the inability of citizens to change their government, extrajudicial killings by security forces and police brutality and impunity. In August 2005, King Mswati III signed a new constitution, but this maintains a ban on political parties. Arrest and detention can be arbitrary. There are restrictions on freedoms of speech, press, assembly, association, and movement. There are also restrictions on worker rights, and the use of child labour is widespread. The death penalty is retained in Swaziland, but no executions have been carried out since 1982.

LOCAL GOVERNMENT

Administratively, Swaziland is divided into four regions: Hhohho, Manzini, Lubombo and Shiselweni. The administrators of each region report to the Deputy Prime Minister. The country is further divided into 55 Tinkhundla centres (made up from 273 tribal areas). Leaders of each Tinkhundla centre report to a Regional Council which oversees the activities of each Inkundla management council. Each city and town is governed by a City Council and Town Board consisting of both elected members and members appointed by the Minister of Housing and Development.

AREA AND POPULATION

Area and Population
Swaziland is situated in southern Africa. A landlocked country, it is almost entirely surrounded by South Africa but has an eastern border with Mozambique. The land is mainly hilly or mountainous with some rolling plains. The area of Swaziland is 17,363 sq. km. The climate varies from near temperate to tropical.

To view a map, consult
http://www.lib.utexas.edu/maps/cia08/swaziland_sm_2008.gif

Population
The population was estimated in 2010 at 1.186 million, with an average annual growth rate of 1.1 per cent for the period 2000-10. Approximately 79 per cent live in rural areas and 21 per cent in urban areas. The capital city is Mbabane and Lobamba is the royal and legislative capital.

English and SiSwati are the official languages, but some African languages are also spoken.

Births, Marriages, Deaths
Estimated figures for 2010 put the birth rate at 29.4 per 1,000 population and the death rate at 14.3 per 1,000 population. The infant mortality rate is around 55 per 1,000 live births in 2010. Life expectancy was 60 years but now that Swaziland has the highest recorded incidence of HIV infection, life expectancy has fallen. In 2005, life expectancy was an estimated 42 years but by 2009 it was estimated to have risen to 49 years. Healthy life expectancy is 42 years. The total fertility rate was estimated at 3.4 per female.

An estimated 5 per cent of the population is over 60 years, and 38 per cent under 15. The median age is 19 years. (Source: http://www.who.int, World Health Statistics 2012)

Public Holidays 2014
1 January: New Year Day
18 April: Good Friday
21 April: Easter Monday
19 April: King's Birthday
25 April: National Flag Day
5 May: Labour Day
29 May: Ascension Day
22 July: Birth of Late King Sobhuza
Aug/Sept.: Reed Dance Day (Umhlanga)*
6 September: Independence Day (Somholo Day)
Dec/Jan: Incwala Ceremony
25 December: Christmas Day
26 December: Boxing Day
* The dates of the Umhlanga and Incwala ceremonies vary according to local sightings of the moon.

EMPLOYMENT

Figures for 2007 estimated the workforce at 458,000. The Swaziland unemployment rate is estimated at 40 per cent. The largest employment sectors are services (30 per cent), agriculture (21 per cent) and finance (10 per cent). An estimated 70 per cent of the population are believed to be below the poverty line.

BANKING AND FINANCE

Currency
The unit of currency is the Lilangeni (plural Emalangeni). The South African Rand is also legal tender in the kingdom.

The financial centre is Mbabane.

GDP/GNP, Inflation, National Debt
Swaziland's economy was traditionally based on agriculture, but manufacturing and mining have developed. Most of the more developed economic activity is run by non-Africans, and an estimated 70 per cent of the population is thought to live in poverty. This is beginning to change. The leading export-earner is the sugar cane industry. This has been adversely affected by EU reforms of the industry. The manufacturing industry faces competition from Asia. The global economic crisis has meant that customs revenues have fallen steeply and the country is currently experiencing a fiscal crisis. Swaziland requested assistance from the IMF and the ADB but was not able to meet their conditions for receiving aid and its economic situation remains extremely serious.

GDP was put at US$2,612 million in 2005, rising to US$2,648 million in 2006, 2,724.57 in 2007 and 2,900 million in 2009. GDP was US$3 billion in 2011, The growth rate was 2.1 per cent in 2007, 2.4 per cent in 2008 and 0.4 per cent in 2009. The growth rate was estimated to be 2 per cent in 2010, falling to 0.5 per cent in 2011. Per capita GDP was an estimated US$5,000 in 2011.

Inflation was estimated at 6.3 per cent in 2006 and 6.8 per cent in 2007, 12.5 per cent in 2008 and 7.5 per cent in 2009. Inflation was estimated to be 6 per cent in 2011.

Total external debt in 2006 was US$493.68 million. Total debt service was US$41.66 million. (Source: ADB)

Balance of Payments / Imports and Exports
Exported goods includ soft drink concentrates, sugar, cotton, pulp and canned fruits. Imported goods include chemicals, clothing, machinery petroleum products and foodstuffs. Swaziland's largest trading partner is South Africa. Trade is also carried out with the EU, Japan and Mozambique.

External Trade, US$ millions

	2005	2006	2007
Trade balance	73.01	90.72	35.29
Exports	1,826.82	1,895.99	1,972.42
Imports	1,753.82	1,805.27	1,937.14

Source: African Development Bank

Exports were estimated to be US$1.4 billion in 2010 and imports cost US$1.6 billion.

Central Bank
Central Bank of Swaziland, PO Box 546, Warner Street, Mbabane, Swaziland. Tel: +268 40 43221/2/3, fax: +268 40 48530, URL: http://www.centralbank.org.sz
Chairman & Governor: M G Dlamini

Chambers of Commerce and Trade Organisations
Federation of Swaziland Employers & Chamber of Commerce, URL: http://www.business-swaziland.com/

MANUFACTURING, MINING AND SERVICES

Primary and Extractive Industries
All mineral resources are held in trust by the king. Coal, industrial minerals, base metals, quarried stone, asbestos, iron ore, gold are mined, mining of diamonds ceased in 1996. Asbestos production, despite a reduction, remained the leading export earner. There are no reported oil or gas reserves. Swaziland has to import all oil to meet its needs 4,000 barrels per day in 2011.

Energy
Over 50 per cent of Swaziland's electricity comes from hydro sources. An estimated 500 million kWh were produced in 2010 and 1.6 billion kWh of electricity consumed. The deficit was imported from South Africa.

Manufacturing
Swaziland's manufacturing industry is based on the processing of agricultural and forestry products and includes sugar refining, ginned cotton, wood pulp, processed foods and textiles. Figures for 2007 show that the manufacturing sector contributed around 32 per cent of GDP.

Service Industries
Tourism is becoming increasing important to the Swaziland economy and approximately 300,000 visitors arrive each year mainly from Europe and South Africa.

Agriculture

50 per cent of the rural land is held in trust by the king and farmed on a subsistence basis by small farmers. Agriculture is the mainstay of the economy, with sugar, cotton, maize, pineapple, corn, tobacco, peanuts and citrus fruits the main products. An extensive forestry sector provides commercially grown wood for export. Production in recent years has been severely hit by drought. Estimated figures for 2011 show that agriculture contributed just over 8.0 per cent of GDP and 70 per cent of the population were engaged in the sector.

Agricultural Production in 2010

Produce	Int. $'000*	Tonnes
Sugar cane	164,185	5,000,000
Indigenous cattle meat	39,004	14,439
Cow milk, whole, fresh	13,185	42,250
Roots and tubers, nes	9,406	55,000
Grapefruit (inc. pomelos)	8,214	42,500
Oranges	8,214	42,500
Pineapples	7,554	26,500
Indigenous chicken meat	6,374	4,475
Maize	4,519	68,000
Indigenous goat meat	4,435	1,851
Almonds, with shell	2,951	1,000
Indigenous pigmeat	2,856	1,858

* unofficial figures
Source: http://faostat.fao.org/site/339/default.aspx Food and Agriculture Organization of the United Nations, Food and Agricultural commodities production

FAOSTAT figures from 2003 show that Swaziland had 580,000 head of cattle and buffalo and 449,000 head of sheep and goats.

COMMUNICATIONS AND TRANSPORT

Travel Requirements

Citizens of the USA, Canada, Australia and the EU require a passport valid for at least six months beyond the length of stay; most visitors to Swaziland enter through South Africa and are therefore strongly encouraged to have several unstamped visa pages left in their passports. Nationals of most of the countries listed above do not require a visa for stays of up to two months, the exceptions being Austrians (who can obtain a visa on entry), and citizens of Bulgaria, Czech Republic, Estonia, Hungary, Latvia, Lithuania, Romania, Slovak Republic and Slovenia, who do require a visa. A return or onward ticket is also an entry requirement.

Other nationals should contact the embassy to check visa requirements.

International Airports

There is one international airport at Matsapa.
Royal Swazi National Airways Corporation, PO Box 939, Mbabane, Swaziland. Tel: +268 86146/7, fax: +268 86156, URL: http://www.royal-swazi.com/index.html, the company ceased operating as an airline in 1999 but still trades as a ticket agency.

Railways

Work on a 137-mile railway line (3 ft. 6 in. gauge) was completed by the end of 1964. The line runs from the iron ore mine on the western border, through the centre of the country to Goba, where it connects with the Mozambique line to the port of Maputo. There are spur lines to the Matsapa industrial estate, just outside Manzini. A rail link that runs north-south connects the Eastern Transvaal network with the South African ports of Durban and Richard's Bay. Total length of track is 301 km.
Swaziland Railway, PO Box 475, Mbabane, Swaziland. Tel: +268 404 7211/2/3, fax: +268 404 7210, e-mail: swazirail@iafrica.sz

Roads

Recent figures show that Swaziland has around 3,600 km of roads many of which connect with South Africa. Many bus routes connect Swaziland with Johannesburg, Durban or Cape Town in South Africa and Maputo in Mozambique. Vehicles are driven on the left.

HEALTH

Swaziland's National Health Policy was established in 1983 and has set up hospitals and rural clinics accessible to all. There are an estimated 176 hospitals, clinics and health centres. These are run both by the government and private enterprise. There are also over 160 outreach clinics. In 2009, there were 21 hospital beds per 10,000 population.

According to the latest WHO figures (2000-10), there were an estimated 171 doctors, 6,828 nurses and midwives, 4,000 community and traditional health workers, 32 dentistry personnel, 110 environment and public health workers, and 70 pharmaceutical personnel. In 2009, the government spent approximately 10.1 per cent of its total budget on healthcare, accounting for 66.5 per cent of all healthcare spending. External resources accounted for over 11 per cent. Total expenditure on healthcare equated to 6.7 per cent of the country's GDP. Private

expenditure accounted for over 33 per cent, of which approximately 42 per cent was out-of-pocket. Per capita expenditure on health was approximately US$169, compared to US$75 in 2000.

Swaziland has the world's highest HIV/AIDS infection rate. In an effort to stop the spread of AIDS, in 2001 the King issued a decree that men were not allowed to sleep with teenage girls. The ban was to last for five years but was lifted a year early in 2005. According to 2009 figures, the HIV/AIDS incidence rate was 1,184 per 100,000 population and the prevalence rate was an estimated 15,605 per 100,000 population.

In 2010, an estimated 71 per cent of the population had sustainable access to improved drinking water sources. An estimated 57 per cent of the population had sustainable access to improved sanitation.

The infant mortality rate in 2010 was 55 per 1,000 live births. The child mortality rate (under 5 years) was 78 per 1,000 live births. The main causes of childhood mortality are: HIV/AIDs (23 per cent), diarrhoea (7 per cent), pneumonia (14 per cent) and prematurity (12 per cent). (Source: http://www.who.int, World Health Statistics 2012)

EDUCATION

Education is not compulsory or free in Swaziland, although most children do attend primary school. In 1996 there were 540 primary schools with 201,901 pupils. In the same year there were also 120 secondary schools teaching some 49,164 pupils. Schools are either government funded, aided or private.

Figures for 2007 show that 87 per cent of primary school aged children attended school, 86 per cent of males and 88 per cent of females, just 29 per cent of secondary school aged children attended, 27 per cent of females and 32 per cent of males and 5 per cent of students were in tertiary education. That year adult literacy was recorded at 83.8 per cent, 84.0 per cent for males and 83.7 per cent for females, this figure rose to 94.0 per cent, 91.9 per cent for males and 96.1 per cent for females amongst the 15-24 age group. In 2006, 24.4 per cent of total government expenditure went on education. (Source: UNESCO, UIS)

RELIGION

Around 88 per cent of the population profess Christian beliefs, with the remaining population following indigenous beliefs. There are also small Muslim and Hindu communities.

Swaziland has a religious liberty rating of 9 on a scale of 1 to 10 (10 is most freedom). (Source: World Religion Database)

COMMUNICATIONS AND MEDIA

State control of the media is rigorous and freedom of expression is restricted. Criticism of the king is not tolerated.

Newspapers

There are two daily newspapers published in Mbabane, Swaziland: The Swazi Observer, (URL: http://www.observer.org.sz/) and the Times of Swaziland, (URL: http://www.times.co.sz/).

Broadcasting

About 95 per cent of the population have access to a radio and this is therefore the medium which communicates with the most people. Swaziland's government-run Broadcasting and Information Services department is responsible for radio and television broadcasts. In 2006 an estimated 18 per cent of households had a television.
Swaziland Television Authority, PO Box A146, Swazi Plaza, Mbabane, Swaziland. Tel: +268 43036, fax: +268 42093
Swaziland Broadcasting Information Service, URL: http://www.gov.sz/home.asp?pid=2568

Telecommunications

The telecommunications system is fairly modern. In 2008 there were an estimated 44,000 telephone mainlines in use and 450,000 mobile phones. Recent figures show that there are around 48,000 internet users.

ENVIRONMENT

Main environmental issues for Swaziland include overgrazing of land leading to soil degradation and erosion. There are limited supplies of drinkable water compounded by droughts. Wildlife is suffering from over-hunting. Swaziland is party to several international environmental agreements, namely, Biodiversity; Climate Change; Climate Change Kyoto Protocol; Desertification; Endangered Species; Hazardous Wastes; Ozone Layer Protection. Swaziland has signed but not ratified the Law of the Sea.

According to figures from the EIA, in 2010, Swaziland's emissions from the consumption of fossil fuels totalled 1.11 million metric tons of carbon dioxide.

SWEDEN
Kingdom of Sweden
Konungariket Sverige

Capital: Stockholm (Population estimate: 800,000)

Head of State: King Carl XVI Gustaf (Sovereign) (page 1400)

National Flag: Light blue, charged with a cross yellow, the upright one-third from the hoist.

CONSTITUTION AND GOVERNMENT

Constitution
It is laid down in the new constitution, which entered into force in 1975, that Sweden is a representative and parliamentary democracy. Parliament (the Riksdag) is declared to be the central organ of government. The executive power of the country is vested in the Government, which is responsible to Parliament. The King is Head of State, but he does not participate in the government of the country. Since 1971 Parliament has consisted of one chamber. It has 349 members, who are elected for a period of four years in direct, general elections. Election is by universal suffrage from age 18. The manner of election to the Parliament is proportional. The country is divided into 28 constituencies. In these constituencies 310 members are elected. The remaining 39 seats constitute a nationwide pool intended to give absolute proportionality to parties that receive at least four per cent of the national votes. A party receiving less than four per cent of the national votes can participate in the distribution of seats in a constituency, as long as it has obtained at least 12 per cent of the votes cast in that constituency.

To consult the constitution, please visit: http://www.sweden.gov.se/sb/d/3288

International Relations
Sweden is famous the world over for her neutrality, remaining so throughout the two world wars. In 1995 Sweden became a member of the European Union but like Denmark and the UK has not adopted the Euro as the official currency. Sweden has no plans to join NATO although is a member of NATO's Partnership for Peace.

Sweden has close relations with her Nordic neighbours and is a member of the Nordic Council of Ministers and enjoys a close relations with the newly independent Baltic States and is a member of the Council of Baltic Sea States.

Recent Events
In September 2003 Foreign Minister Anna Lindh was stabbed and later died in what appeared to be a motiveless attack while shopping in a Stockholm department store. Ms Lindh had been the face of the 'Yes to the Euro campaign'. A few days after the death of Anna Lindh the planned referendum on whether Sweden should adopt the Euro as its currency went ahead. The result of the vote was 56 per cent of voters saying no to the Euro and 42 per cent saying yes.

Elections held in September 2006 were won by a conservative coalition led by Fredrik Reinfelt. Apart from nine years, the previously governing Social Democrat Party had been in power since 1932. A week after the announcement of the new cabinet, trade minister Maria Borelius resigned following allegations of tax evasion.

In November 2008 Sweden became the 24th EU member to ratify the EU's Lisbon Treaty.

In February 2009, the Swedish government reversed a 30 year old policy to phase out nuclear power judging new reactors would secure future energy supplies and fight climate change.

Elections took place in September 2010. The ruling centre-right coalition fell just short of a majority in parliamentary elections. The far right anti-immigration party, Swedish Democrats, won seats in the parliament for the first time. Prime Minister Reinfeldt formed a new minority government in October.

In December 2010, a suicide bombing was carried out by an Iraq-born Islamic extremist, this was the first time Sweden experienced such an attack. The attacker was targeting Christmas shoppers but he was the only fatality.

In December 2011 the car manufacturer Saab filed for bankruptcy, they had unsuccessfully tried to find a buyer.

In January 2012 the leader of the opposition Social Democrat Party, Haakan Juholt, resigned following increasing criticism and a drop in support.

The defence minister Sten Tolgfors resigned in March 2012 over controversial plans to build a weapons plant in Saudi Arabia.

Legislature
The unicameral parliament has 349 members who are directly elected for a four year term. **Sveriges Riksdag**, 10 012, Stockholm, Sweden. Tel: +46 8 786 4000, fax: +46 8 786 6143, e-mail: riksdagsinformation@riksdagen.se, URL: http://www.riksdagen.se

Cabinet (as of July 2013)
Prime Minister: Fredrik Reinfeldt (page 1502)

Minister for Health & Social Affairs: Goran Hagglund (page 1436)
Minister for Finance: Anders Borg (page 1392)
Minister for Employment: Hillevi Engstrom
Minister for Information Technology and Regional Affairs: Anna-Karin Hatt
Minister for Education, Deputy Prime Minister: Jan Bjorklund (page 1389)
Minister for Enterprise: Annie Lööf
Minister for Defence: Karin Enström
Minister of Justice: Beatrice Ask (page 1380)
Minister of Culture & Sport: Lena Adelsohn Liljeroth (page 1372)
Minister of European Affairs: Birgitta Ohlsson (page 1489)
Minister for the Environment: Lena Ek (page 1419)
Minister for Foreign Affairs: Carl Bildt (page 1388)
Minister for Gender Equality Issues: Maria Arnholm
Minister for Infrastructure: Catharina Elmsäter-Svärd
Minister for Children and Care for the Elderly: Maria Larsson
Minister for Integration: Erik Ullenhag
Minister for Rural Affairs: Eskil Erlandsson
Minister for Public Administration and Housing: Stefan Attefall
Minister of Trade: Ewa Bjorling
Minister for Migration and Asylum Policy: Tobias Billstrom (page 1389)
Minister for International Development Cooperation: Gunilla Carlsson
Minister of Social Security: Ulf Kristersson
Minister of Financial Markets: Peter Norman

Ministries
Prime Minister's Office, 103 33 Stockholm, Sweden. Tel: +46 (0)8 763 1000, fax: +46 (0)8 723 1171, URL: http://www.sweden.gov.se/sb/d/2058
Ministry of Agriculture, Drottninggt. 21, 103 33 Stockholm, Sweden. Tel: +46 (0)8 405 1000, fax: +46 (0)8 206496, URL: http://jordbruk.regeringen.se/inenglish/index.htm
Ministry of Culture, Jakobsgt. 26, 103 33 Stockholm, Sweden. Tel: +46 (0)8 405 1000, fax: +46 (0)8 216813, URL: http://kultur.regeringen.se/inenglish/index.htm
Ministry of Defence, Jakobsgt. 9, 103 33 Stockholm, Sweden. Tel: +46 (0)8 405 1000, fax: +46 (0)8 723 1189, URL: http://forsvar.regeringen.se/inenglish/index.htm
Ministry of Education and Research, URL: http://utbildning.regeringen.se/inenglish/index.htm
Ministry of the Environment, Tegelbacken 2, 103 33 Stockholm, Sweden. Tel: +46 (0)8 405 1000, fax: +46 (0)8 241 1629, URL: http://miljo.regeringen.se/english/english_index.htm
Ministry of Finance, Drottninggt. 21, 103 33 Stockholm, Sweden. Tel: +46 (0)8 405 1000, fax: +46 (0)8 217386, URL: http://finans.regeringen.se/inenglish/index.html
Ministry of Foreign Affairs, Gustav Adolfstorg 1, POB 16121, 103 23 Stockholm, Sweden. Tel: +46 (0)8 405 6000, fax: +46 (0)8 723 1176, URL: http://www.utrikes.regeringen.se/inenglish/index.htm
Ministry of Health and Social Affairs, Jakobsgt. 26, 103 33 Stockholm, Sweden. Tel: +46 (0)8 405 1000, fax: +46 (0)8 723 1191, URL: http://www.social.regeringen.se/inenglish/index.htm
Ministry of Justice, Rosenbad 4, 103 33 Stockholm, Sweden. Tel: +46 (0)8 405 1000, fax: +46 (0)8 202734, URL: http://justitie.regeringen.se/inenglish/index.htm
Ministry of Labour, Drottninggt. 21, 103 33 Stockholm, Sweden. Tel: +46 (0)8 405 1000, fax: +46 (0)8 207369, URL: http://www.sweden.gov.se/sb/d/8517
Ministry of Enterprise, Energy and Communications, Jakobsgt. 26, 103 33 Stockholm, Sweden. Tel: +46 (0)8 405 1000, fax: +46 (0)8 118943, URL: http://www.sweden.gov.se/sb/d/2167
Ministry of Integration and Gender Equality, Fredsgaten8, 10333 Stockholm, Sweden. Tel: +46 8405 1000, URL: http://www.sweden.gov.se/sb/d/8366

Elections
Elections were held in September 2006. Although the Social Democratic Party remained the largest party it lost out to forming the government to the coalition led by Fredrik Reinfeldt of the Moderate Party. The coalition known as the new Alliance for Sweden included the Moderate Party, the Liberal Party and the Christian Democrat Party.

The most recent parliamentary election was held in September 2010. Prime Minister Fredrik Reinfeldt's centre-right coalition narrowly failed to win a majority but remained the largest party and it was expected that Reinfeld would form a coalition with the Greens. Following the election street protests were held as the right wing Sweden Democrats party won 20 seats, the first far right party to win seats in Sweden's parliament.

The following table shows the seats won in recent elections:

Party	Seats 2002	Seats 2006	Seats 2010
Social Democrats	144	130	112
Left Party	30	22	19
Greens	17	19	25
Centre Party	22	29	23
Liberal Party	48	28	24
Christian Democrats	33	24	19
Moderate Party	55	97	107
Swedish Democrats	-	-	20

Political Parties

Centrepartiet (Centre Party), Bergst. 7B, POB 22107, 104 22 Stockholm, Sweden. Tel: +46 (0)8 617 3800, fax: +46 (0)8 652 6440; URL: http://www.centerpartiet.se
Chairman: Annie Lööf

Folkpartiet Liberalerna (People's Liberal Party), POB 6508, 113 83 Stockholm, Sweden. Tel: +46 (0)8 674 1600, fax: +46 (0)8 673 2591; URL: http://www.folkpartiet.se
Chairman: Jan Björklund

Sverigedemokraterna (Social Democrats), Sveavägen 68, 105 60 Stockholm, Sweden. Tel: +46 (0)8 700 2600, URL: http://wwwsverigedemokraterna.se
Chairman: Jimmie Åkesson

Kristdemokraterna (Christian Democrats), Målargt. 7, POB 451, 101 29 Stockholm, Sweden. Tel: +46 (0)8 243825, fax: +46 (0)8 219751; URL: http://www.kristdemokraterna.se
Chairman: Göran Hägglund

Miljöpartiet de Gröna (Green Party), Gamla stan, Prästgatan 18 A, Box 2136, 103 14 Stockholm, Sweden. Tel: +46 (0)8 545 22450, URL: http://www.mp.se
Co-Leaders: Gustav Fridolin and Åsa Romson

Moderata Samlingspartiet (Moderate Party), Moderaterna, Box 2080, Stora Nygatan 30, 103 12 Stockholm, Sweden. Tel: +46 (0)8 676 8000, e-mail: info@moderat.se, URL: http://www.moderat.se
Chairman: Fredrik Reinfeldt

Vänsterpartiet (Party of the Left), Kungsgt. 84, 112 93 Stockholm, Sweden. Tel: +46 (0)8 654 0820, fax: +46 (0)8 653 2385; URL: http://www.vansterpartiet.se
Chairman: Jonas Sjöstedt

Piratpartiet (Pirate Party), http://www.piratpartiet.se
Leader: Anna Troberg

Sverigedemokraterna (Sweden Democrats), URL: http://www.sverigedemokraterna.se
Leader: Jimmie Åkesson

Diplomatic Representation

Embassy of the United States of America, Dag Hammarskwölds Väg 31, S-115 89 Stockholm, Sweden. Tel: +46 (0)8 783 5300, fax: +46 (0)8 661 1964, URL: http://stockholm.usembassy.gov
Ambassador: Mark Francis Brzezinski (page 1396)

British Embassy, Skarpögatan 6-8, POB 27819, 115 93 Stockholm, Sweden. Tel: +46 (0)8 671 3000, fax: +46 (0)8 662 9989, URL: http://ukinsweden.fco.gov.uk/en/
Ambassador: Paul Johnston (page 1451)

Embassy of Sweden, 1501 M Street, Suite 900, N.W., Washington, DC 20005, USA. Tel: +1 202 467 2600, fax: +1 202 647 2699, URL: http://www.swedenabroad.com/Washington
Ambassador: Jonas Hafström (page 1436)

Embassy of Sweden, 11 Montagu Place, London, W1H 2AL, United Kingdom. Tel: +44 (0)20 7917 6400, fax: +44 (0)20 7917 6475, URL: http://www.swedenabroad.com/en-GB/Embassies/London/
Ambassador: Nicola Clase (page 1406)

Permanent Mission to the UN, 885 Second Avenue, 46th floor, New York, N.Y. 10017-2201, USA. Tel: +1 212 583 2500, fax: +1 212 832 0389, e-mail: sweden@un.int, URL: http://www.swedenabroad.com
Ambassador: Marten Grunditz

Swedish Royal Family

The Royal family holds a ceremonial role. In 1976 King Carl XVI Gustaf (page 1400) married German-Brazilian Silvia Sommerlath and the couple have three children: Crown Princess Victoria (b.1977), Prince Carl-Philip (b.1979) and Princess Madeleine (b.1982). Crown Princess Victoria married Olof Daniel, now H.R.H. Prince Daniel, on 19 June 2010. Crown Princess Victoria gave birth to a baby girl, Princess Estelle, in February 2012. Princess Estelle is second in line to throne. The Swedish Royal Court also includes Princess Lilian (b. 1915) and Princess Birgitta (b. 1937), married to Prince Johann Georg of Hohenzollern.

LEGAL SYSTEM

The Court System - Sweden has a three-tier hierarchy of courts: the district courts (*tingsrätt*), the intermediate courts of appeal (*hovrätt*), and the Supreme Court (*Högsta domstolen*). There are around a hundred district courts, varying in size from very small, with only one or two judges, to much larger courts such as the one in Stockholm which is served by a large number of judges. The chief judge of a district court has the title *lagman*.

In the Swedish judicial system, district courts play the dominant role. They hear all criminal and civil cases regardless of severity. There are two supreme courts of judicature for the whole kingdom.

Sweden has six courts of appeal, and around ten per cent of cases heard in the district courts are passed to them. Cases in the appeal courts are usually heard by three judges sometimes assisted by a lay assessor.

Appeals from the courts of appeal are heard by the Supreme Court, subject to special permission. (Source: Swedish Institute)

The government respects the rights of its citizens, though there are occasional instances of alleged excessive force by police. Prisons can be overcrowded, and pretrial detention can be lengthy. The death penalty was abolished in 1921.

Supreme Court (Högsta domstolen), URL: http://www.domstol.se/

Discrimination Ombudsman, URL: http://www.do.se/
Parliamentary Ombudsman, URL: http://www.jo.se/

LOCAL GOVERNMENT

For purposes of general administration, the country is divided into 21 counties (*län*). Head of each county state administration is a Governor (*landshövding*) as representative of the Government, who is appointed for six years, and a board of 14 members, elected by the County Council. Each county (except the County of Gotland) has its County Council (*landsting*), the members of which are elected for four years by universal suffrage. These councils meet annually to deal with housing, road networks, water and energy distribution and cultural and leisure activities. The communes of Göteborg, Malmö and Gotland have a separate administration in this respect.

The other administrative body is the Municipality (*kommun*) of which there are 290. The municipalities are responsible for providing such services as schools, social services, building and issuing building permits and some environmental duties. In recent years they have received state compensation for taking on responsibility for refugees from abroad. (Source: Swedish Institute)

The most recent local elections took place in 2010.

The counties and their populations in December 2011 are shown in the following table:

County	Population
Stockholm County	2,091,473
Uppsala	338,630
Södermanland	272,563
Östergötland	431,075
Jönköping	337,896
Kronoberg	184,654
Kalmar	233,090
Gotlands	57,308
Blekinge	152,979
Skåne	1,252,933
Halland	301,724
Västra Götaland	1,590,604
Värmlands	272,736
Örebro	281,572
Västmanland	254,257
Dalarna	276,565
Gävleborg	276,130
Västernorrland	242,155
Jämtland	126,299
Västerbotten	259,667
Norrbotten	248,545
Total	**9,482,855**

Source: Statistics Sweden

AREA AND POPULATION

Area
Sweden has an area of 450,000 sq. km, and is bordered by Norway and Finland. Most of the land is flat or rolling with a mountainous area along the border with Norway. The highest peak is at Kebnekaise (2111m, 6,9226 ft.). Half of the land surface is forested and there are 100,000 lakes and many islands. The largest lake in Europe is the Vanern lake in Sweden. To the south of the lakes the land is mainly plateau and low lying plains. The climate in the south of the country is temperate with cold cloudy winters and cool summers. The northernmost part of the country is in the Arctic circle.

To view a map, consult http://www.lib.utexas.edu/maps/cia08/sweden_sm_2008.gif

Population
The population estimates for November 2012 put the total population at 9,551,781 a 0.75 per cent rise on the previous year. The increase is primarily due to immigration. Figures for 2011 put the population at 9,482,855. Figures for 2011 show that 96,467 immigrants arrived and 51,179 people emigrated. (Source: Statistics Sweden). 85 per cent of the population is in the southern half of the country.

The population of the major cities is as follows: Stockholm, 1,571,000, Göteborg, 768,000 and Malmö, 503,000.

Swedish is the language spoken and there are two minorities: the Finnish-speaking people of the north east and the Sami (Lapp). Recent figures put the Sami population between 17,000 and 20,000.

Births, Marriages, Deaths
In 2011, there were an estimated 111,000 births and 90,000 deaths. Unusually in 2010 more boys than girls were born that year; 59,385 boys and 56,256 girls. Life expectancy from birth is 79 years. 2010 saw the arrival of 98,801 immigrants and the departure of 48,853 emigrants. In 2006, an estimated 8,951 asylum seekers applied for citizenship from Iraq, 1,760 from Serbia and Montenegro and 1,066 from Somalia.

In 2007, 44,692 marriages took place and 19,025 divorces. (Source: Statistics Sweden).

Public Holidays, 2014
1 January: New Year's Day
6 January: Epiphany
18 April: Good Friday
21 April: Easter Monday
1 May: Labour Day
29 May: Ascension Day

SWEDEN

9 June: Whit Monday
21 June: Midsummer Eve
22 June: Midsummer Day
31 October: All Saints' Eve
1 November: All Saints' Day
25 December: Christmas Day
26 December: Boxing Day
Holidays falling on a weekend are not observed on the following Monday.

EMPLOYMENT

The following table shows the number of persons employed by economic sector in recent years.

Employed Persons by Industry

Industry	2010	2011
Agriculture, forestry & fishing	96,000	93,000
Manufacturing, mining, quarrying, electricity & water	602,000	612,000
- Manufacturing of machinery & transport equipment	280,000	286,000
Construction	305,000	312,000
Wholesale & retail trade	560,000	567,000
Transportation	242,000	238,000
Accommodation & food services	153,000	144,000
Information & communication	181,000	196,000
Financial intermediation, business activities	709,000	737,000
Public administration, etc.	274,000	280,000
Education	494,000	504,000
Health & social work	700,000	723,000
Personal services & cultural activities	225,000	223,000
Other	6,000	13,000
Total	4,546,000	4,642,000

Source: Statistics Sweden

In December 2012, the total number of employed people was 4,663,000 (aged 15-74 years), whilst the number of unemployed people was estimated at 371,000. The unemployment rate was 7.4 per cent of the work force. Youth unemployment is recorded as the second highest in the EU, following Italy.

Sweden actively encourages women to return to the workforce after having children by providing a publicly funded childcare system. In 2001 this was expanded to provide pre-school education for the children of those unemployed on a fee capped system.

BANKING AND FINANCE

Currency
One Swedish krona = 100 öre

Sweden held a referendum in September 2003 to decide on adopting the Euro as the national currency or remaining with the Krona. 56 per cent voted against adopting the Euro.

GDP/GNP, Inflation, National Debt
Until the mid-1970s, Sweden (the largest economy in Scandinavia) had an exceptional economic growth rate, which was surpassed only by Japan. This growth can largely be attributed to the development of Swedish industrial enterprises. Since the 1970s GNP has fallen to below average when compared to other OECD countries. In the early 1990s Sweden was hit by recession, but has recovered well; in 1993 the government budget was at a record deficit of 12 per cent of GDP, by 2003 a surplus of 2 per cent of GDP was forecast. The Swedish economy is today highly dependent on a limited number of very large international companies for example, Volvo, Saab, Electrolux and Ericsson. In 1992 the United Nations estimated that of the then 35,000 multinational corporations in the world, approximately 2,700 had their headquarters in Sweden. Swedes pay high taxes but in return enjoy one of the best welfare systems in the world.

Figures for 2010 put GNI at 3,407,447 million krona, rising to 3,564,197 million krona in 2011.

The global economic downturn has effected Sweden as banks tighten controls on lending. The car industry has suffered and the government approved a bail out package worth Skr28bn at the end of 2008. The manufacturing industry across the board has suffered with growth declining by 6.0 per cent in 2008. The Swedish economy went into recession in 2008 mainly because of falling exports. In 2010 the economy began to bounce back and GDP growth was estimated to be 4.0 per cent and 3.5 per cent in 2011. The growth was due to strong public sector finances and an increase in exports particularly of machinery, transport equipment as well as furniture and wood products. During 2012 GDP grew during the first half of the year and although growth slowed in the second half it was still positive. The first quarter of 2013 showed that growth was increasing.

The following table shows Gross Domestic Product at current prices in recent years. Figures are in million Krona.

Year	GDP	Growth %
2000	2,265,447	4.5
2001	2,348,419	1.3
2002	2,443,630	2.5
2003	2,544,867	2.3

- continued

2004	2,660,957	4.2
2005	2,769,375	3.2
2006	2,944,480	4.3
2007	3,126,018	3.4
2008	3,204,320	-0.6
2009	3,105,790	-5.0
2010	3,337,531	6.6
2011*	3,502,534	3.9

Source: Statistics Sweden Statistical Yearbook * Provisional figures

The following table shows GDP by expenditure approach at current prices.

GDP by Economic Activity at Current Prices in Million Krona

Sector	2009	2010	2011*
Producers of Goods	709,856	834,087	878,339
Agriculture, forestry & fishing	46,142	50,029	54,898
Mineral extract	10,858	28,022	30,766
Manufacturing	417,945	494,175	515,497
Electricity, water & gas	99,285	109,812	106,503
Construction	138,917	152,049	171,275
Producers of Services	1,393,110	1,458,928	1,553,705
Wholesale & retail trade	314,192	338,805	357,996
Hotels & restaurants	39,296	40,666	42,814
Transport & storage	137,336	142,422	152,474
Information and communication	143,335	154,345	165,394
Financial intermediation	121,268	117,505	118,287
Real estate, business activities	263,924	253,552	268,135
Professional, scientific, technical & admin. activities	238,116	264,195	291,237
Education, health & social work	94,177	103,303	110,680
Personal and art services	41,466	44,135	46,688

*provisional figures
Source: Sweden in Figures 2013, SCB

The inflation rate was 3.4 per cent in April 2008 and estimated to be an average of 2.9 per cent in 2009, figures for the end of 2011 put inflation at 2.3 per cent.

Foreign Investment
Sweden received over SEK150 billion of foreign direct investment in 1998. Since 1992 Finland has accounted for the most investment, followed by the US, Norway and the Netherlands.

Balance of Payments / Imports and Exports
Total Exports and Imports at Current Prices in SEK Millions in Recent Years

Year	Export	Import	Balance
2007	1,139,674	1,034,450	105,224
2008	1,194,411	1,097,903	96,509
2009	995,144	911,379	83,765
2010	1,138,167	1,069,445	68,721
2011	1,213,946	1,141,610	73,336

Source: Sweden in Figures, 2013

The following tables show the value of main exports and main destination of exported goods:

Exports by important SITC commodity groups in SEK million

SITC commodity group	2010 (Jan.-Nov.)	2011 (Jan.-Nov.)
Food, beverages & tobacco	48,763	49,774
Wood & paper products	119,088	118,993
Minerals	116,292	134,609
Chemicals, rubber products	135,125	128,961
Mineral fuels, electric current	78,811	87,505
Machinery, transport equipment	459,150	518,198
Furniture	15,120	15,547

Source: Statistics Sweden

Exports to largest trade partners in SEK million (Jan.-Nov.)

Country	2010	2011
Germany	104,224	111,373
Norway	104,080	104,979
UK	76,826	77,806
USA	76,060	70,327
Denmark	68,508	68,173
Finland	64,895	67,458
Netherlands	50,151	54,805
France	50,716	51,613
Belgium	41,962	49,903
China	32,292	36,328
Poland	26,484	29,281
Italy	29,926	29,039
Russia	18,545	26,084
Spain	20,543	21,567
Australia	13,615	15,227

- continued

Turkey	11,731	15,190

Source: Statistics Sweden

Machinery, petroleum, chemicals and motor vehicles are the main imports. Germany is Sweden's largest trading partner. The following tables show the value of main exports and main country of origin of imported goods:

Imports by important SITC commodity groups in SEK million

SITC Commodity Group	2010 (Jan.-Nov.)	2011 (Jan.-Nov.)
Food, beverages and tobacco	86,966	90,410
Wood & paper products	29,939	30,277
Minerals	90,013	98,734
Chemicals, rubber products	123,267	128,608
Mineral fuels, electric current	129,968	147,964
Machinery, transport equipment	408,428	436,644
Furniture	14,160	14,405

Source: Statistics Sweden

Imports from largest trade partners in SEK million (Jan.-Nov.)

Country	2010	2011
Germany	175,552	191,344
Norway	88,189	88,142
Denmark	81,248	84,611
Netherlands	63,535	64,419
UK	55,078	61,975
Russia	45,632	56,278
Finland	51,490	55,693
France	44,838	46,694
China	39,717	40,913
Belgium	37,996	40,662
USA	31,409	31,539
Italy	28,611	30,950
Poland	28,467	30,080
Estonia	10,319	18,852
Ireland	12,413	17,906
Spain	11,854	13,538

Source: Statistics Sweden

Central Bank
Sveriges Riksbank, Brunkebergstorg 11, Stockholm, Sweden. Tel: +46 (0)8 787 0000, fax: +46 (0)8 210531, e-mail: registratorn@riksbank.se, URL: http://www.riksbank.se Governor: Stefan Ingves

Chambers of Commerce and Trade Organisations
Stockholm Chamber of Commerce, URL: http://www.chamber.se/en/start
Stockholm Stock Exchange Ltd, URL: http://omxgroup.com/nordicexchange
Exportrådet (Trade Council), URL: http://www.swedishtrade.se

MANUFACTURING, MINING AND SERVICES

Primary and Extractive Industries
The Swedish mining industry is mainly concerned with metal ores. The mining industry accounts for 1.0 per cent of the market value of Sweden's total industrial production and employs 0.5 per cent of the total industrial labour force. Iron ore production (lump ore, fines, concentrates and pellets) amounts to 20 million tonnes per year. The production of sulphide ores - containing such minerals as sulphur, copper, lead, zinc, arsenic as well as small amounts of silver and gold - is 18.5 million tonnes. In addition, about 6 million tonnes of limestone are quarried, mostly for use in the cement industry.

The iron and copper industries formerly relied on the production of semi-finished goods for export but, over time, emphasis shifted to the domestic manufacture of iron and non-ferrous metal goods, which gave rise to the modern Swedish engineering industry. The most important iron ore deposits are found in the Kiruna-Malmberget district, with proven reserves of approximately 3,000 Mt of iron ore. Sweden's biggest copper mine, Aitik, is also situated in this district. In the Skellefteå district extending from Boliden in the east to the mountains in the west, and in the mountain range along the Norwegian border there are sulphide ore deposits. Sweden also has large deposits of uranium.

Energy
Producing no oil, gas or coal of its own Sweden must import all of its energy raw materials and has concentrated on developing domestic sources such as hydropower. Around 15 per cent of Sweden's energy supply is generated by its hydroelectric plants, mainly situated on the northern rivers. Coal and coke (imported) makes up around 7 per cent of requirements and over 40 per cent comes from imported oil. 15 per cent of energy (50 per cent of electrical energy) comes from Sweden's 12 nuclear reactors. Following a referendum on the use of nuclear power in 1980, a decision was made to decommission the nuclear power stations; the first was shut down in 1999 followed by the closure of a second one in 2005. Early in 2006 Sweden began talks on reducing its dependency on oil. A committee has been set up consisting of many concerned groups including manufacturers, farmers, industrialists and academics. The committee will be looking into other ways of producing energy such as wind and wave power as well as bio fuels from the extensive forests. In 2009 the government announced it would revisit the idea of nuclear power and that the phasing out of its existing plants would be put on hold with the possibility of new replacement plants being built. This is in the early discussion stages at present and any new plants would not be state funded.

In 2006, domestic supply of energy was 1,353.5 petajoules. An estimated 1,325.3 petajoules was imported and 527.6 petajoules exported. Total inland consumption was estimated at 1,448.0 petajoules. Mining, quarrying and manufacturing accounted for 565.1 petjoules, transport 359,7 petajoules and housing etc 523.1 petajoules of which wood fuel was 49.9 petajoules.

In 2005 there were 1,848 power stations with an total installed capacity of 33,661 MW. Capacity broke down thus: water power 16,276 MW, windpower 496 MW, nuclear power 9,461 MW, conventional thermal power 7,426 MW. Total gross electricity generated in 2006 was 143,369 GWh. This broke down as water power 61,728 GWh, wind power 987 GWh, nuclear power 66,977 GWh, conventional thermal power 13,677 GWh. An estimated 17,547 GWh was imported.

Capacity of Installed Generators, MW

Production	2008
Hydro power	16,489
Nuclear power	8,839
Conventional thermal power	8,342
Wind power	935
Total	34,604

Source: Statistics Sweden

Manufacturing
Manufacturing plays a major role in exports, and recent figures show that it accounted for 80 per cent of the total exports. The engineering industry accounts for nearly half of the sector with the pharmaceutical industry being the fastest growing area. Sweden numbers among the world's biggest spenders on industrial R&D in relation to output, and this is due to the fact that Swedish industry is operated by a few very large companies, such as Electrolux, Ericsson and Volvo, rather than lots of small ones. The dominant role of a few large companies is especially apparent in manufacturing; more than one third of Sweden's labour force is employed in companies that have at least 500 employees, and nearly half of all employees in the engineering industry work for multinational companies.

Swedish industry was characterised in 1998 by a series of foreign mergers and acquisitions: the pharmaceuticals giant Astra merged with the UK's Zeneca to become AstraZeneca; Volvo sold its car division to another UK company, Ford; and the paper company Stora merged with the Finnish company Enso, becoming StoraEnso.

Recent figures show that manufacturing accounts for 22 per cent of GDP and is showing an annual growth rate in the region of 7 per cent. Manufactured goods dominate the exports; 80 per cent of all merchandise exports in 2000 were of manufactured goods. The engineering section of the manufacturing sector accounts for over 50 per cent of production, followed by the wood and paper sector. Pharmaceuticals have increased in importance to the economy in recent years and production now accounts for 12 per cent of the total manufacturing output. Food processing accounts for 7 per cent and iron and steel production accounts for 5 per cent.

Market Value of Industrial Production by Industry in SEK Million

Industry	2009	2010
Mines & quarries & manufacturing Industry	1,290,925	2,422,886
Mines & quarries	23,653	42,718
Food product, beverage & tobacco industry	135,429	134,723
Textiles & textile products, leather & leather products	9,406	10,437
Wood & wood products	72,777	79,703
Pulp, paper & paper products & printers	134,537	142,797
Coke & refined petroleum products	14,680	12,498
Chemicals, chemical products & man made fibres	121,103	119,824
Rubber & plastic products	34,018	38,170
Other non-metallic mineral products	29,335	32,591
Basic metals	102,867	129,560
Fabricated metal products, machinery & equipment	567,314	628,559
Manufacturing industry n.e.c.	45,806	46,036

Source: Statistics Sweden

Service Industries
There were over 3.2 million visitors to Sweden in 2006 generating US$10,437 million.
Swedish Tourist Authority, Biblioteksgatan 11, Box 7087, S-103 87 Stockholm, Sweden. Tel: +46 (0)8 678 3400, fax: +46 (0)8 678 0425, e-mail: kansli@tourist.se, URL: htp://www.visitsweden.com

Agriculture
Cultivated acreage comprises about 2.8 million hectares, i.e. less than one-tenth of the country; use is also made of non-arable land for grazing. The distance between the northernmost and southernmost points of Sweden is 1,574 km, and agricultural conditions vary widely between these two extremes; the growing season in the extreme south is 240 days, while in the far north it is under 120 days. Roughly 3 per cent of the economically active population is employed in agriculture, which contributes about 2 per cent of Sweden's GDP. In 2010, there were an estimated 71,091 agricultural holdings.

Sweden is more than 80 per cent self-sufficient in food. Figures for 2006 show that there are around 1.59 million head of cattle in Sweden, including 387,530 dairy cows, 505,466 sheep and lambs, over 1.68 million pigs and 6.17 million poultry. In Sami communities there were an estimated 261,404 grazing reindeer. Dairy and meat production in 2006 was 3.17 million tonnes of milk, 133,000 tonnes of beef, 4,000 tonnes of veal, 4,000 tonnes of mutton and lamb, 1,000 tonnes of horsemeat, 264,00 tonnes of pork, 96,000 tonnes of poultry meat and 99,000 tonnes of eggs.

SWEDEN

Selected Crop Yield in Tons

Crop	2010	2011
Winter wheat	1,873,100	1,985,800
Spring wheat	269,900	260,900
Rye	117,600	126,500
Winter barley	81,200	65,200
Spring barley	1,151,100	1,343,900
Oats	559,300	692,000
Triticale	158,700	107,200
Mixed grain	68,600	68,900
Peas	54,000	42,800
Field beans	31,100	53,000
Table potatoes	542,900	584,000
Sugar beets	1,976,200	2,493,200
Winter rape	222,100	173,500
Spring rape	54,100	74,000
Spring turnip rape	2,500	2,300
Oil flax	23,600	23,000

Source: Statistics Sweden

Organic Farming, Total Production in Metric Tonnes

Crop	2010	2011
Winter wheat	40,600	48,200
Spring wheat	28,500	33,600
Winter rye	4,300	4,600
Spring barley	36,000	36,700
Oats	50,400	63,500
Triticale	8,200	8,000
Mixed grain	24,000	26,500
Peas	5,000	4,500
Field beans	13,100	23,000
Winter rape	2,900	2,200
Table potatoes	11,700	12,700

Source: Statistics Sweden

Forestry
The forestry industry is important, making up about 5.5 per cent of GDP. Sweden has a vast supply of spruce, pine and other softwoods, which provide for a highly developed sawmill, pulp, paper and wood product industry. 60 per cent of forest products are exported. The coastline is 2,862 km in length, and Sweden has always had an extensive fishing industry, governed by the restrictions of international fishing zones. Over 50 per cent of forested land is owned by private individuals, nearly 40 per cent by forest companies and only 3 per cent is state owned.

Gross Fellings by Assortments. Figures in Millions of Cubic Metres

Product	2006 (provisional)
Saw logs	28.3
Pulpwood	27.3
Fuelwood of stemwood	5.9
Other roundwood	0.5
Total net fellings	67.6

Source: Sweden in Figures 2006, SCB

Fishing
In 2006, the total salt water yield of fish was 261,9745 tons worth 1,012,520 krone. The most significant catches were baltic herring 67,023 tons (207,208,00 krone), cod 11,497 tons (193,832,000 krone), Norway lobster 1,095 tons (109,961000 kr.), and prawns 2,361 tons (98,052,000 kr.). In 2006 there were 1,691 registered professional fishermen, and 1,589 fishing craft.

Aquaculture production was estimated in 2006 as: rainbow trout 6,116 tonnes, salmon 3 tonnes, eels 191 tonnes, char 444 tonnes, total food fish 6,754 tonnes, mussels 1,791 tonnes, crayfish 5 tonnes.

COMMUNICATIONS AND TRANSPORT

Travel Requirements
Citizens of the USA, Canada and Australia require a passport valid for three months beyond the length of stay but do not need a visa for stays of up to 90 days. EU citizens do not require a passport if they are carrying a valid national Identity Card, and do not require a visa for stays of up to 90 days. Other nationals should contact the embassy to check visa requirements.

Sweden is a signatory of the Schengen Agreement; with a Schengen visa, a visitor can travel freely throughout the Schengen zone, with few border stops and checks. See http://www.eurovisa.info/SchengenCountries.htm for details.

National Airlines
Scandinavian Airlines System (SAS), http://www.sas.se

International Airports
Stockholm-Arlanda, URL: http://www.lfe.se
Stockholm Bromma Airport, URL: http://www.lfe.se
Gothenburg Landvetter Airport, URL: http://www.lfe.se
Swedish Civil Aviation Administration (Luftfartsverket), URL: http://www.lfe.se

In 2011 there were 517,080 scheduled and non-scheduled flights, of which 272,298 were domestic flights. Loaded and unloaded freight in 2005 amounted to 153,722 tonnes and mail 31,980 tonnes.

The busiest airports were Stockholm-Arlanda (5,319,845 passengers), Stockholm-Bromma (1,505,877 passengers), Goteborg-Landvetter (1,346,135 passengers) and Malmo (Source: Statistics Sweden).

Railways
The total length of lines as of 2011 was 11,206 km, of which 8,119 was electrified. In 2011 Swedish railways carried 187 million passengers and 68 million tons of freight (Source: Statistics Sweden). Stockholm has a subway and tram network.

Roads
Figures for 2011 show that there were 215,952 km of roads in Sweden. Vehicles drive on the right. In 2011 public expenditure on maintenance and construction of roads was 22,493 SEK million. As of 2011 there were 4,401,000 passenger cars on the road, 548,000 lorries, 14,000 buses, 189,000 caravans, 321,000 tractors and 305,000 motorcycles. In 2006 the most popular make of car on the road that year was Volvo with 991,347, followed by Volkswagen with 413,832, Saab with 365,489 and Ford with 304,450. In January 2008, new registrations of cars amounted to 19,434 (a decrease of 15.4 per cent from January 2007). In the same month 3,503 new lorries were registered (a decrease of 7.6 per cent compared to the previous year.)

In July 2000 the Öresund Fixed Link was opened linking Malmo in Sweden with Copenhagen in Denmark. The link consists of four kilometres of tunnel and eight kilometres of bridge and carries vehicles and trains. (Source: Sweden in Figures 2006, SCB)

Ports and Harbours
The major ports are Brofjorden, Trelleborg, Gothenburg, Malmo, Halmstad, Kalmar and Helsingborg. In 2006, 39.9 million tonnes passed through Gothenburg, 18.6 million tonnes through Brofjorden, 11.4 million tonnes through Trelleborg, 9 million through Malmo and 7.6 million through Karlshamn.

In 2005 total net turnover for water transport was 36,656 million SEK. The total size of the merchant fleet 10 2011 was 402 vessels.

The total number of vessels that entered Sweden in 2006 was 72,517, with a gross tonnage of 942.3 million tonnes. The total number of passengers was 14.9 million.

HEALTH

Sweden has a comprehensive social welfare system and residents are covered by the national health insurance scheme, paid for through taxes. Hospital care is available at county and regional level. There are 80 county hospitals and 10 regional hospitals, with a combined total of approximately 26,300 beds. Health care is the responsibility of the county councils. The system is subsidised with 90 per cent of the costs being met by the county councils. Dental care is provided free for young people up 19 years of age.

Provisional figures from 2011 show that there are 30,200doctors (318 per 100,000 population), 72,300 nurses and midwives, 36,000 assistant nurses, 5,800 physiotherapists and 4,100 dentists.

Figures for 2008 show that total expenditure on health care was the equivalent of 9.4 per cent of GDP. General government expenditure on health accounted for 78.1 per cent of total expenditure on health and private expenditure for 16.8 per cent (out-of-pocket expenditure 93 per cent). Total per capita expenditure on health amounted to US$4,858 in 2008, compared to US$2,277 in 2000.

Most deaths are caused by heart and circulatory system diseases. In 2009 the infant mortality rate (probability of dying before first birthday) was 2 per 1,000 live births and the child (under-five years old) mortality rate was 3 per 1,000 live births. The main causes of death in the under-fives are: prematurity (7 per cent), pneumonia (5 per cent), congenital abnormalities (29 per cent) and diarrhoea (1 per cent).

All the population have access to improved drinking water and sanitation. (Source: WHO, 2011)

EDUCATION

According to 2010 figures, 8.53 per cent of GDP was spent on education.

Pre-school Education
All children aged six and under are eligible for pre-school education, which is optional for the children but compulsory for municipal authorities. Responsibility for pre-school education is vested in the National Board of Health and Welfare. According to estimates for 2010-11, 103,529 children attended pre-primary school.

Primary/Secondary Education
Primary and secondary school is compulsory for nine years and is divided into three levels: junior, intermediate and senior. Figures for 2006 show that 656,383 children attended primary school and 373,764 attended lower secondary and 727,098 attended secondary school. This represents 99 per cent of the population for girls and boys. The great majority of these schools are run by municipal authorities and are free of charge. Nor is any charge made for teaching materials, school meals, health care or school transport (for children living a long way away from school). The pupil: teacher ratio in primary school is 10:1.

There are a very small number of private schools.

The existing upper secondary school system came into being in 1971, with the amalgamation of gymnasium, continuing school and vocational school. It is divided into lines of two or three years duration. Some of these are vocational, while others lead on to further education. Upper secondary school also includes many directly vocational specialised courses of varying duration. The entire system of upper secondary schooling is now undergoing a process of development. Figures for 2006 show that 353,334 pupils attended upper secondary school.

Higher Education

A unified educational system was created in 1977 the Swedish Higher Educational Act, which integrated institutions which had previously been administrated separately. Higher education in free of charge. This new 'högskola' included not only traditional university studies but also those of various former professional colleges, as well as a number of study programmes previously offered by the secondary school system. One of the goals of the 1977 university reform was to introduce an increased element of vocational training as well as widening admission into Swedish higher education. In 2007 the Higher Education system was reformed and this strata of education was divided into three levels, basic level (grundnivå), advanced level (avancerad nivå) and graduate level (forskarnivå). The basic level is for students coming straight from the end of secondary education, the advanced level is for students who have obtained a degree and the graduate level is for students who have a Swedish degree at advanced level or who have completed at least four years of full-time study with at least one year at the advanced level, or foreign students who already have a degree.

Undergraduate training is available in the form of general, local or individual study programmes, supplementary study programmes or separate courses. General study programmes are intended to meet more permanent educational needs and are being directed towards a wide range of professions (e.g. the training of physicians, economists, lawyers etc.). Local study programmes are offered on the basis of special needs in the area or region (e.g. management for small manufacturers and traders). Individual study programmes may be arranged for individual students or groups of students. Specialised continuation courses are offered after the completion of general study programmes (e.g. the further training of remedial teachers). Separate courses are available to persons with special study interests or to those people who are interested in further training.

A Certificate of Education (B.Sc., M.Sc., UC, etc.) is awarded on completion of a study programme. This certificate states the number of courses taken as well as the points and grades obtained on each course in the study programme. Postgraduate training is given at the universities: the Royal Institute of Technology in Stockholm, the Karolinska Institute, the Stockholm Institute of Education, the Stockholm School of Economics, Chalmers University of Technology and Lulea, University College and Institute of Technology. (Source: UNESCO)

RELIGION

The church law was formulated in 1686. Fundamental to this law was the fact that Sweden was an evangelical nation and that the Swedes should profess the evangelical faith. 85 per cent of the population belong to the Church of Sweden. Recently the ties between church and state have been loosened and in 2000 the final disestablishment of the Church of Sweden took place. Other religions are represented with 16,000 Jews, 250,000 Muslims, 40,000 Buddhists and 13,500 Hindus.

Sweden has a religious liberty rating of 9 on a scale of 1 to 10 (10 is most freedom). (Source: World Religion Database)

COMMUNICATIONS AND MEDIA

Newspapers
Expressen, URL: http://www.expressen.se
Dagens Nyheter, URL: http://www.dn.se
Aftonbladet, URL: http://www.aftonbladet.se

Göteborgs-Posten, URL: http://www.gp.se
Svenska Dagbladet, URL: http://www.gp.se
Sydsvenskan Dagbladet, URL: http://www.sydsvenskan.se

Broadcasting
Until recently the public broadcaster had a virtual monopoly on broadcasting.Public Television is run by Sveriges Television and public radio by Radio Sveriges. The main television competitor is TV4 which was launched in 1992. Public radio is run by Sveriges Radio. Commercial radio stations have operated since 1993 and there are now more than 100. The government aim was to complete a switch to digital broadcasting in 2008.
Sveriges Television (SVT), URL: http://svt.se/ (Public, operates terrestial networks SVT1 and SVT2, news channel SVT24)
TV4, URL: http://www.tv4.se/ (commercial, terrestial)
TV3, URL: http://www.tv3.se/ (commercial, satellite)
Kanal5, URL: http://kanal5.se/web/guest/hem (commercial, satellite)
ZTV, URL: http://www.ztv.se/ (commercial, satellite)
Sveriges Radio, URL: http://www.sr.se (public radio, operates P1,P2,P4 and P4 stations)
Rix FM, URL: http://www.rixfm.se (commercial)
NRJ, URL: http://www.radioplay.se/#/nrj (commerical)
Mix Megapol, URL: http://www.mixmegapol.se/karta (commercial)

Telecommunications
Estimates for 2011 show over 5.1 million telephone lines in use and over 11 million mobile phones. It was estimated that in 20107, over 90 per cent of the population had home access to the internet.

ENVIRONMENT

The Swedish government established the Stockholm Environment Institute in 1989; amongst its policies are pollution taxes, financial encouragement for car recycling, the phasing out of nuclear power and encouragement of alternative sources of energy. The main goals of Swedish environmental policy are to protect human health, conserve biological diversity, manage natural resources and protect natural landscapes. Acid rain and the damage it does to soils and lakes are particular concerns for Sweden.

In 2006, an estimated 47,625,000 tonnes of CO_2 were emitted (compared to 51,614,000 in 1990). An estimated 400,000 tonnes of CO_2 equivalent of methane were emitted in 2005 and 1,458,000 tonnes of CO_2 equivalent of nitrous oxide were emitted. Figures for 2010 show that carbon dioxide emissions totaled 62.74 million tonnes up from 50.72 million tonnes in 2009.

Sweden is party to the following international agreements: Air Pollution, Air Pollution-Nitrogen Oxides, Air Pollution-Persistent Organic Pollutants, Air Pollution-Sulfur 85, Air Pollution-Sulfur 94, Air Pollution-Volatile Organic Compounds, Antarctic-Environmental Protocol, Antarctic-Marine Living Resources, Antarctic Treaty, Biodiversity, Climate Change, Climate Change-Kyoto Protocol, Desertification, Endangered Species, Environmental Modification, Hazardous Wastes, Law of the Sea, Marine Dumping, Ozone Layer Protection, Ship Pollution, Tropical Timber 83, Tropical Timber 94, Wetlands, and Whaling.

SPACE PROGRAMME

The Swedish National Space Board is the central governmental agency responsible for activities relating to space and remote sensing. Its three main tasks are: to carry out R&D especially in the areas of space and remote sensing; to distribute government grants; and the facilitation of international co-operation. The total budget of the agency is approximately 700 million Swedish krona per annum. Sweden is a member of the European Space Agency.
Swedish National Space Board (SNSB), URL: http://www.snsb.se

SWITZERLAND
The Swiss Confederation
Schweizerische Eidgenossenschaft / Confédération Suisse / Confederazione Svizzera

Capital: Berne (Population estimate, 2010: 121,631)

Head of State: Ueli Maurer (page 1472)(President of the Swiss Confederation, 2013)

Vice President: Didier Burkhalter ((page 1397)Vice President, 2013)

National Flag: Red, with a white cross couped

CONSTITUTION AND GOVERNMENT

Constitution
Following the dissolution of the Helvetic Republic in 1803 a new Constitution called 'Act of Mediation' was given to Switzerland by Napoleon. In 1815 the Congress of Vienna recognised the independence of the Confederation, and the neutrality of Switzerland was guaranteed by Austria, Great Britain, Portugal, Prussia and Russia. A new Federal Constitution was adopted in 1848 which was in turn superseded by the constitution of 1874.

The government is in the hands of the Federal Council, which is appointed every four years at the first session of the Federal Assembly after the election in autumn. It consists of seven members and they jointly govern the country. One of them in turn takes the chair for one year and is called the President of the Confederation. In choosing the Federal Council the various regions of the country, languages, religions and parties are taken into consideration. The president and vice-president of the Confederation are elected by the Federal Assembly, but this is a mere matter of routine, as the former vice-president invariably becomes president, being next on the list of the Federal Council, which is drawn up by an old-established rule. The president cannot dismiss his colleagues; there can be no Cabinet crises and no votes of censure. Neither the Parliamentary vote nor referendum can cause the Council to resign.

To consult the constitution, please visit: http://www.admin.ch/ch/e/rs/c101.html

President of the Swiss Confederation, 2013: Ueli Maurer (page 1472)
Vice President of the Swiss Confederation, 2013: Didier Burkhalter (page 1397)

Two peculiar features of Swiss democracy are the 'referendum' and the 'initiative'. A bill approved by the Federal Assembly must, by the constitution, be submitted to the referendum. It comes into force only if no petition is made against it within 90 days. If a petition is submitted bearing the signature of no less than 50,000 citizens, a referendum is held and the final decision as to whether it shall become law rests with the people. Citizens have another means by which they can actively take part in the affairs of the country, namely by the 'initiative'. By this means the people, given the support of 100,000 signatures, can demand that the Federal Constitution shall be amended or totally or partially revised. Should the Federal Constitution be amended, not only is the consent of the majority of people required in every case, but a majority of the cantons must be obtained also. This 'double majority' is settled by first determining the majority of votes, and the proportion of votes for and against the motion in each separate canton. If there is a majority of votes as well as majority of cantons in favour of the motion, it then becomes law. Recent referendums held have been on whether Switzerland should join the EU and UN and in March 2002 Switzerland became the 190th member of the United Nations.

International Relations
Switzerland has been a member of the European Free Trade Association (EFTA) since 1959 and a member of the World Trade Organisation (WTO) since 1995, but is not a member of the EEA or EU. Although two referendums held in 2005 approved membership of the EU Schengen and Dublin agreements which allows passport-free travel to member countries and cooperation on crime and asylum issues, the second referendum approved opening the job market to the recent member nations of the EU. Switzerland has a long history of neutrality which would be at odds with some of the EU's foreign policy. Switzerland is not a member of NATO but does have close links with the NATO Partnership for Peace activities.

Recent Events
In June 2005 a referendum approved the joining of the EU Schengen and Dublin agreement. This would mean Switzerland becoming part of the EU 'Passport Free Zone' and the sharing of information with EU members on crime and asylum applications. A referendum held in September 2006 backed plans to strengthen asylum laws.

In early 2007 the former directors of Swissair, the national airline which collapsed in 2001, were tried in court on charges of mismanagement, fraud and falsifying documents. All were cleared.

In October 2007, Switzerland held a general election. The Swiss People's Party (SVP) increased its majority in the parliament, but left the governing coalition in December. Christoph Blocher was forced from his cabinet seat as the head of the Federal Department for Justice and Police. The election campaign had been marred by rows over SVP posters using the slogan 'kick out the black sheep' which was aimed at the deportation of foreigners found guilty of crimes. Since 1959 Switzerland has been governed by what came to be known as the 'magic formula': up until 2003, the Federal Council was made up of two members from the Social Democrats, two members from the Free Democrats, two members from the Christian Democrats and one

member from the Swiss People's Party. The number of members from each party was not based on the number of votes the party had received. In the 2003 election, the SVP received more votes than the Free and Social Democrats parties, and were given a second seat; the Christian Democrats lost one of theirs. In the 2007 election, the SVP won 29 per cent of the vote, but, following the anti-immigration election campaign, parliament refused to elect the SVP leader Christoph Blocher to the cabinet. This resulted in the withdrawal of the SVP from the coalition. Parliament did elect SVP member Eveline Widmer-Schlumpf to the cabinet, but the SVP would not recognise her position or that of fellow SVP cabinet member Samuel Schmid. In December 2008 the SVP rejoined the coalition when Ueli Maurer was elected to the Federal Council.

In October 2008 Libya cancelled all oil deliveries and withdrew assets from Swiss banks after Colonel Gaddafi's son Hannibal and his wife were arrested for assault but charges were later dropped.

In November 2009 the Swiss voted in favour of a referendum to ban the building of minarets in Switzerland. The referendum was tabled by the Swiss People's Party, (SVP), as they saw minarets as a sign of Islamisation. In recent years the rising number of immigrants has become an issue in Swiss politics, more than 57 per cent of voters and 22 out of the 26 cantons supported the ban.

In November 2010 Switzerland held a referendum on the proposal that any foreigners would automatically be deported if they have committed a serious crime. The electorate approved the proposal.

In a referendum in February 2011, voters rejected tighter gun controls.

In April 2012, the government re-imposed immigration quotas on workers from central and eastern EU countries.

In January 2013, Wegelin, Switzerland's oldest bank (established in 1741) announced it was closing permanently after pleading guilty in a New York court to helping Americans evade their taxes. The bank was fined US$57.8 million and announced it would cease operations after payment of the fine.

Legislature
The supreme legislative authority is the Federal Assembly, made up of two chambers: the National Council (*Nationalrat*) and the Council of States (*Ständerat*).

Upper House
The Nationalrat/Conseil National (National Council) is elected by the people. The number of Councillors used to vary according to the population, but continued growth of the population has forced the government to set a maximum of 200 on the National Council seats. Members serve a four year term. Each canton has at least one representative.
Nationalrat, Parlamentsgebäude, 3003 Berne, Switzerland. Tel: +41 31 322 9711, fax: +41 31 322 4241, URL: http://www.parlament.ch
President: Maya Graf

Lower House
The Ständerat/Conseil des Etats (Council of States) consists of 46 members, two sitting for each canton for a four year term. Three cantons are divided into two half-cantons each - Unterwalden, by a very old tradition, into Obwalden and Nidwalden; Appenzell into Catholic Innerrhoden and Protestant Ausserrhoden; and Basle, after the fierce conflict between town and country in the 1830s, into Basle City and Basle Country. Each one of these half-cantons is as independent a state as any canton, but in federal matters they have only half a vote and hence only one seat in the Council of States. This gives rise to a curious situation, since the Canton of Basle City, with 235,000 inhabitants, has only one vote, while the canton of Uri, with only 34,000 inhabitants, has two votes.
President: Filippo Lombardi

The Federal Assembly, Parlamentsgebäude, 3003 Berne, Switzerland. Tel: +41 (0)31 322 8790, fax: +41 (0)31 322 5374, URL: http//:www.parlament.ch

---

Cabinet (as at June 2013)
Head of the Federal Department of Home Affairs: Alain Berset (page 1388)
Head of the Federal Department of Foreign Affairs: Didier Burkhalter (page 1397)
Head of the Federal Department for Public Economy: Johann Schneider-Ammann (page 1509)
Head of the Federal Department of Finance: Eveline Widmer-Schlumpf
Head of the Federal Department of Environment, Transport, Communications and Energy: Doris Leuthard (page 1463)
Head of the Federal Department of Justice and Police: Simonetta Sommaruga (page 1517)
Head of the Federal Department of Defence, Civil Protection and Sports: Ueli Maurer (page 1472)
Head of Chancellery: Corina Casanova (page 1401)

Ministries
Office of the President, URL: http://www.admin.ch/
Federal Chancellery, Federal Palace, Bundesgasse West, 3003 Berne, Switzerland. Tel: +41 (0)31 322 3791, fax: +41 (0)31 322 3706, e-mail: webmaster@admin.ch, URL: http://www.bk.admin.ch
Federal Department of Finance, Bernerhof, Bundesgasse 3, 3003 Berne, Switzerland. Tel: +41 (0)31 322 2111, fax: +41 (0)31 322 6187, URL: http://www.efd.admin.ch
Federal Department of Foreign Affairs, Bundeshaus West, 3003 Berne, Switzerland. Tel: +41 (0)31 322 2111, fax: +41 (0)31 323 4001, URL: http://www.eda.admin.ch
Federal Department of Home Affairs, Inselgasse 1, 3003 Berne, Switzerland. Tel: +41 (0)31 322 8041, fax: +41 (0)31 322 7901. URL: http://www.edi.admin.ch
Federal Department of Justice and Police, Bundeshaus West, 3003 Berne, Switzerland. Tel: +41 (0)31 322 2111, fax: +41 (0)31 322 7832, URL: http://www.ejpd.admin.ch
Federal Department of Economic Affairs, Bundeshaus Ost, 3003 Berne, Switzerland. Tel: +41 (0)31 322 2007, fax: +41 (0)31 322 2194, e-mail: info@gs-evd.admin.ch, URL: http://www.evd.admin.ch
Federal Department of Defence, Civil Protection and Sports, Bundeshaus Ost, 3003 Berne, Switzerland. Tel: +41 (0)31 324 5058, fax: +41 (0)31 31 324 5104, URL: http://www.vbs.admin.ch
Federal Department of Environment, Transport, Communications and Energy, Bundeshaus-Nord, 3003 Berne, Switzerland. Tel: +41 (0)31 322 5511, fax: +41 (0)31 324 2692, e-mail: info@gs-uvek.admin.ch, URL: http://www.uvek.admin.ch

Political Parties
FDP Freisinnig-Demokratische Partei der Schweiz/PRD Parti Radical Démocratique Suisse (Radical Democrats), Postfach 6136, 3001 Berne, Switzerland. Tel:+41 (0)31 320 3535, fax: +41 (0)31 320 3500, e-mail: gs@fdp-prd.ch, URL: http://www.fdp-prd.ch
Leader: Fulvio Pelli
SP Sozialdemokratische Partei der Schweiz/Parti Socialiste Suisse (Social-Democrats), Spitalgasse 34, 3001 Berne, Switzerland. Tel: +41 (0)31 329 6969, fax: +41 31 329 6970, URL: http://www.sp-ps.ch
Leader: Christian Levrat
CVP Christlichdemokratische Volkspartei der Schweiz/PDC Parti Démocrate-Chrétien Suisse (Christian-Democratic People's Party), Postfach 5835, Berne 3001, Switzerland. Tel: +41 (0)31 357 3333, fax: +41 (0)31 352 2430, e-mail: info@cvp.ch URL: http://www.pdc.ch
Leader: Christophe Darbellay
SVP Schweizerische Volkspartei/UDC Union Démocratique du Centre (Swiss People's Party), Bruckfeldstrasse 18, 3000 Berne 26, Switzerland. Tel: +41 (0)31 302 5858, fax:+41 (0)31 301 7585, e-mail: gs@svp.ch, URL: http//www.svp.ch
Leader: Toni Brunner
E-CSP Christlich-soziale Partei/PCS Parti Chrétien-Social (Christian Socialist Party), Eichenstrasse 79, 3184 Wünnewil PC 87-132107-4, Switzerland. E-mail: info@csp-pcs.ch, URL: http://www.csp-pcs.ch
Leader: Monika Bloch Süss
EDU Eidgenössisch-Demokratische Union/UDF Union Démocratique Fédérale (Union of Federal Democrats), Postfach, 3607 Thun 7, Switzerland. Tel: +41 (0)33 222 3637, fax: +41 (0)33 222 3637, e-mail: info@edu-udf.ch, URL: http://www.edu-udf.ch
Leader: Hans Moser
Lega dei Ticinesi (Ticino League), casella postale 2311, 6901 Lugano, Switzerland. Tel: +41 (0)91 971 3033, fax: +41 (0)91 972 7492
Leader: Giuliano Bignasca
Grüne Partei der Schweiz/Parti écologiste suisse (Green Party), Waisenhausplatz 21, 3011 Berne, Switzerland. Tel: +41 (0)31 312 6660, fax: +41 (0)31 312 6662, e-mail: gruene@gruene.ch / verts@verts.ch, URL: http://www.gruene.ch / http://www.verts.ch
Leader: Ueli Leuenberger
SD Schweizer Demokraten/DS Démocrates Suisses (Swiss Democrats), Postfach 8116, 3001 Berne, Switzerland. Tel: +41 (0)31 974 2010, fax: +41 (0)31 974 2011, e-mail: info@schweizer-demokraten.ch, URL: http://www.schweizer-demokraten.ch
Leader: Bernhard Hess
PST Parti suisse du Travail/PdAS Partei der Arbeit der Schweiz (Worker's Party), case postale 232, 1211 Genève 8, Switzerland. Tel: +41 (0)22 322 2299, fax: +41 (0)22 322 2295, URL: http://www.pst.ch / www.pda.ch
Leader: Nelly Buntschu
EVP Evangelische Volkspartei der Schweiz/PEV Parti évangélique suisse (Evangelical People's Party), Postfach 7334, 8023 Z
rich, Switzerland. Tel: +41 (0)1 272 7100, fax: +41 (0)1 727 1437, e-mail: info@evppev.ch, www.evppev.ch
Leader: Ruedi Aeschbacher
GB Grünes Bündnis/AVeS Alliance Verte et Sociale, Postfach 6411, 3001 Berne, Switzerland. Tel: +41 (0)31 301 8209, fax: +41 (0)31 302 8878, e-mail: gbbern@infodelta.ch, www.gb-aves.ch
BDP/PBD Conservative Democratic Party of Switzerland, URL: http://www.bdp.info
President: Hans Grunder

Elections
All Swiss citizens over the age of 18 are eligible to take part in the elections to the National Council. The most recent parliamentary elections took place in October 21 2011. The results are shown below:

Party	Seats
Swiss People's Party (SVP)	56
Social Democrats (SP)	46
Free Democratic Party (FDP)	30
Christian Democrats (CVP)	31
Green Party	15
Green Liberal Party (GLG/PVL)	12

- continued

Conservative Democratic Party (BDP/PBD)	9
Others	1

The Swiss People's Party lost some ground but remained the largest party.

Ueli Maurer was elected to the post of president for 2013.

Diplomatic Representation
Embassy of the United States of America, Jubiläumsstrasse 95, 3005 Berne, Switzerland. Tel: +41 (0)31 357 7011, fax: +41 (0)31 357 7344, URL: http://bern.usembassy.gov
Ambassador: Donald S. Beyer Jr. (page 1388)
British Embassy, Thunstrasse 50, 300 Berne 15, Switzerland. Tel: +41 (0)31 359 7700, fax: +41 (0)31 359 7701, URL: http://ukinswitzerland.fco.gov.uk/en
Ambassador: Sarah Gillett (page 1430)
Embassy of Switzerland, 2900 Cathedral Ave, NW, Washington, DC 20008, USA. Tel: +1 202 745 7900, fax: +1 202 387 2564, e-mail: Vertretung@was.rep.admin.ch, URL: http://www.eda.admin.ch/washington
Ambassador: Manuel Sager
Embassy of Switzerland, 16-18 Montagu Place, London, W1H 2BQ, United Kingdom. Tel: +44 (0)20 7616 6000, fax: +44 (0)20 7724 7001, e-mail: Vertretung@lon.rep.admin.ch, URL: http://www.swissembassy.org.uk
Ambassador: Anton Thalmann
Permanent Representative of Switzerland to the United Nations, 633 Third Avenue, 29th Floor, New York, NY 10017, USA. Tel: +1 212 286 1540, fax: +1 212 286 1555, e-mail: Vertretung-UN@nyc.rep.admin.ch, URL: http://www.eda.admin.ch/missny
Ambassador: Paul Seger

LEGAL SYSTEM

Switzerland has a civil law system, influenced by customary law.

The Federal Court, the supreme federal tribunal, has its seat at Lausanne. The 38 Federal judges are elected by the Federal Assembly for a period of six years. This court, which has four divisions, is the supreme court of Switzerland, and according to the constitution the three official languages of Switzerland must be represented in the court.

The Federal Court is divided into six different branches: two constitutional divisions which are charged with the highly political duty of protecting the rights of the citizen, but have no power to examine federal laws for their constitutionality; two Civil Courts which are mainly used as courts of appeal; the Bankruptcy Court; and the Criminal Law Division or Court of Cassation.

The government respects the rights of its citizens. Switzerland abolished the death penalty in 1942.

Federal Supreme Court, URL: http://www.supreme-court.ch

Federal Commission against Racism, URL: http://www.ekr.admin.ch/

LOCAL GOVERNMENT

Switzerland is divided into 26 autonomous cantons, each of which has its own constitution and its own legislative and executive bodies. They are sovereign in so far as their sovereign rights are not limited by the Federal constitution.

There are a number of small cantons, Appenzell I. Rh, Nidwalden and Obwalden, in which a convocation of the citizens takes place annually in the form of a *Landsgemeinde* or folkmoot (open-air parliament). At the appointed time, the citizens assemble in the public place of the capital of the canton. They can take part in the discussion, decide by a show of hands which laws and financial measures are to be enacted, and elect the members of the government.

Most cantons have given up this form of direct democracy but citizens still have far-reaching rights concerning direct participation in the life of the canton beyond the right to elect officials. In a number of cantons every law enacted by the Canton Council must be submitted to the people for approval. In other cantons a referendum may be brought into operation. This means that, if a sufficient number of signatures is collected by the citizens among themselves, they have the right to demand that a law approved by the Legislative Assembly be submitted to the vote of the people. Swiss citizens can also propose new laws within the canton by right of the 'initiative'.

The following table shows the resident populations of the Cantons in 2011.

Canton	Population	Capital
Zurich	1,392,396	Zurich
Berne	985,046	Berne
Lucerne	381,966	Lucerne
Uri	35,382	Altdorf
Schwyz	147,904	Schwyz
Obwalden	35,885	Sarnen
Nidwalden	41,311	Stans
Glarus	39,217	Glarlus
Zug	115,104	Zug
Fribourg	284,668	Fribourg
Solothurn	256,990	Solothurn
Basle-City	186,255	Basle

SWITZERLAND

- continued

Basle-County	275,360	Liestal
Schaffhausen	77,139	Schaffhausen
Appenzell A.Rh	53,313	Herisau
Appenzell I.Rh	15,743	Appenzell
St. Gallen	483,156	St. Gall
Graubünden	193,388	Chur
Aargau	618,298	Aarau
Thurgau	251,973	Frauenfeld
Ticino	336,943	Bellinzona
Vaud	725,944	Lausanne
Valais	317,022	Sion
Neuchâtel	173,183	Neuchâtel
Geneva	460,534	Geneva
Jura	70,542	Delémont

Source: Swiss Federal Statistical Office

A further aspect of local government is the commune, of which there are 2,551. They have a large measure of self-government especially in matters like utilities. Within the commune, every citizen has a share in the administration and is expected to play his part as an active member of the commune. All citizens have the right to vote on political matters.

AREA AND POPULATION

Area

Switzerland has common frontiers with Italy (a frontier of 734 km in length), France (572 km), Germany (346 km), Austria (165 km) and Liechtenstein (41 km). The total surface area is 41,285 sq. km, of which 12,523 sq. km (30.3 per cent) is forest or woods, 10,166 sq. km (24.6 per cent) is cultivated land, 5,646 sq. km (13.7 per cent) is used for mountain farming, 2,418 sq. km (5.9 per cent) is settled, 8,806 sq. km (21.3 per cent) is unused and the rest (1,726 sq. km - 4.2 per cent) of the country's land area is made up of rivers and lakes. Altogether 60 per cent of the country is mountainous, (the highest peaks are Monte Rosa at 4,634 metres and Mischabel at 4,545 metres), ranges consisting of the Alps and Jura surround a central plateau made up of hills, plains and lakes including Lake Geneva (surface area 581 km³), Constance, Neuchatel and part of Lake Maggiore. The rivers Rhone, Rhine, Aare and Reuss flow through Switzerland. According to the Swiss Federal Statistic Office (SFSO), the area covered by settlements has grown by approximately 15 per cent since the early 1980s. Buildings account for roughly half of this settled area, transport infrastructure for a third, while the rest is divided between industry, landfills, recreational area and parks.

The climate is temperate with variations according to altitude. Winters are cold with either snow or rain. Summers are warm and humid.

To view a map, please consult http://www.lib.utexas.edu/maps/cia08/switzerland_sm_2008.gif

Population

The estimated total resident population at the end of 2011 was 7,954,662. In 2011, the most densely populated city was Zurich with 377,000 inhabitants, followed by Geneva with 188,200, Basle with 164,500, Berne with 125,700 and Lausanne with 129,400.

A number of languages are spoken in Switzerland; 64 per cent speak German, 20 per cent French, 6 per cent Italian, and 1 per cent Romansch. Nine per cent speak other languages.

Births, Marriages and Deaths

The birth rate in Switzerland had been falling and the population is ageing which is leading to concerns for the future particularly in the area of social security. Live births were recorded at 74,494 in 2007, down from the 1997 figure of 80,584, however, the number of births recorded in 2009 rose to 78,286, 80,290 in 2010 and 80,808 in 2011. The number of deaths recorded in 2008 was 61,233, down from the 1997 figure of 62,839 the number of deaths in 2009 was recorded at 62,476, 62,649 in 2010 and 62,091 in 2011. Approximately 42,083 marriages took place in 2011and 17,566 divorces were recorded. In 2007, 165,634 immigrants arrived and 90,175 people emigrated. (Source: SFSO)

Public Holidays 2014

1 January: New Year's Day
2 January: New Year holiday
18 April: Good Friday
21 April: Easter Monday
1 May: Labour Day
29 May: Ascension Day
9 June: Whit Monday
1 August: National Day
24 December: Christmas Eve (pm only)
25 December: Christmas Day
26 December: St. Steven's Day
31 December: New Year's Eve (pm only)

EMPLOYMENT

Most jobs in Switzerland are held in the tourist industry, followed by the manufacturing, industry and energy sectors; financial services such as insurance and banking; health and social work; construction. The following table gives employment statistics in recent years.

Employment by Economic Activity

Sector	2007	2008
Agriculture, hunting, forestry & fishing	164,000	171,000
Mining & quarrying, manufacturing & utilities	668,000	680,000

- continued

Construction	276,000	266,000
Wholesale & retail trade & repairs	552,000	564,000
Hotels & restaurants	154,000	155,000
Transport, storage & communications	218,000	222,000
Financial intermediation	238,000	244,000
Real estate, renting & business activities	505,000	517,000
Public administration & defence, compulsory social security	216,000	219,000
Education	326,000	343,000
Health & social work	515,000	540,000
Other community, social & personal service activities	284,000	300,000
Other	7,000	8,000

Source: Copyright © International Labour Organization (ILO Dept. of Statistics, http://laborsta.ilo.org)

The recent rise in unemployment figures is mainly attributable to the global economic downturn, particularly in western European and US markets with which the Swiss economy is closely linked. Unemployment is higher amongst unskilled workers and is slightly higher amongst the French- and Italian-speaking population. Unemployment has also been higher in recent years amongst those workers aged 15-25. Figures for 2007 put the unemployment rate at 3.7 per cent, 3.4 per cent in 2008, 4.1 per cent in 2009, 4.2 per cent in 2010, 3.6 per cent in 2011 and 3.7 per cent in 2012.

Figures from Swiss Federal Statistical Office put the number of persons employed in 2012 at 4,759,000 of which 2,622,000 were male and 2,138, were females, 3,402,000 were Swiss nationals and 1,358,00 were foreigners. That year an average of 170,000 people were unemployed.

BANKING AND FINANCE

Currency

One Swiss franc (Sfr) = 100 rappen or centimes

GDP/GNP, Inflation, National Debt

During the 1990s the Swiss economy grew very slowly but began to improve in 1997, recording a growth rate of 3.0 per cent in 2000. The effects of the global downturn in economic growth then began to be felt and figures for 2002 show that GDP grew by only 0.1 per cent. The Swiss economy is heavily based on foreign trade. The average annual increase in GDP between 1975-90 was 2.0 per cent, between 1990-96, average increase was 0.0 per cent and the average increase between 1996-2000 was 2.3 per cent.

Along with the rest of the world Switzerland has experienced the global downturn of the economy and the Swiss economy was forecast to be in recession in 2009 with economic growth that year predicted at 0.0 per cent. Switzerland has not fared as badly as some economies and in 2008 the economy showed growth of 1.9 per cent also that year Switzerland was ranked as the second most competitive economy by the World Economic Forum. Figures for 2010 showed that the Swiss economy grew by 2.6 per cent but was expected to slow again in 2011 in response to other global economies and the strength of the franc. The rate fell to 1.9 per cent in 2011. Forecast figures for economic growth were put at 1.7 per cent for 2013 and 2.0 per cent for 2014.

Switzerland is famous for its large banking sector and it is this which is contributing to the fall in the economy. One of its largest banks, UBS, suffered losses following the collapse of the American sub-prime mortgage sector and had to be helped out by the government and the Swiss National Bank. The tourism, banking, engineering, and insurance sectors are the main contributors to the economy.

GDP at current prices

Year	SF billion
2003	451
2004	465
2005	479
2006	508
2007	541
2008	568
2009	554
2010*	574
2011*	587

*Provisional figures
Source: Swiss Federal Statistical Office 2013

Gross Value Added by Industries, figures in Millions of Swiss francs (current prices)

Classification	2010*	2011*
Agriculture, forestry & fishing	4,336	4,308
Mining & quarrying	893	807
Manufacturing	100,183	102,016
Energy supply, water supply, waste management	11,456	11,450
Construction	29,509	31,072
Trade; repair of motor vehicles	91,688	91,634
Transportation & storage	22,970	24,203
Information & communication	21,903	22,601
Accommodation & food service activities	11,666	11,479
Financial & insurance service activities	59,846	60,520

- continued

Real estate activities, professional, scientific & technical activities	39,774	41,278
Administrative & support service activities	9,497	9,937
Public administration	55,662	57,181
Education	2,736	2,785
Human health & social work activities	33,916	35,007
Arts, entertainment, recreation & other services	8,865	8,642
Activities of households as employers and producers for own use	38,110	40,018
Total before adjustment	543,009	554,940
Taxes on products	32,210	34,920
Subsidies on products	-2,906	-3,075
Total after adjustment	574,314	586,784

* provisional figures
Source: SFSO April 2013

Estimated figures for 2008 put inflation at 2.4 per cent, -0.8 per cent in 2009 and -0.6 In April 2012.

Public debt in 2001 as a percentage of GDP was 49.6. National debt for 2000 was estimated to be CHF 207.5 billion and CHF 253.2 in 2005.

Foreign Investment
Most foreign investment comes from the European Union.

Balance of Payments / Imports and Exports
Switzerland is the EU's second largest customer, after the USA. Around 80 per cent of Switzerland's imports come from the EU and it comes third after the USA and Japan in supplying goods and services to the EU. Around 60 per cent of exports go to EU countries. Principal exports of Switzerland are chemicals, machinery and electronics, high precision instruments, including watches, jewellery, metals and agricultural goods. Principal imports include machinery, chemicals and vehicles.

The following table shows the value of foreign trade in recent years of key goods in million francs.

Product	1990	2010	2011
Imports			
Agricultural & forestry products	8,095	13,398	13,319
Textiles, clothing, shoes	8,806	5,956	8,880
Chemicals	10,625	37,787	37,435
Metals	9,025	14,379	14,715
Machinery, electronics	19,794	31,438	30,680
Vehicles	10,230	16,581	16,838
Instruments, watches	5,786	18,620	18,088
Total Imports	96,611	183,436	184,540
Exports			
Agricultural & forestry products	2,998	8,498	8,439
Textiles, clothing, shoes	4,984	3,386	3,249
Chemicals	18,422	75,909	74,647
Metals	7,537	12,739	13,034
Machinery, electronics	25,527	36,435	36,889
Vehicles	1,485	4,013	4,672
Instruments, watches	13,330	36,971	41,254
Total	88,257	203,484	208,203

Source: SFSO, Statistical Data on Switzerland 2013

2009, Key Trading Partners in Million Francs

Country	Imports	Exports
Germany	59.5	42.0
Italy	19.2	16.3
France	15.9	14.9
USA	9.2	21.3
Great Britain	6.4	10.0
China	6.3	8.8
Austria	8.0	6.6
Netherlands	8.0	5.2
Spain	5.2	5.8
Japan	4.1	6.7

Source: SFSO, Statistical Data on Switzerland 2013

Central Bank
Banque Nationale Suisse, PO Box 4388, Börsenstrasse 15, CH-8022 Zurich, Switzerland. Tel: +41 (0)1 631 3111, fax: +41 (0)1 631 3911, e-mail: snb@snb.ch, URL: http://www.snb.ch
Chairman of the Governing Board: Thomas J. Jordan (page 1451)

Stock Exchanges
Bern Stock Exchange, URL: http//www.bernerboerse.ch
Swiss Stock Exchange, URL: http//www.swx.com

Chambers of Commerce and Trade Organisations
Zentralschweizerische Handelskammer URL: http//www.cci.ch
Schweizerische Zentrale fur Handelsförderung / Swiss Office for Commercial Expansion (OSEC), URL: http//www.osec.ch
Camera di commercio dell'industria e dell'artigianato del Cantone Ticino, URL: http//www.cciate.ch

Chambre du commerce et d'industrie de Genève, URL: http//www.ccig.ch
Chambre de commerce et d'industrie du Jura, URL: http//www.cci.ch/jura
Chambre neuchâteloise du commerce et de l'industrie, URL: http//www.cnci.ch
Chambre vaudoise du commerce et de l'industrie, URL: http://www.cci.ch

Trade Unions
Schweizerischer Gewerkschaftsbund, URL: http//www.sgb.ch

MANUFACTURING, MINING AND SERVICES

Primary and Extractive Industries
Switzerland has hardly any mineral deposits worth exploiting. In 2005, only 4,300 people were employed within the mining and quarrying industry.

Energy
Due to the lack of fossil fuels in the country the Swiss rely heavily on the one resource that is plentiful in the country: hydropower. There are approximately 450 hydropower stations which provide about 60 per cent of Swiss electricity production. The exploitation of nuclear energy as a source for generating electricity began in the 1960s and there are now five operational reactors: Beznau I, Beznau II, Mühleberg, Gösgen, and Leibstadt. Plans for further nuclear power stations have been abandoned due to opposition.

The Swiss reactor centre at Wurenlingen has operated under government direction since 1960, and has the following main research facilities: swimming-pool reactor SAPHIR, engineering test reactor DIORIT, sub-critical assembly MINOR, a hot laboratory and assorted test laboratories for physics metallurgy and other sciences. The Société Nationale pour l'Encouragement de la Technique Atomique Industrielle is also developing a heavy-water moderated pressure tube reactor.

The following table shows the breakdown of final consumption according to energy resource in 2009 Terajoules.

Source	Terajoule
Crude oil	483,280
- Used for combustion	190,210
- Used as fuel	293,070
Electricity	206,980
Natural gas	106,340
Coal & coke	6,290
Wood, charcoal	35,660
District heating	16,060
Household & industrial waste	10,640
Other renewable energy sources	12,310
Total	877,560

Source: SFSO, Statistical Yearbook 2011

Figures for 2011 show that Switzerland produced 62.9 billion kWh of electricity, 40.6 per cent came from nuclear power stations, 30.3 per cent from hydro electricity storage power stations, 23.4 per cent from hydroelectricity turbine power stations, and 5.6 per cent from conventional thermal power.

Most of the oil that Switzerland imports came from Libya and Nigeria but in October 2008 Libya cancelled all oil deliveries after Colonel Gaddafi's son Hannibal and his wife were arrested for assault. Charges were later dropped. Natural gas is also imported using European pipelines and accounts for around 9 per cent of energy consumption.

Manufacturing
The main products of the Swiss manufacturing sector are machine tools, precision tools, vehicle construction, electrical engineering, light engineering, chemical and pharmaceuticals, optics and watch making.

2008 figures show that the Swiss metal industry has a total work force of 109,300. The main product groups are steel, aluminium, foundries, metal construction, metal products and metal processing. The Swiss oil and chemical industry had a total work force in 2005 of 68,500. The main product groups within the chemical industry were basic chemical products, pharmaceuticals, dyestuffs and industrial auxiliaries, soaps, cosmetics, detergents, other end products (including photochemicals) and plastics.

In the field of precision engineering Switzerland is famous for its watches and chronometres, computers, electronic and optical products; figures for 2008 show that around 115,600 people were employed in this area.

Recent figures show the Swiss food, beverages and tobacco industry has a workforce of over 66,500. The main product groups of this industry are meat products, dairy products, confectionery and chocolates, bakery products, coffee and tea products, soups, vinegars, mustards, pasta products, brewery products, mineral water, soft drinks and tobacco products.

The Swiss textiles and clothing industry has a workforce of approximately 18,300. The main products of this industry are knitted articles, embroidered goods, textile finishing, apparel and lingerie, jersey and knitwear; leather articles and footwear.

The Swiss wood, paper, publishing and printing industry has a workforce of about 80,500. The main products of this industry are paper products (paper, cardboard, raw material for corrugated cardboard) and printed products (books, newspapers, magazines). The Swiss wood and furniture industry has been adversely affected by environmental factors. As a result of severe storms wood prices have fallen drastically. The main products of this industry are forest products, wood and furniture (sawmill products, plywood and particle board, joinery products, wood products and furniture).

SWITZERLAND

The following table shows annual average industrial production in recent years, 1995 =100:

Industry	2007	2008	2009
Food & beverages & tobacco	101.8	105.8	102.0
Textiles & garments	92.5	82.4	67.9
Leather goods & footwear	61.1	61.7	46.6
Timber working & processing (excl. furniture)	126.2	124.9	119.1
Paper, cardboard, publishing & printing	103.5	101.1	91.9
Chemical industry	283.3	279.8	295.7
Rubber & plastics	142.2	143.6	118.3
Other products of non-metallic minerals	206.2	204.0	183.7
Metal working & processing	127.4	124.6	107.6
Machinery	132.2	136.4	103.3
Electronics, precision mechanics, optical equipment, watches	152.1	163.4	145.8
Vehicle manufacture	103.7	107.9	94.7
Other industrial output	114.2	112.9	96.4
Total industrial output	148.6	150.6	137.8

Source: SFSO, Statistical Yearbook 2011

Service Industries

Due to its excellent skiing facilities Switzerland has a large tourist industry, employing approximately 23.7 per cent of the workforce. Most recent figures show that chalets and holiday apartments provide most of the accommodation for tourists with 360,000 beds, followed by hotels and spas with 263,000 beds, collective establishments with 222,000 beds, campsites with 206,000 places and youth hostels with 6,000 beds. There are over 64 million overnight stays in Switzerland every year. (Source: SFSO)

Provisional figures for 2011 show Switzerland had 15.6 million visitors including domestic tourism, generating receipts of CHF 15,577 million. Visitors mainly come from Germany, USA, UK, Japan, France, Netherlands and Italy.

Switzerland Tourism, Tödistrasse 7, PO Box 8027, Zurich, Switzerland. Tel: +41 (0)1 288 1111, fax: +41 (0)1 288 1205, e-mail: postoffice@switzerland.com, URL: http//www.myswitzerland.com

A large proportion of the service sector is made up banking and insurance companies. Recent figures show that Switzerland has over 370 banks and banking contributes over 7 per cent of GDP. For years Switzerland has been known for its discreet banking system. Although secrecy regarding accounts still exists, anonymity has been abolished. The following table shows the number of banks and their assets at the end of 2011.

Bank Categories	No.	Assets, mill. CHF
Cantonal Banks	24	499,385
Major Banks	2	1,466,696
Regional & savings banks	66	101,117
Raiffeisen Banks *	1	155,889
Other Banks	174	508,637
Branches of Foreign Banks	32	56,813
Private Banking	13	54,398
Total	312	2,792,935

* = an assoc. with 470 mem. banks
Source: SFSO

Agriculture

Recent figures show that over 170,000 people are engaged in agriculture. Most of the holdings are medium-sized to small: 6,819 farms have less than 3 hectares; 15,529 between 3 and 10 hectares; 22,521 between 10 and 20 hectares; 18,075 between 20 and 50 hectares; 1,522 over 50 hectares.

Only around a quarter of Switzerland can be used for agriculture. Total agricultural land in 2009 was 1,056,000 hectares. Recent figures show that around 11 per cent of agricultural land is used for organic farming.

There were 708,000 head of cattle in 2009 and 1,557,000 pigs. (Source: SFSO)

Agricultural Output in 2011

Product	%
Crop output	42.6
Cereals	3.8
Forage plants	9.5
Vegetables and horticultural products	14.2
Fruits & grapes	5.6
Wine	4.2
Other crop outputs	5.2
Animal output	47.4
Cattle	12.2
Pigs	8.7
Milk	21.2
Other animals & animal products	5.2
Agricultural services output	6.5
Non-agricultural secondary activities	3.5

Source: SFSO Statistical Data on Switzerland 2013

The total value of production of agricultural products in 2011 was 10,166 million CHF up from 10,081 million CHF in 2010.

Forestry

Figures for 2009 showed that forest area covered 1,255,141 hectares. That year 4,879,701 m³ of timber was produced 68.6 per cent was softwood and 31.4 per cent was hardwood.

COMMUNICATIONS AND TRANSPORT

Travel Requirements

Citizens of the USA, Canada and Australia require a passport valid for three months beyond the length of stay but do not need a visa for stays of up to 90 days. EU subjects holding a valid national identity card, providing not taking up employment, did not require a passport or a visa for stays of up to 90 days, however in December 2008 Switzerland joined the EU's Schengen Agreement.

Passengers arriving at Basle or Geneva airports can enter either France or Switzerland, provided their documents for the country of entry are in order; both airports have two different exits, one to France and one to Switzerland. Therefore passengers can exit to the French part of the airport with a valid French or Schengen visa, if required.

National Airlines

SWISS Air Line Ltd, previously, Swissair-Schweizerische Luftverkehr A.G. (declared bankrupt in 2001), URL: http://www.swiss.com

International Airports

Geneva International Airport - Cointrin, URL: http://www.gva.ch
Zurich Airport, URL: http://www.surich-airport.com
Federal Office for Civil Aviation, URL: http://www.bazl.admin.ch/

Railways

The Swiss Federal Railways carry 270 million persons and up to 45 million tons of freight every year over a network of approximately 5,000 km.

In October 2000 work began on a tunnel through the Gottard mountain range. At 36 miles it will be the longest rail tunnel in the world, and will run from Erstfield south of Zurich to Bodio north of the Italian border. Completion is set for 2016.

Geneva, Basle, Bern, Neuchâtel and Zürich all have tram and light railway networks.

SBB/CFF (Swiss Federal Railways), URL: http://www.sbb.ch
BLS Loetschbergbahn AG, URL: http://www.bls.ch
Schweizerische Südostbahn AG, URL: http://www.suedostbahn.ch
Furka-Oberalp-Bahn, URL: http://www.fo-bahn.ch
Chemin de Fer du Jura (Jura Railways), URL: http://www.cj-transport.ch
Montreux-Oberland Berneois (Golden Pass), URL: http://www.goldenpass.ch
Rhätische Bahn (Rhaetian Railway), URL: http://www.rhb.ch
Centovalli Railway, URL: http://www.centovalli.ch

Roads

The road network in Switzerland covers an estimated total of 71,297 km with over four million registered vehicles. Vehicles are driven on the right.
Bundesamt für Strassen/Office fédéral des routes, (Federal Office for Roads), URL: http://www.astra.admin.ch

The following table compares road traffic figures for 2000 and 2009.

Road Traffic	2000	2009
Passenger cars	3,545,247	4,009,602
Goods vehicles	278,518	327,808
of which delivery trucks	227,316	276,236
Motorbikes	493,781	642,777

Source: SFSO

Shipping

Despite being a landlocked country, Switzerland does have a merchant shipping industry of some 30 ships. Basel, on the Rhine, is used as the home port.

HEALTH

Health insurance is compulsory in Switzerland. The Swiss health service is beginning to feel the effects of an ageing population. Figures for 2009 show that life expectancy in Switzerland is approximately 84 years for females and 80 years for males. The main causes of adult mortality, for both females and males, are cardiovascular diseases and cancer.

Figures for 2009 show that total expenditure on health care was the equivalent of 11.4 per cent of GDP. General government expenditure on health accounted for 59.7 per cent of total expenditure on health and private expenditure for 40.3 per cent (out-of-pocket expenditure 75.7 per cent, private pre-paid plans 21.9 per cent). Total per capita expenditure on health amounted to US$5,108 in 2009, compared to US$3,519 in 2000.

Figures from 2000-10 show that there are 29,680 doctors (40.7 per 10,000 population), 116,249 nurses and midwives (159.6 per 10,000 population), 3,987 dentists (5.5 per 10,000 population) and 4,235 pharmaceutical personnel. There were approximately 53 hospital beds per 10,000 population.

In 2009 the infant mortality rate (probability of dying before first birthday) was 4 per 1,000 live births and the child (under-five years old) mortality rate was also 4 per 1,000 live births. The main causes of death in the under-fives are: prematurity (17 per cent), congenital abnormalities (27 per cent), and pneumonia (1 per cent).

All the population have access to improved drinking water and sanitation. (Source: WHO)

EDUCATION

Each canton is more or less responsible for the education it provides, and there is therefore no one centralised system. However certain common characteristics can be defined and in recent years reforms have taken place to include a nationally recognised vocational university qualification.

Pre-school Education
In all cantons children have the 'right to receive pre-school education' for at least one year (sometimes two) before they start their compulsory education. Pre school education is not compulsory, however, and with the exception of certain special institutions, it is free.

Primary/Secondary Education
Compulsory education lasts for nine years, from the age of six or seven to 15 or 16. Some cantons offer a tenth school year. Students are taught in the language they speak either French, German or Italian. In all cantons, compulsory education comprises primary (four to six years) and lower secondary (three to five years) education. At the outset of secondary school students are streamed according to ability. Pupils then have the choice of moving on to Secondary level II or vocational training. Secondary level II consists of sixth form colleges, diploma middle schools and vocational training that involves practical training with a company, coupled with regular attendance at a vocational college.

Higher Education
There are currently seven universities of applied sciences which have emerged from the former Higher Schools of Engineering and Architecture, Economics and Business Administration, Design, Social Work, Health, Music and Fine Arts, two Federal Institutes of Technology and 10 cantonal universities of which Basle is the oldest, having been founded in 1460.

Number of Students in Education

Educational Level	2009-10
Pre-education	147,200
Primary	492,508
Lower secondary	289,636
Upper secondary	315,548
Postsecondary but non-tertiary education	16,353
First stage of tertiary education	228,519
Second stage of tertiary education	20,120
Unclassifiable	12,524

Source: SFSO

Figures for 2006 from UNESCO show that 16.3 per cent of total government expenditure went on education (5.6 per cent of GDP) of which 39 per cent went on secondary education, 29 per cent on primary education and 27 per cent on tertiary education.

RELIGION

There is no State religion. The constitution has declared religious belief to be a private matter in which the State has no right to interfere but which has a right to the protection of the State against the domination of any other religious community. Recent figures show that approximately 46 per cent of the population is Roman Catholic, while 40 per cent is Protestant. (Source: SFSO) Switzerland is home to some 315,000 Muslims, 26,000 Buddhists, 24,000 Hindus and has a Jewish community of around 18,000.

Switzerland has a religious liberty rating of 8 on a scale of 1 to 10 (10 is most freedom). (Source: World Religion Database).

In November 2009 the Swiss voted in favour of a referendum to ban the building of minarets in Switzerland. The referendum was tabled by the Swiss People's Party, (SVP), as they saw minarets as a sign of Islamisation. In recent years, the rising number of immigrants has become an issue in Swiss politics, more than 57 per cent of voters and 22 out of the 26 cantons supported the ban.

Bishops' Conference: URL: http://www.kath.ch/
Federation of Swiss Protestant Churches (Schweizerischer Evangelischer Kirchenbund, Fédération des Eglises protestantes de la Suisse): URL: http://www.sek.ch / www.feps.ch
Schweizerischer Israelitischer Gemeindebund/Fédération suisse des communautés israélites (Swiss Federation of Jewish Communities): URL: http://www.swissjews.org

COMMUNICATIONS AND MEDIA

Newspapers
Recent figures show that daily newspapers have a total circulation of approximately 2,691,800 copies per day. Although the country has a wide range of print media, more and more daily newspapers are merging due to a shift in advertising expenditure from print to other media. There is full editorial freedom in the press and generally operates along linguistic and regional lines. The market is now dominated by free papers. (Source: SFSO)

Main newspapers read in German, French and Italian are:
Tages Anzeiger, URL: http://www.tagesanzeiger.ch
Tribune de Geneve, URL: http://www.tdg.ch
Il Corriere del Ticino, URL: http://www.cdt.ch
Neue Zürcher Zeitung, URL: http://www.nzz.ch
Le Temps, URL: http://www.letemps.ch

Broadcasting
Swiss Broadcasting Corporation, URL: http://www.srgssrideesuisse.ch
SF-DRS, German-language public broadcaster. URL: http://www.drs.ch/www/de/drs/nachrichten.html
RTSI, Italian-language public broadcaster. URL: http://www.rsi.ch/home.html
RSR, French-language public broadcaster. URL: http://www.rsr.ch

Telecommunications
The Post Office, Telephones and Telegraphs Operations is the largest employer in the country with one or more post offices for each local authority and approximately 62,000 employees. The telephone system is a state monopoly administered by the Federal Posts. Recent figures estimate that there are over 4.5 million telephone connections, with an additional 811,000 mobile phones in use. (Source: SFSO).

Recent figures show that Switzerland had 4 million internet users in the first quarter of 2008. Over 75 per cent of households have a PC and at the end of 2007 there were 2.3 million broadband connections. Figures for 2010 show that over 80 per cent of the population are internet users.

ENVIRONMENT

Current threats to the environment are air and water pollution, damage to forests, soil erosion and extermination of flora and fauna.

Switzerland is a party to the following international agreements: Air Pollution, Air Pollution-Nitrogen Oxides, Air Pollution-Persistent Organic Pollutants, Air Pollution-Sulfur 85, Air Pollution-Sulfur 94, Air Pollution-Volatile Organic Compounds, Antarctic Treaty, Biodiversity, Climate Change, Climate Change-Kyoto Protocol, Desertification, Endangered Species, Environmental Modification, Hazardous Wastes, Marine Dumping, Marine Life Conservation, Ozone Layer Protection, Ship Pollution, Tropical Timber 83, Tropical Timber 94, Wetlands, and Whaling. Switzerland has signed but not ratified the Law of the Sea agreement.

According to figures from the EIA, Switzerland's total carbon dioxide emissions in 2010 were 45.55 million metric tons.

SPACE PROGRAMME

Switzerland's space policy is based around the following: development of space applications to improve the quality of life; commitment to space exploration; scientific, technological and industrial contributions to make Switzerland a competitive and significant partner. It is a member of the European Space Agency. In 2012, Switzerland announced it was planning to launch a cleanup satellite to clear orbital debris.

STATES OF THE WORLD

SYRIA

Syrian Arab Republic

Al Jumhuriya al Arabiya as Suriya

Capital: Damascus (Population estimate, 2011: 2 million)

Head of State: Bashar al-Assad (President) (page 1373)

Vice President: Farouk al-Shara

Vice President: Najah al-Attar

Assistant Vice President: vacant

National Flag: Three equal horizontal colours red, white and black with two green five angled stars at the centre of the white.

CONSTITUTION AND GOVERNMENT

Constitution

Syria became a fully independent country in 1946. It came under army dictatorship in 1949, headed by Brigadier Adib Shishakly. Through 1950 and 1951, Lieutenant-Colonel Shishakly maintained a cabinet and worked through civilian ministers. The Constituent Assembly drafted a Constitution, which was passed in September 1950. In December 1951, Lieutenant-Colonel Shishakly carried out a second *coup d'état*, and ruled as dictator until February 1954 when he was overthrown in a coup. Arab nationalist and socialist elements came to power.

Political instability, the parallelism of Syrian and Egyptian policies, and the appeal of Egyptian President Gamal Abdel Nasser's leadership in the wake of the 1956 Suez crisis created support in Syria for union with Egypt. On 22 February 1958 Syria and Egypt formed the United Arab Republic but Syria seceded, following a military coup in September 1961, and reestablished itself as the Syrian Arab Republic. Various coups followed. On March 8, 1963, leftist Syrian Army officers established a National Council of the Revolutionary Command (NCRC), a group of military and civilian officials who assumed control of all executive and legislative authority. The takeover was engineered by members of the Arab Socialist Resurrection Party (Ba'ath Party), which had been active in Syria and other Arab countries since the late 1940s. On February 23, 1966, a group of army officers carried out a successful, intra-party coup, dissolved the cabinet and the NCR, and designated a regionalist, civilian Ba'ath government. On November 13, 1970, Minister of Defense Hafiz al-Asad affected a bloodless military coup, ousting the civilian party leadership and assuming the role of prime minister.

Hafiz Al-Asad died in June 2000, after 30 years in power. Parliament immediately amended the constitution, reducing the mandatory minimum age of the President from 40 to 34 years old, which allowed his son, Bashar Al-Asad to be eligible for nomination by the ruling Ba'ath party. On July 10, 2000, Bashar Al-Asad was elected President by referendum.

The president, approved by referendum for a 7-year term, is also Secretary General of the Ba'ath Party and leader of the National Progressive Front (a coalition of ten political parties authorized by the regime). The president has the right to appoint ministers, declare war and states of emergency, issue laws (which require ratification by the People's Council), declare amnesty, amend the constitution, and appoint civil servants and military personnel. The Emergency Law, which effectively suspends most constitutional protections for Syrians, has been in effect since 1963. The Syrian constitution of 1973 requires that the president be Muslim but does not make Islam the state religion.

Following unrest in 2011, there are reports the constitution is to be revised, lessening the power of the Ba'ath Party.

International Relations

Syria has good relations with Iran; the two countries signed a memorandum of defence understanding in June 2006. In November 2006 Syria and Iraq agreed to restore diplomatic relations after almost 25 years, and in January 2007 President Talabani visited Damascus. In December 2006, the two countries signed a Memorandum of Security Understanding aimed at improving border security and combating terrorism and crime; however, Iraq would like more commitment from Syria in preventing Iraqi and Arab elements based in Syria from contributing financially or militarily to the insurgency in Iraq.

Syria's relations with Turkey have improved since resolution of the problem of the Kurdish PKK terrorist groups based in Syria.

Syria brought an end to the civil war in Lebanon in the 1980s, but maintained a military presence there up until April 2005, despite the UN Security Council Resolution of September 2004 requiring all foreign forces to withdraw from Lebanon. Syria is suspected of involvement in the murder of the former Lebanese Prime Minister and critic of Syria, Rafic Hariri; he and 19 others were killed in a car bomb attack in February 2005. A UN International Independent Investigation Commission (UNIIIC) was set up to look into the attack, and reported that it was unlikely that the murder of Hariri could have been carried out without the knowledge of Syrian intelligence. In October 2008, Syria established diplomatic relations with Lebanon for first time since both countries became independent in the 1940s.

Syria has been in conflict with Israel since the war of 1967, when Israel annexed the Golan Heights from Syria. The country has been under a state of emergency ever since. Negotiations in January 2000 broke down when Israel refused to accept a Syrian condition that it must

withdraw from the Golan Heights. Approximately 1,000 Israeli settlers live there. President Bashar al-Asad claims to be committed to achieving peace with Israel, though Syria's support for Palestinian groups appears to contradict this aim.

Syria has been widely condemned internationally for its actions following the Arab Spring.

Recent Events

After thirty years of rule, President Hafez Assad died in June 2000 leaving his son, Bashar Assad, as his successor. Bashar Assad was inaugurated as President of Syria on 17 July 2000 after winning over 97 per cent of the vote in a referendum. The turnout was 94 per cent.

In May 2004 the USA announced economic sanctions against Syria in response to Syria's alleged support for terrorism, and its failure to stop militants entering Iraq. The UN Security Council called for all foreign forces to leave Lebanon but Syria continued to deploy its troops in the country. In February 2005 the former Lebanese prime minister, Mr Hariri, was killed in Beirut and Syria was accused of involvement. In April Syria claimed to have withdrawn all troops from the Lebanon. In October, a UN report confirmed that Syrian officials were the key suspects in the murder of Mr. Hariri, but Syria denied involvement.

In July 2006, Israel's bombardment of Lebanon caused an influx of refugees to Syria. In November 2006 Iraq and Syria restored diplomatic relations after nearly a quarter century, and in March the following year, the European Union reopened dialogue with Syria. In September 2007, the Israeli air force carried out an attack on a military site in northern Syria. Following talks in Paris, Syria and Lebanon agreed to re-open embassies, and diplomatic relations were formally re-established in October 2008.

A car bomb attack on the outskirts of Damascus, on the 27th September 2008, left at least 17 people dead and 14 wounded. The blast happened near buildings used by security forces at an intersection leading to an important Shia shrine.

In July 2009, the US Special Envoy, George Mitchell, visited Syria for talks with President Assad on peace in the Middle East. In February 2010, the US posted its first ambassador to Syria for five years. However, in May 2010, the US renewed sanctions against Syria.

Demonstrations and political unrest swept through the Arab world in early 2011 including Syria where the situation quickly deteriorated. The government has responded to political demonstration with force. There have been some attempts to calm the situation with political concessions but not enough to appease the protestors. In March 2011 the cabinet resigned. On April 3 President Assad asked the former minister for agriculture Dr Adel Safar to form a new government.

The situation became increasingly bloody. Human rights groups estimated that 500 people had been killed during the month. The government responded with force and in May tanks entered Deraa, Banyas, Homs and the outskirts of Damascus. As the unrest continued, in June the government announced a crack down on what it termed an armed insurrection in the north of the country. Troops were sent to the towns of Jisr al-Shughour, Maarat al-Numan and Khan Sheikhoun. Thousands were forced to flee into neighbouring Turkey.

In a vain attempt to gain control, the government made some concessions to the protesters; an emergency law which had been in place since 1963 was lifted and many detainees were released under a conditional amnesty. Protesters continued to demand greater political freedom, an end to corruption, and more action on poverty.

Following mass demonstrations in Hama, President Assad sacked the governor of the province and sent in troops: many people were killed. In August 2011 the EU announced further sanctions and the USA and the EU called for President Assad to step down. The casualties continued to increase: more than 3,000 people have been reported killed during the unrest.

In October 2011, Syrian opposition groups said they had formed a united common front and launched a joint National Council. Burjahm Ghalioun, a French based academic, was named chairman.

On 2 November 2011 Syria accepted a peace plan proposed by the Arab League to try and end seven months of violence. Terms included an end to violence and killing; release of recently detained prisoners; withdrawal of security forces from cities; access to media and human rights groups; and government-opposition dialogue to begin within two weeks. However, violence continued. In late November the Arab League suspended Syria from its membership and approved sanctions against Syria including freezing of assets and an embargo on investments. In December 2011 Syria agreed to allow observers from the Arab league into the country. It also released 700 detainees from prison. Thousands of people in Homs lined the streets to greet the observers.

In January 2012 a suicide bomber killed 26 people in Damascus, the government announced it would respond with force. In February the UN proposed a resolution condemning Syria's crackdown on anti-government protestors, the resolution failed to pass as China and Russia vetoed the proposal. On February 6, government forces began artillery fire on the city of Homs which has been seen as a anti-government stronghold. It was finally taken by Syrian forces after a month-long bombardment in which up to 700 people were reported killed. The former head of the UN, Kofi Annan, was dispatched to Syria to propose a peace plan and ceasefire. After several days of negotiations, Syria said it would agree to the peace-plan and withdraw security forces from populated areas within 48 hours of a ceasefire. However, the violence continued with hundreds of people killed in clashes between rebels and the government. On 8 April the government announced that the army would not withdraw until it had received written guarantees from the rebels that they would cease all violence. The rebels refused so to do, saying they did not recognise the government as legitimate.

However, despite the truce, the violence is continuing. It was reported in May 2012 that shelling by Syrian forces in the town Souran had killed over 30 people including children. There were further reports of atrocities: on 27 May over 100 people were reported to have been killed in Houla, allegedly by Syrian heavy weaponry. This was denied by the government who blamed the deaths on terrorists. A further 30 people were reported to have been killed in Hama and violence continues in te city of Aleppo. The UN Security Council condemned Syria and called on the government to withdraw its heavy weaponry from residential areas.

In June 2012, a Turkish military jet was shot down over its coast by Syria, Turkey asked for a meeting with NATO to discuss the incident.

On July 9, Kofi Annan, the UN and Arab League's envoy to Syria, began talks with President Assad including the possibility of a transitiaonal unity government

On July 18, a suicide bomber attacked the security headquarters in Damascus. The defence minister Gen. Daoud Rajiha was killed along with his deputy, President Assad's brother-in-law Assef Shawkat. The national security chief and interior minister were also believed to have been badly hurt. In one of the bloodiest days of the conflict, an estimated 200 people were killed. Following the suicide attack violence spread to other cities in Syria, including Aleppo. The government launched attacks on the city to recapture it but made only limited headway.

Early in August the UN General Assembly passed a resolution demanding that President Assad resign. High profile defections were reported mostly notably that of the prime minister, Riad Hijab. The minister for health, Wael Nader al-Halaqi, was appointed prime minister on 9 August. Lakhdar Barhimi replaced Kofi Annan as the new UN-Arab League envoy.

In September 2012 Turkey called for the UN to set up refugee camps within Syria, Syrian rebels said any camps would need to be protected by international air cover. Later that month both the UK Prime Minister David Cameron and the US Secretary of State Hillary Clinton, called on the UN Security Council to renew its efforts to tackle the crisis in Syria.

In October 2012, the UN-brokered a ceasefire during the Islamic holiday of Eid al-Adha, but this broke down following continued government attacks.

Figures from the Syrian Arab Red Crescent in 2012 showed that 2.5 million people had been displaced within Syria.

In November 2012 the Israeli military fired on Syrian artillery units after several months of occasional shelling from Syrian positions across the Golan Heights, this was the first such return of fire since the Yom Kippur War of 1973.

Later that month several major opposition forces came together as the National Coalition for Syrian Revolutionary and Opposition Forces at a meeting which took place in Qatar. The meeting also included the Syrian National Council. Some Islamist militias including the Al-Nusra and Al-Tawhid groups, refused to join the Coalition. In December the coalition was recognised as the legitimate representative of the Syrian people by the US, UK, France, Turkey and the Gulf States.

In January 2013, Syria accused Israeli jets of attacking a military research centre near Damascus.

In February 2013, seven new ministers were appointed.

In March 2013, Syrian warplanes bombed the northern city of Raqqa after control was seized by rebels. The US and Britain pledged non-military aid to the rebels. France and Britain proposed lifting the European Union arms embargo. The Rebel National Coalition elected an interim 'prime minister', technocrat Ghassan Hitto.

In April 2013, the US and Britain asked for an investigation into reports that Syrian government forces had used chemical weapons.

In April 2013, the prime minister Wael Nader al-Halqui, survived a bomb attack in Damascus.

In April 2013, the chairman of the Opposition National Coalition, Moaz al-Khatib resigned, he complained of manipulation by foreign backers. Socialist George Sabra, the leader of the older opposition Syrian National Council replaced him.

In May 2013, the EU announced it would not renew its arms embargo to Syria, potentially permiting the arming of rebels. As fighting continued, the government and Heznollah forces recpatured the strategically-significant-important of Qusair. The EU said it would not renew its arm embargo on the Syria rebels.

In May 2013, France said it had evidence that the government had used sarin nerve gas in attacks on both rebels and civilians.

In June 2013 at the G8 summit in Ireland, leaders agreed to increase humanitarian aid and strengthen diplomatic pressure for peace talks.

Legislation
The legislature is unicameral. The chamber, the People's Council (Majlis al-Sha'ab), has 250 members who are directly elected for a four-year term. There are 15 multi-seat constituencies; 167 seats are guaranteed for the National Patriotic Front. Syria is a single-party state.
Majlis al-Sha'ab (People's Assembly), Damascus. Tel: +963 11 2226 127, fax: +963 11 2246 495, email: peoplecouncil@net.sy, URL: http://syria-people-counsel.org

Cabinet (as at June 2013)
Prime Minister: Wael Nader al-Halaqi (page 1374)
Minister of Foreign Affairs, Minister of Expatriate Affairs: Waleed Al-Muallem (page 1376)
Defence Minister: Gen. Fajad Al-Freij
Minister of Interior: Mohamad Ibrahim Al-Shaar
Minister of Finance: Ismail Ismail
Minister of the Industry: Adnan As-Sahni
Minister of Health: Saad Assalam al-Nayef
Minister of Agriculture and Agrarian Reform: Ahamd Al-Qadri
Minister of Foreign Trade and Economy: Mohammad Mhabak
Minister of Public Works: Hussein Arnus
Minister of Electricity: Imad Mohammed Deeb Khamis
Minister of Petroleum and Mineral Resources: Sleiman Abbas
Minister of Local Administration: Omar Ibrahim Ghalawanji
Minister of Information: Omran Al-Zohbi
Minister of Presidential Affairs: Mansur Azzam
Minister of Culture: Lubana Mushaweh
Minister of Education: Hazwan Al-Wazz
Minister of Justice: Najem Hamad al-Ahmad
Minister of Higher Education: Mohammad Yahia Moalla
Minister of Transport: Mahmoud Saeed
Minister of Water Resources: Bassam Hana
Minister of Awqaf (Religious Trusts): Abdul-Sattar al-Sayed
Minister of Telecommunications and Technology: Imad Abdul-Ghani Sabbouni
Minister of Social Affairs: Kinda Shmat
Minister of Labour: Hassan Hijazi
Minister of Trade and Consumers: Qadri Jameel

Ministries
Office of the President, Mouhajreen, Presidential Palace, Abu Rumanch, Al-Rashid Street, Damascus, Syria. Tel: +963 11 223 1112, URL: http://www.basharassad.org/
Office of the Prime Minister, Shahbandar Street behind Central Bank, Damascus, Syria. Tel: +963 11 222 6001, fax: +963 11 223 3373
Ministry of Agriculture and Agrarian Reform, Jabri Street, Hejaz Street, Damascus, Syria. Tel: +963 11 222 2513, URL: http://www.syrianagriculture.org/
Ministry of Awqaf (Religious Endowments), Meysar Sayda Hafiza Square, Damascus, Syria. Tel: +963 11 441 9080, fax: +963 11 441 9969
Ministry of Telecommunications and Technology, Parliament Avenue, Damascus, Syria. Tel: +963 11 222 7033, fax: +963 11 224 6403
Ministry of Commerce, Economy and Foreign Trade, Meysalun Avenue, Bawabet el Salheya, Damascus, Syria. Tel: +963 11 221 3513, e-mail: econ-min@net.sy, URL: http://www.syrecon.org
Ministry of Culture, Rawda Str., Damascus, Syria. Tel: +963 11 333 8633, fax: +963 11 332 0804,
Ministry of Defence, Ommayad Square, Damascus, Syria. Tel: +963 11 372 0934
Ministry of Education, Abdul Rahruan Shabander Street, Damascus, Syria. Tel: +963 11 4448000, URL: http://www.syrianeducation.org
Ministry of Electricity, Victoria, Barada Bank, Damascus, Syria. Tel: +963 11 222 9654, fax: +963 11 222 3686
Ministry of the Environment, Salihiyeh, Damascus, Syria. Tel: +963 11 222 6000, fax: +963 11 333 5645
Ministry of Health, Parliament Ave, Damascus, Syria. Tel: +963 11 333 9601, fax: +963 11 222 3085, e-mail: health-min@net.sy
Ministry of Finance, Julce Jamal Street, Near CEntral Bank, Damascus, Syria. Tel: +963 11 219603, e-mail: mof@net.sy, URL: http://www.syrecon.org
Ministry of Foreign Affairs and Expatriates, Mouhajreen-Shora, Damascus, Syria. Tel: +963 11 333 1200, URL: http://www.ministryofexpatriates.gov.sy
Ministry of Housing, Youself Al Azmeh Square, Damascus, Syria. Tel: +963 11 221 7571, e-mail: mhu@net.sy
Ministry of Industry, Yousuf Al-Azmeh Square, Damascus, Syria. Tel: +963 11 223 1845, e-mail: min-industry@syria.net; URL: http://www.syrianindustry.org
Ministry of Information, Mezzeb Al-Baath Newspaper, Damascus, Syria. Tel: +963 11 666 4601, e-mail: moi@net.sy, URL: http://www.moi-syria.com
Ministry of Interior, Merjeh Circle, Barada River Bank, Damascus, Syria. Tel: +963 11 221 9401, fax: +963 11 222 3428
Ministry of Oil and Minister al Resources, Al-Adawi, Damascus, Syria. Tel: +963 11 445 1624, e-mail: mopmr@net.sy, URL: http://www.mopmr-sy.org
Ministry of Tourism, Victoria, Fourai Str. Damascus, Syria. Tel: +963 11 221 5916, fax: +963 11 224 2636, e-mail: min-tourism@mail.sy, URL: http://www.syriatourism.org
Ministry of Transport, Abou Roumaneh Avenue, Damascus, Syria. Tel: +963 11 333 6801, fax: +963 11 332 3317, URL: http://www.min-trans.net
Ministry of Irrigation, Fardou Street, Damascus, Syria. Tel: +963 11 222 1400, fax: +963 11 332 0691, URL: http://www.irrigation-sy.com/
Ministry of Justice, Nasr Avenue, Damascus, Syria. Tel: +963 11 221 4101, fax: +963 11 224 6250
Ministry of Labour and Social Affairs, Meysalun Avenue, Damascusm Syria. Tel: +963 11 222 5948, fax: +963 11 224 7499
Ministry of Local Administration, Youssef Al-Azmeh Square, Sanaa Street, Damascus, Syria. Tel: +963 11 231 8682, fax: +963 11 231 7949

Elections
The most recent presidential election was in May 2007 when Bashar al-Assad was re-elected for a second seven year term in office by parliament. This was followed by a referendum to confirm parliament's unanimous choice.

The most recent parliamentary elections were held in May 2012 and for the first time were contested by opposition parties. The Ba'ath party (and its allies) won with a large majority.

SYRIA

Political Parties

Arab Socialist Renaissance (Ba'ath) Party; National Progressive Front (allies of the Ba'ath Party). The age of suffrage is 18.

Diplomatic Representation

American Embassy, All operations suspended in February 2012. Abou Roumaneh, Al-Mansur St, No. 2, Damascus, Syria. Tel: +963 11 333 1342, fax: +963 11 2247938, URL: http://damascus.usembassy.gov/
Ambassador: vacant
British Embassy, All operations suspended March 2012. Kotob Building, 11 Mohamed Kurd Ali Street, Malki, PO Box 37, Damascus, Syria. Tel: +963 11 373 9241, fax: +963 11 373 1600, URL: http://ukinsyria.fco.gov.uk/en/
Ambassador: vacant
Syrian Embassy, 2215 Wyoming Avenue NW, Washington, DC 20008. Tel: +1 202 232 6313, fax: +1 202 234 9548, URL: http://www.syrianembassy.us
Chargé d'Affaires: Zouheir Jabbur
Syrian Embassy, 8 Belgrave Square, London, SW1X 8PH. Tel: +44 (0)20 7245 9012, fax: +44 (0)20 7235 4621, URL: http://www.syrianembassy.co.uk
Chargé d'Affaires: Ghassan Dalla
Permanent Mission of the Syrian Arab Republic to the UN, 820 Second Avenue; 15th Floor, New York , NY 10017, USA. Tel: +212 661 1313, fax: +212 983 4439, URL: http://www.un.int/syria/
Permanent Representative: Bashar Ja'afari, Ph.D

LEGAL SYSTEM

The legal system is based partly on French law and partly on Syrian statutes. Petty crimes are dealt with by peace courts and more serious cases go to courts of first instance. There are civil and criminal appeals courts, the highest being the Court of Cassation. The Supreme State Security Court tries political and national security cases and the Economic Security Court tries cases involving financial crimes; both of these courts operate under the state of emergency rules overriding constitutional defendants' rights.

Shari'ah courts apply Islamic law in cases involving personal status. The Druze and non-Muslim communities have their own religious courts.

With regard to human rights, the citizens of Syria cannot change their government, and an atmosphere of government corruption and impunity prevails. There have been recent instances of unlawful killings, and members of the security forces have tortured and abused prisoners. Arrests and detentions can be arbitrary, and citizens have been detained incommunicado. The authorities ignore privacy rights and there are restrictions on freedoms of speech, press, assembly, and association. The government discriminates against minorities, particularly the Kurds and the Ahvazis, and severely restrict workers' rights. Following the civil uprising the government launched a draconian crack-down on protests. The UN has accused the government of gross human rights abuses including murder, torture and rape. The attorney-general resigned in 2011 after witnessing mass executions.

Syria retains the death penalty, with can be used in cases of treason, murder, political acts such as bearing arms against Syria, desertion of the armed forces to the enemy and acts of incitement under martial law or in wartime, violent robbery, rape; verbal opposition to the government and membership of the Muslim Brotherhood. In 2010, seventeen people were reported to have been executed. Hundreds of people are believed to have died in extrajudicial executions since the civil uprising began.

LOCAL GOVERNMENT

Syria is divided administratively into 13 Mohafaza (province/county) and the city of Damascus. Each Mohafaza is divided into Manatika, and these Manatika are further divided into smaller units called Nahia. Each Nahia covers a number of villages, a village being the smallest administrative unit. In all there are 60 Mantika and 206 Nahia. Damascus City is a Mohafaza in its own right. Each Mohafaza is headed by a Mohafaz (Governor), appointed by the President and assisted by an elected provincial council. Each Mantika is headed by a Mudir el-Mantika; and a Nahia is represented by a Mudir el-Nahia. The villages are represented by one or more Mokhtars: village headmen who are responsible for the village and the surrounding farms. Mohafazat Centres are the chief cities after which the Mohafaza are named.

Despite the civil unrest, the most recent local elections were held in December 2011. More than 43,000 candidates competed for more than 17,000 seats. The elections were held under reformed rules. Turnout was very low, thought to be because of security concerns and in protest at the political situation.

Administrative Divisions

Mohafazat	Cities	Mantikas	Nahias
Damascus City	1	-	-
Damascus	22	9	27
Aleppo	8	8	31
Homs	7	6	17
Hama	5	5	17
Lattakia	4	4	17
Deir-ez-Zor	3	3	11
Idleb	7	5	19
Hasakeh	5	4	11
Al-Rakka	4	3	7
Al-Sweida	3	3	9
Dar'a	8	3	14
Tartous	5	5	22

- continued

Quneitra	2	2	4
Total	84	60	206

Source: Syrian Central Bureau of Statistics

AREA AND POPULATION

Area

Syria lies on the east coast of the Mediterranean Sea, bounded by Turkey to the north, Iraq to the east, Palestine and Jordan to the south, and Lebanon and Israel to the west. Israel occupied Syria's Golan Heights in 1967 and formally annexed them in 1981. Syria covers an area of 71,498 sq. miles; the western part of the country is mountainous, whilst the east comprises a semiarid plateau. The summers are hot and dry, and the winters bring rain.

To view a map, consult http://www.un.org/Depts/Cartographic/map/profile/syria.pdf

Population

In 2010, the population was estimated to be 20.4 million, with an average annual growth rate of 2.4 per cent for the period 2000-10. There are a further 20,000 Arabs living on the Golan Heights. Most people live in 1967 in the Euphrates River valley and along the coastal plain. An estimated 55 per cent of the population lives in urban areas. The most populated city is Aleppo, with around five million inhabitants. The city of Damascus has an estimated 2 million inhabitants, with a further two million living in the surrounding areas. Overall population density is about 140 per sq. mile. Tens of thousands of people were believed to have fled the fighting in the city over 2012.

Arabs, including some 500,000 Palestinian and up to 1.3 million Iraqi refugees, make up 90 per cent of the population. Kurds make up 9 per cent, and there are communities of Armenians, Circassians and Turkomans.

Arabic is the official language although French, English, Kurdish, Armenian, Aramaic and Circassian are also spoken.

Births, Marriages, Deaths

Estimated figures suggest that the birth rate in 2010 was 22.8 births per 1,000 people, whilst the death rate stood at 4.1 per 1,000 people. Infant mortality was 14 per 1,000 live births and the total fertility rate is estimated at 2.9 children per woman. Average life expectancy is 71 years for Syrian men, whilst women can expect to live for 76 years. Healthy life expectancy is put at 63 years. In 2010, an estimated 37 per cent of inhabitants were under the age of 14, and 6 per cent were 60 years and over. The median age is 21 years. (Source: http://www.who.int, World Health Statistics 2012)

Public Holidays 2014

1 January: New Year's Day
14 January: Mawlid al-Nabi (Prophet's Birthday)*
8 March: Revolution Day
17 April: Evacuation Day
6 May: Martyr's Day
29 June: Beginning of Ramadan*
29 July: Eid al-Fitr (End of Ramadan)*
6 October: October Liberation Day
5 October: Eid al-Adha* (Festival of the Sacrifice)
25 October: Muharram (Islamic New Year)*
3 November: Ashura
25 December: Christmas
*Islamic holiday based on lunar observation, variable

EMPLOYMENT

In 2008 the workforce was estimated to be around 5.5 million. Estimates on the unemployment rate vary between nine per cent and 20 per cent of the workforce. It is estimated that around 200,000 people join the workforce each year and there are fears that the economy cannot keep pace with population growth. Government and public sector employees constitute over a quarter of the total labour force. Government officials acknowledge that the economy is not growing at a pace sufficient to create enough new jobs annually to match population growth.

The three major employment sectors are services (66 per cent, including government employees who make up over 25 per cent of the total work force), agriculture (19 per cent) and industry (14 per cent).

BANKING AND FINANCE

Currency

The currency used in Syria is the Syrian Pound or Lira. There are 100 piasters to one Lira or Syrian Pound.

GDP/GNP, Inflation, National Debt

The economy has been adversely affected by the current political situation and unrest. Economic sanctions have been imposed by the Arab League, the EU, the USA and Turkey. Trade has been badly affected and sectors including tourism, oil and farming have contracted.

The Syrian economy is based principally on agriculture and oil, both sectors subject to uncertainties due to changes in oil prices and rain dependency respectively. The oil sector provides around 50 per cent of government revenues and about 40 per cent of its export receipts. Agriculture accounts for around 25 per cent of GDP and almost 20 per cent of employment. The present government is taking steps to diversify the economic base in preparation for the end of oil reserves; it is thought that Syria will be soon be a net importer of petrol. Before the conflict, financial services, construction, telecommunications, non-oil industry and trade were becoming increasingly important.

The government was also moving the country from a state-run economy towards a more market-based system, but progress was slow; privatisation of government enterprises is rejected for idealogical reasons, and major sectors continue to be state-controlled. The banking sector has seen rapid expansion since legalisation of private banking in 2001 and foreign exchange controls were reformed; in 2003 the government decriminalised private sector use of foreign currencies and in 2005, it allowed private banks to sell specific amounts of foreign currency to Syrian citizens and to the private sector for the purpose of financing imports. The current conflict has seen many investors withdraw their money. It is believed that the Syrian government has used a significant proportion of the country's hard currency reserves to prop up the pound, pay wages and for fuel subsidies.

Despite a decrease in oil production prior to the conflict, high oil prices buoyed the economy and provided short-term relief to problems in the non-oil sectors. GDP was estimated to be US$23 billion in 2006, real GDP growth averaging 5.5 per cent over the period 2003-2007. Figures for 2008 put GDP growth at 5.2 per cent. GDP was estimated to be US$59 billion in 2010 with a growth rate of 5 per cent. Due to the conflict, official figures are not available: GDP was estimated to be US$55 billion in 2011. The economy contracted further in 2012 by up to 20 per cent.

Inflation was estimated at over 4 per cent in 2011. Inflation is rising and was over 10 per cent in Q1 2012. Some estimates put it as high as 40 per cent. In Feburary 2012 the government doubled customs duties.

Current foreign debt is estimated to be around $6.8 billion.

Balance of Payments / Imports and Exports
The total volume of trade (imports plus exports) has grown from 48 per cent of GDP in 2000 to 60 per cent in 2006. Syria's export revenues amounted to US$13.6 billion in 2008, and were dominated by oil and minerals which accounted for around 40 per cent of total exports. Other major exported products include food and agricultural products, cotton and textiles. Syria exports mainly to Italy (19.6 per cent), France (8.8 per cent) and Saudi Arabia (8.7 per cent).

Imports cost the country $17.2 billion in 2008, and included refined petroleum products, food and agricultural products, machinery, transport equipment, chemicals and base metals. The main suppliers were China (6.5 per cent), Egypt (5.2 per cent) and South Korea (4.2 per cent).

Sanctions were imposed in 2011 by various bodies and countries including the Arab League, the EU and the USA.

Central Bank
Central Bank of Syria (Banque Centrale de Syrie), Altajrida Al Mughrabia Square, Damascus, Syria. Tel: +963 11 2212642, fax: +963 11 224 8328, URL: http://www.banquecentrale.gov.sy
Governor: Dr. Adib Mayaleh

Chambers of Commerce and Trade Organisations
Damascus Chamber of Commerce, URL: http://www.dcc-sy.com
Aleppo Chamber of Commerce, URL: http://www.aleppochamber.com/

MANUFACTURING, MINING AND SERVICES

Primary and Extractive Industries
The mining and quarrying industry is small. Main deposits under exploitation are bitumen, sodium chloride, natural asphalt and phosphate but it is believed there are also deposits of lead, copper, chrome and other minerals. Petrol and petroleum products are among Syria's main exports.

Total oil production in Syria was at its peak in 1995, at approximately 600,000 barrels a day. This figure had fallen to 426,000 barrels per day in 2008 and is expected to continue to fall as oil fields reach maturity. In 2009, it was estimated at 399,870 bbl/d. Consumption in 2009 was forecast to be 268,000 barrels per day, and Syria exported around 131,000 barrels per day in the same year. Proven oil reserves were estimated at 2.5 billion barrels as at the beginning of 2009. Syria has approximately 130 producing oil wells. It is anticipated that oil reserves could be exhausted within nine years. The Syrian Government is confronting this with increased investment in oil exploration (no new fields have been discovered since 1992) and production. Offshore exploration is underway. Syria is also starting to change from oil-fired to gas-fired electrical power plants.

International political pressure on Syria and the economic sanctions imposed in 2004 by the U.S. government, under the provisions of the Syria Accountability Act, has deterred much needed foreign investment in the oil sector. More sanctions were imposed in 2011 in response to the government crackdown on political opposition. Figures for 2011 show that production had fallen to 330,820 barrels per day, consumption was 25,000 barrels perday and exports were 72,820 barrels per day.

Syria has two state-owned refineries located at Homs and Banias. At present, production from these refineries is around 239,865 barrels a day. Syria has announced plans to construct two new refineries and increase refining capacity by around 380,000 bbl/d. The projects have been delayed by lack of foreign investment. In June 2011, Syria and Iraq signed an agreement to repair the existing 800,000 bbl/d pipeline system and to build two new pipelines including a 1.5 million bbl/d pipeline to transport heavy crude oil and a 1.25 milion bbl/d pipeline to carry light crude oil. Refining capacity in 2012 had fallen to 240,000 barrels per day. (Source: Energy Information Administration, EIA)

Syria has proven gas reserves of around 9.0 trillion cubic feet, mostly owned by the Syrian Petroleum Company (SPC). In 2010 Syria produced an estimated 316 billion cubic feet of natural gas, all of which was used domestically. There are plans to increase natural gas production in order to use it instead of oil in power generation, saving oil for exportation. Expansion of the gas network includes pipeline construction deals with Turkey and Azerbaijan. Syria, Iran and Iraq signed an agreement for construction of a 3,100 mile pipeline that would be able to transport 1.4Tcf/y of natural gas from Iran for export to Europe. Figures for 2011 show that 278 billion cubic feet were produced and consumption were 287 billion cubic feet. (Source: EIA)

Energy
Total energy consumption was an estimated 0.859 quadrillion Btu in 2009 and total production was 1.41 quadrillion Btu.

In 2009, Syria had electricity generating capacity of 8.2 GW, fueled mainly by oil and gas. Hydroelectricity accounted for 1.5 GW. Syria is in the process of converting oil-fired power plants to natural-gas-fired plants, in order to free up oil for export; around half of Syria's power plants now run on gas.

In 2009, Syria consumed 28.87 billion kWh, of the total 40.86 billion kWh produced. Syria had planning to increase capacity by some 3,500 megawatts by 2010. However, lack of capital investment has slowed progress. In order to attract the necessary capital, Syria recently opened the sector to Independent Power Projects (IPPs), and three projects are now ongoing.

In addition to the construction of new power plants, Syria is converting oil-fired power plants to natural-gas-fired plants, in order to free up oil for export. Around fifty per cent of Syria's power plants run on gas at present. A program of wind turbines is currently being developed, and Syria may collaborate with the EU on solar technology.

Syria's power grid is linked to that of several neighboring countries, including Jordan and Lebanon. (Source: EIA)

Manufacturing
Manufacturing in Syria combines the traditional with the modern; textiles and hides; food packaging, beverages and tobacco; cement; brassware; furniture making; paper printing and binding; chemical industries and products, including the refining of petroleum; non-mineral products; main natural industries; and manufactured mineral products and equipment.

Service Industries: Tourism
Syria is hoping to develop tourism as a major part of its economy. The number of visitors to Syria has risen from 815,000 in 1995 to around 4.2 billion in 2006. Most tourists (approximately 70 per cent) are from the Arab states. People travel from Greece and Turkey to shop at lower prices. However, the political climate continues to discourage visitors from Western Europe and the US.

Agriculture
The Government has made the agricultural sector a priority in recent years, in an effort to make the country self-sufficient in food, to improve export earnings and to slow down migration to the cities. Whilst most farms are privately owned, the government maintains control through the marketing and transportation infrastructure.

Some 75 per cent of Syria's land is used for agriculture; 29 per cent is arable and 46 per cent is used for pasture. The Government has invested in massive irrigation systems, especially in the north, to increase output. In 2002, 95 per cent of water resources was used for agriculture (though only 23 per cent of all arable land was irrigated). In 2003, there were 23 tractors and one harvester/thresher per 1,000 hectares. As a result of its efforts in this sector, Syria has gone from a net importer to an exporter of foodstuffs. Agricultural exports accounted for 19 per cent of total export revenue.

Agricultural Production in 2010

Produce	Int. $'000*	Tonnes
Indigenous sheep meat	790,851	290,455
Olives	768,995	960,400
Cow milk, whole, fresh	453,425	1,453,000
Tomatoes	427,327	1,156,300
Wheat	407,567	3,083,100
Cotton lint	320,428	224,200
Indigenous chicken meat	268,620	188,584
Sheep milk, whole, fresh	250,393	643,000
Anise, badian, fennel, corian	227,169	41,100
Almonds, with shell	215,716	73,100
Pistachios	188,838	57,500
Grapes	186,176	325,700

* unofficial figures
Source: http://faostat.fao.org/site/339/default.aspx Food and Agriculture Organization of the United Nations, Food and Agricultural commodities production

Climate change is resulting in a decrease in agriculture production and is adversely affecting the food security target of the government. In 2008, Syria had to import wheat for the first time since the early 1990s.

SYRIA

COMMUNICATIONS AND TRANSPORT

Travel Requirements
Citizens of the USA, Canada, Australia and the EU require a passport valid for at least six months and a visa unless in transit within 24 hours (and holding onward documentation and not leaving the airport). For stays of over 15 days, visitors should apply for a visa extension from the Emigration and Passport Department. Other nationals should contact the embassy to check visa requirements.

The government of Syria rigidly enforces restrictions on prior travel to Israel and refuses entry or transit to passengers holding a passport containing a visa for Israel, a stamp indicating an Israel-Jordan border crossing; or evidence of entry at Sharm El Sheikh, Rafha, Gaza or Nablus. The absence of entry stamps from a country adjacent to Israel, which the traveler has just visited, may lead Syrian immigration officials to refuse admittance. Entry into Syria via the land border with Israel is not possible.

Syria charges a departure tax.

National Airlines
Syrian Arab Airlines, established 1946.
URL: http://www.syriaair.com/SAA/HomepageEn.aspx

International Airports
Syria has three international airports, Damascus International Airport, Aleppo International Airport and Lattakia International Airport. There are over 100 airports in Syria, 29 of which are hard-surfaced. Over 5 million passengers used Damascus International Airport in 2010.

Railways
The railway network extends over 2,000 km.

Roads
The total road work network extends over 68,000 km. Vehicles are driven on the right.

Ports and Harbours
The main ports are Latakia and Tartous, Baniyas and Jablah.

HEALTH

The country has a system of both private and free medical care. State hospitals provide medical care for those unable to pay. In recent years, as a result of government efforts to provide universal health coverage, there have been many improvements in the health sector. According to UN estimates, the percentage of the population with access to health services rose from 76 per cent in the mid 1980s to almost 90 per cent in 2000. In 2009, the government spent approximately 6.0 per cent of its total budget on healthcare, accounting for 46 per cent of all healthcare spending. An estimated 0.8 per cent of expenditure is from external resources. The remainder of healthcare expenditure is private, out-of-pocket expenditure. Total expenditure on healthcare equated to 3.5 per cent of the country's GDP. Per capita expenditure on health was approximately US$95. In 2005-10, there were 30,702 physicians (15 per 10,000 population), 38,070 nurses and midwives, 16,169 dentistry personnel (7.9 per 10,000 population), 16,579 pharmaceutical personnel (8.1 per cent).

The infant mortality rate dropped from 123 per 1000 live births in 1970 to 14 in 2010 and the under-fives mortality rate to 16 per 1,000 live births. Chronic under nutrition has been falling rapidly in urban areas since 1996, but in rural areas some 28.6 per cent of children under five years are classified as stunted and 10 per cent underweight. A programme of vaccinations against diseases such as cholera, measles, polio and tuberculosis has covered between 97 and 100 per cent of the population, and there has been a dramatic reduction of communicable diseases.

According to the latest WHO figures, in 2010 approximately 90 per cent of the population had access to improved drinking water. In the same year, 95 per cent of the population had access to improved sanitation. (Source: http://www.who.int, World Health Statistics 2012)

EDUCATION

Schooling consists of six years of primary education followed by a 3-year general or vocational training period and a 3-year academic or vocational programme. Primary education is free and compulsory from ages six to 11 years old. In recent years government expenditure on education has increased and education from grades 1 - 9 have become compulsory and free. Secondary education, split into two three-year segments, lasts from 12 to 18 years old. Over 95 per cent of schools are state run.

Around 11 per cent of Syrian children attend pre-primary schools. 97 per cent of boys and 92 per cent of girls of the relevant age group are enrolled in primary schools. These percentages fall to 64 and 61 respectively in secondary education.

There are several universities, two of the largest at Damascus and Aleppo. There are approximately 170,000 students enrolled in higher education and an estimated 4,000 students at universities abroad, mainly in Europe and the USA.

The adult literacy rate in 2006 is estimated to have risen to 89 per cent for men and 75 per cent for women over the age of 15. Within the age group 15-24, the literacy rate is higher, at around 95 per cent for men, and 91 per cent for women. Both figures are above the regional average of 86.7 per cent. (Source: UNESCO, UIS, Feb. 2009)

RELIGION

The state religion is Islam. Religious freedom is provided for by the Constitution and formally recognised religious minorities are generally respected and can practise their faith. Sunni Muslims make up 74 per cent of the population, Alawite, Druze and other Muslim sects a further 16 per cent. There is a substantial Christian minority in Syria (10 per cent), and 3 per cent of the people are Druze. There are very small Jewish communities in Damascus, Al Qamishli, and Aleppo, totalling some 100 people.

Syria has a religious liberty rating of 4 on a scale of 1 to 10 (10 is most freedom). (Source: World Religion Database)

COMMUNICATIONS AND MEDIA

Freedom of the press is limited: the government and ruling party control and own much of the media. After the succession of President Bashir Al-Assad, the press enjoyed some freedom. Stricter laws have since been imposed. Self censorship is common and the press is also censored. Criticism of the president is not allowed. There is strict control of the interent and many websites are blocked.

Newspapers
The main newspapers in terms of circulation are: Al Baath, Tichrin (http://www.tishreen.info), Syria Times (http://syriatimes.tishreen.info) and Al Thawra (URL: http://www.thawra.com/). All are based in Damascus and have a circulation of approximately 75,000.

Broadcasting
Syrian TV operates two terrestrial and one satellite television channel, broadcasting in Arabic, English and French. PRivate TV netowrks and radio stations do operate but may not transmit news. Pan-Arab TV stations are popular.
Syrian TV, URL: http://www.rtv.gov.sy/

Syrian Arab Republic Radio is the state-run radio station. In 2005, Al-Madina FM, the country's first private radio station, was launched, but it cannot transmit news or political content. Several private radio stations now operate.

Telecommunications
The system is undergoing improvements and its coverage of rural areas is also being expanded. The number of fixed-line connections has increased considerably since 2000, and the mobile service has also grown rapidly; in 2010 there were approximately 4 million mainline telephones in use, and 11 million mobile phones. Use of the internet more than doubled over 2006-08, from 1.5 million users to 3.5 million. By 2011 it was estimated to be over 4.5 million. The internet has been widely used by the opposition to tell the outside world of the situation in Syria. Social media and the internet have been widely used by protesters. However, the government exercises strict internet censorship and blocks many sites.

ENVIRONMENT

The major environmental problems in Syria include deforestation, overgrazing, soil erosion, desertification, water pollution and water supply. Most water basins are under stress, and water deficits are expected to worsen, due to large and unsustainable water usage in agriculture and an expected increase in urban water demand.

Syria is a party to the following agreements: Biodiversity, Climate change; Climate Change-Kyoto Protocol, Desertification, Endangered Species, Hazardous waste, Ozone layer protection, and Wetlands. It has signed but not ratified Environmental Modification.

According to figures from the EIA, in 2010, Syria's emissions from the consumption of fossil fuels totalled 63.10 million metric tons of carbon dioxide. (Source: EIA)

TAJIKISTAN

Republic of Tajikistan

Jumkhurii Tojikiston

Capital: Dushanbe (Population estimate: 600,000)

Head of State: Emamoli Rakhmon (President) (page 1500)

National Flag: Three horizontal stripes of red, white and green, charged with a crown and seven stars, all in gold in the centre.

CONSTITUTION AND GOVERNMENT

Constitution

Originally an Autonomous Republic within the Uzbek SSR, Tajikistan became a constituent republic of the USSR on 5 December 1929. The Tajik SSR included the Gorny Badakhshan Autonomous Region.

In the era of perestroika, the Supreme Soviet granted legal status to the Tajik language in July 1990 and subsequently declared the republic a sovereign state. Following the Moscow coup on 19-21 August 1991 Communist Party property was nationalised. Rakhmon Nabiyev was sworn in as President on 2 December and formed a government in December 1992.

Tajikistan became a signatory to the Commonwealth of Independent States on 21 December 1991, and this was ratified on 25 December. In September 1992, however, President Nabiyev was removed from office following his replacement of the Communist government with a Revolutionary Coalition Council. After the ensuing outbreak of civil war, Nabiyev's government resigned. Following the imposition of a state of emergency, a ceasefire was signed in December 1996 between President Rakhmonov and insurgent leader Sayed Abdullo Nuri.

A new Tajikistan Constitution was agreed in November 1994 by 90 per cent of the electorate and had the immediate effect of increasing the President's powers. It was amended in 1999 when a presidential term of seven years was set, which was non-renewable. A referendum was held in June 2003 to decide if President Rahmonov could run for two further seven year terms. Over 90 per cent of the vote was in favour. The referendum was criticised by the opposition.

To consult the constitution, please visit: http://www.wipo.int/wipolex/en/details.jsp?id=10268

International Relations

Tajikistan has good relations with the EU and US. Tajikistan and Russia did a deal whereby Russia wrote off around $250 million of bilateral debt in exchange for investment in the Tajik hydro-electric and aluminium industries. Tajikistan generally has good relations with neighbouring countries.

Recent Events

President Rakhmonov ordered the population to drop Russian-style surnames in 2007 to break with the nation's Soviet past. He removed the Russian suffix "-ov" from his own surname, and is now known as President Rakhmon.

The winter of 2007-08 proved to be the worst for fifty years, with millions of people trying to survive without heat, water or electricity in temperatures well below zero. Furthermore, there were severe food shortages, and the cost of food tripled over the winter, partially due to rising world prices. In February, the Tajik government appealed for emergency aid.

In 2009, Tajikistan agreed that the US military could transport non-military supplies to Afghanistan through its territory.

Elections to the Assembly of Representatives took place on 28 February 2010 and elections for the National Assembly took place on 28 March 2010.

In January 2011 Tajikistan settled a long-standing dispute with China by agreeing to give up some land.

Upper House

The National Assembly or *Majlisi Milli*, has a total of 33 members, 25 of whom are indirectly elected. The others are appointed by the president and serve a five year term.
National Assembly, Dushanbe, Tajikistan. Tel: +922 372 212366

Lower House

The Assembly of Representatives, or *Majlisi Namoyandagon*, has a total of 63 members who are elected for a term of five years.
Assembly of Representatives, Rudaki Ave. 42, Dushanbe, Tajikistan. Tel: +922 372 212366, URL: http://www.parlament.tj/

Cabinet (as at June 2013)
Prime Minister: Oqil Oqilov (page 1490)
First Deputy Prime Minister: Matlubkhon Davlatov
Deputy Prime Minister: Rugiya Atoyevna Ourbonova
Deputy Prime Minister for the Economy: Murodali Alimardonov
Minister of Foreign Affairs: Hamrokhon Zarifi (page 1543)
Minister of Defence: Col.-Gen. Sherali Khayrulloyev
Minister of Internal Affairs: Ramazon Rakhimov

Minister of Justice: Rustam Mengliyev
Minister of Education: Abdujabbor Rahmonov
Minister of Economic Development and Trade: Sharif Rahimzoda
Minister of Transport: Nizom Hakimov
Minister of Finance: Safarali Namiddinov
Minister of Labour and Social Welfare: Mahmadamin Mahmadaminov
Minister of Agriculture and Environmental Protection: Oosim Rahbarovich Oosimov
Minister of Land Improvement and Water Economy: Rahmat Bobokalonov
Minister of Culture: Mirzoshohrukh Asrorov
Minister of Industry and Energy: Sherali Gulov
Minister of Health: Nusratullo Fayzullovevich Salimov
Chairman, State Committee on National Security: Gen. Saimumin Yatimov
Chairman, State Committee on State Property: Davlatali Saidov
Chairman, State Committee for Environmental Protection: Khursandgul Zikirov

Ministries

Office of the President, 80 Rudaki Street, Dushanbe, Tajikistan. Tel: +992 372 212911, fax: +992 372 216971, URL: http://www.president.tj/
Ministry of Transport, 14 Ainy Str., Dushanbe 734023, Tajikistan. Tel: +992 372 211713, fax: +992 372 212003, e-mail: mtdh@tajik.net, mintrans@tajnet.com, URL: http://www.mintrans.tajnet.com/
Ministry of Environmental Protection and Water Resources, Bokhtar Street 12, Dushanbe, Tajikistan. Tel: +992 372 211839, fax: +992 372 211839
Ministry of Foreign Affairs, e-mail: info@mfa.tj / admin@mfa.tj, URL: http://mid.tj/
Ministry of Defence, 59 Bokhtar St., Dushanbe, Tajikistan. Tel: +992 372 211809
Ministry of Internal Affairs, 29 Gorky St., Dushanbe, Tajikistan. Tel: +992 372 211071, fax: +992 372 246879
Ministry of Justice, 25 Rudaki Str., Dushanbe, Tajikistan. Tel: +992 372 214405
Ministry of Education, 13 Chekhov St., Dushanbe, Tajikistan. Tel: +992 372 233392
Ministry of Economy and Trade, 44 Rudaki Street, Dushanbe, Tajikistan. Tel: +992 372 216914, fax: +992 372 213754
Ministry of Communications, 57 Rudaki Street, Dushanbe, Tajikistan. Tel: +992 372 212284, fax: +992 372 214739
Ministry of Finance, 3 Academicians Rajabovs St., Dushanbe, Tajikistan. Tel: +992 372 273941
Ministry of Agriculture, 44 Rudaki Street, Dushanbe, Tajikistan. Tel: +992 372 211596
Ministry of Land Improvement and Water Economy, 78 Rudaki Street, Dushanbe, Tajikistan. Tel: +992 372 211012
Ministry of Culture, 34 Rudaki St., Dushanbe, Tajikistan. Tel: +992 372 210305
Ministry of Labour, Employment and Social Welfare, 5/2 A. Navoi St., Dushanbe, Tajikistan. Tel: +992 372 361837
Ministry of Health, 69 Shevchenko St., Dushanbe, Tajikistan. Tel: +992 372 213064
Ministry of Emergency Situations and Civil Defence, 59 Bokhtar Street, Dushanbe, Tajikistan. Tel: +992 372 231778

Elections

The last presidential elections were held in November 2006. President Rakmonov retained power in elections that were criticised by observers as being neither free nor fair. The next elections are due to take place in November 2013.

Elections to the Assembly of Representatives took place on 28 February 2010. Early results suggested that the ruling People's Democratic Party had won with over 70 per cent of the vote. The results suggested that the People's Democratic Party of Tajikistan won 55 seats, and the following all won two seats: Islamic Renaissance Party of Tajikistan, the Communist Party of Tajikistan, the Agrarian Party of Tajikistan and the Economic Reform Party. International observers deemed that the election did not meet international standards and that there were widespread occurrences of electoral fraud.

Political Parties

People's Democratic Party of Tajikistan; United Tajik Opposition (UTO); Islamic Rebirth Party; Communist Party; Democratic Party; Socialist Party; Social Democratic Party.

Diplomatic Representation

Tajik Embassy, 26-28 Hammersmith Grove, London, W6 7BA, UK. Tel: +44 (0)208 834 1003, e-mail: infor@tajembassy.org.uk, URL: http://www.tajembassy.org.uk/
Ambassador: Erkin Kasymov
US Embassy, 109-A Ismoili Somoni Ave., Dushanbe, Tajikistan, Tel: +992 37 229 2000, fax: +992 37 229 2050, e-mail: usembassydushanbe@state.gov, URL: http://dushanbe.usembassy.gov/
Ambassador: Kenneth E. Gross Jr.
British Embassy, 65 Mirzo Tursunzade Street, Dushanbe 734002, Tajikistan, Tel: +992 37 224 2221, fax:+992 37 227 1726, URL: http://ukintajikistan.fco.gov.uk/en/
Ambassador: Trevor Moore
Embassy of the Republic of Tajikistan, 1005 New Hampshire Ave.., NW, Washington, D.C. 20037, USA. Tel: +1 202 223 6090, fax: +1 202 223 6091, URL: http://www.tjus.org/
Ambassador: Nuriddin Shamsov
Permanent Mission to the United Nations, 136 East 67th Street, New York, NY 10021, USA. Tel: +1 212 744 2196, fax +1 212 472 7645, URL: http://www.un.int/wcm/content/site/tajikistan/
Permanent Representative: Sirojidin Aslov

TAJIKISTAN

LEGAL SYSTEM

The legal system is based on civil law, and influenced by the traditions of Islamic law. Tajikistan's independent judicial power is exercised by the Constitutional Court, the Supreme Court, the Supreme Economic Court, the Military Court, the Court of Gornyi Badakhshan Autonomous Region, and regional courts. Judges' terms are currently five years.

The government's human rights record is poor. The right of the people to change their government is limited. There have been recent instances of torture and abuse by security forces with impunity, and there is widespread official and societal corruption. Prison conditions are life-threatening, and pretrial detention can be lengthy. There is restricted freedom of speech, press, association and religion. Tajikistan retains the death penalty for some cases of murder and rape, terrorism and genocide. The most recent execution took place in 2004.

Constitutional Court, URL: www.constcourt.tj/eng/

LOCAL GOVERNMENT

Tajikistan is divided into two provinces or *viloyats*, Viloyati Khatlon (Qurghonteppa) and Viloyati Sughd (Khujand). Tajikistan also has one autonomous province or *viloyati mukhtor*, Kuhistoni Badakhshon, (Gorno-Badakhshan). Assemblies of people's deputies represent those living in regions, towns and districts. Such assemblies, elected for five years, are headed by a chairman, who is the President's representative.

AREA AND POPULATION

Area

Tajikistan is situated in the south-east of Central Asia. It shares its eastern and southern frontiers with the People's Republic of China and Afghanistan, Uzbekistan is to the west and Kyrgyzstan to the north. Its area is 143,100 sq. km. The Tien Shan and Pamir mountains occupy 93 per cent of the area (with nearly half of the mountains more than 3000 m high). The climate is extreme continental with very cold winters and hot dry summers.

To view a map, consult http://www.un.org/Depts/Cartographic/map/profile/tajikist.pdf

Population

World Health Organisation estimates placed the population at 6.879 million in 2010 with an annual population growth rate of 1.1 per cent for the period 2000-10. Approximately 70 per cent are Tajik, 25 per cent Uzbek, 3.5 cent Russian and the remainder Tatar, Kirghizian and others. The population is young; recent figures show that approximately 37 per cent of the population is below 15 years of age. Just 5 per cent are aged over 60 years. The median age was estimated at 20 years in 2010.

Most of the population live in the flatter areas of the country, notably the Ferghana Valley, the Gissar and the Vakhsh Valleys, and the Khatlon region. There are 18 towns; those with a population of over 100,000 are Dushanbe (582,500) and Leninabad. An estimated 26 per cent of the population lives in urban areas.

The official language is Tajik but Russian is widely spoken especially in urban areas.

Births, Marriages, Deaths

The population growth rate was estimated at 1.1 per cent over the period 2000-10, with an estimated 2010 birth rate of 27.9 births per 1,000 population and a death rate of 6.0 deaths per 1,000 population. Average life expectancy from birth in 2009 was 66 years for males and 69 years for females. Healthy life expectancy in 2007 was 57 years. The infant mortality rate in 2010 was 52 per 1,000 live births (down from 91 per 1,000 live births in 2004). The total fertility rate for women was 3.3 in 2010. (Source: http://www.who.int, World Health Statistics 2012)

Public Holidays 2014

1 January: New Year's Day
14 January: Birth of the Prophet*
8 March: International Women's Day
21 March: Persian New Year
5 May: International Labour Day
9 May: Victory Day
27 June: National Unity Day
9 September: Independence Day
29 July: Eid al-Fitr, Ramadan ends *
5 October: Eid al-Adha, Festival of the Sacrifice *
6 November: Constitution Day
* Islamic holidays depend on the sighting of the moon and so dates can vary.

EMPLOYMENT

Figures for 2006 show a labour force of 2,185,000. Participation in the labour force is 54 per cent. Of the 2,137,000 employed, 1,432,000 were engaged in the agricultural sector and 118,000 in industry. An estimated 48,000 were unemployed. The unemployment rate for 2004 and 2005 was 2.0 per cent it rose in 2006 to 2.2 per cent and 2.5 per cent in 2007. Estimated figures for 2009 put the labour force at 2.1 million with an unemployment rate of 2.1 per cent.

Total Employment by Economic Activity

Occupation	2004
Agriculture, hunting & forestry	1,361,000
Mining & quarrying	11,700

- continued	
Manufacturing	114,500
Electricity, gas & water supply	17,300
Construction	296,000
Wholesale & retail trade, repairs	202,100
Hotels & restaurants	23,800
Transport, storage & communications	64,400
Financial intermediation	18,900
Real estate, renting & business activities	16,600
Public admin. & defence; compulsory social security	70,600
Education	122,800
Health & social work	62,800
Other community, social & personal service activities	57,200
Households with employed persons	3,400
Other	9,500

Source: Copyright © International Labour Organization (ILO Dept. of Statistics, http://laborsta.ilo.org)

BANKING AND FINANCE

Currency
The unit of currency was the Tajik Rouble of 100 copeks. In October 2000 a new currency was introduced: the Somoni of 100 dirams.

GDP/GNP, Inflation, National Debt
Tajikistan is the poorest of the former Soviet republics and relies heavily on aid from Russia and remittances from Tajiks working abroad, particularly in Russia. Its infrastructure is poor: the rationing of electricity means many industries and IT cannot operate effectively. Most of the exports come from one aluminium plant (TALCO). Some 60 per cent of the population live below the poverty line; consequently many Tajiks work abroad and their remittances are a crucial part of the economy. One of the main aims of the government is to introduce economic stability which it hopes will then encourage foreign investment.

Of the 15 former Soviet Republics, Tajikistan has the lowest per capita GDP. In 2009 GDP was estimated at US$4.5 billion rising to US$5.50 billion in 2010. Figures for per capita GDP in 2009 was US$765. The growth rate that year was 3.4 per cent.

The agricultural sector contributes around 21 per cent of GDP, industry, 25.5 per cent and services, 53.6 per cent.

GDP by industrial origin at current market prices (million Somoni)

Origin	2008	2009	2010
Total	17,706.9	20,628.5	24,704.7
-Agriculture	3,517.9	3,827.0	4,630.6
-Manufacturing, Mining, Electricity, gas and water	2,515.8	2,957.4	3,113.1
-Construction	1,832.6	2,098.4	2,524.0
-Trade	3,573.4	4,340.0	4,711.3
-Transport and communications	1,782.2	2,264.9	1,900.5
-Finance	343.1	438.7	74.5
-Public administration	406.5	619.3	611.7
-Others	1,674.0	2,040.1	4,541.1
Net factor income from abroad	7,781.5	4,898.8	..
GNI	25,488.4	25,527.3	..

Source: ADB

GDP was estimated to be US$6 billion in 2011.

Inflation in 2009 was put at 6.4 per cent rising to 7.0 per cent in 2010. It rose to 9.1 per cent for 2011. Inflation was estimated to be 6.4 per cent in 2012.

Total debt was estimated at US$2.1 billion in 2011.

Balance of Payments / Imports and Exports
Major export products are cotton, aluminium, textiles, electricity and fruits, and the major import products are fuel, chemicals, machinery and foodstuffs. The following table shows external trade figures in recent years.

Exetrnal Trade, million US $

	2008	2009	2010
Exports, fob	1,409	1,010	1,195
Imports, cif	3,273	2,570	2,658
Trade balance	-1,864	-1,560	-1,463

Source: Asian Development Bank

Main export partners (2010) for Tajikistan are the Turkey (US$257 million), Russia (US$105 million), Uzbekistan (US$73.5 million), Iran US$51.8 million) and China (US$50.9 million). Top import partners include China (US$1,513 million), Russia (US$817 million), Kazakhstan (US$286 million) and Uzbekistan (US$129 million).

Central Bank
National Bank of the Republic of Tajikistan, PO Box 734025, Prospect Rudaki 23/2, Dushanbe, Tajikistan. Tel: +992 3772 217858, fax: +992 3772 212602, URL: http://nbt.tj/en
Chairman: Shirinov Abdujabbor

MANUFACTURING, MINING AND SERVICES

Primary and Extractive Industries

Lignite, oil, gas, lead, zinc, antimony, mercury, tungsten, molybdenum, bismuth and gold have all been found in Tajikistan. Proven oil reserves stood at 12 million barrels in 2012. Oil production was 0.22 thousand barrels per day in 2011. Consumption in 2011 was estimated to be 43.00 thousand barrels per day. Natural gas production was estimated at 1 billion cubic feet in 2011. Estimated consumption that year was put at 47 billion cubic feet with natural gas imports of 6 billion cubic metres. Figures for 2010 show that Tajikistan produced 218,000 metric tons of hard coal, compared to 105,000 metric tons in 2006 and 47,000 metric tons in 2003.

Energy

The energy infrastructure is poor and energy supply has been limited to four hours per day outside of the capital. In the winter of 2007/08 Tajikistan experienced an energy crisis when severe power shortages forced industries to shut down, rationing of energy in the capital and no supply of electricity in many rural areas. The opening of the Santuga hydro-electric plant in 2008 should dramatically improve the energy situation. At present, electricity is sometimes rationed during the winter.

Hydro-electric power stations make up the foundation of the Republic's power engineering. In 2010, electricity generation was 16.2 billion kilowatt hours of which 4.4 billion kWh was exported. Industry consumes almost two-thirds. The first unit of the Santuga-1 hydro-electric station finally came into operation in January 2008. Construction was suspended in the 1990s with the outbreak of civil war. Talks with Russia on completing construction began in 2003 and a deal was signed in 2004. The second unit became operational in July 2008 and the third in November. Construction began in the late 1980s but was beset by delays. The station currently generates some 4.5 million kWh per day and daily supply of electricity to the regions should be increased to eight hours. The estimated capacity of the power station is 670 MW and will generate an estimated 2.7 billion kWh per annum. Russia has a 75 per cent stake in the station.

Manufacturing

The manufacturing industry is hampered by poor facilities and during the winter month electricity is sometimes rationed which severely disrupts production. Most of the manufacturing plants from the Soviet era are no longer operational but have not been replaced. The industry is further hampered by poor energy supply. Non-ferrous metallurgy is developed, and the Republic produces farm machinery, household refrigerators, pipe fittings, transformers, cables and mineral fertilizers. Cotton ginning, carpet making and the production of cotton and silk are among principal activities of the textile industry and account for 9 per cent of exports. Other well developed branches of industry are vegetable canning, the production of vegetable oils and fats, cement and wine making. The TALCO alimuminum plant accounts for 75 per cent of exports.

Agriculture

Recent figures show that the area under cultivation was 4.3 million hectares, of which 75,200 hectares was private subsidiary agriculture and 19,000 hectares was commercial agriculture. Towards the end of 2000, Tajikistan's food production was under threat due to a prolonged drought. Following the severe winter of 2007/08, farmers were expected to face a difficult year with no stock or money to fund the 2008 planting.

Estimated figures for 2011 show that agriculture contributed 21 per cent of GDP, and employed nearly 50 per cent of the labour force.

Tajikistan is a principal producer of fine staple cotton. Essential oils and oil-bearing crops, grain (wheat, barley and rise) and tobacco are cultivated. Vegetables, fruit, grapes, melons and gourds are extensively grown. Animal husbandry (sheep, goats, cattle and horses) is concentrated in the mountain areas. Yaks are bred in the eastern part of the Pamir range.

Agricultural Production in 2010

Produce	Int. $'000*	Tonnes
Cotton lint	146,208	102,300
Tomatoes	124,913	338,000
Indigenous sheep meat	106,843	39,240
Potatoes	106,147	760,139
Cow milk, whole, fresh	104,272	602,000
Indigenous cattle meat	77,372	28,642
Wheat	75,236	857,545
Grapes	71,051	124,299
Onions, dry	62,380	297,000
Apples	48,342	156,600
Carrots and turnips	45,534	184,000
Vegetables fresh nes	40,439	214,600

* unofficial figures
Source: http://faostat.fao.org/site/339/default.aspx Food and Agriculture Organization of the United Nations, Food and Agricultural commodities production

COMMUNICATIONS AND TRANSPORT

Travel Requirements

Citizens of the USA, Canada, Australia and the EU require a passport valid for at least six months beyond the length of stay and a visa. Passport and visa regulations for all the CIS states are liable to change at short notice and therefore all travellers are advised to contact the nearest Tajikistan Embassy or Consulate for up-to-date details.

National Airlines

Tajik Airlines have signed an agreement with the UK company Euro Global Aviation of Britain to set up a new carrier under the name of TAL airlines. Routes include London-Dushanbe-Delhi and Dushanbe-London-Los Angeles.

Tajik Air State Airline, Titova Str., 32/1, Dushanbe, 734006, Republic of Tajikistan. Tel: +992 3772 223283, URL: http://www.tajikair.tj/eng

International Airports

Major airports are located at Pyandzh and in the capital Dushanbe.

Railways

The total length of the railway system in 2004 was 482 km. The system consists of three lines with a fourth planned from Kulyab to Kurgan-Tyube. Currently the lines run from Dushanbe via Kurgan-Tyube and Shaartuz to the Uzbekistan/Afghanistan border at Termez; one runs from Dushanbe, via Kurgan-Tyube to Tugul on the Afghanistan border; and one from Samarkand, via Khojand to the Fergana Valley. A train journey to Moscow takes five days crossing and crosses through Uzbekistan, Turkmenistan and Kazakhstan.

Roads

The total length of roads is an estimated 27,770 km, of which 17,700 are hard-surfaced. Vehicles are driven on the right.

Waterways

A ferry crossing runs between Afghanistan and Tajikistan across the Pyanj river but this service is likely to come to an end as the US funds a bridge across the river.

HEALTH

In 2009, the government spent approximately 5.9 per cent of its total budget on healthcare, accounting for 24.9 per cent of all healthcare spending. Private expenditure accounts for 75.1 per cent of total expenditure on health. External resources account for 8.9 per cent of total expenditure. Total expenditure on healthcare equated to 5.9 per cent of the country's GDP. Per capita expenditure on health was approximately US$44, compared with US$6 in 2000.

According to recent figures, a total of 1,105 hospitals exist within Tajikistan. In 2000-10 there were 61 hospital beds per 10,000 population. Figures for 2005-10 show that there are 14,459 physicians (21.0 per 10,000 population), 36,490 nurses and midwives (53 per 10,000 population), and 1,150 dentistry personnel. There are 52 hospital beds per 10,000 population.

In 2010, 64 per cent of the population had sustainable access to an improved water source and 94 per cent of the population had sustainable access to improved sanitation.

In 2010, the infant mortality rate (probability of dying by first birthday) per 1,000 live births was 52. The under-five mortality rate was 63 per 1,000 live births. The most common causes of death for the under-fives in 2010 were: prematurity (17 per cent), pneumonia (17 per cent), and diarrhoeal diseases (9 per cent). In 2005-11, an estimated 39.2 per cent of children were classified as stunted and 15 per cent as underweight. (Source: http://www.who.int, World Health Statistics 2012)

EDUCATION

Primary education lasts for four years, beginning at seven years of age. In 2007, 99 per cent of boys and 95 per cent of girls were enrolled in primary school. The pupil / teacher ratio in primary school was 22:1. Secondary education lasts for up to seven years, and begins at 11 years old, and in 2007, 87 per cent of boys and 75 per cent of girls were enrolled. Education up until the age of 17 is compulsory, free higher education was abolished in 2001. Tajik is the language of instruction but some private schools teaching in Russian and Uzbek do exist, Russian is a compulsory subject at secondary school. Sixteen per cent of children enroll in tertiary education. In 2007, 18.2 per cent of total government expenditure was spent on education of which 54 per cent went on secondary education.

In 2004 the Aga Khan, leader of the world's Ismaili Muslims announced plans for a university to be built in the Pamir mountains which would benefit people living in the mountains of Tajikistan as well as Afghanistan, China, Kyrgyzstan, Uzbekistan, Iran, Turkey and Pakistan. It was hoped that the first students would enroll in 2007.

In 2007 the average adult literacy rate was 99.6 per cent. (Source: UNESCO)

RELIGION

The main religion in Tajikistan is Islam with 85 per cent Sunni Muslim, 5 per cent Shi'a (Ismaili) Muslim and 10 per cent other including Orthodox Christians and Jews.

Tajikistan has a religious liberty rating of 5 on a scale of 1 to 10 (10 is most freedom). (Source: World Religion Database)

COMMUNICATIONS AND MEDIA

The constitution provides for freedom of the press but is not widely observed. The government controls most printing presses. Defamation is a criminal offense. There are reports of harassment of journalists.

Newspapers

Tajikistan has over 200 newspapers, including government owned and those issued by political parties. Government papers include Jumhuriyat, Khalq Ovozi and Narodnaya Gazeta. The People's Democratic Party publishes Minbar-i Khalq.

Broadcasting

Television is the most popular medium. There are four national state channels: Shabakai Yakum (TV Channel One); TV Channel Safina (URL: http://www.safina.tj/); Children's TV Channel Bahoriston; and TV News Channel Jahonnamo. Jahonnamo started broadcasting in November 2008 and will cover some 60 per cent of the country. There are more than 10 independent TV stations. Foreign stations are available through cable. Russian programmes are popular.

Radio coverage extends throughout the country. There are four national state radio stations: Tajik Radio (URL: http://radio.tojikiston.com/), Radio Tajikistan, Radio-i Dushanbe and Radio Farhang. Radio Farhang (Culture) started broadcasting in November 2008.

Telecommunications

There is limited fixed line availability but mobile phone coverage now extends to all major cities and town. Figures for 2008 estimated 250,000 telephone lines to be in use. In 2008 there were estimated to be 3.5 million mobile phones. Tajikistan has around 600,000 internet users.

ENVIRONMENT

The main environmental issues affecting Tajikistan are inadequate sanitation facilities, increasing levels of soil salinity, industrial pollution, excessive pesticides, over-utilisation of water from the basin of the shrinking Aral Sea.

In 2003, carbon dioxide emissions were 0.7 metric tons per capita compared to 3.7 metric tons in 1992. In 2010, Tajikistan's emissions from the consumption of fossil fuels totalled 6.68 million metric tons of carbon dioxide. (Source: EIA)

On an international level Tajikistan is a party to international conventions on: Biodiversity, Climate Change, Climate Change-Kyoto Protocol, Desertification, Environmental Modification, Ozone Layer Protection and Wetlands.

TANZANIA

United Republic of Tanzania

Jamhuri ya Muungano wa Tanzania

Capital: Dodoma (Seat of Government, population estimate: 326,000); Dar-es-Salaam, (Commercial capital, population estimate: 2,500,000)

Head of State: H.E. Jakaya Mrisho Kikwete (page 1456)

Vice-President: Dr Mohammed Gharib Bilal

President of Zanzibar: Ali Mohamed Shein (page 1513)

National Flag: A wide, yellow-bordered black band running diagonally from bottom left to top right, green above the band and blue beneath.

CONSTITUTION AND GOVERNMENT

Constitution

The United Republic of Tanzania was formed by the Union of the former Republic of Tanganyika and the People's Republic of Zanzibar. The Articles of Union were signed on 22 April 1964 by Mwalimu Julius K. Nyerere, on behalf of the Government of the Republic for Tanganyika, and the late Sheikh Abeid Amani Karume, on behalf of the Government of the People's Republic of Zanzibar.

The Articles of Union were subsequently approved and ratified by the Parliament of Tanganyika and the Revolutionary Council of Zanzibar. The union came into being officially on 26 April 1964.

At the time of the Union, the existing constitution of the Republic of Tanganyika was adapted to form an interim constitution of the United Republic. This constitution was repealed by the Interim Constitution of Tanzania enacted in 1965, which was in turn repealed in 1977, being replaced by a Permanent Constitution which provided for two vice presidents.

Further revision of the constitutions for both the United Republic and Zanzibar occurred in 1985 defining Zanzibar's position in the union more clearly, and making provision for a president who is head of state and commander-in-chief and chief minister who then appoint the Supreme Revolutionary Council from the elected House of Representatives. The presidential term is five years, renewable only once.

In 1992 during the Party National Conference there was a unanimous decision to establish Tanzania as a multi-party state. The first multi-party elections (two by-elections) took place in 1994. Both were won by the Chama Cha Mapinduzi (CCH). The current amended Constitution provides for only one vice president who shall be the principal assistant to the president on all Union matters. The constitution was controversially amended again in 2000, to allow for ten members of parliament to be nominated by the President.

To consult the Constitution, please visit: http://www.tanzania.go.tz/constitutionf.html

International Relations

Tanzania is a member of the East African Community and of the Commonwealth. Tanzania is currently home to up to 300,000 refugees as a result of conflicts in neighbouring countries. There are an estimated 153,000 Burundians and around 127,000 Congolese in the country. The number of refugees was considerably higher until recent years, when many returned home following resolutions of conflict within their countries.

Recent Events

In August 2006, the African Development Bank announced that it would cancel US$640 million of Tanzania's debt as a result of the country's improved economic record. In 2008 the president sacked his cabinet following a corruption scandal. The Central Bank governor, Daudi Ballali, was also sacked after reports that the bank made improper payment of £60 million to local companies. The cabinet was further re-shuffled in May 2008.

In November 2009 an agreement was signed between Tanzania, Kenya, Uganda, Rwanda and Burundi bringing into being a common market agreement allowing free movement of people and goods across the East African Community.

In January 2011, two people were killed during a demonstration demanding the release of opposition leader, detained ahead of a rally against government corruption.

In May 2012, six ministers including the ministers of finance, energy and trade, were sacked over allegations of corruption.

In October 2012, over 120 people were arrested over attacks on churches in Dar Es Salaam after an alleged desecration of a copy of the Qur'an.

Legislature

The National Assembly, (Bunge) consists of 323 members, 232 of which are directly elected 75 appointed women, five members are elected from Zanzibar, a maximum of 10 can be presidential nominees and finally the Speaker. All members serve a five-year term. Zanzibar has its own House of Representatives, with 59 members, (nine appointed women), which legislates on internal matters.

National Assembly, PO Box 941, Dodoma, Tanzania. Tel: +255 26 232 2761, fax: +255 26 232 4218, e-mail: tanzparl@parliament.go.tz, URL: http://www.bunge.go.tz/bunge/bunge.asp

Cabinet (as at June 2013)

Prime Minister: Mizengo Kayanza Peter Pinda (page 1495)
Minister of State in the President's Office (Civil Society): Stephen Wassira (page 1534)
Minister of State in the President's Office (Good Governance): George Mkuchika
Minister of State in the President's Office (Public Service Management): Celina Komabani
Minister of State in the Vice-President's Office (Union Affairs): Samia Suluhu Hassan
Minister of State in the Vice-President's Office (Environment): Terezya Hoviza
Minister of State in the Prime Minister's Office (Regional Administration and Local Government): Hawa Ghasia
Minister of State in the Prime Minister's Office (Policy, Co-ordination and Parliamentary Affairs): William Lukuvi
Minister of State in the Prime Minister's Office (Investment): Dr. Mary Michael Nagu
Minister of Home Affairs: Dr Emmanuel Nchimbi (page 1484)
Minister for Justice & Constitutional Affairs: Mathias Chikawe (page 1404)
Minister for Finance & Economics: Dr William Mgimwa
Minister of Foreign Affairs: Bernard Membe
Minister of Defence: Shamsi Nahodha
Minister of Industry and Trade: Dr Abdalla Kigoda
Minister of Natural Resources and Tourism: Khamis Juma Kagasheki
Minister of Energy and Mineral Resources: Sospeter Muhongo
Minister of Works: Dr John Magufuli
Minister of Transport: Dr Harrison Mwakyembe
Minister of Labour and Employment: Gaudensia Mugosi Kabaka
Minister for Health & Social Welfare: Dr Hussein Mwinyi
Minister for Communication, Science and Technology: Prof. Makame Mnyaa Mbarawa
Minister for Education & Vocational Training: Dr. Shukuru Kawambwa
Minister of Community Development, Gender & Children: Sophia Simba
Minister of Information, Youth, Culture & Sports: Dr. Fenella Mukangara
Minister of Livestock & Fisheries Development: David Mathayo David
Minister of Water: Prof. Jumanne Maghembe
Minister of Lands, Housing and Human Settlement Development: Prof. Anna Tibaijuka
Minister of Agriculture, Irrigation, & Food Security: Christopher Chiza
Minister for East African Co-operation: Samwel Sitta
Minister without Porfolio: Mark Mwandosya (page 1483)

Ministries

Office of the President, State House, Magogoni Road, P O Box 9120, Dar es Salaam, Tanzania. Tel: +255 22 211 6898, URL:

Office of the Vice-President, State House, P O Box 9120, Dar es Salaam, Tanzania. Tel: +255 22 211 3857, fax: +255 22 2113856, e-mail: makamu@twiga.com

Office of the Prime Minister, Magogoni Road, P.O. Box 3021, Dar es Salaam, Tanzania. Tel: +255 22 211 2850 fax: +255 22 211 3439, URL: http://www.tanzania.go.tz/government

National Planning Commission, Kivukoni Front, P O Box 9242, Dar es Salaam, Tanzania. Tel: +255 22 211 2681, email: pc@plancom.go.tz

Civil Service Department, Kivukoni Front, P O Box 2483, Dar es Salaam, Tanzania. Tel: +255 22 213 0122, fax: +255 22 213 1365, e-mail: ps-csd@intafrica.com

Ministry of Finance, Box 9111, Dar es Salaam, Tanzania. Tel: +255 22 211 1174, fax: +255 22 211 0326, URL: http://www.mof.go.tz/

Ministry of Foreign Affairs and International Cooperation, P O Box 9000, Dar es Salaam, Tanzania. Tel: +255 22 211 1906, fax: +255 211 6600, URL: http://www.mof.go.tz/

Ministry of Industries and Trade, Lumumba Road, P O Box 9503, Dar es Salaam, Tanzania. Tel: +255 22 2181397 / 2180418, fax: +255 22 2182481 / 2112527

Ministry of Home Affairs, Ohio/Ghana Avenue, P O Box 9223, Dar es Salaam, Tanzania. Tel: +255 22 2112034-9, fax: +255 22 2139675

Ministry of Justice and Constitutional Affairs, Kivukoni Road, P O Box 9050, Dar es Salaam, Tanzania. Tel: +255 22 2117099 / 2111906

Ministry of Agriculture and Food Security, Kilimo Rd, P.O. Box 9192, Dar es Salaam, Tanzania. Tel: +255 22 2862480, fax: +255 22 2862077, e-mail: psk@Kilimo.go.tz, URL: http://www.agriculture.go.tz/

Ministry of Livestock Development and Fisheries, PO Box 9152, Dar es Salaam, Tanzania. Tel: +255 22 286 1910, fax: +255 22 286 1908, URL: http://www.mifugo.go.tz/

Ministry of Works, Holland House, Garden Avenue P O Box 9423, Dar es Salaam, Tanzania. Tel: +255 22 2111553 / 2117153, fax: 255 22 2113335 / 2116893

Ministry of Communication and Transport, Tancot House, PO Box 37650, Dar es Salaam, Tanzania. Tel: +255 22 2114426, URL: http://www.moct.go.tz/

Ministry of Community Development, Women's Affairs and Children, Kivukoni Front, P O Box 3448, Dar es Salaam, Tanzania. Tel: +255 22 211 1459, fax: +255 22 211 0933, URL: http://www.mcdgc.go.tz/

Ministry of Education, Magogoni Road, P O Box 9121, Dar es Salaam, Tanzania. Tel: +255 22 211 0403, fax: +255 22 2113271, e-mail: ps-moec@twiga.com

Ministry of Science, Technology and Higher Education, Msasani Road, P O Box 2645, Tanzania. Tel: +255 22 2666376, fax: +255 22 211 2533, e-mail: msthe@msthe.go.tz, URL: http://www.msthe.go.tz/

Ministry of Water and Livestock Development, Sokoine/Mkwepu Road, P O Box 9153, Dar es Salaam, Tanzania. Tel: +255 22 2117153-9, fax: +255 22 37138 / 37139, e-mail: Dppmaj@raha.com

Ministry of Energy and Minerals, Sokoine/Mkwepu Street, P O Box 2000/9152, Dar es Salaam, Tanzania. Tel: +255 22 2137138 / 211 7156, fax: +255 211 6719, e-mail: madini@africaonline.co.tz

Ministry of Defence, Ismani Road, P O Box 9544, Dar es Salaam, Tanzania. Tel: +255 22 211 7153, fax: +255 22 211 6719, URL: http://www.modans.go.tz/

Ministry of Health and Social Welfare, Samora Avenue, P O Box 9083, Dar es Salaam, Tanzania. Tel: +255 22 2120261, fax: +255 22 213 9951, e-mail: moh@cats-net.com

Ministry of Lands and Human Settlements Development, Ardhi House, Kivukoni Front, P O Box 9132, Dar es Salaam, Tanzania. Tel: +255 212 1241, fax: +255 22 211 3224, e-mail: Ps-Ardhi@africaonline.co.tz, URL: http://www.ardhi.go.tz/

Ministry of Natural Resources and Tourism, P O Box 9372, Dar es Salaam, Tanzania. Tel: +255 22-2111061-4, fax: +255 22 21106004, e-mail: mipango.mnrt.@twiga.com

Ministry of Information, Culture and Sports, URL: http://www.hum.go.tz

Ministry of Infrastructure, PO Box 9144, Dar Es Salaam. Tel: +21 37650, URL: http://www.infrastructure.go.tz/

Ministry of Public Safety and Security, URL: http://www.policeforce.go.tz/

Ministry of Labour, URL: http://www.kazi.go.tz/

Cabinet (as of June 2013)

President of Zanzibar and Chairman of the Revolutionary Council: Dr Ali Mohammed Shein

Vice-President: Seif Sharif Hamad

Vice-President: Seif Ali Iddi

Minister of State in the President's Office: Dr Mwinyihaji Makame

Minister of State for Finance, Economic Affairs & Development Planning: Omar Yussuf Mzee

Minister of State for Public Services and Good Governance: Haji Omar Kheri

Minister in the Office of first Vice-President: Fatma Abdulhabib Fereji

Minister in the Office of Second Vice-President: Mohamed Aboud Mohamed

Minister without portfolio: Suleiman Othman Nyanga

Minister without portfolio: Haji Faki Shaali

Minister without portfolio: Machano Othman Said

Minister for Constitutional Affairs and Justice: Aboubakar Khamis Bakar

Minister for Infrastructure and Communication: Hamad Masoud Hamad

Minister of Education and Professional Training: Ramdani Abdulla Shaabana

Minister for Health: Juma Duni Haji

Minister for Social Welfare, Women and Children's Development: Zainab Omar Mohamed

Minister for Information, Culture, Tourism and Sports: Mbarouk Abdilahi Jihad Hassan

Minister for Lands, Housing, Water and Energy: Ali Juma Shamhuna

Minister for Agriculture and Natural Resources: Suleiman Othuman Nyanga

Minister for Trade, Industries and Marketing: Nassor Ahmed Mazrui

Minister for Livestock and Fishing: Said Ali Mbarouk

Minister for Labour, Economic Empowerment and Co-operatives: Haroun Ali Suleiman

Ministries

Zanzibar Government portal: URL: http://zanzibar.go.tz/

Zanzibar President's Office, State House, P O Box 776, Zanzibar, Tanzania. Tel:+255 54 3182/30814, fax: +255 54 33788, URL: http://www.ikuluzanzibar.go.tz/

Chief Minister's Office, P O Box 239, Zanzibar, Tanzania. Tel: +255 54 30806/31826/31126/32566, fax: +255 54 33788

Ministry of Planning and Investment, P O Box 874, Zanzibar, Tanzania. Tel: +255 54 30806/31117/32566

Ministry of Education, P O Box 394, Zanzibar, Tanzania. Tel: +255 54 32828/32498

Ministry of Agriculture, Livestock and Natural Resources, P O Box 159, Zanzibar, Tanzania. Tel: +255 54 30206/32840

Ministry of Water, Construction, Energy and Environment, P O Box 238, Zanzibar, Tanzania. +255 54 33056

Ministry of Finance, P O Box 1154, Zanzibar, Tanzania. Tel: +255 54 31169/31170/31172, fax: +255 54 32659

Ministry of Communications and Transport, P O Box 266, Zanzibar, Tanzania. Tel: +255 54 32841/30934

Ministry of Information, Culture, Tourism and Youth,P O Box 456 and 722, Zanzibar, Tanzania. Tel: +255 54 30193/32562/32321

Ministry of Health, P O Box 236, Zanzibar, Tanzania. Tel: +255 54 30189/31071/32579

Ministry of Trade, Industry and Marketing, P O Box 601, Zanzibar, Tanzania. Tel: +255 54 31142-3/32100, fax: +255 54 31870

Elections

Suffrage is universal at 18.

Legislative and presidential elections were held in 2000. Benjamin Mkapa was re-elected as president with over 70 per cent of the vote. The Chama Cha Mapinduzi party won a majority in the National Assembly of 202 seats.

In the 2000 presidential election for Zanzibar, Abeid Amani Karume beat the CUF candidate, Seif Sharif Hamad. The election was marred by violence and 16 people died. CUF members boycotted the legislature in protest and were subsequently banned from parliament. In 2001 the CCM and the CUF parties signed an agreement calling for electoral reforms and an inquiry into the deaths. Changes to the constitution in 2002 meant that both parties were able to nominate members to the Zanzibar Electoral Commission (ZEC). In May 2003 the ZEC held by-elections to fill the vacant seats which included those resulting from the boycott. The elections were judged to be fair.

Presidential and parliamentary elections took place on 14 December 2005 for the mainland and on 30 October 2005 for Zanzibar. Jakaya Mrisho Kikwete of the ruling Revolutionary Party of Tanzania (CCM) won the presidential election. The CCM retained an overall majority in the National Assembly, taking appproximately 80 per cent of the seats.

The most recent presidential elections took place on 31 October 2010. The incumbent candidate, Jakaya Mrisho Kikwete, was re-elected with over 60 per cent of the vote. His closest rival, Wilbrod Slaa, won 26 per cent of the vote. Ali Mohamed Shein, the former vice-president, was elected as president of Zanzibar. Turnout was relatively low at 43 per cent. Opposition parties have alleged intimidation and fraud.

The most recent legislative elections also took place on 31 October 2010. Opposition parties made gains but not enough to challenge the ruling Revolutionary Party of Tanzania. The seats break down thus: CCM 251 seats; Chadema 45 seats; CUF 31 seats; others 30 seats.

The next presidential and parliamentary elections are due to take place in October 2015.

Political Parties

Chama Cha Mapinduzi (CCM); Civic United Front (CUF-Chama Cha Wananchi); Chama Cha Demokrasia na Maendeleo (CHADEMA);The Union for Multiparty Democracy of Tanzania (UMD); National League for Democracy (NLD); Tanzania People's Party (TPP); United People's Democratic Party (UPDP); National Reconstruction Alliance (NRA); Popular National Party (PONA); Tanzania Democratic Alliance (TADEA); Tanzania Labour Party (TLP); The United Democratic Party (UDP)

Diplomatic Representation

High Commission of the United Republic of Tanzania, 3 Stratford Place, London WlC 1AS , United Kingdom. Tel: +44 (0)20 7569 1470, fax: +44 (0)20 7495 8817, URL: http://tanzaniahighcommission.co.uk/
Ambassador: Peter Kallaghe

Embassy of the United Republic of Tanzania in USA, 2139 R Street, NW, Washington DC 20008, USA. Tel: +1 202 939 6125, fax: +1 202 797 7408, e-mail: balozi@tanzaniaembassy-us.org, URL: http://www.tanzaniaembassy-us.org
Ambassador: H.E Mwandaidi S. Maajar

British High Commission, Umojo House, Garden Avenue, PO Box 9200, Dar es Salaam, Tanzania. Tel: +255 22 211 0101, fax: +255 22 211 0120, e-mail: bhc.dar@africaonline.co.tz, URL: http://www.britishhighcommission.gov.uk/tanzania
High Commissioner: Diana Melrose (page 1476)

US Embassy, PO Box 9123, 686 Old Bagamoyo Road, Msasani, Dar Es Salaam, Tanzania, Tel: +255 22 2668001, fax +255 22 2668238, e-mail: embassyd@state.gov, URL: http://tanzania.usembassy.gov
Ambassador: Alfonso E. Lenhardt

Permanent Mission of the Republic of Tanzania to the UN, URL: http://www.tanzania-un.org/
Permanent Representative: Tuvako Manongi

LEGAL SYSTEM

The legal system is based on a combination of common law, customary law and Islamic law.

The judiciary consists of the Court of Appeal, the High Courts for mainland Tanzania and Zanzibar, and the Judicial Service Commission for mainland. Magistrates Courts and Primary Courts. The High Court has full jurisdiction in all civil and criminal cases and has exclusive jurisdiction in questions as to the interpretation of the Constitution. In cases other than

TANZANIA

questions relating to the interpretation of the Constitution, appeals go from the High Court to the Tanzania Court of Appeal. A Commercial Court was established in 1999 as a division of the High Court.

In Zanzibar, the court system consists of the High Court, Kadhis Courts and Magistrates Courts. Zanzibar shares the Court of Appeal with mainland Tanzania.

The Judicial Service Commission consists of: the Chief Justice and a further Justice of the Court of Appeal, the Principal Judge of the High Court, and two members appointed by the President. The Tanzania Law Reform Commission is responsible for the review of the country's laws.

Human rights issues continue in Tanzania; there have been recent cases of excessive force used against inmates and suspects, and police impunity. There is widespread police corruption, as well as judicial corruption and inefficiency. Prison conditions are life threatening. There are restrictions on the freedom of speech and of the press. Under Tanzania laws, murder and high treason are punishable by a death sentence, though no executions have taken place since before 1998.

At least 28 albino people have recently been murdered in what were believed to be ritual killings. 47 suspected perpetrators of the killings were arrested, but by the end of 2008 no-one had been prosecuted. The Tanzania Albino Society criticized the lack of prosecutions and the lack of a long-term comprehensive government plan to prevent such killings.

Court of Appeal, URL: http://www.judiciary.go.tz
Commission for Human Rights and Good Governance, URL: http://chragg.go.tz/

LOCAL GOVERNMENT

Tanzania is divided in 26 regions or *Mikoa*, (five in Zanzibar), they are Arusha, Dar-es-Salaam, Dodoma, Iringa, Kagera, Kigoma, Kilimanjaro, Lindi, Manyara, Mara, Mbeya, Morogoro, Mtwara, Mwanza, Pemba North, Pemba South, Pwani, Rukwa, Ruvuma, Shinyanga, Singida, Tabora, Tanga, Zanzibar Central - South, Zanzibar North and Zanzibar Urban-West. There are 133 councils (also called local government authorities) throughout Tanzania and Zanzibar. On the mainland there are three types of urban authority: city, municipal and town councils. In rural areas there are two levels of authority, firstly district councils and secondly village council and township authorities. Local governments are responsible for law and order in their area and as well as economic and development planning.

AREA AND POPULATION

Area
The United Republic of Tanzania encompasses the mainland formerly known as Tanganyika as well as the islands of Zanzibar, Pemba and Mafia in the Indian Ocean. Mainland Tanzania is located on the east coast of Africa between Lake Victoria, Lake Tanganyika, and Lake Nyasa and the Indian Ocean.

Its total land area is 945,000 square kilometres, including 60,000 square kilometres of inland water. Mainland Tanzania covers 881,000 square kilometres and Zanzibar 2,000 square kilometres. Tanzania shares a border with eight other countries: Kenya and Uganda in the north; the Democratic Republic of Congo; Rwanda and Burundi in the west; and Zambia, Malawi and Mozambique in the south. Africa's highest mountain, Mount Kilimanjaro is situated in the north east of the country. The largest lake in Africa, Lake Victoria is situated in the north forming part of the border with Uganda. Africa's deepest lake, Lake Tanganyika is situated in the east and forms the border with the Democratic Republic of Congo.

The climate is temperate on the coast and semi-temperate inland.

To view a map, visit http://www.un.org/Depts/Cartographic/map/profile/tanzania.pdf

Population
The population in 2010 was estimated to be 44.841 million, one million of whom live in Zanzibar. The annual growth rate was estimated at 2.8 per cent over the period 2000-10.

Approximately 26 per cent of the population lives in urban areas. The main towns and populations are Dar es Salaam (commercial capital), with an estimated population of 2,500,000; Dodoma (political capital), 326,000; other large towns include Mwanza, 380,000; Tanga, 250,000; Zanzibar Town, 254,600; Zanzibar North and Central, 118,000; Zanzibar South and West, 254,000; Mbeya, 1,790,800; Arusha, 270,484; Pemba North, 167,000 and Pemba South, 155,000. an estimated 76 per cent of the population is rural. Population density is very varied, from 3 people per sq. mile in the dry regions to 347 per sq. mile in Zanzibar.

Kiswahili is the official language though English and other African languages are also spoken. The majority of the population (95 per cent) is of Bantu origin.

Births, Marriages, Deaths
In 2010, the birth rate was 41.4 per 1,000 population and the death rate was 11.6 per 1,000 population. Infant mortality was 50 per 1,000 population in 2010 (compared to 103 per 1,000 live births in 2003). In 2009 the total fertility rate was 5.5 per female. Life expectancy in 2009 was 55 years (53 years for males and 58 years for females). Healthy life expectancy is 45 years. Approximately 45 of the population was under 15 years old in 2009 and an estimated 5 per cent of the population were over 60 years old. The median age was 18 years in 2010. (Source: http://www.who.int, World Health Statistics 2012)

Public Holidays 2014
1 January: New Year's Day
12 January: Zanzibar Revolutionary Day
14 January: Birth of the Prophet*

18 April: Good Friday
21 March: Easter Sunday
26 April: Union Day
6 May: International Labour Day
7 July: Industrial Day
29 June: Ramadan begins*
29 July: Eid al-Fitr, (Ramadan ends)*
8 August: Farmers' Day
5 October: Eid al-Adha, (Festival of the Sacrifice)*
25 October: Ashura*
9 December: Independence Day
25 December: Christmas Day
26 December: Boxing Day

Public holidays (except for Easter) in Tanzania remain the same every year. If any of the public holidays fall on Saturday or Sunday then the public holiday would be the following Monday. * Islamic holidays depend on the sighting of the moon and so can vary.

EMPLOYMENT

Agriculture, most of which is subsistence farming, provides a living for nearly 85 per cent of the population. An estimated 57.8 per cent of the population live below the poverty line. The unemployment rate in 2006 was put at 4.3 per cent. Estimated figures for 2010 put the labour force at 23.0 million.

Total Employment by Economic Activity

Occupation	2006
Agriculture, hunting & forestry	13,185,100
Fishing	209,600
Mining & quarrying	104,900
Manufacturing	565,100
Electricity, gas & water supply	17,000
Construction	211,500
Wholesale & retail trade, repairs	1,572,700
Hotels & restaurants	377,500
Transport, storage & communications	258,100
Financial intermediation	17,500
Real estate, renting & business activities	82,000
Public admin. & defence; compulsory social security	184,700
Education	225,600
Health & social work	105,200
Other community, social & personal service activities	126,500
Households with employed persons	701,500

Source: Copyright © International Labour Organization (ILO Dept. of Statistics, http://laborsta.ilo.org)

BANKING AND FINANCE

The financial centre is Dar-es-Salaam.

Currency
The standard unit of currency is the Tanzania shilling. 1 Tsh = 100 cents.

GDP/GNP, Inflation, National Debt
Agriculture dominates Tanzania's economy, accounting for nearly 50 per cent of GDP. Tourism is beginning to grow in significance to the economy and is now the second largest foreign exchange earner. Exports of gold and diamonds have grown in recent years and exports now account for half of the country's GDP. Tanzania has benefitted from foreign aid from the World Bank, the IMF and bilateral donors. There have been recent economic reforms and investment in infrastructure. In 200, Tanzania received a Millennium grant worth US$698 million. Despite the global economic crisis, Tanzania has not entered into recession.

Tanzania has experienced steady growth. Figures for 2011 estimated GDP at US$23.4 billion reflecting a growth rate of 6.3 per cent,

The economy is very dependent on agriculture which makes up 48 per cent of GDP. Industry contributes 15.4 per cent and services 36 per cent. Mineral production has increased over the last 10 years and now provides over 3 per cent of GDP and accounts for over 50 per cent of Tanzania's exports.

Inflation was estimated at 7 per cent in 2010, rising to over 12 per cent in 2011.

Balance of Payments / Imports and Exports
Estimated figures for 2009 put export earnings at US$2.75 billion (compared to US$2.2 billion in 2007). Imports in 2008 cost an estimated US$6 billion.

Main exports are gold diamonds, tanzanite, coffee, tea, cotton sisal, cashew nuts, tobacco, flowers, seaweed and fish. Major export markets are the UK, Germany, India, Japan, Italy and the Far East. Major imports are petroleum, consumer goods, machinery and transport equipment, and chemicals. Most imports come from the UK, Germany, India, Italy, the US, the UAE, Hong Kong, Singapore, South Africa and Kenya.

In March 2004 the presidents of Uganda, Kenya and Tanzania signed a customs pact designed to harmonise external tariffs and boost trade.

Central Bank
Bank of Tanzania, PO Box 2939, 10 Mirambo Street, Dar es Salaam, Tanzania. Tel: +255 22 110945-7, fax: +255 22 112671, e-mail: info@hq.bot-tz.org, URL: http://www.bot-tz.org Governor & Chairman of the Board: Prof. Benno Ndulu

Chambers of Commerce and Trade Organisations
Tanzania Chamber of Commerce, Industry and Agriculture, URL: http://www.tccia.co.tz/
Tanzania Investment Centre, URL: http://www.tic.co.tz/

MANUFACTURING, MINING AND SERVICES

Primary and Extractive Industries
Minerals in order of importance are: diamonds, gold, gemstones including Tansanite, tin, ornamental stones (art stones and amethystine quartz), and salt. Studies are now being undertaken of the large deposits of iron ore, coal, and gold deposits in the Ruvuma, Iringa and Mbeya regions. Gemstones are exploited in the Northern regions of Tanzania.

More money was invested in 1998 in non-ferrous mineral exploitation in Tanzania than any other African nation. The first commercial gold mine started operating in November 1999. 2001 saw the opening of the huge Bulyanhulu mine near Mwanza. The mine is owned by the Barrick Gold Corporation and Canadian company who hope to mine up 400,000 ounces of gold per annum. Overall production of gold in Tanzania was estimated to reach 2 million ounces by 2003. Total estimated gold deposits in Tanzania stand at around 30 million ounces. It is hoped that mining will boost foreign exchange earnings by 50 per cent.

Tanzania has three cement factories. The largest cement plant at Wazo Hill produces approximately 600,000 tons of cement per year; the Tanga cement factory which started production in 1980 produces 500,000 tons per year; and the Mbeya cement plant started production in 1981 with a capacity of 250,000 tons per year.

Energy
An oil refinery is in operation at Dar es Salaam, with a crude oil capacity of 15,000 bbl/d per day. The late 1960s saw the establishment of several mills in the textile industry, mainly under the umbrella of the National Development Corporation. Tanzania has no proven oil reserves of its own although some exploration has been carried out. Offshore exploration began in 1999. In 2011, Tanzania consumed 43,000 barrels of oil per day, all imported.

Tanzania has proven natural gas reserves of 800 billion cubic feet. In 2004, the Songosongo gas field came online and will be used to generate electricity. Traditionally electricity was produced by hydro electric generation, a system which could fail during periods of low rainfall. Gas production in 2011 Tanzania was 30 billion cubic feet all consumed domestically. Coal reserves are estimated to be 220 million short tons. Coal production in 2000 was 0.105 million short tons.

Tanzania has an electric installed capacity of 0.984 GWe and in 2010 generated 4.30 billion kWh.

Manufacturing
The decade after the achievement of independence saw the establishment and expansion of many industries within the manufacturing sector. In 2002, industry contributed 8.3 per cent to GNP.

Apart from the brewing, plastics, enamelware, metal, and plywood industries, new industries have been established for the manufacture of car tyres, fertilizers, steel, soluble coffee, textiles, meerschaum pipes, leather, farm implements, sisal bags, and processing of cashew nuts.

Most of the large industrial firms belong to the state owned National Development Corporation, which is the principal government investment institution for the development of the manufacturing and mining sector. It has over forty operating groups and associate companies. The registered companies include those involved in the garment, aluminium, galvanised iron sheet, hydrogenised vegetable oil, and glass industries.

Service Industries
There has been a steady rise in the amount of visitors to Tanzania from 187,000 in 1991 to 622,000 in 2006, generating receipts of US$950 million.

Agriculture
With over 90 per cent of the population living in rural areas, the economy is predominantly agricultural. It accounts for nearly 60 per cent of GDP. About 40 million hectares is available for agricultural production and livestock. Of that only 6 million hectares is cultivated, and only about 15 per cent of the country has access to water, with very little controlled irrigation. This means that most crops are dependent on the weather.

Tanzania is the second largest producer of sisal in the world. Other main crops are: coffee, cotton, tea, tobacco, oil-seeds, sugar, maize, beans and pulses, rice, wheat, cashew nuts, copra and pyrethrum. It is estimated that for some crops production is at similar levels to thirty years ago. To overcome this problem, in the 2000-01 budget provision of US$250 million was made, to be used to promote cash crop and food production amongst small scale farmers.

In 2003, it was announced that the government wished to boost coffee production from around the average 40-50,000 metric tonnes produced annually. In order to do this Tanzania is experimenting with replacing existing coffee bushes with more disease resistant varieties.

Agricultural Production in 2010

Produce	Int. $'000*	Tonnes
Bananas	823,686	2,924,700
Indigenous cattle meat	788,018	291,710
Maize	563,004	4,736,190
Beans, dry	536,956	950,000
Cow milk, whole, fresh	514,901	1,650,000

- continued

Cassava	437,927	4,392,170
Rice, paddy	289,832	1,104,890
Vegetables fresh nes	282,662	1,500,000
Mangoes, mangosteens, guavas	194,729	325,000
Cotton lint	157,212	110,000
Plantains	133,537	660,000
Groundnuts, with shell	126,918	300,000

*unofficial figures
Source: http://faostat.fao.org/site/339/default.aspx Food and Agriculture Organization of the United Nations, Food and Agricultural commodities production

Local forests contain substantial quantities of timber, both hard and softwoods and there are considerable exports. Tanzania is the second largest exporter of beeswax in the world. It also exports large numbers of mangrove poles to the Persian Gulf area.

Forestry Production in 2004

Product	1000 Cubic Metres
Industrial roundwood	2,314
Sawn wood	24
Woodfuel	21,505
Wood-based panels	4
	1000 Tonnes
Paper, paperboard	25
Wood charcoal	1,328
Wood pulp	54

Source: FAOSTAT, Food & Agriculture Organization of the United Nations

There are extensive fisheries in operation on Lakes Tanganyika and Victoria and on the sea coast. The FAO put the total catch for 2010 at 160 tonnes.

COMMUNICATIONS AND TRANSPORT

Travel Requirements
Citizens of the USA, Canada, Australia and the EU require a passport valid for six months and a visa. Cypriots and Maltese people do not need a visa for stays of up to three months, and British citizens can obtain a tourist visa on entry, but all other visitors should obtain a visa before travelling. Other nationals should contact the embassy to check visa requirements. It is advisable to have proof of yellow fever innoculation.

International Airports
There are 53 airports and landing strips maintained or licensed by the government, of these, three are of international standard and seven are capable of accommodating Fokker Friendship aircraft. Kilimanjaro, Julius Nyerere International Airport, and Dar es Salaam International Airport, Dar-es-Salaam and Kilimanjaro International Airport are capable of accommodating the Boeing 747 jumbo-jet airliner. Domestic charter services are operated by two companies.
Air Tanzania, URL: http://www.airtanzania.com
Precision Air, URL: http://www.precisionairtz.com

Railways
The Tanzania Railway Corporation operates road services, lake steamer services and the railways. There is a main line from Dar-es-Salaam to Kigoma (783 miles) and other lines from Tabora to Mwanza (237 miles), and Tanga to Moshi and Arusha (272 miles). There are also two other branch lines.

A 1,860-mile Tanzania-Zambia railway is in operation. The Tanzania Railway Corporation provides regular and frequent services to all the more important towns within the territory, and the neighbouring countries of Kenya and Uganda.

In 2012, Tanzania's first commuter railway service opened in Dar-es-Salaam. One route covers 25 km between the Mwakanga and Tazara railway stations and another track runs between Ubungo-Maziwa and City railway stations. The trains will mainly run during the morning and evenings and are part of a government plan to ease road congestion.

Roads
Motor traffic is possible over 25,000 miles of road during the dry season and at almost all times over 21,000 miles of road. Vehicles are driven on the left. In 2003 a major road building and repair programme was announced, it is hoped that this improvement to the infrastructure will improve trade. The EU is one of the largest contributors to the scheme.

Ports and Harbours
Tanzania has four main ports, Dar es Salaam, which has 11 deep water berths, Mtwara, Tanga and Zanzibar. A ferry service is operated several times a day between Dar es Salaam and Zanzibar carrying goods and passengers. Ferries carrying freight and passengers operate on Lake Victoria, there is a passenger service between Dar es Salaam and Zanzibar and one between Mwanza and Kenya (Kisumu). Lake Tanganyika and Lake Nyasa are also used as waterways.

HEALTH

Recent figures show that Tanzania has 183 hospitals and 3,286 dispensaries. In 2006 there were an estimated 11,000 hospital beds. Dar es Salaam houses the Muhimbili Medical Centre, the country's teaching hospital and referral centre. According to WHO figures, in 2000-10 there were 300 doctors (0.1 per 10,000 population), 9,440 nurses and midwives (2.4 per 10,000 population), 81 pharmacists, 1,831 environment and public health workers, and 230 dentists. In 2009, total expenditure on health as a percentage of GDP was 5.5 per cent. Per capita total expenditure on health was US$22 in 2008. Expenditure on health represents

TANZANIA

12.9 per cent of general government expenditure. Government expenditure accounts for 66 per cent of total health expenditure. External resources contribute over 50 per cent of total expenditure. Private expenditure amounts to 33.9 per cent of total expenditure, of which 41 per cent was out-of-pocket and 10.1 per cent prepaid plans.

According to 2009 figures, the HIV/AIDS prevalence in adults was 5.6 per cent. Approximately 70 per cent of pregnant women with HIV/AIDS and 30 per cent of people with advanced HIV infection received antiretroviral therapy.

In 2010, the infant mortality rate was 50 per 1,000 live births and the under-5 mortality rate was 76 per 1,000 live births. An estimated 10 per cent of newborns were registered as underweight at birth. In 2005-11, 42.5 per cent of children aged 5 or less were classified as stunted for age and 16.2 per cent underweight. In 2010, 9 per cent of deaths among children under 5 years old were due to diarrhoeal diseases, HIV/AIDS 6 per cent, malaria 11 per cent, prematurity 15 per cent, and pneumonia 15 per cent. An estimated 16 per cent of infants sleep under insecticide treated nets. The immunization rate for measles now stands at over 90 per cent. In 2007 the former president of the United States, Bill Clinton, launched a programme to make subsidised malaria drugs available. Tanzania was chosen to pilot the scheme and an estimated 58 per cent of people received anti-malarial treatment.

In 2010, an estimated 53 per cent of the population had sustainable access to improved drinking water and 10 per cent of the population had access to improved sanitation. (Source: http://www.who.int, World Health Statistics 2012)

EDUCATION

The education system is based on the principle of 'Self-Reliance', first introduced by President Nyerere in 1969, whereby learning is structured to equip the student with the best skills to benefit himself and his society. The basic aims propounded in this system are:
a) to equip learners with knowledge, skills and attitudes for tackling social problems;
b) to prepare the young for work in Tanzania's predominantly agricultural society;
c) to enable learners to know, appreciate and develop a Tanzanian culture that perpetuates the national heritage, individual freedom, responsibility and tolerance and pays respect to its elders.

Primary/Secondary Education
Primary education generally starts at the age of seven years and lasts for seven years. Universal primary education was introduced in 1977. Since that time, all children aged 7 to 12 years are eligible for enrolment. The illiteracy rate was reduced to 31 per cent during a four-year campaign initiated in 1972. Due to lack of funding the programme collapsed. In 2001 the government again announced plans to start free primary education for all children. Enrolment rates have dramatically improved. Figures from UNESCO Institute for Statistics (UIS) in 2006 show that 97 per cent of girls and 98 per cent of boys were enrolled in primary school (compared to an average of 50 per cent enrolment in 1999). The pupil / teacher ratio was estimated at 52:1. An estimated 74 per cent of children complete their primary education and 46 per cent go onto secondary education.

Secondary education lasts six years, the first year normally beginning at the age of 14. Except for private secondary schools where ministry controlled school fees are paid, all education in Tanzania up to the level of university is paid for by the government. Private schools are established and managed according to directives issued by the Ministry of Education. The enrolment rate was estimated at 25 per cent in 2006.

Higher Education
Tanzania has six universities, the University of Dar-es-Salaam, the Sokoine University of Agriculture, Muhimbili University College of Medical Sciences (in Dar-es-Salaam), and University College of Lands, Architecture and Survey. An Open University was established in 1995 for distance education and in 1998 the University of Zanzibar at Zanzibar town opened. The tertiary enrolment rate was estimated at 5 per cent in 2006.

The adult literacy rate is estimated at 72.3 per cent (79.0 per cent males, 65.9 per cent females). The youth literacy (15-24 years) rate is 77.5 per cent (78.9 per cent males, 76.2 per cent females). Source: UNESCO

RELIGION

An estimated 40 per cent of the population is Muslim the majority being Sunni Muslims. There is a large Muslim community to be found chiefly in the coastal areas. Zanzibar is approximately 95 per cent Muslim. Among the immigrant Indian population the majority are Hindus, Sikhs and Muslims. An estimated 53 per cent of the population is Christian. Traditional beliefs are followed by an estimated 13 per cent of the population.

Tanzania has a religious liberty rating of 7 on a scale of 1 to 10 (10 is most freedom). (Source: World Religion Database)

COMMUNICATIONS AND MEDIA

Until the 1990s the media was state controlled.Since the advent of multi-party politics newspapers have proliferated. A private television station started up in 1994 and state-run television launched in 2001. Radio remains the dominant media. There are no private broadcasters or newspapers in Zanzibar.

Newspapers
Uhuru, URL: http://www.uhuru.info
Daily News, government-owned, URL: http://www.dailynews-tsn.com
The Guardian, URL: http://www.ippmedia.com/ipp/newspapers/index.html
Business Times, URL: http://www.bcstimes.com/
Tanzania Daima, URL: http://www.freemedia.co.tz/daima

Broadcasting
State television is run by the Tanzania Broadcasting Corporation. Televisheni ya Taifa (TVT) and Zanzibar TV are both state run stations, there are also four private TV broadcasters. Several private networks exist including Independent Television (ITV) (URL: http://www.ippmedia.com/ipp/television/index.html) owned by IPP. Satellite television has been available since 2001.

Radio Tanzania operates a high and a low power transmitter in Dar-es-Salaam, broadcasting daily in English and Kiswahili. This and Radio Tanzania-Zanzibar are government run. Many private radio stations exist and international news is available. Among the independent radio stations are Radio One, and Capital Radio, and two Christian stations Radio Tumaini and Radio Sauti ya Injili.

Telecommunications
The system is poor but is being modernised. Mobile-phone coverage is much greater and increasing rapidly. Figures from 2009 estimate there are over 175,000 phone lines in use and 14 million mobile phones.

By 2009, an estimated 520,000 people had access to the internet.

ENVIRONMENT

Environmental issues include soil degradation, deforestation and desertification. Tanzania also suffers from occasional droughts which have adverse effects on wildlife. Wildlife is also threatened by illegal hunting and trade, including the illegal ivory trade. A large proportion of the country is given over to the national parks and game reserves including the Serengeti National Park, Gombe National Park and Ngorongoro Park.

Tanzania is a party to the following international agreements: Biodiversity, Climate Change, Climate Change-Kyoto Protocol, Desertification, Endangered Species, Hazardous Wastes, Law of the Sea, Ozone Layer Protection, and Wetlands.

According to figures from the EIA, in 2010 Tanzania's emissions from the consumption of fossil fuels totalled 7.57 million metric tons of carbon dioxide.

THAILAND
Kingdom of Thailand
Prathet Thai

Capital: Bangkok (Population estimate, 2011: 11,500,000)

Head of State: King Bhumibol Adulyadej (Rama IX) (Sovereign) (page 1372)

National Flag: Divided fesswise, red, white, blue, white red, the blue stripe twice the width of each white or red

CONSTITUTION AND GOVERNMENT

Constitution
The first independent Thai kingdom was established in Sukothai in 1238 and thrived until the late 14th century when it was incorporated into the rising Ayutthaya kingdom. Ayutthaya lasted as a capital from 1350 to 1767 and was ruled by 33 successive kings. In 1767 it fell to the Burmese but was recovered seven months later by Phraya Taksin, a former general in the Ayutthaya army. Taksin became king and was succeeded by King Phraphutthayotha Chulalok or Rama I who founded the Chakri Dynasty of which the present monarch is the ninth king.

Succession is in the male line, according to the Kot Monthien Bal 'Law of the Land' on Succession, as revised 11 November 1920. However, Section 20 of the 1978 Constitution stipulates that, in certain circumstances, an exception to the Kot Monthien Bal laws may be made to allow the succession of a female to the throne.

Thailand is a constitutional monarchy. Government is conducted by an appointed prime minister and cabinet who exercise their authority with the consent of the army as well as that of the legislature. Political parties' efforts to play a greater part in government, and military resistance to these efforts, have been a perennial source of domestic tension. Since Thailand switched from absolute to constitutional monarchy in 1932 there have been 14 coups or attempted coups.

In August 2007, the people of Thailand voted by referendum in favour of a new constitution. The draft document limits future prime ministers to two terms in office and makes it easier to impeach them.

To consult the constitution, please visit: http://www.parliament.go.th/files/library/b05-b.htm

Recent Events
There is a history of unrest in the southern part of the country, the situation had calmed down during the 1980s but 2004 saw a resurgence of violence. The population of the area is predominantly Muslim and the violence has been mainly directed at Buddhists. There are three provinces in the south, Pattani, Yala and Narathiwat which have a large Muslim population. Pattani was originally the capital of the Pattani sultanate, an independent Muslim kingdom which became part of Thailand early in the 20th century.

On 26 December 2004 the west coast of Thailand was hit by a massive tsunami that devastated countries around the Indian Ocean. The earthquake that triggered the wave occurred off the coast of Sumatra, Indonesia. The death toll for Thailand was more than 5,000 people with nearly 2,000 being foreign visitors.

In March 2005 Thaksin Shinawatra began his second term as PM after his party's landslide victory in February's elections. In response to violent unrest in the south, the PM was given new powers to counter suspected Muslim militants in the region. By November more than 1,000 people had died in the region since January 2004.

Prime Minister Thaksin called a snap election in April 2006, following protests and allegations of corruption against him. The election was boycotted by the opposition and the government won, but the result was subsequently annulled, leaving a political vacuum. On the 19th August, PM Thaksin was ousted by a military coup led by the army commander-in-chief, General Sonthi Boonyaratglin. General Surayud Chulanont was chosen to replace him pending elections in December 2007. Although the coup was condemned internationally, the King endorsed the leadership who call themselves the Council for National Security. In May the political party Thai Love Thai Party was banned because of electoral irregularities. In August 2007 a referendum was held and a new military-drafted constitution was approved. In October 2007 General Sonthi Boonyaratglin became Deputy Prime Minister in charge of internal security.

In January 2008, eight Thai soldiers were killed in the southern province of Narathiwat, by suspected Muslim separatist rebels. The rebels are fighting for an Islamic state. Over 2,700 people have been killed since the violence escalated in early 2004. In 2007, Human Rights Watch warned that the violence was turning increasingly brutal, with the majority of victims innocent civilians.

In December 2007, general elections took place, and the People Power Party (PPP), viewed as a successor to the banned Thai Rak Thai party, won most seats. A new coalition government was announced in January 2008. In February, Thaksin Shinawatra returned from exile. His corruption trial began in July, and in August he fled to Britain after failing to appear at court.

In July 2008, relations with neighbouring Cambodia became tense when 40 Thai soldiers crossed the frontier into Cambodia following the arrest of three Thai protestors near the Preah Vihear temple. Ownership of the temple has long been a sensitive issue between the two countries; in 1962, the International Court of Justice awarded it to Cambodia. Tension increased when Cambodia applied for World Heritage status for the temple, which was approved by Unesco early in July. The application was controversially endorsed by the Thai Foreign Minister, Noppadon Pattama, who resigned after a court ruled he had breached the constitution. By mid-July, over 500 Thai and 1,000 Cambodian soldiers had been stationed on opposite sides of disputed land near Preah Vihear temple. On the 22nd July, Cambodia asked the UN Security Council for an emergency meeting to resolve the stand-off with Thailand.

On the 26th August, supporters of the People's Alliance for Democracy (PAD) invaded government buildings and a state-run television station in Bangkok, vowing to keep some 30,000 supporters on the streets until the government falls. Thousands of protesters blocked key roads into the city, accusing Prime Minister Samak of running the country on behalf of former Prime Minister Thaksin Shinawatra. The security forces refused to intervene for the government, raising suspicions that the PAD had backers inside the armed forces. On the 2nd September, Prime Minister Samak Sundaravej declared a state of emergency. The PAD protesters occupying the government's building refused to move. The Thai election commission recommended that Mr Samak's People Power Party be disbanded over claims of vote-buying in the December elections. On the 9th September, the court ordered Samak to resign for violating constitution by being paid for a second job as a TV chef. Parliament selected Somchai Wongsawat to take over as prime minister but the demonstrations continued resulting in the deaths of 16 protesters.

On the 15th October, at least two Cambodian soldiers were killed when Thai and Cambodian troops skirmished near the disputed Preah Vihear temple on the border. Thailand implicitly accused Cambodia of planting further mines in the already heavily mined area, claiming a number of new Russian-made mines have been found buried in the ground and that two Thai soldiers had their legs blown off earlier in the month.

In November the anti government demonstrations reached crisis point when thousands of PAD protesters demanded the resignation of the government. On December 2nd a Thai court ruled that Prime Minister Somchai Wongsawat must step down due to election fraud. The Constitutional Court ruling used to force him from office also disbanded the People Power Party for electoral fraud and leaders of the party were banned from politics for five years. The first deputy prime minister, Chaowarat Chandeerakul took over the post as caretaker prime minister and, on December 15 parliament elected opposition leader Abhisit Vejjajiva to the post.

On the 8th June 2009, militants killed at least 10 people and wounded 12 more when they opened fire on worshippers in a mosque in Narathiwat province, southern Thailand. The imam was among the dead. Over 3,700 people have died during a five-year insurgency in southern Thailand's mainly Muslim provinces. Thailand annexed the three provinces of Narathiwat, Yala and Pattani in 1902. Attacks targeted people perceived to be collaborating with the Bangkok government, or are aimed at forcing Buddhist residents from the area in order to establish an Islamic state.

In March 2010 protesters against the government again took to the streets, they carried phials of their own blood which they spilt outside the government headquarters and the prime minister's private residence. A few days later thousands of protesters dressed in red shirts flooded the streets of Bangkok, calling for the government to step down and call fresh elections. Protests by the Red Shirts continued and in April 2010 Prime Minister Abhisit declared state of emergency in Bangkok. On April 9 protestors clashed with police and 21 people were killed. As a result the army chief called for the parliament to be dissolved. Election officials have also recommended Prime Minister Abhisit's party be disbanded over accusations of illegal donations. Violence continued but the protests ended in May when the army stormed the protestors' barricades. However the state of emergency which had been in existence was extended in July amid fears of renewed violence.

In January 2011, Cambodia charged two Thai citizens with espionage after they crossed the countries' disputed border in December. Tension between the two nations further increased in February when Thai and Cambodian forces exchanged fire across the disputed border area near the Preah Vihear temple. Both sides agreed to allow Indonesian monitors in, in an effort to prevent further clashes. However, in April fighting broke out between Cambodian and Thai forces across the border near two disputed Hindu temples of Ta Moan and Ta Krabey, later the fighting spread to the area of Preah Vihear temple.

Elections for the post of prime minister took place in July 2011 and were won by Yingluck Shinawatra.

In June 2012 anti-government protestors blockaded parliament to try to prevent discussion on a posposed reconciliaton bill and amnesty. The group feared that such a move would allow the return of the ousted prime minister Thaksin Shinawatra.

Civil discontent continued: in November 2012 several thousand protestors were dispersed by police. The protestors were calling for the overthrow of the prime minister.

THAILAND

In December 2012, the former prime minister Abhisit Vejjajiva was charged with responsibility for the death of a civilian shot by troops during anti-government protests in 2010.

The leader of the CTP party and minister of tourism and sports died in January 2013.

Legislature

A new constitution was drafted in 1997 which made provision for a directly elected senate. The Senate had previously been made up of appointed members; it now consists of 200 directly elected members who serve a six year term. The new constitution also changed the structure of the House of Representatives: instead of deputies in the House of Representatives being from multi-member constituencies, 400 deputies now represent single member constituencies and 100 deputies are elected by proportional representation from party lists. An election commission was appointed to oversee elections. The new constitution was promulgated in October 1997.

Upper House

Wuthisapha, Senate, National Assembly, U Thong Nai Road, Bangkok 10300, Tel: +66 2 559 5639, URL: http://www.parliament.go.th

Lower House

Rathasapha, House of Representatives, National Assembly, U Thong Nai Road, Bangkok 10300, Tel: +66 2 357 3100, URL: http://www.parliament.go.th

Cabinet (as at March 2013)
Prime Minister: Yingluck Shinawatra
Deputy Prime Minister, responsible for the Ministry of the Interior: Chalerm Yubumrung (page 1542)
Deputy Prime Minister, Minister of Finance: Kittirat na Ranong (page 1457)
Deputy Prime Minister, Minister of Tourism and Sports: currently vacant
Deputy Prime Minister, Minister of Foreign Affairs: Surapong Towichukchaikul (page 1527)
Deputy Prime Minister, Minister of Education, Social and Legal Affairs: Phongthep Thepkanchana (page 1524)
Deputy Prime Minister, Minister of Water Management: Plodrasob Surassawadee
Minister in the Office of the Prime Minister: Surawit Khonsomboon
Minister in the Office of the Prime Minister: Kritsana Seehalak
Minister of Commerce: Bonsong Teriyapirong
Minister of Defence: Sukampol Suwanatat
Minister of the Interior: Jarapong Ruangsuwan
Minister of Agriculture: Yukol Limthong
Minister of Education: Suchart Thadathamrongvej
Minister of Public Health: Pradit Sinthwanarong
Ministry of Industry: Prasert Boonchaisuk
Minister of Justice: Pracha Promnok
Minister of Energy: Pongsak Rensomboonsuk
Minister of Labour: Phadermchai Sasomsap
Minister of Transport: Chatchachart Sittihphan
Minister of Information and Communication Technology: Captain Anudith Nakornthap
Minister of Natural Resources and Environment: Preecha Rengsomboonsun
Minister of Culture: Sukumol Kunplome
Minister of Social Development and Human Security: Santi Promphat
Minister in the Office of the Prime Minister: Sansanee Nakpong
Minister in the Office of the Prime Minister: Niwattamrong Boonsongpaisal
Minister in the Office of the Prime Minister: Nalinee Taweesin
Minister in the Office of the Prime Minister: Woravat Auapinvakul

Ministries
Office of the King, URL: http://www.kanchanapisek.or.th/
Office of the Prime Minister, Government House, Thanon Nakhon Pathom, Bangkok 10300, Thailand. Tel: +66 (0)2 280 3526, fax: +66 (0)282 8792, URL: http://www.opm.go.th
Ministry of Defence, Thanon Sanamchai, Bangkok 10200, Thailand. Tel: +66 (0)2 222 1211 / 225 0098, fax: +66 (0)2 226 3117, URL: http://www.mod.go.th
Ministry of Cultural Promotion, URL: http://www.culture.go.th/
Ministry of Finance, Thanon Rama VI, Bangkok 10400, Thailand. Tel: +66 (0)2 273 9021, URL: http://www2.mof.go.th/
Ministry of Foreign Affairs, Bangkok, Thailand. Tel: +66 (0)2 225 0096 / 225 7900 / 43, URL: http://www.mfa.go.th
Ministry of Transport, Thanon Ratchadamnoen Nok, Bangkok, Thailand. Tel: +66 (0)2 281 3422
Ministry of Commerce, Thanon Sanamchai, Bangkok 10200, Thailand. Tel: +66 (0)2 221 1831/ 226 0294 / 5, URL: http://www.moc.go.th
Ministry of Energy, URL: http://www.energy.go.th/
Ministry of Interior, Thanon Atsadang, Bangkok 10200, Thailand. Tel: +66 (0)2 222 1141/55, URL: http://www.moi.go.th/
Ministry of Justice, Thanon Rachadaphisek, Chatuchak, Bangkok 10900, Thailand. Tel: +66 (0)2 541 2284 / 91, URL: http://www.moj.go.th
Ministry of Education, Chankasem Palace, Thanon Ratchadamnoen Nok, Bangkok 10300, Thailand. Tel: +66 (0)2 282 9893 / 281 6013, URL: http://www.moe.go.th
Ministry of Public Health, Thanon Tiwanond, Amphoe Muang, Nonthaburi 11000, Thailand. Tel: +66 (0)2 591 8495, URL: http://www.moph.go.th
Ministry of Science, Technology & Environment, Thanon Phra Ram VI, Ratchathewi, Bangkok 10400, Thailand. Tel: +66 (0)2 246 0064 / 246 1382 / 6, URL: http://www.moste.go.th
Ministry of Industry, Thanon Phra Ram VI, Bangkok 10400, Thailand. Tel: +66 (0)2 202 3000 / 4, URL: http://www.tisi.go.th/moi
Ministry of Labour and Social Welfare, Thanon Mitmaitri, Dindaeng, Huai Kwang, Bangkok 10400, Thailand. Tel: +66 2 246 1707, fax: +66 2 245 3375, URL: http://www.molsw.go.th

Main Political Parties
Democratic Party (Phak Prachatipat), 67 Setsiri Road, Samsennai Phayathai, Bangkok 10400, Thailand. E-mail: webmaster@democrat.or.th, URL: http://www.democrat.or.th
People's Power Party (Palang Prachachon), URL: http://www.ppp.or.th
Thai Nation Development Party (Phak Chat Thai).
Great People's Party (Phak Mahachon). Leader: Apirat Sirinawin
Royalist People's Party (Phracharaj). Leader: Sanoh Thienthong
For the Motherland (Pua Paendin). Leader: Suwit Khunkitti
For Thai Party, Pheu Thai party: Leader: Yingluck Shinawatra
For Thai Party (Pheu Thai - PT)
Proud Thais party (Bhum Jai Thai - BJT)

Elections
Following political unrest in the south of the country and allegations of tax avoidance, Prime Minister Thaksin dissolved parliament in February 2006 and called for early elections. Opposition parties boycotted the election and the Thai Love Thai party won, but the courts ruled the election was invalid. New elections were called, while the existing government remained in a caretaker capacity. On 19 September the government was overthrown in a bloodless coup, led by General Sonthi Boonyaratkalin who promised elections within a year. Elections were held in December 2007, and were won by the People Power Party (PPP). In January 2008, the People Power Party (PPP) announced a new coalition government which included five smaller parties.

Senate elections took place in March 2008, voter turnout was low.

The most recent elections were held in July 2011. In a surprise result the Pheu Thai party, led by Yingluck Shinawatra, sister of the ousted prime minister Thaksin Shinawatra won a clear majority with an estimated 265 seats. Although Shinawatra won a majority she opted to included members from the Thai Nation Development Party and the National Development Party for the Homeland in her cabinet. Having won such a clear majority it was not necessary for Shinawatra to form a coalition but the alliance gave her a larger power base making it easier to push policies through government.

Diplomatic Representation
Royal Thai Embassy, 29-30 Queen's Gate, London, SW7 5JB, United Kingdom. Tel: +44 (0)20 7589 2944, fax: +44 (0)20 7823 9695, URL: http://www.thaiembassyuk.org.uk/
Ambassador Extraordinary and Plenipotentiary: H.E. Mr Pasan Teparak (page 1524)
Royal Thai Embassy, Suite 401,1024 Wisconsin Avenue, NW, Washington, DC 20007, USA. Tel: +1 202 944 3600, fax: +1 202 944 3611, e-mail: thai.wsn@thaiembdc.org, URL: http://www.thaiembdc.org/
Ambassador: Chauyong Satchiphanon
British Embassy, 1031 Wireless Road, Lumpini Pathumwan, Bangkok 10330, Thailand. Tel: +66 (0)2 253 0191, fax: +66 (0)2 254 9578, e-mail: info.bangkok@fco.gov.uk, URL: http://ukinthailand.fco.gov.uk/en
Ambassador: Asif Ahmad (page 1373)
US Embassy, 120 Wireless Road, Bangkok 10330, Thailand. Tel: +66 (0)2 205 4000, fax: +66 (0)2 205 4131,URL: http://bangkok.usembassy.gov/
Ambassador: Kristie A. Kenney (page 1455)
Permanent Mission of Thailand to the United Nations, 351 East 52nd Street, New York, NY 10022, USA. Tel: +1 212 754 2230, fax: +1 212 688 3029, e-mail: thailand@un.int, URL: http://www.un.int/wcm/content/site/thailand
Ambassador: Norachit Sinhaseni

LEGAL SYSTEM

The judicial system is independent of government, and Thai law is based on the Constitution and its implementing statutes. Thailand has no juries, and judges preside over the courts. The Thai court system consists of Courts of Justice, Military Courts, Administrative Courts and a Constitutional Tribunal.

The Courts of Justice are located throughout the country and known as Provincial Courts; in Bangkok they are divided into Civil Courts, Criminal Courts, Juvenile Courts, Family Courts, Labour Courts and Tax Courts. There are ten Courts of Appeal, one in Bangkok and nine Regional Courts of Appeal that hear appeals from the Provincial Courts. The highest court is the Supreme Court (Dika), located in Bangkok. It receives appeals on questions of law and in some cases on questions of fact from the Courts of Appeal, as well as direct appeals from Specialized Courts. The Dika Court has about 60 to 70 justices, including the President (Chief Justice) and Vice Presidents.

In terms of government respect of human rights, the security forces continue to use excessive force against suspects, and police have been linked to disappearances and unlawful killings. Police corruption is thought to be widespread. Prisons are overcrowded. The government limits freedom of speech, of the press, and of assembly. Thailand retains the death penalty. The Thai authority resumed executions in 1995 after an eight-year moratorium. The most recent execution took place in 2009. Every convicted prisoner has the right to petition the King for a pardon.

Supreme Court of Thailand, URL: http://www.supremecourt.or.th/ (Thai only)

Office of the National Human Rights Commission of Thailand, URL: http://www.nhrc.or.th/

LOCAL GOVERNMENT

The country is divided into four administrative regions and 76 provinces or Changwads, which are sub-divided into 877 districts and 7,255 tambon administrative units. Each Changwad is governed by a Provincial Governor and each Amphur by a Nai Amphur, both being appointed by the Ministry of the Interior. Municipalities are governed by an elected Municipal Council and Provincial Governors can call upon the advice of an elected Provincial Council. Metropolitan Bangkok is governed by an elected Governor.

AREA AND POPULATION

Area

Thailand has borders with Malaysia (in the south), Laos (in the north-east), Cambodia (in the east) and Myanmar (Burma, in the west). Southern Thailand is a peninsular bounded to the east by the Gulf of Thailand and to the west the Andaman Sea. Its area is 513,115 sq. km. The climate is warm and humid with a rainy season from about June to October and a relatively dry season for the remainder of the year. The average temperature is between 23.7°C and 32.5°C.

The north of Thailand is a mountainous region with forests, ridges and deep narrow alluvial valleys. The central area, where the Chao Phraya river basin is found, is a lush and fertile valley and, as the richest and most extensive rice-producing area, is often called the 'Rice Bowl of Asia'. Undulating hills are to be found along the Karat Plateau of the north-east region where the harsh climate often results in floods and droughts. The south is a hilly to mountainous peninsula with thick forests and rich mineral deposits.

To view a map, consult http://www.un.org/Depts/Cartographic/map/profile/thailand.pdf

Population

The population was estimated to be 69.122 million in 2010, with an average annual growth rate of 0.9 per cent over the period 2000-10. An estimated 34 per cent of the population live in urban areas, 9.6 per cent in Bangkok (the only city of significant size) and 5.7 per cent in other cities. Major cities include Chiang Mai, Chon Buri, Khon Kaen, Nakhon Ratchasima and Songkhla. The population is made by of Thai 75 per cent; Chinese, 14 per cent; and 11 per cent of other origin.

Births, Marriages, Deaths

Estimated figures for 2010 put the birth rate at 12.1births per 1,000 population and 10.2 deaths per 1,000 population. Life expectancy in 2009 was 66 years for males and 74 years for females. Healthy life expectancy was 62 years. The government has sponsored a successful programme of family planning which has seen the birth rate fall from 3.21 per cent in 1960 to 1.8 per cent in 2008. In 2010 the median age was 34 years. An estimated 21 per cent of the population was aged 14 years or less and an estimated 13 per cent aged over 60. (Source: http://www.who.int, World Health Statistics 2012)

The official language is Thai, although English is widely understood.

Public Holidays 2014

1 January: New Year's Day
14 February: Makha Bucha Day*
7 April: Chakri Day
13-14 April: Thai New Year
1 May: Labour Day
5 May: Coronation Day
13 May: Visakha Bucha
11 July: Asahna Bucha
12 August: Queen's Birthday
23 October: Chulalongkorn Day
5 December: King's Birthday
10 December: Constitution Day
31 December: New Year's Eve

* Holidays depend on the Buddhist Lunar Calendar and so vary.

EMPLOYMENT

Before the Asian financial crisis in 1997, unemployment in Thailand was around three per cent; however, the unemployment rate rose to 4.4 per cent in 1997, 4.0 per cent in 1998 and as high as 5.3 per cent in 1999. Figures for 2000 showed the rate to be 3.2 per cent (1.1 million people) falling to 1.5 per cent (554,000 people) in 2003. The following table shows employment figures in recent years:

Sector	2005	2006	2007
Labour force	36,120,000	36,429,000	36,942,000
Employed	35,257,000	35,686,000	36,249,000
Agriculture	13,617,000	14,171,000	14,306,000
Manufacturing	5,588,000	5,504,000	5,619,000
Mining	56,000	58,000	63,000
Others	15,996,000	15,953,000	16,261,000
Unemployed	663,000	552,000	508,000
Unemployment rate	1.8	1.5	1.4

Source: Asian Development Bank

Total Employment by Economic Activity

Occupation	2008
Agriculture, hunting & forestry	15,641,400
Fishing	425,600
Mining & quarrying	55,000
Manufacturing	5,231,400
Electricity, gas & water supply	103,100
Construction	2,012,100
Wholesale & retail trade, repairs	5,634,900

- continued

Hotels & restaurants	2,353,200
Transport, storage & communications	1,090,500
Financial intermediation	396,200
Real estate, renting & business activities	717,000
Public admin. & defence; compulsory social security	1,303,300
Education	1,097,500
Health & social work	720,400
Other community, social & personal service activities	818,900
Households with employed persons	196,100
Extra-territorial organisations & bodies	1,400
Other	38,500
Total	37,836,600

Source: Copyright © International Labour Organization (ILO Dept. of Statistics, http://laborsta.ilo.org)

BANKING AND FINANCE

Currency

One Baht = 100 satangs

GDP/GNP, Inflation, National Debt

Thailand's economy is developed using five year plans; the Eighth Economic and Social Development Plan (1997 - 2001) had to be considerably revised after the collapse of the economy. This period saw opening of the market and increased foreign investment. Economic growth was strong, averaging over 5 per cent. Economic growth slowed in 2005-07 because of political instability and the effect of the 2004 Tsunmani. The global economic crisis has also affected Thailand's export-based economy and growth contracted in 2008 and 2009. Although the economy initially rebounded it was further hit in 2010 by poor agricultural harvests and floods. The government has announced plans to spend £40 billion on infrastructure and the economy is expected to recover in 2012 and 2013.

GDP, current market prices, billion baht

Sector	2008	2009	2010
GDP at current market prices	9,080	9,042	10,103
-Agriculture	1,050	1,037	1,255
-Mining	315	307	346
-Manufacturing	3,164	3,088	3,599
-Electricity, gas and water	262	278	297
-Construction	259	246	269
-Trade	1,288	1,273	1,324
-Transport & communications	645	647	688
-Finance	571	585	639
-Public Administration	399	416	440
-Others	1,126	1,166	1,246
Net factor income from abroad	-324	-353	-436
GNI at current market prices	8,757	8,689	9,667

Source: Asian Development Bank

GDP was estimated to be US$318.5 billion in 2010, rising to US$345 billion in 2011. Growth was estimated to be 5.1 per cent in 2011. GDP growth is forecast to be 4 per cent in 2012.

The inflation was estimated to be 2.3 per cent in 2007, 5.4 per cent in 2008, -0.9 per cent in 2009, 3.2 per cent in 2010 and 3.0 per cent in 2011. Inflation rose to 3.6 per cent in December 2012, driven partly by rising food costs

Total outstanding debt was US$63,067 million in 2007. Debt service was US$8,758 million in the same year. External debt rose to a record high of US$119 billion in 2012.

Foreign Investment

In an attempt to rescue the Thai economy, the government has relaxed many controls over foreign investment, including permitting the majority participation of foreign investors in any financial institution for up to ten years.

Currency Restrictions

Foreign currency may be brought in or out of the country unrestricted; if the money is in the form of investment loans etc, it must be either deposited in a foreign currency account or changed into baht within 15 days of entering the country. The taking of Thai currency out of the country is restricted to 50,000 baht per person, except if travelling to Vietnam, Myanmar, Malaysia, Cambodia or Laos, when the limit is 500,000 baht per person (2012).

Balance of Payments / Imports and Exports

Export growth has been high in recent years. The following table shows the trade balance in recent years. Figures are in billion bhat:

Trade	2008	2009	2010
Exports, fob	5,831.1	5,155.1	6,120.9
Imports, cif	5,845.4	4,485.9	5,681.3
Trade balance	-14.3	669.1	439.6

Source: ADB

Thailand's most significant export trade partners (2010) were China (US$20,424 million), Japan (US$20,424 million), the US (US$20,243 million), and Hong Kong (US$13,136 million). There is also trade with the European Union. Top importers were Japan (US$38,320 million), China (US$24,528 million) and the US (US$10,884 million). Top export groups are computers and their components, textile products, electrical appliances, integrated circuits & parts, vehicle parts & accessories, precious stones & jewellery, processed foods and rice. Principal

THAILAND

imports include machinery and parts, vehicles, chemicals, crude oil and fuels and iron and steel. (Source: ADB) Imports were estimated to be US$200 billion in 211 and exports were US$210 billion.

Central Bank
Bank of Thailand, 273 Samsen Road, Bangkhunprom, Bangkok 10200, Thailand. Tel: +66 2 2835353, fax: +66 2 2800449, e-mail: webmaster@bot.or.th, URL: http://www.bot.or.th
Governor & Chairman: Mr Prasarn Trairatvorakul

Chambers of Commerce and Trade Organisations
Thai Chamber of Commerce, URL: http://www.thaichamber.org/default.asp
American Chamber of Commerce in Thailand, URL: http://www.amchamthailand.com/acct/asp/default.asp

MANUFACTURING, MINING AND SERVICES

Primary and Extractive Industries
The oil industry is currently run by the Petroleum Authority of Thailand (PTT), although the government intended to begin its privatisation by the end of 2001. Thailand has five oil refineries, with a combined capacity (as at 2008) of 729,000 barrels per day. As of 1 January 2008, the country has proven oil reserves of 460 million barrels. In 2008, production was an estimated 228,000 barrels per day, of which 38 per cent was of crude oil. In the same year domestic consumption was 942,000 barrels per day meaning that Thailand is an oil importer as well as producer.

The country also has proven natural gas reserves - as at 1 January 2007 of 14,750 billion cubic feet, production that year was put at 897 billion cubic feet and consumption 1,247 billion cubic feet. Domestic demand for this resource, most of which is used for generating electricity, fell in tandem with the fall of the baht. Since then the government introduced a policy to encourage more consumers to use natural gas. Thailand's largest producer of gas is Unocal Thailand.

Recent figures estimate that Thailand has recoverable coal reserves of 1.4 billion short tons; as of 2002 it produced 22.0 million short tons per annum. Several other minerals are mined in Thailand, including tin, tungsten, iron ore, lead ore, antimony, manganese, barite and fluorite ore.

Energy
In 2006, Thailand produced 130.68 billion kWh of electricity, and consumed 123.91 billion kWh.

At present the Office of Atomic Energy for Peace (OAEP) provides research and development in nuclear technology and nuclear safety as well as nuclear services to both the government and private sectors from the following facilities: the Thai Research Reactor; 1/Modification (TRR-1/MI); 2 MW Steady State/2,000 MW Pulsing TRIGA MARK III; Cobalt - 60 Irradiator (AECL Gamma Beam 650/50,000); Physical, Biological Sciences Laboratories and Electronic Laboratories and Workshop. EGAT first proposed to construct Thailand's first nuclear power plant a decade ago, but this project never got off the ground due to financial constraints and has since been shelved indefinitely.

Electricity is distributed in Bangkok and the surrounding area by the Metropolitan Electricity Authority (MEA), and in the rest of the country by the Provincial Electricity Authority (PEA).

Manufacturing
Industrialisation in Thailand began chiefly in the 1960s and was characterised as being mainly a substitute for imports; but by the 1970s manufacturing became more export-oriented, with a growth in the manufacture of intermediate and capital goods. Manufacturing in Thailand mainly revolves around the electronic industry, textiles and garments. Growth in the exports of manufactured exports reached 24.8 per cent in 1995, although the economic crisis in subsequent years has since seen these rates slow considerably. Following the collapse of the Baht in 1997, loans from the IMF were used for the re-structuring of the manufacturing sector. Priority was given to small and medium sized enterprises. The following table shows manufacturing production in recent years. Figures are in metric tons:

Product	2005	2006	2007
Cement	37,871.7	39,408.2	35,668.3
Sugar	5,028.4	5,719.4	7,344.0
Synthetic fibre	809.0	725.4	674.6
Tin plate	228.1	301.5	238.9
Galvanized iron sheet	283.6	297.7	247.2

Source: Asian Development Bank

Service Industries
Since 1982 tourism has been Thailand's highest generator of income, with figures for 1998 showing 7,843,000 visitors generating US$59 billion, rising to 11,737,000 visitors in 2004. Following the devastation caused by the 2004 tsunami, tourist figures were expected to fall in 2005 but had risen in 2006 to 13,822,000.

Agriculture
Agriculture has traditionally been Thailand's main industry. Over 40 per cent of the land is under agricultural use with main crops being rice, tin, rubber, maize sugar and tapioca. More than 10 per cent of Thailand's fish catch comes from the sea. Growth in agricultural exports reached 23.7 per cent in 1995 while growth in exports of fish and related products reached 4.8 per cent the same year; again the economic crisis has since seen these rates slow considerably. In order to assist the industry, the Bank of Thailand has stipulated that 20 per cent of all commercial bank deposits are lent to farmers. (Source: Thai Embassy) In 2004/05, Thailand was hit by a severe drought, and therefore agricultural production was set to fall.

Agricultural Production in 2010

Produce	Int. $'000*	Tonnes
Rice, paddy	7,909,097	31,597,200
Natural rubber	3,490,733	3,051,780
Cassava	2,298,781	22,005,700
Sugar cane	2,259,442	68,807,800
Indigenous chicken meat	1,736,181	1,218,880
Mangoes, mangosttens, guavas	1,528,235	2,550,600
Indigenous pigmeat	1,431,253	931,053
Other bird eggs, in shell	1,139,267	395,000
Indigenous cattle meat	621,797	230,178
Palm oil	560,140	1,287,510
Pineapples	548,617	1,924,660
Hen eggs, in shell	485,607	585,500

* unofficial figures

Fishing
FAO figures for 2010 put the total catch at 1,827,199 tonnes.

COMMUNICATIONS AND TRANSPORT

Travel Requirements
Citizens of the USA, Canada, Australia and most of the EU require a passport valid for six months beyond the length of stay, sufficient funds and return/onward tickets but do not need a visa for stays of up to 30 days. The exceptions are nationals of Bulgaria, Romania and Malta who do need a visa and nationals of Cyprus, Czech Republic, Estonia, Hungary, Latvia, Liechtenstein, Lithuania, Poland, Slovak Republic and Slovenia who may apply for visas on arrival for stays of up to 15 days. The duration of stay in Thailand for persons who enter Thailand without a visa cannot exceed 90 days during any six-month period, counting from the date of first entry. Other nationals should contact the embassy to check visa requirements.

National Airlines
In early 1960 the former Thai Airways Company was reorganised and a new company, Thai Airways International, was formed, with SAS participation, to take over international services, leaving Thai Airways Company to operate internal services and a few routes to neighbouring countries.

Thai Airways International Ltd., URL: http://www.thaiair.com

International Airports
Suvarnabhumi Airport (Also known as New Bangkok International Airport), opened in 2006. Bangkok has a another international airport (Don Muang, also known as Old Bangkok International Airport), about fifteen miles from the city centre.

Railways
Recent figures show the length of track open to traffic is over 4,600 km. The three main lines all start in Bangkok, one ends in Chiang Mai, the second in Nong Khai and Ubon Ratchathani, and the third near the Malaysian border at Padang Besar and Sunai Kolok. A rail link connects Thailand with Kuala Lumpur in Malaysia, and then continues to Singapore.

Around 86 million passengers us the railway system each year. In 1999 the Bangkok Transit System (BTS) came into operation. This consists of two routes the Sukhumvit and the Silom routes. Both routes use the Rama 1 Road central station. Another system is under construction is the underground Metropolitan Rapid Transit (MRT) which will eventually connect with the BTS.
State Railways of Thailand, URL: http://www.thailandrailway.com

Roads
Recent figures show the total length of road is over 189,000 km including, approximately 54,000 km of highways and 135,000 km of rural roads. Vehicles drive on the left. The North-East Highway (158 km) was finished in 1958; the East-West Highway (130 km) in 1960 and the Nakorn Rajsima-Hongtsi Highway in 1965.

Ports and Harbours
Thailand's major port is Bangkok which takes ocean going vessels up to 12,000 tons dead weight and is fast approaching the limit of its capacity. There are deep water ports at Songkhla and Phuket; other major ports include Pattani and Si Racha. The naval base of Sattahip has been leased to the Ports Authority to ease congestion.

Ferry services run from Phuket to Indonesia stopping at islands on the way. Ferries also run Satun in southern Thailand to the Malaysian island of Langkawi.

Thai Maritime Nav. Co. Ltd., 59 New Road, Yanawa District
Thai Petroleum Transports Co. Ltd., 355, Soontornkosa Road, Postbox 2172, Klong Toey, Bangkok. Tel: +66 249 0259
5 Vessels
Juha Maritime Co. Ltd., 2nd Floor, Silom Building, 302, Silom Road Postbox 2362, Bangkok 10500. Tel: +66 234 7920/4
3 Vessels

HEALTH

The Ministry of Public Health has taken major responsibility for the delivery of health services in Thailand. The government owns and operates 70 per cent of hospitals while those in the private sector have fewer beds and are located mainly in urban areas. There is a health service in every tambon (group of villages), a hospital of 10-90 beds in every district and a hospital of 200-500 with specialised care in every province.

In 2009, the government spent approximately 13.3 per cent of its total budget on healthcare, accounting for 74.6 per cent of all healthcare spending. Private expenditure amounted to 25.4 per cent of total expenditure. Total expenditure on healthcare equated to 4.2 per cent of the country's GDP. Per capita expenditure on health was approximately US$160, compared with US$66 in 2000. Figures for 2000-10 show that there are 18,918 physicians (3 per 10,000 population), 96,704 nurses and midwives (15.2 per 10,000 population), 4,129 dentistry personnel, 7,413 pharmaceutical personnel, 2,151 environment and public health workers. There were approximately 22 hospital beds per 10,000 population.

In 2010 the infant mortality rate (probability of dying before first birthday) was 11 per 1,000 live births and the child (under-five years old) mortality rate was 13 per 1,000 live births. The main causes of death in the under-fives are: prematurity (24 per cent), pneumonia (9 per cent), congenital anomalies (27 per cent), birth asphyxia (8 per cent), diarrhoea (3 per cent), and HIV/AIDS (1 per cent). In the period 2000-09 an estimated 15.7 per cent of children (under five-years-old) were classified as stunted and 7.0 per cent as underweight. Approximately 8 per cent of children were classified as overweight.

According to the latest WHO figures, in 2010 approximately 96 per cent of the population had access to improved drinking water and to improved sanitation. (Source: http://www.who.int, World Health Statistics 2012)

EDUCATION

Primary education is compulsory for children from the age of seven to 14 and is free in the public and municipal schools.

Figures from UNESCO for 2007 show that 94 per cent of male and female student were enrolled in primary school and 72 per cent of males students and 81 per cent of female students were enrolled in secondary school. Around 50 per cent of tertiary aged students go onto further education.

The Chulalonghorn University was founded at Bangkok in 1917 and the Thammasat University in 1934. Other universities are the University of Medical Science, founded in 1888, and more recently the University of Agriculture and the University of Fine Arts, all in Bangkok. There is also a University at Chiang Mai in North Thailand. New universities have been set up in the North-East, at Khon Kaen, and in the South at Songkhla. An Open University was established in Bangkok in 1972. A programme of adult education was introduced in 1940.

In 2007, 20.9 pre cent of total government expenditure went on education, 34 per cent of which went on primary education and 19 per cent on secondary education. That year literacy figures were put at 94.1 per cent for adults and 98.2 per cent for youth (aged 15-24).

RELIGION

Recent figures show that 87 per cent of the country is Buddhist while six per cent is Muslim.

Thailand has a religious liberty rating of 6 on a scale of 1 to 10 (10 is most freedom). (Source: World Religion Database)

COMMUNICATIONS AND MEDIA

Most of the national television and radio networks are controlled by the government and military. The press is free to criticise the government but there is self-censorship on issues relating to the military, the judiciary and the monarchy.

Newspapers
Most newspapers are privately run.
Bangkok Post, English, URL: http://www.bangkokpost.co.th
The Nation, English, URL: http://www.nationmultimedia.com
Thai Rath, Thai, URL: http://www.thairath.co.th
Daily News, Thai, URL: http://www.dailynews.co.th

Broadcasting
Most of the terrestial TV networks are either government or military controlled. All are required to broadcdast office news programmes. Satellite and cable TV subscription services are available. Hundreds of government, commercial and community radio stations operate.
Thai TV3, government-owned, URL: http://www.tv3.co.th/
TV5, URL: http://portal.tv5.co.th/
Thai Public Broadcasting Service, URL: http://www.thaipbs.or.th/

Telecommunications
Thailand's telecommunications system is of a good quality especially in urban areas. The mobile phone service is expanding rapidly. Over 7 million land lines are in operation and 62 million mobile phones.

Estimates from 2010 show that over 16 million people in Thailand are regular internet users.

ENVIRONMENT

Tropical logging was banned in 1989 in an effort to protect the rainforest. The government sets incentives to the private sector for reforestation and has set a target for forest area to cover 40 per cent of the country's total land area.

The Chuan government introduced the 'polluter pays' principle by which the parties responsible for particular environmental damage are held accountable for their actions and are called upon to either repair the damage or reimburse the government. The government has also been working in co-operation with the business sector to protect, maintain and monitor the environment; there is considerable water pollution from factory run-off and air pollution from vehicular emissions.

In 2006, Thailand's emissions from the consumption of fossil fuels totalled 245.04 million metric tons of carbon dioxide.

SPACE PROGRAMME

The Geo-Informatics and Space Technology Development Agency (URL: http://www.gistda.or.th/gistda_n/en/) is responsible for is the space research organisation responsible for remote sensing and technology development satellites. Thailand has been involved in satellite remote sensing since the launch of the NASA ERTS-1 programme in 1971 under the National Research Council of Thailand. The Council became the Thailand Remote Sensing Centre in 1979. The Thailand Ground Receiving Station was set up in 1972 and was the first of its kind in southeast Asia. The Thailand Earth Observation satellite was launched from Russia in 2008.

STATES OF THE WORLD

TIMOR-LESTE
Democratic Republic of Timor-Leste
República Democrática de Timor-Leste

Capital: Dilly (Dili) (Population estimate: 156,000)

Head of State: José Maria Vasconcelos (Taur Matan Ruak) (page 1412)

Flag: The flag is formed by two superimposed triangles with their bases at the hoist; the black triangle, of a height equal to one-third of the flag's length, is superimposed on the yellow, whose height is equal to half the length of the flag. There is a white star in the centre of the black triangle; the remainder of the flag is red.

CONSTITUTION AND GOVERNMENT

History
East Timor, the eastern half of the Timor Island came under Portuguese control in 1904. The rest of the island was ceded to the Indonesians by the Dutch in 1949. In East Timor the process of decolonisation was crippled by the civil war that broke out in 1974 between three political movements - the Timor Democratic Union (UDT), the Revolutionary Front for the Independence of East Timor (Fretilin) and the Timor Popular Democratic Association (APODETI). In 1974 the Portuguese authorities were forced to leave the territory, following a failed coup by the Timor Democratic Union. Fretilin subsequently declared the independence of East Timor.

On 7 December 1975 Indonesia intervened and occupied the territory. Portugal asked the United Nations to intervene and the Security Council demanded the withdrawal of the Indonesian forces. In spite of the strong military presence by the Indonesians and an intensive programme of transmigration transferring Indonesian citizens to East Timor, Indonesia was not able to curb resistance to her rule among the East Timorese.

Portugal and the UN never recognised the Indonesian annexation. The UN considered Portugal to be the Administering Power over the territory until the East Timorese were able to exercise their rights freely. In order to find an internationally acceptable solution to the problem, Portugal and Indonesia agreed to resume talks under the auspices of the UN Secretary General. In 1999 at talks between the UN, Indonesia and Portugal, Ali Alatas, the foreign minister, announced that Indonesia would grant independence to East Timor.

A referendum offering a choice between autonomy and full independence from Indonesia was held in September 1999. 78.5 per cent of the population voted for independence and 21 per cent voted for autonomy under Indonesian rule. The UN reported that more than 98 per cent of eligible voters went to the polls. Violence from pro-Indonesia militias followed the referendum, causing over 600 deaths and displacing some 200,000 East Timorese to West Timor.

TIMOR-LESTE

In October 1999 the Indonesian House of Representatives accepted the result of the referendum and a coalition government of East Timorese leaders and UN administrators was formed in July 2000. In October, the 36-member National Council (NC) was set up to replace the National Consultative Council (NCC) and form the basis of a future assembly. The president of the East Timor National Council (appointed by the UN) was Manuel Carrascalao. The Transitional Cabinet was replaced on 20 September 2001 by the 24-member East Timorese Council of Ministers of the Second Transitional Government.

Following the referendum, then President B.J. Habibie accepted the role of UN peacekeeping troops in East Timor and a month later, newly-elected President Abdurrahman Wahid officially gave the UN authority to administer East Timor. In October 1999 the administration of East Timor was assumed by the UN under the auspices of the United Nations Transitional Administration for East Timor (UNTAET). On 31 January 2002 the UN Security Council voted to extend UNTAET's mandate until East Timor's independence on 20 May 2002. Following independence, UNTAET became the UN Mission of Support in East Timor (UNMISET). The mandate has been extended several times, currently until 2012.

Following independence, the government requested that the state be known as Timor-Leste and not East Timor.

Constitution
On 30 November 2001 the Constituent Assembly voted to approve the structure of East Timor's first draft constitution. East Timor's first constitution was signed into force by the Constituent Assembly on 22 March 2002. East Timor became independent on 20 May 2002.

According to the 2002 Constitution, the head of state is the president, directly elected by universal adult suffrage for a five-year term. The head of government is the prime minister, appointed by the president, who nominates the Council of Ministers.

To consult the constitution, please visit: http://www.gov.east-timor.org/constitution/constitution.htm

International Relations
Timor-Leste maintains good relations with Indonesia, and the two countries have set up a Commission for Bilateral Co-operation, to address social and border issues, trade and finance matters, educational and cultural affairs, transport and telecommunications and legal matters. The Government of Timor-Leste contributed humanitarian assistance to the Indonesian victims of the 2004 tsunami, and the Indonesian Government sent aid to help those displaced by the unrest in Dili in 2006.

Timor-Leste enjoys strong links with Australia and Portugal, for historical and geographical reasons. Other significant links are with Japan, the UK, the USA, Thailand, the Philippines, Singapore, Malaysia and New Zealand. The country wishes to join ASEAN (the South East Asian grouping); it joined the United Nations on September 27, 2002 and it became a member of the Non Aligned Movement (NAM) on 24 February 2003.

Recent Events
In May 2005, the UN peacekeeping mission (UNMISET) was wound up, but a small follow-on special mission, (the UN Office in Timor-Leste) was set up to monitor progress over the year to May 2006. A UN report concluded that the perpetrators of the massacres following the independence referendum in 1999 had not been brought to justice; the Indonesian special court had acquitted most of the 18 suspects.

In April 2005, the newly elected Indonesian President visited Timor-Leste, and a border agreement was signed. Agreement was also reached with Australia over the division of revenues from oil and gas deposits in the Timor Sea.

A Truth and Friendship Commission (TFC) accord was signed by the governments of Timor-Leste and Indonesia in August 2005. Its remit was to look into the events surrounding the 1999 referendum, and to settle alleged human rights abuses in East Timor. Both sides agreed that the Commission should have precedence over any UN-backed international tribunal. The final report by the Truth Commission was published in July 2008; it blamed Indonesia for the human rights violations in the run-up to East Timor's independence in 1999. President Susilo of Indonesia expressed "deep regret" but stopped short of an apology.

In May 2006, violence flared when 600 striking soldiers were sacked from the army. At least 30 people were killed and 150,000 others forced from their homes. In June there were calls for the resignation of Prime Minister Alkatiri for triggering the violence by sacking the soldiers as well as for allegations that he had armed civilians to intimidate his opponents. President Gusmao publicly told Alkatiri to quit; the popular Foreign Minister, Sr. Ramos-Horta resigned, and the President threatened to do the same. Sr.Alkatiri resigned on 26th June, and Sr. Ramos-Horta was appointed Acting Prime Minister, then Prime Minister. In August 2006, a UN peacekeeping mission, Unmit, was set up. In January 2007, the former interior minister Rogerio Lobato was found guilty of arming civilians during the unrest; he claimed to be acting on the orders of Mr Alkatiri when he supplied weapons to a rebel leader.

There were further riots in March 2007, following a request from President Gusmao to the Australian peacekeepers that they arrest Maj. Reinado, a renegade officer accused of stealing weapons in attacks on police posts. Maj. Reinado was jailed over his role in the riots of 2006 but he escaped in a mass breakout from a Dili prison. On 11th February 2008, President Jose Ramos-Horta was shot by rebel soldiers led by Maj. Reinado, and put into an induced coma before being airlifted to Australia for treatment. Maj. Reinado died in the attack. Prime Minister Gusmao was targeted in a separate attack, but was unharmed. President Ramos-Horta returned to Dili in April. On 29th April 2008, the new leader of the rebel soldiers, Gastao Salsinha, and eleven others surrendered, following talks with the authorities, and thus brought to an end the rebellion that began in May 2006.

The deputy prime minister resigned in September 2010.

Timor-Leste applied to join ASEAN in March 2011.

José Maria Vasconcelos (Taur Matan Ruak) was elected president in April 2012 and was sworn into office in May.

The UN officially ended its peacekeeping mission in December 2012.

Legislature
On 31 January 2002 the 88-member Constituent Assembly voted to become Timor-Leste's first legislature once the Constitution had been approved. Members serve a five year term. URL: http://www.parliament.east-timor.org

Cabinet (as at June 2013)
Prime Minister: Xanana Gusmão (CNRT) (page 1435)
Deputy Prime Minister, Minister of Social Welfare and Sport: Fernando Lasama
Presidency of the Council of Ministers: Hermenegild Pereira Alves
Minister of Foreign Affairs: José Luis Guterres (page 1435)
Minister for Finance: Emilia Pires (page 1496)
Minister of Administration: Jorge Teme
Minister for Commerce, Industry and the Environment: Antonio da Conceicao
Minister for Education: Bendito Freitas
Minister for Justice: Dionisio Babo-Soares
Minister of Defence: Cirilo Jose Christopher
Minister of Public Works: Gastao Sousa
Minister of Transportation and Telecommunication: Pedro Lay
Minister of Petroleum and Natural Resources: Alfredo Pires
Minister of Agriculture and Fisheries: Mariano Assanami Sabino
Minister of Health: Sergio Lobo
Minister of Tourism: Francisco Kaluadi
Minister of Social Solidarity: Isabel Guterres

Ministries
Office of the President, Palacio das Cinzas, Kaikoli, Dili, Timor Leste. Tel: +670 333 9011, e-mail: op@gov.east-timor.org, URL: http://www.timor-leste.gov.tl
Office of the Prime Minister, Government Palace, President Nicolau Lobato Avenue, Dili, Timor-Leste. Tel: +670 331 2210, e-mail: mail@primeministerandcabinet.gov.tp, URL: http://www.pm.gov.tp
Ministry of Foreign Affairs and Cooperation, GPA Building 1, Ground Floor, Rua Avenida Presidente Nicolau Lobato, Dili, Timor-Leste. Tel: +670 333 9600, fax: +670 333 9025, e-mail: foreign.affairs@gov.east-timor.org, URL: http://www.mfac.gov.tp
Ministry of Justice, Avenida Jacinto Candido, Caicoli, Dili, Timor-Leste. Tel: +670 333 1161, fax: +670 332 9349, e-mail: mj@mj.gov.tl, URL: http://www.mj.gov.tl
Ministry of Agriculture, Forestry and Fisheries, E-mail: agriculture@gov.east-timor.org, URL: http://www.maf.gov.tl/
Ministry of Finance, Bldg. No. 5, Government House, Dili, Timor-Leste. Tel: +670 333 9546, e-mail: info@mopf.gov.tl, URL: http://www.mopf.gov.tl/
Ministry of Economic Affairs. Edifício Fomento, 2 andar, Rua D. Aleixo Corte Real, Mandarim, Dili, Timor-Leste. Tel: +670 333 9039, URL: http://timor-leste.gov.tl
Ministry of Education. Rua de Vila Verde, Dili, Timor-Leste. Tel: +670 333 9654, e-mail: education@gov.east-timor.org, URL: http://timor-leste.gov.tl
Ministry of Internal Administration. E-mail: internal.admin@gov.east-timor.org
Ministry of Health. Rua de Caicoli, Caixa Postal 374, Dili, Timor-Leste. Tel: +670 390 322467, fax: +670 390 3325189, e-mail: ministerforhealthtl@yahoo.com, URL: http://www.minsau.gov.tl/
Ministry of Infrastructure. Avenida Bispo de Madeiros 8, Mercado Lama, Dili, Timor-Leste. Tel: +670 333 9355, fax: +670 331 9349, e-mail: info@mtcop.gov.tl, URL: http://timor-leste.gov.tl
Ministry of Agriculture and Fisheries, Rua Presidente Nicolau Lobato 5, Comoro, Dili, Timor-Leste. Tel: +670 331 0418, e-mail: agriculture@gov.east-timor.org, URL: http://www.maf.gov.tl
Ministry of Defence and Security, Edificio 2, 1 Andar, Palaco do Governo, Avenida Presidente Nicolau Lobato, Dili, Timor-Leste. Tel: +670 333 1190, URL: http://www.mindef.tl
Ministry of Finance, Edifício 5, 1 andar, Palaco do Governo, Avenida Presidente Nicolau Lobato, Dili, Timor-Leste. Tel: +670 333 9510, e-mail: itds@mopf.gov.tl, URL: http://www.mof.gov.tl
Ministry of Foreign Affairs, Avenida de Portugal, Praia dos Coqueiros, Dili, Timor-Leste. Tel: +670 333 1234, fax: +670 331 9025, e-mail: foreign.affairs@gov.east-timor.org, URL: http://www.mfac.gov.tp
Ministry of Social Solidarity, Rua de Caicoli, Dili, East Timor. Tel: +670 333 9582, URL: http://www.mss.gov.tl
Ministry of State Administration and Territorial Planning, Rua Jacinto Candido, Dili, Timor-Leste. Tel: +670 331 0395, e-mail: komunikasaun@estatal.gov.tl, URL: http://www.estatal.gov.tl
Ministry of Tourism, Commerce and Industry, Edifício do Fomento, Rua Dom Aleixo Corte Real, Mandarim, Dili, Timor-Leste. Tel: +670 333 1206, URL: http://www.turismotimorleste.com

Political Parties
National Congress for Timorese Reconstruction (CNRT), newly formed 2007 by ex-President Xanana Gusmão (page 1435)
Frente Revolucionária do Timor Leste Independente (Fretilin, Revolutionary Front of Independent East Timor)
Partido Democrático (PD, Democratic Party)
Partido Social Democrata (PSD, Social-Democratic Party) **Associação Social-Democrata Timorense** (ASDT, Timorese Social-Democratic Association), Coalition of the Timorese Social-Democrat Association and the Social Democrat Party (ASDT-PSD)
União Democrática Timorense (UDT, Timorese Democratic Union)
Klibur Oan Timor Asuwain (KOTA, Association of Timorese Heroes)

Elections

Timor-Leste's first democratic elections took place on 30 August 2001 when hundreds of thousands of Timorese voted to elect members of the Constituent Assembly. Fretilin won 57.3 per cent of the vote.

Timor-Leste's first presidential election was held on 14 April 2002. The two candidates were Francisco da Amaral and Xanana Gusmão. Xanana Gusmão, running as an independent, won 82.7 per cent of the vote and was declared President-Elect on 17 April 2002. The first Presidential elections since independence took place on 9th April 2007. Preliminary results gave Francisco Guterres of the Fretilin Party the lead, ahead of the incumbent Prime Minister Jose Ramos-Horta. Sr. Ramos-Horta won the second round, with 69 per cent of the vote.

The most recent presidential election took place in March 2012; President Jose Ramos-Horta was defeated in the first round and said he would hand over power in May. In the second round of voting in April, the former guerrilla leader Taur Matan Ruak defeated Opposition leader Francisco Guterres.

The most recent parliamentary elections took place on 7 July 2012. Prime Minister Xanana Gusmao's party won but not with an outright majority necessitating a coalition. The CNRT took 30 seats, Fretilin 25 seats, PD 8 seats and Frenti-Mudança 2 seats.

Diplomatic Representation

The British Mission to Timor-Leste was closed in October 2006. Enquiries should be addressed to the British Embassy in Jakarta, Indonesia, URL: http://ukinindonesia.fco.gov.uk/en/
Ambassador: Martin Canning (page 1400)

US Embassy, Avenida de Portugal, Praia dos Coqueiros, Dili, Timor-Leste. Tel: +670 332 4684, fax: +670 331 3206, URL: http://timor-leste.usembassy.gov/
Ambassador: Judith Fergin

Embassy of Timor-Leste, 4201 Connecticut Avenue, Suite 504, NW, Washington DC 20008, USA. Tel: +1 202 966 3202, fax: +1 202 966 3205, URL: http://www.timorlesteembassy.org/
Chargé d'Affairs: Constancio da Pinto

Permanent Representative of the Democratic Republic of Timor-Leste to the United Nations, 866 Second Avenue, 9th Floor, New York, NY 10017, USA. Tel: +1 212 759 3675, fax: +1 212 759 4196, e-mail: timor-leste@un.int, URL: http://www.timor-leste-un.org/
Ambassador: Sofia Mesquita Borges

LEGAL SYSTEM

Over the course of 2000, a number of judicial and legal entities were established: the Timor-Leste Prosecutor General's Office, a Defender Service, 4 District Courts (in Dili, Baucau, Suai, and the Oecussi enclave), and a Court of Appeals. The Supreme Court of Justice is Timor-Leste's highest court, and comprises one judge appointed by the National Parliament and the remainder appointed by the Superior Council for the Judiciary. The Supreme Court has the power of judicial review. There are also military courts and a High Administrative, Tax and Audit Court. The district courts have jurisdiction over criminal and non-criminal offenses referred to as "ordinary crimes," whereas special panels within the Dili District court have exclusive jurisdiction over "serious criminal offenses." The Court of Appeal in Dili is composed of two international judges and one Timor-Leste judge. A Superior Council of Magistrates was established in February 2003.

Because the justice system did not have the capacity to prosecute claims against those responsible for the violence between 1974 and 1999, the Commission for Reception, Truth, and Reconciliation (CRTR) was set up in 2002. Its remit was to enable the victims and perpetrators of the violence to uncover the truth about human rights abuses in an effort to promote national healing and to allow the perpetrators of the less serious crimes to atone through doing community service.

In 2005, a joint Truth and Friendship Commission (TFC) accord was signed by the governments of Timor-Leste and Indonesia, to look into the events surrounding the 1999 referendum and to settle alleged human rights abuses in East Timor. The final report by the Truth Commission was published in July 2008; it blamed Indonesia for the human rights violations in the run-up to Timor-Leste's independence in 1999. President Susilo of Indonesia expressed "deep regret" but stopped short of an apology.

Whilst the government generally succeeds in controlling the national security forces, but there were problems with discipline and accountability; police often use excessive force and made arbitrary arrests. The judiciary is understaffed, depriving citizens of a fair trial, and conditions in camps for internally displaced persons are unsafe and unhealthy.

Capital punishment was abolished in 2002.

LOCAL GOVERNMENT

Administratively, Timor-Leste is divided into 13 districts (capital in brackets): Aileu (Aileu); Ainaro (Ainaro); Ambeno (Oecussi); Baucau (Baucau); Bobonaro (Maliana); Cova Lima (Suai); Dili (Dili); Ermera (Ermera); Lautem (Los Palos); Liquica (Liquica); Manatuto (Manatuto); Manufahi (Same); and Viqueque (Viqque).

AREA AND POPULATION

Area

Timor, of which Timor-Leste is a part, is a large island in the Malay Archipelago, off the north-west coast of Australia, about 700 km from Port Darwin. Timor-Leste includes the territory of Oecussi-Ambeno, which extends for about 60 km to a depth of 25 km along the

middle of the northern coast of Indonesian Timor. The total land area of the province is 17,222 sq. km (6,649 sq. miles) within which is the mainland (14,609 sq. km), the territory of Oecussi-Ambeno (2,461 sq. km), and the islands of Ataúro (144 sq. km) and Jaco (8 sq. km).

Timor-Leste's climate is tropical, with rainy and dry seasons. The terrain is mountainous.

To view a map of the area, please consult http://www.un.org/Depts/Cartographic/map/profile/timor.pdf

Population

In 2010, the population was estimated to be 1.124 million with an average annual growth rate of around 3.0 per cent. Approximately 46 per cent of the population is aged under 15 years and 5 per cent over 60. The median age is 17 years. Population density is 70 people per square kilometre and 72 per cent of the people live in rural areas

In 2010, the birth rate was estimated to be 38.5 per 1,000 people, whilst the death rate was 6.2 per 1,000 inhabitants. The fertility rate was estimated to be 6.2 children per woman in 2010, and life expectancy is 67 years (64 for men and 69 for women). Healthy life expectancy is estimated to be 53 years. The infant mortality rate in 2010 was 46 deaths per 1,000 children. (Source: http://www.who.int, World Health Statistics 2012)

Ethnically, the population is made up of about 54 per cent Malay and Papuan, 12 per cent Mambai, 10 per cent Makasi, 8 per cent Kemak, 8 per cent Galoli, and 8 per cent Tokodede.

The colonial education system and Indonesian occupation over 23 years means that around 13 per cent of the people speak Portuguese, 43 per cent speak Bahasa Indonesia, and 5.8 per cent speak English. Tetum, the most common of the local languages, is spoken by approximately 91 per cent of the population. The linguistic diversity is enshrined in the country's constitution, which designates Portuguese and Tetum as official languages and English and Bahasa Indonesia as working languages.

Public Holidays 2014

1 January: New Year's Day
18 April: Good Friday
1 May: Labour Day
20 May: Independence Day
15 August: Assumption of the Blessed Virgin Mary
30 August: Constitution Day
20 September: Liberation Day
1 November: All Saints Day
12 November: Santa Cruz Massacre
8 December: Immaculate Conception
25 December: Christmas Day

EMPLOYMENT

2001 estimates put the labour force participation rate at just 56 per cent. The agricultural sector employs about 90 per cent of the work force. There are severe shortages of trained personnel to staff newly established institutions, which hinders progress. The few urban areas cannot provide adequate jobs for the country's growing labor force. Unemployment and underemployment combined are estimated to be as high as 70 per cent, and there is little prospect of this improving in the short term.

In 2007, it was estimated that about 70 per cent of paid employment was within the public sector, public works, or nongovernment organisations.

BANKING AND FINANCE

On 24 July 2002 Timor-Leste became the 184th member of the International Monetary Fund (IMF) and the World Bank.

Currency

Timor-Leste's currency, following independence from Indonesia, is the Portuguese escudo. This replaced the Indonesian rupiah.

GDP/GNP, Inflation, National Debt

Timor-Leste is one of Asia's poorest countries and is reliant on foreign aid. About 80 per cent of the infrastructure was destroyed during the violence of 1999. Many cities do not have a dependable electrical service; health and literacy indicators are among the lowest in Asia. However, the country has made progress in setting up an infrastructure, producing a National Development Plan and establishing the institutions required to rebuild the economy, create employment opportunities, and reestablish essential public services.

Vast offshore oil and gas fields in the Timor Sea hold potential; Timor-Leste and Australia agreed to share revenues, and in 2005 the government created a petroleum fund to invest oil revenues in the country's development. Substantial revenues from petroleum production are now deposited in the Petroleum Fund and invested abroad. Only the estimated sustainable income is withdrawn by the government each year to finance expenditures. Figures for 2010 showed that that Petroleum Fund assets reached US$6 billion.

Before the latest civil unrest, in 2006, the economy was expanding and there were indications that some development challenges were being met. The 2006 rioting damaged coffee production at peak harvest time, investment projects were suspended, capital left the country and commercial activity was restricted.

TIMOR-LESTE

GDP decreased by two per cent in 2002, and again by two per cent in 2003. 2004 and 2005 saw growth of 1.8 per cent and 0.8 per cent respectively. The economy contracted again in 2006, by 5.8 per cent overall (non-oil GDP fell by 1.6 per cent). However, 2007 saw the strongest growth for several years, at 7.8 per cent. Improved civil conditions, demand from international forces based in the country and expansion of the public spending programme contributed to this growth. GDP (excluding hydrocarbons and UN operations) grew by 11 per cent in 2008, 12.9 per cent in 2009 and was estimated to grow by 6.1 per cent in 2010. Per capita GDP was estimated to be US$589 in 2010. GDP was estimated to be US$1 billion in 2011.

Services continue to be the highest contributor to GDP, at around 52.6 per cent in 2007. The agriculture sector accounted for 31.5 per cent and industry contributed 15.9 per cent in the same year.

Inflation, as measured by the consumer price index, rose from 1.8 per cent in 2005 to 4 per cent in 2006, and then leapt to 8.7 per cent in 2007, largely due to shortfalls in domestic food production and rising rice prices in the region. In February 2007, food prices rose by 26.4 per cent, before subsiding. Inflation was estimated at 9 per cent in 2011.

GDP by industrial origin at current market prices (figures in US$ million)

Sector	2006	2007
Agriculture	116.6	124.7
Mining	1.9	2.2
Manufacturing	8.7	10.2
Electricity, gas and water	5.0	6.0
Construction	29.8	44.4
Trade	25.4	31.0
Transport and communications	25.4	31.0
Finance	28.8	33.6
Public administration	185.2	112.6
Total GDP	326.8	395.5

Source: Asian Development Bank

Balance of Payments / Imports and Exports
Imports grew by 20.8 per cent in 2010 and imports by 1 per cent.

External Trade, million US$

	2008	2009	2010
Exports, fob	49.2	34.5	41.7
Imports, cif	268.6	295.1	298.1
Trade balance	-219.4	-260.6	-256.4

Source: ADB

Timor-Leste exports coffee, oil and natural gas. Its main market is Korea. Main import commodities were petroleum products and construction materials from Vietnam, Indonesia and China.

Central Bank
Central Bank of Timor-Leste, URL: http://www.bancocentral.tl/en/main.asp

Chambers of Commerce and Trade Organisations
Chamber of Commerce of Timor Leste, URL: http://www.ccitl.org.tl/execsumma.html

MANUFACTURING, MINING AND SERVICES

Primary and Extractive Industries
Timor-Leste has natural resources in the form of petroleum, natural gas, gold, manganese and marble.

A $1,400 million gas exploitation plant in the Timor Gap was approved in February 2000. In July 2001 the Australian government and the East Timor Transitional Administration agreed an arrangement whereby Timor Leste will receive 90 per cent of the revenues from oil and gas reserves in the Timor Sea. Revenues are likely to be in the region of US$90 million per year and will be received over the period 2004 to 2019. In 2004, officials complained that some of the newest and largest oil and gas fields are not included in the arrangement with Australia; agreement was reached between the two governments in 2005.

In 2005, the government created a petroleum fund to manage and invest oil revenues and to ensure that such funds are invested in the country's development.

In 2011 Timor-Leste produced 83.74 thousand barrels per day all of which was crude, just 3.00 thousand barrels per day were used domestically the rest went for export.

Manufacturing
Timor-Leste's manufacturing sector is based mainly on soap manufacturing, handicrafts and woven cloth. In 2006, manufacturing industry contributed almost 12.8 per cent of the country's GDP.

Service Industries
The service sector is Timor-Leste's largest contributor towards GDP, accounting for around 55 per cent in 2006.

Agriculture
Timor-Leste's economy is primarily agricultural and most East Timorese live in rural areas. However, the country is prone to drought, floods, locusts and landslides and the islands are vulnerable to earthquakes and tropical cyclones. The country suffers food shortages, arising from low agricultural output and limited alternative means of earning income in rural areas.

The main products are coffee, copra, palm oil, rice, wax and hides. The sector generates 90 per cent of Timor Leste's exports, largely due to coffee exports. Agriculture employs about 64 per cent of the population and contributed 27.0 per cent of GDP in 2011.

Agricultural Production in 2010

Produce	Int. $'000*	Tonnes
Rice, paddy	29,487	112,925
Meat nes	26,167	19,800
Maize	18,823	148,891
Indigenous pigmeat	15,004	9,760
Coffee, green	13,594	12,653
Roots and tubers, nes	7,986	46,700
Beans, dry	4,750	8,200
Mangoes, mangosteens, guavas	3,665	6,117
Cassava	3,573	34,200
Vegetables fresh nes	3,562	18,900
Indigenous cattle meat	2,728	1,010
Avocados	2,384	3,440

* forecast figures
Source: http://faostat.fao.org/site/339/default.aspx Food and Agriculture Organization of the United Nations, Food and Agricultural commodities production

Fishing
FAO forecast figures for 2010 put the total catch at 3,125 tonnes.

COMMUNICATIONS AND TRANSPORT

Travel Requirements
Visitors from the USA, Canada, Australia and the EU require a passport valid for at least six months beyond the intended date of departure, as well as a visa. An entry permit valid for 30 days can be obtained on arrival, and this can be extended.

Nationals not referred to above should contact the embassy to check visa requirements.

International Airports
Dili airport runs services to Darwin, Australia, three times a week via an Australian airline.

There are eight airports in Timor-Leste, three of which are paved. There are also 9 heliports.

Roadways
There are 5,000 km of roads, half of which are tarmacked. A bus service runs between Dili and Kupang in West Timor, Indonesia

HEALTH

A $12.7 million grant towards Timor-Leste's health service was agreed between UNTAET and the World Bank on 7 June 2000. However, medical services in the country are severely restricted. The basic infrastructure for immunization has been re-established and coverage is improving. An estimated 41 per cent of the population lives in poverty. In 2009, the government spent approximately 7.8 per cent of its total budget on healthcare (down from 12.7 per cent in 2000), accounting for 66.1 per cent of all healthcare spending. Total expenditure on health care equated to 11.9 per cent of the country's GDP. Per capita expenditure on health was US$65 in 2009. Figures for 2000-10 show that there are 79 physicians (1 per 10,000 population), 1,795 nurses and midwives (22 per 10,000 population), 45 dentists, 14 pharmaceutical personnel, 10 community health workers and 22 environment and public health workers.

Common diseases suffered include malaria, dengue fever, and Japanese encephalitis. In 2010 there were 87 reported cases of leprosy, 48,137 of malaria, and 50 cases of measles. In 2009 the infant mortality rate (probability of dying before first birthday) was 46 per 1,000 live births and the child (under-five years old) mortality rate was 55 per 1,000 live births. The main causes of death in the under-fives are: prematurity (19 per cent), pneumonia (20 per cent), birth asphyxia (13 per cent), diarrhoea (8 per cent), malaria (4 per cent) and measles (9 per cent). The immunization rate was 73 per cent for measles in 2008. Malnutrition is a serious concern for children under five. In the period 2005-11 an estimated 55.7 per cent of children (under five-years-old) were classified as stunted and 45.3 per cent as underweight.

In 2010, an estimated 69 per cent of the population had access to safe water. An estimated 47 per cent of the population had access to adequate sanitation facilities. (Source: http://www.who.int, World Health Statistics 2012)

EDUCATION

Figures for 2007 show that 62 per cent of girls and 64 per cent of boys are enrolled in primary schools. In primary schools that year the pupil:teacher ratio was 31:1.

The infrastructure of schools was severely damaged during the post referendum violence, and many teachers and school managers went into exile. Less than half the population is literate and there are huge skills gaps in the workforce.

RELIGION

Portuguese influence during the centuries of colonial rule resulted in around 85 per cent of the population identifying itself as Christian the majority of whom are Roman Catholic, though some of those who consider themselves Catholic practice a mixed form of religion that includes local animist customs. There are also Protestant, Muslim, Hindu and Buddhist communities. In 2005, there were major protests over government proposals to end compulsory religious education in schools.

Timor-Leste has a religious liberty rating of 6 on a scale of 1 to 10 (10 is most freedom). (Source: World Religion Database)

COMMUNICATIONS AND MEDIA

Newspapers
The newspaper market is hindered by poor infrastructure and a high level of illiteracy. Timor Leste's newspapers include the Jornal Nacional (weekly: URL: http://www.semanario.tp), the Timor Post, and Suara Timor Lorosae (URL: http://www.suaratimorlorosae.com)

Broadcasting
Radio stations include Radio Falintil, Radio UNTAET and Radio Nacional de Timor Leste (RTL). The national television station is Televisao de Timor Leste (TVTL).

Public radio reaches around 90 per cent of the population; public TV broadcasting reaches a lower percentage of households.

Post and Telecommunications Service
The postal service began operations on 28 April 2000. The telecommunications service, damaged during the violence associated with independence, is rudimentary and limited to urban areas. In 2008, there were an estimated 2,800 mainline telephones and an estimated 100,000 mobile phones in use. In 2009, there were around 1,800 internet users.

ENVIRONMENT

The main environmental issue for Timor-Leste is deforestation and soil erosion caused by the widespread use of slash and burn agriculture.

Timor Leste is a party to the following environmental agreements: Biodiversity, Climate Change, Climate Change-Kyoto Protocol and Desertification.

Figures for 2010 show that carbon dioxide emissions from the consumption of fossil fuels was 0.40 million tons. (Source: EIA)

TOGO
Republic of Togo
République Togolaise

Capital: Lomé (Population estimate: 500,000)

Head of State: Faure Gnassingbé (President) (page 1431)

National Flag: Parti of five fesswise, alternately green and yellow; a canton red charged with a star five-pointed white

CONSTITUTION AND GOVERNMENT

Constitution
Togo formed part of the German Togoland which was surrendered to the Allies in August 1914. After four years of Anglo-French administration the territory was divided and placed under a League of Nations Mandate, the western part being allotted to Great Britain and the largest eastern area to France. Both areas became United Nations Trust Territories in 1946. On 24 August 1956 French Togo became a Republic with limited autonomy within the French Union.

The United Nations General Assembly voted on 14 November 1958 for the abolition of the Trusteeship on the establishment of complete independence. This was achieved on 27 April 1960.

The former Prime Minister, Sylvanus Olympio, was elected as President and a new Constitution adopted on 9 April 1961. On 13 January 1963 Olympio was assassinated by a group of army officers. The National Assembly was dissolved and the Constitution suspended by the provisional Government of Nicolas Grunitzky. Grunitzky became President on 10 May 1963 when a new Constitution and National Assembly came into force. Political difficulties led to the overthrow of Grunitzky himself by the army on 13 January 1967.

Political activity was suspended by the National Reconciliation Committee which ran the country for three months until the Commander-in-Chief of the Togolese army, Lt. Colonel (later General) Gnassingbé Eyadéma, named himself President on 14 April 1967. In May it was agreed that all former political parties would cease their political activities. A Constitutional Committee was established to advise on the future constitution of the country, and on the eventual return to civilian rule. A single political party, the Rassemblement du Peuple Togolais, was formerly inaugurated in November 1970. General Eyadéma was confirmed as president by a referendum held in January 1972.

In 1991, surrendering to pressure for a multi-party system, General Eyadéma convened a conference to address the matter. From this a new prime minister was elected. A referendum approved a new constitution in 1992. Eyadéma was elected under the first multi-party presidential elections in August 1993 and re-appointed in 1998. This result was contested by the opposition.

Togo's prime minister, Eugène Koffi Adoboli, resigned in August 2000 following a no-confidence vote in parliament. President Eyadema then appointed Gabriel Messan Agbeyome Kodjo as prime minister. In 2002 a vote was held in parliament to change the constitution to allow President Edadéma to stand for re-election. He was declared the winner of the 2003 election.

To view the 1992 Constitution, amended in 2002 (in French), please visit: http://www.assemblee-nationale.tg/spip.php?rubrique4

International Relations
Togo is a member of the Economic Community of West African States (ECOWAS), West African Economic and Monetary Union (UEMOA), African Union (AU) and the Organisation of Islamic Conference (OIC). Togo has close relations with France and Germany. Relations with the UK are limited. Generally it has good relations with its West African neighbours.

Recent Events
President Edadéma died in February 2005 having been president of Togo since 1967. The constitution states that on the death of the president the speaker of the house should assume power, however the House of Assembly voted to remove Speaker Fambare Natchaba Ouattara, who was out of the country at the time, and approve the appointment of President Edadéma's son, Faure Gnassingbé. The assembly also voted to change the constitution to allow him to stay in power for the duration of his late father's term which was due to end in 2008, instead of having an election within 60 days of the president's death. However, after international pressure the government announced that presidential elections would take place in April 2005. Faure Gnassingbé duly won the election. Violence erupted after the result amidst allegations of vote rigging. The Constitutional Court later upheld the result.

President Faure Gnassingbé initially rejected calls for a coalition government, but later appointed Edem Kodjo from a moderate opposition party as prime minister. No member of the main opposition party, the United Forces for Change, was appointed to the cabinet. In September 2006, Yawovi Agboyibo was named as prime minister with responsibility for forming a unity government and organising elections. In May 2007 parliamentary elections were postponed from June 2007 to 5 August 2007, and then again to mid-October.

At the end of September 2007, Togo made an urgent appeal for food and medicine to help deal with flooding that affected almost half the countries in Africa. Around 20,000 people were made homeless by the floods in Togo, and over twenty died. The European Union offered 2 million euros to help in the relief operations in Togo, Ghana and Burkina Faso, three of the worst hit countries.

The Union of Forces for Change (UFC) led by Gilchrist Olympio, having expected to be given the premiership, refused to co-operate with the new government, although its first vice president did enter the government as a senior minister. The minister for economic affairs, finance and privatization was replaced on 15 March 2007. Agboyibo offered his resignation as prime minister on 13 November after the elections. Komlan Mally was appointed to the post of prime minister in December 2007. He named a new cabinet on which did not include the UFC. Mally resigned from the post in September 2008 and was replaced by Gilbert Houngbo, a non-party diplomat.

Presidential elections took place in 2010 and were won by the incumbent Faure Essozimna Gnassingbé. After the presidential elections of 2010 Houngbo offered his resignation as prime minister on 4 May and was reappointed on 7 May. The new cabinet included members of the UFC; however the national executive threatened to expel from the party any member who accepted a cabinet position.

In September 2011, Kpatch Gnassingbe, the half-brother of President Gnassingbe, was sentenced to prison for plotting a coup.

In June 2012, demonstrators protested against reforms to the electoral code which they allege favour the ruling party.

The prime minister, Gilbert Houngbo, resigned in July 2012. The then minister for commerce, Kwesi Ahoomey-Zunu, was named prime minister. His government was named on 31 July 2012.

Legislature
Togo has a unicameral legislature, the National Assembly is made up of 81 directly elected members who serve a five year term.
National Assembly, (Assemblée Nationale), Palais des Congres, PO Box 327, Lomé, Togo. URL: http://www.rdd.tg/assemblee
President: El Hadj Abass Bonfoh

TOGO

Cabinet (as at June 2013)

Prime Minister: Kwesi Ahoomey-Zunu (page 1373)
Minister of State, Minister of Education: Solitoki Magnim Esso (page 1422)
Minister of State, Minister of Foreign Affairs and Co-operation: Elliot Ohina (page 1489)
Minister of Health: Charles Agba
Minister of Water, Sanitation and Rural Irrigation: Bissoune Nabagou
Minister of Territorial Administration, Decentralisation and Local Collectivities: Gilbert Bawara
Minister of Economy and Finance: Adji Otéth Ayassor (page 1380)
Minister of Tourism: Padumhèkou Tchao
Keeper of the Seals, Minister of Justice: Tchitchao Tchalim
Minister of Security and Civil Protection: Col. Damehane Yark
Minister of Development, Handicrafts, Youth and Youth Employment: Mme Victoire Sidéného Tomegah-Togbe
Minister of Public Works: Ninsao Gnofame
Minister of Higher Education and Research: Octave Broohm
Minister of Social Action and National Solidarity: Mme Afi Ntifa Amenyo
Minister of Civil Service and Administrative Reform: Kokou Dzifa Adjeoda
Minister of Agriculture, Livestock and Fishing: Col. Oura Koura Agadazi
Minister of Technical Education and Professional Training: Hamadou Bouraima-Diabacte
Minister of the Environment and Forest Resources: Dédé Ahoéfa Ekoue
Minister of Transport: Dammipi Noupokou
Minister for the Promotion of Women: Mme Patricia Dagban-Zonvide
Minister of Labour, Employment and Social Security: Yacoubou Koumadio Hamadou
Minister of Human Rights, Consolidation of Democracy: Doris Rita de Souza
Minister of Trade and Promotion of the Private Sector: Bernadette Léguézim-Balouki
Minister of Industry and Technological Innovation: François Agbéviadé Galley
Minister of Sport and Leisure: Bakalawa Fofana
Minister of Post and Telecommunications: Mme Cina Lawson
Minister of Urban Affairs: Komlan Nunyabu
Minister in the Office of the President, responsible for Town Planning and Development: Kokou Semodji
Minister of Arts & Culture: Fiatuwo Kwadjo Sessenou
Minister of Communication: Djimon Ore
Deputy Minister to the Ministry of Agriculture, Livestock and Fishing: Gourdigou Kolani

Ministries

National Assembly, BP 327, Lomé, Togo. Tel: +228 222 5791/ 5061, fax: +228 222 1168, e-mail: assemblee.nationale@tg.refer.org, URL: http://www.assemblee-nationale.tg
Office of the President, Palais Présidentiel, ave de la Marina, Lomé, Togo. Tel: +228 221 1951 / 2701 / 3405, fax: +228 221 2436, e-mail: presidence@republicoftogo.com, URL: http://www.republicoftogo.com/
Office of the Prime Minister, BP 1161 Lomé, Togo. Tel: +228 221 1564 / 2952 / 3931, fax: +228 221 3753, e-mail: info@republicoftogo.com, URL: http://www.primature.gouv.tg/
Ministry of Foreign Affairs and Co-operation, BP 900, Place du Monument aux Morts, Lomé, Togo. Tel: +228 221 2910, fax: +228 221 3974, URL: http://www.diplomatie.gouv.tg/
Ministry of Agriculture, Livestock and Fisheries, BP 12175, Lomé, Togo. Tel: +228 221 0305, fax: +228 221 8792, URL: http://www.maeptogo.tg/
Ministry of Commerce, Industry, Transport and the Development of the Free Zone, BP 383, Lomé, Togo. Tel: +228 221 2025, fax: +228 221 0572
Ministry of National Education and Research, BP 12175, Lomé, Togo. Tel: +228 221 3926 / 222 0983, fax: +228 221 0783
Ministry of Vocational and Professional Training, BP 389, Lomé, Togo. Tel: +228 223 1300 / 1400 / 1408, fax: +228 221 6812
Ministry of the Interior, Security and Decentralisation, Lomé, Togo. Tel: +228 222 5712 / 5716, fax: +228 222 6150 / 2184
Ministry of Justice, Lomé, Togo. Tel: +228 221 2653 / 5491, fax: +228 222 2906, URL: http://www.justice.gouv.tg/
Ministry of Regional Integration and Relations with Parliament, Lomé, Togo. Tel: +228 221 7315 / 7300, fax: +228 221 7251
Ministry of of Public Health, Social Affairs, the Promotion of Women and the Protection of Children, BP 386, Lomé, Togo. Tel: +228 221 3524 / 3801 / 2514, fax: +228 222 2073
Ministry of Ecomomy & Finance, BP 387, Lomé, Togo. Tel: +228 221 0037 / 2371, fax: +228 221 2548, URL: http://www.finances.gouv.tg/
Ministry of Civil Service, Labour and Employment, BP 372, Lomé, Togo. Tel: +228 221 4183 , fax: +228 222 5685, URL: http://www.fonctionpublique.gouv.tg/
Ministry of Development, Handicrafts, Youth and Youth Employment, BP 40 Lomé, Togo. Tel: +228 221 2247 / 221 2352, fax: +228 222 4228, URL: http://www.mindevbase.tg/
Ministry of the Environment and Forests, Lomé, Togo. Tel: +228 221 5658 / 2897 / 3078, fax: +228 221 0333
Ministry of Communication, BP 40, Lomé, Togo. Tel: +228 221 2930 / 4802, fax: +228 221 4380
Ministry of Tourism, BP 1177, Lomé, Togo. Tel: +228 221 3990 / 4007, fax: +228 221 8927, URL: http://www.togo-tourisme.com/
Ministry of Defence and Veterans, Lomé, Togo. Tel: +228 221 2605 / 2812, fax: +228 221 8841

Political Parties

Action Committee for Renewal (CAR); Rally of the Togolese People (RPT); Union of Forces for Change (UFC).

Elections

Presidential elections took place on 1 June 2003. President Gen. Gnassingbe Eyadema retained power. The constitution was changed in 2002 so that he could stand for a third term. The main opposition candidate, Gilchrist Olympio, was banned from taking part because he was in exile.

Legislative elections for the parliaments 81 seats were held in 1994 and then 1999. However, the elections were widely boycotted and the government promised to hold them again. Elections were subsequently announced in September 2002 and held on 27 October 2002. Although the major opposition parties boycotted them, turnout was still high. The Rally of the Togolese People (RPT) won another large majority.

Following the death of President Eyadema, his son, Faure Gnassingbé, was controversially instated as president. Following international pressure, a presidential election was held in April 2005. Faure Gnassingbé received 1.4 million votes (60 per cent of the votes), while main opposition candidate Emmanuel Bob Akitani won 841,000 votes (38 per cent of votes cast). The result was disputed by the opposition and the elections were marred by violence. Thousands fled to Benin. Mr Akitani declared himself the winner, and alleged he should have won 70 per cent of the vote. In May 2005 the Constitutional Court declared Mr Gnassingbé the winner.

The most recent presidential election took place on 4 March 2010. It was won by the incumbent president, Faure Gnassingbé, with over 60 per cent of the vote. His closest rival, Jean-Pierre Fabre took 34 per cent of the vote and former prime minister Yawovi Agboyibo took just 3 per cent of the vote. The victory was confirmed on 18 March 2010 by the Constitutional Court.

In May 2007 parliamentary elections were postponed from June 2007 to 5 August 2007, and then to mid-October. There were over 2,000 candidates, with 32 parties and 41 lists of independent candidates. The ruling Rally of the Togolese People (RPT) won a majority of 50 seats. The remaining seats were won by opposition parties: the Union of the Forces of Change (UFC) gained 27 seats and the Action Committee for Renewal (CAR) gained four seats.

The legislative election due in October 2012 did not take place.

Diplomatic Representation

US Embassy, Angle Rue Kouenou et Rue 15 Beniglato, B.P. 852, Lomé, Togo. Tel: +228 22 12994, fax: +228 22 17952, URL: http://togo.usembassy.gov/
Ambassador: Robert Whitehead
British Embassy (All Staff Resident in Accra, Ghana) URL: http://www.ukinghana.fco.gov.uk
Ambassador and Consul-General: Peter Jones (page 1451)
Togolese Embassy, 2208 Massachusetts Ave, NW, Washington, DC 20007, USA. Tel: +1 202 234 4212, fax: +1 202 232 3190
Ambassador: Kadangha Limbiya Bariki
Togolese Embassy, 8 Rue Alfred Roll, 75017 Paris, France. Tel: +33 43 80 12 13, fax: +33 43 80 90 71
Permanent Representative of Togo to the United Nations, 112 East 40th Street, New York, NY 10016, USA. Tel: +1 212 490 3455 / 3456, fax: +1 212 983 6684, URL: http://www.untogo.org/About/The-Permanent-Mission
Permanent Representative: Kodjo Menan (page 1476)

LEGAL SYSTEM

The judicial system blends African traditional law and the French law and court system. A Constitutional Court is the highest court in constitutional matters. The Supreme Court sits in Lomé; there is also a sessions court (Court of Assizes), and Appeals Courts. Courts of first instance are divided into civil, commercial, and correctional chambers, and there are specialist tribunals, such as labour and children's tribunals. Village chiefs or Councils of Elders can try cases in rural areas. There is a separate Constitutional Court.

Despite the independence of the judiciary enshrined in the 1992 Constitution, most judges are under the control of the executive. There are serious human rights problems in Togo, including harsh prison conditions, and torture of detainees; arbitrary arrests and lengthy pretrial detention; restrictions on the press, and on freedom of assembly and movement; and corruption. The judicial system suffers from a lack of personnel and is vastly overburdened.

During 2008, the government created a Truth, Justice, and Reconciliation consultation process in order to facilitate forgiveness and reconciliation, aid the fight against corruption and judicial impunity, and reinforce national unity in the country. Use of the death penalty officially came to an end in June 2009.

National Human Rights Commission, 37 rue 74, Tokoin Dournasséssé, BP 322, Lomé, Togo. Tel: +228 221 7879, fax: +228 221 2436, URL: http://www.cndh-togo.org

LOCAL GOVERNMENT

For administrative purposes Togo is divided into five regions: Des Plateaux, Des Savanes, De La Kara, Du Centre and Maritime. These regions are further divided into 30 prefectures.

AREA AND POPULATION

Area

Togo is situated between Ghana and Benin, on the west coast of Africa with Burkina Faso on its northern border. Its coastline lies on the Gulf of Guinea. It has an area of 56,600 sq. km. The north of the country is semi-arid while the south is tropical.

To view a map, please consult http://www.lib.utexas.edu/maps/cia08/togo_sm_2008.gif

Population

In 2010 the population was estimated at 6.028 million with an annual growth rate of 2.3 per cent over the period 2000-10. The median age is 20 years old. Approximately 40 per cent of the population is aged under 15 years old and just 5 per cent aged over 60 years. The population is divided into three basic ethnic groups: in the south, the Ewe, Mina and Ouatchi; in the central region, the Akposso-Adele; and in the north, the Kabre. There are at least 27 different kinds of tribal groups, and about 2,000 Europeans in the country. Major towns include the capital, Lomé, Sokode, Palime, Atakpame, Bassari and Tsevie. An estimated 43 per cent of people live in urban areas.

The official language is French. Kabre, Ewe, Cotocoli and Hausa are also spoken.

Births, Marriages, Deaths

Estimated figures for 2010 put the birth rate at 32 births per thousand population and 9.6 deaths per thousand population. Infant mortality is an estimated 66 deaths per 1,000 live births in 2010. Neonatal mortality is an estimated 32 per 1,000 live births. In 2008 the maternal mortality ratio was 350 per 100,000 population. The average fertility rate per woman was 4.1 in 2010. Average life expectancy in 2009 was 57 years for males and 61 years for females. Healthy life expectancy is 49.00 for males and 52.0 for females. (Source: http://www.who.int, World Health Statistics 2012)

Public Holidays 2014

1 January: New Year's Day
13 January: Liberation Day
21 April: Easter Monday
27 April: Independence Day
5 May: Labour Day
29 May: Ascension Day
9 June: Whit Monday
15 August: Assumption Day
1 November: All Saint's Day
25 December: Christmas Day

EMPLOYMENT

In 2007 the workforce was estimated at 2.5 million. The agriculture sector employed around 66 per cent of the workforce, industry 5 per cent, and the service sector 28 per cent.

BANKING AND FINANCE

Currency

The currency is the CFA franc.

GDP/GNP, Inflation, National Debt

Togo is one of the world's poorest countries. Its small-scale industrial sector has been in decline for many years. Phosphate mining was for many years the mainstay of the economy but has declined in recent years as easily accessible reserves have been used up. The sector was briefly privatised but the state took back control in 2003. The state also raised income through development of its main port activity and processed incoming goods ready for re-export and this is now the major export sector. It is hoped that the economy will be boosted by the recently completed West Africa Gas pipeline. The government is trying to implement economic and structural reforms. A new investment law was passed in 2012. A court of accounts and a general financial inspectorate have also been created as part of the government's efforts to combat corruption. A programme to modernise state bureaucracy began in 2012.

GDP

	2005	2006	2007
GDP, US$ million	2,109.47	2,216.19	2,537.25
GDP growth rate, %	1.2	2.0	2.3
GNI per capita, US$	350	350	..

Source: African Development Bank

GDP was estimated to be US$3.6 billion in 2011. Per capita income was estimated to be US$950.

The agriculture sector makes up approximately 47 per cent of GDP, the industry sector, 25 per cent and the service sector 27 per cent.

Inflation was 3.7 per cent in 2011. It was estimated to be 2.5 per cent in 2012 , forecast to rise slightly to 3 per cent in 2013.

Total external public debt was US$1,564.85 million in 2006. (Source: AFDB) Following some cancellation of its debts, Togo's government debt stood at approximately 25 per cent of GDP in 2010.

Balance of Payments / Imports and Exports

Principal exports include phosphates, cocoa, coffee and cotton and the main imported goods are petroleum products, machinery and equipment. Togo's main trading partners are the EU, mainly France and the Netherlands, China, Ghana, France, Cote d'Ivoire, Benin and Burkina Faso. In 1989 Togo launched a duty-free export processing zone (EPZ).

External Trade, US$ million

	2005	2006	2007
External Trade	-346.91	-427.25	-495.29

- continued

Imports	596.09	609.86	655.02
Exports	943.00	1,037.11	1,150.32

Source: African Development Bank

Exports were estimated to be US$859 million in 2010 and imports US$1.5 billion.

Foreign Aid

In 2010, Togo reached a HIPC debt relief completion and 95 per cent of its debt was written off. Togo is working with the IMF on economic reform.

Central Bank

Banque Centrale des Etats de l'Afrique de l'Ouest, PO Box 3108, Avenue Abdoulaye Fadiga, Dakar, Senegal. Tel: +221 8 390500, fax: +221 8 239335, e-mail: webmaster@bceao.int, URL: http://www.bceao.int
Governor: Tiémoko Meyliet Kone

MANUFACTURING, MINING AND SERVICES

Primary and Extractive Industries

Exploitation of phosphate has contributed massively to export earnings in the past. Togo is the fourth largest producer of phosphate in the world and its mines have been privatised. Production of phosphate was 2.7 million tonnes in 1997 but fell to an estimated 1.3 million in 2002. The fall is partly due to the decline in easily accesible deposits and lack of investment. Togo also has limestone and marble deposits.

Togo has no oil resources of its own and in 2011 imported 26,000 barrels per day to meet its needs.

Energy

In 2010, Togo generated 0.13 billion kWh of electricity and consumed 0.68 billion kWh. Togo's electricity is produced by thermal and hydroelectric stations.

Agriculture

Togo's economy is based principally on agriculture and Togo is self sufficient in basic foods. The principal products are cocoa, coffee, palm oil, palm kernels, cotton and groundnuts. Vegetables, manioc, maize, yams and rice are grown for local consumption. Coffee, cocoa and cotton are the principal agricultural exports which, between them, account for about 85 per cent of total exports. Coconut tress are harvested for copra. Agriculture contributes around 46 per cent of GDP and employs 65 per cent of the population.

Agricultural Production in 2010

Produce	Int. $'000*	Tonnes
Yams	162,961	710,481
Cocoa beans	105,407	101,500
Cassava	94,931	908,755
Maize	78,754	638,129
Beans, dry	43,390	76,190
Indigenous chicken meat	40,452	28,399
Sorghum	31,870	244,674
Rice, paddy	29,626	110,109
Vegetables fresh nes	25,816	137,000
Indigenous cattle meat	24,973	9,245
Cotton lint	20,009	14,000
Groundnuts, with shelf	18,778	46,496

* unofficial figures
Source: http://faostat.fao.org/site/339/default.aspx Food and Agriculture Organization of the United Nations, Food and Agricultural commodities production

COMMUNICATIONS AND TRANSPORT

Travel Requirements

Citizens of the USA, Canada, Australia and the EU require a valid passport and a visa, unless in transit and leaving with 24 hours and not leaving the airport. All nationals can obtain an entry visa on arrival in Togo for a maximum stay of up to seven days. Passports need to be handed in on arrival (except for passports of nationals of Schengen countries) and collected along with the visa from the police station the following day. Vaccination against yellow fever may be required before entry. Nationals not referred to above are advised to contact the embassy to check visa requirements.

Railways

Togo has around 520 km of railway, including links from Lomé to Atakpamé and Blitta, and along the coast to Aného. Trains are not currently running.

Roads

There are approximately 7,500 km of roads, most of which are unpaved. Buses routes connect Togo with Burkina Faso, Ghana, and Benin. Vehicles are driven on the right.

Ports and Harbours

There are ports at Lomé and Kpémé. In 2001 it was announced that the port at Lomé would be expanded to become a container handling port. It was expected to become operational in 2004. Ferry services run along the coast.

TONGA

HEALTH

Health care is provided by the state although many costs are born by the public. In 2009, the government spent approximately 11.4 per cent of its total budget on healthcare, accounting for 43 per cent of all healthcare spending. External resources contributed 13.6 per cent and private, largely out-of-pocket expenditure contributed the rest. Total expenditure on healthcare equated to 7.4 per cent of the country's GDP. Per capita expenditure on health was approximately US$41.

Latest figures from the WHO (2005-10) show that there were 349 doctors (1 per 10,000 population), 1,816 nurses and midwives (2.7 per 10,000 population), 19 dentists and 11 pharmaceutical personnel and 68 public and environmental health workers. There were an estimated 9 hospital beds per 10,000 population.

In 2018, the infant mortality rate (probability of dying before first birthday) was 66 per 1,000 live births and the child (under-five years old) mortality rate was 103 per 1,000 live births. The main causes of death in the under-fives are: prematurity (13 per cent), pneumonia (16 per cent), birth asphyxia (9 per cent), diarrhoea (10 per cent), malaria (18 per cent) and HIV/AIDS (3 per cent). In the period 2000-09 an estimated 17.3 per cent of children (under five-years-old) were classified as stunted and 21.1 per cent as underweight.

In 2009 an estimated 3.2 per cent of the population had HIV/AIDS. Approximately 18 per cent of pregnant women with HIV/AIDS and 19 per cent of people with advanced HIV infections received antiretroviral therapy coverage. The immunization rate for measles is now approximately 84 per cent. Approximately 35 per cent of children sleep under insecticide-treated nets.

In 2010, an estimated 61 per cent of the population had sustainable access to improved drinking water sources and an estimated 13 per cent of the population had sustainable access to improved sanitation. (Source: http://www.who.int, World Health Statistics 2012)

EDUCATION

Primary education is compulsory and lasts for six years. In 2007, 72 per cent of girls and 82 per cent of boys were enrolled in primary school. Secondary education lasts for 7 years and figures for 2002 show that an estimated 40 per cent of boys and 21 per cent of girls were enrolled in secondary school. Figures for 2007 put five per cent of the population in tertiary education. In 2007 the adult literacy rate was 57 per cent. UNESCO figures from 2007 show that 17.2 per cent of government spending went on education.

RELIGION

Around 32 per cent of the population follow traditional beliefs, 47 per cent are Christian and 20 per cent are Muslims. There is also a small Bahai community.

Togo has a religious liberty rating of 9 on a scale of 1 to 10 (10 is most freedom). (Source: World Religion Database)

COMMUNICATIONS AND MEDIA

The constitution provides for freedom of expression but there have been incidences of legal action and harassment against journalists. In 2002 a law was passed which made it illegal to imprison those who commit press offences. Private newspapers, televisioon stations and community radio stations do exist.

Newspapers
Togo-Presse, government run, daily,
URL: http://www.editogo.tg/presse.php?rubrique=Politique
Le Liberté, daily, private, URL: http://www.libertetg.com/
Le Regard, private, weekly; **Le Combat du Peuple**, private, weekly; **Nouveau Combat**, private, weekly; **Carrefour**, private, weekly

Broadcasting
The main television station is the state-run Television Togolaise (URL: http://www.tvt.tg/tvt/). There are approximately 80 radio stations including two state run radio stations, Radio Kara and Radio Lomé (URL: http://www.radiolome.tg/), privately-run radio stations and Radio France Internationale, which broadcasts to Lomé. Several private radio and tv stations were closed after the installation of Fauré Gnassingbe as president in 2005.

Figures for 2008 estimate that there were 140,900 main lines and 1.5 million mobile phones. There were an estimated 350,000 internet users. The internet system is relatively undeveloped with poor connectivity.

ENVIRONMENT

The use of slash and burn agricultural techniques and the use of wood for fuel makes deforestation a major concern.

Togo is a party to the following international agreements: Biodiversity, Climate Change, Climate Change-Kyoto Protocol, Desertification, Endangered Species, Law of the Sea, Ozone Layer Protection, Ship Pollution, Tropical Timber 83, Tropical Timber 94, Wetlands and Whaling.

According to figures from the EIA, in 2010 Togo's emissions from the consumption of fossil fuels totalled 3.17 million metric tons of carbon dioxide.

TONGA
Kingdom of Tonga
Pule'anga Tonga

Capital: Nuku'alofa (Population estimate, 2010: 34,000)

Head of State: King George Tupou VI (page 1528)

National Flag: Red with a white square canton, bearing a red cross centred in the canton

CONSTITUTION AND GOVERNMENT

Constitution
Tonga, also known as the Friendly Islands, is an independent, constitutional monarchy. Its constitution dates from 1875, with relatively little amendment, and is based on the British model, providing for a Government consisting of the Sovereign, a Privy Council and Cabinet, a Legislative Assembly and a Judiciary. In 2003 the constitution was amended to give the king greater power and state control of the media was increased.

The chief executive body is the Privy Council, presided over by the Sovereign and comprising the Prime Minister, Ministers and the Governors of Vava'u and Ha'apai. The Privy Council advises the Sovereign on affairs of State and in intervals between meetings of the legislature makes ordinances which become law if confirmed by the next meeting of the legislature and endorsed by the Sovereign. Lesser executive decisions are taken by the Cabinet, which consists of the Privy Council members, presided over by the Prime Minister.

A tripartite committee consisting of ministers, nobles, and people's representatives was established in June 2007 with the aim of finding a consensus on political reform. Following reforms in 2010 the majority of MPs (17) will be elected by popular vote. From 2010, the prime minister is also elected by parliament.

To consult the constitution, please visit: http://legislation.to/Tonga/DATA/PRIN/1988-002/ActofConstitutionofTonga.pdf

Recent Events
In August 2005, a long strike was held by public sector workers which led to street protests and demands for political reform. In March 2006 Fred Sevele became the country's first prime minister to be elected and not appointed by the King; this followed the resignation of Prince Ulukalala Lavaka Ata. Rioting broke out in November 2006 following protests about the lack of democratic reforms; a state of emergency was declared following the destruction of part of the business district and several deaths. In the following February, foreign aid was pledged to rebuild the business district.

King Tupov IV died in September 2006 after a long illness. He was succeeded by his son King George Tupov V. King George Tupov V has promised reforms including the ending of the near-absolute power of the monarchy.

In March 2009 a huge underwater volcano erupted near the volcanic islands of Hunga Tonga and Hunga Ha'apai. The intensitiy was such that geologists wondered if a new permanent island would be formed.

In November 2009 a committee on constitutional reform recommended introducing a popularly elected parliament and that the monarchy should be restricted to a more ceremonial role. In November 2010 Tonga held its first vote for a popularly elected parliament.

On March 18 2012, King George Tupou V died. He was succeeded by his brother Crown Prince Tupouto'a Lavaka.

International Relations
Tonga is an active member of the Pacific Islands Forum and hosted the forum in October 2007. It is also an active member of the UN and the Commonwealth. Tonga was admitted to the World Trade Organisation as its 150th member (observer) in December 2005. It became a full member in 2007.

Legislature

The unicameral Legislative Assembly or *Fale Alea* has 26 seats in total. Following the 2010 reforms, 17 MPs are directly elected and nine seats are for hereditary nobles. The speaker is appointed by the sovereign. Elected members serve three-year terms. The House usually sits between May and November.
Legislative Assembly, PO Box 901, Nuku'alofa, Tonga. Tel: +676 87 23565, fax: +676 87 24626

Privy Council (as of March 2013)
Prime Minister, Minister for Foreign Affairs, Police & Fire Services, and Information and Communication: Lord Tu'ivakano
Deputy Prime Minister, Minister for Infrastructure: Lord Samiu Vaipulu (page 1530)
Privy Councillor for Finance and National Planning: Lisiate 'Aloveita Akolo
Privy Councillor for Labour, Commerce and Small Industries: Isileli Pulu
Privy Councillor for the Interior: Lord Vaea
Privy Councillor for Lands, Survey and Natural Resources, Environment and Climate Change: Lord Ma'afu
Privy Councillor for Education and Training: Dr. the Hon. Rev. Ana Taufe'ulungaki
Privy Councillor for Health: Lord Tu'iiafitu
Privy Councillor for Public Enterprises and Justice: Clive Edwards
Privy Councillor for Tourism, Trade & Labour: Vilami Latu
Privy Councillor for Revenue Services: Fe'ao Vakata
Privy Councillor for Agriculture, Food, Forests & Fisheries: Sangster Saulala
Governor of Vava'u: Lord Fulivai
Governor of Ha'apai: Lord Havea Tu'iha'angana

Ministries
Palace Office, P.O. Box 6, Nuku'alofa, Kingdom of Tonga. Tel: +676 25063, fax: +676 24102
Government Portal: URL: http://www.pmo.gov.to
Prime Minister's Office, Taufa'ahau Road, P.O. Box 62, Nuku'alofa, Kingdom of Tonga. Tel: +676 24644, fax: +676 23888, e-mail: minister@mca.gov.to, URL: http://www.pmo.gov.to
Ministry of Agriculture, Food, Fisheries and Forestry, Vuna Rd, P.O. Box 14, Nuku'alofa, Kingdom of Tonga. Tel: +676 23038, fax: +676 24271 / 23093, e-mail: maf-hq@maf.gov.to, URL: http://www.pmo.gov.to
Ministry of Civil Aviation, Salote Rd, P.O. Box 845, Nuku'alofa, Kingdom of Tonga. Tel: +676 24144 / 24045, fax: +676 24145, e-mail: info@mca.gov.to, URL: http://mca.gov.to
Ministry of Education, 2nd Floor, Government Building, Vuna Rd, P.O. Box 61, Nuku'alofa, Kingdom of Tonga. Tel: +676 23511 / 23903, fax: +676 23866, e-mail: moe@kalianet.to, URL: http://www.tongaeducation.gov.to/
Ministry of Finance & National Planning, Treasury Building, Vuna Road, P.O. Box 87, Nuku'alofa, Kingdom of Tonga. Tel: +676 23066, fax: +676 26011, e-mail: minfin@kalianet.to, URL: http://www.finance.gov.to/
Ministry of Fisheries, Vuna Rd, Sopu o Taufa'ahau, Kolomotu'a, P.O. Box 871, Nuku'alofa, Kingdom of Tonga. Tel: +676 21399 / 23753, fax: +676 23891, e-mail: fisheries@tongafish.gov.to
Ministry of Foreign Affairs, Level 4, Reserve Bank Building, Salote Rd, P.O. Box 821, Nuku'alofa, Kingdom of Tonga. Tel: +676 23600, fax: +676 23360, e-mail: secfo@minofa.gov.to, URL: http://minofa.gov.to
Ministry of Health, Vaiola Hospital, Taufa'ahau Rd., Tofoa, P.O. Box 59 , Nuku'alofa, Kingdom of Tonga. Tel: +676 23200, fax: +676 24291, e-mail: mohtonga@kalianet.to, URL: http://www.health.gov.to
Ministry of Justice, Bank of Tonga Building, Railway Rd, P.O. Box 85, Nuku'alofa, Kingdom of Tonga. Tel: +676 24055 / 25671, fax: +676 23098, URL:http://www.pmo.gov.to
Ministry of Labour, Commerce and Tourism, Fasi-moe, Afi Free Wesleyan Church Building, Salote Rd, Fasi-moe-afi, P.O. Box 110, Nuku'alofa, Kingdom of Tonga. Tel: +676 23688, fax: +676 23887, e-mail: secretary@mlci.gov.to, URL: http://www.pmo.gov.to
Ministry of Lands, Survey and Natural Resources, Level 3, Government Building, Vuna Road, P.O. Box 5, Nuku'alofa, Kingdom of Tonga. Tel: +676 23611, fax: +676 23216, e-mail: minlands@kalianet.to, URL: http://www.lands.gov.to/
Ministry of Police, Fire Services and Prisons, Police Training Centre, Hala Maui Kisikisi, Longlongo, P.O. Box 8, Nuku'alofa, Kingdom of Tonga. Tel: +676 23233, fax: +676 23226
Office of the Governor of Ha'apai, Holopeka Rd., Pangai, Ha'apai, Kingdom of Tonga. Tel: +676 60005, fax: +676 60004
Office of the Governor of Vava'u, P.O. Box 39, Neiafu, Vava'u, Kingdom of Tonga. Tel: +676 70070, fax: +676 70501

Elections
The last legislative elections were held in April 2008. Pro-democracy candidates won all nine of the elected seats in the nation's parliament. The government proposed reforms for 2010, when the majority of representatives in parliament were to be elected. The election took place in November 2010, the Democratic party, led by Akalisi Pohiva won 12 of the 17 seats, independents won the other five seats. Nine seats are reserved for the land owning nobility and noble Lord Tu'ivakano with the support of the independents beat Akalisi Pohiva in a vote for the post of Prime Minister.

Political Parties
Democratic Party of the Friendly Islands (DPFI); Human Rights and Democracy Movement (HRDM); People's Democratic Party (PDP).

Diplomatic Representation
Tongan High Commission, UK, 36 Molyneaux Street, London, W1H 6AB, England. Tel: +44 (0)20 7724 5828, fax: +44 (0)20 7723 9074, e-mail: fetu@btinternet.com
Head of Mission: Sione Sonata Tupou
Envoy to Tonga, US, staff resident in Fiji, URL: http://tonga.usvpp.gov
Ambassador: Frankie Annette Reed
British High Commission, Staff resident in Fiji, URL: http://ukinfiji.fco.gov.uk/en/
High Commissioner: Roderick Drummond (page 1418)
Embassy of Tonga, 51st Street, NY 100022, USA. Tel: +1 917 369 1025
Ambassador: Taumoepeau Tupou

Permanent Representative of the Kingdom of Tonga to the United Nations, 250 East 51st Street, New York, N.Y. 10022, USA. Tel: +1 212 917 369 1025, fax: +1 212 917 369 1024, URL: http://www.un.int/tonga
Ambassador: Taumoepeau Tupou

LEGAL SYSTEM

The law derives from the 1875 Constitution of 1875, legislative statutes and English common law.

The judiciary is independent of the king and the executive branch, although Supreme Court justices are appointed by the king, and the king has the power to commute a death sentence.

Tongan courts consist of a Land Court, which hears all land claims, the Magistrates' Courts, which hear minor civil and criminal cases. Appeals are made to a Supreme Court, which exercises jurisdiction in major civil and criminal cases, and then to the Court of Appeal, the appellate court of last resort. The Supreme Court and the Privy Council sit as the Court of Appeal. The Privy Council has jurisdiction over cases on appeal from the Land Court dealing with titles of nobility and estate boundaries. In addition, the court system consists of a court martial for the Tonga Defense Services, a court tribunal for the police force, and a court of review for the Inland Revenue Department.

Citizens cannot change their government. There is some degree of government corruption. Tonga retains the death penalty for murder and treason, though no executions have taken place since 1982.

LOCAL GOVERNMENT

Town and district officers are elected by the people. Town officers represent the Central Government in a village and district officers have authority over a group of villages.

AREA AND POPULATION

Area
The islands of Tonga are situated in the Southern Pacific east of Fiji. There are approximately 171 islands, only 36 of which are inhabited. The area of Tonga is 270 sq. miles (700 sq. km) including inland waters. The largest inhabited islands are Tongatapu (99.2 sq. miles or 257 sq. km), Vava'u (34.6 sq. miles or 89.7 sq. km), 'Eua (33.7 sq. miles or 87.3 sq. km) and Lifuka (4.6 sq. miles or 11.8 sq. km). Most of the islands are formed either of a limestone base with an uplifted coral formation, or limestone overlying a volcanic base.

The climate is tropical, with a warm season from December to May and a cooler season from June to November. Natural hazards include cyclones (November to April), earthquakes and occasional offshore volcanic activity.

To view a map, consult http://www.lib.utexas.edu/maps/cia08/tonga_sm_2008.gif

Population
As of 2010, the population was an estimated 104,000 with an annual growth rate of about 0.6 per cent over the period 2000-10. An estimated 23 per cent of the population live in urban areas. Population density is 126 persons by square km.

The Tongans are Polynesian. English is the official language but Tongan is also spoken.

Births, Marriages and Deaths
In 2010 the crude birth rate was 27.2 per 1,000 population and the crude death rate was 6.7 per 1,000 population. The total fertility rate of women was estimated at 3.9 in 2010. Life expectancy was an estimated 72 years for males and 70 for females in 2009. Healthy life expectancy was 63 years in 2007. In 2009, the infant mortality rate was 17 per 1,000 live births and the neonatal morality rate was 9 per 1,000 live births. The median age is 21 years old. An estimated 37 per cent of the population is under 15 years old and 8 per cent over 60. (Source: http://www.who.int, World Health Statistics 2012)

Public Holidays 2014
1 January: New Year's Day
18 April: Good Friday
20April: Easter Sunday
21 April: Easter Monday
25 April: ANZAC Day
4 June: Independence Day
12 July Birthday of HM King George Tupov V
4 November: Constitution Day
4 December: King Tupou I Day
25 December: Christmas Day
26 December: Boxing Day

EMPLOYMENT

Figures for 2007 put the labour force at 40,000, nearly 32 per cent of whom are employed in the agricultural sector, 30 per cent in industry and 37 per cent in the service sector. The unemployment rate for 2004 was estimated at 12 per cent.

TONGA

BANKING AND FINANCE

Currency
Tonga's currency consists of Pa'anga ($T banknotes) and seniti (cents). Tonga converted to decimal currency in 1967. Australian currency was used before the introduction of Tongan currency.

GDP/GNP, Inflation, National Debt
Industrial origin of GDP in recent years follows. Figures are in thousand Pa'anga and for the fiscal year ending 30 June:

Industrial Origin	2008	2009	2010
GDP by industrial origin	661,480	650,109	671,928
-Agriculture	106,089	111,623	119,537
-Mining	2,076	2,123	1,712
-Manufacturing	47,730	45,537	44,167
-Utilities	16,747	17,979	17,255
-Construction	38,729	40,332	41,408
-Trade	79,379	88,218	91,181
-Transport & communications	26,293	25,351	25,913
-Finance	61,435	53,269	52,131
-Public administration	77,290	81,194	89,140
-Others	110,439	113,777	117,385
Net factor income from abroad	14,256	13,358	7,634
GNI	675,736	663,467	679,562

Source: Asian Development Bank

The structure of GDP 2009 output was agriculture 19.0 per cent, industry 18.0 per cent and services 63.0 per cent. GDP grew by 0.7 per cent in 2008, compared to 0.2 per cent in 2007 and 3.0 per cent in 2006, but in response to the global economic downturn GDP growth was put at -1.0 per cent in 2009 and 0.3 per cent in 2010. Per capita GDP was 5,257 pa'anga in 2008. GDP was estimated at US$435 million in 2011.

GDP was estimated at 9 per cent in 2011.

Tonga's external debt was estimated at US$335 million in 2012. China has provided loans amounting to US$200 million, one to develop the business district and a US$80 million loan for road improvements.

Foreign Investment
Tonga receives external aid from a number of overseas sources including Australia, New Zealand, Britain, Germany, Japan, Asian Development Bank, the EU and the United Nations.

Balance of Payments / Imports and Exports
Organised markets trade in Nuku'alofa: the Vuna market with its cold storage offers meat, fish and ice, while Talamahu market offers produce grown by local farmers.

Tonga regularly experiences an adverse balance of trade, offset to some extent by invisible earnings from such sources as remittances from overseas, tourism, donations, gifts and so on. The trade balance in recent years is shown in the following table. Figures are in thousand Pa'anga and for a calendar year:

External Trade	2008	2009	2010
Exports, fob	15,800	15,100	15,300
Imports, cif	307,000	309,300	285,800
Trade balance	-291,200	-294,200	-270,500

Source: Asian Development Bank

Japan, Australia, Fiji, New Zealand and the USA are Tonga's largest overseas markets. In 2010 exports to the US amounted to an estimated US$2.3 million, to Hong Kong US$3.4 million and Fiji US$1.1 million. The main importers were Fiji (US$53.6 million), New Zealand (US$46.8 million), the US (US$22.7 million) and Australia (US$11.6million). The agricultural sector accounts for 90 per cent of exports. Vanilla is growing in importance as an export commodity. Other exported produce include fish, squash, tropical fruits, and vegetables and kava.

Principal Exports by Commodity

Commodity	2003	2004	2005
Squash	13,793	9,237	8,318
Fish	9,439	5,754	4,024
Vanilla beans	6,130	913	335

Source: Asian Development Bank

Tonga's main imports are flour, fresh and canned meat, canned fish, dairy products, tobacco, cotton piece goods, drapery, motor cars, motor cycles, machinery and petroleum products. Australia and New Zealand are the biggest suppliers, chiefly of food.

Foreign reserves in 2008 were estimated to be US$69.8 million.

Central Bank
National Reserve Bank of Tonga, PO Box 25, Nuku'alofa, Tonga. Tel: +676 24057, fax: +676 24201, e-mail: nrbt@reservebank.to, URL: http://www.reservebank.to/
Governor: Mrs Siosi Mafi

Development Bank
Tonga Development Bank, URL: http://www.tdb.to/

MANUFACTURING, MINING AND SERVICES

There were 107 societies on the Register of Co-operative Societies at the end of June 1974, the fourteenth full year of co-operative development. The co-operatives include produce market/consumer companies, thrift and credit societies as well as manufacturing enterprises. Although agriculture is the major resource of the country, little progress has been made in the formation of co-operatives in that area. However, increasing interest has been shown in consumer co-operation.

Primary and Extractive Industries
Oil seepages were confirmed on 'Eua and Tongatapu in 1968. In 1970 a consortium of foreign oil companies was formed to carry out land and offshore exploration but so far there have been no significant strikes. Otherwise no minerals have been discovered. In 2011 Tonga imported 1,000 barrels per day to meet its needs.

Energy
During 2010 Tonga generated 0.04 billion kWh of electricity all of which is consumed domestically. Electricity is mainly generated by thermal power stations. There are diesel generators on Tongatapu, 'Eua, Ha'apai and Vava'u.

Manufacturing
Import replacement-type industries are showing a recent modest growth and include roofing materials, concrete blocks, fencing, furniture, biscuits, lumber, baking, prefabricated housing, pipe, soft drinks, meat processing and sandals. Export oriented industries are limited to desiccated coconut, coconut buttons and consumer charcoal. Handicraft items include tapa cloth, wood carvings, mats, baskets and shell jewellery.

Service Industries
Tourism is relatively small, but growing. It experienced a 15 per cent annual growth during the recent worldwide recession. Modern accommodation is adequate and emphasis is being placed on transportation facilities.

Agriculture
Among the products grown for local consumption are yams, taro, cassava, groundnuts, sweet potatoes, vegetables, maize, tobacco, sugar-cane, avocado pears, pineapples, water melons, mangoes and citrus fruits. Since the growing of vanilla began in 1968, a growing quantity has been exported. Squash (pumpkin) is now a large export commodity with Japan taking almost the whole crop.

A coconut-industry development scheme was started in 1965 to increase the production of copra. The Government is carrying out measures to control and eradicate such pests as banana scab moth, coconut pest, and rhinoceros beetle. Because rats damage the majority of crops, the government has been operating a sustained programme of rodent research and control since 1970. A Kava Council has recently been formed to promote and protect the industry, as it is one of the fastest growing industries in Tonga. The council is currently drafting guidelines regarding quality control and organic planting methods.

Agricultural Production in 2010

Produce	Int. $'000*	Tonnes
Coconuts	7,431	67,200
Pumpkins, squash and gourds	3,770	21,500
Vanilla	3,320	200
Indigenous pigmeat	2,457	1,598
Vegetables fresh nes	1,093	5,800
Indigenous cattle meat	965	357
Cassava	857	8,200
Fruit fresh nes	803	2,300
Fruit, tropical fresh nes	777	1,900
Taro (cocoyam)	764	3,600
Lemons and limes	753	1,900
Yams	727	5,500

* unofficial figures

Source: http://faostat.fao.org/site/339/default.aspx Food and Agriculture Organization of the United Nations, Food and Agricultural commodities production

Although there has been little commercial development of the fishing industry, the abundant supply of fish in Tongan waters is an important source of food. There is also some deep sea fishing. In order to increase fish exports the government has recently held workshops focusing on the quality of service provided by the fisheries. Emphasis has also been placed on encouraging the promotion of less popular varieties of seafood to increase the market. Tongan waters are rich in tuna. FAO figures for 2010 put the total catch at 3,125 tonnes.

The major types of livestock are pigs, goats and poultry, but the number of heads of cattle kept are increasing, thereby reducing beef imports. Horses are kept for domestic use.

Limited areas of forest on 'Eua and Vava'u supply timber for local use and consideration is being given to the development of forest resources.

COMMUNICATIONS AND TRANSPORT

Travel Requirements
Citizens of the USA, Canada, Australia and most of the EU require a passport valid for six months and sufficient funds for the duration of their stay but do not need a visa; they can obtain a visitor's visa free of charge on arrival, which is valid for 31 days. Citizens of Bulgaria, Czech Republic, Estonia, Hungary, Latvia, Lithuania, Poland, Romania, Slovak Republic and Slovenia do need a visa, unless in transit and not leaving the airport. Other nationals should contact the embassy to check visa requirements.

International Airports
The airport is at Fua'amotu, 14 miles (22.4 km.) from Nuku'alofa. Airstrips on Vava'u and 'Eua are now in use for flights to and from Nuku'alofa. In 2004 Royal Tongan Airways ceased operations due to financial failures. Air New Zealand, Air Pacific and Pacific Blue offer international flights. Peau Vava'u (URL: http://www.peauvavau.to) and Airlines Tonga offer domestic flights (http://www.airlinestonga.com).

Roads
There are 3,083 km of roads including primary-national (757 km), secondary-regional (463 km) and other roads (1,873 km). Of these, 500 km are bitumen-paved, 650 km are all-weather gravel roads and the rest mainly unimproved earth roads. Vehicles are driven on the left. The Public Works Department is responsible for the construction and maintenance of all major roads, and the Divisional Commissioners are in charge of all minor roads within their respective Division.

Shipping
The Pacific Navigation Company of Tonga maintains regular inter-island and external services. Vessels of the Bank Line call every six weeks to load copra for Britain and the continent.

Ports and Harbours
Nuku'alofa and Neiafu are the ports of call for regular passengers and cargo services from New Zealand via Fiji. At both these ports vessels can tie up at the wharf. At Pangai on Lifuka, which is a port of entry for copra collection, ships anchor about a mile from the jetty.

A development project is currently under way to upgrade the harbours. These plans include the reconstruction of the Funa Harbour, the resealing of the Queen Salote Wharf and its access road and the building of a waste oil storage facility and new marina. A new pilot boat is also to be purchased for the Funa Harbour.

HEALTH

Medical facilities are supplied by the government and Tonga has modern hospitals in the towns of Nuku'alofa, Vava'u and Ha'apai as well as a system of health centres. In 2009, the government spent approximately 11.4 per cent of its total budget on healthcare, accounting for 79.3 per cent of all healthcare spending. External resources account for 11.6 per cent of total expenditure. Total expenditure on healthcare equated to 4.6 per cent of the country's GDP. Per capita expenditure on health was approximately US$142.

According to the latest WHO figures, in 2005-10, there were an estimated 58 doctors in Tonga (5.6 per 10,000 population), 400 nurses and midwives (39.8 per 10,000 population), 37 dentistry personnel and 15 pharmaceutical personnel. There were 26 beds per 10,000 population.

In 2010, the infant mortality rate was 13 per 1,000 live births and the under-five mortality rate was 16 per 1,000 live births. The most common causes of mortality in the under-fives are prematurity (22 per cent), pneumonia (9 per cent) and diarrhoea (3 per cent). In 2010, all the population were believed to have sustained access to improved drinking water and 96 per cent to improved sanitation. (Source: http://www.who.int, World Health Statistics 2012)

EDUCATION

The government has received funds from the Japanese government under the Japan Grant Assistance for Grassroots Project for the building of classrooms at state run primary schools and colleges. Education is free and compulsory up to the age of 14. In 2005 the enrolment rate for primary education was estimated at over 90 per cent. Tonga has a literacy rate of 99 per cent. Most students following higher education do so overseas.

RELIGION

The religion of Tonga is mainly Methodist. The official Church is the Free Wesley Church with the Sovereign at its head. Sunday is very much a day for the church and rest. There are small Bahai and Hindu communities.

Tonga has a religious liberty rating of 9 on a scale of 1 to 10 (10 is most freedom). (Source: World Religion Database)

COMMUNICATIONS AND MEDIA

The constitution was amended in 2003 to increase state control of the media and to limit the right of courts to review royal decisions. State-owned broadcasters tend to support government policy and there is little independent coverage. Criticism of the government is published but there are allegations of harrassment of journalists.

Newspapers
Newspapers include the Tonga Chronicle (government-owned weekly), Times of Tonga (private) URL: http://www.timesoftonga.com/, and Matangi Tonga, (bi-monthly), URL: http://www.matangitonga.to/

Broadcasting
There are two state-owned television stations and two privately owned stations. The public service Television Tonga went on air in 2000. Satellite and cable TV is also available. There are two state-owned (Radio Tonga 1 and Kool FM) and three privately-owned radio stations. **Tonga Broadcasting Commission**, Television Tonga, URL: http://www.tonga-broadcasting.com/).
Tonga Radio, private, URL: http://www.tongaradio.com/

Telecommunications
A new system has recently been installed converting the old analogue system to digital, thus improving the service. Increased competition is also helping the expansion and improvement. In 2008 there were an estimated 25,500 main telephone lines and 50,000 mobile phones. An estimated 8,400 people use the internet.

ENVIRONMENT

Due to land clearance for settlements and agricultural use, deforestation is now an issue in Tonga. Over hunting also threatens the marine turtle population. There is also some damage to coral reefs.

Tonga is party to the following international agreements: Biodiversity, Climate Change, Climate Change-Kyoto Protocol, Desertification, Law of the Sea, Marine Dumping, Marine Life Conservation, Ozone Layer Protection and Ship Pollution.

According to figures from the EIA, in 2010 Tonga's emissions from the consumption of fossil fuels totalled 0.16 million metric tons of carbon dioxide.

STATES OF THE WORLD

TRINIDAD AND TOBAGO
Republic of Trinidad and Tobago

Capital: Port of Spain (Population estimate, 2009: 57,000)

Head of State: H.E. Anthony Carmona (page 1400)

National Flag: On a red field a white-edged black diagonal band from the upper hoist side to the lower fly side

CONSTITUTION AND GOVERNMENT

Constitution
Trinidad and Tobago became an independent member of the Commonwealth on 31 August 1962, by virtue of the Trinidad and Tobago Independence Act. An Order made under the Act provides for a new Constitution for Trinidad and Tobago, with effect from that date, including provision for the executive government, the legislature, the judicature and the public service. The Constitution also contains provisions relating to citizenship of Trinidad and Tobago and fundamental rights and freedoms of the individual.

In 1973, Trinidad and Tobago became a signatory to the Treaty establishing the Caribbean Community (CARICOM). On 1 August 1976 Trinidad and Tobago was declared a Republic within the Commonwealth of Nations, with a President replacing the Monarch as Head of State. Under its new constitution, legislative power is vested in the Parliament, consisting of the President, the Senate and the House of Representatives. The President is elected for a term of five years by the Electoral College, which consists of all members of the Senate and the House of Representatives.

A draft constitution was laid as a paper in the House of Representatives in August 2006. To read the draft, please visit: http://www.opm.gov.tt/documents/20060818_draft_constitution.pdf

Upper House
The Senate comprises 31 members, all of whom are appointed by the President: 16 in accordance with the advice of the Prime Minister, six in accordance with the advice of the Leader of the Opposition and nine at the President's discretion. All senators vacate their seats on the dissolution of Parliament.
Senate, Parliament, Red House, Abercromby Street, PO Box 878, Port of Spain, Trinidad. Tel: +1 868 623 8366, fax: +1 868 625 4672, e-mail: administration@ttparliament.org, URL: http://www.parliament.gov.tt

Lower House
The House of Representatives is made up of the elected representatives of 36 electoral constituencies and the Speaker of the House. Elections are held at least every five years. The Prime Minister is appointed by the President from the ranks of the majority party in the House of Representatives.

TRINIDAD AND TOBAGO

House of Representatives, Parliament, Red House, Abercromby Street, PO Box 878, Port of Spain, Trinidad. Tel: +1 868 623 2565, fax: +1 868 625 4672, e-mail: administration@ttparliament.org, URL: http://www.parliament.gov.tt

Tobago

The Legislature of Tobago is unicameral, the House of Assembly has 15 members, 12 are elected and three are chosen by the house. Members serve a four year term. The most recent elections in Tobago were held in January 2009.

International Relations

Trinidad and Tobago has good relations with its Caribbean neighbours and its trading partners (North America and Europe). There was a recent dispute with Barbados over a maritime boundary. It is the most industrialised country of the English-speaking Caribbean and is a leader within Caricom. It joined the Commonwealth and UN in 1962 and was the first Caribbean country to join the Organisation of American States.

Recent Events

In 2007, the former prime minister Basdeo Panday was charged with corruption. Snap elections were held in May 2010 and Kamla Persad Bissesar became the country's first female prime minister.

In August 2011, a state of emergency was imposed following an increase in violent crime.

In November 2011, the prime minister Kamla Persad-Bissessar said a plot had been discovered to assassinate her and several ministers.

Cabinet (as at June 2013)

Prime Minister: Kamla Persad-Bissessar (UNC) (page 1494)
Attorney General: Anand Ramlogan (UNC) (page 1500)
Minister of Foreign Affairs: Winston Dookeran (COP) (page 1417)
Minister of Planning: Bhoendradatt Tewarie
Minister of Public Administration: Carolyn Seepersad-Bachan (COP)
Minister of Food Production: Devant Maharaj (COP)
Minister of Science & Technology: Rupert Griffith (UNC)
Minister of the People and Social Development: Glen Ramdharsingh (UNC)
Minister of National Security: Emmanuel George (UNC)
Minister of Health: Dr Fuad Khan (page 1456)
Minister of Education: Tim Goopeesingh (UNC)
Minister of Tertiary Education: Fazal Karim
Minister of Sports: Anil Roberts (COP)
Minister of Local Government, Works & Infrastructure: Surujrattan Rambachan (UNC) (page 1500)
Minister of Legal Affairs: Prakash Ramadhar (COP) (page 1500)
Minister of Gender, Youth & Child Development: Marlene Coudray (UNC)
Minister of Labour and Small and Micro Enterprises: Errol McLeod (UNC)
Minister of Tourism: Stephen Cadiz (UNC)
Minister of Arts and Multiculturalism: Lincoln Douglas (UNC)
Minister of Community Development: Winston Peters (UNC)
Minister of Energy and Energy Industries: Kevin Ramnarine (UNC)
Minister of Public Utilities: Nizam Baksh (UNC)
Minister of Transport: Chandresh Sharma (UNC)
Minister of Justice: Christlyn Moore (page 1479)
Minister of Trade, Industry & Investment, Minister in the Ministry of Finance: Vasant Bharath (page 1388)
Minister of Housing: Roodial Moonilal (UNC)
Minister of Tobago Development: Delmon Baker (TOP)
Minister of the Environment & Water Resourcs: Ganga Singh
Minister of National Diversity: Clifton de Coteau
Minister of Communication: Jamal Mohammed
Minister of Finance and Economy: Larry Howai
Minister in the Ministry of Environment & Water Resources: Ramona Ramdial
Minister in the Ministry of Food Production: Jairam Seemungal
Minister in the Ministry of National Diversity & Social Integration: Embau Moheni

---

Ministries

Office of the Prime Minister, Level 16, Eric Williams Finance Building, Eric Williams Complex, Independence Square, Port of Spain, Trinidad and Tobago. Tel: +1 868 652 2045, fax: +1 868 653 0262, URL: http://www.opm.gov.tt

Ministry of the Attorney General, Cabildo Chambers, Cor. Sackville & St. Vincents St., Port of Spain, Trinidad and Tobago. Tel: +1 868 623 7010/625 6531, fax: +1 868 625 0470, URL: http://www.ag.gov.tt/

Ministry of Agriculture, Land and Marine Resources, URL: http://www.agriculture.gov.tt

Ministry of Finance, Level 8, Eric Williams Finance Building, Port of Spain, Trinidad and Tobago. Tel: +1 868 627 9692/9693, fax: +1 868 627 6108, URL: http://www.finance.gov.tt/

Ministry of Community Development, Culture and Gender Affairs, ALGICO Building, Jerringham Ave., Belmont, Port of Spain, Trinidad and Tobago. Tel: +1 868 625 3012, URL: http://www.cdcga.gov.tt

Ministry of Education, Hayes Street, St. Clair, Port of Spain, Trinidad and Tobago. Tel: +1 868 622 2181, fax: +1 868 628 7818, URL: http://www.moe.gov.tt

Ministry of Energy and Energy Industries, Level 9, Riverside Plaza, Corner of Besson and Piccadilly Streets, Port of Spain, Trinidad and Tobago. Tel: +1 868 623 6708, fax: +1 868 623 2726, URL: http://www.energy.gov.tt/

Ministry of Finance, URL: http://www.finance.gov.tt/

Ministry of Foreign Affairs, Knowsley Building, 1 Queens Park West, Port of Spain, Trinidad and Tobago. Tel: +1 868 623 4116, fax: +1 868 627 0571, URL: http://www.foreign.gov.tt/

Ministry of Labour and Enterprise Development, Level 15, Riverside Plaza Cor. Besson & Piccadilly Sts., Port of Spain, Trinidad and Tobago. Tel: +1 868 623 2931, fax: +1 868 627 8488, URL: http://www.labour.gov.tt/

Ministry of Legal Affairs, 72-74 South Quay. Port of Spain, Trinidad and Tobago. Tel: +1 868 625 4586, fax: +1 868 625 9803, URL: http://www.legal.gov.tt

Ministry of Health, Corner of Duncan Street and Independence Square, Port of Spain, Trinidad and Tobago. Tel: +1 868 627 0010/12/14, fax: +1 868 623 9628, URL: http://www.health.gov.tt

Ministry of Justice, Tower C, Levels 19-21, International Waterfront Complex, #1 Wrightoson Road, Port of Spain. Tel: +1 868 625 5878, fax: +1 868 623 5596, URL: http://www.moj.tt

Ministry of Local Government, Kent House, Long Circular Road, Maraval, Trinidad and Tobago. Tel: +1 868 628 1325, fax: +1 868 622 7410, URL: http://www.localgov.gov.tt/

Ministry of National Security, Temple Court, 31-33 Abercromby St., Port of Spain, Trinidad and Tobago. Tel: +1 868 623 2441, fax: +1 868 625 3925, URL: http://www.nationalsecurity.gov.tt

Ministry of Planning, Housing and the Environment, Level 14, Eric Williams Plaza, Independence Square, Port of Spain, Trinidad and Tobago. Tel: +1 868 623 4308, fax: +1 868 623 8123, URL: http://www.mphe.gov.tt/home/

Ministry of Science, Technology and Tertiary Education, Nahous Building, Patra STreet, St James, Trinidad and Tobago. URL: http://www. stte.gov.tt

Ministry of Social Development, Port of Spain, Trinidad and Tobago. URL: http://www.socialservices.gov.tt

Ministry of Sport &Youth Affairs, ISSA Nicholas Bldg, Cor. Frederick & Duke Sts, Port of Spain, Trinidad and Tobago. Tel: +1 868 625 5622 4, fax: +1 868 623 4507, URL: http://www.msya.gov.tt/home/

Ministry of Tourism, 45A-45C St Vincent St., Port of Spain, Trinidad and Tobago. Tel: +1 868 627 0002, fax: +1 625 6404, URL: http://www.tourism.gov.tt

Ministry of Trade, Industry and Industry, Levels 9,11-17, Nicholas Tower, 63-65 Independence Square, Port of Spain, Trinidad & Tobago. Tel: +1 868 623 2931, fax: +1 868 627 8488, e-mail: mti-info@gov.tt, URL: http://www.tradeind.gov.tt/

Ministry of Works and Transport, Corner Richmond and London Streets, Port of Spain, Trinidad and Tobago. Tel: +1 868 625 1225, fax: +1 868 627 9886, URL: http://www.mowt.gov.tt/general/homepage.aspx

Elections

The most recent general election was held in May 2010; it was won by the People's Partnership a coalition made up of the United National Congress (UNC), the Congress of the People (COP) and the Tobago Organisation of the People (TOP). Kamla Persad-Bissessar, leader of the UNC was sworn in as Trinidad and Tobago's first female prime minister.

Indirect presidential elections were held in March 2013 and Mr Justice Anthony Carmona was duly elected president.

Political Parties

People's National Movement (PNM), URL: http://www.pnm.org.tt
United National Congress (UNC), URL: http://www.unc.org.tt
Congress of the People (COP), URL: http://www.coptnt.com/ver03/index.php
United National Congress (UNC), URL: http://www.unc.org.tt

Diplomatic Representation

US Embassy, 15 Queen's Park West, Port of Spain, (PO Box 752), Trinidad and Tobago. Tel: +1 868 622 6372, fax:+1 868 628 5462, URL: http://trinidad.usembassy.gov/
Ambassador: Beatrice Welters

British High Commission, 19 St. Clair Avenue, St Clair, Port of Spain, Trinidad and Tobago. Tel: +1 868 622 2748, fax: +1 868 622 4555, e-mail: csbhc@opus.co.h, URL: http://ukintt.fco.gov.uk/en
Ambassador: Arthur Snell

High Commission of the Republic of Trinidad and Tobago, 42 Belgrave Square, London, SW1X 8NT, United Kingdom. Tel: +44 (0)20 7245 9351, fax: +44 (0)20 7823 1065, URL: http://www.tthighcommission.co.uk
High Commissioner: Garvin Nicholas

Embassy of the Republic of Trinidad and Tobago, 1708 Massachusetts Avenue, N.W., Washington D.C. 20036-1975, USA. Tel: +1 202 467 6490 fax: +1 202 785 3130, URL: http://ttembassy.cjb.net/
Ambassador: Neil Parsan

Permanent Mission of the Republic of Trinidad and Tobago to the United Nations, 820 Second Avenue, 5th Floor, New York, N.Y. 10017, USA Tel: +1 212 697 7620 fax: +1 212 682 3580, URL: http://www.un.int/wcm/content/site/trinidadandtobago
Ambassador: Rodney Charles

LEGAL SYSTEM

Judicial power is vested in the Supreme Court, which consists of the High Court of Justice and the Court of Appeal. The High Court comprises the Chief Justice and between six and 16 Puisne Judges. The Court of Appeal comprises the Chief Justice and six Justices of Appeal.

Until 2003, appeals could be referred to the Judicial Committee of the Privy Council in the UK, London, but these are now directed to the Caribbean Court of Justice.

The government respects the rights of its citizens, but there have been recent instances of police killings during arrests or in custody. Prison conditions are poor. Trinidad and Tobago retains the death penalty; the last executions took place in 1999.

Judiciary of Trinidad and Tobago, URL: http://www.ttlawcourts.org/
Supreme Court Chief Justice: The Hon. Mr Justice Ivor Archie

Office of the Ombudsman of the Trinidad and Tobago, 132 Henry Street, Port of Spain, Trinidad. Tel: +868 624 3121-4, URL: http://www.ombudsman.gov.tt/

LOCAL GOVERNMENT

There are 14 Municipal Corporations established under the Municipal Corporations Act 21 of 1990 as amended by Act 8 of 1992 with responsibility for the Local Government functions. Each of the 14 Municipal Corporations in Trinidad has an elected Council, comprising Councillors and Aldermen. Councillors are directly elected for three-year terms at Local Government elections, and Aldermen are elected by the Councillors to join the Council for the same term of office. A Municipal Council is both a local general assembly and a policy-making body for the towns and communities under its jurisdiction. It is empowered to make policies and Bye-laws in relation to its functions for the local area. In 2004 a Draft Policy Paper on Local Government Reform was published. It proposed the reform and decentralization of the system with more autonomy, and mechanisms to promote greater citizen participation in Local Government.

AREA AND POPULATION

Area

The islands of Trinidad and Tobago are to be found in the Southern Caribbean, seven miles eastward of Venezuela and separated from South America by the Gulf of Paria, into which fall the northern mouths of the Orinoco. They cover a total area of 5,128 sq. km (1,980 sq. miles), with Trinidad occupying 4,828 sq. km (1,864 sq. miles) and Tobago 300 sq. km (116 sq. miles). The terrain is largely flat, with some hills and low mountains. The highest point is El Cerro del Aripo at 940 m.

The capital is the Port of Spain, located on Trinidad, and the two principal towns, found on the same island, are San Fernando and Arima. Trinidad is the business centre of the islands, with the focus of activity in the Port of Spain. Tobago, by contrast, is a tranquil island. The climate is tropical. The average maximum temperature is 31.2°C and the minimum 22.3°C, with an average of 7.3 hours of sunshine daily. The average monthly rainfall is 130.1 mm (5.2 inches). The rainy season is June to December.

To view a map of Trinidad and Tobago, please consult http://www.lib.utexas.edu/maps/cia08/trinidad_tobago_sm_2008.gif

Population

The cultural make-up of Trinidad and Tobago is very diverse. The original inhabitants of Trinidad were mainly Arawak and those of Tobago Carib. The European population is chiefly English, Portuguese, French and Spanish. Other nationalities are Chinese, Africans, Syrians, Lebanese, Americans, Venezuelans, indigenous Amerindians and a large number of East Indians (mainly immigrants from Northern India). This large mixture of races has led to a varied cultural life, the diversity of which is reflected at all levels of society, particularly in costume, colloquial language, architecture and place names.

The official language is English but Hindi, Chinese, French and Spanish are also used.

The population of Trinidad and Tobago in 2009 was estimated at 1.33 million with an average annual growth rate of 0.4 per cent. The population of Port of Spain is approximately 300,000. Approximately 14 per cent of the population live in urban areas.

Births, Marriages and Deaths

The infant mortality rate was estimated at 31 per 1,000 live births in 2009. The neonatal mortality rate was estimated at 23 per 1,000 births in 2009. The maternal mortality rate was estimated at 45 per 100,000 births in 2008. Total fertility for females was 1.6 in 2009.

Life expectancy at birth in 2009 was estimated at 66 years for males and 75 years for females. Healthy life expectancy was estimated at 59 years and 64 years respectively in 2007. In 2009, the median age was 30 years. Approximately 21 per cent of the population was aged less than 15 years and 10 per cent over 60 years old. (Source: WHO)

Public Holidays 2014

1 January: New Year's Day
18 April: Good Friday
21 April: Easter Monday
1 May: Labour Day
30 May: Indian Arrival Day
19 June: Corpus Christi
1 August: Emancipation Day
31 August: Independence Day
25 December: Christmas Day
26 December: Boxing Day

EMPLOYMENT

Total Employment by Economic Activity

Occupation	2008
Agriculture, hunting & forestry	22,900
Fishing	21,100
Manufacturing	55,100
Electricity, gas & water supply	7,900
Construction	108,500
Wholesale & retail trade, repairs & hotels	108,500
Transport, storage & communications	41,200
Financing, real estate. renting & business activities	52,500
Community, social & personal services	179,500
Other	700

Source: Copyright © International Labour Organization (ILO Dept. of Statistics, http://laborsta.ilo.org)

BANKING AND FINANCE

Currency

The unit of currency is the Trinidad and Tobago dollar (TT$).

GDP/GNP, Inflation, National Debt

Following economic reforms, Trinidad and Tobago has experienced over 15 years of consecutive growth. Recent government policy has been to try and widen the economic base and reduce dependency on oil and gas as a countermeasure to the slump in oil prices of the 1980s and dwindling reserves and so has encouraged diversification into tourism, manufacturing and agriculture. Gas reserves are expected to be depleted by 2019. As of 2008, Trinidad and Tobago was the fifth largest exporter of liquid natural gas in the world and the largest exporter of methanol and ammonia.

The following table shows make up of GDP in 2006.

Sector	Percentage
Crude oil, natural gas, petrochemicals	20.6
Financial services	7.5
Transport, storage, communication	4.0
Government	1.5
Manufacturing	11.8
Construction & quarrying	14.5
Tourism	5.0
Utilities	2.2
Agriculture	0.6
Education, cultural services	9.4
Hotels and guesthouses	1.7
Distribution, incl. restaurants	3.2

GDP was estimated to be US$22 million in 2011.

Average inflation has been relatively high in recent years; the rise is particularly driven by rising food prices. It reached 10 per cent in 2005, falling to 8 per cent in 2006. It was estimated at 7.9 per cent in 2007 and reached 10 per cent in 2008 and fell to 7.5 per cent in 2009. Drivers include rising food prices, wage demands and increased government spending. Inflation was estimated to be 10 per cent in 2010, rising to 12.5 per cent by 2012.

External debt was estimated at US$4.6 billion in 2011.

Balance of Payments / Imports and Exports

The main exports are in crude petroleum, petroleum products, sugar, cocoa beans, coffee beans, methanol, iron and steel (bars and rods), fertilizers, urea, asphalt and manufactured products. The major trading nations are the United States of America, which accounts for 50 per cent of exports, the EU, EURATOM and Canada. Main imports include manufactured goods, food, live animals, machinery and transportation equipment. Major trading nations for imports are the United States of America (30 per cent), Latin America, EU, and Japan. Estimated figures for 2010 put export earnings at US$12.7 billion and the costs of imports as US$8.1 billion.

Free Trade Area of the Americas

Trinidad and Tobago one oef 34 standing members of the Free Trade Area of the Americas which as of 2012 has not been implemented (URL: http://www.ftaa-alca.org/)

Central Bank

Central Bank of Trinidad and Tobago, PO Box 1250, Eric Williams Plaza, Independence Square, Port of Spain, Trinidad & Tobago. Tel: +1 868 6254835, fax: +1 868 6274696, e-mail: library@central-bank.org.tt, URL: http://www.central-bank.org.tt
Governor: Jwala Rambarran

MANUFACTURING, MINING AND SERVICES

Primary and Extractive Industries

The petroleum industry is the country's major economic sector and the sector provides employment for nearly four per cent of the working population. The chief mineral products are asphalt, obtained from the asphalt lake at La Brea, crude oil, petroleum and natural gas. Trinidad is also the leading exporter of ammonia and methanol.

In January 2008 the total proven oil reserves were put at 728 billion barrels, proven natural gas reserves in 2007 were put at were put at 18,770 billion cubic feet. Further oil exploration, both off- and on-shore is underway. In 2008 Trinidad and Tobago produced 163,520 barrels of oil per day of which 114,280 barrels per day were crude oil. The remainder was mostly natural gas liquids. It consumed and estimated 41,000 barrels per day, and was thus able to export a large quantity of oil. Crude oil producers include BHP Biliton and the state-owned Petrotrin. Most oil production is off-shore. In 2005 production began at the Greater Angostura field, off the northeast of Trindiad. This field contains an estimated 310 million barrels of reserves.

Production of natural gas has increased dramatically in recent years. In 2007 it produced 1.3 billion cubic feet. Year on year growth is over 10 per cent. Trinidad and Tobago is one of the largest LNG exporters in the world.

Manufacturing

The manufacturing sector provided over 7 per cent of the GDP in 2002. In 1998 the iron and steel industry recorded increases in output in all three of its product lines during the third quarter. The largest was in the production of billets, which reached a record of 128.6 thousand tonnes. The figure for wire rods was 103.8 thousand tonnes and direct reduced iron (DRI)

TRINIDAD AND TOBAGO

amounted to 179.5 thousand tonnes. Significantly high levels of export were also achieved in this period. The production of petro-chemicals is the largest manufacturing area. Other manufactured products include processed food and beverages.

Service Industries
Tourism is a substantial source of revenue in Trinidad and Tobago. In 2006, 463,000 people visited the country generating receipts of US$593 million.

Agriculture
Recent figures show that agriculture employed 8.1 per cent of the working population. Agriculture contributed 0.6 per cent in 2006. Lack of grazing grass has hampered the development of the dairy farming industry. To counteract this, pangola grass was introduced about thirty years ago and the dairy industry is being developed. In addition, advances have been made in the knowledge of cattle management, and a beef industry is emerging based on pangola grass grazing.

Agricultural Production in 2010

Produce	Int. $'000*	Tonnes
Indigenous chicken meat	92,246	64,761
Fruit fresh nes	17,312	49,600
Indigenous pigmeat	4,614	3,001
Hen eggs, in shell	3,566	4,300
Indigenous cattle meat	2,674	990
Bananas	2,197	7,800
Citrus fruit, nes	1,989	4,400
Coconuts	1,839	16,635
Pineapples	1,753	6,150
Cow milk, whole, fresh	1,560	5,000
Taro (cocoyam)	1,527	7,200
Oranges	1,005	5,200

* unofficial figures

Source: http://faostat.fao.org/site/339/default.aspx Food and Agriculture Organization of the United Nations, Food and Agricultural commodities production

The sugar industry has been declining in recent years and in 2003 the state owned sugar company, Caroni, closed with the loss of 8,000 jobs. In 2007 plans were announced to close the island's sugar industry completely as it could no longer compete commercially following cuts in European subsidies.

Figures from the FAO for 2010 put the total catch was put at 13.931 tonnes.

COMMUNICATIONS AND TRANSPORT

Travel Requirements
Citizens of the USA, Canada, Australia and the EU require a passport valid for six months beyond the length of stay, a return ticket to their country of residence and sufficient funds for the duration of their stay. Non-tourist visitors must have a work permit, student permit, missionary permit or a ministry permit. Australians need a visa, but citizens of the USA, Canada and most of the EU do not require a visa for stays of up to three months; the exceptions are nationals of Bulgaria, the Czech Republic, Estonia, Hungary, Latvia, Lithuania, Poland, Romania, the Slovak Republic and Slovenia who can stay for up to one month without a visa. Other nationals should contact the embassy to check visa requirements.

National Airlines
BWIA International Airways Ltd (Trinidad and Tobago), the National carrier, provides regular scheduled departures from London to Trinidad and to Tobago. It also operates services from Frankfurt, Stockholm, Zurich, Cologne and Munich. British Airways provides regular scheduled flights from London to Trinidad and other carriers fly to New York, Toronto and Miami where there are connecting flights to Trinidad.

International Airports
There are two international Airports, one at Piarco in Trinidad, Piarco International Airport and one at Crown Point near Scarborough, the chief town of Tobago, which is undergoing expansion. There are several flights a day between Trinidad and Tobago. Four small airports also exist.
Airports Authority, Airports Administration Centre, Piarco International Airport, Caroni North Bank Road, Piarco P.O. Box 1273, Port of Spain. Tel: +1 868 644 8047, fax: +1 868 669 2319

Roads
The total road network is 8,260 km, of which 2,000 km is national highways and 50 km is motorways. Vehicles are driven on the left.

A state operated bus service runs throughout the country as well as a good taxi service.
Public Transport Service Corporation: URL: http://www.ptsc.co.tt

Railways
A light-railway system is being evaluated.

Shipping
Ships call at Trinidad from Canada, America, South America, Europe, South Africa and Australia. Over 4,000 ships enter the harbours of Trinidad and Tobago every year with a total net registered tonnage of approximately 32,000,000. A regular car ferry service operates between Trinidad and Tobago with a travel time of 5 hours. A ferry also operates the two main cities of Trinidad, Port-of-Spain in the north and San Fernando in the south.
Port Authority of Trinidad and Tobago: URL: http://www.patnt.com
Shipping Corporation of Trinidad and Tobago (SCOTT), Port of Spain, Trinidad and Tobago.

Ports and Harbours
The major ports in Trinidad are Port of Spain, Pointe-à-Pierre and Point Lisas. Tobago's port is Scarborough. Port of Spain has a deep water crane and a special container berth.
Port Authority of Trinidad and Tobago, Port of Spain, Trinidad and Tobago.

HEALTH

Five new hospital facilities are currently under construction or have been opened outside of the capital in an effort to decentralise the healthcare system. As well as the public health service there is also a private healthcare system with some health insurance schemes. In 2009, the government spent approximately 9.6 per cent of its total budget on healthcare, accounting for 60.6 per cent of all healthcare spending. Total expenditure on healthcare equated to 5.8 per cent of the country's GDP. Per capita expenditure on health was approximately US$848, compared with US$245 in 2000. According to latest WHO estimates (2005-10) there are 1,543 doctors (12 per 10,000 population), 4,677 nurses (36 per 10,000 population), and 294 dentistry personnel. There are an estimated 25 hospital beds per 100,000 population.

In 2010 the infant mortality rate (probability of dying before first birthday) was 24 per 1,000 live births and the child (under-five years old) mortality rate was 27 per 1,000 live births. The main causes of death in the under-fives are: prematurity (29 per cent), congenital abnormalities (24 per cent), pneumonia (7 per cent), HIV/AIDS (3 per cent) and diarrhoea (1 per cent). In the period 2000-09 an estimated 17.3 per cent of children (under five-years-old) were classified as stunted and 21.1 per cent as underweight. The estimated rate of HIV prevalence in adults aged 15+ years is 1.5 per cent.

In 2010, 94 per cent of the population used improved drinking water and 92 per cent of the population had access to improved sanitation. (Source: http://www.who.int, World Health Statistics 2012)

EDUCATION

Government operated and assisted schools are run in Trinidad and Tobago from junior to secondary and senior comprehensive level. Trinidad and Tobago has three universities the University of the West Indies, the University of Trinidad and Tobago and the University of the Southern Caribbean in addition to a Technical and Vocational College where full and part-time first and higher degrees can be taken.

Compulsory primary education begins at six years of age and ends at 12, whilst secondary education begins at 12 years of age and ends at 16 or 17. Education is free even at degree level. Recent figures suggest that there are some 476 primary schools, 101 secondary schools and the three universities. Figures for 2007 showed that the primary school enrolment rate was estimated at over 90 per cent with over 70 per cent of secondary age children enrolled at secondary schools. (Source: UNESCO)

Literacy in Trinidad and Tobago is estimated at 98 per cent. Figures from 2007 show that 13.4 per cent of government spending went on education.

RELIGION

The main religious denominations are Roman Catholic (31 per cent), Anglican (12 per cent), Hindu (24 per cent), Muslim (7.2 per cent), Presbyterian (3.4 per cent). The rest of the population is made up of other Christian groups, spiritualists, Baha'is and Buddhists.

Trinidad and Tobago has a religious liberty rating of 9 on a scale of 1 to 10 (10 is most freedom). (Source: World Religion Database)

COMMUNICATIONS AND MEDIA

Freedom of expression is guaranteed by the constitution.

Newspapers
Newsday, URL: http://www.newsday.co.tt/
Trinidad Guardian, URL: http://www.guardian.co.tt/
Trinidad and Tobago Express, URL: http://www.trinidadexpress.com/
Three weekly political papers are also published **The Punch**, **The Bomb** and **The T'n'T Mirror** (URL: http://www.tntmirror.com/)

Broadcasting
The state-owned broadcaster NBN closed in 2005 and was replaced by the Caribbean New Media Group (CNMG). It operates a television network (C) and two radio stations. The main private company is TV6 (http://www.trinidadexpress.com/index.pl/tv6_news). It is owned by Caribbean Communications Network (URL: http://www.ccngroup.com/)

Telecommunications
Both international and domestic services are good. Figures for 2008 estimate that there were 307,000 telephone lines in use and 1.5 million mobile phones. An estimated 227,000 people are internet users.

ENVIRONMENT

Main environmental concerns are water pollution from agricultural chemicals, industry and raw sewage, oil pollution, deforestation and soil erosion.

Trinidad and Tobago is a party to the following international treaties: Biodiversity, Climate Change, Climate Change-Kyoto Protocol, Desertification, Endangered Species, Hazardous Wastes, Law of the Sea, Marine Dumping, Marine Life Conservation, Ozone Layer Protection, Ship Pollution, Tropical Timber 83, Tropical Timber 94, Wetlands.

In 2006, Trinidad and Tobago's emissions from the consumption of fossil fuels totalled 47.23 million metric tons of carbon dioxide.

Environmental Management Authority, URL: http://www.ema.co.tt/

TUNISIA
Republic of Tunisia
Al Jumhuriya at Tunisiya

Capital: Tunis (Population estimate, 2009: 759,000)

Head of State: Moncef Marzouki (Interim President) (page 1472)

National Flag: A crescent and red, five-pointed star, centred on a white disk on a red background

CONSTITUTION AND GOVERNMENT

Constitution
Formerly a French Protectorate, Tunisia was granted home rule in 1955 and independence in 1956. The President is assisted by an Advisory Body, the Council of the Republic.

On 25 March 1956 the first general elections took place. These resulted in the return of the National Front, which secured all the 98 seats of the (then) Constituent Assembly. On 8 April a government was formed with M. Habib Bourbuiga as Prime Minister. On 13 April the Constituent Assembly adopted Article 1 of the new Tunisian Constitution.

On 25 July 1957 the Tunisian National Assembly unanimously decided to abolish the monarchy, proclaim Tunisia a Republic, and appoint the Prime Minister, M. Habib Bourguiba, the Head of State and President of the Republic. On 30 July a new government was formed. M. Bourguiba was re-elected President in 1959, 1964, 1969, and 1974. In March 1975 M. Bourguiba's election as President for life was ratified by the National Assembly.

On 7 November 1987 M. Bourguiba was deposed by M. Zine El Abidine Ben Ali and the new regime made moves to liberalise government, the economy, the press and the party system. The Constitution was amended in April 1988 to abolish the "President for life" section and introduce other reforms. The president is responsible to the Chamber of Deputies. He appoints the Council of Ministers.

The General and Presidential elections in April 1989 returned President Ben Ali and the ruling Rassemblement Constitutionnel Democratique (RCD) to power with an overwhelming majority. A referendum held on 26 May 2002 approved the creation of a second legislative chamber as well as changes to the presidential term; the president may now be elected to the post up to five times, while the permitted age of candidates was raised. The changes also provided judicial immunity for a president during and after his presidency.

Following the popular mass protests of January 2011 and the subsequent flight into exile of the president, the Constitutent Assembly (elected October 2011) began to draft a new constitution. A provisional constitution was approved by the Constituent Assembly on 11 December 2011 and came into force immediately while the Assembly considered the final version.

To consult the constitution, please visit: http://www.wipo.int/wipolex/en/details.jsp?id=7201

International Relations
Tunisia follows a moderate, non-aligned course in its international relations. It is active in its support of the Middle East Peace Process, playing a moderating role in the negotiations for a comprehensive Middle East peace.

Tunisia and Algeria resolved a longstanding border dispute in 1993 and have cooperated in the construction of a natural gas pipeline through Tunisia that connects Algeria to Italy. Tunisia's relations with Libya have been erratic in the past, but in recent years, the government has been careful to maintain positive bi-lateral relations, supporting the lifting of UN sanctions against Libya in 2003. Libya is becoming a major trading partner.

Tunisia supports the development of the Arab Maghreb Union (UMA), which includes Algeria, Morocco, Mauritania, and Libya, and has played a positive role in trying to resolve tensions between some member countries.

Tunisian peacekeepers have participated in UN operations in Cambodia, Namibia, Rwanda and Burundi. Tunisian soldiers are currently serving in the Democratic Republic of Congo, Eritrea and Kosovo.

Recent Events
Militant Islamists became a matter of concern in Tunisia following a bomb attack on the tourist resort of Djerba in 2002. Nineteen people were killed and there was a dramatic drop in tourist numbers. In December 2006, May Elherbi was elected leader of the The Progressive

Democratic Party, the first time a woman has been elected in Tunisia to such a post. In January 2007, the security forces clashed with Islamist militants; the Interior Minister said that the Salafist militants had come from Algeria.

On December 17 2010 a student, Sidi Bouzid, set himself on fire in a protest about the lack of jobs in Tunisia. His actions sparked a series of protests about unemployment and the running of the country. By December 28th the protests had spread to the capital Tunis. Many people were killed during the continuing protests and on January 12 the Interior Minister was sacked. The president also announced that he would stand down in 2014. This promise was not enough to stop the rioting and on January 14 President Ben Ali dissolved the government and stepped down; he is now in exile in Saudi Arabia. On January 17 a new Unity Government was announced but protests continued as demonstrators felt that too many of the old government ministers had kept their jobs. The speaker of the parliament Fouad Mebazza, became interim president. In February, Prime Minister Ghannouchi bowed to pressure and resigned and a new interim government was appointed.

Interim President Mebazza announced details of new elections for the Constitutional Council to take place on 24 July, this date was later amended to 23 October to allow the electoral commission more time to prepare. The election was for constituent assembly which will then write a new constitution that will pave the way for legislative and presidential elections. The new assembly will have to decide if Tunisia will have a presidential or parliamentary system, and whether a separation of religion and state becomes law. Since the overthrow of President Ben Ali, 81 political parties have registered.

The interim government ran the country until the October elections. Although constitutionally the role of interim president is limited to 60 days, Mr Mebazza said he would stay in office until the elections. Once elected, the Constitutional Council may appoint a new government or ask the current interim government to stay on until presidential and parliamentary elections take place. The interim government immediately implemented changes including the dismantling of the infamous political police and state security apparatus.

During the protests it has been estimated that 220 people have been killed.

An international warrant for President Ben Ali's arrest has been issued and he will be tried in absentia. Among the charges against him are voluntary manslaughter, drug-trafficking, abuse of power, corruption and charges relating to the killing of some protesters during January's uprising. He has denied all the charges against him. The trials began to take place in June and he and his wife Leila were sentenced to 35 years in prison for embezzlement and misuse of state funds. In July he was convicted on charges of possessing illegal drugs and weapons and sentenced to 15 years in prison.

Parliamentary elections took place in October 2011. The Ennahda party won most seats but not an overall majority. The National Assembly which will draft a new constitution met for the first time in November 2011. The new president and prime minister were sworn in on December 2011.

In June 2012 former president Ben Ali was sentenced *in absentia* to life in prison, for the deaths of protesters in the 2011 revolution. He is currently in exile in Saudi Arabia.

Demonstrations were held in Tunis in August 2012 against the draft constitution which reduces women's rights.

In February 2013, opposition politician Chokri Belaid was shot dead. The political party En-nahda denied responsiblity. Also that month Prime Minister Hamadi Jebali announced plans for a technocrat cabinet, this plan was rejected and Jebali resigned. Interior Minister Ali Larayedh was confirmed as the new prime minister and a new cabinet was formed on 8 March 2013.

Legislature
Government is a bicameral system. Chamber of Councillors was first elected in July 2005, following a referendum on the reform of the Constitution in May 2002, and its first plenary session took place on 16th August 2005. The 112 member Chamber is composed of 71 elected members and 41 members who are nominated by the President. Members serve a six year term with half of the members elected or nominated every three years. The elected members are representatives of different regions and there are also representatives from the National Business Federation (UTICA) and the Farmers' and Fishermen's Union (UTAP). Those nominated by the President are national figures, many from civil society.
Chamber of Councillors, Le Bardo, Tunis, Tunisia

TUNISIA

The Chamber of Deputies *Majlis al-Nuwaab* has 189 directly elected members who serve a five year term. 20 per cent of the seats are reserved for the opposition. The Chamber is an arena for debate on national policy but it does not originate legislation.
Chamber of Deputies, 2000 Le Bardo, Tunis, Tunisia. Tel: +216 71 510200, fax: +216 71 510289, URL: http://www.chambre-dep.tn

---

Cabinet (as at June 2013)
Prime Minister: Ali Laarayedh (page 1459) (En-Nahda)
Minister of Foreign Affairs: Othman Jarandi (Ind) (page 1449)
Minister of the Interior: Lofti Ben Jeddou (Ind) (page 1386)
Minister of Human Rights and Transitional Justice: Samir Dilou (page 1415)
Minister of Women's Affairs: Sihem Badi
Minister of Finance: Elyes Fakhfakh
Minister of National Defence: Rachid Sabbagh
Minister of Trade: Abdelwahab Matar
Minister of Regional Development: Jameleddine Gharbi
Minister of Employment and Vocational Training: Naoufel Jamali
Minister of Justice: Nadir Ben Ammou
Minister of Religious Affairs: Noureddine Khadmi
Minister of Agriculture: Mohamed Ben Salem
Minister of Education: Salem Abyadh
Minister of Industry: Mehdi Jomaa
Minister for Transport: Abdelkarim Harouni
Minister of Communication Technologies: Monqi Marzouk
Minister of Equipment & the Environment: Mohamed Salmane
Minister of Transport: Karim Harouni
Minister of Social Affairs: Khalil Zaouia
Minister of Culture: Mehdi Mabrouk
Minister of Public Health: Abdellatif Mekki
Minister of Youth and Sports: Tarek Dhiab
Minister of Tourism: Jamel Gamra
Minister of Higher Education: Moncef Ben Salem
Minister of State Property: Slim Ben Hamidene

Ministries

Ministry portal: http://www.ministeres.tn/
Office of the Prime Minister, place du Gouvernement, 1020 Tunis, Tunisia. Tel: +216 71 565 400, URL: http://www.pm,.gov.tn
Ministry of Agriculture, Environment and Mineral Resources, 30 rue Alain Savary, 1002 Tunis, Tunisia. Tel: +216 71 786833, e-mail: mag@ministeres.tn
Ministry of Communication and Technology, 3 bis, rue d'Angleterre, 1000 Tunis, Tunisia. Tel: +216 71 359000, URL: http://www.mincom.tn/
Ministry of Culture, URL: http://www.culture.tn/
Ministry of Defence, Boulevard Bab M'Nara, 1030 Tunis, Tunisia. Tel: +216 71 560244, URL: http://www.defense.tn/ar/index.php
Ministry of Education, Ave. Ouled Haffouz, 1030 Tunis, Tunisia. Tel: +216 71 240133, URL: http://www.education.gov.tn/
Ministry of Higher Education & Scientific Research, URL: http://www.mes.tn/
Ministry of the Environment & Sustainable Development, Centre Urbain Nord, boulevard de la terre, 1080 Tunis, Tunisia. URL: http://www.environnement.nat.tn/
Ministry of Finance, Place du Gouvernement, 1008 Tunis, Tunisia. Tel: +216 71 571888, URL: http://www.finances.gov.tn/
Ministry of Foreign Affairs, Avenue de la Ligue des Etats Arabes, Tunis, Tunisia. Tel: +216 71 847500, URL: http://www.diplomatie.gov.tn/
Ministry of Human Rights, URL: http://www.tunisie.gov.tn
Ministry of Industry & Technology, Immeuble Beya, 40 Rue 8011, Montplaisir, 1002 Tunis, Tunisia. e-mail: contact@mit.gov.tn, URL: http://www.industrie.gov.tn/fr/home.asp
Ministry of Justice and Human Rights, 31 Avenue Bab Benat, 1006 Tunis, Tunisia. Tel: +216 71 561440, URL: http://www.e-justice.tn/
Ministry of Public Health, Bab Saadoun, 1006 Tunis, Tunisia. Tel: +216 71 560545, URL: http://www.santetunisie.rns.tn/
Ministry of Religious Affairs, Ave. Bab Benat, Tunis, Tunisia. Tel: +216 71 570147, e-mail: mar@ministeres.tn
Ministry of State Affairs, 19 ave. du Paris, 1000 Tunis, Tunisia. Tel: +216 71 341644, URL: http://www.mdeaf.gov.tn/
Ministry of Tourism, 37 ave. Kheireddine Pacha, 1002 Tunis, Tunisia. Tel: +216 71 890070, URL: http://www.tourisme.gov.tn/
Ministry of Transport, 13 Rue Borjine, 1073 Montplaisir, Tunisia. Tel: +216 71 905 026, fax: +216 71 901 559, e-mail: mtr@ministeres.tn, URL: http://www.transport.tn/
Ministry of Youth and Sport, URL: http://www.sport.tn/

Elections

Parliamentary and presidential elections were held in October 2004. The ruling Democratic Constitutional Rally (RCD) remained in power with over 87.7 per cent of the vote, and 152 of the 189 seats. The main opposition parties include the Movement of Socialist Democrats and the Party of Political Unity. Presidential elections also took place in October 2004. President Ben Ali was re-elected for a fourth term, with 94.5 per cent of the vote.

Both presidential and legislative elections took place on 25 October 2009. President Ben Ali was re-elected for a fifth term with an overwhelming majority. His ruling party, the Constitutional Democratic Rally (RCD), also won an overwhelming majority in the Chamber of Deputies.

Following the uprisings, legislative elections were held on 23 October 2011. En-Nahda won 89 seats, the CPR 29, PP 26, Ettakatol 2 and the PDP 16.

Moncef Marzouki won the presidential election held by the Constituent Assembly on 12 December 2011. Mr Marzouki won 153 votes, others 3. There were 2 abstentions and 44 blank votes.

Legislative elections are expected to take place between October and December 2013.

Suffrage is universal from the age of 20.

Political Parties
Over 80 political parties are now registered.
En-nahdhda, URL: http://www.ennahdha.tn/
Rassemblement Constitutionnel Démocratique (RCD), E-mail: info@rcd.tn, URL: http://www.rcd.tn (dissolved 2011)
Ettakatol Party (Forum for Labour and Liberties), URL: http://www.ettakatol.org/ar
Democratic Progressive Party (PDP), URL: http://www.pdp.tn/
Congress for the Republic (CPR), URL: http://mottamar.com/

Diplomatic Representation
Embassy of Tunisia, 1515 Massachusetts Ave., NW, Washington, DC 20005, USA. Tel: +1 202 862 1850, fax, +1 202 862 1858, URL: http://tunisia.embassyhomepage.com/
Ambassador: currently vacant
Embassy of Tunisia, 29 Prince's Gate, London, SW7 1QC, UK. Tel: +44 (0)20 7584 8117, fax: +44 (0)20 7225 2884, URL: http://tunisia.embassyhomepage.com/
Ambassador: Nabil Ammar
US Embassy, Berges du Lac, 1053 La Goulette, Tunis, Tunisia. Tel: +216 71 107000, fax: +216 71 107-090, URL: http://tunisia.usembassy.gov/
Ambassador: Jacob Walles
British Embassy, Rue du Lac Windermere, Les Berges du Lac, Tunis 1053, Tunisia. Tel: +216 71 108700, fax: +216 71 108749, URL: http://ukintunisia.fco.gov.uk/en/
Ambassador: Chris O'Connor
Permanent Mission to the UN, 31 Beekman Place, New York, NY 10022, USA. Tel: +1 212 751 7503
Permanent Representative: Mohamed Khaled Khiari

LEGAL SYSTEM

The law in Tunisia is based on French civil law and Islamic law.

The Tunisian court system consists of the regular civil and criminal courts (including the courts of first instance), courts of appeal and the Court of Cassation, the nation's highest appeals court; as well as the military tribunals within the Defense Ministry. The latter try cases involving military personnel and civilians accused of national security crimes. A military tribunal consists of a civilian judge from the Supreme Court as well as four military judges.

The law permits trial in absentia of fugitives from the law. Both the accused and the prosecutor may appeal decisions of the lower courts.

Tunisia is a leader in the Arab world in promoting the legal and social status of women. A Personal Status Code was adopted shortly after independence in 1956, which gave women full legal status (allowing them to run and own businesses, have bank accounts, and seek passports under their own authority). It also, for the first time in the Arab world, outlawed polygamy.

The citizens' ability to change their government is limited, and there have been recent reports of brutality by security forces. Arrests and detentions can be arbitrary, and security forces often act with impunity. The government infringes on citizens' privacy rights and imposes restrictions on freedoms of speech, press, assembly, and association. Corruption is widespread.

Following the Arab Spring and the overthrow of President Zine al-Abidine Ben Ali, commissions were set up to investigate corruption, human rights abuses during the uprising. Tunisia created a ministry to deal with transitional justice. The Technical Commission for the Elaboration of the Draft Law was formed in May 2012 and drew up a draft law on transitional justice but the transitional justice process has slowed.

Tunisia retains the death penalty, but there is a de facto moratorium on executions. Human rights groups have been trying to get the abolition of the death penalty inscribed into the new constitution which is currently being drafted. In April 2013, Rached Ghannouchi, the head of the ruling Islamist party, backed the death penalty.

Judicial Portal, URL: http://www.e-justice.tn/index.php?id=331
Higher Committee on Human Rights and Fundamental Freedoms, 85 avenue de la Liberté, 1002 Tunis Belvédère, Tunisia. Tel: +216 71 783 858, fax: +216 71 784 037, URL: http://www.droitsdelhomme.org.tn/en/

LOCAL GOVERNMENT

Tunisia is divided into 24 governorates (counties), Ariana, Beja, Ben Arous, Bizerte, Gabes, Gafsa, Jendouba, Kairouan, Kasserine, Kebili , Kef , Mahdia, Manouba, Medenine, Monastir, Nabeul, Sfax, Sidi Bou Zid, Siliana, Sousse, Tataouine, Tozeur, Tunis and Zaghouan. Municipal elections were held in May 2010. The governors are appointed by the president.

AREA AND POPULATION

Area
Tunisia is situated on the north coast of Africa. It borders the Mediterranean Sea to the north, having a coastline of 800 miles. Algeria is to the west and Libya to the east. Its area is 63,378 sq. miles, 164,450 sq. km. Major cities include Tunis, Sfax, Bizerte and Sousse. Whilst in the north and along the coastal regions there is arable land, the south of Tunisia is predominantly semiarid or desert. Summers are hot and dry, and the winter months are mild and rainy.

To view a map, consult http://www.lib.utexas.edu/maps/cia08/tunisia_sm_2008.gif

Population

The population in 2009 was an estimated 10.481 million, with an average annual population growth rate of 1.0 per cent over the period 2000-10. Approximately 67 per cent of the population lives in urban areas. The population density is approximately 152 people per sq. mile. Recent figures show that Tunisia has a young population, with an estimated median age of 29 years. An estimated 23 per cent of the population was aged 14 years or less and 10 per cent over 60 years.

The official language is Arabic though French is also spoken.

Births, Marriages, Deaths

Average life expectancy in 2009 was 73 years for men and 77 years for women. In 2010 the estimated birth rate was 17.1 per 1,000 people and the death rate was 5.4 per 1,000 people. Infant mortality rate in 2010 was an estimated 14 deaths per 1,000 children. The total fertility rate was 2.0 per female. (Source: http://www.who.int, World Health Statistics 2012)

Public Holidays 2014

1 January: New Year's Day
14 January: Birth of the Prophet*
8 March: Women's Day
20 March: Independence Day
9 April: Martyr's Day
5 May: Labour Day
29 June: Beginning of Ramadan*
25 July: Republic Day
8 August: Women's Day
29 July: Eid al-Fitr (End of Ramadan)*
7 November: New Era Day
5 October: Eid al Adha (Festival of the Sacrifice)*
25 October: Al Hijra (Islamic New Year)
* Islamic holiday dates are dependent on the sighting of the moon and so can vary

EMPLOYMENT

Estimates for 2010 put the total available workforce at around 3.7 million and unemployment was around 143per cent according to official estimates, though it is widely believed to be considerably higher is some regions. Underemployment remains a problem and there is a shortage of skilled workers. More than twice as many men form part of the workforce as women. In 2010, an estimated 18 per cent of the working population were employed in agriculture, over 30 per cent in industry and around 50 per cent in the service sector.

Tunisia has a young, well educated population; recent estimates indicate that 55 per cent of the population is under the age of 25. This would suggest that the unemployment rate could grow over the next few years.

BANKING AND FINANCE

The financial centre is Tunis.

Currency

The unit of currency is the dinar which consists of 1,000 millimes.

GDP/GNP, Inflation, National Debt

The Tunisian economy is based on agriculture, tourism, mining, manufacturing and tourism. The economy enjoyed years of growth but under the presidency of Zine el Ben Ali it began to falter. Unemployment rose and civil unrest increased. The president was overthrown in 2011. The new government has severe economic challenges to overcome: it must stabillize the economy, bring down unemployment and reduce poverty.

Whilst growth stalled following the war in Iraq and a severe drought in the region, during the period 2000-2004 average growth in GDP was 4.6 per cent per annum. In 2005, economic growth slowed to 4 per cent, but, in the year 2006, GDP was estimated at US$25,498 million, representing 5.2 per cent growth on the previous year, due to increased tourism. In 2008, as an oil importer, Tunisia's economy was adversely affected by rising oil prices. The service industry is the greatest contributor to GDP, accounting for some 55 per cent. Industry contributed 33 per cent and agriculture, around 12 per cent. Figures for 2010 put GDP at US$44 billion with a growth rate of 3 per cent. Growth fell to 1 per cent for 2011, caused in part by falling tourism revenues due to the revolution and falling remittances from abroad. GDP was estimated at US$45.5 billion in 2011.

In 2006, inflation rose to 4.5 per cent. Driven by soaring fuel prices, it reached 5.1 per cent in 2008. In 2010 it was estimated at 4.5 per cent, rising to 5.5 per cent in 2011.

Tunisia's large expatriate population of around one million people makes a significant contribution to the economy; in 2010, remittances from abroad amounted to an estimated US$1.6 million per year.

External debt in 2010 totalled US$23 billion.

Foreign Investment

In May 2006, the government announced that revenues from its privatization programme (launched in 1987) had reached US$1.9 billion. US$1.4 billion of this was foreign capital, EU member states being a major source. The Persian Gulf states have also been major investors, particularly in the telecommunications, real estate, and energy sectors. In 2010, the government passed a law allowing foreign franchises in key sectors including retail and tourism.

Balance of Payments / Imports and Exports

In 1995 Tunisia signed an Association Agreement with the EU, effective from 2008, which eliminates customs tariffs and other trade barriers on a wide range of goods and services. In 2001 Tunisia, Egypt, Jordan and Morocco agreed to set up the Great Arab Free Trade Zone, ahead of the 2010 target for trade barriers to end in the Euro-Mediterranean area. Tunisia is a member of the WTO.

In 2011, exports earned an estimated US$17 billion, up from an estimated US$14.4 billion in 2009. France was the largest single importer of Tunisian merchandise (approx. 30 per cent), followed by Italy and Germany. Overall, Europe imported over 80 per cent of all Tunisian exports. Main exports were agricultural goods, hydrocarbons, phosphates and chemicals, textiles and mechanical goods.

Imports in 2011 cost US$22 billion,up from US$19 billion in 2009. Approximately 80 per cent of all Tunisian imports came from Europe. France was the main supplier in 2011 (20 per cent), followed by Italy (18 per cent), Germany and Spain. Main import products are hydrocarbons, textiles, chemicals and machinery and equipment.

Central Bank

The Central Bank of Tunisia controls monetary policies, distribution of credit, foreign exchange currency reserves and the making of proposals to enhance the balance of payments.
Banque Centrale de Tunisie, PO Box 777, 25 Rue Hédi Nouira, 1080 Tunis Cedex, Tunisia. Tel: +216 1 340588, fax: +216 1 354214, e-mail: bct@bct.gov.tn, URL: http://www.bct.gov.tn
Governor: Chédly Ayari

Business Addresses

Tunis Stockmarket: URL: http://www.bvmt.com.tn
Union Tunisienne de l'Industrie, du Commerce, et de l'Artisanat: URL: http://www.utica.org.tn
Agency for the Promotion of Industry, URL: http://www.tunisianindustry.nat.tn

MANUFACTURING, MINING AND SERVICES

Primary and Extractive Industries

Tunisia had proven oil reserves of 430 million barrels as at the beginning of January 2012. In 2011, oil production was about 70,0700 barrels per day, most of which was crude oil, and consumption was 93,000 barrels per day. However, refining capacity remained at 34,000 barrels per day, so the country is an importer of refined oil products.

The main oil fields are El Borma in the desert region bordering Algeria and the Ashtart field offshore in the Gulf of Gabes. Other oil fields include the Ezzaouia, Belli, Sidi Kilani and Rhamoura. Exploration is taking place in other regions including offshore in the Gulf of Hammamet. In February 2006, Tunisia came to an agreement with Malta over a long-disputed oil exploration area; the countries will jointly develop the continental shelf area that lies between them.

Substantial reserves of gas (an estimated 2.75 trillion cubic feet in 2006), have led the Tunisian Government to promote the use of natural gas. It is estimated that it represents approximately 44 per cent of initial consumption in 2005, in comparison with just 14 per cent in 2003. Around two-thirds of the natural gas reserves are located offshore. In 2011, 68 billion cubic feet of gas were produced, and 131 billion cubic feet were consumed.

Energy

In 2010, Tunisia's power generating capacity was 3.65 GWe. 96 per cent of the country now has access to electricity; the country generated 15.14 billion kWh in 2010, and consumed 13.29 billion kWh. Tunisia is developing renewable energy resources, such as wind farming, both independently and in conjunction with the Global Environment Facility. The country is also part of the trans-Maghreb project which aims to link the power grids of all Maghreb countries to those of the European Union.

Total energy consumption in Tunisia rose to 0.307 quadrillion btu in 2009.

Manufacturing

Tunisian industry is largely concentrated around Tunis. The sector has diversified from its original mining and agricultural base and new industries have been developed to meet domestic demand and reduce imports. It is estimated that manufacturing contributed 33 per cent of GDP in 2006 and employed approximately 33 per cent of the workforce. Principal manufacturing growth has been in textiles, plastics, electro-mechanical and electronic components, building materials, automotive assembly and component manufacture, and domestic electrical goods. Over 90 per cent of textiles production are exported, providing a major source of foreign currency revenue.

Service Industries

The services sector contributed some 55 per cent of GDP in 2006 and employed over 44 per cent of the workforce in 2003. Tourism is a main source of income, representing around 20 per cent of currency receipts. It is also a major employment sector. During 2006, 6.5 million tourists visited Tunisia bringing in US$1.5 billion. There are approximately 600 establishments offering accommodation, with over 161,500 beds in total. The majority of tourists come from France, Britain, Germany, Italy, Algeria and Libya.
Tunisian National Tourism Board, URL: http://www.tourismtunisia.com

Agriculture

This is an important sector of the Tunisian economy, contributing an estimated 11 per cent of GDP in 2011 and employing some 18 per cent of the workforce. The main crops are wheat, barley, olives, wine grapes, dates, sugar beets, citrus fruits and vegetables. The main exports are olive oil and dates. Cultivation takes place mostly in the lowland areas and particularly in the north.

TUNISIA

Agricultural Production in 2010

Produce	Int. $'000*	Tonnes
Olives	701,736	876,400
Tomatoes	406,520	1,100,000
Cow milk, whole, fresh	330,473	1,059,000
Almonds, with shell	185,911	63,000
Indigenous chicken meat	159,387	111,897
Indigenous cattle meat	140,481	52,003
Indigenous sheep meat	136,276	50,050
Chillies and peppers. green	131,812	280,000
Wheat	112,792	822,100
Grapes	80,598	141,000
Hen eggs, in shell	75,267	90,750
Dates	66,622	145,000

* unofficial figures

Source: http://faostat.fao.org/site/339/default.aspx Food and Agriculture Organization of the United Nations, Food and Agricultural commodities production

The mountains in the north-west are forested with cork, oak and pines. Olives are grown in the Sahel region on the southern coastal area where it is drier. The southern interior of the country is desert where cultivation is restricted to oases.

Fishing
Tunisia has an extensive coastline and seafood such as prawns, squid, pilchards, mackerel and cuttlefish form an important source of income. In 2010 the FAO put the total catch at 97,743 tonnes.

COMMUNICATIONS AND TRANSPORT

Travel Requirements
Citizens of the USA, Canada, Australia and the EU require a passport valid for six months beyond the length of stay and sufficient funds for the duration of their stay, but most do not need a visa for stays of up to 90 days. US citizens and Germans can stay for up to four months without a visa, but Greeks can only stay for one month. Australians do need a visa, as do Cypriots. Nationals of the Czech Republic, Estonia, Latvia, Lithuania, Poland and the Slovak Republic must travel on a recognised package holidays. Other nationals should contact the embassy to check visa requirements

National Airlines
Tunis Air is the principal airline.
Tunisair, 7 Boulevard du 7 Novembre, Tunis Carthage, 2035, Tunisia. Tel: +216 1 700100, fax: +216 1 700897, URL: http://www.tunisair.com

International Airports
Tunis-Carthage International Airport, near Tunis and Habib Bourguiba, Skanes-Monastir near Monastir and the main airports serving Tunisia. Altogether there are 30 airports in Tunisia, 14 of which have paved runways.

Railways
There are approximately 2,245 km of railway operated by the Société National des Chemins de Fer Tunisiens (SNCFT), URL: http://www.sncft.com. Tunis has a subway system, Métro Léger de Tunis, consisting of four lines although there are plans for expansion.

Roads
The Tunisian road network covers about 25,000 km of primary and secondary roads. Vehicles are driven on the right.

Shipping
Tunis-La Goulette is the main port. Other ports are Sfax, Sousse, Gabes, Zarzis and Bizerte. The Tunisian ports deal with 11,800 arrivals and departures of ships, carrying 280,000 passengers and 18,800 tons of freight. Ferry services run between Tunis and Malta, the Italian ports of Sicily, Naples and Genoa and Marseille in France.

HEALTH

Tunisia has made great progress in the health care sector and was the only country in Africa, apart from Mauritius, to achieve the "health for all by the year 2000" goals set out by the WHO. The upgrading of basic health care has enabled Tunisia to almost eradicate polio, and mandatory vaccination against hepatitis B has been implemented nationwide. Recent figures show over 160 government hospitals and nearly 2,000 health centres and clinics are in operation. Currently the private sector accounts for over half the country's health expenditure through private health facilities. In 2009, the government spent approximately 10.7 per cent of its total budget on healthcare, accounting for 54.9 per cent of all healthcare spending. Private expenditure accounted for 45.1 per cent (87 per cent out-of-pocket) and external resources 1.2 per cent. Total expenditure on healthcare equated to 6.4 per cent of the country's GDP. Per capita expenditure on health was approximately US$243 in 2009.

Figures for 2005-10 show that there are 12,535 physicians (12 per 10,000 population), 34,551 nurses and midwives (32 per 10,000 population), 2,528 dentistry personnel (2.4 per 10,000 population), 2,106 pharmaceutical personnel, 890 environment and public health workers. There were approximately 21 hospital beds per 10,000 population.

In 2010 the infant mortality rate (probability of dying before first birthday) was 14 per 1,000 live births and the child (under-five years old) mortality rate was 16 per 1,000 live births. The main causes of death in the under-fives are: prematurity (29 per cent), pneumonia (7

per cent), malaria (11 per cent), congenital anomalies (23 per cent), birth asphyxia (11 per cent), and diarrhoea (3 per cent). In the period 2005-11 an estimated 9.0 per cent of children (under five-years-old) were classified as stunted and 3.3 per cent as underweight.

According to the latest WHO figures, in 2008 approximately 99 per cent of the urban population and 84 per cent of the rural population had access to improved drinking water. In the same year, 96 per cent of the urban population and 64 per cent of the rural population had access to improved sanitation. (Source: http://www.who.int, World Health Statistics 2012)

EDUCATION

Free education is provided for all those of school-going age and is compulsory for all children between the ages of six to 16 years. There are some 1,460 secondary schools in Tunisia and 13 universities and a further 160 higher education establishments. In 2007, 95 per cent of the relevant age-group attended primary school, and around 67 per cent enrolled in secondary school in 2004. 29 per cent went on to tertiary education. Tunisia has invested heavily in education and the number of students enrolled at university rose from 41,000 in 1986 to over 360,000 in 2006. In 2006, 20.5 per cent of total government expenditure was spent on education.

The literacy rate for men was approximately 86.4 per cent in 2007, but dropped to 69 per cent for women, though significant progress is being made following a drive to increase female school attendance. The literacy rate among 15-24 year olds that year was 97.0 per cent for men and 94.3 for women.

RELIGION

Approximately 99 per cent of Tunisians are Muslims and there is a Muslim university at Tunis. There is a small, mainly Roman Catholic, Christian community. There has been a Jewish population on the southern island of Djerba for 2000 years, and there is still a small Jewish population in Tunis and other cities, mainly descendants of those who fled Spain in the late 15th century.

Tunisia has a religious liberty rating of 4 on a scale of 1 to 10 (10 is most freedom). (Source: World Religion Database)

COMMUNICATIONS AND MEDIA

Although the constitution guarantees press freedom, the government controls the press and broadcasting. Self-censorship is common and breaking the press code can result in prison sentences or high fines. There are reports of reporters being intimidated.

Newspapers
Tunisia has several daily, weekly and regional newspapers. La Presse (http://www.lapresse.tn) and Al-Horria are owned by the ruling RCP. Other newspapers include Le Quotidien (http://www.lequotidien-tn.com) and Nouvelles de Tunisie (http://www.infotunisie.com). **Tunis Afrique Press Agency (TAP)**, URL: http://www.tap.info.tn/en/index.php

Broadcasting
The government controls most of the broadcast media. The state-run Tunisian Radio and Television Establishment operates two national television networks, several national radio networks and some regional radio stations. There are also private radio stations. Foreign satellite TV channels are available.
Tunisian Radio and Television Establishment (ERTT), URL: http://www.radiotunis.com

Telecommunications
The system is good for the region and is in the process of being upgraded. The network is completely digitalised and internet access is possible throughout the country. Figures for 2008 show that there were 1.2 million main telephone lines in use and 8,5 million mobile phones. There are approximately 2.8 million users. Tunisia closely monitors internet use and sites that criticise the government are often blocked.

ENVIRONMENT

Tunisia is currently losing 20,000 ha of productive land per annum due to erosion, desert encroachment, salinisation, flooding and urbanisation. In order to preserve its ecology eight national parks, one national archaeological park and 19 natural reserves have been created.

Carbon dioxide emissions reached 22.24 million metric tons in 2005, equivalent to 2.21 metric tons per capita. The USA produced 20.14 metric tons per capita in the same year. In 2010, Tunisia's emissions from the consumption of fossil fuels totalled 18.72 million metric tons of carbon dioxide. (Source: EIA)

Tunisia is a party to the following international environment agreements: Biodiversity, Climate Change, Climate Change-Kyoto Protocol, Desertification, Endangered Species, Environmental Modification, Hazardous Wastes, Law of the Sea, Marine Dumping, Ozone Layer Protection, Ship Pollution, Wetlands.

SPACE PROGRAMME

The National Commission of Outer Space was created in 1984 and the National Center of Cartography and Remote Sensing in 1988. Tunisia also played a significant role in the launch of Arabsat satellite.

TURKEY
Republic of Turkey
Turkiye Cumhuriyeti

Capital: Ankara (Population estimate, 2011: 4.9 million)

Head of State: Abdullah Gul (President) (page 1435)

National Flag: Red, charged towards the hoist with a white crescent, horns to the fly, and between them a five-pointed white star.

CONSTITUTION AND GOVERNMENT

Constitution
Turkey is a Republic. The current constitution dates from 1982, but has been amended since. It allows for a seven year presidential term and a unicameral legislature. Executive power is held by the Prime Minister and the Council of Ministers. The Prime Minister is appointed by the President. The Council of Ministers are appointed by the President but nominated by the Prime Minister. Legislative power is held by the Turkish Grand National Assembly, which consists of 550 deputies.

In October 2007 a referendum voted in favour of replacing indirect presidential elections with direct presidential elections. Under existing rules the president must be elected with a two-thirds majority. The President serves a seven-year non-renewable term. Under the new law, from 2014, the presidential term will be reduced to five years.

The government has put forward a series of constitutional reforms which it believes are necessary if Turkey is to join the EU. However, in July 2010 the Constitutional Court annulled several measures which would have curbed the power of the judiciary and the army. The remaining proposals will be put to a referendum. The proposals include improving individual rights and the rights of children, the elderly and disabled; civilian courts will have the power to try military personnel for crimes against the state; workers will be allowed to join more than one union; Parliament will have more power to appoint judges. The referendum was held in September and early indications were that it was approved with around 58 per cent of the vote. Many of those that voted against the referendum were based in western looking cities who feared that the new constitution would give the government too much influence over the judiciary. In May 2012, a parliamentary committee began working on a constitution which would be more civilian based.

To consult the constitution, please visit: http://www.byegm.gov.tr

International Relations
Turkey became a member of the Council of Europe in 1949 and NATO in 1952. Turkey wishes to become a member of the EU. At the 2002 Copenhagen summit several countries were formally invited to join, however Turkey failed in its bid. At the 2004 Brussels Summit, Turkey was invited to start the accession negotiations on 3 October 2005 with the objective of full membership. The EU opened formal talks with Turkey in June 2006.

In 2009, Turkey and Armenia agreed to normalise their relations. Parliament will have to ratify the accord. Turkey has stipulated that a resolution of the Nagorno-Karabakh issue is a pre-condition of opening the border.

Cyprus
Under British rule in the 20th Century the Greek Cypriots and Turkish Cypriots became polarised. The island was granted independence in 1960 after Greek and Turkish communities reached agreement on a constitution. Britain retained sovereignty over two military bases. However tensions escalated when Greek Cypriots proposed amendments threatening power-sharing arrangements. The UN sent a peace-keeping force in 1964. In 1974 the Greek Cypriot Archbishop Makarios was deposed in a coup backed by Greece's military junta. In response Turkey sent troops to protect the Turkish Community living there and enforced a partition of the island. Diplomatic attempts to resolve the situation failed and in 1983 this area was named the Turkish Republic of Northern Cyprus, but is only recognised by Turkey. In late 2001 meetings took place between the leaders of Greek Cypriot and Turkish Cypriot communities with the aim of arriving at a peaceful settlement to the problem, especially as Cyprus and Turkey had both applied for EU membership and Cyprus was set to join earlier than Turkey.

Greek Cyprus had been in negotiations to join the European Union since 1995. In January 2002 Greek Cypriot leader Clerides and the Turkish Cypriot leader Rauf Denktash agreed to a series of talks in the UN controlled buffer zone. The talks were prompted by the imminent entry of Greek Cyprus to the EU. In 2002, the Secretary General of the UN, Kofi Annan, presented a peace plan for Cyprus which set out Cyprus as a federation with two equal states with a rotating presidency. The deadline for an agreement was set at March 2003. No agreement was reached at that time, as the Greek Cypriots felt that not enough refugees would be able to return to their homes and the Turkish Cypriots felt they would have to concede too much land. A referendum was held in April 2004 on the proposed UN reunification plan, which both sides had to agree. The Turkish Cypriots voted for reunification, but the Greek Cypriots voted overwhelmingly against the plan. On 1 May 2004 Greek Cyprus - without Turkish Northern Cyprus - became a member of the EU.

Recent Events
In January 2004 a protocol was signed banning the death penalty regardless of the crime committed. This was seen as a big step towards EU membership. In December 2006 membership talks were partially suspended when Turkey refused to allow access to its ports and airports by Cypriot traffic.

In April 2007 large protests took place as secularists took to the streets to protest against reports that prime minister Erdogan, who is seen to have Islamist sympathies, was to stand for president. Later that month Mr Erdogan nominated Abdullah Gul as the Justice and Development Party (AKP) candidate for president. An Assembly vote was held on April 27 but was boycotted by opposition parties; although Abdullah Gul won a majority he did not gain the two thirds majority needed for election. The vote was repeated on May 8 and again it was boycotted by the opposition, and Gul withdrew his candidature.

Parliament then voted to change the constitution so that the president could be directly elected by the electorate rather than by Assembly. President Sezar vetoed this twice; approval would have necessitated a referendum within a set number of days. Parliament then voted to bring the date of the referendum forward so that parliamentary and presidential elections could be held together. This was also vetoed by President Sezar. An early parliamentary election was held on July 22 and the AKP were returned to power. A caretaker cabinet was established until outgoing President Sezar asked Prime Minister Erdogan to form a new government which was then approved by President Gul following his election on August 28.

In October 2007, voters in a referendum backed plans to have future presidents elected by popular vote instead of by parliament.

In December 2007 Turkey launched a series of airstrikes against fighters from Kurdish PKK rebel groups situated in Iraq. In February 2008 Turkish troops entered northern Iraq to look for Kurdish rebels they said were hiding across the border. They insisted that only Kurdish PKK members would be targeted. Airstrikes against alleged Kurdish targets continue.

In March 2008 the Chief Prosecutor of the Appeals Court filed a law suit at the Constitutional Court for closure of the governing AK party, accusing them of violating secular principles. In July, the petition failed by a narrow margin and no members were banned although party funding was cut.

Turkey was elected to hold a non-permanent seat on the UN Security Council for 2009-2010. Turkey took on the rotating presidency in June 2009.

The government introduced some measures into parliament in December 2009 to increase Kurdish language rights and reduce the military presence in the mainly-Kurdish south-east.

Over thirty officers were charged with conspiracy to overthrow the government relating to an alleged plot in 2003.

In May 2010 nine Turkish activists aboard an aid flotilla destined for Gaza were killed by Israeli commandos. The commando raid was internationally condemned.

In July 2010 the courts indicted 196 people who were accused of plotting to overthrow the governments, among those accused were military officers both serving and retired. Also that month the leader of the PKK Murat Karayilan said that if given greater political and cultural rights they would be willing to disarm, no replay was received from the government.

In September 2010 a referendum was held on constitutional reform, the reforms asked for amendments to increase parliamentary control over the army and judiciary.

In November 2010 the controversial Wikileaks website published alleged confidential cables revealing that France and Austria had been deliberately blocking Turkey's EU membership negotiations.

The AKP retained power in the parliamentary election held in June 2011.

A suspected bomb blast killed three people and wounded 15 in the capital Ankara in September 2011. In October, PKK rebels killed 24 Turkish troops near the border, the worst attack against the military for over 10 years.

In January 2012, the former head of the armed forces, Gen. Ilker Basbug, was arrested over an alleged attempted coup.

In June 2012, eight Turkish soldiers were killed in a PKK attack in southern Turkey. The army retaliated by attacking PKK rebel bases in northern Iraq. In the same month Syria shot down a Turkish jet that had strayed into Syrian territory. Turkey said that if Syrian troops approached its borders they would be seen as a military threat and it would act accordingly.

In September 2012 three generals were jailed for 20 years for plotting an alleged coup in 20003. A further 300 officers were also sentenced.

Tension continued to rise with Syria. The Turkish parliament authorised military action inside Syria after Syrian mortar fire killed five people in a Turkish border town in October 2012.

TURKEY

On May 28 2013, a demonstration was held to protest against the demolition and development of Gezi Park, a green area in Taksim Square, central Istanbul. The development plans include a replica Ottoman era style barracks and a mosque. Protestors feel that the area is a rare green space and the city is already well served with places of prayer. Some of the demonstrators stayed to 'occupy' the square, but riot police moved against them with water cannon and tear gas. This triggered a huge protest with people flocking to the square. Solidarity protests then sprang up in over 75 towns and cities and public sector trade unions held a sympathy strike. The protests carried on into June and over 5,000 protesters have been injured as well as 600 police officers. Although the protests started as a demonstration to save the park other issues have come to the fore including the fear of 'creeping Islamisation' a few days before the protests a bill had been passed to ban the late night sale of alcohol. The anger is focused against Prime Minister Erdogan who has also tried to change the constitutional ban on the Islamic headscarf. Prime Minister Erdogan refused to give into the protestor's demands although he did agree to meet with a group of activists for talks. Riot police continued to move against the protestors and towards the end of June the protesters had been evicted. In early July records were released that showed that in June a court had ruled against the development of the square.

Legislature
The unicameral legislature consists of 550 directly elected members who serve a five-year term.
Turkish Grand National Assembly (Türkiye Büyük Millet Meclisi), Ankara, Turkey. Tel: +90 312 420 5151, fax: +90 312 420 6756, e-mail: gensek@tbmm.gov.tr, URL: http://www.tbmm.gov.tr

Cabinet (as at July 2013)
Prime Minister: Recep Tayyip Erdogan (page 1421)
Deputy Prime Minister: Bulent Arinc (page 1379)
Deputy Prime Minister: Ali Babacan (page 1381)
Deputy Prime Minister: Besir Atalay
Deputy Prime Minister: Bekir Bozdag
Minister of Justice: Sadullah Ergin (page 1421)
Minister for the Family and Social Policy: Fatma Sahin
Minister of European Union Affairs: Egemen Bağış (page 1381)
Minister of Industry, Science and Technology: Nihat Ergun (page 1421)
Minister of Labour and Social Security: Faruk Celik (page 1402)
Minister for the Environment and Urban Planning: Erdogan Bayraktar
Minister for Foreign Affairs: Prof. Dr. Ahmet Davutoğlu (page 1413)
Minister of the Economy: Mehmet Zafer Caglayan (page 1398)
Minister of Energy and Natural Resources: Taner Yildiz (page 1541)
Minister of Youth and Sports: Suat Kilic
Minister of Agriculture, Food and Animal Husbandry: Mehmed Mehdi Eker (page 1420)
Minister of Customs and Trade: Hayati Yazici (page 1541)
Minister of the Interior: Muammer Guler
Minister of Development: Cevdet Yilmaz (page 1541)
Minister of Culture and Tourism: Omer Celik
Minister of Finance: Mehmet Simsek (page 1515)
Minister of Education: Nabi Avci
Minister of National Defence: Ismet Yilmaz
Minister of Forestry and Water Affairs: Veysel Eroglu (page 1421)
Minister of Health: Mehmet Muezzinoglu
Minister of Transport: Binali Yildirim

Ministries
Office of the President, Cumhurbaskanligi Kosku, Cankaya, Ankara, Turkey. Tel: +90 312 468 5030, fax: +90 312 427 1330, e-mail: cumhurbaskanligi@tccb.gov.tr, URL: http://www.cankaya.gov.tr
Prime Minister's Office, Basbakanlik, Vekaletler Caddesi, 06573 Bakanliklar, Ankara, Turkey. Tel: +90 312 413 7000, fax: +90 312 417 0476, e-mail: hiliskiler@basbakanlik.gov.tr, URL: http://www.basbakanlik.gov.tr
Ministry of Justice, Adalet Bakanligi, 06659 Kizilay, Ankara, Turkey. Tel: +90 312 417 7770, fax: +90 312 417 3954, e-mail: info@adalet.gov.tr, URL: http://www.adalet.gov.tr
Ministry of Defence, Milli Savunma Bakanligi, Balanliklar, Ankara, Turkey. Tel: +90 (9)312 417 6100, URL: http://www.msb.gov.tr/
Ministry of the Interior, Icisleri Bakanligi, Bakanliklar, Ankara, Turkey. Tel: +90 312 425 7214, fax: +90 312 418 1795, e-mail: iladi@icisleri.gov.tr, URL: http://www.icisleri.gov.tr
Ministry of Foreign Affairs, Yeni Hizmet Binasi, 06100 Balgat, Ankara, Turkey. Tel: +90 312 292 1000, fax: +90 312 287 3869, e-mail: webmaster@mfa.gov.tr, URL: http://www.mfa.gov.tr
Ministry of Finance, Maliye Bakanligi, Dikmen Caddesi, Ankara, Turkey. Tel: +90 312 425 0080, fax: +90 312 425 0058, e-mail: bshalk@maliye.gov.tr, URL: http://www.maliye.gov.tr
Ministry of Education, Milli Egitim Bakanligi, Ankara, Turkey. Tel: +90 312 425 5330, fax: +90 312 417 7027, e-mail: info@meb.gov.tr, URL: http://www.meb.gov.tr
Ministry of Public Works and Housing, Bayindirlik ve Iskan Bakanligi, Vekaletler Caddesi 1, 06100 Ankara, Turkey. Tel: +90 312 410 1000, fax: +90 312 418 0406, URL: http://www.bayindirlik.gov.tr
Ministry of Health, Saglik Bakanligi, Mithatpasa Caddesi 3, 06410 Sihhiye, Ankara, Turkey. Tel: +90 312 435 6440, fax: +90 312 431 4879, e-mail: adres@saglik.gov.tr, URL: http://www.saglik.gov.tr
Ministry of Transport, Ulastirma Bakanligi, Hakki Turayliç Caddesi 5, Emek, Ankara, Turkey. Tel: +90 312 212 4416, fax: +90 312 212 4930, URL: http://www.ubak.gov.tr
Ministry of Agriculture, Food and Animal Husbandry, Tarim ve Köy Isleri Bakanligi, Milli Müdafa Caddesi 20, Kizilay, Ankara, Turkey. Tel: +90 312 424 0580, fax: +90 312 417 7168, e-mail: admin@tarim.gov.tr, URL: http://www.tarim.gov.tr
Ministry of Labour and Social Security, Ismet Inönü Bulvari 42, Emek, Ankara, Turkey. Tel: +90 312 296 6000, fax: +90 312 212 7230, e-mail: webmaster@csgb.gov.tr, URL: http://www.calisma.gov.tr/

Ministry of Industry and Trade, Sanayi ve Ticaret Bakanligi, Tandogan, Ankara, Turkey. Tel: +90 312 286 2006, fax: +90 312 286 5325, e-mail: alicoskun@sanayi.gov.tr, URL: http://www.sanayi.gov.tr
Ministry of Energy and Natural Resources, Enerji ve Tabii Kaynaklar Bakanligi, Konya Yolu, Bestepe, Ankara, Turkey. Tel: +90 312 223 6134, fax: +90 312 222 9405, e-mail: webmaster@enerji.gov.tr, URL: http://www.menr.gov.tr
Ministry of Culture and Tourism, Kultur ve Turizm Bakanligi, Atatürk Bulvari 29, 06050 Opera, Ankara, Turkey. Tel: +90 312 309 0850, fax: +90 312 312 4359, e-mail: info@kulturturizm.gov.tr, URL: http://www.kulturturizm.gov.tr
Ministry of Environment and Urban Planning, Çevre ve Orman Bakanligi, Söğütözü Caddesi 14/E, Ankara, Turkey. Tel: +90 312 207 5000, fax: +90 312 215 00 94, URL: http://www.cevreorman.gov.tr
Ministry of National Defence, Milli Savunma Bakanligi, 06100, Ankara, Turkey. Tel: +90 312 425 4596, fax: +90 312 418 4737, e-mail: info@msb.gov.tr, URL: http://www.msb.gov.tr

Political Parties
Adalet ve Kalkinma Partisi (AK) Justice and Development Party, founded in 2001. URL: http://www.akparti.org.tr/
Leader: Recep Tayyip Erdogan (page 1421)
Cumhuriyet Halk Partisi (CHP) Republican People's Party, Cevre Sok. 38, Ankara, Turkey. Tel: +90 (9)312 468 5969, fax: +90 (9)312 468 5969, e-mail: chpbim@chp.org.tr, URL: http://www.chp.org.tr
Leader: Kemal Kılıçdaroğlu
Anavatan Partisi (ANAP) Motherland Party, 13 Cad. 3, Balgat, Ankara, Turkey. Tel: +90 (9)312 286 5000, fax: +90 (9)312 286 5019, URL: http://www.anap.org.tr
Leader: Erkan Mumcu
Demokratik Sol Parti (DSP) Democratic Left Party, Fevzi Çakmak Cad. 17, Besevlar, Ankara, Turkey. Tel: +90 (9)312 212 4950, fax: +90 (9)312 212 4188, e-mail: info@dsp.org.tr, URL: http://www.dsp.org.tr
Leader: Masum Turker
Demokrat Parti (Formerly the Dogru Yol Partisi (DYP) True Path Party), Akay Cad. 16, Ankara, Turkey Tel: +90 (9)312 419 1818, fax: +90 (9)312 417 6090, URL: http://www.dyp.org.tr
Milliyetci Hareket Partisi (MHP) Nationalist Action Party, Karanfil Sokak 69 06640 Bakanliklar, Ankara, Turkey. Tel: +90 (9)312 417 5060, fax: +90 (9)312 417 5060, URL: http://www.mhp.org.tr
Demokratik Toplum Partisi, is a Kurdish political party, URL: http://www.dtpgm.org.tr/
Genc Parti, (Young Party), founded in 2002, URL: http://www.habergenc.com/

Several parties including **Devrimci Halk Kurtulus Cephesi (Revolutionary People's Liberation Front)**, **Refah Partisi (RP) Welfare Party**, (formerly led by the ex-prime minister, Necmettin Erbakan, currently in jail), **Hadep**, (largest Kurdish Party), **KADEK** (formerly known as the PKK, Kurdistan Workers' Party), (outlawed party led by Abdullah Ocalan, now in prison, convicted of treason) are banned as terrorist organisations.

Elections
Voting is by universal suffrage of citizens over the age of 18. Parliamentary elections are held every five years. Parties must gain more than 10 per cent of the vote in order to be eligible for seats in parliament.

In the elections of November 2002, The Justice and Development Party (AKP), won a landslide victory with 363 seats, with only the social-democratic Republican People's Party (CHP), gaining more than 10 per cent of the vote (178 seats) as the main opposition party. Since the election several members of the AKP and CHP have defected to other parties resulting in the ANAP, DYP, SHP and HYP having enough members to gain parliamentary representation. Elections were held in July 2007; the Justice and Development Party were returned to power with 47 per cent of the vote.

The most recent legislative election took place on 12 June 2011. The Islamist party the AKP retained its overall majority in the Assembly. Breakdown of results was as follows: AKP 326 seats; CHP 135 seats; MHP 53 seats; independents 36 seats.

The most recent presidential election took place in 2007. In the third round on voting on 28 August 2007 Abdullah Gul received 339 votes and was elected president. In future the President will be elected by popular vote instead of by the National Assembly. The next presidential election is due in August 2014.

Diplomatic Representation
Embassy of the United States of America, 110 Ataturk Blvd, Ankara, Turkey. Tel: +90 312 455 5555, fax: +90 312 468 6131, URL: http://turkey.usembassy.gov
Ambassador: Francis J. Ricciardone, Jr.
British Embassy, Sehit Ersan Caddesi 46/A, Cankaya, Ankara, Turkey. Tel: +90 312 455 3344, fax: +90 312 455 3351, URL: http://ukinturkey.fco.gov.uk/en
Ambassador: David Reddaway
Embassy of the Republic of Turkey, 3535 Massachusetts Ave., NW, Washington, DC 20008, USA. Tel: +1 202 612 6700, fax: +1 202 612 6744, e-mail: contact@turkishembassy.org, URL: http://www.washington.emb.mfa.gov.tr/
Ambassador: Namık Tan (page 1523)
Embassy of the Republic of Turkey, 43 Belgrave Square, London, SW1X 8PA, United Kingdom. Tel: +44 (0)20 7393 0202, (press: 1207 235 6968), fax: +44 (0)20 7396 6666, e-mail: embassy.london@mfa.gov.tr, URL: http://london.emb.mfa.gov.tr/
Ambassador: Ahmet Unal Cevikoz (page 1402)
Turkish Mission to the United Nations, 821 United Nations Plaza, New York, NY 1007, USA. Tel: +1 212 949 0150, fax: +1 212 949 0086, e-mail: turkey@un.int., URL: http://www.un.int/turkey/
Ambassador and Permanent Representative to the UN: Yasar Halit Cevik

LEGAL SYSTEM

The basic principle of the independence of the judiciary is set out in the Turkish Constitution.

The justice system is overseen by the Supreme Council of Judges and Public Prosecutors. Judges and public prosecutors cannot be dismissed or retired before the age prescribed by the Constitution. Personnel matters for judges and public prosecutors are within the exclusive jurisdiction of the Supreme Council of Judges and Public Prosecutors, which is itself composed of judges.

The court system is classified into five main sections: the Constitutional Court; the Court of Jurisdictional Disputes; Civil and Criminal Courts; Administrative Courts; and finally Military Courts.

The Constitutional Court is the highest court in Turkey and consists of eleven regular and four substitute members, all appointed by the President. It has powers to try the President, members of the Government and members of the High Courts. It reviews legislation and oversees the constitutionality of laws.

The Court of Jurisdictional Disputes delivers final judgments in disputes between civil, administrative and military judicial branches concerning their jurisdiction and decisions. The Court is headed by a president appointed by the members of the Constitutional Court. There are a further 12 regular and 12 substitute members.

Civil and criminal courts are organised in a three-tier system: Court of Cassation; Regional Courts; and Courts of First Instance. The Court of Cassation is the last instance court of appeal. It is composed of 32 chambers, 21 of which are civil and 11 penal. Each court chamber has a president and four judges. The Court of Cassation hears appeals, whether by the Public Prosecutor or by the party concerned, against the decision of a lower court. The Regional Courts of Appeal were introduced in 2007 and have civil and criminal divisions. Each Regional Court of Appeal has a Chief Prosecutor's office. They may approve or reverse the decisions of the Courts of First Instance. The First Instance Courts are basic judicial authorities that settle both civil and criminal disputes. The Criminal Courts of first instance deal with crimes with a sentence of over two years. Those with a sentence less than two years are dealt with by Peace Criminal Courts.

The administrative courts are the Council of State, the Regional Administrative Courts and the Administrative and Tax Courts. The Council of State is the last instance court for reviewing judgements given by administrative courts appointed by the High Council of Judges. It also tries specific cases, including examination of draft regulations. The Regional Administrative Courts are composed of one presiding judge and two members, appointed by the High Council for Judges. They examine decisions from tax courts, and settle disputes on competence and jurisdiction among administrative and tax courts. Administrative courts deal with disputes on administrative legislation and tax courts deal with tax disputes.

Military courts try military personnel for military offences and offences connected with military service.

As of March 2009 there were 134 High Criminal Courts Centres, 708 court houses, and 7,751 Courts, Public Prosecutor Services and Enforcement Offices. Within the civil judiciary there are 5,951 judges and 3,739 public prosecutors. There are a further 818 administrative judges in administrative courts.

The government generally respects the rights of its citizens, though serious problems persist. In recent years, there have been cases of torture and beatings, as well as unlawful killings, by security forces. There is severe overcrowding in prisons, and trials can be excessively long. The government limits freedom of expression through the use of numerous laws; the penal code prohibits insulting the government, the state, or the "Turkish nation". Limitations on freedom of expression is applied to the internet; access to websites was blocked on almost 1,500 occasions in 2008. Non-Muslim religious groups are restricted in practicing their religion openly.

The new Civil Code, which entered into force in January 2002, strengthened the position of women both within the family and within society. The Code abolished the supremacy of men in marriage. The death penalty was abolished in 2004.

Supreme Court of Turkey, URL: http://www.yargitay.gov.tr/english/aboutus.php
President: Ali Alkan

LOCAL GOVERNMENT

The biggest administrative division in Turkey is the *il* (province), of which there are 81: Adana, Adiyaman, Afyonkarahisar, Agri, Aksaray, Amasya, Ankara, Antalya, Ardahan, Artvin, Aydin, Balikesir, Bartin, Batman, Bayburt, Bilecik, Bingol, Bitlis, Bolu, Burdur, Bursa, Canakkale, Cankiri, Corum, Denizli, Diyarbakir, Duzce, Edirne, Elazig, Erzincan, Erzurum, Eskisehir, Gaziantep, Giresun, Gumushane, Hakkari, Hatay, Icel, Igdir, Isparta, Istanbul, Izmir, Kahramanmaras, Karabuk, Karaman, Kars, Kastamonu, Kayseri, Kilis, Kirikkale, Kirklareli, Kirsehir, Kocaeli, Konya, Kutahya, Malatya, Manisa, Mardin, Mugla, Mus, Nevsehir, Nigde, Ordu, Osmaniye, Rize, Sakarya, Samsun, Sanliurfa, Siirt, Sinop, Sirnak, Sivas, Tekirdag, Tokat, Trabzon, Tunceli, Usak, Van, Yalova, Yozgat, and Zonguldak.

The provinces are divided into *ilçe*, (county), *bucak*, (province) and *köy, (village)*. A *bucak* is the union of a certain number of villages - the smallest administrative units - under one administrator. The highest Administrative Officers in the *il*, *ilçe* and *bucak* and *köy* are the *vali* (governors), the *Kaymakam*, *bucak muduru*, and *muhtar* respectively. Villages are administered by an elective Council of Elders consisting of five to 12 members according to the population of the village. The *muhtar* who is the chairman of the Council of Elders, is

at the same time representative of the central government. The *vali* is the head of the central administrative organization within the *il* and the chairman and executive organ of the Provincial Administrative Council.

Municipalities are a form of local government of which the authority and field of action are limited by the boundaries of the town or city concerned. There are over 2,000 municipalities. Municipal government is conducted under the responsibility of the Municipal Council and Mayor, elected by the people. The Mayor is assisted by a Permanent Committee, which is composed of members of the Municipal Council, and which is always in session.

Local elections are held every five years. The most recent were held on 30 March 2009. The ruling AKP party won approximately 39 per cent of the vote (compared with 47 per cent in the 2007 general election). At least five people were killed in election-related violence.

AREA AND POPULATION

Area

Turkey is situated between the Black Sea to the north and the Mediterranean Sea to the south-west. It borders Greece and Bulgaria to the north-west, and Georgia, Armenia and Azerbaijan to the north-east; Iran is on its eastern border, and Iraq and Syria are to the south. Turkey has an area of 814,578 sq. km and it straddles Europe and Asia. The length of Turkey's land borders is 2,875 km and it has 8,333 km of coastline. Turkey is a predominantly mountainous country, its highest point being Mount Ararat at 5,166 metres. The rivers Euphrates and Tigris flow through Turkey.

The climate is mainly temperate, with hot, dry summers and mild, wet winters. The climate is harsher in the interior of the country.

An approximate 30 per cent of the land is used for arable farming, four per cent for permanent crops and the rest for other use.

Earthquakes are a natural hazard. In August 1999 Turkey suffered a huge earthquake measuring 6.8 on the Richter scale. Its epicentre was the industrial area near Izmet and more than 17,000 people died. This was followed by a further quake in November. February 2002 saw another large quake centred on the town of Bolvadin in which 42 people died. A smaller earthquake occurred in May 2003 in the Bingol area when over 160 people were killed.

To view a map, consult http://www.lib.utexas.edu/maps/cia08/turkey_sm_2008.gif

Population

Figures for 2010 put the total population at 72.752 million with an average annual growth rate of 1.3 per cent over the period 2000-10. Population density in 2006 was approximately 93 persons per sq km. The capital city Ankara has a population of around 5 million, other major cities include Istanbul, with a population of 13 million (2012); Izmir, with a population of 3.5 million; and Bursa, with a population over 2 million. About 69 per cent of the population live in urban areas. The population is concentrated in the west and along the coastal areas.

The official language is Turkish.

Kurds

There are some 12 million Kurds in Turkey. For the last 15 years there has been a struggle led by the Kurdistan Worker's Party (PKK) for Kurdish self rule. The leader of the Kurds, Abdullah Ocalan, was sentenced to death in 1999 for treason by the Turks, but the death sentence was suspended in 2000, pending a ruling by the European Court of Human Rights. Ocalan now faces life imprisonment. The PKK is banned as a terrorist organisation. Official figures put deaths caused by the PKK at 30,000. Kurdish demands include a lifting of the restriction on broadcasting and education in the Kurdish language. These reforms were approved by parliament in 2002, as part of moves toward EU membership, and broadcasts began in 2004.

Births, Marriages, Deaths

The 2010 birth rate was 17.9 per cent and the death rate is 4.9 per cent. The fertility rate has decreased to 2.1. (Source: WHO) In 2002, there were 447,820 marriages and 51,096 divorces. Deaths recorded in 2003 were 184,330.

Average life expectancy in 2009 was estimated to be 75 years (72 years for males and 77 years for females). In 2007, healthy life expectancy was estimated to be 64.0 years for males and 67 years for females. In 2010, an estimated 26 per cent of the population were aged 14 years or under, 64 per cent were aged between 15 and 59 years; and 9 per cent were aged 60 years and over. The median age was 28 years. (Source: http://www.who.int, World Health Statistics 2012)

Public Holidays 2014

1 January: New Year's Day
14 January: Birth of the Prophet*
23 April: National Sovereignty and Children's Day
19 May: Commemoration of Atatürk and Youth and Sports Day
29 June: Ramadan begins*
29 July: Eid al-Fitr, Ramadan ends*
30 August: Victory Day
5 October: Eid Al Adha (Festival of the Sacrifice)*
25 October: Islamic New Year*
29 October: Republic Day
* Islamic holidays depend on the sighting of the moon and so dates can vary.

TURKEY

EMPLOYMENT

Figures for 2010 put the workforce at 24.7 million with an unemployment rate of 12.4 per cent. Unemployment fell to an average 9.8 per cent in 2011 (urban rate 11.9 per cent, rural areas 5.8 per cent). The number of unemployed iundividuals was estimated at 2,625,000, down from 3,046,000 in 2010. Employment rose from an estimated 22,594,000 to 24,110,000 in 2011. An estimated 1.2 million Turks work abroad.

Employment by Economic Activity

Sector	2008
Agriculture, hunting, fishing & forestry	5,016,000
Mining & quarrying	115,000
Manufacturing	4,235,000
Electricity, gas & water supply	92,000
Construction	1,241,000
Wholesale & retail trade & repairs	3,575,000
Hotels & restaurants	998,000
Transport, storage & communications	1,089,000
Financial intermediation	260,000
Real estate, renting & business activities	910,000
Public administration & defence, compulsory social security	1,265,000
Education	921,000
Health & social work	594,000
Other community, social & personal service activities, households with employed persons, other	883,000

Source: Copyright © International Labour Organization (ILO Dept. of Statistics, http://laborsta.ilo.org)

BANKING AND FINANCE

Currency
The Turkish Lira was redenominated on 1st January 2005; the new currency unit is New Turkish Lira (YTL). The sub-unit of New Turkish Lira is New Kurus (YKr).
1 New Turkish Lira = 100 New Kurus

In 2006/07, after the withdrawal of old TL notes and coins, the New Turkish Lira (YTL) reverted to the Turkish Lira.

GDP/GNP, Inflation, National Debt
Turkey is an emerging market economy and is now largely developed and industrialized. Since the economic crisis of 2001, Turkey has experienced strong economic growth. Following the crisis, the IMF agreed to two economic packages. The first was a standby assistance package of US$18.6 billion. The second package in 2005 was for US$10 billion over three years. In return, Turkey agreed to introduce reforms including cutting state spending and subsidies, reforming the banking system, lowering inflation and increasing the privatisation of state-owned industries. Workers' foreign exchange remittances, which reach an annual average of three billion dollars, are an important source of income. There are estimated to be more than 1.2 million Turkish workers abroad. GDP was estimated to be US$520 billion in 2006 and US$650 billion in 2007. The estimated growth rate was 6.9 per cent in 2006 and 4.6 per cent in 2007. Growth was estimated at 3.2 per cent in 2008. Per capita GDP was US$7,500 in 2006 and US$9,200 in 2007, rising again to US$9,818 in Q1 2009.

Turkey was believed to be well-placed to survive the current global economic crisis. The economy contracted in the first quarter of 2009 but expanded by approximately 5 per cent in the second quarter. Estimated figures for 2009 put GDP at US$618 billion rising to US$641 billion in 2010, reflecting growth rates of -4.7 per cent in 2009 and 6.8 per cent in 2010. GDP was estimated at US$750 billion in 2011.

In 2003, an estimated 19 per cent of the population were living below the poverty line.

GDP by sector breaks down to: agricultural production, 9.0 per cent; industrial production, 26 per cent; and service sector 65 per cent.

In accordance with the economic stability and anti-inflation policies adopted since 1998, Turkey initiated a comprehensive macroeconomic programme in the beginning of 2000. The programme was extended to 2004, following talks with the IMF. As a result, interest rates and inflation took a downward trend. The wholesale price index and the consumer price index decreased to 30.8 per cent and 29.7 per cent, respectively, as of the end of 2002. By 2005 the inflation rate was estimated at 7.7 per cent, rising to 9.5 per cent in 2006 before falling to 8.5 per cent in 2007. Inflation rose again in 2008 to 10.6 per cent, fell to 6.5 per cent in 2009 and rose to 7.5 per cent in 2010. Inflation was estimated to be 7.4 per cent in Q42012.

The current account deficit grew to 10 per cent of GDP in 2011. External debt was estimated to be US$97 billion in 2012.

Turkey had an estimated $18.3 billion in net foreign direct investment in 2008, falling, because of the global economic crisis, to $7.7 billion in 2009.

Balance of Payments / Imports and Exports
Main exports include petroleum products, ready-to-wear clothes, tobacco, minerals, and dried fruits and nuts. Exports were estimated to have risen to US$113.9 billion in 2010 and US$141.5 billion in 2011. Imports were estimated to have risen to US$185.9 billion in 2010 and US$233.7 billion in 2011. Major trade partners include Germany, China, the US, Russia, Japan, France and Italy.

Banking
Monetary policies in Turkey are directed by the Central Bank of the Republic of Turkey. The Central Bank has the authority to issue banknotes. The Central Bank is also responsible for implementing the monetary policy, regulating money supply, extending loans to banks, forming the instruments of the monetary policies, achieving price stabilisation and harmonising the applications in the banking sector with international standards and European Union norms.

Central Bank
Banque Centrale de la République de Turquie SA (Turkiye Cumhuriyet Merkez Bankasi; - Central Bank of the Republic of Turkey), Istiklal Cad 10, Ulus, 06100 Ankara, Turkey. Tel: +90 312 507 5000, fax: +90 312 507 5640, e-mail: info@tcmb.gov.tr, URL: http://www.tcmb.gov.tr
Governor: Dr Erdem Basci (page 1384)

Chambers of Commerce and Trade Organisations
Union of Chambers of Commerce, Industry, Maritime Commerce and Commodity Exchanges of Turkey, URL: http://www.tobb.org.tr

MANUFACTURING, MINING AND SERVICES

Primary and Extractive Industries
Turkey is a country rich in mineral deposits and produces about 60 different minerals. One of Turkey's richest mineral resources is boron and Turkey holds 63 per cent of the world's reserves. Other minerals that are found in abundance in Turkey are: prelate, pumice, feldspar, barite, magnesite, sodiumsulphate, rock-salt, trona, trontium salts, zeolite, sepiolite, marble, quartzite, emery, bauxite, and lignite.

Almost 150 million tons of minerals worth US$2.2 billion are produced each year compared to an estimated world total of 7 billion tons worth US$400 billion. Turkey's leading exports are primarily boron salts followed by chromium, magnesite and marble.

Crude oil and natural gas continue to be the most important products in the mining sector. As of January 2012 Turkey had proven oil reserves of 270 million barrels. Estimated figures for 2011 show that production was around 56,500 barrels per day. In the same year Turkey consumed 706,000 barrels per day, approximately 90 per cent of which was imported. Oil accounts for around 40 per cent of Turkey's energy needs but natural gas is growing in importance to the sector. Oil imports come mainly from Russia, Iran, and Saudi Arabia. Libya, Iraq and Syria also supply lesser quantities. Russia has been the top supplier since 2007. Exploration of potential fields under the Aegean Sea has been limited because of disputes with Greece.

Turkey is becoming an increasingly important player in the transit of oil and gas. Several new pipelines have become operational in recent years. The Baku-Tbilisi-Ceyhan pipeline opened in 2006 and delivers 1 milllion b/d of petroleum. In 2007 the South Caucasus Pipeline started delivering natural gas from Azerbaijan to Turkey. A pipeline with Greece also became operational in November 2007. Work on the Samsun-Ceyhan pipline which would transport oil from the Black Sea port of Samsun to Ceyhan on the Mediterranean coast began in 2007. This pipeline would ease pressure on the Bosphorous and will have an initial capacity of 1 million bbl/d.

As of January 2011, Turkey had proven gas reserves of 218 billion cubic feet. In 2011, estimated production was 27 billion cubic feet and consumption was 1.5 trillion cubic feet in 2011. There are 14 gas fields in Turkey, the largest gas field is Marmara Kuzey, an offshore field in the Sea of Marmara/ Currently Turkey has import agreements with Russia, Iran, Algeria and Nigeria. The gas sector which is dominated by the company Botas is undergoing a slow privatisation process. Botas dominates the market although 78 per cent is legally open to competition. Botas has a monopoly over the domestic distribution and supply, although it is meant to be opening this up.

Turkey's major refineries are TPAO: Aliaga-Izmir (200, 000 bbl/d capacity), Izmit (230,000 bbl/d), Kirikkale (100,000 bbl/d), Atas: Mersin (162,000 bbl/d), and Batman (22,3000 bbl/d).

Recoverable coal reserves were estimated to be 2,.6 billion short tons in 2008. Coal production in 2010 was 80 million short tons and consumption was 109 million short tons. (Source: EIA)

Energy
Primary energy sources such as anthracite coal, lignite, petroleum, natural gas, hydroelectric and geothermal energy, wood, animal and plant residues and solar and wind energy are used for energy consumption in Turkey. Electrical energy and coke are used as secondary energy sources. During the Seventh Five-Year Development Plan implemented between 1996 and 2000, primary energy production increased by 1.3 per cent per year. Approximately 74 per cent of the energy demands in Turkey are met through foreign sources. Petroleum has the largest share in foreign sources. In recent years, the use of natural gas has also significantly increased.

In view of the increasing energy demand in Turkey as well as the harmonization process with the EU, and integration with the global economy, the Electricity Market Law went into effect on March 3, 2001 and the Natural Gas Market Law on May 2, 2001. With the termination of the preparatory periods envisioned in these laws, the New Electricity Market opened on 3 September 2002 and the Natural Gas Market on 2 November 2002.

The total electrical power production capacity of Turkey in 2009 was 5,218 GWe. Total electricity production was 201 billion kWh and total consumption was 170 billion kWh. Conventional thermal sources contributed 81 per cent and hydro-electric most of the remainder. The government is considering nuclear power as an option.

Manufacturing

The weaving and clothing industry form a large part of Turkey's exports and hence the cotton industry is the largest sub sector of industry as a whole. 70 per cent of all textile and apparel manufacturing goes for export and the industry employs around 4 million people; the manufacturing of leather goods accounts for over two per cent of the manufacturing output. Other important industries include plastics, chemicals, petrochemicals, petroleum products, fertilizer, cement, glass, electrical machinery, electronics, cars, ship building and aircraft manufacturing.

Production Value in Manufacturing Industry in 2005

Industry	YTL
Food, products & beverages	27,553,938,202
Tobacco products	2,265,693,408
Textiles	12,920,831,149
Wearing apparel	5,876,868,900
Leather & leather products	762,872,658
Wood & wood products excl. furniture	2,053,125,559
Paper & paper products	3,301,905,832
Publishing & printing	1,273,137,684
Coke, refined petroleum products, nuclear fuel	15,844,252,906
Chemicals & chemical products	16,727,488,843
Rubber & plastic products	7,874,308,648
Other non-metallic products	11,593,458,001
Basic metals	22,057,767,745
Fabricated metal products, excl. machinery & equipment	3,983,999,855
Machinery & equipment n.e.c.	8,712,419,256
Office, accounting & computing machinery	445,565,257
Machinery & equipment n.e.c.	4,098,989,044
Radio, television & communication equipment	5,191,435,257
Medical & optical instruments, watches & clocks	329,749,219
Vehicles, trailers & semi-trailers	22,161,029,570
Other transport equipment	562,218,619
Furniture manufacturing n.e.c.	3,220,257,553
Total manufacturing industry	178,811,313,165

Source: Turkish Statistical Institute

Service Industries

There is a government drive to increase the number of tourists visiting Turkey. In 2003 there were 13,341,000 visitors generating receipts of US\$ 1,935 million. In 2005, a total of 21.1 million tourists visited Turkey. Tourism revenue accounts for 5.7 per cent of GDP. The government had a target of 30 million tourists and US\$30 billion in tourism revenues by 2010.

Agriculture

The geographic and regional climatic conditions in Turkey are very suitable for producing agricultural products and Turkey, in consequence, is one of the few self-sufficient countries in the world in terms of agricultural production, especially the production of food items.

Almost 16 per cent of the country's land consists of meadows and pastures, 26 per cent is forest and 35 per cent is arable lands. There were 14.8 million hectares of cultivated and sown lands in 1940; by 2001 this had increased to 26.4 million. Dry agriculture is carried out on 83.5 per cent of these cultivated and sown lands, while irrigated agriculture is carried out on 16.5 per cent. Field crops and fruits comprise almost three quarters of the agricultural products and wheat is the most widespread field crops. Turkey is a leading exporter of hazelnut, fig and apricot production; fourth in fresh vegetables, grape and tobacco production and seventh in wheat and cotton production. Tea is also grown and in 2004, 76,632 hectares were under tea plantations.

Animal husbandry production comprises approximately 25 per cent of total agricultural production.

Agricultural Production in 2010

Produce	Int. \$'000*	Tonnes
Cow milk, whole, fresh	3,894,553	12,480,100
Tomatoes	3,157,603	10,052,000
Wheat	2,808,038	19,660,000
Grapes	2,432,230	4,255,000
Indigenous chicken meat	2,064,251	1,449,200
Olives	1,132,995	1,415,000
Apples	1,099,576	2,600,000
Hazelnuts, with shell	961,745	600,000
Chillies and peppers, green	935,255	1,986,700
Indigenous cattle meat	786,962	291,319
Sugar beet	771,762	17,942,100
Potatoes	720,204	4,548,090

*unofficial figures

Source: http://faostat.fao.org/site/339/default.aspx Food and Agriculture Organization of the United Nations, Food and Agricultural commodities production

COMMUNICATIONS AND TRANSPORT

Travel Requirements

Citizens of the USA, Canada, Australia and most of the EU require a passport valid for three months beyond the length of stay; nationals of Belgium, France, Germany, Greece, Liechtenstein, Italy, Luxembourg, Malta, The Netherlands, Spain and Switzerland can enter with a national ID card if it is valid for one year. Tourists and business visitors from Australia, Austria, Belgium, Canada, Ireland, Italy, Malta, The Netherlands, Portugal, Slovenia, Spain,

the UK and USA can obtain an entry visa for a fee, for stays not exceeding three months. Citizens of the Greek Cypriot Administrative Region, Estonia, Hungary, Latvia, Lithuania, Poland, Romania and Slovak Republic can buy an entry visa for stays not exceeding one month. Bulgarians do not require a visa for stays up to three months, but do require a visa for transit and for entry at certain points in Turkey, and should check with the consulate.

Other nationals should contact the embassy to check visa requirements.

Transport System

The transportation sector together with the communications sector in Turkey constitutes almost 14 per cent of the GDP. Ninety per cent of domestic cargo is transported by road. 3.5 per cent goes by rail, 4.5 per cent by waterway and 2 per cent by pipeline. 95 per cent of domestic passenger transportation is overland. Airways mostly carry domestic passengers, and waterways mostly cargo.

National Airlines

Turk Hava Yollari (THY, Turkish Airlines), URL: http://www.thy.com.tr
The Turkish Airlines Corporation (THY), a state enterprise, is the biggest airline corporation in Turkey. In 2008 Turkish Airlines joined Star Alliance. THY had 180 planes in 2012. THY carried more than 32.6 million passengers and 387,000 tons of cargo in 2011.
Air Alfa Hava Yollari, URL: http://www.airalfa.com.tr

The General Directorate of the State Airports Enterprises (DHMI) (URL: http://www.dhmi.gov.tr/) operates 45 airports.

The following airports are open for international and domestic flights (scheduled and charted): Atatürk (URL: http://www.ataturkairport.com/eng/index.php), Esenboğa, Adnan Menderes, Antalya, Dalaman, Adana, Trabzon, Milas-Bodrum, Süleyman Demirel and Nevşehir-Kapadokya. Ataturk Airport is expected to have passenger traffic of 26 million for 2008.

Bursa-Yenişehir, Denizli-Çardak, Çorlu, Erzurum, Gaziantep, Kars, Kayseri, Konya, Samsun-Çarşamba, Van Ferit Melen Airports are open for international unscheduled and domestic flights.

A further 16 airports (Adıyaman, Ağrı, Çanakkale, Diyarbakır, Elazığ, Erzincan, Kahramanmaraş, Körfez, Malatya, Mardin, Muş, Siirt, Sivas, Şanlıurfa, Tokat and Uflak) are for domestic flights only.

Roads

Figures from 2010 show that Turkey had 1,892 km of motorway, 31,446 km of state highways, 30,368 km of provincial roads and 285,739 km of village roads. In 2006 there were 5,400,440 cars, 318,954 minibuses, 152,712 buses, 1,259,867 cargo vehicles and 647,420 trucks on the roads. (Source: Turkish Statistics Institute). Vehicles drive on the right.

Railways

The Republic of Turkey State Railroads Enterprise (TCDD) carries passengers and cargo over 10,940 km of railways and 8,671 km of these are main lines. Nearly 97 per cent of these lines are single lines. Almost 19 per cent of the lines are electrical and 23 per cent are operated by signal. Five percent of the lines are double lines and 0.3 per cent are triple lines. Railways were responsible for 2 per cent of the total passengers and 4 per cent of the total cargo transported in Turkey in 2002. Istanbul and Ankara both have small subway systems.
Turkish Railways, URL: http://www.tcdd.gov.tr

Shipping

The maritime lines continue to be dominant in international cargo transportation. The total length of coastlines in Turkey is 8,333 km. Approximately 72 per cent of imports and 95 per cent of exports are made over waterways. Three per cent of the intercity transport is by sea. In 2001, 31 per cent of the total 113.4 million tons of haulage was carried by Turkish vessels and 69 per cent by foreign vessels. The total tonnage of the Turkish maritime fleet is 9,650,796 DWT, with 3,196 vessels, 86 of which belong to the public sector and 3,110 to the private sector. The average age of the fleet is 18.33 years.

Ports and Harbours

The major ports of Turkey are at Istanbul, Iskenderun, Mersin and Izmir.

Ferry services operate crossing the Dardenelles at Gallipoli, from Çanakkale to Eceabat and Gelibolu to Lapseki. Ferry services are also in operation from Bostanci, Kadiköy, Kartal, Yalova and Büyükada Island to Bakirköy, Karaköy, Yenikapi, Yalova, Avcilar and Bandirma. Deniz. **Istanbul Fast Ferries**, URL: http://www.ido.com.tr

HEALTH

The public sector continues to provide a major portion of the health services in Turkey. A total of 93.3 per cent of patient beds and almost all protective health services belong to the public sector. Private healthcare is developing. In 2009, the government spent approximately 12.8 per cent of its total budget on healthcare (up from 9.8 per cent in 2000), accounting for 75.1 per cent of all healthcare spending. Total expenditure on healthcare equated to 6.7 per cent of the country's GDP. Per capita expenditure on health was approximately US\$575, compared with US\$205 in 2000.

In 2005-10 there were 118,641 doctors (15.4 per 10,000 population), 49,357 nurses and midwives (6.4 per 10,000 population), 25,201 pharmacists (approx. 3.3 per 10,000 population), 20,589 dentists (approx 2.7 per 10,000 population) and 19,304 environment and public health workers. There were 25 hospital beds per 10,000 population.

In 2010 the infant mortality rate (probability of dying before first birthday) was 12 per 1,000 live births and the child (under-five years old) mortality rate was 13 per 1,000 live births. The main causes of death in the under-fives are: prematurity (24 per cent), pneumonia (11

TURKEY

per cent), congenital anomalies (23 per cent), birth asphyxia (7 per cent) and diarrhoea (1 per cent). In the period 2000-09 an estimated 15.6 per cent of children (under five-years-old) were classified as stunted and 3.5 per cent as underweight.

According to the WHO, in 2010, 100 per cent of the population had sustainable access to improved drinking water and an estimated 90 per cent of the population had sustainable access to improved sanitation. (Source: http://www.who.int, World Health Statistics 2012)

EDUCATION

Primary education includes the education and training of children in the 6-14 age-group. Primary education is compulsory for all citizens and is free of charge. Primary education institutions consist of eight-year schools. Uninterrupted education is carried out in these schools and a primary school diploma is given to graduates. Provisional figures for the 2004-05 school year show that 10,565,389 students were educated in 35,611 primary schools by 401,288 teachers.

There are two types of secondary education. The first is general secondary education and the second is vocational-technical secondary education. In the 2004-05 school year a total of 1,937,055 students were educated in 2,939 general secondary schools by 93,209 teachers, that year 1,102,394 students were educated in 3,877 vocational and technical secondary schools by 74,405 teachers. (Source: Turkish Statistical Institute) The majority of secondary school students attend state school but private schools are available.

Figures for 2009 from UNESCO show that 97 per cent of girls and 98 per cent of boys were enrolled in primary education, 71 per cent of girls and 77 per cent of boys were enrolled secondary school and 46 per cent of the population of tertiary age were enrolled in tertiary education. An estimated 99 per cent of pupils complete primary education.

Recent figures show that there are 76 universities, 53 of which are public and 23 of which are private, 627 faculties, 238 schools of higher education, 290 institutes and 603 vocational schools of higher education. There were 1,894,079 students, including those attending the open university, educated by 74,134 instructors in the 2002-2003 academic year.

The number of academic personnel being educated abroad by private and public scholarships is 12,702 at the graduate level, 6,020 at the post graduate level, making a total of 18,722.

Adult literacy in 2009 was 90.8 per cent (male 96.4 per cent; female 85.3 per cent). For the age group 15-24 years the literacy rate was 97.8 per cent (99.0 per cent for males and 96.6 per cent for females).

In 2004, public expenditure on education was 4.0 per cent of GDP, of which 40 per cent went on primary education, 34 per cent on secondary and 26 per cent on tertiary education. (Source: UNESCO)

In June 2012, the government said it would allow the teaching of Kurdish as an optional course in schools.

RELIGION

Almost 99 per cent of the population of Turkey is Muslim. The remaining 1 per cent is composed of Orthodox Christians, Catholics, Protestants and other denominations. There is religious freedom in the country and secularism is one of the basic principles which is embedded in the Constitution of the Republic of Turkey.

Religious affairs are organized under the Directorate of Religious Affairs which is attached to the Prime Ministry and responsible for the administration of religious affairs. The function of this organization is to carry out activities related to the beliefs of the Islamic religion; the principles of worship and morality; to enlighten society on the subject of religious issues, and to manage the places of worship.

Turkey has a religious liberty rating of 4 on a scale of 1 to 10 (10 is most freedom). (Source: World Religion Database)

COMMUNICATIONS AND MEDIA

Newspapers
In the past there have been sanctions against journalists. Some of the most repressive have been lifted in order to try to meet EU entry requirements. It still a crime to insult Turkish national identity and this code has been used to punish journalists. The Dogan group is the leading media conglomerate.

Hurriyet, URL: http://www.hurriyet.com.tr/anasayfa
Milliyet, URL: http://www.milliyet.com.tr
Yeni Asir, URL: http://www.yeniasir.com.tr
Sabah, URL: http://www.sabah.com.tr (English)
Cumuriyet, URL: http://emedya.cumhuriyet.com.tr/eCumhuriyet/m/
Turkish Daily News, URL: http://www.turkishdailynews.com.tr/ (English)

Approximately 3,450 periodicals, half of them weekly, are published in Turkey. The average daily circulation of local newspapers varies between 1,000 and 15,000. The total circulation of magazines is around 2.3 million.

Broadcasting
In 1994, the constitution was amended to preserve the autonomy and impartiality of the Turkish Radio and Television Corporation (TRT), the state broadcaster. The Supreme Council of Radio and Television (RTÜK) was founded at this time to determine the principles to which broadcasting is subject and to manage the allocation of new broadcasting licences. Kurdish language broadcasts were banned for many years, but have been permitted since 2004.

TRT television broadcasts are made in several different channels, namely TRT-1, TRT-2, TRT-3, TRT-4, TRT-GAP, TRTINT and TRT-TÜRK. TRT has several main radio stations under operation, as well as local stations. Kurdish-language TRT-6 was launched in 2009. The shortwave Service of TRT, "The Voice of Turkey," puts out programs in English, French, German, Serbo-Croat, Bulgarian, Greek, Romanian and Arabic. The national radio-link system is also linked to Eurovision. Furthermore, TRT started in 2004 to broadcast programs in languages of various ethnic communities living in Turkey, including Arabic, Kurdish and Bosnian. In addition to the official radio and television corporation (TRT), there are numerous private television and radio stations. The first television to break the monopoly was Star TV. Popular private television stations include Star TV, Show TV and Kanal D.

Turkish Radio and Television (TRT), URL: http://www.trt.net.tr/wwwtrt/anasayfa.aspx
Star TV, URL: http://www.startv.com.tr/
Show TV, URL: http://www.showturk.tv/
Kanal D, URL: http://www.kanald.com.tr/

Telecommunications
The telecommunications network is undergoing much modernizatrion and expansion. A network of technologically advanced intercity trunk lines have been constructed, using both fiber-optic cable and digital microwave relay. Remote rural areas are reached by a domestic satellite system. In 2009, there were an estimated 16 million landlines and 62 million mobile phones. In 2009 there were an estimated 27.3 million internet users.

ENVIRONMENT

Main environmental concerns for Turkey include marine pollution especially in the Bosporus Straits, which takes a large amount of shipping carrying oil. Dramatically increased industrialisation in recent years has meant an increase in carbon emissions and deforestation. Air pollution is a problem in urban areas. In 2004, Turkey's per capita carbon emissions were approximately 3 metric tons. Total emissions from consumption of fossil fuels reached 263.54 million metric tons of CO_2 in 2010. It was ranked 24th in the world that year. (Source: EIA)

Turkey participates in the Black Sea Environment Program and cooperates with the littoral countries. It ratified the Kyoto Protocol in 2004. Turkey maintains joint efforts with many countries within the framework of bilateral environmental cooperation agreements to protect the Mediterranean Sea. Turkey is a party to the following international agreements: Air Pollution, Antarctic Treaty, Biodiversity, Climate Change, Desertification, Endangered Species, Hazardous Wastes, Ozone Layer Protection, Ship Pollution, Wetlands. Turkey has signed, but not ratified the convention on Environmental Modification.

SPACE PROGRAMME

The government set up a Space Technologies Directorate in November 2011. Currently under the supervision of the Transport Ministry it is planned that it will become the country's first National Space Agency. The state scientific research institute Tübitak currently works with the Federal Russian space agency Roscosmos, the German aerospace centre DLR, the British National Space Centre and the Netherlands space office NSO. It is planned that a total of 17 Turkish satellites will come into orbit from 2012 to 2020. Göktürk II, an electro optical reconnaissance and obervation satellite, is due to launch in 2012 and Göktürk I and Türksat 4A (communications satellites) in 2013.

TURKMENISTAN
Republic of Turkmenistan
Türkmenistan

Capital: Ashgabat (formerly Ashkhabad) (Population estimate, 2009: 900,000)

Head of State: Gurbanguly Berdymukhamedov (President) (page 1387)

National Flag: Green, with five basic carpet patterns and two crossed olive branches appear on a wine coloured stripe near the hoist. Five, five-pointed white stars appear on the larger, green part, in the left corner

CONSTITUTION AND GOVERNMENT

Constitution
In August 1990 the Republic's Supreme Soviet adopted a declaration of independent sovereignty, having been a full republic of the Soviet Socialist Republic since 1925. A referendum vote for independence followed on 26 October 1991 and was approved by the Turkmenian Supreme Soviet on the following day.

Turkmen independence was recognised by the EU and the USA in December of that year. Membership of the UN followed on 2 March 1992. Turkmenistan was a signatory to the Commonwealth of Independent States agreement of 21 December 1991, which was ratified by the Supreme Soviet on 26 December.

The constitution of May 1992 established the president as the head of state and provided for a unicameral legislature. Political activity and opposition parties were not allowed and political gatherings were only permitted if approved by the government. The age of suffrage is 18.

On 28 December 1999 the constitution was amended giving President Saparmurat Atayevich Niyazov the right to be a lifetime president; he died in December 2006.

A new constitution was adopted in September 2008. The existing People's Council, made up of 2,500 tribal elders and local lawmakers, was abolished and parliament increased to 120 seats. The president may now choose regional governors and mayors and appoint the electoral commission. The revised constitution also provides for multiple political parties. Parliament's powers were also increased.

For further details on the constitution, please consult:
http://www.turkmenistanembassy.org/turkmen/business/const.html

Recent Events
In July 2007, Russia, Kazakhstan and Turkmenistan agreed to build a new pipeline north of the Caspian Sea which will ensure Russian access to Turkmen gas.

Turkmenistan cut gas supplies to Iran in January 2008, blaming a technical fault and Iran's failure to pay for supplies. Iran claimed that Turkmenistan wanted to double the price of its gas.

In April 2009, Turkmenistan accused Russia of causing an explosion on a gas pipeline, Russia denied the accusation. In December of that year Turkmenistan opened a pipeline exporting gas to China and in January 2010 a second pipeline was opened, exporting gas to Iran. In November 2010 Turkmenistan agreed to supply gas to Europe.

President Berdimuhammedov was re-elected president in February 2012 with over 95 per cent of the vote.

Legislature
Under the 2008 Constitution the Parliament (Majlis) became unicameral, with an increased membership of 125 members, directly elected for a five-year term.

The Parliament (Majlis), 17 Neutral Turkmenistan Street, 744000 Ashgabat, Turkmenistan. Tel: +993 12 353125, fax, +993 12 353147

Cabinet (as at March 2013)
President and Chair of the Council of Ministers: Gurbanguly Berdimuhammedov (page 1387)
Deputy Chair, Minister of Foreign Affairs: Rashid Meredov (page 1476)
Deputy Chair, responsible for Transport & Communications: Akmyrat Yegeleyew
Deputy Chair, responsible for Culture and the Media: Byagul Nurmyradova
Deputy Chair, responsible for Economy and Finance: Annamuhammet Gocyyew
Deputy Chair, responsible for Construction: Samuhammet Durdylyyew
Deputy Chair, responsible for Agriculture & Water Resources: Annageldi Yazmyradow
Deputy Chair, responsible for Energy & Industry: Rozymyrat Seyitgulyyew
Deputy Chair, responsible for Energy-Sector Work with Foreign Firms: Yagsygeldi Kakayew
Deputy Chair, responsible for Oil and Gas: Baymyrat Hojamuhammedow
Deputy Chair, responsible for Education, Health, Religious Affairs, Tourism, Science: Sapadurdy Toyilev
Minister of Defence: Begench Gundogdiyev
Minister of Labour and Social Protection: Bekmyrat Mesrepowic Samyradow
Minister of National Security: Yaylym Berdiyew

Minister of Finance: Dovletgeldy Sadkykov
Minister of Industry: Babanyyaz Italmazow
Minister of Culture: Gunca Mammedova
Minister of Oil and Gas and Mineral Resources: Muhammetnur Halylow
Minister of Interior Affairs: Iskander Mulikow
Minister of Energy: Myrat Artykow
Minister of Justice: Begenc Carryyew
Minister of Natural Resources and Environmental Protection: Babageldi Annabayramow
Minister of Education: Gulsat Mammedova
Minister of Agriculture: Rejep Bazarov
Minister of Water Resources: Seyitmrat Taganov
Minister of Trade and Foreign Economic Relations: Batyr Abayew
Minister of Construction: Jumageldi Baryramow
Minister of Communications: Bayramgeldi Owezow
Minister of Railways: Bajram Annameredov
Minister of the Textile Industry: Saparmyrat Batyrow
Minister of Economic Development: Babamrat Taganow
Minister of Health and the Pharmaceutical Industry: Gurbanmammet Elyasow

Ministries
Office of the President, Presidential Palace, ul. 2001 24, 744000 Ashkhabad, Turkmenistan. Tel: +993 12 354534, fax: +993 12 354388
Office of the Chair of the Council of Ministers, ul. 2001 24, 744000 Ashkhabad, Turkmenistan. Tel: +993 12 354534, fax: +993 12 354388
Ministry of Agriculture, ul. Azady 63, 744000 Ashkhabad, Turkministan. Tel: +993 12 336691, fax: +993 12 350518, e-mail: minselhoz2004@online.tm
Ministry of Communications, ul. Bitarap 40, 744014 Ashkhabad, Turkmenistan. Tel: +993 12 352152, fax: +993 12 350595, e-mail: mincom@telecom.tm, URL: http://www.mct.gov.tm
Ministry of Construction and Construction Materials, ul. Alisher Navoi 56, 744000 Ashkhabad, Turkmenistan. Tel: +993 12 512359, fax: +993 12 475069, e-mail: mpsmt@online.tm
Ministry of Culture and the Media, ul. Pushkina 14, 744000 Ashkhabad, Turkmenistan. Tel: +993 12 353560, fax: +993 12 353560
Ministry of Defence, ul. Galkynysh 4, 744000 Ashkhabad, Turkmenistan. Tel: +993 12 352259, fax: +993 12 391944
Ministry of Economics and Development, ul. Nurberdy Pomma 4, 744000 Ashkhabad, Turkmenistan. Tel: +993 12 510563, fax: +993 12 511823, e-mail: minekonom@online.tm
Ministry of Economy and Finance, ul. Nurberdy Pomma 4, 744000 Ashkhabad, Turkmenistan. Tel: +993 12 510563, fax: +993 12 511823, e-mail: omeft@online.tm
Ministry of Education, ul. Gerogly 2, 744000 Ashkhabad, Turkmenistan. Tel: +993 12 355803, fax: +993 12 398811
Ministry of Energy and Industry, ul. Nurberdy Pomma 6, 744000 Ashkhabad, Turkmenistan. Tel: +993 12 353870, fax: +993 12 393512, e-mail: kuwwat@online.tm
Ministry of Environmental Protection and Natural Resources, ul. Kemine 102, 744000 Ashkhabad, Turkmenistan. Tel: +993 12 354312, fax: +993 12 511613
Ministry of Foreign Affairs, pr. Magtymkuly 83, 744000 Ashkhabad, Turkmenistan. Tel: +993 12 266211, fax: +993 12 253583, e-mail: mfatm@online.tm
Ministry of Health and Pharmaceutical Industry, pr. Magtymkuly 90, 744000 Ashkhabad, Turkmenistan. Tel: +993 12 356047, fax: +993 12 355032, e-mail: healthtm@online.tm
Ministry of the Interior, pr. Magtymkuli 85, 744000 Ashkhabad, Turkmenistan. Tel: +993 12 251328, fax: +993 12 393739
Ministry of Justice, ul. Alisher Navoi 86, 744000 Ashkhabad, Turkmenistan. fax: +993 12 394410
Ministry of Labour and Social Protection, ul. 2003 3, 744000 Ashkhabad, Turkmenistan. Tel: +993 12 253003
Ministry of National Security, pr. Magtymkuli 85, 744000 Ashkhabad, Turkmenistan. Tel: +993 12 402764, fax: +993 12 391944
Ministry of Oil, Natural Gas and Mineral Resources, ul. Neutral Turkmenistan 28, 744000 Ashkhabad, Turkmenistan. Tel: +993 12 393827, fax: +993 12 393821, e-mail: ministryoilgas@online.tm
Ministry of Railways Administration, Saparmurat Turkmenbashy shayoly 7, 744000 Ashkhabad, Turkmenistan. Tel: +993 12 355545, fax: +993 12 392874, e-mail: tde@online.tm
Ministry of Road Transport and Highways, ul. Baba Annanov 2, 744000 Ashkhabad, Turkmenistan. Tel: +993 12 474992, fax: +993 12 470391, e-mail: tcentr@online.tm
Ministry of the Textile Industry, ul. Armadurdyev 52, 744000 Ashkhabad, Turkmenistan. Tel: +993 12 510303, fax: +993 12 355442, e-mail: textile@online.tm
Ministry of Trade and Foreign Economic Relations, ul. Gerogly 1, 744000 Ashkhabad, Turkmenistan. Tel: +993 12 351047, fax: +993 12 357324, e-mail: mtfer@online.tm
Ministry of Water Resources, ul. A. Niyazov 30, 744000 Ashkhabad, Turkmenistan. Tel: +993 12 390615, fax: +993 12 398539

Elections
President Saparmurad Niyazov, the former Communist party leader, was re-elected by 99.5 per cent of the voters in elections held on 21 June 1992. He was further endorsed in January 1994 when, following a referendum, 99.99 per cent of voters favoured the extension of his term of office to 2002. In 1999 legislation was amended granting him the exclusive right to

TURKMENISTAN

being a lifetime president. In December 2006 Presdient Niyazov died of heart failure and Gurbanguly Berdimuhammedov was announced the winner of presidential elections held in February 2007. He was re-elected with over 95 per cent of the vote in February 2012.

Turkmenistan is a single-party state; the only political party, the Democratic Party of Turkmenistan is the still the only party legally allowed to hold power and all election candidates belong to either it or state-affilliated organisations. Elections took place in December 2008 under the rules of the new constitution.

Political Parties
The Democratic Party of Turkmenistan is the only political party that exists. However the revised constitution of 2008 should pave the way for more political parties.

Diplomatic Representation
Embassy of Turkmenistan, 2207 Massachusetts Avenue, NW Washington, DC 20008, USA. Tel: +1 202 588 1500, fax: +1 202 588 0697, e-mail: turkmen@mindspring.com, URL: http://www.turkmenistanembassy.org/
Ambassador: Meret Bairamovich Orazov
Embassy of Turkmenistan, 131 Holland Park Avenue, London, W11 4UT. Tel: +44 (0)20 7610 5239 fax: +44 (0)20 7751 1903, URL: http://turkmenembassy.org.uk/
Ambassador: Yazmurad N Seryaev (page 1512)
British Embassy, 3rd Floor, 301-308 Office Building Four Points Ak Altin Hotel, Ashgabat, Turkmenistan. Tel: +993 12 363462, fax: +993 12 363465, e-mail: beasb@online.tm, URL: http://ukinturkmenistan.fco.gov.uk/en/
Ambassador: Keith Allan (page 1375)
US Embassy, 9 1984 Street, Ashgabat, Turkmenistan. Tel: +993 12 350045, fax: +993 12 392614, e-mail: irc-ashgabat@iatp.edu.tm, URL: http://turkmenistan.usembassy.gov/ (page 1493)
Ambassador: Robert E. Patterson
Permanent Representative of Turkmenistan to the United Nations, 866 United Nations Plaza, Suite 424, New York, NY 10017, USA. Tel: +1 212 486 8908, fax: +1 212 486 2521, URL: http://www.un.int/wcm/content/site/turkmenistan
Ambassador: Dr Aksoltan Atayewa

LEGAL SYSTEM

The Turkmenistan legal system is in the process of reform, following the collapse of the Soviet Union. At present it is based on civil law, the Constitution being the supreme law of the land. There are also Islamic influences. Judicial power lies with the Supreme Court, a High Commercial Court, and Military and other courts. Judges are independent, though appointed by the president for terms of five years.

The government human rights record remains poor. There is restriction of political and civil liberties. There have been recent instances of torture, arrests can be arbitrary; and detentions prolonged. There are restrictions on freedom of speech, press, assembly, association and religion. Turkmenistan abolished the death penalty in 1999.

LOCAL GOVERNMENT

Turkmenistan has five administrative territorial bodies, known as velayats, Ahal Welayat (Ashgabat), Balkan Welayat (Balkanabat), Dashoguz Welayat (formerly Dashowuz), Lebap Welayat (Turkmenabat, formerly Chardjou/Charjew), Mary Welayat. Balkan, Akhal, Mary, Lebap and Dashkhovuz. These are subdivided into a further 50 districts, or etraps. Local elections took place in December 2010.

AREA AND POPULATION

Area
Turkmenistan lies in south-western Central Asia, facing the Caspian Sea in the west. It borders Kazakhstan to the north-west, Uzbekistan to the east and Iran and Afghanistan to the south. The Republic's area is 488,100 sq. km., comparable to the size of France, and its density is 8 inhabitants per sq. km. The land is flat; 80 per cent is taken up by sandy plains. On the eastern shore of the Caspian Sea lie the Major and Minor Balkan ranges. The Amu Darya river crosses Turkmenistan from east to west. The climate is sub-tropical desert.

To view a map, visit http://www.un.org/Depts/Cartographic/map/profile/turkmeni.pdf

Population
Latest WHO figures put the total population at an estimated 5.042 million in 2010. The annual population growth rate was estimated at 1.1 per cent over the period 2000-10. The median age was 25 years. Approximately 29 per cent of the population is aged 14 years or less. Approximately 6 per cent is aged 60 years or older. An estimated 50 per cent of people live in urban areas, with 900,000 living in the capital Ashgabat. Other major cities include: Dashoguz, Mary and Turkmenbashi. The majority of the population are Turkmen (77 per cent), the remainder being Russian (6.7 per cent) and Uzbek (9.2 per cent), with a smaller proportion of Kazakhs, Ukrainians, Armenians, Azerbaijanis, Belujis and Tartars.

In 2010, the crude birth rate was 21.6 per 1,000 population and the crude death rate was 8.7 per 1,000 population. In 2009, life expectancy at birth was 60 for males and 67 for females. Healthy life expectancy in 2007 was estimated at 53.0 for males and 57 for females. The infant mortality rate was estimated at 47 per 1,000 live births in 2010. In 2008 the maternal mortality rate was estimated at 130 per 100,000 live births. The fertility rate of women was estimated at 2.4 in 2010. (Source: http://www.who.int, World Health Statistics 2012)

The official language is Turkmen (72 per cent) although Russian (6.7 per cent), Uzbek (9.2 per cent), Kazakh (2 per cent) and other languages (5.1 per cent) are also spoken.

Public Holidays 2014
1 January: New Year
12 January: Memory Day
19 February: National Flag Day
8 March: International Women's Day
22 March: Novruz Bairam (Turkmen New Year)
8 May: Heroes Day
9 May: Victory Day
18 May: Constitution Day
29 July: End of Ramadan
6 October: Remembrance Day
5 October: Eid al-Adha*
27-28 October: Independence Day
* Islamic holidays depend on the sighting of the moon and therefore dates can vary.

EMPLOYMENT

The labour force was estimated at 2.09 million in 2004 with unemployment estimated at 60 per cent. The main employment sector is agriculture, which employs around 693,000 people. Other major sectors include education, culture and arts, employing 171,900; construction, employing 163,500; and industry (including manufacturing), which employs 154,300. The private sector currently employs approximately 22 per cent of the labour force.

Turkmenistan implemented an unemployment compensation scheme in April 1991; however, this was withdrawn six months later. At present there is no unemployment benefit. In 2004, 30 per cent of people were estimated to be below the poverty line.

BANKING AND FINANCE

Currency
1 Turkmen manat = 100 tenge.
The manat, replaced the Russian rouble in 1993.

GDP/GNP, Inflation, National Debt
The Turkmenistan economy hasd been boosted by its energy resources. It has large reserves of natural gas and oil. Turkmenistan reneogtiated prices for its oil exports to Russia and is trying to develop new export markets. There has been little economic reform and little privatisation. The agricultural sector is dominated by cotton production but the industry has been hindered by by a decline in production, over-intensive cultivation and out-of-date techniques.

In 2008, GDP reached an estimated US$28.8 billion, representing annual growth of 7.5 per cent, and per capita GDP stood at US$5,800. Growth was estimated at 11 per cent in 2007. The recent growth of GDP is attributable to increased production of gas, oil and wheat. In 2009, agriculture contributed 16.3 per cent to GDP, industry 42.7 per cent and services 41.0 per cent.

GDP by industrial origin at current market prices, million Manats

	2007	2008	2009
Total	27,000.0	43,638.0	49,464.8
Agriculture	5,090.8	5,288.3	7,940.3
Mining, Manufacturing, Electricity, gas and water	8,481.9	19,203.3	17,350.2
Construction	1,699.7	3,887.7	3,483.9
Trade	1,346.7	1,719.5	2,351.8
Transport & communications	2,046.0	2,635.0	3,592.4
Finance, Public admin.,Others	8,025.7	10,286.3	14,074.8

Source: Asian Development Bank

Turkmenistan's economy was one of the fastest growing in 2011 with a growth rate of 14.7 per cent. GDP was estimated at UD$27 billion in 2011.

The inflation rate dropped from 17 per cent in 1998 to 15 per cent in 1999 and 11 per cent in 2000. In 2005, it was estimated at 10.5 per cent, rising to 11 per cent in 2006. Estimates for 2007 put it over 30 per cent, falling to 12 per cent in 2008, 0.1 per cent in 2009, 3.5 per cent in 2010 and it was forecast to be 5.0 per cent in 2011.

Total outstanding debt was US$517 million in 2010.

Foreign Investment
The Law of Foreign Investment was implemented in 1993 offering tax incentives and protection from changes in legislation to foreign investors. Turkmenistan joined the World Bank in 1992.

Balance of Payments / Imports and Exports
Balance of Payments, million US$

	2007	2008	2009
Merchandise exports, fob	9,114.0	11,786.0	14,500.0
Merchandise imports, cif	3,780.0	5,363.0	6,600.0
Trade balance	5,334.0	6,423.0	7,900.0

Source: Asian Development Bank

The main exports are natural gas, cotton, petroleum products, textiles. During 1998, 58 per cent of oil products and 82 per cent of natural gas products were exported. Since 1998 Turkmenistan has suffered from a lack of export routes for its oil and gas, and exports fell.

However, due to the worldwide high prices for oil and gas, export earnings for these commodities remain high. In 2006 the country agreed a deal with China to construct a new natural gas pipeline. The main imports were machinery, equipment, chemicals and foodstuffs.

Direction of Trade, million US$

	2008	2009	2010
Exports, total	**9,943.0**	**2,954.7**	**3,105.3**
Turkey	353.9	297.8	351.2
UAE	269.0	182.9	228.2
Iran	222.6	151.3	188.8
Italy	275.6	56.0	177.9
Afghanistan	193.8	169.6	174.2
Imports, total	**5,290.5**	**6,472.6**	**5,978.8**
Russia	891.3	1,031.3	1,287.0
Turkey	729.2	1,039.6	1,253.1
China	883.3	1,007.5	574.3
UAE	538.9	366.4	457.2
Germany	290.7	393.2	357.0

Source: ADB

Central Bank

Central Bank of Turkmenistan, 22 Bitarap Turkmenistan Street, 744000 Ashgabat, Turkmenistan. Tel: +993 1 2353667 / 1 2510673, fax: +993 1 2355470 / 1 2510812, URL: http://www.cbt.tm/
Chairman: Tuvakmammed Japarov

MANUFACTURING, MINING AND SERVICES

Primary and Extractive Industries

Proven oil reserves amount to approximately 600 million barrels with the major fields being Kotur-Tepe and Nebit-Dag. Further reserves are in the Caspian Sea region, although at present there is some dispute as to which countries bordering the inland Caspian Sea have what rights. Oil production in 2010 was 223,430 barrels per day. Consumption was estimated at 196,740 bb/d. An estimated 78,000 bbld were exported. The two main refineries are Chardzhou and Turkmenbashi with a combined capacity to produce 236,970 barrels per day. A lubricants blending plant has also been built in Turkmenbashi. Two new projects have recently been implemented to increase oil production. The first involves bringing 160 idle wells back into operation by installing compressor stations and pipeline infrastructure to revive the wells. Once operational they are projected to yield 200-500 thousand tons of oil annually. The second project is to construct diesel fuel hydro-refinement units which would help to supply the European market with diesel.

Mineral extraction is the mainstay of the Turkmen economy. Chemical products in the country include iodine, bromine, sodium sulphate, Glauber's salt, potassium and rock salts, sulphur and sulphuric acid. There are also raw reserves of non-ferrous metals, marble onyx and the rare metals gold and platinum. By far the greatest opportunity for Turkmenistan's future expansion lies with its massive reserves of natural gas located in the Amu-Dar'ya and Murgab regions. There are currently natural gas reserves of 265 trillion cubic feet. During 2011 an estimated 2,338 billion cubic feet of natural gas were produced and 710 billion cubic feet were consumed. In 2006 Turkmenistan agreed a deal with China to build a pipeline to supply Turkmen natural gas to China and supply started in 2009. In 2007 Turkmenistan, Russia and Kazakhstan agreed on the construction of a pipeline to carry 10 billion cubic metres of natural gas. Traditionally exports of oil and gas have gone to Russia at reduced prices, but in March 2008 Russia agreed to pay Turkmenistan European-level prices for gas starting in 2009. Turkmenistan opened a second gas pipeline to Iran in January 2010 and in November of that year said it would supply gas to the Nabucco pipeline, meaning EU countires were less reliant on gas from Russia. In December 2010 Turkmenistan agreed to build a pipeline which will carry gas across Afghanistan to Pakistan and India although the logisitics of this plan were not given at the time.

Manufacturing

Turkmenistan is the second largest producer of raw cotton in the former Soviet Union, exporting 97 per cent of its output. The engineering industry manufactures centrifugal oil pumps and heavy-duty ventilators for the chemical industry. The textile industry is engaged in the processing of cotton, wool and cocoons. Hand-woven carpets are a traditional handicraft. For the majority of products, however, it is dependent on imports from Russia.

In common with the other smaller former Soviet republics, measures have been taken to liberalise all prices other than those for bread, milk, butter and meat, and to privatise a number of farmholds. In preparation for economic expansion, co-operation agreements were signed with Turkey and Iran and considerable plans for joint enterprises with foreign companies have been forged. These cover a number of industries from textiles to energy and tourism.

Energy

In 2009 Turkmenistan produced 15.86 billion kWh of electricity of which 11.12 billion kWh were consumed. There are four power stations: Bezrie, Marie, Krasnovodsk and Sedei. Nearly all of Turkmenistan's electricity is produced from fossil fuels.

Agriculture

The total area of land under cultivation is around 31.0 million hectares. In a country where two-thirds of the land is desert, the Kara-kum Canal, 1,069 km long, provides just enough water for agricultural areas requiring irrigation.

Cotton growing is the main branch of agriculture. Varieties of fine staple cotton are cultivated, although recent poor harvests have hampered production. Rice, wheat, and barley are also grown and many farms cultivate fruit, grapes, melons, gourds and vegetables. Four per cent of land use is arable and 65 per cent pasture.

Estimated figures for 2011 put the contribution of the agriculture sector to GDP as 8.0 per cent with 48.0 per cent of the population employed in the sector.

Agricultural Production in 2010

Produce	Int. $'000*	Tonnes
Cotton lint	514,513	360,000
Indigenous cattle meat	399,520	147,895
Indigenous sheep meat	353,027	129,656
Cow milk, whole, fresh	236,277	2,150,000
Wheat	154,879	3,000,000
Cottonseed	149,341	650,000
Grapes	138,560	242,400
Tomatoes	120,108	325,000
Wool, greasy	72,699	38,000
Hen eggs, in shell	41,470	50,000
Potatoes	38,735	245,000
Rice, paddy	37,647	144,600

* unofficial figures

Source: http://faostat.fao.org/site/339/default.aspx Food and Agriculture Organization of the United Nations, Food and Agricultural commodities production

A major trend in animal husbandry is the breeding of Astrakhan sheep. Other than sheep, cattle, camels, horses and goats are raised. Silkworm breeding has long been a tradition in the area. In 2003, there were 860,000 cattle and buffaloes and 6,370,000 sheep and goats. 65 per cent of land is used as pasture.

Recently 620 imported planters, cultivators and three wheeled tractors were purchased to assist the crop farmers. To increase rice production the areas allocated to rice cultivation were increased and the government offered 49.5 billion manat credit for the purchase of rice-seeds. Rice farmers were also offered a fixed discount of 50 per cent for the purchase of seeds, fertilizer, chemicals and transport services.

COMMUNICATIONS AND TRANSPORT

Travel Requirements

Citizens of the USA, Canada, Australia and the EU require a passport valid for six months and a visa. Other nationals should contact the embassy to check visa requirements. Visa regulations within the CIS are liable to change at short notice and all prospective travellers are advised to contact the nearest Turkmenistan embassy well in advance of intended date of departure. Visitors must register with the State Service of Turkmenistan for the Registration of Foreign Nationals if staying for more than three days. The World Health Organization recommends vaccinations against diphteria, hepatitis A and B, measles, mumps, polio, rubella, tetanus, typhoid and varicella.

National Airlines

Turkmenistan State Airline, Ashkhabad Airport, 744008, Turkmenistan. Tel: +993 12 256084
Turkmenistan Airlines, 80 Magtymguly Street, Ashgabat, Turkmenistan. Tel: +993 12 254857, URL: http://www.turkmenistanairlines.com

International Airports

Airports are located regionally in four areas and in the capital Ashkhabad. Twenty-two airports have paved runways. Airspace is controlled by the following regulatory body.
National Department of Civil Aviation, Turkmenia, 744008, Ashkhabad, Turkmenistan. Tel: +993 12 251052, fax: +993 12 254402

Railways

The total length of the railway system according to recent figures was 2,440 km. No trains cross the border but connections are available to Russia and Iran.

Roads

The total length of motor roads is 24,000 km, of which 19,500 km are hard-surfaced. Vehicles are driven on the right.

Ports and Harbours

The main port is at Turkmenbashi. There are 1,300 km of waterways. The merchant navy comprises seven ships (four cargo, two petroleum tankers and one cargo).

HEALTH

In 2009, the government spent approximately 9.9 per cent of its total budget on healthcare, accounting for 59.2 per cent of all healthcare spending. Private expenditure on health accounted for 40.8 per cent of general government expenditure on health. Total expenditure on healthcare equated to 2.5 per cent of the country's GDP. Per capita expenditure on health was approximately US$92, compared with US$45 in 2000. According to the WHO, in 2000-10 there were an estimated 12,176 doctors (23.9 per 10,000 population), 22,551 nurses and midwives (44.2 per 10,000 population), 953 pharmacists (1.9 per 10,000 population), and 7021 dentists (1.4 per 10,000 population). There were 40 hospital beds per 10,000 population.

In 2008, 97 per cent of the urban population had access to improved drinking water sources. In the same year, 99 per cent of the urban population and 97 per cent of the rural population have access to improved sanitation.

TUVALU

The infant mortality rate (probability of dying before age one) in 2010 was 47 per 1,000 live births. The child mortality rate (under 5 years) was 56 per 1,000 live births. The main causes of childhood mortality are: prematurity (21 per cent), diarrhoea (8 per cent), and pneumonia (16 per cent), birth asphyxia (10 per cent) and congenital anomalies (10 per cent). (Source: http://www.who.net, World Health Statistics 2012)

EDUCATION

Recent figures indicate that there are some 1,800 general schools accommodating 800,000 pupils. There are 38 special schools with 35,000 pupils, 14 higher education establishments with 42,000 students and 90 technical colleges. Due to a shortage of skilled workers in the country, a large-scale operation of sending young professionals abroad for further education is in operation. In 2003 the government brought to an end free tuition to university.

Primary education lasts for four years and begins at seven years of age. Compulsory secondary education was recently reduced from 11 years to nine years. Most teaching is carried out in Turkmen, some schools teach in Russian, Uzbek and Kazakh, but this is to be phased out and many ethnic Russian teachers have been dismissed leaving a teaching shortage.

The literacy rate is estimated at 99.5 per cent.

RELIGION

The constitution provides for freedom of religion and does not establish a state religion. However, in practice, the government monitors all forms of religious expression. The Sunni Muslim religion is practiced by 89 per cent of the population and Eastern Orthodox by 9 per cent. The religious board which reports to the President is comprised of an equal number of Muslim and Christian representatives.

Amendments to the law on religious organizations adopted in March 2004 reduced membership requirements from 500 to 5. All groups must register in order to gain legal status with the government. As of January 2006, there were two main religons registered (Sunni Islam and Russian Orthodox Christianity) and nine minority religious groups.

Turkmenistan has a religious liberty rating of 4 on a scale of 1 to 10 (10 is most freedom). (Source: World Religion Database)

COMMUNICATIONS AND MEDIA

While the constitution provides for freedom of the press, there is virtually no freedom of the press or of association. The government has full control of all media and restricts foreign publications. All aspects of the Turkmenistan media are government run. International satellite TV is available but is subject to censorship. Internet access is controlled by state bodies and Turkmentelecom.

Newspapers
The two main government daily papers are: **Turkmenistan** (in Turkmen) and **Neytralni Turkmenistan** (Neutral Turkmenistan) (in Russian) (URL: http://www.tmpress.gov.tm/). Both are published from the Ashgabat Press House, Ashgabat, Turkmenistan. Other newspapers include **Watan**, **Galkynys**, **TurkmenDunyasi** and **Adalat**.

Broadcasting
Turkmen TV operates four networks. International satellite television is available. Programmes are censored before being rebroadcast. It also broadcasts two radio stations. There are over 20 radio stations broadcasting in Turkmenistan and over 1.2 million radios are in use.

Telecommunications
The telecommunications network is poor and modernization is slow. In 2008 there were an estimated 480,000 telephone lines in operation and 1 million mobile phones. Turkmentelecom and other state organisations control internet access. In 2008, it was estimated that there were 75,000 internet users.

ENVIRONMENT

The main environmental issues affecting Turkmenistan are the contamination of soil and groundwater with agricultural chemicals and pesticides, salinisation and water-logging of soil due to poor irrigation methods, Caspian Sea pollution, diversion of a large share of the flow of the Amu Darya into irrigation contributes to the river's inability to replenish the Aral Sea, and desertification.

Turkmenistan is party to the following international agreements: Biodiversity, Climate Change, Climate Change-Kyoto Protocol, Desertification, Hazardous Wastes and Ozone Layer Protection.

According to the EIA, in 2010, Turkmenistan's emissions from the consumption of fossil fuels totalled 62.05 million metric tons of carbon dioxide up from 56.55 million metric tons the previous year.

SPACE PROGRAMME

The Turkmenistan National Space Agency was set up in 2011 to co-ordinate the country's space research programme. An agreement on space exploration was reached with China in 2011. Turkmenistan plans to launch its own satellite in 2014 from Sichan spaceport in China. The satellite will operate for 15 years.

TUVALU

Capital: Funafuti (Population estimate: 5,000)

Head of State: H.R.H. Elizabeth II (Sovereign) (page 1420)

Governor General: Sir Iakoba Taeia Italeli

National Flag: Light blue with Union Jack in top left-hand corner, and with nine stars on the right representing the nine atolls.

CONSTITUTION AND GOVERNMENT

Constitution
Until 1 October 1975 Tuvalu formed part of the Ellice Islands part of the then Gilbert and Ellice Islands Colony (GEIC). The decision to separate from the Gilberts and rename as Tuvalu, was made by the islanders at a referendum held in 1974 and had the full agreement of the Gilbert Islands Government. Independence from Britain was achieved on 1 October 1978, the third anniversary of separation.

The Queen of the United Kingdom is the head of state. She is represented by the Governor General who is appointed by the Queen on the advice of the Prime Minister. The constitution provides for a cabinet of four Ministers and a member of the House of Assembly. MPs vote on the position of prime minister. To view the Constitution, please visit: http://www.tuvaluislands.com/const_tuvalu.htm

Recent Events
Tuvalu is a special member of the Commonwealth, and in September 2000 became the 189th member of the UN.

Current disputes concerning Tuvalu becoming a republic have led to the forming a constitutional review committee to canvass the public on the abandoning of colonial ties.

In 2000 Tuvalu agreed to lease its internet domain name of .tv to a North American company for US$50m over 12 years.

In December 2000 the prime minister, Ionatana Ionatana, died while in office. Faimalaga Luka was elected to succeed him and took office in February 2001. Luka lost a vote of no confidence in 2001 and Koloa Talake became prime minister. A general election was held in 2002 and Saufatu Sopoanga was elected prime minister. He resigned in October 2004 following a vote of no confidence. Maatia Toafa succeeded him to office.

Tuvalu applied to the International Monetary Fund for membership in January 2009 and the request is under consideration.

Like many pacific nations Tuvalu took a keen interest in the 2009 Copenhagen Climate Conference; it rejected the climate pact as inadequate.

In December 2010, Prime Minister Maatia Toafa lost a vote of no confidence and was replaced by Willy Telavi.

In January 2011 the government introduced emergency laws banning public meetings after protesters demanded the resignation of the minister of finance.

A state of emergency was declared in October 2011 because of a severe shortage of fresh water.

Legislature
The Tuvalu Parliament consists of a single chamber called the House of Assembly with 15 members, who are directly elected for a four-year term. There are no political parties but the parliament divides into government and opposition.
House of Assembly, (Palamene O Tuvalu), Vaiaku, Funafuti, Tuvalu. Tel: +688 20250
Speaker: Kamuta Latasi

Cabinet (as at May 2013)
Prime Minister, Minister of Home Affairs: Willy Telavi (page 1524)
Minister for Communications, Transport & Public Utilities: Kausea Natano
Minister of Foreign Affairs: Apisai Ielemia
Minister of Finance: Lotoala Metia
Minister of Education: Dr Falesa Pito
Minister of Health: Taom Tanukale
Minister of Natural Resources: Isaia Italeli

Ministries

Governor General's Office, Tel: +688 20715, fax: +688 20843
Office of the Prime Minister, Tel: +688 20100, fax: +688 20820, URL: http://www.tuvaluislands.com/
Ministry of Home Affairs and Labour, Tel: +688 20172, fax: +688 20821
Ministry of Natural Resources and Environment, Tel: +688 20827, fax: +688 20826
Ministry of Finance and Economic Planning, Tel: +688 20202, fax: +688 20842
Ministry of Health and Social Welfare, Tel: +688 20403, fax: +688 20832
Ministry of Education and Culture, Tel: +688 20407
Ministry of Tourism, Trade and Commerce, Tel: +688 20182
Ministry for Works, Communications and Energy, Tel: +688 20052, fax: +688 20722

Elections

All citizens over the age 18 are entitled to vote. The last legislative elections were held in August 2006 and Apisai Ielemia became prime minister. The most recent elections were held on 16 September 2010. Ten out of the 15 candidates retained their seats. The incumbent prime minister, Apisai Ielemia retained his seat, however Maatia Toafa who was prime minister for two years between 2004-06 was elected as prime minister. A new cabinet was appointed. Mr Toafa was ousted in a no-confidence vote after only three months in power and replaced by Willy Telavi.

Diplomatic Representation

Tuvaluan Consulate, UK, Tuvalu House, 230 Worple Road, London, SW20 8RH, England. Tel: +44 (0)20 8879 0985, fax: +44 (0)20 8879 0985
Consul: Ifthkir Ayaz
US Embassy, URL: http://suva.usembassy.gov/
Ambassador: Frankie A. Reed
British High Commission, (All staff resident in Suva, Fiji), URL: http://ukinfiji.fco.gov.uk/en/
High Commissioner: Martin Fidler
Tuvalu at the United Nations, URL: http://www.tuvaluislands.com/un.html
Ambassador: H.E. Afelee Pita

LEGAL SYSTEM

The law is based on Acts of the Tuvalu Parliament, certain English Acts, common law and customary law.

The eight Island Courts have limited jurisdiction over both Tuvaluans and non-Tuvaluans in civil and criminal matters. A senior magistrate visits Tuvalu two or three times a year to hear more serious cases and appeals. A Chief Justice also visits twice a year to preside at sessions of the High Court of Tuvalu. The High Court has jurisdiction to consider appeals from the magistrates' courts and the Island Courts. Appeals from the High Court are to the Court of Appeal in Fiji or, in the ultimate case, to the Judicial Committee of the Privy Council in Britain.

The government respects the rights of its citizens. The death penalty has been abolished, and no execution has been carried out since independence was declared in 1978. In 2008 Tuvalu co-sponsored the Resolution on a Moratorium on the Use of the Death Penalty at the UN General Assembly.

LOCAL GOVERNMENT

There is a Town Council on Funafuti and Island Councils on the seven other main islands which are responsible for local affairs. Each council is made up of six members.

AREA AND POPULATION

Area

Tuvalu, formerly the Ellice Islands, comprises the nine low-lying islands of Nanumea, Nanumanga, Nuitao, Nui, Vaitupu, Nukufeatu, Funafuti, Nukulaela, and Niulakita. They are located slightly to the south of the equator between Micronesia and Melanesia, approximately 1,000 km north of Fiji. They are spread over 0.5 million sq. miles of ocean and have an aggregate land area of about 26 sq. km. The climate is tropical. The rainy season is November-March.

To view a map, consult http://www.lib.utexas.edu/maps/cia08/tuvalu_sm_2008.gif

Population

The population was approximately 10,000 in 2010 with a population density of about 373 per square km. The annual population growth was approximately 0.4 per cent over the period 2000-10. Approximately 50 per cent of the population lives in urban areas.

The Tuvaluan language is related to Samoan. A Gilbertese dialect, introduced by invaders several hundred years ago, is spoken on Nui. English is used throughout the islands. Ethnically, Tuvaluans are Polynesian. There are a few other races in the archipelago.

Births, Marriages, Deaths

Life expectancy at birth in 2009 was 64 years (64 years for males and 63 years for females). Healthy life expectancy at birth in 2007 was 58 years. An estimated 32 per cent of the population is under 15 years old, and 9 per cent over 65 years of age. The infant mortality rate in 2010 was 23 per 1,000 births and the neo-natal mortality rate was 10.5 per 1,000 live births. The fertility rate was estimated at 3.2 per female in 2009. (Source: http://www.who.int, World Health Statistics)

Public Holidays 2014

1 January: New Year's Day
17 March: Commonwealth Day
18 April: Good Friday
20 March: Easter Sunday
11 May: Gospel Day
9 June: Queen's Birthday
5 August: National Children's Day
1 October: Independence Day
14 November: Prince of Wales' Birthday
25 December: Christmas Day
26 December: Boxing Day

EMPLOYMENT

Recent figures estimate the workforce to be 3,615. An estimated 70 per cent of the official workforce are employed in the public sector. Most of the population is not part of the official work force and work in agriculture and fishing sectors, mainly at a subsistence level. About 1,200 Tuvaluans work abroad (Nauru) in the phosphate industry and as seamen, sending most of their wages home. Youth unemployment is growing. Per capita income is estimated at US$2,000.

BANKING AND FINANCE

Currency

Australian currency is legal tender, although Tuvalu also has its own dollar coins in circulation.

GDP/GNP, Inflation, National Debt

Tuvalu's economy suffers because of its remote location and lack of natural resouces. The economy is based on fishing and subsidence farming. The public sector accounts for 70 per cent of GDP. Remittances from abroad are a major souurce of income. The lack of infrastructure has hindered any significant development.

GDP by Industrial Origin at Current Prices, AU$000

Industry	2007	2008
Total	33,650	35,322
Agriculture	7,268	7,693
Mining	39	40
Manufacturing	251	388
Electricity, gas & water	200	200
Construction	2,809	2,452
Trade	4,453	4,620
Transport & communications	1,833	1,887
Finance	4,864	5,467
Public administration	5,035	5,423
Others	4,982	5,050

Source: Asian Development Bank

Per capita GDP was estimated to be Aus$3,426 in 2008. GDP was estimated to be US$35 million in 2011. The service sector is the largest contributor to GDP, at 67.6 per cent; agriculture contributes 23.2 per cent and industry 9.3 per cent. Annual growth was estimated at 4.9 per cent in 2007 and 1.3 per cent in 2008. The government is hoping to reform the public sector which accounts for 70 per cent of GDP.

Inflation was estimated at 5.64 per cent in 2006. It fell slightly to 5.3 per cent in 2008, 3.8 per cent in 2009, 3.5 per cent in 2010 and was forecast at 4.2 per cent in 2011.

Foreign Investment

With little economic activity of its own, Tuvalu survives mainly by the granting of foreign fishing rights and by receipt of extensive financial aid from abroad. Australia is the principal source of finance for the Tuvaluan expenditure budget. There are little or no savings or investments.

Significant aid donors include Australia, Britain, New Zealand, the European Development Fund (EDF), the United Nations Development Programme (UNDP), Canada, Japan, and Germany. In 1987 the Tuvalu Trust Fund was set up to help the government achieve greater financial autonomy and develop the infrastructure. The Fund was set up with contributions from the UK, Australia and New Zealand, followed by Japan and the Republic of Korea, and these governments have continued to make contributions.

Balance of Payments / Imports and Exports
External Trade in Thousand Aus$

Year	Exports, fob	Imports, cif	Balance
2001	32	6,769	-6,737
2002	252	20,362	-20,110
2003	147	24,043	-23,896
2004	182	15,499	-15,499
2005	80	16,908	-16,828
2006	130	17,903	-17,773
2007	120	18,503	-18,383

Source: Asian Development Bank

Main exported goods are copra, stamps, and handicrafts. Main imported goods are food, animals manufactured goods, fuels and machinery. The main trading nations for Tuvalu are the UK, Fiji, Japan, New Zealand, Australia, China, Italy, Poland and Germany.

TUVALU

Internet addresses for Tuvalu end in .tv. A company called dotTV now sells Tuvaluan websites to people, particularly television companies, who wish to have .tv as part of their address. Tuvalu hoped to earn US$4million per annum for the twelve-year lease (2000-2012) but earnings have not been this high.

Major Banks
The National Bank of Tuvalu, is a joint venture between the Tuvalu Government and Westpac Banking Corporation.
PO Box 13, Vaiaku, Funafuti, Tuvalu. Tel: +688 20803 / 20804, fax: +688 20802 / 20864, e-mail: nbt@tuvalu.tv
Development Bank of Tuvalu, Teone, Funafuti, Tuvalu; Tel. +688 20850 / 20198, fax: +688 20850

MANUFACTURING, MINING AND SERVICES

Energy
An estimated 4,226,000 kWh of electricity were consumed in 2005.

Agriculture
Agriculture provides subsistence for most of the population. Copra production, pork and poultry processing and goat tending are all important. The government encourages planting of improved hybrid crops by the smallholder, particularly crops of indigenous vegetables.

In 1990 a severe cyclone devastated Tuvalu by destroying plantation crops, buildings and the homes of many inhabitants. Cyclone Kelo severely damaged the Islands of Niulakita and Nukulaelae in 1997.

Agricultural Production in 2010

Produce	Int. $'000*	Tonnes
Coconuts	254	2,300
Indigenous pigmeat	175	114
Fruit, tropical fresh nes	172	420
Bananas	113	400
Vegetables fresh nes	104	550
Indigenous chicken meat	71	50
Roots and tubers, nes	27	160
Hen eggs, in shell	25	30
Honey, natural	15	6

* unofficial figures
Source: http://faostat.fao.org/site/339/default.aspx Food and Agriculture Organization of the United Nations, Food and Agricultural commodities production

A South Pacific Commission study on fishing concluded that there were plentiful bait fish and possibly skipjack in the waters around Tuvalu. In 1993 the total catch weighed approximately 1,460 tonnes. The fishing vessel Te Tautai, a gift from the Japanese, operates in and around Tuvalu waters. Licensing fees from foreign fishing vessels have increased. Forecast figures from the FAO put the total catch in 2010 at 11,324 tonnes.

Service Industries
There is very little tourism and only one hotel. Visitors numbered 639 in 1995. The tourism industry is hindered by the remoteness of the location.

COMMUNICATIONS AND TRANSPORT

Travel Requirements
Citizens of Canada, Australia and most of the EU require a passport valid for six months, sufficient funds, proof of accommodation and an onward/return ticket but do not need a visa for stays of up to 30 days. Entry permits for one-month stays are issued on arrival. Citizens of Bulgaria, Cyprus, Czech Republic, Estonia, Hungary, Latvia, Lithuania, Malta, Poland, Romania, Slovak Republic and Slovenia do require a visa, as do US citizens, unless their passport was issued by the Marshall Islands. Transit passengers continuing their journey within 24 hours and not leaving the airport transit lounge do not need a visa. Other nationals should contact the embassy to check visa requirements.

International Airports
Fiji Air, a domestic operator in Fiji, flies between Suva and Funafuti, the only airfield, three times a week. The Airline of the Marshall Islands connects Tuvalu with Nadi, Fiji and Tarawa in Kiribati once a week.

Roads
Tuvalu has only a few roads made from impacted coral and supplemented by dirt tracks, New roads have been built using monies from the sale of Tuvulu's .tv internet domain.

Shipping
The port of entry is Funafuti, which has a deep-water lagoon 20 km by 16 km with three entrance passages. A deep-water wharf, provided with Australian aid of nearly $2.7 million, allows ships drawing up to 5m to come alongside. A ferry service to the islands operates from Funafuti.

HEALTH

There is a hospital on Funafuti with 56 beds and dispensaries on all the islands. In 2009, the government spent approximately 10 per cent of its total budget on healthcare (up from 5.0 per cent in 2000), accounting for 94.7 per cent of all healthcare spending. Total expenditure on healthcare equated to 14.3 per cent of the country's GDP. Per capita expenditure on health was approximately US$396, compared with US$161 in 2000. According to the WHO, in 2005-10 there were 12 doctors (10.9 per 10,000 population), 64 nurses and midwives (58.2 per 10,000 population), 2 dentists and 1 pharmacist. There are an estimated 56 hospital beds per 10,000 population. In 2010, an estimated 98 per cent of the population had sustainable access to improved drinking water sources and 85 per cent sustainable access to improved sanitation. There are occasional outbreaks of mosquito-borne dengue fever but no reported cases of malaria. (Source: http://www.who.int, World Health Statistics)

EDUCATION

Primary/Secondary Education
There are primary schools on each of the nine islands, and a secondary school at Motofoua on Vaitupu. These are financed by the government and administered jointly by the Government and the Tuvalu Church.

All children in Tuvalu attend primary school. Children enter school at the age of six and those selected transfer to the secondary school at ages eleven to thirteen. The primary schools consist of nine classes and are each staffed by trained teachers. The teacher-pupil ratio is 1:24. Secondary education goes to School Certificate level. All Tuvaluans requiring advanced training have to attend courses overseas. Education between the ages of 6 and 15 is free and compulsory.

Vocational Education
Community training centres were established in all islands during the period 1979-83. The main objective of these centres is to provide basic skills and training appropriate to the rural way of life for children who do not go on to secondary education. Subjects taught include English, mathematics, local history and customs, woodwork, metal work, cooking and sewing.

The literacy rate is estimated at 95 per cent.

RELIGION

Most of the islanders are adherents of the Church of Tuvalu, which is a Christian church. There are a small number of followers of the Seventh Day Adventist Church and the Baha'i faith.

Tuvalu has a religious tolerance rating of 7 on a scale of 1 to 10 (10 is most freedom). (Source: World Religion Database)

COMMUNICATIONS AND MEDIA

Media freedom is respected.

Newspapers
A government publication, the Tuvalu Echoes, is published once a fortnight and Te Lama, a religious publication, is published monthly. The government published a news/fact sheet called Sikuleo o Tuvalou. The government also produces an online news service, Tuvalu News.
Tuvalu News, URL: http://www.tuvalu-news.tv/

Broadcasting
Radio Tuvalu is state-run. Satellite is available and offers foreign TV stations.

Telecommunications
There are radiotelephone communications between each island. International calls may be made by satellite. In 2008 there were estimated to be 1,500 main lines in use and 2,000 mobile phones. Recent estimates put the number of internet users at 4,000. Tuvalu has exploited its internet suffix 'tv'; licenses of the suffix have brought in several million dollars of revenue.

ENVIRONMENT

Climate change is of particular concern to Tuvaluans, especially in respect of rising sea levels; the highest point on Tuvalu is only 4.5 metres above sea level. As a result of this problem Tuvalu and New Zealand came to an agreement in October 2001 that New Zealand will accept an annual quota of Tuvaluan refugees escaping from rising sea levels. A land and sea-level monitoring station has been commissioned. In 2009, Taiwan offered to help Tuvalu deal with rising sea levels. Tuvalu is one of the few countries to recognise Taiwan.

There is also no potable water and water needs are met by catchment systems. There is one desalination plant with plans to build another. In October 2011, a state of emergency was declared because of a severe shortage of fresh water. The affected areas included Funafuti. Tuvalu has been experiencing a drought blamed on La Nina weather systems.

Tuvalu is party to the following international treaties: Biodiversity, Climate Change, Climate Change-Kyoto Protocol, Desertification, Law of the Sea, Ozone Layer Protection, Ship Pollution, Whaling.

UGANDA
Republic of Uganda

Capital: Kampala (Population estimate, 2011: 1.42 million)

Head of State: Lt.-Gen. Yoweri K. Museveni (President) (page 1483)

Vice President: Edward Kiwanuka Sekandi (page 1519)

National Flag: The national flag is six horizontal stripes of black, yellow, red, and a white central disc bearing a representation of the Balearic Crested Crane - the national symbol

CONSTITUTION AND GOVERNMENT

Constitution
Uganda became internally self-governing on 1 March 1962. In the general election which followed, the Democratic Party Government was defeated by the Uganda People's Congress alliance with the Kabaka Yekka movement. Dr. A.M. Obote, president of the Uganda People's Congress, took office as prime minister on 1 May 1962.

A further series of constitutional talks were held in London in June 1962 to pave the way for complete independence on 9 October 1962. Under the new constitution, known as 'The Constitution of Uganda (First Amendment) Act, 1962', Uganda became an Independent Sovereign State on 9 October 1963. On that date, the governor-general, who was the Queen's representative, was replaced by a Ugandan head of state - the president. On 15 April 1966 Dr. A.M. Obote, formerly prime minister of Uganda, was sworn in as president.

On 8 September 1967, a new constitution was enacted by Parliament sitting as a Constituent Assembly. Under the new constitution, the country became a republic with an executive president who was head of state, head of government and Commander-in-Chief of the Armed Forces. The institutions of Kings and Constitutional Rulers were abolished.

In January 1971 there was a military coup and Dr A.M. Obote and his government were replaced by the regime of Field-Marshal Idi Amin Dada, Military Head of State and Government and Commander-in-Chief of the Armed Forces, who appointed a Council of Ministers of the Military Government of the Second Republic of Uganda. On 2 February 1971, General (as he then was) Amin announced the suspension of some sections of the constitution. He also amended the constitution to give himself absolute power. Over the course of several years the economy weakened whilst internal oppression increased. Some 300,000 opponents are believed to have died under his rule. 50,000 Asians were also expelled. In 1978 Ugandan troops made an incursion into Tanzanian territory. It was repulsed by Tanzanian troops and fighting continued until they captured Kampala in April 1979. Amin subsequently fled the country.

Shortly after Amin's departure a short-lived ministerial-style administration, the National Consultative Commission (the NCC), was established under the presidency of Mr Yusuf Lule. The NCC then replaced Mr Lule with Mr G. Binaisa who was himself removed in May 1980. The country was governed by a military commission until elections took place. In December 1980, however, President Milton Obote's Uganda People's Congress won an election contested by four parties, with the Democratic Party forming the main opposition party in Parliament. Obote was deposed by forces led by Brigadier Basilio Okello on 27 July 1985. A Military Council was formed, chaired by General Tito Okello, sections of the constitution suspended and Parliament dissolved. An appeal was made to all opposition parties and groups to lay down their arms and participate in forming a broad based civilian cabinet which would pave the way for elections a year later. However violence and internal repression continued. 100,000 people are believed to have died.

In 1986 the National Resistance Movement formed a coalition bringing together the various political organisations in Uganda including the Uganda People's Congress, Democratic Party, Uganda Freedom Movement, Federal Democratic Movement and Uganda National Rescue Front. The coalition seized control of the country and Yoweri Museveni was installed as president.

In 1995 a new constitution was promulgated replacing the 1967 constitution. According to the Constitution, the administrative structure of Uganda consists of the executive, headed by the president, the legislature and the judiciary. The President is the Head of State and Commander-in-Chief of the Armed Forces. The president is elected every five years for a maximum of two terms.

In June 2000 Ugandans voted in a referendum to decide whether to return to multi-party politics or retain the current "no party" system. They voted to continue with the "no-party" system. The referendum was criticised for its low turnout and unfair restrictions. In 2002 the Constitutional Review Commission began to review the 1995 constitution. A report was published in March 2004. The Cabinet suggested a number of changes including the introduction of a multi-party system. The presidential term was also under review, with the possibility of removing the two term limit.

In July 2005 the constitution was amended to abolish the presidential term limits.

For further information on the constitution, please visit: http://www.parliament.go.ug/images/abridged_constitution_2006.pdf

International Relations
Uganda is a member of the Commonwealth and the East African Community. As a member of the InterGovernmental Authority on Development Uganda has peacekeeping trooped stationed in Somalia. In recent years, relations have been strained between Uganda and the Democratic Republic of Congo (DRC); in August 2007 Uganda and the DRC agreed to try to defuse a border dispute. As a result of disputes with the DRC, relations neighbouring Rwanda have suffered, but meetings with the Rwandan president have eased tensions.

Recent Events
Since the mid eighties the Lord's Resistance Army (LRA) has been resisting President Museveni's government in northern Uganda. The organisation was involved in a campaign of intimidation and was believed to be responsible for the abduction of 20,000 children. The violence displaced well over a million people. It was thought that the aim of the LRA was to run the country based on the Ten Commandments from the Bible. In August 2002 President Museveni tried to broker a cease fire so that peace talks could begin, but the offer was refused. In March 2003 LRA leader Joseph Kony tried to initiate a ceasefire but fighting soon broke out. Talks between the LRA and the government began in July 2006 and the following month a truce was signed. However, subsequent peace talks were marred by regular walk-outs. A permanent ceasefire was agreed in February 2008, but Joseph Kony refused to sign a peace deal in April, possibly because he was seeking guarantees about arrest warrants from the International Criminal Court (ICC). Over the following months, he was reported to have looted villages and abducted civilians from the Central African Republic, Sudan and Congo.

In February 2004 a group of opposition parties announced they were forming a coalition in an attempt to win the next general election. The G7 coalition included the Democratic Party, the Ugandan People's Congress and the Reform Agenda. In May 2005 the National Assembly voted to hold a referendum on whether to return to multiparty politics ahead of elections in 2006. As a result, the first multiparty elections for 25 years took place in February 2006.

In September 2007 a state of emergency was imposed when severe flooding caused widespread devastation.

The government and the Lord's Resistance Army (LRA) signed a permanent ceasefire in February 2008. However the ceasefire was not supported by the leader, Joseph Kony, who also failed to sign a peace deal in November. An offensive was launched against various LRA bases. In March 2009 the Ugandan army began to withdraw from the DRC where it had pursued rebels from the LRA.

In June 2010, a corruption investigation began into the activities of Vice-President Gilbert Bukenya, the Foreign Minister Sam Kutesa and several other ministers over the alleged theft of US$25 million.

In July 2010 a Somali Islamist group Al-Shabab claimed a responsibility for two bomb attacks in Kampala that killed over 70 people.

Treason charges against opposition leader Kizza Besigye were dropped in October 2010 by the Constitutional Court. Mr Besigye ran for president in the February 2011 elections won by the incumbent Mr Musevni. Mr Besigye denounced the result as a sham. Mr Besigye was arrested several times in the following months over protests against rising prices.

In September 2011, a Kenyan court ordered the release of the LRA commander Thomas Kwoyelo. In May 2012, the army captured a senior LRA commander, Caesar Achellam. Thousands of refugees fled into Uganda to escape fighting from neighbouring DR Congo.

In November 2012, Uganda announced it was to withdraw from UN international missions, in response to allegations that it had been arming Congolese rebels.

Legislature
The National Assembly consists of 276 members who serve a five year term. 214 are elected by constituencies and 62 are elected indirectly to represent certain groups e.g. women, workers and the disabled.
National Assembly, Parliamentary Buildings, PO Box 7178, Kampala, Uganda. Tel: +256 4134 7440, fax: +256 4123 1296, e-mail: mail@parliament.go.ug, URL: http://www.parliament.go.ug

---

Cabinet (as at June 2013)
Prime Minister: Amama Mbabazi
First Deputy Prime Minister and Minister of Public Service: Henry Kajura
Second Deputy Prime Minister and Leader of Government Business in Parliament: Gen. Moses Ali
Minister of Foreign Affairs: Sam Kahamba Kutesa (page 1459)
Minister of Security: Wilson Mukasa
Minister for the Presidency: Frank Tumwebaze
Minister of Gender, Labour & Social Affairs: Mary Karooro Okurut
Minister responsible for General Duties in the Office of the Prime Minister: Tarsis Kabwegyere
Minister of Agriculture, Animal Industry and Fisheries: Tress Bucyanayandi
Minister of Defence: Crispus W.C.B. Kiyonga
Minister of Relief and Disaster Management: Hilary Onek (page 1489)
Minister of Education and Sports: Jessica Alupo
Minister of Energy and Mineral Development: Irene Muloni
Minister of Internal Affairs: Nyakairima Aronda

UGANDA

Minister of Finance: Maria Kiwanuka (page 1457)
Minister of Public Works and Transport: Abraham Byandaala
Attorney General: Peter Nyombi
Minister of Justice and Constitutional Affairs: Major Gen. Kahinda Otafiire
Ministry of Trade and Industry: Amelia Kyambadde
Minister of Tourism and Wildlife: Maria Mutagamba
Minister of Water and the Environment: Ephraim Kamuntu
Minister of Lands, Housing and Urban Development: Daudi Migereko
Minister of Health: Ruhakana Ruganda
Minister of Communications and Information Technology: John Nasasira Mwoono
Minister of Local Government: Adolf Mwesige
Minister without Portfolio in Charge of Political Mobilization: Richard Todwong
Minister for Karamoja: Janet Kataaha Museveni
Minister, Office of the Prime Minister: Kabwegyere Tarsis

Ministries

The Office of the President, PO Box 7168 Kampala, Uganda. Tel: +256 41 345915, fax: +256 41 346102, e-mail: info@statehouse.go.ug, URL: http://www.statehouse.go.ug/
The Office of the Vice-President, PO Box 7359, Kampala, Uganda. Tel: +256 41 345915, fax: +256 41 346102, e-mail: vp@statehouse.go.ug, URL: http://www.statehouse.go.ug/
The Office of the Prime Minister, PO Box 341, Kampala, Uganda. Tel: +256 41 259081/232575, fax: +256 41 242341
The Office of the First Deputy Prime Minister, PO Box 7048, Kampala, Uganda. Tel: +256 41 233922/244975/230911/258252/257525, fax: +256 41 258722
Ministry of Defence, PO Box 7069, Kampala, Uganda. Tel: +256 41 270331/9, fax: +256 41 245911
Ministry of Agriculture, Animal Industry and Fisheries, PO Box 102, Entebbe, Uganda. Tel: +256 42 20981/9, fax: +256 42 21042/21047, e-mail: info@agric.go.ug, URL: http://www.agriculture.go.ug
Ministry of Gender, Labour and Social Development, PO Box 7168, Kampala, Uganda. Tel: +256 41 233484/235294/233463, fax: +256 41 234290
Ministry of Education and Sports, PO Box 7063, Kampala, Uganda. Tel: +256 41 234440, fax: +256 41 234194, e-mail: mine@starcom.co.ug, URL: http://www.education.go.ug
Ministry of Finance, Planning and Economic Development, Appollo Kaggwa Rd, Plot 2/4, P O Box 8147, Kampala, Uganda. Tel: +256 41 235051, fax: +256 41 230163, e-mail: finance@starcom.co.ug, URL: http://www.finance.go.ug
Ministry of Health, Kitante Road, P.O. Box 7272, Kampala, Uganda. Tel: +256 42 340884, fax: +256 42 340887, e-mail: info@health.go.ug, URL: http://www.health.go.ug
Ministry of Information, P O Box 7142, Kampala, Uganda. Tel: +256 41 254461, fax: +256 41 256888, e-mail: ugabro@infocom.co.ug
Ministry of Internal Affairs, Crested Towers, P O Box 7084, Kampala, Uganda. Tel: +256 41 233814/ 231031, fax: +256 41 231188 / 231641, e-mail: immigi@infocom.co.ug, URL: http://www.immigration.go.ug/
Ministry of Justice and Constitutional Affairs and the Office of The Attorney General, Parliament Building, P O Box 7183, Kampala, Uganda. Tel: +256 41 230538, fax: +256 41 254829, e-mail: mojca@africaonline.co.ug, URL: http://www.justice.go.ug
Ministry of Water, Lands and Environment, P O Box, 7096, Kampala, Uganda. Tel: +256 41 342931/3, fax: 256 41 230891, e-mail: mwle@mwle.go.ug, URL: http://www.mwle.go.ug/
Ministry of Local Government, Uganda House, P O Box 7037, Kampala, Uganda. Tel: +256 41 341224, fax: +256 41 258127 / 347339, e-mail: info@molg.go.ug, URL: http://www.molg.go.ug
Ministry of Energy and Minerals, Amber House Plot No. 29/33, P O Box 7270, Kampala, Uganda. Tel: +256 41 234733, fax: +256 41 234732 , e-mail: psmemd@energy.go.ug, URL: http://www.energyandminerals.go.ug/
Ministry of Public Service, Buganda Road, P O Box 7003, Kampala, Uganda. Tel: +256 41 251003, fax: +256 41 255467, e-mail: mps_feedback@mail.com, URL: http://www.publicservice.go.ug/
Ministry of Tourism, Trade and Industry, Plot 1, Parliament Avenue, P O Box 4241, Kampala, Uganda. Tel: +256 41 243947/256395, fax: +256 41 245077
Ministry of Works, Housing and Communications, Airport Road, P O Box 10, Entebbe, Uganda. Tel: +256 42 320101, fax: +256 42 320135, e-mail: mowhc@utlonline.co.ug, URL: http://www.miniworks.go.ug
Ministry of Foreign Affairs, Parliament Avenue, P.O.Box 7048 Kampala. Tel: +256 41 345661 / 257525 / 258252, fax: +256 41 258722 / 232874, e-ail: info@mofa.go.ug, URL: http://www.mofa.go.ug

Political Parties

Democratic Party (DP); Forum for Democratic Change (FDC); National Resistance Movement (NRM); Uganda People's Congress (UPC).

Elections

Suffrage is universal at 18. The most recent presidential elections were held in February 2011. Yoweri K. Museveni was re-elected with over 68 per cent of the vote. The most recent parliamentary elections were also held in February 2011 and Museveni's party won 258 of the 351 seats. The next elections are due in 2016.

Diplomatic Representation

American Embassy, 1577 Ggaba Road, P.O. Box 7007, Kampala, Uganda. Tel: +256 41 259792, fax: +256 41 259794, URL: http://kampala.usembassy.gov
Ambassador: Scott DeLisi (page 1414)
British High Commission, 4 Windsor Loop, PO Box 7070, Kampala, Uganda. Tel: +256 31 231 2000, e-mail: bhcinfo@starcom.co.ug, URL: http://www.ukinuganda.fco.gov.uk
High Commissioner: Alison Blackburne (page 1396)
Ugandan Embassy, 5911 16th Street NW, Washington, DC 20011, USA. Tel: +1 202 726 7100, fax: +1 202 726 1727, e-mail: ugembassy@aol.com, URL: http://www.ugandaembassy.com
Ambassador: Perezi K. Kamunanwire

High Commission of the Republic of Uganda, Uganda House, 58-59 Trafalgar Square, London, WC2N 5DX. Tel: +44 (0)20 7839 5783, fax: +44 (0)20 7839 8925, URL: http://www.ugandahighcommission.co.uk/
High Commissioner: Mrs Joan Kakima Nyakatuura Rwabyomere
Permanent Mission of the Republic of Uganda to the United Nations, Uganda House, 336 East, 45th Street, New York, NY 10017, USA. Tel: +1 212 949 0110, fax: +1 212 687 4517, URL: http://www.ugandamissionunny.net/
Ambassador: Adonia Ayebare

LEGAL SYSTEM

The legal system is based on English common law and customary law. Whilst the president has some control over the appointment of judges, the courts are largely independent.

The chief magistrate's court which hears appeals from magistrate courts, and further appeals are heard by the High Court, which has full criminal and civil jurisdiction. It consists of the chief justice and a number of puisne justices. The Court of Appeal hears appeals from the High Court, and is also a Constitutional Court. The Deputy Chief Justice, assisted by seven judges, heads the Court of Appeal. The Supreme Court stands out at the top of the judicial pyramid as a final Court of Appeal. It consists of the Chief Justice and six other Justices. The decisions of the Supreme Court form precedents followed by all lower courts.

A military court system handles offenses involving military personnel. Village resistance councils (RCs) handle petty disputes involving land ownership and debts. Their decisions can be appealed at magistrate's courts, but such appeals are rare, due to cost considerations and ignorance of the right to appeal.

The Chief Justice and other judges are appointed by the president on the advice of the Judicial Service Commission. Judges may not be removed from office before the retiring age except for physical or mental incapacity or for misconduct.

The government's human rights record is poor. There have been unlawful killings, as well as torture and abuse of suspects by security forces in recent years. There is official impunity. Arrests and detentions can be arbitrary, and prison conditions are harsh. There are restrictions on freedoms of speech, press, assembly, association, and religion. Official corruption is widespread.

Uganda retains the death penalty, though no civilian executions have been carried out since 1999. In January 2009, the Supreme Court ruled in a case involving more than 400 death row inmates that, whilst *mandatory* death penalty is unconstitutional, the death penalty is constitutional, but said it was unreasonable to keep convicts on death row for more than three years. Therefore most of the prisoners involved in the case had their sentences commuted to life in prison. In 2012, Uganda ruled out the death penalty as a punishment for some homsosexual acts.

Judiciary of Uganda, URL: http://www.judicature.go.ug/
Chief Justice: Hon. Justice Benjamin Odoki

Human Rights Commission, Plot 20-24, Buganda Road, Box 4929, Kampala, Uganda. + 256 41 348007, e-mail: uhrc@uhrc.ug, URL: http://www.uhrc.ug/

LOCAL GOVERNMENT

The number of districts in Uganda has increased in recently. As of 2011, Uganda is divided into 111 districts and one city (the capital city of Kampala) across four administrative regions. Most districts are named after their main commercial and administrative towns. Each district is further divided into counties and municipalities.The head elected official in a district is the Chairperson of the Local Council. A county is made up of several sub-counties. Each county is represented in the national parliament in Kampala by an elected member (an MP). Executive committee members of all the sub-counties constitute the local council. They then elect an executive committee from among themselves. These committees have limited powers, except in municipalities, which they run. A sub-county is made up of a number of parishes which in turn are made up of a number of villages. Each parish has a local council committee, made up of all the chairman from the village committes in the parish. The parish is mainly run by a parish chief. A village is the lowest political administrative unit. A village usually consists of between 50 and 70 households. Each village will be run by a local council.

AREA AND POPULATION

Area
Uganda is situated in central Africa. It borders Sudan in the north, Kenya to the east, Lake Victoria, Tanzania and Rwanda in the south and Democratic Republic of Congo to the west. With an area of 238,462 sq. km, including 39,000 sq. km of swamps and 95,823 sq. km of water, Uganda is comparable in size with the United Kingdom. The area of Africa that Uganda is situated in is often known as the Great Lakes. 20 per cent of Uganda itself is made up of lakes it contains Lake Kwania and Lake George and Lakes Albert. Edward and Victoria form borders with neighbouring countries. Uganda contains rain forest and is mountainous in the western region. The equator runs through Uganda. The climate is tropical, mainly rainy with two dry seasons (December to February and June to August). The northeast has semi-arid conditions.

To view a map, consult http://www.un.org/Depts/Cartographic/map/profile/uganda.pdf

Population
The population is grouped into three large ethnic groups - the Bantu found in central, southern and western Uganda and in some districts of the eastern region; the Nilotics in northern Uganda; and the Nilo-Hamites in eastern and north-eastern Uganda.

The population in 2010 was estimated at approximately 33.425 million with an average annual growth rate of 3.2 per cent over the period 2000-10. The population is predominantly rural. There are several large towns and an estimated 21 per cent live in urban areas. In 2011 the population of Kampala was approximately 1.42 million, Kampala is both the administrative and commercial centre of Uganda. Entebbe (population 43,000) shares with Kampala the functions of administration. Jinja is the largest industrial town (population 65,000). Mbale is the largest town in the eastern region, with a population of about 54,000. Gulu is the largest in the northern region with a population of about 38,000 people. In 1998, population density was 85.3 people per square km. Uganda is also a temporary home to over 200,000 refugees mainly from Sudan, Rwanda and the Democratic Republic of Congo.

English is the official language used in schools, government transactions and courts of law. Kiswahili and Luganda are widely spoken and understood. In addition to these languages each of the major tribes in Uganda is identified by its own language or dialect.

Births, Marriages, Deaths
In 2010, there were an estimated 45.2 births per 1,000 population and 13.1 deaths per 1,000 population. The average female fertility rate was 6.1 children. The average life expectancy at birth in 2009 was 48 years for males and 57 years for females. Healthy life expectancy is respectively 41 and 44 years. The median age in Uganda is 16 years old. Over 48 per cent of the population are aged 14 years or younger and 4 per cent over 60. (Source: http://www.who.int, World Health Statistics 2012)

Public Holidays 2014
1 January: New Year's Day
26 January: Liberation Day
8 March: International Women's Day
18 April: Good Friday
21 April: Easter Monday
5 May: Labour Day
3 June: Uganda Martyrs Day
9 June: National Heroes Day
29 July: Eid al-Fitr*
9 October: Independence Day
5 October: Eid al-Adha*
25 December: Christmas Day
26 December: Boxing Day
* Islamic holidays depend on the sighting of the moon and so dates can vary.

EMPLOYMENT

Estimated figures for 2010 show that the labour force numbered 15.5 million, the national unemployment rate was recently estimated at 3.5 per cent and the underemployment rate was 16.9 per cent. The majority of the population (82 per cent) are employed in the agriculture sector.

BANKING AND FINANCE

Currency
The unit of currency is the Uganda New Shilling of 100 cents.

GDP/GNP, Inflation, National Debt
Uganda's economy is based around agriculture which is the main livelihood of over 80 per cent of the poopulation. Growth has been fairly steady in recent years and needs to average approximately 7 per cent per year to meet the UN Millennium poverty-reduction goals.

Aid dependency, outstanding debts and insufficient tax resources have in the past hindered Uganda's economic growth rate. Corruption also remains a problem. Growth is also affected by climatic conditions as Uganda can experience both heavy rain and severe droughts. The country has experience good growth over the last 10 years, helped by politcal stability, liberal reforms and the discovery of oil. GDP growth was estimated at 6.3 per cent in 2003 and 5.6 per cent in 2004 below the UN 7 per cent target. Growth in 2007 was estimated at 7 per cent. Oil reserves have been found in Uganda and are estimated to be at least 2 billion barrels. It is currently estimated that small scale production may begin in 2016. GDP was estimated at US$14 billion in 2008 and per capita GDP was US$440. GDP rose to US$16 billion in 2009 and to US$17 billion by 2011.

In 2009, services contributed 48 per cent to GDP, agriculture and manufacturing 29 per cent each.

The inflation rate has decreased dramatically since 1991, from 54 per cent in 1991 to 5.8 per cent in 2000. It rose to 7.3 per cent in 2006, fell to 6.4 per cent in 2007 and averaged 7.0 per cent in 2008 and 2009. Inflation was estimated to be 27 per cent in 2011.

External debt in 2006 was estimated to be US$1,106.50 million. (Source: AFDB) Increased government borrowing has led to a rapid rise in the total external debt; it was estimated at UD$4 billion in 2012 (24 per cent of GDP). It is forecast to continue to rise and is expected to be equivalent to over 30 per cent of GDP by 2015.

Foreign Aid
Despite many recent improvements, Uganda is still one of the poorest countries in the world with 30 per cent of the population living under the poverty line. Uganda was the first country to receive HIPC debt relief in 1998. Debt relief is worth about US$100 million per annum. Debt service is around 10 per cent of domestic revenue.

Balance of Payments / Imports and Exports
Uganda's main exports are coffee, cotton, iron and steel, tea and fish, main imports include fuel, vehicles and medical supplies. Coffee is the primary source of foreign exchange earnings. Main export trading partners are EU, Kenya, Japan, South Africa, UK and the USA. Main import trading partners are OPEC countries, EU, India, Kenya, South Africa and the US. Over 40 per cent of imports come from Kenya.

External Trade, US$ million

	2005	2006	2007
Trade balance	-821.60	-1,102.10	-1,245.25
Exports	786.30	889.40	954.29
Imports	1,607.80	1,991.50	2,199.54

Source: African Development Bank

Exports amounted to US$3.1 billion in 2009 and imports cost US$4.3 billion. In 2011, exports were estimated at US$2.5 billion and imports at US$4.5 billion.

Uganda, Kenya and Tanzania formed a trading union called the East African Community. This was dissolved in 1977 due to political differences between the nations but re-established in 2001 and will now work together to form a common market. In March 2004 the presidents of Uganda, Kenya, and Tanzania signed a customs pact designed to harmonise external tariffs and boost trade.

Central Bank
Bank of Uganda, PO Box 7120, 37-43 Kampala Rd, Kampala, Uganda. Tel: +256 41 258441/6 / 41, 258060/9, fax: +256 41 230878 / 41 233818, e-mail: info@bou.or.ug, URL: http://www.bou.or.ug
Governor: Emmanuel Tumusiime-Mutebile

Chambers of Commerce and Trade Organisations
Uganda National Chamber of Commerce & Industry, URL: http://www.chamberuganda.com/

MANUFACTURING, MINING AND SERVICES

Primary and Extractive Industries
The contribution of the mining industry to Uganda's economy has declined since copper mining (the nation's second foreign exchange earner in the 1960s), ended in the 1970s.There were plans to privatise and re-open the large Kilembe copper mine in 1999. The country's mineral potential is significant. Private prospecting of gold is carried out in the western and north-eastern parts of the country and Uganda has some of the world's largest phosphate deposits (over 200 million tons). Other major minerals found in Uganda include iron ore, tin, magnetite, graphite, phosphate and cobalt. In 2004 the government announced plans to invest in development and restructuring of the mining industry.

Energy
Oil exploration has been taking place in the west of the country with promising results. Recently oil reserves have been discovered in Uganda but the size and viability have yet to be assessed. It is throught that the Lake Albert rift basis contains more than 3.5 billion barrles of which 1.2 billion is recoverable. Approximatley 40 per cent of areas with potential oil deposits have been explored so far. It is aiming to start production in 2016. Uganda has no proven reserves of gas, and relies heavily on imported fuels for most of its commercial needs. Around 15,000 barrels a day of oil are imported from refineries in Kenya. Energy is also provided by hydroelectric power, mainly from the Owen Falls Dam at Jinja whose generating capacity is 150 mW. Some of this is exported to Kenya and Tanzania. Generating capacity is being increased in anticipation of an up-turn in industrial demand and planned cuts in oil imports. Uganda consumed 2.19 billion kWh of electricity and generated 2.41 billion kWh during 2010. In 1999 the government made the decision to develop solar energy and in 2002 a project was launched to build the Bujagali hydroelectric project which includes a dam on the River Nile. Construction started in 2007 and phase 1 (64 MW) opened in 2010. As of 2012, the government was seeking investment for phase 2 which would provide a further 64 MW.

Manufacturing
The industrial sector in Uganda is underdeveloped, largely as a result of the civil war in 1980s and the expulsion of Uganda's Indian population who largely ran the manufacturing sector, but the sector has recently experienced high growth rates. Most of the industries are based on agriculture, especially the sectors of food processing, coffee, beer, sugar, beverages, tobacco, textiles, cement, timber and paper. Of these industries, food processing is the largest. Recent growth in the sector has been held back by poor performance in the agro-processing sector. In recent years, the production of footwear, soap, plastics, brick and cement production, as well as steel and steel products, has been developed.

Tourism
Tourism is recovering in Uganda and there were 115,000 visitors during 1994 rising to 539,000 in 2006.

Agriculture
Agriculture is important to Uganda's economy. It contributes around 22 per cent of GDP. 80 per cent of Ugandans make a living out of agriculture. Most of the farming is on small holdings but there are some large plantations for cash crops which include coffee, tea, tobacco and sugarcane as well as maize, beans, soya beans, sesame, sunflowers, groundnuts and cassava. The country has attained self-sufficiency in food production by growing a wide range of agricultural crops, most notably grains and horticultural crops. Animal husbandry, too, forms a major part of the economy of Uganda. Cattle, goats, sheep, pigs and poultry are kept along traditional lines. Of these, cattle are the most important. Due to the slump in commodity

UGANDA

prices, the Ministry of Finance has initiated a programme of diversification and privatisation. Non-traditional agricultural exports e.g. simsim, and vanilla, are being encouraged, to reduce dependence on coffee.

Agricultural Production in 2010

Produce	Int. $'000*	Tonnes
Plantains	1,478,755	9,550,000
Cassava	551,774	5,282,000
Cow milk, whole, fresh	371,353	1,190,000
Indigenous cattle meat	353,056	130,695
Beans, dry	245,670	455,000
Sweet Potatoes	214,349	2,838,000
Coffee, green	174,046	162,000
Indigenous pigmeat	173,877	113,110
Maize	171,252	1,373,000
Bananas	168,979	600,000
Vegetables fresh nes	143,215	760,000
Millet	136,675	850,000

* unofficial figures

Source: http://faostat.fao.org/site/339/default.aspx Food and Agriculture Organization of the United Nations, Food and Agricultural commodities production

Forestry
Uganda has 7.5m ha. of forest which produce timber.

Fishing
Fishing and fish products industry is economically important and Uganda and figures show that the catch in 2010 was 413,800 tonnes.

COMMUNICATIONS AND TRANSPORT

Travel Requirements
Citizens of the USA, Canada, Australia and the EU require a passport valid for six months from date of entry, sufficient funds and a return/onward ticket, as well as a visa, apart from citizens of Cyprus and Malta. Transit passengers do require a visa, which is obtainable on entry if they are leaving within 24 hours, holding confirmed tickets and travel documents and not leaving the airport. Other nationals and all journalists should contact the embassy to check visa requirements.

Evidence of yellow fever vaccination may be required.

National Airlines
Uganda Airlines, URL: http://www.swiftuganda.com/uac/quhom/html

International Airports
Entebbe international airport is on the main trunk route through Africa, and air services link it to the main centres in Europe, Asia and other parts of Africa. There are five other airports with paved runways.

Railways
Over 1,200 km of railway extends from Pakwach on Lake Albert to Kasese near Lake George via several northern towns, then via Tororo and Lake Victoria and Kampala. Unganda Railways is not currently running a passenger service. The service to Kenya run by Kenyan Railways has resumed after a break of 15 years.

Roads
There is a road network of over 27,540 km radiating from Kampala. Many roads including the Northern Corridor route have recently been repaired. Some 2,000 km are paved. Vehicles are driven on the left.

Ports and Harbours
The main ports are Entebbe, Jinja and Port Bell. The main waterways are Lake Victoria, Lake Albert, Lake Kyoga, Lake George, Lake Edward, Victoria Nile and the Albert Nile.

HEALTH

Health facilities, which are adequate except in the north of the country, are mostly provided by non-governmental organisations. Approximately 50 per cent of the population have access to health services.

In 2009, the government spent approximately 13.6 per cent of its total budget on healthcare (up from 7.3 per cent in 2000), accounting for 21.8 per cent of all healthcare spending. External resources account for over 20.4 per cent of health expenditure. Total expenditure on healthcare equated to 8.5 per cent of the country's GDP. Per capita expenditure on health was approximately US$44. Figures for 2005-10 show that there are 3,361 physicians (1.2 per 10,000 population), 37,625 nurses and midwives (13 per 10,000 population), 762 pharmaceutical personnel, 440 dentistry personnel and 1,042 environment and public health workers. There are an estimated 5 hospital beds per 10,000 population.

According to the latest WHO figures, in 2010 approximately 72 per cent of the population had access to improved drinking water. In the same year, 32 per cent of the urban population had access to improved sanitation.

The infant mortality rate in 2010 was 63 per 1,000 live births. The child mortality rate (under 5 years) was 99 per 1,000 live births. The main causes of childhood mortality are: prematurity (13 per cent), diarrhoea (10 per cent), pneumonia (17 per cent), malaria (13 per cent), and HIV/AIDs (7 per cent). In the period 2005-11, an estimated 38.7 per cent of children aged

under five were considered to be stunted and 16.4 per cent underweight. An estimated 9 per cent of children sleep under insecticide-treated nets. An estimated 6.5 per cent of the population have HIV/AIDS. An estimated 39 per cent of people with advanced HIV infection and 53 per cent of HIV-infected pregnant women receive antiretroviral therapy coverage. (Source: http://www.who.int, World Health Statistics 2012)

EDUCATION

The education system in Uganda is arranged into three categories, primary (seven years), secondary (six years), and university (three to five years). Secondary schools offer a four-year course leading to the Uganda General Certificate of Education, awarded by the East African Examinations Council.

The primary school enrolment rate in 2007 was 96 per cent for girls and 93 per cent for boys, primary education is free for up to four children per family. Figures for the same year show that secondary school enrolment was 18 per cent of girls and 20 per cent of boys.

There are more than 32 secondary schools offering a further two-year course leading to the "A" level, the Uganda Advanced Certificate of Education. Secondary schools offer not only academic but also practical subjects like woodwork, metalwork, agriculture, commerce, home economics, etc. The object in diversifying the curriculum is to ensure that young people leaving school will be equipped, not only with academic knowledge and training, but also with practical skills.

Great efforts are being made to increase the output of trained teachers. Primary Training Colleges have a capacity of 3,500. Better rates of pay are attracting large numbers of boys and girls wishing to study for the profession. Of the 13,645 teachers in Uganda's schools about 12,406 are African.

There are five universities in Uganda. Makerere University is the oldest university in East Africa. The Christian University of East Africa was inaugurated in November 1992. The other universities are Mbarara University of Science and Technology, Mbale Islamic University, and Uganda Martyrs University.

In 2003 the adult literacy was approximately 70 per cent.

RELIGION

There is no state religion in Uganda. Two religions are officially accepted by the Uganda Government, the Christian faith, which consists of the Protestant and Orthodox Roman Catholic denominations, and the Islamic faith. Around 85 per cent of the population are Christian and 11 per cent Muslim, the remainder follow traditional beliefs, Buddhism, Jainism, Hinduism, Judaism, Baha'ism or Sikhism.

Uganda has a religious liberty rating of 7 on a scale of 1 to 10 (10 is most freedom). (Source: World Religion Database)

COMMUNICATIONS AND MEDIA

There is significant independence in the print media and criticism of the government is published. Radio remains the most popular media. Private broadcasting has flourished since a relaxing of state control in 1993.

Newspapers
The Monitor, URL: http://www.monitor.co.ug, English daily; Uganda Confidential: English bi-weekly; The New Vision, URL: http://www.newvision.co.ug/; The East African, Regional English weekly for East Africa; The Citizen, English weekly; The People, English weekly; The Crusader, English tri-weekly; The Star, English Daily; Tarehe Sita, military publication; Ngabo, Luganda daily; The Weekly Observer, URL: http://www.observer.ug/.

Broadcasting
Uganda Television and Radio Uganda were restructured in 2005 and the Uganda Broadcasting Corporation was formed. UBC is still owned by the government but is part financed by license fees and commercial activities. The number of radio and television stations has increased and currently stands at some 150 radio stations and over 30 TV stations, mainly based around the capital.
Uganda Broadcasting Corporation, (Radio Uganda and Uganda Television) public, URL: http://ubconline.co.ug/

Telecommunications
The telecommunications infrastructure is being improved. The mobile cellular service has expanded rapidly. There are 168,500 million lines in use and figures for 2008 an estimated 8.5 million mobile phones were in use. In 2008 there were an estimated 2.5 million regular internet users.

ENVIRONMENT

Main environmental concerns are deforestation, overgrazing, soil erosion, draining of wetlands, and plant infestation of Lake Victoria. The government is implementing institutional reforms in an attempt to maintain sustainable development. It set up a new body, the National Environmental Management Authority (NEMA), which has ministerial supervision and is chaired by the prime minister.

Street protests were held in 2007 when the government announced that a sugar cane company could develop part of the Mabira National Park for sugar cane production.

Uganda is a party to the following international agreements: Biodiversity; Climate Change; Desertification; Endangered Species; Hazardous Wastes; Law of the Sea; Marine Life Conservation; Nuclear Test Ban; Ozone Layer Protection; Wetlands.

According to figures from the EIA, in 2010 Uganda's emissions from the consumption of fossil fuels totalled 2.01 million metric tons of carbon dioxide.

UKRAINE
Ukrayina

Capital: Kyiv (Kiev) (Population estimate 2011: 2,790,000)

Head of State: Viktor Yanukovych (President) (page 1540)

National Flag: The flag is made up of two equal horizontal stripes of blue and yellow.

CONSTITUTION AND GOVERNMENT

Constitution

Ukraine was taken over by the Bolsheviks in 1919 with the establishment of the Ukrainian Soviet Socialist Republic. The People's Movement of the Ukraine, *Rukh*, was founded in June 1989. Its objectives were the restoration of the Ukraine's linguistic and cultural identity, the achievement of political liberalisation, and greater autonomy for the republic. The Ukraine's Supreme Soviet declared the republic sovereign in July 1990. Ukraine's independence from the USSR was confirmed by a referendum held in December 1991, and the state was an original signatory to the Commonwealth of Independent States (CIS) agreement on 9 December 1991.

The Supreme Soviet of the Crimean Autonomous Republic declared independence within the Ukraine on 4 September 1991, following the Ukrainian Supreme Soviet's adoption of a resolution on independence on 24 August 1991. A constitutional treaty in 1995 gave more power to the President both in economic policy making and over government personnel. Ukraine's present-day constitution, which replaces its Soviet predecessor, was accepted by the 450-seat *Verkhovna Rada*, Ukraine's highest legislative body, in June 1996. It established Ukraine as an independent, democratic, sovereign and unitary state in which the people are ruled by law and exercise their power through the *Verkhovna Rada* and local government.

The head of state is the president, directly elected by universal suffrage. The term of office is five years.

A constitutional referendum in April 2000 supported changes in the constitution to allow for the dissolution of Parliament if it did not form a majority or adopt a budget. It also supported a reduction in the number of deputies from 450 to 300 and introduced a bicameral legislature. In December 2000 these changes were blocked by Parliament.

Following the unrest that followed the 2004 election, constitutional reforms were agreed in 2006 whereby some of the powers of the president were transferred to the prime minister and parliament. The president appoints the prime minister, subject to parliamentary approval, and on the advice of the prime minister appoints the Council of Ministers. The prime minister is head of government and accordingly chairs the Council of Ministers. Constitutional amendments passed in December 2004 and adopted on 1 January 2006 to increase the powers of the Supreme Council were overturned by the Constitutional Court in October 2010.

To consult the constitution, please visit: http://www.rada.kiev.ua/const/conengl.htm

International Relations

Following the break up of the former USSR, relations between Ukraine and Russia were strained but in 1997 a Bi-lateral Treaty on Friendship and Co-operation was signed by the two presidents. There is some dispute between the two countries over Tuzla Island in the Derch Straight between the Azov and Black seas but negotiations to solve the dispute are under way. Following President Yushchenko's election in 2004 relations again became strained as he pursued a pro-western policy, seeking to improve relations with NATO and the EU. However Prime Minister Yanukovych pursued a pro-Russia agenda and relations improved culminating in an agreement for Ukraine to receive a gas supply from Russia. The Ukraine is an associate member of the Commonwealth of Independent States and is also a member of GUAM, an economic co-operation of Georgia, Ukraine, Azerbaijan and Moldova.

Recent Events

In May 2002 Ukraine confirmed that it would abandon neutrality and apply for NATO membership. It also wishes to join the EU.

Controversial elections were held in 2004 amidst allegations of vote rigging and poisoning. Observers reported that there was widespread vote rigging and supporters of the opposition candidate Viktor Yushchenko took to the streets to protest in what became known as the Orange Revolution. The Supreme Court annulled the election result and a fresh election was held on December 26; Viktor Yushchenko was declared the winner. In February 2005 he appointed Yulia Tymoshenko as prime minister, but her government was dismissed in September following infighting and allegations of corruption.

Elections took place in March 2006, resulting in a coalition victory for the President's pro-Russian rival, Viktor Yanukovych. However, the President refused to nominate him Prime Minister. Over the ensuring months, the President sought compromise from Mr Yanukovych's Party of Regions on several issues, including Ukraine's bid to join the EU and NATO, and threatened to call new elections if agreement could not be reached. In July the parties of President Yushchenko, Yulia Tymoshenko and the Socialists agreed to form a coalition but this collapsed. The Socialists then agreed to form a coalition with Viktor Yanukovychs's Party, the Party of Regions, along with the Communists. This coalition nominated Victor Yanukovych

as prime minister. President Yushchenko reluctantly accepted the nomination rather than force new elections. The political relationship between the president and prime minister was fragile and President Yushchenko issued a decree to dissolve parliament and hold elections in June 2007. The Government and parliament did not recognise the decree and applied to the Constitutional Court to rule on its legality. Eventually a compromise was reached and elections were held on 30 September 2007. There was no clear winner, although pro-Russian parties gained a narrow majority. In December, Yulia Tymoshenko was appointed prime minister, in coalition with President Yushchenko's party.

The coalition was never plain sailing and in September 2008 the Our Ukraine party left the coalition after the Tymoshenko Bloc joined forces with the Party of Regions over a package of laws which President Yushchenko feared would threaten presidential powers. On September 16 the speaker of the parliament officially announced that the coalition had ended. After the parties failed to agree on a new coalition President Yushchenko dissolved parliament and called for early elections. As the country's economic crisis worsened, in December he postponed the elections. A new coalition was formed between the factions of Prime Minister Yuliya Tymoshenko's bloc, Our Ukraine-People's Self-Defence and Bloc of Lytvyn.

Ukraine has been affected by the 2008-09 global economic crisis. In October 2008 the IMF offered a US$16.5 billion (£10 billion) loan.

In late 2008 relations deteriorated with Russia in a dispute over unpaid gas supply bills. Russia finally cut supplies in January 2009. The dispute was settled after a two-week halt in supply.

Presidential elections took place on 17 January and 7 February 2010. The incumbent president Mr Yanykovych won. Despite opposition protests the elections were judged to be fair. Mr Yanykovych took office on 25 February 2010.

Political instability continued and on 28 January 2010 the minister of the interior was dismissed by parliament. The cabinet then appointed him as deputy interior minister and acting minister. This appointment was subsequently challenged in court. Prime Minister Tymoshenko and her government lost a vote of confidence in parliament on 3 March. Ms Tymoshenko resigned and the former deputy prime minister, Okeksander Turchynov, took over as acting prime minister. In March 2010 President Yanukovych appointed Mukola Azarov to the post of prime minister. Mr Azarov is an ethnic Russian who does not speak Ukrainian fluently which has made people suspicious of him in the past. Prime Minister Azarov formed a coalition with the Communists and the centrist Lytvyn Bloc. In the following months several ministers were dismissed. On 13 October two deputy prime ministers were removed from the cabinet, reducing the number of deputy prime ministers to three, the total specified in the 1996 constitution.

In October 2010 the constitutional court overturned restrictions on presidential power introduced in 2004. In December 2010, as part of political reform, the cabinet was restructured and reduced to 17 members including the prime minister.

In December 2010, the former prime minister Yuliya Tymoshenko and the minister of the interior Yurit Kutsenko were charged with corruption. Both claimed their innocence, and accused the government of politically motivated charges.

In March 2011, the former president Leonid Kuchma was charged with the 2000 murder of journalist Georgiy Gongadze. In April, the former interior minister official Olexiy Pukach went on trial for the killing. He is alleged to have confessed to the murder.

The former prime minister Yuliya Tymoshenkowas found guilty of abuse of power in October 2011 and jailed. In April 2013, the European Court of Human Rights ruled unanimously that her arrest and detention in 2011 was unlawful.

There were multiple resignations and cabinet reshuffles throughout 2011 and 2012. Most recently, in February 2012, the finance minister became the first deputy prime minister and new ministers of finance and economic development were appointed. A new minister for environmental protection was named in April 2012.

In May 2012 the government postponed a summit of Central and East European leaders after several presidents and officials said they would boycott it over the treatment of Ms Tymoshenko who has alleged she was beaten in prison. There were calls for a boycott of the Euro 2012 football championship which Ukraine co-hosted in June. All teams took part but several political leaders did not attend.

In July 2012 a law was passed in parliament giving the Russian language, regional language status, this led to hundreds of protesters taking to the streets

Parliamentary elections took place in October 2012.

Several ministers resigned in November 2012. A substantial cabinet reshuffle took place in December 2012 with several new appointments.

UKRAINE

In April 2013, the European Court of Human Rights ruled that the arrest and detention of Yulia Tymoshenko in 2011 was unlawful.

Legislature
The *Verkhovna Rada* or Supreme Council, is the sole chamber whose 450 members are elected for a four-year term, half of them by simple majority and half by party list. A new law passed in November 1999 stated that future elections will be entirely by party list.
Verkhovna Rada 5, M. Grushevskoga St, 01008 Kiev, Ukraine. Tel: +380 44 293 0486, URL: http://www.rada.gov.ua
Speaker: Volodymyr Lytvyn, leader of Lytvyn bloc

Cabinet (as at June 2013)
Prime Minister: Mykola Azarov (page 1381)
First Deputy Prime Minister, responsible for Agriculture, Food, Economic development, Trade, Finance, Revenues and Social Policies: Serhiy Arbuzov
Deputy Prime Minister, Minister for the Infrastructure & Regional Development: Oleksander Vilkul
Deputy Prime Minister, Minister for Ecology, Natural Resources, Energy: Yuriy Boyko
Deputy Prime Minister: Kostyantyn Hryschenko
Minister for Regional Policy, Construction and Housing: Hennady Temnyk
Minister of Health: Raisa Bohatyriova
Minister of the Interior: Maj.-Gen. Vitaliy Zakharchenko
Minister of the Environment and Natural Resources: Oleh Proskuriakov
Minister of Social Policies: Natalya Korolevskaya
Minister for Foreign Affairs: Leonid Kozhara
Minister of Economic Development and Trade: Ihor Prasolov
Minister of Agrarian Policy: Mykola Prysyahnyuk
Minister of the Education & Science: Dmitry Tabachnik
Minister of Youth & Sports: Ravil Safiullin
Minister of Justice: Oleksandr Lavrinovich
Minister of Defence: Pavlo Lebedev
Minister of Culture and Tourism: Leonid Novokhatko
Minister of Energy and Coal Industry: Eduard Stavyskyi
Minister of Emergencies: Mykhaylo Bolotsky
Minister of Finance: Yurii Kolobov
Minister of Revenues and Duties: Oleksandr Klymenko
Minister without Portfolio: Olena Lukash

Ministries
Office of the President, vul. Bankova 11, 01220 Kiev, Ukraine. Tel: +380 44 255 6128, fax: +380 44 293 1001, URL: http://www.president.gov.ua
Office of the Prime Minister, vul. Hrushevskoho 12/2, 01008 Kiev, Ukraine. Tel: +380 44 253 5762, fax: +380 44 253 5762, e-mail: pr@kmu.gov.ua, URL: http://www.kmu.gov.ua
Cabinet Office, 12/2 Hrushevsky Street, 01019 Kiev, Ukraine. Tel: +380 44 226 2289, URL: http://www.kmu.gov.ua
Ministry of Foreign Affairs, 1 Mykhailivska Square, 01018 Kiev, Ukraine. Tel: +380 44 212 8675, fax: +380 44 226 3169, e-mail: zsmfa@mfa.gov.ua, URL: http://www.mfa.gov.ua
Ministry of Finance, 12/2 Hrushevsky Street, 01008 Kiev, Ukraine. Tel: +380 44 293 5263, fax: +380 44 293 8243, e-mail: infomf@minfin.gov.ua, URL: http://www.minfin.gov.ua
Ministry of the Economy, 12/2 Hrushevsky Street, 01008 Kiev, Ukraine. Tel: +380 44 253 9394, fax: +380 44 226 3181, e-mail: meconomy@me.gov.ua, URL: http://www.me.gov.ua
Ministry for Environmental Protection and Nuclear Safety, vul. Uritskoho 35, 01601 Kiev, Ukraine. Tel: +380 44 206 3100, fax: +380 44 206 3107, e-mail: secr@menr.gov.ua, URL: http://www.menr.gov.ua
Ministry for Family and Youth Issues, 14 Desyatynna Street, 252025 Kiev, Ukraine. Tel: +380 44 228 5631, fax: +380 44 228 5540, e-mail: press@dksm.gov.ua, URL: http://www.kmu.gov.ua/sport/control
Ministry of Agro-Industrial Complex, 24 Khreschatyk Street, 01001 Kiev, Ukraine. Tel: +380 44 226 3466, fax: +380 44 229 5786, e-mail: ministr@minapk.kiev.ua, URL: http://www.minagro.gov.ua
Ministry of Coal Mining Industry, 4 Khmelnytskyi Street, 01001 Kiev, Ukraine. Tel: +380 44 228 0372, fax: +380 44 228 2131, e-mail: dsher@mvp.gov.ua, URL: http://www.mvp.gov.ua/mvp/control/uk/index
Ministry of Culture and Tourism, vul. Ivana Franko 19, 01601 Kiev, Ukraine. Tel: +380 44 235 2378, fax: +380 44 225 3257, e-mail: info@mincult.gov.ua, URL: http://www.mincult.gov.ua
Ministry of Defence, vul. Hrushevskoho 30/1, 01021 Kiev, Ukraine. Tel: +380 44 253 1156, fax: +380 44 226 2015, e-mail: pressmou@pressmou.kiev.ua, URL: http://www.mil.gov.ua
Ministry of Education, 10 Peremohy Avenue, 01008 Kiev, Ukraine. Tel: +380 44 226 2661, fax: +380 44 274 1049, e-mail: info@mon.gov.ua, URL: http://www.mon.gov.ua
Ministry of Energy, 30 Khreschatyk Street, 01601 Kiev, Ukraine. Tel: +380 44 221 4364, e-mail: kanc@mintop.energy.gov.ua, URL: http://www.mpe.energy.gov.ua
Ministry of Extraordinary Situations and Chernobyl Issues, 55 Honchara Street, 01030 Kiev, Ukraine. Tel: +380 44 221 4364, e-mail: kanc@mintop.energy.gov.ua, URL: http://www.mpe.energy.gov.ua
Ministry of Health Care, 7 Hrushevskyi Street, 01021 Kiev, Ukraine. Tel: +380 44 253 6975, e-mail: moz@moz.gov.ua, URL: http://www.moz.gov.ua
Ministry of Industrial Policy, 3 Surykova Street, 03035 Kiev, Ukraine. Tel: +380 44 246 3220, e-mail: mail@industry.gov.ua, URL: http://industry.kmu.gov.ua/control/en/index
Ministry of Justice, 13 Arch. Horodetskyi Street, 01001 Kiev, Ukraine. Tel: +380 44 228 3723, fax: +380 44 228 3723, e-mail: themis@minjust.gov.ua, URL: http://www.minjust.gov.ua
Ministry of Labour and Social Policy, vul. Esplanada 8/10, 01023 Kiev, Ukraine. Tel: +380 44 226 2445, fax: +380 44 220 0098, URL: http://www.mlsp.gov.ua
Ministry of the Interior, 10 Acad. Bohomoltsia St, 01024 Kiev, Ukraine. Tel: +380 44 226 2004, fax: +380 44 291 1733
Ministry of Transport, vul. Peremohy 14, 01135 Kiev, Ukraine. Tel: +380 44 235 9770, fax: +380 44 268 2202, e-mail: com@mintrans.kiev.ua, URL: http://www.mintrans.kiev.ua

Ministry of Construction, Architecture, Housing and Utilities, vul. Velyka Zhytomyrska 9, 01025 Kiev, Ukraine. Tel: +380 44 226 2208, e-mail: komitet@build.gov.ua, URL: http://www.minbud.gov.ua/main
Office of the Cabinet of Ministers, vul. Hrushevskoho 5, 01019 Kiev, Ukraine. Tel: +380 44 226 2246, fax: +380 44 293 0211, URL: http://www.kmu.gov.ua
Ministry of Emergency Situations, vul. Honchara 55, 01030 Kiev, Ukraine. Tel: +380 44 247 3050, fax: +380 44 226 3216, e-mail: main@mns.gov.ua, URL: http://www.mns.gov.ua
Ministry of Infrastructure, vul. Peremohy 14, 01135 Kiev, Ukraine. Tel: +380 44 235 9770, fax: +380 44 268 2202, e-mail: com@mintrans.kiev.ua, URL: http://www.mintrans.kiev.ua
Ministry of Regional Development, Construction and Housing, vul. Velyka Zhytomyrska 9, 01025 Kiev, Ukraine. Tel: +380 44 278 4947, fax: +380 44 278 8390, e-mail: press@minregionbud.gov.ua, URL: http://www.minregionbud.gov.ua
Ministry of Social Policy, vul. Esplanada 8/10, 01023 Kiev, Ukraine. Tel: +380 44 226 2445, fax: +380 44 220 0098, e-mail: info@mlsp.gov.ua, URL: http://www.mlsp.gov.ua

Political Parties
Party of the Regions, URL:http://www.partyofregions.org.ua/eng
People's Movement of Ukraine (RUKH) URL: http://www.nru.org.ua/en
Our Ukraine - People's Self Defence, URL: http://www.razom.org.ua/set/en
Lytvyn Bloc, Leader: Volodymyr Lytvyn
Yulia Tymoshenko Bloc, URL: http://www.tymoshenko.com.ua/eng/index
Communist Party of Ukraine (CPU), URL: http://www.kpu.kiev.ua/Main/index.htm

Elections
Presidential elections were held in October 2004. The result of the first round put Viktor Yushchenko just 0.5 per cent ahead of Viktor Yanukovych and a second round was held at the end of November. The result was Mr. Yanukovych 49.4 per cent and Mr. Yushchenko 46.6 per cent. The supporters of Viktor Yushchenko rejected the result and appealed to the Supreme Court amidst allegations of vote rigging and poisoning, which was later confirmed by Mr. Yushchenko's doctors in Austria. Over 100,000 protesters took to the streets for several days. On December 3 the Supreme Court announced that it would annul the result and that fresh elections would be held on December 26. Viktor Yushchenko was declared the winner with 51.9 per cent over Viktor Yanukovych's 44.2 per cent. The result effectively divided Ukraine between the pro-Russian and pro-Western camps. Viktor Yanukovych challenged the result of the second election but the Supreme Court rejected his challenge.

A parliamentary election was held on 26th March 2006. The pro-Russian Party of Regions became the largest party in government, led by Viktor Yanukovych. Three other blocs (the Yuliya Tymoshenko, Our Ukraine and the Socialist Party) tried to form a coalition, but, in July 2006, the Socialist Party announced that it would ally itself with the Party of Regions. Viktor Yanukovych was nominated Prime Minister, and a new cabinet was formed. However, the power sharing agreement was fragile and by March 2007 a political crisis was looming; in April President Yushenko dissolved the parliament and further elections took place in September 2007.

Although Prime Minister Viktor Yanukovych's Party of Regions won the most seats, it could not find enough allies to create a coalition. The new government is a coalition of Bloc Yulia Tymoshenko and Victor Yushchenko's Our Ukraine - People Self Defence party.

After the coalition broke down in September 2008 President Yushchenko dissolved parliament and called for early elections. As the country's economic crisis worsened, in December he said the elections were no longer a priority. A new coalition was formed between the factions of Prime Minister Yuliya Tymoshenko's bloc, Our Ukraine-People's Self-Defence and Bloc of Lytvyn.

Presidential elections were held in February 2010, early indications put the result as President Yanukovych winning 48.9 per cent of the vote and Julia Tymoshenko winning 45.4 per cent. Mrs Tymoshenko said she would contest the decision saying she suspected electoral fraud but overseas observers said the elections had been carried out in a fair and free manner. Mr Yanykovych took office on 25 February 2010.

Prime Minister Tymoshenko and her government lost a vote of confidence in parliament on 3 March 2010. Ms Tymoshenko resigned and the former deputy prime minister, Okeksander Turchynov, took over as acting prime minister, before President Yanukovych appointed Mykola Azarov to the post.

Parliamentary elections took place in October 2012. the governing Party of Regions won the elections and the far-right Freedom party also did well, Outside observers expressed concern about the conduct of the election.

Diplomatic Representation
British Embassy, 01025 Kiev Desyatinna 9, Kiev, Ukraine. Tel: +380 44 462 0011, fax: +380 44 462 0013, e-mail:ukembinf@sovam.com, URL: http://ukinukraine.fco.gov.uk/en/
Ambassador: Mr Simon Smith
US Embassy 4 Hlybochtska, 254053 Kiev 53, Ukraine. Tel: +380 44 490 4000, fax: +380 44 244 7350, URL: http://kiev.usembassy.gov
Ambassador: John F. Tefft
Ukrainian Embassy, 60 Holland Park, London, W11 3SJ, United Kingdom. Tel: +44 (0)20 7727 6312, fax: +44 (0)20 7792 1708, URL: http://uk.mfa.gov.ua/ua
Ambassador: Volodymyr Khandogiy
Ukrainian Embassy, 3350 M Street NW, Washington, DC 20007, USA. Tel: +1 202 333 0606, fax: +1 202 333 0817, URL: http://www.mfa.gov.ua/usa/en/
Ambassador: Olexander Motsyk
Permanent Mission of Ukraine to the United Nations, 220 East 51 Street, New York, NY 10022, USA. Tel: +1 212 759 7003, fax: +1 212 355 9455, e-mail: uno_us@mfa.gov.ua, URL: http://www.mfa.gov.ua/un
Ambassador: Yuriy Sergeyev

LEGAL SYSTEM

Ukraine's judicial system was inherited from that of the Soviet Union and the former Ukrainian SSR, and has undergone major reforms in recent years.

The judicial system of Ukraine consists of four levels of courts of general jurisdiction, namely: local courts of criminal and civil jurisdiction; Appeal courts (including navy, military, economic and administrative); High courts with specialized jurisdiction (covering administrative, economic and commercial cases) and the Supreme Court, which covers all cases. There is also a Constitutional Court of Ukraine which assesses whether legislative acts of the Parliament, President, Cabinet or Crimean Parliament are in line with the Constitution of Ukraine.

Judges in Ukraine retain their positions permanently, with the exception of Constitutional Court justices and initial judicial appointments, which the President creates and which last for five years.

The police and penal systems continue to be sources of serious human rights concerns. Serious corruption persists in all branches of government, including the judiciary. There have been recent instances of torture by law enforcement personnel, and prison conditions are harsh. Discrimination against Roma continues, and there is a serious people trafficking problem. There are restrictions on workers' ability to form and join unions. In 2008, the Ministry of the Interior established human rights monitoring departments in all regions to monitor human rights performance by police during the year.

Ukraine abolished the death penalty in 2000.

Supreme Court of Ukraine, URL: http://www.scourt.gov.ua/
President: Petro Pylypchuk

LOCAL GOVERNMENT

Ukraine is divided administratively into 24 *Oblast* regions, as well as the Autonomous Republic of the Crimea. The cities of Kiev and Sevastopol are responsible directly to central government. Local communities exercise their power through regional and provincial councils, each headed by a chairman, which are elected directly for four years. Local elections took place in 2010.

Provinces and their size

Name	Area (sq. km)
Cherkaska	20,900
Chernihivska	31,900
Chernivetska	8,100
Dnipropetrovska	31,000
Donetska	26,500
Ivano-Frankivska	13,900
Kharkivska	31,400
Khersonska	28,500
Khmelnytska	20,600
Kyivska	28,900
Kirovohradska	24,600
Luhanska	26,700
Lvivska	21,800
Mykolaivska	24,600
Odeska	33,300
Poltavska	28,800
Rivnenska	20,100
Sumska	23,800
Ternopilska	13,800
Vinnytska	26,500
Volynska	20,200
Zakarpatska	12,800
Zaporizhska	27,200
Zhytomyrska	29,900

AREA AND POPULATION

Area

The Ukraine lies in the south-west of what was formerly the USSR. It is bordered by Poland in the north-west, and by Slovakia, Hungary and Romania in the west. In the south it faces the Black and Azov Seas, with Belarus to the north, and Russia bordering the north and east. The Ukraine occupies a total area of 603,700 sq. km. The majority of Ukraine is made up of the steppes, or fertile plains and plateaux.

The climate is temperate continental moving towards Mediterranean on the southern coast line. There is more precipitation in the west and north, less in the south and east. Summers are generally warm, hotter in the south. Winters are cool, colder in the north.

To view a map, consult http://www.lib.utexas.edu/maps/cia08/ukraine_sm_2008.gif

Population

The population was estimated to be 45.548 million in 2010, with a density of around 84 people per sq. km. The population growth rate was estimated at -0.7 per cent over the period 2000-10.

Some 35 million (68 per cent) live in Ukraine's urban areas. The capital, Kiev, has a population of about 2.8 million. Other principal towns with populations over 1 million are Kharkov, Donesk, Dnepropetrovsk, and Odessa. An estimated 32 per cent of the population live in rural areas.

The population is made up of 77 per cent Ukrainians, 17 per cent Russians, 1 per cent Jews, and 4 per cent of other races, including Belarusians, Moldovans, Hungarians, Bulgarians, Poles and Crimean Tatars.

The official language is Ukrainian. Other languages spoken are Russian, Romanian, Polish and Hungarian.

Births, Marriages, Deaths

In 2010 the birth rate was estimated at 10.8 births per thousand population and the death rate at 16.6 per 1,000 population. The total fertility rate in 2010 was 1.4 children per female. Average life expectancy at birth in 2009 was 62 years for men and 74 years for women. Healthy life expectancy in 2007 was 55 years for males and 64 years for females. The median age was 39 years in 2010. Approximately 14 per cent of the population is aged less than 15 years and 21 per cent over 60 per cent. (Source: http://www.who.int, World Health Statistics 2012)

Public Holidays 2014

1 January: New Year's Day
7 January: Orthodox Christmas
8 March: International Women's Day
21 April: Easter Sunday
1 & 2 May: Labour Day
9 May: Victory Day
15 June: Orthodox Pentecost
28 June: Constitutional Day
24 August: Independence Day

EMPLOYMENT

Recent figures put the workforce at around 23 million. The unemployment rate in 2007 and 2008 was 6.4 per cent , rising to 8.0 per cent in 2010.

Total Employment by Economic Activity

Occupation	2008
Agriculture, hunting, fishing & forestry	3.322,100
Mining & quarrying, manufacturing, electricity, gas & water supply	3,871,400
Construction	1,043,400
Wholesale & retail trade, repairs, hotels & restaurants	4,744,400
Transport, storage & communications	1,465,800
Financial intermediation	394,900
Real estate, renting & business activities	1,150,400
Public admin. & defence; compulsory social security	1,067,500
Education	1,702,400
Health & social work	1,369,900
Other community, social & personal service activities. household with employed persons, other	840,100

Source: Copyright © International Labour Organization (ILO Dept. of Statistics, http://laborsta.ilo.org)

BANKING AND FINANCE

Currency

One Hryvnya (UAH) = 100 kopiykas

GDP/GNP, Inflation, National Debt

Ukraine was the most important economic part of the former Soviet Union. It generated more than 25 per cent of the Soviet agricultural output and was also an important industrial region. Following independence in 1991, the Ukraine government put in a framework for privatisation but its economic and structural reforms faltered and output fell dramatically. Ukraine is dependent on Russia for its energy. In 2009, Ukraine agreed to 10-year gas supply contracts with Russia which ended its era of cheap prices. Despite political instability the economy enjoyed several years of economic growth prior to the worldwide economic crisis. Like many countries, Ukraine went into recession in 2009. The Ukraine reached an agreement with the IMF for a US$16 billion stand-by arrangement but the agreement faltered due to the lack of progress in reform. A new agreement with the the IMF was reached in 2010 aimed at developing fiscal sustainability, reform of the gas sector and reform of the banking system. The economy came out of recession in 2010 and 2011.

Between independence in December 1991 and the year 2000, the Ukraine experienced negative real GDP growth rates; real GDP as at June 1999 was at just 40 per cent of 1990 levels. In the first half of 2000 the economy began showing signs of growth, as reforms took hold, and by the end of that year growth of 5.7 per cent had been recorded.

Figures for 2001 showed growth estimated at 9.1 per cent, reflecting an expansion in export markets to countries other than the traditional market of Russia, and increased domestic demand for goods. Figures for 2003 put GDP at around US$50 billion, with an estimated growth rate of 9.3 per cent for that year. Economic growth slowed in 2005 to 2.6 per cent but rose again in 2006. Figures for 2006 put GDP at US$106 billion, a growth rate of 7.0 per cent. In 2007, GDP was estimated at US$142.5 billion with an annual growth rate of 7.6 per cent.

UKRAINE

However, Ukraine has been affected by the 2008 global economic crisis. In 2008, there was a drop in demand for steel and the price of the country's main export thus collapsed. As the crisis deepened many foreign investors pulled out of Ukraine. In 2008, the IMF offered Ukraine a US$16.5 billion (£10 billion) loan to help it through the crisis. Figures for 2009 put GDP at US$115 billion recording a growth rate that year of -14.0 per cent. Growth for 2010 was estimated to be 4.3 per cent and GDP was estimated to be US$136 billion. GDP per capita was estimated to be US$6,698 in 2010. GDP was estimated at US$165 billion in 2011.

Inflation reached over 10,000 per cent in 1993. The inflation rate rose to over 30 per cent in 1999 following devaluations in the Hryvnya after the Russian rouble crisis. It has remained high; estimated figures for 2000 put the inflation rate at 25 per cent, falling to 6 per cent in 2001. In 2007 inflation rose to 12.5 per cent, and 25.1 per cent in 2008 before falling in 2009 to 16.8 per cent and 10 per cent in 2010.

Foreign Investment
Ukraine's shift to a market economy is continuing to move slowly and is hindered by poor corporate governance and corruption. The IMF granted a three-year $2.2 billion loan in September 1998 after Parliament allowed the President to reduce the budget deficit. However, the Government has not passed legislation on privatisation, tax reform, bankruptcy laws and energy sector restructuring, which does not assist in attracting foreign investment, although the Ukraine has publicly stated that it is looking for such investment. As a result of the poor economic environment, Ukraine has a received a cumulative foreign investment of approximately $2.69 billion, among the lowest in the region.

Ukraine has received loans from the IMF intended to modernise the financial sector. In 2001, the IMF delayed part of the handover of funds due to the slow pace of economic reforms. Several foreign investors pulled out of Ukraine during the 2008/09 global economic crisis. Ukraine has also suffered following the global financial crisis. In 2008, the global demand for its steel declined sharply, causing the price of one of its main exports to fall. Several investors pulled out as the value of Ukrainian currency fell. The IMF offered Ukraine a loan of US$16.5 billion to aid its economy.

Balance of Payments / Imports and Exports
The estimated value of exports of goods and services in 2011 was estimated at US$68 billion and for the cost of imports at US$80 billion. The main export products are metals (which make up 40 per cent), chemicals, machinery and transport equipment and food products, whilst the main import products are energy, machinery and parts, transportation equipment, chemicals, plastics and rubber. Ukraine's main trading partners are Europe, Belarus, China, Russia, Turkey and Turkmenistan.

Ukraine has had recent problems with its energy trading with Russia. The dispute came to a head in January 2009 when the Russian energy giant Gazprom halted gas supplies to Ukraine over alleged debts. Ukraine agreed a new tariff and supplies resumed. The dispute affected supplies to other European countries.

Central Bank
National Bank of Ukraine, 9 Instytutska St, Kiev 01008, Ukraine. Tel: +380 44 253 0180, fax: +380 44 230 2033, e-mail: postmaster@bank.gov.ua URL: http://www.bank.gov.ua Governor: Ihor Sorkin

Chambers of Commerce
Ukrainian Chamber of Commerce and Industry, URL: http://www.ucci.org.ua/en/about.html
The Chamber of Commerce in Ukraine, URL: http://www.chamber.ua

MANUFACTURING, MINING AND SERVICES

Primary and Extractive Industries
Ferrous metallurgy is of primary importance in the Ukraine. Mercury, iron ore, titanium, zirconium, and other non-ferrous metals and alloys are also among the Republic's output. The Donets Coal Basin comprises the country's main coal deposits. Oil, natural gas and peat are produced.

Coal
Coal production accounts for almost half of Ukraine's domestic energy production. However, production has been declining, and by 1998 coal production was less than half of what it was in 1990. The decline in production was caused mainly by the fall in domestic demand during this period, resulting from the closing of heavy industry as Ukraine's economy contracted during the 1990s. Despite loans from the World Bank and government subsidies many mines remain unprofitable. In 2000, coal production was at 90.2 million short tons and consumption was 97.1 million short tons; by 2010, coal production had fallen to an estimated 60.1 million short tons. Consumption that year was estimated at nearly 70 million short tons. Ukraine's mining industry is plagued by a poor safety record and industrial action as well as slow progress on deregulation. In 2001, there were nearly 300 deaths in the coal mining industry. Recent figures show that although Ukraine has the seventh largest coal resources in the world underinvestment in the industry means that Ukraine is a net coal importer.

Oil and Gas
In early 1998, President Kuchma formed a single state-owned oil and gas company by joining the smaller state-owned oil and gas companies, and creating Naftogaz Ukrainy. It controls oil and gas production and marketing, as well as the national oil and gas pipeline network, one of the country's largest sources of revenue. Ukraine's national program 'Oil and Gas of Ukraine to the year 2010' was developed to meet at least half of the country's oil and gas needs within the next ten years. Under this plan, foreign investment in Ukraine's oil and gas sectors has been limited to joint venture agreements rather than privatisation. At present, Russia and Turkmenistan supply Ukraine with the oil and gas it needs, but non-payment by Ukraine led to problems such as blockades. In January 2009 Russia halted gas supplies to Ukraine over its debts. Ukraine subsequently agreed new tariffs and supply recommenced.

Ukraine's geographical position and a well developed oil pipeline system means that it is a transit country for Russian exports of gas to Europe, and with development could play a large role in aiding the export of oil from Azerbaijan and Kazakhstan to European markets.

As at January 2011, Ukraine had proven oil reserves of 400 million barrels, but only produced 81,800 barrels per day (48,000 barrels of which were crude), while consuming 328,000 barrels per day. Ukraine's six oil refineries are currently operating well under capacity. Capacity is estimated at 880,000 bbl/d. In order to boost trade in oil, the Yuzhnyy oil terminal near Odessa was constructed. Privatisation of Ukraine's oil refineries is currently underway; Russia's LUKoil is one of the companies that bought a stake.

Although Ukraine has large deposits of natural gas (39.6 trillion cubic feet) it only produced 699 billion cu ft in 2011 while consuming 2,281 billion cu ft per year and therefore relies heavily on imported gas for its domestic needs. (Source: EIA)

Energy
Ukraine is not self sufficient in its energy requirements and has to import petroleum and natural gas from Russia, Turkmenistan and Kazakhstan. At present there are four nuclear power stations in Ukraine; the Chernobyl plant was closed down in December 2000 following aid from the West. The Dnieper chain of hydropower stations includes the Dnieper Hydropower Station and power stations in Dneprodzerzhinsk, Kakhovka, Kremenchug, Kanev and Kiev.

Estimated total energy consumption in 2009 was 4.7 quadrillion Btu and total production was 3.087 quadrillion Btu. 50 per cent of Ukraine's electricity is generated from thermal power plants, 40 per cent by nuclear power and the remainder from hydro-electric plants. In 2009, net generation of electricity was 165 billion kWh and net consumption was 138.3 billion kWh. These figures had risen to a net generation of 176 billion kWh in 2010 and consumption of 150 billion kWh. Production of electricity is hampered by poor infrastructure which is in need of investment, Ukraine has the generating ability to supply twice its needs in electricity. (Source: EIA)

Manufacturing
The Ukraine's engineering industry manufactures metal-cutting machine tools, farm machinery, ocean-going vessels and river boats, motor vehicles, and motor cycles. Other important industries produce electrical equipment, automation devices, cameras, medical equipment, mineral fertilizers, synthetic fibres, dyes and rubber products.

Service Industries
Figures for 2000 show that Ukraine had 4.2 million visitors. This figure rose to 18.9 million visitors in 2006.

Agriculture
Ukraine has very fertile soil in the central and southern areas of the country, which led at one time to it being called the bread basket of Europe. There were originally three belts of vegetation - forest in the north, forest-steppe in the middle, and steppe in the southern part of the country. However, much of this has been replaced by cultivated crops. Ukraine is a major producer and exporter of a wide variety of agricultural products including wheat and sugar beets. Other crops include potatoes, vegetables, fruit, sunflowers and flax. Livestock raising is also important. Recent figures show the area under cultivation was 41.8 m ha., and there were 17.7m cattle, 9.5m pigs, and 1.8m sheep and goats. The area of forested land was 10,782.2 thousand ha. Estimated figures for 2011 put the contribution of agriculture to GDP at 10.0 per cent, with 16 per cent of the labour force employed by the sector.

Agricultural Production in 2010

Produce	Int. $'000*	Tonnes
Cow milk, whole, fresh	2,926,258	10,977,200
Sunflower seed	1,816,832	6,771,500
Wheat	1,806,809	16,851,300
Indigenous chicken meat	1,224,647	859,759
Indigenous cattle meat	1,155,014	427,565
Potatoes	1,149,478	18,705,000
Indigenous pigmeat	961,478	625,457
Hen eggs, in shell	793,642	973,900
Maize	699,443	11,953,000
Tomatoes	674,343	1,824,700
Barley	394,413	8,484,900
Sugar beet	370,996	13,749,000

* unofficial figures
Source: http://faostat.fao.org/site/339/default.aspx Food and Agriculture Organization of the United Nations, Food and Agricultural commodities production

Fishing
FAO figures for 2010 put the ttal catch at 186,021 tonnes.

COMMUNICATIONS AND TRANSPORT

Travel Requirements
Citizens of the USA, Canada, Australia and the EU require a passport valid for at least one months beyond the length of stay. Most do not require a visa for visits not exceeding 90 days, the exceptions being citizens of Australia, Bulgaria and Romania, who should apply before travelling. Travellers should note that Ukrainian visas are not valid in the Russian Federation, and Russian Federation visas are not valid in Ukraine.

Nationals not mentioned above should check visa requirements with the Ukraine embassy.

National Airlines
Air Ukraine, URL: http://www.airukraine.com
Air Urga, URL: http://www.urga.com.ua

International Airports

Airports are situated in 20 locations regionally and in the capital Kiev, which has an international airport, Kyiv Boryspil International Airport, and a domestic airport, Kyiv Zhuliany. Airspace is regulated by the following bodies.

Committee on Airspace Use Pobedy Prospect 14, 01035 Kiev, Ukraine. Tel: +380 44 216 4755/216 4782

Ukraine State Department of Air Transport, Pobedy Prospect 14, 01035 Kiev, Ukraine. Tel: +380 44 226 3163/220 3163

Berdiansk City Airport, Berdiansk City, Ukraine. Tel: +380 6153 35440

Krivoi Rog Airport, 324052 Krivoi Rog, Dnepropetrovskaya, Ukraine. Tel: +380 564 291941, fax: +380 564 270563

Lutsk Airport, 263003 Lutsk, Ukraine. Tel: +380 3322 46147, fax: +380 3322 46007

Mariupol Airport, Mariupol, Ukraine. Tel: +380 629 652187/353376

Zaporozhye Airport State Company, 330022 Zaporozhye, Ukraine. Tel: +380 612 641924, fax: +380 612 629043/604356

Railways

The total length of the railway system in 2003 was just under 23,000, of which 9,250 km were electrified. The railways carries an average of 501 million passengers and 293 million tonnes of freight.

Ukrainian Railways, URL: http://www.uz.gov.ua

Kiev, Kharkiv and Dnipropetrovsk have Metro systems.

Roads

The total length of hard-surfaced motor roads in 2003 was 164,000 km. Vehicles drive on the right.

Ports and Harbours

Foreign trade is to a great extent routed through the sea ports of Odessa, Nikolayev, Ilyichyovsk, Zhdanov and Kherson. In 1997, 2 million passengers and 9 million tonnes of freight were carried by inland waterways mainly on the Dnieper River.

Ferry services run from Istanbul, Georgia, Varna (Bulgaria) to Odessa or to Crimea.

HEALTH

In 2009, the government spent approximately 8.9 per cent of its total budget on healthcare, accounting for 55.0 per cent of all healthcare spending. Private expenditure accounts for 45.0 per cent of total expenditure on health (over 93 per cent out-of-pocket expenditure). Total expenditure on healthcare equated to 7.8 per cent of the country's GDP. Per capita expenditure on health was approximately US$200, compared with US$36 in 2000. In 2005-10, there were 144,174 doctors (32.5 per 10,000 population), 383,130 midwives and nurses (85.9 per 10,000 population), 22,257 pharmaceutical personnel (5 per 10,000 population) and 19,169 dentists (4 per 10,000 population). There are an estimated 87 hospital beds per 10,000 population.

The infant mortality rate in 2009 was 13 per 1,000 live births. The child mortality rate (under 5 years) was 15 per 1,000 live births. The most common causes of death among children aged 5 or less were prematurity (16 per cent), pneumonia (12 per cent), diarrhoea (2 per cent) and HIV/AIDs (1 per cent). In 2000-09, approximately 22.9 per cent of children aged less than 5 were classified as stunted and 4.1 per cent as underweight. Approximately 26.5 per cent were classified as overweight.

In 2010, an estimated 98 per cent of the population had sustainable access to improved drinking water sources and 94 per cent of the population had sustainable access to improved sanitation. (Source: http://www.who.int, World Health Statistics 2012)

EDUCATION

Education is compulsory.

An estimated 90 per cent of children are enrolled in pre-primary education. Although primary education is compulsory, attendance was estimated at 90 per cent in 2006. An estimated 1 per cent of pupils repeated some primary education in 2000. In 2006 the pupil / teacher ratio in primary schools was 17 to one. Completion of primary education is estimated at 100 per cent. Enrolment in secondary education in 2007 was estimated at 85 per cent of girls and 84 per cent of boys, down by 5 per cent from 2002 levels of enrolment. Enrolment in tertiary education is estimated at 76 per cent.

In 2007, 20.2 per cent of total government expenditure went on education.

The literacy rate is 99.8 per cent. (Source: UNESCO)

RELIGION

Religious Ukrainians are predominantly (approx. 73 per cent) Eastern Orthodox (Ukrainian Orthodox Church). An estimated 4.4 per cent of the population are Roman Catholics, 2 per cent Protestant, 2.1 per cent Muslim and 0.4 per cent Jewish.

Ukraine has a religious tolerance rating of 6 on a scale of 1 to 10 (10 is most freedom). (Source: World Religion Database)

COMMUNICATIONS AND MEDIA

There has been greater press freedom since the Orange Revolution in 2004. However, since the election of Viktor Yanukovch as head of state there have been reports of press freedom violations.

Newspapers

Most newspapers are privately owned. Under the former President Leonid Kuchma several opposition papers were closed and several investigative journalists died in suspicious circumstances. A parliamentary commission set up to investigate the murder of the journalist Georgiy Gongadze accused Mr Kuchma of involvement in his kidnapping, a charge denied by the former president.

Main daily mass circulation newspapers include:

Fakty i Kommentarli, URL: http://www.facts.kiev.ua

Segodnya, URL: http://www.segodnya.ua

Vecherniye Vesti, URL: http://www.vv.com.ua

Silski Visti, URL: http://www.silskivisti.kiev.ua

Den, URL: http://www.day.kiev.ua (English language)

Ukrayinska Pravda, URL: http://www.pravda.com.ua/, Online news

Broadcasting

Ukraine has a state run television company, the National TV Company of Ukraine. There are also several commercial stations. Inter TV and Studio 1+1 are national channels. Commercial channels include STB, Novy Kanal and ICTV and 5 Kanal.

National TV Company of Ukraine, URL: http://www.1tv.com.ua/

Inter TV, URL: http://intertv.com.ua/en/about.html

Studio 1+1, http://www.1plus1.ua/generalinfo

One state run radio broadcaster, National Radio Company of Ukraine operates three networks (http://www.nrcu.gov.ua/), UT1, UT2 and UT3 there are also several hundred commercial stations including Russkoye Radio (URL: http://www.rusradio.com.ua/) and Europa Plus (URL: http://www.europaplus.com.ua/).

Telecommunications

The landline system has improved since independence when it was antiquated and in need of repair. The mobile sector has expanded much more rapidly. In 2010 there were an estimated 13 million landline telephones in operation and 54 million mobile phones. The mobile phone market is saturated with more than 100 phones per 100 population.

Figures for 2009 indicate that some 8 million Ukrainians are internet users.

ENVIRONMENT

Major environmental issues include inadequate supplies of water suitable for drinking; air and water pollution; deforestation, and radiation contamination in the north east as a result of the accident at the Chernobyl Nuclear Power Plant in 1986. In June 2000 talks between President Clinton of the USA and President Kuchma resulted in the establishment of a date for the closure of Chernobyl power station. The plant closed on 15 December 2000, ending years of dispute over compensation for the closure between Ukraine and the West.

Ukraine is party to the following environmental conventions: Air Pollution, Air Pollution-Nitrogen Oxides, Air Pollution-Sulfur 85, Antarctic-Environmental Protocol, Antarctic-Marine Living Resources, Antarctic Treaty, Biodiversity, Climate Change, Climate Change-Kyoto Protocol, Desertification, Endangered Species, Environmental Modification, Hazardous Wastes, Law of the Sea, Marine Dumping, Ozone Layer Protection, Ship Pollution, Wetlands. It has signed, but not ratified: Air Pollution-Persistent Organic Pollutants, Air Pollution-Sulfur 94, Air Pollution-Volatile Organic Compounds.

In 2009, Ukraine's emissions from the consumption of fossil fuels totaled 260 million metric tons of carbon dioxide, this rose to 275 million metric tons in 2010. (Source: EIA)

SPACE PROGRAMME

Much of the former Soviet Union's industry was based in Ukraine. However, despite this the Ukrainian space agency has been slow to develop. The National Space Agency of Ukraine (NKAU) was established in 1992. Now known as the State Space Agency of Ukraine, it has an annual budget of approximately $250 million. Ukraine has been responsible for over 100 launches into space including six satellites, most recently the Sich-2 research satellite. Current programs include a co-operation with Brazil to supply launch rockets for Brazil's Alcantera Space Port. It is also working on a satellite to fly around the moon with an estimated launch date of 2017.

State Space Agency of Ukraine, URL: http://www.nkau.gov.au

UNITED ARAB EMIRATES

Al Imarat al Arabiya al Muttahida

Capital: Abu Dhabi (Population estimate: 1 million)

Head of State: Sheikh Khalifa bin Zayed al-Nahyan (President) (page 1389)

Vice-President: Sheikh Mohammed bin Rashid al-Maktoum (page 1376)

National Flag: A red vertical stripe one quarter of the length of the flag near the staff, three horizontal stripes green white and black from top to bottom.

CONSTITUTION AND GOVERNMENT

Constitution

The United Arab Emirates, formerly the Trucial States, is a federation established in 1971 of the following seven Emirates: Abu Dhabi, Dubai, Sharjah, Ajman, Umm al Qaiwain, Ras al Khaimah and Fujairah. The federal system of government is composed of a Supreme Council, made up of the rulers of each of the emirates. A Cabinet or Council of Ministers, a Parliamentary body, the Federal National Council in which is vested legislative and executive powers, and an independent judiciary, at the peak of which is the Federal Supreme Court. The president and vice president are elected from among its number by the Supreme Council of Rulers, which is formed by the hereditary rulers of the seven states.

To consult the constitution, please visit: http://www.mfnca.ae/?lang=en&m=options&act=content_detail&content_id=438

International Relations

The UAE is currently in dispute with Iran over the sovereignty of the Abu Musa and Greater and Lesser Tunb Islands in the Persian Gulf.

Recent Events

On November 1 2004, Sheikh Zayad announced a new cabinet. For the first time it included a female member Shaikha Lubna al-Qasimi as Minister of Economy and Planning. Sheikh Zayad bin Sultan Al Nahyan died on 2 November 2004. He had been president of the United Arab Emirates since independence in 1971 and was succeeded by his eldest son, Sheikh Khalifa bin Zayed al-Nahyan.

In December 2006 the United Arab Emirates held its first elections, to elect half of the country's Federal National Council. Just one per cent of the population were selected by the rulers to vote.

France signed a deal with the UAE in January 2008 which permitted France to establish a permanent military base in Abu Dhabi.

In July 2008 the UAE cancelled Iraq's entire debt to it of US$7 million.

In November 2009 one of Dubai's leading companies, the investment conglomerate Dubai World, requested a moratorium on debt repayments. This action fuelled fears in the financial markets that it would default on billions of dollars debt held abroad. The result was a fall in the Dubai index of 20 per cent. In December neighbouring emirate Abu Dhabi, gave Dubai US$10 billion to help pay off its debts.

In January 2010 the Burj Khalifa tower opened in Dubai as the world's tallest building.

The UAE joined the international military operation in Libya in March 2011.

In April 2011, it was reported that a number of activists were imprisoned after signing an online petition asking for reforms. They were pardoned and released in November 2011.

In November 2011, the UAE confirmed its support for the Palestinian request to gain international recognition as a full member of the UN.

In April 2012, it was reported that a member of the ruling family in Ras al-Khaimah was put under house arrest after calling for political openess.

In January 2013, the trial began of 94 people accused of trying to seize power. The Attorney General said the accused had links to foreign groups such as the Muslim Brotherhood.

Supreme Council (as at March 2013)
Head of State, Ruler of Abu Dhabi: H.H. President Sheikh Khalifa bin Zayed al-Nahyan (page 1389)
Ruler of Dubai: Sheikh Mohammed bin Rashid al-Maktoum (page 1376)
Rule of Sharjah: H.H. Dr Sheikh Sultan bin Mohammed Al Qassimi
Ruler of Ras al-Khaimah: H.H. Sheikh Saud bin Saqr Al Qasimi
Ruler of Umm al'Qaiwain: H.H. Sheikh Saud ibn Rashid Al Mu'alla
Ruler of Ajman: H.H. Sheikh Humaid bin Rashid Al Nuaimi
Ruler of Fujairah: H.H. Sheikh Hamad bin Mohammed Al Sharqi

Legislature
The unicameral Federal National Council has 40 appointed members representing the separate emirates according to population: Abu Dhabi and Dubai both have eight members; Sharjah and Ras al-Khaimah both have six members; and Fujairah, Umm al-Qaiwain, and Ajman all have four members. It has a consultative and legislative role. Members serve a two year term.

Federal National Council, *Majlis Watani Itihad*, PO Box 836, Abu Dhabi, UAE. Tel: +971 2 681 2000, fax: +971 2 681 2846, e-mail: fncuae@emirates.net.ae URL: http://www.almajles.gov.ae
Speaker: Saeed Mohammed Al Kindi
The Council of Ministers is led by the prime minister appointed by the Supreme Council of rulers. Each state is represented by at least one minister, with the senior posts being allocated to the larger emirates. The Council of Ministers initiates legislation for ratification by the Supreme Council of Rulers, which is also the policy making body and meets formally about once a year.

Cabinet (as at March 2013)
Prime Minister, Minister of Defence and Vice President: Sheikh Mohammed bin Rashid al-Maktoum (page 1376)
Deputy Prime Minister and Minister of the Interior: Sheikh Sultan bin Zayed Al-Nahyan
Deputy Prime Minister and Minister of Presidential Affairs: Sheikh Mansour bin Zayed Al-Nahyan
Minister of Finance: Sheikh Hamdan bin Rashid Al-Maktoum
Minister of Foreign Affairs: Shaikh Abdullah bin Zayed al-Nahyan
Minister of Higher Education and Scientific Research: Shaikh Hamdan bin Mubarka al-Nahyan
Minister of Education: Humaid Mohammed Obeid Al Qattami
Minister of Economy and Industry: Sultan bin Sayed al-Mansouri
Minister of Health: Abdul Rahman Mohammed al-Owais
Minister of Energy: Suhai bin Mohammed Faraj al-Mazroui
Minister of Public Works: Dr Abdullah bin Mohammed Balhaif al-Nuaimi
Minister of Justice: Hadef bin Juaan al-Dhaheri
Minister of Labour: Saqr Ghabbash Said Ghabbash
Minister of Cabinet Affairs: Mohammed Abdullah Al Garqawi
Minister of Social Affairs: Mariam Mohammed Khalfan al-Roumi
Minister of Foreign Trade: Shaikha Lubna bint Khalid al-Qasimi
Minister of Environment and Water: Rashid Ahmad Bin-Fahad
Minister of Development and International Co-operation: Shaikha Lubna bint Khalid al-Qasimi
Minister of Culture, Youth and Commmunity Development: Shaikh Nahyan bin Mubarak al-Nahyan
Ministers of State
Minister of State for Foreign Affairs: Anwar Mohammed Gargash
Minister of State for Finance: Ubayd Hamil al Tayir
Minister of State without Portfolio: Maytha Salim al-Shamisi
Minister of State without Portfolio: Rim Ibrahim Al-Hashimi
Minister of State without Portfolio: Sultan bin Ahmed Sultan al-Jaber
Minister of State without Portfolio: Abdullah bin Mohammed Ghubash

Ministries
Ministry of State for Finance & Industry, P.O. Box 433, Abu Dhabi, U.A.E. Tel: +971 2 672 6000, fax: +971 2 666 3088, e-mail: mofi@uae.gov.ae, URL: http://www.fedfin.gov.ae
Ministry of Defence, P.O. Box 46616, Dubai, U.A.E. Tel: +971 2 446 1300, fax: +971 2 446 3286, URL: http://www.mod.gov.ae/
Ministry of Foreign Affairs, P.O. Box 1, Abu Dhabi, U.A.E. Tel: +971 2 444 4071, fax: +971 2 449 4994, e-mail: mofa@mofa.gov.ae, URL: http://www.mofa.gov.ae
Ministry of Information & Culture, P.O. Box 17, Abu Dhabi, U.A.E. Tel: +971 2 445 3000, fax: +971 2 445 2504, e-mail: mininfex@emirates.net.ae, URL: http://www.uaeinteract.com
Ministry of Planning, P.O. Box 904, Abu Dhabi, U.A.E. Tel: +971 2 627 1100, fax: +971 2 626 9942, e-mail: mop@uae.gov.ae, URL: http://www.uae.gov.ae/mop
Ministry of Higher Education & Scientific Research, P.O. Box 45253, Abu Dhabi, U.A.E. Tel: +971 2 642 8000, fax: +971 2 642 7262, e-mail: mohe@uae.gov.ae, URL: http://www.uae.gov.ae/mohe
Ministry of Economy & Commerce, P.O. Box 901, Abu Dhabi, U.A.E. Tel: +971 2 626 5000, fax: +971 2 621 5339, e-mail: economy@emirates.net.ae, URL: http://www.economy.gov.ae
Ministry of State for Supreme Council Affairs, P.O. Box 545, Abu Dhabi, U.A.E. Tel: +971 2 632 3900, fax: +971 2 634 4225
Ministry of Interior, P.O. Box 398, Abu Dhabi, U.A.E. Tel: +971 2 441 4666, fax: +971 2 441 4938, e-mail: moi@uae.gov.ae, URL: http://moi.uae.gov.ae/moiwebportal
Ministry of Health, P.O. Box 848, Abu Dhabi, U.A.E. Tel: +971 2 633 4716, fax: 971 2 672 6000, e-mail: postmaster@moh.gov.ae, URL: http://www.moh.gov.ae
Ministry of Energy, P.O. Box 59, Abu Dhabi, U.A.E. Tel: +971 2 627 4222, fax: +971 2 626 9738, e-mail: mopmr@uae.gov.ae, URL: http://www.uae.gov.ae/moew
Ministry of State for Cabinet Affairs, P.O. Box 899, Abu Dhabi, U.A.E. Tel: +971 2 681 1113, fax: +971 2 681 2968, e-mail: csb@csb.ae, URL: http://www.csb.gov.ae
Ministry of Agriculture and Fisheries, P.O. Box 213, Abu Dhabi, U.A.E. Tel: +971 2 666 2781, fax: +971 2 665 4787, e-mail: maf@uae.gov.ae, URL: http://www.uae.gov.ae/mar
Ministry of Communications, P.O. Box 900, Abu Dhabi, U.A.E. Tel: +971 2 665 1900, fax: +971 2 665 1691, e-mail: moc@moc.uae.gov.ae, URL: http://www.uae.gov.ae/moc
Ministry of Public Works & Housing, P.O. Box 878, Abu Dhabi, U.A.E. Tel: +971 2 665 1778, fax: +971 2 666 5598, URL: http://www.mpw.ae
Ministry of Education & Youth, P.O. Box 295, Abu Dhabi, U.A.E. Tel: +971 2 6213800, fax: +971 2 631 3778, URL: http://www.education.gov.ae
Ministry of Justice & Islamic Affairs & Awqaf, P.O. Box 260, Abu Dhabi, U.A.E. Tel: +971 2 681 4000, fax: +971 2 681 0680, e-mail: moj@uae.gov.ae, URL: http://www.uae.gov.ae/moj

Ministry of Labour & Social Affairs, P.O. Box 809, Abu Dhabi, U.A.E. Tel: +971 2 667 1700, fax: +971 2 666 5889, e-mail: minister@mol.gov.ae, URL: http://www.mol.gov.ae

Elections

There are no legal political parties in the UAE. Power rests with the seven hereditary sheikhs, also known as emirs. In December 2006 around 7,000 people were selected to vote in the country's first elections when half of the Federal National Council was elected.

Diplomatic Representation

Embassy of the United Emirates, 30 Prince's Gate, London SW7 1PT. Tel: +44 (0)20 7581 1281, fax: +44 (0)20 7581 9616, e-mail: information@uaeembassyuk.net, URL: http://www.uaeembassyuk.net/
Ambassador: Abdulrahman Ghanem Almutaiwee (page 1376)
Embassy of the United Arab Emirates, 3522 International Court, NW, Suite 400, Washington DC 20008, USA. Tel: +1 202 243 2400, fax: +1 202 243 2432, URL: http://www.uae-embassy.org/
Ambassador: Yousef Al Otaiba (page 1376)
British Embassy, PO Box 248, Abu Dhabi, United Arab Emirates. Tel: +971 2 6326600, fax: +971 2 6318138, e-mail: chancery@abudhabi.mail.fco.gov.uk, URL: http://ukinuae.fco.gov.uk
Ambassador: Dominic Jermey
US Embassy, Al Sudan Street, Abu Dhabi, PO Box 4009, United Arab Emirates. Tel: +971 2 436691, fax: +971 2 434771, e-mail: usembabu@emirates.net.ae, URL: http://abudhabi.usembassy.gov
Ambassador: Michael H. Corbin
Permanent Mission to the UN, 305 East 47th Street, 7th Floor, New York, NY 10017, USA. Tel: + 1 212 371 0480, URL: http://www.un.int/uae
Permananet Representative to the UN, New York: Ahmed al-Jarman

LEGAL SYSTEM

The law is heavily influenced by French, Roman, Egyptian and Islamic law. The constitution guarantees an independent judiciary.

The judicial system consists of the Federal Supreme Court and Federal Courts of First Instance. The Supreme Court has jurisdiction in constitutional matters, and is made up of five judges who are appointed by the Supreme Council of Rulers. There are three main branches within the court structure: civil, criminal and Islamic law. In all Emirates other than Dubai and Ras Al Khaimah, final appeal is to the federal Supreme Court located in Abu Dhabi.

Dubai and Ras Al Khaimah are not part of the federal judicial system. These two emirates have their own court systems, which are not subject to the federal Supreme Court. The court structure in Dubai is comprised of the following courts: the Court of First Instance, the Court of Appeal and the Court of Cassation. The Court of First Instance includes the Civil Court, the Criminal Court and the Sharia Court.

The Sharia court is the Islamic court in the UAE and is primarily responsible for civil matters between Muslims. Sharia courts have the exclusive jurisdiction to hear family disputes, including matters involving divorce, inheritances, child custody, child abuse and guardianship of minors. The federal Sharia court may also hear appeals of certain criminal cases including rape, robbery, driving under the influence of alcohol and related crimes.

In terms of human rights, citizens cannont change their government. There have been reports of torture, and flogging is a judicially sanctioned punishment. Arrest and detention can be arbitrary.The government restricts civil liberties, including freedom of speech, press, assembly, association, and religion.

The UAE retains the death penalty. Death sentences may be appealed to the ruler of the emirate in which the offense is committed, or to the president of the federation, although in the case of murder, only the victim's family may commute a death sentence. The government normally negotiates with victims' families for the defendant to offer financial compensation, or diya, to receive their forgiveness and commute death sentences. The most recent execution was reported to have taken place in 2011.

LOCAL GOVERNMENT

The United Arab Emirates is made up of seven emirates, Abu Dhabi, Dubai, Sharjah, Ajman, Umm al Qaiwain, Ras al Khaimah and Fujairah. Each of the emirates has its own local government, which varies in size depending on a number of different factors including area, population and development.

Abu Dhabi, as the largest and most populous emirate, has its own governing body, the Executive Council, which is chaired by the Crown Prince Sheikh Khalifa bin Zayed Al Nahyan, and is divided into an Eastern and Western regions, it is made up of 60 members from the emirates main tribes and families. Both regions are headed by an official called the Ruler's Representative. The main cities, Abu Dhabi and Al Ain, are administered by Municipalities, each of which nominate a Municipal Council. Administration in the emirate is run by a number of local departments dealing with services such as public works, water and electricity, finance, and customs.

Other emirates have adopted a similar pattern of local government with Sharjah devolving some authority on a local basis to three branches headed by deputy chairmen.

In smaller or more remote settlements the ruler and government may choose a local representative, an emir or wali, to act as a conduit through which the concerns of the local inhabitants can be directed to the government. In most cases, these are tribal figures. A rulers representative is located on the terminal island of Das.

AREA AND POPULATION

Area

The combined area of the Emirates is 32,000 sq. miles. The largest is Abu Dhabi with 32,400 sq. miles (83,600 sq. km). It is bordered to the north by the Arabian Gulf, to the East by the Gulf of Oman and the Sultanate of Oman, to the south by Saudi Arabia, and to the West by Qatar. The terrain is generally flat, coastal plain, rolling sand dunes and desert wasteland. There are mountains in the east. The climate is dry sub-tropical with hot summers (May to October) and high humidity near the coast.

To view a map of the UAE, please consult:
http://www.lib.utexas.edu/maps/cia08/united_arab_emirates_sm_2008.gif

Population

The population in 2010 was estimated at 7.512 million giving a density of approximately 45 people per sq km. The annual population growth rate was 9.1 per cent over the period 2000-10. Recent figures show that less than 20 per cent of the population are UAE citizens. The official language is Arabic. English, Farsi and Hindi are also spoken. Over 78 per cent of the population lives in urban areas. (Source: http://www.who.int, World Health Statistics 2012)

The following table shows the population in 2003 for each emirate.

Emirate	Area in Sq. Km	Population
Abu Dhabi	67,340	1,591,000
Dubai	3,885	1,204,000
Sharjah	2,590	636,000
Ras al-Khaimah	168	195,000
Ajman	259	235,000
Fujairah	1165	118,000
Umm al-Qaiwain	777	62,000

Births, Marriages, Deaths

In 2010 the birth rate was estimated at 13.1 births per 1,000 population, and the death rate at 1.2 deaths per 1,000 population. Average life expectancy from birth in 2009 was 77 years for males and 79 years for females. Healthy life expectancy in 2007 was 68 years. The median age in 2010 was 30 years. Approximately 17 per cent of the population are aged less than 15 years old and 1 per cent over 60 years old. The infant mortality rate in 2009 was 7 per 1,000 live births. The maternal mortality rate was 54 per 100,000 live births. The total fertility rate was 1.7 per adult female in 2010. (Source: http://www.who.int, World Health Statistics 2012)

Public Holidays 2014

1 January: New Year
14 January: Prophet's Birthday*
27 May: Al Esra Wa Al-M'iraj (Ascension of the Prophet)*
29 July: Eid Al-Fitr*
5 October: Eid Al-Adha*
3 November: Accession of Sheikh Khalifa bin Zayed al-Nahyan
2 December: National Day
25 December: Christmas (Christian holiday)
*Islamic holidays are based on the sighting of the moon and so vary from year to year.

EMPLOYMENT

The government is seeking to encourage the replacement of the predominantly expatriate workforce with UAE nationals. According to figures from 2006, from a workforce of 2.6 million, expatriates made up 96 per cent of the private sector workforce.

Total Employment by Economic Activity

Occupation	2008
Agriculture, hunting & forestry	72,460
Fishing	6,000
Mining & quarrying	35,928
Manufacturing	160,456
Electricity, gas & water supply	25,199
Construction	227,856
Wholesale & retail trade, repairs	300,364
Hotels & restaurants	72,459
Transport, storage & communications	132,586
Financial intermediation	58,727
Real estate, renting & business activities	147,894
Public admin. & defence; compulsory social security	170,300
Education	83,943
Health & social work	48,573
Other community, social & personal service activities	59,268
Households with employed persons	236,545
Extra-territorial organisations & bodies	3,826
Other	3,766
Total	1,846,150

Source: Copyright © International Labour Organization (ILO Dept. of Statistics, http://laborsta.ilo.org)

UNITED ARAB EMIRATES

BANKING AND FINANCE

Currency
The UAE Dirham was introduced as legal currency replacing the Bahrain dinar in Abu Dhabi and the Qatar/Dubai riyal in other emirates.
1 UAE dirham (Dh) = 100 fils

GDP/GNP, Inflation, National Debt
The economy of the United Arab Emirates is based predominantly on the production of oil and gas, but in recent years the UAE has encouraged other industries and now has a successful tourist industry as well as a thriving free trade zone. The global recession has affected the economy with the construction sector being particularly hard hit. In order to counter the global recession, the government is trying to diversify the economy. Figures from 2006 suggest that economic growth of non oil and gas sectors was around 18.0 per cent. GDP at 2007 estimates was put at US$198 billion, showing a growth rate of 6.3 per cent. Per capita GDP for that year was put at US$45,300. In 2009, GDP was estimated to be US$250 billion. In 2011, it was estimated to be US$340 billion with a growth rate of 5 per cent.

Services contribute some 55 per cent of GDP, oil 37 per cent, manufacturing and mining 12 per cent. Agriculture contributes just 1 per cent.

Inflation was estimated to be 1.6 per cent in 2009, falling under 1 per cent in 2010. It remained at under 1 per cent in 2011.

Foreign Investment
In order to encourage direct foreign investment UAE now has several established free zones with over 6,000 companies operating in them.

Balance of Payments / Imports and Exports
Figures for 2011 show that the total earned from exports and re-exports was an estimated US$275 billion. The total cost of imports for that year was estimated at US$199 billion. Around 17 per cent of exports go to Japan. Other main export destinations are South Korea, India, Singapore and Oman. Imports come mainly the US, Japan, the UK, Germany and South Korea. Main exports are crude oil and natural gas. The main imports are manufactured goods, food, transportation, equipment and machinery.

The UAE continues to try to lessen its dependence on oil based products and find new markets for export goods such as aluminium products.

Central Bank
Central Bank of the United Arab Emirates, PO Box 845, Al Bateen Area, Bainoona Street, Abu Dhabi, UAE. Tel: +971 2 6652220, fax: +971 2 6668621 / 2 6652504, URL: http://www.centralbank.ae
Governor: Sultan bin Nasir al-Suwaydi

Chambers of Commerce and Trade Organisations
Abu Dhabi Chamber of Commerce & Industry, URL: http://www.abudhabichamber.ae
Ajman Chamber of Commerce, URL: http://www.ajmanchamber.ae/en/home
Dubai Chamber of Commerce & Industry, URL: http://www.dubaichamber.com/
Fujairah Chamber of Commerce, Industry and Agriculture, URL: http://www.fujcci.ae
Ras Al Khaimah Chamber of Commerce, Industry and Agriculture, URL: http://www.rakchamber.com
Sharjah Chamber of Commerce & Industry, URL: http://www.sharjah.gov.ae

MANUFACTURING, MINING AND SERVICES

Primary and Extractive Industries
Figures from 2012 show that the United Arab Emirates has oils reserves of 97.8 billion barrels, most of which is located in Abu Dhabi. In 2011, 3.0 million barrels per day were produced of which 2.6 million barrels was crude oil. The crude distillation capacity is over 463,000 barrels per day. and total oil refinery capacity is 773,000 barrels per day

Abu Dhabi has 1,064 producing oil wells and is by far the biggest oil producer in the UAE. Its output is about 84 per cent of the total and its reserves exceed 93 per cent of the country's oil reserves of 98 billion barrels (just under 10 per cent of the world total). Oil companies from Japan, France, Britain and other countries own up to 40 per cent of the energy sector in Abu Dhabi, making the UAE the only Gulf oil producer to have kept foreign partners on a production-sharing basis. More than half of Abu Dhabi's oil production comes from the Abu Dhabi Company for Onshore Operations (ADCO) which is amongst the ten largest oil firms worldwide. The second main producer is the Abu Dhabi Marine Operating Company (ADMA-OPCO).

There is an extensive offshore oil drilling programme with 220 wells lined up for exploration. Each of the seven emirates as a constitutional right controls its own oil production.

Most of the oil is destined for Far East markets, primarily Japan. The Abu Dhabi National Oil Company has two refineries: the Emirates National Oil Company has one in Dubai's Jebel Ali Free Zone; and the UAE has two other refineries at Umm al-Nar and Fujairah. A further private refinery is planned for Dubai. Some oil refining is done abroad, for example by the Austrian firm OMV and at the Pak-Arab refinery in Pakistan.

In 2012, the UAE began operating an oil pipeline which bypasses the Strait of Hormuz. In the past Iran has often threatened to closed the strait.

UAE has gas reserves estimated at 228 trillion cubic feet, the fourth largest reserves in the world. Gas production in 2011 was an estimated 1.8 trillion cubic feet. Consumption of natural gas was an estimated 2.1 trillion cubic feet in 2010. Gas exports in 2005 were 201

billion cubic feet but the UAE is now a gas importer. All gas reserves in Abu Dhabi are owned by the Abu Dhabi National Oil Company on behalf of the government. Recent figures show that current gas reserves will last for up 170 years.

In 1998 the Dolphin project was launched. Its aims are to develop links for a gas infrastructure through several pipelines between the UAE, Qatar and Oman, and eventually to Pakistan. The first gas from the North Field wells began flowing in 2007. The Al Ain Fujairah gas pipeline came online in 2008 and exports gas from Qatar to Oman. The Taweelah Fujairah gas pipeline is currently still under construction.

The Emirates have reserves of copper, talc, and manganese but they are not exploited.

Energy
In 2010, electricity production was estimated at 91.8 billion kilowatthours with consuption at 85.1 billion kilowatthours. Capacity has being expanded. It stands at 23.25 GWe. Plans are also underway to build a regional power grid between the countries of the Gulf Cooperation Council (GCC). 97 per cent of UAE's electricity is produced by gas turbines, with the remainder produced by diesel and steam turbines.(Source: EIA)

Manufacturing
Industrial development has been fostered in order to create a more stable economy and break the previous dependency on oil revenue. The main non-oil activities are government services, trade, restaurants and hotels, construction, manufacturing and the financial, banking and insurance sector. Development is centred on free-trade zones. On the basis of oil production, a number of related and down-stream industries have been established, among them: metal industry particularly the aluminium industry, chemical, petroleum, coal, rubber and plastics industries as well as a textile and clothing industry. The construction industry is so large it is estimated that half of the world's cranes are situated in the United Arab Emirates and one of the current projects is the construction of the Burj Dubai. On completion this building will be the tallest building in the world (800 metres).

Service Industries
Tourism has also been promoted on the basis of the need to diversify the sources of national income. In Dubai revenue from tourism may soon overtake that gained from oil. To further develop its tourist industry, plans are underway to expand the national airline and airports to cope with an expected 10 million visitors arriving annually by 2010. The ultimate capacity is to be 50 million. Dubai has the only seven star hotel in the world and is currently building an underwater hotel as well as the world's largest theme park. Figures for 2006 show that the UAE had 7.1 million visitors generating expenditure of US$4.9 billion.

Agriculture
The area under cultivation in the UAE at one time was 40,000 ha. This has now grown to approximately 2.3 million hectares. The development of the agricultural sector is hampered by poor soil and above all low rainfall. Therefore efforts have been made to introduce plant varieties suitable for the country's climate and conditions. Main crops include tomatoes, squash and cabbages. Date and fruit trees occupy almost 50 per cent of the total. The UAE is now 100 per cent self sufficient in dates and fish, nearly 60 per cent sufficient in vegetable production, and over 30 per cent in meat production and nearly 20 per cent in poultry.

Agricultural Production in 2010

Produce	Int. $'000*	Tonnes
Dates	365,153	775,000
Indigenous camel meat	67,970	32,432
Tomatoes	60,978	32,432
Indigenous chicken meat	54,954	38,580
Indigenous goat meat	30,992	12,935
Hen eggs, in shell	21,647	26,100
Indigenous cattle meat	19,068	7,059
Camel milk, whole, fresh	14,457	42,400
Indigenous sheep meat	14,200	5,215
Goat milk, whole, freh	14,094	42,000
Mangoes, mangosteens, guavas	10,785	18,000
Cow milk, whole, fresh	7,333	23,500

* unofficial figures
Source: http://faostat.fao.org/site/339/default.aspx Food and Agriculture Organization of the United Nations, Food and Agricultural commodities production

Fishing
In 1997 there were 17,286 fishermen, resulting in a total fish catch of 114,358 tonnes. In an effort to stop overfishing in UAE waters, in 2001 the government brought in a law that all fishing boats in the area must have a UAE captain. Figures for 2002 put the total catch at 97,574 tonnes, falling to 79,610 in 2010.

COMMUNICATIONS AND TRANSPORT

Travel Requirements
Citizens of the USA, Canada, Australia and most of the EU require a passport valid for three months from the date of arrival (six months for business travel) but do not need a visa for stays of up to 30 days. The exceptions are nationals of Bulgaria, Cyprus, Czech Republic, Estonia, Hungary, Latvia, Lithuania, Malta, Poland, Romania, Slovak Republic and Slovenia, who do need a visa. Transit passengers of these EU countries do not need a visa if holding valid onward or return documentation and not leaving the airport for up to 12 hours. Other nationals should contact the embassy to check visa requirements.

The government of the United Arab Emirates refuses entry and transit to those holding transit documents issued from Lebanon or the Syrian Arab Republic, and travel documents issued by the Coalition Authority in Iraq, should their visas be obtained through an associate in the UAE.

The embassy usually only issues visas for diplomatic or certain business visits. Visas for tourists, family visitors and business travellers must be arranged via the sponsor - i.e. the hotel/package tour operator or UAE resident/company concerned. This includes transit visas.

National Airlines
Emirates Airline, Dubai. URL: http://www.emirates.com

International Airports
The international airports at Abu Dhabi, Dubai, Sharjah, Al Ain, Fujairah and Ras al Khaimah are served by nearly twenty international airlines as well as the major freight contractors, while an air-taxi service was initiated in June 1976. Dubai Airport is rapidly growing and has its own Free Zone and handled 16 million passengers in 2002. Airstrips exist in the oil fields and in Sharjah. The airport at Abu Dhabi has been developed with the addition of a second runway and 60,000 sq. metres of new facilities, which should increase the capacity by one and a half times. In 2006 it handled 6.8 million passengers. The airport is currently undergoing expansion. A temporary expansion will cater for an additional 3 million passengers. The final airport which should be completed by 2010 should be capable of handling 20 million passengers initially with an aim of 50 million capacity.
Abu Dhabi International Airport, URL: http://www.dcaauh.gov.ae
Dubai International Airport, URL: http://www.dubaiairport.com

Railways
A subway system is due to come into operation in Dubai in 2009.

Roads
There are no railways in the UAE, but a sophisticated road network now links all of the Emirates and is being extended both to the Liwa Oasis in southern Abu Dhabi and along the coast towards the border with Qatar in the west. Paved highways total 3,326 km. Vehicles drive on the right.

Shipping
A number of shipping companies make regular calls to Emirates ports including the British India Steam Navigation Company, the British India Company, Holland Persian Gulf, DDG Hansa and Maersk Line. Most services are to Dubai although Abu Dhabi is now also becoming an important port of call. There are 15 commercial ports, and each emirate has its own port as well as many fishing harbours. Some of the ports have associated Free Zones: Jebel Ali in Dubai; Ahmed bin Rashid in Umm al-Qaiwain; Hamriyah Free Zone in Sharjah; the Fujairah Free Zone; and Ras al-Khaimah Free Zone. A Free Zone on Saadiyat Island is under construction. Traffic at UAE ports has increased by an average of eight per cent per year in recent years, leading to some form of expansion at most facilities.

HEALTH

UAE has a comprehensive health care service and the healthcare system has been rated by the UNDP as among the best in the world.

In 2009, the government spent approximately 8.8 per cent of its total budget on healthcare (up from 7.6 per cent in 2000), accounting for 76.9 per cent of all healthcare spending. Total expenditure on healthcare equated to 4.4 per cent of the country's GDP. Per capita expenditure on health was approximately US$1,704, compared with US$885 in 2000. Latest figures from the WHO show that in 2005-10 there were 9,215 doctors (19.3 per 10,000 population), 19,529 nurses (40.9 per 10,000 population), 2,053 dentistry personnel and 2,817 pharmaceutical personnel. There were 19 hospital beds per 10,000 population.

In 2010 the infant mortality rate (probability of dying before first birthday) was 6 per 1,000 live births and the child (under-five years old) mortality rate was also 7 per 1,000 live births. The main causes of death in the under-fives are: prematurity (40 per cent), congenital anomalies (27 per cent), birth asphyxia (9 per cent), pneumonia (2 per cent) and diarrhoea (1 per cent).

In 2010, all the population had access to improved drinking water sources and an estimated 98 per cent of the population had access to improved sanitation. (Source: http://www.who.int, World Health Statistics 2012)

EDUCATION

Education is state funded and compulsory, and there is a private sector which caters for 40 per cent of pupils. The system has four tiers, kindergarten for children ages four and five years, primary for ages six to eleven, intermediate for ages 12-14 and secondary for ages 15-17. There are now five universities including the Zayed University, which is women only. Grants are available for students who wish to study abroad.

In the period 2002-03 there were 1,208 schools and 40,278 teachers. Student enrolments were as follows: kindergarten 74,811; primary 266,224; preparatory 153,009; secondary 98,021; special needs education 1,632; religious and technical 2,975; literacy and adult education 21,330. There were a total of 16,128 university students (3,737 males; 12,391 females).

In 2007, 91 per cent of boys and 90 per cent of girls were enrolled in primary school and 81 per cent of boys and 84 per cent of girls were enrolled in secondary school. The pupil / teacher ratio in primary school is 17:1. Approximately 20 per cent go to tertiary education. (Source: UNESCO)

The literacy rate for adults in 2007 was 90.0 per cent, for the age group 15-24 years the rate is 95.0 per cent. On average 25.0 per cent of government spending goes on education.

RELIGION

The constitution is based on the state religion of Islam. Recent figures show that 76 per cent of the population are Muslim, 12 per cent are Christian, and around six per cent Hindu.

The UAE has a religious liberty rating of 6 on a scale of 1 to 10 (10 is most freedom). (Source: World Religion Database)

COMMUNICATIONS AND MEDIA

The constitution allows for freedom of expression but there is strong regulatory control of the media. There is censorship of foreign publications. Most broadcasters practise self-censorship especially with regard to politics and the ruling families. The government filters websites for political, religious and sexual content.

In 2012, the government outlawed online mockery of the government and attempts to organise public protests through social media.

Newspapers
Publications must be licensed.
Al Bayan, URL: http://www.albayan.co.ae/
Khaleej Times, URL: http://www.khaleejtimes.co.ae/
Gulf News, URL: http://www.gulf-news.com/

Broadcasting
Abu Dhabi (URL: http://www.emi.co.ae/home.asp), Dubai (URL: http://www.dubaitv.gov.ae/), Sharjah (URL: http://www.sharjahtv.ae/)and Ajman (URL: http://www.ajmantv.com/) all have television stations. There are six satellite television stations. Each emirate has its own radio station. Most broadcasters are government-owned but satellite television provides access to pan-Arab channels. The official news agency is Emirates News Agency (http://www.wam.org.ae/).

Telecommunications
There are an estimated 1.5 million landlines in use. Figures from 2008 estimate that there are 9.4 million mobile phone subscribers. ETISALAT have a US$500 m project for the Al Thuraya Satellite to be built by Hughes which will make UAE the first Arab country to have a communications satellite for GSM mobile phones. It will have a capacity of 2.5 m lines. Figures for 2009 estimate that the UAE has a high internet usage with 3.2 million users.

ENVIRONMENT

The UAE's islands and coasts have been inspected for inclusion on the UNESCO World Heritage list. They support 90 per cent of the western Arabian Gulf's breeding population of osprey, 60 per cent of the entire Gulf's population of sooty falcon and at least a third of the population of bridled tern, white cheeked tern and Saunder's little tern. Seven out of the world's twelve colonies of Socotra cormorant are here too.

The Environmental Research and Wildlife Development Agency (ERWDA) is responsible for environmental issues. A new law requires businesses to co-ordinate with and gain certificates of approval from the Agency for all projects that impact the environment. The marine environment is another priority with endangered species such as dugong and turtles being protected by law.

In 2003, there were an estimated 131.9 million metric tons of energy-related carbon dioxide emissions (natural gas 57 per cent, oil 43 per cent). Per capita energy related energy emissions were 44.1 metric tons in 2003. In 2010, the UAE's emissions from the consumption of fossil fuels totalled 199.37 million metric tons of carbon dioxide. (Source: EIA)

UAE is party to the following agreements: Biodiversity, Climate Change, Climate Change-Kyoto Protocol, Desertification, Endangered Species, Hazardous Wastes, Marine Dumping, Ozone Layer Protection. The UAE has signed but not ratified the Law of the Sea.

SPACE PROGRAMME

DubaiSat-1, a remote sensing statlelite, was launched in 2009. It was funded by the UAE government at a cost of $50 million and built by South Orea. A second satellite, capable of producing higher resolution images, is expected to be launched in 2012. Aabar Investments, a private company based in Dubai, has a significant investment in Virgin Galactic.

UNITED KINGDOM

United Kingdom of Great Britain and Northern Ireland

Capital: London (Population estimate: 7,825,500)

Head of State: Her Majesty Queen Elizabeth II (Sovereign) (page 1420)

National Flag: Union Jack - dark blue, charged with the White Cross of St. Andrew (Scottish flag) and the Red Cross of St. Patrick (Irish flag). The colours are counter-changed and surmounted by the Red Cross of St. George (English flag) which is bordered with white.

CONSTITUTION AND GOVERNMENT

Constitution

There is no single written document defining the British Constitution. It is a structure based on a number of statutes, laws, traditions and customs assembled over many centuries. The Constitution can be amended through Acts of Parliament; one of the earliest changes, dating from 1215, is known as *Magna Carta,* which provides among other things for the equality of all men before the law. One of the latest was the Statute of Westminster, 1931, by which legislative autonomy was granted to the Dominions.

Britain is a constitutional monarchy in which the crown is hereditary. The Act of Settlement 1701 secured the Protestant succession to the throne. When the Sovereign leaves the realm, Counsellors of State are appointed to carry out the chief official functions of the monarch, including the holding of Privy Councils and signing of Acts passed by Parliament. The normal procedure is to appoint as Counsellors of State the members of the Royal family of full age who are next in succession to the throne.

The executive power belongs to the Sovereign, but it is entrusted to the Cabinet, which consists of the most important Ministers of the Crown, presided over by the Prime Minister. When it is known which Parliamentary party has a majority, or is able to command a majority of supporters in a newly elected House of Commons, the Sovereign calls the leader of that Party to become Prime Minister and form a government. The Prime Minister chooses the other ministers and these are then officially appointed by the Sovereign. In 2011 Commonwealth leaders agreed to change succession laws so that sons and daughters of any future UK monarch would have an equal right to the throne.

The UK's legislative power resides in the Parliament, which consists of the Monarchy, the House of Lords and the House of Commons.

Parliament's main functions are law-making, authorising taxation and public expenditure, and examining the actions of the Government. Most of this work is carried out, in both Houses, by a system of debates. During their passage through Parliament measures relating to public policy are called 'Bills'. The great majority are Government Bills, introduced by a minister; a few, (known as Private Members' Bills) are sponsored by individual members on their own initiative, but not many of these become law. Bills can be introduced in either House, except for Money Bills which impose taxation, and can only be introduced in the House of Commons.

When the Bill is introduced it normally receives its formal 'first reading', after which it is printed and circulated to members. At the 'second reading' the Bill is debated and if it passes this stage it is sent to a Committee, where details are discussed and amendments generally made. Finally the Bill is given a 'third reading' by the House and if passed is then sent to the other House. When a Bill has passed through all its parliamentary stages, it receives Royal Assent. It then becomes an Act of Parliament and law. Royal Assent may be given by the Sovereign in person or, periodically, by Royal Commission, but is usually declared by their Speakers (presidents) to both Houses.

Normally a Bill is passed by both the House of Commons and the House of Lords. A Bill which originates in the House of Lords cannot become law unless it is passed by the House of Commons, whereas a Bill passed in the Commons can become law under certain circumstances even if rejected by the Lords. The Lords cannot reject a Money Bill and they can merely delay for one year any other Bill which they do not support.

All laws are theoretically the laws of the Sovereign, which the judges cannot question, and therefore Parliament is free to legislate as it wishes. It can make new laws and alter the old ones, but it follows that a subsequent Parliament can alter the laws made by its predecessor.

International Relations

The United Kingdom enjoys close relations with many countries throughout the world, primarily through its former Empire, the successor of which The Commonwealth brings together many nations. The UK is a member of the EU, NATO and also has permanent seat on the UN Security Council. The UK and USA are strong allies both culturally and militarily, and the UK supported the US-led war in Iraq The UK also has troops operating in Afghanistan.

Recent Events

In September 1997 referendums were held in Scotland and Wales on whether there was support for establishing separate assemblies. Both countries voted for devolution and in 1999 the Scottish and Welsh Assemblies were inaugurated.

The Belfast Agreement, concerning the future of Northern Ireland, and subsequently known as the Good Friday Agreement, was signed on 10 April 1998 by the governments and major political parties of Ireland and the United Kingdom. The Agreement made provision for a referendum, which was held on 22 May 1998 in the Republic of Ireland and in Northern Ireland. Approximately 94 per cent of those who voted in the Republic voted in favour of the

agreement, as did approximately 71 per cent of those who voted in Northern Ireland. The referendum in the Republic of Ireland also asked if the constitution should be amended to end the territorial claim on Northern Ireland.

The Good Friday agreement provided for the devolution to a 108-member Northern Ireland Assembly of a range of executive and legislative powers (the executive arm of this body to be known as the Northern Ireland Executive), the creation of a North-South Ministerial Council (accountable to both this Assembly and the Oireachtas), and a British-Irish Council to represent the Irish Government, the British Government, and the devolved assemblies of Northern Ireland, Scotland and Wales. Elections for the Assembly were held on 25 June 1998, each member representing a constituency and being elected by proportional representation. The first meeting of the Assembly took place at Stormont on 2 July 1998.

In 2001 following the destruction of the Twin Towers in New York on September 11, Prime Minister Tony Blair pledged support for the US fight against terrorism and British troops took part in airstrikes in Afghanistan. In March 2003 the UK joined the US led campaign into Iraq to hunt for and destroy Weapons of Mass Destruction believed to be in Iraq. In the UK there were several large protests against the war and Foreign Secretary Robin Cook resigned his post in protest. On July 7 2005, 52 people were killed and 700 injured when suicide bombers protesting against the war in Iraq detonated bombs on the transport system in London.

In May 2007 Prime Minister Tony Blair announced his resignation as leader of the Labour Party and the post of Prime Minister. The announcement had been expected for some time as he had always said he would stand down after winning a third election. Chancellor of the Exchequer Gordon Brown was always believed to be the natural successor and following the announcement no challenger could gain enough support to stand in an election against him.

A diplomatic row developed between Britain and Russia, following the death of Aleksandr Litvinenko, a former Russian Security Service Officer, in November 2008. Litvinenko had become a critic of the Kremlin and was living in exile in London. Britain wanted Andrei Lugovoi, a former KGC agent, extradited to face murder charges, but Moscow refused.

Sir Menzies Campbell resigned as leader of the Liberal Democrats on 15 October 2007. Nick Clegg was elected to succeed him. In January 2008 Works and Pensions Secretary Peter Hain resigned from his post, resulting in a reshuffle of the cabinet.

Towards the end of 2007 in response to global credit concerns one of Britain's largest mortgage lenders, Northern Rock, suffered problems with funding, leading in turn to a lack of confidence in the bank. In September the bank applied for and received emergency financial support from the Bank of England. Customers were not reassured by this action and Britain saw its first run on a bank for many years. By the end of 2008 the global credit crunch had really taken hold and three of Britain's largest banks were part-nationalised in a £37 billion rescue package. The government also pumped millions into the financial system to prop up the failing economy.

In May 2008 the UK held local elections; the Labour Party suffered its worst defeat for 40 years.

British MPs can claim expenses for rent and mortgages on second homes and money to furnish them, as many MPs have to spend a large amount of their time living away from their home in their constituencies. In May 2009 a series of revelations showed how the expenses had been abused by members of all the main parties. By the beginning of June the scandal had become so large that several MPs announced that they would not be standing for re-election and Jacqui Smith, the first female Home Secretary, was the first of a number of ministers to leave the cabinet. Three MPs and two members of the House of Lords were later charged with fraud and subsequently found guilty and jailed.

In November 2009 the Chilcott enquiry began led by Sir John Chilcott. The enquiry was to learn the lessons of the Iraqi Conflict. The former prime minister Tony Blair and members of his cabinet at the time of the invasion were called to appear before the hearing.

In January 2010 the British economy officially came out of recession when economic growth was recorded at 0.1 per cent.

A General Election was held on 6 May 2010. The Conservative Party won the most seats but not enough to win a majority. Conservative leader David Cameron subsequently became Prime Minister after forming a coalition with the Liberal Democrats. It is the UK's first coalition government since 1945. Gordon Brown, the outgoing prime minister, resigned as leader of the Labour Party. Ed Miliband was later elected Labour Party leader in September 2010. Within days of announcing his cabinet, David Cameron was forced to carry out a minor reshuffle following the resignation of the new chief secretary to the Treasury, David Laws, over more expenses allegations. Danny Alexander moved from the Scottish Office to replace Mr Laws and Michael Moore was appointed the new secretary of state for Scotland.

On June 2nd 2010 a man in Cumbria, North West England, went on a killing spree armed with two rifles. He killed 12 people and wounded 11. Incidents like this are rare in the UK as the country has strict gun control laws. The government has announced a further review of the laws.

In October 2010 the Coalition published its public spending cuts plan aimed at reducing the UK's budget deficit. Government departments face an average of 19 per cent four-year cuts. Widespread protests took place against cuts in the education budget and the increase in tuition fees.

In May 2010 the UK and France signed a military and nuclear accord. Under the terms of the new treaty, France and the UK will co-operate in testing nuclear weapons and will share some military resources.

In March 2011 the UK became involved in the UN-led international intervention in the conflict in Libya.

In May 2011 a referendum was held on electoral reform, the question being, should the current electoral system (first-past-the-post) for the House of Commons be replaced with the alternative vote (AV) system. The vote was one of the key aims for the Liberal Democrats on becoming coalition partners with the Conservatives. The majority of voters rejected the proposal.

On July 7 2011 it was announced that after 168 years in print, the Sunday newspaper the News of the World would close following allegations of phone hacking and making payments to the police for stories. The paper was owned by Rupert Murdoch's News Corporation who at that time was bidding to take full ownership of the satellite broadcaster BSkyB, the bid was then abandoned. As the scandal unfolded the revelations of phone hacking progressed from celebrities to victims of crimes and their families, the scandal then moved to the USA where it was alleged that the phones of victims and families of the 9/11 disaster had been hacked into. Further resignations followed including Rebekkah Brookes who had been the editor at the time of the alleged hacking, Sir Paul Stephenson the Metropolitan Police Commissioner and James Murdoch. Rebekkah Brookes was one of several people arrested in March 2012 over the alleged hacking.

In August 2011 riots and looting in London were triggered by the killing of a man by police. The unrest spread to several other cities and the cost of the damage was estimated to be more than £200 million.

The Secretary of State for Energy and Climate Change, Chris Huhne, resigned in February 2012 over charges relating to an alleged speeding incident.

In March 2012, as part of the Queen's Diamond Jubilee celebrations, three towns were given city status. They are Chelmsford in England, St Asaph in Wales and Perth in Scotland.

In April 2012, the British economy recorded its second consecutive quarter of negative growth resulting in a return to recession.

In June 2012, HM Queen Elizabeth II celebrated her Diamond Jubilee.

The Olympic and Paralympic Games were held in London in August and September 2012 respectively.

In October 2012 the British and Scottish governments agreed on the terms for a referendum in Scotland concerning Scottish independence. The referendum will be held in the autumn of 2014 and the question asked will be, Should Scotland be an independent country?

In January 2013 Prime Minister David Cameron proposed the possibility of a referendum on whether the UK should leave the European Union, the referendum would not take place until after the next general election. Both the Liberal Democrats and the Labour Party opposed the idea.

Upper House
The House of Lords consists of hereditary peers, life peers, two archbishops and 24 senior bishops of the Church of England. Through its Appellate Committee, the House acts as the highest court of appeal in the country.

Having initiated 'Stage One' reforms in 1998, wherein the rights to sit in the House of Lords of all but 92 of the hereditary peers were removed, the Government's intention to establish a Royal Commission on the Reform of the House of Lords was announced in The Queen's Speech on 24 November 1998. The members of the Royal Commission were formally appointed by Royal Warrant on 18 February 1999 and the Commission, chaired by Lord Wakeham, met for the first time on 1 March 1999. A series of public meetings were held during the early summer to discuss not only possible changes to the House's role, functions, powers, procedures and composition, but also whether there is a case for a unicameral Parliament instead. The Royal Commission was asked to report its findings by 31 December 1999. The main proposed reforms were that members be chosen by an independent appointment commission, no party should have an overall majority, the second house should have 550 members, up to 195 of those to be elected, and all faiths and ethnic minorities to be fairly represented. After the 2001 election it was announced that further reforms were needed to create a second house 'better equipped' to act with the House of Commons. In May 2002 it was announced that a joint committee of the two houses would decide on the powers and structure of the upper house. In February 2003 the two houses voted on seven options for the upper house ranging from a fully appointed house, a fully elected house and five combinations of differing percentages of appointed and elected members. All seven options were rejected. In the Queen's speech following the General Election in May 2005, the reform of the House of Lords was again referred to, but no definite plans were mentioned. Early in 2007 a further attempt was made to reform the House of Lords, under the proposal MPs were asked to vote on whether they wanted a fully elected House or a fully appointed House with several options between, the vote was taken in March and two options came out ahead, the option for a wholly elected house and the option for 80 per cent to be elected and 20 per cent appointed. It was further proposed that the number of members sitting in the house would be 540 and those appointed if any would serve a term of 15 years. A cross party group was to be set up to discuss what reforms would be adopted but of course any decision made would eventually have to before the existing House of Lords.

In May 2012 at the state opening of Parliament the government set out its plans for the continuing House of Lords Reform. It set out plans for a smaller second house that would be made up of mostly elected members. These members would be elected a third at a time with older members leaving in stages. The number of members has not been agreed but many

think it will be 300, half of the number of MPs. Other matters for discussion include how the elections will take place and what form of proportional representation will be used, how big the regional constituencies will be and would Bishops still be members and if so how many.

House of Lords, London SW1A 0PW, United Kingdom. Tel: +44 (0)20 7219 3107, fax: +44 (0)20 7219 5979, e-mail: hlinfo@parliament.uk, URL: http://www.parliament.uk
Leader of the House of Lords: Lord Hill of Oareford CBE (page 1442)
Shadow Leader of The House of Lords: The Rt Hon Baroness Royall of Blaisdon (page 1506)

Lower House
The House of Commons consists of 659 Members of Parliament (MPs), each representing one of the country's 659 constituencies by a system of 'first past the post' or an absolute majority of votes cast. MPs are elected by the voters in each of these constituencies, MPs serve a term of five years although elections can be called before the end of a term. British citizens over the age of 21 can stand as an MP. The House of Commons elects its own Speaker, who presides over debates but does not vote unless the voting is equal, in which case the Speaker gives the casting vote in accordance with rules which preclude an expression of opinion upon the merits of the question. In the absence of the Speaker, one of three deputies presides.

House of Commons, London SW1A 0AA, United Kingdom. Tel: +44 (0)20 7219 3000, e-mail: hcinfo@parliament.uk, URL: http://www.parliament.uk
Speaker of the House of Commons: John Bercow (page 1387)

In December 1997 plans were announced to implement Scotland's first parliament in 300 years after a referendum in September of the same year. 75 per cent of the 70 per cent of the electorate who voted were in favour of a Scottish parliament. Elections for the 129-seat parliament were held on 6 May 1999; it was officially opened by the Queen on 1 July 1999 and is now fully operational. A Bill creating a Scottish parliament, with powers to vary income tax by up to three pence on standard income tax rate, received Royal Assent in 1998. Another important change is that the Scottish parliament will now have control over Scotland's criminal and civil law.

Sovereignty rests ultimately with Westminster and the Queen remains head of state for the whole United Kingdom. Key matters remain the responsibility of Westminster including foreign policy, defence, macroeconomic policy and national security.

Cabinet (as at June 2013)
Prime Minister, First Lord of the Treasury and Minister for the Civil Service: Rt. Hon. David Cameron (Con) (page 1399)
Deputy Prime Minister, Lord President of the Council (with special responsibility for political and constitutional reform): Rt. Hon. Nick (page 1406) Clegg (LD) (page 1406)
First Secretary of State, Secretary of State for Foreign and Commonwealth Affairs: Rt. Hon. William Hague (Con) (page 1436)
Chancellor of the Exchequer: Rt. Hon. George Osborne (Con) (page 1490)
Lord Chancellor, Secretary of State for Justice: Rt. Hon. Chris Grayling (Con) (page 1433)
Secretary of State for the Home Department; and Minister for Women and Equalities: Rt. Hon. Theresa May (Con) (page 1472)
Secretary of State for Defence: Rt. Hon. Philip Hammond (Con) (page 1437)
Secretary of State for Business, Innovation and Skills: Rt. Hon. Dr Vincent Cable (LD) (page 1398)
Secretary of State for Work and Pensions: Rt. Hon. Iain Duncan Smith (Con) (page 1418)
Secretary of State for Energy and Climate Change: Rt. Hon. Edward Davey (LD) (page 1412)
Secretary of State for Health: Rt. Hon. Jeremy Hunt (Con) (page 1445)
Secretary of State for Education: Rt. Hon. Michael Gove (Con) (page 1432)
Secretary of State for Communities and Local Government: Rt. Hon Eric Pickles (Con) (page 1495)
Secretary of State for Transport: Rt. Hon. Patrick McLoughlin (Con) (page 1475)
Secretary of State for Environment, Food and Rural Affairs: Rt. Hon. Owen Paterson (Con) (page 1492)
Secretary of State for International Development: Rt. Hon. Justine Greening MP (Con) (page 1433)
Secretary of State for Culture, Media and Sport: Maria Miller (Con) (page 1477)
Secretary of State for Northern Ireland: Rt. Hon. Theresa Villiers (Con) (page 1531)
Secretary of State for Scotland: Rt. Hon. Michael Moore (LD) (page 1479)
Secretary of State for Wales: David Jones (Con) (page 1451)
Chief Secretary to the Treasury: Rt. Hon. Danny Alexander (LD) (page 1374)
Minister without Portfolio (Minister of State): Rt. Hon. Kenneth Clarke QC (Con) (page 1405)
Leader of the House of Lords, Chancellor of the Duchy of Lancaster: Rt. Lord Hill of Oareford (Con) (page 1442)
Minister without Portfolio (Minister of State): Rt. Hon. Grant Shapps (Con) (page 1513)
Also Attending Cabinet
Minister for the Cabinet Office, Paymaster General: Rt. Hon. Francis Maude (Con) (page 1472)
Minister for Government Policy: Rt. Hon. Oliver Letwin (Con) (page 1463)
Minister of State (Universities and Science), Dept. for Business, Innovation and Skills: Rt. Hon. David Willetts (Con) (page 1537)
Leader of the House of Commons, Lord Privy Seal: Rt. Hon. Andrew Lansley CBE (Con) (page 1460)
Parliamentary Secretary to the Treasury and Chief Whip: Rt. Hon. Sir George Young (Con) (page 1541)
Senior Minister of State (Jointly Foreign and Commonwealth Office and Department for Communities and Local Government): Rt. Hon. Baroness Warsi (Con) (page 1534)
Minister of State (Jointly Cabinet Office and Department for Education): Rt. Hon. David Laws (LD) (page 1461)
Also invited to attend Cabinet Meetings when required
Attorney General: Dominic Grieve (Con) (page 1433)

STATES OF THE WORLD

UNITED KINGDOM

Government Ministers and Undersecretaries (as at June 2013)Attorney Generals's Office
Solicitor General: Oliver Heald (Con) (page 1440)
Office of the Advocate General for Scotland
Advocate General for Scotland: Rt. Hon. Lord Wallace of Tankerness QC (LD) (page 1533)
Department for Business, Innovation and Skills
Minister of State (Minister for Universities and Science): David Willetts (Con) (page 1537)
Minister of State: Michael Fallon (Con) (page 1423)
Minister of State (Trade & Investment) (Jointly with the FCO): Lord Green of Hurstpierpoint (page 1433)
Parliamentary Under Secretary of State: The Viscount Younger of Leckie (Con) (page 1542)
Parliamentary Under Secretary of State: Jo Swinson (LD) (page 1522)
Parliamentary Under Secretary of State (Jointly with the Department of Education): Matthew Hancock (Con) (page 1437)
Cabinet Office
Minister for the Cabinet Office and Paymaster General: Rt. Hon. Francis Maude (Con) (page 1472)
Minister for Government Policy: Rt. Hon. Oliver Letwin (Con) (page 1463)
Minister of State (Jointly with the Department of Education): Rt. Hon. David Laws (LD) (page 1461)
Parliamentary Secretary: Nick Hurd (Con) (page 1445)
Parliamentary Secretary: Chloe Smith (Con) (page 1516)
Minister without Portfolio (Minister of State): Rt. Hon. Kenneth Clarke QC (Con) (page 1405)
Minister without Portfolio (Minister of State): Rt. Hon. Grant Shapps (Con) (page 1513)
Department for Communities and Local Government
Senior Minister of State (Faith and Communities) (Jointly with the FCO): Rt. Hon. Baroness Warsi (Con) (page 1534)
Minister of State (Housing): Mark Prisk (Con) (page 1498)
Parliamentary Under Secretaries of State: Nicholas Boles (Con) (page 1391), Rt. Hon. Don Foster (LD) (page 1426), Brandon Lewis (Con) (page 1463), Baroness Hanham (Con) (page 1437)
Department for Culture, Media and Sport
Parliamentary Under Secretaries of State: Ed Vaizey (Con) (page 1530), Helen Grant (Con), (page 1432) Jo Swinson (LD) (page 1522)
Ministry of Defence
Minister of State: Rt. Hon. Andrew Robathan (Con) (page 1503)
Minister of State: Rt. Hon. Mark Francois (Con) (page 1426)
Parliamentary Under Secretaries of State: Dr Andrew Murrison (Con) (page 1483), Philip Dunne (Con) (page 1418), Lord Astor of Hever (Con) (page 1380)
Department for Education
Minister of State (Jointly with the Cabinet Office): Rt. Hon. David Laws (LD) (page 1461)
Parliamentary Under Secretaries of State: Lord Nash (Con), (page 1484) Matthew Hancock (Con) (page 1437), Edward Timpson (Con) (page 1525), Elizabeth Truss (Con) (page 1527)
Department for Energy and Climate Change
Minister of State: Gregory Barker (Con) (page 1383)
Minister of State: Michael Fallon (Con) (page 1423)
Parliamentary Under Secretary of State: Baroness Verma (Con) (page 1531)
Department for Environment, Food and Rural Affairs
Minister of State: David Heath (LD) (page 1440)
Parliamentary Under Secretaries of State: Richard Benyon (Con) (page 1387), Lord De Mauley (Con) (page 1414)
Foreign and Commonwealth Office
Senior Minister of State (Jointly with Department of Communities and Local Government): Rt. Hon. Baroness Warsi (Con) (page 1534)
Minister of State (Europe and NATO): David Lidington (Con) (page 1464)
Minister of State (South East Asia / Far East, India and Nepal, Latin America, Falklands, Australasia and Pacific, Commonwealth): Rt. Hon. Hugo Swire (Con) (page 1522)
Minister of State (Trade and Investment): Lord Green of Hurstpierpoint (Con) (page 1433)
Parliamentary Under Secretaries: Mark Simmonds (Con), (page 1515) Alistair Burt (Con) (page 1397)
Department of Health
Minister of State: Norman Lamb (LD) (page 1459)
Parliamentary Under Secretaries of State: Anna Soubry (Con) (page 1518), Daniel Poulter (Con) (page 1497), Lord Howe (Con) (page 1444)
Home Office
Minister of State (Immigration): Mark Harper (Con) (page 1438)
Minister of State (Policing) (jointly with the Ministry of Justice): Damian Green (Con) (page 1433)
Parliamentary Under Secretaries of State: James Brokenshire (Con) (page 1394), Lord Taylor of Holbeach (Con) (page 1523)
Department for International Development
Minister of State: Alan Duncan (Con) (page 1418)
Parliamentary Under Secretary of State: Lynne Featherstone (LD) (page 1423)
Ministry of Justice
Minister of State: Rt. Hon. Lord McNally (LD) (page 1475)
Minister of State (jointly with the Home Office): Damian Green (Con) (page 1433)
Parliamentary Under Secretaries of State: Helen Grant (Con) (page 1432), Jeremy Wright (Con) (page 1539)
Office of the Leader of the House of Commons
Leader of the House of Commons, Lord Privy Seal: Rt. Hon. Andrew Lansley (Con) (page 1460)
Parliamentary Secretary (Deputy Leader of the House): Rt. Hon. Tom Brake (LD) (page 1393)
Office of the Leader of the House of Lords
Leader of the House of Lords, Chancellor of the Duchy of Lancaster: Rt. Hon. Lord Hill or Oareford (Con) (page 1442)
Deputy Leader of the House of Lords: Lord McNally (LD) (page 1475)

Northern Ireland Office
Minister of State: Mike Penning (Con) (page 1494)
Scotland Office
Parliamentary Under Secretary of State: Rt. Hon. David Mundell (Con) (page 1482)
Department for Transport
Minister of State: Rt. Hon. Simon Burns (Con) (page 1397)
Parliamentary Under Secretaries of State: Norman Baker (LD) (page 1382), Stephen Hammond (Con) (page 1437)
HM Treasury
Financial Secretary: Rt. Hon. Greg Clark (Con) (page 1405)
Exchequer Secretary: David Gauke MP (Con) (page 1429)
Economic Secretary: Sajid Javid (Con) (page 1449)
Commercial Secretary: Lord Deighton KBE (Con) (page 1414)
Parliamentary Secretary to the Treasury and Chief Whip: Rt. Hon. Desmond Swayne (Con) (page 1522)
Wales Office
Parliamentary Under Secretaries of State: Stephen Crabb (Con) (page 1410), Baroness Randerson (LD) (page 1500)
Department for Work and Pensions
Minister of State: Mark Hoban (Con) (page 1442)
Minister of State: Steve Webb (LD) (page 1535)
Parliamentary Under Secretaries of State: Lord Freud (Con) (page 1427), Esther McVey (Con) (page 1475)

Shadow Cabinet (as at July 2013)
Leader of Her Majesty's Official Opposition: Rt. Hon. Ed Miliband (page 1477)
Shadow Deputy Prime Minister; Party Chair; Shadow Secretary of State for Culture, Media and Sport: Rt. Hon. Harriet Harman (page 1438)
Shadow Chancellor of the Exchequer: Rt. Hon. Ed Balls (page 1382)
Shadow Foreign Secretary: Rt. Hon. Douglas Alexander (page 1374)
Shadow Secretary of State for the Home Department, Shadow Minister for Women and Equalities: Rt. Hon. Yvette Cooper (page 1408)
Shadow Lord Chancellor, Secretary of State for Justice: Rt. Hon. Sadiq Khan (page 1456)
Shadow Chief Whip: Rt. Hon. Rosie Winterton (page 1538)
Shadow Secretary of State for Health: Rt. Hon. Andy Burnham (page 1397)
Shadow Secretary of State for Education: Stephen Twigg (page 1529)
Shadow Secretary of State for Business, Innovations and Skills: Chuka Umunna (page 1529)
Shadow Secretary of State for Defence: Rt. Hon. Jim Murphy (page 1482)
Shadow Secretary of State for Communities and Local Government: Rt. Hon. Hilary Benn (page 1387)
Shadow Leader of the House of Commons: Angela Eagle (page 1419)
Shadow Secretary of State for Energy and Climate Change: Rt. Hon. Caroline Flint (page 1425)
Shadow Secretary of State to the Treasury: Rachel Reeves (page 1501)
Shadow Secretary of State for Transport: Maria Eagle (page 1419)
Shadow Secretary of State for Work and Pensions, Policy Review Coordinator: Rt. Hon. Liam Byrne (page 1398)
Shadow Secretary of State for International Development: Ivan Lewis (page 1464)
Shadow Secretary of State for Environment, Food and Rural Affairs: Mary Creagh (page 1410)
Shadow Minister of State (Cabinet Office): Jon Trickett (page 1527)
Labour Party Deputy Chair; Campaign Coordinator: vacant
Shadow Secretary of State for Northern Ireland: Vernon Coaker (page 1407)
Shadow Secretary of State for Scotland: Margaret Curran (page 1411)
Shadow Secretary of State for Wales; Chair of the National Policy Forum: Owen Smith (page 1517)
Shadow Leader of the House of Lords: Rt Hon Baroness Royall of Blaisdon (page 1506)
Lords Chief Whip: Lord Bassam of Brighton (page 1384)
Also attending Shadow Cabinet Meetings
Shadow Minister for Care and Older People: Liz Kendall (page 1455)
Shadow Minister without Portfolio (Cabinet Office): Michael Dugher (page 1418)
Shadow Attorney-General: Emily Thornberry (page 1525)
Shadow Minister without Portfolio (Cabinet Office): Lord Wood of Anfield (page 1539)
Policy Review Coordinator: Jon Cruddas (page 1410)

Scottish Parliament, Edinburgh EH99 1SP, United Kingdom. Tel: +44 (0)131 348 5000, fax: +44 (0)131 348 5601, URL: http://www.scotland.gov.uk
Presiding Officer: Tricia Marwick (page 1472)

National Assembly of Wales, Cardiff Bay, Cardiff, CF99 1NA, United Kingdom. Tel: +44 (0)29 2082 5111, fax: 44 (0)29 2089 8229, URL: http://www.wales.gov.uk
First Minister: Rt. Hon Carwyn Jones (page 1451)

Northern Ireland Office, 11 Millbank, London, SW1P 4PN, United Kingdom. URL: http://www.nio.gov.uk
Northern Ireland Office, Stormont Estate, Belfast, BT4 3SH, United Kingdom. Tel: +44 (0)28 9052 0700
Northern Ireland Assembly, Parliament Buildings, Stormont, Belfast BT4 3XX, United Kingdom. Tel: +44 (0)28 9052 1333, fax: +44 (0)28 9052 1961, e-mail: info.office@niassembly.gov.uk, URL: http://www.ni-assembly.gov.uk

Ministries
Office of HM the Queen, Buckingham Palace, London, SW1 1AA, UK. Tel: +44 (0)20 7930 4832, URL: http://www.royal.gov.uk/
Prime Minister's Office, 10 Downing St. London SW1A 2AA, UK. Tel: +44 (0)20 7270 1234, URL: http://www.number-10.gov.uk

Office of the Chancellor of the Exchequer, 11 Downing Street, London, SW1 2AA, UK. Tel: +44 (0)20 7270 3000, fax: +44 (0)20 7270 5663, e-mail: public.enquiries@hm-treasury.gov.uk, URL: http://www.hm-treasury.gov.uk

Cabinet Office, 70 Whitehall, London SW1A 2AS, UK. Tel: +44 (0)20 7276 0527, URL: http://www.cabinetoffice.gov.uk / http://www.dpm.cabinetoffice.gov.uk

Attorney General's Office, 20 Victoria Street, London, SW1H 0NF. Tel: +44 (0)20 7271 2492, e-mail: correspondenceunit@attorneygeneral.gov.uk, URL: http://www.attorneygeneral.gov.uk

Department of Business, Innovation and Skills, 1 Victoria St, London SW1H 0ET, UK. Tel: +44 (0)20 7215 5000, URL: http://www.bis.gov.uk

Department for Communities and Local Government, Eland House, Bressenden Place, London, SW1E 5DU, UK. E-mail: contactus@communities.gov.uk, URL: http://www.communities.gov.uk

Department of Culture, Media and Sport, 2-4 Cockspur St, London SW1Y 5DH, UK. Tel: +44 (0)20 7211 6200, e-mail: enquiries@culture.gov.uk, URL: http://www.culture.gov.uk

Ministry of Defence, 5th Floor, Zone A, Main Building, Whitehall, London SW1A 2HB, UK. Tel: +44 (0)20 7218 9000, URL: http://www.mod.uk

Department for Education, Castle View House, East Lane, Runcorn, Cheshire, WA7 2GJ, UK. Tel: +44 (0)370 000 2288, URL: http://www.education.gov.uk

Department for Energy and Climate Change, 3 Whitehall Place, London, SW1A 2AW, UK. Tel: +44 (0)300 060 4000, e-mail: correspondence@DECC.gsi.gov.uk, URL: http://www.decc.gov.uk

Department of Environment, Food and Rural Affairs, Nobel House, 17 Smith Street, London SW1P 3JR, UK. Tel: +44 (0)20 7238 6951, e-mail: defra.helpline@defra.gsi.gov.uk, URL: http://www.defra.gov.uk

Foreign and Commonwealth Office, King Charles St. London SW1A 2AH, UK. Tel: +44 (0)20 7008 1500, URL: http://www.fco.gov.uk

Department of Health, Richmond House, 79 Whitehall, London SW1A 2NS, UK. Tel: +44 (0)20 7210 4850, URL: http://www.dh.gov.uk

Home Office, Direct Communications Unit, 2 Marsham Street, London SW1P 4DF, UK. Tel: +44 (0)20 7035 4848, e-mail: public.enquiries@homeoffice.gsi.gov.uk, URL: http://www.homeoffice.gov.uk

Department for International Development, 1 Palace Street, London SW1E 5HE, UK. Tel: +44 (0)845 300 4100, e-mail: enquiry@dfid.gov.uk, URL: http://www.dfid.gov.uk

Ministry of Justice, 102 Petty France, London SW1H 9AJ, UK. Tel: +44 (0)20 3334 3555, e-mail: general.queries@justice.gsi.gov.uk, URL: http://www.justice.gov.uk

Department for Transport, Great Minster House, 33 Horseferry Road, London SW1P 4DR, UK. Tel: +44 (0)300 330 3000, URL: http://www.dft.gov.uk

Department for Work and Pensions, Caxton House, Tothill Street, London SW1H 9DA, UK. Tel: +44 (0)20 7712 2171, fax: +44 (0)20 7340 4000, e-mail: ministers@dwp.gsi.gov.uk, URL: http://www.dwp.gov.uk

Her Majesty's Treasury, 1 Horse Guards Road, London SW1A 2HQ, UK. Tel: +44 (0)20 7270 5000, e-mail: public.enquiries@hm-treasury.gov.uk, URL: http://www.hm-treasury.gov.uk

Lord Chancellor's Department, House of Lords, London SW1A 0PW, UK. Tel: +44 (0)20 7210 8500, URL: http://www.lcd.gov.uk

Northern Ireland Office, 11 Millbank, London SW1P 4PN, UK. Tel: +44 (0)28 9052 0700, URL: http://www.nio.gov.uk

Scotland Office, Dover House, Whitehall, London SW1A 2AU, UK / 1 Melville Crescent, Edinburgh, EH3 7HW.Tel:+44 (0)20 7270 6754 (London) / +44 (0)131 244 9010 (Edinburgh), URL: http://www.scotlandoffice.gov.uk

Wales Office, Gwydyr House, Whitehall, London SW1A 2NP, UK. Tel: +44 (0)20 7270 0534, URL: http://www.walesoffice.gov.uk

Privy Council Office, 2 Carlton Gardens, London, SW1Y 5AA, UK. Tel: +44 (0)20 7270 5310, e-mail: pcosecretariat@pco.gov.uk, URL: http://www.privy-council.org.uk

Office of the Leader of the House of Commons, CGI, 1 Horse Guards Road, London, SW2A 1HQ, UK. Tel: +44 (0)20 2776 1005, e-mail: leader@commonsleader.x.gsi.gov.uk, URL: http://www.cabinetoffice.gov.uk/

Office of the Leader of the House of Lords, Room 20, House of Lords, London, SW1A 0PW, UK. Tel: +44 ()20 7219 3200, fax: +44 (0)20 7219 3051, e-mail: psleaderofthelords@cabinet-office.x.gsi.gov.uk, URL: http://www.cabinetoffice.gov.uk

Whips' Office (House of Commons), 12 Downing Street, London SW1A 2AA, UK. Tel: +44 (0)20 7219 4400, fax: +44 (0)20 7270 2015, URL: http://www.lordswhips.org.uk/

Office of the Advocate General for Scotland, Dover House, Whitehall, London, SW1A 2AU, UK. Tel: +44 (0)20 7270 6810, URL: http://www.oag.gov.uk

Church Estates Commissioner's Office, Church House, Great Smith Street, London SW1P 3AZ, URL: http://www.cofe.anglican.org/about/churchcommissioners/

Chancellor of the Duchy of Lancaster, 1 Lancaster Place, London WC2E 7ED, UK. URL: http://www.duchyoflancaster.co.uk/

Political Parties

Main political parties are:

Labour Party, 16 Old Queen Street, London SW1H 9HP, United Kingdom. Tel: +44 (0)8705 900 200, e-mail: info@new.labour.org.uk, URL: http://www.labour.org.uk

Leader: Ed Miliband (page 1477)

Conservative and Unionist Party, Conservative Campaign Headquarters, 25 Victoria Street, London SW1H 0DL, United Kingdom. Tel: +44 (0)20 7222 9000, fax: +44 (0)20 7222 1135,

URL: http://www.conservatives.com

Leader: David Cameron (page 1399)

Liberal Democrat Party, 4 Cowley Street, London, SW1P 3NB, United Kingdom. Tel: +44 (0)20 7222 7999, fax: +44 (0)20 7799 2170, URL: http://www.libdems.org.uk

Acting Leader: Nick Clegg (page 1406)

Democratic Unionist Party, 91 Dundela Avenue, Belfast, BT4 3BU, United Kingdom. Tel: +44 (0)28 9047 1155, fax: +44 (0)28 9047 1797, e-mail: info@dup.org.uk, URL: http://www.dup.org.uk

Leader: Peter Robinson (page 1504)

Green Party, 1a Waterlow Road, London, N19 5NJ, United Kingdom. Tel: +44 (0)20 7272 4474, fax:+44 (0)20 7272 6653, e-mail: gptyoffice@gn.apc.org, http://www.greenparty.org.uk

Leader: Natalie Bennett (page 1387)

Plaid Cymru, 18 Park Grove, Cardiff CF10 3BN, United Kingdom. Tel: +44 (0)29 2064 6000, fax: +44 (0)29 2064 6001, URL: http://www.plaidcymru.org

Leader: Leanne Jones

Scottish National Party (SNP), 6 North Charlotte Street, Edinburgh, EH2 4JH, United Kingdom. Tel: +44 (0)131 226 3661, fax: +44 (0)131 225 9597, e-mail: snp.hq@snp.org.uk, URL: http://www.snp.org.uk

Leader: Alex Salmond (page 1507)

Sinn Féin, 44 Parnell Square, Dublin 1, Republic of Ireland. Tel: +353 (0)1 872 6932, fax: +353 (0)1 873 3441, URL: http://www.irlnet.com/sinnfein/index.html

President: Gerry Adams (page 1372)

Social and Democratic Labour Party (SDLP), 121 Ormeau Road, Belfast BT7 1SH, United Kingdom. Tel: +44 (0)28 9024 7700, fax: +44 (0)28 9023 6699, URL: http://www.sdlp.ie

Leader: Margaret Ritchie (page 1503)

Ulster Unionist Party, 3 Glengall Street, Belfast BT12 5AE, United Kingdom. Tel: +44 (0)28 9032 4601, fax: +44 (0)28 9024 6738, URL: http://www.uup.org

Leader: Mike Nesbitt

United Kingdom Independence Party (UKIP), 123 New John Street, Birmingham, West Midlands B6 4LD. Tel +11 (0)121 333 7737, URL: http://www.ukip.org

Leader: Nigel Farage (page 1423)

Veritas, 109-110 Bolsover Street, London W1W 5NT, United Kingdom. Tel: +44 (0)20 7631 3757, fax: +44 (0)20 7436 9957, e-mail: mail@veritasparty.com, URL: http://www.veritasparty.com

Leader: Therese Muchewicz

Elections

The most recent General Election took place on May 6 2010. Although the Conservative Party won most votes and seats, it fell short of the 326 seats needed for an outright majority. After several days of negotiations the Conservative Party and the Liberal Democrats formed a coalition government, the first in the UK since World War II. David Cameron, leader of the Conservatives, became Prime Minister and Nick Clegg, leader of the Liberal Democrats, became Deputy Prime Minister. In the 2010 election The Greens won a seat in the UK parliament for the first time.

Voting in general elections is open to those over the age of 18.

The following table shows the full result of the 2001, 2005 and 2010 general elections:

British Parliament Election Results

Party	2001	2005	2010
Conservative Party	166	197	306
Labour Party	413	356	258
Liberal Democrat Party	52	62	57
Scottish National Party	5	6	6
Plaid Cymru	4	3	3
Ulster Unionist Party	6	1	
Democratic Unionist Party	5	9	8
Social Democratic & Labour Party	3	3	3
Sinn Féin	4	5	5
Green Party	-	-	1
Alliance Party	-	-	1
Others	1	3	1

Elections to the European Elections

In a radical change announced in October 1997, the Government proposed that the elections for the European Parliament in 1999 should be held under a proportional representation system. The proposals meant that the United Kingdom was divided into 12 voting areas. Scotland, Wales and Northern Ireland all form their own individual region and voters nominate a party rather than an individual.

The following tables show the number of seats in the European Parliament by electoral region and number of seats won in the elections of June 2009 by party:

Number of Seats by Electoral Region

Region	Number of Seats
Eastern	7
East Midlands	6
London	9
North East	3
North West	9
South East	10
South West	7
West Midlands	7
Yorkshire and Humber	6
Scotland	7
Wales	4
Northern Ireland	3

UK MEP Election Results - June 2009

Party	Number of Seats
Conservative Party	26
Labour Party	13
Liberal Democrat Party	11
UK Independence Party	13
Green Party	2
Scottish National Party	2
Plaid Cymru	1

UNITED KINGDOM

British National Party   2
Sinn Féin   1
Democratic Unionist Party   1

Diplomatic Representation

Embassy of the United States of America, 24-31 Grosvenor Square, London W1A 1AE, United Kingdom. Tel: +44 (0)20 7499 9000, fax: +44 (0)20 7409 1637, URL: http://www.usembassy.org.uk
Chargé d'Affaires: Barbara J. Stephenson
British Embassy, 3100 Massachusetts Avenue NW, Washington, DC 20008, USA. Tel: +1 202 588 6500, fax: +1 202 588 7870, URL: http://ukinusa.fco.gov.uk/
Ambassador: Sir Peter Westmacott KCMG LVO (page 1536)
United Kingdom Mission to the United Nations, PO Box 5238, New York, NY 10150-5238, USA. Tel: +1 212 745 9200, fax: +1 212 745 9316, URL: http://ukun.fco.gov.uk/en/
Permanent Representative: Mark Lyall Grant

Reigning Royal Family

The British Royal Family are members of the Anglican House of Windsor.

By a royal proclamation on 17 July 1917 King George V abandoned all German styles and titles for himself and the royal family and adopted the house and family name of Windsor. Succession is in both male and female lines, in which case a daughter would take precedence over her father's brother and more distant male relatives. In February 1998 the Queen agreed that the law should be changed to give females equal rights to succeed to the throne.

The members of the family have the title prince or princess of Great Britain and Ireland, Royal Highness, but this style was limited by King George V to children and grandchildren of the sovereign in the male line, and the eldest grandson of the Prince of Wales.

HM Queen Elizabeth II, (page 1420) Queen of the United Kingdom of Great Britain and Northern Ireland and of her other Realms and Territories, Head of the Commonwealth, Defender of the Faith, was born in 1926 and is the elder daughter of King George VI (born 14 December 1895, died 6 February 1952). Elizabeth succeeded to the throne on the death of her father; married in 1947, Lieut. Philip Mountbatten, RN (created Duke of Edinburgh, Earl of Merioneth, and Baron Greenwich, 19 November 1947; further created Prince of Great Britain, 22 February 1957) formerly Prince of Greece and Denmark (born at Corfu, 10 June 1921), only son of late Prince Andrew of Greece and Denmark.

The Queen has four children:
Prince Charles Philip Arthur George, Prince of Wales, Duke of Cornwall, Duke of Rothesay (page 1403) , (page 1409)married Lady Diana Spencer at St. Paul Cathedral on 29 July 1981 who became Princess of Wales (separated 1992, divorced 1996, died 1997). Prince Charles has two sons, Prince William Arthur Philip Louis, Duke of Cambridge (page 1399) (born 1982) and Prince Henry Charles Albert David (born 1984 and known as Harry). Prince Charles married Mrs Camilla Parker Bowles at the Guildhall, Windsor on 9 April 2005, her title is HRH Duchess of Cornwall (page 1409). The wedding of Prince William to Catherine Middleton took place in Westminster Abbey on 29 April 2011 and the couple are now to be known as the Duke and Duchess of Cambridge. At the end of 2012 it was announced that the Duke and Duchess of Cambridge were expecting their first child, who will third in line to the throne.

HRH The Princess Royal (Anne Elizabeth Alice Louise) (page 1378); born in 1950, married, first, in 1973 to Capt. Mark Phillips, marriage dissolved 1992. Second marriage in 1992 to Commodore Timothy Laurence, RN. The Princess Royal has two children from the first marriage, Peter Mark Andrew and Zara Anne Elizabeth.

Prince Andrew Albert Christian Edward, Duke of York (page 1541) (created 23 July 1986) born 1960, married Sarah Ferguson (page 1424) in 1986 (separated 1992, divorced 1996). The Duke of York has two daughters, Princess Beatrice Elizabeth Mary and Princess Eugenie Victoria Helena.

Prince Edward Antony Richard Louis, Earl of Wessex (page 1535) (created 19 June 1999) born 1964, married Sophie Rhys Jones (page 1535) (now Countess of Wessex) in June 1999. The Earl and Countess have one daughter Lady Louise Alice Elizabeth Mary and one son James Alexander Philip Theo, Viscount Severn.

Queen Elizabeth had one sister, Princess Margaret Rose, 1930-2002, who had a son and a daughter.

Mother of the Queen: Queen Elizabeth The Queen Mother, daughter of Claude George, 14th Earl of Strathmore and Kinghorne; born at St. Paul's Waldenbury, Hitchin, 4 August 1900; married to King George VI at Westminster Abbey, 26 April 1923. Died March 2002 aged 101.

LEGAL SYSTEM

The United Kingdom operates under the Common Law, with separate legal systems for England and Wales, Northern Ireland and Scotland. The Common Law works under a system of precedent whereby judges develop the law through their decisions. The intentions of Parliament and the Executive are represented through primary legislation (Statute) and secondary legislation (Statutory Instrument). Separate Acts of Parliament apply for Scotland.

The supreme judicial authority and highest court of appeal for England, Wales, Scotland and Northern Ireland until 2009 was the House of Lords. Sitting as a judicial body, the House of Lords consisted of a minimum quorum of three members (though usually five attend) drawn from the Lord Chancellor, the Lords of Appeal in Ordinary and Peers who held high judicial office as defined by the Appellate Jurisdiction Act 1876.

There is a Judicial Committee of the Privy Council which is the highest court of appeal for certain independent members of the Commonwealth and for the British dependencies, and has limited jurisdiction in certain matters (for example, appeals by members of the medical and kindred professions against decisions of their disciplinary bodies) in Britain. Those who sit on the Committee hold or have held high judicial office in Britain or in the Commonwealth and are Privy Counsellors.

The Supreme Court

The Supreme Court is the highest court in all matters under English law, Northern Irish law and Scottish civil law. It is the court of last resort and highest appellate court in the United Kingdom; although the High Court of Justiciary remains the supreme court for criminal cases in Scotland. The Supreme Court was established as part of the Constitutional Reform Act of 2005 and came into being in October 2009. It has assumed the judicial functions of the House of Lords, which were exercised by the Lords of Appeal in Ordinary. The Supreme Courts jurisdiction over devolution matters had previously been held by the Judicial Committee of the Privy Council. The Supreme Court has 12 Justices, they are completely separate from Government and Parliament and as a result no longer participate in House of Lords business.
The Supreme Court of the United Kingdom, Parliament Square, London, SW1P 3BD, United Kingdom. URL: http://www.supremecourt.gov.uk
President: The Rt. Hon. the Lord Neuberger of Abbotsbury (page 1485)

Justices of the Supreme Court: Lord Hope of Craighead, Vice President; (page 1443) Baroness Hale of Richmond; (page 1436) Lord Mance; (page 1470) Lord Kerr of Tonaghmore; (page 1456) Lord Clarke of Stone-cum-Ebony; (page 1406) Lord Wilson of Culworth; (page 1538) Lord Sumption; Lord Reed; Lord Carnwath; Rt. Hon. Lord Hughes of Ombersley; The Right Hon Lord Toulson

England and Wales

Below the House of Lords, the Supreme Court of England and Wales handles civil and criminal matters. It comprises the Court of Appeal, the High Court of Justice which has civil jurisdiction and the Crown Court which has predominantly criminal jurisdiction. The Court of Appeal consists of a civil division, which hears appeals from the High Court and the County Courts, and a criminal division, which hears criminal appeals from the Crown Court.

The Civil Division of the Court of Appeal consists in practice of the Master of the Rolls, who is President of the Division, and the Lords Justices of Appeal. In the Criminal Division, which is normally presided over by the Lord Chief Justice or a Lord Justice of Appeal, Judges of the Queen's Bench Division sit with Lords Justices. The High Court has three divisions - Chancery, Queen's Bench, and Family. The Chancery Division is headed by the Lord Chancellor with a Vice-Chancellor. It deals (*inter alia*) with the construction of wills, settlements, trusts and mortgages. There is a separate Patents Court within the Chancery Division, as well as a Companies Court, a Restrictive Practices Court, Court of Protection and High Court of Justice in Bankruptcy. The Queen's Bench Division consists of the Lord Chief Justice, as president, plus judges. There is a separate Admiralty Court and Commercial Court within the Queen's Bench Division. The Family Division is headed by a President.

The High Court judges on circuit at first- and second-tier Crown Court Centres try the more serious criminal cases. At first-tier centres they also try civil actions which fall within the competence of the Queen's Bench Division and defended divorce cases. Civil actions in the Chancery Division may be heard at designated first-tier centres.

In addition to the High Court judges there are Circuit judges who normally sit in the Crown Court and the county courts, and Recorders, experienced members of the legal profession, who undertake to sit as judges for a number of days each year.

County Courts have jurisdiction covering virtually the whole range of civil proceedings including divorce. Their powers are generally similar to the High Court. In the more common actions (eg contract and tort) they can deal with any claim although the more substantial complex and important cases will be transferred to the High Court for trial. Where the County Courts exercise specialist jurisdiction (eg trusts and property law) this is subject to a pecuniary limit although parties may agree to waive such a limit. From County Courts an appeal goes to the Court of Appeal.

On the criminal side, beneath the Crown Court there are the magistrates' courts for the summary trial of offences. These offences are, in general, dealt with by lay justices exercising summary jurisdiction. The 450 Magistrates Courts in England and Wales deal with over 90 per cent of all criminal cases, although in some cases a defendant can opt to be judged by a jury. Justices of the Peace are appointed by the Lord Chancellor. In the case of more serious offences, defendants are sent for trial to the Crown Court. In London and some large towns, the summary jurisdiction is also exercised by legally qualified magistrates called stipendiaries. So many offences have been placed by statute within the competence of the justices and the stipendiaries that the limits of their jurisdiction are impossible to lay down. In the case of customs offences, for example, they may impose very heavy penalties. But in general, prison sentences of not more than six months and fines not exceeding £5,000 may be imposed by magistrates. Magistrates courts also have jurisdiction over certain civil and family cases.

The Crown Court hears appeals and committals for sentence from the magistrates' courts and also tries more serious cases. Appeal may be made to the Criminal Division of the Court of Appeal. The largest Crown Court for Greater London is the Central Criminal Court, which sits in the Old Bailey. At the Crown Court all criminal trials are tried in open court by a judge and jury consisting of 12 members of the public.

When a person's means are insufficient to pay for legal advice and assistance, legal aid may be granted. It may be granted to parties to civil proceedings and, where it is in the interests of justice that a defendant to criminal proceedings be legally represented, it may be granted or, if the charge is murder, it must be granted. If it is granted a solicitor and, if necessary, Counsel will be assigned and the assisted person may be required to make a contribution towards the costs.

In each county the Crown is represented by Her Majesty's Lord Lieutenant, who as Keeper of the Rolls, is the Chief Magistrate in the County. Assisted by an advisory committee, he recommends to the Lord Chancellor the names of persons for appointment as Justices of the Peace. Each county has a sheriff who is responsible for an under-sheriff. It is the duty of the under-sheriffs to execute High Court Writs. Another officer of the Crown is the Coroner, whose duty it is to inquire into cases of sudden death or death of a suspicious nature. He also adjudicates on questions of treasure trove.

The final element in the justice system is the Tribunal. Tribunals usually hear cases covering specific areas of law. They often have a panel consisting of one or more judges or other legally qualified members aided by lay members who are normally experts in that particular field. Some examples of the most important tribunals are the Employment Appeals Tribunal (which itself hears appeals from Industrial Tribunals), the Agricultural Land Tribunal and the Lands Tribunal. Other tribunals hearing appeals covering, for example, social security, child support and medical and disability matters, are supervised by the Independent Tribunal Service.

In June 2003, as part of a cabinet reshuffle, the posts of Welsh and Scottish Secretaries were absorbed into other departments and the ancient role of Lord Chancellor was abolished. At the same time, it was announced that a new supreme court should be established. Lord Falconer, in his role as head of the new Department of Constitutional Affairs, assumed the Lord Chancellor's duties for the transitional period.

In May 2007 it was announced that the Home Office would divide. The Home Office remains in place, its responsibilities being terrorism, security, immigration and policing. A new Ministry of Justice was created and is responsible for prisons and probation services.

Scotland

Control over Scotland's criminal and civil law was passed to the new Scottish Parliament in July 1999.

Civil Rights

The government respects the rights of its citizens, though there have been instances of police misconduct and occasional abuse of suspects and detainees by police. The prisons can be overcrowded and the prison infrastructure is inadequate.

The death penalty for murder was abolished in 1969 in Great Britain, and in 1973 in Northern Ireland. The last executions were carried out in 1964, though the death penalty for espionage remained until 1971, and capital punishment for treason and piracy with violence remained on the statute book until 1998.

Equality and Human Rights Commission, URL: http://www.equalityhumanrights.com

LOCAL GOVERNMENT

England is divided into 56 unitary authorities, Bath and North East Somerset; Bedford; Blackburn with Darwen; Blackpool; Bournemouth; Bracknell Forest; Brighton and Hove; Bristol; Central Bedfordshire; Cheshire East; Cheshire West and Chester; Cornwall; County Durham; Darlington; Derby; East Riding of Yorkshire; Halton; Hartlepool; Herefordshire; Isle of Wight; Isles of Scilly; Kingston upon Hull; Leicester; Luton; Medway; Middlesborough; Milton Keynes; North East Lincolnshire; North Hertfordshire; North Lincolnshire; Northumberland; Nottingham; Peterborough; Plymouth; Poole; Portsmouth; Reading; Redcar and Cleveland; Rutland; Shropshire; Slough; South Gloucestershire; Southampton; Southend on Sea; Stockton on Tees; Stoke on Trent; Swindon; Telford and the Wrekin; Thurrock; Torbay; Warrington; West Berkshire; Wiltshire; Windsor and Maidenhead; Wokingham; York. A unitary authority is a single tier of local government responsible for the functions of a local government in its area some authorities cover a county and some towns and cities.

There are also 34 two-tier authority areas (district and county councils) and 33 London Boroughs for local governing. District councils are run by directly elected councillors, of whom there are about 21,000 in England and Wales. Elections are every four years, although district councils may opt to have annual elections for one third of their councillors in the years when county council elections are not being held. At the lowest local level there are parish councils (England) and community councils (Wales), which carry out local functions benefiting their areas, and for which they depend on district council funds.

Capital expenditure is normally financed by borrowing. Sources of income to finance current expenditure are government grants in the form of a block grant determined in relation to each authority's resources and assumed spending needs and other income from grants and services. Around 25 per cent of income is raised from the council tax.

Broadly speaking the functions of the counties are for needs covering wide areas whereas those of the districts are of a more local nature. County functions include structure planning, development plans governing the preparation of local plans, traffic, transport and highway functions, fire and police services, consumer protection and refuse disposal. The counties also deal with functions which may require a substantial catchment to ensure economical use of facilities, such as education, social services, and libraries.

With their high population density, Metropolitan districts are clearly suited to dealing with these services as well. There is an overlap between counties and all districts in the provision of museums, recreational facilities and tourism. District councils' functions include local planning and development control, minor urban roads, car parks, local transport systems, housing, refuse collection, food safety and hygiene, clean air, building regulations, markets and fairs.

The Local Government Commission is responsible for reviews of the current system and its boundaries.
Local Government Commission for England, URL: http://www.local.gov.uk/

Local government in Scotland and Wales became the responsibility of the Scottish Parliament from July 1999 and the Welsh Assembly from May 1999 respectively. Wales has 22 unitary authorities, Scotland has 32 local government areas each of which has a council, and Northern Ireland has 26 local government districts. The councils of the local government districts in Northern Ireland are not responsible for the same functions as those in the rest of the country for example they do not have responsibility for education, road building or housing.

In 1997 the Government published legislation to allow a referendum to take place in May 1998. London voters had the chance to decide whether they wanted an elected mayor for the capital and assembly. The turnout was only 30 per cent of the electorate and the results were 77.97 per cent in favour and 22.03 per cent against an elected mayor and assembly for London. The election for the mayor took place on 4 May 2000, and was won by Ken Livingstone standing as an Independent. The London Assembly is the elected body which oversees and debates the mayor's decisions. The London Assembly assumed its responsibilities on 3 July 2000. The most recent elections were in May 2012 and were won by the Conservative candidate, Boris Johnson, narrowly beating the Labour candidate Ken Livingstone.

London Assembly, URL: http://www.london.gov.uk

London Assembly
Mayor: Boris Johnson (page 1450)
Darren Johnson (Chair); Tony Arbour; Jeanette Arnold; Gareth Bacon; John Biggs; Andrew Boff; Victoria Borwick; James Cleverly; Tom Copley; Andrew Dismore; Len Duvall; Roger Evans; Nicky Gavron; Darren Johnson; Jenny Jones; Stephen Knight; Kit Malthouse; Joanne McCartney; Steve O'Connell; Caroline Pidgeon; Murad Qureshi; Dr Onkar Sahota; Navin Shah; Valerie Shawcross; Richard Tracey; Fiona Twycross.

AREA AND POPULATION

Area
The United Kingdom is situated off the north coast of the continental mainland of Europe. It consists of England (130,423 sq. km.), Scotland (77,080 sq. km.) and Wales (20,766 sq. km.) on the main island (collectively known as Great Britain) and the six counties of Northern Ireland (13,483 sq. km.) on the other island, the southern half of which is the Republic of Ireland. The total area of the United Kingdom is 242,514 sq. km. Total coastline is 12,429 km. The UK lies between the North Atlantic Ocean and the North Sea, the south coast of England is separated from the northwest coast of France 22 miles away by the English Channel but they are linked by the Channel Tunnel. The main rivers of Britain are the Thames, Severn, Dee, Tweed and Clyde. Among the highest points are Snowdon in Wales (1,085 metres), Ben Nevis in Scotland (1,344 metres) and Scafell Pike (Cumbrian Mountains, 977 metres). Scotland ,Wales the north of England and the Southwest are more mountainous with the midlands, south and east of the country being hilly or of lowland terrain with the fens in the east of the country being the lowest point some of which is up to four metres below sea level. Mountain ranges of the UK include in Scotland, the Cairngorms, Cheviot Hills, Scottish Highlands, Southern Uplands and Grampian Mountains. In Wales, the Brecon Beacons, Cambrian Mountains, Snowdonia, Black Mountains and Preseli Hills. England is home to the Chilterns, Cotswolds, Dartmoor, Lincolnshire Wolds, Exmoor, Lake District, Malvern Hills, Mendip Hills, North Downs, Peak District, Pennines, Salisbury Plain, South Downs, Shropshire Hills and the Yorkshire Wolds and Northern Ireland has the Mourne Mountains, Antrim Plateau and Sperrin Mountains.

The UK enjoys a temperate climate with warm summers and cool winters. As an island the climate is influenced by the surrounding seas and so the summers are cooler than mainland Europe and the winters milder. The wettest region of the UK is the Lake District in the northwest of England with an average annual rainfall of 2,000 mm. The warmest region of the UK is the south of England in particular the counties of Kent, Sussex, Hampshire and Dorset. In November 2009, the Lake District and surrounding area and parts of southern Scotland were hit by severe flooding when over 310 mm of rain fell in 24 hours, hundreds of homes were flooded and one bridge collapsed completely with several others becoming unsafe.

To view a map, please consult:
http://www.lib.utexas.edu/maps/cia08/united_kingdom_sm_2008.gif

Population
The most recent census was taken in 2011, the population was provisionally put at 63.2 million this showed a 4.1 million increase since the the previous census in 2001.

The following figures show recent population statistics.

UK Mid Year Population (millions)	1984	1994	2004	2011*
UK total	56.5	57.8	59.8	63.1
England	47.0	48.2	50.0	53.0
Scotland	5.1	5.1	5.0	5.2
Wales	2.8	2.8	2.9	3.0
Northern Ireland	1.6	1.6	1.7	1.8

*provisional
Source: Office of National Statistics

The total population for the UK according to the 2011 census was provisionally put at 63,182,000. Experts have recently projected that the population will continue to rise until 2036 when it will reach an estimated peak of 65 million before beginning to decline. The population growth rate at the 2001 census was 0.27 per cent per year. Recent statistics show that 3.8 million of the population are of an ethnic minority.

UNITED KINGDOM

The United Kingdom's ten most densely populated cities are: London with a population in 2011 of 8,173,941; Birmingham, 1,073,045; Leeds, 751,485; Glasgow, 593,000; Sheffield, 552,698; Bradford, 552,452; Liverpool, 466,415; Manchester, 4503,127; Edinburgh, 477,000; Bristol, 428,234. Figures from March 2011 put the population density at 2.6 persons per hectare.

The following figures show the estimated resident population by area for March 2011:

Area	Population
North East	2,596,886
North West	7,052,177
Yorkshire & the Humber	5,283,733
East Midlands	4,533,222
West Midlands	5,601,847
East	5,846,965
South East	8,634,750
London	8,173,941
South West	5,288,935
Total England	53,012,456
Scotland	5,295,000
Wales	3,063,456
Northern Ireland	1,810,863

Source: Office of National Statistics

Births, Marriages, Deaths
Vital statistics for in recent years

	2008	2009
Births	794,400	790,200
Deaths	579,700	559,600
Marriages	273,200	266,900
Divorces	136,000	126,500
Immigration	590,000	567,000
Migration	427,000	368,000

Source: National Statistics Office

Figures for the year mid 2010 to mid 2011 show that the population change due to births and deaths was 239,000, up from 227,000 the previous year. Population change due to net migration during 2010-11 was 235,000, up from 218,000 the previous year.

Public Holidays 2014
1 January: New Year's Day
2 January: New Year (Scotland only)
17 March: St. Patrick's Day (Northern Ireland only)
18 April: Good Friday
21 April: Easter Monday
5 May: May Day
26 May: Spring Bank Holiday
12 July: Battle of the Boyne (Orangemen's Day) (Northern Ireland only)
4 August: Summer Bank Holiday (Scotland only)
25 August: Summer Bank Holiday (England, Wales and Northern Ireland only)
25 December: Christmas Day
26 December: Boxing Day
Holidays falling on a Saturday or Sunday are observed the following Monday

EMPLOYMENT

In common with many countries, the UK has been hit by the global economic downturn and credit crisis, which has affected the labour market as companies are forced to close or downsize. Figures for May 2009 show that 2.2 million people were unemployed, a rise of 592,000 on the previous year, resulting in an unemployment rate of 7.1 per cent. Unemployment for the quarter July - September 2009 was 7.8 per cent. The worst affected areas have been the West Midlands, North East England, London and North West Yorkshire, with the retail, banking and insurance, manufacturing and construction sectors being badly hit. Unemployment figures for the fourth quarter of 2010 showed that the unemployment rate was 7.9 per cent. Figures for the first quarter of 2011 showed that unemployment figures had fallen slightly to 2.45 million unemployed, down from 2.47 million in the previous quarter. Figures for the first quarter of 2012 showed that unemployment had risen to 2.67 million, giving an unemployment rate of 8.4 per cent. Figures for the first quarter of 2013 showed that the unemployment rate had fallen to 7.8 per cent or 2.52 million people.

The following tables show recent figures for employment in the UK:

Employment Status of the Workforce, (thousands)

Employment status	Q1 2012	Q1 2013
Employees	24,892	25,280
Self-employed	4,163	4,176
Unpaid family workers	97	105
Gov. supported training & employment programmes	123	147
Total in employment	29,274	29,708
of whom:		
Full time workers	21,275	21,680
Part time workers	7,999	8,028
Workers with a second job	1,141	1,098

Figures from the Office for National Statistics are for spring and are seasonally adjusted

The trend in employment in recent years has seen a decrease in traditional areas of employment such as manufacturing, energy and water, (reflecting the decline of the coal industry), and an increase (prior to the 2008 economic slowdown) in the service and financial sectors, as shown in the following table.

Workforce Jobs by Industry

Industry	Oct.-Dec. 2011	Oct.-Dec. 2012
Agriculture, forestry & fishing	440,000	375,000
Mining & quarrying	65,000	69,000
Manufacturing	2,547,000	2,628,000
Electricity, gas, steam & air conditioning supply	118,000	112,000
Water supply, sewerage, waste & remediation activities	191,000	199,000
Construction	2,059,000	1,989,000
Wholesale, retail trade & repairs	4,816,000	4,881,000
Transport & storage	1,505,000	1,584,000
Accommodation & food services	2,005,000	2,064,000
Information & communication	1,238,000	1,312,000
Financial & insurance activities	1,120,000	1,157,000
Real estate activities	483,000	503,000
Professional scientific & technical activities	2,432,000	2,566,000
Admin. & support activities	2,527,000	2,498,000
Public admin & defence; social security	1,605,000	1,579,000
Education	2,756,000	2,759,000
Health & social work activities	4,029,000	4,084,000
Arts, entertainment & recreation	867,000	863,000
Other services	825,000	801,000
People employed by households etc.	69,000	77,000
All in employment	31,696,000	32,102,000

Source: Office for National Statistics

Employment rates vary throughout the country. The following table shows the number of people of working age claiming unemployment benefit and the change on the previous year:

Regional unemployment percentage rates

Region	May 2013	Change on previous year
England		
- North East	88,569	-4,799
- North West	187,906	-12,389
- Yorkshire & Humber	157,887	-7,712
- East Midlands	102,214	-8621
- West Midlands	156,251	-8,275
- East	108,282	-7,975
- London	213,302	-14,149
- South East	126,806	-14,154
- South West	81,189	-8,158
England	1,222,406	-86,232
Wales	75,791	-2,742
Scotland	134,410	-7,417
United Kingdom	1,495,758	-94,950

Source: Office of National Statistics

A Jobseeker's Allowance scheme was introduced in October 1996, replacing the previous Unemployment Benefit and Income Support for the unemployed. The Allowance is based on income, and is available to unemployed people aged over 18 who are available to work 40 hours a week, and who have paid a specified amount of National Insurance contributions. The Employment Service runs Job Centres throughout the country, which provide services and programmes designed to help the unemployed. In 1998 the New Deal schemes were introduced; these were aimed specifically at getting the young and long term unemployed back into the workplace. In June 2001 a new Department for Works and Pensions was set up. At the beginning of 2002, the DWP announced strategies for helping more people to get jobs; these included *Step Up*, a programme to provide jobs in areas of high unemployment, *Ambition Programmes*, training and recruitment programmes which are industry specific and *Progress2work*, which aims to help drug misuser's back into the workforce.

The UK's main employers' organisation is the Confederation of British Industry (CBI), which acts as the representative of British industry, and advises the Government on industrial policies.
Confederation of British Industry (CBI), Centre Point, 103 New Oxford Street, London WC1A 1DU, United Kingdom. Tel: +44 (0)20 7379 7400, fax: +44 (0)20 7240 1578, URL: http://www.cbi.org.uk

A large proportion of employees in the UK are members of a trade union. Most trade unions are affiliated to the Trades Union Congress, which holds annual meetings with representatives of the affiliated unions, to discuss matters of importance to its members.
Trades Union Congress (TUC), URL: http://www.tuc.org.uk
General Secretary: Frances O'Grady (page 1489)
Scottish Trades Union Congress, URL: http://www.stuc.org.uk
Wales Trades Union Council, URL: http://www.wtuc.org.uk

BANKING AND FINANCE

Currency
One £ Sterling = 100 pence

On 1 January 2002 the European Community began using the euro as its single currency. Only the member states of the UK, Denmark and Sweden have not adopted the euro as their national currency. The Government of the UK has not ruled out joining the single European currency but has stated that this will not happen until five economic tests are met: namely, a sustainable convergence between Britain and the economies of the single currency; sufficient flexibility to cope with economic change; the effect on investment; the impact on the UK financial services industry; benefit to employment.

GDP/GNP, Inflation, National Debt

Gross National Product and Gross Domestic Product recorded the fifteenth consecutive year of growth in 2006. During the 1970s the average GDP growth was 2.4 per cent, 2.3 per cent in the 1980s and 2.1 per cent during the 1990s. GDP growth was recorded at 2.8 per cent in 2002; 3.3 per cent in 2004; 1.8 per cent in 2005; 2.8 per cent in 2006 and 3.0 per cent in 2007. Forecast figures for 2008 and 2009 estimated that GDP would rise by an estimated 1.8 per cent. However, the 2009 figure was later revised and the economy was expected to experience negative growth of -1.0 per cent. This was in reply to the global economic downturn and credit crunch where the UK economy was responding to the downturn in the US economy and a reduction in consumer spending. At the end of 2007, Britain experienced its first run on a bank for many years; the Northern Rock bank was subsequently nationalised in February 2008. In October 2008 three other major banks, the Royal Bank of Scotland, Halifax and TSB were partly nationalised in order to save them and millions of pounds was pumped into the financial system by the government in an effort to prop up the ailing economy. The Bank of England cut interest rates to try to stimulate the economy and has also added £50 billion of new money into its £125 billion programme of quantitative easing. The government also introduced a car scrappage scheme to try to stimulate the motor industry. The government had forecast the economy would rebound in 2010 but the Bank of England warned that any recovery in 2010 will be fragile. The economy officially came out of recession in Q4 of 2009 when GDP was put at 0.1 per cent, ending six consecutive months of negative growth. GDP grew by just over 1.0 per cent in the first quarter of 2010 but fell to -0.5 per cent later in the year. Overall growth in GDP was put at 1.8 per cent in 2010. Figures for the first quarter of 2011 put GDP growth at 0.5 per cent, 1.8 per cent higher than the first quarter of 2010. Growth in real GDP was put at 0.8 per cent in 2011. In April 2012, the British economy recorded its second consecutive quarter of negative growth resulting in a return to recession, a fall in production in the construction industry was a major factor. In the first quarter of 2013 the economy grew by 0.3 per cent thus avoiding falling into recession for the third time in five years, the growth was put down to increased North Sea oil and gas output.

Following the general election in May 2010, the new Conservative government presented an emergency budget to deal with the UK's debt crisis. There were various amendments to taxes including a rise in VAT from 17.5 per cent to 20 per cent in January 2011, it was estimated that this alone would raise around £13 billion a year. Spending was to be cut. Measures include pay freezes in the public sector. The balance of spending cuts to tax rises would be 77 per cent to 23 per cent.

The following table shows figures for Gross National Income and Gross Domestic Product at market prices in recent years (figures are in £million):

Year	GNI	GDP
2000	974,732	975,294
2001	1,027,915	1,019,838
2002	1,091,479	1,068,599
2003	1,155,265	1,136,596
2004	1,220,159	1,199,881
2005	1,275,061	1,262,710
2006	1,334,091	1,333,157
2007	1,417,878	1,412,119
2008	1,476,869	1,440,931
2009	1,423,812	1,401,863
2010	1,479,042	1,427,087
2011	1,539,733	1,441,248
2012	1,540,596	1,445,178

Source: Office of National Statistics

The following table shows Gross Value Added in recent years by industry groups at current basic prices. Figures are in £ million:

Sector	2009	2010
Agriculture, hunting, forestry & fishing	8,030	7,569
Mining & quarrying	25,876	28,804
Manufacturing	126,739	130,611
Electricity, gas, steam & air conditioning supply	21,146	17,259
Water supply; sewerage, waste managment	15,173	14,887
Construction	87,373	90,685
Wholesale & retail trade, repairs	137,682	140,171
Hotels & restaurants	35,228	36,936
Transportation and storage	61,870	60,232
Information & communication	77,099	86,278
Financial & insurance activities	126,894	115,161
Real estate activities	90,414	119,691
Administrative & support service activities	56,101	59,155
Public administration & defence; compulsory social security	68,037	68,756
Education	85,677	88,152
Health & social work activities	99,329	104,930
Arts, entertainment & recreation	19,405	21,225
Other services	17,089	16,446
Activities of households	5,315	6,549
Total	1,256,932	1,301,118

Source: Office of National Statistics

In recent years, annual underlying inflation (RPIX) has ranged between 2.0 and 3.5 per cent. Consumer Prices Index inflation (CPI) was recorded at 1.3 per cent in February 2004 falling to 1.1 per cent in March. RPIX figures for those months were 2.3 and 2.1 per cent respectively. In March 2007, inflation rose to 3.1 per cent before falling in April to 2.8 per cent but still above the 2.0 per cent baseline target set by the government. Figures for 2008 forecast that inflation would rise above the 2.0 per cent baseline target. In March 2009 inflation was recorded to have fallen below zero per cent the first time the UK had experienced negative inflation since 1960. The fall in inflation was mainly attributed to the fall in oil prices and the reaction to the cut in VAT that the government had introduced to stimulate consumer spending. Towards the end of 2009 inflation had begun to rise again and in April 2010 had reached 3.7 per cent its highest rate for 17 months. Inflation was forecast to be as high as 5.0 per cent in 2011 (mainly due to rising fuel prices) but would fall again in 2012 and 2013. At the beginning of 2012 inflation was recorded at 3.5 per cent. In April 2013 inflation had fallen to 2.4 per cent but rose again in May to 2.7 per cent. Forecast figures put inflation rising to a possible peak of 3.0 per cent towards the end of 2013 before falling steadily for the next two years.

Gross debt was estimated to be over 80 per cent of GDP in 2010 (compared to nearly 44 per cent of GDP in 2007).

Foreign Investment

Approximately 15 per cent of the country's jobs are with foreign-owned firms, perhaps partially due to the fact that the UK's labour costs are the fourth lowest in Western Europe (after Spain, Portugal and Greece). Foreign firms account for over 30 per cent of UK manufacturing investment. Foreign direct investment reached a high of £91 billion in 2005. Figures for 2009 show that inward investment was £45.7 billion and outward investment was £21.2 billion.

Balance of Payments / Imports and Exports

The UK is the sixth largest exporter of goods and the second largest exporter of services. EU countries account for over half of the UK's imports and exports, with Germany being the largest trading nation, followed by France and the Netherlands. The largest non-EU trading partner is the USA.

The following tables show external trade in goods and services in £ million over recent years:

Trade	2011	2012
Exports of goods	299,073	300,456
Exports of services	193,382	187,972
Total	492,455	488,428
Imports of goods	399,303	406,799
Imports of services	117,299	117,783
Total	516,602	524,582
Balance of trade in goods	-100,230	-106,343
Balance of trade in services	76,083	70,189
Total	-24,147	-36,154

Source: Office of National Statistics

External Trade by Commodity 2012, in £ million

Commodity	Exports	Imports
Food, beverages & tobacco	17,818	36,552
Basic materials	8,486	10,820
Oil	39,684	53,844
Other fuels	4,339	11,445
Semi manufactured goods	85,383	99,344
Finished manufactured goods	140,481	191,010
Unspecified goods	4,265	3,784
Total	300,456	406,799

Source: Office of National Statistics

External Trade by Services 2012, in £ million

Service	Exports	Imports
Transportation	23,400	20,195
Travel	23,026	33,134
Communiations	6,400	4,191
Construction	1,486	898
Insurance	13,078	2,102
Financial	44,454	10,544
Computer & information	9,149	4,501
Royalities & license fees	7,151	5,107
Other business	55,396	32,517
Personal, cultural & receational	2,160	588
Government	2,272	4,006
Total	187,972	117,783

Source: Office of National Statistics

The top 10 trading partners for imports and exports of goods in 2011 are shown in the following tables:

Countries	£ million
Exports	
United States	39,817
Germany	32,467
Netherlands	23,607
France	22,196
Republic of Ireland	17,848
Belgium & Luxembourg	16,333
Italy	10,030

UNITED KINGDOM

- continued

Spain	9,712
China	9,300
Sweden	6,323

Source: Office of National Statistics

Countries	£ million
Imports	
Germany	50,471
China	31,542
USA	28,799
Netherlands	28,437
Norway	25,222
France	23,053
Belgium & Luxembourg	20,074
Italy	13,933
Republic of Ireland	13,083
Spain	11,542

Source: Office of National Statistics

Central Bank

Bank of England, Threadneedle Street, London, EC2R 8AH, UK. Tel: +44 (0)20 7601 4444, fax: +44 (0)20 7601 4771, e-mail: enquiries@bankofengland.co.uk, URL: http://www.bankofengland.co.uk
Governor: Mark Carney (page 1400)

Financial Ombudsman Service, South Quay Plaza, 183 Marsh Wall, London, E14 9SR, UK. Tel: +44 (0)20 7964 1000, fax: +44 (0)20 7964 1001, e-mail: enquiries@financial-ombudsman.org.uk, URL: http://www.financial-ombudsman.org.uk

Major Banks

The Royal Bank of Scotland, PO Box 31, 42 St. Andrew Square, Edinburgh, EH2 2YE, UK; Tel: +44 131 556 8555, fax: +44 131 557 6565, URL: http://www.rbs.co.uk
Barclays Bank plc, 54 Lombard Street, London EC3P 3AH, UK. Tel: +44 (0)20 7699 5000, fax: +44 (0)20 7699 2460, URL: http://www.barclays.co.uk, http://www.barclays.com
Lloyds TSB Bank plc, 71 Lombard Street, London EC3P 3BS, UK. Tel: +44 (0)20 7626 1500, URL: http://www.lloydstsb.com
Abbey National plc, Abbey National House, 2 Triton Square, Regent's Place, London NW1 3AN, UK. Tel: +44 (0)20 7612 4000, fax: +44 (0)20 7224 5306, e-mail: marketing@ants.co.uk, URL: http://www.abbeynational.com
National Westminster Bank Plc, 135 Bishopsgate, London, EC2M 3UR, UK. Tel: +44 (0)20 7375 5000, fax: +44 (0)20 7375 5050, URL: http://www.natwest.com / http://www.rbs.co.uk
HSBC Bank plc, 27-32 Poultry, London EC2P 2BX, UK. Tel: +44 (0)20 7260 8000, fax: +44 (0)20 7260 7065, URL: http://www.hsbc.co.uk
HBOS plc, PO Box No 5, The Mound, Edinburgh, EH1 1YZ, UK. URL: http://www.hbosplc.com
Halifax plc, (now subsidiary of HBOS Group) Trinity Road, Halifax, HX1 2RG, UK. Tel: +44 (0)1422 333333, fax: +44 (0)1422 333000, URL: http://www.halifax.co.uk
Bank of Scotland, (now subsidiary of HBOS Group) The Mound, Edinburgh EH1 1YZ, United Kingdom. Tel: +44 (0)131 442 7777, fax: +44 (0)131 243 5437, URL: http://www.bankofscotland.co.uk
Nationwide Building Society, Nationwide Hse, Pipers Way, Swindon, Wilts SN38 1NW, UK. Tel: +44 1793 513513, fax: +44 1793 455218, URL: http://www.nationwide.co.uk
Standard Chartered Bank, 1 Aldermanbury Square, London, EC2V 7SB, UK. Tel: +44 20 7280 7500 / 20 7457 7500, fax: +44 20 7280 7791, URL: http://www.standardchartered.com
Cheltenham and Gloucester PLC, Barnett Way, Gloucester, GL4 3RL, United Kingdom. Tel: +44 (0)1452 372372, fax: +44 (0)1452 373955, e-mail: general-enquiries@CGdirect.demon.co.uk, URL: http://www.cheltglos.co.uk

Saving Organisation

National Savings and Investments, Charles House, 375 Kensington High St, London, W14 8SD, United Kingdom. Tel: +44 (0)845 964 5000, URL: http://www.nsandi.com

Banking and Finance Organisations

British Bankers' Association, Pinners Hall, 105-108 Old Broad St, London, EC2N 1EX, United Kingdom. Tel: +44 (0)20 7216 8800, fax: +44 (0)20 7216 8811, URL: http://www.bba.org.uk
Institute of Financial Services, IFS House, 4-9 Burgate Lane, Canterbury, Kent CT1 2XJ, United Kingdom. Tel: +44 (0) 1227 818609, fax: +44 (0) 1227 786696, e-mail: customerservices@ifslearning.com, URL: http://www.ifslearning.com

Stock Exchange

London Stock Exchange, Old Broad St, London, EC2N 1HP, United Kingdom. Tel: +44 (0)20 7797 1000, fax: +44 (0)20 7334 8930, URL: http://www.londonstockexchange.com

Supervisory Bodies

Financial Services Authority, 25 The North Colonnade, Canary Wharf, London, E14 5HS, United Kingdom. Tel: +44 (0)20 7676 1000, fax: +44 020 7676 1099, URL: http://www.fsa.gov.uk
Investment Management Regulatory Organisation Ltd. (IMRO), Lloyds Chambers, 1 Portsoken St, London, E18 BT, United Kingdom. Tel: +44 (0)20 7676 1000, fax: +44 (0)20 7680 0550, URL: http://www.imro.co.uk
Securities and Investment Institute, Centurion House, 24 Monument St, London, EC3R 8AJ, United Kingdom. Tel: +44 (0)20 7645 0600, fax: +44 (0)20 7645 0601, URL: http://www.sii.org.uk

Government Agencies

Forestry Commission, 231 Corstophine Road, Edinburgh, EH12 7AT, United Kingdom. Tel: +44 (0)131 334 0303, fax: +44 (0)131 334 3047, e-mail: enquiries@forestry.gov.uk, URL: http://www.forestry.gov.uk
Competition Commission, Victoria House, Southampton Row, London WC1B 4AD, United Kingdom. Tel: +44 (0)20 7271 0100, fax: +44 (0)20 7271 0367, URL: http://www.competition-commission.gov.uk
Office of Fair Trading, Field House, Breams Bldgs, London, EC4A 1PR, United Kingdom. Tel: +44 (0)20 7211 8000, fax: +44 (0)20 7211 8800, URL: http://www.oft.gov.uk
United Kingdom Atomic Energy Authority, Harwell, Oxfordshire, OX11 0RA, United Kingdom. Tel: +44 (0)1235 820220, fax: +44 (0)1235 436401, URL: http://www.ukaea.org.uk

Development Organisations

Countryside Agency, John Dower House, Crescent Place, Cheltenham, United Kingdom. Tel: +44 (0)1242 521 381, fax: +44 (0)1242 584 270, URL: http://www.countryside.gov.uk
Scottish Enterprise, 120 Bothwell St, Glasgow, G2 7JP, United Kingdom. Tel: +44 (0)141 248 2700, fax: +44 (0)141 221 3217, e-mail: scotentcsd@scotent.co.uk, URL: http://www.scottish-enterprise.com
Welsh Development Agency, Principality House, The Friary, Cardiff, CF1 4AE, United Kingdom. Tel: +44 (0)1443 845500, fax: +44 (0)1443 845589, URL http://www.wda.co.uk

Chambers of Commerce and Trade Addresses

International Chamber of Commerce (ICC), 14-15 Belgrave Square, London SW1X 8PS, United Kingdom. Tel: +44 (0)20 7838 9363, fax: +44 (0)20 7235 5447, URL: http://www.iccuk.net
London Chamber of Commerce and Industry, Swan House, 33 Queen Street, London EC4R 1AP, United Kingdom. Tel: +44 (0)20 7248 4444, fax: +44 (0)20 7489 0391, URL: http://www.londonchamber.co.uk
British Chambers of Commerce, 65 Petty France, London SW1H 9EU, United Kingdom. Tel: +44 (0)20 7565 2000, fax: +44 (0)20 7565 2049, e-mail: info@britishchambers.org.uk, URL: http://www.chamberonline.co.uk
Confederation of British Industry, Centre Point, 103 New Oxford Street, London, WC1A 1DU Tel: +44 (0)20 7379 7400, URL: http://www.cbi.org.uk/home.html
Department of Trade and Industry, 123 Victoria Street, London SW1H 0NN Tel: +44 (0)20 7215 5000, fax: +44 (0)20 7215 6739, URL http://www.dti.gov.uk
UK Department of Trade and Industry's Export Control Organisation, Kingsgate House, 66-74 Victoria Street, London SW1E 6SW Tel: +44 (0)20 7215 5000, fax: +44 (0)20 7215 8564, URL: http://www.berr.gov.uk/europeandtrade/strategic-export-control
Export Market Information Centre, URL: https://www.uktradeinvest.gov.uk/
Her Majesty's Board of Customs and Excise, Tel: +44 (0)20 7620 1313, fax: +44 (0)20 7865 4944, URL: http://customs.hmrc.gov.uk
Patent Office, Central Enquiry and The Marketing and Information Directorate, Room 1LO2, Concept House, Cardiff Road, Newport, Gwent, NP10 8QQ Tel: +44 (0)645 500505, fax: +44 (0)1633 813600, URL: http://www.patent.gov.uk/search
Scottish Trade International, 120 Bothwell Street, Glasgow, G2 7JP Tel: +44 (0)141 228 2633/2869, fax: +44 (0)141 221 3712, URL: http://www.sdi.co.uk
Institute of Export, 64 Clifton St, London, EC2A 4HB, United Kingdom. Tel: +44 (0)20 7247 9812, fax: +44 (0)20 7377 5343, URL: http://www.export.org.uk

MANUFACTURING, MINING AND SERVICES

Primary and Extractive Industries

The UK's proven oil reserves in January 2012 were 2.8 billion barrels which are mainly located in the centre of the North Sea, east of the British Isles; major fields include East Brae, Brent, Forties and Magnus. As the UK's North Sea sector is mature, however, much of UK oil activity is now focused on developing new fields in the North Sea, such as Foinaven, Durward and Ross, and the Jade, Blake and Keith fields. Production started in 2001 in the Graben area off the coast of Scotland with the Elgin/Franklin platform. This may be the last big North Sea platform.

Production has fallen from 2.95 million barrels per day, (of which 2.68 million barrels per day was crude oil in 1999) to an estimated 1.15 million barrels per day in 2011 (1.0 million barrels of crude oil). The North Sea sector is mature, having an annual depletion rate of six per cent while average discovery sizes are down to the 50-million-barrel range. At its peak, it is estimated that the UK used to experience one billion barrel finds regularly (Source: US EIA). The costs of development and operating in the UK's North Sea sector are relatively high by world standards.

Wytch Farm is Europe's largest onshore oilfield. It has reserves estimated at 500 million barrels and is located in Dorset.

Figures for 2011 put consumption of oil at 2.8 million barrels per day making the UK an importer of oil to the tune of 1.3 million barrels of oil per day. The United Kingdom does export oil, mainly to the United States, Netherlands, France and Germany. Most of the oil exported to the Netherlands is not for consumption but is sold on. (source: US EIA).

Most of the UK's natural gas reserves (an estimated 9.0 billion cubic feet) are also located in the North Sea, in fields such as Britannia, Leman and Indefatigable. In 2011 the UK's consumption of natural gas was 2,849 billion cubic feet and production was 1,546 billion cubic feet. (source: US EIA).

Gas supply is split into regions: Eastern, East Midlands, Northern, North Eastern, North Thames, North Western, Scotland, Southern, South Eastern, South Western, Wales and West Midlands. Ofgas is the industry regulator. Competition was introduced to the gas industry throughout the country in stages through the course of 1998. In 1999 Ofgas became Ofgem, a combined gas and electricity regulatory body.

The United Kingdom became a gas importer in 2004 became an importer of oil around 2005. The government has begun a programme of import infrastructure including liquefied natural gas re-gasification terminals, maximizing the production from marginal fields and investing in energy conservation and renewable sources of energy.

Regulatory Authority

Office of Gas and Electricity Markets (OFGEM), URL: http://www.ofgas.gov.uk/ofgem/index.jsp

As of 2010 the UK produced an estimated 19.6 million short tons of coal per year down from 45.5 million short tons in 1998. In 2010 consumption was 55.3 million short tons down from the 2003 figure of 68.81 million short tons per year but up slightly on the 2009 figure of 53.2 million short tons. The industry is entirely in the private sector, and recent figures show there are 29 underground mines including 16 deep mines in production and 56 open cast mines, together employing 11,200.

Energy

The following tables show figures for the UK's energy sector:

Production of Primary Fuels in mil. tonnes of oil equiv.	1995	2000	2007
Coal	32.8	19.6	10.7
Petroleum	142.7	138.3	84.2
Natural Gas	70.8	108.4	72.1
Primary electricity	21.7	20.2	14.9
Renewable energy	1.7	2.3	4.0
Total production	269.7	288.7	185.9

Source: National Office of Statistics

Inland Energy Consumption, in mil. tonnes of oil equiv.	1995	2000	2007
Coal	48.9	37.9	40.8
Petroleum	75.4	75.9	75.6
Primary electricity	23.1	21.4	15.4
Natural gas	69.2	95.6	90.0
Renewables and waste	1.7	2.3	4.4
less energy used by fuel producers & losses in distribution	68.0	74.7	71.0
Total consumption by final users	150.4	158.3	154.9

Source: National Office of Statistics

Final Energy Consumption by Class of Consumer by 2007

Sector	Mil. tonnes of oil equiv.
Agriculture	0.9
Iron & steel industry	1.7
Other industries	30.0
Railways	1.4
Road transport	42.8
Water transport	1.6
Air transport	14.0
Domestic	44.0
Public administration	6.7
Commercial & other services	11.8

Source: Office of National Statistics

Britain's household electricity market was opened to competition in the summer of 1998 and since then any regional electricity company has been allowed to sell electricity in any region. The following companies are regional electricity companies in the UK: Scottish Hydro-Electric, Scottish Power, Northern Ireland Electricity, Norweb, Northern Electric, Yorkshire Electricity, East Midlands Electricity, Manweb, Midlands Electricity, Eastern Electricity, London Electricity, Seeboard, Southern Electric (the last independent regional company), SWEB (South Western Electricity) and Swalec.

Around 79 per cent of the UK's produced electricity is generated by thermal plants. As of 2003 the UK had 13 operational nuclear power stations generating 22.2 per cent of all electricity used. Britain's nuclear fuel policy is currently under review. One per cent of Britain's electricity in generated from hydropower. Thermal production is now moving away from coal and towards natural gas. Figures for 2006 show that 157,382 gigawatt hours of electricity were generated by conventional thermal power stations including gas, oil and renewables (not hydro), 75,451 gigawatt hours were produced by nuclear power stations and 7,680 from hydro-electric stations. In May 2010 the government announced possible plans for an offshore wind turbine production facility that would be built on the east coast or North East England, if the plans go ahead the turbines could come online in 2015. A wind farm consisitng of 195 turbines is under consideration off the south coast of England.

Energy companies include:
British Energy PLC, URL: http://www.british-energy.com
International Power plc, URL: http://www.anpower.com
Powergen PLC, URL: http://www.powergenplc.com
National Grid , URL: http://www.nationalgrid.com/uk
Scottish Power, URL: http://www.scottishpower.plc.uk/pages

AEA Technology undertakes a programme of research and development on all aspects of atomic energy, and particularly research and development in support of the application of nuclear energy to electricity generation. It is a principal adviser to the Government on nuclear energy.

Water

Ofwat is the water industry regulator.
Office of Water Services (OFWAT), URL: http://www.ofwat.gov.uk

Manufacturing

Figures for late 2011 show that manufacturing employed 2.8 million people up from the early 2009 figure of 2.6 million people but down from 3.1 million people in 2005, and in 2007 generated £154,919 million of gross value added. Although still an important contributor to the economy, manufacturing is in decline and has been since the recession in the early 1990s.

The manufacturing sector has been hit by the 2008-09 recession and productivity fell by 3.4 per cent in the fourth quarter of 2008 from the previous quarter, productivity in the third quarter fell by 0.8 per cent. Figures for April 2013 showed that manufacturing output fell by 0.5 per cent over the year from April 2012, the main industries contributing to the fall were chemicals and chemical products, rubber and plastic products and food, beverage and tobacco products.

Total turnover for manufacturing in the UK in recent years

Year	£ million
2008	401,830.6
2009	357,041.4
2010	385,346.4
2011	404,848.0
2012	400,116.3

Source: Office of National Statistics

Britain is the world's tenth largest steel-producing nation, although it is an industry in decline. Total production of crude steel in 2006 amounted to 13.90 million tonnes down from the 2000 figure of 15.15 million tonnes. 2003 saw a slight rise in production, mainly attributable to the resumption of normal work at the Port Talbot plant in South Wales. Production has also been bolstered by an increase in demand for steel products from the construction sector which continues to grow. The major areas of steel production are Wales, Scotland and northern England, and substantial primary production of steel takes place in the Midlands. Around half of the steel produced is exported. Britain is also a major producer of specialized alloys for high-technology requirements in the aerospace, electronic, petrochemical, nuclear and other fuel industries. Almost all manufacturing is carried out by private business. Figures for 2007 showed that there were 27,685 enterprises producing basic and fabricated metal. Figures for 2003 show that Britain exported 6.2 million tonnes of steel, 10 per cent more than in the previous years. Traditional markets for British steel were among the EU countries but growing markets now include China and the Middle East. Corus is the seventh largest steel company in the world and in the UK it employs 24,600 and produces nearly 90 per cent of the UK's total steel production. Following the economic slowdown in 2008, the steel making giant Corus announced over 2,000 jobs would have to go at its Teeside plant in North East England. The plant was mothballed in 2010 but in April 2012 the plant was re-opened and many of the old workforce re-employed. The UK bcame a net importer of steel in 2010, following the resumption of production in Teeside, imports have fallen slightly.

Production of Steel in Thousand Tonnes

Crude Steel	2005	2006
Rods & bars for reinforcement	790	902
Wire rods & other rods & bars in coil	1,035	962
Hot rolled bars in lengths	1,142	1,249
Bright steel bars	233	226
Light sections other than rails	130	149
Heavy sections	1,414	1,527
Hot rolled plates, sheets & strip in coil & lengths	5,823	6,010
Cold rolled plates & sheets	2,769	2,726
Cold rolled strip	131	98
Tinplate	471	421
Other coated sheet	1,644	1,773
Tubes & pipes	932	993

Source: National Statistics Office

Britain's chemicals industry is the third largest in western Europe and the fifth largest in the western world. Nearly half of its production of principal products is exported. Traditionally, Britain has been a major producer of basic industrial chemicals, such as inorganic and basic organic chemicals, plastics and fertilisers. Although these sectors still make up about 38 per cent of the industry's output, the most rapid growth in recent years has been in the production of speciality and 'problem-solving' chemicals, especially pharmaceuticals, pesticides and cosmetics. The value of chemicals produced increased by nearly 5 per cent in the early 1990s, and exports of chemicals were worth £46.9 billion in 2009. Turnover of basic pharmaceutical products and preparations in 2012 was £15,385.2 million, paints, varnishes, printing links and mastics was £3,607.3 million, soap and detergents, cleaning and polishing goods, perfumes and toilertries, £6,574.2 million and other chemical products, 5,580.6 million.

Expansion in recent years of plastics production has mainly been in thermoplastic materials, of which the most important are polyethylene, polyvinyl chloride, polystyrene and polypropylene. The main types of man-made fibre manufactured by UK industry are regenerated cellulosic fibres such as viscose and the major synthetic fibres such as nylon polyamide, polyester and acrylics. Extensive research continues to produce a wide variety of innovative products with characteristics designed to meet market needs, such as anti-static and flame retardant fibres. More specialist products include the aramids (with very high thermal stability and strength), elastanes (giving very high stretch and recovery), melded fabrics (produced without the need for knitting or weaving), and carbon fibres (for the aerospace industry as well as the motor vehicle and sports goods industries).

Britain has a long tradition of shipbuilding but remains only minimally active in the construction, conversion and repair of merchant vessels, warships and offshore structures. The largest sector is the building of warships, including both nuclear-powered and diesel-electric submarines, frigates, glass-reinforced plastics vessels, fast patrol craft and specialist naval auxiliaries. As well as meeting all the needs of the Royal Navy, the warship yards build and convert ships for overseas governments. Figures for 2012 put the turnover of the building of ships and boats at £4,781.4 million, up from £4,407.6 million in 2011.

Britain's aerospace industry is the third largest in the world, with a turnover of approximately £21,000 million. EOver the past decade, the industry has doubled its productivity, doubled its turnover and trebled its exports in real terms. As the largest British exporter of manufactured goods, British Aerospace manufactures an extensive range of aerospace, space and electronic products. It has developed its own family of civil aircraft.

Figures for 2006 showed that 1.44 million motor vehicles were produced in the UK, 1.10 million of which were for the export market. Manufacturers sales of motor vehicles was put at £22.5 million in 2004. Companies with operations in the UK include MG Rover, Nissan, Toyota, Peugeot, Honda, BMW, Ford, General Motors and Volkswagen. In 2005 MG Rover went bankrupt with the loss of 6,000 jobs; the plant in the Midlands has since been brought by the Chinese firm Nanjing. In early 2006 the General Motors-owned Vauxhall plant in Cheshire announced the loss of 900 jobs. The car industry was severely hit by the 2009 recession, sales of new cars fell by 28 per cent and several firms closed for some weeks as there was such a slow market. The government introduced a scheme whereby you could trade in any car older than 10 years and receive £2,000 towards buying a new car in the hope this would boost the motor trade. Figures for 2012 put the manufacturing turnover of motor vehicles, trailers and semi trailers at 54.778.3 million up from £52,939.0 in 2011.

The paper, printing and publishing sector has been growing in recent years; figures for 2003 show that 6.2 million tonnes of paper was produced, 1.3 million tonnes of which went for export. Improvements have been made in the use of recycled materials; in 2003 nearly 67 per cent of material for UK newspapers was from recycled material. Book publishing is a large export earning sector with earnings amounting to £1.3 billion in 2003, the largest markets for publications being the USA and the Republic of Ireland.

The following table shows UK manufacturing turnover at current basic prices by selected industry, figures in £ million:

Industry	2011	2012
Processing & preserving of fish, molluscs, fruit & veg.	9,745.0	10,0967
Bakery & farinaceous products	10,392.3	10,508.1
Other food products	16,997.4	16,278.2
Textiles	5,514.4	5,564.2
Leather & leather products	1,036.4	919.6
Wood & wood products excl. furniture	7,256.9	6,886.5
Paper & paper products	10,871.7	10,429.6
Printing & reproduction of recorded media	11,507.4	10,429.6
Basic pharmaceutical products & preparations	16,293.0	15,385.2
Rubber & plastic products	21,533.7	22,084.4
Other basic metals excl. iron & steel	8,088.2	7,857.9
Fabricated metal products excl. weapons & ammunition	29,498.3	30,332.2
Machinery & equipment not elsewhere classified	38,203.3	39,441.2
Computer, electronic & optical equipment	20,476.2	20,547.5
Other transport equipment	2,032.8	2,193.9
Total manufacturing	404,848.0	400,351.5
Total turnover for services in GB	1,646,854.8	1,697,367.2

Source: Office of National Statistics

Service Industries

Service industries account for over 70 per cent of GDP, with financial services alone representing approximately 15 per cent of GDP.

Tourist figures for 2001 were expected to be down following the outbreak of foot and mouth disease, and international travel figures for the end of 2001 and beginning of 2002 were expected to be down following the terrorist attack in America on 11 September 2001. The final figures showed that visitors to the UK in 2001 fell by nine per cent on 2000 figures, to 22.8 million, but increased to 32.5 million in 2007. Spending by visitors was recorded at £11.3 billion in 2001, £11.7 billion in 2002 and £15.9 billion in 2007. In 2007, 70.0 million visits overseas were made by UK residents who spent a total of £35.4 billion.

Visits to the UK by overseas residents also fell in 2009, but at a slower rate, down 6.3 per cent from the 31.9 million made in 2008 to 29.9 million. Visits of UK residents that year numbered 58.6 million. Visitor numbers were expected to increase dramatically in 2012 when London hosted the Olympic games and the number of visitors to the UK for the Olympics was put at 698,000.

Agriculture

Agriculture is very important to the United Kingdom; 29 per cent of the UK's land is arable, and 48 per cent is used as meadows and pastures. The UK has over 65 per cent self sufficiency in all food production and around 75 per cent self sufficiency in indigenous food production. The sector in 2011 employed around 41,000 people compared to 48,000 in 2008, and contributes nearly £8 billion to the economy. The UK has around 300,000 farm holdings with an average size of 56.4 hectares.

Between 2000 and 2003 there were controlled studies carried out into the production of Genetically Modified (GM) crops. Oilseed rape, maize and beet were tested, having been modified to be resistant to certain herbicides. The government announced that GM crops would not be commercially grown until all the results have been assessed.

The following table shows selected crop production in recent years, figures are in thousand tonnes:

Agricultural Crops	2009	2010
Wheat	14,079	14,879
Barley	6,668	5,252
Oats	744	685
Sugar beet	8,457	6,484
Potatoes	6,396	6,045
Horticultural Crops		
Cabbage	233.8	248.4
Carrots	718.7	747.9
Onions	354.9	364.4
Peas (shelled weight)	110.6	126.6
Lettuce	110.6	126.6
Tomatoes	86.8	89.8
Dessert apples	121.1	124.7
Soft fruit	15.06	145.7

Source: Office of National Statistics

The following figures show how selected agricultural land is used in the UK:

Agricultural Land Use in Thousand Hectares

Agricultural Land	2011
Wheat	1,968
Barley	968
Oilseed rape	705
Potatoes	146
Vegetables	129
Orchard fruit	24
Total agricultural area	18,702

Source: Office of National Statistics

The following table shows recent livestock figures:

Livestock in '000s

Sector	2000	2010	2012
Cattle and calves	11,135	10,112	9,726
- dairy	2,336	1,847	1,802
- beef	1,842	1,657	1,600
Pigs	5,047	4,460	4,221
Sheep and lambs	na	21,295	22,913
Fowls	169,773	163,867	na

Source: Office of National Statistics

Livestock production (primarily for meat) in £ million

Produce	2007	2008
Cattle	1,626.1	2,069.6
Pigs	736.3	858.2
Sheep	637.4	822.1
Poultry	1,207.4	1,482.3
Livestock products		
Milk	2,823.5	3,450.0
Eggs	410.1	523.6

Source: Office of National Statistics

In 2000 British agriculture was hit by the BSE epidemic which saw exports of animals and meat products fall dramatically. That year saw the wettest autumn for over 200 years and widespread flooding meant farming was dealt another blow. In February 2001 the United Kingdom was hit by an outbreak of Foot and Mouth Disease, the first big outbreak since 1967, and by September 2001 there had been 2,020 cases confirmed. The government introduced a policy of culling animals on the affected farms and the surrounding area in an effort to stop the disease spreading. By September 2001, 9,395 premises had been affected and 3,177,000 sheep, 597,000 cattle, 139,000 pigs, 2,000 goats and 500 deer had been culled.

The Forestry Commission is the national forestry authority in Great Britain. The Commissioners give advice on forestry matters and are responsible to the Secretary of State for Scotland, the Minister of Agriculture, Fisheries and Food and the Secretary of State for Wales. Timber production, landscape amenity, environmental protection and employment are all forestry policy objectives. The Commission's activities also include wildlife and flora conservation, plant health, research, and the provision of facilities for recreation. 2,745,000 hectares of the UK's land is forest and woodland.

The UK fishing fleet provides around 60 per cent of British supplies of sea fish and is an important source of coastal employment and income. Cod, haddock, sole, plaice, whiting and herring are the main species targeted by vessels fishing in the North Sea. Cod and haddock and other demersal fish plus nephrops and mackerel are targeted off the west coast of Scotland. In the Irish Sea, and within south western and southern sea areas, sole, plaice, cod, whiting, mackerel and nephrops continue to be important. The UK's distant water fleet fish in Norwegian, Greenland and Svalbard waters. Recent figures show that roughly 485,000 tonnes of fresh, frozen, cured fish, shellfish, and fish and shellfish preparations are imported per annum.

The fishing fleet consists of some 5,829 registered vessels. Most of these are under 12.19 metres. Shore based industries such as fish processors are important employers at all major ports. Generally the fishing industry within the UK is contracting, though it remains an important source of employment in areas where there are little alternative forms of income. The following table shows a summary of the UK fishing industry:

Fishing Industry	1991	2000	2006
No. of vessels	11,411	7,818	6,372
No. of fishermen	n/a	15,121	12,934
Quantity landed '000 tonnes	787	748	614
Value £ million	496	550	610
Household consumption '000 tonnes	418	442	524

Source: National Office of Statistics

COMMUNICATIONS AND TRANSPORT

Travel Requirements
Citizens of the USA, Canada and Australia require a passport valid for three months beyond the length of stay, but do not require a visa for stays of up to six months, though they are advised to have a return ticket or proof of sufficient funds to support themselves for the duration of their stay.

EU citizens do not require a passport if holding a valid national ID card, and do not require a visa. Under the European Economic Area Agreement, European Economic Area nationals are granted the same rights to enter, live and work in the UK as EU citizens. The right of residence is granted to a European Economic Area national provided they have sufficient funds to support themselves. Please contact a British Consulate for further details.

A passport is not required for travel between Great Britain and Ireland, Northern Ireland, the Channel Islands or the Isle of Man. Passengers transiting the UK on route to the Republic of Ireland are advised to hold return tickets.

Other nationals should contact the embassy to check visa requirements.

Customs Restrictions
There are limits on goods brought into the UK, and these limits differ slightly depending on whether or not they are brought in from an EU country.
HM Customs and Excise, URL: http://www.hmce.gov.uk

As from 2001, dogs and cats were permitted to enter the UK without six months of quarantine. A trial of the scheme was set up for 2000 and in February the first dog using a pet passport arrived at Dover port. Dogs and cats must be vaccinated against rabies, fitted with an identification microchip and have health certificates. For more details, contact the Department of Environment, Food and Rural Affairs.

National Airlines
The largest British airlines are:
British Airways, URL: http://www.britishairway.com
Services are international, regional and domestic scheduled and charter passenger and cargo.
Virgin Atlantic Airways, URL: http://www.virgin-atlantic.com
Services are international scheduled passenger.
British Midland Airways Ltd, URL: http://www.flybmi.com
Thomsonfly, URL: http://www.thomsonfly.com
Monarch Airlines, URL: http://www.flymonarch.com
easyJet Airline Company Limited, URL http://www.easyjet.com

International Airports
BAA plc (formerly British Airports Authority) operates seven of the country's airports: Heathrow, Gatwick, Stansted, Southampton, Glasgow, Edinburgh and Aberdeen, and is the world's largest commercial airport operator. It handles over 71 per cent of the UK's air passenger traffic (amounting to 93.6 million terminal passengers and 75.7 million international passengers in 1996) and over 80 per cent of the UK's cargo. BAA was privatised in 1987, and is responsible for airport management, infrastructure projects, commercial facilities and property. In 2009 it was announced that BAA should sell off three of its airports beacuse of monopoly issues, the airports to be sold were Gatwick, Stanstead and Edinburgh.
BAA plc, URL: http://www.baa.com

The Civil Aviation Authority (CAA) has responsibility for the regulation of the British air transport industry. Its functions include the licensing of air transport services by British operators and the regulation of the safety of civil aviation operators and the aircraft used. The CAA runs the National Air Traffic Services Ltd (NATS) jointly with the Ministry of Defence.
Civil Aviation Authority, URL: http://www.caa.co.uk

Figures for 2008 show that 601,700 scheduled flights were operated by UK airlines and 193,400 chartered flights.

London Heathrow Airport, URL: http://www.baa.co.uk/main/airports/heathrow
Heathrow opened in 1946, and accommodates 90 airlines. It is the world's busiest airport, seeing 1,100 flights per day. Heathrow is also the Europe's number one cargo handling airport. In March 2008 a fifth terminal was opened at a cost of over £4.0 billion. It is for the sole use of British Airways.
London Gatwick Airport, URL: http://www.baa.co.uk/main/airports/gatwick
Gatwick is the UK's second largest airport.
Manchester Airport plc, URL: http://www.manairport.co.uk/web.nsf

Glasgow Airport, URL: http://www.baa.co.uk/main/airports/glasgow
Birmingham International Airport, URL: http://www.bhx.co.uk
London Stansted Airport, URL http://www.baa.com/main/airports/stansted
Edinburgh Airport, URL: http://www.baa.com/main/airports/edinburgh
Newcastle International Airport, URL: http://www.newcastleairport.com
Belfast International Airport, URL: http://www.belfastairport.com
London Luton Airport, URL: http://www.london-luton.co.uk

Railways
In 1996 Britain's railways were privatised, reorganising the former British Rail into smaller regional units. By January 1997 there were 74 sales agreed or franchises awarded, 14 businesses on the market, one sales process commenced and two to be sold. There are currently 24 operating companies, some of which are franchised to private operators. These operating companies lease trains from three private rolling stock leasing firms. The signalling, track and infrastructure equipment is owned by Network Rail (Railtrack's replacement) which also operates 14 stations, owns 2,500, and which publishes the national rail timetable. For further details of the country's holding companies and operating companies, please contact OPRAF (details below).

Franchises must publish a passenger charter setting out reliability, punctuality and service standards. If the standards are not met, the firm may be liable for passenger compensation. The Health and Safety Executive (independent body) oversees rail safety standards. The Rail Users' Consultative Committee assists passengers with issues regarding train operators, their services and stations.

In recent years Railtrack has been criticised on its safety record and since 1996 there have been seven serious accidents resulting in the deaths of 50 people. A report into the crash at Ladbroke Grove, London, in October 1999, which resulted in the deaths of 31 people, criticised both Railtrack and one of the operators, Thames, and put forward 88 recommendations for improvement. In 2002 Network Rail took over from Railtrack plc after that company was put into administration.

Provisional figures estimate there to be 17,200 km of railway, including London regional transport and other urban rail systems. Total Passenger journeys undertaken in 2006-07 was 2,396 million (Source: Office for National Statistics).

London, Glasgow, Liverpool and Newcastle all have subway systems. Manchester has a tram system and a system is currently being laid in Edinburgh.

Rail Regulator, URL: http://www.rail-reg.gov.uk
Office of Passenger Rail Franchising (OPRAF), Tel: +44 (0)20 7940 4200
The Associated Society of Locomotive Engineers and Firemen (ASLEF), URL: http://www.aslef.org.uk
Network Rail, URL: http://www.networkrail.co.uk
National Rail Enquiries: URL: http://www.nationalrail.co.uk

Metropolitan Transport
London Regional Transport (LRT), URL: http://tube.tfl.gov.uk
The Anglo-French consortium Eurotunnel runs a train service under the English Channel between England and the Continent. The Channel Tunnel opened in 1994, and runs passenger trains, trains carrying cars, and freight trains.
Eurotunnel, URL: http://www.eurotunnel.com/ukcmain

Roads
Until 2003 Britain had no motorway tolls, with roads funded by car taxes. The first 27-mile stretch of toll motorway was opened off the M6 in the West Midlands in 2003, with drivers opting to pay the toll and avoid one of the busiest motorway stretches in the country. Recent statistics show that there are over 3,475 km of motorways in use (an increase of over 60 per cent in the last 20 years). Recent figures show that the total length of roads in Britain is approximately 398,350 km. Vehicles are driven on the left.

In order to reduce the number of cars in London, the London Assembly introduced a Congestion Charge. Vehicles travelling in parts of central London are charged £8 a day. The scheme was introduced in February 2003 and initial results show that traffic has been reduced by 15 per cent.

Highways Agency, URL: http://www.highways.gov.uk

The Department of Transport is responsible for all the country's road planning, rehabilitation and safety, and the Highways Agency, which is part of the Department of Transport, is responsible for building the country's roads.

The following table shows passenger transport by mode of transportation in billion passenger kilometres:

Transport	2003	2006
Road		
- Buses & coaches	47	50
- Cars, vans & taxis	677	686
- Motorcycles, mopeds & scooters	6	6
- Pedal cycles	5	5
Road total	735	747
Rail	49	55
Air	9	10
All modes of transport	793	812

Inland Waterways
British Waterways, URL: http://www.britishwaterways.co.uk

UNITED KINGDOM

Shipping

At the end of 2002, the UK-owned merchant trading fleet (trading vessels over 100gt) numbered an estimated 590 ships as well as 40 passenger ships.

Ports and Harbours

Ports are owned by private companies, public trusts and local authorities and the largest port owner is Associated British Ports with 23 of the UK's ports.

The following table shows the UK's major ports and the cargo in tonnes they handled in 2003:

UK Ports

Port	Million Tonnes
London	51.0
Forth	38.7
Grimsby and Immingham	55.9
Tees and Hartlepool	53.8
Sullom Voe	26.4
Milford Haven	32.7
Southampton	35.8
Liverpool	31.7
Felixstowe	22.2
Dover	18.8

Source: Office of National Statistics

The UK's major passenger/car ferry ports are Dover (40 per cent of the total), Portsmouth (12 per cent), Holyhead (6 per cent) and Belfast (5 per cent).

Associated British Ports, URL: http://www.abports.co.uk/
The Baltic Exchange, URL: http://www.balticexchange.com
British Ports Association, URL: http://www.britishports.org.uk
Port of London Authority URL: http://www.portoflondon.co.uk

Tourism

British Tourist Authority, URL: http://www.bta.org.uk
Scottish Tourist Board, URL: http://www.visitscotland.com
Wales Tourist Board, URL: http://www.tourism.wales.gov.uk

HEALTH

The Department of Health sets out general health policies and is responsible for all health services in England. The Department is split into four main areas:
(i) NHS (National Health Service) Executive, which administers local health resources and advises the Government on policy development;
(ii) Public Health Group, concerned with policies for widespread disease prevention, and overall public health;
(iii) Social Health Group supports local authorities and social services;
(iv) Departmental Resources and Services Group, which manages the Department overall.

There are 100 health authorities in England. The government has recently introduced the idea of Polyclinics whereby more procedures such as minor surgery could be carried out at polyclinics (large health centre) rather than patients having to travel to hospital.

The UK's General Practitioners in practice number 48,281 (2009). There are approximately 22,000 general dental practitioners employed by the health service, as well as 377,000 nurses, midwives and health visitors.

Government expenditure for the NHS for in 2009 was £90 billion, up from £82.2 billion in 2004-05 and £90.5 billion in 2005-06. It was expected to rise to £100 billion in 2010.

1998 saw the introduction of NHS Direct, a telephone service manned by nurses, which enables patients to phone for advice, information and direction to the appropriate service to help them. In 2000-01 the service received 3.42 million calls. In July 2000 the Government announced a set of reforms for the National Health Service. Among these was an increase in spending, more medical staff to be recruited and waiting lists to be cut.

In 2011, the government announced a proposed major reform of the NHS. Under the plans, GPs and other clinicians would have much more responsibility for budgets and greater competition from the private sector would be encouraged. However, in the wake of widespread criticism, the government is reviewing some parts of the plan. The NHS has been asked to make savings of up to £20 billion by 2015.

EDUCATION

Education is compulsory and free for all children aged between five and 18. Most schools are state-run and are under the management of local authorities. Independent schools, with approximately 7 per cent of pupils, are run without public funding.

Pre-school Education

There are many nursery schools for children under the age of five, although this education is not compulsory in the UK. In 1998 a voucher scheme was introduced for children aged 4 to contribute towards pre-school education, so raising the number of children receiving nursery/pre-school education. By April 2004 the government guaranteed a nursery place to every child. Figures for the academic year 2008-09 show that there were 3,209 state run nursery schools with 28,900 pupils and 1,600 teachers.

Primary/Secondary Education

Primary education takes children from age five to 11, and is usually broken down into two stages: infant school from age five to age seven, then junior or middle school until aged 11. Pupils are tested on their progress throughout primary school.

Secondary education is for pupils aged 11 to 16. GCSEs (General Certificate of Secondary Education) are taken by all pupils in their final year of secondary school, and the results of these determine any further education. In 2009-10, 53 per cent of the relevant population of 15 year olds achieved five or more A* to C grade GCSEs, compared with 44 per cent in 2007-08. (source: Office for National Statistics).

Before 1989 secondary schools received funding from local education authorities. After this date they had the option to be funded directly by the Department of Education, and become grant maintained, which gives them the status of self governing.

Number of Schools 2008-09

School	UK
State nursery	3,209
State primary	21,568
State secondary	4,183
Non maintained schools	2,547
Universities	127

Source: Office of National Statistics

Once compulsory secondary school is over, pupils can attend Sixth Form College, which may be a separate school or part of a secondary school; this form of further education is non-compulsory. A-Level courses take two years and the grades determine entrance qualifications for university. A/S-Level qualifications take one year to complete, and are often counted as half an A-Level in terms of university entrance. In 2000 a new AS-level was introduced whereby students take a wider range of subjects during the first year and then narrow this down for the second year. The first time students applied for university places based on the results of AS-levels was summer 2002.

In 1998 the payment of tuition fees was introduced for British universities, these are paid back once the student has graduated and is earning over £21,000. Prior to 1998 students applied for grants to cover fees and living expenses and these did not have to be paid back.

Figures from UNESCO for 2007 show that 73 per cent of young children were enrolled in pre-primary education, 98 per cent of girls and 97 per cent of boys were enrolled primary education, 93 per cent of girls and 90 per cent of boys were enrolled in secondary education and 59 per cent of the population of tertiary age were enrolled in tertiary education.

Higher Education

As a result of the Further and Higher Education Act (1992), the UK's former polytechnics opted to become universities, and there are now 88 universities (including the Open University, an institution for mature students where degrees are taken mainly by correspondence course). Since the 1998/99 academic year, new students in further education must pay tuition fees, depending on family income. The existing means-tested maintenance grants were replaced by maintenance loans in the 1999/2000 academic year, a portion of which will also be means-tested.

Vocational Education

UK vocational qualifications include City and Guilds, RSA, BTECs and GNVQs. GNVQs, or General National Vocational Qualifications, are open to people aged over 16 and offer a choice of learning methods. There are three levels: foundation (equivalent to four grade D-G GCSEs); intermediate (equivalent to four or five grade A-C GCSEs); and advanced (equivalent to two A levels). Foundation and intermediate GNVQs take one year's full time study, whilst the advanced takes two years. NVQs and SVQs (National and Scottish Vocational Qualifications) are based on national standards of competence and describe an individual's work performance. Qualification is in five levels.
National Council for Vocational Qualifications, Tel: +44 (0)20 7509 5555.
Teacher Training Agency, URL: http://www.tta.gov.uk

Office for Standards in Education, Children's Services and Skills, URL: http://www.ofsted.gov.uk

RELIGION

The UK is predominantly Christian, with approximately 27 million people being Anglican. The Church of England is the state church in England. It has two provinces, Canterbury and York, which are each headed by an archbishop, and each province is split into 44 dioceses. The General Synod takes any Church of England decisions. In 1992 it voted that female priests should be accepted. On July 7 2008 the Synod voted to consecrate women as bishops, it was feared the move could lead to a split in the church with traditionalists refusing to accept the authority of a female bishop. A series of safeguards were to be discussed further in the hope that a compromise could be reached which would mean that clergy would not feel it necessary to leave the church.

The Anglican Church (Church in Wales) is the established church in Wales, while Scotland's is the Scottish Episcopal Church. There are around nine million Roman Catholics in the UK.

General Synod of the Church of England, URL: http://www.cofe.anglican.org
Archbishop of Canterbury: Justin Welby (page 1535)
Lambeth Place, London, SE1 7JU. Tel: +44 (0)20 7928 8282, fax: +44 (0)20 7261 9836
Archbishop for York: Dr John Sentamu (page 1512)
Bishopthorpe Palace, Bishopthorpe, York, YO23 2GE Tel:+44 (0)1904 707021, fax: +44 (0)1904 709204
The Church in Wales, Tel: +44 (0)29 2023 12638, fax: +44 (0)29 2038 7835

Archbishop of Wales: Dr Barry Morgan (page 1480)
Esgobty, St. Asaph, Clwyd
The Church of Scotland: 121 George Street, Edinburgh, EH2 4YN Scotland.
Diocesan Centre, 21A Grosvenor Crescent, Edinburgh, EH12 5EL Tel: +44 (0)131 538 7044
The Catholic Bishops' Conference of England and Wales: URL: http://www.catholic-ew.org.uk
Archbishop of Westminster: The Most Reverend Vincent Nichols
Archbishop's House, Ambrosden Avenue, Westminster, London, SW1P 1QJ. Tel: +44 (0)20 7798 9033
Bishops' Conference of Scotland: General Secretariat, 64 Aitken Street, Airdrie ML6 6LT, Scotland. Tel: +44 (0)1236 764061, fax: +44 (0)1236 762489
President of the Bishops' Conference, His Eminence Keith Patrick Cardinal O'Brien, Archbishop of St Andrews and Edinburgh
Irish Catholic Bishops Conference: URL: http://www.catholicbishops.ie
Cardinal Archbishop of Armagh and Primate of All Ireland, Cardinal Seán Baptist Brady

As part of the 2011 census the population was asked about its religious beliefs. Although it was not compulsory to answer this part of the census. The following table shows the results for England and Wales:

Religion	Persons
Christian	33,242,175
Buddhist	247,743
Hindu	816,633
Jewish	263,346
Muslim	2,706,066
Sikh	423,158
Other religion	240,530
No religion	14,097,229
Not stated	4,038,032

Source: Office of National Statistics

London Central Mosque Trust, URL: http://www.iccuk.org/
Buddhist Society, URL: http://www.thebuddhistsociety.org/
Chief Rabbi of the United Hebrew Congregations of the Commonwealth, URL: http://www.chiefrabbi.org/
Rabbi: Dr Jonathan Sacks
Sikh Missionary Society, URL: http://www.gurmat.info/

COMMUNICATIONS AND MEDIA

Newspapers
The Press Complaints Commission is an independent body formed to manage public complaints.
Press Complaints Commission, URL: http://www.pcc.org.uk

The UK's main daily papers are as follows:
The Sun, URL: http://www.thesun.co.uk
Daily Mirror, URL: http://www.mirror.co.uk
Daily Mail, URL: http://www.dailymail.co.uk
Daily Express, URL: http://www.express.co.uk
Daily Telegraph, URL: http://www.telegraph.co.uk
Daily Record, URL: http://www.dailyrecord.co.uk
Daily Star, URL: http://www.dailystar.co.uk
The Times, URL: http://www.timesonline.co.uk
Evening Standard, (London only) URL: http://www.thisislondon.co.uk
The Guardian, URL: http://www.guardian.co.uk
The Independent, URL: http://www.independent.co.uk
Financial Times, URL: http://www.ft.com
Sunday Express, URL: http://www.express.co.uk
The Independent on Sunday, URL: http://www.independent.co.uk
The Mail on Sunday, URL: http://www.mailonsunday.co.uk
The Observer, URL: http://www.observer.co.uk
Scotland on Sunday, URL: http://www.scotlandonsunday.com
Sunday Mirror, URL: http://www.sundaymirror.co.uk
Sunday People, URL: http://www.people.co.uk
Sunday Telegraph, URL: http://www.sundaytelegraph.co.uk
The Sunday Times, URL: http://www.sundaytimes.co.uk

Business Journals
The main weekly business magazines in the UK are:
The Economist, URL: http://www.economist.com
The Spectator, URL: http://www.spectator.co.uk/the-magazine/
New Statesman & Society, URL: http://www.newstatesman.co.uk
Investors Chronicle, URL: http://www.investorschronicle.co.uk

UK Publishing Media, URL: http://www.publishingmedia.org.uk/orgs.htm
Periodical Publishers' Association Ltd., URL: http://www.ppa.co.uk
Scottish Newspaper Publishers' Association, URL: http://www.snpa.org.uk

Broadcasting
The UK's regulating body for commercially-funded television is OFCOM. It is the regulator for UK communications industries, with responsibilities across television, radio, telecommunications and wireless communications services. It replaced the BSC, the ITC, OFTEL, the Radio Authority and the Radiocommunications Agency in December 2003.
Office of Communications (OFCOM), URL: http://www.ofcom.org.uk
The Broadcasting Standards Commission monitors all national broadcasting regulations and deals with public complaints.

Television
The UK has five national terrestrial television channels; two are run by the British Broadcasting Corporation (BBC) and require a licence, and three are commercial. BBC1 is a general, popular channel; BBC2 is a general channel; ITV is a commercial station operated regionally and mainly competing with BBC1; Channel Four is less mainstream; Channel Five is the newest station, launched in April 1997.

There are also digital, satellite and cable television stations available, the largest broadcaster here being BSkyB, which has two general entertainment channels, sports channels, and a news channel. Digital terrestrial TV includes a number of free-to-view channels, including BBC News 24. As of 2012 all television signals are satellite, cable and digital, analogue telelsion reception having been phased out.

There are five national radio stations: BBC Radio 1, 2, 3, 4 and 5. Radio 1 plays new and pop music and is aimed at an audience age of approximately 20-35. Radio 2 is aimed at an older audience but has a wide variety of programmes, including current affairs, comedy and various types of music. Radio 3 plays classical music and broadcasts documentaries. Radio 4 has political and news programmes, as well as lighter, magazine programmes, and Radio 5 is the country's sports and news network. The BBC also provides the World Service, as well as approximately 40 local radio stations. There are many more commercial local radio stations, including a wide variety in the London area, for example, Virgin Radio, Capital Radio, GLR, Kiss FM, Talk FM, Classic FM.

Digital radio is also on the increase. There are digital-only radio services.

The BBC operates under two constitutional documents - its Royal Charter and the Licence and Agreement. The Charter gives the Corporation legal existence, sets out its objectives and constitution, and also deals with such matters as advisory bodies. Under the Royal Charter, the BBC must obtain a licence from the Home Secretary, which specifies terms, conditions and programme finance. It cannot carry advertising or express its own editorial opinion about current affairs or matters of public policy other than broadcasting. The BBC is governed by a board of governors whose members are appointed by the Privy Council on the advice of the Government. They are ultimately responsible for maintaining programme standards. There are 12 BBC Governors including the Chairman, Vice-Chairman and the National Governors for Scotland, Wales and Northern Ireland. Governors usually serve for five years.

British Broadcasting Corporation (BBC), URL: http://www.bbc.co.uk
BBC World Service, URL: http://www.bbc.co.uk/worldservice/
BBC Television, URL: http://www.bbc.co.uk
ITV, URL: http://www.itv.com
Channel Four Television Corporation, URL: http://www.channel4.com
Channel Five Broadcasting, URL: http://www.five.tv
British Sky Broadcasting, URL: http://www.sky.com
MTV Networks Europe, URL: http://www.mtveurope.com
Cable Communications Association, URL: http://www.cable.co.uk

Postal Service
The Post Office comprises four separate businesses - Royal Mail, Post Office Counters Ltd, Parcelforce and SSL - which together form the UK's national postal administration. The Post Office is both a public corporation and one of the UK's largest commercial organisations. It has a turnover of almost £6 billion a year and directly employs almost 190,000 people, and 18,000 subpostmasters and subpostmistresses.

Royal Mail handles over 72 million letters each working day, while Post Office Counters Ltd, with almost 20,000 post offices, is the largest retailer in Europe. Parcelforce carries 140 million parcels every year and Subscription Services Ltd (SSL) is one of the UK's market leaders in the provision of customer management and telemarketing services.

In March 2001 The Post Office became a state owned limited company and changed its name to Consignia. A further name change in 2002 was made resulting in the Royal Mail Group.
Royal Mail Group plc, URL: http://www.royalmail.com

Telecommunications
UK telecommunications companies need an operating licence, which lays out specifics such as targets and prices. The main companies offering national and international fixed line services are British Telecommunications, AT&T and Mercury Communications. Although British Telecommunications is the chief player, it now has around 150 competitors for national services. There are also cable companies, such as Nynex. The increasing number of mobile network operators include Vodafone, Cellnet, Mercury One 2 One, and Orange.

Recent figures show that there were over 33 million landlines in use and over 81 million mobile phones are use. An estimated 51.4 million use the internet.

ENVIRONMENT

The governmental Department of the Environment is responsible for the country's environmental protection, among other duties. The Environment Agency was set up in 1995 under the Environment Act as a public body sponsored by the Department of the Environment to protect the environment and to set objectives for development. The Agency undertakes pollution control procedures and monitors the extent of pollution.

Policies and increasing public awareness has seen a fall in air emissions. For example, in 1982 there were over 7 million tonnes of carbon monoxide emissions, reduced to 4.6 million in 1996. Sulphur dioxide emissions in 1996 were just over 2.0 million tonnes, down from 4.2 million tonnes in 1986, while emissions of black smoke were down from 561,000 tonnes in 1982 to 338,000 tonnes in 1996. The United Kingdom is working towards increased use of renewable energy sources, and it was hoped that electricity generated from sources such as solar and wind will increase to ten per cent by 2010.

UNITED KINGDOM

It was announced in 1997 that road users with vehicles emitting high levels of pollution would be liable to automatic fines. Reported incidents in water pollution fell in the UK in 1996 by 10 per cent to 32,400 incidents, 156 of which were serious. The Environment Agency reports that chemicals are the main pollutants, and that the largest polluters are the water and sewerage industry, the agriculture industry and the construction industry.

The following table shows estimated atmospheric emissions on a national accounts basis in thousand tonnes:

Air emissions	2005
Carbon monoxide	2,498.45
Greenhouse gases*	733.446
Acid rain precursors**	3,211.75
Volatile organic compounds***	1,074.62
Benzene	17.24
Butadiene	2.68
Lead	121.47
Cadmium	7.26
Mercury	7.752

* = '000 tonnes of carbon dioxide equivalent
** = '000 tonnes of sulphur dioxide equivalent
*** = exc. methane, inc. benzene & 1,3-butadiene
Source: Office of National Statistics

Figures from 2010 show that total greenhouse gas emissions in 2009 were 363,472,000 tonnes and total acid rain precursor emissions were 2,211,000 tonnes.

Environment Agency, URL: http://www.environment-agency.gov.uk

Environment Protection Economics Division, URL: http://www.defra.gov.uk/environment/index.htm
Environment Policy Department, URL: http://www.dfid.gov.uk
Natural England, URL: http://www.naturalengland.org.uk

The UK is a party to the following international agreements: Air Pollution, Air Pollution-Nitrogen Oxides, Air Pollution-Persistent Organic Pollutants, Air Pollution-Sulfur 94, Air Pollution-Volatile Organic Compounds, Antarctic-Environmental Protocol, Antarctic-Marine Living Resources, Antarctic Seals, Antarctic Treaty, Biodiversity, Climate Change, Climate Change-Kyoto Protocol, Desertification, Endangered Species, Environmental Modification, Hazardous Wastes, Law of the Sea, Marine Dumping, Marine Life Conservation, Ozone Layer Protection, Ship Pollution, Tropical Timber 83, Tropical Timber 94, Wetlands, and Whaling.

SPACE PROGRAMME

Britain's space programme is reviewed and updated every year by the British National Space Centre (BNSC), a body which brings together the UK's Government departments and research councils. The current plan focuses on earth observation, competitive commercial industry and the development of the research programme. Britain is a member of the European Space Agency and part of the national space plan encourages its focus on promoting European competitiveness.

The annual budget for space is approximately £180 million, half of which is spent on Earth observation, 26 per cent on space science, 12 per cent on satellite communication and 3 per cent on technology and transportation. The industry employs around 6,500 people.

British National Space Centre (BNSC), URL: http://www.bnsc.gov.uk

NORTHERN IRELAND

Capital: Belfast (Population estimate: 281,000)

CONSTITUTION AND GOVERNMENT

Constitution
Northern Ireland is currently subject to the same fundamental constitutional provisions which apply to the rest of the United Kingdom. In the Northern Ireland Constitution Act 1973 and the Northern Ireland Act 1982, Parliament provided for a measure of devolved government in Northern Ireland. This arrangement was last in force in January 1974 following agreement between the Northern Ireland Political parties to form a power sharing Executive, although this arrangement collapsed in May that year.

Recent History
After January 1974 Northern Ireland was governed by 'direct rule' under the provisions of the Northern Ireland Act 1974. This allowed Parliament to approve all laws and placed the Northern Ireland departments under the direction and control of a UK Cabinet Minister, the Secretary of State. Attempts were made by successive governments to find a means of restoring a widely acceptable form of devolved government to Northern Ireland. A 78 member Assembly was elected by proportional representation in 1982, but four years later this was dissolved.

The Secretary of State and the four Northern Ireland political parties (the Alliance Party, the Social Democratic and Labour Party, the Ulster Unionist Party and the Democratic Unionist Party), together with the Irish Government, embarked upon a talks process in 1991. The Prime Minister and the Taoiseach made a Joint Declaration on 15 December 1993. The Declaration reaffirmed existing constitutional principles and agreed that Sinn Féin would be free to join legitimate constitutional dialogue with the Governments on condition of a cessation of violence. A ceasefire was then declared by the IRA in August 1994.

Multi-party talks were halted when the Irish Republican Army (IRA) ended its 17-month ceasefire on 10 February 1996. Sinn Féin issued a statement saying that the IRA had been particularly disturbed by the British Government's apparent dismissal of the independent Mitchell Commission's report on Northern Ireland, their insistence on holding elections to a constitutional convention, and the precondition that the IRA should begin decommissioning weapons. The British and Irish governments wanted multi-party talks to continue and Prime Minister John Major agreed in May 1996 not to stall talks over the issue of decommissioning weapons and to refer to the Mitchell Report as the basis for future progress.

The Peace Process
The Belfast Agreement, concerning the future of Northern Ireland, and subsequently known as the Good Friday Agreement, was signed on 10 April 1998 by the Governments and major political parties of Ireland and the United Kingdom. The Agreement made provision for a referendum, which was held on 22 May 1998 in the Republic of Ireland and in Northern Ireland. Approximately 94 per cent of those who voted in the Republic voted in favour of the agreement, as did approximately 71 per cent of those who voted in Northern Ireland. The referendum in the Republic of Ireland also asked if the constitution should be amended to end the territorial claim on Northern Ireland.

The agreement provided for the devolution to a 108-member Northern Ireland Assembly of a range of executive and legislative powers (the executive arm of this body to be known as the Northern Ireland Executive), the creation of a North-South Ministerial Council accountable to both this Assembly and the Oireachtas, and a British-Irish Council to represent the Irish Government, the British Government, and the devolved assemblies of Northern Ireland,

Scotland and Wales. Elections for the Assembly were held on 25 June 1998, each member representing a constituency and being elected by proportional representation. The first meeting of the Assembly took place at Stormont on 2 July 1998.

The Belfast Agreement also made provision for a British-Irish Agreement which is a British-Irish Intergovernmental Conference to deal with any bilateral issues between the two Governments, and includes members of the new Northern Ireland Assembly when dealing with non-devolved issues relating to Northern Ireland.

However, the IRA's reluctance to decommission its weapons until Sinn Féin sat in the Assembly, and the Ulster Unionists' subsequent refusal to sit in the Assembly with Sinn Féin until decommissioning occurred, meant that the process stalled. On 11 February 2000 an order was signed by the then Secretary of State for Northern Ireland, Peter Mandelson, suspending the Assembly and Executive. In May 2000 the Assembly and Executive were reinstated amidst renewed talks on decommissioning. The IRA issued a statement that it was ready to start a decommissioning process. Former ANC official Cyril Ramaphosa and former Finnish President Martti Ahtisaari were appointed as independent inspectors and in June reported that they had seen IRA arms dumps and that the weapons could not be used. At the end of July 2000, as part of the 1998 Good Friday Agreement, the remaining paramilitary prisoners held in Northern Ireland were released, most from the Maze Prison; a total of 428 paramilitary prisoners were released before serving their full prison terms.

On 1 July 2001 David Trimble announced his resignation as the Northern Ireland Assembly's first minister as from 11 August, over what he saw as the IRA's failure to decommission its weapons. Reg Empey was appointed interim caretaker until elections could take place for new first and deputy ministers.

On 6 August 2001, the head of the decommissioning body, General John de Chastelain, announced that the IRA had set out 'satisfactory' plans to put its weapons 'beyond use'. In response, David Trimble insisted that he required evidence of 'actual' IRA arms decommissioning. On 10 August, Northern Ireland Secretary John Reid suspended the Northern Ireland Assembly for what was hoped would be a brief period to allow pro-agreement parties more time to resolve the issue of decommissioning. A deadline of 21 September was set. Two days before the deadline a statement issued by the IRA indicated that it was working with the decommissioning body. On 21 September the assembly was again suspended due to the failure to reinstate a first minister. On 23 October an announcement by the IRA said that it has begun putting arms beyond use. The Independent International Decommissioning Commission confirmed this.

The elections for the post of First Minister took place in November. David Trimble was re-elected only after a deal was struck with pro-agreement Alliance Party members.

In April 2002 arms inspector General John de Chastelain confirmed that more IRA weapons had been put beyond use. In spite of this, violence continued during the year and again threatened the peace process. In September 2002 David Trimble announced he would pull his Ulster Unionist Party out of the Power sharing executive if the Republicans did not show they had rejected violence. In October he announced again he would pull out if the British Government did not expel Sinn Féin. Sinn Féin's Stormont offices were raided during a police investigation into the into alleged intelligence gathering by republicans. On 4 October the then Northern Ireland Secretary John Reid announced the suspension of the Northern Ireland Assembly.

Against the background of a suspended Northern Ireland Assembly, the 26 November 2003 elections saw Ian Paisley's DUP overtake the Ulster Unionists as Northern Ireland's largest party. Sinn Fein also took more seats than its nationalist rival, the SDLP. The DUP won 30 seats, Sinn Fein 24, the SDLP 18, and the Alliance 6. Three MLAs later moved over from the UUP to the DUP, giving this latter party 33 seats.

Talks were held in September 2004 at Leeds Castle, in an attempt to end violence and broker power sharing in Northern Ireland. Following two months of negotiations, the British and Irish governments presented their proposals to the DUP and Sinn Féin. Ian Paisley stated in December that it was unrealistic to set deadlines for a political deal when the IRA has still not discussed decommissioning with General de Chastelain. Gerry Adams recommended that Sinn Féin accept the proposals.

Following a multi-million pound bank raid on the Northern Bank in Belfast in December 2004 the Chief Constable of the PSNI, Hugh Orde, told a news conference in January 2005 that he believed the IRA was responsible. While Sinn Fein accused Mr Orde of 'bias', Irish Prime Minister Bertie Ahern said that trust and confidence in the peace process had been damaged as a result of the raid, and the DUP called on the British government to continue the peace process without republicans. Tony Blair said that progress in the Northern Ireland process was possible but there must be 'a definitive end to all forms of paramilitary or criminal activity.'

In the General Elections of May 2005, the Ulster Unionist Party lost five seats, and David Trimble resigned as their leader. A new Northern Ireland Secretary, Peter Hain, was appointed by a third successive Labour government in Westminster. Sir Reg Empey became the new leader of the UUP in June 2005.

On 28 July 2005 the IRA issued a statement saying that the leadership had formally ordered an end to the armed campaign. Two independent witnesses one catholic one protestant were to verify that arms had been decommissioned. The statement went on to say "all Volunteers have been instructed to assist the development of purely political and democratic programmes through exclusively peaceful means".

Policing

As part of the reforms set out by the Good Friday Agreement, and in an effort to de-politicise the police force, The Royal Ulster Constabulary was re-named at midnight on 28 October 2001 and became the Police Service of Northern Ireland. It was endorsed by Catholics, Protestants and Republicans and the new police board included members from all parties with seats in the Assembly Executive. In June 2004, 14.9 per cent of regular officers in the police service were Catholic (up from 7.6 per cent in March 2001); the Government plans for this figure to reach 30 per cent by 2011.

In February 2010 following weeks of negotiations Assembly members voted to approve the transfer policing and justice powers to the Stormont Assembly. This took place on April 12 and Alliance leader David Ford was selected as Northern Ireland's new justice minister making him the first local politician to take responsibility for justice and policing in 38 years. At the time David Ford was being elected a bomb exploded outside an army base in Holywood, County Down which houses MI5's Northern Ireland headquarters. The Real IRA claimed responsibility.

Reinstatement of the Northern Ireland Assembly

The suspension of the Northern Ireland Assembly came into effect on October 4 2002 in response to allegations of a republican spy ring. In March 2006 the British Government proposed emergency legislation that allowed the recall of the Assembly in May and set a deadline of November 24 2006 for the formation of a power-sharing executive. The Assembly met on May 15. If all parties could reach an agreement and elect an executive, then the devolved government would be reinstated; if the November deadline was reached without agreement, the assembly members salaries and allowances would be stopped. The British and Irish governments would then work together to negotiate partnership arrangements to implement the Good Friday Agreement. Before the Assembly met for the first time, the leader of the Progressive Unionist Party, David Ervine, was approached to join the Ulster Unionist group. Although he would still remain leader of his party, it would mean that if the Assembly was successful in forming a new government the Unionists would gain another ministerial post at the expence of Sinn Féin. The assembly was recalled on May 15 and parties were given six weeks to elect an executive. Gerry Adams of Sinn Féin nominated Ian Paisley (leader of the DUP), but he refused until Sinn Féin met its obligations. In October 2006 multi party talks took place at St Andrews in Scotland and a roadmap was unveiled, called the St Andrews Agreement. The agreement gave a deadline of 26 March 2007 for a new executive to be established. On November 16 a transitional government was established which would sit until elections took place which were set for March 7 2007. On November 24, the Transitional Assembly met to hear if the DUP or Sinn Féin had any ministerial choices to put forward. Elections duly took place on March 7 and the DUP became the largest party with 36 seats and Sinn Féin came second with 28 seats. Direct rule ended at midnight. A power sharing government was agreed to by the leaders of the leading parties on 26 March and the new government took office on May 8 2007.

Recent Events

In April 2008 First Minister Dr. Ian Paisley announced that he would retire as first minister and his position as leader of the Democratic Unionist Party (DUP) in May 2008, but would continue as an MP and MLA for North Antrim. Peter Robinson was elected by the DUP to become the leader of the party.

On March 7 2009 two British soldiers were shot dead at Massereene Army base in Antrim. Mark Quinsey and Patrick Azimka were the first soldiers to be murdered in Northern Ireland for 12 years. The Real IRA claimed responsibility for the attack. The Real IRA is a group which split from the Provisional IRA in 1997 when the IRA began actively working towards the peace process. Two days later Police Constable Stephen Carroll was shot by dissident republicans in Country Armargh while on duty. Again the first policeman to be killed in such a manner for 12 years.

In January 2010 First Minister Peter Robinson announced he was standing down from the position for six weeks, to give himself time to clear his name over an allegation surrounding his wife Iris's financial conduct. Iris Robinson, an MP in her own right, did not stand for re-election. Peter Robinson lost his Westminster seat in the May 2010 election.

During the winter of 2010 Northern Ireland in common with the rest of the UK suffered a severe cold snap, between the Christmas and New Year period the cold was too much for the aging water infrastructure and many pipes burst, up to 40,000 people were without water some for as much as 12 days.

Constable Ronan Kerr was killed on 2 April 2011 when a bomb exploded under his car outside his home in Omagh, County Tyrone. No group claimed responsibility but dissident republicans were blamed. Also that month a 500lb bomb was left in a van at an underpass on the main Belfast to Dublin Road in Newry.

In July 2012, the Northern Ireland Auditor General announced that land deals done by the public Housing Executive had been made without proper valuations or approval, potentially costing the public millions of pounds.

Protesters took to the streets of Belfast in December 2012, and protests became increasingly violent. Demonstrators had taken to the streets in protest at proposed changes to the number of days the Union Flag will be flown over the parliament buildings.

In June 2013, the G8 summit was held in Northern Ireland, the main resolutions from the talks were calls for peace talks aimed at ending the conflict in Syria, which were hoped to be held in Geneva. The leaders also signed a declaration pledging to fight tax evasion.

Legislature

The Northern Ireland Assembly consists of 108 elected members. Six members are elected to each of the 18 constituencies used for elections to the Westminster parliament. Following elections the Members of the Legislative Assembly or MLA's elect a First Minister and Deputy First Minister, who then lead the Executive Committee of Ministers. Ministers are selected using the d'Hondt proceedure, so that parties with a significant number of seats are entitled to at least one minister; following the 2007 election, this meant that there were four ministers from the DUP, three minister from Sinn Féin, two UUP ministers and one from the SDLP. Unless the Assembly is dissolved, elections will take place every five years on the first Thursday in May.

Northern Ireland Assembly, Parliament Buildings, Stormont, Belfast, BT4 3XX, United Kingdom. Tel: +44 (0)28 9052 1333, fax: +44 (0)28 9052 1961, e-mail: info.office@niassembly.gov.uk, URL: http://www.niassembly.gov.uk
Speaker: William Hay (page 1439)

Northern Ireland Executive (as at June 2013)
First Minister: Peter Robinson (DUP) (page 1504)
Deputy First Minister: Martin McGuinness (SF) (page 1474)
Minister of Finance and Personnel: Sammy Wilson (DUP) (page 1538)
Minister of Agriculture and Rural Development: Michelle O'Neill (SF) (page 1489)
Minister of Culture, Arts and Leisure: Carál Ní Chuilín (SF) (page 1486)
Minister of Education: John O'Dowd (SF) (page 1488)
Minister of Enterprise, Trade and Investment: Arlene Foster (DUP) (page 1426)
Minister of the Environment: Alex Attwood (SDLP) (page 1380)
Minister of Health, Social Services and Public Safety: Edwin Poots (DUP) (page 1497)
Minister of Employment and Learning: Dr Stephen Farry (Alliance) (page 1423)
Minister for Regional Development: Danny Kennedy (UUP) (page 1455)
Minister for Social Development: Nelson McCausland (DUP) (page 1473)
Minister for Justice: David Ford (Alliance) (page 1426)
Junior Ministers jointly accountable to the First Minister and Deputy First Minister: Jonathan Bell (DUP) and Jennifer McCann (SF)

Northern Ireland Office, 11 Millbank, London SW1P 4PN, United Kingdom. URL:http://www.nio.gov.uk
Secretary of State for Northern Ireland: Rt Hon. Theresa Villiers (page 1531)
Minister of State: Michael Penning (page 1494)

Ministries

Northern Ireland Office, 11 Millbank, London, SW1P 4QE, United Kingdom. Tel: +44 (0)20 7210 3000, fax: +44 (0)20 7210 0254, URL: http://www.nio.gov.uk
Northern Ireland Office, Stormont Castle, Belfast, BT4 3ST. Tel: +44 (0)28 9052 0700, fax: +44 (0)28 9052 8473, URL: http://www.nio.gov.uk
Department of Agriculture and Rural Development, Dundonald House, Belfast, BT4 3SF. Tel: +44 (0)28 9052 0100, fax: +44 (0)28 9052 5544, URL: http://www.dardni.gov.uk
Department of Culture, Arts and Leisure, Interpoint, 20-24 York Street, Belfast, BT15 1AQ. Tel: +44 (0)28 9025 8825, URL: http://www.dcalni.gov.uk
Department of Enterprise, Trade and Investment, Netherleigh House, Massey Avenue, Belfast, BT4 2JP. Tel: +44 (0)28 9052 9475, fax: +44 (0)28 9052 9550, URL: http://detini.gov.uk
Department of Employment and Learning, Adelaide House, 39-49 Adelaid Street, Belfast BT2 8FD. Tel +44 (0)28 9025 7777, URL: http://www.delni.gov.uk
Department of Education, Rathgael House, Balloo Road, Bangor, Co. Down, BT19 7PR. Tel: +44 (0)28 9127 9279, fax: +44 (0)28 9127 9100, URL: http://www.deni.gov.uk
Department of the Environment, Clarence Court, Adelaide Street, Belfast, BT2 8GB. Tel: +44 (0)28 9054 0540, URL: http://www.northernireland.gov.uk/env.htm
Department of Health and Social Services, Castle Buildings, Belfast, BT4 3PP. Tel: +44 (0)28 9052 0000, URL: http://www.dhsspsni.gov.uk
Northern Ireland Civil Service, Central Secretariat, Stoney Road, Belfast. BT4 3SFX. Tel: +44 (0)28 9052 0700, fax: +44 (0)28 9052 8135, URL: http://www.nics.gov.uk

UNITED KINGDOM

Political Parties

Alliance Party, 88 University Street, Belfast, BT7 1HE, United Kingdom. Tel: +44 (0)28 9032 4274, fax: +44 (0)28 9033 3147, e-mail: alliance@allianceparty.org, URL: http://www.allianceparty.org
Leader: David Ford (page 1426)

Democratic Unionist Party, 91 Dundela Avenue, Belfast, BT4 3BU, United Kingdom. Tel: +44 (0)28 9065 4479, fax: +44 (0)28 9065 4480, e-mail: info@dup.org.uk, URL: http://www.dup2win.com
Leader: Peter Robinson (page 1504)

Sinn Féin, 44 Parnell Square, Dublin 1, Republic of Ireland. Tel: +353 (0)1 872 6100, fax: +353 (0)1 873 3074, e-mail: sinnfein@iol.ie, URL: http://www.sinnfein.ie
President: Gerry Adams (page 1372)

Social Democratic and Labour Party , 121 Ormeau Road, Belfast BT7 1SH, United Kingdom. Tel: +44 (0)2890 247700, fax: +44 (0)2890 236699, e-mail: sdlp@indigo.ie, URL: http://www.sdlp.ie
Leader: Dr Alasdair McDonnell MP MLA (page 1474)

Ulster Unionist Party, Cunningham House, 429 Holywood Road, Belfast, BT4 2LN, United Kingdom. Tel: +44 (0)28 9076 5500, fax: +44 (0)28 9076 9419, e-mail: uup@uup.org, URL: http://www.uup.org
Leader: Mike Nesbitt

Progressive Unionist Party, 182 Shanklin Road, Belfast, BT13 2BL, United Kingdom. Tel: +44 (0)28 9032 6233, fax: +44 (0)28 9024 9602, e-mail: central@pup-ni.org.uk, URL: http://progressiveunionistparty.org
Leader: Billy Hutchinson (page 1446)

Traditional Unionist Voice, 139 Holywood Road, Belfast, BT4 3BE, County Down, Northern Ireland. URL: http://www.tuv.org.uk
Leader: Jim Allister QC (page 1375)

Elections

The first election for the 108-member Assembly were held on 25 June 1998, and the next elections were due to take place on 29 May 2003, but were postponed. The British Government felt that any result would not provide a firm basis for power sharing. The elections eventually took place in November 2003. Following the suspension of the Assembly, elections were again held in March 2007. The most recent elections were held in May 2011, the results of which are shown in the table below along with previous elections.

Party	1998	2003	2007	2011
UUP	28	27 *	18	16
SDLP	24	18	16	14
DUP	20	30 *	36	38
Sinn Féin	18	24	28	29
Alliance	6	6	7	8
UKUP	5	1	0	0
PUP	2	1	1	0
Independent	1	1	0	1
Others	5	0	1	1
Green Party	0	0	1	1

* Three of the MLAs elected to the Assembly in November later moved to the DUP, resulting in the DUP having 33 seats and the UUP having 24.

The results of the May 2010 Westminster parliamentary general election are shown in the table below:

Party	No. of MPs	Change
Democratic Unionists (DUP)	8	-1
Sinn Féin (SF)	5	0
Social Democratic & Labour (SDLP)	3	0
Alliance Party	1	+1
Other	1	+1

Northern Ireland elects 18 MPs to the Westminster parliament.

The province sends three MEPs to Europe. In the European parliamentary elections held in June 2009. The DUP, the UCUNF and Sinn Féin each won a seat. The UCUNF or Ulster Conservatives and Unionists - New Force, is an electoral alliance between the Ulster Unionist Party and the Conservative Party convened for the 2009 European election.

LEGAL SYSTEM

The Supreme Court of Judicature of Northern Ireland was established by the Government of Ireland Act 1920 and reconstituted by the provisions of the Judicature (Northern Ireland) Act 1978. It now consists of the Court of Appeal, the High Court and the Crown Court. There are at present four Lord Justices in the Court of Appeal headed by the Lord Chief Justice who is also president of the High Court in which there are currently six puisne judges. Judges are appointed by the crown.

By virtue of the County Courts (Northern Ireland) Order 1980 and the County Court Divisions Order (Northern Ireland) 1990, Northern Ireland is divided into seven county court divisions with 13 county court judges. The county court has a general civil jurisdiction to hear and determine any action (with the exception of defended divorce and any action in which the title to any fair, market or franchise is in question, or any admiralty matter) in which the amount claimed or the value of specific articles claimed does not exceed £10,000. The county court has jurisdiction to hear undefended petitions for divorce. The county court also hears appeals from magistrates' courts.

There are four District Judges who have jurisdiction to deal with most defended and undefended actions. An appeal from the decision of a District Judge lies with the High Court. There is also provision enabling the District Judge to deal by an informal arbitration procedure

with small claims. By virtue of the Magistrates Courts (Northern Ireland) order 1981 and the Petty Sessions Districts Order (Northern Ireland) 1990, Northern Ireland is divided into 22 Petty Sessions Districts. There are 17 full time and 13 deputy resident magistrates presiding over the magistrates' courts which sit daily in Belfast and at intervals varying from four times per week to once per month outside Belfast, depending on the volume of work. There is also the Enforcement of Judgments Office, and the coroners courts, which investigate circumstances of sudden, violent or unnatural deaths.

The Lord Chief Justice of Northern Ireland, Royal Courts of Justice, Belfast, BT1 3JF. Tel: +44 (0)28 9023 8594, fax: +44 (0)28 9023 3508, URL: http://www.courtsni.gov.uk/en-GB/AboutUs/RCJ/
The Honourable Sir Declan Morgan

Northern Ireland Human Rights, URL: http://www.nihrc.org/

LOCAL GOVERNMENT

26 District Councils are responsible for the provision of a wide range of local services. They have in both a representative role in which they send forward representatives to sit as members of statutory bodies such as the Northern Ireland Housing Executive, the Fire Authority, Health and Social Services Boards and the Education and Library Boards. These representatives also have a consultative role under which Government Departments and the Northern Ireland Housing Executive have a statutory obligation to consult them regarding the provision of regional services for which these bodies are responsible. Northern Ireland differs from the rest of the United Kingdom in the way its local authorities are financed. In the rest of the UK revenue is raised through taxes; in Northern Ireland revenue is raised through a system of domestic rates on homes and commercial rates on business properties. Each district fixes its own rate annually through district councils. The Northern Ireland Assembly fixes a regional rate.

The following table shows the 26 district councils their area and population at the 2011 census:

District	Area Sq. Km.	Population
Antrim	421	53,428
Ards	380	78,078
Armagh	671	59,340
Ballymena	360	64,044
Ballymoney	416	31,244
Banbridge	451	48,339
Belfast	110	280,962
Carrickfergus	81	39,114
Castlereagh	85	67,242
Coleraine	486	59,067
Cookstown	514	37,013
Craigavon	282	93,023
Derry	381	107,877
Down	649	69,731
Dungannon	772	57,852
Fermanagh	1,699	61,805
Larne	336	32,180
Limavady	586	33,536
Lisburn	447	120,165
Magherafelt	564	45,038
Moyle	494	17,050
Newry & Mourne	898	99,480
Newtownabbey	151	85,139
North Down	81,000	78,937
Omagh	1,130	51,356
Strabane	862	39,843

Source: National Statistics Office

A review of public administration, initiated by the NI Assembly in 2002, recommended a reduction in the number of local councils from 26 to 10. A decision will be made now that devolution is resumed.

AREA AND POPULATION

Area

Northern Ireland covers an area of 13,576 sq. km. and consists of six counties, Antrim, Armagh, Down, Fermanagh, Londonderry and Tyrone. Lough Neagh is situated near the centre of Northern Ireland and at 151 square miles (392 sq km) it is the largest freshwater lake in the UK. There are significant uplands and generally low-lying hills. The highest point is Slieve Donard in the Morne Mountains which reaches 849 metres. The climate is temperate maritime, wetter in the west.

To view a map of Northern Ireland, please consult:
http://www.lib.utexas.edu/maps/cia08/united_kingdom_sm_2008.gif

Population

As at the 2011 census the resident population was 1,810,863 up from the mid 2008 figure of 1,775,000, and 1,689,300 in 2001. According to recent figures, Belfast is the largest population centre with 280,962 inhabitants, followed by Lisburn with 120,165, Derry with 107,877, and the Newry and Mourne area with 99,480. As part of the Queen's Golden Jubilee celebrations in 2002, Lisburn and Newry were both given city status, joining Belfast Armargh and Londonderry as Northern Ireland cities. Figures for the year 2002 indicate the first positive migration figure for a decade, standing at 100 immigrants. Figures for the year 2007-08 put net migration at 5.300 falling to 2,100 in the year 2008-09.

Births, Marriages, Deaths

Figures for the year 2011 show that there were 25,273 live births and 14,204 deaths. 8,366 marriages took place that year along with 89 civil partnerships, 2,343 divorces were recorded that year. Figures for 2011 put the birth rate at 14.0 per thousand population and the death rate at 7.9 per thousand population. (National Statistics Office).

English is the official language and around 167,000 people (10 per cent of the population) speak or write Irish.

Public Holidays 2014

As UK with the addition of:
17 March: St. Patrick's Day
12 July: Battle of the Boyne

EMPLOYMENT

There has been a steady decline in unemployment since 1992 when unemployed persons totalled over 100,000. Between 1998 and 2003, the unemployment figure fell from approximately 8 per cent to around 5 per cent. Figures for 2004 put the work force at 750,000. Of these, 712,000 were employed, giving an unemployment rate of 5 per cent, just above the unemployment rate for the UK as a whole (4.8 per cent). Figures for 2008 show that 793,000 people were employed, falling to 747,000 in 2009 and rising to 777,000 in 2010. The unemployment figure for 2008 was 3.9 per cent, rising to 6.5 per cent in 2009 and 6.6 per cent in 2010.

In response to the global economic downturn the economy of Northern Ireland has shrunk. In March 2009 it was reported that the number of people claiming unemployment benefit had risen by 75.7 per cent over a 12 month period. The increase in March 2009 over the number in March 2008 was 18,100 meaning 42,000 were unemployed. Figures for April 2011 show that 59,200 people were unemployed, the highest figure for 13 years. Jobs in the construction sector have been particularly hard hit, figures from 2011 show that the number of jobs in construction had fallen to 35,700. By April 2012 the unemployment rate had reached 6.9 per cent and rose to 8.4 per cent in April 2013, compared with the UK figure of 7.9 per cent.

Figures for 2012 show that of a total economically active population of 259,000, 685,000 people were employees, 106,000 were self employed and 9,000 were on government schemes. That year 58,000 were unemployed.

The following table shows how the working population was employed in June 2010:

Sector	% Employed
Agriculture, fishing & forestry	4.3
Production industries	10.6
Construction	7.5
Electricity, water & gas supply	0.4
Construction	6.2
Wholesale & retail trade, repairs	16.9
Transportation & storage	3.8
Accommodation & food service	5.9
Information & communication	1.9
Financial & insurance activities	2.4
Real estate activities	1.1
Professional scientific & technical activities	3.5
Admin. & support service activities	5.6
Education, health & social work activities	24.1
Public admin. & defence, arts & entertainment, other services	12.2
Source: National Statistics Office	

BANKING AND FINANCE

Currency

One Pound Sterling (£) = 100 pence

GDP/GNP, Inflation, National Debt

In common with the rest of the UK, Northern Ireland has been feeling the effects of the global economic downturn and banking crisis. In March 2009 it was reported that its economy had shrunk faster that the other UK regions.

Figures for 2006 put Gross Value Added at £26.4 billion, equivalent to 2.3 per cent of GVA for the UK as a whole. Growth over the year was 5.6 per cent. In 2009 Gross Value Added was £28.2 billion, equivalent to 2.3 per cent of GVA for the UK as a whole which a growth rate of -2.0 per cent.

Total Gross Value Added

Year	£ million	Per capital £'000
2000	19,210	11,415
2001	20,150	11,928
2002	21,164	12,474
2003	22,466	13,195
2004	23,933	13,993
2005	25,017	14,508
2006	26,787	15,381
2007	28,445	16,170
2008	28,700	16,188

- continued

2009	28,256	15,795
2010	29,155	15,651
2011*	29,870	na

*provisional
Source: National Statistics Office

Figures from 2004 show that manufacturing contributed 16 per cent of GVA, above the figure of 14 per cent for the UK as a whole. The contribution of the agriculture, hunting, forestry and fishing sector was also greater than that of the UK as a whole, at 2.7 per cent compared to 1 per cent. Inflation was put at nearly 5 per cent in 2001 but fell to around 2.6 per cent by 2003. Figures for February 2011 show that inflation had risen to 4.4 per cent, considerable higher than the target of 2.0 per cent. Around 2.2 per cent of the United Kingdom GDP comes from Northern Ireland.

The following table shows Gross Value Added in recent years by industry groups at current basic prices. Figures are in £ million:

Sector	2010
Agriculture, hunting, forestry & fishing	330
Mining & quarrying	122
Manufacturing	4,469
Electricity, gas, steam & air conditioning supply	267
Water supply; sewerage, waste management	398
Construction	2,004
Wholesale & retail trade, repairs	3,779
Accomodation and food service activities	860
Transportation and storage	1,089
Information & communication	888
Financial & insurance activities	1,282
Real estate activities	2,325
Professional, scientific & technical activities	1,126
Administrative & support service activities	899
Public administration & defence; compulsory social security	2,955
Education	2,438
Human helath and social work activities	3,097
Arts, entertainment & recreation	403
Other service activities	372
Activities of households	55
Total	29,155

Source: Office of National Statistics

Foreign Investment

Figures for 2000 show that there are around 500 foreign-owned businesses in the region. In 2001, there were 164 foreign-owned manufacturing enterprises, employing some 38,645 people, a slight decrease on the figure for the previous year. Early in 2002, Invest Northern Ireland was set up to promote investment; total commitments to invest £410 million were made in 2003-04, bringing the overall total to £1 billion. 2,750 new business have been established with support from Invest NI. The province also received about €1 billion from the EU Structural Funds allocation up to 2006, and a further €531 million from the EU Programme for Peace and Reconciliation in Northern Ireland and the Border Region of the Republic of Ireland (PEACE II).

Balance of Payments / Imports and Exports

Figures for 2009 show that total exports of goods reached £5,142 millions, and total imports reached £5,014 millions. The EU is the most important trading partner, North America is the second most important partner.

The main traded commodities were from the machinery and transport sector, accounting for 43 per cent of exports and 30 per cent of imports. Manufactured goods totalled 18 per cent of exports and 19 per cent of imports. Food and live animals were the third largest sector of traded commodities, amounting to 15 per cent of imports and 10 per cent of exports.

The following table gives a breakdown of foreign trade for Northern Ireland in 2009.

Exports	£ million	Percentage
All export trade	5,142	
To the EU	3,047	59.3
Outside the EU	2,095	40.7
Imports		
All import trade	5,014	
From the EU	2,888	57.6
Outside the EU	2,126	42.4

Source: National Statistics Office

Figures for the year 2006-07 show that manufacturing export sales earned £11.2 billion, of which £5.1 billion went to countries outside the UK.

Economic Assistance

Taxation in Northern Ireland is largely imposed and collected by the United Kingdom Government. After deducting the cost of collection and of Northern Ireland's contributions to the European Community, the balance, known as the Attributed Share of Taxation, is paid over to the Northern Ireland Consolidated Fund (NICF). Northern Ireland's revenue is insufficient to meet its expenditure and is supplemented by a grant in aid from the United Kingdom Government. Since devolution in 1999, the attributed share of taxation and grant in aid have become a single block grant.

Chambers of Commerce and Trade Organisations

Confederation of British Industry (CBI), URL: http://www.cbi.org.uk/northernireland
LEDU (Northern Ireland Small Business Agency), URL: http://www.ledu-ni.com

UNITED KINGDOM

Northern Ireland Chamber of Commerce and Industry, URL: http://www.nicci.co.uk
Economic Research Institute of Northern Ireland (ERINI), URL: http://www.niec.org.uk
Invest Northern Ireland, URL: http://www.investni.com

MANUFACTURING, MINING AND SERVICES

Primary and Extractive Industries
Minerals extracted in Northern Ireland include basalt and igneous rock; grit and conglomerate; limestone; sand and gravel and others. Recent figures show that 1,700 people were employed in the mining and quarrying sector.

Manufacturing
In 2001, manufacturing accounted for 19 per cent of GDP. The electrical and electronic industries are well represented in Northern Ireland, and there is a long established aircraft industry. A wide range of food, drink and tobacco goods are produced, and this too is an sector in expansion. The textile industry contains a wide range of activities including spinning and weaving, hosiery, man-made fibre production and carpets. Figures from 2004 show that manufacturing contributed 16 per cent of GVA above the figure of 14 per cent for the UK as a whole. Northern Ireland's tradition of ship building has also fallen into decline. The following table shows the provisional value of manufacturing sales in the year 2010-11:

Product	£ million	Percentage
Food, beverages & tobacco	8,287	52.1
Electrical equipment	808	5.1
Other machinery & equipment	853	5.4
Motor vehicles & trailers	356	2.2
Other transport equipment	1,045	6.6
Rubber & plastics	760	4.8
Basic metals	70	0.4
Fabricated metal products	701	4.4
Non-metallic minerals	532	3.3
Other manufacturing	101	0.6
Paper & paper products	219	1.4
Chemicals & chemical products	296	1.9
Furniture	268	1.7
Textiles	189	1.2
Wearing apparel	142	0.9
Leather & related products	5	0.0
Wood & products of cork	282	1.8
Printing & reproduction of recorded media	114	0.7
Pharmaceutical	235	1.5
Computer, electronic & optical	595	3.7
Repair & installation of equipment	56	0.4
Total	15,914	100

Source: NISRA

Service Industries and Tourism
Figures for 2011 show that 1.5 million overseas residents spent at least one night in Northern Ireland and spent an estimated £368 million that year. During the same year 1.9 million Northern Ireland residents took trips within Northern Ireland spending £171 million.

Northern Ireland Tourist Board, URL: http://www.discovernireland.com

Agriculture
Each year, at the beginning of June, the Department of Agriculture surveys all farms to ascertain changes in cropping patterns and in the numbers of the different types of livestock on farms. Since the beginning of the decade, the main changes have been a decline in the number of dairy cows and a continued expansion in the number of beef cows; a rise in the number of ewes and poultry; a decrease in the total area of horticultural crops with more land being devoted to flowers or shrubs; fewer farm owners. Figures for 1987 showed that Northern Ireland had a total of 36,960 farms; this had fallen in 1997 to 32,119 of which 551 were classed as large. In 2010 there were 24,471 farms, 1,493 of which were classed as large. The number of farms in 2012 was put 24,295 of which 1,558 were classed as large. The total number of people employed in farming fell from 53,300 in 2004 to 47,500 in 2012.

Exports fell by 11 per cent in the period 1996-97, due to the BSE crisis. In 2001 when the UK was hit by an outbreak of foot and mouth Northern Ireland had four confirmed outbreaks. (Source: DARD). Cattle and milk account for around three-quarters of the output of livestock and livestock products.

Crop Areas in 2012

Crop	Hectares
Grass	779,842
Oats	1,979
Wheat	9,995
Barley (Winter)	5,923
Barley (Spring)	20,211
Mixed corn	259
Potatoes	4,150
Fruit	1,531
Vegetables	1,260

Source: NISRA

Livestock Numbers in 2012

Livestock	000 Head
Dairy cows	295.4
- continued	
Beef cows	279.2
Sheep & lambs	1,969.9
Horses & ponies	12.0
Goats	3.1
Pigs	426.9
Poultry	19,198.2

Source: NISRA

COMMUNICATIONS AND TRANSPORT

International Airports
Belfast International Airport, the main civil airport for Northern Ireland, is managed by Northern Ireland Airports Ltd., part of the TBI plc group of companies. In 2008 the airport handled 5,223,000 passengers and 36,000 tonnes of freight, making it one of the busiest airports in the United Kingdom. Direct scheduled services are available from Belfast International Airport to London (Heathrow), London (Gatwick), East Midlands, Birmingham, Manchester, Glasgow, Aberdeen, Edinburgh, Amsterdam, Brussels, Shannon and New York. Charter flights operate direct to USA and Canada and to most European destinations. Airlines using Belfast International Airport include British Airways, Easyjet and Maersk Air.
Belfast International Airport Ltd, URL: http://www.belfastairport.com/en

Belfast City Airport, two miles east of the city centre, carries two million passengers per annum to 20 destinations within the UK and Northern Ireland. In 2006 it was announced that Belfast City Airport was to be renamed after footballing legend George Best who was born in the city. The City of Derry Airport near Londonderry provides services to 14 destinations in the UK and four European destinations, handling 2,187,000 passengers in 2007 and 1,000 tonnes of freight. Enniskillen Airport supports seasonal services to Zurich for Crossair and Jersey for British Airways, and operates an air taxi service to destinations in Ireland, UK and Europe.
George Best, Belfast City Airport, URL: http://www.belfastcityairport.com

Flights to airports in Northern Ireland were suspended for several days in April 2010 due to a cloud of volcanic ash originating from a volcanic eruption under the Eyjafjallajokull glacier in Iceland.

Railways
Northern Ireland Railways (NIR) provides rail service within the Province and cross-border services to Dublin in partnership with Irish Rail. The railway system is 229 miles long and is basically a suburban network providing a commuter service for the Greater Belfast area with long-distance spurs to Londonderry and Dublin, although it also handles freight mail and parcels. In 1997 a high speed rail link between Belfast and Dublin was launched to reduce journey time between the cities by a third. Figures for 2001-02 show that 6.3 million passenger journeys were undertaken generating receipts of £15.4 million (source: NISRA)
Northern Ireland Railways Co. Ltd., URL: http://www.translink.co.uk

Roads
Co-ordinating their transport services with NIR under the service brand name of Translink are Citybus Ltd and Ulsterbus Ltd. The first operates within the Greater Belfast Area while the second operates services throughout the rest of Northern Ireland. The Department of Environment currently administers a licensing system for hauliers with the object of maintaining national and European standards necessary for the safe operation of vehicles and fair competition between hauliers. As at 2008 there were 1,024,396 vehicles on the roads.
Northern Ireland Transport Holding Co. (NITHCO), URL: http://www.translink.co.uk/nithco.asp
Translink Ltd., URL: http://www.translink.co.uk

Shipping
There are regular passenger vehicle and freight services from Belfast and Larne to various ports in Great Britain while freight services operate from Londonderry and Warrenpoint. A summer only passenger vehicle service between Ballycastle and Campbeltown was in operation between 1997 and 1999, and there are plans for this service to be reinstated. A major programme of works at all four harbours is at present assisted by the European Regional Development Fund. Figures for 2008 show that 23.5 million tonnes of freight was handled by ports in Northern Ireland, down from the 2006 figure of 24.5 million tonnes.

Ports and Harbours
The main port is Belfast; in 1997 it handled 60 per cent of Northern Ireland's trade and 25 per cent of Ireland's trade. There is also a major port at Derry.

HEALTH

There are five Health and Social Care Trusts with 57,500 staff members. In 2008/09 there were 1,148 GPs with a ratio of 62 GPs per 100,000 patients and 819 dentists. In 2008/09 there were approximately 500,000 inpatient and day case admissions to hospital, 1.5 million outpatient attendances and 750,000 emergency attendances.

The median age is 71.6 for males and 78.2 for females. The Northern Ireland recorded a death rate of 8.1 deaths per 1,000 population in 2009.

Department of Health and Social Services and Public Safety, URL: http://www.dhsspsni.gov.uk

EDUCATION

Education in Northern Ireland is mainly administered centrally by the Department of Education for Northern Ireland (DENI) and locally by the five Education and Library boards. Each Education and Library Board is the local education authority for its area. The education and library boards provide primary and secondary schools, special schools and institutions of further education, and meet the running costs (excluding teachers' salaries) of voluntary schools other than voluntary grammar schools.

The Boards also identify and make provision for children with special educational needs; award university and other scholarships; provide milk and meals, as well as free books and transport for pupils; enforce school attendance; provide an advisory and support service for the curricula of all schools in their areas; regulate the employment of children and young people; secure the provision of recreational and youth service facilities, and develop comprehensive library services for their areas. Board expenditure is funded 100 per cent by the DENI. Within the schools sector, the Council for Catholic Maintained Schools is responsible for employing teachers in Catholic maintained schools, and promoting the effective control and management by Boards of Governors of these schools.

Education in Northern Ireland is organised on similar lines to that in England and Wales, though with some important structural differences. The different kinds of school are as follows: controlled schools - provided by the five education and library boards; Catholic-maintained schools; voluntary grammar schools; integrated schools - a new category of school created by the Education Reform (NI) Order of 1989 where roughly equal numbers of Protestant and Catholic children are taught together in either grant-maintained integrated schools which have their expenditure met by the department, or controlled-integrated, funded through the education and library board. As of October 1997 there were 32 integrated schools with total enrolments of over 8,154 pupils (roughly 2 per cent of all pupils in Northern Ireland). Recent figures show that despite the idea of an integrated education becoming more popular, around 95 per cent of students still attend either a Catholic or Protestant school.

As in England and Wales, a common curriculum has been put in place for pupils in grant-aided schools in Northern Ireland, with formal assessment in the compulsory subjects at ages 8, 11, 14 and 16, against specified attainment targets. As well as religious education and six areas of study, the common curriculum includes a number of compulsory educational (cross-curricula) themes, for example, education for mutual understanding and cultural heritage. The Northern Ireland education system provides free education for all children of compulsory school age (age 4 to 16) as well as for those who stay on until age 18.

In recent years the number of school age children had been falling but figures between the years 2010-11 and 2011-12 the number increased from 321,717 to 322,019.

Nursery education
Figures for the year 2011-12 showed that 5,911 children attended nursery school.

Primary Education
Primary education is for children between the ages of four and 11. Figures for 2011-12 showed that 164,812 children were enrolled at primary school.

Secondary Education
Secondary (including grammar) schools are for pupils aged 11 to 16/18. In 2011-12 146,747 pupils attended secondary schools.

Higher Education
Higher education in Northern Ireland is provided by The Queen's University of Belfast, the University of Ulster (operating on four main campuses at Coleraine, Jordanstown, Belfast and Londonderry), and 17 colleges of further education. Under the Education Reform Order

1989, responsibility for the further training of teachers rests mainly with the five Education and Library Boards, and is conducted at the universities and two colleges of education, Stranmillis and St. Mary's.

Special Education
The Education and Library Boards also provide education for children up to the age of 19. As of 2011-12 there were 41 special schools (including three hospital schools) with 4,549 pupils. (All education figures: DENI and NISRA)

RELIGION

According to 2001 Census figures, 40 per cent of the population are Catholic, 21 per cent are Presbyterian, 15 per cent attend the Church of Ireland and four per cent are Methodist. Six per cent belong to other Christian religions, 0.3 per cent follow other, non-Christian religions and the remaining 13.7 per cent do not follow a religion, or are unwilling to state their religion.

The Irish Council of Churches, URL: http://www.irishchurches.org
President: Most Rev. Richard Clarke
Vice President: Rev. Fr. Godfrey O'Donnell
Archbishop of Armagh and Primate of All Ireland (The Church of Ireland), URL: http://www.ireland.anglican.org/
Most Rev. Alan Harper

COMMUNICATIONS AND MEDIA

Newspapers
Belfast Telegraph, URL: http://www.belfasttelegraph.co.uk
News Letter, URL: http://www.newsletter.co.uk
Irish News, URL: http://www.irishnews.com

Broadcasting
British Broadcasting Corporation (BBC), URL: http://www.bbc.co.uk/northernireland
Ofcom, URL: http://www.org.uk
Ulster Television plc, URL: http://www.utvmedia.com

BBC Radio Ulster, URL: http://www.bbc.co.uk/radioulster
BBC Radio Foyle, URL: http://www.bbc.co.uk/radiofoyle
Downtown Radio (commercial) URL: http://www.downtown.co.uk/

ENVIRONMENT

The Environment and Heritage Service, an executive agency of the Department of the Environment for Northern Ireland, is responsible for the implementation of the government's environmental strategy and policies in Northern Ireland. The Service's remit extends from pollution control to consideration of the natural environment and protection of the built heritage.

In 2000, greenhouse gas emissions were measured as follows: Carbon Dioxide (CO_2), 16,133 kilotonnes; Methane (CH_4), 133 kilotonnes; and Nitrous Oxide (N_2O), 11 kilotonnes.

In the Service's 2000 report, the overall quality of 96 per cent of monitored river stretches were described as very good to fair.

SCOTLAND

Capital: Edinburgh (Population estimate: 495,300)

National Flag: Dark blue background with white cross of St Andrew (The Saltire)

CONSTITUTION AND GOVERNMENT

In December 1997 plans were announced to implement Scotland's first parliament in 300 years, after a referendum in September of that year. 75 per cent of the 70 per cent of the electorate who voted were in favour of a Scottish Parliament. Elections for the 129-seat parliament were held on 6 May 1999; at the election votes were cast for two parliaments: one based on the Westminster Parliament constituencies, and one for one of 56 regional members. The Parliament was officially opened by the Queen on 1 July 1999.

The Scottish Executive is headed by the First Minister who is nominated by the parliament. The First Minister then appoints the ministers.

The areas of responsibility of the parliament are education, law and order, transport, social work, local government, tourism, economic development and financial assistance to industry, health, agriculture and the environment, planning and housing, sport and culture.

Sovereignty rests ultimately with Westminster and the Queen remains head of state for the whole United Kingdom. Key matters remain the responsibility of Westminster including foreign policy, defence, macroeconomic policy and national security. Scotland elected 72 MPs to Westminster who represent their constituencies on these reserved matters. This number was reduced by boundary changes to 59 MPs at the May 2005 election.

Recent Events
The SNP announced that they wished to hold a referendum in 2010 on constitutional changes for Scotland which would pave the way for independence. While the Scottish Government's favoured policy is independence, it acknowledges that there is support within Scotland for a range of positions on increased responsibilities for the Scottish Parliament. In order to reflect this as fully as possible, the Scottish Government is consulting on a referendum which would put two questions to the people of Scotland. A draft referendum bill consultation paper was issued in June 2010. The bill presents two options: firstly a question about the extension of the powers and responsibilities to the Scottish Parliament short of independence, and secondly a question about whether the Scottish Parliament should also have its powers extended to enable independence to be achieved. However, the bill for the referendum was not put to an immediate vote.

A further announcement about extending the powers of the Scottish parliament took place in November 2010. Under the terms of the proposed legislation Scotland would control a third of its budget and would be able to raise half of its income tax as of 2015. Stamp duty and landfill tax may also be devolved. The block grant which the UK government pays to Scotland, currently worth about £30 billion, will be cut. Under the new bill Scotland would have the power to set its own drink driving limits and national speed limits and new procedures for Scottish criminal cases that go to the UK Supreme Court. On May 1 2012 the Bill was given Royal Assent making it law but the new powers will not be in place until 2016.

Referendum on Independence
In February 2010 the Scottish government published a draft bill of its proposed referendum on Independence. Following the May 2011 election The Scottish National Party which won with 69 seats moved forward with its plan for a referendum, and officially launched its plan

UNITED KINGDOM

for independence at its conference in October 2011. In January 2012 the Consultation paper on the referendum was signed off at Bute House in Edinburgh and Alex Salmond announced the referendum would be held in the autumn of 2014. Discussions were then set up to debate the exact nature of the question, at first it was suggested it should be. "Do you agree that Scotland should be an independent country?" On October 15 2012 the Edinburgh Agreement was signed by Prime Minister David Cameron and First Minister Alex Salmond, under the agreement a single Yes/No question on Scotland leaving the United Kingdom would be asked and it also allowed for 16 and 17 year olds to take part in the vote. The question asked will be, "Should Scotland be an independent country?"

Legislature

Scotland elects 129 Members of the Scottish Parliament (MSPs) to the Scottish parliament for a term of four years, 73 members are constituency MSPs and 56 are regional MSPs. Seven regional MSPs represent each of the eight regions, Central Scotland; Glasgow; Highlands and Islands, Lothians; Mid Scotland and Fife; North East Scotland; South of Scotland; West of Scotland. This means that every person in Scotland is represented in the Parliament by one constituency MSP and seven regional MSPs and ensures that seats won reflect the proportion of votes a party has received.

Scottish Parliament, Edinburgh EH99 1SP, United Kingdom. Tel: +44 (0)131 348 5000, fax: +44 (0)131 348 5601, URL: http://www.scotland.gov.uk
Presiding Officer: Tricia Marwick (page 1472)

The newly constructed Scottish Parliament at Holyrood in Edinburgh was officially opened in October 2004. In 2003, an inquiry was launched into the completion time and cost of construction which was around £335 million over budget.

Scottish Executive (as at May 2013)
First Minister: Alex Salmond (page 1507)
Deputy First Minister, Cabinet Secretary, Health and Wellbeing: Nicola Sturgeon (page 1521)
Cabinet Secretary for Education & Lifelong Learning: Michael Russell (page 1506)
Minister for Parliamentary Business: Joe FitzPatrick
Cabinet Secretary, Finance and Sustainable Growth: John Swinney (page 1522)
Minister for Environment and Climate Change: Paul Wheelhouse
Minister for Culture and External Affairs: Fiona Hyslop (page 1446)
Minister for Housing, Transport and Veterans: Keith Brown (page 1395)
Minister for Commonwealth Games and Sport: Shona Robison
Cabinet Secretary, Justice: Kenny MacAskill
Minister for Energy, Enterprise and Tourism: Fergus Ewing
Minister for Community Safety and Legal Affairs: Roseanna Cunningham
Lord Advocate: Frank Mulholland
Minister for Public Health: Michael Matheson
Minister for Children and Young People: Aileen Campbell
Minister for Learning, Science and Scotland's Languages: Dr Alasdair Allan
Minister for Youth Employment: Angela Constance
Cabinet Secretary for Rural Affairs and the Environment: Richard Lochhead
Minister for External Affairs and International Development: Humza Yousaf
Minister for Local Planning: Derek MacKay
Cabinet Secretary for Health and Well Being: Alex Neil
Solicitor General: Lesley Thomson

Ministries

Office of the First Minister, St. Andrew's House, Regent Road, Edinburgh, EH1 3DG, Scotland. Tel: +44 (0)131 556 8400, URL: http://www.scotland.gov.uk/
Scottish Executive Education Department, Education Department, Scottish Executive Victoria Quay, Edinburgh, EH6 6QQ, Scotland. Tel: +44 (0)131 556 8400, URL: http://www.scotland.gov.uk/About/Departments/ED
Scottish Executive Justice Department, 1W.11 St Andrew's House, Regent Road, Edinburgh EH1 3DG, Scotland. Tel: +44 (0)131 244 2120 , URL: http://www.scotland.gov.uk/About/Departments/JD
Scottish Executive Rural Affairs Department, Pentland House, 47 Robb's Loan, Edinburgh, EH14 3DG, Scotland. Tel: +44 (0)131 556 8400, URL: http://www.scotland.gov.uk/who/dept_rural.asp
Scottish Executive Health Department, St. Andrew's House, Regent Road, Edinburgh EH1 3DG, Scotland. Tel: +44 (0)131 556 8400, URL: http://www.scotland.gov.uk/About/Departments/HD
Scottish Executive Development Department, Area 3-H Victoria Quay, Edinburgh, EH6 6QQ, Scotland. Tel: +44 (0)8457 741741, URL: http://www.scotland.gov.uk/About/Departments/DD
Scottish Executive Enterprise, Transport and Lifelong Learning Department, 6th Floor Meridian Court, Cadogan Street, Glasgow, G2 6AT, Scotland. Tel: +44 (0)141 248 4774, URL: http://www.scotland.gov.uk/About/Departments/ETLLD
Scottish Executive Environment and Rural Affairs Department, Scottish Executive, Room 440, Pentland House, 47 Robb's Loan, Edinburgh EH14 1TY, Scotland. Tel: +44 (0)131 556 8400, URL: http://www.scotland.gov.uk/About/Departments/ERAD
Scottish Executive Finance and Central Services Department, St. Andrew's House, Regent Road, Edinburgh EH1 3DG, Scotland. Tel: +44 (0)131 244 5598, URL: http://www.scotland.gov.uk/About/Departments/FCSD

Elections

The first Scottish Parliament was elected on 6 May 1999. The most recent election results from the 5 May 2011 election are shown below:

Party	Seats 2011
Scottish National Party	65
Labour Party	32
Conservative Party	11
Liberal Democrat Party	4
Others	3

Following the 2003 election, the Labour and Liberal Democrat parties formed a coalition. At the May 2007 election, voters were asked to vote on one ballot for MSPs using the traditional X and on a separate ballot sheet for local councillors using numbers. Over 140,000 ballots were believed to have been filled in incorrectly and therefore not counted and an inquiry was to take place. On May 11 the Scottish Nationalist Party and the Green party signed an agreement that the Greens would support Alex Salmond as first minister in return for backing a climate change bill as an early measure, and a Green MSP nomination to chair a committee.

The most recent election was held in May 2011. The Scottish National Party won a decisive victory and its leader Alex Salmond announced that there would now probably be a referendum on Scottish independence.

Seventy-three of the Members of the Scottish Parliament (MSPs) are elected by their constituency and 56 are elected by a regional vote to ensure that seats won reflect the proportion of votes a party has received.

Scotland currently returns 59 MPs to Westminster. Scotland elects eight members to the European Parliament. The most recent Westminster election took place on May 6 2010.

LEGAL SYSTEM

Control over Scotland's criminal and civil law was passed to the new Scottish Parliament in July 1999.

Scotland has a separate legal system and judiciary. Under the Scottish legal system the Lord Advocate undertakes the prosecution on behalf of the public, unlike the English legal system where the prosecution is undertaken on behalf of the police or individual citizens. Any crimes are reported to the office of the Procurator Fiscal, who then decides whether to prosecute. The Procurator Fiscal's office also does the work of a coroner's office.

The supreme civil court in Scotland is the Court of Session, from which there is no appeal except to the House of Lords. It is divided into two Houses, the Inner with thirteen judges and the Outer with nineteen. The Inner House has two Divisions with four judges in each. The judges of the Outer House sit in separate courts and from them appeals are sent to a Division of the Inner House.

The supreme criminal court in Scotland is the High Court of Justiciary, which sits in Edinburgh and in certain circuit towns. Its jurisdiction extends throughout Scotland and includes all categories of crime not specifically reserved to another court. It has concurrent jurisdiction with the sheriff court over most crimes, but has exclusive jurisdiction over treason, murder, rape, deforcement of messengers and breach of duty by Magistrates. The judges of the High Court are the same persons as the judges of the Court of Session.

The High Court is both a trial court and an appeal court. When it sits as the Court of Appeal, it consists of at least three judges in appeals against conviction and at least two judges in appeals against sentence. Its decisions are final and not subject to review.

The principal local courts are the 49 Sheriff Courts with both civil and criminal jurisdiction. In civil matters these courts provide the advantage of justice locally administered and the saving of expense. There is no pecuniary limit to their jurisdiction. Appeals are taken to the Sheriff Principal or to the Court of Session. The criminal jurisdiction of the sheriff is limited by the fact that he cannot award any higher punishment than three years imprisonment. Minor offences are dealt with by the District Courts, overseen by a Justice of the Peace or Magistrate.

There is also a Land Court to try land disputes and a Land Valuation Appeals Court. Matters concerning heraldry are heard by the Court of the Lord Lyon.

Under the Scottish legal system juries consist of 15 members and they must reach a majority decision. Three verdicts are available to the Jury, guilty, not guilty or not proven.

LOCAL GOVERNMENT

Under a new structure of local government which, in terms of the Local Government (Scotland) Act 1994, came into administrative effect on 1 April 1996, Scotland was divided into 32 council areas, including three island areas. Each of these council areas is divided into electoral wards. One councillor is elected to represent each electoral ward on the council for three-year terms. Local government in Scotland became the responsibility of the Scottish Parliament from July 1999. The councils are responsible for areas including education, social work, roads, public transport and planning, libraries, police and fire services and leisure. Local councillors sit in office for four years, and up until the election held in May 2003, councillors were elected by the traditional first past the post method. The 2007 election used the Single Transferable Vote, a system of proportional representation for the first time. The most recent elections were held on May 3 2012.

The councils and their estimated populations in mid 2011 census (March 2011) are set out in the following table.

Council Area	Population
Aberdeen City	222,800
Aberdeenshire	253,000
Angus	116,000
Argyll & Bute	88,200
Clackmannanshire	51,400
Dumfries & Galloway	151,300
Dundee City	147,300
East Ayrshire	122,700
East Dumbartonshire	105,000

- continued

East Lothian	99,700
East Renfrewshire	90,600
City of Edinburgh	476,600
Eilean Siar (Western Isles)	27,700
Falkirk	156,000
Fife	365,200
Glasgow City	593,200
Highland	232,100
Inverclyde	81,500
Midlothian	83,200
Moray	93,300
North Ayrshire	138,200
North Lanarkshire	337,800
Orkney Islands	21,400
Perth & Kinross	146,700
Renfrewshire	174,900
Scottish Borders	113,900
Shetland Islands	23,200
South Ayrshire	112,800
South Lanarkshire	313,800
Stirling	90,200
West Dumbartonshire	90,700
West Lothian	175,100

Source: Office for National Statistics

AREA AND POPULATION

Area

Scotland forms the northern part of the British Isles, and covers an area of around 77,925 sq. km (30,415 sq. miles), including its 790 islands, which include the Western Isles, Orkneys and Shetland. Some 130 of Scotland's Islands are inhabited. It borders to the south England, to the east the North Sea and to the north and west the Atlantic Ocean. There are three physical regions; the Southern Uplands, the Central Lowlands, and the Highlands. The Southern Uplands largely consist of rolling moors. The Central Lowlands has the best farming land. The Highland coast has many long, narrow sea lochs and numerous islands. There are two major mountain ranges in the highlands: the North West Highlands and the Grampians. The highest mountain is Ben Nevis (1,343 metres).

The climate is temperate and oceanic, very changeable. Although milder than other areas on similar latitudes, the temperatures are generally lower than in the rest of the UK. The western highlands are the wettest part of the country with over 3,000 mm of rain per annum.

To view a map of Scotland, please consult:
http://www.lib.utexas.edu/maps/cia08/united_kingdom_sm_2008.gif

Population

The population on the last census day (27 March 2011) was put at 5,295,400 up from the 2001 figure of 5,062,011. Scotland now has seven. Stirling was given city status as part of the Queen's Golden Jubilee celebrations in 2002 and Perth was given city status as part of the Queen's Diamond Jubilee celebrations in 2012. The cities and their populations were recently put at: Edinburgh, 486,120; Glasgow, 592,120; Aberdeen, 217,120; Dundee, 144,290; Inverness, 56,660; Stirling, 89,850. Scotland has the lowest population density in the UK, averaging around 64 people per sq. km. The official language is English, and legally so is Gaelic, which is spoken by around 80,000 of the population.

Births, Marriages, Deaths

Provisional figures for 2011 put live births at 58,590. The number of deaths that year was 53,661. That year, 29,135 marriages took place and there were 9,862 divorces and 554 civil parterships. (Source: National Statistics Office). Since 2003 the population has shown a slight increase; although there has been a rise in the birthrate, the population increase is more attributable to a rise in the number of people choosing to live in Scotland. For example change in population between mid 2009 and 2010 was a rise of 28,100 persons of which 5,200 were from natural increase and 22,900 from net migration and other changes.

Public Holidays 2014

1-2 January: New Year
18 April: Good Friday
21 April: Easter Monday
5 May: May Day Holiday
26 May: Spring Bank Holiday
4 August: Summer Bank Holiday
30 November: St Andrew's Day
25 December: Christmas Day

EMPLOYMENT

Figures for January 2007 showed that 2,512,000 people were employed, the highest number employed for 15 years. Unemployment was put at 5.2 per cent. Figures for early 2008 put the number of employed persons at 2,536,000 and unemployment was recorded at 4.9 per cent. In response to the global economic downturn Scotland has recently suffered a series of job losses resulting in the unemployment rate in the first quarter of 2009 rising by 0.5 per cent on the previous quarter's figure of 5.2 per cent. In the second quarter of 2009 the unemployment rate was recorded at 5.9 per cent. In April 2010 the unemployment rate had risen to 7.8 per cent (208,000 people) although this rate was still lower than the unemployment rate for the UK as a whole which stood at 8.0 per cent. Unemployment for the first quarter of 2011 was put at 8.1 per cent, ahead of the UK figure of 7.8 per cent. This had risen to 8.0 per cent in the third quarter of 2011. Figures for the beginning of 2012

showed that from Dec. 2011-Feb. 2012 the unemployment rate was 8.1 per cent which was below the UK average of 8.3 per cent. Figures for the quarter December 2012 to February 2013 show that of a workforce of 2,627,000; 2,432,000 were employed and 196,000 were unemployed, giving an unemployment rate of 7.4 per cent.

The following table shows the number of people employed by sector:

Employee Jobs by Sector

Sector	Dec. 2010	Dec. 2011
Agriculture, forestry & fishing	47,000	50,000
Mining & quarrying	33,000	31,000
Manufacturing	187,000	190,000
Electricity, gas, steam & air conditioning supply	16,000	19,000
Water, supply, sewerage, waste & remediation activities	18,000	17,000
Construction	176,000	172,000
Wholesale & retail trade, repairs	377,000	370,000
Transport & storage	108,000	130,000
Accommodation & food service activities	182,000	187,000
Information & communication	72,000	73,000
Financial & insurance activities	100,000	90,000
Real estate activities	31,000	27,000
Professional scientific & technical activities	173,000	190,000
Administrative & support service activities	199,000	197,000
Public admin. & defence, compulsory social security	157,000	149,000
Education	206,000	197,000
Health & social work activities	374,000	358,000
Arts, entertainment & recreation	69,000	71,000
Other service activities	73,000	70,000
All jobs	2,596,000	2,589,000

BANKING AND FINANCE

Currency

One £ Sterling = 100 pence
Scotland also issues its own banknotes in denominations of £1, £5, £10, £20, £50 and £100

GDP/GNP, Inflation, National Debt

Gross value added in recent years is shown below. Figures are in £ billion at current basic prices.

GVA	Scotland	UK
2000	67.3	841.5
2001	70.2	883.4
2002	74.0	930.7
2003	78.5	981.7
2004	82.0	1,005.3
2005	88.0	1,115.1
2006	93.3	1,177.2
2007	98.5	1,247.7
2008	103.5	1,295.6
2009	102.5	1,255.7
2010	105.6	1,274.8

Source: Office for National Statistics

The following table shows Gross Value Added in recent years by industry groups at current basic prices. Figures are in £ million:

Sector	2010
Agriculture, hunting & fishing	725
Mining & quarrying	3,427
Manufacturing	12,594
Electricity, gas, steam & air conditioning supply	2,671
Water supply; sewerage, waste management	1,668
Construction	7,572
Wholesale & retail trade, repairs	10,756
Hotels & restaurants	3,223
Transportation and storage	5,109
Accommodation & food service activities	3,583
Information & communication	3,682
Financial & insurance activities	8,831
Real estate activities	7,640
Professional, scientific & technical activities	6,252
Administrative & support service activities	4,433
Public administration & defence; compulsory social security	6,195
Education	7,064
Health & social work	10,608
Arts, entertainment & recreation	1,725
Other services	1,260
Activities of households	287
Total	106,080

Source: Office of National Statistics

Figures for 2005 put GVA at £86 billion. In 2006 the sector which recorded the largest growth was the Financial Services sector which grew by 8.1 per cent; the sector with the lowest growth was Mining and Quarrying which recorded a growth of -9.3 per cent.

UNITED KINGDOM

Budget
The Scottish Parliament is allocated most of its budget money from the UK Parliament. The budget for the year 2011-12 was £24.8 million.

Balance of Payments / Imports and Exports
Selected Scottish Exports by Industry in Recent Years £million

Sector	2007	2008
Agriculture, forestry and fishing	170	180
Mining, quarrying & extraction of petroleum	635	615
Manufacture of food products and beverages	3,180	3,435
Manufacture of textiles and textile products	255	300
Manufacture of pulp, paper & paper products	325	310
Manufacture of coke, refined petroleum products & nuclear fuel, Manufacture of chemicals & chemical products	2,895	3,465
Manufacture of fabricated metal products, except machinery & equipment	530	580
Manufacture of machinery & equipment	1,190	1,360
Manufacture of office machinery & computers	455	300
Business services	1,950	2,335
Manufacture of medical, precision & optical instruments, watches & clocks	735	705
Total Exports	19,000	20,660

Source: Office for National Statistics

The following table shows Scottish trade with the rest of the world not including exports to the rest of the UK in 2008.

Scottish Exports Worldwide

Area	£million
USA	3,100
Netherlands	1,635
France	1,535
Germany	1,300
Spain	995
Ireland	960
Norway	610
Italy	540
Sweden	520
Belgium	495
Switzerland	415
Denmark	380
UAE	360
Japan	300
China	295
Singapore	245
Australia	235
Greece	230
Nigeria	230
Canada	230

Source: Office for National Statistics

Figures for 2005 show that 31 per cent of Scotland's imports came from countries within the European Union not including the rest of the UK. 28 per cent came from countries in Asia and Oceania, 20 per cent from North America and 7 per cent from non-EU Western European countries, 3 per cent came from non-EU Eastern European countries and four per cent from the Middle East and Africa. Figures for 2003 show that Scotland's export earnings were £13.2 billion, while imports cost £8.2 billion. Figures from 2010 show that Scottish exports earned £14,658 million while imports cost £11,244 million.

Banking
Like the rest of Europe, Scotland has been experiencing the recent global economic downturn and banking crisis. One of the UK's largest banks is based in Scotland, The Royal Bank of Scotland (RBS). In February 2009 the RBS (URL: http://www.rbs.co.uk) announced that its total losses in 2008 were £24.1 billion (US$34.2 billion); this was the largest loss ever posted by a UK bank. Approximately 2,300 jobs were expected to be lost. Much of the banks loss was due its purchase of Dutch bank ABN Amro in 2007. The British treasury said it would be injecting £13 billion to help bail out the bank.

MANUFACTURING, MINING AND SERVICES

Primary and Extractive Industries
The oil reserves of the UK are almost all off the coast of Scotland in the North Sea. Devolution has had no effect on North Sea oil and gas which still come under the jurisdiction of the United Kingdom as a whole.

Figures for 2008 show that the North Sea Oil fields have reserves of around 3.6 billion barrels. In 2008 an estimated 1,58 thousand barrels of oil per day were produced (down from the 2007 figures of 1.68 thousand barrels per day). The North Sea has natural gas reserves of around 17 trillion cubic feet and figures for 2008 estimate production at 2.5 trillion cubic feet. The North Sea fields are considered mature and it is unlikely that many large fields still remain undiscovered, although exploration is being undertaken. EIA figures for 2011 show that the UK had 2.9 billion barrels of proven crude oil reserves, produced 1.4 million barrels per day and consumed 1.6 million barrels per day.

After years of being a net exporter of oil and gas, the UK began importing crude oil and natural gas in 2005. Scotland is the largest producer of hydrocarbons in the European Union and accounted for 64 per cent of the EU's total oil production in 2010. It has been estimated recently that oil and gas reserves of up to 24 billion barrels could still be recovered. Recent estimates show that Scotland accounted for 78 per cent of total UK hydrocarbon production in 2011-12.

Manufacturing
Traditional Scottish manufacturing industries include steelmaking, heavy engineering and shipbuilding. These have gradually been replaced in importance by chemicals, electronics and engineering in the vehicle and aircraft sectors. The electronics sector employed over 40,000 people in 2000 and electrical and instrument engineering exports earned £10 million in that year. Whisky production remains an important industry earning around £2 billion a year; Scotland has 90 distilleries. Figures for 2008 show that manufacturing exports from Scotland were worth £14 billion. The manufacturing sector contributes around 18 per cent of GDP. The following table shows the gross value added of selected manufactured products in recent years, figures are in £ million.

Product	2008	2009
Food products, beverages and tobacco	3,708	3,961
Textiles and textile products	285	224
Leather & leather products	25	30
Wood & wood products	457	295
Paper and paper products	339	267
Coke and refined petroleum products	10	11
Chemicals & chemical products	1,316	1,328
Basic pharmaceutical products & pharmaceutical preparations	214	198
Rubber & plastic goods	513	370
Other non-metallic products	425	280
Basic metals & fabricated metal products	1,586	1,337
Machinery & other equipments	943	997
Electrical equipment	208	210
Transport equipment	442	649
Other manufactured products	209	181

Source: National Statistics Office

Service Industries
Figures from 2008 show that Scotland's business services sector earned £2.3 billion in export earnings and £1.4 billion from wholesale and retail trade, £0.6 billion from financial intermediation and (source: Scottish Statistics)

Tourism
Nearly three million overseas visitors came to Scotland in 2007. Figures for 2007 show that tourist expenditure amounted to £4,203 million.

Agriculture
The following table shows principal crop production in £ million:

Crops	2007*	2008*
Wheat	96.600	130.419
Barley	222.998	243.397
Oats	14.628	12.868
Triticale	1039	0.718
Vegetables	92.472	100.368
Fruit	62.704	68.031
Flowers & nursery stock	56.161	46.537
Potatoes	211.028	192.983

*provisional
Source: National Statistics Office

The following table shows head of livestock in recent years:

Livestock	2011	2012
Cattle	1,803,937	1,788,470
Sheep	6,801,134	6,735,974
Pigs	346,253	324,044
Poultry	14,526,394	14,693,992
Deer	5,977	6,121
Horses	763	860
Goats	3,756	3,783

Source: Scottish Statistics

Forestry
Around 60 per cent of the UK's timber production is based in Scotland and supports a growing industry of panel production and pulp and paper processing.

Fishing
Fishing has always been an important part of the Scottish economy, although it has declined in recent years. Scotland produces the largest amount of farmed salmon in the EU and lands 66 per cent of the total UK catch. Figures for 2005 show that the number of fishing vessels in Scotland has fallen to 2,400 from 3,000 in the 1990s.

COMMUNICATIONS AND TRANSPORT

International Airports
Glasgow Airport, Paisley PA3 2ST, United Kingdom. Tel: +44 (0)141 887 1111, fax: +44 (0)141 848 4586, URL: http://www.glasgowairport.com

Edinburgh Airport, Edinburgh EH12 9DN, United Kingdom. Tel: +44 (0)131 333 1000, fax: +44 (0)131 334 3470, URL: http://www.edinburghairport.com

Figures for 2008 show that 3,290,000 passengers passed through Aberdeen airport, 8,992,000 through Edinburgh airport, 8,135,000 through Glasgow airport and 2,414,000 through Prestwick airport.

Railways
Scotland has around 2,700 km of railtrack. Glasgow has a subway system and Edinburgh is currently building a tram system.

Roads
Scotland has around 53,500 km of public roads including 371 km of motorway. Figures for 2008 show that 2,248,000 cars were licensed in Scotland.

Ports and Harbours
The main Scottish ports, are Clyde, Forth, Sullom Voe and Orkneys. Ferries run from the mainland to all Scottish islands, Ireland and Northern Ireland.

HEALTH

Health care is now the responsibility of the Scottish Executive Health Department and Social Work Services Group. The healthcare system is fully integrated: it is accountable to Scottish ministers and delivered by NHS Scotland's 14 health boards. The health boards work though community health and planning partnerships with public services and local authorities. Special health boards provide national services including NHS Education Scotland and NHS 24. In 2011, the estimated public health workforce amounted to 132,000, including an estimated 68,000 nurses and midwives and 8,500 doctors. An estimated 7,000 practitioners including GPS, dentists, opticians and community pharmacists.

EDUCATION

Since devolution, education comes under the jurisdiction of the Scottish Executive Education Department (SEED) including policy for pre-school and school education, children and young people, and arts, culture and sport.

Local authorities are responsible for providing school education in their areas. What are known as state schools in England and Wales are called public schools in Scotland. Like education in England and Wales, education in Scotland is compulsory up until the age of 16 and is free. Figures for the academic year 2007/08 from the National Statistics Office show that there were 2,194 publicly funded primary schools, and 385 publicly funded secondary schools. Scotland also had 117 non maintained (private) schools and 223 special schools. Scotland has 13 universities.

The examinations system in Scotland is different to that in England and Wales. At the age of 16 pupils sit Standard Grade of the Scottish Certificate of Education exams. Most pupils take Standard Grades in eight subjects. Until 2002 pupils then went on to take the Higher

Grade Certificate (Highers) and the Certificate of Sixth Year Studies (CSYS). This has now been phased out in favour of National Qualifications which aims to bring together academic and vocational qualifications.

Higher Education
Scotland has 25 universities including the Open University of Scotland. Degree courses last on average for four years as opposed to three years in the rest of the country. Fees are charged for university education for students not living in Scotland but the fees are lower than those charged for English and Welsh universities.

In 2007 the Scottish Government launched its Skills for Scotland initiative, under the plan areas where change was required were set out: a focus on individual development, a response to the needs of the economy and the demand of employers and the creation of cohesive structures.

Her Majesty's Inspectorate of Education, Scotland, URL: http://www.hmie.gov.uk

RELIGION

The established Church in Scotland is the Church of Scotland, a Presbyterian denomination.
Church of Scotland, URL: http://www.churchofscotland.org.uk/
Scottish Episcopal Church, URL: http://www.scotland.anglican.org/
Catholic Bishops' Conference of Scotland, URL: http://www.bpsconfscot.com/
President of the Bishops' Conference: Archbishop Philip Tartaglia

COMMUNICATIONS AND MEDIA

Newspapers
The Scotsman, URL: http://www.scotsman.com
Daily Record, URL: http://www.dailyrecord.co.uk
Scotland on Sunday, URL: http://www.scotlandonsunday.com

Broadcasting
The BBC provides television programmes through its BBC Scotland outlet as well as radio coverage from Radio Scotland. There is also a commercial broadcaster, Scottish TV (STV). Commercial radio in Scotland is provided by Clyde 1 which is based in Glasgow and the Edinburgh based Forth One.

In 2008, BBC Scotland and the Scottish government-funded MG Alba launched a Gaelic broadcasting service consisting of a digital TV channel BBC Alba, BBC Radio nan Gaidheal and BBC Alba Online.

ENVIRONMENT

Scotland is home to four World Heritage Sites and two National Parks (Loch Lomond and the Trossachs, and the Cairngorms).

WALES

Capital: Cardiff (Population estimate: 336,238)

Flag: Divided in half horizontally, upper half white, lower half green. A large red dragon is centred.

CONSTITUTION AND GOVERNMENT

In 1997 a referendum was held in Wales to decide the question of whether Wales should have its own assembly. The result was a narrow victory for supporters of a Welsh Assembly. 50.3 per cent of the electorate turned out to vote and of those 559,419 agreed with the proposal and 552,698 were against. First elections for the 60-seat Assembly were held on 6 May 1999, and the first session of the Welsh Assembly was opened by the Queen on 26 May 1999. The Welsh Assembly does not have such extensive powers as the Scottish Assembly but has responsibility over health, education, local government and economic development.

Recent Events
On December 10 2009 Carwyn Jones (page 1451) took over the position of first minister from Rhodri Morgan who resigned from the post after nearly 10 years.

In June 2011 an explosion and fire at the Chevron oil refinery in Pembrokeshire left four people dead and one seriously injured.

Legislature
Once the Assembly members have been elected, they must elect from amongst themselves the First Minister, *Prif Ysgrifennydd y Cynulliad*, who is the leader of the Cabinet and the political leader of the Assembly. The First Minister is responsible for appointing the Assembly Ministers, who make up the Cabinet. Members serve a four year term.

On March 1st 2006, the new Senedd building was opened, Senedd being Welsh for parliament or senate. The new building is next door to the old Assembly building and cost £67 million. It was designed with the environment in mind, with a renewable energy system and a system for the collection and use of rain water.
National Assembly of Wales, Cardiff Bay, Cardiff, CF99 1NA, United Kingdom. Tel: +44 (0)29 2082 5111, fax: 44 (0)29 2089 8229, URL: http://www.wales.gov.uk

Presiding Officer: Rosemary Butler (page 1398)

Cabinet (as at May 2013)
First Minister: Carwyn Jones (page 1451)
Leader of the House, Minister of Finance: Jane Hutt (page 1446)
Minister for Children, Education and Lifelong Learning: Leighton Andrews (page 1378)
Minister for Environment and Sustainable Development: John Griffiths (page 1434)
Minister forHousing and Regeneration: Carl Sargeant (page 1508)
Minister for Economy, Science and Transport: Edwina Hart (page 1438)
Minister for Business, Enterprise and Technology: Edwina Hart (page 1438)
Minister for Health and Social Services: Mark Drakeford
Counsel General: Theodore Huckle QC
Minister for Local Government and Government Business: Lesley Griffiths (page 1434)
Minister for Natural Resources and Food: Alun Davies
Minister of Communities and Tackling Poverty: Huw Lewis (page 1463)

Deputy Ministers
Deputy Minister for Skills: Jeff Cuthbert (page 1411)
Deputy Minister for Social Services: Gwenda Thomas (page 1525)

Ministries
All state departments are based at Cardiff Bay, Cardiff, CF99 1NA, United Kingdom. Tel: +44 (0)29 2082 5111, fax: +44 (0)29 2089 8229, URL: http://www.wales.gov.uk/index.htm

Elections
Elections for the Welsh Assembly take place every four years. The electorate cast two votes, one for their constituency member - this is counted on a first-past-the-post basis (there are 40 constituency members) and the second vote towards the election of the 20 additional members. There are four additional members for each of the five electoral regions and they are elected by a system of proportional representation, ensuring that each party is represented according to the number of votes it received.

The first election to the Welsh Assembly was held on 6 May 1999. The most recent election was held on 5 May 2011. The results were as follows:

UNITED KINGDOM

Following the 2007 election the Labour Party was the largest party, it did not win enough seats for a majority government and sought a coalition partner. However, talks collapsed and a minority government was formed. In July 2007 a coalition was agreed between Labour and Plaid Cymru, and a new cabinet was announced.

Wales also returns 40 MPs to Westminster and is represented in the European Parliament by four MEPs. The most recent election for the Westminster Parliament took place in May 2005; the Labour Party won 29 seats, the Liberal Democrats, four seats, Plaid Cymru, three seats, the Conservative Party, three seats and one independent. The most recent Westminster election took place on May 6 2010.

In May 2011 Wales had a referendum the question was, do you want the Assembly now to be able to make laws on all matters in the 20 subject areas it has powers for. The result was 63.5 per cent in favour and 36.5 per cent voted no.

Political Parties
Plaid Cymru, 18 Park Grove, Cardiff CF10 3BN, United Kingdom. Tel: +44 (0)29 2064 6000, fax: +44 (0)29 2064 6001, URL: http://www.plaidcymru.org
President: Leanne Wood (page 1539)
Welsh Labour Party, Transport House, 1 Cathedral Road, Cardiff CF1 9HA, United Kingdom. Tel: +44 (0)29 2087 7700, fax: +44 (0)29 2022 1153
URL: http://www.welshlabour.org.uk
National Assembly Labour Party Leader: Carwyn Jones (page 1451)
Welsh Conservative Party, 4 Penlline Road, Whitchurch, Cardiff, CF14 2XS, United Kingdom. Tel: +44 (0)29 2061 6031, URL: http://www.welshconservatives.com
Leader: Andrew RT Davies
Welsh Liberal Democrats, Bay View House, 102 Bute Street, Cardiff Bay, Cardiff CF10 5AD, United Kingdom. Tel: +44 (0)29 2031 3400, URL: http://welshlibdems.org.uk
Leader: Kirsty Williams (page 1537)

LEGAL SYSTEM

At present in Wales there 35 petty sessional divisions which are responsible for Magistrates Courts and youth justice. Wales has one Crown Court which sits at any one of ten centres. This court hears serious criminal cases. There are 23 County Courts which hear civil cases. More serious civil cases are heard at Cardiff, Chester and Swansea. Commercial cases will be heard at a specialist Mercantile Court which is planned for Cardiff.

For further details of the legal system in Wales please see the legal system section under United Kingdom.

LOCAL GOVERNMENT

Under a new structure of local government, Wales's original eight county and 37 district councils, established in 1974, were abolished and replaced with 22 unitary authorities on 1 April 1996. Local government became the responsibility of the Welsh Assembly from May 1999. Councillors are elected every four years, and areas of responsibility include local planning and development control, minor urban roads, car parks, local transport systems, housing, refuse collection, food safety and hygiene, clean air, building regulations, markets and fairs. The most recent elections took place on 3 May 2012.

At the more local level, there are Community Councils, which carry out local functions benefiting their areas.

The following table shows the 22 unitary authorities and their estimated populations in 2010.

Unitary Authority	Population
Isle of Anglesey	69,460
Blaenau Gwent	69,262
Bridgend	137,201
Caerphilly	174,476
Cardiff	348,977
Carmarthenshire	186,010
Ceredigion	78,216
Conwy	112,666
Denbighshire	99,213
Flintshire	150,908
Gwynedd	119,461
Merthyr Tydfil	56,066
Monmouthshire	89,177
Neath Port Talbot	139,810
Newport	141,032
Pembrokeshire	119,962
Powys	134,661
Rhondda, Cynon, Taff	236,573
Swansea	235,805
Torfaen	90,647
Vale of Glamorgan	127,503
Wrexham	136,103

Source: Statistics for Wales

Welsh Local Government Association, URL: http://www.wlga.gov.uk

AREA AND POPULATION

Area
Wales covers an area of 20,734 sq. km, and is surrounded on three sides by sea: to the north, the Irish Sea; to the west St. George's Channel; to the south the Bristol Channel. Wales has a coastline of over 1,200 km (750 miles). It shares its eastern border with the English counties of Cheshire, Shropshire, Worcestershire and Gloucestershire. The highest mountain in Wales is Snowdon (Yr Wyddfa), situated in the northwest and is 1,085 m (3,560 ft) high. The climate is temperate with annual rainfall of approximately 1,296 mm.

To view a map of Wales, please consult:
http://www.lib.utexas.edu/maps/cia08/united_kingdom_sm_2008.gif

Population
Figures for the 2011 census put the population of Wales at 3.06 million, showing a growth of 153,300 in the ten years since the previous census. The census showed tht he median age was 41, 18 per cent of the population (563,000) were aged over 65, 25,000 of which over 90. The census showed that 178,000 were children aged under 5. Estimated figures for 2011 put the population at 3,024,000. In mid 2010 the population of Wales was 3,006,400 up from the 2005 figure of 2,950,128. This equates to 4.9 per cent of the total population of the UK and is an increase on the 2001 census figure of 2,903,100. Population density in 2010 was put at 145 people per sq km. The official languages are English and Welsh. Recent figures show that 21 per cent of the population can speak Welsh. Two thirds of the population live in the south of Wales. Wales now has six cities, Cardiff, St. David's, Swansea, Bangor, Newport and St Asaph. Newport was given city status by the Queen in the 2003 Golden Jubilee celebrations, St Asaph was given city status by the Queen in the 2012 Diamond Jubilee celebrations.

Births, Marriages, Deaths
Figures from 2010 show that there were 35,952 live births giving a birth rate of 12 per 1,000 population. Figures for mid 2009-10 show that there were 35,300 live births and 30,600 deaths, recording a natural change of 4,600 net migrtaion during that period was 2,500. Provisional figures for 2007 put the number of marriages at 13,500 and the number of divorces at 6,900. In 2007 the net migration figure to Wales from the rest of the UK was 7,300. In 2010 268 civil partnerships ceremonies took place.

EMPLOYMENT

Figures for the year ending 31 December 2012 showed that the number of people in employment was 1,319,300 and the number unemployed 119,100 giving an unemployment rate of 8.3 per cent.

The following table shows provisional figures of how the workforce was employed:

Sector	Dec. 2010	Dec. 2011
Agriculture, hunting, forestry & fishing	33,000	32,000
Mining & quarrying	2,000	2,000
Electricity, gas, steam & air conditioning supply	6,000	7,000
Water supply, sewerage, waste & remediation services	10,000	12,000
Manufacturing	144,000	143,000
Construction	94,000	95,000
Wholesale & retail trade & repairs	209,000	215,000
Transport & storage	55,000	51,000
Accommodation & food service activities	86,000	101,000
Information & communication	28,000	26,000
Financial & insurance activities	31,000	31,000
Real estate activities	14,000	15,000
Professional scientific & technical activities	50,000	65,000
Admin. & support service activities	85,000	82,000
Public admin. & defence, compulsory social security	86,000	84,000
Education	130,000	135,000
Human health & social work activities	192,000	208,000
Arts, entertainment & recreation	42,000	37,000
Other service activities	43,000	37,000

Source: Statistics Wales

Wales has been hard hit by the global economic downturn. The unemployment rate for the year ending September 2007 was 5.5 per cent, 5.8 per cent in 2008, 8.1 per cent in 2009 and the year ending 30 September 2010 it was 8.2 per cent.

BANKING AND FINANCE

GDP/GNP, Inflation, National Debt
Gross Value Added

Year	£ million	£ per head
2001	33,658	11,565
2002	35,355	12,115
2003	37,299	12,735
2004	38,993	13,247
2005	40,485	13,723
2006	42,424	14,323
2007	44,932	15,097
2008	45,388	15,179
2009	44,371	14,794
2010*	46,320	15,407
2011*	47,340	15,696

The following table shows Gross Value Added in recent years by industry groups at current basic prices. Figures are in £ million:

Sector	2010
Agriculture, hunting, forestry & fishing	154
Production	9,632
Construction	3,286
Wholesale, retail, transport, hotels & food	8,515
Information & communication	1,425
Financial & insurance activities	2,255
Real estate activities	3,867
Professional, scientific & technical activities; admin. & support service activities	3,348
Public admin. defence, education & health	12,338
Other service activities	1,497

Source: Office of National Statistics

Foreign Investment
Investment from companies outside Wales has brought around £14 billion to the Welsh economy, and overseas-owned manufacturing companies employ around 74,000 people.

Balance of Payments / Imports and Exports
Exports in 2012, provisional figures in £ million

Product sector	Q1	Q2	Q3	Q4
Food & live animals	37.6	35.5	44.9	45.7
Beverages & tobacco	2.2	2.9	1.9	1.3
Crude materials, inedible, excl. fuels	12.4	11.1	11.5	10.7
Minerals, fuels, lubricants	1,084.8	1,117.1	1,020.5	244.3
Animals & vegetables oils etc.	0.1	0.1	0.2	0.1
Chemicals & related products	331.9	314.0	305.9	267.5
Manufactured goods	463.1	454.1	468.4	464.8
Machinery & transport equipment	1,180.4	1,136.0	1,084.4	1,103.4
Miscellaneous manufacatured goods	181.8	182.7	179.3	193.3
Commodities not classified elsewhere	24.2	18.6	22.6	22.6
Total	3,318.9	3,272.3	3,139.9	2,353.9

Source: Statistics Wales

The main destinations for Welsh exports are the USA, Germany, Ireland, Belgium and France.

MANUFACTURING, MINING AND SERVICES

Primary and Extractive Industries
Wales traditionally had a large coal mining industry based in the south Wales valleys and north eastern Wales. Although both coal mining and steel production have fallen in recent years, the steel industry is still an important part of the economy; 4.7 million tonnes of steel was produced in 2001, 35 per cent of the total UK output.

The following table shows the value of mining and quarrying of energy producing material to Welsh Gross Value Added:

Year	£ million
1996	103
2000	41
2001	46
2002	39
2003	35
2005	41
2006	46
2007	47

Source: National Statistics Office

Energy
Wales has a nuclear power station at Wylfa in Anglesey, two combined cycle gas turbine plants, two pumped-storage plants and a coal-fired power station. Plans are under way to re-open a coal-fired power station in Newport, build a combined heat and power plant at Shotton and a gas-fired plant at Port Talbot. Figures for 1997 show that Wales produced around 16,000 gWh. Wales has some small scale commercial wind farms and hydro-electric schemes in operation. Plans for a large scale wind farm in north Wales, about 10 miles from the Denbighshire and Conwy coastline, have been approved whilst another wind farm near Porthcawl in South Wales has met with local opposition. In March 2009 work began on a controversial new gas fired power station, the 2,000 MW is located in Pembrokeshire at a cost of £1 billion.

Manufacturing
Wales has seen a decline in its traditional manufacturing base such as steel production. Newer industries have now become important to the economy, notably the vehicle components industry and electronic and electrical industries. Manufacturing makes up 27 per cent of the Welsh GDP compared with just 19 per cent in the UK as a whole. The following table shows the value of the manufacturing sector to Welsh Gross Value Added:

Year	£ million
1996	7,896
2000	7,566
2001	7,429
2002	7,244
2003	7,084
2004	7,147
2005	7,368
2006	7,558
2007	7,904

Source: National Statistics Office

The following table shows the indices of production and construction in percentage, 2009 = 100:

Product	2010	2011	2012*
Mining & quarrying	100.4	126.4	134.2
Food, beverages & tobacco	101.6	95.8	96.1
Textiles, wearing apparal & leather	104.8	105.5	137.2
Wood, paper products & printing	93.0	98.7	90.4
Coke & refined petroleum products	91.8	94.2	87.5
Chemicals & pharmaceuticals	108.1	101.6	109.3
Rubber & plastics & other non-metallic minerals	98.3	90.2	100.9
Basic metals & metal products	87.5	82.0	80.7
Computer & electronic products	126.5	121.5	97.2
Machinery & equipment n.e.c.	140.4	150.4	160.8
Transport equipment	100.5	110.7	102.1
Other manufacturing and repair	113.1	108.4	113.8
Engineering & allied industries	114.9	119.3	106.7
Other manufaturing	105.7	102.5	106.1

Source: National Statistics Office

Tourism
Tourism is a large contributor to the Welsh economy. Figures for 2003 show that visitors spent £1.7 billion.

Agriculture
The following table shows the value of the agriculture, hunting, forestry and fishing sector to Welsh Gross Value Added:

Year	£ million
1996	568
2000	541
2001	487
2002	525
2003	529
2004	435
2005	314
2006	234
2007	202

Source: National Statistics Office

Agricultural Land Use in '000 hectares

Land Use	2010	2011
Total area on agricultural holdings of which	1,710	1,713
Arable land	190	206
Rough grazing	410	404
Permanent grassland	1,021	1,045

Livestock

Livestock	2011
Sheep	8,619,400
Dairy cows	275,200
Non-dairy breeding herd	236,800
Pigs	25,800

Source: Wales in Figures

Production of Crops '000 tonnes

Crop	2008	2009*
Wheat	133.0	139.7
Barley	112.3	133.6
Oats	22.6	23.2
Potatoes	74.6	92.6
*provisional		

Source: Nat. Assembly for Wales: Statistics for Wales

Figures for 2008 show that Wales had 857 registered producers or businesses involved in organic produce.

UNITED KINGDOM

In February 2001 the United Kingdom was hit by foot and mouth disease which led to many animals being slaughtered in order to contain the outbreak. Between February and June Wales had a reported 93 cases.

COMMUNICATIONS AND TRANSPORT

International Airports
Wales has an international airport at Rhoose, just outside Cardiff. It handled 42,000 aircraft in 2006 and over two million passengers. In 2006 plans were unveiled to expand the airport; if the plans go ahead, it is estimated that the number of passengers travelling annually would rise from 1.8 million to 8.0 million by 2030.

Railways
Wales has over 1,700 km. of railways.

Roads
The road network covers over 34,031 km. and includes 4,400 km. of motorway. Recent figures show that 1,697,800 vehicles are licensed.

Ports and Harbours
Main ports in Wales include Milford Haven, Holyhead and Cardiff. There were 8,859 ship arrivals in 2006.

HEALTH

Figures for 2000-01 show that Wales has 135 National Health Service hospitals and seven private hospitals. The Welsh Assembly decides on spending priorities for the NHS. Figures for 2010 show that there were 1,991 general practitioners, 5,330, hospital medical staff including 2,042 were consultants, there were 28,168 nursing, midwifery and health visitors and 1,310 dentists.

EDUCATION

Education (excepting university level) is the responsibility of Secretary of State for Wales. The education system is run on the same lines as England with children starting primary school in the term that they reach five years old. Primary education lasts until the pupil is 11 when they transfer to secondary school. At 16 secondary school pupils sit their General Certificate of Secondary Education, (GCSEs) and can then opt for higher education taking two year Advanced (A Level courses) prior to university or college. The main difference between Welsh and English education is the language of instruction; up to 450 Welsh primary schools have most or all teaching in the Welsh language, as do 22 per cent of secondary schools.

Wales has 12 universities, like the rest of the country fees are payable.

Office of Her Majesty's Inspectorate for Education and Training in Wales, URL: http://www.estyn.gov.uk/home.asp

The following tables shows the number of schools and pupils (LEA schools) in Wales in 2010, (source: Wales in Figures):

School	Number	Pupils
Nursery	25	1,672
Primary	1,462	257,445
Secondary	223	203,907
Special	43	4,117
Independent	64	9,222

RELIGION

Like the rest of the UK Wales is predominantly Christian, and has its own Archbishop, denominations include the Church in Wales, Presbyterian, Catholicism, Baptist and Congregational churches. Non Christians, including Buddhists, Hindus, Jews, Sikhs and Muslims, are mainly situated in the cities.
The Church in Wales, URL: http://www.churchinwales.org.uk/
Archbishop of Wales: Most Reverend Dr Barry Morgan

COMMUNICATIONS AND MEDIA

Newspapers
Wales has one national newspaper the Western Mail, URL: http://www.walesonline.co.uk

Broadcasting
The BBC provides television programmes in Welsh and provides two radio station, BBC Radio Wales and BBC Radio Cymru which broadcasts programmes in Welsh.

There are several commercial radio stations serving Wales including: 103.2 & 97.4 Red Dragon; 96.4 The Wave; Swansea Sound;102.1 Swansea Bay Radio; Nation Radio; Radio Ceredigion; Real Radio.

ENVIRONMENT

Wales has three National Parks: Snowdonia, the Brecon Beacons and the Pembrokeshire coast.

Figures for 2005 show that 48.5 million tonnes of Carbon Dioxide Equivalent were produced by Wales, down from the 1999 figure of 54.4 million tonnes. (Wales in Figures)

CHANNEL ISLANDS

CONSTITUTION AND GOVERNMENT

Constitution
The Channel Islands are a group of small islands and islets off the north-west coast of France. The main islands are Jersey, Guernsey, Alderney and Sark. They are the only portions of the Dukedom of Normandy now belonging to the British Crown. There are two representatives of the Sovereign in the islands, the Lieutenant-Governors of Jersey and of Guernsey and the other islands. These representatives are also Commanders-in-Chief.

LEGAL SYSTEM

Although part of the United Kingdom, each of the Channel Islands has its own legal system and courts based on common law concepts from French-Norman and English law. The islands are not part of the European Union and are therefore not subject to EU legislation. The legal community comprises of locally qualified solicitors and advocates, and foreign lawyers. Both local and foreign lawyers can advise on trusts, corporate and finance law, but only locally qualified Jersey lawyers can appear before the courts.

AREA AND POPULATION

Area
The islands lie in the English Channel just off the coast of France. The total area of the islands is 48,491 acres.

The population of the different islands by the census of 2001 was as follows: Jersey, 87,186; Guernsey, 59,807; Alderney's population was estimated as 2,000; Sark's population was estimated at 450, Herm had 97 residents and Jethou, 3. Recent estimated figures put the total population of the islands at 160,000.

The official languages are French and English. The native language *Patois* is spoken by a small number of islanders.

To view a map of the islands, please consult:
http://www.lib.utexas.edu/maps/cia08/united_kingdom_sm_2008.gif

BANKING AND FINANCE

Channel Islands Stock Exchange (URL: http://www.cisx.com) serves the international finance centres of Guernsey and Jersey.

MANUFACTURING, MINING AND SERVICES

Service Industries
The main contributor to the economy is the finance industry (banking, insurance and trusts). Tourism now extends over much of the year and contributes over a quarter of GNP.

Agriculture
There are manufacturing and horticultural activities. The main agricultural activities are dairy products, flowers and potatoes.

COMMUNICATIONS AND TRANSPORT

National Airlines
Regular air links are maintained between Jersey, Guernsey, and England mainly through London and the south of England. A local air service connects Jersey, Guernsey and Alderney.

Shipping
There is a regular passenger shipping service between Jersey, Guernsey, England (Weymouth nearly every day) and France. Locally operated passenger shipping services connect the islands with France (St Malo). Cargo vessels operate between Jersey, Guernsey, Poole and Portsmouth. Alderney and Sark have privately operated services connecting them with Guernsey.

COMMUNICATIONS AND MEDIA

Broadcasting
There is one television network exclusive to the islands, Channel Television (http://www.channelonline.tv/channelonline/) with regular news stories and features.

GUERNSEY

Bailiwick of Guernsey

Chief Town: St Peter Port (Population estimate: 16,500)

Lieutenant Governor: Air Marshal Peter Walker, CB, CBE

National Flag: The Red Cross of St. George on a white background with a Guernsey Cross (being a representation of the cross on the banner of William of Normandy) in gold on the Red Cross.

CONSTITUTION AND GOVERNMENT

The Lieutenant Governor is Her Majesty's personal representative. The other key offices are those of the Bailiff and Deputy Bailiff, who preside over the States of Deliberation and the Royal Court, and HM Procureur (Attorney General) and HM Comptroller (Solicitor General), who are the legal advisers to the Crown and the States. The Bailiwick is not represented in the UK Parliament. Acts of Parliament do not apply in the Bailiwick unless extended by Order in Council. The UK Government is responsible for the Bailiwick's international representation.

The legislature of Guernsey is called the States of Deliberation. The States, as constituted under the Reform (Guernsey) Laws, 1948 to 1998, consisted of 45 People's Deputies, elected for four years by popular vote; 10 *Douzaine* Representatives, nominated by the parish councils or *Douzaines*; and two Alderney Representatives.

In May 2004 the system was reformed, in order to make the legislature more efficient and improve communication between departments, the 43 committees became 10 departments and four main committees. Each department is headed by a minister all of whom will sit on the Policy Council. There is now an elected Chief Minister who is the Guernsey States representative and will chair the Policy Council, a deputy chief minister will act in his or her absence. The number of elected states members has fallen from 57 to 45. Elections took place in April 2004 after which the changes came into force. The most recent elections took place in April 2008.

States of Deliberation, Sir Charles Frossard House, La Charroterie, St. Peter Port, GY1 1FH, Guernsey, Channel Islands. URL: http://www.gov.gg

> **Policy Council (as at June 2013)**
> *Chief Minister:* Peter Harwood
> *Deputy Chief Minister and Home Minister:* Jonathan P. Le Tocq
> *Treasury and Resources Minister:* Gavin St. Pier
> *Education Minister:* Robert Sillars
> *Commerce and Employment Minister:* Kevin Stewart
> *Social Security Minister:* Allister Langlois
> *Health and Social Service Minister:* Mark H. Dorey
> *Environment Minister:* Roger Domaille
> *Housing Minister:* David B. Jones
> *Culture and Leisure Minister:* Mike O'Hara

Policy Council, St Charles Frossard House, La Charroterie, St Peter Port, Guernsey, GY1 1FH, Channel Islands. Tel: +44 (0)1481 717000, fax: +44 (0)1481 713787, e-mail: policycouncil@gov.gg, URL: http://www.gov.gg

Alderney

Alderney is one of the principal islands of the Bailiwick of Guernsey and is a self-governing and democratic territory. Its legislature is the States of Alderney, which is made up of a President and ten States Members. The President chairs the monthly meetings and stands for election every four years. States Members are in office for a term of four years, and every other year there is an "Ordinary" election at which five of the members may offer themselves for re-election, the most election was held in 2006. Routine matters of Government are dealt with by three Committees, these being Policy & Finance, General Services and Building & Development Control. A small Civil Service team supports the elected members and is responsible for the administration of legal matters, the Island's Treasury and overall public affairs. Two members of the Alderney States also sit on the Guernsey States.

The States of Alderney, PO Box 1, Alderney, GY9 3AA, Channel Islands. Tel: +44 (0)1481 822811, fax: +44 (0)1481 822436, email: states@alderney.net, URL: http://www.alderney.gov.gg
President (December 2012-December 2016): Stuart Trought

Sark

The small island of Sark has its own constitution that dates back over 400 years and is self-governing. The governing body is called the *Chief Pleas*, and is overseen by the *Seigneur*, and also consists of a judge, *Seneschal*, and deputies who are elected every three years. The island is divided into 40 tenements and anyone owning a tenement was also entitled to a seat. The Chief Pleas meets around four times a year. In 2006 a vote was held to determine the future make up of the government. It was decided that landowners would now be reserved 14 seats, which would be elected and 14 seats would be made up of elected people's deputies, therefore the total number of seats would be reduced from 52 to 28.

In December 2008 Sark held its first General Election for the office of Conseillers of the Chief Pleas. Sir David and Sir Frederick Barclay, who own the neighbouring island of Brecqhou as well as having business interests in the islands and on the mainland object to the hereditary post of seigneur, as well as the seneschal who acts as both chief judge and the speaker in the island's government and wanted sweeping reforms. The election did not go the way they

hoped and so they threatened to pull out their businesses on the island including hotels, restaurants and building firms which would leave about a quarter of the population unemployed.

In 2010, the parliament decided to split the feudal role of seneschal of Sark as both president of the government and chief judge.

Office of the Seigneur, La Chasse Marette, Sark, Channel Islands, GY10 1SF. Tel: 44 (0)1481 832118, e-mail: seigneur@gov.sark.gg, URL: http://www.gov.sark.gg
Seigneur: Mr. Michael Beaumont OBE
Seneschal: Jeremy La Trobe-Bateman

LEGAL SYSTEM

Although part of the United Kingdom, Guernsey has its own legal system and courts based on common law concepts from French-Norman and English law. Guernsey is not part of the European Union and are therefore not subject to EU legislation. The legal community comprises of locally qualified solicitors and advocates, and foreign lawyers.

Justice is administered by the Royal Court consisting of the Bailiff, the Jurats and certain Court officials. The Guernsey Court of Appeal hears appeals from the Royal Court in civil and criminal cases. Cases in the Magistrate's Court are heard by a Magistrate or Acting Magistrate sitting alone. The Acting Magistrates are normally appointed from among the Jurats. The Lieutenant-Governor's jurisdiction includes not only Guernsey but also its dependencies: Alderney, Sark and the remaining islets.
Bailiff: Geoffrey Rowland

The Island of Sark has its own court, the *Seneschal's Court*, which has jurisdiction over both civil and criminal cases. The Seneschal is both judge and jury.
Office of The Senechal, Sark, Channel Islands. Tel: +44 (0)1481 832097

LOCAL GOVERNMENT

The Island of Guernsey is divided into ten parishes each of which is headed by a Senior and Junior Constable. The parishes are Castel, Forest, St Andrew, St Martin, St Peter, St Peter Port, St Sampson, St Saviour, Torteval and Vale.

AREA AND POPULATION

Area
The Island of Guernsey is 24.3 sq. miles and it is situated in the English Channel between England and France. There are low hills in the southwest of the island. Winters are mild and summers generally cool. To view a map, please consult http://www.lib.utexas.edu/maps/cia08/guernsey_sm_2008.gif

Alderney
This, the third largest of the Channel Islands, lies about 20 miles north-east of Guernsey. The island covers an area of 1,962 acres. The main town is St Annes.

Sark
This small island lies about eight miles to the east of Guernsey. The area of Sark, including Great and Little Sark, Brecqhou, is 1,348 acres.

Herm, Jethou. Lihou and Brecqhou
Herm Island is around one and a half miles long and half a mile wide, and along with Lihou is owned by the States of Guernsey. Jethou is leased by the States of Guernsey from the Crown, and Brecqhou is the territory of Sark.

Population
The resident population in 2009 was estimated at 65,800. At the time of the 2001 census, the population was 59,807 and, of these, 38,425 were born in Guernsey. Alderney had a population of about 2,000; Sark had a population of about 450; Herm had a population of 97; and Jethou had a population of three.

Births, Marriages, Deaths
In 2009 the birth rate was estimated to be 8.5 per 1,000 population and the death rate to be 10 per 1,000 population. Life expectancy in 2009 was estimated to be 78 years for males and 84 years for females.

EMPLOYMENT

Employment by Economic Sector in March 2009

Sector	Employed
Manufacturing	1,239
Construction	3,964
Utilities	365
Transport	1,160
Hostelry	2,005
Supplier/wholesale	678

UNITED KINGDOM

- continued

Retail	3,844
Personal service	859
Recreation/cultural	475
Finance & legal	7,508
Business services	1,643
Information	768
Health	1,261
Education	364
Public admin.	5,229
Non-profit	267
Other	35
Total	31,664

Guernsey Statistical Office

Figures for June 2009 showed that 431 people were registered as unemployed.

BANKING AND FINANCE

GDP/GNP, Inflation, National Debt
Provisional figures put GDP at £1,665 million in 2007. Per capita GDP was £24,538 in 2005. Figures for March 2007 put inflation at 4.8 per cent. (Source: URL: http://www.gov.gg)

The States Income on Revenue Account was £310 million and th Expedniture on Revenue Account was £292 miillion in 2005.
Guernsey Financial Services Commission, URL: http://www.gfsc.gg

MANUFACTURING, MINING AND SERVICES

Energy
Gas consumption has increased from 77.921 million kilowatt hours to 101.5 million kilowatt hours and the consumption of bottled gas also increased from 1.523 tonnes in 1977 to 3,109 tonnes in 1999. Electricity sales also increased for the same period from 149.175 million kilowatt hours to 273.013 million kilowatt hours. Most of Guernsey's electricity is supplied from France by cable link.

Manufacturing
There are 40 companies active in a variety of engineering, electronics and other light industries, with a total export value of £65,795,000. Figures for 2007 show that the manufacturing sector employed 1,239 people.

Service Industries
The financial services sector accounts for one-third of Guernsey's economy, or if professional services are included, nearly 44 per cent. A low rate of tax and other incentives make it attractive. Guernsey has become Europe's largest centre for offshore insurance activity in the last ten years. Guernsey has around 80 licensed banks and had deposits of nearly £53 billion at the end of 1998. The sector employs 6,000 people.

Tourism
The value of tourism to the island's economy has only increased slightly since 1991, when it stood at £46.9 million compared with just over £50 million in 1998. Over the same period, contribution to GDP decreased from 5.6 per cent in 1991 to 5 per cent in 1998. During the 1990s the number of leisure and business visitors rose slightly from 408,000 in 1992 to 449,000 in 1998. There has also been a noticeable increase in the number of visitors from continental Europe; 8,000 per year visited between 1983 and 1985, rising to 72,000 between 1996 and 1998. Tourism supports around 20 per cent of jobs on the island.

Tourism in Guernsey was suffering in 1998 and 1999, mainly as a result of the state of the British economy and the value of sterling abroad which reduced the number of visitors from within the British Isles. The withdrawal of flights from two British and one Dutch airport also affected tourism. As a result, there was expected to be a reduction of around 5-7 per cent in the number of visitors in 1999 compared with 1998, but the European market has yet to be fully exploited. There was expected to be a steady recovery of the British tourism market in 2000 with the recovery of the UK economy, with a projected rise of 5-10 per cent in the number of visitors to Guernsey from the UK compared with 1999. Figures for 2006 showed that Fuernsey had a total of 316,000 visitors.

States of Guernsey Tourist Board, URL: http://www.visitguernsey.com

Agriculture
Approximately 25 per cent of Guernsey's total land area is used for agriculture. The main income derives from horticultural products, predominantly flowers and tomatoes. The total value of flowers in 1998 was £34.06 million. Flower exports were down by 6.2 per cent in volume terms in 1999. Export prices were therefore expected to fall as prices have not risen to compensate for the decline in volume. Exports of plant production were expected to rise by 10-20 per cent in 1999, and to double by 2000 as a result of the implementation of significant expansion and investment plans by several of the larger companies. In 1998, 2,449 tonnes of tomatoes were produced, worth £3.24 million.

There were 35 dairy units in 1999, with 1,970 cows and 1,292 heifers, which produced 9.883 million litres of milk.

COMMUNICATIONS AND TRANSPORT

International Airports
Passenger movements by air were 859,000 in 1999.

Roads
In 1998 there were 43,242 motor vehicles in Guernsey.

Shipping
There are two harbours: Peter Port and St Sampsons. Although freight entering the harbour of Peter Port has steadily increased the amount going through St Sampsons has decreased to the extent where it now only deals with bulk cargos and fuel shipments. Ships entering the ports in 1994 totalled 205,994 metric tonnes of cargo. Passenger movements by sea were 346,000 in 1999. Ferries run between Guernsey and the other Channel Islands as well as mainland UK and France.

HEALTH

In 2006 there were 16 practising physicians per 1,0000 population. Approximately half were working in primary care. No tertiary level care is available on the island. Life expectancy was estimated at 83.4 years in 2007. Diseases of the respiratory and circulatory systems accounted for most admissions to bed-days in hospitals. Cardiovascular and ischemic heart disease were the main causes of death between 2004-08. The infant mortality rate was estimated to be 3.55 deaths per 1,000 live births.

EDUCATION

There are four schools providing education up to GCSE Advanced Level. Two - Elizabeth College for boys (675) and the Ladies College (542) - are considered as equivalent to direct grant grammar schools; a third is an independent convent school for girls (Blanchelande College, 175 pupils); whilst the other one is a wholly maintained co-ed grammar school (764). In addition there are four secondary schools, plus a College of Further Education, 17 schools providing primary education, four special schools and two private schools. In 1999 the total enrolment figure for primary schools was 4,959, of which 4,352 were in state primary schools, 516 in private schools and 91 in special schools. In the same year the total enrolment figure for secondary schools was 3,752, with 2,702 at state schools, 969 at private schools and 81 at special schools. At Guernsey College for the period 1996-98 there were 215 full time pupils, 3,120 in day release and evening classes and 2,498 at the evening class centre. Education expenditure in 1999 was £38.919 million.

RELIGION

Guernsey is a deanery of the diocese of Winchester. Besides ten rectories, which are in the gift of the Crown, there are several other livings of the Church of England. There are also Roman Catholic and Nonconformist churches.

COMMUNICATIONS AND MEDIA

Newspapers
Guernsey Evening Press and Star, URL: http://www.guernsey-press.com/
Guernsey Globe, URL: http://www.thisisguernsey.com/

Broadcasting
Radio and TV licensing is overseen by the Office of Communications in the UK. Terrestial broadcasts from the UK are available and satellite television is available. The signal will begin switching to digital in 2010. There are two radio stations, Island FM and BBC Radio Guernsey.

Telecommunications
In 2008 it was estimated there were over 45,000 land lines in operation and nearly 44,000 mobile phone subscriptions. Estimates suggest 46,000 internet users.

JERSEY

Bailiwick of Jersey

Chief Town: St. Helier (Population estimate: 28,000)

Lieutenant Governor: Gen. Sir John McColl

National Flag: Argent a Saltire Gules in the honour point an Escutcheon also Gules thereon three Lions passant guardant Or ensigned by an Ancient Crown of Gold.

CONSTITUTION AND GOVERNMENT

Constitution

Jersey is a Crown Dependency and is not part of the UK, nor is it a colony, but it owes allegiance to the British Crown and the UK is responsible for Jersey's defence and international relations. It is not represented in the UK parliament, whose Acts only extend to Jersey if expressly agreed by the Island that they should do so.

The legislature of the island is called 'The States of Jersey', members of which are elected by the population, male and female. The States comprises the Bailiff who is President of the Assembly, the Lieutenant-Governor, 12 Senators, the Constables (Connétables) of the 12 parishes of the Island, 29 Deputies, the Dean of Jersey, the Attorney-General and the Solicitor-General. They all have the right to speak in the Assembly, but only the 53 elected members (the Senators, Connétables and Deputies) have the right to vote; the Bailiff who is appointed by the Crown and acts as Speaker, has a casting vote.

For further information on the constitution, please visit: http://www.cab.org.je/.

Elections took place most recently on 19 October 2011.

The States of Jersey (as of June 2013)
Bailiff, President of the Assembly: Michael Cameron St. John Birt (page 1389)
Deputy Bailiff: William James Bailhache QC
Dean of Jersey: The Very Reverend Robert Frederick Key, B.A.
H.M. Attorney-General: Timothy John Le Cocq QC
Greffier of the States: Michael Nelson de la Haye
Deputy Greffier of the States: Anne Harris
Viscount: Michael Wilkins

Ministers (as at June 2013)
Chief Minister: Sen. Ian Gorst
Minister for Economic Development: Sen. Alan MacLean
Minister for Education, Sport and Culture: Dep. Patrick Ryan
Minister for Home Affairs: Sen. Ian Le Marquand
Minister for Health and Social Services: Dep. Anne Pryke
Minister for Housing: Dep. Andrew Green MBE
Minister for Planning and Environment: Dep. Robert Duhamel
Minister for Social Security: Sen. Francis Le Gresley MBE
Minister for Transport and Technical Services: Dep. Kevin Lewis
Minister for Treasury and Resources: Sen. Philip Ozouf

Government Portal: URL: http://www.gov.je
Office of the Lieutenant Governor, URL: http://www.jersey.com/governmenthouse/About/Pages/default.aspx

LEGAL SYSTEM

Although part of the United Kingdom, Jersey has its own legal system and courts based on common law concepts from French-Norman and English law. The island is not part of the European Union and are therefore not subject to EU legislation.

Justice is administered by the Royal Court, consisting of the Bailiff and 12 Jurats (magistrates). There is a final appeal in certain cases to the Sovereign in Council. There is also a Court of Appeal, which consists of the Bailiff and two judges. Minor civil and criminal cases are dealt with by a stipendiary magistrate.

Jersey abolished the death penalty in 2006.

Bailiff: Michael Birt

LOCAL GOVERNMENT

The Island of Jersey is divided into 12 parishes: Grouville, St. Brelade, St. Clement, St. Helier, St. John, St. Lawrence, St. Martin, St. Mary, St. Ouen, St. Peter, St. Saviour and Trinity, each of which is presided over by an elected Connétable, who deals with issues relating to civil matters, and by a Rector who oversees issues relating to ecclesiastical affairs.

AREA AND POPULATION

Area

Jersey is the largest of the Channel Islands with an area of 118.2 sq. km., situated 14 miles off the north-west coast of France and 85 miles from the English coast. The climate is temperate.

To view a map of Jersey, please consult: http://www.lib.utexas.edu/maps/cia08/jersey_sm_2008.gif

Population

The population according to the 2001 census was 87,186. Figures for 2001 showed that the population density was 750 people per square kilometer, with a third of all residents living in the parish of St Helier. Births in 2004 numbered 1,056 and deaths 748. Figures for mid-2006 showed that the population had risen to 88,200, mainly due to people moving to the island to fill posts in essential services such as health and education. In 2011 the population was estimated to be over 97,500. The median age was estimated to be 40 years with 15 per cent aged 65 years and over. The most recent census was held in 2011 and the population of Jersey was 97,857.

The official language of Jersey has been English since 1960, before which time the official language was French, although this remains a second official language. A Norman-French patois, Jerriais, is also occasionally spoken.

EMPLOYMENT

The following table from Jersey Statistics shows employment by sector in December 2008:

Sector	Employed
Financial and legal activities	13,400
Wholesale and retail trades	8,420
Construction	5,250
Education, health & other services	5,130
Hotels & restaurants	4,590
Other business activities	3,470
Transport, storage & communications	2,670
Agriculture & fishing	1,530
Manufacturing	1,370
Computer & related activities	530
Utilities	530

BANKING AND FINANCE

Currency

Jersey issues its own notes and coinage. The denominations are the same as English notes and coins which are also legal tender on the Island, but designs are unique to Jersey and there is still a £1 note.

GDP/GNP, Inflation, National Debt

Jersey is economically self-sufficient and does not receive subsidies from, nor pays contributions to the UK or the EU. The public revenues of the Island are raised by income tax, by duties paid on certain goods and by other tazes. VAT is not charged in the Channel Islands. Jersey also has Double Taxation Arrangements with theUK and Guernsey. It also has its own Customs and Excise Service.

Figures for 2007 show that Gross Value Added (GVA) was £4.1 billion, GNI was £3.7 billion and GDP was £2.61 billion. The GNI per head of population was £41,000. Figures for 2011 put GVA at £3.6 billion.

The state General Funds income was £559 million. Net revenue expenditure was £480 million and income tax returns was £430 million. (Source: http://www.gov.je)

Contribution to GVA by sector (2011)

Sector	%
Finance Industry	50
Other business activities	15.5
Public administration	8.8
Wholesale and retail	7.4
Construction	6.5
Tourism	3.6
Agriculture	1.3
Manufacturing	1.5

Jersey Financial Services Commission

The 'Commission' is a statutory corporate body that is responsible to the States of Jersey. There are eight commissioners, which include practitioners from within the finance industry, users of the industry and representatives of the public interest.
Jersey Financial Services Commission, URL: http://www.jerseyfsc.org/

MANUFACTURING, MINING AND SERVICES

Jersey is a service based economy with very little manufacturing or quarry activity. The key industry is finance, accounting for half of the economic output. Traditional industries such as agriculture and tourism are facing strong international competition.

UNITED KINGDOM

Tourism
In 2007 Jersey had 375,860 staying visitors and 94,050 day trippers, Revenue from tourism for that year was £234 million compared to £238 million in 2002. The total number of registered establishments hotel and guest house bedrooms in 2004 was 13,693.

Jersey Tourism, URL: http://www.jersey.com

Agriculture
Nearly half of all land in Jersey is used for agricultural purposes. The total output of agriculture exports in 2007 was over £30 million. The main crops grown are potatoes and tomatoes. Dairy farming is important to the economy. Value of fish landed was £6,100,000 in 2003. Figures for 2007 show that the make up of agricultural exports was: potatoes, 78 per cent; tomatoes, 14 per cent; other vegetables, 4 per cent; narcissus, 2 per cent; other flowers, 1 per cent; sweet peppers, 1 per cent. (Source: http://www.gov.je/EconomicDevelopment)

COMMUNICATIONS AND TRANSPORT

Jersey Transport Authority, PO Box 843, St Helier, Jersey, JE4 0UT, Channel Islands. Tel: +44 (0)1534 603730, fax: +44 (0)1534 603731

International Airports
The Jersey Airport is situated at St. Peter. It covers approximately 375 acres.

Aircraft Movements (2004)

Aircraft Movements	No.
Total aircraft movements	71,648
Passengers	1,496,805

Shipping
All vessels arriving in Jersey from outside Jersey waters report at St. Helier or Gorey on first arrival. There is a harbour of minor importance at St. Aubin. The number of commercial vessels entering St. Helier in 2004 was 2,924 with a total of 404,951 passengers (excluding yachtsmen). The number of visiting yachts in 2004 was 7,652.

Ferries run between the Channel Islands as well as to the south coast of England and France.

HEALTH

Jersey has a higher proportion of doctors per population than the UK, and one of the highest levels in Europe at 28 doctors per 100 population. Life expectancy was estimated at 81.4 per cent in 2011. The infant mortality rate was estimated at 4 per 1,000 live births.

EDUCATION

In total, there are 24 primary schools, plus two SEN schools (including Victoria College and Jersey College for Girls) and seven secondary schools (including VC and JCG). Victoria College, which is a Headmaster's Conference School, and the Jersey College for Girls have independent governing bodies. There are local facilities for further and part-time education in a wide range of cultural and vocational subjects and a scheme of awards to students attending universities and other institutions of further education in the United Kingdom.

Figures for private schools as of March 2005 were as follows: pre-school 1; primary 7; secondary 3.

Pupil figures (March 2005)

School	No. of pupils
Primary	
Non-fee paying	5,059
Primary SEN	60
Fee paying (VC and JCG)	646
Private	1,321
Total	7,086
Secondary	
Non-fee paying	3,618
Secondary SEN	78
Fee paying (VC and JCG)	1,369
Private	1,087
Total	6,152

RELIGION

Jersey is a Deanery attached to the Diocese of Winchester. There are twelve Rectorial Parishes, which are in the gift of the Crown. There are also six district Churches which are in the gift of other patrons. There are also Methodist and Roman Catholic Churches and Churches of various other Denominations. There is a Jewish Community with a Synagogue.

COMMUNICATIONS AND MEDIA

Newspapers
Jersey Evening Post, URL: http://www.jerseyeveningpost.com/

Broadcasting
Jersey is in the process of switching from an analogue signal to digital. BBC Jersey (URL: http://www.bbc.co.uk/jersey/) provides local television news. There is an independent television station in Jersey which services the other Channel Islands. Satellite television is also available. There are two local radio stations, BBC Radio Jersey, which opened in 1982, and an independent radio station, Channel 103 (URL: http://www.channel103.com/).

Telecommunications
The system is still state-owned. It is in the process of being modernised. Main lines in use were estimated at 74,000 in 2008 and mboile phones at 83,000. An estimated 29,000 were internet users in 2008.

ENVIRONMENT

Jersey's surface area in 118.2 square kilometres and is divided into 12 civil parishes, ranging in size from St Clement at 4.2 square kilometres to St Ouen at 15 square kilometres. In 1997 more than one fifth of the land area was developed, one fifth was grassland and less than one third arable.

In 2003, final energy demand in Jersey was nearly 2.2 TWh. Most of the energy required to meet Jersey's primary energy needs are imported.

ISLE OF MAN

Capital: Douglas (Population estimate: 26,000)

Head of State: Her Majesty Queen Elizabeth II (page 1420)

Lieutenant Governor: Adam Wood

Flag: Red flag charged with three conjoined armoured legs in white and gold.

CONSTITUTION AND GOVERNMENT

Constitution
The Isle of Man is a small island in the Irish Sea, almost midway between England and Ireland. The Queen is the head of state and has the title Lord of Mann. She is represented by a Lieutenant Governor. The Island is not bound by Acts of the United Kingdom Parliament, unless specially mentioned in them. It has its own Legislature called Tynwald consisting of the Legislative Council and the House of Keys. Under the chairmanship of the President of Tynwald the Legislative Council consists of the Bishop of Sodor and Man, the Attorney-General, and eight members appointed by the House of Keys, one of whom is elected to be President of the Council. The Isle of Man is autonomous and does not belong to the EU but enjoys a special relationship under Protocol 3, which allows for free trade in agricultural and manufactured products with member countries.
The House of Keys consists of 24 members, elected by the adult population. The six sheadings, or divisions, return nine of these members, the capital, Douglas, returns eight, Onchan returns three, Ramsey returns two, and Peel and Castletown send one member each to the House of Keys. The Council of Ministers consists of the Chief Minister and the ministers of the nine major Departments of Government. The House of Keys is elected every five years. When Bills have been passed by both branches of the Legislature they are submitted for Royal Assent.

For further information on the constitution, please visit: http://www.gov.im/isleofman/constitution.xml

Tynwald
Legislative Buildings, Douglas, IMI 3PW, Isle of Man. Tel: +44 (0)1624 685500, fax: +44 (0)1624 685504, e-mail: enquiries@tynwald.org.im, URL: http://www.tynwald.org.im
President of Tynwald: Clare Christian BSc MLC
Deputy President: Stephen Rodan SHK
Clerk of Tynwald: R.I.S. Philips LLB
The Lord Bishop of Sodor and Man: Canon Robert Paterson

House of Keys
Speaker of the House: Hon. Stephen Charles Rodan BSc MR Pharm S SHK
Secretary to the House of Keys: R.I.S. Phillips LLB

Council of Ministers (as at June 2013)
Chief Minister: Hon. Allan Bell
Minister of Health: Hon.. David M. Anderson
Minister of Education and Children: Hon. Timothy Crookall
Minister of Economic Development: Hon. John Shimmin (page 1514)
Minister of Food, Agriculture and the Environment: Phil Gawne
Minister of Community, Culture and Leisure: Hon. Graham Cregeen
Minister of Social Care: Hon. Chris Robertshaw
Minister of the Treasury: Hon. Eddie Teare
Minister of Home Affairs: Hon. Juan Watterson
Minister of Infrastructure: Hon. David Cretney

Ministries
Government portal: URL: http://www.gov.im

Lieutenant Governor's Office, Government House, Onchan, IM3 1RR, Isle of Man. Tel: +44 (0)1624 620146, fax: +44 (0)1624 663707, URL: http://www.gov.im/cso/crown/office_gov.xml
The Treasury, Government Office, Douglas IM1 3PG, Isle of Man. Tel: +44 (0)1624 685685, fax: +44 (0)1624 685538, e-mail: treasuryadmin@gov.im, URL: http://www.gov.im/treasury
Attorney General's Chambers, New Wing, Victory House, Prospect Hill, Douglas IM1 3PP, Isle of Man. Tel: +44 (0)1624 685452, fax: +44 (0)1624 629162
Clerk of the Tynwald's Office, Government Office, Douglas IM1 3PG, Isle of Man. Tel: +44 (0)1624 685685
Chief Minister's Office, Government Office, Douglas IM1 3PG, Isle of Man. Tel: +44 (0)1624 685685, fax: +44 (0)1624 626416

Departments

Government portal, URL: http://www.gov.im
Department of Agriculture, Fisheries and Forestry, Murray House, Douglas IM1 3PG, Isle of Man. Tel: +44 (0)1624 685839, fax: +44 (0)1624 685851, URL: http://www.gov.im/daff/
Department of Education, St. George's Court, Upper Church Street, Douglas IM1 2SG, Isle of Man. Tel: +44 (0)1624 685820, fax: +44 (0)1624 685834, URL: http://www.gov.im/education
Department of Health, Markwell House, Market Street, Douglas IM1 2RZ, Isle of Man. Tel: +44 (0) 1624 685028, fax: +44 (0) 1624 685130, URL: http://www.gov.im/health/
Department of Home Affairs, Homefield, 88 Woodbourne Road, Douglas, IM2 3AP Isle of Man. Tel: +44 (0)1624 623355, fax: +44 (0)1624 621298, URL: http://www.gov.im/dha/
Department of Tourism and Leisure, Sea Terminal, Douglas IM1 2RG, Isle of Man. Tel: +44 (0)1624 686801, URL: http://www.gov.im/tourism
Department of Trade and Industry, Illiam Dhone House, 2 Circular Road, Douglas, IM1 1PQ, Isle of Man. Tel: +44 (0)1624 685675, fax: +44 (0)1624 685683, URL: http://www.gov.im/dti
Department of Infrastructure, Douglas, Isle of Man. Tel: +44 (0)1624 686600, URL: http://www.gov.im/transport/

Elections

Elections are held every five years, the most recent being in November 2011. As of 2006, residents aged 16 and 17 are eligible to vote.

LEGAL SYSTEM

The Manx legal system is unique to the island but is based on English common law principles. Criminal law, as well as contract, tort and family law, are all very similar to English law, but taxation law, company law and financial supervision laws have been developed to meet the specific requirements of the Island.

The High Court has three separate divisions, The Chancery Division, Common Law Division and the Family Division. The Court of General Gaol deals with criminal cases, and the Summary Courts include Magistrate, Juvenile and Licensing Courts. There are two High Court Judges, *Deemsters*, who have jurisdiction over all criminal and civil matters and also sit at the Manx Appeal Court along with a Judge of Appeal and an English QC.

LOCAL GOVERNMENT

For administrative purposes the Isle of Man is divided into 24 local authorities, consisting of four town authorities, two district authorities, three village authorities and 15 parish authorities.

AREA AND POPULATION

Area

The island, which lies in the Irish Sea between Ireland and England, is about 33 miles in length and has a maximum width of 13 and a half miles. It covers an area of 141,263 acres (227 sq. miles). A smaller island called the Calf of Man is situated off the southern tip. The climate is temperate with cool summers and mild winters.

To view a map of the island, please consult:
http://www.lib.utexas.edu/maps/cia08/isle_of_man_sm_2008.gif

Population

Figures from the 2001 census show that the population of the Isle of Man was 76,315, an increase of over 9 per cent from the 1991 census. 19 per cent was aged 15 or under and 19 per cent was retired. Around a third of the population, 25,347, were resident in the capital Douglas. Main towns include Onchan with a population of 8,656, Ramsey (6,874), Peel (3,819), Port Erin (3,218) and Castletown (2,958). The population was estimated to be 84,000 in 2011. Life expectancy in 2011 was estimated to be 79 years for males and 82 years for females. The median age was 42 years.

Public Holidays 2014

Public holidays in the Isle of Man are the same as for the UK with the addition of:
6 June: TT Race
6 July: Tynwald Day

EMPLOYMENT

The unemployment rate in 2006 was put at 2.4 per cent.

Total Employment by Economic Activity

Occupation	2006
Agriculture, hunting & forestry	699
Fishing	111
Mining & quarrying	82
Manufacturing	2,096
Electricity, gas & water supply	605
Construction	3,239
Wholesale & retail trade, repairs	5,103
Hotels & restaurants	1,538
Transport, storage & communications	3,208
Financial intermediation	6,824
Real estate, renting & business activities	4,706
Public admin. & defence; compulsory social security	2,706
Education	2,794
Health & social work	4,250
Other community, social & personal service activities	2,680
Households with employed persons	153
Other	19

Source: Copyright © International Labour Organization (ILO Dept. of Statistics, http://laborsta.ilo.org)

BANKING AND FINANCE

Currency

The Isle of Man uses Sterling in common with the rest of the UK, but produces its own coins and notes.

GDP/GNP, Inflation, National Debt

The Isle of Man is an established finance centre. In order to encourage investment, there is a zero rate business tax strategy. It is currently in its 25th year of consecutive growth.

Income generated in basic sectors (current prices)

Sector	2005/06	%	2006/07	%
Manufacturing	138,949	8	135,587	7
Finance	599,806	35	670,688	36
Construction	140,487	8	134,124	7
Agriculture & Fisheries	19,013	1	19,177	1
Public Administration	75,085	4	84,982	5
Prof. & Scientific services	305,775	18	347,521	19
ICT	43,080	3	43,939	2
Tourist industry	97,490	6	98,648	5
Other services	289,554	17	314,707	17
Total	1,709,240	100	1,849,373	100

Source: Treasur, Economic Affairs Div.

GDP per capita was £22,587 in 2006/07, compared to £19,430 for the UK as whole.

In 2006 the inflation rate was 3.0 per cent, rising to 4.2 per cent in 2007, and 5.2 per cent in 2008.

The Government is aiming to provide a capital investment programme of almost £300 million over the next five years to aid health, water and the sewerage system, without raising taxes.

Tax

Standard rate income tax is 12 per cent levied on the first £10,000 and 18 per cent on the balance. Single person's income tax allowance is £7,700 and the combined allowance for a married couple is £15,400. Companies are liable at 20 per cent on their taxable income. The rate of tax is lower than mainland UK and as such the Isle of Man has been viewed at a tax haven. In 2000 the Isle of Man was one of the 35 countries named by the OECD as a tax haven. The countries named had until 2003 to co-operate with the OECD in having more transparent banking and tax arrangements and to reform their programmes by 2005.

Trade Restrictions

The Isle of Man has a 'special relationship' with the European Community and participates in the principle of free trade within the Community. The Isle of Man does not contribute to EC funds and is not eligible for aid from these funds.

Business Addresses

Financial Supervision Commission, URL: http://www.gov.im/FSC/
Isle of Man Customs & Excise, URL: http://www.gov.im/customs
Chamber of Commerce, URL: http://www.iomchamber.org.im/

MANUFACTURING, MINING AND SERVICES

Primary and Extractive Industries

Some slate, sand and limestone quarrying is carried out.

Energy

Gas is supplied by **Manx Gas Ltd**, URL: http://www.manxgas.com.
Manx Electricity Authority, URL: http://www.gov.im/MEA
Isle of Man Water Authority, URL: http://www.gov.im/water

STATES OF THE WORLD

UNITED KINGDOM

Manufacturing

Government policy has been to diversify the economy. A variety of grants and loans has been offered to industry satisfying certain environmental criteria and this has led to the development of a sound manufacturing base. Manufacturing contributes around 6 per cent to the island's GDP and products include aerospace products, laser optics, industrial diamonds, electronics, plastics and precision engineering.

Service Industries

The tourist industry provides about 6 per cent of National Income, and although an important employer of labour it is far less dominant than in the past. There has been rapid growth in the banking, financial and professional services sector, which employs one fifth of the workforce and contributes over one-third of the National Income. In recent years online gambling sites have moved to the Isle of Man and have started contributing to the economy. The film industry has also made contributions with several films using the island for locations.

Agriculture

The traditional industries of agriculture and fishing now employ 4 per cent of the total workforce and contribute 2 per cent of Manx National Income. Main agricultural exports include meat, cheese, flowers and cereals. Over 4,000 hectares are given over to cereal production and the island has 13,000 cows and 66,000 ewes.

COMMUNICATIONS AND TRANSPORT

Visa Information

British and Republic of Ireland citizens do not require a passport or visa to visit. EU citizens require their ID cards and visitors from non EU countries require a passport and should check with the Island regarding visa requirements before travelling.

International Airports

The airport of the Isle of Man is Ronaldsway Airport at Castletown and around 700,000 passengers a year pass through it. Daily sea and air services operate between the Island and various points in the United Kingdom and Eire.
Ronaldsway Airport, URL: http://www.gov.im/airport

Airlines include BA, Euromanx Ltd and Flybe.
BA, http://www.ba.com
Flybe, URL: http://www.flybe.com

Roads

The total length of road is approximately 450 miles.

Railways

There are 15 miles of steam railway still operating and 23 miles of double track for electric trams.

Ports and Harbours

The main port is Douglas, which can accommodate roll-on roll-off ferries as well as cargo ships, and has deep water berths. The main sea routes are Douglas to Liverpool, Douglas to Heysham, Douglas to Belfast and Douglas to Dublin.
Harbour Authority, URL: http://www.gov.im/harbours
Marine Administration, URL: http://www.gov.im/dti/shipping

HEALTH

The main hospital is Noble's Hospital, a 314 bed facility. There is also a Cottage Hospital at Ramsey. Life expectancy is estimated at 78.8 years. The infant mortality rate was estimated at 5.37 deaths per 1,000 live births. A reciprocal health agreement with the UK ended in 2011 and visitors to the Isle of Man including UK citizens will now be expected to pay for treatment (excluding immediate necessary and emergency treatment).

EDUCATION

There are 34 primary schools, five comprehensive co-educational secondary schools, one special school and a college of further education. In addition, King William's College and the Buchan School for girls are public schools, the college being independent and co-educational.

COMMUNICATIONS AND MEDIA

Newspapers

The Isle of Man Newspapers publishes three weekly title: Isle of Man Examiner, Isle of Man Courier and The Manx Independent.
Isle of Man Newspapers, URL: http://www.iomtoday.co.im/

Broadcasting

Radio and television is licensed by the Isle of Man Communications Commissions. Ofcom overseas frequencies. Commercial radio exists: Manx Radio is a public broadcaster funded by advertising and government grants. No local TV station exists but radio and television services received via relays from British broadcasters.
Manx Radio, public broadcaster, URL: http://www.manxradio.com

ANGUILLA

Principal Town: The Valley (Population estimate: 1,400)

Governor: H.E. Mr Alistair Harrison (page 1438)

Flag: British blue ensign with dolphin badge coat of arms in the fly

CONSTITUTION AND GOVERNMENT

Until December 1980 Anguilla was *de jure* part of the Associated State of St. Kitts, Nevis and Anguilla, but was administered as a separate British dependent territory under the Anguilla (Constitutional) Order 1976 made under the powers conferred by the Anguilla Act 1971. It is now formally a separate overseas territory with a separate Constitution and ministerial form of Government under HM Governor as provided for in the 1982 Constitution. The Governor is thus still responsible for external affairs, defence and internal security, while most government functions are in the hands of an Executive Council headed by a Chief Minister. The constitution was amended in 1990. In 2006 a Constitutional and Electoral Reform Commission was set up to look into the Constitutional reform process.

To consult the constitution, please visit:
http://www.gov.ai/documents/Anguilla%20Constitution%20Draft%202009.pdf

International Relations

Anguilla is a self-governing UK Overseas Territory and as a result has close ties with the UK. Anguilla is an associate member of CARICOM and the Organisation of Eastern Caribbean States.

Recent Events

From 1958 to 1962 Anguilla was administered by the United Kingdom as a single federation with St Kitts and Nevis. Anguillans felt they were unfairly represented by the government based in St. Kitts and wished to keep their close links with the UK. They wanted to separate from the federation with St Kitts. Anguilla came under direct British rule in the 1970s and became a separate British Dependent Territory in 1980.

Legislature

The Anguillan legislature is unicameral with the House of Assembly consisting of 12 members, seven are directly elected, two are nominated and the Attorney General, Deputy Governor and the speaker. Members serve a term of five years.
House of Assembly, The Valley, Anguilla. URL: http://www.gov.ai

> **Executive Council (as at May 2013)**
> *Chairman (The Governor):* H.E. Mr Alistair Harrison (page 1438)

> Chief Minister, Minister for Finance, Economic Development, Investment and Tourism: Hubert Hughes (page 1445)
> Deputy Chief Minister and Minister for Social Development: Edison Baird
> Minister for Infrastructure, Communications, Utilities, Housing, Agriculture and Fisheries: Evans Gumbs
> Minister for Home Affairs, Natural resources, Lands and Physical Planning: Jerome C. Roberts

Ministries

Most ministries are based at The Secretariat, The Valley, Anguilla. Tel: +1 264 497 2451, URL: http://www.gov.ai

Political Parties

Anguilla National Strategic Alliance
Anguilla United Front (Anguilla National Alliance and Anguilla Democratic Party), URL: http://www.unitedfront.ai/
Anguilla United Movement
Anguilla Progressive Party
Anguilla Strategic Alliance

Elections

The most recent election took place in February 2010. The Anguilla United Movement won four of the seven seats, coming to power for the first time in 10 years, beating the ruling United Front party. The next election is due in March 2015.

LEGAL SYSTEM

The Law of Anguilla is based on the Common Law of England. There is also local legislation. Anguilla comes under the jurisdiction of the Eastern Caribbean Supreme Court.

The judiciary consists of a Magistrate's Court, a High Court and the Court of Appeal of the Eastern Caribbean Supreme Court of Justice. There is a final right of appeal to the Privy Council in the UK. The Attorney General, Customs and the Royal Anguilla Police Force are accountable to the Governor.

The following Human Rights Conventions have been extended to Anguilla as a British Overseas Territory: European Convention on Human Rights (ECHR), UN Convention against Torture (UNCAT), UN Convention on the Rights of the Child (UNCRC), UN Convention on the Elimination of Racial Discrimination (CERD). Anguilla has not yet requested that the Convention on the Elimination of Discrimination Against Women be extended to cover the island.

AREA AND POPULATION

Area

Like St. Kitts and Nevis, Anguilla was probably first sighted by Columbus in 1493. It was colonised in 1650, and has remained British since then. The island is 16 miles long, and has a maximum width of three miles. There are several small uninhabited off-shore islands - Dog, Scrub and Sombrero Islands being the main ones. Anguilla forms the northern tip of the Leeward Islands in the eastern Caribbean and is situated five miles north of St Martin and 25 miles east of the British Virgin Islands. It is a flat island of coral limestone rock formation covered with low scrub, with a few plantations of fruit trees. In common with most other Caribbean low lying coraline islands, water is a scarce resource. The average annual temperature is 80F and the average annual rainfall is 36 inches.

To view a map, consult http://www.lib.utexas.edu/maps/cia08/anguilla_sm_2008.gif

Population

The population was estimated to be 16,500 in 2011 with an estimated annual growth rate of 2.2 per cent. The capital, The Valley, has a population of around 1,400. The birth rate was estimated to be 13 per 1,000 population and the death rate 4.4 per 1,000 population. Life expectancy was estimated to be 80 years.

Public Holidays 2014

1 January: New Year's Day
18 April: Good Friday
21 April: Easter Monday
1 May: Labour Day
9 June: Whit Monday
30 May: Anguilla Day
9 June: Celebration of the Birthday of HM The Queen
4 August: August Monday (start of Carnival week)
10 August: Constitution Day
14 August: August Thursday
19 December: Separation Day
25 December: Christmas Day
26 December: Boxing Day

EMPLOYMENT

The majority of the working population is employed in the commerce and service sectors. The unemployment rate was estimated at 8.0 per cent in 2002.

The following table shows how the population was employed in 2001.

Employment by Occupation

Occupation	2001
Professional, technical & related workers	369
Administrative & managerial	551
Clerical & related workers	569
Sales workers	842
Service workers	1,314
Agriculture	270
Production workers, transport & labourers	1,639
Other	90
Total	5,644

Source: International Labour Organization

BANKING AND FINANCE

Currency

The unit of currency is the Eastern Caribbean Dollar. The US$ is also accepted.

GDP/GNP, Inflation, National Debt

There are limited but up-market tourist facilities. Other sectors contributing to the national income are agriculture and fisheries, banking and insurance. Anguilla has a growing offshore finance sector. GDP is made up of 78 per cent service sector, 18 per cent industry and four per cent agriculture. Estimated figures for 2006 put GDP at US$158.2 million, giving a per capita figure of US$9,710. Growth that year was an estimated 15.4 per cent. Estimated figures for 2009 put GDP at US$297.2 million, giving a per capita figure of US$18,623. GDP grew by -13.1 per cent that year. Per capita GDP was estimated at US$12,500 in 2008. The inflation rate in 2010 was put at 1.1 per cent.

Balance of Payments / Imports and Exports

Estimated figures for 2010 put exports earnings at US$11.5 million down from US$26.0 million in 2009. Figures for 2010 put trade and investment with the UK as exports to Anguilla: £563, 260 and imports from Anguilla, £185,661. Main trading partners are the USA and Eastern Caribbean countries. The main exported goods are lobster, fish, rum, livestock, salt, and concrete blocks. Estimated figures for 2010 put the cost of imports at US$175 million up from US$152 million in 2009. Main imported goods are fuels, foodstuffs, manufactured good, chemicals, trucks, and textiles.

MANUFACTURING, MINING AND SERVICES

Tourism

Tourism provides over 40 per cent of the island's revenue and the beaches are a popular tourist attraction. Recent figures show that Anguilla has around 107,000 visitors mainly from the USA and other Caribbean countries.

Financial Industries

The offshore financial services industries is a growing business sector and currently provides approximately £2 million in revenue.

Agriculture

Approximately 400 tonnes of fish, lobster and crayfish are caught annually. In 1997 an offshore fisheries development project was started. Anguilla has a 200 nautical mile fishing exclusion zone. Vegetables and a small amount of tobacco are grown on the island.

COMMUNICATIONS AND TRANSPORT

Travel Requirements

Anyone travelling to Anguilla require a passport valid for at least six months except nationals of the USA who require an original birth certificate and official photo ID. A visa is not required by US, Australian, Canadian and EU citizens

Airports

Flight connections are maintained through Wallblake Airport. Anguilla has tarred and gravel/earth roads totalling about 80 miles. The main port is Road Bay.

Roads

Vehicles are driven on the left.

Ports and Harbours

Ferry services operate to nearby St Martin/St Maarten, Blowing Point Ferry Terminal is a port of entry.

HEALTH

The health care delivery system consists of a public and private sector. The public sector services include primary health care and secondary health care. Each of Anguilla's five health districts has a health center providing primary health care and basic core services, including maternal and child health, family planning, immunization, nutrition advice, care of the elderly, management of chronic diseases, health education, and environmental health. Basic medical clinics are conducted semiweekly by a medical doctor. There is a 36-bed hospital. Patients requiring specialized hospital care are referred to neighboring islands at the expense of the Government.

In 2000, medical professionals included: 9 doctors, 40 nurses, 2 dentists, 4 dental therapists/nurses, 3 dental assistants, 3 pharmacists, and 5 environmental health officers. Approximately 14 per cent of the government's budget is spent on health care.

EDUCATION

Education in Anguilla between the ages of 5 and 17 is compulsory. There were six government primary schools and one secondary school with a total of about 2,650 pupils in 1998. According to UNESCO figures, government spending on education in 2005 was the equivalent of 4.0 per cent of GDP or 14 per cent of total government expenditure of which 50 per cent was spent on secondary education.

RELIGION

The majority of the population belongs to the Christian faith (90 per cent), the main denominations being Anglican and Methodist. Approximately 0.6 per cent of the population is Muslim. Anguilla has a religious tolerance rating of 10 on a scale of 1 to 10 (10 is most freedom). (Source: World Religion Database)

COMMUNICATIONS AND MEDIA

Newspapers

There are two weekly news papers, The Light (URL: http://www.thelightanguilla.com) and The Anguillian (URL: http://www.anguillian.com).

Broadcasting

There is a privately owned 24 hour cable television service using US satellite programming. Both government-owned and independent radio stations broadcast on the island.
Radio Anguilla, URL: http://www.radioaxa.com/

Telecommunications

The island's telecommunications network is linked by submarine cable to many other islands in the eastern Caribbean. There is microwave radio relay to Saint Martin. Recent figures show that there are over 26,000 mobile phones in use and some 6,200 landlines.

Recent figures show that in 2009 Anguilla had approximately 3,700 regular internet users.

ENVIRONMENT

Anguilla has one of the most important, largely unbroken, coral reefs in the eastern Caribbean. It is also susceptible to hurricanes from June to November.

BERMUDA

Capital: Hamilton (Population estimate: 3,400)

Governor: George Fergusson (page 1424)

Flag: Red with the British red ensign in the upper hoist-side quadrant with shield of arms in the fly

CONSTITUTION AND GOVERNMENT

Constitution
According to the Spanish navigator and historian Ferdinand d'Oviedo, who sailed close to the islands in 1515, they were discovered by Juan de Bermudez, after whom they were named. No steps were taken to form a settlement on the islands and they were still uninhabited when, in 1609, Admiral George Somers' ship, the 'Sea Venture', was wrecked on one of the sunken reefs which surround the islands. The Virginia Company was granted an extension of the charter by King James I to include the islands within its dominion but shortly afterwards the Company sold the islands for the sum of £2,000 to a new body of adventurers called 'The Governor and Company of the City of London for the Plantation of the Somers' Islands'. The Bermuda parliament dates from 1620. The government of the Colony passed to the Crown in 1684.

To consult the constitution, please visit: http://www.ombudsman.bm/links.html.

International Relations
Bermuda is a member of the Commonwealth and has strong trade links with the USA.

Recent Events
In 1995 there was a referendum on independence: 25 per cent of the voters voted for, and over 73 per cent voted against independence. In 2004 Alex Scott called for a debate on the issue of independence and the Bermuda Independence Commission was formed. An opinion poll on the subject was carried out in 2007 and support for self governance was 25 per cent.

In October 2010, Ewart Brown stood down as Premier and the PLP elected Finance Minister Paula Cox to succeed him.

Legislature
A new constitution was introduced on 8 June 1968. The Governor, appointed by the Crown, retains responsibility for external affairs, defence, the police and internal security. The Cabinet and the Premier are appointed from the House of Assembly except that a maximum of two Ministers must be appointed from the Senate. The House is elected under universal adult suffrage, on the basis of two Members from each of 20 constituencies. The senate consists of five senators appointed by the Premier, three by the Opposition Leader and three at the Governor's discretion.
URL: http://www.gov.bm

Cabinet (as at June 2013)
Premier and Minister of Finance: Hon. Craig Cannonier, JP
Deputy Premier, Minister of Public Safety: Hon. Michael Dunkley, JP
Attorney General and Minister of Legal Affairs: Hon. Mark Pettingill JP
Minister of Environment and Planning: Hon. Sylvan Richards JP
Minister of Health and Seniors: Hon. Patricial Gordon-Pamplin JP
Minister of Education: Senator Hon. Nalton Brangman JP
Minister of Finance: Hon. Edward. T. Richards JP
Minister of Home Affairs: Senator Hon. Michael Fahy JP
Minister of Transport and Tourism: Hon. Shawn Crockwell, JP
Minister of Economic Development: Dr. The Hon. Grant Gibbons, JP
Minister of Community and Cultural Development: Hon. Wayne Scott JP
Minister of Home Affairs: Hon. Michael Fahy JP
Minister without Portfolio: Hon. Leah K. Scott JP

Ministries
Government portal, URL: http://www.gov.bm
Ministry of Education, Dundonald Place, 14 Dundonald Street, Hamilton, Bermuda. Tel: +441 278 3300, URL: http://www.moeb.bm
Ministry of Telecommunications and E-Commerce, FB Perry Building, 2nd Floor, 40 Church Street, Hamilton HM12, Bermuda. Tel: +441 292 4595, e-mail: getelecom@gov.bm, URL: http://www.mtec.bm/portal/server.pt

Political Parties
Progressive Labour Party (PLP), Alaska Hall, 16 Court Street, Hamilton, HM 17, Bermuda. Tel: +441 292 2264, fax: +441 295 7890, email: infp@plp.bm, URL: http://www.plp.bm
Leader: Hon. Paula Cox
One Bermuda Alliance (alliance of the United Bermuda Party and the Bermuda Democratic Alliance), URL: http://www.oba.bm
Leader: Senator Craig Cannonier

Elections
The most recent election was held in December 2012. The One Bermuda Alliance party won 19 seats, and the Progressive Labour Party won 17 seats.

Representative of the Foreign & Commonwealth Office
Deputy Governor's Office, Government House, 11 Langton Hill, Pembroke HM 13, Bermuda. Tel: +1 441 292 2587, fax: +1 441 295 3823, email: depgov@ibl.bm

LEGAL SYSTEM

The legal system is based upon English Common Law. Together with a number of tribunals, Bermuda has a three-tier court system consisting of a Magistrates Court, with a mainly criminal jurisdiction; a Supreme Court, with a civil and criminal jurisdiction, and a Court of Appeal. There is a further right of appeal to the Privy Council in London.

The government respects and protects its citizens' human rights. Bermuda officially abolished the use of the death penalty and judicial corporal punishment on 23 December 1999.

Office of the Ombudsman, URL: http://www.ombudsman.bm/

LOCAL GOVERNMENT

Bermuda is divided into nine parishes or counties (Devonshire, Hamilton, Paget, Pembroke, Sandy's, Smith's, Southampton, Warwick and St. George's) and two cities. The city of Hamilton is in central Pembroke Parish and the much older town of St.George is in eastern St. George's Parish. Both have elected mayors and councillors.

AREA AND POPULATION

Area
The Bermudas are a group of 138 small islands, roughly in the form of a fish-hook, measuring about 21 miles in length and two miles wide at the widest point, with a total land area of 22 sq. miles. The largest is Great Bermuda, or Main Island, which is a mile wide on average and 14 miles long. The next five largest islands are Boaz, Ireland, Somerset, St. David's and St. George's. They are situated in the north-west of the Atlantic Ocean about 600 miles (965 km) ESE of Cape Hatteras in North Carolina, and divided into nine parishes or counties. The principal islands are connected by bridges and causeways.

The climate is sub-tropical and is generally warm and humid. Strong winds occur in winter. The terrain is composed of low-lying hills and fertile valleys.

To view a map, consult http://www.lib.utexas.edu/maps/cia08/bermuda_sm_2008.gif

Population
Estimated figures for 2011 put the population at 64,722. The population of the city of Hamilton is about 3,400, the other large conurbation is St George with a population of 3,300. The official language is English and there is a large Portuguese speaking community.

Births, Marriages, Deaths
The birth rate is 11.6 births per 1,000 of the population and the total fertility rate is 1.7 children born per woman. The death rate is 7.3 per 1,000 and the infant mortality rate, 2.5 per 1,000 live births. The net migration rate is seven migrants per 1,000. Life expectancy is 77 years for males and 83 for females.

Public Holidays 2014
1 January: New Year's Day
18 April: Good Friday
20 April: Easter Day
26 May: Bermuda Day
16 June: National Heroes Day
31 July: Emancipation Day / Match Day (Thursday proceeding first Monday in August)
1 August: Somers Day (second day of Cup Match)
1 September: Labour Day
11 November: Remembrance Day
25 December: Christmas Day
26 December: Boxing Day

EMPLOYMENT

The estimated workforce is 38,370 with an unemployment rate of 2.1 per cent. Around 22 per cent of the workforce are employed in the clerical sector, 20 per cent in the service sector and only around 3 per cent are employed in agriculture and fishing. 12 per cent are employed in administrative and managerial roles and 18 per cent in professional and technical roles.

BANKING AND FINANCE

Currency
The unit of currency is the Bermuda dollar which has parity with the US dollar. US currency is acceptable throughout the community.

GDP/GNP, Inflation, National Debt
Bermuda's economy is based upon international finance and tourism. It is a well-regulated offshore financial centre. It has one of the highest per capita incomes in the world. The tourism industry has contracted in recent years. There is very little manufacturing which has resulted in a large trade deficit.

In 2005, GDP was estimated to be US$4.8 billion, indicating a growth rate of 9.0 per cent. Figures for 2006 put GDP at US$5.4 billion, giving a per capita figure of US$83,935; growth that year was 5.4 per cent. In 2007, GDP was US$5.8 billion with a growth rate of 4.6 per cent. Per capita GDP was US$91,500 in 2007. Figures for 2009 put GDP at US$5.9 billion, reflecting a growth rate of -2.5 per cent. Estimated figures for December 2010 put the GDP at US$5.6 billion, a growth rate of -2.5 per cent and giving a per capital figure of US$56,523. Tourism and the service sector (reinsurance) are the largest earners.

Inflation in 2006 averaged 4.6 per cent. It fell to 5.2 per cent in 2007. Estimates for 2009 put it at 2.0 per cent in 2010 and 2011.

Balance of Payments / Imports and Exports
Estimated figures for 2007 put exports (including re-exports) at US$27 million and imports at US$1.1 billion. The main exported commodity is re-exports of pharmaceuticals, whilst the main imported products are food, clothing, machinery, live animals, chemicals and transport. The US is Bermuda's largest trading partner, and accounts for over US$825 million of imported goods. The UK, Canada and Caribbean are also important trading countries.

Foreign Investment
Bermuda Government policy welcomes offshore operations and investments. Over12,000 international companies are based in Bermuda. Its industry capital base exceeds US$35 billion.

Central Bank
Bermuda Monetary Authority (BMA), Burnaby House, 26 Burnaby Street, Hamilton HM 11, Bermuda. Tel: +1 441 295 5278, fax: +1 441 292 7471, e-mail: info@bma.bm, URL: http://www.bma.bm

MANUFACTURING, MINING AND SERVICES

Manufacturing
Bermuda has no heavy industry. A few light manufacturing industries and some quarrying exist. Products include structural concrete products, paints, perfumes, and furniture.

Service Industries
Tourism is Bermuda's second major industry and, with financial services, forms the basis of the island's economy. In 2000 some 537,577 visitors arrived in Bermuda. This figure fell to 482,670 visitors in 2003. More than 93 per cent of business and holiday visitors come from North America (85 per cent from USA and 8 per cent from Canada).

Agriculture
Only 20 per cent land in Bermuda can be used for agriculture. Bermuda has a small fishing industry and limited agricultural output. Most food is imported, which results in a high cost of living. However, the standard of living is also high, on a par with (if not above) the United States. Main agricultural products include bananas, citrus fruits, flowers and vegetables.

Agricultural Production in 2010

Produce	Int. $'000*	Tonnes
Vegetables fresh nes	452	2,400
Cow milk, whole, fresh	437	1,400
Hen eggs, in shell	299	360
Potatoes	169	1,000
Indigenous chicken meat	159	112
Indigenous pigmeat	115	75
Bananas	104	370
Carrots and turnips	95	380
Indigenous cattle meat	78	29
Tomatoes	52	140
Cabbages and other brassicas	20	130
Onions, dry	13	60

* unofficial figures
Source: http://faostat.fao.org/site/339/default.aspx Food and Agriculture Organization of the United Nations, Food and Agricultural commodities production

Fishing
Bermuda has internationally recognized maritime claims to an exclusive fishing zone of 200 nautical miles and a territorial sea of 12 nautical miles. In 1996 this was changed to an exclusive economic zone.

FAO figures for 2010 put the total catch at 382 tonnes down from 416 tonnes in 2009.

COMMUNICATIONS AND TRANSPORT

International Airports
Direct daily flights are available between Bermuda and the United States, Canada, and the United Kingdom, with excellent connections to the rest of the world and land at Bermuda International Airport. The civil air terminal is served by American Airlines, Air Canada, British Airways, Delta Airlines, Eastern Air Lines, Continental Airlines and US Air.

Roads
Use of motorised vehicles has only been permitted in Bermuda since 1946. Vehicles drive on the left. All vehicles are limited as to size and engine capacity and private cars are limited to one car per household. In addition to cars, local residents ride auxiliary and motor cycles and motor scooters limited to 100cc. Importation of cars is limited to original owners of cars which are no more than six months old.

Shipping
Regular weekly cruise ship service is available from April to November from New York with irregular services out of other eastern seaboard US cities, Canada, the West Indies and the United Kingdom. Air and sea freight services are regularly available in and out of Bermuda. Bermuda has ports at Hamilton and Saint George.

Ferry services operate around Bermuda travelling to Hamilton Harbour and the Great Sound, Somerset and the Dockyard, and the Dockyard and St. George.

HEALTH
Bermuda has one modern general hospital, the King Edward VII Memorial Hospital (KEMH). Most cases can be dealt with there. When the hospital is unable to deal with certain cases, patients are transported to the US (usually Boston or Baltimore). There are plenty of GPs and dentists on the island. There is also a psychiatric hospital, St Brendan's. As of 31 December 2008 there were 710 people aged 22-44 years diagnosed with HIV/AIDS. In 2009, there were an estimated 155.3 new cases per million population. Circulatory diseases accounted for 41 per cent of all deaths. The infant mortality rate has stabilised since the 1950s and in 2009, it was estimated at 2.46 deaths per 1,000 live births. Total health expenditure accounted to 8.5 per cent of GDP; government expenditure accounted for 29 per cent of total expenditure. Per capita expenditure in 2007 was approximately US$7,900.

EDUCATION
Schooling is compulsory for all children between the ages of five and sixteen years and is available free in maintained (Government run) schools. There are also aided (financially assisted by Government) schools and four private fee-paying schools. The Bermuda school system is based on the British system with single sex and coeducational schools available at most levels. There are kindergartens and nursery schools, primary and secondary schools and a Bermuda College complex which offers education at the post-secondary and college levels. There are no boarding schools. The Bermuda College consists of the Department of Hotel Technology (all aspects of hotel training); the Department of Academic Studies (for university entrance into US, Canadian and British colleges and universities) and the Department of Commerce and Technology (commercial, mechanical, industrial, etc.). Figures from UNESCO for 2006 show that the equivalent of 1.2 per cent of GDP was spent on education.

RELIGION
Approximately 89 per cent of the population is Christian. Recent figures estimate that 23 per cent of the population are Anglican; approximately 11 per cent are members of the African Methodist Episcopal Church and another 15 per cent are members of the Roman Catholic Church, seven per cent are Seventh Day Adventists and four per cent are Methodist. Altogether, some 21 denominations were represented. Bermuda has a religious tolerance rating of 10 on a scale of 1 to 10 (10 is most freedom). (Source: World Religion Database)

COMMUNICATIONS AND MEDIA

Newspapers
The Royal Gazette (daily), URL: http://www.theroyalgazette.com; The Mid-Ocean News, (weekly); The Bermuda Sun, Hamilton, (bi-weekly), URL: http://www.bermudasun.org

Broadcasting
Bermuda supports three television stations and 10 radio stations. Cable and satellite subscription is available.

Telecommunications
The telephone system is generally good. Estimated figures for 20086 show that nearly 58,000 land lines were in use and over 80,000 mobile phones. Recent figures show Bermuda has around 50,000 internet users.

ENVIRONMENT
As one of the most densely populated territories on earth, Bermuda takes the protection of its remaining rural environment very seriously and there are numerous national parks. Bermuda enacted one of the earliest environmental protection acts in the world with a 17th century act to protect turtles. In July 2000, the entire Bermuda economic exclusion zone (EEZ) was designated as a whale sanctuary.

In 2006, Bermuda's emissions from the consumption of fossil fuels totalled 0.66 million metric tons of carbon dioxide.

SPACE PROGRAMME
Bermuda has no space programme although it is the headquarters for a number of companies involved in space, such as Iridium and Intelsat.

BRITISH INDIAN OCEAN TERRITORY

Capital: Diego Garcia

Commissioner: Peter Hayes (resident in the UK)

Administrator: John McManus

Flag: A Union flag at the top corner, hoist side, on a background of 11 blue and white wavy lines. The coat of arms in the fly depicts a palm tree with a crown.

CONSTITUTION AND GOVERNMENT

The territory encompasses six atolls of the Chagos Archipelago and consists of 55 islands, the largest of which is Diego Garcia. Discovered in the sixteenth century by Vasco da Gama, the islands were claimed in the eighteenth century by France as a possession of Mauritius. Britain captured Mauritius in 1810 and France ceded the territory to Britain under the Treaty of Paris in 1814. The treaty covered Mauritius and its dependencies, which included the Seychelles and the islands of the Chagos Archipelago. The dependencies were administered from Mauritius up until 1903 when the Seychelles group of islands were formed into a separate Crown Colony. The Chagos islands continued to be administered by Mauritius until, under an agreement between the Mauritius Council of Ministers and the UK, they became part of the British Indian Ocean Territory in 1965 along with the islands of Aldabra, Farquhar and Desroches, formerly of the Seychelles group.

The purpose of the British Indian Ocean Territory was to provide military facilities for the UK and USA. In 1966, work began on providing military sites; the copra plantations were bought and closed down, and the entire population of Diego Garcia was moved to Mauritius, the Seychelles and the UK. A treaty was signed in 1971 between the UK and the USA leasing the island of Diego Garcia to build an air and naval base. In June 1976 the islands of Aldabra, Farquhar and Desroches were returned to the Seychelles. Since then, the British Indian Ocean Territory has consisted of only the Chagos Archipelago.

Since the 1980s, successive Mauritian governments have asserted a sovereignty claim to the islands, arguing that under international law the agreement to detach the islands was illegal.

The islanders (Chagossians) who were removed have always asserted their right to return to the islands and have taken their case to the British High Courts of Justice. They won judgements in 2000, 2002 and 2007; the British Government appealed against the decisions but lost. In May 2006, the High Court ruled that the Order-in-Council was unlawful, and that

the Chagossians could return to the Chagos Archipelago. The Court of Appeal confirmed the ruling in May 2007. The islanders were granted the right to visit Diego Garcia for humanitarian purposes and to tend the graves of their ancestors. The islanders continue to argue for their permanent resettlement.

In 2002, a feasibility study was carried out on whether it would be possible for the Chagossians to return. The study found that life on the outer islands would be precarious and the islanders would need substantial support from the British government, which it was not prepared to give. The US have argued that, since the 9/11 attacks, security issues mean that they would want to limit who can be on the islands.

AREA AND POPULATION

Area
The area of the Chagos Archipelago covers 54,400 sq km of which just 60 km is land and is located in the Indian Ocean about 1,770 km east of Mahe in the Seychelles. The islands are flat and low with a high point of just 15 metres.

The climate is tropical, generally hot and humid but moderated by trade winds.

To view a map, please consult:
http://www.lib.utexas.edu/maps/cia08/british_indian_ocean_sm_2008.gif

Population
In 1965, when the islands were detached, the population of 1,200 were removed; it is estimated that they and their descendents now number about 4,000. In 2012 it was estimated that around 2,800 UK and US military and civilian contract workers were located on Diego Garcia.

BANKING AND FINANCE

Currency
Both the UK pound and US dollar are accepted.

GDP/GNP Inflation, National Debt
Before the population of the islands were removed they made their livings from fishing, farming and copra production.

BRITISH VIRGIN ISLANDS

Capital: Road Town, Tortola (Population estimate: 9,400)

Head of State: HM Queen Elizabeth (page 1420)

Governor: Boyd McCleary CMG (page 1473)

Flag: British blue ensign with the coat of arms in the fly, depicting St. Ursula with a lamp and 11 eleven other lamps representative of her 11,000 virgin followers, with a scroll beneath bearing the word 'vigilate'.

CONSTITUTION AND GOVERNMENT

Constitution
The British Virgin Islands is a British Overseas Territory. Under the Constitution, which came into force on 1 June 1977, the Governor has responsibility for defence and internal security and external affairs. The Constitution, amended in 2000, provided for an Executive Council and a Legislative Council headed by a Chief Minister. In June 2007 a new constitution came into force, providing for a ministerial system of Government with the Governor at its head. The post of Chief Minister was replaced by a Premier who is appointed by the Governor from among elected politicians.

To consult the full constitution, please visit: http://www.bvi.org.uk/government/constitution2007

International Relations
As a British Overseas Territory the British Virgin Islands (BVI) enjoy a close relationship with the UK. The British government is responsible for the BVI's external relations. The BVI is an associate member of the Organisation of Eastern Caribbean States and the Caribbean Community.

Recent Events
In 2002 the British Overseas Territories Act was passed and grants British citizenship to the islanders, who can hold British passports and may work in the UK and EU.

Legislature
The House of Assembly consists of 13 seats; one member is elected from each of the nine districts and a further four by a territory-wide or At-Large vote. All serve five-year terms. The speaker and Attorney General are also members of the Assembly. The Governor appoints as

Premier the person who, in his opinion, is best able to command a majority in the Legislative Council (Legco). The Executive Council (Exco) is appointed by the Governor from members of the Legislative Council, and the Premier appointed from members of the Executive Council. **Virgin Islands Government**, URL: http://www.bvi.gov.vg

Executive Council (as at June 2013)
Premier, Minister of Finance and Tourism: Dr The Hon. D. Orlando Smith OBE
Deputy Premier, Minister for Natural Resources and Labour: Dr the Hon. Kendrick Pickering
Minister for Health and Social Development: Hon. Ronnie Skelton
Minister for Education and Culture: Hon. Myron Walwyn
Minister for Communications and Works: Hon. Mark Vanterpool
Attorney General: Dr Christopher Malcolm

Political Parties
National Democratic Party (NDP); Virgin Islands Party (VIP).

Elections
In the 2007 election, the Virgin Islands Party, (VIP), won seven District seats and three At-Large seats, gaining power from the National Democratic Party (NDP). The most recent election took place in November 2011, the NDP won nine seats and the VIP won 4.

LEGAL SYSTEM

The law is based on British common law. The court system is made up of a Magistrates Court, a High Court and a Circuit Court of Appeal of the Eastern Caribbean Supreme Court, with final appeal to the Judicial Committee of the Privy Council in England.

The government respects the human rights of its citizens, though there are cases of lengthy pretrial detention. The death penalty was officially abolished in 1991.

AREA AND POPULATION

Area
The Virgin Islands were discovered in 1493 by Columbus who named them after St. Ursula and her 11,000 virgins. They are an archipelago adjacent to Puerto Rico and the US Virgin Islands. The islands form the northern extremity of the Leeward Islands in the eastern Caribbean. The total area is approximately 153 sq. km.

There are 36 islands and islets of which 16 are uninhabited. The islands are: Anegada; Beef Island; Bellamy Cay; Buck Island; Carvel Rock; Cockroach Island; Cooper Island; Dead Chest Cay; Dead Chest Island; Diamond Cay; Dog Islands; Drowned Island; East Seal Dog Island; Eustatia Island; Fallen Jerusalem Island; Flanagan Island; Frenchman's Cay; George Dog Island; Ginger Island; Great Camanoe; Great Dog Island; Great Thatch; Great Tobago Island; Green Cay; Guana Island; The Indians; Jost Van Dyke; Little Anegada; Little Camanoe; Little Cay; Little Jost Van Dyke; Little Seal Dog Island; Little Sisters; Little Thatch; Little Tobago; Little Wickmans Cay; Marina Cay; Mosquito Island; Nanny Cay; Necker Island; Norman Island; Old Jerusalem Island; Oyster Rock; Pelican Island; Peter Island; Prickly Pear; Round Rock; Saba Rock; Salt Island; Sandy Cay; Sandy Spit; Scrub Island; Spanish Island; Tortola; Virgin Gorda; West Dog Island; Whale Rock. The largest islands are Tortola, Virgin Gorda, Anegada and Jost Van Dyke. Tortola is home to the capital, Road Town. The islands have an exclusive fishing zone of 200 nautical miles.

Some of the islands are coral and therefore relatively flat. Others are volcanic and hilly.

The climate is sub-tropical.

To view a map of the islands, please consult:
http://www.lib.utexas.edu/maps/cia08/british_virgin_islands_sm_2008.gif

Population
The estimated population in 2009 was 24,500, with a growth rate of 1.8 per cent. Around 75 per cent of the population live on the largest island, Tortola.

Estimated Age structure (2005)

Age group	Total	Male	Female
0-14 years	4,758 (21%)	2,400	2,358
15-64 years	16,722 (74%)	8,607	8,115
65 years and over	1,163 (5%)	614	549
Total	22,643	11,621 (51%)	11,022 (49%)

The official language is English.

Life expectancy in 2009 was estimated as 76 years for males and 78 years for females. The median age was 32 years.

Public Holidays 2014
1 January: New Year's Day
3 March: Lavity Stoutt's birthday
10 March: Commonwealth Day
18 April: Good Friday
21 April: Easter Monday
9 May: Whit Monday
14 June: Queen's Birthday
1 July: Territory Day
4 August: Carnival
21 October: St. Ursula's Day
14 November: Prince Charles' Birthday
25 December: Christmas Day
26 December: Boxing Day

EMPLOYMENT

Employment by economic activity, 2005

Sector	No. of employees
Agriculture, hunting and forestry	78
Fishing	14
Mining and quarrying	37
Manufacturing	404
Electricity, gas and water supply	145
Construction	1,260
Wholesale and retail trade; Repair of motor vehicles and personal and household goods	1,624
Hotels and restaurants	2,573
Financial intermediation	797
Real estate, renting and business activities	1,307
Public administration and defence; Compulsory social security	5,142
Education	1,119
Health and Social work	141
Other community, social and personal service activities	724
Private household with employed persons	404
Not classifiable by economic activity	9
Total	16,232

Source: Copyright © International Labour Organization (ILO Dept. of Statistics, http://laborsta.ilo.org)

BANKING AND FINANCE

Currency
The currency is the US dollar.

GDP/GNP, Inflation, National Debt
In 2010, GDP per capita was estimated to be US$30,282, growth in 2011 was put at 3.05 per cent. The service sector contributes over 90 per cent of GDP. The estimated inflation rate in 2011 was 4.1 per cent.

Balance of Payments / Imports and Exports
External debt in 1996 measured US$34.8 million. In 2002, the value of exports was US$25 million, the principal export commodities being rum, fresh fish, fruit, livestock, gravel and sand. Exports to the UK were worth £32.64 million and imports £13.94 million in 2003. Major imports are building materials, automobiles, foodstuffs and machinery. The main trading partners are the US Virgin Islands, Puerto Rico and the USA.

MANUFACTURING, MINING AND SERVICES

Energy
In 1996, 42 million kWh of electricity was produced, entirely from fossil fuels.

Manufacturing
The islands also receive revenue from light industries, construction, rum and concrete blocks.

Service Industries
The islands' main sources of income are tourism (in particular yacht chartering) and offshore finance. Tourism accounts for 45 per cent of the national income, helping to make the economy one of the most affluent in the Caribbean. The islands receive around 290,000 visitors per year. During the mid-1980s, the Government began offering offshore registration to companies wanting to incorporate in the islands, and incorporation fees generate substantial revenue. It was estimated that 250,000 companies had registered by the end of 1997. The adoption of a comprehensive insurance law in 1994, which provides confidentiality with regulated statutory gateways for investigation of criminal offences, makes the islands even more attractive to international business.

Agriculture
Agricultural Production in 2010

Produce	Int. $'000*	Tonnes
Indigenous cattle meat	374	139
Indigenous sheep meat	194	71
Bananas	121	430
Indigenous goat meat	86	36
Fruit fresh nes	31	90
Indigenous pigmeat	31	20
Coconuts	4	40

* unofficial figures
Source: http://faostat.fao.org/site/339/default.aspx Food and Agriculture Organization of the United Nations, Food and Agricultural commodities production

Exports of fish and agricultural products (fruit, vegetables, livestock and poultry) contribute to the national income. Raising of livestock is the most important agricultural activity as poor soils limit the islands' ability to meet domestic food demand. The main imports are food and beverages, technical products and building materials.

Fishing
FAO figures for 2010 put the total catch in 1,200 tonnes.

COMMUNICATIONS AND TRANSPORT

International Airports
There are three airports, two of which have paved runways. Terrance B. Lettsome International Airport, is located on Beef Island just off Tortola.

Roads
There are over 176 km of paved roads.

Ports and Harbours
There is a harbour at Road Town. The islands have several yachting marinas. Ferry services operate between the islands.

HEALTH

There is one hospital, Peebles Hospital, with 50 beds and 13 health clinics. Life expectancy in 2009 was estimated at 77.3 years. The infant mortality rate was estimated to be 14.6 deaths per 1,000 live births. Major causes of mortality and morbidity include circulatory disorders, diabetics, cancer, and substance abuse.

EDUCATION

Primary and secondary education is available, free of charge and compulsory. Fifteen primary schools and one comprehensive secondary school (The BVI High School) in Tortola are directly maintained by the Government. Secondary education programmes are also offered in Virgin Gorda and Anegada. There are also private primary and pre-primary schools and a private secondary school. In 1994, a total of 2,855 pupils were enrolled in all primary and pre-primary schools and 1,363 pupils were enrolled in secondary school programmes. The H.L. Stoutt Community College, founded in 1990, offers a range of programmes to associate degree level, and higher degrees can be obtained from associate institutions in the USA.

UNITED KINGDOM

Figures for 2007 show that 94 per cent of girls and 93 per cent of boys were enrolled in primary school and 89 per cent of girls and 79 per cent of boys were enrolled in secondary school. That year 14.6 per cent of total government expenditure went on education, of which 38 per cent went on secondary education and 27 per cent on primary education.

RELIGION

The majority of the population belongs to the Christian faith (84 per cent), the main churches being Methodist (46 per cent), Anglican (21 per cent), Adventist, Baptist, and Roman Catholic. Approximately 1.2 per cent of the population is Hindu and 1.2 per cent Muslim. The British Virgin Islands has a religious tolerance rating of 10 on a scale of 1 to 10 (10 is most freedom). (Source: World Religion Database)

COMMUNICATIONS AND MEDIA

The media is free to criticise the government and a wide variety of views appear.

Newspapers
There are three newspapers published weekly, Island Sun, URL: http://islandsun.com; BVI Beacon, URL: http://www.bvibeacon.com/main; BVI Stand Point, URL: http://www.vistandpoint.com

Broadcasting
There are no public broadcasters but a private TV station and radio stations exist. Multichannel satellite televison is available through cable.

Telecommunications
It was estimated that in 2008 there were over 18,000 land line telephones and over 23,000 mobile phones is use. It is estimated that 4,000 people are regular internet users.

ENVIRONMENT

There are limited natural fresh water resources. Except for a few seasonal streams and springs on Tortola, most of the islands' water supply comes from wells and rainwater catchment.

In 2006, the British Virgin Island's emissions from the consumption and flaring of fossil fuels totalled 0.10 million metric tons of carbon dioxide.

CAYMAN ISLANDS

Capital: George Town (Grand Cayman, population estimate: 26,000)

Governor: H.E. Duncan Taylor CBE (page 1523)

Flag: Blue with British ensign, top left, with the coat of arms in the fly

CONSTITUTION AND GOVERNMENT

Constitution
Under the Constitution which came into effect on the 22 August 1972, the Governor, appointed by Britain, administers the Islands on the advice of an Executive Council. The Governor must accept their advice unless there are special reasons, though he has reserved powers in regard to national security, external affairs and the civil service. A constitutional review was begun in 2001 and a new constitution was drafted in 2002 which would allow for a chief minister replacing the existing post of Leader of Government Business, a full ministerial government and a bill of rights, this draft has been put on hold. A new constitutional review began in 2007.

The Executive Council consists of three members appointed by the Governor and four members elected by the Legislative Assembly.

To consult the constitution, please visit: http://www.constitution.gov.ky/portal/page?_pageid=1961,1&_dad=portal&_schema=PORTAL.

International Relations
The Cayman Islands is a British Overseas Territory and therefore has close ties with the UK. The Cayman Islands are an associate member of CARICOM.

Recent Events
In December 2012 Premier McKeeva Bush was arrested following investigations into corruption. He was charged with misuse of a government credit card and importing explosive materials. He denied all charges and refused to resign his position, parliament then passed a vote of no confidence in him.

In May 2013, along with Anguilla, Bermuda, the British Virgin Islands, Montserrat and the Turks and Caicos Islands, the Cayman Islands signed an agreement on sharing of tax information with Britain, France, Germany, Italy and Spain.

Legislature
The Legislative Assembly is composed of 15 elected members who represent the six districts of the island, and three official members (the Chief Secretary, the Financial Secretary and the Attorney-General), presided over by the Speaker. Following a resolution passed in September 1990, the first speaker was appointed, effective from the first meeting in the 1991 Session of the Legislature. The life of the House is four years. A full review of the Constitution took place in January 1991. This resulted in amendments to the 1972 Constitution which proposed the addition of three seats, bringing the number of elected representatives to 15 and the introduction of a ministerial system.
Legislative Assembly, Government Administration Building, Elgin Avenue, George Town, Grand Cayman, Cayman Islands. Tel: +1 345 949 7900, URL: http://www.gov.ky

---
Executive Council (as at June 2013)
Premier, Minister of Home Affairs: Aiden McLaughlin
Deputy Premier, Ministser of Tourism and District Administration: Moses Kirkconnell
Minister of Finance, Development and Planning: Marco Archer
Minister of Health, Works, Agriculture and Community Affairs: Kurt Tibbetts
Minister of Financial Services: Wayne Panton
Minister of Education and Sports: Osbourne Bodden
Minister of Labour and Gender Affairs: Tara Rivers

Ministries
Government portal, URL: http://www.gov.ky/
All government and ministerial offices are located at

Government Administration Building, Elgin Avenue, Georgetown, Grand Cayman, Cayman Islands. Tel: +1 345 949 7900, fax: +1 345 949 4131

Elections
The most recent election was held in May 2013. The opposition People's Progressive Movement won, putting the incumbent United Democratic Party (UDP) in opposition.

Political Parties
United Democratic Party; People's Progressive Movement

LEGAL SYSTEM

The Cayman Islands' legal system is based on English common law. The highest court is the Grand Court, which has unlimited civil and criminal jurisdiction. The lower court is the Summary Court. The Court of Appeal comprises jurists from Jamaica and the Bahamas. Final appeals can be taken to the Privy Council in London.

The government respects the civil rights of its citizens, though there have been instances of discrimination against homosexuals. Homosexual acts between consenting adults were decriminalised in 2000, but a 2009 draft constitution has been criticised for deliberately excluding gay rights. The death penalty was officially abolished in 1991.

Judicial Portal, URL: http://www.judicial.ky/courts/the-grand-court

LOCAL GOVERNMENT

The Cayman Islands are divided into six districts, George Town, West Bay, Bodden Town, Cayman Brac, Little Cayman, Northside and East End. The Governor is represented in Little Cayman and Cayman Brac by a District Commissioner.

AREA AND POPULATION

Area
The Cayman Islands consist of three islands, Grand Cayman, Little Cayman and Cayman Brac, which have a total area of around 260 sq. km. The principal island, Grand Cayman, is about 286 km. from Jamaica and lies to the west of Cayman Brac and Little Cayman. It is about 35 km. in length and ranges from 6.5 to 13 km. in breadth with an area of 124 sq. km. The islands are low-lying, surrounded by coral reefs.

The climate is tropical with hot, rainy summers (May to October) and cooler, drier winters (November to April). The Cayman Islands are in an area prone to hurricanes and in September 2004 they were hit by Hurricane Ivan. 80 per cent of buildings were damaged, many of them made uninhabitable.

To view a map of the islands, please consult:
http://www.lib.utexas.edu/maps/cia08/cayman_islands_sm_2008.gif

Population
The population was estimated at 55,000 in 2010, with a growth rate of 2.4 per cent. The majority of the population lives on Grand Cayman with 1,822 living on Cayman Brac and 115 on Little Cayman. The language spoken is English. The capital, George Town, has a population of around 15,000.

Births, Marriages, Deaths
Estimated figures for 2009 put the birth rate at 12.4 births per 1,000 population and the death rate at 4.9 deaths per 1,000 population. In 2004 the net migration rate was put at 18.6 migrants per 1,000 population. Life expectancy at birth is 77.8 years for men and 83.1 years for women, an average of 80.4 years. Figures for 2006 show that around 520 marriages took place. The total fertility rate was estimated to be 1.8 births per female.

Public Holidays 2014
1 January: New Year's Day
27 January: National Heroes Day
5 March: Ash Wednesday
18 April: Good Friday
21 April: Easter Monday
18 May: Discovery Day
June: Queen's Birthday
6 July: Constitution Day
9 November: Remembrance Day
25 December: Christmas Day
26 December: Boxing Day

EMPLOYMENT

The following table shows how the labour force was employed in 2008:

Employment by sector

Occupation	Employed
Agriculture, fishing & forestry	697
Mining, quarrying & manufacturing	790
Electricity, gas & water supply	553
Construction	5,796
Wholesale, retail trade & repairs	4,732
Hotels & restaurants	4,300
Transport, storage & communications	1,687
Financial intermediation	3,773
Real estate, renting & business activities	5,020
Public administration & defence	2,095
Education, health & social work	2,971
Other community, social & personal services	1,912
Households with employed persons	2,752
Other	370
Total	37,450

Source: Copyright © International Labour Organization (ILO Dept. of Statistics, http://laborsta.ilo.org)

The unemployment rate for 2007 was 3.8 per cent rising to 4.0 per cent in 2008.

BANKING AND FINANCE

Currency
The unit of currency is the Cayman Islands dollar. The financial centre is George Town.

GDP/GNP, Inflation, National Debt
The Cayman Islands enjoy one of the highest standards of living of all the Caribbean islands. GDP per capita was estimated at CI$42,687 in 2010, whilst growth was 1.0 per cent. The composition of GDP is as follows: agriculture, 1.4 per cent; industry, 3.2 per cent; and services, 95.4 per cent, of which the financial services sector makes up around 40 per cent and tourism 35 per cent. Figures for 2008 put GDP growth at 1.1 per cent. The estimated inflation rate in 2011 was 3.4 per cent.

Balance of Payments / Imports and Exports
The value of exports in 2007 was estimated at $25 million, consisting mainly of turtle products and manufactured consumer goods, principally shipped to the USA. Imports amounted to an estimated $1.057 billion, mainly of foodstuffs and manufactured goods. The principal import partners are the US, Trinidad and Tobago, UK, Netherlands Antilles and Japan. Figures for 2010 put export earnings (fob) at CI$1.1 million and import costs (cif) at CI$688.3 million. UK exports to the Cayman Islands in 2010 were £23.6 million and Cayman Islands exports to the UK were £48.0 million.

Central Bank
Cayman Islands Monetary Authority, PO Box 10052 APO, Elizabethan Sq, George Town, Grand Cayman, Cayman Islands. Tel: +1 345 949 7089, fax: +1 345 945 1145, e-mail: admin@cimoney.com.ky, URL: http://www.cimoney.com.ky
Chairman of the Board: George McCarthy

MANUFACTURING, MINING AND SERVICES

Energy
Electricity production in 2006 was 490 million kWh, entirely from fossil fuels.

Service Industries
The main pillars of the economy are tourism and the finance industry. The main government revenue is generated from import duties, company, bank and trust licence fees and stamp duties. The Islands' status as an international offshore finance centre had, by the end of 1997, produced 594 bank and trust companies, 450 captive insurance companies, 1,685 licensed or registered mutual funds and 41,173 registered companies. Banking assets are more than US$500 billion. A stock exchange was opened in 1997.

Recent figures show that some 1.2 million people visited the Cayman Islands. US$394 million was generated by international tourism in 1996, accounting for around 70 per cent of GDP and 75 per cent of foreign currency earnings. The tourist industry is aimed at the luxury market and caters mainly to visitors from North America. About 90 per cent of the islands' food and consumer goods must be imported. Cayman Islands is a popular stop-off point for cruise ships.

Agriculture
The main agricultural products are vegetables including pumpkins, leafy vegetables, sweet potatoes and yams. Fruits grown include bananas, plantains, mangoes, melon and citrus fruits. Livestock and turtles are also farmed.

Agricultural Production in 2010

Produce	Int. $'000*	Tonnes
Bananas	55	195
Citrus fruit, nes	27	60
Honey, natural	25	10
Mangoes, mangosteens, guavas	18	30
Avocados	14	20
Yams	8	30
Pumpkins, squash and gourds	7	40
Plantains	4	20
Hen eggs, in shell	4	5
Vegetables fresh nes	4	20
Tomatoes	4	10
Coconuts	1	10

* unofficial figures
Source: http://faostat.fao.org/site/339/default.aspx Food and Agriculture Organization of the United Nations, Food and Agricultural commodities production

Fishing
FAO figures for 2010 put the total catch 125 tonnes.

COMMUNICATIONS AND TRANSPORT

Travel Requirements
Citizens of the USA, Australia and the EU require a passport valid for at least six months except nationals of Canada and the UK who have another proof of nationality. A visa is not required by US, Australian, Canadian and EU citizens apart from nationals of Bulgaria, Cyprus, Czech Republic, Estonia, Latvia, Lithuania, Malta, Poland, Romania, Slovak Republic and Slovenia who do require a visa. Cruise ship passengers do not require visas to enter the Cayman Islands. Nationals not referred to above are advised to contact the Passport Office to check visa requirements.

National Airlines
Cayman Airways operates internal flights to Cayman Brac and external flights to Miami, Orlando, Houston, Tampa, Atlanta, Honduras and Jamaica.
Cayman Airways, URL: http://www.caymanairways.com/home/home.php

International Airports
The Owen Roberts International Airport in Grand Cayman was opened in 1985 and the Gerrard Smith International Airport in Cayman Brac was opened in 1988. There is also another airport with an unpaved runway.

Roads
There are about 406 km of roads in Grand Cayman and Cayman Brac, 304 km of which are paved. All districts are connected by roads of high standard. Vehicles are driven on the left in the islands.

Shipping
Motor boats operate on a regular basis between the Cayman Islands, Jamaica, Costa Rica and Florida. In 1994 there were 820 vessels registered at George Town. There are ports at Cayman Brac and George Town.

HEALTH

There is a general hospital at George Town with over 100 beds and the Chrissie Tomlinson Hospital on Grand Cayman has 18 beds. In addition, there is a dental clinic, four district clinics and a hospital with 19 beds at Cayman Brac. Figures for 2009 show that there were approximately 100 doctors, 220 nurses including midwives, and 14 dentists. Life expectancy was estimated at 80.4 years in 2009. The infant mortality rate was 6.94 deaths per 1,000 live births.

EDUCATION

Education is provided free and is compulsory up to the age of 16. There are several government schools and 12 private schools which are mainly church affiliated. Enrolment in all schools in 2006 was 7,017. Tertiary education is provided by University College of the Cayman Islands, as well as a law school and the International College of the Cayman Islands, St. Matthews University offers courses in medicine and vetinerary science. Distance learning is offered by the University of the West Indies. Adult literacy is 98 per cent. Figures from UNESCO for 2006 show that the equivalent of 2.6 per cent of GDP was spent on education/

RELIGION

The religion is predominantly Christian (84 per cent of the population), with Anglican, Roman Catholic and Presbyterian churches on the islands. There are also very small Baha'i, Hindu, Buddhist, Jewish and Muslim communities.

The Cayman Islands has a religious liberty rating of 10 on a scale of 1 to 10 (10 is most freedom). (Source: World Religion Database)

COMMUNICATIONS AND MEDIA

Newspapers
The Caymanian Compass, URL: http://www.caycompass.com
Cayman Net News, URL: http://www.caymannetnews.com

Broadcasting
Four television stations broadcast in Cayman Islands as well as cable and satellite stations which offer a variety of US and international stations. Radio Cayman is government owned, several private radio stations also broadcast.
CITN Cayman 27, private, URL: http://www.cayman27.com.ky/
Radio Cayman, government, URL: http://www.radiocayman.gov.ky
Z-99, private, URL: http://z00.ky

Telecommunications
Recent figures suggest that there are over 38,000 telephone lines and 33,000 mobile phones in use on the Islands. Recent figures show the islands have approximately 23,000 regular internet users.

ENVIRONMENT

The Cayman Islands' government is engaged in a number of environmental projects to protect its indigenous wildlife and flora. A botanical park and bird sanctuary exists on Grand Cayman. The National Trust is involved in preserving wildlife and flora, whilst the Caymen Islands Turtle Farm is increasing the Green Sea Turtle population. There is also a Ramsar site, the Booby Pond Nature Reserve, on Little Cayman.

There are no natural fresh water resources. Drinking water supplies must be met by rainwater catchment.

In 2006, the Cayman Island's emissions from the consumption of fossil fuels totalled 0.42 million metric tons of carbon dioxide.

FALKLAND ISLANDS

Capital: Stanley (Population estimate, 2010: 2,200)

Commander-in-chief: Nigel Haywood (page 1439)

Flag: British blue ensign with the coat of arms in the fly

CONSTITUTION AND GOVERNMENT

Constitution
There are conflicting claims to the discovery of the Falkland Islands and navigators of several countries have been credited with first sightings. However, of the various claims, only that of the Dutch sailor Sebald van Weert in 1600 is conclusively authenticated. Both the Spanish claims (Magellan in 1520 and Camargo in 1540) and the English (Captain John Davies in 1592 and Sir Richard Hawkins in 1594) rest on imprecise evidence. The first known landing was made by a Briton, Captain John Strong, on 27 January 1690.

The present constitution dates from 1985 but a new constitution will come into force in January 2009. The constitution clarifies the division of powers between the executive council and the islands' governor. It is now enshrined in the constitution that the governor must abide by the advice of the executive council on matters of domestic policy although the governor can ignore the advice in the interests of good governance, or in matters relating to external affairs, defence or the administration of justice.

International Relations
The Falkland Islands is a UK Overseas Territory and has close links with the UK. Since the Falklands war in 1982, British soldiers have been stationed on the islands.

Recent Events
In February 2010 British company Desire Petroleum, began drilling for oil in the territorial waters of the Falkland Islands. Argentina strongly opposed the drilling and threatened to take "adequate measures" to stop British oil exploration in what it calls contested waters around the islands. Argentina also sought support from other Latin American countries.

In June 2012 it was announced that the Falkland Islanders would take part in a referendum in the first half of 2013. The referendum would be on the 'political status' of the islands in an effort to end the dispute with Argentina over sovereignty. The referendum was held and the result was almost unanimous in voting in favour of remaining a British overseas territory.

Falklands War
The Islands have been definitively and continuously administered by Britain since 1833, interrupted only briefly by the conflict of 1982 with Argentina. Argentine forces landed on the Falklands on 2 April 1982 claiming *Las Islas Malvinas* as their own. British troops were then sent to the islands and British victory was declared on 20 June 1982. 655 Argentinian and 255 British servicemen were killed in the conflict. Following the war, a two-hundred mile exclusion zone was established around the islands. In 1994, the Argentine Government re-stated their claim to the Falkland Islands by including a provision to that effect in their Constitution, but the British and Falkland Islands governments have always rejected it, claiming it lacks both historical and legal substance. Despite this, efforts to normalise relations with Argentina have since been made, and talks resulted in a joint statement agreed in July 1999.

In recent years Argentina's approach towards the Falklands has deteriorated recently. In 2003 Argentina imposed a ban on chartered aircraft flying from, or through, their airspace to the Falkland Islands and in 2008 they introduced legislation which was designed to penalise fishing companies operating in both Argentine and Falkland Island waters.

Legislature
The Falkland Islands are a self-governing entity within the overseas territories of the United Kingdom. The current Falkland Islands Constitution was adopted in 1985, under whose terms eight Legislative Councillors are elected every four years, five from Stanley and three from Camp. Each year, the Legislative Councillors elect three of their number to stand as members of the Executive Council. The Governor is advised by the Executive Council over which he presides, which comprises the three elected members and two ex-officio members, the Chief

Executive and Financial Secretary. The Commander British Forces Falkland Islands and the Attorney General may also attend Executive Council meetings. The present constitution dates from 1985, was amended in 1998 and is currently under review.

The Legislative Council, which is chaired by the Governor, who also acts as Speaker, is made up of the eight elected Councillors and two ex-officio members, again the Chief Executive and the Financial Secretary. As with the Executive Council, the Commander British Forces, Commodore Richard Ibbotson, and the Attorney General, David Lang QC, may attend. Defence and Foreign Affairs remain the responsibility of the British Government.
URL: http://www.falklands.gov.fk

Legislative Council (as at June 2013)
Governor: Nigel Haywood
Chief Executive: Keith Padgett
Members: Stanley area: The Hon. Dick Sawle, The Hon. Jan Cheek, The Hon. Gavin Short, The Hon. Barry Elsby, The Hon. Mike Summers. Camp area: The Hon. Roger Edwards, The Hon. Sharon Halford, The Hon. Ian Hansen

---

Elections
The most recent election took place on 5 November 2009, the next election is due by November 2013.

LEGAL SYSTEM

Petty cases are first heard by a Summary Court, consisting of a panel of justices of the peace (upstanding members of the community). More serious cases are heard in the Magistrate's Court, by a Senior Magistrate, who is usually a UK qualified lawyer. He adjudicates both simple criminal and civil matters as well as very serious criminal matters or complex civil cases. The Senior Magistrate also hears appeals from the Summary Court.

At the head of the judiciary on the Falkland Islands is a Supreme Court, presided over by a non-resident Chief Justice. The most serious criminal and civil matters are reserved for the Supreme Court. In civil matters there is no jury but in criminal matters, the defendant can elect trial by judge and jury or judge alone. Only cases involving murder, manslaughter, rape, piracy, treason and arson are heard before the Supreme Court.

From the Supreme Court, appeals are sent to the Falkland Islands Court of Appeal, in London, and appeals from this Court can be sent to the Privy Council.

AREA AND POPULATION

Area
The Falkland Islands are an archipelago of some 700 islands situated in the South Atlantic Ocean about 400 miles from the South American mainland, 430 miles north east of Cape Horn. They comprise two main Islands (East and West Falkland) and some 700 smaller islands. The total land area is some 4,700 square miles (12,173 sq km). South Georgia, 800 miles south east of the Falklands, and the South Sandwich Islands, 470 miles south east of South Georgia, are a separate overseas territory, but are administered from Stanley for the sake of convenience. The terrain is rocky hills with some boggy, rolling plains. The climate is cold marine with strong westerly winds and frequent precipitation.

To view a map of the islands, please consult:
http://www.lib.utexas.edu/maps/cia08/falkland_islands_sm_2008.gif

Population
The population of the Falkland Islands is almost exclusively of British birth or descent. The census of 2006 showed a civilian population of 2,955, of whom 2,300 lived in Stanley, 78 per cent of the population is under 55 years of age. The Camp is the local term for the areas outside Stanley. Since the Falklands conflict there has also been a sizeable British garrison committed to the defence of the Islands; however, their numbers, along with the 534 contractors based at Mount Pleasant, are not included in the census. The population was estimated to be 3,100 in 2009.

Public Holidays 2014
1 January: New Year's Day
18 April: Good Friday
21 April: Easter Monday
9 June: Queen's Birthday
14 June: Liberation Day
7 October: Spring Holiday
8 December: Battle Day
25 December: Christmas Day
26 December: Boxing Day
27-28 December: Christmas Holiday
31 December: New Year's Eve (Government Depts. only)

EMPLOYMENT

The 2001 census put the workforce at 2,050. Professional and technical positions that cannot be filled from local resources are normally recruited from the UK on supplemented salaries and fixed term contracts. It is the Government's mainly policy to increase local salaries to a level that is in line with UK salaries over the next few years. Since the changes to the fishing industry were introduced the Falkland Islands have enjoyed full employment.

The Falkland Islands General Employees Union (GEU) is registered under the Trade Unions and Trade Disputes Ordinance. It has the character of a general workers union and is an affiliate of the International Confederation of Trade Unions.

BANKING AND FINANCE

Currency
Both British and local coinage (Falkland Island pound) and bank notes are used.

GDP/GNP, Inflation, National Debt
It is estimated that the GNP of the Islands tripled between 1985 and 1987 as a result of declaring the 150 nautical miles around the islands the Falkland Islands Interim Conservation and Management Zone (FICZ). Figures for 2007 put GDP at approximately £104 million. Fishery sector accounts for 60 per cent of GDP and approximately 35 per cent of income. Exploration drilling for oil in Falklands waters is expected to start in 2010. Cruise tourism is a growing industry, bringing in £4.2 million during the 2008-09 season. Landbased tourists spent an estimated £3.2 million. (Source: http://www.falklands.gov.uk)

Foreign Investment
Following the 1982 conflict, Britain announced the provision of £31 million of financial aid. The final part of this was spent in 1992. Since then no further financial aid has been provided. The Islands are now self-sufficient in all areas except defence.

MANUFACTURING, MINING AND SERVICES

In the past, economic development was hindered by the lack of natural resources on the Falklands, the small size of the population, and the remoteness of external markets. Wool was the traditional mainstay of the economy and principal export. Since 1982 there has been considerable diversification. The fishing industry has been developed, creating the mainstay of government income. As a result of this the Falklands are financially self-sufficient.

Primary and Extractive Industries
A long term prospect is oil and gas development in the South Atlantic; although evidence of hydrocarbon deposits have been found in is not yet known if it will financially viable to recover them. Minor traces of gold have been found in streams as well as minerals such as zircon, rutile and garnate in some sands.

Energy
The Falkland Islands Development Corporation (FIDC) has been instrumental in the formation of an Energy Advisory Committee. Petroleum product imports have been increasing by an average of 1,000 tonnes per year, and a primary object of the Committee is to reduce dependence upon expensive imported resources. More efficient use of energy and the increased use of alternative and more environmentally friendly forms of energy, such as hydro, wind and solar power, are key objectives. Around 40 per cent of generated power now comes from wind turbines.

Manufacturing and Service Industries
Sustainable diversification of the economy, import substitution, added value of the Islands exports and the provision of local services all flow from the development of the industrial/service sector. FIDC has assisted in the establishment of a number of businesses in construction and building, manufacturing, food production, retailing and professional services, and on West Falkland a wool and spinning mill has been established. On the edge of Stanley there is a growing light industrial, commercial and retail development under the management of the FIDC. This project is seen as a major contribution to the private sector.

Tourism
Over 30,000 day visitors from cruise ships visited the islands annually, and this was expected to rise to 50,000 during the 2006-07 cruise season. During the 2007-08 season 62,203 cruise ship passengers visited. The Islands' basic infrastructure can now support a tourism industry and is actively seeking visitors from Europe and the Americas. The Islands are a haven for birdwatchers, wildlife enthusiasts, lifestyle travelers, and photographers. The islands also attract military historians and anglers.

Recently a visitor and heritage centre has been built in Stanley and hotel accommodation is being improved.

Falkland Islands Tourist Board, URL: http://www.visitorfalklands.com; http://www.tourism.org.fk/home.htm

Agriculture
The Falkland Islands farmland extends to around 1,140,500 hectares, now consisting of about 90 farms, which are mostly family units with an average 13,500 hectares. There were estimated to be 707,596 sheep, 4,439 cattle and 1,188 horses, and in 2001 the islands took delivery of reindeer with a view to producing reindeer meat. The Falkland Islands is the world's first totally organic food-producing country. There are plans to develop exports of beef, pork, mutton and lamb from local herds and flocks. A modern abattoir has been opened. The Falklands are well placed to gain from rising demand in Europe for organic produce. A hydroponic market garden is used to grow produce, up to 65 per cent of which goes for export. .

Agricultural Production in 2010

Produce	Int. $'000*	Tonnes
Wool, greasy	4,209	2,200
Indigenous sheep meat	2,206	810
Cow milk, whole, fresh	468	1,500
Indigenous cattle meat	423	157
Indigenous chicken meat	11	8

* unofficial figures
Source: http://faostat.fao.org/site/339/default.aspx Food and Agriculture Organization of the United Nations, Food and Agricultural commodities production

Fishing
Since 1982, the pace of economic development has accelerated dramatically. The rapid growth resulted from the influx of aid from Britain but more recently from the development of fisheries. The size of fisheries revenues and their subsequent careful investment has enabled much-needed improvements to be made in infrastructure and the promotion of tourism and other enterprises which will assist in the diversification of the economy. The activity generated has resulted in full employment and an increase in salaries and wages.

In February 1987, the 150 nautical mile Falklands Interim Conservation and Management Zone (FICZ) was introduced in response to concern about the increasing levels of uncontrolled fishing in the south-west Atlantic (SWA). The immediate effect of this was a reduction in vessels fishing in Falkland waters from around 600 to around 200, with all vessels now fishing within the zone requiring a licence from the Falkland Islands Government (FIG). The main resources in the fishery are two species of squid: *Illex argentinus* and *Loligo gahi*. In addition, there are a number of finfish species. The fishery generates around £20 million per year in licence fees, of which £5 million is spent on policing, research and administration. FIG's Fisheries Department is responsible for administering the fishery. The income is entirely dependent on the use of fish stocks; however, the policy is always to conserve stocks and in some years the fisheries have been closed early in order to meet conservation targets. A South Atlantic Fisheries Commission (SAFC) has been established involving Britain and Argentina to explore ways of improving conservation of migratory and straddling stocks. 75 per cent of the catch is squid destined for the European and Far Eastern markets. In 1990 the FICZ was extended to 200 nautical miles. FAO figures for 2010 put the total catch at 99,560 tonnes.

COMMUNICATIONS AND TRANSPORT

Airlines
Lan Chile now operate weekly flights between the Falklands and the South American mainland at Santiago, Chile, with a monthly stop in Argentina. There is a regular RAF flight to and from the UK, on which civilians can travel.

Air transport within the islands is provided by the Falkland Islands Government Air Service (FIGAS). There are some 40 grass and beach airstrips serving almost every settlement in the Islands.

Roads
The network of roads in the Islands is expanding. There are now currently 50 km of surfaced roads on the Islands, as well as over 400 km of unsurfaced roads. This includes the 80 km of road from Stanley to Mount Pleasant Airport and Goose Green, the largest civilian settlement outside Stanley.

Shipping
A chartered cargo vessel plies between Britain and the Falklands about once a month. Freight is normally transported around the Islands by the coastal ship, MV 'Tamar FI', which carries fuel and other supplies to farms and outlying islands, collecting wool for the return trip for subsequent onward shipment to the UK by charter vessel. The 'Tamar' makes occasional voyages to Chile for the collection of stores and it has two double cabins that can be booked by passengers. Communications with South Georgia and the South Sandwich Islands and the British Antarctic Territory are maintained, when ice conditions allow, by the Royal Research Ships James Clark Ross and Bransfield, and by the ice patrol ship HMS Endurance.

Freight and shipping services are currently available through three agents:
H.R. Shipping Services Ltd, TDK House, 5/7 Queensway, Redhill, Surrey, RH1 1YB, United Kingdom. Tel: +44 (0)1737 769055, fax: +44 (0)1737 765916
Jepperson Heaton Ltd, 1st Floor, Charrington House, The Causeway, Bishops Stortford, Herts, CH23 2ER. Tel: +44 (0)1279 461630, fax: +44 (0)1279 461631
Wilson & Co. (UK) Ltd, Units 5 & 6, Parkway Trading Estate, Cranford Lane, Hounslow, Middlesex, TW5 9QA. Tel: +44 (0)20 8814 7000, fax: (0)20 8814 7077

UNITED KINGDOM

HEALTH

The Falkland Islands Government (FIG) Health Service is responsible for preventative and curative medical services in the Islands. The Chief Medical Officer is also responsible for advising FIG on health policy matters. The general standard of health within the Islands is good. Most services, including prescriptions, are free to residents. The Government reserves the right to alter charges when it is deemed appropriate.

The King Edward VII Memorial Hospital, Stanley's only hospital, has 27-beds and includes an acute care wing, a primary care wing, a one-bed maternity unit and a two-bed intensive care unit, with facilities for out-patients and community health care. All medical services for the Islands are run from the hospital, including a general practitioner service for Stanley and a routine and emergency flying doctor service for farm settlements. Full surgeon and anesthetist cover is provided 24 hours a day on a rotational basis. The RAF provide an aeromedical evacuation service to Chile or the UK for the seriously ill.

EDUCATION

Education is free and compulsory for all 5-16 year olds. The Falkland Islands Government provides staff, equipment and supplies for education throughout the Islands, has a primary and secondary school in Stanley and operates three small settlement schools on large farms. Other rural pupils are taught individually or in families. In Stanley, the two schools are of UK standard using English methods and examination systems. The primary school has 18 teaching staff with 190 pupils of 5-11 years and 30 pupils of pre-school age. The Falkland Islands Community School has 18 specialist teaching staff and 150 pupils in the 11-16 age group. Many teachers come from Britain, Australia or New Zealand, in addition to local teachers, all of whom have received training in the UK. Provision is for education up to GCSE level on the Islands, after which pupils may progress to GCE 'A' level and tertiary education in the UK. There are now a total of 40 students attending British universities, polytechnics and sixth-form colleges. (Source: Falkland Islands Government)

RELIGION

Religion on the Islands is predominantly Anglican but there is also a Roman Catholic and a United Free Church in Stanley.

COMMUNICATIONS AND MEDIA

Newspapers
The Penguin News, URL: http://www.penguin-news.com

Broadcasting
British Forces Broadcasting provides a television service to the Islands. There is a local radio service through Falkland Islands Broadcasting Service (FIBS) as well as "Calling the Falklands" from the BBC World Service. The British Forces Broadcasting Service (BFBS) provides a multi-channel satellite television service. A Cable TV service is also in operation.
Falkland Islands Radio Service, URL: http://www.firs.co.fk/
BFBS Radio Falklands, forces radio, URL: http://bfbs-radio.com/index.ph

Telecommunications
The internet is available on the island and most households are connected.

ENVIRONMENT

The Falkland Islands contain exceptional wildlife which the Government and population are committed to sustain and nurture. Species of particular interest include large colonies of albatross, penguins and other seabirds of international conservation importance. The Falkland Flightless Steamer Duck - which is unique to the Islands, the Ruddy-headed Goose, the Striated Caracara and the Black-throated Finch, are all threatened elsewhere. Marine mammals such as sea lions, fur seals and elephant seals all breed on the Islands. Some 15 species of whales and dolphins can be found in the waters around the islands. 14 of around 160 native flowering plants are found nowhere else in the world, and Tussac grass grows at least 10 feet tall, providing vital shelter for many native birds.

In 2001, the Government issued its three year 'Island Plan', the first comprehensive blueprint since Lord Shackleton's report in the early 1980s. The report sets out ten policies including protecting and treasuring the unspoiled nature of the environment, aiming for environmental sustainability in the long term.

Central to environmental protection are the activities of Falklands Conservation, a registered charity to which FIG makes considerable donations for research each year. Falklands Conservation takes action for nature in the Falkland Islands, working with bird and habitat conservation organisations in a global partnership, called BirdLife International. URL: http://www.falklands-nature.demon.co.uk

In 2006, the Falkland Islands' emissions from the consumption of fossil fuels totalled 0.04 million metric tons of carbon dioxide.

GIBRALTAR

Governor and Commander-in-Chief: Vice Admiral Sir Adrian Johns KBE, CBE (page 1450)

Chief Minister: Hon. Fabian Picardo (page 1495)

National Flag: White with a red stripe along the bottom, red triple-towered castle with a gold key descending from the gateway.

CONSTITUTION AND GOVERNMENT

Constitution

Gibraltar was captured by British forces under Admiral Sir George Rooke in 1704 and was ceded by Spain to Great Britain by the Treaty of Utrecht in 1713. Under the Gibraltar Constitution Order in Council 1964, there was a Gibraltar Council, a Council of Ministers and a Legislative Council consisting of a speaker appointed by the Governor, 11 elected members and two ex-officio members, the Attorney-General and the Financial Secretary. At Constitutional talks held in Gibraltar in July 1968, agreement was reached with local leaders on the lines of certain constitutional changes.

These were incorporated into the new 1969 constitution which is contained in the Gibraltar Constitution Order 1969 and which came into effect on 11 August 1969. The new constitution replaced the Legislative Council by a House of Assembly consisting of a Speaker, 15 elected members, the Attorney-General and the Financial and Development Secretary, and formalised the devolution of responsibility for certain defined domestic matters to the Council of Ministers who are appointed from among the elected members of House of Assembly by the Governor in consultation with the Chief Minister, who is also appointed by the Governor. The elected members of the House of Assembly serve a four-year term. The Constitution also made provision for the abolition of the City Council, which dealt with municipal affairs and public utilities. The Governor retains direct responsibility for matters relating to defence, external affairs and internal security.

The preamble to the Order in Council (to which the Constitution is an annex) contains the following: 'Whereas Gibraltar is part of Her Majesty's dominions and Her Majesty's Government has given assurance to the people of Gibraltar that Gibraltar will remain part of Her Majesty's dominions unless and until an Act of Parliament otherwise provides, and furthermore, that Her Majesty's Government will never enter into arrangements under which the people of Gibraltar would pass under the sovereignty of another state against their freely and democratically expressed wishes...'

Gibraltar joined the European Community in 1973, by virtue of Article 227(4) of the Treaty of Rome, as a dependent territory of the United Kingdom. As part of its accession, Gibraltar opted to be excluded from the provisions of the Common Agricultural Policy, the Customs Union (CCT) and Value Added Tax.

In 1999 consultations began to modernise the constitution, a Select Committee was formed, the proposals raised by the committee formed the basis for discussions between delegates of the Gibraltar Assembly and the British Government. A referendum was held on November 30 2006 to approve the changes and more than 60 per cent of those who voted, voted to approve the new constitution which came into force on January 2 2007. Under the new constitution Gibraltar has a larger say in areas such as external affairs, defence, security and public service, areas previously overseen by the Governor. The House of Assembly is now known as the Gibraltar Parliament which will determine its own size. Under the constitution Gibraltar will now create a new Police Authority.

To consult the constitution, please visit: http://www.gibraltarlaws.gov.gi/constitution.php.

Recent Events

Following the re-opening of communications between Britain and Spain regarding Gibraltar, a series of meetings was held and the negotiations became known as the Brussels Process. In 1997 the Spanish Foreign Minister proposed joint sovereignty, with full sovereignty passing eventually to Spain. Following public and political opposition, this path was rejected. In 2002, in order to show their strength of feeling, a referendum was held and 99 per cent of Gibraltarians voted to remain a British dependency. By February 2003, no agreement had been reached apart from the promise by both countries to work together for a resolution in the future. Under the terms of the Utrecht agreement, if Britain gives up sovereignty of Gibraltar, it automatically reverts to Spain; self-government is therefore not an option. Under an agreement with the British government from 1969, any agreement must go to a referendum of the Gibraltarians. In 2004, Britain and Spain agreed for the first time to allow Gibraltar its own voice in a new forum to discuss its future, and in 2006, all three parties reached a series of agreements allowing easier border crossings and improved transport and communications between Spain and Gibraltar. In the same year passenger flights began between Gibraltar and Spain.

In July 2010, Gibraltar announced it was ending the tax-free offshore status for locally-registered companies operating outside Gibraltar, it would came into force in January 2011.

Legislature

The Gibraltar Parliament consists of the speaker who is non-elected and is appointed by parliament and at least 17 elected members who serve a four year term. The Chief Minister is appointed by the Governor.

House of Assembly, 156 Main Street, Gibraltar. Tel: +350 78420, fax: +350 42849, URL: http://www.gibraltar.gov.gi
Speaker: Hon. Haresh K. Budhrani QC
There is a London based Government of Gibraltar office: 179 The Strand, London WC2R 1EH, United Kingdom. Tel: +44 (0)20 7836,0777, e-mail: info@gibraltar.gov.uk

Cabinet (as at April 2013)
Chief Minister, Minister of Economy and Finance: Hon. Fabian Picardo (page 1495)
Deputy Chief Minister and Minister for Planning and Lands, Political, Democratic and Civic Reform: Hon. Dr Joseph Garcia
Minister for Education, Financial Services, Gaming, Telecommunications and Justice: Hon. Gilbert Licudi
Minister for Health & Environment: Hon. Dr John Cortes
Minister of Tourism, Public Transport and the Port: Hon. Neil Costa
Minister for Housing and the Elderly: Hon. Charles Bruzon
Minister for Equality and Social Services: Hon. Samantha Sacramento
Minister of Enterprise, Training and Employment: Hon. Joe Bossano (page 1392)
Minister of Sports, Culture, Heritage and Youth: Hon. Steven Linares
Minister of Traffic, Health and Safety and Techical Services: Hon. Paul Balban

Elections

The most recent general election in Gibraltar took place in December 2011. It was won by an alliance of the Gibraltar Socialist Labour Party (GSLP) and the Liberal Party.

Election Results

Party	% of Votes Cast	Seats
Gibraltar Socialist Labour Party / Liberal Party	48.8	10
Gibraltar Social Democrats	46.7	7

In addition to the elected members, the House of Assembly has an appointed Speaker and two ex-officio members (the Attorney General, the Hon. R.R. Rhoda QC, and the Financial and Development Secretary, T.J. Bristow). A Mayor of Gibraltar is elected by the elected members of the Assembly.

Political Organisations

Gibraltar Liberal Party (GLP) (formed in 1991), URL: http://www.liberal.gi
Leader: Dr Joseph Garcia
Gibraltar Social Democrats (GSD) (formed in 1989 and holds a majority of seats in the House of Assembly), URL: http://www.gsd.gi
Leader: Peter Caruana (page 1401)
Gibraltar Socialist Labour Party (GSLP) (formed in 1976 and is the official opposition party in alliance with the Gibraltar Liberal Party), URL: http://www.gslp.gi
Leader: Fabian Picardo

All parties advocate self determination for Gibraltar.

LEGAL SYSTEM

Gibraltar law is based on English law and UK parliamentary acts which apply to Gibraltar. The 1969 Gibraltar Constitution provided for the protection of the fundamental rights and freedoms of the individual and the maintenance of a Supreme Court with unlimited jurisdiction to hear and determine any civil or criminal proceedings under any law.

The judiciary consists of a Court of Appeal, the Supreme Court, the Court of First Instance and the Magistrates' Court. The Supreme Court of Gibraltar follows the rules of procedure of the English Supreme Court. Appeals lie to the Gibraltar Court of Appeal and from there on a point of law only to the Privy Council in London. As a territory within the European Union, European Union legislation has the same effect as in any member state and references to the European Court on questions of law can be made. Most Gibraltar lawyers qualify in England. The Chief Justice is appointed by the Governor of Gibraltar on the advice of the British Foreign and Commonwealth Office.

Much of Gibraltar's commercial legislation has been enacted to provide a favourable climate for the financial services industry. For example, Gibraltar law on banking secrecy, and the confidentiality of off-shore company management is much stricter than that of the United Kingdom.

The Supreme Court of Gibraltar, 277 Main Street, Gibraltar
Acting Chief Justice: Anthony Dudley

AREA AND POPULATION

Area

Gibraltar is situated in latitude 36°07'N and longitude 05°21'W, and stands out steeply from the adjoining Spanish territory to which it is connected by a sandy isthmus about 1.7 km. long and 0.8 km. wide. The Rock runs from north to south for a length of nearly 5 km. It is 1.2 km. wide and has a total area of 6.5 sq. km. Its highest point is 426 metres. Gibraltar is of significant strategic importance, standing at the mouth of the Mediterranean Sea, and is only 12 miles from the North Coast of Africa. The Strait of Gibraltar links the Mediterranean Sea and the North Atlantic Ocean.

There are no permanent natural water supplies in Gibraltar. The main sources of water supply are the distillation plants which purify sea water or large concrete or natural rock water catchments that collect rain water.

The climate is Mediterranean.

To view a map, consult http://www.lib.utexas.edu/maps/cia08/gibraltar_sm_2008.gif

Population

Figures for 2011 put the population at 29,752 of whom approximately 24,288 were British Gibraltarian, 3,042 UK British and 2,422 non-British, with main ethnic groups including Genoese, Portuguese, Maltese and Spanish. Population density is 4,577 per sq km. English is the official language and Spanish is also spoken.

Births, Marriages and Deaths

In 2011, there were estimated to be 442 births, 241 deaths and 990 marriages.

Life expectancy at birth in 2009 was estimated at 77 years for males and 83 years for females. The median age was 33 years.

Public Holidays 2014

1 January: New Year's Day
17 March: Commonwealth Day
18 April: Good Friday
21 April: Easter Monday
1 May: May Day
26 May: Spring Bank Holiday
2 June: Queen's Birthday
25 August: Late Summer Bank Holiday
9 September: Gibraltar National Day
25 December: Christmas Day
26 December: Boxing Day

EMPLOYMENT

More than 70 per cent of the economy is in the public sector, so any change in government spending has a major impact on the level of employment. In October 2011 the total number of employee jobs was 22,247. At that time the principal areas of employment were community, social and personal services, 5,291; trade, restaurants and hotels, 4,224; construction, 3,434; manufacturing, 464; electricity and water, 299; other, 8,535. Figures for 2007 put unemployment at below five per cent. Figures at July 2010 put employment at 20,450 down by 59 on the 2009 figure which had been a record high level.

BANKING AND FINANCE

Currency

The legal tender currency is UK sterling. Also legal tender are Government of Gibraltar Currency Notes of £50, £20, £10 and £5 denominations, as well as Gibraltar Government coinage.

GDP/GNP, Inflation, National Debt

Gibraltar's economy is a service economy. Revenue is largely generated from an extensive shipping trade, offshore banking and Gibraltar's position as an international conference centre and tourist destination. The financial sector accounts for 15 per cent of GDP, and the British military presence now contributes around 8 per cent to the local economy, greatly reduced from previous years when the British Ministry of Defence maintained a larger presence. Further sources of revenue are tourism, shipping services fees, internet gaming accounts and duties on consumer goods.

Inflation in January 2008 was recorded at 2.8 per cent, 3.4 per cent in January 2010 and 3.7 per cent in January 2012.

Figures for 2005 put GDP (at factor cost) at £655.88 million, rising to £739.06 million in 2007. It was estimated at £803 million in 2007, £869 million in 2008. Figures for 2009 put growth at 5.5 per cent. The final GDP figure for 2009-10 was £998.36 million. provisional figures for the year 2011-12 put economic growth at 8.3 per cent. GDP consists of approximately 25 per cent from government, 15 per cent from retail, 12 per cent from internet gaming, 10 per cent from construction, 10 per cent for business services and real estate, 8 per cent from financial services and 8 per cent from the Ministry of Defence. Per capita GDP was estimated at £27,468 in 2008 and £29,025 in 2009.

Net public debt was put at 19.6 per cent of GDP in 2010-11 and 26.8 per cent in 2011-12.

Balance of Payments / Imports and Exports

Figures for 2011 show that imports cost a total of £541.2 million (excluding fuel) and exports earned £153.8 million recording a visible trade deficit of £455.6 million. Britain is Gibraltar's main trading partner providing 27 per cent of imported goods followed by Spain, the Netherlands and Germany. As agricultural production is negligible foodstuffs account for around eight per cent of imports, as Gibraltar has to import all its fuel this accounts for 77 per cent of the value of total imports. Gibraltar's exports mainly consist of re-exported petroleum and petroleum products and manufactured goods particularly wines, spirits, malt and tobacco. (Source: Gibraltar Statistics Abstract)

UNITED KINGDOM

MANUFACTURING, MINING AND SERVICES

Energy
Gibraltar is dependent on imported petroleum for its energy supplies. Mineral fuels comprised around 71 per cent of the value of total imports in 2009. In 2011, 164.3 million kWh of electricity was produced.

Manufacturing
The industrial sector including manufacturing (ship repair building and repair and fish canning), construction and power employs around 16 per cent of the working population. Since the closure of the Royal Naval Dockyard the contribution of ship repair to the economy has fallen.

Service Industries
Tourism, port services and banking make an important contribution to the economy. The financial sector employs 12 per cent of the working population. Some Spanish banks have established offices in Gibraltar, encouraging the growth of the territory as an 'offshore' banking centre, whilst the absence of taxes for non-residents has also encouraged the use of Gibraltar as a financial centre.

There were 18 banks authorised to conduct banking business in Gibraltar as at March 2007. In 1989 the Financial Services Commission was established to regulate financial activities. There are four building societies.

The economy is primarily dependent upon service industries and port facilities with income being derived from tourism, transhipment, and, perhaps most importantly, in terms of growth, the provision of financial services. Recent figures show that the financial services sector contributes about 22 per cent of GDP.

Gibraltar's tourist attractions include its climate, beaches and a variety of amenities. Following the reopening of the border with Spain in February 1985, the resumption of traffic by day-visitors contributed to the expansion of the tourist industry. Revenue from tourism totalled around £230.5 million in 2007. In that year over 8 million tourists (including day-visitors) visited Gibraltar. There are an estimated 900 hotel beds in Gibraltar. Gibraltar is a popular stop off for cruise ships. Estimated figures for 2011 show that 10,100,000 people visited Gibraltar generating revenue of £279.41 million.

Gibraltar Tourist Board, URL: http://www.gibraltar.gov.uk/main.php

Agriculture
Gibraltar lacks agricultural land and natural resources, and the territory is dependent on imports of foodstuffs and fuels.

COMMUNICATIONS AND TRANSPORT

International Airports
North Front Airport; scheduled flights are operated by British Airways, (GB Airways) to London (Gatwick), Manchester and Casablanca and by Monarch Airlines to London (Luton) and Manchester and by Iberia to Madrid. Figures for 2011 show that 189,529 passengers arrived by air and 193,484 departed. Not including military freight 16 tonnes of freight were loaded and 111 tonnes unloaded.

Railways
There are no railways in Gibraltar, other than in the dockyard area.

Roads
There are 50 km of paved road. Figures for 2006 show that there were 14,637 private vehicles on the roads, over 7,000 motorcycles, 1,391 goods vehicles, 99 buses and 112 taxis. Vehicles are driven on the right.

Shipping
The Strait of Gibraltar is a principal ocean route between the Mediterranean and Black Sea areas and the rest of the world.

The Port of Gibraltar offers protected longside berths to merchant shipping in addition to an anchorage capable of accommodating the largest ships afloat. The port is used by many long distance liners, has drydock facilities and a commercial ship-repair yard. The Port of Gibraltar is a popular port of call for vessels calling for bunkers taking on supplies, change of crew, repairs or any other ancillary requirement. Tax concessions are available to ship-owners who register their ships at Gibraltar.

There is a regular ferry service between Gibraltar and Tangiers in Morocco and Gibraltar and Algeciras in Spain.

Ports and Harbours
The Strait of Gibraltar is a major ocean route. Figures for 2011 show that the total number of merchant vessels arriving at the port of Gibraltar was 10,349. Cruise ship arrivals rose in 2011 but fell slightly in 2012 possibly due to the global economic downturn.

HEALTH

Health care is organised by the Gibraltar Health Authority. The authority operates a Group Practice Medical Scheme which is paid for by contributions, and this enables registered persons to access free medical treatment.

St. Bernard's hospital provides out-patient and in-patient treatment for acute medical and surgical cases. It is equipped with a total of 166 beds including a maternity section and two wards for elderly patients. Facilities also exist for specialist medical services to be obtained outside Gibraltar where such services are beyond the scope of local resources. The King George V Psychiatric Unit can treat up to 60 patients. Out-patient clinics are also provided. A Health Centre houses the General Practice Surgeries. The child welfare and school medical services, makes provision for immunisation and vaccination. The school dental service clinic and health visitors are also housed in this centre. A programme of visits by consultants from the United Kingdom cover certain specialities which are not provided by staff permanently employed in Gibraltar. These include, for example, Paediatric Neurology, Plastic Surgery and Cardiothoracic Surgery.

Registered persons and their dependants can obtain medicines prescribed by a doctor employed by the Authority from Scheme Pharmacists on the payment of a nominal fee.

Total expenditure for the Gibraltar Health Authority for the financial year 2011-12 was £87.3 million.

Heart disease and cancers each account for 25 per cent of all deaths. Lung cancer is the most frequent cause of death from cancer in men, followed by breast cancer in women. The most significant contributory cause of lung cancer is tobacco smoking.

EDUCATION

Free compulsory education is provided for children between ages 5 and 15 years. The medium of instruction is English. The Comprehensive system was introduced in September 1972. Gibraltar has 15 play groups and nursery schools, and there were 11 primary and two comprehensive schools in academic year 2009-10. Primary schools are mixed and divided into first schools for children aged 4-8 years and middle schools for children aged 8-12 years. The comprehensives are single sex. In addition, there is one Services primary school and one private primary school. A new, purpose-built Special School for severely handicapped children aged 2-16 years was opened in 1977, and there are four Special Units for children with special educational needs (one attached to a first school, one to a middle school and one at each secondary school), three nurseries for children aged 3-4 years and an occupational therapy centre for handicapped adults. In September 1997, a new observation and assessment centre was opened at the special school to monitor the progress of pre-school children with special education needs.

Technical and vocational education and training is available at the Gibraltar College of Further Education managed by the Gibraltar Government. In September 2011, there were 2,993 pupils at Government Primary Schools, 458 at private and 103 at the Services School, 24 at the Special School, 1,077 at the Boys' Comprehensive School, and 1,000 at the Girls' Comprehensive. There were 309 students in the Gibraltar College of Further Education. Scholarships are made available for universities, teacher-training and other higher education in the UK. Government expenditure on education in the year ending 31 March 2012 was £29.9 million.

RELIGION

The religion of the civil population is mostly Roman Catholic. There is one Anglican and one Roman Catholic Cathedral as well as two Anglican and six Roman Catholic churches, one Presbyterian and one Methodist church, four Synagogues and two Mosques. According to the 2001 Census, 76.9 per cent of the population were Roman Catholic, 6.9 per cent Muslim, 6.9 per cent Church of England, 2.4 per cent Jewish and 1.7 per cent Hindu.

Gibraltar has a religious liberty rating of 10 on a scale of 1 to 10 (10 is most freedom). (Source: World Religion Database)

COMMUNICATIONS AND MEDIA

Newspapers
Newspapers include:
Gibraltar Chronicle, daily, URL: http://www.chronicle.gi
Panorama, URL: http://www.panorama.gi
Insight Magazine, monthly, URL: http://www.insight-gibraltar.com

Broadcasting
Television services are provided by the Gibraltar Broadcasting Corporation (GBC). GBC Radio (Radio Gibraltar) broadcasts in English and Spanish for 24 hours daily, including commercial broadcasting. Television and radio broadcasts from Spain can also be received.
GBC Television, URL: http://www.gbc.gi/

Telecommunications
Figures for January 2012 show that there were 23,616 fixed exchange lines and an estimated 32,273 mobile phones. An estimated 10,996 customers have access to the internet.

ENVIRONMENT

In 2006 Gibraltar's emissions from the consumption of fossil fuels totalled 4.47 million metric tons of carbon dioxide.

MONTSERRAT

Capital: Plymouth (devastated by the volcano); Brades Estate is currently the seat of government

Governor: Adrian Davis (page 1413)

Deputy Governor: Alric (Jim) Taylor

Flag: A British blue ensign with the shield of arms in the fly depicting a woman with a harp embracing a cross

CONSTITUTION AND GOVERNMENT

Constitution
Under the Constitution of 1989 the government of Montserrat is carried out by the Governor in conjunction with a Legislative and an Executive Council. In 1989 the Constitution of Montserrat was consolidated into a single document. Montserrat is internally self-governing although the Governor retains responsibility for security, external affairs, defence, public service and offshore finance. Under the 1999 White Paper Partnership for Progress and Prosperity the British Government invited all the Overseas Territories to make proposals to review and modernise their constitutions. The Montserrat Constitutional Commissioners submitted their report in 2002 and based on this talks have been held in Montserrat in 2006 and 2007. In 2010, the Constitution was modified, replacing the office of Chief Minister with the office of Premier, and the Executive Council with a Cabinet.

To consult the constitution, please consult: URL: http://constitution.gov.ms/

International Relations
Montserrat is a British Overseas Territory and as such as close ties with the UK. Montserrat is also a member of CARICOM and the Organisation of Western Caribbean States.

Recent Events
On 18 July 1995, Chances Peak volcano erupted for the first time in 350 years. Thousands had to be evacuated, some went to safe areas in the north of the islands and some left for the UK, the USA and other Caribbean islands.

On 25 June 1997 the Soufriere Hills volcano erupted. Two-thirds of the island was rendered uninhabitable and 19 people are killed. The capital of the island, Plymouth had to be abandoned. Rescuers and aid could only reach the island by helicopter or boat as the airport was destroyed. The following year Britain announced that Montserratians could apply for permanent residence in the UK. In July 2001 the volcano erupted again, the island suffered further volcanic eruptions in July 2003 and a more major eruption in February 2010. Some areas were evacuated as a result and the volcano is now considered to be in a state of 'pause'.

In July 2005 Gerald's Airport was opened; it replaced the W H Bramble airport which was destroyed in the 1997 volcanic eruption.

Governor Adrian Davis was sworn in on 8 April 2011.

In June 2012 the opposition leader, Donaldson Romeo, filed a motion of no confidence in the administration of Premier Reuben Meade following several controversial decisions including the raising of import tariffs. Mr Meade also referred to Monstserrat as no longer being a colonised country.

In May 2013, Monsterrat was one of several UK overseas territories to sign an agreement on sharing tax information with the UK, France, Germany, Italy and Spain as part of a drive against tax evasion.

Legislature
The legislative council was made up of 14 members: a Speaker, seven elected members, two nominated members and the Attorney General and Financial Secretary. Following the volcanic eruption, nearly five of the constituencies became unoccupied. In 1999 a reform commission recommended that the nominated membership of the Assembly be abolished and the elected membership be increased from seven to nine. Since the volcano eruption, interim government buildings and ministries have been located in Brades Estate in the Carr's Bay area.
Government Headquarters, 8 Farara Plaza, Brades, Montserrat, West Indies. Tel: +1 664 491 2365/2444, fax: +1 664 491 6234, e-mail: admin@gov.ms, URL: http://www.gov.ms
Governor's Residence, URL: http://ukinmontserrat.fco.gov.uk/en/about-us/

Cabinet (as at June 2013)
President: Adrian Davis (page 1413)
Premier: Reuben Meade
Deputy Premier & Minister of Communications and Works: Charles T. Kirnon
Minister of Education, Health, Sports and Social Services: Colin Riley
Minister of Agriculture, Lands, Housing & the Environment: Easton Taylor-Farrell

---

Government portal: URL: http://www.gov.ms
Office of the Premier: URL: http://ocm.gov.ms
Ministry of Finance, URL: http://finance.gov.ms
Ministry of Health, URL: http://moh.gov.ms/
Ministry of Agriculture, Lands, Housing and the Environment, URL: http://www.malhe.gov.ms/

There was a re-organisation of ministries as part of the ongoing restructuring process and inception of the new Constitution Order. The Ministry of Economic Development & Trade merged with the Ministry of Finance.

Political Parties
Movement for Change and Prosperity (MCAP), URL: http://www.mcap.ms/
New People's Liberation Party (NPLM)
Montserrat Democratic Party, URL: http://www.mdp.ms/

Elections
Following the devastating volcanic eruptions of 1997, four and a half of the seven constituencies were uninhabited at the time of the election. In 1999 the Governor commissioned a report on this, and the first past the post system that had been in existence was slightly modified. There is now one constituency using a modified first past the post system and the elected membership has been increased from seven to nine. An election was held in May 2006 resulting in a coalition of the Montserrat Democratic Party led by Lowell Lewis and the New People's Liberation Movement.

The most recent election was held in September 2009; the Movement for Change and Prosperity led by Reuben Meade won six of the nine seats. Elections are next due to take place in 2014.

LEGAL SYSTEM

The law of Montserrat is English Common law and locally enacted legislation. It is administered by a magistrates court and the Eastern Caribbean Supreme Court (ECSC), with a non-resident puisne judge serving Montserrat. Criminal cases are heard by the Assizes and civil cases are referred to the High Court. In both criminal and civil cases, there is the right of appeal to the Court of Appeal with the ultimate right of appeal to the Privy Council in England.

LOCAL GOVERNMENT

Montserrat is divided into three administrative parishes: Saint Anthony, Saint Georges and Saint Peter.

AREA AND POPULATION

Area
The island was discovered by Columbus in 1493 and named by him after a monastery in Spain, and came under English control in 1632 when predominantly Irish settlers arrived. It is situated 27 miles south west of Antigua and is about 11 miles in length and seven miles in breadth and is predominantly mountainous. The southern half of the island, including the capital Plymouth, has been devastated by the Soufriere Hills Volcano, which erupted in 1995. A further eruption took place in July 2003. Since the volcanic eruptions a safe zone has been created. The dome of the Soufriere Hills volcano began to grow in 2005 and there was increased volcanic activity in 2006 and early 2007, and the designated safe area has now been moved back resulting in some relocation of residents. Homeowners whose properties lie in the unsafe area have to obtain permission to visit.

The climate is tropical.

To view a map, consult http://www.lib.utexas.edu/maps/cia08/montserrat_sm_2008.gif

Population
The population has decreased dramatically since 1995 because of volcanic eruptions. In 2006, there were an estimated 4,655 people living on the island with a further 8,000 living abroad. Most Montserratians that left after the eruption moved to the UK, where they were given temporary residence; this was later made permanent. Others moved to the island of Antigua and the USA, mainly New York and Boston, but the temporary residence they were granted in the US has since been revoked. The problem for many is that although they may wish to return is that there is little to return to, either in terms of housing or employment. Massive eruptions in 1997 led to the island facing an uncertain future, although development is being carried out in the north. British aid, from the start of the crisis in July 1995 to March 2001, totaled £134 million. A further £55 million was committed until 2003. By 2011 the population was estimated to be just over 4,483. Life expectancy was estimated to be 72 years.

The official language is English.

Public Holidays 2014
1 January: New Year's Day
17 March: St Patrick's Day
18 April: Good Friday
21 April: Easter Monday
5 May: Labour Day
9 June: Whit Monday
2 June: Queen's Birthday
18 July: Anniversary of Soufrière Hills Volcano Eruption
4 August: August Monday
25 December: Christmas Day
26 December: Boxing Day
31 December: Festival Day

EMPLOYMENT

The unemployment rate has been estimated at 13 per cent.

UNITED KINGDOM

BANKING AND FINANCE

Currency
The unit of currency is the Eastern Caribbean Dollar.

GDP/GNP, Inflation, National Debt
There is limited economic activity on the island. Activities include mining, construction, financial services and tourism.

GDP in 2006 was estimated at EC\$106 million giving a per capita figure of EC\$22,800 and a growth rate of -2.83 per cent. GDP was recorded at EC\$91.60 million in 2003 and EC\$94.7 in 2004. The service sector is the largest contributor to GDP. Inflation in 2006 was put at 1.0 per cent.

Balance of Payments / Imports and Exports
Figures for 2006 put the value of exports to the UK at EC\$533,485 and imports from the UK at EC\$4,100,000.

MANUFACTURING, MINING AND SERVICES

The economy has been severely hit by volcanic activity which began in July 1995. The main industries are financial services and construction. Tourists are beginning to return to the island. Prior to the volcanic eruption, efforts had been made to develop agriculture-based industries. Main agricultural produce includes cabbages, tomatoes, carrots, cucumbers, peppers and onions. There is also some livestock. Estimated figures for 2011 show that agriculture contributed just 1.6 per cent of GDP. The fishing industry is, as yet, under-developed. FAO figures for 2010 put the total catch 24 tonnes. Tourism had formed a large part of the economy.

Agricultural Production in 2010

Produce	Int. \$'000*	Tonnes
Indigenous cattle meat	1,945	720
Cow milk, whole, fresh	585	1,875
Fruit fresh nes	150	430
Indigenous pigmeat	100	65
Indigenous chicken meat	94	66
Mangoes, mangosteens, guavas	90	150
Indigenous sheep meat	68	25
Indigenous goat meat	62	26
Hen eggs, in shell	58	70
Tomatoes	55	150
Bananas	48	170
Vegetables fresh nes	47	250

* unofficial figures
Source: http://faostat.fao.org/site/339/default.aspx Food and Agriculture Organization of the United Nations, Food and Agricultural commodities production

COMMUNICATIONS AND TRANSPORT

Airports
There is a helicopter service from Montserrat to Antigua. In 2005 Gerald's Airport opened, replacing the W.H. Bramble Airport which was destroyed by volcanic activity, there are five return flights per day between Montserrat and Antigua by fixed wing aircraft operated by Winair.

Roads
There were 126 miles of surfaced main roads. Vehicles are driven on the left.

Ports and Harbours
The main port is at Little Bay; the port at Portsmouth is currently abandoned. A ferry service operates from Little Bay to Antigua.

HEALTH

A well equipped 30 bed hospital provides a 24 hour casualty service. Anyone requiring specialist medical attention may need to travel to a neighbouring island. Life expectancy at birth is estimated at 73 years. The infant mortality rate is estimated at 16.08 deaths per 1,000 live births.

EDUCATION

Nursery, primary and secondary education are available on the island. Education in free and compulsory between the ages of 5 and 14. Figures from UNESCO for 2007 show that 91 per cent of young children were enrolled in pre-school, 96 per cent of girls and 89 per cent of boys were enrolled in primary school and 96 per cent of girls and 95 per cent of boys were enrolled in secondary school.

RELIGION

The majority of the population belongs to the Christian faith, the main churches being Anglican, Methodist, Roman Catholic, Pentecostal and Seventh Day Adventists.

Montserrat has a religious liberty rating of 10 on a scale of 1 to 10 (10 is most freedom). (Source: World Religion Database)

COMMUNICATIONS AND MEDIA

Newspapers
Montserrat has a weekly newspaper, The Montserrat Reporter, URL: http://www.themontserratreporter.com

Broadcasting
Radio Montserrat (URL: http://www.zjb.gov.ms/, is a public broadcaster and two more radio stations exist. Cable and satellite television are available.

Telecommunications
A modern and digitilized telephone system provides links worldwide. In 2008 there were estimated to be 2,800 landlines in operation and 3,000 mobile phones. An estimated 1,200 people were internet users.

ENVIRONMENT

Studies are currently underway to determine the effect of the volcanic eruption on Montserrat's biodiversity. A separate project to monitor the Montserrat's climate has been running for a number of years.

In 2006, Montserrat's emissions from the consumption of fossil fuels totalled 0.07 million metric tons of carbon dioxide. (Source: EIA)

PITCAIRN ISLANDS

Capital: Adamstown (Population estimate: 50)

Governor: Vicki Treadell (page 1527)

Flag: British blue ensign with the coat of arms in the fly

CONSTITUTION AND GOVERNMENT

Constitution
Pitcairn was discovered by Carteret in 1767. In 1790, Fletcher Christian landed with eight of the 'Bounty' mutineers and 18 Tahitians of whom 12 were women. After ten years of strife and murder, the small community settled down under the leadership of John Adams and its existence remained unknown until 1808. On two occasions the island was evacuated but each time people returned. Pitcairn is a British colony by settlement and its constitutional history began in 1838 when a formal constitution was first introduced. In 1898 it came within the jurisdiction of the High Commissioner for the Western Pacific, and in 1952 administration was transferred to the Governor of Fiji. When Fiji became independent on 10 October 1970, the governorship of the islands was transferred to the British High Commissioner in New Zealand.

The Pitcairn Constitution Order 2010 was made on 10 February by Her Majesty in the Privy Council and was expected to come into force in March. Under the terms of the new Constitution a Fundamental Rights chapter is included. The role of the Island Council is established in the Constitution and obliges the Governor, in normal circumstances, to consult with the Island Council before making laws. The independent role of the Pitcairn courts and judicial officers is set out amd it also guarantees the independence of the public service.

To consult the constitution, please visit: http://www.government.pn/Pitcairn%20Islands%20Constitution%20Order%202010.pdf

International Relations
Pitcairn is a British Overseas Territory and as such receives funding for projects from the Department for International Development. Pitcairn has strong links with New Zealand and its nearest neighbour French Polynesia. Pitcairn is a member of the Secretariat of the Pacific Community.

Recent Events
In September 2004 a trial began of seven of the male Pitcairn Islanders, on charges of sexual abuse of under-age girls. The men won the right to be tried on the island and judges and lawyers travelled from New Zealand for the trial. Four of the men received prison sentences, two were sentenced to community service and one was acquitted. Since the absence of four members of the community could have a considerable impact on life on the island, a prison was built on the island to accommodate those given a custodial sentence, and the prisoners are let out to perform vital tasks such as manning the longboat which goes out to passing ships. The convicted men appealed against their sentences but the appeal was rejected by the Privy Council in October 2006. Since the court case the UK government have spent several million pounds improving the infrastructure. In November 2006 Pitcairn got its first full time policeman on the island.

In December 2010, the current mayor, Michael Warren, was charged with several counts of possessing child pornography.

Legislature

The Island has its own elected Island Council headed by the Island Magistrate and it also has a mayor. Elections are held annually. Visitors to the islands must obtain a licence to land and reside from the office of the Commissioner for Pitcairn Islands, based in Auckland.
Island Council, URL: http://www.government.pn

Island Council (as at June 2013)
Mayor 2010-13: Michael Warren
Deputy Mayor: Simon Young
Elected Council Members: Jay Warren, Brenda Christian, Michele Christian, Jacqui Christian, Kerry Young

LEGAL SYSTEM

The Pitcairn Islands has its own court, presided over by a magistrate who is elected every three years.

AREA AND POPULATION

Area

Pitcairn Island lies 25° 04' S. and 130° 06' W., about half way between Panama and New Zealand and is volcanic in origin. The land is fertile but there is little surface water. Pitcairn is rugged and the coast is rocky and has steep cliffs. Bounty Bay is the only landing point for boats and longships from the island have to go out to passing ships to bring in goods and visitors. The remaining three islands of the Pitcairn Group, Henderson, Ducie and Oeno, are uninhabited. Henderson Island is now classified as a World Heritage Site.

The climate is tropical, hot and humid, eased by southeast winds. The rainy season lasts from November to March.

To view a map, consult http://www.lib.utexas.edu/maps/cia08/pitcairn_sm_2008.gif

Population

As of 2011, the population was 50. The first birth to take place on the island for 17 years took place in 2003. The Islanders, all of whom live in or around Adamstown, are all descended from mutineers from HMS Bounty (1790) and the Tahitian Islanders who accompanied them. There are two official languages, English and Pitkern, which is a mixture of old English and Tahitian.

Public Holidays 2014

23 January: Bounty Day
14 June: Queen's Birthday (2nd Saturday in June)

EMPLOYMENT

The population is self employed. Some jobs such as manning the long boats which went out to passing ships traditionally belonged members of one family but since 2006 these jobs have been open to all members of the community.

BANKING AND FINANCE

Currency

The unit of currency is the New Zealand dollar.

Balance of Payments / Imports and Exports

There is no system of taxation on the islands but each islander over the age of 15 must perform some public work each month in lieu of taxes.
The economy is based on the sale of postage stamps, handicrafts, dried fruit and, more recently, honey production. Pitcairn is looking into selling its internet domain of .pn to increase income. In recent years the sale of postage stamps has gone into decline. The Islanders trade handicrafts, fruit and vegetables with visiting ships. Main imported goods include fuel, machinery and foodstuffs.

MANUFACTURING, MINING AND SERVICES

Energy

At present power in generated by diesel generators and that is rationed to 10 hours per day. Plans to improve life on the islands include the provision of wind turbines to generate electricity which would be available 24 hours a day.

Manufacturing

Local handicrafts are made on the island and are sold through the internet and to visiting ships.

Agriculture

Agriculture is at the subsistence level. Main crops include bananas, citrus fruits, vegetables, yams and sugarcane. Some fruit and vegetables are traded with visiting ships. Fishing takes place on a subsistence level. Goats and chickens are kept by the islanders.

Tourism

Tourism is encouraged as a way of boosting the island economy and visitors from passing cruise and container ships can be ferried to the island in the islands longboats. There are plans to promote the islands as an eco tourist destination.

COMMUNICATIONS AND TRANSPORT

Roads

The steep track that leads from the landing stage to Adamstown has recently been concreted.

Ports and Harbours

There is a harbour at Bounty Bay. The amount of shipping passing the Pitcairn Islands has been falling, leaving the islands more and more isolated. Investigations are underway to try and find some way of combating the isolation of the islands, and a new shipping supply route between French Polynesia and Pitcairn came into operation in 2006. Recently Pitcairn received £1.9 million from the Department for International Development to repair the jetty and slipway. There are also plans for a joint Department for International Development and EU funded project to build a breakwater near the Bounty Bay harbour.

HEALTH

The health care system is subsidized. Facilities are limited but include a fully-equipped medical centre which includes an x-ray room and a dental room. Health care is financed by the United Kingdom DFID.

EDUCATION

Primary education has been compulsory for over 150 years and a Government school is conducted by a teacher recruited from New Zealand. A new school building has recently been completed. In 2007, eight children attended the school.

RELIGION

Some of the islanders are active members of the Seventh Day Adventist Church which is in the charge of a resident minister from overseas.

COMMUNICATIONS AND MEDIA

Newspapers

The Pitcairn Miscellany

Telecommunications

Communication is primarily dependent on a well-equipped Government radio station which provides telephone, telex and facsimile links with the rest of the world via satellite. Supplies are brought three times a year by scheduled cargo vessels. Other cargo vessels make unscheduled stopovers. A project funded by the Department for International Development has provided a television service and internet access. Each household now has a phone connection.

SAINT HELENA AND DEPENDENCIES

St Helena
Capital: Jamestown (Population estimate, 2008: 720)
Governor: H.E. Mark Capes (page 1400)

Ascension
Capital: Georgetown (Population, estimate: 530)
Governor: H.E. Governor Mark Capes (resides on St Helena)
Administrator: Colin Wells

Tristan da Cunha
Capital: Edinburgh of the Seven Seas
Governor: H.E. Governor Mark Capes (resides on St Helena)
Administrator: Alex Mitham

CONSTITUTION AND GOVERNMENT

Constitution of St Helena

St. Helena was discovered by the Portuguese navigator Joao da Nova in May 1502, but no permanent settlement was made. It became a port of call for ships of various nations voyaging between the East Indies and Europe. On 5 May 1659 it was annexed and occupied by Captain John Dutton who was sent out by the East India Company for that purpose. A charter was issued to the East India Company for its possession by Charles II in December 1673 and it remained in the Company's possession until 22 April 1834, when it was brought under the direct government of the Crown by an Act of Parliament. Napoleon Bonaparte was exiled to St. Helena in 1815 where he remained until his death in 1821.

The current Constitution came into force in 2009 and replaces the outdated Constitution of 1988. It includes a bill of rights which will permit people to complain in the local courts on human rights issues, instead of having to go to the European Court of Human Rights in Strasbourg. The Governor's power has also been reduced whilst more power has been passed to elected Councillors.

To consult the constitution, please visit: http://www.sainthelena.gov.sh/data/files/resources/541/Constitution-of-St-Helena-Ascension-and-Tristan-da-Cunha.pdf

Legislature

Saint Helena has a Unicameral Legislature, the Assembly is made up of the speaker, three ex officio members and 12 elected members, who serve a four year term. The Governor exercises executive authority and is advised by the Executive Council and the elected Legislative Council. The Executive Council is made up of the Governor, three ex officio officers, and five elected members of the Legislative Council. The whole island will become a single Electoral Constituency at the 2013 elections. Each voter will be able to select up to 12 candidates in the election.

Outgoing Executive Council (as at June 2013)
Acting Chief Secretary: Gillian Francis
Hon. Financial Secretary: Paul Blessington
Hon. Attorney General: Kenneth Baddon
Hon. Rod Buckley MLC
Hon. Cyril Gunnell MLC
Hon. Mervyn Yon MLC
Hon. Tara Thomas MLC
Hon. Tony Green MLC

Mr Colin Owen is due to succeed Paul Blessington as Financial Secretary in September 2013.

Constitution of Ascension

A British military force took possession of the Island in 1815 when Napoleon was exiled to St Helena. The Royal Navy and later the Royal Marines occupied the island until 1922 (HMS Ascension). The Eastern Telegraph Company (later Cable and Wireless) then occupied Ascension until 1964 when an Administrator was appointed. Ascension was strategically important both in World War II, when the airport was built, and during the Falklands conflict.

Ascension is a dependency of St. Helena. The Administrator acts on behalf of the Governor who resides in St Helena. The St Helena Legislative and Executive Councils have no jurisdiction over Ascension. There are two advisory bodies: the Ascension Island Management Group composed of Senior Managers of the organisations resident on the island, and the Administrator's Forum comprising representatives of the employees of these organisations. In June 2000 the British Government published the Report on Ascension Island by consultants from the University of Portsmouth which made recommendations about the future governance of Ascension Island. The island is to move away from its company town and military status and move towards a more modern system of democratic government on a par with other Overseas Territories. The constitution is currently being developed in consultation with the islanders.

Constitution of Tristan da Cunha

The administrator acts on behalf of the Governor who resides in St Helena. The St Helena Legislative and Executive Councils have no jurisdiction over Tristan da Cunha. The Administrator is advised by an Island Council comprising three appointed members and eight elected members; one elected member must be a woman. Tristan da Cunha, Nightingale, Inaccessible and Gough Islands were made dependencies of St Helena by Letters Patent dated 12 January 1938. The islands, of which Tristan da Cunha is the principal, are situated midway between South America and South Africa. Tristan da Cunha itself is a volcano rising 6,760 feet above sea level with a crater lake near its summit. A British military force took

possession of the island when Napoleon was exiled to St Helena. When the garrison was withdrawn in 1817, William Glass, a corporal of artillery, and his wife, elected to remain. They were joined by two ex-Navy men, Alexander Cotton and John Mooney. They, with certain shipwrecked sailors, became the founders of the present settlement.

Legislature

Executive and legislative authority is reserved to Her Majesty but is ordinarily exercised by others in accordance with the provisions of the Constitution. The Constitution provides for a Governor and Commander-in-Chief of St. Helena and its Dependencies (Ascension Island and Tristan da Cunha). There is a Legislative Council for St. Helena, consisting of the Speaker, three ex-officio members (the Chief Secretary, the Financial Secretary and the Attorney General) and 12 elected members. The elected members choose five of their own number to chair the Council Committees. An Executive Council advises the Governor who, ordinarily, must follow such advice. The Executive Council consists of the ex-officio members of the Legislative Council and the five Chairmen of Council Committees. Although a member of both the Legislative Council and the Executive Council, the Attorney General does not vote on either. Executive and legislative functions for the Dependencies are exercised by the Governor.

Legislative Assembly, URL: http://www.sainthelena.gov.sh

Elections

The Legislative Council was dissolved by the governor Mark Capes in April 2013. Elections are scheduled to take place in Saint Helena on 17 July 2013. At the time of going to press, the results were not known.

Government sites

Ascension Island, URL: http://www.ascension-island.gov.ac/
St. Helena, URL: http://www.sainthelena.gov.sh/

LEGAL SYSTEM

The St Helena legal system is based on English common law and statutes.

The judicial system comprises four courts namely the Court of Appeal, Supreme Court, Magistrate's Court and Juvenile Court. Lay Magistrates deal with the majority of court cases. The Supreme Court of St. Helena is headed by a UK-based chief justice with full criminal and civil jurisdiction who visits the Island once a year to deal with matters outside the Magistrates' jurisdiction. Trial is by a jury of eight. The Court of Appeals sits either in the UK or on St Helena, when necessary, to deal with civil and criminal appeals. The Attorney General is the Government's principal legal advisor.

AREA AND POPULATION

Area

St. Helena lies in the South Atlantic Ocean, latitude 15° 5', 5° 45' W, 702 miles south-east of Ascension Island and about 1,200 miles from the south-west coast of Africa. It is 10.5 miles long and 6.5 miles broad, covering an area of 47 sq. miles. The capital and the only town on the island is Jamestown. The language of the island has always been English and the English way of life is firmly established.

To view a map of St. Helena, please consult:
http://www.lib.utexas.edu/maps/cia08/saint_helena_sm_2008.gif

Ascension is volcanic in origin with a central peak rising to 2,800 feet, with or little or no vegetation except at the highest point. Parts are barren but with increasing precipitation vegetation is rapidly spreading to most areas. The climate is sub-tropical. The total area of Ascension is 97 sq. km. It is situated 1,296 km. north-west of St Helena, 1,504 km. from mainland Africa and 2,232 km. from Brazil.

Tristan da Cunha is 38 sq. miles, included in the Tristan da Cunha group of islands are Nightingale, Inaccessible and Gough Island.

Population

The population of St Helena was approximately 4,500 in 2008. There is a resident population in Ascension of 880 and there are currently an estimated 264 residents of Tristan da Cunha.

Births, Marriages, Deaths

In 2010 the birth rate per 1,000 was estimated to be 11 and the estimated death rate per 1,000 was 6.9. The median age is an estimated 39 years. Life expectancy was estimated to be 77.5 years.

EMPLOYMENT

Of the resident population in Ascension, most are employees of Ascension Island Services, the BBC, US base and RAF contractors. Employment on Tristan da Cunha is centred on farming and fishing. Recent figures show that around 1,700 St. Helenians work offshore, mainly in Ascension, the Falkland Islands and mainland UK.

Total Employment by Economic Activity (St. Helena)

Occupation	2008
Agriculture, hunting & forestry	122
Fishing	33

- continued

Mining & quarrying	8
Manufacturing	115
Electricity, gas & water supply	113
Construction	190
Wholesale & retail trade, repairs	385
Hotels & restaurants	36
Transport, storage & communications	237
Financial intermediation	20
Real estate, renting & business activities	185
Public admin. & defence; compulsory social security	157
Education	112
Health & social work	178
Other community, social & personal service activities	217
Households with employed persons	17
Extra-territorial organisations & bodies	5
Total	2,130

Source: Copyright © International Labour Organization (ILO Dept. of Statistics, http://laborsta.ilo.org)

BANKING AND FINANCE

Currency
The St. Helena pound (equivalent to sterling) which equals 100 pence.

The unit of currency on Tristan da Cunha is the pound sterling. There are no other banks other than a Post Office Saving facility. Financial transactions are undertaken by the Tristan Treasury Department.

For the first time in its history, revenue for Ascension Island is now raised through taxes; it receives no aid from Britain.

GDP/GNP, Inflation, National Debt
The territory has scarce natural resources and the main economic sector is agriculture (mainly fishing) and tourism. Estimates put GDP at US$30 million in 2011. Per capita GDP was estimated at US$2,990. As of 2012, discussions were ongoing into investments into the infrastructure, including laying of a data cable to enable broadband and an airport (due to open in 2016).

Balance of Payments / Imports and Exports
Total imports on St Helena in 2004 were estimated at £45 million. Imported items were foodstuffs, fuel, liquor, machinery, motor vehicles, clothing, building materials, cigarettes and tobacco. Fish, coffee, a small amount of timber and handicrafts are the only export products. Exports were estimated to be US$19 million in 2004.

On Tristan da Cunha crayfish, exported to world markets, is the mainstay of the economy. Potential exists for the export of mineral water and limited tourism, but requires outside investment.

MANUFACTURING, MINING AND SERVICES

Energy
Five wind turbines were constructed in 2010 to provide up to 30 per cent of its electricity needs.

Tourism
Tourism is being developed in St Helena and Tristan da Cunha. Approximately 950 visitors come to the island each year. An airport is under construction which should boost visitor numbers to 29,000. The airport is due to open in 2016.
Tourist Office, e-mail: StHelena.Tourism@helanta.sh, URL: http://www.sthelenatourism.com

Agriculture
The main crops are maize, potatoes, sweet potatoes, apples, peaches and vegetables. Livestock numbers in 1997 were cattle, 692; sheep, 798; goats, 1,061; poultry, 7,399; pigs, 295.

Fishing
Fish of many kinds are seasonally plentiful in waters around St. Helena and, since the opening of a cold store in 1977, local demand has been met. Exports of frozen skipjack and tuna began in 1979 and salt-dried skipjack in 1981. During 1999, 64 tonnes of fish were exported at a value of £97,315. Tristan da Cunha's fishing industry is dependent on the lobster catch. Recently a fish freezing facility has been opened in St. Helena.

COMMUNICATIONS AND TRANSPORT

There is no airport or airstrip in St Helena and no railway. Supplies are brought to the island by the ship. The UK government confirmed in 2012 that it would provide £300 million for an airport on the island. The proposed site is on the eastern coast of the island at Prosperous Bay Plain; the airport will have a runway of 2,250 metres. The airport should be completed by 2015/16.

There is an airport on the US base at Ascension which can handle all aircraft. A twice weekly RAF Tristar service linking the UK to the Falkland Islands transits Ascension and there is a weekly US military air service between Florida, Antigua and Ascension.

There is no airport on Tristan da Cunha and all cargo and passengers rely on infrequent shipping services from Cape Town. A lack of proper harbour facilities inhibits development.

Shipping
The only port in St Helena is Jamestown, which is an open roadstead with a good anchorage for ships of any size. The St. Helena Shipping Company provides a passenger/cargo service from the United Kingdom and South Africa, which is subsidised by Britain at over £1m each year. The RMS "St Helena" visits Cape Town, Ascension and St Helena.
RMS St Helena, URL:http://rms-st-helena.com/

There is a monthly shipping service in Ascension. It takes 14 days to sail from the UK to St. Helena, two days to sail from Ascension Island and seven days to sail from Cape Town, South Africa.

HEALTH

There is a hospital located at Jamestown, St Helena. A small hospital and contract doctor provide a free medical service to all islanders on Tristan da Cunha. Life expectancy was estimated at 78.7 in 2011. The infant mortality rate was estimated at 16.4 per 1,000 live births.

EDUCATION

Education on St Helena is compulsory and free for all children between the ages of five and 15. The standard of work at the Prince Andrew School is geared to 'IGCSE' and 'AICE' level requirements of the University of Cambridge Local Examination Syndicate (UCLES).

There is a free public library in Jamestown financed by the Government and managed by a committee and a mobile library service to certain country districts.

On Tristan da Cunha there is one school, for children aged four to 15, which provides free, compulsory education up to UK GCSE level.

RELIGION

The islands are predominantly Christian. Anglican, Baptist, Seventh-Day Adventist, Roman Catholic and Jehovah's Witness communities exist. The is a small Bahai community.

Saint Helena has a religious liberty rating of 10 on a scale of 1 to 10 (10 is most freedom). (Source: World Religion Database)

COMMUNICATIONS AND MEDIA

Newspapers
The St Helena Herald and the St Helena Independent are published weekly and available at: http://www.news.co.sh/
The Islander is published weekly for the Ascension Islands. The Tristan Times is also published.

Broadcasting
There are no local television stations but satellite TV stations are rebroadcast terestially.

Four radio stations broadcast in the area.
Radio St Helena, publicly funded and operated by St Helena News Media Services, URL: http://www.news.co.sh/
Saint FM, a private station operated by St Helena Media Productions, broadcasts are relayed to Ascension and the Falkland Islands. URL: http://www.saint.fm/
Volcano Radio is broadcast on Ascension Island.
Atlantic FM is broadcast on Tristan da Cunha.

Telecommunications
There are estimated to be 2,300 landlines in operation. There are estimated to be 1,000 internet users. As of 2013, St Helena does not have broadband. In January 2013, the UK government rejected a request for £10 million for a fibre optic cable.

ENVIRONMENT

In 2006, Saint Helena's emissions from the consumption of fossil fuels totalled 0.01 million metric tons of carbon dioxide.

SOUTH GEORGIA AND SOUTH SANDWICH ISLANDS

Administrative Centre: King Edward Point

Commissioner: Nigel Haywood (page 1439)

CONSTITUTION AND GOVERNMENT

Constitution
Captain Cook landed on South Georgia in 1775 and in subsequent years the islands became popular with seal hunters of many nationalities. Great Britain annexed the territories in 1908. Argentina made formal claim to South Georgia in 1927 and to the South Sandwich Islands in 1948. In 1955 the United Kingdom unilaterally submitted the dispute over sovereignty to the International Court of Justice, which decided not to hear the application in view of Argentina's refusal to submit to the Court's jurisdiction. South Georgia housed a British Antarctic Survey Base (manned by 22 scientists and support personnel) until it was invaded in April 1982 by Argentine forces, who occupied the island until its recapture by British forces three weeks later. The South Sandwich Islands were uninhabited until the occupation of Southern Thule in December 1976 by about 50 Argentine personnel, said to be scientists. They remained until removed by British forces in June 1982. Under the provisions of the South Georgia and South Sandwich Islands Order 1985, the territories ceased to be governed as Dependencies of the Falkland Islands on 3 October 1985 and became separate dependencies. The Governor of the Falkland Islands is, ex officio, Commissioner for the territories.

Office of the Commissioner
Government House, Stanley, Falkland Islands. URL: http://www.sgisland.gs/

LEGAL SYSTEM

All South Georgia is Crown Land. Legal and financial arrangements are the responsibility of the Commissioner. Laws, proclamations and official business are notified through The South Georgia and the South Sandwich Islands Gazette.

LOCAL GOVERNMENT

Local administration is the responsibility of the Commissioner, and is delegated to the Marine Officer at King Edward Point.

AREA AND POPULATION

Area
South Georgia, an island of 3,592 sq. km (1,387 sq. miles), lies about 1,300 km (800 miles) east-south-east of the Falklands group. The South Sandwich Islands, which have an area of 311 sq. km (120 sq. miles), lie about 750 km (470 miles) south-east of South Georgia. The islands are largely covered by ice and snow with some sparse vegetation. A fisheries conservation and management regime was established in 1993. Fishing in the waters including a 200 mile Maritime Zone around South Georgia and the South Sandwich Islands is now subject to a licensing arrangement.

To view a map, please consult:
http://www.lib.utexas.edu/maps/cia08/south_georgia_sm_2008.gif

Population
There is no indigenous population, although there was until 2001 a small military garrison on South Georgia (Grytviken). The British Antarctic Survey has two manned research stations at King Edward Point and Bird Island. Government Officers and museum curators are stationed on the islands during the summer months. The eleven South Sandwich Islands are uninhabited.

BANKING AND FINANCE

Estimated figures for 2006 show that Government revenue amounted to £4.4 million from fishing licenses, customs and harbour dues, trans-shipment fees and the sale of stamps. Government expenditure for that year was put at £4.5 million, spent on administration, research, fisheries protection and production of stamps. Some fishing takes place in adjacent waters, and there is a potential source of income from harvesting fin fish and krill. Figures for 2009 put Government revenue at £5.4 million and Government expenditure that year at £4.6 million.

MANUFACTURING, MINING AND SERVICES

Tourism
Visitors to the islands can only get there by sea. Members of the International Association of Antarctica Tour Operators have greater access to landing sites. About 30 vessels visit each year. Approximately 2,000 visitors come to the island each year.

Fishing
In order to protect its fisheries the islands have a maritime jurisdiction of 200 nautical miles.

COMMUNICATIONS AND TRANSPORT

Ports and Harbours
South Georgia is only accessible by sea. There is a harbour at Grytviken.

COMMUNICATIONS AND MEDIA

Telecommunications
There is a coastal radiotelephone station at Grytviken.

ENVIRONMENT

The South Georgia government is responsible for the care of South Georgia. They work with organisations such as British Antarctic Survey, IAATO and CCAMR to preserves its fragile environment. South Georgia is host to significant numbers of animals and birds. The government commissions a detailed report every few years to assess the biodiversity of the island and the surrounding area.

Current environmental problems include the spread of rodents. Whole areas have been decimated by brown rats and other rodents, believed to have arrived as stowaways on sealing and whaling boats. Their arrival has had a devasting effect on native bird populations. Experts believe the problem will get worse; glaciers form a natural barrier which control rodent invastion. However, the glaciers as rapidly shrinking as a consequence of global warning.

TURKS AND CAICOS ISLANDS

Capital: Cockburn Town, Grand Turk (Population estimate: 5,500)

Head of State: HRH Queen Elizabeth II (page 1420)

Governor: Peter Beckingham (page 1385)

Flag: British blue ensign with the shield of arms in the fly

CONSTITUTION AND GOVERNMENT

Constitution
The 1988 constitution provided for a Governor (appointed by the Queen), who is responsible for foreign affairs, defence, internal security and offshore finance. The governor also works on the advice of the Executive Council. A Legislative Council also exists which consists of a Speaker, 13 Elected Members, three Appointed Members and three Official Members. The Legislative Council was elected every four years. A Chief Minister and five other Ministers were drawn from the Legislative Council (Legco) and they, with the Governor and the three Official Members, constituted the Executive Council (Exco).

A new constitution came into effect in August 2006. The post of Chief Minister was abolished and replaced by that of Premier. A new post, that of Deputy Governor was created and the former Executive Council was renamed the Cabinet. Following the election in 2007 the Legislative Council was to be renamed the House of Assembly and was to consist of 21 members, 15 of whom were to be elected and four nominated, there was also to be one ex-offico member (the Attorney General) plus the Speaker.

In 2009, the UK government ruled that the islands's government was too corrupt and imposed direct rule. In June 2012 the UK government announced fresh elections would be held in November 2012. A new constitution came into force on 15 October 2012.

To consult the constitution, please visit: http://www.lawsconsolidated.tc

International Relations
The Turks and Caicos Islands is a British Overseas Territory and therefore has strong links with UK. The British Government is responsible for the islands external relations, defence and internal security. The islands also have close relations with Jamaica.

Recent Events
The 2008 Hurricane Season was particularly severe. Hurricane Hanna battered the Turks and Caicos Islands for four days. Hurricane Ike followed soon afterwards, and damaged 80 per cent of homes on Grand Turk.

In 2009 Governor Richard Tauwhare announced a Commission of Enquiry would look into allegations of government corruption. Politicians were accused of selling crown land for personal gain and misusing public funds. Premier Misick denied the charges of corruption levelled against him, and said that removal of the territory's sovereignty was tantamount to being re-colonized. Micheal Misick resigned on 23 March and was replaced by Galmo Williams. In August, the islands' administration was suspended for up to two years, and power transferred to British-appointed Governor Wetherell. A new constitution came into force and the islands returned to home rule after elections took place in November 2012.

Cabinet (as at June 2013)
Premier: Dr Rufus Ewing (page 1422)
Minister of Finance, Investment & Trade: Charles Washington Misick (page 1478)
Minister of Education, Youth, Sport & Culture: Akierra Misick
Minister of Environment, Home Affairs & Agriculture: Amanda Misick
Minister of Government Support Services: George Lightbourne
Minister of Health & Human Services: Porsha Stubbs-Smith
Minister of Border Control and Labour: Ricardo Don-Hue Gardiner

Government Addresses
Government information: URL: http://www.gov.tc/
Governor's Office, Government House, Grand Turk. Tel: 649 946 2308, fax: 649 946 2903, e-mail: govhouse@tciway.tc
Deputy Governor's Office, South Base, Grand Turk. Tel: 946 2702, fax: 649 946 2886, e-mail: cso@gov.tc

Elections
The elections were held in May 2007. The ruling Progressive National Party was returned to power, winning 13 of the 15 seats. The UK government imposed direct rule in 2009. The state was deemed fit to return to home rule in 2012.

General elections took place on 9 November 2012; The PNP won 8 seats and the PDM 7.

Political Parties
People's Democratic Movement (PDM)
Progressive National Party (PNP), URL: http://www.mypnp.tc/, Leader: Galmo Williams
United Democratic Party (UDP)

LEGAL SYSTEM

The legal system is based on English common law, and comprises a Supreme Court and a Court of Appeal. There is provision for appeal to the Privy Council in London. The Attorney General, the Chief Justice, the Senior Crown Counsel and the Legal Draughtsman are all British technical co-operation officers.

Supreme Court, URL: http://www.gov.tc

AREA AND POPULATION

Area
The Turks and Caicos Islands are situated about 100 miles north of the Dominican Republic and Haiti, 50 miles east of Inagua in the Bahamas, of which they are geographically an extension. There are over 40 islands of which six are inhabited: Grand Turk, Salt Cay, South Caicos, Middle Caicos, North Caicos and Providenciales (sometimes known as Provo). The islands cover an estimated area of 193 sq. miles. The principal island is Grand Turk on which the capital is situated.

The terrain is flat with marshes and mangrove swamps. The Islands lie in the Trade Winds but have an excellent climate. The average temperature varies from 17°C - 27°C in the winter and 24°C - 32°C in the summer and humidity is generally low. Average rainfall is 21 inches per annum.

To view a map of the Islands, please consult http://www.lib.utexas.edu/maps/cia08/turks_caicos_islands_sm_2008.gif

The language spoken is English, with Creole spoken by Haitians.

Population
The population has increased from 12,350 in 1990 to 20,200 at the 2001 census and to an estimated 44,500 in 2011. This figure includes about 6,000 non-nationals, mainly from Haiti and the Dominican Republic. Providenciales is now the largest island in terms of population, with 15,000 inhabitants. Grand Turk has a population of around 3,000 and North and South Caicos have a population of around 1,000 each. The population growth rate was estimated to be 3.4 per cent.

Life expectancy was estimated to be 79 years in 2011.

Public Holidays 2014
1 January: New Year's Day
17 March: Commonwealth Day
18 April: Good Friday
21 April: Easter Monday
25 May: National Heroes' Day
8 June: Queen's Official Birthday
25 September: National Youth Day
13 October: Columbus Day
10 December: International Human Rights Day
25 December: Christmas Day
26 December: Boxing Day

EMPLOYMENT

The average unemployment rate is currently about 5.5 per cent, although this varies from island to island. Whilst some islands have up to 20 per cent unemployment, Providenciales enjoys full employment and is the centre for tourism and the financial services industries.

Total Employment by Economic Activity

Occupation	2007
Agriculture, hunting & forestry	111
Fishing	126
Mining & quarrying	16
Manufacturing	246
Electricity, gas & water supply	192
Construction	4,306
Wholesale & retail trade, repairs	1,729
Hotels & restaurants	4,065
Transport, storage & communications	846
Financial intermediation	515
Real estate, renting & business activities	2,384
Public admin. & defence; compulsory social security	2,298
Education, health & social work	771
Other community, social & personal service activities	1,190
Households with employed persons	376
Other	416
Total	19,857

Source: Copyright © International Labour Organization (ILO Dept. of Statistics, http://laborsta.ilo.org)

BANKING AND FINANCE

Currency
The unit of currency is the U.S. dollar.

GDP/GNP, Inflation, National Debt
GDP at market prices was put at US$578 millions in 2005 with a growth rate of 17.47 per cent. Estimated figures for 2006 put the figure at US$617 million, a growth rate of 23.4 per cent. GDP was estimated at US$632 million in 2007 with an estimated growth rate of 11.2 oer cent. Inflation averages around 4 per cent per annum. It was estimated at 3.7 per cent in 2007. The construction, mining & quarrying sector contributes around 25 per cent of GDP, financial services and the education sector around 18 per cent each, with hotels and restaurants contributing around 16 per cent.

Foreign Investment
The TCI economy relies predominantly on offshore finance and tourism. Foreign investors come mainly from Canada, the UK and the US. Major private investment sectors are tourism, property development, real estate, international finance and fishing, most of which can be found on the island of Providenciales.

Balance of Payments / Imports and Exports
In 2006, imports cost US$497,761,708 and exports earned US$17,610,457 giving a trade balance of US$-480,151,251. UK exports in 2000 generated £Stg.0.86 million, whilst UK imports in the same year cost £Stg.0.25 million. In 2007, export revenue was estimated at US$16 million with imports costing an estimated US$580 million.

The main export is seafood products. Main imports are food, beverages, tobacco and construction materials. The US is the main trading partner.

MANUFACTURING, MINING AND SERVICES

Manufacturing
Some small manufacturing takes place on the islands including production of food and drink, including bottled water, cement blocks for the construction industry and handicrafts.

Service Industries
Tourism and offshore finance are now the largest sectors of the economy. Tourist numbers have increased from 52,000 in 1992 to just under 176,130 in 2005 and 248,300 in 2006. More than half of the visitors travelling to the islands come from the USA.

Agriculture
Crops grown include corn, beans, cassava and citrus fruits.

Fishing
Fishing provides virtually the sole visible export and consists mainly of conch, both dried and fresh, and lobster, and is centred in South Caicos. Figures for the 2003-04 season showed that the total catch for lobster was over 610,000 lbs and for conch over 1.5 million lbs.

COMMUNICATIONS AND TRANSPORT

Travel Requirements
Citizens of the Australia and the EU require a passport valid for six months but do not need a visa for stays of up to 30 days. Nationals of Canada and the USA do not require a passport if carrying proof of identity (birth certificate and photo ID). Other nationals should contact the embassy to check visa requirements.

International Airports
There are three international airports, one on Grand Turk, one on South Caicos and one on Providenciales. There are regular flights to Miami, Atlanta, New York, Boston and Toronto and there are plans to establish a regular direct flight from London. Regular flights between the islands are available.

Shipping
There is a direct shipping service to the USA (Miami).

UNITED STATES OF AMERICA

Ports and Harbours
Harbours are located at Grand Turk and Providenciales.

HEALTH

Grand Turk houses the main government hospital, and a smaller hospital exists on Providenciales. Nurses and midwives are stationed on the smaller islands where regular weekly visits are made by government doctors. A private medical system also exists. Enrolment in the National Health Insurance Plan is mandatory for all those who are employed or who reside permanently in the Turks and Caicos Islands. Contributions amount to 2.5 per cent of the employees' salary with another 2.5 per cent contributed by the employer (2011). Life expectancy at birth was estimated at 79.1 years. The infant mortality rate was 11.9 deaths per 1,000 live births.

EDUCATION

Education is free and compulsory in the government primary schools and secondary schools between the ages of 5 and 14. There are also several private primary and high schools. Figures for the year 2002-03 show that 1,669 students were enrolled at primary school and 1,108 at high schools. Figures from USESCO for 2005 show that 11.8 per cent of total government expenditure went on education, 41 per cent of which went on secondary education and 20 per cent on primary education.

RELIGION

Christianity is the main religion (94 per cent of the population) and many churches are represented.

The Turks and Caicos Islands have a religious liberty rating of 10 on a scale of 1 to 10 (10 is most freedom). (Source: World Religion Database)

COMMUNICATIONS AND MEDIA

Newspapers
The islands have a two weekly publications, the Turks and Caicos Free Press, URL: http://www.tcifreepress.com and the Turks and Caicos Weekly News, URL: http://www.tcweeklynews.com

Broadcasting
Radio Turks and Caicos (URL: http://www.rtc107fm.com/) is run by the government. Some 15 private radio stations also exist. Multi-channel televison is available through satellite and cable.

Telecommunications
A comprehensive system is fully digitialised. An estimated 3,700 land lines are in operation and 25,000 mobile phones.

ENVIRONMENT

In order to preserve ecosystems and wildlife habitats, some areas of the Turks and Caicos Islands have been designated as protected areas.

The islands have a limited fresh water supply and so rely on collected rainwater.

In 2006, the Turks and Caicos Island's emissions from the consumption and flaring of fossil fuels totalled 0.01 million metric tons of carbon dioxide. (Source: EIA)

UNITED STATES OF AMERICA

Capital: Washington, DC (Population estimate, 2011: 617,996)

Head of State: Barack Obama (page 1488) (President)

Vice-President: Joseph R. Biden (page 1388)

National Flag: Thirteen red and white horizontal stripes (representing the 13 original colonies) with a dark blue rectangle in the top left corner showing 50 white stars (representing each state)

CONSTITUTION AND GOVERNMENT

Constitution
The United States of America is a federal union of 50 states, the Federal District of Columbia, a commonwealth (Puerto Rico), and 13 dependent areas (American Samoa, Baker Island, Guam, Howland Island, Jarvis Island, Johnston Atoll, Kingman Reef, Midway Islands, Navassa Island, Northern Mariana Islands, Palmyra Atoll, Virgin Islands and Wake Island). Its basic law is the Constitution which was adopted on 4 March 1789 following the Declaration of Independence of 1776. The Constitution prescribes the structure and method of national government together with its field of authority and that of the individual states. All government in America, therefore, has the dual character of both Federal and State Government.

The basic principle of American government is the separation of the three branches: legislative, executive and judicial, with a system of checks and balances.

Twenty-seven amendments have so far been added to the original Constitution of seven articles. The first ten amendments, known as the Bill of Rights, were added in a group in 1791 and enshrine the following rights: the freedom of religion, speech, lawful assembly, and the petitioning of government (Amendment I); the right to bear arms (II); the quartering of soldiers in peace time (III); the security of persons, houses, papers, and effects against unreasonable searches and seizures (IV); the right to trial by jury for capital offences, the right not to be tried for the same offence twice, the right not be a witness against oneself in a criminal case, and the right to compensation if private property is taken for public use (V); the right to trial by jury and counsel for defence in all criminal prosecutions (VI); the right of trial by jury for common law suits (VII); the right not to have excessive bail levied, excessive fines imposed, or cruel punishments inflicted (VIII); the rights of the people in addition to those enumerated in the Constitution (IX); and the right of the states and the people to powers not delegated by the Constitution or prohibited by the states (X).

The eleventh amendment deprives the federal courts of jurisdiction over suits against States instituted by citizens of other states or foreign countries. The twelfth amendment defines the method of electing the President and Vice-President. The thirteenth amendment abolished slavery.

The fourteenth and fifteenth defined citizenship and gave the vote to all male citizens (adopted 1868 and 1870). There were no more amendments until 1913, when the Federal Government, by the sixteenth amendment, gained the power to levy income tax. The seventeenth defined the procedure for the election of Senators. The eighteenth was the Prohibition Law, repealed by the twenty-first. The nineteenth gave the vote to women, and was adopted in 1920. The twentieth defines the terms of President and Vice-President, and also of the Senators and Representatives.

The twenty-second amendment, adopted in 1951, makes it impossible for any President to hold office for more than two terms. The twenty-third amendment, adopted in 1961, gives to the residents of the District of Columbia (the seat of government) the right to vote in the election of the President and Vice-President. The twenty-fourth amendment, adopted in 1964, provides that the right of citizens to vote in federal elections shall not be denied or abridged for failure to pay a poll tax or any other tax.

The twenty-fifth amendment, adopted in 1967, provides for the office of Acting President in case of the inability of the President to discharge the powers and duties of his office. It also provides for the nomination by the President of a Vice-President when there is a vacancy in the office of Vice-President. The twenty-sixth amendment, ratified in 1971, provides that the right of citizens over the age of 18 to vote shall not be abridged on account of age. The twenty-seventh amendment, ratified in 1992, provides that no law, varying the Compensation for the services of Senators and Representatives, shall take effect until an election of Representatives shall have intervened.

To consult the constitution, please visit:
http://www.house.gov/house/Constitution/Constitution.html

Executive
The President heads the executive branch of the government and is elected for a maximum of two consecutive four-year terms. The President must be a native-born citizen of the United States and at least 35 years old. The chief presidential duty is the implementation of the government's programme as directed in the Constitution and in laws made by Congress. In addition, the President recommends to Congress much major legislation and the amounts of money which should be appropriated to carry out government functions. The President also has the right to veto legislation passed by Congress, although Congress in turn may enact legislation over the President's veto by a two-thirds majority vote. The President is also Commander-in-Chief of the Armed Forces. The presidential cabinet is formed by the heads of the various executive departments, known as Secretaries, who are appointed by the President for an indefinite term. Cabinet officers may not serve in the Congress while they hold posts in the executive branch of the Government.

Recent Events
In May 2001 the United States was temporarily voted off two key United Nations committees: the UN Human Rights Commission and the International Narcotics Control Board. It was believed that the votes reflected concern by some UN members at 'bias' on the part of the US in the Middle-East crisis and could also have been a response to the US rejection of the Kyoto Protocol on climate change.

The 11 September 2001 terrorist attacks on the World Trade Center and the Pentagon caused an estimated 3,124 deaths, of which 2,891 were in New York City, 189 in Virginia, and 44 in Pennsylvania (Source: National Center for Health Statistics). On 8th October President Bush issued an Executive Order creating the Office for Homeland Security (OHS).

On 7 June 2002 President Bush announced changes to America's security agencies, giving the Department of Homeland Security overall responsibility for more than 100 agencies. The Cabinet-level department is responsible for analysing intelligence from government agencies such as the CIA, FBI and the National Security Agency. Its remit is also to protect nuclear power plants, road, rail and air systems, and to prepare for possible nuclear, biological and chemical attacks.

In early 2003 diplomatic efforts to resolve the issue of weapons of mass destruction in Iraq ended and, following its failure to obtain the agreement of the UN Security Council to military action, the US led forces against Iraq on 20 March 2003. Saddam Hussein's regime collapsed in April 2003 and was replaced by the Coalition Provisional Authority. No weapons of mass destruction were found. Immediate priorities for the Authority were the reconstruction of Iraq's infrastructure and the re-establishment of Iraqi rule. A 25-member Iraqi Governing Council was chosen by the US administration in Iraq, and was first convened on 14 July 2003.

Iraq's first post-war cabinet was announced on 1 June 2004. Its 24 members were nominated by the US-appointed Governing Council, and included Iyad Allawi as prime minister and Ghazi Yawer as president. The US Coalition Provisional Authority handed over sovereignty to the interim Iraqi government at the end of June 2004. Elections for a Transitional National Assembly were held at the end of January 2005. Over 8 million Iraqis voted in the election. 275 Representatives took office, among them 80 women.

On Monday 29th August 2005, Louisiana, together with neighbouring Gulf Coast states Mississippi and Alabama, was hit by Hurricane Katrina. The strength five hurricane, with winds exceeding 150 km/h, wrecked havoc. New Orleans was especially hard hit; flood defences were breached, causing flooding in 80 per cent of the low-lying areas of the city. Approximately 100,000 people were in the area when the hurricane hit and thousands of people died during the hurricane and its aftermath. In February 2006, a Congressional report stated that all levels of the US government were responsible for poor response to the Katrina disaster, citing organisational paralysis and a failure of initiative.

In the mid-term elections in November 2006, the Democrats won the majority of seats in both the Senate and the House of Representatives. Analysts pointed to the President's policy on Iraq as being a major factor in the election results, but also highlighted domestic issues such as the economy and corruption.

In January 2007, President Bush ordered more than 20,000 extra troops to Iraq, to join the 132,000 already stationed there. He also announced the funding of an aid and reconstruction programme (to the sum of US$1 billion), and the setting of political benchmarks for the Iraqi government, among other measures. Over the period March 2003-December 2006, more than 3,000 US soldiers had been killed, and more than 22,000 injured. Over the same period, more than 55,000 Iraqi people died (some estimates claim that the figure is well over 100,000), most of whom were civilians.

On 16 April 2007, a gunman killed 32 people on the Virginia Tech University campus, before killing himself. Six months previously, five children at an Amish school in Pennsylvannia were killed by a gunman. In December 2007, a teenager shot dead eight people in a Nebraska shopping centre before killing himself. The US Supreme Court considered Americans' right to bear arms in 2008, for the first time in almost 70 years. A case (District of Columbia v. Heller), heard by the US Supreme Court on 18th March 2008, ruled that a ban on handguns in Washington DC was unconstitutional; the private possession of handguns had been prohibited in the nation's capital since 1976, while rifles and shotguns had been required to be locked away or dismantled. The exact meaning of the constitutional right to keep and bear arms has been argued for many years; the June ruling enshrines the individual right to own guns, and will limit efforts to reduce their role in American life.

September 2007 saw the beginnings of a financial crisis as details of so-called 'sub-prime' lending started to emerge; US mortgage companies had made hundreds of billions of dollars of loans to individuals with poor credit histories. These debts were then packaged and sold on to financial institutions around the world, who then sold them on to pension funds and hedge funds. Uncertainty about the extent of exposure to bad debts led to a reluctance on the part of financial institutions to risk further debt, and a lending crunch, which in turn depressed the US housing market and construction industry.

In March 2008, Bear Stearns, Wall Street's fifth largest investment bank, received emergency funding. The bank had been at the centre of the US mortgage debt crisis. The Federal Reserve cut interest rates sharply to ease the credit crunch. However, the US housing market went into freefall, with prices dropping and repossessions rising. Most economists believed that the US economy had moved into recession.

The number of United States military personnel killed in Iraq passed the 4,000 mark on the 22nd March, days after the 5th anniversary of the US-led invasion. Roadside bombs accounted for 44 per cent of deaths in 2007. President Bush and Republican presidential nominee John McCain rejected the idea of a full withdrawal until Iraq is able to defend itself; the Democrat nominee, Barack Obama, pledged an early end to the war.

In April 2008, Citigroup reported a loss of $5.11 billion in the first quarter of 2008 (lower than the $9.8 billion loss in the last quarter 2007). The bank said it would be cutting 9,000 jobs (on top of the 4,200 job losses announced in January) as the credit crisis continued to take its toll on the biggest US bank. Merrill Lynch announced losses of $1.96 billion in the first quarter of 2008, and unveiled plans to cut about 4,000 jobs worldwide.

In July, the government announced measures to shore up the country's two largest mortgage finance companies, Freddie Mac and Fannie Mae, whose share prices had plummeted. The two companies own or guarantee almost half of the total US home loans, amounting to over $5 trillion of debt. On the 7th September, the Federal Government announced that it had taken over the two companies; President Bush said the firms had posed "an unacceptable risk" to the US and global economies.

On 14th July, following another oil price increase (to $147 per barrel), President Bush lifted an executive ban on drilling for oil in most US coastal waters. He asked Congress to end its separate ban on drilling, in order to reduce US dependence on oil imports. Since 1981, a congressional moratorium has prohibited oil and gas drilling along the east and west coasts and in the eastern Gulf of Mexico. The executive drilling ban was introduced in 1990 by President W. Bush, and extended by President Clinton. Environmentalists argue that offshore drilling would take ten years to have any effect on oil supply and would exacerbate climate change.

On the 9th September, President Bush announced that, with reduced levels of violence in Iraq, about 8,000 US troops would be withdrawn by February 2009, and 4,500 would be sent to Afghanistan.

On the 15th September, Lehman Brothers, the fourth-largest US investment bank, filed for bankruptcy protection. The bank had incurred losses of billions of dollars in the US mortgage market. On the same day, Merrill Lynch agreed to be taken over by Bank of America. The news led to sharp falls in share prices around the world. The Federal Reserve bailed out insurance giant AIG. US Federal Reserve chief Ben Bernanke urged Congress to support a proposed $700bn (£378bn) bail-out of the financial markets. On the 29th September, Congress voted against the bail-out; around two-thirds of Republicans and 95 Democrats objected to rescuing irresponsible rich bankers at a cost to the poor taxpayers. Share prices around the world slumped. On Wall Street the share index saw its biggest daily points fall ever, down 770.

On the 2nd October, the House of Representatives reluctantly passed the $700bn rescue bill. The package was aimed at buying up the bad debts of failing financial institutions on Wall Street. The Bail-Out Bill included increased protection for saving deposits, increased child tax credits, more aid for hurricane victims, tax breaks for renewable energy use and higher starting limits to alternative minimum tax. On the 16th October, the government announced a $250bn plan to purchase stakes in a wide variety of banks in an effort to restore confidence in the sector.

Presidential and general elections took place on the 4th November 2008. Democrat Barack Obama won the Presidency with 364 Electoral College votes to Republican John McCain's 162 Electoral College votes. In the Congressional elections, the Democrats increased their Senate majority by at least six seats, but fell short of the 60 needed to stop blocking tactics by Republicans. They also increased their majority in the House of Representatives by 23 seats to give a total 255, leaving the Republicans with 174.

On 24th November, the government announced a $20 billion rescue plan for banking giant Citigroup after its shares plunged by more than 60 per cent the previous week. The plan followed a $25bn injection of public funds in the bank in October. Following a crisis in the vehicle industry, in mid December, the government said it would provide $17.4bn in loans to help General Motors and Chrysler survive; President Bush said allowing the US car industry to fail would not be "a responsible course of action". The government will use part of the $700bn originally pledged to rescue US banks.

On the 20th January 2009, President Barack Obama was inaugurated as the USA's 44th president and its first black leader amid celebrations by millions of supporters. Within hours of the inauguration, he asked for military tribunals at Guantanamo Camp to be suspended for 120 days. Three days later, he ordered that the camp be closed within a year, and ordered a review of military trials for terror suspects and a ban on harsh interrogation methods.

On the 10th February, the Senate voted 61-37 to pass an economic stimulus plan expected to cost some $838bn (£573bn). The plan was later reconciled with the House of Representative's version. At the same time, the Treasury Secretary proposed a bank bail-out plan worth some $1.5 trillion.

On the 18th February, President Obama committed up to 17,000 more US troops to the operation in Afghanistan, and at the beginning of March, he announced that around 100,000 troops would be brought home from Iraq by the end of August 2010, with up to 50,000 staying on until the end of 2011.

On the 23rd March, the government announced details of a Public-Private Investment Programme to buy up to $1 trillion worth of troubled mortgages to help repair banks' balance sheets. The Treasury pledged between $75bn and $100bn (from the $700bn Troubled Asset Relief Program), to the programme, and said the private sector would also contribute.

In March 2009, a US soldier was sentenced to 35 years in prison for murdering four Iraqi detainees in 2007. The detainees were shot and dumped in a Baghdad canal in retribution for an attack on an US patrol in the Iraqi capital in which two soldiers had died.

On the 4th June, President Barack Obama gave a keynote speech in Cairo, saying that the "cycle of suspicion and discord" between the United States and the Muslim world must end. He made a number of references to the Qur'an and called on all faiths to live together in peace. On the key issue of Israeli settlements in the West Bank, Mr Obama said "there can be no progress towards peace without a halt to such construction".

In September 2009, President Obama shelved plans for controversial bases in Poland and the Czech Republic in a review of missile defence in Europe. The US had signed a deal with Poland to site 10 interceptors near the Baltic Sea, and with the Czech Republic to build a radar station on its territory. The review revealed the need to switch strategy to defending against the short- and medium-range missiles that Iran could use to target Europe, and a defence system using sea and land-based interceptors is now planned

In December 2009, President Obama ordered the federal government to take over a currently empty maximum-security prison in Illinois prison for the transfer of prisoners from Guanténamo Bay.

In March 2010, the House of Representatives passed President Obama's controversial Health Reform Bill by 219 votes to 212, with no Republican backing. The Bill will extend coverage to 32 million more Americans. New taxes will be imposed on the wealthy, and restrictive insurance practices such as refusing to cover people with pre-existing medical conditions will be outlawed. However, Republicans argue that the measures are unaffordable and represent a government takeover of the health industry.

On the 20th April 2010, following an explosion on the BP-operated Deepwater Horizon oil rig, between 12,000 and 19,000 thousand barrels of oil per day began to leak into the Gulf of Mexico. Eleven men were killed in the explosion, and the Louisiana coastline, with its environmentally-sensitive wetlands and shrimp and oyster beds was threatened by the resultant slick. The states of Louisiana, Mississippi, Alabama and Florida were affected by the spill, and one third of the Gulf's federal waters were closed to fishing.

In June 2010, ten alleged Russian spies were arrested on suspicion of working as illegal agents for the Russian government.

In the November 2010 mid-term elections the Republicans regained control of the House of Representatives.

In May 2011 US forces killed Osama bin Laden, the leader of Al-Qaeda. He was found in the Pakistani city of Abbottabad.

In August 2011 Republicans and Democrats fought to agree a deal on the national debt. At one point it was feared that the US would not meet its obligations and would default on its debt repayments. A last minute compromise was reached with a US$2.4 trillion debt increase agreed but this was linked to spending cuts.

In September 2011, the 1993 policy banning open homosexuality in the US military was repealed. The US Congress voted to repeal the law in September 2010. The bill was introduced under the administration of President Clinton to replace an outright ban on gay people serving in the military.

Vice-President Joe Biden visited Iraq in November 2011, ahead of the scheduled departure of US troops at the end of December. There has been a recent upsurge of violence with over 70 people killed in the month. Troop withdrawal was one of President Obama's key election pledges. There are currently approximately 14,000 US troops in Iraq; this will fall to fewer than 200 at the end of 2011. At the height of the campaign, there were over 170,000 US troops in the country.

In December 2011, the former Illinois Governor Rod Blagojevich was sentenced to 14 years in prison for trying to sell Barack Obama's Senate seat.

In March 2012, an American soldier named as Sgt. Robert Bales was alleged to have carried out an attack in Afghanistan in which he murdered 16 Afghan villagers including women and children. The attack has prompted fresh calls for the withdrawal of US troops.

In May 2012 the former Massachusetts governor Mitt Romney won the Republican nomination for the 2012 presidential election. He is the USA's first Mormon presidential candidate. In August Mr Romney announced that Paul Ryan, (page 1507) Congressman for Wisconsin would be his running mate for the position of vice president.

In September 2012, the US ambassador to Libya was killed when the consulate in Benghazi was stormed.

In October 2012, more than 100 people were killed when Hurricane Sandy hit the East Coast. New York City was badly hit. At least 40 people were killed in the city, subways were flooded, homes destroyed and there were lengthy power outages.

On 6 November 2012, President Obama narrowly won the presidential election.

In December 2012, a man killed 20 children and six adults at an elementary school in Connecticut. President Obama announced plans for a ban on assault rifles. Any significant gun control reform would need to be passed by Congress.

The US avoided the 'fiscal cliff' of huge tax rises and spending cuts after the House of Representatives passed the bill by 257 votes to 167 in January 2013.

President Barack Obama was inaugurated for his second term of office as US president on 21 January 2013.

In March 2013, the defence secretary, Chuck Hagel, announced that the US would bolster its missile defences after threats from North Korea. The last phase of the US European Missile Defence programme in eastern Europe was scrapped to help fund the new programme.

In April 2013, a bomb attack at the Boston Marathon killed three bystanders including an eight-year-old boy and injured 260 others. The attack was allegedly carried out by two brothers Dzhokhar and Tamerlan Tsarnaev, ethnic Chechens who emigrated to the US in 2002. One of the alleged perpetrators was killed trying to escape, the other was captured alive. The surviving brother, Dzhokhar Tsarnaev, has been charged with conspiring to use a weapon of mass destruction.

In May 2013, Edward Snowden, a former employee of the CIA, fled to Hong Kong after revealing alleged extensive internet and phone surveillance by US intelligence under a surveillance programme known as Prism. Mr Snowden has since fled to Moscow and is believed to be seeking asylum elsewhere. The US filed various espionage charges against him and as of June 2013 was seeking his extradition.

Legislature
The Congress holds America's legislative power, and is made up of the Senate and the House of Representatives. Congress sits for two years. The 113th Congress convened on the 3rd January 2013 and runs until 3rd January 2015.

Included in the powers of Congress are the powers to assess and collect taxes, to regulate foreign and interstate commerce, to coin money, to establish post offices and post roads, to establish courts inferior to the Supreme Court, to declare war and to raise and maintain an army and navy. A further Congressional power is the right to propose amendments to the Constitution whenever two-thirds of both chambers shall consider it necessary. Should two-thirds of the State legislatures demand changes in the Constitution, it is the duty of

Congress to call a constitutional convention. Proposed amendments, however, are not valid until ratified by the legislatures or by conventions of three-quarters of the states, as one or other mode of ratification may be proposed by Congress.

This method of granting different powers to the different chambers prevents the possibility of any one section obtaining too much power. The House of Representatives, for example, has the sole right of instituting impeachment proceedings against the President, Vice-President or other civil officers, but the Senate has the sole right of trying such impeachment. Senators and Representatives cannot be impeached, but each chamber may expel a member by a two-thirds vote.

The Constitution also imposes prohibitions on Congress. No export duty can be imposed. Ports of one state cannot be given preference over those of another state. No title of nobility may be granted.

The work of preparing and considering legislation is carried out mainly by committees of both chambers of Congress. In addition to the Standing Committees in each chambers, there are special committees, and several congressional commissions and joint committees composed of members of both chambers.

Senate
The Senate is composed of 100 members, two from each state, who are elected for a term of six years. Senators are voted for by the electorate. One-third of the Senate is elected every two years. Senators must be aged over 30 years, and a US citizen for at least nine years. They must be resident in the state they represent. Under the Constitution, the Senate is granted certain powers not accorded to the House of Representatives. The Constitution also makes the Vice President of the United States the President of the Senate. However, the President Pro Tempore usually presides over the Senate.

The Senate approves or rejects major Presidential appointments by majority vote, and treaties must be ratified by a two-thirds vote. The President may call a special session of the Senate even when the House is not sitting.

Senate committees are created by the Senate at the beginning of each Congress. As of 2013, there were 20 committees, 68 sub committees and four joint committees.

Following the 2010 elections, the Senate was composed of 51 Democrats, 47 Republicans and two Independents. One third of the seats were elected on 6 November 2012. The Democrats marginally increased their lead in the Senate. Following this partial election the Senate breaks down thus: Democrats 53 seats, Republicans 45 and independents 2 seats. The 113th Congress was sworn in in January 2013.
United States Senate, Hart Senate Office Building, Washington, DC 20510-4103, USA. Tel: +1 202 224 3121, URL: http://www.senate.gov/

113th Congress Senate Leadership (as at March 2013)
President of the Senate: Joseph Biden (D) (page 1388)
President Pro Tempore: Patrick Leahy (D) (page 1461)
Majority (Democrat) Leader: Harry Reid (Nevada) (page 1502)
Assistant Majority Leader (Democratic Whip): Dick Durbin (Illinois) (page 1418)
Minority (Republican) Leader: Mitch McConnell (Kentucky) (page 1473)
Assistant Minority Leader (Republican Whip): John Cornyn (R) (page 1409)

House of Representatives
The House of Representatives consists of 435 members, four delegates (American Samoa, the District of Columbia, Guam and the Virgin Islands), and one resident commissioner (Puerto Rico). The number representing each state is based on population, but every state is entitled to at least one Representative. The Constitution limits the number of Representatives to no more than one for every 30,000 population. Members are chosen by the electorate for two-year terms, all terms running for the same period. A Representative must be resident in the state from which they are chosen. A Representative must be at least 25 years of age and must have been a citizen for at least seven years.

One Resident Commissioner is elected to the House of Representatives from the Commonwealth of Puerto Rico. This Commissioner takes part in the discussions, serves on committees, but has no vote. A delegate from the District of Columbia (which, as the capital, is a Federal district rather than a state) is elected by the qualified voters of the District. He likewise participates in debates and committee work but does not have a vote. He and the Resident Commissioner of Puerto Rico may, however, introduce legislation. The territories of Guam, the Virgin Islands, and American Samoa each have a non-voting delegate, elected by the qualified voters of the respective territories.

The House of Representatives is granted the sole right of originating all bills for the raising of revenue. The President and Speaker of the House of Representatives is, constitutionally, the next in line to the Vice-President in presidential succession.

At the time of the 112th Congress, the House was composed of 242 Republicans and 193 Democrats. Following the 2012 elections, the Republicans retained control of the House: 243 Republicans and 201 Democrats.

The House has 20 Standing Committees, four Joint Committees and one Permanent Select Committee on Intelligence.

House of Representatives, 436 Cannon House Building, Washington, DC 20515-6501, USA. Tel: +1 202 224 3121, URL: http://www.house.gov/

113th Congress House of Representatives leadership (as at March 2013)
Speaker of the House of Representatives: John Boehner (Ohio) (page 1391)
Majority Leader: Eric Cantor (Virginia) (page 1400)
Majority Whip: Kevin McCarthy (California) (page 1473)
Chairman, Republican Conference: Cathy McMorris Rodgers (R) (page 1504)

Chairman, Republican Policy Committee: James Lankford (R) (page 1460)
House Minority Leader: Nancy Pelosi (D) (California) (page 1493)
House Minority Whip: Steny H. Hoyer (D) (Maryland) (page 1444)
Democratic Whip: James E. Clyburn (South Carolina) (page 1407)
Democratic Caucus Chairman: Xavier Becerra (page 1385)

Cabinet (as at June 2013)

President of the US: Barack Obama (page 1488)
Vice President of the US: Joseph R. Biden (page 1388)
Secretary of State: John Kerry (page 1456)
Secretary of the Treasury: Jack Lew (page 1463)
Secretary of Defence: Chuck Hagel (page 1436)
Attorney General: Eric H. Holder Jr. (page 1442)
Secretary of the Interior: Sally Jewell (page 1449)
Secretary of Agriculture: Thomas J. Vilsack (page 1532)
Secretary of Commerce: Penny Pritzker (page 1498)
Acting Secretary of Labor: Seth D. Harris (page 1438)
Secretary of Health and Human Services: Kathleen Sebelius (page 1510)
Secretary of Housing and Urban Development: Shaun Donovan (page 1417)
Secretary of Transportation: Ray LaHood (page 1459)
Secretary of Energy: Dr Ernest Moniz (page 1479)
Secretary of Education: Arne Duncan (page 1418)
Secretary of Veterans Affairs: Eric K. Shinseki (page 1514)
Secretary of Homeland Security: Janet Napolitano (page 1484)

The following positions also have cabinet rank (as at June 2013)

White House Chief of Staff: Denis McDonough (page 1474)
Environmental Protection Agency, Acting Administrator: Robert Perciasepe (page 1494)
Office of Management & Budget, Director: Sylvia Burwell (page 1397)
United States Trade Representative: Michael Froman (page 1427)
United States Ambassador to the UN: Ambassador Susan Rice (page 1502)
Council of Economic Advisers, Chairman: Alan B. Krueger (page 1459)
Small Business Administration: Karen G. Mills (page 1477)

Deputy Secretaries (as at March 2013)

Department of State: William Burns
Department of the Treasury: Neal S. Wolin
Department of Defence: Ashton B. Carter
Department of Justice: James Cole
Department of the Interior: David J. Hayes
Department of Agriculture: Dr. Kathleen Merrigan
Department of Commerce (Acting): Rebecca Blank
Department of Labour: Seth D. Harris
Department of Health and Human Services: Bill Corr
Department of Housing and Urban Development: Maurice Jones
Department of Transport: John Porcari
Department of Energy: Daniel Poneman
Department of Education: Tony Miller
Department of Veteran Affairs: W. Scott Gould
Department of Homeland Security: Jane Holl Lute

Ministries

Executive Office of the President, The White House, 1600 Pennsylvania Avenue NW, Washington, DC 20500, USA. Tel: +1 202 456 1414, fax: +1 202 456 2461, URL: http://www.whitehouse.gov/

Office of the Vice President, The White House, 1600 Pennsylvania Avenue NW, Washington, DC 20500, USA. Tel: +1 202 456 1414, fax: +1 202 456 2461, URL: http://www.whitehouse.gov/

Department of Agriculture, 1400 Independence Ave., SW, Washington, DC 20250, USA. Tel: +1 202 720 2791, e-mail: agsec@usda.gov, URL: http://www.usda.gov

Department of Commerce, 1401 Constitution Ave., NW, Washington, DC 20230-0001, USA. Tel: +1 202 482 2000, URL: http://www.commerce.gov/

Department of Defence, 1400 Defense Pentagon, Washington, DC 20301-1400, USA. Tel: +1 703 541 3343, URL: http://www.defenselink.mil/

Department of Education, 400 Maryland Ave., SW, Washington, DC 20202-0498, USA. Tel: +1 202 401 2000, URL: http://www.ed.gov/index.jsp

Department of Energy, 1000 Independence Ave., SW, Washington, DC 20585, USA. Tel: +1 202 586 5575, URL: http://www.energy.gov

Department of Health and Human Services, 200 Independence Ave., SW, Washington, DC 20201, USA. Tel: (toll free) +1 877 696 6775, URL: http://www.hhs.gov

Department of Homeland Security, 3801 Nebraska Ave. NW, Washington, DC 20528, USA. Tel: +1 202 282 8000, URL: http://www.dhs.gov/index.shtm

Department of Housing and Urban Development, 451 Seventh Street, SW, Washington, DC 20410, USA. Tel: +1 202 708 1112, URL: http://www.hud.gov

Department of the Interior, 1849 C Street, NW, Washington, DC 20240, USA. Tel: +1 202 208 3100, e-mail: feedback@ios.doi.gov, URL: http://www.doi.gov/

Department of Justice, 950 Pennsylvania Ave., Washington, DC 20530-0001, USA. Tel: +1 202 514 2001, e-mail: AskDOJ@usdoj.gov, URL: http://www.justice.gov

Department of Labor, Frances Perkins Building, 200 Constitution Avenue, NW, Washington, DC 20210, USA. Tel: +1 202 693 6000, URL: http://www.dol.gov

Department of State, 2201 C Street, NW, Washington, DC 20520, USA. Tel: +1 202 647 4000, URL: http://www.state.gov

Department of Transportation, 1200 New Jerset Ave, SE, Washington, DC 20590, USA. Tel: +1 202 366 4000, URL: http://www.dot.gov

Department of the Treasury, 1500 Pennsylvania Ave., NW, Washington, DC 20220, USA. Tel: +1 202 622 2000, URL: http://www.treasury.gov

Department of Veterans' Affairs, 810 Vermont Ave., NW, Washington, DC 20420, USA. Tel: +1 202 273 5700, fax: +1 202 273 6705, URL: http://www.va.gov

Other Executive Offices

National Security Council, Old Executive Office Bldg, 17th Street and Pennsylvania Ave., NW, Washington, DC 20504, USA. Tel: +1 202 456 9271, URL: http://www.whitehouse.gov/nsc/

Office of the Director of National Intelligence, Washington, DC 20511, USA. Tel: +1 703 733 8600, URL: http://www.dni.gov
Director: James R. Clapper (page 1405)

Office of National Drug Control Policy, Drug Policy Information Clearinghouse, PO Box 6000, Rockville, MD 20849-6000, USA. Tel: 800 666 3332, URL: http://www.whitehouse.gov/ondcp
Director: R. Gil Kerlikowske (page 1456)

Office of the US Trade Representative, 600 17th Street, NW, Washington, DC 20508, USA. Tel: +1 202 395 3230 (Public and Media Affairs), fax: +1 202 395 4549, URL: http://www.ustr.gov/

Council of Economic Advisors (CEA), The White House, 1600 Pennsylvania Ave NW, Washington, DC 20502, USA. Tel: +1 202 395 5034, URL: http://www.whitehouse.gov/administration/eop/cea/
Chairman: Alan Krueger (page 1459)

Office of Management and Budget (OMB), 725 17th Street, NW, Room 9026, Washington, DC 20503, USA. Tel: +1 202 395 3080, fax: +1 202 395 3888, URL: http://www.whitehouse.gov/omb/

National Economic Council (NEC), The White House, Washington, DC 20502, USA. URL: http://www.whitehouse.gov/administration/eop/nec/
Director of the National Economic Council and Assistant to the President for Economic Policy: Gene Sperling (page 1518)

Bureau of Indian Affairs, Department of the Interior, Washington DC, 20240, USA Tel: +1 202 208 3710, fax: +1 202 501 1516, URL: http://www.bia.gov/
Deputy Assistant Secretary: Larry Roberts

Central Intelligence Agency (CIA), Office of Public Affairs, Washington, DC 20505, USA. Tel: +1 703 482 0623, fax: +1 703 482 1739, URL: http://www.cia.gov
Director: John Brennan (page 1394)

Council on Environmental Quality, 722 Jackson Place, NW, Washington, DC 20503, USA. Tel: +1 202 395 5750, fax: +1 202 456 6546, URL: http://www.whitehouse.gov/ceq/
Chairman: Nancy Sutley (page 1522)

Environmental Protection Agency (EPA), Ariel Rios Building, 1200 Pennsylvania Avenue, NW, Washington, DC 20460, USA. Tel: +1 202 272 0167, URL: http://www.epa.gov/
Acting Administrator: Bob Perciasepe (page 1494)

Office of Administration, Dwight D. Eisenhower Executive Office Building, 727 17th Street, NW, Washington, DC 20503, USA. Tel: +1 202 395 7235, URL: http://www.whitehouse.gov/oa/

Federal Bureau of Investigation (FBI), Edgar Hoover Building, 935 Pennsylvania Avenue, NW, Washington, DC 20535-0001, USA. Tel: +1 202 324 3000, URL: http://www.fbi.gov/
Director: Robert Mueller, III (page 1481)

Federal Election Commission (FEC), 999 E Street, NW, Washington, DC 20463, USA. Tel: +1 202 694 1100 fax: +1 202 219 3880, URL: http://www.fec.gov/
Chairman: Ellen Weintraub (page 1535)

Federal Emergency Management Agency (FEMA), 500 C Street, SW, Washington, DC 20472, USA. Tel: +1 202 566 1600, URL: http://www.fema.gov/
Administrator: W.Craig Fugate (page 1427)

Federal Labor Relations Authority (FLRA), 607 14th Street, NW, Washington, DC 20424-0001, USA. Tel: +1 202 482 6560, URL: http://www.flra.gov/index.html
Chairman: Ernest DuBester (page 1418)

National Aeronautics and Space Administration (NASA), 300 E Street SW, Washington, DC 20024-0210, (Postal address: NASA Headquarters, Washington, DC 20546-0001) USA. Tel: +1 202 358 0000, URL: http://www.nasa.gov/
Administrator: Charles F. Bolden, Jr (page 1391)

Nuclear Regulatory Commission (NRC), Office of Public Affairs, Washington D.C. 20555, USA. Tel: +1 301 415 8200, URL: http://www.nrc.gov
Chairman: Allison M. Macfarlane (page 1468)

Small Business Administration (SBA), 409 Third Street, SW, Washington, DC 20416, USA. Tel: +1 202 205 6740, fax: +1 202 205 6913, URL: http://www.sbaonline.sba.gov/

United States Agency for International Development (USAID), Ronald Reagan Bldg, 1300 Pennsylvania Ave, NW, Washington, DC 20523-1000, USA. Tel: +1 202 712 4810, URL: http://www.usaid.gov/
Inspector General: Rajiv Shah (page 1512)

United States International Trade Commission (USITC), 500 E Street, SW, Washington, DC 20436, USA. Tel: +1 202 205 2000, URL: http://www.usitc.gov

United States Postal Service (USPS), 475 L'Enfant Plaza, SW, Washington. DC 20260-0010, USA. Tel: +1 202 268 2000, fax: +1 202 268 4860, URL: http://www.usps.gov
Postmaster-Gen. and CEO: Patrick Donahoe (page 1416)

United States Trade and Development Agency (USTDA), 1000 Wilson Boulevard, Suite 1600, Arlington, VA 22209, USA. Tel: +1 703 875 4357, fax: +1 703 875 4009, URL: http://www.ustda.gov/
Director: Leocadia I. Zak (page 1542)

Political Parties

The main parties are:

Democratic Party, Democratic National Committee, 430 S. Capitol Street, SE, Washington, DC 20003, USA. Tel: +1 202 863 8000, URL: http://www.democrats.org/
Chairman, DNC: Debbie Wassernann

Republican Party, Republican National Committee, 310 First Street, SE, Washington, DC 20003, USA. Tel: +1 202 863 8500, URL: http://www.rnc.org/
Chairman, RNC: Reince Priebus

Reform Party of the USA, P. O. Box 660675 #3995, Dallas, Texas 79604, USA. Tel: +1 972 275 9297, fax: +1 972 231 2502, e-mail: info@reformparty.org, URL: http://www.reformparty.org
Chairman: David Collison

Tea Party, California Office, 24338 El Toro Road, Suite E-108 Laguna Woods, CA 92637, URL: http://www.teaparty.org/

UNITED STATES OF AMERICA

Communist Party USA (CPUSA), 235 West 23rd Street, 7th Floor, New York, NY 10011, USA. Tel: +1 212 989 4994, fax: +1 212 229 1713, e-mail: cpusa@cpusa.org, URL: http://www.cpusa.org/

Green Party of the United States, PO Box 57065, Washington, DC 20037, USA. Tel: +1 202 319 7191, fax: +1 202 319 7192, e-mail: info@greenpartyus.org, URL: http://www.gp.org/

Green Party USA, PO Box 408316, Chicago, IL 60640, USA. E-mail: info@greenparty.org, URL: http://www.greenparty.org/

Elections

Presidential and Federal elections were held in November 2008; 35 Senate seats and all the House of Representative seats were contested. The main presidential candidates were Republicans John McCain, Mitt Romney, Mike Huckabee and Rudy Giuliani and Democrats Hillary Clinton, John Edwards and Barack Obama. Rudy Giuliani and John Edwards withdrew in January 2008 following disappointing results in the first four state primaries. By mid-March 2008, Barack Obama (page 1488)was leading Hillary Clinton (page 1406) in the Democrat race, whilst John McCain (page 1473) had won the Republican nomination. Hilary Clinton conceded defeat in June, and pledged her support for Barack Obama's campaign. Barack Obama named Joe Biden (page 1388) his running mate. John McCain announced that the Governor of Alaska, Sarah Palin (page 1492), was the Republican candidate for Vice-President.

Barack Obama won the presidency with 52.6 per cent of the popular vote, and 364 electoral College votes (well over the 270 required to win); John McCain won 46.1 per cent of the popular vote, and the remaining 162 Electoral College votes, and independent candidates won 1.1 per cent of the popuar vote, but no electoral College votes. Barack Obama was inaugurated on the 20 January 2009.

The Democrats won a clear victory over their Republican opponents in both houses of Congress. In the Senate, they gained eight seats, and they gained 21 seats in the House of Representatives. Turnout was reported to be extremely high in what many Americans felt was an historic election; it was thought that 130 million Americans had voted, the highest number since 1960.

Mid-term elections for the House of Representatives and partial elections for the Senate took place in November 2010. Thirty-seven out of the 100 Senate seats were up for election. Although the Democrats suffered losses they retained overall control of the Senate with 51 seats. The Republicans gained six seats (and now have a total of 47). Two seats are independent. The Republican party made large gains, taking at least 63 seats from the Democrats and regained control of House of Representatives with the best result for the Republican party in approximately 70 years. Republicans also did well in the gubernatorial elections.

Presidential, full House of Representatives elections and partial Senate elections took place on November 6 2012. Barack Obama won the popular vote in 26 states and the District of Columbia, amounting to 332 electoral votes. His opponent Mitt Romney won the popular vote in 24 states taking 206 electoral votes.
President Obama's second term of office commenced in January 2013.

The Republicans retained control of the House of Representatives taking 234 seats. The Democrats won 201. The Democrats slightly increased their control of the Senate after partial elections: Democrats 53 seats, Republicans 45 seats, independent 2 seats. The 113th Congress was sworn in in January 2013.

Diplomatic Representation

Embassy of the United States of America in the UK, 24 Grosvenor Square, London W1A 1AE, United Kingdom. Tel: +44 (0)20 7499 9000, URL: http://www.usembassy.org.uk/index.html
Ambassador to the Court of St. James: currently vacant
Chargé d'Affaires ad interim: Barbara J. Stephenson
Embassy of the United States of Ame rica in Canada, 490 Sussex Drive, Ottawa, Ontario K1N 1G8, Canada. Tel: +1 613 238 5335, URL: http://canada.usembassy.gov
Ambassador: H.E. David Jacobson (page 1448)
Embassy of the United Kingdom, 3100 Massachusetts Avenue, NW, Washington, DC 20008, USA. Tel: +1 202 588 6500, fax: +1 202 588 7870, URL: http://ukinusa.fco.gov.uk
Ambassador: Peter Westmacott (page 1536)
US Mission to the United Nations, 799 United Nations Plaza, New York, NY 10017-3505, USA. Tel: +1 212 415 4000, fax: +1 212 415 4053, URL: http://www.usunnewyork.usmission.gov/
Permanent Representative: Dr. Susan Rice (page 1502)
Delegation of the European Commission to the United States, 2300 M Street, NW, Washington, DC 20037, USA. Tel: +1 202 862 9500, fax: +1 202 429 1766, URL: http://www.eurunion.org/
Head of the European Commission Delegation to the United States: João Vale de Almeida (page 1530)

For information regarding US Embassies abroad, please refer to the relevant state.

LEGAL SYSTEM

The United States judiciary consists of both State and Federal systems. The Supreme Court of the United States is the highest court in the country, below which are two further levels of Federal Court: trial courts and Appellate Courts. The Appellate Courts system consists of 12 regional Circuit Courts of Appeals and one US Court of Appeals for the Federal Circuit. The Trial Courts system comprises 94 US District Courts, the US Bankruptcy Court, the US Court of International Trade, and the US Court of Federal Claims. Federal courts outside the judicial branch include Military Courts, the Court of Veterans Appeals, and the US Tax Court.

The Supreme Court deals with original cases involving a foreign dignitary, or with the state as a party. Any other case only goes to the Supreme Court on appeal from another court. The Supreme Court comprises a Chief Justice and eight Associate Justices, who are appointed for life by the President with the advice and consent of the Senate. A Justice or Judge may retire at the age of 70 after serving for 10 years as a Federal Judge or at age 65 after 15 years service. The Supreme Court convenes annually from the first Monday in October until June the following year.

There are two special trial courts with nationwide jurisdiction: the Court of International Trade, which consists of a Chief Judge, eight Judges, and three Senior Judges, and deals with cases involving international trade and customs issues; and the United States Court of Federal Claims, which consists of a Chief Judge, 11 Judges, 12 Senior Judges, and six Special Masters, and deals with claims for money damages against the US, disputes over federal contracts, and claims against the federal government for the unlawful 'appropriation' of private property.

The US Tax Court consists of the Chief Judge, 16 Judges, seven Senior Judges, and 10 Special Trial Judges (including one Chief Special Trial Judge).

Supreme Court of the United States, Supreme Court Building, One First Street, NE, Washington, DC 20543, USA. Tel: +1 202 479 3211, URL: http://www.supremecourt.gov/
Chief Justice: John G Roberts (page 1503)
Associate Justices: Antonin Scalia (page 1509), Anthony M. Kennedy (page 1455), Clarence Thomas (page 1525), Ruth Bader Ginsburg (page 1381), Stephen G. Breyer (page 1394), Samuel A. Alito Jr. (page 1374), Sonia Sotomayor (page 1518), Elena Kagan (page 1453)

United States Court of Appeals for the Federal Circuit, URL: http://www.cafc.uscourts.gov/
Chief Circuit Judge: Randall R. Rader (page 1499)
United States Court of Federal Claims, URL: http://www.uscfc.uscourts.gov/
Chief Judge: Emily C. Hewitt (page 1441)
United States Court of International Trade, URL: http://www.cit.uscourts.gov/
Chief Judge: Donald C. Pogue (page 1496)
United States Tax Court, URL: http://www.ustaxcourt.gov/
Chief Judge: John O Colvin (page 1408)

The District Courts are the 94 Federal courts of original jurisdiction. Each state has at least one of these courts, and there is also one each in the District of Columbia, Puerto Rico, US Virgin Islands, Northern Mariana Islands and Guam. Appeals from these District Courts are referred to one of 13 intermediate appellate courts, known as courts of appeals, and the US Court of Appeals for the Federal Circuit.

Each state has a system of courts which is independent of the Federal system. These courts cover all state matters from civil disputes to crime. Cases may be taken on appeal from the highest state court to the Federal Supreme Court, either when it is claimed that the State has denied the appellant his federal constitutional rights, or when the case is such that it comes under Federal jurisdiction because it involves a Federal question.

The Municipal Court system of a city usually includes police courts, and a civil court. Many states also have special courts such as the Probate Court, Juvenile Court, Court of Domestic Relations and Courts of Small Claims. State law varies on such matters as divorce, licensing and procedure, but no state may make a law which conflicts with the Constitution.

The Right to Bear Arms

The exact meaning of the constitutional right to keep and bear arms has been argued for many years. Following the 1999 shooting at Colorado's Columbine High School, the right to carry arms, enshrined in the Second Amendment of the Federal Constitution, became the subject of debate. The case of District of Columbia v. Heller, heard by the US Supreme Court in March 2008, ruled that a ban on handguns in Washington DC was unconstitutional; the private possession of handguns had been prohibited in the nation's capital since 1976, while rifles and shotguns had been required to be locked away or dismantled. Gun laws across the US will be affected by this ruling, as it enshrines the individual right to own guns, and will limit efforts to reduce their role in American life. In January 2013, following the Sandy Hook school shooting in which 20 children and six adults died, President Obama announced proposals to improve the control of firearms, including the introduction of mandatory background checks for all gun sales, a new stronger ban on assault weapons, a ban on armour-piercing bullets and the limiting of magazines to 10 rounds. However, in April 2013 the Senate failed to advance a bill to expand background checks.

The Death Penalty

As of April 2013, 17 states and the District of Colombia have banned the death penalty completely. Texas is now the only state where a sentence of Life without Parole is not available.

The Supreme Court issued a ruling ending the execution of those with mental retardation, in June 2002. The ruling overturned a previous vote 13 years previously.

In March 2005, the US Supreme Court effectively put an end to the execution of juveniles (those under 18 years old). The Court ruled that the death penalty for those who had committed their crimes at under 18 years of age was cruel and unusual punishment and hence barred by the Constitution.

In January 2007, a New Jersey Commission on the death penalty recommended that it be abolished in the State, and replaced with life imprisonment without the possibility of parole, to be served in a maximum security facility. The Commission also recommended that any cost savings resulting from the abolition of the death penalty be used for benefits and services for survivors of victims of homicide. On March 18, 2009, New Mexico Governor Bill Richardson signed a bill to repeal the death penalty. Illinois repealed the death penalty in 2011 and Connecticut in 2012. In both New Mexico and Connecticut the repeal is not retroactive. California narowly chose to retain the death penalty in 2012.

Since the resumption of the death penalty in 1976, the US has executed a total of 1,329 prisoners (April 2013). Forty-three executions were carried out in 2012, the same number as 2011. As of April 2013, 9 people had been executed in 2013 with a further 16 scheduled for the rest of the year. There was a peak of 98 in 1999. Texas has carried out the most executions of all the states. In 2012, the following states carried out executions: Texas (15), Arizona (6), Oklahoma (6), Mississippi (6), Ohio (3), Florida (3), South Dakota (2), Delaware (1), Idaho (1). States which had carried out executions in 2013 (as at April 2013) were Florida, Georgia, Ohio, Oklahoma, Texas (4), and Virginia. At least 77 people received the death penalty during 2012, substantially lower than the number in the mid-1990s. As of 2012, there were 3,146 death row inmates.

Guantanamo

In June 2006, three detainees committed suicide at the detention camp at Guantanamo Bay, Cuba, prompting further calls for its closure. The camp was set up in 2002 to hold suspected terrorists during the Afghanistan campaign. Overall, 775 prisoners were held in Guantanamo, approximately 420 of whom were released without charge. Over a fifth of those held have been cleared for release, but it has been difficult to persuade countries to accept them; in May 2008, the US government said that 36 previous inmates had returned to terrorist activities, or were suspected of having returned to terrorism. The camp was criticised for holding inmates without trial and for mistreatment of detainees. The Pentagon argued that international law allows them to hold 'enemy combatants' without charge or trial for the duration of hostilities, and that the detainees were not entitled to the protections of the Geneva Conventions. In June 2006, the US Supreme Court ruled against the Administration, and the detainees were then granted protection under the Geneva Convention. In December 2006, legislation was passed to establish military commissions, and the following month the Defense department outlined new rules that would allow terror suspects to be imprisoned on the basis of hearsay or coerced testimony. In March 2007, hearings began to determine whether key suspects could be deemed enemy combatants and face military trials. The hearings were held with no defence lawyers present. In June 2008, the US Supreme Court ruled that foreign suspects held in Guantanamo Bay had the right to challenge their detention in US civilian courts. Following the election of President Obama in December 2008, Defense Secretary Robert Gates ordered plans to be drafted for the closure of the detention centre by the end of January 2010. In February 2009, a US federal appeals court rejected the release of 17 Guantanamo Bay detainees onto US soil, on the grounds that the judiciary could not make decisions on immigration. China had requested the return of 17 Uighurs (Chinese Muslims), to try them for alleged separatist activities. In May, White House officials announced that military trials for some of the detainees at Guantanamo Bay would go ahead, a decision that angered civil rights groups. On the 20th May 2009, Congress rejected President Obama's move to fund the closure of Guantanamo, amid concern over moving inmates to the US. On Jan 7, 2011, President Obama signed the 2011 Defense Authorization Bill which contains provisions preventing the transfer of Guantanamo prisoners to the mainland or to other foreign countries, and thus effectively means Guananamo remains open.

LOCAL GOVERNMENT

State government follows much the same pattern as Federal Government. Each state has its own Constitution and, with the exception of Nebraska, a two-chamber legislature. The states are entitled to make their own laws providing these do not conflict with the main Constitution. Most state legislatures meet annually. Each state has a Governor, elected by popular vote, whose term varies from two to four years. The state is entitled to its own police and militia, has authority over education, public works, roads and development, and has its own state courts and legal system. In every state except North Carolina the Governor has the power to veto acts of the legislature, but the latter may over-rule the veto if it can muster the required number of votes.

The states are subdivided into counties (parishes in Louisiana), townships, cities, villages and special areas, such as school districts, water-control districts and forest-preserve areas. Each of these political subdivisions has its own administration suitable for the type of area covered (urban or rural), but the administrations have no authority of their own. Authority flows only from the state. Counties administer state laws and have fairly wide powers in the fields of health, education, taxation and so on, besides being the electoral area for the election of state officials. Towns and villages are more limited in their local government. Cities are usually governed under a charter from the state legislature, although many have recently been granted the privilege of framing their own charters within the state constitution. In all cases officials are elected, not appointed by the state government.

For further details on each state please see their separate entries following this country entry.

AREA AND POPULATION

Area

The USA makes up most of the North American continent, and has a total area of 3,794,083.06 sq. miles, of which 3,537,438.44 sq. miles is land and 256,644.62 sq. miles is water. In terms of land area only, the United States is third largest country in the world, behind Russia and China, and just larger than Canada. The USA is bordered in the north by Canada and in the south-west by Mexico. Alaska, the largest of the States, lies to the northwest of Canada, whilst the southernmost State, Hawaii, lies in the Pacific Ocean.

Moving from east to west, the Atlantic coastal plain gives way to hills and the Appalachian Mountains, which separate the eastern seaboard from the Great Lakes and the prairies and Great Plains of the Midwest. The Rocky Mountains to the west of the Plains run the length of the US, exceeding altitudes of 14,000 feet in some parts. To the west of the Rockies is the Great Basin and the Mojave desert, and finally the Sierra Nevada and Cascade mountain ranges run parallel to the Pacific coast.

The highest point in the USA is Mount McKinley in Alaska, at 20,320 ft., and the lowest point is Death Valley in California, at -282 ft. The Mississippi-Missouri River runs mainly north-south through the centre of the country, and is the world's fourth longest river system.

To view a map of the USA, please consult:
http://www.lib.utexas.edu/maps/united_states/united_states_pol02.pdf

The United States is subject to most climate types, ranging from humid continental in the northeast to tropical in the southeast (Florida and Hawaii), arid in the deserts of the southwest, alpine in the mountains and subarctic in Alaska. The southern states on the Gulf of Mexico are prone to hurricanes, whilst the Midwest sees most of the world's tornadoes.

Population

The US is the third most populated country in the world, behind China and India; around 4.52 per cent of the world population lives within the USA and its territories. According to the 2010 Census, the population was 308,745,538. The population was estimated to be 313,914,040 as at the beginning of July 2012. Over the period 2000-2009, the population grew by 9.1 per cent. The US Census Bureau estimated that the 300 million mark was reached on 17th October 2006, 39 years after reaching 200 million people. The population grew by 1.7 per cent from 2010 to 2012. The average population density was estimated at 88.08 people per sq. mile in 2012. The most densely populated state is District of Colombia and the least Alaska.

The following table shows the current distribution of the population by region:

Distribution of Population by Region, July 2010-July 2012

Region	2010 (Census)	2011 (E)	2012 (E)
Northeast	55,317,240	55,597,816	55,761,091
Midwest	66,927,001	67,145,089	67,316,297
South	114,555,744	116,022,230	117,257,221
West	71,945,553	72,822,851	73,579,431
Total	308,745,538	311,591,917	313,914,040

Source: US Census Bureau

Annual Figures for the Resident Population for the United States by State: 2000 to July 1, 2012

Geographic Area	Census 2000	Census 2010	July 1 2012 (E)
Alabama	4,447,100	4,779,736	4,822,023
Alaska	626,932	710,231	731,449
Arizona	5,130,632	6,392,017	6,553,255
Arkansas	2,673,400	2,915,918	2,949,131
California	33,871,648	37,253,956	38,041,430
Colorado	4,301,261	5,029,196	5,187,582
Connecticut	3,405,565	3,574,097	3,590,347
Delaware	783,600	897,934	917,092
District of Columbia	572,059	601,723	632,323
Florida	15,982,378	18,801,310	19,317,568
Georgia	8,186,453	9,687,653	9,919,945
Hawaii	1,211,537	1,360,301	1,392,313
Idaho	1,293,953	1,567,582	1,595,728
Illinois	12,419,293	12,830,632	12,875,255
Indiana	6,080,485	6,483,802	6,537,334
Iowa	2,926,324	3,046,355	3,074,186
Kansas	2,688,418	2,853,118	2,885,905
Kentucky	4,041,769	4,339,367	4,380,415
Louisiana	4,468,976	4,533,372	4,601,893
Maine	1,274,923	1,328,361	1,329,192
Maryland	5,296,486	5,773,552	5,884,563
Massachusetts	6,349,097	6,547,629	6,646,144
Michigan	9,938,444	9,883,640	9,883,360
Minnesota	4,919,479	5,303,925	5,379,139
Mississippi	2,844,658	2,967,297	2,984,926
Missouri	5,595,211	5,988,927	6,021,988
Montana	902,195	989,415	1,005,141
Nebraska	1,711,263	1,826,341	1,855,525
Nevada	1,998,257	2,700,551	2,758,931
New Hampshire	1,235,786	1,316,470	1,320,718
New Jersey	8,414,350	8,791,894	8,864,590
New Mexico	1,819,046	2,059,179	2,085,538
New York	18,976,457	19,378,102	19,570,261
North Carolina	8,049,313	9,535,483	9,752,073
North Dakota	642,200	672,591	699,628
Ohio	11,353,140	11,536,504	11,544,225
Oklahoma	3,450,654	3,751,351	3,814,820
Oregon	3,421,399	3,831,074	3,899,353
Pennsylvania	12,281,054	12,702,379	12,763,536
Rhode Island	1,048,319	1,052,567	1,050,292
South Carolina	4,012,012	4,625,364	4,723,723
South Dakota	754,844	814,180	833,354
Tennessee	5,689,283	6,346,105	6,456,243
Texas	20,851,820	25,145,561	26,059,203
Utah	2,233,169	2,763,885	2,855,287
Vermont	608,827	625,741	626,011
Virginia	7,078,515	8,001,024	8,185,867
Washington	5,894,121	6,724,540	6,897,012
West Virginia	1,808,344	1,852,994	1,855,413
Wisconsin	5,363,675	5,686,986	5,726,398
Wyoming	493,782	563,626	576,415

Source: US Census Bureau

UNITED STATES OF AMERICA

In 2008, 20.2 per cent of the population was 14 years or under, 67 per cent was aged between 15 and 64 years, and 12.8 per cent were over 65 years old. The median age in 2011 was 37.3 years. Average life expectancy at birth in 2010 was estimated to be 75.7 years for men and 80.8 years for women. It is projected to rise to 77.1 years for males and 81.9 years for females by 2025.

Of the 2009 resident population, some 151,449,490 were male and 155,557,060 were female. According to the 2010 Census, 72.4 per cent of the population were white alone, 12.6 per cent were black or African American alone, 0.9 per cent American Indian or Alaska Native alone, 4.8 per cent Asian alone, and 0.2 per cent native Hawaiian and other Pacific Islander. Approximately 2.9 per cent people (9.009 million) were of two races. Some 50,477,594 people were of Hispanic or Latino origin. There are more than 20 different American Indian tribes, the largest being the Cherokee, who make up 20 per cent of the total. More than 500,000 different American Indian languages are spoken. English is the main language in the US although Spanish is also widely spoken.

The US had 117,538,000 households in 2010; The average household size was 2.59 people. In 2005, it was estimated that approximately 13.3 per cent of Americans lived below the poverty line. Some 12.5 per cent (37,960,935) of the US population was born abroad, and well over three million American citizens live abroad. More than 100,000 are resident in the following countries: Mexico, Canada, United Kingdom, Germany, Israel, Italy, Philippines.(Source: U.S. Census Bureau)

Births, Marriages, Deaths

The US Census Bureau estimated that in 2010 there were around 3,999,386 births and 2,468,435 deaths. The crude birth rate in 2010 was 13.0 births per 1,000 population and the fertility rate was 64.1 newborns per 1,000 women aged 15-44 years. Approximately 8.1 per cent were born with a low birthweight. The 2010 preliminary death rate was 7.995 deaths per 1,000 population. The infant mortality rate was 6.15 infant deaths per 1,000 live births in 2010, down slightly from 6.8 per 1,000 in 2005. (Source: National Center for Health Statistics)

Provisional data for 2009 show that there were 6.8 marriages per 1,000 inhabitants (down from 7.3 in 2007) (2,080,000 marriages). The divorce rate was static, at 3.5 per 1,000 population in 2009 (though this figure excludes data from California, Georgia, Hawaii, Indiana, Louisiana and Minnesota). The median age for marriage is 24.5 for women and 26.7 for men. Recent figures show 12 per cent of adults live alone. Seven out of every 100 couples remain unmarried. In 12 per cent of divorce cases, children remain under the care of the father. (Source: National Center for Health Statistics)

Same-sex marriage in the United States first became legal in the U.S. state Massachusetts in 2004. As of June 2013, 12 states had legalised same-sex marriage: Connecticut, Delaware, Iowa, Maine, Maryland, Massachusetts, Minnesota, New Hampshire, New York, Rhode Island, Vermont, and Washington, D.C. Same-sex marriage was briefly permitted in California before being overturned in November 2008. They are now recognised on a conditional basis.

Public Holidays 2014

1 January: New Year's Day
20 January: Martin Luther King's Birthday (observed on 3rd Monday in January)
17 February: George Washington's Birthday (observed on 3rd Monday in February)
18 April: Good Friday (observed by most states)
26 May: Memorial Day (observed on last Monday in May)
4 July: Independence Day
1 September: Labor Day (observed on 1st Monday in September)
13 October: Columbus Day (observed on 2nd Monday in October)
11 November: Veterans' Day
27 November: Thanksgiving Day (observed on 4th Thursday in November)
25 December: Christmas Day

Should a holiday fall on a Sunday then the following Monday is generally observed; if the holiday falls on a Saturday then it is generally observed on the previous Friday.

EMPLOYMENT

Between the beginning of the recession in December 2007, and the end of March 2009, 5.1 million jobs were lost, with almost two-thirds (3.3 million) of the decrease happening between November 2008 and March 2009. There were predictions that national unemployment figures would reach 10 per cent of the workforce before levelling out, and this figure was reached in November 2009 with the construction, manufacturing, and information sectors being hardest hit. Unemployment fell back to 9.7 per cent in January -March 2010 (up from 7.7 per cent a year earlier), as temporary help services and health care continued to add jobs. Employment within federal government also rose, with the hiring of temporary workers for Census 2010. March was the first month in two years in which most private-sector industries added jobs. However, employment continued to fall in the financial and information sectors. Over the year 2012, unemployment was put at 8.1 per cent, an unemployment level of 12.5 million. The unemployment rate in March 2013 was 7.6 per cent.

Employment figures 2007-13 (not seasonally adj.)

Year	Workforce (000)	Employed (000)	Unemployed (000)	Unempl. rate %
March 2007	153,051	146,320	6,731	4.4
March 2008	153,908	146,086	7,822	5.1
March 2009	154,142	140,721	13,421	8.7
March 2010	153,960	138,767	15,192	9.9
March 2011	153,358	139,643	13,716	8.9
March 2012	154,707	142,020	12,686	8.2
March 2013	155,028	143,286	11,742	7.6

Source: US Dept. of Labor

Employment according to race (not seasonally adjusted) is shown on the following table:

Employment according to race, ('000s)

Employment	March 2012
White non-instit. population	192,688
Civilian labour force	124,156
Employed	113,877
Unemployed	10,279
Unemployment rate (%)	8.3
Black or African American non-instit. population	**29,005**
Labour force	17,705
Employed	14,837
Unemployed	2,740
Unemployment rate (%)	15.5
Asian non instit. population	**11,301**
Civilian labour force	7,410
Employed	6,881
Unemployed	529
Unemployment rate (%)	7.1

Source: Bureau of Labor Statistics

The following table shows annual average non-farm employment levels according to industry sector ('000s):

Employment by industry sector (non-farm) ('000s) (Seasonally adjusted)

Industry	March 2012	March 2013 (p)
Total nonfarm	133,285	135,195
Total private	111,344	113,330
Goods-producing	18,402	18,652
Mining and Logging	852	869
Construction	5,640	5,802
Manufacturing	11,910	11,981
Wholesale Trade	5,640.8	5,732.7
Retail Trade	14,799.1	15,017.0
Transportation and warehousing	4,387.5	4,467.1
Utilities	553.6	558.1
Information	2,679	2,704
Finance and Insurance	5,815.5	5,871.3
Real estate and rental and leasing	1,947.1	1,973.0
Professional and business services	17,796	18,329
Education and health services	20,221	20,586
Leisure and hospitality	13,684	13,975
Other services	5,418	5,465
Government	21,941	21,865

Source: Bureau of Labor Statistics

Over the year to March 2013, unemployment decreased in 40 states and increased in eight states. Nevada recorded the highest unemployment rate among the states (9.7 per cent), followed by (Illinois 9.5) and Mississippi & California (9.4 per cent). North Dakota again registered the lowest unemployment rate, at 3.3 per cent, followed by Nebraska (3.8 per cent). (Source: Bureau of Labor Statistics, April 2013)

BANKING AND FINANCE

Currency
One US$ = 100 cents
US$ 1,000,000,000 = US$1 billion

GDP/GNP, Inflation, National Debt
The US is the world's leading economic power. Following a recession in 2000, 'real' GDP (dollar chained to 2000 value) grew by 3.6 per cent over 2004 before slowing to 2.9 per cent in 2006, due to higher inflation caused by the high cost of oil and a high current account deficit of 6.4 per cent of GDP. Real GDP grew by just 2 per cent over 2007, to $11,523.9 billion.

2007 saw the beginnings of a credit crisis, caused by bad debt in financial institutions. US mortgage companies had made hundreds of billions of dollars of inappropriate loans (sub-prime lending). The debts were sold in packages to financial institutions around the world, and thence to pension funds and hedge funds. The financial institutions, unaware of the extent of the bad debt in their individual portfolios, were unwilling to lend further. The result was a depressed US housing market, and a general economic slowdown, which had a knock-on effect around the world. The US government approved a range of measures, including fiscal stimulus, banking sector support and measures to help home-owners. The federal deficit is likely to rise by around US$787 billion over the next ten years. In April 2009, President Obama said that the recession was easing. In November 2010, in an attempt to keep interest rates from rising and undermining the recovery, the US Federal Reserve Bank announced it was to purchase $600 billion worth of US Government bonds.

Real GDP increased by just 0.4 per cent over 2008, to $13,312.2 billion (chained 2005). Over 2009, real GDP declined by 2.4 per cent (to $12,990.3 billion), due to downturns in business investment, exports, capital investment and consumer spending. However, whilst real GDP contracted by six per cent over the first quarter 2009, by the fourth quarter, the economy was beginning to pick up, and real GDP grew by 5.9 per cent. Current dollar GDP grew by 2.6 per cent over 2008 (to $14,441.4 billion), but contracted by 1.3 per cent over 2009 (to $14,258.2 billion). There were two quarters of negative growth in 2009, but in 2010, growth has ranged between 3.8 per cent and 1.8 per cent. Growth in Q4 of 2010 was 3.1 per cent and growth in the Q1 of 2011 was estimated to be 1.8 per cent. Factors in the slowdown include: slow down of exports, increased imports, reducted consumer spending, decreased government spending and a slowing of business investments. These factors were in part mitigated by increased inventory investment. Growth grew at an annual rate of 2.2 per cent in March 2012, down from 3 per cent in Q4 2011. Growth as a whole was 2.2 per cent over 2012. Growth has remained low: it was 0.4 per cent in Q4 2012, rising to 2.5 per cent in Q1 2013. This was lower than the 3 per cen that had been predicted and growth is expected to remain low as spending cuts are due to come into effect. The growth in Q1 2013 was driven by consumer spending. Federal government spending and investment fell by 8.4 per cent in Q1.

Real GDP increased in 43 states in 2011 and the District of Colombia, led by national growth in manufacturing, professional, scientific & technical services, and information services. North Dakota (7.6 per cent), Oregon (4.7 per cent), West Virginia (4.5 per cent) and Texas (3.3 per cent) saw the highest growth rates. Wyoming (-1.2 per cent) had the lowest rate, followed by Mississippi (-0.8 per cent) and Alabama (-0.8 per cent). (Source: Bureau of Economic Analysis, BEA)

The following table shows GDP - value added by industry.

GDP by Industry (billions of current dollars)

Industry	2009	2010	2011	2012
GDP	13,973.7	14,498.9	15,075.7	15,684.8
Private industries	12,056.7	12,532.3	13,081.8	13,657.6
Agriculture, forestry, fisheries & hunting	142.4	157.6	173.5	168.6
Mining	221.7	251.9	289.9	285.2
Utilities	264.7	284.5	297.9	304.3
Construction	542.9	523.3	529.5	558.7
Manufacturing	1,540.1	1,630.5	1,731.5	1,866.7
Wholesale Trade	766.3	799.0	845.1	897.9
Retail Trade	846.8	876.0	905.7	949.1
Transport and warehousing	396.6	422.6	447.9	469.3
Information	604.8	612.2	646.6	690.6
Finance and insurance	1,093.6	1,157.3	1,159.3	1,242.3
Real Estate and rental and leasing	1,848.3	1,864.5	1,898.8	1,926.3
Professional & business services	1,693.2	1,769.6	1,883.9	1,952.4
Educational services	163.1	166.4	174.2	179.9
Health care and social assistance	1,062.4	1,102.7	1,136.9	1,164.8
Arts, entertainment, and recreation	130.6	139.4	148.0	153.3
Accommodation and food services	394.8	418.6	443.1	471.6
Other services, except government	344.4	356.0	369.9	376.7
Government	1,917.0	1,966.6	1,993.8	2026.2

Source: Bureau of Economic Analysis, May 2013

Per capita income for the US was US$42,070 in 2011, down on $47,040 in 2010. Per capita real GDP ranged from US$63,159 in Delaware to a low of US$28,293 in Mississippi. (Source: Bureau of Economic Analysis, BEA)

The US Census Bureau reported that in 2010 approximately 46.2 million Americans were living in poverty, the highest figure in 50 years.

The Consumer Price Index for All Urban Consumers (CPI-U) rose by just 2.7 per cent over the year to March 2012; the rise was largely due to significant increases in overall energy prices, in particular gasoline and fuel oil prices.

Foreign Investment

The main host countries and regions of US direct investment in 2011 are shown on the following table:

Country	$ million
Total	4,155,551
Canada	318,964
Europe	2,307,697
-United Kingdom	-549,399
-The Netherlands	-595,139
-Luxembourg	-335,279
Latin America & Other Western Hemisphere	831,151
-Brazil	71,101
-Mexico	91,402
-Bermuda	579,014
Africa	56,632
Middle East	35,905
Asia & Pacific	605,202
-Australia	136,249
-Japan	116,533
-Singapore	116,616

Source: Bureau of Economic Analysis, May 2013

Foreign Direct Investment in the US, 2011

	$ million
Total	2,547,828
Canada	210,864

- continued	
Europe	1,811,875
-Germany	215,938
-Netherlands	240,036
-Switzerland	211,700
-United Kingdom	442,179
Latin America and Other Western Hemisphere	85,695
Africa	4,281
Middle East	25,363
Asia and Pacific	409,749
-Japan	289,490

Source: Bureau of Economic Analysis, May 2013

Balance of Payments / Imports and Exports

The trade deficit, a measure of international trade in goods and services, decreased from $696.7 billion in 2007 to $381.3 billion in 2009 (revised), but rose to US$599.9 billion in 2011. It fell to US$539.5 billion. As a percentage of U.S. gross domestic product, the goods and services deficit was 2.7 per cent in 2009, down from 4.8 per cent in 2008.

Trade Balance, 2009-12 ($million)

Imports/Exports	2009	2010	2011	2012
Goods	-505,758	-645,124	-738,413	-735,313
Services	126,603	150,387	178,533	195,799
Balance	-379,154	-494,737	-559,880	-539,514

Source: Bureau of Economic Analysis, May 2013

Major imported goods include crude oil and refined petroleum products, consumer goods, machinery, industrial raw materials, food and beverages. Major export products include cars, capital goods, industrial supplies and raw materials, agricultural products, consumer goods, and services.

The following table shows imports and exports of goods (seasonally adjusted) by principal end-use commodity category, in millions of dollars:

Export/Import of Goods by Principal End-Use Category, ($m)

Commodity	2010	2011
Exports		
- Foods, feeds & beverages	107,699	126,220
- Industrial supplies	390,741	500,342
- Capital goods	445,910	492,988
- Automotive vehicles etc.	111,858	133,116
- Consumer goods	165,754	174,957
- Other	56,177	52,809
Imports		
- Foods, feeds & beverages	91,721	107,460
- Industrial supplies	601,321	755,807
- Capital goods	449,313	510,737
- Automotive vehicles etc.	225,210	254,609
- Consumer goods	483,343	514,061
- Other	61,134	65,150

Source: US BEA, May 2013

Top trading partners in 2010 included: EU (21 per cent), Canada (15 per cent), China (12 per cent), Mexico (10 per cent), and Japan (6 per cent). Top trading partners in 2012 included Canada, China and Mexico.

Top Trading Partners, Export, Imports, Dec. 2012, year to date

	Exports	Imports	Total	%
Total All Countries	1,547.1	2,275.0	3,822.2	100
Canada	292.4	324.2	616.7	16.1
China	110.6	425.6	536.2	14.0
Mexico	216.3	277.7	494.0	12.9
Japan	70.0	146.4	216.4	5.7
Germany	48.8	108.5	157.3	4.1
United Kingdom	54.8	54.9	109.8	2.9
Korea, South	42.3	58.9	101.2	2.6
Brazil	43.7	32.1	75.8	2.0
Saudi Arabia	18.1	55.7	73.8	1.9
France	30.8	41.6	72.4	1.9

Source: US Census Bureau, May 2013

Top import partners in 2012 were Canada, China, Mexico, Japan and Germany. Top export partners were Canada, Mexico, China, Japan and the UK.

US Trade Representative (Acting): Ambassador Demetrios Marantis
URL: http://www.ustr.gov/

The relaxing of US import duties in October 2000 gave 58 countries in Africa, Central America and the Caribbean greater duty-free access to the US market. However, 14 African countries were excluded as a result of their political or economic records: Angola, Burkina Faso, Burundi, the Democratic Republic of Congo, Comoros, Equatorial Guinea, Gambia, Ivory Coast, Liberia, Somalia, Sudan, Swaziland, Togo, and Zimbabwe.

UNITED STATES OF AMERICA

On 15 November 1999 a bilateral agreement was completed between the US and the People's Republic of China in which China was allowed into the World Trade Organisation (WTO). Early in 2000, despite opposition, the US Congress agreed to 'permanent normal trade relations' with China to allow the US to receive the full benefit of China's entry to the WTO.

Top Ten Companies 2012
The ranking is based on revenues. It excludes state-owned enterprises.
Exxon Mobil, URL: http://www.exxon.mobil.com
Walmart Stores, URL: http://www.walmart.com/
Chevron Corporation, URL: http://www.chevron.com
ConocoPhillips, URL: http://www.conocophillips.com/
General Motors, URL: http://www.gm.com
General Electric, URL: http://www.ge.com
Berkshire Hathaway, URL: http://www.berkshirehathaway.com
Fannie Mae, URL: http://www.fanniemae.com/
Ford Motor, URL: http://www.ford.com
Hewlett-Packard, URL: http://www.hp.com

Several companies made huge losses in 2009, notably American International Group (AIG) who lost $99,289 million, Fannie Mae and Freddie Mac ($58,707 million and $50,119 million respectively), General Motors ($30,860 million - largest loss ever in the car industry - due to gas prices and a fall in truck and SUV sales.), Merril Lynch ($27 billion for subprime lending) and Citigroup ($27 billion- also for subprime lending).

Central Bank
The Federal Reserve System consists of the Board of Governors, the Federal Open Market Committee, 12 Federal Reserve Banks, their branches and regional offices.
Federal Reserve System, 20th Street and Constitution Avenue, NW, Washington, DC 20551, USA. Tel: +1 202 452 6400, URL: http://www.federalreserve.gov
Chairman of the Board of Governors: Ben S. Bernanke (page 1387)

Major Banks
Bank of America, URL: https://www.bankofamerica.com
Citibank NA, URL: http://www.citibank.com
J.P. Morgan Chase, http://www.jpmorganchase.com
World Bank Group, URL: http://www.worldbank.org.
President: Dr Jim Yong Kim (page 1449)
Wells Fargo Bank NA, URL: http://www.wellsfargo.com
SunTrust Bank, URL: http://www.suntrust.com

Chambers of Commerce and Trade Addresses
US Chamber of Commerce, URL: http://www.uschamber.com/
Council of American States in Europe (CASE), URL: http://www.case-europe.com
British-American Business Council (BABC), URL: http://www.babc.org/
US and Foreign Commercial Service, URL: http://www.buyusa.gov
Federation of International Trade Associations, URL: http://www.fita.org/
Washington Council on International Trade, URL: http://wcit.org/
American Federation of Labor and Congress of Industrial Organisations (AFL-CIO), URL: http://www.aflcio.org/

Stock Exchanges
US Securities and Exchange Commission, URL: http://www.sec.gov
New York Stock Exchange, NYSE Euronext, URL: https://nyse.nyx.com/
Boston Stock Exchange, Inc. (NASDAQ OMX BX),
URL: http://www.nasdaqtrader.com/Trader.aspx?id=Boston_Stock_Exchange
Chicago Stock Exchange, URL: http://www.chx.com
Philadelphia Stock Exchange (NASDAQ OMX PHLX),
URL: http://www.phlx.com/

MANUFACTURING, MINING AND SERVICES

Primary and Extractive Industries
Coal, iron ore, copper, lead, zinc, silver, tungsten, molybdenum, gold and mercury are mined in the United States. Other essential minerals are also produced, including petroleum, natural gas, bauxite, sulphur, lime, salt, clays and slate. Some of America's natural resources have been depleted in recent years, however, and as a result the country imports lead, zinc and copper. Total non-fuel mineral production is estimated at approximately $30 billion per year.

The US is the world's second largest coal producer and has the world's largest coal reserves, estimated at 484.5 billion short tons as at 1st January 2011, though just 258,619 million short tons are recoverable, and recoverable reserves at producing mines totalled 19.23 billion short tons. Of the reserve base, 257.2 billion short tons are bituminous coal, 177 billion short tons are sub-bituminous coal, 42.8 billion short tons are lignite (brown coal), and 7.5 billion short tons are anthracite. The coal industry is composed of establishments primarily engaged in producing or developing bituminous coal or lignite at surface mines, bituminous coal or lignite at underground mines, or anthracite coal. The industry includes auger mining, strip mining, culm bank mining, and other surface mining, as well as coal preparation plants engaged in cleaning, crushing, screening, or sizing. It also includes establishments primarily engaged in performing coal-mining services for others on a contract or fee basis.

Coal is produced from three main geographical areas: Appalachia (390 million short tons in 2008, up 6.5 per cent on 2007), the Interior (146 million short tons, down one per cent on 2007) and the Western Region (633 million short tons, little change over the year). Over half of US coal is produced in three states: Wyoming (35.7 per cent of the US total), West Virginia and East Kentucky. A total of 25 US states produce coal from about 1,325 mines.

The US coal industry produced a record-breaking 1,171,809 million short tons of coal in 2008, up by 2.2 per cent on the previous year when 1,146,635 million short tons was produced. It fell to 1,072.752 million short tons in 2009 but rose to 1,085.281 million short tons in 2010 and to 1,094.3 million short tons in 2011.

Domestic coal consumption rose from 997.478 million short tons in 2008 to 1,003.1 million short tons in 2011. 1,040,580 million short tons of coal were used in electricity generation.

Imports totalled reached a high of 36.3 million short tons in 2007. supplies came mainly from Colombia. In 2010, imports were estimated at 19.4 million short tons and 13.1 million short tons in 2011. Exports reached 59,190,613 short tons in 2009, and were destined mainly for Canada (17,488,248 short tons) and Europe (29,169,004 short tons). In 2010, exports reached 81.7 million short tons, rising to 107.3 million short tons in 2011.

The major US coal companies include: Peabody Holding Co., Inc.(the world's largest private-sector coal company, URL: www.peabodyenergy.com/); Consol Energy Inc.(URL: www.consolenergy.com/); & Rio Tinto Co. (URL: http://www.riotinto.com).

Oil
The crude petroleum and natural gas industry is made up of establishments engaged in operating oil and gas fields. Such activities include exploration for crude petroleum and natural gas; drilling, completing and equipping wells; operation of separators, emulsion breakers, de-silting equipment; and all other activities incident to making oil and gas marketable up to the point of shipment from the producing property. This industry also includes production of oil through the mining and extraction of oil from oil shale and oil sands, and the production of gas and hydrocarbon liquids through gasification, liquefaction, and pyrolysis of coal at the mine site.

Proven reserves were 25.2 billion barrels in January 2010 (up on the January 2008 figure of 19.18 billion barrels), and are largely concentrated in four states: in 2009, Texas had 5,006 million barrels, Alaska had 3,556 million barrels, Gulf of Mexico Federal Offshore reserves totalled 3,464 million barrels and California had reserves of 2,835 million barrels. In 2004 the United States had a total of 500,000 producing oil wells, the majority of which were considered 'stripper' wells producing just a few barrels per day. Reserves are increasing with the extension of horizontal drilling and hydraulic fracturing in shale formations.

Production has declined annually since 1985, due to rising exploration and production costs and the lowering of oil prices, but the USA remains the third top oil producer, behind Russia (9.9 million barrels per day) and Saudi Arabia (9.76 million barrels per day). In 2009, production was estimated to be 9.147 million barrels per day. Oil production was estimated at 2.0 billion barrels in 2010. The top six crude oil-producing states are Texas (over 20 per cent), Alaska, California, Louisiana, Oklahoma, and New Mexico. Production on Federal offshore-leases in the Gulf of Mexico averages around 1.3 million barrels per day, about 25 per cent of total U.S. production.

Production from deepwater wells in the Gulf of Mexico has been increasing rapidly, and now accounts for around two-thirds of total U.S. Gulf output. Large fields include the Hoover-Diana development, the Atlantis project, and the Thunder Horse (previously "Crazy Horse") field - the largest single field ever discovered in the Gulf of Mexico, which came online in January 2005, with an anticipated peak oil output of 250,000 barrels per day. In 2010, a gas leak and subsequent explosion occured on the Deepwater Horizon oil rig working on the Macondo exploration well. An estimated 4.9 barrels of crude oil were released, causing an environmental catastrophe.

Over 2009, consumption fell to an estimated 18.7 million barrels per day, making the USA the largest consumer in the world. Some 58 per cent of US oil demand is met through imports. Almost half of oil imports come from the American continent and the Caribbean; over 2007, Canada supplied over 18 per cent, Mexico supplied over 11 per cent, and Venezuelan imports amounted to just over ten per cent. Saudi Arabia supplied 11 per cent and Nigeria, 8.4 per cent. America is ranked first in the world for refinery capacity (17.67 million bbl/d per day) in 2009.

In January 2009, newly-elected President Obama called for the US to become energy independent, saying its reliance on foreign oil and global warming posed threats. He called for greater fuel efficiency and an "energy economy" aimed at creating millions of jobs. He also ordered a review of whether states can set car emission standards. The Environmental Protection Agency (EPA) must now review its refusal of a waiver which had previously allowed California to set its own - stricter - vehicle emission and fuel efficiency standards. President Obama's statement that the US would lead on climate change was a clear move away from his predecessor's sceptical view of global warming.

Shale
With the advent of shale exploitation, it is predicted that the US will become the world's top oil producer by 2015-20. New extraction techniques such as hydraulic fracking and horizontal drilling mean that huge hydrocarbon reources are now recoverable. Reserves of shale gas were estimated at 36,805 billion cubic feet and production at 2,226 billion cubic feet in 2010.

Natural Gas
At the beginning of January 2009 the US had estimated proven reserves of wet natural gas reserves of 273 trillion cubic feet, around 3 per cent of world gas reserves, ranking it fifth in the world. In 2010, reserves were estimated to be 317.6 Tcf; the increase is driven by shale gas. Reserves of dry natural gas were estimated at 304.6Tcf in 2010. The US natural gas industry operated 452,768 gas and gas condensate wells in 2007. Dry natural gas production in 2009 was 20.580 billion cubic feet rising to 21,577 billion cu ft in 2010. The largest natural gas states are Texas, Louisian, Oklahoma, Colorado and Pennnsylvania.

Consumption of natural gas reached a peak in 2000 at 23.3 trillion cubic feet, before levelling out, and beginning to decline. In 2009, although consumption fell to 22,816 billion cu ft, it was still ranked first in the world for consumption. Consumption was an estimated 24,088 billion cu ft in 2010. Natural gas is currently used as follows: industrial 6.6 trillion cubic feet (tcf); electric power 6.6 tcf; residential 4.8 tcf and commercial 3.1 trillion cubic feet.

Net natural gas imports reached an estimated 4.6 trillion cubic feet in 2007, most (3.78 trillion cubic feet) originating from Canada. Over the period 1990-2004, natural gas consumption increased by around 16 per cent; consumption and imports are expected to increase substantially in coming decades, largely due to additional natural-gas-fired electric power plants. Imports were an estimated 2,604 billion cu ft in 2010.

Oil and gas exploration is banned on Montana's Rocky Mountain Front, the Continental Shelf along coastal California, in the Gulf of Mexico off Florida and offshore North Carolina. The major US oil companies are Exxon Mobil, Texaco, Shell, Atlantic Richfield (ARCO), and ConocoPhillips. (Source: US Energy Information Administration)

American Gas Association, URL: http://www.aga.org
National Petroleum Council, URL: http://www.npc.org
National Mining Association, URL: http://www.nma.org

Energy
The US is the world's second largest energy producer. In 2010, power generation reached an estimated 75 quadrillion Btu. Total energy consumption was 98 quadrillion btu in 2010, of which total petroleum products 19,180 thousand bbl/d, natural gas 24,385 billion cu ft and 1,003,066 thousand short tons of coal. Per capita energy consumption was 317 million Btu. Installed capacity was 1,039 million kW in 2010. (Source: EIA)

Electricity Net Generation by source, selected years, billion kWh

Source	1990	2000	2010	2011 (p)
Fossil Fuels				
- Coal	1,594.0	1,966.3	1,847.3	1,734.3
- Petroleum	126.5	111.2	37.1	28.2
- Natural Gas	372.8	601.0	987.7	1016.0
- Other Gas	10.4	14.0	11.3	11.3
Nuclear Electric	576.9	753.9	807.0	790.2
Hydroelectric pumped storage	-3.5	-5.5	-5.5	-5.9
Renewable Energy				
-Conventional hydroelectric power	292.9	275.6	260.2	325.1
-Biomass	45.8	60.7	56.1	56.7
-Geo-thermal	15.4	14.1	15.2	16.7
-Solar/PV	0.4	0.5	1.2	1.8
-Wind	2.8	5.6	94.7	118.7
Other	3.6	4.0	12.9	11.1
Total	**3,037.8**	**3,802.1**	**4,125.1**	**4,105.7**

Source: Energy Information Administration

Nuclear
The United States has the most nuclear capacity of any nation. Net nuclear electric power generation has grown from 576.86 billion kilowatthours (kWh) in 1990 to 806.42 billion kWh in 2007. Nuclear power accounts for over 19 per cent of total generated power in the US. In 2007, there were 104 nuclear generating units; of these, 69 are categorized a pressurized water reactors (PWRs) and 35 units are boiling water reactors (BWR). Cost and safety issues as well as environmental dangers have meant that no new reactor has come on line since May 1996 and there are no plans to build any new reactors. The current Administration has been supportive of nuclear expansion, emphasizing its importance in maintaining a diverse energy supply. About 40 per cent of nuclear output is supplied by five states: Illinois, Pennsylvania, South Carolina, North Carolina, and New York. As an independent agency, the Nuclear Regulatory Commission (NRC) is responsible for monitoring public safety and regulates use of nuclear energy and nuclear materials. In 2011, production was estimated at 8.259 quadrillion Btu. Consumption was estimated also at 8.250 quadrillion Btu. (Source: EIA)

Renewables
During 2007, renewable energy sources provided 351.3 billion kWh of electricity (down from 357.5 billion kWh in 2005). Hydropower is currently the leading renewable energy source used by electric utilities to generate electric power. Other sources are biofuels, solar, wind and geothermal energy. Over 60 per cent of hydroelectricity is supplied by four states: Washington, California, Oregon and New York. In 2011, renewable energy production was estimated at 9.236 quadrillion Btu and consumption at 9.135 quadrillion Btu. (Source: US Energy Information Administration)

American Public Power Association, URL: http://www.publicpower.org/
Nuclear Regulatory Commission (NRC), URL: http://www.nrc.gov
Electric Power Research Institute (EPRI), URL: http://www.epri.com

Water
American Water Works Association, URL: http://www.awwa.org
Association of Metropolitan Water Agencies, URL: http://www.amwa.net

Manufacturing
Manufacturing was the second largest contributor to GDP in 2012, after services (excl. government). Figures show that manufacturing GDP reached US$1,866.7 billion in 2012, up from US$1,731.5 billion in 2011. In 2011, the largest subsector in terms of GDP was chemical products (US$253.5 billion) followed by computer and electronic product manufacturing ($227.0 billion) and the food, beverage and tobacco sector (US$215.0 billion).

Overall, Value Added (VA) in manufacturing fell by 2.7 per cent over 2008; durable goods manufacturing declined by 1.3 per cent whilst non-durable goods manufacturing fell by 4.7 per cent. The construction sector declined for the 4th consecutive year; having fallen by 4.1 per cent in 2006 and by 11.2 per cent in 2007, it fell by 5.6 per cent in 2008. This was largely due to the slump in the housing market and the financial crisis caused by subprime lending. (Source: BEA, Industry Economic Accounts)

Approximate figures for manufacturing establishments in the four regions of the country are: northeast - 83,000; midwest - 73,000; south - 113,000; west - 86,000.

The petrochemical industry consists of plastic materials, synthetic resins, and non-vulcanisable elastomers; plastic materials and synthetic resins, synthetic rubber, cellulosic and other man-made fibres; man-made organic fibres; surface active agents, finishing agents, sulfonated oils; cyclic organic crudes and intermediates, and organic dyes and pigments; industrial organic chemicals; nitrogenous fertilisers and carbon black. Inorganic chemicals are predominantly basic chemicals (also called heavy, bulk, or commodity chemicals) such as chloralkalis, industrial gases, acids, salts, inorganic compounds, and rare earth metal salts. The major US consumers of inorganic chemicals are the automotive, housing, paper, packaging, pharmaceutical, paint and inks, and fertiliser industries. Plastics make up the largest category of materials used in the US, as they continue to displace metal, glass, paper, wood, and other materials. Packaging industries continue to be the largest consumers of plastic materials, followed by transportation, electronic, construction, medical equipment, and sporting goods industries. Processing petrochemical feedstocks and intermediate chemicals are used to produces plastic resin. Ethylene is the major feedstock utilised, followed by benzene and propylene.

The chemical industry is one of the largest US industries, producing more than 50,000 different chemicals and formulations in more than 12,000 US chemical plants. Chemicals and allied products is currently the highest manufacturing sector to contribute to the Gross Domestic Product. There are over one million people directly employed in US chemical production, and chemicals from the United States are sold in more than 180 countries. The industry has consistently had a positive trade balance and currently there are at least 20,000 different chemicals involved in two-way trade. The chemical industries sector covers inorganic and organic chemicals (including industrial gases and pigments), plastic resins and synthetic rubber, drugs and pharmaceuticals, soaps and other detergents, cosmetics, paints and coatings, agricultural chemicals (including fertilisers and pesticides), adhesives and sealants, explosives, printing inks, and a variety of miscellaneous chemicals (including essential oils, salt, distilled water, etc).

The textiles industry employs four per cent of all manufacturing workers and five per cent of all production workers in the US and is a major employer of women and minorities. Textile mills are located in every state with the greatest concentration in the Carolinas and Georgia, which combined account for 60 per cent of the industry's employment.

A combination of fierce Asian competition, an evaporation of bank financing for car buyers and a collapse in consumer confidence caused a slump in the car manufacturing sector between 2006 and 2008. Detroit's "big three" - GM, Ford and Chrysler - were badly hit. An estimated 400,000 jobs were lost among motor manufacturers, dealers and suppliers. In 2008, the US carmaker General Motors sold fewer vehicles than Japan's Toyota, ending its 77-year reign as the world's top-selling car firm. GM's North American sales fell by 11 per cent, and its European sales fell by seven per cent. In December 2008, the White House agreed a $17.4 billion bail-out package for GM and rival Chrysler, and in March 2009 President Obama announced tax incentives for Americans to buy new cars. However, he delayed a decision on $21 billion in extra bailout money, demanding far more radical reform proposals from the carmakers. At the end of April 2009, Chrysler filed for Chapter 11 bankruptcy protection (which allowed them to rearrange their finances while still trading), and formed an alliance with Fiat. The partnership with Fiat created the world's sixth largest carmaker.

Service Industries
The non-government services sector is the largest contributor to the US GDP; growth over 2008 was led by professional, scientific, and technical services, information, and health care and social assistance. Over the year, private services-producing industries achieved 1.6 per cent growth. The largest GDP sectors in 2012 were real estate, rental and leasing ($1,926.3 billion), finance and insurance ($ 1,242.3 billion), and professional and business services ($1,954.2 billion). Health care and social assistance contributed US$1,164 billion. Government services accounted for US$2,026.2 billion.

The number of people employed in the services industry is shown on the following table:

Services Industry Employment, annual average ('000s)

Sector	2006	2007
Trade, transport and utilities	26,276	26,608
Information	3,038	3,029
Finance and Insurance	8,328	8,308
Professional and business	17,566	17,962
Education and Health	17,826	18,327
Leisure and hospitality	13,110	13,474
Other non-govt. services	5,438	5,491
Government services	21,974	22,203
Total	**113,556**	**115,402**

Source: US Bureau of Economic Analysis

Tourism
Tourism is one of the US's largest employers, employing some 7.7 million people in 2011. Real spending on travel and tourism increased by 3.0 per cent in 2010 and by 3.5 per cent in 2011. Traveller accommodations fell 8.8 per cent in 2009. Employment in tourism was 5.33 million in 2010 (down from 5.876 million in 2005). Inbound tourism increased 11.4 per cent in 2010 and outbound tourism increased 2.7 per cent. Total travel expenditure in the

UNITED STATES OF AMERICA

US amounted to US$704.4 billion in 2009, and was forecast to be US$817 billion in 2011 and US$851 billion in 2012. There were 55 million international visitors to the US in 2009; this was forecast to rise to 64.9 million in 2012. (Source: BEA)

Agriculture
The US agricultural sector's (farms) contribution to GDP amounted to US$138.7 billion in 2011, up from US$124.8 billion in 2010. Around 1,438,000 people were employed in the agriculture sector in 2007; the number of workers have been falling since 2003, when 1,578,000 were employed in agriculture.

According to the US Department of Agriculture, the number of farms in the US was estimated at 2.2 million in 2011, down from 2,088,790 in 2006. US farmland was around 917 million acres in 2011, down by 1.85 million acres from 2010. The average size of a farm was an estimated 420 acres. The 2007 gross income from cattle and calves, hogs and pigs, and sheep and lambs for the U.S. totalled $65.5 billion, up two per cent from 2006. Cattle and calves accounted for 76 per cent of this total. Cash receipts from marketings of milk during 2007 totalled $35.4 billion, 51.4 per cent higher than 2006.

The state of California generates the most revenue from agriculture (over $25 billion), followed by Texas, Iowa, Nebraska and Illinois. The country is divided into various zones, or belts, according to the best conditions to grow certain crops such as cotton, wheat and fruit.

Corn is the leading US crop, both in volume and value. In recent years about one-fifth of all harvested US cropland has been in corn. Production takes place largely in the Lake States and the Northern Plains, with 17 states accounting for more than 90 per cent of output. In 2008, around 85,982,000 acres were dedicated to corn fields and they produced 12.1 billion bushels, with a value of US$47.3 billion.

Soybeans and other oilseeds comprise one of the fastest growing agricultural sectors in both the US and the rest of the world. The United States accounts for about one-half of world soybean production and for about two-thirds of world trade in soybeans.

The US's third leading field crop in terms of production value is wheat. Production was 2.49 billion bushels in 2008. State-by-state production is more widely dispersed than for other major field crops, but production by class or type of wheat is concentrated in different regions.

US cotton, the fourth largest crop, accounts for about 70 per cent of world cotton production. As a significant earner of foreign exchange, about 25 per cent of global cotton output generally moves in export channels with the United States, the countries of the former Soviet Union, Australia and Pakistan accounting for about 60 per cent of world trade. Much of this cotton is exported to countries in the Far East where it is processed into textile goods and shipped primarily to markets in the United States and Europe. Production was an estimated 16.3 million bales in 2011/12. Seed cotton, which contains cottonseed and lint (fibre), ranks fifth among major field crops in value of farm production. Cotton lint production accounts for about 90 per cent of the income derived from seed cotton; by-products include cottonseed and linters. Seeds are crushed for oil and the remaining meal is fed to livestock. Linters, the short fuzz on the seed, are used in padding materials and as a source of cellulose for making rayon, plastics, and other products. Major markets for cotton lint include domestic and foreign textile mills.

Sorghum, barley and rice are all major US crops. Sorghum is grown mainly on the central and southern plains, in Texas, Kansas, Nebraska, and Missouri, and almost all of it is used for animal feed. Barley is grown on the northern plains and in Pacific regions; its primary use is livestock feed, especially for dairy cattle and wintering beef cattle. Rice is grown in the five southern states of Arkansas, Louisiana, Mississippi, Missouri, and Virginia. A total of 255.3 million cwt was produced in 2010-11.

About 80 per cent of the sugar consumed in the United States is produced domestically (42 per cent from sugarbeets, 38 per cent from sugarcane). Sugarcane is grown in Florida, Hawaii, Louisiana, and Texas. Tobacco is a major US crop, produced in about 21 states. The number of tobacco farms fell from 197,764 in 1974 to 56,977 in 2002. North Carolina and Kentucky have nearly two-thirds of the US tobacco acreage. Production rose from 787,653,000 lbs in 2007 to 800,527,000 lbs in 2008.

The three largest US vegetable crops in terms of production are lettuce, onions and carrots, which together constitute 40 per cent of total production. The three most valuable crops, accounting for 36 per cent of total value, are potatoes, tomatoes, and lettuce. The US is among the world's top producers of fruits and tree nuts, which together produce 13 per cent of US farm cash receipts for all agricultural products in 2002. Highest fruit production is for grapes, oranges, apples and bananas, and for tree nuts, production is highest for almonds, pecans and walnuts.

Livestock
Dairy products account for about 11 per cent of total cash receipts from all farm commodities. Whilst it is produced and processed in every state, approximately half of the total US milk production comes from Wisconsin, California, New York, Minnesota, and Pennsylvania. Large dairy farms with 1,000-2,000 cows are common in Florida and the west (primarily California, Arizona, and New Mexico), but dairy operations of this size are rare elsewhere. The US cattle herd peaked around the end of the 1970s when there were over 130 million cattle. Texas farms the most cattle (14 million), followed by Nebraska (6.7 million), Kansas, Oklahoma and California. The United States has the largest fed-cattle industry in the world, and is the world's largest producer of beef. Calves and cattle totalled 90.8 million head in 2012. The sheep and wool industry has declined dramatically in recent years. As of 2012, there were estimated to be 5.345 million head and only 80,000 sheep operations. As of 2012, there were an estimated 64.9 million head of hogs and pigs.

The US is the world's largest poultry producer and the second-largest egg producer and exporter of poultry meat. US poultry meat production totals over 43 billion pounds annually, mainly turkey meat & the total farm value of the poultry production exceeds $20 billion. The top five turkey-producing States are Minnesota, North Carolina, Missouri, Arkansas, and Virginia. Over 90 billion eggs annually are produced per annum.

Forestry
Of the total 2.3 billion acres of land in the United States, 731 million acres, or one-third, is forested. About 28 per cent of all commercial forestland is in federal, state or municipal ownership. About 14 per cent is owned by the forest industry, and 58 per cent by private landowners. The Government currently has a forest plan to provide a stable timber economy as well as protecting the environment. As a result of this programme, 870 million board feet of timber has been harvested.

The Forest Service of the US Department of Agriculture protects and manages 191 million acres of forest and rangeland in the National Forest System. The Government has allocated six types of federal land, to maintain forest growth: riparian reserves (2.2 million acres mainly by wetlands); adaptive management areas (1.5 million acres, where new forest management techniques are tried out); matrix lands (4.9 million acres outside of reserves, available for timber harvest); congressionally withdrawn areas (7 million acres of National Parks where timber harvest is prohibited); late-succession reserves (7.1 million acres where late successional cutting is prohibited); and administratively withdrawn areas (1.7 million acres divided into areas for research and for recreation). Unemployment in the timber industry is high. In 2011, the forestry, fishing and related activities sector contributed $34.9 billion to the US economy. (Source: BEA)

Fishing
The fishing industry is in decline; Just 9 per cent of seafood eaten in the US is caught domestically. Further restrictions to catch allowances came into force in 2013. Alaska pollock was the most important fish in quantity and value in 2010 (1,960 million pounds). Other important fish in the US are menhaden (1,470 million pounds), salmon (790 million pounds), cod, flounder, crab, shrimp, lobster and tuna. Major species such as pacific hake, menhaden, pollock, pink and red salmon are decreasing. In 2010, 80 per cent of commercial catch was finfish but shellfish represented more than 50 per cent of revenue. Crab was the highest revenue earner (approx. US$575 million), followed by salmon (US$555 million) and scallops (US$455 million). The aquaculture industry is fairly limited. Production of farm raised fish and shellfish in 2009 was approximately 725 million pounds with a revenue of US$1.2 billion. In 2009, imports of edible fish products amounted to US$14.8 billion.

In 2011, the forestry, fishing and related activities sector contributed $34.9 billion to the US economy. (Source: BEA)

COMMUNICATIONS AND TRANSPORT

Travel Requirements
Citizens of Australia, Canada and the EU require a passport normally valid for six months from the date on which the holder enters the USA. For nationals included in the Visa Waiver Program (under which nationals must travel on a valid passport, for holiday, transit or business purposes only and for a stay not exceeding 90 days), passports must be valid for at least 90 days from date of entry. Travellers who do not have a machine-readable passports will require a valid USA entry visa, and holders of passports issued between October 2005 and October 2006 should check with the Embassy that their passport are valid for visa free travel under the Visa Waiver Program.

A visa is not required by nationals of Australia, Canada, Brunei, New Zealand, South Korea, Taiwan and most Europeans, for stays of up to 90 days; the exceptions are nationals of Bulgaria, Cyprus, Poland & Romania, who do require a visa. A visa is also required by Immigrants of Canada and British residents of Bermuda. Transit passengers require a transit visa.

For more information, and to apply online please visit the following website at https://esta.cbp.dhs.gov. Subjects of all countries are advised to contact the embassy to check visa requirements.

National Airlines
The largest American airlines offering international services are:
American Airlines, URL: http://www.aa.com
Services are international, regional and domestic scheduled passenger. Combined fleet of approximately 900.
United Airlines, URL: http://www.united.com/
Services are international, regional and domestic scheduled passenger. United Airlines employs approximately 55,000 and has a fleet of around 620.
Delta Airlines, URL: http://www.delta.com
Delta Airlines and Northwest Airlines merged in early 2009, becoming the world's largest carrier now known as Delta. Services are international, regional and domestic scheduled passenger and cargo. More than 350 destinations in nearly 70 countries, and more than 160 million customers served annually.
US Airways, URL: http://www.usairways.com
Services are international, regional and domestic scheduled and charter passenger and cargo. Part-owned by British Airways.

International Airports
The busiest internal route in the USA is New York to and from Chicago (around 3 million passengers per year). The top three US international airports for passenger traffic are Atlanta (top worldwide), Chicago (second worldwide), and Los Angeles (fifth worldwide).

Amarillo International Airport, URL: http://airport.amarillo.gov/
Atlantic City International Airport, URL: http://www.sjta.com/acairport/, 1.4 million passengers per annum

Dallas/Fort Worth International Airport (DFW), URL: http://www.dfwairport.com/, 60 million passengers per annum

Denver International Airport, URL: http://www.flydenver.com/, 53 million passengers per annum

Detroit Metropolitan Airport, URL: http://www.metroairport.com/, 30 million passengers per annum

El Paso International Airport, URL: http://www.elpasointernationalairport.com/, 3 million passengers per annum

Fort Worth Meacham International Airport, URL: http://www.meacham.com/, 11 million passengers per annum

George Bush Intercontinental Airport/Houston, URL: http://www.fly2houston.com/, 40 million passengers per annum

Hartsfield Atlanta International Airport, URL: http://www.atlanta-airport.com/, 92 million passengers per annum

Los Angeles International Airport, URL: http://www.lawa.org/welcomelax.aspx, 61 million passengers per annum

Lubbock Preston Smith International Airport, URL: http://www.flylia.com/, 500,000 passengers per annum

McCarran International Airport, URL: http://www.mccarran.com/, 40 million passengers per annum

Newark International Airport (EWR), URL: http://www.panynj.gov/airports/newark-liberty.html, 34 million passengers per annum

O'Hare International Airport, URL: http://www.flychicago.com/ohare/en/home/, 66.8 million passengers per annum

Philadelphia International Airport (PHL), URL: http://www.phl.org/, 31 million passengers per annum

San Francisco International Airport, URL: http://www.flysfo.com/web/page/index.jsp, 45 million passengers per annum

Sea-Tac International Airport, URL: http://www.portseattle.org/seatac/, 32.8 million passengers per annum

Sky Harbor International Airport, URL: http://phoenix.gov/AVIATION/, 40 million passengers per annum

Spokane International Airport, URL: http://www.spokaneairports.net/, 3.1 million passengers per annum

America's regulatory body for civil aviation is the Federal Aviation Administration (FAA). The National Transport Safety Board monitors and holds enquiries into air accidents.

Federal Aviation Administration (FAA), URL: http://www.faa.gov
Air Transport Association of America, URL: http://www.airlines.org/

Railways

Railways connect all the main towns or cities as well as providing, by connecting roads, several transcontinental routes. They are all of standard gauge except for 46 miles of narrow gauge in the west. Railways in the United States are, with a few exceptions, owned and managed by private companies, but the rates and fares charged are regulated by the Interstate Commerce Commission (ICC), a federal agency.

There are 7 Class 1 railroads (defined on the basis of operating revenue in excess of £346.8 million): BNSF Railway, CSX Transportation, Grand Trunk Corporation, Kansas City Southern Railway, Norfolk Southern Combined Railroad Subsidiaries, Soo Line Railroad, and Union Pacific Railroad. Together they account for approximately 90 per cent of the carloads handled by the railroad industry. The freight railroad industry encompasses more than 500 smaller carriers (independent of Class 1 railroads), including local, regional, and switching and terminal railroads. Intercity rail passenger service is provided by Amtrak, a quasi-government corporation that handles approximately 22 million passenger trips per year across 43 states.

The rail industry employed approximately 167,5000 people in 2006. There are over 94,900 miles of railroad, and 162,000 miles of railtrack in operation. Freight revenue in 2006 reached US$50.3 billion and net income stood at $6.5 billion.

Many cities have subways systems, elevated track systems (els) or light transit systems to move passengers effectively. Cities with such systems are Atlanta; Baltimore; Boston; Buffalo; Charlotte; Chicago; Cleveland; Dallas; Denver; Detroit; Houston; Jacksonville; Las Vegas; Los Angeles; Miami; Minneapolis/St. Paul; New York City; Newark; Philadelphia; Pittsburgh; Portland; Sacramento; St. Louis; Salt Lake City; San Diego; San Francisco; San José; San Juan; Washington.

Federal Railroad Administration, URL: http://www.fra.dot.gov
AMTRAK (National Railroad Passenger Corporation), URL: http://www.amtrak.com
Association of American Railroads, URL: http://www.aar.org/

Roads

The most widely used means of personal transport in the United States is the privately owned automobile. The individual states build and repair main roads within their borders, and also receive funds for construction for designated federal-aid highway systems from the Federal Government. Design standards are announced by the American Association of State Highway and Transportation Officials and approved by the Federal Highway Administration for use on federal-aid highway projects. State and federal gasoline taxes, state vehicle registration fees, and general taxes provide the money for building and maintaining highways. Federal law provides that Federal funds be matched in varying proportions with state funds for the costs of planning, engineering, right-of-way acquisition, and construction of highways. Other costs, such as maintenance and policing, are borne entirely by the states and local agencies.

Figures for 2010 show that there were over 4 million miles of highways in the USA. Approximately 47,000 miles of this are interstate highways. Texas has the largest amount of roads in any state (294,491 miles). Thirty states, including Puerto Rico, have toll facilities. Most interstates have no tolls but approximately 2,900 miles of Interstates are tolled in 21 states. At the end of 2011, there were some 246 million registered vehicles, and 210 million

licensed drivers. Over 3 trillion vehicle miles were travelled in 2009. In 2010, 16.1 billion tons of freight worth US$14.9 trillion were transported. (Source: http://www.fhwa.dot.gov/policy/)

The regulating authority is the Federal Highway Administration.
Federal Highway Administration, URL: http://www.fhwa.dot.gov

Ports and Harbours

The following table shows 2009 tonnage for the top ten US ports by tonnage traded.

Port	State/s	Total tonnage (millions)
South Louisiana	LA	212.7
Houston	TX	211.3
New York/New Jersey	NY, NJ	144.7
Long Beach	CA	72.6
Corpus Christi	TX	68.2
New Orleans	LA	68.1
Beaumont	TX	67.7
Huntingdon	Tristate	59.2
Los Angeles	CA	58.4
Hampton Roads	VA	59.4

Source: U.S. Army Corps of Engineers

Ocean Shipping

Federal Maritime Commission (FMC), URL: http://www.fmc.gov
Maritime Administration, URL: http://www.marad.dot.gov/

Associations

American Association of Port Authorities, URL: http://www.aapa-ports.org/
American Maritime Congress, URL: http://www.americanmaritime.org/
Chamber of Shipping of America, URL: http://www.knowships.org/

HEALTH

Personal health care is paid for privately in the United States, with five out of six employees covered by group health insurance policies, often contributed to by the employer. In 2011, an estimated 78.7 per cent of Americans had some health-care coverage, according to National Center for Health Statistics (NCHS). Health insurance coverage is lowest amongst the Hispanic population. Overall, in 2011, approximately 21 per cent (48.2 million) of persons aged <=65 years in the United States had no health insurance coverage at the time of interview. Approximately 61 per cent of the population aged less than 65 years had private insurance. Over 40 per cent of people over two years of age are covered by private dental insurance.

There is a wide variety of health plans available. One way of funding personal health care is a Health Maintenance Organization (HMO), which is a group of physicians who provide medical care for a lump sum paid in advance. There are nearly 700 HMOs, and approximately 30 million people belonging to them. Medical costs in the USA are high due to physicians' fees and hospital costs, the latter of which the Government has tried to limit. Physicians charge a patient a fee per visit, and usually work contractually or at least one hospital. Once a patient is admitted to hospital, fees are charged per day; costs are incurred by facilities and machines used.

There are two social health care programmes in the United States, Medicare and Medicaid. The first is for citizens over the age of 65, and disabled people, and subsidizes medical costs. Medicaid funds basic medical services for those with very low incomes - those receiving cash welfare are entitled to Medicaid. Currently around 45.2 million people are covered by Medicare, but this figure could increase by 30 per cent over the next 20 years, and the average cost of health care may increase by up to 50 per cent. In May 2009, new estimates indicated that the Medicare trust fund will run out of money by 2017, and is already running at a deficit. In July 2009, President Obama presented a reform bill to extend healthcare insurance to the 46 million people in the US who are currently uninsured. The US Congress was strongly divided over the healthcare bill, but it was eventually passed in March 2010, with amendments. Healthcare coverage will now be expanded to cover 32 million of the currently uninsured, and insurers can no longer deny coverage to those with pre-existing conditions.

According to latest figures from the CDC, the US spends about $2.5 trillion per year (2009) on its healthcare system - which includes private, federal or employer schemes. This represents around 17.6 per cent of the country's GDP - nearly double the OECD average. Per capita health expenditure amounted to US$8,086 in 2009. The breakdown of expendiutre amounts to: hospital care: 30.5 per cent; nursing home care: 5.5 per cent; physician and clinical services: 20.3 per cent; prescription drugs 10.1 per cent; An estimated 47 per cent of health care expenditure is from public funds.

Hospitals are funded by a state or sometimes national government agency, a profit organisation, or by a non-profit organisation such as a religious group. According to the latest WHO figures, the Government accounts for 47.7 per cent of total health expenditure, whilst the private sector makes up the remaining 54.9 per cent. Social security expenditure accounts for 86.4 per cent of government health expenditure. In the private sector, around 62.7 per cent of expenses are paid through pre-paid plans, and 23.4 per cent are paid out-of-pocket.

According to WHO estimates, in 2000-10, there were 793,649 doctors (27 doctors per 10,000 inhabitants), 2,927,000 nurses and midwives (98 per 10,000 population), 463,663 dentists (16 per 10,000 population) and 249,642 pharmaceutical personnel (9 per 10,000 population). In the same period there were 31 hospital beds per 10,000 population. In 2004, there were 2.7 community hospital beds per 1,000 (down on previous years), and 15,995 nursing homes, with 1.7 million beds (also down on previous years).

UNITED STATES OF AMERICA

Population ageing is a growing concern. In 2008, 38.9 million people were over sixty-five years old, and it is estimated that this number will increase to 89 million within thirty years. The Health and Human Services Department has a budget of $252.4 billion dollars specifically for programmes and services for older Americans. In 2009, 24 per cent of those aged 65 or more were considered to be in fair or poor health. Approximately 6.4 per cent of these people needed help or care from others.

In the year 2011, around 1 million people were living with HIV/AIDs in the USA, and approximately 200,000 died of the disease. Approximately 21 per cent are believed to be unaware of their condition. It is estimated that 56,3000 Americans become infected with HIV each year and more than 18,000 die of HIV/AIDs each year.

Obesity, a matter for growing concern, affected 35.9 per cent of adult Americans (aged 20+) in 2009-10. It has increased dramatically in the period 1990-2010. Those qualifying had a body mass index of over 30.0 kg/m2. According to the National Centre for Health Statistics, a further 33.3 per cent of Americans were considered overweight. In 2009-10, 18.4 per cent of adolescents aged 12-19, 18.0 per cent of children aged 6-11 years and 12.1 per cent of those aged 2-5 years were considered overweight. The same source estimates that 31 per cent of adult Americans exercised regularly in 2007. From 1987 to 2001, diseases associated with obesity accounted for 27 per cent of the increases in US medical costs. Medical costs associated with obesity were estimated at $147 billion in 2006. No state had met the national target of less than 15 per cent of the population. In 2010, 12 states had an obesity prevalence of 30 per cent or more. In 2000, all state levels were lower than 30 per cent. By state, obesity prevalence ranged from 21 per cent in Colorado to 34.0 per cent in Mississippi.

In June 2009, President Obama signed into law America's strongest anti-smoking measure ever, and the US Food and Drug Administration can now regulate the content and marketing of tobacco products. 22.3 per cent of men and 17.4 per cent of women were regular smokers in 2007 (down on previous years), and approximately 440,000 Americans die each year of smoking-related illnesses.

Medicare, URL: http://www.medicare.gov/
Medicaid, URL: http://medicaid.gov/

EDUCATION

Schooling is compulsory throughout the United States, and is governed locally by state, curriculum, funding, teaching, and educational policies are set by locally elected school boards. In the autumn of 2011, there were some 3.7 million elementary and secondary school full-time teaching staff in the public sector. In the private sector, there were 6 million pupils and 500,000 teachers. The school-age population is expected to continue to rise. The number of public school teachers has risen faster than the number of students over the decade, resulting in an estimated average pupil/teacher ratio of 15.2:1 in 2011, (down from 16.0:1 in 1990). The average salary for public school full time teachers in 2010 was $56,069 (Current dollars).

Enrollment in elementary and secondary schools ('000s)

	Total	Pre-kindergarten - grade 8	Grades 9-12
Public			
2008	49,266	34,286	14,980
2009	49,373	34,418	14,955
2010*	49,306	34,637	14,668
2015*	50,659	35,829	14,830
2020*	52,666	37,444	15,222
Private			
2008	5,707	4,365	1,342
2009	5,488	4,179	1,309
2010*	5,398	4,092	1,306
2015*	5,176	4,042	1,134
2020*	5,273	4,216	1,056

Source: National Center for Education Statistics
* Projected

Pre-school Education
Education before the age of six is not compulsory. However, over the period 1985-2005, enrollment in pre-kindergarten increased by 585 per cent, and by 2007, two-thirds of 3-5-year-olds were enrolled in preprimary education (nursery school and kindergarten). In 2011, an estimated 1.1 million children were estimated to attend public prekindergarten and 3.8 million were enroled in kindergarten

Primary/Secondary Education
Elementary school (primary) generally starts at the age of six and runs through grades 1-8. Grades nine to 12 are spent in High Schools, covering the ages 14-17.

Enrolment in America's Elementary schools reached 32.16 million in 2007, and 17.08 million students were enrolled in High School. Hispanic students now make up 1 in 5 public school students, but these students as well as other minority students are disproportionately clustered in high-poverty schools.

An increasing number of children are home-schooled, 1.5 million children in 2007 - up 74 per cent from 1999 figures.

Total expenditure on elementary and secondary education for the year 2008-09 was estimated at $661 billion (4.6 per cent of GDP).

Higher Education
In the Fall of 2007, there were 4,339 post-secondary degree-granting institutions in the USA. Undergraduate enrolment for the year totalled some 15,603,800 students, 8,876,200 of whom were women. 64.4 per cent of the 2007 student population were white/non-Hispanic, whilst 13.4 per cent were black, 12.3 per cent were Hispanic and 6.7 per cent were Asian/Pacific Islander. 2.1 per cent were non-resident aliens. Graduate enrolment totalled 2,293,600, of whom 1,383,300 were women, and 12.2 per cent were non-resident alien. In 2010, college enrolment was estimated to be 20.6 million, higher than any previous year, and was expected to continue to rise in the period 2010-19.

In 2011-12, it was estimated that 1.7 million Bachelor degrees were conferred, together with 696,000 Masters and 74,700 doctorates. Between 2000-10, it was estimated that around 32 per cent of Americans over the age of 25 had completed a Bachelor's Degree: the state with the highest percentage of BAs was the District of Columbia (44 per cent), followed by Massachusetts (36 per cent) and Colorado (35 per cent). The lowest ranking state was West Virginia, at 17 per cent.

The most popular fields of study in 2007 were business related studies, social sciences and education. There has been a noticeable decline in engineering and mathematics over the decade.

Expenditure on postsecondary degree-granting institutions reached some $432 billion in 2008-09 academic year, equivalent to 3 per cent of the US GDP.

RELIGION

The separation of church and state is a primary American principle, and there is no established state Church in the USA. The legal structure makes no provision for automatic membership in any religious group, and the Constitution further provides that 'no religious test shall ever be required as a qualification to any office or trust under the United States'. The same restriction is imposed upon the legislatures of the 50 states. Support of religious institutions is voluntary, and the government gives no funds to churches.

In a poll of 228,182,000 American adults taken in 2008, 173,402,000 professed to be Christian (57,199,000 Catholic), 2,680,000 said they were Jewish), 1,349,000 said they were Muslim and 1,189,000 professed to be Buddhist. There were 582,000 Hindus, 186,000 Native Americans 49,000 Baha'ists, 56,000 Taoists and 25,000 Scientologists amongst the many other religious groups.

In April 2008, Pope Benedict XVI became the first pope to visit the White House in 30 years. He also visited Ground Zero in New York and addressed the UN.

National Council of the Churches of Christ in the USA, URL: http://www.ncccusa.org
The Episcopal Church in the USA, URL: http://www.episcopalchurch.org
National Conference of Catholic Bishops, URL: http://www.usccb.org/
Buddhist Churches of America, URL: http://buddhistchurchesofamerica.org/home/
Islamic Cultural Center of New York, URL: http://www.islamicculturalcenter-ny.org/
American Jewish Congress, URL: http://www.ajcongress.org/

COMMUNICATIONS AND MEDIA

The USA has a highly-developed mass media. Television is the main medium and Fox news is the dominant US cable news network. Freedom of expression is guaranteed by the constitution and some broadcast stations give airtime to extreme views.

Newspapers
The US newspaper industry is currently experiencing one of the worst financial crisises in its history; advertising revenues have plummeted partly in response to the economic downturn and also in the change of readership patterns with consumers turning to the internet. Between 2008 and 2010 eight major newspaper chains went bankrupt and several newspapers ceased publication. Some newspapers have become web only. Congress has debated the issue. As of 2012, there were an estimated 1,500 daily newspapers in the US.

Daily newspapers with the largest circulations are:
Wall Street Journal, URL: http://public.wsj.com/home.html
USA Today, URL: http://www.usatoday.com/
New York Times, URL: http://www.nytimes.com/
Los Angeles Times, URL: http://www.latimes.com/
Washington Post, URL: http://www.washingtonpost.com/
New York Daily News, URL: https://www.nydailynews.com/
Chicago Tribune, URL: http://www.chicagotribune.com/
San Jose Mercury News, URL: http://www.mercurynews.com/
New York Post, URL: http://www.nypost.com/
Houston Chronicle, URL: http://www.chron.com/
Dow Jones and Co. Inc., URL: http://www.dj.com/
Hearst Corporation, URL: http://www.hearst.com/newspapers/index.php

Business Journals
The largest business journals in the USA are:
Time, URL: http://www.time.com/time/
Newsweek, URL: http://www.newsweek.com/
US News and World Report, http://www.usnews.com/
Business Week, URL: http://www.businessweek.com/
Forbes Magazine, URL: http://www.forbes.com/

Broadcasting

Public broadcasting is partly-government funded. The main national broadcast television networks are: ABC, CBS, NBC, Fox, UPN, Univision, Public Broadcasting System (PBS), Telemundo, TBN.

NBC is the largest commercial network with over 200 affiliate stations, followed by CBS and ABC. The largest commercial Spanish-language network, Univision, has over 120 affiliate stations and airs original programming, as well as programmes imported from Mexico and Venezuela. Telemundo is the second-largest commercial Spanish-language network, and operates in Mexico and Puerto Rico as well as in the USA.

Television stations and their programmes are monitored by the Federal Communications Commission (FCC), which also issues licences. Cable television stations are not monitored by the FCC, although it does regulate competition between broadcasters and cable TV owners. A cable television system operates under a franchise obtained from a city government, then a station is licensed by the FCC. There now many cable channels, broadcasting an assortment of programmes from films to sport, such as HBO, MTV, VH1, Disney, Discovery, Weather Channel and CNN. Pay TV broadcasts by charging the viewer for each programme watched. Public television broadcasts to a small audience, even though it is received by most household televisions. The switchover to digital took place in 2009.

Capital Cities/American Broadcasting Companies, Inc., URL: http://abc.go.com/
Colombia Broadcasting System Television Division, URL: http://www.cbs.com/
National Broadcasting Co., Inc., URL: http://www.nbc.com/
Public Broadcasting Service (PBS), URL: http://www.pbs.org
Turner Broadcasting System, URL: http://www.turner.com
CNN, URL: http://edition.cnn.com/
Fox, URL: http://www.fox.com/
National Association of Broadcasters (NAB), URL: http://www.nab.org/
National Cable and Telecommunications Association (NCTA), URL: http://www.ncta.com/
Federal Communications Commission (FCC), URL: http://www.fcc.gov/
Univision, URL: http://www.univision.com
Telemundo, URL: http://www.telemundo.com

Radio

As of 2013, there were some 10,000 commercial radio stations in the USA.
National Public Radio, URL http://www.npr.org/
Clear Channel (large commercial broadcaster), http://www.clearchannel.com/
Colombia Broadcasting System Radio Division (CBS), URL: http://www.cbs.com

Postal Service

The US Postal Service is a semi-autonomous federal agency set up in 1970 by the Postal Reorganization Act. It is one of America's largest employers, with approximately 545,000 regular employees. In 2008, revenues reached $75 billion. As well as the first class service (overnight to metropolitan areas and three days or less coast to coast), the Postal Service also offers Express Mail (next-day delivery) and Priority Mail (low-cost, two-day delivery). The rates and policies are determined by nine governors who are appointed by the President of the United States with Senate consent. These governors appoint the Postmaster General and the Chief Executive of Postal Services. There are approximately 33,000 post offices in the USA, and the US Postal Service collects, sorts and transports 151 million pieces of post per day, six days a week. . The Postal Service also runs the country's largest civilian fleet of vehicles. Mail volume has fallen by 20 per cent in the last three years and this trend is expected to continue. Since 2006, mail processing facilities have been reduced by 27 per cent. The Postal Service is looking to reduce costs by $20 billion by 2015.
United States Postal Service, URL: http://www.usps.com

Telecommunications

There are approximately 500 long-distance telephone companies, the largest being AT&T (URL: http://www.att.com). Some of these companies own their own lines, but the smaller firms can buy the service from the larger companies and sell on to the customer, thereby omitting the need to have their own switches and lines. State Government Agencies set prices for local telephone services, and other services within a state.

The Federal Communications Commission is an independent government agency regulating interstate and foreign communications by radio, television, wire, satellite and cable.
Federal Communications Commission (FCC), URL: http://www.fcc.gov

In 2011, there were an estimated 145 million fixed line telephones in use, and around 290 million mobile phones in circulation

Internet

By 2011, there were around 270 million internet users, more than 78 per cent of the population. An estimated 75 per cent of Americans use social networks and blogs. Over 60 per cent use Facebook.

ENVIRONMENT

Although the American Constitution does not directly deal with environmental issues, policies are formulated from it. Citizens are entitled to information concerning the environmental impact any Government action may have. America's chief environmental problems are greenhouse gas emissions, air pollution resulting in acid rain, limited fresh water resources, water pollution from the run-off of pesticides, and desertification.

Emissions

China overtook the USA as the largest emitter of carbon dioxide through fossil fuel flaring, with 6,017.69 million metric tons in 2006. US per capita carbon emissions were an estimated 19.87 metric tons in the same year, down from 20.27 metric tons in 2005, but well above the world average of 4.48 metric tons

Energy-related carbon dioxide emissions, 2000-2011 (Billion Metric Tons CO2)

	Billion Metric tons	% +/- on previous year
2000	5.867	3.3
2005	5.997	0.4
2010	5.607	3.3
2011	5.471	-2.4

Source: Energy Information Administration

The EIA estimates that US total carbon dioxide emissions will to rise to over 6,300 million metric tons by 2035.

Energy-related CO2 emissions by source and sector for the US, 2011 (million metric tons) (p)

Sources	Residential	Commercial	Industrial	Transport.	Electric Power	Source total
Coal	1	5	151	0	1,718	1,874
Natural Gas	256	171	419	39	411	1,296
Petroleum	78	49	345	1,802	25	2,299
Other[1]	..	..	..	..	11	11
Electricity[2]	827	767	567	4	..	..
Sector Total	1,162	992	1,482	1,845	2,166	5,481

Source: EIA
(p) - preliminary
1 - Misc. wastes & from geothermal power generation
2 - Electricity-related CO2 emissions based on electricity use for both sector & electric power emissions

The US is now the second largest single source of anthropogenic greenhouse gas emissions in the world (following China) accounting for around 20 per cent of total emissions. At the 1992 earth summit the US pledged to reduce greenhouse gas emissions to 1990 levels by the year 2000. This was reassessed at the 1997 Kyoto summit in Japan when a new target of a 7 per cent reduction on 1990 levels by 2012 was set. However, George W. Bush signalled his intention to satisfy the future energy needs of the US through a greater reliance on fossil fuels and nuclear power. The US has not implemented the Kyoto Protocol; however the Bush Administration initiated other environment improvement schemes: tax incentives to encourage the use of clean, renewable energies, the Climate Change Research Initiative and sponsorship of a project to create the world's first coal-based, zero-emissions electricity and hydrogen power plant. The Clear Skies Bill legislated to cut power plant emissions of sulphur dioxide, nitrogen oxides and mercury.

The administration of Barack Obama has set a goal of generating 25 per cent of US energy from renewable sources by 2025 through investing in solar, wind, biofuels, and geothermal power. In June 2009, the climate change bill was passed in Congress, obliging US industry to reduce carbon dioxide emissions and other greenhouse gases. Licences will grow increasingly restrictive over time, pushing up the price of carbon emissions while persuading industry to adopt cleaner ways of making and consuming energy. Democrats on the Senate Environment and Public Works Committee ignored a Republican boycott and used their majority to approve the legislation in November 2009.

Environmental Agreements

The US is a party to the following international environmental agreements: Air Pollution, Air Pollution-Nitrogen Oxides, Antarctic-Environmental Protocol, Antarctic-Marine Living Resources, Antarctic Seals, Antarctic Treaty, Climate Change, Desertification, Endangered Species, Environmental Modification, Marine Dumping, Marine Life Conservation, Ozone Layer Protection, Ship Pollution, Tropical Timber 83, Tropical Timber 94, Wetlands, Whaling. The US has signed, but not ratified, the following: Air Pollution-Persistent Organic Pollutants, Air Pollution-Volatile Organic Compounds, Biodiversity, Climate Change-Kyoto Protocol, Hazardous Wastes.

The US has laws such as the Clean Air Act which is designed to protect public health; Clean Water Act to address national water pollution issues; Endangered Species Act to protect wildlife suffering from decline in population; and the Comprehensive Environmental Response, Compensation and Liability Act which set up a fund for the EPA to monitor and clean hazardous substances.

In April 2010, an environmental disaster occurred following an explosion on the Deepwater Horizon rig situated in the Gulf of Mexico. The leaking of 12,000-19,000 barrels of oil a day formed a slick measuring some 100 miles by 45 miles within a week of the explosion, during which time it was not possible to stop the oil being pumped into the sea. Despite various attempts to stop the leak, it was not until the beginning of June that BP succeeded in reducing the spillage to around 9,000 barrels per day. The Louisiana coastline, with its environmentally-sensitive wetlands and shrimp and oyster beds, was threatened by America's's worst environmental disaster ever, threatening hundreds of species of fish, birds and other wildlife in one of the world's richest marine environments. The states of Mississippi, Alabama and Florida were also affected.

In 2011, BP was ordered to pay out $25 million for an 200,000 gallon oil spill in Alaska in 2006. The settlement also required BP Alaska to develop a system-wide program to manage pipeline integrity for the company's 1,600 miles (2,500km) of pipeline on the North Slope at an estimated cost of $60 million.

UNITED STATES OF AMERICA

SPACE PROGRAMME

The US space programme is researched and administered by NASA, created in 1958. Its aims are to be at the forefront of space exploration and development, as well as to progress scientific knowledge of the earth, universe, solar system and environment. NASA's mission also includes aeronautics research and development.

Recent missions have included a number of Space Shuttle launches, the launch of the Viking and Mars Pathfinder spacecraft, the Hubble Space Telescope, and numerous communications satellites. In 2000 the US and Russia established a permanent human presence in space with the International Space Station. On Feb. 1, 2003, the space shuttle Columbia broke apart on re-entry into Earth's atmosphere, killing all seven crew members. The final launch of the space shuttle took place on 8 July 2011 from the Kennedy Space Center. Its final mission before retirement was to take more than 3.5 tonnes of supplies to the International Space Station.

In November 2011 NASA launched an Atlas 5 rocket carrying a MarsScience Laboratory rover. The robot cost US$2.5 bn and is the most capable machine to be sent to Mars. It will study whether the planet is capable of supporting life forms.

As of 2013, NASA's work is organized into four mission directorates:
-**Aeronautics:** Air transportation system; air traffic congestion; safety and environmental issues.
-**Human Exploration & Operations:** International Space Station operations, commercial space flights, human exploration
-**Science:** studying the Earth, solar system and the unvierse beyond
-**Space Technology:** development of advanced technology

Current research includes: the Mars rover Curiosity; Juno is travelling towards Jupiter and Cassini is in orbit around Saturn. NASA is working towards a goal of landing a human on Mars.

The Budget request for 2013 was $17.7 billion including $699 million for space technology, $3,933 million for exploration, and $4187 million on space operations.

NASA operates from its headquarters in Washington, DC, 10 field installations around the country, as well as partnerships with contractors and other space agencies. It employs 20,000 civil servants.

NASA research centres are located in a number of states:
Ames Research Centre, Moffett Field, California. URL: http://www.arc.nasa.gov
Dryden Flight Research Centre, Edwards Air Force Base, California. URL: http://www.dfrc.nasa.gov
Glenn Research Centre, Lewis Field, Cleveland, Ohio. URL: http://www.nasa.gov/glenn/home/index.html
Goddard Space Flight Centre, Greenbelt, Maryland. URL: http://www.nasa.gov/centers/goddard
Jet Propulsion Laboratory, Pasadena, California. URL: http://www.jpl.nasa.gov
Johnson Space Centre, Houston, Texas. URL: http://www.nasa.gov/centers/johnson/ URL: http://www.spacecenter.org
Kennedy Space Centre, Cape Canaveral, Florida. URL: http://www.kennedyspacecenter.com
Langley Research Centre, Hampton, Virginia. URL: http://www.larc.nasa.gov
Marshall Space Flight Centre, Huntsville, Alabama. URL: http://www.msfc.nasa.gov
Stennis Space Centre, Bay St. Louis, Mississippi. URL: http://www.sssc.nasa.gov
Wallops Flight Facility, Wallops Island, Virginia. URL: http://www.nasa.gov/centers/wallops/home/index.html
White Sands Test Facility, White Sands, New Mexico.http://www.nasa.gov/centers/wstf/home/index.html

National Aeronautics and Space Administration (NASA), URL: http://www.nasa.gov/

ALABAMA

Capital: Montgomery (Population, Census 2010: 205,764)

Head of State: Robert Bentley (R) (Governor) (page 1387)

State Flag: A crimson cross of St Andrew on a white field

CONSTITUTION AND GOVERNMENT

Constitution
Alabama entered the Union on 14 December 1819. According to the 1901 Constitution, the governor heads the executive branch of government assisted by 14 other elected executive officials: lieutenant governor, attorney-general, state auditor, secretary of state, state treasurer, eight members of the board of education (the superintendent is appointed), and commissioner of agriculture and industries. All are elected by the people for four-year terms.

Alabama elects two Senators and seven Representatives to the US Congress, Washington, DC. The Senators serve a six-year term, whilst the Representatives serve for two years.

To consult the state constitution, please visit: http://www.legislature.state.al.us/CodeOfAlabama/Constitution/1901/Constitution1901_toc.htm

Recent Events
On 29th August 2005, states on the Mexican Gulf, including Alabama, were hit by Hurricane Katrina. With winds exceeding 150 km/h, approximately 200 kilometres of coastline was affected. Storm surges from the sea caused flooding which affected areas several kilometres inland. Mobile was the worst hit city in the state; some 400,000 homes and businesses were left without electricity and parts of the city were badly flooded. On 1st March 2007, a tornado struck Alabama and neighbouring Georgia, causing major damage and killing seven people.

In 2007, the Alabama Legislature passed a resolution expressing "profound regret" over slavery and its lingering impact.

Legislature
Alabama's bicameral legislature consists of the Senate and the House of Representatives. The legislature meets in annual Regular Sessions consisting of no more than 30 Legislative days over a 105 calendar day period. Alabama's legislature convenes at different times of the year over a four-year period (Quadrennium) as follows: first year - first Tuesday in March; second year - first Tuesday in February; third year - first Tuesday in February; fourth year - second Tuesday in January.

Upper House
The Senate has 35 members who are elected every four years. The Lieutenant-Governor of Alabama is also President of the Senate. Each Senator represents some 120,000 people.
Senate, Alabama State House, 11 South Union Street, 7th Floor, Montgomery, Alabama 36130, USA. Tel: +1 334 242 7800, URL: http://www.legislature.state.al.us/senate/senate.html

Lower House
The House of Representatives has 105 members who are also elected every four years. Each member of the House represents about 40,000 people.

House of Representatives, Alabama State House, 11 South Union Street, 5th & 6th Floors, Montgomery, Alabama 36130, USA. Tel: +1 334 242 7600, URL: http://www.legislature.state.al.us/house/house.html

---

Executive Branch Officials (as of April 2013)
Governor: Dr Robert Bentley (R) (page 1387)
Lieutenant Governor: Kate Ivey (R)
Secretary of State: Beth Chapman (R)
Attorney General: Luther Strange (R)
State Treasurer: Y. Boozer (R)
State Auditor: Samantha Shaw (R)
Commissioner of Agriculture and Industry: John McMillan (R)
Superintendent of Education: Tommy Bice

Legislature (as at April 2013)
President of the Senate: Kate Ivey (R)
President Pro Tem of the Senate: Del Marsh (R)
Secretary of the Senate: D. Patrick Harris
Speaker of the House: Mike Hubbard (R)
Speaker Pro Tem of the House: Victor Gaston (R)
Clerk of the House: Jeff Woodard

US Senators: Jeff Sessions (R) (page 1512) and Richard C. Shelby (R) (page 1513)

Ministries
Office of the Governor, State Capitol, Room N-104, 600 Dexter Avenue, Montgomery, AL 36130, USA. Tel: +1 334 242 7100, fax: +1 334 242 0004, URL: http://www.governor.state.al.us/
Lieutenant-Governor's Office, 11 South Union Street, Suite 725, Montgomery AL 36130, USA. Tel: +1 334 242 7900, fax: +1 334 242 4661 e-mail: info@ltgov.state.al.us, URL: http://www.ltgov.state.al.us/
Office of the Attorney General, Alabama State House, 11 South Union Street, Third Floor, Montgomery, AL 36130, USA. Tel: +1 334 242 7300, URL: http://www.ago.state.al.us/
Office of the Secretary of State, PO Box 5616, Montgomery, Alabama 36130, USA. Tel: +1 334 242 7200, fax: +1 334 242 4993, URL: http://www.sos.state.al.us/
Office of the State Treasurer, State Capitol, Room S-106, Montgomery, AL 36130-2510, USA. Tel: +1 334 242 7500, fax: +1 334 242 7592, e-mail: alatreas@treasury.state.al.us, URL: http://www.treasury.state.al.us/
Department of Agriculture and Industries, Richard Beard Building, 1445 Federal Drive, Montgomery, AL 36107-1100, USA. (Mailing address: PO Box 3336, Montgomery, AL 36109-0336) Tel: +1 334 240 7100, fax: +1 334 240 7190, e-mail: commone@agi.state.al.us, URL: http://www.agi.state.al.us/
Department of Corrections, 1400 Lloyd Street, Montgomery, AL 36107, USA. Tel: +1 334 240 9500, fax: +1 334 353 3891, e-mail: webmaster@doc.state.al.us, URL: http://www.doc.state.al.us/
Department of Economic and Community Affairs (ADECA), 401 Adams Avenue, Montgomery, AL 36103, USA. Tel: +1 334 242 5100, fax: +1 334 242 5099, e-mail: info@adeca.state.al.us, URL: http://www.adeca.alabama.gov/
Department of Education, 50 North Ripley Street, PO Box 302101, Montgomery, Alabama 36104, USA. Tel: +1 334 242 9950, e-mail: webpost@alsde.edu, URL: http://www.alsde.edu/

Department of Environmental Management (ADEM), 1400 Coliseum Blvd. Montgomery, AL 36110 (mailing address: Post Office Box 301463, Montgomery, AL 36130-1463), USA. Tel: +1 334 271 7700, fax: +1 334 271 7950, URL: http://www.adem.state.al.us/
Department of Finance, 105-N State Capitol/600 Dexter, Montgomery, AL 36104, USA. Tel: +1 334 242 7160, fax: +1 334 353 3300, e-mail: inquiry@finance.state.al.us, URL: http://www.finance.state.al.us/
Department of Human Resources, 50 N. Ripley Street, Montgomery, AL 36130, USA. Tel: +1 334 242 1310, fax: +1 334 242 1086, e-mail: ogapi@dhr.state.al.us, URL: http://www.dhr.state.al.us/
Department of Labour, 100 North Union Street, Suite 620, Montgomery, AL 36130, USA. Tel: +1 334 242 3460, fax: +1 334 240 3417, URL: http://dir.alabama.gov/
Department of Public Safety, 500 Dexter Avenue (PO Box 1511), Montgomery AL 36130, USA. Tel: +1 334 242 4371, fax: +1 334 242 4385, URL: http://www.dps.alabama.gov/Home/
Department of Transport, 1409 Coliseum Boulevard, Montgomery, AL 36130, USA. Tel: +1 334 242 6356, URL: http://www.dot.state.al.us/

Political Parties
Alabama Democratic Party, URL: http://www.aladems.org/
Alabama Republican Party, URL: http://www.algop.org/

Elections
Elections took place in November 2010 for the following statewide positions: Governor, Lieutenant Governor, seven US Representatives, Attorney General, all State Senators and Representatives, Secretary of State, State Treasurer, State Auditor, Commissioner of Agriculture and two Public Service Commissioners. Governor Robert Riley was ineligible to stand in the November 2010 Gubernatorial elections. Robert Bentley, a member of the Alabama State House of Representatives, won the race.

The most recent state legislative elections took place in November 2010 when the Republicans took control of both houses. The Republicans took 63 seats in the House and the Democrats 43. Seats in the Senate are split: Republicans 22, Democrats 12, Independent 1.

US Senator Richard Shelby was re-elected in November 2010. US Senator Jeff Sessions was re-elected in November 2008 and will be up for re-election in 2014.

LEGAL SYSTEM

Alabama's court system comprises the Supreme Court, the Court of Civil Appeals, the Court of Criminal Appeals, 40 Circuit Courts, 68 Probate Courts, 67 District Courts, and 257 Municipal Courts.

The Supreme Court is Alabama's highest court, having both judicial and administrative responsibilities. The court deals with cases where the amount in dispute exceeds $50,000. In addition to the Chief Justice there are eight associate justices who are all elected for terms of six years.

The Court of Civil Appeals and the Court of Criminal Appeals both have five judges each and submit appeals to the Supreme Court.

The Chief Justice of the Supreme Court, Roy Moore, was dismissed in November 2003 following his refusal to follow federal court orders to remove a monument bearing the Ten Commandments he had erected outside the state Supreme Court. The federal court ruled that the monument violated the constitutional separation of church and state.

Alabama is an alcoholic beverage control state, and the government holds a monopoly on the sale of alcohol. Counties can declare themselves "dry"; the state does not sell alcohol in those areas.

Capital punishment is legal in Alabama. As of January 2013 there were 202 inmates on death row, of whom five were women. Six people were executed in 2011 and five in 2010. No-one was executed in 2012. The governor has the power to grant clemency. According to the DPIC the murder rate stands at 5.7 per 100,000 population.

In January 2013, the Supreme Court recognized the unborn as persons deserving of legal protections.

Supreme Court, 300 Dexter Avenue, Montgomery, AL 36104-3741, USA. Tel: +1 334 242 4609, fax: +1 334 242 0588, e-mail: cspear@alalinc.net, URL: http://www.judicial.state.al.us/supreme
Chief Justice: Chuck Malone
Court of Civil Appeals, 300 Dexter Avenue, Montgomery, Alabama 36104, USA. Tel: +1 334 242 4093, e-mail: cspear@alalinc.net, URL: http://www.judicial state.al.us/civil
Presiding Judge: William C. Thompson
Court of Criminal Appeals, 300 Dexter Avenue, Montgomery, Alabama 36104, USA. Tel: +1 334 242 4590, e-mail: cspear@alalinc.net, URL: http://www.judicial.state.al.us/criminal
Presiding Judge: Samuel Welch

LOCAL GOVERNMENT

Administratively, Alabama is divided into 67 county governments and, according to the 2007 census, 458 municipal governments. There are no town or township governments. In addition, there are 131 school district governments and 529 special district governments.

AREA AND POPULATION

Area
Alabama is located in the south of the US, east of Mississippi, west of Georgia, and south of Tennessee. Alabama covers a total area of 52,419.02 sq. miles, of which 50,744.00 sq. miles is land and 1,675.01 sq. miles is water.

To view a map of the state, please consult
http://www.lib.utexas.edu/maps/us_2001/alabama_ref_2001.pdf

Population
Latest Census Bureau estimates put the 2012 population at 4,822,023, up on the mid-2010 figure of 4,779,736, up 0.5 per cent. The population is estimated to reach 4,874,243 by 2030. In 2011, 6.3 per cent of the population was under 5 years, 26.5 per cent under 18 years and 14 per cent over 65 years. An estimated 51.5 per cent of the population is female. Population density in 2010 was estimated as 94.4 per sq. mile. The counties with the largest population numbers are Jefferson County (658,466 at the time of the 2010 Census), Mobile County (412,992), and Madison County (334,811). Alabama's largest cities are Birmingham (212,237 according to the 2010 Census), Montgomery (205,764), and Mobile (195,111). According to the 2010 census, 68.5 per cent of the population is white, and 26.2 per cent black.

Births, Marriages, Deaths
The US Census Bureau (Population Division) provisionally puts the number of births over 2010 at 60,050, and the number of deaths at 48,038, giving a natural population increase of 12,012 residents. Net migration added a further 16,363 inhabitants, most coming from other parts of the USA, resulting in an overall population increase of 31,244 people.

The infant mortality rate in 2007 was 9.89 deaths under 1 year per 1,000 live births, (the second highest rate in the US) and the neonatal rate was 6.27. There were an estimated 39,035 marriages in 2008 (down on the previous year) and 19,509 divorces (also down on the figure for 2007). The median age is 37.9 years, and life expectancy at birth is 73.9 years.

Public Holidays
As well as observing US bank holidays, the counties of Baldwin and Mobile, Alabama, also celebrate the following:
4 March 2014: Mardi Gras Day

EMPLOYMENT

Alabama's total civilian labour force in December 2012 was 2,157,000, of which 2,004,300 were employed and 152,600 were unemployed. The unemployment rate was 7.1 per cent, down on 2010. (Source: Bureau of Labor Statistics, preliminary figures)

The following table shows preliminary December 2012 non-farm wage and salary jobs, (seasonally adjusted) according to industry:

Industry	No. of jobs	Change over 12 months %
Logging and mining	11,900	-4.8
Construction	74,300	-0.1
Manufacturing*	247,000	3.4
Trade, transport and utilities	367,800	0.1
Information	21,500	-6.9
Financial activities	94,600	2.0
Professional and business services	220,700	2.5
Educational and health services	219,900	1.0
Leisure and hospitality	172,300	2.1
Other services	83,000	3.0
Government	366,900	-2.4
TOTAL	1,879,900	0.7

* not seasonally adjusted
Source: Bureau of Labor Statistics

BANKING AND FINANCE

GDP/GNP, Inflation, National Debt
Alabama's Gross Domestic Product (current dollars) rose from $172.6 billion in 2010 to US$173.1 billion (ranked 26th in the US). Alabama contributed 1.2 per cent of total US GDP. Real GDP contracted by 0.8 per cent in 2011 (US average rate for the year 1.5 per cent). In 2011, the largest industry was government (17.5 per cent of Alabama GDP).

Gross Domestic Product, according to industry, is shown on the following table ($million):

Industry	2009	2010	2011
Agriculture, forestry, fishing and hunting	2,170	2,140	2,171
Mining	2,295	2,389	2,303
Utilities	5,044	5,311	5,102
Construction	7,654	7,617	6,875
Manufacturing	23,844	24,823	25,949
Wholesale Trade	9,120	9,254	9,638
Retail Trade	12,169	12,763	13,053
Transportation and warehousing	4,344	4,569	4,712
Information	3,971	3,878	4,043
Finance and insurance	8,962	10,370	10,904
Real estate, rental and leasing	16,817	15,866	15,098
Educational services	929	960	995
Health care and social services	12,343	13,003	13,404

UNITED STATES OF AMERICA

Other non-government services	25,944	27,492	28,468
Government	29,094	29,786	30,308
TOTAL	164,753	170,219	173,122

Source: Bureau of Economic Analysis, Feb. 2013

In 2011, the state's average per capita personal income was estimated at $34,880 (down on the national average of US$41,560), up 3.5 per cent from 2010. Per capita GDP was US$32,208 in 2010, compared to the US average of $42,346.

The annual Consumer Price Index for the South urban area (all items) was 211.3 in 2010, rising to 218.6 in 2011 and 223.2 in 2012. (1982-84 = 100). (Source: Bureau of Labor Statistics)

Balance of Payments / Imports and Exports
Alabama's export revenue rose from $12,355 million in 2009 to US$15,502 million in 2010 and US$17,854 million in 2011, up 15.2 per cent on the previous year. Exports from Alabama constituted 1.2 per cent of US total exports. (Source: US Census Bureau, Foreign Trade Division)

The following table shows the top five export products in 2011 according to revenue:

Product	Export Revenue ($m)
Bituminous coal, not agglomerated	2,195
Pass.Vehicle com-ig int com eng > 3000 cc	1,557
Pass.Vehicle com-ig int com eng > 2500 cc	1,487
Pass Veh. Spk.lg. int. com rcpr p eng >1500	1,192
Polycarbonates	550

Export trading partners in 2011, according to revenue, are shown on the following chart:

Country	Revenue ($m)	+/- % 2010-11
Total	17,854	15.2
Canada	3,306	4.4
China	2,308	20.4
Germany	1,953	9.4
Mexico	1,717	52.7
Japan	716	45.9

Source: US Census Bureau, Foreign Trade Division

Total Alabama imports amounted to US$17,426 million, up 17 per cent in 2010, representing 0.8 per cent of the US total in 2011. Top imports include petroleum and motor vehicle accessories and parts. Main suppliers include South Korea (19.3 per cent), Germany (13.0 per cent), China (11.2 per cent), Canada (10.0 per cent) and Japan (9.6 per cent).

Chambers of Commerce and Trade Organisations
Montgomery Area Chamber of Commerce, URL: http://www.montgomerychamber.com/
Birmingham Business Alliance, URL: http://birminghambusinessalliance.com/
Business Council of Alabama, URL: http://www.bcatoday.org

MANUFACTURING, MINING AND SERVICES

Primary and Extractive Industries
According to the BEA, Alabama's mining industry contributed an estimated $2,303 million towards the state's 2011 GDP. The major sector in 2010 was non-oil and gas extraction $1,299. Oil and gas extraction earned $830 million, and support activities for mining earned $260 million.

Alabama's most valuable minerals are coal, natural gas, petroleum, and limestone. Jefferson, Tuscaloosa, and Walker counties in north-central Alabama produce most of the state's coal. The coal is a bituminous variety that is taken from both underground and surface mines. Natural gas and petroleum are obtained mainly from wells in the south-western part of the state. Large limestone quarries lie near Birmingham and Huntsville. Limestone is used primarily to make cement and roadbeds. Alabama is among the leading states in mining bauxite and marble. The state's other mineral products include clays, salt, and sand and gravel.

Alabama's crude oil reserves were estimated to be 42 million barrels in 2010 (0.2 per cent of US total). From a total of 854 oil wells and seven rotary rigs, Alabama's oil industry produced around 7,145,000 barrels of crude oil in 2010 (0.4 per cent of US total). Total petroleum consumption totalled 109.7 million barrels over 2009, 63,500 thousand barrels of which was used as motor gasoline. Crude oil refinery capacity as of 1 Jan. 2012 was 120,100 bbl/d.

Dry proved reserves of natural gas fell were estimated to be 2,629 billion cu. ft (1.1 per cent of US total) in 2010. Reserves of natural gas plant liquid were estimated to be 68 million barrels. There were 7,063 producing gas wells in 2011. Marketed production was 195,581 million cu ft million cubic feet in 2010 whilst consumption was 531,243 million cu ft in 2009.

Recoverable coal reserves were 306 million short tons in 2010 (1.6 per cent of US total), with total production at 19.07 million short tons. There were 49 mines in 2007, 41 of which were surface mines. An estimated 4,258 people were employed in the coal mining industry in 2009. (Source: EIA)

Energy
Alabama's total energy production was 1,420 trillion Btu in 2010 (1.9 per cent of US total). Alabama's total energy consumption was 1,960 trillion Btu in 2010 (2.0 per cent of US total). Per capita energy consumption was 410 million Btu in 2010, ranking it 12th in the US.

Alabama's electric power industry net summer capacity was 32,417 MW (3.1 per cent of US total) in 2010. Alabama is a net exporter of electricity, with coal as its primary generating fuel. Total net electricity generation was 11,427,000 MWh in Oct. 2012 (3.7 per cent of US total).

Alabama was ranked sixth in the US in 2010 in net electricity generation from renewable sources, of which conventional hydroelectric power supplied 79 per cent.

There are two nuclear power plants; Browns Ferry and Joseph M. Farley. The three reactors at the Browns Ferry nuclear power plant have a combined generating capacity of 3,310 MW, one of the highest capacities among US nuclear power plants. (Source: EIA)

Manufacturing
Manufacturing is Alabama's second largest contributor towards GDP accounting for $25,949 million in 2011 (down from $28,608 million in 2007). Top manufacturing sectors in 2010 were motor vehicle and parts ($1,893 million), primary metal manufacturing ($2,156 million), chemical manufacturing ($2,635 million), fabricated metal manufacturing ($2,045 million) and paper manufacturing ($2,989 million).

The automotive industry is the most important sector in Alabama, with over 300 manufacturers, including Mercedes Benz, Hyundai and Honda. The aerospace industry is another significant sector, and ranks 11th in the US in terms of Department of Defense Prime Contracts.

The state's most important chemical products are used by industry, but chemical fibres, fertilisers, and insecticides are also produced. In 2004, the chemicals sector employed around 10,300 people and exported goods to the sum of $1.7 billion.

Service Industries
The services industry is Alabama's top contributor to its Gross Domestic Product. The leading sector in 2011 was real estate (an estimated $15,098 million). Other major contributors were health care and social assistance ($13,404 million) and professional and technical services ($11,113 million).

Tourism
The accommodation and food services sector contributed $4,696 million towards the 2011 GDP while the arts, entertainment and recreation sector contributed $579 million.

Agriculture
Agriculture contributed an estimated US$2,171 million towards the 2011 state GDP (up from US$2,072 million in 2009). In 2010, the crops and animals sector earned $1,609 million, whilst forestry, fishing, and related activities generated $530 million.

According to the latest Department of Agriculture overview, Alabama's farms numbered 48,500 in 2010, up from 45,112 at the time of the 2002 Census. Total land area of the state's farms was 9,000,000 in 2010, slightly down on the 2002 figure, whilst the size of the average farm had fallen from 199 acres in 2002 to 186 acres in 2010. The total farm receipts amounted to $5.7 billion, of which livestock, poultry and products generated $4.55 billion, up on $4.19 billion the previous year. Alabama was ranked 3rd in peanuts and 10th in cotton production. There were an estimated 1.23 milllion head of cattle on 1 Jan. 2011. An estimated 1.03 billion birds were marketed and 2.18 billion eggs were produced. Poultry make up nearly 70 per cent of cash receipts.

Alabama has an annual fish catch valued at about $40 million. The Gulf of Mexico provides most of the catch. Shrimps are Alabama's most valuable saltwater seafood. Grain-fed catfish, raised in artificial ponds on farms, are an important new food crop. Alabama ranks 6th in the USA in terms of aquaculture.

COMMUNICATIONS AND TRANSPORT

International Airports
Most of Alabama's air traffic uses the Birmingham, Huntsville, and Mobile airports.
Birmingham International Airport, URL: http://www.bhamintlairport.com

Railways
Four major rail lines provide freight service in Alabama. Passenger trains serve Birmingham and two other cities in the state.

Roads
Alabama has about 97,000 miles (156,000 km) of roads and highways.

Ports and Harbours
About 1,350 miles (2,173 km) of navigable waterways cross the state. They include a section of the Gulf Intracoastal Waterway between Brownsville, Tex. and Carrabelle, Fla. This section is about 60 miles (97 km) long. The Black Warrior-Tombigbee-Mobile river system, 453 miles (729 km) long, is the longest navigable waterway in Alabama. The Tennessee River connects northern Alabama with the Mississippi River system. The 234 mile (377 km) long Tennessee-Tombigbee Water was completed in 1985. This canal links the port at Mobile with inland ports on the Tennessee and Ohio rivers. Alabama has several built dock facilities. Mobile, on Mobile Bay, is Alabama's only seaport. The Alabama State Docks at Mobile can handle about 35 ocean-going vessels at a time.

HEALTH

Recent statistics show that Alabama has 129 general hospitals, with a total of 20,895 beds; 235 assisted living facilities, with 5,609 beds; 182 home health agencies; and 50 hospices. Additionally, in 2009, there were an estimated 3.2 community hospital beds per 1,000 resident population. In 2010, there were an estimated 227 nursing homes and 26,656 beds. In 2009, there were approximately 27.4 physicians per 10,000 population and in 2008, 2,032 dentists; There are an estimated 34,000 nurses, 641 nurse practitioners; and 31 certified nursing midwives.

In 2012, an estimated 32 per cent of the adult population were considered obese (4th nationally). In 2012, an estimated 17.6 per cent of the population were living in poverty (US average is 14.3 per cent). An estimated 13.6 per cent of the population in the period 2007-09 were without health insurance coverage (US average 15.8 per cent). Alabama reported 9,738 HIV/AIDS cases from the beginning of the epidemic to the end of 2008. Alabama reported 594 cases of HIV/AIDS in 2009. Alabama has the 17th highest rate of TB, 3.8 per 100,000 population. The most common causes of death are heart disease, malignant neoplasms and cerebrovascular diseases. (Source: Center for Disease Control and Prevention)

EDUCATION

Primary/Secondary Education
Alabama established its public school system in 1854. Like most Southern States, Alabama had separate schools for whites and blacks. In 1954, the Supreme Court of the United States ruled that school segregation was unconstitutional. In 1963, Alabama began to desegregate its public schools and, by 1973, most schools were integrated.

In 2009-10, there were 748,889 elementary and secondary students (rising to an estimated 749,000 in 2011) in 1,628 schools. There were 47,492 teachers, and the pupil/teacher ratio was 15.77 to one. In 2007-08, total expenditure on state elementary and secondary education was $7.9 billion, whilst education revenues amounted to$7.7 billion.

Higher Education
Alabama had 75 degree conferring institutions in 2011, 39 of which were public. They included the University of Alabama, the University of South Alabama, the University of West Alabama, and Alabama State University. In 2010-11, there were 131,066 male students and 180,674 women students enrolled. 56,455 degrees/certificates were awarded, including 25,868 Bachelors, 11,291 Masters and 2,079 Doctorates. (Source: National Center for Education Statistics)

COMMUNICATIONS AND MEDIA

Newspapers
Approximately 100 newspapers, including about 30 dailies, are published in Alabama, together with some 75 periodicals. Newspapers include: The Mobile Register (founded in 1813, is Alabama's oldest newspaper), Birmingham News, Birmingham Post-Herald, Huntsville Times, and Montgomery Advertiser.
Alabama Press Association, URL: http://www.alabamapress.org/
Mobile Register, URL: http://www.al.com

Broadcasting
WAPI of Birmingham is Alabama's oldest commercial radio station. It began in 1922 in Auburn as WMAV. WVTM-TV, the state's first television station, was established in Birmingham in May 1949 as WABT-TV. In 1955, Alabama began operating the first state-owned educational television system in the United States. This system, called Alabama Public Television Network, has stations in several cities, and reaches every county in the state. Alabama has about 220 radio stations and 38 television stations.

ENVIRONMENT

Alabama's primary electricity generating fuel is coal, hence the state's high emissions of carbon dioxide. Emissions by the electric power industry in 2010 totalled 79.34 million metric tons of carbon dioxide (9th in US), 217,903 metric tons of sulfur dioxide and 66,190 metric tons of nitrogen oxide. In 2010, there were 12,683 alternative fueled vehicles in use (1.4 per cent of the US total). Ethanol consumption amounted to 4,415,000 barrels in 2011. (Source: EIA)

SPACE PROGRAMME

The Marshall Space Flight Center, part of NASA, is based at Huntsville, Alabama. The Centre has been a key contributor to many significant NASA programs during the Agency's 45-plus-year history. It now manages the key propulsion hardware and technologies of the space shuttle and is developing the next generation of space transportation and propulsion systems. It is also researching science and hardware development for the International Space Station and managing projects and scientific endeavors to benefit space exploration.

Marshall Space Flight Center, URL: http://www.nasa.gov/centers/marshall/home/index.html

ALASKA

Capital: Juneau (City and borough population, Census 2010: 31,275)

Head of State: Sean Parnell (R) (Governor) (page 1492)

National Flag: A blue background on which appear seven gold stars of the constellation the Great Bear, and a larger star representing the North Star

CONSTITUTION AND GOVERNMENT

Constitution
Alaska was established as the 49th State of the Union on 3 January 1959. The Constitution was adopted by the Constitutional Convention on 5 February 1956, ratified by the people on 24 April 1956, and became operative on 3 January 1959. According to its terms the governor heads the executive branch as one of two elected executive officials. The other is the Lieutenant Governor. Both are elected by the people of Alaska for terms of four years. The Lieutenant Governor serves in the same capacity as a Secretary of State.

Alaskans elect two Senators and one At-Large Representative to the US Congress, Washington, DC. The Senators serve a six-year term, whilst the Representatives serve for two years.

To view the state constitution, please visit: http://ltgov.state.ak.us/constitution.php

Legislature
Alaska's bicameral legislature consists of the Senate and House of Representatives. The first session of the 28th Legislature ran from 21 January 2013 to April 14, 2013. The second session runs from 21 January 2014 to 20 April 2014.
Alaska State Legislature, State Capitol, Juneau, Alaska 99801-1182, USA. Tel: +1 907 465 3701 (Senate Secretary), +1 907 465 3725 (Chief Clerk of House), fax: +1 907 465 2832 (Senate Secretary), fax +1 907 465 5334 (Chief Clerk of House), URL: http://www.legis.state.ak.us/

Upper House
The State Senate has 20 members, one from each Senate district, who are elected for four years. Half of the Senate's membership stands for election every two years. With just 20 Senators, the Alaska Senate is the smallest legislative chamber in the United States. Unlike in other states, the Lieutenant Governor of Alaska does not preside over the Senate. Instead, the Lieutenant Governor oversees the Alaska Division of Elections, fulfilling the role of Secretary of State.

Lower House
The House of Representatives has 40 members, one from each election district, who are elected for two years. Following the November 2008 elections the House was divided into 22 Republican seats and 18 Democrat seats. In November 2010, the Republicans gained one seat from the Democrats.

Elected Executive Branch Officials (as at May 2013)
Governor: Sean Parnell (R) (page 1492)
Lieutenant-Governor: Mead Treadwell

Legislature (as at April 2013)
President of the Senate: Charlie Huggins Stevens (R)
Senate Majority Leader: John Coghill (D)
Senate Minority Leader: Johnny Ellis (R)
Speaker of the House: Mike Chenault (R)
House Majority Leader: Lance Pruitt (R)
House Minority Leader: Beth Kerttula (D)

US Senators: Lisa Murkowski (R) (page 1482) and Mark Begich (D) (page 1386)

Ministries
Office of the Governor, PO Box 110001, Juneau, AK 99811-0001, USA. Tel: +1 907 465 3500, fax: +1 907 465 3532, URL: http://www.gov.state.ak.us/
Office of the Lieutenant Governor, 3rd Floor State Capitol, 120 4th Street, Room 311, Juneau, Alaska (PO Box 110015, Juneau, AK 99811-0015), USA. Tel: +1 907 465 3520, fax: +1 907 465 5400, URL: http://www.ltgov.state.ak.us
Department of Administration, 10th Fl., State Office Bldg., P.O. Box 110208, Juneau, AK 99811. Tel: +1 907 465 2200, URL: http://www.doa.alaska.gov
Department of Commerce, Community and Economic Development, PO Box 110804, Juneau, Alaska 99811, USA. Tel: +1 907 465 2500, URL: http://www.dced.state.ak.us
Department of Corrections, 802 3rd Street, Douglas, Alaska 99824, USA. Tel: +1 907 465 4652, URL: http://www.correct.state.ak.us/
Department of Education and Early Development, 801 West 10th Street, Suite 200, Juneau, Alaska 99801, USA. Tel: +1 907 465 2800, fax: +1 907 465 3452, URL: http://www.eed.state.ak.us/
Department of Environmental Conservation, 410 Willoughby Avenue, Suite 105, Juneau, AK 99801-1795, USA. Tel: +1 907 465 5066, fax: +1 907 465 5097, URL: http://www.dec.state.ak.us
Department of Fish and Game, 1255 W 8th Street, Juneau, AK 99802-5526, USA. Tel: +1 987 465 4100, URL: http://www.adfg.state.ak.us
Department of Health and Social Services, 350 Main Street, Room 204, PO Box 11061, Juneau, AK 99811-0601, USA. Tel: +1 907 465 3030, fax: +1 907 465 3068, URL: http://dhss.alaska.gov/Pages/default.aspx

UNITED STATES OF AMERICA

Department of Labour and Workforce Development, PO Box 21149, Juneau, Alaska 99802-1149, USA. Tel: +1 907 465 2700, fax: +1 907 465 2784, URL: http://www.labor.state.ak.us/home.htm
Department of Law, Tel: +1 907 465 3600, URL: http://www.law.state.ak.us
Department of Military Affairs, Tel: +1 907 428 6003, URL: http://www.ak-prepared.com/dmva
Department of Natural Resources, Tel: +1 907 269 8400, URL: http://www.dnr.state.ak.us
Department of Public Safety, Tel: +1 907 465 4222, URL: http://www.dps.alaska.gov
Department of Revenue, Tel: +1 907 465 2300, URL: http://www.revenue.state.ak.us
Department of Transportation and Public Facilities, 3132 Channel Drive, Juneau AK 99801-7898, USA. Tel: +1 907 465 3900, URL: http://www.dot.state.ak.us/

Political Parties
Alaska Democratic Party, URL: http://www.alaskademocrats.org/
Republican Party of Alaska, URL: http://www.alaskarepublicans.com/

Elections
In the mid-term elections in November 2006, the Republican Sarah Palin was voted Governor of Alaska, with over 48 per cent of the vote. She left office in July 2009, 18 months before the end of her term, and was succeeded by her Lieutenant Governor, Sean Parnell. He was re-elected in November 2010.

In state legislative elections, held on 6th November 2012, the Republicans now hold 25 of the 40 seats in the House of Representatives (a gain of one seat) and the Democrats 15. The Republicans also made gains in the Senate and now hold 13 of the 20 seats in the Senate, up from 10 in 2012. The Democrats won 7, down from 10.

The most recent elections to the US Senate took place in November 2010 and were won by the Democrats. The Republicans initially contested the result but Republican candidate Joe Miller conceded defeat in December 2010.

LEGAL SYSTEM

The Alaskan court system consists of four levels of courts: the Supreme Court, the Court of Appeals, the Superior Court, and the District Court. The system is headed by the Supreme Court, consisting of the Chief Justice, who is appointed by the governor and serves a single three-year term, and four Justices. The Court of Appeals comprises a Chief Judge, who serves a two-year term, and two judges. The Superior Court is headed by four Presiding Judges and 30 judges who serve courts in Alaska's four judicial districts. The District Court has 17 judges.

In Fiscal Year 2009, 154,372 new cases were filed in superior court and district court. During this same period, the trial courts disposed of 156,329 cases. The superior court's caseload amounted to 20,303 new cases. The district court's caseload amounted to 134,240 new cases.

Alaska does not have the death penalty. According to the DPIC the murder rate is 4.4 per 100,000 population.

Supreme Court, URL: http://www.state.ak.us/courts/ctinfo.htm
Chief Justice: Dana Fabe
Justices: Daniel Winfree, Craig Stowers, Peter Maassen, Joel H. Bolger
Alaska Court of Appeals, URL: http://www.state.ak.us/courts/ctinfo.htm
Chief Judge: David Mannheimer

LOCAL GOVERNMENT

According to the 2007 Census, Alaska is divided into 14 boroughs and 11 geographical Census Areas which encompass the 'Unorganized Borough'. Owing to the low population density, most of the land is located in the Unorganized Borough which is administered directly by the state government. Over 57 per cent of Alaska's area has this status, affecting over 13 per cent of the population. According to the 2007 Census Bureau survey of local governments, there are 14 county governments, three consolidated city-borough governments (Anchorage, Juneau, and Sitka), and 148 sub-county municipal governments. There are also 15 special districts. Public school systems number 54.

The borough governments are comparable to county governments other than the fact that they do not cover the entire state area. They are classified as home-rule, first, second or third class, according to their governmental powers. Generally, they are administered by a borough assembly.

Municipal governments are classified as home-rule cities, first or second class cities, according to the population. They are administered by a city government.

AREA AND POPULATION

Area
The largest state in the US, Alaska covers an area of 663,267.26 sq. miles, of which 571,951.26 sq. miles is land and 91,316.00 sq. miles is water. Alaska has more coastline than all the other U.S. states combined. Separated from the rest of the USA by around 500 miles of British Columbia (Canada), Alaska is an exclave of the United States. The state is bordered by the Yukon Territory and British Columbia to the east, the Gulf of Alaska and the Pacific Ocean to the south, the Bering Sea, Bering Strait, and Chukchi Sea to the west and the Arctic Ocean to the north. Alaska's territorial waters touch Russia's territorial waters in the Bering Strait, as the Russian and Alaskan islands are only 3 miles apart.

Alaska has the highest point in the USA, with Mount McKinley (20,320 feet).

In March 2009, the Mount Redoubt volcano erupted, sending a cloud of ash 15km into the air. The volcano, some 166km from Anchorage, last erupted over a four-month period from 1989 to 1990. Ash from the explosion fell on towns north of Anchorage.

To view a map, please consult http://www.lib.utexas.edu/maps/united_states/alaska_90.jpg

Population
The estimated population in 2012 was 731,449 according to US Census Bureau statistics, up from 723,860 in 2011. The population is expected to reach 867,674 by 2030. The population increased by 13.3 per cent over the period 2000-10. Alaska ranks 47th in terms of state population and has the lowest population density in the US: 1.2 persons per sq. mile. The area with the largest population is Anchorage Municipality, with 291,826 inhabitants in 2010. Juneau city and borough had a population of 31,275 in 2010, whilst Fairbanks city had 31,535 inhabitants. An estimated 7.5 per cent of the state population was under 5 years in 2011, 26.1 per cent under 18 years and 8.1 per cent over 65 years. Approximately 48 per cent of the population is female.

Native Alaskans - including Eskimos, Aleuts, and Indians - make up an estimated 14.8 per cent of the state's population.

Births, Marriages, Deaths
The US Census Bureau, Population Division, estimated that there were 11,471 births and 3,728 deaths in 2010. The fertility rate for females aged 15-44 years was 80 per 1,000. The death rate was 524.9 per 100,000 population. Infant deaths numbered 72 in 2007, equivalent to a rate of 6.51 infant deaths per 1,000 live births. Provisional estimates indicate that there were 5,774 marriages and 2,953 divorces in 2007.

Public Holidays
As well as celebrating US holidays Alaska also observes the following days:
31 March: Seward's Day (commemorates the signing of the treaty by which the United States bought Alaska from Russian in 1867)
18 October: Alaska Day (the anniversary of the formal transfer of the territory and the raising of the US flag at Sitka in 1867)

EMPLOYMENT

According to preliminary figures from the BLS, Alaska's total civilian labour force was 363,500 in December 2012, of which 339,400 were employed and 24,200 were unemployed. The unemployment rate was 6.6 per cent.

The following table shows seasonally adjusted non-farm wage and salary employment according to industry in December 2012 (preliminary figures):

Industry	No. of Jobs	Change over 12 months %
Mining and Logging	17,000	5.6
Construction	14,500	-2.7
Manufacturing	10,600	-4.5
Trade, transport and utilities	64,500	1.9
Information	6,400	0.0
Financial activities	14,900	0.0
Professional and business services	27.300	-0.7
Educational and health services	47,000	3.5
Leisure and hospitality	31,600	-1.6
Other services	10.900	2.8
Government	84,000	-0.7
TOTAL	328,700	0.6

Source: Bureau of Labor Statistics

BANKING AND FINANCE

GDP/GNP, Inflation, National Debt
Alaska's Gross Domestic Product (current dollars) reached an estimated US$51.4 million in 2011 and the state was ranked 44th in the USA in this respect in 2010. In 2010, Alaska contributed 0.3 per cent of US total GDP. In 2010, GDP rose by 1.9 per cent. In 2011, it grew by 2.5 per cent, compared to the national change of 1.5 per cent. The largest industry in 2011 was mining (24.5 per cent of total GDP), followed by government (19.3 per cent).

GDP per Industry, figures in millions of dollars

Industry	2009	2010	2011
Agriculture, forestry, fishing, hunting	277	268	289
Mining	9,471	10,192	12,573
Utilities	614	634	600
Construction	1,889	1,882	1,832
Manufacturing	1,582	1,841	2,112
Wholesale Trade	1,008	1,072	1,111
Retail Trade	1,877	1,994	2,060
Transportation & warehousing	4,771	4,891	5,074
Information	1,072	1,066	1,130
Finance & insurance	1,559	1,961	1,946
Real estate, rental and leasing	4,027	3,912	3,877
Educational services	127	130	132
Health care and social assistance	2,594	2,818	3,023
Other non-government services	5,022	5,386	5,676

- continued

Government	9,369	9,665	9,941
TOTAL	45,260	47,713	51,376

Source: Bureau of Economic Analysis, Feb. 2013

The average per capita real GDP in the state was US$61,853 in 2011, more than the US per capita GDP of $42,470. The Alaskans had the 3rd highest national per capita GDP in 2011. Per capita personal income reached $45,655 in 2011. (Source: BEA)

The annual Consumer Price Index for the Anchorage urban area (all items) rose from 195.144 in 2010 to 201.427 in 2011 to 205.8 in 2012 (1982-84 = 100). (Source: Bureau of Labor Statistics).

Balance of Payments / Imports and Exports

Alaska's exports were valued at US$4,155 million in 2010 (up 25.5 per cent on the previous year) and at US$5,325 million in 2011 (up 28 per cent) and contributed 0.4 per cent of the USA's total exports in 2011. Major exports are fish products, crude oil and natural gas, metal mining, forest products, chemicals and allied products.

The following table shows merchandise export revenue from the top five international destinations in 2011:

Destination	2010 ($m)	2011 ($m)	+/-% 2010-11
China	921	1,477	60.3
Japan	1,218	1,086	-10.8
South Korea	477	642	34.6
Canada	390	586	50.2
Germany	174	261	49.9

Source: US Census Bureau, Foreign Trade Division

Top five export products in 2011, according to revenue, are shown on the following table:

Product	$m
Zinc ores and concentrates	972
Fish fillets, frozen	519
Lead ores and concentrates	495
Fish meat, excl. fish steaks and fillets, frozen	319
Pacific salmon, nesoi	293

Source: US Census Bureau, Foreign Trade

Imports totalled US$1,826 million in 2011, compared with US$1,476 million in 2010, an increase of 23.7 per cent. Main imported products are oil, crude oil and copper ores and concentrates. Top suppliers are Canada (30.8 per cent), China (21.8 per cent) and South Korea (20.4 per cent).

Chambers of Commerce and Trade Organisations

Alaska State Chamber of Commerce, URL: http://www.alaskachamber.com/
Alaska Department of Community and Economic Development, URL: http://www.dced.state.ak.us/
Anchorage Economic Development Corporation (AEDC), URL: http://www.aedcweb.com/

MANUFACTURING, MINING AND SERVICES

Primary and Extractive Industries

According to the BEA, the mining industry is the largest contributor towards Alaska's Gross Domestic Product, accounting for $12,573 million of the state GDP in 2011 (up from $10,192 million in 2010). In 2010, the oil and gas extraction sector contributed $7,835 million, all other mining accounted for $1,101 million, and support activities earned $1,256 million. Oil revenues contribute almost 85 per cent of Alaska's state budget.

Alaska is a leading supplier of crude oil. Proven reserves of crude oil were 3,722 million barrels in January 2010, ranking the state 2nd in the US (excluding Federal Offshore reserves). Reserves are approximately 16 per cent of US total. Crude oil production was 0.6 million barrrels bbl/d in 2011, ranking the state 2nd in the US (excl. offshore production). Alaska accounts for almost 10.9 per cent of US oil production and 17.2 per cent of total US crude oil proven reserves. There are 1,769 wells in production, and seven rotary rigs. Refining capacity was an estimated 384,792 barrels per day. Demand for petroleum products is low in Alaska. Oil consumption in 2009 totalled 45.4 million barrels.

There are six main oil fields in Alaska: Prudhoe Bay, Kuparuk, Milne Point, Endicott, Cook Inlet and Lisburne. Prudhoe Bay is the highest yielding oil field in the USA, producing around 264,000 barrels per day.

Dry natural gas reserves were estimated at 8,838 billion cubic feet (2.9 per cent of the US total) in 2010. In 2010, there were also 288 million barrels of natural gas plant liquids. There were 277 natural gas producing wells in the same year, and marketed dry production reached 397,077 million cubic feet. Total natural gas consumption in 2010 was 333,316 million cubic feet, down from 427,288 million cubic feet in 2000. Industry was the largest consumer by a large margin and a sizeable proportion was used for generating electricity.

Other major mining sectors are coal, silver, zinc and gold. In 2011, there was one surface coal mine in Alaska, producing 2,149,000 short tons of coal (0.2 per cent of US total). (Source: EIA)

Energy

Alaska's total energy consumption in 2008 was 630 trillion Btu., whilst production fell to 1,743 trillion Btu in 2010. Per capita energy consumption in 2010 was 899 million Btu, ranking the state 2nd in the US, where the national average per capita consumption was approximately 361 million Btu. Total energy consumption amounted to 642 trillion Btu in 2010, of which petroleum 48.8 million barrels, natural gas 332,723 million cu ft,

Most Alaskan consumers are not linked to large, interconnected grids through transmission and distribution lines. An interconnected grid exists in the populated areas (from Fairbanks to south of Anchorage); however, rural communities rely on their own power sources, almost exclusively using diesel electric generators.

Natural gas fuels around three-fifths of Alaska's electricity generation, and hydroelectric power supplies more than one-fifth. Petroleum and coal each account for nearly one-tenth of net electricity generation. Alaskans also operate one of the Nation's largest fuel cell systems, in Anchorage, and the world's largest battery storage system.

Alaska's electricity generating fuels are gas (60.8 per cent of industry generation in 2006), hydroelectric (18.3 per cent), petroleum (11.5 per cent) and coal (9.2 per cent). More than 50 hydroelectric power plants supply Alaskan communities. Alaska's renewable energy sources also include a 200-KW geothermal plant at Chena Hot Springs and two small wind farms. Net summer capacity in 2010 was 2,067 MW (0.2 per cent of US total).

Plans are being discussed to develop two small nuclear facilities to help meet demand. (Source: EIA)

Manufacturing

The manufacturing industry contributed an estimated $2,112 million towards the 2011 Gross Domestic Product (up from $1,841 million in 2010). The largest GDP-earning sectors in 2010 were petroleum and coal product manufacturing ($928 million) and food, beverage and tobacco product manufacturing ($645 million).

Service Industries

The services industry is Alaska's third largest industry. The highest revenue comes from the transportation and warehousing sector, which earned $5,074 million in 2011. Real estate, rental and leasing sector contributed an estimated $3,877 million towards state GDP in 2011, and other main service sectors included health services ($3,023 million) and professional and technical services ($2,234 million).

Tourism

Alaska receives over 1.1 million visitors per year and the sector employs around 26,000 people, approximately 13 per cent of the state's total number of employees. The accommodation and food sector contributed an estimated $1,244 million towards Alaska's GDP in 2011, whilst the arts, entertainment and recreation sector accounted for $299 million.

Agriculture

The agriculture, forestry and fisheries industry contributed around $289 million towards Alaska's 2011 GDP, up from $268 million in 2010. In 2010, the forestry, fishing and related activities sector contributed $256 million, whilst the farms (crop and animal production) sector contributed $12 million.

In 2007, according to the Census of Agriculture, Alaska had 689 farms, up from 609 in 2002, covering some 881,585 acres. The average size of a farm is 1,285 acres. In 2010 the number of farms was estimated at 680. In 2010, net farm income for crops amounted to $23.8 million, animal ouput was $6.3 million, and services and forestry $7.985 million. Alaska is ranked 50th in the USA for agricultural product revenue. Greenhouse goods are the state's largest agricultural earner. As of Jan. 2011, there were an estimated 13,500 cattle and 1,200 hogs. (Source: USDA)

The forestry industry has 28 million acres of commercial forest which supplies logs, lumber and pulp to world markets. The Tongass National Forest covers 16.8 million acres and the Chugach National Forest covers 4.8 million acres.

Alaska's fishing industry produces in the region of 6 billion pounds of seafood per year. The state is ranked 12th in terms of aquaculture, and earned $28.5 million in 2007. The industry's main harvest is salmon.

COMMUNICATIONS AND TRANSPORT

National Airlines

Alaska Airlines, URL: http://www.alaskaair.com
Yute Air Alaska, URL: http://www.yuteair.com/

International Airports

Two international airports service Alaska: Anchorage International Airport and Fairbanks International Airport. More than 4.87 million people used Anchorage International Airport in 2004 and 4.9 billion pieces of freight were transported through the airport in the same year.
Anchorage International Airport, URL: http://www.dot.state.ak.us/external/aias/aia/aiawlcm.html
Fairbanks International Airport, URL: http://www1.dot.state.ak.us/faiiap/

Railways

The Alaska Railroad runs from the Kenai Peninsula in the south, to Anchorage in the north and toNenana and Fairbanks in the interior. The railroad has been a state-owned corporation since 1985. The railroad was originally built in 1914, to provide transport for gold and other minerals from the interior to port, for onward shipping. Today, 75 per cent of the activities of the corporation revolve around freight transport.
Alaska Railroad Corporation, URL: http://www.akrr.com/

UNITED STATES OF AMERICA

Shipping
Passenger and vehicle ferries connect Haines to Juneau and Skagway.
Alaska Marine Highway, URL: http://www.dot.state.ak.us/amhs/

Ports and Harbours
For the Inside Passage route, there are ferry ports in Bellingham, Prince Rupert, Ketchikan, Wrangell, Petersburg, Sitka, Juneau/Auke Bay, Haines and Skagway. For south central and south west routes there are ferry terminals in Anchorage, Cordova, Homer, Seldovia, Seward, Valdez and Kodiak.
Haines Ferry Terminal. URL: http://haines.ak.us/hainesweb/

HEALTH

Figures published by the National Centre for Health Statistics, (NCHS) indicate that there were 24.2 doctors (including osteopaths) per 10,000 Alaskans in 2009 (compared with the overall US average of 27.4 per 10,000 citizens). In 2008, there were 505 dentists (7.4 per 10,000 population). In 2009, there were 2.2 community hospital beds per 1,000 people. In 2010, there were 15 nursing homes, with a total of 682 beds. In the same period there were 641 residents. Over the period 2007-09, it was estimated that 18.6 per cent of Alaskans had no health insurance cover. (Source: NCHS, Health, USA, 2012)

Alaska reported 730 HIV/AIDS cases cumulatively from the beginning of the epidemic through to December 2008. Alaska ranked 44th in the cumulative number of cases reported by end 2008. Alaska ranked 3rd in cases of TB (7.3 per 100,000 population). Due to vaccination programmes, between 2000 and 2005 reports of acute hepatitis A fell by 71 per cent, and reports of Hep.B decreased by 43 per cent. In 2008, vaccination rates were 64 per cent. In 2011, 65 per cent of Alaskans were overweight or obese, and some 26 per cent were obese (30th in US). (Source: National Center for Chronic Disease Prevention and Health Promotion) It was estimated that in 2007-11, 9.5 per cent of Alaskans were living in poverty, much lower than the US average of 14.3 per cent.

EDUCATION

Primary/Secondary Education
In the year 2009-10 there were an estimated 131,661 primary and secondary school students attending state schools (falling to an estimated 129,000 in 2011). There were 516 elementary and secondary schools. Teachers numbered 8,083 in the same year, and the teacher/pupil ratio was 16.3 to one. In 2007-08, total state revenue from education was $2.3 billion, and current expenditure on public education reached $2.3 billion.

Higher Education
In 2010-11, there were seven degree granting institutions in Alaska, the main one being the University of Alaska. An estimated 19,645 women and 12,761 men were enrolled. In the same year, 4,625 degrees were conferred, of which 1,619 were Bachelors, 681 were Masters degrees and 45 were doctorates. (Source: National Center for Education Statistics)

COMMUNICATIONS AND MEDIA

Newspapers
Alaska's newspapers include: Alaska Star, Anchorage Daily News, The Anchorage Press, Bush Blade, Capitol City Weekly and The Boat Broker, Fairbanks Daily News-Miner, Frontiersman, Juneau Empire, The Nome Nugget.
Anchorage Daily News, URL: http://www.adn.com/news/alaska/

Business Journals
The Alaska Journal of Commerce, URL: http://www.alaskajournal.com/

Telecommunications
Alaska Power and Telephone. Provides service to communities located above the Arctic Circle, in the Wrangell Mountains and throughout the islands of Southeast Alaska. URL: http://www.aptalaska.com/
GCI Cable. URL: http://www.gci.com/

ENVIRONMENT

Because of Alaska's reliance on gas and hydro as primary electricity generating fuels, toxic emissions from the electricity generating industry are relatively low, totalling (2010) 4.125 million metric tons of carbon dioxide, 3,015 metric tons of sulfur dioxide and 16,028 metric tons of nitrogen oxide. Alaska ranked 46th in 2010 in the US in terms of power industry emissions of carbon dioxide. Approximately 2,712 alternative-fuelled vehicles were in use in 2010. Approximately 770,000 barrels of ethanol were consumed in 2011. (Source: EIA)

ARIZONA

Capital: Phoenix (Population, Census 2010: 1,445,632)

Head of State: Janice K. Brewer (R) (Governor) (page 1394)

State Flag: The lower half is blue, the upper half is divided into 13 alternate colour segments, seven of red and six of yellow. Superimposed on the centre of the flag is a copper coloured five-pointed star

CONSTITUTION AND GOVERNMENT

Constitution
Arizona entered the Union on 14 February 1912 as the 48th state. The executive branch of government is headed by the governor, who is assisted by nine other elected officers: the attorney general, secretary of state, state treasurer, state mine inspector, superintendent of public instruction, and four corporation commissioners. All but the corporation commissioners hold office for a maximum of two consecutive four-year terms. The four corporation commissioners serve a single term of six years. The state mine inspector is the only elected mine inspector in the US. Arizona elects two Senators to the US Senate and eight Representatives to the US House of Representatives.

To consult the state constitution, please visit: http://www.azleg.state.az.us/Constitution.asp

Legislature
Arizona's bicameral legislature is composed of the Senate and the House of Representatives. Elections are held every even-numbered year.

Upper House
The Senate has 30 members who are elected every two years. Following the 2012 elections, Arizona's Senate was composed of 17 Republicans and 13 Democrats.
Arizona State Senate, Capitol Complex, 1700 West Washington, Phoenix, AZ 85007-2890, USA. Tel: +1 602 926 3559 (Info Desk), fax: +1 602 926 3429, URL: http://www.azsenate.gov/

Lower House
The House of Representatives has 60 members who are elected every two years. Following the 2012 elections, the House was composed of 36 Republicans and 24 Democrats.
Arizona House of Representatives, Capitol Complex, 1700 West Washington, Phoenix, AZ 85007-2890, USA. Tel: +1 602 926 4221 (Info Desk), fax: +1 602 542 4511, URL: http://www.azhouse.gov/

Elected Executive Branch Officials (as at April 2013)
Governor: Janice Brewer (R) (page 1394)
Secretary of State: Ken Bennett

Attorney General: Tom Horne
State Treasurer: Doug Ducey
Superintendent of Public Instruction: John Huppenthal
State Mine Inspector: Joseph A. Hart
Corporation Commissioners: Brenda Burns, Bob Stump, Gary Pierce, Susan Bittersmith, Bob Burns

---

Legislature (as at April 2013)
President of the Senate: Andy Biggs (R)
Senate Majority Leader: John McComish (R)
Majority Whip: Adam Driggs (R)
President Pro-tempore: Gail Griffen (R)
Minority Leader: Leah Landrum Taylor (D)
Minority Whip: Anna Tovar (D)
Speaker of the House: Andy Tobin (R)
House Majority Leader: David Gowan, Sr (R)
House Minority Leader: Chad Campbell (D)

US Senators: Jeff Flake (R) (page 1425) and John McCain (R) (page 1473)

Ministries
Office of the Governor, State Capitol Executive Tower, 1700 West Washington, Ninth Floor, Phoenix, AZ 85007, USA. Tel: +1 602 542 4331, fax: +1 602 542 1381, URL: http://www.governor.state.az.us
Office of the Attorney General, 1275 W. Washington Street, Phoenix, AZ 85007, USA. Tel: +1 602 542 5025, fax: +1 602 542 4085, URL: http://www.azag.gov/
Office of the Secretary of State, 1700 W Washington, 7th Floor, Phoenix, AZ 85007-2888, USA. Tel: +1 602 542 4285, e-mail: sosadmin@sos.state.az.us, URL: http://www.azsos.gov/
Office of the State Treasurer, 1700 West Washington Street, 1st Floor, Phoenix, Arizona 85007, USA. Tel: +1 602 604 7800, fax: +1 602 542 7176, e-mail: ingo@aztreasury.gov, URL: http://www.aztreasury.gov/
Office of the Superintendent of Public Instruction, Arizona Department of Education, 1535 West Jefferson Street, Bin 2, Phoenix, Arizona 85007, USA. Tel: +1 602 542 5460, fax: +1 602 542 5440, URL: http://www.ade.state.az.us/administration/superintendent/
Office of the State Mine Inspector, 1700 West Washington, Fourth Floor, Phoenix, AZ 85007-2805, USA. Tel: +1 602 542 5971, fax: +1 602 542 5335, e-mail: Admin@mi.state.az.us, URL: http://www.asmi.state.az.us/
Arizona Department of Agriculture, 1688 West Adams, Phoenix, AZ 85007, USA. Tel: +1 602 542 4373, URL: http://www.agriculture.state.az.us/

Arizona Department of Commerce, 1700 W. Washington, Suite 600, Phoenix, AZ 85007, USA. Tel: +1 602 771 1100, URL: http://www.azcommerce.com/
Department of Education, 1535 W. Jefferson, Phoenix, AZ 85007, USA. Tel: +1 602 542 5393, URL: http://www.azed.gov/
Department of Environmental Quality, 1110 W. Washington Street, Phoenix, AZ 85007, USA. Tel: +1 602 207 2300, URL: http://www.adeq.gov
Department of Health Services, 150 North 18th Avenue, Phoenix, Arizona 85007, USA. Tel: +1 602 542 1000, fax: +1 602 542 0883, URL: http://www.azdhs.gov/
Department of Transportation, 206 South 17th Avenue, Mail Drop 101A, Room 135, Phoenix, Arizona 85007, USA. Tel: +1 602 712 7011, URL: http://www.azdot.gov

Political Parties
Arizona Democratic Party, URL: http://www.azdem.org/
Republican Party of Arizona, URL: http://www.azgop.org/

Elections
In the November 2012 legislative elections, all 30 Senate seats were up for election. The Republicans still hold the majority but lost 4 seats: 17 seats compared to the Democrats' 13 seats. In the House of Representatives all 60 seats were up for election. The Republicans lost four seats (36 Republican seats and 24 Democrat seats).

In 2006, the Democrats' Janet Napolitano won a second term in the Governor's office. Governor Janice Brewer took over the post mid-term when the incumbent governor, Janet Napolitano, (page 1484) was appointed US Secretary of Homeland Security, in January 2009. Governor Brewer was re-elected in November 2010.

Three state executive positions (three officers within the Arizona Corporation Commission) were up for election on 6 November 2012. Two incumbents, Paul Newman and Sandra Kennedy lost their positions. Incumbent Bob Stump, former Senate president Bob Burns and Susan Bitter-Smith were elected for four-year terms.

LEGAL SYSTEM

Arizona's court system consists of the Supreme Court, the Court of Appeals (Division One and Division Two), the Superior Court (seven, one per county), Justice of the Peace Courts, and Municipal Courts. There are a total of five justices at the Supreme Court, including the Chief Justice. The Chief Justice is selected by fellow justices to serve a term of five years, whilst the remaining four justices serve for terms of six years.

Arizona still uses the death penalty. As of January 2013, 128 inmates were on death row of which three were women. Six people were executed in 2012. The murder rate is 6.4 per 100,000 population. In 2006, Arizona became the first state to reject an anti-gay marriage amendment in midterm elections. Although same-sex marriage is illegal in Arizona, the amendment would have denied legal or financial benefits to unmarried homosexual or heterosexual couples. In 2008, Arizona passed an amendment to the state constitution to define marriage as a union of one man and one woman.

Supreme Court, URL: http://www.azcourts.gov/
Chief Justice: Rebecca White Berch
Vice Chief Justice: Scott Bales
Justice: A. John Pelander, Robert M. Brutinel, Ann Scott Timmer
Court of Appeals (Division One), URL: http://azcourts.gov/coa1/Home.aspx
Chief Judge: Lawrence F. Winthrop
Court of Appeals (Division Two), URL: http://www.appeals2.az.gov/
Chief Judge: Joseph W. Howard

LOCAL GOVERNMENT

Arizona is divided into 15 county governments and 90 incorporated cities or towns which have their own governments in the form of a city or town council. In addition Arizona has 239 school district governments, 301 special purpose governments, and 14 dependent public school systems.

There are also a number of Indian reservations in Arizona representing, amongst others, the Apache, Navajo, Hopi, and Mohave tribes. The state of Arizona does not tax Indian lands, Indian owned property on reservations, or incomes derived by Indians if derived from reservation sources.

AREA AND POPULATION

Area
Arizona is located in the West of the US, west of New Mexico, south of Utah, and east of California and Nevada. Arizona's total area is 113,998.30 sq. miles, of which 113,634.57 sq. miles is land and 363.73 sq. miles is water.

To view a map of the state, please consult http://www.lib.utexas.edu/maps/us_2001/arizona_ref_2001.jpg

Population
The 2010 census put the population at 6,392,017, down on the mid-2009 estimate of 6,595,778. By comparison, the population increase over the year 2008-09 was the 7th largest in terms of numbers, and was largely due to migration to the state. Since 2000, the population has grown by 28.6 per cent, the nation's fifth highest percentage increase. In 2012, the population was estimated to be 6,553,255. The population is expected to reach 10.7 million

by 2030. An estimated 6.9 per cent of the population is under 5 years, 25.1 per cent under 18 years and 14.2 per cent is aged over 65 years. According to the Census, 50.3 per cent of the state population is female.

According to the 2010 Census, approximately 65.9 per cent of the population is white, 6.5 per cent is black, 2.2 per cent American Indian and 3.2 per cent Asian. Approximately 40.8 per cent of the population is of Hispanic or Latino origin.

The population of Arizona ranks 14th in the USA. Arizona's population density is around 57.2 people per sq. mile. The county with the greatest number of inhabitants is Maricopa County, with a population of 3,072,149. Arizona's capital and county seat is Phoenix, with a population density of 2,781.9 people per sq. mile. Native Indian groups make up about 6 per cent of Arizona's population, and include the Hopi and the Navajo.

Births, Marriages, Deaths
According to the latest US Census Bureau (Population Division) reports (CDC), there were 87,477 births in 2010 and 46,762 deaths. The fertility rate was 69.3 per 1,000 women aged 15-44 years and the death rate was 731.6 per 100,000 population. The infant mortality rate in 2007 was 6.9 deaths of infants under the age of one for every 1,000 live births. Marriages and divorces in 2007 numbered 39,495 and 24,515 respectively, both up on the figure for 2006.

EMPLOYMENT

Of a total civilian labour force of 3,019,700 in December 2012, Arizona had 2,781,400 people in employment, and 238,300 registered unemployed. The unemployment rate in the same month was 7.9 per cent. (Source: US Bureau of Labor Statistics, preliminary figures)

Provisional non-farm wage and salary employment (seasonally adjusted) in December 2012, according to industry, is shown on the following table:

Industry	No. of employed	Change over 12 mths. %
Mining and logging	11,800	0.0
Construction	119,800	6.2
Manufacturing	152,700	2.4
Trade, transport and utilities	487,700	2.7
Information	36,600	-2.7
Financial activities	171,100	2.5
Professional and business services	356,600	4.3
Educational and health services	367,300	2.4
Leisure and hospitality	262,600	2.6
Other services	87,800	-1.9
Government	417,000	1.6
TOTAL	2,479,300	2.7

Source: Bureau of Labor Statistics

BANKING AND FINANCE

GDP/GNP, Inflation, National Debt
Arizona's Gross Domestic Product (current dollars) rose from $249,824 million in 2010 to an estimated $258,447 million in 2011. In 2009, the state was ranked 4th in the US in terms of GDP value. Real GDP contracted by 0.6 per cent (below the US growth rate of two per cent), representing a sharp fall from the state's growth rates of 8.7 per cent in 2005 and 6.7 per cent in 2006. GDP rose by 0.7 per cent in 2010.

The following table shows state Gross Domestic Product according to industry (millions of current dollars):

Industry	2009	2010	2011
Agriculture, forestry, fishing	1,520	1,920	2,319
Mining	3,644	4,199	5,303
Utilities	5,721	5,619	5,164
Construction	12,985	11,739	12,086
Manufacturing	18,022	20,131	21,827
Wholesale Trade	13,429	13,463	14,061
Retail Trade	18,235	18,692	19,397
Transportation & warehousing	6,827	7,029	7,440
Information	6,593	6,391	6,603
Finance & Insurance	19,364	22,095	22,830
Real Estate	40,092	37,671	37,191
Educational services	2,555	2,812	2,973
Health care and social assistance	19,993	21,139	22,012
Other non-government services	43,373	44,758	46,664
Government	33,210	32,166	32,621
TOTAL	245,664	249,824	258,447

Source: Bureau of Economic Analysis, Feb. 2013

Arizona's per capita personal income averaged $35,062 (84 per cent of national average of US$41,560), up 3.8 per cent from 2010. The state's per capita real GDP in 2011 was $35,032 per annum (national per capita GDP US$42,070).

The annual Consumer Price Index (CPI) for the Phoenix urban area (all items) rose from 117.5 in 2009 to 118.2 in 2010 and 121.48 in 2011. (Dec. 2001 = 100). (Source: Bureau of Labor Statistics)

UNITED STATES OF AMERICA

Balance of Payments / Imports and Exports

Total export revenue rose from \$15,636 million in 2010 to \$17,793 million in 2011, indicating an increase of 13.8 per cent. An estimated 1.2 per cent of the US total export revenue originated from Arizona in 2011. Major export products are electrical machinery, machinery, aircraft and spacecraft, medical instruments (including optical equipment) and plastics. (Source: US Census Bureau, Foreign Trade Division).

The top five export trading partners in 2011, according to export revenue, are shown on the following table:

Country	2010 ($m)	2011 ($m)	+/-% 2010-11
Mexico	5,053	5,972	18.2
Canada	1,961	2,135	8.9
China	1,037	1,003	-3.3
Japan	624	837	34.2
UK	658	793	20.5

Source: US Census Bureau

Total imports amounted to \$17,659 million in 2011, up from \$15,263 million in 2010, up 12.5 per cent on the previous year and accounting for 0.8 per cent of the US total. Main imports include processors and controllers, tomatoes and electronic circuits. Main suppliers are Mexico (35.1 per cent), China (13.9 per cent) and Japan (9.7 per cent).

Chambers of Commerce and Trade Organisations

Arizona Chamber of Commerce, URL: http://www.azchamber.com/
Arizona Department of Commerce, URL: http://www.azcommerce.com/
Greater Phoenix Chamber of Commerce, URL: http://www.phoenixchamber.com/index.cfm

MANUFACTURING, MINING AND SERVICES

Primary and Extractive Industries

According to the BEA, mining contributed \$5,303 million towards Arizona's 2011 Gross State Product (up from \$4,199 million in 2010). In 2010, \$4,090 million came from the non-oil and gas mining sector, and \$107 million was earned through support activities. Just \$2 million came from oil and gas extraction.

Arizona's major mined resources include oil, natural gas, liquified petroleum gas (LPG) and salt. Arizona's crude oil reserves account for less than one per cent of US crude oil reserves. In 2010 crude oil production from Arizona's 19 producing oil wells was around 40,000 barrels per year. Total petroleum consumption in 2010 fell slightly to 98.6 million barrels, most of which was used as motor gasoline (62.3 million barrels).

Arizona has five gas wells. Marketed natural gas production was 168 million cu ft in 2010. Natural gas consumption increased from 205,235 million cubic feet in 2000 to 393,039 million cubic feet in 2007. Consumption fell to 289,357 million cu ft in 2011 (1.2 per cent of US total). The electric power sector dominates natural gas consumption in Arizona, using approximately three quarters of the State supply. A new natural gas-fired power plant in Coolidge was completed in 2011.

Arizona's coal production takes place primarily in the Black Mesa Basin. In 2011, coal production was 8,111,000 short tons of coal. Consumption of coal amounted to 23,719 thousand short tons in 2011 (2.4 per cent of US total). (Source: EIA)

Energy

Total energy production was 588 trillion Btu in 2010 (0.8 per cent of US total). Arizona's total energy consumption was 1,400 trillion Btu in 2010, (1.4 per cent of US total). Per capita energy consumption in 2010 was 218 million Btu, ranking the state 46th in the US.

Arizona is a net exporter of electricity. The primary generating fuel is coal, which was used in approximately 42 per cent of power generation in 2011. Nuclear generation accounted for 24 per cent of generation, natural gas 25.4 per cent, and hydroelectric 7.1 per cent. Net summer capability in 2010 was 26,392 MW.

The Palo Verde nuclear generating station, the largest in the US, is located on a 4,050 acre site near Wintersburg, Arizona, and serves about four million people. It is rated at 3,937 net MW.

Arizona requires that 15 per cent of the electricity consumption in 2025 should come from renewable energy sources. In 2011, 9 per cent of net electricity generation came from renewable resources, mainly the Glen Canyon and Hoover Dams. As of January 2012, its solar photovoltaic installations had a capacity of 273 MW (3rd in the US). (Source: EIA)

Manufacturing

Manufacturing is the fourth largest contributor to Arizona's GDP, accounting for an estimated \$21,827 million in 2011 (up from \$20,131 million in 2010). The largest sectors in 2010 were computer and electronic equipment (\$7,921 million), transport equipment other than motor vehicles and parts (\$2,850million), and chemical manufacturing (\$1,450 million).

Service Industries

The services industry is Arizona's largest contributor to GDP. In 2010, the most important sector in terms of revenues was the real estate and rental and leasing sector (\$37,191 million). The finance and insurance sector contributed an estimated \$20,830 million. Professional and technical services and health services were also important contributors to GDP in 2010, contributing \$16,021 million and \$22,012 million respectively.

Tourism

In 2010 revenue from the accommodation and food sector reached an estimated \$9,015 million, whilst arts, entertainment and recreation earned around US\$2,386 million. More than 2.26 million people visited Arizona's state parks in 2004 and over 11.5 million people visited its national parks. 4.7 million people visited the Grand Canyon. There were nearly 633,000 visitors from overseas, 22 per cent of whom were from the UK.
Arizona Office of Tourism, URL: http://www.arizonaguide.com/home.asp

Agriculture

The agriculture, forestry, fishing and hunting sector contributed an estimated \$2,319 million towards Arizona's GDP in 2011 (up from \$1,920 million in 2010). Farming contributed \$1,464 million in 2010, whilst forestry, fishing and related activities contributed \$457 million in the same year.

According to the USDA 2007 Census of Agriculture, Arizona's farms number around 15,600, (up from around 8,500 in 1997, whilst total farmland is down from 27,169,627 acres in 1997 to around 26,100,000 acres. The average size of a farm has fallen from 3,194 acres in 1997 to 1,673 acres in 2007. Arizona's mild climate and sunshine make it a major crop-growing state. Major crops include cotton, broccoli, cantaloupe, cauliflower, lettuce, melon, dry onions, grapefruit, apples and grapes. As of 1 Jan. 2011, there were 870,000 cattle and calves, 165,000 hogs and pigs and 150,000 shepp.

The total value of agricultural products sold in 2007 reached \$3.2 billion. Of this, crops earned \$1.9 billion whilst livestock, poultry and their products earned \$1.3 billion.

COMMUNICATIONS AND TRANSPORT

International Airports

Arizona's international airports include Phoenix Sky Harbor International Airport, Tucson International Airport and Yuma International Airport. The air transport sector has been hit by the global economic downturn; in February 2009 just over 2.8 million passengers used Phoenix Sky Harbor airport (down 14.4 per cent on February 2008), and 18.934 tons of cargo were handled (down 18.8 per cent on the previous February). Aircraft operations were down by 17.2 per cent.
Phoenix Sky Harbor International Airport, URL: http://www.phxskyharbor.com/index.html
Yuma International Airport, URL: http://yumainternationalairport.com/
Tucson Airport Authority, URL: http://www.tucsonairport.org

HEALTH

National Centre for Health Statistics figures indicate that there were 22.6 doctors (including osteopaths) per 10,000 inhabitants in 2009 (compared with the national average of 27.4). In the same year, there were 2.0 community hospital beds per 1,000 residents, and, in 2010, 16,460 beds in 139 nursing homes. There were an estimated 3,302 dentists in 2008 (5.1 per 10,000 population). It was estimated that 19.1 per cent of people aged 18-64 did not have health insurance cover in 2007-09.

In 2007, 8.4 per cent of adults suffered from diabetes, compared to the national average of eight per cent. In 2012, 64.8 per cent of adults were overweight and just 24.3 per cent were obese (body mass index 30.0+), the national average is 26.2 per cent; the obesity prevalence was up from 19.2 in 2000. In 2007, almost 30 per cent of adults exercised for over 20 minutes at least three times per week. Almost 20 per cent of the population are smokers. According to the US Census Bureau, in the period 2007-11 an estimated 16.2 per cent of the state's inhabitants lived in poverty, compared to 14.1 per cent nationally.

Arizona reported 11,747 HIV/AIDS cases from the beginning of the epidemic to the end of 2008, ranking it 21st highest among the 50 states. In 2009, 540 further cases were diagnosed. Arizona has one of the nation's highest teen pregnancy and teen birth rates. (Source: National Center for Chronic Disease Prevention and Health Promotion)

EDUCATION

Primary/Secondary Education

According to US NCES figures, there were 1,077,831 pupils enrolled in the state's public elementary and secondary schools during the 2009-10 academic year. There were 2,325 schools, with a total of 51,947 teachers. The overall teacher/pupil ratio was 1: 20.7.

State revenue from education in 2007-08 reached US\$10.3 billion, whilst current state expenditure on education was \$10.3 billion.

Higher Education

Arizona's higher education institutions include: Arizona State University, Arizona State University West, Grand Canyon University, Northern Arizona University, University of Arizona. There are 84 degree granting institutions altogether. For the academic year 2010-11, 305,782 men were enrolled and 522,849 women. An estimated 158,822 degrees were conferred in 2010-11, 44,339 of which were Bachelors, 34,856 were Masters and 2,684 were Doctorates. (Source: National Center for Education Statistics)

COMMUNICATIONS AND MEDIA

Newspapers

Arizona newspapers include: Arizona Daily Star, Tucson; Arizona Business Gazette, Phoenix; The Business Journal, Phoenix; The Daily Territorial, Tucson; New Times, Phoenix; and The Tucson Citizen, Tucson. The Arizona Republic is the largest newspaper in the Greater Phoenix Area and has a circulation of around 500,000.
Arizona Newspapers Association, URL: http://www.ananews.com/

The Arizona Republic, URL: http://www.azcentral.com/

Business Journals
The Business Journal, URL: http://phoenix.bcentral.com/phoenix/

ENVIRONMENT

Arizona's electricity industry relies on coal as a primary fuel source. As a result carbon dioxide emissions are high; in 2010, approximately 55.683 million metric tons of carbon dioxide emissions were produced (ranking it 15th in US), 33,371 metric tons of sulfur dioxide and 57,244 metric tons of nitrogen oxide. Arizona's first refinery is expected to become operational in 2012 and will be specifically designed to produce clean petroleum fuels such as CARB3 (California Air Resources Board fuel specification), Arizona Clean Burning Gasoline, and ultra-low sulfur gasoline. Arizona has one ethanol plant with a capacity of 55 million gallons per year. Current (2011) ethanol consumption is 7,523 thousand barrels. Approximately 39,343 alternative-fuelled vehicles were in use. (Source: EIA)

ARKANSAS

Capital: Little Rock (Population, Census 2010: 193,524)

Head of State: Mike Beebe (D) (Governor) (page 1385)

State Flag: A white rhombus containing four blue, five-pointed stars and the word 'ARKANSAS' also in blue, with a wide blue border emblazoned with 25 white, five-pointed stars on a red background

CONSTITUTION AND GOVERNMENT

Constitution
Arkansas became the 25th State of the Union on 15 June 1836. According to the 1874 constitution, the executive branch of state government is headed by the governor assisted by six other elected officials: lieutenant governor, secretary of state, attorney general, auditor of state, treasurer of state, and land commissioner. All are elected for a maximum of two four-year terms.

Arkansas sends two representatives to the US Senate and four representatives to the US Congress.

To view the state constitution, please visit:
http://www.arkleg.state.ar.us/data/constitution/ArkansasConstitution1874.pdf

Recent events
On 3rd May 2008, at least eight people were killed when violent storms and tornadoes swept across the central United States. At least two dozen people were injured, and some 350 homes were damaged. Around 6,000 homes and businesses lost power. Other states affected included Kansas, Missouri, Oklahoma and Texas.

Legislature
The Arkansas legislature is known as the General Assembly and consists of the Senate and House of Representatives. The present Arkansas Constitution calls for the General Assembly to meet for 60 days each odd-numbered year. Members serve in the state legislature part-time.

Upper House
The State Senate consists of 35 members, all elected for four years. Each Senator represents about 76,380 people. Following the 2012 elections, the Senate was divided into 14 Democrat seats and 21 Republican seats. The Lieutenant Governor also serves as the Senate President, to be replaced in times of absence by the Senate President Pro Tempore.
Arkansas State Senate, Room 320, State Capitol, Little Rock, AR 72201, USA. Tel: +1 501 682 2902 / 6107, URL: http://www.arkansas.gov/senate

Lower House
The State House of Representatives consists of 100 members who are elected for two years. Each member of the House represents a district with an average population of about 26,730. Following the 2012 elections, the House was split: 54 Democrat members to 46 Republicans. **Arkansas State House of Representatives**, Room 350, State Capitol, Little Rock, AR 72201, USA. Tel: +1 501 682 6211 / 7771, URL: http://www.arkansashouse.org/

Elected Executive Branch Officials (as at April 2013)
Governor: Mike Beebe (D) (page 1385)
Lieutenant Governor: Mark Darr (D)
Secretary of State: Mark Martin (D)
Attorney General: Dustin McDaniel (D)
Auditor of State: Charlie Daniels (D)
Treasurer of State: Martha Schoffner (D)
Land Commissioner: John Thurston (R)

Legislature (as at April 2013)
President Pro Tem of the Senate: Michel Lamoureux
Majority Leader of the Senate: Eddie Joe Williams
Minority Leader of the Senate: Keith Ingram
Speaker of the House: Davy Carter (R)
Speaker Pro Tempore: Darrin Williams (D)
Majority Leader: Bruce Westerman (R)
Minority Leader: Greg Leding (D)

US Senators: John Boozman (R) (page 1391) and Mark Pryor (D) (page 1498)

Ministries
Office of the Governor, State Capitol, Room 250, Little Rock, AR 72201, USA. Tel: +1 501 682 2345, fax: +1 501 682 3597, URL: http://governor.arkansas.gov/Pages/default.aspx
Office of the Lieutenant Governor, State Capitol, Suite 270, Little Rock, AR 72201-1061, USA. Tel +1 501 682 2144, fax: +1 501 682 2894, e-mail: winrock@state.ar.us, URL: http://www.ltgovernor.arkansas.gov/
Office of the Attorney General, 323 Center Street, Suite 200, Little Rock, AR 72201, USA. Tel: +1 501 682 2007, e-mail: oag@ag.state.ar.us, URL: http://www.arkansasag.gov/
Office of the Secretary of State, State Capitol, Room 256, Little Rock, AR 72201, USA. Tel: +1 501 682 1010, URL: http://www.sos.arkansas.gov/Pages/default.aspx
State Treasury, URL: http://www.arkansasag.gov/
Department of Economic Development, One State Capitol Mall, Little Rock, AR 72201, USA. Tel: +1 501 682 1121, fax: +1 501 682 7394, URL: http://www.state.ar.us
Department of Education, 4 Capitol Mall, Little Rock, Arkansas 72201, USA. Tel: +1 501 682 4475, e-mail: gmorris@arkedu.k12.ar.us, URL: http://www.arkansased.org/
Department of Environmental Quality, 8001 National Drive, Little Rock, AR 72209, USA. (Mailing address: PO Box 8913, Little Rock, AR 72219) Tel: +1 501 682 0744, URL: http://www.adeq.state.ar.us/
Department of Finance and Administration, 1509 W. 7th Street, Room 401, DFA Building, Little Rock, AR 72201, USA. Tel: +1 501 682 2242, fax: +1 501 682 1029, URL: http://www.dfa.arkansas.gov/
Department of Labour, 10421 West Markham, Little Rock, Arkansas 72205, USA. Tel: +1 501 682 4500, fax: +1 501 682 4535, URL: http://www.labor.ar.gov
State Highway and Transportation Department, (PO Box 2261, Little Rock, Arkansas 72203) 10324 Interstate 30, Little Rock, Arkansas 72209, USA. Tel: +1 501 569 2000, fax: +1 501 569 2400, URL: http://www.arkansashighways.com/

Political Parties
Arkansas Democratic Party, URL: http://www.arkdems.org/
Republican Party of Arkansas, URL: http://www.arkansasgop.org/

Elections
Following the General Election in November 2006, Democrat Mike Beebe was elected Governor of Arkansas with 55.6 per cent of the vote, having defeated the Republican Asa Hutchinson. Governor Beebe was re-elected in November 2010 with over 60 per cent of the vote.

The state elections were held in November 2012. The Democrats lost several seats to the Republicans but retained their majority with 54 seats to the Republicans' 46. Following the November 2012 state senate election, the Democrats lost their majority. They now hold 14 seats, and the Republicans 21 seats.

LEGAL SYSTEM

The Arkansas court system consists of the Supreme Court, the Court of Appeals, Circuit Courts, District Courts and City Courts.

The Supreme Court comprises a Chief Justice and six Associate Justices, all elected for a term of eight years. The Court of Appeals consists of a Chief Justice and 11 justices, all elected for a term of eight years. Circuit Court Judges number 115, each in one of 28 circuits for a six-year term of office. In addition, there are 124 District Courts with 115 Judges, and 114 City Courts with 87 Judges.

Arkansas has the death penalty. The current death row population stood at 39 in February 2013. Twenty-seven people have been executed since 1976. The murder rate is 4.7 per 100,000 population. (Source: DPIC)

Arkansas voters banned same sex marriages and there are strict limitations on abortions. The state Constitution holds that 'No person who denies the being of a God shall hold any office in the civil departments of this State, nor be competent to testify as a witness in any Court', despite the US Supreme Court finding that a similar clause in the Maryland Constitution violated the First and Fourteenth Amendments of the US Constitution.

Supreme Court, URL: http://courts.state.ar.us/courts
Chief Justice: James Hannah
Court of Appeals, URL: http://courts.state.ar.us/courts
Chief Judge: Larry D. Vaught

UNITED STATES OF AMERICA

LOCAL GOVERNMENT

According to the Census Bureau 2007 survey of local governments, Arkansas is divided into 75 county governments and 502 sub-county general purpose governments. All 502 sub-county governments are municipal. There are no town or township governments. In addition, there are 971 special purpose governments, of which 724 are special district governments and 247 are school district governments.

AREA AND POPULATION

Area
Arkansas is situated in the south of the US, east of Oklahoma and Texas, west of Tennessee and Mississippi, south of Missouri, and north of Louisiana. Arkansas has a total area of 53,178.62 sq. miles, of which 52,068.17 sq. miles is land and 1,110.45 sq. miles is water.

To view a map of the state, please consult:
http://www.lib.utexas.edu/maps/us_2001/arkansas_ref_2001.pdf

Population
According to the US Census Bureau the 2012 population was an estimated 2,949,131, up from 2,938,582 in 2011. Over the period 2000-10 the population increased by 9.1 per cent. The population is expected to reach 3.24 million by 2030. The population density is estimated at 58.84 persons per sq. mile. The capital, Little Rock, the largest city in Arkansas, had a 2010 population of 193,524. The county with the greatest number of inhabitants is Pulaski County (382,748 in 2010), followed by Washington County (203,065), and Benton County (221,339). An estimated 6.7 per cent of the population is under 5 years (2011), 24.2 per cent under 18 years and 14.6 per cent is aged over 65 years. According to the Census, 50.9 per cent of the state population is female. An estimated 77 per cent of the population is white, and 15.4 per cent black.

Births, Marriages, Deaths
Preliminary US Census Bureau (Population Division) (CDC) data puts the number of births in the year 2010 at 38,540 and the number of deaths at 28,91. Provisional US Census Bureau data for 2007 put the number of marriages at 33,741 (down on 2006), and the number of divorces at 16,793 (up on 2006). There were 7.66 infant deaths per 1,000 live births in the year 2007.

Public Holidays
In addition to celebrating national holidays, the people of Arkansas celebrate Daisy Gatson Bates Day, on the 3rd Monday in February, coinciding with the official calendar date for George Washington's Birthday. Daisy Gatson Bates was a civil rights activist and journalist.

EMPLOYMENT

Arkansas had a total civilian labour force in December 2012 of 1,355,000, of which 1,258,800 were employed and 96,200 were unemployed. The unemployment rate was 7.1 per cent, lower than the national average of 7.8 per cent in December 2012. (Source: BLS, preliminary figures)

The following table shows preliminary figures for December 2012 non-farm wage and salary employment according to industry (seasonally adjusted):

Industry	No. of Jobs	12 mth change %
Mining and logging	11,100	2.8
Construction	43,900	-5.6
Manufacturing	155,500	-0.3
Trade, transport and utilities	238,500	0.6
Information	14,100	-0.7
Financial activities	46,500	-2.7
Professional and business svcs.	116,400	-0.9
Educational & health services	171,600	2.1
Leisure and hospitality	102,800	3.6
Other services	45.0	3.4
Government	223,600	1.2
TOTAL	1,169,000	0.7

Source: Bureau of Labor Statistics

BANKING AND FINANCE

GDP/GNP, Inflation, National Debt
Arkansas state Gross Domestic Product (GDP) rose from (current dollars) $102,235 million in 2010 to $105,846 million in 2011 (ranking it fifth in the US). Real GDP rose by 2.3 per cent in 2010, just below the national average growth rate in 2010. Arkansas was ranked 34th in the US for its 2010 GDP. The largest industry was government (14.2 per cent GDP).

The following table shows GDP according to industry (millions of current dollars):

Industry	2009	2010	2011
Agriculture, Forestry, Fisheries and hunting	2,650	2,612	2,818
Mining	1,820	2,046	2,365
Utilities	2,499	2,634	2,500
Construction	4,190	3,998	3,904
Manufacturing	13,463	14,611	15,408
Wholesale Trade	6,651	6,913	7,189
Retail Trade	7,098	7,579	7,835

- continued

Transportation & warehousing	4,075	4,260	5,546
Information	3,613	2,560	2,686
Finance & insurance	4,464	5,018	5,051
Real estate	10,969	10,891	11,201
Educational services	525	542	573
Health care & social assistance	8,109	8,481	8,793
Other non-government services	14,170	21,603	13,978
Government	14,584	15,250	15,000
TOTAL	98,879	102,235	105846

Source: Bureau of Economic Analysis, Jan. 2013

Per capita personal income in 2011 was estimated at US$33,370, up 4.2 per cent on the previous year; the state was ranked 47th in the USA in terms of per capita income. In 2009, per capita real GDP rose to US$32,191 and rose again to $32,678 in 2010.

The annual Consumer Price Index (CPI) for the South urban area (all items) rose from 211.3 in 2010 to 218.6 in 2011 and to 223.2 in 2012 (1982-84 = 100). (Source: Bureau of Labor Statistics).

Balance of Payments / Imports and Exports
Arkansas' export revenue fell in 2010 to $5,219 million before rising by 7.4 per cent to $5,607 million in 2011. Export revenue from the state represents 0.4 per cent of the US total export revenue. Main export commodities include civilian aircraft and parts, military equipment, cotton and agricultural products. The top five international export markets, according to 2011 revenue, are shown on the following table (figures in $m):

Country	2010 ($m)	3011 ($m)	+/-% 2010-11
Canada	1,383	1,396	0.9
Mexico	544	679	24.8
China	336	413	23.1
Japan	334	214	-36.1
South Korea	145	195	34.7

In 2011, imports amounted to $7,208 million compared to $6,758 million in 2010, up 6.7 per cent on the year and representing 0.3 per cent of US total. The main imports are crude oil & airplane parts. Main suppliers are China (26.8 per cent), France (19.5 per cent), Canada (17.9 per cent), Mexico and Germany.

Chambers of Commerce and Trade Organisations
Arkansas Economic Development Commission, URL: http://www.arkansasedc.com/
Arkansas State Chamber of Commerce, URL: http://www.arkansasstatechamber.com/

MANUFACTURING, MINING AND SERVICES

Primary and Extractive Industries
A wide variety of minerals is found in Arkansas, including bauxite, oil, coal, and lignite. There is also an abundant supply of low-volatile and semi-anthracite coal. According to the BEA, in 2011, the mining sector contributed $2,365 million towards the state GDP, an increase on the 2010 figure of $2,046 million. In 2010, most of the revenue came from oil and gas extraction ($1,054 million) followed by from support activities for mining ($754 million). The balance of $238 million came from non-oil and gas extraction.

Proven crude oil reserves were 40 million barrels in 2010 (0.2 per cent of US total). Arkansas had a total of 6,913 producing oil wells and 35 rotary rigs in operation in 2009, producing around 5.73 million barrels in 2010. Oil production in Arkansas accounts for 0.3 per cent of US crude oil production. Total petroleum consumption in 2009 reached 64.8 million barrels, over half of which was motor gasoline. Crude oil refinery capacity was 90,500 bbl/d in 2012.

Arkansas' dry gas reserves were estimated at 14,178 billion cubic feet in 2009, up from 1,663 billion cubic feet in 2003. Natural gas plant liquid reserves amounted to 2 million barrels. Gas wells numbered 8,388 in 2011. Marketed natural gas production amounted to 1,072,212 million cu ft in 2011 (4.5 per cent of US total). Total consumption was 271,512 million cubic feet in 2010.

In 2007, there were two coal mines in Arkansas, producing a total of 83,000 short tons (up a massive 357 per cent on 2006). In 2010, 113,000 short tons were produced in 2011. (Source: EIA)

Energy
Total energy production in 2010 was 1,256 trillion Btu (1.7 per cent of US total). Total energy consumption in 2009 was 1,055 trillion Btu (1.1 per cent of the US total), whilst per capita energy consumption was 365 million Btu (17th in the US).

Arkansas is a net exporter of electricity with coal as its primary generating fuel. In 2011, coal accounted for approximately 52 per cent of electricity generation, with nuclear power accounting for 22 per cent, natural gas 19 per cent, hydroelectric three per cent, and other renewables 2.8 per cent. Net summer capability in 2010 was 15,981 MW (1.5 per cent of US total). Net generation in 2006 was 52,168,703 MWh (27th in US).

Arkansas has a single nuclear power plant, Arkansas Nuclear One, which consists of two reactors. Owned and operated by Entergy Arkansas, Inc., the plant is located in an 1,100 acre site in Pope County. Unit 1 is a 836 net MWe pressurised water reactor, whilst Unit 2 is an 858 net MWe pressurised water reactor; together they produced 15,232,577 MWh of electricity in 2006. (Source: EIA)

Manufacturing

Manufacturing is Arkansas' second largest contributor to GDP, accounting for an estimated $15,408 million in 2011 (up from $14,611 million in 2010). Various manufactured goods are produced in Arkansas including a wide range of household goods and mechanical parts. Food products comprise the largest manufacturing industry, producing $3,282 million in 2010, followed by paper manufacturing ($1,977 million) and fabricated metal products ($1,875 million). Manufacturing employment is generally in decline. (Source: BEA)

Service Industries

Services is Arkansas' largest contributor to Gross Domestic Product. In 2011, the highest revenue-producing sector continued to be real estate, rental and leasing ($11,201 million). Other major sectors include health services ($8,793 million), finance and insurance ($5,051 million) and professional services ($4,354 million). (Source: BEA)

Tourism

The accommodation and food services sector of the services industry contributed $2,716 million in 2011 (up from $2,590 million the previous year), whilst the arts, entertainment and recreation sector contributed $419 million. (Source: BEA)

Arkansas Department of Parks and Tourism, URL: http://www.arkansas.com/

Agriculture

Agriculture, forestry and fisheries contributed an estimated $2,818 million towards the 2011 state GDP (up from $2,612 million in 2010). Crop and animal production contributed $2,159 million in 2010 whilst forestry, fishing and related activities contributed $452 million in the same year. (Source: BEA)

According to the National Agricultural Statistics overview for 2010, Arkansas had a total of 49,300 farms, covering a total land area of 13,700,000 acres (down from 14,507,096 acres in 2002). The average size of a farm was 278 acres, down from 306 acres in 2002. Total market value of agricultural products sold in 2008 was estimated to be $7.5 billion, of which $4.6 billion was generated by livestock, poultry and products, and $2.9 billion was generated by crops, including greenhouse and nursery crops. Arkansas has been the number one broiler-producing state in the US since 1972. The state produces approximately 45 per cent of the rice grown in the US, harvesting more than a million acres each year. Arkansas ranks in the top ten states in the production of soybeans, grain sorghum, catfish, turkeys, grapes, and cotton, much of which is exported. There are approximately 1,720,000 head of cattle and calves and 160,000 hogs and pigs.

Over half of Arkansas, 17.7 million acres, is covered by timber - almost all of it of commercial quality and available for that purpose. Softwoods, mostly shortleaf and loblolly pine, comprise 42 per cent of the standing saw timber. The remaining percentage is in hardwoods, with oak predominating. There are currently more than 980 Arkansas manufacturing firms, from small to huge, producing wood products. Over 34,000 Arkansans are employed in the forest industry.

COMMUNICATIONS AND TRANSPORT

International Airports

Arkansas is served by major airlines with scheduled passenger and freight service to larger cities and an efficient network of commuter lines to smaller cities. Arkansas has 90 public use airports. Approximately 30 of these have facilities and runways long enough to accommodate most business jets. Located throughout the state, these 30 airports are equipped for both day and night operations, and most have instrument approaches available.

Railways

Four major rail systems serve Arkansas on more than 2,500 miles of track within the state. Their comprehensive rail service includes carload, trailer on flat car, container on flat car, and mini-bridge shipments. Single line service is available to 26 states. Most major areas of North America can be served using no more than two railroads.

Roads

Interstate-40, which remains virtually ice-free year-round, crosses the centre of the state. It is the most travelled interstate in the nation and the country's major east-west corridor. Interstate-30 connects Arkansas with important Southwest and Texas markets. Interstate-55 links Arkansas to the Gulf of Mexico and, in the north, to St. Louis and Chicago.

Shipping

Arkansas has 1,000 miles of navigable waterways that link the state with America's 22,202 miles of navigable inland waters and with the ports of the world. The McClellan-Kerr Arkansas River Navigation System is the second largest project ever undertaken by the U.S. Army Corps of Engineers. This project allows barge traffic to use a 450-mile long, nine-foot channel on the Arkansas River which runs from Tulsa, Oklahoma, to the Mississippi River on Arkansas' eastern border. At the heart of the McClellan-Kerr System is the Port of Little Rock, officially designated Foreign Trade Zone 14. At the port, goods may be processed or stored without payment of inventory taxes or custom duties. Foreign and domestic materials may be reassembled, repackaged, processed, used in manufacturing, stored, or simply held tax-free with duties delayed until sold or moved out of the zone.

HEALTH

The National Centre for Health Statistics put the rate of doctors (including osteopaths) per 10,000 population at 20.4 in 2009 (compared with the US average of 27.4). There were 1,125 dentists in 2008 (3.9 per 10,000 population). Arkansas has 3.3 community hospital beds per 1,000 residents (US average is 2.6 beds) and a total of 232 nursing homes, with 24,548 beds.

In 2007-09, 17.7 per cent of adults of Arkansas had no health insurance cover, higher than the US state average of 15.8 per cent. In the period 2007-11 around 18.4 per cent of the population were living in poverty (national rate 14.3 per cent). In 2012, some 66.3 per cent of the adult population was overweight, and 30.1 per cent were obese. Arkansas reported 4,436 HIV/AIDS cases from the beginning of the epidemic to the end of 2008, ranking it 32nd highest among the US states. A further 133 cases were reported in 2009. The TB infection rate was 2.9 per 100,000 persons. (Source: CDC)

EDUCATION

Primary/Secondary Education

Arkansas currently has 1,145 elementary and secondary public schools. There were 480,559 pupils enrolled in the year 2009-10 (rising to an estimated 495,000 in 2011) and the total number of teachers was 37,240, giving a pupil/teacher ratio of 12.9.

Total current state expenditure reached $4.8 billion, whilst revenues from education reached $4.7 billion in 2007-08.

Higher Education

Arkansas has 51 post-secondary degree-conferring institutions, 33 of which are public. In 2010-11, there were 68,943 men enrolled and 99,409 women. In 2010-11, 34,833 degrees were conferred, 12,523 of which were Bachelors, 4,126 were Masters and 804 Doctorates.(Source: National Center for Education Statistics)

Undergraduate programs are offered in all fields, whilst masters and doctoral programs are offered at the University of Arkansas at Fayetteville, the University of Arkansas for Medical Sciences, the University of Arkansas at Little Rock, and Arkansas State University.

Vocational Education

As part of a Vocational Education Programme more than 300 school districts in Arkansas offer both general and occupationally specific courses in their high schools. Tech Prep Certification denotes academic and technical competency for students who are not aiming to go to college.

RELIGION

Most Arkansans are Protestant, but the state has a smaller representation of Catholic, Jewish, Muslim and other religions.

COMMUNICATIONS AND MEDIA

Newspapers

Arkansas' daily newspapers include: the Arkansas Democrat-Gazette, Little Rock (URL: http://www.arkansasonline.com); The Morning News of Northwest Arkansas, Springdale; The Sentinel-Record, Hot Springs; Malvern Daily Record; The Courier, Russellville; The Benton Courier; El Dorado News-Times; Times-Herald, Forrest City; Harrison Daily Times; Newport Daily Independent.

Broadcasting

Radio and television broadcasting networks in Arkansas blanket the state with news coverage. There are 131 commercial radio stations in Arkansas and 10 non-commercial radio stations. Additionally, Arkansas has 15 commercial television stations and eight non-commercial television stations.

Telecommunications

Digital switching networks and transmission routes provide state-of-the-art communications.

ENVIRONMENT

The Arkansas electricity industry relies primarily on coal as a generating fuel, and carbon dioxide emissions are high as a consequence. In 2010, 34.02 million metric tons of carbon dioxide emissions were produced (1.4 per cent of US total, US rank 28th), 74,060 metric tons of sulfur dioxide and 40,490 metric tons of nitrogen oxide.

In 2008, there were 4,538 alternative-fuelled vehicles in use (0.5 per cent of US total). Ethanol consumption was estimated to be 2.9 million barrels in 2011. (Source: EIA)

UNITED STATES OF AMERICA

CALIFORNIA

Capital: Sacramento (Population, Census 2010: 466,488)

Head of State: Jerry (Edumund G.) Brown Jr. (D) (Governor) (page 1395)

State Flag: The Bear Flag: a white background with a red bar running along the bottom; in the centre of the flag is the image of a grizzly bear (the state animal) underneath which are the words 'California Republic'; in the top left hand corner of the flag is a single red star

CONSTITUTION AND GOVERNMENT

Constitution

California entered the Union on 9 September 1850. The original Constitution was ratified by the people on 13 November 1849. The 1849 Constitution was revised on 7 May 1879 with the addition of nine new articles. Since 1911 California's voters have agreed more than 425 amendments to the 1879 Constitution.

According to the 1879 Constitution, the governor heads the executive branch of government together with 12 elected constitutional officers: lieutenant governor, secretary of state, attorney general, state treasurer, state controller, insurance commissioner, superintendent of public instruction, and the five-member board of equalization. The lieutenant governor, attorney general, controller, secretary of state, and treasurer are all elected by the voters of the state at the same time as the governor. All serve a maximum of two four-year terms. The superintendent of public instruction is a non-partisan post.

California elects two US Senators and 53 US Representatives to the US Congress in Washington, DC.

To consult the state constitution, please visit: http://www.leginfo.ca.gov/const-toc.html

Recent Events

On the 2nd December 2008, Governor Arnold Schwarzenegger declared a fiscal emergency to tackle the state's $11.2bn (£7.5bn) deficit; there were fears that the state could run out of cash by early 2009. Mr Schwarzenegger said that the current shortfall could swell to $28bn over the next 18 months if no action was taken. The previous state legislature failed to reach agreement on a series of spending cuts and tax increases, and the November elections produced little change to its political make-up.

On February 20th 2009, Gov. Arnold Schwarzenegger signed the state budget; the initiatives would allow the state to borrow $5 billion against future lottery sales and shift $830 million in taxes collected for children's health care and mental health programs to the general fund. Californian voters rejected all but one of the budget measures, passing the one freezing the pay of elected officials. Gov Schwarzenegger had warned that, if the measures were not passed, California's deficit would swell to $21.3 billion, and further spending cuts would be required, such as a shortening of the school year by 7.5 days and an end to health care for 225,000 low-income children.

A report published in November 2009 estimated that the state would have to confront a budget deficit of nearly $21 billion over the following 18 months. Analysts suggested a tax increase but Gov. Schwarzenegger opposed that route. Serious spending cuts may not be possible since California already spends the minimum on education and health-care allowable to qualify for federal stimulus dollars. In January 2010, Gov. Schwarzenegger went to Washington to request federal government funds. He argued that California, home to some of the nation's highest wage earners, has been paying more in taxes to the federal government than it receives in return.

Legislature

California's bicameral legislature consists of the State Senate and the State Assembly.

Upper House

The Senate has 40 members elected for four-year terms, half being elected every two years. Each Senator represents nearly 847,000 people. Following the 2012 elections, the Senate had 26 Democrats and 12 Republicans. Under the terms of the California State Constitution, the Lieutenant Governor is also the President of the Senate.
California State Senate, State Capital, Sacramento, California, USA. Tel: +1 916 445 4251 (Secretary of the Senate), URL: http://senate.ca.gov/

Lower House

The Assembly has 80 members, all elected for two years. Following the 2012 elections, there were 56 Democrats and 24 Republicans.
California State Assembly, State Capitol, PO Box 942849, Sacramento, CA 94249-0000, USA. Tel: +1 916 319 2856 (Chief Clerk), URL: http://www.assembly.ca.gov/

> **Elected Executive Branch Officials (at at April 2013)**
> *Governor:* Edmund Gerald (Jerry) Brown Jr (D) (page 1395)
> *Lieutenant Governor:* Gavin Newsom Dardenne (D)
> *Secretary of State:* Debra Bowen (D)
> *Treasurer:* Bill Lockyer (D)
> *State Controller:* John Chiang (D)
> *Attorney General:* Kamala D Harris
> *Superintendent of Public Instruction:* Tom Torlakson (D)
> *Insurance Commissioner:* Dave Jones
> *Board of Equalization:* Betty Yee, George Runner, Michelle Steele, Jerome Horton, John Chiang

> **Legislature (as at April 2013)**
> *President of the Senate:* Lt. Gov. Gavin Newsom
> *President Pro Tem of the Senate:* Darrell Steinberg (D)
> *Senate Majority Leader:* Ellen M. Corbett (D)
> *Senate Minority Leader:* Bob Huff (R)
> *Speaker of the Assembly:* John A. Perez (D)
> *Speaker Pro Tem of the Assembly:* Nora Campos (D)
> *Assembly Majority Leader:* Chris R. Holden (D)
> *Assembly Republican Leader:* Connie Conway (R)

> **US Senators:** Barbara Boxer (D) (page 1393) and Dianne Feinstein (D) (page 1424)

Ministries

Office of the Governor, State Capitol Building, Sacramento, CA 95814, USA. Tel: +1 916 445 2841, fax: +1 916 445 4633, URL: http://gov.ca.gov/
Office of the Lieutenant Governor, URL: http://www.ltg.ca.gov/
Office of the Attorney General, Department of Justice, Public Inquiry Unit, PO Box 944255, Sacramento, CA 94244-2550, USA. Tel: +1 916 322 3360, fax: +1 916 323 5341, URL: http://oag.ca.gov
Office of the Secretary of State, 1500 11th Street, Sacramento, California 95814, USA. Tel: +1 916 653 6814, URL: http://www.sos.ca.gov/
Department of Food and Agriculture, Office of Public Affairs, 1220 N Street, Sacramento, CA 95814, USA. Tel: +1 916 654 0466, fax: +1 916 654 0403, URL: http://www.cdfa.ca.gov/
Office of the State Treasurer, 915 Capitol Mall, Room 110, Sacramento, California 95814, USA. Tel: +1 916 653 2995, URL: http://www.treasurer.ca.gov
Office of the State Controller, P O Box 942850, Sacramento, California 94250-5872, USA. Tel: +1 916 445 2636, URL: http://www.sco.ca.gov
Business and Economic Development Programme, Office of the Secretary, 980 9th Street, Suite 2450, Sacramento, CA 95814-2719, USA. Tel: +1 916 322 5400, fax: +1 916 323 5440, URL: http://business.ca.gov
Department of Education, 1430 N Street, Sacramento, CA 95814, USA. Tel: +1 916 319 0800, URL: http://www.cde.ca.gov/
Resources Agency, 1416 Ninth Street, Suite 1311, Sacramento, CA 95814, USA. Tel: +1 916 653 5656, fax: +1 916 653 8102, URL: http://resources.ca.gov/
Department of Conservation, 801 K Street, MS 24-01, Sacramento, California 95814, USA. Tel: +1 916 322 1080, fax: +1 916 445 0732, URL: http://www.conservation.ca.gov/
Department of Health Care Services, 1501 Capitol Avenue, Suite 2101, Sacramento, CA 95814 (PO Box 942732, Sacramento, CA 94234-7320), USA. Tel: +1 916 445 4171, URL: http://www.dhcs.ca.gov/
Department of Transport (CALTRANS), 1120 N Street, Sacramento (PO Box 942873, Sacramento, CA 94273-0001), USA. Tel: +1 916 654 5266, fax: +1 916 653 3291, URL: http://www.dot.ca.gov/

Political Parties

California Democratic Party, URL: http://www.cadem.org/
California Republican Party, URL: http://www.cagop.org/

Elections

In Autumn 2003, Gary Davis became the first Californian governor to be removed from office mid-term, following his posting of a $38 billion deficit. On 7 October 2003 Hollywood actor Arnold Schwarzenegger was elected Governor of California with 48.6 per cent of the votes, beating Cruz M. Bustamante (D) who received 31.5 per cent of votes. He was re-elected to the post in 2006, with 55.9 per cent of the votes. Governor Schwarzenegger was ineligible to stand in the November 2010 elections. Democrat Jerry Brown won with over 54 per cent of the vote.

Legislative elections were last held in November 2012. Elections took place in 20 out of 40 state senate seats. In the state Senate, the Democrats retained the majority (Democrats 26, Republicans 12), and in the state Assembly they also increased their majority (56 Democrats and 24 Republicans).

LEGAL SYSTEM

California's judiciary is the largest in the United States, with some 1,600 judges (compared to the US federal system which has 840). It is supervised by the seven Justices of the Supreme Court of California.

The California judicial system comprises the Supreme Court, Courts of Appeal (six districts, 19 divisions, and 105 justices), and 400 Trial Courts (1,499 judges). The Trial Courts include Family Courts, Juvenile Courts, Criminal Courts, Small Claims Courts and Traffic Courts. California is divided into six appellate court districts. The Governor appoints the Supreme Court Chief Justice and the six associate judges, whose appointments are confirmed by the Commission of Judicial Appointments, by the public at the next general election and by voters after the judges' twelve-year terms.

California has the largest "Death Row" population in the country but executions are currently on hold indefinitely as human rights issues are addressed. As of January 2013 there were 724 inmates on Death Row including 19 women, the highest number of inmates awaiting the death penalty in the USA. After the gas chamber was ruled unlawful in 1994, lethal injection became the only permitted method of excution. The last execution took place in 2006. In 2012, voters narrowly voted to retain the death penalty.

In early 2004, San Francisco became the first place in the US where gay couples were able to marry after the city's Mayor Gavin Newsom authorised same-sex marriage licences, claiming the state legislation was discriminatory. However, in August 2004, California's Supreme Court ruled the mayor had overstepped his authority and nullified the hundreds of marriages. In May 2008, California's Supreme Court ruled that a state law banning marriage between same-sex couples was unconstitutional and California became the second state to allow same sex marriages. Same sex marriages were permitted between June and November 2008. However, following appeals, the status was changed: same sex unions may now have the rights of marriage but the term 'marriage' may not be applied.

California Court system portal: URL: http://www.courts.ca.gov/
Supreme Court: URL: http://www.courts.ca.gov/supremecourt.htm
Chief Justice: Tani Cantil-Sakauye
Associate Justices: Joyce L. Kennard, Kathryn Mickle Werdegar, Ming W. Chin, Marvin R. Baxter, Goodwin Lu, Carol A. Corrigan

LOCAL GOVERNMENT

According to the US Census Bureau, California has 57 county governments and 478 sub-county or municipal governments (cities and towns). The city and county of San Francisco is designated as a consolidated government, although counted as a municipal government for census purposes. In addition, there are also 2,765 special districts, 1,044 school district governments, and 58 dependent public school systems.

California State Association of Counties, URL: http://www.csac.counties.org

AREA AND POPULATION

Area
California is located on the Pacific coast in the far west of the US, south of Oregon, west and south-west of Nevada, and west of Arizona. The area covered by California is 163,695.57 sq. miles, of which 155,959.34 sq. miles is land and 7,736.23 sq. miles is water. California is the third largest state in the USA in size, after Alaska and Texas.

The Central Valley, the state's agricultural heartland, is surrounded on all four sides by mountain ranges. The Sierra Nevada range includes Yosemite Valley, Sequoia National Park and Lake Tahoe. About 45 per cent of the state is forested, and 25 per cent of the state is made up of deserts, including the Mojave Desert (famous for Death Valley, the hottest point in the USA). California is also reknowned for earthquakes due to a number of faults, in particular the San Andreas Fault. It is vulnerable to tsunamis, droughts, Santa Ana winds, wildfires and has several volcanos.

Most of California has a Mediterranean climate. However, the mountain ranges have snow in the winter and more rain. Northwestern California has a temperate climate.

To view a map of the state, please consult:
http://www.lib.utexas.edu/maps/us_2001/california_ref_2001.pdf

Population
California is the most highly populated state in the US, and in 2005 the state population represented 12.5 per cent of the total US population. According to the 2010 Census, the population was 37,253,956, up on the mid-2009 estimate of 36,961,664. California's population grew by 10 per cent over the period 2000-10. The population was estimated at 38,041,430 in 2012. The 2009 population density was estimated at 235.6 people per sq. mile. By 2030, the population is expected to reach 46,444.861. An estimated 6.7 per cent of the population is under 5 years, 24.6 per cent under 18 years and 11.7 per cent is aged over 65 years. According to the Census, 50.3 per cent of the state population is female.

The following table shows the five most populated Californian cities:

Top Five City Populations, 2011

City	County	City Population
Los Angeles	Los Angeles	3,819,702
San Diego	San Diego	1,326,179
San Jose	Santa Clara	967,487
San Francisco	San Francisco	812,826
Fresno	Fresno	501,362
Source: US Census Bureau		

According to the 2010 Census, 57.6 per cent of the population is white, 6.2 per cent black, 37.6 per cent of Hispanic or Latino origin, and 13 per cent Asian.

Births, Marriages, Deaths
The US Census Bureau, Population Division (CDC), estimated that in 2010 there were 510,198 births and 234,012 deaths, giving a natural increase of 276,186 people. In 2009, net migration of 66,802 people (165,600 people came from outside the country, whilst 98,798 left the state). The fertility rate was 64.8 per 1,000 women aged 15-44 years and the death rate was 628.3 per 100,000 population. The infant mortality rate in 2007 was 5.2 infant deaths per 1,000 live births. Marriages in 2007, according to provisional data, numbered 225,832, up on previous years.

Public Holidays
In addition to the national holidays celebrated in the USA, Californians observe Cesar Chavez's birthday, on March 31st.

EMPLOYMENT

California leads the USA in human resources. It not only has a greater population and a higher number of people employed than any other state, but it also leads the states in the number of scientists and engineers, as well as research and development activities.

Preliminary indicators show that California's civilian labour force in December 2012 was 18,468,300, of which 16,663.400 were employed and 1,804,900 were unemployed. The unemployment rate was estimated at 9.8 per cent, higher than the national average of 7.8 per cent.

The following table shows preliminary figures for December 2012 non-farm wage and salary employment according to industry (seasonally adjusted):

Industry	No. of Jobs	Change over 12 months %
Mining and logging	28,100	-0.7
Construction	582,700	4.4
Manufacturing	1,231,200	-0.9
Trade, transportation, and utilities	2,736,400	1.8
Information*	468,200	4.7
Financial activities	782,400	2.4
Professional and business services	2,213,400	2.3
Educational and health services	1,913,600	2.9
Leisure and hospitality	1,606,000	3.9
Other services	478,100	-1.7
Government	2,358,700	-1.3
TOTAL	14,398,800	1.6

Source: US Bureau of Labor Statistics
*Not seasonally adjusted

BANKING AND FINANCE

GDP/GNP, Inflation, National Debt
According to different sources, if California were an independent nation, its economy would currently be ranked between 7th and 10th in the world. California's Gross Domestic Product continues to be the largest in the US, and accounts for around 13 per cent of the national total GDP. Current-dollar GDP rose from $1,846,757 million in 2008 to $1,891,363 million in 2009. It rose to $1,901,088 million in 2010 and $1,958,904 million in 2011. Real GDP grew by just 0.4 per cent in 2008 (lower than the US average growth of 0.7 per cent) and a significant drop on the growth rate of 3.8 per cent in 2007. This was due to continued and significant contractions in the construction industry (down 0.5 per cent), in the finance and insurance sector (down 0.48 per cent), as well as in agriculture and the retail industry. Although growth was still lower than the US average of 2.6 per cent, real GDP growth rate reached 1.8 per cent in 2010, rising to 2 per cent in 2011.

The following table shows Gross Domestic Product according to industry (millions of current dollars):

Industry	2009	2010	2011
Agriculture, forestry and fishing	25,853	29,270	31,757
Mining	15,046	16,222	20,668
Utilities	28,742	28,005	28,231
Construction	62,083	57,387	58,959
Manufacturing	203,067	214,340	229,862
Wholesale Trade	94,903	121,955	131,299
Retail Trade	109,152	116,756	121,416
Transport and warehousing	42,278	42,988	44,203
Information	118,235	125,272	136,046
Finance and insurance	102,335	110,308	111,505
Real estate	317,239	295,649	293,755
Educational services	18,280	19,266	20,471
Health care and social assistance	116,376	123,895	129,413
Other Non-government services	353,983	376,375	400,960
Government	221,265	221,598	224,720
TOTAL	1,828,836	1,877,568	1,958,904

Source: US Bureau of Economic Analysis, Feb. 2013

Per capita real GDP rose from $42,578 in 2010 to $46,041 in 2011, still below 2009 levels and ranking it 12th in the US.

The annual Consumer Price Index (CPI) for the Los Angeles-Riverside-Orange County urban area (all items) rose from 231.9 in 2011 to 236.7 in 2012 (1982-84 = 100). For the San Francisco-Oakland-San Jose urban area (all items) the annual CPI rose from 233.4 in 2011 to 242.8 in 2012. For the San Diego urban area (all items) the annual CPI rose from 245.4 in 2010 to 252.9 in 2011. (Source: Bureau of Labor Statistics)

Balance of Payments / Imports and Exports
California is ranked first in the US for its merchandise export revenue, which fell from $159,122 million in 2011, an increase of 11.1 per cent on the previous year. (Source: US Census Bureau, Foreign Trade Division).

The top ten international destinations in 2011 according to export revenue are shown on the following table:

Destination	2010 ($m)	2011 ($m)	+/-% 2010-11
Mexico	20,949	25,805	23.1

UNITED STATES OF AMERICA

- continued

Canada	16,198	27,269	6.6
China	12,469	14,188	13.8
Japan	12,180	13,096	7.5
Korea, South	8,027	8,426	5.0
Hong Kong	6,757	7,664	13.4
Taiwan	6,518	6,245	-4.2
Germany	5,122	5,310	3.7
United Kingdom	4,181	4,573	10.8
The Netherlands	4,126	4,139	-0.6

Source: US Census Bureau

The top five commodity types in 2011, according to export revenue, are shown on the following table:

Commodity	Value ($m)
Civilian aircraft, engines, equipment and parts	5,432
Parts & accessories for ADP machines/units	4,938
Diamonds, non-industrial, worked	4,829
Machines for recp/convr/trans/regn of voice/image/data	3,997
Oil (not crude) from petrol & bitum mineral etc	2,919

Source: US Census Bureau

Total California imports amounted to US$327,135 million in 2010, up 21 per cent and representing 17.1 per cent of the US total. Imports rose to $351,583 million in 2011, up 7.4 per cent. Main imports were crude oil, vehicle parts, data processing machines and reception apparatus for television.

US imports by top five state of Final Destination

	2011 ($m)	%+/-
China	120,118	5.9
Japan	39,838	-2.4
Mexico	33,641	2.7
Canada	20,512	-5.2
South Korea	11,780	-2.9

Source: US Census Bureau

Chambers of Commerce and Trade Organisations
California Chamber of Commerce, URL: http://www.calchamber.com/
California Association for Local Economic Development, URL: http://www.caled.org/

MANUFACTURING, MINING AND SERVICES

California has several significant economic regions: Hollywood is renowned in the world entertainment industry; the California Central Valley is strong in agriculture; Tech Coast and Silicon Valley are known for computer and high tech. industries and there is a thriving wine sector based in the Napa Valley, Sonoma Valley and the Santa Barbara and Paso Robles areas.

Primary and Extractive Industries
Mining contributed an estimated $20,688 million towards California's 2011 Gross Domestic Product (up from $16,222 million in 2010). The sector generating the most revenue in 2010 was oil and gas, which contributed $13,190 million, whilst non-oil and gas mining contributed $1,399 million, and support activities for the sector accounted for $1,633 million. (Source: BEA)

Gold was the economic resource which led California's early development. From 1848 to 1975, California's gold mines yielded an estimated $2.5 billion in revenue. Over the last few years, however, gold production has declined by some 85 per cent, compared to a national decrease of 28 per cent over the same period. In 2005, 65,300 troy ounces of gold was mined from California's remaining four mines (down from 88,800 troy ounces the previous year), yielding revenues of $29 million (down from $36.3 million in 2004).

California is ranked 4th in the US (including Federal Offshore) for its crude oil reserves and crude oil production. Crude oil reserves were 2,938 million barrels in 2010 (down from 3,435 million barrels in 2005), representing 12.6 per cent of US crude oil reserves. California's oil industry produced around 201,381 thousand barrels in 2010, from a total of 51,481 producing oil wells and 45 rotary rigs, representing 10.1 per cent of US crude oil production. Production has been falling steadily over the years; in 1985, oil production reached a peak of 394,002 thousand barrels; by 1995, production had fallen to 278,977 thousand barrels and by 2005 it was down to 230,294 thousand barrels. The highest oil producing counties (in order of production volume) are Kern, Los Angeles, Ventura, Fresno, and Orange. Total petroleum consumption in 2010 was 653.3 million barrels (9.3 per cent of total US consumption), over half of which (346.9 million barrels) was used as motor gasoline. Over 96,000 barrels were used as jet fuel and 90.4 million barrles as distillate fuel. California ranks third in the USA in petroleum refining capacity and accounts for more than a tenth of total US capacity. Due to falling production, foreign suppliers now provide over two-fifths of the crude oil refined in California. In 2012, the crude oil refinery capacity was 1,955,971 bbl/d (11.3 per cent of US total).

California had reserves of dry natural gas totalling 2,647 billion cubic feet in 2010 (ranking it 13th in the US), up from 2,450 billion cubic feet in 2003. As with crude oil production, California natural gas production is in decline. However, supply has remained relatively stable due to increasing amounts of natural gas shipped from the Rocky Mountains. Production (natural gas- marketed) was 276,575 million cubic feet in 2009 (down from 352,044 million cubic feet in 2005). Natural gas consumption in 2010 was 2,153,498 million cubic feet (8.8 per cent of the US total); the highest consumption was by manufacturing industry and by the power generation industry.

Reserves of natural gas plant liquids were estimated at 114 million barrels in 2010.

Energy
California was ranked 9th in the US in 2010 for total energy production (2,525 trillion btu). California accounted for 8.0 per cent of the US total energy consumption (7,826 trillion Btu in 2010), but 48th in the US for per capita energy consumption (210 million Btu in 2010).

California's primary electricity generating fuel is natural gas, accounting for around 48.8 per cent of industry generation in 2011. Nuclear power contributed 21.2 per cent, hydroelectric 14.1 per cent, other renewables 13.9 per cent, coal less than 1 per cent. Net summer capability in 2010 was 67,328 MW (6.5 per cent of US total), and net generation in 2009 was 16.88 MWh (4.7 per cent of US total).

California has two nuclear reactors: Diablo Canyon, in San Luis Obispo County, and San Onofre, in San Diego County. In 2006 their summer capacity was 2,240 MW and 2,150 MW respectively.

Manufacturing
California has the largest manufacturing complex in the nation. Manufacturing is also California's third largest contributor towards Gross Domestic Product, accounting for $229,862 million in 2011 (up from $214,340 million in 2010). The top sectors in 2010 were computer and electronic products ($65,629 million), petroleum and coal products ($36,614 million), food, beverage and tobacco products ($20,756 million), & chemical manufacturing ($20,624 million). (Source: BEA)

Service Industries
The services industry is California's top contributor towards GDP. In 2011, the major service sectors were real estate ($293,755 million), professional and technical services ($185,132 million), retail trade ($121,416 million), finance and insurance ($111,505 million), health care and social assistance ($129,143 million) and information ($136,046 million). Government accounted for $224,720 million of state GDP. (Source: BEA)

Tourism
Tourism is a significant factor in the Californian economy. In 2004, California was ranked first in the USA with regard to visitors to parks and recreation areas, registering some 77,049,000 visitors. The accommodation and food services sector of the services industry contributed $54,749 million in 2011, whilst the arts, entertainment and recreation sector contributed $26,297 million. (Source: BEA) California's fourth largest employer, tourism supports jobs for nearly 900,000 people and generates $5.2 billion in state and local tax revenues.
California Division of Tourism (CalTour), URL: http://gocalif.ca.gov/state/tourism/

Agriculture
The agriculture, forestry, hunting and fisheries industry contributed $31,757 million towards California's 2011 GDP (an increase of $29,270 million in 2010). The top sector in 2010 was farming ($22,302 million); forestry, fishing and related activities earned $6,968 million. (Source: BEA)

Agriculture is a major resource in the Golden State. According to the USDA Agricultural Overview, there were 82,700 Californian farms in 2010. Total farmland in 2010 was 25,400,000 acres (down from 27,000,000 acres in 2002) and the average size of a Californian farm stood at 311 acres (down from 312 acres).

Fresno County provides the most agricultural products, followed by Tulare and Monterrey Counties. California ranked first in the US in terms of total agricultural income in 2007. The state produces field crops, fruit and nut crops, vegetables, seeds, flowers and ornamentals, livestock and poultry products. In 2007, of the total cash farm income of $33.88 billion, crops accounted for $22.9 billion and livestock earned $10.98 billion. As of Jan. 2011, there were 5.15 million head of cattle and calves, 105,00 hogs and pigs and 610,000 sheep.

In January 2007, Governor Arnold Schwarzenegger declared a state of emergency in 10 counties, after citrus crops were badly damaged by ice-storms. As much as three-quarters of the crop was destroyed; flowers, vegetables and other fruit were also affected.

Major timber producing counties are Humboldt, Mendocino and Siskiyou. There are approximately 16.6 million acres of timberland, of which 5.36 million are designated timber production zones.

Major fish harvests include sardine, mackerel, tuna, herring, squid and crab. Primary fish catching counties are Los Angeles, Santa Barbara, Monterey, Eureka and San Francisco.

COMMUNICATIONS AND TRANSPORT

International Airports
Airports in the state are located at major cities: Burbank, King City, Los Angeles, Oakland, Orange County, Palo Alto, Paso Robles, Sacramento, San Diego, San Francisco, San Jose, San Luis Obispo and Santa Barbara. Los Angeles International (LAX) handled 59,542,151 passengers in 2008, and is the sixth busiest airport in the world.
Los Angeles International Airport, URL: http://www.lawa.org/lax/welcome.htm
San Francisco International Airport, PURL: http://www.flysfo.com/
San Jose International Airport, URL: http://www.sjc.org

Roads

California has a total of 170,599 miles of roads, of which 66,184 miles are county roads, 68,489 miles are city streets and 15,239 miles are state highways. In 2005, the number of vehicles on the roads were recorded as follows: passenger vehicles, 21,546,000; commercial vehicles, 7,590,000; trailers, 2,936,000 and motorcycles, 608,000. With 527 cars per 1,000 inhabitants in 2003, California ranked 7th in the USA in car ownership. Intercity bus travel is provided by Greyhound and Amtrak Thruway Coach.

Railways

Amtrak California provides intercity rail travel, whilst subway and light rail networks operate in Los Angeles (Metro Rail) and San Francisco (MUNI Metro). There are light rail systems in San Jose, San Dieg, Sacramento, and Northern San Diego County. Commuter rail networks serve the San Francisco Bay Area, Greater Los Angeles, and San Diego County.

Construction of a 700 mile high speed rail system was approved by the voters during the November 2008 general election.

Shipping

California's major seaports are the Port of Los Angeles and the Port of Long Beach in Southern California, which combine to create the largest seaport in the USA, handling around a quarter all container cargo traffic in the USA. The Port of Oakland handles trade from the Pacific Rim.

HEALTH

The National Center for Health Statistics estimated that there were 26.4 doctors (including osteopaths) per 10,000 population in 2009, below the national average of 27.4 doctors per 10,000 residents. In 2008, there were 27,922 dentists (7.6 per 10,000 population). There were 1.9 community hospital beds per 1,000 population in 2009. In 2010, there were 1,239 nursing homes with a total of 121,697 beds. It was estimated that 18.9 per cent of Californians aged 18-64 did not have health-care coverage (higher than the national average of 15.8 per cent). An estimated 14.4 per cent of Californians live in poverty (marginally higher than the US average of 14.3 per cent).

Am estimated 60.7 per cent of adults were considered overweight in 2012, and 24.0 per cent were considered obese; both these figures were lower than the national average. California reported 160,293 HIV/AIDS cases from the beginning of the epidemic to the end of 2008, and ranked 2nd highest in the cumulative number of reported AIDS cases. In 2009, a further 3,776 cases were reported in 2009. California also has the second-highest rate of TB, 7.3 per 100,000 persons. (Source: CDC)

EDUCATION

Primary and Secondary Education

There were 10,286 schools in California during the academic year 2009-10. Enrolment in Californian elementary and secondary schools was 6,263,449, the largest enrolment nationally. There were 313,795 classroom teachers, and a ratio of one teacher to 19.96 pupils, well above the national average of one to 15.38. Revenue from education reached $71.2 million in 2007-08, whilst current expenditure on state schools was $73.9 million.

Higher Education

There are 454 degree granting institutions in California. In 2010-11, 1.23 million men enrolled, together with 1.5 million women. An estimated 440,163 degrees/certificates were awarded, of which 164,239 were Bachelors, 65,050 were Masters and 16,382 were Doctorates. (Source: National Center for Education Statistics)

COMMUNICATIONS AND MEDIA

Newspapers

California Newspaper Publishers Association, URL: http://www.cnpa.com
Los Angeles Times, URL: http://www.latimes.com/
Los Angeles Independent, URL: http://www.laindependent.com/

Business Journals

Sacramento Business Journal, URL: http://sacramento.bcentral.com/sacramento/
San Francisco Business Times, URL: http://sanfrancisco.bcentral.com/sanfrancisco/

Broadcasting

Main television stations in Los Angeles include: KABC (ABC); KCBS (CBS); KNBC (NBC); KMET (World TV); KTTV (Fox); as well as nine independent stations. Main television stations in San Francisco include: KFWU, KGO and KNTV (all ABC); KPIX (CBS); KTVU (Fox); KDTV (Univision).

ENVIRONMENT

A number of air pollutants, byproducts of industrial processes, have an impact on the health of Californians. Air monitoring has shown that over 90 per cent of inhabitants breathe in unhealthy levels of air pollutants during the year.

Emissions of carbon dioxide from California's electricity generating industry reached 55.41 million metric tons in 2010 (down from 59,389,000 metric tons in 2006), ranking the state 16th in the US respectively. In 2010, approximately 2,522 metric tons (down from 4,000 metric tons in 2008) of sulphur dioxide and 79,589 metric tons (compared to 82,000 metric tons in 2008) of nitrogen oxide were also produced.

In January 2008, California filed a lawsuit against the US federal government, in an attempt to force car manufacturers to conform to tougher cuts in greenhouse gas emissions. The Californian authorities are aiming for a 30 per cent reduction in motor vehicle greenhouse gas emissions by 2016 through the strengthening of fuel efficiency standards. California claims it faces dangerous consequences from global warming, including to its mountain snowpack, which supplies a third of the state's drinking water, and to miles of coastline and levees threatened by rising sea levels.

California leads the nation in electricity generation from non-hydroelectric renewable energy sources, including geothermal power, wind power, fuel wood, landfill gas, and solar power. The State has also introduced strict fuel requirements for normal petrol cars, and most motorists are required to use a special blend called California Clean Burning Gasoline (CA CBG). California uses ethanol as a gasoline oxygenate additive, and the state is now the largest ethanol fuel market in the USA. In 2010, 144,569 alternative fueled vehicles in use (15.4 per cent). In 2011, 30.468 million barrels of ethanol were consumed (9.9 per cent of US total). As of 2012 there were four ethanol plants in operation. (Source: EIA)

SPACE PROGRAMME

Four of NASA's facilities are located in California: Ames Research Centre, Moffett Field; Dryden Flight Research Centre, Edwards; Jet Propulsion Laboratory, Pasadena; and Moffett Federal Airfield, Mountain View.
NASA, URL: http://www.nasa.gov/

COLORADO

Capital: Denver (Population, Census 2010: 600,158)

Head of State: John Hickenlooper (D) (Governor) (page 1441)

State Flag: Three horizontal and equal strips, the outer two blue and the inner one white, on which, one fifth of the length of the flag from the staff end, is superimposed a circular red 'C', inside which is a golden disc

CONSTITUTION AND GOVERNMENT

Constitution

Colorado entered the Union on 1 August 1876 as the 38th State. The executive branch of government consists of the governor and four other elected officials: lieutenant governor, secretary of state, attorney general, and state treasurer. In addition, the State Board of Education - consisting of the Commissioner, Chairman, Vice Chairman and five members - are elected on a partisan basis for terms of six years.

Colorado sends two senators and seven representatives to the US Congress. Following the 2000 Census, Colorado gained an extra Congressional seat from 2002.

To view the state constitution, please visit:
http://www.colorado.gov/dpa/doit/archives/constitution/index.html

Legislature

Colorado's bicameral legislature comprises the Senate and House of Representatives.

Senate/House of Representatives, Colorado State Capitol, 200 East Colfax, Denver CO 80203, USA. Tel: +1 303 866 2904 (House), +1 303 866 2316 (Senate), URL: http://www.leg.state.co.us/

Upper House

The Senate has 35 members who are elected for four years, one-half retiring every two years. Following the November 2012 elections, the Senate was composed of 29 Democrat seats and 16 Republican seats.

Lower House

The House of Representatives has 65 members who are elected for two years. Following the November 2012 elections, the House was composed of 37 Democrats and 28 Republicans, giving the Democrats control.

Elected Executive Branch Officials (as at April 2013)
Governor: John Hickenlooper (D) (page 1441)
Lieutenant Governor: Joseph Garcia (D)
Secretary of State: Scott Gessler (R)
Attorney General: John Suthers (R)
State Treasurer: Walker Stapleton (R)

Legislature (as at April 2013)
President of the Senate: John P. Morse (D)
President Pro Tempore: Lucia Guzman (D)
Senate Majority Leader: Morgan Carroll (D)
Senate Minority Leader: Bill Cadman (R)

UNITED STATES OF AMERICA

Speaker of the House: Mark Ferrandino (D)
Speaker Pro Tempore: Claire Levy (D)
House Majority Leader: Dickey Lee Hullinghorst (D)
House Minority Leader: Mark Waller (R)

US Senators: Mark Udall (D) (page 1529) and Michael F. Bennet (D) (page 1387)

Ministries
Office of the Governor, 136 State Capitol, Denver, CO 80203-1792, USA. Tel: +1 303 866 2471, fax: +1 303 866 2003, URL: http://www.colorado.gov/governor
Office of the Lieutenant Governor, 200 E Colfax, Room 130, Denver 80203, USA. Tel: +1 303 866 2087, fax: +1 303 866 5469, URL: http://www.colorado.gov/ltgovernor/index.html
Office of the Secretary of State, 1560 Broadway, Suite 200, Denver, CO 80202, USA. Tel: +1 303 894 2200, fax: +1 303 869 4860, URL: http://www.sos.state.co.us/
Department of Agriculture, 700 Kipling St., Suite 4000, Lakewood, CO 80215-5894, USA. Tel: +1 303 239 4100, fax: +1 303 239 4125, URL: http://www.colorado.gov/ag
Department of Corrections, 2862 South Circle Drive, Colorado Springs, Colorado 80906-4195, USA. Tel: +1 719 579 9580, fax: +1 719 226 4455, URL: http://www.doc.state.co.us/
Department of Education, 201 East Colfax Avenue, Denver, Colorado 80203-1704, USA. Tel: +1 303 866 6600, fax: +1 303 830 0793, URL: http://www.cde.state.co.us/
Department of Labour and Employment, 1515 Arapahoe Street, Tower 2, Suite 400, Denver, CO 80202-2117, USA. Tel: +1 303 318 8000, fax: +1 303 318 8048, URL: http://www.coworkforce.com/
Department of Law / Attorney General's Office, 1525 Sherman, 5th Floor, Denver CO 80203, USA. Tel: +1 303 866 4500, fax: +1 303 866 5691, URL: http://www.coloradoattorneygeneral.gov/
Department of Public Health and Environment, 4300 Cherry Creek Drive South, Denver, Colorado 80246-1530, USA. Tel: +1 303 692 2000, fax: +1 303 782 0095, URL: http://www.colorado.gov/
Department of Transportation, 4201 E. Arkansas Avenue, Denver, CO 80222, USA. Tel: +1 303 757 9011, e-mail: Info@dot.state.co.us, URL: http://www.coloradodot.info/
State Treasury, 140 State Capitol, Denver, CO 80203, USA. Tel: +1 303 866 2441, fax: +1 303 866 2123, URL: http://www.colorado.gov/treasury

Political Parties
Colorado Democratic Party, URL: http://www.coloradodems.org/
Republican Party of Colorado, URL: http://www.cologop.org/

Elections
Elections took place in November 2006 for the following statewide positions: Governor, Attorney General, Treasurer, Secretary of State and three Board of Education members as well as 18 State Senators and all 65 State Representatives. All seven US Representative seats were also up for election. Bill Ritter retained the governorship. Mr Ritter was not eligible to stand in the November 2010 election which was won by Democrat John Hickenlooper with 51 per cent of the vote.

In the November 2012 legislative elections, the Democrats lost one seat in the Senate (Democrats 19, Republicans, 16 seats). In the State House of Representatives, the Democrats retook the House and now have 37 seats compared to 28 for the Republicans.

LEGAL SYSTEM

Colorado has a total of 22 judicial districts, and approximately 256 justices and judges. Colorado's court system comprises the Supreme Court, the Court of Appeals, District Courts and County Courts. The Supreme Court's seven Justices are appointed by the Governor for a term of ten years and may be retained by popular vote. The Court of Appeals has a total of 22 judges, whilst the District Courts have 125 judges and the County Courts 118 judges.

Colorado has the death penalty. Only one person has been executed since 1976. As of January 2013, four inmates are currently on death row. An attempt to repeal the death penalty failed by one vote in 2009.

Supreme Court, Colorado State Judicial Building, 2 East 14th Avenue, 4th Floor, Denver, CO 80203, USA. Tel: +1 303 837 3790, URL: http://www.courts.state.co.us
Chief Justice: Michael L. Bender
Justices: Gregory J. Hobbs, Jr., Nancy Rice, Nathan Coats, Allison Eid, Monica Marquez, Brian Boatright
Court of Appeals, Colorado State Judicial Building, 2 East 14th Avenue, 3rd Floor, Denver, Colorado 80203, USA. Tel: +1 303 837 3785, URL: http://www.courts.state.co.us/coa
Chief Judge: Janice B. Davidson

LOCAL GOVERNMENT

According to the US 2007 local government census, for administrative purposes Colorado is divided into 62 county governments and 270 sub-county, or municipal, governments. In addition, there are 180 school district governments and 1,414 special district governments.

Colorado Department of Local Affairs, URL: http://www.dola.state.co.us/

AREA AND POPULATION

Area
Colorado is located in the west of the US, south of Wyoming, north of New Mexico, east of Utah, and west of Kansas and Nebraska. The total area of Colorado is 104,093.57 sq. miles, of which 103,717.53 sq. miles is land, and 376.04 sq. miles is water. Colorado is the only

U.S. state that lies entirely above 1,000 meters. The highest point in the state (and the entire length of the Rocky Mountains) is the summit of Mount Elbert at 14,440 feet. Colorado has more than 100 mountain peaks that exceed 4,000 meters. However, almost half of the state is made up of great plains which enjoy little rainfall and are used principally for ranching. The Continental Divide runs along the crest of the Rockies; this separates the watersheds that drain into the Pacific Ocean from those river systems which drain into the Atlantic Ocean.

The climate of Colorado is affected by the Rocky Mountains; conditions vary from semi-arid continental on the plains, to alpine in the Rocky Mountains.

To view a map of the state, please consult:
http://www.lib.utexas.edu/maps/us_2001/colorado_ref_2001.pdf

Population
According to the 2010 Census the 2010 population was 5,029,196, up from the mid-2009 estimate of 5,024,748. Since the Census of 2000, the population of Colorado has grown by 16.9 per cent (compared to the US average of 9.7 per cent) and is expected to reach 5.8 million by 2030. The population was estimated to be 5,187,582 in 2012. Average population density in 2007 was estimated at 47.6 people per sq. mile in Colorado, compared with 95.6 per sq. mile for the whole of the US. An estimated 6.7 per cent of the population is under 5 years (2011), 24.0 per cent under 18 years and 11.3 per cent is aged over 65 years. According to the Census, 49.9 per cent of the state population is female. According to the 2010 Census, 81.3 per cent of the population is white, and 4.0 per cent black. Approximately 20.7 per cent of the population is of Hispanic or Latino origin.

Births, Marriages, Deaths
The US Census Bureau (Population Division) (CDC) data puts the total number of births in 2010 at 66,355 and the number of deaths at 31,465, giving a natural population increase of 34,980 inhabitants. The fertility rate was 64.7 per 1,000 females aged 15-44 years and the death rate was 625.6 per 100,000 population. Net migration in 2009 contributed a further 48,669 residents. Infant mortality was 6.12 deaths per 1,000 live births in 2007. Marriages and divorces in 2007 numbered 29,206 and 21,178 respectively.

Public Holidays
In addition to national US holidays, the people of Colorado celebrate Colorado Day on 1st August. It is the day when, in 1876, Colorado became a state.

EMPLOYMENT

In December 2012, according to provisional figures, Colorado had a total civilian labour force of 2,726,000, of which 2,517,800 were employed and 208,200 were unemployed. The unemployment rate was 7.6 per cent, slightly lower than the national average of 7.8 per cent. Employment in most sectors was hit by the recession in 2010; jobs in the construction sector fell by 22.2 per cent, whilst mining jobs fell by 20.4 per cent. Manufacturing was also hard hit.

Preliminary figures for non-farm wage and salary employment in December 2012, according to industry, are shown on the following table:

Sector	No. of employed	Change over 12 months %
Mining and logging	28,700	3.6
Construction	119,500	6.0
Manufacturing	133,400	3.3
Trade, transport and utilities	407,400	1.5
Information	68,200	-3.4
Financial activities	147,000	2.6
Professional and business services	353,400	2.7
Educational and health services	282,400	3.1
Leisure and hospitality	282,100	2.6
Other services	96,500	3.3
Government	398,000	0.9
TOTAL	2,316,600	2.3

Source: Bureau of Labor Statistics

BANKING AND FINANCE

GDP/GNP, Inflation, National Debt
Colorado's Gross Domestic Product (current dollar) rose from $253,101 million in 2010 to $264,308 million in 2011. Real GDP grew by 1.4 per cent over 2010, lower than the US average per state of 2.6 per cent. In 2010, Colorado was ranked 39th in the US for its GDP.

The following table shows estimated Gross Domestic Product according to industry (figures in $million):

Industry	2008	2009	2010
Agriculture, forestry, fishing	2,158	2,282	2,576
Mining	8,361	9,273	10,953
Utilities	3,194	3,446	3,249
Construction	10,289	9,369	9,462
Manufacturing	16,959	19,103	20,595
Wholesale trade	12,513	12,841	13,746
Retail trade	14,037	14,663	15,150
Transport	6,336	6,402	6,565
Information	20,420	21,178	22,652
Finance and insurance	15,923	17,402	17,492
Real estate	32,859	31,010	31,089
Educational services	1,848	1,945	1,979

- continued

Health care and social assistance	15,226	16,026	16,652
Other non-govt. services	47,773	54,767	58,197
Government	30,608	32,086	33,478
TOTAL	244,422	253,101	264,308

Source: Bureau of Economic Analysis, Feb. 2013

Per capita GDP was $45,792 in 2011. In 2011 per capita income rose to US$44,053, up from an estimated $42,226 in 2010. The Consumer Price Index (CPI) for the Denver-Boulder-Greeley area rose from 212.5 in 2010 to 220.3 (1982-84=100). (Source: Bureau of Labor Statistics)

Balance of Payments / Imports and Exports

Total Colorado imports amounted to $11,346 million in 2010, up 31.5 per cent on the previous year. In 2011, imports amounted to $11,745 million, up 3.4 per cent on the previous year. Colorado's imports accounted for 0.5 per cent of US imports. Main imports are crude oil, reception apparatus for TV and phones for cellular and wireless networks. Main suppliers are Canada (32.9 per cent), China (16.5 per cent), Mexico, Germany and Switzerland.

Colorado's total exports amounted to $6,727 million in 2010, up 14.6 per cent from 2009. In 2011, exports amounted to $7,332 million, up 9 per cent on the previous year. Colorado's share of total US export revenue was 0.5 per cent in 2011.

The following table shows the top five export products in 2010 according to export revenue:

Product	Revenue ($m) 2010
Meat of bovine animals	307
Medical, surgical, dental, vet. instr. and appliances.	261
Civilian aircraft, engines, equipment and parts	240
Comp. with pyrimidine or piperazine ring	198
X-ray film in rolls	187

Source: US Census Bureau

The top five export trading partners in 2010-11, according to revenue, are shown on the following table:

Country	2010 ($m)	2011 *$m)	+/-% 2010-11
Canada	1,660	1,541	-7.2
Mexico	590	755	28.0
China	559	635	13.7
Japan	318	393	23.5
Netherlands	331	316	-4.5

Chambers of Commerce and Trade Organisations
Colorado Springs Chamber of Commerce, URL: http://www.coloradospringschamber.org/
Colorado Office of Economic Development and International Trade, URL: http://www.advancecolorado.com/

MANUFACTURING, MINING AND SERVICES

Primary and Extractive Industries
Colorado's mineral resources are considerable. Among the most plentiful are coal, gold, crude oil, gas and carbon dioxide. Recent statistics indicate that the state annually produces around $375 million worth of minerals, including gold, silver, zinc, molybdenum, gypsum, sand and gravel, and crushed stone.

Colorado's mining industry contributed an estimated $10,953 million towards the State Gross Domestic Product in 2011 (up from $9,273 million in 2010). In 2010, $5,695 million was earned through oil and gas extraction, $1,873 million from other mining and $1,705 million from support activities. (Source: BEA) Employment in the natural resources and mining sector was around 29,000 in March 2008.

Two of the USA's largest oil fields are found in Colorado; proven oil reserves were 386 million barrels in 2010. Colorado's oil industry had a total of 9,733 producing oil wells and 72 rotary rigs in operation in 2011 which produced around 30,870,000 barrels of crude oil. Crude oil refinery capacity was 103,000 bbl/d in 2011. Total petroleum consumption in 2009 reached 89.8 million barrels, of which 50.8 million barrels were motor gasoline.

Colorado's oil shale deposits, concentrated in the Piceance Basin in the western part of the State, hold an estimated 1 trillion barrels of oil (as much oil as the entire world's proven oil reserves); however, extraction of oil from shale remains highly speculative.

Colorado is one of the top natural gas-producing states, accounting for around 5 per cent of national production. Coalbed methane accounts for just over half of the state's production. Dry proved reserves of natural gas rose from 17,149 billion cubic feet in 2006 to 24,119 billion cu ft in 2010. In 2010, reserves of natural gas plant liquids amounted to 879 million barrels. There were 30,101 gas wells in 2011 (5.8 per cent of US total), and 1,578,379 million cu ft of natural gas were marketed. Total consumption of natural gas was 501,438 million cu ft in 2010 (2.1 per cent of US total). Colorado uses only about two-fifths of its natural gas production, the remainder going to California and to Midwest markets.

Colorado's coal industry had recoverable reserves of 225 million short tons in 2010 (1.2 per cent of US total), and produced a total of 26,890 thousand short tons in 2011. Total coal consumption fell from 19,779 thousand short tons in 2007 to 17,674,000 short tons in 2009. (Source: EIA)

Energy
Colorado's total energy production was 2,483 trillion Btu in 2010 (0.6per cent of US total). Total energy consumption was 1,452 trillion Btu in 2009 (1.5 per cent of US total). Per capita energy consumption was 301 million Btu in 2010, ranking the state 32nd in the US. The USA average state per capita consumption was an estimated 312 million Btu in 2011.

Colorado's electricity power industry had a net summer capability of 13,777 MW in 2009 (1.3 per cent of US total). The primary generating fuel in 2011 was coal (66.7 per cent) followed by natural gas (17.8 per cent), other renewables (11.6 per cent), and hydroelectric (3.9 per cent). (Source: EIA)

Manufacturing
The manufacturing industry contributed an estimated $20,595 million towards Colorado's GDP in 2011 (up from $19,103 million in 2010). In 2010, the largest sectors were computer and electronic product manufacturing ($4,868), food and tobacco products ($3,223 million) and chemical manufacturing ($1,943 million). (Source: BEA)

Service Industries
The services industry is Colorado's greatest contributor to GDP. In 2011, the highest revenue-producing sector was real estate, rental and leasing, which accounted for $31,089 million. Other major sectors were professional and technical services ($25,652 million), information ($22,652 million), and health and social assistance ($16,652 million). (Source: BEA)

Tourism
The accommodation and food services sector contributed $8,767 million towards the 2011 GDP, whilst the arts, entertainment and recreation services sector contributed $2,921 million. (Source: BEA)
Colorado Tourism Office, URL: http://www.colorado.com/

Agriculture
Colorado's agriculture industry contributed $2,576 million towards the state's 2011 GDP (up from $2,047 million in 2010). In 2010 the largest sector was the farming sector, earning some $2,047 million, whilst forestry, fishing and related activities earned $235 million. (Source: BEA)

According to the latest USDA Census of Agriculture, Colorado's farms numbered 36,100 in 2010, up from 31,361 in 2002. Total farmland was 31,200,000 acres in 2010, down from 32,349,832 acres in 1997, and the average size of a farm in Colorado fell from 993 acres in 2002 to 864 acres in 2010. Main crops include: Sheep, goats and products thereof (ranked 2nd in the USA), cattle (ranked 5th in the US), wheat for grain (ranked 7th), proso millet (ranked 1st), corn, hay, fruit and vegetables. As of 1 Jan. 2011, there were approximately 2.65 million head of cattle and calves, 720,000 hogs & pigs and 370,000 sheep.

The total value of agricultural products sold in 2007 was over $6 billion; crops accounted for over 1.9 billion, whilst livestock, poultry and products thereof earned some $4.07 billion.

COMMUNICATIONS AND TRANSPORT

International Airports
Denver International Airport (DIA) is the second largest airport in the world at 53 sq. miles. It is also the 10th busiest airport in the world, handling over 51 million passengers in 2008. In the same year, there were 625,884 aircraft operations through the airport.
Denver International Airport, URL: http://www.flydenver.com/

Railways
Denver has three major federal railways serving it: the Burlington Northern Railroad, the Santa Fe Railway, and the Union Pacific/Southern Pacific Railroad. The state has more than 3,000 miles of Class One tracks.

Roads
Colorado's highway system is over 9,100 miles and has 22,522 lane miles. In total, Colorado has 953 miles of Interstate Highways which centre on the north-south interstate, the I-25, and the east-west interstate, the I-70.

HEALTH

The National Centre for Health Statistics estimated that there were 26.8 doctors (including osteopaths) per 10,000 people in 2009 (compared with the US average of 27.4). In 2008, there were 3,212 dentists (6.5 per 10,000 population). In the same year, there were 2.1 community hospital beds per 1,000 residents. In 2012, there were 210 nursing homes in the state in 2010, with 20,259 beds.

In 2012, some 56.8 per cent of adults were considered overweight, and 21.0 per cent were obese; both figures were considerably lower than the national averages of 63 per cent and 26.2 per cent respectively. Colorado reported 9,639 HIV/AIDS cases from the beginning of the epidemic to the end of 2008, and ranked 23rd highest among the 50 states in the cumulative number of reported AIDS cases by end 2008. In 2009, a further 348 cases were reported. In 2008, Colorado had the 31st highest rate of TB among states in the US, 2.1 per 100,000 persons. Alcohol consumption is higher than the national average, but homicides and heart disease-related deaths are well below the national average. In 2007-11, around 15.9 per cent of adults (18-64) had no health insurance cover (higher than the US average of 15.8 per cent). According to the US Census Bureau, an estimated 12.5 per cent of people live in poverty (lower than the US average of 14.3 per cent). (Source: CDC)

UNITED STATES OF AMERICA

EDUCATION

Primary/Secondary Education
The number of students in Colorado's 1,817 public elementary and secondary schools was 832,368 during the educational year 2009-10. During the same year, there were 49,060 teachers working in the state schools and the teacher/pupil ratio was one to 16.97.

During the academic year 2007-08, revenue from education reached $8.1 billion, and current expenditure on state schools reached $8.9 billion.

Higher Education
In 2010-11 there were 86 degree granting institutions in Colorado, 28 of which were publicly run. There were 156,856 men enrolled and 199,798 women. An estimated 72,595 degrees were conferred in 2010-11, of which 29,560 were Bachelors, 13,054 were Masters and 2,205 were Doctorates. (Source: National Center for Education Statistics)

COMMUNICATIONS AND MEDIA

Newspapers
Colorado has 25 daily newspapers, including: the Denver Post, Rocky Mountain News, Colorado Springs Gazette, The Daily Camera, Jefferson County Transcript Online, Montrose Daily Press, and the Aspen Times.

The Denver Post, URL: http://www.denverpost.com/
The Colorado Springs Business Journal, URL: http://www.csbj.com/
The Denver Business Journal, URL: http://www.bizjournals.com/

Broadcasting
There are 19 network television stations in Colorado, seven of which are in the capital, Denver. They include: KRMA (run by PBS); KMGH (CBS); KUSA (NBC); KBDI (PBS); KDVR (Fox); and KCNC (independent). The state also has 13 public radio stations.

ENVIRONMENT

Colorado's electricity industry relies mainly on coal as a generating fuel. According to EIA data, in 2010, its carbon dioxide emissions were 40.5 million metric tons of carbon dioxide (compared to 38,988,708 metric tons in 2009 and 41,847,000 metric tons in 2006), ranking it 24th in the US and accounting for 1.7 per cent of the US total. Sulfur dioxide emissions were 44,876 metric tons in 2010 (compared to 43,184 metric tons in 2009) and nitrogen oxide emissions amounted to 55,063 metric tons (compared to 54,296 metric tons in 2009).

Colorado has five ethanol plants with a combined capacity of 125 million gal per year. Approximately 19,356 alternative-fuelled vehicles were in use in 2010. Ethanol consumption was 3.39 million barrels in 2011. (Source: EIA)

CONNECTICUT

Capital: Hartford (Population, Census 2010: 124,775)

Head of State: Dan Malloy (D) (Governor) (page 1470)

State Flag: An azure blue field with a gold and silver border in the centre of which appears the armorial bearings in argent white. Under the shield appears a white streamer with a gold and brown border on which appears the motto: 'Qui Transtulit Sustinet' ('He Who Transplanted Sustains Us')

CONSTITUTION AND GOVERNMENT

Constitution
Connecticut is one of the original 13 states of the Union, having joined on 9 January 1788. According to the Constitution, the governor heads the executive branch of government, assisted by five other elected officials: the lieutenant-governor, secretary of the state, treasurer, comptroller and attorney general. All are elected by the people for four-year terms. The lieutenant governor also serves as the president of the Senate.

Connecticut currently sends two senators and five representatives to the US Congress. Connecticut's six congressional districts were reduced to five in 2002 following re-districting.

To view the state constitution, please visit: http://www.sots.ct.gov/RegisterManual/SectionI/ctconstit.htm

Legislature
Connecticut's bicameral legislature consists of the Senate and the House of Representatives.

Upper House
The Senate has 36 members who are elected for two years. The Lieutenant Governor also serves as the President of the Senate. Following the 2012 elections, the Senate was divided as follows: 22 Democrats and 14 Republicans.
Senate, State Capitol, Room 305, Legislative Office Building, Hartford, Connecticut 06106-1591, USA. Tel: +1 860 240 0500 (Clerk), URL: http://www.cga.ct.gov

Lower House
House of Representatives has 151 members who are elected for two years. Following the 2012 elections, the House was divided into 98 Democrat seats and 53 Republican seats.
House of Representatives, State Capitol, Room 109, Legislative Office Building, Hartford, Connecticut 06106-1591, USA. Tel: +1 860 240 0400 (Clerk), URL: http://www.cga.ct.gov

---

Elected Executive Branch Officials (as at April 2013)
Governor: Dannel. Malloy (D) (page 1470)
Lieutenant Governor: Nancy Wyman (D)
Secretary of the State: Denise Merrill (D)
Attorney General: George Jepsen (D)
State Treasurer: Denise L. Nappier (D)
State Comptroller: Kevin Lembo (D)

General Assembly (as at April 2013)
President Pro Tem of the Senate: Donald E. Williams Jr (D)
Senate Majority Leader: Martin Mooney (D)
Senate Minority Leader: John McKinney (R)
Speaker of the House: Brendar Sharkey (D)
Majority Leader of the House: Joe Aresimowicz (D)
Minority Leader of the House: Lawrence F. Cafero, Jr. (R)

US Senators: Richard Blumenthal (page 1390) (D) and Chris Murphy (D) (page 1482)

Ministries
Office of the Governor, State Capitol, 210 Capitol Avenue, Hartford, CT 06106, USA. Tel: +1 860 566 4840, URL: http://www.state.ct.us/governor/
Office of the Secretary of the State, 210 Capitol Avenue, Suite 104, Hartford, CT 06106, USA. Tel: +1 860 509 6000, URL: http://www.sots.state.ct.us/
Office of the State Treasurer, 55 Elm Street, Hartford, CT 06106, USA. Tel: +1 860 702 3000, URL: http://www.state.ct.us/ott/
Office of the State Comptroller, 55 Elm Street, Hartford, Connecticut 06106, USA. Tel: +1 860 702 3300, fax: +1 860 702 3319, e-mail: comptroller.wyman@po.state.ct.us, URL: http://www.osc.state.ct.us/
Office of the Attorney General, 55 Elm Street, Hartford, Connecticut 06106 (PO Box 120, Hartford, Connecticut 06141-0120), USA. Tel: +1 860 808 5318, fax: +1 860 808 5387, e-mail: Attorney.General@po.state.ct.us, URL: http://www.ct.gov/ag
Department of Agriculture, 765 Asylum Avenue, Hartford, CT 06105, USA. Tel: +1 860 713 2500, fax: +1 860 713 2514, e-mail: ctdeptag@po.state.ct.us, URL: http://www.state.ct.us/doag/
Department of Children and Families, 505 Hudson Street, Hartford, CT 06106, USA. Tel: +1 860 550 6300, URL: http://www.state.ct.us/dcf/
Department of Correction, 24 Wolcott Hill Road, Wethersfield, CT 06109, USA. Tel: +1 860 692 7480, fax: +1 860 692 7783, e-mail: doc.pio@po.state.ct.us, URL: http://www.ct.gov/doc/site/default.asp
Department of Economic and Community Development, 505 Hudson Street, Hartford, CT 06106, USA. Tel: +1 860 270 8000, e-mail: DECD@po.state.ct.us, URL: http://www.ct.gov/ecd/site/default.asp
Department of Education, 165 Capitol Avenue, Hartford, CT 06145, USA. Tel: +1 860 713 6548, URL: http://www.state.ct.us/sde/
Department of Environmental Protection, 79 Elm Street, Hartford, CT 06106-5127, USA. Tel: +1 860 424 3000, e-mail: dep.webmaster@po.state.ct.us, URL: http://dep.state.ct.us/
Department of Public Health, 410 Capitol Avenue, PO Box 340308, Hartford, Connecticut 06134-0308, USA. Tel: +1 860 509 8000, URL: http://www.dph.state.ct.us/
Department of Transportation, 2800 Berlin Turnpike, Newington, CT 06131-7546, USA. Tel: +1 860 594 2000, URL: http://www.ct.gov/dot/

Political Parties
Connecticut Democratic Party, URL: http://www.ctdems.org
Connecticut Republican Party, URL: http://www.ctgop.org/

Elections
In the 2012 state legislative elections the Democrats retained their control of the Senate but their majority was reduced by one seat (22 seats compared to the Republican's 14). In the House of Representatives, the Democrat majority was reduced by one seat (Democrats 98, Republicans 43).

In the November 2010 gubanatorial election Governor Rell did not run for election. Democrat Dan Malloy narrowly beat Republican Tom Foley with 50 per cent of the vote to 49 per cent.

LEGAL SYSTEM

Connecticut's court system comprises the Supreme Court, the Appellate Court, the Superior Court, and the Probate Court.

The Supreme Court is Connecticut's highest court and consists of a Chief Justice and six Associate Justices. The Associate Justices are approved by the General Assembly on nomination by the Governor and serve for a term of eight years. All terms expire by limitation of age at 70.

The Appellate Court consists of nine judges, one of whom is appointed Chief Judge by the Chief Justice.

The Superior Court is divided into four main trial divisions: civil, criminal, family and juvenile. Superior Court Judges (four Chief Administrative Judges and 13 Administrative Judges) are nominated by the Governor and appointed by the General Assembly for an eight-year term.

Each Probate Court has a single judge who is elected for four years by voters in each of the 123 probate districts.

In April 2012 Connecticut abolished the death penalty for future cases. Death sentences already passed remain in place. As of January 2013 there were 11 people on death row. The most recent execution took place in 2005. According to the DPIC the murder rate is 3.6 per 100,000.

Same-sex marriage is legal in the state.

Supreme Court, URL: http://www.jud.ct.gov/index.asp
Senior Justice: Chase T. Rogers
Justices: Flemming Norcott, Richard Palmer, Peter Zarella, C. Ian McLachlan, Dennis Eveleigh, Lubbie Harper Jr, Senior Justice: Christine Vertefeuille
Appellate Court, Chief Judge: Alexandra Di Pentima

LOCAL GOVERNMENT

Unlike most other states, Connecticut does not have county government. Although the state is divided into counties, county government was abolished in 1960. Counties are, however, still used by the state to organize its judicial and state marshall system.

Connecticut has 149 towns, which serve as the local political subdivision of the state and 30 municipal governments. There are also 21 cities, most of which have a merged city-town government. There are also nine incorporated boroughs which may provide additional services to a section of town. In addition, there are 453 special district governments, 17 school district governments, and 149 dependent public school systems.

Town elections, city elections and borough elections take place biennially, in odd years, usually in May or November.

Department of Economic and Community Development, URL: http://www.ct.gov/ecd/site/default.asp

AREA AND POPULATION

Area
Connecticut is located in the north-east of the US in New England, south of Massachusetts, west of Rhode Island, and east of New York State. To the south is Long Island Sound. Its total area is 5,543.33 sq. miles, of which 4,844.80 sq. miles is land and 698.53 sq. miles is water. The highest peak in Connecticut is Bear Mountain.

To view a map, consult http://www.lib.utexas.edu/maps/united_states/connecticut_90.jpg

Population
According to the 2010 Census, the 2010 population of Connecticut at 3,574,097, up from the mid-2009 estimate of 3,518,288. Over the period 2000-10, the population grew by 4.9 per cent. The population is expected to reach 3.69 million by 2030. In 2012, the population was estimated to be 3,590,347. Connecticut's population density is the fourth largest in the USA, at 722.6 people per sq. mile. Fairfield County has the greatest number of inhabitants, with a 2010 population of 916,829, whilst Hartford County has 894,014 inhabitants. The state's largest city, Bridgeport, had a population of 144,229. Approximately 5.5 per cent of the population is under 5 years (2011), 22.4 per cent under 18 years and 14.4 per cent is aged over 65 years. According to the 2010 Census, 51.3 per cent of the state population is female. According to the 2010 Census, approximately 77.6 per cent of the population is white, and 10.1 per cent black. An estimated 13.4 per cent of the population are of Hispanic or Latino origin.

Births, Marriages, Deaths
The US Census Bureau (CDC) estimated the number of births in 2010 at 37,708, and the number of deaths at 28,692, giving a natural population increase of 9,016 people. The net fertility rate was 54.5 per 1,000 women aged 15-44 years and the death rate was 802.8 per 100,000 population. Net migration in 2009 amounted to 3,498 people. Infant deaths numbered 276 in 2007, equivalent to a rate of 6.63 deaths per 1,000 live births. Provisional figures suggest that there were 17,328 marriages and 10,714 divorces in 2007.

State Public Holidays
In addition to celebrating the national holidays, the state of Connecticut celebrates Lincoln Day on February 12th.

EMPLOYMENT

Preliminary figures indicate that Connecticut's total civilian labour force in December 2012 numbered 1,873,300, of which 1,712,900 were in employment and 160,500 were unemployed. The unemployment rate was 8.6 per cent, above the national rate of 7.8 per cent in December 2012. (Source: Bureau of Labor Statistics)

The following table shows preliminary figures for December 2012 non-farm wage and salary employment (seasonally adjusted) according to industry:

Industry	No. of Employed	Change over 12 months %
Logging and mining	600	20.0

- continued

Construction	49,100	-0,2
Manufacturing	163,800	-0.6
Trade, transport and utilities	293,100	-0.7
Information	32,000	1.3
Financial activities	130,300	-1.8
Professional and business services	192,200	-2.1
Leisure and hospitality	139,200	0.6
Other services	60,600	1.0
Government	234,100	-1.2
TOTAL	1,623,400	0.0

Source: Bureau of Labor Statistics

BANKING AND FINANCE

GDP/GNP, Inflation, National Debt
GDP was US$230.1 billion in 2011, ranked 24th in the US. The growth rate was 2.0 per cent. The largest industry was finance and insurance (19.4 per cent).

The following table shows the state's Gross Domestic Product according to industry (figures in $million):

Industry	2009	2010	2011
Agriculture, forestry & fishing	321	296	304
Mining	44	58	55
Utilities	4,022	3,872	3,539
Construction	5,944	5,707	5,803
Manufacturing	23,502	23,278	25,008
Wholesale Trade	11,608	11,774	12,345
Retail trade	11,109	11,573	11,925
Transport	3,483	3,420	3,555
Information	8,525	8,691	9,069
Finance and insurance	36,119	42,753	44,611
Real estate	29,838	28,948	29,869
Educational services	4,041	4,165	4,299
Health care and social assistance	17,458	18,273	18,788
Other non-govt. services	36,277	38,018	39,910
Government	21,245	20,519	21,009
TOTAL	213,534	221,347	230,090

Source: Bureau of Economic Analysis, Feb. 2013

Per capita personal income in the state averaged an estimated $57,902 in 2011, up 4.4 per cent on 2010 and above the national average of $41,560 and one of the highest in the USA. Connecticut per capita GDP amounted to $56,242, in 2011 one of the highest in the US.

The annual Consumer Price Index (CPI) for the New York-Northern New Jersey-Long Island, NY-NJ-CT-PA urban area (all items) rose from 236.8 in 2010 to 247.7 in 2011.(1982-84 = 100). (Source: Bureau of Labor Statistics)

Balance of Payments / Imports and Exports
Total Connecticut imports amounted to $18,620 million in 2010, up 12.2 per cent. They rose by 28.8 per cent to $24,028 million in 2011. State imports account for 1.1 per cent of total US imports. Main imports are turbo jet and turboproller parts, silver and light oils. Main suppliers are Mexico, Canada and China.

Total export revenue rose from $16,056 million in 2010 to $16,212 million in 2011, an increase of 1.0 per cent. The state contributes 1.1 per cent of the national total export revenue. (Source: US Census Bureau, Foreign Trade Division).

Merchandise export revenue in 2010-11, according to the top five international trading partners, is shown on the following table:

Country	2010 ($m)	2011 ($m)	+/-% 2010-11
France	2,226	1,971	-11.4
Canada	1,622	1,717	5.8
Germany	1,268	1,384	9.1
Mexico	989	1,098	11.0
China	1,024	983	-4.0

Source: US Census Bureau

The top five export products in 2010, according to export revenue, are shown on the following table (figures in $ million):

Product	Revenue ($m)	+/-2009-10
Civilian aircraft, engines, equipment and parts	6,178	10.1
Wheat (other than durum wheat) and meslin	522	89.8
Helicopters of an unladen weight exceeding 2000 Kg	328	-0.3
Soybeans	238	-39.5
Oil (not crude) from petrol & bitum mineral etc	223	202.4

Source: US Census Bureau

Chambers of Commerce and Trade Organisations
Connecticut Economic Resource Centre, Inc., URL: http://www.cerc.com/
Department of Economic and Community Development, URL: http://www.ct.gov/ecd
Connecticut Business and Industry Association, URL: http://www.cbia.com/home.htm

UNITED STATES OF AMERICA

MANUFACTURING, MINING AND SERVICES

Primary and Extractive Industries
The mining industry contributed an estimated $55 million (down from $58 million in 2010) in 2011. Top mining sectors in 2010 were non-oil and gas mining ($53 million) and support activities ($5 million). (Source: BEA)

Connecticut has no reserves of crude oil, production capability or refineries. There are no reserves of natural gas in Connecticut.

Energy
Total energy production in 2010 was 200 trillion Btu (0.3 per cent of the US). Total energy consumption was 754 trillion Btu in 2010 (0.8 per cent of the US total). Per capita energy consumption in the same year was 211 million Btu, ranking the state 47th in the US. Total petrol consumption in 2010 totalled 63.87 million barrels, over half of which (34.9 million barrels) was in the form of motor gasoline. Natural gas consumption was an 299,710 million cubic feet in 2011. Coal consumption was 325,000 short tons in 2011.

Connecticut's electricity industry relies on nuclear energy, which accounted for 36 per cent of industry generation in 2011. Natural gas accounted for 57 per cent of industry generation. Net summer capability in 2010 was 8,284 MW (0.8 per cent of US total), whilst net generation in 2008 was 34,681,736 MWh (37th in the US).

Nearly half of Connecticut's net electricity generation comes from Connecticut's Millstone nuclear reactor.

Connecticut has set a target of generating 20 per cent of the State's electricity fron renewable energy resources by 2020. Approximately 3 per cent net electricity's generation came from renewable energy in 2011.

In June 2007, Connecticut adopted a renewable portfolio standard that requires 27 per cent of the State's electricity to be generated from renewable sources by 2020. In 2008, Connecticut ranked in the top-ten States for solar power capacity within the United States. However, in 2010, renewable sources contributed less than 2.8 per cent of the state's total electricity generation.

Manufacturing
Manufacturing is Connecticut's fourth largest contributor to GDP, accounting for an estimated $25,008 million in 2011 (up from $23,278 million in 2010). Top manufacturing sectors in 2010 were chemical products ($4,049 million), transport equipment other than motor vehicle and ancilliaries ($4,989 million), fabricated metal products ($3,098 million) and electrical equipment ($1,498 million). (Source: BEA) Connecticut leads the USA in the production of aircraft engines, helicopters, submarines, pharmaceuticals, optical and medical instruments, and electronic components. Manufacturing employment fell by around six per cent over the year to March 2009.

Service Industries
The services sector is the greatest contributor to Connecticut's GDP. In 2011, the most important subsector was finance and insurance, accounting for an estimated $44,611 million. Real estate and renting saw revenues of around $29,869 million, whilst professional and technical services contributed around $16,858 million to state GDP, and health care and social assistance accounted for an estimated $18,798 million. (Source: BEA)

Tourism
The arts, entertainment and recreation services sector contributed $1,590 million towards the 2011 state GDP, continuing an upward trend. The accommodation and food services sector contributed $4,709 million in 2010, up from $4,945 million in 2009. (Source: BEA) **Connecticut Commission on the Arts, Tourism, Culture, History and Film, Tourism Division**, URL: http://www.tourism.state.ct.us/

Agriculture
Connecticut's agriculture, forestry and fisheries industry contributed an estimated $304 million towards the 2011 GDP (up from $296 million in 2010). In 2010, crop and animal farming contributed $247 million, whilst forestry, fishing and related activities produced $49 million. (Source: BEA)

According to USDA National Agricultural Statistics Service, there were a total of 4,900 farms in Connecticut in 2010, covering some 400,000 acres. The average size of a farm in 2010 was 82 acres. Top exported agricultural goods were tobacco (7th largest producer in the US), poultry, dairy produce and fruits and preparations. As of 1 Jan. 2011, there were an estimated 49,000 cattle and calves, 3,400 hogs & pigs.

In 2007, the total value of agricultural products sold reached some $551,553,000; most was earned through the sale of crops ($401,372,000) and the remaining revenue came from livestock and poultry products ($150,181,000).

COMMUNICATIONS AND TRANSPORT

International Airports
Connecticut has six state-owned airports including Bradley International Airport at Windsor Locks. The state also has 25 commercial airports, eight commercial heliports, 52 private heliports, five private seaplane bases, two commercial seaplane bases, and 28 private airports.

Bradley International Airport, URL: http://www.bradleyairport.com/

Railways
There are 12 railroads, 570 route miles of active trackage and 822 track miles of active trackage (including multi-track commuter mainlines and Amtrak lines).

Roads
Connecticut's state highway system has a total length of 4,101.54 miles with 726.07 miles of divided lane highways. It has 3,731.84 state maintained routes, and 369.70 state maintained access road and ramps. Connecticut is crossed by a number of Interstate highways, including I-95, running along Connecticut's Long Island Sound shoreline; I-91, running north from New Haven; I-84, running north-east through Hartford; and I-395, running south along the eastern border of Connecticut.

Shipping
Connecticut's ferry services include the Bridgeport to Port Jefferson Ferry, from Bridgeport, CT, to Port Jefferson, NY; the Chester to Hadlyme Ferry, crossing the Connecticut River; the Glastonbury/Rocky Hill Ferry, an open flatboat towed across the Connecticut River; the Block Island and New London Ferry, a car ferry linking New London with Block Island, RI; the New London to Fishers Island Ferry, an NY ferry; the New London to Montauk Ferry, an NY ferry; and the New London to Orient Point, NY, Ferry.

HEALTH

The National Centre for Health Statistics estimated that there were 36.8 doctors per 10,000 inhabitants in 2009 (well above the US average of 27.4). In 2008, there were 2,610 dentists (7.5 per 10,000 population). In 2009, there were 2.3 community hospital beds per 1,000 people (below the US average of 2.6 beds), and 239 nursing homes with 29,255 beds.

According to figures published by the Center for Disease Control (CDC), Connecticut reported 16,127 HIV/AIDS cases from the beginning of the epidemic to the end of 2008, and ranked 16th highest in the cumulative number of reported cases by end 2008. In 2009, a further 308 cases were reported. Connecticut scores below the national average in many health risk surveys such as those measuring the nation's obesity, homicides, breast cancer deaths and diabetes among adults. In 2012, 59.6 per cent of the adult population were considered overweight and 22.5 per cent obese. An estimated 10.5 of the population had no healthcare insurance over the period 2007-11.

EDUCATION

Primary/Secondary Education and Vocational Education
In the academic year 2009-10, there were 1,178 schools in the state. 563,985 pupils attended public elementary and secondary schools. There were 43,592 teachers and the teacher/pupil ratio stood at one to 12.94.

Connecticut earned some $9.4 billion in education revenues in 2007-08, and spent $9.6 billion on state education.

Higher Education
In the year 2010-11, there were 47 degree-granting institutions in Connecticut, 22 of which were public. An estimated 82,122 men enrolled, together with 110,657 women. 38,740 degrees/certificates were conferred, of which 19,680 were Bachelors, 8,639 were Masters and 1,834 were doctorates. (Source: National Center for Education Statistics)

COMMUNICATIONS AND MEDIA

Newspapers
Connecticut has 19 daily newspapers, including: Connecticut Post, The Bristol Press, The News-Times, Greenwich Time, The Hartford Courant, Journal Inquirer, Record-Journal, The Advocate, and The Chronicle.
Connecticut Post, URL: http://www.connpost.com/

Business Journals
The Hartford Business Journal, URL: http://www.hbjournal.com/

Broadcasting
There are 11 network television stations in Connecticut, amongst which are: WEDW, WEDH, WFSB, WTIC, WRDM. There are also 39 FM radio stations in the state.

ENVIRONMENT

According to EIA statistics, Connecticut's electricity industry emissions of carbon dioxide reached 9,201,364 metric tons in 2010, up from 8,046,088 in 2009, ranking the state 41st in the US. In 2010, sulfur dioxide emissions amounted to 2,032 metric tons and emissions of nitrogen oxide amounted to 7,092 metric tons. Connecticut requires the use of reformulated motor gasoline blended with ethanol, and there are now over 5,400 alternative-fueled vehicles in use. Ethanol consumption amounted to 4.05 million barrels in 2010. In 2008, the state ranked among the top-ten states for solar power capacity. (Source: EIA)

DELAWARE

Capital: Dover (Population, Census 2010: 36,047)

Head of State: Jack A. Markell (D) (Governor) (page 1471)

State Flag: A background of colonial blue on which is placed a buff coloured diamond bearing the state coat of arms, below which appear the words 'December 7, 1787', the date Delaware ratified the federal Constitution

CONSTITUTION AND GOVERNMENT

Constitution

Delaware was one of the original 13 states of the Union and was first to ratify the United States Constitution, on 7 December 1787. The first Constitution was adopted in 1792, whilst the present constitution was adopted in 1897, amended many times since. Under the terms of the current constitution the governor heads the executive branch of government assisted by five other elected officials: the lieutenant governor, attorney general, state auditor of accounts, insurance commissioner, and state treasurer.

Delaware sends two Senators and one At Large Representative to the US Congress, Washington, DC.

To view the state constitution, please visit: http://www.state.de.us/facts/constit/welcome.htm

Legislature

The bicameral parliament, or General Assembly, consists of an upper and a lower house: the Senate and the House of Representatives. Delaware's General Assembly is composed entirely of part-time legislators. The Assembly meets from the second Tuesday of January until 30 June.

Delaware General Assembly, Legislative Hall, Dover, DE 19901, USA. Tel: +1 302 744 4114, URL: http://legis.delaware.gov/

Upper House

The Senate has 21 members who are elected for four-year terms; one-half of Senate seats are contested in each general election. The lieutenant governor also serves as the president of the senate. Senators can serve an unlimited number of terms. Following the 2012 elections, 13 Senate seats were held by the Democrats and 8 by the Republicans.

Senate, Legislative Hall, 411 Legislative Avenue, Dover, DE 19901, USA. Tel: +1 302 744 4129 (Secretary of the Senate), URL: http://legis.delaware.gov/

Lower House

The House of Representatives has 41 members who are elected for two years. Following the 2012 elections, the House of Representatives was composed of 27 Democrats and 14 Republican seats.

House of Representatives, Legislative Hall, 411 Legislative Avenue, Dover, DE 19901, USA. Tel: +1 302 744 4087 (Chief Clerk), URL: http://legis.delaware.gov/

Elected Executive Branch Officials (as at June 2013)

Governor: Jack Markell (D) (page 1471)
Lieutenant Governor: Matthew Denn (D)
Attorney General: Joseph R. (Beau) Biden (D)
State Auditor of Accounts: R. Thomas Wagner, Jr. (R)
Insurance Commissioner: Karen Weldin Stewart (D)
State Treasurer: Chipman Flowers Jr (D)

Legislature (as at June 2013)

President of the Senate: Lt. Gov. Matt Denn (D)
President Pro Tempore of the Senate: Patricia M. Blevins (D)
Senate Majority Leader: David B. McBride (D)
Senate Minority Leader: Gregory F. Lavelle (R)
Speaker of the House: Peter C. Schwartzkopf (D)
House Majority Leader: Valerie Longhurst (D)
House Minority Leader: Daniel B. Short (R)

State Senators: Chris Coons (D) (page 1408) and Thomas Carper (D) (page 1401)

Ministries

Office of the Governor, Tatnall Building, William Penn Street, 2nd Floor, Dover, DE 19901, USA. Tel: +1 302 744 4101, fax: +1 302 739 2775, URL: http://governor.delaware.gov/
Office of the Lieutenant Governor, Tatnall Building, William Penn Street, Dover, DE 19901, USA. Tel: +1 302 577 8787, URL: http://ltgov.delaware.gov/
Office of the Secretary of State, 401 Federal Street, Suite 3, Dover, DE 19901, USA. Tel: +1 302 739 4111, fax: +1 302 739 3811, URL: http://sos.delaware.gov/default.shtml
State Treasurer's Office, Thomas Collins Building, 2nd Floor, 540 S. Dupont Highway, Dover, DE 19901, USA. Tel: +1 302 744 1000, fax: +1 302 739 5635, URL: http://treasury.delaware.gov/
Department of Agriculture, 2320 S. DuPont Highway, Dover, DE 19901, USA. Tel: +1 302 698 4500, fax: +1 302 697 6287, URL: http://dda.delaware.gov/
Office of the Attorney General, Carvel State Office Building, 820 N. French Street, Wilmington, DE 19801, USA. Tel: +1 302 577 8400, fax: +1 302 577 6630, URL: http://attorneygeneral.delaware.gov/
Department of Services for Children, Youth and their Families, 1825 Faulkland Rd, Wilmington, DE 19805-1195, USA. Tel: +1 302 633 2655 e-mail: info.dscyf@state.de.us, URL: http://kids.delaware.gov/
Department of Education, John G. Townsend Bldg, 401 Federal Street, Suite 2, Dover, DE 19901, USA. Tel: +1 302 739 4601, fax: +1 302 739 4654, URL: http://www.doe.state.de.us

Office of the Secretary of Finance, Thomas Collins Building, 540 S. DuPont Highway, 3rd Floor, Dover, DE 19901, USA. Tel: +1 302 744 1100, fax: +1 302 739 5000, URL: http://finance.delaware.gov/
Office of the Secretary of Health and Social Services, 1901 N. Du Pont Highway, Main Building, New Castle, DE 19720, USA. Tel: +1 302 255 9040 / +1 302 744 4550, fax: +1 302 255 4429, URL: http://www.dhss.delaware.gov/dhss/
Office of the Secretary of Labour, 4425 North Market Street, 4th Floor, Wilmington, Delaware 19802, USA. Tel: +1 302 761 8085, URL: http://www.delawareworks.com/
Department of Natural Resources and Environmental Control, 89 Kings Highway, Dover, DE 19901, USA. Tel: +1 302 739 4506, URL: http://www.dnrec.delaware.gov/
Department of Transportation, 800 Bay Road, PO Box 778, Dover, DE 19903, USA. Tel: +1 302 760 2080, URL: http://www.deldot.net/

Political Parties

Delaware Democratic Party, URL: http://www.deldems.org/
Republican State Committee of Delaware, URL: http://www.delawaregop.com/

Elections

General Elections took place in November 2012 for all of the Senate's 21 seats. In the State Senate the Democrats retained their majority but lost one seat (Democrats 13, Republicans 8). In the State House of Representatives all seats were contested. The Democrats increased their majority by one seat (27 Democrats, 14 Republicans).

Elections for State Governor took place in November 2012. The incumbent governor, Jack Markell (D), won the post with 69 per cent of the vote. The Insurance Commissioner, Karen Weldin Stewart (D), was also re-elected.

LEGAL SYSTEM

The judiciary of Delaware comprises the following courts: Supreme Court, Court of Chancery, Superior Court, and Courts of Limited Jurisdiction (Family Court, Court of Common Pleas, Justice of the Peace Courts, and Alderman's Courts).

The Supreme Court's Chief Justice and four Associate Justices are all appointed by the Governor, with confirmation by the Senate, for twelve-year terms.

The budget of the Supreme Court in 2010 was $3,140,700, the Court of Chancery $3,012,700, and the Superior Court $21,257,200.

There are currently 17 men on death row in Delaware. The most recent execution took place in 2005. According to the DPIC the murder rate is 5.3 per 100,000.

Supreme Court of Delaware, 55 The Green, PO Box 476, Dover, DE 19903, USA. Tel: +1 302 739 4155, fax: +1 302 739 3751, URL: http://courts.delaware.gov
Chief Justice: Myron T. Steele
Justices: Randy J. Holland, Carolyn Berger, Jack B. Jacobs, Henry duPont Ridgely

LOCAL GOVERNMENT

For administrative purposes, Delaware is divided into three county governments (Kent, New Castle, and Sussex) and 57 sub-county general purpose governments. All 57 of the sub-county governments are municipal. There are no town or township governments. In addition, there are 19 school district governments and 259 special district governments.

AREA AND POPULATION

Area

Delaware is situated on the eastern seaboard of the US. The states nearest Delaware are New Jersey, Maryland and Pennsylvania. The total area of Delaware is 2,489.27 sq. miles, of which 1,953.56 sq. miles is land and 535.71 sq. miles is water. Delaware is the second-smallest state in the US, after Rhode Island, and almost all of it is a part of the Atlantic Coastal Plain.

To view a map of the state, please consult:
http://www.lib.utexas.edu/maps/us_2001/maryland_delaware_ref_2001.pdf

Population

According to the 2010 Census, the 2010 population was 897,934, up on the mid-2009 estimate of 885,122. Since the time of the last official Census in 2000, Delaware's population has grown 14.6 per cent. The population is expected to reach 1.012 million by 2030. In 2012, the population was an estimated 917,092. An estimated 6.1 per cent of the population is under 5 years (2011), 22.6 per cent under 18 years and 14.7 per cent is aged over 65 years. According to the Census, 51.6 per cent of the state population is female. According to the 2010 Census, approximately 68.9 per cent of the population is white, and 21.4 per cent is black. Approximately 8.2 per cent of the population is of Hispanic or Latino origin. The population density in 2007 was estimated at 446.8 inhabitants per sq. mile, ranking 6th highest in the US. According to the 2010 census, New Castle County is the most populated county, with 538,479 inhabitants, followed by Sussex County, with 197,145, and Kent County, with 162,310.

UNITED STATES OF AMERICA

Births, Marriages, Deaths
US Census Bureau (CDC) data puts the number of births in 2010 at 11,364 and there were an estimated 7,706 deaths over the same period. Net migration in 2009 amounted to 4,596 people (mainly from other parts of the USA). In 2007, infant deaths numbered 91, equivalent to an infant mortality rate of 7.48 deaths per 1,000 live births. In 2007, there were an estimated 4,749 marriages and 3,858 divorces.

EMPLOYMENT

Of Delaware's December 2012 seasonally adjusted civilian labour force of an estimated 441,800, a total of 411,300 were in employment, whilst 30,500 were unemployed. The unemployment rate in December 2012 was 6.9 per cent, below the national average of 7.8 per cent. (Source: Bureau of Labor Statistics, preliminary figures)

The following table shows preliminary December 2012 non-farm wage and salary employment (seasonally adjusted) according to industry:

Industry	No. of employed	Change over 12 months %
Construction, logging and mining	17,900	-5.8
Manufacturing	25,400	0.0
Trade, transport and utilities	77,000	2.3
Information	5,400	-6.9
Financial activities	44,200	1.8
Professional and business services	54,100	-1.6
Educational and health services	69,800	3.1
Leisure and hospitality	42,800	1.7
Other services	19,200	0.5
Government	63,100	-2.3
TOTAL	418,900	0.4

* not seasonally adjusted
Source: Bureau of Labor Statistics

BANKING AND FINANCE

GDP/GNP, Inflation, National Debt
Delaware's Gross Domestic Product (current dollars) rose from $62,280 in 2010 to $65.8 million and was ranked 40th in the US. Real GDP rose by 1.6 per cent over 2011. The largest sector was finance and industry accounting for 38.9 per cent of GDP.

The following table shows GDP according to industry (millions of current dollars):

Industry	2009	2010	2011
Agriculture, forestry, fishing & hunting	286	279	*
Mining	4	4	*
Utilities	884	899	770
Construction	1,635	1,594	1,711
Manufacturing	4,289	4,403	4,442
Wholesale trade	2,002	2,042	2,200
Retail trade	2,363	2,474	2,538
Transportation and warehousing	746	715	724
Information	1,151	1,090	1,071
Finance and insurance	21,881	24,796	25,585
Real estate	6,664	6,411	6,374
Educational services	331	335	341
Health care and social assistance	3,686	3,834	4,034
Other Services	8,481	9,089	9,653
Government	5,743	6,043	5,999
TOTAL	60,148	64,010	65,755

* = not disclosed
Source: Bureau of Economic Analysis, Feb. 2013

Delaware enjoys one of the highest per capita real GDP in the USA. In 2009, per capita real GDP was $62,080. In 2010, it was estimated to be $62,459. Per capita personal income was $41,449 in 2011, up 5.1 per cent from 2010.

The annual Consumer Price Index (CPI) for the Philadelphia-Wilmington-Atlantic City, PA-NJ-DE-MD, urban area (all items) rose from 233.8 in 2011 to 238.1 in 2012 (1982-84=100). (Source: Bureau of Labor Statistics)

Balance of Payments / Imports and Exports
Total imports amounted to $12,166 million in 2011, up 25.1 per cent on the previous year. Delaware's imports account for 0.6 per cent of total US imports. Main imports include nucleic acids and salts, medicaments, light oils and bananas. The top five suppliers in 2011 were the UK (30.7 per cent), Belgium (11.4 per cent), Russia, China and Iraq.

Total export revenue rose from $4,966 million in 2010 to $5,510 million in 2011, up 11.0 per cent. State export revenue accounted for 0.4 per cent of the US total. The top five international export destinations in 2010-11, according to revenue, are shown on the following table:

Country	2010 ($m)	2011 ($m)	+/- % 2010-11
Canada	1,286	1,501	16.7
UK	973	929	-4.5
China	362	465	28.4

- continued

Japan	339	373	10.1
Germany	298	263	-11.6

The top five export products in 2010, according to revenue, are shown on the following table:

Product	Revenue $m
Medicaments nesoi, measured doses, retail pk. nesoi	1,804
Phy. Chem. Ins/Appr.	259
Plates etc, noncell, nt rein plastics NESOI	211
Parts for machines of heading 8464	141
Mach. for recp/convr/trans/regn of voice/image/data	131

Chambers of Commerce and Trade Organisations
Delaware State Chamber of Commerce, URL: http://www.dscc.com/

MANUFACTURING, MINING AND SERVICES

Primary and Extractive Industries
Primary resources include sand, gravel and magnesium compounds. The mining industry contributed $4 million towards Delaware's Gross Domestic Product in 2011.

Delaware has no oil reserves. Crude oil refining capacity was 182,200 bbl/d in 2012. Total petroleum consumption in 2010 was 17.6 million barrels, over half of which (10.3 million barrels) was in the form of motor gasoline.

Delaware produces none of its own natural gas. Total natural gas consumption rose from 54,825 million cu ft in 2010 to 79,716 million cu ft in 2011. (Source: EIA)

Energy
Total energy production amounted to 3 trillion Btu in 2010. Total energy consumption in 2010 was 256 trillion Btu (0.3 per cent of US total). Per capita energy consumption in the same year was 285 million Btu (34th in the US).

Electric power industry net summer capability in 2010 was 3,389 MW (0.3 per cent of the US total), and net electricity generation in 2008 was 7,182,179 MWh (46th in the US). Natural gas accounted for 86 per cent of industry generation in 2011. Coal contributed 0.5 per cent.

Delaware currently produces minimal renewable energy, but plans to increase renewable energy generation are in development including the potential development of an offshore wind farm. In July 2007, Delaware expanded its renewable portfolio standard to require that 25 per cent of the state's electricity be generated from other renewable sources with 3.5 per cent from photovoltaic sources by 2025.

Manufacturing
Manufacturing is Delaware's fourth largest contributor to Gross State Product, accounting for an estimated $4,442 million in 2011 (down from $4,403 million in 2010). Top sectors in 2010 were chemical products ($1,126 million), food products ($724 million), petroleum and coal products manufacturing ($537 million) and computer and electronic products ($642 million). Other manufactured goods include rubber and plastics products, and fabricated metal products. (Source: BEA)

Service Industries
The services industry dominates Delaware's economy. The major sector is finance and insurance, which contributed $25,895 million to state GDP in 2011. The real estate, renting and leasing sector fell to $6,374 million in 2011, whilst health care and social assistance accounted for $4,034 million. Professional and technical services amounted to $4,393 million. (Source: BEA)

Tourism
The accomodation and food services sub-sector of the services industry contributed $1,190 million in 2011 (up from $1,151 million in 2010), whilst the arts, entertainment and recreation sector contributed $458 million. (Source: BEA)
Delaware Tourism Office, URL: http://www.visitdelaware.net/index.html

Agriculture
Agriculture, forestry and fisheries contributed an estimated $279 million towards Delaware's Gross Domestic Product in 2010. In 2009, farming earned $262 million whilst forestry, fishing and related activities produced a revenue of $17 million. (Source: BEA)

According to the latest USDA Census of Agriculture, Delaware had a total of 2,480 farms in 2010, and farmland covering some 490,000 acres (down from 543,176 acres in 2002). The average size of a farm in Delaware fell from 227 acres in 2002 to 198 acres in 2010.

At the end of 2010, the state had 18,000 head of cattle and 5,500 hogs and pigs. Broilers, soybeans, corn, and milk are the primary agricultural produce whilst the fishing industry produces crabs and clams. In 2007, total income from agricultural products reached $1.083 billion; crops earned $210,635,000 whilst livestock products earned $872,400,000. Broilers earned over $51 million of the state's farming income in 2008 and the state ranked 8th nationally in poultry and product exports. Delaware's main agricultural crop is soybeans and its main fruit crop is apples. Sussex County produces over 70 per cent of all agricultural income.

COMMUNICATIONS AND TRANSPORT

Roads
The Delaware Memorial Twin Bridges (the world's longest dual span suspension bridge) is operated by the Delaware River and Bay Authority, a bi-state agency the responsibility of Delaware and New Jersey.

Shipping
The Cape May-Lewes Ferry System operates between Delaware and New Jersey and is also the responsibility of the Delaware River and Bay Authority.

HEALTH

The National Centre for Health Statistics estimated that there were 26.2 doctors per 10,000 residents in 2009, lower than the US average of 27.4. In 2008, there were 403 dentists (4.6 per 10,000 population). In 2010, there were 47 nursing homes, with 4,990 beds. In 2009 there were also 2.4 community hospital beds per 1,000 residents. Around 11.8 per cent of the population of Delaware have no health insurance cover, and 11.2 per cent are considered to be living in poverty, well below the national level of 14.3 per cent. (Source: National Center for Health Statistics)

An estimated 63.4 per cent of the adult population of Delaware is considered overweight, and 28 per cent are considered obese; both figures are slightly above the national rates. Delaware reported 4,028 HIV/AIDS cases from the beginning of the epidemic to the end of 2008, ranking it 33rd highest among the 50 states. An estimated 144 further cases were reported in 2009. The TB infection rate was 2.6 per 100,000 population. (Source: http://www.cdc.gov/nchhstp)

EDUCATION

Primary/Secondary Education
Total student enrolment in Delaware's 237 public elementary and secondary schools in year 2009-10 was 126,801. There were 8,640 teachers working in the public sector, giving a student to teacher ratio of 14.68 to one.

The state earned an estimated $1.69 billion from education in 2007-08, and total current expenditure on state education reached an estimated $1.79 billion over the same period.

Higher Education
In the academic year 2010-11, Delaware had 11 degree conferring institutions, five of which were public. There were 32,915 women enrolled, but only 22,259 men. In the same period, 10,879 degrees/certificates were conferred, of which 5,505 were Bachelors, 2,452 were Masters and 528 were Doctorates. (Source: National Center for Education Statistics)

COMMUNICATIONS AND MEDIA

Newspapers
Delaware's daily newspapers include the Delaware State News, in Dover, and The News Journal, in Wilmington. Non-daily newspapers include The Wave, Dover Post, Newark Post, Delaware Coast Press, and New Castle Business Ledger.

Delaware Coast Press,
URL: http://www.delmarvaheadlines.com/delawarecoastpress/index.html

ENVIRONMENT

In 1993, the State of Delaware became one of the first jurisdictions to become a "Clean City" in the US Department of Energy's Clean Cities Program. The state requires the use of reformulated motor gasoline blended with ethanol. In 2010, there were 2,922 alternative-fueled vehicles in use (0.3 per cent of US total). Ethanol consumption was 952,000 barrels in 2011 (up from 880,000 barrels in 2008), accounting for 0.3 per cent of US total.

Delaware's electricity industry emissions of carbon dioxide reached 7,223,767 metric tons in 2007, ranking the state 43rd in this regard. By 2009, they had fallen to 4,143,240 metric tons (46th in US). They amounted to 4,187,304 metric tons in 2010 (45th in the US). Sulfur dioxide emissions amounted to 13,152 metric tons and nitrogen oxide emissions were 4,814 metric tons. (Source: EIA)

DISTRICT OF COLUMBIA

Capital: Washington (Population, Census 2010: 601,723)

Mayor: Vincent C. Gray (D) (page 1433)

District Flag: Along the top of the flag are three red, five-pointed stars; underneath the stars are two red bars, one above the other

CONSTITUTION AND GOVERNMENT

Constitution
The District of Columbia is the seat of Government of the United States. It became a municipal corporation on 21 February 1871. The land was ceded by the states of Maryland and Virginia as a site for the National Capital. Congress first met there in 1800. The District of Columbia became self-governing following legislation passed by Congress and signed by the President on 24 December 1973. The District of Columbia Self-Government and Governmental Reorganization Act of 1973 effected a changeover from the former Presidential appointed Mayor-Commissioner and nine-member DC Council form of government to the current elected Mayor and elected 13-member DC Council government. This system was effective from 2 January 1975.

Local government is administered by the elected Mayor and an elected 13-member District of Columbia Council. The Mayor, who is elected for four years, has the principal responsibility for carrying out the municipal programmes, providing City leadership and is the official spokesman for the District of Columbia. He is assisted by a City Administrator, who is appointed by the mayor. In addition to the Mayor and DC Council, the following officials are elected: one Congressional Representative (with no voting rights), a three-person Congressional Delegation (two shadow senators, and one shadow representative), the nine-member Board of Education, Advisory Neighbourhood Commissioners for the District of Columbia's eight Wards, and the five-member District of Columbia Financial Responsibility and Management Assistance Authority (DCFRA).

The lack of voting rights for the District of Columbia Congressional Representative, despite the fact that residents pay federal taxes, led to renewed demands for an end to 'taxation without representation', a principle enshrined in the Declaration of Independence. In 1978 Congress approved a constitutional amendment giving the DC Congressional Representative voting rights; however, the amendment was not supported by the requisite three-quarters of the states. The issue remains contentious.

US Congressional Representative, Delegate: Eleanor Holmes Norton (D) (page 1487)
US Shadow Representative: Mike Panetta
US Shadow Senator: Michael D. Brown
US Shadow Senator: Paul Strauss

Legislature
The 13-member DC Council is the legislative branch of the local government and is composed of a Chairman, four at-large members, and eight Ward members (one from each of the city's eight wards). The Council is elected for four years on a staggered basis.

Legislation is enacted by the Council and signed by the Mayor. However, the legislation cannot take effect for 30 legislative days, during which time both the Senate or the House may by resolution disapprove it. From 20 June 1874, until the passage of the 23rd Amendment to the US Constitution was ratified on 3 April 1961, there was no suffrage in the District of Columbia except the election of delegates to the National Party Conventions nominating candidates for President and Vice-President. Under the 23rd Amendment to the Constitution, District residents are entitled to vote for the US President. On 22 April 1968, the President signed a bill allowing the citizens of the District of Columbia to elect an 11-member Board of Education. On 22 September 1970, legislation was enacted authorising the election of a non-voting delegate from the District of Columbia to the US House of Representatives.

In 2010, Democrats had the majority in the unicameral Council of DC (11 Democrats, one Republican and one Independent)

Council of the District of Columbia (as at April 2013)
Chairman: Phil Mendelson (D)
Chairman Pro Tempore: Kenyan McDuffie
Member, At-Large: Anita Bonds
Member, At-Large: David Grosso
Member, At-Large: David Catania
Member, At-Large: Vincent Orange
Member, Ward One: Kenyan McDuffie
Member, Ward Two: Jim Graham
Member, Ward Three: Jack Evans
Member, Ward Four: Mary M. Cheh
Member, Ward Five: Muriel Bowser
Member, Ward Six: Tommy Wells
Member, Ward Seven: Yvette M. Alexander
Member, Ward Eight: Marion Barry

Mayor's Cabinet
Mayor: Vincent C. Gray (D) (page 1433)
Deputy Mayor: Beatriz Otero
Deputy Mayor: Victor L. Hoskins
Chief of Staff: Chris Murphy
Attorney General: Irvin B. Nathan
City Administrator: Allen Lew
Deputy Mayor, Education (Acting): Abigail Smith

Mayor Adrian Fenty lost a Democratic primary in August 2010 to former City Council Chairman Vincent Gray who assumed the role in January 2011.

Kenyan McDuffie was elected onto the Council in May 2012 after Harry Thomas Jr. stepped down over corruption allegations.

UNITED STATES OF AMERICA

Ministries

Executive Office of the Mayor, John A. Wilson Building, 1350 Pennsylvania Avenue, NW, Suite 600, Washington, DC 20004, USA. Tel: +1 202 727 2980, fax: +1 202 727 0505, URL: http://mayor.dc.gov/

Government of the District of Columbia, John A. Wilson Building, 1350 Pennsylvania Avenue, NW, Washington, DC 20004, USA. Tel: +1 202 727 1000, URL: http://www.dc.gov/

Council of the District of Columbia, John A. Wilson Building, 1350 Pennsylvania Avenue, NW, Washington, DC 20004, USA. Tel: +1 202 724 8000, fax: +1 202 347 3070, e-mail: dccouncilmembers@dccouncil.washington.dc.us, URL: http://www.dccouncil.washington.dc.us/

Office of the DC Auditor, 717 14th Street, NW, Suite 900, Washington, DC 20005, USA. Tel: +1 202 727 3600, fax: +1 202 724 8814, e-mail: odca@dc.gov, URL: http://www.dcauditor.org/

Office of the Secretary, John A. Wilson Building, 1350 Pennsylvania Avenue, NW, Suite 419, Washington, DC 20004, USA. Tel: +1 202 727 6306, fax: +1 202 727 3582, URL: http://os.dc.gov

Department of Consumer and Regulatory Affairs, 941 N. Capitol Street, NE, Washington, DC 20002, USA. Tel: +1 202 442 4400, fax: +1 202 442 9445, URL: http://dcra.dc.gov

Emergency Management Agency, 2000 14th Street, NW, Washington, DC 20009, USA. Tel: +1 202 727 6161, fax: +1 202 673 2290, URL: http://dcema.dc.gov

Department of Employment Services, 609 H Street, NE, Washington, DC 20002, USA. Tel: +1 202 724 7000, fax: +1 202 724 5683, URL: http://does.dc.gov

Department of Health, 825 North Capitol Street, NE, Washington, DC 20002, USA. Tel: +1 202 671 5000, fax: +1 202 442 4788, URL: http://dchealth.dc.gov

Office of Human Rights, 441 4th Street, NW, Suite 570N, Washington, DC 20001, USA. Tel: +1 202 727 4559, fax: +1 202 724 3786, URL: http://ohr.dc.gov/

Political Parties

District of Columbia Democratic State Committee, URL: http://www.dcdemocraticparty.org/

Republican Party of the District of Columbia, URL: http://dcgop.com

Elections

The most recent elections took place in November 2010. Four wards of the DC council were elected, as well as the Chairman of the Council, an at-large member, a US Senator, a US Representative and the mayor.

In November 2006, Adrian Fenty (D) won the office of Mayor with 89 per cent of the vote, and Vincent Gray (D) won Chairmanship of the Council of DC. In the November 2010 mayoral elections Vincent Gray won the vote to become mayor.

LEGAL SYSTEM

The court system of the District of Columbia consists of the Court of Appeals and the Superior Court. The Court of Appeals is the highest court within the District of Columbia and is headed by the Chief Judge, eight Associate Judges, and eight Senior Judges. The Court of Appeals is the court of last resort of the District of Columbia and has a criminal division and four civil divisions: the Civil Actions Branch, the Civil Assignment Branch, Small Claims, and Landlord and Tenant. There are close to 100 judges in the two courts as well as 24 magistrate judges and a professional staff of approximately 1,200. The Courts' fiscal year 2011 annual budget was $243 million plus the $55 million for the Defender Services budget for indigent representation.

The District of Columbia does not have the death penalty. The murder rate is 24 per 100,000 population.

In May 2009, the City Council voted to recognise same-sex marriages conducted in other US states. As Washington DC is not a state, the decision had to be approved by Congress. Marriages began in March 2010.

Court of Appeals, URL: http://www.dccourts.gov/internet/welcome.jsf
Chief Judge: Eric T. Washington
Superior Court, URL: http://www.dccourts.gov/superior
Chief Judge: Lee F. Satterfield

LOCAL GOVERNMENT

The District of Columbia has one sub-county general purpose, or municipal, government and one special district government. Eight wards make up the city of Washington, DC, within which are 37 Advisory Neighbourhood Commissions (ANCs) representing over 120 neighbourhoods. In addition, there are two dependent public school systems.

AREA AND POPULATION

Area

The District of Columbia is located in the north-east of the US, on the south-west border of Maryland, north-east of Virginia, The total area of the District of Columbia is 68.34 sq. miles, of which 61.40 sq. miles is land and 6.94 sq. miles is water. DC is divided into eight Wards and includes the following neighbourhoods: Adams Morgan, Brookland, Capitol Hill, Downtown, Dupont Circle, Georgetown, Lafayette Square, Southwest, and U Street/Shaw.

To view a map of the state, please consult:
http://www.lib.utexas.edu/maps/world_cities/washington_baltimore.jpg

Population

According to the 2010 Census, the population was 601,723, up on the mid-2009 estimate of 599,657. District of Columbia has the second smallest population in the USA, the smallest being Wyoming. Between the official Census of 2000 and 2010, the population increased by 5.2 per cent. The population is expected to fall to 433,414 by 2030. It was estimated at 632,323 in 2012. The state's population density was estimated at 9,581.4 people per sq. mile in 2007. An estimated 5.9 per cent of the population is under 5 years, 17.0 per cent under 18 years and 11.4 per cent is aged 65 years or older. According to the 2010 Census, approximately 38.5 per cent of the population is white, and 50.7 per cent black. Approximately 9.1 per cent of the population is of Hispanic or Latino origin.

Births, Marriages, Deaths

The US Census Bureau, Population Division, estimated that there were 9,165 births and 4,672 deaths in 2010, giving a natural population increase of 4,493. Net migration in 2009 amounted to 6,550 people. The fertility rate was 56.5 per 1,000 females aged 15-44 years. The death rate was 776.4 per 100,000 population. There were 116 infant deaths in 2007, equivalent to a rate of 13.09 per 1,000 live births. Provisional NCHS data puts the number of marriages and divorces in 2007 at 2,143 and 962 respectively.

Public Holidays

In addition to US national holidays, the residents of the District of Columbia observe Emancipation Day on 16th April.

EMPLOYMENT

According to preliminary figures from the BLS, the District of Columbia's total civilian labour force in December 2012 (seasonally adjusted) was 367,300, of which 336,300 were employed and 31,100 were unemployed. The unemployment rate was 8.5 per cent, down from 12 per cent in January 2010, but higher than the US average of 7.8 per cent. The following table shows provisional figures for non-farm wage and salary employment in DC in December 2012:

District of Columbia employment according to industry

Industry	No. of Jobs	12-month change (%)
Construction, logging and mining	13,300	7.3
Manufacturing	1,000	-0.3
Trade, transport and utilities	26,500	-2.6
Information	18,000	-3.7
Financial activities	27,100	1.1
Professional and business services	150,800	-0.7
Educational and health services	120,800	1.6
Leisure and hospitality	61,900	-2.5
Other services	70,300	2.3
Government	245,900	-1.1
Total Nonfarm Employment	**735,600**	**-0.3**

*not seasonally adjusted
Source: US Bureau of Labor Statistics

Major industries in terms of employment are: business, professional, financial and association services; biomedical research, and health service; hospitality, entertainment, tourism, and specialty retail; universities, education, and research; and information, technology and telecommunications. DC's major employers include: Georgetown University, George Washington University, Washington Hospital Centre, Howard University, Children's Medical Centre, Washington Post, Potomac Electric Power Company, George Washington University Hospital, and American University.

BANKING AND FINANCE

GDP/GNP, Inflation, National Debt

Total state Gross Domestic Product (current dollars) was $107.6 billion in 2011. Real GDP grew by 3.5 per cent over the year 2010, higher than the US overall rate of 2.6 per cent, and by 1.6 per cent in 2011. The government sector dominated the economy (34.9 per cent).

Gross Domestic Product according to industry, is shown on the following table (millions of current dollars):

Industry	2009	2010	2011
Agriculture	*	*	*
Mining	0	0	0
Utilities	1,409	1,343	1,252
Construction	952	930	1,091
Manufacturing	220	242	268
Wholesale trade	813	881	927
Retail trade	1,044	1,158	1,168
Transport and warehousing	326	269	265
Information	5,262	5,087	5,344
Finance and Insurance	4,379	4,997	5,105
Real Estate	8,179	7,694	7,918
Educational services	2,928	2,961	3,019
Health care and social assistance	4,420	4,709	4,955
Other Services	34,283	43,446	36,550
Government	34,056	36,725	37,564
TOTAL	98,272	103,546	107,593

Source: Bureau of Economic Analysis, Feb. 2013
* Not disclosed

1198

The estimated per capita income in 2011 was $73,783, 178 per cent higher than the average US per capita income of $41,560. In 2011, per capita real GDP in the state was $148,291, some three times that of the US average ($42,070). In 2010 it rose to $150,079. The annual Consumer Price Index (CPI) for the Washington-Baltimore, DC-MD-VA-WV, urban area (all items) rose from 142.2 in 2010 to 146.9 in 2011. (1982-84 = 100). (Source: Bureau of Labor Statistics)

Balance of Payments / Imports and Exports
Total District of Columbia imports amounted to $444 million, down from $667 million in 2010 and $1,156 million in 2009. Imports fell by -33.5 per cent in 2011, representing less than 0.1 per cent of the US total.

Total exports amounted to $1,039 million in 2011, down 30.8 per cent on the 2010 figure of $1,501 million. The District of Columbia contributes around 0.1 per cent of the US total export revenue (Source: US Census Bureau, Foreign Trade Division)

The following table shows 2011 export revenue according to the top five international destinations (US Census Bureau):

Destination	2010 ($m)	2011 ($m)	+/-% 2010-11
UAE	429	282	-34.1
Pakistan	276	215	-22.3
Morocco	16	118	500+
UK	239	84	-64.8
Bahrain	178	45	-74.9

The top five export products in 2010, according to export revenue, are shown on the following table (figures in $million):

Product	Revenue
Bomb mines, other amunition etc	352
Parts of airplanes or helicopters	325
Helicopters (unladen weight exceeding 2000 Kg)	185
Civilian aircraft, engines, equipment and parts	98
Pt. elec. mach & appr. with indiv. functions	58

Major Banks
The headquarters of four international banks are located in Washington DC: the International Monetary Fund, the International Bank for Reconstruction and Development (World Bank), the International Finance Corp (IFC), and the International Development Association (IDA).
International Monetary Fund, URL: http://www.imf.org
Managing Director: Christine Lagarde (page 1459)
International Bank for Reconstruction and Development (The World Bank), URL: http://www.worldbank.org
President: Dr Jim Yong Kim (page 1449)
International Finance Corp (IFC), URL: http://www.ifc.org/
President: Dr Jim Yong Kim (page 1449)
International Development Association (IDA), URL: http://www.worldbank.org/ida
President: Dr Jim Yong Kim (page 1449)
Multilateral Investment Guarantee Agency (MIGA), URL: http://www.miga.org
President: Dr Jim Yong Kim (page 1449)
Export-Import Bank of the United States, URL: http://www.exim.gov
President and CEO: Fred P. Hochberg

The National Capital Bank of Washington, URL: http://www.nationalcapitalbank.com/

Chambers of Commerce and Trade Organisations
DC Chamber of Commerce, URL: http://www.dcchamber.org
Baltimore/Washington Corridor Chamber of Commerce, URL: http://www.baltwashchamber.org/

MANUFACTURING, MINING AND SERVICES

Primary and Extractive Industries
The District of Columbia has no oil industry and relies on outside supplies to meet its requirements. The state's total petroleum consumption was 4 million barrels in 2010, of which gasoline consumption accounted for 2.5 million barrels. With no natural gas reserves, DC relies on supplies from other states. Total natural gas consumption in 2010 was 32,976 million cubic feet. (Source: EIA)

Energy
Total energy production was 1 trillion Btu in 2008, ranking it 51st in the US. Its total energy consumption was 185 trillion Btu in 2010 and was ranked 28th in the US for its per capita energy consumption (307 million Btu in 2010).

The District of Columbia is a net importer of electricity, with petroleum as its sole generating fuel. Net summer capability in 2010 was 790 MW (51st in the US).

In 2005, the District adopted a renewable portfolio standard that requires utilities to provide 20 per cent of retail electricity sales from renewable sources by 2020. (Source: EIA)

Manufacturing
Manufacturing contributed an estimated $268 million towards the 2011 Gross Domestic Product (down from $242 million in 2010). The largest GDP-earning sectors in 2010 were chemical products ($60 million), petroleum and coal products manufacturing ($70 million), printing and related support activities ($31 million), and computer and electronic products ($31 million).

Service Industries
The services industry is the District of Columbia's largest contributor towards GDP. In 2011, the Government was the largest single contributor to state GDP, accounting for $37,564 million. The highest earning industry was that of professional and technical services ($23,574 million), and real estate revenue contributed $7,918 million.

Tourism
Top visitor attractions in Washington, DC, include: the National Air and Space Museum, the National Gallery of Art, the National Museum of American History, the Arlington National Cemetery, the US Holocaust Memorial Museum, the Vietnam Veterans' Memorial, the Library of Congress, the Jefferson Memorial, the White House, the Washington Monument and the US Supreme Court.

In 2003, 16.4 million people visited Washington. Tourism sustains 260,000 jobs. The accommodation and food services sector contributed $3,549 million towards the 2011 state GDP, whilst the arts, entertainment and recreation sector contributed $811 million.
Washington, DC Convention and Tourism Corporation, URL: http://www.washington.org

Agriculture
The District of Columbia's small agricultural industry contributed around $1 million towards the 2008 state GDP.

COMMUNICATIONS AND TRANSPORT

International Airports
The District of Columbia has two international airports: Washington Dulles International Airport and Baltimore/Washington International Airport (BWI). Washington Dulles had 27 million passengers in 2005, travelling on forty airlines to 108 destinations - 37 of them international. 636,978.500 lbs of freight passed through the airport in the same year. Dulles employs more than 18,800 people and generates $6.2 billion annually in business revenues.
Washington Dulles International Airport, URL: http://www.metwashairports.com/Dulles

Railways
Amtrak runs from Washington's Union Station to 44 states in the US, from major east coast cities to many in the west. Metroliner is Amtrak's high speed service, linking Washington, DC, with New York City in three hours and Philadelphia in just under two. Other railway companies that serve DC include: Metrorail, Maryland Rail Commuter, and Virginia Railway Express. The Washington Metropolitan Area Transit Authority operates rail and bus services within Washington, DC, as well as to Maryland and Virginia.
Washington Metropolitan Area Transit Authority, URL: http://www.wmata.com/default.cfm

Roads
Washington, DC, is served by six Interstate Highway systems. It is linked to all east coast cities by the I-95.

HEALTH

Recent National Center for Health Statistics estimates indicate that in 2009 there were 73.8 doctors per 10,000 of the population in 2009, considerably higher than the US average of 27.4 doctors per 10,000). In 2008, there were 634 dentists (10.7 per 10,000 population). In 2009, there were 5.8 community hospital beds per 1,000 residents (US average 1.8), and 19 nursing homes, with a total of 2,775 beds. According to the Center for Disease Control, in 2007-09, 10.6 per cent of DC inhabitants did not have health-care coverage. According to the US Census Bureau, an estimated 18.2 per cent were considered to be living in poverty.

District of Columbia reported 19,684 HIV/AIDS cases from the beginning of the epidemic to the end of 2008. A further 556 cases were reported in 2009. The disease has now reached epidemic proportions, with three per cent of over-12s infected. This is probably an underestimate, as many residents may be unaware that they are infected. Those most infected groups are black men, and people aged between 40 and 49. The infection rate puts Washington DC on a par with Uganda. The Department of Health is tackling the epidemic by promoting testing, preventing transmission by providing free condoms and needle exchanges, and doing more for those already living with HIV/Aids. The TB rate was 9.1 per 100,000 persons in 2008. The adult obesity rate in 2012 was 22.2 per cent and 56.4 per cent were considered overweight.

EDUCATION

Primary/Secondary Education
The District of Columbia has a total of 238 elementary and secondary schools, and enrolled 69,433 pupils during the year 2009-10. There were 6,370 teachers, and the pupil / teacher ratio was 10.9 to one.

The District's total state education expenditure reached $1.59 billion during the academic year 2007-08, and revenues reached $1.36 billion.

Higher Education
The District of Columbia's 20 degree conferring institutions include: Gallaudet College; Georgetown University; George Washington University; Howard University; American University; Catholic University of America; University of the District of Columbia. An estimated 52,120 men and 84,731 women enrolled during 2010-11. In the same period, 23,215 degrees/certificates were awarded, of which 8,927 were Bachelors, 9,285 were Masters and 3,394 were Doctorates. (Source: National Center for Education Statistics)

COMMUNICATIONS AND MEDIA

Newspapers
The District of Columbia's newspapers include: The Washington Post; City Paper; Legal Times; Intowner Newspaper; Afro-American Newspapers; Washington Times Newspapers; The Washington Inquirer; and Washington Hispanic.
The Washington Post, URL: http://www.washingtonpost.com/
Washington Times Newspapers, URL: http://www.washtimes.com/

Broadcasting
Washington's six television stations are: Channel 4 (NBC); Channel 5 (Fox); Channel 9 (CBS); Channel 7 (ABC); Channel 50 (Warner Bros.); and Channel 32 (PBS). Washington also has eight FM radio stations and two AM stations.

ENVIRONMENT

According to EIA statistics, emissions of carbon dioxide from DC's electricity generating industry in 2010 reached 190,742 metric tons, ranking it 50th among the US states. Emissions of sulfur dioxide amounted to 797 metric tons and emissions of nitrogen oxide reached 367 metric tons.

In 2005, the District adopted a renewable portfolio standard that requires utilities to provide 20 per cent of retail electricity sales from renewable sources by 2020.

In 2010, an estimated 12,050 alternative-fueled vehicles were in use (1.3 per cent of US total) and, in 2011, 165,000 barrels of ethanol were consumed (0.1 per cent of US total). (Source: EIA)

FLORIDA

Capital: Tallahassee (Population Census 2010: 181,376)

Head of State: Rick Scott (R) (Governor) (page 1510)

State Flag: A white background in the centre of which appears the state seal; red bars one fifth of the hoist extend from each corner towards the centre. The state seal depicts a female Native American scattering flowers; behind her is a steamboat on water, a cocoa tree, and the sun's rays shining over land in the distance; circling the seal are the words 'Great Seal of the State of Florida: In God We Trust'

CONSTITUTION AND GOVERNMENT

Constitution
Florida entered the Union on 3 March 1845 as the 27th state. The constitution originated in 1885 and was revised in 1968. Florida is the only one of the 50 states to have a governor as well as its own Cabinet of four elected state executives: governor, attorney general, commissioner of agriculture, and chief financial officer. All are elected for terms of four years. The governor can serve two terms in succession. The lieutenant governor is elected on the same ticket as the governor. With effect from the 2002 election, the position of state comptroller was renamed chief financial officer. With effect from January 2003 the following executive positions were abolished by Florida's voters: secretary of state, state treasurer/insurance commissioner, and state education commissioner.

Floridians elect two Senators and 25 Representatives to the US Congress, Washington, DC.

To consult the state constitution, please visit:
http://www.leg.state.fl.us/Statutes/index.cfm?Tab=statutes&submenu=-1

Recent Events
Hurricane Katrina hit Florida on the night of the 25-26th August 2005, leaving approximately one million homes without electricity. On the 25th October in the same year, Hurricane Wilma killed six people in Florida, and caused extensive damage. An evacuation had been ordered in advance, but many chose to remain. The state was declared a major disaster area.

In March 2013, Lt. Gov. Jennifer Carroll (R), the first African-American woman to serve as a lieutenant-governor, resigned amid a gambling and racketeering scandal. Ms Carroll has not been charged with any wrong doing. The governor has said a replacement will not be appointed immediately.

Legislature
Florida's legislature consists of the Senate and the House of Representatives. The legislature meets on an annual basis for a 60-day session. In addition, there may be special and extended sessions.

Upper House
The 40 members of the Senate are elected to serve four-year terms. Half of the senate members are elected every two years. Currently, on the basis of one senator for every 300,000 residents, the senate consists of 40 seats. Following the 2012 elections, the Senate was composed of 26 Republicans and 14 Democrats.
Senate, Senate Office Building, The Capitol, 404 South Monroe Street, Tallahassee, Florida 32399-1100, USA. Tel: +1 850 487 5270 (Secretary of the Senate), e-mail: leg.info@leg.state.fl.us, URL: http://www.flsenate.gov

Lower House
The House of Representatives currently has 120 representatives who are elected to two-year terms. Elections take place in even-numbered years. Following the 2012 elections the House was composed of 74 Republicans and 46 Democrats.
House of Representatives, 1201 The Capitol, 402 South Monroe Street, Tallahassee, FL 32399-1300, USA. Tel: +1 850 488 6026, fax: +1 850 488 4732, e-mail: leg.info@leg.state.fl.us, URL: http://www.myfloridahouse.com/

Elected Executive Branch Officials (as at June 2013)
Governor: Rick Scott (R) (page 1510)
Lieutenant Governor: currently vacant
Attorney General: Pam Bondi (R)
Chief Financial Officer: Jeff Atwater (R)
Commissioner of Agriculture and Consumer Affairs: Adam Putnam (R)

Legislature (as at June 2013)
President of the Senate: Don Gaetz (R)
Senate Majority Leader: Lizbeth Benacquisto (R)
Senate Minority Leader: Christopher L. Smith (D)
Speaker of the House: Will Weatherford (R)
House Majority Leader: Stephen L. Precourt (R)
House Democrat Leader: Maria Lorts Sachs (pro tempore) (D)

US Senators: Marco Rubio (R) (page 1506) and Bill Nelson (D) (page 1485)

Ministries
Office of the Governor, PL 05 The Capitol, 400 South Monroe Street, Tallahassee, FL 32399-0001, USA. Tel: +1 850 488 5152, fax: +1 850 487 0801, URL: http://www.flgov.com/
Office of the Attorney General, The Capitol PL-01, Tallahassee, FL 32399-1050, USA. Tel: +1 850 414 3300, fax: +1 850 487 2564, e-mail: ag@oag.state.fl.us, URL: http://myfloridalegal.com/
Department of Agriculture and Consumer Services, The Capitol, Tallahassee, FL 32399-0800, USA. Tel: +1 850 488 3022, URL: http://www.freshfromflorida.com/
Department of Education, Turlington Building, Suite 1514, 325 West Gaines Street, Tallahassee, Florida 32399-0400, USA. Tel: +1 850 245 0505, fax: +1 850 245 9667, URL: http://www.fldoe.org/
Department of Environmental Protection, 3900 Commonwealth Boulevard, Tallahassee, Florida 32399, USA. Tel: +1 850 245 2118, fax: +1 850 245 2128, URL: http://www.dep.state.fl.us/
Department of Health, 2585 Merchants Row Boulevard, Tallahassee, FL (4052 Bald Cypress Way, Bin# A00, Tallahassee, FL 32399-1701), USA. Tel: +1 850 245 4321, e-mail: health@doh.state.fl.us, URL: http://www.doh.state.fl.us/
Department of State, RA Gray Building, 500 S. Bronough, Tallahassee, FL 32399-0250, USA. Tel: +1 850 245 6500, e-mail: secretaryofstate@dos.state.fl.us, URL: http://www.dos.state.fl.us/
Department of Transportation, 605 Suwannee Street, Tallahassee, Florida 32399-0450, USA. Tel: +1 850 414 4100, fax: +1 850 488 6155, URL: http://www.dot.state.fl.us/

Political Parties
Florida Democratic Party, URL: http://www.fladems.com/
Republican Party of Florida, URL: http://www.rpof.org/

Elections
Legislative elections last took place in November 2012; in the Senate the Republicans retained the majority but lost two seats (Republicans 26 seats, Democrats 14 seats). In the House of Representatives, the Republicans retained their already large majority but lost seven seats (Republicans 74 seats, Democrats 46 seats).

Elections took place in November 2010 for federal, state, and county offices that included Governor and the Lieutenant Governor. Republican Rick Scott narrowly defeated Democrat Alex Sink, the state's current CFO. Jennifer Carrol (R) won the race to be Lieutenant Governor.

In the November 2010 election to the US Senate, Republican Marco Rubio, the former Florida House Speaker, beat former Governor Charlie Crist who was running as an independent and the Democrat candidate Kendrick Meek. Mr Rubio was supported by the Tea Party movement.

LEGAL SYSTEM

Florida's court system consists of the Supreme Court, District Courts of Appeal, Circuit Courts, and County Courts. Florida's 67 counties are divided into five court districts of 20 circuits. As well as the Supreme Court Chief Justice there are six associate justices. All are nominated for six-year terms and must submit to voters of the state for a merit retention vote to remain in office.

Capital punishment is legal in Florida either by electrocution or lethal injection. Seventy-one executions have taken place since 1976. Two execution took place in 2011 and three in 2012. In January 2013 there were 411 people (three women) on death row. According to the DPIC the murder rate is 5.2 per 100,000 population.

Supreme Court of Florida, URL: http://www.flcourts.org/
Chief Justice: Ricky Polston
Justices: Peggy A. Quince, Barbara Pariente, R. Fred Lewis, Jorge Labarga, James E.C. Perry, Charles Canady

LOCAL GOVERNMENT

Administratively, Florida is divided into 66 county governments and 411 sub-county general purpose governments. All 411 sub-county governments are municipal, including the City of Jacksonville (comprising Duval County and the City of Jacksonville). No town or township governments exist in Florida. County governments are administered by a governing body known as the board of county commissioners. Florida's municipal governments comprise its cities, towns and villages. In addition, there are 1,052 special districts and 95 school districts.

Florida Association of Counties, URL: http://www.fl-counties.com/

AREA AND POPULATION

Area
Florida is located in the south-east of the US. It forms a peninsular between the Gulf of Mexico and the North Atlantic, and borders Georgia and Alabama in the north. The total area covered by Florida is 65,754.59 sq. miles, of which 53,926.82 sq. miles is land, and 11,827.77 sq. miles is water.

Florida is the most hurricane-prone US state; indeed it is rare for a hurricane season to pass without any impact in the state by at least a tropical storm. August to October is the most likely period for a hurricane. It also experiences more lightning strikes than any other state.

To view a map of Florida, please consult:
http://www.lib.utexas.edu/maps/us_2001/florida_ref_2001.pdf

Population
According to the 2010 US Census, the population was 18,801,310, up from the mid-2009 estimate of 18,537,969. The population was estimated at 19,317,568 in 2012. Florida has the fourth highest population in the USA (after California, Texas and New York). Florida's total population has increased by 17.6 per cent since 2000 and is expected to reach 28,685,769 by 2030. The state's population density in 2010 was 350.6 persons per sq. mile, the 8th highest density in the USA. The population of the capital, Tallahassee, was estimated at 182,965 in 2011. The county with the highest number of inhabitants is Miami-Dade County. An estimated 5.6 per cent of the population is under 5 years, 21.0 per cent under 18 years and 17.6 per cent is aged over 65 years. According to the Census, 51.1 per cent of the state population is female. According to the 2010 Census, approximately 75 per cent of the population is white, and 16 per cent is black. Approximately 22.5 per cent of the population is of Hispanic or Latino origin.

Births, Marriages, Deaths
The number of births recorded in 2010 was 214,590, giving a fertility rate of 60.3 per 1,000 population. There were 173,791 deaths over the same period, giving a natural population increase of 40,799 inhabitants. Net migration amounted to 56,202 people in 2010, mainly from outside the USA. The infant mortality rate was 7.1 deaths per 1,000 live births in 2007. Provisional 2007 data puts the number of marriages at 157,610 and the number of divorces at 86,367.

Public Holidays
In addition to the public holidays celebrated nationally, Floridians have Pascua Florida Day, on April 2nd.

EMPLOYMENT

According to provisional figures, Florida's total civilian labour force in December 2012 was 9,347,400, of which 8,598,500 were employed and 748,900 were unemployed. The unemployment rate was 8.0 per cent, higher than the overall unemployment rate for the US rate of 7.8 per cent. (Source: Bureau of Labor Statistics)

The following table shows preliminary figures for December 2012 non-farm wage and salary employment according to industry:

Non-farm wage and salary employment by industry

Industry	No. of Employed	12-month change (%)
Mining and Logging*	5,600	0.0
Construction	318,700	-2.1
Manufacturing	314,800	0.5
Trade, transportation and utilities	1,542,400	1.5
Information	129,300	-3.0
Financial activities	483,900	-0.8
Professional and business services	1,082,400	1.7
Educational and health services	1,137,200	1.2
Leisure and hospitality	988,500	3.1
Other services	301,500	-1.5
Government	1,083,800	-1.0
TOTAL	7,388.100	0.7

Source: US Bureau of Labor Statistics
Not seasonally adjusted

BANKING AND FINANCE

GDP/GNP, Inflation, National Debt
Florida's Gross Domestic Product (GDP) rose from $736,065 million in 2010 to $745.3 billion, ranking it 4th in the US. Real GDP grew by 0.5 per cent over the year 2011, after a fall in 2009 largely due to slowdowns in the construction and finance and insurance industries,

sectors that had benefited from a strong housing market earlier the decade. Florida accounted for approximately 5.2 per cent of the US total GDP in 2010, and was ranked 4th in the US. The largest industry is real estate.

The following table shows Gross Domestic Product according to industry (millions of current dollars):

Industry	2009	2010	2011
Agriculture, forestry and fishing	5,561	6,075	6,288
Mining	982	983	1,545
Utilities	16,218	15,611	14,805
Construction	34,644	31,110	29,989
Manufacturing	35,863	36,441	38,338
Wholesale Trade	44,157	45,335	47,713
Retail Trade	53,000	55,887	58,199
Transportation and warehousing	20,711	21,008	22,108
Information	29,274	29,634	31,482
Finance and Insurance	47,183	51,598	52,947
Real estate	129,152	121,161	117,383
Educational services	6,936	7,366	7,911
Health care and social assistance	60,675	63,698	66,2564
Other non-govt. services	147,232	154,411	161,986
Government	94,596	95,748	97,307
TOTAL	721,184	736,065	754,255

Source: Bureau of Economic Analysis, Jan. 2013

Per capita GDP was $34,689 in 2011. In 2011, the average personal income per capita was estimated at $39,636 in Florida, up 3.4 per cent from 2010.

The Consumer Price Index (CPI) for the Miami-Fort Lauderdale area (all items) rose from 231.7 in 2011 to 235.2 in 2012. The annual CPI for the Tampa-St. Petersburg-Clearwater, FL, urban area (all items) rose from 193.5 in 2010 to 198.9 in 2011 (1982-84 = 100). (Source: Bureau of Labor Statistics)

Balance of Payments / Import and Exports
Florida's total import costs amounted to $56,250 million in 2010, up 23.0 per cent. In 2011, they rose by 16.1 per cent to $65,292 million, representing 3.0 per cent of US total imports. Main imports include oil, gold and phones for cellular networks. As of 2011, main suppliers included China (17 per cent), Mexico (8.3 per cent), Japan, Canada & Colombia.

Florida's total export revenue in fell from $54,238 million in 2008 to $46,888 million in 2009, a fall of 13.6 per cent. In 2010, total export revenue amounted to $56,159 million in 2010, up 23.0 per cent. In 2011, it rose by 17.2 per cent to $64,904 million, representing 4.4 per cent of US total exports. (Source: US Census Bureau, Foreign Trade Division).

Total export revenue in 2010-11, according to the top five international destinations, is shown on the following table:

Destination	2010 ($m)	2011 ($m)	+/-% 09-10
Switzerland	5,012	7,291	45.5
Brazil	4,749	5,277	11.1
Venezuela	3,464	4,493	29.7
Canada	3,862	4,068	5.3
Colombia	2,522	2,847	12.9

Source: US Census Bureau

The top five export products in 2010, according to export revenue ($ million), are shown on the following table:

Product	Revenue ($m)
Waste and scrap of precious metal nesoi	4,307
Civilian aircraft, engines, equipment and parts	4,100
Phones for cellular networks of for other wireless ntwks	1,737
Diammonium Hydrogenorthophosphate	1,492
Parts for automatic data processing machines and units	1,089

Source: US Census Bureau

Chambers of Commerce and Trade Organisations
Florida Chamber of Commerce, URL: http://www.flchamber.com/
Greater Miami Chamber of Commerce, URL: http://www.miamichamber.com/
Tallahassee Area Chamber of Commerce, URL: http://talchamber.com/

MANUFACTURING, MINING AND SERVICES

Primary and Extractive Industries
Florida's mining industry contributed $1,545 million towards the Gross Domestic Product in 2011, down from $983 million in 2010. Revenues came from the following sectors in 2010: non-oil and gas mining ($838 million), oil and gas mining ($105 million) and support activities ($40 million). (Source: BEA)

Although Florida has no oil refineries it does have proven oil reserves of 18 million barrels (2010). Geologists believe that there may be large oil and gas deposits off Florida's western coast. The state had 59 producing oil wells in 2011 and one rig. Production averaged 1,999,000 barrels per month in 2012. Total petroleum consumption was 330.1 million barrels (4.7 per cent of the US total) in 2010, 193.2 million barrels of which was in the form of motor gasoline (6.0 per cent of the US total).

UNITED STATES OF AMERICA

Florida has reserves of dry natural gas amounting to 56 billion cubic feet in 2010; however the state relies on imports to meet its requirements. Marketed natural gas production amounted to 15,125 million cu ft in 2011. Florida's natural gas consumption has grown rapidly in recent years, due primarily to increasing demand from the electric power sector; consumption rose to 1,158,522 million cu ft in 2010 (4.9 per cent of the US total).

Florida receives most of its natural gas supply from other Gulf Coast States via two major interstate pipelines: the Florida Gas Transmission line, which runs from Texas through the Florida Panhandle to Miami, and the Gulfstream pipeline, an underwater link from Mississippi and Alabama to central Florida. (Source: EIA)

Energy
Total energy production was 510 Trillion Btu in 2010 (0.7 per cent of US total). Florida's total energy consumption was 4,382 trillion Btu in 2010 (4.5 per cent of US total), and 43rd in the US for its per capita energy consumption (at 233 million Btu in 2010). The US average per capita consumption in 2010 was 316 million Btu, falling to an estimated 312 million Btu in 2011. Florida's per-household consumption of electricity is among the highest in the United States, largely due to the demand for air-conditioning in the hot and humid climate.

Natural gas replaced coal as Florida's primary generating fuel in 2003, though coal continues to account for a large proportion of electricity generation. In 2011, natural gas accounted for approximately 64 per cent, followed by coal at 20 per cent and nuclear (10.7 per cent). Hydroelectricity accounted for just 0.1 per cent in 2008, and other renewables contributed two per cent. Net summer capability in 2010 was 59,147 MW (5.7 per cent of US total) and net monthly generation (Oct.) in 2012 was 18,496 thousand MWh. 387,000 MWh of electricity was generated from renewables in Oct. 2012.

Florida has three nuclear power plants: Crystal River, St. Lucie, and Turkey Point. An estimated 1,513 thousand MWh was produced monthly (Oct.) in 2012.

Renwable energy accounted for 2.2 per cent of Florida's total net electricity generation. Ir ranked 3rd out of the US states for net electricity generation from solar energy.

The State does not have a renewable portfolio standard but has adopted energy standards that require major facility projects in the State to be constructed to high energy efficiency standards in order to reduce energy use. Florida is a leading producer of oranges and there is a planned facility that would make 4 million gallons of ethanol from citrus waste. (Source: Energy Information Administration)

Manufacturing
Manufacturing contributed $38,388 million towards the 2011 state GDP, up from $36,441 million in 2010. The top sectors in 2010 were food products ($4,931 million), electronic and computer products ($8,087 million), and chemical manufacturing ($2,613 million). (Source: BEA)

Service Industries
Florida's services sector is the largest contributor towards state GDP. In 2011, real estate, rental and leasing was the largest single sector, accounting for $117,383 million. The retail sector accounted for $58,199 million, whilst health care and social assistance contributed $66,254 million. Finance and insurance ($52,947 million) and professional and technical services ($54,672 million) were also significant economic contributors. The Government sector accounted for $97,307 million in 2011 (up from $95,748 million in 2010). (Source: BEA)

Tourism
Tourism is one of Florida's largest industries; in 2005, a record 85.8 million tourists visited the state. The accommodation and food services sector contributed an estimated $32,926 million towards the 2011 GDP, whilst the arts, entertainment and recreation sector contributed $13,576 million. (Source: BEA)
Governor's Office of Tourism, Trade & Economic Development (OTTED), URL: http://oir.dos.state.fl.us/

Agriculture
The agriculture, forestry and fisheries industry contributed $6,288 million towards Florida's 2011 GDP, up from $6,075 million in 2010. The farms sector contributed $4,414 million in 2010, whilst forestry, fishing and related activities contributed $1,661 million. (Source: BEA)

According to the latest official USDA Census of Agriculture, Florida's farms numbered 47,500 in 2010, up from 44,081 in 2002. Total farmland was 9,250,000 acres, slightly down from 2002, and the average size of a farm fell from 236 acres in 2002 to 195 acres in 2010.

Florida is the world's leading citrus producing area; in 2003-04, the state produced around 79 per cent of the USA's oranges, tangerines, tangelos and grapefruit. The state ranks seventh in the USA in terms of overall horticulture, with greenhouse and nursery sales of over $6 billion per annum. Main crops are vegetables (especially tomatoes), sugarcane, avocados, watermelons, peanuts, and strawberries. As of 1 Jan. 2011, there were 1.63 million cattle and calves and 15,000 hogs & pigs. The value of livestock and poultry products sold in 2007 reached $1.5 billion, and total value of agricultural products sold was $7.78 billion in the same year.

COMMUNICATIONS AND TRANSPORT

International Airports
Florida has 13 international airports. Bay County International Airport is located in the north-west of Florida; Jacksonville International Airport is in the north-east; Daytona Beach International Airport and Melbourne International Airport are in the central-east; Orlando International Airport is in central Florida; Clearwater International Airport, Bradenton International Airport and Tampa International Airport are in the central-west; Southwest Florida International Airport is in the south-west; and Palm Beach International Airport, Fort

Lauderdale/Hollywood International Airport, Miami International Airport and Keywest International Airport are in the south-east. Notable federal facilities include: John F. Kennedy Space Center, Cape Canaveral, Eglin Air Force Base and Pensacola Naval Air Station.

Miami International Airport was ranked 3rd in the USA (31st in the world) in terms of the number of international passengers, 14.7 million in 2006, and 15th in the USA (27th in the world) in total number of passengers, 32.5 million. During 2006, 1.98 million tons of cargo was handled (an increase of 4.3 per cent on the previous year), and 384,477 aircraft movements were recorded (a rise of 0.8 per cent over the previous year).
Miami International Airport, URL: http://www.miami-airport.com/

Railways
Florida's railway system consists of more than 2,880 miles of track.

Roads
Florida has over 39,050 miles of state highway lanes and more than 11,150 bridges. Tolls operate in 670 traffic lanes in Florida, including the Florida Turnpike, the ferry service and three bridges.

HEALTH

According to statistics published by the National Center for Health Statistics, in 2009, there were 26.0 doctors (including osteopaths) per 10,000 residents of Florida, slightly below the US average of 27.4 per 10,000. In 2008, there were 9,741 dentists (5.3 per 10,000 population). In 2009, there were 2.9 community hospital beds per 1,000 residents (above the US average of 2.6), and there were 678 nursing homes, with a total of 82,226 beds. Around 20.9 per cent of Floridians had no health insurance cover in 2007-09. An estimated 14.7 per cent were living in poverty.

Floridians have a slightly lower than US average rate of obesity, at 24.6 per cent of adults (2012). An estimated 64.2 per cent of adults are categorised as overweight. Florida reported 117,612 HIV/AIDS cases from the beginning of the epidemic to the end of 2008, ranking it 3rd highest among the US states. A further 5,401 cases were diagnosed in 2009. The TB rate of infection was 5.2 per 100,000 population, the sixth highest in the US. (Source: http://www.cdc.gov/nchhstp/).

EDUCATION

Primary/Secondary Education
Florida's pre-kindergarten to twelfth grade public education system enrolled 2,634,522 students in the 2009-10 academic year. There were 4,253 schools. There were 186,827 teachers, and a teacher/pupil ratio of one to 14.3. Total current state education expenditure for the year 2007-08 reached $31.5 billion, whilst revenue was $29.3 billion.

Higher Education
In the year 2010-11, there were 223 degree-conferring institutions in Florida, 43 of which were public. 436,350 men enrolled and 616,871 women. In the same period, 252,115 degrees and certificates were conferred, of which 83,471 were Bachelors, 29,762 were Masters and 9,107 Doctorates. (Source: National Center for Education Statistics)

COMMUNICATIONS AND MEDIA

Newspapers
Florida has 36 daily newspapers, including Key West Citizen, Miami Herald, Orlando Sentinel, Florida Today, Palm Beach Post, Tampa Tribune, St. Petersburg Times, Daytona Beach News-Journal, Northwest Florida Daily News, Florida Times-Union, The News Herald, Tallahassee Democrat, Sun Sentinel, and Naples Daily News.
Florida Press Association, URL: http://www.flpress.com/
Miami Herald, URL: http://www.miami.com/mld/miamiherald/
The Florida Times-Union, URL: http://jacksonville.com/

Broadcasting
There are 57 television networks in Florida, including seven in Miami, nine in Orlando, six in West Palm Beach, six in Tampa, four in Tallahassee, and six in Fort Myers.

ENVIRONMENT

Now that natural gas is replacing coal as a major generating fuel, emissions from Florida's electricity generating industry gradually being reduced. According to EIA statistics, emissions of carbon dioxide amounted to 123.8 million metric tons in 2010 (ranking it 2nd out of US states). An estimated 159,795 metric tons of sulfur dioxide were emitted in 2010 (down from 219,347 metric tons in 2009)and 100,971 metric tons of nitrogen oxide were also produced (compared to 115,829 metric tons in 2009).

In 2010, there were 33,693 alternative-fueled vehicles in use in Florida (3.6 per cent of the US total). Floridians used some 19,710,000 barrels of ethanol in 2010 (compared to 17,043,000 barrels in 2009), 6.4 per cent of the US total. Florida is a leading producer of oranges and researchers are attempting to derive ethanol from citrus peel waste. (Source: EIA)

SPACE PROGRAMME

NASA's John F. Kennedy Space Centre (KSC) is located on the east coast of Florida between Jacksonville and Miami. KSC is the launch site from which manned spaceflights to the moon have taken place and from which, more recently, the Space Shuttle has taken off. Missions include repairs to the Hubble Space Telescope, construction of the International Space Station, and orbiting the Chandra X-ray observatory.

Florida Space Authority, URL: http://www.spaceflorida.gov/
Kennedy Space Center, URL: http://www.nasa.gov/centers/kennedy/home/index.html

GEORGIA

Capital: Atlanta (city population, Census 2010: 420,003)

Head of State: Nathan Deal (R) (Governor) (page 1413)

State Flag: Three horizontal bands of equal width, the top and bottom bands scarlet, the centre band white. In the upper left of the hoist is superimposed a blue square on which appears the state seal of Georgia.

CONSTITUTION AND GOVERNMENT

Constitution

Georgia is one of the original 13 states of the Union (2 January 1788). The 1983 Constitution stipulates that the governor, the state's chief executive officer, is elected for a four-year term and can serve for an additional term. The governor is assisted by the following directly-elected executive officials: lieutenant governor, secretary of state, attorney general, state school superintendent, commissioner of insurance (formerly comptroller general), commissioner of agriculture, commissioner of labour, and five public service commissioners. All are elected for terms of four years. The lieutenant governor also serves as the president of the Senate.

Georgia has two Senators at the US Senate and 13 Representatives at the US House of Representatives. Senators serve six-year terms, while Representatives serve two-year terms. Following re-apportionment in 2002 the number of Congressional Districts in Georgia was increased from 11 to 13, and the number of Congressional seats raised accordingly.

To view the state constitution, please visit: http://sos.georgia.gov/elections/2003_constitution.pdf

Recent Events

On 1st April 2009, the Georgian Senate passed Resolution 632 by a vote of 43-1; this means that the only crimes the federal government can prosecute are treason, piracy and slavery. The resolution goes on to endorse the theory that states have the right to abridge constitutional freedoms of religion, press and speech. The resolution also endorses "nullification," the legal concept that states have the power to ignore federal laws that they believe exceed the powers granted under the Constitution. The resolution states that if Congress, the president or federal courts take any action that exceeds their constitutional powers, the Constitution is rendered null and void and the United States of America is officially disbanded. For example, if the federal government enacts "prohibitions of type or quantity of arms or ammunition," the country is disbanded. The bill was introduced on the penultimate day day of the legislative session, and it is thought that most Georgian senators did not have time to read it through. A similar resolution was introduced in the Georgia House but not voted on.

Legislature

The Georgia General Assembly, first formed in 1777, is made up entirely of part-time members, all elected for a two-year term, with both House and Senate apportioned by population. Legislators convene on the second Monday in January each year for a 40 day session. Deficit spending is prohibited.

Upper House

The Senate has 56 members, all elected for two years. Each of Georgia's senators represents about 146,000 people. Following the 2012 elections, the Georgia Senate is composed of 38 Republicans and 18 Democrats.
Senate, Secretary of the Senate, 353 State Capitol Atlanta, Georgia 30334, USA. Tel: +1 404 656 5040, URL: http://www.legis.state.ga.us/

Lower House

The House of Representatives has 180 members who are elected for two years. Each of its Representatives acts on behalf of about 30,000 people. Following the 2010 elections, the House was composed of 111 Republicans, 68 Democrats and 1 Independent.
House of Representatives, Clerk of the House, 309 State Capitol Building, Atlanta, GA 30334, USA. Tel: +1 404 656 5015, URL: http://www.legis.state.ga.us

Elected Executive Branch Officials (as at April 2013)
Governor: Nathan Deal (R) (page 1413)
Lieutenant Governor: Casey Cagle (R)
Secretary of State: Brian Kemp (R)
Attorney General: Sam Olens (R)
Superintendent of Schools: Dr John D. Barge (R)
Commissioner of Agriculture: Gary Black (R)
Commissioner of Insurance and Safety Fire: Ralph Hudgens (R)
Commissioner of Labour: Mark Butler (R)
Public Service Commissioners: Lauren McDonald Jr. (R) (Chairman), Doug Everett (R), Chuck Eaton (R), Stan Wise (R), Tim Echols (R)

General Assembly (as at May 2013)
President of the Senate: Lt. Gov. Casey Cagle (R)
President Pro Tem of the Senate: David Shafer (R)

Majority Leader of the Senate: Chip Rogers (R)
Minority Leader of the Senate: Steve Henson (D)
Speaker of the House: David Ralston (R)
Majority Leader of the House: Larry O'Neal (R)
Minority Leader of the House: Stacey Abrams (D)

US Senators: Saxby Chambliss (R) (page 1402) and Johnny Isakson (R) (page 1447)

Ministries

Office of the Governor, 203 State Capitol, Atlanta, Georgia 30334, USA. Tel: +1 404 656 1776, fax: +1 404 657 7332, URL: http://gov.georgia.gov/
Office of the Lieutenant Governor, 240 State Capitol, Atlanta, GA 30334, USA. Tel: +1 404 656 5030, fax: +1 404 656 6739, URL: http://www.ltgov.georgia.gov/
Office of the Secretary of State, 214 State Capitol, Atlanta, GA 30334, USA. Tel: +1 404 656 2881, fax: +1 404 656 0513, e-mail: sosweb@sos.state.ga.us, URL: http://sos.georgia.gov/
Office of the Attorney General, 40 Capitol Square, SW Atlanta, Georgia 30334-1300, USA. Tel: +1 404 656 3300, URL: http://law.ga.gov/
Department of Agriculture, 19 Martin Luther King, Jr. Drive, SW, Atlanta, Georgia 30334, USA. Tel: +1 404 656 3685, fax: +1 404 651 7957, URL: http://agr.georgia.gov/
Department of Community Health, 2 Peachtree Street, NW, Atlanta, GA 30303, USA. Tel: +1 404 656 4507, fax: +1 404 651 6880, URL: http://www.dch.georgia.gov
Department of Defence, Confederate Avenue, PO Box 17965, Atlanta, GA 30316-0965, USA. Tel: +1 404 624 6001, URL: http://www.gadod.net/
Department of Education, 2054 Twin Towers East, Atlanta, GA 30334, USA. Tel: +1 404 656 2800, fax: +1 404 651 6867, e-mail: help.desk@doe.k12.ga.us, URL: http://www.doe.k12.ga.us/
Environmental Facilities Authority, 2090 Equitable Building, 100 Peachtree Street, NW, Atlanta, GA 30303-1911, USA. Tel: +1 404 656 0938, fax: +1 404 656 6416, URL: http://www.gefa.org/
Department of Industry, Trade and Tourism, PO Box 1776, Atlanta, GA 30301, USA. Tel: +1 404 656 3545, fax: +1 404 651 8579, e-mail: klangston@georgia.org, URL: http://www.georgia.org
Department of Labour, 148 Andrew Young International Blvd. NE, Atlanta, GA 30303-1751, USA. Tel: +1 404 656 3045, fax: +1 404 656 4843, e-mail: GDOL@dol.state.ga.us, URL: http://www.dol.state.ga.us
Department of Natural Resources, 2 Martin Luther King, Jr. Drive, SE, Suite 1252, East Tower, Atlanta, GA 30334, USA. Tel: +1 404 656 3500, URL: http://www.gadnr.org/
Department of Revenue, 1800 Century Center Blvd., NE, Suite 2225, Atlanta, Georgia 30345-3205, USA. Tel: +1 404 417 4477, fax: +1 404 417 4327, URL: http://www.gatax.org
Department of Transportation, No. 2 Capitol Square, SW, Atlanta, GA 30334, USA. Tel: +1 404 656 5267, fax: +1 404 463 6336, URL: http://www.dot.ga.gov

Political Parties

Democratic Party of Georgia, URL: http://www.democraticpartyofgeorgia.org/
Georgia Republican Party, URL: http://www.gagop.org/

Elections

Elections for Georgia's governor and other elected executive and judicial officials (including lieutenant governor, secretary of state, attorney general, state school superintendent, commissioner of agriculture, commissioner of insurance, commissioner of labour, and public service commissioner) last took place in November 2010. The Republican Sonny Perdue was ineligible for re-election. Republic Nathan Deal, a former member of Congress, defeated the Democrat candidate and former governor, Roy Barnes. Mr Deal won 53 per cent of the vote against 43 per cent for Mr Barnes. Casey Cagle was re-elected Lieutenant Governor.

Following the November 2012 general election, in the state Senate the Republicans increased their majority by three seats (Republicans 38, Democrats 18), whilst in the state House of Representatives, the Republicans increased their majority by five seats (Republicans 119, Democrats 60, one Independent).

Elections also took place for two state executive positions (two officers on the Georgia Public Service Commission. Two incumbent officers, Chuck Eaton and Stan Wise, were both re-elected.

LEGAL SYSTEM

Georgia's court system consists of the Supreme Court, Court of Appeals, Superior Courts, State Courts, Juvenile Courts, Probate Courts, Magistrate Courts, Municipal Courts, and Special Courts.

The Supreme Court consists of the Chief Justice, the Presiding Justice and five Justices. All are elected for terms of six years by popular vote.
Supreme Court, URL: http://www.gasupreme.us
Chief Justice: Carol W. Hunstein
Presiding Justice: Hugh Thompson
Justices: Robert Benham, P.Harris Hines, Harold Melton, David E. Nahmias, Keith Blackwell

UNITED STATES OF AMERICA

According to the DPIC, 52 people have been executed since 1976. The most recent execution took place in September 2011. The current death row population is 97 including one woman. The murder rate is estimated to be 5.8 per 100,000 population.

The Court of Appeals comprises three divisions and 12 judges elected for six-year terms: the Chief Judge, four Presiding Judges, and seven Judges.
Court of Appeals of Georgia, URL: http://www.gaappeals.us/
Chief Judge: John Ellington

LOCAL GOVERNMENT

For local government purposes Georgia is divided into 154 county governments, usually called the Board of Commissioners; some have a Sole Commissioner. Georgia only defines cities as local units of government. Every incorporated town, no matter how small, is legally a city. Municipal government takes the form of mayor-council, commission, or council-manager governments. There are 180 school district governments.

Georgia's County Commissioners form the Association of County Commissioners, as well as the Georgia Municipal Association and the Atlanta Regional Commission. There are also Regional Development Centres in the Central Savannah River Area, Coastal Georgia, Lower Chattahoochee, Middle Flint, Middle Georgia, and Southwest Georgia.

Department of Community Affairs, URL: http://www.dca.state.ga.us

AREA AND POPULATION

Area
Georgia is situated in the south of the US, south-west of South Carolina, east of Alabama, north of Florida, and south of North Carolina and Tennessee. Georgia's total area is 59,424.77 sq. miles, of which 57,906.14 sq. miles is land and 1,518.63 sq. miles is water. Georgia has five major geographic regions: the Blue Ridge Mountains to the north-east, the Piedmont in the centre of the state, the Cumberland Plateau and the Ridge and Valley Province to the north-west, and the Coastal Plain in the south.

To view a map of the state, please consult:
http://www.lib.utexas.edu/maps/us_2001/georgia_ref_2001.pdf

Population
According to the 2010 Census, the population was 9,687,6530, down from the mid-2009 estimate of 9,829,211. Since the official Census in 2000, the population of Georgia has grown by 18.3 per cent. The population was estimated at 9,919,945 in 2012. The population is expected to reach 12.0 million by 2030. The population density was 168.4 people per sq. mile in 2010. The county with the greatest number of inhabitants is Fulton County with a 2010 population of 920,581 and a population density of 1,748 people per sq. mile. Atlanta is the largest city, with a 2011 (E) population of 432,427 and a population density of 3,154.3 persons per sq. mile. An estimated 7.0 per cent of the population is under 5 years, 25.4 per cent under 18 years and 11 per cent is aged over 65 years. According to the Census, 51.2 per cent of the state population is female. According to the 2010 Census, approximately 59.7 per cent of the population is white, and 30.5 per cent is black. Approximately 8.8 per cent of the population is of Hispanic or Latino origin.

Births, Marriages, Deaths
The US Census Bureau estimates that there were 133,947 births in 2010 and 71,263 deaths over the same period. The fertility rate was an estimated 64.6 per 1,000 women aged 15-44 years and the death rate was an estimated 735.6 per 100,000 population. An estimated 53,950 people immigrated into the state in 2009. Most of the immigration to the state was from other parts of the USA. The 2007 infant mortality rate was 8.0 infant deaths per 1,000 live births. Provisional NCHS data puts the number of marriages in 2007 at 64,034, down on the previous year.

EMPLOYMENT

The total civilian labour force in December 2012 was estimated to be 4,804,500, of which 4,390,500 were employed and an estimated 413,900 were unemployed. The unemployment rate was 8.6, down from 10.0 per cent in December 2010 but higher than the national rate of 7.8 per cent. (Source: BLS, preliminary figures)

The following table shows December 2012 non-farm wage and salary employment according to industry (preliminary figures):

Employment Sector	No. employed	Annual change (%)
Logging and mining*	8,500	-2.3
Construction	139,400	-2.5
Manufacturing	363,700	3.0
Trade, transport and utilities	848,800	2.6
Information	99,700	4.9
Financial activities	207,800	0.7
Professional and business svcs.	581,300	4.4
Educational and health svcs.	516,700	2.8
Leisure and hospitality	392,400	3.2
Other services	151,400	-0.1
Government	661,400	-1.5
TOTAL	3,971,100	1.9

*Not seasonally adjusted
Source: US Bureau of Labor Statistics

BANKING AND FINANCE

GDP/GNP, Inflation, National Debt
Georgia's Gross Domestic Product (GDP) rose from $403,230 million in 2010 to $418,943 million in 2011. Real GDP contracted by 0.6 per cent in 2008, mainly due to declines in manufacturing and construction, as well as in finance and insurance. It rose to $403,070 million in 2010, an increase of 1.4 per cent. It grew by 1.7 per cent in 2011. Georgia was ranked 11th in the US for its 2011 GDP. The following table shows estimated GDP according to industry (millions of current dollars):

Industry	2009	2010	2011
Agriculture, forestry, fishing and hunting	3,526	3,563	3,747
Mining	417	407	406
Utilities	8,435	8,467	8,010
Construction	15,987	15,028	14,972
Manufacturing	42,001	42,241	47,007
Wholesale Trade	28,254	29,463	30,820
Retail Trade	24,035	25,396	26,206
Transport & warehousing	14,941	15,502	16,345
Information	25,482	23,931	25,709
Finance and insurance	25,685	30,371	31,190
Real Estate	48,025	45,000	44,799
Educational services	4,234	4,429	4,587
Health care and social assistance	25,689	27,068	28,089
Other non-govt. services	69,798	73,793	78,153
Government	56,843	58,393	58,922
TOTAL	395,194	403,230	418,943

Source: Bureau of Economic Analysis, Feb. 2013

Personal income averaged $35,979 per capita in 2011, 87 per cent of national average. In terms of GDP per capita, Georgians earned $37,270 in 2011, compared to the US where the average was $42,070). Atlanta's annual Consumer Price Index (CPI) rose from 209.1 in 2011 to 212.8 in 2012. (1982-84 = 100). (Source: Bureau of Labor Statistics)

Balance of Payments/ Imports and Exports
Georgia's imports cost $467,269 million in 2011, up 11.8 per cent from the $60,176 imports cost in 2010. Georgia's imports represented 3.0 per cent of US total imports. Main imports are medicaments and medical equipment and vehicle parts. Main suppliers include China (21.8), Germany (15.3), Mexico, South Korea and Japan.

Georgia's exports generated $28,950 million in 2010, up 21.9 per cent. Exports rose to $34,776 million in 2011, up 20.1 per cent. Georgia contributed 2.3 per cent of the US total export revenue in 2011. The following table shows the top five export goods, according to export revenue, in 2010:

Product	$m
Civilian aircraft, engines, equipment and parts	4,026
Chemical woodpulp, soda etc., N.Dis.S.Bl & Bl Conif	1,174
Gas turbine parts nesoi	840
Chicken cuts and edible offal, frozen	687
Pass veh. spk-ig int com rcpr p eng >1500	571

Source: US Census Bureau

Merchandise export revenue in 2010-11, according to international trading partner, is shown on the following table:

Country	2010 ($m)	2011 ($m)	+/-% 10-11
Canada	5,116	6,394	25.0
China	2,388	3,182	33.3
Mexico	1,940	1,979	2.0
Singapore	795	1,485	86.7
Japan	1,195	1,217	1.8

Source: US Census Bureau

Chambers of Commerce and Trade Organisations
Georgia Department of Industry, Trade & Tourism, URL: http://www.georgia.org
Georgia Chamber of Commerce, URL: http://www.gachamber.com/

MANUFACTURING, MINING AND SERVICES

Primary and Extractive Industries
According to the figures from the BEA, mining contributed an estimated $406 million towards Georgia's Gross Domestic Product in 2011. In 2010, the non-oil and gas sector contributed $385 million and the support activities accounted for $21 million. (Source: BEA)

Georgia has no proven crude oil reserves or production and relies entirely on exports of oil from other states. Crude oil refinery capacity as of January 2012 was 28,000 bbl/d (0.2 per cent of US total). Total petroleum consumption over 2010 reached 200.7 million barrels (2.9 per cent of the US total consumption), over 112.1 million barrels of which were in the form of motor gasoline (3.5 per cent of total US consumption).

There are no reserves of natural gas in Georgia. Consumption rose from 530,154 million cu ft (2.2 per cent of US total) in 2010 to522,874 million cu ft (2.1 per cent of US total) in 2011. (Source: EIA)

Energy

Georgia's total energy production was 559 trillion Btu in 2010 (0.7 per cent of the US total). Georgia's total energy consumption was 3,156 trillion Btu in 2010 (3.2 per cent of the US total). Per capita energy consumption in the same year was 325 million Btu, ranking Georgia 24th in the US.

Georgia's primary generating fuel is coal, which accounted for approximately 36 per cent of electricity generation in 2011 (down from 63 per cent in 2006). Nuclear energy accounted for an estimated 28 per cent, natural gas 30 per cent, hydroelectric 2.5 per cent and other renewables 2.5 per cent of US total (2010). Monthly net capability Georgia contributes 3.5 per cent of US total (2010). Monthly net generation (Oct.) in 2012 was 9,344 thousand MWh.

Georgia has two nuclear power plants: Edwin I. Hatch and Vogtle. The Edwin I. Hatch plant is located near Baxley on a 2,244-acre site, and comprises two 924-net MWe boiling water reactors operated by Southern Nuclear Operating Company. Electricity generating capability by the Edwin I. Hatch plant is around 1,752 MW. The Vogtle plant is located in Burke County near Augusta, and comprises two 1,148 net MWe pressurised water reactors also operated by Southern Nuclear Operating Company. Generating capacity is around 2,301 MW. (Source: Energy Information Administration)

Manufacturing

Georgia was largely an agricultural state until the 1950s when industry became predominant. Manufacturing remains a major contributor to the state economy. In 2011, the sector accounted for $47,007 million (up from $42,421 million in 2010). The top manufacturing sectors in 2010 were food and tobacco products ($9,723 million), chemical manufacturing ($4,245 million), and textile mills ($3,969 million). (Source: BEA)

Service Industries

The services sector as a whole is Georgia's highest contributor to GDP. In 2011, the highest revenues came from the Government sector ($58,922 million), real estate ($44,790 million) and the wholesale trade ($30,820 million). Professional and technical services accounted for $31,049 million, information services generated $25,709 million, and health care and social services earned $28.089 million. (Source: BEA)

Tourism

Georgia's 48 state parks receive over 12 million visitors, and 48 million people visit the state each year. The accommodation and food services sector of the services industry contributed $12,379 million towards the 2011 GDP, whilst the arts, entertainment and recreation sector contributed $2,846 million. (Source: BEA)

Agriculture

The agriculture industry contributed $3,747 million to the GDP in 2011, down from $3,563 million in 2010. In 2010, crop and animal production accounted for $2,824 million, and forestry, fishing and related activities contributed $739 million. (Source: BEA)

Georgia's farms numbered 49,000 in 2006, according to the latest NASS Census, and covered a total area of 10.8 million acres. The average size of a farm in 2002 was 220 acres. Georgia ranks first in the USA for pecans, peanuts and broilers. Tobacco, cotton, canteloupes, squash, corn and cucumbers are also principal crops. Around 64 per cent of Georgia's total land area, some 24 million acres, is forested. Cash receipts amounted to $7.34 billion in 2010 of which broilers $3.32 billion and chicken eggs $438 million. Cotton amounted to $792 million, peanuts $401 million and vegetables and melons $603 million.

COMMUNICATIONS AND TRANSPORT

International Airports

Atlanta's Hartsfield International Airport terminal is one of the world's largest and busiest airports. There are 1,800 flight operations daily to 180 cities in the US, Europe, Central America and Asia. Twenty-nine passenger airlines and 23 freight carriers serve Atlanta. Over 2006, the airport handled 84.8 million passengers and handled 738,180 metric tons of cargo. There were 976,447 aircraft operations in total.
Hartsfield Atlanta International Airport, URL: http://www.atlanta-airport.com/
Savannah International Airport, URL: http://www.savannahairport.com/

Railways

Norfolk Southern Corporation and CSX Transportation have a combined network of 5,000 miles.

Roads

There are 1,244 miles of interstate highways, 18,000 miles of federal and state highways, and 110,000 miles of public roads.

Ports and Harbours

Deepwater ports are located at Savannah and Brunswick. Savannah has outstanding container facilities, loading-unloading capabilities, and abundant storage.

The Georgia Ports Authority, URL: http://www.gaports.com

HEALTH

The National Center for Heath Statistics estimated that there were 21.3 doctors per 10,000 inhabitants of Georgia in 2009 (lower than the US average of 27.4) and, in 2008, 4,260 dentists (4.4 per 10,000 population). In 2009, there were 2.6 community hospital beds per 1,000 residents (US average was 2.4) and, in 2010, there were a total of 360 nursing homes, with 39,960 beds. The Center for Disease Control estimated that some 18.6 per cent of Georgians did not have health care cover in 2007-09.

Georgia reported 38,300 HIV/AIDS cases from the beginning of the epidemic to the end of 2008, ranking it 6th highest among the US states. In 2009, 1,606 further cases were reported. The TB rate of infection was 4.9 per 100,000 population, the 8th highest in the US. The state exceeds the US average in terms of both overweight adults (64.8 per cent) and obesity among adults (29.6 per cent). (Source: Center for Disease Control).

EDUCATION

Primary/Secondary Education

In the year 2009-10, there were 2,607 elementary and secondary public schools in the state. Enrolments in the public elementary and secondary sector numbered 1,667,685, and there were 115,918 teachers working in the sector, representing a ratio of one teacher to 14.3 students.

Current expenditure for state education reached $19.007 billion in 2007-08, whilst revenues stood at $18.6 billion.

Higher Education

The University System of Georgia, the responsibility of the Board of Regents, includes four research universities, two regional universities, 13 state colleges and universities, and 15 two-year colleges. There are 132 degree-conferring institutions in Georgia, 67 of which are public. In 2010-11 there were around 213,914 men enrolled and 318,579 women. Over the year, 121,819 degrees/certificates were conferred, of which 42,452 were Bachelors, 16,304 were Masters and 3,958 were Doctorates. (Source: National Center for Education Statistics)

COMMUNICATIONS AND MEDIA

Newspapers

Georgia has 17 daily newspapers, including: Atlanta Journal-Constitution, Atlanta; The Daily Tribune News, Cartersville; The Daily Herald, Jonesboro; Athens Banner-Herald/Daily News, Athens; Columbus Ledger-Enquirer, Columbus; and Thomson South Georgia Newspapers, Valdosta.
Georgia Press Association, URL: http://www.gapress.org/
The Atlanta Journal-Constitution, URL: http://www.accessatlanta.com/partners/ajc/

Broadcasting

There are 36 television networks in Georgia, of which nine are in Atlanta and five are in Columbus. Atlanta's television stations include: WSB (part of ABC), WAGA (Fox), WGTV (PBS), WXIA (NBC), WTBS (independent), WPBA (PBS), WATL (WB), WGNX (CBS), and WUPA (UPN).
Georgia Public Television, URL http://www.gpb.org/

Telecommunications

The state's telephone and other communication services are provided by Southern Bell, General Telephone, and 36 other telephone companies.

ENVIRONMENT

Georgia's electricity generating industry relies primarily on coal as a generating fuel. The state accounted for 3.5 per cent of total US emissions of carbon dioxide in 2010: 82,591,913 metric tons, up from 77,022,270 metric tons in 2009, ranking it 8th out of US states. It also accounted for 4.9 per cent of sulfur dioxide emissions (264,774 metric tons), compared to 294,594 metric tons in 2009. In 2010, nitrogen oxide emissions amounted to 79,274 metric tons, accounting to 3.1 per cent of US total (compared to 73,879 metric tons in 2009).

In 2010, there were 26,451 alternative-fuel vehicles in use in Georgia (2.8 per cent of the US total), and ethanol consumption rose to 11,221,000 barrels in 2011, up from 9,914,000 barrels in 2009 (3.7 per cent of the US total). There were two ethanol plands in 2012. (Source: EIA)

HAWAII

Capital: Honolulu (Urban population, Census 2010: 337,256)

Head of State: Neil Abercrombie (D) (Governor) (page 1371)

State Flag: Eight horizontal stripes and the British Union Jack. The eight stripes represent the eight major islands.

CONSTITUTION AND GOVERNMENT

Constitution
Hawaii was admitted as the 50th state of the Union on 21 August 1959. According to the 1950 Constitution, Hawaiians elect two executive officials: the Governor and the Lieutenant Governor. Both serve no more than two consecutive four-year terms and must be from the same political party.

Hawaiians elect two Senators and two Representatives to the US Congress, Washington, DC. The Senators are elected for six years and the Representatives for two years.

To view the state constitution, please visit: http://www.hawaii.gov/lrb/con/

Legislature
Hawaii's bicameral legislature consists of the Senate and House of Representatives. The legislature convenes annually, commencing on the third Wednesday in January and lasting a maximum of 60 working days.
State Legislature, State Capitol, 415 South Beretania Street, Honolulu, HI 96813, USA. URL: http://www.capitol.hawaii.gov/

Upper House
The Senate's 25 members are elected for staggered four-year terms. Following the 2012 elections the Senate was composed of 24 Democrats and 1 Republicans.
State Senate, Hawaii State Capitol, 415 South Beretania Street, Honolulu, Hawaii 96813, USA. Tel: +1 808 586 6720 (Senate Chief Clerk), fax: +1 808 586 6719 (Senate Chief Clerk), URL: http://www.capitol.hawaii.gov/

Lower House
The House of Representatives has 51 members who are elected for two years. Following the 2012 elections the House was divided into 44 Democrat seats and 7 Republican seats.
State House of Representatives, Hawaii State Capitol, 415 South Beretania Street, Honolulu, Hawaii 96813, USA. Tel: +1 808 586 6400 (House Chief Clerk), fax: +1 808 586 6401 (House Chief Clerk), URL: http://www.capitol.hawaii.gov/

Elected Executive Branch Officials (as at April 2013)
Governor: Neil Abercrombie (D) (page 1371)
Lieutenant Governor: Shan Tstusui (D)

State Officials (as at April 2013)
Acting State Auditor: Jan K. Yamane
Attorney General: David M. Louie
Director of Finance: Kalbert K. Young

Legislature (as at April 2013)
President of the Senate: Donna Mercado Kim (D)
Senate Majority Leader: Brickwood Galuteria (D)
Senate Minority Leader: Sam Slom (R)
Speaker of the House: Joseph M. Souki (D)
House Majority Leader: Scott K. Saiki (D)
House Minority Leader: Aaron Ling Johanson (R)

US Senators: Mazie Hirono (D) (page 1442)and Brian Schatz (D) (page 1509)

Ministries
State Government portal, URL: http://portal.ehawaii.gov/landing/
Office of the Governor, Executive Chambers, Hawaii State Capitol, Honolulu, HI 96813, USA. Tel: +1 808 586 0034, fax: +1 808 586 0006, e-mail: http://www.hawaii.gov/gov/gov/email, URL: http://governor.hawaii.gov/
Office of the Lieutenant Governor, Executive Chambers, Hawaii State Capitol, Honolulu, Hawaii 96813, USA. Tel: +1 808 586 0255, fax: +1 808 586 0231, e-mail: ltgov@hawaii.gov, URL: http://www.hawaii.gov/ltgov/
Department of Agriculture, 1428 S. King Street, Honolulu, HI 96814, USA. Tel: +1 808 973 9560, fax: +1 808 973 9613, URL: http://hdoa.hawaii.gov
Department of Budget and Finance, 250 South Hotel Street, No. 1 Capitol District Building, Honolulu, HI 96813 (PO Box 150, Honolulu, HI 96810) USA. Tel: +1 808 586 2355, fax: +1 808 586 2377, e-mail: HI.BudgetandFinance@hawaii.gov, URL: http://budget.hawaii.gov/
Department of Business, Economic Development and Tourism, 1 Capitol District Building, 250 S. Hotel Street, Honolulu, Hawaii 96813 (PO Box 2359, Honolulu, Hawaii 96804), USA. Tel: +1 808 586 2423, fax: +1 808 587 2790, http://hawaii.gov/dbedt/info/economic/
Department of Education, Queen Lili'uokalani Building, 1390 Miller Street, Honolulu, Hawaii 96813, USA. Tel: +1 808 586 3310, fax: +1 808 586 3320, URL: http://doe.k12.hi.us/
Department of Health, 1250 Punchbowl Street, Honolulu, Hawaii 96813, USA. Tel: +1 808 586 4400, fax: +1 808 586 4444, URL: http://health.hawaii.gov/

Department of Land and Natural Resources, Kalanimoku Building, 1151 Punchbowl Street, Honolulu, HI 96813, USA. Tel: +1 808 587 0400, fax: +1 808 587 0390, e-mail: dlnr@hawaii.gov, URL: http://dlnr.hawaii.gov/
Department of Transport, Aliiaimoku Hale, 869 Punchbowl Street, Honolulu, HI 96813, USA. Tel: +1 808 587 2160 (Public Affairs), fax: +1 808 587 2313 (Public Affairs), URL: http://hidot.hawaii.gov/

Political Parties
Democratic Party of Hawaii, URL: http://www.hawaiidemocrats.org
Republican Party of Hawaii, URL: http://www.gophawaii.com

Elections
Elections were held in November 2010 for the following: Governor, one US Senator, 2 US Representatives, 13 state Senators and all 51 state Representatives. Governor Linda Lingle (R) was ineligible to stand. Democrat Neil Abercrombie beat the Republican candidate, Lt-Gov. James 'Duke' Aiona, with 58 per cent of the vote compared to 41 per cent for Mr Iona. Democrat Brian E. Schatz won the race to become Lt.-Governor.

Following the November 2012 legislative elections, the Democrats maintained their majority in the Senate (Democrats 24 seats, Republicans, 1). They increased their control of the House by two seats (Democrats 44 seats, Republicans 7).

In the US Senate elections, Senator Daniel Akaka did not run for re-election. Mazie Hirono (D) was elected. The Lt-Gov. Brian Schatz (D) was appointed to the US Senate following the death of Daniel Inouye who died in December 2012. Shan Tsutsui was ppointed Lt.Governor on 27 December 2012.

LEGAL SYSTEM

Hawaii's court system consists of the Supreme Court, the Intermediate Court of Appeals, Land and Tax Appeal Courts, Circuit Courts, Family Courts, and District Courts.

The Supreme Court has a Chief Justice and four Associate Justices who are appointed initially to a ten-year term of office. Those retained by the Judicial Selection Commission receive tenure until their retirement at 70. The Intermediate Court of Appeals consists of the Chief Judge and four Associate Judges who sit in panels of three. Like the Supreme Court Justices, Appeals Court Judges are appointed initially for a ten-year term of office and must retire at the age of 70.

Hawaii does not have the death penalty.

Same-sex unions are recognised.

Supreme Court, URL: http://www.courts.state.hi.us/
Chief Justice: Mark E. Recktenwald
Associate Justices: Paula A. Nakayama, Simeon R. Acoba Jr., Richard Pollack, Sabrina McKenna
Intermediate Court of Appeals, URL: http://www.courts.state.hi.us/
Chief Judge: Craig H. Nakamura
Judges: Daniel R. Foley, Alexa D. M. Fujise, Katherine Leonard, Lawrence Reifurth, Lisa Ginoza

LOCAL GOVERNMENT

Hawaii is divided into three county governments - Hawaii, Kauai, and Maui - and one municipal government - Honolulu. Each of the counties has an elected mayor. The city and county of Honolulu is administered by a consolidated city-county government. Kalawao County is the only area regarded as neither a county nor a municipality. Its only governing official is a county sheriff. Hawaii also has 15 special district governments and one dependent public school system.

AREA AND POPULATION

Area
Hawaii is located in the north central Pacific Ocean nearly 2,500 miles from the west coast of the US. Comprising 137 separate islands, Hawaii has a total land area of 10,930.98 sq. miles, of which 6,422.62 sq. miles is land and 4,508.36 sq. miles is water.

To view a map, consult http://www.lib.utexas.edu/maps/us_2001/hawaii_ref_2001.pdf

Population
According to the 2010 Census, the state population was 1,360,301, up on the mid-2009 estimate of 1,295,178. In 2012, the population was estimated at 1,392,313. The population of Hawaii grew by 12.3 per cent between 2000 and 2010 and is expected to reach 1.47 million by 2030. Population density in 2010 was estimated at 211.8 persons per sq. mile. The capital, Honolulu, is the largest city in Hawaii, with 337,256 in 2010, and a population density of 5,572.5 people per sq. mile. An estimated 6.4 per cent of the population is under 5 years, 22.2 per cent under 18 years and 6.4 per cent is aged over 65 years. According to the Census, 49.8 per cent of the state population is female. According to the 2010 Census, approximately 24.7 per cent of the population is white, 1.6 per cent is black, 38.6 per cent is Asian, 10 per cent is Native Hawaiian and Other Pacific Islander. Approximately 8.9 per cent of the population is of Hispanic or Latino origin.

Births, Marriages, Deaths

US Census Bureau data indicates that there were 18,988 births in 2010 and 9,627 deaths, giving a natural population increase of 9,361 people. Net emigration amounted to 1,265 in 2009. The infant mortality rate in 2007 was 6.5 infant deaths per 1,000 live births. According to provisional statistics, there were 27,316 marriages in 2007.

Public Holidays

In addition to the holidays celebrated with the rest of the US, Hawaii also celebrates Prince Jonah Kuhio Kalanianaole Day on 26 March; King Kamehameha I Day on 11 June and Statehood Day (Third Friday in August).

EMPLOYMENT

According to provisional figures, of the December 2012 total civilian labour force of 646,800, around 613,300 people were employed and an estimated 33,500 were unemployed. The unemployment rate was 5.2 per cent, lower than the overall US rate of 7.8 per cent. (Source: Bureau of Labor Statistics)

December 2012 non-farm wage and salary employment (provisional figures)

Industry	No. of Jobs	12-month change (%)
Mining, logging and construction	29,400	6.5
Manufacturing	13,800	4.5
Trade, transport and utilities	115,800	3.9
Information*	8,500	4.9
Financial activities	28,000	2.2
Professional and business services	74,100	-1.2
Educational and health services	77,300	0.9
Leisure and hospitality	110,900	4.4
Other services*	25,900	-1.1
Government	124,800	-0.1
Total non-farm employment	608,400	2.0

*Not seasonally adjusted
Source: Bureau of Labor Statistics

BANKING AND FINANCE

GDP/GNP, Inflation, National Debt

Hawaii's total Gross Domestic Product (GDP) (current prices) amounted to $67.0 billion, ranking it 38th in the US. Real GDP contracted by 0.2 per cent in 2011.

Gross Domestic Product (US$ millions-current)

Industry	2009	2010	2011
Agriculture, forestry and fishing	431	447	452
Mining	22	17	15
Utilities	1,424	1,574	1,557
Construction	3,895	3,653	3,738
Manufacturing	1,152	1,252	1,368
Wholesale Trade	1,902	1,929	1,986
Retail Trade	4,260	4,508	4,649
Transport & warehousing	2,415	2,490	2,611
Information	1,482	1,640	1,547
Finance and Insurance	2,383	2,468	2,424
Real estate	11,924	11,236	10,940
Educational services	712	731	731
Health care & social assistance	4,210	4,382	4,499
Other non-govt. services	12,430	13,282	13,926
Government	15,610	15,991	16,548
TOTAL	64,251	65,599	66,991

Source: Bureau of Economic Analysis, Feb. 2013

Average per capita personal income in Hawaii was estimated at $42,925 in 2011. In 2011, per capita real GDP amounted to $42,171, lower than the US average of $42,070. The annual Consumer Price Index (CPI) for the Honolulu urban area (all items) rose from 234.8 in 2010 to 243.6 in 2011 (1982-84 = 100). (Source: Bureau of Labor Statistics)

Balance of Payments, Imports/Exports

Total Hawaii imports cost $4,743 million in 2010, up 22.0 per cent. Imports rose to $5,974 million in 2011. This represents a 0.3 per cent share of total US imports. Imports include crude oil, airplane and other accessories, and vehicle parts. Main suppliers include Saudi Arabia (15.0 per cent), Russia (13.7 per cent), Indonesia (13.1 per cent), Thailand & Vietnam.

Annual merchandise export revenue rose from $684 million in 2010 to $884 million in 2011, a massive increase of 29.2 per cent. There were large increases in the export of airplane and other aircraft, and parts thereof, and in copper and ferrous waste and scrap. This accounts for 0.1 per cent of total US exports. (Source: US Census Bureau, Foreign Trade Division)

Merchandise Export Revenue 2010-11

Destination	2010 ($m)	2011 ($m)	+/-% 10-11
Canada	26	138	438.6
Australia	139	125	-10.4
China	63	100	58.3

- continued

Singapore	63	96	51.3
South Korea	15	95	+500

Source:
http://www.census.gov

Top five export products ($ million)

Product	2010
Civilian aircraft, engines, equipment and parts	218
Light Oils, not crude from petroleum and bituminous mineral	87
Ferrous waste and scrap	47
Parts of airplanes or helicopters, nesoi	33
Water, mineral & aerated natrl/artfcl nt swtn/flav	24

Source: US Census Bureau

Chambers of Commerce and Trade Organisations

The Chamber of Commerce of Hawaii, URL: http://www.cochawaii.com
Chinese Chamber of Commerce of Hawaii, URL: http://www.chinesechamber.com/
Hawaii Island Chamber of Commerce, URL: http://www.hicc.biz/
Kaua'i Chamber of Commerce, URL: http://www.kauaichamber.org/
Maui Chamber of Commerce, URL: http://www.mauichamber.com/

MANUFACTURING, MINING AND SERVICES

Primary and Extractive Industries

Hawaii's mining industry contributed $15 million towards the 2010 Gross Domestic Product (down from $76 million in 2007). Non-oil and gas mining was the only significant contributor. (Source: BEA)

Hawaii has no domestic oil industry other than two refineries, nine ports and one rotary rig. Apart from jet fuel, used principally by the military installations in Hawaii, consumption of petroleum products is low. Crude oil refinery capacity as of 1 January 2012 was 147,500 bbl/d. In 2009 total petroleum consumption reached 40.8 million barrels; 9.9 million barrels were in the form of motor gasoline, 6.1 million barrels distillate fuel, and 9 million barrels were used for jet fuel (1.7 per cent of total US consumption).

Hawaii relies entirely on the supply of natural gas from outside the state, having no reserves of its own. Total consumption of natural gas rose was 2,627 million cubic feet in 2010. (Source: EIA)

Energy

Total energy production in 2010 was 16 trillion Btu. Hawaii's total energy consumption was 272 trillion Btu in 2010, whilst its per capita energy consumption ranks it 49th in the US (200 million Btu in 2010).

Net summer capability in 2010 was 2,536 MW (0.2 per cent of the US total). Net monthly generation (Oct.) in 2012 was an estimated 907,000 MWh (of which petroleum 690,000 MWh, coal-fired 131,000 MWh and other renewables 67,000 MWh). A planned wave-to-energy project could supply up to 2.7 MW of electricity to Hawaii. In June 2009, Hawaii extended its renewable electricity portfolio standard to require utilities to generate 10 per cent of their net electricity sales from renewable sources by the end of 2010, rising to 40 per cent by 2030. Approximately 25 per cent of its renewable net electricity generation came from geothermal energy in 2011. Hawaii has the world's largest commercial electricity generator feuled by biofuels. Solar photovoltaic capacity increased by 150 per cent in 2011, ranking 11th among US states for PV capacity. (Source: EIA)

Manufacturing

Manufacturing contributed $1,368 million towards Hawaii's 2011 GDP (down from $1,252 million in 2010). The top sectors in 2010 were food and kindred products ($324 million), and petroleum and coal products ($556 million).

Service Industries

The services industry is Hawaii's largest contributor towards GDP. In 2011, apart from the government sector ($16,548 million), the real estate, rental and leasing sector had the highest revenues ($10,940 million), followed by health care and social assistance ($4,499 million).

Tourism

The accommodation and food services sector contributed $5,416 million towards Hawaii's GDP in 2011 whilst the arts, entertainment and recreation services sector contributed $651 million.
Hawaii Visitors and Convention Bureau, URL: http://www.gohawaii.com/

Agriculture

Agriculture, forestry and fishing contributed $452 million towards Hawaii's Gross Domestic Product in 2011, up from $447 million in 2010. In 2010, animal and crop production accounted for $404 million whilst forestry, fishing and related activities contributed $44 million.

According to the latest figures from the USDA, Hawaii's farms numbered 7,500 in 2008. Total farmland was 1,110,000 acres and the average size of a Hawaiian farm fell from 236 acres in 2006 to 148 acres in 2008. Total market value of agricultural products sold in 2008 was estimated at $513,526,000. Crop sales accounted for $429,916,000 of the total value and livestock sales accounted for $83,711,000.

Major crops include sugar, pineapples and melons, flowers & nursery products and macadamia nuts. Hawaii ranked first in the USA for revenues from macadamia nuts and coffee.

UNITED STATES OF AMERICA

COMMUNICATIONS AND TRANSPORT

National Airlines
Almost all scheduled inter-island travel is by air. There were two main inter-island airlines, Aloha Airlines and Hawaiian Airlines, until March 2008 when Aloha Airlines ceased operations. It had been hit by high fuel prices and competition from the recently formed Go! airline. There are now three main operators, as well as smaller companies Island Air and Pacific Wings serve the minor airports and provide air freight service between the islands.

Hawaiian Airlines, URL: http://www.hawaiianair.com/Pages/Index.aspx
Go!, URL: http://www.iflygo.com/
Mokulele Airlines, URL: http://www.mokuleleairlines.com/

International Airports
Hawaii's international airport is based at Honolulu. According to recent annual statistics, Honolulu International Airport recently carried over 9.12 million passengers on 372,099 aircraft operations.
Honolulu International Airport, URL: http://www.honoluluairport.com/

Roads
There are four federal highways, all located on Oahu, and a system of state highways which encircle each main island. Honolulu has a public transit system, known as TheBus.

Sea
A ferry service known as TheBoat began operations in 2007, running from Barber's Point to Aloha Tower Marketplace daily. Norwegian Cruise Lines provides an inter-island cruise service between the islands.

HEALTH

The US National Center for Health Statistics estimated that there were 31.8 doctors (including osteopaths) per 10,000 population in 2009, higher than the US of 27.4. In 2008, there were 1,039 dentists (8.1 per 10,000 population). In 2009 there were 2.3 community hospital beds per 1,000 residents, and 48 nursing homes, with 4,303 beds. According to the US Center for Disease Control, 7.8 per cent of Hawaiians had no health-care coverage in 2007-09, one of the lowest rates in the US where the overall rate is 15.8 per cent. It is estimated that 10.2 per cent of Hawaiians live in poverty, again well below the US rate of 14.3 per cent.

Hawaii reported 3,189 HIV/AIDS cases from the beginning of the epidemic to the end of 2008, ranking it 34th highest of the US states. In 2009, there were 34 further reported diagnoses. The TB rate of infection was 9.6 per 100,000 population, the highest of the 50 states. The obesity rate was 22.7 per cent in 2012 (compared to the national rate of 26.2 per cent) and the overweight rate was 56.4 per cent. An estimated 14 per cent of adolescents were overweight. (Source: CDC)

EDUCATION

Primary/Secondary Education
Over the academic year 2009-10, there were 291 elementary and secondary schools in Hawaii. 180,196 students were enrolled and there were 11,404 teachers, equivalent to a teacher/pupil ratio of one to 15.8.

Current state education expenditure reached $2.342 billion in 2007-08, whilst revenues were $2.541 billion. The average salary for a classroom teacher was $44,273 in 2004.

Higher Education
There were 20 degree-awarding institutions of which 10 were public. There were 31,359 men and 43,450 women enrolled in Hawaii's 20 degree-granting colleges and universities in the 2010-11 academic year, the large majority attending the University of Hawaii. Degrees/certificates were awarded to 11,732 students over the year, of which 5,401 were Bachelors, 2,028 were Masters and 381 were Doctorates. (Source: National Center for Education Statistics)

COMMUNICATIONS AND MEDIA

Newspapers
Hawaii's daily newspapers include: the Hawaii Tribune-Herald, in Hilo; West Hawaii Today in Kailua-Kona; Maui News, Wailuku; Honolulu Advertiser and the Honolulu Star-Bulletin, Honolulu; The Garden Island, Lihue.
Hawaii -Tribune Herald, URL: http://www.hilohawaiitribune.com/

Business Journals
Pacific Business News, URL: http://pacific.bcentral.com/pacific/

Broadcasting
Nineteen of Hawaii's 22 television stations are based in Honolulu and are owned by Fox, ABC, NBC, CBS, PBS, and Independent.

ENVIRONMENT

Hawaii's electricity generating industry primarily uses petroleum rather than coal and therefore its emissions of carbon dioxide are relatively low (ranked 42nd in the US in 2010). EIA statistics show that carbon dioxide emissions fell from 8,661 thousand metric tons in 2009 to 8,286,666 metric tons (0.3 per cent of US total). An estimated 16,747 metric tons of sulfur dioxide and 20,892 metric tons of nitrogen oxide were also produced, down on the 2009 figures of 22,280 metric tons of sulfur dioxide and 22,440 metric tons of nitrogen oxide.

In June 2009, Hawaii extended its renewable electricity portfolio standard to require utilities to generate 10 per cent of their net electricity sales from renewable sources by the end of 2010, increasing to 40 per cent by 2030.

Hawaii has some of the most powerful waves per square meter in the world, and many wave energy projects are being put into effect off the coasts.

In 2010, an estimated 5,949 alternative-fueled vehicles were in use and ethanol consumption was put at 1,261 thousand barrels (0.4 per cent of US total). (Source: EIA)

IDAHO

Capital: Boise (Population, Census 2010: 205,671)

Head of State: C. L. 'Butch' Otter, Governor (page 1491)

State Flag: A blue background bordered by a gilt fringe, in the centre of which is the State Seal of Idaho. The words 'State of Idaho' appear underneath the Great Seal in gold block letters on a red band

CONSTITUTION AND GOVERNMENT

Constitution
Idaho was admitted to the Union on 3 July 1890 as the 43rd state. The executive branch of state government consists of the governor and six other elected officials: lieutenant governor, secretary of state, state controller, state treasurer, attorney general, and state superintendent of public instruction. All are elected for four-year terms.

Idaho is divided into 35 Legislative Districts and elects two Senators and two Representatives to the US Congress in Washington, DC. To view the state constitution, please visit: http://www3.state.id.us/idstat/const/constTOC.html

Legislature
Idaho's bicameral legislature consists of the Senate and the House of Representatives.

Upper House
The Senate has 35 members who are elected for a term of two years. The lieutenant governor is also the president of the Senate. Following the 2012 elections, the Senate was composed of 29 Republicans and 6 Democrats.
Senate, State Capitol Building, Room 351, PO Box 83720, Boise 83720-0081, USA. Tel: +1 208 332 1300, fax: +1 208 334 2320, URL: http://legislature.idaho.gov/senate/senate.htm

Lower House
The House of Representatives has 70 members (the Idaho constitution requires House members to number twice the members of the Senate) who are also elected for a term of two years. Following the 2012 elections, the House of Representatives consisted of 57 Republican seats and 13 Democrat seats.
House of Representatives, State Capitol Building, Room 309, PO Box 83720, Boise 83720-0038, USA. Tel: +1 208 332 1111 (Speaker), fax: +1 208 334 2491 (Speaker's Office), URL: http://www2.state.id.us/legislat/

Elected Executive Branch Officials (as at April 2013)
Governor: C. L. 'Butch' Otter (R) (page 1491)
Lieutenant Governor: Brad Little (R)
Secretary of State: Ben Ysursa (R)
State Controller: Brandon Woolf (R)
State Treasurer: Ron Crane (R)
Attorney General: Lawrence Wasden (R)
Superintendent of Public Instruction: Tom Luna (R)

Legislature (as at April 2013)
President of the Senate: Brad Little (R)
President of the Senate Pro Tem: Brent Hill (R)
Senate Majority Leader: Bart Davis (R)
Senate Democratic Leader: Michelle Stennett (D)
Speaker of the House: Scott Bedkle (R)
House Majority Leader: Mike Moyle (R)
House Minority Leader: John Rusche (D)

US Senators: Mike Crapo (R) and (page 1410) James E. Risch (R) (page 1503)

Ministries

Office of the Governor, State Capitol, West Wing, 700 West Jefferson, 2nd Floor, PO Box 83720, Boise, Idaho 83720-0034, USA. Tel: +1 208 334 2100, fax: 1 208 334 2175, URL: http://www.gov.idaho.gov/ourgov

Office of the Lieutenant Governor, Statehouse, Room 225, PO Box 83720, Boise, ID 83720-0057, USA. Tel: +1 208 334 2200, fax: +1 208 334 3259, URL: http://www.ltgov.illinois.gov

Office of the Attorney General, Statehouse, Room 210, 700 W. Jefferson Street, PO Box 83720, Boise, ID 83720, USA. Tel: +1 208 334 2400, fax: +1 208 334 2530, URL: http://www.ag.idaho.gov/index.html

Department of Agriculture, 2270 Old Penitentiary Rd., Boise 83712 (PO Box 790, Boise 83701), USA. Tel: +1 208 332 8500, fax: +1 208 334 2170, URL: http://www.agri.state.id.us

Department of Commerce, 700 West State Street, PO Box 83720, Boise, Idaho 83720-0093, USA. Tel: +1 208 334 2470, fax: +1 208 334 2631, URL: http://www.commerce.idaho.gov

Department of Correction, 1299 N. Orchard Street, Suite 110, PO Box 83720, Boise, ID 83720-0018, USA. Tel: +1 208 658 2000, URL: http://corrections.state.id.us/

Department of Education, 650 West State Street, PO Box 83720, Boise, Idaho 83720-0027, USA. Tel: +1 208 332 6800, URL: http://www.sde.idaho.gov/

Department of Finance, 700 W. State St., 2nd Floor, PO Box 83720, Boise, ID 83720-0031, USA. Tel: +1 208 332 8000, fax: 208 332 8097, URL: http://www.finance.idaho.gov/

Department of Labour, 317 W. Main St., Boise, ID, 83735-0600, Tel: +1 208 332 3570, fax: +1 208 334 6300, URL: http://www.labour.idaho.gov/

Office of the Secretary of State, 700 W Jefferson, Room 203, PO Box 83720, Boise ID 83720-0080, USA. Tel: +1 208 334 2300, fax: +1 208 334 2282, URL: http://www.sos.idaho.gov/

Office of the State Controller, 700 W. State St., 5th Floor, PO Box 83720, Boise, ID 83720-0011, USA. Tel: +1 208 334 3100, fax: +1 208 334 2671, URL: http://www.sco.idaho.gov/

Office of the State Treasurer, State Capitol Building, Rooms 101-109, PO Box 83720, 700 W. Jefferson, Room 102, Boise, Idaho 83720-0091, USA. Tel: +1 208 334 3200, fax: +1 208 332 2960, URL: http://www.sto.idaho.gov/

Office of the Superintendent of Public Instruction, 650 W. State Street, Room 200, PO Box 83720, Boise, ID 83720-0027, USA. Tel: +1 208 332 6800, fax: +1 208 334 2228, URL: http://www.sde.idaho.gov/

Department of Transportation, 3311 W. State St., Boise (PO Box 7129, Boise 83707-1129), USA. Tel: +1 208 334 8000, fax: +1 208 334 3858, URL: http://www.itd.idaho.gov

Political Parties

Idaho Democratic Party, PO Box 445, 988 S. Longmont, Suite 110, Boise, ID 83706, USA. Tel: +1 208 336 1815, fax: +1 208 336 1817, e-mail: info@idaho-democrats.org, URL: http://www.idaho-democrats.org/

Republican Party of Idaho, Box 2267 Boise, Idaho 83701-2267, USA. Tel: +1 208 343 6405, fax: +1 208 343 6414, URL: http://www.idgop.org/

Elections

Elections for Idaho's state constitutional officers last took place in November 2010. The incumbent Republican candidate, C.L. 'Butch' Otter, won the governorship with 59 per cent of the votes. Legislative elections last took place in 2012; in the Senate, the Republicans increased their majority by one seat: 29 Republicans and 6 Democrats. In the House of Representatives, the partisan split remained the same (57 Republicans to 13 Democrats).

In the US Senate, Mike Crapo was re-elected as senator in November 2010.

LEGAL SYSTEM

Idaho is divided into seven judicial districts. Idaho's court system is headed by the Supreme Court, which consists of a Chief Justice and four Associate Justices, all elected for six-year terms. The Court of Appeals Division of the Supreme Court comprises a Chief Judge and two Associate Judges who are also elected for six-year terms. The District Courts have 39 district judges who are elected for terms of four years. The Magistrates Divisions of the District Courts are staffed by 83 magistrate judges who serve initial terms of 18 months and subsequent terms of four years subject to appointment by district magistrates. The Small Claims Departments operate within the Magistrates Divisions of the District Courts.

Capital punishment is legal in Idaho and three people have been executed since 1976; one person was executed in 2011 and one in 2012. The current death row population is 13, including one women. According to the DPIC the murder rate is 1.3 per 100,000 population.

Supreme Court, URL: http://www.isc.idaho.gov
Chief Justice: Roger Burdick
Justices: Daniel Eismann, Jim Jones, Warren E. Jones, Joel Horton
Court of Appeals, URL: http://www.isc.idaho.gov
Chief Judge: Sergio Gutierrez
Judges: Karen Lansing, David Gratton, John Melanson

LOCAL GOVERNMENT

For state elections Idaho is divided into 35 Legislative Districts each of which elects three legislators. For administrative purposes Idaho is divided into 44 county governments and 200 subcounty general purpose governments. All 200 subcounty governments are municipal governments. In addition, there are 116 school district governments and 880 special district governments or authorities.

AREA AND POPULATION

Area

Idaho is located in the West of the US, with Canada to the north, Wyoming and Montana to the east, Nevada and Utah to the south, and Oregon and Washington state to the west. The total area of Idaho is 83,570.08 sq. miles, of which 82,747.21 sq. miles is land and 822.87 sq. miles is water.

To view a map of the state, please consult:
http://www.lib.utexas.edu/maps/us_2001/idaho_ref_2001.pdf

Population

According to the 2010 Census, the state population was 1,567,582, down from the mid-2009 estimate of 1,545,801. Population was estimated at 1,595,728 in 2012. The population grew by 21.1 per cent over the period 2000 to 2010, the fifth highest growth rate in the US. The population is expected to reach 2.96 million by 2030. Idaho's population density is estimated at 19.0 persons per sq. mile. Ada County is the most highly populated county, with 392,365 inhabitants at the time of the 2010 Census, and a population density of 272.8 people per sq. mile; followed by Canyon County, with 188,923. The cities with the greatest number of inhabitants are Boise City (205,671), Nampa, Pocatello, Idaho Falls, Meridian, Coeur d'Alene and Twin Falls.

According to the 2010 Census, 7.8 per cent of the population is under 5 years, 27.4 per cent under 18 years and 12.4 per cent is aged over 65 years. According to the Census, 49.9 per cent of the state population is female. According to the 2010 Census, approximately 89.1 per cent of the population is white, and 0.6 per cent is black. Approximately 11.2 per cent of the population is of Hispanic or Latino origin.

Births, Marriages, Deaths

The US Census Bureau estimated that the number of births in 2010 was 23,198 (fertility rate of 75.7 per 1,000 women aged 15-44 years) and the number of deaths over the same period was 11,429 (giving a death rate of 729.1 per 100,000 population), giving a natural population increase of 11,769 people. Emigration amounted to 3,734 inhabitants in 2009. The infant mortality rate in 2007 was 6.8 infant deaths per 1,000 live births, down from 7.2 in 2003. In 2007, there were an estimated 15,373 marriages (up on previous years) and 7,372 divorces (also down on previous years).

Public Holidays

In addition to the national holidays, the people of Idaho celebrate Idaho Human Rights Day on January 19th.

EMPLOYMENT

Idaho's total civilian labour force in December 2012 numbered 774,800 (p), of which 724,000 were employed and 50,800 were unemployed. The unemployment rate was 6.6 per cent, below the national average of 8.3 per cent.

The following table shows provisional December 2012 non-farm wage and salary employment according to industry:

Industry	No of Jobs	12 month change (%)
Logging and mining	3,600	-2.7
Construction	31,000	1.0
Manufacturing	57,700	3.4
Trade, transportation, utilities	126,500	1.9
Information	9,700	4.3
Financial activities	29,000	-0.3
Professional and business services	76,200	-0.1
Educational and health services	92,100	5.5
Leisure and hospitality	60,900	4.6
Other services	21,900	3.8
Government	115,300	0.3
TOTAL	623,900	2.2

Source: Bureau of Labour Statistics

BANKING AND FINANCE

GDP/GNP, Inflation, National Debt

Idaho's Gross Domestic Product (GDP) (current dollars) rose from $56,038 in 2010 to $57.9 billion in 2011, a growth rate of 0.6 per cent. Idaho ranked 42nd nationally in terms of 2011 real GDP.

The following table shows Gross Domestic Product according to industry ($m):

Industry	2009	2010	2011
Agriculture, forestry and fishing	2,468	2,785	3,379
Mining	617	763	848
Utilities	880	1,019	991
Construction	2,661	2,563	2,455
Manufacturing	6,539	7,518	7,881
Wholesale Trade	2,775	2,870	3,023
Retail Trade	4,087	4,238	4,360
Transport & warehousing	1,478	1,550	1,576
Information	1,143	1,125	1,146
Finance and insurance	2,667	2,836	2,824
Real estate	6,932	6,524	6,499

UNITED STATES OF AMERICA

Educational services	366	385	403
Health care and social assistance	4,094	4,403	4,685
Other non-govt. services	9,117	9,562	9,945
Government	7,860	7,894	7,913
TOTAL	53,683	56,038	57,927

Source: Bureau of Economic Analysis

The average per capita personal income was estimated at $32,881 in 2011, 79 per cent of US average. Per capita GDP rose from $32,264 in 2010 to $32,469 in 2011, still well below the US average of $42,070. The annual Consumer Price Index (CPI) for the West urban area (all items) rose from 227.5 in 2011 to 232.4 in 2012 (1982-84 = 100). (Source: Bureau of Labor Statistics)

Balance of Payments / Imports and Exports

Idaho's total import costs amounted to $4,126 million in 2010, up 29.2 per cent. Imports rose to $4,860 million in 2011, up 17.8 per cent. Idaho's imports represent a 0.2 per cent share of the US total imports. Main suppliers include Singapore (23.1 per cent), Canada (18.1 per cent), China, Japan and Taiwan. Top import commodities include electronic circuits, machine accesories, semi-conductor devices and oil.

Idaho's export revenue rose from $,5157 million in 2010 to $5,905 million in 2011, a rise of 14.5 per cent. Idaho's export revenue represents 0.4 per cent of the total US export revenue.

The top five export products in 2010, according to export revenue, are shown on the following table:

Product	Revenue ($m)
Memories, electronic integrated circuits	1,822
Electronic integrated circuits	425
Airplane and ot a/c, unladen weight >15,000 Kg	270
Parts & accessories for ADP machines & units	212
Silver, semimanufactured	198

Source: US Census Bureau

Idaho's top five international export markets, according to 2011 export revenue, are shown on the following table:

Country	2010 ($m)	2011 ($m)	+/- 10-11
Canada	1,173	1,649	40.5
Taiwan	628	761	21.3
Singapore	792	610	-23.1
South Korea	502	532	6.0
China	445	398	-10.7

Source: US Census Bureau

Chambers of Commerce and Trade Organisations
Idaho Department of Commerce, URL: http://commerce.idaho.gov/
Idaho City Chamber of Commerce, URL: http://www.idahocitychamber.com/

MANUFACTURING, MINING AND SERVICES

Primary and Extractive Industries
Idaho is known as the 'Gem State', mining 72 types of precious and semi-precious minerals. Other minerals mined include rock phosphate, lead, zinc, gold and molybdenum. Activity is concentrated in the following areas: Shoshone County in the north, southeast Idaho, and the central mountains. In the north, the Silver Valley is one of the ten major mining areas in the world. The Wallace and Kellog are the largest silver mines in the US.

Mining contributed $848 million towards Idaho's Gross Domestic Product in 2011, up from $763 million in 2010. The non oil and gas extraction sector accounted for $733 million in 2010, whilst support activities accounted for $22 million, and oil and gas extraction $9 million. (Source: BEA)

Idaho has no reserves of crude oil, no crude oil production and no producing oil wells. No refineries are located in the state. Total petroleum consumption in 2009 was 28.4 million barrels, over half of which (16.4 million barrels) was motor gasoline.

Idaho does not produce its own natural gas. Consumption in 2009 was 83,329 million cu ft, most of which was used in industry and in power generation. (Source: EIA)

Energy
Idaho's total energy production was 136 trillion Btu in 2010. Idaho's total energy consumption in 2010 was 534 trillion Btu. Per capita energy consumption in the same year was 340 million Btu, ranking Idaho 21st in the US.

Idaho's primary generating fuel is hydroelectric (Net summer capability in 2010 was 3,990 MW (0.4 per cent of US total). Total monthly (Oct.) electricity generation was 987,000 MWh in 2012, of which hydroelectric 556,000 MWh, natural gas-fired 213,000 MWh, coal-fired 6,000 MWh, and other renewables 212,000 MWh. Wind generation increased three-fold in 2011, providing 8.2 per cent of net electricity generation. In 2011, 92 per cent of its net electricity generation came from renewable energy resources. In 2010, 52 per cent of the electricity consumed in the state was imported from other states. (Source: EIA)

Manufacturing
Manufacturing is Idaho's third largest contributor to its GDP, accounting for $7,881 million in 2011 (up from $7,518 million in 2010). The top earning sectors in 2010 were computer and electronic products ($4,199 million), food products ($1,276 million) and fabricated metal products ($329 million).

Service Industries
Within the services sector, the top contributors to GDP in 2011 were government ($7,913 million), real estate ($6,499 million), professional and technical services ($4,210 million) and health services ($4,685 million).

Tourism
Tourism is another large industry in Idaho. In 2011 the accommodation and food services sector contributed $1,509 million towards Idaho's GDP, whilst the arts, entertainment and recreation sector contributed $435 million. While significant throughout the state, the industry is particularly important in the Coeur d'Alene, McCall and Sun Valley areas.
Idaho Department of Parks and Recreation, URL: http://www.idahoparks.org/

Agriculture
Agriculture, forestry, fishing and hunting contributed $3,379 million to the state GDP of 2011, up slightly on the 2010 figure of $2,785 million. Crop and animal production contributed $2,417million in 2010, whilst forestry, fishing and related activities accounted for $369 million.

According to latest USDA estimates, Idaho's farms numbered 25,200 in 2006. Total farmland was around 11,400,000 acres and the average size of an Idaho farm was 452 acres, both down on 2002 figures. Major livestock and poultry products, in order of the number of farms producing them, are cattle and calves, beef cows, milk cows, hogs and pigs, sheep and lambs. Major crops harvested, in order of the number of farms producing them, are wheat for grain, barley for grain, dry beans, potatoes, sugar beets for sugar, and hay-alf and silage.

In terms of employment, the sector continues to contract; the major agricultural sector is crop production which employs just over 9,200.

Idaho produces 29 per cent of the nation's potato crop, and the state is ranked second in overall vegetables harvested. 77 per cent of the nation's commercial trout comes from Idaho.

In 2007, the total value of agricultural products sold reached $5.68 million; $2.3 million was from sales of crops and nursery products, and $3.36 million was from livestock and poultry, and their products.

Forestry, including forest-related manufacturing of wood products, is a major industry, and is concentrated in northern Idaho. Since the early 1980s the industry has restructured and invested heavily in new technology. In 2004, there were some 21,821,000 acres of forested land, and 17,053 people worked in forest-bases industry.

COMMUNICATIONS AND TRANSPORT

National Airlines
National airlines serving Idaho include Delta, Northwest, United and Southwest.

International Airports
Idaho is serviced only by regional airports which are situated at most major cities. They include Boise Air Terminal, Idaho Falls Airport, Lewiston Airport, Moscow Pullman Airport, Pocatello Airport, and Friedman Memorial Airport. The nearest international airport is Spokane International Airport in Washington state.
Spokane International Airport URL: http://www.spokaneairports.net/

Ports and Harbours
The Port of Lewiston is one of the major ports facilitating the export of grain via the Snake and Columbia Rivers.

HEALTH

The National Center for Health Statistics estimates that there were 18.49 doctors per 10,000 residents of Idaho in 2009 well below the US average of 27.4. In 2008, there were an estimated 890 dentists (5.8 per 10,000 population). In 2009, there were 2.2 community hospital beds per 1,000 residents, and, in 2010, there were 79 nursing homes with 6,153 beds.

According to the Center for Disease Control, some 14.9 per cent of the state population does not have health-care coverage (2007-09), below the national rate of 15.8 per cent. According to the US Census Bureau, it was estimated that 14.3 per cent of the residents were living in poverty. Obesity among adults was put at 26.5 per cent. In 2012, an estimated 62 per cent of people were considered overweight. Idaho reported 676 HIV/AIDS cases from the beginning of the epidemic to the end of 2008, ranking it the 45th highest state. In 2009, a further 32 cases were diagnosed. The TB rate of infection was 0.7 per 100,000 population (47th in the US). (Source: http://www.cdc.gov/)

EDUCATION

Primary/Secondary Education
In the academic year 2009-10, there were 755 public elementary and secondary schools, attended by a total of 276,299 students. There were 15,201 teachers, giving a ratio of one teacher to 18.2 students. Total state education expenditure for the 2007-08 year amounted to $2.324 billion whilst revenue reached $2.167 billion.

Higher Education
In 2010-11, Idaho had 15 state colleges and universities, including the University of Idaho, Boise State University and Idaho State University. An estimated 37,252 men and 47,198 women were enrolled, split fairly evenly across the three main universities. The total number of degrees/certificates awarded over the year was 16,344, including 9,466 Bachelors, 1,680 Masters and 306 Doctorates. (Source: National Center for Education Statistics)

COMMUNICATIONS AND MEDIA

Newspapers
Idaho's newspapers include The Times-News, Idaho Statesman, and Idaho Press Tribune.
The Idaho Statesman, URL: http://www.idahostatesman.com/
The Times-News, URL: http://www.magicvalley.com/
Idaho Newspaper Association, URL: http://www.idahopapers.com/

Broadcasting
Idaho Public Television (IPT), part of the Public Broadcasting Service, is the state's broadcasting network proving television through the resources of five stations: KISU for Pocatello; KUID for Moscow; KAID for Boise; KCDT for Coeur d'Alene; and KIPT for Twin Falls.

ENVIRONMENT
Idaho's electricity generating industry produces some of the lowest emissions in the US. Hydroelectric power plants supply roughly four-fifths of Idaho's electricity generation, and in 2006, Idaho imposed a two-year moratorium on proposals for new coal-fired power plants, and all subsequent proposals have been rejected. Emissions of carbon dioxide rose to 1,024,183 metric tons in 2009, up from 1,014,966 metric tons in 2007. Emissions rose to 1,213,214 metric tons in 2010, ranking it 49th highest among the US states. An estimated 6,642 metric tons of sulfur dioxide and 4,134 metric tons of nitrogen oxide were also produced in 2010, compared to an estimated 4,622 metric tons of sulfur dioxide and 2,013 metric tons of nitrogen oxide in 2009.

An estimated 5,511 alternative-fueled vehicles in use in 2010 (0.6 per cent of US total). There is one ethanol plant with a capacity of 54 million gallons per year. Ethanol consumption was 1,106,000 barrels in 2011 (up from 791,000 barrels in 2009), accounting 0.2 per cent of US total. (Source: EIA)

ILLINOIS

Capital: Springfield (Population, Census 2010: 116,250)

Head of State: Patrick Quinn (D) (Governor) (page 1499)

State Flag: A white background in the centre of which is the state seal. The state seal depicts a bald eagle on a boulder holding in its beak a streamer on which appears the state motto: 'State sovereignty, national union'; the eagle holds in its claws a shield with thirteen bars and thirteen stars; there are two dates inscribed on the boulder: '1818' and '1868' (the date of Illinois' statehood and the state seal); below the seal appears the word 'Illinois' in blue capital letters.

CONSTITUTION AND GOVERNMENT

Constitution
Illinois entered the Union on 3 December 1818, the 21st State to join. The Governor heads the executive branch of government assisted by five other elected constitutional officers: the lieutenant governor, secretary of state, attorney general, comptroller, and treasurer. Elected executive officers serve four-year terms.

Illinois elects two Senators to the US Senate for six years and 18 Representatives to the US House of Representatives for two years. To view the state constitution, please visit: http://www.ilga.gov/commission/lrb/conmain.htm

Recent Events
In November 2008, Illinois senator, Barack Obama, was elected President of the USA.

In December 2008, US prosecutors charged Governor Rod Blagojevich with trying to sell the Senate seat left vacant by Barack Obama; the governor has sole authority to select Mr. Obama's successor. Federal investigators had been working on a case against Mr Blagojevich for several years and charged him with a number of offences including soliciting a bribe. He was also charged with illegally threatening to block state aid to the company that owns the Chicago Tribune newspaper, which filed for bankruptcy the day before Mr. Blagojevich was detained. Three of the state's governors have been jailed on corruption charges in the last 35 years. Mr. Blagojevich was impeached at the end of January, and he was replaced as governor by Patrick Quinn, the Lieutenant Governor.

Legislature
Illinois' bicameral legislature consists of the Senate and the House of Representatives.

Upper House
The State Senate has 59 members. Senate districts are divided into three groups, of which one or two are elected every two years for either a two or four year term. Following the November 2012 elections, the Senate was composed of 40 Democrats and 19 Republicans. **State Senate**, Secretary of Senate, Capitol Building, Floor 004, Room 401, Springfield, IL 62706, USA. Tel: +1 217 782 5715, URL: http://www.ilga.gov/senate/

Lower House
The State House of Representatives has 118 members who are elected every two years for a two-year term. Following the November 2012 elections, the House of Representatives consisted of 71 Democrats and 47 Republicans.
House of Representatives, Office of the Clerk, Capitol Building, Floor 003, Room 300, Springfield, IL 62706, USA. Tel: +1 217 782 7996, URL: http://www.ilga.gov/house/

Elected Executive Branch Officials (as at April 2013)
Governor: Patrick Quinn (D) (page 1499)
Lieutenant Governor: Sheila Simon
Attorney General: Lisa Madigan (D)
Secretary of State: Jesse White (D)
State Comptroller: Judy Baar Topinka (R)
State Treasurer: Dan Rutherford (R)

General Assembly (as at April 2013)
President of the Senate: John Cullerton (D)

Senate Majority Leader: James F. Clayborne Jr. (D)
Senate Minority Leader: Christine Radogno (R)
Speaker of the House: Michael J. Madigan (D)
House Majority Leader: Barbara Flynn Currie (D)
House Minority Leader: Tom Cross (R)

US Senators: Richard J. Durbin (D) (page 1418) and Mark Kirk (R) (page 1457)

Ministries
Office of the Governor, 207 State House, Springfield, Illinois 62706, USA. Tel: +1 217 782 0244, fax: +1 217 524 4049, URL: http://www2.illinois.gov/gov/Pages/default.aspx
Office of the Lieutenant Governor, 214 State House, Springfield, Illinois 62706, USA. Tel: +1 217 782 7884, fax: +1 217 524 6262, e-mail: ltgov@gov.state.il.us, URL: http://www2.illinois.gov/ltgov/Pages/default.aspx
Office of the Attorney General, 500 S. Second, Springfield, Illinois 62706, USA. Tel: +1 217 782 1090, fax: +1 217 524 4701, e-mail: attorney_general@state.il.us, URL: http://www.ag.state.il.us/
Office of the Comptroller, 201 Capitol, Springfield, IL 62706-0001, USA. Tel: +1 217 782 6000, e-mail: webmaster@mail.ioc.state.il.us, URL: http://www.ioc.state.il.us/
Office of the Secretary of State, 213 Capitol Building, Springfield, Illinois 62756, USA. Tel: +1 217 782 2201, URL: http://www.cyberdriveillinois.com/
Office of the State Treasurer, 219 State House, Springfield, Illinois 62706, USA. Tel: +1 217 782 2211, fax: +1 217 782 2777, URL: http://www.treasurer.il.gov/
Department of Agriculture, State Fairgrounds, PO Box 19281, Springfield, IL 62794-9281, USA. Tel: +1 217 782 2172, fax: +1 217 785 4505, e-mail: pio@agr.state.il.us, URL: http://www.agr.state.il.us/
Department of Children and Family Services, 406 East Monroe, Springfield IL, 62701-1498, USA. Tel: +1 217 785 2509, URL: http://www.state.il.us/dcfs/index.shtml
Department of Commerce and Community Affairs, 620 E. Adams, Springfield, Illinois 62701, USA. Tel: +1 217 782 7500, e-mail: director@commerce.state.il.us, URL: http://www.commerce.state.il.us/
Board of Education, 100 N. First, Room S-404, Springfield, IL 62777, USA. Tel: +1 866 262 6663, e-mail: ssnodgra@smtp.isbe.state.il.us, URL: http://www.isbe.state.il.us/
Department of Labour, 1 W. Old State Capitol Plaza, Springfield, Illinois 62701, USA. Tel: +1 217 782 6206, fax: +1 217 782 0596, e-mail: idol@mail.state.il.us, URL: http://www.state.il.us/agency/idol/
Department of Natural Resources, One Natural Resources Way, Springfield, IL 62702-1271, USA. Tel: +1 217 782 6302, e-mail: pio@dnrmail.state.il.us (Office of Public Affairs), URL: http://www.dnr.state.il.us/
Department of Public Health, 535 W. Jefferson, Springfield, Illinois 62761, USA. Tel: +1 217 782 4977, fax: +1 217 782 3987, e-mail: mailus@idph.state.il.us, URL: http://www.idph.state.il.us/
Department of Transportation, 2300 S. Dirksen Parkway, Springfield, Illinois 62764, USA. Tel: +1 217 782 7820, URL: http://www.dot.state.il.us/

Political Parties
Illinois Democratic Party, URL: http://www.ildems.com/
Illinois Republican Party, URL: http://www.ilgop.org/

Elections
Elections for the state constitutional officers took place in November 2006. Democrat Rod Blagojevich won a second term as state Governor. In January 2009, Governor Blagojevich was impeached over allegations of corruption. He was replaced by Patrick Quinn (page 1499). In a tight race in 2010 Governor Quinn narrowly defeated the Republican candidate Bill Brady by 47 per cent to 46 per cent. Sheila Simon (D) was elected Lt.-Governor.

The most recent legislative elections were held in November 2012. In the Senate, the Democrats increased their majority by five seats (Democrats 40 seats, Republicans 19). In the House of Representatives, the Democrats also increased their majority: (Democrats 71, Republicans 47). All 118 seats were up for election.

UNITED STATES OF AMERICA

LEGAL SYSTEM

Illinois' court system consists of the Supreme Court, the Appellate Court, and Circuit Courts. As well as the Supreme Court Chief Justice, there are six Associate justices. All serve terms of office of ten years.

Supreme Court: Supreme Court Building, Springfield, IL 62701, USA. Tel: +1 217 782 2035 (Clerk), URL: http://www.state.il.us/court/SupremeCourt/
Chief Justice: Thomas Kilbride
Justices: Charles Freeman, Robert Thomas, Rita Garman, Lloyd Karmeier, Anne Burke, Mary Theis

In January 2003 outgoing governor George Ryan declared a moratorium on the death penalty in the state, and commuted the sentences of all 167 prisoners on death row to life imprisonment. Illinois had restored capital punishment in 1977, and George Ryan came to office as a supporter of the death penalty. However, a commission he set up found that death sentences were given disproportionately, in particular to those from ethnic minorities and the poor. A total of 13 death row prisoners were found to have been wrongfully convicted in the state since the US resumed executions in 1977. In 2011, the Governor Pat Quinn abolished the death penalty on the grounds that the justice system could execute innocent people. The 15 men who were on Illinois's death row had their sentences commuted to life in prison with no hope of parole.

The murder rate is currently 5.5 per 100,000 population.

Same-sex unions are recognised in the state. As of 2013, legislation legalising same-sex marriage was under discussion in the state senate.

LOCAL GOVERNMENT

According to the Census Bureau 2007 survey of local governments, Illinois' local government system consists of 102 county governments and 2,731 sub-county general purpose governments. Of the 2,731 sub-county governments, 1,299 are municipal governments - comprising cities, towns and villages - and 1,432 are township governments. In addition, there are 4,161 special purpose governments, of which 3,249 are special districts and 912 are school districts.

Rahm Emanuel was elected the 55th Mayor of Chicago in February 2011.

AREA AND POPULATION

Area
Illinois is located in the mid-west of the US, south of Wisconsin, west of Indiana, east of Iowa and Missouri, and north of Kentucky. At its northeastern tip is Lake Michigan. The Mississippi River forms the state's western border with Missouri and Iowa and the Ohio River forms its southern border with Kentucky. The total area of Illinois is 57,914.38 sq. miles, of which 55,583.58 sq. miles is land and 2,330.79 sq. miles is water.

To view a map of the state, please consult:
http://www.lib.utexas.edu/maps/us_2001/illinois_ref_2001.pdf

Population
According to the 2010 Census, the population was 12,830,632, down on the mid-2009 estimate of 12,910,409. In 2013, the population was estimated to be 12,875,255. Illinois is the fifth most populous state in the USA. Between 2000 and 2010, the population grew by 3.3 per cent. The population is expected to reach 13.4 million by 2030. Illinois' population density was estimated at 231.7 inhabitants per sq. mile in 2010. The population of the capital, Springfield, was 116,020 in 2010, whilst the city of Chicago had a population of 2,695,598. According to the 2010 Census, 6.5 per cent of the population is under 5 years, 24.4 per cent under 18 years and 12.5 per cent is aged over 65 years. According to the Census, 51 per cent of the state population is female. Approximately 71.5 per cent of the population is white, and 14.5 per cent is black. Approximately 15.8 per cent of the population is of Hispanic or Latino origin.

Births, Marriages, Deaths
The US Census Bureau estimated that there were 165,200 births in 2010 and 99,931 deaths, giving a natural population increase of 65,269 people. Approximately 12,410 people emigrated to Illinois in 2009. The infant mortality rate was 6.7 infant deaths per 1,000 live births in 2007. Marriages and divorces, according to provisional 2007 data, numbered 75,292 and 32,819 respectively.

Public Holidays
As well as the national holidays, the people of Illinois celebrate Abraham Lincoln's birthday, on 12th February.

EMPLOYMENT

Illinois' estimated total civilian labour force in December 2012 numbered 6,645,300, of which 6,068,700 were employed and 576,600 were unemployed. The unemployment rate was 8.7 per cent, above the overall national rate of 7.8 per cent. (Source: US Bureau of Labor Statistics)

Preliminary employment figures per industry - December 2012

Industry	No. of employed	12 month change (%)
Logging and mining	9,300	0.0
Construction	182,700	-4.5
Manufacturing	593,400	2.9

- continued

Trade, transport and utilities	1,145,100	0.3
Information	97,900	-1.9
Financial activities	366,200	1.6
Professional and business svcs.	859,300	2.5
Educational and health svcs.	865,200	0.9
Leisure and hospitality	534,800	2.9
Other services	238,000	-3.8
Government	824,800	-0.9
TOTAL	5,717,900	0.7

Source: US Bureau of Labour Statistics

BANKING AND FINANCE

GDP/GNP, Inflation, National Debt
Illinois' Gross Domestic Product (GDP) (current dollars) rose from $646,794 million in 2010 to $670,727 million in 2011, a growth rate of 1.9 per cent. In 2010, Illinois was ranked 5th in the US in terms of GDP, and contributed 4.4 per cent of the US total.

GDP (millions of current dollars)

Industry	2009	2010	2011
Agriculture, forestry, fishing and hunting	5,807	5,493	7,115
Mining	1,832	1,897	1,605
Utilities	11,568	11,705	10,968
Construction	23,360	21,337	21,712
Manufacturing	74,212	79,600	86,586
Wholesale trade	41,392	43,014	46,050
Retail Trade	35,236	38,001	39,734
Transport and warehousing	21,087	21,965	23,140
Information	21,484	21,092	22,345
Finance and insurance	61,398	68,932	68,616
Real estate	85,533	81,809	81,599
Educational services	8,428	8,874	9,259
Health care and social assistance	45,027	47,043	48,129
Other services	122,485	130,294	137,688
Government	64,258	65,744	66,179
Total	623,128	646,794	670,727

Source: Bureau of Economic Analysis, Jan. 2013

Estimated per capita income in 2011 was $43,721 per annum. Illinois's per capita real GDP was $45,231 in 2011, higher than the US average of $42,070.

The annual Consumer Price Index (CPI) for the Chicago-Gary-Kenosha, IL-IN-WI, urban area (all items) rose from 218.7 in 2011 to 222.0 in 2012 (1982-84 = 100). The annual CPI for the St. Louis, MO-IL, urban area rose from 209.8 in 2011 to 214.8 (1982-84 = 100). (Source: Bureau of Labor Statistics)

Balance of Payments / Imports and Exports
Total Illinois imports cost $122,048 million in 2011, up from $108,489 million in 2010, a rise of 12.0 per cent. Main imports include crude oil, phones for cellular or other wireless networks, medicaments and portable digital automatic data processing machines. Main suppliers include Canada (29.3 per cent), China (18.8 per cent), Mexico, Japan and South Korea.

Total export revenue amounted to $64,823 million in 2011, up 29.5 per cent from the 2010 total of $50,058 million. Illinois earned 4.4 per cent of the USA total export revenue in 2011.

Export revenue according to product, 2010

Product	($m)
Dumpers for off-highway use	2,408
Pass vehicles. spk-ig int com rcpr p eng >1500 Nov 3m cc	975
Civilian aircraft, engines and parts	964
Medical surgical, dental, vet. instruments & appliances	871
Soybeans, whether or not broken	814

Top five export destinations, 2010-11

Country	2010 ($m)	2011 ($m)	+/-% 10-11
Canada	15,021	19,472	29.6
Mexico	4,268	5,722	34.0
China	3,178	3,892	22.4
Australia	2,373	3,699	55.9
Brazil	2,066	2,553	23.5

Chambers of Commerce and Trade Organisations
Illinois State Chamber of Commerce, URL: http://ilchamber.org/
Illinois Department of Commerce and Community Affairs, URL: http://www.commerce.state.il.us/
The Greater Springfield Chamber of Commerce, URL: http://www.gscc.org
Chicagoland Chamber of Commerce, URL: http://www.chicagolandchamber.org

MANUFACTURING, MINING AND SERVICES

Primary and Extractive Industries

Illinois' mining industry contributed $1,605 million towards the 2011 Gross Domestic Product (down from $1,897 million in 2010). The top earning sectors in 2010 were non-oil and gas ($1,573 million), support activities for mining ($148 million), and oil and gas extraction ($176 million). (Source: BEA)

Illinois' chief mineral extract is coal, which covers 65 per cent of the state. Recoverable coal reserves in 2011 were 2,311 million short tons. Illinois' recoverable coal reserves account for some 12 per cent of total US coal reserves. In 2007, there were 21 working coal mines, employing 3,977 miners. Production was 37,770 thousand short tons in 2011 (3.4 per cent of the US total). The state has around 12 per cent of the nation's bituminous coal reserves. Mineral production also includes fluorspar, tripoli, lime, sand, gravel, and stone.

Illinois is the top petroleum refiner in the Midwest, with a combined crude oil distillation capacity of 973,600 barrels per day. Proven crude oil reserves were 64 million barrels in 2010. With a total of 15,719 producing oil wells and one rig, production was around 834,000 barrels in 2010. Crude oil refinery capacity as of 1 Jan. 2011 was 939,600 bbl/d (5.4 per cent). Total petrol consumption in 2009 reached 239.6 million barrels (3.5 per cent of the US total), as follows: motor gasoline, 117.2 million barrels (3.6 per cent of US total); distillate fuel, 43.4 million barrels (3.3 per cent of US total); liquified petroleum gas (LPG), 20.1 million barrels (2.7 per cent of US total); and jet fuel, 25.5 million barrels (4.9 per cent of US total). Illinois is one of the top producers of ethanol in the US.

In 2011, Illinois had 40 operating gas wells; 1,121 million cubic feet of natural gas was marketed over the year. Total natural gas consumption in 2010 was 939,970 million cu ft, equivalent to 4.0 per cent of the US total. The residential sector leads natural gas demand in Illinois, with more than four-fifths of Illinois households using it as their primary energy source for home heating. (Source: EIA)

Energy

Total energy production in 2010 was 2,085 trillion Btu (2.8 per cent of the US total). Total energy consumption in 2010 was 3,937 trillion Btu. Per capita energy consumption in 2010 was 307 million Btu (28th in the US).

Illinois is a net exporter of electricity. The primary source of industry generation in 2011 was nuclear power (50 per cent) followed by coal (44 per cent), and natural gas (1.3 per cent). Net summer capability in 2010 was 44,127 MW (4.2 per cent of the US total). Monthly (Oct.) net generation in 2012 was 15,466 thousand MWh (4.9 per cent of the US total), of which nuclear 7,923,000 MWh (13.3 per cent of US total), coal-fired 6,310,000 MWh, natural gas-fired 340,000 MWh, other renewables 821,000 MWh and petroleum-fired 6,000 MWh. Of the five largest electricity generating plants in Illinois, four are nuclear powered and one is petroleum/coal-fired.

Nuclear power accounts for almost half of Illinois electricity generation and over a tenth of all the nuclear power generated in the USA. With 11 operating reactors at six nuclear power plants, Illinois ranks first in nuclear generating capacity and generation in the US. Illinois' electricity-producing nuclear reactors are: Braidwood, Byron, Clinton, Dresden, LaSalle County, and Quad Cities. Braidwood, operated by Commonwealth Edison Co., is the second largest electricity-producing plant according to generating capability, with a 2006 net summer capability of 2,330 MW. (Source: EIA)

Manufacturing

Manufacturing is Illinois' second largest contributor to GDP, accounting for $86,586 million in 2011 (up from $79,600 million in 2010). The top earning sectors in 2010 were machinery ($16,172 million), food, beverage and tobacco products ($10,376 million), fabricated metal products ($8,593 million) and chemical manufacturing ($9,142 million). Illinois ranks highly in the production of construction machinery, farm equipment, radio and television sets, cellular phones, nuts and bolts, commercial printing, surgical appliances, metal stamping, sanitary food containers, electric transformers and coils, confectionery, environmental controls and food products. The state ranks third in micro and nano technology research.

Service Industries

The services sector is the largest area of economic activity. Government services earned an estimated $66,179 million in 2011; the real estate and financial sectors saw revenues of $81,599 million and $68,616 million respectively. Professional and technical services earned $58,807 million of the state GDP and health care and social services contributed an estimated $48,129 million.

Tourism

The accommodation and food sector contributed $18,406 million towards the state's 2011 GDP, up from $17,418 million in 2010. The amusement and recreation services sector contributed $5,536 million.

Agriculture

The agriculture, forestry and fisheries industry contributed an estimated $7,115 million towards the state's 2011 GDP, up from $5,493 million in 2010 when crops and animal production accounted for $5,213 million and forestry, fishing and related activities contributed $281 million.

In 2008, there were 75,900 farms, covering over 26.7 million acres. The average size of a farm was 352 acres in 2008. Major crops are corn, soybeans, and wheat, and cover 90 per cent of farming acreage.

Illinois ranked second in the USA in terms of corn and soybean production in 2008, and fourth in terms of pig production. Total cash receipts from farming in 2007 totalled $11.679 billion; of this crop fariming accounted for $9.6 billion (82 per cent) whilst livestock and poultry accounted for $2.1 billion (18 per cent). Corn made up 59 per cent of crop receipts, whilst soyabean contributed 33 per cent.

The US Forest Administration oversees 4.27 million acres of national forest in Illinois.

COMMUNICATIONS AND TRANSPORT

International Airports

Chicago O'Hare International Airport is ranked 2nd in the world in terms of passenger numbers. In 2008 the airport handled around 73 million passengers, handled 1.4 billion pieces of cargo, and saw 992,000 aircraft operations. Chicago O'Hare covers over 7,500 acres, has more than 160 aircraft gates and four terminal buildings.
Chicago O'Hare International Airport, URL: http://www.ohare.com/
Chicago Midway International Airport handles around 17 million passengers per year.

Railways

Nearly every North American railway meets at Chicago, making it one of the largest and most active rail hubs in the world. There are 35 stations in Illinois and 47 railroad companies. The major rail service operators from Chicago are: California Zephyr (to San Francisco); Capitol Ltd and Cardinal (to Washington); City of New Orleans (to New Orleans); Empire Builder (Portland and Seattle); International (Toronto); Kentucky Cardinal (Indianapolis and Jeffersonville); Lake Country Ltd (Wisconsin); Southwest Chief (Albuquerque and Los Angeles); Texas Eagle (San Antonio); and Three Rivers (New York and Philadelphia). Within the city and its northern suburbs, there is an extensive commuter network, the Chicago Transit Authority's 'L' system.

Roads

There are over 35,000 miles of primary state highway systems and more than 2,150 miles of interstate highway.

Shipping

Illinois has around 1,118 miles of navigable waterways. The state is linked to both the Atlantic Ocean (via the St. Lawrence and the Great Lakes) and the Gulf of Mexico.

There are 13 port districts and 93 public water terminals, as well as over 200 private terminals, for shippers in Illinois.

HEALTH

The National Center for Health Statistics estimated that in 2009 there were 28.0 doctors (including osteopaths) per 10,000 inhabitants of Illinois. In 2008, there were an estimated 8,192 dentists (6.3 per 10,000 population). In 2009, there were 2.6 community hospital beds per 1,000 residents, and, in 2010, there were an estimated 787 nursing homes with 101,061 beds.

In 2008, the Center for Disease Control estimated that 13.7 per cent of the inhabitants of Illinois did not have health insurance cover. An estimated 13.1 per cent were living in poverty. The obesity rate was estimated at 28.2 per cent for adults and 15.5 per cent among those under 18 years. An estimated 62.2 per cent of adults were considered overweight. Illinois reported 37,880 HIV/AIDS cases from the beginning of the epidemic to the end of 2008, and ranked 8th highest in the cumulative number of reported HIV/AIDS cases. A further 1,202 cases were diagnosed in 2009. The overall rate of TB was 3.6 per 100,000 population, the 19th highest in the US. (Source: CDC).

EDUCATION

Primary/Secondary Education

Illinois elementary and secondary schools are the responsibility of the State Board of Education. In the 2009-10 school year, there were 4,453 public elementary and secondary schools in the state in which 2,104,175 students were enrolled . There were 138,483 teachers at Illinois' public schools in 2009-10, and the teacher /pupil ratio was one to 15.2.

Revenues from education during 2007-08 amounted to over $25.43 billion, whilst current expenditure on state schools exceeded $25.25 billion.

Higher Education

Illinois has the third largest community college system in the States, with 181 higher education institutions, 60 of which are public. In the academic year 2010-11, 389,808 men enrolled and 511,016 women. In the same year, 192,536 degrees/certificates were awarded, of which 70,847 were Bachelors, 41,458 were Masters and 7,625 were Doctorates. (Source: National Center for Education Statistics)

RELIGION

In Illinois there are over 625,100 'Christian Church Adherents' and 268,000 followers of Judaism.

COMMUNICATIONS AND MEDIA

Newspapers

Illinois daily newspapers include: the Chicago Sun-Times; the Chicago Tribune; The State Journal-Register, Springfield; the Shelbyville Daily Union; Commercial News, Danville; The News-Gazette, Champaign; The Daily Herald, Arlington Heights; The Pantagraph, Bloomington; Star Courier, Kewanee; The Daily Register, Harrisburg; Register-News, Mount Vernon.
Illinois Press Association, URL: http://www.il-press.com/
Chicago Tribune, URL: http://www.chicagotribune.com/
Chicago Sun-Times, URL: http://www.suntimes.com/
The State Journal-Register, URL: http://www.sj-r.com/

Broadcasting

Seven of Illinois' television stations are based in Chicago, three in Springfield, three in Quincy, three in Peoria, and three in Rockford.

ENVIRONMENT

For its 2010 electricity power industry emissions of carbon dioxide, Illinois was ranked 6th in the US. In 2009, carbdon dioxide emissions fell to 98,974,783 metric tons from 105,765,973 metric tons in 2007. They rose again to 103,127,834 metric tons in 2010, ranking it In the same year 231,534 metric tons of sulfur dioxide and 82,559 metric tons of nitrogen oxide were produced.

There are around 32,438 alternative-fueled vehicles in use in the state (3.5 per cent of the US total). Illinois is one of the top producers of ethanol in the Nation; the state has 12 ethanol plants, with the capacity to produce 1,480 million gallons per annum (11 per cent of the US total). As of 2010, ethanol consumption stood at 11,566,000 barrels per year (3.8 per cent of the US total). (Source: EIA)

INDIANA

Capital: Indianapolis (Population, Census 2010: 820,445)

Head of State: Mike Pence (R) (Governor) (page 1493)

National Flag: A blue background in the centre of which appear 19 gold or buff stars around a gold or buff torch; 13 of the stars form an outer circle, whilst five stars form a half circle below the torch; the 19th star, slightly larger than the others, represents Indiana and appears above the torch flame; above this star is the word 'Indiana'; three rays radiate from the torch.

CONSTITUTION AND GOVERNMENT

Constitution

Indiana entered the Union on 11 December 1816 as the 19th state. The present Constitution was approved on 10 February 1851 and was adopted by the electorate with effect from 1 November 1851. The governor of the state holds ultimate executive power and serves a term of four years. The governor is assisted by six other elected executive officials: the lieutenant governor, secretary of state, attorney general, state treasurer, state auditor, superintendent of public instruction.

Indiana sends two Senators and nine Representatives to the US Congress, Washington, DC. Senators serve six-year terms, while Representatives serve two-year terms.

To view the state constitution, visit: http://www.law.indiana.edu/uslawdocs/inconst.html

Legislature

Indiana's legislature, the General Assembly, consists of the Senate and the House of Representatives. The General Assembly meets for a 60 day session every odd-numbered year, and a 30 day session every even-numbered year.

Upper House

The Senate has 50 members who are elected for four years. In November 2012 the Senate was composed as follows: 37 Republicans, 13 Democrats.
Indiana State Senate, 200 W. Washington Street, Indianapolis, IN 46204-2785, USA. Tel: +1 317 232 9400, URL: http://www.in.gov/legislative/

Lower House

The House of Representatives has 100 members who are elected for two years. In November 2012 the House was divided as follows: 31 Democrats, 69 Republicans.
Indiana House of Representatives, 200 W. Washington Street, Indianapolis, IN 46204-2786, USA. Tel: +1 317 232 9600, URL: http://www.in.gov/legislative/

Elected Executive Branch Officials (as of April 2013)
Governor: Mike Pence (R)
Lieutenant Governor: Sue Ellspermann (R)
Attorney General: Greg Zoeller (R)
Superintendent of Public Instruction: Glenda Ritz (D)
Secretary of State: CharlieWhite (R)
State Treasurer: Richard E. Mourdock (R)
State Auditor: Tim Berry (R)

Legislature (as at April 2013)
President of the Senate: Lt. Gov. Sue Ellspermann (R)
President Pro Tem of the Senate: David C. Long (R)
Majority Floor Leader of the Senate: Brandt Hershman (R)
Minority Leader of the Senate: Timothy Lanane (D)
Speaker of the House: Brian Bosma (R)
Majority Leader of the House: Bill Friend (R)
Minority Leader of the House: Scott Pelath (D)

US Senators: Dan Coats (R) (page 1407) and Joe Donnelly (D) (page 1416)

Ministries

Office of the Governor, Statehouse Room 206, 200 W. Washington Street, Indianapolis, IN 46204, USA. Tel: +1 317 232 4567, fax: +1 317 232 3443, URL: http://www.in.gov/gov/
Office of the Lieutenant Governor, 333 State House, 200 West Washington Street, Indianapolis, IN 46204, USA. Tel: +1 317 232 4545, URL: http://www.in.gov/lgov/
Office of the Secretary of State, State House, Room 201, Indianapolis, IN 46204, USA. Tel: +1 317 232 6531, e-mail: aa@sos.state.in.us, URL: http://www.in.gov/sos/

Office of the Auditor of State, Room 240 State House, 200 West Washington Street, Indianapolis, Indiana 46204-2793, USA. Tel: +1 317 232 3300, fax: +1 317 233 2794, URL: http://www.in.gov/auditor/
Office of Indiana Attorney General, Indiana Government Center South, 5th Floor, 302 W. Washington Street, Indianapolis, IN 46204, USA. Tel: +1 317 232 6201, fax: +1 317 232 7979, URL: http://www.in.gov/attorneygeneral
Department of Education, Room 229, State House, Indianapolis, Indiana, 46204-2798, USA. Tel: +1 317 232 6610, fax: +1 317 232 8004, URL: http://www.doe.in.gov
Department of Environmental Management, Indiana Government Center North, 100 N. Senate, PO Box 6015, Indianapolis, IN 46206-6015, USA. Tel: +1 317 232 8603, URL: http://www.in.gov/idem/
Department of Labour, Indiana Government Centre - South, 402 W. Washington Street, Room W195, Indianapolis, IN 46204, USA. Tel: +1 317 232 2655, fax: +1 317 233 3790, URL: http://www.in.gov/dol/
Department of Natural Resources, 402 W. Washington Street, Indianapolis, IN 46204, USA. Tel: +1 317 232 4020, fax: +1 317 233 6811, e-mail: http://www.in.gov/dnr/contact/, URL: http://www.in.gov/dnr/
Indiana Tourism Division, Indiana Department of Commerce, One North Capitol, Suite 700 Indianapolis, IN 46204-2288, USA. Fax: +1 317 233 6887, URL: http://www.in.gov/enjoyindiana/
Department of Transportation, 100 N. Senate Avenue, Room IGCN 755, Indianapolis, IN 46204, USA. Tel: +1 317 232 5533, URL: http://www.in.gov/indot/

Political Parties

Indiana Democratic Party, One North Capitol, Suite 200, Indianapolis, IN 46204, USA. Tel: +1 317 231 7100, URL: http://www.indems.org
Indiana Republican Party, 47 South Meridian Street, 2nd Floor, Indianapolis, IN 46204, USA. Tel: +1 317 635 7561, URL: http://www.indgop.org

Elections

Elections for Secretary of State took place in November 2010. Gubernatorial elections took place in November 2012. The incumbent Republican Mitchell E Daniels Jr., was constitutionally ineligible to stand for a third term. The election was won by the Republican congressman Mike Pence.

The legislative elections held in November 2012 resulted in the Republicans increased their majority in the House (Republicans 69, Democrats 31), whilst in the Senate, the partisan split remained the same (37 Republicans and 13 Democrats).

In the November 2012 elections to the US Senate, Joe Donely (D) beat the Republican candidate Richard Mourdock.

Elections for the positions of Governor, Lt. Governor, Attorney General, and Supterintendent of Public Instruction also took place in November 2012.

LEGAL SYSTEM

Indiana's court system consists of the Supreme Court, the Court of Appeals, the Tax Court, Trial Courts, and local circuit courts. Constitutional amendment allows the Supreme Court five non-partisan Judges, comprising a Chief Justice and four Associate Justices. Judges are appointed for an initial two-year term. Voters then can approve or reject an additional ten-year period.

The Court of Appeals consists of 15 judges, from which one is selected as chief judge. The Court of Appeals has five districts.

Twenty people have been executed in Indiana since 1976, most recently one man was executed in 2009. The current death row population is 12 (including one woman). According to the DPIC the murder rate is 4.5 per 100,000 population.

Supreme Court, URL: http://www.in.gov/judiciary/supreme/
Chief Justice: Brent E. Dickson
Justices: Robert Rucker, Steven David, Mark Massa, Loretta Rush
Court of Appeals, URL: http://www.in.gov/judiciary/appeals/
Chief Judge: Margret G. Robb
Indiana Tax Court, URL: http://www.in.gov/judiciary/tax/
Judge: Martha Blood Wentworth

LOCAL GOVERNMENT

Indiana's local government system consists of 91 county governments. County officials are elected to four year terms, and have limited authority to impose county-wide income taxes, excise taxes, and property taxes.. The counties are divided into townships, which have their own municipal or township governments. County governments are usually administered by a board of commissioners. There are three levels of city government: first, second or third class, according to population numbers. According to the 2007 US Census Bureau figures, there were 567 municipal governments and 1,008 township governments. There were 293 school district governments.

Association of Indiana Counties, Inc., URL: http://www.indianacounties.org
Indiana Association of Cities and Towns, URL: http://www.citiesandtowns.org/
Department of Local Government Finance, URL: http://www.in.gov/dlgf/

AREA AND POPULATION

Area
One of the Great Lakes states, Indiana is located in the midwest, south of Michigan, north of Kentucky, to the east of Illinois, and to the west of Ohio. Indiana's total area is 36,417.73 sq. miles, of which 35,866.90 sq. miles is land and 550.83 sq. miles is water.

To view a map of the state, please consult:
http://www.lib.utexas.edu/maps/us_2001/indiana_ref_2001.pdf

Population
According to the Census 2010, the population was 6,483,802, a slight fall on the mid-2009 estimate of 6,423,113. Population was estimated to be 6,537,344 in 2012. Between 2000 and 2010, the population of Indiana has increased by 6.6 per cent and is expected to reach 6.8 million by 2030. The population density is estimated at 181 inhabitants per sq. mile. Indianapolis is the most highly populated city, and the most highly populated county is Marion County. According to the 2010 Census, 6.7 per cent of the population is under 5 years, 24.8 per cent under 18 years and 13 per cent is aged over 65 years. According to the Census, 50.8 per cent of the state population is female. Approximately 84.3 per cent of the population is white, and 9.1 per cent is black. Approximately 6 per cent of the population is of Hispanic or Latino origin.

Births, Marriages, Deaths
The US Census Bureau (CBC) estimated the number of births in 2010 at 83,940 and the number of deaths at 56,743, giving a natural population increase of 27,197. Net migration amounted to 2,389 people in 2009. The infant mortality rate was 6.7 per 1,000 live births in 2007. Provisional NCHS data puts the number of marriages in 2007 at 51,219.

EMPLOYMENT

Indiana's estimated total civilian labour force was 3,158,900 in December 2012, of which 2,899,200 were in employment and 259,800 were unemployed. The unemployment rate was 8.2 per cent, higher than the national average of 7.8 per cent.

The following table shows provisional figures for December 2012 non-farm wage and salary employment according to industry:

Industry	No. of Jobs	12 month change (%)
Logging and Mining	6,500	-3.0
Construction	128,100	1.4
Manufacturing	490,400	3.7
Trade, Transport and Utilities	564,700	2.6
Information	34,000	0.3
Financial Activities	128,300	-0.9
Professional and Business Svcs.	290,500	0.2
Educational and Health Svcs.	432,900	2.2
Leisure and Hospitality	293,800	4.3
Other Services	109,100	-0.4
Government	428,900	0.8
TOTAL	2,906,800	2.0

Source: US Bureau of Labor Statistics

BANKING AND FINANCE

GDP/GNP, Inflation, National Debt
Indiana's total Gross Domestic Product (current dollar) was $278.1 billion in 2011 and ranked 17th in the US. Real GDP rose by 4.6 per cent in 2010, the third highest growth rate in the US. It grew by 1.1 per cent in 2011. Manufacturing is Indiana's highest producing sector (15.0 per cent of GDP), followed by government and real estate.

Gross State Product according to industry is shown on the following table (figures in $million):

Industry	2009	2010	2011
Agriculture, forestry, fishing and hunting	3,629	3,753	4,580
Mining	1,015	1,102	867
Utilities	5,592	5,905	5,463
Construction	9,349	9,377	10,079
Manufacturing	59,304	69,102	74,230
Wholesale Trade	13,214	13,555	14,231
Retail Trade	15,657	16,425	16,984

- continued			
Transport & warehousing	8,488	8,849	9,187
Information	5,636	5,551	5,599
Finance and insurance	16,450	18,603	18,914
Real estate	26,029	24,863	24,744
Educational services	2,504	2,605	2,722
Health care & social assistance	20,821	21,825	22,655
Other non-govt. services	35,249	37,565	33,583
Government	27,623	28,197	28,080
Total GSP	250,562	267,277	278,128

Source: Bureau of Economic Analysis, Feb. 2013

Estimated per capita income in 2011 was $35,689 per annum, 86 per cent of national average. Per capita real GDP was estimated at $36,970 in 2011, down on $37,495 in 2009, and down on the US average of $42,070.

The annual Consumer Price Index (CPI) for the Cincinnati-Hamilton, OH-KY-IN, urban area (all items) rose from 211.1 in 2011 to 216.3 in 2012 (1982-84 = 100). The annual CPI for the Chicago-Gary-Kenosha, IL-IN-WI, urban area (all items) rose from 218.1 in 2011 to 222.0 in 2012. (Source: Bureau of Labor Statistics)

Balance of Payments / Imports and Exports
Indiana's imports rose from $25,287 million in 2009 to $33,153 million in 2010, an increase of 31.1 per cent. Imports rose to $39,515 million in 2011, up 19.2 per cent. Main imports include motor vehicle parts and medical parts. Suppliers include Canada (16.8 per cent, 2011), Ireland (15.8 per cent), China (13.8 per cent), Japan (12.1 per cent) and Mexico (9.2 per cent).

In 2010, export revenue rose to $28,745 million, up 25.5 per cent. Indiana accounted for 2.2 per cent of total US export revenue in 2010. Imports rose to $32,282 million in 2011, up 12.3 per cent.

Export revenue in 2010, according to the top five destinations, is shown on the attached table:

Destination	2010 ($m)	2011 ($m)	+/-% 10-11
Canada	10,685	11,808	10.5
Mexico	2,614	3,280	25.5
Germany	1,831	1,944	6.2
Japan	1,197	1,289	7.7
France	1,408	1,231	-12.6

US Census Bureau, Foreign Trade Statistics

The top five export products in 2010, according to export revenue, are shown on the following table ($ million):

Product	Revenue ($m)
Medicaments meaured doses, retail pk. nesoi	2,516
Gear boxes for motor vehicles	1,519
Motor Vehicles Trans. Gds. Spk. ig. incp. eng.	1,069
Trailers and semi-trailers for housing and camping	949
Civilian aircraft, engines and parts	813

US Census Bureau, Foreign Trade Statistics

Chambers of Commerce and Trade Organisations
Indiana Chamber of Commerce, URL: http://www.indianachamber.com
Indianapolis Chamber of Commerce, URL: http://www.indychamber.com/

MANUFACTURING, MINING AND SERVICES

Primary and Extractive Industries
According to the BEA, mining contributed $867 million towards Indiana's Gross Domestic Product in 2011 ($1,102 million in 2010). In 2010, $1,065 million was from non-oil and gas extraction, $19 million was from support activities for mining, and $18 million was from oil and gas. The principal minerals mined are coal, petroleum and cement.

Indiana had proven crude oil reserves of 8 million barrels in 2010. With 2,856 producing oil wells and one rig, Indiana's oil industry produced around 1,835,000 barrels of crude oil in 2009. Total petroleum consumption was 144.7 million in 2010, 71.4 million of which was in the form of motor gasoline (2.1 per cent of the national total). There are two refineries in the state, with a combined distillation capacity of 363,500 barrels per day (2.1 per cent of the US total).

Indiana's natural gas industry had a total of 914 gas wells in 2010, from which it produced 9,075 million cubic feet of natural gas in 2011. Total consumption in 2011 was 630,705 million cubic feet.

Indiana is one of the leading States in both per capita and total coal consumption. In 2007, Indiana had 27 underground and surface coal mines in operation, employing some 2,683 miners. Recoverable reserves stood at 654 million short tons in 2011 (3.4 per cent of US total). Total coal production in 2010 was 34,950 thousand short tons.

Indiana has major ethanol production potential. It currently has two ethanol plants with several more under construction. (Source: EIA)

UNITED STATES OF AMERICA

Energy

Indiana's total energy production was 991 trillion Btu in 2010 (1.3 per cent of US total). Indiana's total energy consumption was 2,871 trillion Btu in 2010 (2.9 per cent of US total). Per capita energy consumption in 2010 was 442 million Btu, ranking the state 10th in the US.

Indiana is a net exporter of electricity whose primary generating fuel is coal. Coal accounted for over 80 per cent of electricity generation in 2012, with natural gas representing two per cent and other gases accounting for 2.2 per cent. Net summer capability in 2010 was 27,638 MW. Total net monthly (Oct.) electricity generation was 8,577 thousand MWh in 2012, of which coal-fired 6,943,000 MWh. The five largest electricity generating plants (according to generating capability) are: Gibson (coal), Rockport (coal), RM Schahfer (coal), AES Petersburg (coal), and Clifty Creek (coal). Indiana has no nuclear power plants. Indiana's first utility-scale wind project was installed in 2008. (Source: EIA)

Manufacturing

Manufacturing makes the largest contribution towards Indiana's GDP, an estimated $74,230 million in 2011 (up from $69,102 million in 2010). The largest sectors in 2010 were chemicals products ($16,644 million), motor vehicles and equipment ($8,086 million), primary metal manufacturing ($6,203 million), and machinery manufacturing ($5,369 million). Indiana is the leading producer in the US for a diverse range of goods including: raw steel, motor homes, radio and television sets, electrical coils and transformers, truck and bus bodies, wood office furniture, engine electrical equipment, elevators and escalators, household refrigerators and vehicular lighting.

Service Industries

The service sector is the second largest contributor to state GDP. Government services ($28,080 million), real estate ($24,744 million) and health care and social assistance ($22,625 million) were the best performing sectors in 2010, followed by wholesale and retail trade and the financial sector.

Tourism

The arts, entertainment and recreation sector contributed an estimated $3,065 million towards the 2011 GDP, up from $3,117 million in 2010. The accommodation and food sector contributed around $6,809 million in 2011.
Indiana Tourism Division, URL: http://www.IN.gov/enjoyindiana/

Agriculture

Agriculture, forestry and fisheries contributed an estimated $4,580 million towards Indiana's GDP in 2011 (up from $3,753 million in 2010). The crop and animal production sector accounted for $3,500 million in 2010, whilst the forestry, fishing and related activities sector accounted for $253 million.

Figures published by the NASS indicate that Indiana had a total of 62,000 farms in 2010, covering around 14,800,000 acres; both figures were down over the decade. The average size of a farm in 2010 was 239 acres. Major livestock products include cattle and calves, and hogs and pigs. Major crops harvested include soybeans, wheat and corn. In 2007, the state ranked fifth in the US for grains, oilseeds, dry beans, and dry peas sales, and fifth for hogs and pigs. In Jan. 2011, there were 850,000 cattle and calves, 3.65 million hogs and pigs, and 50,00 sheep.

In 2007, the state earned a total of $8.27 billion in agricultural products sold, ranking 10th in this regard. Crops and greenhouse produce made some $5.3 billion, (ranking 8th in the US), whilst livestock and products thereof earned some $2.95 billion.

COMMUNICATIONS AND TRANSPORT

National Airlines
American Trans Air, URL: http://www.ata.com

International Airports
Indianapolis International Airport is served by the following major airlines: American, American Trans Air, America West, ComairLink, Continental, Delta, Northwest, Skyway, Southeast, TWA, United, US Airways, and Western Pacific.
BAA Indianapolis International Airport, URL: http://www.indianapolisairport.com

Railways
The Indiana rail network has more than 3,250 miles of mainline track. Major railway companies operating in Indiana include: CSX Transportation, Norfolk Southern, and Conrail.

Roads
Indiana is known as the 'Crossroads of America' because of the number of interstate highways that cross the state. The I-69 links the manufacturing north-east with the Great Lakes and Detroit; the I-65 runs down the middle of Indiana from north to south; the I-80 and I-90 cross the northern sector of the state; whilst the I-70 and I-74 cross from east to west. Indianapolis, where most of the interstate highways converge, is circled by the I-465.

Ports and Harbours
The state of Indiana transports over 70 million tons of cargo by water each year and ranks 14th among all U.S. states. Indiana's water borders include 400 miles of access to the Great Lakes/St. Lawrence Seaway (via Lake Michigan) and the Inland Waterway System (via the Ohio River). Indiana's major port is the Port of Indiana. Located at Burns Harbour on Lake Michigan, it handles 6 million tons of domestic freight per year. In addition, two ports are located on the Ohio River.

The Ports of Indiana is a quasi-governmental organization that operates a statewide system of ports, foreign trade zones and economic development programs under the authority of the Indiana Port Commission.

The state's three major public ports are Burns Harbour (on Lake Michigan) and Southwind Maritime Centre and Clark Maritime Centre both on the Ohio River.

Ports of Indiana, URL: http://www.portsofindiana.com

HEALTH

The National Center for Health Statistics estimated that there were 22.3 doctors (including osteopaths) per 10,000 people in 2009, well below the US average of 27.4. In 2008, there were an estimated 3,009 dentists (4.7 dentists per 10,000 population). In 2009, there were 2.7 community hospital beds per person, and, in 2010, there were 506 nursing homes, with 57,721 beds. It was estimated that 12.6 per cent of the state population had no health-care coverage in 2007-09. An estimated 14.1 per cent of the population were living in poverty in 2007-11.

Obesity levels are slightly higher than the national average; in 2012, 65.9 per cent of adults are considered overweight and 29.6 per cent of adults obese. Indiana reported 9,186 HIV/AIDS cases from the beginning of the epidemic to the end of 2008, and ranked 24th in terms of the cumulative number of reported cases. A further 425 cases were diagnosed in 2009. The overall rate of TB was 1.9 per 100,000 population. (Source: CDC)

EDUCATION

Primary/Secondary education
During the school year 2009-10 there were 1,989 elementary and secondary schools in Indiana. 1,046,661 students enrolled for the year. There were 62,258 teachers registered, a ratio of one teacher to 16.8 students.

In 2007-08, total revenue from education came to around $12.295 billion, whilst total expenditures on state education reached $10.638 billion.

Higher Education
For the academic year 2010-11, there were 109 higher education institutions in the state, 80 of which were privately run. 195,918 male students enrolled, together with 245,376 women. In the same year, 83,658 degrees/certificates were awarded, of which 41,687 were Bachelors, 13,673 were Masters and 3,250 were Doctorates. (Source: National Center for Education Statistics)

COMMUNICATIONS AND MEDIA

Newspapers
Indiana's daily newspapers include: Indianapolis Star and News; Shelbyville News; The News-Dispatch, Michigan City; The Journal Gazette, Fort Wayne; The News-Sentinel, Fort Wayne; Wabash Plain Dealer.
The Hoosier State Press Association, URL: http://www.indianapublisher.com
The Indianapolis Star, URL: http://www.starnews.com

Business Journals
Indianapolis Business Journal, URL: http://www.ibj.com/

Broadcasting
Seven of Indiana's television stations are based in Indianapolis, four are based in Fort Wayne, five in Evansville, and three in Terre Haute.

ENVIRONMENT

Almost all of Indiana's electricity generation is fueled by coal. In 2007 Indiana's electricity generating industry emissions of carbon dioxide reached 124,295,100 metric tons (5 per cent of the US total). In 2010 emissions of carbon dioxide fell to 103,127,834 metric tons, from 111,112,991 metric tons in 2009 and was ranked 6th in the US. Its emissions accounted for 4.3 per cent of US total. An estimated 231,534 metric tons of sulfur dioxide and 82,559 metric tons of nitrogen oxide were also produced.

Indiana currently has 13 ethanol plants, and the capacity to produce 906 million gallons per year (6.7 per cent of the US total). The state consumes 2.3 per cent of the US total consumption of ethanol (7,136,000 barrels). In 2010, there were 12,949 alternative-fueled vehicles in use. Indiana's first utility-scale wind project was installed in 2008 in Benton County. (Source: EIA)

IOWA

Capital: Des Moines (Population, Census 2010: 203,433)

Head of State: Terry Branstead (R) (Governor) (page 1393)

State Flag: Three vertical stripes - blue, white and red. On the centre white stripe is an eagle carrying in its beak blue streamers on which is written the state motto: 'Our liberties we prize, and our rights we will maintain.' Underneath the streamers is inscribed the word 'Iowa' in red

CONSTITUTION AND GOVERNMENT

Constitution

Iowa entered the Union on 28 December 1846 as the 29th State. The governor heads the executive branch of state government assisted by six other elected officials: lieutenant governor, secretary of agriculture, attorney general, auditor of state, secretary of state, and treasurer of state. According to the 1857 Constitution, the governor, lieutenant governor, secretary of state, auditor of state, and treasurer of state all serve terms of four years.

Two Senators are elected to the US Congressional Delegation for six years and five Representatives are elected for a term of two years. To view the state constitution, please visit: http://www.legis.state.ia.us/Constitution.html

Legislature

Iowa's legislature, the General Assembly, consists of the Senate and the House of Representatives.

Iowa General Assembly, State Capitol Building, East 12th & Grand, Des Moines, IA 50319, USA. Tel: +1 515 281 5301 (Senate), +1 515 281 5381 (House of Representatives), URL: https://www.legis.iowa.gov/index.aspx

Upper House

The Senate has 50 members who are elected for four years, half returning every two years. Following the November 2012 elections, the Senate was split between 26 Democrats and 23 Republicans. There was one vacancy.

Lower House

The House of Representatives has 100 members who are elected for two years. Following the November 2012 elections, the House was composed of 47 Democrat seats and 53 Republican seats.

Elected Executive Branch Officers (as at April 2013)
Governor: Terry Branstead (R) (page 1393)
Lieutenant Governor: Kim Reynolds (R)
Secretary of State: Matt Schultz (R)
Attorney General: Tom Miller (D)
Auditor of State: currently vacant
Treasurer of State: Michael Fitzgerald (D)
Secretary of Agriculture: Bill Northey (R)

General Assembly (as at April 2013)
President of the Senate: Pam Jochum (D)
President Pro Tem of the Senate: Steven J. Sodders (D)
Senate Majority Leader: Michael Gronstal (D)
Senate Minority Leader: Bill Dix (R)
Speaker of the House: Kraig Paulsen (R)
Speaker Pro Tem of the House: Steven N. Olson (R)
House Majority Leader: Linda Upmeyer (R)
House Minority Leader: Kevin McCarthy (D)

US Senators: Chuck Grassley (R) (page 1432) and Tom Harkin (D) (page 1438)

Ministries

Office of the Governor, State Capitol, Des Moines, IA 50319, USA. Tel: +1 515 281 5211, fax: +1 515 281 6611, e-mail: http://www.governor.state.ia.us, URL: http://www.governor.state.ia.us/

Office of the Attorney General, 1305 E. Walnut Street, Des Moines IA 50319, USA. Tel: +1 515 281 5164, fax: +1 515 281 4209, e-mail: webteam@ag.state.ia.us, URL: http://www.state.ia.us/government/ag

Office the Auditor of State, Hoover State Office Building, Level A, Des Moines, Iowa 50319-0001, USA. Tel: +1 515 281 5503, fax: +1 515 281 6137, e-mail: info@auditor.state.ia.us, URL: http://www.auditor.iowa.gov/index.html

Office of the Secretary of State, Room 101, State Capitol, Des Moines, IA 50319, USA. Tel: +1 515 281 8993, URL: http://www.sos.state.ia.us

Office of the Treasurer of State, State Capitol Building, Des Moines, IA 50319, USA. Tel: +1 515 281 5368, fax: +1 515 281 7562, e-mail: treasurer@tos.state.ia.us, URL: http://www.treasurer.state.ia.us

Department of Agriculture, IDALS, Wallace State Office Building, 502 E. 9th Street, Des Moines, Iowa 50319, USA. Tel: +1 515 281 5321, e-mail: agri@idals.state.ia.us, URL: http://www.agriculture.state.ia.us/secretary.htm

Department of Economic Development, 200 E. Grand Avenue, Des Moines, IA 50309, USA. Tel: +1 515 242 4700, fax: +1 515 242 4809, e-mail: info@ided.state.ia.us, URL: http://www.state.ia.us/ided/index.html

Department of Education, Grimes State Office Building, 14 East 14th Street, Des Moines, IA 50319-0146, USA. Tel: +1 515 281 5294, fax: +1 515 242 5988, e-mail: webmaster@ed.state.ia.us, URL: http://www.state.ia.us/educate/index.html

Department of Natural Resources, 502 E. 9th Street, Wallace State Office Building, Des Moines, IA 50319-0034, USA. Tel: +1 515 281 5918, e-mail: webmaster@dnr.state.ia.us, URL: http://www.iowadnr.com/

Department of Public Health, IDPH, Lucas State Office Building, 321 E. 12th Street, Des Moines, IA 50319, USA. Tel: +1 515 281 7689, URL: http://www.idph.state.ia.us

Department of Transport, 800 Lincoln Way, Ames, IA 50010, USA. Tel: +1 515 239 1101, fax: +1 515 239 1639, URL: http://www.dot.state.ia.us

Iowa Workforce Development, 1000 East Grand Avenue, Des Moines, IA 50319-0209, USA. Tel: +1 515 281 5387, URL: http://www.iowaworkforce.org

Political Parties

Iowa Democratic Party, 5661 Fleur Drive, Des Moines, IA 50321, USA. Tel: +1 515 244 7292, fax: +1 515 244 5051, e-mail: iadems@iowademocrats.org, URL: http://www.iowademocrats.org

Republican Party of Iowa, 621 East Ninth Street, Des Moines, Iowa 50309, USA. Tel: +1 515 282 8105, fax: +1 515 282 9019, e-mail: iowagop@iowagop.org, URL: http://www.iowagop.org/

Elections

Gubernatorial elections were last held in November 2010. The incumbent governor, Democrat Chester (Chet) Culver (D) was defeated by the Republican Terry Branstead. Mr Branstead gained 53 per cent of the vote compared to 42 per cent for Mr Culver. State Senator Kim Reynolds was elected Lieutenant Governor.

In legislative elections held in 2012, the partisan split in the Senate was as follows (Democrats 26, Republicans 23, one vacancy), whilst in the House of Representatives, the Democrats made gains but did not overturn the Republican majority (Democrats 47, Republicans 53).

LEGAL SYSTEM

Iowa's court system consists of two appellate courts - the Iowa Supreme Court and the Iowa Court of Appeals - and District Courts in Iowa's eight judicial districts. Under the adopted constitutional provision there are six Supreme Court justices and a Chief Justice and nine Court of Appeals judges. Supreme Court justices are normally retained for a term of eight years. Appointments are made by the governor from a list of nominees submitted by the State Judicial Nominating Commission.

On April 3, 2009, the Iowa Supreme Court decided that the state's law forbidding same-sex marriage was unconstitutional; Iowa thus became the third state in the U.S. and first in the Midwest to permit same-sex marriage.

The death penalty was abolished in 1965. The murder rate is estimated at 1.3 per 100,000 population.

Supreme Court, URL: http://www.iowacourts.gov/
Chief Justice, Supreme Court: Mark S. Cady
Justices: David Wiggins, Daryl Hecht, Brent Appel, Thomas Waterman, Edward Mansfield, Bruce Zager

Iowa Court of Appeals, URL: http://www.iowacourts.gov/
Chief Judge, Court of Appeals: Larry Eisenhauer

LOCAL GOVERNMENT

Iowa is divided into 99 county governments and 947 sub-county general purpose governments, known as incorporated places. All of Iowa's sub-county governments are municipal. There are 380 school district governments.

Iowa State Association of Counties, URL: http://www.iowacounties.org/

AREA AND POPULATION

Area

Iowa is located in the mid-west of the US, south of Minnesota, north of Missouri, east of South Dakota and Nebraska, and west of Wisconsin and Illinois. Iowa's total area is 56,271.55 sq. miles, of which 55,869.36 sq. miles is land and 402.20 sq. miles is water.

To view a map, consult http://www.lib.utexas.edu/maps/us_2001/iowa_ref_2001.pdf

Population

According to the 2010 Census, the 2010 population was 3,046,355, up on the mid-2009 figure of 3,007,856. In 2012, the population was estimated to be 3,074,186. The population increased by 4.1 per cent between 2000 and 2010. The population is expected to reach 2.955 million by 2030. Population density in the state is around 54.5 people per square mile. The population of the capital Des Moines is 203,433 making it the largest city in Iowa. Next is Cedar Rapids with a population of around 126,326. The county with the greatest number of inhabitants is Polk County (430,640 according to the 2010 Census), followed by Linn County (211,226), and Scott County (165,224).

In 2011, 6.5 per cent of the population was under 5 years, 23.7 per cent under 18 years and 14.9 per cent is aged over 65 years. According to the Census, 50.5 per cent of the state population is female. Approximately 91.3 per cent of the population is white, and 2.9 per cent is black.

UNITED STATES OF AMERICA

Births, Marriages, Deaths
The US Census Bureau (Population Division) estimates that there were 38,719 births in 2010 and 27,745 deaths, giving a natural population increase of 10,974 people. Net migration amounted to 1,054 residents in 2009. The infant mortality rate in 2007 was 5.5 deaths per 1,000 live births. Marriages and divorces in 2007, according to provisional data, numbered 20,061 (up on 2006) and 7,770 (down on 2007) respectively.

EMPLOYMENT

Of Iowa's estimated civilian labour force of 1,638,500 in December 2012, a total of 1,558,600 were in employment, and around 80,000 were unemployed. The unemployment rate was 4.9 per cent, considerably lower than the national rate of 7.8 per cent. (Source: Bureau of Labor Statistics)

Provisional figures for non-farm wage and salary employment for December 2012 are shown on the following table:

Industry	No. of Jobs	12 month change (%)
Logging and mining	2,300	4.5
Construction	67,000	5.3
Manufacturing	218,500	3.4
Trade, transport and utilities	299,700	-1.3
Information	27,600	0.7
Financial activities	102,100	2.3
Professional and business services	123,800	0.8
Educational and health services	219,000	0.6
Leisure and hospitality	129,100	1.6
Other services	56,900	1.1
Government	248,200	0.2
TOTAL	1,494,200	1.0

Source: Bureau of Labor Statistics

BANKING AND FINANCE

GDP/GNP, Inflation, National Debt
Iowa's GSP (current dollar) rose an estimated $142,282 million in 2009 to $142,698 million in 2010. GDP was $149.0 billion in 2011 and ranked 30th in the US. Real GDP rose by 3.4 per cent in 2010 and by 1.9 per cent in 2011. The largest industry was finance and industry.

State GDP by Industry, ($million)

Industry	2009	2010	2011
Agriculture, forestry and fishing	7,309	7,684	9,875
Mining	93	92	99
Utilities	2,437	2,489	2,395
Construction	4,833	4,662	4,820
Manufacturing	23,123	25,660	27,642
Wholesale Trade	7,479	7,722	8,211
Retail Trade	8,111	8,493	8,744
Transportation and warehousing	4,556	4,782	4,943
Information	3,996	3,949	4,086
Finance and Insurance	15,286	18,444	18,706
Real Estate	13,749	13,110	14,104
Educational services	1,242	1,275	1,293
Health care and social assistance	9,427	9,863	10,307
Other non-government services	10,324	16,220	16,986
Government	16,179	16,450	16,775
TOTAL	133,134	140,945	148,986

Source: Bureau of Economic Analysis, Feb. 2013

Estimated per capita income in 2011 was $41,156. Per capita real GDP fell from $43,644 in 2009 to $41,859 in 2010, below the US average of $42,346. The annual Consumer Price Index (all items) for the Midwest urban area rose from 214.7 in 2011 to 219.1 in 2012. (1982-84=100). (Source: Bureau of Labor Statistics)

Balance of Payments / Imports and Exports
Imports rose to $7,014 million in 2010, up 14.9 per cent from 2009. Imports rose to $8,240 million in 2011, up 16.2 per cent. Iowa's imports represent 0.4 per cent of the US total imports. Imports include natural gas, potassium chloride, rapeseed, swine and engineering parts. Top suppliers include Canada, China, Mexico, Germany and Japan.

Total export revenue fell from $12,125 million in 2008 to an estimated $9,042 million in 2009, a decrease of 25.4 per cent. Export revenue rose to $10,880 million in 2010, up 20.3 per cent and rose further to $13,307 million, up 22.3 per cent. Iowa contributed 0.9 per cent of the total US export revenue. (Source: US Census Bureau, Foreign Trade Division).

Over 1,400 Iowa companies export to over 150 countries worldwide. The following table shows the top five export products in 2010 together with their values:

Product	Value ($m)
Tractors	745
Soybeans	513

- continued

Frozen meat of swine	436
Corn (Maize), other than seed corn	401
Soybean oil cake & other solid residues	313

The following table shows export revenue according to international trading partner in 2010-11:

Country	2010 ($m)	2011 ($m)	+/-% 10-11
Canada	3,435	4,083	18.9
Mexico	1,833	2,182	19.1
Japan	599	976	14.5
Germany	363	594	24.0
China	479	574	-4.2

Trade Organisations
Iowa City Area Chamber of Commerce, URL: http://www.iowacityarea.com/

MANUFACTURING, MINING AND SERVICES

Primary and Extractive Industries
The mining industry contributed $99 million towards the 2011 state's Gross Domestic Product (up from $92 million in 2010 but still down on $271 million in 2007). In 2010, non oil and gas mining contributed $89 million, and support activities accounted for $3 million. (Source: BEA)

The most important commercial mineral resources are limestone, sand and gravel, and gypsum. Iowa has no crude oil reserves, crude oil production or refineries. Total petroleum consumption in 2009 reached 86.3 million barrels, 41.0 million barrels of which was in the form of motor gasoline. Iowa is the nation's largest producer of ethanol.

Iowa has no natural gas production. Consumption in 2009 was 311,093 million cubic feet. Natural gas supplies nearly one-fifth of the State's energy demand. About two-thirds of Iowa's households use natural gas as their primary home heating fuel. (Source: EIA)

Energy
Iowa's total energy production was 677 trillion Btu in 2010. Iowa's total energy consumption of 1,492 trillion Btu in 2010 (1.5 per cent of the US total). Per capita energy consumption of 489 million Btu in 2010, ranked the state 5th in the US.

Net summer capability in 2010 was 14,592 MW and net monthly (Oct.) generation in 2012 was 4,249 thousand MWh, of which coal-fired 2,713 thousand MWh, renewables 1,368 thousand MWh, natural gas-fired 56 thousand MWh, nuclear 57 thousand MWh and petroleum-fired 9 thousand MWh. Iowa's primary generating fuel is coal, which accounted for over 60 per cent of industry generation in 2011, with nuclear power contributing 9 per cent. Hydroelectric accounted for 2 per cent, and other renewables made up over 20 per cent.

Iowa is a leading State in electricity generation from wind turbines. Iowa's single nuclear plant, Duane Arnold, is located in Palo, eight miles northwest of Cedar Rapids. It has a total capacity of 566 net MWe. (Source: EIA)

Manufacturing
Manufacturing is the greatest source of personal income in Iowa and the largest contributor towards the state GDP. In 2011 manufacturing accounted for $27,642 million (up from $25,660 million in 2010). The largest earning sectors in 2010 were machinery manufacturing ($6,415 million), chemical products ($3,304 million), and food, beverage and tobacco products ($6,275 million).

Service Industries
The service sector plays a major part in the economy of Iowa. Of particular significance are the finance and insurance industry (accounting for $18,706 million of the state GDP in 2011) and real estate ($14,104 million). Health care and social assistance contributed $10,307 million towards state GDP, and government services accounted for $16,775 million.

Tourism
The arts, entertainment and recreation sector of the services industry earned $1,167 million in 2011, whilst the accommodation and food sector contributed $3,093 million.
Iowa Tourism Office, IURL: http://www.traveliowa.com/

Agriculture
Iowa's agriculture, forestry and fisheries industry contributed $9,875 million towards the 2011 state GDP (up from $7,684 million in 2010). In 2010, the farms sector accounted for $7,364 million, whilst the forestry, fishing and hunting services sector contributed $320 million.

Around 89 per cent of Iowa's land area is dedicated to farming. There were an estimated 92,600 farms in 2008, whilst total farmland area was around 30,800,000 acres. The average size of a farm in 2008 was 333 acres (smaller than in previous years). In 2007, Iowa ranked first in production of sales of hogs and pigs, 2nd in the sale of grains, oilsees, dry beans and dry peas, and fourth in the sale of sheep, goats and their products. Iowa is also a significant producer of honey and wine.

Farm commodities earned the state $20.4 million in 2008, the third highest in the US. Crops earned the state some $10.3 million, whilst the value of livestock, poultry and their products reached $10.07 million.

COMMUNICATIONS AND TRANSPORT

International Airports
Iowa has 113 publicly-owned airports, including eight with commercial service and 103 general aviation airports.
Des Moines International Airport, URL: http://www.dsmairport.com/

Roads
The state is crossed by four interstate highways: I-35 from north to south; I-80 from east to west; I-29 from the northwest to the southwest; and I-380 from the northeast to the eastern I-80. At the beginning of 2006, there were 114,332.277 miles of roads in the state, and, in 2000, 1.3 million vehicles were registered in Iowa.

Railways
There are two major rail routes running through Iowa, both operated by Amtrak: the California Zephyr runs through the south from Chicago to close to San Francisco; the Southwest Chief runs from Chicago to Los Angeles.

HEALTH

The National Center for Health Statistics estimated that there were 21.6 doctors (including osteopaths) per 10,000 citizens of Iowa, below the national average rate of 27.4 doctors. In 2008, there were an estimated 1,600 dentists (5.3 per 10,000 population). In 2009, there were 3.4 community hospital beds per 1,000 people (above the US average of 2.6), and, in 2010, there were 443 nursing homes, with 32,842 beds.

Over 2007-09, it was estimated that 10.0 per cent of Iowans had no health care coverage, well below the US rate of 15.8 per cent. An estimated 11.9 per cent of the population were below the poverty level in 2007-11. Obesity affected 28.4 per cent of adults (above the US rate of 26.2 per cent), and 65.4 per cent were considered overweight. Iowa reported 1,936 HIV/AIDS cases from the beginning of the epidemic to the end of 2008, and ranked 40th in terms of the cumulative number of reported AIDS cases.

EDUCATION

Primary/Secondary Education
Iowa state had 1,501 elementary and secondary schools, in which 491,842 students enrolled in the 2009-10 academic year. In the same period, there were 35,842 teachers, equating to a teacher/pupil ratio of one to 13.7. Revenues from education reached $5.297 billion, whilst expenditures on state education reached $5.29 billion in 2007-08 year.

Higher Education
Iowa has 66 degree-conferring colleges and universities, of which 19 are public and 47 are private. An estimated 137,809 men were enrolled in 2010-11, together with 212,822 women. In the same year, 62,746 degrees/certificates were conferred, of which 30,323 were Bachelors, 7,452 were Masters and 2,744 were Doctorates. (Source: National Center for Education Statistics)

COMMUNICATIONS AND MEDIA

Newspapers
Iowa's newspapers include: Iowa City Daily Iowan, Iowa City Icon, Iowa Falls Times-Citizen, Iowa State Daily, Iowa Farm Bureau, Des Moines Register, Des Moines Today, and Fort Madison Daily Democrat.
Iowa Newspaper Association, URL: http://www.inanews.com

Broadcasting
Iowa's television stations include: KCCI TV 8 CBS, KDSM TV 17 Fox, IPTV 11 Public Television, WHO TV 13 NBC and WOI TV 5 ABC, all in Des Moines. There are also two stations in Cedar Rapids, two in Davenport, and two in Sioux City.
Iowa Public Television, URL: http://www.iptv.org/

ENVIRONMENT

Iowa's electricity industry is primarily dependent on coal as a generating fuel and carbon dioxide emissions are high. In 2007, these reached 45,834,877 metric tons. By 2009, carbon dioxide emissions fell to 42,977,893 metric tons but emissions rose to 47,211,320 metric tons in 2010 (2.0 per cent of US total), ranking it 20th in the US. An estimated 107,935 metric tons of sulfur dioxide (2.0 per cent of US total) and 49,963 metric tons of nitrogen oxide were also produced (2.0 per cent of US total). This compares to the 2009 estimated emissions of 92,180 metric tons of sulfur dioxide and 45,095 metric tons of nitrogen oxide.

Iowa is the leading state in electricity generation from wind turbines, and the largest producer of ethanol in the US, with 39 plants (over 18 per cent of the US total) and capacity of 3,595 million gallons per year (26 per cent of the US total). In 2011, ethanol consumption was 2,525,000 barrels (0.8 per cent of US total). There were an estimated 7,708 alternative-fueled vehicles in use (0.8 per cent of US total) in 2010. (Source: EIA)

KANSAS

Capital: Topeka (Population, Census 2010: 127,473)

Head of State: Sam Brownback (R) (Governor) (page 1395)

State Flag: A dark blue background in the centre of which is the state seal. Above the seal is the state crest: a sunflower on a blue and gold twisted bar. Below the seal is the word 'Kansas' in gold block lettering.

CONSTITUTION AND GOVERNMENT

Constitution
Kansas' constitution was ratified on 29 January 1861 when it entered the Union as the 34th State. According to the constitution the Executive Branch comprises six state officers elected for four-year terms: the governor, lieutenant governor, secretary of state, attorney general, state treasurer, and commissioner of insurance.

Kansas elects two Senators and four Representatives to the US Congress in Washington, DC. Senators serve six-year terms, whilst Representatives serve two-year terms.

To view the state constitution, please visit: www.kslib.info/ref/constitution

Legislature
The Legislature consists of the Senate and House of Representatives. Legislative sessions begin the second Monday in January and last for 90 days.
Kansas State Legislature, Kansas State Capitol, 10th and Jackson, Topeka, Kansas 66612, USA. URL: http://www.kslegislature.org/

Upper House
The Senate has 40 members who are elected for four years and represent about 63,000 Kansans. Following the 2012 elections for all 40 seats, the Senate was divided into 31 Republican seats and 9 Democrat seats.
State Senate, Capitol, 300 SW 10th Street, Topeka, KS 66612-1504, USA. Tel: +1 785 296 2456 (Secretary), fax: +1 785 296 6718 (Secretary), URL: http://www.kslegislature.org/

Lower House
The House of Representatives has 125 members who are elected for two years and represent some 19,000 Kansans. Following the 2012 elections the House was composed of 92 Republicans and 33 Democrats.
State House of Representatives, 300 SW 10th Street, Statehouse STE 477-W, Topeka, KS 66612, USA. Tel: +1 785 296 7633 (Chief Clerk), URL: http://www.kslegislature.org/cgi-bin/house/index.cgi

Elected Executive Branch Officials (as at April 2013)
Governor: Sam Brownback (R) (page 1395)
Lieutenant Governor: Jeff Colyer (R)
Secretary of State: Kris Kobach (R)
Attorney General: Derek Schmidt (R)
State Treasurer: Ron Estes (R)
Insurance Commissioner: Sandy Praeger (R)

Legislature (as at April 2013)
President of the Senate: Susan Wagle (R)
Vice President of the Senate: Jeff King (R)
Senate Majority Leader: Terry Bruce (R)
Senate Minority Leader: Anthony Hensley (D)
Speaker of the House: Ray Merrick (R)
Speaker Pro Tem of the House: Peggy Mast (R)
House Majority Leader: Jene Vickery (R)
House Minority Leader: Paul Davis (D)

US Senators: Jerry Moran (R) (page 1480) and Pat Roberts (R) (page 1503)

Ministries
Office of the Governor, Capitol, 300 SW 10th Ave., Ste. 212S, Topeka, KS 66612-1590, USA. Tel: +1 785 296 3232, fax: +1 785 368 8788, e-mail: http://www.ksgovernor.org/comment.html, URL: http://www.ksgovernor.org/
Office of the Lieutenant Governor, Capitol Building, Rm 222 S, 300 SW 10th Avenue, Topeka, KS, 66612-1504, USA. Tel: +1 785 296 2213, fax: +1 785 296 5669, URL: http://www.kansas.gov
Office of the Attorney General, 120 SW 10th Avenue, 2nd Floor, Topeka, Kansas 66612-1597, USA. Tel: +1 785 296 2215, fax: +1 785 296 6296, URL: http://ag.ks.gov/home/
Office of the Secretary of State, Memorial Hall, 1st Floor, 120 SW 10th Avenue, Topeka, KS 66612-1594, USA. Tel: +1 785 296 4564, e-mail: kssos@kssos.org, URL: http://www.kssos.org/main.html
Office of the State Treasurer, Landon State Office Building, 900 SW Jackson, Suite 201N, Topeka, KS 66612-1235, USA. Tel: +1 785 296 3171, URL: http://kansasstatetreasurer.com/
Department of Agriculture, 109 SW 9th Street, 4th Floor, Topeka, KS 66612-1280, USA. Tel: +1 785 296 3556, fax: +1 785 296 8389, URL: http://www.ksda.gov//
Department of Commerce, Curtis State Office Building, 1000 SW Jackson, Suite 100, Topeka KS, 66612-1354, USA. Tel: +1 785 296 3481, fax: +1 785 296 5055, URL: http://www.kansascommerce.com/

UNITED STATES OF AMERICA

Department of Corrections, Landon State Office Building, 900 SW Jackson, Suite 404N, Topeka, Kansas 66612-1284, USA. Tel: +1 785 296 3317, URL: http://www.doc.ks.gov/
Department of Education, 120 SE 10th Avenue, Topeka, KS 66612-1182, USA. Tel: +1 785 296 3201, fax: +1 785 296 7933, e-mail: webmaster@ksde.org, URL: http://www.ksde.org
Department of Health and Environment, Curtis State Office Building, 1000 SW Jackson, Topeka, KS 66612, USA. Tel: +1 785 296 1500, fax: +1 785 368 6368, e-mail: info@kdhe.state.ks.us, URL: http://www.kdhe.state.ks.us/
Department of Transportation, Docking State Office Building, 915 SW Harrison 7th Floor, Topeka KS, 66612-1568, USA. Tel: +1 785 296 3566, URL: http://www.ksdot.org/
Division of Emergency Management, 2800 SW Topeka Boulevard, Topeka, KS 66611-1287, USA. Tel: +1 785 274 1409, fax: +1 785 274 1426, URL: http://www.kansastag.gov/kdem_default.asp

Political Parties

Kansas Democratic Party, 700 SW Jackson Street, Suite 706, Topeka, KS 66603 (PO Box 1914, Topeka, KS 66601), USA. Tel: +1 785 234 0425, fax: +1 785 234 8420, e-mail kdp@ksdp.org, URL: http://www.ksdp.org/
Kansas Republican Party, 2025 SW Gage Boulevard, Topeka, KS 66604, USA. Tel: +1 785 234 3456, fax: +1 785 228 0353, e-mail: republicanparty@ksgop.org, URL: http://www.ksgop.org

Elections

Following elections in November 2012, the partisan split within both Houses remained the same. In the House the Republicans held their 92 seats to the Democrats 33 seats. In the Senate 2012 elections, the partisan split was as follows: Republicans 31, Democrats 9.

Constitutional elections last took place for the Governor, Secretary of State, Attorney General, State Treasurer, and State Insurance Commissioner in November 2010. The Democrats' Kathleen Sebelius retained the governorship for a second term in 2006. However, in April 2009 she resigned the position in order to become US Secretary of Health and Human Services. She was replaced by Mark V. Parkinson. In the November 2010 elections, US Senator Sam Brownback was elected with 63 per cent of the vote. Jeff Colyer (R) was elected as Lt.-Governor.

LEGAL SYSTEM

The Kansas court system consists of the Supreme Court, the Court of Appeals, District Courts, and Municipal Courts. In addition to the Chief Justice, there are six Supreme Court Associate Justices. The Governor makes the appointment from a list of three nominees furnished by the Supreme Court nominating commission. After he/she has served one year in office the justice must be approved by the electorate vote at the next general election. Six years is then the term of office.

The Kansas intermediate appellate court, the Court of Appeals comprises 10 judges nominated by the Supreme Court Nominating Commission and appointed to four-year terms by the Governor.

There are 105 District Courts, one for each county. The District Courts are trial courts, with general jurisdiction over civil and criminal cases. Municipal, or city, courts deal with alleged breaches of city ordinances committed within city limits. Such cases usually involve traffic and other minor offences.

Kansas has the death penalty but no-one has been executed since 1976. The current death row population is 10. According to the DPIC the murder rate is 3.5 per 100,000 population.

Kansas Supreme Court, URL: http://www.kscourts.org/
Chief Justice: Hon. Lawton R. Nuss
Justices: Marla Luckert, Carol Beier, Eric Rosen, Lee Johnson, Dan Biles, Nancy Moritz

LOCAL GOVERNMENT

For administrative purposes, Kansas is divided into 104 county governments and 1,980 sub-county general purpose governments. Of the sub-county governments, 627 are municipal governments (incorporated cities) and 1,353 are town or township governments. In addition there are 316 school district governments and 1,531 special district governments.

Kansas Association of Counties, URL: http://www.kansascounties.org/

AREA AND POPULATION

Area
Kansas is located in the Midwest, north of Oklahoma, south of Nebraska, east of Colorado, and west of Missouri. The total area of Kansas is 82,276.84 sq. miles, of which 81,814.88 sq. miles is land and 461.96 sq. miles is water.

To view a map of the state, please consult:
http://www.lib.utexas.edu/maps/us_2001/kansas_ref_2001.pdf

Population
According to the 2010 Census, the state population was 2,853,118, up on the figure of 2,797,375 in mid-2008. In 2012, it was estimated to be 2,885,905. The Kansas population grew by 6.1 per cent between 2000 and 2010. The population is expected to reach 2.94 million by 2030. The total population density is estimated at 34.9 persons per sq. mile. The county with the greatest number of inhabitants is Johnson County with 544,179 in 2010, followed by Sedgwick County, at 498,365. The largest city in Kansas is Wichita, with 384,445 inhabitants in 2011; the capital, Topeka, has 128,888 inhabitants.

According to the 2010 Census, 7.2 per cent of the population is under 5 years, 25.5 per cent under 18 years and 13.2 per cent is aged over 65 years. According to the Census, 50.4 per cent of the state population is female. Approximately 83.8 per cent of the population is white, and 5.9 per cent is black. Approximately 10.5 per cent of the population is of Hispanic or Latino origin.

Births, Marriages, Deaths
The Census Bureau estimated that there were 40,649 births in 2010 and 24,502 deaths, giving a natural population increase of 16,147 people. Net migration added an estimated 3,761 residents in 2009. The infant mortality rate in 2007 was 7.9 infant deaths per 1,000 live births. Marriages and divorces in 2007, according to provisional data, numbered 18,564 and 9,157, respectively.

EMPLOYMENT

Preliminary figures indicate that the total civilian labour force was 1,490,000 in December 2012, of which 1,409,600 were in employment and 80,400 were unemployed. The unemployment rate was 5.4 per cent, below the US average of 7.8 per cent.

The following table shows provisional figures for December 2012 non-farm wage and salary employment according to industry:

Industry	No. of jobs	12 month change (%)
Logging and mining	8,900	1.1
Construction	53,500	0.9
Manufacturing	167,400	2.8
Trade, transport and utilities	251,900	-0.2
Information	24,800	-7.5
Financial activities	73,600	2.8
Professional and business services	162,600	6.4
Educational and health services	187,200	1.5
Leisure and hospitality	113,700	-2.2
Other services	52,700	1.2
Government	254,400	-0.2
TOTAL	1,350,700	1.1

Source: Bureau of Labor Statistics

BANKING AND FINANCE

GDP/GNP, Inflation, National Debt
The state's Gross Domestic Product (GDP) (current dollars) rose from $124,921 million in 2009 to $127,170 million in 2010. Real GDP was put at $130 billion in 2011 and ranked 31st in the US that year. Real GDP rose by 2.1 per cent in 2010 and by 0.5 per cent in 2011.

GDP according to industry (millions of current dollars)

Industry	2009	2010	2011
Agriculture, forestry and fishing	4,216	4,612	5,136
Mining	1,351	1,472	1,849
Utilities	2,471	2,639	2,755
Construction	4,165	4,062	3,933
Manufacturing	16,078	17,370	18,433
Wholesale Trade	7,637	7,910	8,029
Retail Trade	7,946	8,324	8,641
Transport and warehousing	4,290	4,418	4,711
Information	6,515	5,806	5,780
Finance and insurance	7,798	8,426	8,662
Real estate	12,208	11,794	11,982
Educational services	751	770	809
Health care and social assistance	9,470	9,898	10,028
Other non-government services	17,987	19,103	20,173
Government	18,705	19,471	20,001
TOTAL	121,589	126,074	130,923

Source: Bureau of Economic Analysis, Feb. 2013

Average per capita income was $40,883 in 2011. Per capita real GDP was $41,933 in 2011, below the US average of $42,070. The annual Consumer Price Index (all items) for the Kansas City, MO-KS, urban area rose from 213.5 in 2011 to 218.5 in 2012. (1982-84=100). (Source: Bureau of Labor Statistics)

Balance of Payments / Imports and Exports
In 2010, imports fell to $10,833 million, down 8.9 per cent on 2009. Imports fell again in 2011 to $9,792 million, down 9.6 per cent, representing 0.4 per cent of the US total. Main imports include crude oil, radio navigational aid apparatus and airplane parts. Main suppliers include China, Canada, Taiwan, Germany and Mexico.

Export revenue fell from $12,514 million in 2008 to $8,917 million in 2009, an decrease of 28.7 per cent. In 2010, exports rose to $9,905 million in 2010, up 11.1 per cent. They rose again in 2011 to $11,598 million, up 17.1 per cent. Kansas exports amount to 0.8 per cent of US total. (Source: US Census Bureau, Foreign Trade Division). Major export products are transport equipment, food and similar products, industrial machinery and equipment, instruments and similar products, chemicals and kindred products, rubber and plastic products, fabricated metals, leather and leather products.

Top five export products in 2010 are shown on the following table:

Top five export products

Product	Revenue ($ million)
Civilian aircraft, engines, equipment and parts	2,001
Meat of bovine animals, boneless, fresh or chilled	398
Dog and cat food, put up for retail sale	396
Passenger vehicles, spk-ig. int. com rcpr p eng >1500 Nov 3m cc	353
Wheat (other than Durum) and Meslin	351

Source: U.S. Census Bureau

The following table shows the top five merchandise export destinations in 2010-11, according to revenue:

Exports according to destination

Market	2010 ($m)	2011 ($m)	+/-% 10-11
Canada	2,552	2,566	0.5
Mexico	1,280	1,626	27.0
China	527	668	26.9
Japan	586	665	13.6
Nigeria	243	587	141.4

Source: US Census Bureau

Chambers of Commerce and Trade Organisations

Kansas Chamber of Commerce and Industry, URL: http://www.kansaschamber.org/
Wichita Area Chamber of Commerce, URL: http://www.wichitakansas.org/
The Kansas City Kansas Area Chamber of Commerce, URL: http://www.kckchamber.com/

MANUFACTURING, MINING AND SERVICES

Primary and Extractive Industries

The Kansas mining industry is one of the top ten in the US states in the production of minerals. Salt is the state's most plentiful mineral. Also produced are helium and natural gas. The state has two surface coal mines which produced 229,000 short tons in 2008.

Mining contributed $1,849 million towards the Kansas Gross Domestic Product in 2011 (up from $1,472 million in 2010), oil and gas being the largest sector ($802 million in 2010). Non-oil and gas earned $205 million in 2010, and support activities for mining contributed $465 million.

Kansas had proven crude oil reserves of 295 million barrels in 2010, 1.3 per cent of total US crude reserves. A total of 56,009 oil wells and 28 rotary rigs produced 259 million barrels of crude oil in 2009 (1.3 per cent of total US production). Monthly (Oct.) production was 3,847,000 barrels (1.8 per cent of US total) in 2012. The state has three refineries, with a combined capacity of 339,200 barrels per day. Total petroleum consumption stood at 76.8 million barrels in 2009, 29 million of which was in the form of motor gasoline, 17.9 million barrels in distillate fuel and 16.3 million barrels in liquified petroleum gas (LPG).

The Kansas natural gas industry had dry natural gas reserves of 3,673 billion cubic feet in 2010 and natural gas plant liquids reserves of 195 million barrels. Marketed production was 309,124 million cubic feet in 2011, from a total of 25,758 natural gas producing wells. Consumption of natural gas rose from 286,427 million cubic feet in 2007 to 282,594 million cu ft in 2010. Kansas's industrial sector consumes almost half of the natural gas used. Nearly three-fourths of Kansas households use natural gas as their primary energy source for home heating.

Coal is mined at two surface mines in Kansas. Production fell 1.3 per cent, from 426 thousand short tons in 2006 to 420 thousand short tons in 2007. It was estimated to be 133,000 short tons in 2010, falling to 37,000 short tons in 2011. (Source: EIA)

Energy

Total energy production was 816 trillion Btu in 2010 (1.1 per cent of US total). Total energy consumption in 2010 was 1,165 trillion Btu (1.1 per cent of US total). Per capita energy consumption in the same year was 408 million Btu, 13th in the US.

Kansas is a net exporter of electricity, with coal as its primary generating fuel. Net summer capability in 2010 was 12,543 MW and net monthly (Oct.) generation in the 2012 was 3,699 thousand MWh, of which coal-fired 2,182,000 MWh, nuclear 900,000 MWh, 451,000 MWh, renewables (excluding hydroelectric) and petroleum-fired 2,000 MWh.

Kansas is a leading State in electricity generation from wind power resources. Kansas' single nuclear plant is the Wolf Creek Generating Station which occupies a 9,818 acre site near Burlington. The station is a 1,170 net MWe capacity pressurised water reactor. In 2004 the plant's net summer capability was 1,166 MWh of electricity. In May 2009, Kansas adopted a renewable portfolio standard that requires utilities to acquire one-tenth of their energy from renewable sources by 2011 and one-fifth by 2020. In 2011, 8 per cent of net electricity generation came from wind energy. (Source: EIA)

Manufacturing

Manufacturing is Kansas' second largest contributor to state GDP, accounting for $18,433 million in 2011 (up from $17,370 million in 2010). Major sectors in 2010 were non-motor transport equipment ($3,474 million), food, beverage and tobacco products ($3,277 million), machinery manufacturing ($1,629 million) and chemical products ($1,482 million).

Service Industries

Services is the largest contributor to the state GDP. Key sectors in 2011 included government services ($20,001 million), real estate ($11,982 million - slightly down on 2010), health care and social assistance ($10,028 million), and information ($5,780 million).

Tourism

The accommodation and food sector of the services industry contributed $3,316 million towards the 2011 state GDP (up from $4,350 million in 2010). The arts and entertainment services sector contributed $542 million (up from $506 million in 2010).
Kansas Travel Information Centers, URL: http://www.travelks.com/

Agriculture

The agriculture, forestry and fishing industry contributed an estimated $5,136 million of Kansas' GDP in 2011 (up from $4,612 million in 2010). The farms sector accounted for $4,350 million in 2010, whilst the forestry, fishing and hunting services sector contributed $262 million. (Source: Bureau of Economic Analysis)

Over 91 per cent of land in Kansas is used for agriculture. Kansas farms numbered around 65,500 in 2010, and occupied a total land area of 46,200,000 acres. The average size of a farm was 705 acres, a reduction on past years.

Major crops produced in Kansas are wheat, hay and sunflowers. The major livestock product is beef (sales of cattle and calves are the second highest in the USA). In 2007, the state ranked fifth in the US for the market value of its agricultural products sold, at $14 million; the value of crops was $4.88 million, whilst livestock, poultry and their products earned $9.5 million. As of 1 Jan. 2011, there were 6.3 million cattle and calves, 1.8 million hogs and pigs, and 70,000 sheep. (Source: National Agricultural Statistics Service)

COMMUNICATIONS AND TRANSPORT

Airports

Witchita Mid-Continent Airport is the only major commercial airport in the state. Travellers in the east of Kansas use Kansas City International Airport, whilst those in the far west use Denver International Airport. Manhattan Regional Airport, in Rily County, is due to begin commercial flights in August 2009.

Railways

Some 5,500 miles of railway track is operated by two types of rail carrier in Kansas: major mainline carriers and the smaller Shortlines. Kansas ranks fourth in the nation in terms of the total number of rail miles. Kansas railway operators include: Atchison, Topeka and Santa Fe; Kansas City Southern. Farm products is the main commodity transported by Class I rail carriers originating from Kansas.

Roads

US Route 69 runs north and south through Kansas, from Minnesota to Texas. Kansas has the second largest state highway system in the country after California, due to the high number of counties and county seats (105). There are 133,386 miles of roads in the state, of which 123,630 are rural and 9,756 are urban. A total of 2,207.84 million vehicles use Kansas' roads annually.

Ports and Harbours

The Kansas water freight industry operates primarily on the Missouri River. Five cities run a total of 17 commercial terminals on the river: Kansas City, Wolcott, Leavenworth, Atchison, and White Cloud. Terminals include Leavenworth Municipal Dock, Kansas City, Kansas Public Terminal, American Compressed Steel Company, Missouri River Queen, Atchison Municipal Dock, and White Cloud Grain Company.

HEALTH

The National Center for Health Statistics estimated that there were 24.1 doctors per 10,000 population in 2009 (below the national average of 27.4 doctors). In 2008, there were 1,413 dentists (5.0 per 10,000 population). In 2009, there were 3.6 community hospital beds per 1,000 residents (above the US average), and, in 2010, 340 nursing homes with 25,598 beds.

The Center for Disease Control (CDC) estimated that some 12.7 per cent of the people of Kansas had no health care cover over the period 2007-09. An estimated 11.6 per cent of the population was living in poverty over the period 2007-11. Kansas reported 3,121 HIV/AIDS cases from the beginning of the epidemic to the end of 2008, and the state ranked 35th highest in the cumulative number of reported cases. The overall TB rate was 2.0 per 100,000 population, ranking the state 32nd highest. Obesity levels in 2012 were 63.7 per cent and an estimated 29.4 per cent were overweight.

At the beginning of June 2009, prominent US abortion doctor, Dr George Tiller, was shot dead at his church in Wichita, Kansas. He had been vilified by anti-abortionists, as his clinic is one of just three in the US to perform abortions after 21 weeks.

EDUCATION

Primary/Secondary Education

According to National Center for Education Statistics figures for the year 2009-10, Kansas had 474,489 students in 1,458 public elementary and secondary schools and there were 34,700 teachers. The ratio of teachers to pupils was one to 13.67.

In the 2007-08 academic year, total expenditure on state education reached $5.161 billion whilst revenues reached $5.528 billion.

UNITED STATES OF AMERICA

Higher Education

For the year 2010-11, Kansas had 67 institutions offering higher education, 33 of which were public. A total of 93,819 men were enrolled for the year, together with 117,024 women. 42,309 degrees/certificates were conferred over the year, 17,835 of which were Bachelors, 6,722 were Masters and 1,388 Doctorates. (Source: NCES)

COMMUNICATIONS AND MEDIA

Newspapers

Kansas' daily newspapers include: Kansas City Kansan; The Topeka Capital-Journal; The Journal-World, Lawrence; Wichita Eagle; The Morning Sun, Pittsburg; Dodge City Daily Globe; Augusta Daily Gazette; The Daily Reporter, Derby; and El Dorado Times.
The Kansas Press Association, URL: http://www.kspress.com
Kansas City Kansan, URL: http://www.kansascitykansan.com
Dodge City Daily Globe, URL: http://dodgeglobe.com

Broadcasting

Most of Kansas' television stations are located in Wichita, where there are six, and Topeka, where there are four.

ENVIRONMENT

The primary generating fuel for Kansas' electricity industry is coal. According to EIA figures, in 2010 emissions of carbon dioxide reached 36,320,932 metric tons (down from 36,207,066 metric tons in 2009), ranking the state 26th in the US. Sulfur dioxide emissions fell from an estimated 46,772 metric tons in 2009 to 41,048 metric tons in 2010 and nitrogen oxide emissions rose from 45,814 metric tons in 2009 to 45,946 metric tons in 2010.

There were 10 ethanol plants in Kansas (4.8 per cent of the US total) in 2011 with a capacity to produce 437 million gallons per year (3.2 per cent of the US total). Ethanol consumption amounted to 2,758,000 barrels in 2011, 0.9 per cent of the US total. Kansas ranks among the top ten wind-producing states. (Source: EIA)

KENTUCKY

Capital: Frankfort (Population estimate, 2010: 25,527)

Head of State: Steve Beshear (D) (Governor) (page 1388)

State Flag: A navy blue background in the centre of which is the state seal - an image of two men shaking hands; inside the seal is the motto 'United We Stand, Divided We Fall'; under the seal is an image of the state flower, the Goldenrod.

CONSTITUTION AND GOVERNMENT

Constitution

Kentucky entered the Union as the 15th State on 1 June 1792. The state has had four constitutions: the first adopted in 1792, the second in 1799, the third in 1850, and the fourth (and current constitution) in 1891.

According to the terms of the 1891 constitution, the Chief Executive of Kentucky is the Governor, elected for a four-year term. The governor is assisted by six other elected executive branch officials: lieutenant governor, secretary of state, attorney general, auditor of public accounts, state treasurer, and state agricultural commissioner. Executive branch officials are also elected for terms of four years. Executive policy is enacted by 14 cabinets: Economic Development; Education, Arts and Humanities; Families and Children; Finance and Administration; Health Services; Justice; Labour; Natural Resources and Environmental Protection; Personnel; Public Protection and Regulation; Revenue; Tourism Development; Transportation; and Workforce Development.

Kentucky elects five Representatives and two Senators to the US Congress in Washington, DC.

To view the state constitution, please visit: http://www.lrc.ky.gov/Legresou/Constitu/intro.htm

Legislature

The legislative General Assembly consists of two houses: the Senate and the House of Representatives. Sessions of the General Assembly take place annually. In even-numbered years the General Assembly convenes from the first Tuesday in January and sessions last no longer than 60 working days. In odd-numbered years sessions convene from the first Tuesday in January and last no longer than 30 days.
Kentucky Legislature, Public Information Office, Capitol Annex Room 023, Frankfort, KY 40601, USA. Tel: +1 502 564 8100, fax: +1 502 564 2144, URL: http://www.lrc.ky.gov/

Upper House

The Senate has 38 members who are elected for four years, one-half retiring every two years. Nineteen seats were up for election in 2012. Following the 2012 elections the Kentucky General Assembly, the Senate was composed of 22 Republicans, 14 Democrats, one independent and one vacancy.

Lower House

The House of Representatives has 100 members who are elected for two years. Following the 2012 elections, the House was made up of 55 Democrats and 45 Republicans.

Elected Executive Branch Officials (as at April 2013)
Governor: Steve Bashear (D) (page 1388)
Lieutenant Governor: Jerry Abramson (D)
Secretary of State: Alison Lundergan Grimes (D)
Attorney General: Jack Conway (D)
State Treasurer: Todd Hollenbach (D)
State Auditor: Adam Edelen (D)
State Agricultural Commissioner: James Corner, Jr. (R)

Legislature (as at April 2013)
President of the Senate: Robert Stivers (R)
President Pro Tem of the Senate: Katie Kratz Stine (R)
Senate Majority Floor Leader: Damon Thayer (R)
Senate Minority Floor Leader: R.J. Palmer (D)
Speaker of the House: Greg Stumbo (D)
Speaker Pro Tem of the House: Larry Clark (D)

House Majority Floor Leader: Rocky Adkins (D)
House Minority Floor Leader: Jeff Hoover (R)

US Senators: Rand Paul (R) (page 1493) and Mitch McConnell (R) (page 1473)

Ministries

Office of the Governor, 700 Capitol Avenue, Suite 100, Frankfort, KY 40601, USA. Tel: +1 502 564 2611, fax: +1 502 564 2849, e-mail: http://www.governor.ky.gov/contact, URL: http://governor.ky.gov
Office of the Lieutenant Governor, 700 Capitol Ave., Suite 142, Frankfort, KY 40601, USA. Tel: +1 502 564 2611, fax: +1 502 564 2849, URL: http://ltgovernor.ky.gov
Office of the Attorney General, The Capitol, Suite 118, 700 Capitol Avenue, Frankfort, Kentucky 40601-3449, USA. Tel: +1 502 696 5300, fax: +1 502 564 2894, URL: http://www.ag.ky.gov
Office of the Auditor of Public Accounts, 105 Sea Hero Road, Suite 2, Frankfort, KY 40601, USA. Tel: +1 502 573 0050, fax: +1 502 573 0067, USA. Tel: +1 502 564 5841, fax: +1 502 564 2912, URL: http://www.auditor.ky.gov
Office of the Secretary of State, 700 Capital Avenue, Suite 152, State Capitol, Frankfort, KY 40601, USA. Tel: +1 502 564 3490, fax: +1 502 564 5687, URL: http://www.sos.ky.gov
Office of the State Treasurer, 183 Capitol Annex, Frankfort, KY 40601, USA. Tel: +1 502 564 4722, URL: http://www.kytreasury.com
Department of Agriculture, Capitol Annex, Room 188, Frankfort, Kentucky 40601, USA. Tel: +1 502 564 5126, fax: +1 502 564 5016, e-mail: ag.web@kyagr.com, URL: http://www.kyagr.com
Cabinet for Economic Development, 2400 Capital Plaza Tower, 500 Mero Street, Frankfort, KY 40601, USA. Tel: +1 502 564 7140, URL: http://www.thinkkentucky.com/
Department of Education, 500 Mero Street, Frankfort, KY 40601, USA. Tel: +1 502 564 4770, e-mail: webmaster@kde.state.ky.us, URL: http://www.education.ky.gov/
Department for Environmental Protection, 14 Reilly Road, Frankfort, KY 40601, USA. Tel: +1 502 564 2150, fax: +1 502 564 4245, e-mail: dep@ky.gov, URL: http://www.dep.ky.gov/
Department for Local Government, Capital Complex East Building, 1024 Capital Center Drive, Suite 340, Frankfort, KY 40601, USA. Tel: +1 502 573 2382, fax: +1 502 573 2512, URL: http://www.dlg.ky.gov/
Transportation Cabinet, 200 Mero Street, Frankfort, KY 40622, USA. Tel: +1 502 564 4890, fax: +1 502 564 4809, URL: http://www.transportation.ky.gov/

Political Parties

Kentucky Democratic Party, 190 Democrat Drive, Frankfort, KY 40601-9229 (PO Box 694, Frankfort, KY 40602), USA. Tel: +1 502 695 4828, fax: +1 502 695 7629, URL: http://www.kydemocrat.com/
Republican Party of Kentucky, The Mitch McConnell Building, Capitol Avenue at Third Street, PO Box 1068, Frankfort, KY 40602, USA. Tel: +1 502 875 5130, fax: +1 502 223 5625, e-mail: webmaster@rpk.org, URL: http://www.rpk.org/

Elections

Elections for the state's executive officers including the Governorship took place in November 2011. The incumbent governor Steve Bashear retained his position.

Following the 2012 legislative election, the Republicans maintained their majority in the Senate (22 Republicans, 14Democrats, one independent and one vacancy), whilst in the House of Representatives, the Democrats maintained their majority but lost three seats. (Democrats 55, Republicans 45).

LEGAL SYSTEM

Kentucky's court system consists of the Supreme Court, the Court of Appeals, the Circuit Court, the Family Court, and a number of District Courts. The Supreme Court's Chief Justice is elected by the Associate Judges for a term of four years. There are six Associate Justices, all elected for staggered terms of eight years by popular vote. The Court of Appeals comprises a Chief Judge and 13 Judges.

Three people have been executed in Kentucky since 1976 and 424 before. The current death row population is 35 (one female). According to the DPIC the murder rate is 4.3 per 100,000.

Supreme Court, URL: http://courts.ky.gov/courts/
Chief Justice: John D. Minton Jr.
Court of Appeals, URL: http://courts.ky.gov/courtofappeals/
Chief Judge: Glenn E. Acree

LOCAL GOVERNMENT

For administrative purposes Kentucky is divided into 118 county governments. The whole state is encompassed by county government except the area of the former counties Lexington and Fayette. Fayette County consolidated with the City of Lexington to form a single governmental entity known as Lexington-Fayette Urban County. The city of Louisville and Jefferson County consolidated to form the Louisville-Jefferson County Metro Government. These two governments are counted as municipal government rather than country governments in census reporting. There are 419 sub-county general purpose, or municipal, governments. There are no town or township governments. In addition, Kentucky has 175 school district governments and 720 special district governments.
Department for Local Government, URL: http://www.gold.ky.gov/

AREA AND POPULATION

Area
Kentucky is located in the South, adjoining the states of Illinois, Indiana, and Ohio to the north, Tennessee to the south, Missouri to the west, and West Virginia and Virginia to the east and south-east respectively. Kentucky's total area is 40,409.02 sq. miles, of which 39,728.18 sq. miles is land and 680.85 sq. miles is water.

To view a map of the state, please consult:
http://www.lib.utexas.edu/maps/us_2001/kentucky_ref_2001.pdf

Population
According to the 2010 Census, the population was 4,339,367, slightly up on the mid-2009 figure of 4,314,113. Population was estimated to be 4,380,415 in 2012. Kentucky's population grew by 7.4 per cent between 2000 and 2010 and is expected to reach 4.55 million by 2030. Kentucky has a population density of 109.9 people per sq. mile. The largest conurbation is Louisville/Jefferson County Metro, with an estimated population of 597,337 in 2010. The largest city is Lexington-Fayette, Fayette County, with a 2011 population of 301,569. The capital, Frankfort, had a population of 25,527 in 2010.

According to the 2010 Census, 6.5 per cent of the population is under 5 years, 23.6 per cent under 18 years and 13.3 per cent is aged over 65 years. According to the Census, 50.8 per cent of the state population is female. Approximately 87.8 per cent of the population is white, and 7.8 per cent is black. Approximately 3.1 per cent of the population is of Hispanic or Latino origin.

Births, Marriages, Deaths
The US Census Bureau estimated that there were 55,784 births in 2010 and 41,983 deaths, giving a natural population increase of 13,801 people. Net migration (mainly internal) added 10,866 people in 2009. The infant mortality rate was 6.7 deaths per 1,000 live births in 2007. Marriages and divorces in 2007, according to provisional data, numbered 33,598 and 19,677 respectively, both figures down on 2006.

EMPLOYMENT

According to provisional figures from the Bureau of Labor Statistics, Kentucky had a total civilian labour force of 2,091,600 in December 2012, of whom 1,921,900 were in employment and 169,800 were unemployed. The unemployment rate was 8.1 per cent, above the US unemployment rate of 7.8 per cent in December 2012.

The following table shows provisional non-farm wage and salary employment figures for December 2012, according to industry:

Industry	No. of Jobs	12 month change (%)
Logging and mining	20,800	-5.5
Construction	64,500	-3.0
Manufacturing	216,300	0.7
Trade, transport and utilities	377,800	2.6
Information	27,100	2.3
Financial activities	85,600	2.5
Professional and business services	205,100	5.8
Educational and health services	258,500	-0.2
Leisure and hospitality	180,000	4.5
Other services	71,100	1.6
Government	326,500	-0.4
TOTAL	1,833,300	1.6

Source: Bureau of Labor Statistics

BANKING AND FINANCE

GDP/GNP, Inflation, National Debt
Kentucky's gross domestic product (GDP) rose from an estimated $156,553 million in 2009 to $163,269 million in 2010. In 2011, current-dollar GDP was $164.8 billion and ranked 28th in the US. In 2010, real GDP rose by 3.2 per cent. It rose by 0.5 per cent in 2011. The services sector is the greatest contributor to Kentucky's GDP, followed by manufacturing and government.

GDP according to industry (millions of current dollars)

Industry	2009	2010	2011
Agriculture, forestry, fishing and hunting	2,368	1,877	2,144
Mining	4,160	4,407	4,162
Utilities	2,859	3,018	2,814
Construction	5,953	5,572	5,610
Manufacturing	22,657	25,513	27,154
Wholesale Trade	9,541	9,849	10,333
Retail Trade	9,832	10,370	10,565
Transport and warehousing	7,020	7,240	7,337
Information	4,175	4,133	4,389
Finance and insurance	8,100	9,245	9,298
Real estate	14,714	13,957	13,865
Educational services	955	1,006	1,033
Health care and social assistance	13,193	13,897	14,624
Other non-government services	21,080	22,439	23,454
Government	25,386	26,826	28,019
Total	151,994	159,350	164,799

Source: Bureau of Economic Analysis, Feb. 2013

Average per capita annual income was $33,989 in 2011, 82 per cent of national average. In 2011, per capita real GDP was $33,331 compared to the US average per capita real GDP of $42,070.

The annual Consumer Price Index (CPI) for the Cincinnati-Hamilton, OH-KY-IN, urban area rose from 211.1 in 2011 to 216.3 in 2012 (1982-84=100). (Source: Bureau of Labor Statistics)

Balance of Payments / Imports and Exports
Imports rose to $32,077 million in 2010, up 26.6 per cent for 2009. They fell to $31,970 million in 2011, down -0.4 per cent, accounting for 1.4 per cent of US total imports. Main imported commodities include phones, data processing equipment, turbojet parts, digital equipment and medicaments. Main suppliers are China (18 per cent), Canada (14.3 per cent), Japan (11.5 per cent), Taiwan and Mexico.

Export revenue fell from $19,121 million in 2008 to $17,650 million in 2009, a fall of 7.7 per cent. Export revenue rose to $19,343 million, up 9.6 per cent in 2010 and rose by a further 3.8 per cent in 2011 to $20,084 million. Kentucky's share of total US exports is 1.4 per cent.

The top five export products are shown on the following table:

Export revenue by product, 2010

Industry	Revenue ($m)
Civilian aircraft, engines, equipment and parts	3,548
Antisera and blood fractions, Immunity products	673
Passenger vehicles spark-ignition engine, >3000 cc	639
Mtr vehicles trans gds	440
Silicones, in primary forms	408

Kentucky exports over 21 per cent of total US sales of civilian aircraft, engines and parts. The top five export destinations, according to revenue, are shown on the following table:

Top five export destinations, 2010-11

Destination	2010 ($m)	2011 ($m)	+/-% 10-11
Canada	5,878	6,469	10.1
United Kingdom	1,366	1,496	9.5
Mexico	1,281	1,454	13.5
Japan	1,195	1,066	-10.8
Brazil	860	997	16.0

Chambers of Commerce and Trade Organisations
Kentucky Chamber of Commerce, URL: http://www.kychamber.com/

MANUFACTURING, MINING AND SERVICES

Primary and Extractive Industries
Mining contributed $4,162 million towards Kentucky's Gross Domestic Product in 2011 (down from $4,407 million in 2010). Non-oil and gas mining contributed $3,878 million in 2010 and $161 million came from oil and gas. A further $368 million was earned through support activities. (Source: BEA) Kentucky's principal mineral products include coal, crushed stone, natural gas and petroleum.

Kentucky ranks third in the USA in coal production, producing around a tenth of the total US yield. Almost a third of all US coalmines are found in the state; its vast reserves are found in two major coal regions: the Appalachian basin and the Illinois basin. Recent EIA figures estimate that recoverable reserves in 2011 were 1,419 million short tons (7.4 per cent of the US total), whilst in 2011 production was 108,766 thousand short tons (9.7 per cent of US total). There were 417 mines in 2007, 201 of which were underground. Most of the coal is used in the electricity generating industry.

Kentucky's petroleum industry consists of 18,053 producing oil wells and 5 rotary rigs, and has proven crude oil reserves of 15 million barrels (2010). Total crude oil production in 2009 was 2,519,000 barrels. Monthly production in 2012 (Oct.) amounted to 215,000 barrels.

UNITED STATES OF AMERICA

Total petroleum consumption in 2009 was 125.3 billion barrels, 53.2 billion barrels of which was in the form of motor gasoline and 27.7 billion was distillate fuel. Crude oil refinery capacity was 238,500 bbl/d in 2012.

The natural gas industry consisted of 14,632 wells in 2011 (2.8 per cent of US total) with reserves of 2,613 billion cubic feet in 2010. Natural gas plant liquid reserves amounted to 124 million barrels. In 2010. Marketed production was 124,243 million cubic feet in 2011. Natural gas consumption was 232,006 million cubic feet in 2010. Almost half of gas consumption was used by industry. Over two-fifths of Kentucky households use natural gas for home heating.

The state has untapped oil resources in tar sands and black shale rock which could someday be important fuel sources if technological and economic barriers are overcome. Similarly, given the right market conditions, Kentucky, as a major corn-growing state, could significantly increase its ethanol production. (Source: EIA)

Energy
Total energy production was 2,770 trillion Btu (3.7 per cent of US total) in 2010. Kentucky's total energy consumption in 2010 was 1,977 trillion Btu, 2 per cent of US total. Per capita energy consumption in the same year was 455 million Btu, ranking the state 9th in the US.

Kentucky is a net exporter of electricity whose primary generating fuel is coal. Kentucky has no nuclear plants. Net summer capability in 2010 was 20,453 MW, and total monthly (Oct.) net generation in 2012 was 6,996 MWh (petroleum-fired 11,000 MWh, natural gas-fired 93,000 MWh, coal-fired 6,555,000 MWh, hydroelectric 196,000 MWh, other renewables 30,000 MWH. (Source: EIA)

Manufacturing
Manufacturing is Kentucky's second largest contributor to GDP, accounting for $27,154 million in 2011, up from $25,513 million in 2010. The food, beverages and tobacco products was the largest in 2010 ($5,573 million), followed by motor vehicles ($3,158 million).

Service Industries
The services industry is Kentucky's largest industry in terms of contribution to GDP. In 2011, the Government sector was the highest contributor to state GDP, earning an estimated $28,019 million. Real estate accounted for an estimated $13,865 million. Health care and social assistance accounted for $14,624 million, and professional and technical services earned some $7,184 million.

Tourism
The accommodation and food sector contributed an estimated $4,878 million to the 2011 GDP, up from $4,685 million in 2010. Arts and entertainment accounted for around $790 million, down on the previous year's $806 million.
Kentucky Department of Travel, URL: http://www.kentuckytourism.com/index.aspx
Kentucky Tourism Council, URL: http://www.tourky.com/

Agriculture
Kentucky's agriculture, forestry and fishing industry contributed an estimated $2,144 million towards the 2011 state GDP (up from $1,877 million in 2010). The largest sector in 2010 was farming ($1,567 million) whilst forestry, fishing and hunting services earned some $310 million.

Kentucky's farms number 83,000, continuing a downward trend. Farmland covers around 13,700,000 acres (some 54 per cent of the total acreage of Kentucky), and the average size of a farm is 165 acres, according to 2007 estimates.

Cash receipts from crop farming reached $1.47 billion in 2007. Principal crops produced are tobacco (ranked 1st in the US, 2006), corn, and soybeans.

Cash receipts from livestock farming reached $2.96 billion in 2007. Principal livestock products are horses, mules, cattle and calves and dairy products. Sales of horses, including stud fees, was the state's highest agricultural earner in 2007, earning an estimated $1.13 billion.

COMMUNICATIONS AND TRANSPORT

International Airports
Kentucky's largest airport is Louisville International Airport.
Louisville International Airport, URL: http://www.louintlairport.com/
Regional Airport Authority, URL: http://www.flylouisville.com/Default.aspx

Railways
CSX is Kentucky's largest rail line with over 1,900 miles of the 2,447 total miles of rail in the state. More than 79 million tons of coal were transported over the CSX system according to recent statistics. The Norfolk and Southern Railroad has a major north to south route through the state.

Roads
Kentucky has over 73,555 miles of roads and highways within its jurisdiction. This network contains 763 miles of Interstate highways carrying an average of 55,000 vehicles per day and 650 miles of four-lane limited access parkways.

Shipping
Kentucky has six operational public ports on the Ohio River at sites including Hickman, Paducah, Henderson, Lyon County, Owensboro, and Louisville. In addition, 30 private facilities exist which contract out to public freight. The majority of freight transported consists of coal, agricultural products, and industrial commodities.

HEALTH

The National Center for Health Statistics estimated that there were 23.3 doctors per 10,000 population in 2009, below the US average of 27.4 doctors per 10,000 residents. In 2008, there were 2,338 dentists (5.6 per 10,000 population). In 2009, there were 3.3 community hospital beds per 1,000 inhabitants (above the national average of 2.6 beds), and, in 2010, there were 285 nursing homes with 26,063 beds.

Kentucky reported 5,344 HIV/AIDS cases from the beginning of the epidemic to the end of 2008, and ranked 30th in the US in terms of number of cumulative reported cases in 2008. Obesity in adults reported at 31.3 per cent in 2012 and the state's youth obesity rate was also above the national average, at 17.6 per cent. An estimated 66.2 per cent of adults were considered overweight. According to the Center for Disease Control, 15.3 per cent of Kentucky inhabitants did not have any health care cover in 2007-09. According to the US Census Bureau, an estimated 18.1 per cent were living in poverty in 2007-2011. (Source: US Center of Disease Control)

EDUCATION

Primary/Secondary Education
Kentucky provides public education for its students from kindergarten to grade 12 at 1,565 public schools. During the academic year 2009-10, there were 680,089 students and 44,371 teachers. The pupil-teacher ratio for the year was 15.33 to one.

Total state education expenditure for the academic year 2007-08 was $6.8 billion, whilst total revenues reached $6.56 billion.

Higher Education
Many students continue their education at one of Kentucky's 76 higher education establishments, 51 of which are privately run. The largest higher education institution is the University of Kentucky and other major universities include the University of Louisville, Eastern Kentucky University, and Western Kentucky University. In 2010-11, there were 118,876 male students and 159,031 female students enrolled. 61,952 degrees/certificates were conferred, 20,389 of which were Bachelors, 7,976 were Masters and 1,591 Doctorates. (Source: NCES)

COMMUNICATIONS AND MEDIA

Newspapers
Kentucky has 14 daily newspapers, including The Daily News, The News-Enterprise, Glasgow Daily Times, The Gleaner, Kentucky New-Era, The Daily Independent, The Kentucky Post, The Advocate Messenger, and The Ledger Independent.
Kentucky Press Association, URL: http://www.kypress.com/default.asp

Broadcasting
Kentucky has 30 public television stations, four in Bowling Green, seven in Louisville, three in Paducah, and four in Lexington.

ENVIRONMENT

The Kentucky electricity industry's reliance on coal as a primary generating fuel means that carbon dioxide emissions are high, reaching 86,155,115 metric tons in 2008. They rose to 93,159,570 metric tons in 2010. The state ranked 7th in the US in this regard and accounts for 3.9 per cent of US total. An estimated 248,767 metric tons of sulfur dioxide emissions (232,401 metric tons, 2009) and 84,856 metric tons of nitrogen oxide (73,900 metric tons, 2009) were also produced.

Kentucky has two ethanol plants with a capacity of 35.4 million gallons per year (0.3 per cent of US total). Ethanol consumption was 4,883,000 barrels in 2011 (1.6 per cent of the total) and there were an estimated 11,802 alternative-fuelled vehicles in use in 2010. (Source: EIA)

LOUISIANA

Capital: Baton Rouge (Population, Census 2010: 229,493)

Head of State: Bobby Jindal (R) (Governor) (page 1449)

State Flag: A blue background on which appears an image of a pelican feeding her young in the nest; underneath appears the state motto: 'Union, Justice and Confidence'

CONSTITUTION AND GOVERNMENT

Constitution

Louisiana entered the Union on 30 April 1812 as the 18th state. Under the terms of the 1974 Constitution the executive branch of state government is headed by the governor assisted by six other elected officials: lieutenant governor, secretary of state, attorney general, treasurer, commissioner of agriculture and forestry, commissioner of insurance. All are elected for four-year terms. The position of state commissioner of elections and registration was abolished in January 2004.

Louisianans elect seven Representatives and two Senators to the US Congress, Washington, DC.

To view the state constitution, please visit:
http://senate.legis.state.la.us/Documents/Constitution/Default.htm

Recent Events

On Monday 29th August 2005, Louisiana, together with neighbouring Gulf Coast states Mississippi and Alabama, was hit by Hurricane Katrina. The maximum strength five hurricane, with winds exceeding 150 km/h, wrecked havoc. It was the sixth-strongest Atlantic hurricane ever recorded and the third-strongest hurricane on record that made landfall in the United States. New Orleans, lying some six foot below sea level, was especially hard hit; flood defences were breached in three areas, causing flooding in 80 per cent of the low-lying areas of the city. Although a mandatory evacuation had been ordered, approximately 100,000 people were still in the area when the hurricane hit. Evacuation measures were hampered by the massive flooding, and thousands of people had to be airlifted to neighbouring states. Over 1,460 residents of Louisiana were killed by the hurricane, and 1.3 million people were displaced. The reconstruction of New Orleans is anticipated to take many years.

On 24th September 2005, Hurricane Rita hit the Gulf Coast. This time, a mass evacuation had worked, and just six people died as a direct result of the storm. The hurricane caused a storm surge, which caused renewed flooding in New Orleans.

A march against continuing racism was held in Jena, Louisiana, in September 2007; thousands of civil rights protesters marched in support of six black teenagers charged with the attempted murder of a white classmate. The previous year, three white students hung a noose in a tree where white students congregated after a black student asked if he could enjoy its shade. The white students were briefly suspended from school, but not prosecuted.

On the 1st September 2008, Hurricane Gustav hit the US Gulf coast with torrential rain and winds of 110mph. The Louisiana coast had been evacuated; of New Orleans's population of 200,000, just 10,000 remained when the storm hit. Hurricane Gustav destroyed homes and flooded the low-lying areas of Terrebonne, Lafource and St. Mary, but the worst of the hurricane missed New Orleans, where rebuilt levees held back the floodwaters.

In April 2010, an explosion on the BP-operated Deepwater Horizon rig in the Gulf of Mexico and the subsequent spillage of around 12 to 19 thousand barrels of oil a day threatened the Louisiana coastline. The state's environmentally-sensitive wetlands and important shrimp and oyster beds were in the path of the 100-mile by 45-mile oil slick, and there were also fears of damage to fisheries and wildlife in Mississippi, Alabama and Florida. US government agencies and BP set up 100,000 ft of booms to protect coastal areas, but to no avail; rough seas sent five foot waves of oily water over the top of the booms into the mouth of the Mississippi River on the 29th April. The rate of spillage was continued throughout May despite attempts to shut off the leak. By early June, some 10,000 barrels per day were being funnelled into a drilling ship, to be flared or stored, and BP was drilling two rigs as a permanent solution to the leak. The oil slick was America's worst environmental disaster ever, threatening hundreds of species of fish, birds and other wildlife in one of the world's richest marine environments.

Legislature

The legislative branch of state government comprises the Senate and the House of Representatives. The legislature convenes, in odd-numbered years, on the last Monday in March, and the general session lasts for a maximum of 60 legislative days. In even-numbered years the general session convenes on the last Monday in April and lasts for a maximum of 30 legislative days. Extraordinary Sessions were convened in November 2005 and February 2006 to pass legislation relating to recovery following the Hurricane Katrina.

Upper House

The Senate has 39 members elected for four years. During the period of the 2012 Session, the Senate was divided into 24 Democrat seats and 15 Republican seats.
Louisiana State Senate, Post Office Box 94183, Baton Rouge, Louisiana 70804, USA. Tel: +1 225 342 2040, e-mail: websen@legis.state.la.us, URL: http://senate.legis.state.la.us/

Lower House

The House of Representatives has 105 members, also elected for four years. At the time of the 2012 Session the House was composed of 45 Democrats, 58 Republicans and two independents.

Louisiana House of Representatives, State Capitol Building, PO Box 94062, 900 North Third Street, Baton Rouge, Louisiana 70804-9062, USA. Tel: +1 225 342 7263, fax: +1 225 342 8336, URL: http://house.louisiana.gov

---

Elected Executive Branch Officials (as at April 2013)
Governor: Bobby Jindal (R) (page 1449)
Lieutenant Governor: Jay Dardenne (R)
Secretary of State: Tom Schedler (R)
Attorney General: Buddy Caldwell (D)
Treasurer: John Neely Kennedy (R)
Commissioner of Insurance: James J. Donelon (R)
Commissioner of Agriculture and Forestry: Mike Strain

Legislature (as at April 2013)
President of the Senate: John A. Alario (R)
President Pro Tem of the Senate: Sharon Weston Broome (D)
Speaker of the House: Chuck Kleckley (R)
Speaker Pro Tempore: Walt Leger, III (D)

US Senators: David Vitter (R) (page 1532) and Mary Landrieu (D) (page 1460)

Ministries

Office of the Governor, Constituent Services, PO Box 94004, Baton Rouge, LA 70804-9004, USA. Tel: +1 225 342 0991, fax: +1 225 342 7099, e-mail: http://www.gov.state.la.us/govemail.asp, URL: http://www.gov.state.la.us/

Office of the Lt. Governor, Capitol Annex Building, 1051 North Third Street, Baton Rouge, Louisiana 70802 (PO Box 44243, Baton Rouge, LA 70804-4243), USA. Tel: +1 225 342 7009, fax: +1 225 342 1949, e-mail: ltgov@crt.state.la.us, URL: http://www.crt.state.la.us/ltgovernor/

Office of the Attorney General, State Capitol, 22nd Floor, 300 Capitol Drive, Baton Rouge, Louisiana 70804-9005, USA. Tel: +1 225 326 6705, fax: +1 225 342 8703, URL: http://www.ag.state.la.us/

Office of the Secretary of State, State Capitol, PO Box 94125, Baton Rouge, LA 70802 (PO Box 94005, Baton Rouge, LA 70804-9005), USA. Tel: +1 225 342 4479, fax: +1 225 342 5577, URL: http://www.sos.la.gov

Office of the State Treasurer, 900 North Third Street, 3rd Floor, State Capitol, Baton Rouge, Louisiana 70802 (PO Box 44154, Baton Rouge, LA 70804-0154), USA. Tel: +1 225 342 0010, fax: +1 225 342 0046, URL: http://www.treasury.state.la.us/

Division of Administration, PO Box 94095, Baton Rouge, LA 70804-9095, USA. Tel: +1 225 342 7000, fax: +1 225 342 1057, URL: http://www.doa.louisiana.gov

Department of Agriculture and Forestry, 2nd Floor, PO Box 631, Baton Rouge, LA 70821-0631, USA. Tel: +1 225 922 1234, fax: +1 225 922 1253, e-mail: info@ldaf.state.la.us, URL: http://www.ldaf.state.la.us/

Department of Corrections, 504 Mayflower Street, Baton Rouge, LA 70802 (PO Box 94304, Baton Rouge, LA 70804-9304), USA. Tel: +1 225 342 6741, fax: +1 225 342 3095, URL: http://www.corrections.state.la.us

Department of Culture, Recreation and Tourism, PO Box 94361, Baton Rouge, LA 70804-9361, USA. Tel: +1 225 342 8115, fax: +1 225 342 3207, URL: http://www.crt.g2digital.com

Department of Economic Development, Capitol Annex, 1051 N. 3rd Street, Baton Rouge, LA 70802 (PO Box 94185, Baton Rouge, LA 70804-9185), USA. Tel: +1 225 342 3000, fax: +1 225 342 5389, URL: http://www.lded.state.la.us/

Department of Education, PO Box 94064, Baton Rouge, LA 70804-9064, USA. Tel: +1 225 342 3602, fax: +1 225 342 7316, URL: http://www.doe.state.la.us

Department of Environmental Quality, 602 N. Fifth Street, Baton Rouge, LA 70802 (PO Box 4301, Baton Rouge, LA 70821-4301), USA. Tel: +1 225 342 3000, fax: +1 225 342 9095, URL: http://www.deq.state.la.us/

Department of Health and Hospitals, 1201 Capitol Access Road, PO Box 629, Baton Rouge, LA 70821-0629, USA. Tel: +1 225 342 9500, fax: +1 225 342 5568, e-mail: Webmaster@dhh.la.gov, URL: http://www.dhh.state.la.us/

Department of Labour, 1001 North 23rd Street, PO Box 94094, Baton Rouge , LA 70804-9094, USA. Tel: +1 225 342 3111, fax: +1 225 342 3778, e-mail: os@ldol.state.la.us, URL: http://www.ldol.state.la.us

Department of Natural Resources, 617 North Third Street, PO Box 94396, Baton Rouge, LA 70804-9369, USA. Tel: +1 225 342 4500, fax: +1 225 342 2707, URL: http://www.dnr.louisiana.gov

Department of Public Safety, PO Box 66614, Baton Rouge, LA 70896, USA. Tel: +1 225 925 6117, fax: +1 225 925 3742, URL: http://www.dps.louisiana.gov

Department of Revenue, 617 North Third Street, Baton Rouge, LA 70802 (PO Box 201, Baton Rouge, LA 70821), USA. Tel: +1 225 925 7680, fax: +1 225 925 6797, URL: http://www.revenue.louisiana.gov

Department of Social Services, 755 Third Street, Baton Rouge, LA 70802 (PO Box 3776, Baton Rouge, LA 70821), USA. Tel: +1 225 342 0286, fax: +1 225 342 8636, e-mail: Ann.Williamson@dss.state.la.us, URL: http://www.dss.state.la.us/

Department of Transportation & Development, 1201 Capitol Access Road (PO Box 94245), Baton Rouge, LA 70804-9245, USA. Tel: +1 225 379 1200, fax: +1 225 379 1851, URL: http://www.dotd.louisiana.gov/

Department of Wildlife and Fisheries, 2000 Quail Drive, PO Box 98000, Baton Rouge, LA 70898-9000, USA. Tel: +1 225 765 2623, fax: +1 225 765 2607, URL: http://www.wlf.state.la.us/

Office of Emergency Preparedness, 7667 Independence Boulevard, Baton Rouge, LA 70806 (PO Box 44217, Baton Rouge, LA 70804), USA. Tel: +1 225 925 7500, fax: +1 225 925 7501, URL: http://www.loep.state.la.us/

UNITED STATES OF AMERICA

Political Parties
Louisiana Democratic Party, 701 Government Street, Baton Rouge, LA 70802 (PO Box 4385, Baton Rouge, LA 70821), USA. Tel: +1 225 336 4155, fax: +1 225 336 0046, e-mail: info@lademo.org, URL: http://www.lademo.org/
Interim Chairman: Michael McHale
Republican Party of Louisiana, 11440 N Lake Sherwood, Baton Rouge, LA 70816, USA. Tel: +1 225 928 2998, fax: +1 225 408 2798, URL: http://www.lagop.com/
Chairman: Roger F. Villere Jr.

Elections
The most recent gubernatorial election took place in November 2011. The incumbent governor, Republican Bobby Jindal (a former US Congressman), retained the governorship with 54 per cent of the vote. When Mr Jindal was elected into office in 2007 he became the youngest US governor and the first Indian-American to head a state.

Following the November 2011 legislative election, in the state Senate the Republican party gained two seats, resulting in 24 Republicans and 15 Democrats. In the House of Representatives, the results were as follows: Democrats 45, Republicans 58 and two independents).

State executive official elections for one officer on the Louisiana Public Service Commission took place in November 2012.

LEGAL SYSTEM

The state's legal system of civil law is based on French, German and Spanish legal codes and ultimately Roman law. Louisiana's court system comprises the Supreme Court, Courts of Appeal, District Courts, Juvenile and Family Courts, Mayors' Courts, and Justice of the Peace Courts. The Supreme Court consists of the Chief Justice and six Associate Justices. All are elected for a term of ten years by popular vote. Louisiana is divided into six Supreme Court districts, from which one Supreme Court judge is elected.

The death penalty is legal in the Louisiana. A total of 28 people have been executed since 1976, the most recent in 2010. There are currently 88 people on death row, including two women. According to the DPIC, the murder rate is 11.2 per 100,000.

Supreme Court: URL: http://www.lasc.org/
Chief Justice: Bernette Johnson
Associate Justices: Greg Guidry, Jeffrey Victory, Jeannette Theriot Knoll, Marcus Clark, John Weimer, Jefferson Hughes

First Circuit Court of Appeal, URL: http://www.la-fcca.org/
Second Circuit Court of Appeal, URL: http://www.lacoa2.org/
Third Circuit Court of Appeal, URL: http://www.la3circuit.org/
Fourth Circuit Court of Appeal, URL: http://4thcir-app.state.la.us/
Fifth Circuit Court of Appeal, URL: http://www.fifthcircuit.org/

LOCAL GOVERNMENT

For local governments purposes, Louisiana is divided into 60 parishes (counties). Parish government covers the whole state with the exception of the parishes of East Baton Rouge, Lafayette, Orleans and Terrebonne. These parishes are consolidated for governmental purposes with the cites of Baton Rouge, Lafayette, New Orleans and Houma, respectively. The parish governing body is called the police jury, except in parishes that adopt a home-rule charter where it is known as the parish council. There are 303 municipal governments and 69 public school systems, including one dependent public school system.There are also 95 sepcial districts of authorities that are counted as governments. (Source: US Census Bureau)

Louisiana Municipal Association, URL: http://www.lamunis.org/

AREA AND POPULATION

Area
Louisiana is situated in the south of the US, east of Texas, west of Mississippi, and south of Arkansas. Louisiana's total area is 51,839.70 sq. miles, of which 43,561.85 sq. miles is land and 8,277.85 sq. miles is water.

Louisiana is prone to tropical cyclones and major hurricanes, particularly the lowlands around and in the New Orleans area. The state averages over 60 days of thunderstorms a year, more than any other state except Florida. Louisiana also has around 27 tornadoes annually.

To view a map of Louisiana, please consult http://www.lib.utexas.edu/maps/us_2001/louisiana_ref_2001.pdf

Population
According to the 2010 Census, the state population was 4,533,372, up on the mid-2009 estimate of 4,492,076. In 2012, the population was estimated to be 4,601,893. The population has now exceeded its level of 2000 (4,468,968 inhabitants), prior to the mass exodus following Hurricane Katrina in 2005; more than 200,000 homes, mostly in New Orleans and the surrounding area, were destroyed by the hurricane, and some 266,000 people left the area over the following year. Over the period 2000-10, the population increased by 1.4 per cent and is expected to reach 4.8 million by 2030. Population density is around 104.9 people per square mile, and the state ranks 24th in the US.

According to the 2010 Census, 6.9 per cent of the population is under 5 years, 24.7 per cent under 18 years and 12.3 per cent is aged over 65 years. Approximately 62.6 per cent of the population is white, and 32.0 per cent is black. Approximately 4.2 per cent of the population is of Hispanic or Latino origin.

Births, Marriages, Deaths
The US Census Bureau, Population Division, estimated that there were 62,379 births in 2010 and 40,667 deaths, giving a natural population increase of 21,712 people. Net migration accounted for the influx of 18,123 inhabitants (mainly from other parts of the US) in 2009. In 2007, the infant mortality rate for babies under one year was 9.2 per 1,000 births, the fourth highest rate in the US. There were 32,787 marriages in 2007.

Public Holidays
In addition to national holidays, the people of Louisiana celebrate Mardi Gras; in 2014, this will be on 4th March.

EMPLOYMENT

In December 2012, Louisiana had an estimated total civilian labour force of 2,083,100, of which 1,968,200 were employed and 114,800 were unemployed. The unemployment rate was 5.5 per cent, below the overall US rate of 7.8 per cent (Dec. 2012).

The following table shows provisional December 2012 non-farm wage and salary employment, seasonally adjusted, according to industry:

Industry	No. of Jobs	12 month change (%)
Logging and mining	57,600	4.3
Construction	122,400	2.4
Manufacturing	136,800	-2.1
Trade, transport and utilities	384,600	2.4
Information	25,200	6.8
Financial activities	98,300	1.1
Professional and business svcs.	202,600	1.8
Educational and health svcs.	291,700	0.7
Leisure and hospitality	208,800	3.3
Other services	63,000	0.8
Government	359,500	-0.9
TOTAL	1,950,500	1.2

Source: US Bureau of Labor Statistics

BANKING AND FINANCE

GDP/GNP, Inflation, National Debt
Louisiana's Gross Domestic Product (GDP) rose from $208,377 million in 2009 to $218,853 million in 2010. Current dollar GDP was put at $247.7 billion in 2011 and ranked 23rd in the US. Real GDP rose by just 0.5 per cent in 2011. The largest industry was nondurable goods (22.3 per cent of state GDP).

The following table shows Gross Domestic Product according to major industries (millions of current dollars):

Industry	2009	2010	2011
Agriculture, Forestry, Fishing & Hunting	1,659	1,742	1,921
Mining	19,957	23,014	27,445
Utilities	3,916	4,330	4,083
Construction	11,158	10,315	10,771
Manufacturing	34,659	57,142	63,039
Wholesale Trade	9,196	9,362	9,934
Retail Trade	12,704	13,123	13,754
Transport and warehousing	8,000	8,290	8,592
Information	3,775	3,943	4,008
Finance and insurance	7,834	8,560	9,099
Real estate, rental and leasing	19,452	19,255	19,808
Educational services	1,611	1,684	1,771
Health care and social assistance	13,391	14,193	14,787
Other Non-government services	29,649	31,509	32,820
Government	25,380	25,964	25,888
TOTAL	202,342	232,394	247,720

Source: Bureau of Economic Analysis, Feb. 2013

In 2011, the estimated per capita income was $38,549, 93 per cent of national average. In 2011, per capita real GDP was $45,002, compared to the US per capita figure of $42,070. The annual Consumer Price Index (CPI) for all South urban consumers (all items) rose from 218.6 in 2011 to 223.2 in 2012 (1982-84 = 100). (Source: Bureau of Labor Statistics)

Balance of Payments / Imports and Exports
Imports cost $43,508 million in 2009, down 50 per cent on $87,012 million in 2008. Imports rose $60,915 million to 2010, up 40 per cent. They rose further to $82,652 million in 2011, up 35.7 per cent in 2011, representing 3.7 per cent of total US imports. Imports of crude oil rose by 47 per cent and oil by 24.7 per cent. Light oil imports increased by 141 per cent. Main suppliers include Saudi Arabia (22.2 per cent), Venezuela (12.3 per cent), Mexico, Nigeria and Russia.

Export revenue fell by 22.2 per cent in 2009, from $41,908 million in 2008 to $32,616 million. Exports rose to $41,356 million in 2010, up 26.8 per cent. They rose again in 2011 to $54,976 million, up 32.9 per cent. The state earned an estimated 3.7 per cent of the national export revenue. (Source: US Census Bureau, Foreign Trade Division).

The top five export products in 2010, according to revenue, are shown on the following table ($m):

Product	Revenue ($m)
Soybeans, whether or not broken	8,807
Oil (not crude) from petroleum & bituminous mineral	8,176
Corn (maize) other than seed corn	4,976
Soybean Oilcake & other solid residue, whole/not ground	1,262
Light oils & prep (not crude) from petrol & bitum	1,132

Source: US Census Bureau

The following table shows 2010-11 merchandise exports according to the top five destinations:

Destination	2010 ($m)	2011 ($m)	+/-% 10-11
China	6,488	7,282	12.2
Mexico	2,774	5,767	107.9
Japan	3,071	3,855	25.5
Netherlands	2,006	3,131	56.1
Canada	1,968	2,309	17.3

Source: US Census Bureau

Chambers of Commerce and Trade Organisations
Louisiana Department of Economic Development, URL: http://www.lded.state.la.us/
World Trade Center of New Orleans, http://www.wtcno.org/
The New Orleans Regional Chamber of Commerce, URL: http://chamber.gnofn.org
The Chamber of Greater Baton Rouge, URL: http://www.brchamber.org
Central Louisiana Chamber of Commerce, URL: http://www.cenlachamber.org/

MANUFACTURING, MINING AND SERVICES

Primary and Extractive Industries
At $27,445 million in 2011 (up from $23,014 million in 2010), Louisiana's growing mining industry is a major contributor to Louisiana's Gross Domestic Product. The largest sector in 2009 was oil and gas extraction ($16,791 million). Other mining accounted for $406 million and support activities for the sector earned $5,817 million. (Source: BEA)

Louisiana has the one of the highest value mineral production in the States, with over 10 per cent of US petroleum reserves and approximately 19 per cent of US natural gas reserves. Salt production is the highest in the country and the state is a major producer of lime, sulphur and silica sands. Louisiana had two surface coal mines, producing 3,865 thousand short tons of coal in 2011.

A major oil-producing state, Louisiana had proven crude oil reserves of 424 million barrels in 2010, accounting for 1.8 per cent of US total reserves. Louisiana is the USA's fourth largest crude oil producer, behind Texas, Alaska and California. In 2011 there were 19,990 producing oil wells (8.8 per cent of US total) and 165 rotary rigs in operation (2009). Crude oil production in 2010 was 67,527 million barrels. Monthly production (Oct. 2012) was 6,201,000 barrels (2.9 per cent of US total). The crude oil refinery capacity was 3,246,020 bbl/d in 2012 (18.7 per cent of US total). Oil consumption in 2009 was estimated at 264.6 million barrels (3.9 per cent of the US total), as follows: motor gasoline, 54.6 million barrels; distillate fuel, 32,.7 million barrels; liquified petroleum gas, 58.5 million barrels (7.8 per cent of total US total); and jet fuel, 21.3 million barrels (4.1 per cent of US total). The Louisiana Offshore Oil Port is the US's only port able to take deepdraft tankers.

With a refining capacity of more than 3.2 million barrels per day, Louisiana produces more petroleum products than any State apart from Texas. Around 75 per cent of Louisiana's refined petroleum products are exported to other States; most of the remainder is used by the industrial sector, which includes one of the largest petrochemical industries in the country. Louisiana's total and per capita consumption of petroleum products are among the highest in the USA.

Louisiana has proven reserves of dry natural gas of 29,277 billion cubic feet (2010), equating to 9.6 per cent of the US total. Louisiana's offshore natural gas platforms were damaged by hurricanes Katrina and Rita in 2005, and production was curtailed for several months afterward. In 2011, from a total of 21,235 wells, marketed natural gas amounted to 3,029,206 million cubic feet (12.6 per cent). Louisiana has to import natural gas to supplement its domestic production. Total consumption of natural gas was 1,351,147 million cubic feet in 2010 (5.7 per cent of total US consumption). The LNG import terminal at Sabine is the largest LNG import site in the US. Louisiana had natural gas plant liquids reserves of 216 million barrels in 2010. (Source: EIA)

Energy
Total energy production was 3,197 trillion Btu in 2010 (4.3 per cent of US total). Louisiana's total energy consumption was 4,065 trillion Btu in 2010 (4.2 per cent of US total). Per capita energy consumption in the same year was 894 million Btu (3rd in the US). Louisiana's per capita residential electricity consumption is high, due in part to high demand for electric air-conditioning during hot summer months and the widespread use of electricity as the primary energy source for home heating.

Louisiana is a net importer of electricity, with natural gas as its primary generating fuel. Net summer capability in 2010 was 26,744 MW (2.6 per cent of the US total), and monthly (Oct.) net electricity generation in 2012 was 8,296 MWh (2.7 per cent of the US total), of which natural gas-fired 4,600 thousand MWh.

Louisiana has two nuclear reactors: the 936 net MWe-River Bend station, occupying a 3,300-acre site 24 miles north-west of Baton Rouge, and with an approximate generating capability of 978 MW of electricity; and the 1075 net MWe-Waterford unit near Taft, Louisiana. Total summer capacity was 2,154 MW in 2008. (8.2 per cent of state total). Approximately 15,371,000 MWh was generated (16.6 per cent of state total). (Source: EIA)

Manufacturing
Louisiana is a major manufacturing centre for petroleum refining, petrochemicals, pulp, paper, carbon black, ship-building, and offshore oil exploration and drilling equipment. The forestry industry is the second leading manufacturing employer. Manufacturing was Louisiana's second highest earning sector in 2011 contributing an estimated $63,039 million to state GDP (up from $57,142 million in 2010). Top sectors in 2010 were petroleum and coal products ($32,626 million) and chemical manufacturing ($12,314 million).

Service Industries
The services industry is Louisiana's largest contributor to GDP. The top performing sectors in 2011 were government services ($25,888 million), real estate ($19,808 million) and retail ($13,754 million). Other main contributors were health care and social assistance ($14,787 million) and professional and technical services ($11,148 million).

Tourism
The arts, entertainment and recreation sector contributed $2,176 million towards the 2011 GDP (up from $2,126 million in 2010), whilst the accommodation and food sector contributed $6,632 million.
Louisiana Department of Culture, Recreation and Tourism, URL: http://www.crt.g2digital.com

Agriculture
Agriculture, forestry and fishing contributed $1,921 million towards the 2011 GDP, up from $1,742 million in 2010. In 2010 forestry, fishing and related activities accounted for $499 million and crop and animal production contributed $1,243 million towards state GDP.

According to the latest National Agricultural Statistics, Louisiana had a total of 30,000 farms in 2010 and farmland covered some 8,050,000 acres. The average size of a farm fell from 291 acres in 2006 to 268 acres in 2010.

Main crops are cotton, sugarcane, rice. In 2007, the market value of agricultural products sold reached $2.6 billion; crops accounted for $1.6 billion, whilst livestock, poultry and their products accounted for $1 billion. As of 1 Jan. 2011, there were 790,000 cattle and calves and 10,00 hogs and pigs.

Louisiana was ranked fourth in the production of seafood and other fisheries related products. With over a third of the nation's coastal wetlands, Louisiana is the premier waterfowl wintering area in the country.

COMMUNICATIONS AND TRANSPORT

International Airports
As well as New Orleans International Airport Louisiana has the Alexandria International Airport located less than three miles from the port of Alexandria and less than one mile to Interstate 49.
New Orleans International Airport, URL: http://www.neworleansonline.com/business/airport-intro.shtml
Alexandria International Airport, URL: http://www.englandairpark.org/air.htm

Ports and Harbours
Louisiana's location at the mouth of the Mississippi River means that it has access to the industrialised Mississippi River Valley. Louisiana's has six deep-water ports which process over 457 million tons of US goods annually. Major goods shipped include grain, chemicals, coal and general cargo. Louisiana has four of the eleven largest US ports.

Three of the six deepwater ports suffered extensive damage during Hurricane Katrina: New Orleans, Plaquemines and St Bernard. The Port of New Orleans resumed limited operations rapidly, was back to 75 per cent of normal capacity by March 2006. The hurricane also caused oil spills to the east and southeast of New Orleans.

Ports Association of Louisiana, URL: http://portsoflouisiana.org/

HEALTH

The National Center for Health Statistics estimated that there were 25.4 doctors per 10,000 population in 2009, below the US average rate per state of 27.4 doctors per 10,000 people. In 2008, there were 2,066 dentists (4.7 per 10,000 population). In 2009, there were 3.5 community hospital beds per 1,000 residents (above the national average of 2.6 beds), and there were 281 nursing homes, with 36,098 beds.

In 2007-11, Louisiana was thought to have the highest percentage of people living in poverty, at 18.4 per cent. Some 18.2 per cent of 18-64 year olds had no health insurance coverage in 2007-09. Obesity among adults exceeds the national rate, with 31 per cent of over 18 years olds affected. An estimated 65.8 per cent of adults were considered overweight. Louisiana reported 20,319 HIV/AIDS cases from the beginning of the epidemic to the end of 2008, and the state ranked 11th highest in terms of the cumulative number of reported AIDS cases. The overall TB rate was 5.1 per 100,000 population (9th highest in the US).

UNITED STATES OF AMERICA

EDUCATION

The Louisiana education system was seriously affected by Hurricane Katrina, and many schools and colleges were closed due to damage. Displaced students were offered places in many states, some as far afield as Alaska.

Primary/Secondary Education

According to National Center for Education Statistics figures for the academic year 2009-10, 690,915 elementary and secondary students attended 1,678 schools. There were 49,646 teachers, giving a pupil/teacher ratio of 13.9 to one.

Education receipts reached $7.86 billion in the 2007-08 academic year, whilst expenditure on state education was around $7.77 billion.

Higher Education

The state of Louisiana had 74 higher education establishments in the year 2010-11, 39 of which were publicly run. 102,599 male students enrolled for the year, together with 149,254 women. 60,580 degrees/certificates were awarded over the year, 20,893 of which Bachelors, 6,641 were Masters and 2,381 Doctorates. (Source: NCES)

COMMUNICATIONS AND MEDIA

Newspapers

Louisiana has 20 daily newspapers, including The Advocate (URL: http://www.2theadvocate.com/), The Daily News, The Daily Star, The Courier, The Daily Review, The Daily Advertiser, Lake Charles American Press, Daily Comet, Daily Iberian, Ruston Daily Leader, The Times, and Southwest Daily News.
Louisiana Press Association, URL: http://www.lapress.com

Broadcasting

There are 29 network television stations in Louisiana, of which three are in Baton Rouge, six are in New Orleans, three are Alexandria, four are in Lafayette, and five are in Shreveport.

ENVIRONMENT

Louisiana's 2009 emissions of carbon dioxide from its electric power industry were estimated to be 53,225,974 metric tons, down from 54,603,162 metric tons in 2007. They rose to 58,706,086 metric tons in 2010, ranking the state 14th in the US, and accounting for 2.5 per cent of the US total. An estimated 125,805 metric tons of sulphur dioxide (97,719 metric tons, 2009) and 75,394 metric tons of nitrogen oxide (69,175 metric tons, 2009) were also produced. Louisiana accounts for 2.3 per cent of US sulfur dioxide emissions and 3.0 per cent of nitrogen oxide emissions.

Approximately 12,295 alternative-fueled vehicles were in use in 2010 and ethanol consumption in 2011 was estimated to be 5,030,000 barrels (1.6 per cent of US total). In 2012, Louisiana had one ethanol plant with a capacity of 2 million Gal/Year. (Source: EIA)

Hurricane Katrina revealed that the levees and dams built to protect New Orleans have cut off the build-up of sediment that used to be deposited by the Mississippi River. As a result Louisiana has the highest rate of coastal land loss in the US. During the 2005 hurricane, some 15 hectares of wetlands was lost. Furthermore, the continual pumping of water from the city built below sea level has led to subsidence, so that the city has sunk by some 15 ft. since 1878. Scientists warn that global warming, with its attendant rise in sea levels, could cause further damage to the city.

In April 2010, an explosion on the BP-operated Deepwater Horizon rig in the Gulf of Mexico and the subsequent spillage of around 5,000 barrels of oil a day threatened the Louisiana coastline. The state's environmentally-sensitive wetlands and important shrimp and oyster beds were in the path of the 100-mile by 45-mile oil slick. The oil slick could become Americas's worst environmental disaster in decades, threatening hundreds of species of fish, birds and other wildlife in one of the world's richest marine environments.

MAINE

Capital: Augusta (Population, Census 2010: 19,136)

Head of State: Paul LePage (R, Tea Party) (Governor) (page 1462)

State Flag: A blue background in the centre of which is the State of Maine coat of arms: a silver shield bearing the image of a pine tree in front of which lies a moose; on the left of the shield is a farmer resting on a scythe; on the right is a seaman resting on an anchor; under the shield is a banner with the word 'Maine' written in capitals; above the coat of arms appears a red banner on which the motto 'Dirigo' ('I lead') appears in white; above the motto is a gold five-pointed star.

CONSTITUTION AND GOVERNMENT

Constitution

Maine entered the Union 15 March 1820 as the 23rd state. Executive power is held by the governor who serves a maximum of two consecutive four-year terms. Legislative power is held by the General Assembly. In addition to the governor, the executive branch of state government has three constitutional officers: the secretary of state, the state treasurer, and the state attorney general. The secretary of state and the state treasurer are both elected by a joint ballot of state representatives and senators for a term of two years. In addition, there is one statutory officer: the state auditor.

Maine elects two Senators and two Representatives to the US Congress in Washington, DC.

To view the Maine constitution, please visit: http://janus.state.me.us/legis/const/

Legislature

Maine's bicameral legislature consists of the Senate and the House of Representatives.

Upper House

The Senate has 35 members who are elected for two years. Each Senator can serve a maximum of four consecutive terms (eight years). Following the 2012 elections, the Senate was composed of 21 Democrats and 13 Republicans.
Maine State Senate, 3 State House Station, Augusta, ME 04333-0003, USA. Tel: +1 207 287 1540, e-mail: webmaster_senate@legislative.maine.gov, URL: http://www.state.me.us/legis/senate/

Lower House

The House of Representatives has 151 members who are elected for two years. Representatives can serve a maximum of four consecutive terms. There are two additional non-voting members who represent the Penobscot Nation and the Passamaquoddy Tribe. House members represent districts of about 8,443 people. Following the 2012 elections, there were 86 Democrats and 61 Republicans.
Maine House of Representatives, 2 State House Station, Augusta, ME 04333, USA. Tel: +1 207 287 1400, e-mail: Webmaster_House@legislature.maine.gov, URL: http://www.maine.gov/legis/house/

Elected Executive Branch Officials (as at April 2013)
Governor: Paul LePage (R, Tea Party) (page 1462)
Secretary of State: Matthew Dunlap

State Treasurer: Neria Douglass
Attorney General: Janet T. Mills
State Auditor: Pola Buckley

Legislature (as at April 2013)
President of the Senate: Justin Alfond (D)
Majority Leader of the Senate: Seth Goodall (D)
Minority Leader of the Senate: Michael Thibodeau (R)
Speaker of the House: Mark M. Eves (D)
House Majority Leader: Seth Berry (D)
House Minority Leader: Kenneth R. Fredette (R)

US Senators: Susan Collins (R) (page 1407) and Angus King Jr (I) (page 1457)

Ministries
Office of the Governor, 1 State House Station, Augusta, Me 04333-0001, USA. Tel: +1 207 287 3531, fax: +1 207 287 1034, e-mail: governor@maine.gov, URL: http://www.maine.gov/governor/
Office of the Attorney General, Burton M. Cross Building, 6th Floor, Augusta, Maine (Mailing Address: 6 State House Station, Augusta, Maine 04333), USA. Tel: +1 207 626 8800, e-mail: maineag@state.me.us, URL: http://www.maineag.state.me.us/ag/
Department of Audit, Flagg/Dummer Building, Hallowell Annex, 9 Beech Street, Hallowell, Maine, USA (Mailing address: 66 State House Station, Augusta, Maine 04333-0066). Tel: +1 207 624 6250, fax: +1 207 624 6273, URL: http://www.state.me.us/audit/
Office of the Secretary of State, 148 State House Station, Augusta, Maine 04333, USA. Tel: +1 207 626 8400, e-mail: sos.office@state.me.us, URL: http://www.state.me.us/sos
Office of the State Treasurer, 39 State House Station, Augusta, Maine, 04333, USA. Tel: +1 207 624 7477, fax: +1 207 287 2367. e-mail: state.treasurer@Maine.gov, URL: http://www.state.me.us/treasurer/
Department of Agriculture, Food and Rural Resources, Deering Building, AMHI Complex, 28 State House Station, Augusta, ME 04333-0028, USA. Tel: +1 207 287 3871, fax: +1 207 287 7548, URL: http://www.state.me.us/agriculture/
Public Utilities Commission, 242 State Street, 18 State House Station, Augusta, Maine 04333-0018, USA. Tel: +1 207 287 3831, fax: +1 207 287 1039, e-mail: maine.puc@maine.gov, URL: http://www.state.me.us/mpuc/
Department of Administrative and Financial Services, Burton M. Cross Building, 3rd Floor, 78 State House Station, Augusta, ME 04333-0078, USA. Tel: 207 624 7800, fax: +1 207 624 7804, URL: http://www.state.me.us/dafs/
Department of Corrections, Tyson Building, AMHI Campus, Augusta, Maine. (Mailing Address: 111 State House Station, Augusta ME 04333-0111) Tel: +1 207 287 4360, fax: +1 207 287 4370, URL: http://www.state.me.us/corrections/
Department of Economic and Community Development, Burton M. Cross Building, 111 Sewall Street, 3rd floor, Augusta, ME 04333-0059, USA. Tel: +1 207 624 9800, URL: http://www.maine.gov/decd/
Department of Education, 23 State House Station, Augusta, ME 04333-0023, USA. Tel: +1 207 287 5800, fax: +1 207 624 6618, URL: http://www.maine.gov/doe/
Department of Environmental Protection, 17 State House Station, Augusta, ME 04333-0017, USA. Tel: +1 207 287 7688, URL: http://www.maine.gov/dep/index.shtml

Department of Professional and Financial Regulation, 35 State House Station, Augusta, Maine 04333, USA. Tel: +1 207 624 8500, fax: +1 207 624 8690, URL: http://www.maine.gov/pfr/index.shtml
Department of Transportation, Child Street, 16 State House Station, Augusta, ME 04333-0016, USA. Tel: +1 207 624 3000, fax: +1 207 624 3001, URL: http://www.state.me.us/mdot/

Political Parties
Maine Democratic Party, 16 Winthrop Street, Augusta, Maine (PO Box 5258 Augusta, Maine 04332), USA. Tel: +1 207 622 6233, fax: +1 207 622 2657, e-mail: democrats@mainedems.org, URL: http://www.mainedems.org/
Maine Republican Party, 9 Higgins Street, Augusta, ME 04330-6312, USA. Tel: +1 207 622 6247, fax: +1 207 623 5322, e-mail: mainegop@mainegop.com, URL: http://www.mainegop.com/

Elections
In the November 2010 elections, Governor John Balducci (D) was ineligible to stand. The Tea Party republican candidate, Paul LePage, beat several other candidates. Mr LePage is the first Republican to hold the office of governor in Maine since 1992.

In the 2012 US Senate elections, the incumbent senator Olympis Snowe did not seek re-election. The seat was won by Angus King (Ind.).

In the 2012 legislative elections, the Democrats gained seven seats and took back control of the Senate (21 Democrats, 13 Republicans, one independent) in the Senate. The Democrats also took back control of the House of Representatives (Democrats 86, Republicans 61).

LEGAL SYSTEM

Maine's judicial system has three levels of court: the Supreme Judicial Court, Courts of General Jurisdiction (the Superior Court), and Courts of Limited Jurisdiction (District Courts, Probate Courts, and Administrative Courts). The Supreme Judicial Court consists of the Chief Justice and six Associate Judges. The Superior Court comprises 16 Judges each of whom holds court at one of Maine's 16 counties. Each of Maine's counties has one Superior Court, except Aroostook County which has two Superior Courts. All judges are appointed by the Governor for a term of seven years with the exception of Probate judges who are elected by voters from each county for a term of four years.

In 2009, the Maine House of Representatives approved a bill allowing same-sex marriage by 89 votes to 56. However, before the law came into effect, a referendum rejected the bill by 53 per cent to 47 per cent. Voters passed a law legalizing same-sex marraige in December 2012.

The death penalty was abolished in 1887.

Supreme Judicial Court, URL: http://www.courts.state.me.us/
Chief Justice: Leigh Ingalls Saufley
Justices: Ellen Gorman, Warren Silver, Donald Alexander, Jon Levy, Andrew Mead, Joseph Jabar
Chief Justice of the Maine Superior Court: Thomas E. Humphrey

LOCAL GOVERNMENT

According to the latest US Census Bureau 2007 Census of Local Governments, Maine has 16 county governments and 488 sub-county general purpose governments. The county governing body is the board of county commissioners. Of the 488 sub-county governments, 22 are municipal and 466 are town or township governments. There are 299 public school systems; 98 school district governments and 201 dependent public school systems.

Maine Municipal Association, URL: http://www.memun.org/

AREA AND POPULATION

Area
Maine is located in the far north-east of the US, bordering Canada to the north, and New Hampshire to the south-west. Maine's total land area is 35,384.65 sq. miles, of which 30,861.55 sq. miles is land and 4,523.10 sq. miles is water.

To view a map of the state, please consult:
http://www.lib.utexas.edu/maps/us_2001/maine_ref_2001.pdf

Population
The 2010 Census put the population at 1,328,361, up on the mid-2009 estimate of 1,318,301. In 2012, the population was estimated to be 1,329,192. The population of Maine increased by 4.2 per cent over the period 2000-10. The population is expected to reach 1.4 million by 2030. The population density is estimated at 43.1 people per sq. mile. The largest city is Portland city, Cumberland County, with 66,363 inhabitants in 2011. The population of the capital, Augusta, was 19,103 in the same year. The county with the greatest number of inhabitants is Cumberland County, followed by York County, and Penobscot County.

According to the 2010 Census, 5.2 per cent of the population is under 5 years, 20.7 per cent under 18 years and 15.9 per cent is aged over 65 years. Approximately 95.2 per cent of the population is white, and 1.2 per cent is black. Approximately 1.3 per cent of the population is of Hispanic or Latino origin.

Births, Marriages, Deaths
The US Census Bureau (Population Division) estimated that there were 12,970 births in 2010 and 12,750 deaths over the same period, giving a natural population increase of just 220. Net migration away from Maine was -2,109 in 2009. The infant mortality rate in 2007 was 6.3 infant deaths per 1,000 live births. Provisional data puts the number of marriages and divorces in 2007 at 10,095 and 5,897 respectively.

Public Holidays
In addition to the national holidays, the people of Maine celebrate Patriot's Day on April 19th, the anniversary of the battles of Lexington and Concord.

EMPLOYMENT

Preliminary figures indicate that Maine's total civilian labour force was 708,000 in December 2012, of which 656,600 were employed and 51,400 were unemployed. The unemployment rate was 7.3 per cent, lower than the national average of 7.8 per cent.

The following table shows preliminary figures for December 2012 for non-farm wage and salary employment, seasonally adjusted, according to industry:

Industry	No. employed	12 month change (%)
Logging and mining	2,600	-3.7
Construction	23,800	-3.6
Manufacturing	49,000	-1.4
Trade, transport and utilities	116,600	-1.4
Information	7,800	-2.5
Financial activities	31,200	-1.9
Professional and business svcs.	56,900	0.7
Educational and health svcs.	122,700	0.4
Leisure and hospitality	60,300	2.4
Other services	19,800	-2.5
Government	100,800	2,3
TOTAL	591,500	0.0

Source: Bureau of Labor Statistics

BANKING AND FINANCE

GDP/GNP, Inflation, National Debt
Maine's total Gross Domestic Product (GDP) rose from an estimated $51,293 million in 2009 to $51,643 million in 2010. In 2011, current GDP was put at $51.6 billion and ranked 43rd in the US. Real GDP contracted by 0.4 per cent in 2011.

The following table shows Gross Domestic Product according to industry ($m):

Industry	2009	2010	2011
Agriculture, forestry, fishing & hunting	654	654	676
Mining	8	12	5
Utilities	901	923	823
Construction	1,843	1,808	1,897
Manufacturing	5,408	5,580	5,894
Wholesale Trade	2,433	2,462	2,544
Retail Trade	4,233	4,430	4,517
Transportation and warehousing	1,155	1,158	1,165
Information	1,081	1,118	1,022
Finance and insurance	3,786	3,502	3,599
Real estate, rental and leasing	7,061	6,717	6,680
Educational services	632	662	688
Health & social assistance	5,855	5,992	6,174
Other non-government services	7,840	8,325	8,643
Government	7,271	7,332	7,258
TOTAL	50,160	50,674	51,585

Source: Bureau of Economic Analysis, Feb. 2013

The estimated per capita income in Maine was $38,299 in 2011. Per capita GDP in 2009 reached $41,836, but fell to $33,746 in 2011, below the US average of $42,070.

The annual Consumer Price Index (CPI) (all items) for the Boston-Brockton-Nashua (MA-NH-ME-CT) urban area rose from 243.9 in 2011 to 247.7 in 2012 (1982-84 = 100). (Source: Bureau of Labor Statistics)

Balance of Payments / Imports and Exports
Total Maine imports fell from $4,823 million in 2008 to $4,279 million in 2009, a fall of 11.3 per cent. Imports fell to $4,100 million in 2010, a fall of -4.2 per cent. They rose by 6.8 per cent in 2011 to $4,484 million. Maine imports account for 0.2 per cent of US total imports. Main suppliers (2011) included Canada (47.4 per cent), Germany (19.4 per cent), China, UK and the Netherlands.

Export revenue rose from $3,016 million in 2008 to $2,231 million in 2009, a decrease of 26.0 per cent. Exports rose by 41.8 per cent to $3,164 million in 2010 and by 8.1 per cent in 2011 to £3,421 million. Maine exports account for 0.2 per cent of US total exports.

Merchandise export revenue in 2010-11, according to the top five international destinations, is shown on the following table:

UNITED STATES OF AMERICA

Country	2010 ($m)	2011 ($m)	+/-% 10-11
Canada	1,043	1,129	8.2
Malaysia	850	927	9.1
China	333	275	-17.6
South Korea	99	127	28.6
Japan	88	108	23.3

Source: US Census Bureau

The following table shows 2010 export revenue according to the top five export products.

Product	$m
Electronic integrated circuits, nesoi	709
Chemical woodpulp, soda etc	275
Paper, Paperbd., for writ/pring	183
Lobsters, live, fresh, dried, salted	172
Paper, Paperbd, cellulose wadd etc	124

Source: US Census Bureau

Chambers of Commerce and Trade Organisations
Maine State Chamber of Commerce, URL: http://www.mainechamber.org

MANUFACTURING, MINING AND SERVICES

Primary and Extractive Industries
Maine has no oil reserves and little petroleum infrastructure other than a number of crude-oil pipelines. Total petroleum consumption in 2010 fell to 37 million barrels, compared to 42.9 million barrels in 2007, 16.0 million of which was in the form of motor gasoline, and 12.8 million distillate fuel.

With no natural gas supplies of its own, Maine imports all of its requirements, mainly by pipeline from Canada. Consumption fell from 77,574 million cu ft in 2010 to 70,698 million cu ft in 2011. Natural gas is used primarily for power generation. (Source: EIA)

Mining contributed $6 million to the 2008 state GDP.

Energy
Maine's total energy production was 145 trillion Btu in 2010 (0.2 per cent of US total). Maine's total energy consumption in 2010 was 407 trillion Btu (0.4 per cent of US total). Per capita energy consumption in the same year was 307 million Btu, ranking the state 28th in the US.

Maine is a net importer of electricity with natural gas as the primary energy source for industry generation (45 per cent in 2011). Net summer capability in 2010 was 4,430 MW (0.4 per cent of US total), and approximately net monthly (Oct.) generation in 2012 was 1,239,000 MWh (0.4 per cent of US total). Of this, 9,000 MWh was petroleum-fired, 489,000 MWh was natural gas-fired, 6,000 MWh was coal-fired, 277,000 MWh was hydroelectric and 431,000 MWh came from other renewable sources. (Source: EIA)

Manufacturing
Manufacturing accounted for $5,894 million of state Gross Domestic Product in 2011, up from $5,580 million in 2010. Top sectors in 2010 were non-motor vehicle transport equipment ($686 million), paper manufacturing ($949 million), and food, beverage and tobacco products ($735 million).

Service Industries
The services industry is Maine's largest contributor towards its Gross Domestic Product. The main sectors in 2011 were real estate ($6,680 million) and health services ($6,174 million).

Tourism
The accommodation and food sector of the services industry contributed $1,859 million towards the 2011 GDP (up from $1,782 million in 2010). The arts, entertainment and recreation sector contributed $504 million.
Maine Office of Tourism, URL: http://www.visitmaine.com

Agriculture
The agriculture, forestry and fisheries industry contributed $676 million towards Maine's 2011 GDP (down from $654 million in 2010). In 2010, the forestry, fishing and related activities sector contributed $326 million whilst the farms sector contributed $328 million.

The National Agricultural Statistics Service estimated that there were 8,100 farms in Maine farms in 2010. Total farmland was 1,350,000 in 2008, and the average size of a Maine farm was 167 acres in 2010. Maine's major livestock products are cattle and calves, beef cows, and sheep and lambs. As of 1 Jan. 2011 there were 90,000 cattle and calves and 4,700 hogs & pigs. Major crops produced, in terms of acreage, are hay-alf and silage, potatoes, corn for sil or green chop, oats for grain, and vegetables.

In 2008, the market value of agricultural products was $617 million, of which crops earned some $326 million and livestock accounted for $290 million.

COMMUNICATIONS AND TRANSPORT

International Airports
Portland International Jetport, URL: http://www.portlandjetport.org/

Bangor International Airport, http://www.flybangor.com

Railways
The following railways operate a service in Maine: Canadian Pacific Railroad, Canadian National Railroad, CSX Railroad, Norfolk Southern Railroad, Belfast & Moosehead Lek Railroad. Recent statistics put the annual tonnage of freight transported on Maine's railways at 4,012,332 (originated) and 3,887,892 (terminated).

Roads
Over 80 million tons of freight is estimated to have been transported by truck on Maine's roads in 1999.

Ports and Harbours
Three major ports operate in Maine: Port of Portland, Port of Searsport, and Port of Eastport. In 2008, 766 vessels docked in the Port of Portland, and the port handled 14,109,432 tons of cargo.
The Port of Portland, URL: http://www.portofportland.com/

HEALTH

The National Center for Health Statistics estimated that there were 31.6 doctors per 10,000 population in 2009, above the US average of 27.4. In 2008, there were an estimated 657 dentists (5.0 per 10,000 population). In 2009, there were 2.7 community hospital beds per 1,000 residents, and, in 2010, there were 109 nursing homes, with 7,127 beds.

Maine reported 1,2283 AIDS cases from the beginning of the epidemic to the end of 2008, and the state ranked 42nd highest in the cumulative number of reported AIDS cases. The overall TB rate was 0.7 per 100,000 population, the 49th highest rate. In 2012, an estimated 26.8 per cent of the population were considered obese and 62.9 per cent were overweight.

It is estimated that, in 2007-09, some 9.8 per cent of the people of Maine did not have health insurance, below the US state average of 15.8 per cent. It was estimated that 12 .8 per cent of the population were living in poverty in 2007-11, again below the national rate of 14.3 per cent.

EDUCATION

Primary/Secondary Education
In the 2009-10 academic year, there were 662 elementary and secondary schools, with a total pupil enrollment of 189,225. There were 16,275 teachers, giving a pupil/teacher ratio of 11.63 to one, lower than the national average of 15.3 to one.

Total revenues from education amounted to $2.6 billion in the 2007-08 academic year, whilst expenditures on the state system reached $2.3 billion.

Higher Education
There were 32 degree-conferring establishments in Maine in 2010-11, 15 of which were public. In the same year, 28,976 male students enrolled together with 41,194 women. 12,775 degrees/certificates were conferred, of which 7,099 were Bachelors, 1,829 were Masters and 348 were doctorates. The State University of Maine includes the main campus at Orono, branch campuses at Bangor, Southern Maine (Portland and Gorham), Fort Kent, Farmington, Machias, Presque-Isle, and Augusta. (Source: NCES)

COMMUNICATIONS AND MEDIA

Newspapers
Maine has seven daily newspapers: Morning Sentinel (URL: http://www.onlinesentinel.com), Portland Press Herald (URL: http://pressherald.mainetoday.com/), Sun-Journal, The Times Record, Journal Tribune, Kennebec Journal, and Bangor Daily News (URL: http://www.bangornews.com/)

Business Journals
Kennebec Business Monthly, URL: http://www.kennbizmo.com/

Broadcasting
There are 13 television stations in Maine, including four in Bangor, four in Portland and two in Presque Isle. Two are run by NBC, three by CBS, and five by PBS.

ENVIRONMENT

Emissions from Maine's electricity industry are relatively low due to its use of hydroelectricity and other renewable sources as primary generating resources. Emissions of carbon dioxide rose from 4.7 million metric tons in 2007 to 4.95 million metric tons in 2010, ranking the state 44th in the US. Emissions of sulfur dioxide fell from approximately 32,926 metric tons in 2009 to 12,419 metric tons and nitrogen oxide emissions fell from 12,397 metric tons to 8,413 metric tons.

Maine has the highest wood and wood waste power generation capacity in the United States.

In 2010, 1,987 alternative-fueled vehicles were in use and 1,761,000 barrels of ethanol were consumed in 2011. (Source: EIA)

MARYLAND

Capital: Annapolis (Population, Census 2010: 38,394)

Head of State: Martin O'Malley, Governor (page 1489)

State Flag: Maryland's flag is divided into four quarters: the top left and bottom right quarters are divided diagonally by two lines from the bottom right to the top left, and by five vertical lines from left to right, and is coloured alternately black and gold; the top right and bottom left quarters are divided into quarters - alternately red and white - in the centre of which is a cross bottony - also alternately red and white.

CONSTITUTION AND GOVERNMENT

Constitution

Maryland was the seventh of the original 13 states to join the Union (28 April 1788). Under the current Maryland constitution, the Governor is elected by the people for a term of four years. The Lieutenant Governor is elected at the same time as the Governor, also for a period of four years. They are assisted by eight other executive officials: the Comptroller of Maryland, State Treasurer, Attorney General, Secretary of State, Adjutant General, and three-member Board of Public Works (comprising the Governor, the Comptroller of Maryland, and the State Treasurer). All serve terms of four years. The Comptroller and Attorney General are elected by state voters, whilst the Treasurer is elected by both houses of the General Assembly, the Secretary of State is appointed by the Governor and confirmed by the Senate, and the Adjutant General is appointed by the Governor with advice from the Senate.

The Governor's Council, or Cabinet, comprises 22 ex-officio members including the Governor, who chairs the Council, as well as the Lieutenant Governor, the Secretary of State and the secretary of each Executive Branch department. The Council meets on a weekly basis and is responsible for supervising, co-ordinating and directing State government.

Maryland elects two Senators and eight Representatives to the US Congress in Washington, DC. To view the state constitution, please visit: http://www.msa.md.gov/msa/mdmanual/43const/html/const.html

Recent Events

In response to shootings in the US, Maryland joined Massachusetts in imposing stricter controls on handguns. According to legislation agreed by the Maryland House of Delegates, all handguns sold in the state have to include childproof locks, safety warnings and tamper-proof serial numbers.

Legislature

Maryland's bicameral legislature, the General Assembly, consists of the Senate and the House of Delegates, and meets annually for 90 days.

Upper House

The Senate has 47 members elected for four years. Following the 2010 elections, the Senate was composed of 35 Democrats and 12 Republicans.
State Senate, James Senate Office Building, 110 College Avenue, Annapolis, MD 21401, USA. Tel: +1 410 841 3908 (Secretary of the Senate), URL: http://mgaleg.maryland.gov/

Lower House

The House of Delegates has 141 members who are elected for four years. Following the 2010 elections, the House was composed of 98 Democrats, and 43 Republicans.
State House of Delegates, Lowe House Office Building, 84 College Avenue, Annapolis, Maryland, USA. Tel: +1 410 841 3999 (Chief Clerk), URL: http://mgaleg.maryland.gov/

Elected Executive Branch Officials (as at April 2013)
Governor: Martin O'Malley (D) (page 1489)
Lieutenant Governor: Anthony G. Brown (D)
Comptroller of Maryland: Peter Franchot (D)
Attorney General: Douglas F. Gansler (D)
State Treasurer: Nancy K. Kopp (D)
Secretary of State: John P. McDonough

General Assembly (as at April 2013)
President of the Senate: Thomas V. Mike Miller Jr. (D)
President Pro Tem of the Senate: Nathaniel J. McFadden (D)
Senate Majority Leader: Robert Garagiola (D)
Senate Minority Leader: E.J. Piplin (R)
Speaker of the House: Michael Busch (D)
House Majority Leader: Kumar Barve (D)
House Minority Leader: Anthony J. O'Donnell (R)

US Senators: Barbara A. Mikulski (D) (page 1477) and Benjamin L. Cardin (page 1400)

Ministries

Office of the Governor, State House, Annapolis, Maryland 21401-1925, USA. Tel: +1 410 974 3901, fax: +1 410 974 3275, e-mail: governor@gov.state.md.us, URL: http://www.gov.state.md.us
Office of the Lieutenant Governor, State House, Annapolis, MD 21401-1925, USA. Tel: +1 410 974 3901, fax: +1 410 974 5882, URL: www.governor.maryland.gov/ltgovernor/
Office of the Secretary of State, State House, Annapolis, Maryland 21401, USA. Tel: +1 410 974 5521, fax: +1 410 974 5190, URL: http://www.sos.state.md.us
Office of the Treasurer, 80 Calvert Street, Goldstein Treasury Building, Annapolis, Maryland 21404, USA. Tel: +1 410 260 7533, URL: http://www.treasurer.state.md.us

Office of the Attorney General, 200 St. Paul Place, Baltimore, MD 21202, USA. Tel: +1 410 576 6300, e-mail: OAG@oag.state.md.us, URL: http://www.oag.state.md.us/
Department of Agriculture, 50 Harry S. Truman Parkway, Annapolis, MD 21401, USA. Tel: +1 410 841 5700, URL: http://mda.maryland.gov/
Department of Business and Economic Development, 217 East Redwood Street, Baltimore, Maryland 21202, USA. Tel: +1 410 767 6300, URL: http://www.dbed.state.md.us/
Department of the Environment, 1800 Washington Blvd., Baltimore, MD 21230, USA. Tel: +1 410 537 3000, URL: http://www.mde.state.md.us
Department of Health and Mental Hygiene, 201 West Preston Street, Baltimore, Maryland 21201, USA. Tel: +1 410 767 6860, URL: http://dhmh.maryland.gov/SitePages/Home.aspx
Department of Natural Resources, 580 Taylor Avenue, Tawes State Office Building, Annapolis, MD 21401, USA. Tel: +1 410 260 8019, URL: http://www.dnr.state.md.us
Department of Transport, 7201 Corporate Center Drive, PO Box 548, Hanover MD 21076, USA. Tel: +1 410 865 1142, fax: +1 410 865 1334, URL: http://www.mdot.maryland.gov/

Political Parties

Maryland Democratic Party, 188 Main Street, Suite 1, Annapolis, MD 21401, USA. Tel: +1 410 269 8818, fax: +1 410 280 8882, e-mail: webdem@mddems.org, URL: http://www.mddems.org/
Maryland Republican Party, 15 West Street, Annapolis, Maryland 21401, USA. Tel: +1 410 269 0113, fax: +1 410 269 5937, e-mail: info@mdgop.org, URL: http://www.mdgop.org

Elections

Following the November 2010 elections, the Democrats gained two seats from the Republicans (Democrats 35, Republicans 12). In the House of Delegates, the Democrats lost six seats to the Republicans (Democrats 98, Republicans 43).

Elections for Maryland's state constitutional officers last took place in November 2010. The incumbent Governor, Martin O'Malley, retained his position with 57 per cent of the vote.

LEGAL SYSTEM

Maryland's court system consists of the Court of Appeals, the Court of Special Appeals, the Circuit Courts, the District Court of Maryland, and the Orphans' Courts. The Court of Appeals is Maryland's highest court. As well as the Chief Judge, there are six Associate Justices, appointed by the governor and confirmed by the Senate, who serve a term of 10 years. The Court of Special Appeals is Maryland's intermediate appellate court, and has appellate jurisdiction over any reviewable judgement from the circuit and orphan's courts. The Court of Special Appeals comprises a Chief Judge and 12 Associate Judges who are appointed by the Governor and confirmed by the Senate for terms of 10 years.

Maryland has the death penalty. There have been five executions since 1976 and there are currently five people on death row. The most recent execution took place in 2005. The murder rate is 7.4 per 100,000. (Source: DPIC)

Maryland Court of Appeals, URL: http://www.courts.state.md.us/coappeals/index.html
Chief Judge: Robert M. Bell
Judges: Glenn Harrell Jr., Lynne Battaglia, Clayton Greene Jr., Sally Adkins, Mary Ellen Barbera, Robert McDonald
Maryland Court of Special Appeals, URL: http://www.courts.state.md.us/cosappeals/
Chief Judge: Peter B. Krauser

LOCAL GOVERNMENT

For administrative purposes, according to the US Census Bureau, Maryland is divided into 23 county governments and 157 sub-county general purpose governments. All of the sub-county governments are municipal, consisting of cities and towns. Maryland has no town or township governments. There are also 76 special districts, and 39 dependent public school systems.

AREA AND POPULATION

Area

Maryland is situated on the north-east seaboard, south of the District of Columbia, north of Virginia and West Virginia, and west of Delaware. The total area of Maryland is 12,406.68 sq. miles, of which 9,773.82 sq. miles is land and 2,632.86 sq. miles is water. Washington, DC sits on land that was originally part of Maryland. The Chesapeake Bay, covering an area of 1,726 sq. miles, nearly bisects the state, and the counties east of the bay are known collectively as the Eastern Shore.

To view a map of the state, please consult:
http://www.lib.utexas.edu/maps/us_2001/maryland_delaware_ref_2001.pdf

Population

According to the 2010 Census, the population was 5,773,552, up on the mid-2009 estimate of 5,699,478. In 2012, the population was estimated to be 5,884,563. Over the period 2000 to 2010, the population of Maryland grew by 9.0 per cent and is expected to reach 7.0 million by 2030. Maryland's population density is around 594.8 people per sq. mile (the fifth highest in the US).

UNITED STATES OF AMERICA

Most of the population of Maryland lives in the central region of the state, in the Baltimore Metropolitan Area and Washington Metropolitan Area. The population of the capital, Annapolis, was 38,394, according to the 2010 Census, with a population density of 5,344.0 people per sq. mile. Baltimore City had a population of 620,961 and a population density of 7,671.5 persons per sq. mile. The county with the greatest number of inhabitants was Montgomery County, with a population of 971,777 and a population density of 1,978.2 persons per sq. mile in 2010.

According to the 2010 Census, 6.3 per cent of the population is under 5 years, 23.4 per cent under 18 years and 12.3 per cent is aged over 65 years. Approximately 58.2 per cent of the population is white, and 29.4 per cent is black. Approximately 8.2 per cent of the population is of Hispanic or Latino origin.

Births, Marriages, Deaths
The US Census Bureau estimated that there were 73,801 births in 2010 and 43,325 deaths, giving a natural population increase of 30,476 people. Net migration amounted to 8,402 people in 2009. The infant mortality rate in 2007 was 8.0 deaths per 1,000 live births, down from 8.7 deaths per 1,000 live births in 2004. According to provisional data, marriages and divorces in 2007 numbered 35,549 and 17,374 respectively.

Public Holidays
In addition to federal public holidays Maryland also celebrates Maryland Day on 25 March, in commemoration of the first European settlement of the state.

EMPLOYMENT

Preliminary figures indicate that Maryland's total civilian labour force was 3,113,500 in December 2012, of which some 2,906,700 were employed and 206,700 were unemployed. The unemployment rate was 6.6 per cent, lower than the national average of 7.8 per cent. (Source: US Bureau of Labor Statistics)

The following table shows December 2012 non-farm wage and salary employment according to industry:

Industry	No. of Jobs	12-month change (%)
Construction, logging and mining	150,900	2.8
Manufacturing	107,200	-3.2
Trade, transportation, and utilities	442,800	0.1
Information	42,700	-0.5
Financial activities	140,200	-1.7
Professional and business services	420,200	5.3
Educational and health services	426,500	2.0
Leisure and hospitality	237,800	0.7
Other services	119,100	0.7
Government	501,700	-1.8
TOTAL	2,539,100	0.8

Source: Bureau of Labor Statistics

BANKING AND FINANCE

GDP/GNP, Inflation, National Debt
Maryland's total Gross Domestic Product (current dollar) rose from $286,797 million in 2009 to $295,304 million in 2010. GDP (current dollars) amounted to $301.1 billion and ranked 15th in the US. Real GDP rose by 1.9 per cent in 2011. Top contributors were services, real estate and government.

The following table shows Maryland's Gross Domestic Product according to industry (millions of current dollars):

Industry	2009	2010	2011
Agriculture, Forestry, Fishing & Hunting	734	688	737
Mining	143	265	184
Utilities	5,939	6,363	6,459
Construction	13,197	13,327	13,656
Manufacturing	17,052	18,564	19,481
Wholesale Trade	12,674	13,046	13,636
Retail Trade	15,487	16,449	16,841
Transport and warehousing	5,498	5,749	5,905
Information	11,044	11,250	11,489
Finance and insurance	15,974	18,361	18,269
Real estate	48,478	45,914	44,663
Educational services	4,058	4,170	4,344
Health care & social assistance	22,284	23,267	24,480
Other non-government services	58,602	62,127	65,238
Government	51,760	53,808	55,716
TOTAL	283,644	293,349	301,100

Source: Bureau of Economic Analysis, Feb. 2013

The average annual per capita income in Maryland rose to $50,656 in 2011, 122 per cent of national average of $41,560. Per capita real GDP was $45,360 in 2011, above the US average of $42,070. (Source: Bureau of Economic Analysis)

The annual Consumer Price Index (CPI) for the Washington-Baltimore, DC-MD-VA-WV, urban area (all items) rose from 147 in 2011 to 150.2 in 2012 (1982-84=100). (Source: Bureau of Labor Statistics)

Balance of Payments / Imports and Exports
Total Maryland imports fell from $18,454 million in 2008 to $13,342 million in 2009, a fall of 27.7 per cent. Imports rose to $19,820 million in 2010, up 48.6 per cent. They rose to $23,948 million in 2011, up 20.8 per cent. Imports from Maryland account for 1.1 per cent of total US imports. Vehicle parts are the primary import commodity. Main suppliers include (2011) Germany (44.1 per cent), China (20 per cent), Canada, Mexico, and South Africa.

Merchandise exports fell from $11,383 million in 2008 to $9,225 million in 2009, a 19 per cent decrease. Exports rose to $10,163 million in 2010, up 10.2 per cent and rose to $10,852 million, up 6.8 per cent. Maryland exports accounted for 0.7 per cent of total US exports. (Source: US Census Bureau, Foreign Trade Division)

The top five international export destinations in 2010-11, according to revenue, are shown on the following table:

Country	2010 ($m)	2011 ($m)	+/-% 10-11
Canada	1,588	1,690	6.4
China	574	666	16.2
Saudi Arabia	499	554	11.0
South Korea	481	539	12.2
Netherlands	677	515	-23.9

Source: US Census Bureau

The following table shows the top five export products in 2010 according to revenue:

Product	Revenue ($m)
Pass. Veh. spk-ing. Int. Comb. Rcpr. P. Eng. greater than 3,000 cc	819
Medicaments	309
Composite Diagnostic/Lab. reagents	309
Supported catalysts	260
Bituminous coal, not agglomerated	258

Source: US Census Bureau

Chambers of Commerce and Trade Organisations
Maryland Chamber of Commerce, URL: http://www.mdchamber.org/
Maryland Economic Development Corporation, URL: http://www.medco-corp.com/
Baltimore/Washington Corridor Chamber of Commerce, URL: http://www.baltwashchamber.org

MANUFACTURING, MINING AND SERVICES

Primary and Extractive Industries
Maryland's mining industry produces crushed and cut stone, sand and gravel, industrial sand, and clays. The industry contributed $184 million towards the 2011 Gross Domestic Product (down from $265 million in 2010). Top sectors in 2010 were non-oil and gas mining ($224 million), and support activities ($41 million). (Source: BEA)

Maryland has no reserves of oil or production industry. Total petroleum consumption in 2009 fell to 101.7 million barrels, of which 69.4 million was motor gasoline and 19.7 million barrels was distillate fuel.

Maryland no longer produces significant amounts of natural gas. In 2011 there were 8 natural gas producing wells and 34 million cu ft were produced. Consumption was 208,226 million cu feet in 2010. Maryland's residential and commercial sectors dominate gas consumption; almost a half of Maryland households use natural gas for heating.

Maryland had recoverable coal reserves of 36 million short tons in 2011. Total production fell by 54.5 per cent over the year 2007; one underground mine was closed. In 2011, 2,937,000 short tons were produced. (Source: EIA)

Energy
Maryland's total energy production was 246 trillion Btu in 2010. Maryland's total energy consumption was 1,481 trillion Btu in 2010, whilst its per capita energy consumption ranks it 39th in the US (256 million Btu in 2010).

Maryland is a net importer of electricity with coal as its primary generating fuel. Net summer capability in 2010 was 12,516 MW (1.2 per cent of the US total). Net monthly (Oct.) generation in 2012 was approximately 3,258,000 MWh, 1.0 per cent of US total, of which coal-fired 1,501,000 MWh and nuclear 1,302,000 MWh.

Maryland's single nuclear power plant, Calvert Cliffs, is located on a 2,100-acre site at Lusby, and is owned by Constellation Energy Group and operated by Constellation Nuclear. Unit 1 is a 835-net MWe pressurised water reactor, and Unit 2 is an 840-net MWe pressurised water reactor. Their combined summer capacity was 1,735 MW in 2006. (Source: EIA)

Manufacturing
Maryland's manufacturing industry contributed $19,481 million towards the 2011 GDP (down from $18,564 million in 2010). In 2010, the top sectors were chemical products ($4,089 million), food products ($2,918 million), and computer and electronic products ($5,106 million).

Service Industries
The services industry is Maryland's largest contributor towards GDP. Top sectors in 2011 included real estate ($44,663 million), professional and technical services ($34,121 million), health care and social assistance ($24,480 million). Government services accounted for $55,716 million.

Tourism
The accommodation and food sector of the services industry contributed $8,404 million towards Maryland's GDP in 2011, whilst the arts and entertainment services sector contributed $2,387 million.
Maryland Office of Tourism Development, URL: http://www.mdisfun.org/

Agriculture
The agriculture, forestry and fishing industry contributed $737 million towards Maryland's Gross Domestic Product in 2011 (up from $688 million in 2010). In 2010, the farms sector contributed $583 million, whilst the forestry, fishing and related activities sector contributed $105 million.

Maryland's farms numbered 12,800 in 2010 and farmland covered around 2,050,000 acres, down from 2,193,063 acres in 1997. The average size of a Maryland farm was 160 acres in 2010. Principal crops are corn, soybeans, tobacco and truck-farm vegetables. Maryland also produces melons, wheat, poultry and livestock. Poultry and eggs are the largest agricultural revenue producers, earning some $903 million in 2007. The total value of agricultural products sold was $1.8 billion; livestock, poultry and their products accounted for $1.2 billion, whilst crops contributed 629.3 million. As of Jan. 2011, there were 195,000 cattle & calves and 26,000 hogs & pigs.

The annual fish catch is about 86 million pounds, worth almost $47 million. Hard blue crabs and oysters are important commodities. Fifty per cent of the State's area is forest and about half the lumber yield is soft wood.

COMMUNICATIONS AND TRANSPORT

International Airports
Two airports are owned and operated by the state of Maryland: Baltimore/Washington International Airport (BWI) and Martin State Airport. Baltimore Washington International Airport handled some 20.34 million passengers in 2004 (up 3.3 per cent on 2003) and transported 555.3 million pounds of cargo (up 6.9 per cent on 2003). 52 airlines operate from the airport, and there are around 837 daily operations.
Baltimore/Washington International Airport, URL: http://www.bwiairport.com

Railways
The Central Light Rail provides an electric-powered rail service through central Maryland from Timonium, Baltimore County, to Glen Burnie, Anne Arundel County. The Baltimore Metro provides a subway service over 15.5 miles and carries 44,000 passengers a day. The Washington Metrorail links Washington, D.C., Virginia and the suburbs of Maryland. The main rail service in Maryland is run by the Maryland Rail Commuter Service (MARC), which covers three commuter lines linking Baltimore and West Virginia with Washington, D.C.

Ports and Harbours
The Port of Baltimore, located on the Patapsco River, directly employs around 19,000 people and generates approximately $2 billion in business and federal government revenue.
Baltimore Port Administration, URL: http://www.mpa.state.md.us/index.html

HEALTH

The National Center for Health Statistics estimated that there were 40.1 doctors (including osteopaths) per 10,000 population in 2009, one of the highest rates in the US.In 2008, there were 4,138 dentists in 2008 (7.3 per 10,000 population). In 2009, there were 2.1 community hospital beds per 1,000 residents, and 231 nursing homes, with 29,004 beds. The CDC estimated that 13.2 per cent of Maryland residents did not have health care insurance in 2007-09. An estimated 9.0 per cent were living in poverty (well below the national rate of 14.3 per cent) in 2007-11.

Maryland reported 35,725 HIV/AIDS cases from the beginning of the epidemic to the end of 2008, and ranked 9th highest in terms of number of cumulative reported cases. The overall TB rate was 4.9 per 100,000 population (9th highest in the US). An estimated 65.4 per cent of adults were overweight and 27.1 per cent were obese. (Source: Center for Disease Control)

EDUCATION

Pre-school Education
Kindergarten education in Maryland is mandatory.

Primary/Secondary Education
Elementary and secondary education in Maryland is compulsory for children between the ages of 5 to 16. Maryland has 1,475 elementary and secondary schools. Enrolment for the academic year 2009-10 was 848,412 students, for whom there were 58,235 teachers. The ratio for pupils to teachers was 14.57 to one.

Total revenue for education for the year 2007-08 was $13.06 billion whilst expenditures for state education for the year reached $12.7 billion.

Higher Education
There were 62 degree granting institutions in Maryland in 2010-11, 30 of which were publicly run. The most well-known is Johns Hopkins University in Baltimore. In that period, 154,412 male students were enrolled, together with 209,081 women. 68,040 degrees/certificates were awarded, of which 29,065 were Bachelors, 16,019 were Masters and 2,665 Doctorates. (Source: NCES)

COMMUNICATIONS AND MEDIA

Newspapers
Maryland has 10 daily newspapers, including Cumberland Times-News (URL: http://www.times-news.com), The Capital (URL: http://www.hometownannapolis.com/contactcapital.html), The Star Democrat (URL: http://www.stardem.com), The Daily Times, The Herald-Mail, Baltimore Sun, Carroll County Times, Frederick News-Post, and The Prince George's Journal.
Maryland-Delaware-DC Press Association, URL: http://www.mddcpress.com

Business Journals
The Baltimore Business Journal, URL: http://www.bizjournals.com

Broadcasting
There are in the region of 14 television stations in Maryland, seven of which are based in Baltimore.
Maryland Public Television, URL: http://www.mpt.org

ENVIRONMENT

Emissions of carbon dioxide from Maryland's electricity generating industry fell to 25,659,043 metric tons, down from 29,120,746 metric tons in 2007, but rose to 26,369,386 metric tons in 2010, ranking the state 33rd in the US, and accounting for 1.1 per cent of US total, according to EIA statistics. An estimated 45,090 metric tons of of sulfur dioxide and 24,897 metric tons of nitrogen oxide were also produced.

Maryland requires motor gasoline blended with ethanol to be used across the center of the State, including the Baltimore area and the metropolitan area adjacent to Washington, DC. There were 19,887 alternative-fuelled vehicles in 2010 (2.1 per cent of the US total). Ethanol consumption was 5,714,000 in 2011 (1.9 per cent of US total). In April 2008, Maryland accelerated its existing renewable portfolio, requiring that renewable energy generate 20 per cent of the State's electricity by 2022, with 2 per cent of that from solar sources. (Source: EIA)

The Maryland Department of the Environment is concerned with issues such as recycling, maintaining the Port of Maryland, managing mining operations, controlling urban sprawl, combating pollution in the Chesapeake Bay, and cleaning up brownfield sites.

SPACE PROGRAMME

The Goddard Space Flight Center is located in Maryland. It consists of a group of leading scientists whose remit is to increase knowledge of the Earth and its environment, the solar system and the universe through observations from space.
Goddard Space Flight Center, URL: http://www.gsfc.nasa.gov/

MASSACHUSETTS

Capital: Boston (Population, Census 2010: 617,594)

Head of State: Deval Patrick (Governor) (page 1493)

State Flag: A white background bearing in the centre the Massachusetts coat of arms. The coat of arms depicts a Native American holding a bow of gold in his right hand and a an arrow of gold in his left; above his right arm is a silver five-pointed star; above the blue shield on which the Native American stands is a right arm holding a broadsword; around the bottom of the shield is a blue ribbon on which is written the words 'Ense petit placidam sub libertate quietem' ('By the sword we seek peace, but peace only under liberty').

CONSTITUTION AND GOVERNMENT

Constitution
Massachusetts was one of the original 13 states of the Union (the 6th), having joined on 6 February 1788. The Constitution of Massachusetts was ratified in 1780, nine years before that of the United States. According to the 1780 Constitution, the governor heads the executive branch of government along with five other constitutional officers: Lieutenant Governor, Attorney General, Secretary of the Commonwealth, Treasurer and Receiver General, and Auditor. All are elected for a four-year term. The Governor's Council (also known as the Executive Council) consists of the Lieutenant Governor and eight members elected from councillor districts, and is elected for a two-year term.

Massachusetts elects two Senators and 10 Representatives to the US Congress in Washington, DC.

To view the state constitution, please visit: http://www.mass.gov/legis/const.htm

Recent Events
Republican Scott Brown won a surprise victory over Democrat Martha Coakley in the race for the US Senate seat left vacant by the death of Democrat Edward Kennedy. The result robbed the Democrats of their filibuster-proof 60-seat majority in the Senate.

On April 15 2013 two bombs were detonated near the finishing line of the Boston Marathon; three people were killed and many injured. The two bombers were caught on CCTV and a huge manhunt began. The two suspects were named as Tamerlan Tsarnaev, 26 and his younger brother Dzhokhar, aged 19. Three days later following a shoot out with police Tamerlan was killed. Dzhokar was later captured alive. The brothers had come to America with their family ten years previously from Chechnya, Russia.

Legislature
Massachusetts' bicameral legislature, known as the General Court, consists of the Senate and House of Representatives. The 190th General Court runs from 2013 to 2014.

Upper House
The Senate has 40 members who are elected every two years. The Democrats hold the majority of seats in the Senate. Following the November 2012 elections, the state Senate was composed of 36 Democrats and 4 Republicans.
Senate, URL: http://www.malegislature.gov/

Lower House
The House of Representatives has 160 members who are also elected every two years. The Democrats currently hold the majority of seats in the House. Following the November 2012 elections the House is composed of 131 Democrat seats and 29 Republican seats.
House of Representatives, URL: http://www.malegislature.gov/

Executive Officers (as at March 2013)
Governor: Deval Patrick (D) (page 1493)
Lieutenant Governor: Timothy P. Murray (D)
Attorney General: Martha Coakley (D)
Secretary of the Commonwealth: William Francis Galvin (D)
Treasurer: Steven Grossman (D)
State Auditor: Suzanne M. Bump (D)

Governor's Council (as at March 2013)
Charles Cipollini (District 1); Robert Jubinville (District 2);
Marilyn Petitto Devaney (District 3); Christopher Iannella (District 4);
Eileen Duff (District 5); Terrence Kennedy (District 6);
Jennie Caissie (District 7); Michael Albano (District 8)

General Court (as at March 2013)
President of the Senate: Therese Murray (D)
Senate Majority Leader: Stanley Rosenberg (D)
Senate Minority Leader: Bruce E. Tarr (R)
Speaker of the House: Robert A. DeLeo (D)
House Majority Leader: Ronald Mariano (D)
House Minority Leader: Brad Jones, Jr. (R)

US Senators: Elizabeth Warren (D) (page 1534) and William M. Cowan (D) (page 1409)

Ministries
Office of the Governor, State House, Room 360, Boston, MA 02133, USA. Tel: +1 617 725 4005, fax: +1 617 727 9725, URL: http://www.mass.gov/

Office of the Lieutenant Governor, State House, Room 360, Boston, MA 02133, USA. Tel: +1 617 727 7200, fax: +1 617 727 9725, URL: http://www.mass.gov/
Office of the Attorney General, One Ashburton Place, 20th floor, Boston, MA 02108-1698, USA. Tel: +1 617 727 2200, URL: http://www.mass.gov/ago/
Office of the Secretary of the Commonwealth, State House, Room 337, Boston, MA 02133, USA. Tel: +1 617 727 7030, URL: http://www.sec.state.ma.us
Office of the State Auditor, State House, Room 229, Boston, MA 02133, USA. Tel: +1 617 727 2075, fax: +1 617 727 3014, URL: http://www.mass.gov/auditor/
Office of the Treasurer and Receiver General, State House, Room 227, Boston, MA 02133, USA. Tel: +1 617 367 6900, URL: http://www.mass.gov/treasury/
Department of Conservation and Recreation, 251 Causeway Street, Boston, MA 02114-2104, USA. Tel: +1 617 626 1250, fax: +1 617 626 1449, URL: http://www.mass.gov/dcr
Department of Economic Development, One Ashburton Place, Room 2101, Boston, MA 02108, USA. Tel: +1 617 788 3610, fax: +1 617 727 3605, URL: http://www.state.ma.us/econ
Department of Education, 350 Main Street, Malden, MA 02148-5023, USA. Tel: +1 781 338 3000, fax: +1 781 338 3392, URL: http://www.doe.mass.edu
Department of Energy and Environment, 251 Causeway Street, Suite 400, Boston, MA 02114-2104, USA. Tel: +1 617 626 1500, fax: +1 617 626 1505, URL: http://www.mass.gov/eea/agencies/agr/
Department of Public Health, 250 Washington Street, 2nd floor, Boston, MA 02108-4619, USA. Tel: +1 617 624 6000, fax: +1 617 624 5206, URL: http://www.mass.gov/eohhs/gov/departments/dph/
Executive Office of Transportation, 10 Park Plaza, Suite 3170, Boston, MA 02116, USA. Tel: +1 617 973 7000, fax: +1 617 523 6454, URL: http://www.massdot.state.ma.us/

Political Parties
Massachusetts Democratic Party, 56 Roland Street, North Lobby, Suite 203, Boston, MA 02129, USA. Tel: +1 617 776 2676, fax: +1 617 776 2579, URL: http://www.massdems.org/
Massachusetts Republican Party, 85 Merrimac Street, Suite 400, Boston, MA 02114, USA. Tel: +1 617 523 5005, fax: +1 617 523 6311, e-mail: info@massgop.com, URL: http://www.massgop.com

Elections
Legislative elections were last held in November 2012. In the Senate, the Democrats retained their majority : Democrats 36, Republicans 4. In the House of Representatives, they won 131 seats (up 3), whilst the Republicans won 29 seats.

Elections for Governor and State Constitutional Officers (Lieutenant Governor, Secretary of the Commonwealth, Attorney General, State Treasurer, and State Auditor) last took place in November 2010. The Democrat Deval L. Patrick, the first African-American elected governor of Massachusetts, retained his position with 49 per cent of the vote compared to 42 per cent for the Republican candidate Charlie Baker. Tim Murray was re-elected as Lt.-Governor.

In the November 2012 US Senate elections, the Democrat challenger Elizabeth Warren defeated the incumbent Republican Scott Brown. Governor Deval Patrick appointed William (Mo) Cowan as the interim senator to fill the seat vacated by Senator John Kerry (page 1456) on his appointment as Secretary of State to President Obama. Mr Cowan was later elected Senator in June 2013.

LEGAL SYSTEM

Massachusetts' court system consists of the Supreme Judicial Court, the Appeals Court, the Trial Court, the Superior Court, and District, Housing, Juvenile, Land and Probate Courts. The Supreme Judicial Court comprises a Chief Justice and six Associate Justices.

Massachusetts does not have the state death penalty. In 2007, a vote to reinstate the death penalty was defeated. According to the DPIC the current murder rate is 3.2 per 100,000.

In 2004, Massachusetts became the first U.S. state to legally recognize same-sex marriage.

Supreme Judicial Court, URL: http://www.mass.gov/courts
Chief Justice: Roderick L. Ireland
Associate Justice: Francis Spina, Robert Cordy, Ralph Gants, Margot Botsford, Fernande Duffly, Barbara Lenk
Massachusetts Appeals Court, URL: http://www.mass.gov/courts
Chief Justice of the Appeals Court: Phillip Rapoza
Chief Justice for Administration and Management of the Trial Court: Robert A. Mulligan

LOCAL GOVERNMENT

Between 1997 and 2000, the state abolished all but six of its counties. Four of these, Bristol, Dukes, Norfolk and Plymouth, are counted as county governments in census statistics. The area of Nantucket County is identical with those of the town of Nantucket. Nantucket is counted as a town government rather than as a county government. Suffolk County encompasses an area larger than the city of Boston but is substantially consolidated with the city for government purposes. The combined city and county government is counted as a municipal government. In the abolished counties, the county functions were turned over to the state. The county areas continue to serve as political districts for election purposes. There are 531 subcounty general purpose governments, of which 45 are municipal governments and 306 township governments. (Source: US Census Bureau)

AREA AND POPULATION

Area
Massachusetts is located in the north-east of the US, south of Vermont and New Hampshire, north of Connecticut and Rhode Island, and east of New York State. Its total area is 10,554.57 sq. miles, of which 7,840.02 sq. miles is land and 2,714.55 sq. miles is water.

To view a map of the state, please consult:
http://www.lib.utexas.edu/maps/us_2001/new_england_ref_2001.pdf

Population
According to the 2010 Census, the 2010 population was 6,547,629, down from the mid-2009 population estimate of 6,593,587. In 2012, the population was estimated at 6,646,144. Massachusetts' population increased by 3.1 per cent over the period 2000-10. The population is expected to reach 7.0 million by 2030. The population density is estimated at 839.4 people per sq. mile, the third most dense in the US. The capital, Boston, had an estimated population of 625,087 in 2011 and is the largest city in Massachusetts. The county with the greatest number of inhabitants is Middlesex County, with an estimated 1,503,085 in 2010, followed by Worcester County, with 798,552, and Essex County, with 743,159.

According to the 2010 Census, 5.6 per cent of the population is under 5 years, 21.7 per cent under 18 years and 13.8 per cent is aged over 65 years. Approximately 80.4 per cent of the population is white, and 6.6 per cent is black. Approximately 9.6 per cent of the population is of Hispanic or Latino origin.

Births, Marriages, Deaths
The US Census Bureau estimated that there were 72,865 births in 2010 and 52,583 deaths, giving a natural population increase of 20,282 people. Net migration amounted to some 28,132 in 2009. The infant mortality rate in 2007 was 4.9 infant deaths per 1,000 live births. Marriages and divorces in 2007 were estimated at 38,402 and 14,507, respectively.

Public Holidays
In addition to federal holidays, the people of Massachusetts celebrate Patriot's Day on the 19th April, the anniversary of the battles of Lexington and Concord.

EMPLOYMENT

Preliminary figures indicate that Massachusetts' total civilian labour force in December 2012 was 3,474,300, of which 3,240,000 were in employment and 234,300 were unemployed. The unemployment rate was 6.7 per cent, lower than the national average of 7.8 per cent. (Source: Bureau of Labor Statistics)

The following table shows provisional December 2012 non-farm wage and salary employment according to industry:

Industry	No. of Jobs	12-month change (%)
Logging and mining	1,000	-9.1
Construction	106,100	0.3
Manufacturing	254,700	-0.4
Trade, Transportation, and utilities	560,000	1.5
Information	86,200	5.1
Financial activities	206,700	0.9
Professional and business services	501,300	4.8
Educational and health services	675,500	1.1
Leisure and hospitality	314,400	2.0
Other services	123,800	0.8
Government	433,700	0.2
TOTAL	3,263,400	1.6

Source: Bureau of Labor Statistics

BANKING AND FINANCE

GDP/GNP, Inflation, National Debt
Massachusetts' Gross Domestic Product (GDP) (current dollars) rose from $365,182 million in 2009 to $378,729 million in 2010. Current dollar GDP was $391.8 billion in 2011 and ranked 12th in the US. Real GDP rose by 2.2 per cent in 2011. In 2010, Massachusetts accounted for 2.6 per cent of the US total.

Gross Domestic Product, according to industry, is shown on the following table (millions of current dollars):

Industry	2009	2010	2011
Agriculture, forestry, fishing & hunting	743	763	707
Mining	137	119	127
Utilities	5,055	5,051	4,793
Construction	11,034	10,722	11,163
Manufacturing	35,260	41,167	43,255
Wholesale Trade	18,929	19,277	20,242
Retail Trade	16,560	17,548	17,876
Transportation and warehousing	5,836	5,930	6,086
Information	17,127	18,215	19,146
Finance and insurance	35,244	38,247	38,690
Real estate, rental and leasing	52,784	50,319	50,124
Educational services	10,425	10,917	11,338
Health care & social assistance	35,805	37,884	38,980

Other non-government services	81,162	85,990	82,062
Government	34,473	35,699	37,082
TOTAL	360,574	377,846	391,771

Source: Bureau of Economic Analysis, Feb. 2013

The state average per capita personal income rose to an estimated $53,471 in 2011, 129 per cent of the national average. Per capita real GDP rose from $52,175 in 2010 to $52,195 in 2011; the US state average was $42,070.

The annual Consumer Price Index (CPI) for the Boston-Brockton-Nashua, MA-NH-ME-CT, urban area rose from 243.8 in 2011 to 247.7 in 2012 (1982-84 = 100). (Source: Bureau of Labor Statistics)

Balance of Payments / Imports and Exports
Total Massachusetts imports fell from $32,297 million in 2008 to $26,454 million in 2009, a fall of 18.1 per cent. They rose by 16.2 per cent to $30,735 million in 2010 and by 8.7 per cent in 2011 to $33,367 million. Imports from Massachusetts account for 1.5 per cent of US imports. Commodities imported include gold, light oils, electronic circuits and medical parts. Main suppliers are Canada (22.9 per cent), China (15.4 per cent), Mexico, Germany and the UK.

Total export revenue fell from $28,369 million in 2008 to $23,593 million in 2009, a 16.8 per cent decrease. Export revenue rose by 11.5 per cent to $26,304 million in 2010, amd by 5.5 per cent in 2011 to $27,761 million. The state contributed 2.1 per cent of the US 2010 total export revenue.

The following table shows the top five international merchandise export destinations according to 2010-11 revenue:

Destination	2010 $m	2011 $m	+/-% 10-11
Canada	3,242	3,797	17.1
UK	3,213	3,225	0.4
China	2,194	2,084	-5.0
Germany	1,872	2,051	9.5
Japn	2,045	2,034	-0.5

The top five export products in 2010, according to revenue, are shown on the following table:

Product	Revenue ($m)
Gold, non-monetary, unwrought, nesoi	2,063
Processors and controllers, electronic integ. circuits	970
Medical needles, catheters & parts	914
Antisera and other blood fractions, immun.	874
Medical instruments and appliances	871

Source: US Census Bureau, Foreign Trade Statistics

Gold exports rose by over 49 per cent in the 2008-09 period.

Chambers of Commerce and Trade Organisations
Cambridge Chamber of Commerce, URL: http://www.cambridgechamber.org/
Cape Cod Chamber of Commerce, URL: http://www.capecodchamber.org/
Greater Boston Chamber of Commerce, URL: http://www.gbcc.org/
Massachusetts Department of Economic Development, URL: http://www.state.ma.us/econ

MANUFACTURING, MINING AND SERVICES

Primary and Extractive Industries
The mining industry contributed an estimated $127 million towards Massachusetts' 2011 Gross Domestic Product (down from $391 million in 2006). The non-oil and gas sector accounted for $100 million in 2010, with the support activities contributing $18 million. (Source: BEA) Non-metallic minerals mined include: lime, clay, sand and gravel, marble, quartz, silica, granite, limestone, slate and sandstone. Lesser quantities of asbestos, alum, graphite, feldspar and peat have also been mined, as have semi-precious stone such as aquamarine, beryl, and tourmaline.

Massachusetts has no oil reserves, no oil production industry and no refineries. Petroleum consumption fell to 110.2 million barrels in 2009 (down from 125.8 million barrels in 2007), over half of which was in the form of motor gasoline (66.6 million barrels). 30 million barrels was in distillate fuel.

There are no natural gas reserves in Massachusetts. Natural gas consumption fell from 378,068 million cubic feet in 2005 to 370,789 million cubic feet in 2006, before rising to 430,284 million cu ft in 2010. Electric power generators and the residential sector are the leading consumers of natural gas; over two-fifths of households use natural gas as their primary energy source for heating.

There is one nuclear power plant, the Pilgrim, in Plymouth on Cape Cod Bay. It is a 685 net MWe boiling water reactor. Massachusetts also has several small hydroelectric facilities and is one of the Nation's leading producers of electricity from landfill gas and municipal solid waste.

Energy
Massachusetts' total energy production was 103 trillion Btu in 2010 (0.1 per cent of the US total). Massachusetts' total energy consumption was 1,426 trillion Btu in 2009, accounting for 1.5 per cent of the US. Per capita energy consumption was 216 million Btu in the same year, ranking the state 48th in the US.

UNITED STATES OF AMERICA

Massachusetts is a net importer of electricity, with natural gas as its primary energy source. Net summer capability in 2010 was 13,697 MW (1.3 per cent of US total), Net monthly (Oct.) generation in 2011 was 3,240,000 MWh (1.0 per cent of US total). Total net electricity generation in October 2012 was 2,885,000 MWh, of which natural gas-fired 2,090,000 MWh, nuclear 505,000 MWh, coal-fired 44,000 MWh, hydroelectric 69,000 MWh and other renewables 113,000 MWh.

Massachusetts is developing its renewable energy sources. The first offshore wind farm in the US has been proposed in Nantucket Sound. Massachusetts received $25 million in 2009 from the U.S. Department of Energy for the development of the Nation's first large commercial-scale Wind Technology Testing Center. (Source: EIA)

Manufacturing
Manufacturing earned the state $43,255 million in 2011 (up from $41,167 million in 2010). The top sectors in 2010 were computer and electronic products ($15,658 million), chemical manufacturing ($3,934 million) and fabricated metal products ($4,725 million).

Service Industries
The services industry is the largest contributor to Massachusetts' GDP. The top services sectors in 2011 were real estate ($50,124 million), professional and technical services ($47,793 million), finance and insurance ($38,690 million) and health care and social assistance ($38,980 million). Government revenues accounted for $37,082 million of the state GDP.

Tourism
The accommodation and food sector of the services industry contributed $11,274 million towards the GDP in 2011 (up from $10,641 million in 2010), whilst the arts and entertainment sector contributed $3,744 million (up from $3,596 million in 2010).
Massachusetts Office of Travel and Tourism, URL: http://www.massvacation.com/jsp/index.jsp

Agriculture
The agriculture, forestry and fisheries industry contributed $707 million towards the 2011 GDP (down from $763 million in 2010). The forestry, fishing and hunting services sector contributed $434 million in 2010, whilst the farms sector contributed $329 million.

According to the latest USDA Census of Agriculture, Massachusetts' farms numbered 7,700 in 2010, and covered an area of around 520,000 acres. The average size of a Massachusetts farm was 68 acres in 2010. The total market value of agricultural products sold in 2007 was $489,820,000 of which $364,481,000 was generated by crops, including nursery and greenhouse crops, and $125,338,000 was generated by livestock, poultry and products. Massachusetts' major farm products according to income are milk, nursery and greenhouse products, eggs, vegetables, cattle, hogs, sheep, cranberries and fruit. As of Jan. 2011, there were 40,000 cattle & calves and 11,000 hogs & pigs.

COMMUNICATIONS AND TRANSPORT

International Airports
Logan International Airport is located in Boston and is ranked 18th in the USA in terms of passenger numbers. In 2005, 27 million people passed through the airport. The airport processed 742 million pounds of cargo during the same year and there were 409,066 flights.
Logan International Airport, URL: http://www.massport.com/logan

Rail
The Massachusetts Bay Transportation Authority operates commuter rail services to Worcester and Providence on Rhode Island. The Authority also runs subway, bus and ferry systems in the Metro Boston area.

Ports and Harbours
Annually, the Port of Boston receives more than 62 ships calls and handles over 1.3 million tons of cargo. The Black Falcon Cruise Terminal, in the Boston Marine Industrial Park, processes more than 105,000 passengers a year.

HEALTH

The National Center for Health Statistics estimated that there were 43.4 doctors (including osteopaths) per 10,000 population in 2009, ranking the state second in the US, behind District of Columbia. The US state average was 27.4 doctors per 10,000 residents. In 2008, there were 5,442 dentists (8.4 per 10,000 population). In 2009, there were 2.3 community hospital beds per 1,000 residents (below the US average of 2.6 beds per 1,000 people), and, in 2010, there were 427 nursing homes, with 49,175 beds.

The Center for Disease Control estimated that just 5.1 per cent of the population had no health care insurance in 2007-09. In 2007, an estimated 10.7 per cent of the inhabitants were living in poverty (2007-11). Both figures were well below the US average. Massachusetts reported 21,134 HIV/AIDS cases from the beginning of the epidemic to the end of 2008, and ranked 10th highest in terms of number of reported AIDS cases. The overall TB rate was 4.0 per 100,000 population, 14th highest in the US. In 2012, an estimated 59.3 per cent of aduts were overweight and 23 per cent were obese. (Source: Center for Disease Control)

EDUCATION

Primary/Secondary Education
During the year 2009-10, 957,053 students were enrolled in the 1,886 public elementary and secondary schools in Massachusetts. There were 69,909 classroom teachers, giving a ratio of 13.69 students to one teacher.

Total revenues from education in 2007-08 were $14.6 billion, whilst current expenditures for state education amounted to $13.77 billion.

Higher Education
There were 124 institutions of Higher Education in the state for the academic year 2010-11, including Boston University and the Massachusetts Institute of Technology. In the same period, 213,725 male students were enrolled for the year, together with 283,565 women. 110,728 degrees/certificates were conferred, of which 52,223 were Bachelors, 32,136 were Masters and 7,485 were doctorates. (Source: NCES)

COMMUNICATIONS AND MEDIA

Newspapers
Massachusetts' daily newspapers include: the Boston Globe; the Boston Herald; Christian Science Monitor, Boston; The Salem Evening News; Athol Daily News; The Berkshire Eagle, Pittsfield; The Gloucester Daily Times; The Sun Chronicle, Attleboro; Cape Cod Times, Hyannis; and The Eagle-Tribune, Lawrence.
New England Newspaper Association, URL: http://www.nenews.org/
New England Press Association, URL: http://www.nepa.org/
The Boston Globe, URL: http://www.boston.com/globe/

Broadcasting
The state has six television stations in Boston: three in Springfield and one in Needham.

ENVIRONMENT

Emissions of carbon dioxide from Massachusetts' electricity generating industry in 2009 fell to 19,683,325 metric tons (down from 22,247,982 metric tons in 2007), before rising to 20,291,010 metric tons, ranking the state 36th in the USA. Approximately 34,938 metric tons of sulfur dioxide and 17,308 metric tons of nitrogen oxide are also emitted. Coal accounts for a quarter of all electricity generation. A 420-MW wind power project in Nantucket Sound has been proposed; this would be the first offshore wind farm in the USA.

As of 2010, there were 9,154 alternative-fueled vehicles in use. Ethanol consumption stood at an estimated 6,546,000 barrels (2.1 per cent of US total) in 2010. (Source: EIA)

MICHIGAN

Capital: Lansing (Population, Census 2010: 114,297)

Head of State: Rick Snyder (R) (Governor) (page 1517)

State Flag: A field of blue in the centre of which is the state coat of arms. The coat of arms depicts, at the top, an eagle holding an olive branch and arrows, in the centre, a shield depicting a man standing on a grass peninsula; the shield is supported by an elk and a moose; three mottos are inscribed on the coat of arms - E Pluribus Unum (From Many, One), Tuebor (I Will Defend), and Si Quaeris Peninsulam Amoenam Circumspice (If You Seek a Pleasant Peninsula, Look About You).

CONSTITUTION AND GOVERNMENT

Constitution
Michigan entered the Union on 26 January 1837. Four constitutions have since been adopted: 1835, 1850, 1908, and 1963. The most recent constitution became effective on 1 January 1964, and has been amended 17 times. According to the 1963 constitution the governor heads the executive branch of government assisted by three other elected officials: lieutenant governor, secretary of state, and attorney general. Executive branch officials are elected for four-year terms each alternate even-numbered year.

Michigan sends two Senators and 15 Representatives to the US Congress in Washington, DC.

Legislature
Michigan's legislature consists of the Senate and the House of Representatives. To view the state constitution, please visit: http://www.legislature.mi.gov/documents/historical/miconstitution1850.htm

Upper House
The Senate has 38 members who are elected for four-year terms, running parallel with the governor's term of office. Each Senator represents approximately 212,000 to 263,000 people. The Lieutenant Governor also acts as the President of the Senate. Following the November 2010 elections, the Senate is composed of 26 Republican seats and 12 Democrat seats.
Senate, Post Office Box 30036, Lansing, MI 48909-7536, USA. Tel: +1 517 373 2400 (Secretary), URL: http://senate.michigan.gov/

Lower House

The House of Representatives has 110 members (one for each of Michigan's districts), elected in even-numbered years for two-year terms. Each member of the House represents approximately 77,000 to 91,000 people. Each of the House of Representatives' sessions last for two years. The Speaker of the House is elected by members of the majority party. Following the November 2012 elections, the House is composed of 51 Democrats and 59 Republicans. **House of Representatives**, House Office Building, 124 N. Capitol Avenue, Lansing, MI 48933, USA. Tel: +1 517 373 0135, +1 517 373 0135 (Clerk's Office), URL: http://house.michigan.gov/

Elected Executive Branch Officials (as at April 2013)
Governor: Rick Snyder (R) (page 1517)
Lieutenant Governor: Brian Calley (R)
Secretary of State: Ruth Johnson (R)
Attorney General: Bill Schuette (R)

Non-Elected Executive Branch Officials (as at April 2013)
Treasurer: Andy Dillon

Legislature (as at April 2013)
President of the Senate: Brian Calley (R)
President Pro Tem of the Senate: Tonya Schuitmaker (R)
Senate Majority Leader: Randy Richardville (R)
Senate Minority Leader: Gretchen Whitmer (D)
Speaker of the House: Jase Bolger (R)
House Majority Leader: Jim Stamas (R)
House Minority Leader: Tim Greimel (D)

US Senators: Debbie Stabenow (D) (page 1519) and Carl Levin (D) (page 1463)

Ministries
Office of the Governor, PO Box 30013, Lansing, Michigan 48909, USA. Tel: +1 517 373 3400, fax: +1 517 335 6863, URL: http://www.michigan.gov/synder
Office of the Lieutenant Governor, PO Box 30013, Lansing, Michigan 48909, USA. Tel: +1 517 373 6800, fax: +1 517 241 3956, URL: http://www.michigan.gov/ltgov
Office of the Attorney General, G. Mennen Williams Building, 7th Floor, 525 W. Ottawa Street, PO Box 30212, Lansing, MI 48909, USA. Tel: +1 517 373 1110, fax: +1 517 373 3042, URL: http://www.michigan.gov/ag
Office of the Secretary of State, 430 W. Allegan, Lansing, MI 48918, USA. Tel: +1 517 322 1460, fax: +1 517 373 0727, e-mail: secretary@michigan.gov, URL: http://www.michigan.gov/sos/
Department of the Treasury, Treasury Building, 430 West Allegan Street, Lansing 48922, USA. Tel: +1 517 373 3200, fax: +1 517 373 4968, e-mail: MIStatetreasurer@michigan.gov, URL: http://www.michigan.gov/treasury
Department of Agriculture, Constitution Hall, 525 West Allegan Street, Lansing, MI, USA. (Mailing address: PO Box 30017, Lansing, MI 48909) Tel: +1 517 373 1104, fax: +1 517 335 7071, e-mail: mda-info@michigan.gov, URL: http://www.michigan.gov/mdard
Department of Community Health, Lewis Cass Building, Sixth Floor, 320 South Walnut Street, Lansing, MI 48913, USA. Tel: +1 517 373 3740, URL: http://www.michigan.gov/mdch
Department of Licensing & Regulatory Affairs, URL: http://www.michigan.gov/lara
Department of Education, John A. Hannah Building, 608 West Allegan Street, PO Box 30008, Lansing, MI 48909, USA. Tel: +1 517 373 3324, URL: http://www.michigan.gov/mde
Department for Travel & Tourism, 300 N. Washington Square, Lansing, MI 48913, USA. Tel: +1 517 373 9808, URL: http://www.michigan.org/
Department of Environmental Quality, PO Box 30473, Lansing, MI 48909-7973, USA. Tel: +1 517 373 7917, URL: http://www.michigan.gov/deq
Department of Transport, State Transportation Building, 425 W. Ottawa Street, PO Box 30050, Lansing, MI 48909, USA. Tel: +1 517 373 2090, URL: http://www.michigan.gov/mdot

Political Parties
Michigan Democratic Party, 606 Townsend, Lansing, MI 48933, USA. Tel: +1 517 371 5410, fax: +1 517 371 2056, e-mail: midemparty@mi-democrats.com, URL: http://www.michigandems.com/
Michigan Republican Party, 2121 E. Grand River, Lansing, MI 48912, USA. Tel: +1 517 487 5413, fax: +1 517 487 0090, e-mail: http://www.migop.org, URL: http://www.migop.org/

Elections
Governor Jennifer Granholm (D) was ineligible for re-election in the November 2010 elections. Republican Rick Snyder enjoyed a comfortable victory with 58 per cent of the vote. Republican Brian Calley won the vote for Lieutenant Governor.

In the Senate elections of November 2010, the Republicans increased their majority by four seats (Republicans 26, Democrats 12) in the Senate. In the 2012 elections, the Republicans retained control of the House of Representatives but with a reduced majority, (Democrats 51, Republicans 59).

LEGAL SYSTEM

Michigan's highest court is the Supreme Court, followed by the Court of Appeals, the Circuit Courts, 79 Probate Courts, the Court of Claims, 101 District Courts and six municipal courts. The Supreme Court Chief Justice is chosen from the Associate Justices every two years. The six Supreme Court Associate Justices are all elected for a term of eight years by popular vote. A Court of Appeals is located in each of Michigan's four Districts, with seven Judges in each District.

Michigan does not have the death penalty. According to the DPIC, the murder rate is currently 5.7 per 100,000.

Supreme Court, URL: http://courts.michigan.gov/supremecourt/
Chief Justice: Robert P. Young, Jr
Justices: Michael Cavanagh, Marilyn Kelly, Stephen Markman, Diane Hathaway, Mary Kelly, Brian Zahra

LOCAL GOVERNMENT

Administratively, there are three levels of government: statewide, county and township. According to the 2007 US local government census, Michigan is divided into 83 county governments and 1,775 sub-county governments, of which 533 are municpal and 1,242 are townships. There are 456 special districts or authorities.

AREA AND POPULATION

Area
Michigan is located in America's Midwest, north of Indiana and Ohio, east of Wisconsin, between Lake Michigan to the west and Lake Huron and Lake Erie to the east. Michigan's total area is 96,716.11 sq. miles, of which 56,803.82 sq. miles is land and 39,912.28 sq. miles is water.

To view a map of Michigan, please consult:
http://www.lib.utexas.edu/maps/us_2001/michigan_ref_2001.pdf

Population
According to the 2010 Census Bureau put the state population at 9,883,640, down on 9,969,727 in mid-2009. In 2012, the population was estimated to be 9,883,360. Although the state has the eighth largest population in the US, over the period 2000 to 2010, the population of Michigan decreased by -0.9 per cent. Michigan's population density is 174.8 people per square mile.

Detroit, the largest city, had a 2011 population of 706,585 whilst Grand Rapids, the second largest city, had a population of 189,815 people, and the state capital Lansing had 114,605 residents. Wayne County is the largest in terms of population, with a population of 1,802,584 in 2010.

According to the 2010 Census, 6.0 per cent of the population is under 5 years, 23.7 per cent under 18 years and 13.8 per cent is aged over 65 years. Approximately 78.9 per cent of the population is white, and 14.2 per cent is black. Approximately 4.4 per cent of the population is of Hispanic or Latino origin.

Births, Marriages, Deaths
The US Census Bureau estimated that there were 114,531 births in 2010 and 88,021 deaths, giving a natural population growth of 26,510 people, down on the previous year. Emigration amounted to 71,893 people. The infant mortality rate in 2010 was 7.9 infant deaths per 1,000 live births. Marriages and divorces in 2007, according to provisional data, numbered 59,084 and 35,450 respectively.

EMPLOYMENT

Michigan's total civilian labour force in December 2012 was 4,639,500, of which 4,226,900 were employed and 412,600 were unemployed. The unemployment rate was 8.9 per cent; the average US unemployment rate was 7.8 per cent. (Source: Bureau of Labor Statistics)

Preliminary figures for December 2012 non-farm wage and salary employment, according to industry, is shown on the following table:

Industry	No. of employed	12 month change (%)
Logging and mining	7,200	-1.4
Construction	116,700	-5.4
Manufacturing	527,800	3.3
Trade, transport and utilities	721,900	-0.5
Information	52,100	-4.6
Financial activities	197,900	1.5
Professional and business svcs.	566,000	1.1
Educational and health svcs.	628,500	0.4
Leisure and hospitality	376,700	0.4
Other services	169,700	-0.4
Government	608,800	-0.6
TOTAL	3,973,300	0.3

Source: Bureau of Labor Statistics

BANKING AND FINANCE

GDP/GNP, Inflation, National Debt
Michigan's Gross Domestic Product (current dollar) rose from an estimated $368,401 million in 2009 to $384,171 million in 2010. GDP was $385.2 billion in 2011 and ranked 13th in theUS. Real GDP grew by 2.3 per cent in 2011. The largest industry was government (11.9 per cent of GDP). (Source: Bureau of Economic Analysis)

Gross Domestic Product, according to industry, is shown on the following table:

Industry	2009	2010	2011
Agriculture, forestry, fishing & hunting	2,803	3,343	4,045
Mining	930	1,016	1,293
Utilities	8,022	8,331	7,788

UNITED STATES OF AMERICA

Construction	10,358	10,155	10,852
Manufacturing	43,865	54,381	60,984
Wholesale Trade	21,041	22,008	23,579
Retail Trade	25,398	26,050	26,727
Transport and warehousing	8,580	8,972	9,523
Information	9,705	9,650	10,180
Finance and insurance	22,942	25,623	25,446
Real estate and leasing	47,552	44,760	44,842
Educational services	2,960	3,038	3,045
Health care & social assistance	33,204	34,075	35,172
Other non-government services	67,552	70,748	76,065
Government	45,933	46,224	45,707
TOTAL	350,847	368,371	385,248

Source: Bureau of Economic Analysis, Feb. 2013

The average per capita personal income in the state of Michigan rose to an estimated $36,264 in 2011, and, in 2011, per capita real GDP reached $34,166, below the US average of $42,070.

The annual Consumer Price Index (CPI) for the Detroit-Ann Arbor-Flint, MI, urban area (all items) rose from 211.8 in 2011 to 216.1 in 2012 (1982-84 = 100). (Source: Bureau of Labor Statistics)

Balance of Payments / Imports and Exports

Total Michigan imports fell from $90,151 million in 2008 to $59,748 million, a decrease of 33.7 per cent. Imports cost $88,027 million in 2010, up 47.3 per cent. They rose again in 2011, to $104,278 million (up 18.4 million per cent).Total Michigan imports rose to 4.7 per cent of total US imports (up from 3.8 per cent in 2009). Main imports include vehicle parts and crude oil. Main suppliers include Canada (44.7 per cent), Mexico (31.6 per cent), China (5.5 per cent), Japan and Germany.

Export revenue fell from $45,136 million in 2008 to $32,655 million in 2009, a decrease of 27.7 per cent. Exports rose to $44,768 million in 2010, up 37 per cent. In 2011, exports grew by a further 13.9 per cent to $51,003 million.Michigan exports comprised 3.4 per cent of total US export revenue in 2011.

The top five products exported from Michigan in 2010 are shown on the following table:

Product	$m
Passenger vehicles, spk-ignt., Int.Com. Rcpr. P-engine exceeding 3000 cc	3,918
Motor vehicles trans gds, spk-ig. in c.p. eng	3,740
Parts and accessories of bodies of motor vehicles	2,703
Gear boxes for motor vehicles	1,728
Passenger vehicles, spk-ignt., Int.Com. Rcpr. P-engine exceeding 1500 cc	1,457
Gear boxes for motor vehicles	1,308

Source: US Census Bureau, Foreign Trade Statistics

The following table shows 2010-11 merchandise export revenue according to the top five international destinations ($m):

Destination	2010 ($m)	2011 ($m)	+/-%
Canada	22,088	23,578	6.7
Mexico	7,424	8,965	20.7
China	2,181	1,799	23.2
Germany	1,530	1,337	17.6
Japan	1,240	1,160	7.8

Source: US Census Bureau

Chambers of Commerce and Trade Organisations
Michigan Economic Development Corporation, URL: http://medc.michigan.org/
Ann Arbor Area Chamber of Commerce, URL: http://www.annarborchamber.org/
Detroit Regional Chamber, URL: http://www.detroitchamber.com/

MANUFACTURING, MINING AND SERVICES

Primary and Extractive Industries
Mining contributed an estimated $1,293 million towards the state Gross Domestic Product in 2011, up from $1,016 million in 2010. In 2010 the oil and gas sector contributed $125 million, the non-oil and gas sector $707 million, and the support activities sector $184 million.

Fields for extraction of both oil and gas are located in 61 of Michigan's 83 counties.

Michigan's proven oil reserves were 40 million barrels in 2010. From 3,800 producing oil wells and two rotary rigs around 6,438,000 barrels of oil were produced in 2011. Monthly crude oil production was 580,000 barrels in Oct. 2012. Crude oil refinery capacity was 106,000 bbl/d in 2012. Total petroleum consumption in the same year reached 163.6 million barrels, of which 108.9 million was in the form of motor gasoline (3.3 per cent of the US total).

In 2010, Michigan had proven reserves of 2,919 billion cubic feet of dry natural gas and 48 million barrels of natural gas plant liquids. There were some 11,100 gas wells in operation in 2011. Marketed production of natural gas was 138,162 million cubic feet in 2011. Michigan's natural gas consumption is high, at 746,754 million cubic feet in 2010 (3.5 per cent of US total). The residential sector was the greatest consumer; almost four-fifths of households use natural gas as their primary energy source for heating.

Michigan currently has several ethanol and biodiesel production plants in operation, with many more plants currently under construction or planned. (Source: EIA)

Energy
Total energy production was 657 trillion Btu in 2010. Net summer capability in 2010 was 29,831 MW (2.9 per cent of US total). Net monthly generation in Oct. 2012 was 8,365,000 MWh (2.7 per cent of US total), of which 4,222,000 MWh was coal-fired and 2,712,000 MWh was nuclear generated, 1,020,000 MWh was natural-gas fired, 14,000 MWh was petroleum-fired, 66,000 MWh was hydroelectric and other renewable 317,000 MWh. Much of its coal is imported from Wyoming. Biomass from Michigan's 19 million acres of forest provided fuel for 54 per cent of the state's renewable net electricity generation in 2011.

Total energy consumption in Michigan in 2010 was 2,798 trillion Btu (2.9 per cent of US total), with per capita energy consumption 283 million Btu (35th in the US).

Michigan has three nuclear power reactors: Donald C. Cook, a two-unit 1,000 net MWe plant located in Berrion County; the 760 net MWe Palisades plant, located on the eastern shore of Lake Michigan and the 1,101 net MWe Enrico Fermi plant on the shore of Lake Erie 30 miles south west of Detroit. (Source: EIA)

Manufacturing
Michigan, known mainly for its car industry in Detroit, leads the US in automobile manufacturing. As well as transport, the state manufactures non-electric machinery, furniture and appliances, cereal, baby food, chemicals, pharmaceuticals and lumber.

Manufacturing continues to be Michigan's second largest contributor towards Gross Domestic Product, though the sector has seen significant contractions over the past few years. Manufacturing contributed $60,984 million in 2011, up from $54,381 million in 2010. The largest sector in 2010 was motor vehicle, body trailer, and parts manufacturing ($14,788 million). Other sectors of economic significance in 2010 were fabricated metal products ($5,839 million), machinery ($6,003 million), and food, beverage and tobacco products ($5,079 million).

Service Industries
The services industry is Michigan's largest contributor towards GDP. The largest sectors in 2011 were real estate ($44,842 million), professional and technical services ($30,586 million) and health services ($35,172 million). The financial sector rose slightly $25,446 million in 2011. Government revenue contributed an estimated $45,707 million to state GDP.

Tourism
Tourism is a significant industry in Michigan. Major tourist attractions include the Henry Ford Museum, Detroit's car plants, Cranbrook, the State Capitol, the Straits area, Isle Royale, the Porcupine Mountains, Pictured Rocks and Tahquamenon Falls. The arts, entertainment and recreation sector of the services industry contributed $2,932 million towards the 2010 GDP, whilst the accommodation and food sector contributed $10,580 million.

Agriculture
The agriculture industry contributed an estimated $4,045 million towards the state 2011 GDP, down from $3,343 million in 2010 when farming earned $3,007 million and forestry, fishing and related activities saw revenues of $336 million.

According to estimates by the National Agricultural Statistics Service, Michigan had around 54,800 farms in 2009, and farmland covered 10,000,000 acres. The average size of a farm in 2009 was 182 acres, two acres smaller than in the previous year.

More than 50 major commercial crops are produced each season in Michigan. In addition, the state ranks first nationally in the production of blueberries, red tart cherries, dry beans, pickling cucumbers and potted geraniums. Major crops include oats, corn, rye, hay, potatoes, sugarbeets and soybeans. In addition, it produces apples, plums, peaches, grapes, sweet cherries, mushrooms, processing vegetables, potted Easter lilies and spearmint. Michigan's livestock and poultry industry accounts for just under 50 percent of total cash receipts from farming. In 2009, total cash receipts from agricultural produce were $5.58 billion; of this, livestock and products earned $1.9 billion, whilst crops earned $3.67 billion. In 2010, there were an estimated 1.1 million cattle and calves, 80,000 sheep and 1 million hogs and pigs.

Forests cover 49 per cent (19.3 million acres) of Michigan's total land base. These vast forests - two-thirds of which are birch, aspen and oak - provide Michigan with the largest state-owned forest system in the nation. The total timberland, or forest land capable of producing commercial timber, covers 95 per cent of Michigan total forested lands. Michigan has the fifth largest timberland acreage in the continental United States. Michigan's forests contribute significantly to the state's economy. The wood products industry provides 75 per cent of the economic value of the forests while forest-based tourism and recreation make up the remaining 25 per cent.

Michigan borders four of the five Great Lakes, which collectively comprise the largest body of fresh water in the world. In addition, Michigan has over 10,000 inland lakes, and 36,000 miles of rivers and streams. Approximately 1.6 million individuals, including nearly 400,000 non-residents, purchase licences to sport fish in Michigan each year. Anglers under the age of 17, who fish for free, increase the total number of anglers in the state to 2 million. About one-third of Michigan anglers fish on the Great Lakes, while 45 per cent fish inland lakes and 20 per cent fish rivers and streams. Each year Michigan commercial fishermen catch nearly 16 million pounds of fish from the Great Lakes, whitefish accounting for approximately 75 per cent of the total landed value. Native Americans, fishing under federal treaty rights, produce 50 per cent of the catch, by weight, and 55 per cent of the landed value.

COMMUNICATIONS AND TRANSPORT

International Airports
Michigan has a number of international airports including: Kent County International Airport, Kalamazoo-Battle Creek International Airport, Detroit Metropolitan Airport and Oakland County International Airport. The state also has 19 commercial airports and approximately 240 public use airports.

Detroit Metropolitan Airport, URL: http://www.metroairport.com/
Kalamazoo - Battle Creek International Airport, URL: http://www.azoairport.com/
Oakland County International Airport, URL: http://www.oakgov.com/aviation/

Railways
Michigan's railway network is served by six of the nation's largest rail carriers and several short line railroad companies. These rail lines link Michigan with all the major US rail switching yards and with Canada via the Canadian National Railroad Tunnel as well as the Canadian National/Canadian Pacific Railroad Tunnel. The State of Michigan has an extensive rail freight system.

Roads
Michigan has a total of 119,160 miles of roads, of which 9,629 miles are state trunkline, 26,427 miles are county primary roads, 62,700 miles are county local roads, 5,939 miles are city major roads and 14,462 miles are city local roads.

HEALTH

The National Center for Health Statistics estimated that there were 29.2 doctors per 10,000 population in 2009, slightly above the US average of 27.4. In 2008, there were 6,060 dentists (6.1 per 10,000 population). In 2009, there were 2.6 community hospital beds per 1,000 residents, and, in 2010, 428 nursing homes with 47,054 beds.

According to the Center for Disease Control, in 2007-09, 12.8 per cent of the Michigan population had no health-care cover. An estimated 10.7 per cent were living in poverty in 2007-11 (compared to US rate of 14.3 per cent). Michigan reported 16,866 HIV/AIDS cases from the beginning of the epidemic to the end of 2008, and ranked 15th highest nationally in the cumulative number of reported cases. The overall TB rate was 1.9 per 100,000 population, 35th highest in the US. As of 2012, the obesity rate was 66.1 per cent of adults were overweight and 30.9 per cent considered obese. (Source: CDC, 2013)

EDUCATION

Primary/Secondary Education
In the year 2009-10 there were 4,192 primary and elementary schools in Michigan. Enrolment for the year stood at 1,649,082 students and there were 92,621 teachers, giving Michigan a ratio of 17.79 students per teacher, above the US average of 15.38 pupils per teacher.

Revenues from education reached approximately $19.6 billion, whilst current expenditures for state education over the year 2007-08 were $19.7 billion.

Higher Education
Michigan had 107 degree-conferring institutions in the year 2010-11, 45 of which were public. In the same year, enrolment stood at 299,714 male students and 386,335 women. 56,061 Bachelor degrees were conferred during the year, together with 21,726 Masters and 5,589 Doctorates. (Source: NCES)

COMMUNICATIONS AND MEDIA

Newspapers
Michigan's newspapers include the Detroit Free Press, the Detroit News, the Huron Daily Tribune, Grand Rapids Press, the Daily News and the Daily Press.
Michigan Press Association, URL: www.michiganpress.org/
Detroit News, URL: http://www.detnews.com

Broadcasting
The Michigan Association of Broadcasters ranks among its membership 150 radio stations, including AM & FM stations, and 35 television stations. Detroit, Flint and Grand Rapids are among the largest markets.

ENVIRONMENT

Michigan's electricity industry is primarily reliant on coal as a generating fuel. For its 2010 emissions of carbon dioxide, Michigan was ranked 11th; emissions reached 74,749,744 metric tons, around 3.1 per cent of the US total. An estimated 253,812 metric tons of sulfur dioxide were also produced and 88,864 metric tons of nitrogen oxide were emitted, 4.7 per cent and 3.6 per cent of the US total respectively.

Michigan had five ethanol production plants in operation in 2012. As of 2011, ethanol plant capacity amounted to 265 million gal/year, accounting for 2.0 per cent of total US ethanol capacity. In 2010, there were 24,408 alternative-fueled vehicles in use and ethanol consumption was 10,876,000 barrels (3.5 per cent of US total).

Michigan adopted an Integrated Renewable Portfolio Standard (RPS) of 10 per cent by 2015, and the State allows for the authorisation of up to 15 Renewable Energy Renaissance Zones, which offer tax incentives to promote the development of renewable energy facilities. (Source: EIA)

MINNESOTA

Capital: St. Paul (Population, Census 2010: 285,068)

Head of State: Mark Dayton (Governor) (D) (page 1413)

State Flag: A royal blue background bordered with a gold fringe. In the centre of the flag is the state seal: a farmer ploughing a field near the Mississippi River looks at a Native American on horseback. The motto 'L'Etoile du Nord' (Star of the North) appears on the seal. Around the seal is a wreath of lady slippers surrounded by nineteen stars.

CONSTITUTION AND GOVERNMENT

Constitution
Minnesota entered the Union on 11 May 1858. The state constitution was adopted on 13 October 1857, and was generally revised on 5 November 1974. Further amendments were added in 1974, 1980, 1982, 1984, 1988, 1990, 1996 and 1998. Under the terms of the constitution four elected officials assist the governor within the state executive branch: lieutenant governor, secretary of state, attorney general, and state auditor. Minnesota's elected executive officials all serve terms of four years. The position of state treasurer was abolished by Constitutional Amendment with effect from 6 January 2003. The duties of the state treasurer were transferred to the commissioner of finance.

Minnesota elects two Senators and eight Representatives to the US Congress in Washington, DC.

To consult the state constitution, please visit:
http://www.house.leg.state.mn.us/CCO/RULES/MNCON/preamble.htm

Legislature
Minnesota's bicameral legislature consists of the Senate and the House of Representatives.

Upper House
The Senate has 67 members, one representing each of Minnesota's Senate districts. Senators usually serve terms of four years, apart from election years ending in zero when they serve terms of two years to accommodate the US census process of re-districting. Following the November 2012 elections, the Democrats now hold the majority in the Senate. The Senate is now composed as follows: 39 Democrats, 28 Republicans.

Minnesota Senate, State Capitol Building, 75 Rev. Dr. Martin Luther King Jr. Blvd., St. Paul, MN 55155-1606, USA. Tel: +1 651 296 0504, URL: http://www.senate.leg.state.mn.us/

Lower House
The House of Representatives has 134 members, two for each of the Senate districts, elected for two years. Each member of the House represents about 32,650 constituents. The Republicans currently hold the majority of seats. Following the November 2012 elections, the House is divided as follows: 73 Democrats, 61 Republicans.
Minnesota House of Representatives, 100 Rev. Dr. Martin Luther King Jr. Blvd., Saint Paul, MN 55155, USA. Tel: +1 651 296 2146,
URL: http://www.house.leg.state.mn.us/

Elected Executive Branch Officials (as at April 2013)
Governor: Mark Dayton (DFL)
Lieutenant Governor: Yvonne Prettner Solon (DFL)
Secretary of State: Mark Ritchie (DFL)
Attorney General: Lori Swanson (DFL)
State Auditor: Rebecca Otto (DFL)

Legislature (as at April 2013)
President of the Senate: Sandra L. Pappas (DFL)
Senate Majority Leader: Thomas M. Bakk (DFL)
Senate Minority Leader: David W. Hann (R)
Speaker of the House: Paul Thissen (DFL)
House Majority Leader: Erin Murphy (DFL)
House Minority Leader: Kurt Daudt (R)

US Senators: Amy Klobuchar (D) (page 1457)and Alan (Al) Franken (D) (page 1427)

Ministries
Office of the Governor, 130 State Capitol, 75 Rev. Dr. Martin Luther King Jr. Blvd., St. Paul, MN 55155, USA. Tel: +1 651 296 3391, fax: +1 651 296 2089, URL: http://www.governor.state.mn.us/
Office of the Lieutenant Governor, 130 State Capitol, 75 Rev. Dr. Martin Luther King Jr. Blvd., St. Paul, MN 55155, USA. Tel: +1 651 296 3391, fax: +1 651 296 2089, URL: http://mn.gov/governor/dayton/lt-governor/prettner-solon.jsp

UNITED STATES OF AMERICA

Attorney General's Office, 1400 NCL Tower, 445 Minnesota Street, St. Paul, MN 55101, USA. Tel: +1 651 296 3353, e-mail: attorney.general@state.mn.us, URL: http://www.ag.state.mn.us/

Office of the State Auditor, 525 Park Street, Suite 500, Saint Paul, Minnesota 55103, USA. Tel: +1 651 296 2551, fax: +1 651 296 4755, e-mail: stateauditor@osa.state.mn.us, URL: http://www.auditor.state.mn.us/

Office of the Secretary of State, 180 State Office Building, 100 Rev. Dr. Martin Luther King Jr. Blvd., St. Paul, MN 55155, USA. Tel: +1 651 296 2803, fax: +1 651 297 7067, e-mail: secretary.state@state.mn.us, URL: http://www.sos.state.mn.us

Department of Agriculture, 90 West Plato Boulevard, Saint Paul, Minnesota 55107, USA. Tel: +1 651 297 2200, URL: http://www.mda.state.mn.us

Department of Commerce, 85 7th Place East, Suite 500, St. Paul, MN 55101, USA. Tel: +1 651 296 4026, fax: +1 651 297 1959, e-mail: general.commerce@state.mn.us, URL: http://www.commerce.state.mn.us

Department of Education1500 Highway 36 West, Roseville, Minnesota 55113-4266. Tel: +1 651 582 8200, URL: http://www.education.state.mn.us

Department of Employment and Economic Development, 1st National Bank Building, Suite E200, 332 Minnesota Street, St. Paul, MN 55101, USA. Tel: +1 651 297 1291, e-mail: mdes.customerservice@state.mn.us, URL: http://www.deed.sttte.mn.us

Department of Finance, 658 Cedar Street, 400 Centennial Office Building, St. Paul, MN 55155, USA. Tel: +1 651 296 5900, fax: +1 651 296 8685, URL: http://www.finance.state.mn.us

Department of Health, PO Box 64975, St. Paul, MN, 55164-0975, USA. Tel: +1 651 215 5800, URL: http://www.health.state.mn.us

Department of Labour and Industry, 443 Lafayette Road N., St. Paul, MN 55155, USA. Tel: +1 651 284 5000, e-mail: DLI.Communications@state.mn.us, URL: http://www.doli.state.mn.us

Department of Natural Resources, DNR Information Center, 500 Lafayette Road, St. Paul, MN 55155-4040, USA. Telephone: +1 651 296 6157, e-mail: info@dnr.state.mn.us, URL: http://www.dnr.state.mn.us/index.html

Department of Trade and Economic Development, 500 Metro Square Building, 121 East 7th Place, St. Paul, MN 55101-2146, USA. Tel: +1 651 297 1291, fax: +1 651 296 1290, e-mail: dted@state.mn.us, URL: http://www.dted.state.mn.us

Department of Transport, Transportation Building, 395 John Ireland Boulevard, St. Paul, MN 55155, USA. Tel: +1 651 296 3000, e-mail: info@dot.state.mn.us, URL: http://www.dot.state.mn.us

Political Parties
Republican Party of Minnesota, 525 Park Street, Suite 250, St Paul, MN 55103, USA. Tel: +1 651 222 0022, fax: +1 651 224 4122, e-mail: info@mngop.com, URL: http://www.mngop.com/

Minnesota Democratic-Farmer-Labor Party, 255 E Plato Blvd., St. Paul, MN 55107, USA. Tel: +1 651 251 6300, fax: +1 651 251 6325, e-mail: dfl@dfl.org, URL: http://www.dfl.org

Elections
The last elections for the state's constitutional offices were held in November 2010; the incumbent governor Mr Pawlenty did not run for re-election. The contenders were Democrat Mark Dayton, Republican Tom Emmer and Independent Tom Horner. The contest was narrowly won by Mark Dayton.

Following the November 2012 legislative elections, in the Senate the Democrats took control of the House with 39 seats and the Republicans won 28. In the state House of Representatives the Democrats also gained the majority of seats (Democrats 73, Republicans 61). All seats were up for election.

LEGAL SYSTEM

Minnesota's court system has three levels: the Supreme Court, the Court of Appeals, and the trial courts (one in each county). Minnesota's highest state court is the Supreme Court, consisting of the Chief Justice and six Associate Justices, all elected for a term of six years by popular vote. The Court of Appeals' 19 judges consider decisions by the trial courts, which exist in each of Minnesota's 87 counties. A total of 289 judges serve in the trial courts. The 289 district court judges are appointed by the governor and are re-elected to six-year terms on a non-partisan ballot.

Minnesota does not have the death penalty.

Supreme Court: URL: http://www.courts.state.mn.us
Chief Justice: Lorie Skjerven Gildea
Justices: Alan Page, Paul Anderson, Barry Anderson, Christopher Dietzen, David Stras, Wilhelmina Wright
Court of Appeals
Chief Justice: Judge Matthew Johnson

LOCAL GOVERNMENT

For administrative purposes, Minnesota has 87 county governments and 2,647 subcounty general purpose governments. The subcounty governments consist of 854 municipal (city) governments and 1,793 township or town governments. Some actions in the Twin Cities metropolitan area are coordinated by the Metropolitan Council.

Association of Minnesota Counties, URL: http://www.mncounties.org

AREA AND POPULATION

Area
Minnesota borders Canada to the north, Iowa to the south, North Dakota and South Dakota to the west, and Wisconsin to the east. Minnesota's total area is 86,938.87 sq. miles, of which 79,610.08 sq. miles is land and 7,328.79 sq. miles is water. Minnesota's Northwest Angle in Lake of the Woods is the only part of the US states (apart from Alaska) lying north of the 49th Parallel. The state is known as the Land of 10,000 Lakes.

To view a map of the state, please consult:
http://www.lib.utexas.edu/maps/us_2001/minnesota_ref_2001.pdf

Population
According to the 2010 Census the 2010 population of Minnesota was 5,303,925, up on the mid-2009 population estimate of 5,266,214. In 2012, the population was estimated to be 5,379,139. The population grew by 7.8 per cent over the period 2000-10 and is expected to reach 6.3 million by 2030. The population density is around 66.6 people per square mile. The largest county is Hennepin County, with a population estimate of 1,152,425 in 2010. In 2010, the capital, St. Paul, had an estimated population of 285,068 and its 'twin' city of Minneapolis had a population of 382,578. Minnesota's other major cities include: Rochester (106,769), Duluth (86,265) and Bloomington (82,893).

Minnesota is home to a number of Native American communities: seven Anishinaabe (Chippewa, Ojibwe) reservations and four Dakota (Sioux) communities.

According to the 2010 Census, 6.7 per cent of the population is under 5 years, 24.2 per cent under 18 years and 12.9 per cent is aged over 65 years. Approximately 85.3 per cent of the population is white, and 5.2 per cent is black. An estimated 1.1 per cent of the population is American Indian and 4.0 per cent Asian. Approximately 4.7 per cent of the population is of Hispanic or Latino origin.

Births, Marriages, Deaths
The US Census Bureau estimated that there were 68,610 births in 2010 whilst deaths numbered 38,972, giving a natural population growth of 29,638. Net migration amounted to 1,253 people in 2009. The infant mortality rate in 2010 was 5.6 infant deaths per 1,000 live births. There were 29,803 marriages in 2007, according to provisional data.

EMPLOYMENT

Of Minnesota's estimated December 2012 civilian labour force of 2,976,100, the number employed stood at 2,811,300, whilst the number of unemployed was recorded as 164,800. The unemployment rate was 5.5 per cent, below the US average rate of 8.3 per cent.

Preliminary Employment according to industry, December 2012

Industry	No. of employed	12 month change (%)
Logging and mining	6,600	-1.5
Construction	92,800	3.9
Manufacturing	305,000	0.9
Trade, transport and utilities	503,200	1.4
Information	54,100	3.4
Financial activities	178,000	1.8
Professional and business svcs.	339,700	0.5
Educational and health svcs.	494,500	4.9
Leisure and hospitality	231,800	1.4
Other services	118,400	1.8
Government	411,100	0.9
Total non-farm employment	2,735,200	1.9

Source: Bureau of Labor Statistics

BANKING AND FINANCE

GDP/GNP, Inflation, National Debt
Minnesota's total Gross Domestic Product (current dollars) rose from $260,692 million in 2009 to $270,039 million in 2010. In 2011, it was put at $281.7 billion and ranked 16th in the US. Real GDP increased by 3.2 per cent in 2010 and by 1.5 per cent in 2011.

Gross State Product according to industry

Industry	2009	2010	2011
Agriculture, forestry, fishing & hunting	5,341	6,925	8,206
Mining	329	690	936
Utilities	4,157	4,470	4,359
Construction	9,481	8,952	9,531
Manufacturing	31,889	36,830	39,958
Wholesale Trade	16,637	17,351	18,366
Retail Trade	14,054	14,767	15,270
Transportation and warehousing	7,032	7,164	7,505
Information	9,388	9,291	10,106
Finance and insurance	25,100	27,334	28,425
Real estate	33,986	32,105	32,001
Educational services	2,632	2,717	2,827
Health care & social asistance	23,563	24,708	25,031
Other non-government Services	45,673	43,957	49,755

- continued

Government	28,127	27,823	27,436
TOTAL	257,479	270,792	281,712

Source: US Bureau of Economic Analysis, Feb. 2013

Average annual per capita income in the state was $44,560 in 2011, 107 per cent of the national average. In 2011, per capita real GDP was $45,822, compared to the US figure of $42,070.

The annual Consumer Price Index (CPI) for the Minneapolis-St. Paul, MN-WI, urban area (all items) rose from 219.3 in 2011 to 224.5 in 2012 (1982-84=100). (Source: Bureau of Labor Statistics)

Balance of Payments / Imports and Exports
Total Minnesota imports cost $21,192 million in 2009, down 35.9 per cent from $33,036 million in 2008. Imports rose to $26,264 million in 2010, up 23.9 per cent. They rose a further 25.7 per cent in 2011, to $33,124 million. Total Minnesota imports represent 1.5 per cent of US total. Imports include oil, gas, reception appartus for television, medical equipment and clothing. Top suppliers include Canada (39.6 per cent), China (29.1 per cent), Mexico, Germany and Ireland.

Merchandise export revenue fell from $19,186 million in 2008 to $15,532 million in 2009, a decrease of 19 per cent. Exports rose to $18,904 million in 2010, up 21.7 per cent. They rose again in 2011 to $20,319 million, up 7.5 per cent. Minnesota's exports account for 1.4 per cent of the US total.

The top five international export trading partners in 2010-11 are shown on the following table:

Country	2010 ($m)	2011 ($m)	+/- %
Canada	5,429	5,866	8.1
China	1,572	1,310	22.8
Japan	1,133	1,216	15.6
Mexico	977	734	24.4
Germany	782	702	-6.1

Source: US Census Bureau

The top five export products in 2010, according to revenue, are shown on the following table:

Product	$m
Agglomerated iron ores	567
Parts & accessories for ADP machines & units	528
Medical needles, nesoi, catheters etc	449
Civilian aircraft, engines and parts	448
Motor vehicles, trans gds, spl ig in cp eng, gvw nov 5 mtn	436

Source: US Census Bureau

Chambers of Commerce and Trade Organisations
Department of Commerce, URL: http://mn.gov/commerce
Minnesota State Chamber of Commerce, URL: http://www.mnchamber.com
Saint Paul Area Chamber of Commerce, URL: http://www.saintpaulchamber.com/

MANUFACTURING, MINING AND SERVICES

Primary and Extractive Industries
The mining industry contributed $936 million towards the state's 2011 Gross Domestic Product, up from $690 million in 2010. Non-oil and gas mining contributed most towards the GDP in 2010 at $666 million.

Minnesota's main mining industry is iron ore extraction. Currently, the state produces around 47.5 million tons - over 75 per cent of total iron ore production in the US.

Minnesota has no oil industry of its own and imports all its requirements. Total petroleum consumption in 2009 fell to 117.2 million barrels - 61.2 million barrels in the form of motor gasoline and 23.7 million barrels as distillate fuel. Crude oil refinery capacity was 351,200 bbl/d in 2012 (2 per cent of US total).

Minnesota encourages ethanol production and consumption. It is the only state that requires the use of oxygenated motor gasoline blended with 10 per cent ethanol, and also encourages the use of E85 (85 per cent ethanol with 15 per cent gasoline). Minnesota is among the US top producers of ethanol, with over a dozen corn-based production plants.

Minnesota has no producing natural gas industry and relies on imports. Natural gas consumption was 422,969 million cu ft (1.8 per cent of US total). The residential sector is Minnesota's largest natural gas consumer, accounting for nearly two-fifths of consumption. Over two-thirds of households use natural gas as their primary heating fuel during the cold winters. (Source: EIA)

Energy
Minnesota's total energy production was 429 trillion Btu in 2010 (0.6 per cent of US total). Minnesota's total energy consumption in 2010 was 1,867 trillion Btu (1.9 per cent of US total). Per capita energy consumption in the same year was 352 million Btu, ranking the state 20th in the US despite its cold climate.

Net summer capability in 2010 was 14,715 MW (1.4 per cent of US total). Net monthly generation in October 2012 was 4,339,000 MWh (1.4 per cent of US total). Of that total, coal contributed 2,011,000 MWh, nuclear power 1,104,000 MWh, natural gas 240,000 MWh, hydroelectric NW, other renewables 915,000 MWh (4.8 per cent of US total) and petroleum 2,000 MWh. Minnesota has many wind farms and ranks among the leading states in wind power generation. It generated 6.8 million MWh in 2011, an increase of 42 per cent from 2010. The State also generates electricity using conventional hydroelectric dams. (Source: EIA)

Manufacturing
Manufacturing is Minnesota's second largest contributor to GDP, accounting for an estimated $39,958 million in 2011 (up from $36,830 million in 2010). Major manufacturing sectors in 2010 were: fabricated metal products ($3,574 million), computer and electronic products ($6,766 million) and food products ($4,190 million).

Although many of Minnesota's industries are still based on local natural resources - agriculture, food processing, lumber and wood products, tourism - new industries have arisen to fill the needs of a modern economy. Computer equipment, computer-based business services, printing and publishing, health care and other professional services have become the fastest growing sectors of the Minnesota economy.

Service Industries
Services is Minnesota's largest contributor to GDP. The top sectors in 2011 were real estate ($32,001 million), finance and insurance ($28,425 million) and health services ($25,031 million). Professional and technical services contributed $17,996 million to state GDP, and government accounted for $27,436 million.

Tourism
Recent statistics show that Minnesota has an annual number of visitors of just under 26 million. The arts and entertainment sector of the services industry contributed $2,820 million in 2011 whilst the accommodation and food sector contributed $6,936 million.

Agriculture
Agriculture and forestry are also major industries, contributing an estimated $8,206 million towards Minnesota's 2011 GDP (up from $6,925 million in 2010). The farms sector accounted for $6,608 million in 2010, and the forestry, fishing and related activities services sector accounted for $318 million. (Source: BEA)

According to National Agricultural Statistics Service estimates, Minnesota's farms numbered 81,000 in 2010, and covered a land area of 26,900,000 acres. The average size of a farm was 332 acres (down from 346 in 2006). Total market value of agricultural products sold in 2007 was $13 billion - crops accounting for $7 billion and livestock earning some $6 billion. Major agricultural products sold are: corn; soybeans; dairy products; hogs; cattle and calves; turkeys; vegetables, fruit and other crops; wheat; sugar beet; poultry and eggs; grain and oil crops; other livestock and products. As of Jan. 2011, there were 2.38 million cattle and calves, 7.7 million hogs and pigs and 130,000 sheep.

COMMUNICATIONS AND TRANSPORT

National Airlines
Northwest Airlines, URL: http://www.nwa.com

International Airports
Minneapolis-St. Paul (MSP) International Airport is the 8th busiest in the world, providing around 532,240 flights in 2005. MSP is ranked 9th in the states in terms of passenger traffic, transporting some 37.7 million passengers in 2005, an increase of 2.6 on the figure for 2004. More than 251,500 tons of cargo is handled annually.
Minneapolis - St. Paul International Airport, URL: http://www.mspairport.com
Metropolitan Airports Commission, URL: http://www.mspairport.com/MAC/

Railways
Minnesota's railway system has more than 4,650 miles of railway track.

Roads
Three Interstate highways pass through Minnesota: I-35, I-90 and I-94. In addition, the state has over 130,500 miles of highways and streets, with more than 12,000 miles of state trunk highways.

Ports and Harbours
Minnesota has 230 miles of navigable rivers as well as four ports on the Great Lakes which handle just under 70 million tons of freight annually.

HEALTH

The National Center for Health Statistics estimated that there were 28.9 doctors (including osteopaths) per 10,000 population in 2009, slightly above the national state average of 27.4 doctors per 10,000 residents. In 2008, there were 3,174 dentists (6.1 per 10,000 population). In 2009, the state had 3.0 community hospital beds per 1,000 residents, and, in 2010, there were 385 nursing homes with 32,339 beds.

The Center for Disease Control estimated that 8.6 per cent of the state population had no health care insurance in 2007-09, compared to the US average of 15.8 per cent. In 2007-11, an estimated 11 per cent lived in poverty; below the national average of 14.3 per cent. Minnesota reported 5,422 HIV/AIDS cases from the beginning of the epidemic to the end of 2008, and ranked 29th in the cumulative number of reported cases. The overall TB rate was 4.0 per 100,000 population, the 13th highest rate in the US. In 2012, the state's adult obesity rate was 62.3 per cent and an estimated 24.9 per cent of the adult population was considered obese.

EDUCATION

Primary/Secondary Education

According to National Education Statistics, enrolment in Minnesota's 2,478 public schools reached 837,053 for the year 2009-10. There were 52,839 teachers in the public system, and a ratio of 15.84 students per teacher.

In the year 2007-08, revenues from education reached $10.29 billion, whilst current expenditures on state education reached $10.4 billion.

Higher Education

During the academic year 2010-11, there were 113 degree conferring institutions in the state of Minnesota, 43 of which were public. Some 181,461 male students enrolled for the year, together with an estimated 260,820 women. 91,119 degrees/certificates were conferred during the year, of which 31,952 were Bachelors, 21,105 were Masters and 4,173 Doctorates. (Source: NCES)

COMMUNICATIONS AND MEDIA

Newspapers

Minnesota's daily newspapers include: Star Tribune, Minneapolis; St. Paul Pioneer Press; The Post-Bulletin, Rochester; Winona Daily News; Daily Globe, Worthington; Austin Daily Herald; The Daily Journal, Fergus Falls; and The Daily Tribune, Hibbing.

Minnesota Newspaper Association, URL: http://www.mnnewspapernet.org/index.htm
Star Tribune, URL: http://www.startribune.com

Business Journals
Minneapolis/St. Paul CityBusiness, URL: http://www.bizjournals.com/twincities

Broadcasting
Minnesota has more than 20 television stations, three of which are in Minneapolis, three in St. Paul, three in Alexandria, three in Duluth, and two in Austin.

ENVIRONMENT

Emissions of carbon dioxide from Minnesota's electricity generating industry fell to 32,946,107 metric tons in 2010, down from 33,688,934 metric tons in 2009, ranking the state 29th in the US. An estimated 56,597 metric tons of sulphur dioxide and 44,268 metric tons of nitrogen oxide were also emitted. This compares to the 2009 figures of an estimated 64,770 metric tons of sulphur dioxide and 49,208 metric tons of nitrogen oxide were also emitted.

Minnesota is a leading producer of ethanol and had 23 ethanol production plants in 2012 (11 per cent of the US total), with a total capacity of 1,119 million gallons per year (8.3 per cent of the US total). Minnesota requires the use of oxygenated motor gasoline blended with 10 per cent ethanol. Ethanol consumption was 5,797,000 barrels in 2011 (1.9 per cent of US total). (Source: EIA).

MISSISSIPPI

Capital: Jackson (Population, Census 2010: 173,514)

Head of State: Phil Bryant (R) (Governor) (page 1396)

State Flag: A horizontal tricolour, blue, white, then red, with a white-bordered, red square in the top left corner, its width two-thirds that of the flag. The square has a white-bordered, diagonal blue cross with thirteen white, five-pointed stars.

CONSTITUTION AND GOVERNMENT

Constitution

Mississippi entered the Union on 10 December 1817. According to the Constitution (adopted 1 November 1890), the Executive branch of government is headed by the governor assisted by seven other elected officials: the lieutenant governor, secretary of state, attorney general, state treasurer, state auditor, commissioner of agriculture and commerce, and commissioner of insurance. The governor is elected for a maximum of two four-year terms. The remaining executive officers are elected for four-year terms.

Mississippi voters elect two Senators and four Representatives to the US Congress in Washington, DC, for six years and two years, respectively. As a result of redistricting, Mississippi's Congressional Districts have been reduced from five to four.

To view the state constitution, please visit: http://www.sos.state.ms.us/pubs/constitution/constitution.asp

Recent Events

On Monday 29th August 2005, the Gulf coast, including Mississippi, was hit by Hurricane Katrina. Winds of over 150 km/h wrecked havoc, and storm surges caused a 200 km stretch of coastline to be flooded up to several kilometers inland. Biloxi and Gulfport were the worst affected cities; hundreds of homes and businesses were destroyed, a million homes were left without electricity and over 100 people were killed in the storms.

Legislature

The legislature consists of the Senate and House of Representatives. The legislature meets annually for a maximum period of 90 days from the Tuesday after the first Monday in January, except every fourth year when it meets for a maximum of 125 days.

Upper House

The Senate has 52 members elected for a term of four years. The Lieutenant Governor also serves as the President of the Senate and is responsible for appointing all Senate committee members, naming all committee chairmen and vice chairmen, and casting the deciding vote in the event of a tie in the Senate. Following the 2011 elections, the Republicans took control with 31 seats, whilst the Republicans had 21 seats.

Lower House

The House of Representatives has 122 members who are elected for a term of four years. The Republicans hold the majority of seats in the House. Following the November 2011 General Election, the House was composed as follows: 59 Democrat seats, 63 Republicans.

Mississippi Senate and House of Representatives, PO Box 1018, Jackson, MS 39215-1018, USA. Fax: +1 601 359 3935 (Senate), +1 601 359 3728 (House), URL: http://www.mississippi.gov/

Elected Executive Branch Officials (as at April 2013)
Governor: Phil Bryant (R) (page 1396)
Lieutenant Governor: Tate Reeves (R)
Secretary of State: Delbert Hosemann (R)
Attorney General: Jim Hood (D)

State Treasurer: Lynn Fitch (R)
State Auditor: Stacey Pickering
Commissioner of Agriculture and Commerce: Cindy Hyde-Smith (R)
Commissioner of Insurance: Mike Chaney (R)

Legislature (as at April 2013)
President of the Senate: Tate Reeves (R)
President Pro Tem of the Senate: Terry W. Brown (R)
Speaker of the House: Philip Gunn (R)
Speaker Pro Tem of the House: Greg Snowden (R)
Majority Leader: Tba (R)
Minority Leader: Tyrone Ellis (D)

US Senators: Thad Cochran (R) (page 1407) and Roger Wicker (R) (page 1536)

Ministries
Office of the Governor, 501 N West Street, 15th Floor, Woolfolk Building, Jackson, MS 39201 (Post Office Box 139, Jackson, MS 39205), USA. Tel: +1 601 359 3150, fax: +1 601 359 3741, URL: http://www.governorbryant.com/
Office of the Lt. Governor, 315 New Capitol Building, Jackson, MS 39201 (PO Box 1018, Jackson, MS 39215), USA. Tel: +1 601 359 3200, fax: +1 601 359 4054, URL: http://ltgovreeves.ms.gov
Office of the Attorney General, Carroll Gartin Justice Building, 450 High Street, Jackson, Mississippi 39201 (PO Box 220, Jackson, MS 39205), USA. Tel: +1 601 359 3680, URL: http://www.ago.state.ms.us
Office of the Secretary of State, 401 Mississippi Street, Jackson, MS 39201 (PO Box 136, Jackson, MS 39205), USA. Tel: +1 601 359 1350, fax: +1 601 359 1499, URL: http://www.sos.ms.gov/
Office of the State Auditor, 501 N West Street, Suite 801, PO Box 956, Jackson, MS 39201, USA. Tel: +1 601 576 2800, e-mail: auditor@osa.state.ms.us, URL: http://www.osa.state.ms.us/
Department of Agriculture and Commerce, 121 North Jefferson Street, Jackson, MS 39201 (PO Box 1609, Jackson, MS 39215), USA. Tel: +1 601 359 1100, fax: +1 601 354 6290, URL: http://www.mdac.state.ms.us
Department of Corrections, 723 North President Street, Jackson, Mississippi 39202-3097, USA. Tel: +1 601 359 5600, fax: +1 601 359 5624, URL: http://www.mdoc.state.ms.us
Mississippi Development Authority (previously Department of Economic and Community Development), 501 N West Street, Jackson, MS 39201 (PO Box 849, Jackson, MS 39205), USA. Tel: +1 601 359 3449, fax: +1 601 359 2832, URL: http://www.mississippi.org
Department of Education, Central High School, PO Box 771, 359 North West Street, Jackson, MS 39205, USA. Tel: +1 601 359 3513, URL: http://www.mde.k12.ms.us
Department of Environmental Quality, 2380 Highway 80 West, Jackson, MS 39204 (PO Box 20305, Jackson, MS 39289-1305), USA. Tel: +1 601 961 5171, fax: +1 601 354 6965, URL: http://www.deq.state.ms.us
Department of Insurance, P O Box 79, Jackson MS 39205. Tel: +1 601 359 3569, URL: http://www.mid.ms.gov/
Treasury Department, PO Box 138, Jackson, MS 39205-0138, USA. Tel: +1 601 359 3600, URL: http://www.treasury.state.ms.us/
Department of Transportation, 401 North West Street, Jackson, MS 39201 (PO Box 1850, Jackson, MS 39215-1850), USA. Tel: +1 601 359 7001, fax: +1 601 359 7050, URL: http://www.gomdot.com/

Political Parties
Mississippi Democratic Party, 832 North Congress Street, Jackson, MS 39202 (Post Office Box 1583, Jackson, MS 39215), USA. Tel: +1 601 969 2913, fax: +1 601 354 1599, e-mail: Democrats@msdemocrats.net, URL: http://www.msdemocrats.net/

Mississippi Republican Party, 415 Yazoo Street, Jackson, Mississippi 39201, USA. Tel: +1 601 948 5191, fax: +1 601 354 0972, e-mail: chairman@msgop.org, URL: http://www.msgop.org

Elections

Elections for State Constitutional Officers (Governor, Lieutenant Governor, Secretary of State, Attorney General, Auditor, Treasurer, Commissioner of Insurance, and Commissioner of Agriculture and Commerce) last took place on 8 November 2012. Phil Bryant became the new governor.

In the 8 November 2011 General Elections, the Republicans took control of the Senate (Democrats 21 seats, Republicans 31). In the State House of Representatives, the Republicans won 63 seats and the Democrats 59.

LEGAL SYSTEM

Mississippi has a two-tier appellate court system that reviews decisions of law and fact made by the trial courts. The Mississippi Supreme Court is the court of last resort among state courts. Decisions of the Chancery, Circuit and County Courts and of the Court of Appeals may be appealed to the Supreme Court.

The Supreme Court consists of the Chief Justice, two Presiding Justices, and six Associate Justices, all elected for a term of eight years by popular vote. The Court of Appeals comprises the Chief Judge, two Presiding Judges, and seven Judges.

There are 22 Circuit Court districts and 53 Circuit Court judges. The number of Circuit Judges per district ranges from one to four. Circuit Court judges are selected in non-partisan elections to serve four-year terms. There are 20 Chancery Court districts and 49 Chancery Court judges. Mississippi has 21 County Courts and 30 County Court judges. Counties which have a County Court include Adams, Bolivar, Coahoma, DeSoto, Forrest, Harrison, Hinds, Jackson, Jones, Lamar, Lauderdale, Lee, Leflore, Lowndes, Madison, Pearl River, Pike, Rankin, Warren, Washington and Yazoo.

In 2004, Mississippi voters approved a state constitutional amendment banning same-sex marriage and prohibiting Mississippi from recognizing same-sex marriages performed elsewhere. The amendment passed 86 per cent to 14 per cent, the largest margin in any state.

In May 2007, a former Ku Klux Klan member James Seale went on trial in Mississippi, charged with kidnapping and conspiracy in connection with the murders of two black teenagers in 1964. He was found guilty and incarcerated. At the time of the murders of Charles Eddie Moore and Henry Hezekiah Dee, Mr Seale was released from custody, the authorities citing lack of evidence. The FBI is currently re-opening several cold cases from the civil rights era.

Mississippi has the death penalty and 21 people have been executed since 1976. Most recently two people were executed in 2011 and six in 2012. The death row population is 50 including two women. The murder rate is estimated by the DPIC to be 7 per 100,000 population.

Supreme Court, URL: http://www.mssc.state.ms.us
Chief Justice: William L. Waller, Jr.
Presiding Justices: Michael Randolph, Jess Dickinson
Court of Appeals, URL: http://www.mssc.state.ms.us
Chief Judge: L. Joseph Lee
Presiding Justices: Tyree Irving, T. Kenneth Griffis

LOCAL GOVERNMENT

Mississippi is divided into 82 county governments and 296 municipal governments (cities, towns, and villages). Municipalities which have more than 2,000 inhabitants are regarded as cities; those with 300 to 1,999 inhabitants are towns; and those with 50 to 299 inhabitants are villages. In addition, there are 458 special district governments, 164 school district governments and three dependent public school systems.

AREA AND POPULATION

Area

The state of Mississippi is located in the south-eastern United States, bordered on the south by the Gulf of Mexico, on the west by Arkansas, Louisiana and the Mississippi River, on the north by the State of Tennessee, and on the east by Alabama. Mississippi's total area is 48,430.19 sq. miles, of which 46,906.96 sq. miles is land and 1,523.24 sq. miles is water.

To view a map of the state, please consult:
http://www.lib.utexas.edu/maps/us_2001/mississippi_ref_2001.pdf

Winters are mild, intermingled with warm, spring-like days. Average temperature in July is 81 degrees, but more common summer temperatures range into the 90s. Average rainfall is 52 inches, and fall, the time of harvest, is the driest season. Rivers and reservoirs are plentiful. Distinct soil regions range from a large, fertile alluvial plain along the Mississippi River, to rolling hill lands with hardwood forests and ranch lands of prairie and pine forests.

Population

According to the 2010 Census, the state population was 2,967,297, up from 2,951,996 in mid-2009. In 2012, the population was estimated to be 2,984,926. Over the period 2000-10, the population grew by 4.3 per cent and is expected to reach 3.09 million by 2030. Mississippi's population density was 63.2 persons per sq. mile in 2010. The population of the capital, Jackson, was estimated at 175,561 in 2011, making it the largest city in

Mississippi. Other large population centres are located in the Gulf Coast strip and the north-west corridor south of Memphis. The most highly populated counties are Hinds County, Harrison County, Jackson County, and Rankin County.

Mississippians come from diverse ethnic backgrounds - Native Americans, French, Spanish explorers and settlers, the English and early Americans who made the wilderness a home, Scots, Irish, Orientals, Italians, Greeks, and also the Africans who were brought as slaves. According to the 2010 Census, 7.1 per cent of the population is under 5 years, 25.5 per cent under 18 years and 12.8 per cent is aged over 65 years. Approximately 59 per cent of the population is white, and 37 per cent is black. Approximately 2.7 per cent of the population is of Hispanic or Latino origin.

Births, Marriages, Deaths

The US Census Bureau estimated that there were 40,036 births in 2010 and 28,965 deaths, giving a natural population increase of 11,071 people. Net emigration amounted to 3,590 people in 2009. The infant mortality rate in 2007 was 10 infant deaths per 1,000 live births, the second highest rate in the USA. Marriages and divorces in 2007, according to provisional data, numbered 15,729 and 14,164 respectively.

Public Holidays

In addition to observing the same holidays as the rest of the United States, Mississippi also celebrates the following: Robert E. Lee's Birthday (third Monday in January); Confederate Memorial Day (last Monday in April); National Memorial Day and Jefferson Davis' Birthday (last Monday in May).

EMPLOYMENT

Mississippi's total estimated civilian labour force was 1,336,500 in December 2012, of which 1,221,100 were employed and 115,400 were unemployed. The unemployment rate was 8.6 per cent, above the national rate (Dec. 2012) of 7.8 per cent. (Source: US Bureau of Labor Statistics)

The following table shows preliminary figures for December 2012 non-farm wage and salary employment according to industry:

Industry	No. of jobs	12 month change (%)
Logging and mining	9,000	-2.2
Construction	45,300	-5.6
Manufacturing	136,500	2.0
Trade, transport and utilities	215,200	0.7
Information	11,800	0.0
Financial activities	45,100	-0.2
Professional and business svcs.	96,500	2.7
Education & health services	138,300	0.4
Leisure and hospitality	115,800	0.3
Other services	34,400	0.3
Government	244,600	-0.4
TOTAL	1,092,500	0.3

Source: Bureau of Labor Statistics

BANKING AND FINANCE

GDP/GNP, Inflation, National Debt

Mississippi's Gross Domestic Product (GDP) - current dollar - fell from $98,331 million in 2008 to an estimated $95,905 million in 2009. Real GDP increased by 1.1 per cent in 2010 and GDP rose to $97,461 million. In 2011, current-dollar GDP was $97.8 billion and ranked 35th in the US. Real GDP contracted by 0.8 per cent in 2011. The top earning industry was government (18.4 per cent) followed by real estate (8.7 per cent).

GDP, according to industry, is shown below (millions of current dollars):

Industry	2009	2010	2011
Agriculture, forestry, fishing and hunting	1,986	2,428	2,615
Mining	1,074	1,143	1,443
Utilities	2,580	2,702	2,480
Construction	4,906	4,768	4,772
Manufacturing	13,680	14,321	15,134
Wholesale Trade	4,193	4,207	4,363
Retail Trade	7,317	7,671	7,874
Transport and warehousing	3,020	3,141	3,221
Information	1,865	1,923	1,987
Finance and insurance	4,625	5,268	5,176
Real estate	8,854	8,437	8,501
Educational services	651	685	733
Health care & social assistance	6,977	7,328	7,552
Other non-Govt. Services	12,769	13,586	13,997
Government	17,672	17,872	17,960
TOTAL	92,167	95,480	97,810

Source: Bureau of Economic Analysis

Per capita personal income was estimated at $32,000 in 2011, 77 per cent of national average. Per capita real GDP in 2010 fell to $29,318, the lowest in the US when the national average was $42,346.

The annual average Consumer Price Index (CPI) for the south urban area rose from 218.6 in 2011 to 223.2 in 2012. (1982-84 = 100). (Source: Bureau of Labor Statistics)

UNITED STATES OF AMERICA

Balance of Payments / Imports and Exports

Total Mississippi imports cost $13,350 million in 2009, down 24.2 per cent in $17,601 million in 2008. Imports rose 19.3 per cent to $15,922 million in 2010. They rose again in 2011 to $20,469 million in 2011, up 29.6 per cent . Mississippi imports account for 0.9 per cent of total US imports. Main imported commodities include oil, crude. Main suppliers (2011) include Mexico (26.6 per cent), China (14.1 per cent), Colombia (12.2 per cent), Venezuela and Nigeria.

Merchandise export revenue fell from $7,323 million in 2008 to $6,316 million in 2009, a fall of 13.8 per cent. In 2010, exports rose to $8,229 million, up 30.3 per cent. They rose again in 2011 to $10,930 million, up 32.8 per cent. Mississippi exports account for 0.7 per cent of the US total. (Source: US Census Bureau, Foreign Trade Division).

Mississippi's top five export markets in 2010-11, in order of revenue generated, are shown on the following table:

Country	2010 ($m)	2011 ($m)	+/-% 10-11
Canada	1,290	1,763	36.6
Panama	710	1,548	118.0
Mexico	1,157	1,148	-0.8
China	405	502	23.7
Colombia	233	444	90.6

Top five international trade exports in 2010, in order of revenue generated, are shown on the following table:

Product	$m
Oil (not crude) from petrol & bitumen mineral etc.	1,582
Pigments etc. of 80%+ Titanium Dioxide dry wt.	774
Cotton, not carded or combed	451
Chemical Woodpulp, Soda	444
Light oils & prep (not crude) from petrol & bitum	359

Source: US Census Bureau

Chambers of Commerce and Trade Organisations

Jackson County Chamber of Commerce, URL: http://www.jcchamber.com
Mississippi Development Authority, URL: http://www.mississippi.org
Mississippi Economic Council, URL: http://www.msmec.com/

MANUFACTURING, MINING AND SERVICES

Primary and Extractive Industries

Mississippi has substantial energy resources, and mining operations primarily extracting oil, gas, sand, gravel, clay and limestone. The mining industry contributed $1,443 million of Mississippi's 2011 Gross Domestic Product, up from $1,143 million in 2010. The highest-earning sector in 2010 was oil and gas extraction ($643 million), followed by support activities ($456 million). Non-oil and gas mining accounted for $45 million. (Source: BEA)

Mississippi had proven crude oil reserves of 247 million barrels in 2010, 1.1 per cent of the US total crude oil reserves. From a total of 3,339 oil wells and 9 rotary rigs, around 23,642,000 bbl/d were produced in 2010 (1.2 per cent of US total). Monthly (Oct. 2012) production amounted to 2,085,000 barrels. The state's crude oil refinery capacity was 364,000 bbl/d in 2012. Petroleum consumption in 2010 reached 79 million barrels (1.1 per cent of US total), 37.5 million barrels of which were motor gasoline, and 19.8 million barrels distillate fuel.

Reserves of dry natural gas were estimated at 853 billion cubic feet in 2010 (0.3 per cent of US total). Natural gas plants liquids amounted to 4 million barrels in 2010. There were 5,732 gas and gas condensate wells operating in Mississippi in 2010. Marketed natural gas was estimated to be 81,487 million cu ft in 2011. Mississippi has one of the largest natural gas processing plants in the United States, Pascagoula, which serves offshore supplies. Gas consumption was 434,701 million cubic feet in 2011; over half the state's supplies are imported from neighbouring states. A US$1.1 billion liquefied natural gas import terminal opened in October 2011 in Pascagoula.

Coal production amounted to 2,747,000 short tons in 2011 (0.3 per cent of US total). (Source: EIA)

Energy

Total energy production was 446 trillion Btu in 2010 (0.6 per cent of the US total). Mississippi's total energy consumption in 2010 was 1,189 trillion Btu. Per capita energy consumption was 400 million Btu in 2010 and ranking 15th in the USA.

Mississippi is a net importer of electricity, with coal as its primary energy source. Net summer capability in 2010 was 15,691 MW (1.5 per cent of US total). Net monthly generation in October 2012 was 3,930 MWh (1.3 per cent of the US total): natural gas 2,447,000 MWh, nuclear power 1,078,000 MWh, coal-fired 257,000 MWh, petroleum-fired 1,000 MWh, renewables excluding hydroelectric 117,000 MWh.

Mississippi's nuclear power plant, Grand Gulf, is located 25 miles south of Vicksburg, on the banks of the Mississippi River. The station has a capacity of 1,251 MW. It generated 18 per cent of the State's electricity in 2010. (Source: EIA)

Manufacturing

Manufacturing is Mississippi's third largest contributor to GDP, accounting for $15,134 million in 2011 (up on $14,321 in 2010). Top earning sectors in 2010 were petroleum and coal products ($2,540 million), chemical products ($1,101 million), and food, beverage and tobacco products ($1,363 million).

Mississippi consistently ranks among the nation's top states with most favourable business climates.

Service Industries

The services industry is Mississippi's largest contributor towards GDP. Major services sectors in 2011 were: real estate ($8,501 million) and health care and social assistance ($7,552 million). Finance and insurance accounted for $5,176 million, whilst professional and technical services ($3,601 million) also contributed significantly to the state GDP.

Mississippi has a general seven per cent sales tax, in addition to local property and state income taxes. Other government revenues come from motor vehicle and drivers' licences, fishing and hunting licences, fuel taxes, taxes on alcoholic beverages, cigarettes and tobacco, casino gambling and other fees.

Tourism

One of the major sectors of the tourism industry is gaming, accounting for over 35 per cent of total tourism employment. Annual gaming revenues make up a large proportion of the entertainment and recreation GDP, which amounted to $606 million in 2011. The accommodation and food services sector of the services industry contributed $3,832 million towards the 2011 GDP.
Mississippi Development Authority, Division of Tourism Development, URL: http://www.visitmississippi.org

Agriculture

The contribution of agriculture, forestry, fishing and hunting amounted to $2,615 million in 2011. Crop and animal production amounted to $1,996 in 2010 while forestry, fishing and related activities saw revenues of $432 million.

According to the latest USDA National Agricultural Statistics Service Census, Mississippi had around 42,400 farms in 2010, covering an area of some 11,150,000 acres. The average size of a farm was 263 acres in 2010. Crop production is a major sector of Mississippi's agricultural industry. Major revenues come from poultry and egges ($2.4 billion in 2007), forestry, cotton, and catfish. Mississippi is the nation's leading fish producer, and in 2007 the state ranked fifth in terms of poultry and cotton production. As of Jan. 2011, there were 900,000 cattle and calves and 385,000 hogs and pigs.

In 2007, the total value of agricultural products sold reached $4.8 billion; of this, crops earned $1.6 billion, whilst livestock, poultry and their products earned $3.2 billion.

Mississippi's timber industry generates around $1 billion a year and is the second most valuable of the state's commodities. Mississippi has some 17 million acres of forests. In fact, nearly 56 percent of the state's land area is covered by dense, rich woods owned predominantly by private citizens. These forests are a valuable natural resource - with Mississippi leading the nation in the number of trees produced per acre and one of the most prolific timber-producing states east of the Mississippi River. But more than any economic benefit, the forests are a source of recreation for hunting, camping and exploring.

COMMUNICATIONS AND TRANSPORT

International Airports

Mississippi's largest airport is the Jackson International Airport, having amongst its expanded facilities a 280,000 sq. foot cargo apron. Additionally, there are 75 publicly and privately owned airports in Mississippi, with six providing passenger services to cities throughout the south-east.
Jackson International Airport, 1URL: http://www.jmaa.com

Railways

Mississippi has 2,800 miles of railway track and has access to nearly every North American market. The state is the crossroads for several railroad systems, including the main north-south line of the Illinois Central and Amtrak. Jackson is a major rail destination in the export of freight between Canada and Mexico following the linking of three major railroads: Canadian National, Illinois Central and Kansas City Southern. The railway network is closely linked to the state waterways.

Roads

Mississippi's highway systems include 10 federal highways and 685 miles of four separate interstates. A $1.5 billion expansion of the state's highways is presently underway, adding an extra 1,000 miles of multi-lane highways.

Ports and Harbours

Mississippi is reknown for its system of water transportation. Along the 410 miles of the Mississippi River are four ports, two of which are US Customs Ports of Entry. On the Gulf of Mexico coast there are deep water ports at Gulfport and Pascagoula. The newest access to inland water transportation is the Tennessee-Tombigbee Waterway connecting east Mississippi industries with 1,600 miles of inland waterways and the Gulf of Mexico.

HEALTH

The National Center for Health Statistics (NCHS) estimated that there were 17.3 doctors per 10,000 residents in 2009, well below the US state average of 27.4 doctors per 10,000 state inhabitants. In 2008, there were 1,160 dentists (3.9 per 10,000 population). In 2009, there were 4.4 community hospital beds per 1,000 residents (above the US state average of 2.6), and, in 2010, there were 203 nursing homes with 18,589 beds.

According to the Center for Disease Control, an estimated 18.1 per cent of the state population had no health-care coverage in 2007-09, and an estimated 21.6 per cent were living in poverty in 2007-11. Mississippi reported 7,557 HIV/AIDS cases from the beginning of the epidemic to the end of 2008, and ranked 25th in terms of the cumulative number of reported cases. The overall rate of TB was 4.0 per 100,000 population. Obesity levels were notably higher than in the national rates, both in terms of adults (34.0 per cent) and among the young (16.5 per cent). An estimated 67.9 per cent were considered overweight. (Source: CDC)

EDUCATION

Primary/Secondary Education
Enrolment in the state's 1,097 elementary and secondary public schools for the year 2009-10 stood at 492,481. There were 33,103 teachers, and a teacher/pupil ratio of one to 14.88.

In the academic year 2007-08, total education revenue reached $4.388 billion whilst total current expenditure for state education came to $4.273 billion.

Post Secondary Education
The state currently has 40 institutes of higher education, 24 of which are public. In the year 2010-11, 66,882 male students were enrolled, together with 106,254 women. In the same year, 31,692 degrees/certificate were conferred, of which 12,953 Bachelors, 4,203 were Masters and 1,154 were Doctorates. Mississippi's four main universities are the University of Mississippi at Oxford, Mississippi State University at Starkville, the University of Southern Mississippi at Hattiesburg, and Jackson State University in Jackson.

Mississippi also has the nation's first state-supported school for the handicapped, the first co-educational college to grant degrees to women, the oldest land-grant college for black-Americans, the nation's first planned system of community colleges and the first state college for women. (Source: NCES)

RELIGION

Mississippi's population is predominantly Protestant, with smaller representation of Roman Catholic, Greek Orthodox, Jewish, and other religions.

COMMUNICATIONS AND MEDIA

Newspapers
Major newspapers published in Mississippi are The Bolivar Commercial (URL: http://www.bolivarcom.com/), the Daily Journal, the Daily Mississippian, The Democrat, the Jackson Advocate, Mississippi Link, Natchez Democrat, Picayune Item, South Report, and The Sun Herald.
The Clarion-Ledger, URL: http://www.clarionledger.com
Daily Times Leader, URL: http://www.dailytimesleader.com

Business Journals
Mississippi Business Journal, URL: http://www.msbusiness.com/index3.html

ENVIRONMENT

All 82 of Mississippi's counties comply with standards of air quality as required by the US Environmental Protection Agency. Air permits are required under the terms of the Federal Clean Air Act and the National Pollutant Discharge Eliminations System.

Carbon dioxide emissions from Mississippi's electricity generating industry rose from 23,480,603 metric tons in 2009 to 26,845,306 metric tons, ranking the state 32nd in the US, accounting for 1.1 per cent of US total. Approximately 59,043 metric tons of sulphur dioxide (up from 45,406 metric tons in 2009), and 30,608 metric tons of nitrogen oxide (up from 27,458 metric tons in 2009) were also emitted.

In 2010, 10,810 alternative-fueled vehicles were in use (1.2 per cent of US total). As of 2012, there was one ethanol plant in operation. In 2011 the capacity was 54 million Gal/Year. Approximately 3,211,000 barrels of ethanol were consumed in 2011. (Source: EIA)

SPACE PROGRAMME

NASA's Stennis Space Centre is located in South Mississippi, some 45 miles east of New Orleans. The Centre is primarily responsible for the testing of rocket propulsion systems for the Space Shuttle. A multi-agency centre, it is home to over 30 agencies in applied research and technology.
Stennis Space Center, URL: http://www.nasa.gov/centers/stennis/home

MISSOURI

Capital: Jefferson City (Population, Census 2010: 43,079)

Head of State: Jeremiah W. (Jay) Nixon (D) (Governor) (page 1487)

State Flag: Three horizontal stripes: red, white and blue; over the centre stripe is the Missouri coat of arms around which is a blue band with 24 stars. The coat of arms consists of two grizzly bears standing on a scroll which reads 'Salus Populi Suprema Lex Esto' ('Let the welfare of the people be the supreme law'); below the scroll is the date 1820 (the year Missouri became a state) in Roman numerals; the bears hold a shield, on the right hand side of which is the United States coat of arms and on the left of which is a silver crescent moon and a grizzly bear; around the shield is a belt on which are inscribed the words 'United we stand, divided we fall'.

CONSTITUTION AND GOVERNMENT

Constitution
Missouri entered the Union on 10 August 1821 as the 24th state. The 1875 Constitution gives supreme executive power to the Governor. The Governor is assisted by five other elected officials: Lieutenant Governor, Secretary of State, State Treasurer, Attorney General, and State Auditor. All are elected at the presidential elections for a four-year term. The Governor and Treasurer serve a maximum of two terms.

Missourians elect nine Representatives and two Senators to the US Congress in Washington, DC.

To view the state constitution, please visit: http://www.moga.mo.gov/const/moconstn.htm

Legislature
Missouri's bicameral legislature consists of the Senate and House of Representatives. The Legislature meets from early January to mid-May, each legislature lasting two years.

On 3 November 1992 Missourians approved an amendment to the constitution limiting the term members of the Missouri House of Representatives and Missouri Senate may serve to eight years. The amendment limits a member's total legislative service to 16 years.

Upper House
The Senate has 34 members, all elected for four years, one half (17) of whom are elected every two years. Each of Missouri's Senators represents a district of about 164,000 people. Following the 2012 elections, the Senate was composed of 24 Republicans and 10 Democrats. **Missouri State Senate**, State Capitol Building, Jefferson City, MO 65101, USA. Tel: +1 573 751 3766 (Secretary of the Senate), URL: http://www.senate.mo.gov/

Lower House
The House of Representatives has 163 members, elected for two years. Following the 2012 elections, the House was composed of 110 Republicans and 53 Democrats.

House of Representatives, State Capitol Building, 201 West Capitol Avenue, Jefferson City, Missouri 65101, USA. Tel: +1 573 751 3659, URL: http://www.house.mo.gov/

Elected Executive Branch Officials (as at April 2013)
Governor: Jeremiah W. (Jay) Nixon (D) (page 1487)
Lieutenant Governor: Peter Kinder (R)
Secretary of State: Jason Kander (D)
Attorney General: Chris Koster (D)
State Treasurer: Clint Zweifel (D)
State Auditor: Thomas Schweich (R)

General Assembly (as at May 2013)
President of the Senate: Peter Kinder (R)
President Pro Tem of the Senate: Tom Dempsey(R)
Senate Majority Leader: Ron Richard (R)
Senate Minority Leader: Jolie Justus (D)
Speaker of the House: Timothy Jones (R)
Speaker Pro Tem of the House: Jason Smith (R)
House Majority Leader: John Diehl (R)
House Minority Leader: Jacob Hummel (D)

US Senators: Claire McCaskill (D) (page 1473) and Roy Blunt (R) (page 1390)

Ministries
Office of the Governor, Missouri Capitol Building, Room 216, PO Box 720, Jefferson City, MO 65102-0720, USA. Tel: +1 573 751 3222, fax: +1 573 751 1495, e-mail: mogov@mail.state.mo.us, URL: http://www.gov.mo.gov
Office of the Lieutenant Governor, State Capitol Building, Room 121, Jefferson City, Missouri 65101, USA. Tel: +1 573 751 4727, fax: +1 573 751 9422, e-mail: ltgovinfo@ltgov.mo.gov, URL: http://www.ltgov.mo.gov
Office of the Attorney General, Supreme Court Building, 207 W. High Street, PO Box 899, Jefferson City, MO 65102, USA. Tel: +1 573 751 3321, fax: +1 573 751 0774, URL: http://www.ago.mo.gov
Office of Secretary of State, State Capitol, Room 208 or State Information Center, 600 W Main, Jefferson City, MO 65101, USA. Tel: +1 573 751 4936, URL: http://www.sos.mo.gov/
Office of the State Auditor, P.O. Box 869, Jefferson City, Missouri 65102, USA. Tel: +1 573 751 4213, fax: +1 573 751 7984, URL: http://www.auditor.mo.gov/
Office of the State Treasurer, PO Box 210, Jefferson City, MO 65102, USA. Tel: +1 573 751 2411, fax: +1 573 751 9443, URL: http://www.treasurer.missouri.gov/
Department of Agriculture, PO Box 630 Jefferson City, MO 65102, USA. Tel: +1 573 751 4211, e-mail: aginfo@mda.mo.gov, URL: http://mda.mo.gov/
Department of Conservation, (PO Box 180, MO 65102) 2901 W. Truman Blvd., Jefferson City MO 65109, USA. Tel: +1 573 751 4115, fax: +1 573 751 4467, URL: http://mdc.mo.gov
Department of Corrections, PO Box 236, Jefferson City, Missouri 65102, USA. Tel: +1 573 751 2389, fax: +1 573 751 4099, URL: http://www.doc.missouri.gov

UNITED STATES OF AMERICA

Department of Economic Development, 30 W High Street, P O Box 1157, Jefferson City, MO 65102, USA. Tel: +1 573 751 4962, fax: +1 573 751 7258, URL: http://www.ded.missouri.gov

Department of Elementary and Secondary Education, (PO Box 480, Jefferson City, MO 65102) 205 Jefferson Street, Jefferson City, MO 65101, USA. Tel: +1 573 751 4212, fax: +1 573 751 8613, e-mail: pubinfo@dese.mo.gov, URL: http://www.dese.mo.gov/

Department of Health and Senior Services, PO Box 570, Jefferson City, Missouri 65102, USA. Tel: +1 573 751 6400, fax: +1 573 751 6041, URL: http://health.mo.gov/index.php

Department of Labour and Industrial Relations, 3315 West Truman Boulevard, Room 213, PO Box 504, Jefferson City, MO 65102-0504, USA. Tel: +1 573 751 4091 / 573 751 9691, fax: +1 573 751 4135, URL: http://www.labor.mo.gov/

Department of Natural Resources, 205 Jefferson Street, PO Box 176, Jefferson City, MO 65102, USA. Tel: +1 573 751 3443, URL: http://www.dnr.mo.gov/

Department of Transportation, 105 West Capitol Avenue, PO Box 270, Jefferson City, MO 65102, USA. Tel: +1 573 751 2551, URL: http://www.modot.org

Office of Homeland Security, PO Box 809, Jefferson City, MO 65102, USA. Tel: +1 573 522 3007, fax: +1 573 751 7819, URL: http://www.dps.mo.gov/dir/programs/ohs/

Political Parties

Missouri Democratic Party, 208 Madison Street, PO Box 719, Jefferson City, MO 65102, USA. Tel: +1 573 636 5241, fax: +1 573 634 8176, URL: http://www.missouridems.org

Missouri Republican Party, 204 East Dunklin Avenue, PO Box 73, Jefferson City, Missouri 65102, USA. Tel: +1 573 636 3146, fax: +1 573 636 3273, URL: http://www.mogop.org

Elections

Elections for Governor, Lieutenant Governor, Secretary of State, State Treasurer and Attorney General (as well as 9 US Representatives, 17 state Senators and all state Representatives) took place on 6 November 2012. Jay Nixon (D) retained the governorship with 55 per cent of the vote.

In 2012, the Republicans retained control of the Senate, (Republicans 24, Democrats 10). Elections were also held in the Lower House for all 163 seats (Republicans 110, Democrats 53).

In the US Senate elections the incumbent Republican Kit Bond did not stand for re-election. Republican Roy Blunt won an easy victory.

Elections for five state executive positions (Governor, Lt.-Governor, Attorney General, Secretary of State and Treasurer) also took place on 6 November 2012. The incumbent governor, lt. governor, attorney general and treasurer were re-elected. Jason Kander (D) was re-elected to the position of Secretary of State.

LEGAL SYSTEM

Missouri's court system consists of the Supreme Court, the Court of Appeals, and the Circuit Courts. The Supreme Court comprises the Chief Justice and six Associate Justices. The Associate Justices are all appointed for a term of 12 years by the Governor from nominees submitted by judicial commission under non-partisan court plan. Succeeding terms are subject to the ballot of the people, although judges can serve until the age of 70. As of 2013, Missouri had 405 judges and commissioners in ttoal. In the trial courts there are 141 circuit judges, 193 associate circuit judges, and 32 commissioners and deputy commissioners.

Missouri has the death penalty. There have been 68 executions since 1976. The current death row population is 48. The murder rate is 7 per 100,000. (Source: DPIC) The most recent execution took place in 2011.

Supreme Court, URL: http://www.courts.mo.gov
Chief Justice: Richard B. Teitelman
Judges: George W. Draper III, Laura Denvir Stith, Mary Russell, Patricia Breckenridge, Paul Wilson, Zel Fischer

LOCAL GOVERNMENT

According to the 2002 Census Bureau Census of Governments, Missouri has 114 county governments and 1,258 sub-county general purpose governments. Of the 1,258 sub-county governments, there are 946 municipal governments (city, town, and village) and 312 township governments.

Missouri Association of Counties, URL: http://www.mocounties.com

AREA AND POPULATION

Area
Missouri is located in the mid-west of the US, north of Arkansas and Tennessee, south of Iowa, west of Illinois and Kentucky, and east of Kansas and Nebraska. The area of Missouri is 69,704.31 sq. miles, of which 68,885.93 sq. miles is land, and 818.39 sq. miles is water.

To view a map, consult http://www.lib.utexas.edu/maps/us_2001/missouri_ref_2001.pdf

Population
According to the 2010 Census, the state population was 5,988,927, up from the mid-2009 population at 5,987.580. In 2012, the population was estimated to be 6,021,988. Over the period 2000 to 2010, the population of Missouri grew by 7.0 per cent. The population is expected to reach 6.4 million by 2030. The population density is around 87.1 people per sq. mile. The county with the greatest number of inhabitants is St. Louis county. Kansas City is the largest city in Missouri, with an estimated population of 463,202 in 2011; St. Louis follows, with 318,069 inhabitants. The population of the capital, Jefferson City, lags behind with just 43,332 inhabitants.

According to the 2010 Census, 6.5 per cent of the population is under 5 years, 23.8 per cent under 18 years and 14.0 per cent is aged over 65 years. Approximately 82.8 per cent of the population is white, and 11.6 per cent is black. Approximately 3.5 per cent of the population is of Hispanic or Latino origin.

Births, Marriages, Deaths
The US Census Bureau estimated that there were 76,759 births in 2010 and 55,281 deaths, giving a natural population increase of 21,478. Net migration to the state accounted for a further 6,009 residents in 2009. The 2007 infant mortality rate was 7.5 infant deaths per 1,000 live births. Marriages and divorces in 2007, according to provisional data, numbered 39,417 and 22,377 respectively; marriage numbers were down on the previous year, whilst divorce numbers were up.

Public Holidays
In addition to federal holidays, Missourians celebrate Truman Day on 9th May.

EMPLOYMENT

Preliminary figures indicate that Missouri's total civilian labour force was 3,010,800 in December 2012, of which 2,809,900 were in employment and 200,900 were unemployed. The unemployment rate was 6.7 per cent, lower than the national average of 7.8 per cent.

The following table shows December 2012 non-farm employment (seasonally adjusted) according to industry:

Industry	No. of jobs	12 month change (%)
Logging and mining	4,300	0.0
Construction	100,400	2.2
Manufacturing	249,100	0.5
Trade, transport and utilities	510,700	0.9
Information	55,400	-4.5
Financial activities	160,100	3.2
Professional and business svcs.	351,800	5.7
Educational and health svcs.	429,100	3.3
Leisure and hospitality	269,500	0.9
Other services	117,000	0.1
Government	430,600	-1.3
TOTAL	2,672,700	1.5

Source: Bureau of Labor Statistics

BANKING AND FINANCE

GDP/GNP, Inflation, National Debt
Total Gross Domestic Product (GDP) (current dollars) rose from $237,797 million in 2007 to $239,752 million in 2009. In 2010, it reached $244,016 million, up 2.9 per cent. In 2011, it rose to $249.5 billion and ranked 22nd in the US. In 2011, the largest industry was government (12.8 per cent).

The following table shows Gross Domestic Product according to industry (in millions of current dollars):

Industry	2009	2010	2011
Agriculture, forestry, fishing and hunting	3,274	3,353	4,000
Mining	232	244	276
Utilities	4,248	4,602	4,264
Construction	9,666	8,781	8,450
Manufacturing	28,115	29,865	31,904
Wholesale Trade	14,220	14,553	15,055
Retail Trade	15,411	16,052	16,457
Transport and warehousing	8,232	8,217	8,313
Information	13,387	13,430	13,974
Finance and insurance	15,013	16,329	16,506
Real estate	25,596	24,233	23,402
Educational services	2,682	2,741	2,831
Health care & social assistance	20,693	21,557	22,484
Other non-government services	45,089	47,523	49,575
Government	31,505	31,906	32,034
TOTAL	237,364	243,386	249,525

Source: US Bureau of Economic Analysis, Feb. 2013

Average per capita income rose to $37,969 in 2011, 91 per cent of the national average of $41,560. Per capita real GDP fell to $35,952 in 2011, below the national average of $42,070.

The annual average Consumer Price Index (CPI) (all items) for the St. Louis, MO-IL, urban area rose from 209.8 in 2011 to 214.8 in 2012 (1982-84 = 100). (Source: Bureau of Labor Statistics)

Balance of Payments / Imports and Exports
Total Missouri imports amounted $11,403 million in 2009, down 16.9 per cent from the 2008 total of $13,728 million. Imports rose by 12.5 per cent in 2010 to $12,832 million. They rose again in 2011 to $15,698 million, up 22.2 per cent, representing 0.7 per cent of US total imports. Main suppliers are China (22.2 per cent), Canada (20.7 per cent), Mexico (15.9 per cent), Germany and the UAE. Imports include vehicle parts, engineering parts, medicaments

and beer. Export revenue fell from $12,852 million in 2008 to $9,522 million in 2009, a 25.9 per cent reduction. Exports rose by 35.7 per cent to $12,926 million in 2010. Exports rose by 9.5 per cent in 2011 to $14,154 million. Exports account for 1.0 per cent of US exports.

The top five export destinations in 2010-11 are shown on the following table:

Country	2010 ($m)	2011 ($m)	+/-% 10-11
Canada	3,996	4,282	7.2
Mexico	1,304	1,441	10.5
China	987	1,161	17.6
South Korea	655	608	-7.2
Japan	596	591	-0.8

The following table shows 2010 export revenue according to the top five export products:

Product	$m
Pass vehicles spark-ign. engine 1500-3m cc	1,087
Organo-Sulfur compounds, nesoi	528
Motor vehicles trans gds spl ig in CP eng, GVW Nov 5 mtn	460
Parts of airplanes or helicopters, nesoi	346
Civilian aircraft, engines and parts	301
Source: US Census Bureau

Chambers of Commerce and Trade Organisations
Missouri Chamber of Commerce, URL: http://www.mochamber.org
Missouri Enterprise Business Assistance Centre, URL: http://www.missourienterprise.org/
Kansas City Area Development Council, URL: http://www.smartkc.com
St. Louis Regional Chamber and Growth Association (RCGA), URL: http://www.stlrcga.org/
Jefferson City Area Chamber of Commerce, URL: http://www.jcchamber.org/

MANUFACTURING, MINING AND SERVICES

Primary and Extractive Industries
Missouri's mining industry contributed $276 million towards the 2011 GDP (up from $244 million in 2010), the top sector being non-oil and gas mining ($213 million in 2010). (Source: BEA)

Missouri's proven crude oil reserves account for less than one per cent of US proven crude oil reserves. The state's 488 oil wells produced a total of 147,000 barrels of crude oil in 2010. Monthly production was 13,000 barrels in Oct. 2012. Petroleum consumption was 127.0 million barrels in 2010, 73.3 million barrels of which were motor gasoline (2.3 per cent of the US total) and 30.8 million barrels were distillate fuel.

Until 1996 Missouri had a small natural gas industry, with a total of 53 gas and gas condensate wells producing 25 million cubic feet of natural gas annually. With no further supplies of natural gas produced, Missouri is now dependent on natural gas from outside the state. Consumption was 272,166 million cubic feet in 2011. The residential sector accounts for approximately two-fifths of the State's consumption. Nearly three-fifths of Missouri households use natural gas as their primary energy source for home heating.

Missouri has a small coal industry, producing 465,000 short tons of coal in 2011. Coal supplied 82 per cent of Missouri's net electricity generation in 2011. (Source: EIA)

Energy
Total energy production was 1,928 trillion Btu in 2010 (2 per cent of US total). Missouri's energy consumption in 2010 was 1,818 trillion Btu and its per capita energy consumption was 322 million Btu, ranking it 25th in the US.

Missouri is a net exporter of electricity, and uses coal as a primary generating source. Electric power industry net summer capability was 21,739 MW in 2010. Total monthly net electricity generation was 6,717,000 MWh in October 2012 (2.2 per cent of the US total) of which, coal 5,464,000 MWh, nuclear power 912,000 MWh, natural gas 206,000 MWh, hydroelectric 16,000 MWh and other renewables 120,000 MWh. Missouri's nuclear power station is the 1,137 net MWe Callaway plant, located in Callaway County. (Source: EIA)

Manufacturing
Manufacturing is Missouri's second largest contributor to GDP, accounting for $31,904 million in 2011 (up from $29,865 million in 2010). The top manufacturing sectors in 2010 were food products ($5,597 million) and chemical products ($4,428 million). Missouri is among the nation's leaders in lead production.

Service Industries
Services is Missouri's greatest contributor to GDP. In 2011, the largest sectors were real estate ($23,402 million), health services ($22,484 million), finance and insurance ($16,506 million) and professional and technical services ($16,380 million).

Tourism
The arts, entertainment and recreation sector of the services industry contributed $3,266 million of 2011 GDP whilst the accommodation and food services sector accounted for $7,117 million.
Missouri Division of Tourism, URL: http://www.missouritourism.org/

Agriculture
Agriculture in total contributed $4,000 million to the 2011 GDP. The crop and animal production sector contributed $3,084 million in 2010. The farming sector contributed $2,773 million in 2009 whilst the forestry, fishing and related activities accounted for $384 million.

According to the US Department of Agriculture, Missouri had approximately 108,000 farms in 2010, covering some 29,100,000 acres. The average size of a Missouri farm is 269 acres. The state is among the nation's leaders in cattle production. Soybeans are the state's top crop. Agricultural products include hogs, corn hay, cotton, wheat, poultry, eggs, nursery products and tree nut products. As of 1 Jan. 2011, there were 3.95 million cattle and calves, 2.9 million hogs and pigs, and 81,000 sheep.

The total value of agricultural products sold in 2007 was $7.5 billion; $4 billion was earned through the sale of livestock, poultry and their products, whilst $3.5 billion came from the sale of crops.

COMMUNICATIONS AND TRANSPORT

International Airports
Missouri has two international airports: Kansas City International Airport and Lambert-St. Louis International Airport. In 2005, 14.3 million passengers passed through Lambert-St. Louis Airport, up from 13.3 million in 2003 but a fall on the 2000 figure of 20.5 million.

Lambert-St. Louis International Airport, URL: http://www.lambert-stlouis.com
Kansas City International Airport, URL: http://www.kcairports.com

Shipping
A number of ferries cross the Mississippi, linking Missouri with Illinois and Kentucky. Ferries are located at Canton, Winfield, Golden Eagle, Ste. Genevieve, Dorena, and Akers.

Ports and Harbours
Missouri has 11 major ports: Howard/Cooper County; Jefferson County; Kansas City; Mid-America; Mississippi County; New Bourbon; New Madrid County; Pemiscot County; St. Joseph; City of St. Louis; and Southeast Missouri. They handle a combined cargo of around $4.1 billion annually.
Missouri Port Authority Association, URL: http://www.missouriports.org/

HEALTH

The National Center for Health Statistics estimated that there were 26.1 doctors per 10,000 population in 2007, below the national state average of 27.4 doctors per 10,000 residents. In 2008, there were 2,803 dentists (4.7 per 10,000 population). In 2008, there were 3.2 community hospital beds per 1,000 residents of Missouri, and, in 2010, there were 514 nursing homes, with 55,393 beds.

According to the Center for Disease Control, 13.5 per cent of the inhabitants of Missouri had no health-care coverage in 2007-09, and, in 2007-11, 14.3 per cent were living in poverty. Missouri reported 12,447 HIV/AIDS cases from the beginning of the epidemic to the end of 2008, and ranked 20th in terms of the cumulative number of reported cases. The overall TB rate was 1.8 per 100,000 population, ranking it 39th highest in the US. In 2012, an estimated 65.2 per cent of the adult population was considered overweight and 30.5 per cent obese.

EDUCATION

Primary/Secondary Education
School (K-12) enrolment for the 2009-10 school year was 917,982, with the number of teachers standing at 67,795 for the same year. The ratio of teachers to students was one to 13.54. The total number of schools was 2,456.

State revenues from education reached $9.876 billion over the year 2007-08, and expenditure on state education reached $10.09 billion.

Higher Education
For the academic year 2010-11, there were 138 institutes of Higher Education in the state of Missouri, 34 of which were state-run. There were 178,191 men enrolled, together with 246,753 women. In the same academic year, a total of 90,123 degrees/certificates were conferred, of which 39,670 were Bachelors, 19,512 were Master degrees and 3,501 were Doctorates. (Source: NCES)

COMMUNICATIONS AND MEDIA

Newspapers
Missouri has 30 daily newspapers, including St. Louis Post-Dispatch, The Carthage Press, Lebanon Daily Record, Nevada Daily Mail, Springfield News-Leader, Southeast Missourian, Columbia Daily Tribune, Columbia Missourian, The Daily Statesman, The Daily Press Leader, Jefferson City News Tribune, Daily American Republic, and Kansas City Star.
Missouri Press Association, URL: http://www.mopress.com
The Kansas City Star, URL: http://www.kcstar.com

Business Journals
Kansas City Business Journal, URL: http://www.bizjournals.com/kansascity

Broadcasting
There are 24 television stations in Missouri, five in Kansas City, two in Columbia, five in Springfield and four in St. Louis.

ENVIRONMENT

Coal is the main fuel for electricity generation in Missouri, supplying over four-fifths of the electricity market. The resultant emissions are therefore high; emissions of carbon dioxide from the power industry rose from 74,715,725 metric tons in 2009 to 78,814,666 metric tons in 2010, ranking the state 10th in the US, and accounting for 3.3 per cent of US total. Approximately 232,804 metric tons of sulphur dioxide and 56,116 metric tons of nitrogen oxide were emitted.

Just 3 per cent of Missouri's electricity is currently generated from renewable sources - mainly from hydroelectricity generation. However, in 2008 the state adopted a renewable portfolio standard requiring that investor-owned utilities increase their use of renewable sources to 5 per cent by 2014 and to 15 per cent by 2021. Missouri had five ethanol plants in 2010, with a capacity of 261 million gallons per year (1.9 per cent of the US total). Ethanol consumption was 5,422 thousand barrels in 2011 (1.8 per cent of the US total). There were 20,734 alternative-fueled vehicles in use. (Source: EIA)

MONTANA

Capital: Helena (Population, Census 2010: 28,190)

Head of State: Steve Bullock (D) (Governor) (page 1396)

State Flag: A blue rectangle with yellow edges in the centre of which appears a circle bearing the state seal and above which appears the name 'MONTANA' in capitals. The state seal consists of the Montana landscape (mountains, waterfall, Missouri river, hills, trees and cliff) in front of which are three tools: a plough, shovel and pick, and in front of them a banner bearing the words 'ORO-Y-PLATA' (Gold and Silver).

CONSTITUTION AND GOVERNMENT

Constitution
Montana entered the Union on 8 November 1889. According to the 1972 State Constitution, the executive branch of state government is led by the Governor together with eight other elected officials: Lieutenant Governor, Attorney General, Secretary of State, State Auditor, Superintendent of Public Instruction, and five Public Service Commissioners. All serve terms of four years.

Montana elects two Senators and one At-Large Representative to the US Congress in Washington, DC. To view the state constitution, please visit: http://leg.mt.gov/css/mtcode_const/const.asp

Legislature
The state's legislature consists of the Senate and the House of Representatives. Legislative sessions take place every odd-numbered calendar year and last for 90 days, beginning in the first week of January.

The 63rd session of the Montana legislature convened on January 7 2013.

General Legislature, PO Box 201706, Helena, MT 59620-1706, USA. Tel: +1 406 444 3064, fax: +1 406 444 3036, URL: http://leg.mt.gov/css/default.asp
Upper House
The Senate has 50 members all elected for four years (half at each biennial election). The 63rd Senate (January 2013) will have 27 Republican members and 23 Democrats
MT Senate, PO Box 200500, Helena MT 59620-0500. Tel: +1 406 444 4801 (Secretary), fax: +1 406 444 4875, e-mail: rskelton@state.mt.us (Secretary), URL: http://leg.mt.gov/css/default.asp

Lower House
The House of Representatives has 100 members all elected for two years. Following the 2012 elections, the House has a 63-37 Republican majority.
MT House of Representatives, PO Box 200400, Helena MT 59620-0400, USA. Tel: +1 406 444 4819 (Chief Clerk), fax: +1 406 444 4825-, e-mail: marmiller@state.mt.us (Chief Clerk), URL: http://leg.mt.gov/css/default.asp

Elected Executive Branch Officials (as at March 2013)
Governor: Steve Bullock (D)
Lieutenant Governor: John Walsh (D)
Secretary of State: Linda McCulloch (D)
Attorney General: Tim Fox (R)
State Auditor: Monica Lindeen (D)
Superintendent of Public Instruction: Denise Juneau (D)
Public Service Commissioners: Travis Kavulla, Kirk Bushman, Roger Koopman, Bob Lake, Bill Gallagher

Legislature (as at March 2013)
President of the Senate: Jeff Essmann (R)
President Pro Tem of the Senate: Debby Barrett (R)
Senate Majority Leader: Art Wittich (R)
Senate Minority Leader: Jon Sesso (D)
House Majority Leader: Gordon Vance (R)
House Minority Leader: Chuck Hunter (D)
Speaker of the House: Mark Blasdel (R)

US Senators: Max Baucus (D) (page 1385) and Jon Tester (D) (page 1524)

Ministries
Office of the Governor, State Capitol, Helena, MT 59620-0801, USA. Tel: +1 406 444 3111, e-mail: governor@mt.gov, URL: http://www.governor.mt.gov
Lt. Governor's Office, State Capitol, Helena, MT 59620-0801, USA. Tel: +1 406 444 3111, URL: http://www.governor.mt.gov
Office of the Attorney General, Department of Justice, PO Box 201401, Helena, MT 59620-1401, USA. Tel: +1 406 444 2026, fax: +1 406 444 3549, URL: https://doj.mt.gov/
Office of the Secretary of State, Room 260, Capitol, PO Box 202801, Helena, Montana 59620-2801, USA. Tel: +1 406 444 2034, fax: +1 406 444 3976, URL: http://sos.mt.gov/

Office of the State Auditor, 840 Helena Avenue, Helena, MT 59601 (PO Box 4009, Helena, MT 59604-4009), USA. Tel: +1 406 444 2040, fax: +1 406 444 3497, URL: http://www.csi.mt.gov
Office of Public Instruction, PO Box 202501, Helena, Montana 59620-2501, USA. Tel: +1 406 444 3095, URL: http://opi.mt.gov/
Public Service Commission, 1701 Prospect Avenue, P.O. Box 202601, Helena, MT 59620-2601, USA. Tel: +1 406 444 6199, fax: +1 406 444 7618, URL: http://psc.mt.gov/
Department of Agriculture, 303 North Roberts Street (corner of 6th and Roberts), PO Box 200201, Helena, Montana 59620-0201, USA. Tel: +1 406 444 3144, fax: +1 406 444 5409, URL: http://agr.mt.gov/
Department of Commerce, 301 S. Park Avenue, Helena, MT 59601 (PO Box 200501, Helena, MT 59620-0501), USA. Tel: +1 406 841 2700, fax: +1 406 841 2701, URL: http://commerce.mt.gov/
Department of Corrections, 1539 11th Avenue, PO Box 201301 Helena, MT 59620-1301, USA. Tel: +1 406 444 3930, fax: +1 406 444 4920, URL: http://www.cor.mt.gov/default.mcpx
Department of Environmental Quality, 1520 East Sixth Avenue, PO Box 200901, Helena, MT 59620-0901, USA. Tel: +1 406 444 2544, fax: +1 406 444 4386, URL: http://deq.mt.gov/
Department of Labour and Industry, PO Box 1728 Helena MT 59624-1728, USA. Tel: +1 406 444 2840, fax: +1 406 444 1394, URL: http://dli.mt.gov
Department of Transportation, PO Box 201001, 2701 Prospect Avenue, Helena, MT 59620-1001, USA. Tel: +1 406 444 6200, URL: http://www.mdt.mt.gov/

Political Parties
Montana Democratic Party, PO Box 802, Helena, MT 59624, USA. Tel: +1 406 442 9520, fax: +1 406 442 9534, URL: http://www.montanademocrats.org
Montana Republican Party, 1313 N Last Chance Gulch, Helena, MT 59601, USA. Tel: +1 406 442 6469, fax: +1 406 442 3293, URL: http://www.mtgop.org

Elections
Elections took place November 2012 for the following statewide positions: US representative, governor/lieutenant governor, secretary of state, attorney general, state auditor, and superintendent of public instruction. The incumbent Governor Brian Schweitzer was constitutionally unable to stand (term-limited). The outgoing Attorney General, Steve Bullock (D), won the November election.

All one hundred seats were up for election in the Montana House of Representatives. The Republicans retained their sizeable majority but the Democrats gained five seats: Republicans 63, Democrats 37. Following the November 2012 Senate elections, the Democrats gained one seats (Republicans 27, Democrats 23). Twenty-six seats were up for election.

LEGAL SYSTEM

Montana's court system consists of the Supreme Court (seven Justices), four Water Courts (one chief judge, six water judges, six water masters), 56 District Courts (37 judges), Workers' Compensation Court (one judge), 73 Justice of the Peace Courts (73 justices of the peace), three Municipal Courts (three judges), and 92 City Courts (36 judges).

As well as the Chief Justice there are six Supreme Court Associate Justices, all elected for a term of eight years by popular vote. District Court judges serve terms of six years.

Three people have been executed in Montana since 1976, most recently in 2006. According to the DPIC, the murder rate is 2.6 per 100,000. In 2011, the Montana Senate voted to repeal the death penalty. However, the House Judiciary Committee refused to pass the bill onto the Republican House meaning the death penalty will remain on the statute books at least until 2013. As of February 2013, there were two people on death row.

Supreme Court, URL: http://www.courts.mt.gov
Chief Justice: Mike McGrath
Justices: Brian Morris, James Nelson, Beth Baker, Patricia O'Brien Cotter, James A. Rice, Mike Wheat

LOCAL GOVERNMENT

Montana is divided into 54 county governments and 129 sub-county general purpose governments, all of which are municipal governments. In addition, there are 758 Special Districts and 332 School Districts.

Montana Association of Counties, URL: http://www.discoveringmontana.com/maco/
Montana League of Cities and Towns, URL: http://www.mlct.org/

AREA AND POPULATION

Area

Montana is the fourth largest US state and is located east and north of Idaho, north of Wyoming, west of North Dakota and South Dakota, and south of the Canadian border. Montana's total area is 147,042.40 sq. miles, of which the land area is 145,552.43 sq. miles and the water area is 1,489.96 sq. miles.

Montana is best known for its mountainous western region, most of which is part of the Northern Rocky Mountains; however, a surprising 60 per cent of the state is prairie - part of the Great Plains. As well as straddling the Continental Divide, Montana boasts the Triple Divide Peak - the hydrological apex of North America; this is the point at which the Great Divide and the Northern Divide meet, and waters flow to the Pacific Ocean, the Atlantic Ocean via the Gulf of Mexico, and the Arctic Ocean via Hudson Bay. It is the only place on earth where two oceanic divides meet, i.e. where waters from a single point area feed into three different oceans.

To view a map, consult http://www.lib.utexas.edu/maps/us_2001/montana_ref_2001.pdf

Population

According to the 2010 Census, the population was 989,415, a fall on the mid-2009 estimate of 974,989. In 2012, the population was estimated to be 1,005,141. The population of Montana grew by 9.7 per cent over the period 2000-2010 and is expected to reach 1.04 million by 2030. Montana's population density is 6.8 inhabitants per sq. mile, the third lowest in the USA. The county with the greatest population is Yellowstone County, with around 130,000 inhabitants and the largest city is Billings city, Yellowstone County, with around 147,000 inhabitants. The capital, Helena, had a population of around 28,190 in 2010.

According to the 2010 Census, 6.3 per cent of the population is under 5 years, 22.6 per cent under 18 years and 14.8 per cent is aged over 65 years. Approximately 89.4 per cent of the population is white, and 0.4 per cent is black. Approximately 2.9 per cent of the population is of Hispanic or Latino origin.

Births, Marriages, Deaths

The US Census Bureau, Population Division, estimated that there were 12,060 births in 2010 and 8,827 deaths over the same period, giving a natural population increase of 3,233 people. Net migration, mainly from other parts of the USA, added 2,754 inhabitants in 2009. The infant mortality rate in 2007 was 6.4 infant deaths per 1,000 live births. Provisional data indicates that there were 7,126 marriages and 3,553 divorces in 2007, both figures up on the previous year.

EMPLOYMENT

That Montana is a sparsely populated state is reflected in its comparatively small labour force. In December 2012, Montana's total civilian labour force was estimated to be 510,100, of which 480,800 were employed and 29,200 were unemployed. The unemployment rate was 5.7 per cent, lower than the average rate of 7.8 per cent. (Source: US Bureau of Labor Statistics)

The following table shows December 2012 preliminary non-farm wage and salary employment according to industry:

Industry	No. of Jobs	12 month change (%)
Mining and logging	7,900	0.0
Construction	23,500	1.3
Manufacturing	16,900	0.0
Trade, transport and utilities	87,300	0.3
Information	7,500	1.4
Financial activities	20,900	0.0
Professional and business services	43,200	4.6
Education and health svcs.	65,700	2.3
Leisure and hospitality	56,100	3.1
Other services	17,400	7.4
Government	89,000	5.0
TOTAL	435,400	2.6

Source: Bureau of Labor Statistics

BANKING AND FINANCE

GDP/GNP, Inflation, National Debt

Montana's Gross State Product (GSP) rose from $35,954 million in 2009 to $36,067 million in 2010; real GDP rose 1.1 per cent in 2010, below the US average of 2.6 per cent. GDP rose to $38.00 billion (current prices) and ranked 48th in the US. The following table shows the state Gross State Product according to industry (in millions of current dollars):

GDP by industry ($m)

Industry	2009	2010	2011
Agriculture, Forestry, Fishing & Hunting	1,249	1,409	1,612
Mining	1,444	1,562	1,869
Utilities	1,005	993	937
Construction	1,889	1,847	1,883
Manufacturing	1,646	2,121	2,286
Wholesale Trade	1,766	1,792	1,901
Retail Trade	2,429	2,562	2,649
Transport and warehousing	1,523	1,646	1,762

- continued			
Information	874	905	913
Finance and Insurance	1,820	1,941	1,888
Real estate	4,572	4,350	4,456
Educational services	159	162	187
Health care & social services	3,349	3,530	3,629
Other Non-government services	5,197	5,541	5,877
Government	5,935	6,180	6,140
TOTAL	34,856	36,540	37,990

Source: Bureau of Economic Analysis, Feb. 2013

The average annual per capita personal income in the state rose to $36,016 in 2011, 87 per cent of the national average of $41,560. Per capita real GDP fell to $32,041 in 2011; the US average was $42,070.

The annual Consumer Price Index (all items) for the West urban area rose from 227.5 in 2011 to 232.4 in 2012 (1982-84 = 100). (Source: Bureau of Labor Statistics)

Balance of Payments / Imports and Exports

Montana's imports were valued at $3,556 million in 2009, down 43.2 per cent from $6,266 million in 2008. Imports rose to $4,680 million, up 29.9 per cent in 2010 and to $5,615 million in 2011, up 20 per cent. Montana's imports account for 0.3 per cent of the US total. In 2011, the top import was crude oil. Main suppliers include Canada (94.0 per cent), Germany, China, France and Mexico.

Montana's export revenue fell from $1,395 million to $1,053 million in 2009, a decrease of 24.1 per cent. Exports rose to $4,309 million in 2010 and to $1,587 million in 2011, up 14.3 per cent, representing 0.1 per cent of US total. The following table shows the top five export products in 2010:

Sector	Value ($m)
Crude oil from petroleum and bituminous minerals	3,610
Waste and scrap of precious metal.	153
Urea	105
Natural gas, gaseous	81
Propane, liquefied	48

Source: US Census Bureau, Foreign Trade Dept.

Montana's top five international export trading partners in 2010-11 are shown on the following table:

Country	2010 ($m)	2011 ($m)	+/- % 2010-11
Canada	506	598	18.1
South Korea	187	228	21.8
Mexico	80	129	61.2
China	123	119	-2.8
Taiwan	93	66	-29.1

Source: US Census Bureau, Foreign Trade Dept., Feb. 2013

Chambers of Commerce & Trade Organisations

Montana World Trade Centre, URL: http://www.mwtc.org
Billings Area Chamber of Commerce, URL: http://www.billingschamber.com/
Helena Area Chamber of Commerce, URL: http://www.helenachamber.com/

MANUFACTURING, MINING AND SERVICES

Primary and Extractive Industries

Montana is rich in fossil fuel and renewable energy resources. The state holds more than a quarter of the national estimated recoverable coal reserves. There are also large deposits of oil and gas. Rivers flowing from the Rocky Mountains offer considerable hydroelectric power resources, and there is potential for significant wind energy throughout the State.

Montana's mining industry contributed $1,869 million towards GDP in 2011, up from $1,562 million in 2010. Major mining sectors in 2010 were non-oil and gas mining ($1,006 million) and oil and gas extraction ($285 million). Support activities accounted for $270 million of state GDP. (Source: BEA)

Montana has proven crude oil reserves of 369 million barrels (2010), representing 1.6 per cent of the US total reserves. In the same year Montana had a total of 4,412 oil wells and 9 rotary rigs in operation. The state produced 25,308,000 barrels of crude oil in 2010 (1.3 per cent of the US total). Monthly total in 2012 (Oct) was 2,283,000 barrels. Crude oil refinery capacity was 187,600 bbl/d in 2012. Petroleum consumption in 2009 fell to 32.0 million barrels, as follows: over 11.9 million barrels were in the form of motor gasoline and almost 10.2 million barrels were in distillate fuel.

Montana had an estimated 944 billion cubic feet in natural gas in 2010. It had 11 million barrels of natural gas plant liquids. The state had 6,477 gas and gas condensate wells, and 74,624 million cubic feet of natural gas were sold 2011. Consumption was 72,026 million cubic feet.

Montana had recoverable coal reserves of 846 million short tons in 2011, representing 4.4 per cent of the US total reserves. The state has one underground mine and five surface mines. Production was 42,008 thousand short tons in 2011 (3.8 per cent of US total). Coal consumption stood at 9,854 thousand short tons compared to 12,041 thousand short tons in 2007. Most of it was used in the electricity generating industry. (Source: EIA)

UNITED STATES OF AMERICA

Energy
Total energy production was 1,152 trillion Btu in 2010 (1.5 per cent of the US total). Montana's population and total energy demand are low. The state's total energy consumption in 2010 was 401 trillion Btu. It was ranked 14th in the US for its 2010 per capita energy consumption (405 million Btu).

Net summer capability in 2010 was 5,866 MW (0.6 per cent of US total) and net monthly (Oct.) generation in 2012 was 2,330,000 MWh (0.7 per cent of US total). Coal was the primary fuel source (1,605,000 MWh), followed by hydroelectric (5222,000 MWh) and other renewables (119,000 MWh). Montana has no nuclear power plants.

Wind electric power generation grew by 34 per cent in 2011 and supplied 4.2 per cent of the state's net electricity generation. IT has created a Renewable Portfolio Standard for all electricity suppliers to be capable of generating 15 per cent of electricity from renewable energy resources by 2015. (Source: EIA)

Manufacturing
Manufacturing contributed an estimated $2,286 million towards Montana's 2011 GDP, up from $2,121 million in 2010. The major manufacturing sectors in 2010 was petroleum and coal products ($1,056 million).

Service Industries
The services industry is Montana's leading contributor to GDP. Major producing sectors in 2011 were real estate ($4,456 million), health and social assistance ($3,629 million), and professional and technical services ($1,909 million). In 2011, government services contributed $6,140 million to GDP.

Tourism
The accommodation and food sector accounted for $1,368 million of Montana's GDP in 2011, whilst the arts, entertainment and recreation sector contributed $462 million. Millions of tourists visit Glacier National Park, the Battle of Little Bighorn site, and Yellowstone National Park.
Travel Montana, URL: http://travel.state.mt.us/

Agriculture
Montana's agriculture, forestry and fishing industry accounted for an estimated $1,612 million of the 2011 GDP, up from $1,409 million the previous year. The farms sector contributed $1,246 million in 2010, whilst the forestry, fishing and related activities sector contributed $163 million in the same year.

According to the Department of Agriculture statistics , Montana's farms numbered 29,400 in 2010, and occupied around 60,800,000 acres, up from 58,445,000 acres in 1997. The average farm in Montana has an area of 2,068 acres. In 2008, the value of agricultural products sold reached $1.8 billion; $1.5 billion was in the form of livestock, poultry and their products, whilst crops earned around $1.27 billion. As of Jan. 2011, there were 2.5 million cattle & calves, 180,000 hogs & pigs and 230,000 sheep.

Montana's varied climate means that a wide range of agricultural products is produced: beef and dairy cattle, wheat and barley, sheep, pigs, hay, honey, and cherries.

COMMUNICATIONS AND TRANSPORT

International Airports
As well as Missoula International Airport, Montana has 12 state-owned airports, 119 public airports and more than 350 private airports.
Missoula International Airport, URL: http://www.msoairport.org

Railways
As well as national railway companies such as Amtrak, Burlington Northern Santa Fe and Union Pacific Railroad, Montana's own railway companies operating within the state include Montana Rail Link, Montana Western Railway, and Central Montana Rail. Some 92 per cent of the state's agricultural products are transported by rail.

Roads
Montana has in the region of 69,000 miles of public highways and roads. The Montana Department of Transport is responsible for more than 8,000 miles of highway and 2,100 bridges.

HEALTH

The National Center for Health Statistics estimated that there were 23 doctors per 10,000 population in 2009, below the national average of 27.4 doctors per 1,000 people. In 2008, there were 548 dentists (5.7 per 10,000 population). In 2009, there were 3.9 community hospital beds per 1,000 people, and 88 nursing homes, with 6,991 beds. Some 15.7 per cent of adults (18-64 years) had no health insurance in 2007-09. In 2007-11, an estimated 14.6 per cent of the population were considered to be living in poverty.

Montana has one of the lowest rates of heart disease-related deaths in the US, as well as low rate of diabetes and obesity. In 2012, 60.3 per cent of adults were considered overweight and 23 per cent obese. However, Montana has the third highest rate of motor vehicle-related deaths and a high rate of occupational fatalities. Montana reported 466 HIV/AIDS cases from the beginning of the epidemic to the end of 2008, ranking 47th highest among the 50 states. The overall TB rate was 0.9 cases per 100,000 population, again ranking it 49th highest in the US. (Source: CDC)

EDUCATION

Primary/Secondary Education
For the year 2009-10, there were 828 primary and secondary schools in Montana. Total student enrolment for the year was 141,807 and there were 10,521 classroom teachers, giving a ratio of one teacher to 13.48 students, below the US average of one teacher to 15.3 pupils.

Revenues from education for the year reached $1.559 billion in 2007-08, whilst current expenditure on state education was $1.564 billion.

Higher Education
In 2010-11, Montana had 23 degree conferring institutes of Higher Education, 18 of which were public. 24,096 male students enrolled for the year, together with 27,492 women. Over the year, 9,010 degrees were conferred, of which 5,232 were Bachelors, 1,745 were Masters and 309 were doctorates. (Source: National Center for Education Statistics)

COMMUNICATIONS AND MEDIA

Newspapers
Montana's daily and weekly newspapers include: The Montana Standard, Bigfork Eagle, Billings Gazette Online, Billings Outpost, Daily Inter Lake, Havre Daily News, Helena Independent Record, Lake County Leader, Missoula Independent, Tobacco Valley News and Wolf Point Herald-News.
Montana Newspaper Association, URL: http://www.townnews.com/mt/mna
The Montana Standard, URL: http://www.mtstandard.com
The Bigfork Eagle, URL: http://bigforkeagle.com/
Billings Gazette, URL: http://www.billingsgazette.com/

Broadcasting
Montana has 16 network television stations, including KTVH in Helena; KPAX, KUFM, KECI, and KTMF in Missoula; and KRTV, KFBB, and KTGF in Great Falls.

ENVIRONMENT

Carbon dioxide emissions rose from 17,548,159 metric tons in 2009 to 20,369,529 metric tons in 2010, ranking the state 35th in the US, and accounting for 0.9 per cent of US total. Approximately 22,033 metric tons of sulphur dioxide and 21,197 metric tons of nitrogen oxide were also emitted. Montana is a major hydroelectric power producer; currently six of the state's largest generating plants run on hydroelectric power, and there are plans to expand hydroelectric power. The state has a number of wind farms. In April 2005, Montana adopted a renewable portfolio standard requiring that 15 per cent of the State's energy comes from renewable sources by 2015.

As of 2010 there were 3,841 alternative-fueled vehicles in use (0.4 per cent of US total). Ethanol consumption in 2011 was 1,010,000 barrels (0.3 per cent of US total). (Source: EIA)

NEBRASKA

Capital: Lincoln (Population, Census 2010: 258,379)

Head of State: Dave Heineman (R) (Governor) (page 1440)

State Flag: A field of national blue in the centre of which appears the state seal in gold and silver. The state seal shows, in the foreground, a smith, a hammer and an anvil, behind which is a settler's cabin, sheaves of wheat and stalks of corn; behind the cabin is the Missouri River on which appears a steamboat; in the background a train is travelling towards the Rocky Mountains; above the seal appears the words 'Equality Before the Law' in capital letters

CONSTITUTION AND GOVERNMENT

Constitution

Nebraska entered the Union on 1 March 1867. According to the 1875 Constitution, the chief executive is the governor, elected for a term of four years. The governor is assisted by 19 other executive branch officials: lieutenant governor, secretary of state, auditor of public accounts, treasurer, attorney general, five public service commissioners, and nine state board of education members. All are elected for four-year terms.

Nebraska elects a total of five representatives to the US Congress: three Representatives and two Senators.

To view the state constitution, please visit: http://uniweb.legislature.ne.gov/LegalDocs/view.php?page=index_con

Legislature

Until 1937, Nebraska operated a bicameral, partisan legislature. In 1934, Nebraska's voters opted for a single chamber, non-partisan legislature, making it the only state in the US with such a system. Effectively, the House of Representatives was dropped and the Senate retained. Consequently, members of the Unicameral Legislature are still known as senators. The number of senators was increased from 43 to 49 in 1965. The 49 state senators are elected for a maximum of two consecutive four-year terms, with half of the Senate elected every two years.

Nebraska Unicameral Legislature, State Capitol, PO Box 94604, Lincoln, NE 68509-4604, USA. Tel: +1 402 471 2271 (Clerk), URL: http://nebraskalegislature.gov/

Elected Executive Branch Officials (as at April 2013)

Governor: Dave Heineman (R) (page 1440)
Lieutenant Governor: Lavon Heidemann (R)
Secretary of State: John A. Gale (R)
Attorney General: Jon Bruning (R)
Auditor of Public Accounts: Mike Foley (R)
State Treasurer: Don Stenburg (R)
Public Service Commissioners: Frank E. Landis Jr. (R), Anne C. Boyle, Tim Schram (R), Rod Johnson, Gerald L. Vap
State Board of Education: Jim Scheer (President), Robert Evnen, Mark Quandahl, Rebecca Valdez, Patricia Timm, Lynn Cronk, Molly O'Holleran, John Siegler, Dr Roger Breed

Unicameral Legislature (as at April 2013)

President of the Legislature: Lt. Gov. Lavon Heidemann (R)
Speaker of the Legislature: Greg Adams
Chairperson of the Executive Board of the Legislative Council: John Wightman

US Senators: Mike Johanns (R) (page 1450) and Deb Fischer (R) (page 1424)

Ministries

Office of the Governor, State Capitol, 2nd Floor NE, PO Box 94848, Lincoln, NE 68509-4844, USA. Tel: +1 402 471 2244, fax: +1 402 471 6031, URL: http://governor.nebraska.gov/
Office of the Lieutenant Governor, Room 2315, State Capitol (PO Box 94863), Lincoln, NE 68509-4863, USA. Tel: +1 402 471 2256, fax: +1 402 471 6031, URL: http://www.ltgov.ne.gov
Office of the Secretary of State, Suite 2300, State Capitol (PO Box 94608), Lincoln, NE 68509-4608, USA. Tel: +1 402 471 2554, fax: +1 402 471 3237, URL: http://www.sos.state.ne.us/
Office of the State Treasurer, Room 2003, State Capitol, Lincoln, Nebraska 68509-4788, USA. Tel: +1 402 471 2455, fax: +1 402 471 4390, URL: http://www.treasurer.org/
Office of the State Auditor of Public Accounts, State Capitol, Suite 2303, PO Box 98917, Lincoln, Nebraska 68509-8917, USA. Tel: +1 402 471 2111, fax: +1 402 471 3301, e-mail: kwitek@mail.state.ne.us, URL: http://www.auditors.state.ne.us/
Office of the Attorney General, 2115 State Capitol (PO Box 98920), Lincoln, NE 68509-8920, USA. Tel: +1 402 471 2682, fax: +1 402 471 3297, URL: http://www.ago.ne.gov/
Department of Agriculture, 301 Centennial Mall South, 4th Floor, PO Box 94947, Lincoln, NE 68509-4947, USA. Tel: +1 402 471 2341, fax: +1 402 471 2759, URL: http://www.nda.nebraska.gov/
Department of Banking and Finance, Commerce Court 1230 "O" Street, Suite 400, PO Box 95006, Lincoln, NE 68509-5006, USA. Tel: +1 402 471 2171, URL: http://www.ndbf.ne.gov
Department of Economic Development, PO Box 94666, 301 Centennial Mall South, 4th Floor, Lincoln, NE 68509-4666, USA. Tel: +1 402 471 3111, fax +1 402 471 3778, URL: http://www.neded.org
Department of Education, 301 Centennial Mall South, 6th Floor, PO Box 94987, Lincoln, Nebraska 68509-4987, USA. Tel: +1 402 471 2295, fax: +1 402 471 0117, URL: http://www.education.ne.gov/

Department of Environmental Quality, 1200 'N' Street, Suite 400, PO Box 98922, Lincoln, NE 68509-8922, USA. Tel: +1 402 471 2186, fax: +1 402 471 2909, URL: http://www.deq.state.ne.us
Department of Health and Human Services, PO Box 95044, Lincoln, NE 68509-5044, USA. Tel: +1 402 471 2306, URL: http://www.hhs.state.ne.us
Department of Labor, 550 South 16th Street, PO Box 94600, Lincoln, NE 68509-4600, USA. Tel: +1 402 471 9000, fax: +1 402 471 2318, URL: http://www.dol.nebraska.gov
Department of Motor Vehicles, 301 Centennial Mall South, Mall Level, PO Box 94789, Lincoln, NE 68509-4789, USA. Tel: +1 402 471 2281, fax: +1 402 471 9594, URL: http://www.dmv.state.ne.us/
Department of Roads, 1500 Highway 2, PO Box 94759, Lincoln, NE 68509-4759, USA. Tel: +1 402 471 4567, fax: +1 402 479 4325, URL: http://www.transportation.nebraska.gov/

Political Parties

Nebraska Democratic Party, 1327 H Street, Suite 200, Lincoln, NE 68508, USA. Tel: +1 402 434 2180, fax: +1 402 434 2188, e-mail: info@nebraskademocrats.org, URL: http://www.nebraskademocrats.org
Nebraska Republican Party, 1610 N. Street, Lincoln, Nebraska 68508, USA. Tel: +1 402 475 2122, fax: +1 402 475 3541, e-mail: info@negop.org, URL: http://www.negop.org

Elections

Elections for state constitutional posts took place in November 2006. Mike Johanns, the state Governor since 1999, resigned in January 2005 to take up the office of US Secretary of Agriculture. David Heineman, the then Lieutenant Governor, took up the Governorship, and was elected to the post in the November 2006 elections. He was comfortably re-elected in the November 2010 elections as was the Lieutenant Governor Rick Sheehy. Mr Sheehy resigned in February 2013. The governor appointed Lavon Heidemann, a former state senator, as his replacement.

Partial elections for the Nebraska State Senate took place in November 2012.

In the November 6 2012 elections to the US Senate, Republican Deb Fischer defeated the incumbent Ben Nelson.

Elections for two state executive positions (Nebraska Public Service Commission, two officers) also took place. The two incumbent candidates, Frank Landis, District 1 and Tim Schram, District 3, were both re-elected.

LEGAL SYSTEM

Nebraska's court system comprises the Supreme Court, the Court of Appeals, District courts, County courts, Juvenile courts, and Workers' Compensation courts. The Supreme Court is headed by the Chief Justice and six Associate Justices, all elected for a term of six years by merit system. The Court of Appeals consists of a Chief Judge and five judges, all appointed by the Governor for two-year terms. There are 12 District Courts, one for each District.

Nebraska has the death penalty and three people have been executed since 1976. Eleven people are currently on death row. According to the DPIC the murder rate is 3 per 100,000 population.

Supreme Court, URL: http://www.supremecourt.ne.gov
Chief Justice: Michael Heavican
Court of Appeals, URL: http://www.supremecourt.ne.gov/appeals-court/index.shtml?sub2
Chief Justice: Everett Inbody

LOCAL GOVERNMENT

Nebraska has 93 counties. The county governing body is called the board of commissioners, except in counties having township government, where it is called the board of supervisors. There are 530 municipal and 454 township governments. Most cities have a mayor-council form of government. Nebraska City has a commissioner, and others have a council. Most villages are governed by a five-member board of trustees. Nebraska's constitution grants the option of home rule to cities with more than 5,000 residents, but only Lincoln and Omaha have opted to use this. Additionally, there are 1,294 special district governments. There are 288 school district governments, governed by an elected board.

There are four sovereign Native American tribes within Nebraska: the Omaha, Ponca, Santee Sioux and Winnebago. They are governed by tribal constitutions, bylaws, ordinances and laws. The governing bodies are the tribal councils.
Nebraska Association of County Officials, URL: http://www.nacone.org/
League of Nebraska Municipalities, URL: http://www.lonm.org/

AREA AND POPULATION

Area

Nebraska is located in the mid-west of the US, north of Kansas, south of South Dakota, east of Wyoming and Colorado, and west of Iowa and Missouri. Its total area is 77,353.73 sq. miles, of which 76,872.41 sq. miles is land and 481.31 sq. miles is water.

To view a map, consult http://www.lib.utexas.edu/maps/us_2001/nebraska_ref_2001.pdf

UNITED STATES OF AMERICA

Population
According to the 2010 Census, the state population was 1,826,341, up from the mid-2009 population at 1,796,619. The population was estimated at 1,855,525. The population grew by 6.7 per cent over the period 2000-2010. The population is expected to reach 1.82 million by 2030. Nebraska has a population density of 23.8 people per sq. mile. The county with the greatest number of inhabitants is Douglas county. The capital, Lincoln, had an estimated population of 262,341 in 2011. Omaha is the largest city in Nebraska, with a population of 415,068 (E) in 2011.

There are four Native American tribes that have democratic forms of government; the Omaha, Ponca, Santee Sioux and Winnebago tribes are governed by tribal constitutions, bylaws, ordinances and laws. The governing bodies are tribal councils, made up of elected council members. The Omaha, Winnebago and Santee tribes have their own judicial and law enforcement agencies.

According to the 2010 Census, 7.2 per cent of the population is under 5 years, 25.1 per cent under 18 years and 13.5 per cent is aged over 65 years. Approximately 86.1 per cent of the population is white, and 4.5 per cent is black. Approximately 9.2 per cent of the population is of Hispanic or Latino origin.

Births, Marriages, Deaths
The US Census Bureau estimated that there were 25,918 births in 2010 and 15,171 deaths over the same period, giving a natural population increase of 10,747 people. Net migration amounted to 2,113 people in 2009. The infant mortality rate in 2007 was 6.8 infant deaths per 1,000 live births. Marriages and divorces in 2007, according to provisional data, numbered 12,417 (up on 2006) and 5,500 (down on 2006) respectively.

Public Holidays
In addition to public holidays celebrated by the rest of the US, Nebraska also celebrates Arbor Day on the last Friday in April.

EMPLOYMENT

Nebraska's estimated total civilian labour force in December 2012 numbered 1,029,300, of which 990,700 were employed and 38,500 were unemployed. The unemployment rate was 3.7 per cent, one of the lowest rates in the USA. (Source: US Bureau of Labor Statistics)

Preliminary non-farm wage and salary employment in December 2012, according to industry, is shown on the following table:

Industry	No. of jobs	12 month change (%)
Manufacturing	94,600	1.3
Trade, transport and utilities	195,000	-0.9
Information	16,200	-3.6
Financial activities	68,100	-2.0
Professional and business services	105,300	0.8
Educational and health services	141,700	2.6
Leisure and hospitality	81,900	-0.1
Other services	37,000	0.0
Government	168,900	0.0
TOTAL	953,500	0.6

Source: Bureau of Labor Statistics

BANKING AND FINANCE

GDP/GNP, Inflation, National Debt
Nebraska's total Gross Domestic Product (GDP) rose from an estimated $86,439 million in 2009 to $89,786 million; real GDP rose by 1.9 per cent over 2010, below the US average of 2.6 per cent. In 2011, GDP (current prices) amounted to $94.2 billion and ranked 36th in the US. Real GDP grew by 0.1 per cent in 2011, below the national change of 1.5 per cent. In 2011, the largest industry was government (13.1 per cent of US total).

The following table shows Nebraska's Gross Domestic Product according to industry (in millions of current dollars):

Industry	2009	2010	2011
Agriculture, forestry, fishing & hunting	5,386	6,279	7,825
Mining	74	96	136
Utilities	1,479	1,410	1,276
Construction	3,620	3,362	3,222
Manufacturing	9,713	10,382	11,157
Wholesale Trade	4,514	4,637	4,835
Retail Trade	5,037	5,355	5,469
Transportation & warehousing	6,203	6,489	6,646
Information	2,690	2,590	2,845
Finance & Insurance	8,052	9,317	9,332
Real estate	8,215	7,864	7,837
Educational services	759	779	783
Health care & social assistance	6,452	6,753	7,113
Other non-government services	12,217	12,718	13,327
Government	11,467	12,041	12,356
TOTAL	85,874	90,072	94,160

Source: Bureau of Economic Analysis, Feb. 2013

Average annual per capita income in the state of Nebraska rose to $42,450 in 2011. Per capita GDP fell to $43,356 in 2011, compared to the US figure of $42,070. The Consumer Price Index (CPI) (all items) for the Midwest urban area rose from 214.7 in 2011 to 219.1 in 2012. (1982-84 = 100) (Source: Bureau of Labor Statistics).

Balance of Payments / Imports and Exports
Total Nebraska imports amounted to $3,415 million in 2011, up 17.7 per cent on the 2010 total of $2,901 million. Nebraska imports accounted for 0.2 per cent of total US imports in 2011. Main suppliers are China (24.9 per cent), Canada (22.2 per cent), Mexico (9.8 per cent), Germany and Japan. Commodities include manufactured goods, tractors and tractor parts, bovine animals and engine parts.

Merchandise exports fell by 10.0 per cent from $5,412 million in 2008 to $4,873 million in 2009. Exports rose by 19.4 per cent in 2010 to $5,820 million. Exports rose by 30.3 per cent in 2011, up to $7,582 million, representing 0.5 per cent of US total exports. The top five export products in 2010 according to revenue are shown on the following table:

Commodity	Revenue ($m) 2010
Corn (Maize), other than seed corn	438
Combine Harvesters-Threshers	433
Soybeans	359
Meat of bovine animals, boneless, fresh or chilled	339
Natural gas, gaseous	273

US Census Bureau, Foreign Trade Division

The top five export destinations in 2010-11, according to revenue, are shown on the following table:

Destination	2010 ($m)	2011 ($m)	+/-2010-11
Canada	1,607	2,003	24.7
Mexico	1,314	1,870	42.3
Japan	437	537	23.0
China	279	380	36.2
South Korea	271	332	22.3

US Census Bureau

Chambers of Commerce and Trade Organisations
Nebraska Chamber of Commerce and Industry, URL: http://www.nechamber.com/
Nebraska Department of Economic Development, URL: http://www.neded.org
Lincoln Chamber of Commerce, URL: http://www.lcoc.com
Nebraska City Chamber of Commerce, URL: http://www.nebraskacity.com

MANUFACTURING, MINING AND SERVICES

Primary and Extractive Industries
Nebraska's mining industry contributed $136 million towards the 2011 GDP, up from $96 million the previous year. In 2010, $37 million came from oil and gas extraction, $51 million from mining other than oil and gas, and $8 million from support activities. Leading non-fuel minerals mined in Nebraska are portland cement, crushed stone, and construction sand and gravel.

Nebraska had proven crude oil reserves of 10 million barrels in 2010. Nebraska's oil industry produced a total of 2.207 million barrels in 2009. On Oct. 2012 monthly production amounted to 180,000 barrels. There are 1,226 producing oil wells and one rotary rig in operation. Oil consumption over the year 2010 amounted to 41.3 million barrels, 19.8 million barrels of which were motor gasoline and 15.7 million barrels were distillate fuel.

Nebraska's 322 natural gas wells produced a total of 1,959 million cubic feet of natural gas in 2011. Consumption rose from 168,941 million cubic feet in 2010 to 171,773 million cu ft in 2011. Supply is mainly from Rocky Mountain and Midwest natural gas producers. The industrial sector is the State's leading consumer, followed by the residential sector; over two-thirds of Nebraska households use natural gas as the primary fuel for heating.

Coal consumption was 16.7 million short tons in 2010 (1.7 per cent of US total).

Nebraska is among the top producers of corn-based ethanol, which is largely exported to other States, as Nebraska is one of the few States that allow the use of conventional motor gasoline. The State is considering the use of other feedstocks, including native switchgrass and soybean or other vegetable oils, in the expansion of its biofuels program. It recently opened its first biodiesel facility which has a capacity of 5 million gallons per year. (Source: EIA)

Energy
Nebraska's total energy production was 401 trillion Btu in 2010. Nebraska's total energy consumption in 2010 was 844 trillion Btu (0.9 per cent of the US total). Its per capita energy consumption was 461 million Btu (8th in the US).

Nebraska is a net exporter of electricity, its primary generating fuel being coal. Net summer capability in 2010 was 7,857 MW. Total net generation in October 2012 was 2,670,000 MWh (0.9 per cent of the US total), of which coal 2,422,000 MWh, nuclear power 220,000 MWh, hydroelectric 80,000 MWh, other renewables 118,000 MWh. (Source: EIA)

Manufacturing
The manufacturing industry is the third largest contributor towards Nebraska's GDP, accounting for $11,157 million in 2011, an increase on the previous year ($10,382 million). Top sectors include food product manufacturing ($3,330 million) and chemical manufacturing ($1,547 million). Other key manufacturing industries are electrical and other machinery, metal products, printing and publishing, transportation equipment; stone, clay, and glass products; and rubber and plastic products.

Service Industries

The services industry is a key sector of Nebraska's economy and the top contributor towards its GDP. In 2011, the major sectors apart from real estate ($7,837 million) and finance and insurance ($9,332 million) were transport and warehousing ($6,646 million) and health care and social assistance ($7,113 million).

Tourism

Tourism is an important sector of the economy, employing some 43,000 people. The accommodation and food sector of the services industry contributed $1,961 million towards the state's 2010 GDP, whilst the amusement and recreation sector contributed $444 million. Main attractions include the Arbor Lodge State Historic Park, Buffalo Bill Ranch Park and Carhenge.

Nebraska Division of Travel and Tourism, URL: http://www.visitnebraska.org

Agriculture

Nebraska's agriculture industry accounted for an estimated $7,825 million of Nebraska's 2011 GDP, up on the previous year when the sector earned $6,279 million. In 2010, the top sector was farming ($6,066 million). Forestry, fishing and related activities earned $213 million.

According to USDA Census of Agriculture, Nebraska had a total of 47,200 farms in 2010 (down from 54,539 at the time of the 1997 Census of Agriculture), and a total farm land area of 45,600,000 acres. The average size of a Nebraskan farm rose from 841 acres in 1997 to 966 acres in 2010. Total market value of agricultural products sold in 2008 was $15.5 billion, of which $6.8 billion was generated by livestock, poultry and products, and $8.6 billion was generated by crops, including greenhouse and nursery crops. Major livestock products are hogs and pigs, cattle and calves. As of 1 Jan. 2011, there were 6.2 million cattle and calves, 2.15 million hogs & pigs and 74,000 sheep. Major crops harvested are corn for grain or seed, soybeans for beans, and wheat for grain. (Source: National Agricultural Statistics Service)

COMMUNICATIONS AND TRANSPORT

International Airports

The main airports in Nebraska are Omaha, and Lincoln. Some 2.28 million passengers used Nebraska's 296 airports in 2005. In the same year, 226,095 tons of revenue freight were carried through Nebraska's airports.

Railways

Nebraska's railway system includes: Burlington Northern: Nebraska Public Power District, Nebraska Central, Nebkota, Omaha, and Lincoln and Beatrice. Total mainline miles owned by Nebraskan railway companies was recorded in 2004 at 3,692, with 2,726 miles of Class I railway line. 2004 statistics indicate that 24 million tons of freight originated or terminated on Nebraska's railway system.

Roads

Nebraska has a total of 9,959 miles of roads and streets, 481 miles of which are part of the Interstate highway system. In 2006, 2,119,000 vehicles were registered in the state.

Shipping

In 2003, over 1,195,000 short tons of commodities were transported on the Missouri River, between Omaha and Kansas City. In 2002, 125 thousand short tons of commodities were transported on the Missouri between Sioux City and Omaha, down from 250 thousand short tons the previous year. (Source: Nebraska Data Book)

HEALTH

In 2009, Nebraska had 4.1 beds per 1,000 people. In 2010, there were 222 nursing homes in the state, with 16,065 beds. The National Centre for Health Statistics estimated that there were 24.7 doctors (including osteopaths) per 10,000 population in 2009, below the US average of 27.4. In 2008, there were 1,105 dentists (6.2 per 10,000 population).

The Center for Disease Control estimated that 12.2 per cent of Nebraskans had no health-care coverage in 2008, and that 12 per cent were living in poverty in 2007-11 (both figures comfortably below the US average).

Nebraska reported 1,679 HIV/AIDS cases from the beginning of the epidemic to the end of 2008, and ranked 41st in cumulative number of reported HIV/AIDS cases. The overall TB rate was 1.9 per 100,000 population, ranking it 38th highest. Nebraskans have one of the lowest rates of heart-disease-related deaths, but they suffer a higher than average incidence of occupational fatalities. In 2012, 64.1 per cent of the population were considered overweight and 26.9 per cent obese.

EDUCATION

Primary/Secondary Education

In 2009-10, there were 295,368 students enrolled in the state's 1,142 primary and secondary schools. There were 22,256 classroom teachers, giving a ratio of 13.27 pupils per teacher (below the US average of 15.3 pupils per teacher).

In 2007-08, income from education was around $3.286 million, whilst expenditure in the state sector was $3.457 million.

Higher Education

The total number of students enrolled at Nebraska's 43 higher education institutions in 2010-11 was around 62,252 men and 76,393 women. In the same period 25,912 degrees/certificates were awarded, of which 12,596 were Bachelors, 4,364 were Masters and 1,392 were Doctorates. (Source: National Center for Education Statistics)

COMMUNICATIONS AND MEDIA

Newspapers

Nebraska's newspapers with the highest circulation include: Daily Omaha World-Herald, circ. 232,360 (URL: http://www.omaha.com); Sunday Omaha World-Herald, 290,804 (URL: http://www.omaha.com); Daily Lincoln Journal-Star, 81,301; Sunday Lincoln Journal-Star, 82,833; Omaha Catholic Voice (weekly), 68,546; Grand Island Independent (daily), 24,543; Norfolk Daily News, 20,446.

Nebraska Press Association, URL: http://www.nebpress.com

Broadcasting

Nebraska had 148 radio stations in 2003, most in the Lincoln and Omaha areas. There are 25 television stations in Nebraska (excluding cable), six of which are in Omaha. Cable television stations operate in nearly 340 towns across Nebraska, broadcasting to a total of 507,000 people.

Telecommunications

In 2003, there were 1.09 million access telephone lines: 439,500 business lines, and nearly 653,000 residential lines.

ENVIRONMENT

Carbon dioxide emissions rose from 23,899,471 metric tons in 2009 to 24,460,746 metric tons in 2010, ranking the state 34th in the US, accounting for 1.0 per cent of total. Approximately 64,875 metric tons of sulfur dioxide and 40,030 metric tons of nitrogen oxide were also emitted. Nebraska is a top producer of corn-based ethanol, 22 ethanol plants, with a capacity of 1,8139 million gallons per year (13.6 per cent of the US total). Ethanol consumption was 1,472,000 barrels in 2011 (0.5 per cent of US total). In 2010, there were 5,553 alternative-fueled vehicles. (Source: EIA)

NEVADA

Capital: Carson City (Population, Census 2010: 55,274)

Head of State: Brian Sandoval (R) (Governor) (page 1508)

State Flag: A cobalt blue background in the upper left quarter of which appears a silver five-pointed star between two crossed sprays of sagebrush; above the sagebrush is a gold scroll on which appears the words 'Battle Born' in black; below the star and above the sagebrush appears the word 'Nevada'.

CONSTITUTION AND GOVERNMENT

Constitution

Nevada entered the Union as the 36th state on 31 October 1864. According to the state constitution the executive branch of state government consists of the governor and five other elected officials: lieutenant governor, secretary of state, attorney general, controller, and treasurer. All are elected for a four-year term.

Nevada elects three Representatives and two Senators to the US Congress in Washington, DC. To view the state constitution, please visit: http://www.leg.state.nv.us/Const/NvConst.html

Legislature

The legislative branch comprises the Senate and the Assembly. Sessions of the legislature start on the first Monday in February of each odd-numbered year and last no longer than 120 days.

Nevada Legislature, Legislative Building, 401 South Carson Street, Carson City, Nevada 89701-4747, USA. Tel: +1 775 684 6800, fax: +1 775 684 6500 (Senate), +1 775 684 8533 (Assembly), e-mail: senate@lcb.state.nv.us, assembly@lcb.state.nv.us, URL: http://www.leg.state.nv.us/

Upper House

The Senate has 21 members elected for four-year terms, each half elected in separate general elections. The Lieutenant Governor is also President of the Senate. Following the November 2012 elections, the Democrats retained control of the Senate, with 11 seats; the Republicans have the remaining 10 seats.

Nevada Senate, 401 S. Carson St., Carson City, NV 89701, USA. Tel: +1 775 684 1400 (Secretary), e-mail: cclift@lcb.state.nv.us (Secretary), URL: http://leg.state.nv.us/Senate/

Lower House

The Assembly has 42 members elected for a term of two years. Following the 2012 elections, the Assembly was composed of 27 Democrats and 15 Republicans.

UNITED STATES OF AMERICA

Nevada Assembly, 401 S. Carson St., Carson City, NV 89701, USA. Tel: +1 775 684 8555 (Chief Clerk), URL: http://leg.state.nv.us/Assembly/Index.cfm

---

Elected Executive Branch Officials (as at April 2013)
Governor: Brian Sandoval (R) (page 1508)
Lieutenant Governor: Brian Krolicki (R)
Secretary of State: Ross Miller (D)
State Treasurer: Kate Marshall (D)
State Controller: Kim Wallin (D)
Attorney General: Catherine Cortez Masto (D)

Legislature (as at April 2013)
President of the Senate: Lt. Gov. Brian Krolicki (R)
President Pro Tempore: David R. Parks (D)
Senate Majority Leader: Moises Denis (D)
Senate Minority Leader: Michael Roberson (R)
Speaker of the Assembly: Marilyn Kirkpatrick (D)
Speaker Pro Tem of the Assembly: Paul Aizley (D)
Assembly Majority Leader: William Horne (D)
Assembly Minority Leader: Pat Hickey (R)

US Senators: Dean Heller (page 1440)(R) and Harry Reid (D) (page 1502)

Ministries
Office of the Governor, Capitol Building, Carson City, NV 89701, USA. Tel: +1 775 684 5670, fax: +1 775 684 5683, URL: http://gov.nv.gov/
Office of the Lieutenant Governor, 101 N Carson Street, Suite 2, Carson City, NV 89701, USA. Tel: +1 775 684 5637, fax: +1 775 684 5782, URL: http://ltgov.nv.gov/
Office of the Secretary of State, 101 North Carson Street, Suite 3, Carson City, NV 89701-4786, USA. Tel: +1 775 684 5708, fax: +1 775 684 5717, URL: http://nvsos.gov/
Office of the Attorney General, 100 North Carson Street, Carson City, NV 89701-4717, USA. Tel: +1 775 684 1100, fax: +1 775 684 1108, URL: http://ag.nv.us
Office of the State Controller, 101 N Carson Street, Suite 5, Carson City, NV 89701-4786, USA. Tel: +1 775 684 5750, fax: +1 775 684 5695, URL: http://controller.nv.gov/
Office of the State Treasurer, 101 N Carson Street, Suite 4, Carson City, NV 89701, USA. Tel: +1 775 684 5600, fax: +1 775 684 5623, e-mail: statetreasurer@nevadatreasurer.gov, URL: https://nevadatreasurer.gov/index.htm
Department of Agriculture, 350 Capitol Hill Avenue, Reno, Nevada 89502, USA. Tel: +1 775 688 1180, fax: +1 775 688 1178, URL: http://agri.state.nv.us
Department of Business and Industry, 555 E. Washington Avenue, Suite 4900, Las Vegas, NV 89101, USA. Tel: +1 702 486 2750, fax: +1 702 486 2758, URL: http://business.nv.gov
Department of Conservation and Natural Resources, 123 W. Nye Lane, Room 230, Carson City, Nevada 89701-0818, USA. Tel: +1 775 687 4360, fax: +1 775 687 6122, URL: http://dcnr.nv.gov
Department of Cultural Affairs, 716 North Carson Street, Suite B, Carson City, NV 89701, USA. Tel: +1 775 687 8393, fax: +1 775 684 5446, URL: http://nevadaculture.org/
Department of Education, 700 East Fifth Street, Carson City, NV 89701-5096, USA. Tel: +1 775 687 9200, fax: +1 775 687 9101, URL: http://www.doe.nv.gov/
Department of Employment, Training and Rehabilitation, 500 East Third Street, Suite 200, Carson City, NV 89713, USA. Tel: +1 775 684 3849, fax: +1 775 684 3908, URL: http://detr.state.nv.us/
Department of Information Technology, 505 East King Street, Room 403, Carson City, NV 89701, USA. Tel: +1 775 684 5800, fax: +1 775 684 5846, URL: http://it.nv.gov/
Department of Motor Vehicles, 555 Wright Way, Carson City, Nevada 89711, USA. Tel: +1 775 684 4549, fax: +1 775 684 4692, URL: http://nevadadmv.state.nv.us
Department of Public Safety, 555 Wright Way, Carson City, NV 89711-0900, USA. Tel: +1 775 684 4556, fax: +1 775 684 4692, URL: http://dps.nv.gov/
Department of Transportation, 1263 South Stewart Street, Room 201, Carson City, Nevada 89712, USA. Tel: +1 775 888 7000, fax: +1 775 888 7115, URL: http://www.nevadadot.com

Political Parties
Nevada Democratic Party, 1325 E. Vegas Valley Drive, Suite C, Las Vegas, NV 89104, USA. Tel: +1 702 735 1600, fax: +1 702 735 2700, e-mail: info@nvdems.com, URL: http://www.nvdems.com
Nevada Republican Party, 8625 W Sahara Avenue, Las Vegas, NV 89117, USA. Tel: +1 702 258 9182, fax: +1 702 258 9186, e-mail: webmaster@nevadagop.org, URL: http://www.nevadagop.org

Elections
Following the November 2012 general election, the Democrats retained their narrow majority in the State Senate (Democrats 11, Republicans 10). In the state Assembly the Democrats remained the majority party (Democrats 27 seats, Republicans 15 seats).

Constitution elections took place in 2010 for the Governor and the five executive branch officials (Lieutenant Governor, Secretary of State, State Treasurer, State Controller, and Attorney General). Incumbent Republican Jim Gibbons lost the primary election to Brian Sandoval who went onto win the election. Brian Krolicki (R) the incumbent lieutenant governor was re-elected.

LEGAL SYSTEM

Nevada's court system consists of the Supreme Court, District Courts (60 Judges), Justice Courts (64 Judgeships), and Municipal Courts (29 Judgeships). The Supreme Court consists of the Chief Justice and six Associate Justices all elected to six-year terms. Unlike other state supreme courts, the Supreme Court of Nevada does not have the power of discretionary review, and must hear all appeals; consequently, Nevada's judicial system is congested. In 2009, research on the possible jurisdiction of a proposed Nevada Court of appeals was

completed. The research, undertaken by the Nevada Supreme Court at the request of the Nevada Legislature, suggested that the creation of the Nevada Court of Appeals would be beneficial.

Nevada has the death penalty. According to the DPIC, 61 people have been executed since 1976, most recently in 2006. The murder rate is put at 5.9 per 100,000 population. There are currently 79 people on death row.

A law recognising legal recognition of same-sex unions in Nevada was passed in 2009.

Supreme Court, URL: http://www.nevadajudiciary.us/
Chief Justice: Kristina Pickering
Justices: Mark Gibbons, Ron Parraguire, Michael Cherry, James Hardesty, Michael Douglas, Nancy Saitta

LOCAL GOVERNMENT

Nevada has 16 counties and one city: Carson City, Churchill, Clark, Douglas, Elko, Esmeralda, Eureka, Humboldt, Lander, Lincoln, Lyon, Mineral, Nye, Pershing, Storey, Washoe, White Pine. The state is subdivided into 19 sub-county general purpose governments, all of which are all municipal governments (made up of incorporated cities and towns). Nevada has no town or township governments. The county governing body is the board of county commissioners.

Nevada Association of Counties, URL: http://www.nvnaco.org/
Nevada League of Cities and Municipalities, URL: http://www.nvleague.org/NVLeague/

AREA AND POPULATION

Area
Nevada is located in the West, north and east of California, south of Oregon and Idaho, and west of Utah and Arizona. Nevada has a total area of 110,560.71 sq. miles, of which 109,825.99 sq. miles is land area, and 734.71 sq. miles is water area.

Nevada has many north-south mountain ranges (with peaks exceeding 13,000 feet), but is also within both the Great Basin Desert to the north, and the Mojave Desert in the south. Over 80 per cent of the state's area is owned by the federal government.

To view a map, consult http://www.lib.utexas.edu/maps/us_2001/nevada_ref_2001.pdf

Population
According to the 2010 Census, the state population was 2,700,551, up from the mid-2009 estimate of 2,643,085. In 2012, it was estimated at 2,758,931. Over the period 2000-2010, the population of Nevada grew by 35.1 per cent, the highest percentage increase in the USA. The population is expected to reach 4.28 million by 2030. Population density was 24.6 persons per sq. mile. The largest county is Clark County, with 1,951,269 inhabitants in 2010. The capital, Carson City, had a population of 55,439 (e) in 2011, but Las Vegas is the most highly populated city, with 589,317 inhabitants in 2011; over two thirds of the population live in the Las Vegas metropolitan area.

According to the 2010 Census, 6.9 per cent of the population is under 5 years, 24.6 per cent under 18 years and 12.0 per cent is aged over 65 years. Approximately 66.2 per cent of the population is white, and 8.1 per cent is black. An estimated 7.2 per cent is Asian. Approximately 26.5 per cent of the population is of Hispanic or Latino origin.

Births, Marriages, Deaths
The US Census Bureau, Population Division, estimated that there were 35,934 births in 2010 (giving a fertility rate of 63.5 per 1,000 women aged 15-44 years) and 19,623 deaths over the same period (giving a death rate of 726.6 per 1,000 population), giving a natural population increase of 16,311 people. Net migration, mainly international, amounted to 7,168 new residents in 2009. The infant mortality rate in 2007 was 6.4 infant deaths per 1,000 live births. Marriages and divorces in 2007, according to provisional data, numbered 126,354 (5th highest in the US) and 16,593 respectively.

Public Holidays
As well as the national US holidays, the people of Nevada celebrate Nevada Day, on the last Friday in October. It was originally held on 31st October, to commemorate the day Nevada was admitted to the Union, in 1864.

EMPLOYMENT

Nevada's total civilian labour force was estimated at 1,358,300 in December 2012, of which 1,219,500 were employed and 138,800 were unemployed. The unemployment rate was 10.2per cent, one of the highest rates in the US, well above the US average of 7.8 per cent. (Source: US Bureau of Labor Statistics)

The following table shows preliminary figures for December 2012 non-farm wage and salary employment (seasonally adjusted), according to industry:

Industry	No. of jobs	12 month change (%)
Logging and mining	16,300	10.1
Construction	50,800	-4.0
Manufacturing	37,100	-1.9
Trade, transport and utilities	223,100	3.9
Information	12,600	0.0

- continued

Financial activities	51,900	-0.4
Professional and business services	138,000	-0.9
Educational and health services	109,800	5.7
Leisure and hospitality	328,500	1.8
Other services	34,100	-0.6
Government	148,100	1.1
TOTAL	1,150,300	1.7

Source: Bureau of Labor Statistics

BANKING AND FINANCE

GDP/GNP, Inflation, National Debt

Nevada enjoyed faster than average real growth over 2004 to 2006 (8.2 per cent in 2005), largely due to the housing 'bubble'. The US subprime mortgage crisis hit the state especially hard, contributing to an economic slow-down in 2007, and a contraction of 0.6 per cent in real GDP in 2008. Nevada's Gross Domestic Product (GDP) (current dollars) rose from $131,233 million in 2008 to an estimated $126,503 million in 2009. It rose to $125,650 million in 2010 and to $130.4 billion in 2011. Nevada was ranked 32nd in the US for state GDP in 2011. GDP rose by 1.2 per cent in 2011. Gross Domestic Product according to industry is shown on the following table (in millions of current dollars):

Industry	2009	2010	2011
Agriculture, forestry, fishing, hunting	268	277	305
Mining	3,571	4,603	6,505
Utilities	2,355	2,225	2,141
Construction	8,664	6,351	5,392
Manufacturing	5,123	4,872	5,220
Wholesale Trade	4,540	4,442	4,609
Retail Trade	7,734	8,122	8,416
Transportation & warehousing	4,461	4,662	4,986
Information	2,295	2,228	2,373
Finance & insurance	14,192	16,023	15,784
Real estate, rental & leasing	18,283	16,994	16,741
Educational services	452	486	492
Health care & social assistance	6,601	6,839	7,146
Other non-Government services	32,251	34,351	36,663
Government	13,749	13,715	13,593
TOTAL	124,536	126,188	130,366

Source: Bureau of Economic Analysis, Feb. 2013

The average per capita income fell to $36,964 in 2011, 89 per cent of national average of $41,560. Real GDP per capita was put at $41,311 in 2011, when the US average was $42,070.

The collapse of the housing market in Las Vegas (which suffers one of the highest home foreclosure rates in the US), together with declining gaming revenue and higher prices for gasoline and consumer goods led to a 1.2 billion dollar shortfall in the state budget in 2008; Nevada had to use contingency funds of $267 million, and the Governor made large cuts to many state programs.

The annual Consumer Price Index (all items) for the West urban area rose from 227.9 in 2011 to 232.4 (1982-84 = 100). (Source: Bureau of Labor Statistics)

Balance of Payments / Imports and Exports

Nevada's total imports cost $5,280 million in 2009, down -13.5 per cent than $6,106 million in 2008. Imports rose by 14.6 per cent in 2010 to $6,052 million and by 23.2 per cent in 2011 to $7,450 m illion. Nevada's imports accounted for 0.3 per cent of the US imports in 2011. Imports include electronic circuits, machinery and apparatus, coin/token operated games, phones, machine parts and coffee. Suppliers include China (32.4 per cent), South Korea (14.5 per cent), Canada (11.0 per cent), Mexico and Malaysia.

Nevada's merchandise export revenue fell from $6,121 million in 2008 to $5,672 million in 2009, an decrease of 7.3 per cent. They rose by 4.2 per cent in 2010 to $5,912 million, and by 34.9 per cent in 2011 to $7,978 million, representing 0.5 per cent of total US exports. The top five merchandise export destinations in 2010-11, according to revenue generated, are shown on the following table:

Country	2010 ($m)	2011 ($m)	+/-% 10-11
Switzerland	2,425	3,714	53.1
Canada	938	1,273	35.7
China	456	424	-6.9
Mexico	351	321	-8.7
Japan	164	274	67.2

US Census Bureau, Foreign Trade Division

Nevada's top five exports in 2010, according to revenue, are shown on the following table:

Product	Export Revenue ($m)
Gold, non monetary, unwrought nesoi	2,372
Copper ores and concentrates	711
Coin/token operated games; pts. & access.	429
Electronic integrated circuits, nesoi	188
Diamonds, non-industrial, worked	162

US Census Bureau

Chambers of Commerce and Trade Organisations
Las Vegas Chamber of Commerce, URL: http://www.lvchamber.com/
Carson City Chamber of Commerce, URL: http://www.carsoncitychamber.com/
Reno-Sparks Chamber of Commerce, URL: http://www.reno-sparkschamber.org/

MANUFACTURING, MINING AND SERVICES

Primary and Extractive Industries

Nevada's natural resources and mining industry contributed $6,505 million towards Gross Domestic Product in 2011, up from $4,603 million the previous year. In 2010 the largest sector was non-oil and gas mining, which accounted for $4,443 million. Oil and gas extraction contributed $3 million, and support activities accounted for $156 million.

Nevada is the fifth largest gold producer in the world (after Australia, South Africa, China and Peru), accounting for eight per cent of world production in 2006, and 81 per cent of the US total. Gold production has steadily decreased from a high of 8.86 million ounces in 1998 to 6.3 million ounces in 2006. However, price of gold increased over the year, resulting in an increase of almost 25 per cent in the value of Nevada's yield ($3.8 billion). Nevada also leads the USA in the production of silver (10.3 million ounces mined in 2004) and barite, and is the only state that produces magnesite, lithium, and the specialty clays, sepiolite and saponite. Copper mining earned $389 million for the state in 2006 and silver was another major mineral commodity, earning some $98 million in the same year.

From its 70 producing oil wells and three rotary rigs, Nevada's oil industry produced 408 thousand barrels of oil in 2007, mainly from fields in Nye and Eureka counties. By 2009, the number of crude oil producing wells had fallen to 70. Production in 2010 was 427,000 barrels. Monthly crude oil production in October 2012 was 32,000 barrels. Crude oil refinery capacity was 2,000 bbl/d in 2012. Oil consumption in 2010 reached 45.3 million barrels; of this 25.7 million barrels was motor gasoline and 12.0 million was distillate fuel. The state uses a disproportionately large amount of jet fuel (1.6 per cent of the US total), due to demand from two air bases and the airports at Las Vegas and Reno.

Nevada's small natural gas industry produced a total of 3 million cubic feet of natural gas in 2011. Total consumption fell from 259,273 million cu ft to 250,322 million cu ft. Imports come from California and neighboring Rocky Mountain States. Natural gas is used mainly for electricity generation, and over 50 per cent of households use natural gas as their primary energy source for home heating. (Source: EIA)

The hydroelectric Hoover Dam, on the Colorado River, is the state's largest power plant, which supplies markets in southern California, as well as those in Nevada and Arizona. It took less than five years to build during the Great Depression.

Energy

Nevada's total energy production was 52 trillion Btu in 2010. Nevada's total energy consumption in 2010 was 646 trillion Btu (0.7 per cent of the US total) and was ranked 41st in the US for its per capita energy consumption (239 million Btu).

Nevada is a net importer of electricity with net summer capability of 11,421 MW in 2010. Monthly net electricity generation was 3,146,000 MWh (October 2012), of which natural gas 2,215,000 cu ft, coal 513,000 MWh, hydroelectric 103,000 MWh, other renewables 310,000 MWh, and petroleum 2,000 MWh.

Nevada has large geothermal resources and is ranked second (after California) in the generation of electricity from geothermal energy. It is a significant producer of solar energy; 9.1 per cent of Nevada's net electricity came from geothermal and solar energy in 2011. The States's Energy Porfolio Standard requires 25 per cent of electricity to come from renewable energy resources by 2025. In 2011, 16 per cent of net electricity generation came from geothermal, solar and hydroelectric power sources. (Source: EIA)

Manufacturing

The manufacturing industry contributed $5,392 million towards Nevada's GDP in 2011 (up from $4,872 million the previous year). In 2010, the top sectors were food product manufacturing ($487 million), fabricated metal products ($356 million) and plastics and rubber products ($239 million).

Service Industries

The services sector continued to be the main area of economic activity in 2011. Major contributors to state GDP were real estate ($16,741 million) and finance and insurance ($15,784 million).

Tourism

Nevada has a variety of tourist attractions, including historic mining towns, pony express trials, Las Vegas and Reno. The accommodation and food services sector of the tourism industry contributed an estimated $18,256 million in 2011 whilst the arts, entertainment and recreation sector contributed $2,865 million.
Nevada Commission on Tourism, URL: http://www.travelnevada.com/

Agriculture

Nevada's agriculture, forestry and fishing industry contributed $305 million towards the 2010 GDP, up from $277 million in 2010. The major sector in 2010 was crop and animal production (farms) ($243 million), whilst forestry, fishing and related activities accounted for $34 million. (Source: BEA)

Statistics from the USDA Census of Agriculture put the number of farms at 3,100 in 2010, and farmland covered some 5,900,000 acres. The average size of a farm in Nevada fell from 2,081 acres in 2002 to 1,903 acres in 2010. Total receipts for agricultural products sold in 2007 was $513 million, of which $293 million was generated by livestock, poultry and products, and $219 million was generated by crops, including greenhouse and nursery crops. Nevada's agriculture industry mainly produces livestock, with cattle and calves being the

UNITED STATES OF AMERICA

major livestock product. In addition, dairy products, sheep, lambs and hogs are important industry sectors. As of 1 Jan. 2011, there were 460,000 cattle and calves, 1,400 hogs & pigs, and 68,000 sheep. Major crops produced include alfalfa hay, a key Nevada crop, as well as barley, potatoes, oats, wheat, corn, garlic, onions and honey. Fruits and vegetables are also grown.

COMMUNICATIONS AND TRANSPORT

International Airports
According to preliminary figures for 2007, McCarran International Airport, Las Vegas, served 47.7 million passengers over the year, equivalent to at 3.1 per cent increase on the previous year.
McCarran International Airport, URL: http://mccarran.com
Reno/Tahoe International Airport,
URL: http://www.renoairport.com/reno-tahoe/homepage.asp

Roads
Interstate 80 runs through north Nevada, passing through Reno. Interstate 15 runs through the south, and serves Las Vegas. There are also several federal highways.

Railways
The California Zephyr passes through Elko, Winnemucca, Sparks and Reno on its daily service from Chicago to California. Uniion Pacific runs services in the north and south. The CAT (Citizens Area Transit) operates in the Las Vegas metropolitan area. Several hotels run their own monorail lines between each other, and there is a four mile monorail system which services several casinos.

HEALTH

The National Center for Health Statistics estimated that there were 19.8 doctors per 10,000 inhabitants in 2009, well below the national state average of 27.4 doctors per 10,000 people and one of the lowest rates in the USA. In 2008, there were 1,330 dentists (5.1 per 10,000 population). In 2009 there were 1.9 community hospital beds per 1,000 residents (below the US state average of 2.6 beds per 1,000 people), and there were 50 nursing homes, with 5,856 beds.

The Center for Disease Control estimated that some 18.9 per cent of the state's adults had no health-care coverage in 2007-09 (well above the national rate of 15.8 per cent), and that 10.7 per cent were living in poverty in 2007 (below the US average of 13.4 per cent).

Nevada reported 5,481 AIDS cases from the beginning of the epidemic to the end of 2005, and ranked 27th in number of reported AIDS cases in 2005. The state has a lower than average rate of obesity among adults (22.4 per cent, 2012). An estimated 59 per cent of the population were considered overweight.

EDUCATION

Primary/Secondary Education
Student enrolment in Nevada's 663 primary and secondary schools during the 2009-10 year was 428,947 and there were 22,103 teachers. The pupil/teacher ratio was 19.41 to one, above the national average of 15.3 pupils per teacher. Rapid population growth is leading to concerns about overcrowded schools. Nevada is home to the nation's fifth largest school district in the Clark County School District.

In 2007-08, total educational revenue reached $4.364 billion, whilst expenditure on the public sector was $4.477 billion.

Higher Education
In 2010-11, there were 25 higher education establishments including the University of Nevada, Las Vegas; the University of Nevada, Reno; Desert Research Institute; Community College of Southern Nevada; Great Basin College; Truckee Meadows Community College; and Western Nevada Community College. Around 56,435 men enrolled, together with 68,825 women. 16,878 degrees were conferred, of which 7,345 were Bachelors, 2,652 were Masters and 630 were Doctorates. (Source: National Center for Education Statistics)

COMMUNICATIONS AND MEDIA

Newspapers
Nevada's daily newspapers include: Las Vegas Review-Journal; Las Vegas Sun; Nevada Appeal, Carson City; Reno Gazette-Journal; North Lake Tahoe Bonanza, Incline Village; and the Elko Daily Free Press.
Nevada Press Association, URL: http://www.nevadapress.com/
Las Vegas Review-Journal, URL: http://www.lvrj.com/
Las Vegas Sun, URL: http://www.lasvegassun.com/

Broadcasting
Eight of Nevada's television stations are based in Las Vegas, four in Reno, one in Henderson and one in Elko.

ENVIRONMENT

Nevada's primary electricity generating fuel has moved from coal to natural gas over the last few years, and this has reduced air pollution. Emissions fell from 18,294,514 metric tons in 2009 to 17,020,408 metric tons in 2010, ranking it 38th highest of the US states. Approximately 7,161 metric tons of sulfur dioxide and 15,267 metric tons of nitrogen oxide were also emitted.

The state's largest power generating plant, the Mohave Generating Station, (fuelled primarily by coal), was shut down in 2005 for failing to install agreed-upon pollution-control equipment. The State's second largest operating power plant is the hydroelectric Hoover Dam on the Colorado River. Built in less than five years during the Great Depression, the Hoover Dam stands today as a National Historic Landmark.

In June 2009, Nevada established a new renewable portfolio standard (RPS) that requires 25 per cent of the State's electricity come from renewable sources by 2025, with at least 6 per cent coming from solar energy sources by 2016.

In 2010, there were 11,106 alternative-fueled vehicles in use (1.2 per cent of US total). Ethanol consumption was put at 2,904,000 barrels in 2010. (Source: EIA)

NEW HAMPSHIRE

Capital: Concord (Population, Census 2010: 42,695)

Head of State: Maggie Hassan (D) (Governor) (page 1439)

State Flag: A blue background in the centre of which is the state seal surrounded by a wreath of laurel leaves interspersed with nine stars. The state seal consists of the frigate Raleigh on a background of land and water over which the sun is rising; the field of the state seal is encompassed with laurel, around which appears the words: 'Seal of the State of New Hampshire' and '1776'.

CONSTITUTION AND GOVERNMENT

Constitution
New Hampshire, first settled in 1623, is one of the 13 original states of the union, having become the 9th state on 21 June 1788. While the present constitution dates from 1784, there have been 16 state conventions with 49 amendments adopted.

The New Hampshire Executive Council, known as the Governor's Council, comprises the governor and five administrative officers known as 'Executive Councilors', and is responsible for the administration of the executive branch of government. Executive Councilors represent about 225,000 people, and are elected for two years. Individuals nominated by the governor are appointed by the councilors to fill the positions of agency directors and commissioners, judges and the attorney general. New Hampshire does not have a lieutenant governor and so the president of the Senate serves as acting governor in the absence of the governor.

According to the Constitution, the secretary of state and state treasurer are elected by a joint ballot of senators and representatives. The three public utilities commissioners are appointed by the governor and confirmed by the Executive Council. They serve staggered terms of six years.

New Hampshire elects two Senators and two Representatives to the US Congress in Washington, DC.

To consult the state constitution, please visit: http://www.nh.gov/constitution/constitution.html

Legislature
New Hampshire's legislature, known as the General Court, consists of a Senate and a House of Representatives. It sits annually from early January to the end of June. New Hampshire's General Court is known as a 'Citizen Legislature' due to the fact that its members are drawn from a variety of occupations.

Upper House
The Senate comprises 24 members all elected for two years. Senate sessions are held annually, usually from early January to the end of June. There are 24 Senate districts. Districts are based on population. Following the 2012 elections there are 13 Republicans and 11 Democrats.
New Hampshire State Senate, State House, Room 302, 107 North Main Street, Concord, NH 03301-4951, USA. Tel: +1 603 271 2111, fax: +1 603 271 2105,
e-mail: senatecommunications@leg.state.nh.us, URL: http://www.gencourt.state.nh.us/senate/

NEW HAMPSHIRE

Lower House

The House of Representatives consists of 400 members, elected for two years. Its size makes the New Hampshire House the largest legislative body in the US. The Republicans held the majority following the November 2010 election, with 298 seats. The Democrats hold 102 seats.

New Hampshire House of Representatives, State House, 107 North State Street, Concord, New Hampshire 03301, USA. Tel: +1 603 271 2548 (House Clerk), URL: http://www.gencourt.state.nh.us/house/default.html

Executive Council (as at March 2013)
Raymond S. Burton (R), District 1
Colin Van Ostern (D), District 2
Christopher Sununu (R), District 3
Christophe C. Pappas (D), District 4
Deborah Pignatelli (D), District 5

New Hampshire Executive Council, 107 North Main Street, State House, Room 207, Concord, NH 03301-4951, USA. Tel: +1 603 271 3632, fax: +1 603 271 3633, e-mail: gcweb@gov.state.nh.us, URL: http://www.state.nh.us/council/index.html

Executive Branch Officials (as at March 2013)
Governor: Maggie Hassan (page 1439)
Attorney General: Michael A. Delaney
Secretary of State: William M. Gardner (D)
State Treasurer: Catherine A. Provencher
Insurance Commissioner: Roger A. Sevigny
Public Utilities Commissioners: Amy Ignatius (Chairman), Michael D. Harrington, Robert R. Scott

General Court (as at March 2013)
President of the Senate: Peter Bragdon (R)
President Pro Tem of the Senate: Sen. Bob Odell (R)
Majority Leader: Jeb Bradley (R)
Minority Leader: Sylvia Larsen (D)
Speaker of the House: William O'Brien (R)
Majority Leader: Steve Shurtleff (D)
Minority Leader: Gene Chandler (R)

US Senators: Kelly Ayotte (R) (page 1380) and Jeanne Shaheen (D) (page 1512)

Ministries
Office of the Governor, 107 North Main Street, Room 208, Concord, NH 03301, USA. Tel: +1 603 271 2121, fax: +1 603 271 7630, URL: http://www.state.nh.us/governor
Office of the Attorney General, 33 Capitol Street, Concord, NH 03301, USA. Tel: +1 603 271 3658, fax: +1 603 271 2110, URL: http://doj.nh.gov/
Insurance Department, 21 South Fruit Street, Suite 14, Concord, NH 03301, USA. Tel: +1 603 271 22261, +1 603 271 1406, URL: http://www.nh.gov/insurance/
Public Utilities Commission, 8 Old Suncook Road, Concord, NH 03301-7319, USA. Tel: +1 603 271 2431, fax: +1 603 271 3878, e-mail: puc@puc.nh.gov, URL: http://www.puc.state.nh.us
Department of Agriculture, Markets and Food, State House Annex, 25 Capitol Street, Concord, NH 03301, USA. (Mailing address: PO Box 2042, Concord, NH 03302, USA.) Tel: +1 603 271 3551, fax: +1 603 271 1109, e-mail: spaul@agr.state.nh.us, URL: http://agriculture.nh.gov/
Department of Corrections, State Office Park South, 105 Pleasant Street, PO Box 1806, Concord, NH 03302-1806, USA. Tel: +1 603 271 5600, fax: +1 603 271 5643, URL: http://www.nh.gov/nhdoc/
Department of Cultural Resources, 20 Park Street, Concord, NH 03301-6314, USA. Tel: +1 603 271 2540, fax: +1 603 271 6826, URL: http://www.nh.gov/nhculture/
Department of Education, 101 Pleasant Street, Concord, NH 03301-3860, USA. Tel: +1 603 271 3494, fax: +1 603 271 1953, URL: http://www.ed.state.nh.us/
Department of Employment Security, 32 S. Main Street, Concord, NH 03301, USA. Tel: +1 603 224 3311, fax: +1 603 229 4346, URL: http://www.nhes.state.nh.us
Department of Environment Services, 6 Hazen Drive, PO Box 95, Concord, NH 03302-0095, USA. Tel: +1 603 271 3503, fax: +1 603 271 2867, URL: http://www.des.state.nh.us/
Department of Health and Human Services, 129 Pleasant Street, Concord, NH 03301-3857, USA. Tel: +1 603 271 4958, URL: http://www.dhhs.state.nh.us/
Department of Insurance, 21 South Fruit Street, Suite 14, Concord, NH 03301. Tel: +1 603 271 7973, fax: +1 603 271 1406, URL: http://www.nh.gov/insurance
Department of Justice, 33 Capitol Street, Concord, NH 03301, USA. Tel: +1 603 271 3658, fax: +1 603 271 2110, URL: http://doj.nh.gov/
Department of Labour, 95 Pleasant Street, Concord, NH 03301, USA. Tel: +1 603 271 3176, URL: www.nh.gov/labor/
Department of Resources and Economic Development, 172 Pembroke Road, PO Box 1856, Concord, NH 03302-1856, USA. Tel: +1 603 271 2411, fax: +1 603 271 2629, URL: http://www.dred.state.nh.us
Department of State, State Capitol Building, Room 204, Concord, NH 03301, USA. Tel: +1 603 271 3242, fax: +1 603 271 6316, URL: http://sos.nh.gov/
Department of Transportation, John O. Morton Building, 7 Hazen Drive, PO Box 483, Concord, NH 03302-0483, USA. Tel: +1 603 271 3734, fax: +1 603 271 3914, URL: http://www.nh.gov/dot/
Treasury Department, 25 Capitol Street, Room 121, Concord, NH 03301, USA. Tel: +1 603 271 2621, fax: +1 603 291 3922, URL: http://www.state.nh.us/treasury

Political Parties
New Hampshire Democratic Party, URL: http://www.nhdp.org/
New Hampshire Republican State Committee, URL: http://www.nhgop.org

Elections
Elections for State Governor took place on 6 November 2012. The incumbent governor John Lynch chose to retire rather than stand for a fifth term. Democrat Maggie Hassan won the election. Her term began on January 2, 2013.

In the November 2012 Senate elections, the Republicans retained control but with a reduced majority (Republicans 13, Democrats 11). In the House of Representatives the Democrats took back the House: Democrats 221, Republicans 179. Prior to the election, the number of seats was Republicans 288, Democrats 103.

LEGAL SYSTEM

New Hampshire's legal system consists of four types of court: the Supreme Court, the Superior Court, District Courts, and Probate Courts. All judges are nominated by the Governor and Executive Council and can serve until retirement. The Supreme Court comprises the Chief Justice and four Associate Justices. The Superior Court consists of the Chief Justice, 28 Superior Court Justices, and 10 marital masters.

New Hampshire has the death penalty but no-one has been executed since 1976. According to the DPIC the murder rate is 1 per 100,000 population. As of February 2013, one person was on death row.

As of January 1, 2008, civil unions became legal in New Hampshire, giving all the rights associated with marriage to same-sex couples. As of January 2013, same-sex marriages were legal.

Supreme Court, URL: http://www.courts.state.nh.us/supreme/index.htm
Chief Justice: Linda Stewart Dalianis
Senior Associate: Gary E. Hicks
Superior Court, Chief Justice: Tina Nadeau
Administrative Office of the Courts, URL: http://www.courts.state.nh.us/aoc

LOCAL GOVERNMENT

For the purposes of local government, New Hampshire is divided into 10 county governments and 234 sub-county general purpose governments. Of the 234 sub-county governments, 13 are municipalities and 221 are towns. The state retains all powers not specifically granted to municipalities. Local government in the towns centers on town meetings.
New Hampshire Association of Counties, URL: http://www.nhcounties.org/

AREA AND POPULATION

Area
New Hampshire is bounded to the north by Canada, to the east by Maine and the Atlantic, to the south by Massachusetts, and to the west by Vermont. Its total area is 9,349.94 sq. miles, of which 8,968.10 sq. miles is land and 381.84 sq. miles is water.

New Hampshire's climate means that there are cold winters and warm summers. The most extreme weather in the state is found on Mount Washington, where there are winds of 231 miles per hour, an annual average temperature of 27°F, 185 inches of snowfall annually, and an average of only 33 per cent sunshine.

To view a map of the state, please consult http://www.lib.utexas.edu/maps/us_2001/new_england_ref_2001.pdf

Population
According to the 2010 Census, the state population was 1,316,470, down on the mid-2009 population at 1,324,575. In 2012, the population was estimated to be 1,320,718. Over the period 2000-10, the population of New Hampshire grew by 6.5 per cent. The population is expected to reach 1.65 million by 2030. The population density is an estimated 147 people per sq. mile. The county with the greatest number of inhabitants is Hillsborough County, with a population of 400,721 in 2010. The largest city in the state is Manchester, with a 2009 population of 109,830, whilst the capital, Concord, has an estimated 42,733 inhabitants.

According to the 2010 Census, 5.3 per cent of the population is under 5 years, 21.8 per cent under 18 years and 13.5 per cent is aged over 65 years. Approximately 93.9 per cent of the population is white, and 1.1 per cent is black. Approximately 2.8 per cent of the population is of Hispanic or Latino origin.

Births, Marriages, Deaths
The US Census Bureau estimated that there were 12,874 births in 2010 and 10,201 deaths, giving a natural population increase of 2,673. Net emigration resulted in the loss of 815 people in 2009. The infant mortality rate was 5.5 infant deaths per 1,000 live births in 2010. Marriages and divorces in 2007 numbered around 9,364 and 5,070 respectively.

EMPLOYMENT

New Hampshire's total civilian labour force in December 2012 was estimated at 740,500, of which 698,400 were in employment and 42,000 were unemployed. The unemployment rate was 5.7 per cent, lower than the national December 2012 average of 7.8 per cent. (Source: US Bureau of Labor Statistics)

The following table shows December 2012 wage and salary employment according to industry:

Industry	No. of Employed	12-month change (%)
Logging and mining	900	0.0

STATES OF THE WORLD

1257

UNITED STATES OF AMERICA

- continued

Construction	22,000	-1.8
Manufacturing	66,200	0.0
Trade, transportation, and utilities	133,600	0.9
Information	10,800	-3.6
Financial activities	34,400	-0.9
Professional and business services	66,500	1.8
Educational and health services	112,500	-1.4
Leisure and hospitality	64,800	1.3
Other services	23,400	3.1
Government	91,400	-1.5
TOTAL	626,500	0.0

Source: Bureau of Labor Statistics

BANKING AND FINANCE

GDP/GNP, Inflation, National Debt
GDP at current prices was put at $63.6 billion and ranked 41st in the US. Real GDP rose by 1.5 per cent in 2011. The following table shows the state's Gross Domestic Product according to industry (in millions of current dollars):

Industry	2009	2010	2011
Agriculture, forestry, fishing & hunting	162	149	150
Mining	18	20	18
Utilities	1,247	1,244	1,206
Construction	1,801	1,761	1,860
Manufacturing	6,792	7,976	8,524
Wholesale Trade	3,430	3,555	3,735
Retail Trade	4,485	4,755	4,938
Transportation & warehousing	870	881	919
Information	2,267	2,260	2,219
Finance & insurance	5,104	5,750	5,919
Real Estate	9,210	8,638	8,465
Educational services	1,214	1,220	1,237
Health care & social assistance	5,691	5,959	6,162
Other non-Government services	10,471	111,38	11,739
Government	6,206	6,331	6,465
TOTAL GDP	58,967	61,636	63,556

Source: Bureau of Economic Analysis, Feb. 2013

The average per capita income in the state rose to $45,881 in 2011. Real GDP per capita rose from $41,455 in 2010 to $42,915, slightly above the national average was $42,070.

The annual Consumer Price Index (CPI) (all areas) for the Boston-Brockton-Nashua, MA-NH-ME-CT, urban area rose from 243.8 in 2011 to 247.7 in 2012 (1982-84=100). (Source: Bureau of Labor Statistics)

Balance of Payments / Imports and Exports
Total New Hampshire imports amounted to $6,322 million in 2009, down 40.4 per cent from the 2008 total of $10,615 million. Imports rose by 41.6 per cent in 2010 to $8,950 million, and by 30.5 per cent in 2011 to $11,682 million, representing 0.5 per cent of the US total. Imports of light oils rose by over 100 per cent and oil from petrol and bitum mineral rose by over 60 per cent in 2010. Main suppliers include Canada (68.6 per cent), China (7.4 per cent), Mexico, Germany and India.

Total export revenue fell from $3,752 million in 2008 to $3,061 million in 2009, a 18.4 per cent decrease. Exports rose by 42.7 per cent in 2010 to $4,367 million, and fell by -1.6 per cent in 2011 to $4,297 million, representing 0.3 per cent of the US total. The following table shows the top five export products in 2010 according to export revenue:

Industry	Revenue ($m)
Parts of phone sets & oth. app. for trans/recept.	266
Machines for the manufacture of boules or wafers	241
Parts and access. for use with mach. tool nesoi	167
Insulated optical fiber cables	155
Processors and controllers, electronic integ. circt.t	122

Source: US Census Bureau

The top five export destinations in 2010-11, according to revenue generated, are shown on the following table:

Country	2010 ($m)	2011 ($m)	+/-% 10-11
Mexico	1,049	943	-10.1
Canada	538	652	21.2
China	412	338	-18.0
Germany	223	233	4.3
UK	207	200	-3.5

Source: US Census Bureau

Chambers of Commerce and Trade Organisations
Greater Concord Chamber of Commerce, URL: http://www.concordnhchamber.com/
Greater Manchester Chamber of Commerce, URL: http://www.manchester-chamber.org/
Department of Resources and Economic Development, URL: http://www.dred.state.nh.us
Concord Regional Development Corp., URL: http://www.crdc-nh.com/
Plymouth Chamber of Commerce, URL: http://www.plymouthnh.org/

MANUFACTURING, MINING AND SERVICES

Primary and Extractive Industries
Minerals consist mainly of sand and gravel, stone, and clay for building and highway construction. Mining contributed $18 million to New Hampshire's Gross Domestic Product in 2011 (down from $20 million in 2010). In 2010, non-oil and gas mining earned the state $14 million, and support activities accounted for $6 million.

Other than a port and a crude oil pipeline that crosses the state, New Hampshire has no petroleum infrastructure. Petroleum consumption in 2010 fell slightly to 29.8 million barrels, 16.7 million barrels of which was motor gasoline and 7.1 million was distillate fuel.

New Hampshire has no natural gas industry. Consumption rose to 69,222 million cu ft in 2011. Supplies are shipped in from Maine, Canada, and Massachusetts. Whilst state demand remains comparatively low, it has grown in recent years for use in electricity generation; natural gas-fired generation now accounts over a quarter of the State's power production.

Coal consumption was put at 898,000 short tons in 2011 (0.1 per cent of US total). (Source: EIA)

Energy
New Hampshire's total energy production was 152 trillion Btu in 2010 (0.2 per cent of the US). Total energy consumption was 295 trillion Btu and its per capita consumption fell to 224 million Btu (US rank 44).

New Hampshire is a net exporter of electricity, with nuclear fuel its primary energy source. Net summer capability in 2010 was 4,180 MW (0.4 per cent of US total) and net monthly generation in 2012 was 830,000 MWh (Oct. 2012), of which nuclear 17,000 MWh, natural gas-fired 598,000 MWh and coal-fired 2,000 MWh. Hydroelectric energy generated 99,000 MWh and other renewables 107,000 MWh. The largest utility plants are Seabrook (nuclear), Granite Ridge (gas), NAEA Newington Power Facility (gas), Merrimack (coal), Newington (petroleum) and Schiller. The 1,161 net MWe Seabrook nuclear plant is located on the western shore of Hampton Harbour, 11 miles south of Portsmouth, New Hampshire. (Source: EIA)

Manufacturing
Contribution towards GDP rose from $7,976 million in 2010 to $8,524 million in 2011. The top manufacturing sectors in 2010 were computer and electronic products ($2,831 million), and fabricated metal product manufacturing ($1,109 million).

Service Industries
The services industry is New Hampshire's largest contributor towards its GDP. The top sectors in 2011 were real estate ($8,465 million), health care and social assistance ($6,162 million) and finance and insurance ($5,919 million). Professional and technical services earned $4,581 million.

Government Revenues
New Hampshire has no general sales tax or state income tax but does have local property taxes. Other government revenues come from rooms and meals tax, business profits tax, motor vehicle licences, fuel taxes, fishing and hunting licences, state-controlled sales of alcoholic beverages, cigarette and tobacco taxes. The government sector contributed $6,465 million in 2011.

Tourism
The accommodation and food sector of the services industry contributed $2,037 million towards the 2011 GDP (up from $1,962 million in 2010). The arts, entertainment and recreation sector contributed an estimated $536 million.
New Hampshire Division of Travel and Tourism Development, URL: http://www.visitnh.gov/

Agriculture
Agriculture, forestry and fisheries contributed an estimated $150 million towards New Hampshire's GDP in 2011. In 2010, crop and animal production contributed $66 million whilst forestry, fishing and related activities contributed $84 million. (Source: BEA)

According to the USDA Census of Agriculture, New Hampshire's farms numbered 4,150 in 2010, up from 3,900 at the time of the 1997 Census of Agriculture. Farmland covered 470,000 in 2010 and the average size of a New Hampshire farm fell from 118 acres in 1997 to 113 acres in 2010. New Hampshire's cash receipts totalled $199 million in 2008, with crops, and greenhouse and nursery sales reaching $106 million. The chief field crops are hay and vegetables, whilst the chief fruit crop is apples. Major livestock and poultry products, in terms of the number of farms, are cattle and calves, beef cows, layers and pullets, sheep and lambs, milk cows, and hogs and pigs. As of 1 Jan. 2011, there were 34,000 cattle and calves and 3,300 hogs & pigs.

COMMUNICATIONS AND TRANSPORT

International Airports
There are 14 public and 18 private airports. Manchester Airport is the largest airport. In 2003 approximately 3.6 million passengers passed through.
Manchester Airport, URL: http://www.flymanchester.com
Pease International Airport, URL: http://www.peasedev.org/aviation/aviation.htm

Railways
The length of railways in the state is 450 miles.

Roads
In 2003 there were approximately 1.9 million passenger vehicle registrations and 190,000 commercial vehicle registrations.

Ports and Harbours
New Hampshire Port Authority, URL: http://www.state.nh.us/nhport/index.html
The port has a tonnage of 4.1 million tons.

HEALTH

The National Center of Health Statistics estimated that there were 29.3 doctors (including osteopaths) per 10,000 people in 2009 and 817 dentists (6.2 per 10,000 population) in 2008. In 2009, there were 2.2 community hospital beds per 1,000 residents in the same year. There were 79 nursing homes, with 7,692 beds.

It was estimated that some 10.4 per cent of inhabitants had no health insurance in 2007-09 (compared to the US average of 15.8 per cent), and that in 2007-11, 8.0 per cent of the population were living in poverty. Both figures were below the national average.

New Hampshire reported 1,199 HIV/AIDS cases from the beginning of the epidemic to the end of 2008, and ranked 43rd in number of cumulative reported HIV/AIDS cases in 2008. The overall TB rate was 1.4 per 100,000 population, ranking it 42nd highest state in the US. The state has a lower than national average rate of obesity among adults (25.0 per cent). An estimated 62.2 per cent of adults were considered overweight in 2012. (Source: Center for Disease Control)

EDUCATION

Primary/Secondary Education
Enrolments in New Hampshire's 494 public elementary and secondary schools, according to statistics for 2009-10, were 197,140. The total number of teachers in the same year was 15,490. The average student-teacher ratio across the state was 12.73 to one, below the national average of 15.3.

Revenue from education reached $2.6 billion in 2007-08, and expenditure on state education was $2.618 billion.

Higher Education
Enrolment in the 29 degree-awarding institutions of higher education in 2010-11 comprised 31,415 male students and 42,819 women. In the same period 17,821 degrees were awarded, including 9,396 Bachelors, 3,458 Masters and 459 Doctorates. (Source: National Center for Education Statistics)

RELIGION

The Roman Catholic Church is the largest single body. The largest Protestant churches are Congregational, Episcopal, Methodist and United Baptist Convention of NH.

COMMUNICATIONS AND MEDIA

Newspapers
There are seven major daily newspapers in New Hampshire: the Eagle Times, The Telegraph, The Union Leader, Foster's Daily Democrat, Conway Daily Sun, Concord Monitor, Keene Sentinel. There are 13 non-daily newspapers.
Union Leader Corp., URL: http://www.theunionleader.com
The Portsmouth Herald, URL: http://www.seacoastonline.com

Broadcasting
Across the state there are 42 radio stations and five TV stations.

ENVIRONMENT

New Hampshire's carbon dioxide emissions fell to 5,507,060 metric tons in 2009, down from 6,777,318 metric tons in 2007. They rose to 5,551,486 metric tons in 2010. New Hampshire's electricity industry ranked 43rd in the US for carbon dioxide emission in 2010. Emissions of sulfur dioxide amounted to 33,808 metric tons and emissions of nitrogen oxide amounted to 6,267 metric tons. The state produces around 10 per cent of its electricity from hydroelectric power, fuel wood, landfill gas, and municipal solid waste.

In 2007, New Hampshire adopted a renewable portfolio standard that requires 25 per cent of the State's electricity to be generated from renewable sources by 2025. In 2011, 14 per cent of its net electricity generation came from renewable energy.

In 2010, there were 1,925 alternative-fueled vehicles in use (0.2 per cent of US total) and, in 2011, ethanol consumption was 1,327,000 barrels. (Source: EIA)

NEW JERSEY

Capital: Trenton (Population, Census 2010: 84,913)

Head of State: Chris Christie (page 1405) (Governor)

State Flag: A buff background in the centre of which are the arms of the state: a blue shield on which are three ploughs; above the shield is a helmet and above the helmet is the head of a horse; on either side of the shield are the figures of Liberty, carrying the liberty cap on her staff, and Ceres, holding a cornucopia of harvested crops

CONSTITUTION AND GOVERNMENT

Constitution
One of the original 13 states of the Union, New Jersey joined on 18 December 1787. Under the terms of New Jersey's 1947 Constitution (updated by amendments in November 2000) the governor heads the executive branch of government assisted by a cabinet appointed by himself.

New Jersey elects two Senators and 13 Representatives to the US Congress, Washington, DC.

To consult the state constitution, please visit: http://www.njleg.state.nj.us/lawsconstitution/consearch.asp

Recent Events
On the 23 July 2009, over 40 people, including politicians, officials and several rabbis, were arrested in FBI raids on locations in New Jersey and New York. The operation was part of a 10-year probe into corruption and money laundering. Three mayors from the state of New Jersey and two members of the state legislature were among those held. 15 of the suspects, including rabbis and their "associates", were held in connection with alleged international money-laundering. Between 2001 and 2009, more than 130 New Jersey public officials had either admitted to corruption or been found guilty of it.

A state of emergency was declared in seven counties in February 2010, following storms and severe winter weather conditions.

Legislature
The New Jersey legislature consists of the Senate and the General Assembly. Legislators are elected from the 40 legislative districts of New Jersey. The legislature appoints the State Auditor. Each legislative session lasts for a term of two years, usually convening on the second Tuesday in January of each even-numbered year.
Office of Legislative Services, Office of Public Information, Room 50, State House Annex, PO Box 068, Trenton, NJ 08625-0068, USA. Tel: +1 609 292 4840, fax: +1 609 777 2440, URL: http://www.njleg.state.nj.us/

Upper House
The Senate has 40 members who are elected for four years (other than those Senators elected following a ten-year census, who serve terms of two years). The Democrats currently hold the majority of seats in the Senate. At the time of the 215th legislature, the Senate was composed of 24 Democrats and 16 Republicans.
New Jersey Senate, State House, PO Box 099, Trenton, NJ 08625-0099, USA. Tel: +1 609 292 6828 (Secretary of the Senate), URL: http://www.njleg.state.nj.us/Default.asp

Lower House
The General Assembly has 80 members who are elected for two years. At the time of the 215th legislature, the General Assembly consisted of 48 Democrats and 32 Republicans.
New Jersey General Assembly, State House, PO Box 098, Trenton, NJ 08625-0098, USA. Tel: +1 609 292 5135 (Clerk), URL: http://www.njleg.state.nj.us/Default.asp

---

Elected Executive Branch Officials (as at April 2013)
Governor: Chris Christie (page 1405)
Lieutenant Governor, Secretary of State: Kim Guadagno
Secretary, Department of Agriculture: Douglas H. Fisher
Commissioner, Department of Education: Chris Cerf
State Treasurer: Andrew P. Sidamon-Eristoff
Attorney General: Jeffrey S. Chiesa

Legislature (as at April 2013)
President of the Senate: Stephen M. Sweeney (D)
President Pro Tem of the Senate: Nia H. Gill (D)
Majority Leader of the Senate: Loretta Weinburg (D)
Minority Leader: Thomas H. Kean Jr.(R)
Speaker of the Assembly: Sheila Oliver (D)
Speaker Pro Tem of the Assembly: Jerry Green (D)
Majority Leader: Gordon Johnson (D)
Minority Leader: Jon Bramnick (R)

US Senators: Robert Menendez (page 1476) (D) and Frank Lautenberg (D) (page 1461)

Ministries
Office of the Governor, The State House, PO Box 001, Trenton, NJ 08625, USA. Tel: +1 609 292 6000, URL: http://www.state.nj.us/governor
Office of the Attorney General, Richard J. Hughes Justice Complex, 25 Market Street, PO Box 080, Trenton, NJ 08625-0080, USA. Tel: +1 609 292 4925, fax: +1 609 292 3508, URL: http://www.nj.gov/lps/index.html
Office of the Secretary of State, PO Box 300, Trenton, NJ 08625-0300, USA. Tel: +1 609 984 1900, fax: +1 609 292 7665, URL: http://www.state.nj.us/state

UNITED STATES OF AMERICA

Office of the State Treasurer, State House, 1st Floor, PO Box 002, Trenton, NJ 08625, USA. Tel: +1 609 292 5031, fax: +1 609 984 3888, URL: http://www.state.nj.us/treasury
Department of Agriculture, John Fitch Plaza, PO Box 330, Trenton, NJ 08625, USA. Tel: +1 609 292 3976, URL: http://www.state.nj.us/agriculture
Department of Banking and Insurance, 20 West State Street (PO Box 325), Trenton, NJ 08625-0325, USA. Tel: +1 609 292 5360, URL: http://www.state.nj.us/dobi/index.html
Department of Community Affairs, 101 South Broad Street, PO Box 800, Trenton, NJ 08625-0800, USA. Tel: +1 609 292 6055, fax: +1 609 984 6696, URL: http://www.state.nj.us/dca/
Department of Corrections, Whittlesey Road, PO Box 863, Trenton, NJ 08625, USA. Tel: +1 609 292 4036, fax: +1 609 292 9083, URL: http://www.state.nj.us/corrections
Department of Education, 225 East State Street, PO Box 500, Trenton, NJ 08625, USA. Tel: +1 609 292 4469, URL: http://www.state.nj.us/education/index.html
Department of Environmental Protection, 401 East State Street, 7th Floor, East Wing, PO Box 402, Trenton, NJ 08625, USA. Tel: +1 609 292 2885, fax: +1 609 292 7695, URL: http://www.state.nj.us/dep
Department of Health and Senior Services, John Fitch Plaza, PO Box 360, Trenton, NJ 08625, USA. Tel: +1 609 292 7837, fax: +1 609 292 0053, URL: http://www.state.nj.us/health
Department of Human Services, 222 South Warren Street, PO Box 700, Trenton, NJ 08625-0212, USA. Tel: +1 609 292 3717, URL: http://www.state.nj.us/humanservices/index.html
Department of Labour, John Fitch Plaza, PO Box 110, Trenton, NJ 08625, USA. Tel: +1 609 292 2323, fax: +1 609 633 9271, URL: http://lwd.state.nj.us/labor/index.html
Department of Transport, 1035 Parkway Avenue, PO Box 600, Trenton, NJ 08625-0600, USA. Tel: +1 609 530 3535, URL: http://www.state.nj.us/transportation

Political Parties
New Jersey Democratic State Committee, URL: http://www.njdems.org
New Jersey Republican State Committee, URL: http://www.njgop.org

Elections
Legislative elections take place every odd-numbered year and the latest was held in November 2011. In the State Senate the Democrats increased their majority by one seat (Democrats 24 seats, Republicans 16). In the General Assembly, the party division was Democrats 48 Republicans 32.

Gubernatorial elections last took place in November 2009. Republican Chris Christie won a close race against the incumbent Jon Corzine, winning 48.5 per cent of the vote. In November 2005, the people of New Jersey voted on the question of whether to create the office of Lieutenant Governor; 55.7 per cent voted in favour, and in January 2010, Kimberley Guadagno was sworn in as the state's first Lieutenant Governor.

LEGAL SYSTEM

The New Jersey legal system is headed by the Supreme Court, followed by the Superior Court (which includes the Appellate Division), the Tax Court, and the Municipal Courts.

The Supreme Court consists of a Chief Justice and six Associate Justices. All Supreme Court judges are appointed by the Governor and confirmed by the State Senate for an initial term of seven years. If re-appointed they remain in office until retirement at 70.

The State Superior Court includes an Appellate Court, comprising 32 judges, which refers cases to the Supreme Court if no agreement is reached. The Trial Divisions of the Superior Court hear civil, criminal and family cases. The Tax Court hears appeals following County Boards of Taxation decisions and consists of 12 Judges. Municipal Courts and County Courts make up the rest of New Jersey's legal system.

In December 2007, lawmakers in New Jersey approved a bill abolishing the death penalty and replacing it with life imprisonment without parole. It was subsequently signed into law, making New Jersey the first US state to abolish capital punishment since the US Supreme Court reinstated executions in 1976. However, in January 2011, a New Jersey legislator, Sen. Robert Singer, introduced a bill that, if passed into law, would reinstate the death penalty for those convicted of murdering a child, killing a police officer in the line of duty, or committing a fatal terrorist attack. As of January 2013, the death penalty had not been reinstated. According to the DPIC the murder rate per 100,000 population is 4.2.

Supreme Court, URL: http://www.judiciary.state.nj.us/supreme/index.htm
Chief Justice: Stuart Rabner
Justices: Jaynee LaVecchia, Barry Albin, Helen Hoens, Anne Patterson, Ariel Rodroguez, Mary Cuff
Superior Court, Appellate Division: Acting Presiding Judge for Administration: Ariel Rodriguez
Tax Court of New Jersey, URL: http://www.judiciary.state.nj.us/taxcourt/index.htm
Presiding Judge: Patrick DeAlmeida

LOCAL GOVERNMENT

New Jersey is divided into 21 county governments and 566 sub-county general purpose governments. Nineteen of the 21 county governments are governed by a board of chosen freeholders. Both Mercer and Atlantic counties are administrated by county executive governments. The 566 sub-county governments include 324 municipal governments (cities, towns, and boroughs) and 242 town or township governments townships and villages) which are governed by council-manager or commission governments. Towns are generally administered by mayor-council or mayor-committee governments.

New Jersey State League of Municipalities, URL: http://www.njslom.org/

AREA AND POPULATION

Area
New Jersey is located in the north-west of the US, east of Pennsylvania, north of Delaware, and south of New York State. The total area of New Jersey is 8,721.30 sq. miles, of which 7,417.34 sq. miles is land, and 1,303.96 sq. miles is water.

To view a map of the state, please consult:
http://www.lib.utexas.edu/maps/us_2001/new_jersey_ref_2001.pdf

Population
According to the 2010 Census, the 2010 population was 8,791,894, up from the mid-2009 estimate of 8,707,739. In 2012, the population was estimated to be 8,864,590. The population increased by 4.5 per cent over the period 2000-09. The population is expected to reach 9.8 million by 2030. Due to its relatively small size and large population (11th largest in the US in 2009), New Jersey is the most densely populated state in the US (1,195.1 people per sq. mile). The largest cities are Newark (277,140 in 2010), Jersey City (247,597) and Paterson (146,199). The state capital, Trenton, had 84,913 inhabitants in 2010, representing a population decrease since 2000. The most highly populated county is Bergen, with 905,116 inhabitants in 2010.

According to the 2010 Census, 6.2 per cent of the population is under 5 years, 23.5 per cent under 18 years and 13.5 per cent is aged over 65 years. Approximately 68.6 per cent of the population is white, and 13.7 per cent is black. Approximately 17.7 per cent of the population is of Hispanic or Latino origin.

Births, Marriages, Deaths
The US Census Bureau estimated that there were 106,922 births in 2010 and 69,495 deaths over the same period, giving a natural population increase of 37,427 people. Net immigration amounted to 5,670 people in 2009. The infant mortality rate was 5.2 per 1,000 in 2007. Marriages and divorces in 2007 were provisionally estimated at 42,435 and 25,687 respectively.

EMPLOYMENT

New Jersey had an estimated total civilian labour force of 4,621,000 in December 2012, of which 4,177,200 were employed and 443,800 were unemployed. The unemployment rate was 9.6 per cent, higher than the December 2012 national average of 7.8 per cent.

The following table shows preliminary figures for December 2012 non-farm wage and salary employment according to industry:

Industry	No. of employed	12-month change (%)
Logging and mining	1,300	-7.1
Construction	125,300	-2.8
Manufacturing	247,400	-1.5
Trade, transportation, and utilities	831,500	0.9
Information	70,600	0.6
Financial activities	253,500	0.2
Professional and business services	620,800	2.3
Educational and health services	640,500	3.4
Leisure and hospitality	337,500	1.0
Other services	172,400	3.6
Government	621,800	0.3
TOTAL	3,922,600	1.2

Source: Bureau of Labor Statistics

BANKING AND FINANCE

GDP/GNP, Inflation, National Debt
Gross Domestic Product (current dollar) was $487.0 billion in 2011 and ranked 7th in the US. Real GDP contracted by 0.5 per cent over 2011.

Gross Domestic Product according to industry is shown on the attached table (millions of current dollars):

Industry	2009	2010	2011
Agriculture, forestry, fishing, hunting	821	796	800
Mining	77	58	61
Utilities	8,240	9,248	8,506
Construction	15,355	14,714	14,788
Manufacturing	36,819	36,776	38,075
Wholesale Trade	34,592	35,981	37,509
Retail Trade	28,387	29,938	30,890
Transportation and warehousing	14,628	15,274	15,622
Information	21,172	20,828	21,614
Finance and insurance	36,951	41,146	40,623
Real estate	84,200	80,412	76,339
Educational services	4,760	4,890	5,042
Health care & social assistance	36,326	37,801	38,716
Other non-government services	94,959	98,707	103,695
Government	53,072	53,876	54,710
TOTAL	470,358	480,446	486,989

Source: Bureau of Economic Analysis, Feb. 2013

Per capita GDP fell in 2011 to $48,380, above the national average of $42,070. The average per capita income in New Jersey rose to $52,430 in 2011, above the national average of $41,560.

The Consumer Price Index (CPI) for the New York-Northern New Jersey-Long Island, NY-NJ-CT-PA, metropolitan area rose from 247.7 in 2011 to 252.6 in 2012 (1982-84 = 100). (Source: Bureau of Labor Statistics)

Balance of Payments / Imports and Exports

Total New Jersey imports amounted to $94,368 million in 2009, down 29.8 per cent from $134,375 million in 2008. Imports rose by 15.3 per cent to $108,781 million in 2010, represenmting 5.7 per cent of US total. They rose further in 2011 to $125,457 million, up 15.5 per cent. Main imports include crude oil from petroleum, oil, light oils, vehicles and vehicle parts. Main suppliers (2011) included China (13.5 per cent), Canada (30.0 per cent), Japan (6.6 per cent), Germany and the UK.

New Jersey's merchandise export revenue fell from $35,643 million in 2008 to $27,244 million in 2009, a decrease of 23.6 per cent. Exports rose by 18.0 per cent in 2010 to $32,154 million, representing 2.5 per cent of US total and by 18.5 per cent to $38,115 million in 2011. Most of New Jersey's exports are manufactured goods, including pharmaceuticals, chemicals, electronic and electrical machinery, and computer equipment.

The following table shows the top five international export markets in 2010-11 according to revenue:

Country	2010 ($m)	2011 ($m)	+/-% 10-11
Canada	6,254	7,025	12.3
United Kingdom	2,266	2,547	12.4
Mexico	1,515	2,105	38.9
Netherlands	1,102	1,951	77.1
China	1,389	1,855	33.5

Source: US Census Bureau

The top five New Jersey exports in 2010 by industry are shown in the following table:

Industry	Revenue ($m)
Oil (not crude) from petrol & bitum. mineral etc.	1,728
Platinum, unwrought or powder	757
Ferrous waste & scrap nesoi	742
Civilian aircraft, engines and parts	722
Plat wst a scrp nt cntng oth prec mtls	702

Source: US Census Bureau

Chambers of Commerce and Trade Organisations
New Jersey Chamber of Commerce, URL: http://www.njchamber.com/

MANUFACTURING, MINING AND SERVICES

Primary and Extractive Industries
The mining industry contributed $61 million towards New Jersey's GDP in 2011 (a sharp decline from $461 million in 2007). The main sector in 2010 was non-oil and gas mining, which earned $35 million; oil and gas extraction accounted for $11 million, whilst support activities for mining earned $12 million.

New Jersey has no oil producing industry, although it has six petroleum refineries and is traversed by a major pipeline. The New York Harbor area between New York and New Jersey has over 40 million barrels of refined product storage capacity (much of which is in New Jersey), making it the largest petroleum product hub in the United States. Its crude oil refinery capacity was 584,000 bbl/d in 2012 (3.2 per cent of US total). Oil consumption in 2010 fell to 201.7 million barrels (2.9 per cent of US total); most was in the form of motor gasoline (98.5 million barrels and 3.1 per cent of the US total) and distillate fuel (30.7 million barrels - 2.2 per cent of US total).

New Jersey relies on imports of natural gas to satisfy its requirements. Natural gas in New Jersey is used mainly by the residential sector for home heating. Consumption in 2011 was 660,595 million cubic feet.

Coal consumption was 1,976,000 short tons in 2010 (0.2 per cent of US total). (Source: EIA)

Energy
New Jersey's total energy production was 365 trillion Btu in 2010 (0.5 per cent of US total). New Jersey's total energy consumption was 2,448 trillion Btu in 2010 (2.5 per cent of the US total) and was ranked 37th in the US for per capita energy consumption (278 million Btu in 2010). The transportation sector dominates energy consumption in New Jersey, where the average commute time is among the longest in the US.

New Jersey is a net importer of electricity. Net summer capability in 2010 was 18,424 MW (1.8 per cent of the US total). Monthly net generation in 2012 was 4,660,000 MWh (1.5 per cent of US total), of which nuclear 2,365,000 MWh and natural gas-fired 2,050 MWh. Coal-fired power generated 95 MWh and renewables excluding hydroelectric 108,000 MWh. The major plants include PSEG Salem Gnerating Station (nuclear), Bergen (gas), PSEG Liberty Generating, PSEG Hope Creek Generating (nuclear), and PSEG Linden Cogen Plant (gas). New Jersey has three nuclear electricity generating plants: Hope Creek, Oyster Creek, and Salem. In 2006 Hope Creek had a summer capacity of 1,061 MW, Oyster Creek 619 MW, and Salem 2,342 MW.

New Jersey has enacted the US's first offshore wind renewable energy standard, requiring at least 1,100 MW by 2021 in its renewable energy portfolio. (Source: EIA)

Manufacturing
In 2011, the manufacturing sector contributed $38,075 million to the state's GDP, up from $36,776 million the previous year. In 2010, the top sectors were chemical manufacturing ($12,673 million), food, beverage and tobacco products ($3,623 million), computer and electronic product manufacturing ($3,603 million) and petroleum and coal products ($2,137 million).

Service Industries
The services industry is New Jersey's largest contributor towards GDP. Top sectors in 2011 were real estate ($76,339 million), professional and technical services ($46,8789 million), finance and insurance ($40,623 million), and health care and social assistance ($38,716 million).

Tourism
The accommodation and food sector of the services industry contributed an estimated $11,553 million towards the 2011 state GDP, whilst the amusement, gambling and recreation services sector contributed $1,862 million.
Visit New Jersey, URL: http://nj.gov/travel/
Delaware River Region Tourism Council, URL: http://www.visitsouthjersey.com

Agriculture
The agriculture, forestry, fishing and hunting industry contributed $800 million towards the state 2011 GDP. The highest earning sector in 2010 was farming ($602 million), whilst forestry, fishing and related activities earned the state $194 million. (Source: BEA)

Around 17 per cent of New Jersey is used as farmland. According to the USDA Census of Agriculture, there were 10,300 farms in 2010, covering some 730,000 acres. The average size of a farm fell from 85 acres in 1997 to 71 acres in 2010. The total market value of agricultural products was $986,885,000 in 2007, crops generating the major revenue of $851,653,000. As of 1 Jan. 2011, there were 32,000 cattle and calves and 8,000 hogs & pigs.

COMMUNICATIONS AND TRANSPORT

International Airports
There are two international airports in New Jersey: Newark International Airport and Atlantic City International Airport.
Newark International Airport (EWR),
URL: http://www.panynj.gov/aviation/ewrframe.HTM
Atlantic City International Airport, URL: http://www.acairport.com/

Railways
New Jersey's passenger railway and bus system is operated by NJ Transit. It carries over 230,000 rail and light rail passengers a day. There are 11 rail lines and a total of 542 miles of track serving 161 stations and 28 light rail stations.

Roads
North to south routes in New Jersey are provided by the Garden State Parkway and the New Jersey Turnpike. Interstate 80, to the north of the state, links Pennsylvania with New York City. Interstate 78, in central New Jersey, connects Pennsylvania with Newark. The Atlantic City Expressway in the south of the state connects with the Atlantic City Boardwalk. NJ Transit also operates buses.

Shipping
Ferry services are operated by a number of ferry companies including: Cape May-Lewes Ferry, North Cape May; Delafort Ferry; Circle Line, Hoboken; Express Navigation, Atlantic Highlands; Hoboken Ferry Service, Hoboken; New York Waterway, Weehawken; and River Link, Camden-Philadelphia.

Ports and Harbours
Three of New Jersey's ports are among the busiest in the US: New York, NY & NJ; Philadelphia, and Paulsboro, NJ. The Port of New York/New Jersey is the largest port on the East Coast of the USA and has direct access to extensive road and rail networks in the region. In 2005, cargo volumes increased by 7.6 per cent on the previous year, equating to a value of $132 billion. The rise was largely due to increased trade with China (25 per cent over 2005), which accounted for over 22 per cent of the port's volume of business.

HEALTH

There are health departments in all 21 counties run by the Office of Local Health. The National Center for Health Statistics estimated that there were 33.0 doctors (including osteopaths) per 10,000 population in 2009, well above the national state average of 27.4. In 2008, there were 6,925 dentists (8.0 per 10,000 population). In 2009, there were 2.4 community hospital beds per 1,000 residents, and, in 2010, there were 360 nursing homes, with a total of 51,101 beds.

It was estimated that 15.2 per cent of 18-64 year olds had no health-care coverage in 2007-09, and that 9.4 per cent were living in poverty in 2007; both figures were below the national average (15.8 per cent and 14.3 per cent respectively).

New Jersey reported 54,557 HIV/AIDS cases from the beginning of the epidemic to the end of 2008, and ranked 5th in the cumulative number of reported HIV/AIDS cases as of 2008. The overall TB rate was 4.9 per 100,000 population, ranking it 10th highest in the US. The state has below national average obesity levels among adults (23.8 per cent). An estimated 60.7 per cent of adulats were considered overweight. (Source: Center for Disease Control)

UNITED STATES OF AMERICA

EDUCATION

Primary/Secondary Education
Over the academic year 2009-10, there were 2,620 public elementary and secondary schools in New Jersey with a total of 1.396 million students and 115,248 teachers. The teacher/student ratio was one to 12.11.

In 2007-08, New Jersey expenditure on the state school system reached some $26.478 billion, whilst revenues from education in the same year amounted to an estimated $24.892 billion.

Higher Education
In 2010-11 there were some 194,124 male students and 238,003 women enrolled in New Jersey's 66 higher education institutions. In the same year, 75,866 degrees were awarded, including 36,025 Bachelors, 14,146 Masters and 3,011 doctorates. (Source: National Center for Education Statistics)

COMMUNICATIONS AND MEDIA

Newspapers
New Jersey Press Association, URL: http://www.njpa.org
The Times, URL: http://www.nj.com/times
The Star-Ledger, URL: http://www.nj.com/news/ledger
The New Jersey Herald, URL: http://www.njherald.com/

Broadcasting
New Jersey Network (NJN) is the state's telecommunications network and is available to all households whether or not they have cable. It has been broadcasting for 25 years and provides educational, public affairs and entertainment programmes for both radio and television. There are 39 cable television stations and 2.5 million cable subscribers.
NJN Public Television and Radio, URL: http://www.njn.net

ENVIRONMENT

According to EIA statistics, overall emissions of carbon dioxide fell to 16,085,557 metric tons in 2009, down from 20,072,127 metric tons in 2010. Emissions rose to 19,160,136 metric tons in 2010, ranking it 37th in the US. Emissions of sulphur dioxide amounted to 13,954 metric tons and nitrogen oxide amounted to 14,986 metric tons.

In April 2006, an expansion of the State's renewable portfolio standard was approved. This now requires utilities to generate 22.5 per cent of their electricity from renewable sources by 2021, with solar sources generating at least 2 per cent of this standard. In October 2008, the development of a 350-MW wind farm, consisting of 96 wind turbines, off New Jersey's coast was approved. New Jersey is one of 13 states who are part of the Ozone Transport Commission, an organisation set up to combat ground-level ozone in the Northeast and Mid-Atlantic States.

In 2010, 20,942 alternative-fueled vehicles were in use (2.2 per cent of the US total). Ethanol consumption amounted to 10,980,000 barrels in 2011, 3.6 per cent of the US total. (Source: EIA)

NEW MEXICO

Capital: Santa Fé (Population, Census 2010: 67,947)

Head of State: Susanna Martinez (R) (Governor) (page 1471)

State Flag: A yellow background in the centre of which appears the Zia Sun in red.

CONSTITUTION AND GOVERNMENT

Constitution
New Mexico entered the Union on 6 January 1912 as the 47th state. The governor heads the executive branch of government, assisted by six other elected officials: lieutenant governor, attorney general, secretary of state, state treasurer, state auditor, and commissioner of public lands. All elected executive officials serve a maximum of two consecutive four-year terms.

New Mexico elects two Senators and three Representatives to the US Congress in Washington, DC.

To view the state constitution, open the 'New Mexico Statutes and Court Rules' folder at: http://www.nmlaws.org/

Legislature
The Legislature is composed of the Senate and the House of Representatives. The New Mexico legislature meets for annual sessions usually beginning on the third Tuesday in January and lasting for 60 days in each odd-numbered year and 30 days in each even-numbered year.

Upper House
The Senate's 42 members are elected for a period of four years. The Democrats currently hold the majority of seats in the Senate. The Democrats hold the majority of seats in the State Senate. As of November 2012, the Senate was composed of 24 Democrats and 174 Republicans.
Senate, State Capitol, Santa Fe, New Mexico 87501, USA. Tel: +1 505 986 4714 (Chief Clerk), URL: http://www.nmlegis.gov/lcs/

Lower House
The House of Representatives consists of 70 members elected for two years. The Democrats hold the majority of seats in the New Mexico House of Representatives. The Democrats retained control of the House of Representatives in the November 2012 elections.
House of Representatives, State Capitol, Santa Fe, New Mexico 87501, USA. Tel: +1 505 986 4751 (Chief Clerk), URL: http://www.nmlegis.gov/lcs/

Elected Executive Branch Officials (as at April 2013)
Governor: Susana Martinez (R)
Lieutenant Governor: John A. Sanchez (R)
Secretary of State: Dianna J. Duran (R)
State Auditor: Hector H. Balderas (D)
State Treasurer: James B. Lewis (D)
Attorney General: Gary King (D)
Commissioner, State Lands: Ray Powell

Legislature (as at April 2013)
President of the Senate: John Sanchez (R)
President Pro Tem of the Senate: Mary Kay Papen (D)
Majority Leader: Michael S. Sanchez (D)
Minority Leader: Stuart Ingle (R)
Speaker of the House: W. Ken Martinez (D)
Majority Leader: Rick Miera (D)
Minority Leader: Donald E. Bratton (R)

US Senators: Martin Heinrich (D) (page 1440) and Tom Udall (D) (page 1529)

Ministries
Office of the Governor, State Capitol, Room 400, Santa Fe, NM 87501, USA. Tel: +1 505 476 2200, URL: http://www.governor.state.nm.us
Office of the Attorney General, 407 Galisteo Street, Bataan Memorial Building, Room 260, Santa Fe, NM 87501, USA. (Mailing address: PO Drawer 1508, Santa Fe, NM 87504-1508, USA) Tel: +1 505 827 6000, fax: +1 505 827 5826, URL: http://www.nmag.gov/
Office of the Secretary of State, State Capitol North Annex, Suite 300, Santa Fe, New Mexico 87503, USA. Tel: +1 505 827 3600, fax: +1 505 827 3634, URL: http://www.sos.state.nm.us
State Treasurer's Office, 2019 Galisteo, Building K, Santa Fe, NM 87505 (PO Box 608, Santa Fe, NM 87504-0608), USA. Tel: +1 505 955 1120, fax: +1 505 955 1195, URL: http://www.stonm.org
Office of the State Auditor, 2113 Warner Circle, Santa Fe, NM 87505-5499, USA. Tel: +1 505 827 3500, fax: +1 505 827 3512, URL: http://www.saonm.org
Department of Agriculture, MSC 3189, Corner of Gregg and Espina, Box 30005, Las Cruces, NM 88003-8005, USA. Tel: +1 505 646 3007, URL: http://nmdaweb.nmsu.edu
Economic Development Department, PO Box 20003, Joseph M. Montoya Building, 1100 St. Francis Drive, Santa Fe, NM 87504-5003, USA. Tel: +1 505 827 0561, fax: +1 505 827 0211, URL: http://www.gonm.biz/
Department of Public Education, 300 Don Gaspar, Santa Fe, NM 87501-2786, USA. Tel: +1 505 827 5800, URL: http://ped.state.nm.us/ped/index.html
Department of Energy, Minerals and Natural Resources, 1220 S. St. Francis Drive, Santa Fe, NM 87505, USA. (Mailing Address: PO Box 6429, Santa Fe, NM 87502, USA) Tel: +1 505 476 3200, fax: +1 505 476 3220, URL: http://www.emnrd.state.nm.us
Environment Department, Harold S. Runnels Building, 1190 St. Francis Drive, Santa Fe, NM 87502-0110, USA. Tel: +1 505 827 2855, fax: +1 505 827 2836, URL: http://www.nmenv.state.nm.us
Department of Finance and Administration, Financial Control Division, Bataan Memorial Building, Suite 166, 407 Galisteo Street, Santa Fe, NM 87501, USA. Tel: +1 505 827 3681, URL: http://nmdfa.state.nm.us/Financial_Control.aspx
Department of Transportation, 1120 Cerrillos Road, PO Box 1149, Santa Fe, NM 87504-1149, USA. Tel: +1 505 827 5100, URL: http://dot.state.nm.us/content/nmdot/en.html

Political Parties
New Mexico Democratic Party, 1301 San Pedro NE, Albuquerque, NM 87110, USA. Tel: +1 505 830 3650, fax: +1 505 830 3645, e-mail: info@nmdemocrats.org, URL: http://www.nmdemocrats.org
Republican Party of New Mexico, 5150-A San Francisco NE, Suite 101, Albuquerque, NM 87109, USA. Tel: +1 505 298 3662, fax: +1 505 292 0755, e-mail: administrator@rpnm.org, URL: http://www.gopnm.org/

Elections
A General Election took place in November 2010 for the state positions of US Senator, three US Representatives, State Governor, Lieutenant Governor, Secretary of State, State Auditor, State Treasurer, Attorney General, Commissioner of Public Lands, Judge of the Court of Appeals, all 70 State Representatives, Public Regulation Commissioner, three District Judges, and the State Board of Education. The incumbent Governor, Democrat Bill Richardson, was ineligible for re-election and the seat was won by Republican Susanna Martinez with 54 per cent of the vote.

In the November 2012 Senate elections, the Democrats retained control of the Senate but with a reduced majority (24 Democrats and 17 Republicans). In the 2012 elections in the House of Representatives the Democrats retained control with a slightly increased majority (38 Democrats and 32 Republicans).

In the 2012 US Senate election, Jeff Bingaman (D) did not run for re-election. The seat was won by Martin Heinrich (D).

LEGAL SYSTEM

New Mexico's legal system consists of the Supreme Court, the Court of Appeals, 13 District Courts, 54 Magistrate Courts, 83 Municipal Courts and Probate Courts. In addition to the Supreme Court Chief Justice there are four Associate Justices. The Court of Appeals consists of ten judges, who sit in panels of three, and has offices in Santa Fe, Albuquerque, Las Cruces, and Las Vegas. It has a caseload of approximately 900 cases a year. The District Court has a total of 72 Judges, the Magistrate Court has 62, the Bernalillo County Metropolitan Court has 16, the Municipal Court has 83, and the Probate Court has 33.

In 2009, New Mexico became the second US state to repeal the death penalty since it was reinstated in 1976. The death penalty was replaced by life imprisonment without parole. At the time of the abolition, there were two men on death row. One person had been executed since 1976. The murder rate is estimated at 6.9 per 100,000 population.

Supreme Court, URL: http://nmsupremecourt.nmcourts.gov/
Chief Justice: Petra Jiminez Maes
Justices: Patricio Serna, Richard Bosson, Edward Chavez, Charles Daniels
Court of Appeals, URL: https://coa.nmcourts.com/
Chief Judge: Cynthia Foy Castillo
Judges: Linda Vanzi, Michael Vigil, Roderick Kennedy, Robert Robles, Timothy Garcia, Jonathan Sutin, James Wechsler, Michael Bustamente, Cynthia Fry, Miles Hanisee

LOCAL GOVERNMENT

New Mexico's local government consists of 33 county governments and 101 subcounty governments (all of which are municipal governments). There are no town or township governments. The body governing each of the state's county is known as the county board of commissioners. New Mexico's municipal governments are made up of cities, towns, and villages.

New Mexico Association of Counties, URL: http://www.nmcounties.org/

AREA AND POPULATION

Area
New Mexico is located in the West of the US, north and west of Texas, west of Oklahoma, east of Arizona, and south of Colorado. The area of New Mexico is 121,589.48 sq. miles, of which 121,355.53 sq. miles is land, and 233.96 sq. miles is water.

To view a map of the state, please visit:
http://www.lib.utexas.edu/maps/us_2001/new_mexico_ref_2001.pdf

Population
According to the 2010, the population was 2,059,179, up on the mid-2009 estimate of 2,009,671. In 2012, the population was estimated to be 2,085,538. Over the period 2000-10, the population increased by 13.2 per cent and is expected to reach 2.099 million by 2030. New Mexico's population density is 17.0 people per sq. mile. The county with the greatest number of inhabitants is Bernalillo County, with 662,564 in 2010.

According to the 2010 Census, 7 per cent of the population is under 5 years, 25.2 per cent under 18 years and 13.2 per cent is aged over 65 years. Approximately 68.4 per cent of the population is white, and 2.4 per cent is black. An estimated 9.4 per cent is American Indian. Approximately 46.3 per cent of the population is of Hispanic or Latino origin.

Births, Marriages, Deaths
The US Census Bureau estimated that there were 27,850 births in 2010 and 15,931 deaths over the same period, giving a natural population increase of 11,919 people. Net immigration accounted for 8,194 new residents in 2009. The infant mortality rate in 2007 was 6.3 infant deaths per 1,000 live birth. Marriages and divorces in 2007, according to provisional data, numbered 11,229 and 8,434 respectively.

EMPLOYMENT

New Mexico's total civilian labour force was estimated at 933,700 in December 2012, of which 874,100 were in employment and 59,600 were unemployed. The unemployment rate was 6.4 per cent, below the US national average of 7.8 per cent. (Source: US Bureau of Labor Statistics)

Non-farm wage and salary employment according to industry in December 2012 is shown on the following table:

Industry	No. of jobs	12-month change
Logging and mining	21,800	-0.9
Construction	42,000	2.9
Manufacturing	29,800	1.4
Trade, transportation, and utilities	133,400	-0.1
Information*	13,600	-0.1
Financial activities	33,500	-0.6
Professional and business services	96,200	-3.0
Educational and health services	125,700	1.0
Leisure and hospitality	88,500	4.2
Other services	26,600	-0.7

- continued

Government	189,700	-2.6
TOTAL	800,800	-0.4

*Not seasonally adjusted
Source: Bureau of Labor Statistics

BANKING AND FINANCE

GDP/GNP, Inflation, National Debt
New Mexico's total Gross Domestic Product (current dollar) was put at $77.1 billion in 2010 to $79.4 billion in 2011. Real GDP rose by 0.2 per cent in 2011. New Mexico was ranked 37th in the US for its 2011 GDP.

Gross Domestic Product according to industry is shown on the following table (in millions of current dollars):

Industry	2009	2010	2011
Agriculture, forestry, fishing, hunting	990	1,497	1,807
Mining	5,158	5,641	6,189
Utilities	1,392	1,403	1,264
Construction	3,711	3,441	3,387
Manufacturing	4,589	5,466	5,899
Wholesale Trade	2,490	2,551	2,492
Retail Trade	4,986	5,026	5,210
Transportation & warehousing	1,874	1,925	2,067
Information	2,138	2,102	2,184
Finance & insurance	2,863	3,220	3,154
Real estate	9,339	9,036	9,209
Educational services	443	459	486
Health care & social assistance	5,661	5,888	6,075
Other non-government services	13,808	14,130	14,531
Government	15,293	15,309	15,461
TOTAL	74,736	77,095	79,414

Source: Bureau of Economic Analysis, Feb. 2013

New Mexico's per capita real GDP was an estimated $33,857 in 2011, down on the US average of $42,070. The state's average per capita income rose to $34,133 in 2011.

The annual Consumer Price Index for the West urban area (all items) rose from 227.5 in 2011 to 232.4 in 2012 (1982-84 = 100). (Source: Bureau of Labor Statistics)

Balance of Payments / Imports and Exports
New Mexico's imports amounted to $2,000 milllion in 2009, down 12.3 per cent from $2,281 million in 2008. In 2010, they rose by 58.3 per cent to $3,166 million. They fell by -20 per cent in 2011 to $2,531 million, representing 0.1 per cent of total US imports. As of 2011, main suppliers were China (32.8 per cent), Canada (15.4 per cent), Mexico (13.7 per cent), Japan and the Netherlands. New Mexico's export revenue fell from $2,783 million in 2008 to $1,270 million in 2009, a decrease of 54.3 per cent. In 2010, export revenue rose by 21.4 per cent to $1,541 million. It rose by a further 35.7 per cent in 2011 to $2,092 million, representing 0.1 per cent of US total.

Major industry sectors are high technology, manufacturing, processed natural resources and primary goods. The maquila industry (the assembly of products from materials shipped from outside) is supported by the export of plastics, electronics, chemicals, fabricated steel, and wood products. In addition, New Mexico exports paperboard boxes, cartons, shipping crates, foam interpacking, adhesives, glass and packing equipment.

The top five export products in 2010, according to export revenue, are shown on the following table:

Product	($m)
Photosensitive semiconductor devices	108
Civilian aircraft, engines, equipment and parts	64
Chem elem doped, used in electron etc	60
Fuel, lub/cooling med pumps for internal comb. piston engines	48
Taps, cocks etc f pipe vat inc. thermo control.	43

Source: US Census Bureau

The top five international export destinations in 2010-11, according to revenue, are shown on the following table:

Country	2010 ($m)	2011 ($m)	+/-% 10-11
Mexico	429	464	8.2
Israel	21	442	500+
Canada	284	352	24.1
China	72	90	23.8
UK	29	81	182.1

Source: US Census Bureau

Chambers of Commerce and Trade Organisations
New Mexico Economic Development Department, URL: http://www.gonm.biz/
Association of Commerce and Industry of New Mexico, URL: http://aci.nm.org/
Las Vegas-San Miguel Chamber of Commerce, URL: http://www.lasvegasnewmexico.com/
Santa Fe County Chamber of Commerce, URL: http://www.santafechamber.com/

UNITED STATES OF AMERICA

MANUFACTURING, MINING AND SERVICES

Primary and Extractive Industries

New Mexico's major extractive products include oil, gas, coal and humate, and uranium. New Mexico is the third largest natural gas and seventh largest oil producing state, with over 900 oil and gas operators. Mining contributed an estimated $6,189 million towards New Mexico's 2011 Gross Domestic Product (up from $5,641 million in 2010). Top earning sectors in 2010 were oil and gas extraction ($3,849 million) and support activities ($1,049 million).

New Mexico had proven oil reserves of 823 million barrels in 2010 (3.5 per cent of the US total). Its 20,020 oil wells and 79 rotary rigs produced a monthly (Oct) total of 7,570 thousand barrels in 2012 (3.6 per cent of the US total production) in 2010. Oil consumption in 2010 rose to 48.3 million barrels, of which motor gasoline made up 22.6 million barrels and distillate fuel, 14.1 million barrels. Crude oil refinery capacity amounted to 142,900 bbl/d in 2012.

One of the top natural gas-producing states, New Mexico had proven reserves of 15,412 billion cubic feet of dry natural gas in 2010 (5.1 per cent of the US total). Natural gas plant liquids reserves amounted to 764 million barrels. New Mexico's 32,302 gas wells produced a marketed total of 1,237,303 million cubic feet of natural gas in 2011 (5.1 per cent of US total). State consumption of natural gas is relatively low, and most of New Mexico's supply is delivered to markets on the West Coast and in West Texas. In 2011, 246,505 million cubic feet was used by the state.

Recoverable coal reserves were 518 million short tons in 2011, equivalent to 2.7 per cent of the US total reserves. There were three surface mines and one underground mine in the state in 2007. Production rose from 20,991,000 short tons in 2010 to 21,922,000 short tons in 2011 (2.0 per cent of US total). (Source: EIA)

Energy

New Mexico's total energy production was 2,258 trillion Btu in 2010 (3.0 per cent of US total). New Mexico's total energy consumption was 680 trillion Btu in 2010 (0.7 per cent of US total), whilst its per capita energy consumption ranks 23rd in the US (329 million Btu in 2010).

New Mexico is a net exporter of electricity, with coal as its primary generating fuel. Net summer capability in 2010 was 8,130 MW (0.8 per cent of the US total), and net monthly generation in 2012 was 3,051,000 MWh (Oct. 2012), of which coal 2,127,000 MWh, natural gas 681,000 MWh and renewables excl. hydroelectric 229000 MWh. Major electricity generating plants include Four Corners (coal), San Juan (coal), Luna Energy Facility (gas), Cunningham (gas), Escalante (coal), and Rio Grande (gas).

A solar thermal power plant was completed in 2011. New Mexico's installed solar photovoltaic capacity increased from 43 MW in 2010 to 116 MW in 2011. New Mexico produces a small amount of energy from wind resources. In 2007, New Mexico adopted a renewable portfolio standard that requires 20 per cent of an electric utility's power to come from renewable energy sources by 2020. In 2011, renewable energy supplied 6.5 per cent of electricity generated in the State. (Source: EIA)

Manufacturing

Manufacturing accounted for $5,899 million of the state GDP in 2011 (up from $5,466 million in 2010). Top earning sectors in 2010 were computer and electronic products ($3,794 million), and food products ($432 million).

Service Industries

Services is the largest contributor towards state GDP. In 2011, the largest sectors were real estate ($9,209 million), professional and technical services ($6,601 million) and health services ($6,075 million).

Tourism

The accommodation and food services sector contributed an estimated $2,628 million towards New Mexico's GDP in 2011 whilst the arts, entertainment and recreation sector contributed around $431 million.

New Mexico Department of Tourism, URL: http://www.newmexico.org/

Agriculture

New Mexico's agriculture industry contributed an estimated $1,807 million towards the state 2011 GDP, up from $1,497 million in 2010. The farms sector contributed $1,391 million in 2010, whilst the forestry, fishing and related services sector contributed $106 million in the same year.

According to the USDA Census of Agriculture, New Mexico had a total of 21,000 farms in 2010, and farmland covered approximately 43,200,000 acres; the average size of a New Mexican farm, was 2,057 acres in the same year. In 2008 livestock product receipts were approximately $1.6 billion and crop receipts were around $553,000,000. As of 1 Jan. 2011, there were 1,540,000 cattle and calves, 1,500 hogs & pigs, and 110,000 sheep.

COMMUNICATIONS AND TRANSPORT

International Airports

New Mexico has two international airports: Albuquerque International Sunport and Las Cruces International Airport. 6,487,276 passengers used Albuquerque International Sunport in 2006, and around 32,879 tons of freight was handled. The number of passengers has increased by two per cent per annum since 2002.

Albuquerque International Sunport, URL: http://www.cabq.gov/airport/
Las Cruces International Airport, URL: http://www.las-cruces.org/airport/

Roads

New Mexico has long been an important corridor for trade and migration. New Mexico is crossed by the following interstate highways: I-40 east to west through Albuquerque; I-10 east to west from Las Cruces; and I-25 north to Denver. Annual freight traffic by road amounts to 79 million tons.

Railways

New Mexico has 2,100 miles of railway track. Mainline rail companies are Amtrak, Burlington Northern Santa Fe (BNSF), and Union Pacific (UP). Short line railway companies include Santa Fe Southern (SFS), Southwestern (SW), and Texas and New Mexico (TNMR). Annual freight traffic by rail is 30 million tons.

Burlington Northern Santa Fe, URL: http://www.bnsf.com/

HEALTH

The National Center for Health Statistics estimated that there were 23.9 doctors (including osteopaths) per 10,000 population in 2009, below the US average of 27.4. In 2008, there were 916 dentists (4.6 per 10,000 population). In 2009, there were 1.9 community hospital beds per 1,000 New Mexico residents, and there were 70 nursing homes with 6,769 beds.

It was estimated that, in 2007-09, 22.6 per cent of New Mexicans has no healthcare insurance, one of the highest rates in the USA. Around 19 per cent of the state population lived in poverty in 2007-11. However, levels of obesity and weight were lower than the national average. An estimated 25.1 per cent of adults are considered obese and 59.8 per cent overweight. New Mexico reported 2,903 HIV/AIDS cases from the beginning of the epidemic to the end of 2008. The state ranked 36th highest in cumulative number of reported HIV/AIDS cases in 2008. The overall TB rate was 3.0 per 100,000 population, 25th highest in the US. (Source: CDC)

EDUCATION

Primary/Secondary Education

In total, New Mexico had 866 elementary and secondary schools in 2009-10. Enrolment in the same year was 334,419 and there were 22,723 teachers. The state average student-teacher ratio was 14.72 to one.

Revenue over the year 2007-08 reached $3.65 million, whilst expenditure on the state sector was $3.556 million.

Higher Education

New Mexico's state universities and degree-granting institutions, which number 44, include New Mexico State University, Las Cruces; University of New Mexico, Albuquerque; Western New Mexico University, Silver City; Eastern New Mexico University, Portales; New Mexico Highlands University, Las Vegas; and New Mexico Institute of Mining and Technology (New Mexico Tech.), Socorro. In 2010-11 academic year, there were 65,885 male students and 86,867 women enrolled. 21,509 degrees were awarded, including 7,774 Bachelors, 3,057 Masters and 544 Doctorates. (Source: National Center for Education Statistics)

COMMUNICATIONS AND MEDIA

Newspapers

New Mexico's daily newspapers include: Albuquerque Journal, Albuquerque Tribune, Los Alamos Monitor, Roswell Daily Record, The Daily Times, The Independent, and the Santa Fé New Mexican. Weekly newspapers include: the Lincoln County News, the Stateline Tribune, NM Business Weekly, and the Weekly Alibi.

Albuquerque Journal, URL: http://www.abqjournal.com
The Albuquerque Tribune, URL: http://www.abqtrib.com

Broadcasting

Nevada has over 110 radio stations. Albuquerque has 28 stations, Santa Fe has seven, and Roswell has nine. Eleven of New Mexico's 19 television stations are based in Albuquerque; four are based in Roswell. Two are run by CBS, one by Fox, two by NBC, three by PBS.

ENVIRONMENT

New Mexico's primary electricity generating fuel is coal. Emissions of carbon dioxide from its power generating industry fell from 33,502,278 metric tons in 2009 to 29,378,703 metric tons in 2010 and the state ranked 31st in the US in this respect. Emissions of sulfur dioxide amounted to 15,032 metric tons and nitrogen oxide 55,818 metric tons (2.2 per cent of the US total).

In 2010, there were 17,901 alternative-fueled vehicles were in use. New Mexico has one ethanol plant with a capacity of 30 million gallons per year. Ethanol consumption was 1,788,000 barrels in 2011. (Source: EIA)

SPACE PROGRAMME

NASA's White Sands Test Facility, part of the NASA Johnson Space Centre, is located at White Sands, New Mexico. It is responsible for testing rocket propulsion systems, components and materials.

Sir Richard Branson has a long-term lease with the state of New Mexico for a spaceport which will form the headquarters of his Virgin Galactic space tourism business. Virgin Galactic say space flights will cost around $200,000 for a 2.5-hour flight.

NEW YORK STATE

Capital: Albany (Population, Census 2010: 97,856)

Head of State: David Cuomo (D) (page 1411)

State Flag: A blue background in the centre of which appear the arms of New York State. The arms depict the figures of Liberty and Justice standing on each side of a shield; the shield shows a ship and sloop on a river behind a grass shore and in front of a mountain range over which the sun rises; Liberty holds a staff with a Phrygian cap on top; Justice is blindfolded, carrying a sword in one hand and a set of scales in the other; under the two figures appears the State motto 'Excelsior' ('Ever Upward').

CONSTITUTION AND GOVERNMENT

Constitution
One of the original 13 states of the Union (26 July 1788). New York's Constitution was first adopted in 1777. The current Constitution was approved by the people of New York on 8 November 1938. According to the 1938 Constitution, the governor heads the executive branch of state government assisted by three other elected constitutional officers: lieutenant governor, attorney general, and comptroller. All are elected for four-year terms.

New York State elects two US Senators and 29 US Representatives to the US Congress in Washington, DC.

To view the state constitution, please visit: http://www.dos.state.ny.us/info/pdfs/cons2004.pdf

Recent Events
Governor Eliot Spitzer resigned on 14th March 2008, following allegations that he had used a high-priced prostitution service. The Lieutenant Governor, David Paterson, took over the governorship.

Legislature
New York's bicameral legislature consists of the Senate and the Assembly, and meets in session annually.
Upper House
The Senate has 63 members who are elected every two years. The Lieutenant Governor is also the President of the Senate. The Democrats currently hold the majority of seats in the New York Senate. Following the 2012 elections, the Democrats have 33 seats and the Republicans 30. However, after the election, a small group called the Independent Democratic Conference created a third group in the Senate and formed a majority coalition with the Republicans.
Senate, Legislative Office Building, Albany, New York 12248, USA. Tel: +1 518 445 2800, e-mail: surname@senate.state.ny.us, URL: http://www.senate.state.ny.us/

Lower House
The Assembly has 150 members who are also elected every two years. The democrats hold the majority of seats in the Assembly. Following the 2012 elections the Assembly was composed of 105 Democrats, 44 Republicans and one independent.
New York State Assembly, Legislative Office Building, Albany, NY 12248, USA. Tel: +1 518 455 4218 (Public Information Department), URL: http://www.assembly.state.ny.us/

Elected Executive Branch Officials (as at April 2013)
Governor: Andrew Cuomo (D) (page 1411)
State Comptroller: Thomas P. DiNapoli
Attorney General: Eric Schneiderman

Legislature (as at April 2013)
Temporary President of the Senate and Majority Coalition Leader: Dean G. Skelos (R)
Temporary President of the Senate and IDC Coalition Leader: Jeff Klein (IDC)
Speaker of the Assembly: Sheldon Silver (D)
Assembly Majority Leader: Joseph Morelle (D)
Assembly Minority Leader: Brian M. Kolb (R)

US Senators: Charles E. Schumer (D) (page 1510) and Kirsten E. Gillibrand (D) (page 1430)

Ministries
Office of the Governor, State Capitol, Albany, NY 12224-0341, USA. Tel: +1 518 474 8390, URL: http://www.governor.ny.us/
Office of the Lieutenant Governor, State Capitol, Albany, NY 12224-0341, USA. Tel: +1 518 474 4623, URL: http://www.governor.ny.gov/sl2/ltgovernor_bio
Office of the Attorney General, State Capitol Building, Albany, NY 12224-0341, USA. Tel: +1 518 474 7330, fax: +1 518 473 9909, URL: http://www.ag.ny.gov/
Office of the State Comptroller, 110 State Street, Albany, NY 12236, USA. Tel: +1 518 474 4044, URL: http://www.osc.state.ny.us
Department of Agriculture and Markets, 10B Airline Drive, Albany, NY 12235, USA. Tel: +1 518 457 3880, fax: +1 518 457 3087, URL: http://www.agriculture.ny.gov/
New York State Economic Development Council, 19 Dove Street, Suite 101, Albany NY 12210, USA. Tel: +1 518 426 4058, fax: +1 518 426 4059, URL: http://nysedc.org/
Department of Education, Education Building, 89 Washington Avenue, Albany, NY 12234, USA. Tel: +1 518 473 4501 (Office of Communications), fax: +1 518 473 2827 (Office of Management Services), URL: http://www.nysed.gov
Department of Environmental Conservation, 625 Broadway, Albany, NY 12233, USA. Tel: +1 518 402 8540, URL: http://www.dec.ny.gov/
Department of Health, Corning Tower, Empire State Plaza, Albany, NY 12237, USA. Tel: +1 518 486 9002, URL: http://www.health.ny.gov/

Department of State, 41 State Street, Albany, NY 12231-0001, USA. Tel: +1 518 474 4750, fax: +1 518 474 4765, URL: http://www.dos.ny.gov/
Department of Taxation and Finance, Building 9, State Campus, Albany, NY 12227, USA. Tel: +1 518 457 1000 (Chief Information Officer), URL: http://www.tax.ny.gov/
Department of Transportation, Building 5, State Campus, Albany, NY 12232, USA. Tel: +1 518 457 5100, URL: http://www.dot.ny.gov

Political Parties
New York State Democratic Party, URL: http://www.nydems.org/
New York Republican State Committee, URL: http://www.nygop.org/

Elections
The latest state legislative elections were held in November 2012. Democrats took most seats in the election, 33 to the Republican's 30.However a small group of breakaway Democrats formed a new group, the Independent Democratic Conference, and joined the Republicans, creating a coalition majority. The Democrats retained the State House with an increased majority (Democrats 105, Republicans 44, 1 Ind. Party of New York).

The most recent elections for New York State's constitutional officers took place in November 2010. David Paterson did not contest the Governorship for a second term. Democrat Andrew Cuomo, the state Attorney General, defeated the Republican candidate Carl Paladino by a large margin (61 per cent to 34 per cent).

LEGAL SYSTEM

New York State's court system consists of the Court of Appeals, the Appellate Division of the Supreme Court, the Supreme Court, the Court of Claims, the Family Court, 62 Surrogates Courts (one in each county), County Courts, the New York City Civil Court, the New York City Criminal Court, as well as courts for towns and villages outside New York City. New York State is divided into 12 Judicial Districts.

The New York Court of Appeals is the highest court in the state. In addition to the Chief Judge there are six Associate Judges who serve terms of 14 years. All are appointed by the governor and confirmed by the State senate.

New York's legal system is based on English Common Law. Capital punishment is still technically on the books, but there have been no executions since 1963. In total 1,130 people have been executed in the state. The New York Court of Appeals ruled that the death penalty violated the state constitution (People v Stephen LaValle), and the death row was disestablished in 2008. According to the DPIC the murder rate is 4.5 per 100,000.

Same-sex marriage is legal within the state.

Court of Appeals, URL: http://www.courts.state.ny.us/ctapps/
Chief Judge: Jonathan Lippman
Judges: Eugene Piggott, Susan Read, Victoria Graffeo, Robert Smith
Supreme Court, URL: http://www.courts.state.ny.us/appdivhome.htm
New York State Supreme Court, Appellate Division First Department, URL: http://www.nycourts.gov/courts/ad1/index.shtml
Presiding Justice: Luis A. Gonzalez
New York State Supreme Court, Appellate Division Second Judicial Department, URL: http://www.nycourts.gov/courts/ad2/index.shtml
Presiding Justice: Randall T. Eng
Supreme Court, Appellate Division, Third Judicial Department, URL: http://www.nycourts.gov/ad3/
Presiding Justice: Karen Peters
New York State Supreme Court Appellate Division Fourth Department, URL: http://www.nycourts.gov/ad4/
Presiding Justice: Henry J. Scudder

LOCAL GOVERNMENT

For local government purposes the State is divided into 57 county governments, 618 municipal governments, and 929 town governments. There are two classes of town government according to population. The city of New York counts as a municipal government. Additionally there are 680 school district governments and 1,119 special districts or authorities.

New York City consists of five boroughs: Manhattan, The Bronx, Brooklyn, Queens and Staten Island. Rudolph Giuliani stepped down as New York's mayor in November 2001 after serving the maximum two terms of office. He was replaced by Republican millionaire Michael Bloomberg, who was re-elected in 2005 and again in 2009 for the term beginning on January 1, 2010.

Association of Towns of the State of New York, URL: http://www.nytowns.org/
New York State Association of Counties, URL: http://www.nysac.org

UNITED STATES OF AMERICA

AREA AND POPULATION

Area
New York State borders New Jersey and Pennsylvania to the south, Lakes Ontario and Erie to the west, Canada to the north, and Connecticut, Massachusetts, and Vermont to the east. The area of New York State is 54,556.00 sq. miles, of which 47,213.79 sq. miles is land and 7,342.22 sq. miles inland water.

To view a map of the state, please consult:
http://www.lib.utexas.edu/maps/us_2001/new_york_ref_2001.pdf

Population
According to the 2010 Census, the 2010 population was 19,378,102, down from mid-2009 estimate of 19,541,45. The population was estimated at 19,570,261 in 2012. New York State is the third most populated state in the US. Over the period 2000-10, the population grew by 2.1 per cent. The population is expected to reach 19,477,429 by 2030. The population density is estimated at 411.2 people per sq. mile, the 7th highest in the US. Kings County is the largest of New York State's counties. The capital city, Albany, has a population of 97,856, whilst New York City has a population of 8.17 million.

According to the 2010 Census, 6.0 per cent of the population is under 5 years, 22.3 per cent under 18 years and 13.5 per cent is aged over 65 years. Approximately 65.7 per cent of the population is white, and 15.9 per cent is black. An estimated 7.3 per cent is Asian. Approximately 17.6 per cent of the population is of Hispanic or Latino origin.

Births, Marriages, Deaths
The US Census Bureau, Population Division, estimated that there were 244,375 births in 2010 and 146,432 deaths, giving a natural population increase of 97,943 people. Net emigration from the state reached 23,079 people over 2009. The infant mortality rate in 2007 was 5.6 infant deaths per 1,000 live births. Marriages and divorces in 2007, according to provisional data, numbered 130,584 and 55,943 respectively.

EMPLOYMENT

Preliminary figures indicate that New York State had a total civilian labour force of 9,593,400 in December 2012, of which 8,806,600 were employed and 786,800 were unemployed. The unemployment rate was 8.2 per cent, higher than the US rate of 7.8 per cent. (Source: US Bureau of Labor Statistics)

The following table shows December 2012 non-farm wage and salary employment according to industry:

Industry	No. of jobs	12-month change (%)
Logging and mining	5,100	0.0
Construction	300,600	-1.9
Manufacturing	449,400	-1.2
Trade, transportation, and utilities	1,505,200	1.1
Information	252,900	1.0
Financial activities	692,800	0.8
Professional and business services	1,205,300	4.5
Educational and health services	1,774,900	1.9
Leisure and hospitality	787,700	1.9
Other services	379,100	3.0
Government	1,487,600	0.0
TOTAL	8,840,600	1.4

Source: Bureau of Labor Statistics

BANKING AND FINANCE

GDP/GNP, Inflation, National Debt
New York State is one of the largest economies in the world and contributes around 7.7 per cent of US Gross Domestic Product. It has the third highest state GDP in the US (after California and Texas).

New York City is the leading center of banking, finance and communication in the USA and is home to the NYSE, the largest stock exchange in the world by dollar volume. However, it was hard hit by the financial crisis of 2008; the city shed almost 17,000 jobs in the financial industry alone from October 2007 to October 2008.

Total Gross Domestic Product (current dollars) rose from $1,105,020 million in 2007 to an estimated $1,144,481 million in 2008 and to $1,093,219 in 2009. Real GDP rose by just 1.6 per cent in 2008. The finance and insurance sector contracted significantly over the year. In 2010, GDP rose by 5.1 per cent, amounting to $1,159,540 million. In 2011, GDP (current prices) rose to $1,158.0 billion, ranked 3rd in the US. The following table shows Gross Domestic Product according to industry (in millions of current dollars):

Industry	2009	2010	2011
Agriculture, forestry, fishing and hunting	2,006	2,567	2,961
Mining	822	779	767
Utilities	18,285	19,270	18,016
Construction	34,864	33,347	33,929
Manufacturing	63,525	64,454	67,243
Wholesale Trade	52,344	55,304	58,103
Retail Trade	54,761	58,554	60,885
Transport and warehousing	19,583	19,526	20,078
Information	75,541	77,631	83,192

	- continued		
Finance and insurance	167,102	196,970	198,658
Real estate	148,208	137,670	133,910
Educational services	19,801	20,255	20,949
Health care & social assistance	83,915	88,383	91,253
Other non-government services	211,375	229,158	242,691
Government	120,149	124,956	125,333
TOTAL	1,072,311	1,128,823	1,157,969

Source: US Bureau of Economic Analysis

In 2011, per capita income rose to $51,126, 123 per cent of the national average. Per capita real GDP fell to $52,214 in 2011; the US average for the year was $42,070 per annum.

The annual Consumer Price Index (CPI) for the New York-Northern New Jersey-Long Island, NY-NJ-CT-PA, urban area (all items) rose from 247.7 in 2011 to 252.6 in 2012 (1982-84 = 100). (Source: Bureau of Labor Statistics)

Balance of Payments / Imports and Exports
Total New York imports amounted to $92,909 million in 2009, down 26.0 per cent from $125,577 million in 2008. Imports rose by 22 per cent in 2010 to $113,303 million and by 11.9 per cent in 2011 to $127,245 million, accounting for 5.8 per cent of the US total imports. Main import commodities include precious metals and good, gas and oil. Main suppliers include China (17 per cent), Canada (15 per cent), India, Israel and France.

Total export revenue fell from $81,386 million in 2008 to $58,743 million in 2009, a decrease of 27.8 per cent. Exports rose by 18.6 per cent to $69,696 million in 2010 and by a further 21.8 per cent in 2011 to $84,888 million. New York State accounts for 5.7 per cent of total US export revenue.

The top five export products in 2010, according to export revenue, are shown on the following table:

Product	Export Revenue ($m)
Diamonds, non industrial, worked	9,117
Paintings, drawings and pastels by hand	3,959
Jewelry and parts thereof, of other precious metals	3,555
Gold, non-monetary, unwrought	2,751
Civilian aircraft, engines and parts	1,836

Source: US Census Bureau

Merchandise export revenue in 2010-11, according to the top five international destinations, is shown on the following table:

Destination	2010 ($m)	2011 ($m)	+/-% 10-11
Canada	14,693	16,286	10.8
Hong Kong	4,488	8,102	80.5
United Kingdom	4,738	6,501	37.2
Israel	4,184	5,131	22.6
Switzerland	4,232	5,000	18.2

Source: US Census Bureau

Chambers of Commerce and Trade Organisations
Empire State Development, URL: http://www.empire.state.ny.us
Brooklyn Chamber of Commerce, URL: http://www.ibrooklyn.com
Manhattan Chamber of Commerce, URL: http://www.manhattancc.org/
New York City Partnership, URL: http://www.pfnyc.org/
Manufacturers Association of Central New York, URL: http://www.macny.org/
Staten Island Chamber of Commerce, URL: http://www.sichamber.com

MANUFACTURING, MINING AND SERVICES

Primary and Extractive Industries
New York State's mining industry contributed an estimated $767 million towards the state Gross Domestic Product in 2011 (up from $635 million in 2010). The largest sector in 2010 was non-oil and gas extraction ($635 million), followed by support activities ($110 million) and oil and gas extraction ($34 million).

New York's crude oil reserves account for less than one per cent of US crude oil reserves. In 2009, the oil industry had a total of 3,617 producing oil wells. Monthly production was 31,000 barrels of crude oil (Oct. 2012). The New York Harbor area between New York and New Jersey has over 40 million barrels of refined product storage capacity, making it the largest petroleum product hub in the United States. Oil consumption in 2010 fell slightly to 251.1 million barrels, 131.3 million barrels of which was motor gasoline and 62.7 million barrels distillate fuel.

New York's natural gas industry had proven reserves of 281 billion cubic feet in 2010. Production from the state's 6,157 gas wells was 31,124 million cubic feet in 2011. Most of New York's natural gas supply is brought in from other States and Canada. Consumption rose to 1,216,532 million cu ft in 2011, comprising 5.0 per cent of the US total gas consumption. (Source: EIA)

Energy
New York's State total energy production amounted to 876 trillion Btu in 2010 (1.2 per cent of US total). New York State's total energy consumption was 3,728 trillion Btu in 2010 (3.8 per cent of the US total), whilst its per capita energy consumption ranks it 50th in the US (192 million Btu in 2010). Per capita energy consumption is low due to New York City's high percentage of apartment-dwellers and its widely used mass transportation systems.

New York State is a net importer of electricity, with nuclear as its primary generating fuel. Net summer capability in 2010 was 39,357 MW (3.8 per cent of the US total) and net monthly generation in 2012 was 10,774 MWh (3.5 per cent of US total), of this nuclear 3,342,00 MWh, natural gas-fired 4,804,000 MWh (5.2 per cent of the US total), and hydroelectric 1,709,000 MWh. Major power plants include Robert Moses Niagara (hydro), Ravenswood (gas), Nine Mile Point Nuclear Station (nuclear), Oswego Harbor Power (petroleum), and Northport (petroleum, gas).

New York State has four nuclear power stations: Nine Mile Point Nuclear Station, James Fitzpatrick, Indian Point 2, Indian Point 3, and R.E. Ginna. The James Fitzpatrick plant is located near Oswego, is owned by Entergy Nuclear Operations, and produced 6,592,118 MWh of electricity in 2002.

New York's Renewable Portfolio Standard requires that 30 per cent of electricity comes from renewable resources by 2015. In 2011, 24 per cent came from renewable sources. (Source: EIA)

Manufacturing
The state has a large manufacturing sector, which accounted for an estimated $67,243 million towards GDP in 2011 (up from $64,454 million in 2010). The top sectors in 2010 were chemicals ($15,496 million), food products ($8,629 million), machinery manufacturing ($5,415 million), fabricated metal products ($4,132 million), and computer and electronic products ($10,441 million). Printing, nanotechnology, microchip manufacturing and the production of garments, furs, railroad equipment and bus line vehicles are also important industrial sectors. Manufacturing employment has been on the decline since the middle of 1992, when it peaked at 1,446,300.
Manufacturers Association of Central New York, URL: http://www.macny.org/

Service Industries
The services industry is New York State's largest contributor to GDP. In 2011, finance and insurance continued to be the largest-earning sector, at $198,658 million (up from $196,970 the previous year). Other major contributors to state GDP were real estate ($133,910 million), professional and technical services ($112,341 million) and information ($83,192 million). Health care and social assistance accounted for $91,253 million, and government services contributed some $125,333 million.

Tourism
The arts, entertainment and recreation services sector of the services industry contributed an estimated $15,583 million in 2011. The accommodation and food services sector contributed around $33,330 million in 2011, up from $30,526 million in 2010.
New York State Division of Tourism, URL: http://www.iloveny.com

Agriculture
The agriculture, forestry and fisheries industry contributed $2,961 million towards New York State's GDP in 2011 (up from $2,567 million in 2010). The major agricultural sector in 2010 was farming ($2,243 million), followed by forestry, fishing and related activities ($323 million). (Source: BEA)

According to the latest official USDA Census of Agriculture, New York State had a total of 36,600 farms in 2010. Total farm land in the state occupied an area of 7,000,000 acres in 2010, and the average size of a New York farm fell to 193 acres. New York ranks third in income from dairy products and is an important producer of fresh fruits and vegetables, greenhouse and nursery products and wines. The market value of production in 2008 was $4.4 billion. Crops accounted for $1.5 billion, whilst livestock contributed almost $2.8 billion. As of 1 Jan. 2011, there were 1.4 million cattle and calves, 108,000 hogs & pigs and 70,000 sheep.

COMMUNICATIONS AND TRANSPORT

National Airlines
The following airlines provide a service within the state: American Airlines, Continental, United Airlines, and US Airways.
US Airways, URL: http://www.usairways.com/

International Airports
New York State has more than 10 international airports, including: Albany International Airport; Buffalo Niagara International Airport; Greater Rochester International Airport; John F. Kennedy International Airport; La Guardia International Airport; Massena International Airport; Newark International Airport; Ogdensburg International Airport; Stewart International Airport, Newburgh; Syracuse Hancock International Airport; and Watertown International Airport.

Figures for 2003 indicate that JFK International Airport is ranked 11th in terms of domestic passengers and 17th with regard to international passengers (a total of 31.7 million passengers). JFK also handled 1,800,085 short tons of cargo, the fifth largest amount in the domestic market and the 9th largest for international cargo. Newark International Airport was ranked 13th in the US in terms of domestic passenger traffic and 21st for overseas passenger numbers (29.5 million in total). In addition, the airport handled 956,977 tons of cargo, ranking it 9th in the domestic market and 21st in the international market. La Guardia airport was ranked 20th in terms of domestic passengers and 37th with regard to international passengers (nearly 22.5 million passengers in total). The airport handled 28,400 short tons of cargo.
JF Kennedy International Airport,
URL: http://www.panynj.gov/CommutingTravel/airports/html/kennedy.html
La Guardia International Airport,
URL: http://www.panynj.gov/CommutingTravel/airports/html/laguardia.html

Railways
New York has one of the most extensive transportation infrastructures in the country. As well as its famous mass transit subway, New York City has four suburban commuter railroad systems: the Long Island Rail Road, Metro-North Railroad, Port Authority Trans-Hudson, and five of New Jersey Transit's rail lines.

Roads
In May 2009 cars were banned from Times Square in an attempt to reduce pollution and pedestrian accidents. The ban may become permanent.

Shipping
The Port Authority of New York and New Jersey (PANYNJ) operates most of the regional transportation infrastructure, including the bridges, tunnels, airports, and seaports, within the New York-New Jersey Port District. The Port Authority operates the Port Newark-Elizabeth Marine Terminal (third largest amount of shipping of all ports in the USA), the Hudson River crossings and the three crossings that connect New Jersey with Staten Island. The Port Authority Bus Terminal and the PATH rail system are also run by the Port Authority, as are LaGuardia, JFK, and Newark Liberty International Airport.

New York Harbour is the main port facility of New York and New Jersey, and it is the largest oil importing port and second largest container port in the nation. Several cruise lines, commuter ferries and tourist excursion boats operate from the Harbour. The New York State Barge Canal System is 800 miles in length and carries more than two million tons of freight every year. It is the longest internal waterway in the US.
New York State Canal Corporation, URL: http://www.canals.state.ny.us/

HEALTH

The National Center for Health Statistics (NCHS) estimated that there were 37.9 doctors per 10,000 residents in 2009, above the US state average of 27.4. In 2008, there were 14,980 dentists (7.7 per 10,000 population). In 2009, there were 3.1 community hospital beds per 1,000 New Yorkers, and there were 635 nursing homes, with 117,984 beds.

The NCHS estimated that 14.0 per cent of the population had no health care insurance in 2007-09, and that, in 2007-11,14.5 per cent were living in poverty. New York reported 192,753 HIV/AIDS cases from the beginning of the epidemic to the end of 2008, and ranked highest in terms of the cumulative number of reported cases. The overall rate of TB was 6.2 per 100,000 population, the fifth highest rate in the US. The obesity rate for adults was below the national average (23.9 per cent compared to 26.2 per cent nationally). An estimated 60.6 per cent of adults were classified as overweight in 2012.

EDUCATION

Primary/Secondary Education
The University of the State of New York oversees all public primary, middle-level, and secondary education in the state apart from the New York City school system, which is managed by the New York City Department of Education. Enrolment in New York state's 4,717 elementary and secondary schools totaled 2,740,592 students in the year 2008-09. There were some 217,944 classroom teachers and the teacher/student ratio stood at one to 12.6.

In the 2007-08 academic year, the state earned education revenues totaling $52.766 billion and total current expenditure on state education was $51.991 billion.

Higher Education
In 2010-11, some 556,704 male students attended New York State's public colleges and universities, together with around 738,503 women students. New York State has 304 degree-granting institutes of higher education including the State University of New York and the City University of New York. Both Columbia University and Cornell University are located in New York, making it the only state to contain more than one Ivy League school.

In 2010-11, 278,760 degrees/certificates were conferred, including 124,920 Bachelor degrees, 68,259 Masters and 14,155 Doctorates. (Source: National Center for Education Statistics)

COMMUNICATIONS AND MEDIA

Newspapers
The state's daily newspapers include: the New York Daily News; the New York Post, the New York Times; Staten Island Advance; The Times Union, Albany; The Buffalo News; Rochester Democrat and Chronicle; The Citizen, Auburn; and The Saratogian, Saratoga Springs.
New York Press Association, URL: http://www.nynewspapers.com/
New York Newspaper Publishers Association, URL: http://www.nynpa.com/
New York Post, URL: http://www.nypostonline.com/

Broadcasting
Five of New York State's many television stations operate in the New York City area, four are in Syracuse, three in Albany, five in Buffalo, five in Rochester, and four in Binghamton.

ENVIRONMENT

Carbon dioxide emissions from New York State's electricity industry fell from 47,092,408 in 2007 to 38,130,088 metric tons. They rose to 41,583,758 metric tons, ranking the state 22nd in the US, and accounting for 1.7 per cent of the total. Sulfur dioxide emissions amounted to 61,722 metric tons and nitrogen oxide emissions amounted to 44,052 metric tons.

New York is a major hydroelectric power producer, and the state is one of the Nation's top generators of electricity from municipal solid waste and landfill gas. As of 2008, New York ranked among the top 10 States in photovoltaic solar power capacity and now produces substantial amounts of wind energy. By 2010, there were 34,389 alternative-fueled vehicles in use (3.7 per cent of the US total). Ethanol consumption amounted to 14,060,000 metric tons in 2011 (4.6 per cent of the US total). There were two ethanol plants with a 2011 capacity of 164 million gal/year. (Source: EIA)

NORTH CAROLINA

Capital: Raleigh (Population, Census 2010: 403,892)

Head of State: Pat McCrory (R) (Governor) (page 1474)

State Flag: A blue union in the centre of which is a white star with the letter 'N' on the left and the letter 'C' on the right, both in gilt; above the star is a semi-circular gilt scroll on which is written in black letters 'May 20th 1775' (the date of the Mecklenburg Declaration of Independence); below the star is a similar scroll on which is written in black letters 'April 12th 1776' (the date of the adoption of the Halifax Resolves). The fly of the flag consists of two equally proportioned bars, the upper one red, the lower one white.

CONSTITUTION AND GOVERNMENT

Constitution
North Carolina is one of the original 13 states of the Union, having become the 12th state on 21 November 1789. It seceded from the Union over the issue of slavery on 20 May 1861, and, following the Civil War, was re-admitted on 4 July 1868.

Executive power is vested in the governor, who serves a four-year term, with a maximum of two consecutive terms. The governor is assisted by nine other publicly elected officers (known as the Council of State): the lieutenant governor, secretary of state, auditor, treasurer, superintendent of public instruction, attorney general, commissioner of agriculture, commissioner of labour, and commissioner of insurance. All are elected for four-year terms. The lieutenant governor is also the president of the State Senate.

North Carolina elects two Senators and 13 Representatives to the US Congress in Washington, DC.

To view the state constitution, please visit: http://statelibrary.dcr.state.nc.us/nc/stgovt/preconst.htm

Legislature
The General Assembly consists of the Senate and the House of Representatives. It convenes at the beginning of January of each odd-numbered year, and reconvenes the following even-numbered year for a shorter session.
North Carolina General Assembly, Legislative Building, 16 West Jones Street, Raleigh, NC 27603 (Mailing address: Raleigh, North Carolina 27601-1096), USA. Tel: +1 919 733 7928, fax: +1 919 733 2599 (Legislative Building), URL: http://www.ncleg.net

Upper House
The Senate has 50 members who are elected for two years. Following the 2012 elections, the Senate was composed of 18 Democrats and 32 Republicans.

Lower House
The House of Representatives has 120 members who are elected for two years. Following the 2012 elections, the House was composed of 43 Democrats and 77 Republicans.

State Executives (as of June 2013)
Governor: Pat McCrory (R)
Lieutenant Governor: Dan Forest (R)
Secretary of State: Elaine Marshall (D)
Attorney General: Roy Cooper (D)
Treasurer: Janet Cowell (D)
State Auditor: Beth Wood (D)
Superintendent of Public Instruction: June Atkinson (D)
Commissioner of Agriculture: Steve Troxler (R)
Commissioner of Insurance: Wayne Goodwin (D)
Commissioner of Labor: Cherie Berry (R)

Legislature (as at April 2013)
President of the Senate: Lt. Gov. Dan Forest (R)
President Pro Tem of the Senate: Phil Berger (R)
Majority Leader of the Senate: Harry Brown (R)
Minority Leader of the Senate: Martin Nesbitt (D)
Speaker of the House: Thom Tillis (R)
Majority Leader of the House: Edgar Starnes (R)
Minnority Leader of the House: Larry D. Hall (D)

US Senators: Richard Burr (page 1397) (R) and Kay Hagan (page 1436) (D)

Ministries
Office of the Governor, 20301 Mail Service Center, Raleigh, NC 27699-0301, USA. Tel: +1 919 733 4240 / 919 733 5811, fax: +1 919 715 3175 / 919 733 2120, URL: http://www.governor.state.nc.us
Office of the Lieutenant Governor, URL: http://www.ltgov.state.nc.us/

Office of the Attorney General, Old Education Building, 114 W. Edenton Street, Raleigh, NC 27602 (PO Box 629, Raleigh, NC 27602-0629), USA. Tel: +1 919 716 6400, fax: +1 919 716 6750, URL: http://www.ncdoj.com/
Office of the State Auditor, 2 South Salisbury Street, 20601 Mail Service Center, Raleigh, N. C. 27699-0601, USA. Tel: +1 919 807 7500, fax: +1 919 807 7647, URL: http://www.ncauditor.net/
Department of Agriculture and Consumer Services, 2 West Edenton Street, Raleigh, NC 27601, (1001 Mail Service Center, Raleigh, NC 27699-1001) USA. Tel: +1 919 733 7125, URL: http://www.ncagr.com/
Department of Commerce, 301 North Wilmington Street, Raleigh, NC 27699-4301 (4301 Mail Service Center, Raleigh, NC 27699-4301), USA. Tel: +1 919 733 7651, URL: http://www.nccommerce.com/
Department of Correction, 4202 Mail Service Center, Raleigh, NC 27699-4202, USA. Tel: +1 919 716 3700, email: info@doc.state.nc.us, URL: http://www.doc.state.nc.us
Department of Environment and Natural Resources, 1601 Mail Service Center, Raleigh, NC 27699-1601, USA. Tel: +1 919 733 4984, fax: +1 919 715 3060, URL: http://portal.ncdenr.org/web/guest
Department of Health and Human Services, Office of the Secretary, Adams Building, 101 Blair Drive, Raleigh, NC (2001 Mail Service Centre, Raleigh, North Carolina 27699-2001), USA. Tel: +1 919 733 4534, fax: +1 919 715 4645, URL: http://www.ncdhhs.gov/
Department of Labour, 4 W. Edenton Street, Raleigh, NC 27601 (1101 Mail Service Center, Raleigh, NC 27699-1101), USA. Tel: +1 919 807 2796, URL: http://www.nclabor.com/
Department of Public Schools, 301 N. Wilmington St., Raleigh, NC 27601, USA. Tel: +1 919 807 3300, URL: http://www.dpi.state.nc.us/
Department of the Secretary of State, Old Revenue Building, 2 S. Salisbury Street, Raleigh, NC 27601 (PO Box 29622, Raleigh, NC 27626-0622), USA. Tel: +1 919 807 2005, fax: +1 919 807 2020, URL: http://www.secstate.state.nc.us
Department of the State Treasurer, 325 North Salisbury Street, Raleigh, NC 27603-1385, USA. Tel: +1 919 508 5176, fax: +1 919 508 5167, URL: https://www.nctreasurer.com/Pages/default.aspx
Department of Transportation, 1 South Wilmington Street, Raleigh NC, 27611, USA. (Mailing address: 1500 Mail Service Center, Raleigh NC, 27699-1500) Tel: +1 919 733 2520, fax: +1 919 733 9150, URL: http://www.ncdot.gov/

Political Parties
North Carolina Democratic Party, URL: http://www.ncdp.org
North Carolina Republican Party, URL: http://www.ncgop.org

Elections
Elections took place in 2012 for the state constitutional offices. The incumbent Governor, Democrat Beverley Perdue, chose not to stand for re-election. The governorship was won by the Republican candidate Pat McCrory with an estimated 55 per cent of the vote. He took office in January 2013.

The most recent legislative elections took place in November 2012. In the Senate, the Republicans marginally increased their majority (Democrats 18, Republicans 32) whilst in the House of Representatives, the Republicans again increased their majority (Democrats 43, Republicans 77).

LEGAL SYSTEM

The North Carolina legal system consists of the Supreme Court, the Court of Appeals and District Courts. In addition to the Chief Justice, there are six Associate Justices of the Supreme Court, all elected for a term of eight years by popular vote. The Court of Appeals consists of the Chief Judge and 14 Associate Judges. All serve eight-year terms.

North Carolina has the death penalty. The governor has the sole right to grant clemency. Forty-three people have been executed since 1976. There are currently 163 offenders on death row, including four women. According to the DPIC the current murder rate is 5 per 100,000 population.

Supreme Court, URL: http://www.nccourts.org/
Chief Justice: Sarah Parker
Justices: Mark Martin, Robert Edmunds, Paul Newby, Robin E. Hudson, Barbara Jackson, Cheri Beasley
Court of Appeals, URL: http://www.nccourts.org/
Chief Judge: John C. Martin

LOCAL GOVERNMENT

Administratively, North Carolina is divided into 100 county governments and 548 sub-county general purpose governments. The governing body of each county is the County Board of Commissioners who are elected by the people of the county for terms of two to four years. The 548 sub-county governments are all municipal governments, which take two forms: mayor-council or council-manager. Additionally there are 315 special district governments.

AREA AND POPULATION

Area
North Carolina is located on the eastern coast of the US, south of Virginia, north of South Carolina and Georgia, and east of Tennessee. Its total area is 53,818.51 sq. miles (48,710.88 sq. miles of land and 5,107.63 sq. miles of water). There are three distinct geographical areas: the Mountains to the west (including the Appalachians and the Great Smoky Mountains); the Heartland, or Piedmont, in the centre of the state; and, to the east, the Coast.

To view a map of the state, please consult:
http://www.lib.utexas.edu/maps/us_2001/north_carolina_ref_2001.pdf

Population
According to the 2010 Census, the 2010 population was 9,535,483, up from the mid-2009 estimate of 9,380,884. In 2012, the population was estimated at 9,752,073. Over the period 2000-10, the population grew by 18.5 per cent. The population is expected to reach 12.2 million by 2030. North Carolina has an estimated population density of 196.1 people per sq. mile. The capital Raleigh had an estimated population of 416,468 in 2011, making it the second largest city in the state. Charlotte has an estimated population of 751,087, Greensboro 273,425 and Durham 233,252. The county with the greatest number of inhabitants is Mecklenburg county, with a 2010 population of 919,628.

According to the 2010 Census, 6.6 per cent of the population is under 5 years, 23.9 per cent under 18 years and 12.9 per cent is aged over 65 years. Approximately 68.5 per cent of the population is white, and 21.5 per cent is black. Approximately 8.4 per cent of the population is of Hispanic or Latino origin.

Births, Marriages, Deaths
The US Census Bureau estimated that there were 122,350 births in 2010 and 78,773 deaths, giving a natural population increase of 43,577 people. The fertility rate was 62.8 per 1,000 women aged 15-44 years and death rate was 826.1 per 100,000 population. Net immigration totalled 80,319 over 2009 (mainly from other parts of the US). The infant mortality rate in 2007 was 8.5 infant deaths per 1,000 live births. Marriages and divorces in 2007, according to provisional data, numbered 68,131 and 37,412 respectively.

EMPLOYMENT

In December 2012, North Carolina had an estimated total civilian labour force of 4,753,300, of which 4,314,500 were in employment and 438,900 were unemployed. The unemployment rate was 9.2 per cent, higher than the national average of 7.8 per cent. (Source: US Bureau of Labor Statistics)

The following table shows December 2012 non-farm wage and salary employment according to industry:

Industry	No. of employed	12-month change (%)
Logging and mining	5,300	-3.6
Construction	173,800	-2.2
Manufacturing	441,400	1.7
Trade, transportation, and utilities	742,600	2.1
Information	69,600	2.8
Financial activities	202,200	0.6
Professional and business services	534,100	4.6
Educational and health services	566,700	3.0
Leisure and hospitality	414,800	3.1
Other services	155,900	-0.9
Government	698,200	0.0
TOTAL	4,004,600	1.8
Source: Bureau of Labor Statistics

BANKING AND FINANCE

GDP/GNP, Inflation, National Debt
North Carolina's total Gross Domestic Product (GDP) (current prices) rose from $424,562 million in 2010 to $439.9 billion and ranked 9th in the US. In 2008, its GDP was equivalent to 2.9 per cent of the US total GDP. Real GDP grew by 1.8 per cent in 2011.

Gross Domestic Product according to industry, is set out in the following table (in millions of current dollars):

Industry	2009	2010	2011
Agriculture, forestry, fishing & hunting	4,281	4,516	4,846
Mining	207	213	215
Utilities	6,229	6,695	6,298
Construction	15,067	14,321	14,454
Manufacturing	81,343	81,549	86,575
Wholesale Trade	20,110	21,041	22,180
Retail Trade	21,803	23,504	24,044
Transportation & warehousing	8,546	8,703	9,025
Information	11,797	12,054	13,016
Finance & insurance	47,439	51,884	52,599
Real estate	41,171	38,734	38,507
Educational services	4,132	4,362	4,521
Health care & social assistance	27,751	28,629	29,579

- continued			
Other non-government services	61,060	65,871	50,112
Government	60,557	62,486	63,799
TOTAL	411,495	424,562	439,862
Source: Bureau of Economic Analysis, Feb. 2013

The average per capita income in the state rose to $36,210 in 2011, 87 per cent of the national average of $41,560. Per capita real GDP rose to $39,879; the national average was $42,070.

The annual Consumer Price Index (CPI) for the south urban area rose from 218.6 in 2011 to 223.2 in 2012 (1982-84 = 100). (Source: Bureau of Labor Statistics)

Balance of Payments / Imports and Exports
Total North Carolina imports amounted to $37,644 million in 2009, down 21.1 per cent from $47,701 million in 2008. They rose by 13 per cent in 2010 to $42,538 million and by 12.7 per cent in 2011 to $47,860 million. North Carolina 's imports accounted for 2.2 per cent of total US import costs in 2011. Main imports include medicine, digital equipment and parts and clothes. As of 2011, main suppliers included China (19.3 per cent), Mexico (10.0 per cent), Canada (7 per cent), Germany and Ireland.

Total export revenue fell from $25,091 million in 2008 to $21,793 million in 2009, a decrease of 13.1 per cent. In 2010, exports amounted to $24,905 million, up 14.3 per cent. They rose further to $27,009 million in 2011, up 8.4 per cent. North Carolina accounted for 1.8 per cent of total US export revenue in 2011. The major export industry is machinery and computer equipment. Other major exports are transport equipment, chemicals and allied products, textile mill products and apparel, tobacco products, electronic equipment, and agricultural crops.

The following table shows the top five 2010-11 merchandise export destinations according to revenue:

Destinations	2010 ($m)	2011 ($m)	+/-% 10-11
Canada	5,448	6,354	16.6
China	2,238	2,627	17.4
Mexcio	1,828	1,994	9.1
Japan	1,731	1,629	-5.9
Germany	882	1.116	26.5
US Census Bureau, Foreign Trade Statistics

The top five export products in 2010, according to revenue, are shown on the following table:

Product	Revenue ($m)
Civilian aircraft, engines, equipment and parts	1,279
Tobacco	608
Chemical woodpulp, soda etc	595
Uranium enriched U234 etc, plutonium etc	492
Antisera and blood fractions, immun. products	439
Source: US Census Bureau, Foreign Trade Statistics

Chambers of Commerce and Trade Organisations
Charlotte Chamber of Commerce, URL: http://charlottechamber.org
Greater Raleigh Chamber of Commerce, URL: http://www.raleighchamber.org
Greensboro Area Chamber of Commerce, URL: http://www.greensborochamber.com/
North Carolina Department of Commerce, URL: http://www.nccommerce.com/

MANUFACTURING, MINING AND SERVICES

Primary and Extractive Industries
North Carolina leads in olivine and pyrophyllite production, lithium, feldspar and mica. Mining contributed an estimated $215 million to the state's 2011 GDP. Non-oil and gas mining accounted for the largest amount in 2010 ($201 million), whilst support activities earned $10 million.

North Carolina has no oil industry, although a number of major pipelines cross the state. Oil consumption in 2010 fell slightly to 162.8 million barrels, 102.8 million barrels of which were motor fuel (3.2 per cent of the US total).

The state has no natural gas resources and imports its gas requirements. Consumption rose from to 304,146 million cu ft. in 2010 to 307,809 million cu ft in 2011. The industrial sector is the leading natural gas-consuming sector. Nearly a quarter of households use natural gas as their main source of energy for home heating.

Coal consumption amounted to 25,518,000 short tons in 2011 (2.5 per cent of US total). (Source: EIA)

Energy
North Carolina's total energy production amounted to 577 trillion Btu in 2010 (0.8 per cent of US total). North Carolina's total energy consumption amounted to 2,705 trillion Btu in 2010 (2.8 per cent of US total) and 35th in the US for its per capita energy consumption (283 million Btu).

North Carolina is a net importer of electricity, the primary generating fuel being coal. Net summer capability in 2010 was 27,674 MW (2.7 per cent of US total) and net monthly (Oct. 2012) generation was 8,106,000 MWh (2.6 per cent of US total), of this coal-fired 3,379,000 MWh, nuclear 2,961,000 MWh and gas-fired 1,230,000 MWh. Hydroelectric power generated 306,000 MWh and other renewables 205,000 MWh.The major utility plants are NA1, Roxboro

UNITED STATES OF AMERICA

(coal), Belews Creek (coal), McGuire (nuclear), Marshall (coal), and Brunswick (nuclear). North Carolina has three nuclear power plants: Brunswick (two units), McGuire (two units), and Harris (single units).

In 2011, 5.3 per cent of North Carolina's net electricity generation came from renewable energy sources, almost all from conventional hydroelectric power and biomass. (Source: EIA)

Manufacturing
North Carolina's economy, once predominantly agricultural, is increasingly oriented towards manufacturing, the second highest contributor towards the state GDP. In 2011 manufacturing accounted for an estimated $86,575 million, up from $81,849 million in 2010. Top manufacturing sectors in 2010 were food products ($21,039 million) and chemical manufacturing ($17,036 million). Other areas of strength are computer and electronic products ($12,429 million), fabricated metal products ($3,105 million) and machinery ($4,857 million).

Service Industries
The services industry is North Carolina's highest contributor towards its GDP. Top service sectors in 2011 were finance and insurance ($52,599 million), real estate ($38,507 million), and health care and social assistance ($29,579 million). Professional and technical services contributed $23,808 million towards state GDP.

Tourism
The accommodation and food sector of the services industry contributed $10,554 million towards the state 2011 GDP, whilst the arts, entertainment and recreation sector contributed $3,343 million.
North Carolina Department of Commerce, Division of Tourism, Film, and Sports Development, URL: http://www.visitnc.com/index_home.asp

Agriculture
The agriculture, forestry and fishing industry contributed $4,846 million towards North Carolina's GDP in 2011 (up from $4,516 million in 2010). The largest sector in 2010 was crop and animal production ($3,866 million), followed by forestry and fishing ($650 million). (Source: BEA)

According to the latest USDA Census of Agriculture, North Carolina had around 52,400 farms in 2010, down from 59,000 farms at the time of the 1997 Census of Agriculture. Total farmland covered 8,600,000 acres in 2010, down from 9,400,000 acres in 1997. The average size of a farm in North Carolina grew from 160 acres to 164 acres over the decade. Total cash receipts for agricultural products sold in 2008 was $10.3 billion. Livestock, poultry and products generated some $7.7 billion and crops, including greenhouse and nursery crops, generated $2.6 billion. As of 1 Jan. 2011, there were 780,000 cattle and calves, 8.9 million hogs & pigs and 27,000 sheep.

Tobacco is North Carolina's major crop, and the state accounts for some 40 per cent of total national production. Approximately 50 per cent of US cigarettes are produced in North Carolina, making North Carolina the country's top producer. Grapes are another important crop; there are some 350 vineyards in the state. The state ranks second in terms of the value of their hogs and pigs, and sixth in the value of cotton and cottonseed. Other important products include sweet potatoes, peanuts, port and turkey.

COMMUNICATIONS AND TRANSPORT

International Airports
North Carolina is served by three international airports: Wilmington International Airport, Raleigh-Durham International Airport, and Piedmont-Triad International Airport.
Wilmington International Airport, URL: http://www.airport-wilmington.com/
Raleigh-Durham International Airport, URL: http://www.rdu.com/
Piedmont-Triad International Airport, URL: http://www.ptia.org/index.htm

Railways
North Carolina's rail network stretches for some 4,000 miles. There are 12 passenger train services per day linking New York to Florida, New York to New Orleans, and Raleigh to Charlotte. Amtrak has 16 stations in North Carolina.

Roads
In addition to North Carolina's 78,000 miles of state highways, five major interstates run through the state: from north to south, I-77, I-85, and I-95; from east to west, I-26 and I-40.

Ports and Harbours
North Carolina has two deep-water seaports: the Port of Morehead City and the Port of Wilmington.
North Carolina State Ports Authority, URL: http://www.ncports.com/

HEALTH

The National Center of Health Statistics estimated that there were 25.0 doctors per 10,000 inhabitants in 2009, below the US average of 27.4 In 2008, there were 4,183 dentists (4.5 per 10,000 population). In 2009, there were 2.4 community hospital beds per 1,000 residents, and, in 2010, there were 424 nursing homes, with 44,392 beds.

It was estimated that, in 2007-09, 16.6 per cent of the state population aged 18-64 had no health-care cover, and, in 2007-11, 16.1 per cent were thought to be living in poverty. North Carolina reported 19,539 HIV/AIDS cases from the beginning of the epidemic to the end of 2008, and ranked 12th in terms of cumulative number of reported cases in 2008. The TB rate was 3.6 per 100,000 population, 20th highest out of the US states. Approximately 27.8 per cent of adults suffer from obesity, though the youth are less likely to be overweight than the US average. An estimated 64.9 per cent of adults are considered overweight. (Source: CDC)

EDUCATION

Primary/Secondary Education
In 2009-10 there were 2,592 elementary and secondary schools in the state, with a total enrolment of 1,483,397 students. There were 105,046 classroom teachers and the student/teacher ratio was 14 to one.

Over the academic year 2007-08, total revenue from education amounted to $12.4 billion, whilst current expenditure on state education reached $13.38 billion.

Higher Education
In 2010-11 academic year, there were 139 degree conferring institutes in the State of North Carolina. Enrolment for the year was 232,537 men and 336,328 women. 108,270 degrees were awarded, including 46,826 Bachelors, 15,395 Masters and 3,955 Doctorates. (Source: National Center for Education Statistics)

COMMUNICATIONS AND MEDIA

Newspapers
North Carolina's daily newspapers include: The Herald-Sun (http://www.heraldsun.com), The Courier-Tribune (http://www.courier-tribune.com), The News-Argus, Times-News, News and Observer, Roanoke Rapids Daily Herald, Jacksonville Daily News, Independent Tribune, Salisbury Post, The Shelby Star, and Statesville Record and Landmark.
North Carolina Press Association, URL: http://www.ncpress.com
The News & Observer Publishing Co., URL: http://www.news-observer.com
Morning Star, URL: http://starnews.wilmington.net

Broadcasting
There are 27 television stations in North Carolina, seven of which are in Charlotte, four in Wilmington, three in Winston-Salem, and three in Raleigh.

ENVIRONMENT

North Carolina's 2009 electricity industry emissions of carbon dioxide amounted to 64,845,048 metric tons, up from 57,247,200 metric tons. They rose further to 73,240,828 metric tons, ranking the state 13th in the US, and accounting for 3.1 per cent of the US total. In 2010, emissions of sulfur dioxide amounted to 130,673 metric tons (2.4 per cent of US total) and nitrogen oxide 57,407 metric tons (2.3 per cent of total). North Carolina harnesses hydroelectric power from several rivers, and the state ranks among the top 10 States in wind power capacity. In 2010, there were 35,417 alternative-fueled vehicles in use, some 3.8 per cent of the US total. Ethanol consumption amounted to 10,391,000 barrels in 2011 (3.4 per cent of US total).

In 2007, North Carolina adopted a renewable energy and energy efficiency portfolio standard requiring electric utilities to meet 12.5 per cent of retail electricity demand through renewable energy or energy efficiency measures by 2021. (Source: EIA)

NORTH DAKOTA

Capital: Bismarck (Population, Census 2010: 61,272)

Head of State: Jack Dalrymple (Governor) (page 1411)

State Flag: A blue background in the centre of which appears a bald eagle holding an olive branch in one claw and several arrows in the other; in its beak it carries a ribbon on which appear the words 'One nation made up of many states'; on its breast is a shield with 13 alternative red and white stripes, representing the original thirteen states; a design in the shape of a fan appears above the eagle and represents the birth of the United States; above the fan are thirteen gold stars; underneath the eagle is a red scroll on which appear the words 'North Dakota'.

CONSTITUTION AND GOVERNMENT

Constitution

North Dakota entered the Union on 2 November 1889 as the 39th state. Under the current constitution the governor heads the executive branch of government assisted by 12 other elected officials: lieutenant governor, secretary of state, attorney general, state auditor, state treasurer, superintendent of public instruction, insurance commissioner, agriculture commissioner, tax commissioner, and three public service commissioners. Most elected officials serve four-year terms, the exceptions being the agriculture commissioner, the attorney general, the secretary of state, and the tax commissioner, each serving two-year terms, and the public service commissioners, who serve six-year terms.

North Dakota elects two Senators and one At-Large Representative to the US Congress in Washington, DC.

To view the state constitution, please visit: http://www.legis.nd.gov/constitution/const.pdf

Recent Events

At the end of March 2010, North Dakota was declared a federal disaster area as the swollen Red River rose towards its highest levels for more than 100 years, due to an unusually cold winter, followed by a very quick thaw and heavy rain.

Legislature

North Dakota's bicameral legislature is known as the Legislative Assembly and consists of the Senate and the House of Representatives. The Legislative Assembly meets biennially, usually from the second week in January to mid-April.

Legislative Assembly, 600 E Boulevard Ave, 1st Floor, Bismarck ND 58505-0360, USA. Tel: +1 701 328 3373, fax: +1 701 328 3615, URL: http://www.legis.nd.gov/assembly

Upper House

As of 2012, the Senate has 47 members, one elected from each of the 47 senatorial districts for staggered terms of four years. The lieutenant governor also serves as the president of the Senate. Following the 2012 elections, the Senate was composed of 33 Republicans and 13 Democrats.

Lower House

As of 2012, there are 94 members of the House of Representatives who serve staggered terms of four years. Two representatives are elected from each of the state's 47 senatorial districts. Following the 2012 elections the House was composed of 71 Republican seats and 23 Democrat seats.

Elected Executive Branch Officials (as of June 2013)

Governor: Jack Dalrymple (R) (page 1411)
Lieutenant Governor: Drew Wrigley (R)
Secretary of State: Alvin A. Jaeger (R)
Attorney General: Wayne Stenehjem (R)
State Treasurer: Kelly Schmidt (R)
State Auditor: Robert R. Peterson (R)
Insurance Commissioner: Adam Hamm (R)
Commissioner of Agriculture: Doug Goehring (R)
State Tax Commissioner: Cory Fong (R)
Superintendent of Public Instruction: Dr. Wayne G. Sanstead (D)
Public Service Commissioners: Randy Christmann (R), Julie Fedorchak (R), Brian B. Kalk (R)

Legislature (as at April 2013)

President of the Senate: Lt. Gov. Dree Wrigley (R)
President Pro Tem of the Senate: Tim Flakoll (R)
Senate Majority Leader: Rich Wardner (R)
Senate Minority Leader: Mac Schneider (D)
Speaker of the House: Bill Devlin (R)
Majority Leader of the House: Al Carlson (R)
Minority Leader of the House: Kenton Onstad (D)

US Senators: Heidi Heitkamp (page 1440) and John Hoeven (R) (page 1442)

Ministries

Office of the Governor, 600 E. Boulevard Avenue, Dept. 101, Bismarck, ND 58505-0001, USA. Tel: +1 701 328 2200, fax: +1 701 328 2205, URL: http://www.governor.nd.us/
Office of the Secretary of State, 600 E Boulevard Avenue, 1st Floor, Dept 108, Bismarck, ND 58505-0500, USA. Tel: +1 701 328 2900, fax: +1 701 328 2992, URL: http://www.nd.gov/sos/

Office of the Attorney General, State Capitol, 600 E Boulevard Avenue, Dept 125, Bismarck ND 58505-0040, USA. Tel: +1 701 328 2210, fax: +1 701 328 2226, e-mail: ndag@state.nd.us, URL: http://www.ag.state.nd.us/
Office of the State Auditor, 600 East Boulevard, Dept. 117, 3rd Floor, Bismarck, ND 58505-0060, USA. Tel: +1 701 328 2241, fax: +1 701 328 1406, URL: http://www.nd.gov/auditor/
Office of the State Treasurer, State Capitol, 600 East Boulevard Avenue, 3rd Floor, Bismarck, North Dakota 58505-0600, USA. Tel: +1 701 328 2643, fax: +1 701 328 3002, URL: http://www.nd.gov/ndtreas/
Department of Agriculture, 600 E. Boulevard Avenue, Department 602, Bismarck, ND 58505-0020, USA. Tel: +1 701 328 2231, fax: +1 701 328 4567, URL: http://www.nd.gov/ndda/
Department of Commerce, 1600 East Century Avenue, Suite 2, PO Box 2057, Bismarck, ND 58502, USA. Tel: +1 701 328 5300, fax: +1 701 328 5320, URL: http://www.business.nd.gov/
North Dakota Emergency Services, PO Box 5511, Bismarck, North Dakota 58506-5511, USA. Tel: +1 701 328 8100, fax: +1 701 328 8181, URL: http://www.nd.gov/des/
Department of Health, 600 E. Boulevard Avenue, Dept. 301, Bismarck ND 58505-0200, USA. Tel: +1 701 328 2372, fax: +1 701 328 4727, URL: http://www.ndhealth.gov/
Department of Insurance, 600 E Boulevard, 5th Floor, Dept. 401, Bismarck, ND 58505-0320, USA. Tel: +1 701 328 2440, fax: +1 701 328 4880, URL: http://www.nd.gov/ndins
Department of Labour, 600 East Boulevard Avenue, Dept 406, State Capitol, 13th Floor, Bismarck ND 58505-0340, USA. Tel: +1 701 328 2660, fax: +1 701 328 2031, URL: http://www.nd.gov/labor
Department of Public Instruction, North Dakota Capitol Building, 600 E Boulevard Avenue, Dept. 201, Floors 9, 10, and 11, Bismarck, ND 58505-0440, USA. Tel: +1 701 328 2260, fax: +1 701 328 2461, URL: http://www.dpi.state.nd.us/
Department of Transport, 608 East Boulevard Avenue, Bismarck, ND 58505-0700, USA. Tel: +1 701 328-2500, URL: http://www.dot.nd.gov/

Political Parties

North Dakota Democratic-NPL Party, URL: http://www.demnpl.com
North Dakota Republican Party, URL: http://www.ndgop.org/

Elections

Elections took place in November 2012 for constitutional statewide positions. Incumbent Governor Dalrymple won the election for his first full term of office, taking over 60 per cent of the vote.

Following legislative elections in November 2012, the Republican lead in the House of Representatives increased by 2 seats (Republicans 71, Democrats 23). In the Senate, Republicans retained control but with a slightly reduced majority (33 Republicans and 13 Democrats).

In the 2010 elections to the US Senate, Republican John Hoeven had an easy victory and became the first Republican US Senator elected from North Dakota since 1981. In the 2012 elections to the US Senate, the incumbent Kent Conrad (D) chose not to run for re-election. The seat was won by Heidi Heitkamp (D).

LEGAL SYSTEM

The North Dakota judicial system consists of the Supreme Court, the Court of Appeals, District Courts, and Municipal Courts. The Supreme Court consists of the Chief Justice and four associate judges. The Chief Justice is selected by justices of the Supreme Court and serves a term of five years. The associate judges are all elected for a term of ten years by popular vote. The Court of Appeals comprises three judges who serve terms of one year.

North Dakota does not have the death penalty. It was established in 1865 but abolished in 1975. A recent case (People v. Rodriguez) has revived debate in the state after the defendant was sentenced to death. Although North Dakota state courts do not have the death penalty, it is available in the federal system. Rodriguez's trial was held in the U.S. District Court in Fargo. The murder rate is 1.5 per 100,000 population.

Supreme Court, URL: http://www.court.state.nd.us/
Chief Justice: Gerald W. VandeWalle

LOCAL GOVERNMENT

North Dakota is divided into 53 county governments and 1,677 sub-county general purpose governments, according to the Census Bureau 2002 Census of Governments. Of the 1,677 sub-county governments, 357 are municipal (city) governments and 1,320 are town or township governments. Counties are governed by a board of county commissioners, whilst townships are governed by an elected township board. Consolidated townships, or multi-townships, are governed by a board of supervisors.

North Dakota Association of Counties, PURL: http://www.ndaco.org
North Dakota League of Cities, URL: http://www.ndlc.org/

UNITED STATES OF AMERICA

AREA AND POPULATION

Area
North Dakota is located in the mid-west, south of the border with Canada. It lies east of Montana and west of Minnesota. North Dakota's total area is 70,699.79 sq. miles, of which 68,975.93 sq. miles is land and 1,723.86 sq. miles is water.

The western half of the state consists of the Great Plains and the northern part of the Badlands. The state's high point, White Butte at 3,506 feet (1,069 m) is located in the Badlands. The eastern part of the state consists of the flat Red River Valley, which supports extensive agriculture.

To view a map of the state, please visit:
http://www.lib.utexas.edu/maps/us_2001/north_dakota_ref_2001.pdf

Population
According to the 2010 Census, the population was 672,591. In 2012, the population was estimated at 699,628. Over the period 2000-10, the population of North Dakota increased by 4.7 per cent. North Dakota ranks 48th in the US in terms of population size. The population is expected to fall to 606,566 by 2030. The population density is estimated at 9.3 inhabitants per sq. mile (47th in the US). The capital, Bismarck, had an estimated population of 62,655 in 2011, whilst the largest city in the state, Fargo City, had 107,349 inhabitants. The county with the largest population is Cass County, with 149,778 inhabitants in 2010.

There are several American Indian tribes in Montana, each with their own government: the Spirit Lake Dakotah nation; the Standing Rock Sioux tribe; the Mandan, Hidatsa, and Arikara Nation (aka the Three Affiliated Tribes), and the Turtle Mountain Band of Chippewa.

According to the 2010 Census, 6.6 per cent of the population is under 5 years, 22.3 per cent under 18 years and 14.5 per cent is aged over 65 years. Approximately 90 per cent of the population is white, and 1.2 per cent is black. An estimated 5.2 per cent of the population is American Indian. Approximately 2.0 per cent of the population is of Hispanic or Latino origin.

Births, Marriages, Deaths
The US Census Bureau estimated that there were 9,104 births in 2010 and 5,944 deaths, giving a natural population increase of 3,160 people. Net immigration amounted to 1,896 people in 2009. The fertility rate was 70.5 per 1,000 population and the death rate was 883.7 per 100,000 population. The infant mortality rate in 2007 was 7.5 infant deaths per 1,000 live births. Marriages and divorces in 2007, according to provisional data, numbered 4,211 and 1,527 respectively.

North Dakota has an ageing population, the younger people moving to other states to find employment. The older generations live principally in rural and at times remote areas.

EMPLOYMENT

Preliminary figures indicate that North Dakota's total civilian labour force in December 2012 was 392,200, of which 379,600 were in employment and 12,700 were unemployed. The unemployment rate was 3.2 per cent, the lowest rate in the USA, and well below the national average of 7.8 per cent. (Source: US Bureau of Labor Statistics)

The following table shows preliminary figures for December 2011 non-farm wage and salary employment according to industry:

Industry	No. of Employed	12 month change (%)
Logging and mining	22,400	20.4
Construction	27,100	3.8
Manufacturing	24,500	0.4
Trade, transport and utilities	93,600	5.2
Information	7,600	5.6
Financial activities	21,900	0.9
Professional and business services	34,500	7.1
Educational and health services	59,400	3.1
Leisure and hospitality	37,000	3.9
Other services	15,600	0.6
Government	77,700	-1.5
TOTAL	421,300	3.6
Source: Bureau of Labor Statistics

BANKING AND FINANCE

GDP/GNP, Inflation, National Debt
North Dakota's total Gross Domestic Product (GDP) rose from $35,654 million to $40.3 billion in 2011. Real GDP rose by 7.6 per cent in 2011, the highest percentage increase in the US for the year. North Dakota was ranked 46th in the US (including the District of Columbia) for its 2011 GDP. The largest earning sectors were government (12.5 per cent) and real estate.

The state Gross Domestic Product according to industry, is shown on the following table:

Industry	2009	2010	2011
Agriculture, forestry, fishing & hunting	2,868	3,169	3,376
Mining	1,138	1,837	3,130
Utilities	841	872	833
Construction	1,381	1,432	1,719
Manufacturing	2,394	2,579	2,807

- continued

Wholesale Trade	2,286	2,559	3,034
Retail Trade	2,055	2,247	2,430
Transportation & warehousing	1,300	1,508	1,956
Information	1,014	1,016	1,062
Finance & insurance	2,432	3,167	3,307
Real estate, rental, leasing	3,506	3,588	4,219
Educational services	112	115	121
Health care & social assistance	2,682	2,908	3,152
Other non-government services	3,436	3,767	4,152
Government	4,549	4,890	5,031
TOTAL	31,997	35,654	40,328
Source: Bureau of Economic Analysis, Feb. 2013

Average per capita income rose to an estimated $47,236 in 2011. Per capita real GDP rose from $50,096 in 2011, above the national average of $42,070.

The annual Consumer Price Index (CPI) for the Midwest urban area (all items) rose from 214.7 in 2011 to 219.1 in 2012 (1982-84=100). (Source: Bureau of Labor Statistics)

Balance of Payments / Imports and Exports
Total North Dakota imports amounted to $1,983 million in 2009, down 33.5 per cent from $2,982 million in 2008. Imports rose to $2,530 million in 2010, up 27.6 per cent and to $3,474 million in 2011, up 37.4 per cent. State imports represented 0.1 per cent of the US total in 2010. Imports include machinery, medicaments, seeds, medical supplies and oil. Main suppliers included Canada (71.8 per cent), Mexico (4.5 per cent) China, France & Germany.

Merchandise export revenue fell from $2,772 million in 2008 to $2,193 million in 2009, a rise of 35.5 per cent. Exports rose by 15.7 per cent in 2010 to $2,546 million and by 33.8 per cent in 2011 to $3,393 million. State exports represented 0.2 per cent of the US total.

The following table shows 2010-11 merchandise export revenue according to the top five international destinations:

Destination	2010 ($m)	2011 ($m)	+/-% 10-11
Canada	1,570	2,195	39.8
Mexico	166	178	7.4
Belgium	54	89	64.6
Australia	68	83	22.5
Germany	37	68	80.6

North Dakota's top five export products in 2010 are shown on the following table:

Product	($m)
Mech. front-end shovel loaders, self propelled	246
Crude oil from petroleum and bit. minerals	232
Rapeseeed/colza oil & fractions	204
Tractors, NESOI	169
Wheat (other than durum)	148
US Census Bureau, Foreign Trade Division

Chambers of Commerce and Trade Organisations
Bismarck-Mandan Chamber of Commerce, URL: http://www.bismarckmandan.com/
Fargo-Moorhead Convention and Visitors Bureau, URL: http://www.fargomoorhead.org/
North Dakota Department of Economic Development and Finance, URL: http://www.growingnd.com

MANUFACTURING, MINING AND SERVICES

Primary and Extractive Industries
North Dakota's mineral resources include oil and gas, coal, clay, cement rock, sand and gravel, salt, uranium, and volcanic ash. The mining industry contributed an estimated $3,130 million towards North Dakota's GDP in 2011, up from $1,837 million in 2010. The oil and gas extraction sector contributed $689 million, whilst non-oil and gas mining accounted for $289 million and support activities contributed $859 million in 2010.

North Dakota's crude oil reserves were 1,814 million barrels in 2010, 7.8 per cent of US total reserves. From a total of 4,574 producing oil wells and 468 rotary rigs, North Dakota's oil industry produced 23,164,000 barrels monthly (Oct. 12), 11 per cent of the US total. Crude oil refinery capacity was 60,000 bbl/d in 2012. Oil consumption in 2010 was 28 million barrels, most of which was distillate fuel (13.3 million barrels) and motor gasoline (9.7 million barrels).

North Dakota's dry natural gas reserves amounted to 1,667 billion cu ft in 2010. In 2011, there were 157 million barrels of natural gas plant liquids. Its natural gas industry had a total of 239 gas and gas condensate wells operating in 2011, and total marketed production was 97,102 million cubic feet. North Dakota has the distinction of being one of only two states that produce synthetic natural gas - and annually produces over 54 billion cubic feet of gas from coal. Natural gas consumption rose from 66,395 million cubic feet in 2010 to 72,463 million cu ft in 2011.

Recoverable coal reserves stood at 1,183 million short tons in 2011, some 6.2 per cent of the US total. Total production in 2011 fell slightly to 28,231 thousand short tons (2.6 per cent of US total), all of which was from four surface mines. (Source: EIA)

Energy

North Dakota's total energy production amounted to 1,253 trillion Btu in 2010. North Dakota's total 2010 energy consumption amounted to 481 trillion Btu (0.5 per cent of US total) and 4th in the US for its per capita energy consumption (713 million Btu). The state's high per capita consumption is due in part to high heating demand during the winter months.

North Dakota is a net exporter of electricity with coal as its primary generating fuel. Net summer capability in 2010 was 6,118 MW (0.6 per cent of US total) and total net monthly generation was 2,986,000 MWh (Oct. 12), of which coal-fired 2,241,000 MWh, hydro-electric 180,000 MWh and other renewables 553,000 MWh. Major generating plants in 2010 were: Coal Creek (coal), Antelope Valley (coal), Milton R. Young (coal), Leland Olds (coal), and Garrison (hydroelectric). (Source: EIA)

Manufacturing

Manufacturing was the third largest contributor to the state GDP in 2011. The sector earned an estimated $2,807 million (up from $2,579 million in 2010). Top sectors in 2010 were machinery manufacturing ($835 million), food, beverage and tobacco product manufacturing ($641 million) and petroleum and coal products manufacturing ($255 million).

Service Industries

The services industry is North Dakota's largest contributor towards GDP. In 2011, the largest sectors were real estate ($4,219 million), health care and social assistance ($3,152 million), and finance and insurance ($3,307 million).

Tourism

The accommodation and food sector of the services industry contributed $950 million towards the 2011 GDP, whilst the arts entertainment and recreation sector contributed $123 million. Attractions include the Badlands, buffalo, and winter sports.
North Dakota Tourism, URL: http://www.ndtourism.com/
North Dakota Parks and Recreation Department, URL: http://www.ndparks.com/

Agriculture

Agriculture, forestry, fishing and hunting contributed $3,376 million towards the 2011 GDP (up from $3,169 million in 2010). The farms sector accounted for $3,068 million in 2010, whilst forestry, fishing and related services contributed $101 million. (Source: BEA)

The importance of the agriculture sector has diminished over the past twenty-five years; in 1997, agriculture was the highest earning sector, accounting for 18 per cent of state earnings; by 2004, the sector contributed 8 per cent of GDP. The decline in farming has had an impact on the North Dakota society, with the young moving to urban areas leaving an ageing population in the rural areas.

According to the USDA's National Agricultural Statistics Service latest Census of Agriculture, the total number of farms in North Dakota was 31,900 in 2010. Farmland covered 39,600,000 acres, and the average size of a farm was 1,241 acres. Total market value of agricultural products in 2007 was $6.08 billion, of which $5 billion was generated by crops, including greenhouse and nursery crops, and $1.045 billion was generated by livestock, poultry and products. Major livestock products, in terms of the number of farms, include cattle and calves, beef cows and sheep and lambs. As of 1 Jan. 2011, there were 1.7 million cattle and calves, 143,000 hogs & pigs and 78,000 sheep. Major crop products include wheat for grain, hay alf and wild silage, and barley for grain. The state is the largest producer in the U.S. of barley, sunflower seeds, spring and durum wheat for processing, and farm-raised turkeys.

COMMUNICATIONS AND TRANSPORT

International Airports

North Dakota has three international airports, serving around 1.1 million passengers per year, and handling around 10,000 tons of freight.
Grand Forks International Airport, URL: http://www.gfkairport.com/
Hector International Airport, URL: http://www.fargoairport.com/
Minot International Airport, URL: http://minotnd.org/airport/index.html

Railways

North Dakota's railway system is 3,275 miles in total length. Two major railway companies operate in the state: The Burlington Northern Santa Fe Railroad, which runs from east to west; and the CP Rail System (Soo Line), which runs to and from the Port of Vancouver and other Canadian destinations. In addition, the Red River Valley & Western and the Dakota, Missouri Valley & Western run a freight service in the state.

HEALTH

The National Center of Health Statistics estimated that there were 25.2 doctors per 10,000 inhabitants in 2009, below the US average of 27.4. In 2008, there were 329 dentists (5.1 per 10,000 population). In 2009, there were 5.2 community hospital beds per 1,000 residents, the second highest rate in the US, and there were 85 nursing homes, with 6,438 beds.

It was estimated that, in 2007-09, 10.8 per cent of the population aged 18-64 had no health care insurance, and that 12.3 per cent on the people were living in poverty in the period 2007-11.

North Dakota reported 173 HIV/AIDS cases from the beginning of the epidemic to the end of 2008, and the state ranked lowest in the cumulative number of reported cases in 2008. North Dakota reported three cases of TB, representing 0.5 per 100,000 population, the lowest rate in the US. In 2012, an estimated 63.6 per cent of adults were considered overweight and 27.2 per cent considered obese. (Source: Center of Disease Control)

EDUCATION

Primary/Secondary Education

According to 2008-09 National Center for Education Statistics figures, there were 95,073 students in 522 elementary and secondary schools with 8,365 classroom teachers. The pupil/teacher ratio was 11.36 to one. Over the academic year 2007-08, total educational revenues amounted to $1,056 million, whilst current expenditure in state education reached $993million.

Higher Education

In 2010-11 there were a total of 21 degree-conferring institutions, including the University of North Dakota, Mayville State University, Valley City State University, North Dakota State University, North Dakota State College of Science, Minot State University, Williston State College, Dickinson State University, Bismarck State College, and Lake Region State College. During the 2010-11 academic year, some 26,275 male students were registered, together with 28,158 women. 10,797 degrees/certificates were conferred: 5,727 Bachelors, 1,392 Masters and 447 Doctorates. (Source: National Center for Education Statistics)

COMMUNICATIONS AND MEDIA

Newspapers

North Dakota's daily newspapers include: the Bismarck Tribune; The Daily Journal, Devil's Lake; Williston Daily Herald; Grand Forks Herald; The Dickinson Press; and The Forum, Fargo.
North Dakota Newspaper Association, URL: http://www.ndna.com

Broadcasting

Four of North Dakota's television stations are based in Fargo, three in Bismarck, two in Minot, two in Dickinson, and one in Williston. Five are affiliated with CBS, three with PBS, three with NBC, and one with ABC.

Telecommunications

Telecommunications services are provided by 27 telephone companies. Over 38,000 miles of fibre-optic cable are presently in place to carry communications to North Dakota's businesses. In addition, there are five mobile phone companies providing a service via 25 sites. The major telecommunications companies serving North Dakota are AT&T, MCI, US Sprint and WilTel.

ENVIRONMENT

North Dakota relies primarily on coal for its electricity generation. Emissions of carbon dioxide from the state's electricity generating industry fell from 32,608,448 metric tons in 2009 to 31,063,899 metric tons, ranking the state 30th in the US, and accounting for 1.3 per cent of US total. Emissions of sulfur dioxide amounted to 115,641 metric tons and emissions of nitrogen oxide amounted to 52,011 metric tons.

North Dakota leads the US in production of wind energy, with over 20 operational wind power projects. In 2007, North Dakota adopted a voluntary renewable portfolio objective that aims to have one-tenth of electricity generated from renewable sources by 2015.

By 2012, North Dakota had five ethanol plants with a combined capacity of 343 million gal/year. In 2011, ethanol consumption amounted to 857,000 barrels (0.3 per cent of US total). In 2010, the state had 3,930 alternative-fueled vehicles in use. (Source: EIA)

OHIO

Capital: Columbus (Population, Census 2010: 787,033)

Head of State: John Kasich (R) (Governor) (page 1454)

State Flag: On a swallow-tailed shaped flag a background of three red and two white horizontal stripes on which appears, at the staff end, a blue triangle whose apex is located on the centre red stripe; on the triangle are 17 white, five-pointed stars around a red disc on a white circle.

CONSTITUTION AND GOVERNMENT

Constitution
Ohio entered the Union on 19 February 1803 when the US Congress approved its Constitution and admitted it as the 17th state. The current Constitution was ratified in 1851 and last amended in 1999. Under the terms of the Constitution Ohio's executive branch of government consists of the governor and five other elected officials: lieutenant governor, attorney general, auditor of state, secretary of state, and treasurer of state. All elected executive officials serve a maximum of two successive terms of four years. Ohio elects two Senators and 18 to the US Congress in Washington.

To view the state constitution, please visit: http://www.legislature.state.oh.us/constitution.cfm

Legislature
The state's legislature, the General Assembly, consists of the Senate and the House of Representatives. Legislative sessions of the General Assembly open every two years on the first Monday of odd-numbered years.
Ohio General Assembly, Statehouse, Capitol Square, Columbus, Ohio. URL: http://www.legislature.state.oh.us/

Upper House
The Senate consists of 33 members elected for a maximum of two four-year terms, with elections for half the Senate taking place every two years. Each of Ohio's State Senators represents about 330,000 people. Following the 2012 elections, the Senate is composed of 23 Republicans and 10 Democrats.
Senate, Senate Building, Capitol Square, Columbus, Ohio. Tel: +1 614 466 4900, URL: http://www.ohiosenate.gov/senate/index

Lower House
The House of Representatives comprises 99 members elected for two years. Every 10 years, following the Census, the number of Ohio residents is divided by 99 to determine the population for each House district. There are approximately 110,000 residents for each House district. The House is currently composed of 39 Democrats and 60 Republicans.
House of Representatives, 77 South High Street, Columbus, Ohio 43266-0603, USA. Tel: +1 614 466 2575 (Speaker), fax: +1 614 644 9494 (Speaker), URL: http://www.ohiohouse.gov/

Elected Executive Branch Officials (as at April 2013)
Governor: John Kasich (R) (page 1454)
Lieutenant Governor: Mary Taylor (R)
Secretary of State: Jon Husted (R)
Attorney General: Mike DeWine (R)
Treasurer of State: Josh Mandel (R)
Auditor of State: Dave Yost (R)

Legislative Assembly (as at April 2013)
President of the Senate: Keith Faber (R)
President Pro Tem of the Senate: Chris Widener (R)
Majority Leader: Tom Patton (R)
Minority Leader of the Senate: Eric Kearney (D)
Speaker of the House: William Batchelder (R)
Speaker Pro Tem of the House: Matt Huffman (R)
Majority Leader: Barbara Sears (R)
Minority Leader: Armond Budish (D)

US Senators: Sherrod Brown (D) (page 1395) and Rob Portman (R) (page 1497)

Ministries
Office of the Governor, 30th Floor, 77 South High Street, Columbus, Ohio 43215-6117, USA. Tel: +1 614 466 3555, URL: http://www.governor.ohio.gov
Office of the Lieutenant Governor, Vern Riffe Center, 30th Floor, 77 South High Street, Columbus, Ohio 43215, USA. Tel: +1 614 466 3396, URL: http://www.governor.ohio.gov
Office of the Attorney General, State Office Tower, 30 E. Broad Street, 17th Floor, Columbus, OH 43215-3428, USA. Tel: +1 614 466 4320, URL: http://www.ohioattorneygeneral.gov/
Office of the Auditor of State, 88 East Broad Street, PO Box 1140, Columbus, Ohio 43216-1140, USA. Tel: +1 614 466 0370, fax: +1 614 466 4490, URL: http://www.auditor.state.oh.us/
Office of the Secretary of State, 180 E. Broad Street, 16th Floor, Columbus, OH 43215, USA. Tel: 1 614 466 2655, fax: +1 614 466 0649, e-mail: guide@sos.state.oh.us, URL: http://www.sos.state.oh.us/
Office of the State Treasurer, 30 E. Broad Street, 9th Floor, Columbus, Ohio 43215, USA. Tel: +1 614 466 2160, fax: +1 614 644 7313, URL: http://www.tos.ohio.gov/
Department of Agriculture, 8995 East Main Street, Reynoldsburg, Ohio 43068-3399, USA. Tel: +1 614 728 6200, fax: +1 614 466 4346, URL: http://www.ohioagriculture.gov/

Department of Commerce, Division of Administration, 77 South High Street, 23rd Floor, Columbus, OH 43215-6123, USA. Tel: +1 614 466 3636, fax: +1 614 644 8292, URL: http://www.com.state.oh.us
Ohio Development Services Agency, 77 S. High Street, Columbus, OH 43215-6130, USA. (Mailing address: Box 1001, Columbus, Ohio 43216-1001, USA) Tel: +1 614 466 3379, URL: http://development.ohio.gov/
Department of Education, 25 South Front Street, Columbus, Ohio 43215-4183, USA. Tel: +1 614 466 4838, fax: +1 614 387 0964, URL: http://www.ode.state.oh.us
Ohio Environmental Protection Agency (EPA), (PO Box 1049, Columbus, OH 43216-1049) 122 South Front Street, Columbus, OH 43215, USA. Tel: +1 614 644 3020, fax: +1 614 644 3184, URL: http://www.epa.state.oh.us
Department of Health, 246 North High Street, Columbus, OH 43216-0118, USA. Tel: +1 614 466 3543, URL: http://www.odh.ohio.gov/
Department of Transport, 1980 W. Broad Street, Columbus, OH 43223, USA. Tel: +1 614 466 7170, fax: +1 614 644 8662, URL: http://www.dot.state.oh.us

Political Parties
Ohio Democratic Party, URL: http://www.ohiodems.org
Ohio Republican Party, URL: http://www.ohiogop.org

Elections
The most recent elections for Ohio state constitutional officers took place in November 2010. In a surprise result, the incumbent Democrat Gov. Ted Strickland was defeated by former Congressman John Kasich with 47 per cent to 49 per cent. Mary Taylor was elected Lt. Governor.

Elections took place for Ohio's Legislature in November 2012. The Republicans retained their control over the Senate (Republicans 23, Democrats 10) and also maintained their majority in the House of Representatives (Democrats 39, Republicans 60).

LEGAL SYSTEM

The court system in Ohio consists of the Supreme Court (Chief Justice and six Justices), Courts of Appeals in each of the 12 appellate districts (66 Judges), Courts of Common Pleas in each of the 88 counties (comprising four divisions: General, Domestic Relations, Probate, and Juvenile) (375 Judges), 118 Municipal Courts (203 Judges), 47 County Courts (55 Judges), the Court of Claims (Judges assigned by Supreme Court), and a number of Mayors' Courts (approx. 428 Mayors). The Supreme Court's Chief Justice and six Associate Justices are all elected for a term of six years by popular vote.

Ohio has the death penalty and one of the highest execution rates of the US states. According to the DPIC, 49 people have been executed since 1976. Five people were executed in 2011 and four in 2012. Two Democratic representatives introduced legislation to abolish the state's death penalty in March 2011. As of September 2011, there were 148 inmates on death row including one woman. The murder rate is 4.1 per 100,000 population.

Supreme Court, URL: http://www.sconet.state.oh.us/
Chief Justice: Maureen O'Connor
Justices: Paul Pfeifer, Terrence O'Donnell, Judith Ann Lazinger, Sharon Kennedy, Judith French, William O'Neill

LOCAL GOVERNMENT

According to the US Census Bureau, administratively, Ohio is divided into 88 county governments and 2,246 sub-county general purpose governments. Of the 2,246 sub-county governments, 938 are municipal (city and village) governments and 1,308 are township governments. The county governing body is called the board of county commissioners. As of 2007, all counties except Summit County operate in accordance with general statutes. Summit County is the only county to adopt one of the alternate forms (home rule charter). Its governing body is the county council.

AREA AND POPULATION

Area
Ohio is located in the Midwest, north of Kentucky and West Virginia, south of Michigan and Lake Erie, east of Indiana, and west of Pennsylvania. Ohio's area is 44,824.90 sq. miles, of which 40,948.38 sq. miles is land and 3,876.53 sq. miles is water.

To view a map, consult http://www.lib.utexas.edu/maps/us_2001/ohio_ref_2001.pdf

Population
According to the 2010 Census, the 2010 population was 11,536,504, down slightly on the mid-2009 estimate of 11,542,645. In 2012, the population was estimated to be 11,544,225. Over the period 2000-10, the population grew by 1.6 per cent. Ohio has the seventh largest population in the US. The population is expected to reach 11.6 million by 2020, before falling to 11.5 million in 2030. The population density is estimated at 280.5 persons per sq. mile. The county with the greatest number of inhabitants is Cuyahoga County, with a population of 1,280,122 in 2010. The largest city is the capital, Columbus, with 797,434 inhabitants in 2011 (E).

According to the 2010 Census, 6.2 per cent of the population is under 5 years, 23.7 per cent under 18 years and 14.1 per cent is aged over 65 years. Approximately 82.7 per cent of the population is white, and 12.2 per cent is black. Approximately 3.1 per cent of the population is of Hispanic or Latino origin.

Births, Marriages, Deaths
The Population Division of the US Census Bureau estimated that there were 139,128 births in 2010 and 108,711 deaths, giving a natural population increase of 30,417 people. Net emigration from the state totalled 24,443 in 2009. The fertility rate was 62.2 per 1,000 women aged 15-44 years and the death rate was 942.3 per 100,000 population. The 2007 infant mortality rate was 7.7 infant deaths per 1,000 live births. Provisional data for 2007 puts the number of marriages and divorces at 70,905 and 37,858 respectively (both down on previous years).

EMPLOYMENT

Preliminary figures indicate that Ohio had a total civilian labour force of 5,766,400 in December 2012, of which 5,378,800 were in employment and 387,700 were unemployed. The unemployment rate was 6.7 per cent, lower than the national average of 7.8 per cent. (Source: US Bureau of Labor Statistics)

Non-farm wage and salary employment (preliminary figures) in December 2012, according to industry, is shown on the following table:

Industry	No. of jobs	12-month change (%)
Logging and mining	11,200	-6.7
Construction	177,200	3.6
Manufacturing	660,600	2.4
Trade, transportation, and utilities	978,300	1.7
Information	76,400	-1.7
Financial activities	283,100	2.6
Professional and business services	663,400	2.4
Educational and health services	880,800	2.9
Leisure and hospitality	477,600	1.1
Other services	215,800	2.2
Government	760,600	-0.4
TOTAL	5,185,000	1.8

Source: Bureau of Labor Statistics

BANKING AND FINANCE

GDP/GNP, Inflation, National Debt
Ohio's Gross Domestic Product (GDP) rose from $466,930 million in 2010 to $484.0 billion in 2011. Real GDP rose by 1.1 per cent in 2011. In 2011, the state was ranked eighth in the US for its GDP.

The State Gross Domestic Product according to industry is shown on the attached table (millions of current dollars):

Industry	2009	2010	2011
Agriculture, forestry, fishing & hunting	3,523	3,537	4,311
Mining	1,922	1,839	1,933
Utilities	9,632	9,791	8,462
Construction	15,022	14,242	15,215
Manufacturing	66,435	73,936	80,727
Wholesale Trade	27,456	28,402	29,663
Retail Trade	29,835	31,097	32,158
Transportation & warehousing	14,226	14,048	14,480
Information	13,158	13,172	13,667
Finance & insurance	37,040	39,183	39,106
Real estate	51,938	49,336	49,900
Educational services	4,538	4,687	4,786
Health care & social assistance	42,525	44,121	45,168
Other non-government services	79,673	84,147	88,695
Government	54,069	55,390	55,701
TOTAL	450,991	466,930	483,962

Source: Bureau of Economic Analysis, Feb. 2013

The estimated per capita income in Ohio in 2011 was $37,836. Per capital real GDP was $36,283 in 2011, below the national average of $42,070.

The annual Consumer Price Index (CPI) (all items) for the Cleveland-Akron urban area rose from 211.0 in 2011 to 214.7 in 2012 (1982-84 = 100). (Source: Bureau of Labor Statistics)

Balance of Payments / Imports and Exports
Ohio's total imports amounted to $42,912 million in 2009, down 27.6 per cent from $59.311 milllion in 2008. Imports rose by 23.5 per cent to $52,999 million in 2010 and by 12,8 in 2011 to $59,777 million, representing 2.7 per cent of the US total. Imports include vehicle parts, oil and medical supplies. Main suppliers include Canada (27.1 per cent), China (18.8 per cent), Mexico (10.3 per cent), Japan and Germany. Ohio's total exports fell from $45,628 million in 2008 to $34,104 million in 2009, a decrease of 25.3 per cent. Exports rose by 21.7 per cent up to $41,474 million in 2010 and to $46,146 million in 2011, up 11.9 per cent. This represented 3.1 per cent of US total exports.

The following table shows the top five international merchandise export trading partners in 2010-11 according to revenue:

Country	2010 ($m)	2011 ($m)	+/-% 10-11
Canada	17,221	18,795	9.1
Mexico	3,495	4,045	15.7
China	2,289	2,740	19.7
France	1,998	2,436	21.9
Brazil	1,432	1,613	12.6

The top five export products in 2010 according to revenue are shown on the following table:

Product	Revenue ($m)
Civilian aircraft, engines, equipment and parts	4,100
Passenger Vehicle, spk-ign., >1500	1,323
Spark-ignition reciprocal piston engine over 1000 cc	1,048
Passenger Vehicle, spk-ign., >3300	994
Pts & Access of bodies of motor vehicles, nesoi	973

Source: US Census Bureau, Foreign Trade Division

Chambers of Commerce and Trade Organisations
Ohio Chamber of Commerce, URL: http://www.ohiochamber.com/
Greater Columbus Chamber of Commerce, URL: http://www.columbus-chamber.org
Columbus Countywide Development Corporation, URL: http://www.ccdcorp.org
Hudson Area Chamber of Commerce, URL: http://www.hudsoncoc.org/

MANUFACTURING, MINING AND SERVICES

Primary and Extractive Industries
Commodities mined in Ohio include oil and gas, coal, industrial minerals, limestone and dolomite, sand and gravel, sandstone and conglomerate, clay, shale, salt, gypsum and peat. Mining accounted for $1,933 million of Ohio's 2011 GDP (up from $1,839 million in 2010). In 2010 oil and gas extraction contributed $447 million, whilst non-oil and gas mining accounted for $1,007 million and support activities earned $385 million.

According to EIA, Ohio had proven crude oil reserves of 42 million barrels in 2010. From its 29,458 producing oil wells and 11 rotary rigs, Ohio's oil industry had a monthly production of 412,000 barrels (Oct. 12). Crude oil refinery capacity was 528,000 bbl/d in 2012 (3 per cent of US total). Total oil consumption in 2010 was 221.9 million barrels, 117.0 million barrels of which was motor gasoline (3.7 per cent of US total), and 52.1 million barrels in the form of distillate fuel (3.8 per cent of US total). There is current interest in two shale plays - the Marcellus Shale and the Utica Shale.

Ohio had proven natural gas reserves of 832 billion cubic feet (mcf) in 2010. From its 46,717 gas and gas condensate wells, the state produced 78,858 million cubic feet in 2011. Consumption was high, at 820,485 million cubic feet in 2011 (3.4 per cent of US total), and is led by the residential and industrial sectors. Nearly seven-tenths of Ohio households use natural gas as their primary source of energy for home heating.

Ohio's coal industry had recoverable reserves of 258 million short tons in 2011 (1.3 per cent of the US total). Production totalled 28,166,000 in 2011 (2.6 per cent of US total). (Source: EIA)

Energy
Total energy production was 1,036 trillion Btu in 2010 (1.4 per cent of US total). Ohio's total energy consumption in 2010 was 3,834 trillion Btu and it was ranked 22nd in the US for its per capita energy consumption (332 million Btu).

Ohio's electricity generating industry relies primarily on coal as an energy source. Net summer capability was 33,071 MW in 2010 (3.2 per cent of the US total) and net monthly generation was 9,049,000 MWh (Oct. 2012), 2.9 per cent of US total. Of this, coal-fired generated 5,416,000 MWh, nuclear 1,605,000 MWh, natural gas 1,683,000 MWh, hydroelectric 34,000 MWh and other renewables 177,000 MWh. Ohio's largest utility plants are all coal-fired. Major electricity generating plants are: Gen. J.M. Gavin, J.M. Stuart, W.H. Sammis, Conesville, and Muskingum River.

Ohio has two nuclear reactors: the 873-net MWe Davis-Besse single unit reactor, and the 1,169-net MWe Perry plant. The Davis-Besse, is a Pressurised Light Water Reactor located on a 954-acre site in Oak Harbour. The Perry Plant, is a Boiling Water Reactor located on a 1,100-acre site near Cleveland. (Source: EIA)

Manufacturing
Manufacturing is Ohio's second largest contributor to GDP (after services), earning an estimated $80,727 million in 2011 (up from $73,936 million in 2010). Major manufacturing sectors in 2010 were machinery ($7,063), food, beverage & tobacco products ($8,506 million), fabricated metal products ($9,755 million) and chemical manufacturing ($10,004 million).

Service Industries
The largest contributor to Ohio's GDP, the services industry is a key part of the economy. The top sectors in 2011 were real estate ($49,900 million), finance & insurance ($39,106 million) and health care and social assistance ($45,168 million). Professional and technical services accounted for $30,443 million of the state GDP.

Tourism
The accommodation and food services sector of the services industry contributed $12,430 million towards Ohio's GDP in 2011 whilst the arts, entertainment and recreation services sector contributed $3,473 million, both sectors showing increases on the previous year.
Division of Travel and Tourism, URL: http://www.ohiotourism.com/home.asp

UNITED STATES OF AMERICA

Agriculture

The agriculture sector accounted for $4,311 million of Ohio's 2011 GDP, up from $3,537 million in 2011. Farming contributed $3,296 million in 2010, whilst the forestry, fishing and related activities sector contributed $241 million. (Source: BEA)

According to the USDA, Ohio had a total of 74,700 farms in 2010. Total farmland covered 13,700,000 acres, and the average size of an Ohio farm was183 acres in 2010. The total market value of agricultural products sold in 2007 was $6.8 billion (crops accounted for $4.3 billion whilst livestock earned some $2.5 billion). Main crops are corn, grain and soy beans. As of 1 Jan. 2011, there were 1,230,000 cattle & calves, 2.03 million hogs & pigs, and 129,000 sheep & lambs.

COMMUNICATIONS AND TRANSPORT

International Airports

Ohio has 165 public use airports, 16 public use heliports, one public use seaplane landing area, and 1,045 privately owned and used airports and heliports.
Cleveland Hopkins International Airport, URL: http://www.clevelandairport.com/
Port Columbus International Airport, URL: http://www.port-columbus.com

Railways

Ohio's railways cover a total of 5,800 miles of track. There are 32 freight railway companies.

Roads

Four interstate highways cross at Ohio's capital, Columbus: I-270, I-675, I-70 and I-71. Other interstate highways in Ohio are I-271, I-90, I-475, and I-75. The Ohio Turnpike is situated in the north of the state.

Ports and Harbours

In terms of cargo tonnage transported, Ohio is the fourth largest maritime state in the US. The Ohio River covers 450 miles of Ohio's southern and eastern borders, and transports more cargo than the Panama Canal. Ohio has nine commercial ports: Toledo, Marblehead, Sandusky, Huron, Lorain, Cleveland, Fairport Harbor, Ashtabula, and Conneaut. All are maintained by the US Army Corps of Engineers. Almost all of the Lake Erie port traffic is made up of bulk cargoes such as coal, iron ore, and stone.

HEALTH

The National Center for Health Statistics estimated that there were 28.5 doctors (including osteopaths) per 10,000 residents in 2009, above the US average of 27.4. In 2008, there were 6,029 dentists (5.2 per 10,000 population). In 2009, there were 2.9 community hospital beds per 1,000 inhabitants. In 2010, there were 960 nursing homes, with 93,043 beds.

It was estimated that 12.5 per cent of the population had no health care insurance in 2007-09, below the US average of 15.5 per cent. According to the US Census Bureau, in 2007-11, an estimated 14.8 per cent of people lived in poverty.

Ohio reported 17,129 HIV/AIDS cases from the beginning of the epidemic to the end of 2008, and ranked 14th among US states in cumulative number of reported cases in 2008. The TB rate was 1.9 per 100,000 population, the 36th highest rate among the US states. Obesity among adults was slightly higher than the national average, at 29.2 per cent. An estimated 65.0 per cent were classified as overweight. (Source: Center for Disease Control)

EDUCATION

Primary/Secondary Education

Total enrolment in Ohio's 3,895 primary and secondary schools in 2009-10 was 1,764,297. There were 111,377.5 teachers providing a pupil/teacher ratio of 15.84 to one.

Revenues from education during the 2007-08 academic year reached $22.796 billion, whilst current expenditure on state education amounted to $22.362 billion.

Higher Education

Around 310,080 male students and 401,015 women enrolled in higher education during the 2010-11 academic year. There were 215 degree granting institutions, and 135,249 degrees/certificates were awarded, including 19,535 Masters and 1,586 Doctorates. (Source: National Center for Education Statistics)

COMMUNICATIONS AND MEDIA

Newspapers

Ohio's newspapers include the Columbus Dispatch, the Cincinnati Enquirer, the Cincinnati Post, The Plain Dealer, The Times Reporter, The Morning Journal, and The Independent.
The Ohio Newspaper Association, URL: http://ohionews.org
The Columbus Dispatch, URL: http://www.cd.columbus.oh.us
The Cincinnati Post, URL: http://www.cincypost.com

Business Journals

Business First, URL: http://www.bizjournals.com/columbus

Broadcasting

There are 36 state network television stations, including four in Columbus, five in Dayton, four in Cincinnati, five in Toledo, and four in Cleveland. Columbus's network television stations include: WCMH (owned by NBC); WBNS (CBS); WTTE (Fox); and WOSU (PBS).

Cable television stations include The Ohio News Network.
The Ohio News Network, URL: http://www.onnnews.com/onnweb/index.php

ENVIRONMENT

Coal powers almost nine-tenths of net electricity generation in Ohio. Carbon dioxide emissions from Ohio's electricity generating industry rose from 115,065,819 metric tons in 2009 to 121,963,840 metric tons in 2010. The state has the fourth highest carbon dioxide emissions in the US, and accounted for 5.1 per cent of the US total. Furthermore, the state's power generating industry accounted for 11.3 per cent of US sulphur dioxide emissions (610,245 metric tons), and 4.9 per cent of US nitrogen oxide emissions (122,434 metric tons). Ohio is required to comply with the Clean Air Act Amendments of 1990 in respect of sulphur dioxide and nitrogen oxide emissions.

In 2008, Ohio established an alternative energy portfolio standard that requires that at least 25 per cent of all electricity sold in the State come from alternative energy resources by 2025. Renewable sources such as wind, solar, hydroelectric power, geothermal, and biomass must account for at least half of the standard, or 12.5 percent of electricity sold. The other half of the standard can be met through alternative energy resources like third-generation nuclear power plants, fuel cells, energy-efficiency programs, and clean coal technology that can control or prevent carbon dioxide emissions.

In 2012, there were seven ethanol plants with a capacity of 424 million gal/year. Ethanol consumption reached 11,453 thousand barrels in 2011 (3.7 per cent of US total). There were 22,436 alternative-fueled vehicles in use in 2010. (Source: EIA)

SPACE PROGRAMME

NASA's John H. Glenn Research Centre develops communications technologies, propulsion and electrical power systems for NASA's space missions. It aims, through research, technology, and capability development, to advance exploration of the solar system and beyond, while maintaining global leadership in aeronautics.

NASA John H. Glenn Research Centre, URL: http://www.grc.nasa.gov

OKLAHOMA

Capital: Oklahoma City (Population, Census 2010: 579,999)

Head of State: Mary Fallin (R) (Governor) (page 1423)

State Flag: A sky blue background in the centre of which appears an Indian war shield of tan buckskin; on the face of the shield are six white crosses, the Indian symbol for stars; across the shield is an Indian peace pipe and an olive branch; hanging from the shield are seven eagle feathers.

CONSTITUTION AND GOVERNMENT

Constitution
Oklahoma entered the Union on 16 November 1907. Under the current constitution the executive branch of state government is headed by the governor assisted by ten other elected officials: lieutenant governor, attorney general, state treasurer, state auditor and inspector, insurance commissioner, labour commissioner, superintendent of public instruction, and three corporation commissioners. The term of office for the following elected officials is four years: governor, lieutenant governor, state auditor and inspector, attorney general, state treasurer, commissioner of labour, and superintendent of public instruction. The three corporation commissioners serve terms of six years, staggered so that one commissioner is elected every two years.

Oklahoma elects two Senators and five Representatives to the US Congress in Washington.

To view the state constitution, please visit: http://www.lsb.state.ok.us/

Legislature
Oklahoma's bicameral legislature consists of the Senate and the House of Representatives.

Upper House
The Senate has 48 members elected for staggered four-year terms (senators in odd numbered districts being elected two years after those from even numbered districts). Following the 2012 elections, Oklahoma's Senate had 36 Republican senators and 12 Democrats.
Oklahoma State Senate, Oklahoma State Capitol, 2300 N. Lincoln Blvd., Oklahoma City, OK 73105, USA. Tel: +1 405 524 0126, URL: http://www.oksenate.gov/

Lower House
The House of Representatives has 101 members elected for two years. Representatives' terms expire every even-numbered year. Following the 2012 election, there was a Republican majority (Republicans 72, Democrats 29). The House meets annually, sessions beginning on the first Monday in February and ending on the last Friday in May.
Oklahoma House of Representatives, 2300 N. Lincoln Blvd., State Capitol Building, Oklahoma City, OK 73105, USA. Tel: +1 405 521 2733 (Chief Clerk), fax: +1 405 962 7669 (Chief Clerk), URL: http://www.okhouse.gov

---

Elected Executive Branch Officials (as at April 2013)
Governor: Mary Fallin (R)
Lieutenant Governor: Todd Lamb (R)
Secretary of State: Glen Coffee (R)
State Auditor and Inspector: Gary Jones (R)
Attorney General: E. Scott Pruit (R)
State Treasurer: Ken Miller (R)
Superintendent of Public Instruction: Janet Barresi (R)
Labour Commissioner: Mark Costello (R)
Insurance Commissioner: John Doak (R)
Corporation Commissioners: Patrice Douglas (R), Dana Murphy (R), Bob Anthony (R)

Legislature (as at April 2013)
President of the Senate: Lt. Gov. Todd Lamb (R)
President Pro Tem of the Senate: Brian Bingman (R)
Senate Majority Leader: Mike Schultz (R)
Senate Minority Leader: Sean Burrage (D)
Speaker of the House: T.W. Shannon (R)
Speaker Pro Tem of the House: Mike Jackson (R)
House Majority Leader: Pam Peterson (R)
House Minority Leader: Scott Inman (D)

US Senators: Tom Coburn (R) (page 1407) and James M. Inhofe (R) (page 1447)

Ministries
Office of the Governor, 2300 N. Lincoln Blvd., State Capitol Building, Room 212, Oklahoma City, OK 73105, USA. Tel: +1 405 521 2342, fax: +1 405 521 3353, URL: http://www.ok.gov/governor/
Office of the Lieutenant Governor, Room 211, State Capitol Building, 2300 N. Lincoln Blvd., Oklahoma City, OK 73105, USA. Tel: +1 405 521 2161, fax: +1 405 525 2702, URL: http://www.okgov/ltgovernor/
Office of the Attorney General, State Capitol Building, 2300 N. Lincoln Blvd., Suite 112, Oklahoma City, OK 73105, USA. Tel: +1 405 521 3921, fax: +1 405 522 4534, URL: http://www.oag.state.ok.us/
Office of the Secretary of State, 101 State Capitol, 2300 N. Lincoln Boulevard, Oklahoma City, OK 73105-4897, USA. Tel: +1 405 521 3912, fax: +1 405 521 3771, URL: http://www.sos.ok.gov/
Office of the State Auditor and Inspector, Room 100, State Capitol Building, Oklahoma City, OK 73105, USA. Tel: +1 405 521 2732, e-mail: auditor@sai.state.ok.us, URL: http://www.sai.ok.gov/

Office of the State Treasurer, 2300 N Lincoln Blvd., Room 217, Oklahoma City OK 73105, USA. Tel: +1 405 521 3191, fax: +1 405 521 4994, URL: http://www.ok.gov/treasurer
Oklahoma Insurance Department, URL: http://www.ok.gov/oid/
Corporation Commission, 2101 N. Lincoln Blvd., Jim Thorpe Building, Oklahoma City, OK 73105 (PO Box 52000, Oklahoma City, OK 73152-2000) USA. Tel: +1 405 521 2211, URL: http://www.occ.state.ok.us/
Department of Agriculture, Food and Forestry, 2800 N Lincoln Blvd., Oklahoma City, OK 73105-4298, USA. Tel: +1 405 521 3864, URL: http://www.oda.state.ok.us/
Department of Commerce, 900 N. Stiles Avenue, Oklahoma City, OK 73104, USA. Tel: +1 405 815 6552, URL: http://okcommerce.gov
Department of Education, 2500 North Lincoln Boulevard, Suite 112, Oklahoma City, Oklahoma 73105-4503, USA. Tel: +1 405 521 3301, fax: +1 405 521 6205, URL: http://www.ok.gov/sde/
Department of Environmental Quality, 707 N Robinson Oklahoma City, OK 73102 (PO Box 1677, Oklahoma City, OK 73101-1677), USA. Tel: +1 405 702 1000, fax: +1 405 702 1001, URL: http://www.deq.state.ok.us/
Department of Health, 1000 Northeast Tenth Street, Oklahoma City, OK 73117-1299, USA. Tel: +1 405 271 5600, URL: http://www.ok.gov/health/
Department of Labour, 4001 N. Lincoln Blvd., Oklahoma City, OK 73105-5212, USA. Tel: +1 405 528 1500, fax: +1 405 528 5751, URL: http://www.ok.gov/odol/
Indian Affairs Commission, 4545 North Lincoln Blvd., Suite 282, Oklahoma City, OK 73105, USA. Tel: +1 405 521 3828, fax: +1 405 522 4427, URL: http://www.ok.gov/oiac/
Department of Transportation, Transportation Bldg-200 NE 21, Oklahoma City, OK 73105-3204, USA. Tel: +1 405 521 2631, URL: http://www.okladot.state.ok.us/

Political Parties
Oklahoma Democratic Party, URL: http://www.okdemocrats.org
Oklahoma Republican Party, URL: http://www.okgop.com

Elections
The most recent state constitutional elections in Oklahoma were held in November 2010. In for the first time the gubernatorial contest was between two women. The incumbent governor, Democrat Brad Henry, was ineligible to stand. Republican Mary Fallin defeated Lt.-Gov. Jari Askins (D) by 60 per cent to 40 per cent. Ms Fallin is Oklahoma's first female governor. Todd Lamb was elected Lt. Governor.

Elections for two positions at the Oklahoma Corporation Commission took place in November 2012. The two incumbent candidates, Patrice Douglas and Bob Anthony, were both re-elected.

The latest legislative elections took place in November 2012. The Republicans increased their majority in the Senate (Republicans 36, Democrats 12). In the House of Representatives, the Republicans also increased their majority, winning 72 seats to the Democrats' 29.

LEGAL SYSTEM

The Court of Criminal Appeals is the highest court in Oklahoma and consists of a Presiding Judge, a Vice Presiding Judge, and three Judges. Court of Criminal Appeals Judges serve terms of six years. The Supreme Court comprises nine Justices, all of whom sit for six-year terms. The Court of Civil Appeals consists of 12 judges. The District Courts comprise 71 district court judges, 77 associate district judges, and 73 special judges.

Oklahoma has the death penalty. There have been 102 executions since 1976 (as of January 2013), most recently in six in 2012. The current death row population is 62 including one female. According to the DPIC the current murder rate is 5.2 per 100,000.

Court of Criminal Appeals, URL: http://www.oscn.net/oscn/schome/criminal.htm
Presiding Judge: David Lewis
Judges: Arlene Johnson, Clancy Smith, Gary Lumpkin, Charles Johnson
Supreme Court, URL: http://www.oscn.net/oscn/schome/start.htm
Chief Justice: John Reif

LOCAL GOVERNMENT

Oklahoma is divided into 77 counties, each of which is governed by a three-member board of commissioners located in the county seat. There are also 594 sub-county general purpose governments (cities and towns) consisting entirely of municipal governments. Both county and municipal governments collect taxes, employ a separate police force, hold elections, and operate emergency response services within their jurisdiction.

There are 39 Native American tribal governments in the state, each holding limited powers.

AREA AND POPULATION

Area
Oklahoma is located in the south of the US, north of Texas, west of Arkansas and Missouri, south of Kansas, and east of New Mexico. Oklahoma's total area is 69,898.19 sq. miles, of which 68,667.06 sq. miles is land and 1,231.13 sq. miles is water.

To view a map of Oklahoma, please consult:
http://www.lib.utexas.edu/maps/us_2001/oklahoma_ref_2001.pdf

UNITED STATES OF AMERICA

Population

According to the 2010 Census, the 2010 state population was 3,751,351, up on the mid-2009 estimate of 3,687,050. In 2012, the population was estimated to be 3,814,820. Over the period 2000-10, the state population grew by 8.7 per cent and is expected to reach 3.9 million by 2030. The population density is 54.7 persons per sq. mile. Oklahoma County is the largest county in the state, with 718,633 inhabitants in 2010. The capital, Oklahoma City, is the largest metropolitan area, with an estimated 591,967 inhabitants in 2011.

According to the 2010 Census, 7.0 per cent of the population is under 5 years, 24.8 per cent under 18 years and 13.5 per cent is aged over 65 years. Approximately 72.2 per cent of the population is white, and 7.4 per cent is black. Approximately 8.9 per cent of the population is American Indian. Approximately 8.9 per cent of the population is of Hispanic or Latino origin.

Births, Marriages, Deaths

The US Census Bureau, Population Division, estimated that there were 53,238 births in 2010 and 36,529 deaths over the same period, giving a natural population increase of 16,709 people. The fertility rate was 72.3 per 1,000 women aged 15-44 years and the death rate was 973.8 per 100,000 population. Net immigration of 23,685 people amounted to 2009. The provisional infant mortality rate in 2007 was 8.5 infant deaths per 1,000 live births. Marriages and divorces in 2007, according to provisional data, numbered 26,243 and 18,750 respectively.

EMPLOYMENT

Preliminary figures indicate that Oklahoma's total civilian labour force in December 2012 was 1,824,000, of which 1,730,700 were employed and 93,300 were unemployed. The unemployment rate was 5.1 per cent, below the national average of 7.8 per cent. (Source: US Bureau of Labor Statistics)

The following table shows December 2012 non-farm wage and salary employment according to industry (preliminary figures):

Industry	No. of Jobs	12-month change (%)
Logging and mining	54,400	0.9
Construction	69,500	1.3
Manufacturing	137,200	3.8
Trade, transportation, and utilities	294,500	3.8
Information	23,500	-2.1
Financial activities	82,300	4.0
Professional and business services	176,800	1.5
Educational and health services	207,500	-0.7
Leisure and hospitality	150,900	6.2
Other services	59,100	-0.3
Government	344,800	1.6
TOTAL	1,600,500	2.2

Source: Bureau of Labor Statistics

BANKING AND FINANCE

GDP/GNP, Inflation, National Debt

Oklahoma's total Gross Domestic Product (GDP) (current prices) rose from $147,587 million in 2010 to $155.0 billion in 2011. Real GDP rose by 1.0 per cent in 2010, down on the US average of 2.6 per cent. In 2011, the state ranked 29th nationally in terms of GDP.

The State Gross Domestic Product according to industry is shown on the following table (in millions of current dollars):

Industry	2009	2010	2011
Agriculture, forestry, fishing & hunting	1,321	2,287	2,560
Mining	11,976	13,705	15,868
Utilities	3,472	3,660	3,407
Construction	5,202	5,235	5,357
Manufacturing	14,735	16,824	18,632
Wholesale Trade	7,002	6,958	7,571
Retail Trade	9,122	9,782	10,167
Transportation and warehousing	4,630	4,754	4,968
Information	3,962	3,908	4,050
Finance & insurance	7,128	7,702	7,619
Real estate, rental & leasing	14,231	13,876	13,996
Educational services	803	829	860
Health care & social assistance	10,345	10,921	11,439
Other non-government services	19,846	21,048	22,043
Government	26,866	26,098	26,390
TOTAL	140,661	147,587	154,966

Source: Bureau of Economic Analysis, Feb. 2013

The state's average per capita income fell to an estimated $37,679 in 2011. Per capita GDP was $35,381 in 2011; the national average was $42,070.

The annual Consumer Price Index (CPI) for the South urban area (all items) rose from 218.6 in 2011 to 223.2 in 2012 (1982-84=100). (Source: Bureau of Labor Statistics)

Balance of Payments / Imports and Exports

Oklahoma's total imports amounted to $5,301 million in 2009, down 31.8 per cent from $7,775 million in 2008. Imports rose by 23.4 per cent in 2010 to $6,527 million, and by 73.5 per cent in 2011 to $11,324 million, representing 0.5 per cent of total US imports. Imports include oil, vehicle parts and electronics. Main suppliers include Canada (50.9 per cent), China (18.1 per cent), Mexico (7.2 per cent), Japan and Germany. Oklahoma's total merchandise export revenue fell from $5,077 million in 2008 to $4,415 million in 2009, a decrease of 13 per cent. Exports rose by 21.3 per cent in 2010 to $5,353 million and by 16.2 per cent in 2011 to $6,222 million, representing 0.4 per cent of total US exports. The following table shows the top five merchandise export destinations in 2010-11 according to revenue:

Country	2010 ($m)	2011 ($m)	+/-% 10-11
Canada	1,867	1,943	4.1
Mexico	424	525	23.7
Japan	348	404	16.2
China	243	368	51.1
Singapore	121	169	39.9

The top five export products in 2010, according to revenue, are shown on the following table:

Product	2009 ($m)	2010 ($m)	+/-% 09-10
Civilian aircraft, engines, equipment and parts	320	329	2.8
Instruments & appliances for medical surgical dental vet, nesoi	137	166	21.2
Pneumatic tyres for motorcars	169	161	-4.6
Crude oil from petroleum and bituminous minerals	105	156	48.8
Parts for boring & sinking machinery	122	140	14.8

Source: US Census Bureau, Foreign Trade

Chambers of Commerce and Trade Organisations

Greater Oklahoma City Chamber of Commerce, URL: http://www.okcchamber.com
The State Chamber, Oklahoma Association of Business and Industry, URL: http://okstatechamber.com/
Metro Tulsa Chamber of Commerce, URL: http://www.tulsachamber.com
Midwest City Chamber of Commerce, URL: http://midwestcityok.net/

MANUFACTURING, MINING AND SERVICES

Primary and Extractive Industries

Oklahoma is a leading state in the production of fuel minerals. The leading fuel minerals are natural gas, petroleum and coal. Oklahoma is the third highest producer of natural gas in the US and is also a leading producer of the non-fuel minerals, gypsum and tripoli. Mining contributed $15,868 million towards the state GDP in 2011 (up from $13,705 million in 2010). In 2010, oil and gas extraction were the largest sector ($10,125 million) followed by support activities ($3,264 million) and non-oil and gas mining ($316 million).

Oklahoma had proven crude oil reserves of 710 million barrels in 2010, equivalent to 3.1 per cent of the US total. Its 83,621 oil wells and 180 operational rotary rigs produced 8,185,000 barrels monthly (Oct. 2012), 3.9 per cent of total US production. Crude oil refining capacity was 520,700 bbl/d in 2012 (3 per cent of US total). Oil consumption in 2010 was 91.9 million barrels, 43.2 million barrels of which were used as motor gasoline and 22.6 million barrels as distillate fuel.

Oklahoma is one of the top natural gas-producing states in the US; in 2009, over 12 of the 100 largest natural gas fields in the country were found in the state, and dry natural gas reserves stood at 26,345 billion cubic feet in 2010 (8.6 per cent of the US total). Natural gas plant liquids amounted to 1,270 million barrels. Oklahoma's natural gas industry consisted of 41,238 gas and gas condensate wells in 2011, and marketed production reached 1,888,870 million cubic feet (7.9 per cent of the US total) in 2011. Total consumption was 655,936 million cubic feet in 2011 (2.7 of US total). Most is used by the electricity generation and industrial sectors. The state uses less than a third of its production, and the rest is piped to neighbouring states.

Recovering coal reserves at producing mines was estimated at 11 million short tons in 2011. Approximately 1,145,000 short tons of coal were produced in 2011. (Source: EIA)

Energy

Total energy production was 2,546 trillion Btu in 2010, equating to 3.4 per cent of the US total. Oklahoma's total energy consumption amounted to 1,552 trillion Btu in 2010 whilst its per capita energy consumption ranks it 11th in the US (413 million Btu in 2010).

Oklahoma is a net exporter of electricity, with coal as its primary generating fuel. Net summer capability in 2010 was 21,022 MW and total net monthly generation (Oct. 2012) was 5,317 MWh (1.7 per cent of US total), of which, coal-fired 2,360,000 MWh, natural gas-fired 2,104,000 MWh, hydroelectric 48,000 MWh, and other renewables 816,000 MWh. The major electricity generating plants include: Muskogee (coal), Northeastern (coal), Seminole (gas), Sooner, and Redbud Power Plant (gas). In 2011, Oklahoma ranked seventh in net electricity genertaion from wind, which provided 7.1 per cent of the State's net generation. (Source: EIA)

Manufacturing

Manufacturing is Oklahoma's fourth largest contributor to the State GDP, earning an estimated $18,632 million in 2011 (up from $16,824 million in 2010). The largest earning sectors in 2010 were machinery manufacturing ($3,447 million), fabricated metal products ($1,859 million), petroleum and coal products ($3,769 million) and food, beverage and tobacco products ($1,634 million).

Service Industries

The services industry is Oklahoma's greatest contributor towards GDP. The largest sectors in 2011 were real estate ($13,996 million), and health services and social assistance ($11,439 million). The finance and insurance sector contributed $7,619 million.

Tourism

The arts, entertainment and recreation sector of the services industry contributed an estimated $897 million towards GDP. The accommodation and food services sector contributed around $4,048 million, up from $3,833 million the previous year.
Oklahoma Tourism and Recreation Department, URL: http://tourism.state.ok.us/

Agriculture

Agriculture, forestry, fishing & hunting contributed an estimated $2,560 million towards Oklahoma's GDP in 2011 (up on the previous year's $2,287 million). In 2010, the crop and animal production sector accounted for $2,092 million, and the forestry, fishing and related activities sector contributed $195 million. (Source: BEA)

According to the USDA, Oklahoma's farms numbered 86,500 in 2010, and farmland covered around 35,200,000 acres. The average size of an Oklahoma farm was 407 acres. Total market value of agricultural products sold in 2008 was $5.8 billion, of which $4.6 billion was generated by livestock, poultry and products, and $1.1 billion was generated by crops, including greenhouse and nursery crops. Principal farm products are cattle, wheat, dairy products, and broilers. Principal crops are wheat, hay, cotton lint, and sorghum. Oklahoma ranks sixth for cattle and calf production and 5th in terms of wheat acreage. As of 1 Jan. 2011, there were 5.1 million cattle and calves, 2.33 million hogs & pigs and 75,000 sheep.

COMMUNICATIONS AND TRANSPORT

International Airports

Oklahoma's international airport is Tulsa International (TUL). Oklahoma City has the Oklahoma City Expressway Airpark.
Tulsa International Airport, URL: http://www.tulsaairports.com/index.cfm
Will Rogers World Airport, URL: http://www.flyokc.com

Roads

Oklahoma is crossed by three interstate highways: I-35, I-40, and I-44.

Shipping

The McClellan-Kerr Arkansas River Navigation System is a 440-mile waterway linking Oklahoma and the surrounding five-state area with ports on the nation's 25,000-mile inland waterway system, and foreign and domestic ports beyond by way of New Orleans and the Gulf Intracoastal waterway. The Port of Catoosa, near Tulsa, is at the head of the System. The waterway travels along the Verdigris River, the Arkansas River, the Arkansas Post Canal and the White River before joining the Mississippi at Montgomery Point. New Orleans is 600 miles south.

The U.S. Army Corps of Engineers built the system 36 years ago and continues to operate it. In an average year, 13-million tons of cargo is transported on the McClellan-Kerr by barge. This ranges from sand and rock to fertilizer, wheat, raw steel, refined petroleum products and sophisticated petrochemical processing equipment.

HEALTH

The National Center for Health Statistics estimated that there were 21.3 doctors per 10,000 inhabitants in 2009, below the US average of 27.4. In 2008, there were 1,805 dentists (5.0 per 10,000 population). In the same year, there were 3.1 community hospital beds per 1,000 residents, and there were 314 nursing homes, with 28,932 beds.

It was estimated that, in 2007-09, some 16.6 per cent of the state population had no healthcare insurance (one of the highest rates in the US) and that in 2007-11, 16.3 per cent were living in poverty. Oklahoma reported 5,437 HIV/AIDS cases from the beginning of the epidemic to the end of 2008, and ranked 28th in cumulative number of reported cases in 2008. The TB rate was 2.7 per 100,000 population, the 28 highest in the US. Some 30.4 per cent of adults suffer obesity, above the national rate, and 14.1 per cent of the youth are overweight, again above the US average. An estimated 66.3 per cent of the population were overweight. (Source: Center for Disease Control)

EDUCATION

Primary/Secondary Education

In the 2009-10 educational year, Oklahoma had 1,812 elementary and secondary schools with a total enrolment of 654,802 students. With 42,678 classroom teachers, the pupil/teacher ratio was 15.34 to one.

Total revenues for educational year 2007-08 were estimated as $5.482 billion whilst current expenditure on state education reached an estimated $5.4 billion.

Higher Education

Oklahoma had 60 degree-awarding institutes with an enrolment of some 97,524 male students and 123,126 women students in 2010-11. 39,3885 degrees/certificates were awarded in the same year, including 19,535 Bachelors, 5,947 Masters and 1,586 Doctorates. (Source: National Center for Educational Statistics)

COMMUNICATIONS AND MEDIA

Newspapers

Oklahoma's daily newspapers include: The Oklahoman, based in Oklahoma City; Tulsa World; Clinton Daily News; Durant Daily Democrat; Shawnee News-Star; El Reno Tribune; Perry Daily Journal; and The Comanche Times. Non-daily newspapers include: The Journal Record, Oklahoma City; Greater Tulsa Reporter Newspapers; Urban Tulsa; and The Tribune, Bethany.
Oklahoma Press Association, 3URL: http://www.okpress.com/
The Oklahoman, URL: http://www.oklahoman.com

Broadcasting

Seven of Oklahoma's television stations are based in Oklahoma City and eight in Tulsa.

ENVIRONMENT

Oklahoma relies primarily on coal for its electricity generation. Emissions of carbon dioxide from the electricity generating industry fell from 51,986,033 metric tons in 2009 to 49,535,558 metric tons in 2010, ranking the state 17th in the US, accounting for 2.1 per cent of the US total. Emissions of sulfur dioxide amounted to 84,805 metric tons and emissions of nitrogen oxide amounted to 71,029 metric tons.

Oklahoma produces a significant amount of energy from wind resources. Other renewable energy resources - hydroelectric dams and wood and wood-waste - contribute about 7 per cent of the electricity to the Oklahoma power grid.

Ethanol consumption amounted to 3,748 thousand barrels in 2011 and there were 10,493 alternative-fueled vehicles in use in 2010. (Source: EIA)

OREGON

Capital: Salem (Population, Census 2010: 154,637)

Head of State: John Kitzhaber (D) (Governor) (page 1457)

State Flag: A navy blue background in the centre of which is a shield surrounded by 33 gold stars and bearing the state seal. Above the shield are the words 'State of Oregon' in gold capital letters; below the shield appears the date '1859' in gold letters, the date Oregon was admitted to the union. On the reverse side of the flag is depicted a beaver. The state seal depicts, in the upper half, the Oregon forests and mountains, an antlered elk, a covered wagon, a team of oxen, the Pacific Ocean behind which is the setting sun, a departing British man-of-war and an arriving American merchant ship; in the lower half appears a sheaf of wheat, a plough, and a pickaxe.

CONSTITUTION AND GOVERNMENT

Constitution

Oregon entered the Union on 14 February 1859 as the 33rd state. Oregon's Constitution was approved by the people on 9 November 1857 and went into effect on the day the state entered the Union. Amendments were added on 21 May 2002, 17 September 2002 and 5 November 2002. Under the terms of the Constitution executive power is vested in an elected

governor who is assisted by five publicly elected officials: the secretary of state, treasurer, attorney general, commissioner of the bureau of labor and industries, and superintendent of public instruction.

Oregon elects two Senators and five Representatives to the US Congress in Washington, DC. Senators are elected for six years and Representatives for two years.

To consult the state constitution, please visit:
http://bluebook.state.or.us/state/constitution/constitution.htm

Legislature

Oregon's Legislative Assembly consists of two houses: the State Senate and the State House of Representatives. The Legislative Assembly convenes every odd-numbered year, usually on the second Monday in January. Sessions generally last about six months.
Legislative Administration, 900 Court Street NE, Room 140-A, Salem 97301, USA. Tel: +1 503 986 1848, URL: http://www.oregon.gov

UNITED STATES OF AMERICA

Upper House
The State Senate has 30 members elected for four years (half their number retiring every two years). Recent amendments to the Constitution provide for a maximum of two terms, or eight years. Each senator represents a district of about 114,000 people. Following the 2012 elections the Senate was composed of 16 Democrats, 14 Republicans.
State Senate, 900 Court St. NE, Room 233, Salem, OR 97301, USA. Tel: +1 503 986 1851, fax: +1 503 986 1132, URL: http://www.leg.state.or.us/senate/senateset.htm

Lower House
The State House of Representatives has 60 members who are elected for two years. Amendments to the Constitution limit state representatives to a maximum term of six years. Each member of the House represents a district of about 57,000 people. Following the elections in 2012 the House consisted of 34 Democrats and 26 Republicans.
State House of Representatives, 900 Court St. NE, Room H-271, Salem, OR 97301, USA. Tel: +1 503 986 1870 (Chief Clerk), URL: http://www.leg.state.or.us/house/houseset.htm

---

Elected Executive Branch Officials (as at April 2013)
Governor: John Kitzhaber (D) (page 1457)
Secretary of State: Kate Brown (D)
State Treasurer: Ted Wheeler (D)
Attorney General: Ellen Rosenblum (D)
Commissioner of Bureau of Labor and Industries: Brad Avakian

Legislative Assembly (as at April 2013)
President of the Senate: Peter Courtney (D)
President Pro Tem of the Senate: Ginny Burdick (D)
Senate Majority Leader: Diane Rosenbaum (D)
Senate Minority Leader: Ted Ferrioli (R)
Speaker of the House: Tina Kotek (D)
House Republican Leader: Mike McLane (R)
House Democrat Leader: Val Hoyle Kotek (D)

US Senators: Ron Wyden (D) (page 1540) and Jeff Merkely (D) (page 1476)

Ministries
Office of the Governor, 160 State Capitol, 900 Court Street, Salem, Oregon 97301-4047, USA. Tel: +1 503 378 4582, fax: +1 503 378 6827, URL: http://www.oregon.gov/gov/pages/index.aspx
Office of the Secretary of State, 136 State Capitol, Salem OR 97310, USA. Tel: +1 503 986 1500, fax: +1 503 986 1616, e-mail: oregon.sos@state.or.us, URL: http://www.sos.state.or.us
Department of Agriculture, 635 Capitol Street NE, Salem 97301-2532, USA. Tel: +1 503 986 4550, fax: +1 503 986 4747, URL: http://www.oregon.gov/ODA
Department of Consumer and Business Services, 350 Winter Street NE, Salem 97301-3878, USA. Tel: +1 503 378 4100, fax: +1 503 378 6444, URL: http://www.oregon.gov/DCBS/
Department of Corrections, 2575 Center Street NE, Salem 97301-4667, USA. Tel: +1 503 945 9090, fax: +1 503 373 1173, URL: http://www.oregon.gov/doc/Pages/index.aspx
Business Oregon, 775 Summer Street NE, Suite 200, Salem 97301-1280, USA. Tel: +1 503 986 0123, fax: +1 503 581 5115, URL: http://www.oregon.gov/ECDD/
Department of Education, 255 Capitol St. NE, Salem 97310-0203, USA. Tel: +1 503 378 3569, fax: +1 503 378 5156, URL: http://www.ode.state.or.us/
Department of Environmental Quality, 811 SW 6th Avenue, Portland 97204-1390, USA. Tel: +1 503 229 5696, fax: +1 503 229 6124, URL: http://www.oregon.gov/DEQ/
State Forestry Department, 2600 State Street, Salem 97310, USA. Tel: +1 503 945 7200, fax: +1 503 945 7212, URL: http://www.oregon.gov/ODF/
Department of Human Services, 500 Summer Street, NE E15, Salem 97301-1097, USA. Tel: +1 503 945 5944, fax: +1 503 378 2897, URL: http://www.dhs.state.or.us/
Department of Justice, 1162 Court Street NE, Salem 97301-4096, USA. Tel: +1 503 378 4400, fax: +1 503 378 4017, URL: http://www.doj.state.or.us
Department of Land Conservation and Development, 635 Capitol Street NE, Suite 150, Salem 97301-2540, USA. Tel: +1 503 373 0050, fax: +1 503 378 5518, URL: http://www.oregon.gov/lcd/
Department of Transport, 355 Capitol Street NE, Salem 97301-3871, USA. Tel: +1 503 986 3289, fax: +1 503 986 3432, URL: http://www.oregon.gov/odot/
State Treasury, 350 Winter Street NE, Suite 100, Salem, OR 97301-3896, USA. Tel: +1 503 378 4329, fax: +1 503 373 7051, URL: http://www.oregon.gov/treasury/Pages/index.aspx

Political Parties
Democratic Party of Oregon, URL: http://www.dpo.org
Oregon Republican Party, URL: http://www.oregonrepublicanparty.org/

Elections
Elections for Governor, Superintendent of Public Instruction, and State Labour Commissioner, judges of the various Oregon courts, 5 US Representatives, 15 state Senators and all state Representatives took place in November 2006. The incumbent Governor, Democrat Ted Kulongoski, was ineligible for re-election. Democrat John Kitzhaber, a former governor, beat Republican Chris Dudley by 49 per cent to 48 per cent.

The Attorney General John Kruger resigned in June 2012. He was replaced by Ellen Rosenblum (D). The Superintendent of Public Instruction, Susan Castillo, resigned in June 2012, two years before the position was due to be phased out.

Following legislative elections held in November 2012, the Democrats retained control of the Senate (Democrats 16, Republicans 14) and in the House of Representatives, the Democrats regained their majority (Democrats 34, Republicans 26).

LEGAL SYSTEM

Oregon's legal system comprises the Supreme Court, the Court of Appeals, the Tax Court, 36 Circuit Courts (in 27 judicial districts), County Courts, Justice Courts, and Municipal Courts. The Supreme Court consists of the Chief Justice and six Associate Justices. All are elected by popular vote for a term of six years. The Court of Appeals comprises a Chief Judge and nine Associate Judges. The Chief Judge is appointed by the Supreme Court Chief Justice from the ten Judges of the Court of Appeals, whilst the Associate Judges are elected on a non-partisan, statewide basis for terms of six years.

Oregon has the death penalty and there are currently 37 people on death row including one female. The last execution took place in 1997. The murder rate is 2.4 per 100,000 population.

Supreme Court: URL: http://courts.oregon.gov/Supreme/
Chief Justice: Thomas Balmer
Justices: Rives Kistler, Martha Lee Walters, Virginia Linder, Jack Landau, David Brewer, Richard Baldwin
Oregon Court of Appeals, URL: http://courts.oregon.gov/COA/
Chief Judge: Rick Haselton

LOCAL GOVERNMENT

Administratively, Oregon is divided into 36 counties, of which 24 are governed by a board of commissioners of between three and five elected members. The remaining twelve counties are administered by a county court comprising a county judge and two commissioners. Oregon's counties are subdivided into 240 municipalities which are governed by city councils. These have the responsibility of passing laws and adopting resolutions. City councils consist of less than ten members who serve terms of either two or four years. There are four types of city government: council/manager, council/administrator, commission, and mayor/council.

AREA AND POPULATION

Area
Oregon is situated on the west coast of the US, south of Washington state, north of California and Nevada, west of Idaho. Oregon's total area is 98,380.64 sq. miles, of which 95,996.79 sq. miles is land and 2,383.85 sq. miles is water. Oregon boasts 500 km of scenic Pacific Ocean coastline, a broad fertile valley, lush forests of tall evergreen trees, snow-covered mountain peaks, desert plateaux, and North America's deepest and narrowest river gorge. About 87 per cent of Oregonians live west of the Cascade Range of mountains, whilst relatively few live along the coast. Over two-thirds of the population live in counties bordering the Willamette River in the northwest section of the state.

To view a map of the state, please consult:
http://www.lib.utexas.edu/maps/us_2001/oregon_ref_2001.pdf

Population
According to the 2010 Census, the 2010 state population was 3,831,074, up on the mid-2009 estimate of 3,825,657. In 2012, the population was estimated to be 3,899,353. Over the period 2000 to 2010, the population grew by 12 per cent and is expected to reach 4.8 million by 2030. Oregon's population density is estimated at 39.9 persons per sq. mile. The largest county is Multnomah county (735,334 inhabitants in 2010), The capital, Salem, had a 2010 population of 156,244, but the largest city is Portland, with some 593,820 inhabitants.

Births, Marriages, Deaths
The US Census Bureau estimated that there were 45,450 births in 2010 and 31,890 deaths, giving a natural population growth of 13,560 people. Net immigration amounted to 24,772 people in 2009. The fertility rate was 60.4 per 1,000 women aged 15-44 years and the death rate was 832.4 per 100,000 population. The infant mortality rate in 2007 was an estimated 5.8 infant deaths per 1,000 live births. Marriages and divorces in 2007, according to provisional data, numbered 29,351 and 14,844 respectively.

EMPLOYMENT

Oregon's total civilian labour force in December 2012 was 1,958,800, of which 1,794,800 were in employment and 164,000 were unemployed. The unemployment rate was 8.4 per cent, higher than the national average of 7.8 per cent. (Source: US Bureau of Labor Statistics)

Non-farm wage and salary employment (seasonally adjusted) in December 2012, according to industry, is shown on the following table (preliminary figures):

Industry	No. of jobs	12-month change (%)
Logging and mining	6,800	-1.4
Construction	68,300	-3.0
Manufacturing	169,400	3.3
Trade, transportation, and utilities	322,100	2.3
Information	32,400	-0.6
Financial activities	93,700	2.5
Professional and business services	188,800	1.8
Educational and health services	239,800	0.9
Leisure and hospitality	167,700	1.3
Other services	59,300	1.4
Government	290,700	-0.5
TOTAL	1,639,000	1.2

Source: Bureau of Labor Statistics

BANKING AND FINANCE

GDP/GNP, Inflation, National Debt

Oregon's total Gross Domestic Product (current dollars) rose from $185,211 million in 2010 to $194.7 billion. Real GDP rose by 4.7 per cent over the year 2011. Oregon was ranked 25th in the US for its 2011 GDP. Oregon's GDP according to industry is shown on the table below (in millions of current dollars).

Industry	2009	2010	2011
Agriculture, forestry, fishing & hunting	3,217	3,008	3,249
Mining	265	219	230
Utilities	2,343	2,270	2,107
Construction	6,409	6,021	6,372
Manufacturing	39,923	50,905	56,002
Wholesale Trade	9,717	10,051	10,717
Retail Trade	8,393	8,855	9,138
Transport and warehousing	4,211	4,310	4,436
Information	5,304	5,204	5,589
Finance and insurance	8,047	8,896	8,887
Real Estate	23,664	22,287	22,164
Educational services	1,348	1,403	1,489
Health care & social assistance	13,185	13,924	14,742
Other non-government services	24,396	25,747	27,255
Government	21,180	22,110	22,365
TOTAL	171,601	185,211	194,742

Source: Bureau of Economic Analysis, Feb. 2013

The state's average per capita income rose to $37,527 in 2011. Per capita real GDP rose to $48,940 in 2011, compared to the US figure of $42,070.

The annual Consumer Price Index (CPI) (all items) for Portland-Salem, OR-WA, rose from 224.6 in 2011 to 229.8 in 2012 (1982-84=100). (Source: Bureau of Labor Statistics)

Balance of Payments / Imports and Exports

Total Oregon imports amounted to $11,944 million in 2009, down 29.3 per cent from $16,897 million in 2008. They rose by 12.8 per cent to $13,471 million in 2010, and by 22.2 per cent in 2011 to $16,464 million, representing 0.7 per cent of the US total. Imports include vehicle parts, electronics, light oils, airplanes. Main suppliers (2011) were Japan (22.6 per cent), China (18.1 per cent), Canada (17.7 per cent), South Korea and Germany. Oregon's merchandise export revenue fell from $19,352 million in 2008 to $14,907 million in 2009, a fall of 23.0 per cent. Exports rose by 18.5 per cent to $17,671 million in 2010, and by 3.6 per cent in 2011 to $18,310 million, representing 1.2 per cent of the US total. (Source: US Census Bureau, Foreign Trade Division).

The following table shows the top five export destinations in 2010-11 according to revenue:

Country	2010 ($m)	2011 ($m)	+/-% 2010-11
China	4,047	3,178	-21.5
Canada	2,424	2,716	12.0
Malaysia	2,667	2,219	-16.8
Japan	1,367	1,649	20.6
South Korea	937	1,062	13.4

Source: US Census Bureau

The top five export products in 2010, according to revenue, are shown on the following table:

Product	Export Revenue ($m)
Processors and controllers, elec. integrated circuits	5,617
Wheat (other than Durum) and Meslin	1,294
Potassium Chloride	867
Civilian aircraft, engines and parts	419
Soybeans	381

Source: US Census Bureau, Foreign Trade

Chambers of Commerce and Trade Organisations

Portland Development Commission, URL: http://www.pdc.us/
Portland Metro Chamber of Commerce, URL: http://www.portlandalliance.com/
Salem Area Chamber of Commerce, URL: http://www.salemchamber.org/

MANUFACTURING, MINING AND SERVICES

Primary and Extractive Industries

Eastern Oregon has been the site of mining for precious metals. Pumice and other minerals are also mined in Oregon. Oregon has the nation's only nickel mine and smelter and metals processing is an important industry. In 2011 mining contributed $230 million towards Oregon's Gross Domestic Product, down from $219 million in 2010. The top earning sectors in 2010 were non-oil and gas mining ($206 million) and support activities for mining ($7 million).

Oregon has one oil refinery (asphalt plant) and a number of product pipelines linking with oil refineries in Washington state. These apart, Oregon has no oil industry. Oil consumption in 2010 fell slightly to 65.8 million barrels, over half of which was used as motor gasoline.

Oregon has a small natural gas industry with a total of 24 gas and gas condensate wells in 2010. Production was 1,344 million cu ft in 2011. Consumption of natural gas fell from 239,343 million cu ft in 2010 to 199,481 million cu ft in 2011. Natural gas is mainly used for electricity generation, with the industrial and residential sectors, respectively, as the next largest consumers. (Source: EIA)

Energy

Total energy production was 390 trillion Btu in 2010 (0.5 per cent of US total). Oregon's total energy consumption was 977 trillion Btu in 2010 and was ranked 40th in the US for per capita energy consumption (255 million Btu).

Much of Oregon's electrical energy comes from huge hydroelectric dams on the Columbia River. Most of the dams are operated by the United States Army Corps of Engineers (USCE). The state's only nuclear power plant was closed down in 1993 because of the uneconomical nature of generator repair.

Oregon is a net exporter of electricity, with hydro as the primary means of generating power. Net summer capability in 2010 was 14,261 MW (1.4 per cent of the US total) and total net monthly (Oct. 2012) generation was 4,477 MWh (1.4 per cent of US total), of which 2,100,000 MWh was hydroelectric, other renewables 453,000 MWh, 1,518,000 MWh natural gas-fired, 402,000 MWh coal-fired. Major utility plants include John Day (hydro), The Dalles (hydro), Bonneville (hydro), McNary (hydro), and COB Power Partnership (gas). (Source: EIA)

For fuel, Oregon relies on oil from Alaska (via refineries in Washington) and natural gas from Canada. Substantial geothermal and solar energy potential exists in parts of Oregon.

In 2011, 80 per cent of Oregon's net electricity generation was from conventional hydroelectric power plants and other renewable energy resources.

Manufacturing

Manufacturing is Oregon's second largest contributor towards GDP, accounting for an estimated $56,002 million in 2011 (up from $50,093 million in 2010). Top sectors in 2010 were computer and electronic products ($39,768 million) and food, beverage and tobacco products ($2,065 million). Oregon's major economic activities include logging, lumber and plywood manufacturing, agriculture and food processing, tourism, high technology manufacturing, and metals refining and manufacturing. High technology companies based in Oregon include Intel and Hewlett-Packard. Some three-quarters of Portland's high technology employment are based in the Portland area. The state supplies a large share of the nation's lumber and plywood and is active in international trade, especially with Pacific Rim nations.

Service Industries

The services industry is Oregon's largest contributor to GDP. The main earning sectors in 2011 were real estate ($22,164 million), health care and social assistance ($14,742 million), and finance and insurance ($8,887 million).

In terms of Government revenue, Oregon has no general sales tax but does have local property taxes and a state income tax. Other government revenues come from motor vehicle licences, drivers' licences, fuel taxes, fishing and hunting licences, state-controlled sales of alcoholic beverages, cigarette and tobacco taxes, utility and railroad fees, motor vehicle weight-mile taxes, inheritance tax, timber taxes and miscellaneous taxes.

Tourism

Tourism remains a major part of the service industry and an important aspect of the economy. The accommodation and food services sector contributed $4,757 million towards Oregon's 2011 GDP, whilst the arts, entertainment and recreation sector contributed $1,062 million.
Oregon Travel Information Council, URL: http://www.oregontic.com/

Agriculture

Oregon's agriculture, forestry and fishing industry contributed $3,249 million towards the state economy in 2011 (up from $3,008 in 2010). The top sector in 2010 was farming ($1,898 million). Forestry, fishing and related activities earned $1,110 million. (Source: BEA)

According to latest USDA estimates, Oregon's farms numbered 38,800 in 2010, and farmland covered around 16,400,000 acres. The average size of a farm fell from 435 acres in 2006 to 423 acres in 2010. The market value of agricultural products was $4.3 billion ($2.9 billion from crops and around $1.4 billion from livestock). The state is ranked first for field and grass seed crops and third in terms of nursery, greenhouse and floriculture. As of 1 Jan. 2011, there were 1.33 million cattle and calves ,16,000 hogs & pigs and 215,000 sheep.

Logging and processing trees is an important industry in Oregon. Most of the trees harvested are Douglas fir or Ponderosa pine. Oregon is ranked first in the US for cut Christmas trees and is a major source of the nation's lumber and plywood. The state also produces paper from wood chips.

Oregon's fishing fleets are small in comparison to the huge floating factories sailed by some foreign countries. Oregon is known for its Chinook salmon, dungeness crab, and Oregon pink (cocktail) shrimp.

COMMUNICATIONS AND TRANSPORT

International Airports

Oregon's largest airport is the Portland International Airport (PDX). PDX services flights to 120 cities, numerous non-stop flights to Asia and many domestic connections. PDX is the fastest growing airport on the west coast of the United States, and is the only major airport in the region with spare capacity. During January 2005, 941,271 passengers travelled through the airport and 19,501 short tons of cargo were transported via the airport. Other major cities in Oregon have scheduled or charter air service.
Portland International Airport, URL: http://www.portlandairportpdx.com

Railways

Oregon has a total of 2,500 miles of railway track used by some 21 railway companies. Rail freight is in excess of 55 million tons per annum. Passenger services operate between Eugene to Portland; Eugene to Seattle, Washington; Portland to Vancouver, Canada.

UNITED STATES OF AMERICA

Roads

Oregon has a total of almost 86,000 miles of roads and nearly 3.2 million vehicles. US Interstate 5 runs north-south through Oregon's western interior valleys. US Interstate 84 runs east-west along Oregon's northern border with Washington and through the northeast corner of Oregon. The state maintains a modern state highway system.

Ports and Harbours

Oregon has 23 public ports. Three are deep-water ports - Coos Bay, Astoria, and Portland - that export large quantities of forest and agricultural products and import automobiles, metal ores and many other products. Numerous barges filled with agricultural products travel the Columbia River. The Columbia-Snake River system is Oregon's major commercial transport route, and is second in the world for grain exports. In the region of 50 million tons of cargo was transported through Oregon's deep water ports to the mouth of the Columbia River in 1998.

Port of Portland, URL: http://www.portofportland.com/
Oregon International Port of Coos Bay, URL: http://www.portofcoosbay.com/

HEALTH

The National Center for Health Statistics estimated that there were 28.0 doctors (including osteopaths) per 10,000 Oregon residents in 2009. In 2008, there were an estimated 2,574 dentists (6.8 per 10,000 population). In 2009, there were 1.7 community hospital beds per 1,000 inhabitants, below the US average of 2.6 beds per 1,000 people. In 2010, there were 137 nursing homes, with a total of 12,218 beds.

It was estimated that some 16.9 per cent of the state residents had no health care insurance in 2007-09, and that in 2007-11, an estimated 14.8 per cent were living in poverty. Adult obesity rates were average for the US. An estimated 60.3 per cent are classified as overweight and 26.8 per cent are obese. Oregon reported 6,544 HIV/AIDS cases from the beginning of the epidemic to the end of 2008, and ranked 26th highest in cumulative number of reported cases in 2008. The overall TB rate was 2.0 per 100,000 population, the 34th highest in the US. (Source: CDC)

EDUCATION

Primary/Secondary Education

There are currently 1,329 elementary and secondary public schools. In 2009-10, there were 582,839 students and 28,751 classroom teachers, giving a ratio of 20.27 pupils per teacher, much higher than the US average of 15.3 pupils per teacher.

During the 2007-08 academic year, total educational revenues reached $6.18 billion, whilst current expenditure on state education was $6.33 billion.

Higher Education

There are 60 degree-conferring institutions in Oregon. The Oregon University System (OUS) consists of seven colleges and universities the responsibility of the State Board of Higher Education. They include: Eastern Oregon University (La Grande), Oregon Institute of Technology (Klamath Falls), Oregon State University (Corvallis), Portland State University (Portland), Southern Oregon University (Ashland), University of Oregon (Eugene), and Western Oregon University (Monmouth).

In the 2010-11 academic year, around 109,132 male students were registered, together with 134,280 women. 44,070 degrees/certificates were conferred, including 18,873 Bachelor degrees, 6,779 Masters and 1,849 Doctorates. (Source: National Center for Educational Statistics)

RELIGION

Oregon's population is predominantly Protestant, with a smaller representation of Catholic, Jewish, Muslim, and other religions.

COMMUNICATIONS AND MEDIA

Newspapers

The state's major newspaper is The Oregonian, published in Portland. Portland's other newspaper is the Daily Journal of Commerce. Other newspapers published include: Statesman Journal, Salem; The Times, Brownsville; Jefferson Review, Jefferson; The Observer, La Grande; Lake County Examiner, Lakeview; Valley-Times, Milton-Freewater; Dead Mountain Echo and Hwy. 58 Free Press, Oakridge.

Oregon Newspaper Publishers' Association, URL: http://www.orenews.com/
The Oregonian, URL: www.oregonlive.com
Statesman Journal, URL http://www.salemconnect.com
The Bulletin, URL: http://www.bendbulletin.com/

Business Journals

Daily Journal of Commerce, URL: http://www.djc-or.com

Broadcasting

Oregon has 32 commercial television stations, of which five are in Eugene, four are in Medford, nine are in Portland, and three are in Roseburg. There are also 37 public/educational radio and television stations. AT&T Cable Services and Charter Communications are two of the many cable television companies providing a cable TV service to Oregon.

Oregon Association of Broadcasters, URL: http://www.or-broadcasters.org
Oregon Cable Telecommunications Association, URL: http://www.oregoncable.com

ENVIRONMENT

Two-thirds of Oregon's electricity power plants are hydroelectric, making the industry one of the lowest emitters of sulphur dioxide, nitrogen oxides, and carbon dioxide. Emissions of carbon dioxide rose from 9,405,039 metric tons in 2009 to 10,093,990 metric tons (0.4 per cent of US total) in 2010, ranking 40th in the US. In 2010, sulfur dioxide emissions amounted to 15,862 metric tons and nitrogen oxide emissions amounted to 14,666 metric tons. Oregon is a major producer of wind energy, generating approximately 4 per cent of the US total.

In June 2007, Oregon adopted a renewable energy portfolio standard requiring the State's largest utilities to meet 25 per cent of their electric load with new renewable energy sources by 2025.

As of 2011, Oregon had two ethanol plants with a capacity of 40 million gal/year. Ethanol consumption was 4,355,000 barrels in 2011 and there were 12,980 alternative-fueled vehicles were in use. (Source: EIA)

PENNSYLVANIA

Capital: Harrisburg (Population, Census 2010: 49,528)

Head of State: Tom Corbett (R) (Governor) (page 1408)

State Flag: A blue background in the centre of which is the state coat of arms. The coat of arms consists of a shield on which appears a ship, plough and sheaves of wheat; the shield is supported by two horses; under the shield appear the words 'Virtue, Liberty, and Independence'.

CONSTITUTION AND GOVERNMENT

Constitution

Pennsylvania became one of the original 13 states of the Union on 12 December 1787. Its first Constitution was adopted on 28 September 1776. This was replaced by the Constitution of 1790, and then the Constitution of 1838. According to Pennsylvania's Constitution, the governor heads the executive branch of state government assisted by four other elected executive officials: the lieutenant governor, attorney general, treasurer, and auditor general. All serve terms of four years. The secretary of state is appointed by the governor and confirmed by the state Senate.

Pennsylvania elects two Senators and 19 Representatives to the US Congress in Washington, DC. As a result of re-districting following the 2000 Census, Pennsylvania's Congressional Districts were reduced from 21 to 19 with effect from 2002. To view the state constitution, please visit: http://sites.state.pa.us/PA_Constitution.html

Legislature

Pennsylvania's bicameral legislature, the General Assembly, consists of the Senate and the House of Representatives. The General Assembly meets in regular session on an annual basis, usually convening at noon on the first Tuesday in January and adjourning by noon of the first Tuesday of the following year.

Upper House

The Senate has 50 members who are elected for four years. Senators represent districts of around 59,000 people. According to the Constitution the lieutenant governor is also the president of the Senate. Following the 2012 elections, there were 27 Republicans and 23 Democrats serving in the Senate.

Pennsylvania Senate, Main Capitol Building, Harrisburg, PA 17120-0028, USA. Tel: +1 717 787 7163 (Chief Clerk), URL: http://www.pasen.gov/

Lower House

The House of Representatives has 203 members who are elected for two years. Members of the House represent districts of about 240,000 Pennsylvanians. Following the 2012 elections, the House was composed of 110 Democrats and 93 Republicans.

Pennsylvania House of Representatives, Main Capitol Building, Harrisburg, PA 17120-0028, USA. Tel +1 717 787 2372 (Chief Clerk), URL: http://www.house.state.pa.us

---

Executive Branch Officials (as of June 2013)
Governor: Tom Corbett (R) (page 1408)
Lieutenant Governor: Jim Cawley (R)
Attorney General: Kathleen Kane (D)
Treasurer: Rob McCord (D)
Auditor General: Eugene DePasquale (D)
Non-Elected Executive Branch Officials
Secretary of the Commonwealth: Carol Aichele (R)

Legislature (as at April 2013)
President of the Senate: Jim Cawley (R)
President Pro-Tem of the Senate: Joe Scarnati III (R)
Senate Majority Floor Leader: Dominic Pileggi (R)
Senate Minority Leader: Jay Costa (D)
Speaker of the House: Samuel Smith (R)

House Majority Leader: Mike Turzai (R)
House Minority Leader: Frank Dermody (D)

US Senators: Robert J. Casey Jr. (D) (page 1401) and Pat Toomey (R) (page 1526)

Ministries
Office of the Governor, 225 Main Capitol Building, Harrisburg, Pennsylvania 17120, USA. Tel: +1 717 787 2500, URL: http://www.governor.state.pa.us/
Office of the Lieutenant Governor, 200 Main Capitol Building, Harrisburg, PA 17120, USA. Tel: +1 717 787 3300, e-mail: lieutenant-governor@state.pa.us, URL: http://www.ltgovernor.pa.gov/
Office of the Attorney General, 16th Floor, Strawberry Square, Harrisburg, PA 17120, USA. Tel: +1 717 787 3391, fax: +1 717 783 8242, e-mail: info@attorneygeneral.gov, URL: http://www.attorneygeneral.gov
Department of Agriculture, 2301 North Cameron Street, Harrisburg, PA 17110-9408, USA. Tel: +1 717 787 4737, URL: http://www.agriculture.state.pa.us/
Department of the Auditor General, 229 Finance Building, Harrisburg, PA 17120-0018, USA. Tel: +1 717 787 2543, e-mail: auditorgen@auditorgen.state.pa.us, URL: http://www.auditorgen.state.pa.us
Department of Community and Economic Development, 4th Floor, Commonwealth Keystone Building, Harrisburg, PA 17120-0225, USA. Tel +1 717 787 3003, URL: http://www.inventpa.com/
Department of Conservation and Natural Resources, 7th Floor, Rachel Carson State Office Building, PO Box 8767, Harrisburg, PA 17105-8767, USA. Tel: +1 717 787 2869, fax: +1 717 772 9106, URL: http://www.dcnr.state.pa.us
Department of Corrections, 2520 Lisburn Road, PO Box 598, Camp Hill, PA 17001-0598, USA. Tel: +1 717 975 4859, URL: http://www.cor.state.pa.us
Department of Education, 333 Market Street, Harrisburg, PA 17126, USA. Tel: +1 717 783 6788, URL: http://www.pde.state.pa.us//
Department of Environmental Protection, 16th Floor, Rachel Carson State Office Building, PO Box 2063, Harrisburg, PA 17105-2063, USA. Tel: +1 717 783 2300, fax: +1 717 783 8926, URL: http://www.depweb.state.pa.us/
Department of Health, PO Box 90, Health and Welfare Building, Harrisburg, PA 17108, USA. Tel: +1 717 787 1783, URL: http://www.dsf.health.state.pa.us/health/site/default.asp
Department of Labour and Industry, Room 1700, 7th and Forster Streets, Harrisburg, PA 17120, USA. Tel: +1 717 787 5279, URL: http://www.dli.state.pa.us/
Department of State, 302 North Office Building, Harrisburg, PA 17120, USA. Tel: +1 717 787 6458, fax: +1 717 787 1734, URL: http://www.dos.state.pa.us
Department of Transport, Keystone Building, 400 North Street, Harrisburg, PA 17120, USA. Tel: +1 717 787 2838, fax: +1 717 787 1738, URL: http://www.dot.state.pa.us
Department of the Treasury, Room 129 Finance Building, Harrisburg, PA 17120-0018, USA. Tel: +1 717 787 2465, fax: +1 717 783 9760, URL: http://www.patreasury.org

Political Parties
Pennsylvania Democratic Party, URL: http://www.padems.com
Pennsylvania Republican Party, URL: http://www.pagop.org

Elections
The most recent gubernatorial election took place in November 2010. Governor Rendell was ineligible to stand for election. Republican Tom Corbett defeated the Democrat candidate with 55 per cent to 45 per cent.

In the legislative elections of November 2012, the Republicans kept control of the Senate but with a slightly reduced majority (Republicans 27, Democrats 23). The Republicans also kept control of the House of Representatives (Democrats 93, Republicans 110).

Elections for Attorney General, Treasurer and Auditor General took place in November 2012.

LEGAL SYSTEM

Pennsylvania's legal system consists of the Supreme Court; two appellate courts - the Superior Court and the Commonwealth Court; and the Court of Common Pleas. Special courts are the district justices, the Philadelphia Traffic Court, and the Pittsburgh Magistrate Court.

The Supreme Court comprises the Chief Justice and six Justices. They are elected by voters for a term of 10 years.
Supreme Court, URL: http://www.courts.state.pa.us/
Chief Justice of the Supreme Court: Ronald D. Castille
Justices: Thomas Saylor, J. Michael Eakin, Max Baer, Debra McCloskey Todd, Seamus McCaffery, JoanOrie Melvin

The Superior Court of Pennsylvania consists of the President Judge, 13 Associate Judges and 10 Senior Judges.
Superior Court of Pennsylvania, URL: http://www.courts.state.pa.us/
Superior Court President Judge: Correale F. Stevens

The Commonwealth Court consists of the President Judge, eight Associate Judges, and seven Senior Judges.
Commonwealth Court of Pennsylvania, URL: http://www.pacourts.us/T/Commonwealth/
Commonwealth Court President Judge: Dan Pellegrini

Pennsylvania has the death penalty. It has a large death row penalty but most convictions are commuted on appeal. There have been three executions since 1976. As of February 2013, the current death row population stands at 204 including four women. The current murder rate is 5.2 per 100,000 population. (Source: DPIC)

LOCAL GOVERNMENT

The state of Pennsylvania is primarily divided into 66 county governments and 2,564 sub-county general purpose governments. municipalities. Of the 2,562 general purpose governments, 1,016 are municipal and 1,546 are town or township governments. These are further divided into boroughs. There are additionally 1,728 special districts/authorities.
Pennsylvania League of Cities and Municipalities (PLCM), URL: http://www.plcm.org/
Pennsylvania Municipal Authorities Association (PMAA), URL: http://www.municipalauthorities.org/
Pennsylvania State Association of Boroughs (PSAB), URL: http://www.boroughs.org/index.stm

AREA AND POPULATION

Area
Pennsylvania is situated in the north-east of the US, south of New York State, west of New Jersey, east of Ohio, and north of Maryland, Delaware, and West Virginia. Its total area is 46,055.24 sq. miles, of which 44,816.61 sq. miles is land and 1,238.63 sq. miles is water.

To view a map of the state, please consult:
http://www.lib.utexas.edu/maps/us_2001/pennsylvania_ref_2001.pdf

Population
According to the 2010 Census, the state population was 12,702,379, up on the mid-2008 estimate of 12,604,767. The population was estimated to be 12,763,536 in 2012. The state is the sixth most populated in the USA. Over the period 2000-2010, the state population grew by 3.4 per cent. The population is expected to reach 12.7 million by 2030. The population density is estimated at 283.9 people per sq. mile. The county with the greatest number of inhabitants is Philadelphia county (1,526,006 in 2010). The capital, Harrisburg, had an estimated population of 49,673 in 2011, whilst the largest city is Philadelphia, with a 2010 population of 1,536,471.

According to the 2010 Census, 5.7 per cent of the population is under 5 years, 22 per cent under 18 years and 15.4 per cent is aged over 65 years. Approximately 81.9 per cent of the population is white, and 10.8 per cent is black. Approximately 5.7 per cent of the population is of Hispanic or Latino origin.

Births, Marriages, Deaths
The US Census Bureau, Population Division, estimated that there were 143,321 births in 2010 and 124,596 deaths, giving a natural population growth of 18,725 people. Net immigration (mainly from abroad) added a further 19,826 inhabitants, giving an overall population growth of 38,399 people. The fertility rate was 58.7 per 1,000 women aged 15-44 years and the death rate was 980.9 per 100,000 population. The infant mortality rate in 2007 was 7.6 infant deaths per 1,000 live births. Marriages and divorces in 2007, according to provisional data, numbered 71,094 and 35,268 respectively.

EMPLOYMENT

Of a total estimated labour force of 6,558,700 in December 2012, 6,042,000 were in employment and around 516,700 were unemployed. The unemployment rate was 7.7 per cent, slightly higher than the overall US rate of 7.8 per cent. (Source: US Bureau of Labor Statistics)

The following table shows provisional December 2012 non-farm wage and salary employment (seasonally adjusted) according to industry:

Industry	No. of Jobs	12-month change (%)
Logging and mining	40,100	9.0
Construction	218,100	-3.4
Manufacturing	569,600	1.0
Trade, transportation and utilities	1,110,600	0.8
Information	91,300	2.2
Financial activities	311,200	1.2
Professional and business services	726,000	1.9
Educational and health services	1,170,300	-0.2
Leisure and hospitality	527,800	2.9
Other services	253,600	-1.6
Government	732,900	0.0
TOTAL	5,751,500	0.7

Source: Bureau of Labor Statistics

BANKING AND FINANCE

GDP/GNP, Inflation, National Debt
Pennsylvania's Gross Domestic Product (GDP) rose from $558,918 million in 2010 to $578.8 billion. Real GDP increased by 1.2 per cent over 2011. Its GDP was ranked sixth highest in the USA in 2011. The state GDP according to industry is shown on the following table (in millions of current dollars):

Industry	2009	2010	2011
Agriculture, forestry, fishing & hunting	2,663	3,011	3,551
Mining	5,034	6,806	7,413
Utilities	10,672	11,329	11,273
Construction	19,131	18,768	19,732

UNITED STATES OF AMERICA

- continued

Manufacturing	66,011	66,550	70,958
Wholesale Trade	30,717	31,754	34,026
Retail Trade	30,870	32,604	33,321
Transport and warehousing	15,708	16,103	16,571
Information	21,808	21,769	22,561
Finance and insurance	40,614	47,751	47,920
Real estate	67,454	64,846	64,572
Educational services	12,194	12,618	12,857
Health care & social assistance	55,043	57,744	59,916
Other non-government services	102,819	108,687	114,982
Government	56,484	58,577	59,185
TOTAL	537,223	558,918	578,839

Source: Bureau of Economic Analysis, Feb. 2013

The state's annual average per capital income was $42,291 in 2011. Per capita real GDP was $39,272 in 2011; the national average was $42,070.

The annual Consumer Price Index (CPI) for the Philadelphia-Wilmington-Atlantic City, PA-NJ-DE-MD, urban area (all items) rose from 233.8 in 2011 to 238.1 in 2012 (1982-84 = 100). The annual Consumer Price Index (CPI) for the Pittsburgh, PA, urban area (all items) rose from 225.1 in 2011 to 232.9 in 2012 (1982-84 = 100). (Source: Bureau of Labor Statistics)

Balance of Payments / Imports and Exports

Total Pennsylvania imports amounted to $57,900 million in 2009, down 28.8 per cent from the 2008 total of $81,336 million. Imports rose by 29 per cent in 2010, amounting to $74,662 million, and by 19.9 per cent in 2011 to $89,404 million, representing a 4.0 per cent share of the US import total. Imports include oil, vehicle parts & electronics. Main suppliers (2011) include China (17.6 per cent), Canada (14.2 per cent), Nigeria (12.5 per cent), Israel and Germany. Merchandise export revenue fell from $34,649 million in 2008 to $28,381 million in 2009, a decrease of 18.1 per cent. Export revenue rose by 23.1 per cent to $34,928 million in 2010 and by 17.6 per cent in 2011 to $41,075 million, representing 2.8 per cent of US total.

The top five export products in 2010, according to export revenue, are shown on the following table:

Product	Export Revenue ($m)
Bituminous coal, not agglomerated	1,724
Medicaments N.E.S.O.I., measured doses	1,222
Nucleic acids & salts, other heterocyclic cmp., nes	1,025
Vaccines for human medicine	990
Motorcycles, cycles, exceeding 800 cc	705

Source: US Census Bureau, Foreign Trade

The following table sets out Pennsylvania's major export trading partners in 2010-11, according to the value of exports:

Country	2010 ($m)	2011 ($m)	+/-% 2010-11
Canada	10,287	11,518	12.0
China	2,679	3,570	33.2
Mexico	2,392	2,630	9.9
Japan	1,736	2,074	19.4
Germany	1,424	1,815	27.4

Source: US Census Bureau

Chambers of Commerce and Trade Organisations
PA Chamber of Business and Industry, URL: http://www.pachamber.org/
Greater Philadelphia Chamber of Commerce, URL: http://www.gpcc.com/

MANUFACTURING, MINING AND SERVICES

Primary and Extractive Industries
Mining contributed $7,412 million to Pennsylvania's Gross Domestic Product in 2011 (up from $6,806 million in 2010). The top earning sector in 2010 was non-oil and gas mining ($3,441 million), followed by oil and gas extraction ($1,474 million) and support activities for mining ($1,891 million).

Pennsylvania had crude oil reserves of 22 million barrels in 2010. From a total of 19,841 producing oil wells and 110 operational rotary rigs, monthly production was approximately 422,000 barrels in Oct. 2012. Crude oil refinery capacity amounted to 410,000 bbl/d in 2012 (2.4 per cent of US total). Total oil consumption in 2009 reached 243.7 million barrels (3.6 per cent of the US total), 121.8 million barrels of which was as motor gasoline and 59.8 million as distillate fuel.

Pennsylvania had dry natural gas reserves of 13,960 billion cubic feet in 2010 (4.6 per cent of US total). In 2010, there were 81 million barrels of natural gas plant liquids. Pennsylvania's gas and gas condensate wells numbered 54,347, and produced some 1,310,592 million cu ft of marketed natural gas in 2011 (5.5 per cent of US total). Consumption rose from 804,077 million cu ft in 2009 to 859,939 million cu ft (3.6 per cent of the US total). Natural gas is used primarily for residential and industrial use, although its use for electricity generation has grown rapidly in recent years.

Pennsylvania is a major coal-producing State and sells about one-half of its coal output to other States throughout the East Coast and Midwest. The state had total recoverable coal reserves of 558 million short tons in 2010 (3.1 per cent of US total). Production in 2011 amounted to 59,182 thousand short tons (equivalent to 5.4 per cent of US total), most of which came from the state's 50 underground mines. (Source: EIA)

Energy
Pennsylvania's total energy production was 3,051 trillion Btu in 2010 (4.1 per cent of US total). Its total energy consumption amounted to 3,759 trillion Btu in 2010 (3.8 per cent of US total) and is ranked 33rd in the US for its per capita energy consumption (296 million Btu in 2010).

Pennsylvania is a net export of electricity, with coal as its primary generating fuel. Net summer capability in 2010 was 45,575 MW (4.4 per cent of the US total) and total net monthly generation (Oct. 2012) was 16,927 thousand MWh (5.4 per cent of the US total), of which coal-fired 7,096 thousand MWh, nuclear 5,308 thousand MWh and gas-fired 3,868 thousand MWh. Hydroelectric generated 141,000 MWh and other renewables 425,000 MWh. Major utility plants include Bruce Mansfield (coal), PPL Susquehanna (nuclear), Limerick (nuclear), Peach Bottom (nuclear), and PPL Martins Creek (coal).

Three of Pennsylvania's four top electric generating plants run on nuclear power and the State ranks second in the USA in nuclear power generating capacity. Pennsylvania's nuclear reactors are Beaver Valley, Limerick, Peach Bottom, PPL Susquehanna, and Three Mile Island. Three Mile Island 2 was closed in 1979 following a loss of coolant which led to a partial meltdown.

Pennsylvania's Alternative Energy Portfolio Standards require 18 per cent of electricity sold by 2021 to come from renewable or alternative sources. In 2011, renewable energy accounted for 3.3. per cent of total state net electricity generation. (Source: EIA)

Manufacturing
Manufacturing is Pennsylvania's second highest contributor to GDP, earning an estimated $70,958 million in 2011 (up from $66,550 million in 2009). The top sectors in 2010 were chemical products ($10,376 million), primary metal manufacturing ($4,321 million), fabricated metal products ($6,845 million) and food products ($8,086 million).

Service Industries
The services industry is Pennsylvania's highest contributor towards GDP. The top sectors in 2011 were real estate ($64,572 million), health and social assistance ($59,916 million), and finance and insurance ($47,920 million).

Tourism
The accommodation and food services sector of the services industry contributed $13,481 million towards the state GDP in 2011, whilst the arts, entertainment and recreation sector contributed $6,513 million.
Tourism, Film and Economic Development Marketing Office, URL: http://www.experiencepa.com/experiencepa/home.do

Agriculture
The agriculture, forestry and fishing sector contributed $3,551 million towards the 2011 GDP (up from $3,011 million in 2010). The main sector in 2010 was farming ($2,598 million) followed by forestry, fishing and related activities ($413 million). (Source: BEA)

According to the US Department of Agriculture, there were 58,200 farms in Pennsylvania in 2008, and farmland covered an area of 7,650,000 acres. The average size of a Pennsylvanian farm was 131 acres in 2006. In 2008, total receipts from agriculture reached $5.76 billion; crop farming accounted for some 1.93 billion and livestock contributed $3.83 billion. Main crops are corn, hay, mushrooms, greenhouse nursery products, apples, potatoes, oats, wheat, tobacco, barley, peaches. Cattle and calves represent the major livestock product whilst corn for grain or seed represents the major crop harvested. As of 1 Jan. 2011, there were 1.61 million cattle and calves, 1.12 million hogs, 89,000 sheep and 60,5000 goats.

COMMUNICATIONS AND TRANSPORT

International Airports
There are 6 international airports, 6 major airports and 31 foreign and domestic carriers.
Philadelphia International Airport (PHL), URL: http://www.phl.org/

Railways
Pennsylvania has 70 railway companies, 6 of which are class one rail lines, and 5,600 miles of railway track. Pennsylvania's railway system is ranked fourth in the US.

Roads
Pennsylvania's interstate system of highways totals more than 1,500 miles. Of 115,000 miles of streets and highways, 41,000 are state-maintained roadways. The 470-mile Pennsylvania Turnpike opened in 1940 as the first high-speed, multi-lane highway in the United States.

Ports and Harbours
Pennsylvania's location by the North Atlantic, the Great Lakes and the Ohio-Mississippi River system, makes it an important trade destination. There are three ports: the Port of Erie, the Port of Philadelphia and Camden, and the Port of Pittsburgh. Major commodities shipped from the Port of Pittsburgh, the largest inland US port, are coal, petroleum, chemicals, crude materials, primary manufactured goods, food and farm products. In 2002, cargo shipments at the port exceeded 52 million tons.
Port of Pittsburgh Commission, URL: http://www.port.pittsburgh.pa.us
The Port of Philadelphia and Camden Inc., http://www.drpa.org/

HEALTH

The National Center for Health Statistics estimated that there were 33.1 doctors per 10,000 population in 2009, well above the US average of 27.4. In 2008, there were 7,756 dentists (6.2 per 10,000 population). In 2009, there were 3.1 community hospital beds per 1,000 citizens (again, above the US average). In 2010, there were 710 nursing homes, with 88,829 beds.

It was estimated that, in 2007-09, 10.3 per cent of Pennsylvanians had no health-care coverage and, in 2007-11, an estimated 12.6 per cent were living in poverty - both figures are below the national average. Pennsylvania reported 38,217 HIV/AIDS cases from the beginning of the epidemic to the end of 2008, and ranked 7th highest among US states in cumulative number of reported cases in 2008. The TB rate was 3.1 per 100,000 population, the 24th highest rate among US states. Obesity levels were above the national rate among adults: 28.6 per cent were obese and 65 per cent were overweight. (Source: CDC)

EDUCATION

Primary/Secondary Education
In 2009-10, there were 3,292 elementary and secondary schools in Pennsylvania. Enrolments numbered 1,786,103. There were 130,983 classroom teachers employed by public schools and the teacher/pupil ratio stood at one to13.64. Current expenditure for state education reached $25.346 billion in 2007-08, whilst revenues reached $24.79.billion.

Higher Education
According to National Center for Education Statistics (NCES), for the year 2010-11, there were 262 institutes of higher education in the state of Pennsylvania, 61 of which were publicly run. Enrolment for the year comprised around 339,142 male students and 438,981 women. 176,995 degrees/certificates were conferred, including 87,162 Bachelors degrees, 33,902 Masters and 9,135 Doctorates. (Source: National Center for Education Statistics)

COMMUNICATIONS AND MEDIA

Newspapers
Pennsylvania's newspapers include: Philadelphia Inquirer/Daily News, Pittsburgh Business Times, Pittsburgh Post-Gazette, and The Gettysburg Times.

Pennsylvania Newspaper Association, URL: http://www.pnpa.com
Pittsburgh Post Gazette, URL: http://www.post-gazette.com/
Gettysburg Times, URL: http://www.gettysburgtimes.com/

Business Journals
Philadelphia Business Journal, URL: http://www.bizjournals.com/philadelphia/

Broadcasting
The Pennsylvanian Public Television Network (PPTN), an independent agency of the state government, is responsible for the state's television stations as part of a system of program delivery and provides grants for member stations.
The Pennsylvanian Public Television Network (PPTN), URL: http://www.pptn.state.pa.us/
WHYY-TV, URL: http://www.whyy.org/
WQED-TV, URL: http://www.wqed.org/

ENVIRONMENT

Because of the electricity generating industry's reliance on coal, and the lack of environmental restrictions, emissions of sulphur dioxide, nitrogen oxides and carbon dioxide are high. In 2010 they were as follows: carbon dioxide emissions 122,829,611 metric tons (ranked 3rd in the US), sulfur dioxide 387,433 metric tons, and nitrogen oxide 135,887 metric tons.

In 2010, 18,744 alternative-fueled vehicles were in use (2.0 per cent of US total) and ethanol consumption amounted to 9,881 thousand barrels in 2010 (3.2 per cent of the US total). As of 2012, there was one ethanol plant with a capacity of 110 million gal/year. (Source: EIA)

RHODE ISLAND

Capital: Providence (Population, Census 2010: 178,042)

Head of State: Lincoln Chafee (Ind.) (Governor) (page 1402)

State Flag: A white background in the centre of which, and surrounded by 13 golden stars, appears a golden anchor, underneath which, on a blue ribbon, appears the word 'Hope' in gold capital letters; the whole flag is edged with a yellow fringe

CONSTITUTION AND GOVERNMENT

Constitution
Rhode Island was the last of the original 13 colonies to become a state, having joined on 29 May 1790. The Constitution of the State of Rhode Island and Providence Plantations was first adopted in 1842 and has since been amended 42 times. Under the Constitution five state offices were established: Governor, Lieutenant Governor, Attorney General, Secretary of State, and General Treasurer. Elected state officers serve terms of four years and elections are held for their positions every four even-numbered years.

Rhode Island sends two senators and two representatives to the US Congress in Washington, DC.

To view the state constitution, please visit: http://www.rilin.state.ri.us/RiConstitution/

Legislature
Rhode Island's legislature, the General Assembly, is bicameral, comprising a Senate and a House of Representatives. The General Assembly meets annually, usually from the first Tuesday of January.
Rhode Island General Assembly, State House, Providence, RI 02903, USA. URL: http://www.rilin.state.ri.us/

Upper House
In 2003 the number of state Senators was reduced from 50 to 38. The presiding officer is the Senate president, elected by the members of the Senate. Following the November 2012 elections the Democrats held 32 seats, the Republicans 5 and there was one independent.
Senate, State House, Providence, RI 02903, USA. Tel: +1 401 222 6655 (President of the Senate), URL: http://www.rilin.state.ri.us/senators/default.aspx

Lower House
With effect from 2003 the number of members of the House of Representatives was reduced from 100 to 75. Representatives serve terms of two years. The House of Representatives' leader is the Speaker, elected by the membership of the House. Following the November 2012 elections the Democrats held 69 seats and the Republicans 6.
House of Representatives, State House, Providence, RI 02903, USA. Tel: +1 401 222 2466 (Speaker), URL: http://www.rilin.state.ri.us/representatives/default.aspx

Elected Executive Branch Officials (as at April 2013)
Governor: Lincoln D. Chafee (I)
Lieutenant Governor: Elizabeth Roberts (D)
Secretary of State: A. Ralph Mollis (D)
Attorney General: Peter Kilmartin (D)
General Treasurer: Gina Raimondo (D)

General Assembly (as at April 2013)
President of the Senate: M. Teresa Paiva-Weed (D)
Senate Majority Leader: Dominick J. Ruggerio (D)
Senate Minority Leader: Dennis Algiere (R)
Speaker of the House: Gordon Fox (D)
House Majority Leader: Nicolas A. Mattiello (D)
House Minority Leader: Brian Newberry (R)

US Senators: Sheldon Whitehouse (D) (page 1536) and Jack Reed (D) (page 1501)

Ministries
Office of the Governor, 222 State House, Room 115, Providence, RI 02903, USA. Tel: +1 401 222 2080, fax: +1 401 222 8096, e-mail: governor@governor.ri.gov, URL: http://www.governor.ri.gov/
Office of the Lieutenant Governor, 116 State House, Providence , RI 02903, USA. Tel: +1 401 222 2371, fax: +1 401 222 2012, URL: http://www.ltgov.ri.gov
Office of the Attorney General, 150 South Main Street, Providence, RI 02903, USA. Tel: +1 401 274 4400, fax: +1 401 222 1331, URL: http://www.riag.ri.gov
Office of the General Treasurer, State House Room 102, Providence, RI 02903, USA. Tel: +1 401 222 2397, fax: +1 401 222 6140, URL: http://www.treasury.ri.gov/home.htm
Office of the Secretary of State, 82 Smith Street, Room 217, Providence, Rhode Island 02903, USA. Tel: +1 401 222 2357, fax: +1 401 222 1356, URL: http://sos.ri.gov/
Department of Administration, One Capitol Hill, Providence, RI 02908, USA. Tel: +1 401 222 2000, URL: http://www.info.ri.gov
Rhode Island Economic Development Corporation (RIEDC), One West Exchange Street, Providence, RI 02903, USA. Tel: +1 401 222 2601, fax: +1 401 222 2102, e-mail: riedc@riedc.com, URL: http://www.riedc.com/
Department of Education, 255 Westminster Street, Providence, Rhode Island 02903, USA. Tel: +1 401 222 4600, fax: +1 401 351 7874, URL: http://ridoe.net/
Department of Environmental Management, 235 Promenade Street, Providence, RI 02908-5767, USA. Tel: +1 401 222 6800, fax: +1 401 222 3162, URL: http://www.dem.ri.gov/
Department of Health, 3 Capitol Hill, Providence, RI 02908, USA. Tel: +1 401 222 2231, fax: +1 401 222 6548, URL: http://www.health.ri.gov
Department of Transport, Two Capitol Hill, Providence, RI 02903, USA. Tel: +1 401 222 2481, URL: http://www.dot.ri.gov

Political Parties
Rhode Island Democratic Party, URL: http://www.ridemocrats.org/
Rhode Island Republican Party, URL: http://www.rigop.org/

Elections
Elections for Rhode Island's executive officials (Governor, Lieutenant Governor, Secretary of State, State Treasurer, and Attorney General) last took place on 2 November 2010. The Independent former Senator, Lincoln Chafee was elected to the post of Governor.

The most recent legislative elections took place in November 2012. In the Senate, the Democrats increased their majority, (Democrats 32, Republicans 5, Independent 1). In the state House of Representatives, the Democrats increased their majority by three seats (Democrats 69, Republicans six).

UNITED STATES OF AMERICA

LEGAL SYSTEM

Rhode Island's legal system consists of six courts: the Supreme Court, Superior Court, District Court, Family Court, Workers' Compensation Court, and Administrative Adjudication Court (Traffic Court). A number of cities in the state also have municipal courts. The Supreme Court comprises the Chief Justice, four Associate Justices and a General Magistrate.

Rhode Island first abolished the death penalty in 1852. It was reintroduced in 1872, but it never was carried out before being abolished again in 1984.

Civil unions came into law in 2011.

Supreme Court, URL: http://www.courts.ri.gov/courts/supremecourt/default.aspx
Chief Justice: Paul Suttell
Superior Court, URL: http://www.courts.ri.gov/courts/superiorcourt/default.aspx
Presiding Justice: Alice B. Gibney

LOCAL GOVERNMENT

Rhode Island has no county government; instead it is divided into 39 municipalities (8 cities and 31 towns) each of which has its own government. Local government types include: mayor/administrator/manager and council, and town council.

AREA AND POPULATION

Area
Rhode Island is located in the north-east of the US, east of Connecticut, south and west of Massachusetts, with its southern border on the Atlantic coast. Rhode Island is 48 miles long and 37 miles wide, with a total area of 1,545.05 sq. miles (1,044.93 sq. miles of land and 500.12 sq. miles of water).

To view a map of the state, please consult:
http://www.lib.utexas.edu/maps/us_2001/new_england_ref_2001.pdf

Population
According to the 2010 Census , the 2010 state population was 1,052,567, down from the mid-2009 estimate of 1,053,209. In 2012, the population was estimated to be 1,050,292. Over the period 2000-10, the state population grew by 0.4 per cent. The population is expected to reach 1.15 million by 2030. Rhode Island's population density is estimated at 1,018.1 persons per sq. mile, and ranks second in the US (excluding DC). According to 2011 estimates, the largest cities are Providence, the capital (178,053), Warwick (82,361) and Cranston (80,392). The county with the greatest number of inhabitants, according to the 2010 census, is Providence County (626,667).

According to the 2010 Census, 5.5 per cent of the population is under 5 years, 21.3 per cent under 18 years and 14.4 per cent is aged over 65 years. Approximately 81.4 per cent of the population is white, and 5.7 per cent is black. Approximately 12.4 per cent of the population is of Hispanic or Latino origin.

Births, Marriages, Deaths
The US Census Bureau estimated that there were 11,177 births in 2010 and 9,579 deaths, giving a natural population increase of 1,598 people. Net emigration amounted to 3,076 people in 2009. The fertility rate was 52.1 per 1,000 women aged 15-44 years and the death rate was 910.1 per 100,000 population. The infant mortality rate in 2007 was 7.4 infant deaths per 1,000 live births. Marriages and divorces, according to provisional 2007 data, numbered 6,761 and 3,981, respectively, both figures showing a fall on previous years.

Public Holidays
In addition to the national holidays, the people of Rhode Island celebrate Victory Day (V.J. Day) on the second Monday in August.

EMPLOYMENT

Rhode Island's total civilian labour force in December 2012 was 566,200, of which 508,400 were in employment and 57,800 were unemployed. The unemployment rate was 10.2 per cent, one of the highest in the US. (Source: US Bureau of Labour Statistics)

The following table shows December 2012 non-farm wage and salary employment according to industry (preliminary figures):

Industry	No. of Employed	12-month change (%)
Logging and mining*	200	0.0
Construction	15,300	-6.7
Manufacturing	41,200	1.5
Trade, transport and utilities	71,600	-0.3
Information*	10,300	-1.9
Financial activities	31,100	0.3
Professional and business services	55,700	2.6
Educational and health services	103,700	0.2
Leisure and hospitality	49,800	2.5
Government	58,900	-18
TOTAL	458,800	0.2

*Not seasonally adjusted
Source: US Bureau of Labor Statistics

BANKING AND FINANCE

GDP/GNP, Inflation, National Debt
Rhode Island's total Gross Domestic Product (GDP) (current dollars) rose from $48,840 million in 2010 to $50.1 billion, ranking it 45th in the US. Real state GDP rose by 2.8 per cent in 2010 and by 0.7 per cent in 2011. Rhode Island was ranked 45th in the US for its 2010 GDP. State GDP according to industry (in millions of current dollars) is shown on the following table:

Industry	2009	2010	2011
Agriculture, forestry and fishing	74	69	(D)
Mining	30	20	(D)
Utilities	765	778	749
Construction	1,990	1,867	1,875
Manufacturing	3,453	3,737	3,946
Wholesale Trade	2,241	2,343	2,433
Retail Trade	2,565	2,713	2,673
Transport and warehousing	719	708	752
Information	2,016	2,027	2,194
Finance and insurance	6,290	6,199	6,310
Real estate	7,415	7,032	6,936
Educational services	1,317	1,357	1,365
Health care & social assistance	4,816	5,033	5,165
Other non-government services	7,832	8,361	8,751
Government	6,216	6,597	6,854
TOTAL	47,738	48,840	50,091

Source: Bureau of Economic Analysis, Feb. 2013

The state's average annual per capita income was an estimated $43,875 in 2011. Per capita real GDP rose to $41,532 in 2011, compared to the US average of $42,070.

The Consumer Price Index (CPI) (all areas) for the north-east urban area, including Rhode Island, rose from 225.1 in 2010 to 232.9 in 2012 (1982-84 = 100). (Source: Bureau of Labor Statistics)

Balance of Payments / Imports and Exports
Total Rhode Island imports amounted to $5,485 million in 2009, down 26.5 per cent from the 2008 total of $7,452 million. Imports rose by 31.3 per cent in 2010 to $7,202 million, and by 20.5 per cent in 2011 to $8,579 million, representing 0.4 per cent of the US total. Major imports include vehicle engine parts, lightoils and jewellery. Suppliers (2011) were Germany (34.5 per cent), Mexico (!2.4 per cent), China (12.3 per cent), Canada and the UK. Total merchandise exports fell from $1,974 million in 2008 to $1,496 million in 2009, a fall of 24.2 per cent. Exports rose by 30.3 per cent in 2010 to $1,949 million, and by 17.1 per cent in 2011 to $2,282 million, representing 0.2 per cent of the US total. The top five export trading partners in 2011, according to revenue, are shown on the following table.

Country	2010 ($m)	2011 ($m)	+/-% 2010-11
Canada	591	648	9/6
Germany	118	234	98.2
Mexico	136	158	16.1
Turkey	86	134	56.5
Egypt	55	87	57.9

Source: US Census Bureau, Foreign Trade Division

The following table shows the top five products in 2010 according to export revenue:

Product	Export Revenue ($m)
Waste & scrap gold	192
Ferrous waste and scrap N.E.S.O.I	160
Waste & scrap of precious metal	157
Gold compounds	86
Silver powder	74

Source: US Census Bureau, Foreign Trade Division

Chambers of Commerce and Trade Organisations
Greater Providence Chamber of Commerce, URL: http://www.provchamber.com/
Rhode Island Economic Development Corporation (RIEDC), URL: http://www.riedc.com/
Newport County Chamber of Commerce, URL: http://www.newportchamber.com/

MANUFACTURING, MINING AND SERVICES

Primary and Extractive Industries
The mining industry contributed an estimated $20 million towards Rhode Island's 2011 Gross Domestic Product (down from $31 million in 2007).

Rhode Island has little in the way of petroleum infrastructure other than a number of ports for the supply of heating oil. The state receives oil supplies from a single pipeline which runs from Providence to Springfield, Massachusetts. Oil consumption in 2010 fell slightly to 17.5 million barrels, most of it in the form of motor gasoline (8.9 million barrels).

Rhode Island has no natural gas industry and relies entirely on imports. Consumption rose from 94,122 million cu ft in 2010 to 100,467 million cu ft in 2011. Electricity generators and the residential sector are the largest natural gas consumers. (Source: EIA)

Energy

Total energy production was 3 trillion Btu in 2010, one of the lowest state totals in the US. Rhode Island's total energy consumption was 197 trillion Btu in 2010 and was ranked 51st in the US for per capita energy consumption (187 million Btu in 2010).

Rhode Island is a net importer of electricity with natural gas as its primary generating fuel. Net summer capacity in 2010 was 1,782 MW (0.2 per cent of US total) and total net monthly (Oct. 2012) generation was 755,000 MWh, of which 742,000 MWh was natural gas-fired. Renewables (other than hydroelectric) generated 11,000 MWh. The major utility plants are Rhode Island State Energy Partners (gas), Manchester Street (gas), Tiverton Power Plant (gas), Indeck North Smithfield Energy, and Ocean State Power II (gas).

In 2005, Rhode Island adopted a renewable portfolio standard that required State electricity retailers to obtain at least 3 per cent of State-sold electricity from renewable sources by the end of 2006. In 2008, just over 2 per cent of Rhode Island's electricity was generated with renewable sources, including hydroelectric power, municipal solid waste, and landfill gas. (Source: EIA)

Manufacturing

Manufacturing is Rhode Island's third largest contributor to GDP, earning an estimated $3,946 million in 2011 (up from $3,737 million in 2010). The top sectors in 2010 were fabricated metal manufacturing ($384 million) and electronic and computer products ($366 million). Rhode Island is the world's leading costume-jewelry center and the home of the leading silversmiths in the United States. Major manufacturing sectors include toys, on-line lottery systems, computer power supplies and ships and boats, metrology and medical equipment and chemical and biotech products.

Service Industries

The services industry is the state's largest contributor to GDP. The top sectors in 2011 were real estate ($6,936 million), finance and insurance ($6,310 million), health care and social assistance ($5,165 million) and professional and technical services ($2,836 million).

Tourism

Rhode Island is a major tourist destination; its location on the Atlantic coast offers opportunities for sailing and fishing. There are more than 85 marinas, 28 yacht clubs, almost 100 public launch sites, 50 charter and pleasure boats, nine sailing schools and nearly 30 major boating harbours. Over 15 million people visit the state each year. The accommodation and food sector contributed an estimated $1,615 million towards the 2011 GDP, whilst the arts, entertainment and recreation sector contributed $411 million.
Rhode Island Tourism Division, URL: http://visitrhodeisland.com/index_f.html

Agriculture

The agriculture, forestry and fishing industry contributed $69 million towards Rhode Island's 2010 GDP. In 2010 the major sector was forestry, fishing and related activities ($41 million), followed by farming ($28 million). (Source: BEA)

According to the US Dept. of Agriculture, Rhode Island's farms numbered 1,220 in 2010, and farmland covered around 70,000 acres. The average size of a farm has fallen from 71 acres in 2006 to around 57 acres in 2010. Rhode Island's greenhouse and nursery industry dominated the state's agricultural cash receipts in 2007, comprising $55.6 million of the total $65.9 million generated. Major crops are potatoes, hay, corn, apples, and peaches. The Rhode Island Red chicken was bred in the state. As of 1 Jan. 2011, there were 4,900 cattle and calves and 1,800 hogs & pigs.

Rhode Island's fishing industry is an important source of revenue, the most significant catch being that of lobster and quahog. Squid, sea mussel and rock crab are also caught, as are flounder, mackerel and cod.

COMMUNICATIONS AND TRANSPORT

National Airlines

T.F. Green International Airport is served by seven major airlines: Continental, American, Northwest, Delta, United, Southwest and US Air.

International Airports

The newly-expanded T.F. Green International Airport in Providence provides 15 airline gates, 2 commuter gates and parking for 4,000 vehicles. The airport is served by 11 airlines flying to over 20 cities.
T.F. Green International Airport, URL: http://www.pvd-ri.com/

Railways

AMTRAK provides a transcontinental passenger service along the New York-Boston line. The upgraded service now covers the Providence to New York route in two hours. The Providence and Worcester Railroad provides a daily service to Rhode Island's industrial sites. P&W operates a regional freight service between Massachusetts, Rhode Island, Connecticut and New York. It currently has 515 miles of track with the right to operate along the Northeast Corridor between New Haven, Connecticut and the Massachusetts/Rhode island border.
Massachusetts Bay Transportation Authority Information (MBTA), URL: http://www.mbta.com/

Roads

Road access to regional and national areas is provided along Interstate routes I-95, I-195 and I-295. Rhode Island truckers deliver to all states, as well as Mexico and most Canadian Provinces. Same-day deliveries are available to Boston and New York.

Rhode Island Public Transit Authority (RIPTA), URL: http://www.ripta.com/

Waterways
Block Island Ferry, URL: http://www.blockislandferry.com/

Ports and Harbours
Port terminals are located in Providence, East Providence and North Kingstown (Quonset/Davisville). The Quonset/Davisville port at Narragansett Bay has over 10 miles of commercial waterfront.

HEALTH

Rhode Island's healthcare facilities include 14 acute general care hospitals with 5,600 beds; 110 nursing and personal care home facilities with 9,700 beds; and 90 rescue and ambulance squads. The National Center for Health Statistics estimated that there were 37.2 doctors (including osteopaths) per 10,000 people in 2009, higher than the US average of 27.4. In 2008, there were 573 dentists (5.5 per 10,000 population). The state's major hospitals include Lifespan, St. Joseph, Roger Williams, and Care New England. In 2009, there were 2.4 community hospital beds per 1,000 resident population and in 2010, 86 nursing homes with 8,802 beds.

It was estimated that some 11.6 per cent of Rhode Island's adult population had no health-care cover in 2007-09, and, in 2007-11, an estimated 12.8 per cent were living in poverty, both rates comfortably below the national average. Rhode Island reported 2,846 HIV/AIDS cases from the beginning of the epidemic to the end of 2008, and ranked 37th in cumulative number of reported cases over 2008. The TB rate was 3.4 per 100,000 population, the 23rd highest rate among the US states. The state has comparatively low rates of obesity (25.5 per cent) and cigarette smoking, but high levels of adult drinking and chronic liver disease mortality. An estimated 62.9 per cent of the population were considered overweight. (Source: Center of Disease Control)

EDUCATION

Primary/Secondary Education
In 2008-09, enrolment in Rhode Island's 331 public schools totaled 145,118 according to figures published by the National Education Association. There were 11,365 teachers and a teacher/pupil ratio of one to 12.77, one of the lowest in the US. Over the academic year 2007-08, total current expenditure for state education reached $2.1 billion, whilst revenues reached $2.2 billion.

Higher Education
Rhode Island has 13 institutions of higher learning, three public, including Brown University, the University of Rhode Island, the Rhode Island School of Design and Bryant College. In 2010-11, 47, 342 women and 37,331 men enrolled. 17,786 degrees/certificates were conferred, 10,647 of which were Bachelor degrees, 2,396 were Masters and 746 were Doctorates. (Source: NCES)

COMMUNICATIONS AND MEDIA

Newspapers
Major newspapers include: Brown Daily Herald (URL: http://www.browndailyherald.com/), Jamestown Press, Narragansett Times, Newport Daily News, North Providence News, and Providence Business News.
The Providence Journal, URL: http://www.projo.com/

Business Journals
Providence Business News, URL: http://www.pbn.com/

Broadcasting
The Public Telecommunications Authority owns and holds the licence for Rhode Island's public television station WSBE-TV/Channel 36.
Public Telecommunications Authority, URL: http://www.wsbe.org

ENVIRONMENT

Rhode Island's lack of coal-fired electricity generating plants means that its emissions of sulphur dioxide, nitrogen oxides and carbon dioxides are relatively low. However in 2010 electricity industry emissions of carbon dioxide increased from 3,181,021 metric tons in 2009 to 3,217,071 metric tons, although it remained ranked 48th in the US. However, Rhode Island's relatively small area means that it is ranked 7th in the US for carbon dioxide emissions per square mile. Emissions of sulfur dioxide were 49 metric tons and emissions of nitrogen oxide were 2,919 metric tons.

Rhode Island is a member of the Ozone Transport Commission (OTC) which, along with 12 other US states, is working towards nitrogen oxide reductions. A 2007 study stated that 15 per cent of Rhode Island's electricity needs could be met by offshore wind energy.

In 2010, 2,931 alternative-fueled vehicles were in use and, in 2010, ethanol consumption amounted to 1,418 thousand barrels. (Source: EIA)

SOUTH CAROLINA

Capital: Columbia (Population, Census 2010: 129,272)

Head of State: Nikki Haley (R) Governor (page 1436)

State Flag: A blue background in the centre of which is a palmetto tree and in the top left hand corner of which is a white crescent moon.

CONSTITUTION AND GOVERNMENT

Constitution

South Carolina was one of the original 13 states of the Union. On 23 May 1788 South Carolina became the eighth state to ratify the Federal Constitution. It was the first of the Southern states to secede from the Union over the issue of slavery (20 December 1860). The Civil War began the following April.

South Carolina's Constitution specifies that the governor is head of the executive branch of government, elected by the voters of the state for no more than two successive terms of four years each. The governor is assisted by eight other elected executive branch officials: the lieutenant governor, secretary of state, state treasurer, attorney general, comptroller general, state superintendent of education, commissioner of agriculture, and adjutant general. All are elected by the people for four-year terms.

South Carolina elects two Senators and six Representatives to the US Congress in Washington, DC. Senators are elected for six years and Representatives for two years. To view the state constitution, please visit: http://www.scstatehouse.net/scconstitution/scconst.htm

Legislature

The General Assembly consists of the Senate and the House of Representatives.

Upper House

The Senate has 46 members who are elected from 46 single-member districts for four years. The lieutenant governor also serves as president of the Senate. Following the 2012 elections, the Senate was composed of 28 Republicans and 18 Democrats.
Senate, State House, Post Office Box 142, Columbia, SC 29202-0142, USA. Tel: +1 803 212 6200 (Clerk of the Senate),
URL: http://www.scstatehouse.gov/senate.php

Lower House

The House of Representatives has 124 members elected from 124 single-member districts for two years. Following the November 2012 elections the House consisted of 76 Republicans and 46 Democrats.
House of Representatives, Post Office Box 11867, Columbia, SC 29211-1867, USA. URL: http://www.scstatehouse.gov/

Elected Executive Branch Officials (as at April 2013)
Governor: Nikki Haley (R) (page 1436)
Lieutenant Governor: Glenn McConnell (R)
Secretary of State: Mark Hammond (R)
State Treasurer: Curtis M. Loftis (R)
Attorney General: Alan Wilson (R)
Comptroller General: Richard Eckstrom (R)
State Superintendent of Education: Dr Mick Zais (R)
Adjutant General: Major General Robert E. Livingson Jr
Commissioner of Agriculture: Hugh E. Weathers (R)

Legislature (as at April 2013)
President of the Senate: Lt. Gov. Glenn F. McConnell (R)
President Pro Tem of the Senate: John E. Courson (R)
Speaker of the House: Robert W. Harrell (R)
House Majority Leader: Bruce W. Bannister (R)
House Minority Leader: J. Todd Rutherford (D)

US Senators: Tim Scott (R) (page 1510) and Lindsey O. Graham (R) (page 1432)

Ministries Office of the Governor, PO Box 12267, Columbia, SC 29211, USA. Tel: +1 803 734 2100, fax: +1 803 734 5167, URL: http://www.governor.sc.gov
Office of the Lieutenant Governor, State House, 1st Floor, Post Office Box 142, Columbia, SC 29202, USA. Tel: +1 803 734 2080, fax: +1 803 734 2082, URL: http://ltgov.sc.gov/Pages/default.aspx
Office of the Attorney General, Rembert Dennis Building, 1000 Assembly Street, Room 519, Columbia, SC 29201 (Post Office Box 11549, Columbia, SC 29211), USA. Tel: +1 803 734 3970, fax: +1 803 734 4323, URL: http://www.scag.gov/
Office of the Commissioner of Agriculture, PO Box 11280, 1200 Senate Street, Columbia, SC 29211, USA. Tel: +1 803 734 2210, fax: +1 803 734 2192, URL: http://www.agriculture.sc.gov
Office of the Comptroller General, 1200 Senate Street, 305 Wade Hampton Office Building, Columbia, SC 29201 (Post Office Box 11228, Columbia, South Carolina 29211), USA. Tel: +1 803 734 2121, fax: +1 803 734 2064, URL: http://www.cg.sc.gov/
Office of the Secretary of State, Edgar Brown Building, 1205 Pendleton Street Suite 525, Columbia, SC 29201 (PO Box 11350, Columbia, SC 29211), USA. Tel: +1 803 734 2170, URL: http://www.scsos.com/
Office of the State Superintendent of Education, Rutledge Building, 1429 Senate Street, Columbia, South Carolina 29201, USA. Tel: +1 803 734 8500, fax: +1 803 734 3389, URL: http://www.ed.sc.gov/

Office of the State Treasurer, Post Office Box 11778, Columbia, South Carolina 29211, USA. Tel: +1 803 734 2101, URL: http://www.treasurer.sc.gov
Department of Commerce, 1201 Main Street, Suite 1600, Columbia, SC 29201-3200 (PO Box 927, Columbia, SC 29202-0927), USA. Tel: +1 803 737 0400, fax: +1 803 737 0418, URL: http://sccommerce.com
Department of Health and Environmental Control, 2600 Bull Street, Columbia, SC 29201, USA. Tel: +1 803 898 3432, URL: http://www.scdhec.gov/
Department of Health and Human Services, 1801 Main Street, PO Box 8206, Columbia, SC 29202-8206, USA. Tel: +1 803 898 2500, URL: http://www.scdhhs.gov/
Department of Natural Resources, Rembert C. Dennis Building, 1000 Assembly Street, Columbia, SC 29201, USA. Tel: +1 803 734 3888, fax: +1 803 734 6310, URL: http://www.dnr.sc.gov/
Department of Parks, Recreation and Tourism, 1205 Pendleton Street, Room 505 Columbia, SC 29201, USA. Tel: +1 803 734 1700, URL: http://www.scprt.com/
Department of Transportation, 955 Park Street, PO Box 191, Columbia, SC 29202-0191, USA. Tel: +1 803 737 2314, URL: http://www.dot.state.sc.us/

Political Parties
South Carolina Democratic Party, URL: http://www.scdp.org/
South Carolina Republican Party, URL: http://www.scgop.com/

Elections
The most recent elections for South Carolina's constitutional officers (Governor, Lieutenant Governor, Secretary of State, State Treasurer, Attorney General, Comptroller General, State Superintendent of Education, Adjutant General, Commissioner of Agriculture) took place in November 2010. The incumbent Governor, Republican Mark Sanford, was ineligible for re-election and Republican Nikki Haley won the gubanatorial election becoming the first woman and the first Indian-american to become Governor of South Carolina.

Legislative elections were held in November 2012. In the Senate, the Republicans remained the majority party (Republicans 28, Democrats 18). Following the November 2012 elections the House of Representatives consisted of 76 Republicans, 46 Democrats and one vacancy.

LEGAL SYSTEM

The Supreme Court consists of the Chief Justice and four Associate Justices. All are elected by the General Assembly for terms of ten years. The Court of Appeals comprises a Chief Judge and eight Associate Judges, all of whom are elected for staggered terms of six years.

South Carolina has the death penalty. Since 1976, there have been 43 executions, the most recent in 2011. According to the DPIC there the murder rate was 6.1 per 100,000 population. As of January 2013 there were 54 inmates on death row.

Supreme Court, URL: http://www.judicial.state.sc.us/supreme/index.cfm
Chief Justice: Jean Hoefer Toal
Justice: Costa Pleicones, Donald Beatty, John Kittredge, Kaye Hearn
Court of Appeals, URL: http://www.judicial.state.sc.us/appeals/index.cfm
Chief Judge: John Cannon Few

LOCAL GOVERNMENT

South Carolina has 46 county governments and 268 sub-county general purpose governments. Its sub-county governments are all municipal, consisting of cities and towns, and are administered by one of three government types: the mayor-council, the mayor, or the council-manager government.

South Carolina Association of Counties, URL: http://www.sccounties.org/

AREA AND POPULATION

Area
South Carolina is located on the east coast of the US, north-east of Georgia, and south of North Carolina. Its total area is 32,020.20 sq. miles, of which 30,109.47 sq. miles is land and 1,910.73 sq. miles is water.

To view a map of South Carolina, please consult:
http://www.lib.utexas.edu/maps/us_2001/south_carolina_ref_2001.pdf

Population
According to the 2010 Census, the 2010 state population was 4,625,364, up from the mid-2009 estimate of 4,561,242. In 2012, the population was estimated to be 4,723,723. Over the period 2000 to 2010, the state population grew by 15.3 per cent and is expected to reach 5.15 million by 2030. The population density is 153.9 people per sq. mile. The county with the greatest number of inhabitants is Greenville, with a population of 451,225 in 2010. The capital, Columbia, is the largest city in South Carolina, with an estimated population of 130,591 in 2011.

According to the 2010 Census, 6.5 per cent of the population is under 5 years, 23.4 per cent under 18 years and 13.7 per cent is aged over 65 years. Approximately 66.2 per cent of the population is white, and 27.9 per cent is black. Approximately 5.1 per cent of the population is of Hispanic or Latino origin.

Births, Marriages, Deaths
The US Census Bureau estimated that there were 58,342 births in 2010 and 41,614 deaths, giving a natural population increase of 16,728 people. Net immigration (mainly from other parts of the US) totalled 38,745 new residents in 2009. The fertility rate was 62.8 per 1,000 women aged 15-44 years and the death rate was 899.7 per 100,000 population. The infant mortality rate in 2007 was 8.6 infant deaths per 1,000 live births. Marriages and divorces in 2007 were estimated at 31,378 and 14,357 respectively.

EMPLOYMENT

South Carolina's estimated total civilian labour force in December 2012 was 2,149,600, of which 1,969,600 were employed and 180,000 were unemployed. The unemployment rate was 8.4 per cent, down from 9.5 per cent in 2011, but still higher than the national average of 7.8 per cent. (Source: US Bureau of Labor Statistics)

The following table shows December 2011 non-farm wage and salary employment (seasonally adjusted) according to industry (provisional figures):

Industry	No. of Jobs	12-month change (%)
Logging and mining*	3,600	-5.3
Construction	75,40	0.8
Manufacturing	226,100	2.2
Trade, transportation, and utilities	358,500	1.4
Information	27,400	3.8
Financial activities	99,500	2.7
Professional and business services	228,500	0.2
Educational and health services	227,000	4.4
Leisure and hospitality	219,500	3.3
Other services	69,900	0.4
Government	343,700	2.3
TOTAL	1,867,900	1.9

*Not seasonally adjusted
Source: Bureau of Labor Statistics

BANKING AND FINANCE

GDP/GNP, Inflation, National Debt
South Carolina's Gross Domestic Product (current dollars) rose from an estimated $160,374 million in 2010 to $165.8 billion in 2011. State real GDP rose by 1.2 per cent in 2011 and was ranked 26th in the US for its 2011 Gross Domestic Product.

Current dollar Gross Domestic Product according to industry is shown on the following table (millions of current dollars):

Industry	2009	2010	2011
Agriculture, Forestry, Hunting and Fishing	1,156	1,176	1,223
Mining	231	193	226
Utilities	4,491	4,779	4,520
Construction	7,112	6,686	6,592
Manufacturing	23,777	24,084	26,449
Wholesale Trade	8,361	8,583	9,017
Retail Trade	11,804	12,357	12,625
Transport and warehousing	3,423	3,515	3,614
Information	4,247	4,183	4,244
Finance and insurance	8,322	8,826	8,756
Real estate	18,096	16,925	16,705
Educational services	1,105	1,148	1,195
Health care & social assistance	10,154	10,936	11,327
Other non-government services	26,035	28,206	30,114
Government	28,329	28,777	29,181
TOTAL	156,644	160,374	165,785

Source: Bureau of Economic Analysis, Feb. 2013

The state's average annual per capita income was an estimated $33,380 in 2011. Per capita real GDP fell to $30,060 in 2011, below the national average of $42,070.

The annual Consumer Price Index (CPI) for the south urban area (all items) rose from 218.6 in 2011 to 223.4 in 2012 (1982-84 = 100). (Source: Bureau of Labor Statistics)

Balance of Payments / Imports and Exports
Total South Carolina imports amounted to $20,831 million in 2009, down 28.6 per cent from the 2008 total of $29,183 million. Imports rose by 23.1 per cent to $25,644 million in 2010, and by 31.8 per cent in 2011 to $33,837 million in 2011, representing 1.5 per cent of the total. The top import was uranium. Major import suppliers (2011) included Germany (18.3 per cent), China (16.9 per cent), Canada (7.7 per cent), Mexico and Japan. Merchandise export revenue fell by 16.9 per cent, from $19,853 million in 2008 to $16,488 million in 2009. Export revenue rose by 23.3 per cent in 2010 to $20,329 million and by 21.5 per cent in 2011 to $24,697 million. Merchandise export revenue in 2010-11, according to the top five international destinations, is shown on the following table:

Destination	2010 ($m)	2011 ($m)	+/-% 2010-11
Germany	2,944	3,999	35.8
Canada	3,187	3,756	17.9
- continued			
China	2,157	3,001	39.1
Mexico	1,319	1,761	33.5
United Kingdom	1,124	1,413	25.6

Source: US Census Bureau, Foreign Trade Division

The top five export products in 2010, according to export revenue, are shown on the following table:

Product	Export Revenue ($m)
Passenger vehicles spark-ignitition internal combustion reciprocating piston, 1,500-3,000cc	3,690
Gas turbines of a power exceeding 5,000 KW	739
Pass. veh. com-ig. int. comb. eng. over 2,500	657
New pneumatic tyres of rubber, for buses or trucks	638
Gas turbine parts nesoi	515

Source: US Census Bureau, Foreign Trade Division

Chambers of Commerce and Trade Organisations
South Carolina Chamber of Commerce, URL: http://www.sccc.org/
Central Carolina Economic Development Alliance, URL: http://www.cceda.org/

MANUFACTURING, MINING AND SERVICES

Primary and Extractive Industries
Minerals extracted include: vermiculite, kaolin, brick clay, gravel, limestone, peat, sericite, gold, granite, manganese, schist, sand and shale. The mining industry's contribution to Gross Domestic Product in 2011 was an estimated $226 million (down from $193 million in 2010).

South Carolina has no crude oil reserves or oil production industry. Oil consumption in 2009 fell to 103.7 million barrels, 65.6 million barrels of which was motor gasoline and 19 million barrels distillate fuel.

No supplies of natural gas exist in the state and consequently all natural gas requirements are imported. Over a quarter of households use natural gas as their main energy source for home heating, but winters are generally mild and demand is relatively low. Consumption rose from 190,542 million cu ft in 2009 to 219,809 million cu ft in 2010. (Source: EIA)

Energy
South Carolina's total energy production amounted to 652 trillion Btu in 2010 (0.9 per cent of US total). South Carolina's total energy consumption amounted to 1,662 trillion Btu in 2010 (1.7 per cent of US total), whilst its per capita energy consumption ranks it 18th in the US (358 million Btu in 2010).

South Carolina is a net exporter of electricity. Net summer capability in 2010 was 23,982 MW (2.3 per cent of US total) and total net monthly (Oct. 2012) generation was 7,770 thousand MWh (2.5 per cent of US total), of which nuclear 4,381 thousand MWh, coal-fired 1,864 thousand MWh and natural gas-fired 1,338 thousand MWh. Hydroelectric power generated 102,000 MWh and other renewables 141,000 MWh.

The state has four nuclear power plants: Catawba, HB Robinson, Oconee, and Virgil C. Summer. Catawba is a two-unit light water reactor located on a 391-acre peninsula. The three-unit Oconee plant is located near Greenville, and the single-unit HB Robinson plant is located on a 5,000-acre site near Hartsville. The Virgil C. Summer plant is near Jenkinsville, Fairfield County.

In 2011, renewable energy resources accounted for 4.0 per cent of the State's net electricity gneration. It aims to reduce energy use by 20 per cent from 2000 levels by 2020. (Source: EIA)

Manufacturing
Manufacturing is South Carolina's second largest contributor to GDP accounting for an estimated $26,499 million in 2011 (up from $24,084 million in 2010). The top sectors in 2010 were paper manufacturing ($2,432 million), machinery manufacturing ($3,119 million) and chemical products ($3,163 million).

Service Industries
South Carolina's services industry is the largest contributor to GDP. The top sectors in 2011 were real estate ($16,705 million), health care and social assistance ($11,327 million), professional and technical services ($9,277 million) and finance and insurance ($8,756 million).

South Carolina's per capita tax burden is ranked the sixth lowest in the States and, with a five per cent corporation income tax rate, is the lowest in the south-east. In addition, it provides tax credits for new jobs, for corporate headquarters facilities, for providing child care benefits and for investing in infrastructure.

Tourism
About 32 million tourists visit South Carolina a year. The accommodation and food services sector of the services industry contributed $6,294 million towards GDP in 2011, whilst the arts, entertainment and recreation sector earned an estimated $1,111 million, both figures showing increases on the previous year.
Department of Parks, Recreation and Tourism, URL: http://www.discoversouthcarolina.com/

Agriculture

Agriculture, forestry and fishing contributed an estimated $1,223 million towards the GDP in 2011. In 2010, the top sector was farming ($832 million), followed by forestry and fishing and related activities ($344 million). (Source: BEA)

According to the US Dept. of Agriculture, South Carolina had a total of 27,000 farms in 2010, and farmland covered some 4,900,000 acres. The average size of a farm in South Carolina was 181 acres in 2010. South Carolina's major crops are tobacco, cotton and soybeans. Its major livestock products are cattle and calves, beef cows, hogs and pigs, and sheep and lambs. In 2007, the total agricultural product revenue was $2.3 billion, of which $1.5 billion was earned through livestock and poultry sales. As of 1 Jan. 2011, there were 385,000 cattle & calves and 230,000 hogs & pigs. (Source: National Agricultural Statistics Service)

COMMUNICATIONS AND TRANSPORT

National Airlines

National airlines serving South Carolina's international airports include: Air South, ASA, Delta, Midway Connection, Myrtle Beach Jet Express, United Express and US Air.

International Airports

Charleston International Airport, URL: http://www.chs-airport.com/airlineinfo.htm
Myrtle Beach International Airport, URL: http://www.myrtlebeachairport.org/

Ports

The Port of Charleston is one of the busiest container ports along the Southeast and Gulf coasts. The Charleston Customs district ranks as the nation's sixth largest in dollar value of international shipments, with cargo valued at more than $53 billion annually. In 2006, the South Carolina State Ports Authority (SPA) served 2,064 ships and barges through terminals in Charleston, Georgetown and Port Royal. Shippers in two dozen US states use Charleston to access foreign customers and suppliers. Top commodities transported through the port include agricultural products, consumer goods, machinery, metals, vehicles, chemicals and clay products.
South Carolina State Ports Authority, URL: http://www.scspa.com

HEALTH

The National Center for Health Statistics estimated that there were 22.8 doctors (including osteopaths) per 10,000 population in 2009, below the US average of 27.4. In 2008, there were an estimated 2,065 dentists (4.6 per 10,000 population). In 2009, there were 2.7 community hospital beds per 1,000 residents, and, in 2010, there were 184 nursing homes, with 19,474 beds.

It was estimated that around 16.4 per cent of the state population had no health care cover in 2007-09, and that according to the US Census Bureau some 17 per cent were living in poverty in 2007- 11, both rates being well above the US average.

South Carolina reported 15,176 HIV/AIDS cases from the beginning of the epidemic to the end of 2008, and ranked 17th in cumulative number of reported cases in 2008. The TB rate was 4.2 per 100,000 population, the 12th highest rate among the US states. Adult obesity levels were higher than the national average, at 31.5 per cent, and the rate of overweight

youth was also above the US average. An estimated 66.9 per cent of adults were classified as being overweight. Diabetes rates were also above the national average. (Source: Center for Disease Control)

EDUCATION

Primary/Secondary Education

According to figures published by the National Center for Education Statistics for the year 2009-10, South Carolina had 723,143 students enrolled in their 1,2309 elementary and secondary schools. There were 46,979 classroom teachers and the ratio of teachers to students was one to 15.39, below the national average of 15.3.

In the academic year 2007-08, total revenues from education reached $7.7 billion whilst current expenditure on state education was $6.453 billion.

Higher Education

South Carolina has some 75 colleges and universities, 33 public. Universities include the University of South Carolina, Clemson University, and the Medical University of South Carolina. There were some 99,025 male students enrolled for the year 2010-11, and 147,642 women students. In the same year, 45,692 degrees/certificates were conferred, including 21,095 Bachelors, 5,676 Masters and 1,496 Doctorates. (Source: NCES)

COMMUNICATIONS AND MEDIA

Newspapers

Major newspapers in South Carolina include: The Post and Courier, Charleston; The State, Columbia; Florence Morning News, Florence; The Greenville News, Greenville; The Index-Journal, Greenville; The Sun News, Myrtle Beach.
South Carolina Press Association, URL: http://www.scpress.org/main.html
The Post and Courier, URL: http://www.charleston.net/

Broadcasting

South Carolina has some 29 television stations, four in Augusta, three in Charleston, five in Charlotte, three in Columbia, two in Florence, and five in Greenville-Spartanburg. Columbia's television stations include WIS-TV, WOLO-TV and WLTX-TV.

ENVIRONMENT

South Carolina's 2008 electricity generating industry emissions of carbon dioxide rose to 42,490,369 metric tons and were ranked 23rd in the US. South Carolina has adopted energy standards for public buildings and other energy-reduction goals aimed at lowering energy use by 20 per cent from 2000 levels by mid-2020.

Emissions from the electric power industry in 2010 were as follows: carbon dioxide 41,364,022 metric tons (ranked 23rd in the US), sulfur dioxide 105,821 metric tons, and nitrogen oxide 29,832 metric tons.

In 2010, there were 17,577 alternative-fueled vehicles in use. In 2011, ethanol consumption amounted to 6,077 thousand barrels (2.0 per cent of US total). (Source: EIA)

SOUTH DAKOTA

Capital: Pierre (Population, Census 2010: 13,646)

Head of State: Dennis Daugaard (R) (Governor) (page 1412)

State Flag: A background of sky blue in the centre of which appears the state seal surrounded by a golden, serrated sun, around which appear the words 'South Dakota, The Mount Rushmore State'.

CONSTITUTION AND GOVERNMENT

Constitution

South Dakota entered the Union on 2 November 1889. The Constitution gives the Governor executive power assisted by nine elected officers: lieutenant governor, attorney general, secretary of state, state auditor, state treasurer, commissioner of school and public lands, and three commissioners of public utilities. All elected officers other than the public utilities commissioners serve terms of four years. The public utilities commissioners serve staggered terms of six years.

South Dakota elects two Senators (currently two Democrat) and one At-Large Representative (at present Republican) to the US Congress in Washington, DC. South Dakota consists of 35 legislative districts. According to the terms of the Constitution, the district boundaries are re-drawn every ten years to take account of changes in the population.

To view the state constitution, please visit: http://legis.state.sd.us/statutes/index.aspx

Legislature

South Dakota's legislature consists of the Senate and the House of Representatives. The legislature meets annually on the second Tuesday in January, and at the Governor's request. Sessions last for 40 days in odd-numbered years and 35 days in even-numbered years.

Legislative Research Council, Capitol Building, 3rd Floor, 500 East Capitol Avenue, Pierre, SD 57501-5070, USA. Tel: +1 605 773 3251, fax: +1 605 773 4576, URL: http://legis.state.sd.us/

Upper House

The Senate has 35 members, one for each legislative district, who are elected for two years. Following the November 2012 elections the Senate was composed of 28 Republicans and 7 Democrats.

Lower House

The House of Representatives has 70 members, two from each legislative district, who are also elected for two years. Following the November 2012 elections the House was composed of 53 Republicans & 17 Democrats.

South Dakota's 50,000 American Indians are represented by nine Tribal Governments.

Elected Executive Branch Officials (as at April 2013)
Governor: Dennis Daugaard (R) (page 1412)
Lieutenant Governor: Matt Michels (R)
Secretary of State: Jason Gant (R)
Attorney General: Marty Jackley (R)
State Auditor: Steve Barnett (R)
State Treasurer: Richard L. Sattgast (R)
Commissioner of School and Public Lands: Jarrod Johnson (R) (resigning in August 2013)
Commissioners of Public Utilities: Chris Nelson (R) (Chair), Kristie Fiegen (R), Gary Hanson (R)

Vern Larson has been announced as the next Commissioner of School and Public Lands.

Legislature (as at April 2013)
President of the Senate: Matt Michels (R)
President Pro Temp. of the Senate: Bob Gray (R)

Senate Majority Leader: Russell Olson (R)
Senate Minority Leader: Jason Frerichs (D)
Speaker of the House: Brian Gosch (R)
Speaker Pro Tem of the House: Dean Wink (R)
House Majority Leader: David Lust (R)
House Minority Leader: Bernie Hunhoff (D)

US Senators: John Thune (R) (page 1525) and Tim Johnson (D) (page 1450)

Ministries

Office of the Governor, State Capitol, 500 East Capitol Avenue, Pierre, SD 57501-5070, USA. Tel: +1 605 773 3212, e-mail: http://www.state.sd.us/governor, URL: http://www.state.sd.us/governor

Office of the Lt. Governor, Capitol Building, 500 East Capitol Avenue, Pierre, SD 57501-5070, USA. Tel: +1 605 773 3661, URL: sd.gov/governor/aboutmatt.aspx

Office of the Attorney General, 500 East Capitol Avenue, Pierre, SD 57501-5070, USA. Tel: +1 605 773 3215, fax: +1 605 773 4106, URL: http://atg.sd.gov/

Office of the Secretary of State, Capitol Building, 500 East Capitol Avenue, Suite 204, Pierre SD 57501-5070, USA. Tel: +1 605 773 3537, fax: +1 605 773 6580, URL: http://www.sdsos.gov/

Office of the State Auditor, Capitol Building, 2nd Floor, 500 East Capitol Avenue, Pierre, SD 57501-5070, USA. Tel: +1 605 773 3341, fax: +1 605 773 5929, URL: http://www.sdauditor.gov/

Office of the State Treasurer, State Capitol Building, 500 East Capitol Avenue, Pierre, SD 57501-5070, USA. Tel: +1 605 773 3378, fax: +1 605 773 3115, URL: http://www.sdtreasurer.gov/

Public Utilities Commission, Capitol Building, 1st Floor, 500 East Capital Avenue, Pierre, SD 57501-5070, USA. Tel: +1 605 773 3201, fax: +1 605 773 3809, URL: http://puc.sd.gov/

Department of Agriculture, Foss Building, 523 East Capitol Avenue, Pierre, SD 57501-5254, USA. Tel: +1 605 773 5436, fax: +1 605 773 3481, URL: http://sdda.sd.gov/

Department of Revenue and Regulation, 445 East Capitol Avenue, Pierre, SD 57501-3185, USA. Tel: +1 605 773 3311, URL: http://dor.sd.gov/

Department of Corrections, 3200 East Highway 34, Suite 8, c/o 500 East Capitol Avenue, Pierre, SD 57501, USA. Tel: +1 605 773 3478, fax: +1 605 773 3194, URL: http://doc.sd.gov

Department of Education, Kneip Building, 3rd Floor, 700 Governors Drive, Pierre, SD 57501-2291, USA. Tel: +1 605 773 5669, fax: +1 605 773 6139, URL: http://doe.sd.gov/

Department of Environment and Natural Resources, Joe Foss Building, 523 East Capitol, Pierre, SD 57501, USA. Tel: +1 605 773 3151, fax: +1 605 773 6035, URL: http://denr.sd.gov/

Department of Game, Fish and Parks, 523 East Capitol Avenue, Pierre, South Dakota 57501, USA. Tel: +1 605 773 3485, fax: +1 605 773 6245, URL: http://gfp.sd.gov

Department of Health, Health Building, 600 E. Capitol, Pierre, SD 57501-2536, USA. Tel: +1 605 773 3361, fax: +1 605 773 5683, URL: http://doh.sd.gov/

Department of Labor, 700 Governors Drive, Pierre, SD 57501-2291, USA. Tel: +1 605 773 3094, fax: +1 605 773 4211, URL: http://dol.sd.gov/

South Dakota Office of Tribal Government Relations, 302 East Dakota, Pierre, SD 57501, USA. Tel: +1 605 773 3415, fax: +1 605 773 6592, URL: http://www.sdtribalrelations.com/

Political Parties
South Dakota Democrat Party, URL: http://www.sddp.org/
Republican Party of South Dakota, URL: http://www.southdakotagop.com/

Elections
Elections were held in November 2010 for the following state officials: Governor, Lieutenant Governor, Secretary of State, Attorney General, State Auditor, State Treasurer, Commissioner of School and Public Lands, and Public Utilities Commissioner. Former Lt. Governor Dennis Dugaard (R) won the gubernatorial election. Elections for two officers on the South Dakota Public Utilities COmmission took place in November 2012. Both incumbent candidates, Chris Nelson (R) and Kristie Fiegen (R), were re-elected.

Commissioner Johnson announced his intention to resign his position in August 2013. At the time of going to press, no successor had been announced.

In the last legislative elections, held in November 2012, the Republicans kept control of the Senate but with a slightly reduced majority (Republicans 28, Democrats 7). In the House of Representatives, the Republicans increased their majority (Republicans 53 and Democrats 17).

LEGAL SYSTEM

The Supreme Court heads the state's judicial system and consists of a Chief Justice and four Justices. Supreme Court Justices are retained by election every eight years and they represent each of the five Supreme Court districts. The Chief Justice is elected by the five Justices for a term of four years.

The Circuit Court consists of seven Presiding Judges and 31 Circuit court Judges in seven circuits. The 38 circuit court judges are elected by each circuit for a term of eight years. The state's Magistrates Courts are represented in the seven judicial circuits by 10 full-time and four part-time magistrate Judges.

In February 2006, the South Dakota legislature passed a bill supporting jail sentences of five years for doctors who perform abortions. The only exception to this would be if the woman's life were at risk.

South Dakota has the death penalty. The only crime punishable by death is first degree murder. Three executions have taken place since 1976, two in 2012. According to the DPIC the murder rate is 2.8 per 100,000 population.

South Dakota Supreme Court, URL: http://www.state.sd.us/state/judicial
Supreme Court Chief Justice: David Gilbertson
Justices: John Konenkamp, Steven Zinter, Lori Wilbur, Glen Severson

LOCAL GOVERNMENT

South Dakota is divided into 35 legislative districts. Voters within each district elect two representatives and one senator. The state constitution requires that every 10 years legislative district boundaries are redrawn to account for changes in the population of the state so that each citizen receives equal representation.

For administrative purposes, South Dakota is divided into 66 county governments and 1,225 sub-county general purpose governments. Of the 1,225 sub-county governments, 309 are municipal (city and town) governments, and 916 are town or township governments.

AREA AND POPULATION

Area
South Dakota is located in the northern plains of the United States. To the north is North Dakota, to the east Minnesota and Iowa, to the west are Wyoming and Montana, and to the south Nebraska. The Missouri River divides the state in half, from north to south. The eastern half contains rolling plains and fertile farm land, where most crop production occurs. The total area of South Dakota is 77,116.49 sq. miles, 75,884.64 sq. miles of land and 1,231.85 sq. miles of water. South Dakota is 245 miles from north to south, and 380 miles from east to west.

To view a map of South Dakota, please consult:
http://www.lib.utexas.edu/maps/us_2001/south_dakota_ref_2001.pdf

Population
According to the 2010 Census, the 2010 population was 814,180, up from the mid-2009 population at 812,383. In 2012, the population was estimated to be 833,354 people. Over the period 2000-10, the population grew by 7.9 per cent. The population is expected to reach 800,462 by 2030. Population density is estimated to be 10.7 people per sq. mile. The largest counties are Minnehaha county (169,468 in 2010) and Pennington county (100,948). According to 2011 estimates, the largest cities are Sioux Falls (156,592) and Rapid City (67,956, 2010). The capital, Pierre, has a population of around 13,860.

According to the 2010 Census, 7.3 per cent of the population is under 5 years, 24.9 per cent under 18 years and 14.3 per cent is aged over 65 years. Approximately 85.9 per cent of the population is white, and 1.3 per cent is black. Approximately 8.8 per cent of the population is American Indian. Approximately 2.7 per cent of the population is of Hispanic or Latino origin.

Births, Marriages, Deaths
The US Census Bureau estimated that there were 11,811 births in 2010 and 7,100 deaths, giving a natural population increase of 4,711 people. Net immigration amounted to 2,307 people in 2009. The fertility rate was 77.5 per 1,000 women aged 15-44 years and the death rate was 872.0 per 100,000 population. The infant mortality rate in 2007 was 6.4 infant deaths per 1,000 live births. Marriages and divorces in 2007 numbered 6,169 and 14,357 respectively.

EMPLOYMENT

South Dakota's estimated total civilian labour force was 446,300 in December 2012, of which 426,800 were employed and 19,500 were unemployed. The unemployment rate was 4.4 per cent, much lower than the US national average of 7.8 per cent. (Source: US Bureau of Labor Statistics)

Preliminary figures for non-farm wage and salary employment in December 2012, according to industry, are shown on the following table (preliminary figures):

Industry	No. of jobs	12-month change (%)
Logging, mining and construction	19,900	-5.2
Manufacturing	40,800	4.9
Trade, transportation, and utilities	81,600	-1.9
Information	5,900	-6.3
Financial activities	28,600	1.4
Professional and business services	29,100	-1.4
Educational and health services	67,900	2.9
Leisure and hospitality	42,600	3.1
Other services	15,400	-1.9
Government	77,400	-0.6
TOTAL	409,200	0.3

Source: Bureau of Labor Statistics

BANKING AND FINANCE

GDP/GNP, Inflation, National Debt
South Dakota's Gross Domestic Product (GDP) (current prices) rose from $38,215 million in 2010 to $40.1 billion in 2011. Real GDP rose by 0.8 per cent in 2011 and the state was ranked 47th in the US for its 2011 GDP. Gross Domestic Product according to industry is shown on the attached table (in millions of current dollars):

UNITED STATES OF AMERICA

Industry	2009	2010	2011
Agriculture, forestry and fishing	3,301	3,505	4,368
Mining	87	105	119
Utilities	611	660	607
Construction	1,350	1,316	1,325
Manufacturing	3,091	3,284	3,646
Wholesale Trade	2,089	2,202	2,347
Retail Trade	2,523	2,702	2,805
Transport and warehousing	898	932	971
Information	869	880	917
Finance and insurance	6,703	6,362	6,216
Real estate	3,285	3,119	3,262
Educational services	247	262	260
Health care & social assistance	3,290	3,476	3,599
Other non-government services	4,006	4,402	4,580
Government	4,674	5,007	5,095
Total	37,022	38,215	40,117

Source: BEA, Feb. 2013

The state's average annual per capita income was an estimated $44,217 in 2011. Per capita real GDP rose from $41,795 in 2011, compared to the US average of $42,070.

The annual Consumer Price Index (CPI) for the Midwest urban area (all items) rose from 214.7 in 2011 to 219.1 in 2012 (1982-84 = 100). (Source: Bureau of Labor Statistics)

Balance of Payments / Imports and Exports
Total South Dakota imports amounted to $577 million in 2009, down 37.0 per cent from the 2008 total of $916 million. Imports rose by 20.4 per cent in 2010 to $695 million and by 21.6 per cent in 2011 to $433 million. South Dakota's total export revenue fell from $1,654 million in 2008 to $1,011 million in 2009, a fall of 38.9 per cent. It rose by 24.6 per cent in 2010 to $1,259 million, and by 16 per cent in 2011 to $1,460 million, representing 0.1 per cent of the US total.

The top five manufactured export products in 2010-11, according to revenue, are shown on the following table:

Export Product	Value ($m)
Brewing or distilling dregs and waste, w/nt. pellet	103
Meat, swine, hams, shldrs	77
Fats, bovine, sheep or goat, raw or rendered	66
Meat of swine, nesoi, frozen	61
Soybean oilcake & oth. solid residue, wh/not ground	50

Source: US Census Bureau, Foreign Trade Division

The following table shows South Dakota's top five international export trading partners in 2011 according to revenue generated:

Country	2010 ($m)	2011	+/-% 2010-11
Canada	416	522	25.6
Mexico	340	395	16.0
China	43	70	64.2
Japan	52	55	5.7
Germany	54	43	-21.5

Source: US Census Bureau, Foreign Trade Division

Chambers of Commerce and Trade Organisations
South Dakota Chamber of Commerce and Industry, URL: http://www.sdchamber.biz
Sioux Falls Area Chamber of Commerce, URL: http://www.siouxfalls.com

MANUFACTURING, MINING AND SERVICES

Primary and Extractive Industries
The first significant mineral exploration in South Dakota began with the gold rush of 1876 and the state was a significant source of mineral production thereafter, ranking fourth nationally in the production of gold. Other minerals produced include sand and gravel, Sioux quartzite, pegmatite (feldspar, mica and rose quartz), granite and bentonite. Gold production declined in the late 1990s. The Black Hills is the area of most mining, causing environmental controversy, as well as ownership disputes as the local Native American tribe claim that the area and its resources remain theirs.

South Dakota's mining industry contributed an estimated $119 million towards the 2011 Gross Domestic Product, up from $105 million in 2010. In 2010, non-oil and gas extraction was the highest earning sector ($82 million), followed by oil and gas extraction ($20 million) and support activities for mining ($3 million).

South Dakota's 251 oil wells produced a total of 1,606,000 barrels of crude oil in 2010. Monthly production (Oct. 2012) amounted to 143,000 barrels. There are no oil refineries in South Dakota, although a number of petroleum product pipelines cross the state. Oil consumption in 2010 reached 22.0 million barrels, of which 10.4 million barrels was motor gasoline and 7.7 million barrels was distillate fuel.

South Dakota's natural gas industry consisted of 100 gas wells in 2011 which produced 1,848 million cubic feet of natural gas. Total consumption remains low, at 73,606 million cubic feet in 2011, though almost half of the state's households use natural gas as their primary fuel for home heating. (Source: EIA)

Energy
Total energy production amounted to 226 trillion Btu in 2010 (0.3 per cent of US total). Total energy consumption in South Dakota rose to 380 trillion Btu in 2010 (0.4 per cent of US total). Per capita energy consumption of 465 million Btu in 2010 ranks the state 7th in the US.

South Dakota is a net exporter of electricity. Electricity in the state is mainly hydroelectric. Net summer electric power industry capability in 2010 was 3,623 MW (0.3 per cent of US total), and net monthly generation (Oct. 2012) was 1,142,000 MWh (0.4 per cent of the US total). Of this monthly total, 535,000 MWh was hydroelectric, 294,000 was other renewables, and coal-fired 305,000 MWh. Three of the top five utility plants are hydroelectric and are located on the Missouri River. They are operated by the United States Army Corps of Engineers - Missouri River District. Major plants are: Oahe (hydro), Big Bend (hydro), Big Stone (coal), Fort Randall (hydro), and Angus Anson (gas).

South Dakota offers incentives to encourage the increased use of renewable sources for electricity generation. In 2008, the state adopted a voluntary objective to have 10 per cent of all electricity generation produced from renewable sources by 2015. In 2011, wind and hydroelectric power provided 77 per cent of the state's total net electricity fgeneration in 2011. (Source: EIA)

Manufacturing
Manufacturing is South Dakota's fourth largest contributor to GDP, earning $3,646 million in 2011 (up from $3,284 million in 2010). The largest sectors in 2010 were machinery ($637 million) and food, beverage and tobacco products ($350 million).

Service Industries
The services industry is South Dakota's largest contributor to GDP. The largest sectors in 2011 were finance and insurance ($6,216 million), health services ($3,599 million) and real estate ($3,262 million). Government services accounted for $5,095 million.

South Dakota has no personal or corporate income tax, no property tax and no business inventory tax. Over half of the state's revenue comes from the state sales tax of 4 per cent. Other government revenues come from alcohol and cigarette taxes, the bank franchise tax, proceeds from the state lottery, and other sources.

Tourism
The western half of South Dakota in particular draws many tourists. Its rugged terrain is home to buffalo and cattle ranches, gold mining, and the Black Hills. The state has 39 state parks and monuments, including the Mount Rushmore National Monument, the Crazy Horse Monument, Custer State Park and the Badlands, as well as the world's only Corn Palace and Laura Ingalls Wilder's childhood home. The state also has a winter holiday industry.

The accommodation and food services sector of the services industry contributed $1,117 million towards the 2011 GDP, whilst the arts, entertainment and recreation sector contributed $341 million.
South Dakota Department of Tourism and State Development, URL: http://www.travelsd.com/

Agriculture
The agriculture, forestry and fishing industry earned $4,368 million in 2011 (up from $3,505 million in 2010). In 2010, the highest earning sector was farming ($3,380 million), whilst forestry, fishing and related activities accounted for $124 million. (Source: BEA)

According to the US Dept. of Agriculture South Dakota's farms numbered 31,300 in 2010, and farmland covered 43,700,000 acres. The average size of a farm was 1,374 acres. In 2007, the total market value of agricultural products reached $6.57 billion; crops accounted for $3.38 billion, whilst livestock contributed $3.18 billion. The state ranked fifth in the USA for sheep and lamb production, and seventh for cattle and calves. South Dakota is one of the nation's largest producer of forage. As of 1 Jan. 2011, there were 3.7 million cattle and calves, 1.29 million hogs and pigs and 275,000 sheep.

COMMUNICATIONS AND TRANSPORT

Railways
The railroad system in South Dakota is unique because part of it is owned by the state. The state made the purchase to ensure agriculture producers a cost-effective method of transporting their products to market.

Roads
South Dakota has a total of 83,358 miles of state roads, including 678 miles of the three Interstate highways. In addition to I-229, I-90 crosses the southern portion of the state from east to west, and I-29 crosses the state from north to south in the eastern part of the state. There are 5,902 bridges across South Dakota, of which 1,792 are part of the state road system.

HEALTH

The National Center for Health Statistics estimated that there were 23.2 doctors (including osteopaths) per 10,000 people in 2009, below the US average of 27.4. In 2008, there were an estimated 406 dentists (5.0 per 10,000 population). In 2009, there were 5.1 community hospital beds per 1,000 residents, and, as of 2010, there were 110 nursing homes with 7,932 beds.

In 2007-09, some 12.0 per cent of South Dakotans had no health-care cover, and, in 2007-11, an estimated 13.8 per cent were living in poverty. South Dakota reported 297 HIV/AIDS cases from the beginning of the epidemic to the end of 2008, and ranked 48th highest among the

US states in cumulative number of reported cases in 2008. The TB rate was 2.0 per 100,000 population. An estimated 27.2 per cent of adults were classified as obese and 63.6 per cent were classified as overweight. (Source: CDC)

EDUCATION

Primary/Secondary Education
South Dakota has 724 public elementary and secondary schools. In the K-12 sector, enrolment in 2009-10 reached 123,713 and teachers numbered 9,326. The teacher/student ratio stood at one to 13.27 for the year.

In 2007-08, the state spent an estimated $1.18 billion on state primary and secondary education during the year, and overall education revenues reached $1.2 billion.

Higher Education
There were 25 institutes of higher education in 2010-11, 12 of which were public. South Dakota's higher education institutions include: Black Hills State University, Dakota State University, Northern State University, South Dakota State University, and the University of South Dakota. Total enrolment for the year 2010-11 comprised 23,033 male students and 30,309 women. The state conferred 9,638 degrees/certificates during the year, including 4,976 Bachelors, 1,309 Masters and 307 Doctorates. (Source: National Center for Education Statistics)

The National Center for Education Statistics estimated that, in 2004, 87.5 per cent of the population over the age of 24 had graduated high school, and 25.5 per cent had obtained a Bachelors degree or higher.

RELIGION

There is an almost even split between Catholic and Protestant in South Dakota.

COMMUNICATIONS AND MEDIA

Newspapers
The state newspaper with the largest circulation is the Argus Leader published in Sioux Falls. Other newspapers in wide circulation include the Rapid City Journal and the Aberdeen American News.
South Dakota Newspaper Association, URL: http://www.sdna.com/
Argus Leader, URL: http://www.argusleader.com/
Capital Journal, URL: http://www.zwire.com/site/
Rapid City Journal, URL: http://www.rapidcityjournal.com/

Broadcasting
South Dakota Public Broadcasting is the state's radio and television network. Radio stations include: KCSD-FM - SFU, KBHE-FM and TV, KESD-TV and FM.
South Dakota Public Broadcasting (SDPB), URL: http://www.sdpb.org/

Telecommunications
Information technology continues to develop in the state.
Bureau of Information and Telecommunications, URL: http://www.state.sd.us/bit/index.htm

ENVIRONMENT

Emissions from South Dakota's electricity industry are some of the lowest in the USA. Carbon dioxide emissions rose from 3,510,593 metric tons in 2009 to 3,611,180 metric tons, ranking the state 47th in the US. Emissions of sulfur dioxide amounted to 11,912 metric tons and of nitrogen oxide 11,717 metric tons. South Dakota's 15 ethanol producing plants have a capacity of 1,016 million gal/year (7.5 per cent of US total). Ethanol consumption was 969,000 barrels in 2011 (0.3 per cent of US total). In 2010, there were 6,276 alternative-fueled vehicles in use. (Source: EIA)

TENNESSEE

Capital: Nashville (Population estimate, 2008: 626,144)

Head of State: Bill Haslam (R) (Governor) (page 1439)

State Flag: In the centre of a crimson background is a blue circle with a white border, within which are three white stars; a blue bar with a white border appears at the fly

CONSTITUTION AND GOVERNMENT

Constitution
Tennessee entered the Union on 1 June 1796 as the 16th state. Two state constitutions preceded the current 1870 Constitution (1796 and 1835). The third Constitution was written in January 1870 and ratified by the people in March 1870. It was amended in 1953, 1960, 1966, 1972, 1978, and 1988.

According to the 1870 Constitution, the executive branch of state government consists of the governor. Unlike the other US states, Tennessee's constitutional officers form part of the legislative branch of government and, as such, are not elected by the people. The attorney general is part of the judicial branch of government.

Tennessee elects two Senators and nine Representatives to the US Congress in Washington, DC. To view the state constitution, please visit: http://www.state.tn.us/sos/bluebook/online/section5/tnconst.pdf

Recent Events
At the beginning of May 2010, parts of Nashville had to be evacuated when a levee sprang a leak as over 13 inches of rain fell over two days. 13 people were drowned in the flash floods that hit Tennessee.

Legislature
The legislative branch's three constitutional officers are elected by a joint convention of the House and the Senate. They are the secretary of state, elected for a four-year term; the comptroller of the treasury, elected for a two-year term; and the state treasurer, elected for a two-year term.

Tennessee's bicameral legislature, the General Assembly, consists of the Senate and the House of Representatives. The General Assembly convenes in each odd-numbered year, usually starting on the second Tuesday in January, and sits for 90 legislative days, over a period of two years, usually until April or May of each year.

Upper House
The Senate has 33 members who are elected for four years. Senators serve staggered terms, with half the Senate elected every two years. The post of Speaker of the Senate is held by the Lieutenant Governor. Following the November 2012 elections the Senate consists of 26 Republicans (up by six seats) and 7 Democrats.
Office of the Clerk, State Capitol, 2nd Floor, Nashville, TN 37243-0026, USA. Tel: +1 615 741 2720, URL: http://www.legislature.state.tn.us

Lower House
The House of Representatives has 99 members who are elected in even-numbered years for two years. Following the November 2012 elections the Republicans had 71 seats and the Democrats held 27 seats.
Office of the Clerk, Suite 19, Legislative Plaza, Nashville, TN 37243-0181, USA. Tel: +1 615 741 2901, URL: http://www.legislature.state.tn.us

State Constitutional Officers (as at April 2013)
Governor: Bill Haslam (R) (page 1439)
Lieutenant Governor: Ron Ramsey (R))
Comptroller of the Treasury: Justin P. Wilson
Secretary of State: Tre Hargett (R)
State Treasurer: David H. Lillard Jr. (R)
Attorney General and Reporter: Robert E. Cooper Jr.

Legislature (as at April 2013)
Speaker of the Senate: Lt. Gov. Ron Ramsey (R)
Speaker Pro Tem of the Senate: Bo Watson (R)
Senate Majority Leader: Mark Norris (R)
Senate Minority Leader: Jim Kyle (D)
Speaker of the House: Beth Harwell (R)
Democrat Leader: Craig Fitzhugh (D)
Republican Leader: Gerald McCormick (R)

US Senators: Bob Corker (R) (page 1408) and Lamar Alexander (R) (page 1374)

Ministries
Office of the Governor, 1st Floor, State Capitol, Nashville, TN 37243-0001, USA. Tel: +1 615 741 2001, fax: +1 615 532 9711, URL: http://www.tn.gov/governor/
Office of the Attorney General, 425 5th Avenue North, Nashville, TN 37243-0485, USA. Tel: +1 615 741 3491, URL: http://www.tn.gov/attorneygeneral/
Comptroller of the Treasury, 600 Charlotte Avenue, Nashville, TN 37243, USA. Tel: +1 615 741 2501, fax: +1 615 741 7328, URL: www.treasury.state.tn.us/
Office of the Secretary of State, 312 Eighth Avenue North, 6th Floor, William R. Snodgrass Tower, Nashville, TN 37243, USA. Tel: +1 615 741 2078, URL: http://www.tn.gov/sos/
Department of Agriculture, Ellington Agricultural Centre, Box 40627, Melrose Station, Nashville, TN 37204-0627, USA. Tel: +1 615 837 5103, URL: http://www.state.tn.us/agriculture/
Department of Commerce and Insurance, 500 James Robertson Parkway, Suite 660, Nashville, TN 37243, USA. Tel: +1 615 741 1900, URL: http://www.state.tn.us/commerce/
Department of Economic and Community Development, 312 8th Ave. N., 11th Floor TN Tower, Nashville, TN 37243, USA. Tel: +1 615 741 1888, URL: http://www.state.tn.us/ecd/
Department of Education, 6th Floor Andrew Johnson Tower, 710 James Robertson Parkway, Nashville, TN 37243-0375, USA. Tel: +1 615 741 2731, URL: http://www.state.tn.us/education/
Department of Environment and Conservation, 21st Floor, L&C Tower, 401 Church Street, Nashville, TN 37243-0435, USA. Tel: 1 888 891 8332 (US only), URL: http://www.state.tn.us/environment/

UNITED STATES OF AMERICA

Department of Finance and Administration, 312 Eighth Avenue North, 21st Floor, Tennessee Tower, Nashville, TN 37243-0297, USA. Tel: +1 615 741 0320, URL: http://www.state.tn.us/finance/
Department of Health, 425 5th Ave. N., Cordell Hull Building, 3rd Floor, Nashville, TN 37247-0101, USA. Tel: +1 615 741 3111, URL: http://health.state.tn.us/
Department of Labor and Workforce Development, Andrew Johnson Tower, 8th Floor, 710 James Robertson Parkway, Nashville, TN 37243-0655, USA. Tel: +1 615 741 6642, URL: http://www.state.tn.us/labor-wfd/
Department of Transport, James K. Polk Building, 505 Deaderick Street, Suite 700, Nashville, TN 37243-0349, USA. Tel: +1 615 741 2848, fax: +1 615 741 2508, URL: http://www.tdot.state.tn.us/

Political Parties
Tennessee Democratic Party, URL: http://www.tndp.org
Tennessee Republican Party, URL: http://www.tngop.org/

Elections
Elections took place in November 2010 for the positions of Governor, members of the US Senate and US House of Representatives, and members of the State Senate and House of Representatives. The incumbent Governor, Democrat Phil Bredesen, was ineligible for re-election and Republican Bill Haslam won the election.

In the legislative elections of November 2012, the Republicans increased their majority in the Senate (Republicans 26, Democrats 7). In the House of Representatives, the Republicans hold 71 seats and the Democrats 27.

LEGAL SYSTEM

Tennessee's court system consists of the Supreme Court; Intermediate Appellate Courts (the Court of Appeals, the Court of Criminal Appeals); Trial Courts (Circuit Courts, Chancery Courts, Criminal Courts, and Probate Courts); and Courts of Limited Jurisdiction (General Sessions Courts, Juvenile Courts, and Municipal Courts). Tennessee is divided into 31 judicial districts.

The Supreme Court comprises the chief justice and four justices who are elected for a term of eight years by popular vote. The Court of Appeals has 12 justices elected by the Judicial Selection Commission of 15 members for terms of eight years. The Court of Criminal Appeals has 12 judges.

Capital punishment is legal in Tennessee and as of January 2013 there were 89 inmates on death row. The most recent execution took place in 2009. In 2010, Governor Bredesen commuted the sentence of Gail Owens, one of only two women on death row.

Supreme Court, URL: http://www.tsc.state.tn.us/
Chief Justice: Cornelia Clark
Justices: Janice Holder, William Koch, Gary Wade, Sharon Lee

LOCAL GOVERNMENT

For administrative purposes, Tennessee is divided into 92 county governments and 347 sub-county general purpose governments, all of which are municipal governments. There are no town or township governments.

AREA AND POPULATION

Area
Tennessee is situated in the south of the US, west of North Carolina, south of Kentucky, north of Mississippi, Alabama, and Georgia, and east of Arkansas and Missouri. The total area of Tennessee is 42,143.27 sq. miles, of which 41,217.12 sq. miles is land and 926.15 sq. miles is water.

There are six main physiographic regions in Tennessee: the Blue Ridge, the Appalachian Ridge and Valley Region, the Cumberland Plateau, the Highland Rim, the Nashville Basin, and the Gulf Coastal Plain. With Tennessee has the most caves in the USA, with over 8,350 caves registered.

To view a map, consult http://www.lib.utexas.edu/maps/us_2001/tennessee_ref_2001.pdf

Population
Latest Census Bureau estimates put the mid-2010 population at 6,230,852, up on the mid-2009 estimate of 6,296,254. The population was estimated at 6,456,243 in 2012. The population of Tennessee grew by 11.5 per cent over the period 2000-10 and is expected to reach 7.4 million by 2030. The population density is around 153.9 people per sq. mile. The county with the largest number of inhabitants is Shelby County, with a population of 927,6445 in 2010. Tennessee's capital, Nashville, had a 2008 population of 262,144, but the largest city in Tennessee is Memphis, with a 2010 population of 646,889.

According to the 2010 Census, 6.4 per cent of the population is under 5 years, 23.6 per cent under 18 years and 13.4 per cent is aged over 65 years. Approximately 77.6 per cent of the population is white, and 16.7 per cent is black. Approximately 4.6 per cent of the population is of Hispanic or Latino origin.

Births, Marriages, Deaths
The US Census Bureau estimated that there were 79,495 births in 2010 and 59,578 deaths, giving a natural population increase of 19,917 people. Net immigration over 2009 was 30,079 people. The fertility rate was 62.4 per 1,000 females aged 15-44 years and the death rate

was 938.8 per 100,000 population. The infant mortality rate in 2007 was 8.3 infant deaths per 1,000 live births. Marriages and divorces in 2007, according to provisional data, numbered 65,551 and 29,868 respectively, both up on previous years.

Public Holidays
As well as celebrating national public holidays, the people of Tennessee observe Good Friday, Abraham Lincoln Day (12 February), Andrew Jackson Day (15 March) and Statehood Day (1 June).

EMPLOYMENT

Tennessee's total civilian labour force in December 2012 was an estimated 3,115,300, of which 2,879,600 were employed and 235,700 were unemployed. The unemployment rate was 7.6 per cent in December 2012, below the US average of 7.8per cent. (Source: US Bureau of Labor Statistics)

The following table shows preliminary figures for December 2012 non-farm wage and salary employment (seasonally adjusted), according to industry:

Industry	No. of jobs	12-month change (%)
Logging, mining and construction	118,600	3.7
Manufacturing	319,000	4.0
Trade, transportation, and utilities	559,500	0.5
Information	44,000	1.1
Financial activities	131,900	-1.3
Professional and business services	330,500	1.3
Leisure and hospitality	270,300	1.9
Other services	103,200	1.9
Government	440,300	0.2
TOTAL	2,709,900	1.2

Source: Bureau of Labor Statistics

BANKING AND FINANCE

GDP/GNP, Inflation, National Debt
Tennessee's current-dollar Gross Domestic Product rose from $256,194 million in 2010 to $266.5 billion in 2011. Real GDP rose by 3.5 per cent in 2010 and by 1.9 per cent in 2011. Tennessee was ranked 19th in the US for its 2011 GDP. In 2011, the largest industry was government.

The following table shows state Gross Domestic Product according to industry:

Industry	2009	2010	2011
Agriculture, forestry, fishing, and hunting	1,456	1,363	1,600
Mining	253	285	312
Utilities	1,616	1,677	1,557
Construction	8,274	8,227	8,719
Manufacturing	37,256	38,064	40,741
Wholesale Trade	15,390	15,758	16,487
Retail Trade	18,184	19,443	20,294
Transport and warehousing	11,319	11,653	12,170
Information	7,550	7,505	7,978
Finance and insurance	15,502	18,403	18,054
Real estate	26,243	24,999	25,149
Educational services	2,404	2,470	2,548
Health care & social assistance	24,649	26,586	27,902
Other non-government services	43,816	47,269	49,867
Government	31,084	32,493	33,150
TOTAL	244,995	256,194	266,527

Source: Bureau of Economic Analysis, Feb. 2013

The state's average annual per capita income was an estimated $36,567 in 2011. Per capita real GDP was in $36,543 in 2011, well below the national average of $42,070.

The annual Consumer Price Index for the South (all urban consumers) rose from 218.6 in 2011 to 223.2 in 2012 (1982-84 = 100). (Source: Bureau of Labor Statistics)

Balance of Payments / Imports and Exports
Total Tennessee imports amounted to $41,211 million in 2009, down 21.6 per cent from the 2008 total of $52,549 million. US imports rose by 17 per cent in 2010 to $48,200 million and by 14.6 per cent in 2011 to $55,215 million, contributing 2.5 per cent to the US total. Imports include vehicle parts, manufacturing, electronics and medical suppliers. Main suppliers included (2011) China (36.7 per cent), Canada (10.5 per cent), Japan, Mexico and Ireland. Total export revenue fell from $23,238 million in 2008 to $20,428 million in 2009, a decrease of 11.8 per cent. It rose by 26.6 per cent to $25,943 million in 2010, and by 15.6 per cent in 2011 to $29,993 million, representing 2 per cent of the total. (Source: US Census Bureau, Foreign Trade Division).

The top five international trading partners in 2010-11, according to export revenue, are shown on the following table:

Destination	2010 ($m)	2011 ($m)	+/-% 2010-11
Canada	7,210	8,345	15.7
Mexico	3,039	3,810	25.4
China	1,846	1,989	7.8

- continued

Japan	1,339	1,634	22.1
Belgium	467	1,061	127.2

Source: US Census Bureau,
Foreign Trade Statistics

Export revenue according to the top five export products in 2010 is shown on the following table:

Product	Export Revenue ($m)
Instr. and appl. for medical, surgical, dental, vet. uses	1,601
Civilian aircraft, engines, equipment and parts	1,108
Cotton, not carded or combed	989
Port. Digtl. automatic data process. mach., not over 10 kg	716
Passenger vehicles spark-ignition internal combustion reciproc. piston engines >3000 cc	590

Source: US Census Bureau, Foreign Trade Statistics

Chambers of Commerce and Trade Organisations
Memphis Area Chamber of Commerce, URL: http://www.memphischamber.com/
Nashville Area Chamber of Commerce, URL: http://www.nashvillechamber.com/

MANUFACTURING, MINING AND SERVICES

Primary and Extractive Industries
Tennessee's mining industry contributed $312 million towards the Gross Domestic Product in 2011 (up from $285 million in 2010). The main mining revenue came from the non-fuel extraction sector in 2010 ($216 million). Oil and gas extraction amounted to $17 million whilst support activities for mining contributed $51 million to the total. (Source: BEA)

An estimated 25,000 barrels of oil were produced from Tennessee's 280 oil wells and two rotary rigs in October 2012. Crude oil refinery capacity was 180,000 bbl/d in 2012. Oil consumption fell to 130.7 million barrels in 2010, of which 75.0 million barrels was motor gasoline and 27.4 million barrels was distillate fuel. Other resources mined include lignite and oil shale from west, middle and east Tennessee. Minerals produced for the construction industry include dimension stone, crushed stone, limestone and clay.

Tennessee's 210 operating wells produced a total of 4,851 million cubic feet of gas in 2011. Consumption was 255,027 million cu ft (1.0 per cent of US total). Industry is Tennessee's largest natural gas-consuming sector and a third of households use natural gas as their primary home-heating fuel.

Coal production comes mainly from the Cumberland Plateau and Cumberland Regions. Tennessee had 8 million short tons of recoverable coal reserves in 2011. Several mines have closed and production has fallen: from 2,654 thousand short tons in 2007 to 1,547,000 short tons in 2011 (0.1 per cent of US total). (Source: EIA)

Energy
Tennessee's total energy production amounted to 513 trillion Btu in 2010 (0.7 per cent of the US total). Tennessee's total energy consumption amounted 2,251 trillion Btu in 2010 (2.3 per cent of US total), whilst its per capita energy consumption ranks 19th in the US (354 million Btu in 2010).

Tennessee is a net exporter of electricity, with coal as its primary generating fuel. Net summer electric power industry capability in 2010 was 21,417 MW (2.1 per cent of US total) and the net total monthly (Oct. 2012) generation was 5,527 thousand MWh (1.8 per cent of the US total). Of this, 2,920 thousand MWh were coal-fired, 1,239 thousand nuclear, 687 thousand hydroelectric, 89,000 MWh other renewables, and 572 thousand MWh natural gas-fired. Major plants include Cumberland (coal), Johnsonville (coal), Sequoyah (nuclear), Raccoon Mountain (pumped storage), Gallatin (coal) and John Sevier. Tennessee has two nuclear power plants: Sequoyah and Watts Bar. (Source: EIA)

Manufacturing
Manufacturing is Tennessee's second largest contributor to GDP (after services), earning an estimated $40,741 million in 2011 (up from $38,064 million in 2010). Top manufacturing sectors in 2010 were computer and electronic manufacturing ($3,821 million), food, beverage and tobacco products ($6,133 million) and fabricated metal manufacturing ($3,642 million).

Service Industries
The services industry is Tennessee's highest earning sector. The largest sectors in 2011 were real estate ($25,1495 million), health care and social assistance ($27,902 million), finance and insurance ($18,054 million) and professional and technical services ($15,661 million).

Tourism
The tourism sector in Tennessee is worth around $11 billion per annum. In 2004, 43 million overnight stays were recorded, and the state ranks 11th in terms of US visitors. The theme and amusement park 'Dollywood' attracted some 2.4 million visitors in 2004, whilst the Grand Ole Opry House and Museum in Nashville had 662,495 visitors. The accommodation and food sector of the services industry contributed an estimated $8,811 million towards GDP in 2011 (up from $7,760 million in 2009), whilst the arts, entertainment and recreation sector contributed around $2,653 million.
Tennessee Department of Tourist Development, URL: http://www.state.tn.us/tourdev/

Agriculture
Tennessee's agricultural, forestry and fishing industry earned an estimated $1,600 million in 2011 (up from $1,363 million in 2010). The largest sector in 2010 was farming ($1,095 million) whilst forestry and fishing contributed $268 million. (Source: BEA)

According to the US Dept. of Agriculture, Tennessee's farms numbered around 78,300 in 2010, and farmland covered 10,900,000 acres. The average size of a farm in Tennessee was 139 acres. Total agricultural receipts in 2007 rose to $2.6 billion; livestock products contributed $1.46 billion whilst crops accounted for $1.14 billion. Major crops harvested, in order of receipts generated, are soybeans, tobacco, cotton lint, corn, nursery, wheat, floriculture, hay, cottonseed and tomatoes. The state is ranked third in the US for its sales of tobacco and seventh for sales of cotton and cottonseed. Major livestock products are cattle and calves, broilers, dairy products, hogs, eggs, sheep and lambs. As of 1 Jan. 2011, there were 1.99 million cattle and calves, 170,000 hogs & pigs, and 35,000 sheep.

Tennessee's forestry industry uses 13.6 million acres of commercial forest area, half of the area of the state. National forest area covers 640,000 acres. There are 178 species of tree native to Tennessee, 89 per cent of which are hardwoods. The most common type of wood is oak/hickory which makes up 72 per cent of the forest area. The majority of the state's forests, 86.4 per cent, are privately owned. Federal, state and local governments own 13.6 per cent.

COMMUNICATIONS AND TRANSPORT

International Airports
There are two international airports in Tennessee: Memphis International Airport and Nashville International Airport. Memphis is highly ranked in the world for cargo volume, having transported 213,306,549 items of cargo during 2004. The airport also has a high level of aircraft movements, 387,968 operations recorded in 2004. The total number of passengers through Memphis International airport in 2004 was close to 10.5 million.
Memphis International Airport, URL: http://www.mscaa.com/
Nashville International Airport (BNA), URL: http://www.nashintl.com/

Roads
Tennessee's roads cover 85,037 miles. Of that number, 13,522 miles are state highways carrying 75 per cent of all traffic and 1,062 miles carrying 25 per cent of all traffic.

HEALTH

The National Center for Health Statistics estimated that there were 26.2 doctors per 10,000 inhabitants in 2009, slightly below the US average of 27.4. In 2008, there were 3,015 dentists (4.9 per 10,000 population). In 2009, there were 3.3 community hospital beds per 1,000 residents. In 2010, there were an estimated 318 nursing homes with 37,279 beds.

In 2007-09, some 14.9 per cent of the state population had no health-care cover and, in 2007-11, around 16.9 per cent were living in poverty, both figures significantly higher than the US overall rate. Tennessee reported 14,021 HIV/AIDS cases from the beginning of the epidemic to the end of 2008, and ranked 18th in cumulative number of reported cases in 2008. The TB rate was 4.5 per 100,000 population, the 11th highest among the US states. The population is overweight generally (67.2 per cent), and 30.8 per cent of adults suffer from obesity. (Source: Center for Disease Control)

EDUCATION

Primary/Secondary Education
Total enrolments at Tennessee's 1,791 K-12 public school enrolments in the year 2009-10 reached 972,549. There were 65,361 classroom teachers in the state, and a pupil/teacher ratio of 14.88 to one. Educational revenues reached $8.2 billion in 2007-08, whilst current expenditures on the public sector reached $8.49 billion.

Higher Education
There are some 109 institutes of higher education in the state of Tennessee, 87 of which are private and 22 public. The most popular are the University of Tennessee at Knoxville and Memphis State University. For the year 2010-11, there were some 138,470 male students and 194,448 women. 64,215 degrees/certificates were conferred, of which 29,857 were Bachelors, 10,627 were Masters and 2,655 were Doctorates. (Source: National Center for Educational Statistics)

COMMUNICATIONS AND MEDIA

Newspapers
There are approximately 200 newspapers in Tennessee with collective daily morning subscriptions of 650,200, daily evening subscriptions of 382,700 and Sunday subscriptions of 1,112,300. Daily newspapers include: the Daily Herald (URL: http://www.columbiadailyherald.com/), Herald-Citizen (URL: http://www.herald-citizen.com/), the Daily News Journal, the Commercial Appeal, and The Tennessean.
Tennessee Press Association, URL: http://www.tnpress.com

Broadcasting
Over 80 million people currently watch Tennessee's cable television networks, which include Home & Garden Television (HGTV), The Food Channel, and Shop at Home. CBS cable networks include the Nashville Network (TNN) and Country Music Television (CBT).

ENVIRONMENT

Tennessee's electricity generating industry is required under the terms of the Clean Air Act Amendments of 1990 to reduce emissions of sulphur dioxide and nitrogen oxides. In 2010, the electricity industry's emissions of carbon dioxide rose from 43,457,828 metric tons to 48,196,067 metric tons in 2010 (2.0 per cent of the US total), and the state ranked 18th in the US. Emissions of sulfur dioxide and nitrogen oxide were respectively 137,764 metric tons and 32,911 metric tons.

UNITED STATES OF AMERICA

Tennessee is a top hydroelectric power producer, with many power plants located on the Tennessee and Cumberland river systems; hydroelectric power provides over 8 per cent of the state's total electricity production.

The state has two ethanol plants with a capacity of 177 million gal/year. Ethanol consumption amounted to 7,670 thousand barrels in 2011 (2.5 per cent of US total). There were 16,116 alternative fueled vehicles in use in 2010. (Source: EIA)

TEXAS

Capital: Austin (Population, Census 2010: 790,390)

Head of State: Rick Perry (R) (Governor) (page 1494)

State Flag: The Lone Star Flag: a vertical blue band at the hoist end and two horizontal bands at the fly end, the upper white and the lower red; in the centre of the blue band is a white, five-pointed star.

CONSTITUTION AND GOVERNMENT

Constitution

Texas joined the United States on 29 December 1845. According to the 1876 Constitution the Executive Branch of state government is headed by the Governor, who serves a four-year term. There is no limit to the number of terms the Governor can serve. Elections for Governor take place in even-numbered years when there is no presidential election. The Lieutenant Governor deputises for the Governor in case of absence and is also the Constitutional President of the Senate. The Governor is assisted by eight other elected executive officials: the Lieutenant Governor, Comptroller of Public Accounts, Commissioner of Agriculture, Attorney General, Commissioner of the General Land Office, and three Railroad Commissioners. All are elected by the people for four-year terms. The Secretary of State is appointed by the Governor, and serves the same term as the Governor.

Texans elect two Senators and 32 Representatives to the US Congress in Washington, DC.

To consult the state constitution, please visit: http://tlo2.tlc.state.tx.us/txconst/toc.html

Recent Events

Hurricane Rita hit the Gulf Coast on 24th September 2005. An evacuation plan had been implemented, in anticipation of the hurricane hitting Houston and Galveston, but these cities were spared. The town of Sabine Pass was most affected in Texas, with house fires and power lines down. The feared damage to oil refineries in Port Arthur was minimized, following a shut down in advance of the hurricane. However, the disruption to refining capabilities due to the shut down had an impact on oil and gas prices.

In March 2006, the Panhandle region of Texas was devastated by wildfires blazing over some 820,000 acres. Eleven people died, and up to 10,000 livestock were lost.

On 8th April 2008, Texan authorities removed 463 children and 130 women from a compound belonging to a polygamist sect as part of a child abuse inquiry. The property is owned by the Fundamentalist Church of Jesus Christ of Latter Day Saints (FLDS), a breakaway branch of Mormonism. The 10,000-strong sect, which dominates the towns of Colorado City in Arizona, and Hildale, Utah, split from the mainstream Mormon church more than a century ago. Members believe a man must marry at least three wives in order to ascend to heaven. Women are meanwhile taught that their path to heaven depends on being subservient to their husband. On 22nd May, an appeal court ruled that US officials had no right to seize the children; officials had failed to demonstrate that the children were in any immediate danger, which is the only legally allowable reason for taking children from their homes without court proceedings. However, the Court did not immediately order the return of the children to the ranch.

Hurricane Ike hit the island city of Galveston, off the coast of Texas, on the 13th September 2008, with winds of up to 110 mph and a 12 foot storm surge. A state of emergency had been declared in advance, and over a million people had been evacuated from the areas at risk, though over 20,000 people chose to stay. The hurricane cut through Texas before hitting Louisiana and Arkansas, causing eight deaths in total. 17 refineries in the Gulf of Mexico were shut down as a precaution, halting more than a fifth of US oil production.

Legislature

The Texas legislature consists of the Senate and the House of Representatives. Sessions of the legislature take place in odd-numbered years, usually beginning on the second Tuesday in January and lasting for no longer than 140 days.

Upper House

The State Senate has 31 members (one for each of the 31 geographical districts in Texas), who are elected for staggered terms of four years. Following the 2000 Census, new district boundaries meant that there was an average of 675,000 constituents in each district. According to the State Constitution, the President of the Senate is the Lieutenant Governor. Unlike other state senates, the Texas State Senate does not include majority or minority leaders. Following the November 2012 elections the Senate was composed of 19 Republicans and 12 Democrats.
Texas State Senate, 1400 North Congress, Austin, TX 78701 (PO Box 12068, Austin, TX 78711), USA. Tel: +1 512 463 0200, fax: +1 512 463 0326, URL: http://www.senate.state.tx.us/

Lower House

The House of Representatives has 150 members who are elected for a term of two years. Following the November 2012 elections the Republicans maintained a large majority with 95 seats. The Democrats took 55.

Texas State House of Representatives, State Capitol, 1100 Congress, Room E2.180, Capitol Extension, Austin, TX 78701 (PO Box 2910, Austin, TX 78768-2910), USA. Tel: +1 512 463 1000, fax: +1 512 463 6337, e-mail: hseadmin@house.state.tx.us, URL: http://www.house.state.tx.us/

The Texas Legislative Council (TLC) is a legislative branch state agency operating under the guidance of a council of 14 members, consisting of the lieutenant governor, the speaker of the house of representatives, six Senators appointed by the lieutenant governor, the house administration committee chairman, and five members of the House of Representatives appointed by the Speaker. Its function includes the drafting of bills, legal and public policy research, and publishing information.
Texas Legislative Council, 1501 N. Congress Avenue, Austin TX 78701 (PO Box 12128, Austin, TX 78711-2128), USA. Tel: +1 512 463 1151, fax: +1 512 463 0157, URL: http://www.tlc.state.tx.us/

Elected Executive Branch Officials (as at April 2013)
Governor: Rick Perry (R) (page 1494)
Lieutenant Governor: David Dewhurst (R)
Attorney General: Greg Abbott (R)
Comptroller of Public Accounts: Susan Combs (R)
Secretary of State: Esperanza Andrade (D)
State Auditor: John Keel (D)
Texas Land Commissioner: Jerry Patterson (R)
Commissioner of Agriculture: Todd Staples (R)
Railroad Commissioners: Barry Smitherman (Chair) (R), David Porter and Christi Craddock

---

Legislature (as at April 2013)
President of the Texas Senate: Lt. Gov. David Dewhurst (R)
President Pro Tem of the Senate: Leticia Van de Putte (D)
Speaker of the House: Joe Straus (R)

US Senators: John Cornyn (R) (page 1409) and Ted Cruz (R) (page 1411)

Ministries

Office of the Governor, State Insurance Building, 1100 San Jacinto, Austin, Texas 78701 (PO Box 12428, Austin, Texas 78711-2428), USA. Tel: +1 512 463 2000, fax: +1 512 463 1849, URL: http://www.governor.state.tx.us/
Office of the Lieutenant Governor, State Capitol, 100 West 11th Street, Austin, TX 78701 (Capitol Station, PO Box 12068, Austin TX 78711-2068), USA. Tel: +1 512 463 0001, fax: +1 512 463 0039, URL: http://www.ltgov.state.tx.us
Office of the Attorney General, 300 West 15th Street, Austin, TX 78701 (PO Box 12548, Austin, TX 78711-2548), USA. Tel: +1 512 463 2100, fax: +1 512 463 2063, e-mail: cac@oag.state.tx.us, URL: http://www.oag.state.tx.us/
Office of the Secretary of State, 1100 Congress, Suite 1E.8, Austin, TX 78701 (PO Box 12887, Austin, TX 78711-2887), USA. Tel: +1 512 463 5770, fax: +1 512 475 2761, URL: http://www.sos.state.tx.us/
Office of the State Auditor, Robert E. Johnson, Sr. Building, 1501 North Congress Avenue, Suite 4.224, Austin, TX 78701 (PO Box 12067, Austin, TX 78711-2067), USA. USA. Tel: +1 512 936 9500, fax: +1 512 936 9400, e-mail: auditor@sao.state.tx.us, URL: http://www.sao.state.tx.us/
Office of the Comptroller of Public Accounts, Lyndon B. Johnson State Office Building, 111 E. 17th Street, Austin, TX 78774-0100 (PO Box 13528, Austin, TX 78711-3528), USA. Tel: +1 512 463 4000, fax: +1 512 475 0352, URL: http://www.window.state.tx.us/
Texas General Land Office, 1700 N. Congress Ave., Austin, TX 78701-1495, USA. URL: http://www.glo.texas.gov/
Railroad Commission, URL: http://www.rrc.state.tx.us/
Department of Agriculture, Stephen F. Austin State Office Building, Room 1100A, 1700 North Congress Avenue, Austin, TX 78701 (PO Box 12847, Austin, TX 78711), USA. Tel: +1 512 463 7476, fax: +1 512 223 8861, URL: http://www.texasagriculture.gov/
Texas Economic Development, 1700 N. Congress Avenue, Austin, TX 78701 (PO Box 12728, Austin, TX 78711-2728), USA. Tel: +1 512 936 0100, fax: +1 512 936 0440, URL: http://www.texasedc.org/
Texas Commission on Environmental Quality, 12100 Park 35 Circle, Austin TX 78753, (PO Box 13087, Austin, TX 78711-3087) USA. Tel: +1 512 239 1000, fax: +1 512 239 5533, URL: http://www.tceq.state.tx.us
Department of Health, 1100 West 49th Street, Austin, TX 78756-3199 (1100 W. 49th St., Austin, TX 78756-3199), USA. Tel: +1 512 458 7111, fax: +1 512 458 7708, URL: http://www.dshs.state.tx.us/
Parks and Wildlife Commission, 4200 Smith School Road, Austin, TX 78744, USA. Tel: +1 512 389 4800, URL: http://www.tpwd.state.tx.us/
Department of Transportation, 125 East 11th Street, Austin TX 78701-2483, USA. Tel: +1 512 463 8585, fax: +1 512 305 9567, URL: http://www.txdot.gov

Political Parties

Texas Democratic Party, URL: http://www.txdemocrats.org/
Republican Party of Texas, URL: http://www.texasgop.org

Elections

The most recent election for Texas' statewide officials (Governor, Lieutenant Governor, Attorney General, Comptroller of Public Accounts, Commissioner of the General Land Office, Commissioner of Agriculture, and two Railroad Commissioners) took place in November 2010. Incumbent Governor, Republican Rick Perry, won.

In the legislative elections of November 2012, the division of seats remained the same in the state Senate (Republicans 19, Democrats 12), and in the House of Representatives, Republicans were again victorious (Republicans 95, Democrats 55).

In the November 2012 elections, Ted Cruz (R) won the contest for the US Senate.

LEGAL SYSTEM

The Texas legal system comprises: the Supreme Court of Texas, consisting of a Chief Justice and eight justices (elected by the people to staggered six-year terms); the Court of Criminal Appeals, consisting of a Presiding Judge and eight judges; 14 Courts of Appeals (with 80 judges); District Courts (396 judges); 453 County Level Courts (Constitutional County Courts, County Courts at Law and Statutory Probate Courts); 1,224 Municipal Courts; and 838 Justice of Peace Courts.

Although only capital murder is eligible for the death penalty, Texas leads the US in executions - 477 between 1982 and 2011. As of January 2013, 304 inmates were on death row including 10 women. Thirteen executions took place in 2011 and 15 in 2012. As of January 2013, 10 executions were scheduled to take place in 2013. According to the DPIC the murder rate stands at 5 per 100,000 population.

The Texas Ranger Division of the Texas Department of Public Safety is a law enforcement agency with statewide jurisdiction. Over the years, the Texas Rangers have investigated crimes, acted as riot police, protected the Texas governor, tracked down fugitives, and functioned as a paramilitary force at the service of the state.

Supreme Court, URL: http://www.supreme.courts.state.tx.us
Chief Justice: Wallace B. Jefferson
Justices: Nathan Hecht, Dale Wainwright, Paul Green, Phil Johnson, Don Willett, Eva Guzman, Debra Lehrmann, Jeffrey Boyd, John Devine
Court of Criminal Appeals, URL: http://www.cca.courts.state.tx.us
Presiding Judge: Sharon Keller

LOCAL GOVERNMENT

Texas is divided into 254 county governments and 1,209 municipal governments. Each county runs on Commissioners' Court system consisting of four elected commissioners and a county judge. Cities, towns and villages form the state's municipal governments and are divided into three types, according to the number of inhabitants. The largest municipalities are governed by aldermen or city managers, whilst the smaller municipalities are administered by commissioners.

Texas Association of Counties,
URL: http://www.county.org/resources/countydata/index.asp

AREA AND POPULATION

Area

The second largest state in the United States (after Alaska), Texas has a total area of 268,580.82 sq. miles, of which 261,797.12 sq. miles is land and 6,783.70 sq. miles is water. Texas is located in the South of the US, east of New Mexico, west of Louisiana and Arkansas, and south of Oklahoma. The Rio Grande, Red River and Sabine River form natural state borders.

The Texan landscape is diverse, containing prairie, hills and desert. The weather is also variable; the Panhandle has colder winters than North Texas, while the Gulf Coast has mild winters. Most parts of Texas see high temperatures (around 32 °C) in the summer. Some of the most destructive hurricanes in U.S. history have hit Texas, and tornadoes strike Texas more frequently than any other state, averaging around 139 per annum.

To view a map of the state, please consult:
http://www.lib.utexas.edu/maps/united_states/texas_90.jpg

Population

According to the 2010 Census, the 2010 state population was 25,145,561 people, down on the mid-2009 estimate of 24,782,302. The population was estimated to be 26,059,203 in 2012. Texas has the second largest population of the United States, following California. Over the period 2000 to 2010, the state population grew by 20.6 per cent and is expected to reach 33.3 million by 2030. Texas has a population density of 96.3 people per sq. mile, ranking 26th in the US. The US Census Bureau estimated that the 2011 population in the state's largest three cities was as follows: Houston, 2,145,146; Dallas, 1,223,229; San Antonio 1,359,758. The county with the highest population is Harris County, with an estimated 4,092,459 inhabitants in 2010.

According to the 2010 Census, 7.7 per cent of the population is under 5 years, 27.3 per cent under 18 years and 10.3 per cent is aged over 65 years. Approximately 70.4 per cent of the population is white, and 11.8 per cent is black. Approximately 37.6 per cent of the population is of Hispanic or Latino origin.

Births, Marriages, Deaths

The US Census Bureau estimated that there were 386,118 births in 2010 and 166,527 deaths in the same year, giving a natural population increase of 219,591 people. Net immigration amounted to 231,539 inhabitants in 2009. This was the third largest state population increase in percentage terms in the USA, and the largest increase numerically. The 2007 infant mortality rate was 6.3 infant deaths per 1,000 live births, equivalent to 2,480 deaths. Provisional estimates indicate that there were 179,904 marriages in 2007, and 79,469 divorces.

Public Holidays

In addition to observing national holidays, Texans celebrate Confederate Veterans Day on January 19th.

EMPLOYMENT

The December 2012 civilian labour force in Texas was estimated at 12,637,800, of which 11,866,500 were employed and 771,300 were unemployed. The unemployment rate was 6.1 per cent, below the US average of 7.8 per cent. (Source: US Bureau of Labor Statistics)

The following table shows December 2012 non-farm wage and salary employment, according to industry: (preliminary figures)

Industry	No. of employed	12-month change (%)
Logging and mining	259,800	2.5
Construction	591,500	6.6
Manufacturing	850,300	0.7
Trade, transportation and utilities	2,182,000	2.6
Information	190,200	-1.7
Financial activities	651,400	0.8
Professional and business services	1,406,900	3.5
Educational and health services	1,492,100	3.2
Leisure and hospitality	1,111,500	4.5
Other services	388,600	2.6
Government	1,779,700	0.2
TOTAL	10,904,000	2.5

Source: Bureau of Labor Statistics

BANKING AND FINANCE

GDP/GNP, Inflation, National Debt

According to Bureau of Economic Analysis statistics the Texan Gross Domestic Product (current prices) rose from $1,222,904 million in 2010 to $1,308.1 billion in 2011. Real GDP grew by 2.8 per cent in 2010 and by 3.3 per cent in 2011 and the state was ranked second in the US (after California) for its 2011 Gross Domestic Product.

The state Gross Domestic Product according to industry is shown on the following table (millions of current dollars):

Industry	2009	2010	2011
Agriculture, forestry, fishing & hunting	6,144	9,763	9,897
Mining	86,495	97,083	118,578
Utilities	25,248	25,627	24,234
Construction	57,748	55,956	57,970
Manufacturing	138,924	173,199	192,024
Wholesale Trade	74,740	78,620	85,753
Retail Trade	68,432	72,538	76,625
Transport and warehousing	38,862	40,886	43,200
Information	43,682	42,381	44,903
Finance and insurance	73,280	87,617	89,757
Real estate	107,932	105,616	109,657
Other non-government services	190,656	204,246	219,368
Government	138,138	143,966	146,162
TOTAL	1,129,537	1,222,904	1,308,132

Source: Bureau of Economic Analysis, Feb. 2013

The state's average per capita income was an estimated $40,147 in 2011. Per capita real GDP rose from $43,799 in 2010 to $44,788 in 2011, higher than the US average of $42,070.

The annual Consumer Price Index (CPI) for the Dallas-Fort Worth urban area (all items) rose from 207.9 in 2011 to 212.2 in 2012 (1982-84 = 100). The annual CPI for the Houston-Galveston-Brazoria, TX, urban area rose from 200.5 in 2011 to 202.5 in 2012. (Source: Bureau of Labor Statistics)

Texans have one of the lowest state and local tax burdens in the US; there is no state income tax, but the state collects revenue from a sales tax. In terms of federal taxes, Texas is a donor state, receiving $0.94 in benefits for every $1 paid to the federal government in 2005.

Balance of Payments / Imports and Exports

Total Texas imports amounted to $205,711 million in 2009, down $287,276 million in 2008. Imports rose by 29 per cent in 2010 to reach $265,455 million, and by 20 per cent in 2011 to $318,826 million, accounting for 14.4 per cent of the US total. Crude oil accounts for approximately 22.6 per cent of imports. Main suppliers (2011) included Mexico (29 per cent), China (11.4 per cent), Venezuela, Saudi Arabia and Canada. Total merchandise export revenue fell from $192,222 million in 2008 to $162,995 million in 2009, a decrease of 15.2 per cent.

UNITED STATES OF AMERICA

Exports rose by 27 per cent in 2010 to $206,691 million and by 21.3 per cent in 2011 to $251,006 million.. Texas accounted for 17.0 per cent of the US total merchandise export revenue in 2011.

The top five international merchandise export destinations in 2010-11, according to revenue, are shown on the following table:

Country	2010 ($m)	2011 ($m)	+/-% 2010-11
Mexico	72,627	87,393	20.3
Canada	18,755	22.121	17.9
China	10,275	10,932	6.4
Brazil	7,161	10,059	40.5
Netherlands	5,917	8,796	48.7

Source: US Census Bureau,
Foreign Trade Division

The following table shows the top five export products in 2010 according to revenue:

Product	Export Revenue ($m)
Oil (not Crude) from petroleum and bituminous minerals	20,877
Light oils and preparations (not crude) from petrol and bitum.	9,307
Parts for boring or sinking machinery nesoi	5,636
Parts & accessories for ADP machines & units	4,522
Processors and controllers, electronic integ. circuits	4,297

Source: US Census Bureau, Foreign Trade Division

Chambers of Commerce and Trade Organisations
Greater Southwest Houston Chamber of Commerce, URL: http://www.gswhcc.org
Fort Worth Chamber of Commerce, URL: http://www.fortworthchamber.com/
Dallas Regional Chamber, URL: http://www.dallaschamber.org/
Houston County Chamber of Commerce, URL: http://www.houstoncochamber.com/
San Antonio Economic Development Foundation, URL: http://www.sanantonioedf.com/

MANUFACTURING, MINING AND SERVICES

Primary and Extractive Industries
The mining industry contributed $118,578 million towards the 2011 state Gross Domestic Product (up from $97,083 million in 2010). In 2010, the top sector was oil and gas extraction ($76,520 million), followed by support activities for mining ($18,703 million) and non-oil and gas mining ($1,859 million). (Source: BEA)

Petroleum and natural gas are the state's principal mining products. In the year 2009, Texas had the largest proven crude oil reserves in the US at 5,674 million barrels - the second largest after Federal Offshore reserves. The state holds 24.4 per cent of the US total proven reserves. Its 149,102 oil wells and 838 operational rotary rigs produced total of 5,006 million barrels of crude oil in 2009, equivalent to around 24.2 per cent of national production. Monthly production in Oct. 2012 was 65,100 thousand barrels, 30.8 per cent of US total.

Total oil consumption in 2010 equated to 12 per cent of the US total consumption, at 11,770 trillion barrels. The state consumed 290.2 million barrels of motor gasoline (9 per cent of US total) and 142.3 million barrels of distillate fuel (10.3 per cent of the total). 59.4 per cent of the US total requirement of liquefied petroleum gas (LPG) was used in Texas (471.0 million barrels), as well as 11.9 per cent of the nation's requirement for jet fuel (61.8 million barrels). Texas's petroleum refineries can process over 4.76 million barrels of crude oil per day, and account for more than 27.5 per cent of total US refining capacity.

Texas is the Nation's leading natural gas producer, accounting for more than a quarter of total US natural gas production. The dry natural gas industry had reserves of 88,997 billion cubic feet in 2010 (40.6 per cent of the US total). From a total of 100,966 gas and gas condensate wells, marketed gas reached 7,112,863 million cubic feet in 2011, over 29 per cent of national production. Consumption of natural gas rose from 3,344,934 million cu ft in 2010 to 3,646,491 million cu ft in 2011 (15 per cent of US total). Demand is dominated by the industrial and electric power sectors, which together account for more than four-fifths of state consumption.

The state's total recoverable coal reserves in 2011 stood at 736 million short tons, 3.8 per cent of the US total. Production rose from 40,982 thousand short tons in 2010 to 45,904 thousand short tons in 2011 (4.2 per cent of US total). Consumption fell from 105,327 thousand short tons in 2005 to 104,784 thousand short tons in 2007 (9.3 per cent of the US total). (Source: EIA)

Energy
Total energy production amounted to 11,408 trillion Btu in 2010, representing 15.3 per cent of the US total, ranking it first in the US for production. Total energy consumption was 11,770 trillion Btu in 2010 (12 per cent of US total) whilst per capita energy consumption ranks the state 6th in the US (466 million Btu in 2010).

Texas is a net importer of electricity, with natural gas as the primary generating fuel. Net summer capability in 2010 was 108,258 MW (10.4 per cent of US total), and total net monthly (Oct. 2012) electricity generation was 33,398 thousand MWh, representing 10.7 per cent of national total (1st in the US). Of this, coal-fired 12,512 thousand MWh, natural gas-fired 14,953 thousand MWh, nuclear 2,674 thousand MWh, other renewables 2,871 thousand and hydroelectric 41 thousand MWh. Major plants include: WA Parish (coal), South Texas Project (nuclear), Comanche Peak (nuclear), Cedar Bayou (gas), and Martin Lake (coal).

Texas operates two nuclear power plants: Comanche Peak and South Texas Project. Comanche Peak is located in Somerville County and uses water from the Squaw Creek reservoir. Its two units have one pressurised water reactor of 1,150 net MW each. South Texas Project plant occupies a 12,200-acre site near Houston. Its two units have one pressurised water reactor of 1,250 net MWe each. Texas surpassed California as the country's largest wind energy producer in 2006. With over 2,000 wind turbines in West Texas alone, and substantial new wind generation capacity under construction, the state leads the USA in wind-powered generation capacity. Texas was the first US state to reach 10,000 MW of wind-powered capacity.

In 2005, Texas adopted a law requiring 5,880 MW of new renewable generation be built by 2015, representing about 5 per cent of the State's total 2005 electricity demand. (Source: EIA)

Manufacturing
Manufacturing is Texas' second largest contributor to GDP, earning an estimated $192,024 million in 2011 (up from $173,199 million in 2010). The top sectors in 2010 were chemical products ($34,249 million), computer and other electronic equipment ($24,064 million) and petroleum and coal products ($45,203 million).

Service Industries
Services is the largest contributor to Texas' GDP. The top services sectors in 2011 were real estate ($109,657 million), professional and technical services ($92,107 million) and health care and social assistance ($81,953 million). The finance and insurance sector accounted for $89,757 million and the information sector contributed a significant $44,903 million.

Tourism
The accommodation and food sector of the services industry contributed an estimated $35,777 million towards the 2011 GDP, whilst the arts, entertainment and recreation services sector contributed $7,727 million in the same year.
Parks and Wildlife Commission, URL: http://www.tpwd.state.tx.us/

Agriculture
Agriculture, forestry and fisheries contributed an estimated $9,897 million towards Texas' GDP in 2011 (up from $9,763 million in 2010). The farming sector contributed $8,505 million in 2010, whilst the forestry, fishing and related activities sector contributed $1,258 million. (Source: BEA)

According to the latest official USDA Census of Agriculture, Texan farms numbered around 247,500 in 2010 and farmland covered some 130,400,000 acres. The average size of a Texan farm was 527 acres in 2010. In 2007, the market value of agricultural produce was $21 billion, of which livestock accounted for $14.4 billion and crops accounted for $6.6 billion. Texas is ranked first in the US for cattle and calves, sheep and goat rearing, and cotton and cottonseed cultivation. As of 1 Jan. 2011, there were 13.3 million cattle and calves, 660,000 hogs & pigs and 880,000 sheep.

COMMUNICATIONS AND TRANSPORT

International Airports
International airports are located in Texas' three main cities - Dallas, Houston and Austin - as well as a number of other key locations. Dallas/Fort Worth International Airport is one of the top ranking airports in the world for passenger traffic; in 2005, 3,298,531 passengers used the airport, (an increase of 10.7 per cent of the figure for 2004). 460,480 of these passengers were travelling internationally. Over the same year, the airport handled 817,806 items of cargo. The George Bush Intercontinental Airport in Houston is ranked 14th in the world for international passenger traffic; in 2004, the airport served 36 million international passengers and handled 7.8 billion pounds of cargo.

Regional airports include Robert F. Mueller Airport, Austin, Giddings-Lee Airport, Hilton Houston Hobby Airport, Houston Airport Marriott, Austin-Bergstrom International Airport, Victoria Regional Airport, William P. Hobby Airport, Comfort Inn Airport.

Dallas/Fort Worth International Airport (DFW), URL: http://www.dfwairport.com/
George Bush Intercontinental Airport/Houston, URL: http://www.fly2houston.com/iah
Amarillo International Airport, URL: http://www.amarillo-cvb.org/
El Paso International Airport, URL: http://www.citi-guide.com/elp
Fort Worth Meacham International Airport, URL: http://www.meacham.com/
Lubbock International Airport, URL: http://www.flylia.com/

National Airlines
Continental Airlines, URL: http://www.flycontinental.com
Southwest Airlines, URL: http://www.southwest.com

Roads
The state's main arterial highway is Interstate 35, which has high levels of congestion. Interstate 35 runs 1,568 miles north-south from Laredo (just short of the Mexican border) through Fort Worth in Texas to Minnesota (just south of the Canadian border). It is estimated that congestion within Texas will reach unacceptable levels within the next 25 years, assuming a population increase of 12 million people; the building of a toll road, the Trans Texas Corridor, is in early planning stages.

Ports
The three major ports in Texas are Houston, Beaumont and Texas City. They ranked 2nd, 4th and 9th in the US respectively, in terms of freight tonnage handled in 2004. 202 million tons of freight passed through Houston in 2004 (up 5.8 per cent on 2003 figures); Beaumont handled 91.7 million tons (up 4.7 per cent) and Texas City managed 68.3 million tons (up 11.3 per cent)

HEALTH

Texas has over 470 acute care hospitals, 72,000 licensed beds, 57,150 staffed beds, 1,165 nursing homes and 128,994 licensed beds in nursing homes. The National Center for Health Statistics estimated that there were 21.6 doctors per 10,000 Texans in 2009, below the US state average of 27.4. In 2008, there were an estimated 10,936 dentists (4.5 per 10,000 population). In 2009, there were 2.5 community hospital beds per 1,000 population. In 2010, there were 1,173 nursing homes with 130,665 residents.

It was estimated that some 25.5 per cent of the population had no health-care cover in 2007-09, the highest percentage in the US, and that, in 2007-11, 17.0 per cent were living in poverty. One of the causes is the high level of illegal immigration in the state. Obesity affected 31.0 per cent of the adult population, and 65.9 per cent of the population were considered overweight. Texas reported 77,070 HIV/AIDS cases from the beginning of the epidemic to the end of 2008, and ranked 4th highest among the US states in cumulative number of reported HIV/AIDS cases in 2008. The TB rate was 6.2 per 100,000 population, the 4th highest rate in the US. (Source: CDC)

EDUCATION

Primary/Secondary Education
There were 9,232 elementary and secondary schools in Texas in the academic year 2009-10, with 4,850,210 students enrolled and 333,164 teachers. The number of students per teacher stood at 14.56. Total current expenditure on public schools over 2007-08 amounted to $49.8 billion, whilst education revenues reached $45.74 billion.

Higher Education
There are 252 degree conferring institutes of higher education in Texas, including the University of Texas, and the University of Houston. In the year 2010-11, 631,137 male students were enrolled together with 816,731 women. In the same year, 257,752 degrees/certificates were conferred, including 104,657 Bachelors, 39,739 Masters and 9,318 Doctorates. (Source: National Center for Educational Statistics)

RELIGION

Around 28 per cent of Texans are Roman Catholics, 21 per cent are Baptists, 8 per cent are Methodists and 7 per cent are other Christians. Around one per cent follow Judaism and one per cent Islam.

Texas is part of the Evangelical Protestant Bible Belt, and has the highest percentage of people with a religious affiliation in the USA. Houston is home to Lakewood Church, the largest church in the US which is built like a stadium and has a regular congregation of over 43,000 people.

COMMUNICATIONS AND MEDIA

Newspapers
Texan newspapers include: The Capitol Times, The Austin Chronicle, The Dallas Morning News, The Dallas Observer, The Dallas Times, Houston Public News, San Antonio Business Journal.
Texas Press Association, URL: http://www.texaspress.com/
The Dallas Morning News, URL: http://www.dallasnews.com/
Houston Chronicle, URL: http://www.chron.com/

Business Journals
Business journals include: Texas Business, Texas Highways, Texas Lawyer, Oil Report, and Austin Monthly.
Dallas Business Journal, URL: http://www.bizjournals.com/dallas/

Broadcasting
There are currently 1455 broadcasting networks in Texas, of which 600 are radio stations.

ENVIRONMENT

Texas' electricity industry relies mainly on coal and gas as generating fuels, and the state has major refining and manufacturing industries.

Texas has the highest CO^2 emissions of the states; the Texan power-generating industry released almost twice the amount of carbon dioxide as Ohio, the state with the second highest CO^2 emissions. Causes of the state's greenhouse gas emissions include the state's large number of coal power plants and the state's refining and manufacturing industries. Emissions fell in 2009 to 242,864,409 metric tons but rose to 251,409,188 in 2010 (10.5 per cent of US total). Emissions of sulfur dioxide amounted to 430,123 metric tons (8.0 per cent of US total) and emissions of nitrogen oxide amounted to 203,537 metric tons (8.2 per cent of US total).

Texas has three ethanol plants with a capacity of 250 million gal/year, accounting for 1.9 per cent of national capacity in 2011. Ethanol consumption was 26,705 thousand barrels in 2011 (8.7 per cent of US total). There were 115,374 alternative-fueled vehicles in use (12.3 per cent of US total). (Source: EIA)

SPACE PROGRAMME

The NASA Johnson Space Centre is based in Houston, from which the current US space programme operates. The Centre is primarily concerned with the design and development of spacecraft, the training of astronauts, and the planning of future manned space missions.

Texas Aerospace Commission, URL: http://www.tac.state.tx.us/
Johnson Space Center, URL: http://www.nasa.gov/centers/johnson/home/index.html

UTAH

Capital: Salt Lake City (Population, Census 2010: 186,440)

Head of State: Gary R. Herbert (Governor) (page 1441)

State Flag: A blue background with a gold border in the centre of which is the state seal. The state seal consists of a shield on which is perched the American eagle with outstretched wings; the top of the shield is pierced by six arrows below which is a beehive, and on either side of which are sego lilies; at the top of the shield appears the word 'Industry', and below the beehive appears the date '1847'; on either side of the shield is the American flag. The flag was amended in 2011: the shield has changed from blue to white.

CONSTITUTION AND GOVERNMENT

Constitution
Utah entered the Union on 4 January 1896 as the 45th state. The executive branch of government consists of the governor together with four elected officers: lieutenant governor, attorney general, state treasurer, and state auditor.

Utah elects two Senators and three Representatives to the US Congress in Washington, DC.

To consult the state constitution, please visit: http://le.utah.gov/~code/const/const.htm

Legislature
Utah has a citizen legislature rather than a full-time legislature. Its bicameral legislature consists of the Senate and the House of Representatives. The annual session of the legislature usually lasts 45 days, beginning on the third Monday in January.

Upper House
The Senate has 29 members who are elected for four years (about half are renewed every two years). Each senator represents about 60,000 people. Following the 2012 elections, there were 24 Republicans and five Democrats in the Senate.
Utah State Senate, 319 State Capitol, Salt Lake City, Utah 84114, USA. Tel: +1 801 538 1035, fax: +1 801 326 1475, URL: http://www.utahsenate.org/

Lower House
The House of Representatives has 75 members who are elected for two years. Each member of the House represents about 22,900 people. Following the 2012 elections, the House was composed of 61 Republicans and 14 Democrats.
Utah House of Representatives, 319 State Capitol, Salt Lake City Utah 84114, USA. Tel: +1 801 538 1029, fax: +1 801 538 1414, URL: http://le.utah.gov/house2/index.html

Elected Executive Branch Officials (as of June 2013)
Governor: Gary R. Herbert (R) (page 1441)
Lieutenant Governor: Gregory S. Bell (R)
Attorney General: John Swallow (R)
State Treasurer: Richard K Ellis (R)
State Auditor: John Dougall (R)

Legislature (as at June 2013)
President of the Senate: Wayne Niederhauser (R)
Majority Leader of the Senate: Ralph Okerlund (R)
Minority Leader of the Senate: Gene Davis (D)
Speaker of the House: Rebecca Lockhart (R)
House Majority Leader: Brad L. Lee (R)
House Minority Leader: Jennifer M. Seelig (D)

US Senators: Mike Lee (R) (page 1462) and Orrin G. Hatch (R) (page 1439)

Ministries
Office of the Governor, Utah State Capitol Complex, East Office Building, Suite E220, PO Box 142220, Salt Lake City, Utah 84114-2220, USA. Tel: +1 801 538 1000, fax: +1 801 538 1528, e-mail: http://www.governor.utah.gov/goca/form_governor.html, URL: http://www.governor.state.ut.us/
Office of the Lieutenant Governor, Utah State Capitol Complex, East Office Building, Suite E220, PO Box 142220, Salt Lake City, Utah 84114-2220, USA. Tel: +1 801 538 1000, fax: +1 801 538 1557, e-mail: aesmith@utah.gov, URL: http://www.utah.gov/ltgovernor/
Office of the Attorney General, Utah State Capitol Complex, East Office Bldg, Suite 320, SLC UT 84114-2320 (PO Box 142320, SLC UT 84114-2320), USA. Tel: +1 801 538 9600, fax: +1 801 538 1121, e-mail: uag@utah.gov, URL: http://attygen.state.ut.us/

UNITED STATES OF AMERICA

Office of the State Auditor, Utah State Capitol Complex, East Office Building, Suite E310, PO Box 142310, Salt Lake City, Utah 84114-2310, USA. Tel: +1 801 538 1025, fax: +1 801 538 1383, URL: http://www.sao.state.ut.us/
Office of the State Treasurer, 215 State Capitol, Salt Lake City, Utah, 84114, USA. Tel: +1 801 538 1042, URL: http://www.treasurer.state.ut.us/
Department of Agriculture, 350 N. Redwood Road, Salt Lake City, UT 84116 (PO Box 146500, Salt Lake City, UT 84114-6500), USA. Tel: +1 801 538 7100, fax: +1 801 538 7126, e-mail: UDAF-Information@utah.gov, URL: http://www.ag.state.ut.us/
Department of Commerce, 160 East 300 South, PO Box 146701, Salt Lake City, Utah 84114-6701, USA. Tel: +1 801 530 6431, fax: +1 801 530 6446, URL: http://www.commerce.state.ut.us/
Department of Community and Economic Development, 324 South State Street, Suite 500, Salt Lake City, Utah 84111, USA. Tel: +1 801 538 8700, fax: +1 801 538 8888, URL: http://dced.utah.gov/
Department of Corrections, 14717 S Minuteman Drive, Draper, UT 84020, USA. Tel: +1 801 545 5500, fax: +1 801 545 5670, e-mail: corrections@utah.gov, URL: http://www.cr.ex.state.ut.us/
Department of Environmental Quality, 168 North 1950 West, Salt Lake City, Utah 84116 (PO Box 144810, Salt Lake City, UT 84114-4810), USA. Tel: +1 801 536 4400, fax: +1 801 536 4401, URL: http://www.eq.state.ut.us/
Department of Health, PO Box 141010, Salt Lake City, UT 84114-1010, USA. Tel: +1 801 538 6101, URL: http://www.health.state.ut.us/
Department of Transport, 4501 South 2700 West, Mail Stop 141200, Salt Lake City, UT 84114-1200, USA. Tel: +1 801 965 4000, fax: +1 801 965 4391, e-mail: srwebmail@utah.gov, URL: http://www.dot.state.ut.us/

Political Parties
Utah Democratic Party, URL: http://www.utdemocrats.org/
Republican Party of Utah, URL: http://www.utgop.org

Elections
Elections took place in November 2012 for the following statewide positions: Governor and Lieutenant Governor, Attorney General, State Auditor and Treasurer, one US Senator and three US Representatives. The incumbent governor, Republican Gary Herbert, won with 68 per cent of the vote.

Following legislative elections in November 2012, the Republicans retained their majority in the state Senate (Republicans 24 seats, Democrats 5 seats) and in the state House of Representatives, with an increased majority (Republicans 61 seats, Democrats 14 seats).

LEGAL SYSTEM

Utah's court system consists of two appellate courts: the Supreme Court and the Court of Appeals; and trial courts: the District Court, Juvenile Courts, and Justice Courts. Utah is divided into a total of eight judicial districts.

The Supreme Court consists of the Chief Justice and four Associate Justices who serve renewable terms of ten years. The Court of Appeals comprises seven judges who serve terms of six years.

The 2004 General Session of Utah's state legislature repealed the law requiring the firing squad as the means of carrying out the death penalty in the state. Lethal injection is now the sole means of execution. However, abolition of the firing squad is not retroactive and inmates on death row before this date who chose this method, may be allowed an execution in this manner. In June 2010, Ronnie Lee Gardner was granted his wish to be executed by firing squad. It was Utah's first execution in 11 years; seven have been executed since 1976. Nine people remain on death row. The murder rate was 1.9 per 100,000 population.

Supreme Court, URL: http://www.utcourts.gov/courts/sup/
Chief Justice: Matthew Durrant
Associate Chief Justice: Ronald Nehring
Justices: Christine Durham, Thomas Lee, Jill Parrish
Court of Appeals, URL: http://www.utcourts.gov/courts/appell/
Presiding Judge: Carolyn McHugh

LOCAL GOVERNMENT

For administrative purposes Utah is divided into 29 county governments and 242 sub-county general purpose, or municipal, governments (cities and towns). County governments take the form of one of the following: General County, Urban County, Community Council, and Consolidated City and County. Municipal governments are First to Fifth Class according to the number of inhabitants. Conurbations with a population less than 1,000 have a town municipal government.

AREA AND POPULATION

Area
Utah is located in the West, north of Arizona, south of Wyoming and Idaho, east of Nevada, and west of Colorado. Utah's total area is 84,898.83 sq. miles, of which 82,143.65 sq. miles is land and 2,755.18 sq. miles is water.

To view a map, consult http://www.lib.utexas.edu/maps/us_2001/utah_ref_2001.pdf

Population
Latest Census Bureau estimates put the mid-2010 population at 2,595,013, down on the mid-2009 estimate of 2,784,572. The population was estimated to be 2,855,287 in 2012. Over the period 2000-2010, the state population grew by 16.2 per cent (361,844 people),

the third highest percentage increase in the USA. Over the previous decade, the population grew by 16.2 per cent. The population is expected to reach 3.485 million by 2030. Utah has an estimated population density of 33.3 people per sq. mile. The county with the highest population is Salt Lake County, with 1,029,655 inhabitants in 2010. The capital, Salt Lake City, is the largest city, with 186,440 inhabitants in 2010. Other major metropolitan areas are West Valley City (129,480), Provo city (112,488), and Sandy city (87,461).

According to the 2010 Census, 9.5 per cent of the population is under 5 years, 31.5 per cent under 18 years and 9.0 per cent is aged over 65 years. Approximately 86.1 per cent of the population is white, and 1.1 per cent is black. Approximately 13 per cent of the population is of Hispanic or Latino origin.

Births, Marriages, Deaths
The US Census Bureau, Population Division, estimated that there were 52,258 births in 2010 and 14,766 deaths, giving a natural population increase of 37,492. Net immigration amounted to 14,580 in 2009. The infant mortality rate in 2005 was an estimated 5.1 infant deaths per 1,000 live births. Marriages and divorces in 2007, according to provisional data, numbered 22,640 and 8,889 respectively.

Utah's birth rate on average has been 25 per cent higher than the national rate over the past 50 years,

Public Holidays
In addition to observing national holidays, the people of Utah celebrate Pioneer Day on July 24th.

EMPLOYMENT

Utah's estimated total civilian labour force in December 2012 was 1,362,500, of which 1,291,500 were employed and 71,000 were unemployed. The unemployment rate was 5.2 per cent, below the US rate of 7.8 per cent. (Source: US Bureau of Labor Statistics)

The following table shows December 2012 non-farm wage and salary employment (seasonally adjusted) according to industry (preliminary figures):

Industry	No. of Employed	12-month change (%)
Logging and mining	12,400	2.5
Construction	66,500	-2.1
Manufacturing	119,600	3.3
Trade, transportation and utilities	238,500	1.8
Information	31,900	7.0
Financial activities	74,200	6.5
Professional and business services	174,600	5.9
Educational and health services	162,700	1.4
Leisure and hospitality	123,500	8.3
Other services	36,200	5.8
Government	221,000	0.0
Total non-farm employment	1,260,100	3.0

Source: Bureau of Labor Statistics

BANKING AND FINANCE

GDP/GNP, Inflation, National Debt
Utah's total Gross Domestic Product (current prices) was estimated at $119,231 million in 2010 to $124.5 billion. Real GDP grew by 2.0 per cent in 2011 and was ranked 33rd in 2011 for its GDP.

Gross Domestic Product according to industry is shown on the following table (in millions of current dollars):

Industry	2009	2010	2011
Agriculture, forestry, fishing and hunting	376	559	647
Mining	2,321	2,431	2,845
Utilities	1,507	1,570	1,464
Construction	5,736	5,555	5,705
Manufacturing	14,206	16,475	17,608
Wholesale Trade	5,204	5,273	5,826
Retail Trade	7,204	8,205	8,427
Transportation and warehousing	3,853	3,995	4,156
Information	3,873	3,993	4,468
Finance and insurance	11,262	13,921	13,938
Real estate	13,806	13,168	13,571
Other non-government services	18,768	19,896	20,971
Government	15,610	15,861	16,292
TOTAL	112,300	119,231	124,483

Source: Bureau of Economic Analysis, Feb 2013

The state's average per capita income was an estimated $33,509 in 2011. Per capita real GDP rose from $38,452 in 2011, below the national average of $42,070.

The annual Consumer Price Index for the West urban area (all items) rose from 227.5 in 2011 to 232.4 in 2012. (1982-84 = 100). (Source: Bureau of Labor Statistics)

Balance of Payments / Imports and Exports

Total Utah imports amounted to $11,113 million in 2011, up 45.1 per cent from $7656 million in 2010. Imports account for 0.4 per cent of the US total. Gold was the top export in 2011. Exports rose by 33.6 per cent in 2010 to $13,809 million, rising further to $19,034 million in 2011 (up 37.8 per cent). Utah's exports account for 1.1 per cent of the US total.

The top five direct export destinations in 2011 according to export revenue are shown on the attached table:

Country	2010 ($m)	2011 ($m)	+/-% 2010-11
United Kingdom	4,408	6,715	52.3
Hong Kong	947	3,806	301.7
China	1,265	1,375	73.2
Thailand	172	708	8.7
Taiwan	551	697	310

Source: US Census Bureau, Foreign Trade Division

Utah's top five export industries in 2010, according to revenue, are shown on the table below:

Industry	Value ($m)	+/-% 2009-10
Gold, non monetary, unwroughts, NESOI	7,180	33.6
Memories, electronic integrated circuits	1,231	39.0
Food preparations, NESOI	298	43.9
Molybdenum ores and conc., not roasted	279	18.8
Civilian aircraft, engines, equipment and parts	273	9.3

Source: US Census Bureau, Foreign Trade Division

Chambers of Commerce and Trade Organisations
Salt Lake Area Chamber of Commerce, URL: http://www.saltlakechamber.org/

MANUFACTURING, MINING AND SERVICES

Primary and Extractive Industries
Major minerals and gases extracted from Utah's mines include oil, natural gas, coal, beryllium, gilsonite, potash, copper, magnesium, molybdenum, phosphate rock, silver and salt. Utah contains three of the Nation's 100 largest oil fields and two of its 100 largest natural gas fields. Mining contributed an estimated $2,845 million towards the 2011 Gross Domestic Product (up from $2,431 million in 2010). In 2010, the top earning sector was non-oil and gas mining ($1,254 million) followed by oil and gas extraction ($710 million), and support activities ($466 million). (Source: BEA)

Utah's oil industry had proven crude oil reserves of 449 million barrels in 2010 (1.9 per cent of the US total). Utah's 3,146 producing oil wells and 28 operational rotary rigs produced a monthly total of 2,551,000 barrels of oil in 2012 (1.2 per cent of the US total). The state had five oil refineries with a combined refinery capacity of 167,200 barrels per calendar day in 2012. Oil consumption in 2010 fell slightly to 49.3 million barrels, 25.4 million barrels of which was motor gasoline, and 12.9 million barrels was distillate fuel.

Utah's natural gas industry had 6,469 gas producing wells in 2011 and marketed production was estimated at 457,525 million cubic feet (1.9 per cent of US total). Natural gas reserves were estimated to be 6,981 billion cubic feet in 2010, 2.3 per cent of the US total. Natural gas plant liquids reserves amounted to 132 million barrels. Natural gas consumption was 222,166 million cubic feet in 2011. Utah consumes only about one-half of its own production. Almost 85 per cent of homes in Utah are heated by natural gas, the highest proportion in the US. Amoco is the major gas producer in Utah.

The coal industry had recoverable reserves of 201 million short tons in 2011, down from 281 million short tons in 2005. Production of coal in 2011 was 19,648 thousand short tons. Consumption rose from 17,526 thousand short tons in 2007 to 16,913 thousand short tons in 2009 (1.7 per cent of national total), nearly all of which was used in the electric utility industry. (Source: EIA)

Energy
Total energy production amounted to 1,074 trillion Btu in 2010, 1.4 per cent of the US total, ranking it 18th in the US. Total energy consumption in Utah rose to 764 trillion Btu in 2010 and per capita energy consumption amounted to 275 million Btu, ranking the state 38th.

Utah is a net exporter of electricity, with coal as its primary generating fuel. Net summer capability in 2010 was 7,497 MW (0.7 per cent of US total), and total net monthly (Oct. 2012) generation was 3,565 thousand MWh (33rd in the US). Coal accounted for 3,032 thousand MWh, natural gas 375,000 MWh, hydroelectric 60,000 MWh, other renewables 76,000 MWh and petroleum 4,000 MWh. Major utility plants include Intermountain Power P. (coal), Hunter (coal), Huntington (coal), Lake Side Power Plant (Gas) and Bonanza (coal).

In 2008, Utah adopted a voluntary renewable goal to encourage utilities to produce 20 per cent of their energy from renewable sources by 2025. In 2011, 4.7 per cent of net electricity generation came from renewable resources. (Source: EIA)

Manufacturing
The manufacturing industry is the fourth highest contributor to Utah's GDP, accounting for an estimated $17,608 million in 2011 (up from $16,475 million in 2010). The top manufacturing sectors in 2010 were primary metal manufacturing ($3,298 million), computer and electronic product manufacturing ($2,164 million), and chemical products ($1,455 million). (Source: BEA)

Service Industries
The services industry is Utah's largest contributor towards state GDP. Major sectors in 2011 were real estate and rental ($13,571 million), finance and insurance ($13,398 million), professional and technical services ($7,806 million) and health care and social assistance ($7,019 million). (Source: BEA)

Tourism
The accommodation and food sector of the services industry earned an estimated $3,129 million in 2011, whilst the arts, entertainment and recreation sector contributed $936 million to the state GDP. (Source: BEA) There were over 5 million recorded visitors to Utah's national parks. Canyonlands National Park is the largest of these and comprises a desert landscape eroded into canyons by the Colorado River and its tributaries.
State Division of Travel Development/Utah Travel Council, URL: http://travel.utah.gov/index.html

Agriculture
Utah's agriculture, forestry, fishing and hunting industry contributed an estimated $647 million towards the 2011 state GDP (up from $559 million in 2010). The main sector in 2010 was crop and animal production (farms) ($491 million). Forestry, fishing and related activities accounted for $68 million. (Source: BEA)

According to the US Department of Agriculture, Utah's farms numbered 16,600 in 2010 and covered a total land area of around 11,100,000 acres. The average size of a Utah farm was 669 acres in 2010. Total cash receipts for agricultural products sold in 2007 was $1.4 billion, of which livestock, poultry and products generated over $1 billion and crops, including nursery and greenhouse crops, generated $372 million. Major livestock products produced in Utah are cattle and calves, beef cows, and sheep and lambs. Major crops produced, in terms of crop acreage, include hay-alf and silage, wheat for grain, barley for grain, and corn for sil or green chop. As of 1 Jan. 2011, there were 800,000 cattle and calves, 740,000 hogs & pigs, and 280,000 sheep. (Source: National Agricultural Statistics Service)

COMMUNICATIONS AND TRANSPORT

International Airports
Salt Lake City International Airport serves over 21 million passengers a year and is the 22nd busiest airport in the States. Eleven commercial airlines fly to and from the airport.
Salt Lake City Airport Authority, URL: http://www.slcairport.com/

Roads
Utah has over 43,150 miles of local, state, and federal roads and highways. There are three Interstates running through Utah: I-15, which travels north to Idaho and south to Arizona; I-80, which runs from coast to coast; and I-70, which runs from east to west. Interstates 15 and 80 cross in Salt Lake City.

HEALTH

The National Center for Health Statistics estimated that there were 21.0 doctors (including osteopaths) per 10,000 state residents in 2009, lower than the US average of 27.4. In 2008, there were an estimated 1,743 dentists (6.4 per 10,000 population). In 2009, there were 1.8 community hospital beds per 1,000 residents (below the US average of 2.6 beds), and, in 2010, there were 99 nursing homes with 8,255 beds.

It was estimated that some 13.6 per cent of people in Utah did not have health care insurance in 2007-09, and, in 2007-11, an estimated 11.4 per cent were living in poverty. Utah reported 2,494 HIV/AIDS cases from the beginning of the epidemic to the end of 2008, and ranked 38th highest among the US states in cumulative number of reported HIV/AIDS cases in 2008. The TB rate was1.0 per 100,000 population, ranking it 44th highest among the US states. The obesity levels are below the US average: 22.5 per cent of adults and 6.4 per cent of adolescents. An estimated 56.9 per cent of adults were classified as overweight. (Source: CDC)

EDUCATION

Primary/Elementary Education
In the year 2009-10, enrolment in Utah's 1,060 public elementary and secondary schools reached 582,793 students. In the same year, there were 25,473 classroom teachers, giving a teacher/pupil ratio of one to 22.88, well above the national average of one to 15.3.

Educational revenues reached $4.396 billion over the academic year 2007-08, whilst current expenditure on public sector education amounted to $4.57 billion.

Higher Education
There were 41 degree-awarding institutions in 2010-11. Enrolment comprised 117,562 male students and 119,028 women. In the same year, 44,867 degrees/certificates were awarded, including 21,931 Bachelors, 5,804 Masters and 936 Doctorates. (Source: National Center for Educational Statistics).

RELIGION

Around 68 per cent of Utah's population are members of the Church of Jesus Christ of Latter-day Saints, better known as the "Mormons". Mormons have recently become a minority in Salt Lake City, but they tend to dominate in rural areas. The Church has had its headquarters in Salt Lake City since 1847.

UNITED STATES OF AMERICA

COMMUNICATIONS AND MEDIA

Newspapers
Utah's newspapers include: Desert News and Salt Lake Tribune, in Salt Lake City; Daily Herald, Provo; Herald Journal, Logan; Standard Examiner, Ogden; and The Spectrum, St. George.
Utah Press Association, URL: http://www.utahpress.com/
The Salt Lake Tribune, URL: http://www.sltrib.com/
Deseret News Publishing Co., URL: http://deseretnews.com/dn

Broadcasting
Six of Utah's television stations are based in Salt Lake City, whilst Cedar City and Provo have one each.

ENVIRONMENT

In 2010, emissions of carbon dioxide from Utah's electricity generating industry fell from 36,517,504 metric tons to 35,585,762 metric tons, ranking the state 27th in the US, and accounting for 1.5 per cent of the US total. Sulfur dioxide emissions were estimated at 25,495 metric tons and nitrogen oxide emissions 68,088 metric tons (2.7 per cent of US total).

In 2010 there were 10,375 alternative-fueled vehicles in use. In 2010, ethanol consumption amounted to 1,758 thousand barrels. (Source: EIA)

VERMONT

Capital: Montpelier (Population, Census 2010: 7,855)

Head of State: Peter Shumlin (D) (Governor) (page 1514)

State Flag: A blue background in the centre of which appears the state coat of arms: a landscape in the foreground with high mountains of blue in front of a yellow sky; near the base is a pine tree; on the right hand side are three yellow sheaves of grain set diagonally; on the left hand side is a red cow; on a scroll underneath the shield appear the words 'Vermont', in the centre, 'Freedom' on the left side, 'and Unity' on the right.

CONSTITUTION AND GOVERNMENT

Constitution
Vermont entered the Union on 4 March 1791. The Constitution was established on 9 July 1793 and last amended on 21 September 1995. According to the Constitution, Vermont's executive branch of government is headed by the governor, assisted by five elected executive officials: the lieutenant governor, secretary of state, attorney general, state treasurer, and state auditor of accounts.

Vermont elects two Senators and one At-Large Representative to the US Congress in Washington, DC. To view the state constitution, please visit: http://www.leg.state.vt.us/statutes/const2.htm

Legislature
Vermont's bicameral legislature, the Legislative Council, consists of the Senate and the House of Representatives. The legislature meets annually from January to the end of April, usually from Tuesday to Friday.
Vermont Legislative Council, Vermont State House, 115 State Street, Montpelier, Vermont 05633-5301, USA. Tel: +1 802 828 2231, URL: http://www.leg.state.vt.us/

Upper House
The Senate has 30 members who are elected for two years. The lieutenant governor also serves as the president of the Senate. Following elections held on 6th November 2012 the Democrats took 21 seats, the Republicans 7 and the Vermont Progressive Party 2 seats.
Senate, Office of the Secretary of the Senate, 115 State Street, Drawer 33, Montpelier, VT 05633-5501, USA. Tel: +1 802 828 2241, e-mail: sensec@leg.state.vt.us, URL: http://www.leg.state.vt.us/senateMain.cfm

Lower House
The House of Representatives has 150 members who are elected for two years. Following elections held on 6th November 2012 the Democrats had 98 seats, the Republicans 44, the Vermont Progressive Party 4 seats and Independents held 4 seats.
House of Representatives, Office of the House Clerk, 115 State Street, Drawer 33, Montpelier, VT 05633-5501, USA. Tel: +1 802 828 2247, e-mail: hclerk@leg.state.vt.us, URL: http://www.leg.state.vt.us

---

Elected Executive Branch Officials (as at January 2013)
Governor: Peter Shumlin (D) (page 1514)
Lieutenant Governor: Phil Scott (R)
State Treasurer: Beth Pearce (D)
Secretary of State: Jim Condos (D)
Auditor of Accounts: Doug Hoffer (D)
Attorney General: William H. Sorrell (D)

General Assembly (2013-14)
President of the Senate: Lt. Gov. Phil Scott (R)
President Pro Tem of the Senate: John F. Campbell (D)
Majority Leader of the Senate: Philip Baruth (D)
Minority Leader of the Senate: Joseph Benning (R)
Speaker of the House: Shap Smith (D)
Majority Leader of the House: Willem Jewett (D)
Minority Leader of the House: Donald Turner (R)

US Senators: Bernard Sanders (Ind) (page 1508) and Patrick J. Leahy (D) (page 1461)

Ministries
Office of the Governor, 109 State Street, Pavilion, Montpelier, VT 05609-0101, USA. Tel: +1 802 828 3333, fax: +1 802 828 3339, URL: http://www.vermont.gov/governor/
Office of the Lt. Governor, 115 State Street, Montpelier, Vermont 05633-5401, USA. Tel: +1 802 828 2226, fax: +1 802 828 3198, URL: http://ltgov.vermont.gov/

Office of the Attorney General, 109 State Street, Montpelier, VT 05609-1001, USA. Tel: +1 802 828 3171, fax: +1 802 828 5341, e-mail: aginfo@atg.state.vt.us, URL: http://www.atg.state.vt.us/
Office of the Auditor General, 132 State Street, Montpelier, VT 05633-5101, USA. Tel: +1 802 828 2281, fax: +1 802 828 2198, URL: http://auditor.vermont.gov/
Office of the Secretary of State, Redstone Building, 26 Terrace Street, Drawer 09, Montpelier, VT 05609-1101, USA. Tel: +1 802 828 2363, fax: +1 802 828 2496, URL: http://www.sec.state.vt.us/
Office of the State Treasurer, The Pavilion Bldg., 109 State Street, 4th Floor, VT 05609,USA. Tel: +1 802 828 2301, fax: +1 802 828 2772, URL: http://www.vermonttreasurer.gov/
Department of Agriculture, Food and Markets, 116 State Street, Drawer 20, Montpelier, Vermont 05620-2901, USA. Tel: +1 802 828 2416, fax: +1 802 828 3831, URL: http://www.vermontagriculture.com/index.htm
Agency of Commerce and Community Development, National Life Building, North Drawer 20, Montpelier, VT 05620, USA. Tel: +1 802 828 3211, URL: http://accd.vermont.gov/
Department of Economic Development, National Life Building, Drawer 20, Montpelier, VT 05620-0501, USA. Tel: +1 802 828 3080, fax: +1 802 828 3258, URL: http://www.thinkvermont.com/
Department of Education, 120 State Street, Montpelier, VT 05620-2501, USA. Tel: +1 802 828 3135, fax: +1 802 828 3154, URL: http://education.vermont.gov/
Department of Environmental Conservation, Commissioner's Office, 103 South Main Street, 1 South Building, Waterbury, Vermont 05671-0401, USA. Tel: +1 802 241 3808, fax: +1 802 244 5141, URL: http://www.anr.state.vt.us/dec/dec.htm
Department of Finance and Management, 109 State Street, Montpelier VT 05609-0401, USA. Tel: +1 802 828 2376, URL: http://finance.vermont.gov/
Department of Fish and Wildlife, 10 South 103 South Main Street, Waterbury, VT 05671-0501, USA. Tel: +1 802 241 3700, fax: +1 802 241 3295, URL: http://www.vtfishandwildlife.com/
Department of Health, 108 Cherry Street, PO Box 70, Burlington, VT 05402-0070, USA. Tel: +1 802 863 7200, fax: +1 802 865 7754, URL: http://healthvermont.gov/
Department of Labour, National Life Building, Drawer 20, Montpelier, Vermont 05620-3401, USA. Tel: +1 802 828 2288, fax: +1 802 828 2195, URL: http://www.labor.vermont.gov/
Vermont Agency of Transportation, State Office Building, 120 State Street, Montpelier, VT 05603-001, USA. Tel: +1 802 828 2000, URL: http://www.aot.state.vt.us/dmv/dmvhp.htm
Department of Tourism and Marketing, 6 Baldwin Street, Drawer 33, Montpelier, VT 05633-1301, USA. Tel: +1 802 828 3676, URL: http://www.vermontvacation.com/

Political Parties
Vermont Democratic Party, URL: http://www.vtdemocrats.org
Vermont Republican State Committee, URL: http://vtgop.org/

Elections
Elections were held on 6 November 2012 for the positions of Governor and other executive branch officials. The incumbent governor Peter Shumlin was re-elected with 68 per cent of the vote.

Following the elections held in November 2012 in the State House, the Democrats held 98 seats, the Republicans 44, the Progressives 4 and 4 seats were held by independents. In the Senate the Democrats held 21 seats, the Republicans 7 seats and the Vermont Progressive Party 2 seats.

LEGAL SYSTEM

Vermont's court system consists of the Supreme Court, 14 Superior Courts (one in each county), 14 District Courts, 14 Family Courts, 14 Probate Courts, and the Environmental Court. The Supreme Court comprises the Chief Justice and four Associate Justices. There are 12 Superior Courts, one for each county, which cover civil cases. The Superior Court has 12 judges.

In Baker v. Vermont (1999), the Vermont Supreme Court ruled that the state must either allow same-sex marriage or provide a separate but equal status for them. The state legislature chose the second option by creating the institution of civil union. In April 2009 the state legislature overrode the governor's veto to allow same-sex marriage, and in September 2009, Vermont became one of six states in which same-sex couples can marry.

The death penalty was abolished in 1964.

Supreme Court, URL: http://www.vermontjudiciary.org

Chief Justice: Paul Reiber
Associate Justices: John Dooley, Marilyn Skoglund, Brian Burgess, Beth Robinson

LOCAL GOVERNMENT

Administratively, Vermont is divided into 14 county governments and 284 sub-county general purpose governments. The 282 sub-county governments consist of 45 municipal governments (cities and villages), and 237 town governments. The governing body of a town is known as the board of selectmen.

AREA AND POPULATION

Area

Vermont is situated in the north-east of the US, west of New Hampshire, east of New York State, north of Massachusetts, and south of Montreal, Canada. Vermont's total area is 9,249.56 sq. miles, of which 9,614.26 sq. miles is land and 364.70 sq. miles is water. Over 75 per cent of the state is forested, and the rest is covered in meadow, uplands, lakes, ponds, and swampy wetlands. The climate is continental, with warm summers and cold winters.

To view a map of the state, please consult:
http://www.lib.utexas.edu/maps/us_2001/new_england_ref_2001.pdf

Population

According to the 2010 Census, the state 2010 population at 625,741, up from the mid-2009 population at 621,760. In 2012, the population was estimated to be 626,011. Over the period 2000-10, the state population grew by 2.8 per cent. The population is expected to reach 711,867 by 2030. Vermont has an estimated population density of 67.9 persons per sq. mile. Montpelier is the smallest state capital in the USA, with a 2010 population of 7,855 people. When the legislature is in session the city swells to an estimated 15,000 people. The largest city is Burlington, which had a population of 42,417 in 2010. Major counties are Chittenden County (156,545 in 2010), Rutland County (61,642), and Washington County (59,534).

According to the 2010 Census, 5.1 per cent of the population is under 5 years, 20.7 per cent under 18 years and 14.6 per cent is aged over 65 years. Approximately 95.3 per cent of the population is white, and 1.0 per cent is black. Approximately 1.5 per cent of the population is of Hispanic or Latino origin.

Births, Marriages, Deaths

The US Census Bureau (CDC) estimated that there were 6,233 births in 2010 and 5,380 deaths, giving a natural population increase of 853 people. An estimated 554 people emigrated in 2009. The infant mortality rate in 2007 was 5.1 infant deaths per 1,000 live births. Marriages and divorces in 2007, according to provisional data, were recorded at 5,346 and 2,364 respectively.

Public Holidays

In addition to the public holidays observed by the US as a whole, Vermont also celebrates Town Meeting Day (first Tuesday in March), Memorial Day (30 May) and Bennington Battle Day (16 August)

EMPLOYMENT

Vermont's estimated total civilian labour force in December 2012 was 357,200, of which 339,100 were employed and 18,000 were unemployed. The unemployment rate was 5.1 per cent, significantly lower than the national average of 7.8 per cent. (Source: Bureau of Labor Statistics)

The following table shows preliminary December 2012 non-farm wage and salary employment (seasonally adjusted) according to industry:

Industry	No. of Employed	12-month change (%)
Logging and mining*	800	14.3
Construction	14,000	0.0
Manufacturing	30,500	-0.3
Trade, transport and utilities	57,000	0.5
Information*	4,900	0.0
Financial activities	11,900	0.0
Professional and business services	26,600	3.1
Leisure and hospitality	33,800	1.2
Other services	9,500	-3.1
Government	52,100	-1.1
TOTAL	304,600	1.1

*Not seasonally adjusted
Source: US Bureau of Labor Statistics

BANKING AND FINANCE

GDP/GNP, Inflation, National Debt

Vermont's total Gross Domestic Product (current prices) rose from an estimated $25,264 million in 2010 to $25.9 billion in 2011. Real GDP rose by 2.8 per cent in 2010 and by 0.5 per cent in 2011. Vermont was ranked 50th in the US (including the District of Columbia) for its 2011 Gross Domestic Product. GDP according to industry, is shown on the attached table (millions of current dollars):

Industry	2009	2010	2011
Agriculture, forestry, fishing & hunting	269	347	395

- continued			
Mining	51	51	54
Utilities	612	649	600
Construction	913	915	916
Manufacturing	2,486	2,775	2,869
Wholesale Trade	1,119	1,152	1,192
Retail Trade	1,984	2,090	2,170
Transport and warehousing	481	493	509
Information	680	664	675
Finance and insurance	1,426	1,571	1,557
Real estate	3,399	3,245	3,269
Other non-government services	3,934	4,298	4,588
Government	3,586	3,659	3,711
TOTAL	24,427	25,264	25,905

Source: Bureau of Economic Analysis, Feb. 2013

The state's average per capita income was an estimated $41,572 in 2011. Per capita real GDP fell from $36,968 in 2010 to $36,665 in 2011, below the US average of $42,070.

The annual Consumer Price Index for the northeast urban area (all items) rose from 240.9 in 2011 to 245.7 in 2012. (1982-84 = 100). (Source: Bureau of Labor Statistics)

Balance of Payments / Imports and Exports

Vermont's total imports amounted to $3,369 million in 2010. They rose by 22.5 per cent in 2011, reaching $4,137 million. Top 2010 imports include electronics, chocolate and oil. Vermont's export revenue fell from $3,697 million in 2008 to $3,219 million in 2009, a decrease of -12.9 per cent. Exports rose by 32.9 per cent to $4,277 million, in 2010 representing 0.3 per cent of US total exports. Exports rose to $4,257 million in 2011, down -0.5 per cent.

The following table shows 2010-11 export revenue according to the top five international markets:

Country	2010 ($m)	2011 ($m)	+/-% 2010-11
Canada	2,029	1,873	-7.7
China	585	779	33.2
Hong Kong	240	273	13.8
Taiwan	154	202	30.7
South Korea	130	152	16.9

Source: US Census Bureau, Foreign Trade Division

Vermont's top five export products in 2010, according to revenue, are shown on the following table:

Product	Export Revenue ($m)
Processors and controllers, electronic integrated circuits	1,745
Electronic integrated circuits	927
Video games use w tv rceivr & pts	453
Parts & Access. for ADP machines	61
Pts. mach. for work rubber/plast. mfg.	55

Source: US Census Bureau, Foreign Trade Division

Chambers of Commerce and Trade Organisations
Vermont Chamber of Commerce, URL: http://www.vtchamber.com/
Central Vermont Chamber of Commerce, URL: http://www.central-vt.com/chamber/index.html

MANUFACTURING, MINING AND SERVICES

Primary and Extractive Industries
Vermont's mining industry contributed $54 million towards the 2011 state Gross Domestic Product, all of which was from non-fuel mining. The state mines stone, sand, gravel, talc and pyrophyllite, and gemstones.

Vermont has no domestic oil industry, relying on out-of-state supplies for its requirements. Oil consumption in 2010 was 15.7 million barrels, of which 7.6 million barrels was motor gasoline and 4.7 million barrels was distillate fuel.

With no natural gas reserves, Vermont relies on supplies from outside the state, mainly Canada. Natural gas consumption rose from 8,443 million cu ft in 2010 to 8,609 million cu ft in 2011. Vermont has the second lowest natural gas consumption in the USA. The residential sector is the main user. (Source: EIA)

Energy
Vermont's total energy production amounted to 76 trillion Btu in 2010, ranking it 46th in the US. Vermont's total energy consumption was one of the lowest in the USA in 2010 at 148 trillion Btu. Per capita energy consumption ranked the state 42nd in the US in the same year (236 million Btu).

Vermont is a net importer of electricity, with nuclear power as its primary generating fuel, although it is the only state in the US with a wood-fired plant (the J.C. McNeil plant). Net summer capability in 2010 was 1,128 MW (0.1 per cent of the US total), and total net monthly (Oct. 2012) generation was 553 thousand MWh (50th in the US). Of this, nuclear contributed 438 thousand MWh, hydroelectric 86 thousand MWh, and other renewables 28 thousand MWh. Major utility plants are Vermont Yankee (nuclear), J.C. McNeil (other renewables),

UNITED STATES OF AMERICA

Bellows Falls (hydro), Wilder (hydro), and Sheffield (wind). Vermont's single nuclear power plant is Vermont Yankee, a 506 net MWe boiling water reactor located on the western shore of the Connecticut River in Vernon.

In 2008, Vermont adopted a renewable energy goal to produce 25 per cent of the energy consumed in the State from renewable sources by 2025. (Source: EIA)

Manufacturing

Manufacturing is Vermont's second largest contributor towards GDP (after services), accounting for $2,869 million in 2011 (up from $2,775 million in 2010). The top sectors in 2010 were computer and electronic products ($896 million) and food, beverage and tobacco products ($421 million). (Source: BEA)

Service Industries

The services industry is Vermont's largest contributor to its GDP. The top sectors in 2011 were real estate ($3,269 million), health care and social assistance ($2,807 million), finance and insurance ($1,557 million) and professional and technical services ($1,763 million). (Source: BEA)

Tourism

The food and accommodation sector of the services industry accounted for $1,226 million of Vermont's GDP in 2011 whilst the arts, entertainment and recreation sector contributed $229 million. (Source: BEA)
Vermont Department of Tourism and Marketing,
URL: http://www.vermontvacation.com/

Agriculture

Vermont's agriculture, forestry and fishing industry contributed an estimated $395 million towards the GDP in 2011 (up from $347 million in 2010). The farms sector contributed $290 million towards GDP in 2010, whilst the forestry, fishing and related activities sector contributed $56 million. (Source: GDP)

Over 25 per cent of Vermont's land is used agriculturally. According to the US Dept. of Agriculture, Vermont's farms numbered around 7,000 in 2010 and occupied a total land area of 1,220,000 acres. The average size of a Vermont farm was 174 acres in 2010. Cash receipts from farming reached $673.7 millon in 2007; livestock receipts reached $574.4 million whilst crops earned $99 million. Vermont's main agricultural products include maple, hay and corn silage, apples, vegetable and small fruits, Christmas trees and cut flowers. Major livestock products include sheep and lambs, beef, turkey, pork and eggs. Vermont is first in the US for the production of maple syrup, and first in New England for production of milk, hay and corn silage, wool, sheep and lamb. Aquaculture and horse rearing are growing industries. As of 1 Jan. 2011, there were 270,000 cattle and calves and 2,700 hogs and pigs.

COMMUNICATIONS AND TRANSPORT

International Airports

Burlington International Airport is served by seven major airlines: US Air, Delta, Business Express, NorthWestern, American, Continental, and United.
Burlington International Airport, URL: http://www.burlingtonintlairport.com/

Roads

Vermont is crossed by two Interstate Highways: I-91, running north-south; and I-89, running south-east to north-west, from Massachusetts to Montreal, Canada. Vermont Transit is a coach service linking Vermont with Boston, Montreal, and Albany. The Bonanza coach service links New York City with Bennington.

Railways

Vermont has more than 700 miles of railway lines and owns in the region of 300 miles. Vermont's railway companies include: Clarendon & Pittsford Railroad, Green Mountain Railroad Corporation, New England Central Railway, Northern Vermont Railroad, and Vermont Railway Inc. The Vermonter provides a daily service between Washington, DC, New York and St. Albans. The Ethan Allen Express offers a daily service between New York and Rutland.

Shipping

Vermont has two major ferry companies: Lake Champlain Ferries and Fort Ticonderoga Ferry, both linking Vermont with New York State.

HEALTH

The National Center for Health Statistics estimated that there were 35.9 doctors per 10,000 state residents in 2008, above the national average of 27.7 doctors per 10,000 residents. In 2008, there were an estimated 360 dentists (5.8 per 10,000 population). In 2009, there were 2.1 community hospital beds per 1,000 residents (below the US average of 2.6 beds), and, in 2010, Vermont had 40 nursing homes with a total of 3,276 beds.

It was estimated that some 13.6 per cent of the state population had no health care insurance in 2007-09, and that, in 2007-11, 11.3 per cent were living in poverty. Vermont reported 505 HIV/AIDS cases from the beginning of the epidemic to the end of 2008, and ranked 46th highest in cumulative number of reported HIV/AIDS cases in 2008. The TB rate was 1.0 per 100,000 population, ranking it 45 highest among the US states in 2008. Levels of obesity and overweight youth are comfortably below the US rates. An estimated 57.7 per cent of the adult population are classified as overweight and 23.2 per cent of youths. An estimated 23.2 per cent of the population is classified as obese.(Source: CDC)

EDUCATION

Primary/Secondary Education

In the year 2009-10, there were 323 public elementary and secondary schools in Vermont. Enrolment for the year was 92,431, whilst the number of teachers was 8,733, giving a teacher/student ratio of one to 10.58, one of the lowest in the US.

The state's total current expenditure for public schools during 2007-08 year was $1.462 billion, whilst education revenues reached $1.5 billion.

Higher Education

In the year 2010-11, there were 24 institutes of higher education eligible to confer degrees. 18 of them were private and 6 were public. Enrolment for the year comprised 20,417 male students and 24,588 women. 10,218 degrees/certificates were conferred during the year, including 5,888 Bachelors, 2,244 Masters and 381 Doctorates. Vermont's higher education institutions include: University of Vermont (UVM), Norwich University, Community College of Vermont, Southern Vermont College, Trinity College of Vermont, Johnson State College, Marlboro College Vermont, and Vermont Law School. (Source: National Center for Educational Statistics)

COMMUNICATIONS AND MEDIA

Newspapers

Vermont's newspapers include: Vermont Press Bureau and The World, Montpelier; Burlington Free Press; The Other Paper; Charlotte News; Battlebro Reformer; The Chronicle, Barton.
Vermont Times, URL: http://www.vermont-times.com
The Barre Montpelier Times Argus, URL: http://timesargus.nybor.com/
Vermont Life, URL: http://www.vtlife.com/

Broadcasting

Vermont has 12 television stations serving it, three operated by ABC, two by CBS, three by NBC, three by PBS and one by Fox. Stations include: Vermont ETV, WCAX TV, Channel 31, Channel 3, WNNE TV, WPTZ TV, WVNY TV, Channel 22, WWIN TV, Channel 5, and Channel 39.
Vermont Public Radio, URL: http://relay.vpr.net/VPR/

ENVIRONMENT

Nuclear power accounts for around three quarters of the electricity generated within Vermont, a higher share than in any other State. The remaining generation is produced from renewable energy sources, mainly from hydroelectric power and fuel wood. As a result, emissions from the state's power-generating industry are the lowest in the US. In 2010, carbon dioxide emissions fell to 8,016 metric tons. Emissions of sulfur dioxide were 38 metric tons and nitrogen oxide 655 metric tons.

In 2010, there were 2,551 alternative-fueled vehicles in use. In 2011, ethanol consumption amounted to 831,000 barrels (0.3 per cent of US total). (Source: EIA)

VIRGINIA

Capital: Richmond (Population, Census 2010: 204,214)

Head of State: Robert (Bob) McDonnell (Governor) (page 1474)

State Flag: A deep blue field in the centre of which appears the great seal of the Commonwealth: the Roman goddess Virtus dressed as an Amazon holds a sheathed sword in one hand and a spear in the other and stands with one foot on the fallen figure of Tyranny, who holds a broken chain in one hand and a scourge in the other; his crown lies nearby; at the bottom of the seal appears the state motto: 'Sic Semper Tyrannis' ('Thus Always to Tyrants').

CONSTITUTION AND GOVERNMENT

Constitution
Virginia was one of the original 13 states of the Union (26 June 1788). The Virginia Constitution of 1776 confirmed the state's bicameral legislature. According to the present state Constitution, adopted in 1970, three executive branch officials are elected: the governor, lieutenant governor, and attorney general. All are elected for four-year terms. The Governor cannot be elected for consecutive terms. Executive power is carried out by the Governor's Cabinet, consisting of separate secretaries of Administration, Commerce and Trade, Education, Finance, Health and Human Resources, Natural Resources, Transportation, Commonwealth, Public Safety, and Technology.

Virginians elect two Senators to the US Senate for six years and 11 congressmen to the US House of Representatives for two years.

To consult the state constitution, please visit:
http://legis.state.va.us/Laws/search/ConstitutionTOC.htm

Recent Events
In April 2007, Governor Kaine tightened the state's gun laws in response to Cho Seung-hui's killing of 32 people at Virginia Tech earlier in the month. The new law bans the purchase of guns by people found to be dangerous and ordered to have involuntary mental health treatment. In January 2010, a gunman killed eight people in Appomattox.

Legislature
The General Assembly consists of the State Senate and the State House of Delegates. The General Assembly meets annually on the second Wednesday in January. Sessions usually last for no longer than 60 days in even-numbered years, and no longer than 30 days in odd-numbered years.

Upper House
The State Senate has 40 members who are elected for four years. Each Senator represents about 176,000 citizens. At the time of the 2010 legislative session the state Senate was composed of 21 Democrats and 19 Republicans.
Virginia State Senate, General Assembly Building, corner of Ninth and Broad Street, Richmond, Virginia (Post Office Box 396, Richmond, VA 23218), USA. Tel: +1 804 698 7400, fax: +1 804 698 7410 (Clerk's Office), URL: http://virginiageneralassembly.gov/

Lower House
The State House of Delegates has 100 members who are elected for two years. Each member represents about 71,000 citizens. The Republicans hold the majority of seats in the House. At the time of the 2010 legislative session the House consisted of 59 Republicans, 39 Democrats and two Independents.
Virginia State House of Delegates, General Assembly Building, PO Box 406, Richmond, Virginia 23218, USA. Tel: +1 804 698 1619 (Clerk's Office) fax: +1 804 786 6310, URL: http://virginiageneralassembly.gov/

Elected Executive Branch Officials (as at April 2013)
Governor: Robert (Bob) McDonnell (R) (page 1474)
Lieutenant Governor: Bill Bolling (R)
Attorney General: Ken Cuccinelli (R)

General Assembly (as at April 2013)
President of the Senate: Lt. Gov. Bill Bolling (R)
President Pro Tem of the Senate: Walter Stosch (R)
Senate Majority Leader: Thomas K. Norment, Jr (R)
Senate Minority Leader: Richard L. Saslaw (D)
Speaker of the House: William Howell (R)
House Majority Leader: M. Kirkland Cox (R)
House Minority Leader: David Toscano (D)

US Senators: Jim Webb (D) (page 1535) and Mark Warner (D) (page 1534)

Ministries
Office of the Governor, State Capitol, 3rd Floor, Richmond, Virginia 23219, USA. Tel: +1 804 786 2211, fax: +1 804 371 6351, URL: http://www.governor.virginia.gov/
Office of the Lieutenant Governor, 900 E. Main Street, Suite 1400, Richmond, VA 23219, USA. Tel: +1 804 786 2078, fax: +1 804 786 7514, URL: http://www.ltgov.virginia.gov/
Office of the Attorney General, 900 East Main Street, Richmond, VA 23219, USA. Tel: +1 804 786 2071, fax: +1 804 786 1991, e-mail: mail@oag.state.va.us, URL: http://www.oag.state.va.us/
Office of the Auditor of Public Accounts, James Monroe Building, 101 North 14th Street, Richmond, VA 23219, USA. Tel: +1 804 225 3350, fax: +1 804 225 3357, URL: http://www.apa.state.va.us/

Office of the Secretary of Commerce and Trade, Ninth Street Office Building, Suite 723, 202 North Ninth Street, Richmond, VA 23219, USA. Tel: +1 804 786 7831, fax: +1 804 371 0250, URL: http://www.commerce.state.va.us/
Office of the Secretary of the Commonwealth, 830 East Main Street, 14th Floor, Richmond, Virginia 23219, USA. Tel: +1 804 786 2441, fax: +1 804 371 0017, e-mail: socmail@gov.state.va.us, URL: http://www.soc.state.va.us/
Department of Agriculture and Consumer Services (VDACS), 1100 Bank Street, Richmond, Virginia 23219, USA. Tel: +1 804 786 2373, URL: http://www.vdacs.state.va.us/
Department of Business Assistance, 707 East Main Street, Suite 300, Richmond, VA 23219-4068, USA. (Mailing address: Post Office Box 446, Richmond, VA 23218-0798, USA.) Tel: +1 804 371 8200, fax: +1 804 371 8111, URL: http://vdba.virginia.gov/
Department of Conservation and Recreation, 203 Governor Street, Suite 302, Richmond, VA 23219-2094, USA. Tel: +1 804 786 6124, fax: +1 804 786 6141, URL: http://www.dcr.virginia.gov/
Department of Corrections, 6900 Atmore Drive, Richmond, VA 23225 (Post Office Box 26963, Richmond, VA 23261-6963) USA. Tel: +1 804 674 3000, fax: +1 804 674 3536, e-mail: docmail@vadoc.state.va.us, URL: http://www.vadoc.state.va.us/
Department of Education, Monroe Building, 101 N. 14th Street, Richmond, VA 23219, USA. (Mailing address: PO Box 2120, Richmond, VA 23218, USA.) Tel: +1 804 225 2020, URL: http://www.doe.virginia.gov/
Department of Environmental Quality, 629 East Main Street (Post Office Box 10009, Richmond, VA 23240), Richmond, VA 23219, USA. Tel: +1 804 698 4000, fax: +1 804 698 4500, URL: http://www.deq.state.va.us/
Department of Forestry, URL: http://www.dof.virginia.gov/
Department of Game and Inland Fisheries, URL: http://www.dgif.virginia.gov/
Department of Health, 1500 East Main Street, Richmond, Virginia 23219 (PO Box 2448, Richmond, Virginia 23218-2448), USA. Tel: +1 804 786 3561, URL: http://www.vdh.state.va.us/
Department of Labor and Industry, Powers-Taylor Building, 13 South Thirteenth Street, Richmond, VA 23219-4101, USA. Tel: +1 804 371 2327, fax: +1 804 371 2324, URL: http://www.doli.virginia.gov/
Department of Planning and Budget, Ninth Street Office Building, 200 N. 9th Street, Room 418, Richmond, VA 23219-3418, USA. Tel: +1 804 786 7455, fax: +1 804 225 3291, URL: http://www.dpb.virginia.gov/
Department of Rail and Public Transportation, 1313 E. Main Street, Suite 300, PO Box 590, Richmond, VA 23218-0590, USA. Tel: +1 804 786 4440, fax: +1 804 786 7286, URL: http://www.drpt.virginia.gov/
Department of Transportation, 1401 East Broad Street, Richmond, VA 23219, USA. Tel: +1 804 786 2801, URL: http://virginiadot.org/
Department of the Treasury, 101 North 14th Street, James Monroe Building, 3rd Floor, (PO Box 1879) Richmond, VA 23219, USA. Tel: +1 804 225 2142, fax: +1 804 225 3187, URL: http://www.trs.virginia.gov/

Political Parties
Democratic Party of Virginia, URL: http://www.vademocrats.org/
Republican Party of Virginia, URL: http://www.rpv.org

Elections
The most recent Virginia state legislative elections took place in November 2009. Voters elected all 100 members of the Virginia House of Delegates to two-year terms ending in 2011. Following the election, the House is made up of 59 Republicans, 39 Democrats and two independents. In the state Senate, the Democrats hold the majority with 21 seats whilst the Republicans have 19 seats.

Virginia's Executive Constitutional Officers (Governor, Lieutenant Governor, and Attorney General) were last elected in November 2009 and began their four-year terms in January 2010. Governor Tim Kaine was not eligible to stand for re-election. The Governorship was won by former state Attorney General Bob McDonnell, with 59 per cent of the vote, the highest percentage of the vote for Governor since 1961.

LEGAL SYSTEM

Virginia's court system consists of the Supreme Court, the Court of Appeals, Circuit Courts, and District Courts (Combined District Courts, General District Courts, Juvenile and Domestic Courts, and Relations District Courts). The Supreme Court comprises the Chief Justice and six Associate Justices, all elected for twelve-year terms by a majority of the members of each house of the General Assembly. The Court of Appeals comprises 11 judges, elected for eight-year terms by a majority of the members of the General Assembly. The Chief Judge of the Court of Appeals is elected by members of the Court of Appeals and serves a term of four years.

Virginia has the death penalty. As of February 2013 there were 11 inmates on death row in Virginia. 110 executions have been carried out since 1976. The first execution of a woman in nearly 100 years took place in September 2010. One person was executed in 2011 and one in 2012.

Supreme Court, URL: http://www.courts.state.va.us/courts/scv/supreme.html
Chief Justice: Cynthia D. Kinser (term expires 31 January 2022)
Justices: Donald W. Lemons, S. Bernard Goodwyn, LeRoy F. Millette, Jr., William C. Mims, Elizabeth McClanahan, Cleo Powell
Court of Appeals of Virginia, URL: http://www.courts.state.va.us/courts/cav/appeals.html
Chief Judge: Hon. Walter S. Felton

UNITED STATES OF AMERICA

LOCAL GOVERNMENT

For administrative purposes Virginia is divided into 95 county governments and 229 sub-county general purpose governments. All 229 general purpose governments are municipal governments, comprising independent cities and incorporated towns. Whilst towns remain part of the counties in which they are located, cities are independent, levying and collecting their own taxes.

Virginia Association of Counties, URL: http://www.vaco.org/

AREA AND POPULATION

Area
The Commonwealth of Virginia is in the centre of the East Coast of the United States, north of North Carolina, east of Kentucky and West Virginia, and south of Maryland and Washington, DC. The area of Virginia is 42,774.20 sq. miles, of which 39,594.07 sq. miles is land and 3,180.13 sq. miles is water (10,558,653 hectares, including 275,317 hectares of water area). Virginia has 2,400 km of shoreline. The state is renowned for its 'Blue Ridge Mountains', that form part of the Appalachian chain.

To view a map of Virginia, please consult:
http://www.lib.utexas.edu/maps/us_2001/virginia_ref_2001.pdf

Population
According to the 2010 Census, the 2010 state population was 8,001,024, up from the mid-2009 estimate of 7,882,590. The population was estimated at 8,185,867 in 2012. Virginia's population grew by 13.0 per cent over the period 2000-10, and by 14.4 per cent over the decade 1990-2000. The population is expected to reach 9.8 million by 2030. The population density is estimated at 202.6 persons per sq. mile. Seventy per cent of Virginia's population lives in eight metropolitan areas, whilst 60 per cent lives in the three eastern-most metropolitan areas: Northern Virginia, Richmond, and Hampton Roads. Fairfax County was the most populated in 2010, with 1,081,726 inhabitants. The population of the capital, Richmond, was 204,214 in 2010.

According to the 2010 Census, 6.4 per cent of the population is under 5 years, 23.2 per cent under 18 years and 12.2 per cent is aged over 65 years. Approximately 68.6 per cent of the population is white, and 19.4 per cent is black. Approximately 7.9 per cent of the population is of Hispanic or Latino origin.

Births, Marriages, Deaths
The US Census Bureau (CBC) estimated that there were 103,000 births in 2010 and 59,032 deaths, giving a natural population growth of 43,968 people. An estimated 39,166 people moved to the state in 2009. The infant mortality rate in 2007 was 7.8 infant deaths per 1,000 live births. Marriages and divorces in 2007, were recorded at 57,982 and 29,542 respectively.

Public Holidays
In addition to celebrating the national public holidays, Virginians observe Lee-Jackson Day on the Friday preceding the third Monday in January.

EMPLOYMENT

Virginia's estimated total civilian labour force was 4,351,200 in December 2012, of which 4,113,000 were employed and 238,200 were unemployed. The unemployment rate was 5.5 per cent, below the US average of 7.8 per cent. (Source: US Bureau of Labor Statistics)

The following table shows preliminary December 2012 non-farm wage and salary employment (seasonally adjusted) according to industry:

Industry	No. of Jobs	12-month change (%)
Logging and mining	9,800	-10.1
Construction	171,400	-3.3
Manufacturing	226,500	-0.2
Trade, transportation and utilities	631,000	-0.8
Information	71,300	-3.0
Financial activities	194,200	4.8
Professional and business services	668,900	0.7
Educational and health services	496,100	4.6
Leisure and hospitality	358,900	2.4
Other services	190,100	0.4
Government	715,800	0.2
TOTAL	3,734,000	0.8

Source: US Bureau of Labor Statistics

BANKING AND FINANCE

GDP/GNP, Inflation, National Debt
Virginia's total Gross Domestic Product (GDP) rose from $419,365 million in 2010 to $428.9 billion in 2011. Real GDP increased by 2.6 per cent in 2010 and by 0.3 per cent in 2011. Virginia was ranked 10th in the US for its 2011 GDP. The largest industry was government (18.7 per cent of GDP).

State GDP according to industry is shown on the following table (in millions of current dollars):

Industry	2009	2010	2011
Agriculture, forestry, fishing and hunting	1,385	1,423	1,627
Mining	2,023	2,395	2,180

- continued

Utilities	6,410	6,557	5,816
Construction	14,806	14,660	14,623
Manufacturing	34,189	37,392	39,007
Wholesale Trade	15,625	15,816	16,860
Retail Trade	20,774	21,889	22,462
Transportation and warehousing	9,318	9,462	9,569
Information	18,527	17,961	18,002
Finance and insurance	25,684	28,710	29,414
Real estate, rental and leasing	55,860	52,414	50,986
Other non-government services	96,875	102,909	108,177
Government	75,785	78,660	80,020
TOTAL	404,955	419,365	428,909

Source: Bureau of Economic Analysis, Feb. 2013

The state's average per capita income was an estimated $46,107 in 2011. Per capita real GDP fell to $46,408 in 2011, still above the US average of $42,070.

The annual Consumer Price Index (CPI) for the Washington-Baltimore, DC-MD-VA-WV, urban area (all items) rose from 146.97 in 2011 to 150.2 in 2012. (1982-84 = 100) (Source: Bureau of Labor Statistics)

Balance of Payments / Imports and Exports
Virginia's total imports amounted to $20,418 million in 2010, up 9.4 per cent on the previous year. Imports rose by 5.2 per cent in 201, reaching $21,474 million, accounting for 1.0 per cent of US total. Virginia's total export revenue fell from $18,942 million in 2008 to $15,052 million in 2009, a 20.5 per cent decrease. Exports rose by 14.0 per cent to $17,163 million in 2010 and rose by a further 5.4 per cent in 2011 to reach $18,089 million, accounting for 1.2 per cent of the US total.

The following table shows the top five merchandise export destinations in 2010-11 according to revenue:

Country	2010 ($m)	2011 ($m)	+/-% 2010-11
Canada	2,975	2,925	-1.7
China	1,274	1,755	37.7
UK	1,014	1,089	7.4
Mexico	862	901	4.5
Germany	852	866	1.6

Source: US Census Bureau, Foreign Trade Division

The top five export products in 2010, according to revenue, are shown on the following table:

Product	Export Revenue ($m)
Memories, electronic integrated circuits	1,231
Bituminous coal, not agglomerated	971
Civilian aircraft, engines, and parts	577
Kraft paper over 150g/M2, bleach	452
Soybeans	427

Source: US Census Bureau, Foreign Trade Division

Chambers of Commerce and Trade Organisations
Virginia Chamber of Commerce, URL: http://www.vachamber.com/
Virginia Department of Business Assistance, URL: http://www.dba.state.va.us/
Central Fairfax Chamber of Commerce, URL: http://www.cfcc.org/
Greater Richmond Chamber of Commerce, URL: http://www.grcc.com/

MANUFACTURING, MINING AND SERVICES

Primary and Extractive Industries
The mining industry contributed an estimated $2,180 million towards Virginia's GDP in 2011 (up from $2,395 million in 2010). In 2010, the largest earning sector was non-fuel mining, accounting for $1,909 million. This was followed by oil and gas extraction ($309 million), and support activities ($178 million). (Source: BEA)

Virginia had recoverable coal reserves of 348 million short tons in 2011 (1.8 per cent of US total) and the state produced 22,523 thousand short tons (2.1 per cent of US total).

Virginia's oil industry consisted of three producing oil wells and one rotary rig and a 66,300 barrel-per-day oil refinery in 2009. According to EIA figures oil production in 2010 was just 1,000 barrels. Consumption fell to 158.1 million barrels in 2010, of which 90.8 million barrels were motor gasoline and 34.5 million barrels were used as distillate fuel. Virginia uses a disproportionately large amount of jet fuel (12.7 million barrels, 2.4 per cent of the US total).

Virginia had natural gas reserves of 3,215 billion cubic feet in 2010 (1.1 per cent of US total). The state's 7,903 gas wells produced 151,094 million cubic feet of natural gas in 2010. Consumption amounted to 373,262 million cu ft in 2011, 1.5 per cent of US total. Approximately one third of households in Virginia use natural gas as their primary energy source for home heating. (Source: EIA)

Energy
Total energy production amounted to 1,096 trillion Btu in 2010 (1.5 per cent of US total). Virginia's total energy consumption was 2,502 trillion Btu in 2010 (2.6 per cent of US total) and was ranked 27th in the US for its per capita energy consumption (312 million Btu in 2010).

Virginia is a net importer of electricity, with coal as its primary generating fuel. Net summer capability in 2010 was 24,109 MW (2.3 per cent of the US total) and total net monthly generation (Oct. 2012) was 4,859 thousand MWh (29th in the US), of which nuclear 2,380 thousand MWh, coal 634 thousand MWh, natural gas 1,636 thousand MWh, petroleum 21 thousand MWh, hydroelectric 60 thousand and other renewables 174 thousand MWh.

Major electricity generating plants included Bath County (pumped storage), North Anna (nuclear), Possum Point (gas), Chesterfield (coal) and Surry (nuclear), Yorktown and Tenaska. Virginia's three nuclear power plants are North Anna, Surry, and Surry 2. The North Anna plant is located in Louis County, and consists of two pressurised water reactors with a summer capacity of around 1,835 MW of electricity. The Surry nuclear plant is located in Surry County near Williamsburg, and consists of two pressurised water reactors with a capacity of approximately 1,598 MW of electricity.

In 2007, Virginia established a voluntary renewable portfolio goal encouraging utilities to generate 12 per cent of base-year 2007 sales from renewable sources by 2022. In 2011, 5.1 per cent of the state's net electricity generation came from renewable energy, over 50 per cent of which was biomass. (Source: EIA)

Manufacturing
Manufacturing was the third highest contributor to GDP in 2011, earning an estimated $39,007 million (up from $37,932 million in 2010). In 2010, the largest sectors were food products ($14,986 million), chemical manufacturing ($3,090 million) and machinery manufacturing ($3,160 million). (Source: BEA)

Virginia's main manufacturing industries are based on food products, transportation equipment (primarily shipbuilding and truck assembly), printing and publishing, textiles, electronic equipment, industrial machinery and lumber and wood products. Virginia has one of the largest concentrations of high technology industry in the nation with 172,000 people employed in 5,500 establishments. Only California has more people employed in producing pre-packaged and custom software. Other high technology products include prescription drugs, computers, semi-conductors and communications equipment.

Service Industries
The services industry is Virginia's largest sector. The largest earning sectors in 2011 were real estate ($50,986 million), professional and technical services ($60,416 million), finance and insurance ($29,414 million), and health care and social assistance ($26,413 million). The information sector also plays an important economic role, accounting for some $18,002 million in 2011. (Source: BEA)

The primary sources of revenue for Virginia's state government are the corporate income tax, the individual income tax, and the state sales tax. At the local level the primary sources of revenue are the real and personal property taxes and the local sales tax.

Tourism
The accommodation and food services sector of the services industry contributed an estimated $10,583 million in 2011, whilst the arts, entertainment and recreation services sector contributed $2,439. (Source: BEA)
Virginia Tourism Corporation, URL: http://www.virginia.org/

Agriculture
Agriculture, forestry, fishing and hunting contributed an estimated $1,627 million towards Virginia's GDP in 2011 (up from $1,423 million in 2010). The largest sectors in 2010 were crop and animal production (farms) ($1,113 million), followed by forestry, fishing, and related activities ($310 million). (Source: BEA)

According to the US Department of Agriculture Virginia's farms numbered 47,300 in 2010, and covered around 8,050,000 acres. The average size of a Virginian farm was 170 acres. Cash receipts from agricultural sales totalled $2.9 billion in 2007. Livestock, poultry and products accounted for over $2 billion, whilst crops, including greenhouse and nursery crops, accounted for $858 million. Major livestock and livestock products include broilers, cattle and calves, wholesale milk, turkey, hogs, and eggs. Field crops, vegetables, greenhouse and nursery products, fruits and nuts, tobacco, soybeans, peanuts, and grain corn were the major crops products. As of 1 Jan. 2011, there were 1,540,000 cattle and calves, 355,000 hogs & pigs and 90,000 sheep.

Landings of commercially caught finfish and shellfish from the State's Atlantic Coast and Chesapeake Bay amount to almost 330 million kg, and are valued at $108 million dockside, ranking Virginia third among the states in weight landed.

COMMUNICATIONS AND TRANSPORT

International Airports
Eleven commercial airports serve Virginia, including those just across the State line at Bluefield, West Virginia, and Bristol, Tennessee, with scheduled commercial airline service to over 600 direct destinations around the world. Almost 1,100 commercial flights arrive or depart each day from the two airports serving the Washington/Northern Virginia metropolitan area - National and Dulles International. The 11 commercial airports are supplemented by 58 general aviation airports licensed for public use.
Newport News/Williamsburg International Airport, URL: http://www.nwairport.com
Norfolk International Airport, URL: http://www.norfolkairport.com
Richmond International Airport, URL: http://www.flyrichmond.com/
Ronald Regan Washington National Airport,
URL: http://www.metwashairports.com/national
Washington Dulles International Airport, URL: http://www.metwashairports.com/Dulles

Railways
In addition to having 5,321 km of rail network (exclusive of yards and siding), the Commonwealth is a junction point between major north-south rail lines and major east-west rail lines. Two of the nation's largest railroads are headquartered in the State - the CSX Corporation in Richmond and the Norfolk Southern Corporation in Norfolk.

Roads
Virginia's highway system encompasses more than 88,000 km of interstate, primary, and secondary roads. The State's 1,800 km of interstate highways include six major routes traversing Virginia to serve north-south and east-west traffic. Supplementing the interstate system are 3,200 miles of arterial, four-lane highways connecting nearly all communities of 3,500 or more not already on an interstate route.

Shipping
Virginia has three deep-water ports - Hampton Roads, Alexandria on the Potomac River, and Richmond on the James River. Traditionally Hampton Roads is the number one export port in the U.S. Recent figures show that more than 45 million metric tons of foreign trade move through Hampton Roads annually. More than 75 steamship lines link Hampton Roads with more than 250 ports in 100 foreign countries.

HEALTH

The National Center for Health Statistics estimated that there were 27.5 doctors (including osteopaths) per 10,000 state residents in 2009. In 2008, there were 4,640 dentists (6.0 per 10,000 population). In 2009, there were 2.2 community hospital beds per 1,000 residents, and, in 2010, there were 286 nursing homes with 32,152 beds.

It was estimated that 13.4 per cent of Virginians had no health care insurance in 2007-09, above the US average of 15.8 per cent. In 2007-11, an estimated 10.7 per cent lived in poverty. Virginia reported 19,029 HIV/AIDS cases from the beginning of the epidemic to the end of 2008 and ranked 13th in cumulative number of reported HIV/AIDS cases in 2008. The TB rate was 3.8 per 100,000 population, the 18th highest among the US states. The obesity rate was 27.3 per cent for adults. An estimated 60.4 per cent of adults were considered overweight. (Source: CDC)

EDUCATION

Primary/Secondary Education
There were 2,186 elementary and secondary schools in the year 2009-10, with 1,245,340 students and 70,829 teachers. The pupil/teacher ratio was 17.58 to one, compared to the US average of 15.3 to one.

Over the 2007-08 academic year, current expenditure on elementary and secondary public education was $14.885 billion, whilst revenues from education reached $14.5 billion.

Higher Education
There were 129 degree-awarding institutions in 2010-11, 39 of which were public. Enrolment comprised 232,246 male students and 312,790 women. 105,201 degrees/certificates were awarded over the year, including 45,324 Bachelors, 18,889 Masters and 4,633 Doctorates. (Source: NCES)

RELIGION

Virginia's population is predominantly Protestant, with smaller representation of Catholic, Jewish, Muslim, and other religions.

COMMUNICATIONS AND MEDIA

Newspapers
Virginia's major newspapers include the Richmond Times-Dispatch; the Virginian-Pilot, Norfolk; The Daily Progress, Charlottesville; Roanoke Times and World News; Virginian Review, Culpeper; The Free Lance-Star, Fredericksburg; Manassas Journal Messenger; and the Potomac News, Woodbridge.
Virginia Press Association, URL: http://www.vpa.net/index.htm
Richmond Times-Dispatch, URL: http://www.timesdispatch.com/

Broadcasting
Amongst Virginia's many television stations, Richmond has five, Roanoke has five, Portsmouth has three, Harrisonburg has two, and Charlottesville has two. In addition, there are 12 public and two independent radio stations.

ENVIRONMENT

Virginia's primary generating fuel for its electricity industry is coal. Emissions of carbon dioxide rose from 36,160,554 metric tons in 2009 to 39,719,081 metric tons in 2010, ranking the state 25th in the US. Emissions of sulfur dioxide amounted to 119,828 metric tons (2.2 per cent of the US) and emissions of nitrogen oxide amounted to 48,812 metric tons.

The Commonwealth of Virginia had some 27,999 alternative-fueled vehicles in use in 2010 (3.0 per cent of the US total). In 2010, ethanol consumption was 10,315 thousand barrels in 2011 (3.4 per cent of the total US consumption). (Source: EIA)

SPACE PROGRAMME

Established in 1945 under the National Advisory Committee for Aeronautics (NACA), Wallops is one of the oldest launch sites in the world. Located on Virginia's Eastern Shore, Wallops is now NASA's main facility for the management and implementation of suborbital research programmes.

Wallops Flight Facility, URL: http://www.wff.nasa.gov/

WASHINGTON

Capital: Olympia (Population, Census 2010: 46,478)

Head of State: Jay Inslee (D) (page 1447)

State Flag: A dark green background in the centre of which appears the state seal. The state seal consists of a portrait of George Washington within a green circle, around which appear the words 'The Seal of the State of Washington, 1889'.

CONSTITUTION AND GOVERNMENT

Constitution
Washington entered the Union on 11 November 1889 as the 42nd state. The state Constitution was adopted in 1889, and has been amended since. According to the Constitution, executive power is held by the Governor, elected for a four-year term, assisted by eight elected officials who also serve four-year terms: the lieutenant governor, secretary of state, state treasurer, state auditor, attorney general, superintendent of public instruction, commissioner of public lands, and insurance commissioner.

Two senators are elected to the US Congressional Delegation in Washington, DC, for six years and nine representatives are elected for two years. Washington casts 11 electoral votes in presidential elections.

To view the state constitution, please visit:
http://www.leg.wa.gov/LawsAndAgencyRules/constitution.htm

Legislature
Washington's bicameral legislature consists of the Senate and the House of Representatives. Each of Washington's 49 districts is represented by one Senator and two Representatives. Legislatures last two years, and comprise two regular sessions; the first session, (a budget year) begins on an odd numbered year and lasts around 105 days, whilst the second session lasts around 60 days. The 61st Legislature commenced in January 2009.

Upper House
The State Senate has 49 members who are elected for four years, half their number up for re-election every two years. The President of the Senate is the Lieutenant Governor. Following elections held on 6th November 2012 the Democrats held 27 seats and the Republicans 22. **Senate**, Legislative Building, Olympia, WA 98504, USA. Tel: +1 360 786 7550 (Secretary of the Senate), URL: http://www.leg.wa.gov/pages/home.aspx

Lower House
The State House of Representatives has 98 members, two from each legislative district, who are elected for two-year terms. Following elections held on 6th November 2012 the Democrats had 55 seats and the Republicans 43 seats.
Washington State House of Representatives, Legislative Building, 3rd Floor, PO Box 40600, Olympia, WA 98504-0600, USA. Tel: +1 360 786 7750 (Clerk), URL: http://www.leg.wa.gov/pages/home.aspx

---

Elected Executive Branch Officials (as of March 2013)
Governor: Jay Inslee (D)
Lieutenant Governor: Brad Owen (D)
Secretary of State: Kim Wyman (R)
State Treasurer: James L. McIntire (D)
State Auditor: Troy Kelley (D)
Attorney General: Bob Ferguson (D)
Commissioner of Public Lands: Peter Goldmark (D)
Insurance Commissioner: Mike Kreidler (D)
Superintendent of Public Instruction: Randy Dorn (D)

Legislature (as at March 2013)
President of the Senate: Lt. Gov. Brad Owen (D)
President Pro Tempore of the Senate: Tim Sheldon (D)
Senate Majority Leader: Rodney Tom (D)
Senate Minority Leader: Ed Murray (R)
Speaker of the House: Frank Chopp (D)
Speaker of the House Pro Tempore: Jim Moeller (D)
House Majority Leader: Pat Sullivan (D)
House Minority Leader: Richard DeBolt (R)

US Senators: Maria Cantwell (D) (page 1400) and Patty Murray (D) (page 1482)

Ministries
Office of the Governor, PO Box 40002, Olympia, WA 98504-0002, USA. Tel: +1 360 902 4111, fax: +1 360 753 4110, URL: http://www.governor.wa.gov/
Office of the Lieutenant Governor, 220 Legislative Building, PO Box 40400, Olympia WA 98504-0400, USA. Tel: +1 360 786 7700, URL: http://www.ltgov.wa.gov/
Office of the Attorney General, 1125 Washington Street SE, PO Box 40100, Olympia, WA. 98504-0100, USA. Tel: +1 360 753 6200, fax: +1 360 586 7671, e-mail: emailago@atg.wa.gov, URL: http://www.atg.wa.gov/

Office of the Secretary of State, 520 Union Avenue SE, PO Box 40220, Olympia, WA 98504-0220. USA. Tel: +1 360 902 4151, URL: http://www.sos.wa.gov/
Office of the State Treasurer, Legislative Building, PO Box 40200, Olympia, WA 98504-0200, USA. Tel: +1 360 902 9000, fax: +1 360 902 9044, URL: http://www.tre.wa.gov/index.shtml
Office of the State Auditor, Legislative Building, PO Box 40021, Olympia, WA 98504-0021, USA. Tel: +1 360 902 0370, fax: +1 360 753 0646. e-mail: StateAuditor@sao.wa.gov, URL: http://www.sao.wa.gov/
Office of the Superintendent of Public Instruction, Old Capitol Building, 600 S. Washington Street, Olympia, WA 98504, USA. (Mailing address: Old Capitol Building, PO Box 47200, Olympia, WA 98504-7200), USA. Tel: +1 360 725 6000, fax: +1 360 753 6712, URL: http://www.k12.wa.us/
Department of Agriculture, 1111 Washington Street SE, PO Box 42560, Olympia, WA 98504-2560, USA. Tel: +1 360 902 1800, e-mail: poffice@agr.wa.gov, URL: http://agr.wa.gov/
Washington Economic Development Finance Authority (WEDFA), 1000 Second Ave., Suite 2700, Seattle, WA 98104-1046, USA. Tel: +1 206 587 5634, fax: (206) 389-2819, URL: http://www.wedfa.org/
Department of Ecology, 300 Desmond Drive, Lacey, WA 98503, (PO Box 47600, Olympia, WA 98504-7600) USA. Tel: +1 360 407 6000, URL: http://www.ecy.wa.gov/
State Board of Education, Old Capitol Building, PO Box 47206, Olympia, WA 98504-47206, USA. Tel: +1 360 725 6025, fax: +1 360 586 2357, URL: http://www.sbe.wa.gov/
Department of Fish and Wildlife, Natural Resources Building, 1111 Washington Street SE, Olympia, WA 98501, USA. (Mailing Address: 600 Capitol Way N., Olympia, WA 98501-1091, USA.) Tel: +1 360 902 2200, fax: +1 360 902 2230, URL: http://wdfw.wa.gov/
Department of Health, 101 Israel Road SE, Turnwater WA 98501, PO Box 47890, Olympia, Washington, 98504-7890, USA. Tel: +1 360 236 4501, URL: http://www.doh.wa.gov/
Department of Natural Resources, PO Box 47001, Olympia, WA 98504-7001, USA. Tel: +1 360 902 1004, fax: +1 360 902 1775, URL: http://www.dnr.wa.gov
Department of Transportation, 310 Maple Park Avenue SE, PO Box 47300,Olympia WA 98504-7300, USA. Tel: +1 360 705 7000, URL: http://www.wsdot.wa.gov/

Political Parties
Washington State Democrats, URL: http://www.wa-democrats.org/
Washington State Republican Party, URL: http://www.wsrp.org/

Elections
In the legislative elections of November 2012, Democrats retained the majority in the Senate (Democrats 27, Republicans 22). In the House of Representatives, the Democrats majority also kept control (55 Democrats, 43 Republicans).

Elections for Washington's executive officials, US Representatives and State Senators and Representatives also took place in November 2012. The incumbent Governor, Christine O Gregoire decided to retire. The election for governor was won by Jay Inslee (D) with approximately 51.5 per cent of the vote.

LEGAL SYSTEM

The Washington legal system consists of the Washington Supreme Court, the Washington Court of Appeals, Superior Courts, District Courts and Municipal Courts.

The Supreme Court is made up of the Chief Justice, who is elected for a four-year term, and eight Justices, who are elected by judicial ballot for six-year terms. The responsibility of the Supreme Court is to establish whether the constitution, statute or common law has been properly applied and to properly administer the state's judicial system.

The Court of Appeals has three Divisions - Seattle, Tacoma and Spokane - and consists of a Chief Judge, Judges and Commissioners.

There are 29 superior court judicial districts and 159 superior court judges elected for a term of four years. The superior courts are courts of general jurisdiction, dealing with cases over $25,000. The state's district courts number 49 and deal with cases under $35,000.

In 2008, a ban on handguns in Washington DC was ruled unconstitutional by the US Supreme Court. It was the first such case considered by the court in decades and is expected to have effects on gun laws across the US. The ruling enshrined for the first time the individual right to own guns and limits efforts to reduce their role in American life.

Capital punishment is legal in Washington and may be carried out either by hanging or lethal injection. As of January 2013, there were nine inmates on death row. Five people have been executed since 1976, the most recent in 2010. The murder rate was 2.3 per 100,000 population.

Same-sex marriage entered into law in the state in December 2012.

Supreme Court, URL: http://www.courts.wa.gov/appellate_trial_courts
Chief Justice: Barbara A. Madsen

Associate Chief Justice: Charles Johnson, Justices: Susan Owens, Mary Fairhurst, James Johnson, Charlie Wiggins, Steven Gonzalez, Debra Stephens, Sheryl Gordon McCloud

LOCAL GOVERNMENT

Washington is divided into 39 county governments most of which are boards of county commissioners, usually with three members who are elected for terms of four years. King County, which includes metropolitan Seattle, has an elected council and county executive. In addition to the county governments there are 281 municipalities (incorporated cities and towns), most of which are administered by mayor-council governments.

Washington State Association of Counties, URL: http://www.wacounties.org/wsac/index.htm

AREA AND POPULATION

Area
Washington state is located in the far north-west of the US, south of the Canadian border, north of Oregon, west of Idaho. The total area of Washington is 71,299.64 sq. miles, of which 66,544.06 sq. miles is land and 4,755.58 sq. miles is water. Washington's climate varies from mild and humid in the west, to cool and dry in the east. The temperature ranges from 10.5 degrees Celsius on the Pacific coast to 5 degrees in the north-west.

An earthquake measuring 6.8 on the Richter scale struck Washington on 28 March 2001. The epicentre was about 50 km from Seattle city centre, although damage was caused to the state capital Olympia, and was felt as far away as Salt Lake City, Utah, and Vancouver, Canada.

To view a map of the state, please visit:
http://www.lib.utexas.edu/maps/us_2001/washington_ref_2001.pdf

Population
According to the 2010 Census, the 2010 state population was at 6,724,540, up on the mid-2009 estimate of 6,664,195. In 2012, the population was estimated to be 6,897,012. The state population grew by 14.1 per cent over the period 2000-10, and by 21.1 per cent over the decade 1990 to 2000. The population is expected to reach 8.6 million by 2030. Population density is around 101.2 people per sq. mile. Washington's three largest cities (Census 2010) are Seattle (608,660), Spokane (208,916) and Tacoma (198,397). The population of Washington's capital, Olympia, was 46,478 in 2010. The largest county is King County (1,931,249 in 2010).

According to the 2010 Census, 6.5 per cent of the population is under 5 years, 23.5 per cent under 18 years and 12.3 per cent is aged over 65 years. Approximately 77.3 per cent of the population is white, and 3.6 per cent is black. Approximately 11.2 per cent of the population is of Hispanic or Latino origin.

Births, Marriages, Deaths
The US Census Bureau estimated that there were 89,313 births in 2010 and 48,146 deaths, giving a natural population increase of 41,167. Net immigration added an estimated 58,157 people in 2009. The infant mortality rate in 2007 was 4.8 infant deaths per 1,000 live births. Marriages and divorces in 2007, according to provisional data, numbered 41,766 and 28,925 respectively.

EMPLOYMENT

Washington's total civilian labour force in December 2012 numbered 3,463,300, of which 3,200,800 were employed and 262,500 were unemployed. The unemployment rate was 7.6 per cent, slightly down on the US national average of 7.8 per cent. (Source: US Bureau of Labor Statistics)

The following table shows preliminary December 2012 non-farm wage and salary employment, seasonally adjusted, according to industry:

Industry	No. of jobs	12-month change %
Logging and mining	5,500	-6.8
Construction	147,100	6.5
Manufacturing	288,200	4.1
Trade, transportation, and utilities	540,600	2.4
Information	103,100	-0.3
Financial activities	139,700	2.1
Professional and business services	346,600	2.5
Educational and health services	391,400	0.7
Leisure and hospitality	283,700	2.7
Other services	106,200	-0.2
Government	533,600	-0.3
Total non-farm employment	2,885,700	1.8

Source: Bureau of Labor Statistics

BANKING AND FINANCE

GDP/GNP, Inflation, National Debt
Total Gross Domestic Product (GDP) rose from (current dollars) $339,829 million in 2010 to $355.1 billion in 2011. Real GDP rose by 1.6 per cent in 2010 and 2.0 per cent in 2011 and the state was ranked 14th in the US for its 2011 GDP.

Gross Domestic Product according to industry ($m)

Industry	2009	2010	2011
Agriculture, forestry, hunting and fishing	5,575	6,030	6,393
Mining	512	551	710
Utilities	3,626	3,556	3,416
Construction	14,283	12,944	12,883
Manufacturing	37,662	39,123	44,135
Wholesale Trade	17,749	18,458	19,633
Retail Trade	22,170	22,666	25,057
Transport and warehousing	8,981	9,232	9,724
Information	27,414	28,103	31,283
Finance and insurance	16,566	17,490	17,317
Real estate	47,512	44,494	43,123
Other non-government services	54,218	58,228	61,762
Government	51,279	52,194	52,757
TOTAL	331,861	339,829	355,083

Source: Bureau of Economic Analysis, Feb. 2013

The state's average per capita income was an estimated $43,878 in 2011. Per capita real GDP rose to $45,520 in 2011 whilst the US average was $42,070.

The annual Consumer Price Index (CPI) for the Seattle-Tacoma-Bremerton, WA, urban area (all items) rose from 232.8 in 2011 to 238.6 in 2012. (1982-84 = 100). (Source: Bureau of Labor Statistics)

Balance of Payments / Imports and Exports
Total US imports via Washington amounted to $37,647 million in 2009, down 22.1 per cent from $48,343 in 2008. In 2010, imports rose by 12.9 per cent to $42,516 million, and rose, in 2011, by 9.2 per cent to $46,685 million, accounting for 2.1 per cent of total imports. Crude oil was the top import in 2010. Chief suppliers were Canada (30.2 per cent), Chin (18.7 per cent), Japan (11.2 per cent), Russia and Taiwan. Total export revenue rose from $54,498 million in 2008 to $51,851 million in 2009, a fall of 4.9 per cent. Export revenue rose by 2.9 in 2010 to $53,353 million and by 21.4 per cent in 2011 to $64,747 million, representing 4.4 per cent of the US total. The top five export products in 2010, according to revenue, are shown on the following table:

Product	Export Revenue ($m)	+/-% 2008-09
Civilian aircraft, engines, equipment and parts	23,199	-12.1
Soybeans, whether or not broken	4,137	11.3
Corn (maize), other than seed corn	1,946	37.0
Wheat (other than durum wheat) and meslin	1,275	11.8
Oil (not crude) from petrol & bit., min. etc.	1,175	-2.1

Source: US Census Bureau, Foreign Trade Division

The top five export trading partners, according to export revenue, are shown on the following table:

Merchandise export revenue according to destination, 2010-11

Country	2010 ($m)	2011 ($m)	+/-% 2010-11
China	10,303	11,233	9.0
Canada	6,977	8,547	22.5
Japan	6,135	6,468	5.4
South Korea	2,719	3,261	20.0
UAE	961	2,753	186.4

Source: US Census Bureau, Foreign Trade Division

Chambers of Commerce and Trade Organisations
Greater Seattle Chamber of Commerce, URL: http://www.seattlechamber.com/
Olympia/Thurston County Chamber of Commerce, URL: http://thurstonchamber.com/

MANUFACTURING, MINING AND SERVICES

Washington's economy benefits from its geographic location and wealth of natural resources. The state produces a range of agricultural commodities and is home to leading firms in aerospace, forest products, and computer software. Washington's geographic location is an important factor in trade with other regions. The state is the closest mainland US point to Asia, one shipping day closer than California, and is therefore a major transshipment point for commodities moving across the Pacific.

Primary and Extractive Industries
Washington's mines produce coal, gold, silver, copper, lead, zinc, tungsten and other minerals. Metallic minerals are located primarily in the Rocky Mountains, whilst coal is mined in the Cascades region in the west. In 2011, the mining industry contributed an estimated $710 million towards Washington's Gross Domestic Product (up from $551 million in 2010). The top mining sectors in 2010 were non-oil and gas mining ($529 million) and support activities ($21 million). (Source: BEA)

Washington has no indigenous oil production but receives its crude oil from fields in Canada. The state has a crude oil refining capacity of 630,700 barrels per day in 2012 (3.6 per cent of the US total), and is a leading refining centre in the northwest region. Oil consumption in 2010 fell to 138.7 million barrels (2.1 per cent of the US total), 63.4 million barrels of which were motor gasoline and 25.3 million were distillate fuel. Approximately 19.3 million barrels were in the form of jet fuel, which was proportionately high (3.7 per cent of the US total) due to several large Air Force and Navy installations in the state.

Washington state has none of its own natural gas resources. Consumption was 264,568 million cu ft in 2011. The residential sector leads Washington's natural gas consumption, followed by the industrial and electric power generating sectors. (Source: EIA)

Energy
Washington's total energy production was 904 trillion Btu in 2010, ranking the state 21st in the US. Washington's total energy consumption amounted to 2,037 trillion Btu in 2010 (2.1 per cent of US total), whilst its per capita energy consumption of 302 million Btu in 2010 ranks it 31st in the US. The main energy-using sector is transportation, followed by the industrial, residential and commercial sectors.

Much of Washington's electrical energy comes from huge hydroelectric dams on the Columbia River, including the Grand Coulee Dam. Other sources of electricity include a coal burning plant, a nuclear power plant, and experimental wind generators. Net summer capability in 2010 was 30,478 MW (2.9 per cent of US total) and total net monthly (Oct. 2012) generation was 7,546 thousand MWh (9th in the US). Of this, hydroelectric 4,381 thousand MWh, coal 743 thousand MWh, nuclear 833 thousand MWh, natural gas 869 thousand, other renewable 667 thousand MWh. Major electricity generating plants include: Grand Coulee (hydro) (6,809 MW capcaity), Chief Joseph (hydro), Transalta Centralia G (coal), Rocky Reach (hydro), Boundary, and Columbia Generating S (nuclear). Washington's only nuclear power plant is the 1,108 net MWe Columbia (formerly WNP-2).

In 2006, Washington adopted a renewable energy standard that requires all utilities serving at least 25,000 people to produce 15 per cent of their energy from renewable sources by 2020. In 2011, Washington was the leading producer of electricity from hydroelectric sources and produced 29 per cent of US net electricity generation. It ranked sixth out of the US states in net generation of electricity from wind energy in 2011. (Source: EIA)

Manufacturing
Technology based industries are becoming increasingly important in Washington. The Seattle area has become a centre for the biotechnology industry, and the Microsoft Corporation, the world's leading computer software producer, also has its headquarters near Seattle. Other major manufactures include transport equipment, lumber and wood products, paper, food products, industrial machinery, primary metals, printed materials, and precision instruments.

Manufacturing accounted for an estimated $44,135 million of Washington's GDP in 2011 (up from $39,213 million in 2009). The top earning sectors in 2010 were transport equipment apart from motor vehicle, body, trailer and parts manufacturing ($14,914 million), food products ($3,265 million), computer and electronic products ($3,585 million), and petroleum and coal products manufacturing ($5,967 million). (Source: BEA)

Service Industries
The services industry is the largest contributor to Washington's GDP. The top sectors in 2011 were real estate ($43,123 million), information ($31,283 million) and health care and assistance ($24,798 million). Professional and technical services earned some $25,490 million. (Source: BEA)

Washington does not have an income tax but does have a sales tax and local property taxes. Other government revenue comes from lottery ticket sales, licences (driver, motor vehicle, fishing, hunting), sales of alcoholic beverages, timber tax, cigarette and tobacco taxes, and miscellaneous taxes.

Tourism
Tourism plays a significant role in Washington's economy. In all, Washington has 10 national parks/monuments and 218 state parks. Annual attendance at Washington's state parks, according to recent figures, was 25.08 million, whilst its federal parks attracted over 6.84 million. The arts, entertainment and recreation sector of the services industry contributed an estimated $2,700 million towards the 2011 GDP, whilst the accommodation and food sector earned around $10,104 million. (Source: BEA)

Agriculture
The agriculture, forestry and fishing industry contributed $6,393 million towards GDP in 2011 (up from $6,030 million in 2010). The top earning sector in 2010 was farming ($4,337 million); forestry, fishing and related activities earned an estimated $1,693 million. (Source: BEA)

According to the US Department of Agriculture, there were a total of 39,500 farms in Washington state in 2010 covering an area of 14,800 acres. The average size of a farm was 375 in 2008. The state's top commodities include apples (worth $1.7 billion in 2007), milk ($1.06 billion) and wheat ($974.5 million). Washington state ranks first in the US for red raspberries (91.7 per cent of total US production), hops (77.3 per cent), wrinkled seed peas (75 per cent), spearmint oil (74.7 per cent and apples (57.3 per cent) as well as sweet cherries, concord grapes, peppermint oil, plums and processing carrots. As of 1 Jan. 2011, there were 1,090,000 cattle and calves.

Washington benefits from an abundance of forest land which covers over 40 per cent of the state's total land area. Whilst the lumber and forest product industries have fallen over the past two decades, in 2002 the state ranked 5th for revenues from Christmas trees and short rotation woods.

Both commercial and recreational fishing are important in Washington. Salmon and shellfish are the major commercial harvests, and the state ranks among the top in the USA for aquaculture.

COMMUNICATIONS AND TRANSPORT

National Airlines
Alaska Airlines, URL: http://www.alaskaair.com
Spokane Airways, URL: http://www.spokaneairways.com/

International Airports
Washington's largest airport is the Seattle-Tacoma International Airport (Sea-Tac). It is ranked 16th busiest US commercial airport. In 2004, 28,804,554 air passengers used the airport, an increase of 7.5 per cent over the previous year. Air cargo totalled 346,966 metric tons in the same year, and there were 358,894 aircraft operations during the year, an increase of 1.2 per cent on 2003. In addition to the international airport there are 128 public use airports, including 13 offering commercial services.
Seattle-Tacoma International Airport, URL: http://www.portseattle.org
Spokane International Airport, URL: http://www.spokaneairports.net/

Railways
Washington has over 4,000 miles of railway track. Two trans-continental railways service Washington: Burlington Northern Santa Fe (BNSF) and Union Pacific (UP). In addition, there are 14 local service railway companies. Washington is on the major north-south west coast rail line and is the terminus for the major east-west rail line originating in Chicago, Illinois. Most of the goods shipped from the Orient in containers are distributed to the rest of the US via railways from Washington ports.

Roads
Washington has a total of 130,840 km of roads, 1,218 km of which are interstate highways. Four main interstate highways cross the state: I-5, I-405, I-90, and I-82. Interstate 5 runs north-south through Washington starting at the northern border shared with British Columbia, Canada. Interstate 90 runs west-east through Washington and on east to Boston, Massachusetts. Interstate highways I-205 and I-182 provide inter-loop connections serving the Vancouver and Tri-Cities areas respectively.

Shipping
Washington has 15 deep water ports with Seattle, Tacoma, and Longview being the three largest. The combined cargo volume of Seattle and Tacoma Ports ranks them as the second largest port complex in the west and the 11th largest in the world. Seattle and Tacoma receive the majority of the goods imported via container. The containers are then shipped via railroad to the rest of the US. Three of the state's ports have the advantage of reducing the journey time to Asian-Pacific markets by one to two days.
Port of Seattle, URL: http://www.portseattle.org

HEALTH

The National Center for Health Statistics estimated that there were 27.0 doctors (including osteopaths) per 100,000 residents in 2009. In 2008, there were an estimated 4,579 dentists (7.0 per 10,000 population). In 2009, there were 1.7 community hospital beds per 1,000 residents, below the US average of 2.6. In 2010, there were 229 nursing homes with 21,837 beds.

It was estimated that some 12.2 per cent of the population had no health-care insurance in 2007-09, and, in 2007-11, an estimated 12.5 per cent were living in poverty.

Washington reported 12,826 HIV/AIDS cases from the beginning of the epidemic to the end of 2008, and ranked 19th in number of cumulative reported cases in 2008. The TB rate was 3.5 per 100,000 population, the 22nd highest rate among the US states. The obesity rate in adults is 25.5 per cent and 61.1 per cent of adults were considered overweight. (Source: CDC)

EDUCATION

Primary and Secondary Education
Enrolment in the state's 2,368 primary and secondary schools rose to 1,035,347 in 2009-10. Classroom teachers numbered 53,448 in the same year, and the ratio of teachers to pupils stood at one to 19.37, compared to the national average of one to 15.3.

Over the 2007-08 academic year, the state's education revenues totaled $11.1 billion, whilst current expenditure on public education reached $11.59 billion.

Higher Education
During the 2010-11 academic year, there were 85 institutes (of which 43 were public) of higher education in the state, including the University of Washington, Washington State University, Eastern Washington University, Central Washington University, Western Washington University and The Evergreen State College. The number of students enrolled for the 2010-11 academic year stood at 170,066 men and 212,466 women. A total of 88,672 degrees were awarded, including 30,551 Bachelors, 9,766 Masters and 2,366 Doctorates. (Source: NCES)

COMMUNICATIONS AND MEDIA

Newspapers
Washington has several major newspapers including The Seattle Times (URL: URL: http://seattletimes.nwsource.com/), the Seattle Post Intelligencer (URL: http://www.seattlepi.com/), and the Spokesman-Review (URL: http://www.spokesman.com). **Washington Newspaper Publishers' Association**, URL: http://www.wnpa.com/

Business Journals
Seattle Daily Journal of Commerce, URL: http://www.djc.com/

ENVIRONMENT

Emissions of carbon dioxide from Washington's electricity generating industry reached 13,983,610 metric tons in 2010, ranking the state 39th in the US, and accounting for 0.6 per cent of the US total. Emissions of sulfur dioxide amounted to 14,174 metric tons and nitrogen oxide emissions amounted to 20,614 metric tons.

In 2010, there were 17,051 alternative-fueled vehicles in use. In 2011, ethanol consumption was 7,860 thousand barrels (2.6 per cent of US total).

The Washington State Department of Natural Resources is responsible for the state's environment through its Natural Heritage Program, Natural Area Program, Forest Fire Protection and Fire Program Review. The Department of Natural Resources manages designated Natural Resources Conservation Areas, 24 sites of over 55,000 acres of ecosystems, habitats for endangered animals and plants, and scenic landscapes; and Natural Areas Preserves, 47 sites covering a total of 25,000 acres inhabited by rare animals and plants. The Washington Natural Heritage Program is responsible for gathering scientific data on the natural environment. (Source: EIA)

WEST VIRGINIA

Capital: Charleston (Population, Census 2010: 51,400)

Head of State: Earl Ray Tomblin (Governor) (page 1526)

State Flag: A white field with a blue border in the centre of which is the state coat of arms. The coat of arms depicts a farmer and a miner standing behind two crossed rifles which hold the 'Cap of Liberty'; behind them is a stone bearing the date 20 June 1863 (the date on which West Virginia was admitted to the Union); at the top of the coat of arms is a Latin motto 'Montani Semper Liberi' (Mountaineers are Always Free); surrounding the coat of arms is Rhododendron Maximum, the state flower.

CONSTITUTION AND GOVERNMENT

Constitution
West Virginia joined the Union on 20 June 1863, the 35th state to enter. The State Constitution was ratified on 1872. According to the state Constitution the governor heads the executive branch of government as its chief executive. The governor is assisted by five other elected officers: the secretary of state, auditor, treasurer, commissioner of agriculture, and attorney general.

Two senators are elected to the United States Congressional Delegation, Washington, DC, for six years and three congressmen are elected for two years. To view the state constitution, please visit: http://www.legis.state.wv.us/WVCODE/WV_CON.cfm

Legislature
The legislative branch of state government is divided into the Senate and House of Delegates. Sessions of the Legislature take place annually, usually beginning on the second Wednesday in January, and last for 60 consecutive days.
West Virginia State Legislature, 1900 Kanawha Blvd. E., Charleston, WV 25305, USA. Tel: +1 304 347 4836, URL: http://www.legis.state.wv.us/

Upper House
The state is divided into 12 senatorial districts from each of which voters elect two senators. The State Senate has 34 members who are elected for four years. Following elections held on 6th November 2012 the Senate was made up of 25 Democrats and 9 Republicans.

Lower House
The State House of Delegates has 100 members who are elected for two years. Following the election held on 6th November 2012 the house was made up of 54 Democrats and 46 Republicans.

Elected Executive Branch Officials (as at April 2013)
Governor: Earl Ray Tomblin (D) (page 1526)
Secretary of State: Natalie Tennant (D)
Attorney General: Patrick Morrisey (R)
State Auditor: Glen B. Gainer III (D)
State Treasurer: John D. Perdue (D)
Commissioner of Agriculture: Walt Helmick (D)

Legislature (as at April 2013)
President of the Senate: Jeffre Kessler (D)
President Pro Tempore: Larry J. Edgell (D)
Senate Majority Leader: John Unger II (D)
Senate Minority Leader: Mike Hall (R)
Speaker of the House: Rick Thompson (D)
House Majority Leader: Brent Boggs (D)
House Republican Leader: Tim Armstead (R)

US Senators: Joe Manchin III (D) (page 1470) and John D. (Jay) Rockefeller IV (D) (page 1504)

Ministries
Office of the Governor, 1900 Kanawha Boulevard, E., Charleston, WV 25305, USA. Tel: +1 304 558 2000, fax: +1 304 342 7025, URL: http://www.governor.wv.us/
Office of the Attorney General, 1900 Kanawha Boulevard East, Room 26E, Charleston, WV 25305-9924, USA. Tel: +1 304 558 2021, URL: http://www.wvago.gov
Office of the State Auditor, State Capitol, Building 1, Room W-100, Charleston, WV 25305, USA. Tel: +1 304 558 2251, fax: +1 304 558 5200, URL: http://www.wvsao.gov/
Office of the Secretary of State, Building 1, Suite 157-K, 1900 Kanawha Boulevard East, Charleston, WV 25305-0770, USA. Tel: +1 304 558 6000, fax: +1 304 558 0900, e-mail: wvsos@wvsos.com, URL: http://www.wvsos.com/

Office of the State Treasurer, 1900 Kanawha Boulevard East, State Capitol Building 1, Room E-145, Charleston, West Virginia 25305, USA. Tel: +1 304 558 5000, fax: +1 304 558 4097, URL: http://www.wvsto.com
Department of Agriculture, 1900 Kanawha Boulevard East, State Capitol, Room E-28, Charleston, WV 25305-0170, USA. Tel: +1 304 558 2201, fax: +1 304 558 2203, URL: http://www.wvagriculture.org
Bureau of Commerce, State Capitol Complex, Bldg. 6, Rm B0525, Charleston, WV 25305, USA. Tel: +1 304 558 0352, URL: http://www.wvcommerce.org/default.aspx
Department of Education, 1900 Kanawha Boulevard East, Charleston, WV 25305, USA. Tel: +1 304 558 2681, fax: +1 304 558 0048, URL: http://wvde.state.wv.us/
Department of Environmental Protection, 601-57th Street, Charleston, WV 25304, USA. Tel: +1 304 926 0440, fax: +1 304 558 926 0446, URL: http://www.dep.wv.gov/
Division of Tourism, 90 MacCorkle Ave. SW, South Charleston WV 25303, USA. Tel: +1 304 558 2200, URL: http://www.wvtourism.com
Department of Transportation, Division of Highways, Building 5, 1900 Kanawha Boulevard East, Charleston, WV 25305, USA. Tel: +1 304 558 3505, fax: +1 304 558 1004, URL: http://www.transportation.wv.gov

Political Parties
West Virginia State Democratic Executive Committee, URL: http://www.wvdemocrats.com/
Republican Party of West Virginia, URL: http://www.wvgop.org/

Elections
In the 2012 legislative elections, the Democrats lost three seats but still kept control of the Senate (Democrats 25 seats, Republicans 9 seats), and in the state House of Delegates, the Democrats again kept control of the House but with a reduced majority (Democrats 54 seats (down nine), Republicans 46 seats).

Elections were held in November 2012 for Governor, Attorney General, Secretary of State, Treasurer, State Auditor and Commissioner of Agriculture. Incumbent Governor, Earl Ray Tomblin (D), won with 50.5 per cent of the vote. Mr Tomblin was elected into office in a special election in 2011 and was eligible to stand for a full four-year-term of office.

LEGAL SYSTEM

As from 1 January 1976, West Virginia's courts have been united under a single system which is the responsibility of the Supreme Court of Appeals. The judiciary is organised on three levels: the Supreme Court of Appeals, the circuit courts, and the magistrate courts. The Supreme Court of Appeals is a single appellate court present in only 10 US states. The 31 Circuit Courts have a total of 65 circuit judges, whilst the 55 Magistrates Courts have 158 magistrates. Municipal Courts are locally administered and Family Courts, which came into effect on 1 January 2002 following a constitutional amendment, have 35 judges. The Supreme Courts consists of a chief justice and five justices, all of whom are elected for terms of 12 years. Circuit judges are elected for terms of eight years.

The death penalty was abolished in 1965.

Supreme Court of Appeals, URL: http://www.state.wv.us/wvsca/default.htm
Chief Justice: Brent D. Benjamin
Justices: Robin Jean Davis, Margaret Workman, Menis Ketchum II, Allen Loughry II

LOCAL GOVERNMENT

West Virginia is divided into 55 county governments and 232 municipal governments. The county governments are run by county commissions. Municipal governments consist of cities, towns and villages. There are no town or township governments.

AREA AND POPULATION

Area
West Virginia is a southern state on the border with the American north-east. It lies east of Kentucky and Ohio, north-west of Virginia, and south of Pennsylvania and Maryland. The total area of West Virginia is 24,229.76 sq. miles, of which 24,077.73 sq. miles is land and 152.03 sq. miles is water.

West Virginia is known as The Mountain State as it is the only state located entirely within the Appalachian Mountain range, and in which all areas are mountainous. The average elevation is approximately 460 metres above sea level, the highest east of the Mississippi River.

To view a map of the state, please consult http://www.lib.utexas.edu/maps/west_virginia.html

UNITED STATES OF AMERICA

Population
According to the 2010 Census, the total population in 2010 was 1,852,994, up on the mid-2009 estimate of 1,819,777. The population was estimated at 1,855,413. The state population grew by 2.5 per cent over the period 2000-10, and by 0.8 per cent over the decade 1990-2000. The population is expected to fall to 1.72 million by 2030. The population density is estimated at 77.1 people per sq. mile. The county with the greatest number of inhabitants is Kanawha with a population of 193,063 in 2010. The capital, Charleston, had an estimated 2011 population of 51,777, and continues to be the largest city in West Virginia.

According to the 2010 Census, 5.6 per cent of the population is under 5 years, 20.9 per cent under 18 years and 16.0 per cent is aged over 65 years. Approximately 93.9 per cent of the population is white, and 3.4 per cent is black. Approximately 1.2 per cent of the population is of Hispanic or Latino origin.

Births, Marriages, Deaths
The US Census Bureau estimated that there were 20,470 births in the state over 2010 and 21,275 deaths. Net immigration to the state amounted to 5,068 new residents in 2009. The infant mortality rate in 2007 stood at 7.5 infant deaths per 1,000 live births, equivalent to 169 deaths. Marriages and divorces in 2007, according to provisional data, numbered 12,999 and 28,925 respectively, both figures down on the previous two years.

Public Holidays
In addition to the public holidays celebrated by the US, West Virginia also celebrates West Virginia Day, 20 June, to commemorate the date in 1863 when West Virginia became an independent state from Virginia.

EMPLOYMENT

The estimated total civilian labour force in December 2012 was 779,700, of which 718,100 were employed and 61,700 were unemployed. The unemployment rate was 7.9 per cent, lower than the national average of 8.3 per cent. (Source: US Bureau of Labor Statistics)

The following table shows December 2011 non-farm wage and salary employment (seasonally adjusted) according to industry:

Industry	No. of jobs	12-month change
Mining and logging	29,500	-14.5
Construction	34,100	0.0
Manufacturing	47,200	-4.5
Trade, transport and utilities	131,500	-2.6
Information*	10,200	-3.8
Financial activities	26,300	-2.6
Professional and business services	62,700	-0.2
Educational and health services	127,500	2.0
Leisure and hospitality	74,200	0.4
Other services	53,800	-2.4
Government	149,900	-2.3
Total non-farm employment	746,900	-0.7

*Not seasonally adjusted
Source: Bureau of Labor Statistics

BANKING AND FINANCE

GDP/GNP, Inflation, National Debt
West Virginia's Gross Domestic Product (current dollars) rose from $61,934 million in 2010 to $66.8 billion in 2011. Real GDP rose by 4.0 per cent in 2010 and by 4.5 per cent in 2011 and was ranked 39th in the US for its 2011 GDP.

The following table shows the state Gross Domestic Product according to industry (millions of current dollars):

Industry	2009	2010	2011
Agriculture, forestry, fishing and hunting	185	182	185
Mining	5,465	6,086	9,365
Utilities	1,874	1,945	1,707
Construction	2,520	2,518	2,512
Manufacturing	6,033	5,604	6,085
Wholesale Trade	2,763	2,798	2,950
Retail trade	4,380	4,656	4,825
Transport and warehousing	1,825	1,858	1,903
Information	1,447	1,540	1,633
Finance and insurance	2,318	2,484	2,649
Real Estate	5,853	5,714	5,530
Other non-government services	7,911	8,518	9,093
Government	10,903	11,642	11,801
TOTAL	59,601	61,934	66,821

Source: Bureau of Economic Analysis, Feb. 2013

The average annual per capita income in West Virginia was an estimated $33,403 in 2011. Per capita real GDP was $30,056 in 2011; the national average was $42,070.

The annual Consumer Price Index (CPI) for the Washington-Baltimore, DC-MD-VA-WV, urban area (all items) rose from 146.97 in 2011 to 150.2 in 2012. (1982-84 = 100). (Source: Bureau of Labor Statistics)

Balance of Payments / Imports and Exports
Total West Virginia imports amounted to $3,206 million in 2010, up 25.9 per cent on the previous year. They rose to $3,479 million in 2011, up 8.5 per cent, accounting for 0.2 per cent of the US total. Major imports include chemical products, motor vehicle parts and turbo jet parts and equipment. Main suppliers in 2011 were Canada (36.1 per cent), Japan (21.9 per cent), Mexico (10.9 per cent), China and Germany. Export revenue fell from $5,643 million in 2008 to $4,826 million in 2009, a fall of 14.5 per cent. Exports rose by 33.6 per cent to $6,449 million in 2010, accounting for 0.5 per cent of the US total. They rose to $9,034 million in 2011, up 40.1 per cent, accounting for 0.6 per cent of the US total. The following table shows 2010-11 export revenue according to the top five international export destinations:

Destination	2010 ($m)	2011 ($m)	+/-% 2010-11
Canada	1,474	1,537	4.3
Brazil	400	695	73.8
Netherlands	362	692	91.3
India	359	653	81.9
Italy	255	614	141.0

Source: US Census Bureau, Foreign Trade Division

The top five export products in 2010, according to export revenue, are shown on the following table:

Product	Export Revenue ($m)
Bituminous coal, not agglomerated	2,765
Spark ignition,recprcting piston engine over 1000 cc	629
Polyamide-6,-11,-12,-6,6,9,-6,10 or -6,12	227
Civilian aircraft, enginers and parts	191
Drive axles with differential for motor vehicles	146

Source: US Census Bureau, Foreign Trade Division

Chambers of Commerce and Trade Organisations
West Virginia Bureau of Commerce, URL: http://www.boc.state.wv.us/
West Virginia Chamber of Commerce, URL: http://www.wvchamber.com/

MANUFACTURING, MINING AND SERVICES

Primary and Extractive Industries
West Virginia's mining industry earned an estimated $9,365 million in 2011 (up from $6,086 million in 2010). Major mining sectors in 2010 were non-oil and gas mining ($5,181 million), oil and gas extraction ($421 million) and support activities for mining ($485 million). (Source: BEA)

West Virginia is one of the United States' leading producers and exporters of coal, with recoverable reserves of 2,076 million short tons in 2011, 10.8 per cent of the US total. The state had 282 mines and produced 134,662 thousand short tons (12.3 per cent) in 2011. Almost 80 per cent of the coal is exported to other states.

West Virginia's oil industry in 2010 consisted of 3,965 oil wells, 21 rotary rigs, and total reserves of 17 million barrels. Oil production in 2010 reached 1,992 thousand barrels. Monthly oil production (Oct. 2012) was 250,000 barrels, 0.1 per cent of US total. Oil consumption in 2010 was 38 million barrels, 19.5 million barrels of which were motor gasoline and 13.4 million barrels were distillate fuel. Crude oil refinery capacity amounted to 20,000 bbl/d in 2012.

West Virginia's natural gas production makes it one of the top 15 natural gas-producing states. The industry had a total of 56,813 gas producing wells in 2011 with total production at 394,125 million cubic feet. Consumption rose from 113,169 million cu ft in 2010 to 115,363 million cu ft in 2011. The industrial sector is the leading consumer, accounting for almost one-third of the State's consumption. Reserves amounted to 7,000 billion cu ft in 2010, 2.3 per cent of US total. Natural gas plant liquids reserves amounted to 122 million barrels in 2010. (Source: EIA)

Energy
Total energy production amounted to 3,674 trillion Btu in 2010 (4.9 per cent of US total), ranking it 3rd in the US. Total energy consumption in West Virginia was 739 trillion Btu in 2010 (0.8 per cent of US), with per capita energy consumption ranking the state 16th in the US (398 million Btu in 2010).

West Virginia is an energy-exporting state, exporting electricity as well as coal, gas and petroleum. Net summer capability in 2010 was 16,495 MW (1.6 per cent of US total). Monthly net generation (Oct. 2012) was 5,579,000 MWh (20th in the US) (coal 5,376 thousand MWH, hydro-electric 73,000 MWh, other renewables 98,000 MWh, and petroleum 11,000 MWh). Major electricity generating plants include: John E. Amos (coal), Harrison Power Station (coal), Mitchell (coal), and Mt. Storm (coal). West Virginia has no nuclear power plants. (Source: EIA)

Manufacturing
Manufacturing is West Virginia's third highest earning sector (after services and government). The industry contributed an estimated $6,085 million towards the 2011 GDP (up from $5,604 million in 2010). The major sector in 2010 was chemicals and allied products ($2,210 million). (Source: BEA)

Service Industries
The services industry is the largest contributor to GDP. The largest sectors in 2011 were health care and social assistance ($6,249 million) and real estate and rental ($5,530 million). Finance and insurance accounted for $2,649 million, whilst professional and technical services accounted for an estimated $2,776 million. Government GDP contributed an estimated $11,801 million. (Source: BEA)

Taxes are levied at the State, county and municipal levels in West Virginia. Counties administer and collect property taxes. Counties may also impose a hotel occupancy tax on lodging places. Municipalities may levy licence and gross receipts taxes on businesses within the city limits and a hotel occupancy tax on lodging places in the city. At the State level, taxes are levied on businesses and individuals. Certain types of businesses are also subject to other privilege taxes. The State also levies excise taxes on gasoline, cigarettes, soft drinks and alcohol.

Tourism

Tourism is a major industry in West Virginia. There are 35 state parks encompassing approximately 2,900 square miles of forests. In 2004, overnight visitors to the state spent $3.4 billion, an increase of 11.3 per cent over the previous year. Some 41,000 people are employed by the industry. In 2011, the food and accommodation sector contributed an estimated $2,210 million towards state GDP, and the arts, entertainment and recreation sector earned around $374 million. (Source: BEA)

West Virginia Division of Tourism, URL: http://www.wvtourism.com

Agriculture

In 2011 the agriculture industry generated an estimated $185 million in revenues (up from $182 million in 2010). In 2010, the forestry, fishing and related activities sector earned around $74 million, whilst crop and animal production amounted to $108 million. (Source: BEA)

According to the latest official US Department of Agriculture figures, the total number of farms was 23,200 in 2009. Total farmland was around 3,700,000 acres in 2009, whilst the average size of a farm had fallen to 159 acres (down from 176 acres in 1997). In 2007, cash receipts from agriculture reached $479.7 million, of which $398.8 million came from the livestock sector ($234 million from poultry and eggs, and $115.3 million from cattle and calves). As of Jan. 2010, there were 370,000 cattle and calves, 30,000 sheep, 22,500 goats. As of 2009, there were 5,000 hogs and pigs and 82.7 million broilers and 3.3 million turkeys.

West Virginia ranks 8th in terms of apple production, and in 2007 the state produced some 80 million lbs., valued at around $7.39 million.

West Virginia is the third most forested state in the USA, with woodland covering 11.9 million acres. 94 per cent of the woodland consists of hardwood species.

COMMUNICATIONS AND TRANSPORT

International Airports

There are 38 public airport in the state, eight of which operate a scheduled commercial airline service and 30 of which maintain general airfields. The major airports in the state are Raleigh County Memorial Park, Mercer County Airport, Yeager Airport, Benedum Airport, Tri-State Airport, Greenbrier Valley Airport, Morgantown Municipal/Hart Field, Wood County, and Cumberland Regional.

West Virginia Department of Transportation, Aeronautics Commission, URL: http://www.wvdot.com/1_airports/1e_commission.htm

Railways

West Virginia has over 2,600 miles of railway track along with two main freight carriers: CSX and Norfolk Southern. Other freight carriers include Buffalo Creek Railroad; Consolidation Rail; Elk River Railroad Inc.; Nicholas, Fayette & Greenbrier Railroad; South Branch Valley; Strouds Creek & Muddlety; and Winchester & Western. Passenger services are run by AMTRAK and MARC, with routes through West Virginia between Chicago Washington, DC.

West Virginia Department of Transportation, State Rail Authority, URL: http://www.state.wv.us/wvdot/

Roads

Three interstate highways meet at Charleston, I-64, I-77 and I-79. West Virginia also has 37,408 miles of public roads, 34,319 of which are the responsibility of the West Virginia Department of Transportation. Millions of tons of coal are trucked on the state's highways, although the largest amount of coal is shipped by railroads.

Department of Transportation, Division of Highways, URL: http://www.state.wv.us/wvdot/

Shipping

West Virginia is one of only twenty states in the United States with 419 miles of navigable inland waterways. The Ohio, Monongahela and part of the Kanawha all have nine-foot navigation channels. Direct links to the Midwest and the Gulf of Mexico are provided by the Ohio River system, Kanawha, Monongahela, Little Kanawha and Big Sandy rivers. Metropolitan areas which have direct river access include Huntingdon, Charleston, Wheeling, Parkersburg, Weirton, Fairmont and Morgantown. Major products shipped over West Virginia's waterways include coal, coke, chemicals, steel, petroleum products, ores and stone.

West Virginia Department of Transportation, Public Port Authority, URL: http://www.wvdot.com/5_rivers/5d_portauthority.htm

HEALTH

The National Center for Health Statistics estimated that there were 26.1 doctors per 10,000 population in 2009. In 2008, there were 844 dentists (4.7 per 10,000 population). In 2009, there were 4.1 community hospital beds per 1,000 residents, well above the US average of 2.6 beds. In 2010, there were an estimated 127 nursing homes and 10,840 beds.

Figures from the NCHS indicate that some 14.4 per cent of West Virginians had no health-care cover in 2007-09, and, in 2007-11, some17.5 per cent were living in poverty. West Virginia reported 1,718 HIV/AIDS cases from the beginning of the epidemic to the end of 2008, and ranked 40th highest in cumulative number of reported cases in 2008. The TB rate was 1.5 per 100,000 population, the 41st highest among the US states. The state has one of the highest rates of obesity in the US, with 32.5 per cent of adults suffering from it. An estimated 67.4 per cent of adults were overweight. (Source: CDC)

EDUCATION

Primary/Secondary Education

In the year 2010-11, West Virginia had 771 public elementary and secondary schools. 282,662 students enrolled, and there were 20,299 teachers, giving a pupil/teacher ratio of 13.9 to one. Over the year 2007-08, the state spent $2.8 billion on public education, whilst revenue receipts amounted to $3.16 billion.

Higher Education

There were 46 institutes of Higher Education eligible to confer degrees, 23 of which were public. The state's major higher education institutions include West Virginia University, The University of Charleston, Salem-Teikyo University, West Virginia University Institute of Technology, West Virginia State College and West Liberty State College. 70,075 male students enrolled for the year 2010-11, together with 72,409 women. The state conferred 23,473 degrees/certificates, including 12,032 Bachelors, 5,064 Masters and 943 Doctorates. (Source: National Center for Educational Statistics, NCES)

COMMUNICATIONS AND MEDIA

Newspapers

The state's major newspapers are The Charleston Gazette (URL: URL: http://www.wvgazette.com/) and the Charleston Daily Mail (URL: http://www.dailymail.com), both published in Charleston, and The Herald Dispatch (URL: http://www.herald-dispatch.com), published in Huntington. Twenty-two other daily newspapers and many weekly newspapers are published throughout the state.

West Virginia Press Association, URL: http://www.wvpress.org/

Broadcasting

West Virginia has nine commercial television stations and many commercial AM and FM radio stations.

West Virginia Public Radio, URL: http://www.wvpubcast.org/

ENVIRONMENT

Because of West Virginia's reliance on coal for electricity generation (over 90 per cent of industry generation in 2010), emissions from West Virginia's electricity generating industry are high. In 2009, carbon dioxide emissions rose from 65,927,761 metric tons to 74,823,350 metric tons, equivalent to 3.1 per cent of the US total and ranking the state 12th in the US. Sulfur dioxide emissions amounted to 105,270 metric tons (1.9 per cent of US total) and nitrogen oxide emissions amounted to 49,153 metric tons (2.0 per cent).

In 2010, there were 2,600 alternative-fueled vehicles in use and ethanol consumption amounted to 1,868 thousand barrels in 2011. (Source: EIA)

WISCONSIN

Capital: Madison (Population, Census 2010: 233,209)

Head of State: Scott Walker (R) (Governor) (page 1533)

State Flag: A dark blue background in the centre of which appears the state coat of arms. The coat of arms depicts a sailor holding a coil of rope and a miner holding a pick; they support a quartered shield on which appears a plough, a pick and shovel, an arm and hammer, and an anchor; the US coat of arms also appears on the shield, as does the US motto 'E pluribus unum' ('One out of many'); at the base of the shield is a horn of plenty and a pyramid of 13 lead ingots; above the shield is a badger (the state animal) and the state motto 'Forward'.

CONSTITUTION AND GOVERNMENT

Constitution
Wisconsin entered the Union as the 30th state on 29 May 1848. Wisconsin's first Constitution was submitted to the people on 6 April 1847 but was rejected due to disagreement over a number of provisions. A second Constitution was submitted on 13 March 1848 and duly ratified. That Constitution remains in force today, although subject to a number of amendments. According to the Constitution the governor heads the executive branch of government, assisted by five constitutional officers elected for four-year terms by the people: lieutenant governor, secretary of state, state treasurer, attorney general, and superintendent of public instruction. The position of superintendent of public instruction is officially a non-partisan post.

The people of Wisconsin elect eight Representatives and two Senators to the US Congress, Washington, DC. To view the state constitution, please visit: http://www.legis.state.wi.us/rsb/2wiscon.html

Legislature
Wisconsin's bicameral legislature consists of the Senate and the Assembly. The legislature is sworn into office in January of each odd-numbered year and meets in continuous biennial session.

Upper House
The Senate has 33 members who are elected for four years, one-half (16 or 17 alternately) being elected each two years. Following the 2012 elections, the Senate was composed of 15 Democrats and 18 Republicans.
Senate, 119 Martin Luther King, Jr. Boulevard, Suite 501, Madison, Wisconsin, (PO Box 7882, Madison, WI 53707-7882), USA Tel: +1 608 266 2517 (Chief Clerk), URL: http://www.legis.wisconsin.gov/

Lower House
The Assembly has 99 members who are elected for two years. The Republicans also hold the majority of seats in the state Assembly. Following the 2012 elections, the Assembly was made up of 39 Democrats and 60 Republicans.
Assembly, 1 East Main Street, Suite 402, Madison, Wisconsin, (PO Box 8952, Madison, WI 53708-8952), USA. Tel: +1 608 266 1501 (Chief Clerk), URL: http://www.legis.wisconsin.gov

---

Elected Executive Branch Officials (as at April 2013)
Governor: Scott Walker (R) (page 1533)
Lieutenant Governor: Rebecca Kleefisch (R)
Attorney General: J. B. Van Hollen (R)
Secretary of State: Douglas J. LaFollette (D)
State Treasurer: Kurt Schuller (R)
Superintendent of Public Instruction: Tony Evers

Legislature (as at April 2013)
President of the Senate: Michael Ellis (R)
President Pro Tem of the Senate: Joe Leibham (R)
Senate Majority Leader: Scott L. Fitzgerald (R)
Senate Democratic Leader: Chris Larson (D)
Speaker of the House: Robin Vos (R)
House Majority Leader: Scott Suder (R)
House Minority Leader: Peter Barca (D)

US Senators: Ron Johnson (R) (page 1450) and Tammy Baldwin (D) (page 1382)

Ministries
Office of the Governor, 115 East State Capitol, Madison, WI 53702, USA. Tel: +1 608 266 1212, fax: +1 608 267 8983, URL: http://www.wisgov.state.wi.us/
Office of the Lieutenant Governor, Rm. 19 East, State Capitol, Madison, WI 53702, USA. Tel: +1 608 266 3516, fax: +1 608 267 3571, URL: http://ltgov.wi.gov
Office of the Secretary of State, 30 W. Mifflin, 10th Floor, Madison, WI 53702 (PO Box 7848, Madison, WI 53707-7848), USA. Tel: +1 608 266 8888, fax: +1 608 266 3159, URL: http://www.sos.state.wi.us/
Office of the State Treasurer, One South Pinckney Street, 5th Floor, Madison, WI 53707-7871, USA. Tel: +1 608 266 1714, fax: +1 608 266 2647, URL: http://www.statetreasury.wisconsin.gov/
Department of Agriculture, Trade and Consumer Protection, 2811 Agriculture Drive, PO Box 8911, Madison, WI 53708-8911, USA. Tel: +1 608 224 5012, fax: +1 608 224 5045, URL: http://datcp.wi.gov/
Wisconsin Economic Development Corporation (WEDC), URL: http://www.wedc.org

Department of Safety and Professsional Services, URL: http://dsps.wi.gov
Wisconsin Environmental Education Board, 110 College of Natural Resources, University of Wisconsin, Stevens Point, WI 54481, USA. Tel: +1 715 346 3805, fax: +1 715 346 3025, URL: http://www.uwsp.edu/cnr/weeb/
Department of Financial Institutions, 345 W. Washington Avenue, Madison, WI 53703, USA. Tel: +1 608 261 9555, fax: +1 608 261 7200, URL: https://www.wdfi.org/
Department of Justice, PO Box 7857, Madison, WI 53707-7857, USA. Tel: +1 608 266 1221, URL: http://www.doj.state.wi.us/
Department of Natural Resources, 101 S Webster Street, PO Box 7921, Madison Wisconsin, 53707-7921, USA. Tel: +1 608 266 2621, fax: +1 608 261 4380, URL: http://www.dnr.wi.gov/
Department of Public Instruction, 125 S. Webster Street, PO Box 7841, Madison, WI 53707-7841 USA, Tel: +1 608 266 3390, URL: http://dpi.wi.gov/

Political Parties
Democratic Party of Wisconsin, URL: http://www.wisdems.org/
Republican Party of Wisconsin, URL: http://www.wisgop.org/

Elections
Elections for Wisconsin's state constitutional officers took place in 2010 Republican Scott Walker won the gubernatorial election with 52 per cent of the vote. A recall election took place in June 2012 but the incumbent governor held on.

In legislative elections in November 2012, the Republicans remained the majority party in the House of Representatives (Democrats 39, Republicans 60, 1 Independent). In the Senate, the Democrats lost their majority (Democrats 15, Republicans 18).

In the November 2012 US Senate election, the incumbent senator Herb Kohl did not run for re-election. The seat was won by Tammy Baldwin (D).

LEGAL SYSTEM

Wisconsin's court system comprises the Supreme Court, the Court of Appeals, Circuit Courts, and 252 Municipal Courts. The Supreme Court has a Chief Justice and six Associate Justices, all elected for a term of ten years by popular vote. The Court of Appeals has 16 judges who serve six-year terms in four locations: Milwaukee, Waukesha, Madison and Wausau. Circuit Courts operate in 72 counties and employ 246 circuit judges who serve terms of six years. The 252 Municipal Courts have 254 judges.

Capital punishment was abolished in 1853. Only one person has been executed in the State's history.

Supreme Court, URL: http://www.wicourts.gov
Chief Justice: Shirley S. Abrahamson

LOCAL GOVERNMENT

For administrative purposes, Wisconsin is divided into 72 county governments, and 1,851 sub-county general purpose governments. Of the 1,851 sub-county governments, 592 are municipal governments, and 1,259 are town or township governments. Each county government is run by a county board of supervisors, and each town is run by a town board of supervisors. Cities are divided into one of four classes according to population numbers.

Wisconsin Counties Association, URL: http://www.wicounties.org/

AREA AND POPULATION

Area
Wisconsin is located in the mid-west of America on the western edge of the Great Lakes. It is bordered by Illinois and Iowa to the south, Minnesota and Iowa to the west, Lake Michigan to the east, and Lake Superior and the Upper Peninsula of Michigan to the north. The total area of Wisconsin is 65,497.82 sq. miles, of which 54,310.10 sq. miles is land, and 11,187.72 sq. miles is water (of which 10,062 sq. miles is Lake Superior and Lake Michigan).

To view a map of the state, please consult:
http://www.lib.utexas.edu/maps/us_2001/wisconsin_ref_2001.pdf

Population
According to the 2010 Census, the 2010 population was 5,686,986, up on the mid-2009 estimate of 5,654,774. The population was estimated at 5,726,398 in 2012. Over the period 2000-10, the state population rose by 6.0 per cent, whilst over the decade 1990-2000 the population increased by 6.8 per cent. The population is expected to reach 6.15 million by 2030. Population density is an estimated 105 persons per sq. mile. The largest county is Milwaukee County (947,735 inhabitants in 2010). The three largest cities are Milwaukee (594,833 in 2010), the capital, Madison (233,209), and Green Bay (104,057).

According to the 2010 Census, 6.3 per cent of the population is under 5 years, 23.6 per cent under 18 years and 13.7 per cent is aged over 65 years. Approximately 86.2 per cent of the population is white, and 6.3 per cent is black. Approximately 5.9 per cent of the population is of Hispanic or Latino origin.

Births, Marriages, Deaths
The US Census Bureau estimated that there were 68,487 births in 2010 and 47,308 deaths, giving a natural population increase of 21,179 people. Net immigration amounted to 1,126 people in 2009. The infant mortality rate in 2007 was 6.5 infant deaths per 1,000 live births. Marriages and divorces in 2007, according to provisional data, numbered 32,234 and 16,090 respectively.

EMPLOYMENT

Wisconsin's total civilian labour force was 3,060,800 in December 2012, of which 2,858,600 were employed and 202,200 were unemployed. The unemployment rate was 6.6 per cent, lower than the US average of 7.8 per cent. (Source: US Bureau of Labor Statistics)

Preliminary figures for non-farm wage and salary employment in December 2012, according to industry, are shown on the following table:

Industry	No. of Jobs	12-month change
Logging and mining	2,800	-6.7
Construction	89,500	4.3
Manufacturing	450,000	1.7
Trade, transport, and utilities	506,000	-0.6
Information	46,500	1.5
Financial activities	154,200	-1.2
Professional and business services	285,000	2.0
Educational and health services	414,800	0.4
Leisure and hospitality	242,500	-0.4
Other services	132,300	-2.3
Government	405,300	-0.1
TOTAL	2,728,900	0.3

Source: Bureau of Labor Statistics

BANKING AND FINANCE

GDP/GNP, Inflation, National Debt
Wisconsin's Gross Domestic Product (current dollars) rose from an estimated $219,170 million in 2010 to $254.8 billion. Real GDP increased by 1.1 per cent in 2011 and was ranked 20th in the US for its 2011 GDP. The following table shows Gross Domestic Product according to industry (millions of current dollars):

Industry	2009	2010	2011
Agriculture, forestry, fishing & hunting	3,165	4,372	5,347
Mining	418	503	476
Utilities	4,703	4,807	4,358
Construction	8,383	7,952	7,835
Manufacturing	42,485	46,054	50,068
Wholesale Trade	13,347	13,652	14,504
Retail Trade	14,279	14,884	15,314
Transport and warehousing	6,775	6,949	7,190
Information	7,251	7,190	7,593
Finance and insurance	19,499	22,625	22,689
Real Estate	30,273	28,480	27,484
Other non-government services	34,372	36,571	38,977
Government	26,491	26,550	26,9897
TOTAL	209,190	219,170	277,832

Source: Bureau of Economic Analysis, Feb. 2013

The state's average per capita income was an estimated $9,575 in 2011, 95 per cent of the national average. Per capita GDP was $38,822 in 2011; the US average was US$42,070.

The annual Consumer Price Index (CPI) for the Milwaukee-Racine urban area (all items) rose from 216.9 in 2011 to 221.4 in 2012. (1982-84 = 100). (Source: Bureau of Labor Statistics)

Balance of Payments / Imports and Exports
Total Wisconsin imports amounted to $16,532 million in 2009, down 23.4 per cent from the 2008 total of $21,581 million. Imports rose by 19.1 per cent in 2010 to $19,696 million, and rising by 11.4 per cent over 2011 to $21,924 million, representing 1.0 per cent of the US total. Main suppliers were China (24.5 per cent), Canada (18.4 per cent), Mexico (13.8 per cent), Germany and Japan. Main imports included clothing & vehicle parts. Export revenue fell from $20,570 million in 2008 to $16,725 million in 2009, a decrease of 18.7 per cent. Exports rose by 18.3 per cent in 2010 to $19,790 million and rose by 11.4 per cent in 2011 to $22,055 million, contributing 1.5 per cent of the US total. Merchandise export revenue in 2010-11, according to the top five international destinations, is shown on the following table:

Destination	2010 ($m)	2011 ($m)	+/-% 2010-11
Canada	6,053	7,145	18.0
Mexico	2,010	1,987	-1.1
China	1,333	1,381	3.6
Germany	747	879	17.6
Australia	583	762	30.8

Source: US Census Bureau, Foreign Trade Division

The top five export products in 2010, according to revenue, are shown on the following table:

Product	Export Revenue ($m)
Parts and attachments for Derricks etc.	680
Spark-ignt. recprcting piston engine etc >1000 cc	488
Electro-diagnostic apparatus nesoi, and parts etc	391
Parts of phone sets & oth. app. for trans/recep. etc.	343
Wheath (other than durum) & meslin	340

Source: US Census Bureau, Foreign Trade Division

Chambers of Commerce and Trade Organisations
Wisconsin Economic Development Association, URL: http://www.weda.org/
Metro Milwaukee Association of Commerce, URL: http://www.mmac.org/

MANUFACTURING, MINING AND SERVICES

Primary and Extractive Industries
Wisconsin's mining industry contributed an estimated $476 million towards the 2011 Gross Domestic Product (up from $503 million in 2010). In 2010, $501 million was from non-oil and gas extraction, $2 million was from oil and gas mining, and $1 million was from support activities for mining. (Source: BEA)

Wisconsin has no oil industry. Oil consumption in 2010 reached 104.5 million barrels - 58.9 million barrels as motor gasoline and 24.4 million barrels in distillate fuel. It has a crude oil refinery capacity of 38,000 bbl/d. Wisconsin produces a substantial amount of ethanol in the southern and central regions of the State.

There are no natural gas reserves or production in Wisconsin. Natural gas consumption rose from 372,916 million cu ft in 2010 to 393,737 million cu ft in 2011. The residential and industrial sectors lead consumption. Approximately two-thirds of Wisconsin households use natural gas as their primary fuel for home heating. (Source: EIA)

Energy
Total energy production was 341 trillion Btu in 2010, ranking it 26th in the US. Wisconsin's total energy consumption was 1,800 trillion Btu in 2009, and ranked 26th in the US in terms of its per capita energy consumption (316 million Btu in 2010).

Wisconsin is a net importer of electricity whose primary generating fuel is coal. Net summer capability in 2010 was 17,836 MW (1.7 per cent of US total), and total net monthly (Oct. 2012) generation was 4,843 thousand MWh (25th in the US). Of this, coal-fired 2,799 thousand MWh, nuclear 1,304 thousand MWh, natural gas-fired 320 thousand MWh, hydroelectric 105 thousand MWh, other renewables 290 thousand MWh and petroleum-fired 3 thousand MWh. Of Wisconsin's top five electricity generating plants, four use coal and one uses nuclear energy: Pleasant Prairie (coal), South Oak Creek (coal), Columbia (coal), Point Beach (nuclear), Edgewater (coal). Wisconsin has two nuclear power plants: Kewaunee and Point Beach.

In 2006, Wisconsin adopted a renewable portfolio standard that requires utilities to produce 10 per cent of their electricity from renewable sources - including solar, wind, hydroelectric power, biomass, geothermal technology, tidal or wave action, and fuel cell technology that uses qualified renewable fuels - by 2015. In 2011, 8.4 per cent of the state's net electricity generation came from renewable energy resources. (Source: EIA)

Manufacturing
Manufacturing is Wisconsin's largest contributor to GDP, earning an estimated $50,068 million in 2011 (up from $46,054 million in 2010). Major sectors in 2010 were machinery manufacturing ($7,542 million), fabricated metal products ($5,503 million), and food product manufacturing accounted for some $6,118 million. (Source: BEA)

Service Industries
The services industry is the largest contributor to Wisconsin's GDP. In 2010, the top sectors were real estate ($27,484 million) health care and social assistance ($23,326 million) and finance and insurance ($22,689 million). Professional and technical services accounted for $11,850 million, and the government sector accounted for $26,980. (Source: BEA)

Tourism
With its 14,000 lakes, 2,000 trout streams, 5,000 campsites, 6 million acres of hunting land, 42 state parks, 10 state forests, 13 state trails and 4 recreation areas, Wisconsin is a major tourist attraction. The arts, entertainment and recreation sector of the services industry contributed an estimated $1,927 million towards the 2011 GDP, whilst the accommodation and food sector contributed around $6,249 million. (Source: BEA)
Wisconsin Department of Tourism, URL: http://agency.travelwisconsin.com/

Agriculture
Agriculture (including forestry, fisheries, farms, and agricultural services) earned an estimated $5,347 million in 2011 (up from $4,372 million in 2010). The farms sector accounted for $4,082 million in 2010, whilst forestry, fishing and related activities accounted for $344 million. (Source: BEA)

According to the US Department of Agriculture, Wisconsin's farms numbered around 78,000 in 2010. Farmland covered some 15,200,000 acres in 2010. The average size of a farm was195 acres. Total agricultural produce revenue reached $8.9 billion in 2007; livestock, dairy and poultry accounted for $6.2 billion, whilst crops earned some $2.6 billion. Dairy products are the major source of farm income; at the beginning of 2010, the state had 1,262,000 milk cows. In total as of Jan. 2011, there were 3.45 million cattle and calves, 340,000 hogs & pigs, and 90,000 sheep. Wisconsin ranks first in cheese production and second in milk and other dairy produce. The state produces over 25 per cent of the nation's cheese and butter. The state is a top producer of Christmas trees and mink pelts.

UNITED STATES OF AMERICA

COMMUNICATIONS AND TRANSPORT

International Airports
Recent figures show that there are 718 airports in Wisconsin, of which 95 are publicly owned and 446 privately owned. In addition, there are 108 heliports, 28 seaplane bases and 41 military/police airfields.

Railways
Rail freight traffic has increased steadily over the past 70 years to its current figure of 21 billion ton-miles. Conversely, rail passenger traffic has decreased to 146,000 passengers.

Roads
There are currently 111,500 miles of Wisconsin roads, including 11,813 miles of state trunk highways, 19,621 miles of county trunk highways and 77,523 miles of local roads. The number of registered motor vehicles was recently recorded at 4.25 million. The number of vehicle miles travelled annually in the state is more than 51.4 billion.

Ports and Harbours
Bordered by Lake Superior and Lake Michigan, Wisconsin has twelve ports which handle over 40 million tons of cargo per year, valued at over $7 billion. Commodities transported include agricultural products, coal, iron ore, wood pulp, cement and salt. Wisconsin has easy connection to both the Altantic and the Gulf of Mexico via the St. Lawrence Seaway and the Upper Mississippi River system respectively.

HEALTH

The National Center for Health Statistics estimated that there were 26.5 doctors per 10,000 inhabitants in 2009, slightly below the US average of 27.4. In 2008, there were 3,208 dentists (5.7 per 10,000 population). In 2009, there were 2.4 community hospital beds per 1,000 residents. In 2010, there were 392 nursing homes with 36,113.

In the period 2007-11, an estimated 12.0 per cent of the population were below the poverty level. Wisconsin has one of the highest percentage of health-care coverage in the US, with just 9.1 per cent of the population having no health insurance in 2007-09. The state reported 4,999 HIV/AIDS cases from the beginning of the epidemic to the end of 2008, and ranked 31st among US states in the cumulative number of reported cases in 2008. The TB rate was 1.2 per 100,000 population, ranking it 43rd highest among the US states. The adult obesity rate is 26.3 per cent and an estimated 62.8 per cent of adults are considered overweight. (Source CDC)

EDUCATION

Primary/Secondary Education
In the school year 2010-11, a total of 872,436 students enrolled in Wisconsin's 2,292 public elementary and secondary schools. There were 58,426 teachers working in the public school system, and an estimated ratio of pupils to teacher of 14.93 to one.

Expenditure on state education for the year 2007-08 totaled $10.9 billion, whilst revenues amounted to $10.485 billion.

Higher Education
In the period 2008-09, Wisconsin had 84 institutions of higher education eligible to confer degrees. 31 of these were run by the state, and 53 were private. For the academic year 2010-11, 162,895 male students were enrolled, together with 210,333 women. Over the year, 77,735 degrees/certificates were awarded, including 34,110 Bachelors, 9,476 Masters and 2,347 Doctorates. (Source: National Center for Education Statistics)

COMMUNICATIONS AND MEDIA

Newspapers
Wisconsin daily newspaper include: The Capitol Times, Wisconsin State Journal, Herald Times Reporter, The Daily Reporter, Milwaukee Journal Sentinel, The Journal Times, The Daily News and The Daily Tribune.
Wisconsin Newspaper Association, URL: http://www.wnanews.com/
Wisconsin State Journal / Capitol Times, URL: http://www.madison.com/

Broadcasting
Wisconsin has some 16 commercial television stations, seven of which are in Milwaukee. The state also has four educational television stations and 129 commercial radio stations.

ENVIRONMENT

Wisconsin's primary electricity generating fuel is coal, and therefore emissions from its electricity generating industry are high. In 2010 emissions of carbon dioxide rose from 44,233,260 in 2009 to 47,238,443 metric tons (2.0 per cent of the US total), ranking the state 19th in the US. Sulfur dioxide emissions amounted to 144,871 metric tons (2.73 per cent of US) and emissions of nitrogen oxide amounted to 48,766 metric tons (2.0 per cent of US total).

In 2010, Wisconsin had seven ethanol plants with a capacity of 498 million gal/year (3.7 per cent of US total). There were 12,751 alternative-fueled vehicles in use and ethanol consumption amounted to 5,591 thousand barrels in 2011. (Source: EIA)

WYOMING

Capital: Cheyenne (Population, Census 2010: 59,466)

Head of State: Matt Mead (R) Governor (page 1475)

State Flag: A blue background with a thin white border and outside that a larger red border; in the centre of the flag is the shape of a bison in white on which appears the Great Seal. The Seal depicts a draped figure of a woman in the centre holding a staff from which appears a banner with the words 'Equal Rights'; on each side of the figure appears a pillar on each of which is a lamp; encircling the pillars are scrolls with the words 'Oil, Mines, Livestock, Grain'; on each side of the pillars is a male figure, representing the mining and livestock industries; below the draped figure appears an eagle resting on a shield; the shield bears red stripes on a white background and, at the top, on a blue background, a white, five-pointed star on which appears the number 44 (Wyoming being the 44th state to join the Union).

CONSTITUTION AND GOVERNMENT

Constitution
Wyoming entered the Union on 10 July 1890 as the 44th state. The Constitution was adopted on 30 September 1889 and ratified by the people of Wyoming on 5 November 1889. According to the Constitution executive power is vested in the governor and four other elected officials: secretary of state, state auditor, state treasurer, and superintendent of public instruction. All serve terms of four years.

Wyoming elects two US Senators for six-year terms and one At-Large US Representative for a two-year term to the US Congress, Washington, DC.

To consult the state constitution, please visit: http://legisweb.state.wy.us/statutes/statutes.aspx

Legislature
Wyoming's legislature is one of a few in the states composed entirely of part-time legislators. Legislature general sessions take place every odd-numbered year from the second Tuesday in January and usually last for 40 legislative days. Budget sessions take place every even-numbered year, starting on the second Monday in February, and last 20 legislative days.
Wyoming Legislature, Capitol Building, Cheyenne, Wyoming, USA. URL: http://legisweb.state.wy.us/

Upper House
The Senate has 30 members who are elected for four years, 15 retiring every two years. Following the elections on 6th November 2012 the Senate was composed of 26 Republicans and four Democrats.
Wyoming Senate, Capitol Building, Cheyenne, Wyoming, USA. Tel: +1 307 635 0505, URL: http://legisweb.state.wy.us

Lower House
The House of Representatives has 60 members who are elected for two years. . Following elections on 6th November 2012 the House was made up of 52 Republicans and 8 Democrats.
Wyoming House of Representatives, Capitol Building, Cheyenne, Wyoming, USA. Tel: +1 307 872 7110 (House Speaker), URL: http://legisweb.state.wy.us

---

Elected Executive Branch Officials (as at April 2013)
Governor: Matt Mead (R)
Secretary of State: Max Maxfield (R)
State Auditor: Cynthia I. Cloud (R)
State Treasurer: Mark Gordon (R)
Superintendent of Public Instruction: Cindy Hill (R)

Legislature (as at April 2013)
President of the Senate: Tony Ross (R)
Vice President of the Senate: Eli Bebout (R)
Senate Majority Leader: Phil Nicholas (R)
Senate Minority Leader: Christopher Rothfuss (D)
Speaker of the House: Tom Lubnau (R)
Speaker Pro Tem of the House: Rosie Berger (R)
House Majority Floor Leader: Kermit Brown (R)
House Minority Leader: Mary Throne (D)

US Senators: Mike Enzi (R) (page 1421) and John Barrasso (R) (page 1384)

Ministries
Office of the Governor, Wyoming State Capitol, 200 West 24th Street, Cheyenne, WY 82002, USA. Tel: +1 307 777 7434, URL: http://www.governor.wy.gov
Office of the Attorney General, 123 Capitol Building, 200 W. 24th Street, Cheyenne, WY 82002, USA. Tel: +1 307 777 7841, fax: +1 307 777 6869, URL: http://attorneygeneral.state.wy.us/

Office of the Secretary of State, State Capitol Building, Cheyenne, WY 82002-0020, USA. Tel: +1 307 777 7378, fax: +1 777 6217, URL: http://soswy.state.wy.us/

Office of the State Auditor, State Capitol Building, Room 114, Cheyenne, WY 82002, USA. Tel: +1 307 777 7831, fax: +1 307 777 6983, URL: http://sao.state.wy.us/

Office of the State Treasurer, 200 West 24th Street, Cheyenne, WY 82002, USA. Tel: +1 307 777 7408, fax: +1 307 777 5411, e-mail: treasurer@state.wy.us, URL: http://treasurer.state.wy.us/

Office of the Superintendent of Public Instruction, 2300 Capitol Avenue, Hathaway Building, 2nd Floor, Cheyenne, WY 82002-0050, USA. Tel: +1 307 777 7675, fax: +1 307 777 6234, URL: http://www.k12.wy.us/

Department of Administration and Information, Emerson Building, 2001 Capitol Avenue, Room 104, Cheyenne 82002-0060, USA. Tel: +1 307 777 5492, fax: +1 307 777 3696, URL: http://ai.state.wy.us/

Department of Agriculture, 2219 Carey Avenue, Cheyenne 82002-0100, USA. Tel: +1 307 777 7321, fax: +1 307 777 6593, URL: http://wyagric.state.wy.us

Department of Corrections, 700 W. 21st Street, Cheyenne 82002-3427, USA. Tel: +1 307 777 7208, fax: +1 307 777 7479, URL: http://corrections.wy.gov

Department of Education, Hathaway Building, 2nd Floor, 2300 Capitol Avenue, Cheyenne, WY 82002-0050, USA. Tel: +1 307 777 7690 / 307 777 7673, fax: +1 307 777 6234, URL: http://edu.wyoming.gov/Default.aspx

Department of Environmental Quality, 122 West 25th Street, Herschler Building, Cheyenne 82002, USA. Tel: +1 307 777 7937, fax: +1 307 777 7682, URL: http://deq.state.wy.us/

Department of Health, 2300 Capitol Avenue Room 117, Cheyenne, WY 82002, USA. Tel: +1 307 777 7656, fax: +1 307 777 7439, URL: http://www.health.wyo.gov

Department of Transportation, 5300 Bishop Boulevard, Cheyenne 82009-3340, USA. Tel: +1 307 777 4375, fax: +1 307 777 4289, URL: http://dot.state.wy.us/

Wyoming Business Council, 214 West 15th Street, Cheyenne, WY 82002-0240, USA. Tel: +1 307 777 2800, fax: +1 307 777 2838, e-mail: info@wyomingbusiness.org, URL: http://www.wyomingbusiness.org

Political Parties
Wyoming Democratic Party, URL: http://www.wyomingdemocrats.com/
Wyoming Republican Party, URL: http://www.wygop.org/

Elections
Elections were held in November 2010 for state elected officials (Governor, Secretary of State, State Auditor, State Treasurer, and State Superintendent of Public Instruction), US Senator, US Representatives, members of the State Senate and State House of Representatives, Justices of the Supreme Court of Wyoming, District Court Judges, and Circuit Court Judges. The Republican Matt Mead won the Gubernatorial election.

In the legislative elections of November 2012, the partisan split within the Senate remained the same: 26 Republican seats and four Democrats. In the House of Representatives, the Republicans marginally increased their majority with 52 seats going to the Republicans and 8 to the Democrats.

LEGAL SYSTEM

Wyoming's court system consists of the Supreme Court, District Courts in each of Wyoming's 23 counties, Circuit Courts in 16 of Wyoming's 23 counties, Justice of the Peace Courts in the remaining seven of Wyoming's counties, and Municipal Courts.

As well as the Supreme Court Chief Justice, who serves a term of four years, there are four Associate Justices, appointed for eight-year terms. When vacancies occur the Governor appoints new Justices from a shortlist of three supplied by the Judicial Nominating Commission.

In the District Courts there are 22 judges divided into nine judicial districts.

The current death penalty statute was passed in 1977. The only capital crime is first degree murder and the method of execution is lethal injection. Only one person has been executed in the state since 1976. As of January 2013, there was one person on death row.

Supreme Court, URL: http://www.courts.state.wy.us
Chief Justice: Marilyn S. Kite
Justices: Barton Voigt, Michael Davis, E. James Burke, William U. Hill

LOCAL GOVERNMENT

For local government purposes, Wyoming is divided into 23 county governments and 99 municipal (town and city) governments.

The 3,473.272 sq mile Wind River Indian Reservation is shared by the Eastern Shoshone (est. pop. 2,500) and Northern Arapaho (est. pop. 5,000) tribes in the central western Wyoming. It is a sovereign, self-governed land with two independent governing bodies: the Eastern Shoshone Tribal Government and the Northern Arapaho Tribal Government. Six elected council members from each tribe serve on a Joint Business Council to decide matters that affect both tribes.

AREA AND POPULATION

Area
Wyoming is located in the West of the US, south of Montana, east of Utah and Idaho, west of South Dakota and Nebraska, and north of Colorado and Utah. Wyoming's total area is 97,813.56 sq. miles, of which 97,100.40 sq. miles is land and 713.16 sq. miles is water.

The state is characterised by the plateau of the Great Plains broken by a number of mountain ranges. Gannett Peak is the highest mountain in the state, at 7,076 feet . The Continental Divide runs north-south across central Wyoming; rivers east of the divide drain into the Missouri River Basin (and the Gulf of Mexico) whilst those to the west run into the Columbia River or the Colorado River Basin and, from there, the Pacific Ocean.

To view a map of the state, please consult:
http://www.lib.utexas.edu/maps/us_2001/wyoming_ref_2001.pdf

Population
Wyoming has the smallest population in the United States; according to the 2010 Census, the 2010 population was 563,626, up on the mid-2009 estimate of 544,270. The population was estimated to be 576,412 in 2012. The state population grew by 14.1 per cent over the period 2000-10, and by 8.9 per cent over the decade 1990-2000. Wyoming has a population density of 5.8 people per sq. mile (the second lowest in the US, after Alaska). The county with the greatest number of inhabitants is Laramie County (91,738 in 2010). The population of the capital, Cheyenne, was an estimated 60,096 in 2011, making it the largest city in Wyoming.

According to the 2010 Census, 7.1 per cent of the population is under 5 years, 24.0 per cent under 18 years and 12.4 per cent is aged over 65 years. Approximately 81 per cent of the population is white, and 2.8 per cent is black. Approximately 2.4 per cent of the population is American Indian. Approximately 8.9 per cent of the population is of Hispanic or Latino origin.

Births, Marriages, Deaths
The US Census Bureau estimated that there were 7,566 births in 2010 and 4,438 deaths, giving a natural population increase of 3,128 people. Net immigration amounted to 7,553 people in 2009. In 2007, the infant mortality rate was to 76.4 infant deaths per 1,000 live births. Marriages and divorces in 2007 numbered 4,847 and 2,885 respectively.

EMPLOYMENT

Wyoming's total civilian labour force in December 2012 was 303,800, of which 288,900 were employed and 14,900 were unemployed. The unemployment rate was 4.9 per cent, well below the USA overall rate of 7.8 per cent. (Source: US Bureau of Labor Statistics)

The following table shows preliminary December 2012 non-farm wage and salary employment according to industry:

Industry	No. of Jobs	12-month change
Logging and mining	27,100	-2.9
Construction	20,100	-2.9
Manufacturing	8,900	-2.2
Trade, transportation and utilities	53,700	0.4
Information	3,800	-2.6
Financial activities	10,900	2.8
Professional and business services	16,800	-4.5
Educational and health services*	27,600	3.4
Leisure and hospitality	32,100	1.3
Other services	11,400	-5.8
Government	74,100	1.1
TOTAL	286,500	-0.2

*Not seasonally adjusted
Source: Bureau of Labor Statistics

BANKING AND FINANCE

Wyoming has no individual state income tax or corporate income tax.

GDP/GNP, Inflation, National Debt
Wyoming Gross Domestic Product (current prices) was $35,845 million in 2010, rising to $37.6 billion. Real GDP fell by -0.3 per cent in 2010 and by -1.2 per cent in 2011 and was ranked 49th in the US for its 2011 GDP. State Gross Domestic Product, according to industry, is shown below (in millions of current dollars):

Industry	2009	2010	2011
Agriculture, forestry, fishing & hunting	386	442	524
Mining	9,771	10,406	11,043
Utilities	837	887	861
Construction	1,812	1,784	1,657
Manufacturing	1,810	2,169	2,589
Wholesale Trade	1,233	1,226	1,327
Retail Trade	1,962	1,950	2,022
Transport and warehousing	1,929	2,053	2,179
Information	472	484	511
Finance and insurance	881	942	926
Real estate	3,191	3,187	3,386
Other non-government services	3,424	3,519	3,666
Government	4,982	5,122	5,177
TOTAL	34,157	35,845	37,617

Source: Bureau of Economic Analysis, Feb. 2013

The state's average per capita income was an estimated $47,898 in 2011. Per capita real GDP fell to $55,516 in 2011, above the US average of $42,070 per annum.

UNITED STATES OF AMERICA

The annual Consumer Price Index (CPI) for the West urban area (all items) rose from 227.5 in 2011 to 232.4 in 2012. (1982-84=100). (Source: Bureau of Labor Statistics)

Balance of Payments / Imports and Exports
Total Wyoming imports amounted to $1,996 million in 2009, down 47.7 per cent from $3,815 million in 2008. Imports fell by 12.7 per cent in 2010 to $1,743 million, representing a 0.1 per cent share of total US imports. Oil, which is the major import, fell by 23.5 per cent in 2010. Imports rose by 11.1 per cent in 2011 to $1,937 million. Main suppliers include Canada (87.4 per cent), China (5.4 per cent), Germany, UK and Mexico. Export revenue fell from $1,081 million in 2008 to $926 million in 2009, a decrease of 14.3 per cent. Exports rose by 6.2 per cent in 2010 to $983 million. Exports rose by 23.9 per cent in 2011 to $1,219 million, representing 0.1 per cent of total US exports. The following table shows the top five 2010-11 merchandise export countries:

Country	2010 ($m)	2011 ($m)	2010-11% +/-
Canada	238	330	38.5
Brazil	94	101	8.0
Australia	24	82	237.6
Mexico	69	78	12.6
Indonesia	62	71	13.4

Source: US Census Bureau, Foreign Trade Division

The top five export products in 2010, according to revenue, are shown on the following table:

Product	2010 ($m)
Disodium Carbonate	664
Crude oil from pretroleum and bituminous minerals	50
Bentonite, including calcined	29
Rare gases, other than argon	21
Parts for boring or sinking machinery, nesoi	17

Source: US Census Bureau, Foreign Trade Division

Chambers of Commerce and Trade Organisations
Wyoming Business Council, URL: http://www.wyomingbusiness.org
Greater Cheyenne Chamber of Commerce, URL: http://cheyennechamber.org/
Laramie Chamber of Commerce, URL: http://www.laramie.org/

MANUFACTURING, MINING AND SERVICES

Primary and Extractive Industries
Mining makes the largest contribution to Wyoming's GDP, earning an estimated $11,043 million in 2011, up from $10,406 million in 2010. In 2010, the oil and gas mining sector earned the highest revenues, $5,087 million, followed by non-oil and gas mining ($3,767 million) and support activities for mining ($1,552 million). (Source: BEA) As well as oil and gas, Wyoming mines yield coal, bentonite, uranium, trona and soda ash, diamonds, platinum, and palladium.

Wyoming had proven crude oil reserves of 567 million barrels in 2010, accounting for 2.4 per cent of US oil reserves. Its 8,833 oil wells and 48 rotary rigs produced a total of 53,133 thousand barrels in 2010, equivalent to around 2.7 per cent of total US production. Monthly (Oct. 2012) crude oil production amounted to 5,226,000 barrels (2.5 per cent of US total). Crude oil refinery capacity was 165,500 bbl/d in 2012. Oil consumption in 2010 fell to 30 million barrels; of this 15.5 million barrels were distillate fuel and 8.1 million barrels were motor gasoline.

Wyoming is one of the top natural gas-producing states in the USA. The state's natural gas industry consisted of reserves of 35,074 billion cubic feet of dry natural gas (11.5 per cent of the US total) and 26,180 wells in 2011. Marketed production was 2,159,422 million cubic feet. Consumption is low, and the state uses less than a tenth of its production; total consumption of natural gas was 156,454 million cu ft in 2011. Most of Wyoming's gas is sent to markets in the Midwest and California. The Rockies Express Pipeline is due to begin operations shortly and will ease delivery to Midwest markets.

Wyoming is a leading coal producer; the Powder River Basin, most of which lies within Wyoming, is the largest coal-producing region in the USA and accounts for approximately 40 per cent of all coal mined in the United States. Recoverable reserves were estimated to be 6,898 million short tons in 2011, around 35.9 per cent of the US total. The state has 20 coal mines, 19 of which are surface. Total production in 2011 was 438,673 thousand short tons (40.0 per cent of US total). Coal consumption in the state rose to 28,382 thousand short tons in 2007 (2.5 per cent of US total). (Source: EIA)

Energy
Wyoming's total energy production amounted to 10,533 trillion Btu in 2010, ranking it second in the US, and accounting for over 14.1 per cent of US total. Wyoming's total energy consumption amounted to 535 trillion Btu in 2010, whilst its per capita energy consumption ranks it 1st in the US (948 million Btu in 2010).

Wyoming is primarily a net exporter of electricity. Its electricity generating industry relies mainly on coal for production. Net summer capability in 2010 was 7,986 MW (0.8 per cent of US total), and total net monthly generation (Oct. 2012) was 4,412 thousand MWh (27th in the US). Of this, coal 3,924 thousand MWh, natural gas 39 thousand MWh, hydroelectric 23 thousand MWh, other renewables 402 thousand MWh, and petroleum 4 thousand MWh. The five largest utility plants in the state are all coal burning: Jim Bridger, Laramie, Dave Johnston, Naughton and Wyodak. (Source: EIA)

Manufacturing
Manufacturing contributed an estimated $2,589 million towards Wyoming's GDP in 2011 (up from $2,169 million in 2010). The petroleum and coal products sector earned $1,246 million. (Source: EIA)

Service Industries
The service sector is the second largest industry in Wyoming. Major industries in 2011 were real estate ($3,386 million), transport, and warehousing ($2,053 million), and health care and social assistance ($1,533 million). (Source: BEA)

Tourism
In 2011 the food and accommodation sector of the services industry earned around $1,130 million towards Wyoming's GDP, whilst the arts, entertainment and recreation sector earned an estimated $329 million. Wyoming's two major tourist attractions are the Yellowstone National Park (over 3 million visitors in 2003), and Devil's Tower (nearly 400,000 visitors in 2003). It is reknown for its rodeos.
Wyoming Business Council, Travel and Tourism,
URL: http://www.wyomingtourism.org

Agriculture
Wyoming's agriculture, forestry and fishing industry contributed an estimated $524 million towards the 2011 GDP (up from $442 million in 2010). The farming sector accounted for $396million in 2010, whilst forestry, fishing and related activities accounted for $46 million. (Source: BEA)

According to the US Department of Agriculture, Wyoming's farms numbered around 11,000 in 2010 (up from 9,443 at the time of the 1997 Agricultural Census), and covered around 30,200,000 acres. The average size of a farm was 2,745 in 2010 (the largest in the US). In 2007, the value of livestock production reached $943.7 million and crop production was valued at $213.8 million. Major livestock products are cattle and calves, and beef cows. As of Jan. 2011, there were 1.3 million cattle and calves, 99,000 hogs & pigs, and 365,000 sheep. Wyoming ranks second in the US for wool production and breeding sheep, and third for all sheep and lambs. Major crops produced are hay-alf and silage, wheat for grain, and barley for grain.

COMMUNICATIONS AND TRANSPORT

International Airports
Natrona County International Airport, URL: http://www.iflycasper.com/

Railways
There are over 2,000 miles of Class 1 railway lines in operation in Wyoming, as well as more than 45,350 miles of non-Class 1 railway lines.

Roads
Wyoming has over 910 miles of Interstate Highways, in comparison with the overall US total of 46,030 miles. There are also 34,110 miles of public roads and streets. There are nearly 343,100 licensed drivers in the state and 562,050 vehicle registrations.

HEALTH

The National Center for Health Statistics estimated that there were 19.9 doctors per 10,000 population in 2009, below the US average of 27.4. In 2008, there were 266 dentists (5.0 per 10,000 population). In 2009, there were 3.7 community hospital beds per 1,000 residents, well above the US average of 2.6 beds. There were 38 nursing homes, with 2,965 beds.

It was estimated that 14.3 per cent of the state population had no health-care insurance in 2007-09. In 2007-11, 10.1 per cent were living in poverty (one of the lowest US rates). Wyoming reported 266 HIV/AIDS cases from the beginning of the epidemic to the end of 2008, and ranked 49th in cumulative number of reported cases in 2008. The TB rate was 0.9 per 100,000 population, 46th highest state in the US. Obesity levels are below the US average rate, at 25.1 per cent, and the rate of overweight children is well below the national rate, at 9.8 per cent. An estimated 62.9 per cent of adults are classified as overweight. (Source: CDC)

EDUCATION

Primary/Secondary Education
In the year 2009-10, 88,155 students were enrolled in Wyoming's 366 elementary and secondary schools. There were 7,165 teachers and a ratio of pupils to teachers of 12.3 to one, below the national average of 15.3 to one.

The state expenditure on public education was $1.191 billion during 2007-08, and education revenues amounted to $1.6 billion.

Higher Education
In the year 2010-11, there were 11 institutions in the state eligible to confer degrees, eight of which were public. As well as the University of Wyoming, there are several community colleges including: Casper College, Central Wyoming College, Eastern Wyoming College, and Sheridan College. Enrolment in the year 2010-11 comprised 17,480 male students and 19,613 women. 6,910 degrees/certificates were awarded, including 1,791 Bachelors, 388 Masters degrees and 179 Doctorates. (Source: NCES)

COMMUNICATIONS AND MEDIA

Newspapers
Wyoming's daily newspapers include: the Wyoming Tribune-Eagle, Cheyenne, and the Casper Star-Tribune, Casper. Non-daily newspapers include: Wyoming, State Journal, Lander; The Bounty, Sheridan; Douglas Budget, Douglas; Star Valley Independent, Afton; News Letter Journal, Newcastle; and Cody Enterprise, Cody.
Wyoming Press Association, URL: http://www.wyopress.org
Wyoming Tribune-Eagle, URL: http://www.wyomingnews.com
Daily Boomerang, URL: http://www.laramieboomerang.com

Wyoming State Journal, URL: http://www.statejournal.com/

Broadcasting
KTWO is based in Casper and is affiliated with NBC; KGWN is based in Cheyenne and is affiliated with CBS; and KCWC is based in Riverton and is affiliated with PBS.

ENVIRONMENT

Emissions of carbon dioxide from Wyoming's electricity generating industry rose from 44,683,966 metric tons in 2009 to 45,702,951 metric tons in 2010, ranking it 21st in the US. Emissions of sulfur dioxide amounted to 67,422 metric tons and emissions of nitrogen oxide amounted to 61,363 metric tons.

Wyoming has two ethanol plants with a capacity of 7 million gal/year. Ethanol consumption was 525,000 barrels in 2011. In 2010, there were 2,811 alternative-fueled vehicles in use. (Source: EIA)

AMERICAN SAMOA

Capital: Pago Pago

Head of State: Barack Obama (President) (page 1488)

Governor: Lolo Letalu Matalasi Moliga

Lieutenant-Governor: Lemanu Peleti Mauga (page 1472)

Flag: A dark blue background on which appears a white triangle with a red edge; within the triangle is an eagle holding a yellow staff and club

CONSTITUTION AND GOVERNMENT

Constitution
American Samoa is an external territory of the USA, having been given up by the United Kingdom and Germany following the 1889 Treaty of Berlin. The islands of Tutuila and Aunu'u were formally ceded to the United States in 1900, followed by the islands of Ta'u, Ofu, Olosega, and Rose Atoll in 1904. An unincorporated territory of the United States, American Samoa is administered by the Office of Insular Affairs, US Department of the Interior. Its Constitution was drafted in 1966 and came into effect in 1967. In 1977, the American Samoan people elected their first Governor and Lieutenant Governor.

In 1981 American Samoa sent its first non-voting representative to the US Congress.
US Representative: Eni F.H. Faleomavaega (D) (page 1422)

The Constitution of American Samoa makes provision for two elected executive branch officials, the Governor and Lieutenant Governor, as well as an elected legislature. The Governor and Lieutenant Governor are elected for four-year terms.

In November 2008, there was a referendum on a proposal to give the American Samoa Fono the authority to override a veto by the Governor, rather than the US Secretary of the Interior. Any veto powers bestowed on the Fono would require a two-thirds majority in both the American Samoa House of Representatives and the American Samoa Senate before becoming law. 50.1 per cent of voters were against accepting the constitutional amendment.

To consult the full constitution, please visit:
http://www.house.gov/faleomavaega/samoan-constitution.shtml

Recent Events
In March 2013 the US Department of Interior announced it would be reducing its funding by 5 per cent. The DOI provides grants of approximately $23 million per year to help operate local government.

Legislature
American Samoa has a bicameral legislature (the Fono) consisting of the Senate and House of Representatives. Legislative sessions take place twice a year, in January and July, and last for no longer than 45 days. The 33rd legislature commenced in 2013.
Fono, American Samoa Government, Pago Pago, American Samoa 96799 USA. Tel: +1 684 633 4565 (Senate President) / 633 4366 (Chief of House), fax: +1 684 633 1638 (Senate) / 633 1681 (House)

Upper House
The Senate has 18 non-partisan members who are elected from Matai, or heads of the islands, for four-year terms.

Lower House
The House of Representatives consists of 20 non-partisan representatives, elected by popular vote for two-year terms, including a delegate from Swains Island.

Legislature (as at March 2013)
President of the Senate: Gaoteote Palaie Tofau
Speaker of the House: Savali Talavou Ale

Elected Executive Branch Officials (as at March 2013)
Governor: Lolo Letalu Matalasi Moliga
Lieutenant-Governor: Lemanu Peleti Mauga (page 1472)

Cabinet (as at June 2013)
Director of Human and Social Services: Dr Meki Solomona
Acting Director of Administrative Services: Eliki Afalava
Director of Agriculture: Lealao Melila Purcell
Director of Commerce: Keniseli Fa'alupe Lafaele

Director of Education: Dr Salu Hunkin-Finau
Director of Homeland Security: Utualii Iuniasolua Tului Savusa
Director of Human Resources: Sonny Thompson
Attorney General: Afoa Moega Lutu
Director of Marine & Wildlife Resources: Dr Ruth Matagi
Acting Director of Parks & Recreation: Maeataanoa Pili Gaoteote
Acting Director of Public Health: Tuileama Nua
Director of Public Information: Fagafaga Daniel Langkilde
Commissioner of Public Safety: William Haleck
Director of Public Works: Faleosina Voiight
Secretary of Samoan Affairs: Paramount Chief Satele Galu T. Satele

Ministries
Office of the Governor, Executive Office Building, Third Floor, Utulei, Pago Pago American Samoa, 96799, USA. Tel: +1 684 633 4116, URL: http://www.americansamoa.gov
Department of Administrative Services, American Samoa Government, Executive Office Building, Utulei, American Samoa, Pago Pago, AS 96799, USA. Tel: +1 684 633 4158, fax: +1 684 633 1841, URL: http://www.asg-gov.com/departments/as.asg.htm
Department of Agriculture, American Samoa Government, Executive Office Building, Utulei, American Samoa, Pago Pago, AS 96799, USA. Tel: +1 684 699 1497, fax: +1 684 699 4031, URL: http://www.asg-gov.com/departments/doa.asg.htm
Department of Commerce, Executive Office Building, PO Box 1147, Pago Pago, American Samoa 96799, USA. Tel: +1 684 633 5155, fax: +1 684 633 4195, URL: http://www.asdoc.info
Department of Education, Pago Pago, American Samoa 96799, USA. Tel: +1 684 633 5237, fax: +1 684 633 4240, URL: http://www.doe.as/, http://www.asg-gov.com/departments/doe.home/doe.htm
Department of Health, Pago Pago, American Samoa 96799, USA. Tel: +1 684 633 4606, fax: +1 684 633 5379, URL: http://www.asg-gov.com/departments/doh.asg.htm
Department of Human and Social Services, Pago Pago, American Samoa 96799, USA. Tel: +1 684 633 1187, fax: +1 684 633 7449, URL: http://www.asg-gov.com/departments/dhss/dhss.asg.htm
Department of Human Resources, Pago Pago, American Samoa 96799, USA. Tel: +1 684 633 4485, fax: +1 684 633 1139, URL: http://www.asg-gov.com/departments/dhr.asg.htm
Department of Legal Affairs, Pago Pago, American Samoa 96799, USA. Tel: +1 684 633 4163 (Attorney General), fax: +1 684 633 1838, URL: http://www.asg-gov.com/departments/dla.asg.htm
Office of Tourism, Department of Commerce, American Samoa Government, PO Box 1147, Pago Pago, American Samoa 96799, USA. Tel: +1 684 6999411, fax: (684) 9414, URL: http://amsamoa.com/tourism
Department of Treasury, Pago Pago, American Samoa 96799 USA. Tel: +1 684 633 4155, fax: +1 684 633 4100, URL: http://www.asg-gov.com/departments/dtr.asg.htm

Political Parties
Democratic Party of American Samoa, PO Box 5169, Pago Pago, American Samoa 96799, USA. Tel: +1 684 633 4656, fax: +1 684 633 1638
Chairman: Dr. Oneta M. Togafau
Republican Party of American Samoa, Post Office Box 538, Pago Pago, AS96799, USA. Tel: +1 684 633 2288, fax: +1 684 633 4149, e-mail: asgop@mail.com, URL: http://www.gop.com/our-party/
State Chairman: Tautai A.F. Faalevao

Elections
Elections for the Governor, Lieutenant Governor, US Congressional Representative, and members of the State Senate and House of Representatives took place on 2nd November 2010. Democrat Togiola Talailei Tulafono retained the governorship. In the election for the US Congress, Eni F.H. Faleomavaega (D) (page 1422) won his twelfth term of office, with over 53 per cent of the vote.

The 2012 American Samoa gubernatorial election took place on 6 November 2012. The incumbent governor, Togiola Tulafono, was term limited and was unable to stand for re-election. No candidate received a majority of the vote and a runoff election was held on 20 November 2012. Lolo Letalu Matalasi Moliga (Ind.) took 52.9 per cent of the vote, defeating his rival Fao Aitogele Sunia (47.1 per cent).

LEGAL SYSTEM

The head of the judicial branch of the Government of American Samoa, the Chief Justice, is appointed by the US Secretary of the Interior. The Secretary also appoints an Associate Justice who assists the Chief Justice and acts in his behalf when he is not present in the territory. A panel of ten Samoan judges sit with and assist the Chief and Associate Justices in the wide range of cases that come before the High Court. Court proceedings are conducted in Samoan and English, unless the presiding judge stipulates that the hearing be conducted in one

UNITED STATES OF AMERICA

language only. Proceedings in the High Court are conducted, insofar as applicable, in accordance with US Federal Rules of Civil and Criminal Procedure and the most recent edition of the Revised Code of American Samoa.

American Samoa has the death penalty but it is not mandatory.

High Court Chief Justice: Michael Kruse
High Court Associate Justice: Lyle Richmond

American Samoa Bar Association, URL: http://www.asbar.org/

LOCAL GOVERNMENT

American Samoa is divided into three districts (Eastern District, Manu'a District, and Western District) and two atolls (Rose Island and Swains Island). These in turn are subdivided into 74 villages.

AREA AND POPULATION

Area
The islands constituting American Samoa are located 2,300 miles south-west of Hawaii and 2,700 miles north-east of Australia. The total area is about 76 sq. miles which includes seven islands as follows: Tutuila (the main island of about 42 sq. miles); Aunu'u; Swain's Island (an atoll 200 miles north of Tutuila); The Manu'a Group: Ofu, Olosega, Ta'u; Rose Island (uninhabited). The climate is tropical with average temperatures of 80 degrees Fahrenheit. Average annual rainfall is 200 inches.

To view a map, please consult:
http://www.lib.utexas.edu/maps/cia08/american_samoa_sm_2008.gif

Population
American Samoa's population was estimated at 64,827 by mid-2008 (up from 66,900 in 2006). The annual population growth rate was around two per cent over 2007. It was estimated to have risen to over 68,000 in 2012. The population estimates have increased by an average of around 1,500 inhabitants per year since the 2000 census. Recent immigration statistics indicate that many American Samoans are migrating to the US mainland. Over the 2005-06 period, 3,600 local residents moved off-island to further their education, military services and for greater life opportunities. (Source: ASG Department of Commerce, Statistics Division, American Samoa)

Population density is approximately 273 people per sq. km and the median age of the population is 21.3 years (down from 22.8 years in 2005). Unlike most large developed countries where females outnumber males, American Samoa had a gender ratio of about 104 males for every 100 females. The county with the highest population is Lealataua County, followed by Itua County and Sua County. Of American Samoa's year 2000 population, 50,766 lived in urban areas, whilst 6,525 lived in rural areas. Some 91,376 American Samoans have settled in mainland states, most in California (almost 31,500), Washington D.C. (approximately 16,000) and Utah (around 8,000).

Ethnic origin in 2004 was as follows: Samoan (Polynesian) 89 per cent, Caucasian 2 per cent, Tongan 4 per cent and other groups 5 per cent.

Both Samoan and English are spoken in American Samoa.

Births, Marriages, Deaths
Births during 2007 dropped by almost 300 in comparison to 2006, to under 1,500. It is thought that family planning programmes and the active participation of women in the work force have contributed to the fall in the number of births. Deaths remained under 300 and were estimated at 224 in 2010. The crude birth rate for the year 2007 was estimated at 21.7 per 1,000 people and the crude death rate for the same year was four per 1,000 people. In 2010, the number of births was estimated at 1,234. The fertility rate was estimated at 93.5 per 1,000 females aged 15-44 years. Fetal and neonatal deaths numbered 11.8 per 1,000 live births. The number of registered marriages continued to drop (from 202 in 2005 to 171 in 2006.) Life expectancy at birth for men is 68.5 years and for women it is 76.2 years. (Source: ASG Department of Commerce, Statistics Division, American Samoa)

Public Holidays
American Samoans celebrate Flag Day on the 17th April.

EMPLOYMENT

American Samoa's economy is largely based around the tuna canning industry and tourism. Total employment in 2006 was estimated at 17,395, a slight increase of about 50 workers from the 2005 figure of 17,344. There were 5,894 government workers (including authorities), 4,757 cannery workers and 6,744 other private sector employees. Unemployment has increased in recent years. This is partly due to the minimum wage increases mandated by US federal law from which the territory had traditionally been exempt. The minimum wage was rasied from $3.26 an hour in 2007 to US$5.25 in 2010 and to the current US minimum of $7.25 in 2015. One of the territory's two tuna canning operations closed in 2009 with the loss of 2,000 jobs. The remaining operation announced job losses in 2010 saying the territory was no longer competitive. By 2010, the unemployment rate was an estimated 30 per cent.

BANKING AND FINANCE

The American Samoa Government aims to increase the island's economic self-sufficiency, and to broaden the territory's economic base; however, Samoa's remote location, together with limited transportation and periodic and devastating hurricanes have limited expansion and development.

GDP/GNP, Inflation, National Debt
The American Samoan economy is predominantly based on tuna fishing and processing. Growth in the economy was driven by government spending, and private investment, mainly in construction. Following the 2009 earthquake and tsunami, the government has increased is construction spending for the rebuild. Exports have been hit by the global economic crisis. In 2009, GDP was estimated at $714 million and per capita GDP was $12,660. GDP is estimated at $615 million in 2010, with a growth rate of 1.3 per cent. (Source: BEA)

The latest figures available for revenues per industry are shown below:

Revenues per Industrial Sector, 2002

Sector	US$
Construction	44,210,000
Manufacturing	503,854,000
Wholesale trade	86,788,000
Retail trade	154,593,000
Transportation and warehousing	15,530,000
Information	18,741,000
Finance and insurance	28,265,000
Real estate and rental and leasing	9,055,000
Professional, scientific & technical svs.	53,295,000
Administrative and support/waste mgmt.	9,100,000
Educational services	3,320,000
Health care and social assistance	27,535,000
Accommodation and food services	21,335,000
Other services(except administration)	16,489,000
TOTAL REVENUES	**993,940,000**

Source: American Samoa Dept. of Commerce

In 2010, private industries contributed 72 per cent of GDP, of which manufacturing 7 per cent.

Per capita GDP stood at $8,052.00 in 2003. In 2000, around 61 per cent of all persons lived below the national poverty level. One out of every ten families consisted of a single woman with children. 71 per cent of grandparents living within their families were responsible for childcare.

The inflation rate remained relatively low (at 2-4 per cent) over the decade to 2002. However, there was an overall increase in the Consumer Price Index for the year 2003-04 of 7.1 per cent when there were increases were in food and transport costs. In 2005, the inflation rate slowed to 5.2 per cent, and in 2006, it fell to 3 per cent. In 2006, the largest increases were in transport costs, alcohol and tobacco and food. (Source: American Samoan Government, Dept. of Commerce) In 2009, inflation was estimated to be over 15 per cent.

Foreign Investment
After the Government, the largest employers are the two tuna canneries which employ around 4,757 people (around 27.5 per cent of the workforce). Other industries have shown an active interest in establishing plants in American Samoa to take advantage of the territory's duty-free status. United States customs laws add 30 per cent of the value of most finished products in American Samoa. American Samoa is also eligible for favourable tariff treatment under the Generalized System of Preferences of Australia, New Zealand, Japan and the United States.

Balance of Payments / Imports and Exports
American Samoa is heavily dependent on the US for most of its foreign trade. The largest export industry is tuna canning ($431,478,872 in 2006). There was a significant growth area is the pet food sector; its export revenues increased from $7.7 million in 2003 to $42 million in 2004, before falling back to $21,904,190 in 2005 and 7,050,488 in 2006. Total export revenues reached $438.5 million in 2006, up from $373.8 million in 2005, but lower than the 2003-04 peak. Export revenue from goods and services was estimated at $366 million in 2010, down from $536 million in 2009.

In 2006, total imports cost American Samoa $579.2 million, up from 2005 when imports cost $520.7 million. American Samoa's main import trading partners are the US ($13,430,577 in 2006), New Zealand ($31,075,410) and Singapore ($27,172,928). Major import commodities include food, fuel and oil and machinery and parts. In 2000, imports were estimated to cost $502 million in 2010, down from $532 in 2009. The trade balance in 2010 was -$136 million. (Source: BEA)

Central Bank of Samoa, URL: http://www.cbs.gov.ws/

MANUFACTURING, MINING AND SERVICES

Energy
American Samoa has no oil resources of its own and relies entirely on imports. Electricity generation in 2008 reached 190 million kilowatthours, all of which was thermally produced. There are two electricity generating plants: Satala and Tafuna. Consumption was 167 million kWh, up from 121 MWh in 2001. Per capita consumption in 2009 amounted to 130 million Btu per person, compared to the US average of 308 million. American Samoa imported 4.440 thousand bbld, of which distillate fuel 2.800 thousand bbl/d, motor gasoline 0.700 thousand barrels/day, jet fuel thousand 0.600 bbl/d in 2007.

Potential renewable energy sources in this territory include solar, wind, and ocean currents. Trade winds occurring in the winter season result in class 4 wind resources (up to 16.8 miles per hour at 50 meters above ground level) in the ocean surrounding American Samoa. American Samoa is assessing where it may build wind turbines. American Samoa is developing solar energy; its largest solar facility (1.75 MW) is expected to replace 7 per cent of electricty generation from diesel fuel. (Source: EIA)

Tourism

Tourism is one of the main contributors to American Samoa's economy. In 2010, visitor numbers were estimated at 29,060, down approximately 7 per cent on the previous year. Approximately 50 per cent of visitors are from the US. An estimated 12 cruise liners visited in island in 2010.

Office of Tourism, URL: http://www.amsamoa.com/tourism

Agriculture

Despite the government's efforts to modernise this sector, farming is still largely subsistence. With a growing population, some 95 per cent of food is now imported, costing the economy millions of dollars each year. The situation is exacerbated by hurricanes; Heta destroyed around 90 per cent of agricultural product in January 2004.

According to the 2003 Census of Agriculture, there were 7,094 farms in American Samoa (up from 6,473 in 1998), and 19,642 acres of land were dedicated to farming (down from 19,736 in 1998). The average size of a farm fell from 3 acres in 1998 to 2.8 acres in 2003.

Agricultural Production in 2010

Produce	Int. $'000*	Tonnes
Taro (cocoyam)	1,697	10,000
Coconuts	851	7,700
Indigenous pigmeat	484	315
Bananas	310	1,100
Yams	230	1,000
Pineapples	88	310
Cucumbers and gherkins	79	400
Beans, green	50	140
Tomatoes	48	130
Vegetables fresh nes	38	200
Hen eggs, in shell	37	45
Cabbages and other brassicas	36	240

* unofficial figures
Source: http://faostat.fao.org/site/339/default.aspx Food and Agriculture Organization of the United Nations, Food and Agricultural commodities production

In 2006, there were 51 fishing boats in American Samoa, crewed by 153 fishermen. These figures indicate a fall in the industry since the peak of 2003, when there were 74 fishing boats with 222 crew. In 2002, FAO figures show that 6,939 tonnes of fish were caught and this had fallen to 5,261 tonnes in 2010.

COMMUNICATIONS AND TRANSPORT

Travel Requirements

Citizens of Canada, Australia and the EU require a passport valid for at least 60 days beyond the length of stay, documentation for onward travel, sufficient funds to cover their stay and a confirmed accommodation reservation; advance permission to enter must be obtained from the immigration authorities. Some nationals may be able to enter visa-free for up to 90 days. Within the EU, nationals of Bulgaria, Cyprus, Czech Republic, Estonia, Greece, Hungary, Latvia, Lithuania, Malta, Poland, Romania and Slovak Republic do need a visa.

For visits of up to 30 days, US citizens require a passport or other proof of identity, an onward/return ticket and sufficient funds for the duration of the stay. Under the Western Hemisphere Travel Initiative of January 2007, US citizens returning directly from a US territory do not need to present a passport to re-enter the USA. Other nationals should contact the embassy to check visa requirements.

National Airlines

Hawaiian Air is the only airline which provides a commercial air service to Honolulu. Polynesian Airlines, Air New Zealand and Air Pacific provide an air service to New Zealand, Australia, Vanuatu, Tonga, New Caledonia, Tahiti and the Cook Islands, via connections in Western Samoa and Fiji. The numbers of flights, passengers and cargo have fallen over the last few years:

Incoming	2001	2005	2006
Flights	7,953	4,044	4,344
Passengers	94,117	61,262	75,501
Cargo (lbs)	1,721,957	2,027,461	3,034,501
Mail (lbs)	1,522,130	1,145,901	904,379
Outgoing			
Flights	7,953	4,044	4,344
Passengers	92,824	64,596	81,907
Cargo (lbs)	900,241	834,544	3,111,482
Mail (lbs)	1,810,000	279,856	781,750

Source: American Samoa Department of Commerce

Roads

There were 9,215 vehicles registered on the roads in 2006, up from 8,199 in 2005. 7 ,758 vehicles were privately owned. A new $8.9 million road in Ta'u, Manu'a was opened in 2012. The road had suffered from cyclone damage and now includes shoreline protection.

Shipping

There is a monthly ship to New Zealand and luxury liners call at Pago Pago about every five weeks en route to the USA. Sea borne traffic amounted to 16,500 total movements and around 600,000 tons of cargo passed through the port of Pago Pago in 2006. Most vessels that called into port were fishing vessels bringing in tuna for local canning.

HEALTH

The main medical facility in American Samoa is on the island of Tutuila; the LBJ Medical Centre has a 130-beds and offers general medical, emergency and dental facilities.

The main cause of death is heart disease, followed by malignant neoplasm. Main causes of visits to hospital or to the doctor are dengue fever, flu, chicken pox and dog bites. The average life expectancy in 2012 was estimated to be 71.5 years for men and 77.5 years for women.

EDUCATION

Primary/Secondary Education

The number of schools in American Samoa dropped from 140 in 2002 to 124 in 2006. Enrolment, however, continued to rise: in 2000, there were some 19,484 students and in 2006 this number had risen to 21,135. School enrolments according to level of school in 2006 are shown on the following table:

School	No. of enrolments
Total	21,135
Public schools	
Nursery school, pre-school	1,634
Kindergarten	1,028
Grades 1-8	9,335
Grades 9-12	4,551
Private schools	
Nursery school, pre-school	404
Kindergarten	288
Grade 1 to grade 8	1,765
Grade 9 to grade 12	523
College, graduate or professional school	1,607

Source: Dept. of Education, American Samoa Community College

In 2006, there were 460 teachers in elementary schools, and 216 teachers at secondary level. Both figures show a decrease on previous years.

Vocational Education

The American Samoa Community College offers two year college preparatory, vocational, business, clerical, and nursing curricula, as well as a four-year B.Sc. course in education.

RELIGION

The major religions in American Samoa are London Missionary Society or Congregational (50 per cent), Catholic (20 per cent), Mormon, Seven Day Adventist, Bahai and Methodist.

COMMUNICATIONS AND MEDIA

Newspapers

Samoa News, URL: http://www.samoanews.com/
Samoa Journal, URL: http://samoajournal.net/

Broadcasting

American Samoa's public television system provides daily local and US stateside programmes on three separate channels. Multi-channel pay TV is available. In addition, American Samoa has over 10 radio stations.

Postal Service

American Samoa is included within the US postal system.

Telecommunications

The number of mainline telephones has declined in recent years and was estimated to be just over 10,000 in 2010, whilst cell phone users soared to 9,000. The number of internet subscribers rose from 1,400 in 2002 to around 2000 in 2006.

ENVIRONMENT

Total fossil fuel emissions amounted to 1 million metric tons in 2010, all from petroleum. (Source: EIA)

GUAM

Capital: Hagatña (Agana) (Population estimate: 1,100)

Chief of State: President Barack H. Obama (page 1488)

Governor: Eddie Baza Calvo (page 1399)

Lieutenant Governor: Ray Tenorio

Flag: A red border surrounds a blue background in the centre of which is the Great Seal of Guam. The Great Seal, in the shape of a Chamorro sling stone, depicts a coconut tree and a canoe in front of the land mass of Hila'an.

CONSTITUTION AND GOVERNMENT

Constitution
Guam's constitutional status is that of an 'unincorporated territory' of the US. Entry of US citizens is unrestricted, foreign nationals are subject to normal regulations. In 1949 the President transferred the administration of the island from the Navy Department (who held it from 1899) to the Interior Department. The transfer was completed by 1 August 1950, on the passage of the Organic Act, which conferred full citizenship on the Guamanians who had previously been 'nationals' of the US.

The Governor, Lieutenant Governor, and Attorney General constitute the executive arm of the government. All are elected by the people for four-year terms. Guam's electorate was recently empowered to elect an attorney general following legislation from the US Congress and the government of Guam.

Guam's voters elect one non-voting Representative to the US Congress, Washington, DC, for a two-year term.
US Representative: Madeleine Z. Bordallo (D) (page 1391)

Legislature
The Legislature is unicameral and has 15 Senators who serve two-year terms. Its powers are similar to those of an American state legislature. All adults 18 years of age or over are enfranchised.
Guam Legislature, 155 Hesler Street, Hagatna, Guam 96910, USA. Tel: +1 671 472 3409, fax: +1 671 472 3510, URL: http://www.guamlegislature.com/
Speaker: Judith T. Won Pat

Elected Executive Branch Officials (as of March 2013)
Governor: Eddie Calvo (R) (page 1399)
Lieutenant Governor: Ray Tenorio
Attorney General: Leonardo M. Rapadas

Cabinet (as at March 2013)
Governor: Eddie Baza Calvo
Director, Department of Military Affairs: Maj. Gen. Benny Paulino, The Adjutant General
Director, Department of Administration: Benita Manglona
Department of Agriculture: Mariquita Taitague
Director, Agency for Human Resources Development: Alfredo Antolin
President, Department of Chamorro Affairs: Jospeh Artero-Cameron
Director, Department of Corrections: Jose San Agustin
Director, Bureau of Statistics and Plans: Lorilee Crisostomo
Director, Guam Energy Office: Peter Calvo
Director: Department of Integrated Services for Individuals with Disabilities: Benito Servino
Director, Department of Labor: George Santos
Director, Department of Land Management: Serafin Monte Mafnas
Acting Director, Department of Parks and Recreations: Ray Blas Sr.
Director, Department of Public Works: Carl V Dominguez
Director, Department of Revenue & Taxation: John Camacho
Director, Department of Youth Affairs: Adonis Mendiola

Ministries
Office of the Governor, PO Box 2950, Hagatna, Guam 96932. Tel: +1 671 472 8931, fax: +1 671 477 4826, e-mail: governor@ns.gov.gu, URL: http://www.gov.gu/webtax/govoff.html
Office of the Attorney General, Guam Judicial Center, Suite 2-200E, 120 West O'Brien Drive, Hagatña, Guam GU 96910, USA. Tel: +1 671 475 3324, fax: +1 671 472 2493, email: law@mail.justice.gov.gu, URL: http://www.guamattorneygeneral.com/
Office of the Public Auditor, 1208 E. Sunset Boulevard, Tiyan, PO Box 23667, GMF, Guam 96921. Tel: +1 671 475 0393, fax: +1 671 472 7951, URL: http://www.guamopa.org/
Department of Agriculture, 192 Dairy Road, Mangialo, Guam 96923. Tel: +1 671 734 3942, fax: +1 671 734 6569, URL: http://www.agriculture.guam.gov/
Department of Commerce, 102 M Street, Tiyan, Guam 96913. Tel: +1 671 475 0321, fax: +1 671 477 9031, e-mail: commerce@mail.gov.gu, URL: http://www.admin.gov.gu/commerce/
Guam Economic Development Authority, ITC Building, Suite 511, 590 South Marine Drive, Tamuning, Guam 96911. Tel: +1 671 647 4332, fax: +1 671 649 4146, e-mail: help@investguam.com, URL: http://www.investguam.com/
Guam Department of Education, PO Box DE, Hagatña, Guam 96932. Tel: +1 671 475 0461, fax: +1 671 472 5003, e-mail: juanpflores@guam.doe.edu.gu, URL: http://www.doe.edu.gu/
Guam Environmental Protection Agency, 15-6101 Mariner Avenue, Tiyan, PO Box 22439, Barrigada, Guam 96921. Tel: +1 671 475 1658, fax: +1 671 477 9402

Department of Labour, 504 E. Sunset Boulevard, Tiyan, PO Box 9970, Tamuning, Guam 96931. Tel: +1 671 647 6400, fax: +1 671 477 2988, e-mail: connent@ite.net, URL: http://www.labor.gov.gu/
Department of Law, Suite 2-200E Judicial Centre Building, 120 West O'Brien Drive, Hagatna, Guam 96910. Tel: +1 671 475 3324, fax: +1 671 475 2493, URL: http://www.justice.gov.gu
Department of Revenue and Taxation, Government of Guam, Building 13-1 Mariner Avenue, Tiyan, Barrigada, GU 96921, USA. Tel: +1 671 475 1820, fax: +1 671 472 2643, e-mail: revtax@mail.gov.gu
URL: http://www.admin.gov.gu/revtax/index.html

Political Parties
Guam Democratic Party, PO Box 2950, Agana, Guam 96910. Tel: +1 671 472 8931, fax: +1 671 477 6425, URL: http://www.guamdemocrats.us/
Republican Party of Guam, PO Box 2846, Agana, GU 96932. Tel: +1 671 472 3558, fax: +1 671 734 2001, URL: http://www.gop.com

Elections
Adults over 18 years of age are eligible to vote. Guamanians are automatically US citizens but do not vote in US presidential elections.

The most recent election for Guam's constitutional officers (governor, lieutenant governor and attorney general) took place on 2 November 2010. Eddie Calvo won the Governorship for the first time. Ray Tenorio won the position of Lieutenant Governor.

In the legislative elections for all 15 seats, held on the 4th November 2008, the Democrats won a 'super majority' of 10 seats to the Republican's 5 seats; this allowed them to over-ride vetoes by the territory's Republican governor. In the 2010 election put the Democrats won 10 seats. Incumbent Madeleine Bordallo was elected unopposed to Guam's At-large congressional seat.

LEGAL SYSTEM

The Organic Act established a Supreme Court and a Superior Court, whose judges are appointed by the Governor. The Superior Court, a court of general trial jurisdiction, consists of the Presiding Judge and six Judges. Superior Court judges are appointed by the Governor and serve for eight years. The Supreme Court consists of the Chief Justice and two Associate Justices. In addition, there is a US District Court with jurisdiction in matters arising under both federal and territorial law. The District Court judge is appointed by the President subject to Senate approval. Appeals go through the Ninth Circuit Court of Appeals in San Francisco and, if necessary, from there to the US Supreme Court.

Supreme Court, Suite 300, Guam Judicial Center, 120 West O'Brien Drive, Hagatña, GU 96910. Tel: +1 671 475 3162, fax: +1 671 475 3140, e-mail: justice@guamsupremecourt.com, URL: http://www.justice.gov.gu/supreme.html
Chief Justice: Hon. F. Philip Carbullido
Superior Court of Guam, Guam Judicial Center, 120 West O'Brien Drive, Hagatna, Guam 96910. Tel: +1 671 475 3340 (Clerk), URL: http://www.justice.gov.gu/superior.html
Presiding Judge: Alberto C. Lamorena III

AREA AND POPULATION

Area
Guam is the largest and most southern island of the Marianas Archipelago, in 13°' N. lat., 144° 43' E. long. It is located 1,500 miles east of Manila and 3,700 miles west-southwest of Honolulu. Total area is 541 sq. km. Its length is 30 miles and its breadth ranges from 4 to 10 miles. Agana, the seat of government, is about 8 miles from the anchorage in Apra Harbour.

The terrain is of volcanic origin, and the islands are surrounded by coral reefs. There is a relatively flat coralline limestone plateau, with steep coastal cliffs and narrow coastal plains in north, low hills in center and mountains to the south. The climate is tropical maritime, with little difference in temperatures over the year. Rainfall is copious during all seasons, but is greater from July to October.

To view a map, consult http://www.lib.utexas.edu/maps/cia08/guam_sm_2008.gif

Population
Latest estimates put the July 2012 population at 160,000, reflecting a growth rate of less than 1 per cent over the year. The median age is 29.6 years. Population density is about 830 per sq. mile, one of the highest in the US. Nearly one fifth of the population is made up of military personnel and their families. 37 per cent of the islanders are Chamorro, with 26 per cent Philippine, 11 per cent from other Pacific Islands, 6.9 per cent white, 6.3 per cent Asian and 12 per cent of other or mixed race.

The native language is Chamorro. English is the official language and is taught in all schools.

A ten per cent increase in the population is anticipated over the next few years (2010-2014), as the US Federal government carries out its proposal to relocate some 8,000 military personnel from Okinawa to Guam, together with their families.

Births, Marriages, Deaths
According to estimates, the birth rate was 17.5 births per 1,000 population in 2012 and the death rate was 4.9 per 1,000 inhabitants. The estimated fertility rate was 2.5 children per woman, slightly down on previous years. Migration was negligible. The estimated infant mortality rate in 2009 was 6.05 infant deaths (under 1 year old) per 1,000 live infants, continuing a downward trend, and a significant drop from 12.3 in 2004. Life expectancy at birth was estimated to be 78.5 years.

Public Holidays (in addition to USA holidays)
2 March: Guam Discovery Day
21 July: Liberation Day
8 December: Lady of Camarin Day

EMPLOYMENT

The total civilian labour force numbered 63,600 in September 2007, 58,290 of whom were employed, and 5,310 unemployed. The unemployment rate rose from 7.4 per cent in September 2006 to 8.3 per cent in September 2007. The number of employed people reached 61,990 in September 2011, down by 190 since December 2010. The unemployment rate was estimated to be 13.3 per cent in March 2011, falling to 11.8 the following year.

Employment according to industry is shown on the following table:

Employment by industry, December 2008

Industry	No. of employed
Private Sector total:	45,730
- Agriculture, forestry, fishing	350
- Construction	6,460
- Manufacturing	1,700
- Wholesale and retail trade	13,600
- Transport and Public Utilities	4,820
- Finance, insurance, real estate	2,560
- Services	16,240
Public Sector total:	*15,110*
- Federal government	3,760
- Territorial government	11,350
Total Employment	**60,840**

Source: US Bureau of the Census

Growth in construction jobs reached 26 per cent in 2007 and 18 per cent in 2008, largely due to the anticipated increase of military personnel on the island.

BANKING AND FINANCE

GDP/GNP, Inflation, National Debt

Guam's economy is largely based upon tourism, US military spending and the export of fish and handicrafts. Following several years of stagnation and decline, levels of activity in tourism and defence indicated the beginnings of economic recovery and growth over the early years of the millennium. In 2008-09, the negative impact of the global recession on Guam's external investments and inward tourism was tempered by the promise of the relocation of the 8,000 Marines from Okinawa to Guam over the period 2010-2014. This has already benefited the construction industry, and it is anticipated that the military buildup will make Guam's economy more resilient in the long term due to significant federal spending. In 2004, there were some 6,220 personnel on military active duty, 3,922 of whom were with the US Navy.

Per capita GDP was calculated at $22,900 in 2009. The manufacturing sector contributed about 15 per cent towards GTP, whilst the services sector accounted for around 78 per cent and agriculture contributed some 7 per cent.

Gross Domestic Product ($ million)

	2008	2009	2010
GDP	4,335	4,542	4,577
Personal consumption expenditures	2,895	2,904	2,838
Private fixed investment	252	236	233
Net exports of goods and services	-1,422	-1,405	-1,445
-Exports	801	689	675
--Goods	133	98	73
--Services	668	592	603
-Imports	2,223	2,094	2,120
--Goods	2,091	1,967	1,986
--Services	132	127	135
Government consumption expend. & gross invest.	2,620	2,806	2,951
-Federal	1,698	1,857	1,912
-Territorial	913	950	1,039

Source: BEA

Over 2008, the Guam Consumer Price Index went up by 6.2 per cent, slightly down on the previous year's rate of 6.8 per cent. Higher energy costs were the main cause of the increase, and these, together with a fuel surcharge on flights, contributed to a fall in the number of tourists visiting Guam over the year.

Balance of Payments / Imports and Exports
Export revenue for goods amounted to an estimated $73 million in 2010, whilst imports of goods cost an estimated $1,986 million in the same year. Japan received just over 67.2 per cent of Guam's exports in 2005, followed by Singapore at 11.6 per cent and the UK, 4.8 per cent. Singapore is Guam's major import partner (50 per cent of imports in 2005), followed by South Korea (21.4 per cent), Japan (14 per cent) and Hong Kong (4.6 per cent). Main export commodities are refined petroleum products, construction materials and fish, food and beverage products. Major import commodities are petroleum and petroleum products, food, and manufactured goods.

Major Bank
Bank of Guam, URL: https://www.bankofguam.com

Chambers of Commerce and Trade Organisations
Guam Economic Development Authority, URL: http://www.investguam.com/
Guam Chamber of Commerce, URL: http://www.guamchamber.com.gu

MANUFACTURING, MINING AND SERVICES

Primary and Extractive Industries
Guam has no conventional energy resources and imports all of its oil requirements by tankers to meet its energy needs. Jet fuel accounts for most of the oil imports/consumption (2,700 bbl/d), followed by distillate (800 bbl/d), and motor gasoline (2,700 bbl/d). (Source: EIA)

Energy
Primary energy consumption on Guam fell to 0.024 quadrillion Btu in 2008, which equated to 135.309 million Btu per capita. This was well above the Asia and Oceania average per capita energy consumption of 41 million Btu.

Totall electricity installed capacity was put at 1 million kW in 2010. The electricity industry in Guam produced 2 billion kWh of electricity in 2010, all of it from thermal sources. Consumption reached an estimated 1.664 billion kWh, up from 767 million kWh in 2000. Per capita consumption was an estimated at 129 million Btu/person in 2009, compared to 308 million Btu/Person for the US as a whole.

Electricity generating plants include: Cabras 1-4, Dededo, Macheche, Marbo, Piti 7-9, Pulantat, Talofofo, Tanguisson 1 & 2, Tenjo 1-6, and Yigo. All are run by the Guam Power Authority.

In 2011, the Public Utility Commission approved contracts for the first commercial wind and solar projects. They are due to begin operation in 2014-15 and will total 35 MW capacity. Guam's renewable portfolio goal calls for 5 per cent of net electricity sales to come from renewable energy resources by 2015 and 25 per cent by 2035. (Source: EIA)

Manufacturing
Guam has a relatively small manufacturing base, employing just 1,700 people in December 2008. The main manufacturing industries are concrete products, printing and publishing, food processing, ship-repair, petroleum distribution, textiles and handicrafts.Guam Economic Development Authority manages three industrial estates: Cabras Island (32 acres); Calvo estate at Tamuning (26 acres); Harmon estate (16 acres).

Service Industries
The services sector is the highest contributor to Gross Domestic Product, and rivals the Defence sector as an employer; in December 2008 some 16,240 people were employed in the services sector. Hotels and other lodges employed 5,430 whilst other services areas such as transshipment services, engineering and management services, and management and public relations employed 10,390 people.

Tourism
Following decline due to the Asian financial crisis and concerns about terrorism, Guam's tourist industry enjoyed a resurgence, becoming the fastest growing sector of the economy. Guam is a convenient stop-over point for people traveling to Asia and the Pacific from the US. An estimated 1.3 million people visited Guam in 2006, mainly from Japan (over 90 per cent) and Korea (8 per cent). The number of visitors in March 2006 showed an increase of 10 per cent on the same month in 2003. However, following two years of stable numbers, in 2008 there were declines in visitors from Japan (down by nine per cent) and Korea (down 10 per cent) as the recession hit the world economy. Higher energy costs and the introduction of a fuel surcharge also had a negative impact on tourist numbers.
Guam Visitors Bureau, URL: http://www.visitguam.org

Agriculture
In 2005, an estimated 3.64 per cent of the land was used for arable farming, and 18.18 per cent was used for permanent crops. Major products of the island are sweet potatoes, cucumbers, water melons and beans. Livestock includes cattle, hogs and poultry.

Agricultural Production in 2010

Product	Int. $'000*	Tonnes
Coconuts	9,067	82,000
Fruit fresh nes	873	2,500
Hen eggs, in shell	755	910
Roots and tubers, nes	445	2,600
Vegetables fresh nes	377	2,000
Nuts, nes	330	180
Indigenous pigmeat	240	156
Watermelons	239	2,100
Indigenous chicken meat	171	120
Bananas	138	490
String beans	105	110

UNITED STATES OF AMERICA

- continued

Tomatoes	92	250

* unofficial figures

Source: http://faostat.fao.org/site/339/default.aspx Food and Agriculture Organization of the United Nations, Food and Agricultural commodities production

In December 2008, some 350 people were employed in the sector.

COMMUNICATIONS AND TRANSPORT

National Airlines
The airlines that serve Guam are: Air Nauru, Continental Air Micronesia, Japan Airlines, Northwest Orient, Philippine Air, JAL, Gulf Air, ANA, and Air Guam.

International Airports
There were four aiports with paved runways. The AB Won Pat Guam International Airport provides facilities for six airlines who fly to the US, Hawaii, east Asia, Indonesia, the Philippines, Australia, and New Zealand. Over one hundred flights a week take off from the airport.
AB Won Pat Guam International Airport, URL: http://www.airport.guam.net/

Roads
Guam had 1,050 miles of all-weather roads in 2008.

Ports and Harbours
The Port Authority of Guam operates the largest US deepwater port in the Western Pacific. It was established in 1975 and currently handles about two million tons of cargo a year.
Port Authority of Guam, URL: http://portguam.com/

HEALTH

The Guam Memorial Hospital serves both Guam and Micronesia and has around 150 beds. Military personnel are treated at the US Naval Hospital. In addition, there are 12 medical and dental clinics with about 140 doctors and 30 dentists. The major cause of death is heart disease.

EDUCATION

Primary/Secondary Education
Elementary education is compulsory. Guam's public education system has 25 elementary schools, seven middle schools and four public high schools. The private sector includes a number of elementary schools and five high schools. The Seventh Day Adventist Guam Mission Academy operates a school from grades 1 to 12, serving over 100 students. St. John's School provides education for 530 students between kindergarten and the ninth grade.

Enrolment for the academic year 2009-11 totaled 40,373 in the state's public schools. Of this: elementary 17,373, middle school 9,188, senior school 11,757. Military school enrolment totalled 2,055. In 2009, the Department of Education staff included 2,465 teachers and 88 principals and assistants. 2,145 students graduated High School in 2010.

Chamorro Studies courses and bilingual teaching programmes integrate the Chamorro language and culture into elementary and secondary school courses.

Higher Education
The University of Guam, accredited by the Western Association of Schools and Colleges, offers Masters' degrees in public administration and education, in addition to operating a marine research laboratory. The university's Micronesian Area Research Centre holds a large collection of historical documents relating to the Micronesian and Pacific cultures. The university had around 3,550 students, and 367 degrees were awarded in 2003-04. Of Guam's population over 24 years, more than 76 per cent are high school graduates or higher, whilst over 20 per cent have Bachelor's degrees or higher.

Vocational Education
Guam's public further education system includes Guam Community College and a land grant college.

RELIGION

About 85 per cent of the Guamanians are Roman Catholics. Others are Baptists, Episcopalians, Bahais, Lutherans, Mormons, Presbyterians, Jehovah's Witnesses and members of the Church of Christ and Seventh Day Adventists.

COMMUNICATIONS AND MEDIA

Newspapers
Amongst Guam's newspapers are one daily paper, a thrice-weekly newspaper, a number of commercial weekly and monthly papers, as well as a number of military journals.

Broadcasting
Approximately 20 radio stations operate in Guam, including two religious broadcasters, a public station and a news station. There are an estimated 12 TV channels. Television broadcasting stations include: KGTF Public TV, Kuam TV8, KTGM-TV14 and Marianas Cable TV. PBS Guam began the transition to digital broadcasting in 2000.
PBS Guam, URL: http://pbsguam.org/about

Telecommunications
The Guam Telephone Authority operates the local phone service. As of 2010 there were an estimated 65,500 landlines. Most of the island has mobile phone services, and digital cable and high-speed internet are now widely available through either cable or DSL. Fibre optic cable technology links Guam with Hong Kong, Japan, Hawaii, and the Philippines. As of 2010 there were an estimated 90,000 internet users.
Guam Telephone Authority, URL: http://www.admin.gov.gu/gta/

ENVIRONMENT

The 22,900 acre Guam National Wildlife Refuge was established by the US Fish and Wildlife Service and protects a number of endangered bird species. Recently, there has been opposition from Guam leaders to continued federal control of the refuge. The native bird population is endangered by the rapid proliferation of the brown tree snake, an invasive species.

In 2010, carbon dioxide emissions from the consumption of fossil fuels (all petroleum) fell to an estimated 1 million metric tons. (Source: EIA)

NORTHERN MARIANA ISLANDS
Commonwealth of the Northern Mariana Islands

Capital: Saipan (Population estimate: 63,000)

Head of State: President Barack Obama (page 1488)

Head of Government: Eloy S. Inos (page 1447)

Lieutenant Governor: Jude U. Hofschneider (page 1442)

Flag: Blue, with the grey silhouette of a latte stone in the centre, on which a white, five-pointed star is superimposed, and surrounded by a wreath.

CONSTITUTION AND GOVERNMENT

Constitution
The Northern Mariana Islands are a dependency of the United States of America - a commonwealth in political union with the US - known formally as the Commonwealth of the Northern Mariana Islands. The Commonwealth is self-governing, with an elected governor, lieutenant governor and legislature. The governor holds executive authority, and is elected by popular vote for a term of four years.

Legislature
The islands' bicameral legislature is known as the Northern Marianas Commonwealth Legislature, and consists of the Senate and the House of Representatives. The nine Senators are elected for four-year terms, three Senators for each senatorial district. The 18 Representatives are elected from six Precincts for two-year terms.

Senate, Saipan, Northern Mariana Islands. URL: http://www.cnmileg.gov.mp/
President of the Senate: Jude U. Hofschneider (Republican)
Vice President of the Senate: Ralph Dlg Torres (Republican)

House of Representatives, Saipan, Northern Mariana Islands. URL: http://www.cnmileg.gov.mp/
Speaker of the House: Joseph P. Deleon Guerrero (Ind.)
Vice Speaker of the House: Francisco S. Dela Cruz (Ind.)

Up until May 2008, the Northern Mariana Islands did not have a non-voting delegate in the US Congress; instead, it had a Resident Representative with no voting rights. On May 8, 2008, President Bush signed into law Senate Bill 2739 (H.R. 3079), which included the provision for having a member of congress from the Northern Marianas. On January 6, 2009, the first congressman from the CNMI to the U.S. House of Representatives was sworn in; he serves a four-year term.
CNMI Congressman: T.H. Gregorio Kilili Camacho Sablan
URL: http://www.sablan.house.gov

> **Departmental Cabinet Members (as at June 2013)**
> *Secretary, Department of Finance:* Larrisa Larson
> *Secretary, Department of Community and Cultural Affairs:* Laura Ogumoro
> *Secretary, Department of Labor:* Gil M. San Nicolas
> *Secretary, Department of Land and Natural Resources:* Arnold I. Palacios
> *Secretary, Department of Commerce:* Sixto Igisomar
> *Commissioner, Department of Corrections:* Ramon Mafnas
> *Secretary, Department of Public Works:* Martin Sablan

Commissioner, Department of Public Safety: James C. Deleon Guerrero
Attorney General: Joey Patrick San Nicolas
Acting Secretary, Department of Public Lands: Pedros Itibus
Chief Public Defender, Office of the Public Defender: Doug Hartig

Ministries

Office of the Governor, Juan S. Atalig Memorial Building, Isa Drive, Capitol Hill, Caller 10007, Saipan, MP 96950, USA. Tel: +1 670 664 2200, fax: +1 670 664 2211, URL: http://gov.mp/

Department of Commerce, PO Box 10007, Saipan, MP 96950. Tel: +1 670 664 3000, fax: +1 670 664 3010, URL: http://commerce.gov.mp/

Department of Finance, URL: http://www.cnmidof.net/

Division of Environmental Quality, 3rd Floor, Morgen Building, San Jose, PO Box 501304, Saipan, MP 96950, USA. Tel: +1 670 664 8500, fax: +1 670 664 8540, URL: http://www.deq.gov.mp/

Division of Fish and Wildlife, PO Box 10007, Saipan, MP 96950, USA. Tel: +1 670 664 6000/04, fax: +1 670 664 6060, URL: http://www.cnmi-dfw.org/

Office of the Public Auditor, 1236 Yap Drive, Capitol Hill (Mailing Address: PO Box 501399, Saipan, MP 96950), USA. Tel: +1 670 322 6481, fax: +1 670 322 7812, URL: http://www.opacnmi.com/

Political Parties

Covenant Party: Leader - Benigno R. Fitial
Democratic Party: Dr. Carlos S. Camacho
Republican Party: Juan S. Reyes

Elections

Elections for governor and lieutenant governor (who are elected on the same ticket), members of the Senate and House of Representatives took place in 2009. The gubernatorial election was won by Benigno Fitial winning 51.4 per cent of the run-off vote, ahead of Heinz Hofschneider (48.6 per cent).

The most recent legislative elections took place in November 2011. Governor Fitial resigned in February 2013 ahead of an impeachment charge. He was replaced by the lt-governor, Eloy Inos.

LEGAL SYSTEM

The court system consists of the Commonwealth Supreme Court, Superior Court, and Federal District Court.) The Supreme Court is the appellate court of the Northern Mariana Islands, with jurisdiction to hear appeals from final judgments and orders of the NMI Superior Court. All appeals from the NMI Supreme Court go directly to the United States Supreme Court.

The NMI Supreme Court consists of three Justices appointed by the Governor for a term of eight years. A justice wishing to serve another term must receive voter approval in a retention election.

The Northern Marianas does not have the death penalty.

Supreme Court, Chief Justice: Hon. Alexandro Cruz Castro
Superior Court, Presiding Judge: Robert Naraja

Northern Marianas Judiciary, URL: http://www.justice.gov.mp/supreme_court.aspx

LOCAL GOVERNMENT

The Northern Mariana Islands are divided into four municipalities: Northern Islands, Rota, Saipan, and Tinian. Each municipality has a mayor.

AREA AND POPULATION

Area

The Northern Mariana Islands consists of 14 islands situated in the North Pacific Ocean between Hawaii and the Philippines, covering a total area of 477 sq. km. Six islands are inhabited, including Saipan, Rota, and Tinian. The Mariana Islands were formed by underwater volcanoes along the Marianas Trench. Whilst the northern islands are volcanic, the islands to the south are of limestone and fringed with coral reefs. Anatahan is currently an active volcano with the first recorded volcanic eruption on May 10, 2003.

The climate is tropical marine. The dry season lasts from December to June. There is a risk of typhoons from August to November.

To view a map of the Islands, please consult:
http://www.lib.utexas.edu/maps/cia08/northern_mariana_sm_2008.gif

Population

The estimated population in mid-2011 was 46,050 assuming growth of -4 per cent in 2011. The emigration rate was 8.97 per cent. The median age was estimated at 30 years, and life expectancy at birth was 77.08 years. In 2005, 60,600 people (92 per cent of the total CNMI population) lived on the island of Saipan, 2,829 (just over 4 per cent) lived on Tinian and 2,490 (four per cent) lived on Rota island

In 2005, Asians made up around 53 per cent of the CNMI's total population; Pacific Islanders made up around 37 per cent, and Caucasians, less than two per cent. The largest single ethnic group in the CNMI was Philippine at about 30 per cent of the total CNMI population, followed by Chamorro (23 per cent) and Chinese (16 per cent). The Carolinians made up around 5 per cent.

According to the 2000 Census, 24.4 per cent of the inhabitants spoke Philippine languages, 23.4 per cent spoke Chinese, Chamorro was spoken by 22.4 per cent, English by 10.8 per cent and other Pacific island languages were spoken by 9.5 per cent.

Births, Deaths etc.

In 2011, the birth rate was estimated to be 20.7 per 1,000 residents, whilst the death rate was an estimated 3.28 per 1,000 people. The fertility rate was 2.13 children born per woman. There were 6 infant deaths per 1,000 live births.

Public Holidays

Other than Commonwealth Day on January 9, the Northern Mariana Islands observe the same holidays as the US.

EMPLOYMENT

The labour force in 2005 consisted of 38,533 people over the age of 16 years (equivalent to 79.2 per cent of the total population over 16 years). There were 17,729 men and 20,803 women in the labour force. 35,365 people were employed, and 3,168 (8.2 per cent) were unemployed. Of those employed, 26,116 were Asian (13,559 Philippino, and 9,722 Chinese/Taiwanese).

Employment per industry:

Industry	2005
Agriculture, Forestry & fisheries	249
Mining	92
Construction	1,315
Manufacturing	2,681
Transportation, communication and utilities	783
Wholesale trade	279
Retail trade	2,262
Finance, insurance and real estate	705
Professional, scientific and technical mgmnt. of companies	1,657
Education, health and social services	1,946
Arts, entertainment and recreation	1,110
Accommodation, food and bars	3,163
Other services (apart from Public Admin.)	2,326
Public Administration	3,029
Total employed 18 years and over	22,898

Source: 2005 CNMI Household Income and Expenditure Survey

Of the 22,898 people employed, 17,930 were employed privately, 256 were self-employed and 4,626 were employed by the state.

With the gradual introduction of a US minimum wage, from 2009 onwards, substantial population shrinkage is anticipated as many of the migrant workers (who make up some 30 per cent of the population and who do not qualify under the new minimum wage rules) may seek work on neighbouring Guam, where significant economic growth now forecast.

Unemployment was estimated at13.3 per cent in 2011.

In 2012, a public pension plan, the Northern Mariana Islands Retirement Fund, filed for Chapter 11 bankruptcy protection. The assets are estimated at $268 million yet has over $900 million of liabilities. In 2011, it paid US$76 million in retirement benefts, health and life insurance claims and other payments.

BANKING AND FINANCE

Currency
US dollar = 100 cents

GDP/GNP, Inflation, National Debt
The economy of the Northern Mariana Islands benefits considerably from financial assistance from the US. Tourism is the main industry, employing around half the workforce and accounting for around a quarter of GDP. The economy has been struck by a change in regional tourism patterns over recent years; annual tourist entries were exceeding half a million until economic difficulties hit Japan (source of most tourists). The garment industry has diminished as a result of free trade agreements affecting clothing and textiles, and the gradual imposition of a U.S. minimum wage. The CNMI has relied on low wage labour in the past.

According to figures from the BEA, after declining for six years, GDP rose in 2010 by 2.3 per cent. Real GDP per capita was estimated at US$16,494 in 2007, falling to US$13,300 in 2009.

Gross Domestic Product ($ million)

	2008	2009	2010
GDP	851	725	733
Personal consumption expenditure	590	516	531
Private fixed investment	27	27	26
Net exports of goods and services	-109	-164	-194
-Exports	376	218	242
--Goods	172	23	20
--Services	205	195	222
-Imports	485	382	436
--Goods	417	327	379
--Services	69	55	57

UNITED STATES OF AMERICA

- continued

Government consumption, expend. & gross invest.	343	346	370
-Federal	16	21	22
-Territorial	327	325	349

Source: BEA

In the 4th Quarter of 2008, the Consumer Price Index rose to 120.5, (1st Quarter 2003 = 100), up from 114.1 as at the 4th Qtr. 2007. The largest increase was in food, which rose 11.4 points.

Balance of Payments / Imports and Exports

The islands' main export is clothing though revenues have fallen over recent years; in 2002 the sector earned US$831.3 million and by 2007 this figure had fallen to US$307.57 million. In 2008, the figure slumped to $98.22 million. The imposition of a U.S. minimum wage has reduced the industry.

Major import commodities include food, petroleum products, and construction equipment and materials. The islands receive most of their imports from the US and Japan.

As of 2010, exports of goods was estimated at $20 million and import of goods amounted to $379 million.

MANUFACTURING, MINING AND SERVICES

Energy

The Northern Marianas has no conventional energy resources and meets nearly all of its energy needs with petroleum shipped in by tanker. The Northern Marianas imports its petroleum products to meet its energy needs. Petroleum products used include liquefied petroleum gas, motor gasoline, diesel fuel, and distillate fuel oil.

There are diesel-fueled electric power plants operating on the islands of Saipan, Tinian, and Rota, with a total capacity of approximately 125 MW. The Northern Marianas has set up a renewable portfolio standard that requires 50 per cent of net electricity sales to be provided by renewable sources by 2030.

The feasibility of wind power is being assessed. Its first public renewable energy system (one 2.7-kW wind turbine, nine 18-volt solar panels) was installed in a school in February 2009 and will supply power to the school. (Source: EIA)

Manufacturing

The manufacturing sector earned some US$474.4 million in 2002. The garment industry, once the mainstay of the economy and worth around $1 billion, has gone into decline over the last few years following the introduction new trade rules regarding imports into the USA. The last of 34 garment factories closed down in March 2009.

Services

14,600 people were employed in the services sector in 2005 (excluding public administration). The largest employer was the accommodation and food services sector, which employed 3,163 people.

Tourism

Following the demise of the garment industry, the CNMI economy now relies on tourism, but the industry suffered declining tourist numbers; in 2007, there were 389,261 visitors to the Northern Mariana Islands, down from a high of 589,224 in 2004. Hotel occupancy rate fell from 72 per cent to 58.9 per cent over the same period. In 2011, there were an estimated 341,000 tourists of which over 40 per cent were from Japan and over 30 per cent from Korea.

Agriculture

The most recent agricultural census indicates that there were 103 farms on the Islands in 1997, with an average size of 33 acres. Total farming land area was estimated at approximately 117,760 acres. In 1997, 43 per cent of total sales came from vegetables and melons, 25 per cent from poultry and eggs, 14 per cent from livestock, and 9 per cent from fruits and nuts.

In 2002, 384,489 pounds of fish were caught of the CNMI, with a total market value of $888,776. Pelagic fish was the largest group of fish landed (58 per cent), followed by reef fish (34 per cent).

Revenues from agriculture and fishing amounted to around US$1.7 million in 2002 and the sector employed 249 people in 2005.

COMMUNICATIONS AND TRANSPORT

Airports

There are five airports in the Northern Mariana Islands, though only three of them are paved, and just two have runways of 2,438 to 3,047 metres. There is one heliport.

Roads

The islands' road system is about 536 km in length. There was an an average of 1.1 vehicles per household in 2000, and around 20 per cent of households owned two cars. The absence of a public transport system increased the importance of owning a vehicle. The total number of registered motor vehicles fell from 17,900 in 2001 to 17,349 in 2002.

Ports and Harbours

Three ports & terminals exist: Saipan, Tinian and Rota..

HEALTH

The Department of Public Health provides health services in the CNMI. The Commonwealth Health Center on Saipan is the main hospital. It has 76 in-patient beds, and includes a 10-bed psychiatric unit and a 13-unit hemodialysis service center. Recent expansion included a respiratory therapy unit and CAT Scan unit. The Rota and Tinian Health Centers have holding beds, laboratory, x-ray, pharmacy, dental, emergency, and public health services. There are several small, private medical and dental clinics on Saipan, and each inhabited island has a dispensary.

The infant mortality rate was estimated at 6.5 per 1,000 live births. Life expectancy at birth is approximately 75 years at birth.

Approximately 99 per cent of the population have access to improved sanitation and drinking water. (Source: WHO)

EDUCATION

In 2007, there were five government-run elementary schools and one high school on Saipan island, one state-run elementary school on Tinian and one state high school on Rota island. There were a further seven privately-run schools on the islands. Northern Marianas College was established in 1981 to run training programs for government employees. It now provides education in the areas of adult and continuing education, post secondary and adult vocational education and professional development for the people of the Commonwealth.

Enrolment figures in the education system have increased due mainly to natural population growth and immigration. In the year 2010-11 within the public school system, approximately 4,500 pupils were enrolled in elementary school and 5,100 in secondary schools. In the same year there were 477 teaching staff.

By the year 2000, around 75 per cent of the population over the age of 25 had graduated from High School (compared to around 66 per cent a decade earlier); The percentage of those gaining a Bachelor's degree or higher remained steady over the ten years at around 15.5 per cent. (Source: CNMI)

COMMUNICATIONS AND MEDIA

Newspapers

Marianas Variety, URL: http://www.mvariety.com/default.htm
Saipan Tribune, URL: http://www.saipantribune.com

Broadcasting

In 2009, there were 9 radio stations and one television station. Multi-channel satellite television is available on Saipan.

Telecommunications

In 2010, there were around 25,660 mainline telephones in use. By 2004, there were an estimated 20,500 mobile telephones in use. Internet use is on the increase, with some 10,000 users in 2003. In 2011 there were 17 internet hosts.

ENVIRONMENT

Enivronmental concerns include: protection of endangered species and contamination of ground water.

Division of Environmental Quality, URL: http://www.deq.gov.mp/

PUERTO RICO

Commonwealth of Puerto Rico
Estado Libre Asociado de Puerto Rico

Capital: San Juan (Population estimate: 434,000)

Head of State: Barack Obama (page 1488)

Governor: Alejandro Garcia Padilla (page 1428)

National Flag: On a field of five horizontal stripes, red and white countercharged, a blue triangle at the hoist charged with a white star.

CONSTITUTION AND GOVERNMENT

Constitution

The island of Puerto Rico was inhabited by the Tainos when Christopher Columbus arrived in 1493. Spain ruled Puerto Rico for 400 years and imprinted the Hispanic culture on its people.

In 1897 Spain granted Puerto Rico a Charter of Autonomy, establishing a system of self-government. Spain ceded Puerto Rico to the United States through the Treaty of Paris of 10 December 1898 which ended the Spanish-Cuban-American war. After two years of military government, the United States Congress passed the Foraker Act establishing a civil government headed by a Governor appointed by the President, with an Upper House appointed by the Governor, and a Lower House elected by popular vote.

In 1917 the United States granted American citizenship to all Puerto Ricans. In 1946, the first Puerto Rican Governor, Sr. Jesus T. Piñero, was appointed; in 1947 the US Congress granted authority to Puerto Ricans to elect their own Governor, and in 1948 Luis Muñoz Marin became the first elected Puerto Rican Governor. On 25 July 1952 the Commonwealth of Puerto Rico was established as a self-governing community, voluntarily associated to the United States by virtue of US Public Law 600.

The Constitution contains a Bill of Rights, and provides for a government with separation of powers and separation of Church and State. Puerto Ricans have American citizenship, although they do not vote in Presidential elections. There is free trade between Puerto Rico and the United States, and Puerto Ricans are exempt from payment of federal taxes. Defence and international affairs remain a US responsibility.

In a plebiscite held on 23 July 1967, 60.4 per cent of voters ratified the continuation of Puerto Rico as a Commonwealth, 39 per cent voted for incorporation as a State of the United States and 0.6 per cent voted in favour of independence, even though the pro-independence leadership boycotted the plebiscite. In December 1998 a similar vote took place, with the majority of the electorate rejecting plans for full US statehood. Full independence was even less popular. In 2005, the pro-independence rebel leader Filiberto Ojeda Rios was killed in a shoot-out with US federal agents. The handling of the incident angered the islanders. In March 2006, the US Supreme Court rejected an appeal for Puerto Ricans to have the right to vote in US presidential elections.

Puerto Rico is represented in the United States Congress by a Resident Commissioner elected by direct vote for a four-year term. The Commissioner also holds a seat with voice but no vote in the House of Representatives, but otherwise enjoys the same privileges and immunities of other members of Congress.

Resident Commissioner: Pedro Pierluisi (page 1495)

The executive power is vested in a Governor, elected by direct vote for a four-year term, and sixteen executive departments headed by Secretaries appointed by the Governor with the consent of the Senate. In case of temporary absence, disability or death of the Governor he or she is succeeded by the Secretary of State.

To consult the constitution, please visit: http://www.topuertorico.org/constitu.shtml

Recent Events

In May 2006, a budget shortfall led to the closure of schools and many government agencies. Thousands of people protested. Six months later, the government introduced its first sales tax, to help offset the major deficit.

In March 2008, Governor Anibal Acevedo Vila faced nine charges of corruption, linked to allegations of raising and hiding thousands of dollars in illegal election campaign contributions. If found guilty, he could face up to 20 years in jail. The Governor, up for re-election in November, had opposed moves by US Congress that may lead to a loss of Puerto Rican autonomy.

During the 2008 US election campaign, the inequity in Puerto Rico's separate-and-unequal status within the United States came to the fore; it was seen as ludicrous that Puerto Ricans participate in selecting a presidential candidate for whom they cannot ultimately vote. It was also highlighted that, per capita, the Island has sent more active duty forces to Iraq and Afghanistan than all U.S. states except Nevada, yet its people have no voice in choosing their commander in chief. Both Hillary Clinton and Barack Obama support Puerto Rican self-determination.

In June, Governor Acevedo Vila called on the UN Special Political and Decolonisation Committee to back the Puerto Rican right to self-determination, saying that the US had failed to keep promises it made in the 1950s when it gave the island greater self-governing powers in return for remaining a commonwealth. The governing Popular Democratic Party had previously supported the island's commonwealth status, whilst the opposition New Progressive Party favours full integration as the 51st state. The Puerto Rico Independence Party wants to achieve full independence. The resolution, put forward by Cuba and Venezuela, was approved by the UN Committee.

In November 2008, Anibal Acevedo lost the governorship to the New Progressive Party's Luis Fortuño.

In 2012, voters supported a non-binding referendum to become a full US State. Turnout was approximately 80 per cent and approximately 54 per cent voted in favour of a change in its relationship, currently a territory, and over 60 per cent voted yes to full statehood. Any change would require approval from the US Congress.

Legislature

Legislative power is vested in a Legislative Assembly, composed of a 27-seat Senate and a 51-seat House of Representatives. Members of the Legislative Assembly are directly elected every four years by universal adult suffrage, under an electoral system that provides for three types of representation in both the Senate and the House: district-level, at-large, and additional or minority party representation. A total of eleven members are elected on an at-large basis; parties may nominate up to eleven candidates in each house, but voters may choose only one at-large Senate candidate, and one at-large House candidate. The Constitution provides for an increase in the membership of the Senate or the House of Representatives (or both), in the event the majority party obtains over two-thirds of the seats in one or other of the two houses.

In July 2005, Puerto Ricans voted to replace the island's Senate and House of Representatives with a one-house legislature. This has not yet been established and, to date, legislative power continues to be vested in both the Senate (*Senado*) and the House of Representatives (*Cámara de Representantes*).

Upper House

The 27 Senate seats are made up from two senators from each of the eight Senatorial Districts and 12 Senators-at-Large.

Senate of Puerto Rico, PO Box 9023431, San Juan, PR 00902-3431. URL: http://www.senadopr.us

President of the Senate: Thomas Rivera Schatz

Lower House

The House of Representatives is composed of 51 representatives, one for each of the 40 representative districts and 11 elected at-Large. There is a Constitutional provision that allows for the expansion of both houses. Whenever a single political party obtains more than two-thirds of the seats in any house, additional seats are assigned to minority parties in proportion to the votes they obtained during the election. This provision ensures that no single political party exerts excessive control of the legislature.

Camara de Representantes: PO Box 9022228 San Juan, Puerto Rico 00902-2228. Tel: +1 787 721 6040, URL: http://www.camaraderepresentantes.org

---

Cabinet (as at June 2013)

Secretary of the State Department: David Bernier (page 1388)
Secretary of the Department of Economic and Trade Development: Alberto Baco Bague
Secretary of the Department of the Treasury: Melba Acosta
Secretary of the Department of Health: Francisco Joglar Pesquera
Secretary of the Department of Transport and Public Works: Miguel Torres Diaz
Secretary of the Department of Natural Resources: Carmen Guerrero Perez
Secretary of the Department of Consumer Affairs: Nery Adames Soto
Secretary of the Department of Education: Rafael Roman Melendez
Secretary of the Department of Housing: Ruben Rios Pagan
Secretary of the Department of Labor: Vance Thomas
Secretary of Correction and Rehabilitiation: José Negron Fernandez
Secretary of the Department of Agriculture: Myrna Comas Pagan
Secretary of the Department of Justice: Luis Sanchez Betances
Secretary of the Department of Sports and Recreation: Ramon Orta
Secretary of the Department for Family Matters: Idalia Colon Rodon

---

Ministries

Government portal, URL: http://www.fortaleza.gobierno.pr
Office of the Governor, La Fortaleza, PO Box 82, San Juan, PR 00901, Puerto Rico. URL: http://www.fortaleza.gobierno.pr
Office of the Controller, Avenida Ponce de Leon, 105 Esquina Pepe Díaz, Hato Rey, Puerto Rico 00919 (PO Box 366069, San Juan, PR 00936-6069). Tel: +1 787 754 3030, fax: +1 787 751 6768, URL: http://www.ocpr.gov.pr
Office of the Resident Commissioner, 3rd Floor, Dept. of State, P.O.Box 9023958, Washington, DC 20515-5401, USA. Tel: +1 202 225 2615, fax: +1 202 225 2154, e-mail: fortuno@mail.house.gov, URL: http://www.house.gov/fortuno

UNITED STATES OF AMERICA

Agriculture Department, PO Box 10163, Santurce, PR 00909, Puerto Rico. Tel: +1 787 721 2120, fax: +1 787 722 4990, URL: http://www.agricultura.gobierno.pr

Economic Development and Commerce Department, P.O. Box 362350, Hato Rey, PR 00918, Puerto Rico. Tel: +1 787 758 4747, fax: +1 787 753 4094, URL: http://www.ddecpr.com

Consumer Affairs Department, P.O. Box. 41059, Santurce 00940, PR 00940, Puerto Rico. Tel: +1 787 722 7555, fax: +1 787 726 0077, URL: http://www.daco.gobierno.pr

Education Department, Ave. Tnte César González, Esq. Calle Calaf, Tres Monjitas, Hato Rey, PR 00917, (PO Box 190759, Hato Rey, PR 00917). Tel: +1 787 759 2000, fax: +1 787 250 0275, URL: http://www.de.gob.pr

Environmental Quality Board, PO Box 11488, Hato Rey, PR 00918, Puerto Rico. URL: http://www.jca.gobierno.pr

Health Department, P.O. Box 70184, San Juan 00936, Puerto Rico. Tel: +1 787 274 7676, fax: +1 787 250 6547, URL: http://www.salud.gobierno.pr

Housing Department, P.O. Box 21365, Rio Piedras, 00928, Puerto Rico. Tel: +1 787 274 2525, fax: +1 787 258 9263 URL: http://www.vivienda.gobierno.pr

Interior Department, P.O. Box 9020082, San Juan, PR 00902-0082, Puerto Rico. Tel: +1 787 721 7000, fax: +1 787 721 1472, URL: http://www.doi.gov/

Justice Department, P.O. Box 9020192, Miramar 00907, Puerto Rico. Tel: +1 787 721 2900, fax: +1 787 724 3380, URL: http://www.ojp.gov/saa/pr.htm

Labour and Human Resources Department, Edif. Prudencia Rivera Martínez, Piso 21 Ave. Munoz Rivera # 505, Hato Rey 00918, Puerto Rico. Tel: +1 787 754 5353, fax: +1 787 756 1149, URL: http://www.dtrh.gov.pr

Natural Resources Department, P.O. Box 9066600, Santurce 00906, Puerto Rico. Tel: +1 787 724 8774, fax: +1 787 723 4255, URL: http://www.drna.gobierno.pr

Recreation and Sports Department, P.O. Box 9023207, Rio Piedras 00909, Puerto Rico. Tel: +1 787 721 2800, fax: +1 787 728 0313, URL: http://www.drd.gobierno.pr

State Department, P.O. Box 9023271, San Juan 00902, Puerto Rico. Tel: +1 787 722 2121, fax: +1 787 725 7303, URL: http://www.estado.gobierno.pr

Treasury Department, P.O. Box 9024140, San Juan 00902-3271, Puerto Rico. Tel: +1 787 721 2020, fax: +1 787 723 6213, URL: http://www.hacienda.gobierno.pr

Department of Transport and Public Works, P.O. Box 41269, Santurce 00940, Puerto Rico. Tel: +1 787 722 2929, fax: +1 787 728 8963, URL: http://www.dtop.gov.pr

Political Parties

Partido Popular Democrático, P.O. Box 9065788, San Juan, PR 00906. Tel: +1 787 721 2004, URL: http://www.ppdpr.net
Leader: Héctor J. Ferrer Ríos

Partido Nuevo Progresista (PNP), PO Box 1992 Fernández Juncos Station, San Juan, PR 00910 -1992 Tel: +1 787 289 2000, URL: http://www.pnp.org/
Leader: Luis Fortuño

Partido Independentista Puertorriqueño (PIP), Guaynabo Committee, Box 3242, Guaynabo, DR 00970. E-mail: jrbas@independencia.net, URL: http://www.independencia.net
Chairman: Rubén Ángel Berríos Martínez

Elections

The most recent gubernatorial election took place on 6 November 2012. The incumbent Governor, Luis Fortuño, leader of the Partido Nuevo Progresista (PNP), lost to Senator Alejandro Garcia Padilla of the Popular Democratic party. Mr Padilla took 48 per cent of the vote to Mr Fortuno's 47 per cent.

The incumbent resident commissioner, Pedro Pierluisi (PNP) retained his seat.

Parliamentary elections were also held on 6 November 2012. The PPD won 18 out of 27 seats in the Senate. The New Progressive Party won 8 seats and the Puerto Rican Independence Party won one seat. The PPD also won a majority of seats in the House of Representatives, taking 28 out fof the 51 seats. The PNP won 23.

LEGAL SYSTEM

The Supreme Court is at the apex of the judiciary. It is composed of a Chief Justice and eight Associate Justices appointed by the Governor with the consent of the Senate.

The lower judiciary consists of an Appellate Court, Superior and District Courts and Justices of the Peace equally appointed. Aside from the Puerto Rican courts, there is a US Federal Tribunal to address matters of federal jurisdiction. Federal judges are appointed by the President. The Federal Supreme Court is the ultimate authority determining matters of law and jurisprudence with overriding powers over the Federal Tribunal and the Puerto Rican Supreme Court.

US District Court for the District of Puerto Rico, URL: http://www.prd.uscourts.gov
Chief Judge: Hon. Aida Delgado-Colon
Supreme Court of Puerto Rico, URL: http://www.ramajudicial.pr/
Oficina del Procurador del Ciudadano, URL: http://www.ombudsmanpr.com/

LOCAL GOVERNMENT

Puerto Rico is divided into 78 municipalities Adjuntas, Aguada, Aguadilla, Aguas Buenas, Aibonito, Anasco, Arecibo, Arroyo, Barceloneta, Barranquitas, Bayamon, Cabo Rojo, Caguas, Camuy, Canovanas, Carolina, Catano, Cayey, Ceiba, Ciales, Cidra, Coamo, Comerio, Corozal, Culebra, Dorado, Fajardo, Florida, Guanica, Guayama, Guayanilla, Guaynabo, Gurabo, Hatillo, Hormigueros, Humacao, Isabela, Jayuya, Juana Diaz, Juncos, Lajas, Lares, Las Marias, Las Piedras, Loiza, Luquillo, Manati, Maricao, Maunabo, Mayaguez, Moca, Morovis, Naguabo, Naranjito, Orocovis, Patillas, Penuelas, Ponce, Quebradillas, Rincon, Rio Grande, Sabana Grande, Salinas, San German, San Juan, San Lorenzo, San Sebastian, Santa Isabel, Toa Alta, Toa Baja, Trujillo Alto, Utuado, Vega Alta, Vega Baja, Vieques, Villalba, Yabucoa and Yauco.

AREA AND POPULATION

Area

The total area of the Commonwealth of Puerto Rico, including adjacent islands under its jurisdiction, is 3,435 sq. miles. Puerto Rico consists of the main island, the two smaller islands Vieques and Culebra, and a number of islets. The climate is tropical and there is little variation in temperature through the year. The land is mountainous with a coastal plain in the north. San Juan is one of the biggest and best natural harbours in the Caribbean.

To view a map of Puerto Rico, please consult:
http://www.lib.utexas.edu/maps/cia08/puerto_rico_sm_2008.gif

Population

According to government estimates, the population of Puerto Rico was 3,706,690 in July 2011, down from 3,721,978 in July 2010, a decline of 0.5 per cent. It was estimated at 3.67 million in 2012. The median age is 33.5 years for men, and 37 years for women.

The main languages are Spanish and English.

Births, Marriages, Deaths

According to the US Census Bureau, over the 12 months to July 2009, there were 45,598 births and 28,987 deaths, resulting in natural population increase of 16,611 people. 3,876 people left the island, reducing the population increase to 12,735 over the year.

Life expectancy at birth averaged 79 years in 2011. The rate of infant deaths per 1,000 live births was 8.65 in 2009. The fertility rate stood at 1.76 children per woman. The birth rate was estimated at 11.3 births per 1,000 population in 2013 and the death rate was 8.2 per 1,000 population. Marriages in 2008 numbered 19,195 and divorces 14,880.

Public Holidays 2014

1 January: New Year's Day
18 March: Good Friday
21 April: Easter Monday
26 May: Remembrance for the War Dead (last Monday in May)
4 July: USA Independence Day
25 July: Constitution Day
14 October: Discovery of America Day
11 November: Armistice and Veteran's Day
19 November: Discovery of Puerto Rico Day
24 December: Christmas Eve
25 December: Christmas Day

EMPLOYMENT

Puerto Rico's estimated total civilian labour force in December 2012 was 1,266,300, of which 1,088,500 were employed and 177,700 were unemployed. The estimated unemployment rate in December 2012 was 14.0 per cent, significantly higher than the US national average of 7.8 per cent. (Source: Bureau of Labor Statistics)

Employment in December 2011, according to sector, is shown on the following table (preliminary figures):

Industry	No. of Jobs	12 month % increase
Mining, logging and construction	30,000	-12.3
Manufacturing	76,300	-7.6
Trade, transport and utilities	157,500	-4.1
Information	18,400	-0.5
Financial activities	45,000	3.4
Professional and business services	104,900	-0.4
Education and health services	117,300	0.3
Leisure & hospitality	72,300	-0.3
Other services	19,800	5.9
Government	262,600	-2.5
TOTAL	904,100	-2.4

Source: Bureau of Labor Statistics

Labor costs are below the mainland average, but are higher than in other areas of the Caribbean Basin.

BANKING AND FINANCE

Currency
US dollar = 100 cents

GDP/GNP, Inflation, National Debt

Having few natural resources of economic value, Puerto Rico relies heavily on Federal Aid from the US government. Following an economic slowdown over the period 2001-03, Puerto Rico's economy recorded solid growth during 2004 and 2005, shadowing the strength of the US economy. Low interest rates led to an increase in private consumption. In 2006, the economy slowed again, and growth of just 0.5 per cent was recorded over the year. GDP fell by an estimated 1.8 per cent over 2007, and by 2 per cent over 2008, to an estimated $74.15 billion (ppp). It was estimated at US$71.51 billion in 2008, falling to an estimated $68.8 billion in 2009 and declining again to an estimated US$64.8 billion in 2010. The GDP growth rate was estimated at -5.8 per cent in 2010. Services remains the largest sector (54 per cent). Industry contributes 45 per cent and agriculture just 1 per cent.

Per capita GDP was estimated at US$16,300 in 2010.

The inflation rate rose by 7.9 per cent over the year to December 2008. Major increases were recorded in food and beverages (18 per cent) and housing (12.7 per cent). Transport costs fell by 4 per cent. Inflation was estimated to be 3.6 per cent in 2011.

Foreign Investment
To encourage foreign investment the US Commerce Department's Foreign Trade Zones Board agreed to Puerto Rico's industrial parks becoming free trade zones. Under the scheme, businesses working within such zones will not have to pay customs duties on imported raw materials or export taxes on goods shipped to destinations outside the US.

Balance of Payments / Imports and Exports
Major import commodities include machinery and equipment, chemicals, food, fish, clothing, and petroleum products. Total Puerto Rico imports amounted to $18,529 million in 2009, down -4.8 per cent from $19,464 million in 2008. Imports rose by 4.1 per cent to $19,290 million, representing 1.0 per cent of the 2010 total. Imports amounted to $24,465 million in 2011, 1.1 per cent of US total and up 26.7 per cent on the previous year.

The main export commodities are electronics, pharmaceuticals, medical equipment, clothing, tinned tuna, drink concentrates and rum. According to the US Foreign Trade Department, exports grew by 4.9 per cent in 2009, from $19,961 million in 2008 to $20,937 million. Exports rose by 8.8 per cent to $22,784 million in 2010, representing 1.8 per cent of the US total. Exports were an estimated $18,210 million in 2011, -20 per cent down on the previous year and representing 1.2 per cent of the total US amounts.

Excluding trade with the USA, export destinations were as follows:

Exports per destination, 2010-11, $ million

Country	2010	2011	+/-% 2010-11
Belgium	2,707	2,794	3.2
Netherlands	2,804	2,507	-10.6
Japn	1,126	1,763	56.6
UK	1,501	1,113	-25.9
Canada	973	1,111	14.1

Source: US Foreign Trade Department, US Census Bureau

Top US Imports via Puerto Rico, $ million

	2010	2011	% +/-
Ireland	6,799	9,019	36.9
Singapore	1,908	3,621	14.8
Japan	1,772	1,783	7.3
China	766	817	3.3
Canada	583	773	3.2

Source: US Foreign Trade Department, US Census Bureau

Chambers of Commerce and Trade Organisations
Puerto Rico Chamber of Commerce, URL: http://www.camarapr.org

MANUFACTURING, MINING AND SERVICES

Primary and Extractive Industries
Puerto Rico has no reserves of fossil fuels. Imports of crude oil totalled 42,000 barrels a day in 2010 and petroleum products 176 thousand bbl/d in 2010, most of which was used for transport and electricity generation. Oil refining capacity was 78,000 barrels per day at the beginning of 2008, produced by the Caribbean Petroleum Corporation refinery at Bayamon and the Shell Chemical facility in Yabucoa. Puerto Rico also has storage facilities at Proterm, with a capacity of 9 million barrels. Puerto Rico exported 19.233 thousand bbl/d of crude oil in 2007.

Other energy imports include liquified natural gas (27 billion cu ft, 2010) and coal (1,653 thousand short tons, 2010). Puerto Rico imports supplies of liquified natural gas (LNG) from Trinidad and Tobago for its LNG-fired power plant near the city of Ponce. In 2009, 27,000 bbl/d of natural gas were consumed. Puerto Rico's entire annual supply of coal is also imported. In 2011, 1,688 thousand short tons of coal were consumed. (Source: EIA)

Energy
Puerto Rico imports almost all of its energy requirements, although it is able to generate most of its electricity. Oil accounted for around 99 per cent of the state's primary energy mix until the construction of two power plants fuelled by Liquified Natural Gas and coal; oil now accounts for 74 per cent of energy generation. Total energy consumption in 2008 fell to an estimated 0.389 quadrillion Btu in 2008. Per capita consumption was 105 million Btu in 2009. Puerto Rico has one refinery located at Humacao on the east coast.

Puerto Rico generated approximately 21 billion kWh of electricity in 2010, mainly from oil-fired generators, though a small amount was generated by hydroelectric dams (hydroelectric 0.156 billion kWh). The country used 20.6 million kWh. The Puerto Rico Electric Power Authority (PREPA) accounts for most of the electricity generation. Installed generation capacity on the island is currently 6 million kW.

The use of renewable energy is growing and the Puerto Rico Power Authority plans on generating more than 20 per cent of electricity demand from renewable sources by 2035. Currently, Puerto Rico has 100 MW of hydroelectric capacity and uses sugarcane residue as a fuel source in its sugar factories. Puerto Rico also plans to build a biorefinery to produce ethanol, primarily from sugarcane and agricultural waste. In 2007, Puerto Rico was the fifth largest solar thermal energy producer among U.S. States and territories.

Wind energy projects are currently being developed along Puerto Rico's northern and eastern coasts and at some higher parts in the interior of the island. Fifty MW of wind energy capacity became operational by 2012. Other renewable energy projects are being developed or considered, including two waste-to-energy plants, a 135-MW solar project, and a 75-MW ocean thermal energy conversion project. (Source: EIA)

Manufacturing
Manufacturing is the most important sector on the island, contributing some 40.4 per cent of the GDP and employing 98,900 people in 2008. Incentives to attract new industries include the change in status of Puerto Rico's industrial parks to free trade zones where businesses are exempt from customs duties, export tax and storage charges. Main industries include cane sugar, molasses, rum, cement, cigars, distilled spirits, clothing, footwear, textiles, furniture, electrical equipment, toys, cosmetics, chemicals and medicines and canned products. Areas of recent growth include pharmaceuticals, high-tech products, and plastics. Major US companies producing products in Puerto Rico include Intel and Hewlett Packard. (Source: EIA)

Service Industries
The service industry was the most important in terms of employment, accounting for ten per cent to GDP in 2008. The construction section was strong from 1999 to 2007. The island has begun to privatise its utility companies.

Tourism
Tourism is becoming a major industry in Puerto Rico. Provisional figures for visitor numbers in 2006 suggest that around 5.7 million people visited the island, most of them from the USA. There were 2,112.6 hotel registrations over the year, and 1,338,000 people visited from cruise ships. San Juan has become the largest home port for cruise ships in the Caribbean, and the fourth largest in the world. Income from tourism reached over $3.4 million in 2007.

Agriculture
Up until the mid-1990s, agriculture was Puerto Rico's main economic sector. Sugar cane, coffee and tobacco were the main crops. Sugar cane production declined due to low market prices, loss of labour to the US, and pressure to use the land for other purposes. Tobacco production has almost disappeared. Only coffee production remains strong.

Currently, agriculture accounts for only three per cent of labour force and less than one per cent of GDP. The sector concentrates on crops for export to the USA. Coffee is the most valuable crop, followed by vegetables, sugar cane, fruits (pineapples, plantains and bananas), milk, eggs, and livestock (cattle, chickens and pork).

Agricultural Production in 2010

Produce	Int. $'000*	Tonnes
Cow milk, whole, fresh	118,146	378,600
Indigenous chicken meat	74,388	52,224
Indigenous cattle meat	27,824	10,300
Indigenous pigmeat	18,292	11,899
Bananas	15,923	56,539
Plantains	14,440	69,942
Hen eggs, in shell	9,704	11,700
Mangoes, mangosteens, guavas	9,195	15,346
Tomatoes	8,164	22,090
Coffee, green	8,082	7,523
Pineapples	6,570	23,049
Chicory roots	4,544	5,850

* unofficial figures
Source: http://faostat.fao.org/site/339/default.aspx Food and Agriculture Organization of the United Nations, Food and Agricultural commodities production

Fishing
FAO figures for 2010 put the total catch at 1,898 tonnes.

COMMUNICATIONS AND TRANSPORT

Travel Requirements
Citizens of Australia, Canada and the EU require a passport normally valid for six months from the date on which the holder enters the USA. For nationals included in the Visa Waiver Program (under which nationals must travel on a valid passport, for holiday, transit or business purposes only and for a stay not exceeding 90 days), passports must be valid for at least 90 days from date of entry. Travellers who do not have a machine-readable passports will require a valid USA entry visa, and holders of passports issued between October 2005 and October 2006 should check with the Embassy that their passport are valid for visa free travel under the Visa Waiver Program.

A visa is not required by Australians, Canadians and most Europeans, for stays of up to 90 days; the exceptions are nationals of Bulgaria, Cyprus, Greece, Hungary, Lithuania, Malta, Poland, Romania and Slovak Republic, who do require a visa. A visa is also required by Immigrants of Canada and British residents of Bermuda. Transit passengers require a transit visa. Subjects of all countries are advised to contact the embassy to check visa requirements.

International Airports
The Luis Munoz Marin International Airport (LMM) (URL: http://www.prpa.gobierno.pr/) operates from San Juan. Services fly to New York, Miami, and Los Angeles. There are 29 other airports in Puerto Rico, 17 of which have paved runways.

Roads
Puerto Rico's roadways total about 26,670 km. Vehicles are driven on the right.

UNITED STATES OF AMERICA

Shipping
The state-owned shipping company, Navieras, has been privatised, resulting in an estimated 20 per cent fall in shipping costs. A ferry service connects Mayaguez with Santo Domingo in the Dominican Republic, another service connects Puerto Rico with the US Virgin Islands.

Ports and Harbours
There are ten ports, of which the principal are San Juan, Ponce and Mayaguez. San Juan and Ponce handle more than 15 million metric tons of cargo annually.

HEALTH

The Puerto Rico Health Reform (introduced in the 1990s) is a state program providing medical and healthcare services to those who cannot afford private healthcare, through contracts with private health insurance companies. By the end of 2005, the Reform was providing coverage to almost 38 per cent of the population. However, the system has been criticised because of increasing costs; the government has tried to limit services and has eliminated many participants from the program in an effort to curtail expenditures, but, since medical costs are expected to increase, there are serious concerns over the future funding of the program. While campaigning on the island, President Obama promised that Puerto Ricans would receive equal healthcare assistance as the rest of the USA, but questions have since been raised about whether Puerto Ricans will be able to participate in a health insurance clearinghouse intended to reduce costs for Americans living in the 50 states.

In 2004, there were 1,150 hospital doctors and surgeons in Puerto Rico and 900 GPs. There were 180 dentists and 40 obstetrician, and 8,330 nurses.

Heart disease is the leading cause of death in Puerto Rico, and cardiovascular diseases as a whole cause around 29 per cent of deaths. Puerto Rico has the fifth highest annual rate of reported cases of HIV in the USA, at 2,049 cases. At the end of 2005, 17,173 people were suffering from HIV/AIDS, 30.26 per cent of whom were women; over the year, 483 people died of the disease. (Source: Dept. of Health, Puerto Rico)

EDUCATION

Primary/Secondary Education
Education is free and compulsory between the ages of 6 and 17. The Department of Education employs over 45,000 teachers of whom 32,000 are full-time employees, and the remaining are contracted or part-time. The drop-out rate could be as high as 40 per cent.

The literacy rate is 94.1 per cent. Public education is conducted in Spanish and English is taught as a mandatory second language.

Higher Education
Puerto Rico's higher education system has over 50 institutes of higher education. Over 65,000 students attend the University of Puerto Rico, the island's oldest university (founded in 1903). During the period 2004-2008, the UPR conferred 46,987 academic degrees.

RELIGION

There is complete separation of State and Church. 57 per cent of the population are Roman Catholic, 13 per cent are Protestant and the remainder are Jewish or Buddhist.

Puerto Rico has a religious liberty rating of 10 on a scale of 1 to 10 (10 is most freedom). (Source: World Religion Database)

COMMUNICATIONS AND MEDIA

Newspapers
El Nuevo Dia, URL: http://www.elnuevodia.com/diario/home
El Vocero de Puerto Rico, URL: http://www.vocero.com
Primera Hora, URL: http://www.primerahora.com/home
The San Juan Star, URL: http://www.thesanjuanstar.com/

Broadcasting
Over 120 radio stations operate in Puerto Rico, of which three broadcast in English. There are over 30 television stations. Cable subscriptions are also available.

Telecommunications
The modern telephone system is integrated into the US sytsem and has high-speed data capability. In 20110, there were 826,000 mainline telephones and an estimated 3.1 million mobile telephones in use. In 2009, there were around one million internet users in Puerto Rico.

ENVIRONMENT

Puerto Rico's energy-related carbon emissions fell to 31 million metric tons in 2010 (down from 33.3 million metric tons in 2009). Of this, petroleum 26 million metric tons, natural gas 2 million metric tons and coal 4 million metric tons. Per capita energy-related carbon emissions were 9.97 metric tons in 2005.

Puerto Rico has a long-term energy policy that emphasizes a shift towards gas and renewable energy sources. (Source: EIA)

VIRGIN ISLANDS OF THE UNITED STATES

Capital: Charlotte Amalie (Population estimate: 19,000)

Head of State: President Barack Obama (page 1488)
Governor: John deJongh (D) (page 1414)
Lieutenant Governor: Gregory R. Francis (D) (page 1426)

Flag: On a white field appears the American Eagle in yellow bearing the United States shield; the eagle holds a green sprig of laurel in one claw and three blue arrows in the other; on the left of the eagle is the letter 'V' and on its right side is the letter 'I'.

CONSTITUTION AND GOVERNMENT

Constitution
The US Virgin Islands are an unincorporated territory, and are under the sovereignty of the United States, falling under the constitution of the USA and under the administration of the US Secretary of the Interior. The executive power of the Islands is vested in the Governor. The Governor and Lieutenant Governor are elected by the people and serve a maximum of two consecutive four-year terms. Apart from the Board of Elections and Board of Education, the Governor and Lieutenant Governor are the only executive branch officials to be elected.

In 1993 a referendum was held over the issue of the US Virgin Islands' political status. Voters were asked to vote for independence, statehood, commonwealth, or incorporated territory. As only 31.4 per cent of those eligible voted, the result was of interest only. Of those who did vote, over 80 per cent voted for continued territorial status with the US, just over 13 per cent voted for integration with the US, and just under five per cent voted for a removal of US sovereignty.

A single delegate is elected to the US Congress for a two-year term and, other than having no vote on the House floor, has the same powers as delegates on the US mainland.
US Virgin Islands Delegate to Congress: Donna Christian-Christensen (D) (page 1404)

To consult the Revised Organic Act (1954), please visit: http://governordejongh.com/government/documents/Revised-Organic-Act-of-1954.pdf

Legislature
The Revised Organic Act (1954) of the Virgin Islands provides for a unicameral legislative body, designated as the Legislature of the Virgin Islands, and is composed of 15 members known as Senators. The Virgin Islands are divided into two legislative districts: the District of St. Thomas-St. John and the District of St. Croix. Seven senators are elected from each district and the fifteenth senator is elected at large from the Virgin Islands as a whole. Members of the Legislature are elected biennially, the franchise being vested in all residents of the Virgin Islands aged over 20 years, who are citizens of the United States and are able to read and write the English language.

Legislature of the Virgin Islands, St. Thomas, Capitol Building, Charlotte Amalie, St. Thomas, USVI 00804, USA. Tel: +1 340 774 0880, URL: http://www.legvi.org/
Legislature of the Virgin Islands, St. Croix, 1 Lagoon Street Complex, Frederiksted, St.Croix, USVI 00840, USA. Tel: +1 340 773 2424, URL: http://www.legvi.org/
Legislature of the Virgin Islands, St. John, Hill Top Building, Cruz Bay, St. John, USVI 00830, USA. Tel: +1 340 776 6285, URL: http://www.legvi.org/

Elected Executive Branch Officials (as at March 2013)
Governor: John deJongh (D) (page 1414)
Lieutenant Governor: Gregory R. Francis (D) (page 1426)

Cabinet (as at March 2013)
Commissioner, Department of Finance: Angel E. Dawson, Jr.
Attorney General, Department of Justice: Vincent Frazer
Director, Office of Management & Budget: Debra Gottlieb
Commissioner, Department of Education: Dr LaVerne Terry
Commissioner, Department of Public Works: Darryl Smalls
Commissioner, Department of Housing, Parks & Recreation: St. Claire Williams
Acting Commissioner, Department of Police: Rodney Querrard, Sr.
Commissioner, Department of Property & Procurement: Lynn Millin Maduro
Commissioner, Department of Tourism: Beverly Nicholson Doty
Commissioner, Department of Agriculture: Dr Louis Petersen, Jr.
Commissioner, Department of Labor: Albert Bryan, Jr.
Commissioner, Department of Health: Darice Plaskett
Commissioner, Department of Human Services: Christopher Finch
Commissioner, Department of Planning & Natural Resources: Alicia Barnes
Commissioner, Department of Licensing & Consumer Affairs: Wayne Biggs, Jr.
Commissioner, Department of Personnel: Kenneth Hermon, Jr.
Commissioner, Department of Collective Bargaining: Valdemar Hill, Jr.
Commissioner, Department of Internal Revenue Bureau: Claudette Watson-Anderson
Commissioner, Department of Fire Services: Steve Brow
Adjutant General, National Guard: Renaldo Rivera
Director General, VITEMA: Elton Lewis
Inspector General: Steven van Beverhoudt
Director, Department of Veterans' Affairs: Morris Moorehead

Ministries

Office of the Governor, Government House, 21-22 Kongens Gade, Charlotte Amalie, US Virgin Islands, 00802. Tel: +1 340 774 0001 / 773 1404, fax: +1 340 774 1361 / 778 7978, URL: http://www.governordejongh.com/

Office of the Lieutenant Governor, 18 Kongens Gade, Charlotte Amalie, US Virgin Islands, 00802. Tel: +1 340 774 2991 / 773 6449, fax: +1 340 774 6593 / 773 0330, URL: http://www.ltg.gov.vi/

Department of Agriculture, Estate Lower Love, Kingshill, St. Croix, US Virgin Islands 00850. Tel: +1 340 778 0997, fax: +1 340 774 1823, URL: http://www.vifresh.com/

Economic Development Commission and Industrial Park Corporation, 1050 Norre Gade, Government Development Bank Building. PO Box 305038, St. Thomas, USVI 00803. Tel: +1 340 774 8104, e-mail: edc@usvieda.org, URL: http://www.usvieda.org/index.html

Department of Education, 44-46 Kongens Gade, Charlotte Amalie, US Virgin Islands 00802. Tel: +1 340 774 0100, fax: +1 340 779 7153, e-mail: education@usvi.org, URL: http://www.vide.vi/

Department of Finance, 76 Kronprindsens Gade, GERS Building, 2nd Floor, Charlotte Amalie, U.S. Virgin Islands 00802. Tel: +1 340 774 4750, fax: +1 340 776 4028, URL: http://www.usvifinance.info/

Department of Health, 48 Sugar Estate, Charlotte Amalie, U.S. Virgin Islands 00802. Tel: +1 340 774 0117, fax: +1 340 777 4001, URL: http://www.healthvi.org/

Department of Human Services, Knud Hansen Complex Building A 1303, Hospital Ground, St. Thomas, USVI 00802. Tel: +1 340 774 0930, fax: +1 340 774 3466, URL: http://www.dhs.gov.vi/home/index.html

Department of Justice, 48B-50C Kronprindsens Gade, GERS Building, 2nd Floor, Charlotte Amalie, U.S. Virgin Islands 00802. Tel: +1 340 774 5666, fax: +1 340 774 9710, URL: http://www.doj.vi.gov

Deparment of Labor, URL: http://www.vidol.gov/

Department of Licensing and Consumer Affairs, Property and Procurement Building No. 1, Sub Base, Room 205, Charlotte Amalie, U.S. Virgin Islands 00802. Tel: +1 340 774 3130 (St. Thomas) / +1 340 773 2226 (St. Croix), fax: +1 340 776 0675 (St. Thomas), +1 340 778 8250 (St. Croix), URL: http://dlca.vi.gov/

Department of Planning and Natural Resources, Cyril E. King Airport Terminal Building, Charlotte Amalie, US Virgin Islands 00800. Tel: +1 340 774 3320, fax: +1 340 775 5706, URL: http://www.dpnr.gov.vi/

Department of Tourism, 78-123 Estate Contant, Post Office Box 6400, Charlotte Amalie, US Virgin Islands 00802. Tel: +1 340 774 8784, fax: +1 340 774 4390, URL: http://www.visitusvi.com/

Department of Sports, Parks & Recreation, URL: http://www.dspr.vi/

USVI Police Department, URL: http://www.vipd.gov.vi/Home.aspx

Political Parties

Virgin Islands Democratic Party, Post Office Box 2033, Frederiksted, St. Thomas, USVI 00823. Tel: +1 340 773 0495, fax: +1 340 778 1454, e-mail: videms@email.com, URL: http://www.democrats.org

Virgin Islands Republican Party, PO Box 9965, St. Thomas, VI 00804. Tel: +1 340 776 0583, URL: http://www.rnc.org/StateParties

Elections

The last elections to the senate were held in November 2012. In the Virgin Islands' current 30th legislature, the Democratic Party holds 10 of the Senate's 15 seats. The remaining seats are held by independent senators, three of whom are affiliated to the Independent Citizens Movement.

Elections for the posts of Governor and Lt. Governor were held in 2006. John DeJongh was elected governor having won 57.3 per cent of the vote. His main rival, Kenneth Mapp, won 42.7 per cent. The most recent gubernatorial election was held in November 2010, John DeJongh was re-elected to the post.

LEGAL SYSTEM

The Virgin Islands' judicial power lies with the Territorial Court and the US District Court. The Virgin Islands' District Court is a member of the Third Circuit of the US District Courts and has two divisional offices: Division of St. Thomas/St. John and Division of St. Croix. Four judicial officers are assigned to the District, two magistrate judges and two district court judges.

The Virgin Islands do not have the death penalty.

District Court, URL: http://www.vid.uscourts.gov/
Chief Judge: Curtis V. Gomez
Supreme Court, URL: http://www.visupremecourt.org/index.asp
Chief Justice: Rhys S. Hodge

AREA AND POPULATION

Area

The US Virgin Islands are located in the Caribbean Sea about 45 miles east of Puerto Rico and 1,000 miles south-east of Miami. The group comprises the three principal Islands of St. Thomas (28 sq. miles), St. Croix (84 sq. miles), St. John (20 sq. miles) and about 50 smaller islands mostly uninhabited. Charlotte Amalie, the islands' capital, is located on St. Thomas. The Islands were purchased from Denmark in 1916 for $25 million and proclaimed a United States Possession on 25 January 1917.

VIRGIN ISLANDS OF THE UNITED STATES

The islands' geology is volcanic, and the terrain hilly. There are no rivers, streams or lakes. The temperature ranges from 70 to 90 degrees with little humidity. The rainy season lasts from October to mid-December, and the islands suffer the occasional hurricane. Saint Thomas has one of the best natural deepwater harbours in the Caribbean.

To view a map of the US Virgin Islands, please consult http://www.lib.utexas.edu/maps/cia08/virgin_islands_sm_2008.gif

Population

The estimated population of the US Virgin Islands was 105,300 in 2012, indicating a decline of -0.5 over the figure for 2012.

Approximately 56,576 people live on St. Croix, 54,394 people live on St. Thomas, and 4,461 live on St. John. The largest town is Charlotte Amalie town, with around 11,000 inhabitants. The largest subdistrict is Charlotte Amalie subdistrict, with some 18,900 inhabitants. Around 90 per cent of the inhabitants live in urban areas.

The median age in 2008 was 41 years, up from the 2000 median age of 33.4. Life expectancy is now 79.5 years.

The population of the US Virgin Islands is ethnically diverse, and includes African, Puerto Rican, French, Scots, Danish, and Portuguese. Only 49 per cent of the population was born in the Virgin Islands, while 32 percent have migrated from other islands in the Caribbean region. U.S. mainlanders and Puerto Ricans comprise approximately 13 per cent and four percent, respectively, of the total population. The remaining two per cent is a mixture of immigrants from across the world including the Middle East, India and Asia.

English is the official language of the territory, with Spanish and Creole also being spoken.

Births, Marriages, Deaths

The estimated birth rate in 2011 was 11.4 births per 1,000 people (down on the previous year) and the fertility rate was estimated to be 1.8 children per woman. The estimated death rate for the same year was 7 per 1,000 people, whilst the infant mortality rate stood at 7.53 infant deaths per 1,000 live births, down from 13 infant deaths per 1,000 live births in 2001.

Public Holidays

In addition to other US public holidays, the people of the Virgin Islands celebrate Transfer Day, when the Islands were transferred from Denmark to the US, on 27 March in 1917.

EMPLOYMENT

According to the U.S.V.I. Bureau of Labor Statistics, the number of employed people fell by 3.9 per cent from 48,488 in January 2009 to 46,580 in January 2010, whilst the unemployment rate rose by 1.7 per cent over the year. St. Croix has a higher unemployment rate, estimated at 8.7 per cent, compared to 7.5 per cent on St. Thomas and St. John.

The following table shows December 2012 non-farm wage and salary employment according to industry (preliminary figures):

Industry	No. of Employees	12 month % change
Construction, mining and logging*	2,000	0.0
Manufacturing*	1,100	-50.0
Trade, Transport and Utilities	8,500	-1.2
Information*	800	0.0
Financial Activities*	2,400	0.0
Professional and Business Services*	3,600	-2.7
Educational and Health Services*	2,500	-3.8
Leisure and Hospitality	7,400	-1.3
Other Services*	1,200	-33.3
Government	11,400	-5.8
*not seasonally adjusted		
Total Non-farm	42,600	-2.5

Source: US Bureau of Labor Statistics

The largest employer in the US Virgin Islands is federal and territorial government. The agricultural sector is small, with most food being imported.

BANKING AND FINANCE

GDP/GNP, Inflation, National Debt

Historically, the economy was dependent on commercial trade and sugarcane cultivation, but in the 1960s the economy diversified into manufacturing and tourism. Tourism is now the US Virgin Islands' largest industry, contributing around 80 per cent of Gross Territorial Product and employment.

In the past, St. Thomas was a major trading post for European ships passing through the Caribbean; the island has one of the best natural deepwater harbors in the Caribbean and is strategically located on a key route for ships bound for the Panama Canal. Today, St. Thomas is the tourism centre for the Virgin Islands. St. John is known for its national park which covers two thirds of the island. St. John's economy is predominantly dependent on tourism, attracting excursionists and the luxury end of the holiday-makers market. St. Croix's economy used to depend on sugar cane cultivation, but has now diversified into manufacturing and tourism. St. Croix's economy is now based on manufacturing, and depends on petrol and rum exports.

UNITED STATES OF AMERICA

Gross Domestic Product

	2008	2009	2010
Gross Domestic Product	4,255	4,248	4,498
Personal consumption expenditures	2,239	2,328	2,384
Private fixed investment	403	365	380
Change in private inventories	180	210	-167
Net exports of goods and services	318	185	659
-Exports	18,412	10,718	12,935
--Goods	17,255	9,696	11,922
--Services	1,157	1,021	1,031
-Imports	18,094	10,532	12,276
--Goods	17,861	10,310	12,067
--Services	233	223	209
Government consumption, expend. & gross invest.	1,115	1,159	1,243
-Federal	134	150	186
-Territories	981	1,009	1,057

Source: http://www.bea.gov

According to the Virgin Islands Bureau of Economic Research (BER), per capita personal income in 2006 was $19,787, up from $19,211 the previous year. The average annual salary was $35,366 in 2006 and the USVI Consumer Price Index was up 4.9 per cent from 117.6 in 2006 to 123.3 in 2007. (Source: US Virgin Islands Bureau of Economic Research)

Foreign Investment

The US Virgin Islands offer tax incentives, which have encouraged the establishment of service and manufacturing industries. In the services sector, this has mainly been evident in the area of tourism, whilst in the manufacturing sector, oil refining, aluminum production, watch assembly, boat building and high technology electronics are some of the businesses that have been set up.

Balance of Payments / Imports and Exports

Total imports for the year 2009 totalled $9,151 million, down 44.8 per cent over the year, from the total for 2008 of $16,591 million. Imports rose by 15.9 per cent in 2010 to $10,604 million. They rose to $12,284 million in 2011, up 16.8 per cent, accounting for 0.6 per cent of the total. Oil is the primary import. Main suppliers in 2011 were Venezuela (52.7 per cent), Gabon (35.0 per cent), Azerbaijan (7.6 per cent), Norway and Niger. Total exports from the US Virgin Islands fell 55.7 per cent over the year 2008-09, to $1,217 million in 2009 (down from $2,747 million in 2008). Exports rose by 56 per cent in 2010 to $1,899 million, and by 22 per cent in 2011 to $2,316 million, accounting for 0.2 per cent of the US total.

The top export commodities in 2010 were as follows:

Total Virgin Islands Export Commodities, 2010

Description	$ m
Oil (not crude) from petrol & bitum mineral etc	1,641
Toluene	80
Light oils & prep (not crude) from petrol & bitum	30
Petroleum coke, not calcined	29
Jewelry and parts thereof, of oth precious metal	25

Source: US Census Dept.

Total US exports via Virgin Islands, 2010-11

Destination	2010 ($m)	2011 ($m)	+/-% 2010-11
Netherlands	121	779	500+
Canada	10	299	500+
Netherlands Antilles	507	178	-64.9
Guadeloupe	157	139	-11.5
Martinique	63	112	78.8

Source: US Census Dept.

Chambers of Commerce and Trade Organisations

US Virgin Islands Economic Development Commission and Industrial Park Corporation,
URL: http://www.usvieda.org/index.html

MANUFACTURING, MINING AND SERVICES

Primary and Extractive Industries

The US Virgin Islands had a 2012 crude oil refining capacity of 500,000 barrels per day. The Hovensa oil refinery is one of the 10 largest crude oil refineries in the world. Most of the crude oil supplies are imported from Venezuela, but substantial shipments are also imported from Gabon, Nigeria, and Azerbaijan. In 2009, 425,000 bbl/d of crude oil were imported and in 2007, 17.005 thousand bbl/d of petroleum products were imported. The islands' oil refineries serve both local and export markets. In 2008, almost 320,000 barrels per day of petroleum products were shipped to the US mainland from the US Virgin Islands. In 2005, the refining industry produced 488,747 barrels of petroleum products, almost double the production of 2004 (253,560 barrels).

Petroleum consumption in 2010 was 113.5 million gallons. Gasoline consumption accounted for 37.2 million gallons and distillate fuel 18.7 million gallons. The islands import 100 per cent of their coal requirements.

Hovensa, the second largest petroleum refinery in the western hemisphere, is located on St. Croix, and employs around 2,000 people. A joint partnership between Amerada Hess and PDVSA, Venezuela's national oil company, Hovensa and its subcontractors shipped almost US$11.3 billion of refined petroleum products to the US in 2007.

Energy

The islands' electricity production is generated by thermal means. Total electricity installed capacity in 2010 was an estimated 500,000 kWh. Total net electricity generation in 2010 was 1 billion kWh. Electricity consumption in 2008 reached 0.364 quadrillion Btu. Per capita total energy consumption was 1.7 million Btu in 2009.

The Virgin Islands has potential for wind energy generation. The solar project at King Airport (451 KW) started operations in 2011. Solar water heaters are required for all new construction. (Source: EIA)

Manufacturing

Manufacturing is one of the two principal industries of the US Virgin Islands. Mainly located on St. Croix, the chief industries are petroleum refining, production of alumina, the manufacture of rum, and watch assembly operations. The sector showed strong growth in 2006, with petroleum export values and quantities showing significant rises; the cost of refined petroleum rose by 41 per cent over 2005, and production almost doubled. Rum production is the second most significant industry of the sector; in 2007, exported rum excise taxes contributed an estimated US$86.7 million to the overall gross territorial product (GTP). Cruzan VIRIL, Ltd., located on St. Croix, is a top exporter of Cruzan, Old St. Croix and bulk rum to the US. In July 2008, a public-private partnership between the U.S. Virgin Islands Government and Diageo, was authorized, paving the way for Diageo to build a multi-million dollar rum distillery on St. Croix; it is due to begin production in 2012.

Watch manufacturing, in decline over previous years, saw a volume increase of six per cent in 2006.

Following a general decline over the decade to 2003, when employment in the manufacturing industry fell to a low of 2,019 people, employment figures have begun to pick up. In 2006, the sector employed an average of 2,366 people, up nine per cent on the previous year's 2,170 employees.

Service Industries

The services sector contributed some $554.8 million dollars in 2003, an increase on $526.16 million on 2002. The leisure and hospitality sector employed an average of 7,271 people in 2006, up 4.3 per cent on the previous year. Employment in the trade sector increased by 1.5 per cent in the same year, whilst there was stagnation in the financial services sector.

Tourism

Tourism is the principal industry of the US Virgin Islands. Charlotte Amalie is the leading cruise ship destination in the Caribbean and accounts for a substantial retail and wholesale sector of activity. The island of St. Thomas represents the base for a thriving charter boat fleet as well as deep sea sports fishing activity and provides a large number of hotel facilities for the tourist trade. St. John is the location of a large national park with camp grounds and numerous beach areas as well as historic locations. Tourism is the prime source of economic activity on St. Thomas and St. John, and there are plans to increase tourism facilities to St. Croix; Disney Cruise Lines added St. Croix to its 2009 itinerary. The Virgin Islands are the largest duty-free port in the Caribbean.

2.25 million people visited the Islands in 2009 (down 7 per cent on the previous year), of whom 1.68 million were excursionists, mainly on ship. The number of cruise ships stopping at the Islands fell 9.6 per cent, from 685 to 621 over the year. Around 8,033 islanders are employed in the sector.

In 2006, around 75 per cent of overnight visitors were from the US mainland, many of these from New York City. The occupancy rate for the Islands' 1,776,300 room nights available was 60.1 per cent. (Source: USVI Bureau of Economic Research)

Agriculture

The agricultural and aquaculture sector in the Virgin Islands is small or relatively non-existent, comprised of a small number of farmers. All agricultural goods produced on-island are developed for local consumption and sold at various outdoor markets. According to National Agricultural Statistics information, the US Virgin Islands have around 217 farms, covering a total of 5,881 acres in 2007 (the average size of a farm being 26.9 acres). Most agricultural land (5,209 acres) is used for pasture, whilst the majority of farms grow crops.

Agricultural Production in 2010

Produce	Int. $'000*	Tonnes
Indigenous cattle meat	1,486	550
Cow milk, whole, fresh	811	2,600
Indigenous pigmeat	167	109
Hen eggs, in shell	158	190
Indigenous chicken meat	111	78
Indigenous goat meat	49	20
Indigenous sheep meat	38	14

* unofficial figures
Source: http://faostat.fao.org/site/339/default.aspx Food and Agriculture Organization of the United Nations, Food and Agricultural commodities production

Livestock figures were as follows in 2007: cattle and calves 776, sheep and lambs 2,981, goats and kids 2,331, hogs and pigs 1,125, poulty 804.

Virgin Islanders are dependent on imports from the continental U.S. for the majority of their agriculture and aquaculture products. Aquaculture production in the Latin America and the Caribbean region (LAC), is relatively new and cannot yet compete in world export markets.

However, the combination of local demand for fresh products, an ideal climate ideal for year-round production, and available land resource makes this a sector with potential for further development. FAO figures for 2010 put the total catch at 847 tonnes.

COMMUNICATIONS AND TRANSPORT

Airports
There are two airports on the islands, the Cyril E. King Airport (length of the runway -7,000 feet) on St. Thomas and the Henry E. Rohlsen Airport (length of runway recently extended to 10,000 feet) on St. Croix. Several major airlines serve both airports.

There are no airports on St. John or Water Island, and visitors have to use inter-island ferries to reach these islands.

Roads
In 2008, there were 1,260 km of paved road.

Ports and Harbours
The US Virgin Islands are located along the Anegada Passage - a key shipping lane for the Panama Canal. Saint Thomas has one of the best natural deepwater harbors in the Caribbean. The largest port in the islands is located at Charlotte Amalie. There are 14 ports in total over the Islands.

In 2007, 750 cruise ships docked at the Virgin Islands' ports (down from 782 in 2006). The ports handle over a million tons of cargo each year.
Virgin Islands Port Authority, URL: http://www.viport.com

HEALTH

Major hospitals are located on St. Thomas and St. Croix and are operated by the Virgin Islands Department of Health. According to a report published by the Bureau of Economic Research, over 28 per cent of people in the US Virgin Islands (33,000 people) were without health insurance in 2009. This was significantly higher than the rate of uninsurance in 2003, which was 24.1 per cent.
Department of Health, URL: http://www.healthvi.org/
Roy Lester Schneider Hospital, URL: http://www.rlshospital.org/

EDUCATION

Primary/Secondary Education
The US Virgin Islands' public education system is operated by the Government of the Virgin Islands and subsidised by Federal grants. The public education system provides compulsory education from kindergarten to the age of 16. The number of students attending has declined

over recent years, from around 28,000 in 1997 to approximately 23,566 in 2005, before rising 4.5 per cent to 24,638 in 2006. In 2006, 871 pupils graduated High School, down 3.7 per cent on the previous year.

Higher Education
The University of the Virgin Islands offers BA and B.Sc. degrees in 33 subjects, as well as Master's degrees in education, public administration, and business administration. In 2006, there were 364 graduates from the University of the Virgin Islands, up 9.6 per cent on the figure of 323 graduates in 2005.

RELIGION

The principal religious bodies in the islands are the Episcopal Church, Roman Catholic Church, Christian Mission, Hebrew Synagogue, Lutheran Church, Methodist Church, Moravian Church, Reformed Church of America, Salvation Army and Seventh Day Adventists.

COMMUNICATIONS AND MEDIA

Newspapers
Two local newspapers are published on the islands: the Daily News (URL: http://virginislandsdailynews.com/) and the St. Croix Avis.

Broadcasting
The Virgin Islands Public Television System (URL: http://www.wtjx.org/) was established in 1968 and is affiliated to the Public Broadcasting System. It operates WRJX (Channel 12), a local and national programme service to the Virgin Islands. Satellite and multi-channel TV is available. An estimated 24 radio stations operate on the islands.

Postal Service
The US Virgin Islands' post is part of the US Postal Service.

Telecommunications
In 2010, there were an estimated 75,000 main line telephones in the US Virgin Islands and approximately 80,300 mobile cellular phones. The islands have about 30,000 internet users (2009).

ENVIRONMENT

The main environmental concern is the lack of natural freshwater resources; there are frequent droughts, and occasional floods. The US Virgin Islands have been hit by several hurricanes in recent years, as well as the occasional earthquakes.

In 2010, the islands' emissions from the consumption of fossil fuels totalled 12 million metric tons of carbon dioxide. (Source: EIA)

URUGUAY
Oriental Republic of Uruguay
República Oriental del Uruguay

Capital: Montevideo (Population estimate, 2011: 1.7 million)

Head of State: Jose Mujica (page 1481) (President) (EP-FA)

Vice President: Danilo Astori (page 1380) (EP-FA)

National Flag: Parti of nine fesswise, alternatively white and light blue, a canton white bearing a golden sun in splendour with sixteen rays

CONSTITUTION AND GOVERNMENT

Constitution
Uruguay was declared an independent state in 1828. A civil war was waged from 1838 to 1865 between the Whites (conservatives) and the Reds (liberals). The first Constitution was adopted in 1930. From 1 March 1952 to 28 February 1967 a collegiate system of government was in force. The powers formerly wielded by the President were transferred to a National Council of Government of nine members, six from the majority and three from the minority party. However, as a result of a referendum held in conjunction with the elections in November 1966, presidential rule was restored. A violent Marxist urban guerrilla movement, the Tupamaros, launched in the late 1960s, led Uruguay's president to agree to military control of his administration in 1973. By the end of the year the rebels had been crushed, but the military continued to expand its hold throughout the government. A repressive regime ensued until 1985 when a constitutional government was restored.

A Constitution was written in 1967, and amended over the years. Under the present Constitution, executive power is held by a universally elected President, acting with the appropriate Minister or Ministers or the full Council of Ministers (whom he appoints with parliamentary approval and has the power to dismiss). An incumbent president may not stand for immediate re-election. The Constitution provides that there be eleven Ministries.

To view the 1967 Constitution with the amendments of 1989, 1994, 1996 and 2004 (in Spanish), please visit: http://www0.parlamento.gub.uy/palacio3/index1024.asp?e=1&w=1024

International Relations
Uruguay has strong political and cultural links with its neighbours and Europe. It is a founding member of MERCOSUR, a member of the Latin American Integration Association (a trade association) and a member of the Rio Group (an association of Latin American states that deals with multilateral security issues). Uruguay usually adopts a neutral stance in international affairs, though relations with Argentina are strained at present due to the controversial building of a pulp mill on the Uruguayan bank of the Rio de la Plata.

Uruguay is an active member of the UN, and contributes to UN Peacekeeping operations. Uruguay ranks first in the world on a per capita basis for its contributions to the UN peacekeeping forces, with 2,613 soldiers and officers in 13 UN peacekeeping missions. Current deployments include the Democratic Republic of Congo and Haiti. A third of Uruguay's Army staff is currently undertaking peacekeeping activities overseas.

Recent Events
In November 2004, the left-wing presidential candidate, Tabare Vazquez, won the elections, marking a dramatic political shift, and took office in March 2005. His first moves were to sign an energy deal with Venezuela, restore ties with Cuba and announce a welfare package to tackle poverty.

In January 2006, the International Court of Justice rejected a bid by Argentina to suspend the construction of two Uruguayan pulp mills on the grounds that they would cause pollution of the River Uruguay that separates the two neighbours. However, one mill has now been built, causing a diplomatic rift between the two countries; demonstrators regularly block access to bridges linking the Argentina and Uruguay. In November 2007, tens of thousands of Argentines marched to the Uruguayan border in protests against the pulp paper mill following the Uruguayan President's announcement that work could begin at the mill. The Uruguayans argue that the mill is using the latest technology and will not pollute.

URUGUAY

At the end of the year, Uruguay succeeded in paying off its billion-dollar debt to the International Monetary Fund.

In October 2007 Uruguay was one of seven South American nations (Argentina, Brazil, Bolivia, Ecuador, Paraguay, Uruguay and Venezuela) to announce they were setting up a new development bank, the Banco del Sur.

In October 2009, Uruguay's Supreme Court ruled that a law protecting officials of the last military government from prosecution for human rights abuses was unconstitutional. The former military ruler Gregorio Alvarez was sentenced to 25 years in prison for murder and human rights violations. In March 2010, the former president Juan Maria Bordaberry was sentenced to 30 years in prison for murder and violation of the constitution following the 1973 military coup.

In October 2011, Congress voted to overturn an amnesty law that protected officers from prosecution for crimes committed during the military rule from 1975-83.

In October 2012, Uruguay became only the second Latin American country (after Cuba) to legalise abortion. The vote was won with a 17 to 14 majority.

In April 2013, same-sex marriage was legalised. Argentina is currently the only other Latin American country to do so.

Legislature
The Legislature (General Assembly) consists of two houses: the Senate and the House of Representatives. The president, vice-president and members of both Houses are elected together for a five-year term. From June 1973 until 1985, Uruguay was ruled by a military regime with an appointed president and Council of State.

Upper House
The Senate consists of 31 members, 30 of whom are directly elected by the people, on the basis of proportional representation, for a five-year term. The vice president of the Republic is the chairman of the Senate and is the one ex-officio member.
Senate, Asamblea General, Palacio Legislativo, Avenida de las Leyas, Montevideo. Uruguay. Tel: +598 2 400 9111, fax: +598 2 209 7011, e-mail: rintcss@parlamento.gub.uy, URL: http://www.parlamento.gub.uy

Lower House
The House of Representatives has 99 members directly elected on a provincial, or 'departmental' basis, by proportional representation.
House of Representatives, Asamblea General, Palacio Legislativo, Avenida de las Leyas s/n, Montevideo. Uruguay. Tel: +598 2 924 8686, fax: +598 2 924 8774, URL: http://www.diputados.gub.uy

---

Cabinet (as at June 2013)
Minister for Foreign Affairs: Luis Leonardo Almagro Lemes (MPP)
Minister for the Interior: Eduardo Bonomi (MPP)
Minister for Economy and Finance: Fernando Lorenzo (FLS)
Minister for Defence: Eleuterio Franandez Huidobro (CAP-L)
Minister for Agriculture, Livestock and Fisheries: Tabare Aguerre (Ind.)
Minister for Industry, Energy and Mines: Roberto Kreimerman (PS)
Minister for Transport and Public Works: Enrique Pintado (FLS)
Minister for Education and Culture: Ricardo Ehrlich (MPP)
Minister for Public Health: Susana Muniz (PCU)
Minister of Social Development: Daniel Olesker (PS)
Minister for Labour and Social Security: Eduardo Brenta (VA)
Minister for Housing, Territory and Environment: Francisco Beltrame (MPP)
Minister of Tourism & Sport: Liliam Kechichian (AP)

Ministries
Office of the President, URL: http://www.presidencia.gub.uy/
Ministry of National Defence, Edificio "Gral. Artigas" Avda. 8 de Octubre 2628, Uruguay. Tel: +598 2 487 0389 / 480 9707 / 487 2828, fax: +598 2 481 4833 / 487 4425, URL: http://www.armada.gub.uy/
Ministry of the Interior, Esc Mercedes 993, CP 11100, Montevideo, Uruguay. Tel: +598 2 908 9024, fax: +598 2 900 1626, e-mail: webmaster@minterior.gub.uy, URL: http://www.minterior.gub.uy
Ministry of Foreign Affairs, Av. 18 de Julio 1205, Montevideo, Uruguay. Tel: +598 2 902 1010 / 4094 / 4095, fax: +598 2 902 1349, URL: http://www.mrree.gub.uy/
Ministry of Public Health, Av. 18 de Julio 1892, Montevideo, Uruguay. Tel: +598 2 400 1086 / 400 5001 / 400 0101, fax: +598 2 408 5360, e-mail: msp@msp.gub.uy, URL: http://www.msp.gub.uy/
Ministry of Economy and Finance, Colonia 1089 P.3, Montevideo, Uruguay. Tel: +598 2 902 1017 / 902 0863 / 902 0443, fax: +598 2 902 1277, URL: http://www.mef.gub.uy/
Ministry of Transportation and Public Works, Rincon 561, Uruguay. Tel: +598 2 916 0509 / 915 7013 / 915 8333, fax: +598 2 916 1650, URL: http://www.mtop.gub.uy/
Ministry of Education and Culture, Reconquista 535 c/Ituzaingo, Montevideo, Uruguay. Tel: +598 2 915 0103 / 916 1174, fax: +598 2 900 1048, e-mail: webmaster@mec.gub.uy, URL: http://www.mec.gub.uy/
Ministry of Labour and Social Security, Juncal 1511, Montevideo, Uruguay. Tel: +598 2 916 2681 / 915 7140 / 916 3703, fax: +598 2 916 2708 / 3442, e-mail: webmtss@mtss.gub.uy, URL: http://www.mtss.gub.uy/
Ministry of Agriculture, Livestock and Fisheries, Constituyente 1476, Montevideo, Uruguay. Tel: +598 2 410 4155 / 401 3622, fax: +598 2 409 9623, URL: http://www.mgap.gub.uy/
Ministry of Industry and Energy, Rincón 747, Montevideo, Uruguay. Tel: +598 2 902 2289 / 900 2600, fax: +598 2 902 1245, e-mail: ssecmiem@adinet.com.uy, URL: http://www.miem.gub.uy/

Ministry of Housing and Environment, Zabala 1427, Montevideo, Uruguay. Tel: +598 2 915 0211 / 916 3989 / 916 5209, fax: +598 2 916 3914, URL: http://www.mvotma.gub.uy/
Ministry of Tourism, Av. Libertador Brig. Gral. Lavalleja 1409 P.4, 5 y 6., Montevideo, Uruguay. Tel: +598 2 901 3243 / 908 9105, fax: +598 2 902 1624, e-mail: webmaster@mintur.gub.uy, URL: http://www.turismo.gub.uy

Political Parties
Colorado Party (PC), URL: http://www.partidocolorado.com.uy/; Independent Party (PI), URL: http://www.partidoindependiente.org.uy; National Party (PN, or Blancos), URL: http://www.partidonacional.org.uy/sitio.html; Broad Front (coalition), URL: http://www.frenteamplio.org.uy/

Elections
Presidential elections were held in October 2004. Tabare Vazquez Rosas of the Broad Front coalition was elected. The most recent presidential election was held in November 2009 and Jose Mujica of the Broad Front party was elected to the post. President Broad appointed a coalition government.

Legislative elections took place in October 2004 when the coalition party, Frente Amplio, won an overall majority in both houses, 53 seats in the House of Representatives and 17 in the Senate. The most recent parliamentary election took place in October 2009; the governing coalition was returned to power.

Voting is compulsory.

Diplomatic Representation
Embassy of Uruguay, 1st Floor, 125 Kensington High Stree, London W8 5SF, United Kingdom. Tel: +44 (0)20 7937 4170, fax: +44 (0)20 7376 0502, e-mail: emburuguay@emburuguay.org.uk, URL: http://www.uruguay.embassyhomepage.com
Ambassador: Julio Moreira Moran
Embassy of Uruguay, 1913 I St, NW, 3rd Floor, Washington DC, 20006, USA. Tel: +1 202 331 1313/4/5/6, fax: +1 202 331 8142, e-mail: uruwashi@uruwashi.org URL: http://www.uruwashi.org
Ambassador: H. E. Carlos Gianelli Derois
British Embassy, Calle Marco Bruto 1073, 11300 Montevideo (PO Box 16024), Uruguay. Tel: +598 2 622 3630, fax: +598 2 622 7815, e-mail: bemonte@internet.com.uy, URL: http://www.ukinuruguay.foc.gov.uk
Ambassador: Brn Lyster-Binns
US Embassy, Lauro Muller 1776, Montevideo 11200, Uruguay. Tel: +598 (2) 418 7777, fax: +598 (2) 418 8611, URL: http://uruguay.usembassy.gov/
Ambassador: Julissa Reynoso
Permanent Representative of Uruguay to the United Nations, 866 United Nations Plaza, Suite 322, New York, NY 10017, USA. Tel: +1 212 752 8240 / 8241, fax: +1 212 593 0935, e-mail: uruguay@un.int, URL: http://www.un.int/uruguay
Ambassador: H.E. José Luis Cancela Gomez

LEGAL SYSTEM

The legal system is based on Spanish civil law. The judiciary is structurally independent of the executive and this separation of powers is respected in practice. A Supreme Judicial Council supervises the judiciary and nominates Supreme Court justices.

The Supreme Court, the final court of appeal against the judgements of the three Appeal Courts, consists of five judges, and has original jurisdiction in constitutional, international and admiralty cases. In addition, there are Civil, Criminal and Correctional Courts, as well as courts presided over by justices of the peace, juvenile, administrative and labour courts. A parallel military court system operates under its own procedure. When the Supreme Court hears cases involving the military, two military justices join the Court. Civilians are tried in the military court only in time of war or insurrection.

The government respects the rights of its citizens, though prison conditions continue to be poor. Uruguay abolished the death penalty in 1907. The death penalty was abolished in 1969.

In February 2013, the Supreme Court ruled that a law allowing new investigations of dictatorship-era human rights crimes violates the constitution.

Supreme Court, URL: http://www.poderjudicial.gub.uy/

LOCAL GOVERNMENT

Administratively, Uruguay is divided into 19 departments with limited autonomy: Artigas, Canelones, Cerro Largo, Colonia, Durazno, Flores, Florida, Lavalleja, Maldonado, Montevideo, Paysandú, Rio Negro, Rivera, Rocha, Salto, San José, Soriano, Tacuarembó, Treinta y Tres. Each of the departments has its own capital city, Governor *(Intendente)* and Assembly *(Junta)*. Elections took place most recently in 2010.

AREA AND POPULATION

Area
Uruguay is the second smallest country in South America (after Suriname). It shares its borders with Brazil in the north and northeast, Argentina in the west and the River Plate and the Atlantic Ocean in the south and southeast. It covers an area of 176,220 sq. km. The land has no remarkable topographical features and consists mainly of rolling plains crossed by long rivers, with a major elevation of 514 metres at Cerro Catedral. Around three-quarters of the country is grassland, ideal for cattle and sheep raising.

The climate is mild all year round, with temperatures ranging from 22°C to 32°C in summer (December/February) and 5°C to 15°C in winter (June/August).

To view a map, consult http://www.lib.utexas.edu/maps/cia08/uruguay_sm_2008.gif

Population
The population is approximately 3.369 million (2010), with a current growth rate of 0.1 per cent over the period 2000-10. Approximately 92 per cent of the population lives in urban centres, half in Montevideo. Other main cities include Salto with a population in the region of 93,000; Paysandú, 84,000; Ciudad de la Costa, 80,000; Las Piedras, 66,000 and Rivera, 63,000. Approximately 88 per cent of the population is of European origin, mainly from Italy and Spain. People of African descent make up 4 per cent of the population, and 8 per cent are Mestizo.

Uruguay suffers high rates of emigration; over the past twenty years, some 500,000 young and highly qualified people have left the country in search of the higher salaries offered in Europe, Argentina and the United States. It is estimated that up to one-fifth of all Uruguayans now live abroad and the country has the highest proportion of elderly people in the hemisphere. The beginning of this mass emigration coincided with an economic recession. Uruguayan emigrants are skilled compared to the general population and to other Latin American emigrants, having benefited from the country's high quality education system.

The official language is Spanish, but English and French are spoken in the business community and in the government. Brazilero, a mixture of Spanish and Portuguese, is spoken in the border area with Brazil.

Births, Marriages, Deaths
Estimates for 2010 put the birth rate at 14.8 per 1,000 inhabitants and the death rate at 9.9 per 1,000 population. Population growth is currently estimated at 0.1 per cent per year. Infant mortality rate was approximately 11 per 1,000 live births in 2009. Average life expectancy is 76 years. Healthy life expectancy is 67 years. As a result of the low birth rate, high life expectancy, and relatively high rate of emigration of younger people, Uruguay's population is quite mature; an estimated 18 per cent of the population is 60 years or older. Approximately 23 per cent of the population is 14 years old or younger. The median age is 34 years. (Source: http://www.who.int, World Health Statistics 2012)

Public Holidays 2014
1 January: New Year's Day
6 January: Epiphany
4 March: Carnival
18 April: Landing of the 33 Patriots
17 April: Maundy Thursday
18 April: Good Friday
5 May: Labour Day
16 May: Battle of Las Piedras
19 June: Birth of General Artigas
18 July: Constitution Day
25 August: National Independence Day
13 October: Dia de la Raza (Columbus Day)
2 November: All Souls' Day
25 December: Christmas Day

EMPLOYMENT

In 2007, the total workforce aged over 14 years numbered 1,631.353, equivalent to 41.9 per cent of the overall population. Of these, 1,482,100 were employed, excluding army conscripts, and 149,300 (9.2 per cent) were unemployed, the lowest level in ten years. Unemployment among women was twice as high as unemployment among men. In 2010 the unemployment rate was estimated at 6.6 per cent.

Employment by economic sector, 2007, urban areas, 14+

Sector	No. of people employed
Agriculture, Hunting, Fishing, Forestry; Mining and Quarrying	163,300
Manufacturing; electricity, Gas and Water Supply	219,900
Construction	102,100
Wholesale and Retail Trade; Repair of motor vehicles, personal and household goods; Hotels and restaurants	319,200
Transport, Storage and Communications	83,900
Financial Services; Real Estate, Renting and Business Activities	114,400
Public Administration and Defence; Compulsory Social Services	94,400
Education	84,200
Health and Social Work	97,200
Other Community, Social and Personal Services;	75,200
Extra-Territorial Organisations and bodies	
Employees of Private Households	128,200
Not classifiable by economic activity	1,900
Total	**1,482,100**

Source: International Labour Organisation

BANKING AND FINANCE

Currency
The unit of currency is the Uruguayan Peso (1,000 old pesos) of 100 centésimos. The actual circulation medium consists of coins and paper notes issued by the Central Bank. The US dollar is also in circulation and is accepted in many business establishments.

GDP/GNP, Inflation, National Debt
Uruguay's economy suffered in the 1990s and early 2000s but has enjoyed steady growth more recently. The mainstay of the economy is its agricultural exports. Uruguay has managed to steer clear of the global economic downturn, as economic growth was led by private consumption which had grown as a result of recovery in employment and wages. Exports have also increased in recent years.

Whilst privatisations have taken place in recent years, they are still largely opposed. Privatisations have included concessions for cellular telephone networks, a container terminal at the Port of Montevideo, toll roads between Montevideo and other cities, and the Montevideo International airport. The state continues to play an unusually large role in the economy (some 20 per cent of the working population is employed by the state). A referendum promoted by the National Waterworks Union to reverse the partial privatisation of the country's waterworks and sewerage systems was carried. The Government is now studying the feasibility of Public Private Partnerships as an alternative to privatisation.

In 2009 GDP was put at US$31.5 billion reflecting a growth rate of 2.9 per cent , GDP in 2010 was estimated at US$40.6 billion. Economic growth was estimated at 8.0 per cent 2010 and forecast figures for 2011-15 put annual growth in the region of 4.0 per cent. GDP was estimated at UD$45 billion in 2011. The service sector accounted for around 60 per cent of GDP in 2008, followed by industry (23 per cent) and agriculture (9 per cent).

The inflation rate rose from an average of 6.4 per cent in 2006 to an average of 8.5 per cent the following year. In 2008, inflation averaged 9.19 per cent. In 2010, inflation was 6.5 per cent, rising to 8 per cent in 2011.

In December 2006, Uruguay paid off its debt to the International Monetary Fund.

Uruguay has been successful in attracting foreign investment. In 2010, direct foreign investment was estimated at US1.6 billion.

Balance of Payments / Imports and Exports
In 2010, exports earned US$6.7 billion and imports cost US$8.3 billion. Uruguay's main export markets are the USA, Brazil, Argentina, Mexico and Germany. Major export products are wool, meat, leather, fish, furs, and rice. The main suppliers of Uruguay's imports are Brazil, Argentina, United States, China, Venezuela. Major import products include oil, intermediate goods other than fuels, consumer and capital goods.

The import policy of Uruguay is one of freedom from quantitative restrictions and equal treatment of national and foreign investors. Exports are not subjected to taxes, except for a limited number of raw materials. As of 2012, there were 12 free trade zones.

The Treaty of Asunción established the Common Market of the South, Mercosur, in 1991. Its head office is in Montevideo and its members are Argentina, Brazil, Paraguay and Uruguay. Venezuela joined as a full member in 2006, and Bolivia, Chile, Colombia, Ecuador and Perú are associated members. The government actively seeks new trade partners; whilst deciding not to negotiate a Free Trade Agreement with the US at present, the government reached a Trade and Investment Framework Agreement with the US instead. Uruguay is a member of the Latin American Integration Association (ALADI), a trade association that includes 10 South American countries plus Mexico and Cuba.

Central Bank
Banco Central del Uruguay, Diagonal Fabini 777, Montevideo, Uruguay. Tel: +598 2 1967, fax: +598 2 9085629, e-mail: info@bcu.gub.uy, URL: http://www.bcu.gub.uy
President: Mario Bergara Duque

Chambers of Commerce and Trade Organisations
Uruguay-US Chamber of Commerce, URL: http://www.ccuruguayusa.com/
Cámara Nacional de Comercio y Servicios del Uruguay, URL: http://www.camaradecomercio.com.uy

MANUFACTURING, MINING AND SERVICES

Primary and Extractive Industries
All minerals belong to the nation. Silver, copper, lead, manganese, gold, iron and lignite are found, but are not worked to any great extent as they are not found in sufficient quantity to make their production commercially practicable. Marble and granite are quarried.

Uruguay has no proven oil reserves, and the country relies on imports for its oil requirements. According to the EIA, consumption reached around 40,000 barrels per day in 2011. Uruguay imports mainly from Venezuela, on preferential terms. The country has a single oil refinery, the 50,000-bbl/d La Teja facility near Montevideo. It is operated by state-owned Administracion Nacional de Combustibles Alcohol y Portland (ANCAP).

Uruguay has no proven natural gas reserves. In order to diversify its energy sources away from oil and hydroelectricity, Uruguay imports natural gas from Argentina. Natural gas consumption reached three billion cubic feet (Bcf) in 2011. Argentina has recently interrupted its natural gas flows to Uruguay and Chile, due to domestic shortages, raising concerns in Uruguay about the future security of the natural gas supply. Uruguay is negotiating with Bolivia over the construction of a natural gas pipeline between the two countries as an alternative.

URUGUAY

In June 2006, ANCAP announced that the offshore Punta del Este basin may contain up to 2 trillion cubic feet of natural gas reserves. The organisation hopes to start extracting in 2015.

The government body responsible for the control and administration of subsoil resources is DINAMIGE (Dirección Nacional de Mineria y Geología)
Direccion Nacional De Mineria y Geologia (DINAMIGE), URL: http://www.dinamige.gub.uy

Energy

In June 1997, the Uruguayan Parliament approved regulations for its energy sector. It liberated the generation and marketing of electricity, but retained state control over National Electric Power Generation and Transmission Administration (UTE), which distributes electric power.

Uruguay has an electricity generating capacity estimated at 2.5 gigawatts, around 70 per cent of which is hydroelectric and 30 per cent thermal. In 2010, electricity generation reached 10.6 billion kilowatthours (Bkwh), whilst consumption was an estimated 9.12 billion kilowatthours.

Four hydroelectric stations provide most of Uruguay's electricity generation: Terra (152 MW), Baygorria (108 MW), Palmar (333 MW), and Salto Grande (945 MW). The remainder of the country's electricity comes from thermal power plants and oil- and diesel-fired generators. In May 2006, Uruguay and Argentina began a study on a proposed new hydroelectric plant near Salto Grande. Under normal weather conditions, Uruguay's hydroelectric plants fulfill all the country's requirements; however, seasonal variations can leave Uruguay with power shortages, forcing the country to rely upon imports.

Manufacturing

Industry accounted for 23 per cent of GDP in 2007. Types of industry include meat-processing, textiles, wool, leather and leatherware, hides, tobacco and beverages, chemicals, cement and oil refining. The information software industry is growing rapidly.

Service Industries

The services sector accounts for around 60 per cent of GDP.

Figures for 1997 show that there were 2.46 million visitors to Uruguay, generating revenue of US$759 million. During the recession, this figure dropped to a low of 1.35 million visitors in 2003, before climbing to 1.87 million in 2004 and to 1.92 million in 2005. Most visitors are from other parts of Latin America, 1.1 million coming from neighbouring Argentina in 2005.

Agriculture

Uruguay's economy is dependent on agriculture. Although agricultural production accounts for just nine per cent of GDP, the industrial sector is based largely on the processing of agricultural products, which make up more than half of the country's exports. Produce includes meat, rice, citrus fruits, dairy products, fish and sugar cane.

Around 77 per cent (13.5 million hectares) of the land is used for pasture, and 8 per cent (1.3 million hectares) is arable. The country has 3.6 million hectares of soils suitable for forestry and there are currently 670 thousand hectares of natural forests and 350 thousand hectares of plantations. The potential for fishing for Uruguay is extremely varied, running from lakes with access to the ocean, rivers and the coastlines between Punta de Este and Brazil.

In 2007, Uruguay produced 572,748 million tons on cattle meat (valued at Int.$ 1.18 billion) and 36,212 million tons of sheep meat (valued at Int.$71.6 million). Meat exports are an important source of revenue, traditionally accounting for around 40 per cent of total exports. The meat-canning company, Fray Bentos, is based in the country. In 2001 Uruguay suffered an outbreak of Foot and Mouth disease and exports of meat ceased. In 2003 the country was declared free of disease and exports have gradually been increasing. *(Source: FAO, Food and Agriculture Organization of the United Nations)*

Agricultural Production in 2010

Produce	Int. $'000*	Tonnes
Indigenous cattle meat	1,506,282	557,598
Cow milk, whole, fresh	511,367	1,820,750
Soybeans	477,028	1,816,800
Rice, paddy	313,792	1,148,740
Wheat	182,122	1,300,700
Indigenous chicken meat	98,146	68,903
Indigenous sheep meat	93,583	34,370
Wool, greasy	66,385	34,700
Grapes	63,045	110,292
Honey, natural	47,930	19,100
Maize	46,146	529,100
Hen eggs, in shell	43,533	52,488

* unofficial figures
Source: http://faostat.fao.org/site/339/default.aspx Food and Agriculture Organization of the United Nations, Food and Agricultural commodities production

Fishing

FAO figures for 2010 put the total catch at 74,153 tonnes, down from 125,818 tonnes.

COMMUNICATIONS AND TRANSPORT

Travel Requirements

Citizens of the USA, Canada, Australia and most of the EU require a valid passport but do not need a visa. Estonians do need a visa, and citizens of Canada, Ireland, Malta and the USA are only permitted visa-free stays of up to three months. US citizens travelling on diplomatic or official passports do require a visa. Most holders of MERCOSUR ID cards can enter without a visa. Other nationals should contact the embassy to check visa requirements.

International Airlines

Most international airlines operate at the Carrasco International Airport where daily connections with Argentina and Brazil are available. The airport of Carrasco is situated 17 kms from the centre of Montevideo. PLUNA (Primeras Lineas Uruguayas de Navigación Aerea), the state-controlled national airline, flies services to Europe, Argentina, Paraguay and Chile, and covers domestic and limited freight flights with services by the State owned TAMU internal airline. There are 64 airports in Uruguay, eight of them paved.
PLUNA, URL: http://www.pluna.com.uy

Railways

The total railway system consists of over 2,073 km of standard gauge. The railways all converge upon Montevideo.

Roads

There are three international bridges and a road over the Salto Grande dam linking Uruguay to Argentina, and four highway routes to Brazil. Passenger, mail and freight transportation to the interior of the country is handled by a number of bus and truck companies which also offer international services to the countries in the region. The "Southern Cone Axial Way" which directly links Argentina, Brazil and Uruguay, starts from the Brazilian city of Porto Alegre and ends in Buenos Aires. Vehicles are driven on the right.

Shipping

Uruguay's main ports are located along the Atlantic Ocean, the River Plate and the Uruguay River. A government agency, the Administración Nacional de Puertos (A.N.P.), is in charge of their operation. The most important port, Montevideo, has great operating capacity and accounts for a high percentage of the total port traffic in the country. Ports such as Colonia, Nueva Palmira, Fray Bentos and Paysandu, along the Uruguay River, allow the entry of vessels with a draft of up to 6 metres. There are approximately 1,600 km of navigable rivers and inland waterways. Uruguay is part of a Waterway Project shared with Argentina, Brazil, Bolivia and Paraguay, to provide a reliable and efficient transportation system for the Latin American Southern Cone Region. Ferry services run between Colonia del Sacramento and Montevideo and Buenos Aires, Argentina.

HEALTH

Uruguay was one of the first countries in South America to introduce the social welfare system. This was restructured in 1995. A mixed public and private pension scheme was introduced. In 2009, the government spent approximately 8 per cent of its total budget on healthcare, accounting for 65.3 per cent of all healthcare spending. Total expenditure on healthcare equated to 8.4 per cent of the country's GDP. Per capita expenditure on health was approximately US$787 in 2009.

World Health Organization figures for 2005-10 show that there were 13,197 doctors (37.4 per 10,000 population), 19,595 nurses and midwives (55 per 10,000 population), 2,476 dentistry personnel, and 1,877 pharmaceutical personnel. There were 29 hospital beds per 10,000 population.

HIV/AIDS is an increasing problem, but the rate of infected people (0.36 per cent) is still low. There is a compulsory HIV test for pregnant women, which has significantly decreased the incidence of infection from mother to child. The infant mortality rate in 2010 was 9 per 1,000 live births. The child mortality rate (under 5 years) was 11 per 1,000 live births. The main causes of childhood mortality are: prematurity (16 per cent), congenital anomalies (28 per cent), pneumonia (11 per cent), and diarrhoea (2 per cent).

In 2010, all the population had access to improved drinking-water sources and improved sanitation. (Source: WHO)

Uruguay is expected to legalise abortion (during the first trimester of a pregnancy) in 2012.

EDUCATION

Primary and secondary education is free and compulsory for all children, and no fees are payable for university education or for industrial apprenticeship. As a result, even back in 1990, Uruguay had the highest literacy rate on the South American continent and 18.5 per cent had university degrees. Total, adult literacy is estimated to be 97.8 per cent, rising to 98.8 per cent among the 15-24 age group, the highest rate in Latin America.

In recent years, education has been extended to cover children of pre-school age so that 79 per cent of children between 3 and 6 now attend kindergarten schools. All children of the relevant age now attend primary school, where the ratio of pupils to teacher was 20:1 in 2006. Seven per cent of the population repeated a year in 2006. In 2005, 93 per cent of children completed primary school education, and 81 per cent transferred to secondary education. Approximately 46 per cent of the population of tertiary age studied at tertiary level in 2006.

The University of the Republic is the largest University in Uruguay, with around 60,000 students; the University of Uruguay and the University of Montevideo have around 3,850 and 3100 students respectively. The Catholic University of Uruguay is private and has around 2,140 students.

In 2007, 11.6 per cent of government spending went on education. Following the recession of 1998-2002, large numbers of highly skilled people have emigrated to the USA and Europe, and the country is currently not benefiting from its long term investment in education.

RELIGION

There is no state religion and all faiths have complete liberty of worship. The majority of the inhabitants are nominally Roman Catholic, although the majority of Uruguayans do not actively practice a religion.

Uruguay has a religious liberty rating of 9 on a scale of 1 to 10 (10 is most freedom). (Source: World Religion Database)

COMMUNICATIONS AND MEDIA

Freedom of speech and of the press are guaranteed by the constitution with some limits on 'insulting' the nation.

Newspapers
Uruguayans have access to over 100 private daily and weekly newspapers. Some newspapers are owned by, or linked to, the main political parties. Titles include:
El País, URL: http://www.elpais.com.uy, Est.: 1918
La Republica, URL: http://www.diariolarepublica.com, Est.: 1988
Ultimas Noticias, URL: http://www.ultimasnoticias.com.uy, Est.: 1981
El Observador, URL: http://www.observa.com.uy

Broadcasting
There are over 100 radio stations and some 20 television channels in Uruguay. Cable TV is widely available. State-run radio and TV are operated by the official broadcasting service, SODRE.

The main TV stations are: Teledoce (URL: http://www.teledoce.com/home/, Saeta TV Canal 10 and TV Nacional Uruguay (government-owned, URL: http://www.tnu.com.uy/). Main radio stations are: Radio El Espectador (URL: http://www.espectador.com/index_home3.php), Radio Sarandi, AM Libre, Radio Carve, Radio Montecarlo and Radiodifusion Nacional SODRE (government-owned). Most broadcasters are based in Montevideo.

Telecommunications
The system is fully digitalized, better in urban areas. Overall fixed-line and mobile-cellular ownership was 115 telephones per 100 people in 2007. There were an estimated 960,000 mainline phone lines in use and 3.5 million mobile phones. In the same year, 1.3 million Uruguayans were regular internet users.

ENVIRONMENT

Uruguay's main environmental concerns are pollution caused by a Brazilian power station near its border; water pollution from the meat packing and tannery industries; and ineffective waste disposal. Energy related carbon emissions in 2005 were estimated at 6.01 million metric tons, whilst per capita emissions have 1.58 metric tons in 2002 to 1.75 metric tons in 2005. In 2010, Uruguay's emissions from the consumption of fossil fuels totalled 7.27 million metric tons of carbon dioxide. (Source: EIA)

In 1996 a new section was added to the Constitution stating that every person must abstain from "any act which causes depredation, destruction or grave contamination to the environment".

UZBEKISTAN

Republic of Uzbekistan

Ozbekiston Respublikasi

Capital: Tashkent (Population estimate, 2010: 2.3 million)

Head of State: Islam Abduganevich Karimov (President) (page 1454)

National Flag: Five unequal horizontal stripes of light blue, red, white, red and light green with a white crescent and 12 white stars in the top left-hand corner

CONSTITUTION AND GOVERNMENT

Constitution
In September 1989, the Birlik People's Movement was established with a commitment to Uzbekistan's independent sovereignty and to promoting the status of the Uzbek language. Local and republican elections were held in February 1990 and the Communist Party enjoyed considerable success.

The Uzbek republic issued a sovereignty declaration in June 1990. Following the failed coup against Mikhail Gorbachev of 19-21 August 1991, the Uzbek Communist Party broke away from the Communist Party of the Soviet Union. On 31 August 1991, Uzbekistan declared its independence and changed its name to the Republic of Uzbekistan. This was confirmed in a referendum in December 1991 and recognised by the EC and the USA. On 21 December 1991 Uzbekistan was signatory to the Commonwealth of Independent States agreement, and on the 2nd March 1992 Uzbekistan gained membership to the UN.

On 30 December 1991, Islam Karimov won the presidential election, with 86 per cent of the vote. A 1995 referendum extended Karimov's term of office to the year 2000. The Government was reorganised on 13 January 1992 and a new constitution adopted which established Uzbekistan as a secular, democratic and presidential republic with no state ideology or religion.

The President, elected by the people for a term of five years, may hold office for a maximum of two consecutive terms. He has executive power to create and oversee the Cabinet of Ministers, appoint the Chairman and Ministers, and appoint judges of the lower courts and governors of regions.

In January 2002, it was proposed that the presidential term be extended from five to seven years. The proposal was accepted by referendum and came into force in 2005. Following amendments made to the constitution in 2004, the legislature of Uzbekistan became bicameral, consisting of a Lower house, *Oily Majlis* and an upper house, the Senate. There were further amendments in 2011; the prime minister is no longer appointed by the president, but is now nominated by parliament and may be dismissed by a vote of no confidence.

To view the Constitution, please visit: http://www.gov.uz/en/constitution/

International Relations
In 1999 Uzbekistan became a partial member of the Partnership and Cooperation Agreement with the EU; however EU Foreign Ministers decided on a partial suspension of the membership in 2005 following violence in Andizhan and human rights concerns. A ban on technical visits was lifted in November 2007 in an effort to improve dialogue with Uzbekistan.

Ukbekistan has a close relationship with Russia and in 2005 signed a treaty on allied relations. Uzbekistan is a member of CIS Collective Security Treaty Organisation.

Recent Events
Following the terrorist attacks on the Twin Towers in New York on 11 September 2001, Uzbekistan allowed the USA to use its airbases for strikes against Afghanistan. In July 2004, suicide bombers targeted the US and Israeli embassies in Tashkent. Uzbekistan requested that the US leave the base, which they did in November 2005.

In May 2005, protests against the jailing of men accused of Islamic fundamentalism in Andijan turned into a bloodbath, when supporters of the accused broke into the prison and freed them. Witnesses claimed that hundreds of civilians were killed when troops opened fire. The Uzbek government cited a figure of 180, most of whom were soldiers or militants. Islamic fundamentalists were blamed by the president, whilst opponents blamed the president's oppressive rule. The USA threatened to withhold aid unless an enquiry was held; in August the parliament voted to evict the US forces from Uzbekistan. A trial of the 15 alleged leaders of the protest began in September.

In March 2006 a prominent opposition leader, Sanjar Umarov of the Sunshine Uzbekistan Movement, was jailed for alleged economic crimes. In July 2008, Igor Vorontsov a representative of Human Rights Watch organisation was expelled.

In early 2009, the Court sentenced five writers of an Islamic religious newspaper to jail on charges of inciting religious extremism. President Karimov announced that the US would be allowed to transport supplies to Afghanistan through Uzbekistan.

In October 2009 the EU lifted its arms embargo imposed in 2005 after violence in Andijan.

In December that year Uzbekistan said it had set up new power lines and would be withdrawn from the Soviet-era power grid. Tajikistan and Kyrgyzstan rely on the grid and may therefore face energy shortfalls.

In June 2012 the government announced plans to sell many state assets.

Legislature
The government of Uzbekistan was unicameral. Following legislative elections at the end of 1994 and beginning of 1995, the 500-member Supreme Soviet was replaced by the 120-member Supreme Assembly, or Oliy Majlis. Elected for a term of five years, the Supreme Assembly can be dissolved only by the President in conjunction with the Constitutional Court.

The lower house consists of 150 directly elected members who serve a five year term and 15 elected by the econological Movement of Uzbekistan.

UZBEKISTAN

Oily Majlis, Halklar Dustligi 1, 700035, Tashkent, Uzbekistan. Tel: +998 71 139 8746, URL: http://www.parliament.gov.uz

The upper house consists of 101 members, 16 of whom are appointed by the president. The other members are elected by regional departments to represent those regions and serve a five year term. President Karimov is a life member of the senate.
The Senate, 6 Mustakillik Squaere, 700087 Tashkent, Uzbekistan. Tel: +998 71 138 2666, fax: +998 71 138 2901

Cabinet (as at March 2013)
Prime Minister: Shavkat Mirziyoev (page 1478)
First Deputy Prime Minister, Minister of Finance and Head of Economic Sector; Structure and Regional Development: Rustam Azimov
Deputy Prime Minister, Minister for Construction, Industry, Housing and Transport: Batir Zakirov
Deputy Prime Minister, Chair of the Committee for Women's Affairs: Elmira Basithanova
Deputy Prime Minister for the Industrial Sector: Ulugbek Roziqulov
Deputy Prime Minister for the Geology, Fuel and Energy, Chemical and Petrochemical Industries: Gulomion Ibragimov
Deputy Prime Minister for Culture, Education and Healthcare: Adham Ilkamovich Ikromov
Minister of Foreign Economic Relations, Investments & Trade: Elyer Ghaniyev (page 1430)
Minister of the Foreign Affairs: Abdulaziz Kamilov (page 1453)
Minister of the Interior: Bahodir Ahmedovich Matlubov
Minister of Culture and Sports: Minhojiddin Hijimatov
Minister of Agriculture & Water Resources: Zafar Ruziev
Minister of Economics: Galina Saidova
Minister of Health: Anvar Alimov
Minister of Public Education: Ulugbek Inoyatov
Minister of Higher and Secondary Special Education: Bahodir Xodiyev
Minister of Defence: Kabil Berdiev
Minister of Justice: Nigmatilla Tulginovich Yuldoshev
Minister of Emergency Situations: Tursinkhon Khudayberganov
Minister of Labour and Social Security: Aktam Akhmatovich Khaitov

---

Ministries

Government portal: URL: http://www.gov.uz
Office of the Prime Minister, Government House, 5 Mustaqillik Maydoni, 700078 Tashkent, Uzbekistan. Tel: +998 71 239 8295, URL: http://www.gov.uz
Ministry of Foreign Affairs, 9 Uzbekistan Square, 700029 Tashkent, Uzbekistan. Tel: +998 71 133 6475, fax: +998 71 139 1517, e-mail: root@relay.tiv.uz, URL: http://www.mfa.uz/
Ministry of Finance: 5 Mustaqillik Square, 700078 Tashkent, Uzbekistan. Tel: +998 71 133 7073, fax: +998 71 144 5643, e-mail: info@mf.uz, URL: http://www.gov.uz/eng/mf
Ministry of the Economy, 45A Uzbekistan Avenue, 700003 Tashkent, Uzbekistan. Tel: +998 71 139 6320, fax: +998 71 132-63 72, e-mail: mineconomy@mmes.gov.uz, URL: http://www.mineconomy.cc.uz
Ministry of the Interior, 1 Yunus Rajaby Street, 700029 Tashkent, Uzbekistan. Tel: +998 71 139 7336, fax: +998 71 133 8934, URL: http://www.gov.uz/eng/mia/
Ministry of Justice, 32 Sailgokh Street, 700047 Tashkent, Uzbekistan. Tel: +998 71 133 7311, e-mail: adliya@mail.uznet.uz, URL: http://www.minjust.gov.uz
Ministry of Health, 38 Kh Abdullaev Street, 700000 Tashkent, Uzbekistan. Tel: +998 71 67 6244, fax: +998 71 67 6231, e-mail: mutalova@uzpak.uz
Ministry for Emergencies, 4 Kh Asomov Street, Yunush Abad District, 700084 Tashkent, Uzbekistan. Tel: +998 71 139 1685, URL: http://www.gov.uz/eng/mese
Ministry of Higher and Secondary Special Education, 5 Mustaqillik Square, 700078 Tashkent, Uzbekistan. Tel: +998 71 133 1626, fax: +998 71 139 1271, e-mail: oliy@uzsci.net, URL: http://www.edu.uz/high
Ministry of Labour and Social Security, 20A Abdulla Avloni Street, 700100 Tashkent, Uzbekistan. Tel: +998 71 246 9904, fax: +998 71 139 4313, e-mail: mehnat@uzpak.uz, URL: http://www.gov.uz/eng/mlss
Ministry of Education, 5 Mustaqillik Square, 700008 Tashkent, Uzbekistan. Tel: +998 71 139 4111, fax: +998 71 139 1760, e-mail: yazdon@uzsci.net, URL: http://www.mno.edu.uz
Ministry for Emergencies, 4 Kh Asomov Street, Yunush Abad District, 700084 Tashkent, Uzbekistan. Tel: +998 71 139 1685, fax: +998 71 34 4219, URL: http://www.gov.uz/eng/mese
Ministry of Agriculture and Water Resources, 4 Navoiy Street, 700003 Tashkent, Uzbekistan. Tel: +998 71 241 1353, fax: +998 71 241 3292, URL: http://www.gov.uz/eng/mawr
Ministry of Culture and Sports, 30 Navoi Street, 700129 Tashkent, Uzbekistan. Tel: +998 71 144 2623, fax: +998 71 144 1830, e-mail: mincult@dostlink.net, URL: http://www.mincult.uzpak.uz
Ministry of Defence, 100 Academician Abdullaev Street, 700000 Tashkent, Uzbekistan. Tel: +998 71 169 8721, fax: +998 71 268 4867, URL: http://www.gov.uz/eng/md

Political Parties

Adolat (Justice) Social Democratic Party, 11 seats in parliament
Milliy Tiklanish Democratic Partiyasi (MTP, National Democratic Revival Party), 10 seats in parliament
Fatherland Progress Party (Vatan Tarakiyoti) (VTP merged with the National Democratic Party "Fidokorlar" (Fidokorlar Milliy Democratic Partiya), 62 seats in parliament
People's Democratic Party - PDPU (Uzbekiston Halq Democratic Partiya, formerly Communist Party), 50 seats in parliament
Democratic ERK Party of Uzbekistan, URL: http://www.uzbekistanerk.org
Popular Movement Birlik Party, URL: http://www.birlik.net
Ecological Movement of Uzbekistan (EMU)
Uzbekistan Liberal Democratic Party (UzLiDeP)

Elections

The last parliamentary elections took place on 27 December and 10 January 2010. Senate elections took place on 19 January.

The penultimate presidential elections were held on 9 January 2000. Karimov was re-elected although some independent observers stated that the elections were not fairly held. Following an extension of the presidential term, the next presidential election was held in December 2007. President Karimov was re-elected; the opposition claimed the election was a sham.

Diplomatic Representation

Uzbekistan Embassy, 1746 Massachusetts Avenue, NW, Washington, DC 20036, USA. Tel: +1 202 887 5300, fax: +1 202 293 6804, URL: http://www.uzbekistan.org
Ambassador: Ilhomjon Nematov (page 1485)
American Embassy, 82 Chilanzarskaya, 700115 Tashkent, Uzbekistan. Tel: +998 71 120 5450, fax: +998 71 120 6335, URL: http://uzbekistan.usembassy.gov
Ambassador: George Krol
Embassy of the Republic of Uzbekistan, 41 Holland Park, London, W11 2RP, UK. Tel: +44 (0)20 7229 7679, fax: +44 (0)20 7229 7029, e-mail: info@uzbekistanembassy.uk.net, URL: http://www.uzbekembassy.org
Ambassador: Otabek Akbarov
British Embassy, Ul. Gulyamova 67, Tashkent 700000, Uzbekistan. Tel: +998 712 120 6822, fax: +998 712 120 6549, e-mail: brit@emb.uz, URL: http://ukinuzbekistan.fco.gov.uk/en/
Ambassador: George Edgar
Permanent Mission the the United Nations, 801 Second Avenue, 20th Floor, New York, 10017, USA. Tel: +1 212 486 4242, URL: http://www.un.int/wcm/content/site/uzbekistan
Permanent Representative: Murod Asqarov

LEGAL SYSTEM

Although nominally independent of the other branches of government, the courts remain under the control of the executive branch. The procurator general and his regional and local equivalents are both the state's chief prosecuting officials as well as the chief investigators of criminal cases.

Uzbekistan's higher courts comprise the Constitutional Court, the Supreme Court and the High Economic Court. Lower court systems exist at the regional, district, and town levels. Judges are nominated by the President and confirmed by the Oliy Majlis. The key judicial positions are Chairman of the Supreme Court, Procurator-General, and Chairman of the Constitutional Court.

The government's human rights record is poor. There have been recent reports of security forces torturing, and otherwise mistreating detainees under interrogation. Prison conditions remain poor. Prisoners are often held incommunicado for extended periods, and defendants are sometimes deprived of legal counsel. There is a widespread public perception of official corruption. Critics of the government have been subject to harassment, arbitrary arrest, prosecution and psychiatric treatment. The government does prosecute officials for corruption and for the most serious abuses of power, and has recently made legal reforms aimed at preventing abuses. The government controls the media. The government restricts citizens' right to free assembly or association, as well as religious activity.

Uzbekistan abolished the death penalty in January 2008.

Ombudsman for Uzbekistan, URL: http://ombudsman.uz/

LOCAL GOVERNMENT

Uzbekistan is divided into 12 provinces, or violoyats: Andijan; Bukhara; Dijzak; Fergana; Kashkadarya; Khorezm; Namangan; Navoi, Samarkand; Surkhandarya; Syrdarya and Tashkent. There is also an autonomous republic, Karakalpakstan, which has its own directly elected president.

AREA AND POPULATION

Area

The Republic of Uzbekistan is a landlocked country and is situated in the heart of Central Asia and borders Kazakhstan and the Aral Sea in the north, Kyrgyzstan and Tajikistan in the east, Afghanistan and Turkmenistan in the south. It has a total area of 497,400 sq. km (172,742 sq. miles) and a density of 51 inhabitants per sq. km. The terrain is characterised by mountains in the humid south-east and plains in the hot and dry north-west and centre, a large part of which is covered by the Kyzylkum Desert, one of the largest deserts in the world. The population is concentrated in areas of oasis such as the Ferghana valley. Its two main rivers are the Amu Darya and Syr Darya, both of which flow into the Aral Sea. The surface of the Aral Sea has declined in recent years due to irrigation. Extensive canal systems have also changed hydrologic flow patterns.

To view a map, view http://www.un.org/Depts/Cartographic/map/profile/uzbekist.pdf

Population

The population in 2010 was estimated at 27.455 million with an annual growth rate of 1.1 per cent per annum over the period 2000-10. Approximately 36 per cent of the population lives in urban areas. The capital, Tashkent has a population of 2.3 million. There are 226 cities and districts. Those with populations of over 200,000 are Tashkent, Samarkand, Namangan, and Andizhan. An estimated 29 per cent of the population was aged under 15 years old and 6 per cent of the population were aged over 60 years. The median age was 24 years. Uzbeks form 74.7 per cent of the population. The remainder are composed of Russians (6.5 per cent), Tajik (4.8 per cent), Kazakh (4.1 per cent) and 10.1 per cent of other nationalities which include Tatars, Karakalpaks and Koreans.

The official language is Uzbek. Russian, Tajik and Kazakh are also spoken.

Births, Marriages, Deaths
The birth rate in 2010 was estimated at 21.4 per 1,000 live births, and the death rate was 6.6 per 1,000 population. In 2009 life expectancy at birth for males was 66.0 years and 71.0 for females. Healthy life expectancy was 58.0 years for males and 60.0 for females in 2007. (Source: http://www.who.int, World Health Statistics 2012)

Public Holidays 2014
1 January: New Year's Day
14 January: Birth of the Prophet *
8 March: International Women's Day
21 March: Navruz (Persian New Year)
1 May: Labour Day
9 May: Day of Memory and Respect
1 September: Independence Day
29 July: Eid al-Fitr, End of Ramadan *
5 October: Eid-al-Adha, Feast of the Sacrifice *
8 December: Constitution Day
* Islamic holidays are dependent of the sighting of the moon and may vary.

EMPLOYMENT

Figures for 2007 show that Uzbekistan had a workforce of 10,759,000, of whom 10,735,000 were employed and 23,000 were unemployed. The unemployment rate was 0.2 per cent. The workforce can be divided by economic sector as follows: agriculture 41 per cent, trade and services 36 per cent, industry 13 per cent, construction 6 per cent and transport and communications 4 per cent. Estiamated figures for 2010 put the unemployment rate at 1.0 percent.

Labour Force, 2005

Sector	Thousand Employed
Labour force	10,224
Employed	10,196
- Agriculture	2,970
- Industry	1,348
- Others	5,879
Unemployed	27.7
Unemployment rate %	0.3
Labour force annual change %	2.8

Source: Asian Development Bank

BANKING AND FINANCE

Currency
One sum = 100 teen

GDP/GNP, Inflation, National Debt
The Uzbek economy is largely based on gold mining and exports of cotton, making it largely dependent on the prices of these two markets. Growth for 2009 was estimated at 8.1 per cent.

GDP at current market prices by industrial origin is shown in the following table. Figures are in billion sums.

Industrial origin	2007	2008	2009
GDP by industrial origin	28,186.2	33,789.6	48,097.0
-Agriculture	6,116.4	7,974.3	11,126.4
-Mining, manufacturing & utilities	6764.7	7,523.8	10,960.8
-Construction	1550.2	1,745.8	2,527.8
-Trade	2649.5	3,165.0	4,531.8
-Transport & communications	3128.7	3,807.0	5,413.6
-Finance, Public Admin. & others	5299.0	6,228.6	8,951.4
Net factor income from abroad	80.0	95.9	..
GNI at current market prices	28,266.2	33,885.5	48,233.5

Source: Asian Development Bank

In 2010, total GDP was 361,831.2 billion sums. Agriculture contributed 25.6 per cent, industry 31 per cent and services 43 per cent.

Inflation is relatively high. It reached a high of 64.4 per cent in 1994. Inflation was put at 9.7 per cent in 2010 and at 12.5 per cent in 2011.

Estimated figures for 2007 put external debt at US$3,875 million.

Foreign Investment
Annual foreign direct investment in Uzbekistan grew from US$85 million in 1994 to US$264 million in 1997. Currency controls introduced in October 1996 had an adverse affect on foreign investment in Uzbekistan as they did not allow investors full convertibility of the sum into foreign currency. The government has introduced preferential tax rates for foreign investors and customs privileges.

Uzbekistan received aid from the USA following its decision to allow the use of its airbases by the US air force for their post September 11 conflict in Afghanistan. Many countries called for an international inquiry into the violent clashes in Andijan in May 2005, but Uzbekistan refused; the US threatened to withhold aid, and the Uzbekistan parliament voted to demand that US forces leave their base in the south.

Foreign direct investment was estimated at US$825 million in 2010.

Balance of Payments / Imports and Exports
Uzbekistan's leading trading partners are Russia (over 25 per cent of exports and imports), Ukraine, USA, Kazakhstan, Tajikistan, People's Republic of Korea, Germany, Turkey and China. The EU has approximately 20 per cent of exports and imports. The major export products are cotton, gold, natural gas, mineral fertilizers, ferrous metals, textiles, food and motor vehicles and the major import products are grain, machinery, consumer durables and food.

The following table shows the trade balance in recent years. Figures are in US$ million.

External Trade	Exports, fob	Imports, cif	Trade Balance
2008	11,572.9	7,504.1	4,068.8
2009	11,771.3	9,438.3	8,799.7
2010	13,044.5	2,333.0	4,244.8

Source: Asian Development Bank

Central Bank
Central Bank of the Republic of Uzbekistan, 6 Uzbekistan Avenue, 700001 Tashkent, Uzbekistan. Tel: +998 711 336829, fax: +998 712 406558, URL: http://www.cbu.uz
Chairman: Fayzulla Mullajanov

MANUFACTURING, MINING AND SERVICES

Primary and Extractive Industries
Uzbekistan has the largest single gold operation in the world and substantial deposits of gold and non-ferrous metals. 70 tons of gold are produced per year, making Uzbekistan the seventh largest producer in the world. It has the fourth largest reserves which have attracted foreign investment. Other important minerals include uranium, copper, zinc, tungsten, silver, molybdenum and lead. Uzbekistan is the world's fifth largest uranium producer. In 1998, 2,000 tons of uranium were produced, 6 per cent of the world's total, and in 1996, US$11 million of uranium concentrate was exported to the US. The Almalyk Mining and Metallurgical Works currently generates US$300 million in copper and US$10 million in zinc exports per year.

Oil reserves in 2010 in Uzbekistan are put at 590 million barrels, in 2011 Uzbekistan produced 104,000 barrels per day and consumed 147,000 barrels per day. At present 171 oil and gas fields are in operation. Uzbekistan has reserves of 65 trillion cubic feet of gas and produces 2,226 billion cubic feet per day making it the eighth largest producer of natural gas in the world. Further exploration is to be instigated. Uzbekneftegas, a state-owned company, manages oil and gas production and is in partnership with foreign companies for a variety of investment projects in the industry.

Uzbekistan also produces coal, 3.638 million short tons in 2010 but consumed 3.915 million short tons.

Energy
During 2010 48,150 million kilowatt hours of electricity were generated and 44,510 million kilowatt hours consumed. The major power plants are Syr Darya, Tashkent, Angren and Navoi . The majority of electricity is supplied by thermal plants powered by natural gas although some is generated by coal and 25 hydroelectric driven plants.

Manufacturing
The most important manufacturing industries in Uzbekistan are the textile, automotive and aerospace industries, metallurgy, radio and electronics industry, food processing and chemicals. The Uzbek Association for Production of Light Industry Goods produces 90 per cent of textiles with an annual fabric output of 650 million metres. The Uzbek Association of Automobile Enterprises has developed joint ventures with South Korea's Daewoo company. The US$658 million Daewoo-Uzavtosanoat plant in Andizhan began production in 1996 with a goal of reaching levels of 200,000 units per year by 2000. The Chkalov Corporation produces the IL-76 cargo aircraft as well as the IL-114. In the engineering field, Uzbekistan produces motors, cable and wire products, excavators, cranes, lifts, textile and spinning equipment and cotton gins. Agricultural machinery is produced for the former Soviet Union countries. Cement and steel are also produced.

Service Industries
There exists a firm potential for Uzbekistan to develop a tourist industry based on the Silk Road towns of Khiva, Bukhara and Samarkand and in the south-eastern mountains and plains. There are a new set of tourist class hotels in Bukhara, Samarkand and Tashkent. There are currently about 260,000 visitors to Uzbekistan per year.

Agriculture
Agriculture contributes about 22 per cent of GDP. The cotton sector is the most important as Uzbekistan is the world's fifth largest producer and third largest exporter. The government has increased the amount of land dedicated to grain production in order to reduce food imports. Uzbekistan produces and exports large amounts of vegetables; around five million tons are produced annually including tomatoes, peas, lettuce and potatoes. It produces 0.6 million tons of fruit per year which includes apricots, strawberries, melons and apples, as well as 0.6 million tons of grapes. 20,000 tons of raw silk is produced annually as well and 1.5 million units of astrakhans. Land under cultivation covers around 270,000 hectares. The agriculture sector has suffered in recent years as both 2000 and 2001 saw droughts. Source: http://www.uzbekistanembassy.uk

UZBEKISTAN

Agricultural Production in 2010

Produce	Int. $'000*	Tonnes
Indigenous cattle meat	1,796,080	664,876
Cotton lint	1,357,744	950,000
Cow milk, whole, fresh	1,178,963	6,120,000
Tomatoes	867,367	2,347,000
Wheat	809,485	6,730,400
Grapes	564,358	987,300
Cottonseed	541,259	1,900,000
Carrots and turnips	276,195	1,107,000
Indigenous sheep meat	272,230	99,982
Apples	265,167	712,000
Potatoes	238,302	1,629,900
Onions, dry	185,669	884,000

* unofficial figures

Source: http://faostat.fao.org/site/339/default.aspx Food and Agriculture Organization of the United Nations, Food and Agricultural commodities production

COMMUNICATIONS AND TRANSPORT

Travel Requirements
Citizens of the USA, Canada, Australia and the EU require a passport valid for the length of stay, with a blank page for the visa which is required by all except transit passengers leaving within 24 hours and remaining in the transit area. Passport holders of CIS countries do not require a visa.

Tourists will normally have their visa application completed by their travel agent. Visitors staying longer than three days must register with the Ministry of Internal Affairs within three working days; most hotels will automatically do this on behalf of the visitor, but all other travellers are responsible for registering themselves.

Travel within Uzbekistan by rail or land sometimes requires brief exit into neighboring countries and therefore travellers should have multiple-entry Uzbek visas and a proper visa for the neighboring country. Applicants should contact the consular section of the embassy to check visa requirements prior to travelling.

National Airlines
Uzbekistan Airways, 41 Ulitsa Proletarskaya, Tashkent 700061, Uzbekistan. e-mail: info@uzbekistan-airways.com URL: http://www.uzbekistan-airways.com

International Airports
There are over 60 airports of which 34 have paved runways. Airspace is regulated by the following body.
Uzbek State Corporation of Automotive Transport, 700006 Tashkent, Shirokaya str., 6, Uzbekistan.

Andizhan City Airport
Fergana City Airport
Karshi Airport, 730015, Karshi, Uzbekistan.
Kokand Airport, 713000, Kokand, Uzbekistan.
Tashkent City Airport, 700167 Tashkent, Uzbekistan.

Railways
The total length of the railway is 6,700 km. A rail link connects Uzbekistan and Kazakhstan from where connections can be made to Russia and Ukraine. Tashkent has subway and tram systems.

Roads
The total length of roads is 82,000 km, of which approximately 72,000 km is paved. The Friendship Bridge which is located 10 km south of Termiz, links Afghanistan with Uzbekistan. Vehicles are driven on the right.

Waterways
In 2006 there were an estimated 1,100 km of waterways. The main port is at Termiz.

HEALTH

In 2009, the government spent approximately 8.0 per cent of its total budget on healthcare (up from 6.0 per cent in 2000), accounting for 55.9 per cent of all healthcare spending. Total expenditure on healthcare equated to 5.9 per cent of the country's GDP. Per capita expenditure on health was approximately US$73. In the period 2005-10 there were 72,144 physicians (25.6 per 0000 population), 314,079 nurses and midwives (111.5 per 10,000 population), 4,991 dentists and 992 pharmaceutical personnel. There are 46 hospital beds per 10,000 population.

Life expectancy in 2009 was put at 66 years for men and 71 years for women. The infant mortality rate (probability of dying by first birthday) in 2010 was 44 per 1,000 live births. The child mortality rate (under 5 years) was 52 per 1,000 live births. The main causes of childhood mortality are: prematurity (20 per cent), diarrhoea (7 per cent), pneumonia (15 per cent), and birth asphyxia (10 per cent). In the period 2000-09, approximately 19.6 per cent of children aged less than 5 years were classified as 19.6 per cent and 4.4 per cent were underweight. Some 12.8 per cent were classified as overweight.

In 2010, 87 per cent of the population had access to improved drinking water sources and 100 per cent of the population had access to improved sanitation. (Source: http://www.who.int, World Health Statistics 2012)

EDUCATION

Children between six and 17 attend primary and secondary education. General education is compulsory from age 7 to 17 years of age. Figures from UNESCO in 2007 show that 92 per cent of male children were enrolled in primary school and 90 per cent of female children were enrolled in primary school and 90 per cent of girls and 93 per cent of boys were enrolled in secondary school. 10 per cent of the population of tertiary age were enrolled in tertiary education.

RELIGION

The population is predominantly Sunni Muslim (88 per cent) followed by Eastern Orthodox (9 per cent) and other religions (3 per cent). There have been government concerns regarding Muslim fundamentalism in neighbouring Afghanistan and Tajikistan.

Uzbekistan has a religious liberty rating of 2 on a scale of 1 to 10 (10 is most freedom). (Source: World Religion Database)

COMMUNICATIONS AND MEDIA

The government controls most of the media and the newspaper and printing infrastructure. State pre-press laws were abolished in 2002, but self-censorship is common. Internet sites are subject to censorship also. Uzbeks are still able to access foreign sources of information.

Newspapers
Recent statistics show that of the 508 newspapers published, 290 are in the Uzbek language. Of the 77 periodicals published, 55 are in Uzbek.
Newspapers include: Khalq Sozi; Narodnoye Slovo, http://www.narodnoeslovo.uz; Hurriyat; Fidoko; Pravda Vostoka, URL: http://www.pv.uz; Ozbekistan Ozovi

Broadcasting
Television is the most important medium. The Uzbek State Television and Radio Company (URL: http://www.mtrk.uz/en/) is state controlled. There is also a state controlled Yoshlar radio and television station aimed at the youth of Uzbekistan, and several independent television and radio companies.

Telecommunications
The phone system is in need of investment and modernisation and improvements are being made particularly in Tashkent. In 2008 there were estimated to be 1.8 million land lines. Mobile phone subscribership is growing rapidly and was estimated to be 12.7 million in 2008. In 2009, approximately 2.5 million people subscribed to the internet.

ENVIRONMENT

Uzbekistan's major environmental issues are the drying up of the Aral Sea, leading to an increase in the concentrations of natural salts and chemical pesticides which are being blown from the exposed lake bed and causing desertification; water pollution from industrial waste; fertilizers and pesticides; increasing soil salination and soil contamination from agricultural pesticides. The Aral Sea is drying up due to the irrigation of cotton fields.

On an international level Uzbekistan has played a role in conventions on biodiversity, climate change, desertification, endangered species, environmental modification, hazardous waste and ozone layer protection.

According to figures from the EIA, in 2010, Uzbekistan's emissions from the consumption of fossil fuels totalled 114.27 million metric tons of carbon dioxide.

SPACE PROGRAMME

In 2008, Uzbekistan and Russia agreed on an intergovernmental space programme to study the earth and space for peaceful purposes. The programme included development of Uzbekistan's space infrastructure.

VANUATU
Republic of Vanuatu
Ripablik blong Vanuatu

Capital: Port Vila (Population estimate, 2009: 44,040)

Head of State: Iolu Abil (President) (page 1371)

National Flag: The flag is divided horizontally into three parts by a yellow Y shape with a black border. The open end of the Y is closest to the staff. The area above the horizontal division is red and below is green. The triangular area is black with a yellow pig tusk curved around palm leaves

CONSTITUTION AND GOVERNMENT

Constitution
From 1923 onwards administration was in the hands of British and French Resident Commissioners, each with a staff of national officers.

Following a Ministerial meeting between the British and French Governments in November 1974, it was agreed to create a Representative Assembly for the New Hebrides to replace the Advisory Council. This would be elected by universal suffrage and would have wider statutory powers to deal with issues and problems affecting the New Hebrides. It was also agreed to create municipal councils for the towns of Vila and Santo, and community councils in the outlying islands. Elections for the Assembly were held in November 1975.

The first Assembly was dissolved in 1976, following the majority Vanuaaku Pati's refusal to continue to participate on the grounds that the inclusion of reserved seats for economic interests was undemocratic. A general election was held in November 1977, which the party boycotted and set up a 'people's provisional government' in opposition.

In the first half of 1978, the Vanuaaku Pati agreed to take part in an ad hoc committee on electoral reform, and suspended the PPG. Recommendations from the committee included the lowering of the voting age from 21 to 18.

The progressive transfer of government functions to the New Hebrides Government began with the installation of the Council of Ministers. A Government of National Unity was formed in December 1978 to draw up an independence constitution.

The new Constitution was accepted by Britain and France in October 1979, and elections were held in November. The Vanuaaku Pati won a majority in the Representative Assembly and in both Regional Assemblies (on Santo and Tanna). The VP President, Father Walter Lini, became Chief Minister. The New Hebrides became independent as the Republic of Vanuatu on 30 July 1980 and joined the Commonwealth.

The government is headed by a President who serves a five year term. The prime minister leads the government and appoints the Council of Ministers. Parliament is a 52 member unicameral house which is elected by the constituents and sits a four year term. There is also a national Council of Chiefs, called the Malvatu Mauri, which advises government on all issues concerning ni-Vanuatu culture and language.

To consult the constitution, please visit: http://www.parliament.gov.vu/constitution.html

International Relations
Vanuatu has diplomatic relations with over 70 countries. It is a member of the Melanesian Spearhead Group; the Pacific Islands Forum and the Pacific Community, and a supporter of the emerging Pacific Regional Trading Area (PARTA). Vanuatu is also a member of the UN, the Commonwealth, the Organisation Internationale de la Francophonie and is actively seeking membership of the World Trade Organisation.

Recent Events
In 2005, thousands of people on the island of Ambae had to be evacuated after the active volcano, Mount Manaro, began to throw out ash and steam.

In March 2007 a state of emergency was called when rival groups from the islands of Ambrym and Tanna living in a camp outside the capital Port Vila clashed over accusations of witchcraft. Three people died in the fighting.

In November 2009 Prime Minister Edward Natapei was stripped of his parliamentary seat and position because of a technicality. Prime Minister Natapei was absent from parliament for three sittings while attending a Commonwealth summit. He had failed to notify parliament in writing that he would absent which under constitutional rules meant he would lose his seat. A caretaker government was to sit unill a new prime minister was elected.

On December 2 2010 prime minister Edward Natapei was ousted in absentia by a vote of no confidence in parliament, he was replaced by deputy prime minister Sato Kilman. Mr Kilman lost a vote of no confidence in April 2011 and was replaced by Serge Vohor of the UMP. However the Court of Appeal ruled the vote was invalid citing an insufficient majority and Kilman's government was reinstated in May 2011.

The justice minister Ralph Regenvanu was dismissed in January 2012. He was replaced by the Pentecost constituency MP Charlo Salwai.

Legislature
Vanuatu has a unicameral legislature, the parliament has 52 directly elected members who serve a four year term.
Parliament, Parliament House, Port Vila, Vanuatu. Tel: +678 222 29, fax: +678 245 30, e-mail: comparle@vanuatu.com.vu

---

Cabinet (as at March 2013)
Prime Minister: Sato Kilman (PPP)
Deputy Prime Minister, Minister of Commerce, Industry and Tourism: Ham Lini (NUP)
Minister for Justice: Thomas Laken
Minister for Foreign Affairs: Alfred Carlot (page 1400)
Minister of Finance: Charlot Salwai
Minister of Lands and Mines: James Bule
Minister of Agriculture and Livestock: Dunstan Hilton
Minister of Internal Affairs: Toara Daniel Kalo
Minister of Education: Stephen Kalsakau
Minister of Health: Don Ken
Minister of Ni-Vanuatu Business Development: Marcellino Pipite
Minister of Public Utilities and Infrastructure: Tony Nari
Minister of Civil Aviation: Samson Samsen

Ministries
Prime Minister's Office, PO Box 53, Port-Vila, Vanuatu. URL: http://www.governmentofvanuatu.gov.vu
Ministry of Agriculture, Livestock & Fisheries, PO Box, 39, Port-Vila, Vanuatu. Tel: +678 23406, fax: +678 26498
Ministry of Civil Aviation, PMB 057, Port-Vila, Vanuatu. Tel: +678 22790
Ministry of Commerce, Industry and Tourism, PO Box 056, Port-Vila, Vanuatu. Tel: +678 25674, fax: +678 25674, fax: +678 25677
Ministry of Culture, PO Box 036, Port-Vila, Vanuatu. Tel: +678 22252, fax: +678 27064
Ministry of Finance and Economic Management, PO Box 058, Port-Vila, Vanuatu. Tel: +678 23032, fax: +678 27937
Ministry of Foreign Affairs and External Trade, PO Box 051, Port-Vila, Vanuatu. Tel: +678 27750, fax: +678 27832
Ministry of Health, PO Box 042, Port-Vila, Vanuatu. Tel: +678 22545, fax: +678 26113
Ministry of Home Affairs, PO Box 036, Port-Vila, Vanuatu. Tel: +678 22252, fax: +678 27064
Ministry of Justice & Community Affairs, PO Box 036, Port-Vila, Vanuatu. Tel: +678 22252, fax: +678 27064
Ministry of Lands, Mines and Energy, PO Box 007, Port-Vila, Vanuatu. Tel: +678 23105, fax: +678 25165
Ministry of Public Works, PO Box 057, Port-Vila, Vanuatu. Tel: +678 22790, fax: +678 27714
Ministry of Rural Water Supply, PO Box 007, Port-Vila, Vanuatu. Tel: +678 27833, fax: +678 27833, fax: +678 25165
Ministry of Telecommunication & Postal Services, PO Box 011, Port-Vila, Vanuatu. Tel: +678 23266/22790, fax: +678 24495
Ministry of Transport, PO Box 057, Port-Vila, Vanuatu. Tel: +678 22790, fax: +678 27714
Ministry of Women's Affairs, PO Box 091, Port-Vila, Vanuatu. Tel: +678 25099
Ministry for Education, Youth and Sports, PO Box 028, Port-Vila, Vanuatu. Tel: +678 22309, fax: +678 22309

Elections
Following political unrest acting president Roger Abiut dissolved the parliament in May 2004. Early elections were called for July and resulted in a coalition led by the National United Party, who won 18 of the 52 seats. Kalkot Mataskelekele won the presidential election in the following month. The most recent parliamentary elections were held in September 2008 the result of which was a coalition government led by Edward Natapei of the Vanuaaku Pati and Ham Lini of the National United Party as deputy prime minister.

President Mataskelekele's term of office ended on 16 August 2009. The speaker of parliament, Maxime Jorman, took over as acting president until elections. The first round of voting took place on 1 September when no candidate received an overall majority. Voting is by an electoral college comprising MPs and the six provincial governors. Iolu Abil was elected on the third ballot on 2 September 2009 and was immediately sworn in.

Legislative elections took place on 30 October 2012. The VP remained the largest party in the parliament. Breakdown is as follows: VP 8 seats, PPP 6 seats, UMP 5 seats, NUP 4 seats, IG 3 seats, Nag 3 seats, RMC 3 seats, VGC 3 seats, MPP 2 seats, NIPDP 2 seats, other parties 5 sets, independents 4 seats. Following the results, Prime Minister Kilman formed an 11-party coalition government.

Political Parties
Green Confederation (Green); National United Party (NUP); People's Progress Party (PPP); Union of Moderate Parties (UMP); Vanua'aku Pati (VP); Vanuatu Republican Party (VRP).

Diplomatic Representation
Vanuatu has no diplomatic representation in the UK or USA.

VANUATU

British High Commission, KPMG House, Rue Pasteur, Port Vila, Vanuatu. Tel: +678 23100, fax: 678 27153, e-mail: bhcvila@vanuatu.com.vu
High Commissioner: Roderick Drummond (page 1418) (resident in Fiji)
US Embassy, All staff resident in Papua New Guinea, URL: http://portmoresby.usembassy.gov
Ambassador: Walter North (page 1487)
Mission to the United Nations, US, 866 UN Plaza, 4th Floor Room 41, First Avenue and 48th Street, New York, NY 10017, USA.
Permanent Representative: Donald Kalpokas

LEGAL SYSTEM

The legal system is based on British law. The Supreme Court has a chief justice and up to three other judges. An appeal court would require two or more members of the supreme court. The majority of legal matters are dealt with by Magistrate courts. Village or island courts also exist to deal with customary law issues, and are presided over by chiefs.

The government respects the rights of its citizens, though there is some degree of government corruption, arrests have been made without warrants, prison conditions are poor, and the judicial process can be very slow. Vanuatu abolished the death penalty in 1980.

LOCAL GOVERNMENT

Vanuatu is divided into six provinces: Malampa, Penama, Sanma, Shefa, Tefea, and Torba.

AREA AND POPULATION

Area
The total area of Vanuatu, to which are attached the Banks and Torres Islands, is about 860,000 sq km of which 12,336 sq km is land and contains 83 islands. The islands are of volcanic origin. Vanuatu is situated in the Pacific area known as the Ring of Fire and experiences some 2,000 seismic events each year, Vanuatu is also home to nine active volcanoes and in 2005 thousands of people were evacuated after Mount Manaro began to erupt. The climate is tropical, with moderate rainfall from November to April. There are southeast trade winds from May to October. Cyclones may occur from December to April and in an average year Vanuatu will experience two cyclones.

To view a map, consult http://www.lib.utexas.edu/maps/cia08/vanuatu_sm_2008.gif

Population
In 2010 the population was estimated to be 240,000, with an annual growth rate of 2.6 per cent over the period 2000-10, and a population density of 17 people per sq. km. The capital, Port Vila situated on Efate island has a population estimated at 44,040. The other main urban area is Luganville which is on the island of Espiritu Santo, the largest island in the country. The population is approximately 94 per cent ni-Vanuatu, 4 per cent European and 2 per cent other population groups. Many Ni-Vanuatu speak either French or English, and nearly all speak the local language, Bislama.

Births, Marriages, Deaths
According to 2010 estimates the crude birth rate is approximately 29.5 per thousand; the crude death rate is 4.7 per thousand. In 2009 the infant mortality rate was approximately 14 per 1,000 live births. The total fertility rate per woman in 2010 was 3.9. The average life expectancy was 71 years. Healthy life expectancy was 61 years. The median age was 21 years. Approximately 38 per cent of the population is aged less than 15 years and 5 per cent is aged over 60 years old. (Source: http://www.who.int, World Health Statistics 2012)

Public Holidays 2014
1 January: New Year
18 April: Good Friday
21 April: Easter Monday
5 May: Labour Day
29 May: Ascension Day
24 July: Children's Day
30 July: Independence Day
15 August: Assumption
5 October: Constitution Day
29 November: Unity Day
25 December: Christmas
26 December: Family Day

EMPLOYMENT

The work force is approximately 115,000 with over 65 per cent in the agricultural sector, 30 per cent in services and 5 per cent in industry. Recent figures put the unemployment rate at 1.7 per cent.

BANKING AND FINANCE

There is no direct taxation (with the exception of a value added tax on subdivided land sales).

Currency
The unit of currency is the Vatu of one hundred centimes.

GDP/GNP, Inflation, National Debt
Vanuatu has enjoyed good growth in recent years. GDP grew by 7.4 per cent in 2006, 6.8 per cent in 2007 and 4.7 per cent in 2008. Growth was recorded at 0 per cent in 2009 but it returned to growth in 2010 at an estimated rate of 3 per cent. The following table shows the make up of GDP in recent years. Figures are in million Vatu and are at current market prices:

Sector	2007	2008	2009
Totals	55,784	62,753	63,024
Agriculture	11,076	11,722	12,425
Mining	130	24	26
Manufacturing	1,851	2,380	1,915
Electricity, gas and water	1,024	1,300	1,125
Construction	1,284	1,797	3,162
Trade	8,609	9,563	9,392
Transport & communications	5,638	5,979	6,847
Finance	4,119	4,795	4,623
Public administration	7,115	7,964	8,140
Others	10,141	11,032	10,071

Source: Asian Development Bank

Per capita GDP in 2007 was 226,591 vatu. In 2009, agriculture accounts for approximately 21.5 per cent, industry 10.8 per cent and services 68 per cent. Inflation in 2009 averaged 3.6 per cent, falling to 2.8 per cent in 2010

Foreign Investment
The government encourages foreign investment and willingly enters joint ventures with foreign investors. Direct foreign investment was estimated at 44 billion vatu. Most investment is in the tourism and retail sectors. Australia is one of the country' s,ajor foreign aid donors, contributing approximately $73 million in 2012-13.

Balance of Payments / Imports and Exports
Principal items imported include foodstuffs, timber and building supplies, motor vehicles, mineral fuels, and agricultural machinery. The main food imports are canned meat and fish, dairy products, frozen meat, and fresh fruit and vegetables. In 2010, most imports came from Australia (US$73.8 million), followed by Singapore (IS$70.7 million) and Japan (US$51.6 million).

The main export products are copra, beef, veal, cocoa and timber, with markets in Japan, Europe, India, and Australia. Thailand has developed as a major export destination over the last five years and is now the chief export destination (US$121 million). Japan was the second most significant export destination (US$52.3 million). The following table shows the value of foreign trade in recent years, figures are in million vatu:

External Trade	2008	2009	2010
Exports, fob	5,721	6,150	4,718
Imports, cif	31,667	31,086	27,510
Trade Balance	-25,946	-24,936	-22,792

Source: ADB

Exports by Principal Commodity in Million Vatu

Commodity	2005	2006
Copra	126	324
Beef	302	332
Timber	203	306
Cocoa	181	277

Source: Asian Development Bank

Central Bank
Reserve Bank of Vanuatu, PO Box 62, Port Vila, Vanuatu. Tel: +678 23333 / 23110, fax: +678 24231, e-mail: resrvbnk@vanuatu.com.vu, URL: http://www.rbv.gov.vu
Governor: Odo Tevi

MANUFACTURING, MINING AND SERVICES

Energy
Electricity is generated by thermal power stations. Vanuatu generates enough electricity for its own needs (0.06 billion kilowatt hours in 2010.

Manufacturing
Manufacturing has increased its contribution to GDP from 3 per cent in 1983 to over 7 per cent in 1990 and 12 per cent in 2000. Main industries are food processing (particularly meat), wood processing, soap, coconut oil and construction materials. The increase of tourism has also stimulated the handicrafts sector.

Service Industries
Tourism is the biggest earner of foreign exchange and contributes approximately 18 per cent to GDP; it is the fastest growing sector of the economy. In 1998, there were 52,000 visitors to Vanuatu. In 1999, this figure fell to 51,000 a year after Vanuatu was hit by heavy rain and cyclones.

Agriculture
Around 65 per cent of the population are employed in the agricultural sector. The main subsistence crops are yams, taro, manioc, sweet potato and breadfruit. The major cash crops are copra, cocoa, timber, beef and coffee. Copra is currently accountable for over 35 per cent of the country's exports and the agricultural sector contributes over 20 per cent to the GDP. Exports of beef have increased in recent years as beef produced on Vanuatu is strictly organic. FAO figures for 2010 put the total fishing catch at 97,807 tonnes.

Agricultural Production in 2010

Produce	Int. $'000*	Tonnes
Coconuts	45,571	385,000
Roots and tubers, nes	7,634	49,600
Indigenous cattle meat	6,754	2,500
Indigenous pigmeat	5,253	3,417
Bananas	4,506	16,000
Vegetables fresh nes	2,224	11,800
Fruit fresh nes	1,990	5,700
Indigenous chicken meat	1,598	1,122
Groundnuts, with shell	1,308	2,900
Cow milk, whole, fresh	1,030	3,300
Hen eggs, in shell	829	1,000
Fruit tropical fresh nes	531	1,300

* unofficial figures

Source: http://faostat.fao.org/site/339/default.aspx Food and Agriculture Organization of the United Nations, Food and Agricultural commodities production

COMMUNICATIONS AND TRANSPORT

Travel Requirements
Citizens of the Commonwealth countries, the USA and the EU require a passport valid for six months, proof of sufficient funds and a confirmed onward travel documents but do not need a visa for stays of up to 30 days. Other nationals should contact the embassy to check visa requirements.

International Airports
The main airports of Port Vila and Luganville operate international and domestic flights. There are 26 smaller airfields. Daily flights are operated to New Caledonia, thrice-weekly flights to Fiji and once-weekly to Nauru, with connections to Australia, Asia, Europe and the USA.

Roads
There are about 400 miles of roads, 240 miles of these being seasonal earth motor tracks. Vehicles are driven on the right.

Shipping
There are regular services from New Caledonia, Australia, New Zealand and Europe. The main companies are Compagnie Générale Maritime, Sofrana Unilines and Bankline. Shipping services are maintained with Sydney, Australia, Noumea, New Caledonia and Marseilles via the Panama Canal and San Francisco.

Ports and Harbours
There are harbours at Forari, Port-Vila and Santo, (on the island of Espiritu Santo). Ferry services are in operation.

HEALTH

A nominal fee is paid for health care. There is a network of hospitals and clinics on the islands. There is a network of hospitals and clinics on the islands. In 2009, the government spent approximately 16.4 per cent of its total budget on healthcare, accounting for 89.8 per cent of all healthcare spending. Total expenditure on healthcare equated to 4.9 per cent of the country's GDP. Per capita expenditure on health was approximately US$104. Figures for 2005-10 show that there are 26 physicians (1.2 per 10,000 population), 380 nurses and midwives, 3 dentistry personnel, 2 pharmaceutical personnel and 212 community health workers. There are 17 hospital beds per 10,000 population.

In 2010, 90 per cent of the population had access to improved drinking water sources and 57 per cent of the population used improved sanitation.

In 2010, the infant mortality rate was 12 per 1000 live births and the under-five mortality rate was 14 per 1,000 population. Most common causes of death include prematurity (15 per cent), pneumonia (9 per cent), malaria (19 per cent), and diarrhoea (3 per cent). (Source: http://www.who.int, World Health Statistics 2012)

EDUCATION

Under the Condominium government there was no unified educational system; schooling was conducted on both French and English patterns. The present national education network is under review in order to create a uniform system.

Primary education is available for most children. There was a nominal fee charged, but this was abolished for primary level education after independence resulting in an almost 100 per cent attendance rate. However only about 20 per cent of students continue onto secondary level. The University of the South Pacific has an extension centre in Port Vila. Adult literacy was 53 per cent in 2004. Figures from UNESCO for 2007 put primary school enrolment at 86 per cent for girls and 88 per cent for boys, with a teacher to pupil ration of 20:1. Figures from 2003 put spending on education as equivalent to 9.5 per cent of GDP.

RELIGION

Almost 90 per cent population are a combination of Presbyterians, Catholics and Anglicans, while the remainder follow a syncretic sect called John Frum. There are small Muslim and Bah'ai communities.

Vanuatu has a religious liberty rating of 8 on a scale of 1 to 10 (10 is most freedom). (Source: World Religion Database)

COMMUNICATIONS AND MEDIA

Newspapers
The Vanuatu Weekly, a government run newspaper is published weekly. Other newspapers include the Nasara, a private weekly, and the Vanuatu Daily Post (URL: http://vanuatudaily.com/), the Port Vila Presse and the Ni-Vanuatu (private weekly).

Broadcasting
The state-owned Vanuatu Broadcasting and Television Corporation operates Television Blong Vanuatu which broadcasts in French and English. Multi-channel subscription TV is also available. The state-owned broadcaster also operates two radio stations and operate alongside private TV stations.

Telecommunications
Recent estimates (2008) show that around 10,000 land lines are in use in the islands as well as nearly 36,000 mobile phones. Around 17,500 people have internet access.

ENVIRONMENT

Main environmental concerns for Vanuatu are deforestation and access to fresh water.

Vanuatu is a party to the following international agreements: Antarctic-Marine Living Resources, Biodiversity, Climate Change, Climate Change-Kyoto Protocol, Desertification, Endangered Species, Law of the Sea, Marine Dumping, Ozone Layer Protection, Ship Pollution, and Tropical Timber 94.

According to EIA figures, in 2010, Vanuatu's emissions from the consumption of fossil fuels totalled 0.15 million metric tons of carbon dioxide.

VATICAN CITY
The State of the Vatican City
Stato della Città del Vaticano

Capital: Vatican City (Population estimate: 800)

Head of State: Pope Francis I (Sovereign) (page 1426)

National Flag: Divided pale-wise yellow and white, the white bearing the crossed keys of St. Peter and a triple crown in silver and gold

CONSTITUTION AND GOVERNMENT

The State of the City of the Vatican is the territory of the temporal sovereignty of the Holy See, the residence of the Pope, Bishop of Rome, Vicar of Jesus Christ and Supreme Pontiff of the Universal Church. The Papacy is the oldest monarchy in Europe but Vatican City is an entirely new State. It was established by the Lateran Treaty of 11 February 1929, signed in the Palace of the Lateran in Rome by Cardinal Pietro Gasparri, Papal Secretary of State, on behalf of Pope Pius XI, and by Benito Mussolini, Prime Minister of Italy, on behalf of King Victor Emmanuel III. Ratifications were exchanged on 7 June of the same year and all the treaty's provisions thereupon came into force.

No country outside Italy was involved in the treaty negotiations. Four days before the signing, however, the diplomatic corps accredited to the Holy See were invited to the Vatican and informed by Cardinal Gasparri that a treaty had been arranged, and on 9 March they returned to the Vatican to offer their congratulations to the Pope. Great Britain was among the first states to recognise the Pope as Sovereign of Vatican City.

Vatican City is an integral part of the Holy See but in some respects it is a distinct entity, and as a sovereign State it has some unique features. The autonomy of Vatican City as a State depends upon the spiritual sovereignty of the Holy See, and is totally at its service. The temporal sovereignty of the Vatican City State has no other ultimate justification for its existence than that of making it possible for the Pope to exercise his spiritual mission more freely. It deals with other States only in regard to its own internal affairs: with Italy for postal, travel, trade and economic facilities, and with other states for postal and economic matters. It has no parliament and no diplomatic corps of its own. The sovereignty of the Papal State belongs to the Holy See.

All Papal envoys, both those with and those without diplomatic status, represent the Holy See; they are the representatives of the Pope as Supreme Pontiff of the Universal Church. All diplomatic missions 'at the Vatican' - there are 139 embassies - are in fact accredited to the Holy See. By virtue of the treaty, foreign envoys reside in Rome outside Vatican City, with all the normal diplomatic rights guaranteed to them even if their countries have no diplomatic relations with Italy. During the Second World War, the envoys of the Allied nations were accommodated as the guests of the Pope in buildings on Vatican soil, and enjoyed the envoy's right to travel at any time, in peace or war, across Italian territory to their own countries and back to Vatican City, just as the Holy See's diplomatic envoys and couriers of any nationality, as well as Church dignitaries, have the right to go to and from the City.

All that foreign envoys require for this is an endorsement on their passport by a Papal representative in their country of origin; this representative need not possess diplomatic status. Since 16 January 1982 the Holy See's Mission in London has enjoyed full diplomatic status.

In the Lateran Treaty the Holy See declared that 'it wishes to remain and will remain extraneous to the temporal competitions between other states and to international congresses convened for such a purpose, unless the parties in the conflict unanimously appeal to its mission of peace'. The Holy See within Vatican City is thus a perpetual neutral party; the Holy See reserving, however, 'the right in any case to the exercise of its moral and spiritual power', a right which enables the Pope in wartime to continue to speak freely and take whatever action he deems right and necessary to hasten the return of peace or to mitigate the severity of the conflict.

The Lateran Treaty, in spite of its importance, was regarded by Pope Pius XI as secondary, with regard to the religious welfare of Italy, to the Lateran Concordat which was negotiated and signed at the same time. The concordat, in the words of the Pope, 'gave Italy back to God and God back to Italy'; its purpose was 'to regulate the status of Religion and of the Church in Italy'. In its chief provisions, Italy recognised the Catholic faith as the religion of the State and guaranteed its free exercise, recognised the secrecy of sacramental confession, restored Catholic teaching in the state schools and recognised marriage as a sacrament and as indissoluble. One of the principal concessions to Italy was the right to object to - but solely on political grounds - the appointments of bishops who were to govern dioceses in Italy, except the diocese of Rome and the dioceses of the six Cardinal Bishops, which are in the vicinity of Rome. On 18 February 1984 the amended (or 'revised') text of the Concordat was signed by Cardinal Casaroli, Secretary of State, for the Holy See, and Mr. Bettino Craxi, Prime Minister, for the Italian Government. The Holy See is free to appoint Bishops in Italy without any political conditions imposed by the Government. The Bishops and the clergy are responsible for their own maintenance.

Vatican City originated in a territorial sense with the grants of lands to the Pope after the Peace of Constantine in the fourth century, and developed to the point where the Popes, through governors, ruled over territory - the States of the Church - covering more than 16,000

sq. miles with a total population of 3,000,000. Effective sovereignty over these possessions, after a series of seizures, finally came to an end in 1870, when the forces of King Victor Emmanuel entered Rome itself.

The seizure of the Eternal City, the City of the Popes, was the source of what became known as the Roman Question - the dispute between the Holy See and the Kingdom of Italy. Italy, while proclaiming certain immunities for the Pope, officially regarded him as an Italian citizen. Pius IX, the Pope reigning in 1870, refused to accept this position and, unwilling to place himself in the appearance of subjection by stepping upon the territory seized from him, became the 'Prisoner of the Vatican'. Each of his successors - Leo XIII, St. Pius X, Benedict XV and Pius XI - upon his election, made a formal official protest at their position and declined to appear in public outside St. Peter's. Italy made an ill-fated unilateral attempt to settle the dispute by enacting in 1871 the Law of Guarantees. This acknowledged the Pope's person as sacred and inviolable, offered him royal honours and protection, provided for extra-territorial rights for the Vatican and other Papal buildings, and set aside a yearly sum of 3,500,000 lire for the Pope. All this was refused, the Popes maintaining that their sovereignty depended upon divine right and not upon a civil concession. In 1929, after negotiations between the Italian Government and the Holy See, the Lateran Treaty was signed. The Lateran Treaty declared that the Law of Guarantees was abolished and the Roman Question settled permanently. The Treaty gave visible, tangible, territorial witness to the fact of the temporal sovereignty of the Pope and his independence of any state.

St. Peter's Square is part of the Papal State but the Holy See agreed that it shall normally be open to the public and policed by Italian police. The powers of these police cease at the foot of the steps leading to St. Peter's, and they must not mount them or enter the basilica unless invited to do so by the Vatican authorities. When special ceremonies are to be held in the square, they must, unless invited to remain, withdraw beyond the frontier - the line continuing from the outer side of the two arms of Bernini's colonnade which, as it were, embrace the piazza. Outstanding Papal ceremonies here since the treaty include the Coronation of Pope Paul VI (1963) and the closing ceremony of the Second Vatican Council (1965), the proclamation in 1950 of the dogma of the bodily assumption of the Mother of God, and the canonization of Pope Pius X in 1954. In other articles, Italy agreed to assure the Vatican City of an adequate supply of water, to link the State railways with the Vatican railway, and to provide for the connection of the Papal State directly with other states by the telegraphic, telephonic, radio-telegraphic and postal services of Vatican City. Provision was also made for the circulation in Italy of land vehicles and aircraft belonging to Vatican City. Other aircraft are not allowed to fly over the City. Italy undertook not to allow the construction on land adjoining the Papal State of buildings that would overlook Vatican City, and decided to demolish some that were already there. Regarding the person of the Sovereign Pontiff as sacred and inviolable, Italy declared that attempts against his life and incitement to commit such attempts would be punishable by the same penalties as those prescribed for attempts against the person of the King of Italy.

Administration
The head of the Administration of Vatican City, under Pope Pius XI, was a layman, the Marquis Camillo Serafini. He continued in office under Pope Pius XII, but the Pope instituted a commission of five Cardinals, with an ecclesiastic as secretary and a layman with the title of special delegate. The Governor, hitherto subject only to the Pope, now came under the authority of this commission. Since the death of the Marquis Serafini in 1952, the office of Governor has been retained but has remained vacant. A Consultative Council of 30 appointed members (all lay persons with a lay President) was established in March 1968. There are four main Departments, all under the direction of laymen - one for the Vatican Art Galleries and Museum, another for technical services, the third for economic services, and the fourth for the health services.

Vatican citizenship is normally granted by reason of employment by the Holy See. A citizen who ceases to be subject to the Holy See's sovereignty - a Swiss Guard, for example, at the end of his service - loses his citizenship. In such cases the Lateran Treaty provides that Italy shall then regard them as Italian citizens unless they possess citizenship of another country. Catholics are not subjects of the Pope as Sovereign of the State of Vatican City. By virtue of the Lateran Treaty a number of buildings outside the Papal State are recognised as the property of the Holy See and have extra-territorial rights. The chief of these are the Basilica and Palace of the Lateran (the palace was the residence of the Popes for 1,000 years from the beginning of the fourth century; the original palace was the gift of the Emperor Constantine); the Basilica of St. Mary Major; the Basilica of St. Paul Outside-the-Walls; the Pope's summer residence at Castelgandolfo in the Alban Hills; and buildings which house offices of the Roman Curia, whose members - Cardinals, bishops, priests and some laymen - are the closest collaborators of the Pope in the government and administration of the Universal Church.

Extra-territorial rights are enjoyed by any church in any part of Italy if and when the Pope is present at religious ceremonies taking place in them. For the spiritual and religious administration of Vatican City, the Pope has a Vicar-General (distinct from the Cardinal Vicar of Rome). The Cardinal Archpriest of St. Peter's Basilica is also Vicar-General for the spiritual and religious administration of Vatican City.

Vicar-General: Cardinal Angelo Comastri

St. Peter's is not the Pope's cathedral. The title belongs to the Archbasilica of St. John Lateran, on the other side of Rome; it is this church of which a new Pope 'takes possession' soon after his election as Bishop of Rome.

VATICAN CITY

St. Peter's is not the Pope's cathedral. The title belongs to the Archbasilica of St. John Lateran, on the other side of Rome; it is this church of which a new Pope 'takes possession' soon after his election as Bishop of Rome.

Secretariat of State (as at June 2013)
Secretary of State: Cardinal Tarcisio Bertone
Assistant Secretary of State for General Affairs: Archbishop Giovanni Angelo Becciu
Secretary for Relations with States: His Eminence Archbishop Dominique Mamberti
Member: Archbishop Luciano Suriani
Member: Archbishop Marco Dino Brogi

Pontifical Commission for the Vatican City State
President: Archbishop Giuseppe Bertello

Office of the Holiness the Pope, URL: http://www.vatican.va

Elections
On April 2 2005 Pope John Paul II died, having served as Pope for 26 years. Following the funeral, elections were held and Cardinal Joseph Ratzinger was elected on April 19 and chose the name of Benedict XVI.

On February 11 2012, Pope Benedict XVI announced that he would be resigning as Pope on February 28, he felt that at the age of 85 he was too old to carry out his duties. He was the first Pope to resign for nearly 600 years.

Cardinal Bergoglio of Buenos Aires was elected Pope on March 13 2013 and took the name of Francis I. He became the first non-European Pope since the 8th Century and the first Pope from South America.

Only Cardinals under the age of 80 are eligible to vote in papal elections. Following the death of a Pope the College of Cardinals enters the Sistine chapel, in what is known as the Conclave, 15 days after the death. The Cardinals will not come out again until a new Pope is elected, the elections are held in absolute secrecy from the outside world. After being locked inside the chapel, the Cardinals hold up to four ballots each day, two in the morning and two in the afternoon. Each Cardinal writes the name of his chosen candidate on the ballot paper before placing it on the altar, after each ballot the papers are read out and if there is no clear winner the papers are burned and those watching outside can see the smoke, when a Pope has been elected, chemicals are added to the ballot papers to turn the smoke white, so that the watching crowds know a new Pope has been elected. The elected Pope must have received two thirds of the vote

Diplomatic Representation
US Embassy, Villa Domiziana, Via delle Terme Deciane 26, 00153 Rome, Italy
Tel: +39 06 4674 3428, fax: +39 06 575 8346, e mail: usemb.holysee@agora.it, URL: http://vatican.usembassy.gov
Ambassador: Dr. Miguel Humberto Diaz
British Embassy, 91 Via dei Condotti, 1-00187, Rome, Italy. Tel: +39 06 6992 3561, fax: +39 06 6994 0684, e-mail: HolySee@fco.gov.uk, URL: http://ukinholysee.fco.gov.uk/en
Ambassador: Nigel Baker
Apostolic Nunciature in USA, 3339 Massachusetts Avenue, NW, Washington, DC 20008, USA. Tel: +1 202 333 7121
Ambassador: His Excellency Archbishop Carlo Maria Vigano
Apostolic Nunciature in UK, 54 Parkside, London, SW19 5NE, UK. Tel: +44 (0)20 8946 1410, fax: +44 (0)20 8947 2494
Ambassador: His Excellency Antonio Mennini
Permanent Observer to the UN, New York, URL: http://www.holyseemission.org/
Archbishop Francis Assisi Chullikatt

LEGAL SYSTEM

The pope has absolute judicial powers within the city. The laws of the Papal State are based on the Constitution, the Code of Civil Procedure of Vatican City State, Canon law, and Laws enacted by the City's Administration.

Following the creation of the Vatican City State in 1929, there was little separation between the Holy See and the temporal government, but the court system has been reorganized three times since its inception. Currently, there are four levels of the judiciary, dealing with both civil and ecclesiastical cases. The first level courts are responsible for such matters as small claims, traffic tickets, and validation of marriages, and are presided over by one judge. These are followed by Tribunals, whose three judges are appointed by the Pope. They can hear both civil and penal matters, but most criminal cases are referred to the Italian judiciary. Next is the Court of Appeal; all four judges are nominated by the Pope and serve a five-year term. They hear appeals from the Vatican City's Disciplinary Commission, oversee the Vatican's group of lawyers and handle employment issues from the Labour Office of the Apostolic See. Most of the judges are also judges on the Roman Rota. At the top of the judicial system is the Supreme Court of Appeals (Corte di Cassazione), whose president is also the prefect of the Apostolic Signatura, the highest canon law court in the Catholic Church. The other two judges are also cardinals and members of the Apostolic Signatura. The Supreme Court hears appeals from the Court of Appeal and has original jurisdiction over those penal cases against cardinals and bishops which the Pope does not handle personally.

When the Lateran treaties were signed in 1949 Vatican City automatically adopted the laws of Italy, but Pope Benedict XVI announced recently that many of the laws of Italy were in conflict with the Church's teachings. Each Italian law will now be examined before being adopted or rejected by the Vatican.

AREA AND POPULATION

Area
Vatican City covers an area of 108.3 acres or 0.44 sq. km. In the main, it consists of the Vatican Palace and gardens; St. Peter's Basilica (the largest church in the world); a number of other separate churches; numerous other buildings which house, for example, the Vatican Polyglot Press, Vatican Radio, quarters of the Swiss Guard and other forces of the Holy See; and residences for members of the City's administration and employees of the Holy See.

Figures for 2011 put the population at 850 inhabitants. The official languages are Italian and Latin.

To view a map, please consult http://www.lib.utexas.edu/maps/cia08/holy_see_sm_2008.gif

COMMUNICATIONS AND TRANSPORT

Roads
The No. 64 bus from central Rome goes to Vatican City.

EDUCATION

In Italy, in the state schools, everyone has the right to receive adequate instruction in his or her own religion. The Holy See operates several academic institutions which although based in Rome are connected to the Vatican.

RELIGION

Under the revised Concordat, the Catholic Faith is no longer regarded in Italy as 'the religion of the State', but the Italian Government guarantees the freedom to exercise all religions, with due regard to the preservation of public order.

COMMUNICATIONS AND MEDIA

Newspapers
L'Osservatore Romano, F. 1861. Italian; Daily. Semi-official organ of the Holy See. Reports religious matters and general news. Its editorial board and staff number around 20 reporters. Weekly editions are published in English, French, German, Polish, Portuguese and Spanish. URL: http://www.vatican.va/news_services

Broadcasting
Radio-Vatican was founded in 1931. One of the most powerful stations in Europe, it broadcasts on international frequencies, satellite and internet connections. URL: http://www.vaticanradio.org

STATES OF THE WORLD

1345

VENEZUELA
Bolivarian Republic of Venezuela
República Bolivariana de Venezuela

Capital: Caracas (Population estimate, 2010: 3.2 million)

Head of State: Nicolas Maduro Moros (page 1469)

Vice President: Jorge Arreaza (page 1379)

National Flag: A tricolour fesswise, yellow, blue, red. In the centre of the blue band are seven five-pointed white stars forming an arc. To the hoist side of the yellow band is the coat of arms. In 2006, modifications were made; an eighth star was added to the arc and the white horse on the coat of arms now faces left, not right. There was a five-year transition period for the change-over.

CONSTITUTION AND GOVERNMENT

Constitution

Venezuela gained independence from Spain in 1830. Its first democratically elected government came to power in 1947. Under the 1961 constitution, Venezuela is a Federal Republic.

Until December 1999 power was vested in the President who appointed and presided over a Council of Ministers, and was responsible for submitting draft legislation to Congress and appointing members of the cabinet. Legislative power lay in a bicameral National Congress, in which the Senate had 47 elected members and the Chamber of Deputies had 199 life members. The President and National Congress were elected every five years.

In December 1999 a Constitutional Assembly of 131 members re-drafted the 1961 constitution and submitted it to the people of Venezuela in a public referendum. The changes to the old constitution were approved by voters.

According to the terms of the 1999 constitution, the country is now known as the 'Bolivarian Republic of Venezuela'; the president is able to seek re-election for a second term; the presidential term is increased from five years to six years; and the new post of vice president was created. In November 2000 the president was given new powers for one year to bypass congress when enacting laws on finance, infrastructure, personal and legal security, science and technology, the public sector and industry and agriculture. On the 15th February 2009, Venezuelans voted to lift limits on terms in office for elected officials, allowing President Hugo Chavez to stand for re-election in 2012. The presidential term was also increased to seven years.

To consult the constitution, please visit:
http://www.tsj.gov.ve/legislacion/legislacion.shtml (Spanish)

International Relations

Diplomatic relations with the USA have been strained in recent years. President Chávez ordered the expulsion of the U.S. Ambassador on September 11, 2008 in solidarity with the Bolivian government's decision to expel the U.S. Ambassador in La Paz. The U.S. Government ordered the reciprocal expulsion of the Venezuelan Ambassador in Washington. Conversely, commercial ties between the two countries are strong; the USA is Venezuela's most important trading partner. Venezuela is one of the top four suppliers of foreign oil to the United States. Venezuela is a major transit country for cocaine and heroin, and counternarcotics cooperation between the U.S. and Venezuela deteriorated over 2004-05. In August 2005, the Venezuelan authorities accused the U.S. Drug Enforcement Administration (DEA) of espionage and stopped all cooperation with the DEA.

President Chávez champions regional integration and the reduction of US influence in the world. He aims to achieve these through PetroCaribe and PetroSur petroleum initiatives, the South American Community of Nations, and the establishment of the Bolivarian Alternative for the Americas. In 2006, Venezuela officially joined the Southern Common Market, MERCOSUR, though full membership depends on conformity with the bloc's economic regulations. Venezuela has longstanding border disputes with Colombia and Guyana; Venezuela claims roughly three-quarters of Guyana's territory. Venezuela maintains very close relations with Cuba.

Relations with Colombia have been strained in recent years, due to the Colombian government's continued alliance with the USA. Matters reached a crisis point in March 2008, when Colombian armed forces made a cross-border raid into Ecuador, and killed a senior Farc rebel Raul Reyes. President Chavez mobilised troops along Venezuelan-Colombian border. President Uribe of Colombia accused Sr. Chavez of sponsoring and financing the Farc rebels. The crisis was defused when the three leaders met at a Rio Group summit on 7th March.

In recent years, President Chávez has strengthened relations with Iran through economic and social agreements and by publicly supporting Iran's controversial nuclear programme. He has also strengthened ties with Russia and China, and increased the number of Venezuelan embassies in Africa and Asia.

Recent Events

In 1999 President Chavez introduced a constitutional provision allowing for a recall referendum to be held against any elected official after they reach the mid point of their term of office. In 2004 a total of 3.4 million signatures against President Chavez were gathered by the opposition, of which the National Electoral Council ruled only 1.9 million were valid. However, at the end of May 2004, the electoral council ruled that the required number of signatures had been obtained and a referendum was held on 15 August 2004. Mr Chavez won the vote and announced that he would stand for another six-year term at the 2006 elections.

In January 2005 President Chavez began a programme of land redistribution which he said would bring justice for the poor.

In July 2006 Venezuela joined the Latin American trade group, Mercosur. President Chavez also visited several countries to forge new alliances. He made arms deals with the Russians, much to the consternation of the United States who felt that they exceeded Venezuela's defensive needs. He also visited Iran and pledged support.

In January 2007, following his re-election, President Chavez announced further steps towards making Venezuela a socialist state; these included the nationalisation of key industries, such as energy and telecoms, and more state control over the country's Central Bank. He also announced his intention to seek additional powers to legislate by presidential decree. In February, President Chavez threatened to nationalise shops and supermarkets that were selling meat above a government-set price.

In April 2007, there were protests at the President's decision to close the country's oldest private TV station, Rado Caracas Television (RCTV), often critical of the government. Lawyers for RCTV took the case to Venezuela's Supreme Court, and to the Inter-American Court of Human Rights. The case was seen as a fight between a government intent on increasing its control, and those who felt that the freedoms of individuals were being eroded. On 27th May 2007, RCTV ceased public broadcasts, and was replaced by a state-run TV station, amid protests from its supporters.

On May Day 2007, President Hugo Chavez announced his intention to withdraw Venezuela from the International Monetary Fund and the World Bank. As the country has settled its IMF debt, the withdrawal was largely a symbolic gesture. The President aims to set up a 'Bank of the South', backed by Venezuelan oil revenues, which will finance projects in South America.

On the 2nd May, the government announced that it had taken control of the massive Orinoco Belt oil projects as part of the nationalisation drive. Many of the world's biggest oil companies agreed to transfer operational control to the government. The four projects can refine about 600,000 barrels of crude oil a day.

In October 2007, the Venezuelan government began a final debate on more changes to the Constitution, which was then subject to a referendum in December. The changes would remove term limits for the presidency, and extend the term of office from six years to seven, remove the central bank's autonomy and cut the working week. Two days before the debate, President Chavez added 25 amendments to the 33 passed by Congress, including proposals to detain citizens without charge in emergencies. Although there are no opposition politicians in the National Assembly, since most of the anti-Chavez parties boycotted the last election in 2005, some members of parliament questioned the way that the late changes were introduced. In December, 51 per cent of the people voted against the changes to the Constitution in a referendum; this was a major blow to the President's plan to make Venezuela a socialist republic. More than 40 per cent of Venezuelans did not vote.

In December 2007, Venezuela's clocks went back permanently by half an hour. President Chavez effected the change in record time, causing widespread confusion. The change puts Venezuela on its own time zone.

In January 2008, John Walters, director of the US Office of National Drug Control Policy, accused President Chavez of being a "major facilitator" of the cocaine trade, arguing that failure to deal with the problem amounted to complicity. US officials believe that around a third of Colombia's output of 600 tonnes of cocaine a year now passes through Venezuela.

On 2nd March 2008, President Chavez mobilised thousands of troops and tanks to the border with Colombia, in response to the killing by the Colombian military of Farc rebel leader Raul Reyes one mile across the border in Ecuador. He also announced that Venezuela's embassy in Colombia would close. Mr Chavez had been mediating with Farc to secure the release of hostages the rebels hold; six have so far been freed under this initiative. On the 4th March, President Uribe of Colombia said he would ask the International Criminal Court to bring genocide charges against President Chavez, accusing him of sponsoring and financing the Farc rebels. The crisis was defused when the three leaders met at a Rio Group summit on 7th March. A 20-point declaration by the Organization of American States (OAS), including a promise by President Uribe that Colombia's forces would never again violate the territory of its neighbours, sealed the reconciliation.

In May 2008, President Hugo Chavez signed a decree to nationalise Venezuela's biggest steelmaker, Ternium-Sidor. Argentina's Techint, which owns 60 per cent of it, was given until the end of June to hand it over. Since 2006, the Venezuelan government has taken over foreign-controlled companies including cement, telecoms, oil, gas and electricity firms.

In November 2008, Venezuelans voted in elections to choose new state governors and more than 300 mayors across the country. The polls were seen as a critical test for President Chavez; his government's failure to control crime and inflation were voters' main concerns. The opposition won the mayoral election in Caracas, a post viewed as the second most important in the country, as well as five governorships. However, the remaining 17 governorships were retained by Chavez supporters.

On the 15th February 2009, Venezuelans voted to lift limits on terms in office for elected officials, allowing President Hugo Chavez to stand for re-election in 2012. He had argued he needed another ten years in office to consolidate his 'socialist revolution'. Critics believe the result of the referendum will concentrate too much power in the presidency.

On the 22nd March, President Chavez unveiled a series of measures to offset falling oil revenues that account for about 50 per cent of the national budget. He proposed to cut the 2009 budget by 6.7 per cent ($5 billion), based on oil prices at $40 a barrel, not the $60-a-barrel forecast when the budget was drafted. He also pledged salary cuts for senior public officials, but promised to increase the minimum wage by 20 per cent; the collapse in oil prices threatens the high spending social programmes that have made him popular with the poor majority. The announcement came shortly after the government had sent the army to take control of the country's key airports and sea ports. In May, President Chavez sent troops to take over companies that provide services for the oil industry, thereby placing hundreds of boats, several ports and an estimated 8,000 oil workers under state control. The state-owned oil company PDVSA had owed billions of dollars to foreign and local service providers, and argued that the contractors should have lowered their fees in line with the lower oil prices.

In late July 2009, Sweden asked Venezuela to explain how Swedish-made anti-tank rocket launchers, sold to Venezuela in the 1980s, had ended up in the hands of Colombia's Farc rebels. Colombian troops had recovered the weapons in a raid on a Farc camp. Colombia has long claimed that Venezuela has backed the left-wing rebels.

In an attempt to increase revenue from oil exports, President Chavez devalued the bolivar in January 2010, by 17 per cent against the US dollar for key imports and by 50 per cent for no-essential items.

The global economic crisis also affected Venezuela: the economy shrank by 5.8 per cent in the last quarter of 2009.

Parliamentary elections took place in September 2010. The ruling party won but with a reduced majority.

In June 2011 President Chavez undertook surgery for cancer.

In November 2011 the government introduced price controls in an attempt to reduce the high annual inflation rate (currently standing at over 2 per cent).

Venezuela hosted the inaugural meeting of the Community of Latin American and Caribbean States (Celac) in December 2011. The US is excluded from the group. In July 2012, Venezuela became a full member of the trading bloc Mercosur.

The presidential election took place in October 2012. Mr Chavez won a fourth term of office with approximately 55 per cent of the vote. Mr Chavez missed his inauguration in January 2013 due to health reasons. The inauguration was postponed indefinitely.

On March 6 2013 President Chavez died aged 58 of cancer, he had been ill for some time and had undergone several operations in Cuba. Following his death, Vice-President Nicolas Maduro assumed the presidency until an election was held in April, Maduro won the election.

Legislature

Under the terms of the new 1999 constitution the old Constitutional Assembly was dissolved in January 2000 and a new 21-member legislative body appointed by the Constitutional Assembly, the National Legislative Commission, was given the power to draft laws, consider government spending requests and approve international treaties. The National Legislative Commission handed over power to the new, unicameral National Assembly following elections in May 2000.

Venezuela's unicameral legislature is the National Assembly (*Asamblea Nacional*), which has 165 members directly elected for a five-year term.

National Assembly, Palacio Federal Legislativo, Primer Piso, Esq. Monjas a San Francisco, Caracas, Venezuela. Tel: +58 212 483 6780 (President), fax: +58 212 482 9516 (President), URL: http://www.asambleanacional.gov.ve/
President: Cilia Adela Flores

Cabinet (Council of Ministers) (as at June 2013)
Executive Vice President: Jorge Arreaza (page 1379)
Minister of Justice and the Interior: Gen. Miguel Rodriguez Torres
Minister of Finance: Nelson Jose Merentes Diaz (page 1476)
Minister of Defence: Admiral Diego Molero
Minister of Education: Maryann Hanson
Minister of Sport: Alejandra Benitez
Minister of Health: Isabel Iturria (page 1447)
Minister of the Secretariat of the Presidency: Carmen Melendez
Minister of Labour and Social Security: Maria Cristina Iglesias
Minister of Environment and Natural Resources: Dante Rivas (page 1503)
Minister of Higher Education: Pedro Calzadilla
Minister of Penitentiaries: Maria Iris Varela
Minister of Trade: Alejandro Fleming Cabrera (page 1425)
Minister of Tourism: Andres Izarra
Minister of Land Transport: Haiman El Troudi

Minister of Communications & Information: Ernesto Villegas
Minister of Nutrition: Felix Osorio
Minister of Culture: Fidel Barbarito
Minister of Housing & Infrastructure: Ricardo Molina Penaloza
Minister of Indigenous Peoples: Aloha Nunez
Minister of Communal Affairs: Reinaldo Iturriza
Minister of Women's Affairs & Gender Equality: Andreina Tarazon
Minister of Electricity: Jesse Chacon
Minister of Science & Technology: Manuel Fernandez Melendez
Minister of Agriculture and Lands: Yvan Gil

Ministries

Office of the President, Palacio de Miraflores, Avenida Urdaneta, Caracas 1010, Venezuela. Tel: +58 212 810811 / 862 5990 / 862 3079, fax: +58 212 571 0563, e-mail: presidencia@venezuela.gov.ve, URL: http://www.presidencia.gob.ve/
Ministry of the Interior and Justice, Edificio MRI, PB, Avenida Urdaneta, Esquina de Carmelitas, Caracas 1010, Venezuela. Tel: +58 212 575 0010 / 862 9728 / 837675 / 833371, fax: +58 212 861 1967 / 838452, URL: http://www.minjusticia.gov.ve/
Ministry of Foreign Affairs, Edificio MRE, PB, Avenida Urdaneta, Esquina de Carmelitas, Caracas 1010, Venezuela. Tel: +58 212 862 1085 / 814323 / 815730, fax: +58 212 833633, e-mail: ministro@mre.gov.ve, URL: http://www.mre.gov.ve/
Ministry of Finance, Edf Norte, piso 3 oficina 312, Centro Simón Bolívar, Caracas 1010, Venezuela. Tel: +58 212 419406 / 413444 / 419811, fax: +58 212 481 5953, URL: http://www.mh.gov.ve/
Ministry of Defence, Fuerte Tiuna, Conejo Blanco, El Valle, Caracas 1090, Venezuela. Tel: +58 212 693 1405 / 607 1604 / 607 1606, fax: +58 212 662 8829, URL: http://www.mindefensa.mil.ve/
Ministry of Education and Sport, Esquina de Salas, Edificio Ministerio de Educación, Nivel mezzanina, Esquina de Salas, Caracas 1010, Venezuela. Tel: +58 212 564 0025 / 5068692, fax: +58 212 5640370 / 562 0175, URL: http://www.me.gov.ve/
Ministry of Higher Education, URL: http://www.mes.gov.ve/mes/
Ministry of Health and Social Development, Edificio Sur, Piso 9, Centro Simón Bolívar, Caracas 1010, Venezuela. Tel: +58 212 481 9691 / 481 8250, fax: +58 212 483 4016, URL: http://www.msds.gov.ve/
Ministry of Production and Commerce, Avenida Lecuna, Torre Este, Piso 13, Parque Central, Caracas 1010, Venezuela. Tel: +58 212 509 0241 / 509 0272 / 509 0257, fax: +58 212 509 0118 / 509 0305, e-mail: ministro@mpc.gov.ve, URL: http://www.mpc.gov.ve/
Ministry of Labour, Torre Sur, Piso 5, Centro Simón Bolívar, Caracas 1010, Venezuela. Tel: +58 212 481 1368 / 483 4211, fax: +58 212 483 8914, URL: http://www.mintra.gov.ve
Ministry of Energy and Oil, Edificio Petroleos de Venezuela, Torre Oeste, Av. Libertador con Av. Empalme, Urb. La Campiña, Parroquia El Recreo, Caracas 1010, Venezuela. Tel: +58 212 708 7338, fax: +58 212 708 7598, e-mail: dazaroy@hotmail.com, URL: http://www.menpet.gob.ve
Ministry of Environment and Natural Resources, Torre Sur, Piso 18, Centro Simón Bolívar, Caracas 1010, Venezuela. Tel: +58 212 481 7008 / 408 1071 / 408 1076, fax: +58 212 408 1464, URL: http://www.marnr.gov.ve/
Ministry of Planning and Development, Torre Oeste, Piso 26, Avenida Lecuna, Parque Central, Caracas 1010, Venezuela. Tel: +58 212 507 0811, fax: +58 212 573 6419, e-mail: webmaster@mpd.gov.ve, URL: http://www.mpd.gov.ve/
Ministry of Science and Technology, Final Av. Principal Los Cortijos de Lourdes, Edf. Maploca I., Caracas, Venezuela. Tel: +58 212 237 2114 / 4886, fax: +58 212 239 6056, e-mail: mct@mct.gov.ve, URL: http://www.mct.gov.ve/
Ministry of Agriculture and Lands, Av. Lecuna, Torre Este, Piso 6, Parque Central, Caracas 1050, Venezuela. Tel: +58 212 509 0357, fax: +58 212 509 0258, e-mail: estagric@mat.gov.ve, URL: http://www.mat.gob.ve
Office of the Attorney General, Esquinas de Misericordia a Pele El Ojo, Avenida Méjico, Caracas 1010, Venezuela. Tel: +58 212 509 7211, e-mail: mp@fiscalia.gov.ve, URL http://www.fiscalia.gov.ve
Ministry of Culture, Av. Panteón, Foro Libertador, Edif. Archivo General de la Nación, Caracas 1010, Venezuela. Tel: +58 212 509 5600, e-mail: mcu@ministeriodelacultura.gob.ve, URL: http://www.ministeriodelacultura.gob.ve
Ministry of Indigenous Peoples, Av. Universidad, antiguo Edificio Sudeban, piso 8, Caracas 1010, Venezeula. Tel: +58 212 543 1599, fax: +58 212 543 3100, e-mail: atencionalindigena@minpi.gob.ve, URL: http://www.minpi.gob.ve
Ministry of Science, Technology and Intermediate Industry, Esquina El Chorro, Torre MCT, Av. Universidad, Caracas 1010, Venezuela. Tel: +58 212 210 3401, fax: +58 212 210 3536, e-mail: mct@mct.gob.ve, URL: http://www.mct.gob.ve
Ministry of Sports, Av. Intercomunal Montalban, S/N, Urbanización Montalban, La Vega, Distrito Capital, Caracas 1020, Venezuela. Tel: +58 212 443 2682, URL: http://www.mppdeportes.gob.ve
Ministry of Tourism, Edif. Mintur, Av. Francisco de Miranda con Av. Ppal. de La Floresta, Caracas 1010, Venezuela. Tel: +58 212 208 4511, e-mail: webmaster@mintur.gob.ve, URL: http://www.mintur.gob.ve
Ministry of Trade, Torre Oeste de Parque Central, pisos 6-14, Caracas 1010, Venezuela. Tel: +58 212 509 0690, fax: +58 212 730 6502, e-mail: ministro@mincomercio.gob.ve, URL: http://www.mpc.gov.ve
Ministry of Transportation and Communications, Parque Central, Torre Este, Núcleo 3, Piso 34, Avenida Lecuna, Caracas 1010, Venezuela.
Ministry of Women's Affairs and Gender Equality, Boulevard Panteòn, Esquina de Jesuitas Parroquia Altagracia, Torre Bandagro, Pisos 1, 2 y 3, Caracas 1010, Venezuela. Tel: +58 212 860 8214, fax: +58 212 861 9816, URL: http://www.inamujer.gob.ve

Major Political Parties

Coalition for Democratic Unity (MUD) (The main parties included are: Democratic Action (URL: http://www.acciondemocratica.org.ve/); COPEI (URL: http://www.copeivenezuela.com); Movement for Socialism (URL: http://www.masvenezuela.com.ve/); Radical Cause and Red Flag Party (URL: http://bandera-roja.blogspot.co.uk/); Project Venezuela; A New Era (URL: http://www.partidounnuevotiempo.org/inicio/), Justice First (URL: http://www.primerojusticia.org.ve/cms/) and For Social Democracy (URL: http://informe21.com/partido-podemos);

VENEZUELA

Fatherland for All (PPT), URL: http://www.ppt.org.ve/
United Socialist Party of Venezuela (PSUV), URL: http://www.psuv.org.ve

Elections
Voting is mandatory for all Venezuelan citizens over the age of 18.

Venezuela's opposition made gains in regional polls held in November 2008, but President Hugo Chavez's allies held on to 17 of the country's 22 governorships. The opposition took at least three including the two most populous states (Miranda and Zulia), and won the mayoral election in Caracas, a post viewed as the second most important in the country. The president said the outcome was an endorsement of Venezuela's "socialist project". As well as governorships, more than 300 mayoral positions were up for election.

The most recent parliamentary elections took place on 26 September 2010. Unlike the 2005 election there was no boycott by opposition parties and the PSUV accordingly lost a lot of seats. The PSUV won a majority of the first past the post seats and therefore despite a fairly even national vote split between the PSUV and the MUS, the PSUV has a substantial majority in parliament. The PSUV took 48 per cent of the vote and 98 seats (down by 41 from the 2005 election, the MUS took 47 per cent of the popular vote and 67 seats (up 61 from last year) and the PPT 2 seats.

Following the death of President Chavaz in March 2013, Vice-President Nicolas Maduro took over the post until an election could be held. The election was held in April 2013 and Maduro was elected president with 50.7 per cent of the vote against 49.1 per cent for the opposition candidate Henrique Capriles.

Diplomatic Representation
Venezuelan Embassy, UK, 1 Cromwell Road, London, SW7 2HW, United Kingdom. Tel: +44 (0)20 7584 4206, fax: +44 (0)20 7589 8887, e-mail: venezlon@venezlon.demon.co.uk, URL: http://www.venezlon.co.uk
Ambassador: Samuel Moncada
Venezuelan Embassy, 1099 30th Street, NW, Washington DC 20007, USA. Tel: +1 202 342 2214, fax: +1 202 342 6820, e-mail: apaiva@embavenez-us.org, URL: http://venezuela-us.org/
Chargé d'Affaires: Dr Angelo Rivero Santos
British Embassy, Torre La Castellana, Piso 11, Avenida La Principal de la Castellana, La Castellana, Caracas 1061, Venezuela (Postal Address: Embajada Britanica, Apartado 1246, Caracas 1010-A). Tel: +58 21 2 263 8411, fax: +58 21 2 267 1275, fax: britishembassy@internet.ve, URL: http://ukinvenezuela.fco.gov.uk/en
Ambassador: Catherine Nettleton
US Embassy, Calle F con Calle Suapure, Colinas de Valle Arriba, Caracas 1080-A, Venezuela. Tel: +58 212 975 6411 fax: +58 212 975 6710, e-mail: embajada@state.gov, URL: http://caracas.usembassy.gov/
Chargé d' Affaires: James Derham
Permanent Representative of the Bolivarian Republic of Venezuela to the United Nations, 335 East 46th Street, New York, NY 10017, USA. Tel: +1 212 557 2055, fax: +1 212 557 3528, e-mail: venezuela@un.int, URL: http://www.un.int/venezuela/
Ambassador: Jorge Valero Briceño

LEGAL SYSTEM

The judicial branch of government is headed by the Supreme Tribunal of Justice (TSJ) whose 32 justices are appointed by the National Assembly and serve 12-year terms. The judiciary is divided into courts for each main branch of law; Plenary, Constitutional, Political-Administrative, Electoral, Civil, Social and Criminal Cassation Courts. The lower court system consists of Municipal Courts, and Courts of the first instance.

There is also a citizen's branch of federal government, which consists of the attorney general ("fiscal general"), the "defender of the people" or ombudsman, and the comptroller general. The holders of these offices act collectively as the "Republican Moral Council" . Holders of the "citizen power" offices are selected for terms of seven years by the National Assembly.

The human rights situation in Venezuela is currently poor. There have been recent unlawful killings by security forces, as well as arbitrary arrests and intimidation of the political opposition. Discrimination on political grounds has been reported, as well as widespread corruption at all levels of government. The judiciary is seen as corrupt, inefficient, and politicized, and there have been cases of official impunity, and violations of due process.

Venezuela formally abolished the death penalty in 1863, making it the first modern state to do so.

In 2008, a new intelligence law threatened civil liberties as it required Venezuelans to cooperate with intelligence agencies when requested, and allowed security forces to gather evidence through surveillance methods without obtaining a court order. Authorities could withhold evidence from defence lawyers if this was considered to be in the interest of national security. Human rights activists believed that the new law could be used as a weapon to silence those opposed to the government, and that it would violate a suspect's right to a defence. President Chavez withdrew the law in the face of mounting opposition.

Supreme Tribunal of Justice, URL: http://www.tsj.gov.ve/index.shtml (Spanish only)
President: Dr. Luisa Estella Morales Lamuño

Office of the Ombudsman, URL: http://www.defensoria.gob.ve/

LOCAL GOVERNMENT

There are 23 states, Amazonas, Anzoategui, Apure, Aragua, Barinas, Bolívar, Carabobo, Cojedes, Delta Amacuro, Falcón, Guárico, Lara, Mérida, Miranda, Monagas, Nueva Esparta, Portuguesa, Sucre, Táchira, Trujillo, Vargas, Yaracuy and Zulia. There is also one federal district (distrito federal) and one federal dependency (dependencia federal). The federal dependency consists of 11 federally controlled island groups with a total of 72 individual islands. Mayors and governors have been directly elected since 1989. The most recent municipal elections were held in August 2010.

AREA AND POPULATION

Area
Venezuela is situated on the north coast of South America, with Colombia to the west, Brazil to the south and Guyana to the east. Venezuela has a total area of 912,050 sq. km, of which 30,000 sq. km is water, and a coastline of more than 2,800 km.

It is a country of great geographical contrasts, with the Andes mountains and Maracaibo lowlands, the plains in the centre of the country and the Guayana highlands in the south-east. Angel Falls in the Guayana Highlands is the world's highest waterfall. The climate is tropical, with more moderate temperatures in the highlands. The rainy season occurs between May and November.

To view a map, consult http://www.lib.utexas.edu/maps/cia08/venezuela_sm_2008.gif

Population
According to figures from the WHO, the population was estimated at 28.98 million in 2010, with an average annual population growth rate of 1.7 per cent over the period 2000-10. Population density is around 21 persons per sq. km. Nearly 93 per cent of people live in urban areas, with the majority in the northern half of the country. The largest population centre is Caracas, followed by Maracaibo, Ciudad Bolivar, Valencia, Barquisimeto, Maracay, Merida and San Cristobal. Most of the population (62 per cent) is aged between 15 and 60 years, with 29 per cent aged up to 14 years, and 9 per cent aged 61 years or over. The median age is 26 years.

Main ethnic groups are Spanish, Italian, Portuguese, Arab, German, African, and indigenous people. The official language of Venezuela is Spanish but Indian dialects are spoken by about 200,000 Amerindians in the remote interior of the country. Most businesses prefer to speak Spanish, particularly if contacted by letter or fax.

Births, Marriages, Deaths
According to 2010 estimates, the birth rate is 20.6 births per 1,000 population, while the death rate is 4.8 deaths per 1,000 population. Life expectancy at birth in 2009 was 75 years (71 years for men and 78 years for women). Healthy life expectancy is 66 years. The infant mortality rate was 16 deaths per 1,000 live births in 2010, whilst the total fertility rate was 2.5 children born per woman. (Source: http://www.who.int, World Health Statistics 2012)

Public Holidays 2014
1 January: New Year's Day
6 January: Epiphany
4-5 March: Carnival
17 April: Maundy Thursday
18 April: Good Friday
19 April: Declaration of Independence
5 May: Labour Day
24 June: Battle of Carabobo
5 July: Independence Day
24 July: Simón Bolívar's Birthday and Anniversary of the Battle of Lago de Maracaibo
12 October: Dia de la Raza
25 December: Christmas Day

EMPLOYMENT

The population is young and growing, with an estimated 385,000 people entering the workforce each year. According to the Venezuelan National Institute of Statistics, the population aged 15+ stood at 19,310,604 in the first half year 2008. The total work force comprised 12,433,929 (64.4 per cent) people, and 11,469,595 were employed (92.2 per cent). Official statistics suggest a rate of 7.8 per cent unemployment, though unofficial rates are around two per cent higher.

About 18 per cent of the labor force is unionised. The unions are particularly strong in the petroleum and public sectors.

Total Employment by Economic Activity

Occupation	2008
Agriculture, hunting, fishing & forestry	1,005,900
Mining & quarrying	106,800
Manufacturing	1,416,400
Electricity, gas & water supply	54,700
Construction	1,153,700
Wholesale & retail trade, repairs, hotels & restaurants	2,808,900
Transport, storage & communications	1,042,500
Financial intermediation, real estate, renting & business activities	614,000
Community, social & personal services	3,633,800

- continued

Other	26,300
Total	11,863,100

Source: Copyright © International Labour Organization (ILO Dept. of Statistics, http://llaborsta.ilo.org)

BANKING AND FINANCE

Currency
Bolívar Fuerte

One Bolívar = 100 céntimos

In January 2008, the Venezuelan Government adopted the "bolívar fuerte" as its new currency, effectively redenominating the previous currency, the "bolívar," by removing three zeroes (1 bolivar fuerte=1,000 bolívars).

GDP/GNP, Inflation, National Debt
Following a period of economic growth in 2000 and 2001, the Venezuelan economy went into recession in 2002. Initially caused by the devaluation of the Venezuelan Bolívar and a loss of business confidence, the economic decline was compounded by nationwide strikes at the end of 2002 and beginning of 2003 by opponents of the Chavez government. In January 2007, following his re-election, President Chavez announced further steps towards making Venezuela a socialist state; these included the nationalisation of key industries, such as energy and telecoms, and more state control over the country's Central Bank. Several laws have been passed in keeping with his vision. In 2011, President Chavez announced his intention to transfer international reserves deposited in US and European financial institutions to the Venezuelan Central Bank. Over US$6 billion was to be transferred to banks in Brazil, China and Russia.

GDP was estimated at US$315 billion in 2011. Revenue from oil exports account for some 18 per cent of the country's state GDP. The economy has been boosted by strong oil prices and investment in the construction sector, largely social housing.

Foreign debt was an estimated US$50 billion in 2008. It rose sharply over 2010-11 and was estimated at US94.6 billion in 2010. China is a major investor and is estimated to have lent $42.5 billion over the last five years.

The inflation rate (consumer prices) was estimated to be 18.7 per cent in 2007, but was expected to rise sharply to 30 per cent over 2008. It has remained around the 20 per cent mark, and was estimated at 19.9 per cent in 2012.

Foreign Investment
Foreign exchange controls were ended in 1996 after two years, removing what had been the largest block to foreign investment. New foreign investment regulations granted foreign investors the same rights as local ones. These included the removal of a wide range of restrictions in areas such as trademark and patent licenses, distribution agreements and credit. Traditionally, the US has been Venezuela's biggest foreign investor.

Joint ventures with local business are quite common; these and wholly-owned foreign subsidiaries are given the same treatment as domestic businesses. However, there are certain sectors where foreign investment is limited to 20 per cent of the total capital: these include television and radio broadcasting companies, Spanish language newspapers and security firms. Investment in the banking, insurance and fuel sectors is also restricted. On November 13, 2001, President Chavez enacted a new Hydrocarbons Law, which came into effect in January 2002. The new law provided that all oil production and distribution activities would be the domain of the Venezuelan state, with the exception of the joint ventures targeting extra-heavy crude oil production.

Much of the hydrocarbon sector was open to foreign investment until 2007, when the presidency of Hugo Chavez began imposing restrictions in his drive towards nationalising the industry. Some 60 foreign companies from 14 countries invested billions of dollars in heavy oil production, reactivation of old fields and a number of petrochemical joint ventures. Foreign oil companies involved in Venezuela included BP, ChevronTexaco, CNPC (China), ConocoPhillips, ExxonMobil, Repsol-YPF, Shell, Statoil, TotalFinaElf, and Petro-Canada. However, the climate for foreign investment in the oil sector became less attractive in 2006, due to back taxes and a hike in the royalty rate from one per cent to over 16 per cent. In May 2007, the state took over control of four refineries in the Orinoco belt; PDVSA (the state oil company) now controls at least 60 per cent of the projects, which were ceded by ConocoPhillips, Chevron, Exxon Mobil, BP, Statoil and Total.

The country has two free trade zones: the island of Margarita (commercial) and Paraguana (industrial).

Venezuela joined the South American trade bloc Mercosur in July 2006. Its four other members are Brazil, Argentina, Uruguay and Paraguay. Critics believe that Venezuela's membership will hurt its economy and increase tensions within Mercosur. The expanded group now covers about 250 million people and accounts for close to 75 per cent of South America's total gross domestic product (GDP). The government is not in favour of a proposed Free Trade Agreement of the Americas (FTAA), but aims to develop a South American bloc through the expansion of its Bolivarian Alternative for the Americas (ALBA) project.

Balance of Payments / Imports and Exports
Venezuela enjoys a strategic location making it a natural gateway for trade between South America and North America, Europe and Asia. It is a member of the Andean Pact, a free trade zone between Venezuela, Colombia, Ecuador, Peru and Bolivia.

Venezuela's exports earned US$61.0 billion in 2009: petroleum was the main commodity, earning $58.0 billion, followed by aluminium, steel, chemical products, iron ore, cigarettes, fish, cement and paper. Main export markets are the US (57.5 per cent in 2009), The Netherlands (5.2 per cent), Colombia, (4.5 per cent) and Mexico (4.5 per cent).

Imports cost an estimated US$48.55 billion in 2009 and included machinery and transport equipment, manufactured good and construction materials. Main import suppliers were the US (30.2 per cent), Brazil (10.1 per cent), Colombia (9.9 per cent) and Mexico (6.8 per cent). China was also a significant supplier, at 6.7 per cent of the total.

Central Bank
Banco Central de Venezuela, Ave Urdaneta, Esquina de Carmelitas, Caracas 1010, Distrito Federal, Venezuela. Tel: +58 212 8015111, fax: +58 212 8018622 / 212 8611649, e-mail: info@bcv.org.ve, URL: http://www.bcv.org.ve
President: Nelson Merentes

Chambers of Commerce and Trade Organisations
Caracas Stock Exchange, URL: http://www.caracasstock.com/
Venezuelan-American Chamber of Commerce, URL: http://www.venamcham.org/

MANUFACTURING, MINING AND SERVICES

Primary and Extractive Industries
Venezuela is rich in natural resources including iron ore, nickel, gold, diamonds, bauxite, coal and particularly oil. The Las Cristinas gold mine was being developed in a joint venture between the state-owned mining firm CVG and a foreign investor, but the venture was put on hold due to low gold prices.

Venezuela is the largest source of oil supplies in the Western Hemisphere and is currently the only producer with long term potential outside the Middle East and the countries of the former Soviet Union. It is also one of the top four sources of US oil imports (with Canada, Mexico, and Saudi Arabia). Recent figures show that the petroleum industry accounts for a quarter of GDP and over 70 per cent of export earnings. The traditional centre of the country's oil industry is Lake Maracaibo. However, significant reserves are also found in other regions of the country.

Proven oil reserves at the beginning of 2012 were estimated to be over 210 billion barrels, the largest in the Western Hemisphere. In 2006, the US Department of Energy estimated that Venezuela controlled 1.3 trillion barrels, more than the total oil reserves of the rest of the world. Oil production was estimated at 2.47 million barrels per day in 2011, most of which was crude. A barrel of Venezuelan crude oil was worth $50 in February 2006, up from around $20 in the 1990s (and $10 in 1999). Oil consumption was an estimated 980,000 barrels per day in 2011.

Venezuela is currently the world's sixth largest net oil exporter, exporting 1.82 million barrels per day in 2008; major crude oil customers are the US (68 per cent in 2003), Canada, Germany and Spain, as well as eleven Central American and Caribbean countries under the terms of the San Jose Accord and the PetroCaribe agreement of 2005. Much of the crude oil that is exported to the Caribbean is later re-exported as petroleum products to the United States. China is one of the fastest growing destinations of Venezuelan crude oil and petroleum products. Venezuela has recently diversified its petroleum export destinations away from the United States, though the U.S. will probably be Venezuela's biggest market for the foreseeable future.

Venezuela's state-owned oil company is Petróleos de Venezuela S.A. (PdVSA). Following the 2002-03 strike, the company fired some 18,000 workers, causing gaps in the company's technical knowledge and expertise. PdVSA is to contribute US$2 billion per annum to a government-sponsored special development fund in order to finance projects throughout the country, as well as spending some US$2-3 billion on social programs. The climate for foreign investment in the oil sector is becoming less attractive, due to back taxes and a hike in the royalty rate from one per cent to over 16 per cent. Venezuela currently supplies subsidised oil to several South American countries, in return for agricultural and industrial products, and medical services. In 2005 Venezuela joined forces with several Caribbean countries to launch a regional oil company. In 2007, the Venezuelan government took over operations at four refineries in the Orinoco Belt, as part of the drive towards nationalisation.

Venezuela's natural gas reserves are the second largest in the Western Hemisphere (after the US), and the eighth largest in the world. At the beginning of 2011 natural gas reserves were 179 trillion cubic feet. Production was 880 billion cubic feet and consumption was 957 billion cubic feet mean that some gas had to be imported to meet the country's needs. About 70 per cent of Venezuela's natural gas production is used by the oil industry. The government predicts that there will be a general switch to gas in the future, and is spearheading a project to build a gas pipeline from Venezuela down to Patagonia on the southern tip of the continent, cutting through the Amazon rainforest.

Venezuela is the second largest coal producer in Latin America (after Colombia). Most of Venezuela's coal is exported to the eastern United States and Europe. The largest coal producing region in the country is the Guasaré Basin near the border with Colombia. According to recent EIA statistics, Venezuela has coal reserves estimated at 528 million short tons. Production was an estimated 9.6 million short tons in 2010, with consumption at 2.9 million short tons. Venezuela is the third largest net exporter in the Western Hemisphere, exporting to other Latin American countries as well as the US and Europe. Carbozulia, owned by PdVSA, is the largest coal producing company in Venezuela.

The country is extremely rich in mineral resources in the Andes, Perija and coastal mountain ranges, and in the Guayana region in the south-east. The Orinoco Belt holds immense deposits of bitumen, currently estimated at 1.3 trillion barrels. Mineral exploration and development is in the hands of the corporación Venezolana de Guayana (CVG), an autonomous state-owned entity created in 1960, although as of 1997 CVG has been pursuing foreign capital for its operations. Venezuela's excellent resources and geographical position have made it one of the principal mineral raw material producers in Latin America over the last twenty years. (Source: Energy Information Administration)

VENEZUELA

Energy

Total energy consumption in Venezuela was 9.9 quadrillion Btu in 2009. Fuel share of energy consumption in 2005 was as follows: natural gas, 38 per cent; oil, 38 per cent and hydroelectricity, 24 per cent.

At the beginning of 2005, Venezuela had an estimated installed generating capacity of 3.7 gigawatts, most of which was hydroelectric.

Electricity production was an estimated 115.01 billion kilowatthours (kWh) in 2010, with consumption estimated at 91.51 billion kWh. Venezuela has the world's second largest operational hydroelectric dam, the 10-GW Raul Leoni dam on the Caroni River. The largest generating company is the state-owned Electrificación del Caroni (EDELCA), a subsidiary of Corporación Venezolana de Guayana (CVG). (Source: Energy Information Administration)

Manufacturing

Non-petroleum based manufacturing has retained a relatively small share of total output, and accounts for some 16 per cent of GDP and 20 per cent of exports. It is hindered by a lack of private investment. Important industries are textiles, apparel and leather, paper and paper products, steel, aluminium, motor vehicle assembly, cement, paper and non-metallic mineral products.

Tourism

The tourist industry is rapidly expanding and becoming highly profitable. Tourist arrivals have grown 51.5 per cent since 1993. Ecotourism has been the primary growth area, due to the biological diversity of the region. In 2003 there were approximately 337,000 visitors to Venezuela; the largest numbers came from the US (67,000), Germany (42,000) and the Netherlands (36,000) according to the National Institute of Statistics (INE) of Venezuela. The number of tourist arrivals had risen to 748,000 in 2006.

Corporacion deTurismo de Venezuela, Parque Central. Torre Este Piso 37, Caracas 1010, Venezuela. Tel: +58 2 507 8815

Agriculture

Venezuela's tropical climate allows more frequent harvests per year and shorter growing times than in more temperate regions. This is of particular benefit to paper and pulp production and forestry, and means that Venezuela is able to harvest when many of its competitors have exhausted production.

Four per cent of Venezuela land is arable equating to 2,595,000 hectares, and only 17 per cent of that is irrigated. 21 per cent is used for pasture. Figures for 20115 indicate that agriculture accounts for just 4 per cent of GDP and employs under 10 per cent of the workforce. Venezuela is not self-sufficient in agriculture, with the exception of meat, and imports approximately 66 per cent of its food requirements, a quarter of which comes from the USA.

The country's main products are as follows: rice, maize, potatoes, black beans, fruits, sugar cane, plantains, coffee, cocoa beans, tobacco, cotton. Venezuela's vast coastline also gives access to immense fishing resources. Forecast figures from the FAO put the total fish catch at 274,417 tonnes down from 296,266 tonnes in 2008.

Agricultural Production in 2010

Produce	Int. $'000*	Tonnes
Indigenous chicken meat	1,184,053	831,260
Indigenous cattle meat	756,312	279,973
Cow milk, whole, fresh	715,993	2,294,400
Indigenous rabbit meat	472,488	254,305
Rice, paddy	340,662	1,250,000
Sugar cane	292,501	8,907,670
Indigenous pigmeat	260,178	169,250
Hen eggs, in shell	132,536	159,800
Bananas	116,060	412,100
Pineapples	105,866	371,400
Maize	95,810	2,145,000
Plantains	94,620	477,800

* unofficial figures

Source: http://faostat.fao.org/site/339/default.aspx Food and Agriculture Organization of the United Nations, Food and Agricultural commodities production

COMMUNICATIONS AND TRANSPORT

Travel Requirements

Citizens of the USA, Canada, Australia and most of the EU require a passport valid for six months but do not need a visa for stays of up to 90 days if the purpose of their visit is tourism. A Tourist Entry Card (DEX-2) is issued free of charge by authorised air carriers on presentation of valid air tickets (including return or onward ticket) for stays of maximum 90 days. Latvians do need a visa. Other nationals should contact the embassy to check visa requirements.

Non-tourists should consult the Venezuelan Embassy or nearest Venezuelan consulate regarding possible visa requirements for their specific purpose of travel.

Airports

Aviation plays a vital role in Venezuela, especially in opening up access to the vast regions of the interior of the country. There are 11 international, 36 national and 290 private or municipal airports throughout the country. Caracas is served by the Simon Bolivar International Airport also known as Maiquetia Airport (a 40 minute journey away from the city).

International Airlines

Almost all the major European international airlines provide services between Venezuela and the major capitals of the world. The principal Caribbean, Central American and South American airlines operate links with major Latin American cities. Venezuela's recently privatised national airline, VIASA, flies to 21 cities in North and South America and Europe. The company also offers cargo services. AVENSA, a private Venezuelan airline, serves both domestic and international destinations and Aeropostal airlines provides a network of commercial transport to approximately 40 Venezuelan cities as well as many Caribbean destinations and Orlando in the USA.

Avensa, Tel: +58 2 562 3022/ 561 3366/ 562 3360, fax: +58 2 563 0225/ 545 2621
Aeropostal, Tel: +58 2 576 3922/ 4511, fax: +58 2 575 3950
Aserca C.A., Tel: +58 2 953 2729 / 1217, fax: +58 2 953 7228
Zuliana de Aviación, Tel: +58 2 919801 / 919834, fax: +58 2 919634

Railways

Apart from special railway lines (e.g. those of the iron ore mining companies) there are only about 540 km of railway of which the sole line of any importance is the 160 km line running from Puerto Cabello, on the coast, to Barquisimeto and then on to Acarigua. Recent figures show that Caracas' high-speed Metro system carries between 1 million and 1.5 million passengers per day.

Underground Service

C.A. Metro de Caracas, Multicentro Empresarial del Este, Conjunto Miranda, Torre B, Piso 1 al 17, Chacao, Caracas, Venezuela. Tel: +58 2 208 2111, fax: +58 2 261 6880 / 331908

Roads

Venezuela has a total road network of 95,725 km (as of 1997), of which 32,800 km are paved and 28,000 km are gravel, whilst the rest are compacted soil. Venezuela has road links with Colombia and Brazil. Vehicles are driven on the right.

Ports and Harbours

Venezuela has nine seaports that handle commercial cargo traffic. The principal ports are La Guaira, Maracaibo and Puerto Cabello, which together handle 80 per cent of the country's imports and exports. Venezuela also has 33 petroleum ports, which serve as outlets for the oil industry, and two special ports for iron shipments. Control of the ports is now in the hands of the states in which they are situated, some of which have in turn opted to have the ports run by private companies.

There are 7,100 km of inland waterways, of which the Orinoco River is the most important route. The Orinoco River is navigable for 900 miles upstream (150 miles for ocean-going ships).

HEALTH

The current government aims to increase access to basic health services with quality and equity. Under the re-drafted constitution of 1999, the health service is publicly funded. In 2009, the government spent approximately 8.6 per cent of its total budget on healthcare, accounting for 40.0 per cent of all healthcare spending. Private expenditure accounted for 60 per cent of expenditure on health care, 90.6 per cent of it out-of-pocket expenditure. Total expenditure on healthcare equated to 6.0 per cent of the country's GDP. Per capita expenditure on health was approximately US$688.

Figures for 2000-10 show that there are 48,000 physicians (19.4 per 10,000 population), 28,000 nurses and midwives (11 per 10,000 population) and 13,680 dentists. There are approximately 13 hospital beds per 10,000 population.

In 2010 the infant mortality rate (probability of dying before first birthday) was 16 per 1,000 live births and the child (under-five years old) mortality rate was 18 per 1,000 live births. The main causes of death in the under-fives are: prematurity (23 per cent), pneumonia (10 per cent), congenital anomalies (19 per cent), birth asphyxia (9 per cent) and diarrhoea (7 per cent). In the period 2005-11 an estimated 15.6 per cent of children (under five-years-old) were classified as stunted and 3.7 per cent as underweight. (Source: http://www.who.int, World Health Statistics 2012)

EDUCATION

Education in Venezuela is free, universal and compulsory from the ages of five years to 14 years. Recent figures estimate the adult literacy rate at 95.2 per cent (95.4 per cent for men and 94.9 per cent for women). The equivalent of 3.7 per cent of Venezuela's GDP went on education in 2007.

Through the Ministry of Education, the Venezuelan government provides education at all levels. In 2007, 92 per cent of children of the relevant age were enrolled in primary school, whilst 68 per cent of children attended secondary school; both figures are below the regional average. 98 per cent of children complete the full primary course. 52 per cent of the relevant age-group study at tertiary level, well above the regional average of 31 per cent.

In August 2009 the government passed an education law which said that the system should be based on The Bolivarian Doctrine, supporters of the law said this would open up equal education opportunities for everyone but protestors who took to the streets felt the law would allow for socialist indoctrination.

RELIGION

The constitution guarantees freedom of religion. Seventy-eight per cent of Venezuelans are Roman Catholic and 14 per cent Protestant.

Venezuela has a religious liberty rating of 8 on a scale of 1 to 10 (10 is most freedom). (Source: World Religion Database)

COMMUNICATIONS AND MEDIA

Some of the press has been accused of politisation; President Chavez has accused it of being involved in a coup attempt against him. President Chavez himself has come under criticism for creating a hostile atmosphere for journalists. In 2007 he decided not to renew the broadcasting licence of the terrestial station RCTV.

Newspapers
El Nacional, URL: http://www.gate.net/vei/enacel
Ultimas Noticias, URL: http://www.ultimasnoticias.com.ve/
El Universal C.A., URL: http://www.el-universal.com
Economía Hoy, URL: http://www.rapid-systems.com/ECONOMIA-HOY

Broadcasting
There is one government-run radio station and many private commercial stations. There are numerous television broadcast stations, two of which, *Televisoria nacional* and *Televisora Venezolana Social*, are government run.
Venevisión, URL: http://www.venevision.net/
R.C.T.V., URL: http://www.rctv.net/
RCTV has an anti-Chavez leaning, and lost its licence for public broadcasting on 27th May 2007, amid protests from its supporters. It continues to run private, cable programmes. It was replaced by TVES
TVes (Televisora Venezolana Social), state-run television station, established by Pres. Chavez in 2007. URL: http://www.tves.org.ve/
Venezolano de Televisión, URL: http://www.vtv.gov.ve/
Corporación Televen, URL: http://www.televen.com/Televen/home.aspx

Telecommunications
The telephone system in Venezuela is modern and expanding. The rural service has greatly improved recently. According to 2008 estimates there are just over six million main line telephones in use (20 per 100 people), and over 27 million mobile phones (90 per 100 people). Venezuela launched its first telecommunications satellite in 2008.

By 2008, approximately 7 million Venezuelans were regular internet users.

ENVIRONMENT

Venezuela is subject to industrial pollution, floods, rock slides and mud slides, in addition to periodic periods of drought. The state has passed several laws, including the Environmental Crime Law (1992) which reaffirms the Environment Act (1976), and which came into force to conserve, protect and improve the environment.

The Ministry of Renewable Natural Resources plans and operates measures to conserve and protect the country's land, wildlife and water.

Venezuela is a party to the following international environmental agreements: Conventions on Biodiversity, Climate Change, Desertification, Endangered Species, Hazardous Wastes, Marine Life Conservation, Nuclear Test Ban, Ozone Layer Protection, Ship Pollution, Tropical Timber 83, Tropical Timber 94, Wetlands and Whaling. Venezuela has signed but not ratified the Convention on Marine Dumping. The country is not a signatory to the Kyoto Protocol.

According to figures from the EIA, energy-related carbon dioxide emissions were estimated at 142.68 million metric tons in 2004, up on the previous year. Per capita carbon dioxide emissions were an estimated 5.7 metric tons in 2004 (up from 5.4 the previous year), compared with 20.18 metric tons in the US. In 2010, Venezuela's emissions from the consumption of fossil fuels totalled 158.44 million metric tons of carbon dioxide.

SPACE PROGRAMME

Venezuela launched its first communications satellite in 2006. The Venesat-1 telecom satellite, which was launched from China, cost over $250 million and means that thousands of people in remote areas now have access to TV, radio and the internet. A reconnaissance satellite is expected to be launched in 2013.

VIETNAM
Socialist Republic of Vietnam
Công Hòa Xâ Hôi Chu Nghia Viêt Nam

Capital: Hanoi (Population estimate, 2011: 7 million)

Head of State: Truong Tan Sang (President) (page 1508)

Vice President: Ms Nguyen Thi Doan (page 1486)

National Flag: A five-pointed star, centred gold, on a red field

CONSTITUTION AND GOVERNMENT

Constitution
Following the end of the war in 1975 a political consultative conference on national reunification was held in Saigon and preparations began for nationwide elections, which were held in April 1976. The Socialist Republic of Vietnam was proclaimed on 2 July 1976 by the first National Assembly of 488 deputies. The Communist Party's Fourth Congress was held in 1976, a new party constitution was adopted, and the party was renamed the Communist Party of Vietnam (CPV). The highest executive body was the Central Committee, elected by a Party Congress on a national basis.

A policy of economic liberalisation was endorsed after a change in leadership of 1986 and government changes in 1987. A new constitution was adopted in 1992 affirming Communist Party rule but restricting its power to involvement in the daily business of government, whilst the power of the premier and the National Assembly was strengthened.

A new post of President was created; its incumbent would act as commander of the armed forces and appoint the Prime Minister and Chief Justice with National Assembly approval. The President serves a term of five years. The Prime Minister is responsible for the daily handling of the government and has the right to dismiss and nominate members of cabinet with the National Assembly's approval.

The constitution underwrote certain economic liberties: while ownership of land remained in the state's hands, individuals and groups had the right to transfer the use of land they worked, to own the means of production and to engage in private business. Protection for foreign investment was also guaranteed.

The constitution was revised in 2001 introducing some freedom for small scale capitalism.

To consult the constitution, please visit:
http://www.vietnamembassy-usa.org/learn_about_vietnam/politics/constitution

International Relations
Vietnam joined ASEAN in 1995 and in January 2007 became a member of the World Trade Organization. In January 2008, Vietnam took up a two-year, non-permanent seat on the UN Security Council.

Recent Events
The Communist Party of Vietnam held its Tenth Party Congress in April 2006. One of its duties was to choose who would lead Vietnam until 2010. The National Assembly elected a new State President, Nguyen Minh Triet, and a new Prime Minister, Nguyen Tan Dung

In June 2007, President Nguyen Minh Triet visited the USA; it was the first visit by a Vietnamese president since the end of the Vietnam War in 1975.

In December 2009 the World Bank's International Bank for Reconstruction and Development approved a loan of US$200 million to Vietnam, its first to the country.

Also that month pro-democracy activist Tran Anh Kim was given a five and a half-year jail sentence for subversion after allegedly publishing pro-democracy articles on the internet. The following January four activists including the prominent human rights lawyer Le Cong Dinh were jailed on charges of trying to overthrow the government.

In January 2011 one third of the Politburo stepped down at the five-yearly congress. Prime Minister Nguyen Tan Dung was re-elected to the policy-making Central Committee, made up of the party's top 175 officials. Vietnam's 63 provinces increased their representation to 75 members from 53. The head of the national assembly, Nguyen Phu Trong, was elected as party secretary-general.

In October 2011 China and Vietnam signed an agreement on managing the South China Sea dispute.

In October 2012, Nguyen Phu Trong, head of the Communist Party, admitted mistakes over corruption in response to a series of scandals at state-owned businesses. The following month parliament voted in favour of a proposal that elected leaders should face annual confidence votes.

In February 2013, a court jailed over 30 people on subversion charges. Sentences ranged from 10 years to life.

Legislature
Vietnam's unicameral legislature is known as the National Assembly (Quoc-Hoi), and is the only body with constitutional and legislative powers. The Assembly has 500 members who serve a five-year term. It has powers to elect, release from duty, or remove from office the

VIETNAM

President, Vice President, the Chairman of the National Assembly, the Prime Minister, and the President of the Supreme People's Court. The National Assembly holds two sessions a year.
National Assembly, 35 Ngo Quyen, Hanoi, Vietnam. Tel: +84 4 826 5292, fax: +84 4 804 6997, e-mail: qj@vasc.vnn.vn, URL: http://www.na.gov.vn

Communist Party of Vietnam (Dang Cong San Việt Nam) 49 Phan Dinh Phung, Ba Dinh, Hanoi, Vietnam. Tel: +84 4 0804 4060, fax: +84 4 0804 4173, e-mail: dangcongsan@cpv.org.vn, URL: http://www.cpv.org.vn
General Secretary: Nguyen Phu Trong

Cabinet (as at June 2013)
Prime Minister: Nguyen Tan Dung
Deputy Prime Minister: Nguyen Xuan Phuc
Deputy Prime Minister: Vu Van Ninh
Deputy Prime Minister: Hoang Trung Hai (page 1436)
Deputy Prime Minister: Nguyen Thien Nhan
Minister of Defence: Gen. Phung Quang Thanh
Minister of Internal Affairs: Nguyen Thai Binh
Minister of Public Security: Lt.-Gen. Tran Dai Quang
Minister of Justice: Ha Hung Cuong (page 1436)
Minister of Foreign Affairs: Pham Binh Minh (page 1495)
Minister of Planning and Investment: Bui Quang Vinh
Minister of Finance: Dinh Tien Dung
Minister of Industry and Trade: Vu Huy Hoang
Minister of Information and Communications: Nguyen Bac Son
Minister of Natural Resources and Environment: Nguyen Minh Quang
Minister of Agriculture and Rural Development: Cao Duc Phat
Minister of Education and Training: Pham Vu Luan
Minister of Transport: Dinh la Thang
Minister of Construction: Trinh Dinh Dung
Minister of Public Health: Dr Nguyen Thi Kim Tien
Minister of Labour, War Invalids and Social Affairs: Pham Thi Hai Chuyen
Minister of Science and Technology: Nguyen Quan
Minister of Culture, Sport and Tourism: Hoang Tuan Anh
Chair, Committee for Ethnic Minorities: Giang Seo Phu
Governor of the State Bank: Nguyen Van Binh
Inspector General of the Government Inspectorate: Huynh Phong Tran
Chair of the Government Office: Vu Duc Dam

Ministries

Office of the Prime Minister, 1 Hoang Hoa Tham Street, Ba Dinh District, Hanoi, Vietnam. Tel:+84 4 845 8241 / 458261, fax: +84 4 845 5464
Ministry of Agriculture and Rural Development, 2 Ngoc Ha Street, Ba Binh District, Hanoi, Vietnam. Tel:+84 4 3823 5804, fax: +84 4 3823 0381, e-mail: icard@agroviet.gov.vn, URL: http://www.agroviet.gov.vn/
Ministry of Construction, 37 Le Dai Hanh, Hanoi, Vietnam. Tel: +84 4 3826 8271, fax: +84 4 3825 8122
Ministry of Culture, Sport and Tourism, 51-53 Ngo Quyen Street, Hoan Kiem District, Hanoi, Vietnam. Tel:+84 4 826 2945 / 826 2487 / 825 5349, fax: +84 4 826 7101, e-mail: webmaster@vnnews.com, URL: http://www.vnnews.com/
Ministry of Defence, 1 Hoang Dieu, Hanoi, Vietnam. Tel: +84 4 3826 8101, fax: +84 4 3826 5540
Ministry of Education and Training, 49 Dai Co Viet, Hanoi, Vietnam. Tel: +84 4 3826 4085, fax: +84 4 3869 4085
Ministry of Finance, 8 Phan Huy Chu Street, Hoan Kiem District, Hanoi, Vietnam. Tel: +84 4 826 4872 / 826 2356 / 826 2357, fax: +84 4 826 2266, e-mail: webmaster@mof.gov.vn, URL: http://www.mof.gov.vn/
Ministry of Foreign Affairs, 1 Ton That Dam Street, Ba Dinh District, Hanoi, Vietnam. Tel: +84 4 845 8208 / 845 3973 / 845 8321, fax: +84 4 844 5905, e-mail: webmaster@mofa.gov.vn, URL: http://www.mofa.gov.vn
Ministry of Health, 138A Giang Vo, Hanoi, Vietnam. Tel: +84 4 3826 4050, fax: +84 4 3824 3260
Ministry of Industry and Trade, 54 Hai Ba Trung, Hoan Kiem, Hanoi, Vietnam. Tel: +84 4 3825 8311, fax: +84 4 3826 5303, e-mail: bitec@mot.gov.vn, URL: http://www.moi.gov.vn
Ministry of the Interior, Tran Binh Trong, Hanoi, Vietnam. Tel: +84 4 3825 8300, fax: +84 4 3825 4835
Ministry of Justice, 25A Cat Linh, Hanoi, Vietnem. Tel: +84 4 3825 4658, fax: +84 4 3825 4835
Ministry of Labour, War Invalids and Social Affairs, 2 Dinh Le, Hanoi, Vietnam. Tel: +84 4 3825 2236, fax: +84 4 3825 4728
Ministry of Science, Technology and Environment, 39 Tran Hung Dao, Hanoi, Vietnem. Tel: +84 4 3825 2731, fax: +84 4 3825 1518
Ministry of Transport, 80 Tran Hung Dao Street, Hoan Kiem District, Hanoi, Vietnam. Tel: + 84 4 825 4012 / 825 2925 / 825 2309, fax: +84 4 826 7291, URL: http://www.mt.gov.vn/default.aspx
Ministry of Planning and Investment, 2 Hoang Van Thu, Hanoi, Vietnam. Tel: +84 4 3845 8261, fax: +84 4 3823 2494, URL: http://www.khoahoc.vnn.vn/mpi_website
Ministry of Information and Communications, 18 Nguyen Du Strreet, Hanoi, Vietnam. Tel: +84 4 3822 6410, fax: +84 4 3826 3477, e-mail: office@mpt.gov.vn, URL: http://www.mpt.gov.vn
Ministry of Natural Resources and Environment, 164 Tran Quang Khai, Hanoi, Vietnam. Tel: +84 4 3826 8141, fax: +84 4 3825 6929
Ministry of Public Security, Tran Binh Trong, Hanoi, Vietnam. Tel: +84 4 3825 8300, fax: +84 4 3825 4835

Elections

Independent candidates were permitted to stand for the first time after the 1992 elections. The Communist Party of Vietnam held its Tenth Party Congress in April 2006. One of its duties was to choose who would lead Vietnam until 2010. As a result, the National Assembly elected a new State President, Nguyen Minh Triet, and a new Prime Minister, Nguyen Tan Dung.

The most recent legislative election was held in May 2011. The CPV won 458 seats, the VFF 38 seats and independents took four. The most recent presidential election was held on 25 July 2011. Nguyen Tan Dung was reappointed prime minister and his new cabinet was approved. Presidential elections took place in July 2011. Truong Tan Sang was elected with 487 out of 500 votes from the National Assembly.

Political PartiesCommunist Party of Vietnam (Dang Cong San Việt Nam) 49 Phan Dinh Phung, Ba Dinh, Hanoi, Vietnam. Tel: +84 4 0804 4060, fax: +84 4 0804 4173, e-mail: dangcongsan@cpv.org.vn, URL: http://www.cpv.org.vn/
Secretary General: Nong Duc Manh

Diplomatic Representation

British Embassy, Central Building, 31 Hai Ba Trung, Hanoi, Vietnam. Tel: +84 4 936 0500, fax: +84 4 936 0561/ 936 0562, URL: http://ukinvietnam.fco.gov.uk
Ambassador: Antony Stokes
US Embassy, 7 Lang Ha Street, Ba Dinh District, Hanoi, Vietnam. Tel: +84 4 772 1500, fax: +84 4 772 1510, e-mail: irchano@pd.state.gov, URL: http://vietnam.usembassy.gov/
Ambassador: David Shear
Vietnamese Embassy, UK, 12-14 Victoria Road, London, W8 5RD, United Kingdom. Tel: +44 (0)20 7937 1912, fax: +44 (0)20 7937 6108, URL: http://www.vietnamembassy.org.uk
Ambassador: H.E. Vu Quang Minh
Vietnamese Embassy, USA, 1233 20th St., NW, Suite 400, Washington, DC 20036, USA. Tel: +1 202 861 0737, fax: +1 202 861 0917, e-mail: info@vietnamembassy-usa.org, URL: http://www.vietnamembassy-usa.org
Ambassador: Nguyen Quoc Cuong
Permanent Mission of Vietnam to the United Nations, 866 UN Plaza, Suite 435, New York, NY 10017, USA. Tel: +1 212 644 0594, fax: +1 212 644 5732, e-mail: vietnam@un.int, vietnamun@vnmission.com, URL: http://www.un.int/vietnam
Ambassador and Permanent Representative: Le Hoai Trung

LEGAL SYSTEM

The law of Vietnam is based on Confusianism, communist legal theory and French civil law. The judicial system consists of the Supreme People's Court, the local People's Courts and the Military Tribunals. The Supreme People's Court is the highest judicial organ and its president reports to the National Council. Judges are appointed by the National Assembly of Vietnam for five year terms.

Supreme People's Court Presiding Judge: Truong Hoa Binh

The Supreme People's Procuracy ensures compliance with the law of ministries, ministerial institutions, Government and local Government institutions, economic and social organisations, armed and people's units, and ordinary citizens.

Head of the Supreme People's Procuracy: Nguyen Hoa Binh
URL: http://www.vksndtc.gov.vn/tienganh.aspx

The government's human rights record is poor. Citizens cannot change their government, and opposition movements are prohibited. Independent human rights organizations are also prohibited. The government fights political dissent by arresting activists, often denying them a fair trial. There are restrictions on freedom of speech, the press, assembly, movement and association, as well as limited privacy rights. There are significant levels of corruption and impunity within the police force. Prison conditions are severe. The government limits workers' rights and has arrested several labour activists.

Vietnam retains the death penalty, which may be imposed for 29 offences under the Penal Code. These offences include economic crimes, such as fraud, embezzlement, smuggling, counterfeiting and offering bribes; manufacturing, concealing and trafficking in narcotic substances. In 2008, the government presented amendments on some clauses of the Penal Code, removing the death sentence on offences of embezzlement, bribery and production of fake goods, which would reduce the number of capital offences to 12. There were five reported executions in 2011. As of 2013, more than 500 inmates were reported to be on death row.

LOCAL GOVERNMENT

Vietnam is divided into 58 provinces and five municipalities (Can Tho, Hai Phong, Da Nang, Hanoi and Ho Chi Minh). Hanoi has seven inner districts and five suburban districts. The provinces are: An Giang, Bac Giang, Bac Kan, Bac Lieu, Bac Ninh, Ba Ria-Vung Tau, Ben Tre, Binh Dinh, Binh Duong, Binh Phuoc, Binh Thuan, Ca Mau, Cao Bang, Dac Lak, Dac Nong, Dien Bien, Dong Nai, Dong Thap, Gia Lai, Ha Giang, Ha Nam, Ha Tay, Ha Tinh, Hai Duong, Hau Giang, Hoa Binh, Hung Yen, Khanh Hoa, Kien Giang, Kon Tum, Lai Chau, Lam Dong, Lang Son, Lao Cai, Long An, Nam Dinh, Nghe An, Ninh Binh, Ninh Thuan, Phu Tho, Phu Yen, Quang Binh, Quang Nam, Quang Ngai, Quang Ninh, Quang Tri, Soc Trang, Son La, Tay Ninh, Thai Binh, Thai Nguyen, Thanh Hoa, Thua Thien-Hue, Tien Giang, Tra Vinh, Tuyen Quang, Vinh Long, Vinh Phuc, and Yen Bai. Elections for local People's Assemblies took place in 2011.

AREA AND POPULATION

Area
The Socialist Republic of Vietnam covers an area of 329,600 sq. km. It is bordered to the west by Cambodia and Laos, and to the north by China. To the east is the South China Sea. Vietnam has a 3,300 km coastline. Some three quarters of Vietnam is mountainous, with the Truong Son mountain chain running for 1,200 km north to south. The bulk of Vietnam's population is concentrated in the lowlands and particularly the delta areas of Vietnam's two great rivers, the Songkoi (Red River) in the north and the Mekong in the south. The climate is tropical in the south, with monsoons in the north. The hot, rainy season is from May to September, and the warm, dry season runs from October to March.

To view a regional map, please consult:
http://www.un.org/Depts/Cartographic/map/profile/mekong.pdf

Population
Vietnam has a total population estimated in 2010 at 87,848 million, with an average annual population growth rate of 1.1 per cent over the period 2000-10. About 51 per cent of the population are women. Average population density is approximately 252 per sq. km, but in parts of the Songkoi delta it is as high as 1,500 people per sq. km. The capital, Hanoi, has an estimated population of 7 million. The majority of Vietnamese (65 per cent) are aged between 15 and 60 years, with 26 per cent aged up to 14 years, and 9 per cent aged 60 years and over. The median age is 27 years. Figures for 2010 show that 30 per cent of the population lived in urban areas. (Source: http://www.who.int, World Health Statistics 2012)

The government is anxious to reduce population growth - there are extra taxes for couples with more than two children - and to redeploy people from the cities and overcrowded northern lowlands to the highlands and southern areas, depopulated during the war, where New Economic Zones have been set up. Since 1975, 3.5 million people have been relocated.

Vietnam has 54 nationalities. The Viet (Kinh) make up 88 per cent of the population. Amongst the minority groups are the Tay, Thai, Muong, Hoa, Khmer, Nung, Brau, Romam and Odu. Chinese is the largest minority group (2 per cent).

Births, Marriages, Deaths
The birth rate, according to 2010 estimates, was 16.7 births per 1,000 population, whilst the death rate was 6.6 deaths per 1,000 population. Life expectancy in 2009 was estimated at 72 years (70 years for men and 74 years for women). Healthy life expectancy was estimated to be 64 years. The total fertility rate was 1.8 births per female. (Source: http://www.who.int, World Health Statistics 2012)

Public Holidays 2014
1 January: New Year's Day
30 January: Chinese (Lunar) New Year's Eve
31 January: Chinese (Lunar) New Year's Day*
30 April: Saigon Liberation Day
5 May: International Labour Day
19 May: Ho Chi Minh's Birthday
2 September: National Day of the Socialist Republic of Vietnam
* Precise date depends on the lunar calendar

EMPLOYMENT

The American withdrawal and the end of the war left 3.5 million unemployed, 700,000 of whom lived in Ho Chi Minh City. Unemployment was a major problem in the late 1980s as Hanoi reduced the size of its armed forces and attempted to limit budget expenditure by cutting the number of state employees. Estimated figures for 2010 put the unemployment rate at 4.3 per cent.

The following table shows how the workforce has been employed in recent years:

Labour Force, figures in million

Employment	2006	2007
Labour force	44.3	45.1
Employed	43.3	44.2
- Agriculture	22.4	22.3
- Manufacturing	5.6	6.0
- Mining	0.4	0.4
- Others	14.9	15.5
Unemployed	1.0	0.9
Unemployment rate	2.3%	2.0%

Source: Asian Development Bank

BANKING AND FINANCE

In 1975, the political reunification of North and South Vietnam brought together two very different but potentially complementary economies. In the early 1980s Vietnam's economic problems accumulated, unemployment and prices rose, living conditions deteriorated, with the country's economic survival dependent upon Soviet bloc aid. At the Sixth Party Congress in December 1986 the urgent need for renovation (doi moi) was recognised.

Subsequent economic measures in the 1980s were designed to encourage private agricultural production, remove state restrictions on internal trade, and encourage small private businesses and factories. A foreign investment law was introduced in 1987 and rights to property and inheritance were recognised. Along with other south-east Asian countries Vietnam was affected by the economic crisis that swept the region mid-1997. The more market-oriented economy has transformed Vietnam into one of the fastest growing economies in Asia. A

bilateral agreement with the US came into force in 2001. It dramatically increased Vietnam's exports and Vietnam joined the WTO in 2007. To join the WTO, Vietnam revised its trade and investment laws and opened up the economy to foreign investors and exporters. The government still controls major sectors of the econmy but partial privatization plans are being developed. In 2011, the government announced a strategy to restructure the economy by 2015. The reforms include increased public investment, reform of state enterprises and restructuring of finance markets especially the banking system.

Currency
Vietnam's unit of currency is the dong (VND).

GDP/GNP, Inflation, National Debt
Despite the slowdown of the global economy in 2001 and 2002, Vietnam has maintained economic growth, due mainly to its relative isolation from the world economy and therefore its ability to withstand a decline in demand for its exports. Growth has been steady in recent years. Most recently it has been 7.3 per cent in 2003, 7.8 per cent in 2004, 8.4 per cent in 2005, 8.2 per cent in 2006 and 8.5 per cent in 2007. With the global economic crisis it fell to 6.2 per cent in 2008 and 5.3 per cent in 2009. Growth reached 6.8 per cent in 2010 and remained strong in 2011. GDP was put at US$102 billion in 2010. Per capita GDP was 22,907,000 dong in 2010. GDP was estimated at US$120 billion in 2011.

The following table shows GDP by industrial origin in recent years at current market prices. Figures are in Billion Dong.

Sector	2008	2009	2010
GDP, current market prices	1,485,038	1,658,389	1,980,914
-Agriculture	329,886	346,786	407,647
-Mining	146,607	165,310	215,090
-Manufacturing	302,136	333,166	389,807
-Electricity, gas & water	47,169	58,592	70,006
-Construction	95,696	110,255	139,162
-Trade	212,139	244,933	289,089
-Transport & communications	66,359	72,412	85,392
-Finance	27,215	31,617	37,404
-Public administration	113,856	128,904	149,647
-Others	143,975	166,414	197,670
Net factor income from abroad	-48,083	-77,928	-82,250

Source: Asian Development Bank

In 2009, agriculture contributed 22.1 per cent to GDP, industry 39.7 per cent and services 38.2 per cent.

Inflation has been rising in recent years; it was estimated at 3.1 per cent in 2003, 4.5 per cent in 2004, 8.3 per cent in 2005, 12.6 per cent in 2007 and 25.6 per cent in 2008. This is mainly due to the global economic downturn and the inefficiency of some nationalised companies. Inflation was estimated to be 7 per cent in 2012.

Vietnam's national debt was an estimated US$32 million in 2010 (40 per cent of GDP).

Foreign Investment
Foreign companies with operations in Vietnam include British Petroleum, Mitsubishi, Sumitomo, Mobil and Fina. In 1998 foreign investment was US$1,735 million, a fall of 40 per cent on the 1997 figure. Foreign investment fell by a further 30 per cent in 1999, largely due to the Asian financial crisis. Foreign investment seems unlikely to increase until Vietnam improves the business climate for foreign businesses. In 2009, disbursed Foreign Direct Investment was US$10.0 billion.

Over US$2 billion of development assistance for Vietnam was pledged by multilateral and bilateral donors in 2000.

Balance of Payments / Imports and Exports
During the 1980s one third of Vietnam's exports and two thirds of its imports were traded with Comecon, the Soviet bloc trading organisation which Hanoi had joined in 1978. The collapse of the Soviet bloc, and the consequent loss of aid and concessionary credits, forced Hanoi to look elsewhere for trading partners. A bilateral agreement with the US came into force in 2001. It dramatically increased Vietnam's exports and Vietnam joined the WTO in 2007.Major export trading partners now include the US, Japan, Australia, China, Germany, Taiwan, and Singapore. Main import trading partners include China, Japan, Singapore, Republic of Korea, Taiwan, Hong Kong and Thailand.

The trade balance of Vietnam in recent years is shown in the following table:

External Trade in US$ Million

Year	Exports fob	Imports cif	Balance
2008	62,685	80,714	-18,209
2009	57,096	69,949	-12,853
2010	72,192	84,801	-12,609

Source: Asian Development Bank

Main export commodities are shown in the following table. Figures are in US$ million.

Commodity	2005	2006	2007
Textile products	4,772	5,854	7,750
Marine products	2,733	3,358	3,763
Rice	1,407	1,276	1,489
Coffee	740	1,217	1,911
Wood & wood products	1,562	1,943	2,404
Rubber	804	1,286	1,393

VIETNAM

- continued

Coal	669	914	1,000

Source: Asian Development Bank

The value of exports and imports by SITC section is shown in the following tables. Figures are in US$ million. Source: ADB.

Exports	2004	2005	2006
Food & live animals	5,278	6,346	7,509
Beverage & tobacco	174	150	144
Crude materials exc. fuels	831	1,229	1,845
Mineral fuels etc.	6,233	8,358	9,709
Animal, vegetable oil & fats	38	18	19
Chemicals	421	536	792
Basic manufactures	1,890	2,165	2,926
Machines, transport equipment	2,562	3,145	4,195
Misc. manufactured goods	9,055	10,494	12,679
Unclassified goods	3	5	7

Imports	2004	2005	2006
Food & live animals	1,495	1,955	2,299
Beverage & tobacco	163	176	145
Crude materials exc. fuels	1,454	1,623	2,084
Mineral fuels etc.	3,982	5,366	6,699
Animal, vegetable oil & fats	224	188	254
Chemicals	4,694	5,310	6,317
Basic manufactures	8,859	10,172	12,164
Machines, transport equipment	8,737	9,252	10,806
Misc. manufactured goods	1,795	1,899	2,244
Unclassified goods	567	820	1,879

Trading Partners, 2009-10 million US$

	2009	2010
Exports, total	**57,196**	**67,994**
US	11,356	14,444
Japan	6,292	7,432
China	4,909	6,337
Australia	2,277	2,868
Singapore	2,076	1,458
Imports	**69,949**	**95,826**
China	16,441	25,433
Singapore	4,248	8,126
Japan	7,468	8,996
Korea, Rep. of	6,976	7,169
Thailand	4,514	6,430

Source: Asian Development Bank

Central Bank
State Bank of Vietnam, 47-49 Ly Thai To Street, Hanoi, Vietnam. Tel: +84 4 8252831, fax: +84 4 8258385, URL: http://www.sbv.gov.vn
Governor: Nguyen Van Giau

Chambers of Commerce and Trade Organisations
Vietnam Chamber of Commerce and Industry, URL: http://www.vcci.com.vn/
General Department of Customs, URL: http://www.customs.gov.vn/

MANUFACTURING, MINING AND SERVICES

Primary and Extractive Industries
Vietnam has oil and gas deposits offshore. Oil reserves at the beginning of January 2012 were estimated at 4.40 billion barrels an increase on the previous estimates following recent exploration. Oil production rose from an estimated 339,000 barrels per day in 2002 to 403,300 barrels per day in 2004 but fell to 318,120 barrels per day in 2011. Oil consumption rose from 186,000 barrels per day in 2002 to 210,000 barrels per day in 2004 and an estimated 352,000 barrels per day in 2011. Net oil exports were an estimated 67,000 barrels per day in 2005. Figures for 2006 show that Vietnam exported 125,000 barrels per day to Australia, 40,000 to the USA and 30,000 to Japan. The state-owned oil company, PetroVietnam, reports to the Ministry of Industry.

Western oil companies involved in Vietnam include BP, BHP, Conoco, Enterprise, Fina, Idemitsu, IPL, Japan National Oil, Mitsubishi, Mobil, Nexen, OMV, Occidental, Pedco, PetroCanada, Petronas Carigali, Statoil, Sumitomo, and TotalFina. Companies from India and Malaysia have been drilling offshore since 1988. The first oil field, Bach Ha, was developed by a Vietnam/Soviet joint venture (Vietsovpetro) and began pumping in 1986. Vietnam has a small refinery at Ho Chi Minh city, built with French help, which produces diesel fuel.

Vietnam's natural gas industry is predicted to grow as energy consumption in the country rises. Production has risen from an estimated 45,900 million cubic feet in 2001 to 272 billion cubic feet in 2011. Figures for 2011 showed that Vietnam consumed all it produced. The Cuu Long basin is the largest natural gas production area. Natural gas reserves were estimated at 7.0 trillion cubic feet at the beginning of January 2008.

Vietnam has rich deposits of coal including high grade anthracite. Reserves of coal were estimated at 165 million short tons in 2002. Coal production has increased over recent years, doubling between 1994 and 1998, and reaching a peak of 12.6 million short tons in 1997. In recent years production has begun to rise again after slight falls at the end of the 1990s.

In 1998, coal production was an estimated 19.4 million short tons, falling to 10.98 million short tons in 2000, before rising to 11.0 million short tons in 2001 and 18.1 million short tons in 2004. Fgures for 2010 show that production rose to 49.2 million short tons. Consumption has also picked up, falling from 8.3 million short tons in 1998 to 7.3 million short tons in 2001 before rising to 8.1 million short tons in 2004 and 25.7 million short tons in 2010. Exports - mainly to China, Japan, Thailand, the European Union, Mexico and Brazil - have increased. Net coal exports in 2010 were 23.5 million short tons, up from 3.7 million short tons in 2001. The Quang Yen coal field near Haiphong is the largest in Southeast Asia. The company that oversees Vietnam's coal industry is the Vietnam Coal Corporation, Vinacoal.

Other mineral resources include bauxite, iron ore, copper, tin, chromate, granite, marble and clay.

Energy
Vietnam's total energy consumption was estimated at 1.69 quadrillion Btu in 2009. Per capita energy consumption was 9.6 million Btu in 2001, compared with 341.8 million Btu in the US. Fuel share of energy consumption in 2004 was as follows: oil, 50 per cent; coal, 18 per cent; hydro-electricity, 20 per cent: natural gas, 12 per cent.

Vietnam's electricity generation capacity was estimated at 8.3 gigawatts in 2002. Electricity generation rose from 20.6 billion kilowatthours (kWh) in 1998 to 29.8 billion kWh in 2001, of which 39.9 per cent was thermal and 60.0 per cent was hydroelectric. Consumption in 1998 was an estimated 19.2 billion kWh. A government programme is underway to boost power generation, modernise existing power plants, construct new ones and convert existing gas turbine plants from single to multiple fuels. The state power company, Electricity of Vietnam (EVN), is also working to develop a national electricity grid by 2020. Figures for 2010 show that installed electriciy capicity was 115.21 GWe and generation was 90.64 billion Wh with consumption at 85.68 billion kWh.

Manufacturing
Heavy industry is principally concentrated in the north of the country where the government developed key sectors such as electrical power, iron and steel, engineering and chemicals. Until 1975, industrial development in the south was based on light industry. These enterprises were principally concentrated around Saigon (Ho Chi Minh City) and had benefited from the installation of modern machinery. They depended, however, on imported parts and raw materials; in mid-1975 only two thirds were functioning because these were in short supply.

Between 1977 and 1986 the tendency was to downgrade heavy industry in favour of smaller industrial projects serving local needs and agriculture in particular providing local jobs and using home made machines. The 1982 and 1986 State Plans further reduced investment in heavy industry emphasising energy, consumer goods and exports. By the end of the 1980s, shortages of raw materials, power and spare parts meant that most factories were working at less than 50 per cent of capacity. Ho Chi Minh City accounts for one third of industrial output and produces 70 per cent of consumer goods. Industrial production slowed down in 1997 due to a contraction in consumer spending. Light industry is dominant, particularly food processing, textiles and footwear. The textile industry accounts for about 16 per cent of industrial output and is a good source of employment and export earnings. Figures for 2000 showed that 3.5 m,illion people were employed in the manufacturing sector, this had risen to 6.0 million in 2007. The following table shows the manufacturing output in recent years. Figures are in thousand metric tons.

Product	2005	2006	2007
Cement	30,808	30,976	36,400
Chemical fertilizers	2,189	2,176	2,424
Steel	3,403	3,828	4,250
Sugar, sugar syrups	1,175	1,129	1,671
Beer, '000 litres	1,460,600	1,547,900	1,845,000
Liquor, '000 litres	221,096	290,100	316,000
Bricks, million pieces	16,530	19,893	na
Bicycle tubes, '000 pieces	26,848	31,625	na
Bicycle tyres, '000 pieces	20,387	23,455	na
Cigarettes, million packets	4,485	4,030	4,320

Source: Asian Development Bank

Service Industries
In 2006 there were 3.6 million foreign arrivals, up from 1.6 million in 1997, and some 6.5 million domestic visitors to Hanoi.

Agriculture
Vietnam has an estimated 7 million hectares of cultivable land, whilst 50 per cent of the workforce is employed in agriculture. Rice is the main crop. Other important crops include rubber, coffee and tea. Vietnam is the world's third largest exporter of rice with 85 per cent of cultivated land devoted to rice-growing. After the 1975 unification the government modified the cooperative system in the north, providing greater incentives for farmers, while scaling down and later abandoning plans to collectivise agricultural land in the south.

During the 1980s price controls on agricultural products were removed. The government is attempting to expand the cultivated area in order to grow more cash crops. Land reclamation had high priority at the end of the war and New Economic Zones were established in the Central Highlands, the Mekong Delta and the south east.

Agricultural Production in 2010

Produce	Int. $'000*	Tonnes
Rice, paddy	10,697,574	39,988,900
Indigenous pigmeat	4,670,046	3,037,940
Vegetables fresh nes	1,268,717	6,732,700
Coffee, green	1,187,920	1,105,700
Fruit fresh nes	895,098	2,564,500
Cassava	890,199	8,521,670

- continued		
Natural rubber	863,003	754,482
Indigenous cattle meat	748,719	277,162
Indigenous chicken meat	648,557	455,317
Sugar cane	517,885	15,946,800
Bananas	417,208	1,481,400
Mangoes, mangosteens, guavas	343,922	574,000

* unofficial figures

Source: http://faostat.fao.org/site/339/default.aspx Food and Agriculture Organization of the United Nations, Food and Agricultural commodities production

A campaign to encourage stockbreeding has greatly increased herds since 1980.

In 1979, forest land in Vietnam was estimated at 12.6 million ha. and the forests included many varieties of valuable timber. Uncontrolled selling for fuel and land clearance had reduced the forests to less than 6 million hectares by the middle of the 1990s. Conservation and replanting projects have so far failed to prevent continuing deforestation and its serious agricultural consequences.

Fresh water and sea fish are an essential part of the Vietnamese diet and an increasingly important export. FAO figures for 2010 put the total catch at 2,420,800 tonnes.

COMMUNICATIONS AND TRANSPORT

Travel Requirements

Citizens of the USA, Canada, Australia and the EU require a passport valid for at least one month beyond the expiration of the visa, and a visa, apart from nationals of Denmark, Finland, Norway and Sweden who do not require a visa for stays of up to 15 days. Transit passengers continuing their journey within 24 hours, provided holding valid return or onward tickets, do not require a visa. At present, visas can be issued for either groups or individuals.

For security reasons, it is advisable to carry copies of documents rather than originals when in Vietnam.

Visa and passport regulations are very complex and subject to frequent change. It is therefore advisable to contact the consular section at the embassy before any travel to Vietnam.

National Airlines

The national carrier is Vietnam Airlines which operates domestic and international flights. A small Vietnamese carrier, Pacific Airlines, flies to Taipei.
Vietnam Airlines, URL: http://www.vietnamair.com.vn

International Airports

There are international airports at Hanoi, Ho Chi Minh City and Da Nang.

Railways

A coastal line 1,730 km long links Hanoi and Ho Chi Minh city, in 2007 funds were to be made available to develop a high speed link between the two cities. There are also rail links between Hanoi and Haiphong (104km), Hanoi and Lang Son on the Chinese border (175km), and Hanoi and Lao Cai in north western Vietnam (296 km). There are also direct international train services from Nanning and Beijing in China to Hanoi.
Vietnam Railways: URL: http://www.vr.com.vn
Hanoi Railway Station, 120 Le Duan Road, Hanoi, Vietnam. Tel: +84 4 825 2628.
Saigon Railway Station , 01 Nguyen Thong Street, District 3, Ho Chi Minh City, Vietnam. Tel: +84 8 824 5585

Roads

Vietnam has a road network of 105,000 km, of which 15 per cent is paved. In 1989 Route 9 linking Savannakhet in Laos and Hue in Vietnam was completed with Soviet aid. Route 1 links Hanoi via Ho Chi Minh City with the Cambodian border and Phnom Penh. Approval for the construction of a 1,050 mile highway to link the north and south has been granted and was scheduled to be completed by 2003. Long distance buses serve most Vietnamese towns. Vehicles are driven on the right.

Shipping

Haiphong is the main port and can handle ships of up to 10,000 tons. Other ports are at Da Nang, Hon Gai, Vung Tau and Ho Chi Minh City. Vietnam has a merchant fleet of 300 vessels. There is an extensive network of navigable rivers. Canals and other waterways criss-cross the Songkoi and Mekong river deltas.

HEALTH

In 2009, the government spent approximately 7.8 per cent of its total budget on healthcare, accounting for 37.5 per cent of all healthcare spending. Private expenditure accounts for 62.5 per cent of the health expenditure, largely out-of-pocket expenditure. Total expenditure on healthcare equated to 6.9 per cent of the country's GDP. Per capita expenditure on health was approximately US$77.

Figures for 2005-10 show that there are 107,131 physicians (12 per 10,000 population), 88,025 nurses and midwives (10 per 10,000 population) and 28,370 pharmaceutical personnel. There are 31 hospital beds per 10,000 population.

The infant mortality rate in 2010 was 19 per 1,000 live births. The child mortality rate (under 5 years) was 23 per 1,000 live births. The main causes of childhood mortality are: prematurity (18 per cent), diarrhoea (10 per cent), pneumonia (12 per cent), measles (5 per cent) and HIV/AIDS (1 per cent).

According to the latest WHO figures, in 2010 approximately 96 per cent of the population had access to improved drinking water sources. In the same year, approximately 76 per cent of the population had access to improved sanitation.(Source: http://www.who.int, World Health Statistics 2012)

EDUCATION

In 1997 there were 22 million children in education. Of these, 13.2 million were in primary schools, 4.3 million in secondary schools, and 26,000 in colleges and universities. Primary education is free. The adult literacy rate is an estimated 92 per cent. Approximately 80 per cent of the illiterate reside in remote areas. In 1997 the Education Law was implemented by the National Assembly and its aims are to encourage the establishing of semi-public, private schools, private kindergartens, and professional secondary schools and universities. Further it intends to improve the quality of teachers and to upgrade educational management.

About 15 per cent of the state's expenditure is currently allocated to schooling. Figures for 2002 put adult literacy at 91 per cent.

RELIGION

The population is mainly Buddhist (49 per cent). Up to nine per cent of the population are Christian, nearly all Roman Catholic. About three million people belong to the Cao Dai and Hoa Hao sects.

In August 1999 about 200,000 people gathered in La Vang to attend a mass in celebration of the 200th anniversary of a reported sighting of the Virgin Mary. It was estimated that this was the largest public gathering in 24 years that had not been organised by the communist party.

Vietnam has a religious liberty rating of 4 on a scale of 1 to 10 (10 is most freedom). (Source: World Religion Database)

COMMUNICATIONS AND MEDIA

The Communist Party controls the media. Journalists can be fined for spreading 'harmful' information and the government has closed down publications for transgressions. There is strict control of the internet and many sites are filtered.

Newspapers

The Vietnam News Agency is the official news agency of the Vietnamese state and has a network covering 61 cities and provinces, and has 18 international offices. Publications in foreign languages include English, French and Spanish. Nationwide there are 150 newspapers covering various topics.
Nhan Dan (The People), URL: http://www.nhandan.com.vn/english
Quan Doi Nhan Dan (People's Army), URL: http://www.qdnd.vn/qdnd/baongay.qdnd
Le Courrier de Vietnam, URL: http://lecourrier.vnagency.com.vn/

Broadcasting

Television is the most important medium. The Voice of Vietnam is the official broadcasting system of the Vietnamese government, available on five wavelengths and broadcasting in 12 languages. Pay per view TV is also available. Vietnamese Television (VTV) (URL: http://www.vtv.org.vn/home) has four channels. There are also five regional television channels and each of the 61 cities and provinces has its own channel. There are ove r60 radio stations at city and provincial level, approximately 300 stations at district level and more than 8,000 radio relay stations.

Telecommunications

Vietnam's telecommunications modernisation programme began in 1990. The system linking Hanoi and Ho Chi Minh City has been digitalised. There are 29 million telephone main lines in use, with a further 70 million mobile phones. Internet users numbered 23 million in 2009.

ENVIRONMENT

Vietnam is a signatory to the following environmental agreements: Conventions on Biodiversity, Climate Change, Desertification, Endangered Species, Environmental Modification, Hazardous Wastes, Law of the Sea, Ozone Layer Protection, Ship Pollution, and Wetlands. The country has signed, but not ratified, the Nuclear Test Ban. Vietnam is a signatory to the Kyoto Protocol.

Main environmental problems include: water pollution and over fishing, groundwater contamination, urban industrialisation, deforestation and soil degradation.

Vietnam's energy related carbon emissions were estimated in 2001 at 46.19 million metric tons, representing 0.2 per cent of world carbon emissions. Per capita carbon emissions in the same year were estimated at 0.16 metric tons, compared with 20.2 metric tons in the US. Most of Vietnam's carbon emissions come from industry (38 per cent), followed by transport (33 per cent), the residential sector (20 per cent) and the commercial sector (9 per cent). Vietnam's energy industry emits most carbon from oil (59.2 per cent in 2001), followed by coal (33.7 per cent) and natural gas (6.9 per cent). In 2006, Vietnam's emissions from the consumption of fossil fuels totalled 112.80 million metric tons of carbon dioxide, giving it a world ranking of 38. (Source: EIA)

Vietnam's Space Technology Institute (http://www.sti.vast.ac.vn) was inaugurated in 2007. Its functions include the development of satellite technology and equipment, remote sensing technology and space dynamics. Its first communications satellite (VINASAT-1) was launched in 2008 and should cover 90 per cent of the domestic market. A second satellite is expected to be launched in 2012. A small satellite for environmental research was launched in 2010.

YEMEN

Republic of Yemen

Al Jumhuriya al Yamaniya

Capital: Sana'a (Population estimate, 2011: 1.9 million)

Head of State: Gen. Abd Ar-Rabbuh Mansur Hadi (Transitional President)

National Flag: A tricolour of red, white and black

CONSTITUTION AND GOVERNMENT

Constitution
There were formerly two Yemens. The People's Democratic Republic of Yemen consisted of Aden and the former British Protectorate of South Arabia. The kingdom of Yemen, created at the dissolution of the Ottoman Empire, was proclaimed the Yemen Arab Republic in 1962. After years of friction the Yemen Arab Republic and the People's Democratic Republic of Yemen were unified on 22 May 1990. The new constitution covered the economy, defence, human rights, the judiciary, and local government. It established the main governmental institutions, the Presidential Council, the House of Representatives, and the Council of Ministers.

The Presidential Council was created for the transitional period. It has five members and a consultative council of 45 members. The chairman of the Council is Lt. Gen. Ali Abdullah Saleh, the former head of the Yemen Arab Republic. The Council's legislative functions are to issue laws approved by itself and the House of Representatives, to ratify agreements that do not need the House's approval, and to call referenda. The Council may take decisions during the House's recess but these decisions must be submitted to the House's next session and may be overturned. It also has executive functions, which are to suspend a prime minister and to resolve disagreements between a prime minister and a minister.

In 2000 the constitution was amended to extend the President's term from five to seven years.

The Council of Ministers is the executive and administrative wing of the government and is accountable to the Presidential Council and the House of Representatives. It consists of the Prime Minister and his Ministers. The Prime Minister selects ministers in consultation with the Presidential Council. The Council of Ministers executes state policy, which includes preparing bills, drafting decisions, and directing the work of ministries, administrative and public institutions. It also implements the state's financial directives, including the budget.

In March 2011, the president said he would look at reforming the constitution, reforming it from a presidential style of government to a parliamentary system. In November 2011, it was agreed that the transitional president elected in February 2012 would oversee the drafting of a new constitution.

To consult the constitution, please visit: http://www.wipo.int/wipolex/en/details.jsp?id=9622

International Relations
Yemen has good relations with its neighbours. A border dispute with Saudi Arabia was brought to a close recently and a border agreement was signed in 2006.

Recent Events
In October 2000, while in the port of Aden, the US Naval ship USS Cole was badly damaged in a suicide attack that resulted in the deaths of 17 US personnel. In the same month, a bomb exploded at the British Embassy. Four Yemenis who were jailed for the British Embassy attack said it was carried out in solidarity with the Palestinians. In October 2002, a French oil tanker was attacked and damaged when it was rammed by a small boat packed with explosives off the Yemeni coast. Early reports indicated the attack was carried out by Al-Qaeda.

Government troops fought supporters of the dissident cleric, Houssein al Houthi, during the summer of 2004, and claimed to have killed the cleric in September of that year. There was a resurgence of fighting between the two parties in the Spring of 2005, but in May the President announced that the rebel leader had agreed to renounce the violence in return for a pardon. However, low-level insurgency in the north, allegedly to install Shi'ite religious rule, continued over the years, and in January 2008, there were renewed clashes between security forces and rebels loyal to al-Houthi. In April 2008, southern Yemenis protested against an alleged northern bias in state job allocation, and there were clashes with troops. The spring of 2008 saw a series of bomb attacks on police and foreign business and tourism targets.

In September 2008 there was a two car bomb attacks on the US embassy; 16 people were thought to have died, none of them embassy personnel. The bombers were dressed in police uniforms and fired on embassy guards during the attack. The US believed al-Qaeda was

responsible. In October President Saleh announced the arrest of Islamist militant suspects. In February 2009 the government announced it was releasing over 170 suspected members of al-Qaeda on condition of good behaviour.

In April 2010 the British Ambassador's convoy was targeted by a suicide bomber. Ambassador Tim Torlot escaped unharmed and it was believed only the bomber was killed. Yemen accused Al-Qaeda of being behind the attack.

In October 2010 Yemen became the focus of an international terror alert after packages, originating from Yemen, containing explosives were found on cargo planes heading for the USA.

Early in 2011 protests started in several Middle Eastern countries demanding dramatic changes. Anti-government demonstrations also began in Yemen; on February 11, protesters demanded the resignation of President Ali Abdullah Saleh who has been in power for 32 years. President Saleh announced he would not seek another term in office but protesters wanted his immediate resignation. On March 10 President Saleh announced his plans to change the constitution to move to a parliamentary system saying that a referendum would take place later in the year.

President Saleh initially promised not to renew his presidency in 2013 but to hand over power to his deputy within 30 days of a deal being signed, if he were given immunity from prosecution. However President Saleh repeatedly failed to sign the deal, which had been brokered by Gulf states and approved by a coalition of opposition parties.

The demonstrations continued and police snipers fired on a pro-democracy camp in Sanaa; it was believed more than 50 people were killed. Several ministers and military leaders declared their backing for the demonstrators. President Saleh said that the ongoing protests risked the stability of the country and would plunge it into civil war, a state of emergency was imposed. In April the protests continued but President Saleh vowed to remain in office. In May thousands fled the city of Sanaa following clashes between troops and tribal fighters who were supporting the protesters. In June President Saleh was injured in a rocket attack and was flown to Saudi Arabia for treatment. Vice president Abedrabbo Mansour Hadi took over as acting president.

At least 100 people were killed and hundreds reported injured in protests during the month of September 2011. The vice-president, Abedrabbo Mansour Hadia greed a truce following negotiations with western diplomats who had urged an end to the violence. President Saleh returned to Yemen in late September repeating he was committed to handing over power. He called for dialogue and early polls and asked for an end to the violence.

On 30 September 2011 it was reported that senior US-born al-Qaeda leader Anwar al-Awlaki had been killed in the Jawf province of Yemen.

Security forces fired on anti-government protestors in October 2011. Several fatalities were reported. The protestors had been marching to call for President Ali Abudllah Saleh's resignation.

In October 2011, the Yemeni human rights activist Tawakul Karman won the Nobel Peace Prize, together with Ellen Johnson Sirleaf and Leymah Gbowee of Liberia.

In November 2011 Field Marshall Ali Abdullah Saleh (President) signed an agreement whereby he would step down as president and hand over power to his deputy until an early election is held. In return for standing down he will be immune from prosecution in the future. The Vice-President Abdrabbuh Mansour Hadi named a senior opposition figure, Mohammed Basindwa, as interim prime minister. He had to form a national reconciliation government composed of equal numbers of opposition members and Saleh loyalists ahead of early elections to be held on 21 February.

Presidential elections for the transitional president were held on 21 February and were won by the sole candidate Gen. Abd-Rabbu Mansour Hadi. Mr Hadi had been the vice-president under President Saleh. President Saleh formally ceded power to Mr Hadi on 27 February 2012.

In March 2012, more than 100 people were reported killed in clashes between soldiers and militants linked to al-Qaeda. Fifty soldiers were also taken prisoner from an army post. Suicide bombers also targeted military positions in Zinjibar. There have been allegations that some of the fighters are linked to ex-president Saleh. Islamists took control of some parts of the Abyan province in 2011.

In May 2012, at least 90 soldiers were killed in a suicide bomb attack in the capital Sana'a. A further 200 people were injured. Most of the victims belonged to the paramilitary force, the Central Security Organisation. The commander, Yahya Saleh, a nephew of the former president, was later sacked. Later in the month a suicide bomber killed at least 12 people in the northern town of Hazam. The bomber targetted a school where Shia rebels had gathered for prayers. The dead are reported to include one woman and three children.

President Abdrabbuh Mansour Hadi launched a US-backed military offensive to increase his fight against al-Qaeda. The al-Qaeda strongholds of Jaar and Zinjibar were recaptured by the Yemeni army om June 2012. Several hundred militants were reported to have escaped to the town of Azzan in the Shabwa province. At least nine people were killed in attacks which were reported to also involve a US drone. In a further success for the Yemeni army, they also retook the town of Shuqra, Abyan province. Several towns in Abyan have been under the control of Ansar al-Sharia for more than a year.

Clashes between the Republican Guard and forces loyal to the government were reported in the capital, Sanaa, in August 2012. The Republican Guard is under the control of the son of former President Saleh. In the same month, a secessionist leader, Ahmed Abdullah al-Hassani, was arrested on his return to the country after years of exile.

Al-Qaeda was believed to be behind an attack in August 2012 on the government's intelligence headquarters in Aden. At least 14 people, mostly soldiers, were reported to have been killed.

In September 2012, violent protests took place in several Middle East countries following the release of an amateur anti-Islam video made in the USA. In Yemen protesters broke into the US embassy compound in Sanaa. The minister of defence, Muhammad Nasir Ahmad, survived a car attack in Sanaa. Eleven people were killed in the attack.

A Saudi diplomat was shot dead in San'aa in November 2012.

Legislature

The main legislative body is the House of Representatives, based in Sana'a. Its 301 members are elected for a four year term by all Yemeni citizens who are over 18 years old. The House decides the State's laws, adopts the State's budget and approves all general international political and economic treaties. It elects the five members of the Presidential Council and can pass a bill even if the Council disagrees with it, as long as the bill is passed when returned to the House. It can convene after a general election, even though the Presidential Council has not called it to do so. The House also has the right to issue directives to the Government. The Prime Minister and his Ministers may speak in the House if they wish. However, they cannot vote unless they are members.

House of Representatives (Majlis al-Nowab), PO Box 623, Sana'a, Yemen. Tel: +967 1 272 761, fax: +967 1 276 099, e-mail: parliament.SG@y.net.ye, URL: http://www.parliament.gov.ye

---

National Reconciliation Government (as of June 2013)
Prime Minister: Mohammed Salem Basindwa (page 1384)
Minister of Foreign Affairs: Dr Abu-Bakr Abdallah al-Qirbi (page 1376)
Minister of Public Works and Roads: Omar Abdullah al-Kurshumi
Minister of Marine Resources: Awadh Saad al-Saqatri
Minister of Defence: Mohammed Nasir Ahmed
Minister of Electricity & Energy: Saleh Hasan Sumai
Minister of Religious Endowments and Islamic Affairs: Hamoud Mohammed Ubad
Minister of Social Affairs and Labour: Dr Amat al-Razaq Ali Humaid
Minister of Oil and Mineral Resources: Ahmed Abdullah Dares
Minister of Higher Education and Scientific Research: Hisham Sharaf Abdallah
Minister of Youth and Sports: Muammar al-Eryani
Minister of the Interior: Abdul-Qader Qahtan (page 1499)
Minister of the Civil Service: Nabil Shamsan
Minister of Agriculture and Irrigation: Farid Ahmad Mujawar
Minister of Finance: Sakhr Ahmed Al-Wajih
Minister of Technical Education & Vocational Training: Abul-Hafez Nomu'an
Minister of Education: Abdul-Razzaq Al-Ashwal
Minister of Tourism: Qasim Sallam
Minister of Planning & International Co-operation: Mohammed Al-Sa'adi
Minister of Information: Ali Ahmad Muhammad al-Amrani
Minister of Public Health: Ahmed Qassim Al-Ansi
Minister of Human Rights: Huriya Ahmed Mashour
Minister of Telecommunications and IT: Ahmed Obaid Bin Daghr
Minister of Local Administration: Ali Mohamed Al-Yazidi
Minister of Legal Affairs: Mohammad Al-Mikhlafi
Minister of Transport: Wa'ed Abullah Bathib
Minister of Justice: Murshed Ali Al-Arashani
Ministry of Industry and Trade: Saad al-Din Ali in Talib
Minister of Water and the Environment: Abd Razzaz Khaled
Minister of Culture: Abdullah Mandhouq
Minister of Expatriate Affairs: Mujahid Al-Quhali
Minister of Shura Council: Rashad Al-Rassas
Minister of State for Cabinet Affairs: Jawharah Hamoud Thabet (JMP)
Minister of State: Shaif Saghir (GPC)
Minister of State: Hasan Ahmed Sharaf al-Din

Ministries

Office of the President, Zubairy Street, Sana'a, Yemen. Tel: +967 1 273092
Ministry of Foreign Affairs, Alolofi Square, Sana'a, Yemen. Tel: +967 1 276544, URL: http://www.mofa.gov.ye/
Ministry of Finance, Ring Road, Sana'a, Yemen. Tel: +967 1 260375, URL: http://www.mof.gov.ye/
Ministry of Agriculture and Irrigation, Alzira Street, Sana'a, Yemen.
Ministry of Oil and Mineral Resources, PO Box 81, Sana'a, Yemen. Tel: +967 1 202309, fax: +967 1 202 314; URL: http://www.mom.gov.ye/
Ministry of Youth and Sport, Alquiadah Street, Sana'a, Yemen. Tel: +967 1 215653

Ministry of Industry and Trade, PO Box 1804, Sana'a, Yemen. Tel: +967 1 252471, fax: +967 1 251557, e-mail: most@y.net.ye, URL: http://www.most.org.ye/
Ministry of Fisheries, PO Box 19179, Sana'a, Yemen. Tel: +967 1 268580
Ministry of the Interior and Security, Almatar Road, Sana'a, Yemen. Tel: +967 1 252701
Ministry of Planning and International Co-operation, Abaunia Street, PO Box 175, Sana'a, Yemen. Tel: +967 1 250101, fax: +967 1 251 503, URL: http://www.mpic-yemen.org
Ministry of Transport, Altahrir Square, Sana'a, Yemen. Tel: +967 1 260904, URL: http://wadi.transport-hadhramaut.info/
Ministry of Justice, Wadi Dhahr Street, Sana'a, Yemen. Tel: +967 1 252158
Ministry of Information & Planning, Sana'a, Yemen. Tel: +967 1 200050, e-mail: yemen-info@y.net.ye,
Ministry of Awqaf (Religious Endowments) and Guidance, Sana'a, Yemen. Tel: +967 1 274438
Ministry of the Civil Service and Social Security, Sana'a, Yemen. Tel: +967 1 200404, URL: http://www.mocsi.gov.ye
Ministry of Communications and Information Technology, Sana'a, Yemen. Tel: +967 1 331456, fax: +967 1 331457
Ministry of Construction, Housing and Urban Planning, Sana'a, Yemen. Tel: +967 1 202288
Ministry of Defence, Sana'a, Yemen. Tel: +967 1 250330
Ministry of Education, Gamal Abdulnasser Street, Sana'a, Yemen. Tel: +967 1 274548, URL: http://www.moe.gov.ye/
Ministry of Expatriate Affairs, Sana'a, Yemen. e-mail: mia@y.net.ye
Ministry of Human Rights, URL: http://www.mhryemen.org/
Ministry of Public Health, URL: http://www.mophp-ye.org/english/index.html

Elections

The last presidential elections were held in September 2006. Ali Abdullah Saleh was re-elected with 77 per cent of the vote. The most recent parliamentary elections were held in April 2003; the General People's Congress won 238 seats. The largest opposition party is Islah, which gained 46 seats. Elections were due in February 2009 but were postponed for two years while constitutional reforms were discussed.

After President Saleh finally stepped down in November 2011 it was announced that early elections would be held in February 2011. They were postponed and elections for the transitional president finally took place on 21 February. The sole candidate, Abd-Rabbu Mansour Hadi, won with approximately 65 per cent of the vote and was sworn in on 25 February. Mr Saleh ceded power to him on 27 February 2012. New elections are planned for 2014 under the new constitution.

Political Parties

Arab Socialist Ba'ath Party (Ba'ath); General People's Congress (GPC); Nasserite Unionist Popular Organization (NUPO); Yemen Socialist Party (YSP); Yemeni Alliance for Reform (al-Islah)

Diplomatic Representation

British Embassy, 938 Thaher Himiyear Street, Sana'a, Yemen. Tel: + 967 1 308100, fax: +967 1 302454, URL: http://ukinyemen.fco.gov.uk/en
Ambassador: Nicholas Hopton (page 1443)
US Embassy, Sanaa (PO Box 22347), Yemen. Tel: +967 1 303155, fax: +967 1 303182, e-mail: usembassyol@y.net.ye, URL: http://yemen.usembassy.gov/
Ambassador: Gerald Michael Feierstein (page 1424)
Embassy of Yemen, 57 Cromwell Road, London SW7 2ED, United Kingdom. Tel: +44 (0)20 7584 6607, fax: +44 (0)20 7589 3350, URL: http://www.yemenembassy.org.uk/
Ambassador: Abdulla Ali Alradhi
Embassy of Yemen, Suite 705, 2600 Virginia Avenue, NW Washington DC 20037, USA. Tel: +1 202 965 4760, fax: +1 202 337 2017, URL: http://www.yemenembassy.org/
Chargé d'Affaires: Adel Ali Ahmed Alsunaini
Permanent Representative of the Republic of Yemen to the United Nations, 413 East 51st Street, New York, N.Y. 10022, USA.Tel: +1 212 355 1730 / 1731, fax: +1 212 750 9613, URL: http://www.un.int/wcm/content/site/yemen
Permanent Representative to the UN: Jamal Abdallah al-Sallal

LEGAL SYSTEM

All laws are based on the Islamic *Shari'a*. The judiciary is independent of the government. The constitution stipulates that every citizen is subject to the rule of law. Anyone accused of an offence is held for a maximum of 24 hours, after which they should be cross-examined by a judge who decides whether or not to prosecute. Courts of first instance in each district have jurisdiction over personal status, civil, criminal and commercial cases. Appeals go to Courts of Appeal in each of 18 provinces with Civil, Criminal, Matrimonial and Commercial Divisions, each consisting of three-judge benches. Supreme Court is highest court of appeal and sits in Sana; it has eight divisions: Constitutional, Appeals, Scrutiny, Criminal, Military, Civil, Family, Commercial, and Administrative.

There are significant human rights abuses in the Yemen. The citizens' ability to change their government is limited due to corruption and fraud. There have been recent reports of unlawful killings by security forces, as well as torture taking place in prisons. Excessive use of force has been used to curb demonstrations, and arrests can be arbitrary. Judicial weakness and widespread corruption are also problems. There are restrictions on freedom of speech, the press, and peaceful assembly. Critics of the government are intimidated.

Yemen retains the death penalty, and there are reportedly hundreds of people under sentence of death. Over 50 people were reported to have been executed in 2010 and over 40 in 2011.

YEMEN

LOCAL GOVERNMENT

The country is divided into 21 administrative units called governorates which are subdivided into districts and municipal councils. The governors of these are answerable to the Council of Ministers. The governorates are:Abyan, 'Adan (Aden), Ad Dali', Al Bayda', Al Hudaydah, Al Jawf, Al Mahrah, Al Mahwit, Amanat al 'Asimah, 'Amran, Dhamar, Hadramawt, Hajjah, Ibb, Lahij, Ma'rib, Raymah, Sa'dah, San'a' (Sanaa), Shabwah, Ta'izz.

In each governorate there are elected local councils. Local elections were held for the first time in 2001. The most recent elections were held in September 2006. In 2008, parliament voted to cancel local elections scheduled for 2009. They are currently scheduled to take place in 2013.

AREA AND POPULATION

Area
The Republic of Yemen comprises that area of the Arabian peninsula formerly occupied by the Yemen Arab Republic (North Yemen) and the People's Democratic Republic of Yemen (South Yemen). Yemen has an estimated area of 203,850 sq. miles (527,969 sq. km). It is bounded on the west by the Red Sea, on the north by Saudi Arabia, on the east by Oman, and on the south by the Gulf of Aden. Included in the state are the offshore islands of Perim and Kamaran in the Red Sea, and Socotra in the Gulf of Aden. The highlands and central plateau, and the highest portions of the maritime range of what was South Yemen, form the most fertile part of Arabia, with abundant but irregular rainfall. The area of North Yemen is largely composed of mountains and desert, and rainfall is generally scarce.

To view a map, consult http://www.un.org/Depts/Cartographic/map/profile/yemen.pdf

Population
Yemen had an estimated population of 24.053 million in 2010 with an annual average growth rate of about 3.1 per cent for the period 2000-10. An estimated 32 per cent of the population lives in urban areas. The major cities in Yemen are Sana'a, which has an estimated population of 1.9 million, Aden, Al Hudaydah and Ta'izz.

The official language is Arabic.

Births, Marriages, Deaths
Estimated figures for 2010 put the birth rate at 38.1 births per 1,000 population and the number of deaths as 6.5 per 1,000 population. Life expectancy in 2009 was 63 years for males and 67 years for females. Healthy life expectancy was 54 years. As of 2010 the median age was 17 years. Approximately 44 per cent of the population was aged under 15 and 4 per cent over 60. The total fertility rate was 5.2 children per adult female. (Source: http://www.who.int, World Health Statistics 2012)

Public Holidays 2014
1 January: New Year's Day
14 January: Birth of the Prophet*
5 May: Labour Day
22 May: Unity Day
29 July: Eid al-Fitr (end of Ramadan)*
26 September: Revolution Day
5 October: Eid al-Adha (Feast of Sacrifice)*
14 October: National Day
25 October: Islamic New Year*
30 November: Independence Day
* Islamic holidays depend on the sighting of the moon and so dates can vary.

EMPLOYMENT

The workforce constitutes 25 per cent of the population, of which approximately 53 per cent are involved in agriculture, 17 per cent in public services, 4 per cent in manufacturing and 7 per cent in construction. Recent estimates put Yemen's unemployment rate at 30 per cent.

BANKING AND FINANCE

The financial centre is Aden.

Currency
1 Yemeni Rial = 100 Fils

GDP/GNP, Inflation, National Debt
Yemen is the poorest country in the Middle East and both the IMF and World Bank have advised on economic reforms. The economy relies quite heavily on oil production and so is hampered by fluctuations in oil prices. Oil accounts for 85 per cent of export earnings and 33 per cent of GDP. Although tourism has the potential for growth, this has been hindered by the terrorist attacks and civil unrest. The economy has been assisted by economic reforms that the government has implemented, including the reduction of subsidies on oil and electricity, and a privatisation program. Some of the reforms have been unpopular. The government is continuing its programme of reforms in return for borrowing from the International Monetary Fund. In 2003 government reserves had reached US$5 billion. In 2005, there was some social unrest caused by rising food and fuel prices. Subsidies were also cut to meet IMF targets. A liquified natural gas plant export facility became live in 2009.

Figures for 2007 put Gross National Income at US$19.4 billion giving a per capita figure of US$870 per capita. Figures for 2007 put GDP at US$22.5 billion a growth rate of 3.6 per cent up from 3.2 per cent the previous year. In 2010, GDP was put at approximately US$31 billion.

Per capita GDP was US$1,300. The agricultural sector contributes approximately 8 per cent of GDP and the industrial sector approximately 40 per cent and services 53 per cent. GDP was estimated at US$32 billion in 2011.

Inflation reached a peak of 71 per cent in 1995; it had fallen to 10 per cent by 2000 but had risen again to an estimated 11.7 per cent by 2005. Inflation is currently high; it was estimated at 13 per cent in December 2010, rising to 23 per cent in December 2011. Inflation is driven by rising prices and the political unrest.

Foreign Investment
The government has indicated that many state owned businesses will be sold by tender, auction or private subscription. These businesses include farm and agricultural co-operatives, construction companies, power stations, public housing facilities, refineries, a petroleum retail network, shipping companies and telecommunication companies. The government is currently seeking and encouraging foreign investors to partake in these ventures.

Balance of Payments / Imports and Exports
Yemen's major trading partners are China, Japan, Saudi Arabia, Singapore, South Korea, India, Indonesia, United Arab Emirates, Australia and United States. The main exports are crude oil, cotton, coffee, hides, vegetables, dried and salted fish. The main imports are textiles, manufactured consumer goods, petroleum products, sugar, grain, flour, cement, machinery, chemicals and food stuffs. Estimated figures for 2010 put export earnings at US$7.5 billion (oil, US$5.5 billion) . The cost of imported goods in 2010 was an estimated US$9 billion. Exports were an estimated US$
8.5 billion in 2011 and imports US$8.2 billion.

In early 2002 Yemen joined some of the institutions of the Gulf Co-operation Council (GCC).

Foreign Aid
In 2006, international donors met to agree an aid package and some US$4.7 billion was pledged for the period 2007-10. Main aid donors are The Netherlands, Germany, Japan, EU, USA and UK. An IMF program came into place in 2010 but was put on hold in 2011 due to political instability.

Central Bank
Central Bank of Yemen, PO Box 59, Ali Abdul Mughni Street, Sana'a, Yemen. Tel: +967 1 274314-18, fax: +967 1 274082 / 1 274360 / 1 274131, e-mail: info@centralbank.gov.ye, URL: http://www.centralbank.gov.ye
Governor: Mohammed Awad Bin Hammam

MANUFACTURING, MINING AND SERVICES

Primary and Extractive Industries
Yemen has mineral deposits of copper, zinc, iron, gold. silver lead and nickel.

Yemen currently has 3 billion barrels of proven oil reserves. Production in 2011 was put at 163,000 barrels per day with consumption at 162,000 barrels per day. The Aden Refinery Company has a refining capacity of 140,000 barrels per day. Several Western companies are now involved in oil exploration including Hunt Oil, Total and Canadian Occidental Petroleum.

Yemen has natural gas reserves of some 17.0 trillion cubic feet, making it a potentially important gas producer. Most of these reserves are concentrated in the Marib-Jawf fields, which are operated by the Yemen Exploration and Production Company (YEPC), and the Jannah tract, which is operated by Total. Production in 2010 was 340 billion cubic feet up from 220 billion cubic feet in 2010 Consumption in 2011 was 31 billion cubic feet up from 34 billion cubic feet meaning 309 billion cubic feet went for export.

Energy
Figures for 2010 estimated electricity production at 7.29 billion kWh and consumption at 5.51 billion kWh. All of Yemen's energy is oil generated.

Manufacturing
Trade is encouraged by tax and customs concessions. Foreign agencies have assisted in Yemen's development. Since 1958 the American Agency for International Development has given US$358 million for various development projects. The biggest areas of manufacturing are oil refining, food and beverage processing and materials for the construction trade, namely cement, iron and steel and mixed metal products like storage tanks and doors. Other smaller areas of manufacturing include leather goods, textiles and jewellery making.

Services
382,000 visitors went to Yemen in 2006. Tourism could be a growth area but incidences of kidnapping of foreigners has meant that the sector does not realise its full potential.

Agriculture
Agriculture is the main occupation of the inhabitants. This is largely of a subsistence nature, sorghum, sesame and millets being the chief crops, with wheat and barley widely grown at the higher elevations. The Tihama region, besides the Red Sea, has a tropical climate. Amongst the crops from this area are papaya, mango, cotton, dates and palm trees. The western mountain slopes have a sub-tropical to moderate climate with a high fruit yield. On the upper slopes of this region coffee and grains are grown. A wide variety of fruits are grown in the Central Highlands, which have a moderate climate. On the Eastern mountain slopes, which have a moderate to subtropical climate, grains, fruit trees, dates and palms flourish.

Agricultural Production in 2010

Produce	Int. $'000*	Tonnes
Indigenous cattle meat	260,821	96,551
Mangoes, mangosteens, guavas	240,253	400,978
Indigenous chicken meat	204,693	143,704

- continued		
Tomatoes	96,800	261,930
Grapes	95,047	166,278
Cow milk, whole, fresh	94,024	301,300
Indigenous goat meat	76,684	32,004
Sorghum	75,950	507,302
Indigenous sheep meat	75,147	27,599
Hen eggs, in shell	50,261	60,600
Potatoes	47,294	303,380
Onions, dry	47,018	223,860

* unofficial figures

Source: http://faostat.fao.org/site/339/default.aspx Food and Agriculture Organization of the United Nations, Food and Agricultural commodities production

Fishing is an important part of the agricultural sector and a small amount of the catch is now exported. Figures from the FAO for 2010 put the total catch at 191,100 tonnes. Recent figures show that Yemen had an estimated 1.4 million head of cattle and 13.9 million sheep and goats.

COMMUNICATIONS AND TRANSPORT

Travel Requirements
Citizens of the USA, Canada, Australia and the EU require a passport valid for at least six months beyond the length of stay and a visa. Transit passengers continuing their journey within 168 hours, provided holding valid onward or return documentation and not leaving the airport, do not require a visa. All nationals should contact the embassy to check precise visa requirements. As of 2010 visas were not availble on arrival.

The government of the Republic of Yemen refuses entry and transit facilities to holders of Israeli passports, or holders of passports containing visas valid or expired for Israel or any indication, such as entry or exit stamps, that the holder has visited Israel.

Yemeni law requires that all foreigners traveling in Yemen obtain exit visas before leaving the country. The loss of a passport can result in considerable delay to a traveller because Yemeni law requires that the traveller attempt to recover the passport by placing an advertisement in a newspaper and waiting a week for a response. All minor/underage visitors should be accompanied by their legal guardian(s) and/or provide a notarized letter in Arabic of parental consent when obtaining exit visas to depart Yemen.

International Airports
There are four major airports. Sana'a International Airport, 10 miles north of the city, has developed rapidly. Aden International Airport is at Khour Maksar. Hodeidah Airport is southeast of the city and Ta'izz Airport to the northeast.

National Airlines
The national airline, Yemenia, was founded in 1962. It now operates in Europe, Africa and the Middle-East. A merger between Yemenia and Al-Yemda, the former airline of the Peoples Democratic Republic of Yemen, took place in 1996.

Yemenia (Yemen Airways), URL: http://www.yemenia.com
Alyemda (Democratic Yemen Airlines/Alyemen Airlines of Yemen), PO Box 6006, Alyemda Building, Khormaksar Civil Airport, Aden, Republic of Yemen. Tel: +967 (2) 233 811, fax: +967 (2) 233 287

Roads
According to recent figures Yemen has some 69,200 km of roads, main routes accounting for nearly 10,000 km, and secondary routes accounting for 2,491 km. Vehicles are driven on the right. In 1997 there were 29.4 people per vehicle.

Ports and Harbours
Yemen's major ports are: Aden, Hisn an Nushaymah, Al Khalf, Mocha, Nishtun, Ra's Kathib and Salif. Ferry services operate between the ports.

HEALTH

Recent figures show that Yemen has over 60 hospitals as well as a network of medical centres and two maternity centres. In 2008, the government spent approximately 4.3 per cent of its total budget on healthcare, accounting for 26.5 per cent of all healthcare spending. Private expenditure equates to 73.5 per cent, of which 94.5 per cent is out-of-pocket. Total expenditure on healthcare equated to 5.5 per cent of the country's GDP. Per capita expenditure on health was approximately US$63. Figures for 2005-10 show that there are 7,127 physicians (3 per 10,000 population), 13,746 nurses and midwives (6.6 per 10,000 population), 2,638 pharmaceutical personnel, 792 environment and public health workers and 2,372 dentistry personnel. There are 7 hospital beds per 10,000 population.

In 2010, life expectancy at birth was 65 years. In 2010 the infant mortality rate (probability of dying before first birthday) was 57 per 1,000 live births and the child (under-five years old) mortality rate was 77 per 1,000 live births. The main causes of death in the under-fives are: prematurity (18 per cent), pneumonia (22 per cent), birth asphyxia (13 per cent) and diarrhoea (11 per cent). In the period 2000-09 an estimated 57.7 per cent of children (under five-years-old) were classified as stunted and 43.1 per cent as underweight.

According to the latest WHO figures, in 2010 approximately 55 per cent of the population had access to improved drinking water. In the same year, 53 per cent of the population had access to improved sanitation. (Source: http://www.who.int, World Health Statistics 2012)

EDUCATION

Both the Yemen Arab Republic and People's Democratic Republic of Yemen had established education systems before unification, which provided primary, middle, and secondary schools. The government of Yemen is committed to develop the education system to a high level and in 2000, 32.8 per cent of total government expenditure went on education.

Primary/Secondary Education
Primary education is compulsory and lasts between the ages of six to 15. Secondary education begins at 15 and continues for a further three years. Figures from 2004 show that 62 per cent of children completed primary education and 32.8 per cent of government spending went on education. (Source: UNESCO Institute for Statistics (UIS))

Higher Education
There are seven state or public universities located in Sana'a, Aden, Ta'izz, Ibb, Dhamar and Hadramout. In addition Yemen has five private and religious universities.

Adult illiteracy in 2007 was estimated at 58.9 per cent, 77.0 per cent for males and 40.5 per cent for females. In that year the literacy rate rose for youth literacy (15-24 years of age) to 80.4 per cent, 93.4 per cent for males and 66.8 per cent for females.

RELIGION

The majority of the population is Muslim, and most people are Sunni Muslims. There are also small Christian, Jewish and Hindu communities.

Yemen has a religious liberty rating of 3 on a scale of 1 to 10 (10 is most freedom). (Source: World Religion Database)

COMMUNICATIONS AND MEDIA

The government body administers broadcasting through the Public Corporation for Radio and Television. The government also controls some printing presses. There are reports of arrests of journalists and the government has closed down newspapers and websites for their views.

Newspapers
Illiteracy is widespread.
Al Thawreh, URL: http://www.althawranews.net
Al Ayyam, URL: http://www.al-ayyam.info/
Yemen Times, URL: http://yementimes.com/index.shtml

Broadcasting
Broadcasting is government controlled by the Ministry of Information. Republic of Yemen Television has two channels. Republic of Yemen Radio broadcasts on two networks. Due to the high level of illiteracy, television and radio are the main sources of news.

Telecommunications
The problem of installing telephone lines in mountainous areas was overcome by using Canadian solar powered microwave telephones. In 2008 there were estimated to be over 1 million landlines and 3.5 million mobile phones. It is estimated that Yemen had around 370,000 internet users in 2009.

ENVIRONMENT

Yemen's major environmental problems are the scarcity of natural freshwater resources, overgrazing, soil erosion, and desertification.

In 2010 Yemen's emissions from the consumption of fossil fuels totalled 26.50 million metric tons of carbon dioxide. (Source: EIA)

On an international level, Yemen is a party to the following conventions: Biodiversity, Climate Change, Climate Change-Kyoto Protocol, Desertification, Endangered Species, Environmental Modification, Hazardous Wastes, Law of the Sea, Ozone Layer Protection.

STATES OF THE WORLD

ZAMBIA
Republic of Zambia

Capital: Lusaka (Population estimate: 1.7 million)

Head of State: Michael Sata (President) (page 1509)

Vice President: Guy L.Scott

National Flag: Green background with on the lower fly side, an orange eagle in flight over a rectangular block of three vertical stripes in red, black and orange

CONSTITUTION AND GOVERNMENT

Constitution

At the dissolution of the Federation of Rhodesia and Nyasaland on 31 December 1963, Northern Rhodesia (as Zambia was then known) achieved internal self government under a new Constitution. Zambia became an independent Republic within the Commonwealth on 24 October 1964, 75 years after coming under British rule, and nine months after achieving internal self government.

The Constitution, prepared with the colonial power, provided for an opposition and reserved seats for the white electorate. The reserved seats ceased to be occupied after nine years, and in 1973, by the Choma Declaration, the opposition parties merged with the ruling party, UNIP - United National Independence Party.

In July 1973, a new constitution was introduced, making Zambia a one party state. The president, Dr. Kenneth Kaunda who had assumed office on 24 October 1964, was re-elected in 1973, 1978, 1983 and 1988. Following an attempted coup in May 1990, and considerable unrest throughout the country, the government announced a referendum on the introduction of a multi-party system in August 1991; however, this was cancelled due to pressure from organisations. The government announced general and presidential elections to be held on 31 October 1991. Nine new political parties were formed, but the Movement for Multi-Party Democracy (MMD) attracted most of the well known Zambian politicians, many of whom were rebellious ex-ministers of the UNIP government. The MMD won 125 of the 150 seats. President Kaunda won just 24 per cent of the presidential vote, and F.J.T. Chiluba, leader of the MMD, assumed the presidency on 1 November 1991.

The 1991 constitution was amended in 1996 to allow for a multi party political system, a president who can hold office for two five-year terms only and a National Assembly. A new constitution is currently being debated. It failed to pass through Parliament in March 2011 after it failed to garner the two thirds majority required for the Bill to be passed. It can only be brought back to parliament after six months.

To consult the initial draft, please visit: http://www.znbc.co.zm/documents/The_constitution_of_zambia_bill_2010.pdf

International Relations

Zambia enjoys close relations with its neighbours, though these occasionally become strained with Angola and the Democratic Republic of Congo as conflicts in those nations spill over the border. Zambia has been host to refugees from both countries, but most Angolan refugees have now returned home.

China has recently financed and helped build the Tan-Zam railway which provides an export route for Zambia's copper through Dar es Salaam in Tanzania.

Recent Events

In July 2002, former president, Frederick Chiluba, had his immunity from prosecution removed; in 2003 he was arrested and charged with corruption. In September 2004 most of the charges were dropped, but he was later arrested on new charges. In May 2007, the High Court in Britain ruled that Frederick Chiluba and four of his aides had conspired to rob Zambia of approximately $46 million. He was however cleared of corruption in August 2009 after a six-year trial.

In April 2005, the World Bank agreed a package to write off US$3.8 billion, half of Zambia's debt.

In July 2005 there was a challenge to President Mwanawasa's leadership of the Movement for Multiparty Democracy party. The challenge went to a vote; President Mwanawasa received 1,211 votes and his challenger, Enoch Kavindale, received just 68.

In August 2008 President Mwanawasa died in hospital in Paris where he had been taken for treatment after suffering a stroke in June. Vice President Rupiah Banda was elected president in November 2008.

In February 2010, Zambia and China signed a mining cooperation agreement and agreed to set up a joint economic zone.

The former president, Frederick Chiluba, Zambia's first democratically elected president, died on 18 June 2011 aged 68.

Presidential, parliamentary and local elections took place on September 2011. Nationalist Michael Sata of the opposition Patriotic Front defeated the incumbent President Rupiah Bandah.

Legislature

Zambia has a unicameral legislature, made up of a maximum158 members, 150 of whom are directly elected, and up to eight members are appointed by the president. There is the House of Chiefs, which consists of 27 chiefs who act in an advisory capacity and can table resolutions for debate by the General Assembly. All members serve a five year term.

General Assembly, Parliament Buildings, PO Box 31299, Lusaka 10101. Tel: +260 1 292425, fax: +260 1 292252, e-mail: nazambia@zamnet.zm, URL: http://www.parliament.gov.zm
Speaker: Dr Patrick Matibini

Cabinet (as at April 2013)

Minister of Justice: Wynter Munacaambwa Kabimba (page 1452)
Minister of Defence: Godfrey B. Mwamba
Minister of Finance: Dr Alexander B. Chikwanda (page 1404)
Minister of Home Affairs: Edgar Lungu
Minister of Health: Dr Joseph Kasonde
Minister of Foreign Affairs: Effron Lungu (page 1467)
Minister of Agriculture and Livestock: Emmanuel Chenda
Minister of Sports & Youth: Chisimba Kambwili
Minister of Commerce, Trade and Industry: Robert Sichinga
Minister of Information & Broadcasting: Kennedy Sakeni
Minister of Education, Science and Vocational Training: Dr John N. Phiri
Minister of Mines, Energy and Water Development: Prof. Yamfwa Mukanga Yaluma
Minister of Lands & Natural Resources: Wilbur Simuusa
Minister of Local Government & Housing & Environment: Nkandu Luo
Minister of Community Development and Mother and Child Health: Dr Joseph Katema
Minister of Chiefs and Traditional Affairs: Inonge Wina
Minister of Tourism: Sylvia Masbeo
Minister of Transport, Works, Supply and Communications: Christopher Yaluma

Ministries

Office of the President, URL: http://www.statehouse.gov.zm/
Ministry of Local Government and Housing, PO Box 34204, Lusaka, Zambia. Tel: +260 21 1 253077, fax:: +260 21 1 252680, URL: http://www.localgovernment.gov.zm
Ministry of Foreign Affairs, PO Box RW50069, Lusaka, Zambia. Tel: +260 21 1 262666, fax: +260 21 1 250240, URL: http://www.foreignaffairs.gov.zm
Ministry of Agriculture and Co-operatives, Mulungushi House, Independence Avenue, PO Box RW50291, Lusaka, Zambia. Tel: +260 21 1 251537, fax: +260 21 1 252029, URL: http://www.agriculture.gov.zm
Ministry of Finance and National Planning, Finance Building, PO Box RW50062, Lusaka, Zambia. Tel: +260 21 1 250544, fax: +260 21 1 253494, URL: http://www.finance.gov.zm
Ministry of Commerce, Trade and Industry, Kwacha House Annex, Cairo Road, PO Box 31968, Lusaka, Zambia. Tel: +260 21 1 228301, fax: +260 21 1 226673, URL: http://www.commerce.gov.zm
Ministry of Energy and Water Development, Ministerial Headquarters, Lusaka, Zambia. Tel: +260 21 1 263870. fax: +260 21 1 252589, URL: http://www.energy.gov.zm
Ministry of Works and Supply, PO Box 50003, Lusaka, Zambia. Tel: +260 21 1 353244, fax: +260 21 1 254108, URL: http://www.supply.gov.zm
Ministry of Home Affairs, PO Box 50997, Lusaka, Zambia. Tel: +260 21 1 254261, fax: +260 21 1 224656, URL: http://www.homeaffairs.gov.zm
Ministry of Mines and Mineral Developments, PO Box 31969, Lusaka, Zambia. Tel: +260 21 1 252990. fax: +260 21 1 251224, URL: http://www.mines.gov.zm
Ministry of Defence, PO Box RW 17X. Lusaka, Zambia. Tel: +260 21 1 251211, URL: http://www.defence.gov.zm
Ministry of Education, 102 Ridgeway, PO Box RW50093, Lusaka, Zambia. Tel: +260 21 1 227636, URL: http://www.education.gov.zm
Ministry of Health, PO Box 30205, Lusaka, Zambia. Tel: +260 21 1 253040, URL: http://www.health.gov.zm
Ministry of Tourism, Environment and Natural Resources, Electra House, Cairo Road, PO Box 30575, Lusaka, Zambia. Tel: +260 21 1 227645, fax: +260 21 1 222189, URL: http://www.zambiatourism.com
Ministry of Science, Technology and Vocational Training, PO Box 50464, Lusaka, Zambia. Tel: +260 21 1 229673, fax: +260 21 1 252951, URL: http://www.technology.gov.zm
Ministry of Sports, Youth and Child Development, Memeco House 4th Floor, Sapele Road, PO Box 50195, Lusaka, Zambia. Tel: +260 21 1 227158, fax: +260 21 1 223996, URL: http://www.sports.gov.zm
Ministry of Communications and Transport, Ministerial Headquarters, PO Box 50065, Lusaka, Zambia. Tel: +260 21 1 251444, fax: +260 21 1 253260, URL: http://www.communication.gov.zm
Ministry of Community Development and Social Services, Fidelity House, PO Box 31958, Lusaka, Zambia. Tel: +260 21 1 227840, URL: http://www.welfare.gov.zm
Ministry of Information and Broadcasting, PO Box 50200, Lusaka, Zambia. Tel: +260 21 1 227840, fax: +260 21 1 222368, URL: http://www.information.gov.zm
Ministry of Labour and Social Security, PO Box 32186, Lusaka, Zambia. Tel: +260 21 1 227840, URL: http://www.labour.gov.zm
Ministry of Lands, PO Box 30069, Lusaka, Zambia. Tel: +260 21 1 252288, fax: +260 21 1 250120, URL: http://www.lands.gov.zm
Ministry of Justice, PO Box 50106, Lusaka, Zambia. Tel: +260 21 1 251588, URL: http://www.legalaffairs.gov.zm
Environmental Council of Zambia, PO Box 35131, Corner Suez and Church Roads, Plot number 6975, Ridgeway Area., Lusaka, Zambia. E-mail: ecz@necz.org.zm, URL: http://www.necz.org.zm/

Elections

Elections are held every five years for both president and National Assembly. The most recent parliamentary elections were held on 6 October 2006. The MMD won 72 seats, the PF 43, the UDA 28, Independents 3, the ULP 3, the NDF 1. Parliamentary elections are due in 2011.

In the presidential elections Mr Mwanawasa was returned to office with over 70 per cent of the vote. President Mwanawasa died in August 2008 and Vice President Rupiah Banda was elected to the post in November 2008 with a narrow winning margin over his main rival Michael Sata, who alleged fraud.

Presidential, parliamentary and local elections took place on 20 September 2011. Michael Sata was elected as president. In the legislative elections the Patriotic Front won 60 seats, the Movement for Multiparty Democracy won 55 seats and the United Party for National Development won 28 seats. President Sata named a new cabinet. There were minor reshuffles in January and July 2012.

Political Parties

Forum for Democracy and Development (FDD), URL: http://www.fddzambia.com/; Movement for Multiparty Democracy (MMD); Patriotic Front (PF), URL: http://www.patriotic-front.com/; United National Independence Party (UNIP); United Party for National Development (UPND), URL: http://www.upnd-zambia.com/index.php/en/.

Diplomatic Representation

Embassy of the United States of America, Corner Independence and United Nations Avenues, Lusaka, Zambia. Tel: +260 1 250955, fax: +260 1 252225, e-mail: usembass@zamnet.zm, URL: http://zambia.usembassy.gov
Ambassador: Mark Storella (page 1520)
British High Commission, 5210 Independence Avenue, P.O Box 50050, 15101 Ridgeway, Lusaka, Zambia. Tel: +260 1 251133, fax: +260 1 253798, URL: http://ukinzambia.fco.gov.uk/en/
High Commissioner: James Thornton (page 1525)
Embassy of Zambia, 2419 Massachusetts Ave, NW, Washington, DC 20008, USA. Tel: +1 202 265 9717, fax: +1 202 332 0826, URL: http://www.zambiaembassy.org/
Ambassador: Inonge Mbikusita-Lewanika
High Commission of Zambia, 2 Palace Gate, Kensington, London, W8 5NG, United Kingdom. Tel: +44 (0)20 7589 6655, fax: +44 (0)20 7581 1353, URL: http://www.zambiahc.org.uk/
High Commissioner: Lt. Col. (Rtd) Bizwayo Newton Nkunika
Permanent Mission of the Republic of Zambia to the UN, 237 East 52nd Street, New York, NY 10022, USA. Tel: +1 212 758 1110, fax: +1 212 758 1319, URL: http://www.un.int/zambia
Ambassador: Patricia Mwaba Kasese-Bota

LEGAL SYSTEM

The judicial system is based on English common law and customary law. The independence of the judiciary is respected by the government.

The Supreme Court is the highest court in Zambia and serves as the final court of appeal. The chief justice and other eight judges are appointed by the president. There are several High Courts, which hear civil and criminal cases and appeals from the lower courts. Magistrates' Courts hear both original cases and cases appealed by Local Court, which mainly administer customary law, especially cases relating to marriage, property, and inheritance.

The government's human rights record, whilst improving, remains poor in areas such as unlawful killings, torture, and abuse of suspects and detainees by security forces. There is official impunity and government corruption. Arrests can be arbitrary, prison conditions life-threatening and pretrial detentions long. There are restrictions on freedom of speech, press, assembly, and association.

Zambia retains the death penalty for various offenses, but has not executed anyone since 1997 owing to a presidential moratorium that has been upheld by three heads of state.

Judiciay, URL: http://www.judiciary.gov.zm/
Acting Chief Justice: Lombe Chibesakunda

Human Rights Commission, PO Box 33812, Independence Avenue, Lusaka, Zambia.. Tel: +260 211 251327, fax: +260 211 251342, e-mail: phrc@zamnet.zm, URL: http://www.hrc.org.zm/

LOCAL GOVERNMENT

The Ministry of Local Government and Housing sets national policy. There are three City Councils, six Municipal Councils and many Urban, District and Rural Councils. There are Deputy Ministers in charge of each of the nine Provinces, Central, Eastern, Northern, North Western, Southern, Western, Copperbelt, Luapula and Lusaka. The senior civil servant in each province is the Permanent Secretary. The provinces are subdivided into 72 districts.

Local elections took place most recently in September 2011.

AREA AND POPULATION

Area

Zambia is landlocked and has boundaries with Angola, Namibia, Botswana, Zimbabwe, Democratic Republic of Congo, Mozambique, Malawi and Tanzania. Its area is 753,000 sq. km. Most of the country lies on the great Central African plateau, 1,000m to 1,300m above

sea level. The Zambezi river flows through Zambia which is home to the Victoria Falls. The climate is tropical with a rainy season from October to April. Zambia's climate is moderated by its altitude.

To view a map, consult http://www.un.org/Depts/Cartographic/map/profile/zambia.pdf

Population

In 2010, Zambia's population was estimated at 13.089 million with a growth rate of 2.5 per cent for the period 2000-10. Lusaka has a population of about 1.7 million. This includes the residents of peri-urban (shanty) settlements. Over 36 per cent of the population lives in urban areas. Other cities include Livingstone, Kitwe, Kabwe and Ndola. Nearly half the population live in urban areas. Zambia is host to a large number of refugees, from Angola although most of these have now returned home but more recently refugees have arrived from the Democratic Republic of Congo. Zambians come from more than 70 different ethnic groups the largest being the Bemba, the Tonga and the Lozi.

The official language is English. Major local African languages spoken are Bemba, Kaonde, Lozi, Lunda, Luvale, Nyanga and Tonga.

Births, Marriages, Deaths

Estimated figures for 2010 put the birth rate at 45.6 per 1,000 population and the death rate at 15.7 per 1,000 population. The life expectancy rate has fallen in recent years due to the large incidence of HIV infection; recent figures estimate that one million of the population are infected. The average life expectancy in 2009 was 46 years for males and 50 for females. Healthy life expectancy in 2007 was 40 years. The median age is estimated to be 19 years. Approximately 46 per cent of the population is aged under 15 years and 5 per cent over 60. The total fertility rate per woman was estimated at 6.3 in 2010. (Source: http://www.who.int, World Health Statistics 2012)

Public Holidays 2014

1 January: New Year's Day
12 March: Youth Day
18 April: Good Friday
21 April: Easter Monday
1 May: Labour Day
25 May: Africa Freedom Day
26 May: Public Holiday
7 July: Heroes' Day (First Monday of July)
8 July: Unity Day
4 August: Farmers' Day (First Monday of August)
24 October: Independence Day
25 December: Christmas Day

EMPLOYMENT

Figures for 2010 estimated the labour force to be 5.4 million. Recent figures show that 75 per cent of the population is engaged in the agricultural sector with the services sector employing 19 per cent and mining and industry six per cent. Zambia has high unemployment and underemployment rates; estimated figures for 2006 put unemployment at 15 per cent. Millions of Zambians live below the poverty line.

BANKING AND FINANCE

Currency

The Zambian currency is the Kwacha, which is divided into 100 Ngwee. The financial centre is Lusaka.

GDP/GNP, Inflation, National Debt

The economy of Zambia was hard hit during the 1970s and 1980s; it was reliant on its copper exports, and when copper prices fell internationally, the economy suffered. Since 1991 the Zambian government has pursued a course of privatisation, and very few government-owned enterprises now remain. Privatisation of the copper mining industry has been key. Despite corruption and mismanagment the economy has enjoyed a period of sustained growth. The government is looking to diversify the economy including agriculture, tourism, mining and hydropower.

Estimated figures for 2010 put growth at 5.7 per cent. Areas of growth include mining, tourism, construction and the generation of hydro-electric power. In 2007, agriculture contributed 21.4 per cent of GDP, industry 35.3 per cent (of which manufacturing 11.0 per cent), and services 43.3 per cent. GDP was estimated at US$19 billion in 2011.

Inflation has fallen dramatically over the past few years, from 183.8 per cent in 1993 to 17.5 per cent in 2004. In 2005 it was estimated at 18.3 per cent and in 2007 it ran at 8.7 per cent. In 2008, AFDB figures put inflation at 8.58 per cent. It was estimated at 8.6 per cent in 2011.

In 2000 Zambia wished to be considered for the Highly Indebted Poor Country Initiative (HIPC). To qualify, the government had to agree to certain criteria. These were renegotiated in 2003 and although privatisation of large companies such as the national telephone and electricity suppliers was agreed, over-spending on civil service wages delayed the initiative until 2005. In April of that year the World Bank approved a US$3.8 billion debt relief package. In 2007 Zambia has a national debt in excess of US$0.7 billion (5.9 per cent of GDP). Debt service was 0.4 per cent of GDP. (Source: AFDB)

Foreign Investment

Foreign investment is encouraged; there are virtually no restrictions on investors and 100 per cent foreign ownership of enterprises is allowed. Further, there are no exchange controls relating to equity capital although investors are required to incorporate a company or register with the Registrar of Companies and Business Names.

ZAMBIA

Balance of Payments / Imports and Exports

Main export goods are copper (over 60 per cent, 2011), cotton, lead, cobalt, zinc, vegetables and tobacco. Main imported goods are machinery transport equipment, food and fuel. Major trading partners include South Africa, Tanzania, China, Japan Malawi and the UK. China now takes over 30 per cent of exports. Exports were estimated to be US$7.2 billion in 2010 and imports cost over US$5 billion in 2010. Exports rose to an estimated US$8.5 billion and imports to US$6 billion.

Central Bank

Bank of Zambia, PO Box 30080, Bank Square, Cairo Road, Lusaka 10101, Zambia. Tel: +260 1 228888, fax: +260 1 221722, URL: http://www.boz.zm/
Governor & Chairman: Dr Michael M. Gondwe

Chambers of Commerce and Trade Organisations

Zambia Association of Chambers of Commerce and Industry, URL: http://www.zambiachambers.org/

MANUFACTURING, MINING AND SERVICES

Primary and Extractive Industries

Mining represents 5.8 per cent of Zambia's real GDP and 10 per cent of total workforce. The mines produce annually about 450,000 tons of copper and this is 95 per cent of Zambia's exports. Cobalt, zinc, tin, coal, and semi-precious stones are also mined. After the price of copper collapsed in 1975 the economy went into decline. The copper industry was privatised in the 1990s. It was estimated that the copper mines would become exhausted, and rapid strides are being made to diversify the economy, especially in the fields of agriculture, tourism and hydro power.

Zambia Consolidated Copper Mines (ZCCM) was finally privatised in 2000. The company had been making huge losses. Privatisation of the copper mining industry has encouraged new investment and as a result two new mines are scheduled to open and the larger, Konkola Deep, began production in 2007.

Although Zambia has no oil reserves of its own it has a refinery in Ndola. Crude oil is transported there along the Tanzania-Zambia Pipeline from Dar es Salaam. The refinery experienced technical problems in 2005 which led to serious fuel shortages which affected the important copper mining industry and also disrupted deliveries, threatening food shortages in some parts of the country. In 2011, consumption of oil was 19,000 barrels per day, the country's refining capacity that year was 24,000 barrels per day.

Energy

Zambia obtains its electricity from hydroelectric power stations fuelled by the many rivers and lakes in Zambia. Sufficient electricity is produced to export to neighbouring countries, namely Zimbabwe and Botswana. Over a third of the electricity generated is consumed by Zambia Consolidated Copper Mines. In 2010, 11.19 billion kWh of electricity were generated and 7.96 billion kWh were consumed. Approximately 2 billion kWh were exported. Zambia is engaged in a programme of rural electrification by solar energy. Another energy source being explored is ethanol, produced from sugar cane, which would be blended with petrol. In 2010 China agreed to build a second hydroelectric power plant on the Kafue River.

Manufacturing

Manufacturing accounts for 12 per cent of GDP and 11 per cent of total workforce. Manufacturing in the last decade includes textiles from Zambian grown cotton, clothing, shoes, smelting and refining of copper and steel, engineering products, building materials and food canning. Copper based manufacturing includes the manufacature of copper rods, electrical cables and copper wire. Kaufe is the leading industrial town. The Zambian textile industry has begun to feel the effects of cheap imports from Asian countries.

Service Industries

Services represents 48.9 per cent of the country's real GDP. Tourism is a growing industry. About 669,000 tourists visited Zambia in 2006, mostly the Game parks at Kafue, Luangwa, Livingstone and Lake Kariba. As a result of the continued unrest in neighbouring Zimbabwe the tourist industy of Zambia has benefitted especially from tourists wishing to visit the Victoria Falls.
Zambia National Tourist Board, URL: http://www.zamnet.zm

Agriculture

Agriculture accounts for 21 per cent of GDP. Agriculture has a high priority in the Zambian economy. The main crops farmed are maize, cotton, fresh flowers, tobacco, sugarcane, coffee, soya beans and wheat. The beef and poultry industries are growing rapidly. Just 1 per cent of land is irrigated. In 2004, following years of drought, Zambia had one of its largest harvests leaving the country with surplus grain, some was kept in reserve but much was exported.

Agricultural Production in 2010

Produce	Int. $'000*	Tonnes
Maize	387,179	2,795,480
Indigenous cattle meat	164,322	60,829
Tobacco, unmanufactured	142,871	89,700
Cassava	120,310	1,151,700
Sugar cane	114,930	3,500,000
Game meat	77,649	35,700
Groundnuts, with shell	63,148	163,733
Indigenous chicken meat	60,547	42,507
Vegetables fresh nes	52,179	276,900
Cotton lint	41,447	29,000
Hen eggs, in shell	41,055	49,500
Fruit, tropical fresh nes	33,920	83,000

- continued
* unofficial figures
Source: http://faostat.fao.org/site/339/default.aspx Food and Agriculture Organization of the United Nations, Food and Agricultural commodities production

Figures from the FAO for 2004 show that Zambia had 2.6 million head of cattle and 1.4 million sheep and goats. Figures from 2010 put the total fishing catch at 76,396 tonnes.

COMMUNICATIONS AND TRANSPORT

Travel Requirements

Citizens of the USA, Canada, Australia and the EU require a passport valid for six months beyond the expiry date of the visa, and a visa (apart from Irish nationals who can stay for 30 days without a visa). Transit passengers continuing their journey within 24 hours, carrying valid onward or return documentation and not leaving the airport do not need a visa. Other nationals should contact the embassy to check visa requirements.

Travellers transiting through South Africa should ensure that they have at least two blank (unstamped) visa pages in their passports. South African immigration authorities routinely turn away visitors who do not have enough blank visa pages in their passports. Zambian Immigration officials insist visitors carry the original or a certified copy of their passport and their immigration permit at all times.

National Airlines

Zambia Airways, URL: http://www.zambianairways.com

International Airports

Fourteen scheduled airlines operate to the international airport at Lusaka. Lusaka Airport has the capacity to handle 2 million passengers per year.

Railways

The Tazara Railways links Kapiri Mposhi to Dar-es-Salaam, and connects with Zambia's existing rail system, Zambia Railways Ltd. There are railway links to the ports of South Africa. There are approximately 2,200 km of track.

Roads

All main towns are linked by tarred roads, and all main roads within towns are tarred. In total there around 91,500 km of roads of which approximately 20,000 km are tarred. Bus routes link Zambia with Malawi, Zimbabwe and Tanzania. Vehicles are driven on the left.

Waterways

Although Zambia is a landlocked country Lake Tanganika and the Zambezi and Luapula rivers are navigable and ferry services are in operation. There are 2,250 km of navigable waterways.

HEALTH

Although the population has doubled in recent years, the number of health institutions has not kept pace. Recent figures indicate that there are just over 80 hospitals offering a total of 16,000 beds. In addition there are nearly 1,000 health centres with just over 7,000 beds. In 2009, the government spent approximately 15.7 per cent of its total budget on healthcare (up from 9.4 per cent in 2000), accounting for 58.6 per cent of all healthcare spending. Total expenditure on healthcare equated to 6.2 per cent of the country's GDP. Per capita expenditure on health was approximately US$63. Latest figures from WHO (2005-10) estimate that there are 649 doctors (0.6 per 10,000 population), 8,369 nurses and midwives (7.1 per 1,000 population), 56 dentistry personnel, 108 pharmaceutical personnel and 803 environment and public health officers.

HIV and AIDS is a big problem in Zambia and recent estimates put the number of those infected at 13.5 per cent of the adult population, over 56 per cent of whom were female. It has been estimated that nearly 1 million children have lost one or both parents to the disease and life expectancy is currently 49 years (up from 42 in 2000). In 2009 the infant mortality rate (probability of dying before first birthday) was 69 per 1,000 live births and the child (under-five years old) mortality rate was 111 per 1,000 live births. The main causes of death in the under-fives are: prematurity (13 per cent), pneumonia (14 per cent), malaria (13 per cent), diarrhoea (9 per cent), measles (4 per cent) and HIV/AIDS (11 per cent). In the period 2005-11 an estimated 45.8 per cent of children (under five-years-old) were classified as stunted and 14.9 per cent as underweight. Approximately 41 per cent of children sleep under insecticide-treated nets. The immunization rates for common diseases have risen in recent years; the rate for measles is currently 84 per cent.

In 2008, 87 per cent of the urban population and 46 per cent of the rural population had sustainable access to an improved water source. In the same year, 59 per cent of the urban population and 43 per cent of the rural population had sustainable access to improved sanitation. (Source: http://www.who.int, World Health Statistics 2012)

EDUCATION

In theory, primary schooling, which lasts for seven years, is compulsory. Secondary education lasts for five years, two years at lower level, three years at higher level. Figures for 2007 show that of primary school age children, 94 per cent were enrolled at school. Approximately 88 per cent complete primary school. The pupil / teacher ratio for primary education in 2007 was 49:1. For the same year 38 per cent of girls and 44 per cent of boys of secondary school age were enrolled.

The government plans a rapid expansion of secondary school places and the two universities at Lusaka and Kitwe are to be restructured. Technical and Vocational Training, the Correspondence Course Unit, Educational Broadcasting and Television Service and Teacher Training have all been subject to budget cuts, but plans are now being made for development in these departments. International schools have also been established in Lusaka.

In 2007, public expenditure as a percentage of GDP was 1.5 per cent. It represented 14.8 per cent of total government expenditure, 59 per cent of which went on primary education.

Adult literacy in 2007 was put at 80.8 per cent for males and 60.7 per cent for females. In the age group 15-24 years, the literacy rate is 82.4 for males and 67.8 years for females. (Source: UNESCO)

RELIGION

Christianity is the main religion in Zambia. Recent figures suggest that there over 11 million Christians practicing in the country. Islam, Hinduism and Buddhism also have a following in the urban areas. Many traditional beliefs are still held by the rural dwellers.

Zambia has a religious liberty rating of 10 on a scale of 1 to 10 (10 is most freedom). (Source: World Religion Database)

COMMUNICATIONS AND MEDIA

Broadcasting is dominated by state-owned media. Defamation of the president is a criminal offence.

Newspapers
Times of Zambia (state-owned),URL: http://www.times.co.zm/

Zambia Daily Mail (state-owned), URL: http://www.daily-mail.co.zm
The Post, URL: http://www.postzambia.com

Broadcasting
Zambia Radio (Zambia National Broadcasting Corporation, URL: http://www.znbc.co.zm/) broadcasts on short and medium wave. The government-controlled television service is Television-Zambia. There are also several private television stations. Multi-channel subscription TV is available. ZNBC operates three radio networks. Over 20 private radio stations also operate.

Telecommunications
Network coverage of cellular telephone services is improving and a domestic satellite system is being installed to improve the telephone service in rural areas. In 2008 there were an estimated 90,500 mainlines and 3.5 million mobile phones. In 2008 it was estimated that Zambia had around 700,000 internet users.

ENVIRONMENT

The main environmental concerns for Zambia include air pollution and the resulting acid rain in the mineral extraction and refining region. There are also issues with chemical runoff into water and the lack of water treatment presents problems for human health. Poaching is problem particularly of rhinoceros, elephant, antelope, and large cats, several national parks have been established in an effort to protect wildlife.

Zambia is a party to the following international agreements: Biodiversity, Climate Change, Climate Change-Kyoto Protocol, Desertification, Endangered Species, Hazardous Wastes, Law of the Sea, Ozone Layer Protection, and Wetlands.

According to figures from the EIA, in 2006 Zambia's emissions from the consumption of fossil fuels totalled 2.57 million metric tons of carbon dioxide.

ZIMBABWE
Republic of Zimbabwe

Capital: Harare (Population of Greater Harare, 2011 estimate: 2.2 million)

Head of State: Robert Gabriel Mugabe (page 1481) (President) (Zanu-PF)

Vice President: John Nkomo (Zanu-PF)

Vice President: Joyce Mujuru (Zanu-PF)

National Flag: Seven horizontal stripes of green, gold, red, black, red, gold and green. A bird is shown on a red five pointed star on a white triangle its base at the hoist.

CONSTITUTION AND GOVERNMENT

Constitution
The Republic of Zimbabwe came into existence on 18 April 1980 as the successor state to the colony of Southern Rhodesia. The government of Zimbabwe consists of the President and a unicameral parliament. The President is the Head of State, the Head of the Government and Commander-in-Chief of the Defence Forces. The President is directly elected for a period of six years. The unicameral Parliament consists of 150 members. 120 members are elected from constituencies, 10 are traditional chiefs, 8 are provincial governors and 12 are appointed by the President. Parliament elects an outside speaker and a deputy speaker from its members.

In 2005 the constitution was amended to provide for an upper house. The constitution was amended again in 2007 to remove the president's power to appoint 12 MPs. Subject to parliamentary approval he may nominate his successor if he resigned in mid-term. Amendments to the constitution were again under discussion in 2011 and 2013. A referendum on the constitution took place in March 2013. Turnout was low but over 90 per cent voted in favour of the new constitution. The new constitution limits the President to two six-year-terms in office (this does not apply retrospectively to the incumbent) and removes the President's power to veto legislation passed by Parliament. It also establishes an anti-corruption commission, a peace and reconciliation commission. It prohibits legal challenges to the land reform programme.

To consult the constitution, please visit: http://www.copac.org.zw/downloads.html

Recent Events
In 1999 President Mugabe appointed a Constitutional Commission to write a new constitution. The draft constitution was amended by the government to include a section stating the former colonial power (Great Britain) should compensate farmers for land acquired for the resettlement programme. The people rejected the new constitution in a referendum held in February 2000. The ruling ZANU-PF party pushed through an amendment in April 2000 trying to place Britain under an obligation for land compensation.

As part of the Government's 'fast track' programme of land reforms in 2000 squatters began to occupy white owned farms. The idea was to place over 160,000 families on five million hectares of farm land, at the time owned by white farmers, within a four year time frame. By early 2002 the country was suffering from severe food shortages. Government spokesmen blamed the drought but outside observers blamed the disruption to agriculture. In July 2001 following the land seizure programme the IMF and the World Bank cut aid to Zimbabwe. At the end of 2002 it was announced that following the seizure of 35 million acres of land from white farmers, the land seizure programme was now at an end. The once flourishing agricultural sector has since shrunk to a point where many of the population are reliant on grain handouts and the export market has shrunk alongside agricultural production. Millions of workers began leaving Zimbabwe seeking work in other countries particularly South Africa. The decline in agricultural production and loss of some of the workforce has affected the economy to the extent that inflation passed the 1,000 per cent mark, reaching 1,193 per cent, in May 2006. In August 2006, new banknotes were issued with three noughts removed from them.

Following the presidential elections in 2002, which were disputed by outside observers, the Commonwealth decided to suspend Zimbabwe for a year. In December 2003 the suspension was extended to an indefinite period and Zimbabwe announced that it was leaving the organisation.

In May 2005 the government implemented a controversial clean up campaign of shanty towns, which were bulldozed. The government claimed that the shanty towns were centres of lawlessness and the land was needed for development. Other observers claim the shanty towns were demolished as they housed opposition sympathizers. The UN estimated that around 700,000 people were made homeless in the clean up.

In September 2006, there were protests against the government's handling of the economic crisis. Opposition leaders were arrested and have alleged they were tortured. In December, the ruling Zanu-PF Party voted to postpone presidential elections from 2008 to 2010, thereby extending President Mugabe's rule. In March 2007 the opposition leader, Morgan Tsvangirai, was hospitalised after he was a shot at an opposition rally. In July, inflation exceeded 7,000 per cent, but slowed to around 6,500 per cent the following month.

In September 2007, Zimbabwe's parliament passed a compromise bill on constitutional change; it allows presidential and parliamentary elections to take place in 2008, and for President Robert Mugabe (83 years old) to choose a successor in the event that he does not finish his term in office. Members of parliament from both the ruling Zanu-PF and the opposition Movement for Democratic Change (MDC) supported the bill.

Presidential, House of Assembly, Senate and local elections were held on 29 March 2008 amid a backdrop of inflation running at 165,000 per cent and an unemployment rate of 80 per cent. The MDC accused President Mugabe and Zanu-PF of vote rigging. Announcement of the legislative election results was delayed until the 3rd April, when it was revealed that the MDC had won 99 parliamentary seats and the Zanu-PF 97, a faction of the MDC, won 10 seats. No official results for the presidential election were announced until the 2nd May. After a recount of the ballot and verification of the results, the Zimbabwe Electoral Commission announced that Tsvangirai won had won 47.9 per cent and Mugabe won 43.2 per cent, necessitating a run-off election. The elections were followed by widespread violence, which the MDC claims left at least 40 of its supporters dead and scores of others injured. It accused Mugabe's Zanu-PF party of a campaign of intimidation; Zanu-PF blamed the opposition for the violence. A run-off election was scheduled for 27th June. Opposition supporters were the victims of violence and intimidation, leading the head of the observer mission to announce he would not endorse the election if the violence continued. On June 22 Morgan Tsvangirai announced that he would not stand against President Mugabe in the run off election leaving Mugabe to win by default. Tsvangirai said that any poll held in Zimbabwe at this time would not be credible and that he could not stand by and watch the continued acts of violence against and murder of his supporters. Several leaders of other African nations declared their disappointment in the situation in Zimbabwe. Observers of the election held on June 27th said that the election did not reflect the will of the people.

In July 2008 inflation was running at 2 million per cent and a 100 billion dollar note was introduced. When the note was issued, it was enough to buy two loaves of bread, but with inflation rising every day there was soon talk of trillion dollar notes being needed. Morgan Tsvangirai was offered the post of Vice President but with no executive power; his supporters felt this was unacceptable. In September, the Chairman of the MDC, Lovemore Moyo, was elected to the post of speaker of parliament; he is the first opposition MP to hold the post since 1980.

Following months of talks mediated by the South African President Mbeki, a power sharing agreement was signed on September 15 2008. Under the terms of the agreement Robert Mugabe remains president and head of the armed forces, and chairs the cabinet. Morgan Tsvangirai becomes prime minister, chairs the council of ministers and has control of the police force.

In December, there was a devastating outbreak of cholera around Harare; estimates put the death toll at around 600. Cases were also reported in the South African border town of Musina; the town is often the first port of call for Zimbabweans fleeing their country. By January the epidemic had spread to areas outside of Harare and the death toll had been estimated at 2,755 people.

In January 2009 Morgan Tsvangirai returned to Zimbabwe following two months away, and a power sharing agreement was reached. Mr. Tsvangirai became Prime Minister and the cabinet consists of 16 members of the MDC and 15 members of Zanu PF.

In June 2009 Prime Minister Morgan Tsvangirai met with President Obama in Washington who pledged US$73 million in aid to help boost the Zimbabwe economy.

In January 2010 Zimbabwe's High Court rejected a regional court ruling against President Mugabe's land-reform programme and in March a new ruling was brought in that foreign owned businesses had to sell a majority stake to locals.

In September 2010 as consultations on a new constitution got underway, the prime minister Morgan Tsvangirai alleged that Zanu-PF was instigating violence at these meetings. Human rights groups have alleged increased violence against opposition groups. In March 2011 Morgan Tsvangirai said power sharing deal was being undermined by Zanu-PF.

In 2011 some sanctions were eased. The EU eased further sanctions in 2012 although those against President Mugabe remain.

In 2012, the Minister for Higher Education died in October 2012. The same month, the Minister for Energy and Power Development (MDC) was arrested and charged with insulting the president.

In January 2013 President Mugabe and the prime minister, Morgan Tsvangirai, came to an agreement on a new draft constitution. A referendum was held in March 2013 in which the referendum was endorsed. A court has ruled that elections must be held by end July 2013. The new constitution was approved by both houses of parliament in May.

Legislature

Previous to 2005 Zimbabwe had a unicameral legislature. Since a change to the Constitution in 2005, the legislature is now bicameral, consisting of a National Assembly and a Senate. Following the 2008 elections the number of seats was increased. There are now 210 directly elected members in the lower house. The newly created Senate consists of 93 members, 60 of whom are elected, six from each the provinces plus five appointed by the president, ten provincial governors and 18 traditional chiefs. Under the Interparty Political Agreement of January 2009, the president was to appoint five more senators of his own choice, and the MDC six. Those appointed to the posts of vice president, prime minister and deputy prime minister who were not already MPs would become ex-officio members of the House of Assembly. If they were already MPs they were to be replaced by another member of the same party. All members are elected for a five year term.

Parliament, Box CY 298, Causeway, Harare, Zimbabwe. Tel: +263 4 700181, fax: +263 4 252948, URL: http://www.parlzim.gov.zw
Speaker: Lovemore Moyo

A power sharing agreement was signed on September 15 2008. Under the terms of the agreement the cabinet consists of 31 members. The ZANU-PF led by Robert Mugabe, has15 cabinet seats; the MDC led by Morgan Tsvangirai has16 seats and a breakaway faction of the MDC led by Arthur Mutambara has three seats.

Cabinet (as at June 2013)
Commander in Chief of the Defence Forces: President Robert Mugabe (Zanu-PF) (page 1481)
Vice President: Joyce Mujuru (Zanu-PF)
Vice President and Minister for National Reconciliation: John Nkomo (Zanu-PF)
Prime Minister: Morgan Tsvangirai (MDC-T) (page 1528)
Deputy Prime Minist er: Welshman Ncube (page 1484)
Deputy Prime Minister: Thokozani Khupe (page 1456)
Minister of State for National Security in the Office of the President: Sydney Sekeramayi (page 1511)
Minister of State for Presidential Affairs: Didymus Mutasa
Minister of State in the Office of the Prime Minister: Jameson Timba
Minister of Economic Planning and Development: Tapiwa Mashakada
Minister of Finance: Tendai Biti (page 1389)
Minister of Foreign Affairs: Simbarashe Mumbengegwi (page 1482)
Joint Minister of Home Affairs: Kembo Mohadi

Joint Minister of Home Affairs: Theresa Makone
Minister of Agriculture, Mechanization and Irrigation Development: Joseph Made
Minister of Constitutional and Parliamentary Affairs: Eric Matinenga (page 1472)
Minister of Defence: Emmerson Mnangagwa (page 1478)
Minister of Education, Sport, and Culture: David Coltart
Minister of Energy and Power Development: Elton Mangoma
Minister of Environment and Natural Resource Development: Francis Nhema (page 1486)
Minister of Public Works: Joel Gabuza
Minister of Health and Child Welfare: Henry Madzorera
Minister of Higher and Tertiary Education: Currently vacant
Minister of Industry and Commerce: Priscilla Mushonga
Minister of Information Communications Technology: Nelson Chamisa
Minister of Justice and Legal Affairs: Patrick Chinamasa (page 1404)
Minister of Labour and Social Welfare: Paurina Mpariwa
Minister of Lands and Rural Resettlement: Herbert Murerwa (page 1482)
Minister of Local Government, Urban and Rural Development: Ignatius Chombo (page 1404)
Minister of Media, Information and Publicity: Webster Shamu
Minister of Mines and Mining Development: Obert Mpofu
Joint Minister of National Healing and Reconciliation: Moses Mzila Ndlovu
Joint Minister of National Healing and Reconciliation: Sekai Holland
Minister of National Housing: Giles Mutsekwa (page 1483)
Minister of Public Service: Lucia Matibenga
Minister of Public Works: Joel Gabuza
Minister of Regional Integration and International Cooperation: Arthur Mutambbara
Minister of Science and Technology: Prof. Henri Dzinotyiwei
Minister of SMEs: Sithembiso Nyonii
Minister of State Enterprises: Gordon Moyo
Minister of Tourism: Walter Mzembi
Minister of Transport and Infrastructure: Nicholas Goche (page 1431)
Minister of Water Resources Management and Development: Samuel Sipepa Nkomo
Minister of Women's Affairs, Gender and Community Development: Olivia Muchena
Minister of Youth Development, Indigenization and Empowerment: Saviour Kasukuwere

Ministries

Office of the President, Munhumutapa Bldg., Samora Machel Avenue, Private Bag 7700, Causeway, Harare, Zimbabwe. Tel: +263 (0)4 707091, URL: http://www.gta.gov.zw/
Office of the Vice-President, Munhumutapa Bldg, Samora Machel Avenue, Private Bag 7700, Causeway, Harare, Zimbabwe. Tel: +263 (0)4 707091
Office of the Prime Minister, Munhumutapa Building, Samora Machel Avenue, Causeway, Harare, Zimbabwe. URL: http://www.zimbabweprimeminister.org
Ministry of Finance, 2nd Floor, Munhumutapa Bldg, Samora Machel Avenue, Private Bag 7705, Causeway, Harare, Zimbabwe. Tel: +263 (0)4 794571, fax: +253 (0)4 792750, URL: http://www.mofed.gov.zw
Ministry of National Affairs, Employment Creation and Co-operatives, 3rd Floor, ZANU PF Building, Private Bag 7762, Causeway, Harare, Zimbabwe. Tel: +263 (0)4 734691, fax: +263 (0)4 732709
Ministry of Local Government and National Housing, Cnr L Takawira Street and Herbert Chitepo, PO Box CY 441, Causeway, Harare, Zimbabwe. Tel: +263 4 790601, fax: +263 4 708848, URL: http://www.mlgpwud.gov.zw
Planning Commission, 5th Floor, Old Mutual Centre, PO Box 7700, Causeway, Harare, Zimbabwe. Tel: +263 (0)4 796191
Ministry of Lands and Agriculture, Ground Floor, Ngungunyana Building, 1 Borrowdale Road, Private Bag 7701, Causeway, Harare, Zimbabwe. Tel: +263 (0)4 706081/700596, URL: http://www.lands.gov.zw
Ministry of Justice, Legal and Parliamentary Affairs, 5th Floor, Corner House, Leopold Takawira Street, Private Bag 7751, Causeway, Harare, Zimbabwe. Tel: +263 (0)4 737931, fax: +263 (0)4 790901, URL: http://www.justice.gov.zw/
Ministry of State Security, 4th Floor, Chaminuka Building, 5th Street, PO Box 2278, Causeway, Harare, Zimbabwe. Tel: +263 (0)4 700501, URL: http://www.gta.gov.zw/
Ministry of Foreign Affairs, Basement, Munhumutapa Building, Samora Machel Avenue, PO Box 4240, Harare, Zimbabwe. Tel: +263 (0)4 727005, fax: +263 (0)4 705161, URL: http://www.zimfa.gov.zw
Ministry of Education, Sport and Culture, Ambassador House, Union Avenue, PO Box CY 121, Causeway, Harare, Zimbabwe. Tel: +263 4 734071, fax: +263 4 734075, URL: http://www.moesc.gov.zw
Ministry of Defence, 1st Floor, Munhumutapa Building, Samora Machel Avenue, Private Bag 7713, Causeway. Harare, Zimbabwe. Tel: +263 (0)4 700155, fax: +263 (0)4 796762, URL: http://www.mod.gov.zw/
Ministry of Information, Posts and Telecommunications, 10th Floor, Linquenda House, Baker Avenue, PO Box CY 825, Causeway, Harare, Zimbabwe. Tel: +263 (0)4 703891/706891, fax: +263 (0)4 707213, URL: http://www.gta.gov.zw/
Ministry of Public Service, Labour and Social Welfare, 12th Floor, Compensation House, Central Avenue/4th Street, Private Bag 7707, Causeway, Harare, Zimbabwe. Tel: +263 (0)4 790871, fax: +263 (0)4 794568, URL: http://www.pslsw.gov.zw/
Ministry of Transport and Communications, 16th Floor, Kaguvi Building, PO Box CY 595, Causeway, Harare, Zimbabwe. Tel: +263 (0)4 700991, fax: +263 (0)4 708225, URL: http://www.transcom.gov.zw/
Ministry of Environment and Tourism, 14th Floor, Karigamombe Centre, 53 Samora Machel Avenue, Private Bag 7753, Causeway, Harare, Zimbabwe. Tel: +263 (0)4 751720, fax: +263 (0)4 757877, http://www.met.gov.zw
Ministry of Health and Child Welfare, 4th Floor, Kaguvi Building, 4th Street, PO Box 8204, Causeway, Harare, Zimbabwe. Tel: +263 (0)4 730011, fax: +263 (0)4 793634, e-mail: npro_moh@gta.gov.zw, URL: http://www.gta.gov.zw/health.html
Ministry of Home Affairs, 11th Floor, Mukwati Building, Private Bag 7703, Causeway, Harare, Zimbabwe. Tel: +263 (0)4 703641, fax: +263 (0)4 726716, URL: http://www.moha.gov.zw/

Ministry of Industry and Commerce, 13th Floor, Mukwati Building, 4th Street, Livingston Avenue, Private Bag 7708, Causeway, Harare, Zimbabwe. Tel: +263 (0)4 702731, fax: +263 (0)4 729311, URL: http://www.miit.gov.zw

Ministry of Rural Resources and Water Development, 8th Floor, Kurima House, Nelson Mandela Avenue, Private Bag 7769, Harare, Zimbabwe. Tel: +263 (0)4 729223, http://www.water.gov.zw/

Ministry of Higher Education and Technology, 1st Floor, Old Mutual Centre, PO Box UA 275, Union Avenue, Harare, Zimbabwe. Tel: +263 (0)4 796441, fax: +263 (0)4 728730, URL: http://www.mhet.ac.zw/

Ministry of Mines, 6th Floor Zimre Centre, Cnr L Takawira Street/Kwame Nkrumah, Private Bag 7709, Causeway, Harare, Zimbabwe. Tel: +263 4 777022, fax: +263 4 777044, e-mail: minsec@technopark.co.zw, URL: http://www.mines.gov.zw

Ministry of Water Resources and Infrastructural Development, 8th Floor Kurima House, 89 Nelson Mandela Avenue/4th Street, Private Bag CY 7767, Causeway, Harare, Zimbabwe. Tel: +263 4 700596, fax: +263 4 738165, URL: http://www.water.gov.zw

Ministry of Women's Affairs, Gender and Community Development, 8th Floor Kaguvi Building, Cnr. Fourth Street/Central Avenue, Harare, Zimbabwe. Tel: +263 4 4708389, URL: http://www.women.gov.zw

Ministry of Youth Development, Indigenization and Empowerment, 20th Floor Mukwati Building, Cnr Livingstone Avenue/5th Street, Private Bag CY 7762, Causeway, Harare, Zimbabwe. Tel: +263 4 707741, fax: +263 4 723709, e-mail: mydgec@zarnet.ac.zw, URL: http://www.mydgec.gov.zw

Ministry of National Security, Chaminuka Building, 5th Street, PO Box 2278, Causeway, Harare, Zimbabwe. Tel: +263 4 700501, fax: +263 4 732660, URL: http://www.gta.gov.zw

Ministry of Policy Implementation, 9th Floor Old Reserve Bank Building, 76 Samora Machel Avenue, Harare, Zimbabwe. Tel: +263 4 730732, fax: +263 4 796100, URL: http://www.polimp.gov.zw

Ministry of Public Service, Labour and Social Welfare, 12th Floor Compensation House, Cnr Central Avenue/4th Street, Private Bag 7707, Causeway, Harare, Zimbabwe. Tel: +263 4 790871, fax: +263 4 794568, e-mail: mpslsw@gta.gov.zw, URL: http://www.pslsw.gov.zw

Ministry of Science and Technology, 16th-20th Floor Livingstone House, 48 Samora Machel Avenue, Harare, Zimbabwe. Tel: +263 4 727579, URL: http://www.mstd.gov.zw

Ministry of Small and Medium Enterprises and Co-operative Development, Liquenda House, Corner Nelson Mandela/1st Street, Private Bag 7740, Causeway, Harare, Zimbabwe. Tel: +263 4 731002, fax: +263 4 704953, URL: http://www.msmed.gov.zw

Ministry of State Enterprises and Parastatals, Ground Floor Munhumutapa Building, Cnr Samora Machel Avenue/2nd Street, Private Bag 7700, Causeway, Harare, Zimbabwe. Tel: +263 4 707071, URL: http://www.fightcorruption.gov.zw

Elections

Parliamentary elections were held in March 2005 for the House of Assembly and November 2005 for the newly reintroduced Senate. In the House of Assembly elections, the ruling Zanu PF party won 78 of the seats. The results were disputed by the opposition Movement for Democratic Change (MDC), led by Morgan Tsvangirai. The MDC later split over its decision to boycott the poll.

The most recent parliamentary elections were held on March 29th 2008; the opposition Movement for Democratic Change (MDC) defeated President Mugabe's Zimbabwe African National Union-Patriotic Front (ZANU-PF).

Parliamentary elections should take place by 31 July 2013.

Presidential elections were held in March 2002 amid much controversy. The government passed a law restricting freedom of the press, and the leader of the EU team of election observers was expelled. The rest of the EU observers also left. Robert Mugabe won the election, amid accusations of vote rigging, and over opposition leader Morgan Tsvangirai, who had been charged with treason just before the election. The EU and US issued sanctions against Zimbabwe, and the country was suspended from the Commonwealth. Tsvangiri was cleared of all charges by August 2005.

The most recent presidential election was held on 29th March 2008, and the main contenders were again President Mugabe and Morgan Tsvangirai. According to the official results, which were not announced until several weeks after the election amid serious unrest, Morgan Tsvangirai had won the most votes, with Mugabe coming a close second. It was eventually agreed that a run-off election would take place on 27th June, although the MDC claimed that their candidate, Mr. Tsvangirai, had won an overall majority. During the week before the run off election Morgan Tsvangirai withdrew following continued brutality towards and intimidation of MDC supporters. Robert Mugabe won the election unopposed, but observers denounced the poll saying it did not reflect the will of the people.

The next presidential election was due in March 2013 but was postponed. President Mugabe has called the next presidential and parliamentary elections for 31 July 2013.

Political Parties

ZANU-PF Party, Samora Machel & Rotten Row Rd, Harare, Zimbabwe. Tel: +263 4 753329, 753145URL: http://www.zanupfpub.co.zw
Chairman: Robert Mugabe (page 1481)
Movement for Democratic Change, Harvest Hse, 6th Floor, N.Mandela Ave/Angwa St, Harare, Zimbabwe. Tel: +263 (0)91 240023 URL: http://www.mdczimbabwe.org
Chairman: Morgan Tsvangirai (page 1528)

Other parties include: National Alliance for Good Governance (NAGG); Zimbabwe African People's Union (ZAPU), and Zimbabwe African National Union-Ndonga (ZANU-Ndonga)

Diplomatic Representation

Embassy of the USA, 172 Herbert Chitepo Avenue, Harare, Zimbabwe. Tel: +263 4 794521 / 704679, fax: +263 4 796488, URL: http://harare.usembassy.gov/
Ambassador: David Wharton

British Embassy, 3 Norfolk Road, Mount Pleasant, Harare (PO Box 4490), Zimbabwe. Tel: +263 4 338800, fax: +263 4 338827, e-mail: british.info@fco.gov.uk, URL: http://ukinzimbabwe.fco.gov.uk/en/
Ambassador: Deborah Bronnert

Embassy of the Republic of Zimbabwe, 1608 New Hampshire Avenue, NW, Washington, DC 20009, USA. Tel: +1 202 332 7100, fax: +1 202 483 9326
Ambassador: H.E. Machivenyika Mapuranga

Embassy of the Republic of Zimbabwe, Zimbabwe House, 429 The Strand, London, WC2R 0QE, United Kingdom. Tel: +44 (0)20 7836 7755, fax: +44 (0)20 7379 1167
Ambassador: H.E. Gabriel Mharadze Machinga

Permanent Representative of the Republic of Zimbabwe (UN), 128 East 56th Street, New York, 10022, USA. Tel: +1 212 980 9511, fax: +1 212 308 6705, e-mail: zimbabwe@un.int, URL: http://www.un.int/zimbabwe/
Ambassador: H.E. Chitsaka Chipaziwa

LEGAL SYSTEM

The legal system is based on Roman-Dutch law. A Supreme Court, headed by the chief justice, has original jurisdiction over alleged violations of constitutional rights and appellate jurisdiction over other matters. There is a High Court consisting of general and appellate divisions. Below the High Court are regional magistrate's courts with civil jurisdiction and magistrate's courts with both civil and criminal jurisdiction. Customary law cases can be appealed through all levels to the Supreme Court.

The chief justice of the High Court is appointed by the president upon recommendation of the Judicial Service Commission. The Commission also advises the president on the appointment of the other judges.

The government of Robert Mugabe abuses the rights of its citizens. Unlawful killings and other forms of brutality by security forces continue, and these forces torture and intimidate members of the opposition, student leaders, and civil society activists with impunity. Prison conditions are life threatening, and arrests can be arbitrary. There is widespread government corruption, as well as interference in the judiciary, and the government uses repressive laws to suppress freedoms of speech, press, assembly, association, academic freedom, and movement. In 2008, thousands of people were displaced in the wake of election-related violence, and the government impeded NGOs' efforts to assist them. The government's control and manipulation of the political process through violence, intimidation, and corruption obstructed the right of citizens to change their government.

Zimbabwe retains the death penalty. The last execution was in 2005. As of April 2013, there were 77 people on death row. Fears that executions might restart in 2013 have been raised by the appointment of a hangman.

LOCAL GOVERNMENT

Zimbabwe is divided into ten provinces: Bulawayo, Harare, Mashonaland West, Mashonaland Central, Mashonaland East, Manicaland, Masvingo, Matabeleland South, Matabeleland North and Midlands. Each province is governed by a provincial governor appointed by the president. Local administration is by district and town councils.

The Provincial Governors of the Provinces as of 2011 were as follows:
Harare Metropolitan Province: (Acting Governor) Alfred Tome
Bulawayo Metropolitan Province: Cde Cain Mathem
Mashonaland East: Hon. Aneas Chigwedere
Mashonaland Central: Hon. Martin Dinha
Mashonaland West: Hon. Faber Chidarikire
Masvingo: Hon. Titus Maluleke
Matabeleland North: Hon. Sithohokozile Mathuthu
Matabeleland South: Hon. Angeline Masuku
Manicaland: Hon. Christopher Mushowe
Midlands: Hon. Jaison Machaya

AREA AND POPULATION

Area
Zimbabwe is situated in the south of Africa. It borders Zambia to the north, Mozambique to the north-east and east, Botswana to the south-west and South Africa to the south. Zimbabwe covers an area of 390,759 sq. km. It is an entirely land-locked country and lies between 900m and 1,550m in height, dropping sharply to below 500m in the river valleys and rising to 2,592m at the highest point of the eastern highlands. The Zambezi River is in the north of the country and the Limpopo River in the south.

The climate is tropical, with a rainy season from November to March. Rain occurs in the Eastern Highlands throughout the year. Summer temperatures average 30°C, but it is hotter in low-lying areas such as the Zambesi plain. It is cooler in winter with an average daytime temperature of 20°C.

To view a map, consult http://www.un.org/Depts/Cartographic/map/profile/zimbabwe.pdf

Population
The population density is 16 per sq. km. According to the WHO figures, the population in 2010 was estimated to be 12.571 million and the annual average population growth rate was estimated at 0.0 per cent for the period 2000-10. The decline is due to HIV/AIDS and emigration. Figures from 2009 estimate the HIV/AIDS prevalence rate in the adult population (15-49 years) to be 14.3 per cent. In recent years many Zimbabweans have left, mainly for South Africa and Botswana, looking for work.

ZIMBABWE

An estimated 38 per cent of the population live in urban areas. The major cities are Harare with a population of 1,189,103, Bulawayo with a population of 621,724, Chitungwiza, Gweru, Mutare, Kwekwe and Masvingo.

70 per cent of the population are Shona and 20 per cent Ndebele, Shona and Ndebele are the two major indigenous languages while English is the commercial language.

The government drew up land reform measures. Agreement was reached in September 1998 on 157 units of land. The aim was to help the 8 million people living on barren land. However, in the run up to the parliamentary election there was government-supported illegal occupation of farms and the government announced plans to seize more farms without compensation. In 2000, hundreds of white owned farms were occupied by squatters and in 2002, although at that stage the country was facing food shortages, white farmers were ordered to stop working the land. At the end of 2002 the government announced the land seizure programme had ended.

Births, Marriages, Deaths
Estimated figures for 2010 put the birth rate at 29.2 per 1,000 population and the death rate at 13.9 per 1,000 population. The average life expectancy in 2009 was 49 years. Healthy life expectancy was put at 39 years. The median age is 19 years. An estimated 39 per cent of the population is under 15 years old and 6 per cent over 60 years. The fertility rate was estimated at 3.3 per woman in 2010. (Source: http://www.who.int, World Health Statistics 2012)

Public Holidays 2014
1 January: New Year's Day
18 April: Good Friday
21 April: Easter Monday
18 April: Independence Day
5 May: Worker's Day
25 May: Africa Day
11 August: Heroes Day (2nd Monday in August)
15 August: Defence Forces Day
22 December: National Unity Day
25 December: Christmas Day
26 December: Boxing Day

EMPLOYMENT

Agriculture is the main employer, employing about 70 per cent of the population although this sector has suffered since the introduction of the controversial land reform programme. The manufacturing sector employs 16 per cent and mining six per cent. Estimated figures for 2010 put the labour force at 3.8 million. Figures for 2005 put the unemployment rate as high as 80 per cent rising to 93 per cent in 2009.

The main trade union is the Zimbabwe Congress of Trade Unions.
Zimbabwe Congress of Trade Unions: URL: http://www.samara.co.zw/zctu

BANKING AND FINANCE

Currencies
The unit of currency was the Zimbabwean dollar. 1 Z$ = 100 cents. The Zimbabwean dollar was suspended indefinitely in 2009 in an attempt to end hyper inflation. The economy is now multi-currency, mainly the US dollar and the South African rand, but also the euro, the UK pound and the Botswanan pula.

Economic Situation
Despite having a well-developed infrastructure and financial system, the economy has declined over the last 20 years due to poor governance. GDP has declined by 50 per cent. The agricultural sector has been particulary affected by land resettlements and over 50 per cent of the population now receives food aid. In 2008 the budget revenue was US$133 million and Zimbabwe is dependent on aid. Some US$670 million of aid was received in 2008. Aid from the IMF and World Bank has been suspended because of arrears but following the inclusive government between Zanu-PF and the MDC, discussion between the IMF and Zimbabwe has started. Aid is expected to increase if reforms take place. Inflation fell for the first time in 2008 and is now in single digits. The economy has now started to grow helped by better macro-economic management, high global commodity prices and solid performance in the mining and agricultural sectors.

GDP/GNP, Inflation, National Debt
Until recently, GDP had been in decline for 20 years. Estimated figures for 2000 put GDP at US$7.2 million, with a growth rate for 2001 of -8.0 per cent, and -12 per cent in 2002. In 2003 GDP was estimated to be US$3.6 billion. Growth was estimated to be -13.2 per cent in 2004 and -6.5 in 2005. In 2008, GDP was estimated to be US$1.96 billion with a growth rate of -12.6 per cent. Estimated figures for 2009 put GDP at US$1.3 billion with a growth rate that year of -1.3 per cent. Some 80 per cent of the population live on less than US$2 per day. Growth was put at 9.9 per cent in 2011. GDP was estimated at US$9.9 billion in 2011.Growth is expected to be 5 per cent in 2013.

Inflation decreased from 42.1 per cent in 1992 to a low of 18.8 per cent in 1997 but has since risen sharply. By 1999 it had reached 60 per cent, rising in early 2002 to a rate estimated as high as 130 per cent. In 2004 it was estimated to be over 250 per cent and had risen to 1,193 per cent in May 2006. In June 2006 the Reserve Bank began issuing Z$100,000 notes, in order to reduce the amount of paper money people needed to carry around with them. The notes had the equivalent value of just under one US dollar. By February 2008 inflation had reached 165,000 per cent and in January the Reserve Bank began issuing notes in the denomination of 10 million dollars. In July 2008 inflation had reached 2.2 million per cent and 11.2 million per cent in September. The government then announced that certain

wholesale and retailers would be allowed to accept foreign currency. Figures for October 2008 put inflation at 231 million per cent. In December 2008, the Z$100 trillion was launched. In January 2009 the government announced that Zimbabweans could conduct business using foreign currency. In February 2009 the government revalued the dollar, 12 zeros were removed from the currency to take effect immediately. In June 2009 it was announced that retail prices in January and February had fallen slightly for the first time in years. Average inflation for 2009 was put at 9.0 per cent. It was below 5 per cent in 2012.

The external debt was equivalent to 33.0 per cent of the GNI in 2004.

In 1998 the government adopted a Programme for Economic and Social Transformation (ZIMPREST) which aimed at sustaining a high rate of economic growth and development in order to raise the income and the general standard of living. The programme had the support of the IMF and World Bank. Zimbabwe went into arrears with the World Bank in 2000, and with the IMF in 2001. No money from either institution can be released to Zimbabwe until the arrears are cleared. In February 2010 the IMF restored Zimbabwe's voting rights and its eligibility to use resources from the IMF's General Resources Account(GRA), although Zimbabwe still cannot borrow money from the IMF.

Foreign Investment
In recent years Zimbabwe has seen direct foreign investment fall by 99 per cent.

Balance of Payments / Imports and Exports
Goods to the value of an estimated US$2.3 million were exported in 2010. South Africa, DRC, Botswana and China were the main recipients of Zimbabwe's exports. The main exports are tobacco, gold, ferro-alloys, asbestos, sugar, maize, iron and steel, nickel, cotton, textiles and coffee.

The total value of imports in 2010 were an estimated US$3.6 billion, with machinery and transportation equipment making up 41 per cent of this figure. Zimbabwe has turned away from some of its traditional markets and China is now amongst its leading trading partners. South Africa is still the dominant trading partner supplying over 50 per cent of imported goods.

Central Bank
Reserve Bank of Zimbabwe, PO Box 1283, 80 Samora Machel Avenue, Harare, Zimbabwe. Tel: +263 4 703000 / 4 703111, fax: +263 4 706450 / 707800, e-mail: rbzmail@rbz.co.zw, URL: http://www.rbz.co.zw
Governor: Dr Gideon Gono

Chambers of Commerce and Trade Organisations
Zimbabwe National Chamber of Commerce, URL: http://www.zncc.co.zw/

MANUFACTURING, MINING AND SERVICES

Primary and Extractive Industries
Zimbabwe is endowed with a considerable quantity and variety of minerals. Gold remains the most valuable mineral but asbestos, copper and nickel are also significant, while at Hwange there are vast deposits of coal. Recent figures put Zimbabwe's coal reserves at 810 million short tons, figures for 2010 show that 3.304 million shorts tons was produced and consumption 3.095 million short tons leaving 208,000 short tons for export. Other minerals include precious stones, tantalite, magnesite, lithium and limestone. Mining activities account for about 8 per cent of GDP, 6 per cent of employment and 45 per cent of foreign currency earnings.

Energy
Zimbabwe's power consumption is growing by about 6 per cent per year. The Zimbabwe Electricity Supply Authority (ZESA) is responsible for generation and supply. Zimbabwe plans to use solar power to supply electricity to around 500 districts. Each of the sites would need solar systems with generating capacity of 100 kWh or 500 kWh. In 2010, electricity generation stood at 7.81 billion kWh. and consumption was 12.57 billion kWh, 2.04 billion kWh was imported. Additional power is imported from South Africa, Zambia, Mozambique and the Democratic Republic of Congo. Zimbabwe is heavily in debt to South Africa and Mozambique for electricity supply.

Zimbabwe presently consumes around 10,000 barrels of oil per day.

Manufacturing
Manufacturing accounts for about 25 per cent of GDP and 18 per cent of employment. There are a wide range of goods produced including steel and steel products, transport equipment, leather, textiles, tyres, chemicals, forestry products and food.

Service Industries
The number of tourists had been increasing to a level of 1.9 million per year but figures for 1999 showed an 80 per cent fall in visitors. Figures for 2006 showed that the number of tourists had risen to 2.2 million.

Agriculture
Agriculture accounts for 20 per cent of GDP but has been severely affected by the government's land reforms. Of Zimbabwe's total 39 million hectares, 33 million hectares are designated as agricultural land; of this, 16 million hectares are under communal farming systems, 11 million hectares are under large scale commercial farming, 3 million hectares are under resettlement farming and just over 1 million hectares under small scale commercial farming. The Government implemented a resettlement programme where the aim was to settle 162,000 families on 8.3 m hectares of land taken from the 15.5 m hectares of the large scale commercial sector. In November 2002 it was announced that, with the seizure of 35 million acres of previously white-owned farms, the programme was at an end.

Corn and tobacco production have dropped dramatically. Food shortages occurred in 2001 and were blamed variously on drought , floods and poor government management. Zimbabwe's main crops are maize, wheat, tobacco, cotton, sugar and sunflowers. Tobacco accounts for 22 per cent of the country's exports.

Recent figures estimate that the national cattle herd shrank by 90 per cent between 2000 and 2004 and that the production of flue-cured tobacco had fallen from 235m kg to 70 m kg.

Agricultural Production in 2010

Produce	Int. $'000*	Tonnes
Indigenous cattle meat	269,015	99,585
Tobacco, unmanufactured	174,785	109,737
Maize	156,047	1,192,400
Cow milk, whole, fresh	123,451	395,600
Sugar cane	101,795	3,100,000
Indigenous chicken meat	87,737	61,595
Game meat	76,591	35,200
Cotton lint	54,310	38,000
Indigenous pigmeat	47,932	31,181
Groundnuts, with shell	43,376	106,147
Indigenous goat meat	30,794	12,852
Vegetables fresh nes	26,495	140,600

* unofficial figures
Source: http://faostat.fao.org/site/339/default.aspx Food and Agriculture Organization of the United Nations, Food and Agricultural commodities production

COMMUNICATIONS AND TRANSPORT

Travel Requirements
Citizens of the USA, Canada, Australia and the EU require a passport valid for six months beyond the length of stay, with three blank pages. They also require a return ticket and sufficient funds for the intended length of stay, and a visa (apart from citizens of Cyprus, Ireland and Malta who do not need a visa, and transit passengers continuing their journey within six hours, with an onward ticket and not leaving the transit area). Nationals of the following countries may obtain visas valid for up to 90 days on arrival in Zimbabwe: Australia, Austria, Belgium, Canada, Denmark, Finland, France, Germany, Greece, Italy, Luxembourg, The Netherlands, Poland, Portugal, Spain, Sweden, Switzerland, UK and USA. Other nationals should contact the embassy to check visa requirements.

Travellers should keep all travel documents readily available, as well as a list of residences or hotels where they will stay while in Zimbabwe. They must also carry some form of identification at all times.

U.S. citizens who intend to work in Zimbabwe as journalists must apply for accreditation with the Zimbabwean Embassy at least one month in advance of planned travel.

National Airlines
Air Zimbabwe, P.O. Box AP 1, Harare Airport, Harare, Zimbabwe. Tel: +263 4 575111, fax: +263 4 575068, URL: http://www.airzimbabwe.aero

International Airports
There is an international airport in Harare as well as over 400 domestic airports, some of which have paved runways.

Railways
Branch lines connect several mining areas to the main network. The system is being modernised and electrified. The 3,070 km of track is operated by the state-owned National Railways of Zimbabwe. The railway system connects Zimbabwe with Zambia, Mozambique, Botswana and South Africa.

Roads
There are 18,400 km of roads designated as state roads of which 7,757 are hard surfaced. In addition to this there are 77,574 km of roads maintained by local authorities; 5,287 km of roads in municipal areas; 6,000 km of roads under the Ministry of Water and 9,000 km under the National Parks. Bus services run between Harare and Johannesburg and Bulawayo and Johannesburg. Vehicles are driven on the left.

Ports and Harbours
There are ports at Binga and Kariba on Lake Kariba. Ferries run on Lake Kariba.

HEALTH

There are local clinics and hospitals and a private health care system. Each year between December and March a nationwide programme for malaria control is run. In 2007, the government spent an estimated 8.9 per cent of its total budget on healthcare, accounting for 46.3 per cent of all healthcare spending. Total expenditure on healthcare equated to 8.9 per cent of the country's GDP. Per capita expenditure on health was approximately US$79. Figures for 2000-10 estimate that there are 2,086 physicians (2 per 10,000 population), 9,357 nurses and midwives (7 per 10,000 population), 310 dentists, 883 pharmaceutical personnel, and 1,803 environment and public health workers. There were approximately 30 hospital beds per 10,000 population.

According to the latest WHO figures, in 2010 approximately 80 per cent of the population had access to improved drinking water. In the same year, 40 per cent of the population had access to improved sanitation.

In 2010, life expectancy at birth was 49. The infant mortality rate in 2010 was estimated to be 51 per 1,000 live births. The child mortality rate (under 5 years) was 80 per 1,000 live births. The main causes of childhood mortality are: HIV/AIDS (20 per cent, down from 45 per cent in 2000), prematurity (14 per cent), diarrhoea (8 per cent), pneumonia (11 per cent), measles (8 per cent) and malaria (8 per cent).

Zimbabwe has one of the highest rates of Acquired Immunodeficiency Syndrome (AIDS) in the world. Figures for 2009 estimated that approximately 14.3 per cent of the population were infected with the HIV/AIDS virus. An estimated 34 per cent of the people with advanced HIV infection and 56 per cent of HIV-infected pregnant women had antiretroviral therapy. (Source: http://www.who.int, World Health Statistics 2012)

EDUCATION

Primary and secondary education was segregated until 1979. Education in Zimbabwe begins with Early Childhood Education and Care (ECEC) for children up to six. Primary education consists of a seven year period up to 12. Secondary education begins at the age of 14 and lasts for six years. 90 per cent of educational institutions are non-governmental but they receive grants from the government and most teachers are public servants so are paid by the government.

Figures from 2002 show that 82 per cent of boys and 83 per cent of girls were enrolled in primary schools, and 40 per cent of boys and 36 per cent of girls were enrolled in secondary schools. Teacher, student ratio in 2006 was 1 to 38 pupils in primary schools.

Public expenditure on education is around 4.7 of GDP. The literacy rate is estimated to be 76 per cent.

RELIGION

60 per cent of the population follows Christianity, 31 per cent follow indigenous beliefs. There are small Hindu, Muslim, Bah'ai and Jewish communities.

Zimbabwe has a religious liberty rating of 7 on a scale of 1 to 10 (10 is most freedom). (Source: World Religion Database)

COMMUNICATIONS AND MEDIA

All broadcasters and the main newspapers are state controlled. The private press is subject to government pressure. The Daily News is one of the most outspoken papers and is currently subject to a publication ban.

Newspapers
The newly licensed NewsDay was launched in 2010.
The Herald, URL: http://www.herald.co.zw
The Chronicle, government owned. URL: http://www.chronicle.co.zw
The Financial Gazette, privately owned, URL: http://www.fingaz.co.zw
NewsDay, private, URL: http://www.newsday.co.zw/

Broadcasting
As of 2002 there are two national broadcasting channels run by the Zimbabwe Broadcasting Corporation (ZBC) which is state owned. Prior to 2002 there was a private station, Joy TV, which was closed down by the government. ZBC also runs radio broadcasts. Satellite television is available.
Zimababwe State Broadcasting Corporation: URL: http://www.zbc.co.zw

Telecommunications
The system has been in decline and is poorly maintained. It was estimated in 2008 that over 350,000 phone lines were in use and more than 1.6 million mobile phones, that year there were also an estimated 1.4 million internet users

ENVIRONMENT

Main environmental concerns of Zimbabwe include deforestation, soil erosion and land degradation. Zimbabwe's wildlife has also been under threat from poachers, particularly the now rare black rhinoceros.

Zimbabwe is a party to the following international agreements: Biodiversity, Climate Change, Desertification, Endangered Species, Law of the Sea and Ozone Layer Protection.

According to figures from the EIA, Zimbabwe's emissions from the consumption of fossil fuels totalled 8.49 million metric tons of carbon dioxide in 2010.

BIOGRAPHIES

A

AARIAK, Eva; Premier, Government of Nunavut; ***political career:*** Premier, Minister of Executive and Intergovernmental Affairs, Minister Responsible for Immigration, 2008-, also Minister for Aboriginal Affairs, Minister of Education, 2011-; ***professional career:*** Languages Commissioner; Journalist; Businesswoman; ***office address:*** Office of the Premier, Grinnell Place, PO Box 800, Iqaluit, NT X0A 0H0, Canada; ***phone:*** +1 867 979 5822.

AAVIKSOO, Jaak; Minister of Education and Research, Government of Estonia; ***born:*** 11 January 1954, Tartu, Estonia; ***education:*** Tartu State Univ., Physics grad. cum laude, 1976; ***party:*** Union of Pro Patria; Res Publica; ***political career:*** Minister of Culture and Education, 1995; Minister of Education, 1996; Minister of Defence, 2007-12; Minister of Education and Research, 2012-; ***memberships:*** Management Bd.of Assn. of European Universities; Estonian Academic Council; Estonian Research and Development Cncl.; Estonian Informatics Cncl.; Estonian Physics Society; European Physics Society; American Optics Society; ***professional career:*** TA Junior, Senior and Chief Research Specialist, Instit. of Physics of AS, 1976-92; Prof. of Optics and Spectroscopy, Univ. of Tartu, 1992; First Prorector, Univ. of Tartu, 1992-95, Acting Head, Instit. of Experimental Physics and Technology, 1995, Head, 1996-98; Rector, Univ. of Tartu, 1998-2006; ***publications:*** Over 100 research papers and more than 80 published articles between 1976 and 2002.; ***office address:*** Ministry of Education and Research, Munga 18, 50088 Tartu, Estonia; ***phone:*** +372 735 0222; ***fax:*** +372 735 0250; ***e-mail:*** hm@hm.ee; ***URL:*** http://www.hm.ee.

ABAD, Florencio; Secretary of the Budget and Management, Government of the Philippines; ***education:*** LLB., Ateneo de Manila University; ***political career:*** Secretary of Education, Culture and Sports, 2004-05; Secretary of the Budget and Management, 2010-; ***office address:*** Department of Budget and Management, 2nd Floor, DBM Building III, General Solano Street, San Miguel, Manila, Philippines; ***phone:*** +63 2 735 4926; ***fax:*** +63 2 742 4173; ***URL:*** http://www.dbm.gov.ph.

ABBAS, Mohamed Cherif; Minister of War Veterans (Mujahedin), Algerian Government; ***born:*** 1936; ***political career:*** mem., National Liberation Army, 1955-62; mem., FLN,1962-76; mem., commission of foreign relations of FLN, 1976-82; National Sec., National Org. of War Veterans, 1982, Sec. Gen, 1996; Mem., National Consultative Council, 1993; Founding mem., RND, 1996-; Mem., National Council, 1996; Mem., Senate, 1997-99; Minister of War Veterans, 1999-; ***office address:*** Ministry of War Veterans, 2 avenue de Lieutenant Med Benarfa, El Biar, Algiers, Algeria; ***phone:*** +213 (0)21 922355; ***fax:*** +213 (0)21 923516.

ABBAS (ABU MAZEN), Mahmoud; President, Palestinian National Authority; ***born:*** 1935, Safed, Galilee, Palestine; ***education:*** Univ. of Damascus, Syria, BA law, 1958; Orientalism Institute, Moscow, Ph.D. History, 1982; ***party:*** Sec.-Gen., Palestine Liberation Organisation (PLO); ***political career:*** Co-founder, Palestine National Liberation Movement (FATAH), 1965; Head, Department for National and International Relations, PLO, 1984-2000; Pres., PLO Negotiations Affairs Dept., 1994-2003; Prime Minister, Palestinian National Authority, 2003-04; President, Palestinian Authority, 2005-; ***professional career:*** Dir., Human Resources, Qatari Ministry of Education, 1957-70; ***committees:*** Head, Palestinian-Jordanian Jt. Cttee., 1979-; Sec.-Gen., PLO Exec. Cttee., 1996-2004; Pres., first Palestinian Elections Cmn., 1996-2002; Chmn., PLO Exec. Cttee., 2004-; ***publications:*** Zionism; The Bridge of Evil; The Other Face; The Fall of the Netanyahu Government; Religious and Ethnic Polarization in Israel; The Road to Oslo; ***office address:*** Office of the President, Palestinian National Authority, Ramallah, Occupied Palestinian Territories.

ABBE, Denis; Prefect, French Guiana; ***born:*** 1952; ***education:*** Law; ***political career:*** Commissioner, 1978; Dep. Prefect, Ceret; Dep. Prefect, Saint Benoit, 1993; administrator; Sec.-Gen., Sarthe prefecture, 2001; Sec.-Gen., Guadeloupe prefecture, 2003; Dep. Prefect, Antony, 2006; Dep. Prefect, Lorient, 2009; Prefect of Guyana, 2011-; ***office address:*** Prefecture, rue Fiedmond, BP 7008, 97307 Cayenne, Cedex, French Guiana.

ABBOTT, Diane; British, Member of Parliament for Hackney North and Stoke Newington, House of Commons; ***born:*** 27 September 1953, Paddington, London, UK; ***parents:*** Reginald and Julia; ***children:*** James (M); ***education:*** Newnham Coll., Cambridge, MA, History; ***party:*** Labour Party; ***political career:*** Mem., Westminster City Cncl., 1982-86; MP, Hackney North and Stoke Newington, 1987-; entered leadership contest for Labour Party, June 2010; Shadow Minister, Health, Oct. 2010-; ***interests:*** immigration and asylum, race issues, mental health; ***professional career:*** Journalist, Thames TV; Civil Servant; ***committees:*** All Party Parly. Gp., Gun Crime, Race and Community, British Caribbean; mem., Select Cttee., Treasury & Civil Services, 1989-97, Foreign Affairs, 1997-2001; ***publications:*** Various articles in national press; ***office address:*** House of Commons, London, SW1A 0AA, United Kingdom; ***phone:*** +44 (0)20 7219 4426; ***fax:*** +44 (0)20 7219 4964; ***e-mail:*** glennc@parliament.uk; ***URL:*** http://www.dianeabbott.org.uk.

ABDELAZIZ, Mohamed; President, Sahrawi Republic; ***born:*** 1948; ***education:*** Mohammed V University, Rabat, Morocco; ***party:*** Sec.-Gen.Polisario Front, 1976-; ***political career:*** Pres. Sahrawi Republic, 1982-; ***office address:*** Office of the President, Tindouf, Algiers, Algeria.

ABDEL-RASOOL, Ali-Mahmood; Minister of Finance and National Economy, Government of Sudan; ***education:*** Univ. of Khartoum, Sudan; ***party:*** National Congress Party; ***political career:*** Minister of Finance and National Economy, 2010-; ***office address:*** Minister of Finance and National Economy, Nile Street, P.O. Box 700, Khartoum, Republic of Sudan; ***phone:*** +249 11 775969.

ABDUL HALIM, Tuandu; Supreme Head of State and King, Malaysia; ***born:*** 1927; ***political career:*** Sultan of Kedah, 1958-; Deputy King, 1965-70; Head of State of Malaysia, 1970-75; Deputy King, 2006-2011; 14th Head of State of Malaysia, 2011-; ***office address:*** Office of the President, Istana Negara, 50500 Kuala Lumpur, Malaysia; ***phone:*** +60 3 2078 8332.

ABDULLAH, Dr Farooq; Minister of New and Renewable Energy, Government of India; ***political career:*** Chief Minister of Jammu and Kashmir, 1982-84, 1986-90, 1996-2002; Minister of New and Renewable Energy, 2009-; ***office address:*** Ministry of New and Renewable Energy, Shram Shakti Bhavan, Raffi Marg, New Delhi 110 001, India; ***phone:*** +91 11 371 0071.

ABDULLAH, H.E. Yousuf bin Alawi bin; Minister for Foreign Affairs, Oman Government; ***born:*** 1945; ***political career:*** Sec. of State, 1974; Minister for Foreign Affairs, Oman Govt., 1992-; ***professional career:*** Amb. of Oman to Lebanon, 1973; ***office address:*** Ministry for Foreign Affairs, POB 252, Muscat, Oman; ***URL:*** http://www.mofa.gov.om.

ABDULLAH II, HRH King bin al-Hussein; King, Hashemite Kingdom of Jordan; ***born:*** 30 January 1962, Amman, Jordan; ***parents:*** The late King Hussein I of Jordan and Princess Muna Al Hussein; ***married:*** Queen Rania, 10 June 1993; ***children:*** Prince Hussein (M), Princess Iman (F), Princess Salma (F); ***education:*** Islamic Educational Coll., Amman, Jordan; St. Edmund's Sch., Surrey, England; Eaglebrook Sch. & Deerfield Academy, USA; Royal Military Academy, Sandhurst, UK, 1980; Oxford Univ., Special Studies in Middle Eastern Affairs, 1982; Armoured Officers Advanced Course, Fort Knox, Kentucky, USA, 1985; Sch., Foreign Service, Georgetown Univ., Washington, DC, Mid-Career Fellow, 1987; Advanced Study and Research programme in Int. Affairs, part of 'Master of Science in Foreign Svce.' programme; defence resources management, Monterrey Naval Post Grad. Sch., 1998; ***interests:*** to establish comprehensive solution to Arab-Israeli conflict, to institutionalize democratic, political pluralism in Jordan, the modernization of information technology, educational systems in Jordan, a guarantee for women to be included in socio-economic & political life; ***professional career:*** Reconnaissance Troop Leader, 13th/18th Battalion of Royal Hussars, West Germany & England; Platoon Cdr.& Co. Second-in-Command, 40th Armoured Brigade, Jordanian Armed Forces; Cdr., Tank Co., holding the rank of Capt., 91st Armoured Brigade, Jordanian Armed Forces, 1986; Royal Jordanian Air Force Anti-Tank Wing; Cdr., Royal Jordanian Special Forces; Cdr., Royal Jordanian Special Operations; 2nd Company Cdr., 17th Tank Battalion, 1989; 2nd in Command, 17th Tank Battalion, 1989-91; promoted to rank of Major; Armoured Corps Rep., Office of the Inspector General, Jordanian Armed Forces; Battalion Cdr., Second Armoured Cavalry Regiment, 1992; Colonel, 40th Brigade & Dep. Cdr., Jordanian Special Forces, 1993; Cdr., Special Forces, with the rank of Brigadier, 1994; promoted to Major-General, 1998; proclaimed Crown Prince by Royal Decree, 1999; Appointed King of Jordan, Feb.1999-; ***honours and awards:*** a number of decorations from various countries; ***recreations:*** automobile racing, water sports, scuba diving, collecting ancient weapons and armaments; ***office address:*** Royal Palace, Amman, Jordan.

ABE, Shinzo; Former Prime Minister, Government of Japan; ***born:*** 21 September 1954; ***parents:*** Shintaro Abe (dec'd); ***education:*** Seikei Univ., Dept. of Political Science, Faculty of Law, 1977; ***party:*** Leader, Liberal Democratic Party; ***political career:*** MP., 1993-; Dep. Chief Cabinet Secretary, 2000-03; Sec.-Gen., Liberal Democratic Party, 2003-; Chief Cabinet Sec., 2005; Prime Minister, Sept. 2006-Sept. 2007; ***professional career:*** Kobe Steel, Ltd, 1979-82; Executive Assistant, Minister for Foreign Affairs, 1982-93; ***office address:*** Office of the Prime Minister, 1-6-1 Nagata-cho, Chioda-ku, Tokyo 100, Japan; ***phone:*** +81 (0)3 3581 3111.

ABELA, George; President, Government of Malta; ***born:*** 1948; ***education:*** Univ. of Malta; ***political career:*** Dep. Leader, Labour Party Affairs, 1992-98; President of Malta, 2009-; ***professional career:*** Chmn., Malta Football Association, 1982-92; Legal Consusltant; ***office address:*** Office of the President, The Palace, Valletta VLT 2000, Malta; ***phone:*** +356 2122 1221; ***e-mail:*** president@gov.mt; ***URL:*** http://president.gov.mt.

ABERCROMBIE, Neil; American, Governor, Hawaii; ***education:*** Union Coll., Schenectady, NY, US, BA, Sociology; Univ. of Hawaii, US, MA, Ph.D., American Studies; ***party:*** Democrat; ***political career:*** former Mem., State House of Representatives & State Senate, Hawaii; Mem., Honolulu City Cncl., 1988-90; Democratic Whip-at-Large; US House of Representatives, 1986-2010; Governor, State of Hawaii, Nov. 2010-; ***memberships:*** Amnesty International; Life/Foundation/Aids Foundation of Hawaii; ***committees:*** National Security Cttee.; Resources Cttee.; ***office address:*** Office of the Governor, Executive Chambers, Hawaii State Capitol, Honolulu, HI 96813, Hawaii; ***phone:*** +1 808 586 0034; ***URL:*** http://www.hawaii.gov.

ABERDARE, Lord Alastair; Member, House of Lords; ***political career:*** Mem. House of Lords, 2009-; ***interests:*** Wales, arts, culture and heritage, education and skills, trade and technology, small businesses and entrepreneurship; ***office address:*** House of Lords, London, SW1A 0PW, United Kingdom; ***phone:*** +44 (0)20 7219 3000; ***fax:*** +44 (0)20 7219 5979; ***URL:*** http://www.parliament.uk.

ABIL, Iolu; President, Vanuatu; ***political career:*** Cabinet Minister, 1980, Secretary, Ministry of Lands; Interim Ombudsman, 2004; President, 2009-; ***office address:*** Office of the President, Port Vila, Vanuatu.

ABLONCZY, Diane; Canadian, Minister of State for the Americas, Canadian House of Commons; ***education:*** Calgary Univ., B.Ed., 1973, LL.B., 1980; ***party:*** Reform Party; ***political career:*** MP for Calgary, Nose Hill, 1993-; Parly. Sec. to the Minister of Finance, 2007-08; Minister of State for Small Business and Tourism, 2008-10; Minister of State for Seniors, 2010-11; Minister of State for the Americas, 2011-; ***interests:*** human resources dev.; ***professional career:*** Teacher; Farmer; Private Practice Attorney; ***office address:*** House of Commons, Parliament Buildings, Ottawa, ON K1A 0A6, Canada.

ABRAHAM, Judge Ronny; French, Member, International Court of Justice; ***born:*** 5 September 1951; ***languages:*** English; ***education:*** University of Paris I, Diploma in Advanced Studies in Public Law, 1973; Diploma of the Institut d'études politiques of Paris, 1973; Graduate of the École nationale d'administration, 1978; ***interests:*** Jurisdiction; Human rights; Litigation; State responsibility; Treaties; ***memberships:*** Mem., Board of the Société française pour le droit international; Mem., European Group of Public Law; ***professional career:*** *academic career:* Institut d'études politiques of Paris, Professor, -1998; University of Paris X-Nanterre, Associate Professor, 1997-2003; *professional career:* Agent for France in many cases before international and European courts, 1998-2004;

governmental career: Office of Legal Affairs of the Ministry of Foreign Affairs, Assistant Director, 1986-87, Director, 1998-2005; *diplomatic career:* Committee of Experts for the Improvement of Procedures for the Protection of Human Rights of the Council of Europe, Member, 1986-98, Chairman, 1987-89; Joint Consultative Committee of the OECD, Chairman, 1994-98; Member of the French delegation to the UNG; *judicial career:* Judge, ICJ, 2005-; ***publications:*** Droit international, droit communautaire et droit français, 1989; Revue française de droit administratif; Revue générale de droit international public; Revue universelle des droits de l'homme; Annuaire français de droit international; Revue européenne de droit public; ***office address:*** International Court of Justice, The Peace Palace, 2517 KJ The Hague, Netherlands; ***phone:*** +31 (0)70 302 2470; ***e-mail:*** r.abraham@icj-cij.org.

ABRAHAMS, Debbie; MP for Oldham East and Saddleworth, House of Commons; ***born:*** 1960, Sheffield, UK; ***education:*** Univ. of Salford; MA, Univ. of Liverpool; ***political career:*** MP for Oldham East and Saddleworth, Jan. 2011-; ***professional career:*** Public health consultant; Chair, Rochdale Primary Care Trust, 2002-06; Dir., Int. Health Impact Assessment Consortium, Univ. of Liverpool, 2006-10; ***committees:*** Work and Pensions, 2011-; ***office address:*** House of Commons, London, SW1A 0AA, United Kingdom.

ABUSSEITOV, H.E. Kairat; Ambassador, Embassy of Kazakhstan in the UK; ***education:*** Kazakh State Univ.; ***professional career:*** Amb. in the Swiss Confederation, 2004-08; Amb. to the United Kingdom, 2008-; ***office address:*** Embassy of the Republic of Kazakhstan, 33 Thurloe Square, London, SW7 2SD, United Kingdom; ***phone:*** +44 (0)20 7581 4646; ***fax:*** +44 (0)20 7584 8481; ***URL:*** http://www.kazembassy.org.uk.

ADAM, Brian, MSP; Member of Scottish Parliament for Aberdeen North; ***born:*** 10 June 1948, Newmill Banffshire; ***parents:*** James Pirie Adam and Isabel Adam (née Geddes); ***married:*** Dorothy Adam (née Mann), 12 December 1975; ***children:*** Neil (M), James (M), Brian (M), Alan (M), Sarah (F); ***education:*** Aberdeen Univ.; ***party:*** SNP, 1974-; ***political career:*** MSP, Scottish Parl. for North East Scotland, 1999-2003; MSP, Aberdeen North, 2003-11; MP for Aberdeen Donside, 2011-; Minister for Parliamentary Business and Chief Whip, 2011-; ***professional career:*** Clinical Biochemist; ***office address:*** Scottish Parliament, Edinburgh, EH99 1SP, United Kingdom; ***phone:*** +44 (0)131 348 5692; ***fax:*** +44 (0)131 348 5735.

ADAM, Jean-Paul; Minister of Foreign Affairs, Government of the Seychelles; ***education:*** Univ. of Sheffield, BA; Univ. of Manchester, MA; ***political career:*** Dir. Gen, Presidential Affairs, Office of the President, Principal Secretary, Sec. of State, 2009-10; Minister of Foreign Affairs, 2010-; ***professional career:*** diplomat; Second Sec., MFA, 2001-04; ***office address:*** Ministry of Foreign Affairs, P.O. Box 656, "Maison Quéau de Quinssy", Mont Fleuri , Mahé, Republic of Seychelles.

ADAMS, Gerry; Irish, President, Sinn Féin; ***born:*** 1950; ***parents:*** Gerard Adams and Annie Adams (née Hannaway); ***married:*** Colette Adams (née McArode), 1971; ***s:*** 1; ***party:*** Sinn Féin; ***political career:*** Founder Mem. Northern Ireland Civil Rights Assn.; Vice-Pres., Sinn Féin, 1978-83, Pres., 1983-; MP, Belfast West, 1983-91 (did not take seat in Westminster), 1997-2011; MLA, Belfast West, 1998-2010; Elected to the Dail, 2011-; ***honours and awards:*** Thorr Award, Switzerland, 1995; ***publications:*** Peace in Ireland; Falls Memories; Pathway to Peace; Politics of Irish Freedom; Cage 11; The Street and other Stories. Gerry Adams Selected Writings; Before the Dawn (autobiography) 1996; An Irish Voice, 2000; Hope and History, 2004; ***office address:*** Sinn Féin, 44 Parnell Square, Dublin 1, Ireland; ***phone:*** +353 (0)1 872 6932; ***fax:*** +353 (0)1 873 3441; ***e-mail:*** sfadmin@eucom.net.

ADAMS, Luis Inacio Lucena; Attorney General, Government of Brazil; ***education:*** LLM, Faculty of Law, Federal Univ. of Santa Catarina, Brazil; ***political career:*** Attorney General, 2009-; ***professional career:*** Lawyer; ***office address:*** Office of the Attorney General, Ministry of Justice, Esplanada dos Ministerios, Bl. T, 4th Floor, 70064-900 Brasilia DF, Brazil; ***phone:*** +55 (0)61 429 3000; ***fax:*** +55 (0)61 322 6817; ***URL:*** http://www.mj.gov.br.

ADAMS, Nigel; MP for Swlby and Ainsty, UK Government; ***party:*** Conservative; ***political career:*** Dep. regional chmn., Yorkshire and Humber Conservatives 2001-03; MP for Selby and Ainstry, 2010-; PPS to Lord Strathclyde (Leader of the House of Lords), 2010-; ***committees:*** Environment, Food and Rural Affairs, 2010; ***office address:*** House of Commons, London, SW1A 0AA, United Kingdom; ***phone:*** +44 (0)20 7219 3000; ***e-mail:*** nigel.adams.mp@parliament.uk; ***URL:*** http://www.parliament.uk.

ADAMS OF CRAIGIELEA, Baroness Irene; British, Member, House of Lords; ***born:*** 27 December 1947, Paisley, Scotland, United Kingdom; ***children:*** 3; ***party:*** Labour Party, 1965-; ***political career:*** Cllr., Paisley Town, 1970-74; Cllr., Renfrew District, 1974-78; Cllr., Strathclyde, 1979-84; MP, Paisley North, 1992-2005, House of Lords, May 2005-; ***interests:*** Scottish affairs, trade and industry; ***memberships:*** GMB; JP, 1971; ***recreations:*** walking, reading; ***office address:*** House of Lords, London, SW1A 0PW, United Kingdom; ***phone:*** +44 (0)20 7219 3000.

ADAN, Fawziyo Yussuf Haji; Deputy Prime Minister and Foreign Minister, Government of Somalia; ***education:*** John Hopkins Univ.; American Univ. in Paris; ***political career:*** founded political party, Nabad, Dimograadiyad iyo Barwaaqo (Peace, Democracy & Prosperity Party), later disqualified as political party; Deputy Prime Minister and Foreign Minister, 2012-; ***professional career:*** founder, Univ. of Hargeisa, Somalialand; launched RAADTV; Diplomat; ***office address:*** Ministry of Foreign Affairs, Mogadishu, Somalia.

ADEBOWALE, Rt. Hon. Lord Victor Olufemi, CBE MA; Member of House of Lords; ***education:*** Polytechnic of East London; Tavistock Institute, MA, Advanced Organisational Consultancy; ***political career:*** Mem., House of Lords; ***memberships:*** Bd. mem., Audit Commission; Fellow, Sunningdale Institute; Mem., Council for the Institute of Fiscal Studies; Mem., National Employment Panel, 1997-2006; Assoc., Health Service Management Centre; Patron, Nurse Training Council on Alcohol; Pres., International Assoc. of Philosophy and Psychiatry; Mem. of the Board, National School of Government; Chair, London Youth Crime Prevention Board; Hon. Chair, Community Practitioners and Health Visitors Assn.; Chairmanships: Chancellor, Lincoln Univ.; Chair, Aylesbury Estate New Deal for Communitites Programme; Third Sector Task Forces; Departmental Race Equality national mental health steering group; ***professional career:*** Dir., Alchohol Project, 1990-95; CEO Centrepoint, Youth Homelessness Poverty, 1993-2001; Chief Exec., Turning Point, 2001-; ***honours and awards:*** numerous including: Hon. Ph.D in Social Studies, Univ. of Central England; Hon. Doctorate of Letters, Univ. of Lincoln; Hon. Fellowship, London Southbank Univ.; Doctor of the Univ. of East London (Honoris Causa), Univ. of East London; Visting Prof., Lincoln Univ.; Hon. Doctorate, Univ. of Bradford; Hon. Doctorate, Oxford Brookes Univ.; ***publications:*** several, including: New Deal and the Disadvantaged, 1999, DFES; Review of Social Housing, 2000, Inst. Public Policy and Research; regular columnist for Housing Today and Community Care Magazines; ***recreations:*** poet, kite flying, cinema, art, comic collector, music; ***office address:*** House of Lords, London, SW1A 0PQ, United Kingdom; ***phone:*** +44 (0)20 7219 3000; ***fax:*** +44 (0)20 7219 5979; ***e-mail:*** admin@leadershipinmind.co.uk; ***URL:*** http://www.parliament.uk.

ADELSOHN LILJEROTH, Lena; Minister for Culture, Government of Sweden; ***born:*** 1955; ***party:*** The Moderate Party; ***political career:*** MP, 2002-; Minister for Culture, 2006-; ***professional career:*** Journalist; ***office address:*** Ministry of Education, Research & Culture, Government Offices, SE 103 33 Stockholm, Sweden; ***phone:*** +46 (0)8 405 1000.

ADER, Janos; President, Government of Hungary; ***born:*** 1959; ***party:*** Fidesz (co-founder); ***political career:*** MP, 1990-2009; Speaker of the Parliament, 1998-2002; MEP, 2009-12; President, May 2012-; ***office address:*** Office of the President, Sándor Palace, Szent György tér 1, 1014 Budapest, Hungary; ***phone:*** +36 1 224 5000; ***URL:*** http://www.keh.hu.

ADERHOLT, Robert; American, Congressman, Alabama 4th District, US House of Representatives; ***born:*** 22 July 1965; ***married:*** Caroline Aderholt (née McDonald); ***d:*** 1; ***education:*** Univ. of North Alabama; Birmingham Southern Coll.; Cumberland School of Law at Samford Univ.; ***political career:*** Mem., US House of Representatives, 1998-; ***memberships:*** Commission on Security and Cooperation in Europe; ***professional career:*** legal assistant to the governor, 1995-96; Municipal Judge, Haleyville; ***committees:*** House Appropriations Cttee.; ***office address:*** House of Representatives, 1433 Longworth House Office Building, Washington, DC 20515, USA; ***phone:*** +1 202 224 3121.

ADOKE, Justice Mohammed Bello; Minister of Justice and Attorney General, Government of Nigeria; ***born:*** 1963; ***education:*** Bello Univ., law; called to Nigerian Bar, 1986; Zurich; Oxford; ***political career:*** Minister of Justice and Attorney General, 2010-; ***professional career:*** lawyer; arbitrator; Senior Advocate; ***office address:*** Ministry of Justice, Federal Secretariat Complex, Shehu Shagari Way, Maitama, P.M.B 192, Garki, Abuja, Nigeria; ***phone:*** +234 9 523 5208 / 523 5194.

ADULYADEJ, King Phra Baht Somdech Phra Paramindra Maha Bhumibol; Thai, King, Thailand; ***born:*** 5 December 1927, Cambridge, Mass, USA; ***parents:*** H.R.H. Prince Mahidol of Songkla; ***married:*** Mom Rajwongse Ying Sirikit Kitiyakara, 28 April 1950; ***children:*** Ubolratana (F), Crown Prince Vajiralongkorn (M), Maha Chaki Sirindhorn (F), Chulabhorn Valai Laksana (F); ***political career:*** King of Thailand, 1946-; ***professional career:*** Succeeded to throne, 9 June, 1946; ***office address:*** Grand Palace, Bangkok, Thailand.

AFEWERKI, Issaias; Eritrean, President, Eritrea; ***born:*** 1946, Asmara, Eritrea; ***party:*** Eritrean People's Liberation Front; ***political career:*** joined Eritrean Liberation Front (ELF), 1966; Leader fourth regional area, ELF, 1968; Gen. Cmdr., ELF, 1969; founding mem., Eritrean People's Liberation Front (EPLF), now People's Front for Democracy and Justice (PFDJ), 1977; former Asst. Sec.-Gen., Sec.-Gen., 1987; Chair, State Cncl., Nat. Assy.; Sec.-Gen., Provisional Govt. of Eritrea, 1991; assumed power May 1991; elected Pres. by Nat. Assy. June, 1993-; ***professional career:*** engineer; ***office address:*** Office of the President, PO Box 257, Asmara, Eritrea; ***phone:*** +291 (0)1 122132.

AFRIYIE, Adam, MP; Member of Parliament, House of Commons; ***born:*** 1965; ***party:*** Conservative; ***political career:*** MP for Windsor, 2005-; Shadow Minister for Science and Innovation, 2007-10; ***committees:*** Chmn., Parly. Space Cttee., 2010; Chair, Parly. Office of Science and Technology, 2010; Members' Expenses, 2011-; ***office address:*** House of Commons, London, SW1A 0AA, United Kingdom; ***phone:*** +44 (0)20 7219 8023; ***e-mail:*** adam.afriye.mp@parliament.uk.

AGANGA, Olusegun Olutoyin; Minister of Trade and Investment, Government of Nigeria; ***education:*** BSc., Univ. of Ibadan, Nigeria, 1977; BD, Univ. of Oxford, UK, 2000; ***political career:*** Minister of Finance, 2011; Minister of Trade and Investment, 2011-; ***professional career:*** Chartered Accountant; ***office address:*** Ministry of Trade and Investment, Old Federal Secretariat Complex, Are 1, P.M.B. 88, Garki, Abuja, Nigeria; ***phone:*** +234 9 234 1884.

AGIUS, Judge Carmel; Maltese, Vice-President, International Criminal Tribunal for the former Yugoslavia; ***born:*** 1945; ***professional career:*** Head of Maltese Delegation, UN Commission on Crime Prevention and Criminal Justice in Vienna, 1990-2001; Mem., Permanent Court of Arbitration, 1999-2008; Senior Judge, Court of Appeal of Malta; Judge, ICTY, 2001-, Presiding Judge of Trial Chamber 11, presided over the the Brdjanin, Oric, Popovic trials, 2003-10, Vice-Pres., 2011-; ***office address:*** International Criminal Tribunal Yugoslavia, PO Box 13888, 2501 EW The Hague, Netherlands; ***URL:*** http://www.icty.org/.

AGLUKKAQ, Leona; Minister of Health, Government of Canada; ***political career:*** Minister of Health and Social Services, Gov. of Nunavut; Minister of Health, 2008-; Minister for the Federal Economic Development Initiative for Northern Ontario, Gov. of Canada, 2008-10; Minister of Health, Minister of the Canadian Northern Economic Development Agency, 2011-; ***office address:*** House of Commons, Parliament Buildings, Wellington Street, Ottawa K1A 0A6, Ontario, Canada.

AGUIAR BRANCO, José Pedro; Minister of National Defence, Government of Portugal; *education:* Univ. of Coimbra, Law; *party:* Social Democratic Party (PSD); *political career:* MP, 2005-; Chmn., Oporto Municipal Assembly, 2005-09; Minister of Justice; Minister of National Defence, 2011-; *professional career:* lawyer; *office address:* Ministry of Defence, Av. Ilha De Madeira 1, 1400-204 Lisbon, Portugal.

AHMAD, Asif; Ambassador, British Embassy in Thailand; *education:* Durham Univ., UK, 1977; *professional career:* FCO, Head, South East Asia and Pacific Dept., 2008-10; Amb. to Thailand and Laos, 2010-; *office address:* British Embassy, 1031 Wireless Road, Lumpini Pathumwan, Bangkok 10330, Thailand; *phone:* +66 (0)2 253 0191; *fax:* +66 (0)2 254 9578; *e-mail:* info.bangkok@fco.gov.uk; *URL:* http://ukinthailand.fco.gov.uk/en.

AHMAD OF WIMBLEDON, Lord Tariq; Member, House of Lords; *party:* Conservative Party; *political career:* Councillor, London Borough of Merton, 2002-; Vice-Chmn., Conservative Party (Cities), 2008-; Mem. House of Lords, 2011-; *memberships:* Associate, Inst. of Financial Services; Mem., Inst. of Directors; *professional career:* Businessman; *honours and awards:* Raised to the Peerage, 2011-; *office address:* House of Lords, London, SW1A 0PW, United Kingdom; *phone:* +44 (0)20 7219 3000.

AHMED, Lord; Member of the House of Lords; *born:* 24 April 1957, Mirpur Azad Kashmir; *parents:* Haji S. Mohammed and Rashim Bibi; *married:* Sakina Bibi, 14 July 1974; *children:* Ahmar (M), Babar (M), Maryam (F); *languages:* English, Punjabi, Urdu; *education:* BA, Public Admin.; *party:* Labour Party, 1975; *political career:* Chmn., S. Yorks Labour Party; Vice Chmn., S. Yorks Euro-Constituency; Chmn., Sheffield USDAW- Union; Mem., House of Lords; *interests:* human rights, Kashmir, local government, international human rights, democracy, conflict resolution; *memberships:* Kashmir Policy Group; Amnesty International; USDAW, Life Peer; Chmn., Forced Marriage working group; Pres. South Yorkshire Victim Support; Bd. Mem., British Heart Foundation; *professional career:* Business development manager; *committees:* Chmn., All Party Parly. Gp., Financial Exploitation; Chmn., All Party Parly. Gp., Interreligious Dialogue; Founder and Chmn., APPG on entrepreneurship; Chmn., Working Gp on Mosque and Imam training, preventing extremism together.; *office address:* House of Lords, Westminster, London, SW1A 0PW, United Kingdom; *phone:* +44 (0)20 7219 1396; *fax:* +44 (0)20 7219 1384; *e-mail:* ahmedn@parliament.uk.

AHOOMEY-ZUNU, Kwesi; Prime Minister, Government of Togo; *born:* 1958; *political career:* Minister of Territorial Administration; Sec.-Gen. of the Presidency; Minister of Trade, 2011-12; Prime Minister, 2012-; *office address:* Office of the Prime Minister, BP 1161, Lomé, Togo; *phone:* +228 221 1564; *fax:* +228 221 3753; *URL:* http://www.primature.gouv.tg/.

AIGNER, Ilse; Minister of Food, Agriculture and Consumer Protection, Government of Germany; *born:* 1964; *political career:* mem., CSU, 1985-; mem., Bavarian State Assembly, 1994-98; Mem., Bundestag, 1998-; sec. and mem., Presidium of the CSU, 2007-; Federal Minister of Food, Agriculture and Consumer Protection, 2008-; *professional career:* qualified electrician; systems electronics; *office address:* Ministry of Consumer Protection, Food and Agriculture, Wilhelmstrasse 54, 10117 Berlin, Germany; *phone:* +49 (0)30 20060; *URL:* http://www.bmelv.de.

AINSWORTH, Robert; British, MP for Coventry North East, House of Commons; *born:* 19 June 1952, Coventry, United Kingdom; *parents:* Stanley Ewart Ainsworth (dec'd) and Monica Pearl (dec'd); *married:* Gloria Jean Ainsworth, 1974; *party:* Labour Party, 1975-; *political career:* Mem., Coventry City Cncl., 1984-; Dep. Leader, 1987-91; Chmn., Finance Cttee., 1988-92; Government Whip, 1997-2001; Parly. Under Sec. of State at the Home Office, 2001; MP, Coventry North East, 1992-; Dep. Chief Whip, June 2003-07; Minister of State for Armed Forces, 2007-09; Secretary of State for Defence, 2009-May 2010; Shadow Secretary of State for Defence, May 2010-Sept. 2010; *interests:* economics, housing, industrial relations, taxation policy; *memberships:* MSF, 1979-; *professional career:* sheet metal worker; shop steward; TGWU; MSF; *committees:* Foreign Affairs Select Cttee., Nov. 2010-; Arms Export Controls, 2011-; Chair, Jt. Cttee. on the Draft Enhanced Terrorism Prevention & Investigation Measures Bill, 2012-; *clubs:* Bell Green Working Men's Club; Broad St. Old Boy's Rugby Football Club; *recreations:* reading, walking, chess; *office address:* House of Commons, London, SW1A 0AA, United Kingdom; *phone:* +44 (0)20 7270 3000; *e-mail:* hcinfo@parliament.uk.

AKHMETOV, Serik; Prime Minister, Government of Kazakhstan; *education:* Temirtau plant technical college; Degree of engineer-metallurgist, Russian Academy of Management; Doctorate degree in economic sciences; *political career:* Governor of Temirtau, First Deputy Governor of Astana, head of the State Inspection for Administrative Supervision and Personnel Policies at the Presidential Administration, Chmn. of the Board of the Union of entrepreneurs and employers of Kazakhstan 'Atameken', Minister of Transport and Communications of Kazakhstan, Deputy Prime-Minister of Kazakhstan. Governor of Karaganda region, 2009-; First Deputy Prime-Minister of Kazakhstan, 2012; Prime Minister of Kazakhstan, 2012-; *office address:* Office of the Prime Minister, Government House, 010000 Astana, Kazakhstan; *phone:* +7 7172 745400; *URL:* http://www.government.kz.

AKHTAR AZIZ, Dr Zeti; Governor, Bank Negara Malaysia; *education:* Univ. of Malaya, B.Sc., Econ.; Univ. of Pennsylvania, Ph.D, Monetary and International Economics; *professional career:* Research Economist, South East Asian Central Banks (SEACEN) Research and Training Centre, 1979-84; Deputy Manager, Economics Dept., Bank Negara Malaysia, 1985; Chief Rep., Bank Negara Malaysia London Rep. Office, 1989; Chief Economist, Head Econ. Dept., Bank Negara Malaysia, 1994, Assist. Gov., 1995, Deputy Governor, then Acting Gov., Sept. 98- April 2002, Gov.and Chmn. of the Bd. of Dir., Bank Negara Malaysia, 2000-; *committees:* Chwn., Steering Cttee. for the estab. of the Islamic Financial Services Bd. (IFSB); *publications:* Dr. Akhtar Aziz has written extensively on monetary and financial economics, Islamic finance, capital flows, macroeconomic management, financial reforms and restructuring; *office address:* Bank Negara Malaysia, Jalan Dato Onn, P.O. Box 10922, 50929 Kuala Lumpur, Malaysia; *phone:* +60 (0)3 2698 8044; *fax:* +60 (0)3 2691 2990; *e-mail:* info@bnm.gov.my; *URL:* http://www.bnm.gov.my.

AKIHITO, Emperor; Japanese, Emperor of Japan; *born:* 1933, Tokyo, Japan; *parents:* Emperor Hirohito (dec'd) and Emperess Nagako; *married:* Michiko Shoda, 1959; *s:* 2; *d:* 1; *education:* Gakushuin Schs.; Faculty of Politics and Economics, Gakushuin Univ.; *memberships:* Mem., Ichthyological Soc. of Japan; Hon. Mem., Linnean Soc., London; *professional career:* Official investiture as Crown Prince, 1952; succeeded, 7 Jan. 1989; crowned, 12 Nov. 1990; has undertaken visits to 37 countries and travelled widely throughout Japan; *committees:* Hon. Pres. or Patron, Asian Games, 1958; International Sports Games for the Disabled, 1964; Eleventh Pacific Science Congress, 1966; Hon. Sec., International Conference on Indo-Pacific Fish, 1985; *publications:* 25 papers in the journal of Ichthyological Soc. of Japan; *recreations:* taxonomic study of gobiid fish, natural history, conservation, history, tennis; *office address:* Imperial Palace, 1-1 Chiyoda-ku, Tokyo 100, Japan; *phone:* +81 (0)3 3213 1111.

AL-ANKARI, Dr Khalid bin Muhammed; Saudi Arabian, Minister of Higher Education, Saudi Arabian Government; *born:* 1952; *education:* Univ. of Florida, Ph.D., Geography, 1981; *political career:* Dep. Minister of Municipal and Rural Affairs, 1983-84; Minister of Municipal and Rural Affairs, 1990; Minister of Higher Education, 1991-; *professional career:* Asst. Prof., King Saud Univ., 1981-83; *office address:* Ministry of Higher Education, King Faisal Hospital Street, Riyadh 11153, Saudi Arabia; *phone:* +966 1 464 4444; *fax:* +966 1 441 9004.

AL-ASSAD, Bashar; Syrian, President, Syrian Arab Republic; *born:* 11 September 1965, Damascus, Syria; *parents:* Pres. Hafez al-Assad (dec'd); *married:* Asma Assad (née Ahras), 2000; *languages:* English, French; *education:* Univ. of Damascus Medical School; Ophthalmology, Western Eye Hospital, London; *political career:* Nominated for presidency of Syria following the death of his father; Lieutenant-Gen., June 2000, in command of Syria's armed forces; *professional career:* ophthalmologist; *office address:* Presidential Palace, Damascus, Syria.

AL-ASSAF, Dr Ibrahim Bin Abdul Aziz Bin Abdullah; Saudi Arabian, Minister of Finance and National Economy, Saudi Arabian Government; *born:* 28 January 1949, Quassim, Saudi Arabia; *married:* (married); *children:* 4; *education:* King Saud Univ., Riyadh, BA, Econ. and Political Science; Denver Univ., Colorado, USA, MA, Econ.; Colorado State Univ., Fort Collins, Colorado, USA, Ph.D., Econ.; *political career:* Minister of State and mem., Cncl. of Ministers, 1995-96; Minister of Finance and Nat. Economy, 1996-; *professional career:* Lecturer, Principles of Econ., 1971-82; Assoc. Prof., Econ. and Head of the Dept. of Admin. Sciences, King Abdulaziz Military Coll., 1982-86; Guest Lecturer, Coll. of Command and Staff, 1982-83; part time Advisor, Saudi Dev. Fund, 1982-86; Alternate Saudi Exec. Dir., Int. Monetary Fund (IMF), 1986-89; Saudi Exec. Dir., Exec. Bd. of the World Bank Gp., 1989-95; Vice-Governor, Saudi Monetary Agency, 1995; *office address:* Ministry of Finance and National Economy, Airport Road, Riyadh 11177, Saudi Arabia; *phone:* +966 1 405 0000/405 0080; *fax:* +966 1 405 9202.

AL-ATTIYAH, Dr Khalid Bin Mohammad; Minister of Foreign Affairs, Government of Qatar; *born:* 1967; *education:* King Fayssal Aviation College, Aviation Studies, 1987; Beirut Arab Univ., Law, 1993; Masters, Public Law; Doctorate in Law, Cairo Univ.; *political career:* Minister of State for International Co-operation, 2008-13; Minister of Foreign Affairs, 2013-; *professional career:* Fighter pilot, Emiri Air Force, 1987-95; lawyer; Pres., National Cttee. for Human Rights, 2003-08; *office address:* Ministry of Foreign Affairs, Doha, Qatar; *URL:* http://english.mofa.gov.qa.

ALBANESE, Anthony; Minister of Infrastructure and Transport, Australian Government; *political career:* Member for Grayndler; Minister Infrastructure, Transport and Regional Development, 2007-; Minister of Local Government, 2007-; Leader of the House, 2007-; Minister of Infrastructure and Transport, 2010-; Minister for Regional Australia, Regional Development and Local Government, 2013-; *office address:* Office of the Deputy Prime Minister, 3-5 National Circuit, Canberra, ACT 2600, Australia; *phone:* +61 2 6271 5111; *fax:* +61 6271 5414; *URL:* http://www.pm.gov.au.

AL-BASHIR, Field Marshal Omar Hassan Ahmed; Sudanese, President of the Republic and Commander-in-Chief of Armed Forces, Sudanese Government; *born:* 1935; *political career:* Chmn., Revolutionary Command Cncl. for Nat. Salvation; Minister of Defence, 1989-93; Pres. and Prime Minister, 1989-99; President and Commander-in-Chief of Armed forces, 2000-; *professional career:* Overthrew Govt. of Sadiq Al-Mahdi in coup, 1989; *office address:* People's Palace, P.O. Box 281, Khartoum, Sudan; *phone:* +249 1177 6603 / 777583; *fax:* +249 1177 1724 / 787676.

ALBERT II, HSH Prince; Sovereign, Principality of Monaco; *born:* 1958; *parents:* Prince Rainier III (dec'd) and Princess Grace (dec'd) (née Kelly); *married:* Charlene (née Wittstock), 2 July 2011; *languages:* English, French, German, Italian; *education:* Amherst Coll., Massachusetts USA; *political career:* hereditary Prince of Monaco, succeeded his father Prince Rainier III, April 2005; *memberships:* International Olympic Cttee.; *recreations:* winter sports; *office address:* Office of H.S.H. The Prince Albert, Palais de Monaco BP 518, 98015 Monaco-Ville, Monaco.

ALBERT II, His Majesty King; Former King of the Belgians; *born:* 6 June 1934, Brussels, Belgium; *parents:* His Majesty King Léopold III and Queen Astrid (née Princess of Sweden); *married:* Her Majesty Queen Paola (née Ruffo di Calabria), 1959; *children:* Astrid (F), Philippe (M), Laurent (M); *education:* college in Geneva; *interests:* social exclusion, fight against child abuse, education, social security, economy, evolution of armed forces, international and security affairs; *professional career:* Hon. Pres, Belgian Foreign Trade Board, 1962-93; Pres., Belgian Red Cross, 1958-93; Ascended throne of Belgium (sixth King of Belgium), August 9th, 1993, after the death of his brother, King Baudoin, he abdicated in favour of his son Prince Philippe in July 2013; visited the Cncls. of the Communities and the Regions; Cmdr.-in-Chief of the armed forces Gen. and Admiral; takes close interest in the development and restructuring of the armed forces as well as military activities at national and int. levels; has made the following State visits: Luxembourg, Sweden, Spain, 1994, Denmark and Germany, 1995, Finland and Japan, 1996, Norway, Austria, 1997, Russia, Italy,

BIOGRAPHIES

1998, Poland, Portugal, 1999, The Netherlands, Czech Republic, Switzerland, 2000, Greece, 2001, Hungary, 2002; *office address:* Cabinet of the King, Palais Royal/Koninklijk Paleis, rue de Bréderade/Brederodestraat, 1000 Brussels, Belgium; *phone:* +32 (0)2 551 2020.

ALBIG, Torsten; Prime Minister, State Government of Schleswig-Holstein; *born:* 1963; *party:* Social Democratic Party; *political career:* Mayor, Kiel, 2009-12; Minister-President, State of Schleswig-Holstein, 2012-; *professional career:* lawyer; *office address:* Office of the Prime Minister, State Chancellery, Dusternbrooker way 104, 24105 Kiel, Germany; *URL:* http://www.schleswig-holsein.de/.

ALCALA, Proceso ; Secretary of Agriculture, Government of the Philippines; *born:* 1955; *political career:* Secretary of Agriculture, 2010-; *professional career:* Environmentalist; *office address:* Department of Agriculture, D A Building, Elliptical Road Dilman, Quezon City, Philippines; *phone:* +63 2 928 8741; *URL:* http://www.da.gov.ph.

ALDOUS, Peter; MP for Waveney, UK Government; *party:* Conservative; *political career:* Councillor, Waveney District Council 1999-2002; Suffolk County Council: Councillor 2001-05, Dep. Leader, Conservative Grp., 2002-05; MP for Waveney, 2010-; *committees:* Environmental Audit, 2010-; *office address:* House of Commons, London, SW1A 0AA, United Kingdom; *phone:* +44 (0)20 7219 3000; *e-mail:* peter.aldous.mp@parliament.uk; *URL:* http://www.parliament.uk.

AL-DUWAISAN, Khaled; Ambassador, Embassy of the State of Kuwait, London; *born:* 15 August 1947; *education:* Cairo Univ., Egypt, BA, commerce; Univ. of Kuwait, Dip., business admin.; *memberships:* mem., Queen's Tennis Club; *professional career:* Researcher, Ministry of Foreign Affairs, 1970-71; Diplomatic Attaché, 3rd Sec., 2nd Sec., 1971-76; joined Embassy of Kuwait, Washington DC, USA, 1975; 1st Sec., 1976-80, Counsellor, 1980-84; Ambassador to the Netherlands, 1984-90; appointed non-resident Ambassador to Romania, 1988; Co-ordinator with the UN for Iraq/Kuwait demilitarised zone, 1991-93; Ambassador to the UK, 1993-; accredited non-resident Ambassador to Denmark, Norway and Sweden, 1994-; accredited Ambassador to Ireland, 1995-; Advisory Board, Centre of Near and Middle East Studies, School of Oriental and African Studies, 1998; workshop on International Diplomacy in the New Century, Kuwait Foundation for the Advancement of Sciences and John. F. Kennedy School of Government at Harvard Univ.; *committees:* Co-ordinator, Cttee. for the return of stolen property, 1991-93; *honours and awards:* awarded Freedom of the City of London, 2001; Doyen of the Diplomatic Corps, Court of St. James, 2003; Hon. Certificate from Harvard Univ. (Management of Public Sector Projects and Facilities); Presented with an Award of Excellence by the British Business Forum and British Ambassador to Kuwait, in recognition of the outstanding Services to Anglo-Kuwaiti relations, Jan. 2009; Awarded The Lifetime Contribution to Diplomacy in London by Diplomat Magazine, Apr. 2009; Awarded the Three Faiths Forum Gold Medallion, in recognition of inspirational leadership, July 2010; *recreations:* tennis, swimming; *office address:* Embassy of the State of Kuwait, 2 Albert Gate, London, SW1X 7JU, United Kingdom; *phone:* +44 (0)20 7590 3400.

ALEXANDER, Rt. Hon. Danny; Chief Secretary to the Treasury, UK Government; *born:* 15 May 1976; *married:* Rebecca Alexander, July 2005; *education:* PPE, Hons., Oxford Univ.; *party:* Liberal Democrat; *political career:* MP for Inverness, Nairn, Badenoch and Strathspey, 2005-; Shadow Spokesperson, Dept. for Work and Pensions, 2005-07; Shadow Work and Pensions Sec., 2007-08; Chief of Staff to Nick Clegg, 2008-09; Leader's Chief of Staff, 2009-10; Secretary of State for Scotland, 2010; Chief Secretary to the Treasury, 2010-; *interests:* Highlands and Islands issues; housing; benefit reform and pensions; economic policy; European and Middle Eastern affairs; *professional career:* Press Officer, Scottish Liberal Democrats, 1993-95; Dir., Communications, European Movement, 1996-99; Head of Communications, Britain in Europe, 1999-2004; Head of Communications, Cairngorms National Park, 2004-05; *committees:* Scottish Affairs Select Cttee., 2005-08; *recreations:* hill-walking, fishing, travel, sports; *office address:* Scottish Office, Dover House, 66 Whitehall, London, SW1A 2AU, United Kingdom; *phone:* +44 (0)20 7270 3000; *e-mail:* danny.alexander.mp@parliament.uk; *URL:* http://www.scottishsecretary.gov.uk.

ALEXANDER, Rt Hon Douglas; British, Shadow Foreign Secretary, House of Commons; *born:* 1967, Glasgow; *education:* Park Mains High Sch., Erskine, Scotland; Lester B. Pearson Coll., Vancouver, Canada, Intl. Baccalaureate, 1984-86; Edinburgh Univ., Scotland, Politics & Modern History, 1986-88; Univ. of Pennsylvania, Philadelphia, USA, MA (Hons), 1988-90; Edinburgh Univ., LL.B (Dist), 1993; Dip. in legal practice, 1994; *party:* Labour Party 1982-; *political career:* Parly. Researcher & Speechwriter for Gordon Brown MP, 1990; Minister for E-Commerce and Competitiveness, 2001-02; MP for Paisley South, 1997-; Minister of State, Cabinet Office, 2002-03; Minister for the Cabinet Office & Chancellor, Duchy of Lancaster, 2003-04; Minister of State for Trade, Investment and Foreign Affairs, 2004-05; Minister for Europe, May 2005-06; Transport Secretary and Scottish Secretary, May 2006-June 2007; Secretary of State for International Development, June 2007-May 2010; Shadow Secretary of State for International Development, May 2010-Sept. 2010; Shadow Secretary of State for Work and Pensions, Oct. 2010-11; Shadow Foreign Secretary, 2011-; *professional career:* Lawyer; *office address:* House of Commons, London, SW1A 0AA, United Kingdom; *phone:* +44 (0)20 7270 3000; *e-mail:* hcinfo@parliament.uk; *URL:* http://www.parliament.uk.

ALEXANDER, Heidi; MP for Lewisham East, UK Government; *party:* Labour; *political career:* London Borough of Lewisham Council: Councillor 2004-10, Dep. Mayor 2006-10; MP for Lewisham East, May 2010-; *committees:* Communities and Local Government, 2010-; Regulatory Reform, 2010-; *office address:* House of Commons, London, SW1A 0AA, United Kingdom; *phone:* +44 (0)20 7219 3000; *e-mail:* heidi.alexander.mp@parliament.uk; *URL:* http://www.parliament.uk.

ALEXANDER, Lamar; American, Republican Conference Chair, US Senate; *born:* 1940; *married:* Honey; *education:* Vanderbilt Univ.; NY Univ. School of Law; *political career:* Coordinator, Howard Baker Campaign, 1966 and Legislative Asst. to US Sen Baker; Exec. Asst. to White House Cllr. on Congressional Relations, 1969; Mgr., Winfield Dunn Campaign, Tenn., 1970; Transition Coordinator, Gov Winfield; Rep candidate, Gov., Tennessee, 1974; Gov. of Tennessee, 1978-86; Pres., National Governors Assn. 1985-86; Chmn., Southern

Regional Education Bd.; Chmn., Appalachian Regional Comm.; Mem., Education for Economic Growth Task Force of the Education Comn.; Sec. of Education, 1991-93; Senator for Tennessee, US Senate, 2002-; Republican Conference Chair, 2008-; *memberships:* Founding Mem., Tennessee Citizens for Revenue Sharing, 1971; Founding Mem., Tennessee Council on Crime and Delinquency (Chmn., 1973); *professional career:* Private law practice; Political commentator, Nashville TV Station; Pres., Univ. of Tenn., Knoxville, 1987-91; Law Clerk to US Circuit Court of Appeals Judge; *publications:* Six Months Off: An American Family's Australian Adventure; *clubs:* Phi Beta Kappa; *office address:* Office of Senator Lamar Alexander, 455 Dirksen Senate Office Building, Washington, DC 20510, USA; *phone:* +1 202 224 4944; *URL:* http://www.alexander.senate.gov.

ALFANO, Angelino; Deputy Prime Minister, Minister of the Interior, Government of Italy; *born:* 31 October 1970, Agrigento, Italy; *education:* Law; Ph.D., Media Law; *party:* Il Popolo della Liberta; *political career:* MP for Sicily 1; Minister for Justice, 2008-Nov. 2011; Deputy Prime Minister, Minister of the Interior, Apr. 2013-; *office address:* Ministry for the Interior, Palazzo Viminale, Via Agostino Depretis, 00184 Rome, Italy; *fax:* +39 06 482 7630; *e-mail:* info@interno.it; *URL:* http://www.interno.it.

AL-HALAQI, Wael Nader; Prime Minister, Government of Syria; *born:* 1964; *education:* Univ. of Damascus, medicine, gynaecology; *political career:* Minister of Health, 2011-12; Prime Minister, Aug. 2012-; survived assassination attempt April 2013; *professional career:* Director of Health, Daraa; *office address:* Office of the Prime Minister, Shahbandar Street, Damascus, Syria.

AL-HAMAD AL-SABAH, Sheik Jaber Mubarak; Prime Minister, Government of Kuwait; *education:* Kuwait Univ.; *political career:* Deputy Prime Minister and Minister of Defence, 2007-11; Minister of Interior, 2006-11; Prime Minister, 2011-; *office address:* Office of the Prime Minister, PO Box 4, Safat 13001, Kuwait; *phone:* +965 539 1111; *fax:* +965 481 8028.

AL-HASHIMI, Tariq; Vice President, Government of Iraq; *born:* 1942; *education:* BA, 1969, MA, 1978, al Mustansiriyah Univ.; *party:* Iraqi National Movement; *political career:* Second Vice President, 2006-11; First Vice President, May 2011-; *office address:* Office of the Vice President, Baghdad, Iraq.

ALI, Amadou; Deputy Prime Minister, Government of Cameroon; *born:* 1943; *education:* National School of Admin. & Magistracy, Dipl; International Inst. of Public Admin., Paris; *political career:* Sec. Gen., Ministry of Public Service, 1974-82; Delegate General for Tourism, 1982-83; Delegate Gen. ofr National Gendarmerie, 1983-85; Sec. of State for Defence, in charge of National Gendarmerie, 1985-96; Sec. Gen. at the Presidency, 1996-97; Minister Delegate at the Presidency in charge of Defence, 1997-2001; Minister of State, in charge of Justice, Keeper of the Seals, 2001-04; Vice-Pres., Minister of Justice and Keeper of the Seals, 2004-12; Deputy Prime Minister with responsibility for Relations with the Assemblies, 2012-; *office address:* Office of the Deputy Prime Minister, 1000 Yaoundé, Cameroon.

ALI, Rushanara; MP for Bethnal Green and Bow, House of Commons; *education:* Oxford Univ.; *party:* Labour; *political career:* MP for Bethnal Green and Bow, May 2010-; Shadow Minister, International Development, Oct. 2010-; *office address:* House of Commons, London, SW1A 0AA, United Kingdom; *phone:* +44 (0)20 7219 3000; *URL:* http://www.parliament.uk.

ALI AL MADANI, Dr Ahmad Mohammed; Saudi Arabian, President, Islamic Development Bank; *born:* 27 December 1934, Almadinah Almunawarah, Saudi Arabia; *children:* 4; *education:* Cairo Univ., BA, Commerce,1957, LLB, 1959; Univ. of Michigan, Ann Arbor, USA, MA, Public Administration, 1962; State Univ. of New York, Albany, USA, doctorate in Public Administration, 1967; *memberships:* Following Boards of academic institutions: King Abdulaziz Univ. Council, Jeddah; King Saud Univ., Riyadh; Oil and Mineral Univ., Dharan; Islamic Univ., Medina; Imam Mohamed Ben Saud Univ., Riyadh; Administrative Board, Saudi Credit Bank; Administrative Board, Saudi Fund for Development; *professional career:* Director, Scientific Islamic Institute (Aden) 1958-59; Acting Rector, King Abdulaziz Univ. 1967-72; Dep. Minister of Education for Technical Affairs 1972-75; Pres., Islamic Development Bank, 1975-93; Sec. Gen., Muslim World League, 1993-95; Pres., Islamic Development Bank, 1995-; *publications:* Numerous articles and working papers on Islamic economics, banking, and education; *office address:* Islamic Development Bank, POB 5925, Jeddah 21432, Saudi Arabia; *URL:* http://www.isdb.org.

ALIK, Alik L.; Vice President, Government of Micronesia; *born:* 1953; *education:* United States Int. Univ. in Hawaii, 1976; Graceland Coll., Iowa, USA, 1979; *political career:* Vice President, 2007-; *professional career:* Amb. to Fiji, 1989-98; Amb. to Japan, 1998-2003; *office address:* Office of the Vice President, PS53, Palikir, Pohnpei State, 96941, Federated States of Micronesia; *phone:* +691 320 2228; *fax:* +691 320 2785.

ALISON-MADUEKE, Diezani; Minister of Petroleum Resources, Government of Nigeria; *born:* 1960; *education:* UK; Howard Univ., USA; Cambridge Univ., MBA; *political career:* Transport Minister, Gov. of Nigeria, 2007-08; Minister of Mines & Steel Development, 2008-10; Minister for Petroleum Resources, 2010-; *professional career:* Shell Petroleum Dev. Corp., 1992, Exec. Dir., Nigeria, 2006; *office address:* Ministry of Petroleum, Federal Secretariat Complex, Shehu Shagari Way, Maitama, P.M.B 449, Garki, Abuja, Nigeria; *phone:* +234 1 261 4123.

ALITO, Samuel A., Jr.; Associate Justice, US Supreme Court; *born:* 1 April 1950, Trenton, New Jersey; *professional career:* Law clerk for Leonard I. Garth, US Court of Appeals Third Circuit, 1976-77; Assist. U.S. Attorney, District of New Jersey, 1977-81; Assist. to the Solicitor General, U.S. Dept. of Justice, 1981-85; Dep. Assist. Attorney Gen., U.S. Dept. of Justice, 1985-87; U.S.Attorney, District of New Jersey, 1987-90; Judge, US Court of Appeals for the Third Circuit, 1990-2006; Associate Justice, US Supreme Court, 2006-; *office address:* Supreme Court Building, One First Street, NE, Washington, DC 20543, USA; *phone:* +1 202 479 3211; *fax:* +1 202 479 2971; *URL:* http://www.supremecourt.gov/.

ALIYEV, President Ilham Heydar oglu; President, Government of Azerbaijan; ***born:*** 24 December 1961, Baku, Azerbaijan; ***parents:*** Heydar Aliyev; ***languages:*** English, French, Russian, Turkish; ***education:*** Moscow State Univ. of International Relations, First Degree, 1982, Ph.D., History, 1985; ***political career:*** MP, 1995-2003; Dep Chmn., Yeni Azerbaijan party, 1999-2001, First Deputy, 2001-05, Chmn., 2005-; Prime Minister, Aug. 4 to Oct. 15 2003; Pres., Government of Azerbaijan, Oct. 2003-; ***professional career:*** Lecturer, Moscow State Univ. of Int. Relations, 1985-90; private industrial-commercial enterprises, 1991-94; Vice-Pres., State Oil Co. (SOCAR), 1994-2003; ***committees:*** Pres., Nat. Olympic Cttee., 1997; Head, Azerbaijani del. to the Parly. Assembly of the Cncl. of Europe (PACE), 2001-03; Dep. Chmn., PACE, 2003; ***honours and awards:*** Heydar Aliyev Order (the Republic of Azerbaijan); Ihsan Dogramacı Prize for International Relations for Peace (Turkey); The Star of Romania Order (Romania); King Abdul Aziz Order (Kingdom of Saudi Arabia); Order of Honor (Georgia); Grand Cross of the Legion of Honor (France); Sheikhulislam Order (Republic of Azerbaijan); Prepodobniy Sergiy Rodonejskiy first degree Order of Russian Orthodox Church; Grand Cordon Order of Merit (International Military Sport Council); Honorary decoration of International Confederation of Sport Organizations of CIS countries; Highest order of FİLA Sport legend; Grand Cross of Order of Merit of the Republic of Poland (Republic of Poland); Order of Prince Yaroslav Mudry of 1st Class (Ukraine); Mubarak Al-Kabeer Order (Kuwait); Gold medal of the Hellenic Republic (Greece); Badge of Honor of European Fair Play Movement; Order of the Three Stars (Commander of the Grand Cross) (Latvian Republic); Grand Croix de la Légion d'Honneur, France, 2008; Many Hon. Doctorates from universities over the world; ***office address:*** Office of the President, Istiqlaliyyet st. 19, 1066-AZ Baku, Azerbaijan; ***phone:*** +994 (0)12 492 3527; ***e-mail:*** office@apparat.gov.az.

AL-JUBIER, H.E. Adel A.; Ambassador, Embassy of Saudi Arabia; ***born:*** 1962; ***languages:*** English, German; ***education:*** BA, summa cum laude in political science and economics, Univ. of North Texas, USA, 1982; MA, in international relations, Georgetown Univ. USA, 1984; ***professional career:*** Ambassador to the USA, 2007-; ***office address:*** Embassy of Saudi Arabia, 601 New Hampshire Avenue, NW, Washington DC 20037, USA; ***phone:*** +1 202 342 3800; ***fax:*** +1 202 944 5983; ***URL:*** http://www.saudiembassy.net.

AL-KHALIFA, H.E. Shaikh Ali Bin Khalifa; Deputy Prime Minister and Minister of Transport and Communications, Government of Bahrain; ***political career:*** Minister of Transport and Communications, to 2006; Deputy Prime Minister and Minister of Transport and Communications, 2006-; ***office address:*** Ministry of Transportation, PO Box 10325, Manama, Bahrain; ***phone:*** +973 17 534534; ***fax:*** +973 17 537537.

AL-KHALIFA, Shaikh Hamad bin Isa; Emir, State of Bahrain; ***born:*** 28 January 1950, Riffa; ***parents:*** Sheikh Isa Bin Sulman Al Khalifa (dec'd); ***married:*** , 9 October 1968; ***children:*** 4; ***education:*** Leys Public Sch., Cambridge, England; Mons Officer Cadet Sch., England, Graduate, 1968; Sandhurst Academy; Fort Leavenworth, Leadership degree (with honour), 1973; ***memberships:*** Dep. to the Head of the Al Khalifa Family Cncl., 1974; Pres., Supreme Cncl. of Youth and Sports, 1975; Hon. Permanent Mem., Helicopter Club, U.K., 1979; Head, Bahrain Centre for Studies and Research, 1981; ***professional career:*** Crown Prince (heir apparent since 1964) and Commander-in-Chief of the Bahrain Defence Force, 1968-99; succeeded to throne on death of his father, Sheikh Isa Bin Sulman Al Khalifa, March 1999-; ***honours and awards:*** Freedom Medal of Kansas city; National Diploma in military admin, 1972; Military Honour Certificate, USA; ***recreations:*** falconry, golf, fishing, tennis, football, horseriding, aviation; ***office address:*** Rifa'a Palace, PO Box 555, Rifa'a, Bahrain; ***phone:*** +973 17 666666.

AL-KHALIFA, H.E. Shaikh Khalid bin Ahmed; Minister of Foreign Affairs, Kingdom of Bahrain; ***born:*** 24 April 1960; ***married:*** Shaikha Wesal bint Mohamed Al Khalifa; ***education:*** Secondary Education, Islamic Coll., Amman, Jordan, 1978; St. Edward's Univ., Texas USA., B.Sc., History and Political Sciences, 1984; ***political career:*** Minister of Foreign Affairs, Kingdom of Bahrain, 2006-; ***professional career:*** Third Sec., Min. Foreign Affairs, 1985; Dip., Bahrain Embassy, Washington, 1985-94; Chief Liaison Officer, Office of H.E. the Minister of Foreign Affairs responsible for Maritime Delimitation and Territorial Dispute between Bahrain and Qatar., 1995-00; Dir., PR and Info., Crown Prince's Court, August 2000; attended and participated in several conferences and int. meetings as mem. of deleg. accompanying H.H. The Crown Prince and the Foreign Minister; Ambassador Extraordinary and Plenipotentiary, Kingdom of Bahrain, Court of St. James's, Sept. 2001-06, Kingdom of the Netherlands, March 2002-06, Republic of Ireland, May 2002-06, Kingdom of Norway, May 2002-6, Kingdom of Sweden, Nov. 2003-06; ***honours and awards:*** The Bahrain Medal Second Degree in recognition of his contribution as Liasion Officer during Territorial Dispute bet. Bahrain and Qatar, bestowed upon him by H.H. Shaikh Hamad bin Isa Al Khalifa, the Amir, May 2001; ***office address:*** Ministry of Foreign Affairs, PO Box 547, Manama, Bahrain; ***phone:*** +973 17 227555; ***fax:*** +973 17 212603.

AL-KHALIFA, H.H. Shaikh Khalifa Bin Salman; Bahraini, Prime Minister, Government of Bahrain; ***born:*** 25 November 1935; ***political career:*** Pres., Education Cncl., 1956; Acting Sec., Government of Bahrain, 1958; Head, Gov. Finance, 1960; Chmn., Manama Municipality, 1962; Chmn., Bahrain Monetary Cncl., 1965; Chmn., Admin. Cncl., 1966; Prime Minister, Bahrain, 1970-; Hdm Supreme Defence Cncl.; Higher Cncl of the Civil Aviation; Higher Cttee for Projects; Cncl. of Petroleum; Water Resources Cncl.; ***professional career:*** Chmn., Bahrain Monetary Agency; ***honours and awards:*** Khalifite Medallion, Dec. 1979; Order of Sheikh Isa bin Salman Al Khalifa, First Class, Oct. 1999; Hon. Dr., Political Science, Int. Islamic Univ., Malaysia; Hon. Fellowship, Royal Coll. Surgeons, Rep. of Ireland; Honor Medal from Pres. of France, Feb. 2004; Knight Grand Cordon of the Most Exalted Order of the White Elephant, Kingdom of Thailand, Feb. 2004; Hon. Dr. of Letters, Indira Ghandi Nat. Open Univ., Rep. of India, Feb. 2004; ***office address:*** Office of the Prime Minister, PO Box 1000, Manama, Bahrain; ***phone:*** +973 17 253361; ***fax:*** +973 17 533033.

AL-KHALIFA, H.E. Shaikh Mohammed Bin Mubarak; Bahraini, Deputy Prime Minister and Minister of Foreign Affairs, Government of Bahrain; ***born:*** 1935; ***parents:*** Shaikh Murabak Bin Hammad Al Khalifa; ***children:*** 2; ***education:*** American Univ., Beirut; Univs. of Oxford & London, UK; ***political career:*** Head, Political Bureau, 1968-; Dept. of Foreign Affairs, 1969-2006; State Cncl., 1970-; Minister for Foreign Affairs, 1971-2006; Deputy Prime Minister, 2002-; Ministerial Cttees., 2006-; ***office address:*** Ministry of Foreign Affairs, PO Box 547, Manama, Bahrain; ***phone:*** +973 17 227555; ***fax:*** +973 17 212603.

AL-KHALIFA, H.E. Shaikh Ahmed Bin Mohammed; Minister of Finance, Government of Bahrain; ***political career:*** Min. of Finance, Govt. of Bahrain, Aug. 2005-; ***professional career:*** Governor of the Bahrain Monetary Agency and Chairman of the Bahrain Stock Exchange, Aug. 2005; ***office address:*** Ministry of Finance, P O Box 333, Manama, Bahrain; ***phone:*** +973 17 530800; ***fax:*** +973 17 532713; ***URL:*** http://www.mofne.gov.bh.

AL-KHOZAEI, Dr. Khodair; Second Vice President, Government of Iraq; ***education:*** Doctorates in the Philosophy of Islamic Thought and Quranic Studies; ***political career:*** Third Vice President, May 2011; Second Vice President, May 2011-; ; ***professional career:*** Univ. Lecturer; ***office address:*** Office of the Vice President, Baghdad, Iraq.

ALLAN, Keith; Ambassador to Turkmenistan, British Embassy; ***professional career:*** Counter Terrorism Policy Dept., FCO, 1996-97; Dep. Head of Mission, Tashkent, 1997-2000; Central and North West European Dept., FCO, 2000-02; Consul, Kabul, 2002; Dep. Dir., Africa Middle East, FCO, 2002-03; Dep. High Commissioner, Port of Spain, 2003-06; Consul Gen., Miami, 2006-09; Ambasassador, Ashgabat, Turkmenistan, 2010-; ***office address:*** British Embassy, 3rd Floor, 301-308 Office Building Four Points Ak Altin Hotel, Ashgabat, Turkmenistan.

ALLAN OF HALLAM, Lord Richard; British, Member, House of Lords; ***born:*** 1966, Sheffield; ***education:*** Oundle Sch., Northants; Pembroke Coll., Cambridge Univ., BA, Archaology and Anthropology; Bristol Poly., MSc, Info. Technology; ***party:*** Liberal Democratic Party; ***political career:*** Lib. Dem. Spokesman for Community Relations & Business Affairs and on Info. Technology; Mem., Bd., Parly. Office of Science and Technology, to date; active in sev. All Party Gps., inc. the Internet Gp., the Latin America Gp., the Colombia Gp. and the Modernisation Gp.; MP, Sheffield Hallam, 1997-2005; Mem. House of Lords, 2010-; ***interests:*** development of e-democracy and e-government; ***memberships:*** Amnesty International; World Development Movement; Hallamshire Historic Buildings Society and Friends of the Porter Valley; ***professional career:*** Field Archaeologist in Britain, France and the Netherlands, 1984-85; Ecuador, 1988-89; National Health Service, 1991-97; ***committees:*** Chmn., Info. Select Cttee., House of Commons, 1998-2001; Mem., Home Affairs Select Cttee., 1997-98; Mem., Employment Select Cttee., 2000-2001; Mem., Info. Select Cttee. and Liaison Cttee. of the House of Commons, to date; ***trusteeships:*** Trustee, Ind. and Parly. Trust; unpaid Dir., Sheffield City Trust; ***publications:*** written regularly on broad range of technology related subjects; ***office address:*** House of Lords, London, SW1 0AA, United Kingdom; ***phone:*** +44 (0)20 7219 3000; ***e-mail:*** allanr@parliament.uk.

ALLEN, Graham; British, Member of Parliament for Nottingham North, House of Commons; ***born:*** 11 January 1953, Nottingham, United Kingdom; ***parents:*** William Allen and Edna Allen; ***education:*** City of London Polytechnic, BA; Leeds Univ., MA; ***party:*** Labour Party, 1970-; ***political career:*** Research Officer, Labour Party, 1978-83; Cllr., London Borough of Tower Hamlets, 1982-86; Senior Officer, GLC, 1983-84; Nat. Co-ordinator, Political Campaign Fund, 1984-86; Spokesperson on Social Security, Labour Party, 1991; Opposition Spokesman on Home Affairs, Constitution and Democracy, Immigration, 1992; Opp. Spokesman, Transport, 1995; Opp. Spokesperson, Environment, 1996-97; Gov. Whip, 1997-2001; MP, Nottingham North, 1987-; ***memberships:*** TGWU; ***professional career:*** warehouseman, 1971-72; Regional Education Officer, GMBATU, 1986-87; ***committees:*** Liaison, 2010-; Chair, Political & Constitutional Reform, 2010-; ***publications:*** Reinventing Democracy, 1994; The Lost Prime Minister - Being Honest about the UK Presidency, 2002; Early Intervention: Good parents, great kids, better citizens, 2008; ***recreations:*** cricket; ***office address:*** House of Commons, London, SW1A 0AA, United Kingdom; ***phone:*** +44 (0)20 7219 3000; ***e-mail:*** hcinfo@parliament.uk; ***URL:*** http://www.grahamallen.labour.co.uk.

ALLEN, The Hon. Dr. Patrick Linton; Governor-General, Jamaica; ***born:*** 7 February 1951; ***education:*** Moneague Teachers' College, Grad.; Andrews Univ., Michigan, Bachelor's degree in History and Religion, Master's degree in Systematic Theology, 1986, Ph.D. in Education Administration and Supervision, 1998; ***professional career:*** Teacher; Principal, Hillside Primary School; District Pastor, 1986-93; ordained as Seventh-day Adventist pastor, 1989; Andrews Univ., Michigan, Registrar, 1993-98; Pres., Central Jamaica Conference of Seventh-day Adventists, 1998-2009; Pres., West Indies Union Conference of Seventh-day Adventists, 2000-09; Governor-General of Jamaica, 2009-; ***committees:*** Former Mem., Police Civilian Oversight Authority; Strategic Review Implementation Oversight Cttee. for the Jamaica Constabulary Force; Bd. of the Public Broadcasting Corp. of Jamaica. Vice-Chmn., Bible Society of the West Indies; Justice of the Peace, 2003; ***honours and awards:*** CD, 2006; ON, 2009; GCMG, 2009; ***office address:*** Office of the Governor-General, King's House, Hope Road, Kingston 10, Jamaica; ***phone:*** +1 876 927 6424; ***fax:*** +1 876 927 4561.

ALLISTER, James Hugh; Irish, Member, European Parliament; ***born:*** 2 April 1953, Crossgar; ***party:*** Democratic Unionist Party (Northern Ireland), 1971-2007; Traditional Unionist Voice; ***political career:*** mem., European Parl. (6th Term), 2004-09; Leader, Traditional Unionist Party; ***professional career:*** Lawyer; ***office address:*** Traditional Unionist Voice, 139 Holywood Road, Belfast, County Down, BT4 3BE, Northern Ireland; ***URL:*** http://www.tuv.org.uk.

AL-MAHMOUD, H.E. Ahmed Bin Abdulla Bin Zaid; Deputy Prime Minister, Minister of State for the Council of Ministers' Affairs, Government of Qatar; ***education:*** Cairo Univ., BA, Arabic & Islamic Studies, 1976; Central Michigan Univ., USA, MSc., economics, 1981; ***political career:*** Minister of State for Foreign Affairs, 1995-; Chmn., Cttee. on Boundary Issues, 1995-12; Mem., Council of Ministers, 1999; Resp. for Darfur dossier in Qatar mediation for settlement of the Darfur Conflict; Chmn., Qatar Dev. Fund, 2010-12; Dep. PM & Minister of State for the Council of Ministers' Affairs, 2011-; ***professional career:*** Chargé d'Affaires, Embassy of Qatar in Algeria, 1983; Amb. Extraordinary & Plenipotentiary of Qatar to Oman, 1984-86; Amb. Extra. & Pleni. of Qatar to USA, 1987-89; ***office address:*** Office of the Deputy Prime Minister, POB 923, Doha, Qatar.

AL-MAKTOUM, Gen. Sheikh Mohammed bin Rashid; Vice President, United Arab Emirates; *born:* 22 July 1949; *parents:* Rashid bin Saeed Al Maktoum; *political career:* Min. of Defence, to date; Vice president, Prime Minister, Ruler of Dubai, 2006-; *office address:* Ministry of Defence, P O Box 2838, Dubai, United Arab Emirates; *phone:* +971 2 446 1300; *fax:* +971 2 446 3286.

AL-MALIKI, Nouri Jawad; Prime Minister, Government of Iraq; *born:* 1950; *education:* studied Arabic Literature, Baghdad Univ.; *party:* al-Dawa; *political career:* Prime Minister of Iraq, June 2006-; Trade Minister, 2009-; *office address:* Office of the Prime Minister, Baghdad, Iraq.

AL-MANNAI, Jassim; Bahraini, Director General Chairman of the Board, Arab Monetary Fund; *born:* 1948, Bahrain; *parents:* Abdulla Al-Mannai; *languages:* English, French; *education:* Univ. of Paris Sorbonne; Harvard Business Sch., Boston, USA; Chase Manhattan Bank, New York; *memberships:* Bd. of several Gulf and Arab industrial and investment corporations; *professional career:* Ministries of Finance and National Economy and Development and Industry; Exec. Vice Pres., Gulf Investment Corp.; Dir. Gen. Chmn. of the Bd., Arab Monetary Fund (AMF), and Chief Exec., 1994-, and Chmn. of the Bd., Arab Trade Financing Program (ATFP); *honours and awards:* Hon. Degree Award by His Majesty King of Bahrain; the Banking Leadership Personality, 2009 by the World Union of Arab Bankers; The Rafiq Harriri Leadership Award, 2010, by Al-Iktissad Wal-Aamal Grp. ; *office address:* Arab Monetary Fund, PO Box 2818, Abu Dhabi, United Arab Emirates; *phone:* +971 2 634 5354; *fax:* +971 2 633 2089; *e-mail:* dg@amfad.org.ae.

AL-MUALLEM, Waleed; Minister of Foreign Affairs, Government of Syria; *born:* 1941; *political career:* Minister of Foreign Affairs, 2006-; *professional career:* Amb., to the USA, 1990-2000; Amb. to Bucharest, Romania; *office address:* Ministry of Foreign Affairs, Shora, Mhajireen, Damascus, Syria; *phone:* +963 11 333 1200.

ALMUNIA, Joaquin; Commissioner, European Commission; *born:* 17th June 1948, Bilbao, Spain; *children:* 2; *education:* Univ. of Deusto, Bilbao, Law and Econs. graduate; L'Ecole Practique des Hautes Etudes de Paris; Kennedy Sch. of Govt., Harvard Univ., Senior Managers in Government programme; *party:* PSOE; *political career:* Mem., Federal Cttee. of PSOE; mem. Spanish Parliament, 1979-2004; Minister for Employment and Social Security, 1982-86; Minister of Public Administration, 1986-91; Spksmn., Socialist Parly. Gp., 1994-97; Leader, PSOE, 1997-2000; socialist candidate for Prime Minister, 2000; Cmnr. for Economic and Monetary Affairs, European Cmn., 2004-; *professional career:* Assoc. Lecturer, Univ. of Alcala de Henares, Madrid, Employment and Social Security Law; Economist, Cncl. Bureau, Spanish Chambers of Commerce, Brussels, 1972-1975; Chief economist, UGT (Trade Union), 1976-79; *office address:* European Commission, rue de la Loi 200, B-1049 Brussels, Belgium; *phone:* +32 (0)2 299 1111; *fax:* +32 (0)2 80397; *URL:* http://www.europa.eu.int.

ALMUTAIWEE, H.E. Abdulrahman Ghanem; Ambassador Extraordinary and plenipotentiary of the UAE to the UK and Ambassador to Iceland, Embassy of the UAE; *professional career:* Banking; Dir.-Gen., Dubai Chamber of Commerce & Industry; Amb. Extraordinary & Plenipotentiary of the UAE to the Court of St James, 2009-, and the Ambassador of the UAE to Iceland, 2010-; *office address:* Embassy of the UAE, 30 Prince's Gate, London , SW7 1PT, United Kingdom.

AL-NAIMI, Ali Bin Ibrahim; Saudi Arabian, Minister of Petroleum and Mineral Resources, Saudi Arabian Government; *born:* 1935; *education:* LeHigh Univ., USA, B.Sc., Geology; Stanford Univ., USA, M.Sc., Geology; *political career:* Minister of Petroleum and Mineral Resources, 1995-; *professional career:* joined ARAMCO, 1947; Supervisor, Production Dept., Abqaiq, 1969; Asst. Dir., then Dir. of Production, Northern Province, 1972-75; Vice-Pres., Petroleum Affairs, 1978; mem., Bd. of Dirs., 1980; Exec. Vice-Pres., Oil and Gas Affairs, 1981; Pres., Saudi Aramco, 1983; *office address:* Ministry of Petroleum and Mineral Resources, PO Box 757, Airport Road, Riyadh 11189, Saudi Arabia; *phone:* +966 1 478 1661 / 478 1133; *fax:* +966 1 479 3596.

AL NOAIMI, H.E. Dr. Majed bin Ali; Minister of Education, Government of Bahrain; *education:* Doctorate Degree, Univ. of Wales, UK; MA (Hons.), Military Sciences, Military College of Saudi Arabia; MA in Gulf History, Ain Shams Univ., Egypt; BA, History, Univ. of Kuwait; *political career:* Minister of Education; *honours and awards:* His Highness Sheikh Isa bin Salman Al Khalifa's Third Degree; Bahrain's Second Decree; Appreciation of Military Service Decree; Military Duty Decree; A medal on the event of Kuwait's Liberation from the Iraqi invasion; Hawar Decree; *office address:* Ministry of Education, PO Box 43, Isa Town, Bahrain; *phone:* +973 1768 0071; *fax:* +973 1768 0161; *e-mail:* majed.alnoaimi@gmail.com; *URL:* http://www.education.gov.bh.

AL OTAIBA, Ambassador Yousef; Ambassador of the UAE to the USA, Embassy of the UAE; *education:* Cairo American College; Georgetown Univ., Washington, USA; International Fellow, Industrial College of the US Armed Forces, National Defense Univ., Washington; *political career:* Dir., International Affairs, Court of the Crown Prince of Abu Dhabi; Senior counselor to H.H.Gen. Sheikh Mohamed bin Zayed Al Nahyan; *professional career:* Ambassador of the UAE to the US, 2008-; *office address:* Embassy of the UAE , 3522 International Court, NW, Suite 400 , Washington DC 20008, USA.

AL-QIRBI, Dr Abu-Bakr Abdullah; Minister of Foreign Affairs, Government of Yemen; *born:* 1942; *education:* BSc., 1965, BM, 1968, University of Edinburgh, Scotland; Diploma in Tropical Medicine, 1969, Univ. of Liverpool, UK; Diploma in Pathology, 1972, London, Univ., UK; *political career:* Minister of Education, 1993-94; Minister of Foreign Affairs, 2001-; *professional career:* Dean, Sana'a Univ., 1979-87; Vice-Rector, Sana'a Univ., 1982-93; *office address:* Ministry of Foreign Affairs, Alolofi Square, Sana'a, Yemen; *phone:* +967 1 276544; *URL:* http://www.mofa.gov.ye.

AL-SABAH, Shaikh Nawaf Al-Ahmed Al-Jaber; Crown Prince of Kuwait; *born:* 1937; *political career:* Governor, Hawalli, 1962-78; Minister of Interior, 1978-88; Minister of Defence, 1988, 1992-2003; Dep. Prime Minister and Minister of Interior, 2003-; Crown Prince of Kuwait, 2006-; *office address:* Office of the Crown Prince, 13001 Safat, Kuwait City, Kuwait.

AL-SABAH, H.H. Sheikh Sabah Al-Ahmad Al-Jaber; Kuwaiti, Emir of Kuwait; *born:* 1929; *parents:* Amir Sheikh Ahmad Al-Jaber (dec'd); *political career:* Minister of Guidance, 1962; Mem., Cncl. for Constructing; Minister of Foreign Affairs, 1963-91; Acting Minister of Oil and Finance, 1965-67; Acting Minister of Information, 1971-75; Head, Dept. of Social Affairs and Labour and the Dept. of Press and Publications; First Dep. PM and Foreign Minister; Prime Minister, 2003-2006; Emir of Kuwait, 2006-; *committees:* mem., Organising Authority for the Higher Cttee.; *office address:* Office of the Emir, Kuwait City, Kuwait.

AL-SABAH, H.H. Sheikh Salem Abdullah Al-Jaber; Ambassador, Embassy of Kuwait in the US; *born:* 24 September 1957, Kuwait; *parents:* Abdullah Al-Sabah and Leila Merhabi; *married:* Rima Boulos Al-Sabah, 28 January 1988; *children:* Faysal (M), Talal (M), Khaled (M); *languages:* Arabic, English, French; *education:* American Univ. of Beirut, Beirut, Lebanon, BA, Political Science, 1981, and MA, Political Science, 1991; *professional career:* Private Family Business, 1981-86; Diplomat Attaché, Office of the Minister of State for Foreign Affairs, Min. of Foreign Affairs, Kuwait, 1986-91; Third Sec., Perm. Mission of the State of Kuwait to the UN, New York, 1991-94; Second Sec., Perm. Mission of the State of Kuwait to the UN, New York, 1994-97; First Sec., Perm. Mission of the State of Kuwait to the UN, New York, 1997-98; Promoted to Minister Plenipotentiary, 1998; apptd. Amb. of the State of Kuwait to the Republic of Korea, 1998; apptd. Amb. of Kuwait to the USA, 2001-; *honours and awards:* The Order of Diplomatic Service Merit Medal awarded by President Kim Dae-Jung, Pres. of the Republic of Korea; *clubs:* Sports Club; *recreations:* reading, travelling, music; *office address:* Embassy of Kuwait, 2940 Tilden Street, NW, Washington, DC 20008, USA; *phone:* +1 202 966 0702; *fax:* +1 202 364 2868.

AL-SAID, H.M. Sultan Qaboos bin Said; Sultan, Sultanate of Oman; *born:* 18 November 1940, Salalah; *parents:* Sultan Said bin Taimur (dec'd); *education:* Royal Military Academy, Sandhurst; England, Local Government; *political career:* Prime Minister; Minister of Foreign Affairs, Defence and Finance; Sultan, 1970-; *professional career:* served in British Infantry Battalion, Germany; staff appointment, British Army; Chmn., Central Bank of Oman; *honours and awards:* KCMG; Int. Peace Award, Nat. Cncl. on US-Arab Relations; *office address:* Office of the Sultan, Royal Palace, Muscat, Oman.

AL-SAID, H.H. Sayyid Fahad bin Mamoud; Omani, Deputy Minister for Cabinet Affairs, Oman Government; *born:* 5 October 1940, Muscat, Sultanate of Oman; *married:* Berthe Al-Said; *s:* 2; *d:* 3; *languages:* French, English; *education:* Cairo Univ., Economics, 1965; Paris, Political Studies, 1969; *political career:* Minister of State for Foreign Affairs, 1971-73; Minister of Information and Culture, 1973-79; Dep.Prime Minister for Legal Affairs 1979-94; Dep. Prime Minister for Cncl. of Ministers, 1994-; Deputy Minister for Cabinet Affairs; *honours and awards:* Grand Order of Renaissance of Oman, (Sultanate of Oman), other high decorations from UK, France, Italy, Iran, Jordan, Qatar and Egypt; *publications:* many publications relating to History and Culture; *recreations:* classical music, reading and sports; *office address:* Cabinet of the Deputy Prime Minister for the Council of Ministers, Po Box 721, Muscat 113, Oman.

AL-SAUD, HRH King Abdullah Bin Abdul Aziz; Saudi Arabian, King and Prime Minister, Saudi Arabian Government; *born:* 1924, Riyadh, Saudi Arabia; *parents:* King Abd-al-Aziz Al Saud and Fahada bint Asi al-Shuraym; *education:* received formal education from religious scholars and intellectuals; *political career:* Mayor, Holy City of Mecca; Dep. Minister of Defence, 1963; 1st Dep. Prime Minister, 1982-2005; King and Prime Minister, August 2005-; *interests:* domestic and foreign policy; *professional career:* Cmdr., Nat. Guard, 1962-; Crown Prince, 1982-2005; Head, deleg. to the 16th summit conference of the Gulf Co-operation Cncl. (GCC), 1995; *office address:* Royal Court, Riyadh, Saudi Arabia; *phone:* +966 1 488 2222.

AL-SAUD, HRH Prince Met'eb bin Abdulaziz; Saudi Arabian, Minister of Municipal and Rural Affairs, Saudi Arabian Government; *born:* 1931; *education:* Gen. and court education supplemented by private tutoring and reading, religion, econ. and politics; *political career:* Dep. Minister of Defence and Aviation; fmr. Governor of the Holy city of Makkah; visited Arab and European countries; fmr. Interim Minister of Municipal and Rural Affairs; Minister of Housing and Public Works, 1975-2004; Minister of Municipal and Rural Affairs, to date; *committees:* Pres., the Cttee. for Mena Project; *honours and awards:* Various Orders of Merit from Arab and European countries; *office address:* Ministry of Municipal and Rural Affairs, PO Box 955, Riyadh 11136, Saudi Arabia; *phone:* +966 1 402 2268 / 402 2036; *fax:* +966 1 402 2723 / 406 7376.

AL-SAUD, HRH Prince Mohammed bin Nawaf; Ambassador, Embassy of the Kingdom of Saudi Arabia; *born:* 1953; *professional career:* Amb. to Italy and Malta, 1995-98; Amb. to the United Kingdom and Ireland, Dec. 2005-; *office address:* Embassy of the Kingdom of Saudi Arabia, 30 Charles Street, Mayfair, London, W1J 5DZ, United Kingdom; *phone:* +44 (0)20 7917 3000.

AL-SAUD, HRH Price Salman bin Abdulaziz; Crown Prince, Deputy Prime Minister and Minister of Defence, Government of Saudi Arabia; *born:* 1935; *political career:* Acting Governor, 1954; Governor of Riyadh, 1955-1960, 1963-; Minister of Defence, 2011-; Appointed Crown Prince, 2012-; Deputy Prime Minister, 2012-; *office address:* Ministry of Defence, PO Box 26731, Airport Road, Riyadh 11165, Saudi Arabia; *phone:* +966 (0)1 478 5900 / 477 7313; *fax:* +966 (0)1 401 1336; *URL:* http://www.pca.gov.sa.

AL-SAUD, HRH Prince Saud Al-Faisal bin Abdulaziz; Saudi Arabian, Minister of Foreign Affairs, Saudi Arabian Government; *born:* 1942; *education:* Princeton Univ., USA, BA, Econ., 1964; *political career:* Dep. Minister of Petroleum and Mineral Resources, 1971; Minister of Foreign Affairs, 1975-; Head, deleg. of Kingdom of Saudi Arabia to 1976 session of UN Gen. Assembly.; presided over the 5th conference of the Foreign Ministers of Islamic countries, Jeddah, 1976; mem., Saudi deleg. to Arab restricted summit, Riyadh, 1976 and full-scale Arab summit, Cairo, 1976; mem., Saudi deleg. accompanying His Majesty the late King Khalid on state visits to Egypt, Pakistan, Syria, Sudan, France and Belgium; *professional career:* Dep. Governor, Petromin, 1970-71; *office address:* Ministry of Foreign Affairs, Nasseriya Street, Riyadh 11124, Saudi Arabia; *phone:* +966 1 406 7777 / 441 6836; *fax:* +966 1 403 0159.

AL-SISI, Gen. Abdel Fattah; Head of Armed Forces, Minister of Defence, Government of Egypt; *born:* 19 November 1954, Cairo, Egypt; *education:* Egyptian Military Academy, 1977; *political career:* General Commander of Egypt's armed forces and Minister of Defence, Aug. 2012-; *professional career:* Commander of mechanised infantry; Head of information and security at the general secretariat of the Defence Ministry; Military Attache in Saudi Arabia; Chief-of-staff and Commander of the Northern Military Zone; Dir., Military Intelligence and Reconnaissance; *office address:* Ministry of Defence, Sharia 23 July, Kobri el Kubba, CAI 36 Cairo, Egypt; *phone:* +20 (0)2 419 2183; *e-mail:* mod@idsc.gov.eg; *URL:* http://www.mmc.gov.eg.

ALTANKHUYAG, Norov; Prime Minister, Government of Mongolia; *born:* 1958; *political career:* MP; Minister of Agriculture and Industry, 1998-99; Finance Minister, 2004-06; Leader, Democratic Party, 2008-; First Dep. PM, 2008; Prime Minister, 2012; *professional career:* lecturer, National Univ. of Mongolia, maths & physics; *office address:* Office of the Prime Minister, State Palace, Sukhbaatar Square 1, Ulaan Baatar 12, Mongolia; *URL:* http://www.pmis.gov.mn.

AL-THANI, Sheikh Abdullah bin Nasser bin Khalifa; Prime Minister, Minister of the Interior, Government of Qatar; *education:* Sandhurst, 1984; *political career:* Interior Ministry, 1985; Dir., Special Security Forces, 2002; Commander, Interior Ministry's Special Forces, 2004; Prime Minister, Minister of the Interior, 2013-; *office address:* Office of the Prime Minister, POB 923, Doha, Qatar; *URL:* http://www.diwan.gov.qa.

AL THANI, H.H. Sheikh Tamim Bin Hamad Bin Khalifa; Qatari Amir, State of Qatar; *born:* 1980; *education:* Royal Military Academy, Sandhurst, UK; *political career:* Heir Apparent, 2003-2013; Amir of Qatar, June 2013-; *professional career:* Head, Qatar Investment Authority; Chair, 2030 Vision Project; Head, Qatar 2022 Supreme Committee; *office address:* Office of H.H. The Amir, PO Box 923, Doha, Qatar; *phone:* +974 468333.

ALTMAIER, Peter; Minister of the Environment, Nature Conservation and Nuclear Safety, Government of Germany; *education:* LLB, Univ. of Saarland, 1985; *party:* CDU; *political career:* MP, 1994-; Minister of the Environment, Nature Conservation and Nuclear Safety, 2012-; *office address:* Ministry of the Environment, Alexanderstrasse 3, 10178 Berlin, Germany; *phone:* +49 (0)1888 3050; *fax:* +49 (0)1888 305 4375; *e-mail:* service@bmu.de; *URL:* http://www.bmu.de.

ALTON OF LIVERPOOL, Lord David; British, Professor of Citizenship, Liverpool John Moores Univ. and Member of the House of Lords; *born:* 1951; *parents:* Frederick Charles Alton and Bridget Alton (née Mulroe); *married:* Lizzie Bell, 1988; *children:* Padraig (M), Philip (M), James (M), Marianne (F); *languages:* French; *education:* Edmund Campion Sch., Hornchurch; Christ's Coll., Liverpool; *party:* Independent Cross Bencher; *political career:* City Cllr., 1972-80; Dep. Leader, Liverpool City Cncl., Housing Chmn., 1978-79; Nat. Pres., 1979-80, Nat. League of Young Liberals, 1979-80; MP Lib. for Liverpool, Edge Hill 1979-83, Liverpool, Mossley Hill, 1983-97; Alliance Northern Ireland Spokesman, 1983-88; Lib. Spokesman on the Environment Housing and Local Govt., May 1979-81; Home Affairs Spokesman, 1981; Lib. Chief Whip, 1985-87; elevated to House of Lords, 1997-; *interests:* human rights, citizenship, pro-life, Northern Ireland; *memberships:* Vice-Pres. Life, Founder Mem. Movement for Christian Democracy; Vice Pres., Merseyside Cncl. for Voluntary Service; Pres., Liverpool NSPCC; *professional career:* Teacher, 1972-79; *committees:* All Party Friends of CAFOD; Chmn., All Party North Korea; Sec., All Party Sudan; Vice-Chmn., All Party Group on Blood Cord; *trusteeships:* Patron, Jubilee Campaign; Patron, Karen Aid; Bd. Mem., Inst. on Religion and Public Policy, 2002; Patron, Habitat for Humanity; Patron, Jospice; Patron, Liverpool School of Tropical Medicine; Patron, Motec Life; Patron, Asylum Link (Merseyside); Patron, Mersey Kidney Research; Trustee, G.K. Chesterton Institute; *honours and awards:* Visiting Fellow, St. Andrew's Univ.; Michael Bell Memorial Award; Life Peer, created 1997; Knight with Merit of the Constantinian Order, 2002; Knight Commander Order of St. Gregory, 2008; Mysteries of Life Award, 2008; *publications:* What kind of Country? 1987; Whose Choice Anyway? - The Right to Life 1988; Faith in Britain 1991; Signs of Contradiction 1993; Life After Death 1997; Citizen Virtues, 1999; Citizen 21, 2000; Pilgrim Ways, 2001; Passion and Pain, 2003; Euthanasia: Getting to the Heart of the Matter, 2005; Abortion: Getting to the Heart of the Matter, 2005; *office address:* House of Lords, London, SW1A 0PW, United Kingdom; *phone:* +44 (0)151 231 3852; *fax:* +44 (0)151 231 3853; *e-mail:* altond@parliament.uk; *URL:* http://www.davidalton.com.

ALWARD, David; Premier, Government of New Brunswick; *born:* 2 December 1959, Beverley, Massacusetts; *parents:* Reverend Ford and Jean (née Alward); *married:* Rhonda; *children:* Jonathan (M), Benjamin (M); *education:* Bryan Coll., Dayton, TN, BA, Psychology; *political career:* elected as the Progressive Cons. Mem. for Woodstock, 1999, re-elected, 2003; Minister of Agriculture, Fisheries and Aquaculture, 2003-06; Minister for Aboriginal Affairs, 2010; Premier, 2010-; current (2013) portfolios: Pres., Executive Council Office, Minister responsible for the Status of Disabled Persons; Citizens' Engagement; Office of Government Review; *professional career:* worked with Federal Govt., 1982-96; Human Resource Dev. & community Dev. Consultant, 1996-99; volunteer with St. John Ambulance & Meductic Fire Dept.; served on bd. of dirs., Carleton Regional Dev. Cmn., New Brunswick Hereford Assn.; served on local agric. employment bd.; *committees:* served on Centennial Elementary Sch. Parent Advisory Cttee., the Sch. District 12 Stay-in-School Cttee.; *office address:* Office of the Premier, Room 212, Centennial Building, Fredericton, NB, Canada; *phone:* +1 506 453 2144; *fax:* +1 506 453 7407; *URL:* http://www2.gnb.ca/content/gnb/en/departments/premier.html.

AL-ZEBARI, Hoshyar; Minister of Foreign Affairs, Transitional Government of Iraq; *political career:* Minister of Foreign Affairs, Transit. Gov. of Iraq, 2005; Minister of Foreign Affairs, 2005-; Interim Minister of Women's Affairs, 2010-11; *office address:* Ministry of Foreign Affairs, Baghdad International Zone Convention Centre, Baghdad, Iraq.

AMADOU, Marou; Minister of Justice and Keeper of the Seals, Government of Niger; *born:* 1972; *education:* Univ. Abdou Moumoni, Niamey, law; Univ. d'Abomey Calavi, Benin, law; *political career:* Political Activist; imprisoned several times; Pres., Interim Parliament (following coup), 2010; Minister of Justice, Keeper of the Seals, 2011-; *honours and awards:* Chevalier de la Légion d'honneur, 2010; Grand Officier, Ordre National du Niger, 2011; *office address:* Ministry of Justice, BP 466, Niamey, Niger; *phone:* +227 20 723131; *fax:* +227 20 723577; *URL:* http://www.justice.gouv.ne/.

AMANO, Yukiya; Director General, International Atomic Energy Agency; *born:* 1947; *languages:* English, French; *education:* Tokyo Univ., Faculty of Law; *professional career:* April 1972: Joined Japanese Ministry of Foreign Affairs, 1972; Dir., Research Coordination and Senior Research Fellow, Japan Inst. of Int. Affairs, Tokyo, 1988; Dir., OECD Publications and Information Center, Tokyo, 1990; Dir., Nuclear Science Division, Japanese Ministry of Foreign Affairs, 1993; Dir., Nuclear Energy Division, Japanese Ministry of Foreign Affairs, 1993; Counselor, Delegation of Japan to the Conference on Disarmament, Geneva, Switzerland, 1994; Consul General of Japan in Marseilles, France, 1997; Dep. Dir.-Gen., Arms Control and Scientific Affairs, Japanese Ministry of Foreign Affairs, 1999; Chmn., G7 Nuclear Safety Group, 2000; Fellow, Weatherhead Center for Int. Affairs, Harvard Univ., USA, 2001; Governmental Expert on Missiles to the UN Panel, 2001; Governmental Expert on Disarmament and Non-Proliferation Education to the UN Group, 2001; Visiting Scholar, Monterey Inst. of Int. Studies, USA, 2001; Amb., Dir.-Gen. for Arms Control and Scientific Affairs, Japanese Ministry of Foreign Affairs, 2002; Amb., Dir.-Gen. for Disarmament, Non-Proliferation and Science Department, Japanese Ministry of Foreign Affairs, 2004; Chmn., Board of Governors of the IAEA, 2005-06; Chmn., First Session of the Preparatory Committee for the 2010 NPT Review Conference, 2007; Perm. Rep. and Amb. Extraordinary and Plenipotentiary of Japan to the International Organizations in Vienna and Governor to the IAEA, 2005-09; Dir. Gen. IAEA, 2009-; *publications:* Sea Dumping of Liquid Radio Active Waste by Russia (Gaiko Jiho, 1994); La Non Proliferation Nucleaire en Exteme-Orient (Proliferation et Non-Proliferation Nucleaire, 1995); The Significance of the NPT Extension (Future Restraints on Arms Proliferation, 1996); A Japanese View on Nuclear Disarmament (The Non-Proliferation Review, 2002) ; *office address:* International Atomic Energy Agency, Vienna International Centre, Wagramerstrasse 5, PO Box 100, A-1400 Vienna, Austria; *phone:* +43 (0)1 26000; *fax:* +43 (0)1 26007; *e-mail:* Official.Mail@iaea.org; *URL:* http://www.iaea.org.

AMARI, Akira; Minister in charge of Economic Revitalization, Government of Japan; *party:* Liberal Democratic Party; *political career:* Mem., House of Representatives , 1983-; Minister of Labour; Minister of Economy, Trade and Industry, 2006-08; Minister in charge of Economic Revitalization, Minister in charge of Total Reform of Social Security and Tax, Minister of State for Economic and Fiscal Policy, 2012-; *office address:* Ministry of Economy, Trade and Industry, 1-3-1 Kasumigaseki, Chiyoda-ku, Tokyo 100 8901, Japan; *phone:* +81 (0)3 3501 1511.

AMBROSE, Hon. Rona; Federal Minister of Public Works and Government Services, Canadian Government; *languages:* English, French; *education:* BA, Univ. of Victoria; MA, Univ. of Alberta; *party:* Conservative; *political career:* MP, Edmonton-Spruce Grove, Alberta, 2004-; Critic, International Trade, Intergovernmental Affairs; Minister of the Environment, 2006-07; President of the Queen's Privy Council for Canada, Minister of Intergovernmental Affairs and Minister of Western Economic Diversification, 2007-08; Federal Minister of Labour, 2008-10; Federal Minister of Public Works and Government Services, 2010-; Registrar General of Canada, Minister of Western Economic Diversification and Minister of Status of Women; *professional career:* Senior Intergovernmental Officer, Gov. of Alberta Dept. of Int. and Intergovernmental Relations; *committees:* Vice Pres., Cabinet Treasury Board Cttee.; *office address:* House of Commons, Parliament Buildings, Wellington Street, Ottawa, ON K1A 0A6, Canada.

AMESS, David, MP; British, Member of Parliament for Southend West, House of Commons; *born:* 26 March 1952; *married:* Julia Amess (née Arnold); *s:* 1; *d:* 4; *education:* St. Bonaventure's Grammar Sch.; Bournemouth Coll. of Technology, B.Sc., economics; *party:* Conservative Party; *political career:* Joined Conservative party, 1968; Contested Newham North West, 1979; Redbridge Cncl., 1981-85; Vice-Chmn., Housing Cttee., Redbridge Council, 1981-85; MP for Basildon, 1983-97; PPS to Edwina Currie, Michael Portillo and Lord Skelmersdale, all DHSS, 1987-88; PPS to: Michael Portillo, Minister at Department of Transport, Chief Sec., Treasury, Sec. of State for Employment, Sec. of State for Defence, -1997; MP for Southend West, 1997-; *memberships:* Freeman City of London; *professional career:* Teacher, Bethnal Green; Chmn., employment consultancy; *committees:* Chmn., 1912 Club, House of Commons; Mem., Health Select Cttee., 1998-2008; Vice-Chmn., Cons. Health/Social Services Policy Cttee.; Chairman's Panel, 2001-; Blackbench Business, 2012-; *publications:* The Road to Basildon, 1993; Basildon Experience, 1994; *office address:* House of Commons, London, SW1A 0AA, United Kingdom; *phone:* +44 (0)20 7219 3452; *fax:* +44 (0)20 7219 2245; *e-mail:* amessd@parliament.uk; *URL:* http://www.davidamess.co.uk.

AMMON, Peter; Ambassador of Germany to the US, Embassy of Germany; *education:* Frei Univ., Berlin, Economics; *professional career:* Economic Minister, German Embassy, Washington DC, 1999-2001; various diplomatic positions including London, Dakar and New Delhi; Amb. to Paris, 2007-08; State Sec., Foreign Office, -2011; Ambassador to the US, 2011-; *office address:* Embassy of Germany, 4645 Reservoir Road, NW, Washington, DC 20007-1998, USA; *phone:* +1 202 298 4000; *fax:* +1 202 298 4249; *URL:* http://www.germany.info.

AMORIM, Celso; Minister of Defense, Government of Brazil; *born:* 3 June 1942, Santos, State of Sao Paulo; *education:* Brazilian Diplomatic Academy Instituto Rio Branco, 1965; Diplomatic Academy of Vienna, Post grad. in International Relations, 1967; London School of Economics and Political Science, PhD, Political Science and Int. Relations, 1971; *political career:* Minister of External Relations, 2003-10; Minister of Defence, Minister of Civil Aviation, 2011-; *memberships:* Dept. of Foreign Affairs, Inst. of Advanced Studies, Univ.

of São Paulo; *professional career:* Lecturer, Political Science and Internat. Relations, Univ. of Brasilia, 1977; Secretary -General., Foreign Relations, 1993; Minister of Foreign Relations, 1993-94; Perm. Rep. of Brazil to the UN in New York, 1995-99; Perm. Rep. of Brazil to the UN and others Int. Orgs. in Geneva, 1999-2001; Amb. to London, 2001-02; *office address:* Ministry of Defense, Qg/Ex. Bloco A, 40 Pavimento - Smu, 70630-901 Brasilia DF, Brazil; *phone:* +55 (0)61 415 5200; *fax:* +55 (0)61 415 4379; *URL:* http://www.defesa.gov.br.

ANASTASIADES, Nicos; President, Government of Cyprus; *born:* 1946, Limassol, Cyprus; *married:* Andri (née Moustakoudes); *education:* Kykko Pancyprian Gymnasium, 1964; Univ. of Athens, 1969; Univ. of London, Shipping Law, 1971; *party:* Democratic Rally; *political career:* District Sec. of the Youth Org. of the Democratic Rally (DR), 1976-85; Elected to Parl., 1981, 1985, 1991, 1996, 2001, 2006; Vice Pres., 1985-87, and Pres. of the Youth Organisation, 1987-90; Vice Pres. of the DR, 1990-93; Parly. Leader of the Democratic Rally, 1993-97; Dep. Pres. of the DR, 1995-97; Dep. Speaker of the House of Representatives, 1996-; Elected Pres. of the Democratic Rally, 1997, re-elected, 1999, 2003, 2007; President, Feb. 2013-; *professional career:* Practising law in Limassol, 1972-; *office address:* Presidential Palace, Dem, Severis Avenue, 1400 Nicosia, Cyprus; *phone:* +357 22 867400; *fax:* +357 22 663799; *e-mail:* president@presidency gov.cy; *URL:* http://www.presidency.gov.cy.

ANASTASIADES, H.E. Pavlos; Ambassador of Cyprus to the US, Embassy of Cyprus; *professional career:* joined diplomatic service, 1991, several positions, Emb. of Cyprus, Washington, 1993-97; Emb. of Cyprus, Stockholm, 1997-2002; EU Division, MFA, Nicosia, 2002-03; Dir., Foreign Minister's Office, Nicosia, 2003-05; Amb. of Cyprus to Sweden, 2005-10, non-resident Ambassador to Norway, 2006-10 and Latvia; Minister Pleniopotentiary, 2008; Amb. of Cyprus to the US, 2010-, non-resident High Commissioner of Cyprus Canada, 2011-; *office address:* Embassy of Cyprus, 2211 R Street, NW, Washington, DC 20008, USA; *phone:* +1 202 462 5772; *fax:* +1 202 483 6710; *URL:* http://www.cyprusembassy.net/.

ANDERSON, David; MP for Blaydon, House of Commons; *born:* 1953, Sunderland, UK; *education:* Durham Univ.; *party:* Labour; *political career:* MP for Blaydon, 2005-; *professional career:* Coal Mining Industry; Social Worker; Trade Union Representative; *committees:* Backbench Business, 2010, 2012-; Environment, Food & Rural Affairs, 2010-11; Regulatory Reform, 2010-; *office address:* House of Commons, London, SW1P 0AA, United Kingdom; *phone:* +44 (0)20 7219 4348; *e-mail:* andersonda@parliament.uk.

ANDOR, Laszlo; Hungarian, Commissioner, European Commission; *born:* 1966; *education:* Univ. of Economic Sciences, Hungary, MA, Economics; George Washington Univ., USA; Univ. of Manchester, MA, Development Economics; *political career:* Commissioner for Employment, Social Affairs and Inclusion, 2010-; *professional career:* Assoc. Prof., Economic Dept., Corvinus Univ., Budapest; Assoc. Prof., King Sigismund College; Mem., Board of Dirs., European Bank for Reconstruction & Development, 2005-10; *office address:* European Commission, rue de la loi 200, B-1049 Brussels, Belgium; *URL:* http://www.ec.europa.eu.

ANDREW, Stuart; MP for Pudsey, UK Government; *party:* Conservative; *political career:* Councillor, Leeds City Council 2003-10; MP for Pudsey, May 2010-; PPS to Francis Maude, 2012-; *committees:* Welsh Affairs, 2010-; *office address:* House of Commons, London, SW1A 0AA, United Kingdom; *phone:* +44 (0)20 7219 3000; *e-mail:* stuart.andrew.mp@parliament.uk; *URL:* http://www.parliament.uk.

ANDREWS, Leighton; Member of Welsh Assembly; *education:* Univ. of Wales (Bangor); Univ. of Sussex; *political career:* Mem. National Assembly for Wales, May 2003-; Minister for Children, Education and Lifelong Learning, 2009-; Minister for Education and Skills, May 2011-; *office address:* Welsh Assembly, Cardiff Bay, Cardiff, CF99 1NA, United Kingdom; *phone:* +44 (0)29 2082 5111; *fax:* +44 (0)29 2089 8229.

ANIFAH, H.J. Aman; Minister of Foreign Affairs, Government of Malaysia; *party:* United Malays National Organisation; *political career:* MP, 2004-; Dep. Minister of Plantation Industries and Commodities; Minister of Foreign Affairs, 2009-; *office address:* Ministry of Foreign Affairs, 1 Jalan Wisma Putra, Presint 2, 62603 Putrajaya, Malaysia; *phone:* +60 (0)3 8887 4000; *URL:* http://www.kln.gov.my.

ANNAN, Kofi; Ghanaian, Former Secretary General, United Nations; *born:* 8 April 1938, Kumasi, Ghana; *married:* Nane Annan (née Largergren); *children:* Kojo (M), Ana (F), Nina (F); *public role of spouse:* Lawyer and artist; *languages:* English, French, several, African, Languages; *education:* Univ. of Science and Technology, Kumasi, Ghana; Macalester Coll., St. Paul, MN, USA, undergraduate studies, econ., 1961; Institut universitaire des hautes etudes internationales, Geneva, graduate studies, econ., 1961-62; Massachusetts Inst. of Technology, USA, Sloan Fellow, 1971-72, M.Sc., management; *interests:* Armed conflict; Criminal Law; Environment law; Human rights; Organisations; State responsibility; Law of the Sea; Territory/boundaries; Treaties; Responsibility to protect; Use of force; *memberships:* mem. of the Bd., Ghana Tourist Dev. Co., mem., Ghana Tourist Control Bd., 1974-76; fmr. Chmn., Appointment and Promotion Bd., UN; fmr. Chmn., Sr. Review Gp., UN; mem., Admin., Management and Financial Bd., UN; mem., Sec.-Gen.'s Task Force for Peace-keeping, UN; mem., UN Jt. Staff Pension Fund; *professional career:* Diplomatic assignments, including negotiating the repatriation of over 900 int. staff and the release of Western hostages in Iraq, 1990; has served in Addis Ababa, Cairo, Geneva, Ismailia (Egypt), UN HQ in NY, USA; Admin. Officer and Budget Officer, WHO, Geneva, 1962; Man. Dir., Ghana Tourist Dev. Co., 1974-76; Dep. Dir. of Admin., Head of Personnel, Office of the UN High Cmnr. for Refugees, Geneva, 1980-83; Governor, Int. Sch., Geneva, 1981-83; Dir. of Budget, Office of Financial Services, 1984-87; Asst. Sec.-Gen., Office of Human Resources Management, Security Co-ordinator, UN system, 1987-90; Asst. Sec.-Gen., Programme Planning, Budget and Finance and Controller, 1990-92; oversaw the creation of a "situation centre" that monitors UN peace-keeping operations around the clock; Asst. Sec.-Gen., Peace-keeping Operations, UN, 1992-93; Under-Sec.-Gen. for Peace-keeping Operations, UN, 1993-95, 1996; Special Rep. of the Sec.-Gen. to the fmr. Yugoslavia, Special Envoy to NATO, 1995-96; Secretary-General., UN, 1997-2006; currently serves on board of the United Nations Foundation; Chmn., Alliance for a Green Revolution in Africa (AGRA); Chmn., Africa Progress Panel (APP); *trusteeships:*

Chmn., Bd. of Trustees, UN Int. Sch., NY, USA, 1987-95; mem., Bd. of Trustees, Macalester Coll.; *honours and awards:* A number of hon. degrees and awards; *publications:* numerous articles and book chapters incl: Christian Science Monitor; Economist; Financial Times; Foreign Affairs; Foreign Policy; Independent (UK); International Herald Tribune; Le Monde; Los Angeles Times; New York Times; Wall Street Journal; Washington Post; *office address:* Kofi Annan Foundation, POB 157, 1211 Geneva 20, Switzerland; *phone:* +41 22 919 7535; *fax:* +41 22 919 7529; *URL:* http://www.kofiannanfoundation.org.

ANNE ELIZABETH ALICE LOUISE, HRH The Princess Royal; British, Princess Royal; *born:* 1950; *parents:* Prince Philip, Duke of Edinburgh and Queen Elizabeth II; *married:* Timothy Lawrence; Capt. Mark Anthony Peter Phillips, 1973 (div'd 1992); *children:* Peter Mark Andrew (M), Zara Anne Elizabeth (F); *education:* Benenden Schl.; *memberships:* Mem. RNVR Officers Assn.; Hon. Mem., Brit. Equine Veterinary Assn.; Pres. Internat. Equestrian Fedn. 1986-; *professional career:* Col. in chief 14th/20th King's Hussars, Worcestershire and Sherwood Forresters Regt.; 8th Canadian Hussars; Royal Corps of Signals; The Canadian Armed Forces Communications and Electronics Br.; The Royal Australian Corps of Signals; Royal N.Z. Corps of Signals; Royal N.Z. Nursing Corps; The Grey and Simcoe Foresters Militia; Chief Comdt. W.R.N.S. Pres. Benevolent Trust; Hon. Air Commodore RAF Lyneham; Pres. Brit. Acad. Film and TV Arts; Hunters Improvement and Light Horse Breeding Soc.; Save The Children Fund; Windsor Horse Trials; The Royal Sch. for Daughters of Officers of Royal Navy and Royal Marines; Patron of numerous Brit. and worldwide orgns.; official visits throughout the world as Rep. of the Crown; Comdt. in Chief St. John Ambulance and Nursing Cades, Women's Transport Service; Fishmongers Co.; Middle Warden Farriers Co; Hon. Liverman Carmen's Co.; Hon. Freeman Farmers Co.; Loriners Co; Yeoman Saddlers Co.; Chancellor Univ. London; participant in numerous equestrian competitions incl: Montreal Olympics 1976; Horse of the Year Show; Wembley and Badminton Horse Trials; Pres. International Equestrian Fedn. 1986-; *trusteeships:* Pres., Benevolent Trust; *honours and awards:* Freeman, City of London; Recipient Raleigh Trophy, 1971; Silver Medal Individual European Three Day event, 1975; named Sportswoman of Year, Sports Writers Assn.; Daily Express; World of Sport, BBC Sports Personality, 1971; *clubs:* Royal Yacht Squadron; Royal Thames Yacht; Minchinhampton Golf Club; *office address:* Buckingham Palace, London, SW1A 1AA, United Kingdom.

ANSARI, M. Hamid; Vice-President of India, Government of India; *born:* 1 April 1937; *education:* BA (Hons.); MA; *political career:* Vice-Pres. of India, 2007-; *professional career:* joined Indian Foreign Service (IFS), 1961. Positions incl. Amb. to the UAE, 1976-79; Chief of Protocol to Gov. of India, 1980-85; High Commissioner to Australia, 1985-89; Amb. to Afghanistan, 1989-90; Amb. to Iran, 1990-92; Perm. Rep. to the UN, 1993-95; Amb. to Saudi Arabia, 1995-99; *office address:* Vice-President's House, 6 Maulana Azad Road, New Delhi 110 011, India.

ANSIP, Andrus; Prime Minister, Government of Estonia; *born:* 1 October 1956, Tartu, Estonia; *children:* 3; *languages:* Russian, English, German; *education:* Tartu Univ., Estonia, Diploma, Chemistry, 1979; York Univ., UK, business mgmt., 1992; *political career:* Mayor of Tartu, 1998-2004; Minister of Economic Affairs and Communications, 2004-05; Prime Minister of Estonia, 2005-; *professional career:* Head of regional office, Joint Venture Estkompexim, 1988-93; mem., bd. of dirs., Rahvapank (People's Bank), 1993-95; Chmn., Livonnia Privatization IF, 1995-96; mem., bd. of dirs., Fondijuhtide AS, 1995-96; CEO, Fondiinvesteeringu Maakler AS (Investment Fund Broker), 1996-97; Chmn., Tartu Commercial Bank, Tartu Bankruptcy Trustee, 1994-98; Radio Tartu Ltd, 1994-99; *office address:* Office of the Prime Minister, Rahukohtu 3, 15161 Tallinn, Estonia.

ANTHONY, A.K.; Minister of Defence, Government of India; *children:* 2; *party:* Congress Party; *political career:* Chief Minister, Kerala, India; mem., Rajya Sabha; Minister of Defence, 2006-; *office address:* Ministry of Defence, South Block, New Delhi 110 011, India; *URL:* http://mod.nic.ind.

ANTHONY, Dr Kenny D.; Prime Minister, Governor of Saint Lucia; *born:* 8 January 1951, Saint Lucia; *education:* Laborie Boys' Sch., Saint Lucia, 1963-64; Vieux Fort Senior Secondary Sch., Saint Lucia, 1964-68; Saint Lucia Teachers' Coll., Saint Lucia, 1969-71; BSc (1st Class Hons) Govt. and History Univ. of West Indies, 1973-76; LLB, LLM Univ. of West Indies, 1981-85; Ph.D., Univ. of Birmingham, 1985-88; *political career:* Special Advisor, Ministry of Education and Culture, 1979-80; Minister of Education, 1980-81; General Cncl, Caribbean Community Secretariat, Georgetown, Guyana, (on secondment from UWI), 1995-96; elected Leader of the Saint Lucia Labour Party, 1996; Prime Minister, 1997-2006, 2011-; *professional career:* Teacher, Castries Anglican Primary Sch., Saint Lucia, 1968-69; Teacher, Vieux Fort Senior Sch., 1971-73, 1976-78; Part-time Tutor, Introduction to Politics and Public Administration, Faculty of Social Sciences, Univ. of the West Indies, St Augustine, Trinidad, 1978-79; Part-Time Tutor, Introduction to Politics, Univ of West Indies, 1981-83; Asst. Lecturer, Faculty of Law, Univ. of West Indies, 1984-88; Lecturer and Head of Teaching, Dept of Law, 1989-93; Advisor, Regional Constituent Assembly of the Windward Islands, 1990-91; Dir., Caribbean Justice Improvement, Faculty of Law, 1993-94; *committees:* fmr. Mem., Students' Regulations Cttee., Pay and Promotions Cttee., Speakers' Cup Cttee., Cave Hill Campus, Univ. of West Indes; fmr. Mem., Editorial Cttee., Bulletin of Eastern Caribbean Affairs, ISER, Barbados; fmr. Mem., Editorial Cttee., Occasional Papers, ISER, Barbados; fmr. Mem., Law Reform Cttee. of Barbados; fmr. Mem. and Chmn., Editorial Cttee., Caribbean Law Review; Mem., Editorial Cttee., Folk Research Centre Bulletin, Saint Lucia; Mem., Editorial Cttee., Caribbean Education Annual; *publications:* numerous articles on law, 1985-95; *office address:* Prime Minister's Office, 5th Floor, Greaham Louuisy Administrative Building, Waterfront, Castries, St. Lucia; *phone:* +758 468 2111; *URL:* http://www.pm.gov.lc/.

ANTORINI, Christine; Minister for Children and Education, Government of Denmark; *born:* 23 May 1965, Jyllinge, Denmark; *education:* MA, (public administration), Roskilde Univ., 1994; *party:* Social Democratic Party; *political career:* MP, 1998-99, 2009-; Minister for Children and Education, 2011-; *office address:* Ministry of Education, Frederiksholms Kanal 21-25, 1220 Copenhagen K, Denmark; *phone:* +45 3392 5000; *fax:* +45 3392 5547; *e-mail:* uvm@uvm.dk; *URL:* http://www.uvm.dk.

APDAL, YB Datuk Mohd Shafie; Malaysian, Minister of Rural and Regional Development, Malaysian Government; ***born:*** 1957, Semporna; ***political career:*** Sabah Umno Youth Chief, 1992-; Parly. Secy.; Minister of Domestic Trade & Consumer Affairs, -08; Minister for Unity, Culture, Arts and Heritage, 2008-09; Minister of Rural and Regional Development, 2009-; ***professional career:*** fmr. Chmn., North Borneo Timber Berhad; ***office address:*** Ministry of Rural Development, Level 9, Block D9, Parcel D, Federal Government Administrative Centre, 62606 Putrajaya, Malaysia; ***URL:*** http://www.rurallink.gov.my/.

APONTE, Mari Carmen; Ambassador, US Embassy in El Salvador; ***education:*** BA in Political Science, Rosemont Coll.; MA in Theatre, Villanova Univ.; JD, Temple Univ., USA; ***professional career:*** Lawyer; Exec. Dir. of the Puerto Rican Federal Affairs Administration, 2001-04; Amb. to El Salvador, 2010-; ***office address:*** Embassy of the USA, Boulevard Santa Elena, Antiguo Cuscatlán La Libertad, El Salvador; ***phone:*** +503 2278 4444; ***fax:*** +503 2278 6011; ***URL:*** http://sansalvador.usembassy.gov.

AQUINO, Benigno 'Noynoy'; President, Government of the Philippines; ***born:*** 8 February 1960; ***parents:*** Benigno "Ninoy" Aquino (dec'd) and former president Cory Aquino (dec'd); ***education:*** AB Economics, Ateneo de Manila Univ., 1981; ***party:*** Exec. Vice Pres. Liberal Party, 2007-; ***political career:*** Elected to House of Representatives in 1998-2007; Dep. Speaker, House of Representatives, 2004-06; Senator in 2007-10; President, June 2010-; ***committees:*** Chmn., Cttee on Local Government; Vice Chmn., Cttee. on Justice and Human Rights; Cttee. Membership, Accounts; Constitutional Amendments, Revisions of Codes and Laws, Economic Affairs; Education, Arts and Culture; Environment and Natural Resources; Nat. Defense and Security; Peace, Unifications and Reconciliation; Public Works; Trade and Commerce; Urban Planning, Housing and Resettlement; Ways and Means; Youth, Women and Family Relations; ***office address:*** Office of the President, Malacanang Palace, JP Laurel Street, San Miguel 1005, Manila, The Philippines; ***phone:*** +63 2 564 1451 to 80; ***URL:*** http://www.op.gov.ph/.

ARABADJIEV, Alexander; Judge, Court of Justice of the European Union; ***education:*** St. Kliment Ohridski University, Sofia, Bulgaria; ***political career:*** Mem., National Assembly, Bulgaria, 2001-06; ***professional career:*** Judge, District Court, Blagoevgrad, 1975-83; Judge, Regional Court, Blagoevgrad, 1983-86; Judge at the Supreme Court, 1986-91; Judge, Constitutional Court, 1991-2000; Mem., European Commission of Human Rights, 1997-99; Mem., European Convention on the Future of Europe, 2002-03; Observer, European Parliament; Judge, Court of Justice, 2007-; ***office address:*** Court of Justice of the EU, Rue du Fort Niedergrunewald, L-2925, Luxembourg.

ARAUD, Gérard; Permanent Representative of France, United Nations; ***professional career:*** First Sec., Emb. of France in Israel, 1982-84; Forecasting Centre, MFA, 1984-87; Second Counsellor, Emb. of France to the USA, Washington, 1987-91; Under Dir. of Community Affairs, MFA, 1991-93; Diplomatic advisor to the cabinet of the Minister of State, Ministry of Defence, 1993-95; Perm. Rep. to the Perm Delegation of France to NATO, 19995-2000; Dir. of Strategic Affairs, MFA, 2000-03; Amb. Extraordinary & Plenipotentiary in Israel, 2003-06; Sec. Gen. to the Ministry of Foreign and European Affairs, 2006-09; Ambassador, Permanent Rep. of France to the UN in New York, 2009-; ***office address:*** Permanent Mission of France to the UN, One Dag Hammarskjöld Plaza, 245 East 47th Street, 44th Floor, New York, NY 10017, USA; ***URL:*** http://www.franceonu.org/.

ARBUTHNOT, Rt. Hon. James Norwich, MP; British, MP for NE Hampshire, House of Commons; ***born:*** 4 August 1952; ***married:*** Emma (née Broadbent), 1984; ***children:*** Alexander (M), Katherine (F), Eleanor (F), Alice (F); ***public role of spouse:*** District Judge and Crown Court Recorder; ***education:*** Eton Sch.; Trinity Coll., Cambridge, MA (Hons.), Law, 1974; Coll. of Law; ***political career:*** Contested Cynon Valley constituency in 1984 by-election, Gen. Election, 1983; Kensington and Chelsea Borough Cllr., 1978-87; MP, Wanstead & Woodford, 1987-97; PPS to Sec. of State at DTI and to Minister of State for the Armed Forces, 1988-92; Govt. Whip, 1992-94; Parly. Under Sec. of State for Social Security, 1994-95; Minister of State for Defence Procurement, 1995-97; MP, North East Hampshire, 1997-; Opp. Chief Whip House of Commons, 1997-2001; Privy Counsellor, 1998-; Shadow Sec. of State for Trade, 2003-05; ***professional career:*** called to Bar, 1975; practised, Lincoln's Inn, 1976-92; ***committees:*** Intelligence and Security Cttee., 2001-05; Chmn., Defence Select Cttee., 2005-; Mem., Liaison, 2005-; Jt. Cttee. on Security Strategy, 2010-; Chair, Armed Forces Bill, 2011; ***recreations:*** family, music, computers, skiing; ***office address:*** House of Commons, London, SW1A 0AA, United Kingdom; ***phone:*** +44 (0)20 7219 4649.

ARCE CATACORA, Luis Alberto; Minister of Economy and Public Finance, Government of Bolivia; ***languages:*** English, Portuguese; ***education:*** Univ. Mayor de San Andrés, Econ.; Univ. of Warwick, Masters in Econ., 1996-97; ***political career:*** Minister of Finance, 2006-09; Minister of Economy and Public Finance, 2009-; ***professional career:*** Banco Central de Bolivia, 1999-2006; ***office address:*** Palacio de Comunicaciones (piso 19), Avenida Mariscal Santa Cruz, La Paz, Bolivia; ***phone:*** +591 2 392540 / 392779 / 392220; ***fax:*** +591 2 359955.

ARESTIS, George; Judge, Court of Justice of the European Union; ***born:*** 1945; ***education:*** Univ. of Athens, law; Univ. of Kent at Canterbury; ***professional career:*** lawyer, Cyprus, 1972-82; District Court Judge, 1982, Pres., 1995; Administrative President, District Court of Nicosia, 1997-2003; Judge, Supreme Court of Cyprus, 2003; Judge, Court of Justice, 2004-; ***office address:*** Court of Justice of the European Union, Rue du Fort Niedergrunewald, L-2925, Luxembourg.

ARHINMAKI, Paavo; Minister of Culture and Sport, Government of Finland; ***political career:*** Helsinki City Council, Member, 2001-; MP, 2007-; Minister of Culture and Sport, 2011-; ***office address:*** Ministry of Culture and Sport, Meritullinkatu 10, Helsinki, FI-00023 Government, Finland; ***phone:*** +358 295 330 289; ***URL:*** http://www.minedu.fi.

ARINÇ, Bülent; Deputy Prime Minister, Government of Turkey; ***education:*** LLB., Univ. of Ankara, 1970; ***political career:*** Speaker of the Parliament, 2002-07; Deputy Prime Minister, 2009-; ***office address:*** Office of the Deputy Prime Minister, Basbakanlik Necatibey Cad, 108 Ankara, Turkey; ***phone:*** +90 (9)312 413 7000; ***URL:*** http://www.basbakanlik.gov.tr.

ARKWRIGHT, H.E. Paul; Ambassador, British Embassy in The Hague; ***born:*** Bolton, UK; ***education:*** Cambridge Univ.; ***professional career:*** English Teacher in Japan; UK delegation, UN in New York; Amb. to The Netherlands, 2009-; ***office address:*** British Embassy, Lange Voorhout 10, 2514 ED The Hague, Netherlands; ***phone:*** +31 (0)70 427 0427; ***fax:*** +31 (0)70 427 0345; ***e-mail:*** library@fco.gov.uk; ***URL:*** http://www.britain.nl.

ARMSTRONG OF ILMINSTER, Lord , GCB, CVO; Member of the House of Lords; ***born:*** 1927; ***education:*** Eton Coll., Christ Church, Oxford; ***political career:*** Mem. of House of Lords; ***professional career:*** joined the Civil Service in 1950; Principal Private Sec. to the Prime Minister (Edward Heath, then Harold Wilson), 1970-75; Dep. Under Sec. of State at the Home Office, Police and Broadcasting Depts., 1975-77; Permanent Under Sec. of State at the Home Office, 1977-79; Sec. of the Cabinet, 1979-87; Head of the Home Civil Service, 1981-87; retd. from public service, 1987; Chmn., Bd. of Trustees of the Victoria & Albert Museum, London, UK, 1988-98; non-exec. dir., Shell Transport & Trading plc, 1988-97; BAT Industries plc, 1988-97; RTZ plc, 1988-97; Lucas Industries, 1988-93;mChllr. of Hull Univ., 1994-2006; retd. as Chmn. of Bristol & West, plc., end of 1997; Dir., Bank of Ireland, 1997-2001; Chmn., Forensic Investigative Assocs. plc., 1997-2003; non-exec. dir., Iamoold Corp. Ltd., 1997- 2003; Chmn., Bd. of Governors, Royal Northern Coll. of Music, 2000-05; ***trusteeships:*** Trustee, Leeds Castle Foundation, 1988-2007, Chmn., 2001-07; Trustee, Derek Hill Foundation, 2001; Chmn., Sir Edward Heath Charitable Foundation, 2005-; Trustee, Wells Cathedral School Foundation, 2007-; ***office address:*** House of Lords, London, SW1A 0PW, United Kingdom; ***phone:*** +44 (0)20 7219 3000; ***fax:*** +44 (0)20 7219 1259.

ARNADOTTIR, Ragnheidur Elin; Minister of Industry and Commerce, Government of Iceland; ***born:*** 30 September 1967; ***education:*** BA, Univ. of Iceland, 1991; Int. Relations, Georgetown Univ., USA; ***party:*** Independence Party; ***political career:*** MP, 2007-; Minister of Industry and Trade, 2013-; ***office address:*** Ministry of Industry and Innovation, Arnarhváli, 150 Reykjavík, Iceland; ***phone:*** +354 545 8500; ***fax:*** +354 562 1289; ***URL:*** http://eng.idnadarraduneyti.is.

ARNASON, Kristinn; Secretary General, EFTA; ***education:*** Univ. of Oslo, law; Univ. of Exeter; Univ. of Iceland; ***professional career:*** various positions, MFA, 1992-2005, incl. Amb. to Norway, 1999-2003, also to Czech Rep., Egypt, Poland, Slovak Rep.; Amb. & Perm Rep, Permanent Mission of Iceland, Geneva, 2005-12; Sec.-Gen., European Free Trade Assn., 2012-; ***office address:*** EFTA, 9-11 rue de Varembé, CH-1211 Geneva, Switzerland; ***phone:*** +41 (0)22 332 2600; ***e-mail:*** kfa@efta.int.

ARRAN, Earl Arthur Desmond Colquhoun Gore; British, Member of the House of Lords; ***born:*** 1938; ***married:*** Eleanor van Cutsem, 1974; ***d:*** 2; ***public role of spouse:*** D.L.; ***education:*** Eton; Balliol Coll., Oxford; ***political career:*** Mem., House of Lords; ***memberships:*** Pres., Children's Country Holiday Fund; ***professional career:*** 2nd Lieutenant 1st Bn. Grenadier Guards (national Service); Asst. Manager, Daily Mail, 1972-73; Man. Dir., Clark Nelson, 1973-74; Asst. Gen. Mgr., Daily & Sunday Express, 1974; Lord in Waiting, 1987-89; Parly. Under-Secy. of State for the Armed Forces, 1989-92; Parly. Under-Secy. of State, Northern Ireland office (responsible for Agriculture and Department of Health and Social Security), 1992-94; Parly. Under-Secy. Dept. of the Environment, 1994; Dpty. Chief Whip, House of Lords, 1994-95; Non-Exec. Dir., HMV (Thorn/EMI), 1995; Bonhams, 1997; Chmn., Waste Ind. Nast. Training Org. (Winto), 2001; Dir., Weather World, 2005-; ***trusteeships:*** Chelsea Physic Garden; Pres. Children's Country Holidays Fund; ***clubs:*** Turf Club; Beefsteak; Pratt's; White's; ***office address:*** House of Lords, London, SW1A 0PW, United Kingdom.

ARREAGA, H.E. Luis E.; Ambassador, US Embassy in Iceland; ***education:*** MA. in management, PhD in economics, Univ. of Wisconsin, USA; ***professional career:*** Dep. Chief of Mission , Panama; Consul General in Vancouver, Canada; Amb. to Iceland, 2010-; ***office address:*** US Embassy, Laufásvegur 21, 101 Reykjavík, Iceland; ***phone:*** +354 562 9100; ***fax:*** +354 562 9139; ***URL:*** http://www.usa.is.

ARREAZA, Jorge; Vice President, Government of Venezuela; ***born:*** 1973; ***education:*** Univ. Central de Venezuela; Univ. of Cambridge; ***political career:*** Minister of Science and Technology, 2011-13; Vice-Pres. of Venezuela, 2013-; ***office address:*** Office of the Presidency, Palacio de Miraflores, Avenida Urdaneta, Caracas 1010, Venezuela; ***URL:*** http://www.presidencia.gob.ve/.

ARVIZU, H.E. Alexander A.; Ambassador, US Embassy in Albania; ***professional career:*** Dep. Chief of Mission, Phnom Penh, Cambodia, 2000-03; Dep. Chief of Mission, Bangkok, Thailand, 2004-07; Dep. Assist. Sec., responsible for Japan, Korea and Regional Security, 2007-09; Amb. to Albania, 2010-; ***office address:*** Embassy of the United States, Rruga Elbasanit 103, Tirana, Albania; ***phone:*** +355 (0)4 247285; ***fax:*** +355 (0)4 232222; ***URL:*** http://tirana.usembassy.gov.

ASHFIELD, Keith; Minister of Fisheries and Oceans, Government of Canada; ***born:*** 1952; ***political career:*** Mem., New Brunswick Legislative Assembly, 1999-2006; MP Canadian Parliament, 2008-; Minister of State for Atlantic Canada Opportunities Agency, 2008-10; Minister of National Revenue, 2010-11; Minister of Fisheries and Oceans, Minister of the Atlantic Gateway, 2011-; ***office address:*** House of Commons, Parliament Buildings, Wellington Street, Ottawa, Ontario, K1A 0A6, Canada; ***phone:*** +1 613 943 5959.

ASHIRU, Amb. Olugbenga Ayodeji; Minister of Foreign Affairs, Government of Nigeria; ***education:*** Univ. of Lagos; ***political career:*** Minister of Foreign Affairs, 2011-; ***professional career:*** joined Ministry of Foreign Affairs, 1972; Diplomat; Various postings; Amb. to the Democratic People's Republic of Korea, 1991; High Commissioner to South Africa, 2005; ***office address:*** Ministry of Foreign Affairs, Maputo Street, WuseZone 3 , P.M.B 130, Garki, Abuja, Nigeria; ***phone:*** +234 9 523 0491 / 234 4686.

ASHTON OF UPHOLLAND, Baroness; High Representative For Foreign Affairs, European Union; *born:* 1956; *education:* University of London; *political career:* Mem. of House of Lords, 1999-; Parly. Under-Sec. of State, Dept. for Education and Skills, 2001; Parly. Under-Sec., Dept. for Constitutional Affairs, then Ministry of Justice with responsibilities for human rights, freedom of information and equalities; Privy Councillor, May 2006; Leader of the House of Lords and Lord President of the Council, June 2007-Oct. 2008; EU Commissioner for Trade, 2008-09; High Representative For Foreign Affairs, EU, Nov. 2009-; *professional career:* Dir., Business in the Community, 1983-89; Chwmn., Hertfordshire Health Authority, 1998-2001; Vice Pres., National Council for One Parent Families; *office address:* European Commission, rue de la loi 200, B-1049 Brussels, Belgium; *URL:* http://www.europa.eu.int.

ASHWORTH, Jon; MP, House of Commons; *party:* Labour Party; *political career:* Political Research Officer, Labour Party, 2001, Economics and Welfare Policy Officer, 2002-04; MP, Leicester South, May 2011-; Opp. Whip, 2011-; *office address:* House of Commons, London, SW1A 0AA, United Kingdom; *phone:* +44 (0)20 7219 3000; *e-mail:* jon.ashworth.mp@parliament.uk.

ASJES, Ivar; Prime Minister, Government of Curaçao; *party:* Pueblo Soberano (PS); *political career:* Commissioner of Economic Affairs and Tourism, PLKP party; Commissioner of Finance, PS Party; Pres. of Parliament, 2010; Head, PS delegation in parliament, 2012; Prime Minister, 2013-; *office address:* Office of the Prime Minister, Willemstad, Curaçao.

ASK, Beatrice; Swedish, Minister of Justice, Government of Sweden; *born:* 20 April 1956; *parents:* Sven Ask and Anne-Marie Mattsson; *children:* Victor (M), Stefan (M); *languages:* English; *education:* American High Sch.; Upper Secondary Sch.; Uppsala Univ., Int. Econ.; *party:* Moderaterna (Moderates); *political career:* Nat. Chmn., Young Moderates; Stockholm Education Cmnr., 1988-91; Vice Mayor, City of Stockholm, 1988-91; Minister. for Schs. and Adult Education, 1991-94; MP, 1994-; Minister of Justice, 2006-; *professional career:* Organization official, Young Moderates; Asst. Sec. to a Stockholm City Cmnr.; *committees:* Vice-Pres., Parly. Standing Cttee. on Education and Research, 1994-2002; Standing Cttee. on Justice, 2002-; *office address:* Ministry of Justice, Rosenbad 4, 103 33 Stockholm, Sweden; *phone:* +46 (0)8 405 1000; *e-mail:* beatrice.ask@justice.ministry.se.

ASMUSSEN, Jorg; Member of the Executive Board, European Central Bank; *born:* 1966; *education:* Univ. of Milan; Univ. of Bonn; *political career:* Private Sec. to the State Sec., German Federal Ministry of Finance, 1998-99; Head of the Minister's office and Private Secretary to the German Federal Minister of Finance, 1999-2002; Head of European Policy directorate, German Federal Ministry of Finance, 2002-03; Dir. Gen., Financial Market Policy, German Federal Ministry of Finance, 2003-08; State Secretary, German Federal Ministry of Finance, 2008-11; *professional career:* Mem. Exec. Board, European Central Bank, 2012-; *office address:* European Central Bank, Kaiserstrasse 29, D-60311 Frankfurt-am-Main, Germany; *URL:* http://www.ecb.int.

ASO, Taro; Minister of Finance, Government of Japan; *born:* September 1940; *education:* Fac. of Politics and Economics, Gakushuin Univ., 1963; *party:* Leader, Liberal Democratic Party; *political career:* mem., House of Representatives, 1979-; Vice Min. for Educ., Sports, Science and Culture, 1988; Dir., Educ. Div., Liberal Democratic Party (LDP), 1990; Dir., Foreign Affairs Div., LDP, 1992; Minister of State, Econ. Planning Agency, 1996; Dep. Sec.Gen., LDP, 1999; Minister of State, Econ. and Fiscal Policy, IT Policy, 2001; Minister for Public Management, Home Affairs, Post and Telecommunications, 2003; Ministry of Internal Affairs and Communications; Minister of Foreign Affairs, 2005-07; Prime Minister, Sept. 2008-12; Deputy Prime Minister, Minister of Finance, Overcoming Deflation and Counting Yen Appreciation, Minister of State for Financial Services, 2012-; *professional career:* Pres. Aso Industry, 1973; *committees:* Chmn., Standing Cttee. on Foreign Affairs, 1991; Chmn., Special Cttee on Coal Issues, 1991; Chmn., Special Cttee. on Fiscal Structure Reform, 1998; Chmn., Policy Research Cncl., LDP, 2001; *office address:* Ministry of Finance, 3-1-1 Kasumigaseki, Chiyoda-ku, Tokyo 100, Japan; *phone:* +81 (0)3 3581 4111; *URL:* http://www.mof.go.jp.

ASSCHER, Lodewijk; Deputy Prime Minister and Minister of Social Affairs and Employment, Netherlands Government; *born:* 1974; *education:* Univ. of Amsterdam, law, degree, doctorate; *political career:* Amsterdam City Council, 2002-06; Interim mayor, March. - July 2010; Municipal executive, 2010-12; Deputy Prime Minister and Minister of Social Affairs and Employment, Rutte-Asscher gov., Nov. 2012-; *professional career:* Univ. of Amsterdam, researcher, lecturer; *office address:* Ministry of Social Affairs and Employment, Anna van Hannoverstraat 4, Postbus 90801, 2509 LV The Hague, Netherlands.

ASSELBORN, Jean; Deputy Prime Minister, Government of Luxembourg; *born:* 27 April 1949; *education:* Univ. of Nancy II, LLM, 1981; *political career:* Dep., Chamber of Deputies, 1984-; Pres., Parly. gp. Luxembourg Socialist Workers (LSAP), 1989; Pres., Socialist Party, 1997; Vice-Pres.,Chamber of Deputies, 1999-2004; Vice-Pres., European Socialist Party, 2000-04; Minister of Foreign Affairs and Immigration; Deputy Prime Minister, 2004-, also Minister of Foreign Affairs, 2009-; *professional career:* Hospital administrator, Steinfort, 1976; Burgomeister, Steinfort, 1981; *office address:* Ministry of Foreign Affairs and Foreign Trade, 5 rue Notre Dame, 2240 Luxembourg, Luxembourg; *phone:* +352 478 12300; *fax:* +352 22 3144; *e-mail:* officielle.boite@mae.etat.lu; *URL:* http://www.mae.lu/.

ASTOR OF HEVER, Lord; Member of the House of Lords; *born:* 16 June 1946; *married:* Hon. Elizabeth Mackintosh; Fiona Harvey; *children:* Charles (M), Camilla (F), Tania (F), Violet (F), Olivia (F); *languages:* French; *education:* Eton; *party:* Conservative Party; *political career:* House of Lords, 1984-, elected hereditary peer, 1999-; Opp. Whip, 1998-2010; Opp. Spokesperson: Defence, FCO, International Dev., 2003-10; Parly. Under-Sec. of State and Gov. Spokesperson, Ministry of Defence, 2010-; Gov. Whip, 2010-11; *honours and awards:* DL; *office address:* House of Lords, London, SW1A 0PQ, United Kingdom; *phone:* +44 (0)20 7219 5475; *fax:* +44 (0)20 7219 0086; *e-mail:* astorjj@parliament.uk.

ASTORI, Danilo; Vice President, Government of Uruguay; *political career:* Pres. of the Uruguay Assembly; Senator of the Republic, 1990-2005; Minister of Economics and Finance, 2005; Vice President, 2010-; *memberships:* Fmr. Exec. Sec., now Mem., CIEDUR

(Interdisciplinary Development Studies Centre); Fmr. mem., Admin. Bd., Univ. of the Republic; *professional career:* Hon. Prof., Economics, Fac. of Econ. and Admin., Univ. of the Republic; Fmr. Deacon, Fac. of Econ. and Admin., Univ. of the Republic; UN Consultant on economics; Columnist, Economia y Mercados Supplement, El Pais; *committees:* Senate Cttees. on the Treasury, Industry and Energy, Agriculture, Livestock and Fisheries; Mem., Jt. Parly. Cttee. on MERCOSUR; *publications:* Author of many books and articles on economics; *office address:* Office of the Vice President, Avda Dr. Luis Alberto de Herrera 3350, Montevideo, Uruguay; *phone:* +598 2487 2110; *e-mail:* presidente@presiencia.gub.uy; *URL:* http://www.presidencia.gub.uy.

ATAMBAYEV, Almazbek; President, Kyrgyz Republic; *born:* 1956; *party:* Chmn., Social Democratic Party of Kyrgyzstan, 1999-; *political career:* Minister of Industry, Trade and Tourism, 2005-06; Prime Minister, March-Nov. 2007, 2010-11; President, Oct. 2011-; *professional career:* Businessman; *office address:* Office of the President, 720003 Bishkek, Kyrgyzstan.

ATTLEE, Earl , TD; Member of the House of Lords; *born:* 3 October 1956; *married:* Teresa Ahern, 2008; *party:* Conservative Party; *political career:* Mem., House of Lords, to date; Gov. Whip and spokesman for all transport matters in House of Lords; Whip and Jnr. Spokesman for DCLG and Home Office (Immigration); *office address:* House of Lords, London, SW1A 0PQ, United Kingdom; *phone:* +44 (0)20 7219 6071; *fax:* +44 (0)20 7219 5979; *e-mail:* attleej@parliament.uk.

ATTWOOD, Alex; Member of the Northern Ireland Assembly; *born:* 26 April 1959, Belfast; *parents:* Benjamin Attwood and Claire Attwood; *education:* Park Lodge Primary Sch.; St Malachy's Coll.; LLB Queens Univ., Belfast; *party:* Social Democratic and Labour Party; *political career:* Mem. Belfast City Cncl, 1985-; Mem. Forum for Peace and Reconciliation, 1994-95; Mem. Northern Ireland Assembly, 1998-; Minister for Social Development, 2010-11; Minister for the Environment, 2011-; *interests:* justice issues, international affairs; *trusteeships:* John Hume Trust; *clubs:* Towpath Veterans Running Club; *recreations:* marathon running; golf music; cinema; *office address:* Northern Ireland Assembly, Parliament Buildings, Stormont, Belfast BT4 3XX, Northern Ireland; *phone:* +44 (0)28 9052 1130.

AUBOUIN, Michel; Prefect-High Administrator, Wallis and Futuna; *political career:* Dep.-Dir., Territorial Administration, Ministry of the Interior and Sec.-Gen., Prefecture of Essonne; Dir., Arrival, Integration & Citizenship / General Secretariat, Immigration and Integration; Prefect-High Administrator, Wallis and Futuna, March. 2013-; *office address:* Administration Superieure, Havelu, BP 16, 98600 Mata-Utu, Ile de Wallis, Wallis and Futuna.

AUSTIN, Ian; MP for Dudley North, House of Commons; *born:* 1965; *party:* Labour; *political career:* Dudley Borough Councillor 1991-95; MP, Dudley North, 2005-; PPS to the Prime Minister, June 2007-09; Parly. under Sec., Dept. for Communities and Local Gov., 2009-10; Shadow Minister for Communities and Local Government, May-Sept. 2010; Shadow Minister, Culture, Media and Sport, Oct. 2010-11; Shadow Minister, Works and Pension, 2011-; *office address:* House of Commons, London, SW1P 0AA, United Kingdom.

AUSTRIE, Hon. Reginald; Minister of Housing, Lands and Telecommunications, Government of Dominica; *political career:* Minister of Energy; Minister of Communications, Works and Housing; Minister of Housing, Lands and Telecommunications, 2007-; *office address:* Ministry of Communications, Works and Housing, Government Headquarters, Kennedy Avenue, Roseau, Dominica.

AVRAMOPOULOS, Dimitrios; Minister of Foreign Affairs, Government of Greece; *born:* 1953; *party:* New Democracy; *political career:* Mayor of Athens, 1995-2002; Minister of Tourism, 2004-09; Minister of Health and Social Solidarity, 2006-09; Minister of National Defence, Nov. 2011-May 2012; Minister of Foreign Affairs, June 2012-; *office address:* Ministry of Foreign Affairs, 1 Acadimias str., 106 71 Athens, Greece; *phone:* +30 (0)10 368 1000; *e-mail:* mfa@mfa.gr; *URL:* http://www.mfa.gr.

AYASSOR, Adji Otéth, Minister of Finance, Government of Togo; *education:* Univ. of Bordeaux; Univ. de Wisconsin, US; *political career:* Sec. Gen. to the President, 2006; Minister of Finance, Budget and Privatisations, 2007; *professional career:* Lecturer, Law, Univ. de Lomé; Teacher, National School of Administration; *office address:* Ministry of Finance, BP 900, Place du Monument aux Morts, Lomé, Togo; *phone:* +228 221 2910; *fax:* +228 221 3974; *URL:* http://www.diplomatie.gouv.tg/.

AYOTTE, Kelly; Senator for New Hampshire, US Senate; *party:* Republican; *political career:* Mem., US Senate, 2010-; *professional career:* Attorney General, New Hampshire, 2004-10; *committees:* Armed Services; Budget; Commerce; Homeland Security & Governmental Affairs; Special Cttee. on Aging; *office address:* US Senate, 144 Russell Senate Office Building, Washington DC 20510, USA; *phone:* +1 202 224 3324; *URL:* http://www.ayotte.senate.gov.

AYRAULT, Jean-Marc; French, Prime Minister, Government of France; *born:* 25 January 1950, Maulévrier, Maine et Loire, France; *party:* Socialist Party; *political career:* Mem., Assemblée Nationale, 1986-; Deputy of Loire-Atlantique, 1986, re-elected 1988-2012; Mayor of Nantes, 1989-; Pres. of the Socialist Grp. at the Nat. Assembly, 1997-2012; Prime Minister, 2012-; *professional career:* German teacher, 1973-86; *office address:* Office of the Prime Minister, Hôtel Matignon, 57 rue de Varenne, 75700 Paris, France; *phone:* +33 (0)1 42 75 80 00; *fax:* +33 (0)1 42 75 75 04; *URL:* http://www.gouvernement.fr/premier-ministre.

AZAD, Ghulam Nabi; Minister of Health and Family Welfare, Government of India; *born:* 7 March 1949, Village Soti; *parents:* Shri Rahamatullah and Shrimati Basa Begum; *married:* Shrimati Shameem Dev Azad; *education:* Kashmir Univ., M.Sc., Zoology, Srinagar; *party:* Indian National Congress (INC); *political career:* Sec., Block Congress Cttee., 1973-75; Pres., Pradesh Youth Congress, Jammu & Kashmir, 1975-77; mem., Congress Exec. Cttee., J&K Pradish Congress, 1975-85; Pres., District Congress Cttee., Doda, 1975-88; Gen.-Sec., All India Youth Congress, 1977-80, Pres., 1980-82; Pres., All India Muslim Youth Conference, 1978-81; mem., 7th Lok Sabha, 1980-84; Dep. Minister, Ministry of Law, Justice & Company

Affairs, 1982-83, Ministry of Information & Broadcasting, 1983-84; mem., 8th Lok Sabha, 1985-89; Minister, Parly. Affairs, 1984-86; Minister, Home Affairs, 1986; Minister, Food & Civil Supplies, 1986-87; Gen.-Sec., All India Congress Cttee., 1987-92, 1996-; elected to Rajya Sabha, 1990, re-elected, 1996; Minister, Parly. Affairs, 1991-93, 1995-96; Minister, Civil Aviation & Tourism, 1993-96; Minister of Parliamentary Affairs and Urban Development, 2004-06; Minister, Health and Family Welfare, 2009-; ***committees:*** mem., Congress Exec. Cttee., Maharashtra, 1980-; mem., Cttee. on Public Undertakings, 1980-82; mem., Consultative Cttee. for the Ministry of Defence, 1981-82; Chmn., Youth Service Cttee., IX Asian Games, 1982; mem., Special Organising Cttee., IX Asian Games; mem., Consultative Cttee. for the Ministry of Information & Broadcasting; mem., Congress Working Cttee., 1987-; mem., Consultative Cttee. for the Ministry of Home Affairs, 1996-97; mem., Cttee. on Energy, 1998; mem., Central Disciplinary Action Cttee. (A.I.C.C), 1998-; mem., Rajghat Samadhi Cttee., 1998-; mem., Informal Consultative Cttee. for the Northern Railway Zone, 2000-; mem., Joint Parly. Cttee. on the Functioning of Wakf Boards, 2000-; ***recreations:*** gardening, socialising, national integration; ***office address:*** Ministry of Health and Family Welfare, Nirman Bhavan, New Delhi 110 001, India.

AZAROV, Mykola; Prime Minister, Government of Ukraine; ***political career:*** Vice PM, Minister of Finance, 2004; First Dep. Prime Minister, Minister of Finance, 2006-07; Prime Minister, March 2010-; ***professional career:*** Mining Specialist; ***office address:*** Office of the Prime Minister, vul. M.Hrushevskoho 12/2, 01008 Kiev, Ukraine; ***phone:*** +380 44 226 2289; ***fax:*** +380 44 293 2093; ***e-mail:*** web@kmu.gov.ua; ***URL:*** http://www.kmu.gov.ua/.

B

BAALI, Abdallah; Ambassador, Algerian Embassy in the USA; ***born:*** October 19, 1954; ***languages:*** Arabic, English, French, Spanish; ***education:*** Diplomatic Section, National School of Administration, Algiers, Dipl., 1977; New York Univ., Dipl., Contemporary American Politics, 1987; ***professional career:*** Amb. of Algeria to Indonesia, Australia, New Zealand and Brunei Darussalam, 1992-96; Amb., Permanent Mission of Algeria to the United Nations, 1996-2005; Amb. to the USA, 2008-; ***office address:*** Algerian Embassy, 2118 Kalorama Road, NW Washington DC 20008, USA; ***phone:*** +1 202 265 2800; ***fax:*** +1 202 667 2174; ***e-mail:*** embalgus@cais.com; ***URL:*** http://www.algeria-us.org.

BABACAN, Ali; Deputy Prime Minister, Turkish Government; ***born:*** 1967, Ankara, Turkey; ***married:*** Zeynep Babacan; ***children:*** Kerem (M), Dilara (F); ***languages:*** English; ***education:*** TED Ankara College; Industrial Engineering Dept., Middle East Technical Univ.; ***party:*** Justice and Development Party, 2001-; ***political career:*** MP, 2002-; Minister of State in charge of Economy; Minister of Foreign Affairs with responsibility for EU membership negotiations, 2007; Deputy Prime Minister, 2009-; ***interests:*** economy, social problems; ***professional career:*** Industrial Engineer; ***honours and awards:*** Minister of the Year; ***recreations:*** travel; ***office address:*** Turkish Grand National Assembly, Balgat, Ankara, Turkey; ***e-mail:*** ali.babacan@hazine.gov.tr.

BACHELET, Michelle; Chilean, Under Secretary-General and Executive Director, UN Women; ***born:*** September 1951, Santiago, Chile; ***languages:*** English, French, German, Portuguese; ***party:*** Socialist Party; ***political career:*** Minister of Health, -2002; Minister of Defence, 2002-05; President, 2006-March 2010; ***professional career:*** Doctor; Under Secretary-General and Executive Director, UN Women, 2010-; ***office address:*** UN Women, 304 East 45th Street, 15th Floor, New York, NY 10017 , USA; ***URL:*** http://www.unwomen.org/.

BACHOO, Hon. Anil Kumar; Vice President, Minister of Public Infrastructure, Transport and Shipping, Government of Mauritius; ***born:*** 6 September 1953; ***education:*** Delhi Univ., BA Hons.; Mauritius Inst. of Education., Post Grad. Certificate in Education; ***party:*** Leader of Mouvement Socialiste Democrate; ***political career:*** Mem., Nat. Assembly for Flacq/Bon Accueil, 1991-95, 2005-; Minister of Commerce and Marine, 1991-93; Minister of Works, 1994-95; Minister of Public Infrastructure, Land Transport and Shipping, 2000-05; Minister of Environment and National Development Unit, 2005-08; Minister of Public Infrastructure, Land Transport and Shipping, 2008-; Vice-President; ***interests:*** social work; ***professional career:*** Dep. Rector Universal Coll., 1996-2000; ***publications:*** A Modern Approach to Hinduism; ***recreations:*** culture, philosophy; ***office address:*** Ministry of Public Infrastructure, Transport and Shipping, Moorgate House, Sir William Newton Street, Port Louis, Mauritius; ***phone:*** +230 208 0281; ***fax:*** +230 208 7149; ***e-mail:*** webmaster-mpi@mail.gov.mu; ***URL:*** http://publicinfrastructure.gov.mu/.

BACHUS, Spencer; American, Congressman, Alabama 6th District, US House of Representatives; ***born:*** 1947; ***children:*** 5; ***education:*** Auburn Univ., 1969; Univ. of Alabama Law School, 1972; ***party:*** Republican; ***political career:*** Representative, Alabama 6th District, US House of Representatives, 1992-; ***committees:*** Chmn., Financial Services; ***office address:*** House of Representatives, 442 Cannon Building, Washington, DC 20515, USA; ***phone:*** +1 202 224 3121.

BACON, Richard; Member of Parliament for South Norfolk, House of Commons; ***education:*** The King's Sch., Worcester; BSc (Hons), Politics & Economics, London Sch. of Economics; ***party:*** Conservative Party; ***political career:*** MP, Norfolk South, 2001-; ***memberships:*** Conservative Agents Employment Bd.; ***professional career:*** Man. Dir., English Word Factory 1999-; ***committees:*** Public Accounts, 2001-; European Scrutiny, 2003-07; Unopposed Bills (Panel), 2010-; ***office address:*** House of Commons, London, SW1A 0AA, United Kingdom; ***phone:*** +44 (0)20 7219 3000; ***e-mail:*** hcinfo@parliament.uk; ***URL:*** http://www.parliament.uk.

BADER GINSBURG, Ruth ; Associate Justice, US Supreme Court; ***born:*** 15 March 1933, Brooklyn, New York; ***education:*** Cornell Univ., B.A.; Harvard Law School; Columbia Law School, LL.B.; ***memberships:*** fellow, Center for Advanced Study in the Behavioral Sciences, Stanford, California, 1977-78; Women's Rights Project of the American Civil Liberties Union, 1971, Mem., General Counsel, 1973-80, Nat. Bd. of Dirs. 1974-80; ***professional career:*** law clerk, Southern District of New York, 1959-61; Research Assoc. and Assoc. Dir., Columbia Law School Project on International Procedure, 1961-63; Prof. of Law, Rutgers Univ. School of Law, 1963-72, and Columbia Law School, 1972-80; Judge, US Court of Appeals, District of Columbia Circuit, 1980-93; Associate Justice of the Supreme Court, 1993- ; ***office address:*** Supreme Court Building, One First Street, NE, Washington, DC 20543, USA; ***phone:*** +1 202 479 3211; ***fax:*** +1 202 479 2971; ***URL:*** http://www.supremecourt.gov/.

BADRIDZE, H.E. Giorgi; Ambassador, Embassy of Georgia in the UK; ***education:*** Tbilisi State Univ.; Int. Relations and European Studies Dept. of the Central European Univ. in Prague and Budapest; ***professional career:*** Amb. to the UK and Ireland, 2007-; ***office address:*** Embassy of Georgia, London, United Kingdom.

BAGIS, Egemen; Minister for EU Affairs and Chief Negotiator, Government of Turkey; ***born:*** 1970; ***married:*** Beyhan Bagis; ***children:*** 2; ***education:*** BA, Human Resources Management, MA, Public Admin., Baruch Coll., The City Univ., New York; ***party:*** Justice and Development Party; ***political career:*** MP, for Istanbul, 2002-; AK Party Vice Chmn. in charge of Foreign Affairs and Representative Offices; Foreign Policy Advisor to PM Erdogan; Chmn., Turkey-USA Inter-Parly. Friendship Caucus; Dep. Chmn., Turkish Delegation to NATO Parly. Assembly; Minister for EU Affairs and Chief Negotiator, 2009-; ***committees:*** AK Party mem. Central Executive Cttee.; AK Party, mem. Central Decision Making and Admin. Cttee.; Chmn., NATO-PA Subcttee. on Transatlantic Relations; ***honours and awards:*** Italian Cavaliere State Recognition; ***office address:*** Ministry of State, Eski Basbakanlik, Ankara, Turkey; ***phone:*** +90 (9)312 413 7000.

BAGSHAWE, Louise; MP for Corby, UK Government; ***education:*** Christ Church, Oxford Univ.; ***party:*** Conservative; ***political career:*** MP for Corby, May 2010-; ***professional career:*** Author; ***committees:*** Select Cttee. for the Dept. of Culture, Media and Sport; ***office address:*** House of Commons, London, SW1A 0AA, United Kingdom; ***phone:*** +44 (0)20 7219 3000; ***URL:*** http://www.louisebagshawe.net.

BAHA, Abdellah; Minister of State, Government of Morocco; ***born:*** 1954; ***education:*** agricultural engineering; ***political career:*** MP, 2002-; Pres., Justice, Law & Human Rights Commission, 2002-03; Sec. Gen., Parti Justice et Développement (PJD), 2004-; Vice-Pres., Chamber of Reps., 2007; Minister of State, 2012-; ***office address:*** Office of the Prime Minister, Al Méchouar, Essaid, Rabat, Morocco.

BAHR, Danny; Minister of Health, German Government; ***born:*** November 1976; ***party:*** Free Democratic Party; ***political career:*** Parly. State Sec. for the Federal Minister of Health, 2009-11; Minister of Health, 2011-; ***office address:*** Ministry of Health, BM für Gesundheit, 11017 Berlin, Germany; ***phone:*** +49 (0)30 206400; ***fax:*** +49 (0)30 206 404974; ***e-mail:*** postelle@bmg.bund.de; ***URL:*** http://www.bmg.bund.de.

BAILEY, Adrian; Member of Parliament for West Bromwich West, House of Commons; ***born:*** 11 December 1945, Salisbury, UK; ***parents:*** Edward Arthur Bailey and Sylvia Alice; ***married:*** Jill Bailey, 1989; ***education:*** Cheltenham Grammar School; Exeter Univ., BA Hons, Econ. History, 1967; Loughborough College of Librarianship, postgrad. Diploma, Librarianship, 1971; ***political career:*** Labour Candidate, South Worcester constituency, 1970, Nantwich, 1972 (both general elections), Wirral by-election, 1976, Cheshire West European seat, 1979; political organiser, Co-operative Party, 1982-2000; Mem., Sandwell Council (Rowley ward), 1991-2000, Chair of Finance, 1992, Dep. Leader of the Cncl., 1997-2000; MP, 2000-; ***interests:*** manufacturing industry, economics, mutuals and co-op policies, child protection, crime, criminal welfare; ***professional career:*** School teacher; librarian, Cheshire County Council, 1973-82; ***committees:*** Business, Innovation & Skills, 2010-; Liaison, 2010-; Jt. Cttee. on National Security Strategy, 2010-; ***recreations:*** football and cricket supporter, swimming; ***office address:*** House of Commons, London, SW1A 0AA, United Kingdom; ***phone:*** +44 (0)20 7219 6060.

BAIN, Willie; MP for Glasgow North East, British Government; ***education:*** Strathclyde Univ., Scotland; ***party:*** Labour Party, 1995-; ***political career:*** MP for Glasgow North East, Nov. 2009-; Shadow Minister, Transport, May-Oct. 2010; Shadow Minister, Environment, Food and Rural Affairs, Oct. 2010-11; Shadow Minister, Scotland, 2011-; ***interests:*** economy, welare and work, constitutional reform, environment, foreign affairs; ***office address:*** House of Commons, London, SW1A 0AA, United Kingdom; ***phone:*** +44 (0)20 7219 7527; ***e-mail:*** bainw@parliament.uk.

BAINIMARAMA, Commodore Josaia Voreqe (Frank); Prime Minister, Government of Fiji; ***education:*** Marist Brothers High School; ***political career:*** following counter-coup, Head of Interim Military Government of Fiji, 29 May-13 July 2000; Acting President, Fiji, Dec.2006-07; Prime Minister, Minister for Public Service, People's Charter for Change, Information, Provincial Development, Indigenous and Multi-Ethnic Affairs, 2007-; ***professional career:*** joined the Fijian Navy, 1975; various posts and training, 1975-82; Commander, 1982-86; Lieutenant Commander, 1986-87; Commanding Officer of the Fijian Navy, 1988; Acting Chief of Staff, 1997; Chief of Staff, 1998; Commodore, Commander of the Armed Forces, 1998-; Rear Admiral, 2002; reverted to Commodore, 2003; ***office address:*** Office of the Prime Minister, P.O. Box 2353, Government Buildings, Suva, Fiji; ***phone:*** +679 3211 201; ***fax:*** +679 3306 034; ***e-mail:*** pmsoffice@connect.com.fj.

BAIRD, Hon. John R.; Minister of Foreign Affairs, Government of Canada; ***political career:*** Minister of Community and Social Services, also Minister of Francophone Affairs, 1999; Minister Responsible for Children; Minister of Energy, Deputy House Leader and Minister Responsible for Francophone Affairs, Gov. of Ontario, 2003; Pres. of the Treasury Bd., Gov. of Canada, 2006-07; Minister of the Environment, 2007-08; Minister of Transport, Infrastructure and Communities, 2008-10; Leader of the Government in the House of Commons, 2010- Minister of Foreign Affairs, 2011-; ***office address:*** House of Commons, Parliament Buildings, Wellington Street, Ottawa, Ontario, K1A 0A6, Canada.

BAJNAI, Gordon; Leader, Together 2014; *born:* March 5 1968; *education:* MA, Corvinus Univ., Budapest; *political career:* Minister of Economy, 2007-09; Prime Minister, Apr. 2009-10; Founder and Leader, Together 2014; *professional career:* Creditum Financial Consulting Ltd.; European Bank for Reconstruction and Development (London); Man. Dir., CA IB Securities Co.; CEO, Wallis Rt., 2000-05; *office address:* National Assembly, Kossuth Lajos ter 1-3, 1055 Budapest, Hungary; *URL:* http://www.egyutt2014.hu.

BAKER, Frank; Ambassador, British Embassy in Kuwait; *professional career:* FCO, Dep. Dir., Middle East, 2007-10; Amb. to Kuwait, 2010-; *office address:* British Embassy, Arabian Gulf Street, PO Box 2, 13001 Safat, Kuwait City, Kuwait; *phone:* +965 240 3334; *fax:* +965 240 7395; *e-mail:* general@britishembassy-kuwait.org; *URL:* http://ukinkuwait.fco.gov.uk.

BAKER, George S.; Senator for Newfoundland and Labrador, Canadian Senate; *political career:* MP for Gander, Grand Falls; Minister of Veterans Affairs, also Secretary of State (Atlantic Canada Opportunities Agency), 1999-; Senator for Newfoundland and Labrador, 2002-; *office address:* Canadian Senate, Senate Building, 111 Wellington Street, Ontario, K1A 0A4, Canada.

BAKER, Norman; Member of Parliament for Lewes, House of Commons; *born:* 26 July 1957, Aberdeen; *education:* Royal Liberty Sch.; Royal Holloway Coll., Univ. of London, BA, German; *party:* Liberal Democrat Party; *political career:* MP for Lewes, 1997-; House of Commons, Lib. Dem. Environmental Campaigner, 1989-90; Lib. Dem. Shadow Environment Sec.; Shadow Environment and Food and Rural Affairs Sec., 2005-06; Shadow Sec. of the Cabinet Office and Chancellor of the Duchy of Lancaster, 2007; Shadow Sec. of State for Transport, 2007-10; Parly. Under-Sec. of State, Dept. of Transport, 2010-; *professional career:* Leader, Lewes District Cncl., 1991-97; *committees:* Chair, Economic Development and Public Transport Sub-Cttees. on East Sussex County Council, 1993-97; Environmental Audit, 1997-2000; Broadcasting, 2000-01; Jt. Cttee. on Human Rights, 2001-03; *office address:* House of Commons, London, SW1A 0AA, United Kingdom; *phone:* +44 (0)20 7219 2864; *e-mail:* bakern@parliament.uk; *URL:* http://www.normanbaker.org.uk.

BAKER, Steven; MP for Wycombe, UK Government; *party:* Conservative; *political career:* MP for Wycombe, May 2010-; *professional career:* RAF engineer; *committees:* Transport, 2010-; *office address:* House of Commons, London, SW1A 0AA, United Kingdom; *phone:* +44 (0)20 7219 3000; *e-mail:* steve.baker.mp@parliament.uk; *URL:* http://www.parliament.uk.

BAKER OF DORKING, Lord; Member of the House of Lords; *born:* 3 November 1934, Newport; *parents:* Wilfred M. Baker OBE and Amanda Baker (née Harries); *married:* Mary Elizabeth Baker (née Gray Muir), 1963; *education:* St. Paul's, Magdalen Coll., Oxford; *party:* Conservative Party; *political career:* Sec. of State for Environment, 1985-86; Sec. of State for Education and Science, 1986-89; Chmn., Conservative Party and Cllr., Duchy of Lancaster, 1989-90; Home Sec., 1990-92; Mem. of House of Lords, to date; *professional career:* Vice-Chmn., the Cartoon Museum; Chmn., Edge Foundation, 2010-; Chmn., Baking Dearing Educational Trust, 2010-; *committees:* Chmn., HoL, Information Cttee., 2002-06; Mem., Lords House Cttee., 2007-; *honours and awards:* Companion of Honour, 1992; *publications:* Unauthorised Version: Poems and their Parodies (ed.), 1990; Faber Anthology of Conservatism (ed.), 1993; Turbulent Years: My Life in Politics, 1993; Faber Book of War Poetry, 1996; Faber Book of Landscape Poetry, 1999; I Have No Gun But I Can Spit (Ed.), 1980; London Lines (ed.), 1982; Faber Book of English history In Verse (ed.), 1981; The Prime Ministers: An Irreverent Political History in Cartoons, 1995; Kings and Queens - An Irreverent Cartoon history of the Monarchy, 1996; Faber Book of War Poetry, 1996; George IV: A Life in Caricature, 2005; George III: A Life in Caricature, 2007; George Washington's War, 2009; *clubs:* Garrick; Athenaeum; *recreations:* reading, history, collecting political caricatures; *office address:* House of Lords, London, SW1A 0PW, United Kingdom; *phone:* +44 (0)20 7219 3000.

BAKEWELL, Baroness Joan, DBE; Member, House of Lords; *education:* Newnham College, Cambridge Univ.; *party:* Labour Party; *political career:* Mem., House of Lords, 2010-; *professional career:* TV, radio and print journalist, 1960-; *publications:* incl.: The Centre of the Bed, 2004; All the Nice Girls, 2009; She's Leaving Home, 2011; *office address:* House of Lords, London, SW1A 0PW, United Kingdom; *phone:* +44 (0)20 7219 3000.

BALAKRISHNAN, Dr Vivian; Minister of Environment and Water, Government of Singapore; *born:* 1961; *education:* Nat. Univ. of Singapore, Medicine, 1985; post-graduate specialist training in Ophthalmology, admitted as a Fellow of the Royal College of Surgeons of Edinburgh, 1991; *political career:* MP for Holland-Bukit Panjang GRC, 2001-; Minister of State, (National Development), 2002; Minister of State (Trade and Industry), 2003; Acting Minister for Community Development, Youth and Sports and Senior Minister of State, Ministry of Trade and Industry, 2004; Minister of Community Development, Youth and Sports and Minister responsible for entrepreneurship, 2005-11; Minister of the Environment and Water Resources, 2011-; *professional career:* Moorfields Eye Hospital, London, 1993-95;Consultant Ophthalmologist, Singapore Nat. Eye Centre; Medical Dir., Singapore Nat. Eye Centre, 1999; CEO, Singapore General Hospital, 2000-01; *office address:* Ministry of Environment, 40 Scotts Road, Singapore 228231, Singapore; *URL:* http://www.app.mewr.gov.sg.

BALDETTI, Roxanna; Vice President Guatemala, Government of Guatemala; *born:* 13 May 1962, Guatemala City, Guatemala; *education:* BA, Univ. of San Carlos, Guatemala; *party:* Patriot Party; *political career:* Congress of Guatemala, 2004-12; Vice President, 2012-; *professional career:* Elementary school teacher; Journalist; *office address:* Office of the Vice President, Palacio Nacional, 6a calle y 7a avenida, Zona 1, Guatemala City, Guatemala.

BALDOZ, Rosalinda; Secretary of Labour and Employment, Government of the Philippines; *education:* Bachelor of Arts and Science, Bachelor of Laws, and Master on National Security Administration; *political career:* Secretary of Labour and Employment, 2010-; *professional career:* Lawyer; Commissioned Officer with the Rank of Lieutenant Colonel,

Reserve Force, Philippine Army; Mediator-Arbiter, Bureau of Labor Relations (BLR); Labor Arbiter of the Nat. Labor Relations Commissions (NLRC); Dep. Exec. Dir. later Exec. Dir. of the Nat. Conciliation and Mediation Board (NCMB); Undersecretary for Labor Relations and Management Services; Administrator of the Philippine Overseas Employment Administration, (POEA); *honours and awards:* Dept. of Labor and Employment KAPWA Award; *office address:* Department of Labour and Employment, Room 107, Executive Building, San Jose Street, Intramuros, Manila, Philippines; *phone:* +63 2 527 3464; *URL:* http://www.dole.gov.ph.

BALDRY, Tony; British, Member of Parliament for Banbury, House of Commons; *born:* 1950; *parents:* Peter Baldry and Oina Baldry (née Paterson); *married:* Pippa (née Isbell), 2001; *children:* Edward (M), Honor (F); *education:* Leighton Park, MA; Univ. of Sussex, LL.B; *party:* Conservative Party; *political career:* Personal Aide to Margaret Thatcher, Oct 1974 Gen. Election, remained in the office when she became Leader of the Opposition; PPS to John Wakeham, Sec. of State for Energy; PPS, Dept. of Transport and at Foreign and Cmmw. Office, 1985-87; PPS to Lord Privy Seal, Leader of the House and Lord Pres. of the Cncl., 1987-89; Parly Under-Sec. of State for Dept. of Energy, 1990; Under-Sec. of State, Dept. of the Environment, 1990-94; Under Sec. of State, Foreign and Cmmw. Office, 1994-95; Minister of State, Ministry of Agriculture, Fisheries and Food, 1995-97; MP (Cons) for Banbury, 1983-; Second Church Estates Commissioner, 2010-; *interests:* foreign affairs, particularly Asia, Latin America and Middle East; *memberships:* Former Dpty Chmn, Conservative Group for Europe; Chmn., Conservative Parly. Mainstream; *Fellowships:* Chartered Institute of Arbitrators; Chartered Institute of Builders; Chartered Institute of Personnel and Development; Institute of Management; Institute of Directors; Architechture and Surveying Institute; Visiting Fellow, St.Antony's Coll., Oxford, 1998; Fellow of the Royal Society of Arts; Cncl. of Chatham House; Cncl. of the Overseas Development Instit.; Governor, the Cmnwlth. Instit. ; *professional career:* Research Sec., Federation of Conservative Students 1971; Barrister specialising in Construction Law, Commercial Law and Int. Arbitration, 1975-; Head of Chambers; Dir., careers publishing house 1975-; various directorships of a number of public companies in the United Kingdom and abroad; Exec. Partner, Diamond Film Partnership (UK); *committees:* fmr Chmn., Nat. Appeal Cttee. of Nat. Children's Homes; Mem., Select Cttee on Employment; Secy., All Party Hospice Support Gp.; Chmn., the House of Commons Select Cttee. on Int. Dev., 2001-05; Ecclesiastical Cttee., 2010-; *honours and awards:* Robert Schumann Silver Medal, 1975; *clubs:* Carlton; Farmers; Garrick; *office address:* House of Commons, London, SW1A 0AA, United Kingdom; *phone:* +44 (0)20 7219 4476; *fax:* +44 (0)20 7219 5826; *mobile:* +44 (0)7798 840570; *e-mail:* baldryt@parliament.uk; tonybaldry@gmail.com; *URL:* http://www.tonybaldry.com.

BALDWIN, Harriett; MP for West Worcerstershire, British Government; *party:* Conservative; *political career:* MP for West Worcestershire, May 2010-; *interests:* Pensions, economics, social enterprise, financial literacy, micro-finance; *committees:* Work and Pensions, 2010-; *office address:* House of Commons, London, SW1A 0AA, United Kingdom; *phone:* +44 (0)20 7219 3000; *e-mail:* harriett.baldwin.mp@parliament.uk; *URL:* http://www.parliament.uk.

BALDWIN, Tammy; American, Senator, US Senate; *born:* Wisconsin, US; *education:* Smith Coll., Northampton, Massachusetts, 1984; Univ. of Wisconsin Law Sch., JD, 1989-92; *party:* Republican; *political career:* Supervisor, Dane County, 1986-94; Wisconsin State Assembly, 1992; State Rep., Central and South Madison, 1993-99; Representative, Wisconsin 2nd District, US House of Representatives, 1998-; *committees:* Budget; Homeland Security & Governmental Affairs; Health, Education, Labor & Pensions; Special Cttee. on Aging; *office address:* US Senate, 1 Russel Courtyard, Washington, DC 20510, USA; *phone:* +1 202 224 5653; *URL:* http://www.baldwin.senate.gov.

BALLANTYNE, H.E. Frederick N.; Governor-General, St. Vincent and the Grenadines; *born:* 5 July 1936, St. Vincent; *parents:* Samuel Ballantyne and Olive Ballantyne; *married:* Sally-Ann, 14 December 1996; *education:* Howard Univ., Washington, DC., B.Sc. Chemistry, 1959, Magna Cum Laude, Phi Beta Kappa; Syracuse Univ., New York, MD, 1963; Rochester General Hospital, New York, Internal Medicine, 1968-69; Fellowship of Cardiology, 1970-72; Diplomate of American Board of Internal Medicine, 1972; *political career:* Governor-General of St. Vincent and the Grenadines, 2003-; *professional career:* District Medical Officer, St. Vincent, 1965-68; Chief of Medicine and Medical Dir., Kingstown General Hospital, 1971-85; Asst. Dean of Clinical Studies, St Georges Univ. Medical Sch., 1976-85; Chief Medical Officer, 1985-92; Coordinator of Visiting Specialist Programme, Kingstown General Hospital, 1982-; Consultant in Internal Medicine, 1992-; Mem., Editorial Board, Int. Academy of Clinical and Applied Thrombosis/Hemostasis, 1995-2002; Chmn. and Co-owner, Young Island Resorts; Chmn., Ballantyne Enterprises Ltd; *honours and awards:* GCMG; *office address:* Office of the Governor General, Old Montrose, Kingstown, St. Vincent and the Grenadines; *phone:* +784 456 1401; *fax:* +784 457 9710; *e-mail:* govthouse@vincysurf.com; *URL:* http://www.gov.vc/.

BALLS, Rt. Hon. Edward, MP; Shadow Chancellor of the Exchequer, House of Commons; *born:* 1967; *married:* Yvette Cooper; *public role of spouse:* MP for Normanton, Pontefract and Castleford; *party:* Labour/Co-operative ; *political career:* MP for Normanton, 2005-May 2010; Secretary of State for Children, School and Families, June 2007-May 2010; MP for Morley and Outwood, May 2010-; Shadow Secretary of State for Education, May 2010-Sept. 2010; candidate for Labour Party leadership, Sept. 2010; Shadow Secretary of State for the Home Department, Oct. 2010-11; Shadow Chancellor of the Exchequer, 2011-; *office address:* House of Commons, London, SW1P 0AA, United Kingdom.

BALÓI, Oldemiro; Minister of Foreign Affairs and Cooperation, Government of Mozambique; *political career:* Minister of Industry, Trade and Tourism, 1994-99; Minister of Foreign Affairs and Cooperation, 2008-; *professional career:* Dir., International Bank of Mozambique; *office address:* Ministry of Foreign Affairs and Co-operation, C.P. 2787, Avenida Julius Nyerere 4, Maputo, Republic of Mozambique; *phone:* +258 1 491762; *fax:* +258 1 494070; *e-mail:* minec@zebra.uem.mz; *URL:* http://www.minec.gov.mz.

BAN, Ki-Moon; Secretary General, United Nations; ***born:*** 1944, Republic of Korea; ***languages:*** French; ***education:*** Seoul National Univ., BA, international relations; Kennedy School of Gov., Harvard Univ., MA, public administration; ***political career:*** Advisor to Foreign Minister, 1992; Vice Minister for Foreign Affairs, 2000-01; Minister of Foreign Affairs and Trade, 2004-06; ***professional career:*** various positions with UN since 1975, including: First Sec., ROK's Permanent Mission to the UN, Dir. of UN Division, Seoul; Chmn., Prep. Commission for the Comprehensive Nuclear Test Ban Org., 1999; Chef de Cabinet, ROK Presidency of General Assembly, 2001-02; Secretary-General, United Nations, 2007-; ***office address:*** UN Headquarters, First Ave. at 46th Street, New York, NY 10017, USA; ***URL:*** http://www.un.org.

BANDA, Joyce; President, Government of Malawi; ***born:*** 1950; ***party:*** The People's Party; ***political career:*** Minister for Gender, Children's Affairs and Community Services, 2004-06; Minister of Foreign Affairs, 2006-09; Vice-President of Malawi, 2009-12; President of Malawi, 2012-; ***professional career:*** CEO, the Joyce Banda Foundation for Better Education; ***office address:*** Office of the President, Private Bag 301, Lilongwe 3, Malawi; ***URL:*** http://www.malawi.gov.mw/.

BANGGUO, Wu; Chairman, National People's Congress of China; ***born:*** July 1941, Anhui Province, China; ***education:*** Tsinghua Univ., Dept. of Radio Electronics; ***political career:*** Mem., State Cncl., CPC, Leading Party Group, 1999-; Mem., 16th CPC, Central Cttee., 2002-; Mem., 16th CPC Central Cttee., Politboro, 2002-13; Mem., 16th CPC, Central Cttee., Politboro, Standing Cttee., 2002-; Chmn., 10th Standing Cttee.of the National People's Congress, 2003-; ***office address:*** National People's Congress, Great Hall of the People, 100805 Beijing, China.

BANKS, Gordon, MP; MP for Ochil and South Perthshire, House of Commons; ***born:*** 1955; ***party:*** Labour; ***political career:*** MP, Ochil and South Perthshire, 2005-; Shadow Minister, Business, Innovation and Skills, 2010-11; Shadow Minister, Scotland, 2012-; ***office address:*** House of Commons, London, SW1P 0AA, United Kingdom.

BANNSIDE, Lord Ian Richard Kyle, DD, MP, MEP, FRGS; British, Member, House of Lords; ***born:*** 1926; ***parents:*** Rev., James Kyle Paisley and Isabel Paisley (née Turnbull); ***married:*** Eileen Emily Paisley (née Cassells); ***children:*** Kyle (M), Ian (M), Sharon (F), Rhonda (F), Cherith (F); ***education:*** Tech. High School; S. Wales Bible Coll.; Reformed Presbyterian Theol. Coll. Belfast; Ordained, 1946; ***party:*** Democratic Unionist Party; ***political career:*** Mem., Northern Ireland Parliament (Stormont), Bannside, County Antrim, 1970-72, Leader of the Opposition, 1972; MP, Antrim North, 1970-2010; Mem., Northern Ireland Assembly, 1973-74; Mem., Constitutional Convention, 1975-76; Mem., of European Parliament for Northern Ireland, 1979-; Mem., Second Northern Ireland Assembly, 1982-86; MP, Antrim North, 1997-; Mem., North Antrim, Northern Ireland Assembly, 2000-10; Leader (co-founder), Democratic Unionist Party, 1971-; First Minister, Northern Ireland Assembly, May 2007-May 2008; Mem. House of Lords, 2010-; ***memberships:*** International Cultural Soc. of Korea; ***professional career:*** Minister Martyrs Memorial Free Presbyterian Church, 1946- ; Moderator, Free Presbyterian Church, Ulster, 1951; Editor, The Revivalist, 1950-; ***committees:*** Chmn., Public Accounts Cttee., 1972; mem., Rex Cttee. and Political Cttee.; Chmn., Agriculture and Privileges Cttees., 1983-86; ***honours and awards:*** Hon. D.D. Bob Jones Univ.; SC. FGRS; ***publications:*** History of the 1859 Revival, 1959; Christian Foundations, 1960; Exposition of the Epistle to Romans, 1968; Billy Graham and the Church of Rome, 1970; The Massacre of St. Bartholomew, 1974; America's Debt to Ulster, 1976; ***office address:*** House of Lords, London, SW1A 0PW, United Kingdom; ***phone:*** +44 (0)20 7219 3000; ***URL:*** http://www.parliament.com.

BAPPOO, Hon. Sheilabai; Mauritian, Minister of Women's Rights, Child Development and Family Welfare, Government of Mauritius; ***born:*** 1947; ***education:*** Henry Boswell and Queen Elizabeth College, School Certificate; Diploma in Home Economics; ***political career:*** joined MMM Party, 1970, President, 1973; candidate, General Election, 1976; elected Municipal Councellor, MMM Beau Bassin/Rose Hill, 1977-78; joined MSM Party, 1983; MP, 1983-; Minister for Women's Rights and Family Welfare, 1983-86; Minister of Labour and Industrial Relations, Women's Rights and Family Welfare, 1986-; President, Women's Wing of the MSM; Minister of Social Security, National Solidarity and Senior Citizens Welfare and Reform Institutions, 2005-10; Minister of Women's Rights, Child Development and Family Welfare, 2010-; ***professional career:*** Teacher,1966-83 ; ***office address:*** Ministry of Women, Family Welfare & Child Development, C.S.K Building, Corner Remy Ollier/Emmanuel, Anquetil Streets, Port Louis, Mauritius; ***phone:*** +230 240 1377; ***fax:*** +230 240 7717; ***e-mail:*** mwfwcd@mail.gov.mu; ***URL:*** http://women.gov.mu.

BARAKA, Nizar; Minister of Economy & Finance, Government of Morocco; ***education:*** Unic. of Aix-Marseille, France, Ph.D, economics; ***party:*** Istiqal Party; ***political career:*** joined Ministry of Finance, 1996. Various posits. incl. Head, Economic Watch Services, Head, Macro-Analysis, 2006, Dep. Dir., Financial Research & Forecasts, Ministry of Finance & Privatizations; Minister of General & Economic Affairs, 2007-11; Minister of Economy & Finance, 2011-; ***professional career:*** lecturer, Univ. Mohammed V., Rabat; ***office address:*** Ministry of Economy & Finance, Ministry of Economic and Finance, Avenue Muhammad V, Rabat-Maroc, Morocco; ***phone:*** +212 537 763171; ***URL:*** http://www.finances.gov.ma/.

BARAKAUSKAS, Dailis Alfonsas; Minister of the Interior, Government of the Republic of Lithuania; ***born:*** 29 June 1952, Pakruojis District, Republic of Lithuania; ***languages:*** English, Russian, Latvian; ***education:*** Dip.Engineering Kaunas Univ. of Technology, 1970-75; Dip.Economics Vilnius Univ.1989-90; Training course in Breda, Chamber of Commerce and Industry, 1992; Training Courses in Chamber of Commerce and Industry in Germany, Sweden, Great Britain, and the Netherlands, 1993-96; Program on Investment Appraisal and Management, 1999; ***political career:*** Minister of Transport and Communications, 2002; Minister of the Interior, 2012-; ***memberships:*** Mem. of the Presidium of the Association of Lithuanian Regional Chambers of Commerce and Industry, 1992-95 ; Mem. of the Cncl. of the Directorate of the Chambers of Commerce of Belgium and the Baltic States, 1993-97 ; Mem. of the Cncl. of International Chamber of Commerce Lietuva, 1993-98 ; Mem. of the Presidium of Association of Lithuanuan Chambers of Commerce, Industry and Crafts, 1996-00 ; Mem. of the Siauliai, 2000; ***professional career:*** Siauliai Machine Tools Enterprise: Forman, Engineer-programmer, Head of the Program Department, Deputy Cheif Engineer, 1975-89; Director for Marketing and External Commerce of the Enterprise, 1990-91; Director of Saiuliai Regional Chamber of Commerce and Industry, 1992-96; Director General of Chamber of Commerce, Industry, and Crafts of Siauliai, 1999-00; Member of the Seimas of the Republic of Lithuania, 2000-; ***committees:*** Mem. of the Seimas of the Republic of Lithuania; Mem. of the Economic Committee of the Seimas of the Republic of Lithuanaia; Mem. of the European Affairs Committee of the Seimas of the Republic of Lithuania; Head of the Inter-parliamentary Relations Group of the Seimas of the Republic of Lithuania with the United Kingdom of Great Britain and Northern Ireland; Deputy Chairman of the Petitions Commission of the Seimas of the Republic of Lithuania, 2000-; ***office address:*** Ministry of Interior, Sventaragop 2, 2754 Vilnius, Lithuania; ***phone:*** +370 2 271 7130; ***URL:*** http://www.vrm.lt.

BARCLAY, Stephen; MP for North East Cambridgeshire, UK Government; ***education:*** Peterhouse, Cambridge Univ.; The College of Law, Chester, IK; ***party:*** Conservative; ***political career:*** MP for North East Cambridgeshire, May 2010-; ***committees:*** Public Accounts, 2010-; ***office address:*** House of Commons, London, SW1A 0AA, United Kingdom; ***phone:*** +44 (0)20 7219 3000; ***URL:*** http://www.parliament.uk.

BARKER, Gregory; Minister of State, Department for Energy and Climate Change, UK Government; ***married:*** Celeste, divorced 2008; ***education:*** Steyning Grammar Sch.; Lancing Coll; BA (Hons), Modern History, Econ. History & Politics, London Univ.; ***party:*** Conservative Party; ***political career:*** MP, Bexhill & Battle, 2001-; Opposition Whip, 2003-05; Shadow Environment Minister, 2005-08; Shadow Climate Change Minister, 2008-10; Minister of State, Department of Energy and Climate Change, 2010-; ***professional career:*** Dir., Daric plc, 1998-2001; ***committees:*** Mem., Environmental Audit Select Cttee., 2001-05, 2007-10; Broadcasting, 2003-05; ***office address:*** House of Commons, London, SW1A 0AA, United Kingdom; ***phone:*** +44 (0)20 7219 3000; ***e-mail:*** hcinfo@parliament.uk; ***URL:*** http://www.parliament.uk.

BARNETT, Hon. Colin James ; Premier, Government of Western Australia; ***born:*** 15 July 1950, Perth, Australia; ***education:*** Univ. of Western Australia, Masters, Economics; ***political career:*** Mem. for Cottesloe, Western Australian Legislative Assembly, 1990-; Deputy Leader, Western Australian Liberal Party, 1992-2001, Leader, 2001-05, 2008-; Minister for Resources Development and Energy, Minister for Education, Minister for Tourism, 1993-2001; Premier, Western Australia, 2008-; ***professional career:*** Research Officer, Australian Bureau of Statistics, 1973-75; Lecturer in Economics, Western Australian Instit. of Technology (now Curtin Univ. of Technology), 1975-1981; seconded to the Confed. of Western Australian Industry, founding editor of Western Australian Economic Review, and chief economist, 1981-85; Exec. Dir., Western Australian Chamber of Commerce and Industry; ***office address:*** Office of the Premier, 24th Floor, 197 St. George's Terrace, Perth, Western Australia 6000, Australia; ***phone:*** +61 8 9222 9888; ***fax:*** +61 8 9322 1213; ***e-mail:*** wa-government@dpc.wa.gov.au; ***URL:*** http://www.premier.wa.gov.au/.

BARNETT, H.E. Robin; Ambassador, British Embassy in Poland; ***professional career:*** Director, UK Visas 2002-06; British Ambassador to Romania, June 2006-11; Amb. to Poland, 2011-; ***office address:*** British Embassy, Aleje Roz No 1, 00-556 Warsaw, Poland; ***phone:*** +48 22 628 1001; ***fax:*** +48 22 621 7161; ***e-mail:*** britemb@it.com.pl; ***URL:*** http://ukinpoland.fco.gov.uk/en.

BARNIER, Michel; French, Commissioner for Internal Market and Services, European Commission; ***born:*** 1951; ***parents:*** Jean Barnier and Denise Barnier (née Durand); ***married:*** Isobelle Barnier (née Altnaver); ***languages:*** English; ***education:*** Ecole Supérieure de Commerce, Diploma, 1972; ***political career:*** Mem., Savoie General Cncl., 1973; elected to the National assembly as Dep. for Savoie, 1978-93; Chmn., Savoie Gen. Cncl., 1982; worked in private office of Min. for Youth and Sport; Min. of Environment 1993-95; Ministre délégué aux affaires européennes, up to 1997; Senator for Savoie, 1997-; Chmn., French Assn. of the Cncl. of European Municipalities and Regions, 1997-; Pres., Senate Delegation for the EU, 1998-; European Cmn., Regional Policy, 1999-; Minister of Foreign Affairs, to 2005; Minister of Agriculture and Fisheries, 2007-09; European Commissioner for Internal Market and Services, 2010-; ***interests:*** International and European environment; ***memberships:*** Founder, Eco-Croissance (Ecological Growth) Assn., 1992; ***committees:*** Pres. of the Cttee. supporting the candidature and then the organization of the Sixteenth Winter Olympic Games of Albertville and Savoie with Jean-Claude Killy, 1982-92; Special Rapporteur to the National Assembly of the Finance Cttee. for the budget of the Ministry of the Environment and Prevention of Major Technological and Natural Hazards, 1988-93; ***trusteeships:*** Pres., Fondation Internationale d'Action Culturelle eu Nontapre (FACIN); ***publications:*** Vive la Politique 1985; Le défi écologique chacun pour tous 1990; L'Atlas des risques majeurs 1992; ***recreations:*** skiing, jogging; ***office address:*** European Commission, rue de la Loi 200, B-1049 Brussels, Belgium; ***phone:*** +32 (0)2 299 1111; ***URL:*** http://www.europa.eu.

BARON, John; Member of Parliament for Basildon and Billericay, House of Commons; ***born:*** 21 June 1959, Redhill, Surrey; ***parents:*** Raymond Arthur Ernest and Katherine Ruby; ***education:*** Queen's College, Taunton, 1975-77; Jesus Coll., Cambridge; ***party:*** Conservative Party; ***political career:*** MP, Billericay, 2001-10; MP, Basildon and Billericay, 2010-; Shadow Minister for Health, 2003-07; Opposition Whip, 2007-10; ***interests:*** law and order, health, freedom of speech, Europe, treasury, small business; ***memberships:*** Securities Inst.; ***professional career:*** Army, 1984-88; Dir., Henderson Private Investors and then Rothschild Asset Management, 1988-2001; ***committees:*** Foreign Affairs, 2010-; ***recreations:*** tennis, walking, cycling, history; ***office address:*** House of Commons, London, SW1A 0AA, United Kingdom; ***phone:*** +44 (0)20 7219 8138; ***fax:*** +44 (0)20 7219 1743; ***e-mail:*** baronj@parliament.co.uk; ***URL:*** http://www.johnbaron.co.uk.

BARON, Dr Peter; Executive Director, International Sugar Organization; ***born:*** Germany; ***education:*** Germany, Agricultural Economic Degree; ***political career:*** Min. of Agriculture, Food and Forestry, German Govt., Bonn; ***professional career:*** Jr. Lecturer, Technical Univ., Munich, 1967-71; Chmn., UN Sugar Conference, 1992; Exec. Dir., International Sugar Organization, 1994-; ***honours and awards:*** Officer's Cross of the Order of Merit of the Federal Republic of Germany; Officer of the Order of Don Cristobal Colon, (Dominican

Republic); Commander of the Order of the Two Niles, (Sudan); Elected as International Personality 2006 by MasterCana, Brazil; *office address:* International Sugar Organization, 1 Canada Square, Canary Wharf, London, E14 5AA, United Kingdom.

BARRASSO, John; Senator for Wyoming, US Senate; *born:* July 21 1952; *education:* Georgetown Univ., B.Sc., 1974, M.D., 1978; *political career:* Wyoming State Senate, 2002-2007; appointed US Senator, 2007-08; elected US Senator, 2008-; *memberships:* Pres., Wyoming Medical Society; Pres., National Association of Physician Broadcasters, 1988-1989; *professional career:* Casper Orthopedic Associates, 1983- 2007; Chief of Staff, Wyoming Medical Center; *committees:* Energy & Natural Resources; Environment & Public Works; Indian Affairs Cttee.; Foreign Relations; *office address:* US Senate, 307 Dirksen Senate Office Building, Washington, DC 20510, USA; *phone:* +1 202 224 6441; *fax:* +1 202 224 1724; *URL:* http://www.barrasso.senate.gov.

BARRON, Kevin; British, MP for Rother Valley, House of Commons; *born:* 1946, Tadcaster, UK; *parents:* Richard and Edna; *married:* Carol (née McGrath); *children:* Robert Edward (M), Amy Louise (F), Emma Elizabeth (F); *education:* Ruskin Coll., Oxford; *political career:* Parly. Private Sec. to Leader of the Labour Party, Neil Kinnock MP, 1985-88; Chmn., Yorkshire Group of Labour MPs, 1987-; Shadow Minister for Energy, 1988-92; Shadow Employment Minister, responsible for health and safety, 1993-94; responsible for training, regeneration, 1994-95; Originated Private Members' Bill to ban advertising and promotion of tobacco products, 1993, 1994; Shadow Health Minister, Oct 95-Jul 96; Shadow Minister for Public Health, Jul 96-Apr 97; Chmn., All-Party Group on Pharmaceutical Industry, Chmn., All-Party Group on Smoking and Health, May 1997-; MP (Lab) for Rother Valley, 1987-; *interests:* health, public health, environment, intelligence, security; *memberships:* Rotherham and Dist. TUC (Pres.); NUM delegate for Maltby Colliery; Vice Pres., Combined Heat and Power Assn; *professional career:* Coalminer; *committees:* Mem., House of Commons Select Cttee., on Energy, 1983-85; Mem., House of Commons Select Cttee. on the Environment; Chmn., PLP Health Cttee.; Mem., Intelligence and Security Cttee., July 97-2005; Chair, APP British/Bulgaria , 1997-; Chmn., Food Standards Agency Cttee., Feb 99-March 99; Chair All Party Connecting Communities, 2002-07; Chair, Health Select Cttee., 2005-10; Liason Cttee., 2005-; Standards & Privileges Cttee., 2005-10, Chair, 2010-; Chair, All Party Film Grp., 2005-; Chair, All Party Earth Sciences Grp, 2005-2010; Vice Chair, Royal Soc. for the Promotion of Health, 2007-; Vice Pres., Royal Soc. of Health, 2006-; Chair, APPG Pharmacy Group, 2010-; Co-Chair, All Party Health Group, 2010-; *trusteeships:* Trustee/Dir., National Coal Mining Museum for England; *honours and awards:* Privy Council; *recreations:* family outings, fishing, film, football; *office address:* House of Commons, London, SW1A 0AA, United Kingdom; *phone:* +44 (0)20 7219 4432; *e-mail:* barronk@parliament.uk; *URL:* http://www.rothervalley.info.

BARROSO, José Manuel, M.Sc. (Political Science); LL.B; Portuguese, President, European Commission; *born:* 23 March 1956; *parents:* Luís Barroso and Maria Elisabete Durão; *married:* Maria Margarida Pinto Ribeiro de Sousa Uva Barroso; *children:* Luis (M), Guilherme (M), Francisco (M); *education:* Lisbon Univ., LL.D Hons., 1978; Univ. of Geneva, Master, Political Science, 1981; European Univ. Inst., Univ. of Geneva, Dipl.; *political career:* MP (PSD), Lisbon, 1985-87; Secy. of State for Home Affairs, 1985-87; MP, Viseu, 1987 and 1991; Secy. of State for Foreign Affairs and Co-operation 1987-92; Minister of Foreign Affairs, 1992-95; MP, Lisbon, 1995-; Mem., National Council, PSD; Chmn., Commission for Foreign Affairs of the Portuguese Parliament, 1995-99; Party Leader, PSD, 1999-2004; Chmn., PSD Dept. for International Relations; Prime Minister of Portugal, 2002-04; Pres., European Commission, 2004-; *memberships:* National Council of the Social Democratic Party (PSD); *professional career:* Lecturer, Faculty of Law, Lisbon Univ., 1978-; Lecturer, Political Science Dept., Geneva Univ., 1981-85; Visiting Scholar, Univ. of Georgetown, Washington DC, 1985; Visiting Prof., Georgetown Univ., Washington., Dept. of Government, School for Foreign Service, 1996-98; Hd., Dept. of International Relations, Universidade Lusíada, Lisbon, 1995-99, Prof. of International Relations; Leader, International IDEA (Inst. for Democracy and Electoral Assistance), mission to Bosnia, 1996; Advisor of UN to the Project for Peace Process in Africa (Tanzania), Oct. 1997; Ed. Revistat de Ciência Política; *honours and awards:* Recipient of more than 20 decorations including Portugal's Grã-Cruz da Ordem Militar de Cristo, 1996; *publications:* contrib. to collective works, encyclopaedias and international scientific journals, Governmental System and Party System, (joint), 1980; Le Système Politique Portugais face à i'Intégration Européene, 1983; Política de Cooperação, 1990; A Política Externa Portuguesa 1992-93; A Política Externa Portuguesa 1994-95; Uma Certa Ideia de Europa, 1999; Uma Ideia para Portugal, 2000; Mudar de Modelo, 2002; Reformar: Dois Anos de Governo, 2004; *office address:* European Commission, rue de la Loi 200, B-1049 Brussels, Belgium; *URL:* http://ec.europa.eu/index_en.htm.

BARROW, Dean Oliver; Belizean, Prime Minister, Belize Government; *born:* 1951; *education:* Univ. of the West Indies, LLB 1973; Norman Manley Law School, Kingston, Jamaica, Legal Education Cert. 1975; Univ. of Miami School of Law, LLM 1981; Center for Advanced International Studies, Univ. of Miami, MA 1982; *party:* United Democratic Party; *political career:* Mem, House of Reps., 1984-; Minister of Foreign Affairs and Economic Development, 1984-86; Attorney General and Minister of Foreign Affairs and Economic Development, 1986-89; Dep. Prime Minister; Attorney General and Minister of Foreign Affairs and Economic Development 1993-98; Prime Minister, 2008 - ; *professional career:* Belize Public Service, Clerk 1969-70; Assoc., Lindo's Law Firm, Belize 1975-77, Partner 1977; Partner, Barrow and Williams Law Firm, 1989-93; *office address:* Office of the Prime Minister, New Administrative Building, (P O Box 173), Belmopan, Belize; *phone:* +501 (0)822 2346; *fax:* +501 (0)822 3323; *e-mail:* primeminister@belize.gov.bz.

BARROW, Timothy ; Ambassador, British Embassy in Russia; *professional career:* Joined FCO, 1986; Ambassador to Ukraine, 2006-08; UK Rep Brussels, Representative to the Political and Security Committee of the European Union and Ambassador to the Western European Union, 2008-2011; Ambassador to Russia, 2011-; *office address:* British Embassy, Smolenskaya Naberezhnaya 10, 121099 Moscow, Russia; *fax:* +380 44 490 3662; *e-mail:* ukembinf@sovam.cpm; *URL:* http://www.ukinrussia.fco.gov.uk/en.

BARSON, Jackie, MBE; High Commissioner to Papua New Guinea, British High Commission; *professional career:* career diplomat; joined FCO, 1979; various postings incl. Overseas postings to Prague, Belgrade, Abu Dhabi, Malaysia, Copenhagen, Ottawa,

Brussels, Athens; Dep. Head of Mission, Belmopan, 2004; Dep. Dir. of Protocol & Assist. Marshal of the London Diplomatic corps, 2005-09; Commissioner to Papua New Guinea, 2010-; *office address:* British High Commission Port Moresby, Sec 411, Lot 1&2, Kiroki Street, Waigani, NCD, Port Moresby, Papua New Guinea.

BARWELL, Gavin; MP for Croydon Central, UK Government; *party:* Conservative; *political career:* Councillor, Croydon Council 1998-2010; MP for Croydon Central, May 2010-; PPS to Greg Clark, 2011-12; to Michael Gove, Sec. of State for Education, 2012-; *office address:* House of Commons, London, SW1A 0AA, United Kingdom; *phone:* +44 (0)20 7219 3000; *e-mail:* gavin.barwell.mp@parliament.uk; *URL:* http://www.parliament.uk.

BASCI, Dr Erdem; Governor, Central Bank of the Republic of Turkey; *born:* 1966, Ankara, Turkey; *education:* Middle East Technical Univ., 1987, Electrical & Electronics Engineering; Bilkent Univ., MBA, MA, Economics; John Hopkins Univ., MA, Economics; Bilkent Univ., Economics, Ph.D, 1993; *professional career:* Assist. Prof., Bilkent Univ., 1995-2003, Associate Prof., 1999; Dep. Gov., Central Bank of Turkey, 2003-11, Governor, 2011-; *office address:* Central Bank of the Republic of Turkey, Istiklal Cad 10, Ulus, 06100 Ankara, Turkey; *phone:* +90 312 507 5000.

BASESCU, Traian; Romanian, President of Romania; *born:* 4 April 1951, Basarabi, Constanta, Romania; *languages:* English; *education:* Mircea cel Batran Inst., Faculty of Navigation, commercial section, graduate, 1976; Norwegian Acad., Advanced Courses of Management, Industry of Maritime Transport, Norwegian Scholarship, 1995; *party:* Democratic Party; *political career:* Under-Sec. of State, Head, Naval Transportation Dept., Ministry of Transportation, 1990-91; Minister of Transport, 1991-92; Dep., Democratic Party, 1992-96; Vice-Pres., Cmn. for Industry and Services of the Chamber of Deps., 1992-96; Co-ordinating Dir., Petre Roman's electoral campaign, 1996; Minister of Transport, 1996-2000; Mayor of Bucharest; President of Romania, 2004-; *professional career:* Navy Officer, heavy tonnage ships, NAVROM Constanta, 1976-81; Master Mariner, 1987; Head, NAVROM Agency, Antwerpen, Belgium, 1987-89; *office address:* Office of the President, Palatul Cotroceni, Blvd Geniului 1, 76238 Bucharest, Romania; *URL:* http://www.presidency.ro/?lang=en.

BASHIR, Prof. Marie, AC, CVO; Governor, New South Wales; *education:* University of Sydney, Bachelors degree in medicine and surgery, 1956; *political career:* Governor, New South Wales, 2001-; *interests:* refugees, the people of Indo-China, human rights, Australian Aboriginal people; *memberships:* Amnesty International; Life mem., National Trust of Australia; Hon. mem., UN Development Fund for Women; Tandanya National Aboriginal Cultural Centre; Fac. of Community Child Health, Royal Aust. Coll. of Physicians, 1993-; *professional career:* Foundation Dir., Rivendell Royal Prince Alfred Hospital, 1972-87; Area Dir., Community Health Services, Central Sydney Health Service, 1987-93; Clinical Prof. of Psychiatry, Univ. of Sydney, 1993-2001; Area Dir. of Mental Health Services Central Sydney; 1994-2001; Senior Consultant Psychiatrist, Aboriginal Medical Services of Kempsey and Redfern,1996-2001; *trusteeships:* Patron, Sydney Symphony and Opera; *honours and awards:* numerous including: Fellow, Royal Australian and New Zealand Coll. of Psychiatrists, 1971-; Officer of the Order of Australia AO, 1988; Companion of the Order of Australia AC, 2001; Hon. Colonel, The Royal New South Wales Regiment, 2001; Hon. Fellow, Aust. Coll. of Health Service Exec., 2001; Dep. Prior and Dame of the Order of St. John, 2001; Hon. Fellow, Australiasian Coll. of Biomedical Scientists, 2002; Hon. Air Commodore, Sq. 22., Royal Aust. Air Force., 2002; Centenary Medal, 2003; Commander of the Order of the Cedars, Lebanon, 2004; elected one of Australia's 'Living Treasures', 2004; Hon. Fellow, Aust. Coll. of Legal Medicine, 2004; Commander of the Royal Victorian Order, CVO, 2006; Paul Harris Fellow Award, 2006; Honorary Doctorates from five universities; Chancellor, Univ. of Sydney, 2007; Chevalier dans l'Ordre National de la Légion d' Honneur, 2009; *recreations:* Australian social and political history, women's health, early Aust. antique furniture, classical music, opera, Aboriginal art, growing camellias; *office address:* Office of the Governor, Chief Secretary's Building, Level 3, 121 Macquarie Street, Sydney, New South Wales 2000, Australia.

BASINDWA, Mohammed Salem; Prime Minister, Interim Government of Yemen; *political career:* former member of General People's Congress; several cabinet positions including foreign and information minister; left GPC to become independent opposition figure; Interim Prime Minister, Nov. 2011-; *office address:* Office of the Prime Minister, Sana'a, Yemen.

BASS, Karen; Congresswoman, US House of Representatives; *party:* Democrat; *political career:* Congresswoman, California 33rd District, 2010-; *committees:* Budget; Foreign Affairs; *office address:* 408 Cannon HOB, Washington DC 20515, USA; *phone:* +1 202 225 7084; *URL:* http://karenbass.house.gov/.

BASSAM OF BRIGHTON, Rt. Hon. Lord; Lords Chief Whip, House of Lords; *born:* 11 June 1953, Kingston-Upon-Hull; *parents:* Sydney Stevens and Enid Bassam; *married:* Jill Whittaker; *children:* Thomas Harry Whittaker (M), Lauren Stephanie Whittaker (F), Ellen Rose Whittaker (F); *public role of spouse:* Solicitor; *education:* BA Hon, History, Sussex Univ.; MA (Social Work), Kent Univ.; *party:* Labour Party & Cooperative Party; *political career:* Cllr. Brighton Cncl, 1983-96; Brighton & Hove, 1996-99; Leader of Cncl. from 1987-99; Officer, Camden Cncl.; GLC; AA Sec. AMA 1988/97; Head of Environmental Services 1997-98; Parly.-under-Sec., 1999-2001; Govt. Whip, June 2001-08; Chief Whip, 2008-10; Lords Chief Whip, 2010-; *interests:* local government, health, housing, crime and policing, education; *honours and awards:* Peerage 1997; Hon. Alumni Fellow, Univ. of Sussex, 2001; Privy Counsellor; *publications:* Various journal articles; *clubs:* Preston Village Cricket Club; Supporter, Brighton & Hove Albion; *recreations:* cricket, running, travel, watching Brighton & Hove Albion FC and Brove AFC; *office address:* House of Lords, London, SW1A 0PW, United Kingdom; *phone:* +44 (0)20 7219 4918; *fax:* +44 (0)20 7219 5979; *e-mail:* bassam@parliament.uk; stevebassam@msn.com.

BATEMAN, H. E. Peter; Ambassador, Embassy of the United Kingdom in Azerbaijan; *born:* 23 December, 1955; *languages:* French, German, Japanese, Spanish; *education:* St. Peters, Oxford, Modern Languages, 1978 ; *professional career:* European Commission civil servant, 1979-84; Diplomatic Service, 1984-; Head of Commercial Section, Berlin, 1993-98;

Tokyo, 1998-2002; Adj. Exec. Dir. of International Financial Services, City of London, 2003-05; Amb., UK Emb. in Bolivia, 2005-07; Amb., UK Emb. in Luxembourg, 2007-11; UK Amb. to Azerbaijan, 2011-; ***office address:*** Embassy of the United Kingdom, 45 Khagani Street, AZ1010 Baku, Azerbaijan; ***phone:*** +994 (0)12 197 5190; ***URL:*** http://ukinazerbaijan.fco.gov.uk/en.

BAUCUS, Max; Senator for Montana, US Senate; ***born:*** 11 December 1941, Helena, MT, USA; ***married:*** Wanda Baucus (née Minge); ***children:*** Zeno (M); ***education:*** BA, Law degree, Stanford Univ., 1967; ***political career:*** Rep. of Missoula, Montana State Legislature, 1973-74; US House of Representatives, 1974-78; Senator for Montana, US Senate, 1978-; ***professional career:*** US Securities and Exchange Cmn.; Law Practice, Missoula, USA, 1971; Exec. Dir., Cttee. Coordinator, Montana's 1972 Constitutional Convention; ***committees:*** Chmn., Finance; Agriculture; Environment & Public Works; Taxation; ***office address:*** United States Senate, 511 Hart Senate Office Building, Washington, DC 20510, USA; ***phone:*** +1 202 224 2651; ***fax:*** +1 202 224 2262; ***URL:*** http://www.baucus.senate.gov.

BAUDENBACHER, Prof. Dr. Carl; Swiss, President, EFTA Court; ***born:*** 1 September 1947; ***languages:*** German, English, French, Italian, Spanish; ***education:*** University of Berne, 1967-71, Dr iur, 1978; University of Zurich, Habilitation, 1983; ***interests:*** Economic law; Human rights; Organisations; State responsibility; EEA and EU law; Intellectual property law; Competition law; ***professional career:*** *academic career:* Universities of Berne and Zurich, Assistant, 1972-78; Universities of Bochum, Berlin, Tübingen, Marburg, Saarbrücken, Visiting Professor, 1984-86; Max Planck Institute of Intellectual Property Law, Alexander von Humboldt Scholar, 1979-81; University of Kaiserslautern, Professor of private, labour, commercial and economic law, 1987; University of St Gallen, Chair of private, commercial and economic law, 1987-; University of St Gallen Institute of European Law, Managing Director, 1991; University of Geneva, Visiting Professor, 1991; St Gallen International Competition Law Forum, Chairman, 1993-; University of St Gallen, postgraduate program in European and international business law executive MBL-HSG, Founder and Director, 1995; University of Texas School of Law, Visiting Professor, 1993-2002; *diplomatic career:* Expert Adviser to the Liechtenstein Government in EEA matters, 1990-94; *judicial career:*Legal Secretary, Bulach District Court, 1982-84; Member of the Supreme Court of the Principality of Liechtenstein, 1994-95; Judge, EFTA Court 1995-, President, 2003-; ***publications:*** More than 20 books on national, European and international law; Articles: European Law Review; Fordham International Law Journal; Texas International Law Journal; European Law Reporter; Common Market Law Review; Europäische Zeitschrift für Wirtschaftsrecht; Der Betrieb; GRUR International; ***office address:*** EFTA Court, 1, rue du Fort Thüngen, L-1499 , Luxembourg; ***phone:*** +352 42 108 322; ***fax:*** +352 43 4389 422; ***e-mail:*** carl.baudenbacher@eftacourt.lu; ***URL:*** http://www.eftacourt.lu.

BAY LARSEN, Lars; Judge, Court of Justice of the European Union; ***born:*** 1953; ***education:*** Univ. of Copenhagen, political science, law; ***professional career:*** Ministry of Justice; Lecturer, Family Law, Univ. of Copenhagen, 1984-91, Assoc. Prof., 1991-96; Head of Section, Danish Bar Assn., 1985-86; Head of Section, Ministry of Justice, 1986-91; called to the Bar, 1991; Head of Police Dept., 1995-99; Head of Law Dept., Ministry of Justice, 2000-03; Judge, Supreme Court, 2003-06; Judge, Court of Justice of the EU, 2006-; ***office address:*** Court of Justice of the European Union, Rue du Fort Niedergrunewald, L-2925, Luxembourg.

BAYLET, Jean-Michel; French, Leader, Parti Radical Gauche; ***born:*** 1946; ***education:*** Toulouse Univ., Faculty of Law and Social Sciences; ***political career:*** co-founder, with Robert Fabre, of the Radical Left Movement (MRG), Nat. Sec., 1973, Vice-Pres., 1978, Pres., 1983; elected Mayor of Valence d'Agen, 1977-; MP for Tarn-et-Garonne, 1978, re-elected, 1988; Pres., Tarn-et-Garonne Gen. Cncl., 1985; Senator for Tarn-et-Garonne, 1986; Sec. of State to the Min. of Foreign Relations, 1984-86; Sec. of State to the Min. of the Interior, with responsibility for Territorial Organisations, 1988-90; Min.-Delegate, attached to the Min. of Industry and Regional planning, with responsibility for Tourism, 1990- Chmn, Parti Radical Gauche, 1996-; ***professional career:*** Professional journalist; Dir-Gen., publishing company La Dépêche du Midi, 1973-; ***office address:*** Parti Radical Gauche, 13 rue Duroc, 75007 Paris, France; ***URL:*** http://www.planeteradicale.org/.

BAYLEY, Hugh; British, Member of Parliament for York Central, House of Commons; ***born:*** Oxford, United Kingdom; ***parents:*** Michael Bayley and Pauline Bayley; ***married:*** Fenella Jeffers, 1984; ***education:*** Bristol Univ., B.Sc.; York Univ., B.Phil.; ***party:*** Labour Party, 1975-; ***political career:*** Cllr., London Borough of Camden, 1980-86; Parly. Under Sec. of State, Dept. of Soc. Security, 1999-2001; MP, City of York, 1992-10, York Central, 2010-; mem. NATO Parly. Assembly 1997-98 and 2001-, and Chmn. of its Economic and Security Cttee. 2003-, and the Assembly's Cive Pres., 2010-; ***interests:*** health care, economic policy, environment, int. dev., defence; ***memberships:*** York Health Authority, 1988-90; BECTU; Chmn., Westminster Foundation for Democracy; Chmn., UK Branch, Commonwealth Parly. Assn.; ***professional career:*** Nat. Officer, NALGO, 1977-82; Gen. Sec., Int. Broadcasting Trust, 1982-86; Univ. of York Research Fellow in Health Econs., 1986-92; freelance TV Producer; ***publications:*** The Nation's Health, 1995; Long Term Care for the Elderly, 1990; ***clubs:*** SERA; UN Assn.; ***office address:*** House of Commons, London, SW1A 0AA, United Kingdom; ***phone:*** +44 (0)1904 623713.

BAYROU, François; French, Chairman, Union Pour La Démocratie Française; ***born:*** 1951; ***s:*** 2; ***d:*** 4; ***education:*** Lycée in Nay; Montagne Lycée, Bordeaux; Bordeaux III Univ.; Agrégation in Classics; ***political career:*** Mem., Pau General Council, 1982; Mem., Pau Town Council, 1983; elected to the National Assy. as Dpty. for Pyrénés Atlantiques, 1986; Gen-Secy., Union pour La Démocratie Française (UDF), 1991-; Vice-Chmn., Centre des Démocrates Sociaux (CDS), 1991; Chmn., Pyrénées Atlantiques General Council, 1992; Min. of Education, 1993-97; ***publications:*** La Décennie des Mal-Appris 1990 (re-issued 1993); Henri IV - Le Roi Libre 1994; Le droit au sens 1996; ***office address:*** Union pour la Démocratie Française, 133 bis rue de l'Université, 75007 Paris, France; ***URL:*** http://www.mouvementdemocrate.fr/.

BAZOUM, Mohamed; Minister of Foreign Affairs, Government of Niger; ***party:*** Nigerien Party for Democracy and Socialism; ***political career:*** Minister of State for Foreign Affairs, 1995-96; Minister of State for Foreign Affairs, Cooperation, African Integration, and Nigeriens Abroad, 2011-; ***office address:*** Ministry of Foreign Affairs and African Integration, BP 396, Niamey, Niger; ***phone:*** +227 20 722907; ***fax:*** +227 20 735231.

BEAZLEY, H.E. Kim Christian, AC 2009; Australian, Ambassador, Australian Embassy in the USA; ***born:*** 14 December 1948; ***parents:*** the late Hon. Kim Edward Beazley and Betty Beazley; ***married:*** Mary Paltridge, 1974; Susie Annus, 1990; ***education:*** Univ. of Western Australia (MA); Oxford, Rhodes Scholar (MPhil); Tutor and lecturer in Social and Political Theory, Murdoch Univ., Western Australia 1976-80; ***political career:*** Member, Hse. of Reps. 1980-96; Minister for Aviation and Minister Assisting the Minister for Defence 1983-84; Served on Jt. Parly. Cttee. on Public Accts. 1980-81; Jt. Parly. Cttee. on Foreign Affairs and Defence 1980-83; Special Minister of State 1983-84; Vice-Pres. of the Executive Council 1988-91; Leader of the House 1988-96; Minister for Defence 1985-90; Minister for Transport and Communications 1990-91; Minister for Finance 1991, Minister for Employment, Education and Training 1991; Dep. Prime Minister, 1995-96; Leader of the Opposition, 1996-2001, 2005-06; ***memberships:*** Australian Political Science Assn; Int. Inst. for Strategic Studies; ***professional career:*** Mem. Adv. Bd, Army Jl, 2007-; Professorial Fellow, UWA, 2007-10; Chancellor, ANU, 2009-2010; Ambassador to the USA, 2010-; ***publications:*** The Politics of Intrusion, The Superpowers and the Indian Ocean (Jt. author); ***office address:*** Australian Embassy, 1601 Massachusetts Avenue, NW, Washington DC 20036-2273, USA; ***URL:*** http://www.usa.embassy.gov.au.

BEBB, Guto; MP for Aberconwy, UK Government; ***party:*** Conservative; ***political career:*** MP for Aberconwy, May 2010-; ***interests:*** Europe, taxation, reform of the welfare state, devolution, economy, rural development, regeneration policy; ***committees:*** Welsh Affairs, 2010-; Members' Expenses, 2011-; ***office address:*** House of Commons, London, SW1A 0AA, United Kingdom; ***phone:*** +44 (0)20 7219 7002; ***e-mail:*** guto.bebb.mp@parliament.uk.

BECERRA, Xavier; American, Congressman, California 31st District, US House of Representatives; ***education:*** Stanford Univ., BA, Economics, 1980; Stanford Law Sch., jur Dr., 1984; ***party:*** Democrat; ***political career:*** Fmr. Mem., CA Legislature; Congressman, California 31st District, US House of Representatives, 1992-; ***professional career:*** Fmr. Dep. Attorney-Gen., CA Dept. of Justice; ***committees:*** Ways and Means Cttee.; ***office address:*** Office of Representative Xavier Becerra, 1119 Longworth House Office, Washington, DC 20515, USA; ***phone:*** +1 202 224 3121.

BECKETT, Rt. Hon. Margaret Mary, MP; British, MP for Derby South, House of Commons; ***born:*** 15 January 1943, Ashton-under-Lyne; ***parents:*** Cyril Jackson and Winifred Jackson; ***married:*** Leo A. Beckett, 1979; ***public role of spouse:*** Chairman of Lincoln Constituency Labour Party; ***education:*** Notre Dame High Sch., Norwich; Manchester Coll. Science and Technology and John Dalton Polytechnic; Student Apprentice in Metallurgy, AEI Ltd, 1961-62; ***party:*** Labour Party, 1963-; ***political career:*** Political Adviser, Ministry of Overseas Development, 1974; MP (Lab.) for Lincoln, 1974-79; PPS to Rt. Hon. Judith Hart, Min. of Overseas Development, 1974-75; Asst. Govt. Whip, 1975-76; Minister, Dept. of Education, 1976-79; MP (Lab) for Derby South, 1983-; Shadow Minister of Social Security, 1984-89; Shadow Chief Sec. to the Treasury, 1989-92; Mem., Labour Party National Exec. Cttee. (NEC), 1991-; Dpty. Leader of the Labour Party; Shadow Leader of the House and Campaigns Organiser, 1992-94; Leader of the Opposition, 1994; Shadow Minister for Health, 1994-95; Shadow Pres. of Bd. of Trade, 1995-97; Pres., Bd. of Trade, 1997-98; Pres., Cncl. and Leader of the House of Commons, 1998-2001; Sec. of State for Environment, Food and Rural Affairs, 2001-06; Foreign Sec., 2006-07; Minister for Housing, 2008-09; ***memberships:*** Labour National Executive Cttee., 1980-81, 1985-86, 1988-98; Transport and General Workers' Union, 1964-; Transport & General Workers' Union Parly. Labour Party Gp.; National Union of Journalists, BECTU; Fabian Soc.; Anti-Apartheid Movement; Socialist Education Cttee; Labour Women's Action Cttee; Derby Co-op. Party; Socialist Environment & Resources Assoc.; Amnesty Int.; Council of St. George's College, Windsor, 1976-82; Hon. Pres., Labour's Friends of India; ***professional career:*** Experimental Officer, Dept. of Metallurgy, Manchester Univ., 1967-70; Researcher, Labour Party, 1970-74; Principal Researcher, Granad Television, 1979-83; ***committees:*** Chmn., Intelligence and Security Cttee., Jan.-Oct. 2008; mem., UK Parliamentarians for Multilateral Nuclear Disarmament and Non-Proliferation, 2009; Signatory to Global Zero (working for the phased, verified elimination of all nuclear weapons worldwide), 2008; Pres., No2AV Campaign, 2010; Labour Mem., Cttee. on Standards in Public Life, 2010-; Chair, Joint Cttee. on the National Security Strategy, Jan. 2011-; ***publications:*** The Need for Consumer Protection, 1972; The National Enterprise Board; The Nationalisation of Shipbuilding, Ship Repair & Marine Engineering; Relevant Sections of Labour's Programme, 1972 & 1973; Renewing the NHS, 1995; Vision for Growth - A New Industrial Strategy for Britain, 1996; ***clubs:*** Derby Labour Social Club; ***recreations:*** cooking, reading, caravanning; ***office address:*** House of Commons, London, SW1A 0AA, United Kingdom; ***phone:*** +44 (0)20 7219 3000; ***URL:*** http://www.epolitix.com/webminister/margaret-beckett.

BECKINGHAM, H.E. Peter; Governor, Turks & Caicos Islands; ***born:*** Essex, UK; ***married:*** Jill Beckingham; ***public role of spouse:*** Special needs teacher; ***professional career:*** Teacher in Zambia under Nuffield Foundation Scholarship; Decca Record Co.; British Overseas Trade Board, 1974-79; Joined the FCO, 1979-, Dir. British Information Services, New York, Head, Commercial Section, Stockholm, Head, Political Section, Canberra, British Consul General, Sydney and Dir. of Trade and Investment; British Amb. to the Philippines, 2005; Dep. High Commissioner in India-2013; Governor, Tuks & Caicos, 2013-; ***recreations:*** music, golf, tennis; ***office address:*** Office of the Governor, Grand Turk, Turks & Caicos Islands.

BEEBE, Governor Mike; Governor, State of Arkansas; ***born:*** 1946; ***education:*** Arkansas State Univ., Bach. in Political Science, 1968; Univ. of Arkansas, Law, 1972; ***political career:*** State senator, 1982-2006; Attorney General, to 2006; Governor of Arkansas, 2006-; ***office address:*** State Capitol, Room 250, Little Rock, Arkansas, AR 72201, USA; ***phone:*** +1 501 682 2345; ***fax:*** +1 501 682 3597.

BEEBEEJUAN, Hon. Dr. Ahmed Rashid; Deputy Prime Minister, Government of Mauritius; ***political career:*** Minister of Public Utilities, 1998-2000; Dep. Prime Minister, Minister of Infrastructure, Land Transport and Shipping, 2005-08; Dep. Prime Minister, Minister of Renewable Energy, 2008-; ***office address:*** Ministry of Public Infrastructure, Moorgate House, Sir William Newton Street, Port Louis, Mauritius; ***phone:*** +230 208 0281; ***fax:*** +230 208 7149; ***URL:*** http://publicinfrastructure.gov.mu.

BEECHAM, Lord Jeremy; Member, House of Lords; ***party:*** Labour; ***political career:*** Leader of Newcastle City Council; Chmn., Local Government Assn.; Chmn., Nat. Exec. Cttee. of the Labour Party, 2005-06; mem., House of Lords, 2010-; ***professional career:*** Solicitor; ***office address:*** House of Lords, London, SW1A 0PW, United Kingdom; ***phone:*** +44 (0)20 7219 3000; ***fax:*** +44 (0)20 7219 5979; ***URL:*** http://www.parliament.uk.

BEECROFT, H.E. Robert; Ambassador , US Embassy in Iraq; ***education:*** BA, Brigham Young Univ; J.D.,Univ. of California, Berkeley; ***professional career:*** Lawyer; Amb. to Jordan, 2008-12; Amb. to Iraq, 2012-; ***office address:*** US Embassy, Baghdad, Iraq; ***URL:*** http://iraq.usembassy.gov.

BEGG, Anne; British, Member of Parliament for Aberdeen South, House of Commons; ***born:*** Forfar, Angus; ***party:*** Labour Party; ***political career:*** MP for Aberdeen South, 1997-; ***committees:*** Scottish Affairs, 1997-2001; Work and Pensions: Member, 2001-10, Chair, 2010-; Member: Chairmen's Panel/Panel of Chairs, 2002-11, Liaison, 2010-; ***office address:*** House of Commons, London, SW1A 0AA, United Kingdom; ***phone:*** +44 (0)20 7219 2140; ***e-mail:*** anne.begg.mp@parliament.uk.

BEGICH, Senator Mark; Senator for Alaska, U.S. Senate; ***party:*** Democrat; ***political career:*** Mem., Anchorage Assembly, 1988-97; Mayor of Anchorage, 2003-08; US Senator, 2008-; ***memberships:*** National Rifle Assoc.; ***professional career:*** Businessman; ***committees:*** Science, Commerce and Transportation; Armed Services; Veterans Affairs; ***office address:*** US Senate, 144 Russell Senate Office Building, Washington DC, 20510, USA.

BEITH, Rt. Hon. Sir Alan James, MP; British, Member for Berwick-upon-Tweed, British Parliament; ***born:*** 1943; ***parents:*** James Beith and Joan Beith (née Harty); ***married:*** Barbara Jean Beith (née Ward), 1965 (dec'd 1998); Diana Margaret Maddock (Baroness); ***languages:*** French, Welsh, Norwegian; ***education:*** King's Sch., Macclesfield; Balliol and Nuffield Colls., Oxford, B.Litt., MA; ***party:*** Liberal Democrat Party; ***political career:*** MP (Lib.) for Berwick-upon-Tweed, 1973-; Liberal Chief Whip, 1976-85; Dep. Leader of Parly. Liberal Party, 1985-88; Treasury Spokesman, Liberal Democrats, 1988-94; Home Affairs Spokesman, 1994-98; Dep. Leader of Liberal Democrats, 1992-2002; ***professional career:*** Lecturer, Dept. of Politics, Univ. of Newcastle-upon-Tyne, 1966-73; ***committees:*** Mem., Intelligence and Security Cttee., 1994-2008; Mem., Procedure, 2000-01; Mem., Liaison, 2003-10, Chair, 2010-; Chair, Constitutional Affairs/Justice, 2003-; Mem., Liaison (Liaison Sub-Committee), 2006-10; mem., Joint Committee on National Security Strategy, 2010-; ***trusteeships:*** Chmn., Historic Chapels Trust; ***honours and awards:*** Privy Cllr.; Hon. D.C.L., Univ. of Newcastle-upon-Tyne; Knight Bachelor, 2008; ***publications:*** The British General Election of 1964, 1965 (1 Chapter); The Case for the Liberal Party and The Alliance, 1982; Faith in Politics (with J.S. Gummer and E. Heffer), 1987, A View from the North, 2008; ***clubs:*** Nat. Liberal; Athenaeum; Northern Counties (Newcastle); ***recreations:*** walking, music; ***office address:*** House of Commons, London, SW1A 0AA, United Kingdom; ***phone:*** +44 (0)20 7219 3540; ***fax:*** +44 (0)20 7219 5890; ***e-mail:*** cheesemang@parliament.uk.

BELGRAVE, H.E. Eliot, CHB, KA, QC; Governor General of Barbados; ***born:*** 16 March 1931; ***education:*** MA, Univ. of Cambridge, UK; LLB, Univ. of London, UK ; ***political career:*** Acting Governor-General, Nov. 2011-June 2012; Governor-General of Barbados, June 2012-; ***professional career:*** High Court Judge; ***office address:*** Office of the Governor General, Bridgetown, Barbados.

BELKA, Marek; President, National Bank of Poland; ***born:*** 1952; ***education:*** Lodz Univ., Master of Econ., 1972; Columbia Univ., Fulbright Foundation Fellow, 1978-79; Univ. of Chicago, Scholarship from the American Cncl. of Learned Societies, 1985-86; Dr., Econ. Sciences, 1978; Prof., Econ. Sciences, 1994; ***political career:*** Dep. Prime Minister and Minister of Finance, 1997, 2001-02; PM, 2004-05; ***interests:*** macro & micro-economics; ***professional career:*** Prof. at the Chair of Econ., Lodz Univ., 1973-96; Dir., Inst. of Econ. Sciences at the Polish Academy of Sciences, 1993-97; Adviser & consultant in the Finance Min., Privatisation Ministry & Central Planning Office, 1990-96; World Bank Consultant, 1990-96; Econ. Adviser to the Pres., Poland, 1996-97, 1997-2001; Hd., Coalition Cncl. for Int. Co-ordination in Iraq, 2003; Dir. in charge, econ. policy for the Coalition Prov. Authority, 2003; Exec. Sec., UN Economic Commission for Europe (UNECE), 2006-09; Dir., European Dept., IMF, 2009-10; President, National Bank of Poland, 2010-; ***publications:*** author of dozen-odd books and over 100 scholarly articles in Polish and int. press; ***office address:*** National Bank of Poland, Swietokrzyska 11/21, 00-919 Warsaw, Poland; ***URL:*** http://www.nbp.pl/.

BELL, Sir Stuart, MP; British, Member of Parliament for Middlesbrough, House of Commons; ***born:*** 16 May 1938, High Spen, County Durham, United Kingdom; ***parents:*** Ernest Bell and Margaret Rose Bell; ***married:*** Margaret Bell, 1980; ***languages:*** French; ***education:*** Gray's Inn, London; ***party:*** Labour Party, 1964-; ***political career:*** Mem., Fabian Soc.; Cllr., Newcastle City, 1980-1983; MP, Middlesbrough, 1983-; PPS to Dep. Leader, Labour Party, 1983-84; Spokesperson, Labour Party, Northern Ireland, 1984-87; Frontbench Labour Spokesperson on Trade and Industry, 1992-97; ***interests:*** economics, international affairs, law, education, EU, Middle East; ***memberships:*** GMB; Fabian Soc.; Co-operative Soc.; MBATU; ***professional career:*** Colliery Clerk; newspaper reporter; typist; novelist; Barrister-at-Law, 1970-; Conseil Juridique and international Lawyer, Paris, 1970-77; ***committees:*** Second Church Estates Chmn., 1997-10; Chmn., Financial Services Cttee., House of Commons 2000-10; House of Commons Commission, 2000-10; Independent Parliamentary Standards Authority, 2009-10; Ecclesiastical Cttee., 19970; ***publications:*** Paris 69, 1973; How to Abolish the Lords, 1981; Valuation for United States Customs Purposes, 1981; Tony Really Loves Me, 2000; When Salem Came to The Boro, 1988; Pathway to the Euro, 2002; The Honoured Society, 2002; Binkie's Revolution, 2002; Lara's Theme, 2003; Softly in the Dark, 2003; An Ever Closer Union, 2007; The Ice Cream Man and Other Stories, 2007; ***recreations:*** writing novels and short stories ; ***office address:*** House of Commons, London, SW1A 0AA, United Kingdom; ***phone:*** +44 (0)20 7219 3577; ***e-mail:*** contact@stuartbellmp.org.

BELLINGHAM, Henry; Member of Parliament for North West Norfolk, House of Commons; ***born:*** 29 March 1955; ***parents:*** Henry Bellingham and June (née Cloudsley-Smith); ***married:*** Emma Louise, August 1993; ***children:*** James Henry (M); ***languages:*** French, German; ***education:*** Cambridge Univ., law; ***party:*** Conservative Party; ***political career:*** MP for North West Norfolk, 1983-97, 2001-; Conservative Opposition Shadow Industry and Small Businesses Spokesman; Opposition Whip, 2005-06; Opposition Shadow Minister for Justice and Legal Services, 2006-10; Foreign Office Minister for Office of Overseas Territories and Conflict Issues, 2010; Parliamentary Under Secretary of State (Africa and the United Nations), 2011-; ***interests:*** industry, small business, environment, defence; ***professional career:*** Barrister, 1978-84; Company Dir., 1987-2001; ***committees:*** Leader of All Party Environment Select Cttee. 1988-90; All Party N, Ireland Cttee. 2001-02; ***recreations:*** cricket, country sports; ***office address:*** House of Commons, London, SW1A 0AA, United Kingdom; ***phone:*** +44 (0)20 7219 8484; ***fax:*** +44 (0)20 7219 2844; ***e-mail:*** bellinghamh@parliament.uk.

BENEDICT XVI, Pope Emeritus (Joseph Ratzinger); Pope Emeritus; ***born:*** 1927, Markt am Inn, Germany; ***parents:*** Josef Ratzinger and Maria Ratzinger; ***education:*** Traunstein Seminary; ***professional career:*** Required mem. Hitler Youth; German Army, deserted, April 1944, POW 1945; Ordained into the priesthood, 1951; Chair, Dogmatic Theology, Univ. of Teubingen, 1966; Dean and Vice Pres., Regensburg Univ. Bavaria, 1969; made Archbishop of Munich, March 1977; made Cardinal, July 1977; Head, Congregation for the Doctrine of Faith, 1981-; Elected Pope, April 2005-resigned Feb. 2013; Pope Emeritus, March 2013-; ***publications:*** several books inc. Salt of the Earth, The Ratzinger Report, Introduction to Christianity, Milestones; ***office address:*** Mater Ecclesiae , The Vatican, Vatican City, Italy.

BENEDIKTSSON, Bjarni; Minister of Finance and Economic Affairs, Government of Iceland; ***born:*** 26 January 1970; ***party:*** Chmn., Indepedence Party; ***political career:*** MP, 2009-; Minister of Finance and Economic Affairs, 2013-; ***committees:*** Foreign Affairs Cttee., 2009-13; ***office address:*** Ministry of Finance, Arnarhváli, 150 Reykjavík, Iceland; ***phone:*** +354 545 9200; ***fax:*** +354 562 8280; ***e-mail:*** mail@fjr.stjr.is; ***URL:*** http://www.stjr.is/fjr.

BENISHEVA, Bisserka; Ambassador Extraordinary and Plenipotentiary, Bulgarian Embassy in Hungary; ***born:*** 1st December 1953, Bulgaria; ***education:*** Higher Instit. of Economics, Sofia, 1972-77; IMF Instit., Macroeconomic policy, 1990; Centre for Int. and European Economic Law, Greece, 1992; EU Affairs and EU Integration, T.M.C. ASSER Instit., 1998; ***professional career:*** Consultant to Min. of Foreign Trade, 1977-93; Head of the Integration Policy Dept., Min. of Trade, 1993; Plenipotentiary Minister (commercial and econ. issues), Bulgarian Mission to the EU, 1993-97; Member, European Integration Directorate, Min. of Foreign Affairs, 1997-2001; Dep. Chief of Mission, Bulgarian Mission to the EC, 2001-03; Amb. Ex. & Pleni., to Ireland, 2004-11; Amb. Ex. & Pleni., to Hungary, 2012-; Pres., Danube Commission, 2012- ; ***office address:*** Embassy of the Republic of Bulgaria, Budapest, Hungary.

BENJAMIN, Jon; Ambassador, British Embassy in Chile; ***professional career:*** Dep. British Consul General, Dep.Head of Mission and Acting Consul General, British Consul; New York, 2005-08; Amb. to Chile, 2009-; ***office address:*** British Embassy, Avda. El Bosque Norte 0125, Las Condes, Santiago, Chile; ***phone:*** +56 (0)2 370 4100; ***fax:*** +56 (0)2 335 5988; ***e-mail:*** chancery.santiago@fco.gov.uk; ***URL:*** http://www.britemb.cl.

BENJAMIN, Raymond; Secretary General, International Civil Aviation Organization; ***born:*** 1945, Egypt; ***professional career:*** Civil Aviation Administration of France, 1970-1982; Air Transport Officer, European Civil Aviation Conference (ECAC), 1982-82, Deputy Secretary, 1983-89; Chief, Aviation Security Branch, International Civil Aviation Organization (ICAO), 1989-94; Exec. Sec., ECAC, 1994-2007; Special Joint Aviaiton Authorities Training Org., 2008-09; Sec.-Gen., ICO, 2009-; ***office address:*** ICAO, 999 University St, Montreal, Quebec HC3 5H7, Canada; ***phone:*** +1 514 954 8219; ***fax:*** +1 514 954 6077; ***URL:*** http://www.icao.int/.

BENJAMIN OF BECKENHAM, Baroness Floella, OBE DL; Member, House of Lords; ***party:*** Liberal Democrat; ***political career:*** Mem., House of Lords, 2010-; ***professional career:*** Actress; Children's Television Presenter; Governor, Dulwich Coll., 2001-; Mem., Content Board, Ofcom 2003-06; ***office address:*** House of Lords, London, SW1A 0PW, United Kingdom; ***phone:*** +44 (0)20 7219 3000; ***fax:*** +44 (0)20 7219 5979; ***URL:*** http://www.parliament.uk.

BENJAMINSON, Amb. Eric; Ambassador, US Embassy to Gabon and Sao Tome e Principe; ***education:*** Univ. of Oregon; ***professional career:*** entered Foreign Service, 1982; various postings incl. Nigeria & Montreal, Beijing, Sweden; Counselor for Economic Affairs, US Embassy to Belgium, 1999-2003; Dep. Chief of Mission, Ouagadougou, Burkina Faso; Dep. Chief of Mission, US Embassy in Windhoek, Namibia, 2005-08; Minister Counselor for Economic Affairs, US Embassy in Ottawa, Canada, 2008-10; Ambassador to Gabon & the Democratic Republic of Sao Tome and Principe; ***office address:*** US Embassy, Libreville, Gabon; ***URL:*** http://libreville.usembassy.gov.

BEN JEDDOU, Lofti; Minister of the Interior, Government of Tunisia; ***born:*** 1964; ***education:*** Higher Inst. of the Judiciary; ***party:*** Independent; ***political career:*** Minister of the Interior, 2013-; ***professional career:*** magistrate; judge, Court of First Instance, Kef; judge, Court of First Instance, Kasserine; Prosecutor, Trial Court, Kasserine; ***office address:*** Ministry of the Interior, place du Gouvernement, 1020 Tunis, Tunisia.

BENKIRANE, Abdelilah; Prime Minister, Government of Morocco; ***born:*** 1954; ***party:*** Leader, Justice and Development Party, July 2008-; ***political career:*** Prime Minister, Nov. 2011-; ***office address:*** Office of the Prime Minister, Rabat, Morocco; ***URL:*** http://www.pm.gov.ma.

BENN, Rt. Hon. Hilary, MP; British, Shadow Secretary of State for Communities and Local Government, House of Commons; *born:* November 1953; *parents:* Anthony (Tony) Wedgwood Benn and Caroline Benn (dec'd) (née De Camp); *education:* BA, Russian Studies, Sussex Univ., 1974; *political career:* MP for Leeds Central, 1999-; Parly. Under-Sec. of State, DFID, 2001-02; Parly. Under-Sec. of State, Home Office, 2002-03; Minister of State, DFID, 2003; Sec. of State for Int. Dev., 2003-June 2007; Secretary of State for Environment, Food and Rural Affairs, June 2007-May 2010; Shadow Secretary of State for the Environment, Food and Rural Affairs, May 2010-Sept. 2010; Shadow Leader of the House of Commons, Oct. 2010-11; Shadow Secretary of State for Communities and Local Government, 2011-; *committees:* Environment, Transport and the Regions Select Cttee. 1999-2001; Vice-Chair, Backbench Education Cttee. of Labour MPs, 1999-2001; Vice-Chmn., Commission for Africa, 2004-05; *honours and awards:* House Magazine Minister of the Year 2006 and 2007; *publications:* Beyond 2002: long-term policies for Labour (Contribution), 1999; Men who made Labour, 2006 (Contribution); *office address:* House of Commons, London, SW1A 0AA, United Kingdom; *phone:* +44 (0)20 7270 3000; *e-mail:* bennh@parliament.uk; *URL:* http://www.hilarybennmp.com.

BENNET, Senator Michael F.; Senator for Colorado, US Senate; *education:* Wesleyan Univ., BA (Hons).; Yale Law School, Law; *political career:* Superintendent of Denver Public Schools; US Senator for Colorado, 2009- ; *professional career:* Counsel to the Dep. Attorney Gen., US Dept. Justice; MD., Anschutz Investment Co.; Chief of Staff to Denver Mayor John Hickenlooper; *committees:* Finance; Health, Education, Labour and Pensions; Agriculture, Nutrition, and Forestry; *office address:* US Senate, 702 Hart Senate Building, Washington DC 20510, USA; *phone:* +1 202 224 5852; *URL:* http://bennet.senate.gov/public/.

BENNETT, Natalie; Leader, Green Party; *education:* Bachelor of Agricultural Science, Univ. of Sydney, Australia; BA (Hons) in Asian studies, Univ. of New England, Australia; MA, in Mass Communication, Univ. of Leicester, UK; *political career:* Leader of the Green Party, Sept. 2012-; *professional career:* Journalist; Editor, Guardian Weekly, 2007-12; *trusteeships:* Fawcett Society; *office address:* Green Party, 1a Waterlow Road, London, N19 5NJ, United Kingdom; *phone:* +44 (0)20 7272 4474; *URL:* http://www.greenparty.org.uk.

BENNOUNA, Judge Mohamed; Moroccan, Member, International Court of Justice; *born:* 1943; *education:* Doctor of Int. Law; Professor of Int. Law; Diploma, Hague Academy of Int. Law; *professional career:* Ambassador, Perm. Rep. of the Kingdom of Morocco to the United Nations, 2001-06; Judge, International Criminal Tribunal for the former Yugoslavia, The Hague, 1998-2001; Dir. Gen., Arab World Institute (Institut du Monde Arabe, Paris), 1991-98; Amb., Dep. Perm. Rep. to the UN, 1985-89; Professor and later Dean, Faculty of Law, Rabat, Morocco, 1972-84; Founder & first Director, Revue juridique, politique et économique de Maroc, 1976; Visiting Professor at various universities: Tunis, Algiers, Nice, New York, Thessaloniki, Paris; Judge ad hoc of the International Court of Justice, 2002-2005; mem., International Court of Justice, 2006-; *office address:* International Court of Justice, Peace Palace, 2517 KJ The Hague, Netherlands.

BENTLEY, Robert; Governor, State of Alabama; *education:* Univ. of Alabama; *party:* Republican; *political career:* Alabama State House of Reps., 2002-2010; Governor of Alabama, 2011-; *interests:* primary health care; economy; *professional career:* physician; founder of several businesses; *recreations:* mem., First Baptist Chruch Tuscaloosa; Deacon and Sunday school teacher; *office address:* Office of the Governor, State Capitol Room, N-104, 600 Dexter Avenue, Montgomery, AL 36130, USA; *phone:* +1 334 242 7100; *URL:* http://www.governor.alabama.gov/.

BENTON, Joe; British, Member of Parliament for Bootle, House of Commons; *born:* 28 September 1933, Bootle, United Kingdom; *parents:* Thomas Edward Benton and Agnes Wynne; *married:* Doris Irene Benton, 1959; *languages:* Spanish; *education:* Bootle Technical Coll.; Liverpool Sch. of Commerce; *party:* Labour Party; *political career:* Mem., Bootle Borough Cncl. and Sefton MBC, 1970-91; Leader, Labour Group, 1985-90; Spokesperson, education; Opposition Whip, 1993-97; MP, Bootle, 1990-; *interests:* education, housing, social services; *memberships:* Assoc. Mem., Inst. of Personnel Management; Inst. of Linguists; Speaker's Panel of Chairmen, 1992-93, and 1997; Court of Liverpool Univ.; Bd. of Visitors HMP Liverpool, 1974-86; All Party Parly. Groups, British/Irish Group, British/Spanish Group, Sec. of Pro-Life Group; *professional career:* JP; Chmn., of Governors, Hugh Baird Coll. of Technology, 1972-94; Savio High Sch., 1974-90, Chmn., 1985-90; Mem., Management Cttee. of the Apostleship of the Sea; *committees:* Mem., Northern Ireland Affairs Cttee., 2010-; *recreations:* reading, classical music, squash, swimming, cycling; *office address:* House of Commons, London, SW1A 0AA, United Kingdom; *phone:* +44 (0)20 7219 3000; *e-mail:* hcinfo@parliament.uk.

BENYON, Richard; MP for Newbury, House of Commons; *born:* 1960; *party:* Conservative; *political career:* Local Councillor; MP for Newbury, 2005-; Parliamentary Under Secretary of State (Natural Environment and Fisheries), 2010-; *professional career:* Army; Chartered Surveyor; *office address:* House of Commons, London, SW1P 0AA, United Kingdom; *phone:* +44 (0)20 7219 3000.

BERCOW, John; British, Speaker, House of Commons; *born:* 19 January 1963, Edgware, Middlesex, UK; *parents:* Charles Bercow (dec'd) and Brenda Bercow; *children:* Oliver (M), Freddie (M), Jemima (F); *education:* Finchley Manorhill School, London; Univ. of Essex, BA, Government, (First Class Hons.), 1985; *party:* Conservative Party; *political career:* Conservative Councillor, London Borough of Lambeth, 1986-90; Dep. Leader, Conservative Opp. Gp, 1987-89; Special Adviser to Chief Sec. to the Treasury, 1995; Special Adviser to Sec. of State for Nat. Heritage; Conservative Frontbench Spokesman on Education and Employment, 1999-; MP, Buckingham, 1997-; Shadow Chief Secretary to the Treasury, 2001-2002; Shadow Minister for Work and Pensions, 2002; Shadow Secretary of State for International Development, 2003-04; Sec. of State for Children, Schools and Families, 2007-08; Speaker of the House of Commons, June 2009-; *interests:* Education, Britain - EU Relations, Trade and Industry; *professional career:* Merchant banking; Former Dir., Rowland Sallingbury Casey; Former Special Adviser to Ministers; *committees:* Nat. Chmn., Federation of Conservative Students, 1986-87; Vice-Chmn., Conservative Collegiate Forum, 1987; Exec.

of the 1922 Cttee. of Conservative MPs, 1998; Trade and Industry Select Cttee., 1998-99; *honours and awards:* Spectator Magazine Backbencher to Watch Award, 1998; *publications:* Aiming for the Heart of Europe: a Misguided Venture, 1998; Assets: why Tories should change policy on immigration and asylum, 2005; Promote Freedom or Protect Oppressors: the choice at the UN Review Summit, 2005; *recreations:* tennis, squash, swimming, reading, music; *office address:* House of Commons, London, SW1A 0AA, United Kingdom; *phone:* +44 (0)20 7219 3000; *e-mail:* hcinfo@parliament.uk.

BERDYMUKHAMEDOV , Gurbanguly; President, Government of Turkmenistan; *born:* 1957; *political career:* Minister of Health and the Pharmaceutical Industry, 1997; Deputy Chair, Cncl. of Ministers, 2001-07; President, Feb. 2007-; *professional career:* Dentist; *office address:* Presidential Palace, ul. 2001 24, Ashgabat, Turkmenistan; *phone:* +993 12 354534.

BERESFORD, Sir Paul; Member of Parliament for Mole Valley, House of Commons; *born:* 6 April 1946, Levin, New Zealand; *education:* Otago Univ., Dunedin, New Zealand; *party:* Conservative Party; *political career:* Leader, Wandsworth Council, 1982-92; MP, Croydon Central, 1992-97; Parly. Under-Secretary of State, Department of Environment, 1994-97; MP, Mole Valley, 1997-; *professional career:* Dental Surgeon; *committees:* Finance & Services, 2010-; Standards & Privileges, 2010-; Jt. Cttee. on Security, 2010-; *honours and awards:* Knighted, 1990; *office address:* House of Commons, London, SW1A 0AA, United Kingdom; *phone:* +44 (0)20 7219 5018; *e-mail:* dukem@parliament.uk.

BERGER, Luciana; MP for Liverpool, Wavertree, House of Commons; *party:* Labour; *political career:* MP for Liverpool, Wavertree, May 2010-; Shadow Minister, Energy and Climate Change, Oct. 2010-; *committees:* Business, Innovation and Skills Cttee., 2010; Arms Export Controls, 2010; *office address:* House of Commons, London, SW1A 0AA, United Kingdom; *phone:* +44 (0)20 7219 3000; *e-mail:* luciana.berger.mp@parliament.uk.

BERGER, Dr. Maria; Judge, Court of Justice of the European Union; *born:* 19 August 1956, Perg, Austria; *languages:* English, French; *education:* Univ. of Innsbruck, Master of Laws, 1975-79; *party:* Sozialdemokratische Partei Europas (SPE, European Social Democratic Party); *political career:* Fed. Min. of Science and Research, lastly as Dep. Head of Dept., 1984-88; Pres., Young Generation of the SPOE, 1984-87; Specialist on EU matters in the Office of the Federal Chancellor, 1988-89; Head of Dept. for the Integration -Policy Coordination in the Office of the Federal Chancellor (preparation of Austria's accession to the EU), 1989-92; Mem., Municipal Council, for Perg, 1997-2009; MEP 1996-Jan. 2007; Federal Minister for Justice, Jan. 2007-08; *professional career:* Asst. Prof., Inst. of Public Law & Political Sciences, Univ. of Innsbruck, 1979-84; Dep. Head of Division, Austrian Min. of Science & Research, 1984-88; Fed. Chancellery, 1988-92, Head of Division of European Policies Division; EFTA-Surveillance Authority, Geneva & Brussels, 1992-94, Vice-Pres., Donau Universität Krems, 1995-96; Judge, Court of Justice of the European Union, 2009-; *committees:* mem., Legal Affairs & Internal Market Cttee.; Civil Liberties & Home Affairs Cttee.; The European Convention; Joint Parly. Delegation with Czech Rep.; Dep. mem., Cttee. on Constitutional Affairs; Interparliamentary Delegation for Relations with the ASEAN Countries and SAARC; Dep. mem., Interparliamentary Delegation for Relations with Canada; *office address:* Court of Justice of the European Union, Rue du Fort Niedergrunewald, L-2925, Luxembourg.

BERISHA, Prof. Dr Sali; Albanian, Prime Minister, Government of Albania; *born:* 1944, Tropoja; *married:* 2 Chdn; *education:* University of Tirana; *political career:* founded Democratic Party 1990; elected deputy to the Peoples' Assembly 1991; elected President of Republic of Albania 1992-97 (resigned); Prime Minister, Sept. 2005-; *professional career:* Assistant teacher and physician, Clinic of Cardiology, Tirana Hospital 1967; elected member of the European Committee on Medical Scientific Research 1986; *publications:* Numerous research articles on Hemodynamics; *office address:* Office of the Prime Minister, Bulevardi Dëshmorët e Kombit, Tirana, Albania; *phone:* +355 4 250474; *e-mail:* info@km.gov.al; *URL:* http://www.km.gov.al.

BERKEL, Lt. Gov. Gerald; Lieutenant Governor, St. Eustatius; *born:* 1969; *education:* Florida Inst. of Technology; *political career:* Lt. Gov., St. Eustatius, 2010-; *professional career:* Eutel NV, St. Eustatius, 2004-10, MD, 2007-2010; *office address:* Office of the Lieutenant Governor, Oranjestad, Sint Eustatius; *URL:* http://www.statiagovernment.com/.

BERKELEY OF KNIGHTON, Lord Michael Fitzhardinge Berkeley; Member, House of Lords; *political career:* House of Lords, 2013-; *professional career:* Composer; *office address:* House of Lords, London, SW1A 0AA, United Kingdom; *phone:* +44 (0)20 7219 3000.

BERLAKOVICH, Nikolaus; Federal Minister of Agriculture, Forestry, Environment and Water Management, Government of Austria; *born:* 4 June 1961; *languages:* Croatian, English; *education:* Vienna Univ., Natural Resources and Life Sciences,1985; *party:* Austrian People's Party; *political career:* Federal Minister of Agriculture, Forestry, Environment and Water Management, Dec. 2008-; *office address:* Ministry of Agriculture, Forestry, Environment and Water Management, Stubenring 1, 1010 Vienna, Austria; *phone:* +43 (0)1 711000; *URL:* http://www.lebensministerium.at.

BERNANKE, Dr Ben; Chairman, Board of Governors, US Federal Reserve System; *education:* BA, (economics), Harvard Univ. USA, (summa cum laude), 1975; Ph.D., (economics), Massachusetts Institute of Technology, 1979; *political career:* Chairman, Council of Economic Advisers, 2005-06; Chmn., Bd of Governors, Federal Reserve System, 2006-; *committees:* Chmn., Federal Open Market Cttee.; *office address:* Federal Reserve System, 20th Street and Constitution Avenue, Washington, DC 20502, USA; *URL:* http://www.federalreserve.gov/.

BERNARD, Alvin; Minister of State in the Ministry of Foreign Affairs, Government of Dominica; *born:* 1955; *education:* Univ. of Wales; Univ. of East Anglia, UK; *political career:* Minister of State in the Ministry of Foreign Affairs, 2010-; *professional career:* Economist; *office address:* Government Headquarters, Kennedy Avenue, Roseau, Commonwealth of Dominica; *URL:* http://www.government.dm.

BERNATONIS, Juozas; Minister of Justice, Government of Lithuania; ***born:*** 8 September 1953, Kaunas, Lithuania; ***married:*** Vilma Bernatoniene (née Sleinotaite), 1984; ***children:*** Gaile (F); ***public role of spouse:*** Economist; ***languages:*** English, Russian; ***education:*** Faculty of Chemical Technology, Kaunas Inst. of Polytechnics, Graduate, 1976; co-researcher, Research Lab. of Large Molecular compounds at Kaunas Inst. of Polytechnics, 1976-79; employed by the Komsomol, 1979-85; post-grad. student, Prague Sch. of High Politics, 1987-90; Ph.D thesis in Prague, 1990; studied law, Faculty of Law, Vilnius Univ., 1998-2002; obtained Master's Degree in Law, 2002; ***party:*** fmr. Mem., Community Party, Lithuania; Lithuanian Democratic Labour Party, 1990-, after merger of Democratic Labour Party and Social Democratic Party, became Mem., Lithuanian Social Democratic Party; ***political career:*** Head of the Parly. activity gp. of the Lithuanian Democratic Labour Party Secretariat, 1990-92; Advisor of Lithuanian Democratic Labour Party (LDLP) faction of the Supreme Council, the Reconstituent Seimas, 1992; Mem. and Dep. Chmn., Seimas, 1992-96; Dep. Chmn., Seimas, 1993-96; Political Advisor, Pres. Algirdas Brazauskas, 1996-; Advisor to the Pres., 1997-98; desk officer of Pres. Algirdas Brazauskas, 1998-; elected to the Seimas of the Republic of Lithuania, 1998-; won multi-mandate constituency as Mem., Social Democratic Coalition headed by Algirdas Brazauskas, 2000; Mem. Parl. (Seimas) of the Republic of Lithuania, to date; Dep. Chmn., Lithuanian Social Democratic Party, 2001-; Minister of the Interior, 2001-04; Minister of Justice, 2012-; ***interests:*** formation of political strategy of the party; ***professional career:*** fmr. Scientific Worker in the Molecular Research Laboratory, Kaunas Polytechnic Inst; Lawyer; Chemistry Technology Engineer; ***committees:*** Instructor, Science and Education Division of the Central Cttee. of the Lithuanian Communist Party, 1986-87; Dep. Chmn., State and Law Cttee., 1992-93; Mem., Foreign Affairs Cttee., Seimas, 1998-2000; Mem., Law and Law Enforcement Cttee. (Seimas); ***trusteeships:*** National Youth Basketball Team; ***publications:*** co-author of book, Human Rights and Freedoms: The Problems of Compatability between the Laws of the Republic of Lithuania and the Convention of the Protection of the European Human Rights and Main Freedoms; ***recreations:*** reading, theatre, classical music; ***office address:*** Ministry of Justice, Gedimino pr. 30/1 , 2600 Vilnius, Lithuania; ***phone:*** +370 5 266 2980; ***URL:*** http://www.tm.lt.

BERNIER, Dr David; Secretary of State, Government of Puerto Rico; ***education:*** Univ. of Puerto Rico, Natural Science; Medical Sciences School, UPR, Odontology; ***political career:*** Exec. Dir., Office of Youth Affairs, Gov. of Puerto Rico, 2003-04; Sec. , Dept. of Sports and Recreation, 2005; Sec. of State, 2012-; ***office address:*** State Department, P.O. Box 9023271, San Juan 00902, Puerto Rico; ***phone:*** +1 787 722 2121; ***fax:*** +1 787 725 7303; ***URL:*** http://www.estado.gobierno.pr.

BERRIDGE, Baroness Elizabeth; Member, House of Lords; ***party:*** Conservative Party; ***political career:*** Mem., House of Lords, 2011-; ***professional career:*** Personal Injury Barrister; Exec. Dir, Conservative Christian Fellowship; ***office address:*** House of Lords, London, SW1A 0PW, United Kingdom; ***phone:*** +44 (0)20 7219 3000.

BERRY, Jake; MP for Rossendale and Darwen, UK Government; ***party:*** Conservative; ***political career:*** MP for Rossendale and Darwen, May 2010-; PPS to Grant Shapps, 2010-; ***professional career:*** Property and Construction Lawyer; ***office address:*** House of Commons, London, SW1A 0AA, United Kingdom; ***phone:*** +44 (0)20 7219 3000; ***e-mail:*** jake.berry.mp@parliament.uk.

BERSET, Alain; Federal Councillor, Government of Switzerland; ***born:*** 1972; ***education:*** Univ. of Neuchatel, Political Science & Economics, degree, doctorate; ***political career:*** Strategic advisor, Dept. of Economic Affairs of canton Neuchatel; elected to Council of States, Fribourg, 2003-, president, 2008-09; vice-pres., Social Democratic group, 2005-11; elected to Federal Council, 2011; Head, Federal Dept. of Home Affairs, 2012-; ***professional career:*** guest researcher, Hamburg Inst. of International economics; communications advisor; ***office address:*** Federal Department of Home Affairs, Inselgasse 1, 3003 Berne, Switzerland; ***phone:*** +41 (0)31 322 8041; ***URL:*** http://www.edi.admin.ch/.

BERZINS, Andris; President, Latvia; ***born:*** 1944; ***education:*** Riga Polytechnical Institute; Latvian State Univ.; ***party:*** Union of Greens and Farmers; ***political career:*** Supreme Council of the Latvian SSR, 1990-93; ran for Mayor, 2005; MP, 2010-; President of Latvia, 2011-; ***professional career:*** Banker; ***office address:*** Office of the President, Pils Square 3, Riga LV 1900, Latvia.

BESHEAR, Governor Steve; Governor, State of Kentucky; ***born:*** 21 September 1944; ***education:*** Univ. of Kentucky, grad. and law degree; ***political career:*** Mem., Kentucky House of Reps., 1974-79; Attorney General, 1980-84; Lt. Gov. of Kentucky, 1984-88; Democratic nominee, US Senate, 1996; Governor of Kentucky, 2007-; ***professional career:*** Practised law, Lexington, Kentucky, 1987-2007; ***office address:*** Office of the Governor, 700 Capitol Avenue, Suite 100, Frankfort, KY 40601, USA; ***phone:*** +1 502 564 2611; ***fax:*** +1 502 564 2849; ***URL:*** http://governor.ky.gov.

BETHEL, H.E. Eldred E.; High Commissioner, Bahamas High Commission in the UK; ***professional career:*** Reporter; Broadcast Journalist; Consul General to New York, USA, 2002-07; High Commissioner to the UK, 2013-; ***office address:*** High Commission for the Commonwealth of the Bahamas, 10 Chesterfield Street, London, W1X 8AH, United Kingdom; ***phone:*** +44 (0)20 7408 4488; ***fax:*** +44 (0)20 7499 4937; ***URL:*** http://www.bahamashclondon.net/.

BETTS, Clive; British, Member of Parliament for Sheffield, South East, House of Commons; ***born:*** 13 January 1950, Sheffield, UK; ***parents:*** Harold Betts (dec'd) and Nellie Betts (dec'd); ***education:*** Pembroke Coll., Cambridge, BA; ***party:*** Labour Party, 1969-; ***political career:*** Local Govt. Officer; Cllr., Sheffield City, 1976-92; Chmn., Housing, 1980-86; Dep. Leader, 1986-87; Leader, 1986-92; Chmn., AMA Housing Cttee., 1984-89; Vice-Chmn., Assn. of Metropolitan Authorities (AMA), 1988-91; MP, Sheffield Attercliffe, 1992-2010, MP, Sheffield South East, 2010-; Asst. Whip, 1997; Lord Commissioner, 1998-2001; ***interests:*** economic policy, local government, housing; ***memberships:*** TGWU; Anti-Apartheid Movement; ***committees:*** Communities and Local Government, 2010-; Liaison, 2010-; ***recreations:*** Sheffield Wednesday Football Club, cricket, squash; ***office address:*** House of Commons, London, SW1A 0AA, United Kingdom; ***phone:*** +44 (0)20 7219 3000; ***e-mail:*** clive.betts.mp@parliament.uk.

BEVAN, James, CMG; High Commissioner, British High Commission in India; ***professional career:*** FCO, Chief Operating Officer and Dir Gen. for Corporate Affairs, 2007-11; High Commissioner to India, 2011-; ***office address:*** British High Commission, Chanakyapuri, New Delhi 110021, India; ***phone:*** +91 11 2687 2161; ***fax:*** +91 11 2687 2882; ***e-mail:*** postmaster.NewDelhi@fco.gov.uk; ***URL:*** http://ukinindia.fco.gov.uk/en.

BEVANDA, Vjekoslav; Prime Minister, Chairman of the Council of Ministers, Government of Bosnia and Herzegovina; ***born:*** 1956; ***education:*** Univ. of Mostar, 1979; ***political career:*** Minister of Finance, 2007-11; Prime Minister, Chairman, Council of Ministers, 2012-; Minister of European Integration, 2013-; ***office address:*** Office of the Prime Minister, Vojvode Putnika 3, 71000 Sarajevo, Bosnia and Herzegovina; ***phone:*** +387 3366 4941; ***fax:*** +387 3344 3446; ***e-mail:*** kabprem@fbihvlada.gov.ba; ***URL:*** http://www.fbihvlada.gov.ba.

BEYER, Donald; Ambassador, US Embassy in Switzerland; ***education:*** BA, Williams College, USA; ***political career:*** Lieutenant Governor and President of the Senate of Virginia; ***professional career:*** Amb. to Switzerland and Liechtenstein, 2009-; ***office address:*** Embassy of the United States of America, Jubiläumsstrasse 95, 3005 Berne, Switzerland; ***phone:*** +41 (0)31 357 7011; ***fax:*** +41 (0)31 357 7344; ***URL:*** http://bern.usembassy.gov.

BHAGWATI, Dr J.; High Commissioner, Indian High Commission in the UK; ***languages:*** Hindi, English, Spanish; ***education:*** MSc (Physics), St. Stephen's College, Delhi Univ.; MS (Finance), Sloan School, Massachusetts Institute of Technology, USA; Ph.D. (Finance), Tufts University, USA; Executive Development Program, Harvard Business School, USA; ***professional career:*** Amb. to Belgium, Luxembourg and the EU, 2008-12; High Commissioner to the UK, 2012-; ***office address:*** Indian High Commission, India House, Aldwych, London, WC2B 4NA, United Kingdom; ***phone:*** +44 (0)20 7836 8484; ***fax:*** +44 (0)20 7836 4331; ***URL:*** http://hcilondon.in.

BHANDARI, Judge Dalveer; Judge, International Court of Justice; ***born:*** 1947; ***memberships:*** Exec. mem., International Law Assn.; Pres., India International Law Foundation, 2007; ***professional career:*** Rajasthan High Court, 1968-70, 1973-77; Supreme Court of India; Judge, High Court of Delhi, 1991-2004; Chief Justice, Bombay High Court, 2004; Senior Judge, Supreme Court of India, 2005-; Mem., ICJ, 2012-; ***office address:*** International Court of Justice, Peace Palace, 2517 KJ The Hague, Netherlands.

BHARATH, Vasant; Minister of Trade, Industry and Investment, Government of Trinidad & Tobago; ***education:*** Accountancy; LLM; MBA; ***political career:*** MP, 2007; Senator; Minister of Trade, Industry & Investment, 2012-; ***professional career:*** Chartered Accountant; long corporate career in various sectors; Board appointments include; Caribbean Industrial Research Inst.; Trinidad & Tobago Bureau of Standars; Trinidad & Tobago Manufacturers' Association; Chmn., Board, Public Transport Service Corp.; ***office address:*** Ministry of Trade, Industry & Investment, Levels 9,11-17, Nicholas Tower, 63-65 Independence Square, Port of Spain, Trinidad & Tobago; ***phone:*** +1 868 623 2931; ***fax:*** +1 868 627 8488; ***URL:*** http://www.tradeind.gov.tt/.

BICHARD, Lord Michael; Member, House of Lords; ***political career:*** Mem., House of Lords, 2010-; ***professional career:*** Perm. Sec., Dept. for Employment; Perm. Sec., Dept. for Education and Employment; ***office address:*** House of Lords, London, SW1A 0PW, United Kingdom; ***phone:*** +44 (0)20 7219 3000; ***fax:*** +44 (0)20 7219 5979; ***URL:*** http://www.parliament.uk.

BIDEN, Vice-President Joseph R., Jr.; American, Vice-President, US Government; ***born:*** 1942; ***married:*** Jill Tracy Biden; ***education:*** Univ. of Delaware, Newark, Del. (BA Political Science and History); Syracuse Univ. Sch. of Law, Syracuse, New York (JD); ***party:*** Democrat; ***political career:*** US Senator for Delaware, 1972-; Candidate for Democratic Nomination for President, 2008; Candidate for Vice-President, 2008; Vice-Pres., 2009-; ***professional career:*** New Castle County (Delaware) Cncl., 1970-72; Trial Lawyer, Wilmington, Delaware 1968-72; ***committees:*** Ranking Democratic Mem., Foreign Relations Cttee.; Judiciary Cttee.; Co-Chmn., US Senate Caucus on Int. Narcotics Control; Co-Chmn., Senate Democratic Working Gp. on Drugs; Democratic Senatorial Campaign Cttee.; Co-Chmn., Democratic House and Senate Cncl.; US Commission on US/Soviet Relations, Cncl. for Foreign Relations; Chmn., US Delegation on Salt II, Moscow 1979; Vice-Chmn., US Senate Delegation to North Atlantic Assembly; North Atlantic Assembly Special Cttee. on Nuclear Weapons in Europe 1980; ***office address:*** Office of the Vice President, The White House, 1600 Pennsylvania Avenue, NW, Washington DC 20500, USA; ***phone:*** +1 202 456 1414; ***fax:*** +1 202 456 2461; ***e-mail:*** vice.president@whitehouse.gov; ***URL:*** http://www.whitehouse.gov/.

BIENKOWSKA, Elzbieta; Minister of Regional Development, Government of Poland; ***languages:*** English; ***education:*** MA in oriental studies, Jagiellonian Univ., 1989; National School of Public Admin., 1996; Warsaw School of Economics post-graduate MBA, 1998; ***political career:*** Minister of Regional Development and Government Plenipotentiary for Equal Legal Status and with responsibility for Women and Legal Affairs; ***office address:*** Ministry of Regional Development, pl. Trzech Krzyzy 3/5, 00-507 Warsaw, Poland; ***phone:*** +48 22 461 5000; ***URL:*** http://www.mrr.gov.pl.

BILDT, Carl; Swedish, Minister of Foreign Affairs, Government of Sweden; ***born:*** 15 July 1949, Halmstad, Sweden; ***married:*** Anna Maria (née Corazza); ***education:*** Stockholm Univ., 1968-73; ***political career:*** Chmn., Confed. of Liberal and Cons. Students, 1973-74; Chmn., European Democrat Students, 1974-76; Mem., Stockholm County Cncl., 1974-77; Under-Sec. of State for Co-ordination and Planning at the Cabinet Office, 1979-81; MP, 1979; Mem., Submarine Defence Cmn., 1982-83; Mem., 1984 Defence-Policy Cmn., 1984-87; Chmn., Moderate Party, 1986; Chmn., Cons. Gp. in Nordic Cncl., 1988-91; Vice-Chmn., Int. Democrat Union (IDU), 1992; Prime Minister, 1991-94; Co-Chmn., Int. Conference on the Former Yugoslavia, 1995; High Representative for Peace Implementation in Bosnia and Herzegovina, 1996-97; Minister of Foreign Affairs, 2006-; ***memberships:*** Advisory Cncl. on Foreign

Affairs, 1982-; Int. Inst. for Strategic Studies 1988-; ***professional career:*** Editor, Svensk Linje, 1969-73; ***committees:*** Exec. Cttee., Moderate Party, 1981-; Moderate Party's Parly. Gp. Cncl., 1982-; Economic Cttee., Nordic Cncl., 1986-91; ***honours and awards:*** Honorary Knighthood, Knight Commander of the Most Distinguished Order of St. Michael and St. George-KCMG, 1998; Grand Cross Order of Merit of the Federal Republic of Germany, Bonn, 1998; Commander, Honorary Legion at the Elysée Palace, 1997; Grand Officer, the order of Three Stars, Riga, 1997; Commander, the Grand Cross Estonia Terra Mariana Cross, Tallin, 1996; ***publications:*** The Country that Stepped out into the Cold, 1972; A Future in Freedom, 1976; A Citizen of Halland, Sweden and Europe, 1991; Peace Journey in Stockholm, 1997, in Sarajevo, 1998; in Belgrade, 1999 and in London, 1998; ***office address:*** Ministry of Foreign Affairs, Gustav Adolfstorg 1, 103 23 Stockholm, Sweden; ***phone:*** +46 (0)8 405 6000; ***fax:*** +46 (0) 723 1176; ***URL:*** http://www.utrikes.regeringen.se.

BILIRAKIS, Michael; American, Congressman, Florida 9th District, US House of Representatives; ***party:*** Republican; ***political career:*** Congressman, Florida 9th District, US House of Representatives, 1982-; ***professional career:*** Veterans' Affairs Cttee.; Commerce Cttee.; ***committees:*** Veterans' Affairs; Foreign Affairs; Homeland Security; ***honours and awards:*** L. Mendel Rivers Award of Excellence, Air Force Sergeants Assn.; Inspirational Leadership Award, Military Order of the Purple Heart; AMVETS Silver Helmet Award; ***office address:*** House of Representatives, 2269 Rayburn House Office Building, Washington, DC 20515, USA; ***phone:*** +1 202 225 5755.

BILLSTROM, Tobias; Minister of Migration and Asylum Policy, Government of Sweden; ***born:*** 1973; ***education:*** BA, 2000, MA, 2002, Lund Univ., Sweden; ***political career:*** MP, 2002-; Minister of Migration and Asylum Policy, 2006-; ***office address:*** Ministry of Migration and Asylum Policy, Rosenbad 4, 103 33 Stockholm, Sweden; ***phone:*** +46 (0)8 405 1000 .

BILTGEN, François; Minister of Justice, Employment, Culture, Higher Education, Research and Religious Affairs, Luxembourg Government; ***born:*** 1958; ***education:*** Univ. de Paris; Institut d'Etudes Politiques, Paris; ***political career:*** Sec., Christian Social Party, 1983; Town Councillor, Esch-sur-Alzette, 1987, Deputy Mayor, 1997; Mem., Chmaber of Deputies, 1994-; Minister of Employment, Religious Affairs, Relations with Parliament, Communications; Minister of Employment, Culture, Higher Education, 1999-2004; Minister of Labour, Employment and Religious Communities, Culture, Higher Education and Research, 2004-09; Minister of Justice, Minister of the Civil Service and Administrative Reform, Minister of Higher Education and Research, Minister of Communication and Media. Minister of Religion, 2009-; ***office address:*** Ministry of Justice, 13 rue Erasme, L-2939, Luxembourg.

BINGHAM, Andrew; MP for High Peak, UK Government; ***party:*** Conservative; ***political career:*** MP for High Peak, May 2009; ***interests:*** business, pensions; ***committees:*** Works & Pensions, 2010-; ***office address:*** House of Commons, London, SW1A 0AA, United Kingdom; ***phone:*** +44 (0)20 7219 3000; ***e-mail:*** andrew.bingham.mp@parliament.uk.

BINLEY, Brian; MP for Northampton South, House of Commons; ***born:*** 1942; ***political career:*** Local Councillor; MP for Northampton South, 2005-; ***professional career:*** Chmn., BCC Marketing Services; ***office address:*** House of Commons, London, SW10 0AA, United Kingdom; ***phone:*** +44 (0)20 7219 3000; ***e-mail:*** brian.binley.mp@parliament.uk.

BIN MOHAMED, Mustapa; Malaysian, Minister of International Trade and Industry, Malaysian Government; ***born:*** 1950, Bachok Kelantan; ***education:*** Sultan Ismail Coll., Kota Bharu, 1968-69; Melbourne, Australia, BA (Hons) econ.; Colombo Plan Scholarship, First Class; Hubert H. Humphrey Fellowship, Boston MA, USA, MA dev. econ., 1980-82; ***political career:*** Special Officer to the Minister of Finance, 1984-87; Politicial Secy. to Minister of Finance, 1987-91; mem., Senate, 1991; Parly. Secy. to Minister of Finance, 1991; Dep. Minister of Finance, 1994-95; Minister of Entrepreneur Dev., 1995; Minister of Higher Education, 2006-08; Minister of Agriculture and Agro-based Industry, 2008; Minister of International Trade and Industry, 2009-; ***memberships:*** Secy., Malay Assn. of Victoria Australia, 1971-72; Chmn., Advisory Bd. of Kelantan Poverty Eradication Foundation; ***professional career:*** Admin. and Diplomatic Officer, Min. of Finance, 1974-80; Lecturer Intan, 1982-84; ***trusteeships:*** Pulau Pinang Bina Ilmu Foundation; Patron, Malaysia Children Welfare Foundation; ***publications:*** Daim and Razaleigh: A Comparison; Outstanding Decade of Mahathir Leadership; Malaysian Economy: Facts and Fallacy; Towards an Excellent Era; Economics for Politicians; Understanding the Economy; ***office address:*** Ministry of International Trade and Industry, (Kementerian Pertaniuan Antarabangsadu Perindustrian), Blok 10, Kompleks Pejabat Kerajaan, Jalan, 50622 Kuala Lumpur, Malaysia; ***URL:*** http://www.miti.gov.my.

BIN ZAYED AL-NAHYAN, Sheikh Khalifa; Ruler and President, Abu Dhabi; ***born:*** 1948, Al Ain; ***parents:*** HH Sheikh Zayed bin Sultan al-Nahyan; ***political career:*** Crown Prince of Abu Dhabi, 1969-2004; Prime Minister, Minister of Defence and Finance of Abu Dhabi, 1971; Dep. Prime Minister,second UAE Federal Cabinet, 1973; Chmn., Abu Dhabi Exec. Cncl., 1974; President and Ruler, Abu Dhabi, 2004-; ***office address:*** Office of the President, Manhal Palace, P.O.Box 280, Abu Dhabi, United Arab Emirates; ***phone:*** +971 2 665 2000; ***fax:*** +971 2 665 1962.

BIRRU, Girma; Ethiopian, Ambassador, Ethiopian Embassy in Washinton; ***languages:*** Amharic, English, Oromiffa; ***education:*** Addis Ababa Univ., Ethiopia, BA, Economics, 1982; Inst. of Social Studies (ISS), The Hague, Netherlands, MA, Economic Policy and Planning, 1986; ***political career:*** Advisor, Socio-economic Affairs Dept., Office of the Council of Ministers, 1982-87; Sr. Advisor, Bureau of Industry and Handicrafts, 1987-89, Head of Desk (Dept.), 1989-91; Advisor to the Minister in Economic Affairs, Min. of Nat. Defence, 1991-92; Vice Minister of Finance, Admin. and Logistics, Min. of Nat. Defence, 1992; with the rank of Minister, Head of Revenue Admin. Bd., Office of the Council of Ministers, 1994-95; Minister of Econ. Dev. and Co-operation, 1995-2001; Minister of Trade and Industry, 2001-10; ***professional career:*** Amb. to the USA, 2010-; ***publications:*** The Importance of Coffee in Ethiopian Economy (research paper), 1982; The Possible Effect of the Adjustment Role of Delvaluation in Ethiopia (research paper), 1986; ***office address:*** Ethiopian Embassy, 3506 International Drive, NW Washington, DC 20008, USA; ***phone:*** +1 202 364 1200; ***fax:*** +1 202 686 9551; ***e-mail:*** g.birru@telecom.net.et; ***URL:*** http://www.ethiopianembassy.org.

BIRT, Lord John; British, Member of the House of Lords; ***born:*** 10 December 1944; ***education:*** Engineering Science, St. Catherine's College, Oxford; ***political career:*** Mem., House of Lords, 2000-; ***memberships:*** Wilton Park Academic Council; the Media Law Group; Business in the Community's Women's Economic Target Team; ***professional career:*** Granada TV, 1966; produced various current affairs programmes; Dir. of Programmes, London Weekend Television, 1982; Dpty. Dir-Gen. of BBC, 1987-92; Dir-Gen., BBC, 1992-2000; International Cncl., Museum of TV and Radio, NY, 1994-2000; Vice- Pres., Royal Television Society, 1994-2000; Adviser, McKinsey, 2000-05; Prime Minister's Strategy Adviser (UK), 2001-05; Adviser, Terra Firma, 2005-; Adviser, Capgemini, 2006-2010; Chmn., Waste Recycling Group, 2006; Chmn., InGains, 2006-07; Chmn., Maltby Capital, 2008-10; Chmn., Paypal Europe, 2010-; ***committees:*** Exec. Cttee., Broadcasting Research Unit; ***honours and awards:*** Fellow and Vice-Pres., Royal Television Society; Visiting Fellow, Nuffield College, Oxford; Hon. Fellow, St. Catherine's College, Oxford; Hon. Doctorate, Liverpool John Moores University; Emmy Award, US National Academy of Television, Arts and Sciences, 1995; Hon. Fellow, City Univ., Univ. of Wales, Univ. of Bradford, Univ. of Westminster; ***office address:*** House of Lords, London, SW1A 0PW, United Kingdom; ***phone:*** +44 (0)20 7219 3000.

BIRT, Sir Michael Cameron St. John; Bailiff and Chief Justice of Jersey, Government of Jersey; ***born:*** 25 August 1948, Godalming, Surrey, UK; ***parents:*** St John Birt and Mairi Birt; ***married:*** Joan Frances Birt (née Miller); ***education:*** Marlborough Coll., 1961-66; Magdalene Coll, Univ. of Cambridge, 1966-69; ***professional career:*** Barrister in England, 1970-75; Advocate in Jersey, 1976-93; Attorney General of Jersey, 1993-2000; Dep. Bailiff of Jersey, 2000-09; Bailiff and Chief Justice of Jersey, July 2009-; ***honours and awards:*** QC, 1994; ***office address:*** Bailiff's Chambers, Royal Court Building, St Helier, Jersey, JE1 1BA, United Kingdom; ***phone:*** +44 (0)1534 441100; ***fax:*** +44 (0)1534 441137.

BIRTWISTLE, Gordon; MP for Burnley, UK Government; ***party:*** Liberal Democrat; ***political career:*** Burnley Borough Councillor, 1983-; MP for Burnley, May 2010-; ***office address:*** House of Commons, London, SW1A 0AA, United Kingdom; ***phone:*** +44 (0)20 7219 3000; ***e-mail:*** gordon.birtwistle.mp@parliament.uk.

BIRUTIS, Sarunas; Lithuanian, Minister of Culture, Government of Lithuania; ***born:*** 20 September 1961, Slauliar; ***party:*** Group of the Alliance of Liberals and Democrats for Europe; ***political career:*** mem., European Parl., 2004-09; Minister for Culture, 2012-; ***office address:*** Ministry of Culture, J. Basanaviciaus g. 5, 2683 Vilnius, Lithuania; ***phone:*** +370 5 261 9486; ***fax:*** +32 (0)2 284 9671; ***URL:*** http://www.lrkm.lt.

BISHOP OF COVENTRY, The Rt. Rev. the Lord ; Bishop of Coventry; ***education:*** BD., PhD, Univ. of Manchester; St John's College, Nottingham; ***political career:*** Mem., House of Lords, 2012-; ***professional career:*** Ordained, 1981-; Principal, Ridley Hall, Cambridge, 2001-08; Bishop of Coventry. 2008-; ***office address:*** House of Lords, London, SW1A 0PW, United Kingdom; ***phone:*** +44 (0)20 7219 5353.

BISOGNIERO, Claudio; Ambassador of Italy to the US, Embassy of Italy; ***born:*** 1954; ***education:*** Univ. of Rome, Political Science; ***professional career:*** Italian Foreign Service, 1978-; Embassy of Italy in Beijing, 1981; Permanent Mission of Italy to Nato, Brussels, 1984-89; Dipl. Advisor to President Cossiga, 1989-92; First Counselor, Embassy of Italy in Washington, DC, 1992-96; Permanent Mission of Italy to the UN in New York, 1996-99; Home Office, 1999, Dir. Gen. for the Americas, 2005; Deputy Sec. Gen., NATO, 2007-11; Amb. of Italy to the US, 2012-; ***office address:*** Embassy of Italy, 3000 Whitehaven Street, NW, Washington, DC 20008, USA; ***phone:*** +1 202 612 4400; ***fax:*** +1 202 518 2154; ***e-mail:*** stampa@itwash.org; ***URL:*** http://www.ambwashingtondc.esteri.it/ambasciata_washington.

BITI, Tendai; Minister of Finance, Government of Zimbabwe; ***born:*** 1966; ***education:*** Zimbabwe Univ.; ***party:*** Sec. Gen., Movement for Democratic Change; ***political career:*** MP for Harare East; Minister of Finance, 2009-; ***professional career:*** Lawyer; ***office address:*** Ministry of Finance, 2nd Floor, Munhumutapa Bldg, Samora Machel Avenue, Causeway, Harare, Zimbabwe; ***phone:*** +263 (0)4 794571; ***fax:*** +253 (0)4 792750; ***URL:*** http://www.mofed.gov.zw.

BIYA, Paul; President, Republic of Cameroon; ***born:*** 1933; ***married:*** Jean Irène Atyam; ***s:*** 1; ***education:*** Lycée Genéral Leclerc; Lycée Louis-le-Grand, Paris; Faculty of Law, Sorbonne (LLB); Inst. of Political Science, Paris (Diploma); Higher Institute of Overseas Studies, Paris (THEOM); postgraduate Diploma in Public Law; ***political career:*** Chargé de Mission, Presidency of Cameroon, 1962-64; Dir., Cabinet of Minister of Nat. Education, Youth and Culture, 1964-65, Sec.-Gen., 1965-67; Dir., Cabinet of the President, 1967, Sec.-General, then Minister Sec.-Gen., 1968-70, concurrently Dir., of Civil Cabinet; Minister of State, 1970-75; Prime Minister, 1975-79, 1980-82; Pres. of Cameroon, Nov. 1982-; ***memberships:*** Political Bureau; CC of Cameroon National Union, 1975-, Vice-Chmn., 1980-, National Pres., 1983-; ***honours and awards:*** Grand Master of National Orders; Commander, German National Order, Tunisian National Order; Grand Cross of the Senegalese National Order of Merit; Grand Cross of the Legion of Honour, and many other foreign decorations; ***office address:*** Presidence de la République du Cameroon, c/o the Central Post Office, Yaoundé, Cameroon.

BJERRE-NIELSEN, Soren; Chairman of Board of Directors, Danmarks Nationalbank; ***born:*** 1952; ***professional career:*** Accountant; Deloitte & Touche; Group Pres., CFO, Danisco A/S, 1995-2011; Chmn., Board, VKR Holding A/S; Chmn., Board, MT Hojgaard; Mem., Board of Dirs., Danmarks Nationalbank, 1999-, Chmn., 2007-; ***office address:*** Danmarks Nationalbank, Havenegade 5, 1093 Copenhagen K, Denmark; ***URL:*** http://www.nationalbanken.dk.

BJORKLUND, Jan; Deputy Prime Minister, Minister for Education, Government of Sweden; ***born:*** 1962; ***party:*** Liberal Party; ***political career:*** elected exec. of the Liberal Party, 1995; Minister for Schools, 2006-07; Party Leader, Liberal Party, 2007-; Minister for Education, 2007-; Deputy Prime Minister, 2011-; ***office address:*** Ministry of Schools, Government Offices, SE 103 33 Stockholm, Sweden; ***phone:*** +46 (0)8 405 1000.

BLACK OF BRENTWOOD, Lord Guy Vaughan; Member, House of Lords; ***education:*** Peterhouse, Cambridge Univ.; ***party:*** Conservative; ***political career:*** Councillor, Brentwood District Council 1988-92; Mem., House of Lords, 2010-; ***professional career:*** Exec. Dir., Telegraph Media Group; Chmn., Press Standards Board of Finance; Chmn., Commonwealth Press Union Media Trust ; ***office address:*** House of Lords, London, SW1A 0PW, United Kingdom.

BLACKBEARD, Roy; Botswanan, High Commissioner, Republic of Botswana; ***born:*** 16 April 1953; ***languages:*** Afrikaans, English; ***political career:*** Treasurer of the Botswana Democratic Party, 1980-96; Mem. of Parliament for Serone North Constituency, 1989- 1998; Assistant Minister of Agriculture, 1992-94; Min. of Agriculture, 1994-97; ***memberships:*** Mem. of the Central District Council, 1979-89; ***professional career:*** Official Learner Metallurgy, De Beers, 1972-79; Audit Clerk, Price Waterhouse, 1973-74; C.E.O., Blackbeard & Co., June 1974-89; Ranch Manager, 1974-96; High Commissioner, 1998-; ***committees:*** Livestock Industry Advisory Cttee., 1979-89; General Purposes and Finance Cttee., 1979-89; ***office address:*** High Commission of the Republic of Botswana, 6 Stratford Place, London, W1N 9AE, United Kingdom; ***phone:*** +44 (0)20 7499 0031; ***fax:*** +44 (0)20 7495 8595.

BLACKBURNE, H.E. Alison; High Commissioner, British High Commission in Uganda; ***professional career:*** FCO, 1987-; Previous posts in Warsaw, Poland; Stockholm, Sweden; New York, USA; Brussels, Belgium; High Commissioner to Uganda, 2012-; ***office address:*** British High Commission , 4 Windsor Loop, PO Box 7070, Kampala, Uganda; ***phone:*** +256 31 231 2000; ***e-mail:*** bhcinfo@starcom.co.ug; ***URL:*** http://www.ukinuganda.fco.gov.uk.

BLACKMAN, Bob; MP for Harrow East, UK Government; ***party:*** Conservative; ***political career:*** London Borough of Brent Councillor, 1986-; Mem., Greater London Assembly 2004-08; MP for Harrow East, May 2010-; ***committees:*** Communities and Local Government, 2010-; Backbench Business, 2012-; ***office address:*** House of Commons, London, SW1A 0AA, United Kingdom; ***phone:*** +44 (0)20 7219 3000; ***e-mail:*** bob.blackman.mp@parliament.uk.

BLACKMAN-WOODS, Roberta, MP; MP for City of Durham, House of Commons; ***party:*** Labour; ***political career:*** MP for City of Durham, 2005-; PPS to Rt. Hon. Hilary Armstong MP, Chancellor of the Duchy of Lancaster and Minister for the Cabinet Office, to 2007; PPS to Rt. Hon. Des Browne MP, Defence Sec., 2007-10; PPS to the Department of Innovation, Universities and Skills Ministers; Shadow Minister for Civil Society, Oct. 2010-11; Shadow Minister, Communities and Local Government, 2011-; ***interests:*** education, regeneration, foreign affairs and development; ***committees:*** Jt. Cttee., Statutory Instruments 2005-10; Innovation, Universities and Skills Select Cttee., 2007-10; Chwmn., Associate Parly. Grp. for Afghanistan, 2007-; Founder and Chwmn., Balanced and Sustainable Communities All-Party Grp., 2007-; Loss Cttee., -2008; ***office address:*** House of Commons, London, SW1P 0AA, United Kingdom.

BLACKWOOD, Nicola; Member of Parliament, House of Commons; ***political career:*** MP (Oxford West and Abingdon), 2010-; ***interests:*** human rights, home affairs; ***committees:*** Home Affairs, 2010-; ***office address:*** House of Commons, London, United Kingdom; ***phone:*** +44 (0)20 7219 7136; ***e-mail:*** nicola.blackwood.mp@parliament.uk.

BLAIR OF BOUGHTON, Lord Ian; Member, House of Lords; ***education:*** Christ Church, Oxford; ***political career:*** Mem., House of Lords, 2010-; ***professional career:*** Police Officer, 1974-2008; Dep. Commissioner of Police of the Metropolis, 2000-05; Commissioner of Police of the Metropolis, 2005-08; ***office address:*** House of Lords, London, SW1 0AA, United Kingdom; ***phone:*** +44 (0)20 7219 3000.

BLEARS, Hazel; British, MP for Salford and Eccles, House of Commons; ***born:*** 14 May 1956; ***party:*** Labour Party; ***political career:*** Chwn., NW Regional Labour Party; MP, Salford, 1997-2010, Salford and Eccles, 2010-; Minister without Portfolio, May 2006-June 2007; Secretary of State for Communities and Local Government, June 2007-June 09; ***professional career:*** Solicitor; ***office address:*** House of Commons, London, SW1A 0AA, United Kingdom; ***phone:*** +44 (0)20 7219 3000; ***e-mail:*** blearsh@parliament.uk.

BLENCATHRA, Rt. Hon. Lord David; British, Member, House of Lords; ***born:*** 1953; ***party:*** Conservative Party; ***political career:*** MP, Penrith and The Border, 1983-2010; Minister of State, Dept. of the Environment 1992-93; Minister of State, Home Office 1993-97; Opposition Chief Whip, House of Commons, 2001-05; Mem., House of Lords, 2011-; ***honours and awards:*** Raised to the peerage as Baron Blencathra, of Penrith in the County of Cumbria, 2011; ***office address:*** House of Lords, London, SW1A 0PW, United Kingdom; ***phone:*** +44 (0)20 7219 3000.

BLENKINSOP, Tom; MP for Middlesborough South and East Cleveland, UK Government; ***party:*** Labour; ***political career:*** MP for Middlesborough South and East Cleveland, May 2010-; Opposition Whip, 2011; ***committees:*** Environment, Food and Rural Affairs Cttee., 2010-12; Standards & Privileges, 2010-11; Treasury, 2011; Selection, 2012-; ***office address:*** House of Commons, London, SW1A 0AA, United Kingdom; ***phone:*** +44 (0)20 7219 3000; ***e-mail:*** tom.blenkinsop.mp@parliament.uk.

BLOK, Stef; Minister for Housing and the Central Government Sector, Netherlands Government; ***born:*** 1964; ***education:*** Univ. of Groningen; ***party:*** People's Party for Freedom and Democracy (VVD); ***political career:*** Mem., House of Reps., 2002-12; Minister for Housing and the Central Government Sector, Rutte-Asscher gov., Nov. 2012-; ***professional career:*** various positions, most recently, vice pres., corporate banking, ABN AMRO, 1988-98; ***office address:*** Ministry of the Interior and Kingdom Relations, PO Box 20011, 2500 EA The Hague, Netherlands; ***phone:*** +31 (0)77 465 6767.

BLOMFIELD, Paul; MP for Sheffield Central, UK Government; ***married:*** Linda McAvan MEP; ***party:*** Labour; ***political career:*** MP for Sheffield Central, May 2010-; PPS to Shadow Leader of the House of Commons, Oct. 2010-; ***interests:*** universities; housing; skills and employment; social cohesion; ***committees:*** Select Cttee., Business Innovation and Skills, 2010-; ***office address:*** House of Commons, London, SW1A 0AA, United Kingdom; ***phone:*** +44 (0)20 7219 4001; ***e-mail:*** paul.blomfield.mp@parliament.uk.

BLUMENTHAL, Richard; Senator for Connecticut, US Senate; ***born:*** 1946; ***education:*** Harvard College, Phi Beta Kappa, Magna cum Laude; Yale Law School, J.D.; Trinity College, Cambridge; ***political career:*** Mem., Connecticut House of Reps., 1984-87; Mem., Connecticut Senate, 1987-91; elected to US Senate, 2010, sworn in Jan. 2011; ***professional career:*** US Marine Corps Reserves, 1970-76; US Attorney for the District of Connecticut, 1977-81; Connecticut State Attorney General, 1991-2011; ***committees:*** Judiciary; Armed Services; Commerce, Science, and Transportation; Veterans' Affairs; ***office address:*** United States Senate, 702 Hart Senate Office Building, Washington DC 20510, USA; ***phone:*** +1 202 224 2823; ***URL:*** http://www.blumenthal.senate.gov.

BLUNKETT, Rt. Hon. David, MP; British, MP for Sheffield, Brightside and Hillsborough, British Government; ***born:*** 6 June 1947; ***parents:*** Arthur Blunkett (dec'd) and Doris Matilda Elizabeth (dec'd) (née Williams); ***children:*** Alistair Todd (M), Hugh Saunders (M), Andrew Keir (M), William Saunders (M); ***education:*** Sheffield Univ., BA, Political Theory and Institutions, 1972; Huddersfield Holly Bank Coll. of Education, PGCE; ***party:*** Labour Party; ***political career:*** Mem., Sheffield City Council, 1970-88, Leader, 1980-87; Mem., South Yorkshire Metropolitan County Cncl., 1973-77; Mem., Labour Party National Exec.Cttee., 1983-98; MP (Labour) for Sheffield Brightside, 1987-2010, MP for Sheffield, Brightside and Hillsborough, 2010; front bench opposition spokesman on the Environment, 1988-92; Mem., Shadow Cabinet, 1992-97; chief opposition spokesman on Health 1992-94, Education 1994-95, education and employment 1995-97; Vice-Chmn., Labour Party, 1992-93, Chmn., 1993-94; Sec. of State for Education and Employment, 1997-2001; Sec. of State for the Home Office, 2001-04; Sec. of State for Works and Pensions, 2005; ***professional career:*** clerk typist, 1967-69; lecturer and tutor in industrial relations and political administration, Barnsley Coll. of Technology, 1973-87; Dep. Chmn., AMA, 1984-87; ***committees:*** chmn., Family and Community Services Cttee., Sheffield City Cncl., 1976-80; Chmn., Labour Party Cttee. on Local Govt., 1984-92; Mem., Home Policy, Organisation, International, Finance and General Purposes, Communications and Campaign Strategy Cttees.; ***publications:*** On a Clear Day, 1995 (revised 2002); Politics and Progress, 2001; The Blunkett Tapes - my life in the bear pit, 2006; Local Enterprise and Worker's Plans, 1981; Building from the Bottom: the Sheffield Experience, 1983; Democracy in Crisis: the town hall respond, 1987; ***recreations:*** walking, music, sailing, being with friends; ***office address:*** House of Commons, London, SW1A 0AA, United Kingdom; ***phone:*** +44 (0)20 7219 3000; ***e-mail:*** blunkettd@parliament.uk.

BLUNT, Crispin Jeremy Rupert; British, Member of Parliament for Reigate, House of Commons; ***born:*** 15 July 1960; ***parents:*** Maj. Gen. Peter Blunt, CB, MBE, GM and Adrienne (née Richardson); ***married:*** Victoria Ainsley (née Jenkins), 15 September 1990; ***s:*** 1; ***d:*** 1; ***children:*** Claudia (F), Frederick (M); ***education:*** Wellington College; RMA Sandhurst; Univ. College Durham, BA; Cranfield Inst. of Technology, MBA; ***party:*** Conservative Party; ***political career:*** MP, Reigate, 1997-; Opposition Frontbench Spokesman on Northern Ireland, 2001-2002; Opposition Frontbench Spokesman on Trade, Energy and Science, 2002-2003; Opposition Whip, 2004; Parliamentary Under Secretary of State, Ministry of Justice, 2010-12; ***professional career:*** Army Officer, 13/18 Royal Hussars, 1980, UK and Cyprus, 1980-81, BAOR, 1984-85; Regimental Signals Officer/ Ops Officer, BAOR/UK, 1985-87, Sqdn Ldr, 2 i/c UK 1987-89, resigned Cmn., 1990; Representative, Forum of Private Business, 1991-92; Consultant, Politics International, 1993; Special advisor to Sec. of State for Defence, 1993-95; Special advisor to Foreign Sec., 1995-97; ***committees:*** Conservative Middle East Cncl., Conservative Parliamentary Friends of India; Mem, House of Commons, Defence Select Cttee, 1997-00; Environment Select Cttee., 2000-2001; Defence, 2003-04; Finance, 2005-09; ***clubs:*** Reigate Priory cricket; MCC; ***recreations:*** cricket, travel; ***office address:*** House of Commons, London, SW1A 0AA, United Kingdom; ***phone:*** +44 (0)20 7219 2254; ***e-mail:*** crispinbluntmp@parliament.uk.

BLUNT, Roy D.; American, Senator, US Senate; ***born:*** 1950; ***married:*** Roseann Ray Blunt, 1968; ***education:*** Southwest Baptist Univ., BA, History; Southwest Missouri State Univ., MA, History; ***party:*** Republican; ***political career:*** Sec. of State for Missouri, 1984; Congressman, Missouri Seventh District, US House of Representatives, 1997-2010; House Majority Whip, to Jan. 2007; Minority Whip, 2007-09; Mem., US Senate, 2010-; Vice-Chmn., Senate Republican Conference, 2010-; ***memberships:*** Advisory Bd., Federal Election Commn. (USA); Missouri Opportunity 2000 Cmmn. (Co-Chmn.); Red Cross; ***professional career:*** County Clerk, Greene County, Missouri 1973-85; Secy. of State, Missouri 1985-; Chmn. Governor's Advisory Council on Literacy; ***committees:*** Senate Appropriations Cttee.; Commerce, Science & Transportation; Rules & Administration Cttee.; Armed Services; ***honours and awards:*** Springfield, Missouri's Outstanding Young Man of 1980; Missouri's Outstanding Young Civic Leader of 1981; one of the U.S. Jaycees' Ten Outstanding Young Americans for 1986; ***publications:*** Voting Rights Guide for the Handicapped in Missouri; co-author, Missouri Election Procedures: A Layman's Guide; ***clubs:*** Kiwanis Club; Masonic Lodge; Abou Ben Adhem Shrine; ***office address:*** US Senate, 260 Russell Senate Office Building, Washington, DC 20510, USA; ***phone:*** +1 202 224 5721; ***URL:*** http://www.blunt.senate.gov.

BOAKAI, Joseph; Vice President, Government of Liberia; ***born:*** 30 November 1944; ***education:*** College of West Africa; Univ. of Liberia; Kansas State Univ. USA; ***party:*** Unity Party; ***political career:*** Minister of Agriculture, 1983-85; Vice President, 2006-; ***office address:*** Office of the Vice President, EPO Box 9001, Capitol Hill, Monrovia, Liberia.

BOATSWAIN, Hon. Anthony; Minister of Education and Human Resource Development, Government of Grenada; ***political career:*** MP for St. Patrick's West; Minister of Finance, Trade, Industry & Planning, to 2007; Minister of Economic Planning, and Trade and Industry, 2007-08; Minister of Education and Human Resource Development, 2013-; ***office address:*** Ministry of Education and Human Resources Development, Ministerial Complex, Botanical Gardens, Tanteen, St. George's, Grenada; ***phone:*** +1 473 440 2737; ***fax:*** +1 473 440 4115; ***e-mail:*** mail@mined.edu.gd; ***URL:*** http://www.grenadaedu.com.

BODE, Ridvan; Minister of Finance, Government of Albania; ***born:*** 1959; ***party:*** Democratic Party; ***political career:*** MP, Albania, 1996-; Minister of Finance, 1996-97; Gen. Sec., Albanian Democratic Party, 1997-; mem., Steering Cttee., 1997-; mem., National Council, 1997-; Minister of Finance, 2009-; ***office address:*** Ministry of Finance, Bulevardi Gjergj Fishta 6, Tirania, Albania; ***e-mail:*** rbode@minfin.gov.al.

BØDSKOV, Morten; Minister of Justice, Government of Denmark; ***born:*** 1 May 1970, Karup, Denmark; ***education:*** Aalborg Univ.; ***political career:*** MP, 2001-; Minister of Justice, 2011-; ***office address:*** Ministry of Justice, Slotsholmsgade 10, 1216 Copenhagen K, Denmark; ***phone:*** +45 3392 3340; ***fax:*** +45 3393 3510; ***e-mail:*** jm@jm.dk; ***URL:*** http://www.jm.dk.

BOEDIONO, Dr; Vice President, Government of Indonesia; ***political career:*** Minister of Finance, 2001-05; Coordinating Minister for the Economy, 2005-08; Vice President, 2009-; ***professional career:*** Governor, Bank Indonesia, 2008-09; ***office address:*** Office of the Vice President, Jalan Merdeka Selatan 6, Jakarta , Indonesia; ***phone:*** +62 (0)21 363539; ***URL:*** http://www.indonesia.go.id.

BOEHNER, John A.; American, Speaker of the House, US House of Representatives; ***born:*** November 1949, Cincinatti, Ohio, USA; ***education:*** Xavier Univ., B.Sc., 1977; ***party:*** Republican; ***political career:*** Union Township trustee, 1982-84; representative, Ohio state legislature, 1984-90; fmr. House Republican Conference Chmn.; Congressman, Ohio Eighth District, US House of Representatives, 1990-; Majority Leader, HOR, 2006-07; Minority Leader, HOR, 2007-10; Speaker of the House, HOR, 2011-; ***committees:*** Agriculture Cttee.; Education and the Workforce Cttee; House Administration Cttee.; ***office address:*** House of Representatives, 436 Cannon House Building, Washington, DC 20515-6501, USA; ***URL:*** http://www.house.gov.

BOHMER , Maria; Minister of State in the Federal Chancellery, German Government; ***born:*** 1950; ***political career:*** MP, 1990-; Minister of State in the Federal Chancellery and Federal Government Commissioner for Migration, Refugees, and Integration, 2005-; ***professional career:*** Professor, Heidelberg Teachers Coll., 2001-; ***office address:*** Federal Chancellery, Bundeskanzleramt, Willy-Brandt Str. 1 , 10557 Berlin, Germany; ***fax:*** +49 (0)1 888400 2357.

BOKOVA, Irina; Bulgarian, Director-General, UNESCO; ***born:*** 1952; ***education:*** Moscow State Inst; Harvard Univ.; Univ. of Maryland; ***professional career:*** Ambassador of Bulgaria to France and Monaco; Bulgarian Rep., International Organisation of Francophony; Permanent Delgate to UNESCO, 2005-09, Director-General, 2009-; ***office address:*** UNESCO, 7 Place de Fontonoy, 75352 Paris, France; ***URL:*** http://www.unesco.org.

BOLD, Luvsanvandan; Minister of Foreign Affairs, Government of Mongolia; ***born:*** 1962; ***political career:*** activist for democracy; mem., People's Great Khural; mem., State Small Khural, 1990-92; MP, 1996-2000, 2008-; Minister of Defence, 2008; Minister of Foreign Affairs, 2012-; ***office address:*** Ministry of Foreign Affairs, Peace Ave., 71, Ulaan Baatar 210648, Mongolia; ***URL:*** http://www.mfat.gov.mn.

BOLDEN, Charles, Jr; Administrator, NASA; ***political career:*** BSc, electrical science, 1968; Univ. of Southern California, MSc, systems management, 1977; ***professional career:*** US Naval Academy; naval aviator, more than 100 combat missions; 34-year career with the Marine Corps., incl. 14 years at NASA's Astronaut Office; incl. four flights on the space shuttle, commanded two missions; NASA Administrator, 2009-; ***office address:*** NASA, 300 E Street SW, Washington, DC 20024-3210, USA; ***URL:*** http://www.nasa.gov/.

BOLES, Nick; MP for Grantham and Stamford, UK Government; ***party:*** Conservative; ***political career:*** Westminster City Councillor, 1998-2002; MP for Grantham and Stamford, May 2010-; PPS to Minister of State for Schools, 2010-12; Parliamentary Under-Secretary of State (Planning), Dept. for Communities and Local Government, 2012-; ***interests:*** education, local government, foreign affairs; ***office address:*** House of Commons, London, SW1A 0AA, United Kingdom; ***phone:*** +44 (0)20 7219 3000; ***e-mail:*** nick.boles.mp@parliament.uk.

BOLOT, Pascal; Prefect & High Administrator, French Southern & Antarctic Territories; ***born:*** 1960; ***professional career:*** 10-year army career; Ecole Nationale d'Administration, 1993; Ministry of the Interior, Dir. of the Prefect's cabinet, Eastern Pyrenees; Cabinet Dir., High Commissioner of the Republic, French Polynesia, 1997-99; Sec.-Gen., Prefecture Eure-et-Loir, France, 2001; Dep. Prefect, St. Pierre, Reunion; Sec.Gen., Regional Affairs, Mid-Pyrenees, 2006; Ministry of Overseas Territories, 2010; Prefect and High Administrator, French Southern & Antarctic Territories, 2012-; ***office address:*** Office of French Southern & Antarctic Territories, Rue Gabriel Dejean, 97410 Saint Pierre, Réunion; ***URL:*** http://www.taaf.fr.

BONE, Peter; MP for Wellingborough, House of Commons; ***born:*** 19 October 1952, Billericay, Essex; ***children:*** Alexander (M), Helen (F), Thomas (M); ***education:*** Westcliff-on-Sea Grammar Sch.; ***party:*** Conservative Party; ***political career:*** MP for Wellingborough, 2005-; ***professional career:*** Financial Dir, Essex Electronics and Precision Engineering Group, 1977-83;Chief Executive and Dir., High Tech Electronics plc, 1983-90; MD, International travel and realty company 1990-; ***office address:*** House of Commons, London, SW1P 0AA, United Kingdom; ***phone:*** +44 (0)20 7219 3000; ***e-mail:*** bonep@parliament.uk.

BONGO ONDIMBA , Ali Ben; President, Gabon Government; ***born:*** 1959; ***parents:*** Omar Bongo and Patience Dabany; ***education:*** PhD in law, Sorbonne, Paris; ***political career:*** Minister of Foreign Affairs, 1989-91; Minister of National Defence, 1999-2009; President, 2009-; ***office address:*** Office of the President, BP 546, Libreville, Gabon; ***phone:*** +241 172 20 30.

BONI, Yayi; President of Benin; ***born:*** 1952; ***party:*** Independent; ***political career:*** President of Benin, March 2006-; ***professional career:*** Head, West African Development Bank; Chair, African Union, 2012; ***office address:*** Office of the President, BP 1288, Cotonou, Benin.

BONICHOT, Jean-Claude; Judge, Court of Justice of the European Union; ***born:*** 1955; ***education:*** University of Metz, law; Institut d'études politiques, Paris; ***professional career:*** Legal Secretary at the Court of Justice, 1987-91; Judge, 1999-2000, President, Sixth Sub-Division of the Judicial Division, 2000-06, Council of State; Univ. Lecturer, University of Metz and University of Paris I, Panthéon-Sorbonne; Judge, Court of Justice, 2006-; ***office address:*** Court of Justice of the European Union, Rue du Fort Niedergrunewald, L-2925, Luxembourg.

BONINO, Emma; Italian, Minister for Foreign Affairs, Government of Italy; ***born:*** 9 March 1948, Bra (Cuneo); ***languages:*** French, Spanish, English; ***education:*** Bocconi Univ., Milan, Degree in Modern Languages, 1972; Distinguished Visiting Prof., American Univ. of Cairo; ***party:*** Pres., 1991-93, Sec., 1993-94, Transnational Radical Party; ***political career:*** Deputy, Italian Chamber of Deputies, 1976-; elected MEP, 1979, re-elected, 1984, 1999; mem., Presidential Bureau; Head, Italian Govt. delegation to the UN Gen. Assembly for the Moratorium on death penalty initiative, 1994; appointed European Cmnr., 1994; MEP, 2004-06; Minister for International Trade, 2006-08; Minister of Foreign Affairs, Aor, 2013-; ***memberships:*** Head, PARIFA (Italian Parliamentarians against Hunger), 1982; Chair, Parly. Gp., Radical Party; Bd. mem., International Crisis Gp. (ICG); ***professional career:*** Founder, CISA, Information Centre on Sterilisation and Abortion; promoter, referendum which led to the introduction of the legalisation of abortion in Italy; Promoter of a referendum against nuclear energy, 1986; Promoter, int. campaigns: civil and political rights in Eastern Europe, 1987; tribunals on war crimes in the former Yugoslavia and Rwanda, for the establishment of a permanent int. criminal court, 1990, 2002; for the eradication of female genital mutilation (FGM), 2000-02; for the inclusion of women in the interim Govt. of Afghanistan, 2001; ***committees:*** Cttee. on Foreign Affairs, Human Rights, Common Security and Defence Policy; Founder, Head, Assn. Food and Disarmament International, 1978; ***honours and awards:*** Gran Cruz de la Orden de Mayo, 1995; European Personality of the Year, 1996; European Communicator of the Year, 1997; Premio Principe de Asturias, 1998; Order of the Prince Branimir, 2002; Gonfalone d'Argento, 2002; Premio Presidente della Repubblica, 2003; ***office address:*** Ministry of Foreign Affairs, Piazzale della Farnesina 1, 00189 Rome, Italy; ***phone:*** +39 06 36911; ***URL:*** http://www.esteri.it.

BONNER, Jo; Congressman, Alabama Ist District, US House of Representatives; ***born:*** 19 November 1959, Selma, Alabama, USA; ***education:*** Univ. of Alabama, BA, Journalism; ***political career:*** Congressman, Alabama First District, US House of Representatives; Assist. Majority Whip, US House of Representatives; ***committees:*** Ethics; Chair appropriations; ***honours and awards:*** Outstanding Alumnus in Public Relations, Univ. of Alabama; ***office address:*** House of Representatives, 315 Cannon House Office Building, Washington, DC 20515, USA.

BONNICI, Josef; Governor, Central Bank of Malta; ***education:*** Univ. of Malta, economics; Simon Fraser Univ., Canada, MA, Ph.D, economics; Rikkyo Univ., Japan, Doctor of Humanities, Honoris Causa; ***political career:*** Advisor to the prime minister of Malta; Parly. Sec. in Finance; Minister of Economic Services; Mem., European Court of Auditors; ***professional career:*** Professor of Economics, University of Malta; Board Member, Central Bank of Malta; Governor, Central Bank of Malta, 2011-; ***office address:*** Central Bank of Malta, PO Box 378, Castille Place, CMR Valletta 01, Malta.

BOOLELL, Hon. Dr. Arvin; Minister of Foreign Affairs, Mauritius Government; ***born:*** 26 May 1953; ***education:*** Nat. Univ. of Ireland; Royal Coll. of Surgeon, Ireland, LLM RCP, LLM RCS, MB, BCH, BAO (Dublin); ***party:*** Vice Chmn., Mauritius Labour Party; ***political career:*** MP, 1987-; Minister of Agriculture and Natural Resources, 1995; Minister of Agriculture, Fisheries & Co-operatives, 1997; Minister of Agriculture, Food Technology and Natural Resources, 1998-2000; Minister of Agro Industry and Fisheries, 2005-08; Minister of Foreign Affairs, International Trade and Cooperation, 2008-; ***professional career:*** Medical Practitioner, Wales & New Zealand; ***office address:*** Ministry of Foreign Affairs, 5th floor, New Government Centre, Port Louis, Mauritius; ***fax:*** +230 208 8087 / 212 6764; ***e-mail:*** mfa@mail.gov.mu; ***URL:*** http://foreign.gov.mu.

BOOMGAARDEN, H.E. Georg; Ambassador, German Embassy in the UK; ***born:*** 1948; ***professional career:*** Amb. to Nicaragua, 1989-92; Amb. to the Kingdom of Spain, 2003-05; State Sec., Federal Foreign Office, 2005-08; Amb. to the United Kingdom, 2008-; ***office address:*** German Embassy, 23 Belgrave Square, London, SW1X 8PZ, United Kingdom; ***phone:*** +44 (0)20 7824 1300; ***fax:*** +44 (0)20 7824 1435; ***e-mail:*** mail@german-embassy.org.uk; ***URL:*** http://www.german-embassy.org.uk.

BOOTH, H.E. Donald E.; Ambassador, US Embassy in Ethiopia; ***professional career:*** US Ambassador to Liberia, 2005-10; Amb. to Ethiopia, 2010-; ***office address:*** US Embassy, Entoto Street, Addis Ababa, Ethiopia; ***phone:*** +251 (0)1 550666; ***fax:*** +251 (0)1 551328; ***e-mail:*** usemaddis@state.gov; ***URL:*** http://ethiopia.usembassy.gov.

BOOZMAN, John; Senator for Arkansas, US Senate; ***born:*** 10 December 1950, Shreveport, Louisiana; ***married:*** Cathy (née Marley); ***education:*** undergraduate, Univ. of Arkansas, US; Doctorate (O.D.), Southern College of Optometry; ***political career:*** Mem., US House of Representatives, Rep. of the State of Arkansas, 3rd District, -2010; Mem., US Senate, Rep. of the State of Arkansas, Nov. 2010-; ***professional career:*** Optometrist; ***committees:*** Agriculture, Nutrition and Forestry; Appropriations; Environment and Public Works; Veterans' Affairs; ***office address:*** US Senate, 320 Hart Senate Office Building, Washington DC, 20510-4103, USA; ***phone:*** +1 202 224 4843; ***URL:*** http://www.boozman.senate.gov/.

BORDALLO, Madeleine Z.; Congresswoman, Guam, US House of Representatives; ***born:*** 31 May 1933, Graceville, Minnesota; ***parents:*** Christian and Evelyn; ***married:*** Ricardo J. Bordallo, 20 June 1953 (dec'd 1990); ***children:*** Deborah Josephine Bordallo (F); ***public role of spouse:*** former governor of Guam; ***education:*** St. Mary's Coll., South Bend, Indiana, 1952; Assoc. Degree in Music, St. Katherine's Coll., St. Paul, Minnesota, 1953; ***party:*** Democratic Party; Women's Democratic Party of Guam, 1965-94; ***political career:*** Senator, Guam Legislature, 1981-82 1987-88, 1989-90,1992-94; First Woman Lt. Gov. of Guam, 1994-98, 1999-2002; US Congresswoman for Guam, 2003-; ***memberships:*** Federation of Asian Women's Assn., 1959-2000, now Pres.; American Red Cross, Guam Chapter, 1963-, now Fund Drive Chwmn.; Guam Memorial Hospital Volunteers Assn., 1966-; Soroptomist International of Guam, 1978-; and many others, social and religious; ***professional career:*** Sales for KUAM Radio/TV Station, Traffic Mgr., Programme Dir., Women's Dir., hosted radio programmes for Women and Children, 1954-63; First Lady of Guam, 1975-78, 1983-86; Gen. Mgr., Zapatos Inc., 1979-83; Bd. of Dirs., APIL, 1994; Pacific

BIOGRAPHIES

Islands Development Bank Task Force, 1994; Bd. of Dirs., Watergate East, Inc., 2007-2010; ***committees:*** Nat. Cttee. Woman, Nat. Democratic Party, 1964-; Chwmn., Housing and Community Dev., 1987-88; Mem., Guam's Cmn. on Self Determination, 1988-90; Chwm., Cttee. on Health, Ecology and Welfare, 1989-90; Chwm., Cttee. on Education, 1992-94; mem., House Cttee. on Small Business, 2003-06; mem., House Armed Services Cttee., 2003-; mem., Sub Cttee. on Readiness of the House Armed Services Cttee., 2003-; Mem., House Cttee. on Natural Resources, 2003-; Chwn., Sub Cttee. on Fisheries, Wildlife and Oceans, 2007-08; Chwn., Sub Cttee. on Insular Affairs, Oceans and Wildlife, 2009-; Mem., Sub Cttee., on Military Personnel of the House Armed Services Cttee., 2009-; mem., Banking Ctee., 2010-; ***honours and awards:*** Outstanding Young Woman of America, 1966; Hon. Degree, Outstanding Community Service, Coll. of Guam, 1968; "Woman of the Year", Women's Organisation of Guam; Soroptimist Int., "Women Helping Women" Award, 1983-84; 20 Most Influential Leaders in Guam, Latte Magazine; ***publications:*** articles on fashion and travel, Leblon Finatinas Para Guam (Cookbook), 1978; Official Protocal Guide for Guam, 1982; Educational Conference Proceedings, 1994; ***clubs:*** Guam Women's Club, 1959-2000, now Pres.; ***office address:*** US House of Representatives, 427 Cannon HOB, Washington, DC 20515, USA; ***phone:*** +1 202 225 0288; ***fax:*** +1 202 226 0341; ***e-mail:*** madeleine.bordallo@mail.house.gov.

BORG, Anders; Minister of Finance, Government of Sweden; ***born:*** 1968; ***education:*** Univ. of Uppsala; post-grad. studies, Stockholm Univ.; ***party:*** Moderate Party; ***political career:*** Minister of Finance, 2006-; ***professional career:*** Economist; ***office address:*** Ministry of Finance, Drottninggt 21, 103 33 Stockholm, Sweden; ***phone:*** +46 (0)8 405 1000.

BORG, Dr Tonio; Commissioner, European Commission; ***born:*** 1957, Floriana, Malta; ***education:*** Doctor of Laws, Univ. of Malta, 1979; ***political career:*** MP; Minister for Home Affairs and the Environment, 1995-96; Minister of Justice and Home Affairs, 2003-04; Deputy Prime Minister, 2004-07; Deputy Prime Minister and Minister for Foreign Affairs, 2007-12; Commissioner for Health & Consumer Policy, 2012-; ***professional career:*** Lawyer and Lecturer in Law; ***office address:*** European Commission, rue de la loi 200, B-1049 Brussels, Belgium; ***URL:*** http://ec.europa.eu.

BORRIE, Lord Gordon, Kt, QC; British, Member, House of Lords; ***born:*** 13 March 1931, Croydon, Surrey, UK; ***parents:*** Stanley Borrie and Alice Borrie; ***married:*** Dorene Borrie (née Toland), 10 December 1960 (died 2010); ***education:*** Univ. of Manchester, LL.B, LL.M; Barrister-at-Law; ***party:*** Labour Party; ***political career:*** Mem., House of Lords; ***professional career:*** Called to Bar, Middle Temple, 1952; Director-General, Office of Fair Trading, 1976-92; Council of the Ombudsman for Corporate Estate Agents, 1992-98; Chmn., Commission on Social Justice, 1992-94; Dir., Woolwich Building Society, 1992-2000; Dir., Three Valleys Water plc, 1992-03; Dir., Mirror Group Newspapers plc, 1993-99; Dir., Telewest plc, 1994-2001; Dir., General Utilities plc, 1998-03; Chmn., The Advertising Standards Authority, 2001-07; The Accountancy Foundation, 2000-03; Chmn., Council for the Estate Agents Ombudsman, 2007-10; ***office address:*** House of Lords, London, SW1A 0PQ, United Kingdom.

BOSSANO, Hon. Joseph J., B.Sc, BA, MP; Gibraltarian, Minister of Enterprise, Training and Employment, Government of Gibraltar; ***born:*** 1939, Gibraltar; ***married:*** Judith Baker, 1969; Rose Torilla, 1988; ***education:*** Gibraltar Grammar School; University of London, B.Sc., Economics, 1969; University of Birmingham, BA, 1972; ***political career:*** Founder Mem., Integration with Britain Movement and First Gen. Secy., 1965; active in UK student movement, 1966; Secy., London Branch of the Integration with Britain Movement; Mem., Management Committee, Tottenham Constituency Labour Party 1965-68; mem., Integration with Britain Party's (IWBP) 1972 election line-up; elected Opposition Mem. at the House of Assembly; Branch Officer, Transport & General Workers' Union, 1974; resigned from IWBP following British Labour Party rejection of integration, leading his own party, the Gibraltar Democratic Movement (GDM); Leader of the Opposition, 1976 General Elections (4 GDM seats); renamed GDM the Gibraltar Socialist Labour Party (GSLP), 1977; instrumental in achieving parity of wages with Britain in 1978 after 4 years negotiation; Opposition mem., 1980 Election; GSLP leader, 1984 Election (the GSLP now being the sole Party in Opposition, with 7 seats); led GSLP to victory in 1988, with a 58% majority; returned to office in the 1992 General Elections with an increased majority of 73%; Addressed UN Cttee., of 24 in 1992-95 and UN 4th Cttee., 1993-95 where Gibraltar's case for decolonlisation was presented. 1994 presented Gibraltar's case for self-determination before UN Economic, Social & Cultural Rights Cttee., in Geneva; Chief Minister, 1988-96; attended UN Decolonisation seminars in Trinidad & Tobago, Cuba & St. Vincents; addressed UN 4th Cttee., 1999-2005; addressed UN Cttee. of 24, 1999-2006; Leader of the Opposition, 1996-2011; Minister of Enterprise, Training and Employment, 2011-; ***professional career:*** Military service, Gibraltar Regiment; various UK factory posts, 1958-60; joined British Merchant Navy (1960), becoming active in Trade Union affairs; participated in reform movement leading to better representation of the National Union of Seamen; undertook correspondence study with the College of the Sea, obtaining University placements; returned to Gibraltar in 1964, working initially as a bar steward until intensified Spanish restrictions and Gibraltar-UN talks stimulated his political interests; ***office address:*** Office of the Minister of Enterprise, Training and Employment, 156 Main Street, Gibraltar; ***phone:*** +350 78420; ***fax:*** +350 42849; ***URL:*** http://www.gibraltar.gov.gi.

BOSWELL OF AYNHO, Lord Timothy Eric; British, Member, House of Lords; ***born:*** 1942; ***parents:*** Eric New Boswell (dec'd) and Joan Boswell (dec'd) (née Jones); ***married:*** Helen Boswell (née Rees), 1969; ***languages:*** French, German, Italian, (some); ***education:*** New Coll., Oxford, MA, Dip. in Agricultural Econ.; ***party:*** Conservative; ***political career:*** MP (Cons.) for Daventry, 1987-; PPS Financial Sec. to Treasury, 1989-90; Asst. Whip, 1990-92; Lord Cmnr. of HM Treasury (Sr. Whip), 1992; Parly. Under-Sec. of State Dept. for Education, 1992-95; Parly. Sec., Min. of Agriculture, Fish and Food, 1995-; Opposition Spokesman on Treasury matters, 1997, Trade and Industry, 1998-99, Education, Employment and Disabilities, 1999-2001, Pensions and Disabilities, 2001-02; Lifelong Learning, 2002-03; Home and Constitutional Affairs, 2003-04; Work and Pensions, 2004-07; PPS to Party Chmn., 2005-07; Mem., House of Lords, 2010-; ***interests:*** agriculture, education, finance, Europe; ***memberships:*** Agriculture and Food Research Cncl., 1988-90; ***professional career:*** Cons. Research Dept., 1966-73 and Head of Econ. Section, 1970-73; Farmer, 1974-87; Part-time Special Adviser to Min. of Agriculture, 1984-86; Treas., 1976-79, and Chmn., 1979-83, of Daventry Constituency Cons. Assn.; County Chmn., Leics. Northants and Rutland Counties Branch NFU, 1983; Pres., Cncl. of Perry Foundation Agricultural Research, 1984-90; ***committees:*** Chmn., Parly. Panel on Charity Law, 1988-90; Sec., Conservative Backbench Agricultural Cttee., 1987-89; Mem., Agricultural Select Cttee., 1987-89; DIUS Select Cttee., 2007-; ***clubs:*** Farmers; ***recreations:*** country pursuits, travel; ***office address:*** House of Lords, London, SW1A 0AA, United Kingdom; ***phone:*** +44 (0)20 7219 3000.

BOT, Yves; Judge, Court of Justice of the European Union; ***education:*** Faculty of Law, Rouen; Doctor of Laws, University of Paris II, Panthéon-Assas; ***professional career:*** Lecturer, Faculty of Law, Le Mans; Deputy Public Prosecutor, Senior Deputy Public Prosecutor, Public Prosecutor's Office, Le Mans, 1974-82; Public Prosecutor, Regional Court, Dieppe, 1982-84; Deputy Public Prosecutor, Regional Court, Strasbourg, 1984-86; Public Prosecutor, Regional Court, Bastia, 1986-88; Advocate General, Court of Appeal, Caen, 1988-91; Public Prosecutor, Regional Court, Le Mans, 1991-93; Special Adviser to the Minister for Justice, 1993-95; Public Prosecutor at the Regional Court, Nanterre, 1995-2002; Public Prosecutor, Regional Court, Paris, 2002-04; Principal State Prosecutor, Court of Appeal, Paris, 2004-06; Advocate General, Court of Justice, 2006-; ***office address:*** Court of Justice of the European Union, Rue du Fort Niedergrunewald, L-2925, Luxembourg.

BOTTOMLEY, Peter James; British, Member of Parliament for Worthing West, House of Commons; ***born:*** 1944; ***married:*** Virginia Garnett, 1967; ***s:*** 1; ***d:*** 2; ***education:*** Trinity Coll., Cambridge, BA(Econ.); ***political career:*** Conservative MP for Woolwich West, 1975-83, for Eltham, 1983-97; Dept. of Employment, Parly. Under-Sec. of State, 1984-86; Dept. of Transport, Parly. Under-Sec. of State, 1986-89; Parly. Under-Sec. of State, Northern Ireland Office, 1989-90; MP for Worthing West, 1997-; ***memberships:*** Chmn., Family Forum (1979-80); Pres., Conservative Trade Unionists National Advisory Cttee (1978-81); Transport & General Workers Union.; Chmn., Church of England Children's Socy. 1983-84; ***professional career:*** Lorry Driver 1966; Salesman 1967-68; Industrial Relations Officer 1969; Marketing Manager 1970-71; Industrial Consultant 1972-73; Managing Director 1974-75; ***office address:*** House of Commons, London, SW1A 0AA, United Kingdom; ***phone:*** +44 (0)20 7219 3000; ***e-mail:*** bottomleyp@parliament.uk; ***URL:*** http://www.epolitix.com/webminister/peter-bottomley.

BOUCHER, Ambassador Richard A.; American, Deputy Secretary General, OECD; ***born:*** Bethesda, MD, USA; ***married:*** Carolyn Boucher (née Brehm); ***children:*** Madeleine (F), Peter (M); ***public role of spouse:*** Executive, General Motors; ***languages:*** French, Chinese; ***education:*** Tufts Univ., BA, English and French Lit., 1973; George Washington Univ., graduate work in econ.; ***political career:*** Spokesman and Assist. Sec. for Public Affairs; Assist. Sec. of State for South and Central Asia, 2006-09; ***professional career:*** joined Foreign Service, 1977; US Consulate Gen., Guangzhou, 1979-80; China Desk, State Dept.'s Econ. Bureau, Washington DC; Dep. Principal Officer, US Consulate Gen., Shanghai, 1984-86; Sr. Watch Officer, State Dept.'s Operations Center, Washington DC, 1986; Dep. Dir., Office of European Security and Political Affairs, 1987-89; Dep. Press Spokesman, State Dept. under-Secy. Baker, 1989; Spokesman under-Secy. Eagleburger, 1992, Christopher, 1993; US Amb. to Cyprus, 1993-96; US Consul Gen., Hong Kong, 1996-99; US Senior Official for Asia-Pacific Economic Co-operation, 1999; Dep. Sec. Gen., Organisation for Economic Co-operation and Development (OECD), 2009-; ***office address:*** OECD, 2 rue André-Pascal, 75775 Paris Cédex 16, France; ***URL:*** http://www.oecd.org.

BOUDOU, Amado; Vice President, Government of Argentina; ***education:*** National University of Mar del Plata, Argentina; Center for Macroeconomic Studies of Argentina; ***political career:*** Minister of the Economy and Public Finance, 2009-13; Vice President, 2011-; ***office address:*** Office of the Vice President, Balcarce 50, 1064 Buenos Aires, Argentina; ***phone:*** +54 (0)11 4379 5858; ***fax:*** +54 (0)11 4954 4707; ***e-mail:*** webmaster@presidencia.gov.ar; ***URL:*** http://www.presidencia.gov.ar.

BOURAN, H.E. Alia; Ambassador, Embassy of the Hashemite Kingdom of Jordan; ***political career:*** Minister of Environment and Minister of Tourism and Antiquities, 2003-04; Minister of Tourism and Antiquities, 2003-05; ***professional career:*** Amb Ex. & Plen. of Jordan to Belgium, 2001-03, concurrently to Norway, EC and Luxembourg; Amb. Ex. & Plen. of Jordan to the UK, 2006-11; Amb. Ex. & Plen. of Jordan to the US, 2011-; ***office address:*** Embassy of the Hashemite Kingdom of Jordan, 6 Upper Phillimore Gardens, London, W8 7HB, United Kingdom; ***phone:*** +44 (0)20 7937 3685; ***fax:*** +44 (0)20 7937 8795; ***e-mail:*** lonemb@dircon.co.uk; ***URL:*** http://www.jordanembassyuk.org .

BOUTEFLIKA, Abdelaziz; Algerian, President and Minister of National Defence, Republic of Algeria; ***political career:*** Foreign Minister; candidate in presidential elections, 1999; President of the Republic, Minister of National Defence, 1999-; ***professional career:*** General, Algerian Army, now retired; ***office address:*** Office of the President, Présidence de la République, El Mouradia, Algiers, Algeria; ***phone:*** +213 (0)21 691515; ***fax:*** +213 (0)21 691515; ***URL:*** http://www.elmouradia.dz.

BOUTERSE, Dési; President, Government of Suriname; ***born:*** 1945; ***party:*** National Democratic Party; ***political career:*** President of Suriname, August 2010-; ***professional career:*** Army Officer; ***office address:*** Office of the President, Onafhankelijkheidsplein, Paramaribo, Suriname; ***URL:*** http://www.sr.net/users/burpres.

BOWEN, Christopher; Minister of the Treasury, Government of Australia; ***born:*** 1973, New South Wales; ***education:*** BEc (Syd).; ***party:*** ALP; ***political career:*** Member for Prospect, New South Wales, 2004-; Shadow Assistant Treasurer, 2006-07; Shadow Minister for Revenue and Competition Policy, 2006-07; Assistant Treasurer and Minister of Competition Policy and Consumer Affairs, 2007-09; Minister for Financial Services, Superannuation and Corporate Law and Minister for Human Services, 2009-10; Minister for Competition Policy and Consumer Affairs, 2010; Minister for Immigration and Citizenship, 2010-13; Minister of Tertiary Education, Skills, Science and Research, Minister of Small Business, 2013; Minister of the Treasury, 2013-; ***office address:*** Department of the Treasury, Langton Crescent, Parkes, ACT 2601, Australia; ***e-mail:*** department@treasury.gov.au; ***URL:*** http://www.treasury.gov.au.

BOWEN, Hon. Gregory; Minister of Communications and Works, Government of Grenada; ***political career:*** Minister of Communication, Works and Public Utilities; Dep. PM, to 2008; Minister of Communications and Works, Physical Development, Public Utilities, and Information Commuications, 2013-; ***office address:*** Ministry of Works, Communication & Public Utilities, Ministerial Complex, 4th Floor, St. George's, Grenada; ***phone:*** +1 473 440 2821; ***fax:*** +1 473 440 4122.

BOXER, Barbara, BA; Senator for California, US Senate; ***born:*** 1940, Brooklyn, USA; ***education:*** Brooklyn Coll., BA, Econ.; ***party:*** Democrat; ***political career:*** US House of Representatives, 1982-92; US Senator for California, 1993-; Western Regional Democratic Whip; Dep. Asst. Floor Leader; ***professional career:*** Stockbroker; Journalist; Pres., Marin County Bd. of Supervisors, 1976-82; ***committees:*** Environment and Public Works Cttee.; Foreign Relations Cttee.; Commerce, Science and Transportation; Select Cttee. on Ethics; ***honours and awards:*** many honours and recognitions from various organisations; ***office address:*** United States Senate, 112 Hart Senate Office Building, Washington, DC 20510, USA; ***phone:*** +1 202 224 3553; ***URL:*** http://www.boxer.senate.gov/.

BOZIZE, Gen. François; President, Central African Republic; ***political career:*** opposition figure; led unsuccessful coup, 1983; exiled to Togo; presidential candidate, 1993; suspected of involvement in a coup, 2001; took control of part of country before fleeing to Chad; took power in a coup and declared himself president, March 2003; elected president, 2005-; Minister of Defence, 2005-11; Minister of Diplomacy, Justice and Security, 2011-; ***office address:*** Office of the President, Palais de la Renaissance, Bangui, Central African Republic.

BRABAZON OF TARA, Lord Ivon Anthony; British, Member, House of Lords; ***born:*** 1946; ***married:*** Harriet Frances, 1979; ***children:*** Benjamin Ralph (M), Anabel Mary (F); ***education:*** Harrow; ***political career:*** Minister for Shipping, 1986-89; Minister for Aviation & Shipping, 1987-89; Minister of State, Foreign and C'wealth Office, 1989-90; Minister of State, Dept. of Transport, 1990; Minister for Aviation and Shipping, Dept. of Transport,1990-92; Principal Dep., Chmn. of Cttees., 2001-02, Chmn of Cttees., 2002-; Mem., House of Lords; ***memberships:*** Pres., UK Warehousing Assoc.; ***professional career:*** Mem. of London Stock Exchange,1972-84; Lord-in-Waiting (Govt. Whip in House of Lords), 1984-86; ***clubs:*** Royal Yacht Squadron; ***office address:*** House of Lords, London, SW1A 0PW, United Kingdom.

BRADLEY, Karen; MP for Staffordshire Moorlands, UK Government; ***party:*** Conservative; ***political career:*** MP for Staffordshire Moorlands, May 2010-; ***committees:*** Work and Pensions, Select Cttee., 2010-12; Procedure, 2011-12; ***office address:*** House of Commons, London, SW1A 0AA, United Kingdom; ***phone:*** +44 (0)20 7219 3000; ***e-mail:*** karen.bradley.mp@parliament.uk.

BRADSHAW, Ben; British, MP for Exeter, British Government; ***born:*** 30 August 1960, London; ***parents:*** Canon Peter Bradshaw and Daphne Bradshaw (née Murphy); ***married:*** Neal Dalgleish (Partner); ***languages:*** German, Italian; ***education:*** Norwich & Sussex Univ.; ***party:*** Labour Party; ***political career:*** Sec., Labour Movement for Europe; MP, Exeter, 1997-; Parly. Private Sec. to John Denham MP, 2000-01; Under sec. of State at the Foreign Commonwealth Office, 2001-02; Dep. Leader, House of Commons, 2002-03; Under Sec. of State, Dept. for the Env., Food & Rural Affairs, 2003-06; Minister of State, Dept. for the Environment, Food and Rural Affairs, 2006-07; Minister of State, Dept. of Health, and Minister for the South West, 2007-09; Secretary of State for Culture, Media and Sport, 2009-May 2010; Shadow Secretary of State for Culture, Olympics, Media & Sport, May 2010-Sept. 2010; ***interests:*** Europe, foreign policy, transport, environment, electoral reform; ***professional career:*** Journalist; BBC Radio, Devon; BBC's Berlin Correspondent, 3 years; BBC Radio 4; ***committees:*** Ecclesiastical Cttee., 2010-; Jt. Cttee. on Culture, Media & Sport, 2012-; ***honours and awards:*** Hon. Fellow, Humboldt Univ.; ***clubs:*** Whipton Labour Club, Exeter; ***recreations:*** cycling, walking, music, dancing, cooking, family; ***office address:*** House of Commons, London, SW1A 0AA, United Kingdom; ***phone:*** +44 (0)20 7219 6597; ***fax:*** +44 (0)20 7119 0950; ***e-mail:*** bradshawb@parliament.uk.

BRADY, Graham; British, Member of Parliament for Altrincham and Sale West, House of Commons; ***born:*** 20 May 1967, Salford, UK; ***parents:*** John and Maureen (née Birch); ***married:*** Victoria Lowther, 1992; ***children:*** William (M), Catherine (F); ***education:*** Altrincham Grammar School; Law, Univ. of Durham; ***party:*** Conservative Party; ***political career:*** Chmn., Northern Conservative Students, 1987-89, Durham Univ. Conservative Assn., 1987-88; Vice-Chmn., East Berkshire Conservative Assn., 1993-95; MP, Altrincham and Sale West, 1997-; Shadow Employment Minister, 2000-01; Opposition Whip, 2000; Shadow Schools Minister, 2001-03; PPS to Michael Howard, Leader of the Opposition, 2003-07; Shadow Minister for Europe, 2003-07; ***interests:*** education, health, EU; ***professional career:*** Shandwick PLC, Graduate Trainee; Centre for Policy Studies, 1990-92; Public Affairs Dir. The Waterfront Partnership, 1992-97; ***committees:*** Education and Employment Select Cttee., 1997-2001; 1922 Exec. Cttee., 1998-2000, 2007-, Chmn., 2010-; Treasury Select Cttee., 2007-10; Select Cttee., Parliamentary Reform, 2009-10; ***trusteeships:*** Independent governor, Manchester Metropolitan Univ., 2008-; Gov., Westminster Foundation for Democracy, 2009-10; ***recreations:*** family, garden; ***office address:*** House of Commons, London, SW1 0AA, United Kingdom; ***phone:*** +44 (0)20 7219 1260; ***e-mail:*** crowthers@parliament.uk; ***URL:*** http://www.epolitix.com/webminster.graham-brady.

BRADY, His Eminence Cardinal Sean; Irish, Archbishop of Armagh and Primate of All Ireland, Roman Catholic Church; ***born:*** 16 August 1939, County Cavan, Ireland; ***languages:*** Italian, French, Irish, Latin, &, Greek, (reading, knowledge); ***education:*** St. Patrick's Coll., Maynooth, BA, Ancient Classics, 1960; Lateran Univ., Rome, Licentiate in Theology, 1964; Lateran Univ., Rome, Doctorate in Canon Law, 1967; ***professional career:*** Ordained as priest, 1964; Prof., St. Patrick's Coll., Cavan, 1967-80; Vice-Rector, Irish Coll., Rome, 1980-87, Rector, 1987-93; PP, Co. Cavan, 1993-94; Coadjutor Archbishop of Armagh, 1995-96; Archbishop of Armagh & Primate of All Ireland, 1996-, created Cardinal (by Pope Benedict XVI), 24 November 2007-; ***committees:*** Chmn., Standing Cttee. of Irish Episcopal Conference, 1996-; Chmn of Irish Episcopal Conference, 1996-; Chmn. of Episcopal Visitors to Saint Patrick's College, Maynooth, 1996-2001; Mem. of the Holy See's Pontifical Commission for the Cultural Goods of the Church, 2002-; ***honours and awards:*** Honorary Doctorate of Law, Univ. of Ulster, 2002; ***office address:*** Ara Coeli, Cathedral Road, Armagh, BT61 7QY, United Kingdom; ***phone:*** +44 (0)28 3752 2045; ***fax:*** +44 (0)28 3752 6182; ***e-mail:*** admin@aracoeli.com; ***URL:*** http://www.armagharchdiocese.org.

BRAKE, Tom; British, MP for Carshalton and Wallington, House of Commons; ***born:*** 6 May 1962, Melton Mowbray, UK; ***parents:*** Michael Brake and Judith Brake; ***married:*** Candida Brake (née Goulden); ***languages:*** French, Russian, Portuguese; ***education:*** Imperial Coll., London, B.Sc., Physics; ***party:*** Liberal Democrats; ***political career:*** Spokesman for Environment and Transport in London, and Aviation, 1997-99; MP for Carshalton and Wallington, 1997-; Environment and Transport in London, 1999-2001; Shadow Transport Minister, 2001-03; London Spokesman, 2002-03; Lib. Dem. Whip, 2000-03; Shadow Sec. of State for Int. Dev., 2003-05; Shadow Transport Secretary, 2005-06; Local Gov. Spokesman, 2006-07; Olympics Spokesman, 2007-10; London Spokesman, 2007-10; Home Affairs Spokesman, 2008-10; Parly. Sec. (Dep. Leader of the House of Commons), 2012-; ***interests:*** environment, transport, foreign affairs; ***professional career:*** IT Consultant, Cap Gemini, until 1997; ***committees:*** Home Affairs Select Cttee., 2008-10; ***trusteeships:*** Ecolocal; ***recreations:*** sports, travel; ***office address:*** House of Commons, London, SW1A 0AA, United Kingdom; ***phone:*** +44 (0)20 7219 3000; ***e-mail:*** braket@parliament.uk.

BRALEY, Bruce; Congressman, Iowa 1st District, US House of Representatives; ***born:*** 1957, Iowa, USA; ***education:*** Iowa State Univ., B.A, 1980; University of Iowa School of Law, grad. 1983 ; ***political career:*** Congressman, Iowa 1st Dist., 2007-; ***committees:*** Oversight and Government Reform; Veterans' Affairs; ***office address:*** US House of Representatives, 1408 Longworth House Office Building, Washington, DC 20515, USA; ***phone:*** +1 202 225-2911 .

BRAMMERTZ, Serge, DCL, PhD; Belgian; ***born:*** 17 February 1962; ***languages:*** French, German, Dutch; ***education:*** University of Liège, Belgium, Degree in Criminology, 1991, final year/major subject: International Police Cooperation, cum laude; Catholic University of Leuven, Belgium, Preliminary and full degrees in Law, 1985, final year/major subject Comparative Criminal Law, cum laude; Albert Ludwigs Universitaet, Freiburg i Br, Doctorate in Law, 1988, Dissertation on Cross-border Police Cooperation, summa cum laude; ***interests:*** Armed conflict; Criminal Law; Jurisdiction; Human rights; Organisations; State responsibility; Territory/boundaries; Treaties; ***memberships:*** International Association of Magistrates, 1996-; International Association of Prosecutors, 2000-; Editorial Committee of the Revue de droit pénal et de criminologie, 2000; ***professional career:*** *academic career:* University of Liège, Professor, 2001-, Scientific Research Assistant, 1996-2001; Catholic University of Leuven, Research Assistant, Department of Criminal Law and Criminology, 1991-93; *governmental career:* Deputy Prosecutor and Head of the Investigation Division at the ICC, The Hague, 2003-; *diplomatic career:* Involved in the negotiation of bilateral agreements on judicial cooperation (eg Canada, Hong Kong, Thailand), as well as different fora at EU level, eg served as chairman of the European Judicial Network (Belgian Presidency of the EU, 2001); Expert for the Council of Europe and European Commission dealing with the fight against organised crime, fraud and corruption; Expert for the IOM regarding the fight against trafficking in human beings; Participation as a speaker in numerous international conferences on international humanitarian law, terrorism, organised crime, trafficking in human beings, international drugs trafficking and mechanisms for international cooperation;*judicial career:*Federal Prosecutor of the Kingdom of Belgium, Head of Federal Prosecution Office, in charge of conducting investigations into terrorism, organised crime and violations of international rights law, 2002-03; National Prosecutor in charge of coordinating at the national and international level investigation in the area of cross-border organised crime, 1997-2002; Deputy Prosecutor, Court of First Instance in Eupen and Deputy to the Prosecutor-General, Liège Court of Appeal, 1989-99; ***publications:*** Books: Collaboration policière transfrontalière (Cross-border Police Cooperation), co-author, 1993; Grenzüberschreitende polizeiliche Zusammenarbeit am Beispiel der Euregio Maas-Rhein (Cross-border Police Cooperation on the Lines of the Example of the Meuse-Rhine Euregion), 1999; Le droit pénal international (International Criminal Law), in "Recueil de jurisprudence de procédure pénale", 1996; Eurojust: parquet européen de la première génération? (Eurojust: A First-Generation European Prosecution Service?), in "Vers un espace judiciaire pénal européen (Towards a European Criminal Legal Area)", 2000; La coopération judiciaire internationale (International Judicial Cooperation), in "Poursuites pénales et extraterritorialité (Criminal Proceedings and Extra-territoriality)", 2002; Cross-border operational activities, in "Combating Transnational Organised Crime", 2002; Articles: Revue de droit pénal et de criminologie; Zeitschrift für die gesamte Strafrechtswissenschaft; Delikt en Delinkwent; Schriftenreihe der Polizei-Führungsakademie; CUSTODES, Cahiers thématiques de la police et de la justice; Vigiles, Revue de droit de police; ***office address:*** Maanweg 174, 2516 AB The Hague, Netherlands; ***phone:*** +31 (0)70 515 8083; ***e-mail:*** Serge.brammertz@icc-cpi.int; ***URL:*** http://www.icc-cpi.int.

BRANSTEAD, Terry; Governor, State of Iowa; ***political career:*** elected to the Iowa House, 1972, 1974, 1976; Lieutenant Governor of Iowa, 1978; Governor, 1983-99, re-elected 2010; ***professional career:*** Pres., Des Moines Univ., 1999; ***office address:*** Office of the Governor, State Capitol, Des Moines, IA 50319, USA; ***phone:*** +1 515 281 5211; ***URL:*** http://www.governor.iowa.gov/.

BRATUSEK, Alenka; Prime Minister, Government of Slovenia; ***born:*** 1971, Celje; ***political career:*** Ministry of the Economy; Ministry of Finance, 1999, head of its Budget Directorate, 2004; mem., operational working group for presidency preparation for the EU Council; MP, 2011-; Party leader, Positive Slovenia, 2013-; Prime Minister, 2013-; ***office address:*** Office of the Prime Minister, Gregorciceva 20,25, 1000 Ljubljana, Slovenia; ***URL:*** http://www.kpv.gov.si.

BRAY, Angie; MP for Ealing Central and Acton, UK Government; ***party:*** Conservative; ***political career:*** Mem., Greater London Assembly, 2000-08; MP for Ealing Central and Acton, May 2010-; ***committees:*** Transport Select Cttee., 2010; ***office address:*** House of Commons, London, SW1A 0AA, United Kingdom; ***phone:*** +44 (0)20 7219 3000; ***e-mail:*** angie.bray.mp@parliament.uk.

BRAZIER, Julian William Hendy; British, Member of Parliament for Canterbury, House of Commons; *born:* 24 July 1953, Dartford, United Kingdom; *parents:* Lt. Colonel P.H. Brazier and Mrs P.H. Brazier; *married:* Katharine Elizabeth, 1984; *children:* 3; *education:* Wellington Coll., Berkshire; Brasenose Coll., Oxford (Scholar), MA, Maths and Philosophy; London Business Sch., part-time; *party:* Conservative Party; *political career:* Chmn., Oxford Univ. Conservative Assn., 1974; various constituency offices; Parly. Candidate, 1983; MP, 1987-; PPS to Mrs Gillian Shephard, 1990-93; Pres. Conservative Family Campaign, 1995-01; Opposition Whip, 2001; MP, Canterbury, 1997-, re-elected, 2001-; Shadow Minister, Trade and Int. Dev., 2003-05; Shadow Minister, Transport (Airlines and Shipping), 2005-10; *interests:* defence, economics, law and order, family issues; *professional career:* Project Manager, HB Maynard; Int. Management Consultant; Territorial Army; *committees:* Hse. of Commons Defence Cttee., 1997-01, 2010-; *honours and awards:* Territorial Decoration; Spectator, Backbencher of the Year, 1996; *publications:* various papers and pamphlets with the Bow Group and CPS; *recreations:* cross country running; *office address:* House of Commons, London, SW1A 0AA, United Kingdom; *phone:* +44 (0)20 7219 3000; *e-mail:* brazierj@parliament.uk.

BREGU, Majlinda; Minister for European Integration, Government of Albania; *born:* 1974; *political career:* Mem., National Council, Democratic Party, 2004; Mem., Health and Social Issues Parly. Commission, 2005-07; Head, Sub-Commission, Minor and Gender Equality, 2005-07; Head, Albanian Parly. Delegation to European Parliament, 2005-07; Spokesperson, Council of Ministers, 2007-; Minister of European Integration, 2007-; *office address:* Ministry of European Integration, Bulevardi Dëshmorët e Kombit, Tirana, Albania; *e-mail:* majlinda.bregu@mie.gov.al.

BRENNAN, John; Director, Central Intelligence Agency; *education:* Fordham Univ., 1997, political science; American Univ. in Cairo, 1975-76; Univ. of Texas, Austin, Masters, government; *professional career:* CIA, various positions, 1980-2005, incl. Chief of Staff to George Tenet, 1999-2001; Dep. Exec. Dir., -2003, Interim Dir., 2004-05; private sector, 2005-08; Assist. to the President for Homeland Security & Countererrorism, 2008-12; Director, CIA, 2013-; *office address:* Central Intelligence Agency (CIA), Office of Public Affairs, Washington, DC 20505, USA; *phone:* +1 703 482 0623; *URL:* http://www.cia.gov.

BRENNAN, Kevin; Member of Parliament for Cardiff West, House of Commons; *born:* 16 October 1959, Cwmbran; *parents:* Michael Brennan and Beryl Brennan; *education:* Pembroke Coll., Oxford Univ., BA; Univ. Coll. Cardiff, PGCE; Univ. of Glamorgan, M.Sc.; *political career:* Special Advisor to Rhodri Morgan, 2000-2001; MP then First Minister of Nat. Assembly for Wales; MP, Cardiff West, 2001-; Asst. Govt. Whip, 2005-07; Parly. Under-Sec., Dept. for Children, Schools and Families, 2007-08; Parly. Sec., Cabinet Office, 2008-09; Minister of State Dept. for Business, Innovation and Skills, 2009-10; Shadow Minister for Business, Innovation and Skills, May-Sept. 2010; Shadow Minister, Education, Oct. 2010-; *professional career:* Teacher, 1985-94; Researcher, 1995-99; *publications:* Voting the Vision, Huw Edwards and Mary Southcott, 1996; The Money Myth, Rhodri Morgan, 1997; *office address:* House of Commons, London, SW1A 0AA, United Kingdom; *phone:* +44 (0)2920 223207; *fax:* +44 (0)2920 230422; *e-mail:* brennank@parliament.uk; *URL:* http://www.kevinbrennan.co.uk.

BRENTON, H.E. Jonathan; Ambassador, British Embassy in Belgium; *languages:* French, German, Russian; *education:* MA, English Literature, Bristol Univ. UK; MA, English Literature, Boston, Univ., Massachusetts, 1991; PhD., Girton Coll., Cambridge Univ., 1998; *professional career:* Head of Joint Management Office, Brussels, Belgium, 2008-10; Amb. to Belgium, 2010-; *office address:* British Embassy, Rue d'Arlon 85 Aarlenstraat, 1040 Brussels, Belgium; *phone:* +32 (0)2 287 6211; *fax:* ; *e-mail:* info@britain.be; *URL:* http://ukinbelgium.fco.gov.uk/en.

BREWER, Governor Janice K.; Governor, State of Arizona; *political career:* State Rep., 1983-86; State Senator, 1987-96, Majority Whip, 1993-96; Chmn., Maricopa County Board of Supervisors, 1996-2002; Arizona Secretary of State, 2002-09; Governor of Arizona, 2009-; *office address:* Office of the Governor, State Capitol Executive Tower, 1700 West Washington, Ninth Floor, Phoenix, AZ 85007, USA; *phone:* +1 602 542 4331; *fax:* +1 602 542 1381; *URL:* http://www.governor.state.az.us.

BREYER, Stephen G. ; Associate Justice, US Supreme Court; *born:* 15 August 1938, San Francisco, California; *education:* Stanford Univ., AB; Magdalen College, Oxford, B.A.; Harvard Law School, LL.B.; *professional career:* Special Assist., U.S. Attorney General for Antitrust, 1965-67; Assist. Prof., Prof. of Law, Lecturer, Harvard Law School, 1967-94; Assist. Special Prosecutor of the Watergate Special Prosecution Force, 1973; Special Counsel, U.S. Senate Judiciary Cttee., 1974-75, Chief Counsel,1979-1980; Prof., Harvard Univ., Kennedy School of Govt., 1977-80; Judge, US Court of Appeals, First Circuit, 1980-90, Chief Judge, 1990-94; Assoc. Justice, Supreme Court, 1994- ; *committees:* Judicial Conference of the US, 1990-94; US Sentencing Cmn., 1985-89; *office address:* Supreme Court Building, One First Street, NE, Washington, DC 20543, USA; *phone:* +1 202 479 3211; *URL:* http://www.supremecourt.gov/.

BRICQ, Nicole; Minister of Foreign Trade, Government of France; *born:* 1947; *education:* Law; *political career:* Regional Councillor, Ile de France, Mem., Cultural Affairs Cttee.; Mem., Assemblée Nationale, 1997; Mem., Senate, Seine et Marne, 2004-; Minister for Ecology, Sustainable Development & Energy, May-June 2012; Minister of Foreign Trade, 2012-; *office address:* L'Assemblée Nationale, 126 rue de l'université, 75355 Paris, France; *phone:* +33 (0)1 40 63 60 00.

BRIDGEWATER, Pamela E.; Ambassador, US Embassy in Jamaica; *born:* Fredericksburg, Virginia, USA; *education:* Walker-Grant High Sch.; Virginia State Univ., BA, Political Science, 1968; Univ. of Cincinnati, MA, Political Science, 1970; American Univ. Sch. of Int. Service (SIS), 1976; *professional career:* univ. lecturer, Morgan State University, Bowie State University, Voorhees College; joined US Foreign Service, 1980; Office of Global Affairs; Bureau of Oceans and Int. Environmental Affairs; Bureau of European Affairs; Bureau of Intelligence and Research; Attache/Political Officer, Kingston, Jamaica; Vice-Consul, Brussels, Belgium; Political Officer, Pretoria, South Africa, 1990-93; Consul General, Durban, South Africa, 1993-96; Dep. Chief of Mission, Nassau, Bahamas, 1996-99; Amb. to Benin, 2000-2002;

Amb. to Ghana, 2005-08; Amb. to Jamaica, 2010-; *honours and awards:* Doctor of Laws Degree (Honorary), Virginia State Univ., 1997; Charles Cobb Award for Trade Promotion, 2002; *office address:* Embassy of the United States of America, Jamaica Mutual Life Centre, 2 Oxford Road, 3rd Floor, Kingston 5, Jamaica; *phone:* +1 876 935 6053; *e-mail:* opakgn@pd.state.gov; *URL:* http://kingston.usembassy.gov.

BRIGDEN, Andrew; MP for North West Leicestershire, UK Government; *party:* Conservative; *political career:* MP for North West Leicestershire, May 2010-; *committees:* Regulatory Reform, 2010-; *office address:* House of Commons, London, SW1A 0AA, United Kingdom; *phone:* +44 (0)20 7219 3000; *e-mail:* andrew.bridgen.mp@parliament.uk.

BRINE, Steve; MP for Winchester, UK Government; *education:* Univ. of Liverpool; *party:* Conservative; *political career:* MP for Winchester, May 2010-; *professional career:* Radio Journalist; *committees:* Justice, 2011-; *office address:* House of Commons, London, SW1A 0AA, United Kingdom; *phone:* +44 (0)20 7219 3000; *e-mail:* steve.brine.mp@parliament.uk.

BRITO, H.E. Nuno Filipe Alves Salvador e; Ambassador, Portuguese Embassy; *education:* Law Degree, Univ. of Lisbon; *professional career:* Political Dir. of Portugal and co-chair of the Portuguese - US Bilateral Commission, 2008-11; Amb. to the USA, 2011-; *office address:* Embassy of Portugal, 2121 Kalorama Road, NW, Washington, DC 20008, USA; *phone:* +1 202 328 8610; *fax:* +1 202 462 3726; *e-mail:* portugal@portugalemb.org; *URL:* http://www.embassyportugal-us.org.

BRITTAN OF SPENNITHORNE, Rt. Hon. Lord , QC, DL; British, Member, House of Lords; *born:* 25 September 1939; *married:* Diana Brittan (née Peterson), 1980; *education:* Haberdashers' Aske's Sch.; Trinity Coll. Cambridge, MA; Yale Univ. Henry Fellow; *party:* Conservative Party; *political career:* Cons. candidate for North Kensington, 1966 and 1970; MP (Con.) for Cleveland and Whitby, 1974-83; Opp. Spokesman on Devolution and House of Commons Affairs, 1976-78; Opp. Spokesman on Devolution and Employment, 1978-79; Min. of State at the Home Office, 1979-81; Mem., Privy Cncl., 1981; Chief Sec. to the Treasury, 1981-83; Home Sec., 1983-85; MP for Richmond North Yorks, 1983-88; Sec. of State, Trade and Industry, 1985-86; Chmn., Soc. of Cons. Lawyers, 1986-89; Mem., House of Lords; *memberships:* Chmn., Society of Conservative Lawyers, 1986-89; Chmn., Conservative Group for Europe, 2001-04, Pres., 2004-07; Mem. of Business, New Europe Advisory Council, 2007-; *professional career:* Chmn., Cambridge Univ., Cons. Assn., 1960; Pres., Cambridge Union, 1960; Debating tour of USA for Cambridge Union, 1961; Called to Bar, Inner Temple, 1962; Chmn., Bow Gp., 1964-65; Editor, Crossbow, 1966-68; Co Vice-Chmn., Nat. Assn. of Sch. Governors and Mngrs., 1970-78; QC, 1978; Distinguished Visiting Fellow, Policy Studies Inst., 1988; Bencher of the Inner Temple, 1983; Chancellor, Univ. of Teesside, 1993-2005; Vice Chmn, UBS Investment Bank, Chmn., UBS Ltd., 2000-(Leave of absence, Sept. 2010-Feb. 2011); Advisory Dir., Unilever, 2000-04; Consultant, Herbert Smith, 2000,06; Non-Exec., Dir., Unilever Plc and Unilever NV, 2004-; Mem., International Advisory Bd., Total SA, 2004-; Trade Adviser to the PM, Sept. 2010-; *committees:* Mem., Cttee. of British Atlantic Gp. of Young Politicians, 1970-78; Vice-Chmn., Employment Cttee., Parly. Cons. Party, 1974-76; Mem. & Vice-Pres., European Cmn., 1989-99; *trusteeships:* Daiwa-Anglo Japanese Foundation; *honours and awards:* QC, 1978; mem., Privy Council, 1981; Knighthood, 1989; Hon. Degrees: D.C.L., Newcastle and LL.D, Hull, 1990; Doctor honoris causa, Edinburgh, 1991; D.L., Bradford and D.C.L., Durham, 1992; LL.D, Bath, 1992; Doctorate of Econs., Korea Univ. 1997; Life Peerage, 2000; Deputy Lieutenant for North Yorkshire, 2001; *publications:* Millstones for the Sixties (co-author); Rough Justice; Infancy & The Law; How to Save your Schools; A New Deal for Health Care (1988); Defence and Arms Control in a Changing Era (1988); Europe: Our Sort of Community (1989 Granada Guildhall Lecture); Discussions on Policy (1989); Monetary Union: the Issues and the Impact (1989); Hersch Lauterpacht Memorial Lectures, Univ. of Cambridge (1990); European Competition Policy (1992); Europe: The Europe We Need (1994); Globalisation vs. Sovereignty? The European Response, (The 1997 Rede Lecture and Related Speeches); A Diet of Brussels (2000); *clubs:* White's, Carlton, MCC; *recreations:* hill walking, cricket, opera; *office address:* House of Lords, London, SW1A 0PW, United Kingdom; *phone:* +44 (0)20 7568 0305; *e-mail:* leon.brittan@ubs.com.

BRIX, H.E. Emil; Ambassador, Austrian Embassy in the UK; *education:* 1979 Dr.phil, History, 1979; MA, History and English Literature, 1982; Diplomatic Academy, Vienna, 1982 ; *professional career:* Consul-General in Cracow, Poland, 1990-95; Dir. Austrian Cultural Inst., 1995-99; Dir.-Gen., for Foreign Cultural Policies, 2002-10; Amb. to the United Kingdom, 2010-; *office address:* Austrian Embassy, 18 Belgrave Mews West, London, SW1X 8HU, United Kingdom; *phone:* +44 (0)20 7235 3731; *e-mail:* embassy@austria.org.uk.

BROKENSHIRE, James; MP for Old Bexley and Sidcup, House of Commons; *born:* 1968; *party:* Conservative Party; *political career:* Member for Hornchurch, 2005-10, for Old Bexley and Sidcup, 2010-; Shadow Home Affairs Minister, 2006-10; Parliamentary Under-Secretary of State (Minister for Crime Prevention), Home Office, 2010-; *committees:* Constitutional Affairs Select Cttee., 2005-06; *office address:* House of Commons, London, SW1A 0AA, United Kingdom; *phone:* +44 (0)20 7219 8400; *e-mail:* brokenshirej@parliament.uk; *URL:* http://www.jamesbrokenshire.com.

BROOKE, Annette; Member of Parliament for Mid Dorset and North Poole, House of Commons; *married:* ; *d:* 2; *education:* Romford Technical Sch.; London Sch. of Economics, B.Sc., Economics; Hughes Hall Cambridge, Certificate in education; *party:* Liberal Democratic Party; *political career:* Poole Borough Cllr., 1986-; Chair of Planning, 1991-96; Chair of Education, 1996-2000; Chair of Environmental Strategy Working Party, 1995-97; Dep. Leader of Ruling Liberal Democrat Group, 1995-97, 1998-2000, now Group Leader Sheriff, 1996-97, Mayor, 1997-98, Dep. Mayor, 1998-99; Conference Representative for Mid-Dorset and North-Poole Constituency; Mem., ALDC Standing Cttee., 1996-98; Liberal Democrat Parly. Spokesperson for Mid-Dorset and North Poole Constituency since January 1999; MP, Mid Dorset and North Poole, 2001-; Liberal Democrat Whip and a spokeswoman on Home Affairs; spokeswoman on Education and Skills. Parly. spokesperson on all issues concerning children, young people and the family; *memberships:* RSPB, Wessex-Newfoundland Society, Poole Local Agenda 21; fmr of the following, Bd. Mem., Dorset Careers; Sch. Governor; Vice-Chair, Poole Town Management Bd., Mem. of the S.Wessex Area Environment Agency Advisory

Group; ***professional career:*** fmr. Lecturer/Teacher, Economics and Social Sciences for 19 years, Open Univ.; school teacher, 1974-94, Head of Economics, Talbot Heath School for Girls, Bournemouth; ***office address:*** House of Commons, London, SW1A 0AA, United Kingdom; ***phone:*** +44 (0)20 7219 3000; ***e-mail:*** brookea@parliament.uk.

BROOKS, Mo; Congressman, House of Representatives; ***education:*** Duke Univ.; Univ. of Alabama Law School; ***political career:*** Alabama HOR, 1982-1991; Mem., HOR, Alabama 5th District, 2010-; ***professional career:*** law; Madison County District Attorney; ***committees:*** Armed Services, Homeland Security, and Science, Space and Technology; Chairman, Science, Space and Technology subcommittee on Research and Science Education; ***phone:*** +1 202 225 4801.

BROT, Jean-Jacques; High Commissioner, New Caledonia; ***born:*** 1956, Paris, France; ***political career:*** Civil Servant; Sec.-Gen., Prefecture, Eure, 1990; Sec.-Gen., Prefecture of Finistère, 1993; Sec.-Gen., Prefecture of Hauts-de-Seine, 1995; Prefect, Mayotte, 2002; Prefect, Deux-Sèvres, 2005; Prefect, Guadeloupe, 2006; State representative, St. Barthélemy & St.-Martin, 2007; Prefect, Eure-et-Loir, 2007; Prefect, la Vendée, 2010; Prefect, Finistère, 2011; High Commissioner, New Caledonia, 2012-; ***honours and awards:*** Chevalier, Légion d'honneur; Officer, National Order of Merit; ***office address:*** Office of the HIgh Commissioner, BP C5, 98844 Noumea Cedex, New Caledonia; ***phone:*** +687 26 63 00; ***fax:*** +687 27 28 28; ***URL:*** http://www.nouvelle-caledonie.gouv.fr.

BROUN, Paul C., MD; Reprsentative, 10th District of Georgia, US House of Representatives; ***born:*** May 14, 1946, Atlanta, Georgia; ***education:*** Univ. of Georgia, B.Sc. Chemistry, 1967; Medical College of Georgia, Medical Doctor degree, 1971; ***political career:*** Mem., US HOR, 2007-; ***professional career:*** Interne, Good Samaritan Hospital, Portland, Oregon; Residency, Univ. Hospital, Birmingham, Alabama; general medicine, South Georgia; ***committees:*** Homeland Security Cttee.; Science, Space and Technology Cttee.; Natural Resources; ***office address:*** US House of Representatives, 2104 Rayburn House Office Building, Washington, DC 20515, USA; ***phone:*** +1 (202) 225 4101; ***fax:*** +1 (202) 226 0776.

BROWN, Corrine; American, Congresswoman, Florida 3rd District, US House of Representatives; ***education:*** Florida Agricultural and Mechanical Univ., B.Sc., M.Sc.; ***political career:*** Florida State House of Representatives, 1982-92; Congresswoman, Florida Third District, US House of Representatives, 1992-; ***memberships:*** Women's Caucus; Black Caucus; Human Rights Caucus; Progressive Caucus; ***committees:*** Veterans' Affairs Cttee.; Transportation and Infrastructure Cttee.; ***office address:*** House of Representatives, 2444 Rayburn House Office Building, Washington, DC 20515, USA; ***phone:*** +1 202 225 0123.

BROWN, Rt. Hon. (James) Gordon, MP; British, Former Prime Minister, MP for Kirkcaldy and Cowdenbeath, House of Commons; ***born:*** 1951; ***parents:*** Rev. John Brown and Elizabeth Brown; ***married:*** Sarah (née Macaulay), 2000; ***children:*** John (M), James (M); ***education:*** Edinburgh Univ., MA Hons., Ph.D.; ***party:*** Labour Party; ***political career:*** Chmn., Scottish Cncl., Lab. Party, 1983-84; MP (Lab.) Dunfermline East, 1983-2005; MP for Kirkcaldy and Cowdenbeath, 2005-; Opp. Spokesman on Regional Affairs, 1985-87; Shadow Chief Sec. to the Treasury, 1987-89; Shadow Sec. of State for Trade and Industry, 1989-92, for Treasury and Economic Affairs, 1992-97; Chancellor of the Exchequer, 1997-June 2007; Leader of the Labour Party, 2007-10; Prime Minister, First Lord of the Treasury and Minister for the Civil Services, June 2007-May 2010; ***professional career:*** Rector, Edinburgh Univ., 1972-75; Lecturer, Edinburgh University and Caledonian University, 1975-80; Current Affairs Editor, Scottish TV, 1980-83; ***committees:*** Mem., Select Cttee. on Employment, 1983-85; ***trusteeships:*** Chmn., John Smith Memorial Trust; ***honours and awards:*** Privy Counsellor; ***publications:*** (ed) Red Paper on Scotland; (co-ed) Scotland: The Real Divide; Maxton; Where There is Greed: Margaret Thatcher & the Betrayal of Britain's Future (1989); (co-written with James Naughtie) John Smith - Life and Soul of the Party (1994); (co-edited with Tony Wright) Values, Visions and Voices: An Anthology of Socialism (1995); ***recreations:*** reading, writing, football and tennis; ***office address:*** House of Commons, London, SW1A 0AA, United Kingdom; ***phone:*** +44 (0)20 7219 3000; ***e-mail:*** hcinfo@parliament.uk; ***URL:*** http://www.parliament.uk.

BROWN, Jerry (Edmund G.); Governor, State of California; ***born:*** 1938; ***education:*** University of Santa Clara, freshman year, 1955; Sacred Heart Novitiate, Jesuit Seminary, 1956-60; Univ. of California, 1960, BA, Classics; Yale Law School, 1964; ***political career:*** California Secretary of State, 1970; Governor of California, 1974, re-elected 1978; chmn., State Democratic Party, 1989-91; sought the 1992 Democratic Presidential nomination; mayor of Oakland, 1998, re-elected 2002; State Attorney General, 2006; Governor, 2011-; ***professional career:*** law; ***office address:*** Office of the Governor, State Capitol Building, Sacaramento, CA 95814, USA; ***phone:*** +1 916 445 2841; ***URL:*** http://gov.ca.gov/.

BROWN, Keith; Minister of Housing and Transport, Scottish Government; ***education:*** Dundee Univ.; ***political career:*** Trade Union rep., UNISON; Councillor, Clakmannanshire, -2007; mem., EU Ctte. of the Regions; MSP, Ochil Constituency, 2007-; Minister of Education and Lifelong Learning, 2009-11; Minister for Housing and Transport, 2011-; Minister of Veterans, 2013-; ***professional career:*** marine; ***office address:*** Scottish Parliament, Edinburgh, EH99 1SP, Scotland.

BROWN, Lyn, MP; MP for West Ham, House of Commons; ***born:*** 1960; ***party:*** Labour; ***political career:*** MP for West Ham, 2005-; PPS; Assist. Gov. Whip, 2009-10; Opp. Whip, 2010-; ***office address:*** House of Commons, London, SW1P 0AA, United Kingdom.

BROWN, Rt. Hon. Nicholas Hugh, MP; British, MP for Newcastle Upon Tyne East, British Government; ***born:*** 1950, Hawkhurst, Kent, United Kingdom; ***parents:*** R.C. Brown (dec.d) and G.K. Brown (dec'd); ***education:*** Univ. of Manchester, UK, BA, 1971; ***party:*** Labour Party; ***political career:*** Cllr., Newcastle upon Tyne City Cncl., UK, 1980-83; Opp. Spokesman on Legal Affairs, 1984-87, Economic Affairs, 1988, Treasury, 1988-95; Dep. Chief Whip, Labour, 1995-97; Parly. Sec. to the Treasury, & Chief Whip, Labour, 1997-98; MP, Labour, Newcastle upon Tyne East, 1983-; Minister of Agriculture, Fisheries and Food, 1998-2001; Minister of State for Work, 2001-; Re-elected MP for Newcastle upon Tyne East & Wallsend, 2001-10, Newcastle upon Tyne East, 2010-; Parly. Sec. to the Treasury and Chief Whip, Oct. 2008-May 2010; Shadow Parliamentary Secretary and Opposition Chief Whip, 2010; ***professional career:*** fmr. Brand Assist., Proctor & Gamble; Trade Union Officer, General and Municipal Workers' Union Northern Region, 1978-83; ***clubs:*** Shieldfield Working Men's Club; West Walker Social Club; Newcastle Labour Club; ***office address:*** House of Commons, London, SW1A 0AA, United Kingdom; ***phone:*** +44 (0)20 7238 3000; ***e-mail:*** hcinfo@parliament.uk; ***URL:*** http://www.parliament.uk.

BROWN, Russell; British, Member of Parliament for Dumfries and Galloway, House of Commons; ***born:*** 17 September 1951, Annan, Dumfriesshire; ***parents:*** Howard Russell Brown and Muriel Brown (née Anderson); ***children:*** Sarah Ann Kirk (nee Brown) (F), Gillian Brown (F); ***education:*** Annan Academy; ***party:*** Labour Party; ***political career:*** MP, Dumfries, 1997-; Parly. Private Sec. to Leader of House of Lords, June 2002; Shadow Minister, Defence, Oct. 2010-; ***interests:*** employment rights; ***committees:*** Select Cttee. on Deregulation and Regulatory Reform; ***recreations:*** sport, football; ***office address:*** House of Commons, London, SW1A 0AA, United Kingdom; ***phone:*** +44 (0)20 7219 4429 / consituency office: +44 (0)1387 247902; ***e-mail:*** brownr@parliament.uk.

BROWN, Sherrod; American, Senator for Ohio, US Senate; ***education:*** Yale Univ., Russian Studies; Ohio State Univ., MPA, M.Ed.; ***party:*** Democrat; ***political career:*** Ohio State House of Representatives, 1974-90; Ohio Sec. of State, 1990-92; Congressman, Ohio Thirteenth District, US House of Representatives, 1992-2007; US Senator for Ohio, 2007-; ***committees:*** US Senate: Agriculture, Nutrition & Forestry; Banking, Housing & Urban Affairs; Finance; Select Cttee. on Ethics; Veterans' Affairs; ***office address:*** United States Senate, Washington, DC 20510, USA; ***phone:*** +1 202 224 2315; ***URL:*** http://www.brown.senate.gov.

BROWNBACK, Sam, B.Sc, LL.B; American, Governor, State of Kansas; ***born:*** 12 September 1956; ***married:*** Mary Brownback; ***children:*** Abby (F), Andy (M), Liz (F), Mark (M), Jenna (F); ***education:*** Kansas State Univ., B.Sc. (Hons.), Agricultural Economics; Univ. of Kansas, LL.B; ***party:*** Republican; ***political career:*** Sec. of Agriculture for Kansas State; Republican Congressman representing 2nd District of Kansas; White House Fellow, Office of the US Trade Representative; US Senator for Kansas 1996-2010; Governor of Kansas, Jan. 2011-; ***professional career:*** administrator; broadcaster; attorney; teacher; author; lecturer; ***committees:*** Cttee. on Health, Education, Labor and Pensions; Commerce, Science and Transportation Cttee.; Cttee. on Governmental Affairs; Chmn., Subcttee. on Oversight of Govt. Management and the District of Columbia; Cttee. on Foreign Relations; Chmn., Subcttee. on the Middle East; Joint Economic Cttee.; Chmn., Foreign Sub-cttee. on Near Eastern and South Asian Affairs; ***publications:*** co-author of two books and numerous articles; ***office address:*** Office of the Governor, Capitol 300 SW 10th Ave., Suite 212S, Topeka KS 66612, USA.

BROWNE, H.E. Dr Carolyn; Ambassador, British Embassy in Kazakhstan; ***professional career:*** British Embassy in Moscow; UK Mission to the United Nations in New York; Dep. Dir. for Southern European matters, and Dir. of Human Rights Dept., FCO, 1999-2002; UK Rep, to the EU in Brussels, 2003-05; Amb. to Azerbaijan, 2007-12; Amb. to Kazakhstan, 2012-; ***office address:*** British Embassy, Renco Building 6 Floor, 62 Kosmonavtov street, Astana 010010, Kazakhstan; ***phone:*** +7 7172 556200; ***e-mail:*** british-embassy@online.kz; ***URL:*** http://ukinkz.fco.gov.uk/en.

BROWNE, Rt. Hon. Lord Desmond; British, Member, House of Lords; ***born:*** 22 March 1952; ***education:*** Glasgow Univ., LLB; ***party:*** Labour Party; ***political career:*** contested Argyll and Bute, 1992; MP for Kilmarnock and Loudoun, 1997-2010; PPS to Donald Dewar, 1998-99; PPS to Adam Ingram; MP, Kilmarnock and Loudoun, 1997-; Parliamentary Under-Secretary of State, Northern Ireland Office, 2001-03; Minister of State for Work, Dept. for Work and Pensions 2003-04; Minister of State for Nationality, Immigration and Asylum, Home Office, 2004-05; Chief Sec. to the Treasury, 2005-06; Sec. of State for Defence, May 2006-Oct. 2008 and Secretary of State for Scotland, June 2007-Oct. 2008; ***professional career:*** Solicitor; called to the Scottish Bar, 1993; Pres., Commonwealth War Graves Commission, May 2006-08; ***committees:*** Fmr. mem. Select Cttees. on Northern Ireland, 1997-98 and Public Administration, 1999; Mem. Jt. Parly. Cttee on Human Rights, 2001; ***office address:*** House of Lords, London, SW1A 0PW, United Kingdom.

BROWNE, Jeremy; MP for Taunton Deane, House of Commons; ***born:*** 1970; ***party:*** Liberal Democrat; ***political career:*** MP, 2005- (for Taunton, 2005-10, Taunton Deane, 2010-); Shadow Minister for Foreign and Commonwealth Office, 2005-07; Whip, 2006-07; Shadow Minister for Home Affairs, 2007; Shadow Chief Secretary to the Treasury, 2007-10; Minister of State, FCO, 2010-12; ***office address:*** House of Commons, London, SW1P 0AA, United Kingdom.

BROWNING, Baroness Angela Frances; British, Member, House of Lords; ***born:*** 4 December 1946, Reading, England; ***parents:*** Thomas Pearson and Linda Pearson (née Cross); ***married:*** David Browning, 1968; ***children:*** Philip (M), Robin (M); ***education:*** Reading Coll. of Technology; Bournemouth Coll. of Technology; ***party:*** Conservative Party; ***political career:*** Ministerial Appointment, Advisory Cttee. on Women's Employment, Dept. of Employment, 1989-92; Govt. Co-Chwn., Women's Nat. Cmn.; Parly. Sec., Min. of Agriculture, Fisheries & Food, 1994-97; MP, Tiverton, 1992-97; Shadow Sec. of State for Trade and Industry, 1999-2000; Shadow Leader of the House of Commons and Constitutional Affairs, 2001; MP, Tiverton and Honiton, 1997-2010; Dep. Chmn., Conservative Party, 2005-07; Mem., House of Lords, 2010-; ***interests:*** small businesses, taxation, agriculture, special needs, mental health; ***memberships:*** Fellow, Inst. of Sales and Marketing Management; ***professional career:*** Sales and Training Manager,GEC/Hotpoint, 1976-85; Management Consultant, 1985-92; Dir., Small Business Bureau Ltd.; Nat. Chwn., Women into Business, 1988-92; ***committees:*** mem., Parly. Select Cttee. of Agriculture, 1992-94; Joint Sec., Backbench Employment Cttee., 1992-94; Public Accounts, 2004-; Standards and Privileges, 2004-07; ***clubs:*** Thomas Hardy Soc.; ***recreations:*** theatre, opera; ***office address:*** House of Lords, London, SW1A 0AA, United Kingdom; ***phone:*** +44 (0)20 7219 3000.

BRUCE, Fiona; MP for Congleton, UK Government; ***party:*** Conservative; ***political career:*** Warrington Borough Councillor, 2003-; MP for Congleton, May 2010-; ***committees:*** Scottish Affairs Select Cttee., 2010-; ***office address:*** House of Commons, London, SW1A 0AA, United Kingdom; ***phone:*** +44 (0)20 7219 3000; ***e-mail:*** fiona.bruce.mp@parliament.uk.

BRUCE, Malcolm Gray, MP; British, MP for Gordon, House of Commons; ***born:*** 17 November 1944; ***parents:*** David Bruce and Kathleen Bruce (née Delf); ***married:*** Jane Wilson, 1969 (div'd 1992); Rosemary Bruce (née Vetterlein), 1998; ***children:*** Alexander (M), Caroline (F), Catriona (F), Alasdair (M); ***public role of spouse:*** Candidate for Beckenham twice; ***languages:*** French; ***education:*** St. Andrew's Univ., Scotland, Hons Graduate, Economics & Political Science; Strathclyde Univ., Scotland, M.Sc., Marketing; Barrister, Gray's Inn, 1995; ***party:*** Liberal Democrat; ***political career:*** MP, Gordon, 1983-; Spokesman: Scottish Affairs, 1983-85, Energy, 1985-87, Employment, 1987, Trade and Industry, 1987-88; Natural Resources (Energy and Conservation); Leader, Scottish Liberal Democrats, 1988-92; Spokesman: Scottish Affairs, 1990-92, Trade and Industry, 1992-94, Treasury, 1994-99; Chmn., Liberal Democrat Parly. Party, 1999-2001; Delegate to Cncl. of Europe; Shadow Secretary of State for Trade and Industry. 2003-05; ***memberships:*** NUJ; ***professional career:*** Trainee journalist, Liverpool Daily Post, 1966-67; Buyer, Boots the Chemists, 1968-69; Exec., A. Goldberg, Glasgow, 1969-70; Research/ Information Officer, NESDA, Aberdeen, 1971-75; UK Marketing Mgr., Noroil Publishing House, 1975-81; Jt. editor/publisher, Aberdeen Petroleum Publishing Ltd, 1981-84; Rector, Dundee Univ., 1986-89; ***committees:*** Scottish Affairs Select Cttee., 1990-92; Trade and Industry Select Cttee., 1992-94; Treasury Select Cttee., 1997-99; Cttee. on Standards and Privileges, 1999-2001; Liaison, 2005-; International Development, 2005-; Jt. Cttee. on National Security Strategy, 2010-; ***trusteeships:*** Vice Pres., National Deaf Children's Soc., 1990; ***publications:*** Rural Development Energy, Local Enterprise; ***recreations:*** theatre, music, walking; ***office address:*** House of Commons, London, SW1A 0AA, United Kingdom; ***phone:*** +44 (0)20 7219 6233; ***fax:*** +44 (0)20 7219 2334; ***e-mail:*** brucem@parliament.uk.

BRUMMELL, H.E. Paul; High Commissioner, British High Commission in Barbados; ***born:*** 28 August 1965, Harpenden, UK; ***parents:*** Robert George Brummell and June Brummell (née Rawlins); ***education:*** St Albans School; BA, Geography, St Catharine's Coll., Cambridge; ***professional career:*** joined HM Diplomatic Service, 1987; Third later Second Sec., Islamabad, 1989-92; FCO, 1993-94; First Sec., Rome, 1995-2000; Dep. Head, Eastern Dept., FCO, 2000-2001; British Ambassador in Turkmenistan, 2002-05; HM Amb. to Kazakhstan and Non-Resident Amb. to Kyrgystan, 2005-09; British High Commissioner to Barbados and the Eastern Caribbean, 2009-; ***publications:*** Turkmenistan: The Brady Travel Guide, 2005; ***recreations:*** travel, entering writing competitions, glam rock; ***office address:*** British High Commission, Lower Collymore Rock, PO Box 676, Bridgetown, Barbados; ***phone:*** +1 246 430 7800; ***fax:*** +1 246 430 7851; ***e-mail:*** paul.brummell@fco.gov.uk; ***URL:*** http://ukinbarbados.fco.gov.uk/en.

BRUTON, Richard; Irish, Minister for Enterprise, Jobs and Innovation, Government of Ireland; ***born:*** 1953; ***married:*** Susan Meehan; ***education:*** Belvedere Coll., Dublin; Clongowes Wood Coll.; Univ. Coll., Dublin; Nuffield Coll., Oxford, MPhil, Oxon, Economics; MA; BA; ***political career:*** Senator, Agricultural Panel, 1981-82; elected to the Dáil, 1982; Min. of State, Dept. of Industry and Commerce, 1986-87; Fine Gael front bench spokesman on Energy and Communications, 1987-90, on Energy and Natural Resources, 1989-90, on Health, 1992; Min. for Enterprise and Employment, 1994-97; Front Bench Spokesman on Education, Science and the Social Partners, 1997-2000; Dir. of Policy and Press, 2000-2001; Dir. of Policy, 2001-07; Dep. Leader and Spokesperson on Finance, 2002-10; Minister Social Protection, 2011; Minister for Enterprise, Jobs and Innovation, 2011-; ***memberships:*** fmr. Mem., Meath CC, 1979-82; ***professional career:*** Employed with Stokes, Kennedy, Crowley, 1981-82, Cement Roadstone Holdings, 1978-81, with Carroll Industries, 1977-78, with ESRI, 1973-75; ***committees:*** fmr. Mem. Oireachtas Cttee. on Women's Rights and Dáil Cttee. on Enterprise and Economic Strategy, 1993-94; Oireachtas Joint Cttee. on Commercial State Sponsored Bodies, 1987-91; fmr. Mem., Oireachtas Cttee. on Education and Science; fmr. Mem., Orreachtas Cttee. on Public Enterprise; Cttee. on Finance and Public Service, 2002-10; Spokesperson on Enterprise, Jobs and Economic Planning, 2010-; Mem., Oir Cttee. on Enterprise Trade and Innovation, 2010-; ***office address:*** Dáil Éireann, Kildare Street, Dublin 2, Ireland; ***e-mail:*** richard.bruton@oireachtas.ie; ***URL:*** http://www.richardbruton.com.

BRYANT, Chris; Member of Parliament for Rhondda, House of Commons; ***born:*** 11 January 1962, Cardiff, Wales; ***parents:*** Rees Bryant and Anne Grace Bryant (née Goodwin); ***languages:*** French, Spanish; ***education:*** Cheltenham Coll.; Mansfield Coll.; Oxford, MA (Hons), English, 1983; Ripon Coll., Cuddesdon, MA (Hons), Theology, 1986; ***party:*** Labour Party, 1986-; ***political career:*** Frank Dobson's election agent; Labour Party's Local Government Development Officer, 1993; Chair, Christian Socialist Movement: Hackney (London), Councillor, 1993-98; MP, Rhondda, 2001-; Chair of the Labour Movement for Europe, 2002-; PPS to Lord Falconer of Thoroton, 2005-06 PPS to Rt. Hon. Harriet Harmen, 2007-08; Parly. Sec., Office of the Leader of the House of Commons, 2008-09; Shadow Minister for Foreign and Commonwealth Office, 2010; Shadow Minister, Justice, Oct. 2010-11; Shadow Minister, Home Affairs, 2011-; ***interests:*** Europe, media; ***memberships:*** Associate, National Youth Theatre of Great Britain; Coop Party; Amnesty International; Amicus; the Fabians; ***professional career:*** Curate, All Saints, High Wycombe; Youth Chaplain to the diocese of Peterborough; Freelance Author, 1996-98; Head, European Affairs, BBC, 1998-2000; Manager, educational charity, Common Purpose; ***committees:*** Culture, Media and Sport, Select Cttee., 2001-05; Jt. Cttee. on HoL Reform, 2002-10; Public Accounts, 2007; Modernisation of the House of Commons, 2007-10; ***publications:*** Possible Dreams; Stafford Cripps; Glenda Jackson; ***recreations:*** swimming, theatre, gym; ***office address:*** House of Commons, Westminster, London, SW1A 0AA, United Kingdom; ***phone:*** +44 (0)20 7219 8315; ***fax:*** +44 (0)20 7219 1792; ***URL:*** http://chrisbryantmp.co.uk.

BRYANT, Phil; Governor, State of Mississippi; ***education:*** Univ. of Southern Mississippi, cirminal justice; Mississippi College, Political Science; ***party:*** Republican; ***political career:*** Lt Governor, State of Mississippi, 2007-2011, Governor, 2012-; ***professional career:*** State auditor; ***office address:*** Office of the Governor, 501 N West Street, 15th Floor, Woolfolk Building, Jackson, MS 39021, USA; ***URL:*** http://www.governorbryant.com.

BRYCE, H.E. Quentin, AC; Governor-General, Australia; ***born:*** 1942, Brisbane, Australia; ***married:*** Michael Bryce, 1964; ***s:*** 3; ***d:*** 2; ***education:*** Moreton Bay Coll., Brisbane; Univ. of Queensland, BA and LLB; ***professional career:*** Lecturer, Faculty of Law, Univ. of Queensland, 1968-83; Convenor, National Women's Advisory Council, 1982-1984; inaugural Dir., Queensland Women's Information Svce., Office of the Status of Women, Dept. of Prime Minister and Cabinet, 1984-87; Dir., Human Rights and Equal Opportunity Cmn., Queensland, 1987-88; Federal Sex Discrimination Cmnr., 1988-93; founding Chair and Chief Executive Officer, National Childcare Accreditation Cncl., 1993-96; Principal, The Women's Coll., Univ. of Sydney, New South Wales, 1997-2003; Governor, Queensland, 2003-08; Governor-Gen., Australia, 2008-; ***honours and awards:*** Officer of the Order of Australia, 1988; Companion of the Order of Australia, 2003; Dame of Grace of the Most Venerable Order of The Hospital of St John of Jerusalem, 2003; Hon. Doctorate of Laws, Macquarie Univ., New South Wales, 1998; Hon. Doctorate of Letters, Charles Stuart Univ., New South Wales, 2002; Hon. Doctor, Griffith Univ., Queensland, 2003; Hon. Doctor, and Queensland University of Technology in 2004; Hon. Doctor of Laws, Univ. of Queensland, 2006; ***recreations:*** visual arts, literature, opera, women's history; ***office address:*** Government House , Dunrossil Drive, Yarralumla ACT 2600, Australia; ***e-mail:*** governor-general@gg.gov.au; ***URL:*** http://www.gg.gov.au.

BRZEZINSKI, H.E. Mark Francis; Ambassador, US Embassy in Sweden; ***education:*** BA, Dartmouth College, USA; JD, Univ. of Virginia School of Law, USA; Doctorate, Oxford Univ., UK; ***professional career:*** Lawyer; Dir., on the National Security Council in the White House, 1999-2001; Amb. to Sweden, 2011-; ***office address:*** Embassy of the United States of America, Dag Hammarskwölds Väg 31, S-115 89, Stokholm, Sweden; ***phone:*** +46 (0)8 783 5300; ***fax:*** +46 (0)8 661 1964; ***URL:*** http://stockholm.usembassy.gov.

BUCHANAN, Vern; Congressman, Florida Dist. 13, US House of Representatives; ***party:*** Republican; ***political career:*** Mem., US House of Representatives, 2007-; ***committees:*** Ways and Means; ***office address:*** House of Representatives, 1516 Longworth HOB , Washington DC 20515 , USA; ***phone:*** +1 202 225-5015 .

BUCK, Karen; British, Member of Parliament, House of Commons; ***party:*** Labour Party; ***political career:*** MP, Regent's Park and Kensington North, 1997-2010, Westminster North, 2010-; Parly. Sec., Dept. of Transport, 2005-06; Dep. Minister for London, Sept. 2008-2010; Shadow Minister, Work and Pensions, Oct. 2010-11; Shadow Minister, Education, 2011-; ***office address:*** House of Commons, London, SW1A 0AA, United Kingdom; ***phone:*** +44 (0)20 8968 7999; ***fax:*** +44 (0)20 8960 0150; ***e-mail:*** k.buck@rpkn-labour.co.uk.

BUCKLAND, Robert; MP for South Swndon, UK Government; ***party:*** Conservative; ***political career:*** MP for South Swindon, May 2010-; ***committees:*** Mem., Justice Cttee., 2010-; Joint Cttee. on Statutory Instruments 2010-; ***office address:*** House of Commons, London, SW1A 0AA, United Kingdom; ***phone:*** +44 (0)20 7219 3000; ***e-mail:*** robert.buckland.mp@parliament.uk.

BUFFETT, David Ernest; Chief Minister, Norfolk Island Government; ***born:*** 1942; ***political career:*** Mem., Norfolk Legislative Assembly, Speaker, 1994-97, 2000-06; Chief Minister, Norfolk Island, 1979-86; Pres., Legislative Assembly, 1989-92; Chief Minister, Norfolk Island, 2006-07, ; ***office address:*** Ministry of Norfolk Island, Old Military Barracks, Kingston, Norfolk Island.

BULLOCK, Steve; Governor, State of Montana; ***political career:*** Governor, State of Montana, elected 2012, sworn in 2013-; ***professional career:*** Chief Legal Counsel, Montana Sec. of State, 1996; Montana Dept. of Justice; Attorney General, State of Montana, 2009-12; ***office address:*** Office of the Governor, PO Box 200801, Helena MT 59620-0801, USA; ***phone:*** +1 406 444 3111; ***fax:*** +1 406 444 5529; ***URL:*** http://governor.mt.gov/.

BULNES, Felipe; Ambassador to the US, Embassy of Chile; ***born:*** 1969; ***education:*** Catholic Univ. of Chile, law, 1991; Fulbright scholar; Harvard Law School, LL.M; ***political career:*** Minister of Justice, 2010-11; Minister of Education, July-Dec. 2011; ***professional career:*** academic career including Prof. of Civil law, Prof. of Law and Economics, Catholic Univ. of Chile, Adolfo Ibanez Univ; lawyer; Amb. of Chile to the US, to date; ***office address:*** Embassy of Chile, 1732 Massachusetts Ave., NW, Washington, DC 20036, USA; ***phone:*** +1 202 785 1746; ***fax:*** +1 202 887 5579; ***URL:*** http://www.chile-usa.org/.

BURDEN, Richard; British, Member of Parliament for Birmingham, Northfield, House of Commons; ***born:*** 1 September 1954, Liverpool, UK; ***parents:*** Kenneth and Pauline; ***married:*** Jane Slowey (née Perry), 2001; ***public role of spouse:*** Chief Exec., Foyer Federation; ***education:*** York Univ., BA (Hons.), Politics, 1978; Warwick Univ., MA, Industrial Relations, 1979; ***party:*** Co-operative Party; Labour Party, 1980-; ***political career:*** Founder Mem., Bedale Branch, Thirsk and Malton Constituency Labour Party; Founder, Joint Action for Water Services; Fmr. Exec. Mem., Labour Middle East Cncl.; Mem., Cncl. for the Advancement of Arab-British Understanding; Vice Chair, Labour Campaign for Electoral Reform, 1997-; Mem., Make Votes Count, Cncl.; Chair, Parly. Motor Gp.; Jt. Chair, Parly. Advisory Cncl., on Transport Safety, 1994-97; PPS to Jeff Rooker (Minister for Pensions), 1997-2001; Chmn., Britain-Palestine All Party Parly. Gp.; Chmn., Birmingham Gp. of Labour MPs; Rep. West Midlands Regional Assembly; MP, Birmingham Northfield, 1992-; Parly. advisor to Sports Minister on motorsport, 2002-; ***interests:*** motor industry and manufacturing, community regeneration, electoral and constitutional reform, Middle East, International development; ***memberships:*** Socialist Environment and Resources Assn.; TGWU; Socialist Health Assn.; Fabian Soc.; Fellow of Ind. and Parliament Trust, Graduate, Armed Forces Parly. Scheme, (Royal Navy); ***professional career:*** Pres., York Univ. Student's Union, 1976-77; Branch Organiser, NALGO, 1979-81, District Officer, 1981-92; Fmr. Dir., West Northfield Community Assn.; Bd. Mem., Rover Community Action Trust; ***committees:*** Mem., Parly. Standing Cttee., Trade Union Reform and Employment Rights Bill, 1992-93, Job Seekers Bill, 1995; Sec., Parly. Labour Party Trade and Industry Cttee.; Mem., Parly. Labour Party Health Cttee.; Mem., House of Commons Cttee. Examining Tory Housing Policy; Mem., Trade and Ind. Select Cttee., 2001-05; Mem., International Development Select Cttee., 2005-; ***clubs:*** 750 motor club, Austin social club, Kinghurst Labour club, Austin branch British legion; ***recreations:*** motor racing, food, travel; ***office address:*** House of Commons, London, SW1A 0AA, United Kingdom; ***phone:*** +44 (0)20 7219 2318; ***fax:*** +44 (0)20 7219 2170; ***e-mail:*** burdenr@parliament.uk; ***URL:*** http://www.richardburden.com.

BURES, Doris; Federal Minister of Transport, Innovation and Technology, Government of Austria; ***born:*** 3 August 1962 , Vienna; ***party:*** Austrian Socialist Party; ***political career:*** Mem., Federal Parliament, 1990-2007; Federal Mgr., SPÖ, 2000-06; Federal Minister for Women, Media and Civil Service, 2007-08; Federal Minister of Transport, Innovation and Technology, 2008-; ***memberships:*** Pres., Tenants' Assn., 1997-; ***office address:*** Federal Ministry of Transport, Innovation and Technology, Radetzkystrasse 2, 1030 Vienna, Austria.

BURKE, Anna; Speaker, Australian House of Representatives; ***born:*** 1 January 1966; ***party:*** Labor Party; ***political career:*** MP for Chisholm, Victoria, 1998-; Speaker of the Australian House of Representatives, 2012-; ***office address:*** House of Representatives, Parliament House, Canberra, ACT 2600, Australia.

BURKE, Paddy; Chathaoirleach (Chairman), Seanad Éireann; ***born:*** 15 January 1955, Castlebar, Co. Mayo; ***parents:*** Patrick and Marie; ***married:*** Dolores (née Barrett); ***party:*** Fine Gael; ***political career:*** Castlebar Town Cncl.; Mayo County Cncl. 1979; Senator, Seanad Éireann, 1993-; Leas-Chathaoirleach (Deputy Chairman), Seanad Éireann, 2002-11; Chairman, 2011-; ***committees:*** Jt. Transport Cttee. of the Irish Parliament; ***clubs:*** Castlebar Golf Club; Westport Golf Club; ***recreations:*** golf; ***office address:*** Houses of the Oireachtas, Leinster House, Kildare Street, Dublin 2, Ireland; ***phone:*** +353 (0)1 618 3574; ***fax:*** +353 (0)1 618 4570; ***e-mail:*** paddy.burke@oireachtas.ie.

BURKE, Tony; Minister for Immigration, Multicultural Affairs and Citizenship, Minister of Arts, Australian Government; ***education:*** University of Sydney, Arts and Law; ***political career:*** Member for Watson, 2004-; Shadow Minister for Small Business, 2004-05; Shadow Minister for Immigration, 2005-06; Shadow Minister for Immigration, Integration and Citizenship, 2006-07; Minister for Agriculture, Fisheries and Forestry, 2007-10; Minister for Sustainability, Environment, Water, Population and Communities, 2010-; Minister for the Arts, 2013; Minister for Immigration, Multicultural Affairs and Citizenship, Minister of Arts, 2013-; ***office address:*** Department of Immigration and Citizenship, PO Box 25, Belcoonnen ACT 2616, Australia; ***phone:*** +61 2 6274 1111; ***fax:*** +61 2 6225 6970; ***URL:*** http://www.immi.gov.au.

BURKHALTER, Didier; Vice President and Head of the Federal Department of Foreign Affairs, Swiss Government; ***born:*** 17 April 1960; ***education:*** Univ. of Neuchâtel, economics; ***political career:*** elected to Neuchâtel, 1991, president, 1994-95, 1998-99, 2001-03; sat in communal (Hauterive NE), cantonal (Neuchâtel) and federal parliaments; Elected to National Council, 2003; Elected to Council of States, 2007; mem., Swiss delegation to the Parliamentary Assembly of the OSCE, 2005-09; elected to Federal Council, 2009-; Head, Federal Department of Home Affairs, 2009-11; Head, Federal Dept. of Foreign Affairs, 2011-; Vice-President, 2013-; ***professional career:*** various academic functions and private sector positions; ***office address:*** Federal Department of Foreign Affairs, Bundeshaus West, 3003 Berne, Switzerland; ***phone:*** +41 (0)31 322 2111; ***URL:*** http://www.eda.admin.ch.

BURLEY, Aidan; MP for Cannock Chase, UK Government; ***party:*** Conservative; ***political career:*** Councillor, London Borough of Hammersmith and Fulham Council 2006-10; MP for Cannock Chase, 2010-; ***committees:*** Home Affairs Cttee., 2010-11; ***office address:*** House of Commons, London, SW1A 0AA, United Kingdom; ***phone:*** +44 (0)20 7219 3000; ***e-mail:*** aidan.burley.mp@parliament.uk.

BURNHAM, Rt. Hon. Andrew; Shadow Secretary of State for Health, House of Commons; ***married:*** Marie-France van Heel; ***education:*** St Aelred's RC High Sch. Newton-Le-Willows, Merseyside; Fitzwilliam Coll., Cambs. MA (Hons) English; ***party:*** Labour Party; ***political career:*** MP, Leigh, 2001-; PPS to Sec. of State for Home Dept., 2003-05; Parly. Under-Sec. of State, Home Office, 2005-06; Minister of State, Dept. of Health, 2006-07; Chief Sec. to the Treasury, 2007-08; Sec. of State for Culture, Media and Sport, 2008-09; Sec. of State for Health, 2009-10; Shadow Secretary of State for Health, May 2010-Sept. 2010; Shadow Secretary of State for Education and Election Coordinator, Oct. 2010-11; Shadow Secretary of State for Health, 2011-; ***committees:*** Health Select Cttee., 2001-03; ***office address:*** House of Commons, London, SW1A 0PW, United Kingdom; ***phone:*** +44 (0)20 7219 3000; ***e-mail:*** hcinfo@parliament.uk; ***URL:*** http://www.parliament.uk.

BURNS, Conor; MP for Bournemouth West, UK Government; ***party:*** Conservative; ***political career:*** Councillor, Southampton City Council, 1999-2002; MP for Bournemouth West, May 2010-; PPS, Northern Ireland Office, 2010-12; ***committees:*** Education Select Cttee., 2010; ***office address:*** House of Commons, London, SW1A 0AA, United Kingdom; ***phone:*** +44 (0)20 7219 3000; ***e-mail:*** conor.burns.mp@parliament.uk.

BURNS, Simon Hugh McGuigan, MP; British, Minister of State, Department of Health, UK Government; ***born:*** 1952; ***parents:*** Brian Burns (dec'd) and Shelagh Nash; ***married:*** Emma Burns (née Clifford) (Div'd 2000); ***children:*** Amelia (F), Bobby (M); ***education:*** Stamford Sch., Stamford; Worcester Coll., Oxford, BA, Modern History; ***party:*** Conservative; ***political career:*** Political Advisor to Rt. Hon. Sally Oppenheim MP, 1975-81; MP, Chelmsford, 1987-97, Chelmsford West, 1997-2010, Chelmsford, 2010-; PPS Min. of State, Dept. of Employment, 1989-90; PPS, Min. of State, Dept. of Education, 1990-92; PPS Min. for Energy, DTI; PPS to Min. for Agriculture, 1993-94; Asst., Gov't., Whip, 1994-95; Lord Cmnr. to HM Treasury, 1995-96; Parly. Under-Sec. of State, Dept. of Health, 1996-97; Opposition Spokesman on Social Security, 1997-98; Opposition Spokesman on the Environment, 1998-99; Treasurer, 1999-2001; Opposition Spokesman on Health, 2001-2005; Opposition Whip, 2005-2010; Minister of State: Dept. of Health, 2010-12; Dept. for Transport, 2012-; ***interests:*** health; ***professional career:*** Dir., What to Buy Ltd, 1981-83; Policy Exec. Inst. of Dirs., 1983-87; ***committees:*** 1922 Cttee.; Health, 1999-05; Armed Forces, 2005-06; Administration Cttee., 2006-09; Selection, 2007-08; ***trusteeships:*** Chelmsford Cathedral Appeal; ***clubs:*** Patron, Chelmsford Cons.; Essex Club; ***recreations:*** swimming, reading, tennis; ***office address:*** House of Commons, London, SW1A 0AA, United Kingdom; ***phone:*** +44 (0)20 7219 6811.

BURR, Richard; American, Senator, North Carolina, US Senate; ***born:*** 1955, Charlottesville, Virginia, US; ***education:*** R.J. Reynolds High Sch.; Wake Forest Univ.; ***party:*** Republican; ***political career:*** Republican Whip; Congressman, North Carolina Fifth District, US House of Representatives, 1994-05; Senator, US Senate, 2005-; ***committees:*** US Senate: Veterans' Affairs; Finance; Health, Education, Labor & Pensions; Select Cttee. on Intelligence; ***office address:*** US Senate, Hart Senate Office Building, Washington, DC 20510-4103, USA; ***URL:*** http://burr.senate.gov/public/.

BURROWES, David; MP for Enfield Southgate, House of Commons; ***born:*** 1969; ***party:*** Conservative Party; ***political career:*** MP for Enfield Southgate, 2005-; Shadow Minister for Justice, 2007-10; PPS to: Francis Maude as Minister for the Cabinet Office and Paymaster General, 2010, Oliver Letwin as Minister of State, Cabinet Office, 2010-12, Owen Paterson as Secretary of State for Environment, Food and Rural Affairs, 2012-; ***office address:*** House of Commons, London, SW1P 0AA, United Kingdom; ***phone:*** +44 (0)20 1219 3000.

BURSTOW, Paul; British, Minister of State, Department of Health, UK Government; ***born:*** 13 May 1962, Carshalton; ***children:*** Jonathan (M), Katherine (F), Eleanor (F); ***education:*** South Bank Polytechnic, London; ***party:*** Liberal Democrat Party; ***political career:*** MP, Sutton & Cheam, 1997-; Lib. Dem. Spokesman for Older People & Vulnerable Children, Local Gov., Social Services & Community Care; Shadow Spokesman for Health, 2003-05; Spokesperson for London, 2005-06; Chief Whip, 2006-2010; Minister of State (Care Services), 2010-12; ***office address:*** House of Commons, London, SW1A 0AA, United Kingdom; ***phone:*** +44 (0)20 7219 1196; ***e-mail:*** paul@paulburstow.org.uk; ***URL:*** http://www.paulburstow.com.

BURT, Alistair; Member of Parliament for Bedfordshire North East, House of Commons; ***born:*** 1955; ***married:*** Eve Alexandra; ***education:*** Bury GS, Lancashire; Oxford Univ.; Qualified as a solicitor, 1980; ***party:*** Conservative Party; ***political career:*** MP for Bury, 1983-97; MP, Bedfordshire North East, 2001-; Parly. Under-Sec. of State, 1992-95; Minister of State, 1992-97; Minister for Disabled People, 1995-97; Opp. Spokesperson, 2001-02; Shadow Minister for Communities and Local Gov., 2005-08; Opp. Assist. Chief Whip, 2008-10; Parliamentary Under Secretary of State (Afghanistan/South Asia, counter terrorism/proliferation, North America, Middle East and North Africa), 2010-12; ***office address:*** House of Commons, London, SW1A 0AA, United Kingdom; ***phone:*** +44 (0)20 7219 8132; ***e-mail:*** burta@parliament.uk; ***URL:*** http://www.alistair-burt.co.uk.

BURT, Lorely; MP for Solihull, House of Commons; ***married:*** Richard Burt; ***party:*** Liberal Democrat Party; ***political career:*** Local Councillor; MP for Solihull, 2005-; ***professional career:*** Company Dir.; Consultant; ***office address:*** House of Commons, London, SW1A 0AA, United Kingdom; ***phone:*** +44 (0)20 7291 3000.

BURTON, Joan; Minister of Social Protection, Government of Ireland; ***party:*** Labour Party; ***political career:*** TD for Dublin West, 1992-97, 2002-; Minister for Social Protection, 2011-; ***professional career:*** Chartered Accountant; ***office address:*** Department of Social and Family Affairs, Aras Mhic Dhiarmada, Store Street, Dublin 1, Ireland; ***phone:*** +353 (0)1 704 3000; ***fax:*** +353 (0)1 704 3868; ***URL:*** http://www.welfare.ie.

BURWELL, Sylvia; Director, Office of Management and Budget, US Government; ***education:*** Harvard Univ., A.B.; Oxford Univ., BA, Rhodes Scholar; ***political career:*** Clinton administration: Dep. Dir., OMB, Dep. Chief of Staff to the President, Chief of Staff to the Sec. of the Treasury; Staff Dir., National Economic Council; Director, Office of Management & Budget (OMB), 2013-; ***professional career:*** Pres., Global Dev. Program, Bill & Melinda Gates Foundation; Pres., Walmart Foundation, 2012; ***office address:*** Office of Management and Budget, 725 17th Street, NW, Room 9026, Washington, DC 20503, USA; ***phone:*** +1 202 395 3080; ***fax:*** +1 202 395 3888; ***URL:*** http://www.whitehouse.gov/omb.

BUSH, George Herbert Walker; American, Former President, US Government; ***born:*** 12 June 1924, Massachusetts, United States; ***parents:*** Prescott Bush and Dorothy Bush (née Walker); ***married:*** Barbara Bush (née Pierce), 6 January 1945; ***children:*** George Walker (M), John Ellis (M), Neil Mallon (M), Marvin Pierce (M), Dorothy (F); ***education:*** Phillips Acad., Andover, Mass., 1942; Yale Univ., 1948; ***political career:*** Mem. House of Reps. from 7th District of Texas 1967-71; US Perm. Rep. to UN 1971-73; Chmn. Republican Nat. Cttee. 1973-74; Head, US Liaison Office, Peking 1974-75; Dir. Central Intelligence Agency 1976-77; Republican candidate for the Vice-Presidency 1980; Vice-President USA 1981-89; President of the USA 1989-93; ***professional career:*** Pilot USNR 1942-45; Co-founder, Dir. Zapata Petroleum Corp. 1953-59; Pres. Zapata Off Shore Co. 1956-64; Chmn. Board 1964-66; ***honours and awards:*** Gordon Brown Prize for all-round student leadership; Distinguished Flying Cross; Three Air Medals; Necklace of the Most Excellent Order of Mubarak the Great, presented by Amir of Kuwait, 1993; The Most Honourable Order of the Bath - Knight Grand Cross, presented by H.M. Queen of England, 1993; The Grand Cross - special class of the Order of Merit of the Federal Republic of Germany, presented by Chancellor Helmut Kohl, 1994; The Order of the White Lion, presented by Vaclav Havel, Pres. of the Czech Republic, 1999; ***publications:*** Looking Forward (with Victor Gold), 1987; A World Transformed (with General Brent Scowcroft), 1998; All the Best: My Life in Letter and Other Writings, 1999; ***recreations:*** fishing, tennis, golf, jogging, horseshoes, boating; ***office address:*** Bush Presidential Library Center, Texas A & M Univ., Texas A & M Univ. College Station, TX 77843-1145, USA.

BUSH, George W.; American, Former President, United States Government; ***born:*** 6 July 1946, New Haven, CT, USA; ***parents:*** George Herbert Walker Bush and Barbara Pierce Bush; ***married:*** Laura Bush; ***education:*** Yale Univ., BA, 1968; Harvard Univ., MBA, 1975; ***party:*** Republican Party; ***political career:*** Governor, State of Texas, 1994-00; US President, 2000-Jan. 2009; ***professional career:*** F-102 Fighter Pilot, Texas Air Nat. Guard, 1968-73; worked in oil and gas business in Midland, 1975; worked in energy industry until 1986; Snr. Advisor, George H.W. Bush's presidential campaign, 1988; assembled the gp. of ptnrs. who purchased the Texas Rangers baseball franchise, 1989; built the Rangers' new home, the Ballpark at Arlington; Man. Gen. Ptnr., Texas Rangers, until 1994; ***office address:*** Republican Party, 310 First Street, SE Washington, DC 20003, USA; ***phone:*** +1 202 863 8500; ***fax:*** +1 202 863 8820; ***e-mail:*** info@gop.com; ***URL:*** http://www.rnc.org.

BUSSEMAKER, Jet; Minister of Education, Science and Culture, Netherlands Government; ***born:*** 1961; ***education:*** Univ. of Amsterdam, degree, doctorate; ***party:*** Labour Party (PvdA); ***political career:*** Policy Officer, Ministry of Social Affairs and Policy, 1986-88; mem., House of Reps., 1998-; State Sec. for Health, Welfare and Sport, 2007; Minister of

Education, Sciene and Culture, Rutte-Asscher gov., 2012-; ***professional career:*** University of Amsterdam, research assist., researcher, lecturer, 1985-93; VU Univ., 1989-2007; visiting fellow, Harvard Univ.; ***office address:*** Ministry of Education, Culture & Science, Rijnstraat 50, 2515 XP The Hague, Netherlands; ***phone:*** +31 (0)70 412 3456; ***fax:*** +31 (0)70 412 3450.

BUTHELEZI, Chief Mangosuthu Gatsha; South African, Leader, Inkatha Freedom Party; ***born:*** 27 August 1928, Mahlabathini, South Africa; ***parents:*** Chief Mathole Buthelezi and Princess Magogo ka Dinuzulu; ***married:*** Irene Audrey Thadekile Mzila, 2 July 1952; ***s:*** 3; ***d:*** 4; ***education:*** Adams Coll., Amanzimtoti, Certificate, Matriculation, 1944-47; Univ. of Fort Hare, Alice, Cape Province, BA, 1948-50; ***party:*** Leader, Inkatha Freedom Party; ***political career:*** Acting Chief, Buthelezi Tribe, Mahlabathine, 1954-57; Chief, Buthelezi Tribe, 1957-; Chief Exec. Officer, Zululand Territorial Authority, Nongoma, 1970-72; Chief Exec. Cllr., KwaZulu Legislative Assy., 1972-76; Chief Min., KwaZulu, 1976-94; Apptd. Acting Pres. by fmr. Pres. Mandela, numerous occasions; Pres., Inkatha Freedom Party, to date; Mem., Nat. Assembly, South African Govt., 1994-; Minister of Home Affairs, South African Govt., 1994-2004; ***memberships:*** African Nat. Congress Youth League, 1948-50; Cncl. of St. Peter's Seminary, C.P., 1961-63; Inanda Seminary Govt. Cncl., 1972-75; ***professional career:*** Clerk, Bantu Administration, Durban, 1951-52; Clerk, Cowley & Cowley, Durban., 1952; Acting Chief, Buthelezi Tribe, Mahlabathini, 1953-57; Founder, Inkatha; Founder, South African Black Alliance; Chmn., Mashonangashoni Regional Authority, 1968-75; Synthesis (non-party non-racial political study gp.), 1971-; Chancellor, Inst. for Industrial Education, 1971-77; Chmn., Asset Trust Fund, 1971-; Pres., Inkatha yeNkululeko yeSizwe, (Inkatha Freedom Party, 1990) 1975-; Chmn., The Buthelezi Tribal Authority, 1975-; Patron, LEARN Fund, 1975-; Pres., The Rhino and Elephant Foundation of Southern Africa; Pres., KwaZulu Conservation Trust, 1977-; Chancellor, Univ. of Zululand, 1979-2001; ***committees:*** Zululand Diocesan Standing Cttee., 1957-74; ***honours and awards:*** Newsmaker of the Year, South African Soc. of Journalists, 1973; Knight Commander, Star of Africa, Liberia, 1975; Dr. of Law, hon. degree, Univ. of Zululand, 1976; Citation for Leadership, District of Columbia Cncl., US, 1976; Dr. of Law, hon. degree, Univ. of Cape Town, 1978; French National Order of Merit, 1981; George Meany Human Rights Award, The Cncl. of Industrial Organisation of the American Federation of Labour (AFL-CIO), 1982; Apostle of Peace, Pandit Satyapal Sharma of India, 1983; Dr. of Law, hon. degree, Tampa Univ., Florida USA, 1985; Indian Acad. of South Africa Nadaraja Award, 1985; Financial Mail, Man of the Year, 1985; Newsmaker of the Year, Pretoria Press Club, 1985; Honorary Freedom of the City of Pinetown, Natal, 1986; Man of the Year Award, Inst. of Management Consultants of South Africa, 1986; Dr. of Law, hon. degree, Univ. of Boston, MS USA, 1986; Freedom of Ngwelezana, 1988; Unity, Justice and Peace Award, Inkatha Youth Brigade, 1988; Magna Award for Outstanding Leadership, Hong Kong, 1988; King's Cross Award by HM King Zwelithini Goodwill ka Bhekuzulu, Ulundi, 1989; Hon. Dr., Humane Letters, City Univ. of Los Angeles, 1989; Key to the City of Birmingham, Alabama USA, 1989; Bruno H Shubert Foundation: Conservation Award Class 1, 1998; South African Foundation 1988 Award for Excellence and Achievement; Hon. Pres., Inst. for Afro-Indian Relations, 2000; American Conservative Union: Courage under Fire Awards, Washington, DC, 2001; ***publications:*** published works include: Professor ZK Mathews: His Death, The South African Outlook, Lovedale Press, 1968; KwaZulu Development, Black Viewpoint, Black Community Programmes, 1972; Bi-weekly column, syndicated to SA morning newspapers, 1974-75; Inkatha, Reality, Pietermaritzburg, 1975; Transkei Independence, Viewpoint, Black Community Programmes, 1976; South Africa: My Vision of the Future, Weidenfeld and Nicholson, London, 1980; The Constitution, Leadership SA, 1983; South Africa: Anatomy of Black-White Power Sharing: collected speeches in Europe, 1986; books include: Gatsha Buthelezi: Zulu Statesman, Ben Temkin, 1976; Power is Ours, 1979; Der Auftrag des Gatsha Buthelezi Friedliche Befreiung in Sudafrika?, editors - H. Gunther, H. Bechheim, 1981; Usuthu, Cry Peace, Wessel de Kock, 1986; Buthelezi: The Biography, by Jack Shepherd-Smith, 1988; ***recreations:*** music; ***office address:*** Inkatha Freedom Party, Pretoria, South Africa; ***phone:*** +27 (0)12 326 8081; ***fax:*** +27 (0)12 321 6491.

BUTKEVICIUS, Algirdas; Prime Minister, Government of Lithuania; ***political career:*** Minister of Finance, Gov. of Lithuania, to 2004-05; Minister of Transport and Communications, 2006-08; Prime Minister, 2012-; ***office address:*** Office of the Prime Minister, Gedimino pr. 11 , 2039 Vilnius, Lithuania; ***phone:*** +370 5 266 3711; ***URL:*** http://www.lrvk.lt.

BUTLER, Rosemary, AM; Presiding Officer, National Assembly for Wales; ***born:*** 21 January 1943, Much Wenlock; ***education:*** St Julian's High Sch., Newport; ***party:*** Labour Party; ***political career:*** Former Sec. for Education and Children, Nat. Assembly for Wales; Newport Borough Councillor 1973-99; Mayor of Newport 1989-90; Chair, National Assembly's Culture, Welsh Language and Sport Committee 2003-7; Member, European Committee of the Regions 2003-7; Deputy Presiding Officer, May 2007-11; Presiding Officer, May, 2011-; ***professional career:*** Chmn., Nat. Industrial and Maritime Museum Swansea; ***committees:*** Culture, European Affairs & Business Partnership Cttee.; European Cttee. of the Regions; Chair, Culture, Welsh Language and Sport, 2003-07; Deputy Presiding Officer, 2007-; ***office address:*** National Assembly for Wales, Cardiff Bay, Cardiff, CF99 1NA, United Kingdom; ***phone:*** +44 (0)29 2089 8470; ***fax:*** +44 (0)29 2089 8527; ***e-mail:*** rosemary.butler@wales.gov.uk; ***URL:*** http://www.rosemarybutleram.com.

BYLES, Daniel; MP for North Warwickshire, UK Government; ***married:*** Prashanthi Katangoor Reddy; ***party:*** Conservative; ***political career:*** MP for North Warwickshire, May 2010-; ***memberships:*** Fellow of the Royal Geographical Society; ***professional career:*** British Army Officer, 1996-2005; ***committees:*** Energy and Climate Change, Select Cttee., 2010-; Chair, All Party Environment Group, 2012-; Chair, All Party Parliamentary Group for Unconventional Oil & Gas, 2013-; ***office address:*** House of Commons, London, SW1A 0AA, United Kingdom; ***phone:*** +44 (0)20 7219 3000.

BYRNE, Liam; Shadow Secretary of State for Work and Pensions, House of Commons; ***party:*** Labour Party; ***political career:*** MP for Birmingham Hodge, July 2004-; Parly. Sec., Dept. of Health, 2005-07; Minister of State, Home Office and Minister for the West Midlands, 2007-08; Minister for the Cabinet Office and Chancellor of the Duchy of Lancaster, Oct. 2008-09; Chief Secretary to the Treasury, 2009-May 2010; Shadow Chief Secretary to the Treasury, May 2010-Sept. 2010; Shadow Minister for the Cabinet Office, Oct. 2010-11; Shadow Secretary of State for Work and Pensions, 2011-; Policy Review Coordinator, 2012; ***office address:*** House of Commons, London, SW1A 0AA, United Kingdom.

C

CABLE, Rt. Hon. Dr Vincent; British, Business Secretary and President of Board of Trade, UK Government; ***born:*** 9 May 1943; ***parents:*** Leonard Cable and Edith Cable; ***married:*** Rachel Wenban Smith, 2004; Olympia (née Rebelo), 1968 (Dec'd 2001); ***children:*** Paul (M), Aida (F), Hugo (M); ***education:*** Nunthorpe Grammar Sch., York; Cambridge University, BA, Natural Science and Economics; Glasgow University, Ph.D. ; ***party:*** Liberal Democratic Party; ***political career:*** Parly. Candidate, Labour, for Glasgow Hillhead, 1970; City Cllr., Labour, Glasgow, Chmn. of Roads, 1971-74; Parly. Candidate, SDP/Liberal Alliance, for York, 1983, 1987; Special Advisor to Rt. Hon. John Smith, Sec. of State for Trade, 1989; Party. Candidate, Lib. Dem., for Twickenham, 1992; elected MP for Twickenham, 1997-; Lib. Dem. Spokesman for Trade and Industry; Shadow Sec. of State, Trade & Industry, 1999-2004; Shadow Liberal Democrat Chllr.of the Exchequer, 2004-10; Deputy Leader of the Liberal Democrats, Oct. 2007- (Acting Leader (following resignation of Sir Menzies Campbell), Oct. - Dec. 2007); Shadow Chancellor, 2008-May 2010; Business Secretary, Lib. Dem-Conservative coalition government, May 2010-; ***professional career:*** Treasury Finance Officer, Kenya, 1966-68; Lecturer, Economics, Glasgow Univ., 1968-74; First Secretary, Diplomatic Service, Foreign and Commonwealth Office, 1974-76; Dep. Dir., Overseas Development Inst., 1976-83; Special Advisor and Dir., Economic Affairs Division to Commonwealth Sec. Gen., Sir Sonny Ramphal, 1983-89; Group Planning, Shell Int., 1989-93; Head of Int. Economics Programme, Royal Inst. of Int. Affairs, 1993-95; Chief Economist, Shell International, 1995-1997; Occasional Lecturer, London Business Sch., 1996-99; Special Prof., Univ. of Nottingham, 1996-99; Visiting Fellow, Nuffield Coll., Oxford, 2000-; Visiting Fellow, London Sch. of Economics, 2001-; substantial freelance work for the World Bank, OECD, UNCTAD, and ILO, regular writing for the Economist Group, the Independent, and broadcaster ; ***committees:*** Treasury Select Cttee., 1998-99; Chair, All Party Police Grp., 1998-2003; Chmn., All Party Grp. for Victims of Crime, 2005- ; ***honours and awards:*** Fellow, London Sch. of Economics, 2001-04; Fellow, Nuffield Coll., Oxford, 2000-; ***publications:*** The Storm: The World Economi Crisis and What it Means, Atlantic Books, 2009; Free Radical, Atlantic Books, 2009; Tackling the Fiscal Crisis, 2009, Multiple Identities, 2005, Demos; Regulating Modern Capitalism, 2002, Centre for Reform; Globalisation and Global Governance, 2000, Chatham House and Pinter; Global Superhighways, 1996, Chatham House; A New Trade Agenda. Special Edition of Int. Affairs, 1996, Chatham House; Trade Blocks? The Future of Regional Integration, David Henderson, 1996, Chatham House; The Economic Superpowers, 1995, Chatham House; The World's New Fissures, 1995, Demos; Developing with Foreign Investment, B. Persaud, 1989, Croom Helm; Protectionism and Industrial Decline, Hodder and Stoughford; The Commerce of Culture, L.C. Jain and A. Weston, 1980, ODI; The Future of The GSP, A. Hewitt and A. Weston, 1978, ODI; The EU's External Trade Policy and Asia, A. Weston, 1978, ODI; ***recreations:*** ballroom latin dancing; ***office address:*** House of Commons, London, SW1A 0AA, United Kingdom; ***phone:*** +44 (0)20 7219 1106; ***e-mail:*** cablev@parliament.uk; ***URL:*** http://www.vincentcable.org.uk.

CAGLAYAN, Mehmet Zafer ; Minister for the Economy, Government of Turkey; ***born:*** 1957; ***education:*** Gazi Univ., Ankara, 1980; ***political career:*** Minister responsible for Foreign Trade, 2007-11; Minister for the Economy, 2011-; ***professional career:*** Pres., Ankara Chamber of Industry; Vice Pres., The Union of Chambers and Commodity Exchanges of Turkey; ***office address:*** Ministry of the Economy, Balgat, Ankara, Turkey.

CAIRNS, Alun, AM; British, MP, House of Commons; ***born:*** 30 June 1970, Clydach, Swansea, Wales; ***languages:*** Welsh; ***education:*** Ysgol Gyfun Ddwyieithog, Ystalyfera; Univ. of Wales, Master's Degree in Business Admin., specialising in inward investment policy; ***party:*** Conservative; ***political career:*** Regional Mem., South Wales West; Shadow Education Minister, 2007-2008; Shadow Local Government Minister, 2008; Member for Vale of Glamorgan, May 2010-; ***memberships:*** Motor Neurone Disease Assoc.; Just Say No campaign; ***professional career:*** Business Development Consultant, Lloyds TSB Gp.; Broadcaster in English and Welsh; ***committees:*** Public administration, 2011-; ***office address:*** House of Commons, London, SW1A 0AA, United Kingdom; ***e-mail:*** alun.cairns.mp@parliament.uk.

CAITHNESS, Earl Malcolm Ian Sinclair; British, Member of the House of Lords; ***born:*** 1948; ***s:*** 1; ***d:*** 1; ***education:*** Marlborough Coll.; Royal Agricultural Coll., Cirencester; ***political career:*** Govt. Whip, House of Lords 1984; Spokesman, Health and Social Security, Scottish and Foreign Affairs 1984-85; Parly. Under-Secy of State, Dept of Transport, 1985-86; Minister of State, Home Office, prisons and the fire service in England and Wales, UK relations with the Channel Islands and the Isle of Man, 1986-88; Minister of State, Dept. of the Environment; Paymaster General 1989-90; Minister of State, Foreign and Commonwealth Office, Hong Kong, the Far East and South Pacific, 1990-92; Min. of State, Dept. of Transport, aviation and shipping, 1992-94; elected hereditary Peer, House of Lords, 1999; ***professional career:*** Land agent, Savills; Partner, Brown and Mumford 1978; mem., property development co. 1980; consultant and non executive director to various companies 1994-; Chief Exec., Clan Sinclair Trust, 1999; ***committees:*** EC Agricultural Cttee.; Cttee. on Rural Policy 1979-80; ***office address:*** House of Lords, London, SW1A 0PQ, United Kingdom; ***phone:*** +44 (0)20 7219 3000; ***fax:*** +44 (0)20 7219 5979.

CALDEIRA, Vitor Manuel da; President, European Court of Auditors; ***education:*** Universidade Classica, Lisbon, Law, European Inst. of the Faculty of Law, European Studies; ***professional career:*** Assist. Prof., Fac. of Law, Lisbon Univ, 1983-84; Inspectorate Gen. of Finance, Ministry of Finance, 1984-2000, Senior Inspector of Finance, 1989-95, Dep. Inspector General of Finance, 1995-2000; OECD consultant; Mem., European Court of Auditors, 2000-01, Dean, CEAD Group, Mem., Court's Administrative Committee; Pres., European Court of Auditors, 2008-, Pres., Administrative Cttee., 2010-; ***office address:*** European Court of Auditors, 12 rue Alcide de Gasperi, 1615 Luxembourg, Luxembourg.

CALVERT, Ken; American, Congressman, California 44th District, US House of Representatives; ***born:*** 8 June 1953; ***education:*** Corona High Sch., 1971; Chaffey Coll., Alta Loma; San Diego State Univ., Bachelor of Arts, Economics, 1975; ***party:*** Republican; ***political career:*** Congressman, California 44th District, US House of Representatives, 1992 (originally 43rd District, but became 44th due to re-apportionment); ***committees:*** Appropriations; Budget; ***office address:*** House of Representatives, 2201 Rayburn Building, Washington, DC 20515, USA; ***phone:*** +1 202 225 1986.

CALVO, Eddie; Governor, Guam; ***born:*** 1961; ***party:*** Republican; ***political career:*** Senator, Guam legislature, 1998-2002, 2004-2010; Governor of Guam, 2010-; ***office address:*** Office of the Governor, PO Box 2950, Hagatna 96332, Guam; ***URL:*** http://www.gov.gu/.

CAMBRIDGE, HRH The Duke of , KG; ***born:*** 21 June 1982; ***parents:*** HRH Prince Charles, Prince of Wales and The Late Diana, The Princess of Wales; ***married:*** Catherine Middleton, April 29 2011; ***education:*** Eton College; BA, St Andrew's Univ., Scotland, 2005; Army officer training, Royal Military Academy, Sandhurst; ***professional career:*** Patron. Centrepoint charity, 2005-; Second Lieutenant, Household Cavalry (Blues and Royals); RAF Search and Rescue Pilot, Sept. 2010-; ***honours and awards:*** Royal Knight Companion of the Most Noble Order of the Garter, 2008; ***office address:*** Clarence House, London, SW1A 1BA, United Kingdom.

CAMERON, Rt. Hon. David; Prime Minister, British Government; ***married:*** Samantha Cameron (née Sheffield), 1996; ***public role of spouse:*** Creative Dir., Smythson; ***education:*** Eton; Brasenose Coll., Oxford, First Class honours, Politics, Philosophy and Economics, 1988; ***political career:*** worked in Conservative Research Dept., 1988-92; Special Advisor to the Chancellor of the Exchequer and the Home Sec.; MP for Witney, 2001-; Shadow Dep. Leader of the House of Commons, 2003; Dep. chair, Conservative Party, 2003-05; spokesperson, Conservative Party on local Govt. Finance; Shadow Secretary of State for Education and Skills, May-Dec. 2005; Leader of the Conservative Party, 2005-; Leader of the Opposition, Dec. 2005-10; Prime Minister, First Lord of the Treasury and Minister for the Civil Services, May 2010-; ***professional career:*** Head of Corporate Affairs, Carlton Communications PLC, 6 yrs.; ***committees:*** Mem., Home Affairs Select Cttee., 2001-03; Sec. All Party Epilepsy Gp., 2004-; Vice-chmn., Learning Disability Gp., 2005-; Vice-Pres., All-Party America Gp., 2006-; ***recreations:*** tennis, cooking; ***office address:*** Prime Minister's Office, 10 Downing Street, London, SW1A 2AA, United Kingdom; ***phone:*** +44 (0)20 7270 3000; ***fax:*** +44 (0)20 7925 0918; ***URL:*** http://www.number-10.gov.uk.

CAMERON OF DILLINGTON, Lord; Member, House of Lords; ***education:*** Oxford Univ.; ***political career:*** raised to the peerage, 2004; ***professional career:*** Manager, Dillington Estate, 1971-; Chair, Countryside Agency, 1999-2004 ; ***honours and awards:*** knighted 2003; ***office address:*** House of Lords, London, SW1P OPW, United Kingdom.

CAMP, Dave; American, Congressman, Michigan 4th District, US House of Representatives; ***born:*** Midland, Michigan, US; ***education:*** Univ., of Albion, Michigan, B.Sc.; Univ. of San Diego, JD; ***political career:*** state representative, Michigan Legislature; Congressman, Michigan Fourth District, US House of Representatives, 1990-; ***committees:*** Chmn., House Ways and Means Cttee.; ***office address:*** House of Representatives, 137 Cannon House Office Building, Washington, DC 20515, USA; ***phone:*** +1 202 225 3561.

CAMPBELL, Alan; British, Member of Parliament for Tynemouth, House of Commons; ***born:*** 8 July 1957, Consett, Co. Durham, UK; ***parents:*** Albert Campbell and Marian Campbell (née Hewitt); ***married:*** Jayne Campbell (née Lamont); ***s:*** 1; ***d:*** 1; ***education:*** Lancaster Univ., BA Hon., Politics; Leeds Univ., PGCE; Newcastle Polytechnic, MA; ***party:*** Labour Party; ***political career:*** Sec., Northern Gp. of Labour MPs; Parly. Private Sec. to Lord Gus MacDonald, 2001-; MP, Tynemouth, 1997-; PPS to Lord Gus MacDonald, 2001-03; PPS to Rt Hon Adam Ingram, Minister for Armed Forces, 2003-05; Asst. Govt. Whip, 2005-07; Whip (Lord Commissioner of HM Treasury), 2007-08; Parly, Under Sec., Home Office, Oct. 2008-10; Shadow Minister for Home Office, 2010-; ***professional career:*** Head of Sixth Form; ***committees:*** Public Accounts Cttee., 1997-01; Armed Bill, 2005-06; Selection, 2010-; Jt. Cttee. on Security, 2010-; ***office address:*** House of Commons, London, SW1A 0AA, United Kingdom; ***phone:*** +44 (0)20 7219 3000; ***e-mail:*** campbellal@parliament.uk; ***URL:*** http://www.alancampbell.co.uk.

CAMPBELL, Hon. Gordon; High Commissioner, Canadian High Commission in the UK; ***born:*** Vancouver; ***married:*** Nancy Campbell; ***children:*** Geoffrey (M), Nicholas (M); ***public role of spouse:*** Vice Principal, Vancouver School District; ***education:*** Dartmouth College, New Hampshire, USA, 1970; MBA, Simon Fraser Univ., Vancouver, Canada, 1978; ***political career:*** Mayor, Vancouver, 1986-93; Premier, Provincial Gov. of British Columbia, Canada, 2001-11; ***professional career:*** Secondary school teacher in Nigeria (for two years under CUSO); High Commissioner to the United Kingdom of Great Britain and Northern Ireland, Sept. 2011-; ***office address:*** Canadian High Commission, MacDonald House, 1 Grosvenor Square, London, W1X 0AB, United Kingdom; ***phone:*** +44 (0)20 7258 6600; ***fax:*** +44 (0)20 7258 6474; ***URL:*** http://www.london.gc.ca.

CAMPBELL, Gregory; MP for East Londonderry, House of Commons; ***party:*** Democratic Unionist Party; ***political career:*** Mem. Northern Ireland Assembly,1982-86, 2007-; MP for East Londonderry, 2001-; Minister of Culture, Arts and Leisure, 2008-09; DUP spokesperson; ***office address:*** House of Commons, London, SW1A 0AA, United Kingdom.

CAMPBELL, John; Congressman, U.S. Government; ***education:*** Univ. of Calif., BA Econ.; Univ. of Southern Calif., Masters in Business Taxation; ***party:*** Republican; ***political career:*** State Senator, 35th Dist. of Calif., 2004-05; US Congressman, representing 48th Congressional District, 2005-; ***professional career:*** Tax Accountant; Automotive Industry; ***committees:*** Budget; Financial Services; ***office address:*** House of Representatives, 2402 Rayburn House Office Building, Washington DC 20515, USA; ***phone:*** +1 202 225 5611; ***fax:*** +1 202 225 9177.

CAMPBELL, Rt. Hon. Sir (Walter) Menzies, CBE, QC, MP; British, Member of Parliament, House of Commons; ***born:*** 22 May 1941; ***married:*** Elspeth Mary Urquhart, 1970; ***education:*** Hillhead High Sch.; Glasgow Univ., MA, LL.B, Pres. of the Union, 1964-65; Stanford Univ., CA, postgraduate studies in Int. Law; ***party:*** Liberal Democratic Party; ***political career:*** Chmn., Scottish Liberal Party, 1975-77; Parly. candidate, 1974 (twice), 1979, 1983 and 1987; Spokesman for the Liberal Democrats in Parl. on Foreign Affairs, Defence, Europe and Scottish Legal Affairs; MP, North East Fife, 1987-; Shadow Spokesman on Foreign Affairs and Defence; Shadow Spokesman on Foreign Affairs; Dep. Leader of the Liberal Democrats, 2003-06; Shadow Foreign Secretary, 2005-06; Leader of the Liberal Democrats, 2006-07; ***memberships:*** UK delegation to the North Atlantic Assembly, 1989-2007; UK delegation to the UN, 1989 and 1993; UK delegation to the Parly. Assembly of the OSCE, 1992-97 and 1999-2006; ***professional career:*** Competed in the Olympic Games, Tokyo, 1964; Competed in the Cmmw. Games, Jamaica, 1966; Captained the UK athletics team, 1965-66; Holder of the UK 100 metres record, 1967-74; Called to Scottish Bar, Advocate, 1968; Appointed QC, 1982; Chmn., Lyceum Theatre, Edinburgh, until 1987; Mem., Broadcasting Cncl. for Scotland, 1984-87; ***committees:*** Mem., Clayson Cttee. on Liquor Licensing Reform in Scotland; Mem., House of Commons Select Cttee. on Members' Interests, 1987-90; Mem., House of Commons Select Cttee. on Trade and Industry, 1990-92; Mem., House of Commons Select Cttee. on Defence, 1992-99; Foreign Affairs, 2008-; Intelligence and Security Cttee., 2010-; ***trusteeships:*** Scottish Int. Education Trust; ***honours and awards:*** CBE in the New Years Hons., 1987 and to the Privy Cncl., 1999; Knighthood, Services to Parliament, January 2004; ***office address:*** House of Commons, London, SW1A 0AA, United Kingdom; ***phone:*** +44 (0)20 7219 3000; ***e-mail:*** hcinfo@parliament.uk.

CAMPBELL, Ronnie; British, Member of Parliament for Blyth Valley, House of Commons; ***born:*** 14 August 1943, Blyth Valley, United Kingdom; ***married:*** Deirdre Campbell (née McHale); ***s:*** 5; ***d:*** 1; ***party:*** Labour Party; ***political career:*** Cllr., Blyth Borough, 1969-74; Cllr., Blyth Valley, 1974-; MP, Blyth Valley, 1997-; ***interests:*** employment, housing, health, mining; ***memberships:*** NUM, 1965-; ***professional career:*** Miner; Mem., Branch Cttee., NUM; ***committees:*** Chmn., Environmental Health Cttee.; Vice-Chmn., Housing Cttee.; Mem., Select Cttee. on the Parly. Cmnr. for Admin., 1987; Public Administration 1997-2001; Catering, 2001-05; Health, 2005-07; ***recreations:*** restoring old furniture, collecting stamps, political history; ***office address:*** House of Commons, London, SW1A 0AA, United Kingdom; ***phone:*** +44 (0)20 7219 3000; ***e-mail:*** hcinfo@parliament.uk.

CAMPBELL, H.E. Sharon; Ambassador, British Embassy in Costa Rica; ***professional career:*** Dep. Head, FCO Consular Resources Group, 2008-11; Amb. to Costa Rica, 2011-; ***office address:*** British Embassy, San Jose, Costa Rica.

CANCADO TRINDADE, Judge Antonio; Member, International Court of Justice; ***born:*** 17 September 1947, Brazil; ***languages:*** English, French, Spanish, Portuguese, Italian, German; ***education:*** University of Cambridge, PhD, International Law, 1977, thesis: Developments in the Rule of Exhaustion of Local Remedies in International Law, Yorke Prize, LLM in International Law, 1973; Federal University of Minas Gerais, Brazil, LLB, International Law, 1969; International Institute of Human Rights, Strasbourg, Diploma, 1974; Certificates of the Research Centre of the Hague Academy of International Law, 1974, and of the seminar of the ILC, Geneva, 1975; Doctor HC, Central University of Chile, 2003, Catholic University of Peru, 2003, American University of Paraguay, 2004, Universidad de La Plata, 2005; Professor HC, Universidad Nacional Mayor de San Marcos, 2001, Universidad del Rosario, 2005; National Autonomous University of Mexico, Prize 'Isidro Fabela', 2003; State University of Rio de Janeiro, Prize 'José Bonifacio de Andrada', 1999; University of Brasilia, Prize 'Fausto Alvim', 1999; Federal University of Minas Gerais, Prize 'Destaque 2002', 2002; Legal qualification: judge; ***memberships:*** Curatorium of the Hague Academy of International Law, 2004-; Institute of International Law, 1997; ILA, Committee on the Enforcement of Human Rights Law; International Council of Environmental Law; Board of Directors, Inter-American Institute of Human Rights; Board of Directors, International Institute of Human Rights; International Institute of Humanitarian Law; Permanent Member, Associón Argentina de Derecho Internacional; Societé Française pour le Droit International; Instituto Hispano-Luso-Americano de Derecho Internacional, Permanent Member, 1994-, Rapporteur, 1996; ASIL; Indian Society of International Law; Association des Anciens Auditeurs of the Hague Academy of International Law; Brazilian Academy of Juridicial Letters, 2005-; Advisory Board, Asia-Pacific Council on Human Rights Studies, 1998; International Council on Human Rights Policy, 1997; Steering Committee, PICT, 1998-2001; Honorary President, Brazilian Institute of Human Rights; Brazilian Bar Association; Profesor Homenageado of the University of Brasilia, the Catholic University of Minas Gerais, 2002, and of the Tuiuiti University of Curitiba, Brazil, 2002; Editorial Council, Review Arquivos of the Ministry of Justice of Brazil, 1987-; Editorial Board, Brazilian Journal of International Politics, 1993-; Editorial Board, International Newsletter of the University of Sao Paulo, 1997-; ***professional career:*** *academic career:* University of Brasilia, Professor of Public International Law, 1978-, Head of the Department of Political Science and International Relations, 1979-83, Coordinator of the Graduate Course in International Relations, 1985-86; Diplomatic Academy Rio-Branco of Brazil, Professor of Public International Law, 1979-; The Hague Academy of International Law, Lecturer at numerous sessions, 1987-2005, Co-sponsor of the XXIV External Session, 1995, Participant in the 1974 Session; Lecturer at numerous Annual Courses of International Law organised by the OAS Inter-American Juridical Committee, 1981-2004; Lecturer at numerous Annual Study Sessions of the International Institute of Human Rights, 1988-2004; Lecturer at numerous Interdisciplinary Courses of the Inter-American Institute of Human Rights, 1986-2004; Academic Coordinator of Specialised Courses and Seminars and Lecturer in a number of seminars of the Inter-American Institute of Human Rights; Visiting Professor, University of Los Andes, 1981, 1982, Institut des Hautes Etudes Internationales, University of Paris-II, 1988-89, University of Ferrara, 1983 and 1986, University of Lisbon, 1993, Columbia University, 1998, Tulane University, 1999, Universities of Seville and Deusto, 2002, Washington College of Law, 2003 and 2004, Notre Dame University, 2005; Lecturer, Institute of Public International Law and International Relations of Thessaloniki, 1988; Lecturer, Euromediterranean Courses on International Law, Castellon, 1999; Lecturer, International Committee of the Red Cross in Humanitarian Law Seminars, China, 1996; Lecturer, University of Nottingham, Centre for Human Rights, 2002; Lecturer, Universities of Toronto, Externado de Colombia, Quito, Buenos Aires, Montevideo, Simon Bolivar, Milan, Salerno, Turin, Segovia, Warsaw, George Washington, American University, Chile, and the main universities of Brazil, 1982-2005; Lecturer at various institutions, including the Italian Diplomatic Institute, Florence, Institute Artigas of the Ministry of External Relations of Uruguay, Diplomatic Academy Antonio J Quevedo of Ecuador, Diplomatic Academy Andres Bello of Chile, Diplomatic Institute Manuel Maria de Peralta of Costa Rica, Consejo Argentino para las Relaciones Internacionales, 1992-98; Participant in seminars organised, inter alia, by the BIICL, Instituto Universitario Iberoamericano de Estudios Internacionales, Polish Institute of International Relations,

Canadian Council on International Law, Royal Institute of International Relations, ASIL, Max-Planck Institue for International and Comparative Law, 1982-2005; Lecturer at the External Courses (Training of Diplomats) of the Brazilian Diplomatic Academy Rio-Branco in Suriname, Cape Verde and Gabon; Participant as lecturer or rapporteur in numerous international congresses or symposia; professional career: Inter-American Institute of Human Rights, Executive Director, 1994-96, Member of the Board of Directors, 1988-, External Legal Adviser, 1991-94; governmental career: Legal Adviser to the Ministry of External Relations of Brazil, 1985-90; diplomatic career: Delegate to the Regional Meeting of the Latin American and the Caribbean Preparatory of the UN World Conference on Human Rights, 1993, and other satellite meetings of the preparatory process of the second UN World Conference on Human Rights, 1992-93, and to the second UN World Conference on Human Rights, 1993; Head of the Delegation to the Central American Conference on Peace and Development, 1994; Deputy Head of the Delegation of Brazil to the UN Conference on the Law of Treaties between States and International Organisations, 1986; Special Envoy of the Minister of External Relations of Brazil to Chile for Questions Pertaining to Human Rights, 1993-94; Delegate of Brazil to the XXIV General Assembly of the OAS, 1994, to the XIV General Assembly, 1984, to the Conferences on the Institutionalisation of the Latin American Parliament, 1987, to the Joint Meeting of the Group of Contadora and the Group of Support, 1985; Head of the Delegation of Brazil to the third Specialised Conference on Private International Law, 1984; Legal Adviser to the Delegation of Brazil to the UN Conference on the Code of Conduct for Transfer of Technology, 1983; Legal Adviser to the Delegation of Brazil to the sixth Conference of the Brazilian-French Mixed Commission of Demarcation of Limits, 1981; Expert of the UN and Lecturer in the UN Global Consultation on the Right to Development as a Human Right, 1990; Member of the Group of Senior Legal Advisers to UNEP, 1990-92; Member of the Advisory Committee of Experts in International Environmental Law of the UN University, 1984-87; Adviser to UNDP for its project of advisory services to and modernisation of Foreign Offices of Latin American countries, 1988; Adviser of the UNEP for the elaboration of the project of environmental legislation of São Tomé and Principe, 1992; Member of the Group of Jurists of the Comision Sudamericana de Paz entrusted with the elaboration of the first draft of the Treaty of Zone of Peace in South America, 1989 and 1990; Member of the Commission of Jurists of the OAS for Nicaragua, 1993-94; Member of the Commission of Senior Legal Advisers to the UNHCR for the Final Evaluation of the Process of International Conference on Central American Refugees, 1994; Legal Adviser to the Council of Europe in the case concerning the 1995 Minsk Convention on Human Rights of the Community of Independent States, 1995; Member of the Commission of Advisers to UNESCO on the Right to Peace as a Human Right; Research Supervisor of the Project on Humanitarian Law and Customary Law of the International Committee of the Red Cross, 1997; Director of the Brazilian Journal of International Law, 1985-; Co-Director of the Brazilian Journal of Human Rights; Brazil's Corresponding Editor of the International Legal Materials, 1981-; Heleno Fragoso Prize of Human Rights awarded by the Brazilian Bar Association, 2000; World Citizenship Prize of Human Rights non-governmental organisations in Brazil, 1998; judicial career: IACHR, President, 1999-, Vice-President, 1997-99, Judge, 1995-, Judge ad hoc, 1990-94; ***honours and awards:*** Comendador of the Order of Rio-Branco; Great-Cross of the Order of Rio-Branco; Great Medal of the Order of Inconfidencia; Condecoration of the Supreme Court of Justice of Venezuela; ***publications:*** numerous; ***office address:*** International Court of Justice, The Peace Palace, 2517 KJ The Hague, Netherlands.

CANCELLIERI, Anna Maria; Minister of Justice, Government of Italy; ***political career:*** Prefect in Bologna, Vicenza, Catania and Genova; Minister of the Interior, 2011-13; Minister of Justice, 2013-; ***office address:*** Ministry of Justice, Via Arenula 70, 00186 Rome, Italy; ***phone:*** +39 06 5227 8550; ***fax:*** +39 06 482 7630; ***URL:*** http://www.giustizia.it.

CANNING, H.E. Mark; Ambassador, British Embassy in Indonesia; ***education:*** London Univ.; ***professional career:*** Career diplomat, most recently: Amb. to Myanmar, 2006-09; Amb. to Zimbabwe, 2009-11; British Amb. to Indonesia, 2012-; ***honours and awards:*** CMG; ***office address:*** British Embassy, Jl M.H. Thamrin No. 75, Jakarta 10310, Indonesia; ***e-mail:*** british.info@fco.gov.uk; ***URL:*** http://ukinindonesia.fco.gov.uk/.

CANNON, H.E. Nicholas; Ambassador, British Embassy in Albania; ***professional career:*** Joined FCO, 1988; postings to France, Cyprus and Pakistan; Assist. Private Sec. to the PM Tony Blair, 2003-04; Africa Directorate, FCO, 2004-07; Amb. to Rwanda, 2008-11; Amb. to Burundi (non-resident), 2008-11; Amb. to Tirana, Albania, 2012-; ***office address:*** British Embassy, Rruga Skenderbeg 12, Tirana, Albania; ***phone:*** +355 (0)4 234973/4/5; ***URL:*** http://ukinalbania.fco.gov.uk.

CANTOR, Eric; Congressman, Virginia, 7th District, US House of Representatives; ***education:*** George Washington Univ.; Coll. of William and Mary, law degree; Columbia Univ., New York, Master's degree; ***political career:*** Virginia House of Delegates; Congressman, Virginia, Seventh District, US House of Representatives, 2001-; Republican Whip, 2009-10; Majority Leader, 2011-; ***committees:*** House Ways and Means Cttee.; ***office address:*** House of Representatives, 329 Cannon Building, Washington, DC 20515, USA; ***phone:*** +1 202 225 2815.

CANTWELL, Maria; Senator, Washington, US Senate; ***born:*** 1958, Indianapolis; ***parents:*** Paul Cantwell and Rose Cantwell; ***education:*** Miami Univ., Ohio, BA, Public Policy; ***party:*** Democrat; ***political career:*** Elected to the US Congress in Seattle, 1992; Senator, Washington state, US Senate, 2000-; ***professional career:*** Organised coalition to build new library in Mountlake Terrace; Joined a software start-up, 1995; ***committees:*** Commerce. Science and Transportation; Energy & Natural Resources; Finance; Indian Affairs; Small Business and Entrepreneurship; ***office address:*** Office of Senator Maria Cantwell, 717 Hart Senate Office Building, Washington, DC 20510, USA; ***phone:*** +1 202 224 3441; ***URL:*** http://www.cantwell.senate.gov.

CAO, Joseph; Congressman for Louisiana 2nd District, U.S. House of Representatives; ***born:*** March 13, 1967, Saigon, Vietnam; ***education:*** Baylor Univ., Physics; Loyola Univ., studied for the priesthood; New York's Fordham Univ., MA, Philosophy; Loyola Law Sch., Law; ***political career:*** leader, Louisiana Republican Party; Delegate, 2008 Rep. Nat. Convention; Mem., US HOR, 2008- (first Vietnamese-American elected to US Congress); ***professional career:*** Legal Counsel, Boat People S.O.S, Inc.; Mem., Nat. Advisory Cncl. of the US Conf. of Catholic Bishops, 2002; lost home and office in Hurricane Katrina, 2005; Mem., Bd. of Elections, Orleans Parish; ***committees:*** Homeland Security; Transportation and Infrastructure; Oversight and Government Reform. ; ***office address:*** US House of Representatives, 2113 Rayburn HOB, Washington, DC 20515, USA; ***phone:*** +1 202 225 6636; ***URL:*** http://josephcao.house.gov/.

CAPES, H.E. Mark; Governor, St Helena, Ascension and Tristan da Cunha; ***professional career:*** Dep. Governor, Anguilla & Bermuda; Dep. Chief Secretary, Providenciales, 1991-94; CEO, Turks & Caicos, 2009-2011; Governor, St Helena, Tristan da Cunha and Ascension, 2011-; ***office address:*** Office of the Governor, Jamestown, Saint Helena.

CAPPS, Lois; American, Congresswoman, California 23rd District, US House of Representatives; ***born:*** 10 January 1938; ***education:*** Pacific Lutheran Univ., Tacoma, B.Sc., Nursing; Yale Univ., MA, Religion; Univ. of California, Santa Barbara, MA, Education; ***party:*** Democrat; ***political career:*** Congresswoman, California 23rd District, US House of Representatives, 1998-; ***committees:*** House: Energy and Commerce; ***office address:*** House of Representatives, 1707 Longworth House Office Building, Washington, DC 20515, USA; ***phone:*** +1 202 225 3601.

CARDIN, Benjamin L.; American, Senator, United States Senate; ***education:*** Univ. of Pittsburg, BA *cum laude*, 1964; Univ. of Maryland Sch. of Law, 1967; ***party:*** Democrat; ***political career:*** Maryland House of Delegates, 1967-86, Speaker, 1979-86; US House of Representatives, 1987-Jan. 2007; US Senator for Maryland, 2007-; ***professional career:*** Lawyer, private practice; ***committees:*** Environment & Public Works; Foreign Relations; Finance; Small Business & Entrepreneurship; Commission on Security and Co-operation in Europe; ***office address:*** United States Senate, 509 Hart Senate Office Building, Washington, DC 20510, USA; ***phone:*** +1 202 224 4524; ***fax:*** +1 202 224 1651; ***URL:*** http://www.cardin.senate.gov/.

CARDONA, Dr Christian; Minister of the Economy, Investment & Small Business, Government of Malta; ***education:*** Univ. of Malta, Law; IMO International Maritime Inst., International Maritime Law; ***political career:*** MP, 1996-; Minister of the Economy, Investment & Small Business, 2013-; ***office address:*** Ministry of Finance, the Economy and Investment, Maison Demandols, South Street, Valletta VLT 2000, Malta; ***URL:*** http://www.mfin.gov.mt.

CARLOT, Alfred; Minister of Foreign Affairs, Government of Vanuatu; ***born:*** 1959; ***party:*** Natatok; ***political career:*** MP, 2008-12; Minister of Justice, 2011; Minister of Lands, 2011; Minister of Foreign Affairs, 2011-; ***professional career:*** First Sec., Vanuatu UN Mission, NY; ***office address:*** Ministry of Foreign Affairs, PO Box 051, Port-Vila, Vanuatu.

CARL XVI GUSTAF, HM King; Swedish, King of Sweden; ***born:*** 30 April 1946; ***parents:*** Prince Gustaf Adolf and Princess Sibylla of Saxe-Coburg and Gotha; ***married:*** H.M. Queen Silvia (née Sommerlath), 1976; ***children:*** Crown Princess Victoria Ingrid (F), Prince Carl Philip Edmund (M), Princess Madeleine Thérèse (F); ***public role of spouse:*** Queen of Sweden; ***languages:*** English, German, French; ***education:*** Sigtuna; Univ. of Uppsala; Univ. of Stockholm; ***party:*** Non political; ***political career:*** crowned Duke of Jämtland; became Crown Prince, 1950; succeeded to throne Sept. 1973; ***interests:*** technology, agriculture, business enterprise and trade; ***professional career:*** Military Service; ***honours and awards:*** Hon. Dr. degrees, Swedish Univ. of Agricultural Sciences, Stockholm Inst. of Technology and Åbo Academy, Finland; ***recreations:*** outdoor life, skiing, water sports; ***office address:*** Office of the Head of State, Royal Palace, Stockholm, Sweden; ***phone:*** +46 (0)8 402 6000; ***fax:*** +46 (0)8 402 6005.

CARMICHAEL, Alistair; Member of Parliament for Orkney and Shetland, House of Commons; ***born:*** 15 July 1965; ***married:*** Kathryn Jane Eastham; ***children:*** Sandy (M), Simon (M); ***languages:*** French, German; ***education:*** Islay High Sch.; LLB, Dip. LP, Law, Aberdeen Univ.; ***party:*** Liberal Democrat Party; ***political career:*** MP, Orkney and Shetland, 2001-; Lib. Dem. Dep. Spokesperson on Northern Ireland; Home Affairs Spokesperson; Shadow Transport Sec. 2006-07; Shadow Scottish and Northern Ireland Sec., 2007-08, 2009-10; ***interests:*** fishing, energy, farming, maritime issues, renewables, human rights; ***professional career:*** Solicitor, 1996-; ***committees:*** Scottish Affairs Cttee., 2001-05, 2008-10; Public Accounts, 2005-06; Jt. Cttee. on Security, 2010-; ***office address:*** House of Commons, London, SW1A 0AA, United Kingdom; ***phone:*** +44 (0)20 7219 8181; ***fax:*** +44 (0)20 7719 1787; ***e-mail:*** carmichaela@parliament.uk.

CARMICHAEL, Neil; MP for Stroud, UK Government; ***party:*** Conservative; ***political career:*** Northumberland County Councillor, 1989-93; MP for Stroud, May 2010-; ***committees:*** Environmental Audit, 2010-; Education, 2010-; ***office address:*** House of Commons, London, SW1A 0AA, United Kingdom; ***phone:*** +44 (0)20 7219 3000; ***e-mail:*** neil.carmichael.mp@parliament.uk.

CARMONA, H.E. Anthony; President, Trinidad & Tobago; ***born:*** 1953; ***political career:*** Pres., Trinidad & Tobago, 2013-; ***professional career:*** called to the Bar, 1983; Senior State Attorney, 1989; Assist., Dep. Dir. of Public Prosecutions, 1994-99; Appeals, International Criminal for the Former Yugoslavia; International Criminal Tribunal for Rwanda, Arusha; Senior Counsel, 2002; Judge, Supreme Court, 2004; Judge, ICC, 2011; ***office address:*** Office of the President, President's House, St Ann's, Port of Spain, Trinidad and Tobago; ***URL:*** http://www.thepresident.tt/.

CARNEY, John; Congressman, US House of Representatives; ***party:*** Democrat; ***political career:*** Mem., HOR Delaware at Large, 2010-; ***committees:*** Financial Services; ***office address:*** 1249 Longworth HOB, Washington DC 20515, USA; ***phone:*** +1 202 225 4165.

CARNEY, Mark; Governor, Bank of England; ***born:*** Fort Smith, Northwest Territories, Canada; ***education:*** BA, Harvard Univ. USA, economics, 1988; MA, 1993, Ph.D., 1995 economics, Oxford Univ. UK, economics, MA, Ph.D; ***political career:*** Senior Assoc. Deputy Minister of Finance, 2004-08; ***professional career:*** 30 year career, Goldmann Sachs; Dep. Gov., Bank of Canada, 2003-04; Governor, Bank of Canada, 2008-13; Chmn., Financial Stability Board (FSB), 2011-13; Governor, Bank of England, July 2013-; ***office address:***

Bank of England, Threadneedle Street, London, EC2R 8AH, United Kingdom; ***phone:*** +44 (0)20 7601 4444; ***fax:*** +44 (0)20 7601 4771; ***e-mail:*** enquiries@bankofengland.co.uk; ***URL:*** http://www.bankofengland.co.uk.

CARPER, Thomas, BA, MBA; American, Senator for Delaware, US Senate; ***born:*** 1947, Virginia, USA; ***parents:*** Wallace Richard Carper and Mary Jean Carper (née Patton); ***married:*** Martha Carper (née Stacy), 1986; ***children:*** Christopher Tomas (M), Benjamin Michael (M); ***education:*** Whetstone High Sch., Columbus, Ohio, Graduated, 1964; Ohio State Univ., Columbus, BA, 1968; Univ. of Delaware, Newark, MBA, 1975; ***party:*** Democrat; ***political career:*** State Treasurer, Delaware, 1976-83; mem., 98th-102nd Congresses from Delaware, 1983-93; Governor of Delaware, 1993-01; Mem., US Senate, 2001-; ***memberships:*** Chmn., Nat. Governors' Assn.; ***professional career:*** US Navy, 1968-73; Naval Reserve Commander, 1973-; Industrial Dev. Specialist, Econ. Dev., 1975-76; ***committees:*** Homeland Security and Gov. Affairs; Environment and Public Works; Finance; ***trusteeships:*** Delmarva County Boy Scouts Am, 1983-; fund-raising Chmn., Big Bros.-Big Sisters of Delaware, 1985 and 1993; hon. Chmn. Delaware Special Olympics, 1987-90; ***office address:*** Office of Thomas Carper, 513 Hart Senate Office Building, Washington, DC 20510, USA; ***URL:*** http://www.carper.senate.gov/public/.

CARR, Kim; Minister for Innovation, Industry, Science and Research, Government of Australia; ***education:*** MA, Dip. Ed., Univ. of Melbourne; ***political career:*** Senator, 1993-; Minister for Innovation, Industry, Science and Research, 2007-11; Minister for Manufacturing, 2011-12; Minister for Defence Materiel, 2011-12; Minister for Human Services, 2012-13; Minister for Innovation, Industry, Science and Research, Minister for Education, 2013-; ***professional career:*** Secondary School Teacher; ***office address:*** Ministry for Innovation, Industry, Science and Research, PO Box 9839, Canberra, ACT 2601, Australia; ***URL:*** http://www.industry.gov.au.

CARR, Hon. Robert John, BA (Hons); Australian, Minister for Foreign Affairs, Australian Government; ***born:*** 1947; ***married:*** Helena Carr; ***education:*** BA (Hons), NSW; ***political career:*** Chmn. Public Accounts Cttee, 1984; Fmr. Min. for Planning and Environment, 1984-1988; Min. for Consumer Affairs, 1986; Min. for Heritage, 1986-1988; Legislative Assy. Rep. on Council of Univ. of New South Wales, 1984-88; Leader of Opposition, 1988-95; Mem. for Maroubra, 1983, re-elected, 1984, 1988, 1991, 1995; 1999-; Premier of New South Wales, Minister for the Arts and Citizenship, 1999-06; Senator for New South Wales, Minister for Foreign Affairs, 2012-; ***professional career:*** Journalist with ABC Radio current affairs prog, 1969-72; Education Officer for Labor Council, 1972-78; Industrial Relations Reporter for The Bulletin, 1978-83; ***recreations:*** bushwalking, reading; ***office address:*** Department of Foreign Affairs and Trade, R.G. Casey Building, John McEwen Crescent, Barton, ACT, 0221, Australia; ***phone:*** +61 2 6261 1111; ***fax:*** +61 2 6261 1038; ***URL:*** http://www.dfat.gov.au.

CARSON, André; Congressman for Indiana, 7th District, U.S. House of Representatives; ***education:*** Concordia Univ., Wisconsin, Criminal Justice Management; Indiana Wesleyan Univ., Business Management, MA; ***political career:*** Mem., US HOR, 2008-; ***professional career:*** Investigative Officer, Indiana State Excise Police, for nine years; Anti-terrorism unit Indiana Dept. of Homeland Security's Intelligence Fusion Center, 2006-08; ***committees:*** Financial Services; ***office address:*** House of Representatives, 425 Cannon HOB, Washington, D.C. 20515, USA; ***phone:*** +1 202 225 4011; ***fax:*** +1 202 225 5633; ***URL:*** http://carson.house.gov/.

CARSWELL, Douglas; MP for Clacton, House of Commons; ***born:*** 1971; ***parents:*** Wilson Carswell FRCS, OBE; ***education:*** Univ. of East Anglia; King's College London; ***party:*** Conservative; ***political career:*** Conservative Party Candidate for Sedgefield against Tony Blair PM, 2001; Sr. Policy Officer, Conservative Party Policy Unit, reporting to David Cameron MP, 2004-2005; MP for Harwich, 2005-10, for Clacton, 2010-; ***professional career:*** Chief Project Officer, Invesco fund Management, AMVESCAP, 1999-2004; ***publications:*** Direct Democracy: An agenda for a new model party, 2005; Paying for Localism, 2004, Adam Smith Institute; The Plan, 2008; ***recreations:*** riding, swimming, gardening, fencing; ***office address:*** House of Commons, London, SW10 0AA, United Kingdom; ***phone:*** +44 (0)20 7219 3000.

CARTER, David; Speaker, Government of New Zealand; ***born:*** April 1952, Christchurch, New Zealand; ***education:*** B Ag Sci., Lincoln Univ.; ***party:*** National Party; ***political career:*** MP, 1994-1999, 2002-; Minister for Senior Citizens, 1998-99; Minister for Agriculture, Biosecurity and Forestry, 2008-11; Minister for Primary Industries, 2011-13; Minister of Loval Government, 2012-13; Speaker, 2013-; ***office address:*** Office of the Speaker, Parliament Buildings, Private Bag 18888, Wellington 6160, New Zealand.

CARTES, Horacio; President-Elect, Republic of Panama; ***born:*** 1956; ***party:*** Colorado Party, 2009; ***political career:*** President-elect, Panama, 2013-; ***professional career:*** Businessman, controlling stake in various companies incl. agriculture and tobacco; ***office address:*** Office of the President, Palacio de Lopez, Asuncion, Paraguay.

CARUANA, Peter R, QC MP; Leader, Gibraltar Social Democrats; ***born:*** 15 October 1956; ***education:*** Christian Brothers Sch., Gibraltar; Grace Dieu Manor, Ratcliffe Coll., Leicester, UK; Queen Mary Coll., Univ. of London, UK; Cncl. of Legal Education, London, UK; ***party:*** Gibraltar Social Democrats; ***political career:*** mem./party leader, Gibraltar Social Democrats, 1990-91; elected to House of Assembly (by-election), 1991-; Leader of Opposition, Hse. of Assembly, 1992; Chief Minister, 1996; re-elected Chief Min., 2000, 2003 and 2007 ; ***professional career:*** Practitioner in law firm, Triay & Triay, Gibraltar, 1979-90, Partner, Specialising in Commercial and Shipping Law, 1990-95; apptd. Queen's Counsel for Gibraltar, 1998; ***recreations:*** golf, political and current affairs; ***office address:*** Gibraltar Social Democrats, Gibraltar; ***URL:*** http://www.gsd.gi.

CASANOVA, Corina; Chancellor, Swiss Federal Chancellery; ***born:*** 1956; ***education:*** Univ. of Fribourg, law; ***political career:*** Delegate for Information, Parliamentary Services of the Federal Assembly, 1992-96; joined staff of Federal Councillor Flavio Cotti, Federal Department of Foreign Affairs (DFA); Personal advisor to Councillor Joseph Deiss, 1999; Dep. Sec.-Gen., DFA, 2002; Vice-Chancellor, 2005-08, Federal Chancellor, 2008-; ***office address:*** Federal Chancellery, Federal Palace, Bundesgasse West, 3003 Berne, Switzerland; ***URL:*** http://www.bk.admin.ch.

CASEY, Senator Robert; Senator for Pennsylvania, US Senate; ***education:*** Catholic Univ., law, 1988; ***party:*** Democratic Party; ***political career:*** Pennsylvania Commonwealth Auditor General; Commonwealth Treasurer; US Senator, 2007-; ***professional career:*** Lawyer; ***committees:*** Jt. Economic Cttee.; Foreign Relations; Agriculture, Nutrition and Forestry; Health, Education, Labor & Pensions; Special Cttee. on Aging; ***office address:*** United States Senate, 393 Russell Senate Office Building, Washington, DC 20510, USA; ***phone:*** +1 202 224 6324; ***URL:*** http://www.casey.senate.gov.

CASH, William Nigel Paul, MP; British, MP for Stone, House of Commons; ***born:*** 1940; ***parents:*** Paul Trevor Cash and Moyra (née Morrison); ***married:*** Bridget (née Lee), 1965; ***children:*** William (M), Sam (M), Laetitia (F); ***public role of spouse:*** Public Relations and Media Consultant. Dir. of the European Foundation; ***education:*** Oxford Univ. (BA Oxon.); ***political career:*** MP, Stafford, 1984-97, Stone, 1997-; Shadow Attorney General, 2001-03; ***memberships:*** Cons. Small Business Bureau (Vice-Pres.); Law Soc.; ***professional career:*** Qualified as solicitor, 1967; Specialist in Constitutional and administrative law; Partner, Dyson Bell & Co., 1971-79; William Cash & Co., 1979-; Founder and Chairman, The European Foundation; ***committees:*** Chmn., European Scrutiny Cttee., 2010-; Conservative Backbench Cttee European Affairs, 1989-91 (Chmn); All Party Cttee. on East Africa (Chmn.); Select Cttee. on European Legislation; Former member: Cons. Constitutional Cttee., 1984-86 (Vice-Chmn); Standing Cttee. on Financial Services, 1985-86; Standing Cttee. on Banking, 1986-87; Standing Cttee. on Broadcasting, 1989-90; Vice Chmn., All Party Campaign of Jubilee 2000, 1997; Liaison, 2010-; ***publications:*** Against a Federal Europe- The Battle for Britain (1991) and contributor to national newspapers and magazines; Europe The Crunch 1992, The European Journal published monthly by The European Foundation; ***clubs:*** Carlton; Vincents; Beefsteak; ***recreations:*** jazz, history, cricket; ***office address:*** House of Commons, London, SW1A 0AA, United Kingdom; ***phone:*** +44 (0)20 7219 3431.

CASTILLA RUBIO, Luis Miguel; Minister of Economy and Finance, Government of Peru; ***born:*** 1968; ***education:*** McGill Univ., John Hopkins Univ., Ph.D, economics; ***political career:*** Dep. Minister of Finance, 2010-11; Minister of Economy and Finance, 2011-; ***professional career:*** economist; consultant incl. to the World Bank, Andean Dev. Cop., ; lecturer, John Hopkins Univ., Lecturer. Univ., of the Pacific; ***office address:*** Ministry of Economy & Finance, Jr. Junin 339 4th Floor , Lima 1, Peru.

CASTOR, Kathy; Congresswoman, US House of Representatives; ***party:*** Democrat; ***political career:*** Hillsborough County Commissioner, District 1, Florida; Mem., US House of Representatives, for Florida 11th Dist., 2007-; ***professional career:*** Attorney; ***committees:*** Budget; Energy and Commerce; ***office address:*** House of Representatives, 317 Cannon HOB , Washington, DC 20515, USA; ***phone:*** +1 202 225-3376.

CASTRO, H.E. Alicia; Ambassador, Argentine Embassy in the UK; ***political career:*** Member of the Lower House, 1997-2005; ***professional career:*** Air stewardess and chairperson of the Argentine Association of Air Stewards; Amb to Venezuela, 2006-11; Amb. to the UK, 2011-; ***office address:*** Embassy of Argentina, 65 Brook Street, London, W1Y 1YE, United Kingdom; ***phone:*** +44 (0)20 7318 1300; ***fax:*** +44 (0)20 7318 1301; ***URL:*** http://www.argentine-embassy-uk.org/index_eng.shtml.

CASTRO RUZ, Fidel, D-en-D; Cuban, Former President; First Secretary, Partido Comunista de Cuba PCC, Republic of Cuba; ***born:*** 1927; ***married:*** Mirta Díaz Balart, 1948; ***education:*** Havana University; ***political career:*** prospective candidate of the Partido del Pueblo Cubano (Orthodoxo) for a parliamentary seat in the elections banned by Batista, June 1952; led the attack on the Moncado barracks (in Santiago de Cuba); sentenced to 15 years' imprisonment (served for two years, of which seven months were spent in solitary confinement) 1953; in exile in U.S. and Mexico; organized the 26th July movement 1955; landed in Oriente Province to begin the armed fight in the Sierra Maestra Nov. 1956; won the victory over Batista, who fled to the Dominican Republic, Jan. 1959; Prime Minister, 1959-76, Head of State, Pres. of Council of State and Council of Ministers 1976-2008; First Sec., Partido Unido de la Revolución Socialista 1963-65; First Sec., Partido Comunista, 1965- (mem. Political Bureau since 1976); ***professional career:*** With two other partners, established a law practice, 1950; ***publications:*** Ten Years of Revolution (1964); History Will Absolve Me (1968); ***office address:*** Partido Comunista de Cuba, Havana, Cuba.

CASTRO RUZ, General Raul; Cuban, President of the Council of Ministers, Cuban Government; ***born:*** 1931; ***political career:*** Sentenced with his brother Fidel to 15 years imprisonment following the attack on Moncado Barracks 1953; amnestied 1954; returned to Cuba 1956; Chief of the Armed Forces Feb. 1959; Dep. Prime Minister 1960-72; Minister for the Armed Forces,1960-2008; First Dep. Prime Minister 1972-76; First Vice-Pres. of Council of State & Council of Ministers, 1976-2008; Minister of the Revolutionary Armed Forces, to 2008; Mem. of Secretariat & Political Bureau of the Partido Comunista; Council of State President, 2008-; ***office address:*** Office of the President, Havana, Cuba.

CATERIANO BELLIDO, Pedro; Minister of Defence, Government of Peru; ***born:*** 1958; ***education:*** Pontifical Catholic Univ. of Peru; Instituto Universitario Ortega y Gasset, Complutense Univ. of Madrid; ***political career:*** Dep. Minister of Justice, 2001-02; Minister of Defence, 2012-; ***professional career:*** lawyer, constitutional law; Professor of Constitutional Law, Univ. of Lima; ***office address:*** Ministry of Defence, Avenida Arequipa 291, Lince, Lima 14, Peru.

CATON, Martin; British, Member of Parliament for Gower, House of Commons; ***born:*** 15 June 1951; ***education:*** Aberystwyth Coll. of Further Education; ***party:*** Labour Party; ***political career:*** Political Asst. and Researcher to Wales South West MEP; MP, Gower, 1997-; ***interests:*** planning, environment, education; ***professional career:*** Scientific Officer; ***office address:*** House of Commons, London, SW1A 0AA, United Kingdom; ***phone:*** +44 (0)20 7219 5111; ***e-mail:*** martin.caton.mp@parliament.uk.

CAVACO SILVA, President Anibal, Ph.D; Portuguese, President, Republic of Portugal; *born:* 1939; *parents:* Teodoro Gonçalves Silva and Maria Cavaco Silva (née Nascimento Cavaco); *married:* Maria Alves Cavaco Silva; *children:* Bruno (M), Patricia (F); *public role of spouse:* Professor; *languages:* English, French; *education:* Lisbon Univ., grad in economics; Univ. of York, UK, Dept. of Econ., PhD, 1973; *party:* Social Democratic Party (PSD); *political career:* joined Social Democratic Party (PSD), 1974; Min. for Finance and Planning, 1980-81; elected MP (Lisbon), 1980; Chmn., Nat. Cncl. for Planning, 1981-84; mem., PSD Nat. Cncl., 1981; Chmn., Nat. Political Cttee. PSD, 1985-95; re-elected MP 1985; Prime Minister, 1985-95; President of Portugal, 2006-; *memberships:* Int. Inst. of Public Finance; Global Leadership Foundation; mem., Scientific Soc. of the Catholic Univ.; mem., International Inst. of Public Finance; *professional career:* Research Fellow; Lecturer, Faculty of Econ., Lisbon, 1965; Prof., Catholic Univ., Lisbon, 1975-; Full Prof., Faculty of Economy, Univ. Nova, Lisbon, 1979-; Chmn., Bank of Portugal Studies Gp., 1977-85; consultant to the Bank of Portugal, 1996-; *honours and awards:* Dr. Honoris Causa, York Univ., UK, Univ. Coruña; Mem., Royal Acad. of Spain; Joseph Bech Prize, 1991; Freedom Prize, 1995; Carl Bertelsmann Prize, 1995; Robert Schuman medal, 1998; Mediteranneo Inst. Prize, 2009; *publications:* Econ. Effects of Public Debt; Public Finances and Macroeconomic Policy; A Decade of Reforms; Portugal and the Single Currency; The European Monetary Union; several other books and articles; *recreations:* golf, gardening; *office address:* Presidência da Republica, Palacio de Belem, Praça Afonso Albuquerque, 1300 Lisbon, Portugal; *phone:* +351 (0)21 361 4600; *fax:* +351 (0)21 361 4611; *e-mail:* presidente@presidenciarepublica.pt; *URL:* http://www.presidenciarepublica.pt.

CELIK, Faruk; Minister of Labour and Social Security, Government of Turkey; *born:* 1956; *political career:* MP, 2002-; Minister of Works, 2007; Minister of State responsible for Religious Affairs and Int. Co-operation, -2011; Minister of Labour and Social Security, 2011-; *professional career:* Teacher: Businessman; *office address:* Ministry of Labour and Social Security, Inönu Bul. 42 Emek, Ankara, Turkey ; *URL:* http://www.calisma.gov.tr/.

CEVIKOZ, Ahmet Unal; Ambassador to the UK, Turkish Embassy; *education:* Bosphorous Univ.; Free Univ. of Brussels; *professional career:* entered foreign service, 1978; postings to Moscow, Sofia, Bregenz; International Secretariat of NATO, Brussels, 1989; promoted to Ambassador, 2001; Amb. of Turkey to Azerbaijan, 2001-04; Ambassador of Turekyt to Iraq, 2004-06; Dep. Under Sec. for Bilateral Political Affairs, MFA, 2007-10; Amb. of Turkey to the UK, 2010-; *office address:* Turkish Embassy, 43 Belgrave Square, London, SW1x 8PA, United Kingdom; *URL:* http://london.emb.mfa.gov.tr/.

CHAFEE, Lincoln Davenport; American, Governor, Government of Rhode Island; *born:* 26 March 1953, Warwick, USA; *married:* Stephanie Chafee; *education:* Brown Univ., BA, Classics, 1975; Montana State Univ. Horseshoeing Sch., Bozeman; *political career:* Delegate, Rhode Island Constitutional Convention, 1985-86; Warick City Cncl., 1986-92; Mayor, City of Warick, 1992-; US Senator for Rhode Island, 1999-06; Governor, Rhode Island, 2010-; *professional career:* Farrier; Manufacturing Management; Planner, General Dynamics, Quonset Point; Exec. Dir., Northeast Corridor Initiative; *committees:* Mem., Cttee. on the Environment and Public Works; Chmn., Sub-Cttee. on Superfund, Waste Control and Risk Assessment; Mem., Cttee. on Foreign Relations; Chmn., Sub-Cttee. on Western Hemisphere, Peace Corps, Narcotics and Terrorism; *honours and awards:* Francis M. Driscoll Award for Leadership, Scholarship and Athletics; *office address:* Office of the Governor, 222 State House, Room 115, Providence, RI 02903, USA; *phone:* +1 401 222 2080; *URL:* http://www.governor.ri.gov/.

CHAKRABARTI, Sir Suma; President, European Bank for Reconstruction and Development; *born:* 1959, India; *education:* Oxford Univ.; Univ. of Sussex; *professional career:* senior civil servant; UK Treasury; UK Cabinet Office; Head, Dept. for International Dev. UK; Perm. Sec. , Ministry of Justice, UK; Pres., EBRD, 2012-; *office address:* EBRD, One Exchange Square, London, EC2A 2JN, United Kingdom; *URL:* http://www.ebrd.com.

CHALKER OF WALLASEY, Rt. Hon. Baroness Lynda; British, Member of the House of Lords; *born:* 1942, Hitchin, Herts; *parents:* Sidney H.J. Bates and Marjorie K. Randell; *languages:* French, German; *education:* Roedean; Heidelberg Univ.; Westfield Coll., London Univ. and Central Poly; *political career:* MP (Cons.) for Wallasey, 1974-92; Shadow Spokesman on Social Services, 1976-79; Parly. Under-Secy. of State at DHSS for Social Security, 1979-82; Under Secy. of State for Transport, 1982-83; Minister of State of Dept. of Transport, 1983-86; Minister of State for Foreign and Commonwealth Affairs, 1986; Dpty. to Foreign Secy., with responsibility for the Common Market, Western Europe, Trade and Econ. Rels., African, Commonwealth and Personnel Matters, 1987-89; Minister of State for Foreign and Commonwealth Affairs and Minister for Overseas Development, 1989-; fmr. Mem., House of Commons; Mem., House of Lords; *memberships:* Fellow, Royal Statistical Socy.; Fellow, Member of Royal Institute for International Affairs; *professional career:* Kodak Ltd., 1962-63; Unilever Ltd., Research Bureau, 1963-69; Shell Mex & BP Ltd, 1969-72; Louis Harris Int. Inc., 1972-74; Barclays Bank Int., 1976-79; Consultant to the World Bank, 1997-2007; Non-Exec. Dir., Freeplay Energy plc, 1997-2003; chmn. & cncl. mem., London Sch., Hygiene & Tropical Medicine, 1998-2005; Chair, Africa Matters Ltd., 1998; Advisory Dir., Unilever plc/NV, 1998-2007; Chair, Hon. Presidential Investment Council in Nigeria, 2001-; Non-Exec. Dir., Landell Mills Ltd (subsidary of DCI), 1999-2003, DCI (Eire), 2001-03, Ashanti Goldfields Co. Ltd., 2000-08, Group 5 (Pty) Ltd., 2001-; Advisory Bd. mem., Lafarge et Cie, 2003-; *publications:* (jointly) Police in Retreat (1967); (jointly) Unhappy Families (CPC 1971); (jointly) We are Richer than we Think (1978); Africa: Turning the Tide (1989); *office address:* House of Lords, London, SW1A 0PQ, United Kingdom; *phone:* +44 (0)20 7219 3000; *fax:* +44 (0)20 7219 5979.

CHAMBLISS, Saxby; American, Senator for Georgia, US Senate; *education:* University of Georgia, Bachelor's degree in Business Administration, 1966; University of Tennessee College of Law, Juris Doctor degree, 1968; *party:* Republican; *political career:* Congressman, Georgia Eighth District, US House of Representatives; Senator for Georgia, US Senate, 2002-; *committees:* Senate: Select Cttee. on Intelligence; Agriculture, Nutrition & Forestry Cttee.; Armed Services Cttee.; Rules & Administration Cttee.; *office address:* US Senate, 416 Russell Senate Office Building, Washington, DC 20510, USA; *phone:* +1 202 224 3521; *URL:* http://www.chambliss.senate.gov/public/index.cfm.

CHAMPION, Sarah; MP for Rotherham, British Parliament; *education:* Sheffield Univ.; *party:* Labour Party; *political career:* MP for Rotherham, 2012-; *professional career:* Chief Exec., Children's Hospice; *office address:* House of Commons, London, SW1 0AA, United Kingdom; *phone:* +44 (0)20 7219 3000.

CHAN, Florinda da Rosa Silva; MC, Secretary for Administration and Justice, Executive Council of Macau; *born:* June 1954, Macau; *languages:* English, Portuguese, Cantonese, Mandarin; *education:* Univ., Asia International, MA; Univ. of Language, Beijing, Language and Public Administration Course, 1993-94; Nat. Inst. of Public Admin., Beijing, Course in Public Administration; Int. Open Univ. of Asia (Macao), MA, Business Admin.; Univ. of Languages and Culture, Beijing, Chinese Language and Public Admin.; *political career:* joined Macau Govt., 1974, Dir., Economy Services, 1998; Sec. for Admin. and Justice, Office of the Sec. for Admin. and Justice, 1999- ; *office address:* Sede do Governo da RAEM, Avenida da Praia Grande, Macau; *phone:* +853 989 5180/181; *fax:* +853 2872 6880; *URL:* http://portal.gov.mo/.

CHAN, Dr. Margaret ; Director-General , World Health Organization; *education:* Medical Degree, Univ. of Western Ontario, Canada; *professional career:* Dir. of Health of Hong Kong, 1994-2003; Dir., Dept. for Protection of the Human Environment, World Health Organization (WHO), 2003-05; Dir., Communicable Diseases Surveillance and Response, and Rep. of the Dir.-Gen. for Pandemic Influenza 2005; Assistant Dir.-Gen. for Communicable Diseases, 2005; Director-General, WHO, 2006-; *office address:* World Health Organization, 20 Ave Appia, 1211 Geneva 27, Switzerland; *e-mail:* info@who.int; *URL:* http://www.who.org.

CHAN, Sarun; Minister of Agriculture, Forestry and Fishery, Government of Cambodia; *born:* 18 March 1951, Takeo Province, Cambodia; *parents:* Ngor Kin Chan and Kan Lay; *married:* Sok Keo; *languages:* English, Chinese, French, Khmer, Vietnamese; *education:* Cambodia, Sciences Diploma (S.P.C.N.), 1970; Cert. of Agronomy, 1973; Ph.D., Agricultural Science, 2005; Russian Academy of Econ., Correspondence Degree, M.Sc., Economics, 1991; Chamroeun Univ. of Poly-Technology, Phnom Penh, Ph.D., Agricultural Science, 2005; *political career:* MP, National Assembly of Cambodia, 1998-2000; Undersecretary of State, Agriculture, Forestry and Fisheries, 2000-01; Minister of Agriculture, Forestry and Fishery, 2001-; *memberships:* Bd. of Governors, Regional Center for Graduate Study and Research in Agriculture (SEAMEO); Bd. of Govs., Int'l Fund for Agricultural Development (IFAD), 2002-; *professional career:* Researcher, Dept. of Water, Forest and Wildlife, Phnom Penh, 1974-75; Ministry of Commerce, 1979; First Dep. Dir., Dept. of Forestry and Wildlife, Min. of Agriculture, Forestry and Fisheries, 1979-87, Dir., 1987-97; Dean, Royal Univ. of Agriculture, Phnom Penh, 1989-97, Rector, 1997-98; Advisor to Chmn., of the Cambodian National Assembly, 1995-98; Advisor to the PM, 2000-; *committees:* Chmn., PRASAC Steering Cttee., 2001-03; Chmn., Cttee. of Cambodian Peoples Party at the Min. of Agriculture, Forestry and Fisheries, 2001-; *honours and awards:* Ph.D (h.c.), Univ. of Southern California for Professional Studies, 2004; many awards for Work Appreciation, including: Medal for the construction of the National Phnom Tamao Zoo and Wildlife Rescue Center, 2000; National Construction Award Medal for the construction of water irrigation systems in Kampong Cham and Prey Veng provinces, 2001; Royal Decree No. 0203/049, Work Appreciation Award Level Mahasena Medal, 0223 and Monysaraphorn Medal Level Tipaden, for contributions to educational, social and Buddhism sectors in Takeo Province, 2003 ; *publications:* Author of twelve books on aspects of forestry as well as many papers on forestry, fishing and agriculture.; *office address:* Ministry of Agriculture, Forestry and Fisheries, 200 blvd. Preah Norodom, cnr rue Red Cross, cnr Blvd Issarek, Phnom-Penh, Cambodia; *phone:* +855 (23) 211351-2; *fax:* +855 (23) 217320; *e-mail:* maffcab@camnet.com.kh; *URL:* http://www.maff.gov.kh.

CHAN, The Hon. Sek Keong; Chief Justice of Singapore; *born:* 5 November 1937, Ipoh, Perak, Malaysia; *married:* Elisabeth Albyn Chan (née Eber); *d:* 3; *education:* Bachelor of Laws (Hons), Univ. of Malaya in Singapore; *professional career:* Legal Assist., Bannon & Bailey, Federation of Malaya, 1962-1963; Legal Assist., Braddell Brothers, Singapore, Legal Assistant, 1963-66, Partner, 1966-69; Partner, Shook Lin & Bok, Singapore and Federation of Malaya, 1969-76; Partner, Shook Lin & Bok, Singapore, 1969-86; Judicial Commissioner of the Supreme Court, July 1986- June 1988; Mem., Military Court of Appeal, Singapore, 1971-86; Judge of the Supreme Court, 1988-92; Attorney-General of Singapore, 1992-2006; Chief Justice of Singapore, 2006-; Pres. of the Legal Service Commission, 2006-; Chmn., Presidential Council for Minority Rights, 2006-; Pres., Singapore Academy of Law, 2006- ; *honours and awards:* The State Award of Perak conferred by the Sultan of Perak (Darjah Dato' Seri Paduka Mahkota Perak, S.P.M.P.), Perak, 1999; Distinguished Service Order (Darjah Utama Bakti Cemerlang D.U.B.C.),1999; The Order of Temasek (Second Class) (Darjah Utama Temasek), Singapore 2008; Honorary Bencher, Honourable Society of Lincoln's Inn, United Kingdom, 2008; International Jurists Award, 2009 ; *recreations:* reading; *office address:* Supreme Court of Singapore, 1 Supreme Court Lane, Singapore, 178879, Singapore; *URL:* http://app.supremecourt.gov.sg/default.aspx?pgID=40.

CHANG CHIA-JUCH ; Minister of Economic Affairs, Government of Taiwan; *political career:* Commissioner, Taiwan Prov. Gov., 1994-95; Adminstrative Dep. Minister, Ministry of Transportation & Communications, 1995-2005; Minister of Economic Affairs, 2013-; *professional career:* Prof., National Chiao Tung Univ.; Dir-Gen, Inst. of Transportation, Ministry of Transportation & Communications, 1987-1995; Dir-Gen., Civil Aeronautics Admin., 1988; Chmn., Chunghwa Post Co. Ltd., 2003; Pres., Chuang Hua Univ., 2005-08; Chmn., Sinotech Consultants, Inc., 2008-10; Chmn., China Steel Corp., 2008-10; Vice-Chmn., Dev. Financial Holding Corp., 2010-11; Chmn., China Airlines, 2011-13; *office address:* Ministry of Economic Affairs, 15 Foochow Street, Taipei, Taiwan; *URL:* http://www.moea.gov.tw/.

CHANG SHENG-FORD ; Minister of Finance, Government of Taiwan; *born:* 1949; *education:* NTU, BA; National Chengchi Univ., MA, Public Finance; Univ. of Iowa, USA, MA, Economics ; *political career:* Administrative Dep. Minister, MOF, 2007-08; Political Dep. Minister, MOF, 2008-12; Minister of Finance, 2012-; *professional career:* Dep. Dir-Gen., Taxation Agency, MOF, 1992-97; Adjunct Assoc. Prof., Dept. of Accounting, NTU, 1997-; Dir.-Gen., Taipei National Tax Administration, 2000-06; Dir.-Gen., Taxation Agency, MOF, 2006-07; Assoc. Prof., Kainan Univ., 2012-; *office address:* Ministry of Finance, 2 Aikuo West Road, Taipei, Taiwan; *URL:* http://www.mof.gov.tw/.

CHAPMAN, Jenny; MP for Darlington, House of Commons; ***party:*** Labour; ***political career:*** Councillor, Darlington Council, 2007-10; MP for Darlington, May 2010-; Shadow Minister, Justice, 2011-; ***committees:*** Procedure, 2010-; ***office address:*** House of Commons, London, SW1A 0AA, United Kingdom; ***phone:*** +44 (0)20 7219 3000; ***e-mail:*** jenny.chapman.mp@parliament.uk.

CHAPRA, Muhammad Umer, BBA, MBA, Ph.D; Saudi Arabian, Research Advisor, Islamic Research and Training Institute of the Islamic Development Bank; ***born:*** 1 February 1933; ***parents:*** Abdul Karim Chapra and Halima Bai; ***married:*** Khairunnisa Chapra (née Mundia), 1962; ***children:*** Maryam (F), Sumayya (F), Anas (M), Ayman (M); ***languages:*** Urdu, English, Persian, Arabic; ***education:*** Univ. of Sind, 1950; Univ. of Karachi, B.Com (BBA), 1954; Univ. of Karachi, M.Com (MBA), 1956; Ph.D., Univ. of Minnesota, Major: Economics, Minor, Sociology, 1961; ***memberships:*** The Royal Economic Society; American Economics Assoc.; Int. Assn. for Islamic Economics; ***professional career:*** Teaching and Research Asst., Univ. of Minnesota, 1957-60; Asst. Prof., Univ. of Wisconsin, Plattville, 1960-61; Sr. Economist, Institute of Development Economics, Karachi, 1961-62; Reader in Economics, Central Institute of Islamic Research, Karachi, 1962-63; Assoc. Prof., Univ. of Wisconsin, Plattville, 1963-64; Assoc. Prof., Univ. of Kentucky, Lexington, 1964-65; Economic Adviser, Saudi Arabian Monetary Agency, Riyadh, 1965-99; Advisor, Islamic Research and Training Inst., Islamic Dev. Bank, 1999-; ***honours and awards:*** Several merit awards, particularly the Islamic Dev. Bank Award & the King Faisal International Award received in 1990 for his contribution to Islamic Economics and Islamic studies; Gold medal 1989 from Overseas Pakistanis' Inst., for services to Islam and Islamic Economics; ***publications:*** Towards a Just Monetary System, 1985; Islam and The Economic Challenge 1992; Islam and Economic Development, 1993; The Future of Economics: An Islamic Perspective, 2000; Muslim Civilization: The Causes of Decline and the Need for Reform (2008); The Islamic Vision of Development in the Light of Maqasid al-Shari'ah (2008): 10 other books and monographs; over 100 professional papers; 15 book reviews; newspaper articles; ***office address:*** Islamic Research and Training Institute, PO Box 9201, Jeddah 21413, Saudi Arabia; ***phone:*** +966 2 646 6330; ***fax:*** +966 2 637 8927; ***e-mail:*** mchapra@isdb.org; ***URL:*** http://www.muchapra.com.

CHAREST, Hon. Jean, PLQ, MNA; Canadian, Premier, Government of Quebec; ***born:*** 24 June 1958, Sherbrooke, Quebec; ***parents:*** Claude Charest and Rita Charest (née Leonard); ***married:*** Michèle Dionne, 1980; ***children:*** Amélie (F), Alexandra (F), Antoine (M); ***languages:*** French, English; ***education:*** Univ. de Sherbrooke, LL.B., 1980; ***political career:*** MP for Sherbrooke 1984-1998; Asst. Dep. Speaker, 1984-86; Minister of State for Youth, 1986-90; Dep. Govt. Leader, 1988; Minister for Fitness & Amateur Sport, 1988-90; Minister of Environment 1991-93; Dep. Prime Minister 1993; Minister for Industry Science and Technology, 1993; Minister responsible for the Federal Business Dev. Bank, 1993; Leader of Progressive Conservative Party 1993-98; Leader of the Quebec Liberal Party, 1998; MNA for Sherbrooke, 1998-Leader of the Official opposition, 1998-2003; Premier, 2003-; ***memberships:*** Quebec Bar Assn.; Canadian Bar Assn; ***professional career:*** Called to the bar, 1981; Lawyer, Legal Aid Office, 1980-81; Layer, Beauchemin, Dussault, 1984; ***committees:*** Cabinet Cttee. on Planning and Priorities, 1991-93; Vice-Pres., NO Cttee., 1995; ***office address:*** Office of the Premier , Edifice Honoré-Mercier, 3e Étage, 835 Boulevard René-Lévesque Est, Québec, G1A 1B4, Canada; ***phone:*** +1 418 643 5321.

CHARFI, Mohamed; Minister of Justice, Government of Algeria; ***political career:*** Minister of Justice, 2002-; Keeper of the Seals, 2012-; ***professional career:*** Judge, 1972-89; Attorney General, 1989-91; ***office address:*** Ministry of Justice, 8 Place Bir Hamem, El Biar, Algiers, Algeria; ***phone:*** +213 (0)21 921608; ***URL:*** http://www.mjustice.dz.

CHARLES PHILIP ARTHUR GEORGE, H.R.H. The Prince of Wales; British, Prince of Wales; ***born:*** 1948; ***parents:*** Prince Philip, Duke of Edinburgh and Queen Elizabeth II; ***married:*** Camilla, The Duchess of Cornwall (née Shand), April 2005; The Late Diana, The Princess of Wales (née Spencer), July 1981 (div'd 1996); ***children:*** Prince William of Wales (M), Prince Henry of Wales (M); ***education:*** BA, Trinity Coll. Cambridge Univ. 1970; MA, 1975; ***professional career:*** became Duke of Cornwall and Duke of Rothesay, Earl of Carrick, Baron of Renfrew, Lord of the Isles and Prince and Gt. Steward of Scotland, 1952; created Prince of Wales and Earl of Chester, 1958; invested, 1969; Col-in-Chief Royal Regiment Wales, 1969-2006; 22nd Cheshire Regiment, 1977-; Lord Strathcona's Horse (Royal Canadians), 1977-; Parachute Regiment, 1977-; Royal Australian Armoured Corps. 1977-; Royal Regiment of Canada, 1977-; The Royal Gurkha Rifles 1977-; Royal Winnipeg Rifles, 1977-; 1st The Queen's Dragoon Guards; Air Reserve (Canada); The Black Watch (Royal Highland Regiment) of Canada; The Royal Canadian Dragoons; The Royal Pacific Islands Regiment; Col. Welsh Guards, 1975-; Hon. Air Commodore, RAF Valley; Air Commodore in Chief, Royal New Zealand Air Force; Royal Hon. Colonel, The Queen's Own Yeomanry; High Steward Borough Windsor and Maidenhead, 1974-; Pres. Prince's Trust, 1976-; Youth Bus. Trust, 1986-; Royal Acad. Music, 1985-; Chancellor Univ. Wales, 1976-; Col.-in-Chief, Royal Dragoon Guards, 1992; Army Air Corps, 1992; Admiral, Royal Navy, 2006-; General, Army, 2006-, Air Chief Marshall, Royal Air Force, 2006-; Col-in-Chief, The Toronto Scottish Regiment (Queen Elizabeth The Queen Mother's Own), 2005-; Commodore-in-Chief Plymouth, Royal Naval Command, 2006-; Royal Colonel, 51st Highland, 7th Batallion, The Royal Regiment of Scotland (Territorial Army), 2006-; Royal Colonel, The Black Watch, 3rd Battalion The Royal Regiment of Scotland, 2006-; Col-in-Chief The Mercian Regiment, 2007-; The Prince of Wales is Patron or President of more than 400 charities and organisations, including: The Prince's Trust, 1976; The Prince's Scottish Youth Business Trust, 1986; Prime, 1999; Prime-Cymru, 2001; The Prince's Drawing School, 2001; The Prince's School for Traditional Arts, 2004; The Prince's Teaching Institute, 2006; The Prince's Foundation for Children & the Arts, 2003; The Prince's Foundation for the Built Environment, 1992; The Prince's Regeneration Trust, 1997; Turquoise Mountain, 2006; The Great Steward of Scotland's Dumfries House Trust, 2007; Duchy Originals, 1992; North Highland Initiative, 2005; The Highgrove Shop, 2008; Business in the Community, 1985; Scottish Business in the Community, 1985; The Prince of Wales International Business Leaders Forum, 1990; In Kind Direct, 1997; Arts & Business, 2000; The Prince of Wales's Business & the Environment Programme (University of Cambridge), 1994; The Prince's Foundation for Integrated Health, 1998; ***trusteeships:*** Nat. Gallery, 1986-98; Patron, The Queen's Trust for Young Australians, 1977-; ***honours and awards:*** created Knight Order of Garter, 1958, installed 1968; created Knight Grand Cross of The Order of the Bath, 1975; Privy Counsellor, 1977; Knight Order of Thistle, 1977; Order of Merit, 2002; decorated Order of the White Rose, Grand Cross (Finland), 1969; Supreme Order of the Chrysanthemum, Grand Cross (1971); The Order of Orange Nassau, Grand Cross (Netherlands), 1982; Order of the Oak Crown, Grand Cross (Luxembourg), 1972; Order of the Elephant, 1 class only (Denmark), 1974; Order of the Ojasvi Rajanya, Grand Cross (Nepal), 1975; Order of the Southern Cross, Grand Cross (Brazil), 1978; Order of the Seraphim, 1 class only (Sweden), 1975; Knight Order of Australia (Australia), 1981; Order of St Olav, Grand Cross, Military (Norway), 1978; Order of Charles III, Grand Cross (Spain), 1986; The Khalifiyyeh Order, Grand Cross (Bahrain), 1986; Order of The Lion of Malawi, Grand Cross (Malawi), 1985; Order of Merit, Grand Cross (Saudi Arabia), 1986; Military Order of Aviz, Grand Cross (Portugal), 1994; The Star of Ghana, Grand Cross (Ghana), 1977; Order of Merit, King Abdul Aziz Order (Saudi Arabia), 1986; Legion of Honour (France), 1984; Order of Merit (Qatar), 1986; Papua New Guinea Independence Medal (Papua New Guinea), 1975; Inauguration Medal (Netherlands), 1980; Independence Medal (Zimbabwe), 1980; Canadian Forces Decoration (Canada), 1991; The New Zealand 1990 Commemorative Medal (New Zealand), 1990; The Saskatchewan Order of Merit (Canada), 2001; Queen's Golden Jubilee Medal; ***publications:*** The Old Man of Lochnagar, 1980; A Vision of Britain: A Personal View of Architecture, 1989; HRH The Prince of Wales Watercolours, 1990; Highgrove: Portrait of an Estate, 1993; The Prince's Choice: A Selection from Shakespeare by the Prince of Wales, 1995; Travels with the Prince, 1998; The Garden at Highgrove (Candida Lycett Green) 2000; The Elements of Organic Gardening, 2007; ***clubs:*** Royal Navy; ***office address:*** Clarence House, London, SW1A 1BA, United Kingdom; ***URL:*** http://www.princeofwales.gov.uk.

CHARLTON, H.E. Alan; Ambassador, British Embassy in Brazil; ***education:*** Cambridge Univ.; Leicester Univ.; Manchester Univ.; ***professional career:*** Amb. to Brazil, 2008-; ***honours and awards:*** Commander of the Most Distinguished Order of St Michael and St George (CMG); Commander of the Royal Victorian Order (CVO); ***office address:*** British Embassy, Setor de Embaixadas Sul, Quadra 801, Conjunto K, Brasilia DF 70408-900, Brazil; ***phone:*** +55 (0)61 3329 2300; ***fax:*** +55 (0)61 3329 2369; ***e-mail:*** britemb@terra.com.br; ***URL:*** http://www.reinounido.org.br.

CHARME, Alfredo Moreno; Minister of Foreign Affairs, Government of Chile; ***born:*** August 1956, Santiago, Chile; ***education:*** Universidad Católica de Chile; MBA, Univ. of Chicago, USA; ***political career:*** Minister of Foreign Affairs, 2010-; ***professional career:*** Diplomat; ***office address:*** Ministry of Foreign Affairs, Catedral 1158, Santiago, Chile; ***phone:*** +56 (0)2 679 4200; ***URL:*** http://www.minrel.cl.

CHATZIDAKIS, Kostis; Minister of Development, Competitiveness, Infrastructure, Transport and Networks, Government of Greece; ***political career:*** MEP, 1994-2007; MP, 2007-; Minister for Transport and Communication, 2007-09; Minister of Development, 2009-10; Minister of Development, Competitiveness, Infrastructure, Transport and Networks, 2013-; ***office address:*** Ministry of Development, 80 Michalacopoulou str.,, 115 28 Athens, Greece; ***phone:*** +30 9)010 778 8279; ***URL:*** http://www.ypan.gr.

CHEDID, H.E. Antoine; Ambassdor of Lebanon to the US, Lebanese Embassy; ***born:*** 1951; ***professional career:*** joined Foreign Service, 1978, career diplomat. incl. postings to Greece, the US, the UN; most recently: Amb. of Lebanon to Greece, 1998-2000; Consul Gen., NY, 1991-98; Head, Bureau of International Organizations, Conferences and Cultural Relations, MFA, Beirut, 2001-07; Amb. to the US, 2007-; ***office address:*** Embassy of Lebanon, 2560 28th Street, NW, Washington, DC 20008, USA; ***phone:*** +1 202 939 6300; ***fax:*** +1 202 939 6324; ***URL:*** http://www.lebanonembassyus.org/.

CHEEK, Ahmad Shabery; Minister of Communication and Multimedia, Government of Malaysia; ***party:*** United Malays National Organisation; ***political career:*** MP, 2004-; Minister of Information, 2008-09; Minister of Youth and Sports, 2009-13; Minister of Communication and Multimedia, 2013-; ***office address:*** Ministry of Communication and Multimedia, Bhg. Perhubungan Awam Tingkat 4, 50610 Kuala Lumpur, Malaysia.

CHEN WEI-ZEN ; Secretary General, Executive Yuan, Government of Taiwan; ***born:*** 1953; ***political career:*** Dep. Cmmissoner; Dept. of Urban Dev., Taipei City Gov., 1993-95; Dep. Commissioner, Dept. of Construction, Taiwan Prov. Gov., 1995-97, Commissioner, Info Dept. and Dep. Sec.-Gen, 1997-98; Commissioner, Dept. of Urban Dev., Taipei City Gov., 1998-2001, Commissioner, Dept. of Public Works, 2001-05; Dep. Magistrate, Taipei County Gov., 2005-09; Admin. Dep. Minister, Ministry of Transportation and Communications, 2009-10; Dep. Mayor, Taipei City, 2010-13; Sec.-Gen., Executive Yuan, 2013-; ***office address:*** Executive Yuan, 1 Chuanghsiao E. Road, Section 1, Taipei, Taiwan; ***URL:*** http://www.ey.gov.tw.

CHERNOV, Hon. Alex, AC QC; Governor, State of Victoria, Australia; ***born:*** Lithuania; ***education:*** B.Com., LLB (Hons)., Univ. of Melbourne; ***political career:*** Governor of Australia, 2011-; ***professional career:*** Barrister; Judge, Trial Division, Supreme Court of Victoria, 1997; Court of Appeal, 1998; Chancellor, Univ. of Melbourne, 2009; ***honours and awards:*** Officer of the Order of Australia, 2008; Companion of the Order, 2012; ***office address:*** Office of the Governor, Government House Drive, Melbourne, Victoria 3004, Australia; ***URL:*** http://www.governor.vic.gov.au.

CHHON, Keat; Cambodian, Senior Minister, Minister of Economy and Finance, Government of Cambodia; ***born:*** 11 August 1934, Kratie, Cambodia; ***s:*** 1; ***d:*** 1; ***languages:*** English, French; ***education:*** Training, Naval Architect, Marine Engineer, Nuclear Engineer, 1954-61; Economic Development Institute of the World Bank, Washington D.C.; ***political career:*** Minister of Industry/Commerce of RGC, 1967-69; Minister of Prime Minister's Office of the RGUNC, 1970-75; Deputy Prime Minister of the PNGC, 1993; Senior Minister in Charge of Rehabilitation and Development, RGC, 1993; Senior Minister in Charge of Rehabilitation and Development, Vice Chmn. of CDC, Minister of Economy and Finance, 1994-; ***professional career:*** Chief Engineer of Public Works, General Manager of ODEM, 1961-64; Founder and President of Royal Univ. of Kampong Cham, 1964-68; Manager for int. operations of CIEE, 1984-88; Chief Technical adviser of UNIDO, 1988-92; UNDP Consultant, 1992-93; ***office address:*** Ministry of Economy and Finance, 60 rue 92, Phnom Penh, Cambodia; ***phone:*** +855 (0)23 428960; ***URL:*** http://www.mef.gov.kh.

CHICOTY, Georges Rebelo Pinto; Minister of Foreign Affairs, Government of Angola; ***education:*** Univ. of Abidjan, Côte d'Ivoire; Univ. of Paris, France, 1986; ***political career:*** Vice Minister of External Relations; Minister of Foreign Affairs, 2010-; ***professional career:*** Ambassador; ***office address:*** Ministry of Foreign Affairs, Rua Major Kanhangulo, Luanda, Angola; ***phone:*** +244 22 239 4827; ***fax:*** +244 22 239 3246; ***e-mail:*** geral@mirex.gov.ao; ***URL:*** http://www.mirex.gov.ao.

CHIDAMBARAM, Palaniappan; Indian, Minister of Finance, Government of India; ***born:*** 16 September 1945, Kanadukathan in Distt., India; ***parents:*** Shri Palaniappa Chettiar; ***married:*** Nalini Chidambaram, 11 December 1968; ***education:*** Madras Univ., BSc., LLB.; Harvard Univ., MBA; Cambridge, MA, USA; ***political career:*** MP, 1984-; Union Dep. Minister, 1985-86; Union Minister of State, 1986-89 1991-92; 1995-; Minister of Finance, 1990-91; former Minister of Finance, Minister of Company Affairs; Minister of Finance, May 2004-Nov. 2008; Minister of Home Affairs, Nov. 2008-2012; Minister of Finance, 2012-; ***memberships:*** Supreme Court Bar Association; ***professional career:*** Lawyer; Sr. Advocate, Madras High Court; Sr. Advocate, Supreme Court of India; ***committees:*** mem., Consultative Cttee.; mem., Public Accounts Cttee., 1990-91; ***clubs:*** Delhi Gymkhana; ***office address:*** Ministry of Finance, North Block, New Delhi 110001, India; ***phone:*** +91 11 2301 2611; ***e-mail:*** isdea@finance,delhi.nic.in; ***URL:*** http://www.finmin.nic.in.

CHIKAWE, Mathias; Minister for Justice & Constitutional Affairs, Government of Tanzania; ***born:*** 1951; ***education:*** Univ. of Dar es Salaam, LL.B; North Staffs. Poly., UK; Inst. of Social Studies, The Hague, The Netherlands, Int. Law; ***party:*** CCM; ***political career:*** Legal Advisor, Poresident's Office, 1976-85; MP, 2005-; Minister of Good Governance, 2010-; Minister of Justice, 2010-; ***office address:*** Ministry of Justice, PO Box 9120, Dar es Salaam, Tanzania; ***phone:*** +255 713 325 087; ***e-mail:*** mchikawe@parliament.go.tz.

CHIKWANDA, Dr Alexander; Minister of Finance, Government of Zambia; ***education:*** Univ. of Lund, economics; ***party:*** Patriotic Front; ***political career:*** MP; Minister of Finance, 2011-; ***office address:*** Ministry of Finance, Finance Building, PO Box RW50062 , Lusaka, Zambia.

CHILCOTT, H.E. Dominick John; Ambassador, British Embassy in Dublin; ***born:*** 17 November 1959; ***professional career:*** Joined FCO, 1982: Private Secretary to the Foreign Secretary, 1996-1998; UK Rep to the EU (Head of External Relations Section), 1998-2002, Director of Iraqi Planning (later Policy) Unit, 2002-03; Director Europe (Bilateral Relations, Resources & Mediterranean Issues), 2003-05; High Commissioner, Sri Lanka, 2006-08; Dep. Head of Mission, British Embassy in Washington and Permanent Observer to the Organisation of American States, 2008-12; Amb. to Ireland, 2012-; ***office address:*** British Embassy, 29 Merrion Road, Ballsbridge, Dublin 4, Ireland; ***phone:*** +353 (0)1 205 3700; ***e-mail:*** dominick.chilcott@fco.gov.uk ; ***URL:*** http://britishembassyinireland.fco.gov.uk.

CHIN, Young; Minister of Health and Welfare, Government of the Republic of Korea; ***education:*** LL.B., Seoul National Univ., 1975; LL.M., University of Washington School of Law, USA., 1985; ***political career:*** MP, 2004-; Minister of Health and Welfare, 2013-; ***office address:*** Ministry of Health and Welfare, 75 Yulgong-Ro, Jongno-Gu, Seoul 110 793, Republic of Korea; ***URL:*** http://english.mw.go.kr.

CHINAMASA, Patrick; Minister of Justice, Legal and Parliamentary Affairs, Government of Zimbabwe; ***born:*** 25 January 1947, Nyanga, Zimbabwe; ***parents:*** Anthony Chinamasa and Regina Maunga; ***married:*** Monica Chinamasa (née Mutamba); ***children:*** Tinotenda (M), Chengetai (M), Kangai (F), Camuchirai (F); ***languages:*** English, Shona; ***education:*** Univ. of London, BA (Hons.), Law, 1971; Univ. of Zimbabwe, Dipl. in Law, BA, Law; ***political career:*** Minister of Justice, Legal and Parly. Affairs, to date; ***office address:*** Ministry of Justice, Legal and Parliamentary Affairs, Private Bag 7704, Causeway, Harare, Zimbabwe; ***phone:*** +263 (0)4 774620; ***fax:*** +263 (0)4 772933; ***e-mail:*** pchinamasa@gta.gov.zw.

CHINCHILLA, Laura; President, Government of Costa Rica; ***education:*** Univ. of Costa Rica; MA, Georgetown Univ., USA; ***party:*** National Liberation Party; ***political career:*** Vice Minister for Public Security, 1994-96; Minister of Public Security, 1996-98; mem., National Assembly, deputy for the province of San José, 2002-06; Vice President, 2006-08; President, May 2010-; ***office address:*** Office of the President, 520-2010 Zapote, San Jose, Costa Rica; ***phone:*** +506 207 9200.

CHIRAC, Jacques; Ex Officio Member, Conseil Constitutionnel, France; ***born:*** 29 November 1932; ***parents:*** François Chirac and Marie-Louise Chirac (née Valette); ***married:*** Bernadette Chodron de Courcel, 16 March 1956; ***children:*** Laurence (M), Claude (M); ***education:*** Lycées Carnot and Louis-le-Grand, Paris; Institut d'Etudes Politiques de Paris; Summer School of Harvard Univ.; Ecole Nationale d'Administration; ***political career:*** Head of Dept., Gen. Secretariat of Govt., 1962; Head of Dept., Private Office of M. Pompidou, 1962-65; Member of Parliament V.D. Vème for Corrèze (3 cons. Ussel), 1967 (re-elected 1993); Sec. of State for Employment Problems, 1967-68; Sec. of State for Economy & Finance, 1968-71; MP for Corrèze, 1967-; Cabinet of M. Couve de Murville, 1968-69; Minister for Parl. Relations, 1971-72, for Agriculture & Rural Development, 1972-74, of the Interior, 1974; Prime Minister, 1974-76; Sec.-Gen., Union des Démocrates pour la République,1975, Hon. Sec.-Gen. 1975-76; Pres., Rassemblement pour la République, 1976-94; Mayor of Paris, 1977-95; Prime Minister, 1986-88; President of France, 1995-07, Co-Prince of the Principality of Andorra, 1995-07; Mem., Conseil Constitutionnel, France, 2007-; ***professional career:*** Nat. Sch. of Admin. 1957-59; Auditor, Cour des Comptes, 1959; Counsellor, Cour des Comptes, 1965-67; ***honours and awards:*** Grand Croix de la Légion d'Honneur; Grand Croix de l'Ordre National du Mérite; Croix de la Valeur Militaire; Chevalier du Mérite Agricole, des Arts et Lettres, de l'Etoile Noire, du Mérite Sportif, du Mérite Touristique, Médaille de l'Aéronautique; Grand Cross of the Merit of the Sovereign Order of Malte; ***publications:*** Thèses à l'Institut d'Etudes Politiques sur le Développement du Port de la Nouvelle-Orléans, 1954; Discours pour la France à l'Heure du Choix, Editions Stock, 1978; La Lueur de l'Espérance: Réflexion du Soir pour le Matin, Editions La Table Ronde, 1978; Une Nouvelle France, Réflexions 1, Nil Editions, 1994; La France pour Tous, Nil Editions, 1995; ***office address:*** Conseil Constitutionnel, 2 rue de Montpensier, 75001 Paris, France; ***phone:*** + 33 (0)1 40 15 30 00; ***fax:*** +33 (0)1 40 20 93 27; ***URL:*** http://www.conseil-constitutionnel.fr/.

CHISHTI, Rehman; MP for Gillingham and Rainham, UK Government; ***party:*** Conservative; ***political career:*** Councillor, Medway Council, 2003-; Diversity adviser to Francis Maude MP 2006-; MP for Gillingham and Rainham, May 2010-; ***committees:*** Jt. Cttee. on Human Rights, 2010-; ***office address:*** House of Commons, London, SW1A 0AA, United Kingdom; ***phone:*** +44 (0)20 7219 3000; ***e-mail:*** rehman.chishti.mp@parliament.uk.

CHITOUI, Daniel; Vice Prime Minister and Minister of Public Finance, Romanian Government; ***born:*** 1967; ***political career:*** MP, 2008-12; Mem., Parly Cttee. on budget, finance and banking, 2012; Minister of Economics, 2012; Vice Prime Minister and Minister of Finance, 2013-; ***office address:*** Ministry of Public Finance, 17 Apolodor Street, 050741 Bucharest, Romania.

CHIUME, Ephraim Mganda; Minister of Foreign Affairs, Government of Malawi; ***born:*** 1953; ***education:*** B.Sc., UK; ***political career:*** Sec., Democratic Progressive Party; Mem., DPP Governing Council, 2008; MP, 2009; Deputy Minister of Natural Resources and Energy, 2009; Minister of Justice; Minister of Foreign Affairs, 2012-; ***professional career:*** chartered surveyor; ***office address:*** Ministry of Foreign Affairs, P.O. Box 30315, Lilongwe 3, Malawi.

CHO, Yoon-seon; Minister of Gender Equality and Family, Government of the Republic of Korea; ***education:*** Bachelor of Diplomatic Science, Seoul, National Univ., 1988; Master of Laws, Columbia Univ., 2001; ***political career:*** MP, 2008-; Minister of Gender Equality and Family, 2013-; ***professional career:*** Lawyer, 1994-2006; ***office address:*** Ministry of Gender Equality and Family, Cheong gyechonno 8 Jung-Gu, Seoul, Republic of Korea; ***URL:*** http://english.mogef.go.kr.

CHOMBO, Ignatius Morgan Chiminya, B.Sc., M.Sc., Ph.D; Minister of Local Government and National Housing, Zimbabwean Government; ***born:*** 1 August 1952; ***parents:*** Enock Chiminya Chombo and Severina Chiminya Chombo; ***married:*** Marion Chminya Chombo (née Mhloyi); ***children:*** Nimrod (M), Ignatius (M); ***languages:*** English, Shona; ***education:*** Kutama, Dip.; Vanderbelt, B.Sc., M.Sc.; Texas, Ph.D.; ***party:*** Mem., Central Cttee., Zanu PF; ***political career:*** Mem. Parl., Zvimba North; Provincial Governor and Resident Minister, 1992-95; Minister of Higher Education and Technology; Minister of Local Government, Public Works and National Housing, Acting Minister for Higher Education and Technology; Minister of Local Government and National Housing, 2005-; ***professional career:*** Teacher; University Lecturer; ***trusteeships:*** ZIMDEF; Chmn., Mashonaland West Child Survival Foundation; ***recreations:*** golf, football; ***office address:*** Ministry of Local Government, Public Works and National Housing, 9th Floor, Makombe Complex, Private Bag CY 7706, Causeway, Harare, Zimbabwe.

CHOMIAK, Hon. David Walter; Minister of Innovation, Energy and Mines, Government of Manitoba; ***born:*** Winnipeg, Canada; ***married:*** Rita Chomiak; ***political career:*** Mem. of Legislative Assembly for Kildonan, 1995-; Minister of Health and Minister responsible for Sport, 1999-04; Minister of Energy, Science and Technology, 20004-06; Attorney General, Minister of Justice, Keeper of The Great Seal, Minister responsible for Constitutional Affairs, Minister charged with the Administration of The Manitoba Public Insurance Corporation Act, Minister Charged with the Administration of the Manitoba Gaming Control Act, 2006-10; Minister of Innovation, Energy and Mines, 2010-; ***professional career:*** Lawyer; ***office address:*** Ministry of Innovation, Energy and Mines, 104 Legislative Building, 450 Broadway, Winnipeg, MB R3C 0V8, Canada; ***URL:*** http://www.gov.mb.ca/.

CHOPE, Christopher Robert, OBE, MP, LL.B; British, Member of Parliament for Christchurch, House of Commons; ***born:*** 1947; ***parents:*** Judge Robert Chope and Pamela Chope (née Durell); ***married:*** Christine Chope (née Hutchinson), 1987; ***children:*** Antonia Felicity (F), Philip Robert (M); ***education:*** Marlborough Coll.; Univ. of St. Andrew's; Inns of Court School of Law; ***party:*** Conservative; ***political career:*** elected to Wandsworth Council, 1974, Leader, Wandsworth Council 1979-83; former mem., Inner London Education Authority; former mem., Assn. of Metropolitan Authorities; former mem., London Boroughs Assn; MP, Southampton Itchen, 1983-92; PPS to Peter Brooke, 1986; Parly. Under-Secy. of State, Dept. of the Environment, 1986-90; Minister for Roads and Traffic, 1990-92; MP for Christchurch, 1997-; Vice-Chmn., Conservative Party with resp. for Local Gov., 1997; Front Bench Spokesman Environment, Transport and Regions, 1997; Opposition Frontbench Spokesman for Social Security, 1998; Opp. Frontbench Spokesman for the Treasury, 2001; Shadow Minister of State for Transport, 2002; Shadow Minister for Environment & Transport, 2003-05; ***professional career:*** Barrister, Inner Temple; Special Advisor, Ernst and Young, 1992-; ***committees:*** Procedure Select Cttee.; Administration Cttee.; on Speaker's Panel of Chairmen; mem. of Parly Deleg. to the Council of Europe & Jt. Sec. of the 1922 Cttee.; Chmn., Conservative Way Forward; Procedure, 2005-10; Administration, 2006-10; Political and Constitutional Reform, 2010-; ***office address:*** House of Commons, London, SW1A 0AA, United Kingdom; ***phone:*** +44 (0)20 7219 3000.

CHOPIN, Philippe; Prefect, Saint-Barthelemy; ***born:*** 1958; ***education:*** Public law; ***political career:*** long career in civil service; Prefect, Saint-Bathelemy and Saint Martin, 2011-; ***honours and awards:*** Chevalier de la Légion d'Honneur; Chevalier de l'Ordre National du Mérite; ***office address:*** Prefecture, Rue Lupin Brin, Gustavia 97133, Saint-Barthelemy.

CHOQUEHUANCA CÉSPEDES, David; Minister of Foreign Affairs and Culture, Government of Bolivia; ***born:*** 7 May 1961, Cota Cota Baja, Bolivia; ***education:*** Post Grad. studies in History and Anthropology, 1990; Univ. Cordillera, Higher Diploma in the Rights of Indigenous Peoples, 2001-02; ***political career:*** Minister of Foreign Affairs, 2006-; ***office address:*** Ministry of Foreign Affairs, Calle Ingavi esq. Junin, La Paz, Bolivia; ***phone:*** +591 2 371150 / 391999 / 371166; ***fax:*** +591 2 392134 / 365590.

CHOUHAN, Shivraj Singh; Chief Minister, Government of Madhya Pradesh; ***party:*** BJP; ***political career:*** State Assembly; MP, Lok Savbha, 1991-2003; Chief Minister, Madhya Pradesh, 2005-; ***office address:*** Office of the Chief Minister, Bhopal, India.

CHRISTIAN-CHRISTENSEN, Donna Marie; American, Congresswoman At Large for the US Virgin Islands, US House of Representatives; ***education:*** St. Mary's Coll., Indiana, B.Sc.; Washington Sch. of Medicine, Medicine; ***party:*** Democrat; ***political career:*** Acting

Cmnr., Dept. of Health; Congresswoman, US Virgin Islands, US House of Representatives, 1996-; *committees:* 110th Congress HOR Cttees: Natural Resources; Homeland Security; Chwmn., Natural Resources Sub-cttee. on Insular Affairs; Homeland Security Sub-cttees. Emergency Communications, Preparedness and Response and Emerging Threats, Cybersecurity and Science and Technology; Mem., Black Caucus; Chwmn., Black Caucus' Health Braintrust; Mem., Caucus for Women's Issues; Mem., Steering Cttee., Travel and Tourism Caucus; Mem., Rural Caucus; Mem., Friends of the Caribbean Caucus; Mem., Coastal Caucus; Mem., Fire Caucus; Mem., National Guard and Reserve Caucus; *office address:* House of Representatives, 1510 Longworth House Office Building, Washington, DC 20515-5501, USA; *phone:* +1 202 225 1790.

CHRISTIE, Governor Christopher; Governor, State of New Jersey; *born:* 6 September, 1961, Newark, New Jersey; *education:* Univ. of Delaware, BA Political Science, 1984; Seton Hall Univ. School of Law, JD, 1987; *party:* Republican; *political career:* Governor of New Jersey, 2010-; *professional career:* Lawyer; US Attorney for the District of New Jersey, 2002-2008; *office address:* Office of the Governor, State House, PO Box 001, Trenton, NJ 08625, USA; *phone:* +1 609 292 6000; *URL:* http://www.state.nj.us/governor.

CHRISTIE, Hon. Perry Gladstone; Prime Minister, Government of Bahamas; *born:* 1943; *married:* Bernadette Joan Temple; *education:* Eastern Sen. Sch., New Providence; Birmingham Univ.; University Tutorial Coll.; Inner Temple; *political career:* Min. of Agriculture, Trade and Industry, 1990; Prime Minister and Minister of Finance, 2002-07; Prime Minister, 2012-; *professional career:* Represented The Bahamas at the 1960 West Indies Fedn. Games, Kingston and Central American and Caribbean Games, Kingston 1962 Bronze medallist, triple jump); appointed to the Senate by the Prime Minister, the Rt. Hon. Sir Lynden Pindling 1974-77; MP for Centerville 1982-; Minister of Tourism 1982-84; Former ptnr., Christie, Ingraham and Co.; *office address:* Office of the Prime Minister, Sir Cecil Wallace-Withfield Centre, Cabla Beach, PO Box CB-10980, Nassau, Bahamas; *phone:* +1 242 327 5826; *fax:* +1 242 327 5806; *URL:* http://www.opm.gov.bs.

CHRYSOSTOMOS, Archbishop; Archbishop of Nova Justinia and Cyprus; *born:* 10 April 1941, Tala, Pafos District, Cyprus; *education:* Univ. of Athens, School of Theology, 1972; *professional career:* Ordained, Deacon, Nov. 1963; Ordained to the Holy Priesthood, elevated to the rank of Archimandrite and installed as Abbot . Nov. 1972; Ordained and enthroned as Bishop of Paphos, Feb. 1978; Archbishop of Cyprus and Primate of the Autocephalous Orthodox Church of Cyprus. Nov. 2006-; *office address:* PO Box 1130, Archbishop Kyprianos Street, Nicosia, Cyprus; *phone:* +357 (0)2 430696; *fax:* +357 (0)2 432470.

CHU, Dr. Judy; Congresswoman, California 32nd District , U.S. House of Representatives; *education:* BA, Mathematics; Ph.D, Psychology; *political career:* Mem., Calif. State Assembly, 2001-06; Mem., Calif. State Bd. of Equalization, 2006-10, Chwmn., 2008, Vice-Chwmn., 2009; Congresswoman, US HOR, 2009-; *professional career:* Community college professor of psychology, 20 years; Bd. Mem., Garvey School Dist.,1985-88; Monterey Park City Cncl., 1988-2001, Mayor three times ; *committees:* House: Judiciary; Small Business; *office address:* US House of Representatives, 2421 Rayburn HOB, Washington, D.C. 20515, USA; *phone:* +1 202 225 5464; *fax:* +1 202 225 5467; *URL:* http://chu.house.gov/contact/index.shtml.

CHUI SAI ON, Fernando; MC, Chief Executive, Executive Council of Macau; *born:* January 1957, Macau; *education:* California State Univ. of Sacramento, BA, Community Health; Univ. of Oklahoma, USA, MPH and Dr. Ph., Public Health ; *political career:* mem., Cncl. for Youth Affairs, 5th Legislative Assembly, 1992-95; Sec. for Social Affairs and Culture, 1999-; Chief Executive, 2010-; *memberships:* hon. Life-Time Pres., Macau Junior Chamber of Commerce Sr. Mem. Assn.; Chmn., Macau Assn. for the mentally handicapped, and Vice-President, Macau Management Assn.; *professional career:* Principal of Kang Peng Sch. and the Kang Peng Centre of Continuing Education for Professionals, 1992-95; played an active role in many community organisations in Macau; Chief, Medical and Health Department, Tung Sin Tong Charitable Inst.; Exec. Dir. of Macau Kiang Wu Hospital Charitable Assn.; Dir., Macau Eye Bank Fund; Hon. Pres. of Macau Nursing Assn.; *committees:* Mem. of the Exec. Cttee. of China Youth Federation, President of Macau Junior Chamber, 1991; Pres. of the Staff Cttee of Kiang Wu; *office address:* Headquarters of the Government of the Macau Special Administrative Region, Macau; *phone:* +853 989 5148/726886; *fax:* +853 728354.

CHULTEM, Dr Ulaan; Minister of Finance, Government of Mongolia; *political career:* Deputy Prime Minister; Dep. Speaker of Parliament, 2012; Minister of Finance, 2012-; *office address:* Ministry of Finance, Peace Avenue 7a, Ulaan Baatar 210648, Mongolia.

CHUNG, Hong-won; Prime Minister, Government of South Korea; *born:* 1944; *education:* LL.B, College of Law, Sung Kyun Kwan Univ., Seoul, 1971; *political career:* Prime Minister, 2013-; *professional career:* Prosecutor; Pres., Korea Legal Aid Corporation, 2008-11; *office address:* Prime Minister's Office, 77 Sejongno, Jongno-gu, Seoul, South Korea; *phone:* +82 2 737 0094; *fax:* +82 2737 0109; *URL:* http://www.korea.net/Government.

CIOLOS, Dacian; Romanian, Commissioner, European Commission; *born:* 1969; *political career:* Undersecretary of State for European Affairs, Romania, 2007; Agriculture & Rural Development Minister, 2007-08; Head., Presidential Commission on Agricultural Development Public Policy of Romania, 2009-10; Commssioner responsible for Agriculture and Rural Development, 2010-; *office address:* European Commission, rue de la loi 200, B-1049 Brussels, Belgium; *URL:* http://ec.europa.eu.

CLAPPER, James R.; Director, Office of the Director of National Intelligence; *education:* Univ. of Maryland; St. Mary's Univ.; *political career:* Director of National Intelligence, 2010-; *professional career:* career in the US Armed Forces, incl. Lieutenant general , US Air Force and Dir., Defense Intelligence Agency; Also, Assist. Chief of Staff for Intelligence at US Air Force HQ; two combat tours; 73 combat support missions; industry; consultant and advisor to Congress and to the Depts. of Defense and Energy; Dir., National Imagery and

Mapping Agency, 2001 (now the National Geospatial-Intelligence Agency); Principal Staff Assist., Sec. of Defense; *office address:* Office of the Director of National Intelligence, Washington, DC 20511, USA; *phone:* +1 703 733 8600; *URL:* http://www.dni.gov.

CLAPPISON, James; British, Member of Parliament for Hertsmere, House of Commons; *born:* 1956; *married:* Helen; *public role of spouse:* solicitor and university lecturer; *education:* St Peter's School, York; Queen's College, Oxford; Second Class Honours Degree, Philosophy, Politics and Economics; *party:* Conservative Party; *political career:* PPS to Minister of State, Home Office, 1994-95; Parly. Under Sec. of State, Dept. of Environment; MP, Hertsmere, 1992-; Shadow Minister for Work, 2001-2002; *memberships:* National Trust; English Heritage; NSPCC; *professional career:* Barrister; *office address:* House of Commons, London, SW1A 0AA, United Kingdom; *phone:* +44 (0)20 7219 3000; *e-mail:* hcinfo@parliament.uk.

CLARK, Hon. Christy; Premier, Provincial Government of British Columbia; *political career:* Dep. Premier and Minister of Education, 2001-2004; Dep. Premier and Minister of Children and Family Development, 2004-05; Premier, 2011-; *office address:* Office of the Premier, Parliament Buildings, Victoria, BC, V8V 1X4, Canada.

CLARK, Greg; Financial Secretary, HM Treasury, UK Government; *born:* 1967; *party:* Conservative; *political career:* MP for Tunbridge Wells, 2005-; Shadow Secretary of State for Energy and Climate Change, 2009-10; Minister of State, Dept. for Communities and Local Government, 2010-11, Minister of State, Business, Innovation and Skills, 2010-11; Financial Sec., HM Treasury, 2012-; *office address:* House of Commons, London, SW1P 0AA, United Kingdom.

CLARK, Rt. Hon. Helen, MA (Hons.); New Zealander, Administrator, United Nations Development Programme; *born:* 1950, Hamilton; *education:* MA, Hons, Auckland Univ. 1974; Univ. Grants Cttee. post-graduate scholarship, 1976; *party:* New Zealand Labour Party; *political career:* Mem., Labour Party's NZ Exec., 1978-88 and 1989-; MP (Mount Albert), 1981-96; Govt. delegate to the World Conference, 1985; MP (Owairaka), 1996-; held Labour Party offices at all levels; Labour Party's New Zealand Exec., 1978-88; fmr. Pres., Labour Youth Cncl.; fmr. Exec. Mem., Labour Party's Auckland Regional Cncl.; fmr. Sec., Labour Women's Cncl.; fmr. Mem., Policy Cncl.; Minister of Housing, 1987-89; Minister of Conservation, 1987-89; Dep. Prime Minister, Minister of Health, Minister of Labour, 1989-90; Dep. Leader of the Opp. and Spokesperson on Health and Labour, 1990-93; Leader of the Opp., 1993-99; Prime Minister, Minister for Arts, Culture and Heritage, Minister, New Zealand Security Intelligence Service and Ministerial Services, 1999-2008; *interests:* social policy, international affairs, equality for women; *professional career:* Jr. Lecturer, political studies, Auckland, 1973-75 and 1977-81; Administrator, UNDP, 2009-; *committees:* Convenor, Int. Cttee. of the Labour Party's New Zealand Cncl.,1979-; Chmn., Foreign Affairs and Defence Select Cttee.; Chmn., ad hoc Disarmament and Arms Control Select Cttee.; Chmn., fmr. Foreign Affairs Select Cttee.; Govt. Admin. Select Cttee.; Convenor Govt. Caucus Cttee. on External Affairs and Security, 1984-87; Chmn., Cabinet Social Equity Cttee.; Cabinet Policy Cttee.; Cabinet Cttee. on Chief Executives; Cabinet Economic Devt. and Employment Cttee.; Cabinet Expenditure Review Cttee.; Cabinet State Agencies Cttee.; Cabinet Honours Appointments and Travel Cttee.; Cabinet Domestic and External Security Cttee.; Social Services Select Cttee., 1990-93; Labour Select Cttee., 1990-93, Cabinet Policy Cttee., 2000-; *honours and awards:* Annual Peace Prize, Danish Peace Foundation, 1986; *office address:* UNDP, 1United Nations Plaza, New York NY 10017, USA; *phone:* +1 212 906 5000.

CLARK, Katy, MP; MP for North Ayrshire and Arran, House of Commons; *born:* 1967, Kilwinning, Ayrshire, Scotland; *education:* Univ. of Aberdeen, LLB; Univ. of Edinburgh, Dipl. of Legal Practice; *party:* Labour; *political career:* Parly. candidate, Galloway and Upper Nithsdale, 1997; MP for North Ayrshire and Arran, 2005-; *interests:* employment rights, closing the pay gap between men and women, disarmament, women's rights, environmental and poverty issues; *professional career:* Solicitor; *committees:* Scottish Affairs, 2005-10; Procedure Cttee., 2005-10; European Scrutiny Cttee., 2005-10; Business, Innovation & Skills Cttee., 2010-; Environmental Audit Cttee., 2010-; Cttee.on Arms Export Controls, 2010-; Speakers' Panel of Chairs, 2010-; *office address:* Constituency Office, 53 Main Street, Kilbirnie, Ayrshire, KA25 7BX, Scotland.

CLARKE, Rt. Hon. Kenneth Harry, QC, BA, LL.B, MP; British, Minister without Portfolio (Minister of State), UK Government; *born:* 1940; *parents:* Kenneth Clarke and Doris Clarke (née Smith); *married:* Gillian Mary Clarke (née Edwards), 1964; *education:* Nottingham High Sch.; Gonville and Caius Coll., Cambridge; *party:* Conservative Party; *political career:* MP, Rushcliffe, 1970-; Parly. Private Sec., The Solicitor Gen., 1971-72; Asst. Govt. Whip, 1972-74; Lord Cmnr. of Treasury, 1974; Cons. Shadow Spokesman on Health and Social Security, 1974-76, on Industry, 1976-79; Parly. Under Sec. of State, Dept. of Transport, 1979-82; Minister for Health, 1982-85; Privy Cllr., 1983; Paymaster Gen. and Minister of Employment, 1985-87; Chllr. of the Duchy of Lancaster and Minister of Trade and Industry, 1987-88; Sec. of State for Health, 1988-90; Sec. of State for Education and Science, 1990-92; Home Sec., 1992-93; Chllr. of the Exchequer, 1993-97; ran for the Cons. Leadership, 1997, 2001 and 2005; Shadow Sec. of State for Business, Enterprise and Regulatory Reform, Jan. 2009-10; Lord Chancellor and Secretary of State for Justice, 2010-12; Minister without Portfolio (Minister of State), 2012-; *interests:* social services, industry, transport, health, employment, education, legal affairs, treasury/finance; *memberships:* Pres., Cambridge Union, 1963; Chmn., Fed. of Cons. Students, 1963-64; *professional career:* Barrister-at-law, called to the Bar by Gray's Inn, 1963; became QC, 1980; Dir., Independent News & Media Plc. and Independent News & Media, (UK); *committees:* served on many Nat. Cttees. of the Conservative Party; *publications:* Various pamphlets, Bow Group; New Hope for the Regions, 1979; The Free Market and the Inner Cities, 1987; *clubs:* Garrick, The Other, Nottingham CC; *recreations:* football, cricket, motor racing, jazz, birdwatching; *office address:* House of Commons, London, SW1A 0AA, United Kingdom.

CLARKE, Hon. Roger; Minister of Agriculture and Fisheries, Government of Jamaica; *party:* People's National Party (PNP); *political career:* Minister of Agriculture, 1997-2007; Minister of Land, 2006-07; Minister of Agriculture and Fisheries, 2011-; *office address:* Ministry of Agriculture, Hope Gardens, Kingston 6, Jamaica; *phone:* +1 876 927 1731/45; *fax:* +1 876 927 1904.

CLARKE, Thomas, CBE, JP, MP; British, Member of Parliament for Coatbridge, Chryston and Bellshill, House of Commons; ***born:*** 1941; ***education:*** Columba High Sch., Coatbridge; Scottish Coll. of Commerce; ***political career:*** MP (Lab.) for Coatbridge and Airdrie, 1982-83, for Monklands West, 1983-97; Author, Disabled Persons Act, 1986; Front Bench Spokesperson, Scottish Affairs, 1986-87, UK Social Services, 1987-92, on Scotland; Overseas Development Spokesperson, 1993-94; Disabled People's Rights; Minister of State for Film & Tourism, 1997-98; MP, Coatbridge and Chryston, 1997-2005; MP, Coatbridge, Chryston and Bellshill, 2005-; ***professional career:*** Asst. Dir., Scottish Council for Educational Technology (SEO), 1966-82; Mem., Coatbridge Town Cncl., 1964-75; Mem., Monklands Dist. Cncl. 1975-82; Provost of Monklands, 1975-82; Pres., Convention of Scottish Local Authorities, 1978-80; former Nat. Pres., British Assn. of Amateur Cinematographers; ***committees:*** Treasurer, All Party Parly. Overseas Development Group; Former Chairperson, Parly. Labour Party Foreign Affairs Cttee; Administration, 2008-10; Standards and Privileges, 2010-; Joint Committee on the Draft House of Lords Reform Bill, 2011-12; ***honours and awards:*** Commander of the Order of the British Empire, 1980; Justice of the Peace, 1972; ***publications:*** Director, amateur award winning film Give Us A Goal (1972); ***clubs:*** Coatbridge Municipal Golf; Easter Moffat Golf; ***office address:*** House of Commons, London, SW1A 0AA, United Kingdom; ***phone:*** +44 (0)20 7219 6997.

CLARKE OF STONE-CUM-EBONY, Lord Anthony; Justice of the Supreme Court of the United Kingdom; ***born:*** May 1943; ***education:*** King's Coll., Cambridge Univ.; ***political career:*** Mem., Privy Council; Mem., House of Lords, 2009-, as Justice of the Supreme Court, disqualified from participation 2009-; ***professional career:*** Called to the Bar at Middle Temple, 1965; Queen's Counsel, 1979; Recorder in criminal and civil courts, 1985-92; High Court Judge, 1993-98; Lord Justice of Appeal, 1998-2005; Master of the Rolls and Head of Civil Justice in England and Wales, 2005-09; Justice of the Supreme Court, 2009-; ***office address:*** Supreme Court of the United Kingdom, Parliament Square, London, SW1P 3BD, United Kingdom; ***URL:*** http://www.supremecourt.gov.uk.

CLASE, H.E. Nicola; Ambassador, Swedish Embassy in the UK; ***languages:*** English, Mandarin; ***professional career:*** State Sec., Foreign and EU affairs, Swedish Prime Minister's Office, 2006-08; Amb. to the UK, 2010-; ***office address:*** Embassy of Sweden, 11 Montagu Place, London, W1H 2AL, Kingdom; ***phone:*** +44 (0)20 7917 6400; ***fax:*** +44 (0)20 7917 6475; ***URL:*** http://www.swedenabroad.com/en-GB/Embassies/London.

CLEGG, Rt. Hon. Nicholas; Deputy Prime Minister, Leader, Liberal Democrat Party; ***born:*** 7 January 1967; ***parents:*** Nicholas P. Clegg and Hermance Eulalie Clegg (née Van den Wall Bake); ***married:*** Miriam Gonzalez Durante, September 2000; ***languages:*** French, Dutch, Spanish, German; ***education:*** Cambridge Univ., Robinson Coll., MA, Anthropology, 1986-89; Univ. of Minnesota, USA, Political Theory, 1989-90; Coll. D' Europe, Bruges, Belgium, European Affairs, 1991-92; ***political career:*** Trade and Industry spokesman, Lib. Dem. Gp. (ELDR); Chief Whip, UK Lib. Dem. Delegation; MEP, Liberal Democrat, 1999-2004; MP for Sheffield Hallam, 2005-; Lib. Dem. Foreign Affairs Spokesman, 2005; Shadow Home Secretary, 2006; Leader, Liberal Democrat Party, Dec. 2007-; Deputy Prime Minister, Conservative-Lib. Dem. Coalition government, May 2010-; ***professional career:*** Research Asst., Dept. of Political Science, Univ. Minnesota, 1990; Journalist, The Nation Magazine, New York, 1990; Political Consultant, GJW Govt. Relations Ltd., 1992-93; Official, European Cmn., DGIA Programme, 1994-96; Sr. Policy Adviser to the Vice-Pres. of the European Cmn. in Brussels, 1996-99; ***honours and awards:*** Financial Times 1993 David Thomas Prize; ***publications:*** Doing Less to do More, (Centre for European Reform, 2000); Trading for the Future, (Centre for Reform, 2001); Learning from Europe, lessons in Education (2002), CER; Reforming the European Parliament (Foreign Policy Centre, 2003); numerous newspaper articles; ***recreations:*** skiing, mountaineering, theatre, literature; ***office address:*** House of Commons, London, SW1P 0AA, United Kingdom; ***e-mail:*** libdemleader@parliament.uk; ***URL:*** http://www.nickclegg.com.

CLEMENT, Hon. Tony; Canadian, President of the Treasury Board, Government of Canada; ***born:*** Manchester, UK; ***married:*** Lynne Golding; ***public role of spouse:*** Lawyer; ***education:*** Univ. of Toronto, Political Science, Law Degree, 1983-86, called to Bar, 1988; ***political career:*** Pres., Progressive Conservative Party of Ontario, 1990-92; Assistant Principal Sec. to Mike Harris PC Ontario Leader, 1992-95; elected MPP, Brampton South, 1995-99; re-elected, Brampton West - Mississauga 1999-2003; Parliamentary Asst. to the Minister of Citizenship, Culture and Recreation, 1995-97; Ontario Minister of Transportation, 1997-99; Ontario Minister of the Environment, 1999-2000; Ontario Minister of Municipal Affairs and Housing, 1999-2001; Ontario Minister of Health and Long-Term Care, 2001-03; Elected MP, House of Commons, 2006- re-elected 2008-; Minister of Health and Minister for the Federal Economic Development Initiative for Northern Ontario, Gov. of Canada, 2006-08; Minister of Industry, 2008-11; President of the Treasury Board, Minister for the Federal Economic Development Initiative for Northern Ontario, 2011-; ***professional career:*** Lawyer; consultant in Central and Eastern Europe, 1988-92; Counsel, Bennett Jones LLP, 2003-06; Small Business Owner; Visiting Fellow Faculty of Law, Univ. of Toronto, 2003-05; ***committees:*** Chair, Economic and Long Term Growth Cttee. of Cabinet; mem., Planning & Priorities Cttee. of Cabinet; ***office address:*** House of Commons, Parliament Buildings, Wellington Street, Ottawa, Ontario, K1A 0A6, Canada.

CLIFF, Ian, OBE; British, Ambassador, British Embassy in Kosovo; ***born:*** 11 September 1952, Twickenham, UK; ***parents:*** Gerald Shaw Cliff and Dorothy Cliff (née Cameron); ***married:*** Caroline Mary Cliff (née Redman), 1988; ***children:*** Richard Vernon (M), Louise Alexandra (F), Julia Emily (F); ***public role of spouse:*** member of H.M. Diplomatic service; ***languages:*** Arabic, French, German, Serbo-Croatian; ***education:*** Magdalen Coll., Oxford, 1971-74; ***professional career:*** FCO, 1979-82; First Sec., B.E.Khartoum, 1982-85, FCO, 1985-89; First Sec., UK Mission to U.N., New York, 1989-93; Dir., Middle East Exports, DTI, 1993-96; DHM, B.E. Vienná, 1996-2001; British Amb. to Bosnia and Herzegovina, 2001-05; British Amb. to Sudan, 2005-07; Amb. to Kosovo, 2011-; ***honours and awards:*** OBE, 1991; ***publications:*** Various articles in Railway Magazines; ***clubs:*** Midland and Great Northern Joint Railway Soc., Ipswich Transport Soc., Mid Norfolk Railway Presevation Trust; ***recreations:*** railways, philately, music, history; ***office address:*** British Embassy, Ismail Qemali 6, Arberi-Dragodan, Pristina, 10000, Kosovo; ***phone:*** 381 (0)38 254 700; ***fax:*** +381 (0)38 249 799; ***e-mail:*** ian.cliff@fco.gov.uk; ***URL:*** http://ukinkosovo.fco.gov.uk.

CLIFTON-BROWN, Geoffrey, ARICS; British, Shadow Minister for Foreign Affairs, Trade & Investment, House of Commons; ***born:*** 1953; ***education:*** Eton Coll., 1966-70; Royal Agriculture Coll., Cirencester, 1971-73; ***party:*** Conservative Party; ***political career:*** Constituency Vice-Chmn., North Norfolk, 1984, Chmn., 1986-91; Euro Constituency Vice-Chmn., Norfolk, 1990; MP, Cirencester and Tewkesbury, 1992-97; Vice-Chmn., Small Business Bureau, 1995-; PPS to the Rt. Hon. Douglas Hogg, GQ, Minister for Agriculture, Fisheries and Food, 1995-97; MP, Cotswolds, 1997-; Opposition Whip, 1999-2001; Shadow Spokesman on Housing & Planning, 2001-02; Shadow Minister for Local Gov. Housing and Planning, 2002-04; Opposition Whip, 2004-05; Opposition Assistant Chief Whip, 2005; Shadow Minister for Foreign Affairs, 2005-07, Trade & Investment, 2007, International Development, 2007-10, Trade, 2009-10; ***professional career:*** investment surveyor, Jones Lang Wotton Int., London, 1975-79; MD & owner, farming business, Norfolk, 1979-; former gov. of primary school and sixth form college; ***committees:*** Eastern Area Exec. and Agricultural Cttees.; Environmental Select Cttees., 1992-95; Sec., European Affairs Backbench Cttee. and Sec., Housing Improvement, 1992-95; Vice-Chmn., Charities Property Assoc., 1993; Chmn., All Party Gp. on Population, Development and Reproductive Health, 1995-97; Vice-chmn., Euro Atlantic group, 1996; Public Accounts Cttee., 1997-99; Broadcasting, 2000-01; Administration, 2001, 2010-11; Finance and Services, 2005-; Selection, 2005-06, Chair 2010-; Liaison, 2010-; ***publications:*** Privatising the State Pension - Secure Funded Provision for All, Bow Group; ***office address:*** House of Commons, London, SW1A 0AA, United Kingdom; ***phone:*** +44 (0)20 7219 5147; ***e-mail:*** cliftonbrowng@parliament.uk; ***URL:*** http://www.cliftonbrown.co.uk.

CLINTON (B. BLYTHE III), Bill (William) Jefferson; American, Former President of the USA; ***born:*** 19 August 1946, Hope, AR, USA; ***parents:*** William Jefferson Blythe II and Virginia Cassidy Blythe; ***married:*** Hilary Clinton (née Rodham), 11 October 1975; ***children:*** Chelsea (F); ***public role of spouse:*** US Secretary of State; ***education:*** Georgetown Univ., B.Sc., Int. Affairs, 1964-68; Univ. Coll., Oxford Univ. (Rhodes Scholar), UK, 1968-70; Yale Law Sch., JD, 1970-73; ***party:*** Democratic Party; ***political career:*** Intern, office of Arkansas Senator J. William Fulbright; Arkansas Attorney-Gen., 1977-79; Governor, State of Arkansas, 1979-81 and 1983-93; Chmn., Education Cmn. of the States, 1986-87; Pres. of the USA, 1993-01; ***memberships:*** Chmn., Southern Growth Policies Bd., 1985-86; Chmn., Nat. Governors' Assn., 1986-87; Vice-Chmn., Democratic Governors' Assn., 1987-88, Chmn., 1989-90; ***professional career:*** Prof., Univ. of Arkansas Law School, 1974-76; Attorney Gen., State of Arkansas, 1977-79; law firm Wright, Lindsey & Jennings, 1981-83; ***honours and awards:*** Nat. Cncl. of State Human Service Administrators' Assn. Award for Leadership on Welfare Reform; Nat. Energy Efficiency Advocate Award; Nat. Cncl. of Jewish Women, Award for recognition of HIPPY in Arkansas and the nation; Hon. Degree, Northeastern Univ., Boston, 1993; ***recreations:*** playing the saxophone, golf, playing with the family cat called Socks, horseback riding, bike riding, boating; ***office address:*** Democratic Party, 430 S. Capitol St. SE, Washington, DC 20003, USA.

CLINTON, Hillary Rodham; American, Former Secretary of State, US Government; ***born:*** 26 October 1947, Chicago, Illinois, US; ***parents:*** Hugh Ellsworth Rodham and Dorothy Rodham (née Howell); ***married:*** Bill Clinton, 1975; ***children:*** Chelsea Victoria (F); ***public role of spouse:*** Former President of the US; ***education:*** MA, Wellesley College, 1969; BA, Yale Univ., JD, 1973; ***political career:*** Chmn., Presidential Task Force on National Health Care Reform, 1993; Goodwill Ambassador; Mem., US Senate, 2000-09; Presidential Candidate, 2008; US Sec. of State, 2009-Feb. 2013; ***memberships:*** Fellow, American Bar Assn.; Arkansas Bar Assn.; Arkansas Trial Lawyers Assn.; Arkansas Women Lawyers Assn.; American Trial Lawyers Assn.; Pulaski County Bar Assn.; ***professional career:*** Counsel, Impeachment Inquiry Staff, House Cmn. on the Judicary, 1974; Asst. Prof. of Law & Dir., Legal Aid Clinic, Univ. of Arkansas School of Law, Fayetteville 1974-76; Ptnr., Rose Law Firm, Little Rock, Arkansas, 1977-92; Assist. Prof. of Law, Univ. of Arkansas School of Law, Little Rock, 1979-80; ***committees:*** numerous, inc. Hon. Chmn., Presidential Chmn., on the Arts and Humanities, 1993-; Franklin and Eleanor Roosevelt Inst., 1988-92; US Delegate, UN Fourth World Conference on Women, 1995; Senate Cttees: Environment and Public Works; Health, Education, Labor and Pensions; Armed Services; ***honours and awards:*** numerous, inc. Outstanding Layman of the Year, Phi Delta Kappa, 1984; Albert Schweitzer Leadership Award, Hugh O'Brien Youth, Fdn., 1993; Martin Luther King Jr. Award, Prog. Nat. Bapt. Conv., 1994; Greater Washington Urban League Award, 1995; Nat. Breast Cancer Coalition Leadership Award, 1995; Distinguished Service Award, Columbia Univ. Centre of Addiction and Substance Abuse, 1997; Eleanor Roosevelt Living World Award, Peace Links, 1997; ***publications:*** Handbook on Legal Rights for Arkansas Women, 1977; It Takes A Village: And Other Lessons Children Teach Us, 1996; ***office address:*** c/o Democrat Party, 430 S. Capitol Street SE, Washington, DC 20, USA; ***URL:*** http://www.hillaryclintonoffice.com/.

CLOS, Joan; Executive Director, UN Habitat; ***education:*** Universidad Autónoma de Barcelona (UAB), Medicine; University of Edinburgh, Scotland, Public Health and Epidemiology; ***political career:*** Mayor of Barcelona, 1997-2006; Minister of Industry, Commerce and Tourism, 2006-08; ***professional career:*** Spanish Ambassador to Turkey and Azerbaijan; Executive Dir., UN Habitat, 2010-; ***office address:*** UN Habitat, POB 30030 , Nairobi, Kenya; ***URL:*** http://www.unhabitat.org.

CLWYD, Ann, MP; British, Member of Parliament for Cynon Valley, House of Commons; ***born:*** 1937; ***education:*** Univ. Coll., Bangor; ***party:*** Labour Party; ***political career:*** Mem., European Parly. for Mid and West Wales, 1979-84; Mem., Labour NEC, 1983-84; MP, Cynon Valley, 1984-; Frontbench Spokeswoman on Women & Education, 1987-88, and Overseas Development & Cooperation, 1989-92; Shadow Sec. of State for Wales, 1992, for Nat. Heritage, 1992-93; Spokeswoman on Employment, 1993-94, Foreign Affairs, 1994-95; Asst. to John Prescott, 1994-95; Vice-Chair, Parliamentary Labour Party; Chair, All Party Parly. Human Rights Group; Vice-Chair, Inter-Parly. Union; mem., Human Rights Cmn.; Special Envoy to the PM on Human Rights in Iraq, 2003-; ***interests:*** human rights; ***memberships:*** Welsh Hospital Board 1970-74; Welsh Arts Council, Vice-Chairwoman 1975-79; Arts Council of Great Britain 1975-80; ***professional career:*** Broadcaster; Welsh correspondent for The Guardian and The Observer, 1964-79; ***committees:*** House of Commons Select Cttee. on International Development, 1997-2005; Foreign Affairs, 2010-; Arms Export Controls, 2011-; ***honours and awards:*** Back-bencher of the Year, House Magazine Award, 2003, Spectator Award, 2003; ***office address:*** House of Commons, London, SW1A 0AA, United Kingdom; ***phone:*** +44 (0)20 7219 6609; ***e-mail:*** ann.clwyd.mp@parliament.uk.

CLYBURN, James E.; American, Assistant Democrat Leader, US House of Representatives; ***education:*** South Carolina State Univ.; ***party:*** Democrat; ***political career:*** Congressman, South Carolina Sixth District, US House of Representatives, 1992-; Democratic Caucus Chairman, -2006; Democrat Whip, 2007-10; Assist. Democratic Leader, 2011-; ***professional career:*** teacher; employment counsellor; director of two youth and community development projects, Charleston, South Carolina; staff of Governor John C. West, 1971; South Carolina Human Affairs Commissioner, 1974-92; ***committees:*** Chmn., Congressional Black Caucus, 1998-; House Cttee. on Appropriations: Energy and Water Development, Transportation and Treasury, Legislative Branch sub-cttees.; ***office address:*** US House of Representatives, 2135 Rayburn House Office Building, Washington, DC 20515, USA; ***phone:*** +1 202 225 3315.

COAKER, Vernon; British, MP for Gedling, House of Commons; ***born:*** 17 June 1953; ***education:*** Univ. of Warwick; Trent Polytechnic; ***party:*** Labour Party; ***political career:*** MP, Gedling, 1997-; Lord Cmnr., 2005-; Parliamentary Under Sec. of State, Home Office, 2007-08; Minister of State for Policing, Crime and Security, Oct. 2008-09; Minister of State, Department of Children, Schools and Families, 2009-10; Shadow Minister for Education, 2010; Shadow Minister, Home Affairs, Oct. 2010-Oct. 2011; Shadow Secretary of State for Northern Ireland, Oct. 2011-; ***interests:*** social security, animal rights, education; ***professional career:*** Dep. Head Teacher; ***office address:*** House of Commons, London, SW1A 0AA, United Kingdom; ***phone:*** +44 (0)20 7219 3000; ***e-mail:*** coakerv@parliament.uk; ***URL:*** http://www.vernon-coaker-mp.co.uk.

COATS, Dan; Senator, US Senate; ***married:*** Marcia Coats (née Crawford), 1965; ***education:*** Wheaton Coll.; Indiana Univ. Sch. of Law; ***party:*** Republican; ***political career:*** US Army, 1966-68; Assist. Vice Pres., Indiana life insurance company; Indiana Director, Congressman Dan Quayle, 1977-80; Congressman District Dir.; elected to US Congress, 1980; US Representative, 1981-88; US Senator for Indiana 1989-99, 2010-; ***memberships:*** co-chair, Center for Jewish and Christian Values; ***professional career:*** US Army; Legal Intern; Assoc. Editor, Law Review; Attorney in Fort Wayne; Special Counsel, Verner, Liipfert, Bernhard, McPherson and Hand, 1999; US Ambassador to Germany, 2001-05; ***committees:*** Senate: Appropriations; Select Intelligence; Commerce, Science & Transportation; Joint Economic Cttee. (JEC); ***publications:*** The Project for American Renewal and Mending Fences: Renewing Justice Between Gov; ***office address:*** US Senate, Hart Senate Office Building, Washington DC, USA; ***URL:*** http://www.coats.senate.gov.

COBURN, Tom A., MD; American, Senator, US Senate; ***party:*** Republican; ***political career:*** US House of Representatives, 1994-04; mem., US Senate, 2004-; ***professional career:*** Doctor; ***committees:*** US Senate: Finance; Homeland Security & Governmental Affairs; Judiciary; ***office address:*** United States Senate, 172 Russell Senate Office Building, Washington, DC 20510, USA; ***phone:*** +1 202 224 5754; ***URL:*** http://www.coburn.senate.gov.

COCHRAN, Thad; American, Senator for Mississippi, US Senate; ***born:*** 7 December 1937, Pontotoc, Mississippi, USA; ***parents:*** William Holmes Cochran and Emma Grace Cochran; ***married:*** Rose Cochran (née Clayton), 6 June 1964; ***children:*** Clayton (M), Kate (F); ***education:*** Univ. of Mississippi, Sch. of Liberal Arts, BA (major in Psychology, minor in Political Science), 1959; US Navy Sch. of Justice, Newport, Rhode Island, honor student; Sch. of Law, Univ. of Mississippi, 1961; Trinity Coll., Univ. of Dublin, Ireland, postgraduate Jurisprudence and Int. Law, 1963-64; ***party:*** Republican; ***political career:*** Mem., 93rd to 95th congresses for Mississippi; Senator for Mississippi, 1978-; ***memberships:*** American Bar Assn.; Mississippi Bar Assn.; former Chmn., Mississippi Law Inst.; elected Pres., Young Lawyers Div. of the Mississippi Bar Assn. 1971; Mem. of the Bd., US Naval Academy; Mem. of the Bd. of Regents, Smithsonian Inst.; Lawyers' Chmn., Heart Fund and United Givers Fund; Hon. Chmn., Delta Wildlife Foundation; Bd. Mem., Mississippi Opera, Inc.; ***professional career:*** Ensign, Ship's Legal Officer, Officer of the Deck, Commandant of the 8th Naval District, New Orleans, Louisiana 1961, US Naval Reserve; Article Editor, Mississippi Law Journal, 1964; Practised in Jackson, 1965-72; Assoc., Watkins & Eager, 1965-72; ***committees:*** Senate Cttee. on Appropriations; Agriculture, Nutrition and Forestry; Rules & Administration; ***honours and awards:*** Jackson's Young Man of the Year 1971; one of Three Outstanding Men of the Year in Mississippi 1971; Conservationist of the Year in Mississippi, Ducks Unlimited 1994; Conservationist of the Year, North American Waterfowl Fed. 1996; Conservation Achievement Award, Nat. Wildlife Fed. 1996; Hon. degrees from Kentucky Wesleyan Coll., Mississippi Coll., Blue Mountain Coll., Univ. of Richmond; ***clubs:*** Pres., Jackson Men's Y Club; Bd. Mem., Jackson Rotary Club; ***office address:*** United States Senate, 113 Dirksen Senate Office Building, Washington, DC 20510, USA; ***phone:*** +1 202 224 5054; ***e-mail:*** senator@cochran.senate.gov; ***URL:*** http://www.cochran.senate.gov.

COENE, Luc; Governor, National Bank of Belgium; ***born:*** 1947; ***education:*** Ghent Univ., Economics; ***professional career:*** IMF; Chef de cabinet to the PM, Secretary to the Council of Ministers, 1999-2001; Chmn., Board of Dirs., to the Chancellery of the PM and Secretary of the Council of Ministers, 2001-03; Minister of State, 2003-; Vice-Gov., National Bank of Belgium, 2003-09, Gov., 2011-; mem., ESRB, 2011-; Dir., BIS, 2011-; ***office address:*** National Bank of Belgium, Boulevard de Berlaimont 14, B 1000 Brussels, Belgium; ***URL:*** http://www.nbb.be.

COEURÉ, Benoit; French, Member of the Executive Board, European Central Bank; ***education:*** Univ. Paris Diderot; Ecole nationale de la statistique et de l'administration, Paris; ***professional career:*** Economist, INSEE (National Inst. of Statistics & Economic Studies), 1992-95; Economist, French Treasury, 1995-987; Economic adviser to the Dir.-Gen. of the French Treasury, 1997-2002, Head of the Foreign Exchange Policy and Economic Policy Unit, 1999-2001; Dep. Chief Executive, Agence France Trésor, 2002-06, Chief Exec., 2006-07; Head, Multilateral Affairs and Development Dept., French Treasury, 2007-09, Dep. Dir. Gen., 2009-11; Mem. of the Executive Board, European Central Bank, 2012-; ***office address:*** European Central Bank, Kaiserstrasse 29, D-60311 Frankfurt-am-Main, Germany; ***URL:*** http://www.ecb.int.

COFFEY, Ann; British, Member of Parliament for Stockport, House of Commons; ***born:*** 31 August 1946, Inverness, Scotland, United Kingdom; ***education:*** Polytechnic of the South Bank, B.Sc, Sociology; Manchester Univ., M.Sc; PGCE; Certificate of Qualification, Social Work; ***party:*** Labour Party, 1977-; ***political career:*** Cllr., Stockport MBC, 1984-92; Leader, Labour Group, 1988-92; MP, Stockport, 1992-; ***interests:*** health, education, social services, local government; ***recreations:*** reading, walking, cinema; ***office address:*** House of Commons, London, SW1A 0AA, United Kingdom; ***phone:*** +44 (0)20 7219 3000; ***e-mail:*** ann.coffey.mp@parliament.uk.

COFFEY, Dr Thérèse; MP for Suffolk Coastal, UK Government; ***party:*** Conservative; ***political career:*** MP for Suffolk Coastal, May 2010-; ***committees:*** Culture, Media and Sport Select Cttee., 2010-; ***office address:*** House of Commons, London, SW1A 0AA, United Kingdom; ***phone:*** +44 (0)20 7219 3000; ***e-mail:*** therese.coffey.mp@parliament.uk.

COFFMAN, Mike; Congressman, 6th District of Colorado, US House of Representatives; ***party:*** Republican; ***political career:*** Mem., US HOR, Colorado Dist. 6, 2009-; ***committees:*** Armed Services; Natural Resources; Small Business; ***office address:*** House of Representatives, Washington, D.C., USA.

COLEMAN, Dr Jonathan; Minister of Defence, New Zealand Government; ***education:*** Auckland Univ. Medical School; ***party:*** National Party; ***political career:*** MP, 2005-; Minister of Broadcasting and Immigration, 2008-11; Minister of Defence, Minister of State Services, 2011-; ***office address:*** Ministry of Defence, 3rd Floor, Defence House, 15-21 Stout Street, Wellington, New Zealand; ***phone:*** +64 (0)4 496 0270; ***URL:*** http://www.defence.govt.nz.

COLLINS, Damian; MP for Folkestone and Hythe, UK Government; ***party:*** Conservative; ***political career:*** MP for Folkestone and Hythe, May 2010-; PPS to Theresa Viliers as Sec. of State for Northern Ireland, 2012-; ***committees:*** Culture, Media and Sport Select Cttee., 2010-; ***office address:*** House of Commons, London, SW1A 0AA, United Kingdom; ***phone:*** +44 (0)20 7219 3000; ***e-mail:*** damian.collins.mp@parliament.uk.

COLLINS, Jacinta; Australian, Minister for Mental Health and Ageing, Government of Australia; ***born:*** 4 September 1962, Altona, Victoria, Australia; ***education:*** BA (Monash), BSocWK (La Trobe); ***party:*** Australian Labour Party (ALP); ***political career:*** Senator for Victoria, 1995-; Mem., Parly. Deleg. to the 101st IPU Conference, Brussels, Belgium, 1999; Parly. Sec., representing the Shadow Minister for Industrial Relations and Employment, Training and Population, 1998-2001; mem., Opposition Shadow Ministry, 2003;; Shadow Minister for Children and Youth, 2003; Minister for Mental Health and Ageing, 2013-; ***memberships:*** Mem., ACTU Cncl., 1993-;; ***professional career:*** Social Welfare Officer and Research Officer, Shop, Distributive and Allied Employees' Assn., 1980-90, Nat. Industrial Officer, 1991-95; ***committees:*** Mem., ACTU Women's Social Welfare and Occupational Health and Safety Cttees.; Mem., ALP Admin. Cttee., 1989-91; Mem., ALP Status of Women Cttee., 1989-93; Mem., ALP Social Justice Policy Cttee., 1989-92; Caucus Rep., ALP Living Standards and Employment Nat. Policy Cttee.; Senate Standing Cttees., Publications, 1995-98, Regulations and Ordinances, 1995-96, Senators' Interest, 1995-96, 1998-, Jt. House 1995-96, 1997-; Senate Legislative and General Purpose Standing Cttees., Community Affairs, 1995-96; Econ. Reference, 1996-98, Chair, 1996, Legislation, 1997-98; Participating Mem., Econ. Legislation, 1996-97, Legal and Constitutional Legislation, 2000-02; Participating Mem., Employment, Workplace Relations and Education and Community Affairs Legislation, 2002-; Participating mem., Foreign Affairs, Defence and Trade, 2003-; ***office address:*** Department of Health and Ageing, Furzer Street and Bower Street, Woden Town Centre, Canberra, ACT , Australia; ***URL:*** http://www.health.gov.au.

COLLINS, Judith; Minister of Justice, Government of New Zealand; ***education:*** LLB, LLM (Hons), Master of Taxation Studies (MTaxS), Univ. of Auckland; ***party:*** National Party; ***political career:*** MP, 2002-; Minister of Police, Corrections and Veterans' Affairs, 2008-11; Minister of Justice, Minister of Accident Compensation Corporation, Minister of Ethnic Affairs, 2011-; ***office address:*** Ministry of Justice, 10th FLoor, Charles Ferfusson Building, Bowen Stret, Wellington, New Zealand; ***phone:*** +64 (0)4 474 9700; ***e-mail:*** reception@justice.govt.nz; ***URL:*** http://www.justice.govt.nz.

COLLINS, H.E. Michael; Ambassador, Embassy of Ireland in the USA; ***born:*** 25, June 1953, Dublin, Ireland ; ***languages:*** French, Italian; ***education:*** Institute of Public Administration; Trinity College, Dublin, B.Sc., 1978; ***professional career:*** Dept. of Foreign Affairs, 1974-; postings to Rome and New York, as well as home postings, 1974-93; Counsellor, Washington Emb., 1993-95; Amb., Saudi Arabia (Bahrain, Kuwait, Oman, Qatar and the United Emirates), 1995-99; Amb., Czech Republic (and Ukraine), 1999-2001; Second Sec. Gen, Dept. of the Taoiseach, resp. for Int. and EU Affairs and the Northern Ireland Peace Process, 2001-07; Amb., USA, 2007-; ***office address:*** Embassy of Ireland, 2234 Massachusetts Ave, NW, Washington, DC 20008, USA; ***phone:*** +1 202 462 3939; ***fax:*** +1 202 232 5993; ***URL:*** http://www.irelandemb.org/.

COLLINS, Susan, BA; American, Senator for Maine, US Senate; ***born:*** 7 December 1952, Caribou, Maine, USA; ***education:*** St. Lawrence Univ., BA, 1971-75; ***party:*** Republican; ***political career:*** US Senator for Maine, 1996-; ***professional career:*** Business Center Dir.; State Dep. Treasurer; Small Business Admin. Official; State Financial Regulation Cmnr.; Congressional Aide; ***committees:*** Appropriations; Ageing; Intelligence; ***honours and awards:*** Guardian of Small Business Award; Advocate for Education Award, 1998; Advocate of the Year Award; 1999 Legislator of the Year; Congressional Leadership Award; Friend of the Farm Bureau Award; ***office address:*** United States Senate, 172 Russell Senate Office Building, Washington, DC 20510, USA; ***phone:*** +1 202 224 2523; ***e-mail:*** senator@collins.senate.gov; ***URL:*** http://www.collins.senate.gov/.

COLLIS, H.E. Simon; Ambassador, British Embassy in Iraq; ***professional career:*** Amb to the State of Qatar, 2005-07; Amb. to Syria, 2007-12; Amb. to Iraq, 2012-; ***office address:*** British Embassy, PO Box 341, International Zone, Iraq; ***e-mail:*** lonemb@iraqmofamail.net; ***URL:*** http://ukiniraq.fco.gov.uk/en .

COLOME IBARRA, Corps. Gen. Abelardo; Minister of Interior, Government of Cuba; ***political career:*** Minister of the Interior, to date; Vice-Pres., Council of States, 2008-; ***office address:*** Ministry of Interior, Plaza de la Revolución, Havana, Cuba.

COLVILE, Oliver; MP for Plymouth, Sutton and Devonport, UK Government; *born:* 1959; *party:* Conservative; *political career:* MP for Plymouth, Sutton and Devonport, May 2010-; *committees:* Northern Ireland Affairs, 2010-; *office address:* House of Commons, London, SW1A 0AA, United Kingdom; *phone:* +44 (0)20 7219 3000; *e-mail:* oliver.colvile.mp@parliament.uk.

COLVIN, John O.; Judge, US Tax Court; *education:* Univ. of Missouri, A.B., 1968, J.D., 1971; Georgetown University Law Center, LL.M., Taxation, 1978 ; *memberships:* Officer, Tax Section, Federal Bar Assn, 1978-; *professional career:* Admitted to practice law in Missouri, 1971, and District of Columbia, 1974; U.S. Coast Guard, Washington, D.C., 1971-75; Tax Counsel to Senator Bob Packwood, 1975-84; Chief Counsel, 1985-87 and Chief Minority Counsel, 1987-88, U.S. Senate Finance Committee; Adjunct Prof. of Law, Georgetown Univ. Law Center, 1987-; Judge, US Tax Court, 1988-, Chief Judge, 2006-12; *office address:* United States Tax Court, 400 Second Street, NW, Washington, DC 20217, USA; *URL:* http://www.ustaxcourt.gov/.

COMPAORÉ, Captain Blaise; Burkinabe, President, Burkina Faso; *born:* 1950; *political career:* Chair, Popular Front of Burkina Faso, 1987-; Interim Head of State, June-Dec. 1991; Pres., Burkina Faso, 1991-; *professional career:* Former second-in-command to Capt. Thomas Sankara whom he overthrew in a coup in Oct. 1987; *office address:* Office of the President, Ouagadougou, Burkina Faso.

CONAWAY, Mike; Congressman, Eleventh District, Texas, US House of Representatives; *education:* Texas A & M Univ., Commerce, BBA, Accounting, 1970; *political career:* Texas State Board of Public Accountancy, 1995-2002; US House of Representatives, 2004-; *professional career:* Army, Fort Hood; Price Waterhouse & Co.; Chief Financial Officer, Bush Exploration; *committees:* Permanent Select Cttee. on Intelligence; Armed Services; Agriculture; Ethics, Chmn.; *office address:* US House of Representatives, 511 Cannon House Office Building, Washington, DC 20515, USA.

CONDÉ, Alpha; President, Government of Guinea; *born:* 4 March 1938; *political career:* President, Minister of Defence, Dec. 2010-; *professional career:* Political Science Professor, Univ. of Paris; *office address:* Office of the President, State House, Conakry, Guinea; *phone:* +224 30 44 11 47; *URL:* http://www.guinee.gov.gn/1_bienvenue/president.htm.

CONNARTY, Michael; British, Member of Parliament for Linlithgow and East Falkirk, House of Commons; *born:* 3 September 1947, Coatbridge, Lanarkshire, United Kingdom; *parents:* Patrick Connarty (dec'd) and Elizabeth Connarty (dec'd) (née Plunkett); *married:* Margaret Mary (née Doran), 1969; *children:* Bryan (M), Laura (F); *public role of spouse:* Professor of Education; *languages:* French; *education:* Stirling Univ., BA, Econs.; Jordanhill Coll. of Education, DCE Teaching Diploma; *party:* Labour Party, 1964-; *political career:* Cllr., Stirling District, 1977-90; Cncl. Leader, 1980-90; Mem., Scottish Exec. of the Labour Party, 1983-92; PPS to Rt. Hon. Tom Clarke MP; PC Min. for Film and Tourism, 1997-98; MP, Falkirk East, now Linlithgow and East Falkirk, 1992-; *interests:* economic policy, crime, drugs, prisons, Europe, technology, welfare, Northern Ireland; *memberships:* UNITE, convenor, 1972-73; Educational Inst. of Scotland (EIS); Exec. Mem., Central Region EIS, 1976-84; Pres., Central EIS Assoc., 1982-83; Socialist Educational Assoc.; Vice-Chmn., Scottish MAP, 1988-95; Scottish Opera Gp.; *professional career:* Teacher of Econ. and Modern Studies, secondary sch. and special needs; *committees:* Standing Cttees. on Bankruptcy, Scotland, Act 1993, Prisoners and Criminal Proceedings Act 1993, Local Government Etc., Scotland, Act 1994, Children Bill, Scotland, Bill 1995, Lottery Act 1998; Vice-Chair, APG for Chemical Industries; Sec., APG for UK Offshore Oil and Gas Industry; Chair, Parly. Jazz Appreciation Gp.; Information Select Cttee., 1997-2001; mem., European Scrutiny Select Cmn., 1998-, Chmn., 2006-10; Mem., Parliamentary Assembly of the Council of Europe (PACE), 2011-; Mem., Culture, Science and Education Cttee. of PACE, 2011-; *recreations:* family, hillwalking, reading, music, live theatre and concerts; *office address:* House of Commons, London, SW1A 0AA, United Kingdom; *phone:* +44 (0)20 7219 5077; *e-mail:* michael.connarty.mp@parliament.uk; *URL:* http://www.mconnartymp.com.

CONTEH, Major (retd.) Alfred Paolo; Minister of Defence, Government of Sierra Leone; *education:* Law, LLB, LLM; *political career:* Minister of Defence, 2007-; *professional career:* soldier, military service, 1976-92; *office address:* Ministry of Defence, State Avenue, Freetown, Sierra Leone.

COOK, Sarah; Director, United Nations Research Institute for Social Development; *education:* Oxford Univ., BA; LSE, M.Sc.; Harvard Univ., Phd., Public Policy; *professional career:* Research Fellow, Institute of Development Studies, Univ. of Sussex, 1996-2009; Director, UNRISD, 2009-; *office address:* UNRISD, Palais des Nations, 1211 Geneva 10, Switzerland; *URL:* http://www.unrisd.org/.

COONS, Christopher; Senator for Delaware, US Senate; *education:* Amherst College, BA, Chemistry and political science; Yale Law School; Yale Divinity School; *political career:* New Castle County Exec.; Pres., New Castle County Council; mem., US Senate, 2010-; *professional career:* attorney, W.L. Gore & Assoc.; *committees:* Foreign Relations; Judiciary; Energy; Budget; *office address:* United States Senate, 127A Russell Senate Office Building, Washington DC 20510, USA; *phone:* +1 202 224 5042; *URL:* http://www.coons.senate.gov.

COOPER, Rosie; MP for West Lancashire, House of Commons; *born:* 1950; *party:* Labour Party; *political career:* Liverpool City Councillor, 1973-2000; Lord Mayor of Liverpool, 1992-93; MP for West Lancashire, 2005-; PPS to the Rt. Hon. Lord Rooker of Perry Bar (Dept. for Environment, Food & Rural Affairs), May 2006-June 2007; PPS to Ben Bradshaw MP (Minister of State for Health), June 2007-; *office address:* House of Commons, London, SW1P 0AA, United Kingdom.

COOPER, Yvette; British, Shadow Home Secretary; Minister for Women and Equalities, House of Commons; *born:* 20 March 1969, Inverness, Scotland; *parents:* Tony Cooper and June Cooper; *married:* Ed Balls; *public role of spouse:* MP; *education:* Eggars Comprehensive, Alton, Hants, 1980-85; Alton Sixth Form Coll., 1985-87; 1st Class BA Hons., Politics, Philosophy and Economics, Balliol Coll., Oxford Univ., 1987-90; Kennedy Scholar,

one year post-grad. study, Politics and Economics, Harvard Univ., USA, 1994-95; *party:* Labour Party; *political career:* MP, Pontefract, Castleford and Knottingley 1997-; Parly. Under-Sec. of State for Public Health, 1999-2002; Parly. Sec. Lord Chancellor's Dept. 2002-03-; Parly. Under-Sec.of State, Office of Dep. Prime Minister, June 2003-05; Minister of State for Housing and Planning, 2005-07; Minister of State for Department for Communities and Local Government, 2007-Jan. 2008; Chief Secretary to the Treasury, Jan. 2008-09; Secretary of State for Work and Pensions, 2009-May 2010; Shadow Secretary of State for Work and Pensions, May 2010-Sept. 2010; Shadow Foreign and Commonwealth Secretary, Oct. 2010-11; Minister for Women and Equalities, Oct. 2010-; Shadow Home Secretary, 2011-; *interests:* unemployment, child poverty, coal industry; *memberships:* GMB; T & G; *professional career:* Economic Researcher for late John Smith MP, then Shadow Chllr., 1990-92; Policy Advisor to Bill Clinton Presidential Campaign, 1992; Policy Advisor to Labour's Treasury Team, Public Spending, 1993-94; economic columnist and leader writer, The Independent, 1995-97; *committees:* Fmr. Mem.: Education and Employment Select Cttee; Intelligence and Security Cttee.; All party Coalfield Communities Gp.; *office address:* House of Commons, London, SW1A 0AA, United Kingdom; *phone:* +44 (0)20 7219 5080; *e-mail:* coopery@parliament.uk; *URL:* http://www.yvettecooper.com.

COPE OF BERKELEY, Lord , PC, FCA, John Ambrose; British, Member of the House of Lords; *born:* 1937; *parents:* George Cope MC, FRIBA and Catherine Cope (née Spencer); *married:* Djemila Lovell Cope (née Payne), 1969; *d:* 2; *party:* Conservative Party; *political career:* MP (Con) for South Gloucestershire, 1974-83, for Northavon, 1983-97; Govt. Whip, 1979-83, Dep. Chief Whip and Treas. of Her Majesty's Household, 1983-87; Minister of State, Dept. of Employment and Minister for Small Businesses, 1987-89; Minister of State, Northern Ireland Office, 1989-90; Dep. Chmn. and Joint Treasurer, Conservative Party, 1990-92; Paymaster General, 1992-94; Mem. British parly. delegation to Assemblies of Council of greater Europe and Western European Defence Union, 1995-97; Opposition Spokesman for Northern Ireland, 1997-99; Opposition Spokesman for Home Office matters, House of Lords, 1999-2001; Opposition Chief Whip, 2001-07; Mem., British-Irish Parliamentary Assembly, 2008, Co-Chair, 2010-; Mem., House of Lords; *memberships:* Chartered Accountant FCA; *honours and awards:* Privy Cllr, 1988; Knighthood, 1991; Peerage, 1997; *clubs:* Carlton; Beefsteak; *office address:* House of Lords, London, SW1A 0PW, United Kingdom; *phone:* +44 (0)20 7219 3000; *fax:* +44 (0)20 7219 5679; *e-mail:* hlinfo@parliament.uk; *URL:* http://www.parliament.uk.

CORBELL, Simon; Attorney General, Government of Australian Capital Territory; *political career:* Minister for Education, Youth and Family Services, Minister for Planning, Minister for Industrial Relations; Minister of Health, Minister of Planning, 2003-05; Attorney General, Minister for Police and Emergency Services, and Minister for Planning; 2005-07; Attorney General, Minister for Police and Emergency Services, 2007-09; Attorney General, Minister for Police and Emergency Services, Environment, Climate Change and Energy, 2009-, also Minister for Territory and Municipal Services; *office address:* Attorney General's Office, Level 3 GIO House, 250 City Walk, Canberra ACT 2601, Australia; *phone:* +61 2 6207 0500; *fax:* +61 2 6207 0499; *e-mail:* jcs.webadmin@act.gov.au; *URL:* http://www.jcs.act.gov.au/main.html.

CORBETT, Tom; Governor, State of Pennsylvania; *education:* St Mary's Univ. School of Law, San Antonio, Texas; *political career:* Governor, Commonwealth of Pennsylvania, Jan. 2011-; *professional career:* Pennsylvania National Guard, 1971-84; Assist. U.S. Attorney, Western District of Pennsylvania, 1980; private law practice; US Attorney, Western District of Pennsylvania; Attorney General, Pennsylvania, 1995-97, re-elected, 2004; *office address:* Office of the Governor, 225 Main Capitol Building, Harrisburg, Pennsylvania 17120, USA; *phone:* +1 717 787 2500.

CORBYN, Jeremy Bernard; British, Member of Parliament for Islington North, House of Commons; *born:* 1949; *d:* 2; *political career:* MP, Islington North, 1983- ; *professional career:* Organiser for the National Union of Public Employees, 1975-83; *committees:* Social Security, 1991-97; London, 2009-10; Justice, 2011-; *honours and awards:* Beard of the Year, 2001 (Presented by Beard Liberation Front); *office address:* House of Commons, London, SW1A 0AA, United Kingdom; *phone:* +44 (0)20 7219 3545; *fax:* +44 (0)20 7219 2328; *e-mail:* corbynj@parliament.uk.

CORKER, Senator Bob; Senator, United States Senate; *born:* 24 August 1952; *education:* Univ. of Tennessee, BSc. Industrial Management, 1974; *political career:* Cmnr. of Finance and Administration, State of Tennessee, 1995-2001; Mayor of Chattanooga, 2001-06; US Senator for Tennessee, 2007-; *professional career:* Construction business; *committees:* Foreign Relations; Banking, Housing and Urban Affairs; *office address:* United States Senate, 455 Dirksen Senate Office Building, Washington, DC 20510, USA; *phone:* +1 202 224 4944; *URL:* http://www.alexander.senate.gov.

CORLATEAN, Titus; Minister of Foreign Affairs, Government of Romania; *born:* 1968; *education:* Univ. of Bucharest, Ph.D, law; *political career:* MP, Chamber of Deputies, 2004-07; MEP, 2007-08; Senator, 2008-12; Vice-pres., Social Democratic Party, 2010-; Minister of Justice, May-Aug. 2012; Minister of Foreign Affairs, Aug. 2012-; *office address:* Ministry of Foreign Affairs, Aleea Alexandru nr. 31, Sector 1, Bucharest, Romania; *phone:* +40 1 230 2071; *fax:* +40 1 230 7489; *URL:* http://www.mae.ro.

CORMACK, Lord Patrick, BA; British, Member, House of Lords; *born:* 1939; *parents:* Thomas Charles Cormack and Kathleen Mary Cormack (née Harris); *married:* Mary Cormack (née McDonald), 1967; *children:* Charles James Stuart (M), Richard Nicholas Thomas (M); *languages:* French; *education:* Havelock Sch. Grimsby; Univ. of Hull, BA (Hons), 1961; *party:* Conservative Party, 1956-; *political career:* MP, for Cannock ,1970-74, for Staffordshire South West, 1974-83; PPS, Dept. of Health, Social Security, 1970-73; MP, Staffordshire South, 1983-2010; Opp. Spokesman, Constitution Affairs, 1997-2000; Mem., House of Commons Cmn., 2001-05; Member, House of Lords, 2010-; *interests:* foreign affairs & defence, education, arts & heritage, constitutional affairs; *memberships:* Vice-Chmn., Heritage in Danger; Vice-Pres., Historic Churches Preservation Trust; Mem., Cncl. for British Archeology; Mem., Historic Buildings Cncl., 1979-84; Faculty Jurisdiction Cmn. of Church of England; Royal Cmn. on Historical Manuscripts, 1981-2005; mem., Cncl. of Churchill Memorial Trust; Gen. Synod of the Church of England, 1995-2005; *professional career:*

Schoolmaster, 1961-70; Visiting Lecturer, Univ. of Texas, 1984; Visiting Parly. Fellowship, Oxford, 1994; Advisor; Co. Dir.; Writer; Governor of English Speaking Union. 2001-07; ***committees:*** Chmn. All Party Parly. Cttee. for Soviet Jewry, 1971-74; Chmn., All Party Gp. for Widows and Single Parent Families, 1974; Chmn., All Party Heritage Cttee., 1979-2010; Vice-Chmn., Heritage in Danger; Chmn. Cons. Party Arts and Heritage Cttee., 1979-83; Chmn. Cons. Party Forestry Cttee., 1979-83; Select Cttee. on Education, Science & Arts, 1979-83; Mem., Lord Chllr's. Advisory Cttee. on Public Records; Chmn., House of Commons Art Cttee., 1987-2002; Mem., Speaker's Panel of Chmn., 1983-1997; Chmn., Conservative Party Arts Heritage Nat. Advisory Cttee., 1988-97; Visiting Fellow, 1994, Sr. Assoc. Mem., 1995-, St. Antony's Coll.; Visiting Sr. Scholar, Univ. of Hull, 1995-; Foreign Affairs Cttees., 2001-03; Chmn., N. Ireland Affairs Cttee., 2005-; ***trusteeships:*** Historic Churches Preservation Trust, 1972-2005; Tradescant Trust. 1980-2001; chmn., History of Parliament Trust, 2001-; ***honours and awards:*** Hon. Citizen of Texas, 1985; Freeman, City of London, 1980; Fellow, Soc. of Antiquaries, Vice Pres., 1994; Knighted, 1995; Cmdr. of the Order of the Lion, Finland, 1998; Fellow, Royal Historical Society, 2010; Hon. Fellow, Historical Assn., 2010; Hon. Doc. of Letters, Univ. of Hull, 2011; Hon. Doc. of Laws, Catholic Univ. of America, 2011; ***publications:*** Heritage in Danger, 1976; Right Turn, 1978; Westminster Palace and Parliament, 1981; Castles of Britain, 1982; Wilberforce-The Nation's Conscience, 1983; English Cathedrals, 1984; Responsible Capitalism (Ed.), 2009; ***clubs:*** Athenaeum; Arts Club; ***recreations:*** fighting philistines, avoiding sitting on fences; ***office address:*** House of Lords, London, SW1A 0PW, United Kingdom; ***phone:*** +44 (0)20 7219 3000.

CORNWALL, HRH The Duchess of; Duchess of Cornwall; ***born:*** 17 July 1947, London, UK; ***parents:*** Major Bruce Shand and Hon. Rosalind Shand (née Cubitt); ***married:*** HRH Prince Charles, 9 April 2005; Andrew Parker Bowles, 1973 (Div'd 1995); ***children:*** Tom Parker Bowles (M), Laura Parker Bowles (F); ***office address:*** Clarence House, London, SW1A 1BA, United Kingdom.

CORNYN, John; Senator for Texas, US Senate; ***born:*** 2 February 1952, Houston, Texas, USA; ***education:*** Trinity Univ., San Antonio, Texas; St. Mary's School of Law, San Antonio, Texas; Univ. of Virginia Law Sch., Masters of Law, 1995; ***party:*** Republican; ***political career:*** Texas Attorney General, 1999-2002; Senator for Texas, US Senate, 2002-; ***professional career:*** District Court Judge, San Antonio, Texas; elected to Texas Supreme Court, 1990, re-elected 1996; ***committees:*** US Senate: Finance; Judiciary; ***office address:*** Office of Senator John Cornyn, 517 Hart Senate Office Building, Washington, DC 20510, USA; ***phone:*** +1 202 224 2934; ***URL:*** http://www.cornyn.senate.gov.

CORREA, President Rafael; President, Republic of Ecuador; ***born:*** 6 April 1963; ***languages:*** English, French, Kichwa; ***education:*** Univ. Católica de Santiago de Guayaquil, Econ., 1987; Univ. Católica de Lovaina la Nueva, Belgium, MA, Econ., 1991; Univ, de Illinois in Urbana-Champaign, M.Sc., Econ., 1991, Ph.D., Econ., 2001; ***political career:*** Minister of Economic and Financial Affairs, April-August 2005; President of Ecuador, 2007-; ***professional career:*** Various lecturing posts, Univ. Católica de Santiago de Guayaquil, 1983-97; Head Profesor, Dept. of Economics, Univ. "San Francisco de Quito", Ecuador, 1993-2005; Independent Consultant, 2005-2006; ***office address:*** Palacio de Gobierno , García Moreno 1043, Quito, Ecuador; ***phone:*** +593 (0)2 210300; ***fax:*** +593 (0)2 580735; ***URL:*** http://www.presidencia.gov.ec.

CORSEPIUS, Uwe; German, Secretary-General, Council of the European Union; ***born:*** 1960; ***education:*** Univ. of Erlangen-Nuremburg, business studies; Kiel Inst. for World Economics; Kiel Univ., economics, Ph.D; ***professional career:*** Research Fellow, Kiel Inst. of World Economics; economist, German Fed. Ministry of Economics, 1990; economist, IMF, 1992-94; Federal Chancellery, Berlin, 1994-2011, inc. most recently, Dir. Gen., European Policy Advisor to the Federal Chancellor, 2006-11; Sec. Gen., Council of the European Union, 2011-; ***office address:*** Council of the European Union, Rue de la Loi 175, 1048 Brussels, Belgium; ***phone:*** +32 (0)2281 6111; ***fax:*** +32 (0)2281 6934; ***URL:*** http://www.consilium.europa.eu.

CORSTENS, G.J.M.; President, Supreme Court of the Netherlands; ***born:*** 1 February 1946, The Netherlands; ***married:*** Madeleine Mignot; ***children:*** Clarine (F), Hadewych (F), Veerle (F); ***languages:*** French, English, German, Spanish; ***education:*** Master of laws, cum laude, Radboud Univ. Nijmegen, 1969; Doctor of law (Ph.D.), Univ. of Amsterdam, 1974; ***memberships:*** Visiting professor, Univ. of Poitiers (France), 1986; Mem.of the board of the Dutch Law Association, 1983-1986; Mem., Nat. Cttee. for the reform of Criminal Procedure, 1989-93, appointed by the Dutch minister of justice; Pres., Advisory Board of the national research project on criminal procedure, 1998-2003, appointed by the Dutch minister of justice; Mem., editorial board of the Nederlands Juristenblad (the leading general Dutch Law Journal, 1995-2004, president, 2004-2006; Mem., jury of the Spinoza Award (the leading Dutch award for outstanding university professors), 1995-98; Mem., Board of Int. Advisors Int. Judicial Academy, Washington D.C., 2001-; Mem., Koninklijke Hollandsche Maatschappij voor Wetenschappen 1994-; Pres, Advisory Board of the nat. research project on the quality of criminal judgements, 2005-2008; ***professional career:*** Assist. public prosecutor, Amsterdam, 1973-75; Law clerk, District court of Amsterdam, 1975-76; Lawyer, Goudsmit & Branbergen, private law firm, Amsterdam, 1976-77; Public prosecutor, Arnhem, 1977-81; Prof. of criminal law, Catholic Univ. Nijmegen, 1982-95; Justice, Supreme Court of the Netherlands, 1995-2006; Vice-president, Supreme Court of the Netherlands, 2006-08; Pres., Supreme Court of the Netherlands, 2008-; ***honours and awards:*** Officier dans l'Ordre des Palmes académiques; Chevalier dans l'Ordre de la Légion d'honneur; Médaille d'honneur de l'Université de Poitiers; doctor honoris causa, University of Antwerp; ***publications:*** Het Nederlands strafprocesrecht (Handbook on Dutch criminal procedure), 6th edition, Kluwer, Deventer 2008, XXVII + 964 p.;European criminal law (together with Jean Pradel), Kluwer Law International, The Hague/London/New York, 2002, XII + 650 p.; About 300 contributions to Dutch and foreign books and articles in Dutch and foreign law journals, amongst which the following recent publications: Criminal law in the first pillar?, European journal of Crime, Criminal Law and Criminal Justice 2003, p. 131-144; L'équilibre entre le droit d'examiner les témoins et le respect de leur sécurité, Revue pénitentiaire et de droit pénal 2007, p. 949-953; Vers une justice pénale européenne?, in : Le droit pénal à l'aube du troisième millénaire, Mélanges offerts à Jean Pradel, Cujas, Paris 2006, p. 1033 et suiv.; ***office address:*** Supreme Court, Hoge Raad der Nederlanden, Postbus 20303, 2500 EH The Hague, The Netherlands; ***phone:*** +3170 361 1311; ***fax:*** +3170 453 0347.

CORYDON, Bjarne; Minister of Finance, Government of Denmark; ***born:*** 1 March 1973, Kolding, Denmark; ***education:*** MSc., (political science) Aarhus Univ., Denmark, 2000; ***party:*** Social Democratic Party ; ***political career:*** MP for South Jutland, 2011-; Minister of Finance, 2011-; ***office address:*** Ministry of Finance, Christiansborg Slotsplads 1, 1218 Copenhagen K, Denmark; ***phone:*** +45 3392 3333,; ***fax:*** +45 3332 8030; ***e-mail:*** fm@fm.dk; ***URL:*** http://www.fm.dk.

COSTA, Carlos da Silva; Governor, Central Bank of Portugal; ***born:*** 1994; ***professional career:*** Lecturer, Fac. of Economics, Oporto Univ.; Banco Portugues do Atlantico, 1978-, finally, Head, Research Dept. on the economy, 1981-85; Coordinator, Economic & Financial Affairs Dept., Portuguese Perm. Rep. to the EU & Mem., EU Economic Policy Cttee., 1986-92; Gen. Manager, Millennium BCP, 2000-04; Mem., Bd. of Dirs., Euro Banking Assn., 2001-03; Exec. Dir., Caixa Geral de Depositos, 2004-06; Chmn. of the Board, Caixa Geral de Aposentacoes, 2004-06; Chmn. of the Board, Banco Nacional Ultramarino SA, Macao, 2004-06; Pres., Banco Caixa Geral (Spain), 2004-06; Vice-Pres., EIB, 2006-10; Governor, Central Bank of Portugal, 2010-; Mem., Gov. Council, ECB; ***office address:*** Central Bank of Portugal, Rua do Ouro 27, 1100-150 Lisbon, Portugal; ***URL:*** http://www.bportugal.pt.

COSTA, Jim; Congressman, 20th District, California, US House of Representatives; ***education:*** Calif. State Univ., Political Science; ***party:*** Democrat; ***political career:*** State Legislator, California; US House of Representatives, 2005-; ***committees:*** Resources; Agriculture; ***office address:*** House of Representatives, 1004 Longworth House Office Building, Washington, DC 20515, USA; ***phone:*** +1 202 225 3341; ***fax:*** +1 202 225 9308.

COURTNEY, Joe; Congressman, US House of Representatives; ***education:*** Tufts Univ., Boston, grad. 1975; Univ. of Connecticut School of Law, law degree, 1978; ***political career:*** Connecticut General Assembly, 1987-94; Congressman, for Connecticut 2nd Dist., 2007-; ***committees:*** Agriculture; Armed Services Cttee.; ***office address:*** House of Representatives, 215 Cannon House Office Building, Washington, DC 20515, USA; ***phone:*** +1 202 225 2076; ***fax:*** +1 202 225 4977.

COUSIN, Ertharin; Executive Director, World Food Programme; ***professional career:*** Exec. Vice Pres. & CEO, Feeding America; White House Liaison to the State Dept., Clinton Administration; US Amb. to the UN Agencies for Food & Agriculture, Head of the US Mission to the UN Agencies in Rome, 2009-12; Executive Dir., WFP, 2012-; ***office address:*** World Food Programme, Via C.G. Viola 68, Parco dei Medici, 00148 Rome, Italy; ***e-mail:*** wfpinfo@wfp.org; ***URL:*** http://www.wfp.org.

COUVREUR, Philippe Marie A.J.; Belgian, Registrar, International Court of Justice; ***born:*** 29 November 1951; ***languages:*** Dutch, English, French, Italian, Spanish; ***education:*** Facultés Notre-Dame de la Paix, Namur, Candidatures in Law, 1971, First class honours; Université Catholique de Louvain, Licence in Law, 1974, with honours, Diploma of Thomist philosophy, 1974, First class honours; University of London, 1975, International and European Law; University of Madrid, 1976, International and European Law, scholarship from the Spanish Ministry of Foreign Affairs; Université Catholique de Louvain, 1978, European Law; ***interests:*** Air; Armed conflict; Claims; Criminal Law; Dispute settlement; Economic law; Environment law; Jurisdiction; History & theory; Human rights; Litigation; Organisations; State responsibility; Law of the Sea; Space; Territory/boundaries; Treaties; EU law; ***memberships:*** Corresponding Member, Royal Academy of Moral and Political Sciences of Spain; Various national societies of international law; ***professional career:*** *academic career:* Université Catholique de Louvain, Assistant at the Centre of European studies and the Law Faculty, 1976-82, Visiting Senior Lecturer, 1997-; Faculty of Law, University of Ouagadougou, Burkina Faso, Visiting Professor of Law of international organisations, 1980-82; Ecole des Hautes études commerciales, Saint-Louis, Visiting Professor of public international law and comparative constitutional law, 1986-96; *professional career:* Commission of the European Communities, Intern, Legal Service, 1978-79; ICJ, Special Assistant to the Registrar and Deputy-Registrar, 1982-86, Secretary, 1986-94, First Secretary, 1994-95, Principal Legal Secretary, 1995-2000, Registrar, February, 2000-; ***publications:*** Books: La problématique de l'adhésion de l'Espagne aux Communautés européennes, 1978; Articles: Editions de L'Université libre de Bruxelles; Revue belge de droit international; Kluwer Law International; Revue européene de droit international; Société française de droit international; Global Community; Yearbook of International Law and Jurisprudence; Annuaire africain de droit international; Répertoire notarial (droit français); Integracion Lationoamericana; Thesaurus Acroasium; ***office address:*** International Court of Justice, Peace Palace, Carnegie Plein 2, 2517KJ, The Hague, Netherlands; ***phone:*** +31(0)70 302 2349; ***fax:*** +31 (0)70 302 2346; ***e-mail:*** greffier@icj-cij.org; ***URL:*** http://www.icj-cij.org.

COVENEY, Simon, TD; Irish, Minister for Agriculture, Marine and Food, Government of Ireland; ***born:*** 16 June 1972, Cork, Ireland; ***parents:*** Hugh Coveney and Pauline Coveney; ***education:*** Clongowes Wood Coll.; U.C.C.; Gurteen Agricultural Coll., Tipperary; Royal Agricultural Coll., Cirencester; ***party:*** Fine Gael; Group of the European People's Party (Christian Democrats) and European Democrats; ***political career:*** Fine Gael; Mem., elected Mem. of Dáil Éireann (Irish Parl.), 1998-; Fine Gael Spokesperson on Communications, Marine and Natural Resources; MEP, 2004-09; Minister for Agriculture, Marine and Food, Feb. 2011-; ***interests:*** marine, youth, justice; ***professional career:*** agriculture; ***committees:*** Communications, Marine and Natural Resources; ***clubs:*** Royal Cork Yacht Club, Crosshaven Rugby Club; ***recreations:*** rugby, sailing; ***office address:*** Department of Agriculture, Fisheries and Food, Kildare Street, Dublin 2, Ireland; ***phone:*** +353 (0)1 607 2000; ***mobile:*** +353 0878 321755; ***e-mail:*** simoncoveney@oireachtas.ie; ***URL:*** http://www.simoncoveney.ie.

COWAN, William (Mo); Interim Senator for Massachusetts, US Senate; ***party:*** Democrat; ***political career:*** Legal counsel and chief of staff to Gov. Deval Patrick; interim senator, US Senate, Feb. 2013-; ***office address:*** US Senate, 365 Dirksen Senate Office Building, Washington DC 20510, USA; ***phone:*** +1 202 224 2742; ***URL:*** http://www.cowan.senate.gov/.

COWLEY, H.E. Sarah; Ambassador, British Embassy in Latvia; ***professional career:*** FCO, 2005-; Deputy Head, Commercial and Economic Diplomacy Dept.; Amb. to Latvia, 2013-; ***office address:*** British Embassy, 5 J. Alunana Street, Riga, Latvia; ***phone:*** +371 733 8126; ***fax:*** +371 733 8132; ***e-mail:*** british.embassy@apollo.lv; ***URL:*** http://www.ukinlatvia.fco.gov.uk.

COX, Geoffrey; MP for Devon West and Torridge, House of Commons; ***children:*** Charlotte (F), James (M), Jonathan (M); ***education:*** Kings College; ***political career:*** MP for Devon West and Torridge, 2005-; ***memberships:*** NFU; ***professional career:*** Barrister; ***committees:*** Environment, Food and Rural Affairs, 2006-10; Standards & Privileges, 2010-; ***office address:*** House of Commons, London, SW1H 0AA, United Kingdom; ***phone:*** +44 (0)20 7219 3000; ***e-mail:*** coxg@parliament.uk.

COX, Paula, JP, MP; Leader, Progressive Labour Party; ***party:*** Leader, Progressive Labour Party; ***political career:*** Minister of Labour, Home Affairs and Public Safety, 1998-2001; Attorney General and Minister of Justice and Education, 2001-04; Minister of Finance, 2004-12; Deputy Prime Minister, 2006-10; Prime Minister, Minister of Finance, Oct. 2010-12; ***office address:*** Progressive Labour Party (PLP), Alaska Hall, 16 Court Street, Hamilton, HM 17, Bermuda; ***phone:*** +441 292 2264; ***e-mail:*** infp@plp.bm; ***URL:*** http://www.plp.bm.

CRABB, Stephen; MP for Preseli Pembrokeshire, House of Commons; ***born:*** 1973; ***children:*** Ioan (M), Isabelle (F); ***education:*** Bristol Univ., B.Sc. Politics, 1995; London Business School, MBA, 2002-04; ***party:*** Conservative; ***political career:*** MP for Preseli Pembrokeshire, 2005-; Assist. Gov. Whip, 2010-12; Parly. Under Sec. of State, Wales Office, 2012-; Gov. Whip, 2012-; ***interests:*** energy policy; rural and agricultural communities; youth affairs; human rights; India, the Middle East, France and the USA; ***memberships:*** Founding mem., All Party Dairy Industry Gp.; All Party Rural Services Gp.; Vice Chmn., All Party Youth Affairs Gp.; Conservative Party Human Rights Cmn.; ***professional career:*** Research Assist. to Andrew Rowe MP; Parly. Affairs Officer, National Cncl. for Voluntary Youth Services, 1996; Election Observer, OSCE, Bosnia Herzegovina, 1998; Policy and Campaigns Mgr., London Chamber of Commerce & Industry, 1998-2002; Marketing Consultant, 2002-05; ***recreations:*** rugby (playing for the Commons & Lords RFC and the London Business School Alumni), long distance running, mountain biking, skiing, football, Italian cuisine, reading biographies; ***office address:*** House of Commons, London, SW1P 0AA, United Kingdom; ***phone:*** +44 (0)20 7219 3000; ***e-mail:*** crabbs@parliament.uk.

CRAPO, Mike; Senator for Idaho, US Senate; ***married:*** Susan Crapo; ***children:*** Michelle (F), Brian (M), Stephanie (F), Lara (F), Paul (M); ***education:*** Brigham Young Univ., BA, political science, 1973; Harvard Law Sch., Juris Dr. cum laude, 1977; ***political career:*** Idaho's 2nd District Rep., US House of Representatives; Mem., Idaho State Senate; Senator for Idaho, US Senate; ***memberships:*** Idaho & California Bar Assns.; ***professional career:*** Clerkship, 9th Circuit Court of Appeals; Fmr. Ptnr., Law Firm, Holden, Kidwell, Hahn & Crapo; ***committees:*** Senate: Environment and Public Works; Banking, Housing and Urban Affairs; Budget; Indian Affairs; ***office address:*** US Senate, 239 Dirksen Senate Office Building, Washington, DC 20510, USA; ***phone:*** +1 202 224 6142; ***URL:*** http://www.crapo.senate.gov.

CRATHORNE, Lord; Member of the House of Lords and Lord Lieutenant of North Yorkshire; ***born:*** 12 September 1939, Sutton, Surrey; ***parents:*** 1st Lord Crathorne and Nancy Crathorne (née Tennant); ***married:*** the late Sylvia Montgomery, 8 January 1970; ***children:*** Thomas Dugdale (M), Charlotte Dugdale (F), Katharine Dugdale (F); ***education:*** Eton; Trinity Coll., Cambridge Univ., MA, Fine Arts, 1963; ***party:*** Conservative Party; ***political career:*** Mem., House of Lords; ***interests:*** arts and heritage, visual and performing arts, country houses; ***professional career:*** Impressionist Painting Dept. Sotheby & Co., 1966-69; Asst. to Pres., Parke-Bernet Galleries, New York, 1966-69; Independent Fine Art Consultancy, James Dugdale & Associates, 1969-; Lecture tours to the USA, 1969-; Dir., Blakeney Hotels Ltd., 1979-96; Lecture Series 'Aspects of England', Metropolitan Museum, New York, 1981; Australian Bicentennial Lecture Tour, 1988; Dir., Woodhouse Securities Ltd., 1988-99, Cliveden plc., 1996-99, Cliveden Ltd., 1999-2002, Council RSA, 1982-88; Editorial Bd., the House magazine, 1983-; Mem., Univ. Court of the Univ. of Leeds, 1985-97; Exec. Cttee., Georgian Group, 1985-, Chair, 1990-99; Pres., Cleveland Family History Society, 1988-; Cleveland Sea Cadets, 1988-; Hambleton district of CPRE, 1988-; Patron, Cleveland Community Foundation, 1990-; Dep. Chair, Joint Cttee. of National amenity Societies, 1993-96, Chmn., 1996-99; Pres., Cleveland and North Yorkshire Magistrates' Assoc., 1997-; Vice-Pres., The Public Monuments and Sculpture Assoc., 1997-, Yorkshire and Humberside RFCA, 1999-; Pres., North Yorkshire County Scout Council, 1999-; Vice-Pres., North of England RFCA, 2001; FSA, 2009; ***committees:*** Sec., All Party Parly. Arts and Heritage Group; ***trusteeships:*** Georgian Theatre Royal, Richmond, Yorkshire, 1970-; Captain Cook Birthplace Museum Trust, 1978-, Chmn., 1993-; Yorkshire Regional Cttee., National Trust, 1988-94; Vice-Pres. Cleveland Wildlife Trust, 1989-; Patron, Attingham Trust for the Study of the British Country House, 1990-; Patron, British Red Cross North Yorkshire Branch, 1999; ***honours and awards:*** Knight of St. John; ***publications:*** Articles in The Connoisseur and Apollo; Edouard Vuillard, 1967; Cliveden, the Place and The People, 1995; the Royal Cresent Book of Bath, 1998; Co-Author: Tennant's Stalk, 1973; A Present from Crathorne, 1989; Co-Photographer, Parliament in Pictures, 1999; ***clubs:*** Brooks's Club; Pratt's; ***recreations:*** photography, travel with the family, country pursuits, jazz, collecting; ***office address:*** House of Lords, London, SW1A 0PW, United Kingdom; ***phone:*** +44 (0)20 7219 5224; ***fax:*** +44 (0)20 7219 5979; ***e-mail:*** james.crathorne@btconnect.com / crathornej@parliament.uk.

CRATO, Nuno; Minister of Education and Science, Government of Portugal; ***political career:*** Minister of Education and Science, 2011-; ***professional career:*** Scientific Co-ordinator, Cemapre, 2007-11; Prof., Lisbon Tech. Univ., 2007-11; CEO, Taguspark, 2010-2011; Full Prof. of Mathematics & Statistics, Higher Inst. of Economics and Management, Lisbon; ***office address:*** Ministry of Education, Av. 5 de Outubro 107-13, 1069-018 Lisbon, Portugal; ***URL:*** http://www.min-edu.pt.

CRAUSBY, David; British, Member of Parliament for Bolton North East, House of Commons; ***born:*** 17 June 1946, Bury, UK; ***parents:*** Thomas Crausby and Kathleen Crausby (née Lavin); ***married:*** Enid Crausby (née Noon), 1965; ***s:*** 2; ***party:*** Labour Party; ***political career:*** Mem., Bury Cncl., 1979-92; MP, Bolton North East, 1997-; ***professional career:*** Engineer; ***office address:*** House of Commons, London, SW1A 0AA, United Kingdom; ***phone:*** +44 (0)20 7219 4092; ***e-mail:*** crausbyd@parliament.uk.

CRAWFORD, Rick; Congressman, House of Representatives; ***education:*** Arkansas State Univ.; ***party:*** Republican; ***political career:*** Mem., HOR, Arkansas First District, 2010-; ***professional career:*** Military; bomb disposal technician; ***committees:*** Agriculture; Transportation & Infrastructure; ***phone:*** +1 202 225 4076.

CREAGH, Mary, MP; Shadow Secretary of State for Environment, Food and Rural Affairs, House of Commons; ***born:*** 1967, Coventry, UK; ***parents:*** Thomas Creagh and Elizabeth Creagh; ***married:*** Adrian Pulham, 2001; ***children:*** Clement (M); ***languages:*** French, Italian, Spanish; ***education:*** Bishop Ullathorne R.C. Comprehensive School, Coventry; Pembroke Coll., Oxford; LSE; ***party:*** Labour; ***political career:*** Councillor, London Borough of Islington, 1998-2005; Leader, Labour Group, London Borough of Islington, 2000-04; MP for Wakefield, 2005-; PPS to Andy Burnham MP and Lord Philip Hunt, Dept. of Health; Shadow Secretary of State for Environment, Food and Rural Affairs, 2010-; ***interests:*** Europe, employment, social policy, disability issues, Irish community; ***memberships:*** European Movement, 1995-; Fabians, 1995-; Co-operative Party, 1995-; Amnesty International, 1997-; ***professional career:*** Assist. to Stephen Hughes MEP, 1991; Press Officer, European Youth Forum, 1991-95; London Enterprise Agency, 1995-97; Lecturer, Cranfield School of Management, 1997-2005; ***committees:*** Joint Cttee. on Human Rights, 2005-06; ***recreations:*** family, yoga, cycling, swimming, food; ***office address:*** House of Commons, London, SW1A 0AA, United Kingdom; ***phone:*** +44 (0)207 219 6984; ***fax:*** +44 (0)207 219 4257; ***e-mail:*** mary@marycreagh.co.uk; ***URL:*** http://www.marycreagh.co.uk.

CREASY, Dr Stella; MP for Walthamstow, House of Commons; ***party:*** Labour; ***political career:*** Councillor, Waltham Forest Council; Dep. Mayor; Mayor; MP for Walthamstow, May 2010-; Shadow Minister, Home Affairs, 2011-; ***office address:*** House of Commons, London, SW1A 0AA, United Kingdom; ***phone:*** +44 (0)20 7219 3000; ***e-mail:*** stella.creasy.mp@parliament.uk.

CRENSHAW, Ander; Congressman, Florida 4th District, US House of Representatives; ***political career:*** Congressman, Florida 4th District, US House of Representatives, 2000-; ***committees:*** House Appropriations Committee; ***office address:*** US House of Representatives, 127 Cannon House Office Building, Washington DC, 20515, USA; ***phone:*** +1 202 225 2501.

CRISTAS, Assunçao; Minister of Agriculture, the Sea, the Environment and Spatial Planning, Government of Portugal; ***born:*** 1974; ***education:*** Univ. of Lisbon, Law; New Univ. of Lisbon, Law; ***political career:*** MP, 2009-; Dep. Leader, Democratic and Social Centre - People's Party (CDS-PP), 2009-; Minister of Agriculture, the Sea, the Environment and Spatial Planning, 2011-; ***professional career:*** lecturer, New Univ. of Lisbon; Dir., Min. of Justice's Office for Legislative Policy and Planning; law consultant; ***office address:*** Ministry of Agriculture, Rural Development and Food, Praça do Comércio, 1149-010 Lisbon, Portugal; ***URL:*** http://www.min-agricultura.pt.

CROCKART, Mike; MP for Edinburgh West, UK Government; ***education:*** B.Sc., Edinburgh Univ., 1987; ***party:*** Liberal Democrat; ***political career:*** MP for Edinburgh West, May 2010-; ***committees:*** Joint Committee on Human Rights, 2011-; Business, Innovation and Skills, 2012-; Joint Committee on the Draft Enhanced Terrorism Prevention and Investigation Measures Bill, 2012-; ***office address:*** House of Commons, London, SW1A 0AA, United Kingdom; ***phone:*** +44 (0)20 7219 3000; ***e-mail:*** mike.crockart.mp@parliament.uk.

CROSBIE, Hon. John Carnell, PC, OC, OHL, QC; Canadian, Lieutenant Governor , Government of Newfoundland and Labrador; ***born:*** 1931; ***married:*** Jane Ellen Audrey Furneaux, 1952; ***education:*** Queen's Univ., Kingston, Ont. (Hons., BA, Pol. Sci. and Economics) and Dalhousie Law School, Dalhousie Univ., Halifax N.S. (Hons. LLB); Univ. of London (post-grad. Law); ***political career:*** Elected to City Council of St. John's 1965; appointed Deputy Mayor of St. John's 1966; Min. of Municipal Affairs and Housing, Government of Newfoundland and Labrador 1966. Member, House of Assembly, district of St. John's West 1966-76; Min. of Health 1967-68; Re-elected St. John's West 1971; Min. of Finance. Pres. Treasury Board, Min. of Economic Development 1972; Reappointed Min. of Finance & Pres. of Treasury Board 1972-74; Min. of Fisheries & Min. for Intergovernmental Affairs, 1974-75; Min. of Mines & Energy & Min. for Intergovernmental Affairs, 1975-76; Elect. Canadian House of Commons, Dist. of St. John's West, 1976; Min. of Finance, 1979-80; Minister of Justice and Attorney General of Canada 1984-86; Min. of Transport 1986-88; Min. for International Trade 1988-91; Minister of Fisheries and Oceans 1991-; Minister for the Atlantic Canada Opportunities Agency 1991-93; Lieutenant Governor of Newfoundland and Labrador, 2008-; ***memberships:*** Law Socy. of Newfoundland; Canadian Bar Assn.; Canadian Tax Foundation. Progressive Conservative; ***professional career:*** Practised as Barrister and Solicitor in St. John's 1957-66 (partner in firm of Lewis, Aylward & Crosbie); ***honours and awards:*** University Medal: in Political Science (Queen's Univ.) 1953, and in Law (Dalhousie Univ) 1953; Viscount Bennett Fellowship of the Canadian Bar Association 1956-57; ***publications:*** Local Government in Newfoundland (1954) 1972; No Holds Barred: My Life in Politics, 1999; ***office address:*** Office of the Lieutenant Governor, Government House, Military Road, St. John's, NL A1C 5W4, Canada; ***e-mail:*** johncrosbie@gov.nl.ca.

CROUCH, Tracey; MP for Chatham and Aylesford, UK Government; ***education:*** Hull University; ***party:*** Conservative; ***political career:*** MP for Chatham and Aylesford, May 2010-; ***office address:*** House of Commons, London, SW1A 0AA, United Kingdom; ***phone:*** +44 (0)20 7219 3000; ***e-mail:*** tracey.crouch.mp@parliament.uk.

CRUDDAS, Jon; Member of Parliament for Dagenham and Rainham, House of Commons; ***education:*** Oaklands Roman Catholic Comprehensive Sch., Portsmouth; B.Sc., MA, Warwick Univ.; Ph.D., Univ. of Wisconsin, USA; ***party:*** Labour Party; ***political career:*** MP, Dagenham, June 2001-10, Dagenham and Rainham, 2010-; Policy Review Coordinator, 2013-; ***memberships:*** Mem.,TGWU; ***office address:*** House of Commons, London, SW1A 0AA, United Kingdom; ***phone:*** +44 (0)20 7219 3000; ***e-mail:*** cruddasj@parliament.uk; ***URL:*** http://www.parliament.uk.

CRUZ, Ted; Senator for Texas, US Senate; ***party:*** Republican; ***political career:*** Member, US Senate, 2013-; ***professional career:*** lawyer; Solicitor General, Texas; ***committees:*** Commerce, Science & Technology; Armed Services; Judiciary; Special Cttee. on Aging; Rules and Administration; ***office address:*** US Senate, B40B Dirksen Senate Office, Washington 25010, USA; ***phone:*** +1 202 224 2934; ***URL:*** http://www.cornyn.senate.gov.

CRYER, John; British, Member of Parliament for Leyton and Wanstead, House of Commons; ***born:*** 11 April 1964, Darwen, Lancashire; ***parents:*** Bob and Ann; ***married:*** Narinder (née Bains); ***education:*** Oakbank Grammar Sch.; Hatfield Poly., BA, Literature & History; London Coll. of Printing; ***party:*** Labour Party, 1979-; ***political career:*** MP, Hornchurch, 1997-2005; MP, Leyton and Wanstead, 2010-; ***interests:*** Europe, pensions, education, health, public owmership; ***memberships:*** NUJ, T&G, UCATT; ***professional career:*** fmr. Journalist, 1988-97; ***committees:*** Deregulation and Regulatory Reform, 1997-2002; Treasury, 2010-11; ***publications:*** many newspapers and magazine articles; ***clubs:*** RAF Hornchurch Assn., Hornchurch historical soc., Hornchurch swimming club; ***recreations:*** swimming, cricket, cycling, reading, cinema, old cars; ***office address:*** House of Commons, London, United Kingdom; ***e-mail:*** john.cryer.mp@parliament.uk.

CUFER, Uros, Dr.Sc.; Minister of Finance, Government of Slovenia; ***education:*** Univ. Paris IX, economics, Ph.D; ***political career:*** Finance Minister, Government of Slovenia, 2013-; ***professional career:*** Dir., Analysis and Research Dept., Bank of Slovenia, 1999-2004; Dir., Centre for Financial Management, NLB; ***office address:*** Ministry of Finance, Zupanciceva 3, SI-1000 Ljubljana, Slovenia; ***phone:*** +386 1 369 6300; ***URL:*** http://www.mf.gov.si.

CUISIA, H.E. Jose Lampe; Ambassador of the Philippines to the USA, Philippines Embassy; ***education:*** De La Salle Univ.; The Wharton School, Univ. of Pennsylvania; ***professional career:*** Banker; Pres., Philippine National Bank; Chmn., Monetary Board, 1990-93; Governor, Central Bank, 1990-93; Amb. of the Philippines to the USA, 2011-; ***office address:*** Embassy of Paraguay, 2400 Massachusetts Ave., NW, Washington DC 20008, USA; ***phone:*** +1 202 467 9300; ***fax:*** 1 202 467 9417; ***URL:*** http://www.philippineembassy-usa.org/.

CULLEN OF WHITEKIRK, Rt. Hon. the Lord William Douglas, KT; Member, House of Lords; ***political career:*** Mem., House of Lords, 2003-; ***professional career:*** Lord Justice Clerk and Pres. of the Second Division of Court of Session, 1977-2001; Lord Justice General of Scotland and Lord Pres. of the Court of Session, 2001-05; ***office address:*** House of Lords, London, SW1A 0PW, United Kingdom.

CUNNINGHAM, Alex; MP for Stockton North, UK Government; ***party:*** Labour; ***political career:*** Councillor, Cleveland County Council, 1984-97; MP for Stockton North, May 2010-; ***committees:*** Work and Pensions, 2010-11; Armed Forces Bill, 2011; Education, 2011-; ***office address:*** House of Commons, London, SW1A 0AA, United Kingdom; ***phone:*** +44 (0)20 7219 3000; ***e-mail:*** alex.cunningham.mp@parliament.uk.

CUNNINGHAM, H.E. James B.; Ambassador, US Embassy in Afghanistan; ***born:*** Pennsylvania; ***languages:*** French, Italian, Spanish, Mandarin; ***education:*** Syracuse Univ., Political Science and Psychology; ***professional career:*** Postings to Stockholm, Washington and Rome; Sec. Gen., NATO, 1988; Dep. Chief of Staff then Chief of Staff, 1989; Dep. Political Counsellor, US Mission at the UN., 1990-93; Dir., State Dept. Office of European Security and Political Affairs, 1993-95; Dep. Chief., US Embassy in Rome, 1996-99; Acting Permanent Rep. then Permanent Rep. to the UN, 2001-05, Consul General to Hong Kong SAR and Macau SAR, 2005-08; US Amb. to Israel, 2008-12; Amb. to Afghanistan, 2012-; ***honours and awards:*** Hammer Award for innovation in government management; President's Meritorious Service Award; State Dept.'s Superior, Merit and Performance awards; ***office address:*** US Embassy, The Great Masoud Road, Kabul, Afghanistan ; ***phone:*** +93 230 0436; ***fax:*** +93 230 1364; ***e-mail:*** kabulwebmaster@state.gov; ***URL:*** http://kabul.usembassy.gov.

CUNNINGHAM, Jim; British, Member of Parliament for Coventry South, House of Commons; ***born:*** 4 February 1941, Coatbridge, Lanarkshire, United Kingdom; ***parents:*** Adam and Elizabeth; ***married:*** Marion; ***children:*** Andrew (M), Paul (M), Jeanette (F), Jacky (F); ***party:*** Labour Party, 1967-; ***political career:*** Cllr., Coventry City, 1972-; Leader, Labour Group; Chmn., West Midlands Joint Cttee.; MP, Coventry South East, 1992-97; MP, Coventry South, 1997-; Chair of the West Midland Grp. of Labour MPs; PPS to M. O'Brien MP, Solicitor General; ***interests:*** the economy, Europe, local government, industrial legislation; ***memberships:*** MSF; ***professional career:*** Engineer; Shop Steward, Sr. Shop Steward, 1972-; ***committees:*** Select Cttee. Constitutional Affairs, 2003-05; Procedure, 2005-06; Standards & Privileges, 2010-; ***recreations:*** walking, music, reading; ***office address:*** House of Commons, London, SW1A 0AA, United Kingdom; ***phone:*** +44 (0)20 7219 6362; ***e-mail:*** hcinfo@parliament.uk.

CUNNINGHAM, Tony; Member of Parliament for Workington, House of Commons; ***born:*** 16 September 1952; ***parents:*** Daniel Cunningham and Bessie Cunningham; ***married:*** Anne Gilmore; ***education:*** Workington Grammar Sch.; Liverpool Univ.; ***party:*** Labour Party; ***political career:*** Mem. of Allerdale District Cncl., 1987-92; Leader, Allerdale District Cncl., 1992-94; MEP, Cumbria & Lancashire North, 1994-99; MP, Workington, 2001-; Asst. Govt. Whip, 2005-08; Gov. Whip, 2008-11; Opp. Assist. Whip, 2010-11; Shadow Minister, International Development, 2011-; ***professional career:*** teacher; Chief Exec., Human Rights, 1999; ***office address:*** House of Commons, London, SW1A 0AA, United Kingdom; ***phone:*** +44 (0)20 7219 3000; ***e-mail:*** cunninghamt@parliament.uk; ***URL:*** http://www.parliament.uk.

CUOMO, Andrew M.; American, Governor, State of New York; ***born:*** 6 December 1957, Queens, New York City, USA; ***parents:*** Mario Cuomo; ***married:*** Kerry Cuomo (née Kennedy); ***children:*** Cara (F), Mariah (F), Michaela (F); ***education:*** Fordham Univ., BA, 1979; Albany Law Sch., Law degree, 1982; ***political career:*** Asst. Sec. of Housing and Urban Dev., Office of Community Planning and Dev.; Housing and Urban Dev. Sec., 1997-2001; Governor, New York State, 2010-; ***professional career:*** Campaign Mananger, Mario M. Cuomo's campaign for Governor of New York, 1982; Special Asst. to the Governor; Asst. District Attorney, Manhattan; Partner, Law firm of Blutrich, Falcone and Miller; founder, Housing Enterprise for the Less Privileged (H.E.L.P.), 1986; Chmn., New York City Cmn. on the Homeless, 1991; Attorney General, New York State, 2006-2010; ***honours and awards:*** Ford Foundation/Kennedy Sch. Innovations in Govt. Award; American Inst. of Architects Pioneer in Housing Award; New York Univ. Distinguished Community Service Award; Fannie Mae Foundation Award of Excellence; American Red Cross Good Neighbour Award; ***office address:*** Office of the Governor, State Capitol, Albany, NY 12224-0341, USA; ***URL:*** http://www.state.ny.us/governor.

CURRAN, Margaret, MSP; Shadow Secretary of State for Scotland, Scottish Parliament; ***parents:*** James Curran and Rose Curran; ***married:*** Robert Murray; ***education:*** Our Lady & St. Francis, Glasgow; Glasgow Univ., MA, History & Econ. History, 1981; Dundee Coll., C.Ed., Community Education, 1982; ***party:*** Labour; ***political career:*** MSP, Glasgow Baillieston, 1999-; Dep. Minister for Social Justice; Minister for Communities, 2003-04; Minister for Parliamentary Business, 2004-07; Shadow Minister, Work and Pensions, Oct. 2010-11; Shadow Secretary of State for Scotland, 2012-; ***interests:*** social inclusion, housing and community empowerment, women's issues; ***professional career:*** Welfare Rights Worker; Community Worker; Lecturer in Community Education; ***recreations:*** children, cinema, books; ***office address:*** House of Commons, London, SW1A 0AA, United Kingdom; ***e-mail:*** Margaret.Curran.mp@parliament.uk.

CURRIE OF MARYLEBONE, Lord; Member, House of Lords; ***born:*** 9 December 1946; ***parents:*** Kennedy Moir Currie and Majorie Currie (née Thompson); ***married:*** Angela Piers Dumas, 24 March 1995; Saziye Currie (née Gazioglu), 1975 (diss'd 1991); ***children:*** James (M), Tim (M), Simon (M); ***education:*** Univ. of Manchester, B.Sc., Mathematics, 1965-68; Univ. of Birmingham, M.Soc. Sc., Economics, 1969-71; Univ. of London, Ph.D., Economics, 1978; ***party:*** cross-bencher; ***political career:*** Mem. of House of Lords; ***professional career:*** Queen Mary Coll., Univ. of London, 1972-88; London Business Sch., 1988-2000; Dean, Cass Business Sch. (City Univ.), 2001-07; Founding chmn., Ofcom, 2002-09; chmn., International Centre for Financial Regulation, 2009-; Chmn., Semperian Investment Partners, 2008-; Dir., Dubai Financial Services Authority, 2005-; London Philharmonic Orchestra, 2007-; Royal Mail, 207-; BDO, 2008-; ***office address:*** ICFR, 41 Moorgate, London, EC2R 6PP, United Kingdom; ***e-mail:*** dc@davidcurrie.eu.

CUTHBERT, Jeffrey; Assembly Member for Caerphilly, National Assembly of Wales; ***party:*** Labour Party; ***political career:*** National Assembly of Wales mem, for Caerphilly, May 2003-; Dep. Minister for Skills, 2011-; ***office address:*** National Assembly for Wales, Cardiff Bay, Cardiff, CF99 1NA, United Kingdom; ***phone:*** +44 (0)29 2082 5111; ***fax:*** +44 (0)29 2082.

CVIJANOVIC, Zeljka; Prime Minsiter, Government of the Serb Republic; ***born:*** 1967; ***party:*** Alliance of Independent Social Democrats; ***political career:*** Minister of Economic Relations and Regional Cooperation, 2010-13; Prime Minister, 2013-; ***professional career:*** Professor of English; ***office address:*** Office of the Prime Minister, Banja Luka, Republic of Serbia; ***phone:*** +387 9)051 331322.

D

DACIC, Ivica; Prime Minister, Government of Serbia; ***born:*** 1966; ***education:*** Univ. of Belgrade; ***political career:*** Spokesperson, Socialist Party, Party leader, 2006; First Dep. PM, Minister of Internal Affairs, 2008-12; Prime Minister, 2012-; ***office address:*** Office of the Prime Minister, Nermanjina 11, 11000 Belgrade, Serbia; ***phone:*** +381 11 361 7719; ***fax:*** +381 11 361 7609; ***URL:*** http://www.srbijia.gov.rs/.

DADNADJI, Joseph Djimrangar; Prime Minister, Government of Chad; ***party:*** Patriotic Salvation Movement; ***political career:*** Minister of Planning, Development, and Cooperation, 2002-03; Minister of the Environment and Water, 2003-04; Minister of Spatial Planning, Urban Planning, and Housing, 2010-11 Prime Minister, 2013-; ***office address:*** Office of the Prime Minister, PO Box 74, N'Djamena, Chad.

DAKIN, Nick; MP for Scunthorpe, UK Government; ***party:*** Labour; ***political career:*** Councillor and Council Leader, North Lincolnshire Council; MP for Scunthorpe, May 2010-; Opp. Whip, 2011-; ***committees:*** Education Select Cttee., 2010-11; Procedure, 2011-; ***office address:*** House of Commons, London, SW1A 0AA, United Kingdom; ***phone:*** +44 (0)20 7219 3000; ***e-mail:*** nick.dakin.mp@parliament.uk.

DALAI LAMA OF TIBET ; see GYATSO, Tenzin.

DALRYMPLE, Jack; Governor, State of North Dakota; ***born:*** 1948; ***education:*** Yale Univ., 1970, BA, American Studies; ***political career:*** North Dakota legislature, 1985, eight terms; chmn., House Appropriations Cttee.; Lieutenant Governor, 2000-2010; Governor, State of North Dakota, 2010-; ***professional career:*** Farmer; ***office address:*** Office of the Governor, 600 E Boulevard Ave., Dept. 101, Bismarck, ND 58505-0001, USA; ***phone:*** +1 701 328 2200; ***URL:*** http://governor.nd.gov/.

DAMANAKI, Maria; Greek, Commissioner, European Commission; ***born:*** 1952; ***education:*** Tech. Univ. of Athens, Greece, Chemical Engineering; Univ. of Lancaster; ***political career:*** political activist against Greek dictatorship, 1970-74, imprisoned, 1973-74; MP, 1977-93; Vice-Pres., Greek Parliament, 1986-90; Pres., Coalition of Left and Progress, 1991-93; MP, 2000-03; Head, PASOK Party; MP, 2004-09; Commissioner for Fisheries and Maritime Affairs, 2010-; ***office address:*** European Commission, rue de la loi 2000, B-1049 Brussels, Belgium; ***URL:*** http://ec.europa/eu.

DANCZUK, Simon; MP for Rochdale, UK Government; ***party:*** Labour; ***political career:*** Councillor, Blackburn with Darwen Council 1993-2001; MP for Rochdale, May 2010-; PPS, 2011-; ***committees:*** Communities and Local Gov., 2010-; ***office address:*** House of Commons, London, SW1A 0AA, United Kingdom; ***phone:*** +44 (0)20 7219 3000; ***e-mail:*** simon.danczuk.mp@parliament.uk.

DANNATT, Lord Richard, GCB CBE MC; Member, House of Lords; ***political career:*** Mem., House of Lords, 2011-; ***professional career:*** British Army Officer; Chief of General Staff, 2006-09; Constable of the Tower of London, 2009-; ***honours and awards:*** Knight Grand Cross of the Order of the Bath; Knight Commander of the Order of the Bath; Commander of the Order of the British Empire; Military Cross; Queen's Commendation for Valuable Service; ***office address:*** House of Lords, London, SW1A 0PW, United Kingdom; ***phone:*** +44 (0)20 7219 5353.

DANSO-BOAFO, Prof. Kwaku; High Commissioner, Ghanian High Commissioner in the UK; ***education:*** BSc., Suffolk Univ., Massachusetts, USA 1976; MPA, Northeastern Univ., Massachusetts, l977; PhD., Howard Univ., Washington, D.C., USA, 1981 ; ***political career:*** Minister of Health of Ghana, 2000; ***professional career:*** Lecturer, Clark Atlanta Univ., Atlanta, Georgia, 1986-97, 2001-05; Amb. to Cuba, Jamaica, Trinidad and, Nicaragua and Panama, 1997-2000; High Commissioner to the UK, 2010-; ***office address:*** Ghana High Commission, 13 Belgrave Square, London, SW1X 8PN, United Kingdom; ***phone:*** +44 (0)20 7235 4142; ***fax:*** +44 (0)20 7245 9552; ***e-mail:*** enquiries@ghana-com.co.uk; ***URL:*** http://www.ghanahighcommissionuk.com.

DAR, Mohammad Ishaq; Minister of Finance, Government of Pakistan; ***education:*** Gov. College Univ., Lahore; Univ. of the Punjab; ***party:*** Pakistan Muslim League; ***political career:*** MP, 1993-96, 1997-99; Senator; Federal Minister for Finance, 1998-99, 2008, 2013-; ***professional career:*** Accountant; Finance Dir.; Senior Auditor, Auditor General Dept., Tripoli; Financial Advisor; Chm., CEO; Dir., World Bank; Dir., Asian Development Bank; Dir., Islamic Development Bank; ***office address:*** Ministry of Finance, Pakistan Secretariat, Islamabad, Pakistan ; ***URL:*** http://www.finance.gov.pk/.

DARLING, Rt. Hon. Alistair Maclean, MP; British, MP for Edinburgh South West, House of Commons; ***born:*** 1953, London, UK; ***married:*** Margaret McQueen Vaughan, 1986; ***education:*** Loretto Sch.; Aberdeen Univ., LL.B; ***party:*** Labour Party; ***political career:*** Cllr., Lothian Regional Cncl., 1982-87; Chmn., Lothian Regional Transport Cttee., 1986-87; MP, Edinburgh Central, 1987-2005; MP for Edinburgh South West, 2005-; Opp. Front Bench Spokesman on Home Affairs, 1988-92; Opp. Front Bench Spokesman on Treasury and Econ. Affairs, 1992; Shadow Chief Sec. to the Treasury, 1997; Chief Sec. to the Treasury, 1997-; Privy Cllr., 1997-; Sec. of State for Social Security, 1998-2001; Secretary of State for Work and Pensions, 2001-2002; Secretary of State for Transport, 2002-06; Secretary of State for Scotland, June 2003-06; Secretary of State for Trade and Industry, May 2006-June 2007; Chancellor of the Exchequer, June 2007-May 2010; Shadow Chancellor of the Exchequer, May 2010-Sept. 2010; ***interests:*** economic affairs; ***memberships:*** Mem., GMB; ***professional career:*** Solicitor, 1978-82; Advocate, 1984; Governor, Napier Coll., Edinburgh, 1985-87; ***office address:*** House of Commons, London, SW1A 0AA, United Kingdom; ***phone:*** +44 (0)20 7270 3000; ***e-mail:*** hcinfo@parliament.uk; ***URL:*** http://www.parliament.uk.

DAUGAARD, Dennis; Governor, State of South Dakota; ***education:*** Univ. of South Dakota, 1975; Northwetsern Law School, JD, 1978; ***political career:*** Governor, South Dakota, 2010-; ***professional career:*** US Bank, Sioux Falls, 1981-1990, sev. positions, incl. vice-pres.; Dev. Dir., Children's Home Foundation, 1990-2002, Exec. Dir., 2002-09; ***office address:*** Office of the Governor, State Capitol, 500 East Capitol Avenue, Pierre, SD 57501-5070, USA; ***phone:*** +1 605 773 3212; ***URL:*** http://www.sd.gov/governor/.

DAURIS, H.E. James; Ambassador, British Embassy in Peru; ***professional career:*** Dep. Head of Mission, Bogota, Colombia, 2005-0; Amb. to Peru, 2011-; ***office address:*** British Embassy, Torre Parque Mar (Piso 22), Avenida Jose Larco 1301, Miraflores, Lima, Peru; ***phone:*** +51 (0)1 617 3000; ***fax:*** +51 (0)1 617 3100; ***e-mail:*** belima@fco.gov.uk; ***URL:*** http://www.ukinperu.fco.gov.uk.

DA VASCONCELOS, Jose Maria (Taur Matan Ruak); President, Timor-Leste; ***political career:*** Chief of Staff, Falintil guerilla force, 1992, commander-in-chief, 2000; Head of Armed forces (after independence), 2002-11; President, Timor-Leste, May 2012-; ***office address:*** Office of the President, Palacio das Cinzas, Kaikoli, Dili, Timor-Leste; ***URL:*** http://www.timor-leste.gov.tl.

DAVEY, Edward; British, Secretary of State for Energy and Climate Change, UK Government; ***born:*** 25 December 1965, Nottinghamshire; ***parents:*** John George Davey and Nina Davey (née Stanbrook); ***education:*** Jesus Coll., Oxford, BA, PPE; Birkbeck Coll., London Univ., MSc., Economics; ***party:*** Liberal Democrat Party; ***political career:*** Econ. Researcher, Liberal Democrats; Senior Economics Advisor, Lib. Dems., 1989-93; Lib. Dem. Econ. Affairs Spokesman for Tax, Spending & Monetary Policy; Speaker for the London Liberal Democrats on the Economy, Employment and Tourism; MP, Kingston & Surbiton, 1997-; Shadow Chief Sec. to the Treasury; Shadow Office of the Deputy Prime Minister; Shadow Education and Skills Sec., 2005; Shadow Trade and Industry Secretary, 2006-07; Chair of Campaigns and Communications and Liberal Democrat Leader's Chief of Staff, 2007-08; Shadow Secretary of State for Foreign and Commonwealth Affairs, 2007-10; Parly. Under-Sec. of State for Employment Relations and Consumer and Postal Affairs, 2010-12; Secretary of State for Energy and Climate Change, 2012-; ***professional career:*** Management consultants, Omega Ptnrs.; ***committees:*** Lib. Dem. Federal Policy Cttee.; Finance Bill Cttee.; Procedure, 1997-2000; Treasury, 1999-2001; Treasury (Treasury Sub-Committee), 1999-2001; ***honours and awards:*** From Royal Humane Society and British Transport; ***office address:*** House of Commons, London, SW1A 0AA, United Kingdom; ***phone:*** +44 (0)20 7219 3152; ***e-mail:*** daveye@parliament.uk; ***URL:*** http://www.edwarddavey.co.uk.

DAVID, Wayne; MP for Caerphilly, House of Commons; ***born:*** 1 July 1957, Bridgend; ***parents:*** D. Haydn David and Edna A. David; ***married:*** Catherine (née Thomas), 1991 (Div'd. 2008); ***education:*** Cynffig Comprehensive Sch.; Univ. Coll. Cardiff, BA (Hons), History & Welsh History, 1979; Univ. Coll. Swansea, Research in Economic History, 1979-82; Univ. Coll. Cardiff, 1982-83; ***party:*** Labour Party; ***political career:*** MEP, 1989-99; Vice Pres., European Parly. Socialist Gp., 1994-98; Leader, European Parly. Labour Party, 1994-98; MP, Caerphilly, 2001-; PPS for Armed Forces Minister, 2004-06; Assist. Govt. Whip, 2007-08; Parly. Under Sec., Welsh Office, Oct. 2008-May 2010; Shadow Minister for Wales, May-Sept. 2010; Shadow Minister, Foreign and Commonwealth Affairs, Oct. 2010-11; Shadow Minister, Justice, 2011-; ***professional career:*** Teacher; Educationalist; ***committees:*** mem., European Scrutiny Cttee., 2001-07; Bd. Mem., European Movement, 2002-07; Mem., Standards and Privileges Cttee., 2004-05; Pres., Wales Cncl. of the European Movement, 2006; Chmn., Houses of Parly.All Party Grp. on the EU, 2006-07; ***honours and awards:*** Fellow, Cardiff Univ., 1985; ***publications:*** Two pamphlets on the future of Europe; 'Remaining True - A Biography of Ness Edwards', 2006; ***office address:*** Community Council Offices, Newport Road, Bedwas, Caerphilly, CF83 8YB, United Kingdom.

DAVIDSON, Ian; British, Member of Parliament for Glasgow, South West, House of Commons; ***born:*** 8 September 1950, Jedburgh; ***parents:*** Graham Davidson and Elizabeth Davidson (née Crowe); ***married:*** Morag Christine Anne Mackinnon, 21 September 1978; ***children:*** Colin (M), Christine (F); ***education:*** Jedburgh Grammar Sch.; Galashiels Acad.; Edinburgh Univ., Jordanhill Coll., MA (Hons); ***party:*** Labour Party; Co-operative Party; ***political career:*** Cllr., Strathclyde Regional Council, 1978-92; MP, Govan, 1992-97; MP, Pollok, 1997-2005; MP, Glasgow South West, 2005-; ***interests:*** Co-operative Movement, Commonwealth, defence, education, local economic development, local government, Third World and international development, trade & industry, trade unions, shipbuilding, Europe, poverty issues, Euro (against); ***memberships:*** Party Political Gps.: fmr. Chair, Co-operative Party; fmr. Chair, MSF; Sec., Trade Union Gp. of Labour MPs; Sec., Tribune Gp. of MPs; All Party Parly. Gps: Aerospace (fmr. Sec.); Alcohol Misuse; Building Societies & Financial Mutuals; Clothing, Textiles & Footwear; Housing Co-operatives; Local Govt. Cllrs.; New Europe (SEc.); Overseas Territories; Pensions; Royal Marines; Rugby Union Team (Se. and Captain); Scotch Whiskey; Ship Building & Repair Gp. (Sec.); Smoking and Health; Socially Responsible Investment; Works of Art; All Party Aprly. Country Gps.: America; ANZAC; Bermuda (Chmn.); Canada; Cayman Islands; China; Egypt; Falklands; Germany (fmr. Sec.); Gibraltar; India; Japan (Sec.); Republic of Korea; Russia; South Africa; Zimbabwe; Assoc. Gps.: Parly. Lighting Gps.; Sudan; other: British Council (Treasurer); New Europe Advisory Council; ***professional career:*** Sabbatical Chmn., Nat. Assoc. of Labour Students, 1973-74; Pres., Students Assoc., Jordanhill Coll., 1975-76; Researcher for Janey Buchan M.E.P., 1978-92; Manager, Community Service Volunteers 1992-97; ***committees:*** Chmn., Education Cttee., 1986-92; Chmn., C.O.S.L.A., Education Cttee., 1990-92; Mem., Cttee. of Selection; Mem., Public Accounts, 1997-; Backbench Cttees.: Overseas Aid; Trade and Industry; Defence; Scottish Affairs Select Cttee., 2005-; Liaison, 2010-; ***recreations:*** family, rugby, distance running, swimming; ***office address:*** House of Commons, London, SW1A 0AA, United Kingdom; ***phone:*** +44 (0)20 7219 3610.

DAVIES, David; MP for Monmouth, House of Commons; ***born:*** 27 July 1970; ***married:*** Aliz Harnisföger, October 2003; ***children:*** 3; ***languages:*** German, Hungarian, Welsh; ***education:*** Bassaleg Comprehensive, Newport, South Wales; ***party:*** Conservative; ***political career:*** Conservative Group; Mem., Nat. Assembly for Wales, Monmouth; MP for Monmouth 2005-; ***professional career:*** various jobs in Australia, including nightclub promoter, tobacco picker, rickshaw driver; continental lorry driver; manager, family haulage business; Special Constable, British Transport Police; ***committees:*** Home Affairs Cttee., 2007-10; Chmn., Welsh Affairs Cttee., June 2010-; Liaison, 2010-; ***honours and awards:*** Welsh Speaker of the Year, National Assembly for Wales; ***clubs:*** Oriental Club; ***recreations:*** surfing, running, sport; ***office address:*** Constituency Office, 16 Maryport Street, Usk, NP15 1AB, United Kingdom; ***phone:*** +44 (0)1291 672817; ***e-mail:*** david.davies.mp@parliament.uk.

DAVIES, Geraint R.; British, MP for Swansea West, UK Government; ***born:*** 3 May 1960; ***parents:*** David Thomas Morgan Davies and Betty Ferrer Davies; ***married:*** Dr Vanessa Catherine Fry, 1991; ***children:*** Angharad Mair Davies (F), Meirian Sian Davies (F), Eluned Josephine Ferrer Davies (F); ***public role of spouse:*** Senior Lecturer, Economics, Essex Univ.; ***education:*** Llanishen Comprehensive, Cardiff; Jesus Coll., Oxford Univ., BA, PPE, JCR Pres.; ***party:*** Labour Party; ***political career:*** Leader Croydon Cncl., 1986-97; Leader Croydon Cnc. 1996-97; Parly. Candidate, Croydon South, 1987 and Croydon Central 1992; Chair., Labour Finance and Ind. Group, 1997-2001; Vice Chair, 2001-05; MP, Croydon Central, 1997-2005; Parly. Private Sec. Dept. of Constitutional Affairs, 2003-05; MP, Swansea West, 2010-; ***interests:*** local government, housing, trade and industry; ***professional career:*** fmr. marketing manager, and company dir.; ***committees:*** Public Accounts Select Cttee., 1997-2003; Chair, PLP Transport Cttee.; Welsh Affairs, 2010-; Standing Orders, 2011-; Unopposed Bills (Panel), 2011-; ***office address:*** House of Commons, London, SW1H OAA, United Kingdom; ***phone:*** +44 (0)20 7219 3000; ***e-mail:*** geraint.davies.mp@parliament.uk.

DAVIES, Glyn; MP for Montgomeryshire, UK Government; ***party:*** Conservative; ***political career:*** Councillor, Montgomeryshire District Council, 1979-89; MP for Montgomeryshire, May 2010-; ***committees:*** Welsh Affairs Select Cttee., 2010; ***office address:*** House of Commons, London, SW1A 0AA, United Kingdom; ***phone:*** +44 (0)20 7219 3000; ***e-mail:*** glyn.davies.mp@parliament.uk.

DAVIES, Jocelyn; British, Regional Member for South Wales East, National Assembly for Wales; ***born:*** 1959, Usk, Monmouthshire, UK; ***s:*** 1; ***d:*** 2; ***education:*** Newbridge Grammar Sch.; ***party:*** Plaid Cymru (The Party of Wales); ***political career:*** mem., Nat. Assembly for Wales, South Wales East; Dep. Minister for Housing and Regneration; ***interests:*** higher education; ***committees:*** Health & Social Services; Audit; ***office address:*** National Assembly for Wales, S.E. Constituency Office, 10 High Street, Newport, NP20 1PQ, United Kingdom; ***phone:*** +44 (0)1633 220022; ***fax:*** +44 (0)1633 220603.

DAVIES, Philip; MP for Shipley, House of Commons; ***born:*** 5 January 1972; ***parents:*** Peter Davies and Marilyn Davies; ***married:*** Debbie Hemsley, 23 July 1994; ***children:*** Oliver (M), Charlie (M); ***education:*** Univ., of Huddersfield, Historical and Political Studies; ***party:*** Conservative; ***political career:*** Parly. Candidate, Colne Valley, 2001; MP for Shipley, 2005-; ***interests:*** Europe, education, law and order; ***professional career:*** Customer Services and Marketing Manager, ASDA; ***committees:*** Culture, Media and Sport, 2006-;

Modernisation of the House, 2007-10; Backbench Business, 2010-12; Chairmen's Panel/Panel of Chairs, 2010-; Joint Committee on Privacy and Injunctions, 2011-12; ***recreations:*** horse racing; ***office address:*** House of Commons, London, SW1A 0AA, United Kingdom; ***phone:*** +44 (0)20 7219 3000; ***e-mail:*** daviesp@parliament.uk.

DAVIES OF OLDHAM, Rt. Hon. Lord , BA, B.Sc; Member , House of Lords; ***born:*** 9 November 1939; ***parents:*** George William Davies and Beryl Davies; ***married:*** Monica Davies (née Shearing), 1963; ***children:*** Roderick (M), Gordon (M), Amanda (F); ***education:*** Univ. Coll., London, UK; LSE; Inst. of Education, London, UK; ***party:*** Labour Party; ***political career:*** Labour MP for Enfield North, 1974-79; PPS to Rt. Hon. Fred Mulley at Dept. Education and Science, 1975, to Rt. Hon. Edward Short, Lord Privy Seal, 1976 and to Rt. Hon. Joel Barnett, Chief Sec. to the Treasury, 1977; Govt. Whip, 1978-79; Sec., Parly. Labour Party, 1979-92; MP for Oldham Central and Royton, 1992-97; Opposition Spokesperson on Further and Higher Education, 1993-97; Life Peerage, 1997; Govt. Whip, 2000-03; Dep. Chief Whip, House of Lords, June 2003-10; Parly. Under Secretary of State, DEFRA, 2009-10; Shadow Minister of Transport, House of Lords, 2010-; Shadow Treasury Minister, House of Lords, 2010-; ***professional career:*** Teacher, Latymers Sch., 1962-65; Teacher/Principal Lecturer/Asst. Dean, Social Science, Middlesex Poly., UK, 1965-74; Chair, Further Education Funding Cncl., 1998-2000; ***committees:*** Select Cttee. on Nat. Heritage, 1992; ***honours and awards:*** Hon. Dr., Middlesex Univ., UK., 1996; cr. Life Peer, 1997; Privy Counsellor, 2007; ***recreations:*** theatre, literature, golf, cycling; ***office address:*** House of Lords, London, SW1A 0PQ, United Kingdom; ***phone:*** +44 (0)20 7219 1475.

DAVIES OF STAMFORD, Lord Quentin; British, Member, House of Lords; ***born:*** 29 May 1944; ***parents:*** Dr. Michael Ivor Davies (dec'd) and Thelma Davies (dec'd) (née Butler); ***married:*** Chantal Davies (née Tamplin), 1983; ***children:*** Nicholas (M), Alexander (M); ***education:*** Cambridge Univ., BA, MA, History; Harvard Univ., Frank Knox Fellow; ***party:*** Conservative, 1997-2007; Labour Party, June 2007; ***political career:*** MP for Stamford and Spalding, 1987-97; PPS Dept. Education & Science, 1988-90 & Home Office, 1990-91; Conservative Front Bench Spokesman on Pensions, 1998-99; Shadow Paymaster Gen., 1999-2000; Shadow Defence Spokesman, 2000-2001; Shadow Secretary of State for Northern Ireland, 2001-03; MP, Grantham & Stamford, 1997-; Parly. Under Sec., Ministry of Defence, Oct. 2008-10; Mem., House of Lords, 2010-; ***memberships:*** Liveryman Hon. Company of Goldsmiths; Freeman of the City of London; ***professional career:*** Entered Diplomatic Service, 1967; 3rd Sec., FCO, 1967-69; 2nd Sec., Moscow, 1969-72; 1st Sec., FCO, 1972-74; Morgan Grenfell & Co Limited, 1974-, and Dir., 1981-87; Dir., Dewe Rogerson Int., 1987-95; SGE, later Vinci SA, 1999-2001, 2003-; Vinci UK (formerly Norwest Holst, 2001-; Adviser NatWest Securities, then NatWest Markets, 1993-99; Royal Bank of Scotland, 1999-2003; Mem., Cncl., Lloyds of Londn, 2004-; Parly Advr., Chartered Inst, of Taxation, 1993-; ***committees:*** Sec., Conservative Finance Cttee., 1991-97; Mem., Treasury Select Cttee., 1992-98; mem., Standards and Privileges Cttee., 1995-98; European Standing Cttee., 1991-97; European Legislation Cttee., 1997-98; Vice Chmn., Conservative Trade & Industry Cttee., 1997-98; International Development Select Cttee., 2003-; Jt. Chmn. 1997-2005, Chmn.m 2005-, British German Parly Grp.; Vice Chmn: Anglo-French Parly Grp, 1997-; British -Netherlands Parly Grp, 1999-; British-Italian Parly Grp., 2005-; Chmn., Conservative Grp. for Europe, 2006-07; Chmn., City in Europe Cttee, 1975; ***trusteeships:*** Liveryman, Goldsmiths' Co. Trustee and mem. Cncl., Centre for Econ. Policy Res., 1996-; ***honours and awards:*** Freeman, City of London; Freedom of Information Award, 1996; Guardian Backbencher of the Year Award, 1996; Spectator Parliamentarian of the Year Award, 1997; ***publications:*** Britain and Europe: A Conservative View, 1996; ***clubs:*** Beefsteak; Brooks's; Traveller's; Grantham Conservative Club; ***recreations:*** reading, walking, riding, skiing, travel, playing bad tennis, art and architecture; ***office address:*** House of Lords, London, SW1A 0AA, United Kingdom; ***phone:*** +44 (0)20 7219 3000.

DAVIS, Adrian; Governor of Montserrat; ***professional career:*** economist; diplomat; various positions, DFID / ODA, most recently, Country Dir. for North and East Asia, Department for International Development, Beijing, 2007-11; Governor of Montserrat, April 2011-; ***office address:*** Governor's Residence, Brades Estate, Montserrat; ***URL:*** http://ukinmontserrat.fco.gov.uk/en/.

DAVIS, Rt. Hon. David Michael, B.Sc; British, MP for Haltemprice and Howden, Conservative Party; ***born:*** 1948; ***married:*** Doreen Davis; ***education:*** Warwick Univ., 1968-71; Master's Degree in Business, London Business School, 1971-73; Advanced Management Program, Harvard, 1984; ***political career:*** Nat. Chmn., Federation of Conservative Students; MP for Boothferry; PPS, Francis Maude; Asst. Govt. Whip, 1990-93; Parly. Sec. of State, Office of Public Service and Science, 1993-94; Min. of State, Foreign and Cmmw. Office, 1994-97; Chmn. of the Conservative Party, 2001; MP, Haltemprice and Howden, 1997-; Shadow Dep. PM, 2002-03; Shadow Sec. of State for Home, Constitutional and Legal Affairs and Shadow Home Sec., 2003-June 2008, resigned as MP and stood for election to highlight Govt. infringement of civil liberties, incl. 42-day pre-charge detention limit; re-elected July 2008; ***professional career:*** Financial Dir., Manbre and Garton 1976-80; Man. Dir., Tate and Lyle Transport 1980-82; Pres., large Canadian sweetener manufacturer 1982-84; Strategic Planning Dir., Tate and Lyle PLC 1984-87; Non-Exec. Dir., Tate and Lyle PLC 1987-90; ***committees:*** Fmr. Mem., National Union Exec. Cttee.; NUEC Gen. Purposes Cttee.; Chmn. Public Accounts Cttee, 1997-2001; Chmn., Future of Banking Commission, 2010; ***publications:*** BBC Guide to Parliament, Penguin; How to Turn Round a Business, Simon & Schuster; Numerous articles on business and Politics; ***office address:*** House of Commons, London, SW1A 0AA, United Kingdom.

DAVIS, Susan; Congresswoman, California 53rd District, US House of Representatives; ***political career:*** California State Assembly, 1994-2000; Congresswoman, California 53rd District, US House of Representatives, 2000-; ***committees:*** House Armed Services Committee; Education and the Workforce Committee; ***office address:*** US House of Representatives, 1224 Longworth House Office Building, Washington DC, 20515, USA; ***phone:*** +1 202 225 2040.

DAVUTOGLU, Ahmet; Minister of Foreign Affairs, Government of Scotland; ***born:*** 1959; ***education:*** MA, in Public Administration, PhD in Political Science and Int. Relations, Boğaziçi Univ., Istanbul; ***political career:*** Chief Advisor to the Prime Minister: Minister of Foreign Affairs, May 2009-; ***professional career:*** Lecturer and Prof., Marmara Univ., 1993-99; Ambassador; ***publications:*** Alternative Paradigms: The Impact of Islamic and Western Weltanschauungs on Political Theory; The Civilizational Transformation and The Muslim World; Stratejik Derinlik (Strategic Depth); Küresel Bunalim (The Global Crisis) ; ***office address:*** Ministry of Foreign Affairs, Balgat, Ankara, Turkey; ***phone:*** +90 (9)312 287 2555; ***URL:*** http://www.mfa.gov.tr.

DAWALEH, Ilyas Moussa; Minister of Economy and Finance, Government of Djibouti; ***languages:*** Arabic, English, French; ***education:*** BA, in Economic and Social Administration, MA, (DEA) in Marketing and Strategic Management, Univ. François Rabelais of Tours, France; ***political career:*** Minister of Economy and Finance, in charge of Industry and Planning, 2011-; ***professional career:*** Co-founder of the Djibouti Corporates Network (RDE); ***office address:*** Ministry of Economy, Finance, Planning and Privatisation, B.P. 13, Djibouti, Djibouti; ***phone:*** +253 353331; ***e-mail:*** cabmefpp@intnet.d; ***URL:*** http://www.ministere-finances.dj.

DAYTON, Mark; Governor, State of Minnesota; ***born:*** 26 January 1947, Minneapolis; ***children:*** Eric (M), Andrew (M); ***education:*** Yale Univ., Graduated cum laude, 1969; ***party:*** Democratic-Farmer-Labor Party; ***political career:*** Mem., Governor Rudy Perich's staff, 1977, State Commissioner of Economic Dev., 1978; ran for public office, 1982; Minnesota's Commissioner of Energy and Economic Dev., 1983-86; elected State Auditor, 1990-94; Mem., US Senate; US Senator for Minnesota, 2001-07; Governor of Minnesota, 2011-; ***professional career:*** Teacher, 9th grade science, New York City public Schs., 1969-71; Councillor and Administrator, Boston Social Service agency, 1971-75; Legislative Asst., Minnesota Senator Walter Mondale, 1975-77; ***committees:*** Agriculture, Armed Service, Rules and Governmental Affairs Cttees., 2001-; ***office address:*** Office of the Governor, 130 State Capitol, 75 Rev. Dr. Martin Luther King Jr. Blvd, St. Paul, MN 55155, USA; ***URL:*** http://www.governor.state.mn.us.

DEAL, Nathan; American, Governor, State of Georgia; ***education:*** Mercer University, BA, cum laude, 1964; Mercer School of Law, JD, cum laude, 1966; ***political career:*** Georgia State Senate, 1980-92, President Pro-Tempore; Congressman, Georgia 10th District, US House of Representatives, 1992-2010; Governor, State of Georgia, Nov. 2010-; ***professional career:*** US Army; Juvenile Court Judge; ***office address:*** Office of the Governor, 203 State Capitol, Atlanta, Georgia 30334, USA; ***phone:*** +1 404 656 1776; ***URL:*** http://gov.state.ga.us/.

DEAR, Lord; Member, House of Lords; ***party:*** cross-bencher; ***political career:*** Mem., House of Lords, June 2006-; ***professional career:*** Chief Constable, West Midlands Police, 1985-90; HM Inspector of Constabulary, 1990-97; ***office address:*** House of Lords, London, SW1A 0PW, United Kingdom; ***phone:*** +44 (0)20 7219 3576.

DE BOIS, Nick; MP for Enfield North, UK Government; ***party:*** Conservative; ***political career:*** MP for Enfield North, May 2010-; ***committees:*** Public Administration Select Cttee., 2010-11; Justice, 2011; ***office address:*** House of Commons, London, SW1A 0AA, United Kingdom; ***phone:*** +44 (0)20 7219 3000; ***e-mail:*** nick.debois.mp@parliament.uk.

DEBRÉ, Jean-Louis; French, President, Conseil Constitutionnel, France; ***born:*** 30 September 1944, Toulouse, Haute-Garrone, France; ***parents:*** Michel Debré and Anne-Marie Debré (née Lemaresquier); ***married:*** Anne-Marie Engel, 1971; ***children:*** Charles-Emmanuel (M), Guillaume (M), Marie-Victoire (F); ***education:*** Inst. of Political Studies, Paris, diploma; Faculty of Law, Paris, 1st degree, Politicial Science and Public Law, 2nd degree; Nat. Magistrates School, Doctorate in Law; ***party:*** Rassemblement pour la Republique (RPR, Rally for the Republic); ***political career:*** Technical Advisor, then Rep. to office of Jacques Chirac, Minister of Agriculture, 1973-74, Minister of the Interior, 1974, Prime Minister, 1974-76; Principal Private Sec. to Maurice Papon, Minister for Budget, 1978; Dep. for Eure, 1986-; Minister of the Interior, 1995-97; President, National Assembly, 2002-07; Pres., Conseil Constitutionnel, 2007-; ***professional career:*** Asst., Faculty of Law, Paris 1972-75; Dep. Public Prosecutor, High Court, Evry, 1976-78; Magistrate, Central Admin., Min. of Justice, 1978; Examining Judge, High Court, Paris, 1979; ***honours and awards:*** Chevalier of Agricultural Merit; ***publications:*** La Justice au XIXe, 1981; Les républiques des avocats, 1984; Le curieux, 1986; Les idées constitutionnelles du Général de Gaulle, 1974; La Constitution de la vie république, 1974; Le Pouvoir politique, 1977; Le Gaullisme, 1978; Quand les brochets font courir les coupes, 2008; Les oublies de le Republique, 2008; ***recreations:*** tennis, riding; ***office address:*** Conseil Constitutionnel, 2 rue de Montpensier, 75001 Paris, France; ***phone:*** + 33 (0)1 40 15 30 00; ***fax:*** +33 (0)1 40 20 93 27; ***URL:*** http://www.conseil-constitutionnel.fr.

DEBY, General Idriss; Chadian, President, Government of Chad; ***born:*** 1952; ***political career:*** Pres., Chad, 1991-, won first presidential elections, 1996; ***professional career:*** career army officer; helped Hassan Habré topple Goukouki Oueddei, 1982; fled to Sudan after accused of plotting coup, 1989; returned to Chad, 1990, after Hassan Habre forced into Exile; Cmdr. in Chief of the Armed Forces; ***office address:*** Office of the President, PO Box 74, N'Djamena, Chad; ***fax:*** +235 514501/514653; ***e-mail:*** presidence@tchad.td.

DE CASTRO, H.E. Anibal; Ambassador, Embassy of the Dominican Republic in the USA; ***professional career:*** various positions within media and broadcasting incl. Ed., newpaper Ultima Hora, producer, TV, Trialogo, Host, Rumbo TV, Exec. VP, Omnimedia; founding ed., Diario Libre newspaper; Amb. of the Dominican Republic to the UK, 2004-11; non-resident amb., Australia, 207-11, Rep. of Ireland, 2009-11; Amb. of the Dominican Rep. to the US, 2011-; ***office address:*** Embassy of the Dominican Republic, 1715 22nd Street, NW, Washington, DC 20008, USA; ***phone:*** +1 202 332 6280; ***fax:*** +1 202 265 8057; ***URL:*** http://www.domrep.org/.

DE CREM, Pieter; Minister of Defence, Government of Belgium; ***born:*** 22 July 1962; ***education:*** Univ. Catholique de Leuven, Romance Languages; Univ. of Brussels, Int'l. and European Law; ***political career:*** Mayor, Aalter, 1995-; Deputy in the Chamber of Reps., 1995-; Minister of Defence, 2008-; ***office address:*** Ministry of Defence, rue Lambermont 8 , 1000 Brussels, Belgium; ***phone:*** +32 (0)2 550 2811; ***URL:*** http://www.pieterdecrem.be.

DEEN, Mohaded Waheed; Vice President, Government of Maldives; *political career:* Minister for Atoll Affairs; Vice Pres. of the Maldives, 2012-; *professional career:* Owner, Bandos Island Resort; *office address:* Office of the President , Medhuziyaaraiy Magu, Malé 20113, Maldives; *phone:* +960 332 3701; *fax:* +960 332 5500; *e-mail:* info@po.gov.mv; *URL:* http://www.presidencymaldives.gov.mv.

DEENIHAN, Jimmy, TD; Irish, Minister of Arts, Sport and Tourism, Government of Ireland; *born:* September 1952, Listowel, Co. Kerry, Ireland; *parents:* Michael Deenihan and Mary Deenihan; *married:* Mary Deenihan (née Dowling), August 1986; *public role of spouse:* Teacher; *languages:* Gaelic; *education:* St. Michael's Coll., Listowel; St. Mary's College, Twickenham; Nat. Coll. of Physical Education, Limerick, BE.d; *party:* Fine Gael; European People's Party; *political career:* Seanad Éireann, 1982-87; Senator, Taoiseach's nominee, 1983-87; Mem., Kerry County Cncl., 1985-94, 99-; Minister of State, Dept. of Agriculture, Food and Forestry, 1994-97; Fine Gael Spokesperson on Youth and Sport, 1988-93, Tourism and Trade, 1993-97, the office of Public Works; Dail Dep., 1987-; Dáil Éireann 1987-; Opposition spokesperson on Arts, Sport and Tourism; Minister of Arts, Sport and Tourism, Feb. 2011; *interests:* arts, culture, sports, heritage, agriculture, environment; *memberships:* Mem., Kerry County Enterprise Bd., 1992-94; Listowel and Tralee Chambers of Commerce; *professional career:* Teacher, 1975-83; *committees:* Mem., Kerry County Vocational Education Cttee., 1985-91; Rail Restoration Cttee. Listowel, Co. Kerry; Dail Cttee., Finance and Public Service; Joint Cttee. on Arts, Sport and Tourism; *trusteeships:* North Kerry Literary Trust; *honours and awards:* GAA All Star Award, 1981; Four Nat. League medals; Five Railway Cup medals; Five All-Ireland Senior Football Medals; *clubs:* Ballybunion Golf Club; *recreations:* hill walking, golf; *office address:* Department of Arts, Sport and Tourism, 23 Kildare Street, Dublin 2, Ireland; *phone:* +353 (0)1 631 3800; *e-mail:* jdeenihan@eircom.net; *URL:* http://www.arts-sport-tourism.gov.ie.

DEGETTE, Diana; American, Congresswoman, Colorado First District, US House of Representatives; *education:* Colorado College, BA magna cum laude, 1979; New York Univ. School of Law, JD, 1982; *party:* Democrat; *political career:* Colorado House of Representatives, 1992-96; Congresswoman, Colorado First District, US House of Representatives, 1996-, and Democratic Chief Deputy Whip, 2005-; *committees:* House Energy & Commerce Committee; *office address:* US House of Representatives, 1530 Longworth House Office Building, Washington, DC 20515, USA; *phone:* +1 202 225 4431.

DE GUCHT, Karel; Commissioner for Trade, European Commission; *born:* 27 January 1954, Overmere, Belgium; *married:* Mireille Schreurs; *children:* Frédéric (M), Jean-Jacques (M); *education:* Royal Atheneum of Alost, ESS Latin-Math, 1971; Vrije Univ., Brussels, Master at Law, 1976 ; *political career:* Pres., Nat. Liberal Student Union, 1975-77; MEP, 1980-94; President of Vlaamse Liberalen en Demokraten (VLD, Flemish Liberals and Democrats Liberal Party - Flemish Wing), 1999-2004; Member of Flemish Parliament, 1995-2003; Minister of State, 2002-; MP, 2003-; Dep. PM, Minister of Foreign Affairs, 2004-09; European Commissioner for Trade, 2010-; *interests:* European politics and international relations, human rights, education policy; *professional career:* Lawyer; Lecturer in European Law, Univ. of Vrije, Brussels; *recreations:* modern art and architecture; *office address:* European Commission, rue de la Loi 200, B-1049 Brussels, Belgium; *phone:* +32 (0)2 299 1111; *fax:* +32 (0)2 299 1970; *URL:* http://www.europa.eu.

DEIGHTON, Lord Paul Clive; Member, House of Lords; *education:* Trinity Coll., Cambridge Univ.; *party:* Conservative; *political career:* Mem., House of Lords, 2012-; Commercial Sec., HM Treasury, 2012- ; *professional career:* Partner, Goldman Sachs; *office address:* House of Lords, London, SW1A 0AH, United Kingdom; *phone:* +44 (0)20 7219 5353.

DEJONGH, JR., John P. ; Governor, US Virgin Islands; *born:* 13 November 1957, St. Thomas, US Virgin Islands; *married:* Cecile René (née Galiber), 1986; *s:* 2; *d:* 1; *education:* Antioch College, BA, Econ., 1981; *political career:* Chmn., Governing Bd., Virgin Islands Water and Power Authority, 1988-92; Exec. Assist. to Governor Farrelly, 1990-92; Director of Finance and Administration, VI Public Finance Authority, 1990-92; Chmn., VI Economic Recovery Task Force; Co-Chair, Cruise Ship Task Force; Exec. Dir., VI Democratic Party; Governor, US Virgin Islands, 2007-; *professional career:* Tri-Island Economic Devel. Cncl.; Chase Manhattan Bank; Cmnr. of Finance, 1987-90; Sr. Managing Consultant, Public Financial Management plc, 1993; COO & Dir., Lockhart Companies Inc.; Partner, Chilmark Partners, LLC, 2003-; *committees:* Mem., Ind. Development Cmn., 1984; *trusteeships:* Pres., Karen Ingeborg Lockhart Foundation; trustee, Government Employees Retirement System; Mem., Bd. of Dir., Community Foundation of the Virgin Islands (Pres. for three terms); trustee, Antilles School; *office address:* Government House, 21-22 Kongens Gade, Charlotte Amalie 00802, US Virgin Islands; *phone:* +1 340 774 0001 / 773 1404; *fax:* +1 340 774 1361 / 778 7978; *URL:* http://www.gov.vi/html/gov.html.

DEKKER, Sander; State Secretary for Education, Culture and Science, Netherlands Government; *born:* 1975; *education:* Univ. of Leiden; *political career:* The Hague municipal council, 2003-06, portfolio holder for Youth, Education and Sport, 20006-10, portfolio holder for Finance and City Management, 2010-12; State Secretary for Education, Culture and Science, Rutte-Asscher gov., Nov. 2012-; *office address:* Ministry of Education, Culture and Science, Rijnstraat 50, 2515 XP The Hague, Netherlands; *phone:* +31 (0)70 412 3456.

DELATTRE , H.E. François; Ambassador, French Embassy in the USA; *professional career:* Consul General in New York. 2004-08; Amb. to Canada, 2008-11; Amb. to the United States, 2011-; *office address:* Embassy of France, 4101 Reservoir Road, NW, Washington, DC 20007, USA; *phone:* +1 202 944 6000; *fax:* +1 202 944 6166; *URL:* http://www.ambafrance-us.org/.

DELAURO, Rosa; American, Congresswoman, Connecticut Third District, US House of Representatives; *party:* Democrat; *political career:* Congresswoman, Connecticut Third District, US House of Representatives, 1990-; Asst. to Democratic Leader, 1999-; *committees:* House Appropriations Cttee.; *office address:* US House of Representatives, 2262 Rayburn House Office Building, Washington, DC 20515, USA; *phone:* +1 202 225 3661.

DE LIMA, Leila; Secretary of Justice, Government of the Philippines; *born:* 1959; *education:* LLB, San Beda College, 1985; *political career:* Secretary of Justice, 2010-; *office address:* Department of Justice, 2nd Floor, BOJ Main Building, Padre Faura Street, Ermita, Manila, Philippines; *phone:* +63 2 523 8481; *URL:* http://www.doj.gov.ph.

DELISI, H.E. Scott; Ambassador, US Embassy in Uganda; *education:* Univ. of Minnesota, Law School, Juris Doctor; *professional career:* Career diplomat incl. postings to India, Madagascar, Pakistan, Sri Lanka, Botswana; Most recently: US Ambassador to Eritrea, 2004-09; Amb. to Nepal, 2009-12; Amb. to Uganda, 2012-; *office address:* US Embassy, 1577 Ggaba Road, P.O. Box 7007, Kampala, Uganda; *phone:* +256 41 259792; *fax:* +256 41 259794; *URL:* http://kampala.usembassy.gov.

DELVAUX-STEHRES, Mady; Luxembourgeois, Minister of National Education and Professional Training, Luxembourg Government; *born:* 1950, Luxembourg City, Luxembourg; *married:* Michel Delvaux (dec'd); *children:* 3; *education:* Univ. Preparatory Classes, Luxembourg; Univ. of Paris-Sorbonne, Master's degree in Classics; *party:* Parti Ouvrier Socialiste Luxembourgeois, (POSL, Luxembourg Socialist Workers' Party), 1974-; *political career:* Communal Councillor, Luxembourg City, 1987; Elected to Chamber of Deputies for Centre Constituency; MEP; Former Sec. of State for Health, Sec. of State for Social Security, Sec. of State for Physical Education and Sports; Sec. of State for Social Security and Youth to Minister Lahure, 1989; Minister for Social Security, Transport, Post and Communications, 1994-99; Minister of National Education and Professional Training, to date; *professional career:* Teacher; *committees:* Mem., Management Cttee. of Socialist Workers Party, 1984-; *office address:* Ministry of National Education, Professional Training and Sports, 29 rue Aldringen, 1118 Luxembourg, Luxembourg; *phone:* +352 478 5151; *fax:* +352 478 5110; *e-mail:* pisa@men.lu; *URL:* http://www.men.lu/.

DE MAIZIERE, Dr Thomas; Minister of Defence, Government of Germany; *born:* 21 January 1954, Bonn; *education:* Military Service; Law School, Munster, 1974-79; Bar exam, 1982; Univ. of Munster, Doctorate in Law, 1986; *party:* CDU; *political career:* Hd. of Policy Div., Berlin Senate Chancellery, 1985-89; Spokesman, CDU parly gp., Berlin HOR, 1985-89; State Sec., Mecklenburg-Western Pomeranian Ministry of Culture, 1990-94; Head of the State Chancellery of Mecklenburg-Western Pomerania, 1994-98; Advisor and Minister of State and Head of the Saxon State Chancellery, 1999; Saxon Minister of State for Finance, 2001-02; Saxon Minister of State for Justice, 2002-04; Saxon Minister of State for the Interior, 2004-05; Member of the Saxon State Parliament, 2004-05; Head of Chancellery and Federal Minister for Special Tasks, 2005-09; Federal Minister of the Interior & mem., German Parliament, 2009-11; Federal Minister of Defence, 2011-; *professional career:* Assist. to Mayors of Berlin, 1983; *office address:* Ministry of Defence, Stauffenbergstrasse 18, 10785 Berlin, Germany; *URL:* http://www.bmvg.de.

DE MAULEY, Lord; Member, House of Lords; *born:* 30 June 1957; *parents:* the late Colonel Hon. Thomas Maurice Ponsonby TD, DL and Maxime Henrietta Thelinsson; *education:* Eton College; *party:* Conservative Party; *political career:* Member, House of Lords (elected hereditary peer), 2005-; Opposition Whip, 2005; Opposition Spokesperson for: Trade and Industry / Business, Enterprise and Regulatory Reform / Business, Innovation and Skills, 2005, Cabinet Office, 2006; Gov. Whip and Spokesperson on HM Treasury, Business and DEFRA, 2010-12; Work and Pensions, 2011-12; Parly. Under-Sec. of State, Dept. for Environment, Food and Rural Affairs, 2012-; *interests:* China, South-East Asia; *memberships:* FCA, 1990; Fellow, Inst. of Chartered Accountants in England and Wales; *professional career:* Lt. Col., The Royal Wessex Yeomanry (Commanded 2003-04); Dir., Samuel Montagu & Co. Ltd., 1990-93; Standard Chartered Merchant Bank Asia Ltd., 1994-99; Jt. Chmn. & Chief Exec., FixIT Worldwide Ltd., 1999-2006; *recreations:* country sports, woodland management; *office address:* House of Lords, London, SW1A 0PW, United Kingdom.

DEMETRIADES, Panicos; Governor, Central Bank of Cyprus; *education:* Univ. of Essex, economics, BA, MA; Univ. of Cambridge, Ph.D; *professional career:* Economic Research Dept., Central Bank of Cyprus, 1985-90; Lecturer, Univ. of Keele, UK, 1990-95, Senior Lecturer, 1995-96, Reader, 1996-97; Prof. of Financial Economics, South Bank Univ., UK, 1997-2000; Prof. of Financia Economics, Univ. of Leicester, 2000-12.; Governor, Central Bank of Cyprus, 2012-; *office address:* Central Bank of Cyprus, 80 Kennedy Avenue, CY-1395 Nicosia, Cyprus; *URL:* http://www.centralbank.gov.cy.

DEMOTTE, Rudy; Minister-President , Walloon Government, Belgium; *born:* 3 June 1963, Renaix, Belgium; *party:* Parti Socialiste (PS, Socialist Party); *political career:* Community Councillor for Flobecq, 1994-2000; Minister of Economic Affairs and Scientific Research, 1999-2000; Minister for Culture, Budget, the Civil Service, Youth and Sport, Govt. of French Community, 2001-2003; Minister of Social Affairs and Public Health, Government of Belgium, 2003-07; Minister-President, Walloon Gvt., 2008-; Minister-President, French Community, Belgium, 2008-; *office address:* Office of the Minister-President of the Walloon Region, 25-27 rue Mazy, 5100 Jambes, Belgium; *phone:* +32 (0)81 333160; *fax:* +81 (0)81 333166; *e-mail:* dircom@mrw.wallonie.be; *URL:* http://mrw.wallonie.be.

DENDIAS, Nikolaos; Minister of Public Order and Citizen Protection, Government of Greece; *born:* Corfu, Greece; *languages:* English, Italian; *education:* Athens Univ. Law School; L.L.M. Univ. of London, UK; *political career:* MP, 2004-; Minister of Justice, 2009; Minister of Public Order and Citizen Protection, 2012-; *professional career:* Supreme Court Lawyer; *office address:* Ministry of Public Order and Citizen Protection, 4 P. Canellopoulou Str., 10177 Athens, Greece; *phone:* +30 (0)10 692 1675; *URL:* http://www.ydt.gr.

DENHAM, Jeff; Congressman, US House of Representatives; *party:* Republican; *political career:* Mem., HOR, California 18th District, 2010-; *committees:* Natural Resources; Transport and Infrastructure; *office address:* 1605 Longworth HOB, Washington 20515, USA; *phone:* +1 202 225 4540; *URL:* http://denham.house.gov/.

DENHAM, Rt. Hon. John; British, MP, House of Commons; *education:* Southampton Univ., B.Sc. (Hons), Chemistry; *party:* Labour Party, 1975-; *political career:* Cllr., Hampshire County, 1981-89; Cllr., Southampton City, 1989; Parly. Under-Sec. of State, Dept.

of Social Security, 1997; MP, Southampton Itchen, 1992-; Home Office Minister of State (Police & Crime Reduction), 2001-03; Secretary of State for Innovation, Universities and Skills, June 2007-09; Secretary of State for Communities and Local Government, 2009-May 2010; Shadow Secretary of State for Communities and Local Government, May 2010-Sept. 2010; Shadow Secretary of State for Business, Innovation and Skills, Oct. 2010-Oct. 2011; ***interests:*** education, housing, development, north/south financial issues, local democracy and participation; ***office address:*** House of Commons, London, SW1A 0AA, United Kingdom; ***phone:*** +44 (0)23 8033 9807; ***e-mail:*** john@johndenham.org.uk.

DENNY, Ross; Ambassador, British Embassy in Belize; ***born:*** 1955, Southampton, UK; ***political career:*** Deputy Head of Mission, Consul and Director of Trade and Investment, Angola, accredited to the Republic of Sao Tome and Principe, 2002-05; Administrator of Ascencion Island, 2008-11; Amb. to Belize, 2011-; ***office address:*** British Embassy, Avenida Arce 2732, Casilla 697, La Paz, Bolivia; ***phone:*** +591 (0)2 2433424; ***fax:*** +591 (0)2 2431073; ***URL:*** http://ukinbolivia.fco.gov.uk/en.

DE PIERO, Gloria; MP for Ashfield, House of Commons; ***party:*** Labour; ***political career:*** MP for Ashfield, May 2010-; Shadow Minister, Culture, Media and Sport, Oct. 2010-11; Shadow Minister, Home Affairs, 2011-; ***professional career:*** Journalist and TV Presenter; ***office address:*** House of Commons, London, SW1A 0AA, United Kingdom; ***phone:*** +44 (0)20 7219 3000; ***e-mail:*** gloria.depiero.mp@parliament.uk.

DESAI, Lord, Baron Meghnad Jagdischchandra; British, Member of the House of Lords; ***born:*** Baroda, India; ***parents:*** Jagdishchandra and Mandakini; ***married:*** Gail Graham Wilson, June 1970 (Div'd); Kishwar Ahlunalia, July 2004; ***children:*** Sven (M), Tanvi (F), Nuala (F); ***languages:*** English, French, Gujarati, Hindi, Marathi; ***education:*** BA (Hons), MA, Univ of Bombay; Ph.D., Univ of Pennsylvania; ***party:*** Labour Party; ***political career:*** Mem., House of Lords, 1991-; ***professional career:*** Prof. of Economics, London School of Economics; ***honours and awards:*** Life Peer; Padma Bhushan (India); ***office address:*** House of Lords, London, SW1A 0AA, United Kingdom; ***phone:*** +44 (0)207 7274 5561; ***e-mail:*** m.desai@lse.ac.uk.

DE SILVA, Nimal Siripala; Minister of Irrigation and Water Resources Management, Government of Sri Lanka; ***political career:*** Minister of Health and Indigenous Medicine; Minister of Irrigation and Water Resources Management, 2010-; ***office address:*** Ministry of Irrigation and Water Resources, 11 Jawatta Road, Colombo 05, Sri Lanka; ***URL:*** http://www.gpv.lk.

DE VALLERA, Joao; Ambassador, Portuguese Embassy to the UK; ***professional career:*** Amb to Ireland; Amb., to the United States, 2007-10; Amb.to the UK, 2010-; ***office address:*** Embassy of Portugal, 11 Belgrave Square, London, SW1X 8PP, United Kingdom; ***phone:*** +44 (0)20 7235 5331; ***fax:*** +44 (0)20 7245 1287; ***e-mail:*** london@portembassy.co.uk.

DE VIDO, Julio Miguel; Minister of Federal Planning, Public Investment and Services, Government of Argentina; ***education:*** Univ. Nacional of Buenos Aires, Architecture, 1974; ***political career:*** Pres., Federal Taxation Commission, 1995-96 and 2000-01; Govt. Minister in the province of Santa Cruz, 1999-2003; Minister of Federal Planning, Public Investment and Services, 2003-; ***office address:*** Ministry of Federal Planning, Public Investment and Services, Hipólito Yrigoyen 250 , 1310 Buenos Aires, Argentina; ***phone:*** +54 (0)11 4349 5000 / 5010; ***fax:*** +54 (0)11 4318 9432; ***URL:*** http://www.minplan.gov.ar.

DEXTER, Darrell; Premier, Government of Nova Scotia; ***political career:*** Dartmouth City Councillor; MLA, 1998-; Leader, New Democratic Party, 2001-; Premier, June 2009-, also Pres., Executive Council, Chair, Treasury and Policy Board, Minister of Intergovernmental Affairs, Minister of Aboriginal Affairs, Minister responsible for Military Relations; ***professional career:*** lawyer; ***office address:*** Office of the Premier, Halifax, Nova Scotia, Canada; ***URL:*** http://www.gov.ns.ca/premier.

DHIEU DAU, Stephen; Minister of Petroleum and Energy, Government of South Sudan; ***political career:*** Finance Minister; Minister of Trade; Minister of Petroleum and Energy, 2011-; ***office address:*** Ministry of Petroleum and Energy, Juba, South Sudan; ***URL:*** http://www.mpmrss.org.

DHOININE, Ikililou; President, Government of Comoros; ***born:*** 1962, Djoièzi, Comoros; ***political career:*** Deputy President, 2006-11; President, May 2011-; ***professional career:*** Pharmacist; ***office address:*** Office of the President, PO Box 521, Moroni , Comoros; ***phone:*** +269 774 4808; ***fax:*** +269 744 8821; ***URL:*** http://www.beit-salam.km.

DIARRA, Judge Fatoumata Dembele; Judge, International Criminal Court; ***born:*** 1949; ***education:*** LL.B, Dakar Univ.; LLM in private law, Mali École Nationale d'Administration; Graduated from the École Nationale de la Magistrature, Paris; Diploma in the Implementation of Regional and International Standards for the Protection of Human Rights; ***professional career:*** Nat. Director, Mali Justice Department; Judge, International Criminal Tribunal for the former Yugoslavia; First Vice-President, International Criminal Court, March 2009-March 2012; ***office address:*** International Criminal Court, PO Box 19519, 2500 CM, The Hague, The Netherlands; ***phone:*** +31 (0)70 515 8515; ***e-mail:*** FatoumataDembele.Diarra@icc-cpi.int; ***URL:*** http://www.un.org/law/icc.

DI BARTOLOMEO, Mars; Minister of Health and Social Security, Government of Luxembourg; ***born:*** 27 June 1952; ***political career:*** Parly. Sec. LSAP, 1984; Dep., Chambre of Deputies, 1989-04; Mayor, City of Dudelange, 1994-2004; Pres. Southern Region, LSAP, 1999-2004-; Minister of Health and Social Security, 2004-; ***professional career:*** Journalist, Tageblatt, 1972-84; ***office address:*** Ministry of Health, Villa Louvigny, Allée Marconi, L-2120 Luxembourg, Luxembourg; ***phone:*** +352 247 85501; ***fax:*** +352 46 79 63; ***e-mail:*** ministere-santé@ms.etat.lu; ***URL:*** http://www.ms.public.lu/fr/index.html.

DICKSON, H.E. Sarah; Ambassador , British Embassy in Guatemala; ***education:*** MBA; ***professional career:*** Amb. to the Republic of Guatemala and Non-Resident Amb. to the Republic of Honduras, 2012-; ***office address:*** British Embassy, Edificio Torre Internacional, Nivel 11, 16 Calle 00-55, Zona 10, Guatemala; ***phone:*** +502 2380 7300; ***fax:*** 502 2380 7339; ***e-mail:*** embassy@intelnett.com; ***URL:*** http://ukinguatemala.fco.gov.uk/en.

DIJKSMA, Sharon; Minister for Agriculture, Netherlands Government; ***born:*** 1971; ***political career:*** Mem., House of Representatives, 1994-2007; State Sec. for Education, Culture & Science, 2007; Mem., HoR, 2010-12; Sate Sec. for Economic Affairs, 2012, Rutte-Asscher gov., Dec. 2012; Minister for Agriculture, 2013-; ***office address:*** Ministry of Economic Affairs, Agriculture and Innovation, PO Box 20401, 2500 EK The Hague, Netherlands; ***phone:*** +31 77 465 6767; ***URL:*** http://www.government.nl/ministries/eleni.

DIJSSELBLOEM, Jeroen; Minister of Finance, Netherlands Government; ***born:*** 1966; ***education:*** Wageningen Univ.; ***political career:*** Wageningen municipal council, 1994-97; Polit. adviser, Minister of Agriculture, Nature Management and Fisheries, 1996-88, Dep. Head, Advisory, -2000; Mem., House of Reps., 2000-12; Minister of Finance, 2012-; ***office address:*** Ministry of Finance, Korte Voorhout 7, Postbus 20201, 2500 EE The Hague, Netherlands; ***phone:*** +31 (0)70 342 8000.

DILOU, Samir; Minister of Human Rights and Transitional Justice, Government of Tunisia; ***born:*** 1966; ***political career:*** Minister of Human Rights and Transitional Justice, 2012-; Government spokesperson, 2012-; ***professional career:*** political activist; imprisonned; lawyer; founder, Int. Org. to Defend Political Prisoners; ***office address:*** Ministry of Human Rights & Transitional Justice, 31 Avenue Bab Benat, 1006 Tunis, Tunisia; ***phone:*** +216 71 561440; ***URL:*** http://www.e-justice.tn/.

DINENAGE, Caroline; MP for Gosport, UK Government; ***party:*** Conservative; ***political career:*** Councillor, Winchester District Council, 1998-2003; MP for Gosport, May 2010-; ***committees:*** Science and Technology, 2012-; ***office address:*** House of Commons, London, SW1A 0AA, United Kingdom; ***phone:*** +44 (0)20 7219 3000; ***e-mail:*** caroline.dinenage.mp@parliament.uk.

DINKIC, Mladjan; Minister of Finance and Economy, Government of Serbia; ***born:*** 1964; ***political career:*** Minister of Finance, 2004-06; Dep. Prime Minister and Minister and Economy and Regional Development, 2007-11; Minister of Finance & Economy, 2012-; ***professional career:*** Governor, National Bank of Yugoslavia, 2000-03; ***office address:*** Ministry of Economy, 16 Kralja Milana Street, Belgrade, Serbia; ***phone:*** +381 11 361 7599; ***fax:*** +381 11 361 7640.

DIOUF, Abdou; Sengalese, Secretary General, International Organisation of Francophonie; ***born:*** 1935; ***education:*** Lycée Faidherbe; Universities of Dakar and Paris, law and political sciences; ***political career:*** Dep. Sec.-Gen. to the Government, 1960-61; Sec.-Gen., Ministry of Defence, 1961; Gov. Sine-Saloum Region, 1961-62; Principal Sec. to the Minister for Foreign Affairs, 1962-63; Principal Sec. to the President of the Republic, 1963-65; Sec. Gen., of the Presidency of the Republic, 1964-68; Min. of Planning and Industry, 1968-70; Prime Minister of Senegal, 1970-80; Pres., Rep. of Senegal, 1981-2000; Chmn., of O.M.V.S., 1981-82; Pres., Senegambian Confederation, 1982-89; Chmn., and Co-ordinator of the G.15, 1990; Chmn., of the 6th Islamic Conference (OIC), 1991; Sec.-Gen., Departmental Co-ordination of Louga; Mem., Parliament for Louga Department; Dep. Sec.-Gen., UPS; Dep. Sec.-Gen., Socialist Party (PS) of Senegal, then Sec.-Gen.; Chmn., of the Inter African Socialist and Democratic Conference; Vice-Chmn., International Socialist, 1992-; ***professional career:*** Dir., International Technical Co-operation, 1960; Sec.-Gen., International Organisation of Francophonie, to date; ***honours and awards:*** Grand Croix de l'Ordre du Mérite français, 1978; grand Croix de la Légion d'honneur française, 1982; Doctor h.c. title bestowed by fifteen universities in different parts of the world; "Africa Leadership" Prize of the Hunger Project, New York 1987; Hon. Mayor of Tivaouane 1989; Mem. Acad. des Sciences d'Outre-mer, 1997; Grand Prix de l'Académie Française pour la Francophonie, 1997; King Faisal International Prize for services to Islam, 1998; Medal of Merit, FIBA, 1999; Prix Grand Siecle Laurent Perrier, 2003; Grand Croix de l'Ordre National Malgache ; ***office address:*** Organisation Internationale de la Francophonie, 28 rue de Bourgogne, 75007 Paris, France.

DI RUPO, Elio; Belgian, Prime Minister, Government of Belgium; ***born:*** 18 July 1951, Morlanwelz, Belgium; ***languages:*** Dutch, English, Italian; ***education:*** Univ. of Mons, Doctor of Sciences; ***party:*** Parti Socialiste; ***political career:*** Chef de Cabinet, Budget and Energy Min. of Walloon Region, 1982-85; Communal Cllr., Mons, 1982-; MP, 1987; MEP, 1989; Pres., Energy Cmn. (Socialist Party); Senator, 1991; Min. of Education, 1992; Dep. Prime Minister and Minister of Communications and Public Enterprises, 1994-95; Dep. Minister and Minister for Economy and Telecommunications, until 1999; Pres. of Parti Socialiste, 1999-; Minister-Pres., responsible for International Relations, Walloon Govt. 1999-2000, Minister President, Walloon Govt., to 2005-07; Prime Minister, Dec. 2011-; ***professional career:*** Researcher; Chemist; ***office address:*** Office of the Prime Minister, 16 Rue de la Loi, B-1000 Brussels, Belgium; ***phone:*** +32 (0)2 501 0211; ***fax:*** +32 (0)2 512 6953; ***URL:*** http://www.premier.fgov.be.

DJALAL, H.E. Dr Dino Patti; Ambassador of the Republic of Indonesia to the USA, Indonesian Embassy; ***born:*** 1965; ***professional career:*** youth activist; academic; best-selling author; diplomat; Dept. of Foreign Affairs, Indonesia, 1987, posts include Dili, London and Washington DC; Special Staff for International Affairs and Presidential Spokesperson for President Yudhoyono, 2004-2011; Indonesian Ambassador to the US, 2011-; ***office address:*** Embassy of Indonesia, 2020 Massachusetts Ave., NW, Washington, DC 20036, USA; ***phone:*** +1 202 775 5200 ; ***fax:*** +1 202 775 5365; ***URL:*** http://www.embassyofindonesia.org/.

DJANOGLY, Jonathan; Member of Parliament for Huntingdon, House of Commons; ***married:*** Rebecca Jane Silk; ***s:*** 1; ***d:*** 1; ***education:*** University College Sch.; BA (Hons) Law/Politics, Oxford Brookes Univ.,1987; Guildford Coll. of Law, Solicitor, 1988; Corporate Finance Qualification (ICA), 2007; ***party:*** Conservative Party; ***political career:*** MP, Huntingdon, 2001-; Shadow Minister, Home, Constitutional and Legal Affairs, 2004-05; Shadow Solicitor General, 2005-; Shadow Minister, Business, Enterprise and Regulatory

Reform, 2005-10; Parliamentary Under Secretary of State, Ministry of Justice, 2010-; ***professional career:*** Partner, SJ Berwin LLP, 1998-; ***committees:*** Trade and Industry Select Cttee., 2001-05; ***office address:*** House of Commons, London, SW1A 0AA, United Kingdom; ***phone:*** +44 (0)20 7219 3000; ***e-mail:*** jonathan.djanogly.mp@parliament.uk; ***URL:*** http://www.jonathandjanogly.com.

DJOTODIA, Michel; President, Government of the Central African Republic; ***education:*** Studied economics in the former Soviet Union; ***party:*** Leader, Seleka; ***political career:*** Civil servant in the government of Ange-Felix Patasse; Minister of Defence, Jan.-March, 2013; President (self-appointed), Minister of National Defence, Army Restructuring, Veterans and Victims of War, and the Programme for Disarmament, Demobilisation and Reintegration, March 2013-; ***professional career:*** Diplomat in Sudan; ***office address:*** Office of the President, Palais de la Renaissance, Bangui, Central African Republic; ***phone:*** +236 21 61 0323; ***URL:*** http://www.presidence-rca.org.

DJOUDI, Karim; Minister of Finance, Government of Algeria; ***born:*** 1958, Montpellier, France; ***education:*** BA in Economics, Lycee Descartes, Algeris, 1978; MA in Economics, Univ. of Strasbourg, 1983; ***political career:*** Minister of Finance, 2007-; ***professional career:*** Central Dir., Central Bank of Algeria, 1990-99; ***office address:*** Ministry of Finance, Place du Perou, Immeuble Mauretania, Algiers, Algeria; ***phone:*** +213 (0)21 595151; ***URL:*** http://www.finance-algeria.org.

DJUKANOVIC, Milo; Prime Minister, Montenegrin Government; ***born:*** 15 February 1962, Niksic; ***parents:*** Radovan Djukanovic and Stana Djukanovic; ***married:*** Lidija Djukanovic (née Kuc); ***children:*** Blazo; ***languages:*** Russian, English; ***education:*** Univ. of Montenegro, Faculty of Economics; ***party:*** Pres., Democratic Party of Socialists (DPS); ***political career:*** mem., Democratic Party of Socialists, 1979-; Prime Minister, Republic of Montenegro, 1991-93, 1993-96, 1996-98; President, Republic of Montenegro, 1998-2002; Prime Minister, 2003-06; Minister of Defence, 2006, Prime Minister, 2008-10, 2012-; ***interests:*** promotion of democracy, economic reform, European and trans-Atlantic integration; ***recreations:*** basketball; ***office address:*** Office of the Prime Minister of Montenegro, Jovana Tomasevica bb, 81000 Podgorica, Montenegro.

DLAMINI, Rt. Hon. Dr Barnabas Sibusiso; Swazi, Prime Minister, Government of the Kingdom of Swaziland; ***born:*** 15 May 1942; ***education:*** Univ. of Wisconsin, U.S.A., BSc., Chemistry & Mathematics, 1969; Univ. of South Africa, BComm., Economics & Accounting, 1976; New York Univ. USA, MBA, Financial Management, 1982 ; ***political career:*** Senator and Mem. of Parl. 1978-83; Minister of Finance, 1984-92; Exec. Dir with International Monetary Fund (IMF) in Washington D.C., 1992-96; Prime Minister, 1996-2003, 2008-; ***memberships:*** American Inst. of certified Public Accountants, NY, U.S.A.1983; Swaziland Inst. of Accountants, 1985; ***professional career:*** Swaziland Iron Ore Development Company, Ngwenya Mine, Assist. Chemist, Chief Chemist, Metallurgical Superintendent, 1969-77; Coopers & Lybrand, Chartered Accountants, Mbabane, Clerk, Audit Snr, Partner, 1978-84; Exec. Dir., International Monetary Fund, 1996-2003; ***honours and awards:*** Chief Counsellor of the Royal Order of Sobhuza II, by His Majesty King Mswati III, 1989; Order of Brilliant Star with Grand Cordon by President Dr Lee Teng Hui, Republic of China in Taiwan, 1989 ; ***office address:*** House of Assembly, PO Box 37, Lobamba, Swaziland.

DOBBIN, Jim; British, Member of Parliament for Heywood and Middleton, House of Commons; ***born:*** 26 May 1941; ***education:*** Napier Coll., Edinburgh; ***party:*** Labour Party; ***political career:*** Dep. Leader, Rochdale Cncl.; fmr. Chair, District Labour Party; MP, Haywood and Middleton, 1997-; ***interests:*** health, housing, local government; ***professional career:*** microbiologist, retd.; ***committees:*** European Scrutiny, 1998-; Transport, 2010-; ***office address:*** House of Commons, London, SW1A 0AA, United Kingdom; ***phone:*** +44 (0)20 7219 4530; ***e-mail:*** dobbinj@parliament.uk.

DOBBS, Lord (Michael); Member, House of Lords; ***education:*** Christ Church, Oxford Univ. UK, 1971; MA, PhD, Fletcher School, Massachusetts, USA, 1975; ***party:*** Conservative Party; ***political career:*** Advisor to Margaret Thatcher, 1977-79; Government Special Advisor, 1981-86; Conservative Party Chief of Staff, 1986-87; Dep. Chmn., Conservative Party, 1994-95; Mem., House of Lords, 2010-; ***professional career:*** Author; Dep. Chmn., Saatchi & Saatchi, 1983-86; broadcaster & columnist; ***office address:*** House of Lords, London, SW1A 0PW, United Kingdom; ***phone:*** +44 (0)20 7219 3000; ***URL:*** http://www.michaeldobbs.com.

DOBSON, Rt. Hon. Frank Gordon, MP; British, MP for Holborn & St Pancras, House of Commons; ***born:*** 1940; ***married:*** Janet Mary Alker, 1967; ***s:*** 2; ***d:*** 1; ***education:*** Archbishop Holgate's Grammar Sch., York; London Sch. of Economics, B.Sc. (Econ.); ***party:*** Labour Party; ***political career:*** Opp. Spokesman on Education, 1982-83; Shadow Health Min., 1983-88; Opp. Leader of the House and Campaigns Co-ordinator, 1988-89; Shadow Sec. of State for Energy, 1989-92, for Employment, 1992-93; Shadow Transport Sec., 1993-94; Shadow Environment Sec., 1994-97; Sec. of State for Health, 1997-99; MP for Holborn and St. Pancras South (Lab.), 1979-, re-elected MP, 1997-; ***professional career:*** Admin. Work with Central Electricity Generating Bd., 1962-70, and with Electricity Cncl., 1970-75; Asst.-Sec. Local admin. (Ombudsman's Office), 1975-79; ***clubs:*** Covent Garden Community Centre; ***office address:*** House of Commons, London, SW1A 2NS, United Kingdom; ***phone:*** +44 (0)20 7219 3000; ***fax:*** +44 (0)20 7210 5523.

DOCHERTY, Thomas; MP for Dunfermline and West Fife, UK Government; ***party:*** Labour; ***political career:*** MP for Dunfermline and West Fife, May 2010-; ***committees:*** Environment, Food and Rural Affairs Select Cttee., 2010-; Administration, 2010-; Defence, 2010-; Procedure, 2010-; Armed Forces Bill, 2010-11; Arms Export Controls, 2011; ***office address:*** House of Commons, London, SW1A 0AA, United Kingdom; ***phone:*** +44 (0)20 7219 3000; ***e-mail:*** thomas.docherty.mp@parliament.uk.

DODDS, Nigel; Member of Parliament, Northern Ireland Assembly; ***born:*** 20 August 1958, Londonderry; ***parents:*** Joseph and Doreen; ***married:*** Diana (née Harris), 16 August 1985; ***children:*** Mark (M), Andrew (M), Robyn (F); ***public role of spouse:*** Lady Mayoress of Belfast, 1988-89, 1991-92; Constituency Office Manager; ***languages:*** French; ***education:*** Portora Royal, Enniskillien; St John's Coll. Cambridge; ***party:*** Democratic Unionist; ***political career:*** Belfast City Cllr., 1985-; Mem. of NI Assembly, 1998-; Lord Mayor of Belfast, 1988-89, 1991-92; Mem., MP, North Belfast, 2001-; Minister for Social Development, NI Assembly, 2000-02 (NI Assembly suspended); Minister for Enterprise, Trade and Investment, May 2007-08; Minister for Finance and Personnel, 2008-09; DUP Parly. Group Leader, 2010-; Spokesperson, 2010-; ***professional career:*** Barrister, Politician; ***honours and awards:*** OBE; ***office address:*** Northern Ireland Assembly, Parliament Buildings, Stormont, Belfast, BT4 3XX, United Kingdom; ***phone:*** +44 (0)28 9052 1333; ***e-mail:*** doddsn@parliament.uk.

DODIK, Milorad; Serbian, President, Republic of Serbia; ***born:*** March 12, 1959; ***party:*** President, Alliance of Independent Social Democrats; ***political career:*** Prime Minister, 2006-Nov. 2010; President, Nov. 2010-; ***office address:*** Office of the President, Belgrade, Serbia.

DOER, H.E. Gary Albert; Ambassador, Canadian Embassy in USA; ***born:*** Winnipeg, Manitoba; ***married:*** Ginny Devine; ***children:*** Emily (F), Kate (F); ***political career:*** Elected Concordia's MLA, 1986; Min. of Urban Affairs & of Crown Investments; Minister responsible for the Telephone Act, and for the Manitoba Liquor Control Cmn.; elected Leader of the New Democrats 1988; Leader of the Opposition 1990-99; Premier of Manitoba 1999-2009; ***memberships:*** Bd. Mem., Winnipeg Blue Bombers; Bd. Mem., Prairie Theatre Exchange; Bd. Mem., Niagra Inst.; Mem., Bd. of Governors of the Univ. of Manitoba; ***professional career:*** Dep. Superintendent, Vaughan Street Detention Centre; Vice-Pres., Manitoba Special Olympics; Amb. to the USA, October 2009-; ***committees:*** Pres., Manitoba Govt. Employees Assn.; Pres., Boys and Girls Club of Winnipeg; ***office address:*** Embassy of Canada, 501 Pennsylvania Avenue, NW, Washington, DC 20001, Canada; ***phone:*** +1 202 682 1740; ***e-mail:*** canada@canadianembassy.org ; ***URL:*** http://www.canadianembassy.org.

DOHERTY, Pat; Member of the Northern Ireland Assembly for West Tyrone; ***party:*** Sinn Fein; ***political career:*** Mem., Belfast North, 2001-; DUP chief whip, 2001-08; UPD spokesperson, 2005-; ***office address:*** Northern Ireland Assembly, Parliament Buildings, Stormont, Belfast, BT4 3XX, Northern Ireland; ***phone:*** +44 (0)28 9052 1130; ***e-mail:*** doddsn@parliament.uk.

DOMBROVSKIS, Valdis; Latvian, Prime Minister, Government of Latvia; ***born:*** 5 August 1971, Riga, Latvia; ***education:*** Univ. of Latvia, Faculty of Physics and Mathematics, Bachelor's degree in Physics, 1993; Riga Technical Univ., Faculty of Engineering and Economics, Bachelor's degree in Economics, 1995; Meinz Univ. (Germany), Faculty of Physics, studies and development of the experimental part of the Master Paper, 1996; Univ. of Latvia, Faculty of Physics and Mathematics, Master's degree in Physics, 1996; Univ. of Maryland (USA), Dept. of Electrical Engineering, 1998; ***party:*** New Era Party; ***political career:*** Minister of Finance, Nov. 2002-04; MEP, 2004-09; Prime Minister, 2009-; ***professional career:*** Univ. of Maryland (USA), Dept. of Electrical Engineering, lab. assistant, 1997-98; Bank of Latvia, Monetary Policy Board, specialist in macroeconomics, 1998-99; Bank of Latvia, Monetary Policy Board, senior economist, 1999-2001; Bank of Latvia, Monetary Policy Board, chief economist, 2001-2002; ***office address:*** Office of the Prime Minister, Brivibas bulv. 36, Riga 1520, Latvia; ***URL:*** http://www.mk.gov.lv.

DONAGHY, Baroness Rita; Member, House of Lords; ***party:*** Labour; ***political career:*** Mem. House of Lords, 2010-; ***professional career:*** Pres., TUC, 2000; Chair, Industrial Conciliation Service ACAS, 2000-07; ***office address:*** House of Lords, London, SW1A 0PW, United Kingdom; ***phone:*** +44 (0)20 7219 3000; ***fax:*** +44 (0)20 7219 5979; ***URL:*** http://www.parliament.uk.

DONAHOE, Patrick R.; Postmaster General and CEO, United States Postal Service; ***education:*** Univ. of Pittsburgh, BSc., economics; Massachusetts Institute of Technology, Sloan Fellow, MSc.; ***professional career:*** various positions in his long career (35+ years) at USPS, incl. most recently: senior vice pres., HR, vice-pres., Allegheny Area Operations, Dep. Postmaster General & CEO, Postmaster General & CEO, 2010-; ***office address:*** United States Postal Service (USPS) , 475 L'Enfant Plaza, SW, Washington DC 20260-0010, USA; ***phone:*** +1 202 268 2000; ***URL:*** http://www.usps.gov.

DONALDSON, Rt. Hon. Jeffrey, MP; Member of Parliament for Lagan Valley, House of Commons; ***born:*** 7 December 1962, Kilkeel; ***parents:*** James Donaldson and Anne Donaldson (née Charleton); ***married:*** Eleanor Donaldson (née Cousins), 26 June 1987; ***d:*** 2; ***education:*** Diploma in Electrical Engineering; ***party:*** Democratic Unionist Party; ***political career:*** MP for Lagan Valley, 1997-; Ulster Unionist Spokesperson, 1997-03; DUP Spokesperson, 2004-; ***committees:*** Northern Ireland Affairs, 1997-2000; Environment, Transport and Regional Affairs, 2000-01; Regulatory Reform, 2001-05; Joint Committee on Statutory Instruments, 2001-06; Transport, 2004-07, 2009-10; Defence, 2010-; Arms Export Controls, 2011-12; ***honours and awards:*** Privy Council; ***office address:*** House of Commons, London, SW1A 0AA, United Kingdom; ***phone:*** +44 (0)20 7219 3407; ***e-mail:*** jeffreydonaldson.mp@laganvalley.net.

DONNELLY, Joe; Senator for Indiana, US Senate; ***born:*** 29 September 1955; ***education:*** Univ. of Notre Dame, B.A. in Government, 1977; Univ. of Notre Dame Law School, 1981; ***political career:*** Mem., Indiana State Election Board, 1988-89; Congressman, for 2nd Dist. Indiana, 2007-13; Senator, US Senator, 2013-; ***professional career:*** Lawyer, Nemeth, Feeny and Masters, South Bend; ***committees:*** former HOR: Financial Services; Veterans' Affairs; ***office address:*** US Senate, B33 Russell Senate Office Building 1218 , Washington, DC 20510, USA; ***phone:*** +1 202 224 4814; ***fax:*** +1 202 225 6798; ***URL:*** http://www.donnelly.senate.gov/.

DONOGHUE, Judge Joan E.; Member, International Court of Justice; ***professional career:*** various posits, US Dept. of State, 1986-94; Adjunct Prof., Georgetown Univ. Law Center, 1991; Assist. Legal Adviser, US Dept. of State, 1993-2001; Adjunct Prof., George Washington Univ. School of Law, 2005; Principal Deputy Legal Adviser, US Dept. of State, 2007-10; Mem., International Court of Justice, 2010-; ***office address:*** International Court of Justice, Peace Palace, Carnegieplein 2, 2517 KJ The Hague, Netherlands; ***phone:*** +31 (0)70 302 2323.

Don-Dra

DONOHOE, Brian; Member of Parliament for Central Ayrshire, House of Commons; ***born:*** 10 September 1948, Kilmarnock; ***parents:*** George Donohoe and Catherine; ***married:*** Christine Donohoe (née Pawson), 16 July 1973; ***children:*** Graeme (M), Craig (M); ***education:*** Kilmarnock Technical College, Nat. Certificate in Engineering; ***party:*** Labour Party; ***political career:*** Treasurer, Cunninghame South CLP, 1983-91; MP, Cunninghame South, 1992-05; Chair, Scottish Group of Labour MPs, 1996-98; Sec., Irvine Trades Council, 1973-82; MP, Central Ayrshire, 2005-; PPS to Minister of State at Transport; ***interests:*** transport, finance; ***memberships:*** Transport and General Workers Union (TGWU); ***professional career:*** Apprentice Engineer, Ailsa Shipyard, 1965-70; Hunterson Nuclear Power Station, 1977; Draughtsman, ICI Organics Division, 1977-81; Nalgo District Officer 1981-1992; ***committees:*** Aluminium Industry APPG; Chmn., Aviation APPG; Jt. Chmn. First Past the Post APPG; Chair. Fluoridation APPG; Sec ., Gardening and Horticulture APPG; Mem., Motor APPG; Mem., Road Passenger Transport APPG; Mem., Royal Air Force APPG; Sec., Scotch Whisky and Spirits APPG; Mem., Scout APPG; Mem., Shopping APPG; Hon. Sec., America APPG; Mem., Falkland Islands APPG; Vice Chmn., Singapore APPG; Mem., Labour Party Departmental Cttee. for Health; Labour Party Departmental Cttee. for Trade and Industry; Chmn., Parly. Labour Party Transport Cttee.; Rail, Maritime and Transport Workers Union (RMT) Parly. Campaigning Grp.; ***recreations:*** gardening, cycling; ***office address:*** House of Commons, London, SW1A 0AA, United Kingdom; ***phone:*** +44 (0)20 7219 6230; ***fax:*** +44 (0)20 7219 5388; ***mobile:*** +44 07774 646600; ***e-mail:*** brian.donohoe.mp@parliament.uk; ***URL:*** http://www.briandonohoemp.co.uk.

DONOUGHUE, Lord, Baron Bernard, Life Peer; British, Member of the House of Lords; ***born:*** 8 September 1934; ***parents:*** Thomas Joseph Donoughue (dec'd); ***married:*** Carol Ruth Goodman, 1959 (div'd); Lady Sarah Berry, 2009; ***education:*** Lincoln Coll.; Nuffield Coll., Oxford, MA, D.Phil.; Harvard Univ., USA; ***party:*** Labour Party; ***political career:*** Senior Policy Advisor to the PM, 1974-79; Mem., House of Lords, 1985-; House of Lords Opposition Spokesman on Treasury, 1991-92, on Energy, 1991-93, on Nat. Heritage, 1993-97; Minister of Farming Food, 1997-99; ***professional career:*** Editorial Staff, Economist, 1959-60; Sr. Research Officer, Political and Econ. Planning Inst., 1960-63; Sr. Lecturer, London Sch. of Econs., 1963-74; Dev. Dir., Economist Intelligence Unit, 1979-81; Asst. Editor, Times, 1981-82; Head of Research and Investment Policy, Grieveson Grant & Co., 1982-88; Head of Int. Research and Dir., Kleinwort Grieveson Securities Ltd., 1986-88; Visiting Prof. of Govt., LSE, 2000-06; Vice-Chmn., London and Bishopgate Int.; ***committees:*** Stable Staff Enquiry; Future Funding of Racing Enquiry; Greyhound Racing Enquiry; Chmn., Starting Price Regulatory Commission, 2004-; ***trusteeships:*** 1LPH, Dorneywood; ***publications:*** seven books on history and politics; ***clubs:*** Pratt's; ***office address:*** House of Lords, London, SW1A 0PQ, United Kingdom; ***phone:*** +44 (0)20 7219 3000; ***fax:*** +44 (0)20 7219 5979.

DONOVAN, Secretary Shaun; Secretary of Housing and Urban Development, US Government; ***born:*** 24 January 1966, New York; ***education:*** Kennedy Sch.of Government, Harvard, Public Administration; Graduate Sch. of Design, Harvard, Architecture ; ***political career:*** Secretary of Housing and Urban Development, 2009-; ***professional career:*** Community Housing and Preservation Corp.; Mgr., Federal Housing Administration, Prudential Mortgage Capital Co.; Dep. Assist. Sec. for multifamily housing, Dept. of Housing and Urban Development, Clinton administration; Visiting scholar at New York Univ, studying federally assisted housing; Housing Cmnr., Dept. of Housing Preservation and Development, New York City, 2004-08; ***office address:*** Department of Housing and Urban Development, 451 Seventh Street, SW, Washington, DC 20410, USA; ***phone:*** +1 202 708 1112; ***fax:*** +1 202 619 8153; ***URL:*** http://www.hud.gov.

DOOKERAN, Hon. Winston; Trinidadian, Minister of Finance, Government of Trinidad and Tobago; ***born:*** 1943; ***married:*** Shirley Dhrupatie; ***education:*** Univ. of Manitoba, 1966; Univ. of London, 1969; ***political career:*** Minister of Planning and Mobilization, 1986; Minister of Finance, 2010-; ***professional career:*** Lecturer in Economics, UWI, Trinidad 1971-81; Member of Parliament 1981-; numerous public sector appointments; Minister of Planning and Mobilization 1986-; Gov. Inter-American Development Bd & Caribbean Development Bank; Governor of Central Bank of Trinidad and Tobago; ***honours and awards:*** Honorary Doctor of Law, University of Manitoba 1991; ***office address:*** Ministry of Finance, Eric Level 18 Williams Finance Building, Independence Square, Port of Spain, Trinidad and Tobago; ***URL:*** http://www.finance.gov.tt.

DORAN, Frank; British, Member of Parliament for Aberdeen North, House of Commons; ***born:*** 13 April 1949; ***education:*** Dundee Univ., LL.B., Law, 1975; ***party:*** Labour Party, 1973-6; ***political career:*** Frontbench Spokesman on Oil & Gas; MP, Aberdeen South, 1987-92, Aberdeen Central, 1997-2005, Aberdeen North, 2005-; Sec., Trade Union Gp. of Labour MPs; Sec., APG Fisheries; ***professional career:*** Solicitor, 1977-88; ***committees:*** Culture, Media and Sport, 2001-05; Finance and Services, 2005-10; Administration, 2005-10; Liaison, 2005-10; Works of Art, 2011-; ***office address:*** House of Commons, London, SW1A 0AA, United Kingdom; ***phone:*** +44 (0)20 7219 3481; ***e-mail:*** doranf@parliament.uk.

DORDAIN, Jean-Jaques; Director-General, European Space Agency (ESA); ***professional career:*** French National Aerospace Study and Research Agency (ONERA); ESA, 1986-; Dir.-Gen., ESA, 1993-; Exec. Sec., Evaluation Cttee., Japanese Space Agency, 1997; ***honours and awards:*** French Legion of Honour; Ordre National du Mérite; ***office address:*** European Space Agency (ESA), 8-10 rue Mario Nikis, 75738 Paris Cedex 15, France; ***phone:*** +33 (0)1 53 69 71 55; ***fax:*** +33 (0)1 53 69 76 90; ***URL:*** http://www.esa.int.

DOREY, Greg; Ambassador, British Embassy in Ethiopia; ***education:*** MA, Oxford Univ. UK; ***professional career:*** Dep. Head of Mission, British Consulate General in Hong Kong, 2000-04; Amb. to Hungary 2007-12; Amb. to Ethiopia, 2012-; ***office address:*** British Embassy, Fikre Mariam Abatechan Street, Addis Ababa, Ethiopia; ***phone:*** +251 (0)1 612354; ***fax:*** +251 (0)1 610588; ***URL:*** http://www.britishembassy.hu.

DORRELL, Rt. Hon. Stephen James, MP; British, Member of Parliament for Charnwood, House of Commons; ***born:*** 1952; ***education:*** Uppingham Sch., Brasenose Coll., Oxford; ***political career:*** MP, Loughborough, 1979-97; Asst. Whip, 1987-90; Under-Sec. of State for Health, 1990-92; Financial Sec. to the Treas., 1992; Sec. of State for Nat. Heritage, 1994-95; Sec. of State for Health, 1995-97; Opp. Front Bench Spokesman for Education & Employment, 1997-98; MP, Charnwood, 1997-; ***professional career:*** Dir. of Industrial Clothing Co., 1975-87; ***committees:*** Joint Committee on Consolidation, Bills, 2005-; Health, 2010-; Liaison, 2010-; ***office address:*** House of Commons, London, SW1A 0AA, United Kingdom; ***phone:*** +44 (0)20 7219 4472; ***e-mail:*** info@stephendorrell.org.uk; ***URL:*** http://www.stephendorrell.org.uk.

DORRIES, Nadine; MP for Mid Bedfordshire, House of Commons; ***children:*** 3; ***party:*** Conservative; ***political career:*** Advisor to Shadow Home Sec. & Shadow Chancellor of the Exchequer, Oliver Letwin; MP for Mid Bedfordshire, 2005-; ***professional career:*** Nurse; Dir., BUPA; ***committees:*** Education and Skills, 2005-06; Science and Technology, 2007; Innovation, Universities, Science and Technology, 2007-10; Energy and Climate Change, 2009-10; Health, 2010-11; Chairmen's Panel/Panel of Chairs, 2010-; ***office address:*** House of Commons, London, SW1P 0AA, United Kingdom; ***e-mail:*** dorriesn@parliament.uk.

DOS SANTOS, President José Eduardo; Angolan, President, Republic of Angola; ***born:*** 28 August 1942, Luanda, Angola; ***married:*** Ana Paula dos Santos; ***education:*** Graduate in Petrochemical Engineering Oil and Gas, Inst. of Baku, (then in) Russia, 1969; ***political career:*** First Representative of Movimento Popular de Libertacao de Angola (MPLA), Brazzaville, 1963; Mem., Prov. Readjustment Cttee., Northern Front, 1974; Mem., MPLA Central Cttee., and Political Bureau, 1974; Minister of Foreign Affairs, Angola, 1975; First Dep. Prime Minister, 1975-78; Planning Minister and Head of National Planning Commission, 1978-79; President of Angola, 1979-; President and Prime Minister, 1999-2002; President, 2002-; ***professional career:*** Military course in telecommunications, USSR 1969-70; Returned to Angola, joined in war against Portugal 1970-73; Second in Command, Telecommunications Services MPLA Second Politico-Military Region, Cabinda; ***office address:*** Office of the President, Protocolo de Estado, Futungo de Belas, Luanda, Angola; ***phone:*** +244 (0)2 350409; ***URL:*** http://www.angola.org.

DOUGHTY, Stephen; MP for Cardiff South and Penarth, British Government; ***education:*** Oxford Univ.; St Andrews Univ.; ***political career:*** MP for Cardiff South and Penarth, Nov. 2012-; ***professional career:*** Head of Oxfam Cymru; ***office address:*** House of Commons, London, SW1A 0AA, United Kingdom; ***phone:*** +44 (0)20 7219 3000.

DOUGLAS, Hon. Dr Denzil; Prime Minister, Government of St. Kitts and Nevis; ***born:*** 1953; ***education:*** B.Sc., 1977; medical degree; ***party:*** Leader, St Kitts and Nevis Labour Party, 1989-; ***political career:*** Dep. Chmn., St Kitts-Nevis Labour Party, 1987-89, Leader, 1989-; MP, 1989 and Leader of the Opposition; Minister of Foreign Affairs, -2002; Prime Minister, 1995-; also currently (2013) has the portfolio of: Minister of Finance, Sustainable Development, Human Resources Development, Constituencies, and Social Security; ***professional career:*** Private medical practice; ***office address:*** Office of the Prime Minister, Government Headquarters, Basseterre, St. Kitts and Nevis; ***phone:*** +1 869 465 0299; ***fax:*** +1 869 465 1001.

DOWD, Jim; Member of Parliament for Lewisham West and Penge, House of Commons; ***party:*** Labour Party; ***political career:*** MP, Lewisham, 1992-2010, Lewisham and Penge, 2010-; ***committees:*** Health, 2001-10; Science and Technology, 2012-; ***office address:*** House of Commons, London, SW1A 0AA, United Kingdom; ***phone:*** +44 (0)20 7219 4617; ***e-mail:*** dowdj@parliament.uk.

DOYLE, Gemma; MP for West Dunbartonshire, House of Commons; ***party:*** Labour; ***political career:*** MP for West Dunbartonshire, May 2010-; Shadow Minister, Defence, Oct. 2010-; ***committees:*** Energy and Climate Change Select Cttee., 2010; Administration, 2010; Armed Forces Bill, 2011; ***office address:*** House of Commons, London, SW1A 0AA, United Kingdom; ***phone:*** +44 (0)20 7219 3000; ***e-mail:*** gemma.doyle.mp@parliament.uk.

DOYLE, Norman E.; Canadian, Senator, Canadian Senate; ***born:*** 11 November 1945; ***political career:*** Parly. Asst. to A. Brian Pickford, 1981-82, to Minister for Cmn., 1982-84, to Minister of Municipal Affairs, 1984-87, to Minister of Transport, 1987-89, to Minister of Labour, 1989; Opp. Parly. Whip, 1989-93; Opp. Critic on Health and Environment and Lands, 1989-93; Dep. PC Party Whip, 1997; Party Critic, Citizenship and Immigration, 1997-2000; MP for St.John's East, 1997-2008; Senator, 2012-; ***office address:*** Canadian Senate, Senate Building, 111 Wellington Street, Ottawa, ON K1A 0A4, Canada.

DOYLE-PRICE, Jackie; MP for Thurrock, UK Government; ***party:*** Conservative; ***political career:*** MP for Thurrock, May 2010-; ***committees:*** Public Accounts Select Cttee., 2010-; ***office address:*** House of Commons, London, SW1A 0AA, United Kingdom; ***phone:*** +44 (0)20 7219 3000; ***e-mail:*** jackie.doyleprice.mp@parliament.uk.

DRAGHI, Prof. Mario; President, European Central Bank; ***born:*** 3 September 1947, Rome, Italy; ***education:*** Univ. La Sapienza, Rome, Econ., 1970; MIT, Ph.D. Econ.; ***professional career:*** Prof.of Economics, Univ. of Florence, 1981-91; Exec. Dir., World Bank, 1984-90; Economic Advisor, Banca d'Italia, 1990; Dir. Gen., Treasury, 1991-2001; Visiting Fellow, Inst. of Politics, John F. Kennedy School of Govt., Harvard, 2001; Vice Pres. & MD and Mem. of Exec. Cttee., Goldman Sachs Int., 2004-05; Governor, Banca d'Italia, 2006-11; Pres., ECB, 2011-; ***trusteeships:*** Princeton Institute for Advanced Study; the Brookings Institution; ***publications:*** Produttività del lavoro, salari reali, e occupazione (Collana di economia:Sezione 4; 17) 1979; Public Debt Management: Theory & History (co-author) 1990; Transparency, Risk Management and International Financial Fragility: Geneva Reports on the World Economy 4 (co-author) 2004; ***office address:*** European Central Bank, Kaiserstrasse 29, 60311 Frankfurt am Main, Germany; ***URL:*** http://www.ecb.int/.

DRAGNEA, Liviu Nicolae; Vice Prime Minister, Minister of Regional Development and Public Administration, Romanian Government; ***born:*** 1962; ***political career:*** Chmn., Teleorman County Council; Gen. Sec., PSD, 2010-; Minister of Administration & Interior, Emil Bloc cabinet, 2009; Vice Prime Minister, Minister of Regional Development and Public Administration; ***professional career:*** Engineer; ***office address:*** Chamber of Deputies, Palatul Parlamentului, St. Izvor 2-4, Sector 5, 050563 Bucharest, Romania.

BIOGRAPHIES

DRAKE OF SHENE, Baroness Jeannie; Member, House of Lords; ***party:*** Labour; ***political career:*** Mem. House of Lords 2010-; ***professional career:*** Commissioner, Equal Opportunities Commission, 2000-07; Board Mm., Sector Skills Development Agency 2001-08; Mem.,Pensions Commission 2002-06; Commissioner, Equal and Human Rights Commission 2006-09; Governor, Pensions Policy Institute; ***office address:*** House of Lords, London, SW1A 0PW, United Kingdom; ***phone:*** +44 (0)20 7219 3000; ***fax:*** +44 (0)20 7219 5979; ***URL:*** http://www.parliament.uk.

DRAX, Richard; MP for South Dorset, UK Government; ***party:*** Conservative; ***political career:*** MP for South Dorset, May 2010-; ***professional career:*** Soldier; Journalist; ***committees:*** Environment, Food and Rural Affairs, 2010-; ***office address:*** House of Commons, London, SW1A 0AA, United Kingdom; ***phone:*** +44 (0)20 7219 3000; ***e-mail:*** richard.drax.mp@parliament.uk.

DREYER, Malu; Minister President, Rhineland-Palatinate; ***born:*** 1961; ***education:*** Univ. of Mainz, law; ***political career:*** Minister of Social Affairs, Labour, Health & Demography, 2002-12; Minister President, Rhineland-Palatinate, 2013-; ***professional career:*** law; judge; prosecutor; ***office address:*** Office of the Minister-President, Staatskanzlei Rheinland-Pflaz, Postfach 3880, 550238 Mainz, Germany; ***URL:*** http://www.rlp.de.

DROMEY, Jack; MP for Birmingham Erdington, House of Commons; ***married:*** Harriet Harman; ***public role of spouse:*** MP for Camberwell and Peckham, Acting Leader, Labour Party; ***party:*** Labour; ***political career:*** Treasurer of the Labour Party; MP for Birmingham Erdington, May 2010-; Shadow Minister, Communities and Local Government, Oct. 2010-; ***professional career:*** Dep. Gen. Sec., Transport and General Workers Union; ***committees:*** Business, Innovation and Skills, 2010-11; Regulatory Reform, 2010-; ***office address:*** House of Commons, London, SW1A 0AA, United Kingdom; ***phone:*** +44 (0)20 7219 3000; ***URL:*** http://www.parliament.uk.

DRUMMOND, Roderick; High Commissioner to Fiji, British High Commission; ***professional career:*** joined FCO, 1985; Postings in Algeria, Jordan, Syria, Qatar& Saudi Arabia; Dep. Head of Mission, Saudi Arabia, 2009-13; British High Commissioner to Fiji, 2013-; ***office address:*** British High Commission in Fiji, KPMG House, Rue Pasteur, Port Vila, Vanuatu.

D'SOUZA, Baroness Frances, CMG; Member, House of Lords; ***born:*** 18 April 1944, Colwyn Bay, UK; ***married:*** Martin Griffiths, 1985 (Div'd); Stanislaus D'Souza, re-married 2003; ***children:*** Christa Clare (F), Heloise (F); ***education:*** St Mary's Sch. Princethorpe; BSc., Univ. Coll. London; D.Phil., Lady Margaret Hall, Oxford; ***party:*** Labour Party, 1980-2004; ***political career:*** House of Lords, 2004-; Elected Convenor of the Independent Crossbench Peers, 2007-; ***professional career:*** Lecturer; Research Dir.; Human Rights Consultant; ***committees:*** APPG., Zimbabwe, Afghanistan; sat on all major Select Cttees. including: Admin. & Works; Home; Liaison; Privileges; Procedure; Security Jt. Cttee.; Selection; ***trusteeships:*** Zimbiala Trust; ***honours and awards:*** CMG, 1998; Appointed Privy Councillor, July 2009; ***office address:*** House of Lords, London, SW1A 0PW, United Kingdom; ***phone:*** +44 (0)20 7219 8308; ***e-mail:*** dsouzaf@parliament.uk.

DUBESTER, Ernest; Chairman, Federal Labor Relations Authority; ***education:*** Boston College; Catholic Univ. of American School of Law; Georgetown Univ. Law Center; ***professional career:*** National Labor Relations Boarrd; attorney, Highsaw & Mahoney; legislative counsel, AFL-CIO; Mem., Federal Labor Relations Authority, 2009-13, Chmn., 2013-; ***office address:*** ErnestFederal Labor Relations Authority (FLRA), 607 14th Street, NW, Washington, DC 20424-0001, USA; ***URL:*** http://www.flra.gov/index.html.

DUCHESNE, Hon. Pierre; Lieutenant Governor, Government of Quebec; ***born:*** 1940; ***education:*** Chicoutimi Seminary; Univ. Laval, law; ***political career:*** Mem., National Assembly of Québec, 1974-2001, Gen. Sec., 984; Special Advisor to the National Assembly, 2001-03; Lieutenant Governor, 2007-; ***professional career:*** notary; ***office address:*** Lieutenant Governor's Office, 1050 des Parlementaires, Quebec, PQ G1A 1A1, Canada.

DUDDRIDGE, James, MP; MP for Rochford and Southend East, House of Commons; ***born:*** 1971; ***party:*** Conservative; ***political career:*** MP for Rochford and Southend East, 2005-; Opp. Whip, 2008-10; Lord Commissioner and Government Whip, 2010-; ***office address:*** House of Commons, London, SW1P 0AA, United Kingdom.

DUGHER, Michael, MP; MP for Barnsley East, House of Commons; ***party:*** Labour; ***political career:*** MP for Barnsley East, May 2010-; Shadow Minister, Defence Equipment, Support and Technology, 2010-11; PPS to the Leader of the Opposition, Ed Miliband, May-Oct. 2011; Shadow Minister without Portfolio (Cabinet Office), Oct. 2011-; VIce-Chair of the Labour Party, 2012-; ***committees:*** Public Administration Select Cttee., 2010; ***office address:*** House of Commons, London, SW1A 0AA, United Kingdom; ***phone:*** +44 (0)20 7219 7006; ***e-mail:*** michael.dugher.mp@parliament.uk.

DUNCAN, Rt. Hon. Alan; Minister of State, Department for International Development, UK Government; ***born:*** 1957; ***education:*** Beechwood Park Sch.; Merchant Taylors' Sch.; St John's Coll., Oxford; Pres., Oxford Union, 1979; Kennedy Scholar, Harvard Univ; ***party:*** Conservative Party; ***political career:*** MP, Rutland and Melton, 1992-; PPS to Rt. Hon. Sir Brian Mawhinney MP, 1995-1997; Vice-Chmn. of Conservative Party; Parly. Political Sec. to Rt. Hon. William Hague, 1997-98; Opposition Front Bench Spokesman for Health, 1998-99; Opposition front Bench Spokesman for Trade and Industry, 1999-2001; Shadow Minister for Foreign Affairs, 2001-2003; Shadow Sec. of State for Constitutional Affairs, 2003-05; Shadow Sec. of State for Transport, 2005; Shadow Sec. of State for Trade Industry and Energy, 2005-07; Shadow Sec. of State for Business, Enterprise and Regulatory Reform, 2007-09; Shadow Leader of the House of Commons, Jan.-Aug. 2009; Minister of State, Dept. for International Development, 2010-; ***memberships:*** "No Turning Back" group; '92' Group of Conservative MPs; ***professional career:*** Shell International Petroleum and oil trader; Marc Rich & Co., 1982-88; Visiting Fellow, St. Antony's Coll. Oxford, 2002-03; ***publications:*** Saturn's Children-How the State Devours Liberty, Prosperity and Virtue, co-author, Dominic Hobson, 1995; Written or Co-written CPC pamphlets on the welfare state, privatisation, budget policy; An end to illusions, 1993; ***recreations:*** fishing, shooting, skiing, water skiing, travel; ***office address:*** House of Commons, London, SW1A 0AA, United Kingdom; ***phone:*** +44 (0)20 7219 5204; ***e-mail:*** duncana@parliament.uk; ***URL:*** http://alanduncan.org.uk.

DUNCAN, Arne ; Secretary of Education, US Government; ***born:*** 6 November 1964; ***education:*** Univ. of Chicago Laboratory Schools; Harvard, Sociology, 1987; ***political career:*** US Sec. of Education, 2009-; ***professional career:*** Basketball player, Eastside Spectres, Nat. Basketball League, Australia; Dir., Ariel Education Initiative, Chicago, 1992-98; Chicago Public Schools, 1998-08, Dep. Chief of Staff to Schools CEO, 1999-2001, CEO, 2001-08; ***honours and awards:*** Hon. Dr. of Laws, Lake Forest College, 2003; ***office address:*** Department of Education, 400 Maryland Ave., SW, Washington, DC 20202-0498, USA; ***phone:*** +1 202 401 2000; ***fax:*** +1 202 401 0689; ***e-mail:*** customerservice@inet.ed.gov; ***URL:*** http://www.ed.gov/index.jsp.

DUNCAN, Daniel Kublan; Ivorian, Prime Minister, Ivorian Government; ***born:*** 1943; ***political career:*** Office of the Prime Minister, 1990-93; Prime Minister and Minister of Planning and Industrial Development, 119-99; Minister of Foreign Affairs, 2011-12; Prime Minister, Minister of Economy and Finance, 2012-; ***professional career:*** IMF, Washington DC, 1973;BCEAO; ***office address:*** Office of the Prime Minister, 01 BP 1533, Abidjan 01, Côte d'Ivoire; ***phone:*** +225 20 22 0020; ***e-mail:*** pm@primature.gov.ci; ***URL:*** http://www.primature.gov.ci.

DUNCAN SMITH, Rt Hon. Iain; British, Secretary of State for Work and Pensions, UK Government; ***born:*** 9 April 1954, Edinburgh; ***married:*** Elizabeth Wynn Duncan Smith (née Fremantle), 1982; ***political career:*** Contested Bradford West, 1987; MP for Chingford, 1992, Chingford and Woodford Green, 1997-; Shadow Sec. of State for Social Security, 1997-99; Shadow Sec. of State for Defence, 1999-2001; Leader of the Conservative Party, Sept. 2001-Oct. 2003; Secretary of State for Work and Pensions, 2010-; ***professional career:*** Scots Guard Officer; GEC-Marconi; Dir., Property Company; Publishing Dir., Jane's Information Gp.; ***committees:*** Standards in Public Life (Nolan) Select Cttee., 1995-97; Mem., Admin. Select Cttee., 1993-97; Mem., Health Select Cttee., 1993-95; Sec., Conservative Back Bench Foreign and Cmmw. Affairs Cttee., 1992-97; ***publications:*** Five Years and Counting...Britain and Europe's Growing Vunerability to Missile Attack, Game, Set and Match; Who Benefits; Facing the Future; 1994 and Beyond; A Response to Chancellor Kohl; ***recreations:*** rugby, cricket, painting, fishing, family; ***office address:*** House of Commons, London, SW1A 0AA, United Kingdom; ***phone:*** +44 (0)20 7219 2667; ***e-mail:*** hcinfo@parliament.uk.

DUNDERDALE, Kathy; Premier, Government of Newfoundland and Labrador; ***married:*** Peter; ***political career:*** Dep. Mayor, Burin; elected Pres., Newfoundland and Labrador Fed. of Municipalities (NLFM); served as Dir., Canadian Fed. of Municipalities; past pres., PC Party, Newfoundland and Labrador; Minister of Industry, Trade and Rural Development, Minister responsible for Rural Secretariat, 2003-07; Minister of Natural Resources. 2007; Deputy Premier, 2009-10, Premier, 2010-; ***memberships:*** past Chair, Burin Peninsula Roman Catholic School Bd.; ***professional career:*** volunteer, Canadian Paraplegic Assn., the Assn. for Community Living, the Community Alliance for Better Solutions, the Coaltion against violence; ***honours and awards:*** Hon. mem., NLFM; ***office address:*** Office of the Premier, St. John's, NF, Canada; ***phone:*** +1 709 729 3570; ***e-mail:*** premier@gov.nf.ca; ***URL:*** http://www.premier.gov.nl.ca/premier.

DUNNE, Philip; MP for Ludlow, House of Commons; ***party:*** Conservative; ***political career:*** Local Councillor, 2001-07; MP for Ludlow, 2005-; Opposition Whip, 2008-10; Dep. Chmn., Conservative Party, 2008-10; Assistant Government Whip, 2010-12; Parly. Under-Sec. of State, Ministry of Defence, 2012-; ***professional career:*** Farmer; Investment Banker, 1980-2001; co-founder & chmn., Ottakar's plc, 1988-2006; ***office address:*** House of Commons, London, SW1P 0AA, United Kingdom; ***phone:*** +44 (0)20 7291 2388.

DURBIN, Richard J.; Senator for Illinois, US Senate; ***born:*** 21 November 1944, East St. Louis, Illinois, USA; ***parents:*** William Durbin and Ann Durbin (née Kutkin); ***married:*** Loretta Durbin (née Schaefer); ***education:*** St. Louis Univ.; Georgetown Univ., Washington D.C., BS, 1966, JD, 1969; ***party:*** Democrat; ***political career:*** US House of Representatives, representing the 20th Congressional District of Illinois, 1982-96; US Senator for Illinois, 1996-; Assistant Minority Leader and Democratic Whip 2004-Jan. 2007; Assist. Majority Leader and Democratic Whip, 2007-; ***professional career:*** Staff Attorney/legislator, Illinois State Senate; Practitioner of Law; ***committees:*** Judiciary Cttee.; Governmental Affairs Cttee.; Budget Cttee.; Appropriations; Select Cttee. on Intelligence; ***honours and awards:*** Hon. degrees from Millikin Univ. 1994, Lincoln Coll. 1997; "Friend of Agriculture" Award, Illinois Farm Bureau, 2000; ***office address:*** US Senate, 332 Dirksen Senate Office Building, Washington, DC 20510, USA; ***phone:*** +1 202 224 2152; ***fax:*** +1 202 224 2262; ***URL:*** http://www.durbin.senate.gov/.

DURKAN, Mark; MP for Foyle, House of Commons; ***party:*** Social Democratic and Labour Party; ***political career:*** Mem. for Foyle, Northern Ireland Assembly, 1998-2010; Minister of Finance and Personnel, 2000-2001; Dep. First Minister, 2001-02 (NI Assembly suspended); Leader SDLP, 2001-10; MP for Foyle, 2005-; ***office address:*** 23 Bishop Street, Derry, BT48 6PR, Northern Ireland; ***phone:*** +44 (0)2871 360700.

DUVAL, Charles Gaëtan Xavier-Luc; Deputy Prime Minister, Government of Mauritius; ***political career:*** Minister of Industry, Commerce, Corporate Affairs and Financial Services, 2000; Dep. Prime Minister, Minister of Tourism, Leisure and External Communications, 2005-10; Dep. Prime Minister, Minister of Social Integration and Economic Empowerment, 2010-; ***office address:*** Office of the Prime Minister, Independence Street, Port Louis, Mauritius; ***phone:*** +230 207 9595.

E

EACHO III, H.E. William C.; Ambassador, US Embassy in Austria; ***education:*** Graduated Magna Cum Laude, Duke Univ., Durham, North Carolina, (Law and Economy); MBA, with Distinction, Harvard Business School, 1979; ***professional career:*** Business Manager and Entrepreneur; CEO of Carlton Capital Group; Amb. to Austria, 2009-; ***office address:*** US Embassy, Boltzmanngasse 16, A-1090 Vienna, Austria; ***phone:*** +43 (0)1 31339; ***fax:*** +43 (0)1 310 06820; ***e-mail:*** embassy@usembassy.at; ***URL:*** http://vienna.usembassy.gov.

EAGLE, Angela; British, Shadow Leader of the House of Commons, House of Commons; ***born:*** 17 February 1961; ***education:*** St. John's Coll., Oxford Univ., BA (Hons), Philosophy, Politics and Econs.; ***party:*** Labour Party, 1978-; ***political career:*** Mem., Nat. Exec. Women's Cttee.; Chwn., Nat. Conference of Labour Women, 1991; MP, Wallasey, 1992-; Opp. Whip, 1996-97; Parly. Under-Sec. of State, Dept. of the Environment, 1997-98; PPS, Department of Social Security, 1998-2001, Home Office 2001-02; Exchequer Secretary, 2007-09; Minister of State, Department for Work and Pensions, 2009-10; Shadow Minister for Treasury, May-Sept. 2010; Shadow Chief Secretary to the Treasury, Oct. 2010-11; Shadow Leader of the House of Commons, Oct. 2011-; ***interests:*** economy, equal opportunities, employment; ***office address:*** House of Commons, London, SW1A 0AA, United Kingdom; ***phone:*** +44 (0)20 7219 3000; ***e-mail:*** eaglea@parliament.uk; ***URL:*** http://www.angelaeagle.labour.co.uk.

EAGLE, Maria; British, Shadow Secretary of State for Transport, House of Commons; ***born:*** 17 February 1961; ***education:*** Pembroke Coll., Oxford, BA (Hons), Philosophy, Politics and Econs.; Lancaster Gate Coll. of Law, CPE and Law Soc. Finals; ***party:*** Labour Party; ***political career:*** MP, Liverpool Garston, 1997-2010, Garston & Halewood, 2010-; Parly. Sec., Dept. of Educ. and Skills, 2005-06; Parly. Under Sec. of State, Northern Ireland Office 2006-08; Parly. Under Sec. of State, Ministry of Justice, Oct. 2008-09; Minister of State, Department of Justice, 2009-10; Shadow Solicitor General, 2010; Shadow Minister for Justice, 2010; Shadow Secretary of State for Transport, Oct. 2010-; ***interests:*** housing, economy, transport; ***professional career:*** Solicitor; ***office address:*** House of Commons, London, SW1A 0AA, United Kingdom; ***phone:*** +44 (0)20 7219 3000; ***e-mail:*** hcinfo@parliament.uk.

EAMES, Lord; Member, House of Lords; ***born:*** 27 April 1937, Belfast; ***parents:*** Rev. W.E. Eames and Mary Eames (née Alexander); ***married:*** Christine Eames (née Daly), June 1966; ***children:*** Niall (M), Michael (M); ***public role of spouse:*** Human Rights Commissioner for Northern Ireland; ***education:*** Methodist College, Belfast; Belfast Royal Academy; The Queen's Univ., Belfast; Trinity College, Dublin, LL.B, Ph.D; ***political career:*** Mem., House of Lords; ***professional career:*** Domestic Chaplain to Bishop of Down and Dromore, 1970-72; Examining Chaplain to Bishop of Down and Dromore, 1973-75; Elected Bishop of Derry and Raphoe by Electoral College, 1975; Consecrated in Armagh Cathedral, 1975; Bishop of Down and Dromore, 1980; Primate of All Ireland and Metropolitan; ***honours and awards:*** Eight Honorary Doctorates from UK, Irish and USA universities; Freeman of the City of London; Honorary Bencher, Lincoln's Inn; ***publications:*** The Quiet Revolution, the Disestablishment of the Church of Ireland, 1970; Through Suffering, 1973; Chains to be Broken, 1992; ***clubs:*** Athenaeum; ***recreations:*** sport, reading and travel; ***office address:*** House of Lords, London, SW1 0AA, United Kingdom.

EATON, Dame Margaret, OBE; Member, House of Lords; ***political career:*** Mem., House of Lords, 2010-; ***professional career:*** Chair., Local Government Association; ***office address:*** House of Lords, London, SW1A 0PW, United Kingdom; ***phone:*** +44 (0)20 7219 3000; ***fax:*** +44 (0)20 7219 5979; ***URL:*** http://www.parliament.uk.

EDINBURGH, Duke of, HRH Prince Philip, KG, KT, OM, GBE; British; ***born:*** 10 June 1921, Corfu, Greece; ***parents:*** HRH Prince Andrew of Greece and Denmark (dec'd) and HSH Princess Alice of Battenberg (dec'd); ***married:*** Queen Elizabeth II, 1947; ***children:*** Prince Andrew (M), Prince Edward (M), Prince Charles (M), Princess Anne (F); ***education:*** Cheam Sch.; Salem Baden; Gordonstoun; RN Coll., Dartmouth; ***political career:*** Mem., House of Lords, 1947-99; ***professional career:*** Royal Navy, 1939-51; Personal ADC to HM King George VI, 1948-52; Admiral of the Fleet, Field-Marshal and Marshal of the RAF, 1953; Captain General, Royal Marines; PC of Canada, 1957; Colonel, Grenadier Guards, 1975; Chancellor of Univs. of Edinburgh, 1952-, Cambridge, 1977-, Wales, 1948-76, Salford, 1967-91; Pres., Patron or Trustee of numerous orgs including: Nat. Playing Fields Assn., Nat. Maritime Museum, London Youth (The Federation of London Youth Clubs), Automobile Assn., Royal Yachting Assn., 1948-; Variety Clubs Int., City and Guilds of London Inst., Central Cncl. of Physical Recreation, 1951-; Design Cncl., Royal Soc. of Arts, English Speaking Union of the Commonwealth, Outward Bound Trust, Trinity House, 1952; Royal College of Art, Commonwealth Games Federation (until 1990); Duke of Edinburgh's Award Scheme and Duke of Edinburgh's Commonwealth Study Conferences, 1956-; Royal Agricultural Soc. of the Commonwealth, 1958-; Voluntary Service Overseas, World Wildlife Fund (UK) (until 1982); Int. Equestrian Federation, 1964-86; Maritime Trust, 1974-, British Commonwealth Ex-Services League, 1974-; Royal Acad. of Engineering, 1976-; Pres., World Wide Fund for Nature, WWF International, 1976-; Pres., Emeritus, 1997-; ***honours and awards:*** KG; KT; OM; GBE; AC; QSO; FRS; ***publications:*** Author of twelve publications, 1957-94; ***office address:*** Buckingham Palace, London, SW1A 1AA, United Kingdom.

EDMISTON, Lord Robert; Member, House of Lords; ***party:*** Conservative Party; ***political career:*** Mem., House of Lords, 2011-; ***professional career:*** Finance Dir., Jensen Motors; Founder and Chmn., IM Group, IM Properties; ***office address:*** House of Lords, London, SW1A 0PW, United Kingdom; ***phone:*** +44 (0)20 7219 3000.

EDWARDS, Jonathan; MP for Carmarthen East and Dinefwr, House of Commons; ***party:*** Plaid Cymru; ***political career:*** Sheriff of Carmarthen Town; MP for Carmarthen East and Dinefwr, May 2010-; Plaid Cymru Spokesperson for: Business, Innovation and Skills 2010-, Communities and Local Gov., 2010-, Culture, Olympics, Media and Sport 2010-, Transport 2010-, Treasury 2010-; ***committees:*** Welsh Affairs Select Cttee., 2010-; ***office address:*** House of Commons, London, SW1A 0AA, United Kingdom; ***phone:*** +44 (0)20 7219 3000; ***e-mail:*** jonathan.edwards.mp@parliament.uk.

EFENDIYEV, Elchin Ilyas Oglu; Deputy Prime Minister, Government of Azerbaijan; ***born:*** 13 May 1943, Baku; ***parents:*** Ilyas Efendiyev and Tovsiya Efendiyeva; ***married:*** Nushaba Efendiyeva (née Aliyeva), 1972; ***children:*** Gunay (F), Humay (F), Aysu (F); ***public role of spouse:*** Teacher in special music school, named after Bul-Bul; ***languages:*** English, Russian; ***education:*** Baku State Univ., Faculty of Philology, 1960-65; Nizami's Research Inst., Post-Grad studentship, 1967-70; ***political career:*** Dep. of Supreme Council of the Azerbaijan Socialist Republic, 1988; Dep. Prime Minister, Republic of Azerbaijan, 1993-; ***interests:*** believer in peace, independence of Republic of Azerbaijan, democracy, human rights; ***memberships:*** Chmn., Veten Society - creating cultural relations with Azerbaijanis living abroad, 1987-; ***professional career:*** Sr. Scientific officer of Nizami's Research Inst. of Azerbaijan Academy of Sciences, 1969; Scientific Sec. of the Research Inst. of Azerbaijan Academy of Sciences (both Inst. of Linguistics and Inst. of Literature and Language), 1972; Editorial; Bd. of the newspaper 'Edebiyyet ve injescnet' (Literature and Art); Dep. chief of the Bd. of the Union of Writers of Azerbaijan, 1975; Doctor of Philological Sciences, 1997, Professor, 1998; ***committees:*** Chmn., Cmn. on Minors Issues and the Protection of Rights; Chmn., Cmn. on the Adoption of Children; Chmn., State Cmn. on Using Official Language; Fuzuli Int. Award Cmn.; Chmn.,Society of Relations with Compatriots Abroad, 1987; ***trusteeships:*** Trusteeship to gymnasium No 41, Baku city; ***honours and awards:*** Lenin Komsomol's award for novels and short stories, 1982; 'Most Active Author' of newspaper Literaturnaya Gazeta, 1983; Honoured Artist of Azerbaijan, 1984; Order 'Znak Pocheta', 1986; Honour Khalq Yazichisi (People's Writer), 1997; Order 'Istiqhal' (Independence), 2003; ***publications:*** 3 novels, 83 stories and 300 essays and critical articles. Scriptwriter for 9 films and 10 stage plays. Translations of Moliere, Pirandello, R. Bradbury, I Asimov and others. Translations of classic Japanese poetry.; ***recreations:*** traveling; ***office address:*** Office of the Prime Minister, Lermontov St 68, AZ1066 Baku, Azerbaijan; ***phone:*** +994 (0)12 492 7728; ***fax:*** +994 (0)12 492 5273; ***e-mail:*** e.elchin@cabmin.gov.az.

EFFORD, Clive; British, Member of Parliament for Eltham, House of Commons; ***born:*** 10 July 1958; ***party:*** Labour Party; ***political career:*** Cllr., Greenwich; MP, Eltham, 1997-; Shadow Minister, Dept. of Home Affairs, 2011; Shadow Minister, Culture, Media and Sport, 2011-; ***professional career:*** Taxi driver, London; ***office address:*** House of Commons, London, SW1A 0AA, United Kingdom; ***phone:*** +44 (0)20 7219 3000; ***e-mail:*** hcinfo@parliament.uk.

EFREMOVA, Marija; Ambassador, Embassy of Macedonia in the UK; ***education:*** LLB, Faculty of Law, Univ. St. Cyril and Methodius, Skopje, 1986; MA, Int. Environmental Law, Italian Soc. for Int. Org., (SIOI), Rome, Italy, 2007; ***professional career:*** Minister Counselor, Embassy in Rome, Italy, 2002-06; Amb.to London, UK, 2008-; ***office address:*** Macedonian Embassy, Suites 2.1-2.2, Buckingham Court, 75/83 Buckingham Gate, London, SW1E 6PE, United Kingdom; ***phone:*** +44 (0)20 7976 0535; ***e-mail:*** info@macedonianembassy.org.uk; ***URL:*** http://www.macedonianembassy.org.uk .

EIDE, Espen Barth; Minister of Foreign Affairs, Government of Norway; ***born:*** 1 May 1964; ***education:*** Autononmous Univ. of Barcelona, Spain; MA, Political Science, Univ. of Oslo, Norway, 1998; ***political career:*** State Sec. Ministry of Defence, 2005-10; State Sec., Ministry of Foreign Affairs, 2010-11; Minister of Defence, 2011-12; Minister of Foreign Affairs, 2012-; ***office address:*** Ministry of Foreign Affairs, 7 juni plassen 1, PB 8114 Dep, 0032 Oslo, Norway; ***phone:*** +47 2224 3600; ***fax:*** +47 2224 9580; ***e-mail:*** post@mfa.no; ***URL:*** http://www.odin.dep.no/ud.

EISEN, Norman; Ambassador, US Embassy in the Czech Republic; ***education:*** BA (Hons), Brown Univ. USA, 1985; JD (Hons), Harvard Law School, 1991; ***professional career:*** Partner in law firm Zuckerman Spaeder; Special Counsel to the President for Ethics and Government Reform, 2009-11; Amb. to the Czech Republic, 2011-; ***office address:*** US Embassy, Trziste 15, 118 01 Prague 1, Czech Republic; ***phone:*** +420 2 5753 0663; ***e-mail:*** webmaster@usembassy.cz; ***URL:*** http://prague.usembassy.gov.

EK, Lena; Swedish, Minister of the Environment, Government of Sweden; ***born:*** 16 January 1958, Monsteras; ***party:*** Centerpartiet; mem., Bureau, Gp., the Alliance of Liberals and Democrats for Europe; ***political career:*** MEP, 2004-09; Minister of the Environment, 2011-; ***committees:*** mem., Cttee on Industry, Research and Energy; Sub., Cttee on Women's Rights and Gender Equality; Sub., Cttee on the Environment, Public Health and Food Safety; ***office address:*** Ministry of the Environment, Tegelbacken 2, 103 33 Stockholm, Sweden; ***phone:*** +46 (0)8 405 1000; ***URL:*** http://miljo.regeringen.se/english/english_index.htm.

EKANDJO, Jerry; Namibian, Minister for Youth, National Service, Sport & Culture, Namibian Government; ***born:*** 17 March 1947, Windhoek; ***married:*** Loide Ekandjo; ***children:*** Sam Shafiishuna Nujoma (M), Jacobine Kashinga (F), Kristofine Kawiitongonwa (F); ***education:*** Augustineum Coll., 1964-68; ***political career:*** Joined SWAPO, 1969; Branch Chmn., Party Office, Walvis Bay, 1970; Chmn., SWAPO Party Youth League, 1971, re-elected 1973 and 1983-86; arrested and imprisoned because of political activities, Jan.-Apr. 1973, and again Aug. 1973; released in 1981; SWAPO Party Sec. for Information and Publicity, 1987-88; SWAPO Party Field Mobilizer, 1988; Internal Leadership of SWAPO, 1989; SWAPO Party Dep. Head of Voters Registration, 1989; Constituent Assembly of the Rep. of Namibia, 1989-90; Dep. Min. of Regional and Local Govt. and Housing, 1990-95; Dep. Minister of Home Affairs, 1995; Minister of Home Affairs, 1995-04; Minister of Lands and Resettlement, 2004-07; Minister for Regional and Local Government, Housing and Rural Development, 2007-12; Minister of Youth, National Service, Sport & Culture, 2012-; ***professional career:*** Teacher, A.M.E. Community Sch., Gibeon, Namibia 1982-87; ***committees:*** Nat. Exec. Cttee. of the SWAPO Party 1983-89; Central Cttee. of the SWAPO Party Congress; ***office address:*** Ministry of Youth, National Service & Sport, Private Bag 13186, Windhoek, Namibia; ***phone:*** +264 61 293 3111.

EKER, Mehmet Medhi; Minister of Agriculture and Rural Affairs, Government of Turkey; ***born:*** 1956; ***education:*** Ankara Univ., Veterinary Medicine; MSc, Univ. of Aberdeen; Ankara Univ., Inst . of Health Sciences, Ph.D; ***political career:*** Minister of Agriculture and Rural Affairs, 2006-; ***office address:*** Ministry of Agriculture, Milli Mudafaa Cad, 20 Kizilay, Ankara, Turkey.

EL ARABY, Dr Nabil; Egyptian, Secretary General, League of Arab States; ***born:*** 1935; ***education:*** Cairo Univ., Law, 1955; New York Univ. Law School, LLM, JSD; ***political career:*** Minister of Foreign Affairs, 2011; ***professional career:*** Vice-Pres., UN General Assembly, 1993, 1994, 1997; Pres., Security Council, 1966; Amb., Dep. Perm. Rep. to the UN in New York, 1978-81; Amb. to India, 1981-83; Legal Adviser, MFA, 1976-78, 1983-87; Perm. Rep. of Egypt to the UN, Geneva, 1987-91; Perm. Rep. of Egypt to the UN, New York, 1991-99; Judge, Judicial tribunal, Org of Arab Petroleum Exporting Countries, 1990; Mem., Int. Law Commission of the UN, 1999-2001; Mem., ICJ, 2001-06; Dir., Cairo Regional Centre for International Commercial Arbitration, 2008-11; Sec.-Gen., League of Arab States, 2011-; ***office address:*** League of Arab States, PO Box 11642, Maidane Al-Tahrir, Cairo, Egypt; ***URL:*** http://www.lasportal.org.

EL-BADRI, Abdalla; Secretary General, OPEC; ***born:*** 1940, Libya; ***political career:*** Minister of Petroleum, 1990-92; Minister of Oil and Electricity, 1993-2000; Dep. PM, 2000-04; ***professional career:*** Esso; Board Mem., Umm al-Jawabi Oil Co.; Chmn., Waha Oil Co, 1980-83; Chmn., National Oil Corp., 1983-90, 2004-06; Sec.-Gen., OPEC, 2007-; ***office address:*** OPEC, 93 Obere Donaustrasse, A-1020 Vienna, Austria; ***URL:*** http://www.opec.org.

ELBEGDORJ, President Tsakhia; President, Government of Mongolia; ***political career:*** MP, 1990-; co-Leader, Democratic Union Coalition, 1996; Majority Leader, 1996-2000, PM, 1998; Prime Minister, 2004-06; President, 2009-; ***office address:*** State Palace, Sukhbaatar Square 1, Ulan Bator 12, Mongolia; ***e-mail:*** webmaster@presi.pmis.gov.mn; ***URL:*** http://pmis.gov.mn/president.

ELIAS, Edna; Commissioner, Nunavut; ***interests:*** education, Inuit culture and languages; ***professional career:*** teacher; principal, Jimmy Hikok Ilihakvik Primary School; mayor, Kugluktuk; Co-Chair, Northwest Territories Aboriginal Language Task Force; Director, Language Bureau of the Department of Culture and Employment; Supervisor, Family and Community Support Services, High Level, Alberta; worked in child and community development in the Northwest Territories; Nuktitut interpreter and translator; interpreter, Legislative Assembly of Nunavut; Aboriginal and Official Language services for the Government and Legislative Assembly of the Northwest Territories; founder, Edmonton Inuit Cultural Society; Commissioner of Nunavut, May 2010-; ***office address:*** Office of the Commissioner, Box 2379, Iqaluit, Canada; ***URL:*** http://www.commissioner.gov.nu.ca/.

ELIAS , Dame Sian; Chief Justice, Supreme Court of New Zealand; ***education:*** Univ. of Auckland, LLB (Hons); Stanford Univ., USA, JSM; ***professional career:*** admitted to the Bar, 1970; practicing lawyer, Auckland, 1972-; Law Cmnr., 1986-90; Queen's Counsel, 1988; High Court judge, 1995-99, Chief Justice, 1999-2004; Supreme Court Judge, 2004-; ***office address:*** Supreme Court, PO Box 61, Wellington, New Zealand; ***phone:*** +64 4 918 8222; ***fax:*** +64 4 914 3560; ***e-mail:*** supreme court@justice.govt.nz; ***URL:*** http://www.courtsofnz.govt.nz/.

ELIS-THOMAS, Lord, Baron Dafydd, Life Peer; British, Member, House of Lords; ***married:*** Mair Parry Jones; ***s:*** 3; ***public role of spouse:*** simultaneous translator, National Assembly for Wales; ***languages:*** English, Welsh; ***education:*** Univ. of Wales, Bangor, Ph.D., Literary History; Visiting Fellow at St Andrews; Fellow, Int. Centre for Intercultural Studies, Inst. of Education, London; ***party:*** Plaid Cymru (The Party of Wales); ***political career:*** Mem. of Parliament, Meirionnydd Nant Conwy, 1974-92; Pres., Plaid Cymru, 1985-92; Mem., House of Lords, 1992-; Assembly Mem., Meirionnydd Nant Conwy, 1999-2007; Presiding Officer, Nat. Assembly for Wales, 1999-; Privy Councillor, 2004-; Assembly Member, Dwyfor Meirionnydd (following boundary change), 2007-11; ***interests:*** environment; ***memberships:*** Welsh Arts Cncl.; Wales Film Cncl.; Welsh Film Board; BBC's General Consultative Cncl.; Active mem. of the Church in Wales; ***professional career:*** Welsh Studies Tutor, Coleg Harlech, 1971; Lecturer in various cultural and educational subjects, Univ. of Wales colleges, Bangor, Aberystwyth, Cardiff, and the Open Univ.; Chmn. of the Welsh Language Bd., 1993-99; Chair, Sgrin, the New Media Agency; Dir., Oriel Mostyn, the Nat. Botanical Gardens, and MFM Marcher; fmr. journalist and columnist; Pres., Univ. of Wales, Bangor; ***committees:*** HOL Select Cttee. on the European Communities; HOL Sub-Cttees. on the Environment, Consumer Affairs and Public Health; HOC Select and Legislative Cttees.on Education, the Arts, Broadcasting and the Environment; ***trusteeships:*** The Big Issue Foundation, Theatre Bara Caws; ***honours and awards:*** Life Peer, House of Lords, 1992; ***recreations:*** hill walking; ***office address:*** House of Lords, London, SW1A 0AA, United Kingdom; ***e-mail:*** elisthomasd@parliament.uk; dafydd.elis-thomas@wales.gov.uk.

ELIZABETH II, HM Queen of Great Britain and Northern Ireland and of Her other Realms and Territories; British, Queen, Great Britain and Northern Ireland and her Territories; ***born:*** 1926, London, UK; ***parents:*** HM King George VI (dec'd) and HM Queen Elizabeth The Queen Mother (dec'd); ***married:*** HRH Prince Philip, Duke of Edinburgh, 1947; ***children:*** Prince Edward (M), Prince Charles (M), Princess Anne (F), Prince Andrew (M); ***education:*** No.1 Mechanical Transport Training Centre, Aldershot, driving and maintenance course, qualified driver, 1945; ***memberships:*** Girl Guide, 1937, Patrol Leader, 1st Buckingham Palace Guide Co.; joined Sea Rangers, Chief Ranger of the British Empire Rangers, sr. branch of the Girl Guides Assn., 1946; ***professional career:*** Public duties include, 1st radio broadcast, 1940; accompanied the King and Queen on morale raising tours of the country, 1941; 1st official audience receiving Col. Prescott of the Grenadier Guards, 1942; appointed as Col. of Grenadier Guards, 1942; 1st acted as Counsellor of State, 1944; 1st public speech, Hackney, to Governors of the Queen Elizabeth Hosp. for Children, 1944; Nat. Service, Auxiliary Transport Service, 1945, registered as No. 230873 Second Subaltern; took the salute, Trooping the Colour ceremony, 1951; succeeded to the Throne after her father's death, 1952-, crowned 1953; ***office address:*** Private Office, Buckingham Palace, London, SW1A 1AA, United Kingdom.

ELLIOTT, Julie; MP for Sunderland Central, UK Government; ***party:*** Labour; ***political career:*** MP for Sunderland Central, May 2010-; PPS to Caroline Flint, 2010-; ***committees:*** European Scrutiny, 2010-; Business, Innovation and Skills,2011-; ***office address:*** House of Commons, London, SW1A 0AA, United Kingdom; ***phone:*** +44 (0)20 7219 3000; ***e-mail:*** julie.elliott.mp@parliament.uk.

ELLIS, Kate; Minister for Employment Participation and Childcare, Minister for the Status of Women, Government of Australia; ***political career:*** Member for Adelaide, South Australia, 2004-; Minister for Youth; Minister for Sport, 2007-; Minister for Early Childhood Education, Child Care and Youth, 2009-10; Minister for Employment Participation and Childcare, Minister for the Status of Women, 2010-; ***committees:*** Sec., ALP Caucus Cttee. on Economics, 2004-; Mem., ALP National Policy Cttee., 2005-; ***office address:*** Department of Education, Employment and Workplace Relations, GPO Box 9879, Canberra, ACT 2601, Australia; ***phone:*** +61 2 6121 6000; ***fax:*** +61 2 6121 7542; ***URL:*** http://www.deewr.gov.au.

ELLIS, Michael; MP for Northampton North, UK Government; ***party:*** Conservative; ***political career:*** Councillor, Northamptonshire County Council; MP for Northampton North, May 2010-; ***committees:*** Joint Cttee. on Statutory Instruments 2010-; Home Affairs, 2011-; Unopposed Bills (Panel), 2011-; ***office address:*** House of Commons, London, SW1A 0AA, United Kingdom; ***phone:*** +44 (0)20 7219 3000; ***e-mail:*** michael.ellis.mp@parliament.uk.

ELLISON, Jane; MP for Battersea, UK Government; ***party:*** Conservative; ***political career:*** MP for Battersea, May 2010-; ***committees:*** Business Select Cttee., 2010-; ***office address:*** House of Commons, London, SW1A 0AA, United Kingdom; ***phone:*** +44 (0)20 7219 3000; ***e-mail:*** jane.ellison.mp@parliament.uk.

ELLMAN, Louise; Member of Parliament for Liverpool Riverside, House of Commons; ***born:*** 14 November 1945, Manchester, UK; ***parents:*** Harold Rosenberg and Ann Rosenberg; ***married:*** Geoff Ellman, 16th July 1967; ***s:*** 1; ***d:*** 1; ***education:*** Univ. of Hull., BA (Hons); Univ. of York, M.Phil., Social Admin.; ***party:*** Labour Party and Co-operative Party; ***political career:*** Mem. Lancashire County Cncl. 1970-97, Leader, 1981-97; Leader, MP, Liverpool Riverside, 1997-; ***interests:*** transport, public services, Middle East, combating racism and anti-semitism regional policy; ***professional career:*** Counsellor, Open Univ.; further education lecturer; ***committees:*** Mem., Environment, Transport & Regional Affairs Select Cttee., 1997-2001; Transport Select Cttee., 2002-, Chair, 2008-; Liaison, 2008-; ***office address:*** House of Commons, London, SW1A 0AA, United Kingdom; ***phone:*** +44 (0)20 7219 3000; ***e-mail:*** ellmanl@parliament.uk; ***URL:*** http://www.epolitix.com/webminister/louise-ellman.

ELLWOOD, Tobias; MP for Bournemouth East, House of Commons; ***born:*** 1966; ***party:*** Conservative; ***political career:*** MP for Bournemouth East, 2005; Opposition Whip, 2005-07; Shadow Minister for Culture, Media and Sport, 2007-10; PPS; ***committees:*** Environmental Audit, 2005-06; Armed Forces Bill, 2011; ***office address:*** House of Commons, London, SW1P 0AA, United Kingdom; ***e-mail:*** tobias.ellwood.mp@parliament.uk.

ELPHICKE, Charlie; MP for Dover, UK Government; ***party:*** Conservative; ***political career:*** Councillor, London Borough of Lambeth Council, 1994-98; MP for Dover, May 2010-; ***committees:*** Public Administration Select Cttee., 2010-; Jt. Cttee. on Consolidation, 2010-; ***office address:*** House of Commons, London, SW1A 0AA, United Kingdom; ***phone:*** +44 (0)20 7219 3000; ***e-mail:*** charlie.elphicke.mp@parliament.uk.

ELRINGTON, Wilfred; Attorney General, Government of Belize; ***party:*** University of the West Indies; ***political career:*** Attorney-General, Minister of Foreign Affairs and Trade, 2008-10; Minister of Foreign Affairs and Foreign Trade, 2010-12; Attorney-General, Minister of Foreign Affairs and Trade, 2012-; ***professional career:*** Lawyer; Judge; ***office address:*** Office of the Attorney General, Ground Floor, East Block Building, Belmopan, Belize; ***phone:*** +501 822 2504; ***fax:*** +501 822 3390; ***e-mail:*** access@btl.net; ***URL:*** http://www.belizelaw.org.

ELTON, Lord, 2nd Baron. Rodney, TD; British, Member of the House of Lords; ***born:*** 1930; ***married:*** Anne Francis Tilney, 1958 (separated 1979); (Susan) Richenda (née Gurney), 1979; ***s:*** 1; ***d:*** 3; ***education:*** Eton College; New College Oxford; ***political career:*** Contested Loughborough Constituency as Cons. candidate in General Elections of 1966 and 1970; Mem. of the Boyd Comm. to evaluate the Elections in Rhodesia 1979; Succeeded Father, Godfrey Ist Baron Elton of Headington 1973; Opposition Whip, House of Lords 1974-77 and Spokesman 1977-79; Parly. Under-Secy. of State for Northern Ireland 1979-81; DHSS 1981-82; Home Office 1982-84; Minister of State, Home Office 1984-85; Dept. of Environment 1985-86; Dep chmn. Assn. of Conservative Peers 1986-93; Elected Hereditary mem., House of Lords; Dep. Chmn., Cttees.; Dep. Speaker, House of Lords; ***professional career:*** Dir. Wakeley Farm Ltd., 1957-74; Asst. Master Loughborough Grammar School 1962-67; Fairham Comprehensive School Notts., 1967-69; Lect. Bishop Lonsdale Coll. of Education Derby, 1969-72; Dir., Overseas Exhibition Services Ltd. and Building Trades Exhibition Ltd., 1976-79; Dir. & Vice-Chmn., Andry Montgomery Group 1978-79 and 1987-2004; Chmn., Financial Intermediaries, Managers and Brokers Regulatory Assn. 1987-90; Mem., Panel on Takeovers and Mergers, 1987-90; Chmn., Independent Enquiry into Discipline in Schools 1987; Chmn., Intermediate Treatment Fund 1990-93; Founder Chmn., The Divert Trust 1992-99, Pres., 2000-03; Pres., Building Conservation Trust, 1987-90; Licensed Lay Minister of the Church of England, 1998-; ***committees:*** House of Lords Select Cttee. on the scrutiny of delegated powers, 1994-97; on the constitution, 2003-06; Procedure, 2005-2009; Jt. Select Cttee., Ecclesiastical Cttee., 2005-; Jt. Select Cttee. on Conventions, 2007; ***honours and awards:*** Territorial Decoration; Master of Arts (Oxon.); Hon. Fellow, City & Guilds of London; ***clubs:*** Cavalry, Beefsteak, Pratt's; ***office address:*** House of Lords, London, SW1A 0PQ, United Kingdom; ***phone:*** +44 (0)20 7219 3000; ***fax:*** +44 (0)20 7219 5979.

ELYSTAN-MORGAN, Lord, Baron Dafydd, Life Peer; British, Member of the House of Lords; ***born:*** 1932; ***married:*** Alwen, 1959 (dec'd 2006); ***s:*** 1; ***d:*** 1; ***education:*** Bachelor of Law (Hons.), Univ. of Wales; ***political career:*** MP for Cardigan, 1966-74; Contested Cardigan, Oct. 1974; Anglesey, 1979; Chmn., Welsh Parly. Party, 1968-69 and 1973-74; Under Secy. of State Home Office, 1968-70; Mem., House of Lords; ***professional career:*** Solicitor, Partner in Firm North Wales 1958-68; became Barrister at Law 1971; Pres. Welsh

Local Authority Assn. 1967-74; Barrister, Wales and Chester Circuit 1974-87, Asst. Recorder 1978 Recorder 1983; Circuit Judge, 1987-2003; Pres., Univ. of Wales, Aberystwyth, 1997-2007; Pres., Welsh School of Legal Studies, 1997-; ***honours and awards:*** hon. fellow, Univ. College of Wales (1991); ***office address:*** House of Lords, London, SW1A 0PQ, United Kingdom; ***phone:*** +44 (0)20 7219 3000; ***fax:*** +44 (0)20 7219 5979.

EMAN, Michiel; Prime Minister, Government of Aruba; ***education:*** Univ. of the Netherlands Antilles; ***party:*** Aruban People's Party; ***political career:*** Prime Minister, 2009-; ***office address:*** Office of the Prime Minister, Orangstad, Aruba.

EMERENCIA, Lydia; Lieutenant-Governor, Bonaire; ***born:*** 1954, Bonaire; ***education:*** Univ. of Utrecht, Ph.D; Catholic Univ. of Nijmegen, Ph.D; ***political career:*** Lieutenant-Governor, Bonaire, 2012-; ***professional career:*** Rector, Univ. of Aruba; Dir., Center for Research & Dev., Univ. of Aruba, 2010-12; ***office address:*** Office of the Lieutenant-Governor, Kralendijk, Bonaire.

EMERTON, Baroness; Member of the House of Lords; ***born:*** 10 September 1935, Tunbridge Wells, Kent; ***parents:*** George William Emerton and Lily Emerton (née Squirrell); ***education:*** Tunbridge Wells Grammar School for Girls, 1944-53; St George's Hospital, London, State Registered Nurse, 1953-56; Part I & II CMB Midwifery, 1957-58; Battersea Coll. of Tech., London, 1962-64; ***political career:*** Mem. of House of Lords; ***memberships:*** Royal Coll. of Nursing, 1957 to date; appointed Hon. Vice-Pres., Royal Coll. of Nursing, 1993; Assn. of Nurse Administrators, 1970-85; elected Pres., Assn. of Nurse Administrators, 1979; re-elected Pres., Assn. of Nurse Administrators, 1981; Fellow, Royal Society of Arts, 1983; Royal Soc. of Medicine, St. John Ambulance, 1986; Deanery Synod, 1984-86; Fellow, Royal College of Nursing, 2009; Hon. Fellow, Kings College, London, 2009; ***professional career:*** Nursing; Mem., The General Nursing Council including mem., Disciplinary Education & Finance Cttee(s), 1976-80; Mem., shadow English National Board for Nursing, Midwifery & Health Visiting, Dep. Chmn. & Chmn. of Finance Cttee, 1980-83; Mem., English National Board, elected Chmn., 1983-85; Mem., English National Board Chmn. of United Kingdom Central Council for Nursing, Midwifery & Health Visiting, 1985-93; Chmn. of Brighton Health Care NHS Trust, 1994-2000; Lay Mem. of General Medical Council, 1996-2001; Chief Commander of St John Ambulance, 1998-2002; ***trusteeships:*** Burdett Trust for Nursing, Defence Medical Welfare Service, National Assoc. Hospital Community Friend; ***honours and awards:*** Cmdr, Order St. John Ambulance (C.St.J), 1978; Dame Order of the British Empire (DBE), 1989; Hon. Degree, Univ. of Kent, Canterbury, DCL, 1989; Deputy Lieutenant, Kent (DL), 1992; Dame of Grace, Order of St. John Ambulance (D.St.J), 1993; Dame Grand Cross Order of St John 2004; Univ. of Central England, Birmingham, Hon. D.Univ., 1997; Univ. of Brighton, D.Sc., 1997; Fellow, Christ Church Canterbury ; ***office address:*** House of Lords, London, SW1A 0PQ, United Kingdom; ***e-mail:*** audrey.emerton@sja.org.uk.

EMIÉ, H.E. Bernard; Ambassador, French Embassy; ***education:*** Paris Institut d'Etudes Politiques,1979; Ecole nationale d'administration; ***professional career:*** Amb. to the Hashemite Kingdom of Jordan, 1998-2002; Dir., Middle East and North Africa Dept., Ministry of Foreign Affairs, 2002-04; Amb. to Lebanon, 2004-07; Amb. to Turkey, 2007-11; Amb. to the UK, 2001-; ***office address:*** French Embassy, 58 Knightsbridge, London, SW1X 7JT, United Kingdom; ***phone:*** +44 (0)20 7073 1000; ***fax:*** +44 (0)20 7201 1004; ***URL:*** http://www.ambafrance-uk.org.

ENGEL, Natascha; MP for North East Derbyshire, House of Commons; ***born:*** 1967; ***party:*** Labour; ***political career:*** MP for North East Derbyshire, 2005-; ***professional career:*** Journalist and subtitler; ***committees:*** Work and Pensions, 2005-07; Reform of the House of Commons, 2009-10; Chair, Backbench Business, 2010-; Liaison, 2010-; ***office address:*** House of Commons, London, SW1A 0AA, United Kingdom.

ENGLISH, Hon. Bill; New Zealander, Deputy Prime Minister, Government of New Zealand; ***born:*** 30 December 1961, Lumsden, Southland, New Zealand; ***parents:*** Mervyn English and Norah English (née O'Brien); ***married:*** Dr Mary English (née Scanlan), 1987; ***children:*** Luke (M), Maria (F), Thomas (M), Rory (M), Bartholomew (M), Xavier (M); ***education:*** St Patrick's Coll., Silverstream; Otago Univ., B.Com; Victoria Univ., BA (Hons) (1st class); ***party:*** National Party; ***political career:*** Nat. Party Candidate for Wallace, 1990; Minister of Crown Health Enterprises and Assoc. Minister of Education, 1996; Minister of Health in Coalition govt.; Minister of Finance and Minister of Revenue, 1996-99; Treasurer, June 1999; MP for Clutha-Southland; Leader, NZ National Party, 2001-2003; Opposition Spokesman for Education, Spokesman for Finance, 2003; Dep. Leader of the Opposition and Spokesman for Finance, 2005-08; Minister of Infrastructure, 2008-2012; Dep. Prime Minister, Minister of Finance, 2008-; ***professional career:*** farmer, 1980-85; ***office address:*** Parliament Buildings, Wellington, New Zealand; ***phone:*** +64 (0)4 817 6801; ***e-mail:*** b.english@ministers.govt.nz; ***URL:*** http://www.treasury.govt.nz.

ENSIGN, John; Chairman, Republican Policy Committee, US Senate; ***born:*** 25 March 1958; ***married:*** Darlene Sciaretta; ***children:*** Trevor (M), Siena (F), Micheal (M); ***education:*** Univ. of Nevada. Las Vegas, 1979; Oregon State Univ., Bachelor's degree, 1981; Colorado State Univ., Veterinary Medicine, 1985; ***political career:*** elected to US House of Representatives, 1994; Mem., US House of Representatives, 1st District, 1995-99; Senator for Nevada, US Senate, 2001-; Chmn., Republican Policy Cttee., 2009-11; ***professional career:*** Practiced Veterinary Medicine, opened first animal hospital in Las Vegas, 1987-94; owner, South Shores Animal Hospital, Las Vegas, 1994-; ***committees:*** Ways and Means Cttee., 1994; Banking, Housing, Urban Affairs, Commerce, Science and Transportation, Small Business and Special Ageing; ***office address:*** Office of Senator John Ensign, 364 Russell Senate Office Building, Washington, DC 20510, USA; ***phone:*** +1 202 224 6244.

ENSOUR, Dr Abdullah; Jordanian, Prime Minister, Government of Jordan; ***born:*** 1939, Salt, Jordan; ***education:*** American Univ. of Beirut, BA; Wayne State Univ., MA; Sorbonne, Paris, Dr. in human resources planning; ***political career:*** Dep., Balqa; Minister of Foreign Affairs, Planning and Higher Education, 1984-91; Minister of Foreign Affairs, 1991-93; Minister of Industry and Trade, 1993-96; Deputy Prime Minister for Service Affairs and Minister of Information, 1997-2001; appointed Prime Minister, Oct. 2012-; ***professional career:*** Dir. Gen., Budget Dept.; Dir., Income Tax Dept.; ***office address:*** Office of the Prime Minister, PO Box 80, Amman, Jordan; ***URL:*** http://www.pm.gov.jo.

ENZI, Michael B.; American, Senator for Wyoming, US Senate; ***born:*** 1 February 1944, Bremerton, Washington, USA; ***married:*** Diana Enzi (née Buckley), 1969; ***children:*** Amy (F), Emily (F), Brad (M); ***public role of spouse:*** involved in Children Against Land Mine Problems (CHAMPS); ***education:*** Sheridan High Sch., grad., 1962; George Washington Univ., Washington, DC, Accounting degree, 1966; Univ. of Denver, Master's degree, Retail Marketing, 1968; Rapport Leadership Inst., Master Grad. class of Nov. 1997; ***party:*** Republican; ***political career:*** Mayor, Gillette, Wyoming, 1975-82; State Rep., 1987-91; State Senator, 1991-96; Senator for Wyoming, 1997-; ***memberships:*** Elder, Presbyterian Church; Eagle Scout; Human Resources Management Professional, 1993-; ***professional career:*** Wyoming Air Nat. Guard, 1967-73; started small business, NZ Shoes, with wife; Pres., Wyoming Jaycees, 1973-74; founding Bd. of Dirs., First Wyoming Bank of Gillette, 1978-88; Pres., Wyoming Assn. of Municipalities, 1980-82; Accounting Manager and Computer Programmer, Dunbar Well Service, 1985-97; Education Cmn. of the States, 1989-93; Dir., Black Hills Corp., 1992-96; Cmnr., Western Interstate Cmn. for Higher Education, 1995-96; ***committees:*** US Senate: Budget; Finance; Health, Education, Labor and Pensions; Small Business & Entrepreneurship; Homeland Security & Governmental Affairs; ***honours and awards:*** Golden Triangle Award, Nat. Farmer's Union, 2003; True Blue Award, Family Research Cncl., 2003; Outstanding dedication and service to the Wyoming Fed. of Coll. Republicans, 2002; Hero of the Taxpayer Award, Americans for the Tax Reform, 2002, 2001; Spirit of Enterprise, Chamber of Commerce, 2001; American Legion Flag Protection Award, American Legion, 2000; ***recreations:*** hunting, fishing, cycling, reading; ***office address:*** US Senate, 379S Russell Senate Office Building, Washington, DC 20510, USA; ***phone:*** +1 202 224 3424; ***fax:*** +1 202 228 0359; ***e-mail:*** senator@enzi.senate.gov; ***URL:*** http://www.enzi.senate.gov.

EPHREM EMMANUEL, Sebhat; Eritrean, Minister of Defence, Government of Eritrea; ***born:*** 5 September 1950, Asmara, Eritrea; ***parents:*** Lete-Giorgies; ***married:*** Ruth (née Haile), July 1981; ***children:*** Alex (M), Berhe (M), Isabel (F); ***public role of spouse:*** Nurse and Social Works Student; ***education:*** Prince Mekonnen High Sch., Asmara; Haile Sellasie I Univ, Faculty of Medicine, 1969-72; currently studying MBA, Open Univ.; ***party:*** Eritrean People's Liberation Front; ***political career:*** Elected to position of the Polit-Bureau, 1977; Head of The Peoples Organization of the EPLF 1977-87; elected to post of Polit-Bureau 1987; Head of General Staff of he Liberation Army 1987-92; Mayor of Asmara, 1992-93; Post of the Central Cttee. of the PFDJ, 1994; Minister of Health, 1994; Minister of Defence, 1995-; ***professional career:*** Private in Liberation Army; Battalion Commander, 1975; ***honours and awards:*** Four Star General; ***office address:*** Ministry of Defence, PO Box 629, Asmara, Eritrea; ***phone:*** +291 (0)1 115493; ***fax:*** +291 (0)1 124920.

ERDOGAN, Recep Tayyip; Prime Minister, Government of Turkey; ***born:*** 1954, Istanbul, Turkey; ***children:*** 4; ***education:*** Marmara Univ., Coll. of Business; ***political career:*** Mayor of Istanbul; Leader of the Justice and Development Party (AK Partisi); Prime Minister, 2003-; ***office address:*** Prime Minister's Office, Basbakanlik Necatibev Cad, 108 Ankara, Turkey; ***phone:*** +90 (9)312 413 7000; ***URL:*** http://www.basbakanlik.gov.tr.

ERGIN, Sadullah; Ministry of Justice, Government of Turkey; ***born:*** 1964; ***education:*** Ankara Univ., Faculty of Law; ***party:*** founding mem., Justice & Development Party; ***political career:*** Minister of Justice, 2009-; ***professional career:*** lawyer; ***office address:*** Ministry of Justice, Adalet Basbakanlik Necatibey Cad, 108 Ankara, Turkey; ***phone:*** +90 (0)312 417 7770; ***URL:*** http://www.adalet.gov.tr.

ERGUN, Nihat; Minister of Industry and Commerce, Government of Turkey; ***born:*** 1962; ***education:*** Marmara University; ***political career:*** Minister of Industry and Commerce, 2009-; ***office address:*** Ministry of Industry and Commerce, Eskisehir Yolu 154, Ankara, Turkey; ***phone:*** +90 (9)312 286 0365; ***URL:*** http://www.sanayi.gov.tr.

ERJAVEC, Karl; Minister of Foreign Affairs, Government of Slovenia; ***born:*** 1960; ***education:*** Univ. of Ljubljana, law; ***political career:*** mem., Exec. Council, Assembly of Kranj Municipality; State Sec. for Judicial Administration, Ministry of Justice, 2001-04; Minister of Defence, 2004-08; Minister of the Environment & Spatial Planning, 2008; Minister of Foreign Affairs, 2012-; ***professional career:*** Office of the Human Rights Ombudusman, 1995-2000; ***office address:*** Ministry of Foreign Affairs, Presernova 25, Ljubljana 1000, Slovenia.

EROGLU, Veysel; Minister of Environment and Forestry, Government of Turkey; ***born:*** 18 August 1948, Suhut, Afyonkarahisar ; ***parents:*** Ibrahim Eroglu and Emine Eroglu; ***education:*** BSc., 1969, MSc., 1971, Ph.D. 1980, Instanbul Technical Univ.; ***political career:*** MP for Afyonkarahisar, 2007-; Minister of Environment and Forestry; ***professional career:*** Head, State Hydraulic Works, 2003-07; ***office address:*** Ministry of Environment and Forestry, Sögütözü Cad., No: 14/E, Blok A, Kat: 5, 06560, Bestepe, Ankara, Turkey; ***phone:*** +90 (9)312 207 6262; ***e-mail:*** eroglu@cevreorman.gov.tr; ***URL:*** http://www.cevreorman.gov.tr.

ESHOO, Anna; American, Congresswoman, California 14th District, US House of Representatives; ***born:*** 1942, New Britain, Connecticut, USA; ***children:*** Karen (F), Paul (M); ***party:*** Democrat; ***political career:*** Congresswoman, California Fourteenth District, US House of Representatives, 1992-, and At-Large Democratic Whip; ***interests:*** high technology, environment, health care, family issues; ***committees:*** House Energy and Commerce Cttee.; ***honours and awards:*** Legislator of the Year Award from California's Governor's Committee on the Employing of the Disabled, 1989; the Margaret Sanger Community Service Award from San Mateo County Planned Parenthood, 1991; Friend of BAYMEC Award, 1990; 1989 Public Official of the Year, awarded by State Commission on Aging and Easter Seal's 1987 Humanitarian of the Year; ***office address:*** US House of Representatives, 205 Cannon Building, Washington, DC 20515, USA; ***phone:*** +1 202 225 8104.

ESPINOZA, Marisol; Vice President, Government of Peru; ***education:*** Univ. of Piura, Peru; ***party:*** Peruvian Nationalist Party; ***political career:*** Mem. of Congress, 2006-; VIce President, 2011-; ***office address:*** Office of the Vice President, Jirón de la Union, s/n 1ra cuadra, Lima 1, Peru; ***phone:*** +51 1 311 3900; ***fax:*** +51 1 426 6770; ***e-mail:*** webmaster@presidencia.gob.pe; ***URL:*** http://www.presidencia.gob.pe.

ESSO, Solitoki; Minister of State for Primary and Secondary Education, Government of Togo; ***political career:*** elected to National Assembly, 1985; Minister of Communication and Culture; Sec.-Gen., Rally of the Togolese People, 2006; Minister of State fro the Civil Service and Administrative Reform, 2010-12; Minister of State for Primary and Secondary Education, 2012-; ***office address:*** Ministry of National Education, BP 12175, Lomé, Togo; ***phone:*** +228 221 3926; ***fax:*** +228 221 0783.

ESTERSON, Bill; MP for Sefton Central, UK Government; ***party:*** Labour; ***political career:*** MP for Sefton Central, May 2010-; PPS, 2011-; ***committees:*** Environment, Food and Rural Affairs Select Cttee., 2010-11; Communities and Local Gov., 2011-; Unopposed Bills (Panel), 2011-; ***office address:*** House of Commons, London, SW1A 0AA, United Kingdom; ***phone:*** +44 (0)20 7219 3000; ***e-mail:*** bill.esterson.mp@parliament.uk.

ETHELL, Col. (Retd.) The Hon. Donald, OC OMM AOE MSC CD; Lieutenant Governor, Alberta; ***born:*** 1937; ***professional career:*** long and distinguished career in Canadian Armed Forces incl. 14 peacekeeping tours, ret'd. 1993; military advisor;worked for several humanitarian causes incl. Care Canada; Dir., International Cttee. for the Relief of Starvation and Suffering; installed as 17th Lieutenant Governor of Alberta, 11 May 2010; ***honours and awards:*** Mem., Order of Canada; Alberta Order of Excellence; Order of Military Merit; Order of St. John; Meritorious Service Cross for peacekeeping efforts in the Middle East; ***office address:*** Lieutenant-Governor's Office, Calgary, Alberta, Canada.

EUSTICE, George; MP for Camborne and Redruth, UK Government; ***party:*** UKIP 1998-99; Conservative; ***political career:*** Press Sec. to Conservative Leader David Cameron, 2005-07; External relations co-ordinator, Conservative HQ, 2008-; MP for Camborne and Redruth, May 2010-; ***committees:*** Environment, Food and Rural Affairs Select Cttee., 2010-; Joint Committee on Privacy and Injunctions, 2011-12; ***office address:*** House of Commons, London, SW1A 0AA, United Kingdom; ***phone:*** +44 (0)20 7219 3000; ***e-mail:*** george.eustice.mp@parliament.uk.

EVANS, Chris; MP for Islwyn, UK Government; ***party:*** Labour / Co-operative; ***political career:*** MP for Islwyn, May 2010-; ***committees:*** Justice Select Cttee., 2010-; Jt. Cttee., Draft Enhanced Terrorism Prevention, 2012-; Draft Defamation Bill, 2011-; ***office address:*** House of Commons, London, SW1A 0AA, United Kingdom; ***phone:*** +44 (0)20 7219 3000; ***e-mail:*** chris.evans.mp@parliament.uk.

EVANS, Graham; MP for Weaver Vale, UK Government; ***party:*** Conservative; ***political career:*** Councillor, Macclesfield Borough Council, 2000-; MP for Weaver Vale, May 2010-; ***committees:*** Administration, 2011-; ***office address:*** House of Commons, London, SW1A 0AA, United Kingdom; ***phone:*** +44 (0)20 7219 3000; ***e-mail:*** graham.evans.mp@parliament.uk.

EVANS, Jonathan; MP for Cardiff North, UK Government; ***party:*** Conservative; ***political career:*** MP for Brecon and Radnor, 1992-97; Minister for Corporate and Consumer Affairs, Dept. of Trade and Industry, 1994-95; Parly. Sec., Lord Chancellor's Dept., 1995-96; Under Sec. of State for Wales 1996-97; MP for Cardiff North, May 2010-; ***office address:*** House of Commons, London, SW1A 0AA, United Kingdom; ***phone:*** +44 (0)20 7219 3000; ***e-mail:*** jonathan.evans.mp@parliament.uk.

EVANS, Nigel; British, MP for Ribble Valley, House of Commons; ***born:*** 10 November 1957; ***parents:*** Albert Evans and Betty Evans (née Bown); ***education:*** Dynevor Sch.; Univ. Coll., Swansea, BA (Hons), Politics; ***party:*** Conservative Party, 1974-; ***political career:*** Cllr., West Glamorgan County Cncl., 1985-91; Vice-Chmn., Small Business Bureau; MP, Ribble Valley, 1992-; Vice-Chmn., All Party Gp. Networking for Industry; Pres., Country Guardians; Sec., North West Mem. Gp.; Sec., Manufacturing Industry Parly. Gp.; PPS to David Hunt, 1993-95; PPS to Tony Baldry, 1995-96; PPS to William Hague, 1996-97; Mem., Opposition Constitutional Affairs Team; Front Bench Spokesperson for Welsh Affairs, 1997-; Vice-Chmn., Conservative Party, 1999-2001; Shadow Secretary of State for Wales, 2001-03; Vice Chmn., Conservative Party; mem., Council of Europe and the Western European Union; ***interests:*** law and order, media and telecommunications, small business affairs, Europe, defence, education, economy, foreign affairs; ***professional career:*** owner, small retail business; ***committees:*** Fmr. Mem.: Home Affairs Sub-Cttee.; Welsh Select Cttee.; Trade and Industry Select Cttee.; Quadripartite Cttee; ***clubs:*** Carlton; Royal Overseas League; Insitute of Directors; ***office address:*** House of Commons, London, SW1A 0AA, United Kingdom; ***phone:*** +44 (0)20 7219 6939; ***e-mail:*** evansn@parliament.uk; ***URL:*** http://www.nigelmp.com.

EVENNETT, David Anthony, MP; British, MP for Bexleyheath and Crayford, House of Commons; ***born:*** 1949; ***parents:*** Norman Evennett (dec'd) and Irene Evennett (dec'd) (née Turner); ***married:*** Marilyn Evennett (née Smith); ***languages:*** French, German; ***education:*** Buckhurst Hill County High Sch. for Boys; London School of Economics; ***party:*** Conservative Party; ***political career:*** Redbridge BC 1974-78; contested Hackney South and Shoreditch 1979; MP (Con) for Erith and Crayford 1983-97; PPS Dept. for Education, 1992-93; PPS to Secy. of State for Wales 1993-95; PPS to Home Office Min. David Maclean and Lady Blatch 1995-96; PPS to Rt. Hon. Gillian Shephard MP, Secy. of State for Education & Employment, 1996-97; MP for Bexleyheath and Crayford, 2005-; Opposition Whip, 2005-09; Shadow Minister for Universities and Skills, 2009-10; PPS to Michael Gove as Secretary of State for Education, 2010-; ***interests:*** education, employment and the economy; ***memberships:*** National Trust; Richard III Soc.; Bexleyheath Conservative Club; ***professional career:*** Schoolmaster, 1972-74; marine insurance broker, Lloyds, 1974-81; Underwriting Member of Lloyds, 1975-92; Dir., Lloyds Underwriting Agency, 1982-91; Commercial Liaison Manager, Bexley College, 1997-2001; Management lecturer and consultant, 2001-05; ***committees:*** Mem. Select Cttee on Education, Science & The Arts, 1986-92; Mem., Select Cttee. for Education and Skills, 2005-06; Selection, 2012-; ***recreations:*** reading, theatre, cinema, history; ***office address:*** House of Commons, London, SW1A 0AA, United Kingdom; ***e-mail:*** david.evennett.mp@parliament.uk.

EWING, Dr Rufus; Premier, Government of Turks & Caicos Islands; ***education:*** Univ. of the West Indies, medicine, Bachelor of Medicine, Bachelor of Surgery Degree, Doctor in General Surgery; ***party:*** Progressice National Party; ***political career:*** Premier, 2012-; ***professional career:*** Fellow, Royal College of Surgeons, Edinburgh, Scotland; training, Pediatric Genral Surgery, Nova Scotia; Deputy Chief Medical Officer, Myrtle Rigby Health Complex, Chief Medical Officer; pres., Civil Service Association; ***office address:*** Office of the Premier, Grand Turk, Turk & Caicos Islands.

EYYUBOV, Yaqub Abdulla; First Deputy Prime Minister, Government of Azerbaijan; ***born:*** 24 October 1945, Baku, Azerbaijan; ***parents:*** Abdulla Ismayil Eyubov and Gulzar Mehrali Eyubova; ***married:*** Mina Megid Eubova, December 1972; ***children:*** Emin Yagub (M), Farkhad Yagub (M), Orkhan Yagub (M); ***languages:*** Russian, English; ***education:*** Azerbaijan Polytechnical Institute, Faculty of Construction, 1972; ***party:*** New Azerbaijan Party; ***political career:*** Deputy Prime Minister, New Azerbaijan Party, 1999-2003; First Deputy Prime Minister, 2003-; ***memberships:*** Int. Soc. for Soil Mechanics and Geotechnical Engineerings; ***professional career:*** Specialist on Foundation Engineering and Soils Mechanics; Head Laboratory Asst., Postgraduate Student, Dep. Sec., Party Cttee. of the Polytechnic Inst., 1972-75; Head Teacher, Sr. Lecturer, Dep. Dean, Dean, Head of Chair, Pro-rector on Scientific work of the Az. Construction Engineers Univ., 1975-97; Chief, State Committee on 'Gosgortechnadzor', 1997-99; ***committees:*** Head, Nat. Cttee. for Soil Mechanics and Foundation Engineerings (ANCSMFE); ***honours and awards:*** Doctor of Technical Sciences, Prof. in the sphere of Engineering, Academian of the Int. Engineering Academy; ***publications:*** Author of more than 100 scientific works and monographies; ***recreations:*** tennis; ***office address:*** Office of the Prime Minister, Lermontov St 68, 370066 Baku, Azerbaijan; ***phone:*** +994 (0)12 927728.

F

FABIUS, Laurent; French, Minister of Foreign Affairs, Government of France; ***born:*** 1946; ***married:*** Françoise Castro, 1961; ***children:*** Thomas (M), Victor (M); ***education:*** Ecole Normale Superieure, Inst. d'Etudes Politiques, Paris; Agrigation de lettres; Ecole Nationale D'Administration, 1971-73; ***political career:*** Request Master to the Conseil D'Etat, 1981; First Asst. to the Mayor of Grand Quevilly, 1977-95, 2000-08; Nat. Sec., Socialist Party in charge of press, 1979-; Minister with special responsibility for the Minister of Econ. and Finances, in charge of the Budget, 1981-83; Minister of Industry and Research, 1983-84; Pres., Cncl. Regional of Normandy, 1981-82; Prime Minister, 1984-86; Socialist Dep. to Seine-Maritime, 1978-81; 1986-2000, 2002-2012; Pres. of the Nat. Ass., 1988-92; Mem. of European Parl., 1989-91; First Sec. of the Socialist Party, 1992-93; Mayor of Grand Querilly, 1995; Pres., Socialist Parly. Gp., 1995; Pres., Nat. Assy., 1997-2000; Minister for the Economy, Finance and Industry 2000-2002; First Dep. to the Mayor of Grand-Quevilly, 2000; Pres., Conglomeration of Rouen, Elbeuf & Austrberthe, 2010-; Minister of Foreign Affairs, 2012-; ***professional career:*** Auditor 1973; ***honours and awards:*** Grand Cross of the National Order of Merit; ***publications:*** La France Inegale, 1975; Le Coeur du Futur, 1985; C'est en Allant Vers La Mer, 1990; Les Blessures de la Vérité, 1995; ***office address:*** Ministry of Foreign Affairs, 37 quai d'Orsay, 75351 Paris Cédex 07, France; ***phone:*** +33 (0)1 43 17 53 53; ***fax:*** +33 (0)1 43 17 53 53.

FABREGA, Jorge Ricardo; Minister of the Interior, Government of Panama; ***education:*** Univ. de Panama; ***political career:*** Private Sec., Minister of Foreign Relations, 1994-99; Dep. Sec.-Gen., National Assembly, 1999-2004; Dir., Land Transit & Transportation Authority,-2012; Sec.-Gen., Union Patriotica party, to date; Minister of the Interior, 2012-; ***professional career:*** lawyer; ***office address:*** Ministry of the Interior, Calle 29 y Avenida Cuba, Panama City, Panama.

FABRICANT, Michael; British, MP for Lichfield, House of Commons; ***born:*** 12 June 1950, Brighton, UK; ***education:*** Loughborough Univ., B.Sc., Law and Econs., 1970-73; Univ. of Sussex, M.Sc., Systems, 1974; Univ. of South California, USA, Dr., Econs., 1975-77; ***party:*** Conservative Party; ***political career:*** Regional Party Chmn., Brighton, 1986-90; Chmn., Brighton Pavilion Conservatives, 1985-88; Parly. Candidate, South Shields, 1987; Vice-Chmn., Conservative Party Media Cttee.; Mem., Nat. Heritage Select Cttee.; PPS to Financial Sec. to Treasury, 1996-97; MP, Mid-Staffordshire, 1992-97, Lichfield, 1997-; Shadow Minister for Trade and Economic Affairs, 2003-05; Opposition Whip, 2005-; ***interests:*** overseas trade, Eastern Europe, economics, defence; ***memberships:*** Senate Engineering Cncl., 1999-; ***professional career:*** Radio Journalist; ***committees:*** National Heritage Cttee., 1992-97; Joint Vice-Chmn., Back Bench Media Cttee., 1992-97; Culture, Media and Sport Select Cttee., 1997-99, 2001-05; Home Affairs Select Cttee., 1999-2001; Vice Chair, All-Party Internet Group, 1997; Joint Chair All-Party Royal Marines Gp., 1998; mem. various Engineering, Media, and Broadcast Parly. Cttees, 1997; Chmn., Information Cttee., 2001-03; Administration, 2009-10; Selection, 2010-12; ***recreations:*** fell walking, canal boating, reading, skiing, Mozart operas, Archers, eating out; ***office address:*** House of Commons, London, SW1A 0AA, United Kingdom; ***phone:*** +44 (0)20 7219 3000; ***e-mail:*** fabricantm@parliament.uk; ***URL:*** http://www.michael.fabricant.mp.co.uk.

FALEOMAVAEGA, Eni F.H.; Congressman At Large, American Samoa, US House of Representatives; ***born:*** Vailoatai, American Samoa; ***parents:*** Eni Hunkin and Taualai Hunkin; ***married:*** Hinanui Bambridge Cave; ***children:*** 5; ***education:*** Kahuku High Sch., Hawaii, Diploma, 1962; Brigham Young Univ., Provo, Utah, BA Pol. Sci./History, 1966; Univ. of Houston Law Sch., Texas, Juris Doctorate, 1972; Univ. of California, Berkeley, Boalt Hall Sch. of Law, Master of Law, 1973; ***party:*** Democrat; ***political career:*** Admin. Asst. to American Samoa's first elected Representative to Washington, DC, 1973-75; Staff Counsel to House of Representatives Cttee. on Interior/Insular Affairs, 1975-81; Dep. Attorney Gen., American Samoa, 1981-84; Lt. Governor of American Samoa, 1985-88; American Samoa Representative to the US House of Representatives, 1989-; ***professional career:*** US Army, Honourable Discharge 1966-69, Vietnam Veteran; ***committees:*** Natural Resources; Foreign Affairs; ***publications:*** Navigating the Future: A Samoan Perspective in US Pacific Relations, 1995, KIN Publications; ***office address:*** US House of Representatives, 2422 Rayburn House Office Building, Washington, DC 20515, USA; ***phone:*** +1 202 225 8577.

FALLIN, Mary; Governor, State of Oklahoma; ***education:*** Oklahoma State Univ.; ***political career:*** Oklahoma state legislator, 1990-95; Oklahoma Lieutenant Governor, 1995-2006; Mem. US House of Representatives, 2007-10; Governor, State of Ohio, 2010-; ***office address:*** Office of the Governor, 2300 N. Lincoln Blvd., State Capitol Bldg., Room 212, Oklahoma, OK 73105, USA; ***phone:*** +1 405 521 2342; ***URL:*** http://www.governor.state.ok.us/.

FALLON, Michael, MA Hons; British, Member of Parliament for Sevenoaks, House of Commons; ***born:*** 1952; ***s:*** 2; ***education:*** Epsom Coll.; St. Andrews Univ; MA Hons (Classics and Ancient History); ***political career:*** Political asst. to Lord Carrington 1975-77; Conservative Research Dept. 1977-81; MP (Con) for Darlington 1983-92; Parly. Private Sec.to Rt. Hon. Cecil Parkinson MP Sec. of State for Energy 1987-88; Assistant Govt. Whip 1988-90; Parly. Under-Sec., Dept. of Education and Science 1990-92; MP, Sevenoaks, 1997-; Opposition Spokesman on Trade and Industry, 1997, on Treasury, 1997-98; Minister of State for Business and Enterprise, Dept. for Business, Innovation and Skills, 2012-; Minister of State, Dept. for Energy and Climate Change, 2013-; ***professional career:*** Dir., Quality Care Homes PLC 1992-97; Dir., Just Learning Ltd. 1995-; Collins Stewart Tullett, 2004-06; Tullett Prebon, 2006-; Attendo AB, 2008-; ***committees:*** Treasury Select Cttee., 1999-2012; ***publications:*** The Quango Explosion (1978); Sovereign Members? (1982); The Rise of the Euroquango (1982); No Turning Back (1985), co-author; Brighter Schools (1993); ***clubs:*** The Academy; ***office address:*** House of Commons, London, SW1A 0AA, United Kingdom; ***phone:*** +44 (0)20 7219 6482.

FARAGE, Nigel Paul; British, Member of European Parliament; ***born:*** 3 April 1964, Farnborough; ***children:*** Samuel (M), Thomas (M), Victoria (F); ***education:*** Dulwich Coll.; ***party:*** Leader, UK Independence Party; Independence & Democracy Gp.; ***political career:*** MEP for South-East England, 2004-; ***professional career:*** Commodity broker; ***committees:*** mem., Cttee on Int. Trade; Sub. mem., Cttee on Fisheries; ***office address:*** European Parliament, 60 Rue Wiertz, B-1047 Brussels, Belgium; ***fax:*** +32 (0)2 284 9855.

FAREMO, Grete; Norwegian, Minister of Justice and Emergency Preparedness, Norwegian Government; ***born:*** 1955; ***education:*** Degree in Law, Univ. of Oslo, 1978; ***political career:*** Minister of Development Cooperation 1990-92; Minister of Justice 1992; Minister of Defence, 2009-11; Minister of Justice and Emergency Preparedness, 2011-; ***professional career:*** Exec. Officer, Ministry of Finance 1979-80; Directorate for Development Cooperation (NORAD) 1980-84; Head, Cultural Cttee., Labour Party Youth Organisation of Norway (AUF) 1982-84; Mem., AUF International Cttee., 1984; Ministry of Development Cooperation, Head of Department 1984-86; Bd. Mem., Afghanistanhjelpen (Solidarity Organisation for Afghanistan) 1985-86; Aker Eiendom, Chief Negotiating Officer 1986-88, subsequently Aker Brygge, Cultural Dir.; Dpty. Mem., Oslo Municipal Exec. Council 1987-; mem., Labour Party Forum for Art and culture; Bd. Mem., Forum for Art and Culture, Labour Party of Norway 1989-; Dir., Norwegian Labour Press AS 1990; Bd Mem., Oslo Labour Party 1990-; ***committees:*** Council Mem., Norwegian Helsinki Cttee., 1986-; ***office address:*** Ministry of Justice, Akersgaten 42, PB 8005 Dep, 0030 Oslo, Norway; ***phone:*** +47 2224 9090; ***fax:*** +47 2224 9530.

FARR, Sam; American, Congressman, California 17th District, US House of Representatives; ***born:*** 4 July 1941; ***education:*** Willamette University, Salem, Oregon, bachelor of science degree in biology, 1963; Monterey Institute of International Studies; University of Santa Clara; ***party:*** Democrat; ***political career:*** California State Assembly, 1980-93; Congressman, California 17th District, US House of Representatives, 1993-; ***committees:*** House Appropriations Committee; ***office address:*** US House of Representatives, 1221 Longworth House Office Building, Washington, DC 20515, USA; ***phone:*** +1 202 225 2861; ***e-mail:*** samfarr@mail.house.gov.

FARRELLY, Paul; Member of Parliament for Newcastle-under-Lyme, House of Commons; ***born:*** 2 March 1962, Newcastle-Under-Lyme; ***parents:*** Thomas Farrelly and Anne Farrelly (née King); ***married:*** Victoria Jane Perry, 19 September 1998; ***children:*** Joe (M), Aneira Kate (F), Octavia (F); ***public role of spouse:*** Architect; ***languages:*** French, German, Italian; ***education:*** Wolstanton Grammar/Marshlands High Sch., Newcastle-Under-Lyme; St Edmund Hall; BA (Hons) PPE, Oxford Univ., 1981-84; ***party:*** Labour Party; ***political career:*** MP, Newcastle-under-Lyme, 2001-; ***memberships:*** Newcastle Working Men's Club, Cross Heath; ***professional career:*** Manager, Corporate Finance, Barclays de Zoete Wedd, 1984-90; Correspondent, Reuters, 1990-95; Dep. City Editor, Independent on Sunday, 1995-97; City Editor, Observer, 1997-2001; ***committees:*** Unopposed Bills, 2004-; Culture, Media & Sport, 2005-; ***clubs:*** Trentham RUFC, Finchley RFC; Holy Trinity Community Centre; Halmer End Working Men's Club; Commons and Lords, RUFC; ***recreations:*** rugby, football, writing, languages; ***office address:*** House of Commons, London, SW1A 0AA, United Kingdom; ***phone:*** +44 (0)20 7219 8391; ***fax:*** +44 (0)20 7219 1986; ***e-mail:*** paul.farrelly.mp@parliament.uk; ***URL:*** http://www.parliament.uk.

FARRON, Tim; MP for Westmorland and Lonsdale, House of Commons; ***born:*** 1970; ***party:*** Liberal Democrat; ***political career:*** Local Councillor; MP for Westmorland and Lonsdale, 2005-; Shadow Home Office Minister, 2005-07; Parly. Private Sec. to the Leader (Liberal Democrat), 2007-08; Shadow Environment, Energy, Food and Rural Affairs, 2009-10; ***committees:*** Education and Skills, 2005-06; Environmental Audit, 2006-07; European Scrutiny, 2010-; ***office address:*** House of Commons, London, SW1P 0AA, United Kingdom; ***phone:*** +44 (0)20 7219 3000; ***e-mail:*** farront@parliament.uk.

FARRY, Dr Stephen; MLA for North Dowm, Northern Ireland Assembly; ***party:*** Alliance Party of Northern Ireland; ***political career:*** MLA for North Down, 2007-; Mayor of North Down, 2007-; Minister for Employment and Learning, 2011-; ***office address:*** Northern Ireland Assembly, Parliament Buildings, Ballymiscaw, Belfast, BT4 3XX, United Kingdom.

FAULKNER OF WORCESTER, Lord; Deputy Speaker, House of Lords; ***born:*** 22 March 1946; ***parents:*** Harold Faulkner and Mabel Faulkner; ***married:*** Susan Faulkner (née Heyes), 1968; ***education:*** Merchant Taylors' Sch., Northwood; Worcester Coll., Oxford, MA, PPE; Hon. Fellow, 2002; Univ. of Bedfordshire, Hon. DCL; ***party:*** Labour; ***political career:*** parly. candidate, 1970, 1974, 1979 general elections; London Borough cllr., 1971-78; Co-Founder, Parly. Journal The House Magazine; Communications Adviser to Leader of the Opposition and Labour Party (unpaid) in general elections, 1987, 1992, 1997; Mem., House of Lords, 1999-; Dept. Liaison Peer, Cabinet Office, 2001-05; Dept. of the Environment, Transport & the Regions, 2000-01; Lord-in-Waiting (Government Whip), 2009-10; Dep. Speaker, House of Lords, 2010-; ***interests:*** transport, sport, human rights, war heritage; ***memberships:*** Member of various groups, including Government's Advisory Board on World War One Centenary Commemoration, 2012-; draft gambling bill joint scrutiny cttee., Human Rights Gp., Railways Gp., Football Gp., Arts and Heritage Gp., War Heritage Gp., Smoking and Health Gp.; officer Norway, Sweden, Argentina and Taiwan Gps.; ***professional career:*** Research Assist., Labour Party, 1967-69; PR officer, Construction Industry Training Bd., 1969-70; Editor, Steel News, 1971; Account Dir., FJ Lyons Ltd, 1971-73; Dir., PPR International, 1973-76; Founder & Chmn., Camden Assoc (PR), 1976-89; Jt-man. Dir. & Co-proprietor, Westminster Communications Group, 1989-97; Dep. Chmn., Citigate Westminster, 1997-99; gov. relations adviser, 1973-99; communications advisor to the Bishop of Lambeth, 1990; Dir., Cardiff Millennium Stadium plc, 1997-2004, Dep. Chmn., 2004-08; adviser, Littlewoods Leisure, 1999-2003, 2004-09; Strategy Adviser, Alderney Gambling Control Commission, 2005-08, Commissioner, 2013-; Dir., Football Assn. of Wales, 2000-05; Vice Pres., The Football Conference, 2007-09, 2010-; Nat. Assn., for Disabled supporters, 2007-09, 2010-; Die., Worcester Live, 2010-; ***committees:*** various cttees. including recently: Treasurer, All-Party Parly. Railways Group; Mem., Delegated Powers and Regulatory Reform Cttee., 2007-09; mem., Armed Forces Parly. Scheme, 2005-08; ***trusteeships:*** Science Museum Grp., 2011-; Chmn. Railway Heritage Designation Advisory Board, 2013-; Pres., Heritage Railway Assoc., 2010-; Founding Trustee, Football Trust, 1979-82, Sec. 1983-86, First Dep. Chmn., 1986-98; Roy Castle Lung Cancer Foundation; ***honours and awards:*** Hon. LLD Beds (formerly Luton), 2003; Friendship Medal of Diplomacy (Taiwan), 2004; Order of the Brilliant Star with Grand Cordon (Taiwan), 2008; ***publications:*** Holding The Line - How Britain's Railways Were Saved, (Ian Allan 2012); ***clubs:*** Reform; ***recreations:*** traveling by railway, collecting Lloyd George memorabilia, tinplate trains, watching Association Football; ***office address:*** House of Lords, London, SW1A 0PW, United Kingdom; ***phone:*** +44 (0)20 7219 8503; ***fax:*** +44 (0)20 7219 1460; ***e-mail:*** faulknerro@parliament.uk; ***URL:*** http://www.lordfaulkner.net.

FAULKS, Lord Edward Peter Lawless, QC; Member, House of Lords; ***party:*** Conservative; ***political career:*** Mem., House of Lords, 2010-; ***professional career:*** Barrister; ***office address:*** House of Lords , London, SW1A 0PW, United Kingdom; ***phone:*** +44 (0)20 7219 3000; ***fax:*** +44 (0)20 7219 5979; ***URL:*** http://www.parliament.uk.

FAURÉ, Danny; Vice President, Government of the Seychelles; ***political career:*** Minister of Education and Human Resources Development, 2004-06; Minister of Finance, 2006-11; Vice President, Minister of Finance and Trade, Public Administration and Information Communication Technologies, 2011-; ***office address:*** Ministry of Finance, P.O. Box 648, International Conference Centre, Victoria, Mahé, Seychelles.

FAUZI, Gamawan; Minister of Home Affairs, Government of Indonesia; ***education:*** Andalas Univ. School of Law; ***political career:*** Governor of West Sumatera, 2005-2009; Minister of Home Affairs, 2009-; ***office address:*** Ministry of Home Affairs, Jalan Merdeka Utara 7, Jakarta Pusat, Indonesia.

FAYMANN, Werner; Federal Chancellor, Austrian Government; ***born:*** 4 May 1960 , Vienna, Austria; ***education:*** currently studying law; ***political career:*** Mem., Viennese State Parliament & Municipal Cncl., 1985-94; Executive city councillor for housing, housing construction and urban renewal, 1994; Minister of Transport, Innovation and Technology, Jan. 2007-08; Federal Chancellor, Dec. 2008-; ***memberships:*** Pres., Viennese Fund for Provision of Property and Urban Renewal; Vice-Pres., Viennese Business Agency; ***professional career:*** consultant, Zentralsparkasse,1985-88; Dir. & provincial Chmn.,Viennese Tenants' counselling, 1988 ; ***office address:*** Federal Chancellery, Ballhausplatz 2, 1014 Vienna, Austria; ***phone:*** +43 (0)1 531150; ***URL:*** http://www.bka.gv.at.

FEATHERSTONE, Lynne; MP for Hornsey and Wood Green, House of Commons; ***born:*** 20 December 1951, London, UK; ***parents:*** Gladys Ryness (dec'd) and Joseph Ryness (dec'd); ***married:*** Stephen Featherstone, 30 April 1982 (divorced); ***children:*** Jenna (F), Cady (F); ***education:*** Oxford Polytechnic; ***party:*** Liberal Democrat; ***political career:*** Muswell Hill ward, Haringey Cncl., 1998-2006; Leader of the Opposition, Haringey Cncl., 1998-2002; Mem., London Assembly, 2000-05; MP for Hornsey and Wood Green, 2005-; Lib Dem.spokesperson on Police, Crime, Disorder and Prisons, 2005-07; Shadow Sec. of State for International Development, 2007-08; Spokesperson for Youth and Equality, 2007-10; Parliamentary Under Secretary of State: Equalities and Criminal Information, 2010-12; Dept. of International Dev., 2012-; ***interests:*** policing, crime, transport, environment, blogging ; ***professional career:*** Designer; ***committees:*** Environmental Audit Cttee.; ***publications:*** Marketing & Communication Techniques for Architects, 1992, Longman; ***recreations:*** film, writing; ***office address:*** Constituency Office, c/o The Three Compasses, 62 High Street, Hornsey, London, N8 7NX, United Kingdom; ***phone:*** +44 (0)20 8 340 5459; ***e-mail:*** feathersonel@parliament.uk.

FEATHERSTONE, HE Simon; High Commissioner, British High Commission in Malaysia; ***professional career:*** British Ambassador to Switzerland and non-resident Ambassador to the Principality of Liechtenstein, 2004-09; High Commissioner to Malaysia, 2010-; ***office address:*** British High Commission, 185 Jalan Ampang, 50450 Kuala Lumpur, Malaysia; ***phone:*** +60 (0)3 2148 2122; ***fax:*** +60 (0)3 2144 7766; ***e-mail:*** political.kualalumpur@fco.gov.uk; ***URL:*** http://ukinmalaysia.fco.gov.uk/en.

FEDOTOV, Yury; Executive Director, UNODC; ***education:*** Moscow State Institute of International Relations (MGIMO); ***political career:*** Dep. Minister of Foreign Affairs, 2002-05; ***professional career:*** Various diplomatic assignments, 1972-; Amb. to the UK, June 2005-11; Executive Director, United Nations Office on Crime and Drugs, 2010-; ***office address:*** UNODC, Vienna International Centre, P.O. Box 500, A-1400 Vienna, Austria; ***phone:*** +43 1 260 60-0; ***URL:*** http://www.unodc.org.

FEIERSTEIN, Gerald M.; Ambassador to Yemen, US Embassy; *professional career:* career diplomat; joined Foreign Service, 1975; overseas postings incl.: Islambad, Tunis, Riyadh, Peshawar, Muscat, Jerusalem, Beirut; Dep. Chief of Mission, Islamabad, Pakistan, 2008-10; US Amb. to Yemen, 2010-; *office address:* Embassy of the US, PO Box 22347, Sana'a , Yemen.

FEINSTEIN, Dianne; American, Senator for California, US Senate; *born:* 22 June 1933; *married:* Richard C. Blum; *children:* Katherine (F), Annette (F), Heidi (F), Eileen (F); *education:* Stanford Univ., BA, History, 1955; *party:* Democrat; *political career:* San Francisco Bd. of Supervisors, 1970-78, Pres., 1970-71, 1974-75, 1978; Mayor of San Francisco, 1978-88; Candidate for Governor, 1990; US Senator for California, 1992-; *memberships:* Co-Chwn., San Francisco Education Fund's Permanent Fund, 1988-89; Pres., Japan Soc. of Northern California, 1988-89; *professional career:* California Women's Parole Bd., 1960-66; Dir., Bank of California; Mayor, San Francisco, 1978; *committees:* Chmn., Select Cttee. on Intelligence; Appropriations; Judiciary; Rules and Administration; *honours and awards:* 'Most Effective Mayor', City and State Magazine; *office address:* US Senate, 331 Hart Senate Office Building, Washington, DC 20510, USA; *phone:* +1 202 224 3841; *URL:* http://www.feinstein.senate.gov/.

FEKTER, Maria; Austrian, Minister of Finance, Government of Austria; *born:* 1956; *education:* Doctorate of Law, Johannes Kepler Univ., Linz; MA, Business Administration; *political career:* Mem., Attnang-Puchheim local council 1985-; Party Chairwoman, Attnang-Puchheim municipal branch of Austrian People's Party (ÖVP); MP (ÖVP) 1990-] Parly. Under-Secy. of State in Federal Ministry for Economic Affairs 1991; Minister of the Interior, 2008-11; Minister of Finance, 2011-; *professional career:* Niederndorfer & Co. (gravel and ready-made concrete suppliers); co-owner of Niederndorfer company group 1989-; *office address:* Ministry of Finance, Himmelpfortgasse 8, 1015 Vienna, Austria; *URL:* http://www.bmf.gv.at.

FELDMAN OF ELSTREE, Lord; Member, House of Lords; *party:* Conservative Party; *political career:* Conservative Party, Chair, 1985-86, Vice-Pres.1986-,Chair, Nat. Union Exec. Cttee., 1995-96; Party Treasurer 1996- Mem., House of Lords, 2011-; *office address:* House of Lords, London, SW1A 0PW, United Kingdom; *phone:* +44 (0)20 7219 3000; *e-mail:* feldmanb@parliament.uk.

FELLOWES OF WEST STAFFORD, Lord Julian; Member, House of Lords; *education:* Magdalene Coll., Univ. of Cambridge; *political career:* Mem., House of Lords, 2011-; *professional career:* Actor; Screenwriter; Film Director; Chmn., RNIB appeal for Talking Books; *office address:* House of Lords, London, SW1A 0PW, United Kingdom; *phone:* +44 (0)20 7219 3000.

FENN, H.E. Robert; High Commissioner, British High Commission in Brunei Darussalam; *born:* 1962; *education:* Cambridge Univ., UK; *professional career:* Dep. High Commissioner to Cyprus, 2005-09; High Commissioner to Brunei Darussalam, 2009-; *office address:* British High Commission, 2.01, 2nd Floor, Block D, Kompleks Yayasan Sultan Haji Hassanal Bolkiah, Bandar Seri Begawan 8674, Brunei Darussalam; *phone:* +673 (0)2 222231; *fax:* +673 (0)2 234315; *e-mail:* brithc@brunet.bn; *URL:* http://ukinbrunei.fco.gov.uk/en.

FERGUSON, Patricia, MSP; MSP for Glasgow Maryhill, Scottish Parliament; *born:* 24 September 1958, Glasgow, UK; *parents:* John Ferguson and Andrewina Ferguson (née Power); *married:* Bill Butler; *education:* Garnethill Convent, Secondary, Glasgow, UK; *party:* Scottish Labour Party, Co-operative Party; *political career:* MSP, Glasgow Maryhill, 1999-; Minister for Parliamentary Business, 2001-04; Minister, Tourism, Culture and Sport, 2004-07; *office address:* Scottish Parliament, Hollyrood, Edinburgh, EH99 1SP, United Kingdom; *e-mail:* patricia.ferguson.msp@scottish.parliament.uk.

FERGUSON, Sarah, Duchess of York; British, Founder and Life President, Children in Crisis; *born:* 15 October 1959; *parents:* Ronald Ferguson (dec'd) and Susan Wright (dec'd); *married:* HRH Prince Andrew, 1986 (div'd 1996); *children:* Princess Beatrice (F), Princess Eugenie (F); *professional career:* PR; art gallery; publishing; promoter, Weightwatchers; founder, Chances for Children Charity; founder, Children in Crisis.; *office address:* Children in Crisis, 5th Floor, The Towers, 125 High Street, London, SW19 2JR, United Kingdom.

FERGUSSON, Alex, MSP; MSP for Galloway and West Dumfries, Scottish Parliament; *born:* 8 April 1949, Scotland; *parents:* Simon Fergusson and Auriole Fergusson (née Hughes-Onslow); *married:* Merryn Fergusson (née Barthold), 20 June 1974; *languages:* French; *education:* Eton; West of Scotland Agricultural Coll.; *party:* Independent; *political career:* Principal Rural Affairs Spokesman, 2001-03; MSP, South Scotland, 1999-2003; MSP, Galloway and Upper Nithsdale, 2003-11 MSP, Galloway and West Dumfries, 2011-; Presiding Officer, May 2007-11; *interests:* rural affairs; *memberships:* SLF; *professional career:* Farmer, 1970-99; *recreations:* reading, rugby; *office address:* Scottish Parliament, Edinburgh, EH99 1SP, United Kingdom; *phone:* +44 (0)131 348 5636; *fax:* +44 (0)131 348 5932; *e-mail:* alex.fergusson.msp@scottish.parliament.uk.

FERGUSSON, H.E. George; Governor of Bermuda; *parents:* Sir Bernard Fergusson (dec'd); *political career:* Governor, Bermuda, 2012-; *professional career:* Northern Ireland Office, 1978-1991; Head of the Irish Dept., FCO, 1997-99; British Consul-General, Boston, 1999-2003; Head of the Foreign Policy Unit, Cabinet Office, 2003-06; British High Commissioner in New Zealand, 2006-11, Governor, Pitcairn, 2006-; High Cmnr., Cook Islands, 2006-11; *office address:* Office of the Governor, 11 Langton Hill, Pembroke HM13, Bermuda; *phone:* +441 292 3600; *URL:* http://www.gov.bm.

FERNÁNDEZ DE KIRCHNER, President Cristina; President, Government of Argentina; *born:* 19 February 1953, La Plata, Buenos Aires, Argentina; *married:* Néstor Kirchner, 9 March 1975; *public role of spouse:* President of Argentina, 2003-07; *education:* Univ. Nacional de La Plata, Law, 1979; *party:* Peronist Youth Movement; Front for Victory; *political career:* Mem., Santa Cruz provincial legislature, 1989-95; Rep. for Santa Cruz 1995-97, 2001-03; Rep. for Santa Cruz, Chamber of Deputies, 1997-2001; First Lady of Argentina, 2003-07; Senator for Buenos Aires province, 2005-07; President of Argentina,

2007-; *professional career:* practised law in Rio Gallegos; *office address:* Office of the President , Balcarce 50, 1064 Buenos Aires, Argentina; *phone:* +54 (0)11 4344 3600; *fax:* +54 (0)11 4344 3700 / 3800; *e-mail:* webmaster@presidencia.gov.ar; *URL:* http://www.presidencia.gov.ar.

FERREIRA DA COSTA, Gabriel Arcanjo; Prime Minister, Government of Sao Tome and Principle; *political career:* Prime Minister, 2002, 2012-; *office address:* Office of the Prime Minister, Sao Tome e Principe.

FICO, Robert; Prime Minister, Government of the Slovak Republic; *born:* 15 September 1964; *languages:* English, Russian; *political career:* Founder, SMER (Direction-Social Democrats), party, 1999; Leader of Parliamentary Group of SMER, 2002-06; Prime Minister, 2006-10, 2012-; *professional career:* Lawyer; *office address:* Office of the Prime Minister, Mudronova 1, 812 80 Bratislava , Slovak Republic.

FIELD, Frank, MP; British, Member of Parliament for Birkenhead, House of Commons; *born:* 1942; *education:* St. Clement Danes Grammar Sch.; Univ. of Hull; *party:* Labour Party; *political career:* MP (Lab.) for Birkenhead, 1979-; Spokesman for the Opposition on Education, 1979-81; Min. for Welfare Reform, Dept. of Social Security, 1997-98; *professional career:* Teacher in colls. of further education, 1964-69; Dir. Child Poverty Action Gp., 1969-79; Dir., Low Pay Unit, 1974-80; *committees:* Fmr. Chair, Select Cttee. on Social Security; mem., Public Accounts Cttee., 2002-05; Ecclesiastical; *trusteeships:* Chmn., Churches Conservation Trust, 2001-; Non-Exec. Dir., Medicash, 2003-; Chmn., Cathedrals Fabric Cmn., 2005-; *honours and awards:* Hon. Doctorate of Law, Warwick Univ.; Doctorate of Science, Southampton Univ.; Hon. Fellow, South Bank Univ., 2001; Hon. Fellow, Canterbury Christ Church, Univ. Coll., 2002; *publications:* Twentieth Century State Education (ed. jtly.), 1971; Black Britons (ed. jtly.), 1971; Low Pay (ed.), 1973; Unequal Britain, 1974; Are Low Wages Inevitable? (ed.), 1976; Education & the Urban Crisis (ed.), 1976; The Conscript Army: A Study of Britain's Unemployed (ed.), 1976; To Him Who Hath: A Study of Poverty & Taxation (jtly.), 1976; The Wealth Report: A Report on the Rich in 1978 (ed.), 1979; Inequality in Britain: Freedom, Welfare and the State, 1981; Poverty and Politics, 1982; Wealth Report 2 (ed.), 1983; The Minimum Wage: It's Potential and Dangers, 1984; Freedom and Wealth in a Socialist Future, 1987; The Politics of Paradise, 1987; Losing Out: The Emergence of Britain's Underclass, 1989; An Agenda for Britain, 1993; Europe Isn't Working, 1994; Beyond Punishment: Hard Choices on the Road to Full Employability, 1994; Making Welfare Work: Reconstructing Welfare for the Millennium, 1995; How to Pay For the Future: Establishing a Stakeholders' Welfare, 1996; Reforming Welfare, 1997, Social Market Foundation; Reflections on Welfare Reform, 1998; The State of Dependency Welfare Under Labour, 2000, Social Market Foundation; Making Welfare Work, 2001, Transaction; Welfare Titans: How Lloyd George and Gordon Brown Compare, 2002; Debating Pensions, 2002; How Saving Damages Your Retirement, 2003; Neighbours from Hell: The Politics of Behaviour, 2003; *office address:* House of Commons, London, SW1A 0AA, United Kingdom; *phone:* +44 (0)20 7219 3000; *e-mail:* fieldf@parliament.uk.

FIELD, Mark; Member of Parliament for City of London and Westminster, House of Commons; *parents:* Major Peter Field (dec'd) and Ulrike Field (dec'd) (née Peipe); *married:* Victoria Field, Apr. 2007; *children:* Frederick (M); *public role of spouse:* Theatrical Agent; *education:* Reading Sch.; St Edmund Hall, Oxford Univ.; *party:* Conservative Party; *political career:* Councillor, Kensington and Chelsea, 1994-2002; MP, City of London & Westminster, 2001-; Front bench spokesperson, London 2003-05, Treasury (Financial Sec.), May-Dec. 2005, Culture and Arts, 2005-06; *professional career:* Businessman, publishing and recruitment business; Corporate Solicitor with Freshfields; *committees:* Standing Cttees: Proceeds of Crime Act, 2002, Finance Act, 2002, Enterprise Act, 2002; Licensing Act 2003, Housing Act 2004, Railways Act 2005, Finance Act (No.2) 2005, Regulation of Financial Services (Land Transactions) Act 2005, National Insurance Contribution Act 2006, National Lottery Act 2006, Crossrail Act 2008; Finance Act, 2008, Finance Act, 2009, Intelligence & Security Cttee., Sept. 2010-; *publications:* Various Nat. Newspaper articles on economics and financial services, pensions policy, ID cards and civil liberties; Contributing chapters in various political books; *recreations:* cricket, soccer, rock and pop music; *office address:* House of Commons, London, SW1A 0AA, United Kingdom; *phone:* +44 (0)20 7219 3000; *e-mail:* fieldm@parliament.uk; *URL:* http://www.parliament.uk.

FINK, Lord Stanley; Member, House of Lords; *party:* Conservative Party; *political career:* Mem. House of Lords, 2011-; *professional career:* Citibank; CEO, Man Group, 2000-07; Chief Exec., International Standard Asset Management (Isam), 2008-; Co-Treasurer, Conservative Party, 2009-; Chmn., Absolute Return for Kids, 2009-; *office address:* House of Lords, London, SW1A 0PW, United Kingdom; *phone:* +44 (0)20 7219 3000.

FINLAYSON, Chrisopher; Attorney-General, Government of New Zealand; *party:* National Party; *political career:* MP, 2005-; Attorney-General of New Zealand, Minister for Arts, Culture and Heritage, 2008-; *office address:* Office of the Attorney General, 10th, Charles Fergusson Building, Bown Street, Wellington, New Zealand; *phone:* +64 (0)4 494 9700; *URL:* http://www.justice.govt.nz.

FINLEY, Hon. Diane; Minister of Human Resources and Skills Development, Canadian Government; *party:* Conservative; *political career:* MP, House of Commons, 2004-; Critic: Agriculture and Agri Food, 2004-06; Minister of Human Resources and Social Development, 2006-07; Minister of Citizenship and Immigration, 2007-08; Minister of Human Resources and Skills Development, 2008-; *office address:* House of Commons, Parliament Buildings, Wellington Street, Ottawa, ON K1A 0A6, Canada.

FISCHER, Deb; Senator for Nebraska, US Senate; *education:* Univ. of Nebraska-Lincoln; *party:* Republican; *political career:* Nebraska Unicameral, 2004; Senator, US Senate, 2012-; *committees:* Armed Services; Commerce, Science & Transportation; Environment & Public Works; Small Business & Entrepreneurship; Indian Affairs; *office address:* US Senate, 825 Hart Senate Office Building, Washington DC 20510, USA; *phone:* +1 202 224 6551; *URL:* http://www.fischer.senate.gov/.

FISCHER, Dr Heinz; Federal President, Republic of Austria; *born:* 9 October 1938, Graz, Austria; *married:* (married); *education:* Univ. of Vienna. Doctorate of Law, 1956-61; *political career:* Sec., Socialist Parly. Party, 1963-75; Mem., Nationalrat for Constituency of Vienna, 1971-2004; Exec. Floor Leader, Socialist Parly. Party, 1975-83; Dep. Chmn., Socialist Party, 1979-2004; Fed. Minister for Science & Research, 1983-87; Floor Leader, Socialist Parly. Party, 1987-90; Pres., Austrian Nationalrat, 1990-2004; Dep. Chmn., European Socialist Party, 1992-2004; Federal Pres. 2004- ; *professional career:* Lecturer in political science, 1978- ; Full Univ Prof., 1994- ; Vice-Pres., Inst. of Advanced Studies; Pres., Assoc. of Austrian Adults Education Centres (Volkshochschule); *committees:* Foreign Affairs Cncl.; Pres., Austrian Gp., Inter-Parly. Union; *publications:* Numerous books & articles in the field of law & political science; Reflexionen, 3rd Edition, 1999; co-editor of Europäische Rundschau; *office address:* Office of the Federal President, Hofburg, 1010 Vienna, Austria; *phone:* +43 (0)1 534220; *URL:* http://www.hofburg.at.

FISCHER, Prof. Stanley; Governor, Bank of Israel; *born:* 1943; *education:* London School of Economics, B.Sc (Econ) and M.Sc. (Econ), 1962-66; MIT, Ph.D. in economics, 1969; *professional career:* Assist. Prof.of Economics, Univ. of Chicago, to 1973; Assoc. Prof. of Econ., Massachusetts Institute of Technology; Prof. of Econ., 1977; Killian Prof. and Head of Economics, MIT; Vice Pres., Development Economics and Chief Economist, 1988-90; First Dep. MD, International Monetary Fund, 1994-2001; Vice Chair, Citigroup 2002-05; Head of the Public Sector Group, 2004-05; President of Citigroup International; Governor, Bank of Israel, 2005- ; *office address:* Bank of Israel, PO Box 780, Qiryat Ben-Gurion , Jerusalem 91007, Israel; *phone:* +972 2 6552211; *fax:* +972 2 6528805; *e-mail:* webmaster@bankisrael.gov.il; *URL:* http://www.bankisrael.gov.il.

FITZGERALD, Frances, TD; Minister for Children, Government of Ireland; *education:* Univ. College Dublin; London School of Economics; *political career:* TD for the Dublin South-East, 1992-2002; TD for the Dublin Mid-West . Feb. 2011- ; Minister of Children and Youth Affairs, Feb. 2011- ; *professional career:* Social Worker; *office address:* Houses of the Oireachtas, Leinster House, Kildare Street, Dublin 2, Ireland.

FITZGIBBON, Joel; Minister of Agriculture, Fisheries and Forestry, Government of Australia; *education:* Univ. of New England, worked towards an Arts/Law degree; Univ. of Newcastle, Grad. Cert. Business Administration, 2004; *political career:* Mem. for Hunter, 1996- ; various Shadow portfolios, Small Business, Tourism, Banking and Financial Services, Forestry, Mining and Energy, and Assistant Treasurer; Shadow Minister for Defence, to 2007; Minister for Defence, 2007; Minister of Agriculture, Fisheries and Forestry, 2013- ; *professional career:* ran his own small business for 10 year; Councillor, Cessnock City Council; Deputy Mayor, Cessnock City Cncl.; *office address:* Department of Agriculture, Fisheries and Forestry, Edmund Barton Building, Kings Avenue, Barton, ACT 2600, Australia; *phone:* +61 2 6275 3933; *fax:* +61 2 6272 3008; *URL:* http://www.affa.gov.au/index.cfm.

FITZPATRICK, Jim; British, MP for Poplar and Limehouse, House of Commons; *born:* 4 April 1952; *parents:* James Fitzpatrick and Jean F. Fitzpatrick (née Stones); *children:* James (M), Helen (F); *education:* Secondary Sch., Holyrood, Glasgow; *party:* Labour Party; *political career:* PPS, Asst. Govt. Whip; Vice Chamberlain of Her Majesty's Household; MP, Poplar and Canning Town, 1997-2010, Poplar and Limehouse, 2010- ; Parly. Sec., Office of Dep. PM, 2005-07; Parly. Under Sec. of State, Dept. of Transport, 2007-09; Minister of State, Department for Environment, Food and Rural Affairs, 2009-10; Shadow Minister for Environment, Food and Rural Affairs, 2010; Shadow Minister, Transport, Oct. 2010- ; *interests:* anti-poverty strategies, internationalism, regeneration, anti-racism, local gov.; *professional career:* Fire Fighter, London Fire Brigade; *honours and awards:* Fire Service, Long Service (20 Yrs) and good conduct Medal; *clubs:* West Ham Utd. FC; Pres., Millwall Rugby Football Club; *office address:* House of Commons, London, SW1A 0AA, United Kingdom; *phone:* +44 (0)20 7219 6215; *fax:* +44 (0)20 7219 2776; *e-mail:* jim.fitzpatrick.mp@parliament.uk; *URL:* http://www.jimfitzpatrickmp.co.uk.

FLAHERTY, Hon. James; Canadian, Minister of Finance, Government of Canada; *married:* Christine (née Elliott); *political career:* Province of Ontario, Minister of Labour, Solicitor General and Minister of Correctional Services, 1997- ; Solicitor General and Minister of Correctional Services, 1997-99; Attorney General and Minister responsible for Native Affairs, 1999- ; Dpty. Premier and Minister of Finance, 2001; Minister of Enterprise, Opportunity and Innovation, 2001; MP, House of Commons, 2006- ; Minister of Finance, 2006- ; *professional career:* Lawyer; *office address:* Ministry of Finance, l'Esplanade Laurier, 140 O'Connor Street, Ottawa, Ontario, K1A 0G5, Canada; *phone:* +1 613 996 7861.

FLAKE, Jeff; Senator, US Senate; *education:* Brigham Young University, BA, International Relations, MA, Political Science; *political career:* Congressman, Arizona Sixth District, US House of Representatives, 2001-13; Mem., US Senate, 2013- ; *committees:* Judiciary; Energy & Natural Resources; Foreign Relations; Special Cttee. on Aging; *office address:* US Senate, B85 Russell Senate Office Building, Washington DC, 20510, USA; *phone:* +1 202 224 4521; *URL:* http://www.flake.senate.gov.

FLELLO, Robert C.D., MP; MP for Stoke-on-Trent South, House of Commons; *born:* 14 January 1966, Birmingham, UK; *parents:* Alfred Douglas Flello and Valerie Swain; *children:* 2; *education:* Univ. College of North Wales, Bangor ; *party:* Labour; *political career:* MP for Stoke-on-Trent South, 2005- ; PPS to Rt. Hon. Hazel Blears MP; Shadow Minister, Justice, Oct. 2010- ; *interests:* home affairs, defence, regeneration; *memberships:* Cooperative Party; UNITY Trade Union; TGWU; AMICUS; *professional career:* CEO, Malachi Community Trust; Dir., Platts Flello Ltd, 2001-04; Manager, Arthur Andersen, Tax Consultant, Price Waterhouse; Revenue Executive, HM Inspector of Taxes; *committees:* Science & Technology Cttee., 2005-07; Finance & Service, 2010- ; *recreations:* running, reading, motorcycling; *office address:* Constituency Office, 2A Stanton Road, Meir, Stoke-on-Trent, ST3 6DD, United Kingdom; *phone:* +44 (0)20 7219 6744; *e-mail:* flellor@parliament.uk.

FLEMING, John; Congressman, Louisiana 4th Dist., US House of Representatives; *education:* Medicine; *political career:* Congressman, 2008- ; *memberships:* Deacon, Sunday School teacher and School Dept. Dir., First Baptist, Minden; *professional career:* Medical Officer, US Navy; Family physician, to date; *committees:* Armed Services; Natural Resources; *office address:* House of Representatives, 1023 Longworth HOB, Washington, DC 20515, USA; *phone:* +1 202 225 2777; *URL:* http://fleming.house.gov/ .

FLEMING CABRERA, Alejandro; Ministry of Trade, Government of Venezuela; *education:* Central Univ. of Venezuela; Univ. de Marne-Lalvallée, Paris; Univ. de la Sorbonne, Paris, 2005; *political career:* Vice Minister of Foreign Relations with Europe, 2008-10; Minister of Tourism, 2010; Minister of Trade, 2013- ; *professional career:* Ambassador of Venezuela to Belgium-Luxembourg; Perm. Rep. to EU, 2006-08; *office address:* Ministry of Trade, Torre Oeste de Parque Central, pisos 6-14, Caracas 1010, Venezuela; *URL:* http://www.mpc.gov.ve.

FLETCHER, Steven John; Minister of State for Transport, Government of Canada; *born:* 1972; *education:* B.Sc.GE; MBA; *political career:* MP for Charleswood, St. James, Assiniboia, 2004- ; Parly. Sec. for Health, 2006-08; Minister of State for Democratic Reform, 2008-11; Minister of State for Transport, 2011- ; *professional career:* Mining Engineer; *office address:* House of Commons, Parliament Buildings, Wellington Street, Ottawa, Ontario, K1A 0A6, Canada; *phone:* +1 613 943 5959; *fax:* +1 613 992 3674; *URL:* http://www.parl.gc.ca.

FLETCHER, Tom, CMG; Ambassador, British Embassy in Lebanon; *professional career:* Foreign Policy Adviser to Prime Minister David Cameron, and Prime Minister's adviser on Northern Ireland, 2010-11; Amb. to Lebanon, 2011- ; *office address:* British Embassy, Embassies Complex Army Street, Zkak Al-Blat, Serail Hill PO Box 11-471, Beirut, Lebanon; *phone:* +961 4 417007; *fax:* +961 1 990420; *e-mail:* britemb@cyberia.net.lb; *URL:* http://ukinlebanon.fco.gov.uk.

FLIGHT, Lord Howard; British, Member, House of Lords; *born:* 16 June 1948; *parents:* Bernard Flight (dec'd) and Doris Flight (dec'd); *married:* Christabel Norbury, 1973; *children:* Catherine (F), Thomas (M), Josephine (F), Mary Anne (F); *public role of spouse:* Treasurer, Conservative Party; *languages:* French; *education:* Brentwood Sch., Essex, 1959-66; MA, History & Economics, Magdalene Coll., Cambridge, 1966-69; MBA, Univ. of Michigan Business Sch., 1969-71; *party:* Conservative Party; *political career:* Chmn., Cambridge Univ. Conservative Assn., 1969; Vice Chmn., FCS, 1969; Conservative Parliamentary Candidate, Bermondsey Southwark, 1973-77; MP, Arundel and South Downs, 1997- ; Shadow Economic Sec. to the Treasury, 1999-2001; Shadow Paymaster General to the Treasury, 2001-2002; Shadow Chief Secretary of State to the Treasury, 2002-2004; Dep. Chmn., Conservative Party Special Envoy to the City; Mem., House of Lords, 2011- ; *interests:* finance, taxation, education, economic policy, farming, India, Hong Kong; *memberships:* Fellow of the Royal Society of Arts; *professional career:* Investment Adviser, Rothschilds, 1971-73; Manager, Cayzer Ltd., 1973-77; Hong Kong Bank Group, Hong Kong and India, 1977-79; Asst. Dir./Dir., Guinness Mahon, 1979-86; Joint Managing Director, Guinness Flight Global Asset Mngt., 1986-98; Joint Chmn., Investec Asset Mngt., Non-Exec. Dir., 1998-2003; *committees:* Cttee. Mem., Tax Consultative Cttee. to H.M Treasury, 1988-92; Mem., Political Cttee., Carton Club, 1995-97; Exec. Cttee., Team 1000, 1994-96; Mem., HOC Environment Select Cttee., 1997-98; Mem., HOC Social Security Bill Standing Cttee., 1998-99; *trusteeships:* Elgar Foundation; Brentwood School; *publications:* All You Need to Know About Exchange Rates, 1988, Sidgwick & Jackson; *clubs:* Carlton Club, Pratt's, Coningsby Club; *recreations:* skiing, classical music, architecture; *office address:* House of Lords, London, SW1A 0PW, United Kingdom; *phone:* +44 (0)20 7219 3000.

FLINT, Caroline; British, Shadow Secretary of State for Energy and Climate Change, House of Commons; *born:* 20 September 1961; *education:* Univ. of East Anglia, BA Hons., American Literature and History; *party:* Labour Party, 1979- ; *political career:* Chair., Brentford and Isleworth Constituency, 1991-95; MP, Don Valley, 1997- ; Parly. Advisor to the Police Fed. of England and Wales, 1999; Founder and Chair., All Party Parly. Gp. on Childcare, 1998-2003, British-American; PPS to Peter Hain, FCO Minister for Europe at FCO and DTI, 1999-2002; appt., Parly. Under Sec. of State, Home Office; PPS to Dr John Reid, Labour Party Chmn., 2002-03; Minister Without Portfolio, 2002-05; Parly. Under Sec., Minister for Public Health, 2005-07; Minister of State, Dept of Works and Pensions and Minister for Yorkshire and the Humber, 2007-Jan. 2008; Minister for Housing, Jan.-Oct. 2008; Minister for Europe, Oct. 2008-09; Shadow Secretary of State for Communities and Local Government, 2010-11; Shadow Secretary of State for Energy and Climate Change, Oct. 2011- ; *interests:* education, family policy, crime, welfare to work; *professional career:* National Women's Officer, Labour Students, 1980-82; Chair, Working for Childcare; Equal Opportunities Officer, Lambeth Cncl., 1989-91; Welfare and Staff Dev. Officer, 1991-93; Sr. Researcher and Political Officer, GMB Trade Union, 1994-97; *committees:* Mem., Education and Employment Cttee., 1997-99; Exec. Cttee., APG British-American; Mem., Commons Administration Cttee., 2000-03; *recreations:* cinema, family, tap-dancing; *office address:* House of Commons, London, SW1A 0AA, United Kingdom; *e-mail:* caroline.flint.mp@parliament.uk; *URL:* http://www.carolineflint.co.uk.

FLOSSE, Gaston; President, French Polynesia; *born:* 1931; *political career:* President, French Polynesia, 1984-87; Sec. of State with responsibility for the South Pacific, 1986-88; Senator, France, 1988- ; Pres., French Polynesia, 1991-2004, Oct. 2004-March 2005; Feb.-April 2008, 2013- ; *office address:* Office of the President, BP 2551, Papeete, French Polynesia; *phone:* +689 54 34 50; *fax:* +689 41 02 71; *URL:* http://www.presidence.pf.

FLYNN, Paul Phillip, MP; British, MP for Newport West, House of Commons; *born:* 1935; *parents:* James Flynn and Kathleen Flynn (née Williams); *married:* Samantha Flynn (née Douglas), 1985; Anne Harvey, 1962; *children:* James (M), Alex (stepson) (M), Rachel (dec'd 1979) (F), Natalie (stepdaughter) (F); *languages:* Welsh; *education:* Univ. Coll., Cardiff; *party:* Labour Party; *political career:* Front-bench spokesperson on Welsh Affairs, 1987; Front-bench spokesperson on Social Security, 1988-90; re-elected MP, Newport West, 1997- ; *interests:* social security, transport, drugs, pensions, animal welfare, Wales, constitutional reform; *memberships:* Pill Labour and Ringland Labour Clubs; *committees:* Mem., Transport Select Cttee., 1993- ; Mem., Health, Social and Family Affairs Cttee. of the Cncl. of Europe; Mem., Defence Cttee. of the Western European Union; Environmental Audit Cttee., 2003-05; Public Administration Select Cttee., 2005- ; *trusteeships:* Mitzvah Trust; George Shell Trust; *honours and awards:* Gorsedd of Bards; Freedom of Information

Campaign Parly. Award, 1991; Backbencher of the Year Award, Spectator Magazine,1996; New Statesman Elected Rep. Website Award, 2000; ***recreations:*** photography; ***office address:*** House of Commons, London, SW1A 0AA, United Kingdom; ***phone:*** +44 (0)20 7219 3478; ***fax:*** +44 (0)20 7219 2433; ***e-mail:*** paulflynnmp@talk21.com.

FOFANA, Mohamed Said; Prime Minister, Government of Guinea; ***born:*** 1952; ***political career:*** Prime Minister, Dec. 2010-; ***professional career:*** Economist; ***office address:*** Office of the Prime Minister, Conakry, Guinea.

FONSECA, Jorge Carlos; President, Government of Cape Verde; ***born:*** 1950; ***education:*** LLB, Master in Legal Sciences, Univ. of Lisbon, Portugal; ***party:*** Movement for Democracy; ***political career:*** Minister of Foreign Affairs, 1991-93; President, 2011-; ***professional career:*** Lawyer; ***office address:*** Presidência da República, CP 100, Plateau, Praia, São Tiago, Cape Verde; ***phone:*** +238 261 2669 ; ***URL:*** http://www.presidenciarepublica.cv.

FONTES LIMA, Cristina Lopes de Almeida; Deputy Prime Minister and Minister of Health, Government of Cape Verde; ***education:*** Law, Univ., Portugal; Public Administration, MA, USA; ***political career:*** Various positions, MFA; Minister of Justice and the Interior, to 2006; Minister to the Presidency; Minister of Defence and State Reform, 2006-11 Deputy Prime Minister and Minister of Health, 2011-; ***office address:*** Ministry of Health, Praia, Sao Tiago, Cape Verde.

FORD, David; Leader, Alliance Party; ***party:*** Alliance; ***political career:*** mem., South Antrim, Northern Ireland Assembly, 1998-; leader Alliance Party, Oct, 2001-; Minister of Justice, Apr. 2010-; ***office address:*** Northern Ireland Assembly, Department of Justice, Block B, Castle Builidings, Ballymiscaw, Belfast, BT4 3SG, Northern Ireland; ***phone:*** +44 (0)28 9052 1314; ***fax:*** +44 (0)28 9052 2704; ***e-mail:*** david.young@niassembly.gov.uk; private.office@dojni.x.gsi.gov.uk.

FOSTER, Arlene; Minister for Enterprise, Trade and Investment, Northern Ireland Assembly; ***s:*** 1; ***d:*** 1; ***education:*** Queens University in Belfast, LLB Hons, Cert of Prof Legal Studies; ***party:*** Democratic Unionist Party; ***political career:*** MLA, Fermanagh, South Tyrone; Minister for Environment, May 2007-June 2008; Minister of Enterprise, Trade and Investment, June 2008-; ***professional career:*** Solicitor; ***honours and awards:*** Women in Public Life Awards - Devolved Parliamentarian of the Year 2008; ***office address:*** Northern Ireland Assembly, Parliament Buildings, Stormont, Belfast, BT4 3XX, United Kingdom; ***phone:*** +44 (0)28 9052 1333.

FOSTER, Don; British, Member of Parliament, House of Commons; ***born:*** 31 March 1947, Preston, Lancashire, UK; ***education:*** Lancaster Royal Grammar Sch.; Degree, Keele Univ.; Research Masters Degree, Bath Univ.; ***party:*** Liberal Democratic Party; ***political career:*** MP for Bath, 1992-; Liberal Democrat Spokesman for Education, Employment and Training, 1992-1999; Spokesman for Environment, Transport & the Regions, 2000-2001; Liberal Democrat Shadow Sec. of State for Transport, Local govt. and the Regions, 2001-02; Lib. Dem. Shadow Sec. of State for Transport, 2002-03; Lib. Dem. Shadow Sec. of State for Culture, Media and Sport, 2003-10, and Olympics, 2007-10; Parly. Under-Sec. of State, Department for Communities and Local Government, 2012-; ***interests:*** Third World issues; ***memberships:*** Hon. Fellow, Bath Coll. of Higher Education; Mem., Inst. of Physics; Former Pres., Liberal Democrat Youth and Student Movement; Former Hon. Pres., British Youth Cncl.; Pres., Nat. Campaign for Nursery Education; Amnesty Int.; ***professional career:*** Science Teacher, 1969-75; Science Curriculum Project Dir., 1975-80; Science Education Lecturer, 1980-89; Avon County Cncl., 1981; Management Consultant, Pannell Kerr Forster, 1989-92; ***committees:*** Chair, Education Cttee., Avon County Cncl., 1986; Mem., Exec. Cttee., Assn. of County Cncls.; Mem., Education and Employment Select Cttee, 1996-99; ***publications:*** numerous books and articles; ***recreations:*** sport, music, travel, reading; ***office address:*** House of Commons, London, SW1A 0AA, United Kingdom; ***phone:*** +44 (0)20 7219 4805; ***e-mail:*** fosterd@parliament.uk.

FOULKES, Sir Arthur; Governor General, The Bahamas; ***political career:*** elected MP, 1976; Minister of Communications, then Minister of Tourism, 1968; Founder, Free National Movement, 1971; Senator, 1972-82; MP, 1982; ***professional career:*** journalist; High Commissioner to the UK; Amb. to France, Germany, Italy, Belgium and the EU; Amb. to People's Rep. of China, 1999, Amb. to Cuba, 1999; Dir.-Gen., Bahamas Information Services, 2007-; Dep. to the Gov. General, 2007-2010; Governor General of the Bahamas, 2010-; ***office address:*** Office of the Governor, Government Hill, P.O. Box N-8301, Nassau, N.P., Bahamas.

FOULKES, Rt. Hon. Lord George, PC, JP, BSc; British, Member, House of Lords; ***born:*** 21 January 1942; ***parents:*** George Foulkes (dec'd) and Jessie Margaret Arbuthnot Watt Foulkes (dec'd); ***married:*** Elizabeth Anna Foulkes (née Hope), 1970; ***children:*** Jennifer Hope (F), Roderick Shearer (M), Alexander William (M); ***languages:*** Spanish; ***education:*** Keith Grammar Sch.; Haberdashers' Aske's Sch.; Edinburgh Univ., BSc.; ***party:*** Labour Party 1963-; Co-Operative Party, 1965-; ***political career:*** Cllr. and Magistrate, Edinburgh, 1970-75; Cllr., Lothian Regional Cncl., 1974-79; MP (Lab. and Co-op) for Ayrshire South, 1979-83, for Carrick Cumnock and Doon Valley, 1983-2005; Chair, Labour Campaign for a Scottish Parl., 1997; Chair, The John Wheatley Centre; Delegate, Cncl. of Europe, 1979-80; Opposition Spokesman on Foreign Affairs, 1983-92, Defence, 1992-93, Overseas Dev., 1994-97; Parly. Under-Sec. of State for Int. Dev., 1997-2001; Minister of State for Scotland, 2001-02; Pres., Caribbean British Business Cncl., 2003-07; Delegate to Parly. Assembly, 2003-05; House of Lords, May 2005-; Mem., Scottish Parliament, 2007-2011; ***interests:*** foreign affairs, int. dev., defence, Scotland; ***memberships:*** Fabian Soc.; ***professional career:*** Pres., Scottish Union of Students, 1965-67; Mgr., Fund for Int. Student Co-operation, 1967-68; Scottish Organiser, European Movement, 1968-69; Dir., European League for Econ. Co-operation, 1969-70, Enterprise Youth, 1970-73, Age Concern Scotland, 1973-79; ***committees:*** Chmn., Lothian Regional Cncl. Education Cttee. and Education Cttee. on the Convention of Scottish Local Authorities, 1974-79; Mem., House of Commons Select Cttee. on Foreign Affairs, 1980-83; Mem. of the Exec., Inter-Parly. Union (IPU), British Section, 2005-07; Mem., of the Exec., Socialist International, 2004-07; Mem., Intelligence and Security Cttee., 2007-10; Mem., Joint Cttee. on National Security Strategy, 2010-; ***honours and awards:*** JP; Wilberforce Medal, 1998; Privy Counsellor, 2002; ***publications:*** Eighty Years on - History of Edinburgh University SRC 1964; chapters in 'A Claim of Right for Scotland', and 'Football and the Commons People'; ***recreations:*** supporting Heart of Midlothian F.C.; Chmn., Heart of Midlothian F.C., April 2004-05; ***office address:*** House of Lords, London, SW1A 0PW, United Kingdom; ***e-mail:*** foulkesg@parliament.uk.

FOVARGUE, Yvonne; MP for Makerfield, UK Government; ***party:*** Labour; ***political career:*** Councillor, Warrington Borough Council 2004-10; MP for Makerfield, May 2010-; ***committees:*** Health, 2010-11; Selection, 2012-; ***office address:*** House of Commons, London, SW1A 0AA, United Kingdom; ***phone:*** +44 (0)20 7219 3000; ***e-mail:*** yvonne.fovargue.mp@parliament.uk.

FOX, Rt. Hon. Dr Liam; British, MP for North Somerset, UK Government; ***born:*** 1961; ***married:*** Jesme Fox, Dec. 2005; ***education:*** St. Bride's High Sch., East Kilbride; Univ. of Glasgow; ***party:*** Conservative party; ***political career:*** Nat. Vice Chmn., Scottish Young Conservatives, 1983-84; MP, Woodspring, 1992-10, MP, North Somerset, 2010-; PPS to Michael Howard MP, Home Sec., 1993; Asst. Govt. Whip, 1994; Lord Cmnr., Her Majesty's Treasury - Sen. Govt. Whip, 1995; Parly. Under-Sec. of State, Foreign and Commonwealth Affairs Office, 1996-97; Spokesman on Constitutional Affairs; Shadow Sec. of State for Health, 1999-2003; Co-chmn., Conservative Party, 2003-05; Shadow Foreign Secretary, May-Dec. 2005; Shadow Defence Sec., 2005-May 2010; Sec. of State for Defence, May 2010-Oct. 2011, (resigned); ***memberships:*** Royal Coll. of General Practitioners; Mem., Beaconsfield CPC; ***professional career:*** GP; Civilian Army Medical Officer, Divisional Surgeon, St. John's Ambulance; ***committees:*** Mem., Central Cttee. Families for Defence, 1987-89; Mem. Select Cttee. 1992-93; Sec., Conservative Back Bench Health Cttee., 1992-1993; Sec., Conservative West Country Members Cttee., 1992-93; ***clubs:*** Pres., Glasgow Univ. Conservative Club, 1982-83; ***office address:*** House of Commons, London, SW1A 0AA, United Kingdom; ***phone:*** +44 (0)20 7219 3000.

FRAMLINGHAM, Lord Michael; Member, House of Lords; ***born:*** 17 October 1938, Manchester, UK; ***education:*** William Hulme's Grammar Sch., Manchester; Christ Coll., Cambridge; ***party:*** Conservative Party; ***political career:*** Cllr., North Bedfordshire Borough, 1974-77; Parly. Candidate for Manchester, Gorton, 1979; Cllr., Bedfordshire County, 1981-83; PPS to John MacGregor, Min. of State, 1984-85; Chief Sec. to the Treasury, 1985-87; Mem., WEU, 1987-91; Parly. Assembly to the Cncl. of Europe, 1987-91; Second Dep. Chmn., Ways and Means (Dep. Speaker), 1997-; MP, Central Suffolk and North Ipswich, 1983-2010; Mem., House of Lords, 2011-; ***interests:*** agriculture, arboriculture, forestry, countryside, environment, sport; ***committees:*** Mem., Select Cttee. on Agriculture, 1983-84; Select Cttee. on Admin., 1990; ***honours and awards:*** Knighthood, 2001; Raised to the peerage as Baron Framlingham, of Eye in the County of Suffolk, 2011-; ***recreations:*** sailing, golf, gardening, Britain's ancient and historic trees; ***office address:*** House of Lords, London, SW1A 0PW, United Kingdom; ***phone:*** +44 (0)20 7219 3000.

FRANCIS, Gregory R.; Lt. Governor, US Virgin Islands; ***s:*** 1; ***d:*** 3; ***education:*** Univ. of the Virgin Islands, Paralegal Programme, 1984; ***party:*** Democrat; ***political career:*** Dir., Office of Veterans' Affairs, 1999-2001; Administrator of St. Croix, 2001-06; ***professional career:*** served 27 years in US Army, with postings to Germany, Puerto Rico and the Virgin Islands, posts incl. Command Program Support Specialist, Supervisory Military Personal Specialist and Recruiting and Retention Manager; retired from US Army with rank of Chief Warrant Officer, 1999; ***office address:*** Office of the Lt. Governor, 18 Kongens Gade, Charlotte Amalie, 00802, US Virgin Islands; ***phone:*** +1 340 774 2991 / 773 6449; ***fax:*** +1 340 774 6593 / 773 0330; ***URL:*** http://www.ltg.gov.vi/.

FRANCIS, Hywel; British, Member of Parliament for Aberavon, House of Commons; ***born:*** 6 June 1946, Onllwyn, South Wales; ***parents:*** David Francis and Catherine Francis; ***married:*** Mair Georgina Price, 7 September 1968; ***children:*** Samuel (dec'd) (M), Dafydd (M), Hannah (F); ***languages:*** English, French, Welsh; ***education:*** Llangatwg Secondary, 1958-59; Whitchurch secondary, 1960; Whitchurch Grammar, 1960-65; BA (Hons), History, University of Wales, Swansea, 1968, Ph.D., History; ***party:*** Labour Party; ***political career:*** MP, Aberavon, 2001-; ***committees:*** Liaison, 2005-; Chair, Jt. Cttee. on Human Rights, 2010-; ***office address:*** House of Commons, London, SW1A 0AA, United Kingdom; ***phone:*** +44 (0)20 7219 8121; ***fax:*** +44 (0)20 7219 1734; ***e-mail:*** francish@parliament.uk; ***URL:*** http://www.epolitix.com/webminster/hywel-francis.

FRANCIS, Patricia; Executive Director, International Trade Centre; ***professional career:*** business leader; business facilitator; President, Jamaica Trade and Invest, 1996-2006; mem., Jamaican Cttee. for Development; Exec. Dir. , International Trade Centre, 2006-; ***office address:*** International Trade Centre, Palais des Nations, 1211 Geneva 10, Switzerland; ***phone:*** +41 (0)22 730 0111; ***URL:*** http://www.intracen.org/.

FRANCIS I, His Holiness Pope (Jorge Mario Bergoglio); Pope, Bishop of Rome and Head of the Roman Catholic Church; ***born:*** 17 December 1936, Buenos Aires, Argentina; ***parents:*** Mario José Bergoglio and Regina María Sívori; ***education:*** M.Sc. (chemistry) Univ. of Buenos Aires, Argentina; ***professional career:*** Ordained as a Jesuit, 1969; Bishop, 1992-98; Archbishop of Buenos Aires, 1998-2013; Cardinal, 2001-13; Elected Pope, March 13, 2013-; ***office address:*** The Vatican, Vatican City, Italy; ***URL:*** http://www.vatican.va.

FRANCOIS, Mark; MP for Rayleigh and Wickford, House of Commons; ***born:*** 1965, Islington, UK; ***education:*** BA (Hons), History, Bristol Univ.,1986; MA, War Studies, King's Col., London Univ., 1987; ***party:*** Conservative Party; ***political career:*** MP, Rayleigh, June 2001-2010, Rayleigh and Wickford, 2010-; Junior Opposition Whip, July 2002; Shadow Economic Sec. to the Treasury, 2004; Shadow Paymaster General, 2005-07; Shadow Europe Minister, 2007-10; Government Whip (Vice-Chamberlain of HM Household), 2010-12; Minister of State for Defence Personnel, Welfare and Veterans, Ministry of Defence, 2012-; ***professional career:*** Infantry Officer, Territorial Army; Self Employed Consultant; ***committees:*** Environmental Audit Cttee., 2001-05; ***recreations:*** reading, hill walking, history, particularly military history; ***office address:*** House of Commons, London, SW1A 0AA, United Kingdom; ***phone:*** +44 (0)20 7219 3000; ***e-mail:*** mark.francois.mp@parliament.uk; enquiries@rayleighandwickfordconservatives.com; ***URL:*** http://www.markfrancoismp.com; www.rayleighandwickfordconservatives.com.

FRANKEN, Senator Alan (Al); Senator for Minnesota, US Senate; ***born:*** May 21 1951; ***education:*** Harvard, 1973; ***party:*** DFL (Democratic-Farmer-Labor) Party; ***political career:*** US Senator for Minnesota, 2009-; ***professional career:*** comedy writer, author, and radio talk show host; ***committees:*** Health, Education, Labor, and Pension Committee; Judiciary Committee; Committee on Indian Affairs; Energy & Natural Resources; ***office address:*** US Senate, 320 Hart Senate Office Building, Washington, DC 20510, USA; ***phone:*** +1 202 224 5641; ***e-mail:*** info@franken.senate.gov; ***URL:*** http://www.franken.senate.gov/.

FRANKS, Trent; Congressman, Arizona Second District, US House of Representatives; ***political career:*** mem., Arizona House of Representatives; Congressman, Arizona Second District, US House of Representatives; ***committees:*** Armed Services; Judiciary; ***office address:*** US House of Representatives, 1237 Longworth House Office Building, Washington, DC 20515, USA.

FRASER, Murdo, MSP; Member for Mid Scotland and Fife, Scottish Parliament; ***born:*** 5 September 1965, Inverness, Scotland; ***parents:*** Sandy Fraser and Barbara Fraser; ***married:*** Emma Fraser (née Jarvis), 29 July 1994; ***s:*** 1; ***d:*** 1; ***education:*** Inverness Royal Academy, 1977-83; Aberdeen Univ., LLB (Hons), Dip LP, Grad., 1987; ***party:*** Conservative; ***political career:*** MSP for Mid Scotland & Fife, 2001-; Scottish Conservatives Spokesperson on Enterprise and Lifelong Learning, May 2003-07; Scottish Conservatives Deputy Leader, 2005-; Spokesman on Education, 2007-10; Spokesperson on Health, 2010-; ***professional career:*** Solicitor, Ketchen & Stevens WS, Edinburgh, 1990-2001; ***committees:*** Cross-Party Gp. in the Scottish Parl. on Scottish Economy; Audit Cttee.; ***recreations:*** climbing, cycling, football, classic cars, travel, Scottish history, Rangers FC; ***office address:*** Scottish Parliament, Edinburgh, EH99 1SP, United Kingdom; ***phone:*** +44 (0)13 1348 5293 / +44 (0)13 1738 553990; ***fax:*** +44 (0)13 1348 5933; ***e-mail:*** murdo.fraser.msp@scottish.parliament.uk.

FREDERIKSEN, Mette; Minister of Employment, Government of Denmark; ***born:*** 19 November 1977, Aalborg, Denmark; ***education:*** Bachelor of Administration and Social Science, Aalborg Univ., 2007; MA, African Studies, Univ. of Copenhagen, 2009-; ***party:*** Social Democratic Party; ***political career:*** MP, 2001-; Minister of Employment, 2011-; ***office address:*** Ministry of Employment, Ved Stranden 8, 1061 Copenhagen K, Denmark; ***phone:*** +45 3392 5900; ***fax:*** +45 3312 1378; ***e-mail:*** bm@bm.dk; ***URL:*** http://www.bm.dk.

FREEMAN, Lord; Member of the House of Lords; ***born:*** 21 May 1942; ***married:*** Jennifer Freeman, 1969; ***children:*** 2; ***education:*** Balliol Coll. Oxford (PPE), 1964; Institute of Chartered Accountants in England and Wales, 1969; ***party:*** Conservative Party; ***political career:*** MP, 1983-97; Privy Counsellor, 1993; Life Peer, 1997; Parliamentary Sec. Armed Forces, 1985-88; Parly. Sec. Health, 1988-90; Minister of State for Public Transport, 1990-94; Minister of State for Defence Procurement, 1994-95; Cabinet Minister for Public Service, 1995-97 and Chancellor of the Duchy of Lancaster; Special Advisor on Candidate Selection, Conservative Party, 1997-2001; Pres. Reserve Forces and Cadets Assoc., 1999-2010; Mem., House of Lords; ***professional career:*** Chmn., Thales UK PLC.; Chmn., Pricewaterhouse Coopers Advisory Bd., 2001-; ***clubs:*** Carlton Club; ***office address:*** House of Lords, London, SW1A 0PQ, United Kingdom; ***phone:*** +44 (0)20 7219 3000; ***fax:*** +44 (0)20 7219 5979.

FREEMAN, George; MP for Mid Norfolk, UK Government; ***party:*** Conservative; ***political career:*** MP for Mid Norfolk, May 2010-; PPS, 2010-12; Adviser, Life Sciences, 2011-; ***committees:*** Communities and Local Government Select Cttee., 2010; ***office address:*** House of Commons, London, SW1A 0AA, United Kingdom; ***phone:*** +44 (0)20 7219 3000; ***e-mail:*** george.freeman.mp@parliament.uk.

FREER, Mike; MP for Finchley and Golders Green, UK Government; ***party:*** Conservative; ***political career:*** Councillor, London Borough of Barnet Council, 1990-94, 2001-; MP for Finchley and Golders Green, May 2010-; ***committees:*** Communities and Local Government Select Cttee., 2010-11; Scottish Affairs, 2010-; ***office address:*** House of Commons, London, SW1A 0AA, United Kingdom; ***phone:*** +44 (0)20 7219 3000; ***e-mail:*** mike.freer.mp@parliament.uk.

FRENCH, Hon. Robert Shenton; Chief Justice , High Court of Australia; ***professional career:*** Admitted to the bar, 1972-; Barrister and Solicitor, Western Australia 1972-83; Independent Bar, 1983-86; Judge, Federal Court of Australia, 1986-2008; Pres., National Native Title Tribunal, 1994-98; Chief Justice, High Court of Australia, 2008-; ***office address:*** High Court of Australia, Parkes Place, Parkes, Canberra, ACT 2600, Australia; ***e-mail:*** enquiries@hcourt.gov.au; ***URL:*** http://www.hcourt.gov.au/.

FREUD OF EASTRY, Baron David Anthony; Member, House of Lords; ***born:*** 1950; ***education:*** Merton College, Oxford; ***political career:*** Mem., House of Lords, 2009-; Shadow Minister for welfare in the House of Lords, 2009-10; Parliamentary Under-Secretary of State (Minister for Welfare Reform) and Government Spokesperson, Department for Work and Pensions, 2010-; ***professional career:*** Journalist; ***office address:*** House of Lords, London, SW1A 0AA, United KIngdom.

FRICK, Dr Aurelia; Minister of Foreign Affairs, Government of Liechtenstein; ***born:*** September 19 1975; ***education:*** Law, Univ. of Fribourg, Switzerland; Doctorate of Law, Univ. of Basel, Switzerland; ***political career:*** Minister of Foreign Affairs, Minister of Justice, Minister of Cultural Affairs, 2009-13; Minister of Foreign Affairs, Minister of Education, Minister of Culture, 2013-; ***office address:*** Ministry of Foreign Affairs, Heiligkreuz 14, Postfach 684, Vaduz, Liechtenstien; ***phone:*** +423 236 6057.

FRIEDEN, Luc, LL.M; Minister of Finance, Luxembourg Government; ***born:*** 16 September 1963; ***education:*** Univ. of Luxembourg, 1982-83; Queen's Coll., Cambridge Univ., UK, LL.M., 1986-87; Harvard Law School, USA, LL.M, 1987-88; Univ. of Paris-Sorbonne, 1983-86; ***party:*** Christian Social Party; ***political career:*** Dep., Chamber of Deputies, 1994-1998; Minister of Justice, Treasury and Budget, 1998-2004; Minister of Justice, Treasury, Budget & Defence, 2004-06; Minister of Justice, Treasury and Budget, 2006-09; Minister of Finance, 2009-; ***professional career:*** Lawyer; ***office address:*** Ministry of Finance, 3 rue de la Congregation, L-1352 Luxembourg, Luxembourg; ***URL:*** http://www.etat.lu/fl.

FRIEDRICH, Dr Hans-Peter; Minister of the Interior, German Government; ***education:*** Univ. of Augsburg; ***party:*** Christian Social Union; ***political career:*** Mem. of the Bundestag, 1998-; Minister of the Interior, 2011-; ***professional career:*** Lawyer; ***office address:*** Ministry of the Interior, BM des Innern, Alt-Moabit 101, 10559 Berlin, Germany; ***phone:*** +49 (0)1888 6810; ***fax:*** +49 (0)1888 681 2926; ***e-mail:*** poststelle@bmi.bund.de; ***URL:*** http://www.bmi.bund.de.

FROMAN, Michael; US Trade Representative, US Government; ***born:*** 1962; ***education:*** Woodrow Wilson School, Princeton Univ., AB, Public & Int. Affairs; Oxford Univ., Ph.D., International Relations, 1988; Harvard Law School, J.D., 1991; ***political career:*** joined Clinton Administration, 1992; Dir., International Economic Affairs, National Economic Council & National Security Council, 1993-95; Dep. Assist. Sec.for Eurasia & the Middle East, 1996; Treasury Chief of Staff, 1997-99; policy advisor, Barack Obama's 2004 Senate campaign; Dep. Assist. to the President and Dep. National Security Adviser for International Economic Affairs, 2008; US Trade Rep., June 2013-; ***professional career:*** Harvard Law Review; various positions, Citigroup incl. Chief of Staff in the Office of the Chairman and COO, Internet Operating Group, 1999-2001; ***office address:*** Office of the US Trade Representative, 600 17th Street, NW, Washington, DC 20508, USA; ***phone:*** +1 202 395 3230; ***fax:*** +1 202 395 4549; ***URL:*** http://www.ustr.gov/.

FUGATE, William Craig; Administrator, Federal Emergency Management Agency; ***professional career:*** Emergency Manager, Alachua County, Gainesville, Florida, -1997; Bureau Chief for Preparedness and Response for FDEM; Dir., Florida Division of Emergency Management (FDEM); Administrator, FEMA, 2009-; ***office address:*** Federal Emergency Management Agency, Federal Emergency Management Agency (FEMA), 500 C Street, SW, Washington, DC 20472, USA; ***phone:*** +1 202 646 2500; ***URL:*** http://www.fema.gov/.

FÜLE, Stefan; European Commissioner for Enlargement and European Neighbourhood Policy, European Commission; ***born:*** 1962; ***political career:*** First Dep. Defence Minister, Czech Rep., 2001-02; European Affairs Minister, 2009; European Commissioner for Enlargement and European Neighbourhood Policy, 2010-; ***professional career:*** career diplomat; Czech Ambassador to Lithuania, 2000-01; Ambassador of the Czech Republic to the UK, 2003-05; Czech Perm. Rep. to NATO, 2005-09; ***office address:*** European Commission, rue de la Loi 200, B-1049 Brussels, Belgium; ***URL:*** http://www.europa.eu.

FULLANI, Ardian; Governor, Bank of Albania; ***professional career:*** joined State Bank of Albania, 1985, Dep. Dir., Foreign Dept., 1987-90; Hd., Foreign Dept., Albanian Commercial Bank, 1990-92; Dep. Gov., Bank of Albania, 1992-93; Dir., Foreign Dept., 1993-96; Consultancy, 1996-97; Dep. Gen. Manager, Italian-Albanian Bank, 1997-2000, Gen. Mgr., 2000-04; Governor, Bank of Albania, 2004-; ***office address:*** Bank of Albania, (Banka e Shqiperise), Sheshi Skenderbej 1, Tirana, Albania; ***phone:*** +355 (0)4 235568; ***fax:*** +355 (0)4 223558; ***e-mail:*** public@bankofalbania.org; ***URL:*** http://www.bankofalbania.org.

FULLBROOK, Lorraine; MP for South Ribble, UK Government; ***party:*** Conservative; ***political career:*** Councillor, Hart District Council, 2002-04; MP for South Ribble, May 2010-; ***committees:*** Home Affairs Select Cttee., 2010-; ***office address:*** House of Commons, London, SW1A 0AA, United Kingdom; ***phone:*** +44 (0)20 7219 3000; ***e-mail:*** lorraine.fullbrook.mp@parliament.uk.

FULLER, Richard; MP for Bedford, UK Organisation; ***party:*** Conservative; ***political career:*** MP for Bedford, May 2010-; ***office address:*** House of Commons, London, SW1A 0AA, United Kingdom; ***phone:*** +44 (0)20 7219 3000; ***e-mail:*** richard.fuller.mp@parliament.uk.

FUNES CARTAGENA, President Carlos Mauricio; President, El Salvador; ***born:*** 18 October 1959 , San Salvador; ***education:*** Univ. Centroamericana "José Simeón Cañas" (UCA), San Salvador, Literature ; ***party:*** Farabundo Marti National Liberation Front (FMLN); ***political career:*** President of El Salvador, 2009-; ***professional career:*** Journalist; TV host ; ***office address:*** Office of the President, Alameda Nauel Enrique Araujo 5505, San Salvador, El Salvador; ***phone:*** +503 248 9000; ***fax:*** +503 243 9947; ***e-mail:*** casapres@casapres.gob.sv; ***URL:*** http://www.casapres.gob.sv/.

FUREY, Hon. Charles, MHA; Canadian, Senator, Government of Canada; ***education:*** St. Francis Xavier Univ., Antigonish, Nova Scotia, Canada; ***political career:*** MHA, District of St. Barbe, Newfoundland and Labrador, 1985-; fmr. Minister, Dep. of Dev.; fmr. Minister, Tourism and Industry; fmr. Minister, Trade and Technology; Minister, Mines and Energy, 1997-99; Minister of Tourism, Culture and Recreation, 1999; Senator, 1999-; ***office address:*** Canadian Senate, Senate Building, 111 Wellington Street, Ontario ON K1A 0A4, Canada.

G

GAHR STORE, Jonas; Minister of Health and Care Services, Government of Norway; ***born:*** 25 August 1960; ***languages:*** English, French, German; ***education:*** Naval Officers Training School (OMA II), Royal Norwegian Naval Academy, 1979-81; Institut d'Etudes Politiques de Paris, Certificat d'Etudes Politiques de Paris, 1981-82, Diplome de l'Institut d'Etudes Politiques de Paris, 1982-85; ***political career:*** State Sec. and Chief of Staff, Office of the Prime Minister, 2000-01; Minister of Foreign Affairs, Oct. 2005-12; Minister of Health and Care Services, 2012-; ***professional career:*** Teaching Fellow, Harvard Law School, Harvard Negotiation Project, 1985-86; Research Fellow, Norwegian School of Management, Scenarios 2000, 1986-88; Special Adviser to the Prime Minister, Int. Dept., 1989-95; Dir. Gen., Int. Dept., Office of the Prime Minister, 1995-97; Exec. Dir., Head of the Dir. Gen. Office, World Health Organization, 1998-2000; Chmn., ECON Analysis, 2002-03; Sec. Gen., Norwegian Red Cross, 2003-05; ***office address:*** Ministry of Health and Care Services, Teatergata 9, PB 8011, 0030 Oslo, Norway; ***phone:*** +47 2224 9090; ***e-mail:*** postmottak@hod.dep.no.

GAJA, Professor Giorgio; Member, International Court of Justice; ***born:*** 1939; ***education:*** Univ. of Rome, Law, 1960; International Law, 1968; Hon. Doc. of Law, Dickinson Law School, 1985; ***professional career:*** *Academic career:* Prof. of International Law, Univ. of Florence, 1974-2011, Dean of the Law School, 1978-1981; Lecturer, Hague Academy of International Law,1981 and 2011. Part-time Prof., European Univ. Institute, 1980 and 1984-1985. Visiting Prof., John Hopkins Univ., 1977-1978, Univ. of Geneva, 1983 and 1985, Univ. of Paris I, 1989 and 2000, Univ. of Aix-Marseille III, 1992, Univ. of Michigan School of Law,1992, Columbia Law School, 1996, and Graduate Institute of International Studies, 2001; Prof. of International Law, Univ. of Florence, 1974-2011, Dean of the Law School, 1978-1981; Lecturer, Hague Academy of International Law,1981 and 2011. Part-time Prof., European Univ. Institute, 1980 and 1984-1985. Visiting Prof., John Hopkins Univ., 1977-1978, Univ. of Geneva, 1983 and 1985, Univ. of Paris I, 1989 and 2000, Univ. of Aix-Marseille III, 1992, Univ. of Michigan School of Law,1992, Columbia Law School, 1996, and Graduate Institute of International Studies, 2001.
Professional career: Member of the International Law Commission, 1999-2011. Delegate of the Italian Gov. to the Vienna Conference on the Law of Treaties between States and International Organizations and between International Organizations, 1986. Counsel to the Italian Government in the ELSI case before the International Court of Justice; *Judicial career:* Mem., International Court of Justice, 2012-; ***office address:*** International Court of Justice, The Peace Palace, 2517 KJ The Hague, Netherlands; ***phone:*** +31 (0)70 302 2337; ***fax:*** +31 (0)70 364 9928.

GALE, Roger James; British, Member of Parliament for North Thanet, House of Commons; ***born:*** 1943, Poole, Dorset; ***parents:*** Richard Gale and Phyllis (née Rowell); ***married:*** Susan Gabrielle Marks, 1980; ***children:*** Jasper (M), Thomas (M), Misty (F); ***public role of spouse:*** Vice Chair., Conservative Animal Welfare Group and JP; ***languages:*** French; ***education:*** Hardye's School, Dorchester; Guildhall Sch. of Music and Drama (LGM&D); ***party:*** Conservative Party; ***political career:*** MP, North Thanet, 1983-; PPS to the Minister of State For the Armed Forces, 1987-89; Speaker's Panel of Chmn., 1997-; Vice Chmn., Conservative Party, 2001-03; ***memberships:*** Equity; FRAME (former Chmn. 1987-89); British Delegation Council of Europe 1987-89; Western European Union, 1987-89; Hon. Mem., British Veterinary Assn.; ***professional career:*** Freelance broadcasting, 1963-68; PA to Gen. Man., Universal Films, 1968-70; Market Research, Marplan, 1970-72; freelance reporter, BBC Radio London, 1972-73; Producer, BBC Radio Newsbeat, 1973-75; Producer, BBC Radio 4 Today, 1975-76; Dir., BBC Children's Television, 1976-79; Producer/Director, Thames Television (Children's), 1979-82; Editor, Teenage Unit, Thames Television, 1982-83; Chmn., CTU Communications Gp., working party, Trades Unions and Democracy; Member, BBC General Advisory Council, 1992; Pres., Conservative Animal Welfare Group; Chmn., The Try-Angle Awards Foundation; Vice-Pres., St. John's Ambulance (Herne Bay); ***committees:*** Served on Con. Trades Unionists National Cttee.; Vice-Chmn., Backbench Media Cttee; Chmn., Conservative Animal Welfare Gp., 1997-2001 and Patron, 2001-; Chmn., All Party Welfare Gp., 1992-98; Broadcasting Select Cttee.; BTP, 2003-06; Proceedure Cttee. 2007-; ***trusteeships:*** 1st St. John's (Margate) Scouts; ***honours and awards:*** Parliament & Armed Forces Fellowship (1992); Fellow, Industry & Parliament Trust; Police & Parliament Fellowship; Richard Martin Award (RSPCA), 2001; Special Constable, British Transport Police, Oct. 2003; ***clubs:*** Kent County Cricket Club; Lords Taverners'; ***recreations:*** swimming, sailing; ***office address:*** House of Commons, London, SW1A 0AA, United Kingdom; ***phone:*** +44 (0)20 7219 3000; ***e-mail:*** galerj@parliament.uk.

GALLARD, H.E. Jill; Ambassador, British Embassy of Portugal; ***professional career:*** FCO, 1991-; Amb. to Portugal, 2011-; ***office address:*** British Embassy, Rua de Sao Bernardo 33, 1249-082 Lisbon, Portugal; ***phone:*** +351 21 392 4000; ***fax:*** +351 21 392 4185; ***e-mail:*** PPA@Lisbon.mail.fco.gov.uk; ***URL:*** http://www.ukinportugal.gov.uk.

GALLARDON, Alberto Ruiz; Minister of Justice, Government of Spain; ***born:*** 1958; ***political career:*** Councillor, Madrid, 1983; Dep., Regional Assembly, 1987-2004, senator, 1987-2004; Pres., COmmunity of Madrid, 19elected 1995 and 1999; Mayor of Madrid, 2003-2011; Dep., Madrid district, 2011; Minister of Justice, 2012-; ***professional career:*** Attorney at Law; ***office address:*** Ministry of Justice, C/ San Bernardo, 45, 28015 Madrid, Spain; ***phone:*** +34 91 390 4500; ***URL:*** http://www.mjusticia.gob.es/.

GALLOWAY, George, MP; British, Member of Parliament for Bradford West, House of Commons; ***born:*** 1954, Dundee, Scotland; ***parents:*** George Galloway and Sheila Galloway (née Reilly); ***married:*** Elaine Fyffe, 1979 (div'd); ***children:*** Lucy (F), Zein (M); ***education:*** Harris Academy, Dundee; ***political career:*** N.E.C., Scottish Labour Party, 1975-84; Chmn., Scottish Lab. Party, 1981-82; Lab. Party Organiser, 1977-83; Fonder, British Trades Union Friends of Palestine, 1980; Gen. Secy., War on Want, 1983-87; MP (Lab.) for Hillhead, 1987-97; MP, Glasgow Kelvin, 1997- expelled from Labour Party Oct. 2003, Respect Party MP; MP for Bethnal Green and Bow, 2005-10; MP for Bradford West, March 2011-; ***interests:*** defence, foreign affairs; ***memberships:*** Transport and General Workers Union; ***professional career:*** Part time broadcaster, talkSPORT, to date; Founder, Marian Appeal, 1998; Chmn. & Founder, Great Britain - Iraq Soc., 2000-; ***committees:*** Fmr. Sec., All Party Parly. Gp. on Iran; Chmn., Emergency Cttee. on Iraq, 1991; ***honours and awards:*** Hilali-Quaid-Azzam Award for services to Democracy (Pakistan); Hilali-Pakistan (services to Kashmir); ***publications:*** The Ceausescus and the Romanian Revolution, 1991; I'm Not the Only One, 2004 (Penguin); Fidel Castro Handbook, (MQ Publications), 2006; ***office address:*** House of Commons, London, SW1A 0AA, United Kingdom; ***phone:*** +44 (0)20 7219 6940; +44 (0)20 7613 5640; ***fax:*** +44 (0)20 7219 2879; +44 (0)20 7613 5310; ***e-mail:*** gallowayg@parliament.uk; rob@respectcoalition.org.

GAPES, Mike; Member of Parliament for Ilford South, House of Commons; ***born:*** 4 September 1952, Wanstead, UK; ***parents:*** the late Frank Gapes and Emily Gapes; ***education:*** MA, Economics, Cambridge Univ.; Diploma, Industrial Relations, Middlesex Polytechnic; ***party:*** Labour and Co-op; ***political career:*** Research Officer, Int. Dept., Labour Party, 1980-88; Sr. Int. Officer, 1988-92; PPS to the Min. of State, Northern Ireland Office, Paul Murphy, 1997-99; PPS to the Minister of State at Home Affairs, Lord Jeff Rooker, 2001-2; MP for Ilford South, 1992-; ***interests:*** foreign affairs, housing, education, defence; ***professional career:*** VSO teacher in Swaziland, 1971-72; ***committees:*** mem., Foreign Affairs Select Cttee., 1992-97, chmn., 2005-10, mem., 2010-; mem., Defence Select Cttee., 1999-2001, 2003-05; chmn., Westminster Foundation for Democracy, 2002-05; ***recreations:*** music, football; ***office address:*** House of Commons, London, SW1A 0AA, United Kingdom; ***phone:*** +44 (0)20 7219 3000; ***e-mail:*** mike.gapes.mp@parliament.uk.

GARAMENDI, John; Congressman for California, 10th Dist., US House of Representatives; ***education:*** Univ. of California at Berkeley, BA, Business; Harvard Business School, MBA; ***political career:*** Mem., Calif. State Assembly, 1974-76; Senator, Calif. State Senate, 1976-1990, Senate Maj. Ldr.; Calif. Insurance Cmnr., 1991-95, 2003-07; Dep. Sec., US Dept. of the Interior, 1995-98; Lt. Gov., California, 2007-09; Congressman, US HOR, 2009-; ***professional career:*** Rancher; Peace Corps volunteer (teaching and community development, Ethiopia); ***committees:*** Armed Services; Natural Resources; ***office address:*** US House of Representatives, 2459 Rayburn HOB, Washington, DC 20515, USA; ***phone:*** +1 202 225 1880; ***URL:*** http://garamendi.house.gov/.

GARAYEV, Abulfas; Minister of Culture and Tourism, Government of Azerbaijan; ***born:*** 13 November 1956, Baku, Azerbaijan; ***parents:*** Mursal Abulfas and Boyukkhanim Abulfas; ***married:*** Lala Kazîmova, 1983; ***children:*** Suad (F); ***languages:*** Azeri, English, French, Russian, Turkish; ***education:*** Univ. of Foreign Languages, Ph.D., 1978; Academy of Social Sciences, Moscow, 1992; ***political career:*** Minister of Youth and Sport, 1994-2001; Minister of Youth, Tourism and Sport, 2001-06; Minister of Culture and Tourism, 2006-; ***interests:*** international relations, diplomacy, political science, scientific research; ***professional career:*** Teacher, 1978; Military Service, 1978-80; Instructor in organisational dept. of Narimanov District's Communist Party, 1985-87; Head of Propaganda Dept. of Narimanov District's Communist Party, 1987-89; Commercial Dir. Improteks Commers Co., 1992-93; Lecturer, Univ. of Politology and State Admin, Dept. of Culture, 1992-93; Dir. Gen., Improteks Commers Co., 1993-94 ; ***committees:*** Vice-Pres., Nat. Olympic Cttee. of the Republic of Azerbaijan; ***publications:*** Cultural Aspects of Azerbaijani Diaspora in 1918-1930; ***recreations:*** swimming, tennis, hunting; ***office address:*** Ministry of Culture and Tourism, House of Government, Baku - AZ 1000, Azerbaijan; ***phone:*** +994 (0)12 493 4398; ***fax:*** +994 (0)12 493 5605; ***e-mail:*** nazir@mct.gov.az.

GARCIA LINERA, Vice President Alvaro Marcelo; Vice-President, Bolivia; ***born:*** 19 October 1961, Cochabamba, Bolivia; ***education:*** Universidad Nacional Autónoma de México (UNAM), B.Sc., Mathematics, 1985; UNAM, Postgrad. studies in Pure Sciences; ***political career:*** Campaigner for indigenous land rights; arrested and tortured in April 1992; imprisoned without trial or sentence, 1992-95; Vice-Pres., 2005-; ***professional career:*** Professor, Sociology, Social Sciences and Political Science at three Bolivian universities, 1997- ; ***office address:*** Office of the Vice President, Palacio de Gobierno, Plaza Murillo, La Paz, Bolivia; ***phone:*** +591 2 371302 / 359736; ***fax:*** +591 2 367421.

GARCIA-MARGALLO Y MARFIL, José Manuel; Minister of the Home Affairs, Government of Spain; ***born:*** 1944; ***education:*** Law Degree, 1965; LL.M, Harvard, 1972; Univ. of Miguel Hernandez, 2002; ***political career:*** Mem., Congress, 1977-79; MEP, 1994; Minister of Justice, 2012-; ***professional career:*** lawyer; ***office address:*** Ministry of the Interior, Calle Rafael Calvo 33, 28071 Madrid, Spain; ***URL:*** http://www.exteriores.gob.es/.

GARCIA PADILLA, Alejandro; Governor, Puerto Rico; ***born:*** 1971; ***education:*** Univ. of Puerto Rico; Interamerican Univ. of Puerto Rico, law; ***party:*** Democrat; ***political career:*** Sec., Puerto Rico Dept. of Consumer Affairs, 2005-07; Senator, 2008; Governor of Puerto Rico, 2012-; ***professional career:*** lawyer; ***office address:*** Office of the Governor, La Fortaleza, PO Box 82, San Juan, PR 00901, Puerto Rico; ***URL:*** http://www.fortaleza.gobierno.pr.

GARDINER, Barry; British, MP for Brent North, House of Commons; ***born:*** 10 March 1957, Glasgow; ***parents:*** John Flannegan Gardiner and Sylvia Jean Gardiner; ***married:*** Caroline Smith, 29 July 1979; ***children:*** Jesse (M), Cameron (M), Jacob (M), Bethany (F); ***public role of spouse:*** Poet; ***languages:*** French; ***education:*** Univ. of St. Andrew's; Univ. of Cambridge; Harvard Univ., USA, John F. Kennedy Scholarship, 1983; ***party:*** Labour Party; ***political career:*** MP, Brent North, 1997-; Parly. Under-Sec. of State for Northern Ireland, 2004-05; Parly. Under-Sec. of State for Competitiveness, DTI, 2005-06; Parly. Sec. for Biodiversity, Landscape and Rural Affairs, 2006-07; Prime Minister's Special Envoy for Forestry, 2007-08; PPS to Lord Mandelson as Secretary of State for Business, Enterprise and Regulatory Reform/Business, Innovation and Skills, 2009-10; ***interests:*** trade and industry, crime, economy, foreign affairs; ***memberships:*** Chair, Labour Friends of India; ***professional career:*** Arbitrator; Lecturer, Moscow, Russia; ***committees:*** Chair, Broadcasting Select Cttee., Procedure Select Cttee., 1997-2001; Broadcasting, -2001; Energy & Climate Change, 2010-; Environment, Food & Rural Affairs, 2011-; ***trusteeships:*** Parliamentary Contributory Pension Fund; ***publications:*** Philosophical Quarterly + Insurance International; ***recreations:*** hill-walker, birdwatcher; ***office address:*** House of Commons, London, SW1A 0AA, United Kingdom; ***phone:*** +44 (0)20 7219 4046; ***e-mail:*** gardinerb@parliament.uk; ***URL:*** http://www.barrygardiner.com.

GARDINER OF KIMBLE, Lord John; Member, House of Lords; ***party:*** Conservative; ***political career:*** Mem. House of Lords, 2010-; ***professional career:*** Dep. Chief Exec. of Countryside Alliance; ***honours and awards:*** Raised to the peerage as Baron Gardiner of Kimble, 2010; ***office address:*** House of Lords, London, SW1A 0PW, United Kingdom; ***phone:*** +44 (0)20 7219 5353.

GARDNER, Cory; Congressman, US House of Representatives; ***party:*** Republican; ***political career:*** Congressman, HOR, Colorado 4th District, 2011-; ***committees:*** Energy & Commerce; ***office address:*** 213 Cannon HOB, Washington DC 20515, USA.

GARNIER, Edward, QC, MP; MP for Harborough, House of Commons; ***born:*** 26 October 1952; ***parents:*** Colonel William d'Arcy Garnier (dec'd) and The Hon. Lavender d'Arcy Garnier (née de Grey); ***married:*** Anna Caroline Garnier (née Mellows), 17 April 1982; ***children:*** George Edward (M), James William (M), Eleanor Katharine Rose (F); ***languages:*** French; ***education:*** Wellington Coll., Berkshire; Jesus Coll., Oxford; Coll. of Law, London; ***party:*** Conservative Party; ***political career:*** MP for Harborough, 1992-; PPS to Rt. Hon. Alastair Goodlad MP and David Davis MP, Ministers of State, FCO, 1994-95; PPS to Rt. Hon. Sir Nicholas Lyell QC MP, the Attorney General and Sir Derek Spencer QC MP, the Solicitor

Gar-Geo

General, 1995; PPS, Rt. Hon. Roger Freeman MP, Chancellor of the Duchy of Lancaster, 1996; Visiting Parly. Fellow, St. Antony's College, Oxford, 1996-97; Shadow Minister, Lord Chancellor's Dept., 1997-99; Shadow Attorney General, 1999-2001; Shadow Home Affairs Minister, 2005-07; Shadow Minister for Justice, 2007-09; Attorney General, 2009-10; Solicitor General, 2010-12; ***professional career:*** Barrister, 1976; QC, 1995; Crown Court Recorder, 1998; Bencher of the Middle Temple, 2001; ***committees:*** Hon. Sec., Foreign Affairs Forum, 1988-92, vice chmn., 1992-; sec., Conservative House of Commons Foreign Affairs Cttee., 1992-94; mem., Home Affairs Select Cttee., 1992-95; ***publications:*** Contributor to Halsbury's Laws of England, 4th edition (1984), Facing the Future (1993), Bearing the Standard (1991); ***office address:*** House of Commons, London, SW1A 0AA, United Kingdom; ***phone:*** +44 (0)20 7219 3000; ***e-mail:*** garniere@parliament.uk; ***URL:*** http://www.edwardgarnier.co.uk.

GARNIER, Mark; MP for Wyre Forest, UK Government; ***party:*** Conservative; ***political career:*** Councillor, Forest of Dean District Council, 2003-07; MP for Wyre Forest, May 2010-; ***committees:*** Treasury Select Cttee., 2010-; Banking Standards, 2012-; ***office address:*** House of Commons, London, SW1A 0AA, United Kingdom; ***phone:*** +44 (0)20 7219 3000; ***e-mail:*** mark.garnier.mp@parliament.uk.

GAROYIAN, Marios; Leader, Dimokratico Komma; ***born:*** 31 May 1961, Nicosia, Cyprus; ***married:*** Marina Garoyian (née Adamides); ***languages:*** English, Italian, Spanish; ***education:*** Terra Santa College; Univ. of Perugia, Italy, political science; ***political career:*** Pres., Students' Movement Anagennisi of Italy, 1981; First Pres., Students Union of Cypriots of Perugia, 1983; mem., administrative cttee. of POFNE; Pres., Nicosia District Cttee., NEDIK, 1986-92; Sec., Union Dept. of the Party, 1992-; Dir., House of Representatives, President's Office, 1991-2001; Pres. House of Representatives, 2008-11; ***committees:*** mem., Central Cttee. of DIKO, 1988-, mem., Executive Office; ***office address:*** House of Representatives, Dyiavaharlal Nehrou, Omerou Avenue, 1402 Nicosia, Cyprus; ***phone:*** +357 (0)2 303451; ***fax:*** +357 (0)2 366611; ***URL:*** http://www.parliament.cy.

GASINZIGWA, Oda; Minister of Family and Gender Promotion in the Office of the Prime Minister, Government of Rwanda; ***born:*** 1966; ***education:*** Inst. of Development Management, Tanzania, Bachelor's Degree, Local Gov.; Kigali Inst. of Education, MA, Gender and Development; ***political career:*** Sec., National Women Council; Chairperson, National Women Council, 2004; Chief Gender Monitoring Officer, 2008-13; Minister of Family & Gender Promotion in the Office of the Prime Minister, 2013-; ***office address:*** Prime Minister's Office, PO Box 1334, Kigali, Rwanda.

GASPAROVIC, Ivan; President, Slovak Republic; ***born:*** 1941; ***children:*** 2; ***education:*** Comerius Univ., Faculty of Law; ***party:*** fmr. mem., Movement for a Democratic Slovakia; ***political career:*** Speaker, National Council, 1994-98; President, Slovak Republic, June 2004-; ***professional career:*** Lawyer; Lecturer in Law; ***office address:*** Office of the President, Hodozovo nam 1, PO Box 128, 81000 Bratislava, Slovak Republic.

GATES III, William H. (Bill); American, Co-chair, Bill and Melinda Gates Foundation; ***born:*** 28 October 1955, Seattle, USA; ***parents:*** William H. Gates II and Mary Gates; ***married:*** Melinda French Gates; ***children:*** Jennifer (F); ***education:*** Lakeside Sch., North Seattle, USA; Harvard Univ.; ***professional career:*** Chmn., Chief Exec. & Co-founder, Microsoft Corporation; Chairman, 2000-; Chief Software Architect, Microsoft Corp., 2000-08; Co-chair, Bill and Melinda Gates Foundation, 2008-; ***publications:*** The Road Ahead, 1995; Business@ The Speed of Thought; ***recreations:*** reading, golf, bridge; ***office address:*** Bill and Melinda Gates Foundation, PO Box 23350, Seattle, WA 98102, USA; ***phone:*** +1 206 709 3100; ***e-mail:*** info@gatesfoundation.org; ***URL:*** http://www.gatesfoundation.org.

GATETE, Amb. Claver; Minister of Finance & Economic Planning, Government of Rwanda; ***born:*** 1962, Uganda; ***education:*** Univ. of British Colombia, Canada, Agricultural Economics, BSc, MSc; ***political career:*** President's Rep. to Nepad, Oct. 2001; Sec. Gen. & Sec. to the Treasury, Ministry of Finance & Economic Planning, 2003-05; Minister of Finance & Economic Planning, 2012-; ***professional career:*** Economist; various boards of directors; Economist, UN Development Programme, Rwanda, 1997-2000; Amb. to the UK, Ireland and Iceland, 2005-09; Dep. Governor, National Bank of Rwanda, 2009-11, Governor, 2011-13; ***office address:*** Ministry of Finance & Economic Planning, BP 158, Kigali, Rwanda; ***phone:*** +250 55756 / 75113; ***fax:*** +250 57581 / 77581; ***URL:*** http://www.minecofin.gov.rw/.

GAUCK, Joachim; President, Government of Germany; ***born:*** January 1940; ***education:*** Univ. of Rostock; ***political career:*** President, March 2012-; ***professional career:*** Lutheren Pastor; ***office address:*** Office of the Federal President, Bundespraesidialamt, Spreeweg 1, 10557 Berlin, Germany; ***phone:*** +49 (0)30 2000 0; ***fax:*** +49 (0)30 2000 1999; ***e-mail:*** posteingang@bundespraesident.de; ***URL:*** http://www.bundespraesident.de.

GAUKE, David; Exchequer Secretary, HM Treasury; ***born:*** 1971; ***party:*** Conservative; ***political career:*** MP for South West Hertfordshire, 2005-; Shadow Exchequer Secretary to the Treasury, 2007-10; Exchequer Secretary, May 2010-; ***professional career:*** Solicitor; ***office address:*** HM Treasury, 1 Horse Guards Road, London, SW1A 2HQ, United Kingdom.

GAVIN, H.E. Michelle; Ambassador, US Embassy in Botswana; ***education:*** BA, Georgetown Univ., USA; MPhil., Int. Relations from Oxford Univ., UK, (Rhodes Scholar); ***professional career:*** Special Assist. to the President; Amb. to Botswana, 2011-; ***office address:*** US Embassy, PO Box 90, Gaborone, Botswana; ***phone:*** +267 353982; ***fax:*** +267 395 6947; ***e-mail:*** usembgab@mega.bw; ***URL:*** http://botswana.usembassy.gov.

GAZMIN, Voltaire; Secretary of Defence, Government of the Philippines; ***born:*** October 22 1944, Moncada, Tarlac; ***married:*** Rhodora Hernandez; ***children:*** Ezechiel (M), Leandro (M); ***education:*** Philippine Military Academy, 1968; ***political career:*** Secretary of Defence, 2010-; ***professional career:*** Army, Commanding General, Philippine Army, 1999-2000; Amb. to Cambodia, 2002-04; ***office address:*** Department of Defence, Room 301, 3rd Floor, DND Building, Camp Aguinaldo, Quezon City, Philippines; ***phone:*** +63 2 911 6001; ***URL:*** http://www.dnd.gov.ph.

GEENS, Koen; Minister of Finance, Government of Belgium; ***political career:*** Deputy Prime Minister, Minister of Finance and Sustainable Development, Minister responsible for the Civil Service, March 2013-; ***professional career:*** Professor of law and economics, Catholic Univ. of Leuven; ***office address:*** Ministry of Finance, 12 rue de la Loi, 1000 Brussels, Belgium; ***phone:*** +32 (0)2 233 8111; ***fax:*** +32 (0)2 233 8003; ***URL:*** http://www.minfin.fgov.be/.

GEINGOB, Hage Gottfried, LL.D; Namibian, Prime Minister, Namibian Government; ***born:*** 1941; ***education:*** BA (Fordham Univ., NY); MA (International Relations) (New Sch. Social Research, NY); LLD (Hon.) Univ. of Delhi; ***party:*** SWAPO; ***political career:*** SWAPO Rep. for UN and the Americas 1964-71; Asst. SWAPO Rep., Botswana 1963-64; Political Affairs Officer, UN Secretariat 1972-75; Director UN Institute for Namibia, Lusaka 1975-89; Election Director SWAPO 1989; Chmn. Constituent Assembly 1989-90; Prime Minister, Republic of Namibia, 1990-2002; Minister of Trade & Industry, 2008-12; Vice-Pres., SWAPO; Prime Minister, 2012-; ***honours and awards:*** Palmes Academiques (Officer Class) by the French Govt. in recognition of valuable services in education 1980; Ongulumbashe Medal for Bravery and Long Service 1987; Ph.D Honoris Causa by Columbia College, Illinois 1994; Carlos Manuel De Cespedes, the second highest order in Cuba 1994; Order of the Dun, 1st Class by the Govt. of Namibia for providing outstanding political leadership; ***publications:*** Chmn. of the most comprehensive study ever undertaken on Namibia, viz., Namibia: Perspectives for National Reconstruction and Development 1985-86; Chmn., Research Coordination Cttee., twenty-five sectoral policy publications; numerous international articles; ***office address:*** Office of the Prime Minister, Private Bag 13338, Windhoek, Namibia.

GEITHNER, Timothy Franz; Senior Fellow, Council on Foreign Relations; ***born:*** 18 August 1961, New York, USA; ***languages:*** Chinese, Japanese; ***education:*** Dartmouth College, A.B., Government and Asian studies, 1983; Johns Hopkins Univ. School of Advanced International Studies, M.A., International Economics and East Asian studies, 1985; ***political career:*** Secretary for the Treasury, 2009-2013; ***memberships:*** Group of Thirty, 2006; ***professional career:*** Kissinger and Assoc., 1985-88; International Affairs Div., U.S. Treasury Dept., 1988-, Attaché, US Embassy, Tokyo, Dep. Assist. Sec., Int'l. Monetary and Financial policy, 1995-96, Senior Dep. Assist. Sec., Intl. Affairs, 1996-97, Assist. Sec., Intl. Affairs, 1997-98, Under-Sec.of the Treasury for International Affairs, 1998-2001; Dir., Policy Development and Review Dept., IMF, 2001-03; Sr. Fellow, Intl. Economics Dept., Council on Foreign Relations, 2002-03; Pres., Federal Reserve Bank of New York, 2003-08 (arranged the rescue and sale of Bear Stearns, March 2008); Senior Fellow, Council of Foreign Relations, 2013-; ***office address:*** Council on Foreign Relations, The Harold Pratt House, 58 East 68th Street, New York, NY 10065, USA; ***phone:*** +1 212 434 9400; ***URL:*** http://www.cfr.org.

GEOGHEGAN-QUINN, Máire; Irish, European Commissioner for Research and Innovation, European Commission; ***born:*** 1950; ***parents:*** John Geoghegan and Barbara Geoghegan (née Folan); ***married:*** John Quinn; ***languages:*** Irish, French; ***education:*** Scoil Mhuire, Carna, Co. Galway; Coláiste Mhuire, Tourmakeady, Co. Mayo; Carysfort Training Coll., Blackrock, Co. Dublin; ***party:*** Fianna Fáil; ***political career:*** Parly. Secy. to the Minister for Industry, Commerce and Energy 1977; Minister of State at the Dept. of Industry, Commerce and Energy 1978-79; Minister for the Gaeltacht (Irish speaking areas) Dec. 1979-June 1981; Minister for Youth and Sport, Mar.-Nov. 1982; Front Bench Spokesperson for Women's Rights; Minister of State of Dept. of the Taoiseach with special responsibility as Co-ordinator of Govt. Policy and European Community Matters 1987-92; Min. for Tourism, Transport and Communication 1992-93; Minister for Justice 1993-94; ret'd June 1997; European Commissioner for Research and Innovation, 2010-; ***memberships:*** Dáil Eireann for Galway West 1975-; ***professional career:*** Teacher, Ranelagh, Dublin 1970-73; Teacher, Renmore, Galway 1973-75; ***committees:*** Galway Borough Cncl. 1985-91; Chwn., Joint Oireachtas Cttee. on Women's Rights; ***publications:*** The Green Diamond (novel) 1996; ***clubs:*** Bearna Golf & Country Club, Galway; ***office address:*** European Commission, rue de la Loi 200, B-1049 Brussels, Belgium; ***phone:*** +32 (0)2 299 1111; ***URL:*** http://www.europa.eu.

GEORGE, Andrew; Member of Parliament for St. Ives, House of Commons; ***born:*** 2 December 1958, Mullion, Cornwall, UK; ***parents:*** Reginald Hugh George and Diana May George (née Petherick); ***married:*** Jill Elizabeth Marshall, 4 July 1987; ***children:*** Davy Tregarthen (M), Morvah May (F); ***public role of spouse:*** Nurse; ***languages:*** French, Cornish; ***education:*** Mullion and Helston Schs., Cornwall; Univs. of Sussex and Oxford; ***party:*** Liberal Party, 1980-83 and 1987-; Mebyon Kernow (The Cornish Party), 1985-87; ***political career:*** MP for St. Ives, 1997-; Liberal Democrat Shadow Minister Fisheries 1997-2005; Liberal Democrat Disabilities Spokesman, 1999-2001; PPS to Liberal Democrat Leader, Rt. Hon. Charles Kennedy, MP, 2001-02; Shadow Liberal Democrat Farming and Rural Affairs Minister, 2002-05; Shadow Sec. of State for Int. Dev., 2005-06; ***interests:*** economic development, minority rights, racial issues, third world development, environment, Cornish issues, housing, agriculture, fishing; ***memberships:*** Pres., Cncl. Racial Equality, Cornwall; All Party Asthma Gp.; ***professional career:*** Charity worker; Dep. Dir., Cornwall Rural Community Cncl.; Researcher; ***committees:*** Agriculture Select Cttee., 1997-2000; Communities and Local Gov. Cttee.; various All Party Parliamentary Gps., including Vice Chair of Objective One Gp. and Fisheries Gp.; Roma Gp.; Housing and Planning Gp.; Debt, Aid and Trade Gp.; Global T.B. Gp; Health, 2010-; ***trusteeships:*** Pres., West Cornwall Reliant Robin Owners' Club; Pres., Cornish Racial Equality Cncl.; Rural Race Equality Action Project (Trustee); Trelya (Youth Project); ***publications:*** various books on housing, planning and community development; The Natives are Revolting Down in the Cornwall Theme Park, in Cornish Scene, 1986; Cornwall at the Crossroads, 1989; Another Vision of Cornwall, 1992; A View from the Bottom Left-Hand Corner, 2002; ***clubs:*** Commons and Lords Rugby Club; Parly. Football Team and Cricket Club; Leedstown Cricket; Crowntown Football Club; ***recreations:*** all sports, art, walking, gardening, hen keeping; ***office address:*** House of Commons, London, SW1A 0AA, United Kingdom; ***phone:*** +44 (0)20 7219 4588; ***e-mail:*** andrew.george.mp@parliament.uk.

GEORGIADES, Charis; Minister of Finance, Government of Cyprus; ***education:*** Univ. of Reading, UK; ***political career:*** Minister of Labour and Social Insurance, 2013; Minister of Finance, Apr. 2013-; ***office address:*** Ministry of Finance, Ex Secretariat Compound, 1439 Nicosia, Cyprus; ***phone:*** +357 22 601149; ***URL:*** http://www.mof.gov.cy.

BIOGRAPHIES

GEORGIEVA, Kristalina; Bulgarian, Commissioner, European Commission; ***education:*** Univ. of National & World Economy, Sofia, Bulgaria, MA, Ph.D, Economic Science; ***professional career:*** Assoc. Prof., Univ. of National and World Economy, 1977-93; Research Fellow, LSE; Visiting Prof., Univ. of the South Pacific, Fiji; Visiting Prof., Australian National Univ.; various positions, World Bank, 1993-2010, incl. Director, World Bank environmental strategy, policies and lending; Commissioner for International Co-operation, Humanitarian Aid and Crisis Response, 2010-; ***office address:*** European Commission, rue de la loi 2000, B-1049 Brussels, Belgium; ***URL:*** http://ec.europa.eu.

GERMAN, Lord Michael, OBE AM; Member, House of Lords; ***born:*** 8 May 1945, Cardiff, Wales, UK; ***education:*** St Marys Coll., Certificate of Education, 1963-66; Open Univ., BA, 1970-73; Univ. of the West of England, Dip. Education Management, 1973-74; ***party:*** Welsh Liberal Democrat; ***political career:*** Joined Liberal Party, 1974; Leader, Liberal Democrats, Cardiff City Council, 1983-96; Joint Leader of Cardiff City Cncl., 1987-91; Dir., General Election Campaigns in Wales, 1992, 1997; Mem., Federal Party Exec., 1991-99; Leader, Welsh Liberal Democrats Gp., National Assembly for Wales, 1999-; mem., Nat. Assembly for Wales, Regional mem., South Wales East-; Dep. First Minister and Minister for Economic Development; Dep. First Minister and Minister for Rural Development and Wales Abroad, 2002-03; Leader Welsh Liberal Democrats, Nov. 2007-Dec. 2008; Mem. House of Lords, 2010-; ***interests:*** Small businesses; ***professional career:*** Primary Sch. Teacher, Cardiff, UK, 1967-68; Comprehensive Sch. Teacher, Cardiff, 1968-70; Head of Music, Lady Mary High School, Cardiff, 1970-86; Head of Music, Corpus Christi High School, Cardiff, 1986-91; Dir. of the European Division of the WJEC, 1991-99; ***committees:*** Chair, Companies and Communications Cttee., 1990-98, 2010-; Mem., Federal Policy Cttee., 1987-89; Liberal Democrat Federal Exec. Cttee., 2001-02; Lib. Dem. Parly. Cttee. for Work and Pensions, 2010-; ***honours and awards:*** OBE for Public and Political Service, 1998; ***recreations:*** reading, music, travel; ***office address:*** House of Lords, London, SW1A 0PW, United Kingdom; ***phone:*** +44 (0)29 2089 8219; ***fax:*** +44 (0)29 2089 8354; ***URL:*** http://www.parliament.uk.

GHALLAMALLAH, Bouabdellah; Minister of Religious Affairs and Wakfs, Algerian Government; ***born:*** 1934; ***education:*** Univ. of Damascus, Syria, Social Sciences; ***political career:*** elected mem., APN, Minister of Religious Affairs, 1977-99; Minister of Religious Affairs and Endowments, 1999-; ***office address:*** Ministry for Religious Affairs, 4 rue de Timgad, Hydra, Algiers, Algeria; ***phone:*** +213 (0)21 608820; ***fax:*** +213 (0)21 691569.

GHANIYEV, Elyor; Minister of Foreign Economic Affairs, Government of Uzbekistan; ***born:*** 1 January 1960, Syrdaryo Province; ***education:*** Tashkent Polytechnic Inst., 1981; ***political career:*** Dep. Minister for Foreign Economic Relations, 1994-95; First Dep. Minister for Foreign Economic Relations, 1995-97; Minister of Foreign Economic Relations, 1997-2002; Vice Prime Minister, Chmn., Agency for Foreign Economic Relations, 2002-06; Minister of Foreign Affairs, 2006-10, Deputy Prime Minister, -2012; Minister of Foreign Economic Affairs, Investment & Trade, 2010-; ***professional career:*** Prof., Tashkent Polytechnic Inst., 1981-85; Military Service, 1985-90; Head, Protocol Service and Accreditation Dept, Ministry for Foreign Economic Relations, 1992-93; Head, Sector on Foreign Economic Problems, Inst. of Strategic & Interregional Research under the Pres. of the Republic of Uzbekistan, 1993-94; Engineer; ***committees:*** Sr. Advisor, State Cttee. on Foreign Economic and Trade Relations, 1990-92; ***office address:*** Agency for Foreign Economic Relations, 1 Shevchenko str. , 700029 Tashkent, Uzbekistan.

GHIMIRE, Madhav Prasad; Minister of Foreign Affairs and Home Affairs, Government of Nepal; ***born:*** 1961; ***political career:*** Chief Sec. of the Government, 2009-12; Minister of Home Affairs and Foreign Affairs, 2013-; ***professional career:*** long-standing civil service career; ***office address:*** Ministry of Foreign Affairs, Singha Durbar, Kathmandu, Nepal; ***phone:*** +977 1 422 8801; ***fax:*** +977 1 422 7186 .

GHIZ, Robert; Premier, Government of Prince Edward Island; ***education:*** Bishops Univ., BA, Political Science; ***party:*** Leader, Liberal Party of Prince Edward Island; ***political career:*** Premier, 2007-; ***office address:*** Office of the Premier, Fifth Floor, Shaw Building, 95 Rochford Street, P.O. Box 2000, Charlottetown, PE, C1A 7N8, Canada; ***phone:*** +1 902 368 4400; ***fax:*** +1 902 368 4416; ***URL:*** http://www.gov.pe.ca/.

GIBB, Nick; British, Minister of State, Department for Education, UK Government; ***born:*** 1960; ***education:*** Roundhay Sch., Leeds; Thornes House Sch.; Wakefield & Durham Univ.; ***party:*** Conservative Party; ***political career:*** Parly. Candidate, Stoke on Trent, 1992, Rotherham, 1994; MP, Bognor Regis and Littlehampton, 1997-; Shadow Treasury spokesman 1998-99; Shadow Trade & Industry spokesman. 1999-2001; Shadow Minister for Schools, 2005-10; Minister of State, Dept. for Education, 2010-; ***professional career:*** Chartered Accountant; ***committees:*** Public Accounts Cttee. 2001-03; Education and Skills, 2003-; ***publications:*** Author of numerous reports concerning tax, reform and economics; ***office address:*** House of Commons, London, SW1A 0AA, United Kingdom; ***phone:*** +44 (0)20 7219 3000; ***e-mail:*** gibbn@parliament.uk.

GIBSON, H.E. Robert Winnington; High Commissioner, British High Commission in Bangladesh; ***professional career:*** Dep. Head of Mission, Iraq, 2006-07; Dep. High Commissioner and Director UK Trade and Investment Pakistan, 2008-11; High Commissioner to Bangladesh, 2011-; ***office address:*** British High Commission, United Nations Road, Baridhara, Dhaka, Bangladesh; ***phone:*** +880 (0)2 882 2705; ***fax:*** +880 (0)2 882 6181; ***URL:*** http://ukinbangladesh.fco.gov.uk/en.

GIDDINGS, Lara; Premier, Government of Tasmania; ***political career:*** MP, 1996-98, 2002-; Minister for Economic Development and the Arts, 2004-06; Minister for Health and Human Services, 2006-08; Deputy Premier, Attorney General and Minister for Justice, 2008-11; Premier, 2011-; ***office address:*** Office of the Premier, 11th Floor, 15 Murray Street, Hobart, Tasmania 7000, Australia; ***URL:*** http://www.premier.tas.gov.au.

GIFFORD, H.E. Michael; Ambassador, British Embassy in North Korea; ***professional career:*** Amb. to Yemen, 2004-07; Amb. the Democratic People's Republic of Korea, 2012-; ***office address:*** British Embassy, Munsu Dong Diplomatic Compound, Pyongyang, Democratic People's Republic of Korea; ***phone:*** +850 (0)2 381 7980; ***fax:*** +850 (0)2 381 7985; ***URL:*** https://www.gov.uk/government/world/organisations/british-embassy-pyonyang.

GIFFORDS, Gabrielle; Congresswoman, Arizona 8th District, US House of Representatives; ***education:*** Cornell Univ., Master's Degree in Regional Planning, 1996; Scripps College, Fulbright Scholarship to study for a year in Chihuahua, Mexico ; ***political career:*** Senator, Arizona Legislature, 2000-05; Mem., U.S. House of Representatives, 2007- (Serious injured in shooting at constituency meeting, 2011); ***professional career:*** Pres. and CEO, El Campo Tire; ***committees:*** Armed Services; Science, Space and Technology; ***office address:*** House of Representatives, 502 Cannon House Office Building, Washington, DC 20515, USA; ***phone:*** +1 202 225 2542 ; ***fax:*** +1 202 225 0378.

GILBERT, Stephen; MP for St Austell and Newquay, UK Government; ***party:*** Liberal Democrat; ***political career:*** Councillor, Restormel Borough Council, 1998-2002; London Borough of Haringey Council, 2002-06; MP for St Austell and Newquay, May 2010-; ***committees:*** Communities and Local Government Select Cttee., 2010-; ***office address:*** House of Commons, London, SW1A 0AA, United Kingdom; ***phone:*** +44 (0)20 7219 3000; ***e-mail:*** stephen.gilbert.mp@parliament.uk.

GILDERNEW, Michelle; MP for Fermanagh and South Tyrone, Northern Ireland Assembly; ***party:*** Sinn Fein; ***political career:*** Mem., Fermanagh & South Tyrone, Northern Ireland Assembly, 1998, re-elected 2003; MP, 2001-; Minister for Agriculture, Northern Ireland Assembly, May 2007-10; ***interests:*** housing, rural affairs, education; ***office address:*** Constituency Office, Thomas Clarke House, 60 Irish Street, Dungannon, BT70 1QD, Northern Ireland; ***e-mail:*** michelle.gildernew@sinn-fein.ie.

GILL, Stuart; Ambassador, British Embassy in Iceland; ***education:*** Univ. of Kent, Canterbury,UK, 1980; ***professional career:*** Consul-General, Melbourne, Australia, 2008-12; Amb. to Iceland, 2012-; ***office address:*** British Embassy, Laufásvegur 31, 101 Reykjavík, Iceland; ***phone:*** +354 550 5100-2; ***fax:*** +354 550 5105; ***e-mail:*** britemb@centrum.is; ***URL:*** http://ukiniceland.fco.gov.uk/en.

GILLAN, Rt. Hon. Cheryl; Member of Parliament, House of Commons; ***born:*** 21 April 1952; ***parents:*** Major Adam Mitchell Gillan and Mona Elsie (née Freeman); ***married:*** John Coates Leeming, 1985; ***education:*** Cheltenham Ladies College; College of Law, FCIM, Dip M; ***party:*** Conservative Party; ***political career:*** MP, Chesham and Amersham, 1992-; PPS to Lord Privy Seal, 1994-95; Parly Under Sec. of State DFEE, 1995-97; Opposition frontbench spokesman trade and industry, 1997-98; Opposition frontbench spokesman on foreign and commonwealth affairs, and int. dev.1998-2001; Opposition Whip, 2001-03; Shadow Home Office Minister, 2003-05; Shadow Secretary of State for Wales, 2005-May 2010; Secretary of State for Wales, 2010-12; ***professional career:*** International Management Gp., 1976-84; British Film Year, 1984-86; Ernst & Young, 1986-91; Dir., Kidsons Impey, 1991-93; Chmn. Bow Group, 1987-88; ***honours and awards:*** Freeman, City of London, 1991; Liveryman, Marketors Co., 1991; ***clubs:*** RAC; ***recreations:*** golf, music, gardening, animals; ***office address:*** House of Commons, London, SW1A 0AA, United Kingdom; ***phone:*** +44 (0)20 7219 3000; ***e-mail:*** gillanc@parliament.uk.

GILLETT, Sarah; Ambassador, British Embassy in Switzerland; ***professional career:*** Dep. Head of Mission, Brasilia, Brazil, 2000-01; Consul-General, Montreal, Canada, 2002-05; Amb. to Switzerland and Liechtenstein, 2009-; ***office address:*** British Embassy, Thunstrasse 50, 300 Berne 15, Switzerland; ***phone:*** +41 (0)31 359 7700; ***fax:*** +41 (0)31 359 7701; ***URL:*** http://ukinswitzerland.fco.gov.uk/en.

GILLIBRAND, Kirsten; Senator for New York State, US Senate; ***education:*** Dartmouth, Bachelors; UCLA, law; ***political career:*** Special Counsel to the U.S. Sec. of Housing and Urban Development; Mem., House of Representatives, 2007-09; Senator for New York State, US Senate, 2009-; ***professional career:*** Lawyer; ***committees:*** Armed Services; Aging; ***office address:*** US Senate, 478 Russell, Washington, DC 20510, USA; ***phone:*** +1 (202) 224-4451; ***URL:*** http://www.gillibrand.senate.gov.

GILLON, Karen, MSP; British, Member for Clydesdale, Scottish Parliament; ***born:*** 18 August 1967, Edinburgh, Scotland; ***parents:*** Edith Turnbull (née Macdonald); ***married:*** James Gillon, 13 March 1999; ***children:*** James (M), Matthew (M), Johann (F); ***education:*** Jedburgh Grammar Sch.; Univ. of Birmingham; ***party:*** Labour; ***political career:*** Scottish Labour Party Exec., 1997-99; MSP, Clydesdale, 1999-; Convener, Education, Culture and Sport, 2001-03; Shadow Spokesperson on Rural Affairs; ***interests:*** education, public health, sport, social inclusion, Malawi; ***committees:*** Scottish Parl. Environment and Rural Development Cttee.; ***recreations:*** sport, cooking, flower arranging; ***office address:*** 7 Wellgate, Lanark, Scotland, ML11 9DS, United Kingdom; ***phone:*** +44 (0)1555 660526; ***fax:*** +44 (0)1555 660528; ***e-mail:*** karen.gillon.msp@scottish.parliament.uk.

GILMORE, Eamon; Deputy Prime Minister, Government of Ireland; ***born:*** April 1955, Galway, Ireland; ***education:*** University College, Galway; ***party:*** Leader, Labour Party; ***political career:*** Pres., Union of Students in Ireland, 1976-78; Mem., Dublin County Cncl,1985; Minister for State for the Marine, 1994-97; elected to Dail Eireann for Dun Laoghaire, 1989-; Spokespersonon Environment and Local Government; Labour Party Leader, 2007-; Tanaiste (Depuuty Prime Minister), Minister of Affairs and Trade, Feb. 2011; ***memberships:*** Parly .Assembly of the Council of Europe; ***committees:*** Chmn., Labour's Policy Cttee.; Mem., Labour Party Nat. Exec. Cttee.; Mem., Jt. Cttee. on Environment and Local Government, 2002-07; ***office address:*** Department of Foreign Affairs, 80 St. Stephen's Green, Dublin 2, Ireland; ***phone:*** +353 (0)1 478 0822; ***fax:*** +353 (0)1 478 1484; ***URL:*** http://www.dfa.ie.

GILMORE, Sheila; MP for Edinburgh East, UK Government; ***party:*** Labour; ***political career:*** Councillor, Edinburgh City Council 1991-2007; MP for Edinburgh East, May 2010-; PPS, 2011-; ***committees:*** Political and Constitutional Reform Select Cttee., 2010-; Work & Pensions, 2011-; ***office address:*** House of Commons, London, SW1A 0AA, United Kingdom; ***phone:*** +44 (0)20 7219 3000; ***e-mail:*** sheila.gilmore.mp@parliament.uk.

GIOVANNINI, Enrico; Minister of Labour and Social Policy, Government of Italy; ***education:*** Sapienza Univ. of Rome, Italy; ***political career:*** Minister of Labour and Social Policies, Apr. 2013-; ***professional career:*** Prof. of Economics, Univ. of Rome Tor Vergata, 2002-13; Chief Statistician and Dir. of Statistics Directorate of the Organisation for Ecomomic

Co-operation and Development in Paris, 2001-09; Chair of the Conference of European Statisticians, 2011-13; ***office address:*** Ministry of Labour and Social, WelfareVia Veneto 56, 00187 Rome, Italy; ***phone:*** +39 06 36751; ***URL:*** http://www.lavoro.gov.it.

GISCARD D'ESTAING, Valery; French, Ex Officio Member, Constitutional Council; ***born:*** 1926; ***married:*** Anne Aymone de Brantes; ***education:*** Ecole Polytechnique; Ecole Nationale d'Administration; ***political career:*** PPS to Pres. of Council, 1954; Deputy, Puy-de-Dôme, 1956; Re-elected Clermont-North and South-West, 1958, 1962, 1967, 1968-73; Sec. of State for Finance, 1959; Minister of Finance, 1962; Minister of Finance and Economic Affairs, 1962-66, 1969-72 and 1972-74; Pres. of Republic of France, 1974-81; Deputy, Puy-de-Dôme, 1984, 1988-89; Pres., Région d'Auvergne, 1986; Pres., Cmn. of Foreign Affairs, 1987-89; Dpty., European Parliament, 1989-93; Pres., European Movement Intl., 1989; Pres., of the UFD; Deputy, Puy-de-Dome, 1993-; Pres., Cmn. of Foreign Affairs 1993; mem., Constitutional Council, 2004-; ***professional career:*** Armed forces, 1944-45; Inspector of Finance, 1954; ***honours and awards:*** Grand Croix de la Légion d'Honneur; Croix de Guerre, 1939-45; Nansen Medal, 1979; ***publications:*** Démocratie Française, 1976; Deux Français sur Trois, 1984; Le Pouvoir et la Vie, 1988; Le Pouvoir et la Vie, 2nd vol., 1991; Le Passage, 1994; Dans 5 ans l'an 2000, 1995; ***office address:*** Constitutional Council, 2 rue de Montpensier, 75001 Paris, France.

GISKE, Trond; Norwegian, Minister of Trade and Industry, Norwegian Government; ***born:*** 7 November 1966, Trondheim, Norway; ***parents:*** Bjorn Giske and Norunn Giske; ***languages:*** English, French; ***education:*** Univ., Oslo and Trondheim, MA, Economics, Political science and Law, 1997; Part-time study in USA and France; ***party:*** Norwegian Labour Party; ***political career:*** Exec. sec., Trondheim Labour Youth League, 1988; Exec. sec., Sør-Trondelag Labour Youth League, 189-90; Exec. sec., Norwegian Labour League of Youth, 1992-96; Mem., Norwegian Parl., representing the Sør-Trøndelag constituency for the Labour Party, 1997-; Mem., the Storting, 1997-; Minister of Education, Research and Church Affairs, 2000-2001; Minister of Culture and Church Affairs, 2005-09; Minister of Trade and Industry, 2009-; ***committees:*** Mem. of the bd., Labour Party Central Exec. Cttee., 1992-96, 2000-; Cttee. mem., Movement for Social Democrats Against Membership in the European Union; mem., Finance Cttee.; ***office address:*** Ministry of Trade & Industry, Grubbegaten 8, PO Box 8014 Dep, 0030 Oslo, Norway; ***phone:*** +47 2224 9090; ***e-mail:*** postmottak@nhd.dep.no; ***URL:*** http://www.odin.dep.no/nhd.

GJERSKOW, Mette; Minister of Food, Agriculture and Fisheries, Government of Denmark; ***education:*** Graduate in Agronomics, Royal Danish Veterinary and Agricultural Univ., Denmark, 1993; ***party:*** Social Democratic Party; ***political career:*** MP, 2005-; Minister of Food, Agriculture and Fisheries, 2011-; ***office address:*** Ministry of Food, Agriculture and Fisheries, Landbrug og Fiskeri, Slotsholmsgade 12, 1216 Copenhagen, Denmark; ***phone:*** +45 3392 3301; ***e-mail:*** fvm@fvm.dk.

GLASMAN, Lord Maurice; Member, House of Lords; ***education:*** Univ. of York; European Univ. Inst. in Florence; ***party:*** Labour Party; ***political career:*** Mem., House of Lords, 2010-; ***professional career:*** Snr. Lecturer in political theory at London Metropolitan Univ.; ***office address:*** House of Lords, London, SW1A 0PW, United Kingdom; ***phone:*** +44 (0)20 7219 3000.

GLASS, Pat; MP for North West Durham, UK Government; ***party:*** Labour; ***political career:*** Councillor, Lanchester Parish Council; MP for North West Durham, May 2010-PPS, 2011-; ***committees:*** Education Select Cttee., 2010-; ***office address:*** House of Commons, London, SW1A 0AA, United Kingdom; ***phone:*** +44 (0)20 7219 3000; ***e-mail:*** pat.glass.mp@parliament.uk.

GLEAN, Governor Carlyle Arnold; Governor General, Grenada; ***born:*** 11 February 1932; ***parents:*** George Clean and Olive McBurnie; ***married:*** Norma Glean (née DeCoteau), 1955; ***children:*** Carlyle (M), Corinne (F), Susan (F), Patricia (F), Rose Ann (F); ***public role of spouse:*** voluntary social worker; ***education:*** Grenada's Teachers' College, 1964-65; Univ. of Calgary, B.Ed., 1967-70, MA (Ed), 1973; ***party:*** National Democratic Congress, 1988-99; ***political career:*** Senator, 1990-98; Minister of Education, 1990-95; ***interests:*** Education, National Development; ***memberships:*** Catholic Central Board of Management, Education (Hon.); ***professional career:*** Primary School Teacher, 1947-56, 1960-63, 1965-66; Primary School Principal, 1963-64, 1967; Grenada Teachers' College, Lecturer, 1970-74, Principal, 1974-76; various positions Univ. of the West Indies Faculty of Education incl.: Lecturer, 1976-86, mem. of Conservation Ed. Comm., 1978-81; Assist. Chief Examiner, 1979-84; Educational Consultant, 1986-89; Mem., Caricom Working Party on Family Life Education, 1988-89; Governor General of Grenada, 2008-; ***trusteeships:*** founder, Camerhogne Foundation (Grenada) Inc., 2009; trustee, Grenada Univ. of Science and Technology; ***honours and awards:*** GCMG, 2009; ***recreations:*** walking; ***office address:*** Building #5, Financial Complex, The Carenage, St. George's, Grenada; ***phone:*** +1 473 440 2401; ***fax:*** +1 473 440 6688 ; ***e-mail:*** patogg@spiceisle.com.

GLEN, John; MP for Salisbury, UK Government; ***education:*** Oxford Univ.; ***party:*** Conservative; ***political career:*** MP for Salisbury, May 2010-; PPS to Eric Pickles, 2012-; ***committees:*** Defence Select Cttee., May 2010-; Arms Export Control, 2010-; ***office address:*** House of Commons, London, SW1A 0AA, United Kingdom; ***phone:*** +44 (0)20 7219 3000.

GLENARTHUR, Lord; British, Company Director, Audax Global s.a.r.l.; ***born:*** 1944; ***parents:*** Matthew, 3rd Baron Glenarthur and Margaret (née Howie); ***married:*** Susan (née Barry), 1969; ***children:*** Edward Alexander (M), Emily Victoria (F); ***education:*** Eton Coll.; ***political career:*** Lord in Waiting (Govt. Whip in House of Lords), 1982-83; Parly. Under-Sec. of State, DHSS, 1983-85, and Home Office, 1985-86; Min. of State for Scotland, 1986-87; Min. of State, Foreign and Commonwealth Affairs, 1987-89; Mem., House of Lords; ***memberships:*** Fellow of Royal Aeronautical Soc., 1992-2011, Liveryman Guild of Air Pilots and Air Navigators; Fellow Chartered Inst. of Transport and Logistics; Fellow Royal Geographical Soc.; Chmn., European Helicopter Assn., 1996-2003; Chmn., Int. Fed. of Helicopter Assns., 1997-2004; ***professional career:*** Served in British Army, 1963-75; Captain, British Airways Helicopters, 1976-82; Dir., Aberdeen and Texas Corporate Finance, 1977-82; Exec., Hanson plc, 1989-96; Consultant, British Aerospace plc, 1989-99; Chmn., St. Mary's Hospital, Paddington NHS Trust, 1991-98; Chmn., British Helicopter Advisory Bd., 1992-2004, Pres. 2004-; Pres., Nat. Cncl. for Civil Protection, 1991-2003; Dir., the Lewis Gp. PLC, 1993-94; Dep. Chmn., Hanson Pacific Ltd., 1994-98; Consultant, Chevron UK Ltd., 1994-97; Cncl. Mem., The Air League, 1994-2009; Consultant, Hanson plc, 1996-99; Consultant, Imperial Tobacco Group plc, 1996-98; Dir., Millennium Chemicals Inc., 1996-2004; Governor, Nuffield Hospitals, 2000-09; Commissioner, Royal Hospital, Chelsea, 2001-07; Dir., Audax Global s.a.r.l., 2003-; Gov. & Council mem., King Edward VII's Hospital, Sister Agnes, 2010-; ***committees:*** Mem., National Employers Advisory Bd. for HM Reserve Forces, 1996-, Chmn., 2002-; ***trusteeships:*** St. Mary's Hospital, Special Trustees, 1991-2000; ***clubs:*** Cavalry and Guards Club, London; Pratt's; ***recreations:*** fieldsports, gardening, choral singing, barometers, organ playing; ***office address:*** PO Box 11012, Banchory, Kincardineshire, AB31 6ZJ, United Kingdom; ***phone:*** +44 (0)1330 844467.

GLENDONBROOK, Lord Michael (David), CBE; British, Member, House of Lords; ***born:*** 10 February 1942; ***education:*** Mill Hill Sch.; ***party:*** Conservative Party; ***political career:*** Mem., House of Lords, 2011-; ***memberships:*** East Midlands Electricity Bd., 1980-83; East Midlands Regional Bd., Central Independent TV plc, 1981-89; Companion of Royal Aeronautical Soc.; ***professional career:*** Mercury Airlines, Manchester,1963-64; British Midland Airways Ltd, 1964-69, and Gen. Mgr., 1969-72 and Man.Dir., 1972-78; Chmn., British Midland Airways, 1978-2010; Chmn., Channel 4 TV, 1993-97; Chmn., D'Oyly Carte Opera Trust; ***honours and awards:*** Raised to the peerage as Baron Glendonbrook, of Bowdon in the County of Cheshire, 2011; ***clubs:*** Brooks's; ***office address:*** House of Lords, London, SW1A 0PW, United Kingdom; ***phone:*** +44 (0)20 7219 3000.

GLINDON, Mary; MP for North Tyneside, UK Government; ***party:*** Labour; ***political career:*** Councillor, North Tyneside Council 1995-; Dep. Mayor 1998-99, Mayor 1999-2000; MP for North Tyneside, May 2010-; ***committees:*** Environment, Food and Rural Affairs Select Cttee., 2010-; Unopposed Bills (Panel), 2011-; ***office address:*** House of Commons, London, SW1A 0AA, United Kingdom; ***phone:*** +44 (0)20 7219 3000; ***e-mail:*** mary.glindon.mp@parliament.uk.

GNASSINGBÉ, Faure; President, Government of Togo; ***education:*** Univ. Paris-Dauphine, Management Studies, Masters; George Washington Univ., MBA; ***political career:*** Communications and Mines Minister; President of Togo, February 2005-; Minister of Defence, 2007-; ***office address:*** Palais Présidentiel, ave de la Marina, Lomé, Togo; ***e-mail:*** presidence@republicoftogo.com.

GOCHE, Nicholas; Minister of Transport, Government of Zimbabwe; ***born:*** 1946; ***party:*** Zanu-PF; ***political career:*** Minister of National Security (in the President's Office); Minister of Public Service, Labour and Social Welfare, 2005-08; Minister of Transport and Communications, 2009-; ***office address:*** Ministry of Transport and Communications, 16th Floor, Kaguvi Building, Causeway, Harare, Zimbabwe; ***URL:*** http://www.transcom.gov.zw.

GODEC, H.E. Robert F.; Ambassador, US Embassy in Kenya; ***married:*** Lori (née Magnusson); ***public role of spouse:*** retired State Dept. Foreign Service Officer; ***languages:*** French, German; ***education:*** Univ. of Virginia, BA Foreign Affairs; Yale Univ., MA Int. Relations; ***professional career:*** joined the Foreign Service in 1985; Econ. Counselor, US Emb., Nairobi; Assist. Office Dir. for Thailand and Burma, Bureau of East Asian and Pacific Affairs; Dir. for Southeast Asian Affairs, Office of the U.S. Trade Rep.; Acting Dep. Chief of Mission and Minister Counselor for Econ. Affairs, U.S. Embassy Pretoria; Dep.Coordinator for the Transition in Iraq; Dep. Assist. Sec., Bureau of Near Eastern Affairs; Ambassador to Tunisia, 2006-09; Amb. to Kenya, 2012-; ***recreations:*** ultra marathon running; ***office address:*** US Embassy, Mombasa Road, PO Box 30137, Unit 64100, Nairobi, Kenya; ***phone:*** +254 2 537800; ***fax:*** +254 2 537863; ***e-mail:*** ircnairobi@state.gov; ***URL:*** http://nairobi.usembassy.gov.

GODSIFF, Roger D.; British, Member of Parliament for Birmingham Hall Green, House of Commons; ***born:*** 28 June 1946; ***party:*** Labour Party; ***political career:*** fmr. Chmn., Small Heath Young Socialists; Mem., Exec. Cttee., Constituency Treas., Small Heath Labour Party; Cllr., London Borough of Lewisham, 1971-90; Officer of the Labour Group and Chief Whip, 1974-77; Mayor, 1977; MP, Birmingham Small Heath, 1992-97; MP, Birmingham Sparkbrook and Small Heath, 1997-2010, Birmingham Hall Green, 2010-; ***interests:*** foreign affairs, defence, the economy; ***committees:*** Chmn., All Party British Japanese Group; Chmn., All-Party Parly. Kashmir Group, 1992-2004; ***trusteeships:*** Chmn., Charlton Athletic Charitable Trust, 2003-; ***office address:*** House of Commons, London, SW1A 0AA, United Kingdom; ***phone:*** +44 (0)20 7219 3000; ***e-mail:*** godsiffr@parliament.uk.

GOGGINS, Paul; British, Member of Parliament for Wythenshawe and Sale East, House of Commons; ***born:*** 16 June 1953; ***parents:*** John Goggins and Rita Goggins (dec'd); ***married:*** Wyn Goggins (née Bartley), 1977; ***children:*** Matthew (M), Dominic (M), Theresa (F); ***education:*** Manchester Polytechnic, CQSW; ***party:*** Labour Party; ***political career:*** MP, Wythenshawe and Sale East, 1997-; PPS to John Denham, Minister of State and Health, 1998-; PPS to John Denman, 1998-2000; PPS to David Blunkett, 2000-2003; Home Office Minister, 2003-06; Parly Under Sec. of State, Northern Ireland Office 2006-07; Minister of State, Northern Ireland Office, 2007-2010; Shadow Minister for: Cabinet Office, -Sept. 2010, Northern Ireland, -Sept. 2010; ***interests:*** transport, poverty, health, international development; ***professional career:*** Social Worker; ***committees:*** Social Security Select Cttee., 1997-98; Intelligence and Security Cttee., 2010-; ***recreations:*** watching Manchester City, walking, music; ***office address:*** House of Commons, London, SW1A 0AA, United Kingdom; ***phone:*** +44 (0)161 499 7900; ***fax:*** +44 (0)161 499 7911; ***e-mail:*** gogginsp@parliament.uk.

GOLD, Lord David; Member, House of Lords; ***party:*** Conservative Party; ***political career:*** Mem., House of Lords, 2011-; ***professional career:*** Lawyer; Snr. Litigation Partner, Herbert Smith; ***office address:*** House of Lords, London, SW1A 0PW, United Kingdom; ***phone:*** +44 (0)20 7219 3000.

GOLDSMITH, Zac; MP for Richmond Park, UK Government; ***parents:*** Sir James Goldsmith and Lady Annabel Vane-Tempest-Stewart; ***party:*** Conservative; ***political career:*** MP for Richmond Park, May 2010-; ***professional career:*** Environmental journalist; Entrepreneur;

Editor-in-chief and director, The Ecologist; ***committees:*** Environmental Audit, 2010-; ***office address:*** House of Commons, London, SW1A 0AA, United Kingdom; ***phone:*** +44 (0)20 7219 3000; ***e-mail:*** zac.goldsmith.mp@parliament.uk.

GOLODETS, Olga; Deputy Prime Minister of the Russian Federation, Russian Government; ***born:*** 1962; ***education:*** Lomonosov Moscow State Univ., Economics, Ph.D; ***political career:*** Dep. Moscow Mayor for Education and Healthcare, 2010-2012; Mem., Moscow Gov.; Dep. Prime Minister, 2012-; ***office address:*** State Duma, Ok hotny Ryad 1, 103265 Moscow, Russia.

GONSALVES, Hon. Dr Ralph E.; Prime Minister, Government of St. Vincent and the Grenadines; ***born:*** 1945; ***education:*** Univ. of the West Indies, B.Sc., M.Sc.; Univ. of Manchester, UK, Ph.D; Gray's Inn, London; ***party:*** Unity Labour Party; ***political career:*** Leader, Unity Labour Party, 1998-; Prime Minister with additional portfolios, 2001-, as of June 2012, portfolio included: Minister of Finance, Minister of National Security, Grenadine Affairs and Legal Affairs; ***professional career:*** Lawyer; ***office address:*** Office of the Prime Minister, Kingstown, St. Vincent and the Grenadines; ***phone:*** +1 809 456 1703; ***fax:*** +1 809 457 2152; ***e-mail:*** pmosvg@caribsurf.com.

GOODLATTE, Bob; American, Congressman, Virginia Sixth District, US House of Representatives; ***education:*** Washington and Lee University School of Law, graduate; Bates College in Lewiston, Maine, undergraduate degree in Government; ***party:*** Republican; ***political career:*** Congressman, Virginia Sixth District, US House of Representatives, 1992-; ***professional career:*** Lawyer; ***committees:*** Agriculture Cttee.; Judiciary Cttee., Chmn.; ***office address:*** US House of Representatives, 2240 Rayburn House Office Building, Washington, DC 20515, USA; ***phone:*** +1 202 225 5431.

GOODMAN, Helen, MP; MP for Bishop Auckland, House of Commons; ***born:*** 2 January 1958; ***parents:*** Alan Goodman and Hanne Goodman; ***married:*** Charles Seaford, 1988; ***children:*** 2; ***education:*** MA, Philosophy, Politics and Economics, Somerville Coll. Oxford, 1979; ***party:*** Labour; ***political career:*** MP for Bishop Auckland, 2005-; Parly. Sec., Office of the Leader of the House of Commons, 2007-08; Govt. Whips Office, 2008-09; Parly. under Sec., Dept. for Work and Pensions, 2009-10; Shadow Minister for Work and Pensions, 2010; Shadow Minister, Justice, Oct. 2010-11; Shadow Minister, Culture, Media and Sport, 2011-; ***interests:*** economics, environment, children, international dev., human rights, Denmark, Czech Rep.; ***memberships:*** GMB; Amnesty Int.; Christian Socialist Movement; Chair., Camden Co-operative Party; ***professional career:*** Research Assist., Phillip Whitehead MP, 1979-80; Civil Servant, HM Treasury, ending as Head of Strategy Unit, 1980-97; Czechoslovak Prime Minister's Office, 1990-91; Dir. of Commission on Future of Multi-Ethnic Britain, 1998; Head, Strategy Children's Soc., 1998-2002; Chief Exec., Nat. Assn. of Toy and Leisure Libraries, 2002-05; ***committees:*** Select Cttee. on Public Accounts, 2005-07; Ecclesiastical Cttee., 2010-; Procedure, 2010-; ***recreations:*** cooking, family; ***office address:*** House of Commons, London, SW1A 0AA, United Kingdom; ***phone:*** +44 (0)20 7219 4346; ***fax:*** +44 (0)20 7219 0444; ***e-mail:*** goodman@parliament.uk.

GOODWILL, Robert; MP for Scarborough and Whitby, House of Commons; ***party:*** Conservative; ***political career:*** MEP, 1999-2004; MP for Scarborough and Whitby, 2005-; Opposition Whip, 2006-07; Shadow Minister for Transport, 2007-10; Assistant Government Whip, 2010-12; Government Whip, 2012-; ***professional career:*** Farmer; ***office address:*** House of Commons, London, SW1 0AA, United Kingdom; ***phone:*** +44 (0)20 7219 3000; ***e-mail:*** robert.goodwill.mp@parliament.uk.

GOODYEAR, Gary; Federal Minister of Statae for Science and Technology, Government of Canada; ***education:*** Univ. of Waterloo, Canada; ***party:*** Conservative; ***political career:*** MP, 2004-; Minister of State for Science and Technology, 2008-; Minister of State for Federal Economic Development Agency for Southern Ontario, 2010-12; Federal Minister of State for Science and Technology, 2013-; ***professional career:*** Chiropractor; ***office address:*** House of Commons, Parliament Buildings, Wellington Street, Ottawa, Ontario, K1A 0A6, Canada; ***phone:*** +1 613 943 5959.

GORDHAN, Pravin Jamnadas; Minister of Finance, Government of South Africa; ***born:*** April 1949; ***education:*** Univ. of Durban Westville; ***political career:*** Minister of Finance, 2009-; ***office address:*** Ministry of Finance, 240 Vermeulen Street, 26th Floor, corner Andries and Vermeulen Streets, Pretoria 0002, South Africa; ***phone:*** +27 (0)12 323 8911; ***fax:*** +27 (0)12 323 3262; ***URL:*** http://www.finance.gov.za.

GOSAR, Paul; Congressman, House of Representatives; ***party:*** Republican; ***political career:*** Mem., HOR, Arizona 1st District, 2010; ***committees:*** Natural Resources; ***office address:*** House of Representatives, 504 Cannon HOB, Washington DC 20515, USA; ***URL:*** http://gosar.house.gov/.

GOULD, Matthew; Ambassador, British Embassy in Israel; ***professional career:*** Dep. Head of Mission, the British Embassy in Tehran, 2003-05; Principal Private Sec. to the Foreign Sec., 2007-10; Amb. to Israel, 2010-; ***office address:*** British Embassy, 192 Hayarkon Street, Tel Aviv 63405, Israel; ***phone:*** +972 3 725 1222; ***fax:*** +972 3 524 3313; ***e-mail:*** webmaster.telaviv@fco.gov.uk; ***URL:*** http://ukinisrael.fco.gov.uk/en.

GOURDE, Jacques; Parliamentary Secretary, Government of Canada; ***political career:*** MP for Lotbinière, Chures de la Chaudière, Quebec, 2006-; Parly. Sec. to the Minister of Agriculture and Agri-Food, 2006-; Parly. Sec. to the Minister of Natural Resources and Minister for the Canadian Wheat Board, 2007; Parly. Sec. to the Minister of Labour and Minister of the Economic Development Agency of Canada for the Regions of Quebec, 2007-08; Parly. Sec. to the Minister of Public Works and Gov. Services and to the Minister of Nat. Revenue, 2008-; ***professional career:*** Farmer; ***office address:*** House of Commons, Parliament Buildings, Wellington Street, Ottawa K1A 0A6, Ontario, Canada; ***phone:*** +1 613 943 5959; ***fax:*** +1 613 992 3674; ***URL:*** http://www.parl.gc.ca.

GOVE, Rt. Hon. Michael; Secretary of State for Education, House of Commons; ***born:*** 1967; ***party:*** Conservative; ***political career:*** MP for Surrey Heath, 2005-; Shadow Sec. of State for Children, Schools and Families, 2007-May 2010; Secretary of State for Education, May 2010-; ***professional career:*** TV reporter; ***office address:*** Department for Education, Sanctuary Buildings, Great Smith Street, London, SW1 3BT, United Kingdom.

GRABINER, Lord , QC; Member of the House of Lords; ***born:*** 21 March 1945, London; ***parents:*** Ralph and Freda (née Cohen); ***married:*** Jane Aviva (née Portnoy), 1983; ***children:*** Joshua (M), Daniel (M), Samuel (M), Laura (F); ***education:*** Central Foundation Boys' Grammar Sch.; London Sch. of Economics; ***political career:*** Mem., House of Lords; ***interests:*** law reform, trade & industry; ***professional career:*** Commercial Lawyer; BAR, 1968; QC, 1981; Deputy High Court Judge,1994-; ***committees:*** Chmn. Court of Governors, L.S.E; ***honours and awards:*** Life Peer, 1999; ***clubs:*** Wentworth MCC; Garrick; ***recreations:*** golf, theatre; ***office address:*** House of Lords, London, SW1A 0PQ, United Kingdom; ***phone:*** +44 (0)20 7219 3000; ***fax:*** +44 (0)20 7583 2000; ***e-mail:*** agrabinet@oeclaw.co.uk.

GRADE OF YARMOUTH, Lord Michael; Member, House of Lords; ***parents:*** Leslie Grade; ***party:*** Conservative Party; ***political career:*** Mem., House of Lords, 2011-; ***professional career:*** Journalist, Daily Mirror, 1964-66; Dep. Controller, entertainment LWT, 1973; BBC Dir. of programmes, 1986; Chief Exec. channel 4, 1988-97; Chmn. Camelot; Chmn. BBC, 2004-06; Exec. Chmn., ITV plc, 2007-09; ***honours and awards:*** CBE, 1998; ***office address:*** House of Lords, London, SW1A 0PW, United Kingdom; ***phone:*** +44 (0)20 7219 3000.

GRAHAM, Lindsey O.; American, Senator for South Carolina, US Senate; ***education:*** D.W. Daniel High Sch.; Univ. of South Carolina in Columbia, undergraduate and law degrees; ***party:*** Republican; ***political career:*** SC State House of Representatives, 1992-94; Representative, South Carolina Third Congressional District, US House of Representatives, 1994-2002; Senator for South Carolina, US Senate, 2002-; ***professional career:*** US Air Force, 1982-88; established a private law practice, 1988; South Carolina Air Guard, 1989-95; Staff Judge Advocate, McEntire Air National Guard Base; Lt. Colonel, U.S. Air Force Reserves, 1995-; current rank, Colonel; ***committees:*** Appropriations; Armed Services; Budget; Judiciary; ***office address:*** Office of Senator Lindsey Graham, 290 Russell Senate Office Building, Washington, DC 20510, USA; ***phone:*** +1 202 224 5972; ***URL:*** http://www.lgraham.senate.gov.

GRAHAM, Richard; MP for Gloucester, UK Government; ***party:*** Conservative; ***political career:*** Councillor, Cotswold District Council, 2003-07; MP for Gloucester, May 2010-; ***committees:*** Work and Pensions Select Cttee., 2010; ***office address:*** House of Commons, London, SW1A 0AA, United Kingdom; ***phone:*** +44 (0)20 7219 3000; ***e-mail:*** richard.graham.mp@parliament.uk.

GRANT, Helen; MP for Maidstone and The Weald, UK Government; ***party:*** Labour Party 2004-05; Conservative Party, 2006-; ***political career:*** MP for Maidstone and The Weald, May 2010-; Parly. Under-Sec. of State (Women and Equalities), Dept. for Culture, Media and Sport and Ministry of Justice, 2012-; ***committees:*** Justice Select Cttee., 2010-11; ***office address:*** House of Commons, London, SW1A 0AA, United Kingdom; ***phone:*** +44 (0)20 7219 3000; ***e-mail:*** helen.grant.mp@parliament.uk.

GRANT, Hon. John James; Lieutentant Governor, Government of Nova Scotia; ***born:*** January 1936; ***education:*** Mount Allison Univ. Canada; ***political career:*** Lieutenant Governor, 2012-; ***professional career:*** Brigadier-General; Accountant; Volunteer Work; ***office address:*** Government House, 1451 Barrington Street, Halifax, Nova Scotia, B3J 1Z2, Canada.

GRASSLEY, Chuck; American, Senator for Iowa, US Senate; ***born:*** 17 September 1933, New Hartford, Iowa; ***married:*** Barbara Grassley (née Speicher), 1954; ***children:*** Lee, Wendy, Robin, Michele, Jay; ***education:*** Univ. of Northern Iowa, BA, 1955, MA, 1956, Political Science; Univ. of Iowa, Ph.D. work; ***party:*** Republican; ***political career:*** elected to Iowa Legislature, 1958; US House of Representatives, 1974; US Senator for Iowa; ***memberships:*** Farm Bureau; the Butler County and State of Iowa Historical Soc.; Pi Gamma Mu; Kappa Delta Pi; Int. Assn. of Machinists, 1962-71; Int. Parl. Gp. for Human Rights; Masons; Eagles; Baptist Church; ***professional career:*** Farmer; sheet metal shearer, 1959-61; assembly line worker, 1961-71; ***committees:*** Senate: Judiciary Cttee.; Finance Cttee; Agric., Nutrition & Forestry; Budget; Taxation; Caucus on International Narcotics Control; Senate Caucus on Foster Youth; ***honours and awards:*** Taxpayer's Friend Award; Iowa Corn Growers Assn.; Nat. Farmers Union; Nat. Grain and Feed Assn.; Nat. Corn Growers Assn. The American Farm Bureau Fed.; Nat. Telephone Co-operative Assn.; Iowa Farm Bureau; Agricultural Retailers Assn.; Nat. Pork Producers Cncl.; ***office address:*** US Senate, 135 Hart Senate Office Building, Washington, DC 20510, USA; ***phone:*** +1 202 224 3744; ***URL:*** http://www.grassley.senate.gov/.

GRAVES, Sam; Congressman, Missouri Sixth District, US House of Representatives; ***education:*** University of Missouri-Columbia, School of Agriculture, degree in Agronomy; ***political career:*** Congressman, Missouri Sixth District, US House of Representatives, 2000-; ***committees:*** Small Business, Chairman; Transportation and Infrastructure; ***office address:*** US House of Representatives, 1513 Longworth House Office Building, Washington, DC 20515, USA; ***phone:*** +1 202 225 7041.

GRAY, James; Member of Parliament for North Wiltshire, House of Commons; ***born:*** 7 November 1954; ***parents:*** Very Revd. Dr. John R. Gray and Dr. Sheila Gray; ***married:*** Sarah Gray (Div'd 2008); Philippa Mayo (2009); ***children:*** John (M), Olivia (F), William (M); ***education:*** High Sch. of Glasgow, 1966-71; Glasgow Univ., MA (Hons), 1971-75; Christ Church, Oxford, 1975-77; Graduate, Royal Coll. of Defence Studies, 2003; ***party:*** Conservative Party; ***political career:*** Special Advisor to the Sec. of State for the Environment, 1992-95; Dep. Chmn., Wandsworth Tooting Conservative Assn., 1994-96; MP for North Wiltshire, 1997-; Opposition Whip, 2000-2001; Shadow Defence Minister, 2001-2002; Shadow Minister for the Countryside, 2002-05; Shadow Sec. of State for Scotland, 2005; Visiting Parly. Fellow, St. Antony's Coll., Oxford, 2005-06; Parly. Delegate, Cncl. of Europe and Western European

Union, 2007-08; ***memberships:*** Baltic Exchange, 1978-91, Pro bono Member, 1997-; Armed Forces Parly. Scheme, 1997, Postgrad, 2000; Pres., Chippenham Branch, M.S. Society; Pres., Assn. of British Riding Schools; Vice Pres., HAC Saddle Club; Mem., Court of Assistants HAC, 2002-07; Avon Vale Foxhounds; ***professional career:*** Graduate Management Trainee, P&O, 1977-78; Shipbroker and Dept. Man., Anderson Hughes Ltd, 1978-84; Man. Dir., GNI Freight Futures Ltd, 1985-92; Dir., Baltic Futures Exchange, 1989-91; Dir., Westminster Strategy (Public Affairs Consultants), 1995-97; Vice-Chmn., Charities' Property Assn., 2003-09; ***committees:*** Most recently: DEFRA Select Cttee., 2007-10; Procedure, 2010-; Finance & Services, 2010-; ***trusteeships:*** Patron, MS Armed Forces Mutual Support Gp.; Patron, Woodshaw Residents Assn.; ***honours and awards:*** Freeman, City of London; Hon. Mem., Rotary Club, Wiltshire Vale; Hon. Assoc., British Veterinary Assn.; ***publications:*** Futures and Options for Shipping, 1987; Shipping Futures, 1990; Crown vs Parliament: Who decides on Going to War, 2003; Financial Risk Management, 1985; ***clubs:*** seven years service, Honourable Artillery Co.; Chippenham Constitutional Club; Wootton Bassett Conservative Club; Member, Biddestone & Slaughterford Branch, Royal British Legion; Hon. Mem., Rotary Club of the Wiltshire Vale; Pratt's; ***recreations:*** countryside, horse riding, British heritage and local history, the army, China; ***office address:*** House of Commons, London, SW1A 0AA, United Kingdom; ***phone:*** +44 (0)20 7219 6237; ***fax:*** +44 (0)20 7219 1163; ***mobile:*** +44 (0)831 552529; ***e-mail:*** jamesgraymp@parliament.uk.

GRAY, Vincent C.; Mayor, District of Columbia; ***political career:*** Dir., Dept. of Human Services; City Councilman, 2004, Chmn., 2006; Mayor, District of Columbia, Nov. 2010-; ***professional career:*** The Arc of DC; Exec. Dir., Covenant House Washington; ***office address:*** Executive Office of the Mayor, John A. Wilson Building, 1350 Pennsylvania Avenue, NW Suite 600, Washington DC 20004, USA; ***phone:*** +1 202 727 2980; ***URL:*** http://mayor.dc.gov/DC/.

GRAYLING, Chris; Lord Chancellor, Secretary of State for Justice, UK Government; ***married:*** Susan Grayling; ***education:*** Royal Grammar Sch., High Wycombe; Sidney Sussex Coll., BA (Hons) History, Cambridge Univ.; ***party:*** Conservative Party; ***political career:*** MP, Epsom & Ewell, 2001-; Conservative Spokesman on Higher Education; Shadow Leader of the House of Commons, 2005; Shadow Sec. of State for Transport, 2005-07; Shadow Sec. of State for Work and Pensions, 2007-09; Shadow Home Secretary, Jan. 2009-May 2010; Minister of State, Dept. for Work and Pensions, May 2010-12; Lord Chancellor, Secretary of State for Justice, 2012-; ***professional career:*** Dir., Workhouse Ltd, 1993-95; SSVC Group, 1995-97; Burson Marsteller, 1997-2001; ***office address:*** Ministry of Justice, Selborne House, 54 Victoria Street, London, SW1E 6QW, United Kingdom; ***e-mail:*** graylingc@parliament.uk; ***URL:*** http://www.justice.gov.uk.

GRAZIANO DA SILVA, José; Director-General, Food and Agriculture Organization of the UN; ***born:*** 1949; ***education:*** Univ. of Sao Paulo, Agronomy, Rural Economics & Sociology; State Univ. of Campinas, Economics, Ph.D; University College London; Univ. of California; ***political career:*** Leader, Zero Hunger campaign; Minister of Food Safety, Government of Brazil; ***professional career:*** Head, Regional Office for Latin America and the Caribbean, 2006-11; FAO, Dir.-Gen., FAO, 2012-; ***office address:*** FAO, Viale delle Terme di Caracalla, 00153 Rome, Italy; ***phone:*** +39 (0) 6 57051; ***fax:*** +39 (0) 6 5705 3152; ***URL:*** http://www.fao.org.

GREATREX, Tom; MP for Rutherglen and Hamilton West, House of Commons; ***party:*** Labour/Co-operative; ***political career:*** MP for Rutherglen and Hamilton West, May 2010-; Shadow Minister, Scotland, Oct. 2010-11; Shadow Minister, Energy and Climate Change, 2011-; ***committees:*** Energy and Climate Change Select Cttee., 2010; Procedure, 2010-; ***office address:*** House of Commons, London, SW1A 0AA, United Kingdom; ***phone:*** +44 (0)20 7219 3000; ***e-mail:*** tom.greatrex.mp@parliament.uk.

GRECH, Louis; Maltese, Minister for European Affairs and Implementation of the Electoral Manifesto, Government of Malta; ***born:*** 22 March 1947; ***education:*** BA; MA (Oxon); ***party:*** Malta Labour Party; ***political career:*** MEP, 2004-13; Deputy Leader, Malta Labour Party, 2012-; Deputy Prime Minister of Malta, 2013-; Minister of European Affairs and Implementation of the Election Manifesto, 2013-; ***committees:*** mem., Cttee. on Budgets; sub. mem., Cttee. on Regional Dev.; ***office address:*** Parliament, The Palace, CMR 02, Valletta, Malta.

GREEN, Damian; British, Minister of State (Minister for Immigration), UK Government; ***born:*** 1956, South Wales; ***married:*** Alicia (née Collinson); ***education:*** Reading School; Balliol College, Oxford, Philosophy, Politics and Economics (1st class Hons); ***party:*** Conservative Party; ***political career:*** Vice-Pres., Tory Reform Gp., Vice-Chmn., Parliamentary Mainstream; Prime Minister's Policy Unit at 10 Downing Street, dealing with Housing, Local Government, Urban Regeneration, Agriculture, Media and Arts Policy, the National Lottery and Wales, 1992-94; MP, Ashford, 1997-; Conservative Spokesman on Education and Employment, 1998-99; Conservative Frontbench Spokesman on the Environment, 1999-2001; Shadow Secretary of State for Education and Skills, 2001-04; Shadow Secretary of State for Transport, 2004-05; Shadow Minister for Immigration, 2005-10; Minister of State (Minister for Immigration), May 2010-; ***memberships:*** Vice-Chmn., Parliamentary Mainstream; ***professional career:*** financial and business journalist, BBC Radio 4, ITN, 1978-92; Dir., European Media Forum, and independent think tank; ***trusteeships:*** Community Development Foundation; ***publications:*** Annual ITN Budget Factbook, 1984-86; Freedom of the Airwaves, 1990; A Better BBC, 1991; Communities in the Countryside, 1996; The Four Failures of the New Deal, 1998, Regulating the Media in the Digital Age, 1997, European Media Forum; Four Failures of the New Deal, 1998; ***recreations:*** music, football, cricket, cinema; ***office address:*** Home Office, 2 Marsham Street, London, SW1P 4DF, United Kingdom; ***phone:*** +44 (0)20 7035 4848; ***e-mail:*** greend@parliament.uk.

GREEN, Kate; MP for Stretford and Urmston, House of Commons; ***party:*** Labour; ***political career:*** MP for Stretford and Urmston, May 2010-; Shadow Minister, Government Equalities Office, 2011-; ***memberships:*** Magistrate; ***committees:*** Work and Pensions Select Cttee., 2010-11; ***office address:*** House of Commons, London, SW1A 0AA, United Kingdom; ***phone:*** +44 (0)20 7219 3000; ***e-mail:*** kate.green.mp@parliament.uk.

GREEN OF HURSTPIERPOINT, Lord Stephen; Member, House of Lords; ***political career:*** Mem., House of Lords, 2010-; Minister of State for Trade and Investment, Dept. for Business, Innovation and Skills and Foreign and Commonwealth Office 2011-; Gov. Spokesperson, Dept. for Business, Innovation and Skills, 2011-; ***honours and awards:*** Raised to peerage as Baron Green of Hurstpierpoint, of Hurstpierpoint in the County of West Sussex, 2010; ***office address:*** House of Lords, London, SW1 0AA, United Kingdom; ***phone:*** +44 (0)20 7219 3000.

GREENING, Justine; Secretary of State for International Development, UK Government; ***born:*** 1969; ***party:*** Conservative; ***political career:*** Local Councillor, Epping; MP for Putney, 2005-; Shadow Economic Sec. to the Treasury; Vice Chmn., Conservative Party; Shadow Communities and Local Gov. Minister, 2009-10; Economic Secretary, HM Treasury, May 2010-Oct. 2011; Secretary of State for Transport, 2011-12; Secretary of State for International Development, 2012-; ***office address:*** Department for International Development, 94 Victoria Street, London, SW1E 5JL, United Kingdom; ***phone:*** +44 (0)20 7917 7000; ***URL:*** http://www.dfid.gov.uk.

GREENWOOD, Judge Christopher John, CMG, QC, MA, LLB; British, Member, International Court of Justice; ***born:*** 12 May 1955; ***languages:*** English; ***education:*** Cambridge University, BA, 1976, Law, First Class Honours, LLB, 1977, International Law, First Class Honours, MA, 1980; Legal qualification: MA; LLB; Barrister, Middle Temple, 1987; QC, 1999; ***interests:*** Armed conflict; Claims; Criminal Law; Dispute settlement; Economic law; Jurisdiction; Human rights; Litigation; Organisations; State responsibility; Law of the Sea; Territory/boundaries; Treaties; Investment; ***memberships:*** ASIL; BIICL; ILA; International Institute of Strategic Studies; Royal Institute of International Affairs; Board of Editors: BYBIL; Cambridge Studies in International Law; Journal of Armed Conflict and Security Law; International Humanitarian Law Series ; ***professional career:*** *academic career:* Cambridge University, Fellow of Magdalene College, 1978-96, Assistant Lecturer, 1981-84, Lecturer, 1984-86; LSE, Professor of International Law, 1996-; Various visiting professorships, Public International Law; *professional career:* Essex Court Chambers; Principal cases: Lockerbie (Libya v UK) (ICJ); Advisory Opinions on Nuclear Weapons, Legality of Use of Force (Yugoslavia v UK) (ICJ); Armed Activities in the Territory of the Congo (DRC v Rwanda) (ICJ); Armed Activities in the Territory of the Congo (DRC v Rwanda) (New Application) (ICJ); Bankovic v Belgium and Others (ECHR); Kingsley v UK (ECHR); Azinas v Cyprus (ECHR); R v Bow Street Magistrates, ex p Pinochet (Nos 1 and 3) (House of Lords); Kuwait Airways Corp v Iraqi Airways Co (High Court, Court of Appeal and House of Lords); Holland v Lampen-Wolfe (House of Lords); R (Abbasi) v Sec of State for Foreign and Commonwealth Affairs (Court of Appeal); R (Al-Skeini) v Sec of State for Defence (Div Court and Court of Appeal); Occidental Exploration and Production Co v Republic of Ecuador (High Court and Court of Appeal); SGS v Phillippines (ICSID); Impregilo v Pakistan (ISCID); Bayindir v Pakistan (ICSID); Barbados v Trinidad and Tobago (ad hoc); mem., International Court of Justice, 2009-; *judicial career:*Member of ICSID Panel of Arbitrators; Member of the Panel of Arbitrators, Law of the Sea Convention; ***publications:*** Books: Co-Editor, International Law Reports, 1978-; Essays on the Law of War, 2006; Articles: BYIL; ICLQ; Netherlands Year Book of International Law; Israel Year Book of Human Rights; Various others; ***office address:*** International Court of Justice, The Peace Palace, 2517 KJ The Hague, The Netherlands.

GREENWOOD, Lilian; MP for Nottingham South, House of Commons; ***party:*** Labour/Co-operative Party; ***political career:*** MP for Nottingham South, May 2010-; Shadow Minister, Transport, 2011-; ***committees:*** Transport Select Cttee., 2010; Regulatory Reform, 2010-; ***office address:*** House of Commons, London, SW1A 0AA, United Kingdom; ***phone:*** +44 (0)20 7219 3000; ***e-mail:*** lilian.greenwood.mp@parliament.uk.

GREY-THOMPSON OF EAGLESCLIFFE , Baroness; Member, House of Lords; ***political career:*** Mem., House of Lords, 2010-; ***professional career:*** Paralympic athlete; Mem., Sports Council for Wales, 1996-2002; ***honours and awards:*** Dame of the British Empire, 2005; Raised to the peerage as Baroness Grey-Thompson, of Eaglescliffe in the County of Durham, 2010; ***office address:*** House of Lords, London, SW1A 0PW, United Kingdom; ***phone:*** +44 (0)20 7219 3000; ***fax:*** +44 (0)20 7219 5979; ***URL:*** http://www.parliament.uk.

GRIEVE, Rt. Hon. Dominic, MP; British, Attorney General, UK Government; ***born:*** 24 May 1956, London, UK; ***parents:*** W.P Grieve Q.C. and Evelyn Grieve (née Mijouain); ***married:*** Caroline Grieve (née Hutton), 6 October 1990; ***s:*** 2; ***languages:*** French; ***education:*** Westminster Sch.; Magdalen Coll., Oxford; Inns of Court Sch. of Law; ***party:*** Conservative Party; ***political career:*** Parly. Candidate, Lambeth Norwood, 1987; Cllr., Hammersmith and Fulham, 1982-86; PA to Sir Anthony Grant, 1983; Mem., Prime Minister's Campaign Team, 1992; MP, Beaconsfield, 1997-; Conservative Front Bench Spokesman for Scotland, 1999-2001; Home Office, 2001-03; Shadow Attorney-General, 2003-June 2008; Shadow Home Sec., June 2008-Jan. 2009; Shadow Justice Sec., Jan. 2009-10; Attorney General, 2010-; ***interests:*** constitutional affairs, legal affairs, environment, Northern Ireland, foreign affairs; ***professional career:*** Barrister, 1980-; ***committees:*** Mem. Select Cttee. on Environmental Audit, 1997-2001; Statutory Instruments, 1997-2001; ***recreations:*** mountaineering, skiing, fell-walking, architecture and art; ***office address:*** House of Commons, London, SW1A 0AA, United Kingdom; ***phone:*** +44 (0)20 7219 3000; ***e-mail:*** dominic.grieve.mp@parliament.uk.

GRIFFIN, Tim; Congressman, US House of Representatives; ***education:*** Hendrix College; Tulane Law School, new Orleans, JD; Pembroke college, Oxord Univ., UK; ***party:*** Republican; ***political career:*** Mem., House of Representatives, Aksansas 2nd District, 2010-; ***professional career:*** US Army Reserve; ***phone:*** +1 202 225 2506.

GRIFFITH, Nia; MP for Llanelli, House of Commons; ***born:*** 1956; ***party:*** Labour; ***political career:*** Sheriff of Carmarthen, 1977; Dep. Mayor, Carmarthen, 1998; MP for Llanelli, 2005-; Shadow Minister, Business, Innovation and Skills, 2010-11; Shadow Minister, Wales, 2011-; ***committees:*** European Scrutiny, 2005-07, 2010-; Welsh Affairs, 2005-10, 2011-; Joint Committee on Human Rights, 2006-07; Jt. Cttee. on the Draft Climate Change Bill, 2007; ***office address:*** House of Commons, London, SW1A 0AA, United Kingdom; ***e-mail:*** nia.griffith.mp@parliament.uk.

GRIFFITHS, Andrew; MP for Burton, UK Government; ***party:*** Conservative; ***political career:*** MP for Burton, May 2010-; ***committees:*** Political & Constitutional Reform, 2010-; ***office address:*** House of Commons, London, SW1A 0AA, United Kingdom; ***phone:*** +44 (0)20 7219 3000; ***e-mail:*** andrew.griffiths.mp@parliament.uk.

GRIFFITHS, John; British, Minister for Environment and Sustainable Development, National Assembly for Wales; ***born:*** 19 December 1956, Newport, UK; ***married:*** Alison Griffiths (née Hopkins); ***languages:*** Welsh; ***education:*** Dyffryn Comprehensive Sch.; Newport Coll.; Univ. of Wales, Cardiff, Law; ***party:*** Labour; ***political career:*** Mem., Workers Education Assn.; Full Employment Forum; Mem., Co-op party; Gwent County Cllr. 1994-95; Newport County Borough Cllr, 1995-99; apptd. Dep. Minister for Economic Dev., May 2001-; AM, Newport East/Dwyrain Casnewydd, 1999-; Dep. Minister for Health and Social Care, with special responsibilities for older people, 2003-07; Dep. Minister for Education, Special Responsibility of Skills, 2007; Counsel General and Leader of the Legislative Programme; Minister for Environment and Sustainable Development, May 2011-; ***interests:*** education, employment, social inclusion, Europe; ***memberships:*** MSF Trades Union; Community Trade Union; UNITE Union; ***professional career:*** Solicitor; ***recreations:*** sport, reading, travel; ***office address:*** National Assembly for Wales, Cardiff Bay, Cardiff, CF99 1NA, United Kingdom; ***fax:*** +44 (0)29 2089 8308 / 02920 898303.

GRIFFITHS, Lesley; Minister for Local Government and Government Business, Welsh Assembly; ***political career:*** Assembly Member, 2007-; Dep. Minister for Science, Innovation and Skills, 2009-11; Minister for Health and Social Services, 2011-13; Minister for Local Government and Government Business, 2013-; ***office address:*** National Assemby for Wales, Cardiff Bay, Cardiff, CF99 1NA, United Kingdom; ***phone:*** +44 (0)29 2089 8752.

GRIJALVA, Raúl M.; Congressman, Arizona 7th District, US House of Representatives; ***political career:*** Congressman, Arizona 7th District, US House of Representatives, 2002-; ***committees:*** House Education and the Workforce Cttee.; Natural Resources Cttee.; ***office address:*** US House of Representatives, 1440 Longworth House Office Building, Washington, DC 20515, USA.

GRÍMSSON, Dr Ólafur Ragnar, Ph.d; Icelandic, President, Republic of Iceland; ***born:*** 14 May 1943, Ísafjördur, Iceland; ***parents:*** Grimur Kristgeirsson and Svanhildur Ólafsdóttir Hjartar; ***married:*** Gudrun Katrin Thorbergsdóttir (née Þorbergsdóttir), 1974 (dec'd 1998); Dorrit Moussaieff, 2003; ***children:*** Dalla (F), Tinna (F); ***education:*** Reykjavik Higher Secondary Grammar Schl., 1962; Manchester Univ., BA, economics and political science, 1965; Manchester Univ., doctorate in political studies, 1970; ***party:*** Althydubandalag (PA, People's Alliance); ***political career:*** Mem. Brd. of Progressive Party's Youth Federation, 1966-73; Mem. Exec. bd. Progressive Party, 1971-73; Alternate Mem. of Icelandic Parl. 1974-78; Chmn. Exec. bd. of Liberal and Left Alliance, 1974-75; elected to Althingi as Rep. of Reykjavik for People's Alliance Party, 1978 & 1979-93; Chmn. People's Alliance, 1980-83; Mem., Council of Europe Parly. Assembly, 1981-84 and 1995-96, responsible for organising the conference on 'North-South: Europe's Role'; Chmn., later Int. Pres. of the Int. Assoc. Parliamentarians for Global Action, 1984-90, sat on its bd. until 1996; Leader of the People's Alliance parly. group, 1987-95; Min. of Finance, 1988-91; Mem. People's Alliance, 1991, 1995; elected fifth President of Iceland, 1996-, re-elected 2000-, 2004 and 2008; ***memberships:*** Mem., Economic Cncl., 1966-68; Mem., bd. of Icelandic Broadcasting Service, 1971-75; Chmn., Cttee of Relocation of Public Institutions, 1972-75; Chmn., Iceland Social Sciences Assoc. 1975; Vice Chmn., Icelandic Security Comm., 1979-90; Mem. bd. of National Power Co. 1983-88; Chmn., Int. Pres. Parliamentarians for Global Action, 1984-90 & 1990-; Mem., Parliamentarian Assembly of Cncl. of Europe, 1980-84, & 1995; ***professional career:*** Lecturer of Political Science, Univ. of Iceland, 1970; Prof., Univ. of Iceland, 1970-88; responsible for television and radio programs, 1966-70; Mem., Economic Council, 1966-68; sat on the bd. of the Icelandic Broadcasting Service, 1971-75; Chmn., Icelandic Social Sciences Assn., 1975; Vice-Chmn., Icelandic Security Commission, 1979-90; sat on the bd. of the Nat. Power Company, 1983-88; ***committees:*** Chmn., cttee. concerned with the relocation of public institutions, 1972-75; ***honours and awards:*** Indira Gandhi Peace Prize, 1987 on behalf of the Int. Assoc. Parliamentarians for Global Action; also received a number of other int. awards; ***publications:*** various articles and texts on the Icelandic political system; essays on international affairs in foreign periodicals and essay collections; ***office address:*** Office of the President, Soleyjargata1, 150 Reykjavik, Iceland; ***phone:*** +354 540 4400; ***fax:*** +354 562 4802; ***e-mail:*** president@president.is; ***URL:*** http://www.president.is.

GROSNER, Tim; Minister of Trade, Government of New Zealand; ***born:*** Perth, Scotland; ***education:*** Victoria University; ***political career:*** MP, 2005-; Minister of Trade, 2010-; Minister of Climate Change Issues; ***office address:*** Ministry of Trade, Stafford House, 40 The Terrace, Wellington, New Zealand; ***phone:*** +64 (0)4 494 8500; ***URL:*** http://www.mft.govt.nz.

GRUBJESIC, Suzana; Deputy Prime Minister and Minister for EU Integration, Government of Serbia; ***born:*** 1963; ***education:*** Belgrade Univ., Political Sciences; ***political career:*** MP; mem., Administrative Ctte. & Cttee. for European Integration; Deputy Prime Minister for European Integration, 2012-; ***office address:*** Office of the Deputy Prime Minister, Nermanjina 11, 11000 Belgrade, Serbia; ***phone:*** +381 11 361 7580; ***fax:*** +381 11 361 7597.

GRUEVSKI, Nikola; Macedonian, Prime Minister, Government of Macedonia; ***born:*** 31 August 1970, Skopje, Republic of Macedonia; ***parents:*** Talo and Nadezda; ***languages:*** English; ***education:*** Univ., 'St. Kliment Ohridski', Economic Faculty, Prilep, BA, 1994; Univ., 'St. Kiril I Metadji', Economic Faculty, Skopje, Postgraduate Studies in monetary economics, 1996; ***political career:*** Minister without Portfolio, 1998; Minister of Trade of the Republic of Macedonia, 1998; Minister of Finance, Republic of Macedonia, 1999-2002; Pres., Securities Cmn. of the Republic of Macedonia, 2000-02; Pres. Economic Cncl., of the Govt. of the Republic of Macedonia, 2000-02: Prime Minister , 2006-; ***memberships:*** Pres., Brokerage Assn. of the Republic of Macedonia, 1998; Mem., Int. Assn. for Financial Markets, 1998; Mem., Macedonian FOREX Club, 1998; Mem., Reform Cmn. of the Govt. of the Republic of Macedonia, 1999; Mem., Securities Cmn., Govt. of Macedonia, 1999; Mem., Exec. Body of the VMRO-DPMNE; ***professional career:*** Employed at the Balkanska Banka, Skopje, in several depts., 1995-98; Dir. Dept. of liquidity, planning, analysis and securities, Balkanska banka, Skopje, 1998; Certified Legal Appraiser of the original capital of trading companies; Governor, World Bank and EBRD and Chief of Macedonian team for negotiations with the IMF/WB Missions, 1999; Certified Legal Aapraiser of the original capital of trading companies, 1998; financial commentator on several electronic and published media, 1998; accomplished numerous official visits of world-known stock markets and other consulting institutions throughout the world; ***publications:*** 'Macedonian Economy on the Crossroads: on the way to a more sound economy', 1998; Contributes to many articles on economic issues in several newspapers in Macadonia; ***clubs:*** 'Metalija' amateur theatre club; Boxing Club 'Vodno'; ***recreations:*** boxing, basketball; ***office address:*** Office of the Prime Minister, Ilindenska bb, 1000 Skopje, Macedonia; ***phone:*** +389 2 3115 389; ***fax:*** +389 2 3112 561; ***e-mail:*** office@primeminister.gov.mk; ***URL:*** http://www.primemininster.gov.mk.

GRYBAUSKAITÉ, Dalia; President, Republic of Lithuania; ***born:*** 1 March 1956, Vilnius, Lithuania; ***languages:*** English, Polish, Russian; ***education:*** Leningrad Univ., political economics,1983; Moscow Public Science Academy, economics, Ph.D.,1988; Geogetown Univ., Washington DC, School of Foreign Service, Special Prog. for Snr. Execs., 1991; ***political career:*** Programme Mgr., Govt. of Lithuania, 1990; Dir., European Dept., Ministry of Int. Economic Relations, 1991-93; Dir., Economic Dept., MFA, 1993-94; Chwn., Cmmn. for the Co-ordination of Assistance to Lithuania (PHARE and G-24), 1993-94; Chief Negotiator, EU Free Trade Agreement, 1993-94; Dep. Minister, Ministry of Finance, 1999-2000; Dep. Minister, MFA, 2000; Dep. Hd. of Negotiations, EU, 2000; Minister of Finance, 2001-04; European Cmnr. for Financial Programming and Budget, 2004-09; Pres., Republic of Latvia, 2009-; ***professional career:*** Scientific Sec., Inst. of Economics, 1990-91; Envoy Ex and Minister Plen., Mission of Lithuania to the EU; Nat. Assistance co-ordinator, Brussels, 1994-95; Minister Plen., Emb.of Lithuania, USA, 1996-99; Chief Negotiator, IMF, WB, 1999-2000; ***honours and awards:*** Commdr's Cross Order of Grand Duke Gediminas 2003; The Commissioner of the Year 2005 award by The European Voice daily; Special award from the LTU TV3 news service, during the traditional awards ceremony Lietuvos Garbė (Lithuania's Honour), 2006; The Wladislav Grabski award for contribution to business, by Polish Confederation of Private Employers LEWIATAN, 2006; Leader of a partnership 2005 award by the Int.Chamber of Commerce Lithuania, 2006; ***office address:*** Office of the President, Pils laukums 3, Riga LV-1050, Lithuania; ***phone:*** +371 709 2106; ***e-mail:*** chancery@president.lv.

GUAJARDO VILLARREAL, Ildefonso; Secretary of Economy, Government of Mexico; ***education:*** Univ. Autonoma de Nuevo Leon; Arizona State Univ.; Univ. of Pennsylvania, US; ***political career:*** Fed. Rep., 2000-03; Local Rep., State of Nuevo Leon, 2006-09; Fed. Rep., 2009-12; Pres., Commission for Economic & Tourism Dev., 2009; Sec. of the Economy, 2012-; ***office address:*** Secretariat of the Economy, Alfonso Reyes 30, Col. Hipodromo Condesa, Cuauhtemoc, 06179 Mexico, Mexico; ***phone:*** +52 55 5729 9100; ***fax:*** +52 55 5286 1543.

GUARNIERI, Roberto; Venezuelan, Permanent Secretary, Sistema Económico Latinoamericano (SELA) Torre Europa; ***education:*** Degree, Economics, Universidad Central de Venezuela, 1963; MA, Economics, Yale Univ., USA; D. PHIL Candidate, Oxford Univ., Pernbroke Coll., UK; ***memberships:*** rep. in IMF, UNCTAD, Cartagena Agreement, OPEC Special Fund, Caribbean Dev. Bank, Int. Fund for Agricultural Dev. (IFAD); ***professional career:*** Staff mem., Central Bank, Venezuela, 1963; Economic Advisor, Pres, Central Bank, Venezuela, 1967-72; Dir., Economic research, Venezuelan Ministry of Finance, 1972-74; Exec. Dir., World Bank for Costa Rica, El Salvador, Guatemala, Haiti, Honduras, Mexico, Nicaragua, Panama, Peru, Venezuela, 1974; Alternate Dir. & exec. dir., Int. Monetary Fund for Costa Rica, El Salvador, Guatemal, Honduras, Mexico, Nicaragua, Venezeula, 1974-97; Honorary Cllr., Venezuelan Embassy, Washington, 1974-97; Economic Consultant for public sector instns. including SELA, IIMC, 1978-79; Principle Dir., Central Bank of Venezuela, 1980-81; Exec. Vice-Pres., Andean Dev. Corp. (CAF), 1983-88; Economic Adviser, Central Bank, Venezuela, 1994-97; Exec. Pres, Latin American Reserve Fund (FLAR), 1998-2003; Perm. Sec., SELA, 2003-06; Exec. Dir., IMF, 2006-07; Perm. Sec., Latin American and Caribbean Economic System, 2013-; ***honours and awards:*** Civil Merit Awards from the Venezuelan Gov., Orden Libertador Simón Bolívar en el Grado Comendador, Orden Francisco de Miranda en el Segundo Grado, Ordine al Mérito della Repubblica Italiana, Commendatore; ***office address:*** Sistema Económico Latinoamericano (SELA) Torre Europa, piso 4, Av. Fco. de Miranda, Urb. Campo Alegre Caracas 1010-A, Venezuela; ***phone:*** +58 212 955 7111; ***fax:*** +58 212 951 5262; ***e-mail:*** difusion@sela.org; ***URL:*** http://www.sela.org.

GUDMUNSSON, Mar; Governor, Central Bank of Iceland; ***born:*** 1954; ***education:*** Univ. of Göteborg; Univ. of Essex; Univ. of Cambridge; ***professional career:*** Economist, Central Bank of Iceland, 1980-; Economic Adviser, Minister of Finance, 1988-91; Head, Economic Dept., Central Bank of Iceland, 1991-94, Chief Economist & Dir. of Economics Dept., 1994-2004; Dep. Head, Monetary & Economic Dept., Bank for International Settlements; Governor, Central Bank of Iceland, 2009-; ***office address:*** Central Bank of Iceland, Kalkofnsvegur 1, 150 Reykjavik, Iceland.

GUEBUZA, President Armando Emilio; Mozambican, President, Republic of Mozambique; ***born:*** 1943; ***married:*** Maria da Luz Guebeza, 1974; ***s:*** 2; ***d:*** 2; ***party:*** Frelimo Party; ***political career:*** Secy. for Education (Frelimo) 1966-70; National Political Commissar 1970-77; Min. for Internal Administration 1974-75; Min. for Home Affairs 1975-77; Vice Min. for Defence 1977-81; MP 1978-; Resident Min. (Sofala Province) 1981-83; Min. for Home Affairs 1983-84; Min., President's Office 1984-86; Min. for Transport and Communication 1987-; Chmn., SATCC 1987; President, Republic of Mozambique, 2004-; ***memberships:*** Mozambican Writer's Assn.; ***honours and awards:*** Eduardo Mondlane Medal; ***publications:*** Poems and short stories in newspapers; ***office address:*** Office of the President, Avda. Julius Nyerere 1780, Maputo, Mozambique; ***phone:*** +258 1 491121; ***fax:*** +258 1 492065; ***URL:*** http://www.mozambique.mz.

GUELLEH, Ismael Omar; President, Republic of Djibouti; ***born:*** November 1947, Dire Dawa, Ethiopia; ***political career:*** Pres., Rep. of Djibouti, 1999-; ***professional career:*** fmr. head of security; ***office address:*** Office of the President, BP 6, Djibouti, Djibouti.

GUENAIZIA, Abdelmalek; Deputy Prime Minister, Government of Algeria; ***born:*** 1936; ***political career:*** Minister of Defence, 2007-12; Deputy Prime Minister,; ***professional career:*** Chief of Staff of the Army; Amb. to Switzerland, 1992-2005; ***office address:*** Office of the Deputy Prime Minister, rue Docteur Saadane, Algiers, Algeria; ***phone:*** +213 (0)21 731200; ***URL:*** http://www.cg.gov.dz.

GUILDFORD, Bishop of; Member, House of Lords; ***education:*** King's Coll., London Univ.; ***political career:*** Mem., House of Lords, 2010-; ***professional career:*** Bishop Suffragan of Stafford, 1996-2004; Bishop of Guildford, 2004-; ***office address:*** House of Lords, London, SW1A 0PW, United Kingdom; ***phone:*** +44 (0)20 7219 3000; ***fax:*** +44 (0)20 7219 5979; ***URL:*** http://www.parliament.uk.

GUL, Abdullah; President, Republic of Turkey; ***born:*** 1950, Kayseri, Turkey; ***languages:*** English; ***education:*** Fac. of Econ., Istanbul Univ.; Masters and Ph.D., Istanbul Univ.; ***party:*** Justice & Development Party (AKP); ***political career:*** Mem., Turkish Parl., 1991-; Dep. Chmn., Welfare Party (SP); mem., Virtue Party (FP); Dep. Chmn., AKP; Minister of State & Government Spokesman, 1996-97; Prime Minister, 2002-03; Deputy Prime Minister and Minister of Foreign Affairs, 2003-07; President, August 2007-; ***professional career:*** Taught econ., Sakarya Univ., Turkey, 1980-83; Islamic Development Bank, 1983-91; Assist. Prof. of Int. Econ., 1991; ***office address:*** Office of the President, Cumhurbaskanligi Kosku, Cankaya, Ankara, Turkey; ***phone:*** +90 (9)312 468 5030; ***fax:*** +90 (9)312 427 1330; ***URL:*** http://www.abdullahgul.gen.tr; http://www.cankaya.gov.tr.

GUMMER, Benedict; MP for Ipswich, UK Government; ***born:*** February 1978; ***education:*** Cambridge Univ.; ***party:*** Conservative; ***political career:*** MP for Ipswich, May 2010-; ***committees:*** Justice, 2010-; Regulatory Reform, 2010-; ***office address:*** House of Commons, London, SW1A 0AA, United Kingdom; ***phone:*** +44 (0)20 7219 3000; ***e-mail:*** ben.gummer.mp@parliament.uk.

GUNELL, Camilla; Premier, Government of the Aland Islands; ***born:*** 1970; ***party:*** Aland Social (ASD); ***political career:*** Mem., City Council of Mariehamn, 2003-; Mem., Culture Delegation, 1999-2003; Mem., Parliament of Aland, 2003-04, 2008-11; Mem., Aland Legislative Assembly Cttee. on Finance & autonomous political cttee.; Mem., Aland, 2005-07; Chmn., Aland Health, 2010-11; Party leader, Aland Social Democrats Party, 2010-; Premier, 2011-; ***office address:*** Office of the Premier, PB 1060, AX-22111 Mariehamn, Aland Islands; ***phone:*** +358 (0)18 25 370; ***URL:*** http://www.regeringen.ax.

GUNNLAUGSSON, Sigmundur D.; Prime Minister, Government of Iceland; ***born:*** 12 March 1975; ***party:*** Chmn. Progressive Party; ***political career:*** MP, 2009-; Prime Minister, 2013-; ***committees:*** Foreign Affairs Cttee., 2009-13; Foreign Affairs Cttee's Working Group on European Affairs, 2010-13; Delegate to the EFTA and EEA Parly. Cttees., 2009-13; EU-Iceland joint Parly. Cttee., 2010-13; ***office address:*** Office of the Prime Minister, Stjornarradshusinu vid Laekjartorg, 150 Reykjavik, Iceland; ***phone:*** +354 545 8400; ***e-mail:*** forseti@forseti.is.

GURRÍA, José Angel, MA; Mexican, Secretary-General, Organisation for Economic Co-operation and Development; ***born:*** 1950, Tampico, State of Tamaulipas; ***education:*** Schl. of Economics at Univ. Nacional Autónoma de México (UNAM); Leeds Univ. MA in Finance; studied International Relations at Univ. of Southern California and Financial Management at Harvard Univ.; ***political career:*** Under-Secry. for International Affairs at the Secretariat of Finance and Public Credit, 1989-94; Minister of Foreign Affairs, 1994-98; Minister of Finance and Public Credit, 1998-2000; ***professional career:*** President and CEO, Bancomext, Mexico's foreign trade bank (Ex-Im bank) and of Nacional Financiera (NAFIN), Mexico's development bank; Secretary-General, OECD, 2006-; ***office address:*** OECD, 2 rue André-Pascal, 75775 Paris, France; ***URL:*** http://www.oecd.org.

GURRY, Dr. Francis; Director General, World Intellectual Property Organization; ***born:*** 17 May 1951, Australia; ***languages:*** French; ***education:*** Univ. of Melbourne, LL.B, LL.M; Univ. of Cambridge, Ph.D.; ***memberships:*** Vice-Pres., International Federation of Commercial Arbitration Institutions,1996-2004; Centre for Intellectual Property and Information Law, Univ. of Cambridge; Intellectual Property Research Institute of Australia, Univ. of Melbourne; Indian Journal of Intellectual Property; International Review of Industrial Property and Copyright Law (IIC), Munich, Germany ; ***professional career:*** Senior Lecturer in Law, Univ. of Melbourne, 1979-1984; Barrister and Solicitor, Supreme Court of Victoria, Australia; Joined WIPO, 1985; Consultant and Senior Program Officer, Development Cooperation and External Relations Bureau for Asia and the Pacific, 1985-1988; Special Assistant to the Dir.Gen., 1991-1993; Head, Industrial Property Law Section, 1988-1990; Office of the Dep. Dir.Gen., WIPO Arbitration and Mediation Center, 1993 -1997; Acting Legal Counsel, 1996-1997; Legal Counsel, WIPO Arbitration and Mediation Center; electronic commerce, 1997-1999; Assist. Dir., General and Legal Counsel, WIPO Arbitration and Mediation Center, 1999-2003; Dep. Dir.-Gen., WIPO, 2003-2008; Dir.Gen., WIPO, 2008-; Sec.-Gen., International Union for the Protection of New Varieties of Plants (UPOV), 2008-; ***honours and awards:*** Professorial Fellow, Faculty of Law, University of Melbourne, 2001-; ***office address:*** World Intellectual Property Organization, WIPO, P O Box 18, CH-1211 Geneva 20, Switzerland; ***phone:*** +41 (0)22 338 9111; ***URL:*** http://www.wipo.int.

GUSMÃO, Xanana; Prime Minister, Government of Timor-Leste; ***born:*** 20 June 1946, Manatuto, East Timor; ***education:*** Jesuit seminary, Dare; Dili High Sch.; ***party:*** formerly Fretilin (Revolutionary Front for an Independent East Timor); Independent; ***political career:*** guerrilla leader; imprisoned, Indonesia, 1993-99; Pres., East Timor, 2002-07; Founder/Leader, National Congress for Timorese Reconstruction party (CNRT), 2007-; Prime Minister, 2008-; ***professional career:*** Portuguese Army, three years' compulsory service; local government department, colonial administration; ***office address:*** Prime Minister's Office, Dili, East Timor.

GUTERRES, Antonio; Portuguese, UN High Commissioner for Refugees; ***born:*** 1949, Santos-o-Velho, Lisbon; ***education:*** grad. of Engineering, Instituto Superior Técnico, Lisbon; ***party:*** Socialist Party; ***political career:*** Chmn. Industrial Planning Div. Cabinet of Sines Region, 1973; Asst. of Min. without portfolio, 1974-75; Mem. European Integration Cttee, 1976-79; Dir. of Strategic Development of IPE, 1984-85; Dep. of Parl., 1985-; Chmn. Parly. Cttee on Regional Planning, Local Authorities and Environment, 1985-88; Shadow Min. for Industry, 1985-88; Mem. National Bureau of Socialist Party, 1986-88; Pres. of Parly. Grp of Socialist Party, 1988-91; Mem. of Council of State, 1991-; Leader of Socialist Party, Vice-Pres. of Socialist Int.,1992-99, Pres., 1999-; PM, 1995-02; ***professional career:*** Asst. Lecturer of Instituto Superior Técnico, Lisbon, 1973-75; UN High Commissioner for Refugees, 2005-; ***office address:*** Office of the UN High Commissioner for Refugees, Case Postale 2500, CH 1211 Geneva, Switzerland.

GUTHRIE OF CRAIGIEBANK, General The Rt. Hon. Lord Charles Ronald Llewelyn, GCB, LVO, OBE, DL; Member, House of Lords; ***married:*** Kate Guthrie; ***children:*** David (M), Andrew (M); ***education:*** Army Staff Coll., 1972; ***political career:*** Mem., House of Lords; ***memberships:*** council mem. of The International Inst. of Strategic Studies; ***professional career:*** joined Welsh Guards, 1959, served with them and the SAS, United Kingdom, Germany, Libya, The Middle East, Malaysia and East Africa, 1960s; no. of appts., Whitehall and with regiment, London, Northern Ireland and Cyprus, 1972; commanded the Welsh Guards, Berlin and Northern Ireland, 1977-80; served in south Pacific, 1980; commanded an Armoured Brigade, an Infantry Division 1st British Corps, the British Army of the Rhine, and the Northern Army Group; Chief of the General Staff (Head of the Army, 1994); Chief of the Defence Staff and the Principle Military Adviser to two Prime Ministers and three Sec, of State for Defence, 1997-2001; Colonel Commandant, the Intelligence Corps, ten years; retired from the army 2001; Dir., N M Rothschild & Sons Limited, 2001-2010; Visiting Prof., King's Coll., London Univ.; currently Colonel, The Life Guards, Gold Stick to The Queen; ***committees:*** mem., Steering Cttee. of the Centre for Strategic and International Studies, Washington DC; ***trusteeships:*** Pres., The Army Benevolent Fund; Medical Action Research; Federation of London Youth Clubs and Governor of The Charterhouse, Clerkenwell; Hon. Benches, Middle Temple; ***honours and awards:*** Fellow, King's Coll., London; Commander Legion of Merit (USA); ***recreations:*** keen sportsman, played rugby for the army, riding, tennis, opera; ***office address:*** House of Lords, London, SW1A 0PQ, United Kingdom; ***e-mail:*** crlguthrie@gmail.com; ***URL:*** http://www.parliament.uk.

GUTIERREZ, Jose Luis; Minister of Foreign Affairs, Government of Timor-Leste; ***education:*** Univ. of Cambridge; Univ. of Western Cape, South Africa; Malaysian Institute of Diplomacy & International Relations, Inst. of Strategic & International Studies, Portugal; ***political career:*** active mem., National Council of Timorese Resistance; first Ambassador of Timor-Leste to the US, 2002 and first rep. at the UN; Foreign Minister, 2006-07; formed new splinter faction, Fretlin Change, later Frenti-Mudansa; Deputy Prime Minister, 2007; Minister of Foreign Affairs; ***office address:*** Ministry of Foreign Affairs, GPA Building 1, Ground Floor, Rua Avenida Presidente Nicolau Lobato, Dili, Timor-Leste; ***URL:*** http://www.mfac.gov.tp.

GWYNNE, Andrew; MP for Denton and Reddish, House of Commons; ***born:*** 4 June 1974, Manchester; ***parents:*** Richard John Gwynne and Margaret Elisabeth Gwynne (née Ridgway); ***married:*** Allison Louise Gwynne (née Dennis), 28 March 2003; ***children:*** James Brian (M), William Charles (M), Maisie Eleanor (F); ***education:*** N.E. Wales Instit. of Higher Education; Univ. of Salford; ***party:*** Labour; Co-operative Party; ***political career:*** MP for Denton and Reddish, 2005-; PPS to the Rt. Hon. The Baroness Scotland of Asthal, 2005-07; PPS to Rt. Hon. Jacqui Smith MP, Home Secretary, 2007-09; PPS to Rt. Hon. Ed Balls, Secretary of State for Children, Schools and Families, 2009-10; Shadow Minister, Transport, Oct. 2010-11; Shadow Minister, Health, 2011-; ***interests:*** computing, local government, education, regeneration; ***memberships:*** Tameside Metropolitan Borough Cncl., 1996-2008; ***office address:*** House of Commons, London, SW1A 0AA, United Kingdom; ***phone:*** +44 (0)20 7219 4708 / (0)161 320 1504; ***fax:*** +44 (0)161 320 1503; ***e-mail:*** gwynnea@parliament.uk.

GYATSO, Tenzin, His Holiness the 14th Dalai Lama of Tibet; The Dalai Lama, Tibet; ***born:*** 1935, Takster, Tibet; ***education:*** Dr. of Buddhist Philosophy, 1959; ***professional career:*** recognised as the reincarnation of his predecessor, 13th Dalai Lama, 1937; enthroned, Lhasa, 1940; 14th Dalai Lama, 1940-; Head of the State and Govt., 1950; held peace talks with Chmn. Mao Tse-Tung and other Chinese Leaders, Beijing, China, 1954; held a series of meetings with PM Nehru and Premier Chou En-Lai about the deteriorating situation in Tibet following the Chinese invasion, India, 1956; escaped to India, 1959; enunciated a 5 point peace plan for Tibet before the US Congressional Human Rights Caucus, Washington DC, USA, 1987, expanded the idea further at an address at the EP, Strasbourg, France, 1988; ***honours and awards:*** Nobel Peace Prize, 1989; ***publications:*** several books on Buddhism, philosophy, human nature and universal responsibility; 2 autobiographies, My Land and My People; Freedom In Exile; ***office address:*** Thekchen Choeling, McLeod Ganj 176219, Dharamsala, Himachal Pradesh, India.

GYIMAH, Sam; MP for East Surrey, UK Government; ***party:*** Conservative; ***political career:*** MP for East Surrey, May 2010-; PPS to David Cameron as Prime Minister, 2012-; ***interests:*** education, international development, small business; ***committees:*** International Development, 2011-; ***office address:*** House of Commons, London, SW1A 0AA, United Kingdom; ***phone:*** +44 (0020 7219 3000; ***e-mail:*** sam.gyimah.mp@parliament.uk.

GYÖRGY, Dr Matolcsy; Governor, Central Bank of Hungary; ***born:*** 1955; ***political career:*** Political State Sec.& Advisor, Office of the PM, 1990; Minister of Economic Affairs, 2000-02; Minister for National Economy, 2010; ***professional career:*** Researcher, Financial Research Inst., 1985; researcher, Financial Research Plc, 1987; MD, Privatisation Research Inst. (subsequently Institute for Growth), 1991, Dir., 1995-2000, 2002-10; mem., Board of Gov., European Bank for Reconstruction & Development, 1991-94; Founder, Hungarian Economic Development Institute, 2007-10; Gov., Central Bank of Hungary, 2013-; ***office address:*** Magyar Nemzeti Bank, Szabadsag ter 8, 1054 Budapest, Hungary; ***URL:*** http://www.mnb.hu.

H

HABUMUREMYI, Dr Pierre; Prime Minister, Government of Rwanda; ***born:*** 1961; ***political career:*** Exec. Sec., National Electoral Commission; Rep., East African Legislative Assembly, 2008; Minister of Education, Rwandan Government, 2011-Oct. 2011; Prime Minister of Rwanda, 2011-; ***office address:*** Office of the Prime Minister, PO Box 1334, Kigali, Rwanda; ***phone:*** +250 85444 / 77554; ***fax:*** +250 83714 / 76969; ***URL:*** http://www.primature.gov.rw.

HÆKKERUP, Nick; Minister of Defence, Government of Denmark; ***born:*** 3 April 1968, Fredensborg, Denmark; ***education:*** Master of Laws, 1994, Ph.D., Univ. of Copenhagen, Denmark 1998; ***party:*** Social Democratic Party; ***political career:*** MP, 2007-; Minister of Defence, 2011-; ***professional career:*** Lecturer, Univ. of Copenhagen, 1998-2000; ***office address:*** Ministry of Defence, Holmens Kanal 42, 1060 Copenhagen K, Denmark; ***phone:*** +45 3392 3320; ***fax:*** +45 3332 0655; ***e-mail:*** fmn@fmn.dk; ***URL:*** http://www.fmn.dk.

HAFSTRÖM, H.E. Jonas; Ambassador, Embassy of Sweden in Washington DC; ***born:*** 1948; ***education:*** Degree in law, Univ. of Lund; ***professional career:*** Non-Commissioned Reserve Captain, Swedish Army, to date; served as Aide D'Camp to the Swedish Commanding Officer, UN Peace Keeping Operations in the Middle East, 1977; Joined the Foreign Service in 1979; Tehran posting, 1982-84; Washington, DC posting, 1984-86; Foreign policy adviser to Carl Bildt, 1987-1991 and 1994-2000; Foreign policy adviser to PM Carl Bildt, 1991-94; Dep. Dir. for Consular Affairs and Civil Law, MFA, 2000-04; Amb. to Thailand, accredited to Laos, Cambodia and Myanmar, 2004-07; Amb. to the USA, 2007-; ***committees:*** Swedish Defense Cttee.,1998-99; ***office address:*** Embassy of Sweden, 1501 M Street, Suite 900, N.W., Washington, DC 20005, USA; ***phone:*** +1 202 467 2600; ***fax:*** +1 202 647 2699; ***URL:*** http://www.swedenabroad.com/Washington.

HAGAN, Senator Kay; Senator for North Carolina, U.S. Senate; ***education:*** Florida State Univ.; Wake Forest Law School; ***political career:*** North Carolina State Senator, 1998-2008; US Senator, 2008-; ***professional career:*** 10 years at North Carolina National Bank (now Bank of America); ***committees:*** U.S. Senate Small Business & Entrepreneurship; Armed Services; Banking, Housing and Urban Affairs; Health, Education, Labor & Pensions; ***office address:*** US Senate, 521 Dirksen Building, Washington, DC 20510, USA; ***URL:*** http://www.hagan.senate.gov/.

HAGEL, Chuck; Secretary of Defense, US Government; ***born:*** 4 October 1946, North Platte, Nebraska, USA; ***married:*** Lilibet Hagel; ***children:*** Allyn (F), Ziller (M); ***education:*** Brown Inst. for Radio and Television, Minneapolis, Minnesota; Univ. of Nebraska, Omaha; ***party:*** Republican; ***political career:*** US Senator for Nebraska, 1996-Jan 2009; Dep. Whip for the Senate Republicans; Secretary of Defense, 2013-; ***memberships:*** Mem., Council of Foreign Relations; Life mem., American Legion, Veterans of Foreign Wars, Vietnam Veterans of America, Disabled American Veterans, and the Military Order of the Purple Heart; ***professional career:*** US Army, 1968; Newscaster and talk show host, KBON, KLNG, Omaha, Nebraska, 1969-71; Admin. Asst. to Congressman, 1971-77; Manager of Government Affairs, Firestone Tire & Rubber Co., Washington, DC, 1977-80; Pres., Collins, Hagel & Clarke Inc.; Co-founder, Dir. and Exec. Vice-Pres., VANGUARD Cellular Systems Inc.; Co-founder and Chmn., Communications Corp. Int. Ltd; Pres. and CEO, World USO, 1987-90; Dep. Dir. and Chief Operating Officer, G7 Summit, 1990; Pres. and CEO, Private Sector Cncl., Washington, DC, 1990; Pres., McCarthy & Co., Omaha, Nebraska; Chmn. Bd., American Information Systems (AIS); ***committees:*** Senate Cttees. on Foreign Relations, Banking, Housing and Urban Affairs; Select Cttee. on Intelligence; Chmn., Subcttee. on Senate Foreign Relations Int. Economic Policy, Export and Trade Promotion; Chmn., Subcttee. on Senate Banking Int. Trade and Finance; Mem., Advisory Cttee. of the Inst. of politics, Harvard Univ.; Mem., Bd. of the Int. Republican Inst., the German Marshall Fund's Trade and Poverty Forum, and the Cncl. on Foreign Affairs; ***trusteeships:*** served on numerous Bds. of Trustees including Manville Personal Injury Settlement Trust and (as Chmn.), Agent Orange Settlement Fund; Bellevue Univ., Hastings Coll. and Heartland Chapter of the American Red Cross; ***honours and awards:*** many military decorations and honours, including two Purple Hearts; distinguished Alumni Award, Univ. of Nebraska at Omaha, 1988; Hon. Doctor of Laws degree, Creighton Univ., Omaha, Nebraska, 1998; Hon. Dr. of Laws degree of commerce, Bellevue Univ., 2001; small Business Administration's Nebraska Veterans Advocate; Headliner Award, Greater Omaha Chamber of Commerce, 2000; Vietnam Veterans of America honoured him, Legislator of the Year Award, 2000; Horatio Alger Award from Horatio Alger Assoc., 2001; Patriot "Good Scout" Award, Boy Scouts of America, 2001; inducted into Hall of Fame of the Consumers for World Trade; many other awards for service in the Senate; ***office address:*** Department of Defense, OASD(PA)/DPC, 1400 Defense Pentagon, Room 1E757, Washington, DC 20301-1400, USA.

HAGGLUND, Goran; Minister of Health and Social Affairs, Government of Sweden; ***born:*** 1959; ***party:*** Christian Democrat Party; ***political career:*** Mem., Jonkoping Municipal Council, 1982-86; Mem., Riksdag, 1991-2006; Chair, Swedish Christian Democrats, 2004-; Minister of Health and Social Affairs, 2006-; ***office address:*** Ministry of Social Affairs, Jakobsgt 26, 103 33 Stockholm, Sweden; ***phone:*** +46 (0)8 405 1000.

HAGUE, Rt. Hon. William, MP; British, Foreign Secretary, House of Commons; ***born:*** 1961, Rotherham, UK; ***parents:*** Nigel Hague and Stella Hague (née Jefferson); ***married:*** Ffion Jenkins; ***education:*** Degree in Philosophy, Politics and Econ., Magdalen Coll. Oxford, 1982; Business Admin., INSEAD France, 1986; ***party:*** Conservative Party; ***political career:*** Political Advisor to Sir Geoffrey Howe, to Chllr. of the Exchequer and Leon Brittan, then Chief Sec. to the Treasury; MP, Richmond, Yorkshire, 1989-; Sec. of the Conservative Yorkshire Mems., 1989-92; PPS to the Chllr. of the Exchequer, the Rt. Hon. Norman Lamont MP, 1990-93; Under Sec. of State for Social Security, 1993-94; Minister of State for Social Security and Disabled People, 1994-95; Sec. of State for Wales, 1995-97; Shadow Sec. of State for the Welsh Office, 1997; Leader, Conservative. Party, June 1997-2001 (resigned); Shadow Foreign Secretary, 2005-2010; Foreign Secretary, May 2010-; ***interests:*** economics, agriculture; ***professional career:*** Mngr., McKinsey & Co.; ***committees:*** Sec. of the Conservative Backbench Agriculture Cttee., 1989-90; Jt. Cttee. on House of Lords Reform, 2003-10; ***clubs:*** Beefsteak; ***office address:*** Foreign & Commonwealth Affairs Office, King Charles Street, London, SW1A 2AH, United Kingdom; ***URL:*** http://www.fco.gov.uk.

HAHN, Johannes; Commissioner for Regional Policy, European Commission; ***born:*** 1957; ***education:*** Univ. of Vienna, 1987 ; ***party:*** Austrian People's Party; ***political career:*** Federal Minister of Science and Research, 2007-10; European Commissioner for Regional Policy, 2010-; ***office address:*** European Commission, rue de la Loi 200, B-1049 Brussels, Belgium; ***phone:*** +32 (0)2 299 1111; ***URL:*** http://www.europa.eu.

HA HUNG CUONG ; Minister of Justice, Government of Vietnam; ***born:*** 1953; ***education:*** Univ. of International Relations, Moscow, USSR, International Law; Academy of Science, USSR; ***party:*** Communist Party of Vietnam; ***political career:*** Dep. Dir., Dept. of International Law, Ministry of Justice, 1986-88; Mem., Communist Party Cttee., 1998-2003; Dep. Minister of Justice; Party Central Cttee., 2007-; Minister of Justice, 2007-; ***professional career:*** Lecturer & Dep. Dean, International Law, Hanoi Law Univ.; ***office address:*** Ministry of Justice, 25A Cat Linh, Hanoi, Vietnam; ***URL:*** http://www.hahungcuong.net.

HAI, Hoang Trung; Deputy Prime Minister, Government of Vietnam; ***born:*** 27 September 1959, Hanoi, Vietgnam; ***education:*** Hanoi Polytechnic Univ., Bach. of Electrical Eng.; Postgraduate Dip., Power Systems and Power Utility Managment; Trinity College, Dublin, MBA; ***political career:*** Minister of Industry; Dep. Prime Minister, 2008-; ***memberships:*** Central Cttee. of the Communist Party of Vietnam; ***office address:*** Deputy Prime Minister's Office, 1 Hoang Hoa Tham Street, Ba Dinh District, Hanoi, Vietnam; ***phone:*** +84 4 845 8241.

HAILEMARIAM, Desalegne; Prime Minister, Government of Ethiopia; ***education:*** BSc., Addis Ababa Univ., 1988; ***political career:*** MP, 2005-; Deputy Prime Minister, Minister of Foreign Affairs, 2010-; Acting Prime Minister, Aug. Sept., 2012; Sworn in as Prime Minister, Sept. 2012-; ***office address:*** Ministry of Foreign Affairs, PO Box 393, Abbis Ababa, Ethiopia; ***phone:*** +251 11 551 7345; ***fax:*** +251 11 551 4300; ***mobile:*** http://www.mfa.gov.et; ***e-mail:*** mfa.addis@telecom.net.et.

HAIN, Peter, MP; Member of Parliament, House of Commons; ***born:*** 16 February 1950, Kenya; ***parents:*** Walter Vannet Hain and Adelaine Florence Hain (née Stocks); ***married:*** Dr. Elizabeth Haywood, 14 June 2003; Patricia Hain (née Western), 8 February 1975 (div'd); ***children:*** Sam (M), Jake (M); ***education:*** London Univ., B.Sc. (Econ) (first class hons.); Sussex Univ., M.Phil.; ***party:*** Labour Party; ***political career:*** Labour MP for Neath, 1991-; Labour Foreign Affairs Whip, 1995-96; Shadow Employment Minister, 1996-97; Parl. Under-Sec. of State, Welsh Office, 1997-99; Minister of State, FCO, 1999-2001; Minister of State, Dept. Trade and Industry, 2001; Minister for Europe, FCO, 2001-Oct. 2002; Gov. Rep., EU Convention, 2002; Sec. of State for Wales, Oct. 2002; Leader of House of Commons, Lord Privy Seal, June 2003-05; Sec. of State for Northern Ireland, May 2005-June 2007; Secretary of State for Work and Pensions and Secretary of State for Wales, June 2007-resigned Jan. 2008; Secretary of State for Wales, June 2009-May 2010; Shadow Secretary of State for Wales, 2010-12; Chair, National Policy Forum, -2012; ***memberships:*** GMB, Co-Op, Fabians; ***publications:*** Author of 16 books including Ayes to the Left: A Future for Socialism; Sing the Beloved Country; Mandela; ***clubs:*** Royal British Legion, Resolven; ***recreations:*** rock & roll, folk music and walking, rugby, soccer, cricket, motor racing; ***office address:*** House of Commons, London, SW1 0AA, United Kingdom; ***fax:*** +44 (0)1639 641196; ***URL:*** http://www.peterhain.org.

HÄKÄMIES, Jyri; Minister of Economic Affairs, Government of Finland; ***born:*** 1961; ***education:*** Master of Social Sciences; ***party:*** National Coalition Party; ***political career:*** MP, 1999-; Mem., Kotka City Cncl., 2005-; Minister of Defence, Apr. 2007-11; Minister of Economic Affairs, 2011-; ***office address:*** Ministry of Economic Affairs, FI-00131, Helsinki, Finland; ***URL:*** http://www.tem.fi.

HAKEEM, Abdul Rauff; Minister of Justice, Government of Sri Lanka; ***born:*** 1960, Sri Lanka; ***education:*** Royal College Colombo; Univ. of Colombo, LL.B, LL.M; ***party:*** United National Party; ***political career:*** MP; Minister of Port Development & Shipping, and Minister of Eastern Development & Muslim Religious Affairs; Leader, Sri Lanka Muslim Congress; Minister of Justice; ***professional career:*** Attorney; ***office address:*** Ministry of Justice, Superior Courts Complex, Colombo 12, Sri Lanka; ***e-mail:*** minister@justiceministry.gov.lk; ***URL:*** http://www.justiceministry.gov.lk.

HALE OF RICHMOND, Rt. Hon. the Baroness , DBE; Justice of the Supreme Court of the United Kingdom; ***political career:*** Member, House of Lords, 2004-, as Justice of the Supreme Court, disqualified from participation 2009-; ***professional career:*** Barrister; Professor; Law Commissioner; High Court Judge, 1994-99; Lord Justice of Appeal, 1999-2004; Lord of Appeal in Ordinary, 2004-2009; Justice of the Supreme Court, 2009-; ***office address:*** Supreme Court of the United Kingdom, Parliament Square, London, SW1P 3BD, United Kingdom; ***URL:*** http://www.supremecourt.gov.uk.

HALEY, Nikki; Governor, State of South Carolina; ***education:*** Clemson Univ., BSc., Accounting; ***political career:*** South Carolina State legislature, 2004-10; Governor, South Carolina, Nov. 2010-; ***professional career:*** Accounting Supervisor, FCR Inc; ran family multi-million dollar business; ***office address:*** Office of the Governor, PO Box 12267, Columbia, SC 29211-1867, USA; ***phone:*** +1 803 734 5167; ***URL:*** http://www.governor.sc.gov.

HALFON, Robert; MP for Harlow, UK Government; ***party:*** Conservative; ***political career:*** Parish Councillor, 2005-11; MP for Harlow, May 2010-; ***committees:*** Public Administration Select Cttee., 2010-; ***office address:*** House of Commons, London, SW1A 0AA, United Kingdom; ***phone:*** +44 (0)20 7219 3000.

HALL OF BIRKENHEAD, Lord Tony; Member, House of Lords; ***political career:*** Mem., House of Lords, 2010-; ***professional career:*** Mem, Olympics Cultural Advisory Board, Dept. for Culture, Media and Sport, 2006-08; Bd. mem., London Organising Cttee.,

Olympic Games 2009-; Chair, Cultural Olympiad Bd., 2009-; ***office address:*** House of Lords, London, SW1A 0PW, United Kingdom; ***phone:*** +44 (0)20 7219 3000; ***fax:*** +44 (0)20 7219 5979; ***URL:*** http://www.parliament.uk.

HALSDORF, Jean-Marie; Minister of Home Affairs and Defence, Government of Luxembourg; ***born:*** 1 February 1957; ***education:*** Univ. Louis Pasteur, Strasbourg, Doctor of Pharmaceuticals, 1980; ***party:*** Christian-Social Party, CSV; ***political career:*** Deputy, Southern region, 1994-; Secr.Gen, Syndicate of Community Towns of Luxembourg (Syvicol), 2000-; Minister of the Interior and of Land Management, 2004-09; Minister of the Interior and Minister of Defence, 2009-; ***memberships:*** Parly. Assembly of NATO; Regional Cttee. of the EU; Benelux; Interregional Parly. Board; Interparliamentary Consultative Bd. ; ***professional career:*** Pharmacist, Clinique Sacré Cœur de Luxembourg; Burgomeister, Commune of Pétange, 2000; ***committees:*** Pres., Cttee. of the intercommunal Syndicate for the Princesse Marie-Astrid Hospital; ***office address:*** Ministry of Home Affairs, 19 rue Beaumont, Luxembourg L-1219, Luxembourg; ***phone:*** +352 478 4626; ***fax:*** +352 221125; ***URL:*** http://www.miat.public.lu.

HAMDALLAH, Rami; Prime Minister (resigned), Caretaker Transitional Government of Palestinian Authority; ***party:*** independent; ***political career:*** Prime Minister, Palestinian Authority, June 2013 (resigned after 18 days), remaining as caretaker pm until successor is found; ***professional career:*** academic; linguistic prof.; Pres., An Najah National Univ., 1998-; ***office address:*** Office of the Prime Minister, Al-Masyoun, Al-Ma'ahed Street, PO Box 2466, Ramallah, Occupied Palestinian Territories; ***URL:*** http://www.pmo.gov.ps/.

HAMES, Duncan; MP for Chippenham, UK Government; ***party:*** Liberal Democrat; ***political career:*** MP for Chippenham, May 2010-; PPS to Sarah Teather as Minister of State for Children and Families, 2010-11; PSS, to Chris Huhne, Sec. of State for Energy & Climate Change, 2011-12; PPS to Ed Davey, Sec. of State for Energy and Climate Change, 2012; PPS to Nick Clegg, Deputy PM and Lord President of the Council, 2012-; ***office address:*** House of Commons, London, SW1A 0AA, United Kingdom; ***phone:*** +44 (0)20 7219 3000; ***e-mail:*** duncan.hames.mp@parliament.uk.

HAMID, Abdul; President, Government of Bangladesh; ***education:*** BA, Gurudayal Government Coll., Kishoreganj; LLB, Central Law Coll., Univ. of Dhaka; ***political career:*** MP, 1970-2009; Speaker of the National Parliament, 2009-13; President, 2013-; ***professional career:*** Lawyer; ***office address:*** Office of the President, Bangabhaban, Dhaka 1000, Bangladesh; ***phone:*** +880 831 2066; ***URL:*** http://www.bangabhaban.gov.bd.

HAMILTON, David; Member of Parliament for Midlothian, House of Commons; ***born:*** 24 October 1950, Dalkeith, Scotland; ***parents:*** David Hamilton and Agnes Gardner; ***married:*** Jean Hamilton (née Macrae), 1 August 1969; ***children:*** Shirley (F), Isla (F); ***education:*** Dalkeith High Sch., 1962-65; ***party:*** Labour Party; ***political career:*** Councillor, Midlothian Council, 1995-2001; Chair, Strategic Services inc. Economic Development, Strategic Planning and Transportation; COSLA spokesman for Economic Development and Tourism; MP for Midlothian 2001-; Opposition Whip, 2010-; ***interests:*** energy, defence; ***memberships:*** Chair, Midlothian Innovation Technology Trust (MITT); Honoury Mem., Midlothian Artists; ***professional career:*** Miner; Employment Training Scheme Supervisor; Placement Training Officer; Craigmillar Festival Society; Chief Executive, Craigmillar Opportunities Trust; ***committees:*** Dept. of Work and Pensions Cttee., 2003-05; Proceedures Select Cttee.; Work and Pensions Select Cttee., 2001-05, Broadcasting Select Cttee., 2001-05; Scottish Affairs Select Cttee., 2001-05; Defence Select Cttee., 2005-10; European Scrutiny Committee 2005-07; Chair, Scottish Group of MPs, 2008; ***clubs:*** Dalkeith Miners Club; ***recreations:*** theatre, films, local politics, grandchildren; ***office address:*** 95 High Street, Dalkeith, Midlothian, EH22 1HL, United Kingdom; ***phone:*** +44 (0)1316 541585; ***fax:*** +44 (0)1316 541586; ***e-mail:*** hamiltonda@parliament.uk; ***URL:*** http://www.davidhamiltonmp.co.uk.

HAMILTON, Fabian; British, Member of Parliament for Leeds North East, House of Commons; ***born:*** 12 April 1955; ***education:*** Univ. of York, BA (Hons.), Social Sciences; ***party:*** Labour Party; ***political career:*** MP, Leeds North East, 1997-; ***interests:*** racial equality, education, economic development; ***professional career:*** fmr. Taxi driver; fmr. graphic designer; ***committees:*** mem., Foreign Affairs Select Cttee., 2001-10; Political & Constitutional Reform, 210-; Jt. Cttee. on National Security Strategy, 2010-; ***trusteeships:*** National Heart Research Fund; ***office address:*** House of Commons, London, SW1A 0AA, United Kingdom; ***phone:*** +44 (0)20 7219 3493; ***fax:*** +44 (0)20 7219 4945; ***e-mail:*** fabian@leedsne.co.uk.

HAMMOND, Aleqa; Prime Minister, Government of Greenland; ***born:*** 1965; ***languages:*** Danish, English, German, Inuktitut; ***education:*** Arctic College, Nunavut, Canada; ***party:*** Chmn., Siumut Party; ***political career:*** MP, 2005-; Minister of Family and Justice; Minister of Foreign Affairs and Finance; Prime Minister, Minister of Foreign Affairs, 2013-; ***office address:*** Office of the Prime Minister, P.O.Box 1015 , 3900 Nuuk, Greenland; ***phone:*** +299 245000; ***e-mail:*** govsec@nanoq.gl.

HAMMOND, Rt. Hon. Philip; British, Secretary of State for Defence, UK Government; ***born:*** 4 December 1955; ***married:*** Susan Hammond, 1991; ***children:*** Amy (F), Sophie (F), William (M); ***education:*** Shenfield Sch., Brentwood, Essex, 1966-74; Univ. Coll., Oxford (Open Scholarship), 1st Class Hons, PPE, 1977; ***party:*** Conservative Party; ***political career:*** Chmn., East Lewisham Conservative Assn., 1989-96; Parly. Candidate, Newham North East, 1994; MP, Runnymede and Weybridge. 1997-; Opposition Health Spokesman, 1998-2001; Opposition Trade and Ind. Spokesman, Sept. 2001-02; Opposition Local Government spokesman, 2002-05; Shadow Chief Secretary to the Treasury, 2005; Shadow Secretary of State for Work and Pensions, 2005-; Shadow Chief Sec. to the Treasury, 2007-May 2010; Secretary of State for Transport, May 2010-11; Secretary of State for Defence, 2011-; ***interests:*** economics, crime and punishment, social security reform, long-term care of the elderly, promoting an enterprise culture, Britain's place in the world; ***professional career:*** Dir. and Man. Dir. of Cos., distributing medical equipment Germany, Italy and UK; Partner in energy consultancy business with int. Govt. and private sector clients; ***committees:*** fmr. Mem., Select Cttee. for Environment, Transport and The Regions; Mem., European Standing Cttee., 1997-98; Sec., Conservative Party Health Cttee., 1997-98; Opposition Health and Social Services Spokesman, 1998-2001; ***recreations:*** family, restoration of his 500 year old house, cinema, walking in Scotland; ***office address:*** Department of Defence, Main Building, Whitehall, London, SW1A 2HB, United Kingdom; ***e-mail:*** hammondp@parliament.uk; ***URL:*** http://www.mod.uk.

HAMMOND, Stephen; MP for Wimbledon, House of Commons; ***born:*** 4 February 1962, Southampton, UK; ***parents:*** Bryan Norman Walter and Janice Eve (née Yeoman); ***married:*** Sally Patricia Brodie, 14 May 1991; ***children:*** Alice Sophie Jane (F); ***languages:*** French; ***education:*** King Edward VI Sch., Southampton; Queen Mary College, Univ. of London; ***party:*** Conservative Party, 1983-; ***political career:*** Candidate for North Warwickshire, 1997, Wimbledon, 2001; Councillor, London Borough of Merton, 2002-06; MP for Wimbledon, 2005-; Shadow Transport Minister, 2005-10; PPS to Eric Pickles as Secretary of State for Communities and Local Government, 2010-12; Parly. Under Sec., Dept. of Transport, 2012-; ***interests:*** treasury, foreign affairs, environment, education, transport; ***professional career:*** Dir., Dresdner Kleinwort Securities, 1994; Dir., Research Commerzbank; ***committees:*** Financial Bill 2005; NI Contribs Bill, 2005; Regulatory Reform Select Cttee., 2005-08; ***trusteeships:*** Gov., Wimbledon College; ***clubs:*** Wimbledon Village Club; RWGE; Wimbledon Club; ***office address:*** House of Commons, London, SW1A 0AA, United Kingdom; ***phone:*** +44 (0)20 7219 1029/3401; ***fax:*** +44 (0)20 7219 0462; ***e-mail:*** hammondsp@parliament.uk; ***URL:*** http://www.stephanhammondmp.com.

HANCOCK, Hon. David, QC; Canadian, Minister of Human Services, Government of Alberta; ***born:*** 1955, Fort Resolution; ***parents:*** Richard Hancock and Kathleen Hancock; ***married:*** Janet; ***children:*** Ian (M), Janis (F), Janine (F); ***public role of spouse:*** Principal at Edmonton Public School; ***education:*** Univ. of Alberta, BA, Political Science/Econ., 1975, LLB, 1979; ***party:*** Progressive Conservative; ***political career:*** MLA, Edmonton-Whitemud, 1997-; Minister of Intergovernmental Affairs and Aboriginal Affairs, 1997-99; Minister of Justice and Attorney General, 1999-; Govt. House Leader, 2003-04; Minister of Advanced Education, 2004-06; Minister of Health and Wellness, Government House Leader, 2007-08; Minister of Education, 2008-12; Minister of Human Services, Government House Leader, 2012-; ***professional career:*** Partner, Matheson and Company; ***trusteeships:*** Ph. Gamma Delta Educational Foundation of Canada; ***clubs:*** Kilvanis; ***office address:*** Ministry of Human Services, Legislature Building, 10800-97 Avenue, Edmonton, Alberta T5K 2B6, Canada; ***e-mail:*** dave.hancock@gov.ab.ca.

HANCOCK, Matthew; MP for West Suffolk, UK Government; ***party:*** Conservative; ***political career:*** MP for West Suffolk, May 2010-; Parly. Under-Secretary of State, Dept. for Business, Innovation and Skills and Education, 2012-; ***committees:*** Public Accounts Select Cttee., 2010-12; Standards and Privileges, 2010-12; ***office address:*** House of Commons, London, SW1A 0AA, United Kingdom; ***phone:*** +44 (0)20 7219 7186; ***e-mail:*** matthew.hancock.mp@parliament.uk; ***URL:*** http://www.matthewhancock.co.uk.

HANCOCK, Mike; British, Member of Parliament for Portsmouth South, House of Commons; ***born:*** 9 April 1946; ***education:*** Portsmouth Sch.; ***party:*** Liberal Democratic Party; ***political career:*** Lib. Dem. Spokesman for Defence; MP for Portsmouth, 1997-2001; Re-elected MP for Portsmouth South, 2001-; ***memberships:*** Assembly of European Regions; Atlantic Arc.; Western European Union Parliamentary Delegation, NATO Parliamentary assembly; ***professional career:*** District Officer for MENCAP, 1987-97; Dir. BBC Daytime; ***committees:*** Defence Select Cttee., 1999-2001; House of Commons Chairman's Panel, 2000-; ***honours and awards:*** CBE award, 1992; ***office address:*** House of Commons, London, SW1A 0AA, United Kingdom; ***phone:*** +44 (0)20 7219 3000; ***e-mail:*** portsmouthldp@cix.co.uk / hcinfo@parliament.uk.

HANDS, Greg; MP for Chelsea and Fulham, House of Commons; ***born:*** 1965; ***party:*** Conservative; ***political career:*** Councillor, Hammersmith and Fulham Borough Cncl., 1998-2006; MP for Hammersmith and Fulham, 2005-10, Chelsea and Fulham, 2010-; ***office address:*** House of Commons, London, SW10 0AA, United Kingdom; ***phone:*** +44 (0)20 7219 3000.

HANHAM, Baroness Joan; Member of the House of Lords; ***married:*** Dr. Iain William Ferguson, 11 April 1964; ***children:*** James Charles (M), Emma Margret (M); ***education:*** Hillcourt, Glenageary, Co.Dublin; ***party:*** Conservative; ***political career:*** Leader, Royal Borough Kensington & Chelsea, 1989-2000; Mem., House of Lords, 1999-; Shadow Min., Communities and Local Government, 2001-07; Shadow Min., Home Office, 2007-09; Shadow Min., Transport, 2009; Parly. Under-Sec., Dept. Communities and Local Government, 2010-; ***interests:*** local government, health; ***honours and awards:*** CBE, 1998; ***office address:*** House of Lords, London, SW1A 0PQ, United Kingdom; ***phone:*** +44 (0)20 7219 3000; ***fax:*** +44 (0)20 7219 6563.

HANS-ADAM II, Prince; Prince of Liechtenstein; ***born:*** 14 February 1945; ***parents:*** His Serene Highness Prince Franz Josef II of Liechtenstein (dec'd) and Her Serene Highness Princess Gina (dec'd); ***married:*** Countess Marie Kinsky von Wchinitz und Tettau, 30 July 1967; ***children:*** Prince Alois (M), Prince Maximilian (M), Prince Constatin (M), Princess Tatjana (F); ***languages:*** English, French, German; ***education:*** Sch. of Economics and Social Sciences, St. Gallen Coll., Switzerland, Licentiate, 1969; ***interests:*** state economic and financial plans, foreign policy, the economic and political development of Europe; ***professional career:*** Exec. Authority of Liechtenstein, 1984-; Prince of Liechtenstein, 1989-; August 2004 Prince Hans-Adam II appointed Hereditary Prince Alois his permanent deputy in preparation for his succession to the throne; ***office address:*** Schloss Vaduz, FL-9490 Vaduz, Liechtenstein; ***phone:*** +423 238 1200.

HANSEN, Margrethe Vestager ; Danish, Deputy Prime Minister, Minister of Economic Affairs, Danish Government; ***born:*** 13 April 1968; ***children:*** Maria (F), Rebecca (F), Ella (F); ***languages:*** English, French, German; ***education:*** Varde Gymnasium, upper secondary sch. leaving exam., Mathematics-Music branch, 1986; Univ. of Copenhagen, MA, Political Economics, 1993; ***party:*** Radikale Venstre (RV, Social-Liberal Party); ***political career:*** Parly. candidate for Esbjerg for the Social Liberal Party, 1988-92; mem., Social Liberal Party's exec. cttee., 1989-; Nat. Chmn., Social Liberal Party, 1993-97; Minister for Education, 1998-2001 and Church, 1998-2000; mem., Danish Parliament, 2001-; Parly. Leader for the Social Liberal Party, 2007-; Deputy Prime Minister, Minister of Economic Affairs, Minister of the Interior, 2011-; *memberships:* Fomer Mem., Bd. of ID-Sparinvest A/S and Care Denmark; *professional career:* Editor, 'Radikal Politik', Det Radikale Venstre's members' bulletin, 1989-91; Lecturer of Pol. Economics, Copenhagen Univ., 1990-91 & 1992; Stagiaire, European Parl., 1991; Tutor of Pol. Econ., Copenhagen Sch. of Economics & Business Admin. 1992; Economist, Head of Section, Min. of Finance, Dept. of Management & Personnel 1993; Special adviser in Agency for Financial Management and Admin. Affairs, 1995-97; Head of Secretariat in Agency for Financial Management and Admin. Affairs, 1997; *committees:* Social Liberal Party's Exec. Cttee., 1992; Social Liberal Party's EC Cttee., 1992; *publications:* Various articles on political subjects, The EC Agricultural Policy, 1986; Market Segmentation, 1987; Consequences for Employment of Reduced Working Hours, 1988; Social Choice-a fair Electoral Procedure, 1989; Presentation of Economy on TV, 1989; Poverty in the 1980s in Denmark, 1990; Is the African Crisis Political?, 1990; Media Liability, 1991; The Nation State in a European Perspective, 1991; Flexible Specialisation, 1993; *office address:* Ministry of Economic Affairs, Slotholmsgade 10-12, 1216 Copenhagen K, Denmark; *phone:* +45 3392 3350; *fax:* +45 3312 3778; *e-mail:* oem@oem.dk; *URL:* http://www.oem.dk.

HANSON, David; British, Member of Parliament, House of Commons; *born:* 5 July 1957; *parents:* the late Brian Hanson and Glenda Hanson; *children:* Amy (F), Alys (F), Tom (M), Daniel (M); *education:* Hull Univ. UK, BA (Hons), PGCE; *party:* Labour Party; *political career:* Vale Royal Borough Cncl., 1983-92; Leader, Labour Group, 1990-92; Mem., Leadership Campaign Team; MP, Delyn, 1992-; Parly.-under-Sec., Welsh Office, 1999-2001; Whip, 1998-99; PPS, Prime Minister's Office, 2001-05; Minister of State, Northern Ireland Office, 2005-07; Minister of State, Min. of Justice, June 2007-09; Appointed to Privy Cncl., 2007; Minister of State, Home Office, 2009-10; Shadow Minister, Treasury, 2010-11; Shadow Minister, Policing, 2011-; *interests:* local government, civil service, heritage; *committees:* Mem., Welsh Affairs Select Cttee., 1992-96; Sec., PLP Nat. Heritage Cttee., 1994-97; Mem., Public Service Select Cttee., 1996; *office address:* House of Commons, London, SW1A 0AA, United Kingdom; *phone:* +44 (0)20 7219 3000; *e-mail:* david.hanson.mp@parliament.uk.

HANSSON, Ardo; Governor, Eesti Pank; *born:* 1958, Chicago, USA; *education:* Univ. of British Colombia, Canada, economics; Harvard Univ., USA, MA, Ph.D, economics; *professional career:* Research Assist., Univ. of British Columbia, 1980-82; Research Assist, Harvard Univ., 1984-87; Assist Prof., Univ. of British Columbia, 1987-90; UN Univ., 1990-92; Economic Adviser to the PM of Estonia, 1992-94; Research Fellow, Stockholm School of Economics, 1992-96; Economic Adviser to PM, 1997; Mem., Supervisory Board, Eesti Pank, 1993-98; Various posits., World Bank, 1998-2012; Governor, Eesti Pank, 2012-; Mem., Gov. Council, ECB, 2012-; *office address:* Eesti Pank, Estonia bld. 13, 15095 Tallinn, Estonia; *URL:* http://www.eestipank.ee.

HARALD V, HM King; Norwegian, King, Kingdom of Norway; *born:* 21 February 1937, Skaugum, Norway; *parents:* King Olav V (dec.d 1991) and Crown Princess Märtha (dec'd 1954); *married:* Sonja Haraldsen; *children:* Märtha Louise (F), Haakon (M); *education:* Balliol Coll., Oxford, BA, Political Science, History and Economics, 1962; *professional career:* Cavalry Officers' Candidate Sch., Trandum; Military Academy, 1957-59 then compulsory military service; ascended to the throne, 1991; represented Norway at Olympic Games, Gold Cup Races, 1968, Kiel Week Races, 1972; World Champion, Yacht "Fram X", 1987 ; *honours and awards:* Commander in Chief, Norwegian Land and Naval Forces; Army and Air Force General, Admiral of the Norwegian Navy; *recreations:* outdoor pursuits, nature; *office address:* Royal Palace, Oslo, Norway; *URL:* http://www.kongehuset.no/english/vis.html.

HARDARDOTTIR, Eyglo; Minister of Welfare, Government of Iceland; *born:* 12 December 1972; *political career:* MP, 2008-; Minister of Social Affairs and Housing, 2013-; *office address:* Ministry of Welfare, Hafnarhusinu vid Tryggvagotu, 150 Reykjavik, Iceland; *phone:* +354 545 8100; *URL:* http://www.stjr.is/htr.

HARDT, Dr Brent; Ambassador, US Embassy in Guyana; *professional career:* Chargé d'Affaires, to Barbados and the Eastern Caribbean; Dep. Chief of Mission and Chargé d'Affaires, to the Bahamas and the Holy See in Rome; Amb. to the Cooperative Republic of Guyana, Plen. Rep.to the Caribbean Community (CARICOM), 2011-; *office address:* US Embassy, 100 Young and Duke Streets, Georgetown, Guyana; *phone:* +592 226 3938; *fax:* +592 227 0240; *e-mail:* usembassy@hotmail.com; *URL:* http://georgetown.usembassy.gov.

HARKIN, Tom; American, Senator for Iowa, US Senate; *born:* 19 November 1939, Iowa; *married:* Ruth Harkin (née Raduenz), 1968; *children:* Amy (F), Jenny (F); *public role of spouse:* President and Chief Executive Officer, Overseas Private Investment Corporation; *education:* Iowa State Univ., degree in Govt. and Economics; Catholic Univ. of America Law Sch., Washington 1972; *party:* Democrat; *political career:* elected to US Congress, 1974; US Senator for Iowa, 1984-; *memberships:* Mem., American Legion Post 562, Cumming; *professional career:* US Navy, 1962-67, US Naval Reserve, 1967-70; Legal Aid Attorney; *committees:* Senate: Health, Education, Labor & Pensions; Appropriations; Agriculture, Nutrition & Forestry; Small Business & Entrepreneurship; *office address:* US Senate, 731 Hart Senate Office Building, Washington, DC 20510, USA; *phone:* +1 202 224 3254; *fax:* +1 202 224 9369; *e-mail:* tom_harkin@harkin.senate.gov; *URL:* http://www.harkin.senate.gov/.

HARMAN, Rt. Hon. Harriet Ruth, QC, MP; British, Shadow Deputy Prime Minister and Shadow Secretary of State for Culture, Media and Sport, House of Commons; *born:* 1950; *married:* Jack Dromey, 1982; *party:* Labour Party; *political career:* MP (Lab) for Peckham, 1982-97; MP, Camberwell and Peckham, 1997-; Opp. Spokesman on Health and Social Services, until 1992; Opp. Chief Sec. to the Treasury, 1992-97; Sec. of State for Social Security and Minister for Women, 1997-98; Solicitor-General, 2001-05; Minister of State, Dept. for Constitutional Affairs, May 2005-June 2007; Leader of the House of Commons, Lord Privy Seal, Minister for Women, Labour Party Chair, June 2007-May 2010, Acting Leader of the Labour Party, 2010; Deputy Leader and Shadow Secretary of State for International Development, 2010-12; Shadow Deputy Prime Minister, Party Chair, Shadow Secretary of State for Culture, Media and Sport, 2012-; *professional career:* Solicitor in law centre; solicitor, NCCL; *office address:* House of Commons, London, SW1A 0AA, United Kingdom; *e-mail:* hcinfo@parliament.uk.

HARPER, Mark; MP for Forest of Dean, House of Commons; *born:* 1970; *party:* Conservative; *political career:* MP for Forest of Dean, 2005-; Parliamentary Secretary (Political and Constitutional Reform), 2010-12; Minister of State for Immigration, Home Office, 2012-; *office address:* House of Commons, London, SW1P 0AA, United Kingdom; *phone:* +44 (0)20 7219 3000.

HARPER, Hon. Stephen; Prime Minister, Government of Canada; *born:* Toronto, Ontario, Canada; *children:* 2; *education:* Univ. of Calgary, MA; *political career:* Reform Party MP, 1993-97; Conservative lobby grp, 1997-2002; Canadian Alliance MP and Leader of the opposition, 2002-06, Leader of Conservativce Party, the merged Canadian Alliance and Progressive Conservative Party of Canada, 2003-; Prime Minister, Jan. 2006-; *office address:* Office of the Prime Minister, Langevin Building 80 Wellington Street, Ottawa, Ontario, K1A 0A2, Canada; *phone:* +1 613 992 4211; *e-mail:* pm@pm.gc.ca.

HARRINGTON, Richard; MP for Watford, UK Government; *party:* Conservative (Treasurer, 2008-10, Vice-Chmn., 2012-); *political career:* MP for Watford, May 2010-; *committees:* International Development Select Cttee., 2010-; *office address:* House of Commons, London, SW1A 0AA, United Kingdom; *phone:* +44 (0)20 7219 3000; *e-mail:* richard.harrington.mp@parliament.uk.

HARRIS, Rebecca; MP for Castle Point, UK Government; *party:* Conservative; *political career:* Councillor, Chichester District Council, 1999-2003; MP for Castle Point, May 2010-; *committees:* Business, Innovation and Skills Select Cttee., 2010-; Jt. Cttee., Draft Enhanced Terrorism Prevention & Investigation Measures Bill, 2012-; *office address:* House of Commons, London, SW1A 0AA, United Kingdom; *phone:* +44 (0)20 7219 3000; *e-mail:* rebecca.harris.mp@parliament.uk.

HARRIS, Seth D.; Acting Secretary of Labour, US Government; *education:* Cornell Univ.; New York Univ. School of Law; *political career:* Dept. of Labour, Clinton Administration incld. Counselor to the Sec. of Labor and Acting Assistant Sec. of Labor for Policy; Dep. Sec. of Labor, 2009-, Acting Sec., 2013-; *professional career:* Law clerk, US Court of Appearls; Law clerk, US District Court for the District of Maine; Professor of Law, New York Law School; *office address:* Department of Labour, Frances Perkins Building, 200 Constitution Avenue, NW , Washington, DC 20210, USA; *URL:* http://www.dol.gov.

HARRIS, Tom; Member of Parliament for Glasgow South, House of Commons; *born:* Irvine; *education:* Garnock Academy, Kilbirnie; Napier Coll., Edinburgh, HND, Journalism; *party:* Labour Party; *political career:* MP, Glasgow Cathcart, 2001-05, Glasgow South, 2005-; Parly. Under Sec. of State, Dept. of Transport, 2006-08; Shadow Ministerfor Environment, Food & Rural Affairs, 2012-; *professional career:* Chief Public Relations and Marketing Officer, Strathclyde Passenger Transport Executive 1998-2001; *committees:* Transport, 2010-; *office address:* House of Commons, London, SW1A 0AA, United Kingdom; *phone:* +44 (0)20 7219 8237; *e-mail:* tomharrismp@parliament.uk; *URL:* http://www.tomharris.com.

HARRISON, H.E. Alistair; Governor of Anguilla; *born:* 1954; *education:* Classics, Univ. Coll., Oxford; Economics, Univ. of London, 1995; *political career:* Governor of Anguilla, 2009-; *professional career:* British High Commissioner to Zambia, Sept. 2005-08; *office address:* Office of the Governor, Government House, PO Box 60, The Valley, Anguilla.

HARRY, HRH Prince; See Prince Henry of Wales.

HART, Edwina, AM, MBE; Minister for Economy Science and Transport, National Assembly for Wales; *born:* 26 April 1957; *married:* (Married); *party:* Labour Party; *political career:* Mem., National Assembly for Wales (Gower), 1999-; Finance Sec., 1999-2000; Minister for Finance, Local Government & Communities, 2000-2003; Minister for Social Justice and Regeneration, 2003-07; Minister for Social Justice and Regeneration, June 2007; Minister for Health and Social Services, 2007-11; Minister for Business, Enterprise and Technology, 2011-13; Minister for Economy Science and Transport, 2013-; *interests:* economic development, equal opportunities; *memberships:* fmr. Mem. of the following: Broadcasting Council for Wales, 1995-99; Wales Millennium Centre, 1997-99; South West Wales Economic Forum; Employment Appeal Tribunal, 1992-99; Council Univ. of Wales, Swansea, 1998-99; Current Mem., Court of Governors, Univ. of Wales, Swansea, 2000-; T&GWU; ISTC; *professional career:* Ex-Pres., the Banking, Insurance and Finance Union, 1992-94; non-exec. Dir., Chwarae Teg, 1994-99; Representative, Wales TUC General Council, Chmn., 1997-98; fmr. Trade Union Official working with Wales TUC; *committees:* Mem., South West Wales Regional Cttee., 1999-; Chair, Equality of Opportunity Cttee., 2000-02; *honours and awards:* MBE, services to Trade Unionism, 1998; *recreations:* music, literature, cooking; *office address:* National Assembly for Wales, Room A.2.11, Cardiff Bay, Cardiff, CF99 1NA, United Kingdom; *phone:* +44 (0)29 2089 8400; *fax:* +44 (0)29 2089 8524; *e-mail:* edwina.hart@wales.gov.uk.

HART, Simon; MP for Carmarthen West and South Pembrokeshire, UK Government; *party:* Conservative; *political career:* MP for Carmarthen West and South Pembrokeshire, May 2010-; *committees:* Political and Constitutional Reform Select Cttee., 2010-; *office address:* House of Commons, London, SW1A 0AA, United Kingdom; *phone:* +44 (0)20 7219 3000; *e-mail:* simon.hart.mp@parliament.uk.

HARVEY, Nick; British, Minister of State (Minister for the Armed Forces), UK Government; *born:* 3 August 1961, Chandler's Ford, Hampshire; *education:* Queen's Coll, Taunton; Middlesex Univ., BA (Hons), Business Studies, 1983; *party:* Liberal Democratic Party; *political career:* Liberal Agent, Finchley, 1983; contested Barnet Cncl. Seat for the Liberals, 1986; contested Southgate Enfield, 1987; MP, North Devon, 1992-; Lib. Dem. Transport Spokesman, 1992-94; Party Spokesman for Trade and Industry, 1994-97; Lib. Dem. Parly. Spokesman on Constitution (English Regions),1997-99; Lib. Dem. Shadow Health Sec., 1999-2001; Lib. Dem. Shadow Culture, Media and Sport Sec., 2001-03; Shadow Defence Secretary, 2006-10; Minister of State (Minister for the Armed Forces), May 2010-; *memberships:* Greenpeace, Friends of the Earth, Amnesty International; *professional career:* Communications, marketing, City consultants Dewe Rogerson; *committees:* Chmn., Party's Campaigns Cttee., 1994-99; Chmn., Candidates' Cttee., 1993-98; Home

Affairs, 2005-06; Standards & Privileges, 2005-10; *office address:* Ministry of Defence, Main Building, Whitehall, London, SW1A 2HB, United Kingdom; *phone:* +44 (0)20 7218 9000; *e-mail:* mail@nickharveymp.com.

HASANOV, Ali; Deputy Prime Minister, Government of Azerbaijan; *political career:* Deputy Prime Minister, 1998-; *committees:* Chmn., State Cttee. on Affairs of Refugees and Forcibly Displaced Persons, to date; *office address:* Office of the Prime Minister, Lermontov ST 63, 370066 Baku, Azerbaijan; *phone:* +994 (0)12 927728.

HASELHURST, Sir Alan; British, Member of Parliament for Saffron Walden, House of Commons; *born:* 1937; *parents:* John Haselhurst and Alice Haselhurst (née Barraclough); *married:* Angela Haselhurst (née Bailey), 1977; *children:* David (M), Mark (M), Emma (F); *education:* King Edward VI Grammar Sch., Birmingham; Cheltenham Coll.; Oriel Coll., Oxford; *party:* Conservative Party; *political career:* PA to Lord Balniel in gen. elections, 1964 and 1966; MP (Con) for Middleton and Prestwich, 1970-74; MP, Saffron Walden, 1977-; PPS to Sec. of State for Education, 1979-81; Chmn., Ways and Means, 1997-2010; Dep. Speaker, 1997-2010; *memberships:* Hon Sec., All Party Parly. Cricket Gp., Chmn., 2010-; *professional career:* Pres., Oxford Univ. Cons. Assn.; Officer, Oxford Union; Nat. Chmn., YCs, 1966-68; Chmn., Trustees, Community Dev. Foundation, 1986-97; Chmn., C'wealth Youth Exchange Cncl., 1978-81; Privy Counsellor, 1999; *committees:* Chmn., Adminstration Cttee., 2010-; Chmn., Commonwealth Parly. Assn. (UK Branch), 2010-; Commons Cttee. M'ships: Finance and Services, 2008-, Liaison, 2010-, Audit, 2010-, Ecclesiastical, 2010-, Works of Art, 2011-; *honours and awards:* Knighted, 1995; *publications:* Occasionally Cricket, Queen Anne Press, 1999; Eventually Cricket, Queen Anne Press, 2001; Incidentally Cricket, Queen Anne Press, 2003; Accidentally Cricket, Professional and Higher Partnership Ltd., 2009; Unusually Cricket, Professional and Higher Partnership Ltd, 2010; *office address:* House of Commons, London, SW1A 0AA, United Kingdom; *phone:* +44 (0)20 7219 3000; *e-mail:* haselhursta@parliament.uk; *URL:* http://www.siralanhaselhurst.net.

HASELOFF, Dr Reiner; Prime Minister, State Chancellery of Saxony-Anhalt; *born:* 1954; *education:* Humboldt Univ. in Berlin, Ph.D, 1991; *party:* CDU; *political career:* Dep. Dir. Administrator , Wittenberg, 1990-92; Sec., Ministry of Economy and Labour of Saxony-Anhalt, 2002-06, Minister, 2006-11; Minister-President, Saxony-Anhalt, 2011-; *office address:* Office of the Prime Minister, State Chancellery, Hegelstrasse 40-42, 39104 Magdeburg, Germany; *URL:* http://www.sachsen-anhalt.de/.

HASKEL, Lord, Baron Simon, Life Peer; British, Member of the House of Lords; *party:* Labour Party; *political career:* Mem., House of Lords, 1993-; *office address:* House of Lords, London, SW1A 0PQ, United Kingdom; *phone:* +44 (0)20 7219 3000; *fax:* +44 (0)20 7219 5979.

HASLAM, Bill; Governor, State of Tennessee; *education:* Emory Univ., History; *party:* Republican; *political career:* Mayor, Knoxville, 2003-10; Governor, Tennessee, 2010-; *professional career:* Pilot Corp.; *office address:* Office of the Governor, 1st Floor, State Capitol, Nashville, TN 37243-0001, USA; *URL:* http://www.tn.gov/governor/.

HASLER, Adrian; Prime Minister, Government of Liechtenstein; *education:* Univ. of St Gallen; *party:* Progressive Citizens Party; *political career:* MP, 2001-04; Prime Minister 2013-; *professional career:* Economist; Chief, National Police Force, 2004-; *office address:* Office of the Prime Minister, Haus Risch, Aeulestrasse 51, 9490 Vaduz, Liechtenstein.

HASSAN, Maggie; Governor, New Hampshire; *education:* Brown Univ., BA; Northeastern School of Law, JD; *party:* Democrat; *political career:* Senator, New Hampshire, 2004-10, President Pro Tempore and Majority Leader; served on sevearl cttees. including: Commerce; Public and Municipal Affairs; Finance; Energy & Environment; and Economic Development; elected Governor, New Hampshire, Nov. 2012; *professional career:* Attorney; *office address:* Office of the Governor, 107 North Main Street, Room 208, Concord, NH 03301, USA; *URL:* http://www.state.nh.us/governor.

HASTINGS, Doc; American, Congressman, Washington Fourth District, US House of Representatives; *party:* Republican; *political career:* Washington State House of Representatives, 1979-87; Assist. Majority Whip, 1999-; Congressman, Washington Fourth District, US House of Representatives, 1994-; *committees:* Chmn., Natural Resources; Oversight & Government Reform; *office address:* US House of Representatives, 1323 Longworth House Office Building, Washington, DC 20515-4704, USA; *phone:* +1 202 225 5816.

HATCH, Orrin Grant, BS, JD; American, Senator for Utah, US Senate; *born:* 1934, Homestead Park, PA., USA; *parents:* Jesse Hatch and Helen Kamm Hatch; *married:* Elaine Hatch (née Hansen), 1957; *education:* Brigham Young Univ., bachelor's degree; Univ. of Pittsburgh Law Sch., full honors scholarship, Juris Doctorate with honours; *party:* Republican; *political career:* US Senator for Utah, 1977-; *professional career:* Ptnr., Thomson Rhodes & Grigsby, 1962-69; Ptnr., Hatch & Plumb, 1976; *committees:* Finance; Judiciary; Health, Education, Labor and Pensions; *honours and awards:* many awards for actions throughout service in the Senate; five hon. doctorate degrees from law schools and universities; *publications:* several books and articles on his policies and beliefs including: ERA Myths and Realities, 1983; Square Peg: Confessions of a Citizen Senator; has written the lyrics for hundreds of songs and has co-produced seven CDs; *recreations:* poetry, music; *office address:* US Senate, 104 Hart Senate Office Building, Washington, DC 20510, USA; *phone:* +1 202 224 5251; *URL:* http://hatch.senate.gov/.

HAUSIKU, Marco; Namibian, Deputy Prime Minister, Namibian Government; *born:* 1953; *education:* Dobra Training College 1969-72; Augustineum Training College 1972-73; Univ. of Fort Hare 1975-76; *political career:* Minister of Lands, Resettlement and Rehabilitation 1990-1992; Minister of Works, Transport and Communication 1992; Minister of Prisons and Correctional Services; Minister of Labour, 2002; Minister of Foreign Affairs, 2004-10; Deputy Prime Minister, 2010-; *professional career:* Teacher, Shifidi Secondary School 1977-89; joined SWAPO 1976; elected as member of the SWAPO Windhoek Branch; arrested under AG 26 in 1978 and detained for over six months; re-arrested in early 1979 and detained until

January 1980; restricted to house and banned from teaching; arrested under AG.9 in 1982 and detained at Osire, Head SWAPO office Rundu, Kavango 1989-90; *office address:* National Assembly, Parliament Buildings, Private Bag 13323, Windhoek, Namibia; *phone:* +264 61 280 3111.

HAUTALA, Heidi Anneli; Minister for International Development, Government of Finland; *born:* 1955; *education:* MA in horticulture; *party:* Finnish Green Party; *political career:* Member of European Parliament, 2009-11; Minister for International Development, 2011-; *publications:* Venäjä-teesit. Vakaus vai vapaus, 2008; *office address:* Ministry of Foreign Affairs, Merikasarmi, PO Box 176, 00161 Helsinki, Finland; *phone:* +358 (0)9 16005; *URL:* http://www.formin.finland.fi.

HAVARD, Dai; Member of Parliament for Merthyr Tydfil & Rhymney, House of Commons; *born:* 7 February 1950, Quakers Yard, Merthyr Tydfil; *parents:* Edward (Ted) Milner (dec'd) and Eileen (dec'd); *married:* Julia Watts, 1986 (divorced); *education:* St. Peter's Coll., Birmingham; MA, Industrial Relations, Warwick Univ.; *party:* Labour Party; *political career:* MP, Merthyr Tydfil & Rhymney, 2001-; *interests:* defence, industrial relations and working conditions, education - lifelong learning, health, cancer, blood; *memberships:* Co-Operative Party; Merthyr Tydfil Credit Union; BHS; RSPB; NFAS; Bevan Foundation; *professional career:* Trade Union Studies, tutor, 1971-75; self employed trade union researcher, 1975-79; trade union education tutor, 1975-82; Wales Secretary, Amicus MSF, 1982-2001; *committees:* Deregulation and Regulatory Reform Cttee., 2001; European Standing Cttee., 2001-05; Wales Labour Party Joint Policy Cttee., 2001-04; Defence Select Cttee., 2003-10, 2010-; Panel of Chairs, 2011-; *publications:* contributor to academic publications on trade union and economic development; *clubs:* Aberfan Social and Democratic; Commons and Lords Rugby Club; *recreations:* hill walking, horse riding, field archery, Commons and Lords Rugby Club, bird watching; *office address:* House of Commons, London, SW1A 0AA, United Kingdom; *phone:* +44 (0)20 7219 8255; *fax:* +44 (0)20 7219 1449; *e-mail:* havardd@parliament.uk; *URL:* http://www.parliament.uk.

HAWORTH, Lord Alan; Member, House of Lords; *born:* 26 April 1948, Blackburn, Lancashire, UK; *parents:* Jack Haworth and Hima Haworth (née Westhead); *married:* Gill Cole, 1973 (div'd); Maggie Rae, 1991; *public role of spouse:* Matrimonial lawyer, Former Chair of Fabian Society; *party:* Labour; *political career:* Cttee. Officer, Parliamentary Labour Party, 1975-85, Senior Cttee. Officer, 1985-92, Secretary, 1992-2004; mem., House of Lords, 2004-; *interests:* energy, environment, transport, health, foreign affairs, Royal Navy; Countries of interest: Azerbaijan, Georgia, Russia, Iran, Kazakhstan, Kyrgysztan, Tibet, Laos, Cambodia & Vietnam; *memberships:* Munro Society; *professional career:* Registrar of Faculty of Art & Design, North East London Polytechnic, 1972-73, Admin. Assist. to Director of Course Development, 1973-75; *recreations:* mountaineering and hill-walking; completed the Munros 2001 and the Furths 2008; *office address:* House of Lords, London, SW1A 0PW, United Kingdom; *e-mail:* hawortha@parliament.uk.

HAY, William; Speaker, Northern Ireland Assembly; *party:* Democratic Unionist; *political career:* Mayor, Derry City Council, 1993; MLA for Foyle, 1998-; Speaker of the Northern Ireland Assembly, May 2007-; *professional career:* Marine engineering and haulage industries; *office address:* Office of the Speaker, Room 39, Parliament Buildings, Belfast BT4 3XX, Northern Ireland; *phone:* +44 (0)28 90 521130; *e-mail:* speaker@niassembly.gov.uk.

HAYASHI, H.E. Keiichi; Ambassador , Embassy of Japan in the UK; *languages:* English; *professional career:* Minister Plenipotentiary to the UK, 2010-11; Amb. to the UK, 2011-; *office address:* Embassy of Japan, 101-104 Piccadilly, London, W1V 9FN, United Kingdom; *phone:* +44 (0)20 7465 6500; *URL:* http://www.uk.emb-japan.go.jp.

HAYES, John H., MP; British, MP for South Holland and the Deepings, House of Commons; *born:* 23 June 1958; *married:* Susan Hayes (née Hopewell), July 1997; *education:* Colfe's Grammar Sch.; Univ. of Nottingham, BA (Hons), Politics, PGCE, History/English; *party:* Conservative Party; *political career:* fmr. Chmn., Young Conservatives; Chmn., Univ. of Nottingham Conservative Assn.; Chmn., East Midlands Regional Conservative Students; Parly. Candidate (Cons.) for Derbyshire North East, 1987, 1992; County Cllr., Nottinghamshire, 1985-98; County Conservative Spokesperson on Education, 1988-97; MP, South Holland and the Deepings, 1997-; Vice-Chmn., Conservative Party, 1997-; Front Bench Education and Employment Spokesman, 2001-02; Acting Head, Political Section, Office of the Leader of the Opposition, 2000-01; Opposition Pairing Whip, 2001; Shadow Minister for Agriculture and Fisheries, 2002-03; Shadow Minister for Housing and Planning, 2003-05; Shadow Minister for Transport, 2005; Shadow Minister for Vocational Education, 2005-09; Shadow Minister for Universities and Skills, 2009-10; Minister of State, Further Education, 2010-12; Minister of State, Energy, 2012-13; *interests:* education, parties, elections and campaigning, political ideas and philosophy, local government, agriculture, commerce and industry, welfare of the elderly and disabled; *memberships:* Countryside Alliance; Countryside Mem. NFU; Patron, Headway (charity); Vice Chmn., British Caribbean Assn.; *professional career:* Co. Dir., The Data Base Ltd, 1986-99; *committees:* mem., Agriculture Select Cttee., 1997-99; mem., Education Select Cttee., 1998-99; Vice-Chmn., Conservative Backbench Education Cttee., 1997-99; Sec., All Party Acquired Brain Injury Cttee.; Joint Chmn., All Party Disablement Gp., 1998; *publications:* various articles and pamphlets; *clubs:* Carlton Club, London; Spalding Club, Lincolnshire; Spalding Gentleman's Soc., Lincolnshire; *recreations:* arts, history, gardening, antiques, sports, wine, food; *office address:* House of Commons, London, SW1A 0AA, United Kingdom; *phone:* +44 (0)20 7219 3000; *e-mail:* hcinfo@parliament.uk.

HAYTER OF KENTISH TOWN, Baroness Dianne; Member, House of Lords; *party:* Labour; *political career:* Mem., House of Lords, 2010-; *committees:* Mem:, Exec. Ctte., London Labour Part,y 1977-83: Nat. Constitution Cttee., Labour Party 1987-98; Nat. Exec. Cttee., Labour Party, Mem. 1998-, Vice-chair 2006-07, Chair 2007-08; *office address:* House of Lords, London, SW1A 0PW, United Kingdom; *phone:* +44 (0)20 7219 3000; *fax:* +44 (0)20 7219 5979; *URL:* http://www.parliament.uk.

HAYWOOD, HE Nigel; Governor of the Falkland Islands; *education:* New College, Oxford Univ.; Royal Military Academy Sandhurst; *professional career:* British Ambassador to Estonia, 2004-07; Consul-General in Basra, Iraq; Governor of the Falkland Islands,

Commissioner for South Georgia and the South Sandwich Islands, 2010-; ***office address:*** Governor's Office, Government House, Stanley, F1QQ 1ZZ, Falkland Islands; ***URL:*** http://www.falklands.gov.fk.

HEALD, Oliver, MP; British, Solicitor General, Attorney General's Office; ***born:*** 15 December 1954, Reading, UK; ***languages:*** French, German; ***education:*** Reading School; Pembroke Coll. Cambridge, MA (Hons) Law; ***party:*** Conservative Party; ***political career:*** MP, North Hertfordshire, 1992-97; Pensions Minister, 1995-97; MP, North East Hertfordshire, 1997-; Whip, 1997-2000; Opposition Home Affairs Spokesman, 2000-01; Opposition Health Spokesman, 2001-02; Opposition Spokesman for Work and Pensions, 2002-03; Shadow Leader of the House, 2003-05; Shadow Sec. of State for Constitutional Affairs, 2004-07; ***interests:*** employment, pensions, home affairs; ***professional career:*** Barrister, Middle Temple; ***committees:*** Administration, 1998-2000; Modernisation, 2003-05; Work & Pensions, 2007-12; Mem., Cttee. on Standards and in Public Life, 2008-12; Standards and Privileges, 2010-12; Ecclesiastical Cttee., 2010-12; Jt. Cttee. on the Draft House of Lords Reform Bill, 2011-12; ***recreations:*** sports; ***office address:*** House of Commons, London, SW1A 0AA, United Kingdom; ***phone:*** +44 (0)20 7219 6354; ***e-mail:*** healdo@parliament.uk.

HEALEY, John; British, MP, House of Commons; ***born:*** 13 February 1960; ***education:*** Lady Lumley's Comprehensive Sch., Pickering; St Peter's Sch., York; Coll., Cambridge; ***party:*** Labour Party; ***political career:*** MP, Wentworth, 1997-10, Wentworth & Dearne, 2010-; PPS to the Chllr of the Exchequer, 1999-; Under Sec. of State, Adult Skills, DES, 2001-02; Econ. Sec. to the Treasury, May 2002-05; Financial Sec., Treasury, 2005-07; Minister of State, Dept. for Communities and Local Government, 2007-09; Minister of Housing, 2009-10; Shadow Minister for Housing, May- Sept. 2010; Shadow Secretary of State for Health, Oct. 2010-Oct. 2011; ***interests:*** employment, economy, health, social care, local government finance; ***recreations:*** family; ***office address:*** House of Commons, London, SW1A 0AA, United Kingdom; ***phone:*** +44 (0)20 7219 3000; ***e-mail:*** healeyj@parliament.uk.

HEALY, Baroness Anna; Member, House of Lords; ***party:*** Labour; ***political career:*** Government and Political Adviser; Mem., House of Lords, 2010-; ***office address:*** House of Lords, London, SW1A 0PW, United Kingdom; ***phone:*** +44 (0)20 7219 3000; ***fax:*** +44 (0)20 7219 5979; ***URL:*** http://www.parliament.uk.

HEATH, David; Member of Parliament for Somerton and Frome, House of Commons; ***born:*** 16 March 1954, Westbury-sub-Mendip, Somerset; ***education:*** Millfield School, St John's College, Oxford; ***party:*** Liberal Democratic Party; ***political career:*** Lib. Dem. Spokesman; MP for Somerton & Frome, 1997-; Lib. Dem. Spokesman Foreign Affairs, 1997-99, Rural Affairs, 1999-01; Work and Pensions, 2001-02, Science, 2002-03, Lord Chancellors Dept., now, Constitutional Affairs, 2002-05, Home Affairs, 2002-05; Shadow Leader of the House of Commons, 2006-07; Shadow Justice Sec. and Lord Chancellor, 2007-08; Leader of the House of Commons, 2009-10; Parliamentary Secretary (Deputy Leader of the House), 2010-12; Minister of State, Dept. for Environment, Food & Rural Affairs, 2012-; ***professional career:*** Optician, 1979-85; ***committees:*** Foreign Affairs, 1997-01; Science, 2001-03; Standards and Privileges, 2001-05; Modernisation of the House of Commons, 2005-06; Court of Referees, 2007-10; Justice, 2008-10; ***honours and awards:*** CBE, 1989; ***office address:*** Constituency Office, 14 Catherine Hill, Frome, Somerset, BA11 1BZ, United Kingdom; ***phone:*** +44 (0)1373 473618; ***fax:*** +44 (0)1373 455152; ***e-mail:*** davidheath@davidheath.co.uk; ***URL:*** http://www.davidheath.co.uk.

HEATON-HARRIS, Christopher; British, Member of European Parliament; ***born:*** 28 November 1967, Epsom, Surrey; ***party:*** Conservative; ***political career:*** Parly. candidate, 1997; MEP, East Midlands, 2004; MP, Daventry, 2010-; ***interests:*** economic policy, campaign strategy, defence, education, youth policy, Europe, sport; ***committees:*** Public Accounts, 2010-; European Scrutiny, 2010-; ***office address:*** House of Commons, London, SW1A 0AA, United Kingdom; ***e-mail:*** chris.heatonharris.mp@parliament.uk.

HEDDERSON, Tom; Minister for the Environment and Conservation, Government of Newfoundland and Labrador; ***political career:*** Minister of Education; Minister of Tourism, Culture and Recreation, 2006-07; Minister of Intergovernmental Affairs; Minister Responsible for the Volunteer and Non-Profit Sector, 2007-09; Minister for Fisheries and Aquaculture, 2009-10; Minister for Transportation and Works, 2010-12; Minister of Environment and Consultation, 2012-; ***office address:*** Ministry of Environment and Labour, Confederation Building, PO Box 8700, St. John's, NF, A1B 4J6, Canada; ***URL:*** http://www.gov.nl.ca/env.

HEDEGAARD, Connie; European Commissioner for Climate Action, European Commission; ***born:*** 1960; ***education:*** MA, History, Univ. of Copenhagen; ***political career:*** Minister for the Environment, 2004-05; Minister for the Environment and Minister for Nordic Cooperation, 2005-07; Minister for the Climate and Energy, 2007-09; Minister for the UN Climate Change Conference in Copenhagen, 2009; ***professional career:*** Journalist; ***office address:*** European Commission, rue de la Loi 200, B-1040 Brussels, Belgium; ***phone:*** +32 (0)2 298 7874; ***fax:*** +32 (0)2 298 8606; ***URL:*** http://www.europa.eu.

HEDENSTED STEFFENSEN, H.E. Anne; Ambassador , Embassy of Denmark in the UK; ***education:*** MSc., LSE, UK, 1988; MA (Politics), Univ. of Aarhus, Denmark, 1990; ***professional career:*** State Sec., Head of the Trade Council, Amb., Ministry of Foreign Affairs, 2006-09; State Sec., Trade and Corporate Affairs, Min. of Foreign Affairs, 2009-11; Amb. the the UK, 2011-; ***office address:*** Danish Embassy, 55 Sloane Street, London, SW1X 9SR, UK; ***phone:*** +44 (0)20 7333 0200; ***fax:*** +44 (0)20 7333 0270; ***e-mail:*** lonamb@um.dk; ***URL:*** http://www.denmark.org.uk.

HEINEMAN, Governor Dave; Governor, State of Nebraska; ***education:*** US Military Acad., West Point, 1970; ***political career:*** Chief of Staff to fmr. Congressman Hal Daub; Mem. Fremont City Cncl; Nebraska State Treasurer, 1994-2001; Lt. Gov., Nebraska, 2001-05; Governor of Nebraska, 2005-; ***committees:*** Chmn. Nebraska Information Technology Cmn.; Dir., Nebraska Homeland Security; US Homeland Security Advisory Cncl., 2004; ***office address:*** State Capitol, PO Box 94848, Lincoln, 68509-4844, Nebraska, USA; ***phone:*** +1 402 471 2244; ***fax:*** +1 402 471 6031; ***URL:*** http://gov.nol.org.

HEINRICH, Martin; Senator for New Mexico, US Senate; ***party:*** Democrat; ***political career:*** Mem., US HOR, New Mexico 1st Dist., 2009-12; Mem., US Senate, 2013-; ***committees:*** Armed Services; Natural Resources; ***office address:*** US Senate, B40D Dirksen Senate Office Building, Washington, DC 25015, USA; ***phone:*** +1 202 224 5521; ***URL:*** http://www.heinrich.senate.gov/.

HEITKAMP, Heidi; Senator for North Dakota, US Senate; ***party:*** Democrat; ***political career:*** Mem., US Senate, 2013-; ***professional career:*** Attorney-general; ***committees:*** Agriculture; Banking, Small Business; Homeland Security and Governmental Affairs; Indian Affairs; ***office address:*** US Senate, SD-G55 Dirksen Senate Office Building, Washington DC 20510, USA; ***phone:*** +1 202 224 2043; ***URL:*** http://www.heitkamp.senate.gov/.

HELLER, Dean; Senator, US Senate; ***education:*** Univ. of Southern California, Bachelor's Degree in Business Administration, 1985 ; ***party:*** Republican; ***political career:*** Mem. Nevada State Assembly, two terms; Sec. of State, Nevada, three terms; US House of Representatives, 2007-11; Mem., Senate, 2011-; ***professional career:*** Stockbroker and broker/trader, Pacific Stock Exchange ; ***committees:*** Energy and Natural Resources; Commerce, Science & Transportation; Special Cttee. on Aging; ***recreations:*** stockcar racing, basketball, golf, snowboarding; ***office address:*** US Senate, Hart Senate Office Building, Washington, DC 20510, USA; ***URL:*** http://www.heller.senate.gov.

HEMMING, John; MP for Birmingham Yardley, House of Commons; ***political career:*** MP for Birmingham Yardley, 2005-; ***committees:*** Backbench Business, 2010-; Jt. Cttee. on Statutory Instruments, 2010-; Standing Orders, 2011-; ***office address:*** House of Commons, London, SW1P 0AA, United Kingdom; ***phone:*** +44 (0)20 7219 3000.

HENDERSON, Gordon; MP for Sittingbourne and Sheppey, UK Government; ***party:*** Conservative; ***political career:*** Councillor, Kent County Council 1989-93; MP for Sittingbourne and Sheppey, May 2010-; ***committees:*** Regulatory Reform, 2010-; ***office address:*** House of Commons, London, SW1A 0AA, United Kingdom; ***phone:*** +44 (0)20 7219 7144; ***e-mail:*** gordon.henderson.mp@parliament.uk.

HENDRICK, Mark; Member of Parliament for Preston, House of Commons; ***born:*** 2 November 1958, Salford; ***parents:*** Brian Francis Hendrick and Jennifer Hendrick (née Chapman); ***married:*** Yannan Yu; ***languages:*** German, French; ***education:*** Salford Grammar Sch.; Liverpool Polytechnic, B.Sc., Electrical and Electronic Engineering, 1982; Manchester Univ., M.Sc., Computer Science, 1985; Cert. Ed., 1992; Volkshochschule, Hanau, Germany, Zertifikat Deutschals Fremdsprache; ***political career:*** Branch Sec., Salford Co-operative Soc., 1984-94; Councillor, Salford City Cncl., 1987-94; Chair, Eccles Constituency Labour Party, 1990-94; MEP for Central Lancs., 1994-99; MP, Preston, 2000-; Parly. Private Sec. to the Rt. Hon. Margaret Beckett MP, Sec. of State for the Dept. of the Environment, Food and Rural Affairs (DEFRA) and then as Foreign Sec.; PPS to Jack Straw, Sec. of State for Justice and Lord Chancellor; PPS to Ivan Lewis, FCO until May 2010; Opp. Whip, 2010-12; ***interests:*** foreign affairs, defence, European affairs, economic and industrial affairs, int. dev.; ***memberships:*** Hon. mem., Central and West Lancs Chamber of Commerce and Industry; ***professional career:*** AEG Telefunken, 1981; Science and Engineering Research Cncl., 1982; Student Engineer, Min. of Defence, 1987-94; Electronics and Software Design Lecturer, Stockport Coll., 1990-94; ***committees:*** European Scrutiny Cttee., House of Commons, 2001-July 2004; Int. Development Cttee.; Chair, China all-party parly. grp.; International Development, 2009-10; Foreign Affairs, 2012-; ***publications:*** Changing States: A Labour Agenda for Europe, 1996, Mandarin; The Euro and Co-operative Enterprise: Co-operating with the Euro, 1998, Co-operative Press; ***recreations:*** football, boxing, chess; ***office address:*** Constituency Office, PTMC Marsh Lane, Preston, Lancs, PR1 8UQ, United Kingdom; ***phone:*** +44 (0)1772 883575; ***fax:*** +44 (0)1772 887188; ***e-mail:*** hendrickm@parliament.uk; ***URL:*** http://www.prestonmp.co.uk.

HENDRY, Charles; Minister of State, Department for Energy and Climate Change, UK Government; ***political career:*** MP, High Peak, 1992-97; MP, Wealden, 2001-; Opposition Whip 2001-02; Shadow Minister for Young People 2002-05; Shadow Minister for Higher Education 2005; Shadow Minister for Energy, Science and Technology, 2005-10; Minister of State, Dept. for Energy and Climate Change, 2010-12; ***office address:*** House of Commons, London, SW1A 0PQ, United Kingdom; ***phone:*** +44 (0)20 7219 3000.

HENLEY, Baron Oliver Michael Robert Eden; British, Member of the House of Lords; ***born:*** 1953; ***s:*** 3; ***d:*** 1; ***education:*** Clifton Coll.; Durham Univ.; ***political career:*** Pres., Cumbria Assoc. of Local Cncls., 1981-89; Cumbria County Cllr., 1986-89; Lord in Waiting, 1989; Government Whip, House of Lords, 1989; Govt. spokesman on Health, 1989; Parly. Under-Sec. of State, Dept. of Social Security, 1989-; Parly. Under-Sec. of State, Dept. of Employment, 1993-94; Parly. Under-Sec. of State, Min. of Defence, 1994-95; Minister of State, Dept. for Education and Employment, 1995-97; Opposition Spokesman for Home Affairs, 1997-99; Opposition Chief Whip, House of Lords, 1998-2001; Mem., House of Lords; Minister of State (Crime Prevention and Antisocial Behaviour Reduction), 2011-12; ***memberships:*** Chmn., Penrith and Border Conservative Assoc. 1987-89; Pres., Cumbria Wildlife Trust 1988-; ***professional career:*** Called to Bar, 1977; ***clubs:*** Brooks's; Pratt's; ***office address:*** House of Lords, London, SW1A 0PQ, United Kingdom; ***phone:*** +44 (0)20 7219 3000; ***fax:*** +44 (0)20 7219 5979.

HENNESSY OF NYMPSFIELD, Lord Peter; Member, House of Lords; ***political career:*** Mem. House of Lords, 2010-; ***honours and awards:*** Raised to the peerage as Baron Hennessy of Nympsfield, of Nympsfield in the County of Gloucestershire 2010; ***office address:*** House of Lords, London, SW1P 0AA, United Kingdom.

HENNIS-PLASSCHAERT, Jeanine; Minister of Defence, Netherlands Government; ***born:*** 1973; ***party:*** People's Party for Freedom and Democracy (VVD); ***political career:*** Mem., European Parliament, VVD Party, 2004-10; Mem., Dutch House of Reps. 2010-12; Minister of Defence, Rutte-Asscher gov., 2012-; ***office address:*** Ministry of Defence, PO Box 20701, 2500 ES The Hague, Netherlands; ***phone:*** +31 (0)77 465 6767; ***URL:*** http://www.defensie.nl.

HENRI, HRH Grand Duke; Luxembourgeois, Head of State, Grand Duchy of Luxembourg; *born:* 1955; *parents:* HRH Grand Duke Jean and HRH Grand Duchess Joséphine-Charlotte; *married:* María Teresa Mestre y Batista, 1981; *children:* 5; *education:* Univ. of Geneva, Switzerland; Royal Military Academy, Sandhurst, UK; *professional career:* Grand Duke of Luxembourg, October 2000-; *committees:* mem., International Olympic Committee; *office address:* Palais Grand-Ducal, L-2013, Luxembourg.

HENRIKSSON, Anna-Maja; Minister of Justice, Government of Finland; *born:* 7 January 1964; *languages:* Swedish; *education:* Master of Laws, Univ. of Helsinki, Finland; *political career:* MP, 2007-; Minister of Justice, 2011-; *professional career:* Lawyer; *office address:* Ministry of Justice, Eteläesplanadi 10, P.O. Box 1, 00131 Helsinki, Finland; *phone:* +358 (0)9 1825 7605; *fax:* +358 (0)9 1825 7630; *URL:* http://www.om.fi.

HENSARLING, Jeb; Congressman, Texas 5th District, US House of Representatives; *education:* Texas A&M University, BA, economics, 1979; *political career:* State Director for United States Senator Phil Gramm, 1985-89; Executive Director of the National Republican Senatorial Committee, 1991-92; Congressman, Texas 5th District, US House of Representatives, to date; Republican Conference Chmn., 2011-13; *committees:* House Cttee. on Financial Services; *office address:* US House of Representatives, 423 Cannon House Office Building, Washington, DC 20515, USA.

HEPBURN, Stephen; Member of Parliament for Jarrow, House of Commons; *born:* 6 December 1959; *parents:* Peter Hepburn and Margaret Hepburn; *education:* Newcastle Univ., BA (Hons); *party:* Labour Party; *political career:* MP, Jarrow, 1997-; *clubs:* Iona Club; Neon (Civ) Club; *recreations:* sport, reading, music; *office address:* House of Commons, London, SW1A 0AA, United Kingdom; *phone:* +44 (0)20 7219 3000; *e-mail:* hcinfo@parliament.uk.

HERBERT, Governor Gary R.; Governor, State of Utah, USA; *born:* 7 May 1947, Utah, USA; *education:* Brigham Young Univ., Utah; *political career:* Cmr., Utah County Commission, 1990-2004; Lieutenant Gov. of Utah, 2004-09; Gov. of Utah, 2009-; *professional career:* Two year mission for the LDS Church; Utah Army National Guard; Real Estate, Herbert and Associates Realtors; *office address:* Office of the Governor, Utah State Capitol Complex, East Office Building, Suite E220, PO Box 142220, , Salt Lake City, Utah 84114-2220, USA; *phone:* +1 801 538 1000; *fax:* +1 801 538 1528; *URL:* http://www.governor.state.ut.us/.

HERBERT, Rt. Hon. Nick; MP for Arundel and South Downs, House of Commons; *political career:* MP for Arundel and the South Downs, 2005-; Shadow Sec. of State for Justice, 2007-09; Shadow Sec. of State for Environment, Food, and Rural Affairs, Jan. 2009-May 2010; Minister of State for the Home Office and HM Treasury, May 2010-12; *office address:* House of Commons, London, SW1P 0AE, United Kingdom.

HEREFORD, Bishop of; Member, House of Lords; *born:* 15 March 1948, Stanmore, Middlesex; *education:* Corpus Christi College, Cambridge (MA); Cuddesdon Theological College; New College Oxford (Dip. Theol, MA by incorporation); *political career:* Mem. House of Lords, 2009-; *professional career:* Deacon, 1972; Ordained priest, 1973; Assist. curate, St. Edward's, New Addington, 1972-1975; College Chaplain, Christ Church, Oxford, 1975-80; Team Vicar, St John's High Wycombe, 1980-86; Rector of Amersham, 1986-96; Rural Dean of Amersham, 1992-96; Hon. Canon of Christchurch, 1995; Bishop of Warwick, 1996-2004; Bishop of Herford, 2004-; *committees:* Chair, Rural Bishop's Panel, then Rural Affairs Group, 2004-; Mem., West Midlands Life Regional Cultural Consortium, 2002-; Lay Mem., Bd. of the Faculty of A&E Medicine, 2002-; Chair, C. of E. Safeguarding Group, 2002-2011; *trusteeships:* Trustee & Chmn., Amersham United Charities, 1986-96; Founder mem., Chiltern Hundred Housing Assn. Bd., 1988-92; Trustee, Coventry Relate, 2001-04; Trustee, Family Life and Marriage Education (Flame) Network, 2001-09, Co-Chair, 2003-09; Trustee, Eveson Charitable Trust, 2004-; *honours and awards:* FCEM (Hon. Fellow, College of Emergency Medicine, 2000-07); *publications:* The Study of Spirituality (contrib. 1986) and many articles for magazines, as well as broadcasts on radio and television; *office address:* The Bishop's House, Hereford, HR4 9BN, United Kingdom; *e-mail:* bishop@hereford.anglican.org.

HERMON, Lady Sylvia; Member of Parliament for North Down, House of Commons; *born:* 11 November 1955; *parents:* Robert Paisley and Mary Paisley; *married:* Sir John Hermon OBE QPM, 1988; *languages:* French, German; *education:* LL.B, Aberystwyth Univ., Wales, 1977; Part II Solicitors' Qualifying Exams, 1978; *political career:* Ulster Union Executive, 1999; Constituency Chair North Down Unionist Constituency Assoc., 2001-; MP, North Down, 2001-; UUP Spokesperson for: Home Affairs, 2001-, Trade and Industry, 2001-02, Youth and Women's Issues, 2001-05, Culture, Media and Sport, 2002-05; *interests:* policing, human rights, European Affairs, health, education; *memberships:* Chair, North Down Support Grp. Marie Curie Cancer Care 1998-; Friends of Bangor Community Hospital, 2000-; *professional career:* Lecturer European, international and constitutional law, Queen's Univ. Belfast, 1978-88; *committees:* Author and Cttee. mem. addressing Patten Report Criminal Justice Review, 2000; Vice-chair, All Party: Police Grp., 2002, Dignity at Work Grp., 2003; Northern Ireland Affairs, 2005-; *publications:* A Guide to EEC Law in Northern Ireland, 1986, SLS Legal Publications (NI); *recreations:* fitness training, swimming, ornithology, letter writing, proof reading; *office address:* House of Commons, London, SW1A 0PQ, United Kingdom; *phone:* +44 (0)20 7219 8491; *fax:* +44 (0)20 7219 1969; *e-mail:* jamisons@parliament.uk.

HEWITT, Chief Judge Emily C. ; Chief Judge, US Court of Federal Claims; *education:* Cornell Univ., A.B., 1966; Union Theological Seminary, New York City, M. Phil.; Ordained to the diaconate of the Episcopal Church, 1972, ordained to the Episcopal priesthood, 1974; Harvard Law School, 1978; *memberships:* Bar of the Supreme Judicial Court of The Commonwealth of Massachusetts; *professional career:* Assist. Prof. of religion and education, Andover Newton Theological School, Mass.,1973-75; practiced law, Hill & Barlow, Boston, 1978-93; General Counsel US General Services Administration (GSA), 1993-98; Judge, US Court of Federal Claims,1998-, Chief Judge, 2009- ; *committees:* Financial Disclosure Cttee. Judicial Conference, 2006-; *recreations:* long distance race walking (1987 winner of US national race walking medal; marathons include Boston, New York and United States

Marine Corps Marathons); National Park trails hiker ; *office address:* United States Court of Federal Claims, 717 Madison Place, N.W., Washington DC 20005, USA; *URL:* http://www.uscfc.uscourts.gov/.

HEYES, David; Member of Parliament for Ashton under Lyne, House of Commons; *education:* Blackley Technical High Sch.; BA, Social Sciences, Manchester Open Univ., 1987; *political career:* MP, Ashton under Lyne, 2001-; *professional career:* Deputy District Manager, Manchester Citizens Advice Bureaux, 1995-; *committees:* Public Admin., 2001-; Communities and Local Government, 2010-; *office address:* House of Commons, London, SW1A 0AA, United Kingdom; *phone:* +44 (0)20 7219 3000; *e-mail:* hcinfo@parliament.uk; *URL:* http://www.parliament.uk.

HEYHOE FLINT, Baroness Rachael; Member, House of Lords; *born:* 11 June 1939; *married:* M. Derrick, 1971; *education:* Dartford College of P.E., 1957-60; *party:* Conservative Party; *political career:* Mem., House of Lords, 2011-; *memberships:* Vice-Pres., Wolverhampton Wanderers F.C.; MCC Gen. Cttee., 2004-; Hon. Life mem., 1998-; *professional career:* Teacher, Phys. Ed., 1960-64; Mem., English women's cricket, 1960-82, Captain, 1966-78; England Hockey International, 1964; Journalist, Express & Star Wolverhampton, 1965-71; Journalist, Daily Telegraph Sport, 1971-85; Broadcaster; Public Relations Consultant; *committees:* ECB Board, 2009-; *trusteeships:* Wolves Community Trust, 2002-; *honours and awards:* MBE, 1972; OBE, 2009; ICC Hall of Fame, 2010; Life Peerage, 2011; *publications:* Heyhoe (autobiography), 1978; Fair Play (cricket history), 1973; *clubs:* La Manga Club, Spain; South Staffs. Golf Club; *recreations:* golf; *office address:* House of Lords, London, SW1A 0PW, United Kingdom; *phone:* +44 (0)20 7219 3000; *e-mail:* heyhoeflintr@parliament.uk.

HICKENLOOPER, Gov. John; Governor, State of Colorado; *political career:* Mayor of Denver; Gov., Colorado, Nov. 2010-; *professional career:* Geologist; founder, Colorado's first brewpub, The Wynkoop Brewing Co; *office address:* Officeof the Governor, 136 State Capitol, Denver, CO 80203-1792, USA; *phone:* +1 303 866 2471; *URL:* http://www.colorado.gov/governor/.

HIGGINS, Michael D; Irish, President, Ireland; *born:* 1941, Limerick, Ireland; *married:* Sabina Higgins (née Coyne); *public role of spouse:* Founder member of the Focus Theatre and Stanislavsky Studio in Dublin; *education:* Univ. College, Galway; Indiana Univ.; Manchester Univ.; *party:* Dáil Éireann; *political career:* Elected to Dáil 1981 (re-elected 1987); Mem. Galway County Council 1974-85; Alderman, Galway Borough Council 1974-85; Mem., Galway City Council 1985-93; Chmn., Galway County Council Fisheries Bd. 1980-85; Min. for Art, Culture and Gaeltacht 1993-94; Pres., Ireland, 2011-; *interests:* Sociological Assn. of Ireland; American Sociological Assn.; PEN; Irish Writers' Union; *memberships:* Mem., Western Health Board; Chmn., Galway/Mayo Regional Arts Cttee.; mem., Governing Body of Univ. Coll., Galway; Chmn., Galway County Council Fisheries Board, 1980-85; mem., Sociological Assoc. of Ireland and Americal Soliological Assoc.; Patron of several Nat. Organisations, incl. Amnesty Inter., and Irish Council against Blood Sports; *professional career:* Former Lecturer in Political Science and Sociology at Univ. College, Galway; Visiting Professor at Univ. of Southern Illinois; Twice Mayor of Galway; *committees:* Mem., Joint Oireachtas Cttee. on the Irish Language, Women's Rights and Secondary Legislation of the Euro. Communities; *honours and awards:* Sean MacBride Peace Prize of the International Peace Bureau, Helsinki, 1992; *publications:* Contributed widely to political and philosophical journals on many subjects, incl., Ideology, The Sociology of Literature, Clientism in Politics, Regionalism, The Politics of the Media; First collection of poems, The Betrayal, 1990; second collection of poems, Season of Fire, 1993; *recreations:* poetry, human rights activist; *office address:* Office of the President, Aras an Uachtarain, Phoenix Park, Dublin 8, Ireland; *phone:* +353 (0)1 617 1000; *URL:* http://www.president.ie.

HIGGINS, Dame Rosalyn, DBE, QC; British; *born:* 2 June 1937; *languages:* English, French, Dutch; *education:* Cambridge University, BA, 1st Class, 1959, LLB, 1st Class 1962, MA, 1962; Yale Law School, Graduate Fellow, 1959-61, JSD, 1962 Rockefeller Foundation Fellowship, 1961; Certificate of Merit of the ASIL, 1971 and 1995, Honorary Life Membership Award, 1992; British Academy Award, Vols I and II of UN Peacekeeping, 1977-78; Honorary Doctorates from the following universities: Paris XI, 1980, Dundee, 1992, Durham and LSE, 1995, Cambridge, Kent, Essex, Sussex, Greenwich and London City, 1996, Birmingham, Leicester, Glasgow, 1997, Nottingham, 1999, Bath, Paris II, 2001, Oxford, 2002, Reading, 2005; Wolfgang-Friedman Medal for services to International Law, Columbia University, 1985; Harold Weil Medal, New York University, 1995; Yale Law School Medal of Merit, 1997; The Manley O Hudson Medal, 1998; Legal qualification: QC; Bencher of the Inner Temple; *interests:* Dispute settlement; Jurisdiction; Human rights; Litigation; Organisations; State responsibility; Territory/boundaries; Treaties; Immunities; Theory; *memberships:* Institut de Droit International, Associé, 1987, Membre, 1991; BIICL, Chairman of Public International Law Advisory Board, 1992-2005, Vice-President, 2005-; ASIL, Honorary Life Vice-President, 1993; AJIL, Hon Life Member, Board of Editors; Journal of Energy and Natural Resources Law, former Member of the Board of Editors; BYIL, Board of Editors; Pres., British Institute of International and Comparative Law; *professional career: academic career:* Royal Institute of International Affairs, Staff specialist in International Law, 1963-74; LSE, Visiting Fellow, 1974-78; University of Kent, Professor of International Law, 1978-81; University of London, Professor of International Law, 1981-95; *professional career:* Leading cases as counsel include Counsel for 1° Congreso del Partido; The International Tin Council: Winding up, Receivership, Maclaine Watson Action; Westland Helicopters v Arab Organization for Industrialisation; Kuwait Airways Corporation v Iraq Airways Corporation; Case concerning East Timor (Portugal v Australia) (ICJ); Territorial dispute: Libyan Arab Jamahiriya v Chad (ICJ); Questions of Interpretation and Application of the 1971 Montreal Convention arising fom the Aerial Incident at Lockerbie (Libyan Arab Jamahiriya v United Kingdom) (ICJ); Case concerning Gabcikovo-Nagymaros Project (Hungary/Slovakia) (ICJ); Member, Committee on Human Rights under the International Covenant on Civil and Political Rights, 1985-95; Special Rapporteur for new cases, 1989-91; Judicial career: ICJ, 1995-, President, 2006-; Member of Arbitral Tribunal in Arbitration between Eritrea and Yemen: Territorial Sovereignty, 1998; Maritime Delimitation, 1999; President, AMCO Asia/Indonesia, Resubmitted Case, Award on Jurisdiction, 1988, Award on Merits, 1992; President, Iron Rhine Arbitration (Belgium v Netherlands), 2003-05; President, Interpretation of the Award in the Iron Rhine, 2005; President, Capital Power Mauritius I and Energy Enterprises (Mauritius) Company v Republic of India, 2004-05; *honours and awards:* DBE, 1995; Chevalier de l'Ordre des Palmes Académiques, 1988; *office address:* International Court of Justice, Peace Palace, 2517 KJ The Hague, The Netherlands; *phone:* +31 (0)70 302 2415; *fax:* +31 (0)70 302 2409; *e-mail:* r.higgins@icj-cij.org.

HILL OF OAREFORD, Lord; Leader of the House of Lords, House of Lords; *education:* Trinity Coll. Cambridge Univ.; *party:* Conservative; *political career:* Mem., House of Lords, 2010-; Parly Under-Sec. of State and Gov. Spokesperson, Dept. for Education 2010-13; Leader of the House of Lords, 2013-; *office address:* House of Lords, London, SW1A 0PW, United Kingdom; *phone:* +44 (0)20 7219 3000; *fax:* +44 (0)20 7219 5979; *URL:* http://www.parliament.uk.

HILLIER, Meg; MP, House of Commons; *born:* 1969; *party:* Labour/Co-operative; *political career:* Councillor, London Borough of Islington, 1994-2002; GLA mem. for North East London, 2000-04; MP for Hackney South and Shoreditch, 2005-; Parliamentary Under Sec. of State, Home Office, 2007-10; Shadow Minister for Home Office, May-Sept. 2010; Secretary of State for Energy and Climate Change, Oct. 2010-Oct. 2011; *professional career:* Journalist; *committees:* Public Accounts, 2011-; *office address:* House of Commons, London, SW1A 0AA, United Kingdom.

HILLING, Julie; MP for Bolton West, UK Government; *party:* Labour; *political career:* MP for Bolton West, May 2010-; PPS, 2010-12; Opposition Whip, 2012-; *committees:* Transport, 2010-; Standards & Privileges, 2011-; *office address:* House of Commons, London, SW1A 0AA, United Kingdom; *phone:* +44 (0)20 7219 3000; *e-mail:* julie.hilling.mp@parliament.uk.

HILTON OF EGGARDON, Baroness Jennifer; British, Member of the House of Lords; *born:* 12 January 1936, Nicosia, Cyprus; *parents:* John Robert Hilton, CMG and Margaret Frances (née Stephens); *languages:* French; *education:* Bedales School; Manchester Univ., MA, Psychology; *party:* Labour Party; *political career:* Mem., House of Lords, 1991-; *interests:* environment, home affairs, international affairs; *professional career:* Metropolitan Police; *committees:* Science and Technology Cttee.; *honours and awards:* Q.P.M.; *publications:* The Gentle Arm of the Law; Individual Development & Social Experience; *recreations:* gardening, painting, foreign travel; *office address:* House of Lords, London, SW1A 0PQ, United Kingdom; *phone:* +44 (0)20 7219 3000; *fax:* +44 (0)20 7219 5979.

HIMES, Jim; Congressman, 4th District Connecticut, US House of Representatives; *party:* Democrat; *political career:* Mem., US HOR, Connecticut Dist. 4, 2009-; *committees:* Financial Services; *office address:* House of Representatives, Washington, D.C., USA.

HINDS, Damian; MP for East Hampshire, UK Government; *party:* Conservative; *political career:* MP for East Hampshire, May 2010-; PPS, Minister of State for Defence Personnel, 2012-; *committees:* Education Select Cttee., 2010-; *office address:* House of Commons, London, SW1A 0AA, United Kingdom; *phone:* +44 (0)20 7219 3000; *e-mail:* damian.hinds.mp@parliament.uk.

HINDS, Hon. Samuel A.A.; Prime Minister, Government of Guyana; *party:* People's Progressive Party; *political career:* involved in human rights; Prime Minister, 1992-, acted as president following death of President Cheddi Jagan, March 1997; *professional career:* Engineer; *office address:* Office of the Prime Minister, Wights Lane, Kingston, Georgetown, Guyana; *phone:* +592 227 6955; *fax:* +592 226 7573; *URL:* http://www.pm.gov.gv.

HINTZE, Peter; Member of German Bundestag; *education:* Univ. of Bonn, Theology; *party:* CDU; *political career:* Mem., Rhineland Regional Assembly, and of the Rhine-Sieg District Cncl., 1975-79; Fed. Cmnr. for Civic Duty, 1983-90; Dep. Chmn, CDU, Northrhine, Westfalia, 1987-92; Mem., German Parliament (Bundestag), 1990-; Under Sec. of State, Fed. Ministry of Women and Youth, 1991-91; Sec.-Gen., Christian Democratic Union (CDU), 1992-98;Vice Pres., Christian Democratic International and Centrist Democratic International (IDC), 2001-; Vice Pres., European People's Party (EPP), 2002-; Vice Pres., International Democrat Union (IDU), 2002-; Parly. State Sec. to Minister of Econ. and Technology, 2005-; Fed. Gvt. Coordinator, German Aerospace Policy, 2007-; *professional career:* Vicar, Protestant Church, Rhineland, 1977-79; Assist. Pastor, 1979-80; Pastor, Konigswinter Protestant Church, 1980-83; *office address:* Deutscher Bundestag, Platz der Republik 1, D-11011 Berlin, Germany; *phone:* +49 (0)30 227 75238; *fax:* +49 (0)30 227 76764; *e-mail:* peter.hintze@bundestag.de.

HIRONO, Mazie; Senator for Hawaii, US Senate; *education:* Univ. of Hawai'i; Georgetown Univ. Law Center, Washington, D.C., law degree; *party:* Democrat; *political career:* Lieutenant Governor, Hawaii, 1998-2006; Mem., House of Representatives, 2007-13; US Senate, 2013-; *professional career:* Hawai'i State Legislature; *committees:* former HOR Cttees: Education and the Workforce; Transportation and Infrastructure; Ethics; *office address:* US Senate, B-40E Dirksen Senate Office Building, Washington, DC 20510, USA; *phone:* +1 202 224 6361; *fax:* +1 202 224 2126; *URL:* http://www.hirono.senate.gov/.

HITCHENS, Theresa; Director, United Nations Institute for Disarmament Research; *professional career:* journalist; Inside Washington Publishers; Defense News, 1988-2000; Director of Research, British American Security Information Council; Dir., Center for Defense Information; Director, UNIDIR, 2009-; *publications:* several; mem., editorial board, Bulletin of the Atomic Scientists; *office address:* UNIDIR, Palais des Nations, 1211 Geneva 10, Switzerland; *URL:* http://unidir.org/.

HITCHENS, H.E. Tim; Ambassador, British Embassy in Japan; *languages:* French, Japanese; *education:* Christ's Coll., Cambridge, UK, 1983; *professional career:* Dir., Africa Desk, FCO, 2010-12; Amb. to Japan, 2012-; *office address:* British Embassy, 1, Ichiban-cho, Chiyoda-ku, Tokyo 102-8381, Japan; *phone:* +81 (0)3 5211 1100; *fax:* +81 (0)3 5211 3164; *e-mail:* embassy.tokyo@fco.gov.uk; *URL:* http://ukinjapan.fco.gov.uk/en.

HOBAN, Mark; Financial Secretary, HM Treasury; *born:* 31 March 1964, Peterlee, Co. Durham, England; *parents:* Tom Hoban and Maureen Hoban; *married:* Fiona Jane Barrett, 6 August 1994; *education:* St Leonard's RC Comprehensive Sch.; BSc Economics, London Sch. of Economics, 1985; *party:* Conservative Party; *political career:* MP, Fareham, June 2001-; Opposition Whip, 2002-03; Shadow Minister for Education, 2003-05; Shadow Financial Sec. to the Treasury, 2005-10; Financial Secretary, HM Treasury, May 2010-12; Minister of State, Dept. of Work and Pensions, 2012-; *interests:* economy, education; *memberships:* Inst. of Chartered Accountants; Fruiterers Co., 2003; Hon. Vice Pres., Soc. of Maritime Industries, 2003-10; *professional career:* Chartered Accountant; fmr. Senior Manager, PricewaterhouseCoopers; *committees:* Mem., Select Cttee. on Science and Technology, 2001-03; All Party Small Business Gp.; *honours and awards:* Freeman of the City of London, 2003; *office address:* Her Majesty's Treasury, 1 Horse Guard's Road, London, SW1E 2HQ, United Kingdom; *phone:* +44 (0)20 7270 4558; *e-mail:* mail@markhoban.com; *URL:* http://www.markhoban.com.

HODGE, Margaret; MP for Barking, House of Commons; *education:* BSc., economics, London School of Economics, 1966; *party:* Labour Party; *political career:* Leader of Islington Cncl. 1982-92; MP, Barking, 1994-; Parliamentary Under Sec. of State at the DfEE.; Minister for Employment and Equal Opportunities; Minister for Work, 2005-07; Minister of State, Dept. for Culture, Media and Sport, 2007-08; *memberships:* Local Government Commission; Bd. of Governors, LSE; *professional career:* Market research 1966-73, Senior consultant, Price Waterhouse, 1992-94; *office address:* House of Commons, London, SW1A 0AA, United Kingdom; *phone:* +44 (0)20 7219 3000; *e-mail:* info@epolitix.com; *URL:* http://www.epolitix.com/webminister/margaret-hodge.

HODGSON, Sharon; MP for Washington and Sunderland West, House of Commons; *born:* 1966, Gateshead, UK; *married:* Alan Hodgson, 1990; *education:* Newcastle College; TUC National Education Centre; *party:* Labour Party, 1996-; *political career:* Labour Party Organiser, Mitcham & Morden 2000-02; Unison Labour Link Co-ordinator, 2002-04; MP for Gateshead East and Washington West, 2005-10; Government Whip; Previously PPS to Dawn Primarolo, Minister of State for Public Health, Also previously a PPS to Bob Ainsworth, Armed Forces Minister; PPS to Liam Byrne, Border and Immigration Minister; MP, Washington and Sunderland West, 2010-; Shadow Minister, Education, Oct. 2010-; *memberships:* Fabian Society; Co-operative Party; Christian Socialist Movement; *committees:* Parly. Cttee. of the Parly. Labour Party, 2008-09; *office address:* Constituency Office, Suites 1 and 1A Vermont House, Concord, Washington, NE37 2SQ, United Kingdom; *phone:* +44 (0)191 417 2000; *e-mail:* hodgsons@parliament.uk; *URL:* http://www.sharonhodgson.org.

HOEVEN, John; Senator for North Dakota, US Senate; *married:* Mical (Mikey) Hoeven; *children:* Marcela (F), Jack (M); *education:* Dartmouth Coll., Bachelor's degree in history and economics; J.L. Kellogg Graduate Sch. of Management at Northwestern Univ., Master's degree; *political career:* Governor, North Dakota, 2000-10; Senator, US Senate, 2011-; *memberships:* Souris Valley Humane Soc.; *professional career:* Exec. Vice-Pres., First Western Bank, Minot; Pres. and CEO, Bank of North Dakota, 1993; *committees:* Appropriations; Energy & Natural Resources; Agriculture, Nutrition & Forestry; Indian Affairs; *clubs:* Dir., Minot Kiwanis Club; *office address:* US Senate, 120 Russell Senate Office Building, Washington DC 20510, USA; *phone:* +1 202 224 2551; *URL:* http://www.hoeven.senate.gov.

HOEY, Kate; British, MP for Vauxhall, House of Commons; *born:* 21 June 1946; *education:* City of London Coll., B.Sc., Econs.; *party:* Labour Party, 1972-; *political career:* Cllr., London Borough of Hackney, 1978-82, London Borough of Southwark, 1988; Opp. Spokeswoman, Citizens Charter and Women, 1992-93; MP, Vauxhall, 1989-; PPS to Frank Field, Dept. of Social Security, 1997-98; Minister for Sport, 1999-2001; *interests:* sport, environment, the Middle East, housing; *professional career:* Educational Advisor, London football clubs; *office address:* House of Commons, London, SW1A 0AA, United Kingdom; *phone:* +44 (0)20 7219 3000; *e-mail:* hcinfo@parliament.uk.

HOFSCHNEIDER, Jude U.; Lt. Governor of the Northern Marianas; *political career:* Northern Marianas Commonwealth Legislature, Legislative Sec., 2006-08, 2008-10; Senate Floor Leader, 2008-10; Senate Pres., 2013; Lt. Governor, CNMI, 2013-; *office address:* Office of the Lt.-Governor, Juan A. Sablan Memorial Building, Capital Hill, Caller Box 10007, Saipan, MP 96950, Northern Marianas.

HOGAN, Phil; Minister of the Environment, Government of Ireland; *party:* Fine Gael; *political career:* TD for Carlow-Kilkenny, 1989-; Minister for the Environment, Heritage and Local Government, 2011-; *professional career:* Insurance Broker; Auctioneer; *office address:* Department of the Environment, Heritage and Local Government, The Custom House, Dublin 1, Ireland; *phone:* +353 (0)1 888 2000; *fax:* +353 (0)1 888 2888; *e-mail:* press-office@environ.ie; *URL:* http://www.environ.ie.

HOGG, Hon. John; President of the Senate, Government of Australia; *born:* 19 March 1949, Brisbane, Queensland; *education:* Queensland Univ., B.Sc; *party:* Australian Labor Party, 1976-; *political career:* Senator for Queensland, 1996-; ALP Caucus Sec., 2002-; Dep. Pres. of the Senate, 2002-08; President of the Senate, 2008-; *professional career:* Trade union official, Shop Distributive and Allied Employees' Assn., 1976-81; Branch Sec. and Mem., Nat. Exec., 1981-96; Branch Pres., 1996-; *committees:* Chair, ALP National Policy Committee (Government Administration), 1991-94; Temp. Chair of Committees, 1997-2002; Chair of Committees, 2002-08; Chair, Senate Standing Cttees: House, Appropriations and Staffing, Library, 2008-; Chair, Jt. Statutory Cttee. on Broadcasting of Parliamentary Proceedings, 2008-; *office address:* Senate, Parliament House, Canberra, ACT 2600, Australia; *URL:* http://www.aph.gov.au/Senate/.

HOLDER, Eric H. Jr., BA; American, Attorney General, US Government; *born:* 1951; *education:* BA, Columbia College 1969-73; Columbia Law School 1973-76; *political career:* US Attorney General, 2009-; *professional career:* Trial Attorney, Public Integrity Section, Dept. of Justice 1976-88; Assoc. Judge, Superior Court of District of Columbia

1988-93; Attorney for District of Columbia 1993-; ***office address:*** Office of United States Attorney for the District of Columbia, Room 5806A, 555 4th Street , NW, Washington, DC 20001, USA; ***URL:*** http://www.usdoj.gov.

HOLIDAY, Eugene; Governor, Sint Maarten; ***born:*** 1962; ***education:*** Catholic Univ. of Brabant, Tilburg, economics; ***political career:*** Governor, Sint Maarten, 2010-; ***professional career:*** Analyst & policy advisor, Central Bank of the Netherlands Antilles, Head, Research & Monetary PolicyDept., Dep. Director, monetary and economic affairs; managing dir., Windward Island Airways Int. Ltd, 1995; Pres. Dir, Princess Juliana International Airport Operating Co., 1998-2010; ***office address:*** Office of the Governor, Falcon Drive 3, Harbour View, Philipsburg, Sint Maarten; ***phone:*** +1 721 542 1160; ***fax:*** +1 721 542 1187; ***URL:*** http://www.kabgsxm.com/.

HOLLANDE, François; President, Republic of France; ***born:*** 12 August 1954, Rouen, France; ***education:*** École nationale d'administration, Paris, 1980; Institut d'Études Politiques de Paris; ***party:*** Leader, Socialist Party; ***political career:*** Elected Dep., 1988; Sec. of Finance, Economy and Planning Commission; Sec.-Gen., Socialist Party, 1994, National Press Sec. and Spokesperson, 1995; Elected Dep. for Corrèze, 1997; First Dep. Sec., Socialist Party, 1997, First Sec., Nov. 1997-; Mayor of Tulle, 2001-08; Pres. of the General Council of Corrèze, 2008-12; Co-Prince of Andorra, 2012-; President of France, May 2012-; ***professional career:*** Auditor, Auditor General's Dept., 1980-81; ***office address:*** Office of the President, Palais de l'Elysée, 55-57 rue du Faubourg, Saint Honoré, 75008 Paris, France; ***phone:*** +33 (0)1 42 92 81 00; ***fax:*** +33 (0)1 47 42 24 65; ***URL:*** http://www.elysee.fr.

HOLLINGBERY, George; MP for Meon Valley, UK Government; ***party:*** Conservative; ***political career:*** Councillor, Winchester City Council, 1999-; MP for Meon Valley, May 2010-; PPS to Home Sec., 2012-; ***committees:*** Communities and Local Government Select Cttee., 2010-; Works of Art, 2011-; ***office address:*** House of Commons, London, SW1A 0AA, United Kingdom; ***phone:*** +44 (0)20 7219 3000; ***e-mail:*** george.hollingbery.mp@parliament.uk.

HOLLINS, Baroness Sheila; Member, House of Lords; ***political career:*** Mem., House of Lords, 2010-; ***professional career:*** Prof. of Psychiatry of Disability, St George's Univ. of London (part-time); Hon. Consultant Psychiatrist in Learning Disability, SW London and St George's Mental Health Trust, non-clinical and part-time, 2006-; ***honours and awards:*** Raised to the peerage as Baroness Hollins, of Wimbledon in the London Borough of Merton and of Grenoside in the County of South Yorkshire, 2010; ***office address:*** House of Lords, London, SW1A 0PW, United Kingdom; ***phone:*** +44 (0)20 7219 5353.

HOLLOBONE, Philip; MP for Kettering, House of Commons; ***education:*** Dulwich College, Oxford Univ., MA, modern history and economics; ***party:*** Conservative Party; ***political career:*** MP for Kettering, 2005; ***professional career:*** Territorial Army, nine years, latterly as a paratrooper; Finance and investment, 13 years; ***office address:*** House of Commons, London, SW1A 0AA, United Kingdom; ***phone:*** +44 (0)20 7219 8373.

HOLLOWAY, Adam; MP for Gravesham, House of Commons; ***born:*** 1965; ***party:*** Conservative; ***political career:*** MP for Gravesham, 2005-; ***professional career:*** Army Officer; TV Presenter and Reporter; ***committees:*** Defence Select Cttee., 2006-10; Arms Export Controls, 2009-11; ***office address:*** House of Commons, London, SW1P 0AA, United Kingdom; ***phone:*** +44 (0)20 7219 3000.

HOLLOWAY, H.E. Michael; Ambassador, British Embassy in Panama; ***professional career:*** Dir. for Consular Services in Iberia, Spain. 2005-10; Amb. to Panama. 2011-; ***office address:*** British Embassy, MMG Tower, 4th Floor, Calle 53, Marbella, Panama City, Republic of Panama; ***phone:*** +507 297 6550 ; ***URL:*** http://ukinpanama.fco.gov.uk/en.

HOLQUIN, Maria Angela; Minister of Foreign Affairs, Government of Colombia; ***education:*** Université de la Sorbonne, France, 1983; BSc. Political Science, Univ. of Los Andes, Bogotá, Colombia, 1988; ***political career:*** Minister of Foreign Affairs, 2010-; ***professional career:*** Amb. to Venezuela; Amb. to the United Nations; ***office address:*** Ministry of Foreign Affairs, Palacio de San Carlos, Calle 10, No. 5-51, Santafé de Bogotá, Colombia; ***phone:*** +57 1 282 7811; ***fax:*** +57 1 341 6777; ***URL:*** http://www.minrelext.gov.co.

HOLTBY, H.E. Christopher, OBE; Ambassador, British Embassy in Estonia; ***professional career:*** Dep. Head of Security Policy Dept. in the FCO, 2007-11; Amb. to Estonia, 2012-; ***office address:*** British Embassy, Wismari 6, 10136 Tallinn, Estonia; ***phone:*** +372 667 4700; ***fax:*** +372 667 4724; ***e-mail:*** information@britishembassy.ee; ***URL:*** http://ukinestonia.fco.gov.uk/en.

HOMOUD , H.E. Mazen Kemal Homoud ; Ambassador, Embassy of Jordan in the UK; ***professional career:*** Man. Dir. of the Jordan Tourism Board, 2005-07; CEO, Jordan Projects for Tourism, 2007-10; Amb. to the UK, 2011-; ***office address:*** Embassy of the Hashemite Kingdom of Jordan, 6 Upper Phillimore Gardens, London, W8 7HB, United Kingdom; ***phone:*** +44 (0)20 7937 3685; ***fax:*** +44 (0)20 7937 8795; ***e-mail:*** lonemb@dircon.co.uk; ***URL:*** http://www.jordanembassyuk.org .

HONDA, Mike; Congressman, California 15th District, US House of Representatives; ***education:*** San Jose State University, bachelor's degrees in Biological Sciences and Spanish, MA, Education; ***political career:*** Congressman, California 15th District, US House of Representatives, 2000-; ***committees:*** House Appropriations and Budget; ***office address:*** US House of Representatives, 1713 Longworth House Office Building, Washington, DC 20515, USA; ***phone:*** +1 202 225 2631.

HONOHAN, Patrick; Governor, Central Bank of Ireland; ***education:*** Univ. College Dublin; LSE, Ph.D; ***professional career:*** Economist, Central Bank of Ireland, 1976-81, 1984-86; Economist, IMF, 1971-73; Research Prof., Economic and Social Research Inst., 1990-98;Senior Advisor, World Bank; Prof. of International Financial Economics & Development, Trinity College Dublin, 2007-09; Gov., Central Bank of Ireland, 2009-; ***office address:*** Central Bank of Ireland, PO Box 559, Dame Street , Dublin 2, Ireland; ***URL:*** http://www.centralbank.ie.

HOOD, Jim; British, Member of Parliament for Lanark and Hamilton East, House of Commons; ***born:*** 16 May 1948, Lesmahagow, UK; ***education:*** Lesmaghow Higher Grade Sch.; Coatbridge Technical Coll.; Nottingham Univ. WEA; ***party:*** Labour Party; ***political career:*** NUM Branch Pres. and Sec., 1973-84; Leader of Nottinghamshire striking miners, 1984-85; fmr. Cllr. and Official, Nat. Union of Miners; MP, Clydesdale, 1987-2005; MP, Lanark and Hamilton East, 2005- ; ***interests:*** Europe, industry, economy, home affairs, local government, industrial relations, alcohol abuse; ***memberships:*** NUM Branch Pres. and Sec., 1973-84; Leader of Nottinghamshire striking miners, 1984-85; Fellow of the Industry and Parliament Trust; Vice- Chmn., Miners Parliamentary Gp., 1990-91, Chmn., 1991-92; Armed Forces Parlimentary Scheme; ***professional career:*** Miner, Coal-face engineer; ***committees:*** Mem., Commons Select Cttee. on European Legislation, 1987-97; Vice-Chmn., Miners' Parly. Group, 1990-91, Chmn., 1991-92; Chair, Cttee. on European Legislation, 1992-97; Convener, Scottish Group of Labour MPs, 1995-96; Chair, European Scrutiny Cttee. 1997-2007; Chmn., All-Party Parly. Group on ME; Mem. Speaker's Panel of Chairmen, 1997; Mem., Defence Select Cttee., 1997-2001; mem. Liaison Cttee., 1992-2007; Mem., NATO UK Parly. Assembly, 2005-10; Mem. of UK Parly. Assembly to the Council of Europe (COE), 2007-; Mem., Western European Union, 2008-10; ***trusteeships:*** Fellow of the Industry and Parliament Trust; ***office address:*** House of Commons, London, SW1A 0AA, United Kingdom; ***phone:*** +44 (0)20 7219 4585; ***fax:*** +44 (0)20 7219 5872; ***e-mail:*** davidsonh@parliament.uk; ***URL:*** http://www.jimhoodmp.org.uk.

HOPE OF CRAIGHEAD, Lord, Baron James Arthur David, Life Peer; British, Vice President, Supreme Court of the United Kingdom; ***born:*** 27 June 1938; ***parents:*** Arthur H.C. Hope and Muriel Hope (née Collie); ***married:*** Katharine Mary (née Kerr), 1966; ***children:*** William (M), James (M), Lucy (F); ***education:*** The Edinburgh Academy; Rugby Sch.; St. John's Coll., Cambridge; Univ. of Edinburgh; ***party:*** Crossbencher; ***political career:*** Mem., House of Lords, 1995-, As Vice President of the Supreme Court, disqualified from participation 2009-; ***memberships:*** Hon. Fellow, American Coll. of Trial Lawyers, 2000-; ***professional career:*** Advocate at the Scottish Bar; Dean of Faculty, 1986-89; Lord Justice General of Scotland and Lord President of the Court of Session, 1989-96; Lord of Appeal in Ordinary, 1996-2009; Dep. Pres., UK Supreme Court, 2009-; ***committees:*** Mem. Select Cttee. on the European Union, 1998-2001; ***honours and awards:*** PC, 1989; Hon. LLD., Aberdeen, Strathclyde, Edinburgh; Chllr., Univ. of Strathclyde, 1998-; FRSE, 2003; KT, 2009; ***office address:*** UK Supreme Court, Parliament Square, London, SW1P 3BD, United Kingdom; ***phone:*** +44 (0)20 7860 1980; ***fax:*** +44 (0)20 7760 1401.

HOPKINS, Kelvin; British, Member of Parliament for Luton North, House of Commons; ***born:*** 22 August 1941; ***party:*** Labour Party; ***political career:*** MP, Luton North, 1997-; ***professional career:*** Lecturer; ***committees:*** Public Admin., 2011-; European Scrutiny, 2007-; Transport, 2010; ***honours and awards:*** Hon. Fellow, Univ. of Luton; ***office address:*** House of Commons, London, SW1A 0AA, United Kingdom; ***phone:*** +44 (0)20 7219 3000; ***e-mail:*** hcinfo@parliament.uk.

HOPKINS, Kris; MP for Keighley, UK Government; ***party:*** Conservative; ***political career:*** Councillor, Bradford Council, 1998-, MP for Keighley. May 2010-; ***committees:*** Northern Ireland Affairs, 2011-; ***office address:*** House of Commons, London, SW1A 0AA, United Kingdom; ***phone:*** +44 (0)20 7219 3000; ***e-mail:*** kris.hopkins.mp@parliament.uk.

HOPTON, Nicholas; British Ambassador to Yemen, British Embassy; ***professional career:*** career diplomat; joined FCO, 1989; postings incl. Paris, Rome, Morocco, Mauritania; Ambassador to the Republic of Yemen, 2012-; ***office address:*** British Embassy, 938 Thaher Himiyear Street, Sana'a, Yemen; ***phone:*** +967 1 308100; ***fax:*** +967 1 302454; ***URL:*** http://ukinyemen.fco.gov.uk/en.

HORNER, Doug; President of the Tresaury Board, Government of Alberta; ***political career:*** MLA; Minister of Agriculture, Food and Rural Development; Minister of Advanced Education and Technology, 2007-10; Deputy Premier, Advanced Education and Technology, and Minister Liaison to the Canadian Armed Forces, 2010-11; Deputy Prime Minister, 2011-12; President of Treasury Board and Enterprise, Minister Responsible for Corporate Human Resources, 2011-; ***office address:*** Legislative Building, Legislative Building, Room 307, 10800 - 97 Avenue, Edmonton, Alberta, T5K 2B6, Canada; ***phone:*** +1 780 427 2251; ***fax:*** +1 780 427 1349.

HORWOOD, Martin; MP for Cheltenham, House of Commons; ***born:*** 1962; ***education:*** Oxford, Modern History, 1984; ***party:*** Liberal Democrats; ***political career:*** Pres. Oxford Student Liberal Soc.; Chmn., Union of Liberal Students; Councillor, Vale of White Horse District Cncl., 1991-95; MP for Cheltenham, 2005-; Shadow Environment Minister, 2006-10; ***professional career:*** Advertising exec.; Oxfam, UK; Oxfam in India; Dir. of Fundraising, Alzheimer's Soc.; Head of Consultancy, Target Direct; ***committees:*** Select Cttee., Communities and Local Gvt., 2005-07; Chmn., All Party Parly. Gp. for Tribal Peoples; Sec, All Party Parly Gp. on Corporate Responsibility; Environmental Audit Cttee., 2007-10; Jt. Cttee. on Privacy & Injunctions, 2011-12; ***office address:*** House of Commons, London, SW1A 0AA, United Kingdom.

HOSIE, Stewart; MP for Dundee East, House of Commons; ***born:*** 3 January 1963, Dundee; ***married:*** Shona (née Robison); ***children:*** Morag (F); ***public role of spouse:*** SNP Member of the Scottish Parliament for the Dundee East; ***education:*** Carnoustie High School; Higher Diploma, Computer Studies, Bell Street College; ***party:*** SNP; ***political career:*** MP for Dundee East, 2005-; SNP spokesperson, 2005-; Chief Whip, 2007-; ***memberships:*** Mem, MSF union; ***professional career:*** IT consultant, Scottish Telecom; ***committees:*** Treasury, 2010-; ***office address:*** House of Commons, London, SW1P 0AA, United Kingdom; ***phone:*** +44 (0)20 7219 3000; ***e-mail:*** hosies@parliament.uk; ***URL:*** http://www.snp.org.uk.

HOSSEINI, Shamseddin; Minister of Economic Affairs and Finance, Government of Iran; ***born:*** 1967; ***education:*** Ph.D., Islamic Azad Univ.; ***political career:*** Minister of Economic Affairs and Finance; ***professional career:*** University Lecturer; ***office address:*** Ministry of Economic Affairs and Finance, Sour Israfil Street, Babe Homayoon Avenue, Tehran, Iran; ***phone:*** +98 21 3391 6791; ***fax:*** +98 21 390528; ***e-mail:*** info@mofir.com; ***URL:*** http://www.mefa.gov.ir.

HOWARD OF LYMPNE, Lord Michael, QC; British, Member, House of Lords; ***born:*** 1941; ***married:*** Sandra Paul, 1975; ***education:*** Llanelli Grammar Sch.; Peterhouse, Cambridge, BA Hons., Econ. and Law, 1962, LL.B Hons., 1963; ***party:*** Conservative Party; ***political career:*** PPS to the Solicitor Gen., Sir Patrick Mayhew, QC, MP, 1984-85; Parly. Under-Sec. of State, Dept. of Trade and Industry, 1985-87; Minister of State for Local Govt., Dept. of Environment, then Minister of State for Water and Planning, 1987-90, responsible for water privatisation, subsequently for housing, planning, construction industries, new towns, and water; Sec. of State for Employment, Dept. of Employment, 1990-92; PC, 1990-; Sec. of State for the Environment, 1992-93; Home Sec., 1993-97; Opp. Front Bench Spokesman for Foreign and Commonwealth Affairs, 1997-99; MP (Cons.) for Folkestone and Hythe, 1983-2010; Shadow Chancellor, 2001-03; Leader of the Conservative Party, 2003-05; Mem., House of Lords, 2010-; ***professional career:*** Called to the Bar, Inner Temple, 1964; mem. Bow Gp., Chmn., 1970; appointed QC, 1982; ***committees:*** Joint Hon. Sec., cons. Parly. Legal Cttee., 1983-84; Joint Vice-Chmn., Cons. Parly. Employment Cttee., 1983-84; ***office address:*** House of Lords, London, SW1A 0AA, United Kingdom; ***phone:*** +44 (0)20 7219 3000.

HOWARD OF RISING, Lord Greville; Member of House of Lords; ***political career:*** mem., House of Lords, 2003-; Opposition Spokesman Dems, 2008-10; ***office address:*** House of Lords, London, SW1A 0PW, United Kingdom; ***phone:*** +44 (0)20 7219 3000; ***fax:*** +44 (0)20 7219 0620.

HOWARTH, Rt. Hon. George; MP for Knowsley, House of Commons; ***party:*** Labour Party; ***political career:*** MP for Knowsley North and Sefton East, 1997-2010, Knowsley North, 2010-; Parly.-under-Sec., Home Office, 1997-99; Parly.-under-Sec., Northern Ireland Office, 1999-2001; ***committees:*** Intelligency & Security Cttee., 2008-; ***office address:*** House of Commons, London, SW1A 0AA, United Kingdom; ***phone:*** +44 (0)20 7219 3000; ***e-mail:*** george.howarth.mp@parliament.uk.

HOWARTH, (James) Gerald (Douglas); British, Member of Parliament for Aldershot, House of Commons; ***born:*** 12 September 1947, Guildford, UK; ***parents:*** James Howarth (dec'd) and Mary Howarth; ***married:*** Elizabeth Howarth, 1973; ***children:*** Emily (F), Alexander (M), Charlie (M); ***languages:*** French, German; ***education:*** Haileybury & Imperial Service Coll. Junior Sch., Windsor; Bloxham Sch., Banbury (Scholar); Peninsular & Oriental Steam Navigation Company (Utility Steward); Southampton Univ., BA Hons.; ***party:*** Conservative Party; ***political career:*** Sec., Society for Individual Freedom, 1969-71; Dir., Freedom Under Law/founder, The Dicey Trust, 1977; Branch Chmn., Hounslow, Brentford & Isleworth Conservatives, 1978-83; Vice-Chmn., (Political), HBI Conservatives, 1981-83; Cllr., Hounslow London Borough, 1982-83; MP, Cannock and Burntwood, 1983-92; PPS to Parly. Under-Sec. of State, Dept. of Energy, then Housing, 1987-90, to Minister of Housing and Planning, 1990-91 and to the Rt. Hon. Margaret Thatcher, 1991-92; MP, Aldershot, 1997-; Shadow Defence Minister, 2002-10; Parliamentary Under-Secretary of State, Ministry of Defence 2010-; ***interests:*** aviation, defence, home issues, Europe; ***memberships:*** Founder Mem., No Turning Back Gp. of Conservative MPs, 1984; Pres., Air Display Assn., Europe, 2003; ***professional career:*** Commissioned, Royal Air Force Volunteer Reserve, 1968; Bank of America Limited (JV Kleinwort Benson/ Bank of America), 1971-83; Business Development Manager, European Arab Bank, 1977-81; Syndication Manager, Standard Chartered Bank, 1981-83; Advisor, Sukhoi Design Bureau, Moscow, 1992-93; Dir., Taskforce Communications Limited, 1993-95 ; ***committees:*** Sec., Conservative Parly. Aviation Cttee., 1983-87; Mem., Select Cttee. on Sound Broadcasting, 1987-90; Home Affairs Select Cttee., 1997-2001; Vice-Chmn., Parly. Aerospace Gp., 1997; Joint Chmn., All-Party Male Cancers Gp., 1997-2001; Chmn., Lords and Commons Family and Child Protection Gp., 1999; Chmn., 92 Gp. of Conservative MPs, 2001-; Defence Select Cttee. (Vice-Chmn.), 2001-03; Mem., 1922 Exec., 1999-2002; Convenor, All Party RAF Gp., 2005-06; ***trusteeships:*** Fellow, Industry & Parl. Trust (British Aerospace fellow), 1986; ***honours and awards:*** Britannia Airways Parly. Pilot of the Year, 1988; Companion, Royal Aeronautical Soc.; Freeman, Guild of Air Pilots and Air Navigators; ***recreations:*** flying (holder of pilot's licence since age 17), photography, DIY, walking, family; ***office address:*** House of Commons, London, SW1A 0AA, United Kingdom; ***phone:*** +44 (0)20 7219 5650; ***fax:*** +44 (0)20 7219 1198; ***mobile:*** +44 09850 638023; ***e-mail:*** geraldhowarth@parliament.uk.

HOWE, 7th Earl, Frederick Richard Penn Curzon; British, Opposition Spokesman for Health, House of Lords; ***born:*** 29 January 1951, London, UK; ***parents:*** Chambré George William Penn Curzon (dec'd) and Jane Curzon (née Fergusson (dec'd)); ***married:*** Elizabeth Helen (née Stuart), 26 March 1983; ***children:*** Anna (F), Flora (F), Lucinda (F), Thomas (M); ***public role of spouse:*** Deputy Lieutenant for Buckinghamshire; ***education:*** Rugby Sch.; Christ Church, Oxford, MA; ***party:*** Conservative Party; ***political career:*** Mem., House of Lords, 1984-; Govt. Whip, 1991-92; Parly. Under-Sec., Min. of Agriculture, Fisheries and Food, 1992-95; Parly. Under-Sec. of State, Min. of Defence, 1995-97; Opposition Spokesman for Health, HOL, 1997-2010, the Family, 2004-05; Parliamentary Under-Secretary of State (Quality) and Government Spokesperson, Dept. of Health, 2010-; ***interests:*** agriculture, finance, penal affairs; ***memberships:*** Chartered Inst. of Bankers; ***professional career:*** Barclays Bank, 1973-87; Farmer, 1984; Dir., Adam and Co. plc., 1987-90; Dir., Provident Life Assoc. Ltd., 1988-91; Chmn., Lapada, 1999-; ***committees:*** former: All Party Penal Affairs; All Party Gp. on Adoption; All Party Gp. on Abuse Investigations; ***trusteeships:*** Pres., Nat. Soc. for Epilepsy, 1986-; ***recreations:*** music, walking; ***office address:*** House of Lords, London, SW1A 0PQ, United Kingdom; ***phone:*** +44 (0)20 7219 5427; ***fax:*** +44 (0)20 7219 1177.

HOWE OF IDLICOTE, Baroness Elspeth, CBE; Member, House of Lords; ***born:*** 8 February 1932; ***married:*** Lord Howe of Aberavon, August 1953; ***children:*** Caroline (F), Amanda (F), Alexander (M); ***education:*** London Sch. of Economics, BSc.in Social Science and Administration, 1985; ***political career:*** Mem. of the House of Lords, 2001-; ***memberships:*** numerous incl. Inner London Education Authority, 1966-70; East London Partnership, 1988-93; Cncl. of St. George's House of Windsor, 1989-93; Council of the Institute of Business Ethics, 1990-; Lord Chancellor's Advisory Cttee.; Chmn., The Hansard Soc. Cmn. 'Women at the Top', 1990-91; Chmn., MRC Report, The Ethical Conduct of Research on Children, 1991-; Sec. of State for Employment's Working Group on Women's Issues, 1992-97; Mem., NCVO Advisory Cncl., 1998-; Vice-Chmn., The Open University, 2001-03; ***professional career:*** Sec. to Principal, AA School of Architecture, 1952-55; Dep. Chmn., Equal Opportunities Commission, Manchester, Chmn., Commission's Legal Cttee., 1975-79; President, Fed. of Rec. & Empl. Services, 1980-94; Non-Exec. Dir., Kingfisher plc, 1986-2000; Non-Exec. Dir., Legal & General, 1989-97; Non-Exec. Dir., United Biscuits plc, 1988-94; Chairman, The BOC Foundation for the Env., 1990-2003; Chmn., The Broadcasting Standards Commission, 1993-99; ***committees:*** numerous incl. Pres., The Peckham Settlement, 1976-; Gov., LSE, 1985-2007; Patron, Inst. of Business Ethics, 2001-; ***trusteeships:*** The Architectural Assoc., 1987-; The Anne Driver Trust, 1987-; Bd. Mem., Veolia Env. Trust (formerly Onyx), 2003-; ***honours and awards:*** created Baroness Howe of Idlicote, 2001; Hon. Drs., London, 1990, The Open University, 1993, Bradford, 1993, Aberdeen, 1994, Liverpool, 1994, Sunderland, 1995, South Bank, 1995; Hon. Fellow, London Sch. of Economics, 2001; ***publications:*** Articles published for The Times, Financial Times, Guardian, New Society and others., Women on the Board, Susan McRae, 1991, Policy Studies Institute; The Hansard Society Report, Women at the Top, 1990; EOC pamphlet Women & Credit, 1978; CPC pamphlet Under Five, 1966; ***office address:*** House of Lords, London, SW1A 0PW, United Kingdom; ***phone:*** +44 (0)20 7219 6581; ***fax:*** +44 (0)20 7219 1991; ***e-mail:*** howee@parliament.uk.

HOWELL, John, MP; MP for Henley on Thames, House of Commons; ***political career:*** Local Councillor; MP for Henley-on-Thames, June 2008-; PPS, 2010-; ***professional career:*** Businessman; ***office address:*** House of Commons, London, SW1A 0AA, United Kingdom; ***phone:*** +44 (0)20 7219 3000.

HOWIE OF TROON, Lord, Baron William, Life Peer; British, Member of the House of Lords; ***born:*** 2 March 1924; ***parents:*** Peter Howie (dec'd) and Annie Howie; ***married:*** Mairi Sanderson, 1951 ((dec'd 2005)); ***education:*** Marr. Coll., Troon; Royal Technical Coll., Glasgow; ***party:*** Labour Party; ***political career:*** MP, 1963-70; Mem., House of Lords, 1978-; ***memberships:*** Fellow, Industry and Parly. Trust; Fellow, Soc. of Engineers and Scientists, France; Fellow, Inst. of Civil Engineers; Hon. Fellow, Inst. of Structural Engineers; Hon. Fellow, Assn. of Building Engineers; ***professional career:*** fmr. Civil Engineer; fmr. Journalist; fmr. Publisher; Cncl. Mem., Inst. of Civil Engineers, 1965-68; Cncl. Mem., City Univ., 1968-91, Pro-Chllr., 1984-91; Dir. of Internal Relations, Thomas Telford Ltd. 1976-89; ***committees:*** Mem., Cttee. of Enquiry into Engineering Profession, 1977-79; ***office address:*** House of Lords, London, SW1A 0PQ, United Kingdom; ***phone:*** +44 (0)20 7219 3000; ***fax:*** +44 (0)20 7219 5979.

HOWLIN, Brendan; Irish, Minister of Public Expenditure and Reform, Government of Ireland; ***born:*** 1956; ***education:*** CBS, Wexford; St. Patrick's Teachers' Training College, Dublin; ***political career:*** Dáil Dpty. 1987-; Labour Party Spokesman on Health and Youth Affairs 1989; Spokesperson on Health and Women's Rights 1987-89; Mem., Wexford County Council 1985-; Alderman, Wexford Borough Council 1985- (Mayor 1986-87); Min. for Health 93-94; Min. for the Environment 1994-97; Department of Public Expenditure and Reform, Feb. 2011-; ***professional career:*** Teacher; ***office address:*** Department of Public Expenditure and Reform, Government Buildings, Upper Merrion Street, Dublin 2, Ireland; ***phone:*** +353 (0)1 676 7571.

HØYBRÅTEN, Dagfinn; Norwegian, Secretary General, Nordic Council of Ministers; ***born:*** 2 December 1957; ***education:*** Univ. Oslo, MA, Political Science, 1984; ***party:*** Kristeligt Folkeparti (KRF, Christian Democratic Party); ***political career:*** Deputy Chmn., Young Christian Democrats of Norway, 1978-79, Chmn., 1982; Political Advisor to MPs, Stortinget, 1978-81, 83; Political advisor to the Minister of Education and Church Affairs, 1983-86; Mem., Akershus County Cncl., 1983-91; State Sec. in the Min. of Finance and Customs, 1989-90; Minister of Health at the Min. of Health and Social Affairs, 1997-2000; Minister of Health, 2002-2004; Minister, Labour and Social Affairs, 2004-05; Leader, KRF, 2004-11; Sec.-Gen., Nordic Council of Ministers, 2013-; ***memberships:*** Mem., Board of the Norwegian Inst. of Hospital Research, 1992-93; Mem., Board of Governors, Central Bank of Norway, 1991-97; ***professional career:*** Consultant, Chief of Staff, Exec. Dir., Norwegian Assn. of Local and Regional Authorities, 1986, 1988, 1989, 1990-93; Chief Exec., Oppegaard Municipality, 1994-97; Dir. Gen., Nat. Insurance Admin., 1997; ***committees:*** Mem., Exec. Cttee, Christian Democratic Party, 1979-82, 83-97; Mem., Nat. Cttee. of UN's Int.Year of Youth, 1983-85; Chmn., Programme Cttee., Christian Democratic Party, 1986-91; Mem., Goverment's Cttee., on Planning, 1984-86, 1989-90; ***office address:*** Nordic Council of Ministers, Ved Stranden 18, 1061 Copenhagen K, Denmark; ***URL:*** http://www.norden.org.

HOYER, Steny; Democratic Whip, US House of Representatives; ***education:*** Univ. of Maryland, 1963; Georgetown Univ., Law Center, 1966; ***political career:*** Mem., Maryland State Senate, 1966-78; Pres., Senate, 1975-78; State Bd. of Higher Education, 1978-81; Congressman, Maryland Fifth District; Chairman, Democratic Caucus, 1989-95; Democrat Whip, 2002-07; Democrat Leader, 2007-10; Democrat Whip, 2010-; ***memberships:*** Naval Bd. of Visitors; ***committees:*** House Appropriations Cttee.; House Administration Cttee.; ***trusteeships:*** St. Mary's Coll. Bd. of Trustees; ***office address:*** US House of Representatives, 1705 Longworth House Office Building, Washington, DC 20515, USA; ***phone:*** +1 202 224 4131; ***URL:*** http://www.house.gov.

HOYER, Dr Werner; German, President, European Investment Bank; ***born:*** 1951; ***education:*** Cologne Univ., economics; ***party:*** FDP; ***political career:*** Mem., German Bundestag, 1987-2011; Sec.-Gen., FDP, 1993-94; Minister of State (Deputy Foreign Minister), Foreign Office, 1994-98; Minister of State (Deputy Foreign Minister), resp. for Political & Security Affairs, European Affairs, UN and Arms Control, 2009-11; ***professional career:*** Pres., European Investment Bank & Chmn. of its Board of Dirs., Jan. 2012-; ***office address:*** European Investment Bank, 100 boulevard Konrad Adenauer , L- 2950 , Luxembourg; ***URL:*** http://www.eib.org.

HOYLE, Lindsay; Member of Parliament for Chorley, House of Commons; ***born:*** 10 June 1957; ***parents:*** Lord Hoyle of Warrington; ***married:*** Catherine Swindley; ***party:*** Labour Party; ***political career:*** Dep. Leader of Chorley Borough Cncl., 1997-97; Mayor of Chorley, 1997-98; MP, Chorley, 1997-; ***interests:*** trade and industry, sport, defence; ***committees:*** Trade and Industry Select Cttee.; European Scrutiny Cttee.; Dep. Speaker, Chmn. of Ways and Means, 2010; Finance and Services, 2010-; *clubs:* Chorley Cricket Club; Chorley Tennis Club; *recreations:* rugby league, cricket; *office address:* House of Commons, London, SW1A 0AA, United Kingdom; *phone:* +44 (0)20 7219 3000.

HUEBNER, H.E. David; Ambassador, US Embassy in New Zealand; *education:* Princeton Univ., USA; *memberships:* Fellow of the Chartered Institute of Arbitrators; *professional career:* Lecturer; Lawyer, partner at Sheppard Mullin Richter and Hampton LLP; Amb. to New Zealand and the Independent State of Samoa, Dec. 2009-; *office address:* Embassy of the United States of America, 29 Fitzherbert Terrace, Thorndon, Wellington, New Zealand; *phone:* +64 (0)4 462 6000; *fax:* +64 (0)4 499 0490; *URL:* http://wellington.usembassy.gov.

HUGHES, Hubert; Prime Minister, Government of Anguilla; *party:* Anguilla United Movement; *political career:* Prime Minister, 1994-2000, 2010-; *office address:* Secretariat, The Valley, Anguilla; *phone:* +1 264 497 2451; *URL:* http://www.gov.ai.

HUGHES, Simon Henry Ward, MP; British, Liberal Democrats Deputy Leader, House of Commons; *born:* 17 May 1951, Cheshire; *parents:* James Henry Annesley Hughes and Sylvia Hughes (née Ward); *languages:* French; *education:* Christ Coll., Brecon; Selwyn College, Cambridge Univ., BA, 1973, MA, 1978; Inns of Court School of Law; College of Europe, Bruges, Cert. in Higher European Studies; Hon. Fellow, London South Bank University; *party:* Liberal Democratic Party; *political career:* MP (Lib. Dem.) for Southwark and Bermondsey, 1983; Lib & Lib Dem for Southwark and Bermondsey, 1983-1997; Lib Dem for North Southwark and Bermondsey, 1997-2010, Bermondsey and Old Southwark, 2010-; Party Spokesperson on the Environment, 1983-87 & 1990-94; Health, 1987-88, & 1995-99; Education, 1988-90; Lib Dem Spokesperson for London, 1988-1997; Liberal Democrat Dep. Chief Whip, 1988-99; Urban Affairs, Community Relations & Young People, 1994-95; Shadow Home Secretary, 1999-2005; Candidate for Leader of Lib Dems, 1999 & 2006; Candidate for Mayor of London, 2004; Liberal Democrat Federal President, 2004-; Shadow Minister for the Office of the Dep. Prime Minister, 2005-6; Shadow Constitutional Affairs Secretary and Attorney-General, 2006-07; Shadow Leader of the House of Commons, 2007-09; Shadow Sec. of State for Energy and Climate Change, 2009-10; Liberal Democrats Deputy Leader in the House of Commons, 2010-; *interests:* Commonwealth, conflict resolution, environment, faith, human rights, sport, youth issues; *memberships:* Joint Parly. Chair, Council for Education in the Commonwealth; Joint Chair: Nth. Lambeth and Nth. Southwark Sport Action Zone and South Bank Forum; Chair of Governors, St James C of E PS, Bermondsey; Patron, Southwark Playhouse; *professional career:* Barrister, 1974-; Trainee and Mem. Secretariat, Directorate and Comm. on Human Rights, Council of Europe, Strasbourg, 1976-77; *committees:* Modernisation of the House of Commons, 2007-10; Ecclesiastical, 2010-; *trusteeships:* Bacon's College; Mayor's Thames Festival (Chair); Rose Theatre; *publications:* Co-author of: Human Rights in Western Europe (1981); Across the Divide - Liberal Values for Defence and Disarmament (1986); Pathways to Power (1992); Who Goes Where - Asylum: Opportunity not Crisis (2002); Beyond Blair (2006); *recreations:* music, theatre, open air, family & friends; *office address:* House of Commons, London, SW1A 0AA, United Kingdom; *phone:* +44 (0)20 7219 6256; *e-mail:* simon@simonhughes.org.uk; *URL:* http://www.simonhughes.org.uk.

HUGHES OF STRETFORD, Baroness Beverley; British, Member, House of Lords; *born:* 30 March 1950; *education:* Univ. of Manchester; Univ. of Liverpool; *party:* Labour Party; *political career:* Parly.-under-Sec., 1999-; MP, Stretford and Urmston, 1997-2010; Minister of State, 2002-05; Minister for Children, 2005-07; Minister of State, Dept. of Children, Schools and Families and Minister for the North West, 2007-08; Minister of State, Dept. for Children, Schools and Families, 2008-09; Mem., House of Lords 2010-; *interests:* education, health, economic development, social services; *professional career:* Sr. Lecturer, Univ. of Manchester; *office address:* House of Lords, London, SW1A 0AA, United Kingdom; *phone:* +44 (0)20 7219 3000.

HUHTANIEMI, Pekka; Ambassador, Finnish Embassy in the UK; *born:* November 1949; *education:* M.Pol.Sc., Univ. of Helsinki, 1971; *professional career:* Amb. and Perm. Rep., to Geneva, Switzerland, 1998-2003; Amb. to Norway, 2003-05; Amb. to the UK, 2010-; *office address:* Finnish Embassy, 38 Chesham Place, London, SW1X 8HW, United Kingdom; *phone:* +44 (0)20 7838 6200; *fax:* +44 (0)20 7235 3680; *URL:* http://www.finemb.org.uk.

HUITFELDT, Anniken; Minister of Health, Government of Norway; *born:* 1969; *education:* Univ. of Oslo, Political Science and History, 1992; LSE, Geography, 1993; Univ. of Oslo, Postgrad. degree in History; *political career:* Minister for Children and Equality, 2008-09; Minister of Culture, 2009-12; Minister of Health, 2012-; *professional career:* Researcher, Institute for Applied Social Science FAFO, 2000-05 ; *committees:* Mem., Labour Party Central Exec. Cttee., 2002-; Mem., Labour Party Parly. Grp., 2005-; First Dep. Chwmn., Standing Cttee. on Education Research and Church Affairs, 2005-; Hd., Norwegian Labour Party women's network, 2007-; *office address:* Ministry of Health, PB 8019 Dep, 0030 Oslo, Norway.

HUMALA TASSO, Ollanta Moises; President, Peru; *education:* Pontifical Catholic Univ. of Peru; *political career:* led uprising against Alberto Fujimori, 2000, pardoned and allowed to return to military career; founded Peruvian Nationalist Party, 2005; presidential candidate 2006; elected pres., 2011; *professional career:* military; *office address:* Office of the President, 1ra cuadra, Lima 1, Peru; *URL:* http://www.presidencia.gob.pe/.

HUN SEN, Samdech; Prime Minister, Cambodian Government; *born:* 4 April 1951, Kompong Cham Province, Cambodia; *education:* Ph.D., Political Sciences, Hanoi, 1991; *political career:* Foreign Minister, 1979; Dep. Prime Minister & Foreign Minister, 1981-85; Prime Minister & Foreign Minister, 1985-91; Prime Minister & mem., Supreme Nat. Cncl.,1991-93; Prime Minister, 1993-; *professional career:* joined Army, 1970; Fled to Vietnam, 1977; *office address:* Office of the Prime Minister, Phnom Penh, Cambodia.

HUNT, H.E. David; Ambassador , British Embassy in Lithuania; *professional career:* FCO, Dep. Head of Conflict Dept., 2008-11; Amb. to Lithuania, 2011-; *office address:* British Embassy, 2 Antakalnio , 2055 Vilnius, Lithuania; *phone:* +370 5 246 2900; *fax:* +370 5 246 2901; *URL:* http://ukinlithuania.fco.gov.uk.

HUNT, Rt. Hon. Jeremy; Secretary of State for Health, UK Government; *born:* 1966; *party:* Conservative; *political career:* MP for South West Surrey, 2005-; Shadow Sec. of State for Culture, Media and Sport, 2007-May 2010; Secretary of State for Culture, Olympics, Media and Sport, May 2010-12; Secretary of State for Health, 2012-; *professional career:* Man. Dir., Hotcourses Ltd., 1991-2005; *office address:* Department of Health, Richmond House, 79 Whitehall, London, SW1A 2NS, United Kingdom; *phone:* +44 (0)20 7210 3000; *URL:* http://www.doh.gov.uk.

HUNT, Tristram, FRHistS; MP for Stoke-on-Trent, UK Government; *born:* May 1974; *parents:* Lord Hunt of Chesterton; *education:* Trinity College, Cambridge Univ., Univ. of Chicago; *party:* Labour; *political career:* MP for Stoke-on-Trent, May 2010-; *professional career:* Historian; Broadcaster; Columnist; Lecturer on Modern British History, Queen Mary, Univ. of London; *committees:* Political & Constitutional Reform, 2010-; Jt. Cttee. on the Draft House of Lords Reform Bill, 2011-12; Works of Art, 2012-; *publications:* Building Jerusalem; Making our Mark; The Frock-Coated Communist: The Revolutionary Life of Friedrich Engels; *office address:* House of Commons, London, SW1A 0AA, United Kingdom; *phone:* +44 (0)20 7219 3000.

HUNT OF KINGS HEATH, Lord , OBE; Member, House of Lords; *party:* Labour Party; *political career:* Mem. of House of Lords; Parly.-under-Sec., Dept. of Health, 1999-resigned March 17 2003; Parly.-under-Sec., Dept. for Work and Pensions, 2005-06; Minister of State for Dept. of Health, 2007; Parly.-under-Sec. of State, 2007-08; Minister of Strate, Dept. for Environment, Food and Rural Affairs, 2008-09; Shadow Deputy Leader of the House of Lords, 2011-; *honours and awards:* OBE; *office address:* House of Lords, London, SW1A 0PW, United Kingdom; *phone:* +44 (0)20 7219 1475; *fax:* +44 (0)20 7219 6837.

HUNT OF WIRRAL, Rt. Hon. Baron David James Fletcher, MBE, Life Peer; British, Solicitor, Beachcroft LLP; *born:* 1942; *married:* Paddy Orchard, 1973; *children:* Tom (M), Richard (M), Joanna (F), Daisy (F); *education:* Liverpool Coll.; Montpellier Univ.; Bristol Univ., LL.B; *political career:* MP (Cons.) for Wirral, 1976-83; MP for Wirral West, 1983-97; PPS to the Sec. of State for Trade, 1979-81, to Sec. of State for Defence, 1981; Chmn., Cons. Grp. for Europe, 1981-82; an Asst. Govt. Whip, 1981-83, a Lord Commissioner of the Treasury, 1983-84; Vice-Chmn., Cons. Party, 1983-85; Chmn. and Vice-Pres., Cons. Grp. for Europe, 1981-85; Dept. of Energy. Parly. Under Sec. of State, 1984-87; Dpty. Govt. Chief Whip and Treasurer of Her Majesty's Household, 1987-89; Minister for Local Government and Inner Cities 1989-90; Sec. of State for Wales, 1990-93; Privy Counsellor, 1990-; Pres., Tory Reform Group, 1990-97; Pres. Conservative Students, 1994-98; Sec. of State for Employment, 1993-94; Chancellor of the Duchy of Lancaster and Cabinet Minister for Public Service and Science, 1994-95; Pres. All Party Parly. Group on Occupational Safety and Health, 1999-; Mem., House of Lords; *memberships:* Law Society; Fellow, Int. Inst. of Risk and Safety Management; Fellows, Chartered Insurance Institute; Fellow, Institute of Actuaries; *professional career:* Nat. Vice-Chmn., Conservative Students 1966-68; Nat. Chmn., Young Conservatives 1972-73 (Vice-Pres., Nat. Young Cons. 1986-88); mem., S.W. Economic Planning Council 1972-76; Pres., British Youth Council 1977-80; Senior Partner, Beachcroft, 1996-2005; Governor, English Speaking Union, 1999-, and Chmn., 2005-; Chmn. Beachcroft LLP, Financial Services Division, 2002-; Chmn. Assn of Ind. Financial Advisors, 1999-2002; Pres., Chartered Insurance Inst, 2007-08; *committees:* mem., Govt. Adv. Cttee on Pop Festivals 1972-75; *trusteeships:* Holocaust Educational Trust, 1998-; Chmn., Inter Parliamentary Council Against Anti-Semitism; *honours and awards:* Member of the Order of the British Empire, 1973; Observer Mace, 1965-66; received life peerage, 1997; Apptd. to Privy Council, 1990; *publications:* Europe Right Ahead, 1978; A Time for Youth, 1978; Towards 2000 and Beyond, 1990; Right Ahead: Conservatism and the Social Market, 1994; *clubs:* Hurlingham; *office address:* 100 Fetter Lane, London, EC4A 1BN, United Kingdom; *phone:* +44 (0)20 7894 6613; *fax:* +44 (0)20 7894 6158; *e-mail:* lordhunt@beachcroft.com.

HUNTER, Duncan; American, Congressman, California 52nd District, US House of Representatives; *born:* 1948; *political career:* Congressman, California 52nd District, US House of Representatives, 1980; *professional career:* Lawyer; *committees:* Armed Services; Education and the Workforce; Transportation and Infrastructure; *office address:* US House of Representatives, 2265 Rayburn House Office Building, Washington, DC 20515, USA; *phone:* +1 202 224 3121.

HUNTER, Mark; MP for Cheadle, House of Commons; *born:* 25 July 1957, Manchester; *parents:* Arthur Hunter and Elizabeth Hunter (née Trainer); *married:* Leslie Graham; *children:* Robert (M), Francesca (F); *education:* Audenshaw Grammar School; *party:* Liberal Democrat Party; *political career:* Councillor, Stockport Metropolitan Borough Council, 1996-2006, Leader, 2002-05; MP for Cheadle, July 2005-; Lib. Dem. Shadow Minister for: Office of the Deputy Prime Minister, 2005-06, Home Affairs, 2006-07, FCO, 2007; PPS to Nick Clegg as Leader of the Lib. Dems., 2007-10; Lib. Dem. Shadow Minister for Transport, 2008-10; Assistant Government Whip, 2010-; *interests:* local government, foreign affairs; *professional career:* Marketing exec., Guardian Media Group, -2002; *committees:* Trade and Industry Select Cttee., 2005-08; Arms Export Controls, 2007-08; Administration, 2011-; *recreations:* Manchester City Football Club; *office address:* House of Commons, London, SW1A 0AA, United Kingdom; *e-mail:* hunterm@parliament.uk; *URL:* http://www.markhunter.org.uk.

HUPPERT, Julian; MP for Cambridge, UK Government; *education:* Trinity Coll. Cambridge Univ., BA, 2000, Ph.D, Biological Chemistry, 2005; *party:* Liberal Democrats; *political career:* County Councillor; MP for Cambridge, May 2010-; *committees:* Home Affairs, 2010-; Jt. Cttee., Human Rights, 2010-11; *office address:* House of Commons, London, SW1A 0AA, United Kingdom; *phone:* +44 (0)20 7219 3000.

HURD, Nick; MP for Ruislip, Northwood and Pinner, House of Commons; *born:* 1962; *party:* Conservative; *political career:* Chief of Staff to Tim Yeo MP, 2004-05; MP for Ruislip Northwood, 2005-10, Ruislip, Northwood and Pinner, 2010-; Opposition Whip, 2006-08; Shadow Minister for Charities and Social Enterprise and Volunteering, 2008-09; Parly. Sec., 2010-; *office address:* House of Commons, London, SW1A 0AA, United Kingdom.

HURD OF WESTWELL, Lord; Member, House of Lords; ***born:*** 8 March 1930, Marlborough, Wilts, England; ***parents:*** Anthony Richard Hurd and Stephanie Hurd (née Corner); ***married:*** the late Judy Hurd (née Smart), 7 May 1982 (dec'd 2008); Tatiana Elizabeth Michelle Hurd (née Eyre), 10 November 1960 (div'd); ***children:*** Nicholas (M), Thomas (M), Alexander (M), Philip (M), Jessica (F); ***education:*** Scholar at Eton; Trinity Coll., Cambridge, BA (Hon); ***party:*** Conservative Party; ***political career:*** Foreign Sec.; MP, Mid Oxfordshire, 1974-83, Witney, 1983-97; PS, to Rt. Hon. Edward Heath, 1968-70; PS to PM 1970-74; Opposition Spokesman on Foreign Affairs, 1976-79; Minister of State, FCO, 1979-83; Minister of State Home Office, 1983-84; Sec. of State for N. Ireland, 1984-85; Home Sec., 1985-89; Foreign Sec., 1989-95; Mem. of House of Lords; ***memberships:*** Pres., Cambridge Union, 1952; Royal Commission on Lords Reform, 1999; ***professional career:*** HM Diplomatic Service, 1952-66 (Beijing, UK Mission to UN, Rome); Dir., Nat. Westminster Bank Plc, 1995-99; Dep. Chmn., Natwest Markets, 1995-99; Chmn., British Invisibles, 1997-2000; Chmn., Booker Prize for Fiction, 1998; Chmn., Prison Reform Trust, 1997-2001; Dep. Chmn., Coutts and Co., 1998-2009; Senior Adviser, Hawkpoint Partners Ltd., 1998-2010; Co-Pres., R11A; High Steward of Westminster Abbey, 1999; Chmn., Centre for Effective Disputes Resolution (CEDR), 2001-04; Co-Pres., Royal Institute of International Affairs (Chatham House), 2004-10; ***honours and awards:*** OBE, 1974; PC, 1982; CH, 1996; Life Peer, 1997; ***publications:*** Three historical works; Nine Political Thrillers; latest works include: The Search for Peace,1997; The Shape of Ice, 1998; Ten Minutes to Turn the Devil, 1999; Image in the Water, 2001; Memoirs, 2003; Sir Robert Peel, 2007; Choose your Weapons, 2010; ***recreations:*** writing, walking, reading; ***office address:*** House of Lords, London , SW1A0PW, United Kingdom.

HUSNI BIN MOHAMAD HANADZLAH, Ahmad; Second Minister of Finance, Government of Malaysia; ***education:*** University of Malaya; ***political career:*** MP, 1995-; Second Minister of Finance, 2009-; ***office address:*** Ministry of Finance, Kompleks Kementerian Kewangan, Puast Pentadbiran Kerajaan Persekutuun, 62592 Putrajaya, Malaysia; ***phone:*** +60 (0)3 8882 3000; ***URL:*** http://www.miti.gov.my.

HUSSAIN, Lord Qurban; Member, House of Lords; ***party:*** Liberal Democrat Party; ***political career:*** Councilor, Luton Borough Council; Mem., House of Lords, 2011-; ***office address:*** House of Lords, London, SW1A 0PW, United Kingdom; ***phone:*** +44 (0)20 7219 3000.

HUSSAIN BIN ALI MIRZA, H.E. Abdul; Minister of Energy, Oil, Electricity and Water Authority, Government of Bahrain; ***political career:*** Minister of State for Cabinet Affairs, 2005-06; Minister of State and Chairman of the National Oil and Gas Bureau, 2006; Minister of Oil and Gas, 2006-10; Minister of Energy, Oil, Electricity and Water Authority, 2011-; ***office address:*** Ministry of Oil and Gas, PO Box 2991, Manama, Bahrain; ***phone:*** +973 17 714422; ***fax:*** +973 17 715715.

HUSSEIN, Bishar Abdirahman; Director General, Universal Postal Union; ***education:*** Univ. of Nairobi; ***professional career:*** Kenya Posts & Telecommunications Corp, 1984-2002, including postmaster general, 1999-2002; Amb. of Kenya to the UAE, 2002-08; Chair, UPU Council of Administration, 2008-12; Dir.-Gen., UPU International Bureau, 2013-; ***office address:*** UPU, International Bureau, Case postale 13, CH-3000 Berne, Switzerland; ***URL:*** http://www.upu.int.

HUSSEIN-ECE OF HIGHBURY, Baroness Meral; Member, House of Lords; ***party:*** Liberal Democrat; ***political career:*** London Borough of Hackney Council: Councillor 1994-2002; Dep. Leader 1995-96; London Borough of Islington Council. Councillor 2002-10, Cabinet Member for Health and Social Care 2002-06; mem. House of Lords, 2010-; ***professional career:*** Chair, Islington Health Partnership Board, 2002-06; Board mem., Islington Primary Care Trust, 2002-06; Non-exec. Dir., Camden and Islington Mental Health and Social Care Trust, 2002-06; Commissioner, Equality and Human Rights Commission 2009-; ***office address:*** House of Lords, London, SW1A 0PW, United Kingdom; ***phone:*** +44 (0)20 7219 3000; ***fax:*** +44 (0)20 7219 5979; ***URL:*** http://www.parliament.uk.

HUTCHINSON, Billy; Leader, Progressive Unionist Party; ***party:*** Progressive Unionist; Leader, 2011-; ***political career:*** mem., North Belfast, Northern Ireland Assembly, 1998-2003; ***office address:*** Northern Ireland Assembly, Parliament Buildings, Stormont, Belfast BT4 3XX, Northern Ireland; ***phone:*** +44 (0)28 9052 1130.

HUTT, Jane, AM; British, Leader of the House, Minister of Finance, Welsh Assembly Government; ***born:*** 15 December 1949, Surrey, UK; ***parents:*** Prof. Michael S.R. Hutt (dec'd 2000) and Elizabeth Mai Hutt; ***married:*** Michael John Hilary Trickey, 14 July 1984; ***children:*** Jessica Rees (F), Rachel Catrin (F); ***education:*** Univ. of Kent at Canterbury, BA (Hons.), Public and Social Administration, 1967-70; London Sch. of Economics, certificate of qualification in social work, 1971-72; Bristol Univ., M.Sc., Management Development & Social Responsibility, 1993-95: Hon. Fellow, UWIC; ***party:*** Labour Party; ***political career:*** Mem. Nat. Assembly for Wales, Vale of Glamorgan; County Cllr., 1981-93; Minister for Health and Social Services, 1999-2005; Minister for Assembly Business, Children and Equalities, 2005-07; Minister for Budgets and Business Management, May-July 2007; Minister for Children, Education, Lifelong Learning and Skills, July 2007-09; Minister for Budget and Business, 2009-11; Leader of the House, Minister of Finance, 2011-; ***professional career:*** Co-ordinator, Welsh Women's Aid, 1978-88; Director, Tenant Participation Advisory Services, 1988-92; Director, Chwarae Teg (Fair Play), 1992-99; former Welsh mem. on the New Opportunities (UK) Fund; ***office address:*** National Assembly for Wales, Ty Hwyel, Cardiff Bay, CF99 1NA, United Kingdom; ***e-mail:*** jane.hutt@wales.gov.uk.

HWANG, Kyo-ahn; Minister of Justice, Government of South Korea; ***born:*** April 1957; ***education:*** LL.B., College of Law, Sungkyunkwan Univ., 1981; LL.M., Graduate School of Law, Sungkyunkwan Univ., 2006; ***political career:*** Minister of Justice, 2013-; ***professional career:*** Prosecutor; ***office address:*** Ministry of Justice, Building 5, Gwacheon GOvernment of Complex, Jungang-dong 1, Gwacheon-si, Kyunggi-do, Republic of Korea; ***phone:*** +82 503 7023; ***e-mail:*** webmaster@moj.go.kr; ***URL:*** http://www.moj.go.kr.

HYLTON, Anthony; Minister of Industry, Commerce and Investment, Government of Jamaica; ***political career:*** Minister of Foreign Trade, -2002; Minister of Mining and Energy, 2002-08; Minister of Industry, Commerce and Investment, 2011-; ***office address:*** Ministry of Industry, Commerce and Investment, PCJ Building, 36 Trafalgar Rd, Kingston 10, Jamaica; ***phone:*** +1 876 754 5501; ***URL:*** http://www.mct.gov.jm.

HYSLOP, Fiona, MSP; Minister for Culture and External Affairs, Scottish Government; ***party:*** SNP; ***political career:*** MSP, Lothians, 1999-; Cabinet Secretary, Education and Lifelong Learning, 2007-09; Minister for Culture and External Affairs, 2009-; ***office address:*** Scottish Parliament, Edinburgh, EH99 1SP, United Kingdom; ***phone:*** +44 (0)131 348 5000; ***fax:*** +44 (0)131 348 5601.

HYUN, Oh-seok; Minister for Strategy and Finance, Government of South Korea; ***education:*** BA, Business Admin. 1974, MA, Public Admin. 1976, Seoul National Univ.; Ph.D., Economics, Univ, of Pennsylvania, 1984; ***political career:*** Deputy Prime Minister, Minister for Strategy and Finance, 2013-; ***professional career:*** Pres., Korea Development Inst., 2009-13; Mem., Knowledge Advisory Commission, The World Bank, 2012-; ***office address:*** Ministry of Finance and Economy, 1 Jungang-dong, Gwacheon, Gyeonggi Province, South Korea; ***phone:*** +82 2 503 9032; ***fax:*** +82 2 502 9033; ***URL:*** http://english.mofe.go.kr/main.php.

I

IHALAINEN, Lauri; Minister of Labour, Government of Finland; ***born:*** 14 May 1947; ***party:*** Social Democratic Party; ***political career:*** Minister of Labour. 2011-; ***professional career:*** Carpenter; ***office address:*** Ministry of Employment and the Economy, Eteläesplanadi 4, PO Box 32,, Helsinki FI-00023 Government, Finland; ***URL:*** http://www.tem.fi.

ILESIC, Marko; Judge, Court of Justice of the European Union; ***born:*** 1947; ***professional career:*** Prof. of Civil, Commercial and Private Interantional Law; Vice-Dean, Fac. of Law, Univ. of Ljubljana, 1995-2001, Dean, 2001-04; Hon. Judge & Pres. of Chamber at the Labour Court, Ljubljana, 1975-86; Pres., Sports Tribunal of Slovenia, 1978-86; Pres., Arbitration Chamber, Ljubljana Stock Exchange; Arbitrator, Chamber of Commerce of Yugoslavia, -1991; Arbitrator, ICC, Paris; Judge, Board of Appeals, UEFA and FIFA; Judge, Court of Justice, 2004-; ***office address:*** Court of Justice of the European Union, Rue du Fort Niedergrunewald, L-2925, Luxembourg.

ILVES, Toomas Hendrik; Estonian, President, Government of Estonia; ***born:*** 26 December 1953, Stockholm, Sweden; ***parents:*** Endel Ilves and Irene Ilves (née Rebane); ***married:*** Evelin Ilves; ***children:*** Luukas Kristjan (M), Juulia (F), Kadri Keiu (F); ***languages:*** English, German, Spanish; ***education:*** Columbia Univ. NY, USA, BA, 1976; Univ. of Pennsylvania, Philadelphia, USA, MA, Psychology, 1978; ***party:*** Chmn., People's Party, 1998-99; Dep. Chmn., Party Mõõdukad, (Social Democrats), 1999-; Socialist Group in the European Parliament; ***political career:*** Minister of Foreign Affairs, 1996-98 and 1999-2002; Minister of Foreign Affairs, 1999-2002; MP, 2002-04; MEP, 2004-06; President of Estonia, Oct. 2006-; ***interests:*** foreign and security policy, information technology; ***memberships:*** Estonian Students Society (Eesti Üliõpilaste Selts),1995; Trilateral Commission, 2004-06; Board of Trustees of think-tank Friends of Europe 2005; Founder of the Estonian Foreign Policy Institute (Eesti Välispoliitika Instituut), Member of the Executive Committee, 2002; Honorary Member of the Latvian Students Society, Austrums; Mem. of the Board, Viljandi County Municipal Fund; Board of Trustees, Estonian Academy of Arts, 2004-2006; President of the Estonian Special Olympics,1997-2004; Member of the Board of Trustees of Tartu Univ., 1996-2003; European Movement Estonia (EME) Mem. of the Board, Founding Mem., 1999-2004; Honorary Mem. of the Estonian Society in Belgium 2006; ***professional career:*** Research Asst., Dept. of Psychology, Columbia University, 1974-76; Research Asst., Dept. of Psychology, 1979; Asst. to the Dir. and English Teacher, Centre for Open Education Englewood, New Jersey, 1979-81; Arts Administrator, Dir., Vancouver Literary Centre, 1981-83; Lecturer, Estonian Literature and Linguistics, Dept. of Interdisciplinary Studies, Simon Fraser Univ. Vancouver, Canada, 1983-84; Research Analyst, Research and Analysis Dept. Radio Free Europe, Munich, Germany, 1984-88; Dir. Estonian Service, Radio Free Europe, Munich, Germany, 1988-93; Ambassador of Estonia to the USA, Canada and Mexico, 1993-96; Chmn. Bd. North Atlantic Inst., 1998; ***honours and awards:*** Grand Commandeur Legion d'Honneur of the Republic of France, 2001; Third Class Order of the Seal of the Republic of Estonia, 2004; Three Star Order of the Republic of Latvia, 2004; The Collar of the Order of the Cross of Terra Mariana (Estonia), 2006; The Knight Grand Cross of the Order of the Bath of Great Britain, 2006; Order of the White Rose of Finland, 2007; Order of the Golden Fleece of Georgia, 2007; ***publications:*** Compilation of speeches and writings from 1986-2006: Eesti jõudmine. Kõned ja kirjutised aastaist 1986-2006; Varrak, 2006 Tallinn; Articles in Estonian and other newspapers and magazines; ***clubs:*** Rotary, Estonian Nature Fund; ***recreations:*** reading, cooking, farming; ***office address:*** Office of the President, A. Weizenberg; 39, Tallinn 15050, Estonia; ***phone:*** +372 631 6202; ***fax:*** +372 631 6250; ***e-mail:*** vpinfo@vpk.ee; ***URL:*** http://www.president.ee.

IMAMI, Arben; Minister of Defence, Albanian Government; ***party:*** Democratic Party of Albania; ***political career:*** Minister of State for Legislative Reform, Albanian Cabinet, 1998-01; Minister of Justice, 2000-01; Minister of Local Government and Decentralization, 2000-02; Chief of Cabinet of the Prime Minister, 2005-09; Minister of Defence, 2009-; ***office address:*** Ministry of Defence, Ministria e Mbrojtjes, Tirana, Albania; ***phone:*** +355 (0)4 225726; ***e-mail:*** kontakt@mod.gov.al; ***URL:*** http://www.mod.gov.al.

IMBERT, Lord; Member of the House of Lords; ***born:*** 27 April 1933, Folkestone, Kent; ***parents:*** Willaim Henry Imbert and Frances May (née Hodge); ***married:*** Iris Rosina (née Dove), 1956; ***children:*** Simon (M), Elaine (F), Sally-Ann (F); ***languages:*** Russian; ***education:*** Harvey Grammar Sch., Folkestone; ***party:*** Cross Bencher; ***political career:***

Mem., House of Lords; Mem., House of Lords All Party London Gp.; ***interests:*** criminal justice, education; ***memberships:*** Patron, Assoc. osf Security Consultants; ***professional career:*** Commissioner Metropolitan Police, 1987-93; Lord-Lieutenant of Greater London, 1998-2008; Non-Exec., Dir., Securicor plc; Non-Exec., Dir., Camelot Gp. plc; Non-Exec. Chmn. Retainagroup Ltd.; Patron, London Region NCAB; Chmn., Capital Eye Security Ltd.; Mem., Bd. of Inspectorate of the Security Industry; Pres., Richmond Horse Show; Mem., Advisroy Bd., Youth at Risk; Vice Pres., Friend's of St Thomas; Patron, David Jenkinson Appeal Fund (for Chidren with Cancer); Patron, New Romney Old School Trust; Mem., Police Discipline Appeal Tribunals, 1993-98; Vice Pres., Royal Assn. in Aid of Deaf People; ***committees:*** Mem., Public Policy Cttee. of the RAC; ***trusteeships:*** Surrey County Cricket Club Youth Trust, 1993-98. appointed Vice Pres. Surrey Cricket Club, 2004; Community Action Trust; Foundation of St Catherine at Cumberland Lodge, Windsor; Trustee/Dir., Prospect Education Foundation; Police Foundation; ***honours and awards:*** CVO; QPM; ***publications:*** Occasional articles and book reviews; ***clubs:*** Saints and Sinners Club, London; ***recreations:*** bad bridge, talking about my grandchildren; ***office address:*** c/o House of Lords, London, SW1A 0PW, United Kingdom.

INGE, Field Marshal, Lord; Member of the House of Lords; ***parents:*** Raymond Inge and Grace Inge (née Durose); ***married:*** Letitia Marion Inge (née Thornton Berry), 26 November 1960; ***d:*** 2; ***education:*** Wrekin Coll.; RMA Sandhurst; ***political career:*** Chief of Defence Staff, 1994-97; Mem. of House of Lords; ***interests:*** defence; ***trusteeships:*** King Edward VII Hospital Sister Agnes; ***honours and awards:*** KG, GCB; ***office address:*** House of Lords, London, SW1A 0PW, United Kingdom; ***phone:*** +44 (0)20 7219 3000; ***fax:*** +44 (0)20 7219 8602.

INGRAM, Adam; MSP for South of Scotland, Scottish Parliament; ***party:*** SNP; ***political career:*** MSP for South of Scotland, May 2003-; Minister for Children and Early Years, 2007-11; ***office address:*** Scottish Parliament, Edinburgh, EH99 1SP, United Kingdom; ***phone:*** +44 (0)131 348 5720; ***e-mail:*** adam.ingram.msp@scottish.parliament.uk.

INHOFE, James (Jim) M.; Senator for Oklahoma, US Senate; ***married:*** Kay Inhofe; ***children:*** 4; ***education:*** Univ. of Tulsa, Economics degree; ***party:*** Republican; ***political career:*** Oklahoma State House of Representatives, 1996-; State Senate, Minority Leader; Mayor of Tulsa, 1978-84; US House of Representatives; US Senator for Oklahoma, 1994-; ***memberships:*** Pres., Sophomore Class of Senators, 1994-; ***professional career:*** US Army; small businessman (working in aviation, real estate and insurance) for over 30 years; ***committees:*** Standing Cttee. on Armed Services; Standing Cttee. on Environment & Public Works; ***office address:*** US Senate, 453 Russell Senate Office Building, Washington, DC 20510, USA; ***phone:*** +1 202 224 4721; ***URL:*** http://www.inhofe.senate.gov.

INOS, Eloy S.; Governor, Government of the Marianas Islands; ***education:*** Univ. of Guam; ***political career:*** Dir. of Finance, CNMI Gov. under Gov.Tenorio, 1987-90; Dir. of Finance, CNMI Gov. under Gov. Guerrero, 1990-94; Secretary of Finance, CNMI Government, 2006-09; Lt Gov., 2009-13; Governor of the Northern Mariana Islands, Feb. 2013-; ***office address:*** Office of the Governor, Juan A. Sablan Memorial Building, Capital Hill, Caller Box 10007, Saipan, Northern Mariana Islands; ***URL:*** http://gov.mp.

INSLEE, Jay; American, Governor, State of Washington; ***born:*** 9 February 1951; ***party:*** Democrat; ***political career:*** Congressman, Washington First District, US House of Representatives, 1993-95, 1999-2012; Governor, State of Washington, 2012-; ***professional career:*** Attorney, Peter, Fowler and Inslee, Selah, WA, 1976-92; ***committees:*** Energy and Commerce; ***office address:*** Office of the Governor, POB 40002, Olympia, WA 98504-0002, USA; ***URL:*** http://www.governor.wa.gov.

INSULZA, José Miguel; General Secretary, Organisation of American States; ***born:*** 2 June 1943, Chile; ***education:*** Univ. of Chile, Law Degree; Univ. of Michigan, Masters in Political Science; ***political career:*** Under-Sec., then Minister of Foreign Affairs, 1994-99; Mn. of the Interior and Vice Pres. of Chile, 2000-05; ***professional career:*** Professor of Political Theory, Univ. of Chile; Prof., Political Sciences, Catholic Univ., Chile. Exiled during Augusto Pinochet's tenure of power, 1974-88; Amb. for Int'l. Cooperation and Dir. of Mulltilateral Econ. Affairs, Min. of Foreign Affairs, Chile; Sec. Gen., OAS, 2005-; ***office address:*** Organisation of American States, 17th Street & Constitution Avenue, N.W., Washington, DC 20006, USA; ***phone:*** +1 202 458 3000; ***fax:*** +1 202 458 3967; ***URL:*** http://www.oas.org.

IQBAL CHAUDHARY, Ahsan; Minister of Planning and Development, Government of Pakistan; ***born:*** 1958; ***political career:*** Mem., National Assembly; Minister of Education, 2009; Dep.Sec. Gen., PML-N; Minister for Planning & Development, 2009-; ***office address:*** National Assembly, Parliament House, Islamabad, Pakistan; ***URL:*** http://www.na.gov.pk/.

IRRANCA-DAVIES, Huw; Member of Parliament for Ogmore, House of Commons; ***born:*** 22 January 1963, Gower; ***s:*** 3; ***languages:*** English, Welsh; ***education:*** Crewe and Alsager Coll.; Swansea Inst. of HE, M.Sc.; ***party:*** Labour; ***political career:*** MP, Ogmore, 2002-; Parly. Under Sec. of State , Dept. of Work and Pensions, 2007-08; Parly. Under Sec. Dept. for Environment, Food and Rural Affairs, Oct. 2008-May 2010; Shadow Minister for Environment, Food and Rural Affairs, May-Sept. 2010-; Shadow Minister, Energy and Climate Change, Oct. 2010-11, Shadow Minister, Environment, Food and Rural Affairs, 2011-; ***interests:*** Northern Ireland, Middle East, EU, law and order; ***memberships:*** Fabian Soc.; Co-operative Party; Inst. of Leisure and Amenity Management (MILAM); ***professional career:*** Sr. Lecturer, Swansea Inst. of HE; ***committees:*** Former: Proceedures Select Cttee.; PLP, Northern Ireland; Foreign Affairs; Home Affairs; Welsh Grand Cttee. ; ***clubs:*** Patron, Maesteg Celtic Cricket Club; Pres., Ogmore Vale Male Voice Choir; Vice-Pres., British Resorts Assn.; ***recreations:*** family activities, hill-walking, cycling, motorcycling, reading, biographies and historical fiction; ***office address:*** House of Commons, London, SW1A 0PQ, United Kingdom; ***phone:*** +44 (0)20 7219 4027; ***fax:*** +44 (0)20 7219 0134; ***URL:*** http://www.huwirranca-davies.org.uk.

ISAKSON, Johnny; American, Senator for Georgia, US Senate; ***education:*** Univ. of Georgia, BBA, 1966; ***political career:*** State Rep. then State Senator, Georgia, 1976-96; Congressman, Sixth District Georgia, US House of Representatives, 1999-2004; US Senate, 2004-; ***committees:*** US Senate Cttee. on Finance, 2013-; ***office address:*** US Senate, 120 Russell Senate Office Building, Washington, DC 20510, USA; ***phone:*** +1 202 224 3643; ***e-mail:*** isakson.senate.gov/contact.cfm; ***URL:*** http://www.isakson.senate.gov/public/.

ISARESCU, Mugur Constantin; Romanian, Governor, National Bank of Romania; ***born:*** 1 August 1949, Dragasani, Vâlcea County, Romania; ***parents:*** Constantin Isarescu and Aritina Isarescu; ***married:*** Dina Elena , 1975; ***children:*** Ileana-Lacramioara, Costin-Mugur; ***public role of spouse:*** Professor of physics and chemistry; ***languages:*** English, French; ***education:*** Acad. for Economic Studies, Bucharest, 1971, Ph.D, Econs.,1989; ***political career:*** Prime Minister, 1999-2000; ***memberships:*** Pres., Economic, Law and Sociological Sciences Section, Romanian Academy, 2006; Trilateral Cmn.; ***professional career:*** Sr. Fellow and Head of Dept., Inst. for World Economy, Bucharest; Prof. of Int. Finances at Timisoara Univ.; Visiting Prof. with main academic bodies in Romania; Sec. for Economic and Monetary Affairs, Romanian Embassy, Washington D.C., 1990; Govr., Nat. Bank of Romania, Sept. 1990-; ***honours and awards:*** Grand Cross of the Star of Romania, 2000; Grand Cross of the Southern Cross, Brazil, 2000; Grand Officer of the Industrial and Commercial Merit, Romania, 2007; The Order of Saints Constantin and Elena, May 2009, awarded by the Patriarch of the Romanian Orthodox Church; ***publications:*** Author, co-author of 27 books and 15 working papers; ***recreations:*** History, banking and architectural history, vine growing and winemaking, chess, fishing; ***office address:*** National Bank of Romania, 25 Lipscani St, 70421 Bucharest 3, Romania; ***phone:*** +40 1 6130410; ***fax:*** +40 1 3123831; ***URL:*** http://www.bnro.ro.

ISHIHARA, Nobuteru; Minister of the Environment, Japanese Government; ***born:*** 1957; ***education:*** Faculty of Letters, Keio Univ., 1987 ; ***political career:*** House of Representatives, 1990-; Minister of State (Administrative Reform, Regulatory Reform), 2001-02; Minister of Land, Infrastructure and Transport, 2003-05; Minister of the Environment, Minister of State for the Corporation in Nuclear Emergency Preparedness, 2012-; ***professional career:*** Nippon Television Network Corporation ; ***office address:*** Ministry of the Environment, 5 Godochosha, 1-2-2 Kasumigaseki, Chiyoda-ku, Tokyo 100, Japan; ***phone:*** +81 (0)3 3581 3351; ***URL:*** http://www.env.go.jp.

ISSA, Darrell; Congressman, California 49th District, US House of Representatives; ***party:*** Republican Party; ***political career:*** Congressman, California 49th District, US House of Representatives 2000-; ***committees:*** Oversight and Government Reform, Chairman, Judiciary; ***office address:*** House of Representatives, Washington, DC 20515, USA; ***phone:*** +1 202 224 3121.

ISSOUFOU, Mahamadou; President, Republic of Niger; ***born:*** 1952; ***political career:*** Leader, Social Democratic Party; President, Republic of Niger, 2011-; ***office address:*** Office of the President, BP 550, Niamey, Niger; ***URL:*** http://www.presidence.ne.

ITURRIA, Isabel; Minister of Health, Government of Venezuela; ***education:*** Univ. Central de Venezuela, medicine, cardiology; public helath; ***political career:*** Minister of Health, 2013-; ***professional career:*** Hospital Cardiologico Infantil Latinoamericano; ***office address:*** Ministry of Health, Edificio Sur, Piso 9, Centro Simón Bolívar, Caracas 1010, Venezuela; ***URL:*** http://www.msds.gov.ve/.

IVANISHVILI, Bidzina; Prime Minister, Government of Georgia; ***born:*** February 1956; ***party:*** Georgian Dream; ***political career:*** Prime Minnister, Oct, 2012-; ***professional career:*** Businessman; ***office address:*** Office of the Prime Minister, Ingorovka Street 7, Tbilisi 380018, Georgia; ***phone:*** +995 (8)32 935907; ***URL:*** http://www.government.gov.ge/eng.

IVANOV, President Gjorge; President, Government of Macedonia; ***born:*** 1960, Valandovo, Macedonia; ***party:*** Internal Macedonian Revolutionary Organisation - Democratic Party for Macedonian National Unity (VMRO-DPMNE); ***political career:*** President of Macedonia, 2009-; ***professional career:*** Professor of Political Science, Sts. Cyril and Methodius Univ., Skopje, to 2009; ***office address:*** Office of the President, Blvd. Ilinden bb, 1000 Skopje, Macedonia; ***phone:*** +389 2 3118 022 / 3115 455; ***fax:*** +389 2 3112 561 / 3115 285; ***URL:*** http://www.gov.mk/.

IYAMBO, Nicky, MA, MD; Namibian, Minister of Veterans Affairs, Namibian Government; ***born:*** 1936; ***education:*** Döbra Training College, Windhoek; Univ. of Helsinki, Finland; ***political career:*** Joined SWAPO; First Secy., SWAPO, Katutura 1960-64; Official Representative, SWAPO, Finland 1966; Secy. of Education and Culture (SWAPO) 1976-78; Liaison Officer, SWAPO's first Leadership Movement 1989-90; Min. of Health and Social Services 1990-98; Minister for Regional and Local Government and Housing, 1998-2002; Minister for Mines and Energy, 2002-04; Minister of Agriculture, Water and Forestry, 2004-08; Minister of Safety and Security, 2008-10; Minister of Education, 2010-12; Minister of Veterans Affairs, 2012-; ***professional career:*** Postmaster, Katutura Post Office, Windhoek 1963; announcer, Tanzania Broadcasting Corporation; ***committees:*** Mem., Central Cttee., SWAPO 1976-; ***office address:*** National Assembly, Parliament Buildings, Private Bag 13323, Windhoek, Namibia; ***phone:*** +264 61 288 9111.

IZETBEGOVIC, Bakir; President, Government of Bosnia and Herzegovina; ***born:*** June 1956; ***parents:*** Alija Izetbegovic; ***education:*** Univ. of Sarajevo, 1981; ***party:*** Party of Democratic Action; ***political career:*** Mem. Parliament of Bosnia and Herzegovina, 2006-10; Bosniak member, Presidency of Bosnia and Herzegovina, Nov. 2010-; ***professional career:*** Architect; ***office address:*** Office of the President, Musala 5, 71000 Sarajevo, Bosnia and Herzegovina; ***phone:*** +387 3366 4941; ***URL:*** http://www.predsjednistvohih.ba.

J

JAAFAR, Jasim Mohammed; Minister of Youth and Sport, Transitional Government of Iraq; ***political career:*** Minister of Housing and Construction, Transit. Gov. of Iraq, 2005; Minister of Youth and Sport, 2005-; ***office address:*** Ministry of Youth and Sport, Baghdad International Zone Convention Centre, Baghdad, Iraq.

JAASKINEN, Niilo; Advocate General, Court of Justice of the European Union; ***born:*** 1958; ***education:*** Univ. of Helsinki, Law, 1980, doctorate, 2008; ***professional career:*** Lecturer, Univ. of Helsinki, 1980-86; Legal Sec. & Acting Judge, District Court, Rovaniemi, 1983-84; Legal Adviser, European Law Section, Ministry of Justice, then Head, 1990-95; Legal Adviser, MFA, 1989-90; Adviser, Grand Cttee., Finnish Parliament, 1995-2000; Acting Judge, Supreme Administratice Court, 2000-02, Judge, 2003-09; Advocate Gen., Court of Justice, 2009-; ***office address:*** Court of Justice of the European Union, Rue du Fort Niedergrunewald, L-2925, Luxembourg.

JABLONER, Dr Clemens; President, Administrative Court, Austria; ***professional career:*** Vice Pres. of the Verwaltungsgerichtshof (Administrative Court),1991-93; Pres., Verwaltungsgerichtshof, April 1993-; ***office address:*** Verwaltungsgerichtshof, Judenplatz 11, Vienna I, Austria.

JACKSON, Glenda, CBE; British, Member of Parliament for Hampstead and Kilburn, House of Commons; ***born:*** 9 May 1936; ***education:*** RADA; ***party:*** Labour Party, 1978-; ***political career:*** MP, Hampstead and Highgate, 1992-10, Hampstead and Kilburn, 2010-; Parly. Under-Sec. of State, Dept. of Transport, 1997-99 (resigned); ***interests:*** aid for the developing world; ***professional career:*** Actress; ***committees:*** Work and Pensions, 2010-; ***honours and awards:*** various awards for acting, including an Oscar Acadamy Award for 'Women in Love', 1971; ***office address:*** House of Commons, London, SW1A 0AA, United Kingdom; ***phone:*** +44 (0)20 7219 3000; ***e-mail:*** hcinfo@parliament.uk.

JACKSON, Ambassador Jeanine; Ambassador of the US to Malawi, US Embassy; ***professional career:*** retired Colonel of the US Army Reserve; career diplomat: postings in Switzerland, Nigeria, Saudi Arabia, Hong Kong, Kenya and Afghanistan. Most recently: Minster Counselor for Management, US Embassy, Baghdad, 2010-12; Ambassador to Malawi, 2012-; ***office address:*** Embassy of the US, PO Box 30016, Lilongwe 3, Malawi.

JACKSON, Stewart; MP for Peterborough, House of Commons; ***party:*** Conservative; ***political career:*** Local Councillor, for Ealing; MP for Peterborough, 2005-; ***committees:*** Regulatory Reform, 2005-10; Health, 2006-07; Public Accounts, 2012-; ***office address:*** House of Commons, London, SW1P 0AA, United Kingdom; ***phone:*** +44 (0)20 7219 3000.

JACOBS, Marie-Josée; Luxembourgeois, Minister of Family, Integration, Co-operation and Humanitarian Action, Luxembourg Government; ***born:*** 1950, Marnach, Luxembourg; ***languages:*** French, English, German; ***education:*** Saint-Anne Sch., Ettelbruck, Luxembourg; Diploma in Nursing, 1969; Diploma in Nursing-Anaesthesiology, 1973; ***party:*** Christian Union, LCGB; ***political career:*** Mem., northern region, Christian Socialist Party, PCS, 1967; Pres., Christian Social Women; Pres., PCS northern region; Vice-Pres., PCS, national level; Deputy of the northern district, PCS, 1984, re-elected, 1989, 1994; Mem., City Council of Luxembourg City, 1987; Minister of Agriculture, Viticulture and Rural Development, Minister Delegate with Cultural Affairs, 1992-1995; Minister of Family, Minister for the Advancement of Women, Minister for the Handicapped and the Disabled, 1995-99; Minister of Family Affairs, Social Solidarity and Youth, Women, 1999-2004; Minister of Family, Integration & Equal Opportunities, 2004-09; Minister of Family Affairs and Integration, Minister of Co-operation and Humanitarian Action, 2009-; ***committees:*** Pres., Private Employees Section, LCGB, 1980-92; Vice-Pres., LCGB, 1981-92; ***office address:*** Ministry of the Family, 12-14 Avenue Emile Reuter, Luxembourg 2919, Luxembourg; ***fax:*** +352 478 6571.

JACOBSON, H.E. David C.; Ambassador, US Embassy in Canada; ***education:*** Johns Hopkins Univ., B.A.; Georgetown Univ. Law Center, J.D. ; ***professional career:*** Pntr., law firm Sonnenschein, Nath & Rosenthal LLP, 30 years; founder, AtomWorks (fostering nanotechnology in the Midwest); Special Assist. to the Pres., Presidential Personnel; Amb. to Canada, 2009-; ***office address:*** US Embassy, 490 Sussex Drive, Ottawa, Ontario K1N 1G8, Canada; ***phone:*** +1 613 688 5200; ***URL:*** http://canada.usembassy.gov.

JACOBSON, H.E. Tracey Ann; Ambassador, American Embassy in Kosovo; ***education:*** BA, John Hopkins Univ.; MA, John Hopkins Univ. School of Advanced International Studies; ***professional career:*** Foreign Service; most recently, Dep. Chief of Mission, US Embassy in Riga, Latvia, 2000-03; Amb. to Turkmenistan, 2003-06; Amb. to Tajikistan, 2006-09; Amb. to Kosovo, 2012-; ***office address:*** American Embassy, Arberia/Dragodan, Nazim Hikmet 30, Pristina, Kosovo; ***phone:*** +381 38 59 59 3000; ***fax:*** +381 38 549 890; ***e-mail:*** PaPristina@state.gov; ***URL:*** http://pristina.usembassy.gov.

JAGLAND, Thorbjørn; Norwegian, Secretary General, Council of Europe; ***born:*** 5 November 1950, Drammen, Norway; ***married:*** Hanne Grotjord Jagland; ***education:*** Univ. degree, econ, 1975; ***party:*** Labour Party; ***political career:*** Exec. Sec., Norwegian Labour Youth League, Buskerud County, 1973-76; Labour Party Mem., Buskerud County Cncl., 1975-79; Exec. Sec., Norwegian Labour Youth League, 1977-81; Project and Planning Officer, Norwegian Lab. Party, 1981-86; Acting Sec. General, Norwegian Lab. Party, 1986-87; Party Sec., Norwegian Labour Party, 1987-92, Chmn., Norwegian Labour Party, 1992-; Mem., of the Storting, 1996-97; Prime Minister, 1999-2001; Chmn., Labour Party parly. gp., 1996-7; Minister of Foreign Affairs, 2001-2005; President of the Storting, 1992-2002; ***professional career:*** Secretary General, Council of Europe, 2009-; ***committees:*** Chmn., Int. Cttee. Norwegian Lab. Party, 1986-; Mem., Standing Cttee. on Foreign Affairs, 1993-2000, Chmn., 2000-; Chmn., Middle-East Cttee., Socialist Int., 2000-; Vice-Pres., Socialist Int., and Chmn., Middle East Cttee. of the Socialist Int., 1992-2002; Mem., Sharm-el-Sheikh Fact Finding Ctte., 1999-2000; Chmn., Nobel Peace Prize Cttee.; ***publications:*** several articles on defence, security and disarmament issues; Før det blir for sent (Before Too Late), co-author, 1982; Min europeiske drøm (My European Dream), 1990; New Solidarity, 1993; Brev (Letters), 1995; ***office address:*** Council of Europe, Avenue de l'Europe, 67075 Strasbourg Cedex, France; ***phone:*** +33 (0)3 88 41 20 33; ***e-mail:*** private.office@coe.int; ***URL:*** http://www.coe.int.

JAHJAGA, Atifete; President, Government of Kosovo; ***born:*** April 20 1975 , Rashkoc - Gjakova ; ***languages:*** Albanian, English, Serbian; ***education:*** Faculty of Law, Univ. of Prishtina, 2000; Postgraduate certification programme, Police Management and Penal Law, Univ. of Leicester, UK, 2006-07; Postgraduate Certification in Crime Science, Univ. of Virginia, USA, 2007; ***political career:*** President of Kosovo, Apr. 2011-; ***professional career:*** Dep. Gen. Dir. of the Police of Kosovo, 2009-11; ***office address:*** Office of the President, Mother Theresa Street, 10 000 Prishtina, Kosovo; ***URL:*** http://www.president-ksgov.net/.

JAHNATEK, Lubomir; Minster of Agriculture and Rural Development, Slovak Republic; ***born:*** 1954; ***education:*** Slovak Technical Univ., Bratislava; C.Sc., macro-molecular chemistry; ***political career:*** Minister of Economy, Slovak Republic, -2010; Minister of Agriculture and Rural Development, 2012-; ***professional career:*** Production-Technology, Plastika a.s., 1992-2003; Dir., Duslo, a.s., 2003-05; Head of Field Division, Fac. of Material Sciences and Technology, Slovak Technical Univ., 2005-06; ***office address:*** Ministry of Agriculture and Rural Development, Dobrovicova 12, 81266 Bratislava, Slovak Republic.

JAMES, Rt. Revd. Graham; Bishop of Norwich, Anglican Church; ***born:*** 19 January 1951, Torrington, Devon; ***parents:*** Lionel James and Florence James; ***married:*** Julie James (née Freemantle), 1978; ***children:*** Dominic (M), Rebecca (F); ***public role of spouse:*** State registered nurse; ***education:*** Northampton Grammar Sch., Univ. of Lancaster, Univ. of Oxford, Cuddesdon Theological Coll.; ***political career:*** Mem., House of Lords, 2004-; ***professional career:*** Ordained Deacon, 1975; Priest, 1976, Curate at Church of Christ the Carpenter, Dogsthorpe, Peterborough; Priest in charge, then Team Vicar, Christ the King Church, Digswell, Welwyn Garden City, 1979; Selection Sec. and Sec. for Continuing Ministry in Advisory Council for Church's Ministry, 1983-85; Senior Selection Sec., 1985; Chaplain to Archbishop Runcie and Archbishop Carey, 1987-92; Suffragan Bishop, St. Germans in Diocese of Truro, 1993; Bishop of Norwich, 2000-; ***committees:*** Bd. Mem., Countryside Agency, 2001-06; Chmn., Central Religious Advisory Cttee., BBC, 2004-08; Chair, Ministry Division of Church of England, 2006-; Chair, BBC Standing Conference on Religion and Belief, 2009-; ***trusteeships:*** George Bell Inst., 1996-; ***publications:*** New Soundings, 1997; ***clubs:*** Athenaeum, London, Norfolk; Strangers, Norwich; ***recreations:*** theatre, rugby union; ***office address:*** Bishop's House, Norwich, Norfolk, NR3 1SB, United Kingdom; ***phone:*** +44 (0)1603 629001; ***fax:*** +44 (0)1603 761613; ***e-mail:*** bishop@norwich.anglican.org.

JAMES, Margot; MP for Stourbridge, UK Government; ***party:*** Conservative; ***political career:*** Councillor, Kensington and Chelsea Borough Council 2006-08; MP for Stourbridge, May 2010-; ***committees:*** Business, Innovation and Skills Select Cttee., 2010-; Arms Export Control, 2010-; ***office address:*** House of Commons, London, SW1A 0AA, United Kingdom; ***phone:*** +44 (0)20 7219 3000; ***e-mail:*** margot.james.mp@parliament.uk.

JAMES, Sian; MP for Swansea East, House of Commons; ***born:*** 1959; ***party:*** Labour; ***political career:*** MP for Swansea East, 2005-; ***committees:*** Welsh Affairs, 2005-10; Procedure, 2005-10; Crossrail Bill, 2006-07; Constitutional Affairs/Justice, 2006-11; Administration, 2010-; ***office address:*** House of Commons, London, SW1A 0AA, United Kingdom.

JAMIESON, Cathy; MP for Kilmarnock & Loudon, Scottish Parliament; ***party:*** Labour; ***political career:*** MSP, Carrick, Cumnock and Doon Valley, 1999; Minister for Education and Young People: Minister for Justice, 2003-07; MP, Kilmarnock & Loudoun, May 2010-; Shadow Minister, Treasury, 2011-; ***office address:*** House of Commons, London, SW1A 0AA, United Kingdom.

JAMMEH, H.E. Alhaji Dr Yahya A.J.J.; Gambian, President and Secretary General for Defence and Agriculture, Republic of the Gambia; ***born:*** 25 May 1965, Kanilai Village, Western Division, Gambia; ***married:*** Zineb Yahya Jammeh (née Souma); ***children:*** Miriam Yahya Jammeh (F); ***languages:*** English, French, Wolof; ***education:*** Gambia High Sch., Gen. Cert. of Education, GCSEs, 1983; Military Police Officers, Iola, Mandinka, Basic course (MPOBC), Port McCellan, AB, USA, Dip., military science, 1994; ***party:*** Alliance for Patriotic Reorientation and Construction; ***political career:*** Chmn., Armed Forces Provisional Ruling Cncl., Head of State, 1994; ret'd from Army, 1996; Chmn., CILSS, 1997; President of the Republic of Gambia, 1996-; Elected 1st Vice-Chmn. of the Organisation of the Islamic Conference (OIC) during its 9th Meeting of Heads of State and Govt., Doha, Qatar, 2000; Re-Elected for Second Term as Pres. of the Republic of The Gambia, 2001-; ***professional career:*** joined fmr. Gambia Nat. Gendarmerie, 1984, Private to Sergeant, 1986, Cadet Officer, 1987, Commissioned, 1989; Gambia Nat. Army: Special Intervention Unit, 1984-86; Mobile Gendarmerie Special Guards Unit, 1986-87; Gendarmerie Training Sch., Sch. of Presidential Escort, 1987-89; Promoted to Second Lt., 1989; Special Security officer for Visiting Heads of State of the ECOWAS summit, Kairaba Beach Hotel, 1990; Officer In-Charge of ECOWAS Peace Conference for Liberia, Kairaba Beach Hotel, Aug. 1990; Commanding Officer, Mobile Gendarmerie, 1991; Commanding Officer, Military Police Unit, The Gambia Nat. Gendarmerie, 1991; Commanding Officer of GNA Military Police Yundum Barracks, Gambia Nat. Army, 1991; Promoted to Lt., 1992; Officer in-charge of close protection of Pope John Paul II and entourage, and Officer in-charge of VIP security in State functions inc. Heads of State, Feb. 1992; Special Officer in-charge of close protection of Visiting ECOMOG Field Commander, 1993; Chmn., Armed Forces Provisional Ruling Council and Head of State, 1994; Promoted to the Rank of Captain, 1994; Promoted to the Rank of Colonel, 1996; Retired from the Army, 1996; ***committees:*** Chmn., Inter-States Cttee. for the Control of Drought in the Sahel (CILSS); ***honours and awards:*** Hon. Citizen of the State of Georgia, USA, 1993; Hon. Lt. Col. ADC, Alabama State Military, USA, 1994; Grand Cmdr. of the Order Al-Fatah, Libya, 1995; The Order of Brilliant Jade with Grand Cordon, China, 1996; Pan-African Humanitarian Award, The Pan-African Foundation and The World Cncl., 1997; Hon. Admiral, Alabama State Navy, by the Governor of the State of Alabama, 1998; Grand Order of Bravery, Libya, 1998; Islamic Worldwide Grand Prix, The Cheikhna Cheikh Saad Bouh Foundation of Dakar, Senegal, 1998; Dr. of Civil Laws Degree, St. Mary's Univ. Halifax, Canada, 1999; Decorated with Libya's Highest Honour, The African Medal, 1999; Decorated with Orders of

Jar-Jin

The Distiction of Liberia, 2000; Decorated with the Republic of Senegal's highest insignia- Grand Croix de L'Ordre National du Lion, 2001; Nominated as Int. Honourary Consultant of the Federation of World Peace and Love (FOWPAL), 2001; Hon. Fellow, West African Postgrad. College of Pharmacists, 2002; Multiple Paul Harris Fellow, Rotary Fdtn. of Rotary Int., 2002; Military Order of the Collar, Order of Chivalry of the Cross, Italy, 2002; Necklace of Independence Medal, Qatar, 2002; Pedro Kouri Medal, Inst. of Tropical Medicine, Havana, Cuba, 2002; UNESCO award, 2003; ***recreations:*** tennis, soccer, hunting, reading, correspondence, driving and riding motorcycles, music, films, world events, animal rearing; ***office address:*** Office of the President, State House, Banjul, Gambia.

JARANDI, Othman; Minister of Foreign Affairs, Government of Tunisia; ***political career:*** Minister of Foreign Affairs, 2012-; ***professional career:*** career diplomat with postings in Middle East, Africa, Asia and the USA; Councillor, Perm. Mission of Tunisia at the UN, 1990-94; Perm. Rep. of Tunisia to the UN, 2000-02; Amb. of Tunisia to Rep. of Korea, 2002-05; Amb. of Tunisia to Jordan, 2010-12; ***office address:*** Ministry of Foreign Affairs, Avenue de la Ligue des Etats Arabes, Tunis, Tunisia; ***phone:*** +216 71 847500; ***URL:*** http://www.diplomatie.gov.tn/.

JARASIUNAS, Egidijus; Judge, Court of Justice of the European Union; ***born:*** 1952; ***education:*** Univ. of Vilnius, law; Doctor of Legal Science of Law, Univ. of Lithuania; ***political career:*** mem., Supreme Council, Rep. of Lithuania, 1990-92; Mem., Seimas, 1992-96; ***professional career:*** Judge, Constitutional Court of the Rep. of Lithuania, 1996-2005; Lecturer, Fac. of Law, Mykolas Romeris Univ., 1997-2000, Assoc. Prof., 2000-04, Prof., 2004-, Head of Dept., 2005-07, Dean, 2007-10; Adviser, Lithuanian Constitutional Court, 2006-; Judge, Court of Justice of the European Union, 2010-; ***office address:*** Court of Justice of the European Union, Rue du Fort Niedergrunewald, L-2925, Luxembourg; ***URL:*** http://www.curia.europa.eu.

JARRAUD, Michel; Secretary General, World Meteorological Organisation; ***born:*** 1952; ***memberships:*** Fellow of the American Meteorological Society (USA); mem., Société Météorologique de France; mem., The Royal Meteorological Society (UK); mem., African Meteorological Society; Hon. Mem., Chinese Meteorological Society; Hon. Mem., Cuban Meteorological Society. ; ***professional career:*** Dir., European Centre for Medium-Range Weather Forecasts (ECMWF); Dep. Secretary General, World Meteorological Organisation, Secretary General, Jan. 2004-; ***office address:*** World Meteorological Organisation, PO Box 2300, CH 2111 Geneva 2, Switzerland.

JARVIS, Dan, MP; MP for Barnsley, British Parliament; ***party:*** Labour Party; ***political career:*** MP for Barnsley, March 2011-; Shadow Minister, Culture, Media and Sport, 2011-; ***professional career:*** Former Soldier serving in Afghanistan and Iraq; ***office address:*** House of Commons, London, SW1A 0AA, United Kingdom; ***phone:*** +44 (0)20 7219 3000.

JAVID, Sajid; MP for Bromsgrove, UK Government; ***party:*** Conservative; ***political career:*** MP for Bromsgrove, May 2010-; PPS to Minister of Further Education, Skills and Lifelong Learning, 2010-11; PPS to Chancellor of Exchequer, 2011-12; Economic Secretary, 2012-; ***committees:*** Work and Pensions Select Cttee., 2010; Public Accounts, 2012-; ***office address:*** House of Commons, London, SW1A 0AA, United Kingdom; ***phone:*** +44 (0)20 7219 3000; ***e-mail:*** sajid.javid.mp@parliament.uk.

JAY OF PADDINGTON, Rt. Hon. Baroness Margaret Ann; British, Member, House of Lords; ***born:*** 1939; ***parents:*** Rt. Hon. Baron Callaghan of Cardiff, KG; ***married:*** Prof. Michael W. Adler, 1994; ***s:*** 1; ***d:*** 2; ***education:*** Somerville Coll., Univ. of Oxford, UK, BA, Politics, Philosophy and Economics; ***party:*** Labour Party; ***political career:*** Appointed to the HOL, 1992; Opposition Whip, 1992-95; Principal Opposition Spokesperson on Health, 1995-97; Minister of State for Health, 1997-98; Lord Privy Seal, Minister for Women and Leader of the House of Lords, 1998-2001; ***interests:*** health, communications, international affairs and oversesas development; ***memberships:*** Nat. Union of Journalists (NUJ), UK; ***professional career:*** career with BBC TV, UK; Paddington and North Kensington District Health Auth., 1984-93; Kensington & Chelsea & Westminster Health Auth., 1993; Non-Exec. Dir., British Telecom, 2002-08; Mem, Int'l Advisory Bd., Independent News and Media, 2002-; Sr. Non-Exec. Dir., Independent News and Media, 2002-; ***committees:*** House of Lords Select Cttee. on Medical Ethics, 1993-94; Mem., Cttee. on Standards in Public Life, 2003-05; Mem., Council of Overseas Dev. & Institute, 2007-; Corporate Social Responsibility Cttee., British Telecom, 2008-, Non. Exec. Dir, BT Cttee. for Sustainable and Responsible Business, 2008-; Chair, House of Lords Select Cttee. on the Constitution, 2010-; Chair, Advisory Cttee. Bringing Research to Life, Great Ormond Street Hosp., 2010-; Fellow, Industry and Parliament Trust, 2010-; ***trusteeships:*** Founder and Dir., Nat. AIDS Trust, 1988-92; Help the Aged Reaction Trust and Progress; Chmn., The Overseas Development Institute, 2002-07; ***honours and awards:*** Life Peer, cr. 1992; Hon. Fellow, Somerville Coll., Oxford, 1999; Hon. Fellow, South Bank Univ., 1999; Hon. Fellow, Sunderland Univ., 2002; ***publications:*** How Rich Can We Get?, 1972; Battered - The Story of Child Abuse, 1986 (co-author); ***office address:*** House of Lords, London, SW1A 0AA, United Kingdom; ***phone:*** +44 (0)20 7219 3000; ***fax:*** +44 (0)20 7222 1213.

JAYARATNE, Dissanayake Mudiyanselage; Prime Minister, Government of Sri Lanka; ***born:*** June 1931; ***education:*** Faculty of Arts, Univ. of Peradeniya; ***party:*** Sri Lanka Freedom Party (SLFP); ***political career:*** Minister of Land, Agriculture and Forestry, 1994-2000; Minister of Agriculture, Food and Cooperatives, 2000-01; Minister of Post and Telecommunication and Upcountry Development, 2004-05; Minister of Post and Telecommunication and Rural Economic Development, 2005-07; Minister of Plantation Industries, 2007-10; Prime Minister, Buddha Sasana, Minister of Religious Affairs, 2010-; ***office address:*** Office of the Prime Minister, 58 Sir Ernest de Silva Mawatha, Colombo 07, Sri Lanka; ***phone:*** +94 11 257 5317; ***e-mail:*** primeminister@sltnet.lk; ***URL:*** http://www.gov.lk/pm/office.htm.

JELVED, Marianne, M.Ed.; Danish, Minister of Culture, Danish Government; ***born:*** 5 September 1943, Charlottenlund, Denmark; ***education:*** M.Ed., Danish Lang. and Lit., 1979; ***party:*** Radikale Venstre (RV, Social-Liberal Party); ***political career:*** Local cncl. mem. for the Social Liberal Party, Gundsø, 1982-89; MP, "Folketinget" 1987; Chmn. of Social Liberal MPs, 1988; Minister for Economic Affairs, 1993-2002; Minister for Nordic Cooperation, 1994-2002; Minister of Culture, 2012-; ***memberships:*** Mem. of various bds. in teachers' organisations; ***professional career:*** Teacher, various public schs., 1967-89, Royal Danish Sch. of Educational Studies, 1979-87; Dep. Mayor, 1982-85; ***publications:*** Co-author, Brud - Radikale værdier i en forandret tid, 1994; Author and editor of Danish schoolbooks; ***office address:*** Ministry of Culture, Nybrogade 2, 1015 Copenhagen K, Denmark; ***phone:*** +45 3392 3370; ***fax:*** +45 3392 3370; ***e-mail:*** kum@kum.dk; ***URL:*** http://www.kum.dk.

JENKIN, Hon. Bernard; MP for Harwich and North Essex, House of Commons; ***born:*** 9 April 1959, London; ***parents:*** Rt. Hon. Lord Patrick Jenkin of Roding and Monica Jenkin; ***married:*** Anne Jenkin (née Strutt), 24 September 1988; ***education:*** Highgate Sch.; William Ellis Sch.; Corpus Christi Coll., Cambridge, awarded a Choral Exhibition, Hon. Degree in English Literature; Pres., Cambridge Soc., 1982; ***party:*** Conservative Party; ***political career:*** MP for North Colchester, 1992-97, North Essex, 1997-2010, Harwich & North Essex, 2010-; PPS to Rt. Hon. Michael Forsyth, 1995-97; Opposition Front Bench Spokesman for Constitutional Affairs, 1997; Shadow Minister for Transport, 1998-2001; Shadow Sec. of State for Defence, 2001-03; Shadow Sec., State for the Regions, 2003-05; Shadow Minister for Energy, 2005; ***interests:*** economy, trade financial services, small businesses, EU, foreign affairs, defence; ***professional career:*** PA to Sir Hugh Rossi MP, 1979 and 1983; Governor of Central Foundations Girl's Sch. ILEA, 1985-89; Political Advisor to Rt. Hon. Sir Leon Brittan QC, 1986-88; Mngr., Legal and General Ventures Ltd., 1989-92; previously with 3i & Ford Motor Co.; ***committees:*** Social Security Select Cttee., 1993-97; Defence, 2006-10; Arms Export Controls, 2008-10; Chair, Public Administration, 2010-; Liaison, 2010-; Unopposed Bills (Panel), 2010-; ***recreations:*** sailing, music, DIY, fishing, family; ***office address:*** House of Commons, London, SW1A 0AA, United Kingdom; ***phone:*** +44 (0)20 7219 4029; ***e-mail:*** jenkinb@parliament.uk; ***URL:*** http://www.bernardjenkinmp.com.

JENKIN OF KENNINGTON, Baroness Anne; Member, House of Lords; ***party:*** Consesrvative Party; ***political career:*** Mem., House of Lords, 2011-; ***professional career:*** Charity Work; ***office address:*** House of Lords, London, SW1A 0PW, United Kingdom; ***phone:*** +44 (0)20 7219 3000.

JENKINS, Sir John, LVO; Ambassador, British Embassy in Saudi Arabia; ***professional career:*** career diplomat; British Ambassador to Myanmar,1999-2002; British Consul General, East Jerusalem, 2003-06; Ambassador to Damascus, 2006-07; FCO, Dir., Middle East & North Africa, 2007-09; Amb. to Baghdad, 2009-11; UK, Special Rep. to Libya, 2011; Amb. to Saudi Arabia; ***office address:*** British Embassy, PO Box 94351, Riyadh 11693, Saudi Arabia; ***phone:*** ; ***URL:*** .

JENSEN, Siv; Party Chair, Fremsrittspartiet; ***political career:*** Mem, Oslo City Parliament, 1995-99; Mem., Storting, 1997-; First Dep. Chmn., Progress Party, 1995-2006, Chmn., 2006-; ***office address:*** Fremsrittspartiet, POB 8743, 0184 Oslo 1, Norway; ***phone:*** +47 2241 0769.

JEREMIC, Vuk; President, General Assembly; ***political career:*** Political Adviser; Chmn., Foreign Affairs Cttee., Democratic Party, Serbia. 2004; Senior Foreign Policy Adviser to the President of the Rep. of Serbia, 2004-07; Minister of Foreign Affairs, 20078-12; President, General Assembly, 67th session, Sep. 2012-Sep. 2013; ***professional career:*** finance; ***office address:*** General Assembly, UN,, First Ave. at 46th Street, New York, NY 10017, USA; ***URL:*** http://www.un.org/en/ga.

JEWELL, Sally; Secretary of the Interior, US Government; ***education:*** Univ. of Washington; ***political career:*** Secretary of the Interior, 2013-; ***professional career:*** petroleum engineer; commercial banker; private sector, most recently, Chief Operating Officer, Office of Recreation Equipment, Inc. (REI), 2000-05, CEO, 2005; ***office address:*** Department of the Interior, 1849 C Street, NW, Washington, DC 20240, USA; ***phone:*** +1 202 208 3100; ***URL:*** http://www.doi.gov/.

JHA, Parmananda; Vice President, Government of Nepal; ***political career:*** Vice President, 2008-; ***professional career:*** Supreme Court Judge; ***office address:*** Office of the Vice President, Shital Niwas, Maharajganj, Kathmandu, Nepal.

JIHAD, Abdulla; Minister of Finance and Treasury, Government of Maldives; ***political career:*** MMA Governor; Minister of Finance, 2008-10; Civil Service Commission, 2010-12; Minister of Finance & Treasury, 2012-; ***office address:*** Ministry of Finance, Ameeni Magu, Malé 20121, Maldives; ***phone:*** +960 332 2343; ***fax:*** +960 332 4432; ***URL:*** http://www.finance.gov.mv.

JIMINEZ MAYOR, Juan; President of the Council of Ministers (Prime Minister), Government of Peru; ***political career:*** Deputy Justice Minister, interim government, 2001, 2011; Minister of Justice and Human Rights, 2011-; ***professional career:*** Lawyer; ***office address:*** Office of the President of the Council of Ministers, Avenida 28 de Julio no 878, Miraflores, Lima, Peru; ***URL:*** http://www.pcm.gob.be.

JIM YONG KIM, Dr; President, World Bank; ***born:*** 1959, Seoul, South Korea; ***education:*** Brown Univ., USA, A.B. magna cum laude; Harvard Medical School, MD; Harvard Univ., Ph.D, anthropology; ***professional career:*** physician; co-founder, Partners in Health, 1987; Director, HIV/AIDS Dept., World Health Org; founder, Darmouth Centre for Health Care Delivery Science; Pres., Darmouth College; Pres., World Bank Group, July 2012-; ***office address:*** World Bank, 1818 H Street, NW, Washington, DC 20433, USA; ***URL:*** http://www.worldbank.org.

JINDAL, Governor Bobby; Governor, State of Louisiana, USA; ***education:*** Brown Univ., Louisiana; Rhodes Scholar, Oxford Univ., UK, 1994; ***political career:*** State Sec., Dept. of Health and Hospitals, State of Louisiana; 1996-98; Exec. Dir., National Bipartisan Cmn. on the future of Medicare; Pres., Univ. of Louisiana System, State Govt., 1999-2001; Asst. Sec. for Panning and Public School Evaluation, US Dept. of Health and Human Services, 2001-2004; ran for Gov. of Louisiana, 2003; US Congressman, rep. 1st Dist. of Louisiana, 2004-08, Assistant Majority Whip; Governor of Louisiana, 2008-; ***committees:*** Education and the

BIOGRAPHIES

Workforce; Resources; Homeland Security; ***office address:*** Office of the Governor, Constituent Services, PO Box 94004, Baton Rouge, LA 70804-9004, USA; ***phone:*** +1 225 342 0991; ***fax:*** +1 225 342 7099; ***URL:*** http://www.gov.state.la.us/.

JOHANNESEN, Kaj Leo; Prime Minister, Government of the Faroe Islands; ***born:*** 28 August 1964 ; ***party:*** Unionist Party; ***political career:*** MP, 2002-; Leader of the Unionist Party, 2004-; Prime Minister, Sept. 2008-; ***professional career:*** Shipmaster; Sales manager in the industry of fisheries; Independent Businessman; ***office address:*** Office of the Prime Minister, PO Box 64, FO-110 Torshavn, Faroe Islands; ***e-mail:*** info@tinganes.fo; ***URL:*** http://www.tinganes.fo.

JOHANNS, Mike; American, Senator for Nebraska, US Senate; ***born:*** 18 June 1950, Iowa, USA; ***married:*** Stephanie Johanns; ***public role of spouse:*** former Lanchaser County Cmnr. and fmr. State Senator; currently Vice-Pres., External Relations for Nebraska, Kansas and Missouri, ALLTEL; ***education:*** St. Mary's Coll., Minnesota, BA, 1971; Creighton Univ., Nebraska, JD, 1974; ***party:*** Republican Party; ***political career:*** Lancaster County Cmnr.; Lincoln City Cllr.; Mayor, Lincoln, NE, 1991-98; Governor, State of Nebraska, 1999-2005 ; US Secretary of Agriculture 2005-07; US Senator for Nebraska, 2008; ***interests:*** building state's economy, protecting families, reducing size of govt., ensuring health, safety and success of Nebraska's children ; ***memberships:*** Pres., League of Nebraska Municipalities, 1996; ***professional career:*** Judicial Law Clerk for the Hon. Hale McCown; worked at law firm Cronin & Hannon; Ptnr., Nelson, Johanns, Morris, Holdemann & Titus Law Firm; ***committees:*** fmr. Mem., City/County Common and City/County Jt. Budget Cttee.; US Conference of Mayors' Exec. Cttee.; Chmn., Nat. Governor's Assoc. Cttee. on Economic Dev. and Commerce, 2000-2001; State Govt. Rep., Advisory Cttee. to the Export-Import Bank of the US, 2001: Senate, 2013: Agriculture, Nutrition & Forestry; Appropriations; Banking, Housing and Urban Affairs; Veterans' Affairs; ***honours and awards:*** Job Training Partnership Act Presidential Award, outstanding civic leader category, 1993; ***office address:*** US Senate, Washington DC, USA; ***phone:*** +1 202 224 4224; ***URL:*** http://www.johanns.senate.gov.

JOHANNSSON, Sigurour; Minister of Fisheries and Agriculture, Government of Iceland; ***born:*** 20 April 1962; ***education:*** Royal Veterinary and Agricultural College, Copenhagen, Denmark; ***party:*** Progressive Party; ***political career:*** MP, 2009-; Minister of Fisheries and Agriculture, 2013-; ***professional career:*** Farmer; Veterinarian; ***office address:*** Ministry of Industry and Innovation, Skúlagötu 4, 150 Reykjavík, Iceland; ***phone:*** +354 545 8300; ***fax:*** +354 562 1853; ***e-mail:*** postur@hafro.is; ***URL:*** http://www.stjr.is/sjr.

JOHNS, Vice Admiral Sir Adrian, KCB, CBE; Governor and Commander-in-Chief, Gibraltar; ***political career:*** The Governor and Commander-in-Chief, Gibraltar, 2009-; ***professional career:*** Royal Navy in 1973-; Rear Admiral , 2003; Vice Admiral, 2005; Second Sea Lord, 2005-08; ***office address:*** Office of the Governor, The Convent, Gibraltar; ***phone:*** +350 2004 5440.

JOHNSEN, Sigbjørn; Norwegian, Minister of Finance, Norwegian Government; ***born:*** 1 October 1950; ***married:*** Helle Johnsen (née Laier); ***languages:*** English, German; ***education:*** Norwegian Sch. of Management, evening course; ***party:*** Labour; ***political career:*** MP, 1974-90; Vice-Chmn., Norwegian Labour League of Youth, 1975-77; Dep. Chmn., Equal Status Cncl., 1976-83; Del., Cncl. of Europe's Parly. Assy., 1985; Dep. Rep., Nat. Assy. for Labour Hedmark, 1973-76, Perm. Mem., 1976-77, el. Rep., 1977-97; Min. of Finance, 1990-96, 2009-; ***interests:*** economic policy, general; ***professional career:*** Bank Cashier; Dir. of Studies; Accountant; County Governor of Hedmark, 1997-; ***committees:*** Parly. Standing Cttee. on Justice, 1976-77; Standing Cttee. on Local Govt. and Environment, 1977-80; Standing Cttee. of Finance, 1981-90; Standing Cttee. on Defence, 1996-97; Standing Cttee. of Scrutiny and the Constitution, 1997; ***recreations:*** skiing, sports; ***office address:*** Ministry of Finance, Akersgaten 42, PB 8008 Dep, 0030 Oslo, Norway; ***phone:*** +47 2224 9090; ***fax:*** +47 2224 9505; ***URL:*** http://www.odin.dep.no/fin.

JOHNSON, Alan; British, Member of Parliament, House of Commons; ***born:*** May 1950; ***party:*** Labour Party; ***political career:*** Mem., Trade and Industry Select Cttee., 1997; PPS to the Financial Sec. of the Treasury, 1997; MP for Kingston upon Hull West and Hessle, 1997-; PPS to Paymaster General, 1998-99; Parly.-under-Sec., DTI, 1999-01; Minister of State, DTI, 2001-03; Minister of State, DFES, 2003-04; Sec.of State for Work and Pensions, 2004-05; Sec. of State for Trade and Industry, May 2005-May 2006; Sec. of State for Education and Skills, May 2006-June 2007; Sec. of State for Health, June 2007-June 2009; Sec. of State for Home Affairs, June 2009-May 2010; Shadow Home Secretary, May 2010-Sept. 2010; Shadow Chancellor of the Exchequer, Oct. 2010-11; ***interests:*** trade and industry, electoral reform, education, employment law, the Post Office, Northern Ireland; ***professional career:*** Postman; Mem., Branch Cttee., Union of Communication Workers (UCW), Slough, 1973, Chmn., 1976, elected to Nat. Exec. Cncl., 1981, full-time Officer, 1987, elected to Gen.-Sec., 1992, Joint Gen. Sec., CWV, 1995; ***office address:*** House of Commons, London, SW1A 0AA, United Kingdom; ***phone:*** +44 (0)20 7270 3000; ***e-mail:*** johnsona@parliament.uk; ***URL:*** http://www.alanjohnson.org.uk.

JOHNSON, Boris; Mayor of London, Greater London Authority; ***education:*** Eton College; Balliol College, BA, Oxford Univ.; ***party:*** Conservative Party; ***political career:*** MP, Henley, June 2001-08; Shadow Minister for the Arts, 2004; Shadow Minister for Higher Education, 2005-08; Mayor of London, May 2008-; ***professional career:*** Editor, Spectator, 1999-2005; ***office address:*** Office of the Mayor, City Hall, Queens Walk, London, SE1 2AA, United Kingdom; ***phone:*** +44 (0)20 7983 4000; ***URL:*** http://www.london.gov.uk.

JOHNSON, Diana; MP for Kingston upon Hull North, House of Commons; ***born:*** 25 July 1966; ***parents:*** Eric Johnson (Dec'd) and Ruth Johnson ; ***education:*** LL.B, Queen Mary Col., Univ. of London, 1988; ***party:*** Labour Party; ***political career:*** Councillor, London Borough of Tower Hamlets, 1994-2002; mem., Greater London Assembly, 2003-04; MP for Hull North, 2005-10; PPS to Stephen Timms MP, Nov. 2005-07; Govt. Assistant Whip, 2007-09; Parly. under Sec., Dept. for Children, Schools and Families, 2009-10; MP for Kingston upon Hull North, 2010-; Shadow Minister for Health, 2010; Shadow Minister, Home Affairs, Oct. 2010-11; Crime and Security, 2011-; ***interests:*** employment rights, health, education, animal welfare; ***memberships:*** Co-operative Party; Labour Women's Network; TGWU; UNISON; Fawcett Society 2000; Amnesty Int.; Fabian Society; ***professional career:*** Barrister; Paralegal, Herbert Smith Solicitors, 1990; Volunteer/locum lawyer, Tower Hamlets Law Centre, 1991-94; Family Lawyer, McCormacks Solicitors, 1994-95; Legal visiting mem. of the Mental Health Act Commission, 1995-98; Employment, immigration and education lawyer, North Lewisham Law Centre, 1995-; Mem., Metropolitan Police Authority, 2003-04; Non-Exec. Dir., Newham Healthcare Trust, 1998-2001; Employment lawyer, Paddington Law Centre, 1999-2002; Non-Exec. Dir., Tower Hamlets PCT, 2001-05; Nat. Officer, FDA Trade Union, 2002-03; ***committees:*** Public Accounts, 2005; ***recreations:*** theatre, cinema, walking dog; ***office address:*** House of Commons, London, SW1A 0AA, United Kingdom; ***phone:*** +44 (0)20 7219 5647; ***fax:*** +44 (0)20 7219 0959; ***e-mail:*** johnsond@parliament.uk; ***URL:*** http://www.dianajohnson.co.uk.

JOHNSON, Gareth; MP for Dartford, UK Government; ***party:*** Conservative; ***political career:*** Councillor, London Borough of Bexley Council, 1998-2002; MP for Dartford, May 2010-; ***committees:*** Science and Technology, 2012-; ***office address:*** House of Commons, London, SW1A 0AA, United Kingdom; ***phone:*** +44 (0)20 7219 3000; ***e-mail:*** gareth.johnson.mp@parliament.uk.

JOHNSON, Janis G.; Senator for Manitoba, Canadian Senate; ***born:*** 27 April 1946, Winnipeg, Manitoba; ***parents:*** Honourable George Johnson MD and Doris Johnson (née Blondal); ***children:*** Stefan (M); ***education:*** Univ. College, Univ. of Manitoba, BA, Political Science, 1968; ***political career:*** Senator for MB, Canadian Govt., 1990-2008; ***professional career:*** Political strategist, public affairs consultant and writer; ***committees:*** Standing Cttee. on Transport and Communications; ***honours and awards:*** Velia Stern Award, outstanding contribution to student affairs, 1968; Queen's Jubilee Medal, 1977; Professional Women's Award, 1985; Canada 125 medal, 1992; Nat. Volunteer Award, Canadian Special Olympics, 1995; Knight of the Order of the Falcon, Govt. of Iceland, 2000; Queen's Jubilee Medal, 2002; ***clubs:*** Albany Club, Canadian Club, Icelandic Canadian Club, YM-YWCA, Gimli Summer Club; ***recreations:*** art, film, fitness, fly-fishing and travel; ***office address:*** Room 335, East Block, Senate of Canada, Ottawa, Ontario, KIA 0A4, Canada; ***phone:*** +1 613 943 1430; ***fax:*** +1 613 992 5029.

JOHNSON, Joseph; MP for Orpington, UK Government; ***born:*** 1971; ***parents:*** Stanley Johnson MEP and Charlotte Johnson Wahl; ***languages:*** French; ***education:*** Balliol College, Oxford; Université Libre de Bruxelles; MBA, INSEAD, 2000; ***party:*** Conservative; ***political career:*** MP for Orpington, May 2010-; ***professional career:*** Financial Times, with postings in Paris and New Delhi; ***office address:*** House of Commons, London, SW1A 0AA, United Kingdom; ***phone:*** +44 (0)20 7219 3000; ***URL:*** http://www.jo-johnson.com.

JOHNSON, Ron; Senator for Wisconsin, US Senate; ***education:*** Univ. of Wisconsin-Maidson; Harvard Univ.; ***political career:*** Mem., US Senate, 1988-; ***interests:*** children's issues; farming; anti-crime; senior citizens; ***professional career:*** Kohl's grocery and department stores; bought Milwaukee Bucks, 1985; ***committees:*** Budget; Commerce, Science & Transportation; Foreign Relations; Homeland Security & Governmental Affairs; Small Business & Entrepreneurship; ***office address:*** United States Senate, 386 Russell Senate Office Building, Washington DC 20510, USA; ***phone:*** +1 202 224 5323; ***URL:*** http://www.ronjohnson.senate.gov.

JOHNSON, Tim; American, Senator for South Dakota, US Senate; ***born:*** 28 December 1946, Canton, South Dakota, USA; ***parents:*** Van Johnson and Ruth Johnson; ***married:*** Barbara Johnson (née Brooks); ***children:*** Brooks (M), Brendan (M), Kelsey (F); ***education:*** Univ. of South Dakota, Phi Beta Kappa academic hons., MA, Political Science, LL.B; ***party:*** Democrat; ***political career:*** South Dakota House of Representatives, 1978-82; State Senate, 1982-86; US House of Representatives, 1986-1996; US Senator for South Dakota, 1996-; ***professional career:*** Budget Analyst, Michigan State Senate Appropriations Cttee.; Private Law Practice, Vermillion, 1975; ***committees:*** Appropriations; Banking, Housing and Urban Affairs Cttee.; Energy and Natural Resources Cttee.; Indian Affairs; ***honours and awards:*** Outstanding Citizen Award, Vermillion Jaycees, 1979; Billie Sutton Award for Legislative Achievement, South Dakota Democratic Party, 1983; Presidential Export Cncl., 1999; ***recreations:*** cycling, tennis; ***office address:*** US Senate, 136 Hart Senate Office Building, Washington DC 20510, USA; ***phone:*** +1 202 224 5842; ***e-mail:*** tim@johnson.senate.gov; ***URL:*** http://www.johnson.senate.gov.

JOHNSON SIRLEAF, Ellen; President of Liberia; ***born:*** October 1938, Monrovia, Liberia; ***education:*** College of West Africa, Monrovia, Accountancy and Economics; Univ. of Colorado, USA; Harvard Univ, USA, MA in Public Administration; ***political career:*** Finance Minister, 1972-73 under President William Tolbert; fled country when President Tolbert was overthrown; Imprisoned in the 1980s for criticising the military regime of Samuel Doe; initially a supporter of coup led by Charles Taylor, 1989-90 but then became an opponent and stood against Taylor in the 1997 presidential election, coming second to Taylor and again went into exile in Kenya following charges of treason; President of Liberia, 2005-; ***professional career:*** Dir.Citibank, Nairobi 1983-85 (while in exile in Kenya); World Bank; Africa Dir. at the UN Development Programme; Head, Governance Reform Commission, 2003-05; ***office address:*** Office of the President, Executive Mansion, Capitol Hill, PO Box 9001, Monrovia, Liberia; ***e-mail:*** emansion@liberia.net; ***URL:*** http://www.executive-mansion.gov.lr.

JOHNSSON, Anders B.; Swedish, Secretary-General, Inter-Parliamentary Union; ***born:*** 30 November 1948, Lund, Sweden; ***married:*** Kyra Johnsson (née Nuñez de León), 1978; ***children:*** 3; ***languages:*** English, French, Spanish; ***education:*** Faculty of Law, Univ. of Lund, Sweden, BA, Law, 1972; Coll. of Europe, Bruges, Belgium, Certificate of Advanced European Studies, 1973; Faculty of Econs., Univ. of Lund, Sweden, Certificate in Int. Econs., 1974; Faculty of Law, New York Univ., USA, MA, Comparative Jurisprudence, 1975; ***professional career:*** Law Clerk, district Court of Justice, Lund, 1973-74; Asst. Editor, El Sol de Chiapas, Tuxtia Gutierrez, Mexico, 1980-82; UN, 1975-80, 1982-91: Fund-raising officer, UN High Cmn. for refugees, Switzerland; acting Dep. Representative, Khartoum, Sudan, 1976; Head of the UNHCR, Vietnam, 1977-80; UNHCR co-ordinator for Western Honduras, 1982; Asst. Chief of Mission, Islamabad, Pakistan, with responsibility for refugee protection issues, 1983-85; Sr. Legal Advisor in the High Cmnr.'s Office in Geneva, Switzerland, and later Chief of the Gen. Legal Advice Section; Asst. Sec.-Gen., Inter-Parly. Union, 1991-, Dep. Sec.-Gen., 1994; Legal Counsellor; Sec.-Gen., IPU, 1998- ; ***publications:*** several articles published in the International Journal of Refugee Law, including 'The international protection of women refugees' and 'Obligations of refugees'; 'The protection of refugee children and the Convention of the Rights of the Child', paper prepared for the United Nations Centre for Human Rights; 'Critical refugee protection issues in the 1990s', paper prepared for the Fletcher Sch. of Law and Diplomacy (USA); 'The Inter-Parliamentary Union and the Promotion of Representative Institutions', article published in the Journal of Legislative Studies; 'Human rights mechanisms and international parliamentary institutions', article prepared for publication in book edited by the Raoul Wallenberg Inst.; *office address:* Inter-Parliamentary Union, Chemin du Pommier 5, 1218 Grand-Saconnex, Switzerland; *URL:* http://www.ipu.org.

JOHNSTON, H.E. the Rt. Hon. David; Governor General, Government of Canada; *born:* Sudbury, Ontario; *married:* Sharon Johnston; *d:* 5; *education:* LLB, Queen's Univ. 1966; LLB, Univ. of Cambridge, 1965; AB, Harvard Univ., 1963; *political career:* Governor General, of Canada, Oct. 1, 2010-; *professional career:* Assist. Prof., Faculty of Law, Queen's Univ., 1966-68; Law Faculty, Univ. of Toronto, 1968; Dean, Faculty of Law, Univ. of Western Ontario, 197479 In 1979, Principal and vice-chancellor, McGill Univ., 1979; McGill Faculty of Law, full-time prof., 1994; Pres., Univ. of Waterloo. 1999; *office address:* Governor General's Office, Rideau Hall, 1 Sussex Drive, Ottawa. ON, K1A OA1, Canada; *URL:* http://www.gg.ca.

JOHNSTON, H.E. Paul; Ambassador, British Embassy in Sweden; *professional career:* Director, Int. Security for the FCO, 2008-11; Amb. to Sweden. 2011-; *office address:* British Embassy, Skarpögatan 6-8, POB 27819, 115 93 Stockholm, Sweden; *phone:* +46 (0)8 671 3000; *fax:* +46 (0)8 662 9989; *URL:* http://ukinsweden.fco.gov.uk/en.

JOK, John Luk; Minister of Justice, Government of South Sudan; *education:* law; LL.B LL.M, London; *political career:* Minister for Culture, Youth & Sports, Energy & Mining; Dep. rapporteur, National Petroleum Commission; mem., DDR Council; mem., Technical Cttee. which drafted National Constitution of Sudan and the interim Constitution of Southern Sudan; Minister of Justice, 2011-; *professional career:* Chmn. of the Board, Nile Petroleum Corp.; *office address:* Ministry of Justice, Airport Road, Opposite Juba Hotel, Central Equatoria, South Sudan; *URL:* http://www.mojss.org/.

JOLLY, Baroness Judith; Member, House of Lords; *party:* Liberal Democrat Party; *political career:* Chmn., Exec. Cttee. of Liberal Democrats in Devon and Cornwall; Mem., House of Lords, 2010-; *office address:* House of Lords, London, SW1A 0PW, United Kingdom; *phone:* +44 (0)20 7219 3000.

JONATHAN, H.E. Dr Goodluck; President, Government of Nigeria; *born:* 1957, Bayelsa, Nigeria; *education:* B.Sc., in Zoology, M.Sc. in Hydrobiology and Fisheries biology, Ph.D. in Zoology, Univ. of Port Harcourt; *political career:* Governor of Bayelsa State, 2005-07; Vice Pres., 2007-10; President, Chair of the Nat. Economic Council, National Council on Privatization, Nat. Economic Revitalization Cttee. and Nat. Planning Commission, Minister of Power, 2010-; *professional career:* Education Inspector; Lecturer; Environmental Protection Officer ; *office address:* Office of the President, Federal Secretariat Phase II, Shelu Shagari Way, Abuja, Nigeria; *phone:* +234 9 234 1010; *URL:* http://www.nopa.net.

JONES, Alun Ffred, AC, AM; Constituency Member for Caernarfon, National Assembly for Wales; *born:* 29 October 1949, Llanelli, Wales; *parents:* Gerallt Jones and Elizabeth Jane; *married:* Mairan Alwen (née Roberts), 1981 ((dec.)); *children:* Dafydd Gerallt (M), Ifan Alun (M), Gwenllian Haf (F); *languages:* Welsh, English; *education:* Univ. of Wales Coll., Bangor, (Hons); *party:* Plaid Cymru - The Party of Wales; *political career:* Cllr. for Penygroes in the Nantlle Valley & Leader, Gwynedd Cncl., 1996-2003; National Assembly of Wales mem., May 2003-; Minister for Heritage, 2008; *interests:* community development, language planning, economic development; *professional career:* Welsh teacher in Mold; journalist, HTV, Cardiff; director/producer, Nant Films; *committees:* Chair, Environmental Com, 2005-06; *recreations:* cycling, sport, theatre, gardening, books; *office address:* 8 Castle Street, Caernarfon, Gwynedd, LL55 1NS, United Kingdom; *phone:* +44 (0)1286 672076; *e-mail:* alunffred.jones@wales.gov.uk.

JONES, Andrew; MP for Harrogate and Knaresborough, UK Government; *party:* Conservative; *political career:* Councillor, Harrogate Borough Council, 2003-; MP for Harrogate and Knaresborough, May 2010-; PPS, 2010-; *committees:* Regulatory Reform, 2010-; *office address:* House of Commons, London, SW1A 0AA, United Kingdom; *phone:* +44 (0)20 7219 3000; *e-mail:* andrew.jones.mp@parliament.uk.

JONES, Carwyn; British, First Minister, National Assembly for Wales; *born:* 21 March 1967, Swansea, Wales; *parents:* Caron Wyn Jones and Katherine Janice Jones; *married:* Lisa Jones (née Murray), 3 December 1994; *children:* Seren Hâf (F), Ruairi Wyn (M); *languages:* Welsh; *education:* Brynteg Comprehensive; Univ. of Wales, Aberystwyth; Inns of Court, Sch. of Law, London; *party:* Labour; *political career:* constituency Mem. for Bridgend, Nat. Assembly for Wales; Minister for Rural Affairs and Assembly Business, National Assembly for Wales, -2002; Minister for Open Government, 2002-2003; Minister for Environment, Planning and Countryside, 2003-07; Minister for Education, Culture and Welsh Language, June 2007; Counsel General, Leader of the House and Assembly Business and Communications, July 2007-09; Leader of the Labour Party in Wales, Dec. 2009-; First Minister of Wales, Dec. 2009-; *interests:* transport, foreign affairs, economic development; *professional career:* Barrister; *honours and awards:* Hon. Fellow, Bangor Univ.; *publications:* The Future of Welsh Labour, Institute of Welsh Affairs; *recreations:* sport, travel; *office address:* National Assembly for Wales, Cardiff Bay, Cardiff, CF99 1NA, United Kingdom; *phone:* +44 (0)29 2089 8769; *fax:* +44 (0)29 2089 8635; *e-mail:* carwyn.jones@wales.gov.uk.

JONES, David Ian; Secretary of State for Wales, House of Commons; *born:* 1952; *party:* Conservative Party; *political career:* Welsh Assembly Mem. for North Wales, 2002-03; MP for Clwyd West, 2005-; Shadow Minister for Wales 2006-10; Parliamentary Under-Secretary of State, Wales Office 2010-12; Secretary of State for Wales, 2012-; *committees:* Welsh Affairs, 2005-10; *office address:* Welsh Office, Gwydyr House, Whitehall, London, SW1A 2NP, United Kingdom; *phone:* +44 (0)20 7270 0534; *URL:* http://www.walesoffice.gov.uk.

JONES, Graham; MP for Hyndburn, UK Government; *party:* Labour; *political career:* Councillor, Hyndburn Borough Council, 2002-10; Councillor, Lancashire County Council, 2009-; MP for Hyndburn, 2010-; *office address:* House of Commons, London, SW1A 0AA, United Kingdom; *phone:* +44 (0)20 7219 3000; *e-mail:* graham.jones.mp@parliament.uk.

JONES, Helen; British, Member of Parliament for Warrington North, House of Commons; *born:* 24 December 1954; *education:* Univ. Coll., London; Liverpool Univ.; *party:* Labour Party; *political career:* MP, Warrington North, 1997-; Shadow Deputy Leader of the House, Oct. 2010-11; Shadow Minister, Communities and Local Government, 2011-; *professional career:* Solicitor; *office address:* House of Commons, London, SW1A 0AA, United Kingdom; *phone:* +44 (0)20 7219 3000; *e-mail:* hcinfo@parliament.uk.

JONES, Kevan; Member of Parliament for Durham North, House of Commons; *education:* Portland Comprehensive, Worksop; BA (Hons), Government & Public Policy, Newcastle Upon Tyne Polytechnic; *party:* Labour Party; *political career:* Mem., Chief Whip, Newcastle Upon Tyne City Cncl., 1990-2001; MP, Durham North, 2001-; Parly. Under Sec., Ministry of Defence, Oct. 2008-10; Shadow Minister for Defence, 2010-; *office address:* House of Commons, London, SW1A 0AA, United Kingdom; *phone:* +44 (0)20 7219 3000; *e-mail:* kevanjonesmp@parliament.uk; *URL:* http://www.kevanjonesmp.org.uk.

JONES, Marcus; MP for Nuneaton, UK Government; *party:* Labour; *political career:* Councillor, Nuneaton and Bedworth Borough Council, 2005-10; MP for Nuneaton, May 2010-; *office address:* House of Commons, London, SW1A 0AA, United Kingdom; *phone:* +44 (0)20 7219 3000; *e-mail:* marcus.jones.mp@parliament.uk.

JONES, Paul W.; Ambassador, US Embassy in Malaysia; *education:* Cornell Univ.; MA, Univ. of Virginia; Naval War Coll.; *professional career:* Dep. Chief, U.S. Mission to the Org. for Security and Cooperation in Europe; Dep. Chief of Mission in Macedonia; Amb. to Malaysia, 2010-; *office address:* Embassy of the United States of America, 376 Jalan Tun Razak, POB 10035, 50700 Kuala Lumpur, Malaysia; *phone:* +60 (0)3 2168 5000; *fax:* +60 (0)3 2168 4961; *URL:* http://malaysia.usembassy.gov.

JONES, Peter; Ambassador, British Embassy in Ghana; *languages:* Italian; *professional career:* FCO, Director of Migration, 2009-11; High Commissioner to Ghana, non resident ambassador to Togo and Burkina Faso, 2011-; *office address:* British High Commission, Osu Link, off Gamel Abdul Nasser Avenue, Accra, Ghana; *phone:* +233 21 221665; *fax:* +233 21 701 0655; *e-mail:* high.commission@accra.mail.fco.gov.uk; *URL:* http://ukinghana.fco.gov.uk/en.

JONES, Susan; MP for Clwyd South, UK Government; *languages:* Japanese, Welsh; *education:* Univ. of Bristol; Univ. of Cardiff; *party:* Labour; *political career:* Councillor, London Borough of Southwark, 2006-09; MP for Clwyd South, May 2010-; PPS, 2011; Opposition Whip, 2011-; *professional career:* Charity Fundraiser; *committees:* Welsh Affairs, 2010-; *office address:* House of Commons, London, SW1A 0AA, United Kingdom; *phone:* +44 (0)20 7219 3000; *e-mail:* susan.jones.mp@parliament.uk.

JONES OF BIRMINGHAM, Lord Digby; British, Member, House of Lords; *born:* 28 October 1955; *married:* Pat Jones; *education:* Scholarship to Bromsgrove Sch.; Univ. Coll. London, LL.B; *political career:* Minister of State, Foreign and Commonwealth Office and Dept. of Business Enterprise and Regulatory Reform, 2007-08; *memberships:* National Trust; Yorkshire Society; Vice-Pres., UNICEF; Chmn., Cancer Research UK; Corp. Amb. and mem., Royal British Legion; Companion, Instit. of Management, 2000; Advisory Bd., Cmwlth Education Fund, 2000-; Fellow, RSA, 2001; Fellow, Royal Institution, 2002; Fellow, Sunningdale Institute; National Learning and Skills Cncl, 2002-; Skills Alliance, 2002-; Chmn., Birmingham Univ. Business School Advisory Bd., 2004-; Dir., Leicester Tigers, 2005-; *professional career:* Royal Navy; Lawyer, Edge & Ellison, 1978; Partner, Edge & Ellison, 1984; Involved in most of the Merger and Acquisition activity in the West Midlands, late 1980s, early 1990s; Dep. Sr. Partner, Edge & Elliot, 1990; Sr. Partner, Edge & Elliot, 1995, Vice-Chmn. of Corporate Finance, KPMG, 1998-2000; Non-Exec. Dir., several companies, covering sectors such as quarry aggregates, local radio and automotive component manufacture; Dir.General, CBI, 2000-07 (non-renewable 5 year term extended to 7 years); Dir., Business in the Community, 2000-; Non-exec. Dir., Alba plc, 2003-; Non-Exec. dir., mhl support plc, 2004-; Dir., Konigswinter, 2003-; Chmn. of the Int. Business Advisory Board at HSBC, Chmn.of Triumph Motorcycles Limited, and is Corporate Amb. for Jaguar Cars and JCB; *trusteeships:* Birmingham Symphony Orchestra Dev. Trust Charity; Chmn., Birmingham St. Mary's Hospice Appeal; Aston Reinvestment Trust, 2003-; patron, Hospice of Hope, Romania; patron, Lifecycle UK; patron, Canning House Library Appeal; patron, Campaign for Learning; patron, WellChild; patron, Where Next Assn.; *honours and awards:* Freeman of the City of London; Honorary doctorates, Univ. of Central England 2002, Univ. of Birmingham 2002, UMIST 2003, Univ. of Hertfordshire 2004, Univ. of Middlesex 2005, Sheffield Hallam Univ., 2005; Honorary Fellow, Cardiff Univ., 2004; Fellow, Univ. Coll., London, 2004; Knight Bachelor, 2005; Raised to the peerage as Baron Jones of Birmingham, of Alvechurch and of Bromsgrove in the County of Worcestershire, 2007; *recreations:* theatre, skiing, rugby, football, cricket, military history; *office address:* House of Lords, London, SW1A 0AA, United Kingdom.

JONSSON, H.E. Benedikt; Ambassador, Embassy of Iceland in the UK; *born:* November 1954; *education:* BA. hons. (History, Pol. Science, Philosophy), 1979; MA. hobs (Pol. Science), 1982; *professional career:* Amb. to the Russian Federation, Moscow. Armenia, Azerbaijan, Belarus, Georgia, Kazakhstan, Kyrgyzstan, Moldova, Tajikistan, Turkmenistan and Uzbekistan, 2001-06; Perm. Sec. of State, Min. for Foreign Affairs, Reykjavik, 2008; Amb. to the Court of St. James's, 2009-; *office address:* Embassy of Iceland, 2a Hans Street, London, SW1X 0JE, United Kingdom; *phone:* +44 (0)20 7259 3999; *URL:* http://www.iceland.org/uk/the-embassy/Iceland-UK.

JORDAN, Thomas J.; Chairman of the Governing Board, Schwiezerische Nationalbank; *born:* 1963; *education:* Univ. of Bern, economics, Ph.D; Harvard Univ., post-doctoral reseach, economics, Harvard Univ.; *professional career:* Lecturer; Univ. of Bern, Hon. Prof., 2003; Economic Adviser, Swiss Nationl Bank, 1997, Assist Dir., Economic Studies Unit, 1999-2000, Head, Research Unit, Director, 2004, Alternate Mem., Gov. Board & Head, Financial Markets, Dept. III, 2004-07, Mem., Gov. Board, 2007 & Head., Dept. III, 2007-10,

Vice-Chmn., Gov. Board & Management of Dept. II, 2010-12, Chmn. of Governing Board, Head of Dept., 2012-; ***office address:*** National Bank of Switzerland, Bundesplatz 1, 3003 Berne, Switzerland; ***URL:*** http://www.snb.ch.

JOSHI, Bharat; Ambassador, British Embassy in Cameroon; ***professional career:*** Dep. High Commissioner, The Gambia, 1999-2001; Regional Manager, UK Border Agency, Visa Services, for the Gulf and Iran, 2007-09; High Commissioner to Cameroon, non-resident Amb. to the Central African Republic, Chad and Gabon, 2009-; ***office address:*** British High Commission, Avenue Winston Churchill, BP 547, Yaoundé, Cameroon; ***phone:*** +237 222 0545; ***fax:*** +237 222 0148; ***URL:*** http://ukincameroon.fco.gov.uk/en.

JOSHI, C.P.; Minister of Road Transport and Highways, Government of India; ***education:*** BA., (Law); MSc., (Physics); MA, Ph.D., (Psychology); ***party:*** Indian National Congress; ***political career:*** Minister for Rural Development, 2009-11; Minister of Road Transport and Highways, 2011-; Minister of Railways, 2013-; ***professional career:*** Professor; ***office address:*** Ministry of Road Transport and Highways, 1, Parliament Street, New Delhi-110001, India; ***URL:*** http://morth.nic.in/index1.asp?linkid=135&langid=2.

JOSIPOVIC, Ivo; President, Republic of Croatia; ***born:*** 1957; ***education:*** MA, Ph.D., University of Zagreb; ***party:*** Social Democratic Party of Croatia; ***political career:*** MP, 2003-10; President, Jan. 2010-; ***professional career:*** Law Prof.; Classical music composer; ***office address:*** Office of the President, Pantovcak 241, 10 000 Zagreb, Croatia; ***phone:*** +385 1 456 5191; ***e-mail:*** office@president.hr; ***URL:*** http://www.president.hr.

JOSPIN, Lionel Robert; French, Former Prime Minister, Leader, Parti Socialiste; ***born:*** 12 July 1937, Meudon, Hauts de Seine, France; ***married:*** Sylviane Agacinski; ***public role of spouse:*** Lecturer in Philosophy, Institut des Hautes Etudes en Sciences Sociales; ***education:*** Institut d'etudes politiques, Paris, 1956; E.N.A. (Ecole Nat. d'Administration), 1963-65; ***party:*** Socialist Party; ***political career:*** National Secy., Socialist Party with responsibility for education 1973-75, the Third World 1975-79, international relations 1979-81; First Secy., Socialist Party 1981-; Councillor for Paris, 18th District 1977-86; elected Socialist Member of Parliament for Paris, 27th Outer District 1981-86; elected Socialist Member of Parliament, Haute-Garonne 1986; Leader, Parti Socialiste; Minister of National Education, Youth and Sport 1988-92; Prime Minister, 1997-02; ***professional career:*** Sec. to the Minister of Foreign Affairs, 1965-70; seconded to Univ. of Paris XI, Senior Lecturer in Economics, Institut Universitaire de Technology 1970-81; ***publications:*** L'Invention du Possible, 1991, Flammarion; Le Temps de Répondre, 2002, Stock; Le Monde comme je le vois, 2005, Gallimard; L'impasse, 2007, Flammarion; Lionel raconte Jospin, 2010, Le Seuil; ***office address:*** Parti Socialiste, 10 rue de Solférino, 75333 Paris Cédex 07, France.

JOWELL, Rt. Hon. Tessa, MP; British, Member of Parliament, House of Commons; ***born:*** 17 September 1947; ***education:*** St. Margaret's School, Aberdeen; Aberdeen Univ., MA; Edinburgh Univ., Diploma, Social Admin.; ***party:*** Labour Party, 1969-; ***political career:*** Cllr., London Borough of Camden, 1971-86; MP, Dulwich 1992-97; Opp. Whip, responsible for Trade and Industry, 1994-95; Opp. Spokeswoman on Women 1995-96; Opp. Spokesperson on Health 1996-97; MP, Dulwich and West Norwood, 1997-; Minister of State for Public Health, 1997-99; Minister of State for Employment, 1999; Privy Cllr. 1998-; Secretary of State for Culture, Media and Sport, 2001-June 2007; Minister for the Olympics, July 2005-2010; Minister for London, 2009- 2010; Minister for the Cabinet Office, 2009-10; Shadow Secretary of State for Cabinet Office, 2010, 2011; Shadow Minister for the Olympics, 2010-12, also Shadow Minister for London, 2012; ***interests:*** community care, health, social policies, education, trade and employment; ***memberships:*** Mental Health Act Cmn., 1985-90; Visting Fellow Coll., Oxford; ***professional career:*** Child Care Officer; Social Worker; Community Care Dir.; Asst. Dir., MIND, 1974-86; Dir., Community Care Special Action Project, 1987-90; Dir., Joseph Rowntree Foundation Community Care Programme, 1990-92; Governor, Nat. Inst. of Social Work, 1985-97; ***committees:*** Chwn., Social Services Cttee., Housing Management Cttee., Staff Cttee., Assn. of Metropolitan Authorities, 1978-86; Mem., Health Select Cttee., 1992-94; ***office address:*** House of Commons, London, SW1A 0AA, United Kingdom; ***phone:*** +44 (0)20 7219 3000; ***e-mail:*** jowellt@parliament.uk.

JOYCE, Eric; Member of Parliament for Falkirk, House of Commons; ***party:*** Labour Whip, suspended February 2012; Resigned from Labour Party, 2012; ***political career:*** MP, Falkirk West, 2000-05, Falkirk, 2005; Shadow Minister, Northern Ireland, Oct. 2010; ***interests:*** Foreign affairs, international development, defence, trade and industry, higher education, asylum and immigration; ***office address:*** House of Commons, London, SW1A 0PQ, United Kingdom; ***phone:*** +44 (0)1324 638919.

JOYCE, Steven; Minister of Economic Development, Government of New Zealand; ***education:*** Massey Univ., New Zealand; ***party:*** New Zealand National Party; ***political career:*** Minister of Transport, Minister for Communications and Information Technology, 2008-11; Minister for Tertiary Education, 2010-11; Minister of Economic Development, Science and Innovation, Tertiary Education, Skills and Employment, 2011-; ***professional career:*** Managing Director, RadioWorks; ***office address:*** Ministry of Economy, 38-42 Waring Taylor Street, Wellington, New Zealand; ***phone:*** +64 (0)4 472 1253; ***URL:*** http://www.transport.govt.nz.

JUAN CARLOS I DE BORBÓN Y BORBÓN, H.M.; Spanish, King of Spain; ***born:*** 5 January 1938; ***parents:*** Don Juan de Borbon y Battenberg and Dona Maria de las Mercedes de Borbon y Orleas; ***married:*** Princess Sophia of Greece, 1962; ***children:*** Crown Prince Felipe (M), Princess Elena (F), Princess Christina (F); ***education:*** Inst. San Isidro, Madrid, Spain; Colegio del Carmen, Gen. Mil. Academy, Zaragoza; Univ. Madrid; ***professional career:*** King of Spain, 1975-; commander in chief of Armed Forces, 1975-; head, Supreme Council of Defence, 1975-; ***honours and awards:*** numerous honourary degrees and awards; ***office address:*** Office of HM Juan Carlos I de Borbón y Borbón, Palacio de la Zarzuela , Madrid, Spain.

JULIUSSON, Kristjan por; Minister of Health, Government of Iceland; ***born:*** 15 July 1957; ***party:*** Independence Party; ***political career:*** MP, 2007-; Minister of Health, 2013-; ***office address:*** Ministry of Welfare, Hafnarhusinu vid Tryggvagotu, 150 Reykjavík, Iceland; ***phone:*** +354 545 8100; ***fax:*** +354 551 9165; ***URL:*** http://www.stjr.is/htr.

JUMEAU, Ronald Jean; Ambassador, Seychelles Embassy in the USA; ***born:*** 24 January 1957, Dar-es-Salaam, Tanzania; ***parents:*** Esme Jumeau and Monita Jumeau (née Pool); ***children:*** Christine (F); ***languages:*** Creole, English, French; ***education:*** Seychelles College; ***party:*** mem., central cttee., Seychelles People's Progressive Front; ***political career:*** Adviser, Ministry of Education, 1991-93; Dir. of Research, President's Office, 1993-98, Secretary to the Cabinet, 1993-98; Sec., National Economic Consultative Cttee., 1993-98; Sec., 4 inter-ministerial cttees. of the cabinet, 1994-98; Resp. for Parly. Relations, 1995-98; Minister of Agriculture and Marine Resources, 1998-99; Minister of Culture and Information, 2000-Sept. 01; Minister of Environment, Sept. 2001-03; Minister of Environment and Natural Resources, 2004-08; ***professional career:*** Reporter, Gov. Info. Services, 1978-80; First Ed., Seychelles Agence Presse (SAP), 1980-82; Seychelles stringer for Reuters International News Agency, 1980-83; Chief Ed., Seychelles Nation & SAP, 1983-90; Journalism instructor, School of Media Studies, Seychelles Poly., 1986-89; Ambassador to USA, 2008-; ***recreations:*** reading, listening to music, cultural performances and events; ***office address:*** Embassy of the Seychelles, 800 2nd Ave., Suite 400C, New York, NY 10017, USA; ***phone:*** +1 212 972 1785; ***fax:*** +1 212 972 1786.

JUNCKER, Jean-Claude; Prime Minister, Minister of State and Minister of the Treasury, Luxembourg Government; ***born:*** 9 December 1954, Rédange-sur-Attert, Luxembourg; ***parents:*** Jos Juncker and Marguerite Juncker (née Hecker); ***married:*** Christiane Juncker (née Frising), 1979; ***languages:*** German, French, English; ***education:*** Clairefontaine High Sch., Belgium, 1967-74; Michel Rodange High Sch., Luxembourg; Univ. of Strasbourg, Faculty of Law, LLM., 1979; ***party:*** Parti Chrétien Social, (PCS, Christian Social Party), 1974-; ***political career:*** Parly. Sec., Parti Chrétien Social (PCS), 1979-82; Pres., Christian Social Youth, 1979-85; State Sec., Labour and Social Affairs, 1982-84; Elected to Chambre des Députés (Parliament) for Sud Constituency, 1984; Minister of Labour, Minister in charge of budget, 1984-89; Minister of Labour, Minister of Finance, 1989-94; Pres., PCS, 1990-95; Pres., EU of Christian Democratic Workers 1993-95; Minister of Labour, Minister of Finance, 1994-95; Minister of Labour & Employment, 1995-99; Prime Minister, Minister of State, Minister of Finance, 1995-99; Vice-Pres., European People's Party, 1996-99; Prime Minister and Minister of Finance, 1999-04; PM, 2004-; also Minister of State & Minister of Finance, 2004-09; also Minister of State and Minister of the Treasury, July 2009-; ***interests:*** social policy; ***memberships:*** Foreign Assoc. mem., Academy of Ethics and Political Science of the Institute of France; ***professional career:*** admitted to the Bar of Luxembourg, 1980; Governor of the World Bank, 1989-95; Governor, European Bank for Reconstruction & Development, London, 1995-; Governor, Int. Monetary Fund, 1995-; ***committees:*** Pres., Cncl. of Ministers of the EC, Social Affairs & Budget, 1985; Pres., Cncl. of Ministers of the EC, Social Affairs, Economic & Financial Affairs, Budget, 1991; Pres., European Cncl., Cncl. of Ministers of Finance & Economy of the EU, Cncl. of Ministers of Social Affairs of the EU, 1997; Permanent Pres., Eurogroup, 2005-; ***honours and awards:*** Prix 'L'Européen de l'Année, 1997'; Dr hon. causa, Miami Univ., 1998; Prix 'Vision for Europe', Fondation Edmond Israel, 1998; Doctor Honoris Causa, Faculty of Philosophy, Westfälische Wilhelms-Universität, Münster, Germany, 2001 and Univ., Bucarest, Romania, 2003, and the Univ. of Thrace, 2004; Grand Officier de la Légion d'Honneur, Pres. of the French Republic, 2002; Grand-Croix de l'Etoile, 2003; Honorary Citizen, Trier, Germany, 2003 and of Orestiada, Greece, 2004; Charlemagne Prize of Aachen, 2006; elected Assoc. Mem., Académie des sciences morales et politiques de l'Institut de France, 2006; Hon. Senator, European Academy of Scienes and Arts; ***publications:*** a great number of press articles; ***recreations:*** lecturing; ***office address:*** Office of the Prime Minister and Minister of State, Hôtel de Bourgogne, 4 rue de la Congrégation, L-2910, Luxembourg;
URL: http://www.gouvernement.lu/gouvernement/premier-ministre/index.html.

K

KABERUKA, Dr Donald; Rwandan, President, African Development Bank; ***education:*** Tanzania; Glasgow Univ., Scotland, Ph.D, economics; ***political career:*** Minister of Finance and Economic Planning, 1997-2005; ***professional career:*** Banking; International Finance; Pres., African Development Bank, 2005-; ***office address:*** AFDB, 15 Avenue du Ghana, PO Box 323-1002, Tunis-Belvedere, Tunisia; ***phone:*** +216 71 103900.

KABILA, Maj. Gen. Joseph; President, Democratic Republic of Congo; ***parents:*** Laurent Kabila; ***political career:*** President and Minister of Defence, Democratic Republic of Congo, 2001-; ***professional career:*** former guerilla fighter; major-general and chief of staff, Congolese Army; ***office address:*** Office of the President, Mont Ngaliema, Kinshasa, Democratic Republic of Congo.

KABIMBA, Wynter; Minister of Justice, Government of Zambia; ***political career:*** PF Secretary General; MP; Minister of Justice, 2012-; ***memberships:*** Law Assn. of Zambia; ***professional career:*** Advocate, High Court; Advocate, Supreme Court of Zamiba; ***office address:*** Ministry of Justice, PO Box 50106, Lusaka, Zambia.

KABUI, Sir Frank; Governor-General, Solomon Islands; ***born:*** 1946, Solomon Islands; ***education:*** Law degree, Papua New Guinea, 1975; ***professional career:*** Attorney General, 1980-94; Chmn., Law Reform Commission, 1994, 2006-09; High Court Judge, 1998-2006; Governor-General, Solomon Islands, 2009-; ***office address:*** Office of the Governor General, PO Box 252, Honiara, Solomon Islands.

KACHALI, Khumbo Hastings; Vice President, Government of Malawi; ***education:*** Univ. of Cambridge, UK; MSc., Univ. of Derby, UK; ***political career:*** Minister of Industry, Science and Technology, 2004-06; Dep. Minister for Home Affairs and Internal Security, 2006-07; Minister of Youth Development and Sport, 2007-08; Minister of Health, 2008-09; Minister of Transport, 2009-10; Vice President, 2012-; ***office address:*** Office of the Vice President, Private Bag 301, Lilongwe 3, Malawi; ***phone:*** +265 1 789311; ***fax:*** +265 1 788456; ***e-mail:*** opc@malawi.gov.mw; ***URL:*** http://www.malawi.gov.mw.

KAGAN, **Elena;** Associate Justice, Supreme Court of the US; ***born:*** 1960; ***education:*** Princeton Univ., AB, summa cum laude; Worcester College, Oxford Univ., Princeton's Daniel M. Sachs Graduating Fellow, M.Phil; Harvard Law School, JD, magna cum laude; ***professional career:*** law clert to Judge Abner Mikva, US Court of Appeals, DC Circuit, 1986-87; law clerk to Justice Thurgood Marshall, Supreme Court of the US, 1987 term; associate, Williams & Connolly, LLP, Washington, 1989-91; Assist. Prof., Univ. of Chicago Law School, 1991, tenure professor of law, 1995; Assoc. Counsel to President Clinton, 1995-1999, then Dep. Assist. to the President for Domestic Policy and Dep. Dir. of the Domestic Policy Council; Visiting Prof., Harvard Law School, 1999, professor of law, 2001; Charles Hamilton Houston Professor of Law; Dean of Harvard Law School, 2003; Solicitor General of the USA, 2009; Assoc. Justice of the Supreme Court, August 2010-; ***office address:*** Supreme Court of the United States, 1 First Street, NE, Washington DC 20543, USA; ***phone:*** +1 202 479 3000; ***URL:*** http://www.supremecourt.gov/.

KAKABADSE, **Yolanda;** President, World Wide Fund for Nature; ***born:*** 15 September 1948, Ecuador; ***parents:*** Dimitri Kakabadse and Maximina Kakabadse (née Navarro); ***languages:*** English, Spanish; ***education:*** Catholic Univ. of Quito, Educational Psychology; ***political career:*** Minister of Environment, Republic of Ecuador, 1998-2000; ***memberships:*** Mem. of the Bd. of Dirs., the World Resources Inst., 1996-; Mem., the Bd. of the Millennium Ecosystem Assessment, 2000; Mem., Int. Advisory Bd., INBio, 2000-; ***professional career:*** Exec. Dir., Fundación Natura, Quito, 1979-90; coordinated the participation of civil society organisations in the UN Conference for Environment and Development (Earth Summit), Geneva, Switzerland, 1990-92; Pres., The World Conservation Union (IUCN), 1996-2004; Visiting Prof., Yale's Sch. of Forestry and Environment, USA, 2001; Founder and Exec. Pres., Fundación Futuro Latinoamericano, NGO, 1993-2009; President, World Wide Fund for Nature, 2009-; ***trusteeships:*** Mem., Bd. of Trustees of the Ford Foundation, 1997-98 and 2000-; ***honours and awards:*** Insignia of the Nat. Order for Merit as a Commissioned Officer for the Republic of Ecuador, 1990; Global 500 Award of the UN Environment Program, 1991; The Golden Ark Order, bestowed by Prince Bernard of The Netherlands, 1991; Zayed Int. Price for the Environment, 2001; ***office address:*** World Wide Fund for Nature, Avenue du Mont-Blanc, CH 1196 Gland, Switzerland ; ***phone:*** +41 (0)22 364 9111; ***fax:*** +41 (0)22 364 8836; ***URL:*** http://www.wwf.org.

KAKKAR OF LOXBEARE, **Lord Ajay;** Member, House of Lords; ***political career:*** Mem., House of Lords, 2010-; ***professional career:*** Physician; Surgeon; Lecturer ; ***office address:*** House of Lords, London, SW1A 0PW, United Kingdom; ***phone:*** +44 (0)20 7219 3000; ***fax:*** +44 (0)20 7219 5979; ***URL:*** http://www.parliament.uk.

KALINAK, **Robert;** Deputy Prime Minister and Minister of the Interior, Government of the Slovak Republic; ***born:*** 1971; ***education:*** Comenius Univ., Bratislava, law; ***party:*** Smer; ***political career:*** MP, National Council, 2002; Mem., Regional Parliament, Bratislava, 2005; Dep. Prime Minister and Minister of the Interior, 2006-10; Chmn., Special Supervision Cttee. of the National Council of the Slovak Republic, 2010-12; Mem. of the Cttee. of the National Council for Defence and Security, 2001-12; Mem., Perm. Delegation to the Parly. Assembly of NATO, 2010-12; MP, Municipality of Bratislava, 2010-12; Dep. PM and Minister of the Interior, 2012-; ***professional career:*** lawyer; ***office address:*** Ministry of the Interior, Pribinova 2, 812 72 Bratislava, Slovak Republic.

KALJURAND, **Ambassador Marina;** Estonian, Ambassador Extraordinary and Plenipotentiary to the US, Embassy of Estonia; ***born:*** 6 September 1962; ***languages:*** Estonian, Russian, English; ***education:*** Tartu University, Law Faculty, LLM, cum laude, 1986; Estonian School of Diplomacy, Professional Diploma in International Relations, 1992; Tufts University, Fletcher School of Law and Diplomacy, MA, 2005, Fulbright Scholarship; ***interests:*** Jurisdiction; Human rights; Organisations; Territory/boundaries; Treaties; ***memberships:*** ILA, Estonian Branch, founding member, 1996; ***professional career:*** *academic career:* Estonian School of Diplomacy, Lecturer in international law, 1999-2005; Tallinn Economic School, Lecturer in international law, 1995-2005; *governmental career:* Counsellor, Estonian Embassy in Finland, 1996-99; Ministry of Foreign Affairs, Estonia, Director General of the Legal Department and Legal Adviser, 1999-2003, Undersecretary for Legal and Consular Affairs, 2003-05; Ambassador Extraordinary and Plenipotentiary (non-resident) of Estonia to the State of Israel, 2004-06; *Diplomatic career:* Member, Estonian Governmental Delelgation in negotiations on Troops Withdrawal Agreement between Estonia and Russia, 1992-94; Member, Estonian Governmental Delegation in negotiations on Estonian-Russian Border Agreements, 1995-; Head of Estonian Governmental Delegation at CHR Summit, 2003; Head of Estonian Governmental Delegation at different UN and CoE meetings, including human rights conventions supervising bodies (CAT, CEDAW, CCPR, CESR, CERD, CC), 1999-2004; Member, Estonian Governmental Delegation in accession negotiations to the EU; Chair, legal working group in drafting of the Accession Agreement to the EU, 2002-04;Ambassador Extraordinary and Plenipotentiary of Estonia to the Russian Federation, 2005-08; to Kazakhstan (non-resident), 2007-11; Undersecretary for Foreign Economic Relations and Development Aid, 2008-11; Amb., Extraordinary and Plenipotentiary to the US, also to Canada (non-resident), 2011-, to Mexico (non-resident), 2011-; *judicial career:* Member, PCA, 2005-; ***office address:*** Embassy of Estonia, 2131 Massachusetts Avenue, NW, Washington, DC 20008, USA; ***phone:*** +1 202 588 0101; ***fax:*** +1 202 588 0108; ***URL:*** http://www.estemb.org/.

KALLAS, **Siim;** Estonian, Vice President, European Commission; ***born:*** 2 October 1948; ***parents:*** Udo Kallas (dec'd) and Rita Kallas (dec'd); ***married:*** Kristi Kallas, 1972; ***children:*** Ylo (M), Kaja (F); ***languages:*** English, Finnish, Russian, French; ***education:*** Univ. of Tartu, Grad. (cum laude), Finance and Credits, 1972; Post Graduate Univ. of Tartu, 1972-75; ***party:*** Founding Mem. & Fmr. Chmn., Reform Party (R); Hon. Chmn., Reform Party; ***political career:*** Mem., KPSU, 1972-90; Chmn., of the Estonian Central Assn. of Trade Unions, 1989-91; Mem., Reform Party, 1994-; Minister of Foreign Affairs, 1995-96; Riigikogu, 1995 and 1996-99; Elected to the Riigikogu, 1999; Minister of Finance, 1999-02; Prime Minister, 2002-03; mem., Riigikogu, 2003-04; Mem., European Cmn., 2004, Vice Pres., EC, in charge of Administration, Audit and Anti-Fraud, 2004- ; ***memberships:*** EPF; ***professional career:*** Head Specialist, ESSR Min. of Finance, 1975-79; Head, Estonian of Savings Bank Dept., 1979-86; Deputy Editor, 'Rahva Hääl' Newspaper, 1986-89; Chmn., Assn. of Estonian Trade Unions, 1989-91; Pres., Bank of Estonia, 1991-94; ***publications:*** 400 publications; ***recreations:*** reading, tennis, theatre, music, cycling; ***office address:*** European Commission, rue de la Loi 200, B-1049 Brussels, Belgium; ***URL:*** http://ec.europa.eu/.

KALOUSEK, **Miroslav;** Minister of Finance, Government of the Czech Republic; ***born:*** 17 December 1960, Tabor; ***children:*** 2; ***education:*** Institute of Chemical Technology, Prague, 1984; ***party:*** Chmn. of the Christian Democratic Party (KDU-ČSL), 2003-06; Dep. Chmn., TOP 09 party; ***political career:*** MP, 1998-; Expert Adviser of the Vice-Chairman of the Czech Government, 1990-92; Dir. of the Dept. of the Advisors of the Vice-Chairman of the Government, 1992-; Dep. Minister of Defence with responsibility for the budget and acquisitions operations, 1993-98; Minister of Finance, 2007-09; Minister of Finance, 2010-; ***professional career:*** Head of the Investment Section, Mitas Praha; ***committees:*** Chmn.Budget Cttee. of the Chamber of Deputies; mem., advisory cttee of the South-Bohemian Brewery, 1991-92; ***honours and awards:*** The Minister of Finance of the Year 2008 (Emerging Europe) by the journal Emerging Markets; ***recreations:*** history, literature, traveling, film; ***office address:*** Ministry of Finance, Letenská 15, 118 10 Prague 1, Czech Republic; ***phone:*** +420 2 5704 1111; ***fax:*** +420 2 5704 2788; ***URL:*** http://www.mfcr.cz.

KAMARA, **Dr Samura Matthew Wilson;** Minister of Foreign Affairs, Government of Sierra Leone; ***born:*** 1963, Kamalo, Sierra Leone; ***professional career:*** Economist; Gov., Bank of Sierra Leone, -2009; Mem., Board of Governors, African Development Bank; Gov. Islamic Development Bank; Minister of Finance and Economic Development, 2009; Minister of Foreign Affairs & International Cooperation, 2013-; ***office address:*** Ministry of Foreign Affairs & International Cooperation, Gloucester Street, Freetown, Sierra Leone; ***phone:*** +232 22 224778; ***fax:*** +232 22 225615.

KAMIL MOHAMED, **Abdoulkader;** Prime Minister, Government of Djibouti; ***born:*** 1951; ***education:*** Univ. of Limoges, France; ***political career:*** Minister of Agriculture, 2005-11; Minister of Defence, 2011-13; Prime Minister, Apr. 2013-; ***office address:*** Office of the Prime Minister, Djibouti.

KAMILOV, **H.E. Abulaziz;** Minister of Foreign Affairs, Government of Uzbekistan; ***born:*** 1947; ***education:*** History, Ph.D; ***political career:*** Vice-Chair, National Security Service, 1992-94; Dep. Minister of Foreign Affairs, 1994; Minister of Foreign Affairs, 1994-2003; First Dep. Minister of Foreign Affairs, 2010-12; Minister of Foreign Affairs, 2012-; ***professional career:*** various appointments, Ministry of Foreign Affairs, USSR, 1972-88; Counsellor, Uzbekistan Embassy to the Russian Federation, 1991-92; State Advisor to the President, 2003; Amb. of Uzbekistan to the USA, 2003-10; ***office address:*** Ministry of Foreign Affairs, 9 Uzbekistan Street, 700029 Tashkent, Uzbekistan.

KAMP, **Henk G.J.;** Minister of Economic Affairs, Netherlands Government; ***born:*** 23 July 1952, Hengelo; ***education:*** auditor's course, Tax and Customs Administration Training Centre, Utrecht, 1977-80; ***political career:*** Mem., Borculo Municipal Council for the People's Party for Freedom and Democracy (VVD), 1976-94; served as alderman, 1986-; Mem., Gelderland Provincial Council, 1987-94; Mem., House of Representatives of the States Gen., 1994-; Mem., Tweede Kamer; Minister of Housing, Spatial Planning and the Environment, 2002; Minister of Defence, 2002-06; VVD spokesperson on immigration and integration policy, 2006-08; Commissioner for Bonaire, Sint Eustatius and Saba, 2009; Minister of Social Affairs and Employment, 2010-12; Minister of Economic Affairs, Nov. 2012-; ***memberships:*** Mem., regional bd., Manpower Servies Org., Arnhem/East Gelderland; ***professional career:*** worked for two wholesalers in Enschede, Tilburg and Borculo, -1977; Investigator, Fiscal Info. and Investigation Service (FIOD), -1986; ***committees:*** fmr. Mem., Exec. Cttee. of the Achterhoek region; ***office address:*** Ministry of Economic Affairs, Agriculture and Innovation, Postbus 20401, 2500 EK The Hague, Netherlands; ***URL:*** http://www.government.nl.

KAMP, **Randy;** Member of Parliament, Government of Canada; ***born:*** 1953; ***education:*** BA, theology; ***political career:*** MP for Pitt Meadows-Maple Ridge-Mission in British Columbia, 2004-; Parly. Sec. to the Minister of Fisheries and Oceans, 2009-; ***office address:*** House of Commons, Parliament Buildings, Wellington Street, Ottawa K1A 0A6, Ontario, Canada; ***phone:*** +1 613 947 4613; ***fax:*** +1 613 947 4615; ***URL:*** http://www.parl.gc.ca.

KANDIL, **Hisham Mohamed;** Prime Minister, Government of Egypt; ***born:*** 17 September 1962; ***education:*** BSc. in engineering, Cairo Univ., 1984; MA, irrigation and drainage engineering, Utah State Univ. USA, 1988; PhD in biological and agricultural engineering . North Carolina State Univ., USA, 1993; ***political career:*** Minister of Water Resources and Irrigation, 2011-12; Prime Minister, July 2012-July 2013; ***office address:*** Office of the Prime Minister, Sharia Majlis ash-Sha'ab, Cairo, Egypt.

KANDODO, **Ken;** Minister of Defence, Government of Malawi; ***education:*** B.Sc. in Social Science, Univ. of Malawi, 1983; MBA in Finance, Univ. of Strathclyde, Scotland, UK; ***party:*** Democratic Progressive Party; ***political career:*** Minister of Finance, June 2009-12; Minister of Defence, 2012-; ***professional career:*** Consultant for UNICEF; ***office address:*** Ministry of Defence, Private Bag 339, Lilongwe 3, Malawi.

KANE, **Amadou;** Minister of the Economy and Finance, Government of Senegal; ***born:*** 1954; ***political career:*** Minister for Finance and the Economy, 2012-; ***professional career:*** Banking; President / CEO, Banque international pour le commerce et l'industrie du Sénégal (BICIS); ***office address:*** Ministry of Finance and the Economy, rue René Ndiaye, BP 4017, Dakar, Senegal; ***phone:*** +221 33 889 2100; ***fax:*** +221 33 822 41 95; ***URL:*** http://www.finances.gouv.sn.

KAPUYA, **Hon. Prof. Juma Athumani;** Minister of Labour, Employment and Youth Development , Government of Tanzania; ***political career:*** Minister of Education and Culture, Republic of Tanzania; Minister of Labour, Youth Development and Sport; Minister of Defence, 2006-08; Minister of Labour, Employment and Youth Development, 2008-; ***office address:*** Ministry of Labour, Employment and Youth Development , Dar es Salaam, Tanzania.

KARAOGLOU, Theodoros; Minister of Macedonia and Thrace, Government of Greece; ***languages:*** English; ***political career:*** MP, 2004-; Minister of Macedonia and Thrace, 2012-; ***publications:*** Public Intervention, 2007; ***office address:*** Ministry of Macedonia and Thrace, Administratioon Building, 54123 Thessaloniki, Greece; ***phone:*** +30 (0)310 379000; ***e-mail:*** minister@mathra.gr; ***URL:*** http://www.mathra.gr.

KARIMOV, Islam; Uzbek, President, Uzbekistan; ***born:*** 30 January 1938, Samarkand, Uzbekistan; ***married:*** Tatiana Karimova; ***d:*** 2; ***public role of spouse:*** Economist and Scientific Worker; ***education:*** Central Asian Polytechnical Institute; Tashkent Econ. Univ., degrees as an engineer-mechanic and economist; ***political career:*** Minister of Finance, UzSSR, 1983; Dep. Chmn. of Cncl. of Ministers, UzSSR - Cham. of the State Plan Cttee., 1986; President, Uzbek Soviet Socialist Republic, 1990; Chmn. of Cabinet Minister; Pres., Uzbekistan, 1991-; ***memberships:*** Academy of Sciences of Uzbekistan; ***professional career:*** Engineer, Leading Engineer-Constructor, Tashkent Aviation Factory, 1960-66; Chief Specialist, Head of Dept., First Dep. Chmn., State Planning Cttee., 1966-83; Chmn. State Planning Cttee., 1986; ***committees:*** First Sec., Kashkadarya Province Party Cttee., 1986-89; First Sec., Uzbek Communist Party Central Cttee., 1989-91; ***honours and awards:*** Hon. Dr. of Econs., Hon. Dr. and Academician of nine foreign Univ.; Hero of Uzbekistan; The Mustakillik and Amir Temur Awards; ***publications:*** Uzbekistan, its own model of renewal and progress, 1992; Uzbekistan - a State With A Great Future, 1992; On the Priorities of the Economic Policy of Uzbekistan, 1993; Uzbek model of deepening economic reforms, 1995; Stability and Reforms, 1996; Uzbekistan on the Threshold of the 21st Century, 1997; Uzbekistan Striving Towards the 21st Century, 1999; the Spiritual Path of Renewal, 2000; ***recreations:*** tennis; ***office address:*** Office of the President, Uzbekiston Shohkochasi 43, Tashkent 700163, Uzbekistan; ***phone:*** +998 371 139 5325; ***fax:*** +998 371 139 5625; ***e-mail:*** presidents_office@press-service.uz; ***URL:*** http://www.press-service.uz.

KARRAN, H.E. Bayney; Ambassador, Embassy of Guyana; ***languages:*** English, Spanish; ***professional career:*** Attorney; Amb. to Venezuela, 1997-2003; Amb. to the USA, 2003-; ***office address:*** Embassy of Guyana, 2490 Tracy Place NW, Washington, DC, 20008, USA; ***phone:*** + 1 202 265 6900; ***fax:*** +1 202 232 1297; ***e-mail:*** guyanaembassy@hotmail.com; ***URL:*** http://www.guyana.org/govt/embassy.html.

KARTI, Ali Ahmed; Minister of Foreign Affairs, Government of Sudan; ***education:*** Faculty of Law, Univ. of Khartoum; ***party:*** National Congress Party; ***political career:*** Minister of Foreign Affairs, 2010-; ***office address:*** Ministry of Foreign Affairs, P.O. Box 873, Khartoum, Republic of Sudan; ***URL:*** http://www.sudanmfa.com.

KARUGARAMA, Tharcisse; Minister of Justice and Attorney General, Government of Rwanda; ***party:*** RPF; ***political career:*** Politician; Minister of Justice, 2006-; Attorney General, 2007-; ***professional career:*** judge; vice pres., Supreme Court of Rwanda; ***office address:*** Ministry of Justice, PO Box 160, Kigali, Rwanda; ***URL:*** http://www.minijust.gov.rw.

KARZAI, Hamid; President, Islamic State of Afghanistan; ***born:*** 24 December 1957, Kandahar, Afghanistan; ***education:*** Simla Univ., India; ***political career:*** dir. of operations, Afghan National Liberation Front (ANLF), 1982; Transitional President and Chair, Interim Government of Afghanistan, 2001-04; elected President, 2004-; ***office address:*** Office of the President, Kabul, Afghanistan.

KASEL, Jean-Jacques; Luxembourgeois, Judge, Court of Justice of the European Union; ***born:*** 1946; ***education:*** Doctor in Law; Diploma in Administrative Law; ***professional career:*** At the Bar, Luxembourg 1970; Legal Adviser, Bank of Paris and of Netherlands, Luxembourg 1972-73; Attaché, Legation 1973-74; Cllr., Legation 1980-87; First Cllr., 1987; Min. Plen., 1987; Min., International Economic Relations 1973-76; Ambassador to UNESCO and Permanent Representative to OECD 1976-79; Min., Chef de Cabinet of Vice-Pres., 1979-81; Cllr., then Chef de Cabinet of Pres. of European Commission 1981; Dir. of Budget and with rank of Secy-Gen. of Council of Minister of European Community 1981-84; Head of Mission at Permanent Mission to European Community and Dir. of Political Affairs 1984-85; Min., Dir. of Political and Cultural Affairs 1986; Ambassador to Greece (with residence in Luxembourg) 1989; Ambassador and Permanent Representative to European Community 1991-98; Chairman of Coreper, 1997; Ambassador (Brussels, 1998-2002; Permanent Representative to NATO, 1998-2002; Marshal of the Court and Head of the Office of HRH the Grand Duke, 2002-07; Judge, Court of Justice of the European Union, 2008-; ***office address:*** Court of Justice of the European Union, Rue du Fort Niedergrünewald, L-2925, Luxembourg.

KASICH, John R.; American, Governor, State of Ohio; ***education:*** Ohio State Univ., 1974; ***party:*** Republican; ***political career:*** US House of Representatives, 1982-2000; Governor, Ohio, Jan. 2011-; ***professional career:*** MD, Investment Banking Div., Lehman Brothers; Presidential Fellow, Ohio State Univ.; ***office address:*** Office of the Governor, 30th Floor, 77 South High Street, Columbus, Ohio 43215-6117, USA; ***phone:*** +1 614 466 3555; ***URL:*** http://www.state.oh.us/gov.

KASOULIDES, Ioannis; Minister of Foreign Affairs, Government of Cyprus; ***born:*** 10 August 1948, Nicosia; ***languages:*** English, French, German; ***education:*** Studied medicine, Univ. of Lyon; specialised in Geriatrics in London hospitals; ***party:*** Group of the European People's Party (Christian Democrats) and European Democrats; ***political career:*** Pres. and various other posts, Youth of the Democratic Rally Party (NEDISY), 1990-93; Mem., House of Reps. for Nicosia, 1991; Govt. Spokesman, 1993-97; Minister of Foreign Affairs, 1997-03; MEP, 2004-13; Minister of Foreign Affairs, 2013-; ***committees:*** Dep. Pres., Parly. Health Cttee.; Mem., Finance, Budget, Education Cttees.; ***office address:*** Ministry of Foreign Affairs, Dem, Severis Avenue, 1477 Nicosia, Cyprus; ***URL:*** http://www.mfa.gov.cy.

KATAINEN, Jyrki; Prime Minister, Government of Finland; ***born:*** 14 October 1971; ***party:*** National Coalition Party; ***political career:*** Vice Chair, Youth of the European People's Party, 1998-2000; Chmn., Nat. Coalition Party Cncl., 1999-2000; MP, 1999-; Vice-Chair, Nat. Coalition Party Bd. of Dir., 2001-04, Chair, 2004-; Mem., Finnish Delegation to the Parly. Assembly of OSCE, 2004-05; Vice Pres., European People's Party, 2005-; Minister of Finance, 2007-; Deputy Prime Minister, 2010-11; Prime Minister, 2011-; ***committees:*** Chair, Cttee. for the Future, 2003-07; Finnish Broadcasting Co., Admin. Cncl., 2003-05; Parly. Supervisory Cncl., Bank of Finland, 2005-07; Mem., Forum for Int'l Affairs, 2006-07; Chair, Foreign Affairs Cttee., 2007; ***office address:*** Office of the Prime Minister, PO Box 23, 00023 Government, Helsinki, Finland; ***phone:*** +358 9 6611333; ***URL:*** http://www.vn.fi.

KATZ, H.E. Allan J.; Ambassador, US Embassy, Portugal; ***education:*** Univ. of Missouri, B.A.; American Univ., Washington College of Law, J.D.; ***political career:*** Assist. Insurance Cmnr. & General Counsel, Florida Insurance Dept.; General Counsel, U.S. HOR Cmn. on Administrative Review; Legislative Assist. to Congressman Bill Gunter; Legislative Dir. for Congressman David Obey; City Cmnr. City of Tallahassee; Hd., Jt. Planning Bd. ; ***professional career:*** Mging. Ptnr., Katz, Kutter, Alderman & Bryant, P.A.; Bd. Mem., Citizens Property Insurance Corp.; Counsel, Akerman Senterfitt; Ambassador to Portugal, 2009-; ***office address:*** US Embassy, Avenida das Forças Armadas, 1600-081 Lisbon, Portugal; ***phone:*** +351 21 727 3300; ***fax:*** +351 21 727 9109; ***URL:*** http://portugal.usembassy.gov/.

KATZ, Yisrael; Minister of Transportation and Road Safety, Government of Israel; ***political career:*** Minister of Agriculture and Rural Development, to 2006; Minister of Transportation and Road Safety, 2009-; Minister of National Infrastructure, 2013-; ***office address:*** Ministry of Transport, 97 Yaffo Street, Jerusalem 91000, Israel; ***URL:*** http://portal.mot.gov.il/.

KAUFMAN, Rt. Hon. Sir Gerald Bernard, KB, MA, MP; British, Member of Parliament for Manchester, Gorton, House of Commons; ***born:*** 1930; ***parents:*** Louis Kaufman and Jane Pantirer; ***education:*** State Schs., Oxford Univ.; ***party:*** Labour Party; ***political career:*** Parly. Press Liaison Officer, Labour Party, 1965-70; MP (Lab.) for Manchester, Ardwick, 1970-83; Under-Sec. of State, Dept. of the Environment, 1974-75; Under-Sec. of State, Dept. of Industry, 1975; Min. of State, Dept. of Industry, 1975-79; Privy Cllr., 1978; Opp. Spokesman on Environment, 1980-83; Shadow Home Sec., 1983-87; Shadow Foreign Sec., 1987-92; Mem., Royal Cmn. on the Reform of the House of Lords, 1999; MP, Manchester, Gorton 1983-; ***memberships:*** General, Municipal Boilermakers and Allied Trades Union; ***professional career:*** Asst. Gen. Sec., Fabian Soc., 1954-55; Political Staff, Daily Mirror, 1955-64; Political Correspondent, New Statesman, 1964-65; ***committees:*** Mem., Labour Party Nat. Exec. Cttee. (NEC) 1991-92; Chmn., Booker Prize Judges, 1999; Chmn., Nat. Heritage Select Cttee., 1992-97; Chmn., Culture, Media and Sport Select Cttee. 1997-2005; ***honours and awards:*** K.B., 2004; ***publications:*** How to Live Under Labour, The Left; To Build The Promised Land; How to be a Minister; Renewal; My Life in the Silver Screen; Inside the Promised Land; Meet Me In St. Louis; ***office address:*** House of Commons, London, SW1A 0AA, United Kingdom; ***phone:*** +44 (0)20 7219 3000; ***e-mail:*** hcinfo@parliament.uk.

KAWANA, Hon. Dr Albert; Minister for Presidential Affairs, Government of Namibia; ***born:*** 26 March 1956, Katima Mulilo, Namibia; ***parents:*** John Kawana and Easter Kawana; ***children:*** Brown (M), Minnie (F); ***education:*** UN Institute for Namibia, Zambia, Dipl. in Development Studies and Management, 1979; Univ. of Warwick, UK, LL.B, 1983, LL.M, 1984, Ph.D., 1988 ; ***party:*** SWAPO, 1971-; Mem. of SWAPO Central Cttee. 2002-; Mem., SWAPO Secretariat 2002- ; ***political career:*** MP, 2000-; Dep. Minister of Justice, 2000-03; Minister of Justice, 2003; Minister for Presidential Affairs, 2005-; Attorney General, 2009-; ***memberships:*** Planning Advisory Board, 1991-99; Bd. Mem., Namibia's Justice Training Centre, 1993-99; Board for Legal Education, 1993-99; Board of Dirs., NAMDEB Diamond Corp. (Pty) Ltd., 1994-99; ***professional career:*** Research Assist., Univ. of Warwick, 1984-87; Lecturer, UN Inst. for Namibia, 1988-90; Perm. Sec., Ministry of Justice, 1990-99; ***committees:*** Mem., SWAPO party drafting Cttee., 1989; Head, SWAPO Party Election Cttee., 1994 and 1999; Chmn., Cab. Cttee. on Legislation 2003-05; Chmn., Management Cttee., NAMDEB Diamond Corp. Ltd., 1996-99; ***publications:*** Author of several papers presented at international conferences; ***office address:*** Office of the President, Daniel Munamava Street, State House, Private Bag 13339, Windhoek, Namibia; ***phone:*** +264 (0)61 270 7213; ***fax:*** +264 (0)61 245989; ***e-mail:*** akawana@op.gov.na.

KAWCZYNSKI, Daniel; MP for Shrewsbury and Atcham, House of Commons; ***born:*** 1972; ***party:*** Conservative; ***political career:*** MP for Shrewsbury and Atcham, 2005-; ***office address:*** House of Commons, London, SW1P 0AA, United Kingdom; ***phone:*** +44 (0)20 7219 3000.

KAZIMIR, Ing. Peter; Deputy Prime Minister and Minister of Finance, Slovak Government; ***born:*** 1968; ***education:*** Univ. of Economics, Bratislava; ***political career:*** State Sec., Ministry of Finance, 2006-10; Mem., National Council, 2010-12; Vice-Chmn., Finance and Budget Cttee., 2010-12; Vice-Chmn, SMER-SD, 2010; Deputy PM and Minister of Finance, 2012-; ***office address:*** Ministry of Finance, Stefanovicova 5, PO Box 82, 817 82 Bratislava, Slovak Republic; ***URL:*** http://www.finance.gov.sk/.

KEBEDE, H.E. Berhanu; Ambassador, Embassy of Ethiopia in the UK; ***education:*** Addis Ababa Univ., 1978; MA, Free University of Brussels, Development Economics, 1986, Management and Finance,1988.; ***professional career:*** Chargé d'Affaires to the Russian Federation, 2000-02; Amb. to Sweden, Norway, Finland and Iceland, 2002-06; Amb. to UK, 2006-; ***office address:*** Ethiopian Embassy, 17 Prince's Gate, London, SW7 1PZ, United Kingdom; ***phone:*** +44 (0)20 7589 7212; ***fax:*** +44 (0)20 7584 7054; ***URL:*** http://www.ethioembassy.org.uk.

KEBO, Mirsad; Federation Vice President, Presidency of Bosnia and Herzegovina; ***born:*** 1947, Mostar; ***parents:*** Mehmed and Muhiba; ***married:*** Dina mel Cesir; ***children:*** Mehmed (M), Mirdina (F); ***public role of spouse:*** Tourist Association of Bosnia and Herzegovina (Head of Organisational Unit); ***education:*** Grad. Engineer in Chemistry; ***party:*** Vice-pres., Party for Democratic Action, 2001-; ***political career:*** Pres., Canton Sarajevo Assembly, 1996-2000; pres., Canton Sarajevo, 2000-01; representative, House of Representatives, Parl. of Fed., Bosnia and Herzegovina; mem., Cmn. for Human Rights, Parl. of Fed., Bosnia and Herzegovina; Minister for Human Rights and Refugees, Cncl. of Ministers of Bosnia and Herzegovina, 2003-06; Federation of Vice President, 2011-; ***professional career:*** Economy management; Pres., Public Utility Co. (Rad), Sarajevo, 1990-2000; ***committees:*** Fmr. Vice-pres., Cttee. for Housing-public Works and Environment Protection; Chmn., Bosnia and Herzegovina Cncl. of Ministers' Personnel Commission; ***office address:*** Office of the Presidency, Trg Bosne i Hercegovine 1, 71 000 Sarajevo, Bosnia and Herzegovina; ***phone:*** +387 (0)33 471630; ***fax:*** +387 (0)33 206140.

KEDDY, Gerald; Parliamentary Secretary to the Minister of International Trade, Canadian Government; ***political career:*** MP for South Shore, 1997-; Parly. Sec. to the Minister of the Atlantic Canada Opportunities Agency and to the Minister of International Trade, 2007-; ***professional career:*** Farmer; driller in oil industry; Christmas tree producer and exporter; ***office address:*** House of Commons, Parliament Buildings, Ottawa, ON K1A 0A6, Canada.

KEDIKILWE, Hon. Ponatshego H.K., MP; Botswanan, Vice President, Botswanan Government; ***born:*** 1938; ***education:*** Kikuyu College of Social Studies, Univ. of East Africa, Nairobi 1963-64; Univ. of Rochester, NY 1964-65; Univ. of Connecticut 1965-68; Maxwell School of Citizenship and Public Affairs, Syracuse Univ., NY 1968-70; ***political career:*** Asst. Principal, Ministry of Finance and Dev. Planning, 1970-73; Principal Finance Officer, 1973-75; Dir. of Financial Affairs, 1976-77; Permanent Sec., Ministry of Works and Communications, 1977-78; Dir. of Public Service Management, Office of the Pres., 1979-83; MP; Asst. Minister of Finance and Dev. Planning, 1984; Minister of Presidential Affairs and Public Admin., 1985-89; Chmn. of Nat. Education Cmn., 1992; Minister of Commerce and Industry, 1989-94; Minister of Presidential Affairs and Public Admin., 1994-98; Minister of Finance and Development Planning, 1998-99; Minister of Education 1999-2001; Minister of Minerals, Energy and Water Resources, 2007-; Vice President, 2012-; ***memberships:*** Fellow, International Bankers Assn. 1974-; Commonwealth Parly. Assn; Vice-Pres., African Assn. of Public Administration and Management; ***professional career:*** on various boards including Bank of Botswana and Chmn. of Cncl., Univ. of Botswana; ***office address:*** Ministry of Minerals, Energy and Water Resources, Private Bag 005, Gaborone, Botswana.

KEELEY, Barbara; MP for Worsley and Eccles South, House of Commons; ***party:*** Labour; ***political career:*** Councillor, Trafford Borough Cncl., 1995-2004; MP for Worsley, 2005-10, Worsley and Eccles, 2010-; Parly. Sec., Office of the Leader of the House of Commons, 2009-10; Shadow Minister for Health, May-Sept. 2010; Shadow Minister, Communities and Local Government, Oct. 2010-11; ***committees:*** Constitutional Affairs, 2005-06; Finance and Services, 2006-10; Health, 2011-; ***office address:*** House of Commons, London, SW1A 0AA, United Kingdom; ***e-mail:*** keeleyb@parliament.uk.

KEFALOGIANNI, Olga; Minister of Tourism, Government of Greece; ***education:*** LLB, National and Kapodistrian Univ. of Athens, 1997; LLM in commercial and business law, King's College, London Univ., UK 1998; MA in International Affairs, The Fletcher School of Law and Diplomacy, Tufts Univ., USA; ***political career:*** MP, 2007-; Miniser of Tourism, 2012-; ***office address:*** Ministry of Tourism, Bouboulinas 20-22, 10682 Athens, Greece; ***phone:*** +30 210 820 1100; ***URL:*** http://www.mintour.gr.

KEITH, Right Hon. Judge Sir Kenneth James, KBE; New Zealand, Judge, International Court of Justice; ***born:*** 19 November 1937; ***languages:*** English, French; ***education:*** University of New Zealand, LLB 1961; Victoria University of Wellington, LLM, 1964; Legal qualification: QC; ***interests:*** Armed conflict; Dispute settlement; Human rights; Litigation; Organisations; State responsibility; Treaties; ***memberships:*** International Institute of Strategic Studies, 1973-; New Zealand Institute of International Affairs, 1966-; American Law Institute, 2002-; ASIL, 1966-; Institut de Droit International, 1997-; Australian and New Zealand Society of International Law; ILA, New Zealand Branch; International Humanitarian Law Consultant to the New Zealand Red Cross; ***professional career:*** *academic career:* Victoria University of Wellington, Junior lecturer, 1962-63, Lecturer, 1964, Senior Lecturer, 1966-70, Reader, 1971-83, Professor, 1974-91, Professor Emeritus, 1991-; NZ Institute of International Affairs, Director, 1971-73; Osgoode Hall Law School, Visiting Professor, 1981-82; *professional career:* Supreme Court of NZ, Solicitor, 1960, Barrister, 1961, QC, 1994; ICJ, member of NZ legal team, Nuclear Testing cases, 1973, 1974, 1995; *governmental career:* NZ Department of External Affairs, legal division, 1960-62; UN Secretariat, Office of Legal Affairs, 1968-70; Member of NZ Law Commission, 1986-96, President, 1991-96; *diplomatic career:* Leader of NZ delegation to Diplomatic Conference updating Geneva Conventions for the protection of war victims, 1975-76; Member of International Humanitarian Fact-Finding Commission, 1991, President, 2002; *judicial career:* Western Samoan Court of Appeal, 1982-; Cook Islands Court of Appeal, 1982-; Arbitrator in: Rainbow Warrior arbitration, NZ v France, 1989-90, Southern Bluefin Tuna Arbitration, Australia and NZ v Japan; Niue Court of Appeal, 1995-; Judge of the NZ Court of Appeal, 1996-2003; Chair of UPS v Canada (NAFTA), 2000-; Judicial Committee of the Privy Council, London, 1997-; Judge of the Fijian Supreme Court, 2003-; Judge of the NZ Supreme Court, 2004; Judge, ICJ, 2006-; ***publications:*** Books: Essays on Human Rights, editor, 1968; The Extent of the Advisory Jurisdiction of the International Court of Justice, 1971; Defence Perspectives, editor, 1972; International Implications of Race Relations in New Zealand, 1972; Articles: AJIL; Australian Yearbook of International Law; ICLQ; New Zealand Universities Law Review; Victoria University of Wellington Law Review; Texas International Law Journal; Duke Law Journal; Georgetown Immigration Law Journal; Political Science; Human Rights Journal; Cambridge Law Journal; Otago Law Review; Waikato Law Review; ***office address:*** International Court of Justice, Peace Palace, 2517 KJ The Hague, The Netherlands.

KELLY, Chris; MP for Dudley South, UK Government; ***education:*** BA, Oxford Brookes Univ., 1999; MBA, Imperial Coll. Business School, 2003; ***party:*** Conservative; ***political career:*** MP for Dudley South, May 2010-; ***committees:*** European Scrutiny, 2010-; ***office address:*** House of Commons, London, SW1A 0AA, United Kingdom; ***phone:*** +44 (0)20 7219 3000; ***e-mail:*** office@chriskellymp.com.

KENDALL, Liz; MP for Leicester West, UK Government; ***education:*** Queens' College, Cambridge Univ.; ***party:*** Labour Party; ***political career:*** MP for Leicester West, May 2010-; Shadow Minister, Health, Oct. 2010-Oct. 2011; Shadow Minister for Care and Older People, Oct. 2011-; ***committees:*** Education, 2010; ***office address:*** House of Commons, London, SW1A 0AA, United Kingdom; ***phone:*** +44 (0)20 7219 3000; ***e-mail:*** liz.kendall.mp@parliament.uk.

KENNEDY, Anthony M.; Associate Justice, US Supreme Court; ***born:*** 23 July 1936, Sacramento, California; ***education:*** Stanford Univ., B.A.; London School of Economics; Harvard Law School, LL.B.; ***professional career:*** Private practice, California, 1961-75; US Court of Appeals, Ninth Circuit. 1975-1988; Associate Justice, US Supreme Court, 1988-; ***committees:*** Federal Judicial Center, 1987-88; US Judicial Conference; Advisory Panel on Financial Disclosure Reports and Judicial Activities (renamed Advisory Cttee. on Codes of Conduct), 1979-87; Cttee. on Pacific Territories, 1979-90, chair 1982-90; ***office address:*** Supreme Court Building, One First Street,, NE, Washington, DC 20543, USA; ***phone:*** +1 202 479 3211; ***URL:*** http://www.supremecourt.gov/.

KENNEDY, Rt. Hon. Charles Peter, MP; British, MP for Ross, Skye and Lochaber, House of Commons; ***born:*** 25 November 1959, Inverness, Scotland, UK; ***married:*** Sarah (née Gurling), 20 July 2002; ***children:*** Donald (M); ***education:*** Univ. of Glasgow, MA (Hons.), Politics and Philosophy; Fulbright Scholar, Indiana Univ.; ***party:*** Liberal Democrat Party; ***political career:*** MP (SDP) Ross, Cromarty and Skye, 1983-97; Ross, Skye and Inverness West, 1997-2005; Ross, Skye and Lochaber, 2005-; SDP Spokesman on Health and Social Services, 1983-87; Chmn., SDP in Scotland, 1986-88; Lib. Dem. Spokesman on Social Security, 1988-90; Lib. Dem. Spokesman on Health, 1990-92; Lib. Dem. Spokesman on Europe, 1992-97; UK Party Pres., Lib. Dems., 1990-94; Lib Dem. Spokesman and Team Leader, Agriculture and Rural Affairs, 1997-99; Leader, Lib. Dems., 1999-2006 (resigned); ***memberships:*** Gaelic Coll. Appeal Cttee, Isle of Skye (Trustee), 1984-88; Select Cttee on Social Services, 1986-87; World Communications Assn. Youngest MP, 1983-87; ***professional career:*** BBC Journalist/Broadcaster, 1982; Assoc. Instructor, Dept. of Speech Communications, Indiana Univ. 1982-83; ***committees:*** All Party Select Cttee. on Health and Social Services; Commons Select Cttee. for introducing television to the Chamber; Standards & Privileges, 1997-99; Works of Art, 2011-; ***honours and awards:*** British Observer Mace Fox Univ. Debating; ***office address:*** House of Commons, London, SW1A 0AA, United Kingdom; ***phone:*** +44 (0)20 7219 3000; ***e-mail:*** kennedyc@parliament.uk; ***URL:*** http://www.charleskennedy.org.uk.

KENNEDY, Danny; British, Member, Northern Ireland Assembly; ***born:*** 6 July 1959; ***parents:*** John Trevor Kennedy and Mary Ida Kennedy (née Black); ***married:*** Karen Susan Kennedy (née McCrum), 1988; ***children:*** Stephen (M), Philip (M), Hannah (F); ***education:*** Newry High Sch., N.I.; ***party:*** Ulster Unionist; ***political career:*** Councillor, Newry & Mourne District Cncl., 1985, Chmn., 1994-95; mem., N.I. Assembly, 1998; mem., Newry and Armagh, N.I. Assembly; Dep. Leader, UUP Assembly Party, 2005-; Minister for Regional Development, 2011-; ***interests:*** economic development, tourism, education; ***professional career:*** British Telecom., N.I., 1978-98; ***committees:*** Chmn., N.I. Assembly Education Cttee. 2001-03; Bd. of Governors, Newry High Sch., Bessbrook Primary Sch.; mem., Newry & Mourne Local Strategy Partnership; mem., Newry & Mourne District Policing Partnership; ***recreations:*** family, church activities, sport (spectator), reading; ***office address:*** Advice Centre, 107 Main Street, Markethill, Co. Armagh, BT60 1PH, Northern Ireland; ***phone:*** +44 (0)28 3755 2831; ***fax:*** +44 (0)28 3755 2832.

KENNEDY OF SOUTHWARK, Lord Roy; Member, House of Lords; ***party:*** Labour; ***political career:*** Dir., Finance and Compliance, Labour Party; Mem., House of Lords, 2010-; ***office address:*** House of Lords, London, SW1A 0PW, United Kingdom; ***phone:*** +44 (0)20 7219 3000; ***fax:*** +44 (0)20 7219 5979; ***URL:*** http://www.parliament.uk.

KENNEY, Jason; Member of Parliament for Calgary Southeast, Canadian House of Commons; ***political career:*** MP for Calgary Southeast, 1997-; Sec. of State (Multiculturalism and Canadian Identity), 2007-; Minister of Citizenship, Immigration and Multiculturalism, 2008-; ***office address:*** House of Commons, Parliament Buildings, Ottawa, ON K1A 0A6, Canada.

KENNEY, H.E. Kristie A.; Ambassador, US Embassy in the Philippines; ***professional career:*** Diplomat since 1981, most recently: US Amb. to Ecuador; Amb, to the Philippines, 2006-10; Amb. to Thailand, 2011-; ***office address:*** Embassy of the United States of America, 1201 Roxas Boulevard, Ermita 1000, Manila, Philippines; ***phone:*** +63 2 523 1001; ***fax:*** +63 2 522 4361; ***URL:*** http://usembassy.state.gov/manila.

KENNY, Enda, TD; Irish, Taoiseach, Government of Ireland; ***born:*** 1951, Castlebar, Co. Mayo; ***education:*** St. Gerald's Secondary Sch.; St. Patrick's Teachers' Training College; ***political career:*** Former Minister of State at the Depts. of Education and Labour; elected to the Dáil, 1975; Front bench spokesperson on the Gaeltacht, 1982, 1987-88; on Western Development, 1982, on Youth Affairs and Sport, 1977-80; Fine Gael Economic Affairs Cttee., 1991-92; Mem., Executive Cttee. of Inter-Parliamentary Union, 1993-; Chmn., Fine Gael Economic Affairs Cttee., 1991-92; Fine Gael Chief Whip 1992; Minister for Tourism and Trade, 1994-97; Leader, Fine Gael, 2002-; Taoiseach, Feb. 2011; ***memberships:*** Mayo CC, 1975-; ***committees:*** Former Chmn., Mayo Vocational Education Cttee.; West Mayo Vocational Education Cttee; Western Health Bd.; ***office address:*** Department of the Taoiseach, Government Buildings, Upper Merrion Street, Dublin 2, Ireland; ***URL:*** http://www.taoiseach.gov.ie.

KENT, Peter; Minister of State for the Environment, Government of Canada; ***born:*** 1943; ***party:*** Conservative; ***political career:*** MP, 2008-; Minister of State of Foreign Affairs (Americas), 2008-11; Minister of State for the Environment, 2011-; ***professional career:*** Journalist; TV Producer; TV Presenter; ***office address:*** House of Commons, Parliament Buildings, Wellington Street, Ottawa, Ontario, K1A 0A6, Canada; ***phone:*** +1 613 943 5959.

KENYATTA, Uhuru; President, Government of Kenya; ***parents:*** Jomo Kenyatta; ***education:*** Amherst College, USA; ***political career:*** MP for Gatundu South; Minister for Local Government; Dep. Prime Minister, 2008; Minister of Trade, 2008-09; Minister of Finance from, 2009-12; President of Kenya, 2013-; ***office address:*** Office of the President, Harambee House, Harambee Avenue, PO Box 30510, Nairobi, Kenya; ***phone:*** +254 20 227411 ; ***fax:*** +254 20 210150; ***URL:*** http://www.officeofthepresident.go.ke.

KEQIANG, Li; Politburo Standing Committee, Government of China; ***born:*** 1955, Anhui Province, China; ***education:*** Peking Univ., Law; ***political career:*** joined CCP, 1976; Dep. Sec., CCP, Henan Province, 1998; Party Sec., Liaoning Province, 2004-08; Mem., Standing Cttee., CCP Politburo, 2007-; Vice-Premier of the State Council, 2008-13; Mem., Standing Cttee., 8th National People's Congress, 2008-13; Minister for Economic Development, Reform and Prices, 2008-13; ***professional career:*** Manual labour on a commune; ***office address:*** Office of the State Council, Beijing, China.

KERLIKOWSKE, R. Gil; Director, National Drug Control Policy, Office of National Drug Control Policy; *education:* BA, MA, criminal justice; *professional career:* St. Petersburg Police Dept., Florida; Police Commissioner of Buffalo, New York; Dep. Dir., US Dept. of Justice, Office of Community Oriented Policing Services; Chief of Police, Seattle; Dir., Office of National Drug Control Policy, to date; *office address:* Office of National Drug Control Policy, Drug Policy Information Clearinghouse, PO Box 6000, Rockville, MD 20849-6000, USA; *URL:* http://www.whitehouse.gov/ondcp.

KERR OF TONAGHMORE, Lord Brian; Justice of the Supreme Court of the United Kingdom; *born:* February 1948; *education:* St Colman's College, Newry; Queen's Univ., Belfast; *political career:* Member, House of Lords, 2009-, as Justice of the Supreme Court, disqualified from participation 2009-; *professional career:* Barrister; Appointed, Judge of the High Court, 1993; Appointed Lord Chief Justice, 2004; Lord of Appeal in Ordinary, 2009-; Justice of the Supreme Court of the United Kingdom, 2009-; *honours and awards:* Created Baron Kerr of Tonaghmore, of Tonaghmore in the County of Down, June 2009; *office address:* Supreme Court of the United Kingdom, Parliament Square, London, SW1P 3BD, United Kingdom; *URL:* http://www.supremecourt.gov.uk.

KERRY, John F.; Secretary of State, US Government; *born:* 11 December 1943; *married:* Teresa Kerry (née Heinz); *children:* Alexandra (F), Vanessa (F), John (stepson) (M), Andre (stepson) (M), Christopher (stepson) (M); *education:* Yale Univ., 1966; Boston Law Coll., 1976; *party:* Democrat; *political career:* Lt. Governor, 1982; US Senator for Massachusetts, 1984-13; presidential candidate, 2004; Secretary of State, 2013-; *memberships:* active leader, Vietnam Veterans Against War; co-founder, Vietnam Veterans of America; *professional career:* enlisted in the Navy, 1966; *committees:* Senate Banking, Small Business, Commerce, Foreign Relations and Intelligence Cttees.; Chmn., Senate Democratic Steering and Coordination Cttee.; *honours and awards:* Silver Star, Bronze Star, three Purple Hearts for service in the Navy; two Presidential Unit Citations; Nat. Defense Medal; *office address:* Department of State, 2201 C Street, NW, Washington, DC 20520, USA; *phone:* +1 202 647 4000; *URL:* http://state.gov/.

KESTENBAUM, Lord Jonathan; Member, House of Lords; *party:* Labour Party; *political career:* Mem., House of Lords, 2011-; *professional career:* Chief Exec., National Endowment for Science, Technology and the Arts; *office address:* House of Lords, London, SW1A 0PW, United Kingdom; *phone:* +44 (0)20 7219 3000.

KETSO, Hon. Leketekete Victor; Minister of Finance, Government of Lesotho; *political career:* Minister of Finance and Development Planning, 1998-2000; Minister of Finance, 2012-; *office address:* Ministry of Finance, PO Box 395, Maseru, Lesotho; *phone:* +266 2231 0826; *URL:* http://www.lesotho.gov.ls/mnfinance.htm.

KEY, Rt. Hon. John; Prime Minister, Government of New Zealand; *born:* 9 August 1961, Auckland, New Zealand; *married:* Bronagh Key, 1984; *children:* 2; *education:* BCom., in accounting, Univ. of Canterbury, 1981; studied at Harvard Univ., USA; *party:* Leader, National Party, 2006-; *political career:* MP for Helensville, 2002-; National party Finance Spokesperson, 2004-08; Prime Minister, Nov. 2008-; *professional career:* Foreign Exchange Dealer, Elders Finance, Wellington; Bankers Trust, Auckland; Global Head of Foreign Exchange, Merrill Lynch, London; *office address:* Office of the Prime Minister, Level 5, Reserve Bank Building, 2 The Terrace, Wellington, New Zealand; *URL:* http://www.dpmc.govt.nz.

KHAMA, President Seretse Khama Ian; President, Government of Botswana; *parents:* President Sir Seretse Khama; *education:* Sandhurst Officer Training Coll., UK; *party:* Chmn., Botswana Democratic Party (BDP), 2003-; *political career:* Vice President and Minister for Presidential Affairs and Public Administration; Vice-President, 1998-2008; President, Apr. 2008-; *professional career:* Commander, Botswana Defence Force (BDF); *office address:* Office of the President, Private Bag 001, Gaborone, Botswana.

KHAMENEI, Ayatollah al-Udhma Sayyid Ali; Spiritual Leader, Islamic Republic of Iran; *born:* 1939; *political career:* President, 1981-89; Religious Leader and Commander in Chief of the Armed Forces, 1989-; *office address:* Office of the Spiritual Leader, Tehran, Iran.

KHAN, Dr Fuad; Minister of Health, Government of Trinidad & Tobago; *party:* UNC; *political career:* MP, 1995-2007; Dep. Speaker, 1995-2001; Minister of Health, 2001; Mem. of Opposition, 2001-07; MP, 2010-; Dep. Speaker, 2010-; Minister of Health, 2011-; *professional career:* medical doctor, specializing urology; *office address:* Ministry of Health, Corner of Duncan Street and Independence Square, Port of Spain, Trinidad and Tobago; *phone:* +1 868 627 0010; *fax:* +1 868 623 9628; *URL:* http://www.health.gov.tt.

KHAN, Madam Judge Khalida Rachid; Pakistani; *born:* 25 September 1949; *languages:* English, Urdu, Pushto; *education:* Peshawar University, Pakistan, BA, 1967, Political Science, Islamic History, LLB, 1969, International Law, Civil Law, Law of Torts, Company Law; Masters in Political Sciences, 1971; Legal qualification: Judge; *interests:* Criminal Law; Human rights; *memberships:* International Association of Women Judges; *professional career: governmental career:* Solicitor to The Government of NWFP, 1987-89; *judicial career:*Permanent Judge, ICTR, 2003-; Justice of the Peshawar High Court, 1994; Special Judge, Banking Companies, 1992-94; Special Judge, Customs, Taxation & Anti-Corruption, 1989-92; Chairperson, Services Rule Committee, 1980-83; District/Sessions Judge, 1979; Civil/Senior Judge, 1974; *publications:* Articles: Asia/South Pacific Regional Judicial Colloquium; *office address:* International Criminal Tribunal for Rwanda, Arusha International Conference Centre, PO Box 6016, Arusha, Tanzania; *phone:* +255 27 256 5194; *fax:* +255 27 250 4000; *e-mail:* Khanras71@hotmail.com; *URL:* http://www.ictr.com.

KHAN, Nisar Ali; Minister of the Interior, Government of the Pakistan; *political career:* Minister, Ministry of Science and Technology, 1988; Minister of Petroleum and Natural resources, 1990-93, 1997-99; Senior Leader, Pakistan Muslim League; Leader of the Opposition, 2008; Minister of the Interior, 2013-; *office address:* Ministry of the Interior, 4th Floor, Block R, Pakistan Secretariat, Islamabad, Pakistan; *URL:* http://www.interior.gov.pk/.

KHAN, Sadiq; Shadow Lord Chancellor, Shadow Secretary of State for Justice, House of Commons; *born:* 1970; *party:* Labour; *political career:* Councillor, Wandsworth Borough Cncl., 1994-2006; MP for Tooting, 2005-; Parly. Under Sec., Dept. for Communities and Local Gov., 2008-09; Shadow Minister for Transport, May-Sept. 2010-; Shadow Lord Chancellor, Shadow Secretary of State for Justice (with responsibility for political and constitutional reform), Oct. 2010-; *professional career:* Solicitor; *office address:* House of Commons, London, SW1A 0AA, United Kingdom.

KHARGE, Mallikarjun; Minister of Labour and Employment, Government of India; *party:* Indian National Congress; *political career:* MP, 1972-; Minister of Labour and Employment, 2009-; *office address:* Ministry of Labour and Employment, Shram Shakti Bhavan, Raffi Marg, New Delhi 110 001, India; *phone:* +91 11 371 7515; *URL:* http://labour.nic.in.

KHARKAVETS, Andrey; Minister of Finance, Government of Belarus; *political career:* First Dep. Finance Minister; Minister of Finance, 2008-; *office address:* Ministry of Finance, 7 Sovetskaya Street, 220010 Minsk, Belarus; *phone:* +375 17 222 6137; *fax:* +375 17 222 4593; *e-mail:* web_mf@open.by; *URL:* http://www.ncpi.gov.by/minfin.

KHAW BOON WAN ; Minister for National Development, Government of Singapore; *born:* 8 December 1952; *education:* Univ. of Newcastle, Australia under the Singapore Gov. Colombo Plan Scholarship, B.Engineering (Hons) and B.Commerce, 1977; *political career:* Snr. Minister of State for Transport and Information, Communications and the Arts, 2001-03; Acting Minister for Health and Snr. Minister of State for Finance, 2003-04; Minister for Health, 2004-11; Minister for National Development, 2011-; *professional career:* CEO, Nat. Univ. Hospital, KK Hospital and the Singapore General Hospital; *office address:* Ministry of National Development, 5 Maxwell Road, 21/22-00 Tower Block, 069110 Singapore, Singapore.

KHUPHE, Thokozani; Deputy Prime Minister, Government of Zimbabwe; *born:* 1963; *education:* BA, Media Studies; *party:* Vice Pres., Movement for Democratic Change; *political career:* MP for Makokoba, 2000-; Deputy Prime Minister, Feb. 2009-; *office address:* Office of the Deputy Prime Minister, Munhumutapa Building, Samora Machel Avenue, Causeway, Harare, Zimbabwe; *URL:* http://www.zimbabweprimeminister.org.

KIDRON, Baroness Beeban, OBE; Member, House of Lords; *political career:* Mem., House of Lords, 2012-; *professional career:* Film Dir. and Producer; Dir., Bodyline Films Ltd.; Dir., Soho Angel Films Ltd.; Dir., Cross Street Films Ltd.; Governor, British Film Institute; *office address:* House of Lords, London, SW1 0PW, United Kingdom; *phone:* +44 (0)20 7219 5353.

KIIR MAYARDIIT, Salva; President, South Sudan; *born:* 1951; *political career:* Joined Sudanese army following 1972 peace agreement; joined rebels, 1983; Pres., South Sudan (still part of Sudan), 2005-11; Vice-Pres., Sudan (as part of power-sharing agreeement); Leader, Sudan People's Liberation Movement, 2005; Pres., independent South Sudan, 2011-; *office address:* Office of the President, Juba, South Sudan.

KIKWETE, Hon. Jakaya Mrisho; President and Commander in Chief of the Armed Forces, Government of Tanzania; *born:* Bagamoyo, Tanzania; *education:* Economics Degree from the Univ. of Dar es Salaam; *party:* Chama Cha Mapinduzi; *political career:* Minister of Foreign Affairs and Cooperation; President and Commander in Chief of the Armed Forces, 2005-; *professional career:* Military Officer ; *office address:* State House, Magogoni Road, PO Box 9120, Dar es Salaam, Tanzania.

KILROY, Mary Jo; Congresswoman, Ohio 15th Dist., US House of Representatives; *education:* Cleveland State Univ., B.A.; Ohio State Univ., J.D.; *political career:* Mem., Columbus Bd. of Educ., 1991-98; Franklin County Cmnr., 2000-08, Pres., 2005-07; US Congresswoman, 2009-; *committees:* Financial Services - Capital Markets, Insurance and Government Sponsored Enterprises, Housing and Community Opportunity and Oversight and Investigations subcttees; Homeland Security; *office address:* House of Representatives, Washington, DC 20515, USA.

KIM, Jong-un; Supreme Leader of the Party, Government of North Korea; *parents:* Kim Jong-il (dec'd) and Ko Yong-hui (dec'd); *married:* Ri Sol-ju, 2012; *education:* Educated in Switzerland; Kim Il-sung Military Univ.; *party:* Gen. Sec., Korean Workers' Party; *political career:* Supreme Leader of the Party, State and Army; First Secretary of the Korean Workers Party (KWP); Supreme Commander of the Armed Forces; First Chair of the National Defence Commission; Chair of the Central Military Commission of the KWP, 2011-; *office address:* Central Committee of the Workers' Party of Korea, Pyongyang, North Korea.

KIM, Sung Y.; Ambassador, US Embassy in the Republic of Korea; *education:* BA, Univ. of Pennslyvania, USA; LLB, Loyola Univ., Chicago, USA; Master of LAws, London School of Economics, UK; *professional career:* Public Prosecutor, Los Angeles County District Attorney's Office; Head, Office of Korean Affairs, Dept. of State, 2006-08; Amb. to South Korea, 2011-; *office address:* Embassy of the United States of America, 82, Sejong-no, Chongno-ku, Seoul, South Korea; *phone:* +82 2 397 4114; *fax:* +82 2 725 6843; *URL:* http://seoul.usembassy.gov.

KIM, Yong Nam; President of the Presidium of the Supreme People's Assembly, Government of North Korea; *party:* Korean Workers Party; *political career:* Minister of Foreign Affairs, 1983-98; President of the Presidium of the Supreme People's Assembly, 1998-; *office address:* Office of the President of the Presidium of the Supreme People's Assembly, Pyongyang, North Korea.

KIN-CHUNG CHEUNG, Matthew; Secretary for Labour and Welfare, Executive Council of Hong Kong SAR; *professional career:* Joined the Administrative Service, 1979; promoted to the rank of Administrative Officer Staff Grade A1, 2004; Dep. Sec. for Education and Manpower, 1996-99; Commissioner for Labour, 1999-2000; Dir. of Education, 2000-02; Permanent Sec. for Economic Development and Labour Bureau, 2002-07; Sec. for Labour and Welfare, 2007-; ***office address:*** Bureau of Labour and Welfare, Central Government Offices, Lower Albert Road, Hong Kong, Hong Kong SAR; ***phone:*** +852 2810 2318; ***fax:*** +852 2337 3539; ***URL:*** http://www.lwb.gov.hk.

KING, Angus S., Jr.; American, Senator for Maine, US Senate; ***born:*** 31 March 1944, Alexandria, VA, USA; ***married:*** Mary King; ***education:*** Dartmouth Coll., BA, 1966; Univ. of Virginia Law Sch., law degree, 1969; ***political career:*** Governor, Maine, 1994-02; Senator, US Senate, 2012-; ***professional career:*** Aide to Senator William D. Hathaway, ME, 1972-75; Chief Counsel, US Senate Subcttee. on Alcoholism and Narcotics; Attorney, 1975-83; Founded energy conservation co., 1989, Pres., 1989-94; Host of a Maine public television public affairs programme; ***office address:*** US Senate, 188 Russell Senate Office Building, Washington DC 25010, USA; ***phone:*** +1 202 224 5344; ***URL:*** http://www.king.senate.gov/.

KING OF BOW, Baroness Oona; British, Member, House of Lords; ***born:*** 22 October 1967; ***parents:*** Professor Preston King and Hazel Stern; ***married:*** Tiberio Santomarco; ***public role of spouse:*** Media Executive; ***languages:*** French, Italian; ***education:*** York Univ.; Berkeley Univ.; ***party:*** Labour Party; ***political career:*** Political Asst., Glenys Kinnock; GMB Regional Officer; MP, Founder & Chmn., APPG on Genocide Prevention & The Great Lakes Region; MP, Bethnal Green and Bow, 1997-2005; PPS to Sec. of State at DTI, Rt. Hon. Patricia Hewitt MP, 2003-2005; mem., House of Lords, 2011-; ***interests:*** poverty, race, housing, Europe, employment, international development, women's issues, social enterprise; ***memberships:*** Mem. International Dev. Select Cttee.; ***committees:*** Int. Development, 1997-2001; DTLR Select Cttee.- Urban Affairs, 2001-02; Modernisation; ***publications:*** Why we still need Feminism, edited by Natasha Walter; ***recreations:*** languages, music, film, fitness; ***office address:*** House of Lords, London, SW1A 0PW, United Kingdom; ***phone:*** +44 (0)20 7219 3000.

KINNEAR, Ms Meg, LLB, LLM; Canadian, Secretary-General, International Centre for Settlement of Investment Disputes; ***born:*** 30 April 1957; ***languages:*** English, French; ***education:*** Queen's University, BA, 1978; Smith College, 1975; University of Virginia, LLM, 1982; McGill University, LLB, 1981; Legal qualification: Member, Law Society of Upper Canada (Ontario), 1984-; Member, District of Columbia Bar, 1982-; ***interests:*** Claims; Dispute settlement; Economic law; Litigation; Treaties; Arbitration; ***professional career:*** *governmental career:* Senior General Counsel and Director General, Trade Law Bureau, Departments of Justice, Foreign Affairs and International Trade Canada, 1999-2009; Chair, FTAA Negotiating Group on Dispute Settlement, 2002; Secretary-General, ICSID, 2009-; ***publications:*** Books: Investment Disputes under NAFTA, 2006; Federal Court Practice, published annually, 1988-; Crown Liability and Proceedings Act Annotated, 1994; Articles: International Law News; IBA; ***office address:*** ICSID, 1818 H Street, N.W, Washington, DC 20433, USA; ***phone:*** +1 202 458 1534; ***fax:*** +1 202 522 2615.

KIRBY, Simon; MP for Brighton, Kemptown, UK Government; ***born:*** 1964; ***party:*** Conservative; ***political career:*** MP for Brighton, Kemptown, May 2010-; ***committees:*** Environmental Audit, 2010-11; Business, Innovation and Skills, 2010-; Administration, 2011-; ***office address:*** House of Commons, London, SW1A 0AA, United Kingdom; ***phone:*** +44 (0)20 7219 7024; ***e-mail:*** simon.kirby.mp@parliament.uk; ***URL:*** http://www.simonkirby.org.

KIRK, Mark; Senator, Illinois, US Senate; ***education:*** Cornell Univ.; LSE, UK; Georgetown Univ., law; ***party:*** Republican Party; ***political career:*** Mem., US House of Representatives, 2000-10; Mem., US Senate, 2010-; ***professional career:*** lawyer; Baker & McKenzie; World Bank; ***committees:*** Senate Cttees.: Appropriations; Banking, Housing and Urban Affairs; Healthcare, Labor & Pensions; Aging; ***office address:*** Senate, Washington, DC 20515, USA; ***URL:*** http://www.kirk.senate.gov.

KISHIDA, Fumio; Minister of Foreign Affairs, Government of Japan; ***born:*** 1957; ***education:*** Waseda University, Japan, 1982; ***political career:*** Mem., House of Representatives, 1993-; Minister of State for Okinawa and Northern Territories Affairs, Science and Technology Policy, Quality-of-Life Policy, and Regulatory Reform, 2007-08; Minister of State for Consumer Affairs, Minister for Space Policy, 2008-11; Minister of Foreign Affairs, 2013-; ***professional career:*** Long-Term Credit Bank of Japan; ***office address:*** Ministry of Foreign Affairs, 2-2-1 Kasumigaseki, Chiyoda-ku, Tokyo 100, Japan; ***phone:*** +81 3 3580 3311; ***URL:*** http://www.mofa.go.jp.

KISLYAK, Serguey; Russian, Ambassador to the United States, Russian Embassy; ***parents:*** Ivanovitch; ***languages:*** French, English; ***education:*** Physical Institute, Moscow, 1973; Foreign Trade Academy, 1977; ***professional career:*** Permanent Representative to UN, Min. of Foreign Affairs, 1981-85; Russian Embassy to US, 1985-88; Dir., Security and Disarmament Dept. of the Min. of Foreign Affairs, 1995-98; Permanent Representative to NATO; Ambassador to Belgium; Ambassador to the United States, 2008-; ***office address:*** United States Embassy, 2650 Wisconsin Avenue, NW, Washington, DC 20007, USA; ***phone:*** +1 202 298 5700; ***fax:*** +1 202 298 5735; ***URL:*** http://www.russianembassy.org.

KITTIRATT NA-RANONG ; Deputy Prime Minister and Minister of Finance, Government of Thailand; ***born:*** 1958; ***education:*** Chulalongkom Univ., Bachelors, economics, Masters, business administration; ***political career:*** Dep. Prime Minister and Minister of Commerce, 2011-12; Deputy Prime Minister and Minister of Finance, 2012-; ***professional career:*** Pres., Stock Exchange of Thailand; Chmn., National Economics Research Council; Chancellor, Shinawatra Univ.; ***office address:*** Ministry of Finance, Thanon Rama VI, Bangkok 10400, Thailand; ***URL:*** http://www2.mof.go.th/.

KITTMER, H.E. Johm; Ambassador, British Embassy in Greece; ***professional career:*** Attached to Department for Environment, Food & Rural Affairs; Amb. to Greece, 2013-; ***office address:*** British Embassy, Ploutarchou 1, 106 75 Athens, Greece; ***phone:*** +30 (0)10 727 2600; ***fax:*** +30 (0)10 7272734; ***e-mail:*** britania@hol.gr; ***URL:*** http://ukingreece.fco.gov.uk/en.

KITZHABER, John Albert, BA, MD; American, Governor, State Government of Oregon; ***born:*** 1947, Colfax, WA, USA; ***parents:*** Albert Raymond Kitzhaber and Annabel Reed Kitzhaber (née Wetzel); ***education:*** BA, Dartmouth Coll, 1969; MD, Univ. Oregon 1973; ***party:*** Democrat; ***political career:*** Mem., Oregon House of Reps. 1979-81; Mem., Oregon Senate, 1981-95; Pres., 1985, 87, 89, 91, Governor, State of Oregon, 1995-2002, 2010-; ***memberships:*** Mem. American College Emergency Physicians, Douglas County Medical Soc.; Physicians for Social Responsibility; American Council Young Political Leaders; ***professional career:*** Intern, Gen. Rose Meml. Hosp, Denver, 1976-77; Emergency Physician Mercy Hosp. Roseburg, Oregon, 1974-75; ***office address:*** Office of the Governor, 160 State Capitol, 900 Court Street, Salem, Oregon 97301-4047, USA; ***phone:*** +1 503 378 6827; ***URL:*** http://www.governor.oregon.gov.

KIURU, Krista; Minister of Education and Science, Government of Finland; ***born:*** 5 August 1974; ***languages:*** English, Estonian, French, Swedish; ***education:*** Univ. of Turku, Finland; ***party:*** Social Democratic Party; ***political career:*** MP, 2007-; Minister of Transport and Communications, 2011-13; Minister of Education and Science, 2013-; ***professional career:*** Teacher; ***office address:*** Ministry of Education, Meritullinkatu 10, PO Box 380, Helsinki, FI-00023 Government, Finland; ***phone:*** +358 (0)9 1341 7407; ***URL:*** http://www.minedu.fi.

KIWANUKA, Maria; Minister of Finance, Government of Uganda; ***born:*** 1955; ***education:*** Bachelor of Commerce, 1977, Makerere Univ.; MBA, London Business Sch., UK, 1981; ***political career:*** Minister of Finance, Planning and Economic Development, 2011-; ***professional career:*** Financial Analyst; ***office address:*** Ministry of Finance, Appollo Kaggwa Rd, Plot 2/4, P O Box 8147, Kampala, Uganda; ***phone:*** +256 41 235051; ***fax:*** +256 41 230163; ***e-mail:*** finance@starcom.co.ug; ***URL:*** http://www.finance.go.ug.

KLEIST, Kuupik; Leader, Inuit Ataqatigiit Party; ***born:*** March 1958, Qullissat, Greenland; ***party:*** Inuit Ataqatigiit; ***political career:*** MP in the Danish Parliament, 2001-07; Prime Minister of Greenland, June 2009-13; ***office address:*** Inuit Ataqatigiit, Nuuk, Greenland; ***URL:*** http://www.ia.gl.

KLIJNSMA, Jetta; State Secretary for Social Affairs and Employment, Netherlands Government; ***born:*** 1957; ***party:*** PvdA; ***political career:*** mem., The Hague municipal council, 1990-2002; Acting Mayor of the Hague, 2008; State Sec. for Social Affairs and Employment, 4th Balkenende gov., 2008; mem., House of Reps., 2010-12; State Sec. for Social Affairs and Employment, Rutte-Asscher gov., Nov. 2012-; ***office address:*** Ministry of Social Affairs and Employment, Anna van Hannoverstraat 4, 2595 BJ The Hague, Netherlands; ***URL:*** http://www.government.nl/.

KLINE, John; Congressman, Minnesota 2nd District, US House of Representatives; ***party:*** Republican Party; ***political career:*** Congressman, Minnesota 2nd District, US House of Representatives; ***professional career:*** US Marine Corps; ***committees:*** House Armed Services; Education and the Workforce, Chmn.; ***office address:*** US House of Representatives, 1429 Longworth HOB, Washington, DC 20515, USA; ***phone:*** +1 202 225 2271.

KLOBUCHAR, Senator Amy; Senator for Minnesota, US Senate; ***born:*** 1960; ***education:*** Yale, magna cum laude; Univ. of Chicago Law School; ***party:*** Democrat; ***political career:*** Chief Prosecutor, Hennepin County; Senator for Minnesota, 2007-; ***professional career:*** Partner, Dorsey & Whitney; Partner, Gray Plant Mooty; ***committees:*** Agriculture, Nutrition and Forestry Cttee.; Commerce, Science and Transportation; Judiciary; Joint Economic Cttee.; ***office address:*** United States Senate, Washington, DC 20510, USA; ***phone:*** +1 202 224 3244.

KNIGHT, Rt. Hon. Greg; British, Member of Parliament for East Yorkshire, House of Commons; ***born:*** 4 April 1949, Leicester; ***parents:*** Albert George Knight and Isabel Knight; ***education:*** Alderman Newton's Grammar Sch.; London Coll. of Law; ***party:*** Conservative Party; ***political career:*** MP for Derby North, 1983-97; Shadow Dep. Leader, House of Commons, 2001-03; MP Yorkshire East, 2001-; Shadow Minister for Culture, 2003; Shadow Minister for Railways & Aviation, 2003-05; ***professional career:*** Qualified solicitor, -1997; Business Consultant, 1997-2001; ***committees:*** Chmn., All Party Historic Vehicles Group; Chmn., Select Cttee. on Procedure, 2005-12; Treasurer, All-Party British-Spanish Group; Treasurer, British-American Parliamentary Group; Liaison, 2006-12; Administration, 2006-10; Standards and Privileges, 2009-10; Reform of the House of Commons, 2009-10; Joint Committee on the Draft Detention of Terrorist Suspects (Temporary Extension) Bills, 2011; ***honours and awards:*** Privy Cllr., 1995; ***publications:*** Honourable Insults, 1989, Right Honourable Insults, 1998; Naughty Graffiti, 2005; ***recreations:*** classic cars; ***office address:*** House of Commons, London, SW1A 0AA, United Kingdom; ***phone:*** +44 (0)845 090 0203; ***e-mail:*** secretary@gregknight.com; ***URL:*** http://www.gregknight.com.

KNIGHT-SANDS, H.E. Catherine; Ambassador, British Embassy in Montenegro; ***professional career:*** Dep. Head of Mission, Sarajevo, Bosnia and Herzegovina, 2004-07; Political Counsellor, Baghdad, Iraq, 2007-09; Amb. to Montenegro, 2009-; ***office address:*** British Embassy, Ulcinjska 8, Gorica C, 81000 Podgorica, Montenegro; ***phone:*** +382 81 205 460; ***e-mail:*** podgorica@britishembassy.cg.yu; ***URL:*** http://ukinmontenegro.fco.gov.uk/en/.

KNOT, Prof. Klaas; Governor, De Nederlandse Bank; ***born:*** 1967; ***education:*** Univ. of Groningen, economics, Ph.D; ***professional career:*** Economist, De Nederlandsche Bank, 1996-98; Economist, European Dept., IMF, 1998; Head of Banking & Supervisory Strategies Dept., De Nederlandsche Bank, 1999-2002; Dir., Dutch Pensions and Insurance Authority, 2002-04; Dir., Supervisory Policy Division, De Nederlandsche Bank, -2009; Dir. of Financial Markets, Ministry of Finance, 2009-11; Pres., De Nederlandsche Bank, 2011-; Mem., Gov. Council, ECB; ***office address:*** De Nederlandse Bank, Westeinde 1, 1017 ZN Amsterdam, Netherlands; ***URL:*** http://www.dnb.nl.

KNOTT, H.E. Jonathan; Ambassador, British Embassy in Hungary; ***professional career:*** Dep. Head of Mission and Director UK Trade & Investment, British Emb, in Seoul, South Korea, 2008-11; Amb. to Hungary, 2012-; ***office address:*** British Embassy, Harmincad Utca 6, Budapest 1051,, Hungary; ***phone:*** +36 (0)1 266 2888; ***fax:*** +36 (0)1 266 0907; ***e-mail:*** info@britemb.hu; ***URL:*** http://www.britishembassy.hu.

Kob-Kro

KOBEH GONZALEZ, Roberto; President of the Council, International Civil Aviation Organization; ***born:*** 1943; ***languages:*** English; ***professional career:*** Dir. Gen., Air Navigation Services of Mexico, 1978-97; Perm. Rep. of Mexico on the Council of International Civil Aviation Organization (ICAO), 1998-2006; President of the Council, ICAO, 2006-; ***office address:*** International Civil Aviation Organization (ICAO), 999 University St, Montreal, Quebec HC3 5H7, Canada; ***phone:*** +1 514 954 8219; ***fax:*** +1 514 954 6077; ***e-mail:*** icaohq@icao.int; ***URL:*** http://www.icao.int.

KOLOKOLTSEV, Vladimir; Minister of the Interior, Russian Government; ***born:*** 1961; ***education:*** Higher Political School of the Interior Ministry, jurisprudence; ***political career:*** Interior Ministry; Platoon commander, Patrol Guard Service, Interior Ministry's Directorate for the Gagarinsky District Exec. Cttee. of Moscow, 1984; Office of the Criminal Invesigation Dept., Interior Ministry's Directorate for the Kuntsevsky District Exec. Cttee. of Mosw, Dep. Head, 20th Militia Station, Moscow, Head, 8th Militia Station, Moscow, 1989-92; Senior officer, Criminal Investigation Dept. of the Interior Ministry's Main Directorate of Moscow; Head, 108th Militia Station, Moscow; Chief Investigative Officer of the 2nd District Criminal Investigation Dept. of Moscow's Central Administrative Area; Deputy Head, Investigative Bureau; Head, Interior Ministry Directorate for the Orel Region, 2007-09; First Dep. Head, Interior Ministry's Criminal Investigation Dept., 2009; Head, Interior Ministry's Main Directorate for Moscow, 2009; Minister of the Interior, 2012-; ***office address:*** Ministry of the interior, ul. Zhitnaya 16, 117049 , Moscow, Russia.

KOMOROWSKI, Bronislaw; President, Republic of Poland; ***parents:*** Count Zygmunt Leon Komorowski (dec'd); ***education:*** University of Warsaw; ***political career:*** MP, 1991-2010; Minister of National Defence, 2000-01; Vice speaker of the Sejm, 2005-07 ; Speaker of the Sejm, 2007-10; Acting President, April-July 2010; President, July 2010-; ***professional career:*** Historian; ***office address:*** Office of the President, ul. Wiejska 10, 00-902 Warsaw, Poland; ***phone:*** +48 22 694 2900; ***fax:*** +48 22 694 2237; ***URL:*** http://www.sejm.gov.pl.

KOMSIC, Zelijko; Rotating President, Government of Bosnia & Herzegovina; ***education:*** Univ. of Sarajevo, Law; Edmund A. Walsh School of Foreign Service, Georgetown Univ., Washington, USA; ***party:*** SDP; ***political career:*** Amb. to Fed. Rep. of Yogoslavia, 1998-2000; Hd., Municipal Gvt. of Novo Sarajevo, 2000; Dep. Mayor of Sarajevo; Rotating President of Bosnia and Herzegovina, (Croat), 2006-; ***office address:*** Office of the Prime Minister , Musala 5, 71000 Sarajevo, Bosnia & Herzegovina; ***phone:*** +387 3366 4941; ***URL:*** http://www.predsjednistvohih.ba.

KONNEH, Amora; Minister of Finance, Government of Liberia; ***education:*** Penn State Univ., USA; MA, John F. Kennedy School of Gov., Harvard Univ. USA; ***political career:*** Minister of Planning and Economic Affairs, 2008-12; Minister of Finance, 2012-; ***office address:*** Ministry of Finance, Broad Street, PO Box 10-9013, 1000 Monrovia 10, Liberia; ***phone:*** +231 226863; ***URL:*** http://www.mofliberia.org.

KONOVALOV, Alexander; Minister of Justice, Russian Government; ***born:*** 1968; ***education:*** St. Petersburg State Univ., law, Ph.D; ***political career:*** Minister of Justice, 2008-; ***professional career:*** Soviet Armed Forces; Assist. prosecutor, Vyborgsky District, St Petersburg, 1992; investgator, Vyborgsky District, Office of the Public Prosecutor, 1992-94, prosecutor, 1994-97, Dep. Prosecutor, 1997-98; Dep. Prosecutor of St. Petersburg, 2001-05; Prosecutor of Bahkortostan, 2005; President's Plenipotentiary Envoy to the Volga Federal District, 2005; ***office address:*** Ministry of Justice, ul. Zhitnaya 14, 119991 Moscow, Russia; ***phone:*** +7 495 955 5999; ***fax:*** +7 495 916 2903; ***URL:*** http://www.minjust.ru.

KOROMA, Ernest Bai; President of Sierra Leone; ***born:*** 1953; ***party:*** All People's Congress (APC); ***political career:*** Pres., Sierra Leone, 2007-; ***professional career:*** Insurance executive; ***office address:*** Office of the President, State House, Freetown, Sierra Leone; ***URL:*** http://www.statehouse-sl.

KOSKINEN, Jari; Minister of Agriculture and Forestry, Government of Finland; ***born:*** 11 June 1960; ***education:*** MA, (Social Sciences), Univ. of Helsinki, 1988; ***party:*** National Coalition Party; ***political career:*** MP, 1996-; Minister of Agriculture and Forestry, 2002-03, 2011-; ***professional career:*** Farmer; ***office address:*** Ministry of Agriculture and Forestry, Hallituskatu 3A, P.O.Box 30, 00023 Government, Helsinki, Finland; ***phone:*** +358 (0)9 1602299; ***fax:*** +358 (0)9 1602190; ***e-mail:*** name.surname@mmm.fi; ***URL:*** http://www.mmm.fi.

KOUPAKI, Pascal Irenée; Prime Minister, Government of Benin; ***born:*** 1951; ***party:*** Cauri Forces for an Emerging Benin; ***political career:*** Minister of Finance, 2006-07; Minister of State for the Exploration, Development and Evaluation of Public Policy, 2007-11; Prime Minister, 2011-; ***professional career:*** Central Bank of West African States, (BCEAO); International Monetary Fund, (IMF); ***office address:*** Office of the Prime Minister, National Assemby, PO Box 371, Porto-Novo, Benin.

KOZLOVSKIS, Rihards; Minister of Interior, Government of Latvia; ***education:*** Faculty of Law, Univ. of Latvia, 2003; ***political career:*** Minister of Interior, 2011-; ***professional career:*** Lawyer, BBF Consulting Ltd., 2007-11; ***office address:*** Ministry of the Interior, Raina bulv. , Riga LV-1533, Latvia; ***phone:*** +371 6721 9210; ***fax:*** +371 6721 2255; ***e-mail:*** pc@iem.gov.lv; ***URL:*** http://www.iem.gov.lv.

KRAFT, Hannelore; Premier, State of North Rhine-Westphalia; ***born:*** 1961; ***political career:*** SPD Mem., 1994-; Mem., caucus of the SPD Mulheim subdistrict, 1995-2009; Mem., NRWSPD caucus, 2004-; Mem., SPD federal caucus, 2005-; mem., federal SPD party executive, 2007-; SPD Chwn., North Rhine-Westphalia, 2007-; Dep. Chwn., Social Democratic Party of Germany, 2009-; Mem., North Rhine-Westphalia State Parly., 2002-; Leader, SPD parly. group, 2005-10; Minister for Federal and European Relations of the State of North Rhine-Westphalia, 2001-02; Minister for Higher Education & Research, NRW, 2002-05; Premier, State of NRW, 2010-; ***office address:*** Landtag, Platz des Landtags 1, 40221 Dusseldorf, Germany.

KRAJESKI, H.E. Thomas; Ambassador, US Embassy in Bahrain; ***professional career:*** Ambassador of the USA to Yemen, 2004-07; Amb. to Bahrain, 2012-; ***office address:*** US Embassy, Building 979, Road 3119, Block 331, Zinj , Manama, Bahrain; ***phone:*** +973 17 273300; ***fax:*** +973 17 272594; ***URL:*** http://bahrain.usembassy.gov.

KRAMER, Baroness Susan; Member, House of Lords; ***born:*** 1950; ***party:*** Liberal Democrats; ***political career:*** MP for Richmond Park, 2005-10; Shadow Trade and Industry Sec., 2006-07; Shadow Transport Sec., 2007-08; Shadow Sec. of the Cabinet Office and Chancellor of the Duchy of Lancaster, 2008-09; Liberal Democrat Spokesperson for Heathrow; Mem., House of Lords, 2010-; ***office address:*** House of Lords, London, SW1A 0PW, United Kingdom; ***phone:*** +44 (0)20 7219 3000.

KRAMP-KARRENBAUER, Annegret; German, Minister-President, Government of Saarland; ***born:*** 1962; ***party:*** CDU; ***political career:*** Mem., Bundestag, 1988; Minister-President of Saarland, 2011-; ***office address:*** Office of the Minister-President, Am Ludwigsplatz 14, 66117 Saarbrucken, Germany; ***URL:*** http://www.saarland.de.

KRAWETZ, Ken; Deputy Premier, Minister of Finance, Government of Sakatchewan; ***political career:*** MLA, Canora-Pelly, 1995; Interim leader, Saskatchewan Party & Leader of the Opposition, 1997-99, currently Dep. Leader; Dep. Prem., 2007-; Minister of Education, 2007; Minister of Finance, 2010-; ***office address:*** Ministry of Finance, 2350 Albert Street, Regina, SK, S4P 4A6, Canada; ***phone:*** +1 306 787 6768; ***fax:*** +1 306 787 6544; ***URL:*** http://www.finance.gov.sk.ca/.

KRECKÉ, Jeannot; Minister of the Economy and Foreign Trade, Government of Luxembourg; ***born:*** 26 April 1950; ***education:*** Univ. Libre de Bruxelles, Physical and Sports education; courses in economics, accountancy and taxation, USA, 1989; ***political career:*** Deputy, 1989-; Treasurer Gen., LSAP, 1985-; Spokesperson for the State budget, 1996; Minister of the Economy, Foreign Trade and Sport, 2004-09; Minister of the Economy and Foreign Trade, 2009-; ***professional career:*** Teacher, Univ. Libre de Bruxelles, 1973-76; International semi-professional footballer; External Consultant, Mazars, 1994-99, Arthur Andersen, 1999-2003 and Ernst & Young, 2003-04; co-founder and Pres, Luxembourg Alzheimer Assn., to 1997; Head, European Alzheimer Assn., 1996-2001 ; ***recreations:*** transatlantic ship racing; polar navigation; ***office address:*** Ministry of Economy, Foreign Trade and Sport, 6 boulevard Royal , Luxembourg L-2449, Luxembourg; ***phone:*** +352 478 4101; ***fax:*** +352 460448; ***URL:*** http://www.gouvernement.lu/ministeres/meco.

KRISTENSEN, Astrid Krag; Minister for Health and Prevention, Government of Denmark; ***born:*** 17 November 1982; ***education:*** BA, (political science), Univ. of Copenhagen, Denmark, 2007; ***party:*** Socialist People's Party; ***political career:*** MP, 2007-; Minister for Health and Prevention, 2011-; ***office address:*** Ministry for Health and Prevention, Holbergsgade 6, 1057 Copenhagen K, Denmark; ***phone:*** +45 7226 9000; ***e-mail:*** sum@sum.dk; ***URL:*** http://www.sf.dk/astridkrag.

KRISTENSEN, Henrik Dam; Danish, Minister of Transport, Government of Denmark; ***born:*** 31 January 1957, Vorbasse; ***parents:*** Ove Dam Kristensen and Gudrun Dam Kristensen; ***married:*** Bente Dam Kristensen, 1 April 1979; ***education:*** Technical Coll. of Kolding, 1974-75; ***party:*** Socialist Group in the European Parliament; ***political career:*** Candidate of the Social Democratic Party in the constituency of Grindsted, 1984; Member of the Danish Parliament, 1990; Spokesman on Agriculture and Fisheries of the Social Democratic Party, 1992-94; Minister for Agriculture and Fisheries, 1994-96; Minister for Food, Agriculture and Fisheries, 1996-00; Minister for Social Affairs, 2000-2001; MEP, 2004-06; Minister for Transport, 2011-; ***professional career:*** Rural postman in Vorbasse, 1978-90; Advisor to the Workers' Educational Assn. (AOF), 1988-90; ***committees:*** Mem. of the education cttee. of the Local Authorities of Billund, 1984-88; Mem., Country programming Cncl. of Ribe, 1984-90; Mem. of staff of the Danish Refugee Cncl., 1986-87; Mem. of the Cttee. of the Parly. Social Democratic Party, 1991-94; ***office address:*** Ministry of Transport, Frederiksholms Kanal 27, 1220 Copenhagen K, Denmark; ***phone:*** +45 3392 3355; ***fax:*** +45 3312 3893; ***e-mail:*** trm@trm.dk; ***URL:*** http://www.trm.dk.

KRISTJANSDOTTIR, Hanna; Minister of the Interior, Government of Iceland; ***education:*** BA, Univ. of Iceland, 1991; MSc., Univ. of Edinburgh, UK; ***party:*** Independence Party; ***political career:*** Mayor of Reykjavik, 2008-10; Minister of Interior, 2013-; ***office address:*** Ministry of Interior, Skuggasundi, 150 Reykjavík, Iceland; ***phone:*** +354 545 9000; ***fax:*** +354 552 7340; ***e-mail:*** postur@irr.is; ***URL:*** http://www.stjr.is/dkm.

KROES, Neelie; Dutch, Commissioner for Digital Agenda, European Commission; ***born:*** 19 July 1941, Rotterdam, The Netherlands; ***education:*** Erasmus Univ., Rotterdam, MSc. Econ., 1965; ***political career:*** Rotterdam Chamber of Commerce, 1969-71; Mem., Rotterdam Municipal Cncl., 1969-71; MP (Liberal), 1971-77; Dep. Minister for Transport and Public Works, 1977-81; Cabinet Minister of Transport and Public Works, 1982-89; Advisor to European Transport Cmnr., Brussels, Belgium, 1989-91; Cmnr. for Competition, 2004-09; Vice President and Commissioner for Digital Agenda, 2009-; ***memberships:*** fmr. Mem.of the following: Supervisory Bd. Digital Equipment B.V.; Supervisory Bd. Groenveld Transport Efficiency; Bd. of Dirs. SC Johnson Waz Euro Bd.; Supervisory Bd., McDonald's; Governing Bd., Conservation of Nature; Governing Bd., Insurance Authority (Verzekeringskamer); Competiveness Gp. to the Chmn. European Commission; Bd. of Dirs., Brambles Industries Ltd. (Australia); Current Mem.: Supervisory Bd., Cório; Supervisory Bd. Royal Nedloyd; Supervisory Bd., Ballast Nedlam; Supervisory Bd., NCM Holding N.V.; Supervisory Bd. Dirs., Prologis; Supervisory Bd., New Skies Satellites; Supervisory Bd., PriceWaterhouseCoopers; Supervisory Bd. Lucent Technologies B.V. the Netherlands; Governing Bd., AH Vaste Klantenfonds (Ahold); Governing Bd., Royal Trade Fair (Koninklijke Jaarbeurs); Governing Bd., Stichting Int. Human Resources Dev. VNO/NCW; Advisory Bd., Int. Problems (AIV); Governing Bd., Nelson Mandela Children Fund; Governing Bd., Verening Koninlljke Jaarbeurs; ***professional career:*** fmr. of the following: Chmn., Supervisory Bd. Intis B.V., Advisor, Arcadis (Heidemij/Grabowsky), Chmn., Governing Bd. Kunsthal, Lid Raad van Toezicht Veerstichting; Asst. Prof. Transport Economics, Erasmus Univ, Rotterdam, 1965-71; Chmn., Bd. of Directors, NIB Capital N.V.; Chmn., Supervisory Bd. Port Support Int. B.V.; Mem. Bd. of Dirs., VIB, Brambles Industries Ltd, Australia; Advisor, Heidemij/Grabowsky and Poort; Advisor, PriceWaterhouseCoopers; Pres., Nijenrode Univ., 1991-2000; Advisor, Monitor

Company; Non Exec. Bd. Mem., MM02; Non Exec. Dir., P&O Nedlloyd; Chmn., Governing Bd., TBS Mental Hospital De Kijvelanden; Chmn., Governing Bd., Delta Psychiatrical Hospital; Chmn., Governing Bd., Bezinnings Groep Water; Chmn., Governing Poets of all Nations; Chmn., Overlegorgaan Waterbeheer en Noordzee-aangelegenheden; Chmn., Governing Bd. of De Kunsthal, Rotterdam; *honours and awards:* Grand Officer dans l'Ordre de Légion d'Honneur (France), 1984; Grand Cross of the Order of the German Federal Republic, 1985; Grand Officer of the Order of Orange Nassau of the Netherlands, 1989; Doctor Honoris Causa, Hull Univ., UK, 1989; Woman of the Year in Infrastructure, 1993; Int. Road Fed.; The Bintang Mahaputra Adiprana Order, Indonesia, 1993; *office address:* European Commission, rue de la Loi 200, B-1049 Brussels, Belgium; *phone:* +32 (0)2 299 1111; *fax:* +32 (0)2 299 1970; *URL:* http://ec.europa.eu/.

KRUEGER, Alan B.; Chairman, Council of Economic Advisers, US Government; *education:* Cornell Univ., School of Industrial & Labor Relations; Harvard Univ., A.M., economics, Ph.D., economics; *political career:* Chief Economist, US Dept. of Labor, 1994-95; Assist. Sec. for Economic Policy & Chief Economist, US Dept. of Treasury, Obama Administration; Chmn., Council of Economic Advisers and mem. President Obama's Cabinet, 2011-; *professional career:* labor economist; Bendheim Prof. of Economics & Public Affairs, Princeton Univ. (currently on leave); *office address:* Council of Economic Advisers, 1600 Pennsylvania Ave NW, , Washington, DC 20502, USA.

KUAN CHUNG-MING ; Minister without Portfolio, Minister, Council for Economic Planning and Development, Government of Taiwan; *born:* 1956; *education:* Univ. of California, USA, Ph.D, economics; *political career:* Minister without Portfolio, Executive Yuan, 2012-13; Minister without Portfolio, Minister, Council for Economic Planning and Development, 2013-; *professional career:* Assist. Prof. & Assoc. Prof., Dept. of Economics, Univ. of Illinois, 1989-96; Prof., Dept. of Economics, National Taiwan Univ., 1994-99; Dir., National Science Council, 1999-2001; Research Fellow, Inst. of Economics, Academia Sinica, Dir., 2001-07; Chair Prof., Dept. of Finance, NTU, 2009-; Chmn., Commerce Dev. Research Inst., 2010-; *office address:* Executive Yuan, 1 Chuanghsiao E. Road, Section 1, Taipei, Taiwan; *URL:* http://www.ey.gov.tw.

KUDRYCKA, Barbara; Minister of Higher Education and Science, Government of Poland; *party:* Group of the European People's Party (Christian Democrats) and European Democrats; *political career:* MEP, 2004-; Minister of Higher Education and Science, Govt. of Poland, 2008-; *office address:* Ministry of Higher Education, Aleja J.Ch. Szucha 25, 00-918 Warsaw, Poland; *phone:* +48 22 628 0461/ 629 7241; *fax:* +48 22 628 8561 ; *e-mail:* minister@menis.gov.pl; *URL:* http://www.men.waw.pl.

KUMAR, Meira; Speaker, Lok Sabha, House of the People; *born:* 31 March 1945, Patna; *married:* Shri Manjul Kumar, 29 November 1968; *education:* Univ. of Delhi, LLB; Magadh Univ., Bihar, MA; Advanced Dip. in Spanish; *political career:* Ministry of External Affairs, May 2004-09; Speaker, Lok Sabha, 2009-; *publications:* Editor, Pavan Prasad; *clubs:* India International Centre; Rotary Club, New Delhi; *recreations:* writing poems, reading, gardening, painting, travelling; *office address:* Speakers Office, Lok Sabha, Parliament Street, New Delhi 110001, India; *phone:* +91 11 3017 465; *fax:* +91 11 3015 518; *e-mail:* lokmail@parlis.nic.in; *URL:* http://parliamentofindia.nic.in.

KUOC VA, Cheong; Secretary for Security, Executive Council of Macau; *education:* Macau Security Forces Training Coll.; *political career:* Vice-Dir., Public Security Forces Affairs Office, 1997- , Dir., 1999- ; Sec. for Security, 1999-09; Secretary for Economy and Finance, 2009; Secretary for Security, 2009-; *professional career:* Macau Police Force, 1975; *office address:* Central Office of the Chief Executive of Macau SAR, Alameda Dr., Carlos D'Assumpçã, NAPE, Macau; *phone:* +853 797 8111; *fax:* +853 725468; *URL:* http://portal.gov.mo/.

KURODA, Haruhiko; Governor, Bank of Japan; *born:* 25 October 1944; *education:* Univ. of Tokyo, BA Law; Univ. of Oxford, Ph.D Econ.; *political career:* Min. of Finance, 1967-2003; Vice Minister of Finance and Dir.Gen. Int'l Bureau, 1997-03; *professional career:* Professor of Econ., Hitotsubashi Univ., Tokyo; Special Advisor to PM on int. monetary issues, 2003-05; Pres. and Chmn. Bd. of Dirs., Asian Development Bank, 2005-13; Governor, Bank of Japan, 2013-; *office address:* Bank of Japan, 2-1-1 Hongoku-cho, Nihonbashi, Chuo-ku , Tokyo 103-0021, Honshu, Japan.

KUTESA, Sam Kahamba; Minister of Foreign Affairs, Government of Uganda; *education:* LLB (Hons.); *political career:* MP, Mbarara North, 1980-85; Attorney General, 1995-86; Mp, Mawogola, 1996-2001, 2006-; Minister of Finance, 2001-05; Minister of Foreign Affairs, 2005-; *committees:* Lawyer in private practice, 1973-2001; *office address:* Ministry of Foreign Affairs, Parliament Avenue, P.O.Box 7048, Kampala, Uganda; *phone:* +256 41 345661; *fax:* +256 41 258722 / 232874; *e-mail:* info@mofa.go.ug; *URL:* http://www.mofa.go.ug.

KUUGONGELWA-AMADHILA, Hon. Saara; Minister of Finance, Government of Namibia; *born:* 12 October 1967; *education:* Lincoln Univ. USA, B.Sc. Econ., 1994; London Sch. of African and Oriental Studies, M.Sc. Financial Econ., 2000; *party:* SWAPO; *political career:* MP, 2000-; Minister of Finance, 2003-; *professional career:* Dir-Gen., Namibia National Planning Commission, 1995-2003; *committees:* Mem., Political Bureau and Central Cttee., SWAPO; *office address:* Ministry of Finance, Private Bag 13295, Windhoek, Namibia.

KWARTENG, Dr Kwasi; MP for Spelthorne, UK Government; *education:* Trinity Coll., Cambridge Univ.; *party:* Conservative; *political career:* MP for Spelthorne, May 2010-; *committees:* Transport, 2010-; *office address:* House of Commons, London, SW1A 0AA, United Kingdom; *phone:* +44 (0)20 7219 3000; *e-mail:* kwasi.kwarteng.mp@parliament.uk.

KYLLONEN, Merja; Minister of Transport, Government of Finland; *born:* 25 January 1977; *languages:* English; *political career:* MP, 2007-; Minister of Transport, 2011-; *professional career:* Biomedical Laboratory Scientist; *office address:* Ministry of Transport and Communications, Eteläesplanadi 16, PO Box 31, 00023 Helsinki, Finland; *phone:* +358 9 16002; *fax:* +358 9 1602 8596 ; *e-mail:* kirjaamo@mintc.fi.

L

LAARAYEDH , Ali; Prime Minister, Government of Tunisia; *born:* 1955; *party:* Ennahda Movement; *political career:* Spokesperson, Ennahada Movement, 1981-1990, imprisoned; Minister of the Interior, 2011-13; Interim Prime Minister, 2013-; *office address:* Office of the Prime Minister, place du Gouvernement, 1020 Tunis, Tunisia; *phone:* +216 71 565 400; *URL:* http://www.pm,.gov.tn.

LAENSER, Mohammed; Minister of the Interior, Moroccan Government; *born:* 1942, Imouzzar Marmoucha; *education:* National Sch. of Administration (ENAP), high degree; *political career:* Ministry of Post & Telecommunications, 1969, Minister, 1983, 1985; Minister of Agriculture and Rural Development, 2002-07; Minister of State, 2009-11; Minister of the Interior, Jan. 2012-; *honours and awards:* Reda Wissam, First Class; *office address:* House of Representatives, BP 431, Rabat, Morocco.

LAFLAQUIÈRE, Jean-Pierre; High Commissioner, French Polynesia; *born:* 1947, Toulouse, France; *political career:* Civil Servant; Sec. Gen., Prefecture of Guadeloupe, 1997; Sec. Gen., Prefecture, Loire-Atlantique, 2002; Prefect, Rhone, 2005; Prefect, French Guiana, 2006; Prefect, Manche, 2009; High Commissioner, French Polynesia, 2012-; *honours and awards:* Officer of the Légion d'honneur; *office address:* Office of the High Commissioner, 43 Avenue Pouvanaa A. Oopa, BP 115, 98713 Papeete, French Polynesia; *phone:* +689 46 86 86; *fax:* +689 46 86 89; *URL:* http://www.polynesie-francaise.pref.gouv.fr.

LAGARDE, Christine; Managing Director, International Monetary Fund; *born:* 1 January 1956, Paris, France; *education:* Univ. of Paris X-Nanterre, Institut d'Édudes Politiques (IEP), Paris; *political career:* Delegate Minister, Foreign Trade, 2005-07; Minister of Economy, Finance and Industry, 2007-11; Managing Director, IMF, June 2011-; *professional career:* Lawyer to the Court of Appeal of Paris; Pres. of the exec. Cttee., Baker & McKenzie, Chicago, USA, 1999-2004, Pres., Global Policy Cttee., 2004-; *office address:* International Monetary Fund HQ, 700 19th St., Washington, D.C., 20431, USA; *URL:* http://www.imf.org.

LAHOOD, Ray; American, Secretary of Transportation, US Government; *party:* Republican; *political career:* Mem., US House of Representatives, 1994-Jan. 2009; US Secretary of Transportation, 2009-; *committees:* Co-Chmn., Congressional Bipartisan Retreat Cttee.; *office address:* Department of Transportation, 400 7th Street , SW, Washington, DC 20590, USA; *phone:* +1 202 366 4000; *fax:* +1 202 366 5583; *e-mail:* dot.comments@ost.dot.gov; *URL:* http://www.dot.gov.

LAING, Eleanor; Member of Parliament for Epping Forest, House of Commons; *born:* 1958, Paisley; *married:* Alan Laing (divorced); *s:* 1; *education:* BA, LL.B, Edinburgh Univ., 1982; *party:* Conservative Party; *political career:* Special Advisor to Rt. Hon. John MacGregor OBE MP, 1987-96; MP, Epping Forest, 1997-; Opposition Whip responsible for Trade and Ind.; Frontbench Spokesman on Constitutional Affairs, 2000-01; Frontbench Spokesman on Education, 2001; Shadow Minister for Women and Equality, 2004-07; Shadow Minister for Justice, 2007-10; *interests:* education, transport, the economy and the constitution; *professional career:* Practised law in Edinburgh and the City of London, 1983-1989; *clubs:* Agatha Christie Society; *recreations:* golf, music, theatre; *office address:* House of Commons, London, SW1A 0AA, United Kingdom; *phone:* +44 (0)20 7219 3000.

LAJCAK, Miroslav; Minister of Foreign Affairs, Slovak Government; *born:* 1963; *education:* Commenius Univ., Bratislava, Law; *political career:* Dir. Gen., Political Affairs, Ministry of Foreign Affairs, 2005-07; EU Special Representative for Bosnia and Herzeogovina, Jan 2007-09; Minister of Foreign Affairs, 2009-10, 2012-; *professional career:* Ambassador Extraordinary and Plenipotentiary of the Slovak Republic to the Federal Rep. of Yugoslavia (later Serbia and Montenegro), Republic of Albania and the former Yusloglav Republic of Macedonia, 2001-05; Managing Dir., European External action Service, (Europe & Central Asia), Brussels, 2010-2012; *office address:* Ministry of Foreign Affairs, Hlboka cesta 2, 833 36 Bratislava, Slovak Republic; *phone:* +421 2 5978 1111; *URL:* http://www.foreign.gov.sk/.

LAKE, Anthony; Executive Director, UNICEF; *professional career:* Foreign Service Officer, US State Department, 1962; Dir. of Policy Planning, Administration of President Carter, 1977-81; Senior foreign policy adviser, presidential campaign of Bill Clinton, 1991-92; National Security Advisor, 1993-97; DSenior foreign policy adviser, presidential campaign of Barack Obama, 2007-08; Exec. Dir., UNICEF, 2010-; *office address:* UNICEF, UNICEF House, 3 United Nations Plaza, New York, NY 10017, USA; *URL:* http://www.unicef.org/.

LAKSONO, Agung; Co-ordinating Minister for People's Welfare, Government of Indonesia; *education:* Christian Univ. of Indonesia Sch. of Medicine; *party:* Golkar; *political career:* Speaker, Indonesia People's Representative Council, 2004-09; Co-ordinating Minister for People's Welfare, 2009-; *office address:* Ministry for People's Welfare, Jl. Merdeka Barat, no.3, Jakarta Pusat, Indonesia; *e-mail:* biro_informasi@menkokesra.go.id; *URL:* http://www.menkokesra.go.id.

LAMB, Norman; Member of Parliament for North Norfolk, House of Commons; *born:* 16 September 1957; *parents:* Hubert Horace and Beatrice Moira; *married:* Mary Elizabeth (née Green), 14 July 1984; *s:* 2; *education:* Wymondham Coll., Norfolk; Leicester Univ.;

City of London Polytechnic; ***party:*** Liberal Democrat party; ***political career:*** MP, Norfolk North, 2001-; Dep. Spokesman, International Dev., 2001-02; Shadow Treasury Minister, 2002-05; PPS to Charles Kennedy, 2003-05; Shadow Trade and Industry Sec., 2005-06; Leader's Chief of Staff, 2006-07; Shadow Health Secretary, 2007-10; Assist. Gov. Whip and Chief Parliamentary and Political Adviser to the Deputy Prime Minister, 2010-12; Minister of State, Health, 2012-; ***interests:*** constitutional reform, environment, health, international development economy; ***professional career:*** Solicitor and Partner, Steele & Co.; ***committees:*** Treasury Select Cttee., 2003-05; Treasury Sub. Cttee., 2003-10; ***publications:*** Remedies in the Employment Tribunal (Sweet & Maxwell 1998); ***recreations:*** art, football; ***office address:*** Constituency Office, Guyton House, 5 Vicarage Street, North Walsham, NR28 9DQ, United Kingdom; ***phone:*** +44 (0)1692 403752; ***fax:*** +44 (0)1692 500818; ***e-mail:*** normanlamb@hotmail.com; ***URL:*** http://www.normanlamb.org.

LAMBERTZ, Karl-Heinz; Minister-President and Minister for Local Authorities, Government of the German-Speaking Community in Belgium; ***married:*** Sylvie Palotas; ***children:*** Eveline (F), Esther (F); ***education:*** Univ. of Heidelberg, Bach. of Law; ***party:*** Socialistische Partij (SP, Socialist Party); ***political career:*** mem., Parliament of the German-Speaking Community, 1981-; Pres., Socialist Party of the German-Speaking Community of Belgium, 1984-90; Mem., Exec. Bd. of the Socialist Party (PS), 1986-; Minister of Media, Adult Educ., Disabled, Social Aid and Professional Retraining, 1990-95; Minister of Youth, Training, Media and Social Affairs, 1995-99; Minister-Pres., Minister for Employment, Disabled Policy, Media and Sport, Govt. of the German Community in Belgium, 1999-2004; Minister-President, and Minister for Local Authorities, 2004-09; ***professional career:*** Assist. Prof., Law Dept. of the Catholic Univ. of Louvain-La-Neuve, 1976-80; Consultant, Office of the Minister for Institutional Reform, 1980-81; Dep. Mgr., Aerotech Ltd., 1980-81; Consultant for the SRIW, 1981-90; Lecturer, Fac. of Law, UCL, 1988-; ***committees:*** Pres., Council of the German-Speaking Youth, 1975-80; mem., Commission of the Official German Translation of Laws and Decrees, 1975-81; Chmn., Socialist Group in the Council of the German-Speaking Community of Belgium, 1091-90; ***office address:*** Office of the Minister-President, Klötzerbahn 32, B-4700 Eupen, Belgium; ***phone:*** +32 (0)87 596443; ***fax:*** +32 (0)87 554538; ***e-mail:*** karl-heinz.lambertz@dgov.be; ***URL:*** http://www.lambertz.be; www.dglive.be.

LAMBORN, Douglas; Congressman, 5th Dist. Colorado, US House of Representatives; ***education:*** Univ. of Kansas, journalism and law ; ***political career:*** Colorado House and Senate, 1995-2006; Mem., US HOR, 2007-; ***professional career:*** Attorney in private general practice, Colorado Springs; ***committees:*** Veterans' Affairs; Natural Resources; Armed Services; ***office address:*** House of Representatives, 437 Cannon HOB, Washington, DC 20515, USA; ***phone:*** +1 202 225 4422; ***fax:*** +1 202 226 2638.

LAMMY, David; British, MP for Tottenham, House of Commons; ***education:*** King's School, Peterborough; law degree; Harvard Law School; ***party:*** Labour Party; ***political career:*** Greater London Assembly, May-June 2000; MP, Tottenham, June 2000-; Parly. Sec., Dept. for Culture, Media and Sport, 2005-07; Parly. Under Sec., Dept. for Innovation, Universities and Skills, 2007-08; Minister of State, Department for Business, Innovation and Skills, 2008-10; Shadow Minister for Business, Innovation and Skills, 2010-; ***professional career:*** Barrister; ***committees:*** Public Administration, 2001; Procedure, 2001; Ecclesiastical Committee, 2010-; Works of Art, 2011-; Joint Committee on the Draft Defamation Bill, 2011; ***office address:*** House of Commons, London, SW1A 0AA, United Kingdom; ***phone:*** +44 (0)20 7219 3000.

LAMONT OF LERWICK, Lord Norman Stewart Hughson; British, Member of the House of Lords; ***born:*** 1942; ***s:*** 1; ***d:*** 1; ***education:*** Loretto Sch., Musselburgh, Midlothian (scholar); Fitzwilliam Coll., Cambridge, BA, Econ.; ***party:*** Conservative Party; ***political career:*** Chmn., Cambridge Univ., Conservative Assn., 1963; Pres., Cambridge Union, 1964; PA to Rt. Hon., Duncan Sandys MP, 1965; Conservative Research Dept., 1966-68; MP (Cons.) for Kingston-upon-Thames, 1972-1997; PPS to Minister for the Arts, 1974; an Opposition Spokesman on Prices & Consumer Affairs, 1975-76, on Industry, 1976-79; Parly. Under-Sec. of State, Dept. of Energy, 1979-81; Minister of State for Industry, 1981-85; Min. of State for Defence Procurement, 1985-86; Privy Councillor, 1986; Finance Sec. to Treasury, 1986-89, Chief Sec., 1989-90; Chancellor of the Exchequer, 1990-93; Advisor to Romanian Government, 1995-97; Mem., House of Lords, 1998-; ***memberships:*** Chmn., Bow Group, 1972; Vice Pres., Bruges Gp.; Pres., British Romanian Chamber of Commerce; Chmn., British Iranian Chamber of Commerce, 2005-; Chmn. Clan Lamont Soc., 2004-09; ***professional career:*** Merchant Banker, N.M. Rothschild & Son, 1968-79; Dir. Balli Group Plc; Dir., N.M. Rothschild & Sons, 1993-95; Dir., RAB Capital plc, 2004; Chmn., Jupiter Adria plc, 2006-; Chmn., Small Companies Div. Trust, 2006-; Dir., Stanhope Gate Developments; Dir., Pharm, 2008-; ***honours and awards:*** Life Baron, UK, cr. 1998; ***publications:*** Newspaper articles and Bow Group Memoranda; 'Sovereign Britain' (1995); 'In Office' (1999); ***clubs:*** Garrick, White's, Beefsteak; ***office address:*** House of Lords, London, SW1A 0PQ, United Kingdom; ***phone:*** +44 (0)20 7306 2138; ***fax:*** +44 (0)20 7306 2072.

LAMOTHE, Laurent; Prime Minister, Government of Haiti; ***born:*** 1972, Port-au-Prince, Haiti; ***education:*** BA, Barry Univ, Miami, USA; MA, St Thomas Univ.; ***political career:*** Minister of Foreign Affairs, 2011-12; Prime Minister, Minister of Foreign Affairs and Religious Affairs, 2012-; ***professional career:*** Businessman; Co-Founder, Global Voice Group ; ***office address:*** Office of the Prime Minister, Rue Champ-de-Mars, Port-au-Prince, Haiti; ***phone:*** +509 2228 2128; ***URL:*** http://www.palaishaiti.net.

LANCASTER, Mark; MP for Milton Keynes North, House of Commons; ***born:*** 12 May 1970; ***parents:*** Rev. Ron Lancaster MBE and Kathleen Lancaster; ***married:*** Katie Lancaster, 1995 (dissolved); ***public role of spouse:*** Partner, Farrer and Co.; ***education:*** Buckingham Univ., B.Sc., D.Sc.; Exeter Univ., MBA; ***party:*** Conservative; ***political career:*** Local Councillor; MP for Milton Keynes North East, 2005-10, Milton Keynes North, 2010-; ***professional career:*** Man. Dir., Kimbolton Fireworks ; ***committees:*** Office of the Deputy Prime Minister, 2005-06; Defence, 2006; Communities and Local Government, 2008-09; International Development, 2009-10; Armed Forces Bill, 2011; ***honours and awards:*** TD; ***office address:*** House of Commons, London, SW1P 0AA, United Kingdom; ***phone:*** +44 (0)20 7219 3000.

LANDAU, Uzi, MK; Minister of Tourism, Government of Israel; ***born:*** 1943, Haifa; ***education:*** Massachusetts Inst. of Technology, Ph.D; Technicon in Haifa, B.Sc. and M.Sc. degrees; ***party:*** Likud; ***political career:*** Dir.-Gen. of the Min. of Transport; Chmn. Knesset Delegation to the European Parly; Minister of Public Security, 2001-03; Minister Without Portfolio, 2003-04; Minister of National Infrastructure, 2009-12; Minister of Energy and Water, 2012-13; Minister of Tourism, 2013-; ***memberships:*** Mem. of the Bds. of El-Al Israel Airlines, Israel Port Authority and Israel Airport Authority; Mem. of the Bd. for the Protection of Nature; Mem. of the Bd. of Si'ah Vasig Israel Debating Soc.; Mem. of Knesset, 1984; Mem., Israeli Delegation to the Madrid Peace Conference; Mem. Knesset Delegation to the Cncl. of Europe ; ***professional career:*** Systems Analyst; Lecturer, Technicon, Israel Inst. of Technology, Haifa; ***committees:*** 11th Knesset - Mem., Economic Affairs Cttee., State Control Cttee., Immigration and Absorption Cttee., Chmn. Sub-cttee. for Soviet Jewry; 12th Knesset - Chmn., Defense Budget Sub-cttee. Mem., Foreign Affairs & Defense Cttee., Economic Affairs Cttee., Constitution, Law & Justice Cttee.; Chmn. Likud's foreign Affairs and Defense Cttee.; 13 th Knesset - Mem., Economic Affairs Cttee., State Control Cttee., Cttee. on the Min. of Defense and the Idf, Chmn., Sub-cttee. of the State Control, Chmn. Likud's Policy Cttee.; 14th Knesset - Chmn., the State Control Cttee.; ***office address:*** The Knesset, Qiryat Ben-Gurion, Jerusalem 91950, Israel.

LANDRIEU, Mary; Senator for Louisiana, US Senate; ***born:*** 23 November 1955; ***parents:*** Moon Landrieu and Verna Landrieu; ***married:*** Frank Snellings, 1988; ***children:*** Connor (M), Mary Shannon (F); ***party:*** Democrat; ***political career:*** elected to Louisiana House of Representatives, 1979; elected Louisiana State Treasurer, 1987; US Senator for Louisiana, 1997-; ***committees:*** Senate: Appropriations; Small Business & Enterpreneurship; Energy & Natural Resources; Homeland Security & Governmental Affairs; ***office address:*** US Senate, 702 Hart Senate Office Building, Washington, DC 20510-1804, USA; ***phone:*** +1 202 224 5824; ***fax:*** +1 202 224 9735; ***e-mail:*** senator@landrieu.senate.gov; ***URL:*** http://www.landrieu.senate.gov.

LANE-FOX OF SOHO, Baroness Martha; Member, House of Lords; ***party:*** crossbencher; ***political career:*** Mem., House of Lords, 2013-; ***professional career:*** Co-founder, Lastminute.com; ***office address:*** House of Lords, London, SW1 0AA, United Kingdom; ***phone:*** +44 (0)20 7219 3000.

LANG, Rein; Minister of Culture, Government of Estonia; ***born:*** 4 July 1957, Tartu, Estonia; ***languages:*** English, Finnish, Russian; ***education:*** Univ. of Tartu, Fac. of Law, 1980; Fac. of History, 1985; ***party:*** Estonian Reform Party, 1995-; ***political career:*** MP, 2003-; Minister of Foreign Affairs; Minister of Justice, Gov. of Estonia, 2005-12; Minister of Culture, 2012-; ***memberships:*** Assn. of Estonian Broadcasters, 1993-2000; Estonian Union of Journalists, 1994-2001; Creative Council, 1998-2001; ***professional career:*** Consultant, Moscow Bar Assn., Estonian Branch, 1980-86; Dep. Dir., Tallinna City Hall, 1986-89; Dep. Dir., Muusik Club, 1989-90; Chmn., Bd. of Directors, Laulusillad AS, 1990-91; Chmn., Bd.of Dirs. TRIO LSL 1991-97, Chmn., Supervisory Bd. TRIO LSL, 1997-2001; Mem. of various company Supervisory Boards, 1998-2001; Dep. Mayor of Tallinn, 2001-03; ***honours and awards:*** Order of the White Star, 4th Class, 2001; Decoration of the Estonian Police (special class), 2003; Kinght of the National Order of the Republic of France, 2004; Order of the White Star, 2nd Class, 2006; Order of the Lion of Finland - Grand Cross; ***office address:*** Ministry of Culture, Suur Karja 23, 15076 Tallinn, Estonia; ***phone:*** +372 628 2250; ***fax:*** +372 628 2200; ***e-mail:*** min@kul.ee; ***URL:*** http://www.kul.ee.

LANKFORD, James; Congressman, US House of Representatives; ***party:*** Republican; ***political career:*** mem., US HOR, Oklahoma 5th District, 2010-; Chair, Republican Conf. Cttee., 2013-; ***committees:*** Oversight and Government Reform; Transportation and Infrastructure; ***office address:*** 509 Cannon House Office, Washington DC 20515, USA; ***URL:*** http://lankford.house.gov/.

LANSLEY, Rt. Hon. Andrew, CBE; British, Leader of the House of Commons, Lord Privy Seal, UK Government; ***born:*** 11 December 1956; ***parents:*** Thomas Lansley and Irene Lansley; ***married:*** Sally Lansley, 2001; Marilyn Lansley, 1985 (div'd); ***children:*** Katherine (F), Sarah (F), Eleanor (F), Martha (F), Charles (M); ***education:*** Univ. of Exeter, BA, Politics, 1979; ***party:*** Conservative Party; ***political career:*** Dir., Conservative Research Dept., 1990-95; Selected PPC, South Cambridgeshire, Sept. 1995; Campaign Manager, Uxbridge By-Election, July 1997; Vice-Chmn., Conservative Party, 1998-99; Campaign Co-ordinator for the European Elections, May 1999; Shadow Minister for the Cabinet Office and Policy Renewal, 1999-2001; Shadow Chancellor of the Duchy of Lancaster, 1999-2001; MP for South Cambridgeshire, 1997-; Shadow Sec. of State for Health, 2003-May 2010; Secretary of State for Health, 2010-12; Leader of the House of Commons, Lord Privy Seal, 2012-; ***interests:*** economic policy, industry, businesses and small business interests, health policy, local government, transport, constitutional issues, policy making in the Conservative Party; ***memberships:*** Vice-Pres., Local Govt. Assn.; ***professional career:*** Dept. of Trade and Industry, 1979-84; PPS to the Rt. Hon. Norman Tebbit MP, 1984-87; Dep. Dir.-Gen., British Chamber of Commerce, previously Policy Dir. of the British Chamber of Commerce, 1987-90; ***committees:*** Mem., Health Select Cttee., 1997-98; Sec. Backbench Trade and Industry Cttee., Environment Cttee., Transport and the Regions Cttee., 1997-98; Mem., Trade and Industry Select Cttee., 2001-; ***trusteeships:*** Patron, STRADA (Stroke and Action for Dysphasic Adults in Cambridge); Headway; Int. Centre for Child Studies; ASPIRE (Assoc. for Spinal Injury Research Rehabilitation and Reintegration); ***honours and awards:*** CBE, 1996; ***publications:*** A Private Route, 1989; Conservatives and the Constitution, (with R. Wilson) 1997; ***recreations:*** history, travel, biography, films, spending time with children, meeting people; ***office address:*** House of Commons, London, SW1A 0AA, United Kingdom; ***phone:*** +44 (0)20 7219 3000; ***e-mail:*** lansleya@parliament.uk; ***URL:*** http://www.parliament.uk.

LAOLY, Asang; Deputy Prime Minister, Government of Laos; ***political career:*** Minister of the Interior, -2002; Deputy Prime Minister, 2006-; ***office address:*** Ministry of the Interior, National Assembly, 1 That-Luang Square, Vientiane, Laos.

LAPORTE, Pierre; Minister of Finance, Government of the Seychelles; ***political career:*** Minister of Finance, 2012-; ***professional career:*** economist, IMF; Governor, Central Bank of the Seychelles, -2012; ***office address:*** Ministry of Finance, Liberty House, PO Box 113, Central Bank Building, Victoria , Mahé, Republic of Seychelles.

LAQHDAF, Moulaye ould Mohamed; Prime Minister, Government of Mauritania; *political career:* Prime Minister, 2008-; *professional career:* Amb. to the EU in Brussels, 2006-08; *office address:* Office of the Prime Minister, Immeuble du Gouvernement, B.P. 184 Nouakchott, Mauritania; *phone:* +222 529 3743; *e-mail:* mobaba@mauritania.mr.

LARRAIN BASCUÑÁN , Felipe; Minister of Finance, Government of Chile; *education:* Catholic Univ. of Chile; Harvard Univ., USA; *political career:* Minister of Chile, 2010-; *professional career:* Professor, Catholic Univ. of Chile; *office address:* Ministry of Finance, Santiago, Chile.

LARSON, John B.; American, Democratic Caucus Chairman, US House of Representatives; *party:* Democrat; *political career:* Connecticut State Senate, 1990-98; Mem., US House of Representatives, 1999-; Democratic Caucus Chairman, 2009-13; *committees:* Ways & Means; *office address:* House of Representatives, 436 Cannon House Street, Washington, DC 20515-6501, USA; *phone:* +1 202 224 3121; *URL:* http://www.house.gov.

LARUELLE, Sabine; Minister for SMEs, Independents, Agriculture and Middle Classes, Government of Belgium; *born:* 2 June 1965, Huy, Belgium; *education:* Fac. Univ. of Agricultural Studies, Gembloux, 1983-88; Univ. of Liege, Certif. in Management and Administration; Inst. Eco-Conseil, training in environment consultancy; *political career:* Fed. Dep., 2003-; Minister of Agriculture & the Middle Classes, 2003-07; Minister for the Economy, Agriculture and the Self-Employed, 2007-08; Minister of the Small and Medium Sized Enterprises, the Self-Employed, Agriculture and Scientific Policy, 2008-11; Minister for SMEs, Independents, Agriculture and Middle Classes, Dec. 2011-; *professional career:* Researcher at the Luxembourg Univ. Foundation, and consultant for the King Baudoin Foundation, on the Agriculture-Environment relationship; Dir. Gen., Alliance Agricole Belge, 1999-2000; Dir. Gen., Walloon Federation of Agriculture, 2001-2003; *office address:* Ministry of Small and Medium Sized Enterprises, 87 avenue de la Toison d'Or, B-1060 Brussels, Belgium; *phone:* +32 (0)2 250 0303; *fax:* +32 (0)2 219 0914; *e-mail:* info@laruelle.gov.be; *URL:* http://www.sabinelaruelle.be.

LATHAM, Pauline; MP for Mid Derbyshire, UK Government; *party:* Conservative; *political career:* Councillor, Derbyshire County Council, 1987-2002; Derby City Council, 1992-96, 1998-2010; Mayor of Derby 2007-08; MP for Mid Derbyshire, May 2010-; *committees:* International Development Select Cttee., 2010-; *office address:* House of Commons, London, SW1A 0AA, United Kingdom; *phone:* +44 (0)20 7219 3000; *e-mail:* pauline.latham.mp@parliament.uk.

LATRON, Patrice; Prefect, Saint-Pierre et Miquelon; *born:* 1961; *political career:* Aid to Prime Minister, 1994; Dir. of Prefect's cabinet, Ain, 1997; Dir. of Prefect's cabinet, Oise, 1998; Dep. Prefect, Saint-Martin-Saint Barthelemy, 2000; Administrator,2003; Sec.-Gen., Prefecture of Martinique, 2005; Sec.-Gen., Prefecture of Hérault, 2008; Prefect of Saint-Pierre-et-Miquelon, 2011-; *professional career:* Military; Commando training officer; Company Commandant, 9th regiment, Officer; *honours and awards:* Chevalier de la Légion d'Honneur; Chevalier de l'Ordre National du Mérite; *office address:* Prefecture, pl. du Lieutenant-Colonel-Pigeaud, BP 4200, 97500 St-Pierre, Saint-Pierre-et-Miquelon; *URL:* http://www.saint-pierre-et-miquelon.pref.gouv.fr/.

LAUTENBERG, Frank R.; American, Senator for New Jersey, US Senate; *born:* Paterson, New Jersey, USA; *married:* Bonnie Englebardt Lautenberg; *education:* Columbia Univ., degree in econ., 1949; *party:* Democrat; *political career:* US Senator for New Jersey, 1982-2000, 2002-; *professional career:* Co-founder, Chmn., CEO, Automatic Data Processing; *committees:* Environment and Public Works, Appropriations, Commerce, Science, and Transportation; *office address:* Office of Frank R. Lautenberg, 324 Hart Senate Office Building, Washington, DC 20510, USA; *phone:* +1 202 224 3224; *URL:* http://www.lautenberg.senate.gov.

LAVERY, Ian; MP for Wansbeck, UK Government; *party:* Labour; *political career:* Councillor, Wansbeck District Council; MP for Wansbeck, May, 2010-; *committees:* Northern Ireland Affairs, 2010-11; Regulatory Reform, 2010-; Energy and Climate Change, 2010-; *office address:* House of Commons, London, SW1A 0AA, United Kingdom; *phone:* +44 (0)20 7219 3000.

LAVROV, Sergei; Russian, Minister of Foreign Affairs, Government of Russia; *born:* 1950; *education:* Moscow State Institute of International Relations; *political career:* Deputy Minister of Foreign Affairs, 1992-94; Minister of Foreign Affairs, 2004-; *professional career:* Began diplomatic career; Dept. of Int. Orgs., MFA, USSR, 1976-81; First Sec., Counsellor & Senior Counsellor, Permanent Mission of the USSR to the UN, 1981-88; Dep. Head, Dept. of International Economic Relations of Russia, 1988-90; Dir., Dept. of Int. Orgs. & Global Problems of the Russian Foreign Ministry, 1990-92; Perm. Rep. of the Russian Federation to the UN, 1994-2004; *office address:* Ministry of Foreign Affairs, Smolenskaya-Sennaya pl. 32/34, 121200 Moscow, Russian Federation; *phone:* +7 095 244 1606; *fax:* +7 095 230 2130; *e-mail:* ministry@mid.ru; *URL:* http://www.mid.ru/.

LAWS, David; Minister of State, UK Government; *born:* 30 November 1965; *education:* St George's Coll., Weybridge; Double First Class Honours, Economics, Kings Coll., Cambridge; *party:* Liberal Democrat Party; *political career:* MP for Yeovil, 2001-; Lib. Dem. Shadow Defence Spokesman; Shadow Chief Sec., 2002-05; Shadow Work and Pensions Sec., 2005-07; Shadow Children, Schools and Families Secretary, 2007-10; Chief Secretary to the Treasury, 2010, resigned; Minister of State (Jointly Cabinet Office and Department for Education), 2012-; *professional career:* Investment Banking; *committees:* Mem., Treasury Select Cttee.; *office address:* House of Commons, London, SW1A 0AA, United Kingdom; *phone:* +44 (0)20 7219 8413; *fax:* +44 (0)20 7219 8188; *e-mail:* lawsd@parliament.uk; *URL:* http://www.parliament.uk.

LAZAR, Valeriu; Deputy Prime Minister, Government of Moldova; *born:* May 20 1968; *party:* Democratic Party of Moldova; *political career:* Dep. Prime Minister and Minister of Economy, 2009-; *office address:* Ministry of the Economy, Piata Marii Adunari Nationale 1, MD2033, Chisinau, Moldova; *phone:* +373 22 237448; *fax:* +373 22 234064; *e-mail:* minecon@moldova.md; *URL:* http://www.mec.gov.md.

LAZAROWICZ, Mark; Member of Parliament for Edinburgh North & Leith, House of Commons; *s:* 3; *d:* 1; *education:* MA, History, St Andrews Univ., 1976; LL.B, Law Edinburgh Univ.,1992; *party:* Labour Party; *political career:* MP, Edinburgh North & Leith, 2001-; Shadow Minister, International Development, Oct. 2010-11; *office address:* House of Commons, London, SW1A 0AA, United Kingdom; *phone:* +44 (0)20 7219 3000; *e-mail:* lazarowiczm@parliament.uk; *URL:* http://www.parliament.uk.

LEADSOM, Andrea; MP for South Northamptonshire, UK Government; *political career:* Councillor, South Oxfordshire District Council 2003-07; MP for South Northamptonshire, May 2010-; *committees:* Treasury Select Cttee., 2010-; *office address:* House of Commons, London, Sw1A 0AA, United Kingdom; *phone:* +44 (0)20 7219 3000; *e-mail:* andrea.leadsom.mp@parliament.uk.

LEAHY, Patrick J.; American, Senator for Vermont, US Senate; *born:* Montpelier, Vermont, USA; *married:* Marcelle Leahy (née Pomerleau); *children:* Alicia (F), Kevin (M), Mark (M); *education:* St. Michael's Coll., Winooski, grad., 1961; Georgetown Univ. Law Center, Juris Dr., 1964; *party:* Democrat; *political career:* US Senator for Vermont, 1974-; *professional career:* State's Attorney, Chittenden County for eight years; *committees:* Agriculture Cttee.; Judiciary Cttee.; Appropriations Cttee.; *office address:* US Senate, 433 Russell Senate Office Building, Washington, DC 20510, USA; *phone:* +1 202 224 4242; *URL:* http://www.leahy.senate.gov.

LEAKE, H.E. Nicholas; High Commissioner, High Commission in the Mauritius; *professional career:* Joined FCO, 1994; 2nd Sec., Budapest, 1996-2000; 1sr Sec., UKREP Brussels, 2000-02; HM Treasury, 2002-04; FCO/DTI, 2004-05; Dep. Head of Mission, Bulgaria, 2006-10; High Commissioner to Mauritius, 2010-; *office address:* British High Commission, Les Cascades Building, Edith Cavell Street, PO Box 1063, Port Louis, Mauritius; *phone:* +230 202 9400; *fax:* +230 202 9408; *e-mail:* bhc@intnet.mu; *URL:* http://ukinmauritius.fco.gov.uk/en.

LEANCA, Iurie; Prime Minister, Government of Moldova; *born:* 1963; *education:* Moscow State Inst. of Int. Relations, 1993; *party:* Liberal Democratic Party of Moldova; *political career:* Deputy Prime Minister, Minister of Foreign Affairs, and Minister of European Integration, 2009-13; Prime Minister, 2013-; *professional career:* Minister-Counselor, Moldovan Embassy in Washington, D.C, USA, 1993-97; *office address:* Office of the Prime Minister, Piata Marii Adunari Nationale 1, MD2033 Chisinau, Moldova; *URL:* http://gov.md.

LEBEL, Denis; Minister of Transport, Infrastructure and Communities, Minister of State for Canadian Economic Development Agency for the Region of Quebec, Government of Canada; *political career:* Mayor of Roberval, Quebec; MP, 2007-; Minister of State for Economic Development Agency of Canada for the Regions of Quebec, 2008-11; Minister of Transport, Infrastructure and Communities, Minister of State for Canadian Economic Development Agency for the Region of Quebec, 2011-; President of the Queen's Privy Council for Canada, Minister of Intergovernmental Affairs, 2013-; *office address:* House of Commons, Parliament Buildings, Wellington Street, Ottawa, Ontario, K1A 0A6, Canada; *phone:* +1 613 943 5959.

LEBRANCHU, Marylise; Minister of State Reform, Decentralisation and the Civil Service, Government of France; *born:* 1947; *political career:* Regional Cllr., Brittany, 1986-; Town Cllr., Morlaiz, 1995-2003; Mayor of Morlaix, 1995-2004; Vice-Pres., Regional Council of Brittany, 2004-2010; Secretary of State responsible for Small & Medium Companies, Trade, the Craft Industry and Consumption, 1997-2000; Keeper of Seals, Minister of Justice, 2000-02; Deputy, Finistère, 2002-07; Minister for Reform of the State, Decentralisation and Civil Service, 2012-; *office address:* L'Assemblée Nationale, 126 rue de l'Université, 75355 Paris, France; *phone:* +33 (0)1 40 63 60 00; *fax:* +33 (0)1 40 63 77 65.

LEBRETON, Marjory; Leader of the Government in the Senate, Canadian Senate; *education:* Ottawa Business Col.; *party:* Conservative Party; *political career:* Senator for ON, Canadian Govt., 1993-; Leader of the Government in the Senate, 2006-; Minister of State in the Min. of Human Resources and Social Development; Sec. of State for Seniors, 2007-10; *professional career:* Senior Political Advisor and Organiser; *office address:* Senate, Parliament Buildings, Ottawa, ON K1A 0A6, Canada; *phone:* +1 613 943 0756; *e-mail:* lebrem@sen.parl.gc.ca.

LE DRIAN, Jean-Yves; Minister of Defence and Veterans Affair, Government of France; *born:* 1947; *education:* Univ. of Rennes,; *political career:* Dep. Mayor of Lorient, 1977; Minister of the Sea, 1991-92; Minister of Defence and Veterans Affairs, 2012-; *office address:* Ministry of Defence, 14 rue Saint Dominique, 00452 Armees, France; *phone:* +30 (0)1 42 19 30 11; *e-mail:* courrier-defense@defensee.gouv,fr; *URL:* http://www.defense.gouv.fr.

LEE, Dong-phil; Minister of Agriculture, Food and Rural Affairs, Government of the Republic of Korea; *education:* BA, Livestock Management, Yeungnam Univ., 1978; MA, Economics, Seoul National Univ., 1981; Doctoral Degree in Agricultural Economics, Univ. of Missouri, USA, 1991; *political career:* Minister of Agriculture, Food and Rural Affairs, 2013-; *professional career:* Korea Rural Economic Inst. 1980-13, Pres., 2011-13; *office address:* Ministry of Agriculture, Food and Rural Affairs, Government Complex Sejong, Da-Som 2 ro, 94 Euh-Jin Dong, Sejong-si 339-012, Republic of Korea; *phone:* +82 44 201 1001; *URL:* http://english.mifaff.go.kr.

LEE, Brig-Gen. Hsien Loong; Singaporean, Prime Minister, Singapore Government; *born:* 1952; *married:* Ho Ching, 1985; Wong Ming Yang, 1978 ((dec'd)); *s:* 3; *d:* 1; *education:* Univ. of Cambridge, BA Hons, 1974; Univ. of Cambridge, Diploma in Computer Science (Distinction), 1974; US Army Command and General Staff Course, Fort Leavenworth, Kansas, 1978; Harvard Univ., Master of Public Administration, 1979; *party:* Sec.-Gen, People's Action Party; *political career:* Asst. Chief of General Staff (Operations), 1981; Chief of Staff of General Staff, 1982; Dir., Joint Operations Planning Directorate, 1983; Political Sec. to Min. of Defence, 1984; MP (Teck Ghee Constituency), 1984-; Min. of State (Defence) and Min. of State (Trade and Industry), 1985; Min. for Trade and Industry and Second Minister for Defence (Services); Minister for Trade and Industry, 1990-2002; First Asst. Sec.-Gen.; Dep. Prime Minister, 1990-2004; Minister for Finance, 2001-07; Prime Minister, August 2004-; ***professional career:*** Singapore Armed Forces, 1971-84, rose to rank of Brigadier-Gen.; Chmn., Monetary Authority of Singapore, 1998-2004; ***committees:*** elected to the Central Exec. Cttee. of the People's Action Party, 1986; ***recreations:*** reading, walking, classical music; ***office address:*** Prime Minister's Office, Istana Annexe, Orchard Road, Singapore 238823, Singapore; ***phone:*** +65 225 9911; ***fax:*** +65 324 3418.

LEE, Jessica; MP for Erewash, UK Government; ***party:*** Conservative; ***political career:*** MP for Erewash, May 2010-; ***committees:*** Justice Select Cttee., 2010; ***office address:*** House of Commons, London, SW1A 0AA, United Kingdom; ***phone:*** +44 (0)20 7219 3000; ***e-mail:*** jessica.lee.mp@parliament.uk.

LEE, Mike; Senator for Utah, US Senate; ***education:*** Brigham Young Univ.; ***party:*** Republican; ***political career:*** Senator for Utah, US Senate, 2010-; ***professional career:*** law; attorney, Sidley & Austin; Assist. US Attorney, Salt Lake City; General Counsel, Utah; returned to private practice, 2007; ***committees:*** Judiciary; Armed Services; Joint Economic Cttee.; ***office address:*** US Senate, 316 Hart Senate Office Building, Washington DC 20515, USA; ***phone:*** +1 202 224 5444; ***URL:*** http://www.lee.senate.gov.

LEE, Philip; MP for Bracknell, UK Government; ***party:*** Conservative; ***political career:*** MP for Bracknell, May 2010-; ***committees:*** Energy and Climate Change Select Cttee., 2010-; Administration, 2010-; ***office address:*** House of Commons, London, SW1A 0AA, United Kingdom; ***phone:*** +44 (0)20 7219 3000; ***e-mail:*** phillip.lee.mp@parliament.uk.

LEE, Hon. Philip S., C.M., O.M.; Lieutenant Governor of Manitoba; ***born:*** 1944, Hong Kong; ***education:*** Univ. of Manitoba; ***political career:*** Lieutenant Governor of Manitoba, Aug. 2009-; ***professional career:*** Research Chemist; Branch Head Chemist in charge of Winnipeg's Industrial Waste Control Program; ***office address:*** Office of the Lieutenant Governor, Rm. 235 Legislative Building, 450 Broadway Ave., Winnipeg, MB, R3C 0V8, Canada; ***phone:*** +1 204 945 2753; ***URL:*** http://www.lg.gov.mb.ca/index.html.

LEECH, John; MP for Manchester Withington, House of Commons; ***born:*** 11 April 1971, Hastings, UK; ***parents:*** Rev. John Leech and Mrs. Jean Leech; ***education:*** Manchester Grammar School; Brunel University; ***party:*** Liberal Democrat; ***political career:*** Councillor, Manchester City Cncl.; MP for Manchester Withington, 2005-; ***interests:*** housing, planning and transport; ***committees:*** Mem., Transport Select Cttee., 2005-; ***office address:*** House of Commons, London, SW1P 0AA, United Kingdom; ***phone:*** +44 (0)20 7219 3000/(0)161 434 3334; ***fax:*** +44 (0)161 434 3206; ***e-mail:*** leechj@parliament.uk.

LEE HONG-YUAN ; Minister of the Interior, Government of Taiwan; ***born:*** 1956; ***education:*** National Cheng Kung Univ., engineering; Univ. of Iowa, Dept. of Civil & Environmental Engineering, MS, Ph.D; ***political career:*** Commissioner, Taiwan Prov. Gov., 1997; Dir-Gen., Water Resources Dept., Taiwan Prov. Gov., 1997-98; Minister without Portfolio, Executive Yuan, 2011-12; Minister, Public Construction Commission, Excutive Yuan, 2011-12; Minister, Ministry of the Interior, 2012-; ***professional career:*** Assoc. Prof, Dept. of Civil Engineering, National Taiwan Univ., Prof., 1991-; Dep. Magistrate, Taipei County Gov., 2005-09; ***office address:*** Ministry of the Interior, 5 Huschow Road, Taipei, Taiwan; ***phone:*** +886 2 2356 5005; ***fax:*** +886 2 2356 6201; ***URL:*** http://www.moi.gov.tw/.

LE FOLL, Stéphane; Minister of Agriculture, Food and Forests, Government of France; ***born:*** 1960; ***party:*** Socialist Party; ***political career:*** Town Councillor, Longnes, 1983-95; Vice-Pres., Urban Community of Mans, 2001-; Town Councillor, Mans, 2001-MEP, 2004-12; Minister of Agriculture, Food and Forests, 2012-; ***office address:*** Ministry of Agriculture, Food and Forests, 78 rue de Varenne, 75349 Paris, France; ***phone:*** +33 (0)1 49 55 49 55; ***fax:*** +33 (0)1 49 55 40 39.

LEFROY, Jeremy; MP for Stafford, UK Government; ***party:*** Conservative; ***political career:*** Councillor, Newcastle-under-Lyme Borough Council, 2003-07; MP for Stafford, May 2010-; ***committees:*** International Development Select Cttee., 2010-; ***office address:*** House of Commons, London, SW1A 0AA, United Kingdom; ***phone:*** +44 (0)20 7219 3000; ***e-mail:*** jeremy.lefroy.mp@parliament.uk.

LEIGH, Edward Julian Egerton; British, Member of Parliament for Gainsborough, House of Commons; ***born:*** 1950; ***parents:*** Sir Neville Leigh KCVO (dec'd) and Lady Leigh (née Branch); ***married:*** Mary Leigh (née Goodman); ***children:*** Benedict (M), Nicholas (M), Therdore (M), Natalia (F), Tamara (F), Marina (F); ***languages:*** French; ***education:*** St. Philips Sch.; Oratory Sch.; Lycée Français de Londres; Durham Univ; ***party:*** Conservative Party; ***political career:*** Conservative Party Research Dept., 1973-75; Principal Correspondence Sec. to Mrs Margaret Thatcher MP, 1975-76; Parly. Private Sec., Home Office, 1989-90; Under-Sec. of State for Corporate Affairs, Dpt. of Trade and Industry, 1990-93; MP, Gainsborough and Horncastle, 1983-; ***interests:*** foreign affairs, social security; ***memberships:*** Chmn., Nat. Cncl. for Civil Defence, 1981-82; Dir., Coalition for Peace through Security, 1982-83; ***professional career:*** practising barrister, 1976-; ***committees:*** Select Cttees., Agriculture, Defence, 1983-87, 1995-97 and Social Security, 1995-; Chmn., Public Accounts Cttee., 2001-; Vice Chmn., Conservative Party Foreign Affairs Cttee.; ***publications:*** Right Thinking (1979); ***recreations:*** walking; ***office address:*** House of Commons, London, SW1A 0AA, United Kingdom; ***phone:*** +44 (0)20 7219 6480; ***fax:*** +44 (0)20 7219 4883; ***e-mail:*** hcinfo@parliament.uk.

LE JEUNE D'ALLEGEERSHECQUE, H.E. Susan; Ambassador, British Embassy in Austria; ***languages:*** French, German, Spanish; ***professional career:*** Consul General and Counsellor, British Embassy in Washington D.C., 2005-07; Dir., HR and Mem. of Board, FCO, 2007-12; Amb. to Austria, 2012-; ***office address:*** British Embassy, Jauresgasse 12, 1030 Vienna, Austria; ***phone:*** +43 (0)1 716130; ***fax:*** +43 (0)1 7161 32999; ***e-mail:*** info@britishembassy.at; ***URL:*** http://www.britishembassy.at.

LE LUONG MINH ; Secretary-General, ASEAN; ***born:*** 1952; ***political career:*** Assist. Min. of Foreign Affairs, 2007-08; Dep. Min. for Foreign Affairs, -2011.; ***professional career:*** MFA, 1975-; incld. Amb. & Permanent Rep. to the UN, Geneva, 1995; Amb. Extraordinary & Plenipotentiary, Perm. Rep. to the UN, 2004-11; ASEAN Sec.-Gen., 2013-; ***office address:*** ASEAN Secretariat, 70A Jalan Sisingamangaraja, Jakarta 12110, Indonesia; ***URL:*** http://www.asean.org.

LENAERTS, Professor Dr Koen, MJS; Belgian, Vice President, Court of Justice of the EU; ***born:*** 20 December 1954; ***languages:*** Dutch, French, English, German, Spanish; ***education:*** University of Namur, Candidat en droit, 1974, summa cum laude; University of Leuven, Licentiaat in de Rechten, 1977, summa cum laude, with special congratulations of the Jury, PhD, Law, 1982, with a comparative study analysing the constitutional case-law of the European Court of Justice and the American Supreme Court; Harvard University, Master of Laws, 1978, Master in Public Administration, 1979; Harkness Fellow of the Commonwealth Fund of New York, 1977-79; Prize of the Royal Academy of Sciences, Belgium, 1983, for doctoral dissertation; Prize Fernand Collin of the Fondation universitaire, Belgium, 1984, for doctoral dissertation; Legal qualification: Judge; Member of the Brussels Bar, 1986-89; ***interests:*** EU law; ***memberships:*** Academia Europaea, 1988-; Honorary CBR Fellow, Belgian American Educational Foundation, 1977-79; Fellow, Deutscher Akademischer Austausch-Dienst, 1979; ***professional career:*** *academic career:* College of Europe, Bruges, Professor, 1984-89; Harvard University, Visiting Professor of Law, 1989; Belgian Francqui Chair, University of Antwerp, 1998, and Université Libre de Bruxelles, 2000; Vrije Universiteit, Brussels, Chair, 2003-04; University of Michigan Law School, Distinguished Helen DeRoy Fellow, 2005; *professional career:* Law Clerk, Court of Justice of the EC, 1984-85; *judicial career:* Judge, Court of First Instance of the EC, 1989-2003; Judge, Court of Justice of the EU, 2003-, Vice-President, 2012-; ***publications:*** Books: Europees Recht in hoofdlijnen, co-author, 2003; Europees Procesrecht, co-author, 2003; Podstawy Prawa Europejskiego, co-author, 1998; Constitutional Law of the European Union, co-author, 2005; Procedural Law of the European Union, co-author, 2006; Articles: European Law Review; Cahiers de droit européen; SEW Tijdschrift voor Europees en economisch recht; Journal des Tribunaux - Droit européen; Columbia Journal of European Law; Fordham International Law Journal; World Competition. Law and Economics Review; Concurrences, Revue des droits de la concurrence; European Consitutional Law Review; Rechtskundig Weekblad; Europarecht; Common Market Law Review; Yearbook of European Law; ICLQ; Revue trimestrielle de droit européen; ***office address:*** Court of Justice of the EC, Boulevard Konrad Adenauer, L-2925 , Luxembourg; ***phone:*** +352 4303 3553; ***fax:*** +352 4303 3541; ***e-mail:*** Koen.Lenaerts@curia.europa.eu.

LENGSAVAD, Somsavat; Deputy Prime Minister, Government of Lao People's Democratic Republic; ***political career:*** Minister of Foreign Affairs and Dep. Prime-Minister; Deputy Prime Minister, Standing Government Member, 2006-; ***office address:*** Office of the Deputy Prime Minister, National Assembly, 1 That-Luang Square, Vientiane, Laos.

LEPAGE, Paul; Governor, State of Maine; ***education:*** BS, Business Administration in Finance/Accounting; Univ. of Maine, MBA; ***party:*** Republican; ***political career:*** Mayor, Waterville; Governor, Maine, Nov. 2010-; ***professional career:*** private consultancy; Gen. Mgr, Marden's, 1996; businessman; ***office address:*** Office of the Governor, 1 State House Station, Augusta, Maine 04333-001, USA; ***phone:*** +1 207 287 1034; ***URL:*** http://www.maine.gov/governor/lepage/.

LEPIL VON WIREN, Aino; Ambassador, Estonian Embassy in the UK; ***born:*** October 28 1961, Stockholm, Sweden; ***languages:*** English, French, Swedish; ***education:*** Univ. of Surrey, UK, 1985; Faculty of Law, Stockholm Univ., Sweden, 1987; ***professional career:*** Rep. in the European Commission of Human Rights, 1997-99; Secretary of State, 1999-2003; Amb. to Portugal 2003-06; Undersec. of Legal and Consular Affairs, Ministry of Foreign Affairs, 2006-10; Amb. to Israel, 2007-2-10; Amb. to the UK, 2010-; ***office address:*** Estonian Embassy, 16 Hyde Park Gate, London, SW7 5DG, United Kingdom; ***phone:*** +44 (0)20 7589 3428; ***fax:*** +44 (0)20 7589 3430; ***e-mail:*** london@mfa.ee; ***URL:*** http://www.estonia.gov.uk.

LESLIE, Charlotte; MP for Bristol North West, UK Government; ***party:*** Conservative; ***political career:*** MP for Bristol North West, May 2010-; ***committees:*** Education Select Cttee., 2010-12; ***office address:*** House of Commons, London, SW1A 0AA, United Kingdom; ***phone:*** +44 (0)20 7219 3000; ***e-mail:*** charlotte.leslie.mp@parliament.uk.

LESLIE, Christopher; British, Member of Parliament for Nottingham East, House of Commons; ***born:*** 28 June 1972; ***education:*** Univ. of Leeds, BA (Hons), MA, Industrial and Labour Sciences; ***party:*** Labour Party; ***political career:*** fmr. Political Research Asst.; MP, Shipley, 1997-2005; Parly. Under Secretary of State, Office of the Deputy Prime Minister, 2001-05; MP, Nottingham East, 2010-; Shadow Minister, Treasury, Oct. 2010-; ***interests:*** industrial and economic policy, environmental issues, local government; ***professional career:*** Office Admin.; ***office address:*** House of Commons, London, SW1A 0AA, United Kingdom; ***phone:*** +44 (0)115 711 7666; ***e-mail:*** chris.leslie@parliament.uk.

LESTER OF HERNE HILL, The Rt. Hon. Lord Anthony Paul, QC; British; ***born:*** 3 July 1936; ***languages:*** English, French; ***education:*** Cambridge University, BA, 1960; Harvard Law School, LLM, 1962; Honorary Doctorates from Open University, University of Ulster, 1998, South Bank University, 1998, University of Durham, 2001; Legal qualification: Called to the Bar, Lincoln's Inn, 1963; Bencher, Lincoln's Inn, 1985; QC, Bar of NI, 1984; Member, Irish Bar; ***political career:*** Mem., House of Lords, 1993-; ***interests:*** Criminal Law; Jurisdiction; Human rights; Litigation; State responsibility; Treaties; Public law; Employment law; Media law; Commercial law; European law; ***memberships:*** Advisory Board, Institute of European Public Law, Hull University; Board of Directors, Salzburg Seminar, 1996-2000; Legal Advisory Committee, European Roma Rights Centre, Budapest, 1999-, Co-chair of Executive Board, 1999-2001; President, Liberal Democrat Lawyers Association; Co-founder and former Chairman, The Runnymede Trust, 1990-93; Governor, British Institute of Human Rights; National Committee for the 50th Anniversary of the UN Universal Declaration of Human Rights, 1998; Advisory Committee, Centre for Public Law, University of Cambridge, 1999-; JUSTICE, Council Member, 1977-, Executive Board, 1977-2002; Editor-in-Chief, Butterworths' Human Rights Cases; Editorial Board, Public Law; Editorial Board, International Journal of Discrimination and the Law; International Advisory Board, Open Society Institute, 2000-; American Philosophy Society, 2003-; Honorary Member, American Academy of Arts and Sciences, 2002; Vice-President, English Pen, 2006-; ***professional career:*** *academic* *career:* UCL, Honorary visiting Professor of Law and Honorary Fellow; University College Cork, Ireland, Adjunct Professor of Law, 2006; *professional career:* Chairman, Institute for Public Policy Research's Judiciary Working Group on A British Bill of Rights, 1990; Became a Life Peer, 1993; House of Lords Select Committee on the EC Sub-Committee E (Law and Institutions), 1998-2003, 2004-; Joint Select Committee on Human Rights 2000-04; Sub-Committee on the 1996 Inter-Governmental Conference and Joint Committee on Human Rights 2001-04, 2005-; Vice Chair of the All-Party Parliamentary Group on Genocide Prevention 2005-; President, INTERIGHTS (International Centre for the Legal Protection of Human Rights), 1982-; *governmental career:* Special Adviser to the Home Secretary with responsibility for policy advice on human rights, 1974-76; Special Adviser to Standing Advisory Commission on Human Rights for NI, 1975-77; UK legal expert on EEC Commission's Network Committee on Equal Pay and Sex Discrimination, 1983-93; *judicial career:* Former Recorder South Eastern Circuit, 1987 and Deputy High Court Judge; ***publications:*** Books: Shawcross & Beaumont on Air Law, co-editor of 3rd ed, 1964; Race and Law, co-author, 1972; Equal Pay for Work of Equal Value, co-author, 1984; Human Rights: Law and Practice, co-editor of 2nd ed, 2004; Articles: ICLQ; AJIL; Public Law; Colombia Law Review; Current Legal Problems; Industrial Law Journal; Commonwealth Law Bulletin; Statute Law Review; Israel Law Review; New Law Journal; Yearbook of Media and Entertainment Law; Judicical Review; Equal Opportunities Review; European Human Rights Law Review; Judicial Law Review; ***office address:*** Blackstone Chambers, Blackstone House, Temple, London, EC4Y 9BW, UK; ***phone:*** +44 (0)207 404 4712; ***fax:*** +44 (0)207 822 7350.

LETERME, Yves; Deputy Secretary General, OECD; ***born:*** 6 October 1960, Wervik, Belgium; ***married:*** Sofie Haesen; ***children:*** Matthias (M), Thomas (M), Julie (F); ***education:*** Latin-Greek Humanities, Sint Vincentius College, 1973-1979; Bachelor of Laws, Kulak, 1981; Bachelor of Political Sciences, Royal Univ., of Ghent, 1983; Master of Laws, Royal Univ. of Ghent, 1984; Master of Administrative Sciences, Royal Univ. of Ghent, 1985; Graduated, Int. Federalism Study Centre, Nice, 1984; ***political career:*** Parly. assistant, MP Paul Breyne, 1985; CVP (Christian People's Party) sec., for the Ypres district, 1985-87; Worked in the cabinet of the Community Minister Paul Deprez, 1986; Assist. Auditor at the Audit Office, Jan. 1987-Jan. 1989; Pres., CVP, Ypres section, 1988-91; Assist. nat. CVP sec. Feb. 1989-Jan. 1992; Nat. CVP sec. Dec. 1991-Dec. 1992; Admin. European Union Civil Service, Jan. 1993-Dec. 1994; Alderman, Ypres, 1995-2001; Mem., Belgian HOR, 1997-; Minister-Pres. Gov. of Flanders, 2004-07; "Formateur" in charge of forming a new fed. gov., July-Aug.2007 and Sept.-Sec. 2007; Dep. PM, Minister of Budget, Institutional Reforms and Transport, Federal Gov. of Belgium, 2007-08; Prime Minister, March 2008-Jan. 2009; Minister of Foreign Affairs, July 2007-09; Prime Minister, 2009-11; ***professional career:*** Dep. Sec. Gen., Organisation for Economic Co-operation and Development (OECD), 2011-; ***office address:*** OECD, 2 rue André-Pascal, 75775 Paris Cédex 16, France; ***URL:*** http://www.oecd.org.

LETSIE III, King; Sovereign, Kingdom of Lesotho; ***born:*** 17 July 1963; ***parents:*** The late King Moshoeshoe; ***married:*** Queen Motsoeneng, 18 February 2000; ***s:*** 1; ***d:*** 2; ***education:*** Ampleforth College, UK; ***professional career:*** King of Lesotho, 1990 (following deposition of father), Abdicated 1995 to allow return of father, King Moshoeshoe, resumed throne, 1997-; ***office address:*** The Royal Palace, P.O. Box 524, Maseru 100, Lesotho.

LETTA, Enrico; Italian, Prime Minister, Government of Italy; ***born:*** 20 August 1966, Pisa, Italy; ***education:*** BA in Political Science; PhD., International Law; ***party:*** Democratic Party; ***political career:*** Minister for European Policies, Italian Govt., 1998-00; Minister of Industry (Tourism) and Foreign trade, 2000-01; MEP, 2004-06; Chamber of Deputies, 2008-13; President of the Council of Ministers (Prime Minister). Apr. 2013-; ***office address:*** Office of the Prime Minister, Palazzo Chigi, Piazza Colonna 370, 00187 Rome, Italy; ***phone:*** +39 06 67791; ***URL:*** http://www.palazzochigi.it; http://www.governo.it.

LETWIN, Rt. Hon. Oliver; British, Minister of State, Cabinet Office, UK Government; ***born:*** 19 May 1956; ***parents:*** Prof. W. Letwin and Dr. S.R. Letwin (dec'd 1993); ***married:*** Isabel Grace Letwin (née Davidson), 1984; ***children:*** Jeremy (M), Laura (F); ***education:*** Eton; Trinity Coll., Cambridge, MA, Ph.D.; ***party:*** Conservative Party; ***political career:*** Party. Candidate for Hackney North, 1987, Hampstead Highgate, 1992; Mem., Prime Minister's Policy Unit, 1983-86; MP, West Dorset, 1997-; opposition front bench spokesman on constitutional affairs, 1998-99; Shadow Financial Sec. to the Treasury, 1999-2000; Shadow Chief Sec. to the Treasury, 2000-2001; Shadow Sec. of State for Home Affairs, 2001-03; Shadow Chancellor of the Exchequer and Shadow Sec. for Economic Affairs, 2003-05; Shadow Secretary of State for Environment, Food and Rural Affairs, May 2005-06; Chmn. of the Policy Review and Chmn. of the Conservative Research Dept., 2006-; Minister of State, Cabinet Office 2010-; ***memberships:*** FRSA., 1991; ***professional career:*** visiting research fellow, Princeton Univ., 1980-81; research fellow, Darwin, Coll., Cambridge, 1981-82; special adviser, Dept. of Education and Science, 1982-83; Dir., N.M. Rothschild and Sons Ltd., 1991-2009; ***honours and awards:*** Privy Council, 2002; ***publications:*** Ethics, Emotions and the Unity of the Self, 1984; Privatising the World, 1987; Aims of Schooling, 1988; Drift to Union, 1990; The Purpose of Politics, 1998; Numerous articles in journals; ***recreations:*** philosophy, walking, skiing, tennis; ***office address:*** Cabinet Office, 70 Whitehall, London, SW1A 2AS, United Kingdom; ***phone:*** +44 (0)20 7219 3000; ***e-mail:*** charlesa@parliament.uk.

LEUNG, Hon. Chun-ying (CY), JP; Chinese, Chief Executive, Executive Council, Hong Kong SAR; ***born:*** 12 August 1954, Hong Kong; ***married:*** Regina Tong Ching Yee; ***languages:*** English, Putonghua, Cantonese; ***education:*** Bristol, UK, B.Sc., Surveying and Estate Management; ***political career:*** Hong Kong Affairs Advisor, 1992-; Hon. Advisor, Leading Gp., Shanghai Govt. on Land Reform, PRC; Hon. Consultant, Pudong Dev. Leading Bd., Shanghai Govt., PRC; Hon. Advisor, Shenzhen Govt. on Land Reform, PRC; Hon. Advisor, Tianjin Govt. on Land Reform, PRC; mem., Exec. Cncl. of the HKSAR, 1997-, Convenor, 2000-11; Chief Executive, March 2012-; ***memberships:*** mem., Provisional Bd., Land Dev. Corp., 1986-87; mem., Man. Bd., Land Dev. Corp., 1988-96; mem., HK Housing Authority, 1991-97; Bd. mem., HK Industrial Estate Corp., 1992-93; mem., Surveyors Registration Bd., 1993-96; founding mem., The Court, The HK Polytechnic Univ., 1995-97; Pres., HK Inst. of Surveyors, 1995-96; Chmn., Royal Institution of Chartered Surveyors, HK Branch, 1995-96; ***professional career:*** Hon. Sec., One Country Two Systems Econ. Research Inst., 1990-; ***committees:*** mem., Building Cttee. of the HK Housing Authority, 1987-93; Sec. Gen., Basic Law Consultative Cttee., 1988-90; mem., Advisory Cttee. on Private Building Management, 1988-91; mem., Ad hoc Cttee. on Sale of Flats to Sitting Tenant, HK Housing Authority, 1989-91; mem., Land and Building Advisory Cttee., 1990-92; mem., Ad hoc Cttee. to Review the Policy on Housing Subsidy, HK Housing Authority, 1991-93; Convenor, Sub-cttee. on Land and Related Dev., Airport Consultative Cttee., 1993-95; Gp. Leader, Political Sub-Gp. of the Preliminary Working Cttee., 1993-95; mem., Home Ownership Cttee., HK Housing Authority, 1993-97; Vice-Chmn., Preparatory Cttee. for the HKSAR, 1995-; ***office address:*** Office of the Chief Executive, 5/F Central Government Offices, Lower Albert Road, Hong Kong; ***phone:*** +852 2878 3300; ***URL:*** http://www.info.gov.hk/ce.

LEUTHARD, Doris; Federal Councillor for the Environment, Transport, Communications and Energy, Government of Switzerland; ***born:*** 1963; ***married:*** Dr. Roland Hausin; ***political career:*** mem., National Council, 1999-2006; Pres., Christian Democratic People's Party, 2004-06; Head of the Federal Dept. of Economic Affairs, Aug. 2006-09; Vice President, 2009; Pres., Swiss Confederation, 2010; also Federal Councillor for the Environment, Transport, Communications and Energy, 2010-; ***professional career:*** Attorney-at-Law; ***office address:*** Bundeshaus East , 3003 Berne, Switzerland; ***phone:*** +41 (0)31 322 2001; ***fax:*** +41 (0)31 322 2112.

LEUTHEUSSER-SCHNARRENBERGER, Sabine; Federal Minister of Justice, German Government; ***born:*** 26 July 1951, Minden/Westfalen, Germany; ***education:*** Legal studies, Univ. of Göttingen and Bielefeld; First State Exam in Hamm, 1975; Second State Exam, Düsseldorf, 1978; ***political career:*** Mem., FDP, 1978-; Chair, of the FDP district chapter in Starnberg (Bavaria), 1982-2001; Member of the German Federal Parliament (Deutscher Bundestag), 1990-; Chair., FDP Bavararain Expert Cttee for home policiy and legal policy, 1996-2001; FDP Federal Exec. Cttee. (Bundesvorstand), 1991-; Mem., Supervisory Bd. of the GDP (Prasidium), 1997-; FDP Chair. for the Federal State of Bavaria, 2000-; Federal Minister of Justice, Oct. 2009-; ***professional career:*** German Patent and Trade Mark Office (DPMA), 1979-1990; Attorney-at-law in Munich, 1996-; ***committees:*** Dep. Chair., FDP parly. gp.; Federal Parliament Spokesperson on legal policy for the GDP parly. gp.; Chair., FDP parly. cttee. on legal affairs; Dep. mem., parly. cttee. for human rights and humanitarian assistance; Mem. German delegation at the parly. assembly of the Council of Europe; ***office address:*** Ministry of Justice, Justizministerium, 11015 Berlin, Germany; ***phone:*** +49 (0)30 202 570; ***fax:*** +49 (0)30 2025 9525; ***e-mail:*** poststelle@bmj.bund.de; ***URL:*** http://www.bmj.bund.de.

LEVIN, Carl; Senator for Michigan, US Senate; ***born:*** 1934, Detroit, USA; ***married:*** Barbara Levin (née Halpern), 1961; ***children:*** Kate (F), Laura (F), Erica (F); ***education:*** Central High Sch.; Swarthmore Coll., grad. (Hons.), 1956; Harvard Univ. Law Sch., 1959; ***party:*** Democrat; ***political career:*** Detroit City Cncl., 1969, Pres., 1973; US Senator of Michigan, 1978-; ***professional career:*** practised and taught Law in Michigan; apptd. Asst. Attorney Gen. of Michigan, first gen. counsel for the Michigan Civil Rights Cmn., 1964; ***committees:*** Senate Armed Services Cttee.; ***office address:*** US Senate, 269 Russell Senate Office Building, Washington, DC 20510, USA; ***phone:*** +1 202 224 6221; ***URL:*** http://www.levin.senate.gov/.

LEW, Jack; Secretary, Department of the Treasury, US Government; ***political career:*** Dir., Office of Management and Budget, 1998-2001; First Dep. Sec. of State for Mgmt & Resources; Dir., Office of Management and Budget, 2010; Chief of Staff to President Barack Obama, 2011-13; Sec., Dept. of the Treasury, 2013-; ***professional career:*** Exec. VP and CEO, New York Univ; MD & CEO, Citi Global Wealth Management; Citi Alternative Investments; ***office address:*** Department of the Treasury, 1500 Pennsylvania Ave., NW, Washington, DC 20220, USA; ***phone:*** +1 202 622 2000; ***URL:*** http://www.ustreas.gov.

LEWANDOWSKI, Janusz; Polish, Commissioner, European Commission; ***born:*** 13 June 1951, Lublin, Poland; ***married:*** Lidia Lewandowska; ***education:*** Univ. of Gdansk, Masters in Economics, 1974; Gdansk Univ., Ph.D, Econ., 1984; ***party:*** Solidarity, 1980-89; European People's Party (Christian Democrats) and European Democrats; ***political career:*** Min. of Privatisation 1991-93; MP,1997-2004; Observer to the European Parliament, 2003-04; MEP, 2004-; Commissioner for Budget and Financial Programming, 2010-; ***memberships:*** Civic Platform, 2001-; ***professional career:*** Assoc. Prof. of Int. Trade and Maritime Transport, Univ. of Gdansk, 1974-84; Private Consultant and consultant to Polish Ocean Lines, 1984-1991; ***committees:*** Chmn., Program Bd. of the Gdansk Instit. for Market Economics, 1993-; Vice-Chmn., Poland-EU Cttee., 2001-04; Chmn., Cttee. on Budgets, to date; ***publications:*** Series of underground articles "Przeglad Polityczny", 1984-88, Neo-Liberals and the Present Times, 1991, Gdynia; Self-Government in the Solidarity Era, 1984, London; ***recreations:*** Chmn., Athletics Club of Sopot; mountain trekking, football; ***office address:*** European Commission, rue de la Loi 200, B-1040 Brussels, Belgium; ***URL:*** http://www.europa.eu.

LEWIS, Brandon; MP for Great Yarmouth, UK Government; ***party:*** Conservative; ***political career:*** Councillor, Brentwood Borough Council, 1998-2009, Leader 2004-09; MP for Great Yarmouth, May 2010-; Parly. Under-Sec. of State, Dept. for Communities and Local Government, 2012-; ***committees:*** Regulatory Reform, 2010-12; Work and Pensions, 2010-12; ***office address:*** House of Commons, London, SW1A 0AA, United Kingdom; ***phone:*** +44 (0)20 7219 3000; ***e-mail:*** justine.duggan@parliament.uk.

LEWIS, Hon. H. Frank; Lieutentant Governor, Prince Edward Island; ***political career:*** Lieutentant Governor, 2011-; ***professional career:*** Broadcasting industry executive ; ***office address:*** Government House, P.O. Box 846 , Charlottetown, PE, C1A 7L9, Canada; ***phone:*** +1 902 368 5480 ; ***e-mail:*** hflewis@gov.pe.ca.

LEWIS, Huw; Constituency Member for Merthyr Tydfil & Rhymney, National Assembly for Wales; ***born:*** 1964, Aberfan, Wales; ***married:*** Lynne Lewis (née Neagle), 1996; ***children:*** James (M); ***public role of spouse:*** Assembly Mem. for Torfaen; ***education:*** Afon Taf High School, Wales; Edinburgh Univ., UK; ***party:*** Labour; ***political career:*** Mem., Nat. Assembly for Wales, Merthyr Tydfil and Rhymney; fmr. Dep. Minister for Education and Lifelong Learning; Dep. Minister for Children; Minister for Housing, Regeneration and Heritage, 2011-13; Minister of Communities and Tackling Poverty, 2013-; ***interests:*** education, economic regeneration; ***office address:*** National Assembly for Wales, Cardiff Bay, Cardiff, CF99 1NA, United Kingdom; ***phone:*** +44 (0)29 2089 8752; ***fax:*** +44 (0)29 2089 8385.

LEWIS, Ivan; British, Shadow Secretary of State for International Development, House of Commons; ***born:*** 4 March 1967, Prestwich, Manchester; ***parents:*** Joe Lewis and Gloria Lewis (dec'd); ***married:*** Juliette (née Fox), 3 June 1990 (Div'd); ***children:*** Ben (M), Harry (M); ***education:*** William Hulme's Grammar School; Stand College; ***party:*** Labour Party; ***political career:*** Campaigner, Educational Standards in Bury; Cllr. Bury MBC, 1990-98; Cllr., Bury Borough; PPS to Sec. of State for Trade & Industry; Under Sec. of State, Dept. of Education and Skills; MP, Bury South, 1997-; Econ. Sec., Treasury, 2005-06; Parly. Under-Sec. of State, Dept. of Health, 2006-08; Parly. Under-Sec. of State, Dept. of Int. Dev., 2008-09, Minister of State, FCO, 2009-10; Shadow Minister, Foreign and Commonwealth Affairs, May-Sept. 2010; Shadow Secretary of State for Culture, Media and Sport, Oct. 2010-Oct. 2011; Shadow Secretary of State for International Development, 2012-; ***interests:*** culture, media, sport, education, health, social services; ***professional career:*** Chief Exec., Jewish Social Services; ***trusteeships:*** Holocaust Educational Trust; ***recreations:*** walking, reading, supporter of Manchester City FC; ***office address:*** Constituency Office, 381 Bury New Road, Preswich, M25 1AW, United Kingdom; ***phone:*** +44 (0)161 773 5500; ***e-mail:*** ivanlewis@burysouth.fsnet.co.uk; ***URL:*** http://www.ivanlewis.co.uk.

LEWIS, Dr Julian; British, Member of Parliament for New Forest East, House of Commons; ***born:*** 1951, Swansea; ***parents:*** Samuel (dec'd) and Hilda Lewis (dec'd); ***education:*** Balliol Coll., Oxford Univ., MA., 1977; St. Antony's Coll., Oxford Univ., D.Phil., 1981; ***party:*** Conservative Party; ***political career:*** Political Campaigner; Sec. Campaign for Representative Democracy, 1977-78; Dir., Policy Research Assoc., 1985-; Dep. Dir., Conservative Research Dept., 1990-96; MP, New Forest East, 1997-; Opposition Whip, 2001-2002; Shadow Defence Minister, 2002-04; Shadow Minister for the Cabinet Office, 2004-05; Shadow Defence Minister, 2005-10; ***interests:*** defence security, foreign affairs, New Forest issues; ***professional career:*** Research Consultant; Military Historian; Research in Defence Studies, 1975-77, 1978-81; Seaman, Royal Naval Reserve, 1979-82; Research Dir.; Dir., Coalition for Peace Through Security, 1981-85; ***committees:*** Defence Select Cttee., 2000-2001; Welsh Select Cttee., 1998-2001; Vice-Chmn., Conservative Parly. Foreign Affairs, Europe Cttees., 2000-2001; Sec. Conservative Parly. Defence Cttee., 1997-2001; elected mem., exec. of 1922 Cttee., 2001; Intelligence and Security Cttee., 2010-; ***trusteeships:*** British Military Powerboat Trust, 1998-2001, Hon. Pres., 2007-09; ***honours and awards:*** 1st prize, Trench-Gascoigne Essay competition, Royal United Services Institute, 2005, 2007; Dissertation prize, Royal College of Defence Studies, 2006; ***publications:*** Changing Direction: British Military Planning for Post-War Strategic Defence, 1988 (2nd Edition 2003), Univ. paperback edn., (2008); Who's Left?: An Index of Labour MPs and Left Wing Causes, 1992; Labour's CND-Cover Up, 1992; What's Liberal?, 1996; Racing Ace: The Fights and Flights of 'Kink' Kinkead, DSO, DSC, DFC, 2011; ***recreations:*** history, films, music; ***office address:*** House of Commons, London, SW1A 0AA, United Kingdom; ***phone:*** +44 (0)23 8081 4817; ***URL:*** http://www.julianlewis.net.

LEXDEN, Lord Alistair; Member, House of Lords; ***education:*** MA, Peterhouse, Cambridge Univ., 1970; ***party:*** Conservative Party; ***political career:*** Mem., House of Lords, 2011-; ***professional career:*** Lecturer and Tutor, Modern History, Queen's Univ., Belfast, 1971-77; Gen. Sec., Independent Schools Council, 1997-2004; Historian of the Conservative Party, 2009-; ***honours and awards:*** OBE, 1988; ***office address:*** House of Lords, London, SW1A 0PW, United Kingdom; ***phone:*** +44 (0)20 7219 3000.

LI, Keqiang; Premier of the State Council, Government of the People's Republic of China; ***born:*** July 1955; ***education:*** School of Economics, Peking Univ.; ***political career:*** Mem., Standing Cttee., Political Bureau, CPC Central Cttee.; Vice Premier of the State Council and Dep. Sec. of its Leading Party Members' Group; Dir., Three Gorges Project Construction Cttee. and of South-to-North Water Diversion Construction Project Cttee.; head of the leading group of deepening the reform of medical and health care system, State Council, 2008-13; Mem. Standing Committee of the Political Bureau of the CPC Central Committee; Premier of the State Council, March 2013-; ***office address:*** Office of the State Council, Beijing, People's Republic of China; ***phone:*** +86 10 6207 2370.

LI, Yong; Director General, UNIDO; ***political career:*** Assist. Minister of Finance, People's Republic of China, 2000-03; Vice-Minister of Finance, 2013-; ***professional career:*** Exec. Dir., for China in the World Bank Group, 1996-98; Sec. Gen. Chinese Inst. of Certified Public Accountants, 1999-2002; Dir. Gen., UNIDO, 2013-; ***office address:*** Office of the Secretary General, UNIDO, Wagramerstr. 5, PO Box 300, Vienna International Centre, A 1400 Vienna, Austria; ***phone:*** +43 (0)1 260 260; ***e-mail:*** unido@unido.org; ***URL:*** http://www.unido.org.

LI, Yuanchao; Vice President, Government of the People's Republic of China; ***education:*** Doctor of Laws; ***political career:*** Vice President, March 2013-; ***professional career:*** Teacher; ***committees:*** Political Bureau of the CPC Central Cttee. 2013-; ***office address:*** Office of the President, State Council Secretariat, Shong Nan Hai, Beijing, China; ***phone:*** +86 10 6309 8375; ***URL:*** http://www.gov.cn.

LICHFIELD, Bishop of; Member, House of Lords; ***political career:*** Mem., House of Lords, 2009-; ***professional career:*** Rural Dean at Canterbury, 1988-94; Hon. Canon of Canterbury Cathedral, 1992-96; Mem., General Synod, 1995-98; Suffragan Bishop of Southampton, 1996-03; Bishop of Lichfield, 2003-; ***office address:*** House of Lords, London, SW1A 0PW, United Kingdom; ***phone:*** +44 (0)20 7219 3000; ***fax:*** +44 (0)20 7219 5979; ***URL:*** http://www.parliament.uk.

LIDDELL OF COATDYKE, Baroness Helen; British, Member, House of Lords; ***born:*** 6 December 1950; ***married:*** Dr Alistair Liddell; ***education:*** St Patrick's High Sch., Coatbridge; Univ. of Strathclyde, BA, Econs.; ***party:*** Labour Party; ***political career:*** Gen. Sec. of the Scottish Labour Party, 1977-88; MP, Monklands East, 1994-97, Airdrie and Shotts, 1997-; Opp. Spokeswoman on Scotland, 1995-97; Econ. Sec. to the Treasury, 1997; MP, Airdrie and Shotts, 1997-2005; Minister for Education, Scottish Office, 1998-99; Minister for Energy and Competitiveness in Europe, Dept. of Trade and Industry, 1999; Minister of Transport, 1999; Sec. of State for Scotland, 2001-2003; Mem., House of Lords, 2010-; ***professional career:*** Head Econ., Dept., Scottish TUC, 1971-75; Economics Correspondent, BBC Scotland, 1976-77; Dir., Corporate Affairs, Scottish Daily Record and Sunday Mail (1986) Ltd, 1988-92; Chief Exec., Business Venture Programme, 1993-94; writer and broadcaster; High Commissioner to Australia, 2005-10; ***publications:*** Elite, 1990; ***recreations:*** cooking, hill-walking, music, writing; ***office address:*** House of Lords, London, SW1A 0PW, United Kingdom; ***phone:*** +44 (0)20 7219 3000; ***fax:*** +44 (0)20 7219 5979; ***URL:*** http://www.parliament.uk.

LIDDELL-GRAINGER, Ian; Member of Parliament for Bridgwater and West Somerset, House of Commons; ***education:*** Millfield School, Somerset; ***party:*** Conservative Party; ***political career:*** MP, Bridgwater, June 2001-10, Bridgwater and West Somerset, 2010-; ***professional career:*** Man. Dir., group of property management and dev. co's, 1985-; ***committees:*** Jt. Cttee. on Statutory Instruments, 2010-; Works of Art, 2011-; ***office address:*** House of Commons, London, SW1A 0AA, United Kingdom; ***phone:*** +44 (0)20 7219 3000; ***e-mail:*** ianlg@parliament.uk; ***URL:*** http://www.parliament.uk.

LIDEGAARD, Martin; Minister of Climate, Energy and Buildings, Government of Denmark; ***born:*** December 12 1966; ***education:*** MA, (Communication), Roskilde Univ. Centre, 1993 ; ***party:*** Social Liberal Party; ***political career:*** MP, 2001-; Minister of Climate, Energy and Buildings, 2011-; ***office address:*** Ministry of the Environment, Højbro Plads 4, 1200 Copenhagen K, Denmark; ***phone:*** +45 3392 7600; ***fax:*** +45 3332 2227; ***e-mail:*** mim@mim.dk; ***URL:*** http://www.mim.dk.

LIDINGTON, David; Minister of State for the Foreign and Commonwealth Office, UK Government; ***party:*** Conservative Party; ***political career:*** MP, Aylesbury, 1992-; PPS to Michael Howard and William Hague; former Shadow Secretary of State for Environment, Food and Rural Affairs, 2002-2003; Shadow Sec. of State for Northern Ireland, 2003-07; Shadow Minister for Foreign Affairs, 2007-10; Minister of State, FCO, May 2010-; ***office address:*** Foreign and Commonwealth Affairs Office, King Charles Street, London, SW1A 2AH, United Kingdom; ***phone:*** +44 (0)20 7270 1500; ***e-mail:*** davidlidingtonmp@parliament.uk.

LIEBERKNECHT, Christine; German, Minister President, Government of Thuringia; ***born:*** 1958; ***party:*** Christian Democratic Union; ***political career:*** Mem., Thuringian Parliament, 1991-; Minister of Education & Cultural Affairs, 1990-92; Minister of Federal and European Affairs, 1992-94; Minister for Federal Affairs with the State Chancellery, 1994-99; Speaker, Thuringian Parliament, 1999-2004; Minister for Social Affairs, Family & Health, 2008-09; Minister-President of Thuringia, 2009-; ***professional career:*** Pastor, Church District of Weimar, 1984-90; ***office address:*** Freistaat Thuringen, Thuringer Staatskanzlei, Regierungsstrasse 73, 99084 Erfurt, Germany; ***phone:*** +49 361 / 37 900.

LIECHTENSTEIN, Alois, (Hereditary Prince of Liechtenstein); Permanent Representative of Prince Hans-Adam II; ***born:*** 11 June 1968, Zurich, Switzerland; ***parents:*** Prince Hans-Adam II and Princess Marie of Liechtenstein; ***married:*** Sophie Herzogin in Bayern, 3rd July 1993; ***children:*** Prince Joseph Wenzel (m), Prince Georg (m), Prince Nikolaus (m), Princess Marie Caroline (f); ***languages:*** English, French; ***education:*** Royal Military Academy, Sandhurst, UK, 1987; Univ. of Salzburg, Austria, Masters Degree in Law, 1993; ***professional career:*** Second Lieutenant, Coldstream Guards in Hong Kong and London, 1987-88; Arthur Andersen, London, 1993-96; Princely Family Foundations, 1996-; Permanent Representative of Prince Hans-Adam II entrusted with the tasks of the Head of State of Liechtenstein, 2004-; ***office address:*** Schloss Vaduz, FL-9490 Vaduz, Liechtenstein; ***phone:*** +423 238 1200; ***fax:*** +423 238 1201; ***e-mail:*** office@sfl.li.

LIFE, H.E. Vivien; Ambassador , British Embassy in Denmark; ***education:*** MA, (English), Oxford Univ., UK; ***professional career:*** FCO, Head of Dept. concerned with energy and climate change; Amb. to Denmark, 2012-; ***office address:*** British Embassy, Kastelsvej 36/38/40, 2100 Copenhagen Ø, Denmark; ***phone:*** +45 3544 5200; ***fax:*** +45 3544 5293; ***e-mail:*** info@britishembassy.dk; ***URL:*** https://www.gov.uk/government/world/denmark.

LIIKANEN, Erkki Antero; Finnish, Governor, Bank of Finland; ***born:*** 19 September 1950, Mikkeli, Finland; ***married:*** Hanna Liisa Issakainen, 1971; ***children:*** 2; ***education:*** Univ. of Helsinki, Finland, M.Pol.Sc.; ***party:*** Social Democratic Party; ***political career:*** MP 1972-90; Sec.-Gen., Social Democratic Party 1981-87; Minister of Finance 1987-90; ***professional career:*** mem., Supervisory Bd. of Televa Oy 1976-79; Vice-Chmn., Bank Supervisors, nominated by Parliament, 1982-; mem. then Chmn., Supervisory Bd. of Outokumpu, 1980-89; Parly. Cmnr. to the Bank of Finland; Amb. Ex & Plen., Head of Finnish Mission to the EU 1990-94; mem. of the Commission, 1995-2004; Governor, Bank of Finland, 2004-; ***committees:*** Cultural Affairs Cttee. 1972-75; Vice-Chmn, Agriculture and Forestry Cttee. 1977-79; Foreign Affairs Cttee. 1975-90, Chmn. 1983-87; ***office address:*** Bank of Finland, PO Box 160, FIN-00101 Helsinki, Finland; ***phone:*** +358 (0)9 1831; ***fax:*** +358 (0)9 174872; ***e-mail:*** info@bof.fi; ***URL:*** http://www.bof.fi.

LIKINS, Rose; US Ambassador to Peru, US Embassy; ***languages:*** Bulgarian, Spanish; ***education:*** Mary Washington Coll., Fredericksburg, Virginia, Bachelor of Arts (magna cum laude honors), Spanish and Int. Affairs, 1981; ***memberships:*** Phi Beta Kappa and Mortar Board honor societies, Mary Washington Coll.; American Foreign Service Assn.; ***professional career:*** joined US Foreign Service, 1981; consular officer, US Consulate General, Monterrey, Mexico; chief of the political section, US Embassy, Asuncion, Paraguay; Dep. Chief of Mission, US Embassy, Sofia, Bulgaria; Honduras desk officer, Special Asst. to the Dep. Sec. of State, Exec. Assist. to the Under Sec. for Global Affairs, Dir. of the Department's Operations Center, and Dep. Exec. Sec. of the Dept., Bureau of Human Rights and Humanitarian Affairs, Bureau of Intelligence and Research; US Ambassador to El Salvador, 2000-03; US Ambassador to Peru, 2010-; ***honours and awards:*** Meritorious and Superior Honor awards; Horsemen of Madara medal, Government of Bulgaria, 1997; ***office address:*** Embassy of the USA, Avenida Encalada, Cuadra 17, Monterrico, Lima, Peru; ***phone:*** +51 (0)1 434 3000.

LILLEY, Rt. Hon. Peter Bruce, MP; British, Member of Parliament for Hitchen and Harpenden, House of Commons; ***born:*** 1943; ***married:*** Gail Ansell, 1979; ***education:*** Dulwich Coll.; Clare Coll., Cambridge (MA in Natural Sciences and Economics); ***party:*** Conservative Party; ***political career:*** MP (Cons.) for St. Albans, 1983-97; PPS to Minister for Local Govt., 1984; PPS to Chancellor of Exchequer, 1984-87; Economic Sec. to the Treasury, 1987-89, Financial Sec., 1989-90; Sec. of State for Trade and Industry 1990-92; Sec. of State for Social Security, 1992-97; Shadow Chancellor of the Exchequer, 1997-98; Deputy Leader,

Lil-Llw

Conservative Party, 1998-99; MP, Hitchin and Harpenden, 1997-; ***memberships:*** Fellow, Inst. of Petroleum; ***professional career:*** Economic Advisor on underdeveloped countries, 1966-72; Investment Advisor on North Sea Oil and other energy industries, 1972-84; Dir. of Great Western Resources Ltd., 1985-87; Dir. of Greenwell Montagu Stockbrokers, 1986-87; Dir., Flemings Claverhouse Inv. Trust, 1999-; Dir., i-documentsystems plc, 2002-; ***committees:*** Chmn., Globalisation and Global Poverty Policy Cmn., 2006-07; Jt. Cttee. on the Draft Financial Services Bill, 2011-12; ***publications:*** Do you Sincerely Want to Win - Defeating Terrorism in Ulster (1972); Lessons for Power (1974); Delusions of Incomes Policy (co-author) (1977); End of the Keynesian Era (contributor) (1980); Thatcherism: The Next Generation (1989); The Mais Lecture: Benefits and Costs - Securing the Future of Social Security (1993); Winning the Welfare Debate (1995); Patient Power (2000); Common Sense on Cannabis (2001); Taking Liberties (2002); Save our Pensions (2003); Case against Identity Cards (2004); Too Much of a Good thing?-Immigration (2005); ***office address:*** House of Commons, London, SW1A 0AA, United Kingdom; ***phone:*** +44 (0)20 7219 3000; ***e-mail:*** hcinfo@parliament.uk.

LILLIE, H.E. Stephen; Ambassador, British Embassy in the Philippines; ***professional career:*** Consul-General, Guangzhou, China, 1999-2003; Head of the Far Eastern Group at the FCO, 2006-11; Amb. to the Philippines, 2011-; ***office address:*** British Embassy, 120 Upper McKinley Road, McKinley Hill, Taguig City 1634, Metro Manila, Philippines; ***phone:*** +63 2 858 2200; ***fax:*** +63 2 858 2216; ***URL:*** http://www.ukinthephilippines.fco.gov.uk/en.

LILO, Gordon Darcy; Prime Minister, Government of the Solomon Islands; ***born:*** 1965; ***party:*** SIDP; ***political career:*** MP, Western Province of the Solomon Islands, 2001-; Gov. Minister, 2007; Finance Minister, -2011; Prime Minister, 2011-; ***office address:*** Prime Minister's Office, PO Box G1, Honiara, Solomon Islands.

LIM, Hng Kiang; Minister for Trade and Industry, Singapore Government; ***born:*** 9 April 1954; ***married:*** Lee Ai Boon; ***s:*** 2; ***education:*** secondary and pre-univ. education, Raffles Inst.; President's Scholarship, 1973; Engineering degree, Cambridge Univ., 1976; Command and Staff course, Singapore Armed Forces (SAF); MA Public Admin., Kennedy School, Harvard Univ., 1985; ***political career:*** Dep. Sec., Ministry of National Development, 1986; elected one of four MPs for Tanjong Pagar Gp. Representation constituency, 1991; Minister for National Development, 1991-94; Acting Minister for National Development and Sr. Minister for Foreign Affairs, 1994-95; Minister for National Dev. , 1995-99; second Minister for Foreign Affairs, 1995-98; re-elected one of four MPs, West Coast Gp. Representation constituency, 1997; Second Minister for Finance, 1998-2004; Minister for Health, 1999-2004; Minister for Trade and Industry, 2004-; ***memberships:*** Mason Fellow, Kennedy School, Harvard Univ., 1985; fmr. Mem., Nanyang Technological Inst. Cncl. and Mass Rapid Transit Corp. Bd.; fmr. Bd. Mem., People's Assoc.; ***professional career:*** Command and Staff appointments, Singapore Armed Forces, 9 yrs; fmr. Head of the Air Plans Dept., Republic of Singapore Air Force; posted to Ministry of Defence, helped set up dept. to handle military relations, 1986; CEO, Housing and Development Bd., 1991; Dep. Chmn., Monetary Authority of Singapore (MAS), 2001; Bd. Dir., Govt. of Singapore Investment Corporation (GIC), to date; ***recreations:*** swimming, golf; ***office address:*** Ministry of Trade and Industry, 100 High Street, 01-01, The Treasury, 179434 Singapore, Singapore; ***phone:*** +65 6225 9911.

LINDBACK, Peter; Governor, Aland Islands; ***born:*** 1955; ***education:*** Univ. of Helsinki, law; Univ. of Oslo, Maritime Law; ***political career:*** Perm. Sec., Government of Aland, 1987-99; Governor of Aland Islands, 1999-; ***professional career:*** District Court Judge, District Court of Aland, 1984-87; ***office address:*** Office of the Governor, PO Box 58, 22101 Mariehamn, Aland Islands; ***URL:*** http://www.ambetsverket.ax.

LINDE, Luis Maria; Banker, Central Bank of Spain; ***born:*** 1945, Madrid, Spain; ***education:*** Univ. of Madrid, Economics; ***professional career:*** Ministry of Trade; Dep. Dir. Gen., Foreign Dept., Banco de Espana, 1983-87, Dir.-Gen., International Affairs, 1987-2000; Dir., ICO, 1989-92; Dir., Country Risk Dept., Banco de Espana, 2001-04; Exec. Dir., Spain's group, Inter-American Dev. Bank, 2005-08; Council Member, Banco de Espana, 2012; Governor, Bank of Spain, 2012-; ***office address:*** Banca de Espana, Alcalá, 50, 28014 Madrid, Spain; ***URL:*** http://www.bde.es.

LINGFIELD, Lord Sir Robert George Alexander; Member, House of Lords; ***party:*** Conservative Party; ***political career:*** Mem. House of Lords, 2010-; ***professional career:*** Chmn., League of Mercy; Dep. Lieutenant of Greater London; Dir.-Gen., St. John Ambulance; Pro-Chancellor, Brunel Univ.; ***honours and awards:*** Knight Bachelor, 1993; Raised to the Peerage as Baron Lingfield, of Lingfield in the County of Surrey; ***office address:*** House of Lords, London, SW1A 0PW, United Kingdom; ***phone:*** +44 (0)20 7219 3000.

LINIC, Slavko; Minister of Finance, Government of Croatia; ***education:*** Univ. of Rijeka; ***political career:*** Mayor of Rijeka, 1990-2000; Deputy Prime Minister, 2000-03; Minister of Finance, 2011-; ***office address:*** Ministry of Finance, Katanciceva 5, 10000 Zagreb, Croatia; ***phone:*** +385 (0)1 459 1333; ***URL:*** http://www.mfin.hr.

LIN JUNQ-TZER ; Minister without Portfolio, Governor of Taiwan Province, Government of Taiwan; ***born:*** 1944; ***political career:*** Mem., Hsinchu County Council, 1972-77; Delegate, National Assembly, 1981-93; Mem., Legislative Yuan, 1996-2001; Mayor, Hsinchu City, 2001-09; Minister without Portfolio, Executive Yuan and also Governor, Taiwan Province, 2010-; ***office address:*** Executive Yuan, 1 Chuanghsiao E. Road, Section 1, Taipei, Taiwan; ***URL:*** http://www.ey.gov.tw.

LINKEVICIUS, Linas Antanas; Lithuanian, Minister of Foreign Affairs, Government of Lithuania; ***born:*** 6 January 1961, Vilnius, Lithuania; ***languages:*** English, Russian, Polish; ***education:*** Dip. Engineering, Kaunas Polytechnic Inst., 1978-83; ***political career:*** Mem., Council of Labour Democratic Party, 1991-96; Chmn., Labour Youth Union, 1992-93; MP, 1992 (Democratic Labour party); Head of Parly. Deleg. to NATO, 1992-93; Dep. Chmn., Parly. Comn. on Foreign Affairs, 1992-93; Mem., Seimas (Parliament), 1992-96; Minister of National Defence, 1993-96; Advisor to the Minister of Foreign Affairs, Minister for Special Appointments, Special Envoy, 1997; Minister of National Defence, 2000-04; Minister of Foreign Affairs, 2012-; ***memberships:*** Mem., Cncl. of Labour Party, 1991-96; Chmn., Labour Youth Union, 1992-93; ***professional career:*** Engineer; Observer of Lithuanian daily 'Tiesa' 1992-93; Amb. Ex & Plen., Head of Mission to NATO and WEU, 1997-2000; ***office address:*** Ministry of Foreign Affairs, J. Tumo-Vaizganto g 2 , 2600 Vilnius, Lithuania; ***phone:*** +370 5 236 2444; ***fax:*** +370 2 226082; ***URL:*** http://www.urm.lt.

LIN YUNG-LO, (David Yung lo); Minister of Foreign Affairs, Government of Taiwan; ***political career:*** Rep., Taipei Economic & Trade Office, Indonesia, 2003-07; Vice Minister of Foreign Affairs, 2008-10; Rep., Taipei Rep. Office in the EU & Belgium, 2010-12; Minister of Foreign Affairs, 2012-; ***professional career:*** long diplomatic & civil service career, incl. Dir-Gen., Taipei Economic & Cultural Office, Houston, US, 1995-97; Amb. to Grenada & St. Vincent & The Grenadines, 1997-2001; Dir.-Gen., Dept. of European Affairs, MOFA, 2001-03, 2007-08; ***office address:*** Ministry of Foreign Affairs, 2 Kaitakelan Boulevard, Taipei, Taiwan; ***phone:*** +886 2 2348 2999; ***URL:*** http://www.mofa.gov.tw/.

LIPENGA, Hon. Dr. Ken; Minister of Finance, Government of Malawi; ***political career:*** Minister of Tourism, Parks and Wildlife; Minister responsible for Presidential Affairs, 2003-04; Minister of Information, Communications & Tourism; Minister of Trade and Private Sector Development; Minister of Finance, 2012-; ***office address:*** Ministry of Finance, PO Box 30136, Capital City, Lilongwe 3, Malawi; ***URL:*** http://www.malawi.gov.mw/.

LISTER OF BURTERSETT, Baroness Ruth; Member, House of Lords; ***party:*** Labour Party; ***political career:*** Mem., House of Lords, 2011-; ***professional career:*** Emeritus Prof. of Social Policy, Loughborough Univ.; ***office address:*** House of Lords, London, SW1A 0PW, United Kingdom; ***phone:*** +44 (0)20 7219 3000.

LIU, Xiaoming; Ambassador to the UK and Ireland, Embassy of the People's Republic of China; ***education:*** Dalian Univ. of Foreign Languages, China, 1974; MA, in international relations, Tufts University, USA, 1983; ***professional career:*** Amb. to the Arab Republic of Egypt, 2001-03; Amb. to the Democratic People's Republic of Korea, 2006-09; Amb. to the UK and Ireland, 2009-; ***office address:*** Embassy of the People's Republic of China, 49-51 Portland Place, London, W1N 4JL, United Kingdom; ***phone:*** +44 (0)20 9375 / 5726; ***fax:*** +44 (0)20 7636 9756; ***URL:*** http://www.chinese-embassy.org.uk.

LIVERPOOL, 5th Earl of, Edward Peter Bertram Savile Foljambe, UK; British, Member of the House of Lords; ***born:*** 14 November 1944; ***married:*** Lady Juliana Noel, 1970 (dissolved 1994); Marie-Ange dePierredon, 1995 (dissolved 2001); Georgina Lederman, 2002; ***s:*** 2; ***education:*** Shrewsbury School; Perugia Univ., Italy; ***party:*** Conservative Party; ***political career:*** Mem., House of Lords, 1969-; ***professional career:*** Man. Dir., Melbourns Brewery Ltd., 1971-76, Joint Chmn. and Man Dir., 1977-87; Dir., Hilstone Devs. Ltd., 1986-90; Dir., Hart Hambleton plc, 1986-94; Chmn. and Man. Dir., Maxador Ltd., 1987-96; Dir., J.W. Cameron and Co. Ltd., 1987-94; Dir., Naylor Automatics Ltd., 1990-92; Dir., Glastonwise Ltd., 1989-92; Dir., Rutland Management Ltd., 1992-, Chmn., 1994-; ***clubs:*** Turf Club; Pratt's; Air Squadron; ***recreations:*** flying, golf, shooting; ***office address:*** House of Lords, London, SW1A 0PW, United Kingdom; ***phone:*** +44 (0)20 7219 5406; ***fax:*** +44 (0)20 7219 2082.

LIVNAT, Limor; Israeli, Minister of Culture and Sport, Israeli Government; ***born:*** 1950, Haifa; ***education:*** studied Hebrew Literature, Tel-Aviv Univ.; ***party:*** Likud; ***political career:*** ran for the Knesset, 1986; elected to the Knesset, 1992; Dep. Chwn., World Likud Movement, 1992-; chwn., Likud and Benjamin Netanyahu's campaign, 1996 election; Chwn., Parly. Comn. of Inquiry into Domestic Violence, 1995; Vice-Chmn. of World Likud Movement; apptd. Minister of Communications, 1996-99; Minister of Education, 2001-06; Minister of Culture and Sport, 2009-; ***professional career:*** Vice Chwn., Student Union when studying at Tel-Aviv Univ.; served in Israel Defence Forces in the Education and Social Welfare Unit; Advertising and Public Relations; ***committees:*** fmr. Mem. of Knesset Education and Culture Cttee; fmr. Mem. Labour and Social Affairs Cttee.; fmr. Mem., Cttee. on Commercial TV; Chwn., Knesset Cttee. for Advancement of Women, 1993-94; Chwn., Sub-Cttee on Women's Representation; Likud Information Cttee.; Chwn., Knesset Finance Cttee.; Chwn., Inter-Ministerial Cttee. on the Promotion of the Status of Women in Israeli Society; ***honours and awards:*** Amitai Award; Hon. Doctorate, Yeshiva Univ.; ***publications:*** Author of book, Straight to the Point, a compendium of speeches; ***office address:*** Ministry of Culture and Sport, The Knesset, Qiryat Ben-Gurion, Jerusalem 91950, Israel; ***phone:*** +972 2 675 3333; ***URL:*** http://www.knesset.gov.il.

LIVNI, Tzipi, MK; Minister of Justice, Government of Israel; ***born:*** 1958, Israel; ***education:*** Bar Ilan Univ., LL.B. degree; ***party:*** Likud, to 2005; Kadima, 2005-; Head of Kadima Party; ***political career:*** Elected to the Knesset, 1999; Minister of Regional Co-operation; Minister Without Portfolio; Minister of Agriculture; Minister for Immigrant Absorption, 2003-04; Acting Minister, then Minister of Housing and Construction, 2004; Acting Minister of Justice, then Minister for Justice and Immigrant Absorbtion, 2004-06; Dep. Prime Minister and Minister of Foreign Affairs, 2006-09; Leader, Kadima, 2008-; Minister of Justice, 2013-; ***professional career:*** Attorney at Law, private practice, specialising in commercial law, constitutional law and real estate law, for ten years; Officer, IDF; employee, Mossad, 1980-84; Dir. of the Register of Govt. Corps.; Gen. Man., Govt. Companies Authority; ***committees:*** mem. of the Constitution, Law and Justice Cttee., and Cttee. for the Advancement of the Status of Women; ***office address:*** Ministry of Justice, 29 Salah A-din Street, 91010 Jerusalem, Israel; ***phone:*** +972 2 670 8511; ***URL:*** http://www.justice.gov.il.

LLOYD, Stephen; MP for Eastbourne, UK Government; ***party:*** Liberal Democrat; ***political career:*** MP for Eastbourne, May 2010-; ***committees:*** Work and Pensions Select Cttee., 2010-; ***office address:*** House of Commons, London, SW1A 0AA, United Kingdom; ***phone:*** +44 (0)20 7219 3000; ***e-mail:*** stephen.lloyd.mp@parliament.uk.

LLWYD, Elfyn; British, Member of Parliament for Dwyfor Meirionnydd, House of Commons; ***born:*** 26 September 1951, Betws-y-Coed, Wales; ***parents:*** Meirion Lloyd Hughes (dec'd) and Hefina Hughes (dec'd); ***married:*** Eleri Llwyd (née Edwards); ***children:*** Rhodri (M), Catrin (F); ***languages:*** Welsh; ***education:*** Univ. Coll. of Wales, LL.B.(Hons), 1974; Coll. of Law, Chester, Solicitors' Qualifying Exam; ***party:*** Plaid Cymru, (Party of Wales), 1968-; ***political career:*** MP, Meirionnydd Nant Conwy, 1992-2010, Dwyfor Meirionnydd, 2010-; Plaid Cymru Whip, 1995; Plaid Cymru Party Parly. Leader, 1999 ; ***interests:*** civil rights, home affairs, transport, tourism, local government; ***memberships:*** Commonwealth Parly.

BIOGRAPHIES

Assn., 1992; All Party Gp. on Children, 1992; Inter-Parly. Union, 1992; All Party Gp. for the Bar, 1999; memberships since 2001: British-Irish Parly. Body; Nat. Patron Abbeyfield, Wales; Court of Univ. Coll., Wales, Bangor; Court of Univ. Coll., Wales, Aberystwyth; Bd.of Governors, Cardiff School of Medicine; Court of the Nat. Library of Wales; Honourable Soc., Cymmrodorion; Gov., Westminster Foundation for Democracy, 1999-2004; mem., Howard League for Penal Reform, 2010-; ***professional career:*** Partner, Guthrie Jones and Jones, 1978; Hon. Sec., Gwynedd Law Soc., 1980-89; Pres., Gwynedd Law Soc., 1990; solicitor, north Wales Steering Cttee., 1990; legal correspondent, daily Welsh radio current affairs programme, for 8 yrs; regular reviewer of legal books and contributor to television and radio programmes; mem., Gray's Inn- called to Bar, 1997; UNICEF Parly. Amb., 1999; NSPCC Wales Amb., 1999 ; ***committees:*** mem., Select Cttee. on Welsh Affairs, 1992-95 & 1996-2001; mem., Standing Cttee., Welsh Language Bill, 1992-93; mem., Standing Cttee., Local Govt. Wales Bill, 1994; mem., Standing Cttee. on Family Law Bill, 1996; mem., Standing Cttee. on Agricultural Tenancies Bill, Crime Sentences Bill, 1996; mem., Gov. of Wales Bill Standing Cttee., 1996; mem., Standing Cttee. Countryside and Rights of Way Bill, 1999; mem., Standing Cttee. Adoption Bill, 1999; Parly. Standards and Privileges Cttee.; Chmn., Exec. Cttee. of the Royal National Eisteddfod of Wales 2009; Justice Cttee., 2010-; Joint Committee on Privacy and Injunctions, 2011-12; ***clubs:*** various fishing, football and rugby clubs; Club Rotari Bala/Rotary Club; ***recreations:*** choral singing, rugby, football, fishing, pigeon breeding; ***office address:*** Angorfa, Heol Meurig, Dolgellau, LL40 1LN, United Kingdom; ***phone:*** +44 (0)1341 422661; ***fax:*** +44 (0)1341 423990; ***e-mail:*** llwyde@parliament.uk.

LOBO SOSA , Porfirio; President, Government of Honduras; ***born:*** 1948, Trujillo, Honduras; ***education:*** San Francisco Institute of Tegucigalpa; BA, University of Miami, USA; Patrice Lumumba Univ., Moscow, Russia; ***party:*** National Party; ***political career:*** Elected to Congress, 1990-; President of Honduras, Jan. 2010-; ***professional career:*** Rancher; Teacher; Honduran Corporation for Forestry Development, 1990-94; ***office address:*** Casa Presidencial, Blvd. Juan Pablo II, Tegucigalpa, Honduras; ***phone:*** +504 232 1527; ***e-mail:*** ministerio@sdp.gob,hn; ***URL:*** http://www.sdp.gob.hn.

LOCHHEAD, Richard, MSP; Member of Scottish Parliament for North East Scotland; ***born:*** 24 May 1969, Paisley, Scotland; ***education:*** Univ. of Stirling; ***party:*** SNP, 1986-; ***political career:*** MSP, North East Scotland, 1999-; Cabinet Secretary, Rural Affairs and the Environment, 2007-11; ***clubs:*** Forthill Sports Club; ***office address:*** Thainstone Centre, Inverurie, AB51 5WU, United Kingdom; ***phone:*** +44 (0)1467 624795; ***fax:*** +44 (0)1467 625992.

LOCKE, Gary; American, Secretary of Commerce, US Government; ***born:*** 21 January 1950, Seattle, WA, USA; ***married:*** Mona Lee Locke; ***education:*** Yale Univ., undergrad. degree, political science, 1972; Boston Univ., law degree, 1975; ***political career:*** Washington House of Representatives, 1983-93; King County Exec., 1993-96; Governor, State of Washington, 1996-2004 (first Chinese American Governor in USA); Sec. of Commerce, US Govt., 2009-11; ***professional career:*** King County Dep. Prosecuting Attorney; Community Relations Mgr., US West Locke; Partner, law firm Davis Wright Tremaine, 2004-08; Amb., US Embassy, China, 2011-; ***committees:*** fmr. mem., House Judiciary and Appropriations Cttees.; ***office address:*** US Embassy, Xiu Shui Bei Jie 3, Chao Yang District, Beijing 100600, China; ***URL:*** http://beijing.usembassy.gov/.

LODGE, Matthew; Ambassador, British Embassy in Finland; ***professional career:*** Dep. Head of Mission, Baghdad, Iraq, 2007; Amb. to Finland, 2009-; ***office address:*** British Embassy, Itäinen Puistotie 17, 00140 Helsinki, Finland; ***phone:*** +358 (0)9 2286 5100; ***fax:*** +358 (0)9 2286 5262; ***e-mail:*** info@ukembassy.fi; ***URL:*** http://ukinfinland.fco.gov.uk/eni.

LOEAK, Christopher J.; President, Government of the Marshall Islands; ***born:*** November 1952; ***education:*** Hawaii Pacific College; Gonzaga Univ. Sch. of Law; ***political career:*** Politician, 1985-; Minister of Justice, 1988-92; Minister of Social Services, 1992-96; Minister of Education, 1996-89; Minister of Ralik, 1998-99; Minister in Assistance to the Admin. of President Litokwa Tomeing 2008; President, Jan. 2012-; ***office address:*** Office of the President, PO Box 2, MH 96960, Majuro, Marshall Islands; ***phone:*** +692 625 3213.

LOFGREN, Zoe; Congressman, California 16th District, US House of Representatives; ***born:*** 1947; ***education:*** Stanford Univ., 1970; graduated Law School, 1975; ***political career:*** entered Congress, 1995; mem., US House of Representatives; ***professional career:*** admitted to the Bar, 1975; Practised with Law Firm, Webber and Lofgren; Lectured in Law, Santa Clara Sch. of Law; ***committees:*** House: Administration; Judiciary Cttees.; ***office address:*** House of Representatives, 436 Cannon House Street, Washington, DC 20515-6501, USA; ***phone:*** +1 202 224 3121.

LOHMUS, Judge Uno; Estonian, Judge, Court of Justice of the European Union; ***born:*** 30 October 1952; ***languages:*** Estonian, English, Russian; ***education:*** Tartu University, Diploma in Law, 1976; Leningrad University, PhD (Law), 1986; Doctoral Thesis on Qualification of participation in crime; ***interests:*** Criminal Law; Human rights; State responsibility; ***memberships:*** Founding member, Estonian Academic Law Society, 1988-; ILA, Estonian branch, 1998-; Consultative Council of European Judges, 2000-04; Board of Editors, Juridica International; ***professional career:*** *academic career:* Tartu University Faculty of Law, Visiting Professor, 2000-, Human Rights Law, European Law; *judicial career:* Judge, ECHR, 1994-98; Chief Justice, Supreme Court of Estonia, 1998-2004; Judge, European Court of Justice, 2004-; Member, PCA, 2005-; ***publications:*** Books: Commentaries on the Constitution of the Republic of Estonia (in Estonian), co-author, 2002; Human Rights and the Protection thereof in Europe (in Estonian), editor and co-author, 2003Articles: Juridica (in Estonian); ***office address:*** Court of Justice of the European Union, L-2925, Luxembourg; ***phone:*** +352 4303 3880; ***fax:*** +352 4303 3889; ***e-mail:*** Uno.Lohmus@curia.europa.eu.

LONG, Naomi; MP for Belfast East, UK Government; ***party:*** Alliance Party; ***political career:*** Councillor, Belfast City Council, 2001-; Lord Mayor of Belfast 2009-10; MP for Belfast East, May 2010-; ***committees:*** Northern Ireland Affairs, 2010-; ***office address:*** House of Commons, London, SW1A 0AA, United Kingdom; ***phone:*** +44 (0)20 7219 3000; ***e-mail:*** naomi.long.mp@parliament.uk.

LOOMBA, Lord Raj, CBE; Member, House of Lords; ***education:*** D.A.V. Coll., Julllandhar, Inida, 1960; State Univ. of Iowa, U.S.A., 1962 ; ***party:*** Liberal Democrat Party; ***political career:*** Mem., House of Lords, 2010-; ***professional career:*** Exec. Chmn., Rinku Group; Founder, The Loomba Trust; ***office address:*** House of Lords, London, SW1A 0PW, United Kingdom; ***phone:*** +44 (0)20 7219 3000.

LOPES, Carlos Alberto; Minister of Finance, Government of Angola; ***political career:*** Dep. Planning Minister, 2003-10; Minister of Finance, 2010-; ***professional career:*** Accountant; ***office address:*** Ministry of Finance, Largo da Mutamba, Luanda, Angola; ***phone:*** +244 22 233 6095; ***fax:*** +244 22 233 3016; ***e-mail:*** geral@minfin.gov.ao; ***URL:*** http://www.minfin.gov.ao.

LOPRESTI, Jack; MP for Filton and Bradley Stoke, UK Government; ***party:*** Conservative; ***political career:*** Councillor, Bristol City Council, 1999-2007; MP for Filton and Bradley Stoke, May 2010-; ***committees:*** Northern Ireland Affairs, 2010-; Armed Forces, Bill 2011; ***office address:*** House of Commons, London, SW1A 0AA, United Kingdom; ***phone:*** +44 (0)20 7219 3000; ***e-mail:*** jack.lopresti.mp@parliament.uk.

LORD, Jonathan; MP for Woking, UK Government; ***party:*** Conservative; ***political career:*** Councillor, Westminster City Council, 1994-2002; Councillor, Surrey County Council, 2009-11; MP for Woking, May 2010-; ***office address:*** House of Commons, London, SW1A 0AA, United Kingdom; ***phone:*** +44 (0)20 7219 3000; ***e-mail:*** jonathan.lord.mp@parliament.uk.

LORENZETTI, Dr. Ricardo Luis; President, Supreme Court of Justice of Argentina; ***education:*** Univ. Nacional del Litoral de Santa Fe., grad. 1978, LL.D., 1983; ***professional career:*** Lecturer in a number of law faculties in Argentina; Lawyer for 26 years; Judge, Supreme Court of Justice of Argentina, 2004-, Pres., 2007-; ***office address:*** La Corte Suprema de Justicia, Talcahuano 550, Ciudad Autónoma de Buenos Aires, Argentina; ***URL:*** http://www.csjn.gov.ar.

LOTHIAN, Lord (Michael Andrew Foster Jude Kerr); Member, House of Lords; ***born:*** 1945; ***parents:*** The Marquis of Lothian and Antonella (née Newland); ***married:*** Lady Jane (née Fitzalan Howard), 1975; ***children:*** Clare (F), Mary (F); ***languages:*** French; ***education:*** Ampleforth; Oxford Univ., MA Hons.; Edinburgh Univ., LL.B; ***party:*** Conservative Party; ***political career:*** MP (Cons.) for Berwickshire and East Lothian, Feb.-Oct. 1974; Vice-Chmn., Cons. Party in Scotland, 1975-80; Chmn. Cons. Party , Scotland, 1980-83; MP (Cons.), Edinburgh South, May 1979-87; Parly. Under-Sec.of State, Scottish Office, 1983-87; MP (Cons.), Devizes, 1992-2010; Parly. Under-Sec. of State, Northern Ireland Office, 1993-94; Minister of State, Northern Ireland, 1994-97; Shadow Cabinet Front Bench Spokesman for Constitutional Affairs, with overall responsibility for Scottish & Welsh Affairs, 1997-; Party Chairman; Shadow Secretary of State for Foreign and Commonwealth Affairs and Deputy Leader of the Opposition, 2001-05; Shadow Sec. of State for Defence and Dep. Leader of the Opposition, 2005-06; ; ***interests:*** housing, foreign affairs, constitution; ***memberships:*** Faculty of Advocates; Nat. Farmer's Union of Scotland; ***professional career:*** Farmer, writer, businessman; ***committees:*** Select Cttee. on Energy, 1979-83; Commons Public Accounts, 1992-93; Intelligence & Security Cttee.; ***honours and awards:*** Privy Councillor; Created a life peer as Baron Kerr of Monteviot, of Monteviot in Roxburghshire, 2010; ***clubs:*** New (Edinburgh); Beefsteak; ***recreations:*** fishing, folk-singing; ***office address:*** House of Lords, London, SW1A 0AA, United Kingdom; ***phone:*** +44 (0)20 7219 3000.

LOUGHTON, Tim; British, Member of Parliament for East Worthing and Shoreham, House of Commons; ***born:*** 30 May 1962, Eastbourne, East Sussex, England; ***married:*** Elizabeth Loughton (née MacLauchlan), 1992; ***s:*** 1; ***d:*** 2; ***education:*** Univ. of Warwick 1980-83; Clare Coll., Cambridge; ***party:*** Conservative Party; ***political career:*** Chmn., Lewes Young Conservatives, 1978; Vice Chmn., Lewes Constituency Conservative Assoc., 1979; Sec., Warwick Univ. Conservative Assoc., 1981; Candidate, Latchmere Ward, Wandsworth Borough Cncl. Elections; Vice Chmn., Battersea Conservative Assoc., 1990; Candidate for Sheffield Brightside, 1992; London Area Conservative Exec. Cttee., 1993; Dep. Chmn., Battersea Conservative Assoc., 1994; MP, East Worthing & Shoreham, 1997-; Shadow Minister, Dept.of the Environment, Transport and the Regions, 2000-2001; Shadow Health Minister, 2001-07; Shadow Children's Minister, 2003-10; Parliamentary Under Secretary of State (Children and Families), 2010-12; ***memberships:*** Securities and Futures Assoc. Working Party on Training; Court of Sussex Univ.; IEA; Centre for Policy Studies; Treas. Parly. Maritime Grp.; Vice Chmn. Parly. Grp. for Autism; Capt., Lords & Commons Hockey Team; Chmn., All Party Wholesale Financial Services and Markets Grp., 2005-; Chmn., All Party Mental Health Grp., 2005-; Vice Chmn., All Party Cardiac Risk in the Young Grp., 2006-; ***professional career:*** Fund Mgr., Fleming Private Asset Management 1984-2000, Dir., 1992-2000; Gov., Battersea City Technical Coll., 1994-96; Local Authority Appointee to Wandsworth Community Health Cncl.; ***committees:*** Mem., Wandsworth Health Authority Substance Misuse Cttee., 1994-96; Finance Bill Standing Cttee (1997 and 98); Environmental Audit Select Cttee., 1997-2001; Chmn., All Party Parly. Wholesale Financial Services & Markets Grp; Chmn., Parly Mental Health Group; Treasurer, All Party Swiss Group; ***trusteeships:*** Patron St. Barnabas Hospice, Worthing; Patron, League of Friends of Worthing Hospital; Patron of the Worthing Hockey Club; ***office address:*** House of Commons, London, SW1A 0AA, United Kingdom; ***phone:*** +44 (0)20 7219 3000; ***e-mail:*** loughtont@parliament.uk.

LOUISY, H.E. Dame Calliopa Pearlette, GCMG, GCSL, D.St.J, Ph.D., LL.D; Governor General, St Lucia; ***born:*** 8 June 1946, Laborie, St Lucia; ***education:*** Univ., West Indies, Barbados, BA, English and French; Univ. of Laval, Quebec, MA, Linguistics, 1975; Univ. of Bristol, United Kingdom, Ph.D., Higher Educ., 1994; ***political career:*** Governor General, St Lucia, 1997-; ***professional career:*** Teacher, St. Joseph's Convent, 1969-72; Tutor then Principal, St. Lucia 'A' Level College, 1976-86; Dean then Vice Principal and Principal , Sir Arthur Lewis Community Coll., 1986-97; ***committees:*** Int. Cttee. on Creole Studies; Org. for Cooperation in Overseas Development; Indep. Cttee. for OECS Unity; ***honours and awards:*** Canadian Commonwealth Scholarship award, 1972; Grand Cross of the Order of St. Lucia, 1997; Int. Woman of the Year, 1998 and 2001; Fellow, RSA, 1999; GCMG, 1999; Hon. LLD., Univ. of Bristol, 1999; Paul Harris Fellow, 2001; D.St. J., 2001; Dame of the Equestrian Order of St. Gregory the Great, 2002; Doctorate in Arts and Culture, World Univ. Roundtable, 2002; Hon. LLD., Univ. of Sheffield, 2003; Hon. Distinguished Fellow, Univ.

of WI, 2003; Woman of Great Esteem, 2003; Hon. Distinguished Fellow of the Univ. of the West Indies, 2004; Caribbean Liminary Award, American Foundation of the Univ. of the West Indies, 2007; ***publications:*** Whose context for what quality?: Informing Education Strategies for the Caribbean, Compare, Vol 34, No. 3; Globalisation and Comparative Education: A Caribbean Perspective, Comparative Education, Vol 37, No. 4; Higher Education in the Caribbean: Issues and Strategies; Dilemnas of Inside Research in a small country setting: Tertiary Education in Saint Lucia, Qualitative Educational Research in the Developing Countries: Current Perspective, Crossley & Vulliamy, Eds.; The changing role of the small state in Higher Education: a comparison of national and regional initiatives in the Caribbean and the South Pacific; ***recreations:*** the performing arts, language and culture, gardening, small states issues; ***office address:*** Government House, Morne Fortune, Castries, St. Lucia; ***phone:*** +1 758 452 2481; ***fax:*** +1 758 453 2731; ***e-mail:*** govgenslu@candw.lc.

LOVE, Andrew; British, Member of Parliament for Edmonton, House of Commons; ***born:*** 21 March 1949, Greenock, Scotland; ***parents:*** James Love and Olive Love (née Mills); ***married:*** Ruth Rosenthal, 12 March 1983; ***public role of spouse:*** IT Director, Major Charity; ***education:*** BSc. (Hons); FCIS; ***party:*** Labour Party; Co-operative Party; ***political career:*** Parly. Officer, Co-operative Retail Soc.; MP, Edmonton, 1997-; ***interests:*** economy, regeneration; ***memberships:*** FCIS (Chartered Inst. of Co. Secretary's); ***professional career:*** Bd. of Dirs., Greater London Enterprise; ***committees:*** Treasury Select Cttee., 2005-; Parliamentary Commission on Banking Standards, 2012-; ***trusteeships:*** Industrial and Common Ownership Fund; ***clubs:*** Fellow of Royal Soc. of Arts; ***recreations:*** golf, opera, history; ***office address:*** House of Commons, London, SW1A 0AA, United Kingdom; ***phone:*** +44 (0)20 7219 6377; ***fax:*** +44 (0)20 7219 6623; ***e-mail:*** andy.love.mp@parliament.uk; ***URL:*** http://www.andylovemp.com.

LOVELL, Harold; Minister of Finance, the Economy and Public Administration, Government of Antigua and Barbuda; ***political career:*** Minister of Tourism and Civil Aviation, 2004; Minister of Environment and Culture, 2007-09; Minister of Finance, the Economy and Public Administration, 2009-; ***office address:*** Ministry of Foreign Affairs, Queen Elizabeth Highway, St John's, Antigua and Barbuda; ***phone:*** +1 268 462 1052; ***fax:*** +1 268 462 2482; ***e-mail:*** minforeign@candw.ag.

LUCAS, Dr Caroline; MP for Brighton Pavillion, UK Government; ***education:*** BA (1983), PhD (1989), Univ. of Exeter; Univ. of Kansas, 1984; Diploma of Journalism, 1987; ***party:*** Green Party (UK); ***political career:*** MEP for South East England, 1999-2010; MP for Brighton Pavillion, May 2010-; ***committees:*** Environmental Audit, 2010-; ***office address:*** House of Commons, London, SW1A 0AA, United Kingdom; ***phone:*** +44 (0)20 7219 3000; ***URL:*** http://www.carolinelucas.com.

LUCAS, Frank D.; American, Congressman, Oklahoma 3rd District, US House of Representatives; ***party:*** Republican; ***political career:*** Mem., US House of Representatives, 1994-; ***committees:*** House Agriculture (Chmn), Financial Services, and Science, Space and Technology Cttees.; ***office address:*** House of Representatives, 436 Cannon House Street, Washington, DC 20515-6501, USA; ***phone:*** +1 202 224 3121.

LUCAS, Ian; British, Member of Parliament for Wrexham, House of Commons; ***born:*** Gateshead, England; ***parents:*** Colin and Alice; ***married:*** Norah (née Sudd), July 1986; ***children:*** Patrick (M), Ellen (F); ***languages:*** German; ***education:*** New Coll., Oxford Univ.; ***party:*** Labour Party; ***political career:*** Candidate, North Shropshire, 1997; MP for Wrexham, 2001-; Parly. under Sec., Dept. for Business, Enterprise and Regulatory Reform, 2009-10; Shadow Minister for Business, Innovation and Skills, 2010-11; Shadow Minister, Foreign and Commonwealth Affairs, 2011-; ***interests:*** German affairs, manufacturing, industry, criminal justice, digital economy; ***memberships:*** Law Soc.; ***recreations:*** history, art, cinema; ***office address:*** House of Commons, London, SW1A 0AA, United Kingdom; ***phone:*** +44 (0)20 7219 3000; ***e-mail:*** ian.lucas.mp@parliament.uk; ***URL:*** http://www.ianlucas.co.uk.

LUCAS, Dr Jonathan; Director, United Nations Interregional Crime and Justice Research Institute; ***education:*** Univ. of Lyon, France, diploma; Univ. of Newcastle-upon-Tyne, BA; Acadia Univ., Canada, MA; Graduate Institute for International Studies, Geneva Ph.D, International Law/Economics; ***professional career:*** International Labor Org., 1982-84; UN Division of Narcotic Drugs, 1983, various posits.; Chief of the Cmmissions, Secretariat Section (Sec., Commission on Narcotic Drugs, Sec. Commission on Crime Prevention and Criminal Justice), 1998-2004; Rep. of the UNODC Regional Office for Southern Africa, 2004-10; Sec., International Narcotics Control Board, Chief of the INCB Secretariat, 2010-11; Director, UNICRI, 2011-; ***office address:*** UNICRI, Viale Maestri del Lavoro, 10, 10127 Turin, Italy; ***phone:*** +39 (0)11 653 7111; ***fax:*** +39 (0)11 631 3368; ***URL:*** http://www.unicri.it.

LUCAS, Sylvia; Premier, Northern Cape; ***political career:*** Environmental MEC; Acting Premier, Northern Cape, 2013-, Premier, 30 May 2013-; ***office address:*** Office of the Premier, Kimberley, Northern Cape, South Africa; ***phone:*** +27 531 830 9555; ***URL:*** http://www.northern-cape.gov.za.

LUFF, Peter James; British, Member of Parliament for Mid Worcestershire, House of Commons; ***born:*** 18 February 1955, Windsor; ***parents:*** Thomas Luff and Joyce Luff (née Mills); ***married:*** Julia Luff (née Jenks); ***children:*** Oliver (M), Rosanna (F); ***education:*** Corpus Christi Coll., Cambridge, MA, Econs.; ***party:*** Conservative Party, 1970-; ***political career:*** Research Asst. to Rt. Hon. Peter Walker, 1977-80; Head of Private Office to Rt. Hon. Edward Heath, 1980-82; Special Advisor to Lord Young, DTI, 1987-89; MP, Worcester, 1992-97; Mem., Welsh Affairs Select Cttee., 1992-97; PPS to Rt. Hon. Tim Eggar, Minister of Industry and Energy, 1993-96, to Ann Widdecombe, Prisons Minister, 1996-97, to Rt. Hon. Lord MacKay of Clashfern, 1996-97; MP, Worcester, 1992-97; MP, Mid Worcestershire, 1997-; Opposition Whip, 2000-10, Assist. Chief Whip, 2002-05; Parly. Under-Sec. of State for Defence Equipment, Support and Technology, Ministry of Defence, 2010-; ***interests:*** Europe, performing arts, rural issues; ***professional career:*** Dir. and then Man. Dir., Good Relations Ltd., 1982-92; ***committees:*** Chmn., Common Agriculture Cttee., 1997-2000; Chmn., Common Trade and Industry Cttee.; Chmn., Business & Enterprise Cttee., 2005-; Chmn., Business, Innovation & Skills Select Cttee., 2005-10; ***honours and awards:*** Fellow, Inst. Public Relations; ***recreations:*** photography; ***office address:*** House of Commons, London, SW1A 0AA, United Kingdom; ***phone:*** +44 (0)1905 763952; ***e-mail:*** luffpj@parliament.uk.

LUKASHENKO, Alexander Grigoryevich; Belorussian, President, Republic of Belarus; ***born:*** 30 August 1954, Kopys, Orsha District, Vitebsk Province, Belarus; ***married:*** Galina Rodionovna Lukashenko; ***s:*** 2; ***public role of spouse:*** Civil Servant, Shklov District Executive Committee; ***education:*** Mogilev Teacher Training Inst., Historical Faculty, 1975; Belarussian Agricultural Academy, 1985; ***political career:*** People's Dep., Supreme Cncl., 1990-94; C-in-C, Armed Forces; Head, Security Cncl.; Chmn., Supreme Cncl. of the Community of Russia and Belarus, 1996; President, 1994-; ***professional career:*** Army, 1975-77; Admin. Bodies, City of Mogilev, 1977-78; Exec. Sec., Shklov District Branch, All-Union Soc. Knowledge, 1978-80; Army, 1980-82; Dep. Chmn., Collective Farm, Dep. Manager, Building Materials Factory, Dir., Gorodets State Farm, 1982-90; ***committees:*** Pres., Nat. Olympic Cttee., 1997; ***honours and awards:*** Hon. Academician of the Russian Academy of Social Sciences, 1995; M.A. Sholokhov Int. Award, 1997; ***recreations:*** sport, reading; ***office address:*** Office of the President, Karl Marx Street 38, Minsk 220016, Belarus; ***phone:*** +375 (8)172 223217; ***fax:*** +375 (8)172 260610; ***URL:*** http://www.president.gov.by.

LUKIWSKI, Tom; Parliamentary Secretary, Government of Canada; ***born:*** 1951; ***political career:*** MP for Regina, Lumsden, Lake Centre in Saskatchewan, 2004-; Parly. Sec. to the Leader of the Government in the House of Commons and Minister for Democratic Reform, 2006-08; Parly. Sec. to the Leader of the Government in the House of Commons, 2008-; ***office address:*** House of Commons, Parliament Buildings, Wellington Street, Ottawa K1A 0A6, Ontario, Canada; ***phone:*** +1 613 943 5959; ***fax:*** +1 613 992 3674; ***URL:*** http://www.parl.gc.ca.

LUKSIC, Dr. Igor; Deputy Prime Minister, Government of Montenegro; ***born:*** June 1976; ***education:*** Faculty of Economics, Univ. of Montenegro, 1998; Diplomatic Academy of Vienna, Austria, 1999; Ph.D. in economics, Univ. of Montenegro, 2005; ***party:*** Democratic Party of Socialists; ***political career:*** Minister of Finance, 2004-10; Prime Minister, 2010-12; Deputy Prime Minister, 2012-; ***office address:*** Office of the Deputy Prime Minister, Jovana Tomasevica bb, 81000 Podgorica, Montenegro; ***phone:*** +381 81 24 530; ***fax:*** +381 81 242329.

LUMLEY, Karen; MP for Redditch, UK Government; ***born:*** 28 March 1964; ***married:*** Richard Lumley, 1984; ***children:*** Elizabeth (F), Christopher (M); ***party:*** Conservative; ***political career:*** Councillor, Clwyd County Council, 1993-96; Redditch Borough Council, 2001-03; MP for Redditch, May 2010-; ***committees:*** Welsh Affairs Select Cttee., 2010-; ***office address:*** House of Commons, London, SW1A 0AA, United Kingdom; ***phone:*** +44 (0)20 7219 3000; ***e-mail:*** karen.lumley.mp@parliament.uk.

LUMMIS, Cynthia; Congresswoman-at-Large, Wyoming, US House of Representatives; ***party:*** Republican; ***political career:*** Mem., US HOR, Wyoming, 2009-; ***office address:*** House of Representatives, Washington, DC, USA.

LUNDY, Kate; Senator for Australian Capital Territory, Australian Government; ***party:*** Australian Labor Party; ***political career:*** Senator for Australian Capital Territory, 1996-; Shadow Minister for Sport and Recreation, 2006-; Shadow Minister for Local Government, 2006-11; Minister of Sport, 2011-13; Minister of Multicultural Affairs, Assisting for Industry and Innovation, 2011-; ***office address:*** Parliament House, Canberra, ACT 2600, Australia.

LUNGU, Effron; Minister of Foreign Affairs, Government of Zambia; ***party:*** Chama South Patriotic Front (PF); ***political career:*** MP; Deputy Foreign Minister, -2013; Minister of Foreign Affairs, Feb. 2013-; ***office address:*** Ministry of Foreign Affairs, PO Box RW50069, Lusaka, Zambia.

LUO YING-SHAY ; Minister without Portfolio, Minister, Mongolian & Tibetan Affairs Commission, Government of Taiwan; ***born:*** 1951; ***education:*** National Taiwan Univ., LLB; SUNY, MA, Criminal Justice; ***political career:*** Advisor, Taipei City Gov., 2007-10; National Policy Advisor to the President, 2009-11; Minister without Portfolio, 2011-; Minister, Monglian & Tibetan Affairs Commission, 2011-; ***professional career:*** lecturer; attorney-at-law; ***office address:*** Executive Yuan, 1 Chuanghsiao E. Road, Section 1, Taipei, Taiwan; ***phone:*** +886 2356 1500; ***fax:*** +886 2 394 8727; ***URL:*** http://www.ey.gov.tw.

LWAKABAMBA, Prof. Silas; Minister of Infrastructure, Government of Rwanda; ***born:*** Tanzania; ***education:*** Univ. of Leeds, UK, engineering, BSc., Ph.D; ***political career:*** Minister of Infrastructure, 2013-; ***professional career:*** various posits., Fac. of Engineering, Univ. of Dar es Salaam, Professorship, 1981, Head of Dep., Dean; African Regional Centre for Engineering Design & Manufacturing, Nigeria; founding Rector, Kigali Inst. of Science & Technology, 1997; Rector, National Univ. of Rwanda, 2006; Co-chair, Advisory Board, US Africa Higher Education Initiative; Chmn., Gov. Board, Inter-University Council of East Africa; ***office address:*** Ministry of Infrastructure, BP 24, Kigali, Rwanda; ***URL:*** http://www.mininfra.gov.rw.

LYSBAKKEN, Audun; Minister of Children, Equality and Social Inclusion, Government of Norway; ***education:*** Univ. of Bergen; ***political career:*** Mem., Norwegian Parliament, 2001-05; Dep. Chair, Socialist Left Party, 2005; Minister of Children, Equality and Social Inclusion, 2009-; ***professional career:*** Journalist; ***office address:*** Ministry of Children, Equality and Social Inclusion, Akersgata 59 Postboks 8036 Dep, 0030 Oslo, Norway; ***phone:*** +47 9777 3634; ***e-mail:*** postmottak@bld.dep.no.

M

MACDONALD, Lord Kenneth, QC; Member, House of Lords; ***education:*** St Edmund Hall, Oxford Univ., 1974; ***party:*** Liberal Democrat; ***political career:*** Mem., House of Lords, 2010-; ***professional career:*** Barrister; Queen's Counsel, 1997; Dir. of Public Prosecutions, 2003-08; ***honours and awards:*** Knighthood, 2007; Elevated to the peerage, 2010; ***office address:*** House of Lords, London, SW1A 0PW, United Kingdom; ***phone:*** +44 (0)20 7219 3000; ***fax:*** +44 (0)20 7219 5979; ***URL:*** http://www.parliament.uk.

MACEDO, Miguel; Minister of Internal Administration, Government of Portugal; ***born:*** 1959; ***education:*** Univ. of Coimbra, Law; ***political career:*** MP, 5th, 6th, 7th, 8th, 10th and 11th parly. terms; Mem., Braga City Council, 1993-97; Sec. of State for Youth, 11th const. gov.; Sec. of State for Justice, 15th-16th const. gov.; Mem., Braga Municipal Assembly, to date; Minister of Internal Administration, 2011-; ***professional career:*** lawyer; ***office address:*** National Assembly, Palácio de S. Bento, 1249-068 Lisbon, Portugal.

MACEDO, Paulo; Minister of Health, Government of Portugal; ***born:*** 1963; ***education:*** Inst. of Economics & Management, Technical Univ. of Lisbon; AESE Business School, Lisbon; ***political career:*** Minister of Health, 2011-; ***professional career:*** Arthur Andersen; various management positions, Banco Comercial Portugues, 1993-98; Bd. of Dir., Comercila Leasing, 1998-2000; Bd. of Dir., Interbanco, 2000-01; Bd. of Dir., Seguros e Pensoes, 2003-04; Dir.-Gen. of Taxation & Chmn., Tax Admin. Board, 2004-07; Vice-Chmn., Banco Comercial Portugues (BC), Exec. Bd. of Dir., 2008-11; non-exec. vice-chmn of several companies in the BCP Group, 2011; mem., supervisory bd., Bank Millennium, Poland, 2008-11; mem., supervisory bd., Euronext, 2010-11; ***office address:*** Ministry of Health, A. Joao Crisóstomo 9, 1069-062 Lisbon, Portugal; ***URL:*** http://www.min-saude.pt.

MACFARLANE, Allison; Chairman, US Nuclear Regulatory Commission; ***education:*** Univ. of Rochester, BSc., geology; MIT, Ph.D, geology; ***professional career:*** Fellowships, Radcliffe College, MIT, Stanford & Harvard Univs.; Assoc. Prof., environmental science & policy, George Mason Univ.; Blue Ribbon Commission on America's Nuclear Future, 2010-12; Chmn., US Nuclear Regulatory Commission, 2012-; ***office address:*** Nuclear Regulatory Commission (NRC), Office of Public Affairs, Washington DC 20555, USA; ***phone:*** +1 301 415 8200; ***URL:*** http://www.nrc.gov/.

MACFARLANE OF BEARSDEN IN THE DISTRICT OF BEARSDEN AND MILNGAVIE, Lord, Baron Norman Somerville, Life Peer, KT, DL, FRSE; British, Member of the House of Lords; ***born:*** 5 March 1926; ***parents:*** Daniel Robertson Macfarlane and Jessie Lindsay Macfarlane (née Somerville); ***married:*** Margarite Mary Somerville (née Campbell), 1953; ***s:*** 1; ***d:*** 4; ***education:*** High Sch. of Glasgow ; ***party:*** Conservative Party; ***political career:*** Mem., House of Lords, 1991-; ***memberships:*** Pres., Stationers Assoc. of GB and Ireland, 1965; Co. of Stationers of Glasgow, 1968-70; Cncl. mem., CBI Scotland, 1975-81; Chmn., The Fine Art Society PLC, 1976-98 (Hon. Pres. 1998); Court mem., Univ. of Glasgow, 1979-87; Hon. Pres., Charles Rennie Mackintosh Soc., 1988-; Hon. Pres., High Sch. of Glasgow, 1992- (Chmn. Govs., 1979-92); Hon. Patron, Queen's Park F.C.; Vice Pres., Professional Golfers Assoc.; ***professional career:*** Commissioned RA, 1945; served Palestine, 1945-47; founder, N.S. Macfarlane & Co. Ltd., 1949, became Macfarlane Gp. (Clansman) PLC, 1973; Dir.Chmn., 1973-98, Managing Dir., 1973-90, Macfarlane Gp. PLC, Hon Life Pres., 1999; Dir., Glasgow Chamber of Commerce, 1976-79; American Trust PLC, 1984-97; Guinness PLC, 1987-89, JT. Dep. Chmn.,1989-92; Governor, Glasgow Sch. of Art, 1976-87, Hon. Fellow, 1993, Hon. Pres., 2001; Pres., Royal Glasgow Inst. of Fine Arts, 1976-87; Dir., Scottish National Orch., 1977-82; Underwriting Mem., Lloyd's, 1978-97; Bd., Scottish Development Agency, 1979-87; Dir., Clydesdale Bank PLC, 1980-96 (Dep. Chmn., 1993-96); Edinburgh Fund Managers PLC, 1980-98; Dir., Scottish Ballet, 1975-87, Vice Chmn., 1983-87, Pres., 2001-; General Accident Fire & Life Assoc. Corp. PLC, 1984-96; Chmn., Glasgow Development Agency (formerly Glasgow Action), 1985-92; Dir., Third Eye Centre, 1987-91; Chmn. and Hon. Life Pres., United Distillers PLC, 1987-96; Regent RCSE, 1997- ; ***trusteeships:*** Scottish Patron, National Art Collection Fund, 1978-; Trustee, Nat. Heritage Memorial fund, 1978-, Nat. Galls of Scotland, 1986-97; Patron, Scottish Licenced Trade Assoc., 1992-; ***honours and awards:*** KT, 1996; Kt, 1983; Hon. FRIAS, 1984; Hon. LLD, Strathclyde, 1986, Glasgow, 1988, Glasgow Caledonian, 1993, Aberdeen, 1995; HRSA, 1987; HRGI, 1987; Hon. FScotvc, 1991; Hon. FRCPSGlas, 1992; DUniv. Stirling, 1992; Dr (HE) Edinburgh, 1992; Hon. Fellow, Glasgow Sch. of Art, 1993; KT, 1996; DL, Dunbartonshire, 1993; CIMgt, 1996; FRSE; Hon. Life Pres., Macfarlane Gp. PLC, 1999, and United Distillers PLC, 1996; Lord High Commissioner, General Assembly, Church of Scotland, 1992, 1993 and 1997; Winner of Glasgow St. Mungo medal, 2005; Freeman of Dumfries & Galloway, 2006; Goodman Award for Art & Business, 2007; ***clubs:*** Glasgow Art; Royal Scottish Automobile, Glasgow; New (Edinburgh) the Honourable company of Edinburgh Golfers Glasgow Golf; ***recreations:*** golf, cricket, theatre, art; ***office address:*** House of Lords, London, SW1A 0PW, United Kingdom; ***phone:*** +44 (0)20 7219 3000; ***fax:*** +44 (0)20 7219 5979.

MACGREGOR, H.E. Judith; Ambassador, British Embassy in Mexico; ***born:*** 17 June 1952; ***parents:*** John Richard Brown and Beatrice Brown; ***married:*** John Malcolm Macgregor; ***education:*** St Saviour's and St Olave's Grammar School; Lady Margaret Hall, Oxford, BA 1st class Hons, Modern History, 1974; ***professional career:*** entered FCO, 1976; First Sec. Belgrade, 1978-81; FCO, 1981-86; Prague, 1989; Paris, 1992-93; Dep. Hd., Western European Dept., FCO, 1993-95; Counsellor and Head of Security, FCO, 2001-03; FCO Chair, CSSB, 2003-04; British Amb. to the Slovak Republic, 2004-07; Dir., Migration, FCO, 2007-09; Amb to Mexico, 2009-; ***recreations:*** walking, gardening, reading about Central Europe; ***office address:*** British Embassy, Rio Lerma 71, Col Cuauhètmoc, 06500 Mexico City, Mexico; ***phone:*** +52 55 5242 8500; ***fax:*** +52 55 5242 8517; ***e-mail:*** commsec@embajadabritanica.com.mx; ***URL:*** http://ukinmexico.fco.gov.uk/en.

MACK, Connie; Congressman, 14th District, Florida, US House of Representatives; ***education:*** Univ. of Florida, Coll. of Communication, B.Sc.; ***political career:*** Florida House of Representatives, 2000-03, Dep. Majority Leader in 2nd Term; US House of Representatives, 2005-; ***professional career:*** Exec., LTP Management; independent business and marketing consultant; ***committees:*** Foreign Affairs; Oversight and Government Reform; ***office address:*** US House of Representatives, 317 Cannon House Office Building, Washington, DC 20515, USA; ***phone:*** +1 202 225 2536; ***fax:*** +1 202 226 0439.

MACKAY, Peter; Minister of National Defence, Canadian Government; ***born:*** New Glasgow, Nova Scotia, Canada; ***education:*** Acadia Univ., BA, 1987; Dalhousie Law Sch., LL.B, 1990; ***political career:*** MP, 1997- (Central Nova, 2004-); House Leader for the Progressive Conservative Party and critic for the Dept. of Justice, 2002; critic for: Solicitor General, 2002-03, Public Security, 2002-03, Prime Minister, 2003-04; Public Safety & Emergencies, 2004, of the Deputy Prime Minister, 2004-06, Public Safety and Emergency Planning, 2004-06; Minister of Foreign Affairs and Minister of the Atlantic Canada Opportunities Forum, 2006-07; Minister of National Defence and Minister of the Atlantic Canada Opportunities Agency, 2007-09; Minister of National Defence, 2009-; Minister for the Atlantic Gateway, 2009-10; ***memberships:*** Big Brothers- Big Sisters, the Pictou County Senior Rugby Club and The YMCA; Mem., Commonwealth Parly. Assn, Canada-Europe Parly. Assn and Canada-Germany Friendship Gp.; ***professional career:*** Called to the Bar, 1991; Started general law practice, New Glasgow; Thyssen Henschel Co., Kassell, Germany, 1992-93; Crown Attorney, Nova Scotia Govt.; Bd. of Dirs., New Leaf and Tearmann House (home for abused women and children); ***committees:*** Mem. of the Bd. of Internal Economy and The Standing Cttee. on Justice and Human Rights; Asst. Mem. of the Standing Cttees. on Canadian Heritage and Finance; ***office address:*** House of Commons, Room 6485 Centre Block, Ottawa, ON K1A 0A6, Canada.

MACKAY OF DRUMADOON, Lord, Baron Donald Sage, QC, Life Peer, Privy Cllr.; British, Member of the House of Lords; ***born:*** 30 January 1946; ***parents:*** Rev. Donald George Mackintosh Mackay and Jean Margaret Mackay; ***married:*** Lesley Ann Waugh, 1979; ***children:*** Simon (M), Caroline (F), Diana (F); ***education:*** George Watson's Boy's Coll., Edinburgh; Univ. of Edinburgh, LL.B., 1966, LL.M., 1968; Univ. of Virginia, USA, LL.M., 1969; ***party:*** sits as a Cross-Bencher; ***political career:*** Solicitor Gen. for Scot., 1995; Mem., House of Lords, 1995-; Lord Advocate, 1995-97; Govt. Spokesman on Legal Affairs and for the Home, Scottish and Welsh Offices, 1995-97; Official Opposition Spokesman on Constitutional Affairs, Legal Affairs and Scotland, 1997-2000; ***professional career:*** Law Apprentice, 1969-71; Solicitor, Allan McDougall & Co., Edinburgh, 1971-76; Called to the Scots Bar 1976, Q C (Scotland), 1987, Advocate Depute, 1982-85; Mem., Criminal Injuries Compensation Board, 1989-95; Senator of the Coll. of Justice in Scotland, 2000-; ***honours and awards:*** Privy Cllr., 1997; ***clubs:*** Western Club, Glasgow; ***recreations:*** golf, gardening; ***office address:*** Parliament House, Edinburgh, EH1 1RF, United Kingdom; ***phone:*** +44 (0)131 447 1412; ***fax:*** +44 (0)131 447 9863; ***e-mail:*** lord.mackay@scotcourts.gov.uk.

MACKENZIE OF CULKEIN, Lord; British, Member of the House of Lords; ***born:*** 25 February 1940, Stranraer, Scotland; ***parents:*** George MacKenzie and Williamina Budge MacKenzie (née Sutherland); ***married:*** Anna Robertson MacKenzie (née Morrison), 1961 (Dis.); ***children:*** David (M), Catriona (F), Ishbel (F), Morag (F); ***education:*** Leverndale Sch. of Nursing, Glasgow; West Cumberland Sch. of Nursing, Whitehaven; ***party:*** Labour; ***political career:*** Mem. Labour Party Policy Forum; Mem. Labour Party Policy Cmn. on Health; Mem., House of Lords 1999-; ***interests:*** health (particularly nursing), defence, aviation and marine matters, land reform; ***memberships:*** Gov. Mem., RNLI; Gov. Mem., Marine Soc.; National Trust for Scotland; RSPB; ***professional career:*** Student, Leverndale Hosp., 1958-61; Asst. Lighthouse Keeper, Clyde Lighthouses Trust, 1961-64; Post-registration Student Nurse, 1964-66, Staff Nurse, 1966-69, West Cumberland Hosp.; COHSE, Asst. Regional Sec., Yorkshire and East Midlands Region, 1969-70: Regional Sec., 1970-74: National Officer, 1974-83: Asst. Gen. Sec., 1983-87: Gen Sec., 1987-93; Assoc. Gen. Sec., UNISON (following merger of COHSE, NALGO and NUPE), 1993-2000; ***trusteeships:*** Confederation of Health Service Employees (1974) Pension and Assurance Scheme, 1987-; Unison Pension Scheme, 1993-2001; ***honours and awards:*** Lindsay Robertson Gold Medal, Nurse of the Year, 1966; ***publications:*** various articles in nursing and specialist health service press; ***clubs:*** St. Elpheges, Wallington; ***recreations:*** reading, Celtic music, shinty, aviation; ***office address:*** House of Lords, London, SW1A 0PW, United Kingdom; ***phone:*** +44 (0)20 7219 8515; ***fax:*** +44 (0)20 7219 8712; ***e-mail:*** mackenzieh@parliament.uk.

MACKINTOSH, Hon. Gord; Minister of Conservation and Water Stewardship, Government of Manitoba; ***political career:*** Minister of Justice and Attorney General, also Keeper of the Great Seal, Minister responsible for Constitutional Affairs, and Government House Leader 1999-2007; Minister charged with administration of Manitoba Public Insurance Corporation Act, 2001; Minister of Family Services and Housing, 2007-10; Minister of Family Services and Consumer Affairs, 2010-11; Minister of Conservation and Water Stewardship, 2012-; ***office address:*** Ministry of Conservation, Legislative Building, Winnipeg, Manitoba, R3C 0V8, Canada; ***URL:*** http://www.gov.mb.ca/.

MACKLIN, Jenny; Minister of Family, Housing, Community Services and Indigenous Affairs, Australian Government; ***political career:*** Member for Jagajaga; Minister of Family, Housing, Community Services and Indigenous Affairs, 2007-; Minister of Disability Reform, 2013-; ***office address:*** Department of Families, Housing, Community Services and Indigenous Affairs, Box 7788, Canberra, ACT 2610, Australia; ***URL:*** http://www.facsia.gov.au/.

MACLEOD, Mary; MP for Brentford and Isleworth, UK Government; ***party:*** Conservative; ***political career:*** MP for Brentford and Isleworth, May 2010-; PPS to the Rt. Hon. Nick Herbert MP, Minister for Policing and Criminal Justice, Sept. 2010-; ***committees:*** Home Affairs Select Cttee., 2010; ***office address:*** House of Commons, London, SW1A 0AA, United Kingdom; ***phone:*** +44 (0)20 7219 3000; ***e-mail:*** mary.macleod.mp@parliament.uk.

MACLEOD, Sian; Ambassador, British Embassy in the Czech Republic; ***languages:*** Russian; ***professional career:*** Dep. Head of Mission, Moscow, Russian Federation, 2005-07; Amb. to the Czech Republic, 2009-; ***office address:*** British Embassy, Thunovska 14, 118 00 Prague 1, Czech Republic; ***phone:*** +420 2 5740 2111; ***fax:*** +420 2 5740 2296; ***e-mail:*** info@britain.cz; ***URL:*** http://ukinczechrepublic.fco.gov.uk/en.

MACNEIL, Angus; MP for Na h-Eileanan an Iar, House of Commons; ***party:*** Scottish National Party; ***political career:*** MP for Na h-Eileanan an Iar, 2005-; SNP spokesperson, 2005-; ***committees:*** Scottish Affairs, 2005-09; ***office address:*** House of Commons, London, SW1P 0AA, United Kingdom; ***phone:*** +44 (0)20 7219 3000; ***e-mail:*** macneila@parliament.uk.

MACTAGGART, Fiona; British, Member of Parliament for Slough, House of Commons; ***born:*** 12 September 1953; ***party:*** Labour Party; ***political career:*** MP, Slough, 1997-; Shadow Minister, Government Equalities Office, Oct. 2010-11; ***professional career:*** Lecturer; ***committees:*** Public Administration, 1997-98; Education and Skills/Children, Schools and Families, 2006-10; Joint Committee on Human Rights, 2009-10; Health, 2010; Public Accounts, 2011-; ***office address:*** House of Commons, London, SW1A 0AA, United Kingdom; ***phone:*** +44 (0)20 7219 3000; ***e-mail:*** hcinfo@parliament.uk.

MADDEN, Paul; High Commissioner, British High Commission, Australia; ***born:*** 25 April 1959; ***professional career:*** Dept. for Trade and Industry, 1980-84; Private Sec. to Rt. Hon. David Trippier, 1984-85; Private Sec. to Rt. Hon. Michael Howard, 1985-86; Head of Japan desk, DTI, 1986-87; First. Sec., Tokyo, 1988-92; Environment, Science & Energy Dept., FCO, 1992-94; EU Dept., FCO, 1994-96; First Sec., Washington, 1995-2000; Singapore, Dept. High Cmnr., 2000-03; Hd. of Public Diplomacy Policy Dept., FCO., 2003-04; MD, UK Trade and Investment, 2004-06; High Cmnr., Singapore, 2007-10; High Commissioner, Australia, 2011-; ***office address:*** British High Commission Canberra, Commonwealth Avenue, Yarralumla, ACT 2600, Australia; ***phone:*** +61 (0)2 6270 6666; ***fax:*** +61 (0)2 6273 3236; ***e-mail:*** ppa.canberra@fco.gov.uk; ***URL:*** http://ukinaustralia.fco.gov.uk.

MADURO MOROS, Nicolas; President, Government of Venezuela; ***born:*** Caracas, Venezuela; ***political career:*** Founder, Metro Union of Caracas; Founder and Coordinator, Bolivarian National Force of Workers; Deputy to Congress, 1999; Deputy for the Federal District to the National Assembly, 2000-05; Founder Mem., Movimiento V Republica; Coodinator of the Parly. team of the Movimiento V Republica, 2000-01; Pres., National Assembly, 2005-06; Minister of Foreign Affairs, 2006-13; President, April 2013-; ***memberships:*** Parly. Gps. for Friendship with Argentina, Syria and Western Saharan Republic, 2001; Parly. Gp. promoting friendship with China, 2005 ; ***committees:*** Pres., Permanent Cttee. on Integral Social Development, 2000-05; Pres., Mixed Cmn. on Legislative Initiatives to develop Employment, 2002; Mem., Finance Cttee., 2004-05; Mem., Sub-Cttee. on Financial policy, Banking, Insurance and Financial Coordination, 2005; ***office address:*** Office of the President, Palacio de Miraflores, Avenida Urdaneta,, Caracas 1010, Venezuela; ***phone:*** +58 212 862 810811; ***fax:*** +58 212 571 0563; ***e-mail:*** presidencia@venezuela.gov.ve; ***URL:*** http://www.venezuela.gov.ve.

MAELANGA, Manasseh; Minister of Home Affairs, Government of Solomon Islands; ***born:*** 1970; ***political career:*** elected mem., National Parliament of Solomon Islands, 2008-; Minister of Home Affairs and Dep. PM, 2010-; ***professional career:*** Senior police officer; ***office address:*** National Parliament, PO Box G19, Honiara, Solomon Islands.

MAGAN OF CASTLETOWN, Lord George; Member, House of Lords; ***party:*** Conservative Party; ***political career:*** Mem., House of Lords, 2011-; ***professional career:*** Dir., Morgan Grenfell & Co.; Chmn., Carlton Capital Partners; Dep. Chmn., Carlton Corporate Finance; Dep. Treasurer, Conservative Party, 2002-; Conservatiave Party Treasurer; ***office address:*** House of Lords, London, SW1A 0PW, United Kingdom; ***phone:*** +44 (0)20 7219 3000.

MAGNETTE, Paul; Minister of Public Enterprises, Science Policy and Development Co-operation, Government of Belgium; ***born:*** 28 June 1971; ***education:*** ULB, Politics; Cambridge, European Politics; ***political career:*** Walloon Minister of Social Action, Health and Equal Opportunity, 2007-08; Minister of Climate and Energy, 2008-11; Minister of Public Enterprises, Science Policy and Development Co-operation, Minister for Urban Affairs, Dec. 2011-; ***professional career:*** Lecturer, Politics, ULB; Dir., Instit. of European Studies, ULB; ***office address:*** Ministry of Civil Service and Public Enterprises, rue Royale 180, 1000 Brussels, Belgium; ***phone:*** +32 (0)2 210 19 11; ***e-mail:*** info@ingevervotte.be; ***URL:*** http://www.magnette.fgov.be / http://www.meta.fgov.be.

MAHAMA, John; President, Ghanaian Government; ***education:*** BA, in history, 1981, Postgraduate Dip. in Communication Studies, 1986, Univ. of Ghana; ***party:*** National Democratic Congress; ***political career:*** MP, 1997-2009; Minister of Transport and Communications, 1999-2000; Vice President, 2009-12; President, 2012-; ***office address:*** Office of the President, The Castle, PO Box 1627, Osu, Ghana; ***phone:*** +233 21 665 415; ***URL:*** http://www.ghana.gov.gh.

MAHMOOD, Khalid; Member of Parliament for Birmingham Perry Barr, House of Commons; ***party:*** Labour Party; ***political career:*** MP, Birmingham Perry Barr, 2001-; ***office address:*** House of Commons, London, SW1A 0AA, United Kingdom; ***phone:*** +44 (0)20 7219 3000; ***e-mail:*** hcinfo@parliament.uk; ***URL:*** http://www.parliament.uk.

MAHMOOD, Shabana; MP for Birmingham, Ladywood, House of Commons; ***party:*** Labour; ***political career:*** MP for Birmingham, Ladywood, May 2010-; Shadow Minister, Home Affairs, Oct. 2010-11; Shadow Minister, Business, Innovation and Skills, 2011-; ***committees:*** Work and Pensions Select Cttee., 2010; ***office address:*** House of Commons, London, SW1A 0AA, United Kingdom; ***phone:*** +44 (0)20 7219 3000; ***e-mail:*** shabana.mahmood.mp@parliament.uk.

MAIN, Anne; MP for St Albans, House of Commons; ***party:*** Conservative; ***political career:*** Local Councillor; MP for St Albans, 2005-; ***professional career:*** Teacher; ***committees:*** Energy and Climate Change, 2009-10; Chairmen's Panel/Panel of Chairs, 2010-; ***office address:*** House of Commons, London, SW1P 0AA, United Kingdom; ***phone:*** +44 (0)20 7219 3000; ***e-mail:*** maina@parliament.uk.

MAJOR, Rt. Hon. Sir John, KG, CH, PC; British, Former Prime Minister; ***born:*** 29 March 1943; ***parents:*** Late Thomas Major and Gwendolyn Minnie Coates; ***married:*** Dame Norma Christina E. Major (née Johnson), 1970; ***children:*** Elizabeth (F), James (M); ***education:*** Rutlish School; ***party:*** Conservative Party; ***political career:*** Contested St Pancras North, Camden, 1974; MP (Cons.) for Huntingdonshire, 1979-83 and for Huntingdon, 1983-2001; PPS to Ministers of State at the Home Office, 1981-83; Asst. Govt. Whip, 1983-84; Pres., Eastern Area Young Conservatives, 1983-85; a Lord Cmnr. of HM Treasury (Govt. Whip), 1984-85; Parly. Under-Sec. of State for Social Security, 1985-86; Minister of State for Social Security, 1986-87; Chief Sec. to HM Treasury, 1987-89; Secy. of State for Foreign and Commonwealth Affairs, 1989; Chllr. of the Exchequer, 1989-90; Leader of the Conservative Party, 1990-97; Prime Minister and First Lord of the Treasury, 1990-97; ***memberships:*** Mem. Bd, Warden Housing Assn., 1975-83; Associate of the Institute of Bankers; Councillor, London Bor. of Lambeth, 1968-71; Mem., Int. Bd. of Governors, Peres Center for Peace, Israel, 1997-; Mem., InterAction Cncl., Tokyo, 1998-; Pres., Asthma UK, 1998-; Patron, National Forest Foundation, 1998-; Pres., Surrey County Cricket Club, 2000-02; Mem., CCC Cttee., 2001-04, 2005-; Hon. Pres., Sight Savers Appeal, 2001-; Vice Pres., Macmillan Cancer Relief; Vice Pres., Inst. of Sports Sponsorship, 2001-; Mem., Club de Madrid, 2002-06; ***professional career:*** Standard Chartered Bank Ltd., various exec. posts in UK and abroad 1965-79; Mem., London Bor. of Lambeth 1968-71; Mem., European Advisory Bd., The Carlyle Grp., 1998-2005, Chmn. 2001-05; Mem., Bd. of Advisors, Baker Inst., Houston, 1998-2005; Chmn., European Advisory Cncl., Emerson Electric Co, 1999-; Pres., Surrey CCC, 2000-2002; Non-Exec. Dir., Mayflower Corp., 2000-03; Chmn., Ditchley Cncl., 2000-; Sr. Adviser, Credit Suisse, 2001-; Mem., European Bd., Siebel Systems, Inc., 2001-03; Non Exec. Dir., Mayflower Corp. plc, 2000-03; Chmn., Int. Advisory Noard, Nat. Bank of Kuwait, 2007-; ***committees:*** Chmn., Housing Cttee., Lambeth Borough Cncl., 1970-71; Jt. Sec. Cons. Parly. Environment Cttee., 1979-81; ***trusteeships:*** Patron of the following: Wavemakers; Mercy Ships, Prosrate Cancer Charity, Support for Africa, 2000, Deafblind UK, 2002-, Consortium for Street Children, 2002-, Atlantic Partnership, 2001-, Foreign and Commonwealth Office Assoc., 2001-, Professional Cricketers' Assoc., 2001-; 21st Century Trust, 2002-; Goodman Fund, Chicago, 2002-; Norfolk Cricket Umpires and Scores Assoc., 2002-; Vice-Patron, The Atlantic Council of the United Kingdom; British and Commonwealth Cricket Charitable Trust, 2002-; DEMAND, 2004-; Future Ireland, 2004-; Dickie Bird Foundation, 2004-; Atlantic Partnership, 2001-; Tim Parry and Johnathan Ball Trust; ***honours and awards:*** Lord of Her Majesty's Most Honourable Privy Council, 1987; Hon. Bencher, Middle Temple, 1997-; Member of the Order of the Companions of Honour, 1999; Hon. Freeman, Merchant Life Taylors' Company, 2002-; Hon. Vice-Pres., Surrey County Cricket Club; Knight Companion of the Most Noble Order of the Garter, 2005; ***publications:*** John Major: The Autobiography, 1999; More Than A Game, 2007; ***clubs:*** Athenaeum, Carlton; Farmers'; Buck's; Pratt's; Surrey CCC; MCC; ***recreations:*** opera, football, cricket and other sports, music, theatre, reading, travel; ***office address:*** PO Box 38506, London, SW1P 1ZW, United Kingdom.

MAKUCH, Jozef; Governor, Central Bank of the Slovak Republic; ***born:*** 1953; ***education:*** Univ. of Economics, Bratislava; ***professional career:*** Assoc. Prof., Univ. of Economics, Bratislava, 1989, Dean, 1991-94; Board Mem., Narodna Banka Slovenska, 1993-96; Exec. Dir., Research Section, NBS, 1994; Chmn., Financial Market Authority, 2000, Chmn. of Board of Dirs., 2002-05; Visiting Prof., Univ. of Economics, Bratislava, 2012-; Board Mem., Narodna Banka Slovenska, 2006, Exec. Dir., 2007, Governor, 2010-; Mem., Gov. Council, ECB; ***office address:*** Central Bank of the Slovak Republic, Imricha Karvasa 1, 813 25 Bratislava, Slovak Republic.

MALENOVSKY, Professor Dr Jirí, JUDr, CSc; Czech, Judge, European Court of Justice; ***born:*** 15 July 1950; ***languages:*** Czech, French, English, German, Russian; ***education:*** Jan Evangelista Purkyne University (now Masaryk University), Brno, 1974, International Space Law, with honours, CSc, 1984, International terrorism; Charles University, Prague, JUDr, 1975, Status of celestial bodies; Université Libre de Bruxelles, 1987, International customary law; International Committee of the Red Cross, Geneva, 1988, International humanitarian law; Danish Centre of Human Rights, Copenhagen, 1991, European protection of human rights; Legal qualification: Judge; ***interests:*** Criminal Law; Dispute settlement; Human rights; Space; Territory/boundaries; Relationships between public international law, municipal law and European Community Law; ***memberships:*** ILA, Czech branch, 1999-; Scientific Council, International Institute for Human Rights in Strasbourg, 2001-; French Society for International Law, 1994-; Czech Society for International Law, 1994-; ***professional career:*** *academic career:* JEP, Faculty of Law, Senior Lecturer, 1974-90, Public International Law; Masaryk University, Faculty of Law, Associate Professor of International Law, 1990-2001, Professor of Public International Law, 2001-; *governmental career:* Director General, Legal and Consular Affairs, Ministry of Foreign Affairs of the Czech Republic, 1998-2000; *diplomatic career:* Ambassador of the Czech Republic to the Council of Europe in Strasbourg, 1993-98; Chairman of the Group of Rapporteurs of the Ministers' Deputies for Legal Cooperation, 1994-98; Czech delegate to UNGA Sixth Committee, 1999; Member of the Ad Hoc Committee of Legal Advisers on Public International Law of the Council of Europe, 1998-2000; Member of the Committee of Experts for the Improvement of Procedures for the Protection of Human Rights of the Council of Europe, 2000-04, Vice-President, 2003-04; *judicial career:* Judge, Constitutional Court of the Czech and Slovak Federal Republic, 1992; Judge, Constitutional Court of the Czech Republic, 2000-04; Member, PCA, 2000-; Judge, Court of Justice of the European Union, 2004-; ***publications:*** Books: Public International Law, General Part, 4 editions: 1993, 1997, 2001, 2004; Relationship between International Law and Domestic Law in general and Czech law in particular, 2000; Articles: Právník; Proceedings of the Colloquia of the International Institute of Space Law; Revue belge de Droit International; Nordic Journal of International Law; Austrian Journal of Public and International Law; Recht in Ost und West; Cahiers internationaux, CEDIN-Paris; Annuaire française de droit international; Revue québécoise de droit international; Revue universelle des droits de l'homme; ***office address:*** Court of Justice of the European Union, L-2925, Luxembourg; ***phone:*** +352 4303 3864; ***fax:*** +352 4303 3869; ***e-mail:*** jiri.malenovsky@curia.eu.int; ***URL:*** http://www.curia.eu.int.

MALHOTRA, Seema; MP for Feltham and Heston, British Parliament; ***party:*** Labour Party; ***political career:*** MP for Feltham and Heston, Dec. 2011-; ***committees:*** Justice, 2012-; ***office address:*** House of Commons, London, SW1A 0AA, United Kingdom; ***phone:*** +44 (0)20 7219 3000; ***e-mail:*** seema.malhotra.mp@parliament.uk.

MALIELEGAOI, Hon. Tuilaepa Lupesolia'i Neioti Aiono Sailele; Prime Minister, Government of Samoa; ***born:*** 14 April 1945, Samoa; ***parents:*** Malielegaoi Veni and Leasunia Lupeasoliai; ***married:*** Gillian Muriel Meredith, 25 November 1972; ***languages:***

English; ***education:*** Auckland Univ., Bachelor of Commerce, 1968, Master of Commerce 1969; ***party:*** Rights Protection Party; ***political career:*** MP, 1981-; Minister of Economic Affairs, Minister of Transport & Civil Aviation, Assoc. Minister of Finance, 1982; Minister of Finance, 1983-85 & 1988-90; Dep. Minister, Minister of Finance, Trade & Tourism, 1991-98; Prime Minister, Foreign Affairs, Internal Affairs, Finance, Commerce, Trade, Industry, Customs, Audit, Tourism and Police and Prisons, 1998-2001; Prime Minister, Attorney General, Minister of Foreign Affairs, Police and Prisons, Immigration, Public Service Commission, 2001-06; PM, Minister of Foreign Affairs, Foreign Trade, Attorney General, Ministry of the Prime Minister & Cabinet and Immigration, 2006-11; PM, Minster of the Cabinet and Immigration, Foreign Affairs, Attorney General, responsible for Samoa Tourism Authority, Samoa Land Corp., Public Service Commission, 2011-; ***memberships:*** Samoa Soc. of Accountants; ***professional career:*** Partner, Coopers & Lybrand Intl. 1981-82; Treasury Investigating Officer 1970; Dep. Dir., Economic Affairs 1971-73; Dep. Financial Sec., Treasury 1973-78; Expert Intra ACP Trade Transport & Communications ACP 1978-80; Gen. Secretariat, Brussels 1978-80; Chmn. of the Bd. of Governors, ADB 1988; Co-Pres., Joint Cncl., of ACP/EU Ministers 1991; Co-Pres., Joint Cncl. of ACP/EU Ministers 1991 & 92; Chmn., Pacific Ministers of the ACP Gp.; ***clubs:*** Chmn., Samoa Rugby Union; Chmn., Samoa Cricket Assn.; Patron, Australian/Samoa Rules Rugby Football; Patron, Samoa Soccer Assn.; Patron, Samoa Tennis Assn.; mem., Royal Country of Golf Club; ***office address:*** Office of the Prime Minister, PO Box L1861, Apia, Samoa; ***phone:*** +685 23636; ***fax:*** +685 21822.

MALLOY, Dannel P.; Governor, State of Connecticut; ***education:*** Boston College; Boston College Law School; ***party:*** Democrat; ***political career:*** Mayor of Stamford, 1996-2010; Governor of Connecticut, Nov. 2010-; ***professional career:*** law, deputy attorney general, Brooklyn; ***office address:*** Office of the Governor, State Capitol, 210 Capitol Avenue, Hartford CT 06106, USA; ***phone:*** +1 860 566 4840; ***URL:*** http://www.ct.gov/governor.

MALOSSE, Henri; French, President, European Economic and Social Committee; ***born:*** 1954; ***education:*** EIP, Paris; Diplomas Univ. of Munich and Warsaw; ***professional career:*** involved in launch of French Chambers of Commerce and Industry Delegation to the EU, 1979; Prof., Univ. of Kaunas, Lithuania, Warsaw, Poland, Diplomatic Institute of Moscow, Russia; created Masters course on Eeropean public policies, Robert Schuman Univ., Strasbourg, 1993; founded, European Network of Euro Information Centres, 1987; preisdent; Established the European Association of SMEEs; Pres., Employers' Group, 2006-13; Pres., EESC, 2013-; ***office address:*** European Economic and Social Committee, Rue Belliard, 99, B-1040 Brussels, Belgium; ***phone:*** +32 (0)2 546 90 11; ***URL:*** http://www.eesc.europa.eu.

MAMEDOV, Fazil; Minister of Taxes, Government of Azerbaijan; ***born:*** 1964, Shamakhi, Republic of Azerbaijan; ***education:*** Azerbaijan Inst. of National Economy, Finance and Credit, 1985; ***political career:*** Minister of Taxes, 2000-; ***professional career:*** Economist, Head of Cashier's Office, and Economist of Operations Dept., Bank of Industry and Construction, 1987-89; Prof., Hd. of Dept., Technical Sch. of Finance and Credit, 1989-93; Chmn., Bd. of Dirs., 'Unsal' Commercial Bank, 1993; Dir., Agrarian Industrial Joint-Stock Commercial Bank, 1994; Dep. Chief, Chief of Finance Tariff and Currency Control, Dep., Chmn., State Customs Cttee., 1995-99; Chief, Head State Tax Inspection, 1999; Second degree state tax advisor, 2002-; ***office address:*** Ministry of Taxes, L. Landau str., 16, Baku, Azerbaijan; ***phone:*** +994 (0)12 403 8634; ***fax:*** +994 (0)12 403 8971; ***e-mail:*** office@taxes.gov.az.

MANCE, Lord Jonathan; Justice of the Supreme Court of the United Kingdom; ***political career:*** Member, House of Lords, 2005-, as Justice of the Supreme Court, disqualified from participation 2009-; ***professional career:*** Judge of the High Court, Queen's Bench Division, 1993-99; Lord Justice of Appeal, 1999-2005; Lord of Appeal in Ordinary in 2005-09; Justice of the Supreme Court of the United Kingdom, 2009-; ***office address:*** Supreme Court of the United Kingdom, Parliament Square, London, SW1P 3BD, United Kingdom; ***URL:*** http://www.supremecourt.gov.uk.

MANCHIN, Joe, III; Senator, State of West Virginia; ***born:*** Farmington, West Virginia; ***political career:*** Mem. Leg. to 1996; Sec. of State, 2000-2004; Governor, State of West Virginia, 2004-10; US Senator for West Virginia, 2010-; ***committees:*** Energy and Natural Resources; Armed Services; Special Cttee. on Aging; ***office address:*** United States Senate, 303 Hart Senate Office Building East, Washington, DC, 20510-4103, USA; ***phone:*** +1 202 224 3954; ***URL:*** http://www.manchin.senate.gov.

MANDELA, Nelson Rolihlahla, BA, LL.B; South African, Former President, South African Government; ***born:*** 1918; ***married:*** Graça Machel, 18 July 1998; Nomzana Winnie, 1958 (div'd 1996); Evelyn Ntoko, 1944 ((div'd 1957)); ***s:*** 3; ***d:*** 3; ***education:*** Univ. Wits., part time law student; Univ. of Lagos, BA, LL.B, 1990; ***party:*** mem., Nat. Exec. Cmn. of ANC; ***political career:*** Co-founder of African National Congress (ANC) Youth League; Nat. Pres., ANC Youth League; Volunteer-in-Chief in Defiance Campaign of Unjust Laws, 1952; charged with treason along with 154 others, 1956, the Treason Trial ends with acquittal of all defendants, 1961; launch of armed struggle, Mandela appointed Cmdr.-in-Chief of Umkhonto we Sizwe, military wing of ANC; visits Ethiopia, Algeria and London and charged with leaving the country illegally, 1962; charged with treason and sent to Robben Island, 1963; transferred to Pollsmoor Prison, 1982; released from prison, 1990; Leader of Deleg. on talks about Talks with SA Gov., 1990; Dep. Pres., ANC, 1990-91; Pres. of ANC, 1991-97; Pres. of South Africa, 1994-99; ***memberships:*** Patron of numerous organisations; ***professional career:*** Clerk, legal firm in Johannesburg; Chancellor, Univ. of the North, 1992-; ***honours and awards:*** Co-Recipient of Nobel Prize for Peace 1993; ***office address:*** Nelson Mandela Foundation, Private Bag X 70,000, Houghton, 2041, South Africa; ***fax:*** +27 11 728 1111.

MANICKCHAND, Hon. Priya; Minister of Education, Government of Guyana; ***born:*** 13 August 1976, Georgetown, Guyana; ***parents:*** Krishendat Manickchand and Hyacinth Manickchand; ***education:*** Univ. of Guyana, LL.B; Hugh Wooding Law School, Univ. of the West Indies; ***political career:*** Minister of Human Services and Social Security, Sept. 2006-11; Minister of Education, 2011-; ***memberships:*** Guyana Bar Assoc.; Guyana Assoc. of Women Lawyers; ***professional career:*** Attorney-at-Law; Private Practice, 2000-06; Senior Supervising Attorney, Georgetown Legal Aid Clinic, 2003-05; ***clubs:*** Georgetown Cricket Club, Bourda; ***office address:*** Ministry of Education, 26 Brickdam, Georgetown, Guyana; ***e-mail:*** humanservicesministry@yahoo.com.

MANITAKIS, Antonios; Minister of Administrative Reform and e-Governance, Government of Greece; ***born:*** 1944, Thessaloniki, Greece; ***education:*** LL.B., 1968; LL.M., (Administrative Law), 1970, PhD. in Law, 1974, Universite Libre de Bruxelles, Belgium; ***political career:*** Minister of Administrative Reform and e-Governance, 2012-; ***professional career:*** Prof. of Constitutional Law at the Faculty of Law of the Aristotle University of Thessaloniki; Prof. Emeritus of the Aristotle University of Thessaloniki; Pres. of the National Cttee. of Human Rights; Pres. of the Assn. of Greek constitutionalists "Aristovoulos Manesis"; ***office address:*** Ministry of Administrative Reform and e-Governance, Vas Sofias 15, 10674 Athens, Greece; ***phone:*** +30 213 131 3000.

MANN, John; Member of Parliament for Bassetlaw, House of Commons; ***party:*** Labour Party; ***political career:*** MP, Bassetlaw, 2001-; ***committees:*** Treasury Select Cttee.; Chair, All Party Group on Combating Antisemitism; ***office address:*** House of Commons, London, SW1A 0AA, United Kingdom; ***phone:*** +44 (0)20 7219 3000; ***e-mail:*** mannj@parliament.uk; ***URL:*** http://www.johnmannmp.com.

MANNING, Fabian; Senator, Government of Canada; ***political career:*** MP, Newfoundland and Labrador House of Assembly; Senator, 2009-; ***committees:*** Fisheries and Oceans; Nat. Security and Defence ; ***office address:*** Canadian Senate, Senate Building, 111 Wellington Street, Ontario K1A 0A4, Canada.

MANSARAY, Alhaji Minkailu; Minister of Mines & Minerals Resources, Government of Sierra Leone; ***education:*** West African Insurance Inst.; ***political career:*** Mem., National Advisory Cttee., All Peoples' Congress; Minister of Mines and Mineral Resources, to date; ***office address:*** Ministry of Mines & Minerals, 5th Floor, Youyi Building, Brookfields, Freetown, Sierra Leone; ***URL:*** http://www.statehouse-sl.org/ministrymines.htm.

MANSOUR, Interm President Adly Mahmud; Interim President, Government of Egypt; ***born:*** 1945, Ciaro, Egypt; ***education:*** Cairo Univ., 1967; ***political career:*** Interim Pres., July 4 2013-; ***professional career:*** State Council, 1970-; Dep. Pres., Constitutional Court, 1992-2013; Pres., Constitutional Court, 2013-; ***office address:*** Office of the President , Al Etehadia Building, Heliopolis, Cairo, Egypt; ***URL:*** http://www.presidency.gov.eg.

MANSVELD, Wilma; Minister for the Environment, Netherlands Government; ***born:*** 1962; ***political career:*** Sec., Social & Economic Council for the Northern Netherlands, 20001-11; mem., Groningen Provincial Council for the PvdA, 2007-, leader of the PvdA group, 2009-11; Mem., Groningen Provincial Executive, 2011-12; State Secretary for Infrastructure and the Environment, Rutte-Asscher gov., Nov. 2012-; ***office address:*** Ministry of Infrastructure and Environment, Postbox 20901, 2500 EX The Hague, Netherlands; ***phone:*** +31 (0)70456 0000.

MANTEGA, Guido; Minister of Finance, Government of Brazil; ***education:*** Univ. of Sao Paulo, Fac. of Economics and Administration, Economics ; ***political career:*** Head of Office; Municipal Sec. of Planning, 1989-92; Econ. Advisor to Pres. Lula, 1993-2002; Minister of Planning, Budget and Management, 2003-04; Minister of Finance, 2006-; ***professional career:*** Prof. of Economics, Business Admin. Fac., Getúlio Vargas Foundation; Doctor in the Sociology of Development, Univ. of Sao Paulo; Prof. of Econ., Pontificia Catholic Univ. (PUC), 1982-87; Vice Rector, PUC, 1984-87; Pres., National Bank of Economic and Social Development (BNDES), to 2006; ***office address:*** Ministry of Finance, Esplanada dos Ministerios, Bloco P, 70048-900 Brasilia DF, Brazil; ***phone:*** +55 (0)61 412 2000 / 3000 ; ***fax:*** +55 (0)61 226 9084; ***e-mail:*** se.df@fazenda.gov.br ; ***URL:*** http://www.fazenda.gov.br.

MANUEL, Trevor Andrew; South African, Minister in the Presidency, South African Government; ***born:*** 31 January 1956, Cape Town; ***parents:*** Abraham and Philma von Sohnen; ***married:*** Lynne Matthews; ***children:*** Govan (M), Pallo (M), Jaime (M); ***languages:*** Afrikaans, English; ***education:*** Matriculated from Harold Cressy High Sch., Cape Town; Technician's diploma in civil engineering, Peninsula Technikon; Exec. Programme Course, Stanford Nat. Univ., Singapore; ***party:*** African Nat. Congress; ***political career:*** Joined Labour Party Youth, 1967; founding Mem., Western Cape U; elected Regional Sec. and Nat. Exec. Mem., UDF, 1983; founding Mem., United Democratic Front; Nat. Sec., UDF, 1984-88; detained three times between 1985 and 1988 for political activities; elected to Nat. Exec., ANC, 1991; head of the dept. of economic planning of the ANC 1991-94; Minister for Trade and Industry, 1994-96; Minister of Finance, 1996- 2009; Minister in the Presidency, Chair of the National Planning Commission, 2009-; ***professional career:*** practised as technician, -1981; Policy Man., Entrepreneurial and Community Dev., Mobil Foundation, 1989; ***committees:*** Gen. Sec., Cape Areas Housing Action Cttee., 1981; Nat. Exec. Cttee. (NEC) and Nat. Working Cttee. (NWC) of the ANC, 1991-; apptd. to Advisory Cttee., UN Initiative for Trade Efficiency, 1994; ***honours and awards:*** selected by the World Economic Forum as a 'Global Leader for Tomorrow', 1994; awarded the Africa Prize by the German Africa Foundation, jointly with the (then) South African Minister of Finance, Derek Keys, 1994; ***office address:*** Ministry in the Presidency, PO Box 15, Cape Town 8000, South Africa; ***phone:*** +27 (0)12 403 2911; ***fax:*** +27 (0)12 461 4331.

MANZ, Dr Hans Peter; Ambassador, Embassy of Austria, Washington DC; ***education:*** Univ. of Vienna, Law, 1977; ***professional career:*** various diplomatic positions incl. First Sec. and Dep. Chief of Mission, Austrian Emb., Iran, 1985-87; Advisor, MFA, 1987-91, 2000-07; Dep. Chief of Mission, Perm. Mission of Austria to the UN, New York, 1994-99; Austrian Ambassador, Switzerland, 2007-11; Austrian Ambassador, Washington DC, 2011-; ***office address:*** Embassy of Austria, 3524 International Court, NW, Washington DC, 20008, USA; ***phone:*** +1 202 895 6700; ***fax:*** +1 202 895 6750; ***URL:*** http://www.austria.org/.

MAR, Countess of (31st in line from Rundri, 1st Earl of Mar, 1115) Margaret; British, Member of the House of Lords; ***born:*** 19 September 1940; ***parents:*** 30th Earl of Mar; ***married:*** J.H. Jenkin, MA, FRCO; ***d:*** 1; ***political career:*** holder of Premier Earldom of Scot.; Mem., House of Lords, to date; Dep. Speaker/Dep. Chmn., HOL, 1997-2007, 2009-; ***interests:*** agriculture, animal and human health, food production, toxic chemicals;

memberships: Specialist Cheesemakers Assn., 2000-; chmn., Forward-ME, 2008-; **professional career:** Clerical Officer, Civil Service, 1959-63; Sales Superintendant, PO/BT, 1969-82; Lay Governor, The King's Sch., Gloucester, 1984-87; Pres., Avanti, 1987; Farmer, 1982-; **committees:** Lay Mem., Immigration Appeal Tribunal, 1985-2006; Mem., English Advisory Cttee. for Telecoms., 1985-86; HoL Refreshment Cttee., 2006-09; Jt. Cttee.on Statutory Instruments, 2007-10; Pres., Guild of Agricultural Journalists, 2007-10; **trusteeships:** Patron, Dispensing Drs. Assn., 1985-2001; Patron, Worcester Branch, Nat. Back Pain Assn., 1987; Patron of several ME charities; **office address:** House of Lords, London, SW1A 0PQ, United Kingdom; **phone:** +44 (0)20 7219 3000; **fax:** +44 (0)20 7219 5979.

MARCUS, Gill; 1949, Governor, South African Reserve Bank; **party:** SACP, ANC; **political career:** political activist (in exile); Dept. Sec., ANC's Dept. of Information & Publicity, London; returned to South Africa, 1990; ANC Information Dept., 1990; MP, 1994; Dep. Minister of Finance, Gov. of National Unity of Nelson Mandela, 1996-99; **professional career:** Dep. Gov., Reserve Bank, 1999-2004; Chair, Absa Group; Chair, Absa Bank; Gov., Reserve Bank, 2009-; **office address:** South African Reserve Bank, PO Box 427, Pretoria 0002, South Africa.

MARGRETHE II, H.M.; Danish, Queen of Denmark; **born:** 16 April 1940, Amailenborg Palace, Denmark; **parents:** King Frederik IX (dec'd 1972) and Queen Ingrid (dec'd 2000); **married:** Prince Henrik of Denmark H.R.H. (née Henri-Marie-Jean-André Count de Laborde de Monpezat), 10 June 1967; **children:** Crown Prince Frederik (M), Prince Joachim (M); **education:** Zahles Skole, matriculation (private), 1959; Women's Flying Corps Leadership Academy, 1959; Copenhagen Univ., philosophy, 1960; Cambridge Univ., prehistoric archaeology, 1960-61; Aarhus Univ., political science, 1961-62; The Sorbonne, Paris, 1963; London Sch. of Economics, 1965; **memberships:** Pres. of the Royal Nordic Ancient Manuscript Soc; Pres. of Queen Margrethe and Prince Henrik Foundation; Founder of Queen Margrethe II's Archaeological Foundation; Hon. mem., Swedish Royal Academy of Science, History and Antiquities, 1988; Invited mem. of Assn. for Promotion of Skiing, Oslo; **professional career:** Training and voluntary service with Women's Flying Corps., 1958-70; Allied Colonel-in-Chief, The Queen's Regiment (UK), 1972; succeeded to the throne, 1972-; Supreme Commander of the Defence Forces; Allied Colonel-in-Chief, The Princess of Wales's Royal Regiment, 1992; **trusteeships:** The Royal Danish Academy of Sciences and Letters; The Danish Bible Soc.; The Royal Orphanage; **honours and awards:** Royal Fellow, Soc. of Antiquaries of London, 1974; Hon. Dr., (D.LL. hon. caus.), Cambridge Univ., 1975; Hon. Fellow, London Sch. of Economics, 1975; Hon. Dr. Univ. of London, 1980; Hon. Dr., Univ. of Iceland, 1986; Medal of the Headmaster, Paris Univ., 1987; Royal Fellow, Lucy Cavendish Coll., Cambridge, 1989; Mother Tongue Socs. Prize, 1989; Adeil Order, 1990; Royal Fellow, Girton Coll., Cambridge, 1992; Hon. Dr, Oxford Univ., 1992; Hon. Bencher of The Middle Temple, 1992; Hon. Dr. Univ. of Edinburgh, 2000; Hon Freedom of the City of London, 2000; decorated with 56 Danish and foreign orders and medals.; **publications:** Translations of: All Mankind are Mortal (translation), 1981; The Valley, The Fields and The Forest, 1988-89; The Wind on the Moon, 1991; llustrations to The Lord of The Rings, 1977, Norse Legends as Told by Jorgen Stegelmann, 1979, Bjarkenmaal, 1982 and Comedy in Florens, 1990; Cantabile, poems by H.R.H. the Prince Consort, 2000; Costumes and scenography for theatre and ballet, 1987, 1991, 2001, 2009; découpages for television film 2000-09; Exhibitions of works of art, 1988-2010; **office address:** Amalienborg, DK-1257, Copenhagen K, Denmark.

MARKELL, Governor Jack; Governor, State of Delaware, USA; **born:** Newark, Delaware; **education:** Brown Univ., Econ. and Development Studies; Univ. of Chicago, MBA ; **political career:** Delaware State Treasurer, 1998-08; Delaware Governor, 2008- ; **professional career:** Sr. Vice-Pres. for Corporate Development, Nextel; Sr. Mgr., Comcast; Consultant, McKinsey and Co., Inc.; banker, First Chicago Corp.; **office address:** Governor's Office, Tatnall Building, William Penn Street, 2nd Floor, Dover, Delaware 19901, USA; **phone:** +1 302 744 4101; **fax:** +1 302 739 2775; **URL:** http://www.state.de.us/governor/comments.shtml.

MARKOVIC, Dusko; Deputy Prime Minister, Minister of Political Affairs, Minister of Justice, Government of Montenegro; **born:** 1958; **education:** Fac. of Law, Kragujevac, Serbia; **political career:** Sec., Municipal Assembly, Mojkovac, 1986-89, Pres., 1989-91; Sec.-Gen., Montenegrin Gov., 1991-98; MP, Parliament of Montenegro, 1997-98; Dep. Minister of Internal Affairs & Head of the State Security Service, 1998-2005; Dir., National Security Agency, 2005-10; Minister without portfolio in the Government of Montenegro, 2010; Dep. Prime Minister for Political System, Foreign & Interior Policy, 2010; Dep. Prime Minister, Minister of Political Affairs, Minister of Justice, 2012-; **office address:** Ministry of Justice, Vuka Karadzica 3, 81000 Podgorica, Montenegro.

MARKS OF HENLEY-ON-THAMES, Lord Jonathan, QC; Member, House of Lords; **born:** 19 October 1952; **parents:** Geoffrey Marks LDS RCS and Patricia Marks LLB (née Bowman); **married:** Sarah Ann Russell, 1982 (Dissolved 1991); Clementine Medina Cafopoulos, 1993; **s:** 3; **d:** 2; **languages:** French, German; **education:** Harrow; Univ. College, Oxford, BA Hons Jurisprudence; Inns of Court School of Law; **party:** Liberal Democrat; **political career:** Founder mem., SDP, 1971; Mem., Lib Dem. Cttee. for England, 1988-89; Chair, Buckingham Constituency Lib. Dems., 2000-02; Chair, Liberal Democrats Lawyers Assn., 2001-07; Mem., Liberal Democrat Policy Cttee., 2004-2010; Mem., House of Lords, 2011-; **interests:** justice issues, constitutional reform, human rights, education; **professional career:** Called to the Bar, Inner Temple, 1975; QC, 1995; practises mostly in commercial law and family law; visiting lecturer in advocacy, Univ. of Malaya, 1985, 1989-91, Univ. of Mauritius, 1988, Sri Lanka Law College, 1992; **office address:** House of Lords, London, SW1A 0PW, United Kingdom; **phone:** +44 (0)20 7219 3000.

MARLAND, Lord; Member, House of Lords; **born:** 1956; **married:** Penelope Marland (née Lamb), 1983; **children:** Marcus (M), Hugo (M), Allegra (F), Domenica (F); **education:** Shrewsbury; **political career:** former treasurer, Conservative Party; Mem., House of Lords, June 2006-; Treasurer, Boris Johnson's mayoral campaign, 2007; Front Bench Spokesman, House of Lords, Energy, and Climate Change and Constitutional Affairs; Parly. Under Sec. of State, Dept. for Energy and Climate Change, 2010-12; Parly. Under Sec. of State, Dept. for Business, Innovation and Skills, 2012-13; **memberships:** Fellow, RSA; **professional career:** Chmn.; Herriot Ltd, Janspeed Ltd., Clareville Capital Partners LLP: Non-exec. dir.,

Jubilee, Essex Court Mgmt. Co. Ltd; formerly dir., Jardine Lloyd Thompson plc; Chmn./founder, The Sports Nexus; Dir., Insurance Capital Partners LLp; Dir, C&UCO Properties; Dir., Hunter Boot Ltd.; Chmn., Jubilee Holdings Ltd.; Chmn., Tickets for Troops; Pres., Salisbury City FC; **trusteeships:** Treasurer/trustee, Atlantic Partnership; Chmn., Harnham Water Meadows Trust; JP Marland Charitable Trust; Guggenheim UK Charitable Trust; mem., Advisory Bd. of Peggy Guggenheim Museum, Venice; Invercauld Estate; **clubs:** MCC, Brooks; **recreations:** tennis, skiing, shooting, wine, works of art, gardening, watching sport; **office address:** House of Lords, London, SW1A 0PW, United Kingdom; **phone:** +44 (0)20 7219 3000.

MAROIS, Hon. Pauline; Premier, Government of Quebec; **political career:** Chief of Staff for the Minister of State for the Status of Women, 1978; MP, National Assembly, La Peltrie, 1981; MP, National Assembly, Taillon, 1989-2008; Minister of Health and Social Services, 1999; Dep. Premier, Minister of Finance, Minister of Research, Science and Technology, Minister of State for the Economy and Finance, 2003; Premier of Quebec, 2013-; **office address:** Office of the Premier, Québec, Canada; **URL:** http://www.premier-ministre.gouv.qc.ca/.

MARSDEN, Gordon, MP; British, Member of Parliament for Blackpool South, House of Commons; **born:** 28 November 1953; **parents:** the late Harry Marsden and Joyce Marsden; **party:** Labour Party; **political career:** MP, Blackpool South, 1997-; PPS to Sec. of State, Culture, Media, and Sport, 2003-05; Chair, Assoc. Parly. Skills Group, 2005-; PPS, Sec. of State, Communities and Local Government, 2009-10; Shadow Minister, Communities and Local Government, 2010; Shadow Minister, Business, Innovation and Skills, Oct. 2010-; **interests:** education policy, skills and local economies and seaside regeneration, foreign affairs, heritage issues; **professional career:** Open Univ. Lecturer & Tutor, 1977-97; Public Affairs Adviser, English Heritage, 1984-85; Editor, History Today, 1985-97; **committees:** Advisory Cttee., Inst. of Historical Research; **trusteeships:** History Today; History of Parliament; Chair, Future of Europe Trust, 2001-; **publications:** contributes to The Independent, The Times Higher Ed., The Times Educational Supplement; Editor, Victorian Values, 2nd ed. 2000; Contributor, World Encyclopedia of Censorship; **office address:** House of Commons, London, SW1A 0AA, United Kingdom; **phone:** +44 (0)20 7219 1262; **e-mail:** gordonmarsdenmp@parliament.uk.

MARSHALL, Elizabeth; Canadian, Senator, Government of Canada; **born:** 1951, Stephenville Crossing; **married:** Stan Marshall; **education:** Memorial Univ., Newfoundland, B.Sc., Maths; **political career:** served in several sr. positions including: Dep. Minister, Social Services, Dep. Minister of Works, Services, and Transportation, province's Auditor Gen. for 10 yrs.; Minister for Health and Community Services, Newfoundland and Labrador Provincial Gov.; Senator, Gov. of Canada, 2010-; **professional career:** Chartered Accountant, 1979-; **office address:** Canadian Senate, Senate Building, 111 Wellington Street, Ontario K1A 0A4, Canada; **URL:** http://sen.parl.gc.ca.

MARTELLY, Michel; President, Government of Haiti; **born:** 12 February 1961; **political career:** Pres. of Haiti, May 2011-; **professional career:** Musician, known as Sweet Micky; Composer; **office address:** Office of the President, Rue Champ-de-Mars, Port-au-Prince, Haiti.

MARTI, Antoni; Prime Minister, Government of Andorra; **party:** Democrats for Andorra; **political career:** Prime Minister, 2011-; Minister of Culture, 2013-; **professional career:** Architect; **office address:** Consell General, Casa de la Vall, Andorra la Vella, Andorra; **phone:** +376 821234; **fax:** +376 861234; **e-mail:** conseil.general@andorra.ad; **URL:** http://www.consellgeneral.ad.

MARTIN, Archbishop of Dublin and Primate of Ireland Diarmuid; Archbishop of Dublin and Primate of Ireland, Roman Catholic Church; **education:** Univ. College, Dublin, Philosophy; Dublin Diocese Seinary, Clonliffe, Theology; Pontifical Univ. of St. Thomas Aquinas (Angelicum), Rome; **professional career:** Ordained a priest, 1969; Curate, Paish of St. Brigid, 1973-74; Pontifical Cncl. for the Family, 1976; Pontifical Cncl. for Justice and Peace, under-sec 1986-94, Sec., 1994-99; Titular Bishop of Glendalough, 1999-2001; titular Archbishop of Glendalough, 2001-03; Holy See Permanent Observer in Geneva, UN, Specialised Agencies and WTO; Co-Adjutor Archbishop of Dublin, 2003-04; Archbishop of Dublin and Primate of Ireland, 2004-; **office address:** Archbishop's House , Drumcondra, Dublin 9, Ireland; **phone:** +353 (0)1 837 3732; **fax:** +353 (0)836 9796.

MARTIN, Dr Earl Asim; Minister of Public Works, Utilities, Transport and Posts, Government of St Christopher and Nevis; **born:** 1958; **education:** Univ. of Havana, Cuba, medicine; **party:** Labour Party; **political career:** MP, 1993-; Minister of Health & Women's Affairs, 1995; Minister of Health and Environment, 2000; Minister of Public Works, Utilities, Transport and Posts, 2004; Minister of Housing, Public Works, and Utilities, 2010-; Deputy Prime Minister, 2013-; **professional career:** medical doctor; **office address:** Ministry of Public Works, Church Street, Basseterre, St. Kitts and Nevis.

MARTINELLI, President Ricardo; President, Government of Panama; **born:** 11 March 1952, Panama City; **education:** Univ. of Arkansas, USA, degree in Business Administration; INCAE, Costa Rica, Masters in Business Administration; **political career:** Dir., Social Security, 1994-96; Min. for Canal Affairs, 1999-2003; Pres., Democratic Change party, Leader, 2004-; Pres. candidate, 2004; President of Panama, July 2009-; **professional career:** Chmn., Bd. of Dirs. Panama Canal, 1999-2003; Fndr., The Ricardo Martinelli Foundation, 2004; Chmn., Super 99 supermarket chain, to date; **office address:** Office of the President, Presidential Palace, San Felipe, Panama; **phone:** +507 227 4158 / 4157 / 4052; **fax:** +507 227 0076; **e-mail:** ofasin@presidencia.gob.pa; **URL:** http://www.presidencia.gob.pa.

MARTINEZ, Susana; Governor, State of New Mexico; **education:** Univ. of Texas; Univ. of Oklahoma, Law; **professional career:** law; District Attorney, Dona Ana County, New Mexico, 1996-2010; Governor of New Mexico, Jan 1. 2011-; **office address:** Office of the Governor, State Capitol, Room 400, Santa Fe, NM 87501, USA; **phone:** +1 505 476 2200; **URL:** http://www.governor.state.nm.us/.

MARTÍNEZ BONILLA, Hugo; Minister of Foreign Affairs, Government of El Salvador; ***languages:*** English, French; ***education:*** Univ. of El Salvador, Eng.; Univ. of Toulouse, France, Masters in Training and Systems Eng.; Univ. Centroamericana, Dr. Jose Simeon Canas, Masters in Admin. and Business Leadership; Univ. Latinoamericana de Ciencia y Tecnologia, Costa Rica, Masters in Human Resources; ***political career:*** FMLN Substit. Dep. to the Legislative Assembly, 1994-2003; Dep., 2003-; Minister of Foreign Relations, 2009-; ***memberships:*** Consultative Commission of the Min. of Foreign Affairs, 2000-09; ***professional career:*** University posts; ***office address:*** Ministry of Foreign Affairs, Colonia San Benito. Calle Circunvalación, No.227, San Salvador, El Salvador; ***phone:*** +503 243 9648 / 9649; ***URL:*** http://www.rree.gob.sv/.

MARTON-LEFEVRE, Julia; Secretary-General, IUCN; ***born:*** Hungary; ***professional career:*** Exec. Dir., International Council for Science; Exec. Dir., LEAD (Leadership for Environment & Development) International; Rector, Univ. for Peace (UPEACE); Director-General, IUCN, to date; ***office address:*** IUCN, Rue Mauverney 28, 1196 Gland, Switzerland; ***URL:*** http://www.iucn.org.

MARTONYI, János; Hungarian, Minister of Foreign Affairs, Government of Hungary; ***born:*** 1944; ***education:*** Faculty of Law, Szeged, S. Hungary; ***party:*** MSZMP, Fidesz; ***political career:*** Head, International Law Dept., Min. of Trade, 1984-89; Govt. Commissioner in charge of privatization, 1989-90; State Secy., Int. Economic Relations, 1990-91; State Sec., Foreign Ministry, 1991-94; Foreign Minister, 1998-2002, May 2010-; ***memberships:*** European Academy of Sciences and Arts; ***professional career:*** Representative, Foreign Trade Ministry, Brussels, 1979-84; Professor at Law School, Budapest, 1990-; ***office address:*** Ministry of Foreign Affairs, Bem rkp. 47, 1027 Budapest, Hungary; ***URL:*** http://www.mfa.gov.hu.

MARWICK, Tricia, MSP; British, Presiding Officer, Scottish Parliament; ***born:*** 5 November 1953, Fife, Scotland, UK; ***parents:*** John Lee and Mary Lee (née Lynch); ***married:*** , 19 July 1975; ***party:*** Scottish National Party (SNP) 1985-resigned, 2011; ***political career:*** MSP, Mid-Scotland and Fife, 1999-11; SNP Chief Whip and Business Manager, 2004-05; Shadow Minister for Housing, 2005-7; MSP, Mid Fife and Glenrothes, 2011-; Presiding Officer, 2011-; ***interests:*** housing, social issues; ***professional career:*** Public Affairs Officer; ***honours and awards:*** Politician to Watch Award, Herald Newsaper, 1999; ***recreations:*** reading, sport; ***office address:*** Scottish Parliament, Edinburgh, EH99 1SP, United Kingdom; ***phone:*** +44 (0)131 348 5680; ***fax:*** +44 (0)131 348 5944.

MARZOUKI, Moncef; President, Republic of Tunisia; ***party:*** Congress for the Republic (CPR); ***political career:*** human rights campaigner; jailed, 1994 after challenging Mr Ben Ali in presidential election; President, Government of Tunisia, Dec. 2011-; ***office address:*** Office of the President, Tunis, Tunisia.

MASHAM OF ILTON, Baroness Susan, Countess of Swinton; Member, House of Lords; ***born:*** 14 April 1935, Lyth, Caithness, Scotland; ***parents:*** Sir Ronald Sinclair and Reba Inglis; ***married:*** Earl of Swinton, 8 December 1959 (Dec'd 2006); ***children:*** John Charles Yarborough Cunliffe Lister (Adopted) (M), Clare Cunliffe Lister (Adopted) (F); ***public role of spouse:*** Hereditary Peer, House of Lords -1999; County Council Mem. for North Yorkshire; ***languages:*** French, German; ***education:*** Heathfield Sch., Ascot; London Polytechnic; ***party:*** Crossbench Peer; ***political career:*** Mem. of House of Lords; ***interests:*** health and disablility, drug abuse, penal affairs; ***memberships:*** NFU Mem.; Pres., Spinal Injury Association; ***professional career:*** Health Service; ***committees:*** All Party Grps. on: Drug Misuse, 1984; Aids; Penal Affairs, 1975-; Children; Disablement, 1970-; Alcohol Misuse; Breast Cancer, 1993-; Skin, 1994-; Epilepsy, 1994-; Primary Care and Public Health, 1998-; Mem., Sub-Cttee. on Resistance to Antimicrobial Agents of Select Cttee. on Science and Technology, 1997-; Mem., British Cncl. Assoc. Parly Grp., 1999-; Select Cttee., HIV/AIDS, 2011; All Party Groups: Spinal Injuries, Associates Health Group; ***honours and awards:*** Hon. Fellow of the Royal College of General Practitioners, 1981; Hon. Degrees from Open Univ., York Univ., Leeds Univ., Ulster Univ., Leeds Poly., Keele Univ., Teeside Univ., East Anglia Univ.; Freedom of the Borough of Harrogate, 1989; ***publications:*** The World Walks By; ***clubs:*** National Pony Society, Ponies UK; Rare Breeds Assoc.; British Texel Sheep Soc.; Highland Pony Soc.; Nat. Pony Soc.; Yorkshire Wildlife Trust; ***recreations:*** swimming, gardening, breeding highland ponies; ***office address:*** House of Lords, London, SW1A 0PQ, United Kingdom; ***phone:*** +44 (0)20 7219 3000; ***fax:*** +44 (0)20 7219 5979; ***e-mail:*** susan@masham1935.fsnet.co.uk.

MASKEY, Paul; MP for Belfast West, British Parliament; ***political career:*** Cllr., Belfast City Council, 2001-09; MP, Belfast West, 2011-; ***office address:*** House of Commons, London, SW1A 0AA, United Kingdom; ***phone:*** +44 (0)20 7219 3000; ***e-mail:*** paul.maskey.mp@parliament.uk.

MASSERON, Paul; Minister of the Interior, Government of Monaco; ***education:*** Institut d'Etudes Politiques de Paris; Ecole Nationale d'Administration; ***political career:*** Prefect of the Vendée, 1998-2001; Prefect of Upper Rhine, 2001-04; Prefect, Assist. to the Sec.Gen. of the French Ministry of the Interior, 2004-06; Minister of the Interior, 2006-; ***office address:*** Ministry of the Interior, Monaco, Monaco.

MATEPARAE, Rt. Hon. Lt. Gen. Sir Jerry, GNZM, QSO; Governor General of New Zealand; ***education:*** British Army Staff College, 1989; Australian Joint Service Staff College, 1995; Royal College of Defence Studies, 1999; MA, Univ.; Fellow of the New Zealand Institute of Management; ***political career:*** Governor General, Aug. 2011-; ***professional career:*** Regular Force of the New Zealand Army; Graduate, Officer Cadet School at Portsea; Served in both battalions of the RNZIR and with the New Zealand Special Air Service; Commanded a regionally-based combined force Truce Monitoring Group on the island of Bougainville during Operation Belisi in 1998; Chief Observer in southern Lebanon with the United Nations Truce Supervisory Organisation, 1994-95; Joint Commander for New Zealand forces in East Timor, 1999-2001; Chief of Army, 2002; Chief of the New Zealand Defence Force with the rank of Lieutenant General, 2006; ***office address:*** Office of the Governor General, Government House, Private Bag 39995, Wellington Mail Centre, Lower Hutt 5045, Wellington, New Zealand; ***phone:*** +64 (0)4 389 8055; ***URL:*** http://gg.govt.nz.

MATINENGA, Eric; Minister of Constitutional and Parliamentary Affairs, Government of Zimbabwe; ***party:*** Movement for Democratic Change; ***political career:*** MP for Buhera West, 2008-; Minister of Constitutional and Parliamentary Affair, Feb. 2009-; ***professional career:*** Lawyer; ***office address:*** Ministry of Constitutional and Parliamentary Affairs, c/o 5th Floor, Corner House, Leopold Takawira Street, Causeway, Harare, Zimbabwe.

MATO ADROVER, Ana; Ministry of Health, Social Services and Equality, Government of Spain; ***party:*** Group of the European People's Party (Christian Democrats) and European Democrats; ***political career:*** MEP, 2004; Ministry of Health, Social Services and Equality, 2011-; ***office address:*** Ministry of Health, Paseo del Prado 18-20, 28014 Madrid, Spain; ***phone:*** +34 901 400100; ***URL:*** http://www.msc.es.

MATSUI, Doris O; Congresswoman, 5th District, California, US House of Representatives; ***party:*** Democrat; ***political career:*** US House of Representatives, 2005-; ***committees:*** Energy and Commerce; ***office address:*** US House of Representatives, 222 Cannon HOB, Washington, DC 20515, USA; ***phone:*** +1 202 225 7163; ***fax:*** +1 202 225 0566.

MATTHYSEN, H.E. Jan; Ambassador, Belgian Embassy in the USA; ***education:*** Univ. of Ghent, 1973; ***professional career:*** Chargé d'Affaires and Amb. to Belgrade, Serbia, 1994-97; Amb. to Turkey, Azerbaijan and Turkmenistan, 2000-04; Amb. to Thailand, Cambodia, Laos and Myanmar, 2004-09; Amb. to the United States, 2009- ; ***office address:*** Embassy of Belgium, 3330 Garfield Street, NW Washington DC 20008, USA; ***phone:*** +1 202 333 6900; ***fax:*** +1 202 333 5457; ***e-mail:*** Washington@diplobel.org; ***URL:*** http://www.diplobel.us.

MAUDE, Rt. Hon. Francis Anthony Aylmer, MP; British, Minister for the Cabinet Office, Paymaster General, UK Government; ***born:*** 1953; ***married:*** Christina Hadfield, 1984; ***education:*** Corpus Christi Coll., Cambridge Univ.; ***party:*** Conservative Party; ***political career:*** Cllr., Westminster City Cncl., 1978-84; MP (Cons.), Warwickshire North, 1983-92; PPS to Peter Morrison, Minister of State for Employment, 1984-85; Govt. Whip, 1985-87; Minister for Corp. Affairs, 1987-89; Minister of State, Foreign and Cmmw. Office, 1989-90; Financial Sec., Treasury, 1990-92; Opp. Front Bench Spokesman for Nat. Heritage, 1997-98; Chairman, Government's Deregulation Task Force, 1994-97; Shadow Chancellor, 1998-2000; Shadow Sec. of State for Foreign Affairs, 2000-2001; MP, Horsham, 1997-; Chmn., Conservative Party, 2005-07; Shadow Minister for the Cabinet Office and Shadow Chancellor of the Duchy of Lancaster, 2007-May 2010; Minister for the Cabinet Office, Paymaster General, May 2010-; ***professional career:*** non-executive Director, ASDA Group Plc,1992; Dir., Salomon Brothers,1992-93; Managing Dir. Morgan Stanley & Co Ltd, 1993-97; ***committees:*** Vice-Chmn., Housing Cttee., WCC, 1980-83; ***publications:*** No Turning Back (co-author); ***office address:*** Cabinet Office, 70 Whitehall, London, SW1A 2AS, United Kingdom; ***phone:*** +44 (0)20 7270 6000; ***e-mail:*** hcinfo@parliament.uk.

MAUGA, Lemanu Peleti; Lieutenant Governor, American Samoa; ***education:*** American Samoa Community College; Univ. of Hawaii-Manoa; San Diego Univ.; ***political career:*** Senator, 32nd Legislature of American Samoa; ***professional career:*** Over 23 years in military; Vice-Chmn., Bank of American Samoa; ***office address:*** Office of the Lt. Governor, Executive Office Building, Utulei, Pago Pago, American Samoa; ***URL:*** http://americansamoa.gov.

MAURER, Ueli; President, Government of Switzerland; ***party:*** Swiss People's Party; ***political career:*** Head of Federal Department of Defence, Civil Protection and Sports, 2009-12; Vice President, 2012; President, 2013-; ***professional career:*** Major in Swiss Army; ***office address:*** Office of the President, Bundeshaus West, 3003 Berne, Switzerland; ***phone:*** +41 (0)31 332 2111; ***URL:*** http://www.admin.ch.

MAURO, Mario; Minister of Defence, Government of Italy; ***education:*** Univ. Cattolica del Sacro Cuora, Milan, Italy; ***party:*** Civic Choice; ***political career:*** Mem., European Parliament, 1999-13; Minister of Defence, Apr. 2013-; ***office address:*** Ministry of Defence, Gabinetto, Via XX Settembre 8, 00187 Rome, Italy; ***phone:*** +39 06 488 2126/7; ***fax:*** +32 (0)2 284 9075; ***e-mail:*** ministro@difesa.it; ***URL:*** http://www.difesa.it.

MAY, Rt. Hon. Theresa; Home Secretary, UK Government; ***party:*** Conservative Party; ***political career:*** MP for Maidenhead, 1997-; Shadow Sec. of State for Education and Employment, 1999-2001; Shadow Secretary of State for Transport, Local Government and the Regions, 2001; Shadow Secretary of State for Transport, 2002-02; Conservative Party Chairman, 2002-03; Shadow Secretary of State for Environment and Transport, 2003-04, for the Family, 2004-05 and for Culture, Media and Sport, 2005; Shadow Leader of the House of Commons, 2005-09; Shadow Sec. of State for Work and Pensions and Shadow Minister for Women, 2009-10; Home Secretary, May 2010-; ***office address:*** Home Office, 2 Marsham Street, London, SW1P 4DF, United Kingdom; ***phone:*** +44 (0)20 7035 4848; ***e-mail:*** mayt@parliament.uk; ***URL:*** http://www.homeoffice.gov.uk.

MAY OF OXFORD, Rt. Hon. Lord Robert McCredie, OM, AC, Kt; Professor, Oxford University; ***born:*** 8 June 1936, Sydney, Australia; ***married:*** Judith (née Feiner), 3 August 1962; ***children:*** Naomi May (F); ***education:*** trained as physicist/applied mathematician; ***political career:*** Mem., House of Lords; ***interests:*** structure of populations and communities, response to change; ***memberships:*** Foreign Mem., US Nat. Academy of Sciences; Overseas Fellow, the Australian Academy of Sciences; Mem. of various bds., inc. UK Inst. of Sport; ***professional career:*** Chair in Physics, Sydney Univ., 1969-73; Class of 1877 Prof. of Zoology, Princeton Univ., USA, 1973-88; Royal Soc. Research Prof., Oxford, 1988; Chief Scientific Adviser to the UK Govt. and Head, UK Office of Science and Tech., 1995-2000; Pres., The Royal Society, 2000-05; holds Professorship at Oxford Univ. and Imperial Coll., London; Fellow, Merton Coll., Oxford; ***trusteeships:*** fmr. Chmn. of Bd. of Trustees of the Natural History Museum, London; fmr. Trustee of the Royal Botanic Gardens, Kew; fmr. Independent Mem. of the Joint Nature Conservancy Council; fmr. Trustee of WWF, UK; Exec. Trustee, Nuffield Foundation and Cambridge Univ. Gates Trust; ***honours and awards:*** 1996 Crafoord Prize, Royal Swedish Academy of Sciences; Knighted, 1996, Companion of the Order of Australia, 1998, both for 'services to science'; 1998 Balzan Prize Presented by Pres. of Italy; Blue Planet Prize, presented by Asahi Glass Foundation, Japan 2001; Life Peer, House of Lords Appointments Cmn., 2001; Hon. degrees from sev. univs.

inc. Uppsala, Yale, Princeton and Sydney; Order of Merit, 2002; ***office address:*** Univ. of Oxford, Dept. of Zoology, South Parks Road, Oxford, OX1 3 PS, United Kingdom; ***phone:*** +44 (0) 1865 271170; ***fax:*** +44 (0) 1865 281060; ***e-mail:*** robert.may@zoo.ox.ac.uk.

MAYNARD, Paul; MP for Blackpool North and Cleveleys, UK Government; ***education:*** Oxford Univ.; ***party:*** Conservative; ***political career:*** MP for Blackpool North and Cleveleys, May 2010-; PPS to Oliver Letwin as Minister for Government Policy, Cabinet Office, 2012-; ***committees:*** Transport, 2010-; ***office address:*** House of Commons, London, SW1A 0AA, United Kingdom; ***e-mail:*** paul.maynard.mp@parliament.uk; ***URL:*** http://paulmaynard.co.uk.

MBASOGO, Brig. Gen. Teodoro Obiang Nguema; Equatorial Guinean, President, Republic of Equatorial Guinea; ***born:*** 1942; ***education:*** Military Training, Spain; ***party:*** Democratic Party of Equatorial Guinea (PDGE); ***political career:*** Former Dep. Minister of Defence; overthrew former Pres. Macías Nguema in coup, 1979; Head, Supreme Military Cncl., 1979-; Minister of Defence, 1986-; Chmn., African Union; ***professional career:*** Armed Forces; ***office address:*** Office of the President, Malabo, Equatorial Guinea.

MBAYE, Abdoul; Prime Minister, Government of Senegal; ***education:*** Univ. of Dakar, Senegal; Hautes Etudes Commerciales, France; Sorbonne Univ., France; ***political career:*** Prime Minister, Apr. 2012-; ***professional career:*** President, Federation of Associations of Banks and Financial Institutions of the West African Economic and Monetary Union; ***office address:*** Office of the Prime Minister, Immeuble Administratif, ave Léopold Sédar Senghor, BP 4029, Dakar , Senegal; ***phone:*** +221 33 823 1088; ***fax:*** +221 33 822 5578; ***URL:*** http://www.primature.sn.

MBEKI, Thabo Mvuyelwa; South African, Former President, South African Government; ***born:*** 18 June 1942, Idutywa, Transkei, South Africa; ***parents:*** Govan Mbeki and Epainette Mbeki; ***married:*** Zanele (née Dlamini), 1974; ***education:*** Univ. of London, Econ., 1961-62; Univ. of Sussex, Masters, Econ., 1966; ***party:*** African National Congress; ***political career:*** Involved with ANC activities in exile, 1962-1989; Chmn., ANC, 1993; Dep. Pres., South Africa 1994-99; Pres., African National Congress, 1997-; Pres., South Africa, June 1999-Sept. 2008; Chmn., African Union, July 2002-July 2003; ***office address:*** c/o African National Congress, Luthuli House, 54 Sauer Street, Johannesburg, South Africa.

MCCABE, Steve; British, Member of Parliament for Birmingham, Hall Green, House of Commons; ***born:*** 4 August 1955; ***party:*** Labour Party; ***political career:*** MP, Birmingham Hall Green, 1997-10, Selly Oak, 2010-; Assist. Gov. Whip, 2006-07; Gov. Whip, 2008-10; Opp. Whip, 2010; ***committees:*** Home Affairs Select Cttee., 2005-06; 2010-; ***office address:*** House of Commons, London, SW1A 0AA, United Kingdom; ***phone:*** +44 (0)20 7219 4842; ***e-mail:*** mccabes@parliament.uk.

MCCAIN, John Sidney; American, Senator for Arizona, US Senate; ***born:*** 1936, Panama Canal Zone; ***parents:*** John S. McCain Jr.; ***married:*** Cindy McCain (née Hensley), 1980; ***children:*** Meghan (F), Jack (M), Jimmy (M), Bridget (F); ***education:*** US Naval Acad. BS 1958; Nat. War Coll.; ***party:*** Republican; ***political career:*** US House of Representatives, 1982-86; US Senator for Arizona, 1986-; Presidential Candidate, 2008; ***memberships:*** Chmn., Int. Republican Inst. 1993-; ***professional career:*** US Navy 1954-81 (Prisoner of War, Vietnam conflict 1967-73, ret'd. as Captain 1981); ***committees:*** Armed Services; Indian Affairs; Foreign Relations; Homeland Security and Governmental Affairs; ***honours and awards:*** Silver Star; Bronze Star; Legion of Merit; Purple Heart; Distinguished Flying Cross; ***office address:*** US Senate, 241 Russell Senate Office Building, Washington, DC 20510, USA; ***phone:*** +1 202 224 2235.

MCCANN, Michael; MP for East Kilbride, Strathaven and Lesmahagow, UK Government; ***party:*** Labour; ***political career:*** Councillor, South Lanarkshire Council, 1999-; MP for East Kilbride, Strathaven and Lesmahagow, May 2010-; ***committees:*** International Dev., 2010-; ***office address:*** House of Commons, London, SW1A 0AA, United Kingdom; ***phone:*** +44 (0)20 7219 3000; ***e-mail:*** michael.mccann.mp@parliament.uk.

MCCARTHY, Kerry; MP for Bristol East, House of Commons; ***born:*** 1965; ***party:*** Labour; ***political career:*** Councillor, Luton Borough Cncl., 1995-2003; MP for Bristol East, 2005-; Shadow Minister, Treasury, Oct. 2010-2011; Shadow Minister, Foreign and Commonwealth Affairs, 2011-; ***office address:*** House of Commons, London, SW1A 0AA, United Kingdom; ***e-mail:*** kerry.mccarthy.mp@parliament.uk.

MCCARTHY, Kevin; Congressman, 22nd Dist. Calif., US House of Representatives; ***born:*** Bakersfield, Calif.; ***education:*** Calif. State Univ., Business Administration; ***political career:*** Mem., Calif. State HOR, 2002-06; Mem., US HOR, 2007-; Majority Whip, 2011-; ***committees:*** HOR Cttee: Financial Services; ***office address:*** House of Representatives, 1523 Longworth House Office Building, Washington, DC 20515, USA; ***phone:*** +1 202 225 2915 .

MCCARTNEY, Jason; MP for Colne Valley, UK Government; ***party:*** Conservative; ***political career:*** MP for Colne Valley, May 2010-; ***office address:*** House of Commons, London, SW1A 0AA, United Kingdom; ***phone:*** +44 (0)20 7219 3000; ***e-mail:*** jason.mccartney.mp@parliament.uk.

MCCARTNEY, Karl; MP for Lincoln, UK Government; ***party:*** Conservative; ***political career:*** Wrotham Parish Council 1999-2004; MP for Lincoln, May 2010-; ***committees:*** Unopposed Bills (Panel), 2011-; ***office address:*** House of Commons, London, SW1A 0AA, United Kingdom; ***phone:*** +44 (0)20 7219 3000; ***e-mail:*** karl.mccartney.mp@parliament.uk.

MCCASKILL, Senator Claire; Senator for Missouri, United States Senate; ***born:*** 1953; ***education:*** Univ. of Missouri, grad. 1975, law degree, 1977; ***political career:*** Missouri State Legislature, 1983-88; Missouri State Auditor, 1999-2006; Candidate for State Governorship, 2004; US Senator, 2007-; ***professional career:*** Jackson County Prosecutor, 1993-98; ***committees:*** Armed Services; Commerce; HSGAC; Aging; ***office address:*** United States Senate, Washington, DC 20510, USA; ***URL:*** http://www.mccaskill.senate.gov/.

MCCAUL, Michael; Congressman, 10th District, Texas, US House of Representatives; ***education:*** Trinity Univ., BA, Business and History; St. Mary's Univ. Sch. of Law, J.D.; Harvard Univ., School of Govn., grad. Snr. Exec. Fellows Program; ***political career:*** Dep. Attorney General, State of Texas; Snr. Advisor to Texas Governor Rick Perry on Homeland Security; Bush-Cheney Pres. Transitional Team, 2000; Chief of Terrorism and Nat. Security, US Dept. of Justice, Western Judicial Dist. of Texas; US House of Representatives, 2005-; ***committees:*** Homeland Security, Chmn.; Foreign Affairs; Science and Technology; ***office address:*** US House of Representatives, 131 Cannon House Office Building, Washington, DC 20515, USA; ***phone:*** +1 202 225 2401; ***fax:*** +1 202 225 5922.

MCCAUSLAND, Nelson; MLA for North Belfast, Northern Ireland Assemby; ***party:*** Democratic Unionist Party; ***political career:*** MLA for North Belfast, 2003-; Minister of Culture, Arts and Leisure, 2009-11; Minister for Social Development, 2011-; ***office address:*** Northern Ireland Assembly, Parliament Buildings, Ballymiscaw, Belfast, BT4 3XX, United Kingdom.

MCCLEARY, Boyd; Governor, British Virgin Islands; ***education:*** Queen's Univ. Bellfast; ***political career:*** Governor of the British Virgin Islands, 2010-; ***professional career:*** British High Commissioner to Malaysia, 2006-10; ***honours and awards:*** Commander of the Royal Victorian Order, 2004; Companion of the Order of St Michael and St Geroge, 2010; ***office address:*** Governor's Office, PO Box 702, Road Town, Tortola, British Virgin Islands; ***e-mail:*** govoffice.totola@fco.gov.uk; ***URL:*** http://ukinbvi.fco.gov.uk/en.

MCCLINTOCK, Tom; Congressman for California, US House of Representatives; ***party:*** Republican; ***political career:*** Mem., US HOR, California Dist. 4, 2009-; ***committees:*** Budget; Natural Resources; ***office address:*** House of Representatives, Washington DC, USA.

MCCLYMONT, Gregg; MP for Cumbernauld, Kilsyth and Kirkintilloch East, House of Commons; ***party:*** Labour; ***political career:*** MP for Cumbernauld, Kilsyth and Kirkintilloch East, May 2010-; Shadow Minister, Work and Pensions, 2011-; ***committees:*** Science and Technology Select Cttee., 2010-12; Business, Innovation and Skills, 2010; ***office address:*** House of Commons, London, SW1A 0AA, United Kingdom; ***phone:*** +44 (0)20 7219 3000; ***e-mail:*** gregg.mcclymont.mp@parliament.uk.

MCCOLL OF DULWICH, Lord, Baron; British, Professor of Surgery, London University Hospital; ***born:*** 6 January 1933, UK; ***married:*** Jean Lennox (née McNair), 27 August 1960; ***children:*** Alastair (M), Caroline (F), Mary (F); ***public role of spouse:*** Paediatrician; ***education:*** Hutchesons' Grammar Sch., Glasgow; St. Paul's Sch., London, Foundation scholarship in Classics; ***party:*** Conservative Party; ***political career:*** Former PPS to Prime Min. John Major, House of Lords; Opposition Spokesman on Health; Dep. Speaker, House of Lords; Mem., House of Lords, 1989-; ***interests:*** health, forestry; ***memberships:*** FRCS; FRCSE; FACS; ***professional career:*** Professor of Surgery, Guy's Hosp., 1971-98; Prof. of Surgery, Univ. of London, 1971-; ***committees:*** Former Chmn., Government Working Party on ALAC services; ***trusteeships:*** Mercy Ships; Mildmay Centre, Uganda; Wolfson Foundation; ***honours and awards:*** Life peerage, 1989; CBE, 1997; Fellow of King's College, 2001; Hutchesonian Award, 2000; Great Scot Award, 2002; Hon. F.D.S. R.C.S.; ***publications:*** Numerous papers on surgery and intestinal absorbtion; ***recreations:*** forestry; ***office address:*** House of Lords, London, SW1A 0PW, United Kingdom; ***phone:*** +44 (0)20 7219 5141; ***e-mail:*** mccolli@parliament.uk.

MCCONNELL, Mitch, BA; American, Minority Leader (Republican Whip), US Senate; ***born:*** 20 February 1942; ***married:*** Elaine L. Chao McConnell; ***children:*** Elly (F), Claire (F), Porter (F); ***public role of spouse:*** Secretary of Labor; ***education:*** Univ. of Louisville, BA (Hons.); Univ. of Kentucky, Coll. of Law; ***party:*** Republican; ***political career:*** US Senator for Kentucky, 1984-; Assistant Majority Leader (Republican Whip), 2002-Jan. 2007; Minority Leader, 2007-; ***professional career:*** founder and Chmn., Kentucky Task Force on Missing Children; Chief Legislative Asst.; Dep. Attorney Gen.; ***committees:*** Agriculture, Nutrition & Forestry; Appropriations; Rules & Adminstration; ***honours and awards:*** named one of the Outstanding Young Men of the Year in Jefferson County, 1974; one of Kentucky's Outstanding Young Men of the Year, 1977; The Golden Plow, American Farm Bureau, 1996; ***publications:*** frequent contributor of opinion pieces to national newspapers including The New York Times, The Washington Post and The Wall Street Journal; ***office address:*** US Senate, 361-A Russell Senate Office Building, Washington, DC 20510, USA; ***phone:*** +1 202 224 2541; ***URL:*** http://www.mcconnell.senate.gov/.

MCCONNELL OF GLENSCORRODALE, Lord Jack, MSP PC; Member, House of Lords; ***born:*** 30 June 1960, Irvine, Ayrshire, UK; ***parents:*** William McConnell and Elizabeth McConnell; ***married:*** Bridget McConnell; ***children:*** Mark (M), Hannah (F); ***public role of spouse:*** Chief Executive, Culture and Sport Glasgow; ***education:*** Arran High School, UK; Stirling Univ., UK; ***party:*** Labour; ***political career:*** Mem., Stirling District Cncl., 1984-93; Leader of the Cncl., 1990-92; Gen.-Sec., Scottish Labour Party, 1992-98; MSP for Motherwell and Wishaw; Minister for Finance, Scottish Parl., 1999-00; Minister for Education and External Affairs, 2000-2001; First Minister of Scotland, 2001-07; President, Legislative Regions of Europe 2004; UK Prime Minister's Special Representative for Peacekeeping; Mem., House of Lords, 2010-; ***interests:*** Education advisor, Clinton Hunter Development Initiative; ***professional career:*** Maths Teacher, 1983-92; ***honours and awards:*** Fellow, 48 Group Club; Amb., Action for Children UK; Stirling Univ., Doctorate of University; ***recreations:*** golf, gardening; ***office address:*** House of Lords, London, SW1A 0PW, United Kingdom; ***phone:*** +44 (0)207219 3000; ***URL:*** http://www.jackmcconnell.org.

MCCREA, Rev. Dr. Robert Thomas William, DC; British, Member, Northern Ireland Assembly and Member of Parliament; ***born:*** 1948, Stewartstown, Co. Tyrone; ***parents:*** Robert Thomas McCrea (dec'd) and Sarah Jane McCrea (dec'd) (née Whann); ***married:*** Anne Shirley McCrea (née McKnight), 1971; ***children:*** Ian (M), Stephen (M), Sharon (F), Faith (F), Grace (F); ***public role of spouse:*** Former Elected member, Cookstown District Council; ***education:*** Cookstown Grammar Sch.; Theological Hall Free Presbyterian Church of Ulster; Marietta Bible College, Ohio, USA; ***party:*** Democratic Unionist Party; ***political career:*** Mem., N.I. Assembly 1982-85 (D. Cnclr. 1973-, and Chmn. 1977-81 and 2002-03); MP (Democratic Unionist Party) for Mid Ulster, 1983-97; Mem., Mid Ulster, Northern Ireland

Assembly, 1998; MP, South Antrim 2000-01, 2005-; Vice Chmn., DUP Exec. Cncl.; Dep. Whip, DUP Assembly Party; DUP Spokesman for the Environment, Food and Rural Affairs at Westminster; ***memberships:*** Loyal Orange Order; Royal Black Inst.; Apprentice Boys of Derry; ***professional career:*** Northern Ireland Civil Service, Dept. of Health and Social Services; Recording Artist, Gospel Singer; Dir., Daybreak Recording Company. Recipient of silver, gold and platinum discs for record sales; ***committees:*** Fmr. Vice Pres., Assn. of Local Authorities in NI; Fmr. Party spokesman at Westminster on Educ. Health and Social Services, Environment, Disability and Agriculture; Northern Ireland Forum for Political Dialogue, 1996-98; Chmn., Environment Cttee., 1998-2003; Mem., Assembly Cttee. on Procedures, 2002-03; Preparation of Government Cttee.; Assembly Business Cttee.; Northern Ireland Grand Cttee.; Public Accounts Commission; ***trusteeships:*** Calvary Free Presbyterian Church; Board of Govnrs. Magherafelt High Schl; ***honours and awards:*** Hon. Doctorate of Divinity, Marietta Bible College (1989); ***publications:*** (Autobiography) In His Pathway; ***recreations:*** gospel recording artist; ***office address:*** House of Commons, London, SW1A 0AA, United Kingdom; ***phone:*** +44 (0)20 7219 8525; ***e-mail:*** william.mccrea.mp@parliament.uk.

MCCRORY, Pat; Governor, North Carolina; ***political career:*** Councillor, Charlotte; Mayor, Charlotte, 1995 (seven terms); elected Governor, North Carolina, Nov. 2012; ***office address:*** Office of the Governor, 20301 Mail Service Center, Rayleigh, NC 27699-0301, USA; ***URL:*** http://www.governor.state.nc.us.

MCCULLY, Hon. Murray; New Zealander, Minister for Foreign Affairs, New Zealand Government; ***born:*** 19 February 1953, Whangarei; ***married:*** Karen Eula McCully (née Baeyertz) (div'd); ***education:*** Auckland and Victoria Univs., LLB; ***party:*** Nat. Party; ***political career:*** New Zealand Pres., Young Nationals, 1973-75; Dominion Cllr., 1973-76; Dir. of Communications, Nat. Party, 1976-78; Dep. divisional chmn. and on East Coast Bays Electorate Exec., 1980-84; MP, Albany, 1996-2002; Minister of Crown, 1991-2000; MP, East Coast Bays, 1987-; Minister of Foreign Affairs, Sport and Recreation, 2008-; Rugby World Cup, 2008-11; ***professional career:*** Principal of Public Relations firm; Chmn. of Dirs., Northland FM Radio Ltd; qualified Solicitor; ***office address:*** Ministry of Foreign Affairs, Stafford House, 40 The Terrace, Wellington, New Zealand; ***phone:*** +64 4 494 8500; ***URL:*** http://www.mft.govt.nz.

MCCUSKER, Malcolm, AO QC; Premier, Government of Western Australia; ***political career:*** Governor of Western Australia, 2011-; ***professional career:*** Barrister; ***office address:*** Office of the Premier, 24th Floor, 197 St. George's Terrace, Perth, Western Australia 6000, Australia; ***URL:*** http://www.premier.wa.gov.au.

MCDONAGH, H.E. Bobby; Ambassador, Irish Embassy in the UK; ***born:*** 29 June 1954, Washington D.C. USA; ***education:*** Gonzaga Coll., Dublin, Ireland; MA, (Classics), Balliol Coll., Oxford, UK; ***professional career:*** Third Sec., Embassy in Luxembourg, 1980-83; Amb. to Malaysia, accredited to Laos, Thailand and Vietnam, 2000-01; Perm. Rep. to the European Union, Brussels, Belgium, 2005-09; Amb. to London, UK, 2009-; ***office address:*** Embassy of Ireland, 17 Grosvenor Place, London, SW1X 7HR, United Kingdom; ***phone:*** +44 (0)20 7235 2171; ***fax:*** +44 (0)20 7245 6961; ***URL:*** http://www.embassyofireland.co.uk/home/index.aspx?id=33706.

MCDONAGH, Siobhain; British, Member of Parliament for Mitcham and Morden, House of Commons; ***born:*** 20 February 1960; ***party:*** Labour Party; ***political career:*** Cllr., Mitcham and Morden, 1982-97; MP, Mitcham and Morden, 1997-; ***interests:*** housing; ***committees:*** Social Security, 1997-98; Health, 2000-05; Unopposed Bills (Panel), 2004-; London, 2009-10; Education, 2012-; ***office address:*** House of Commons, London, SW1A 0AA, United Kingdom; ***phone:*** +44 (0)20 7219 3000; ***e-mail:*** mcdonaghs@parliament.uk; ***URL:*** http://www.siobhainmcdonagh.org.uk.

MCDONALD, Andy; MP for Middlesbrough, British Parliament; ***born:*** 1958; ***party:*** Labour Party; ***political career:*** MP for Middlesbrough, 2012-; ***office address:*** House of Commons, London, SW1 0AA, United Kingdom; ***phone:*** +44 (0)20 7219 3000.

MCDONALD, H.E. Simon; Ambassador, British Embassy in Germany; ***professional career:*** British Amb. in Tel Aviv, to 2003-06; Amb, to Germany, 2010-; ***office address:*** British Embassy, Wilhelmstrasse 70-71, 10117 Berlin, Germany; ***phone:*** +49 (0)30 20457-0; ***fax:*** +49 (0)30 20457 574; ***e-mail:*** info@britischebotschaft.de; ***URL:*** http://ukingermany.fco.gov.uk/en.

MCDONNELL, Dr Alasdair; Member, Northern Ireland Assembly; ***parents:*** Charles McDonnell and Margaret McDonnell (née McIlhatton); ***married:*** Olivia McDonnell (née Nugent), 6 Febuary 1998; ***children:*** Dearbhla, Ruairi, Oisin, Aileen; ***education:*** UCD Medical Sch.; ***party:*** SDLP, Leader 2011-; ***political career:*** Cllr., Belfast C.C., 1977-2001; Dep. Lord Mayor, 1995-96; new Mem., South Belfast, Northern Ireland Assembly, 1998; MP (at Westminster) for Belfast South, 2005-; ***memberships:*** BMA; ***professional career:*** family doctor; ***office address:*** House of Commons, London, SW1A 0AA, United Kingdom; ***e-mail:*** mcdonnella@parliament.uk.

MCDONNELL, John; British, Member of Parliament for Hayes and Harlington, House of Commons; ***born:*** 8 September 1951; ***party:*** Labour Party; ***political career:*** Sec., Assn. of London Govt.; MP, Hayes and Harlington, 1997-; ***office address:*** House of Commons, London, SW1A 0AA, United Kingdom; ***phone:*** +44 (0)20 7219 3000; ***e-mail:*** mcdonnellj@parliament.uk; ***URL:*** http://www.john-mcdonnell.net.

MCDONNELL, Governor Robert Francis 'Bob'; Governor, Commonwealth of Virginia, USA; ***born:*** 15 June 1954, Pennsylvania, USA; ***education:*** Univ. of Notre Dame (ROTC scholarship), BBA Management, 1976; Boston Univ. MSBA, 1980; Regent Univ. School of Law, M.A./J.D. 1989; ***political career:*** Delegate, Virginia House of Delegates, 1992-2006; Attorney General, 2005-09; Governor, Cmnwlth. of Virginia, 2010-; ***professional career:*** Medical Supply Officer, US Army, 1976-81; American Hospital Supply Corp.; Interned for Congressman Jerry Lewis; retired from army service in 1997, as Lt. Colonel; ***office address:*** Office of the Governor, State Capitol, 3rd Floor,, Richmond, Virginia 23219, USA; ***phone:*** +1 804 786 2211; ***fax:*** +1 804 371 6351; ***URL:*** http://www.governor.virginia.gov/.

MCDONOUGH, Denis; Chief of Staff, US Government; ***education:*** St John's Univ., Minnesota; Georgetown Univ.; ***political career:*** Foreign Policy Adviser for Senate Democratic Leader Tom Daschle; Senior Adviser on foreign policy issues, Presidential Transition Team; Senior Adviser, Barack Obama's 2008 presidential campaign; Dep. National Security Advisor, 2010-13, also, Chief of Staff, National Security Staff; Dep. National Security Advisor for Strategic Communications; Chief of Staff to President Barack Obama, 2013-; ***office address:*** The White House, 1600 Pennsylvania Avenue NW, Washington, DC 20500, USA; ***URL:*** http://www.whitehouse.gov.

MCFADDEN, Rt. Hon. Pat; MP for Wolverhampton South East, House of Commons; ***born:*** 1965; ***party:*** Labour; ***political career:*** Political Secretary to the Prime Minister, Tony Blair, MP, 2002-05; MP for Wolverhampton South East, 2005-; Parliamentary Under-Secretary of State, Cabinet Office, 2006-07; Minister of State, Dept. for Business Enterprise and Regulatory Reform, 2007-09; Minister of State, Dept. for Business, Innovations and Skills, 2009-10; ***committees:*** Treasury, 2011-; Parliamentary Commission on Banking Standards, 2012; ***office address:*** House of Commons, London, SW1A 0AA, United Kingdom; ***e-mail:*** mcfaddenp@parliament.uk.

MCFAUL, H.E. Michael; Ambassador, US Embassy in Moscow; ***education:*** BA, Int. Relations and Slavic Languages, MA, in Soviet and East European Studies. Stanford Univ.; Rhodes scholarship to Oxford Univ., D. Phil. in Int. Relations, 1991; ***professional career:*** Special Assist. to the President and Senior Dir. for Russia and Eurasian Affairs at the National Security Council, 2009-12; Amb. to Russia, 2012-; ***office address:*** US Embassy, Bolshoy Deviatinsky Pereulok No. 8, 121099 Moscow, Russian Federation; ***phone:*** +7 095 728 5000; ***fax:*** +7 095 728 5090; ***URL:*** http://moscow.usembassy.gov.

MCGOVERN, Alison; MP for Wirral South, UK Government; ***education:*** University Coll., London; ***party:*** Labour; ***political career:*** Councillor, London Borough of Southwark Council, 2006-10; MP for Wirral South, May 2010-; PPS to the Right Hon. Gordon Brown MP, 2010-; ***committees:*** House of Commons Int. Development Select Cttee, Nov. 2010-; Works of Art, 2011-; ***office address:*** Constituency Address, 99 New CHester Road, New Ferry, Wirral, CH62 4RA, United Kingdom; ***phone:*** +44 (0)151 645 6590; ***e-mail:*** alison@alisonmcgovern.org.uk; ***URL:*** http://www.alisonmcgovern.org.uk.

MCGOVERN, Jim; MP for Dundee West, House of Commons; ***born:*** 1956; ***party:*** Labour; ***political career:*** MP for Dundee West, 2005-; ***committees:*** Scottish Affairs, 2005-07, 2008-; ***office address:*** House of Commons, London, SW1A 0AA, United Kingdom; ***e-mail:*** mcgovernj@parliament.uk.

MCGUINNESS, Martin; Deputy First Minister, Northern Ireland Assembly; ***party:*** Sinn Féin; ***political career:*** MP, Mid Ulster, 1997-; MLA, Mid Ulster, 1998-; Minister of Education, 1999-2002 (NI Assembly suspended); Dep. First Minister, May 2007-; ***office address:*** Northern Ireland Assembly, Parliament Buildings, Stormont, Belfast, BT4 3XX, Northern Ireland; ***phone:*** +44 (0)28 9052 1130.

MCGUIRE, Anne; Member of Parliament for Stirling, House of Commons; ***married:*** Len McGuire; ***children:*** Paul (M), Sarah (F); ***public role of spouse:*** Chartered Accountant; ***education:*** Our Lady and St. Francis' Secondary Sch., Glasgow; Univ. of Glasgow, MA (Hons.), Politics with History; Notre Dame Teacher Training Coll., Glasgow; ***party:*** Labour Party; ***political career:*** Sr. Mem., Labour Party's Scottish Exec., Chair, 1992-93; MP, Stirling, 1997-; PPS to the Sec. of State for Scotland, 1997-99; Asst. Govt. Whip; 2nd Lord Commissioner, HM Treasury, 2001-02; Parly. Sec. to the Scotland Office, 2002-05; Minister for Disabled People; Parly. Under Sec. of State, Dept for Work and Pensions, 2005-08; Shadow Minister, Work and Pensions, 2011-; ***memberships:*** Fmr. Mem., Children's Panel; ***professional career:*** Dep. Dir., Scottish Cncl. of Voluntary Organisations, Edinburgh; ***committees:*** Public Accounts, 2010-11; ***recreations:*** cooking, reading; ***office address:*** House of Commons, London, SW1 0AA, United Kingdom; ***phone:*** +44 (0)20 7219 5014; ***e-mail:*** anne.mcguire.mp@parliament.uk; ***URL:*** http://www.annemcguiremp.org.uk.

MCINTOSH, Anne; British, Shadow Minister for Education, House of Commons; ***born:*** 20 September 1954, Edinburgh; ***parents:*** Alistair Ballingall McIntosh and Grete-Lise McIntosh (née Thomsen); ***married:*** John Harvey, 19 September 1992; ***public role of spouse:*** Insurance Executive; ***languages:*** Danish, French, German, Spanish, Italian; ***education:*** Harrogate Coll., Yorkshire, 1964-73; Univ. of Edinburgh, LL.B (Hons.), 1973-77; Univ. of Aarhus, Denmark, European Economic Law, 1977-78; Trained at the Scottish Bar, 1980-82, admitted to the Faculty of Advocates, Edinburgh, 1982; ***party:*** Conservative Party; ***political career:*** Mem. Exec. Cncl. of British Conservative Assn. in Belgium, 1987-89; MEP North East Essex, 1989-94; Mem., EP delegation with Norway, 1989-94, Asst. EDG Whip, 1989-92; Pres., Anglia Enterprise in Europe, 1988-99 & Yorkshire First, 1996-; Mem., EP delegation with Poland, 1994-97; Chwmn., EP delegation with Norway, 1994-95; Fellow, Industry and Parliament Trust, BP Plc., 1992-94; Elected to Bureau, British Section, EPP, 1994-97, Parly. Cttee., Czech Republic, 1997-99; MEP, North Essex & South Suffolk, 1994-99; MP, Vale of York, 1997-; Shadow DCMS Spokesman, 2001-02; Shadow Minister for Transport, 2002-03; Shadow Minister for Env. & Transport, 2003-05; Shadow Minister for Work and Pensions, 2005-06; Shadow Minister for Education, with responsiblity for Children, Young People and Families, 2001-07; Shadow Minister for Environment, 2007-; ***interests:*** transport, tourism, legal affairs, animal welfare, Scandinavia, Central and Eastern Europe; ***memberships:*** Yorkshire Agricultural Soc. & Anglo-Danish Soc.; Nat. Eye Research (Yorkshire) Advisory Bd.; ***professional career:*** Trainee with EC Cmn., Brussels, 1978; Legal Adviser, Didier & Assocs., 1979-80; Advocate with European Community Law Office, Belmont, Brussels, 1982-83; Political Adviser, European Democratic Gp., EP, 1983-89; ***committees:*** Mem., European Scrutiny Cttee., 1999-2003; Exec., the 1922 Cttee., 2000-01; Transport Select Cttee., 2003-05; Vice Chmn., All Party Parly. Gp. on Aviation; Chmn., All Party Trans European Network and Infrastructure Gp.; Chmn., All Party Bristish South Africa Gp.; Vice Chmn., All Party Gp. on Diabetes; Select Cttee. on Environment, Family and Food, 2008-; Vice-Chmn., Commonwealth Parliamentary Assn.; Liaison, 2010-; ***trusteeships:*** Patron, Thirsk Museum Soc.; ***honours and awards:*** Hon. Doctorate of Law, Anglia Polytechnic Univ., 1997; ***recreations:*** swimming, reading, cinema; ***office address:*** House of Commons, London, SW1A 0AA, United Kingdom; ***phone:*** +44 (0)20 7219 3541; ***fax:*** +44 (0)20 7219 0972; ***e-mail:*** mcintosha@parliament.uk.

Mck-Mea

MCKECHIN, Ann; MP for Glasgow North, House of Commons; ***born:*** 22 April 1961, Johnstone, Scotland; ***parents:*** William McKechin (dec'd) and Anne McKechin; ***education:*** Sacred Heart High Sch., Paisley; Paisley Grammar Sch., Paisley; LLB, Scots Law, Strathclyde Univ.; ***party:*** Labour Party; ***political career:*** MP, Glasgow Maryhill, 2001-05; MP, Glasgow North, 2005-; Parliamentary Under Secretary of State, Scotland, 2008-10; Shadow Minister for Scotland, May-Oct. 2010; Shadow Secretary of State for Scotland, Oct. 2010-12; ***professional career:*** Solicitor, Partner, Pacitti Jones, Glasgow, 1990-2000; ***committees:*** Scottish Affairs, 2001-05; Standing Orders, 2001-10; Information, 2001-05; International Development, 2005-09, 2010; Business, Innovation and Skills, 2011-; Arms Export Controls, 2012-; ***office address:*** House of Commons, London, SW1A 0AA, United Kingdom; ***phone:*** +44 (0)20 7219 8239; ***fax:*** +44 (0)20 7219 1770; ***e-mail:*** ann.mckechin.mp@parliament.uk; ***URL:*** http://www.annmckechinmp.net.

MCKENZIE, Iain; MP for Inverclyde, British Government; ***born:*** 1959; ***party:*** Labour; ***political career:*** Leader, Inverclyde Council; MP for Inverclyde, June 2011-; ***committees:*** Scottish Affairs, 2011-; Environment, Food and Rural Affairs, 2012-; ***office address:*** House of Commons, London, SW1A 0AA, United Kingdom; ***phone:*** +44 (0)20 7219 3000.

MCKEON, Howard (Buck); American, Congressman, California 25th District, US House of Representatives; ***party:*** Republican; ***political career:*** Mem., US House of Representatives, 1992-; ***committees:*** House: Armed Services, Ranking mem., 2009, Chmn., 2011-; Education and the Workforce Cttee.; ***office address:*** House of Representatives, 436 Cannon House Street, Washington, DC 20515-6501, USA; ***phone:*** +1 202 224 3121.

MCKINLEY, Michael; Ambassador, US Embassy in Colombia; ***professional career:*** Dep. Chief of Mission, US Mission to the EU, Brussels, 2004-07; Amb. to Peru, 2007-10; Amb. to Colombia, 2010-; ***office address:*** US Embassy, Calle 22D Bis # 47-51 (Carrera 45 # 22D-45), Santafé de Bogotá, Colombia; ***phone:*** +57 1 315 0811; ***fax:*** +57 1 315 2197; ***URL:*** http://bogota.usembassy.gov.

MCKINNELL, Catherine; MP for Newcastle Upon Tyne North, House of Commons; ***education:*** University in Edinburgh; ***party:*** Labour; ***political career:*** MP for Newcastle Upon Tyne North, May 2010-; Shadow Solicitor General, Oct. 2010-11; Shadow Minister, Education, 2011-12; Shandow Chancellor, 2012-; ***committees:*** Political and Constitutional Reform, 2010; ***office address:*** House of Commons, London, SW1A 0AA, United Kingdom; ***phone:*** +44 (0)20 7219 3000; ***e-mail:*** catherine.mckinnell.mp@parliament.uk.

MCLACHLIN, The Rt. Hon. Beverley; Chief Justice, Supreme Court of Canada; ***education:*** Univ. of Alberta, Edmonton, B.A. (Hon.), 1965, M.A., 1968 and LL.B, 1968; ***professional career:*** Called to the Alberta Bar, 1969 and the British Columbia Bar, 1971; lawyer, Edmonton, Fort St. John and Vancouver, 1969-74; lecturer, Univ. of British Columbia, Fac. of Law, 1974-81; Judge, Vancouver County Court, 1981; Judge, British Columbia Supreme Court, 1981-85; Judge, British Columbia Court of Appeal, 1985-88; Chief Justice of the British Columbia Supreme Court, 1988-89; Supreme Court Judge, 1989-2000; Chief Justice of Canada, 2000-; ***committees:*** Chwmn., Canadian Judicial Council; Chwmn., Advisory Cncl. Order of Canada; Chwmn., Bd. of Governors, Nat. Judicial Instit. ; ***office address:*** Supreme Court of Canada, 301 Wellington Street, Ottawa, Ontario, K1A 0J1, Canada; ***URL:*** http://www.scc-csc.gc.ca.

MCLEOD, Bob; Premier, Government of Northwest Territories; ***education:*** BA, Univ. of Alberta, Canada; Honours Dip. in Administrative Management, Northern Alberta Inst. of Technology, Edmonton; ***political career:*** Premier, Minister of Executive, Minister of Aboriginal Affairs and Intergovernmental Relations, Minister Responsible for Women and Minister Responsible for New Energy Initiatives, 2011-; ***office address:*** Office of the Premier, PO Box 466, Fort Simpson, NWT, X0E 0N0, Canada; ***phone:*** +1 867 669 2311; ***fax:*** +1 867 873 0169; ***URL:*** http://www.premier.gov.nt.ca.

MCLETCHIE, David, MSP; MSP for Edinburgh Pentlands, Scottish Parliament; ***born:*** 6 August 1952, Edinburgh, Scotland; ***parents:*** James Watson McLetchie and Catherine Alexander McLetchie (née Gray); ***married:*** Sheila Elizabeth McLetchie (née Foster), 4 July 1998; ***children:*** James (M); ***education:*** George Heriot's Sch.; Edinburgh Univ.; ***party:*** Conservative Party; ***political career:*** MSP, Lothians, 1999-2003; MSP, Edinburgh Pentlands, 2003- ; ***interests:*** home affairs, education; ***memberships:*** Law Soc. of Scotland; ***professional career:*** Solicitor, 1976-2005; ***clubs:*** New Club, Edinburgh; Bruntsfield Links Golfing Soc.; ***recreations:*** golf, watching football; ***office address:*** Scottish Parliament, Edinburgh, EH99 1SP, United Kingdom; ***phone:*** +44 (0)131 348 5659; ***fax:*** +44 (0)131 348 5935.

MCLOUGHLIN, Rt. Hon. Patrick Allan; British, Secretary of State for Transport, UK Government; ***born:*** 1957; ***education:*** Staffs. Coll. of Agriculture; ***party:*** Conservative Party; ***political career:*** Mem., Cannock Chase District Council, 1980-87; Mem., Staffordshire County Council, 1981-87; MP, West Derbyshire, 1986-2010, Derbyshire Dales, 2010-; PPS to Mrs Angela Rumbold, 1987-88, and to the Rt Hon Lord Young of Graffham, 1988-89; Parly. Under-Sec. of State for Transport, 1989-92; Under-Sec. of State, Dept. of Employment, 1992-93; Parly. Under-Sec. of State, Dept. of Trade and Industry, 1993-94; Asst. Govt. Whip, 1995; Lord Cmnr. to the Treasury, 1996-97; Opposition Chief Whip in the House of Commons, 2005-10; appointed to Privy Council, May 2005; Parliamentary Secretary to the Treasury 2010-12; Chief Whip 2010-12; Secretary of State for Transport, 2012-; ***professional career:*** Farmer; Coal Miner; ***committees:*** Jt. Secy., Conservative Back Bench Environment Cttee. 1986-88; Mem., National Heritage Select Cttee., 1994; ***office address:*** Department for Transport, Local Government and the Regions, Eland House, Bressenden Place, London, SW1E 5DU, United Kingdom; ***phone:*** +44 (0)20 7219 3000; ***e-mail:*** hcinfo@parliament.uk; ***URL:*** http://www.detr.gov.uk.

MCLUCAS, Jan; Minister for Human Services, Government of Australia; ***political career:*** Shadow Minister; Parliamentary Secretary, 2007-13; Minister for Human Services, 2013-; ***recreations:*** Senator for Queensland; ***office address:*** The Department Human Services, Parliament House, Canberra, ACT 2600, Australia.

MCMURDO, Hon. Justice Margaret A.; President, Court of Appeal, Queensland Supreme Court; ***married:*** Justice Philip McMurdo; ***s:*** 3; ***d:*** 1; ***public role of spouse:*** Judge of the Queensland Supreme Court; ***education:*** Univ. of Queensland, LL.B, 1975; Barrister at law, 1976; ***memberships:*** Women Lawyers Assoc. of Queensland; Australian Institute of Judicial Administration; Australian Judicial Conference; International Assoc. of Women Judges; National Trust of Queensland; Nundah & District Historical Society; ***professional career:*** Clerk, District Court, 1975-; Barrister, Public Defender's Office, 1976-89; Associate, Family Court, 1976; Barrister in private practice, 1989-91; Judge of the District Courts, Queensland, 1991-98; President of the Court of Appeal, Supreme Court of Queensland, 1998; ***clubs:*** Zonta Club of Brisbane; ***recreations:*** visual and performing arts; ***office address:*** P.O. Box 15167, City East, Queensland 4002, Australia; ***phone:*** +61 7 3247 9214.

MCNALLY, Lord, Baron Tom, Life Peer; British, Member, House of Lords; ***born:*** 20 February 1943; ***parents:*** John McNally and Elizabeth McNally (née McCarthy); ***married:*** Eileen Powell, 1970 (Diss); Juliet Hutchinson, 1990; ***children:*** John (M), James (M), Imogen (F); ***education:*** Coll. of St. Joseph, Blackpool; University Coll., London, BSc (Econ.), 1966; Fellow, Univ. Coll., London, 1995; ***party:*** Labour Party; Social Democratic Party, 1981-88; Liberal Democrats, 1988-; ***political career:*** Research Asst., Labour Party, 1967-69; Head of Int. Dept., Labour Party, 1969-74; Political Sec. FCO, 1974-76; Head of Political Office, 10 Downing Street, 1976-79; MP (Lab.) for Stockport South, 1979-83; Mem., House of Lords, 1995-; Dep. Leader, Liberal Democrats, House of Lords, 2001-04, then Leader of Liberal Democrats, House of Lords, 2004-; Lib. Dem. Spokesperson for Constitutional Affairs, 2006-10; Minister of State, Ministry of Justice, May 2010-; Dep. Leader, House of Lords, 2010-; ***memberships:*** Fellow, Inst. of Public Relations (FIPR); Dir., (non-exec.), Governing Bd. of Moody Int. Quality Certification, 1998-; ***professional career:*** Pres., University Coll., London Union, 1965-68; Asst. Gen.-Sec., Fabian Soc., 1966-67; Special Adviser, Foreign & Commonwealth Office, 1974-76; Public Affairs Adviser GEC, 1983-84; Dir.-Gen., British Retail Consortium, 1985-87; Head of Public Affairs, Hill and Knowlton (UK), 1987-93; Head of Public Affairs, Shandwick (UK), 1993-96; Vice-Chmn., Weber Shandwick, 1996-2004; ***honours and awards:*** Fellow, Industry and Parl. Trust; Fellow, Inst. of Public Relations; Fellow, 48 Grp. China Trade Clubs, 2003; Fellow, Univ. Coll., London; Member of the Privy Council, 2004; ***recreations:*** watching sport; ***office address:*** House of Lords, London, SW1A 0AA, United Kingdom; ***phone:*** +44 (0)20 7219 5443; ***e-mail:*** mcnallyt@parliament.uk.

MCNERNEY, Jerry; Congressman, Calif. Dist. 11, US House of Representatives; ***education:*** PhD in mathematics; ***party:*** Democrat; ***political career:*** Mem., US HOR, 2007-; ***professional career:*** National security contractor, Sandia National Laboratories, New Mexico; Senior Engineer, US Windpower, Kenetech; Energy consultant, PG&E, FloWind, the Electric Power Research Institute; CEO, wind turbine manufacturing company, to 2006; ***committees:*** HOR Cttees: Science, Space and Technology; Veterans Affairs; ***office address:*** House of Representatives, 312 Cannon House Office Building, Washington, DC 20515, USA; ***phone:*** +1 202 225 1947.

MCPARTLAND, Stephen; MP for Stevenage, UK Government; ***education:*** BA (Hons) in History; MSc in Technology Management; ***party:*** Conservative; ***political career:*** MP for Stevenage, May 2010-; ***committees:*** Science and Technology, 2011-12; ***office address:*** House of Commons, London, SW1A 0AA, United Kingdom; ***phone:*** +44 (0)20 7219 3000; ***e-mail:*** stephen.mcpartland.mp@parliament.uk.

MCVEY, Esther; MP for Wirral West, UK Government; ***born:*** 1967; ***education:*** MSc., Corporate Governance, Liverpool John Moores Univ., Winner of the North Award for Excellence for her studies; ***party:*** Conservative; ***political career:*** MP for Wirral West, May 2010-; PPS, to Chris Grayling MP, Minister for Employment, 2010-12; Parly. Under-Sec. of State, Dept. of Works and Pensions, 2012-; ***professional career:*** Broadcaster and Businesswoman; Founder, business women's network 'Winning Women'; Established co-operative office and incubator space for new start up businesses; Author, 'If Chloe Can', a school girls career book, distributed for free to girls on Merseyside; Chair, APPG Chemical Industry Association; ***office address:*** House of Commons, London, SW1A 0AA, United Kingdom; ***phone:*** +44 (0)20 7219 3000; ***e-mail:*** esther.mcvey.mp@parliament.uk.

MEAD, Matt; Governor, Government of Wyoming; ***education:*** Trinity Univ.; Univ. of Wyoming, law; ***party:*** Republican; ***political career:*** Governor, Wyoming, 2010-; ***professional career:*** county and federal prosecutor; US Attorney for Wyoming, 2001-07; Rancher; ***office address:*** Office of the Governor, State Capitol, Room 124, Cheyenne, WY 82002, USA; ***URL:*** http://governor.wy.gov/.

MEADE KURIBRENA, José Antonio; Secretary of Foreign Affairs, Government of Mexico; ***born:*** 1969; ***education:*** National Univ. of Mexico, BA, Law; Univ. of Yale, Ph.D, economics; ***political career:*** Secretary of Finance and Public Credit; Energy Sec.; Secretary of Foreign Affairs; ***professional career:*** Banking; ***office address:*** Secretariat of Foreign Affairs, Plaza Juarez 20, piso 22, Col. Centro. Del. Cuahutémoc, C.P. 06010, Mexico Df., Mexico; ***phone:*** +52 55 36866036; ***fax:*** +52 55 36866042; ***URL:*** http://www.sre.gob.mx/.

MEALE, (Joseph) Alan, MP; British, Member of Parliament for Mansfield, House of Commons; ***born:*** 31 July 1949, Bishop Auckland, County Durham; ***parents:*** Albert Meale and Elizabeth Meale (née Catchpole); ***married:*** Diana Meale (née Gilhespy), 1983; ***education:*** St Joseph's RC Sch., Bishop Auckland; Durham Univ.; Ruskin Coll., Oxford; Sheffield Hallam Univ.; ***party:*** Labour Party; ***political career:*** Nat. Employment Dev. Officer, NACRO, 1977-80; Asst. to Gen. Sec., ASLEF, 1979-84; Parly. and Political Adviser to Michael Meacher MP, 1984-87; Shadow Sec. of State for Health, Social Services and Social Security, 1984-87; MP for Mansfield, 1987-; Front Bench Labour Whip (Responsibilities Transport, Social Security and Home Affairs), 1992-94; PPS to Rt. Hon. John Prescott MP 1994-97; Parly. Court of Referees, 1997-; ***interests:*** human rights, drug misuse, sports, Europe, music, unemployment, media, transport, health, social security and home affairs, environment and animal welfare; ***memberships:*** mem., Cncl. of Europe & Western European Union 1999-; Official Rapporteur, Cnl. of Europe, Kyoto Protocol, 2001-; Vice Chmn. Cnl. of Europe Cttee., Sustainable Development, 2002-; Official Rapporteur, Western European Union, Petersburg Tasks, 2001-; Sr. First Vice-pres., Cncl. of Europe Env., Agriculture, Local and Regional Democracy; Fellow and Postgraduate Fellow of the Industry and Parly. Trust;

BIOGRAPHIES

mem., COE Environment Cttee, 2008-10; ***professional career:*** Author; Editor; Dev. Officer; Trade Union Official; Researcher; Political Adviser; Journalist; Cmnr., War Grave Cmn., 2002-; Dir., Portland Training Coll., Mansfield; Chmn., Stags Community Trust, 2002-; ***committees:*** Exec. Inter Parly. Union & Cmmw. Parly. Assoc.; Treas., Cmmw. Parly. Assn. Cyprus (UK) Gp.; Sec., All-Party Animal Welfare Gp.; Sec., Parly. All-Party Greyhound Gp.; Parly. Racing and Bloodstocks Gp.; Former Mem., European Legislation Select Cttee.; Former Mem., Home Affairs Select Cttee.; Ex-Vice-Chmn., PLP Employment Cttee.; Jt. Sec., All-Party Cults Cttee.; Chmn., British Cyprus Cttee.; Vice-Chmn., Parly. Ukraine Cttee.; Founder and Chmn., Parly. Beer Industries Cttee.; Chmn., PLP East Midlands and Central Gps., 1988-95; Parly. Rep., SSAFA (Armed Forces Social Welfare Organisation), 1989-95; War Pensions Bd., 1989-97; Home Affairs, 1990-92, Court of Referees, 1999-2001; Crossrail Bill, 2006-07; Panel of Chairs, 2011-; ***honours and awards:*** Hon. Citizenship of Morphou, Cyprus, Mansfield, USA; Hon. Senatorship of Louisiana, USA; ***publications:*** Author of various publications; ***recreations:*** reading, writing, music, arts, politics, Cyprus, sports and Mansfield Town F.C.; ***office address:*** 85 West Gate, Mansfield, Notts., NG18 1RT, United Kingdom; ***phone:*** +44 (0)1623 660531; ***fax:*** +44 (0)1623 420495; ***e-mail:*** enquiries@alanmeale.co.uk; ***URL:*** http://www.alanmeale.co.uk.

MEARNS, Ian; MP for Gateshead, UK Government; ***party:*** Labour; ***political career:*** Councillor, Gateshead Council, 1983-; MP for Gateshead, May 2010-; PPS to Ivan Lewis, 2011-; ***committees:*** Education Select Cttee., 2010-; Backbench Business, 2010-; ***office address:*** House of Commons, London, SW1A 0AA, United Kingdom; ***phone:*** +44 (0)20 7219 3000; ***e-mail:*** ian.mearns.mp@parliament.uk.

MEDELCI, Mourad; Minister of Foreign Affairs, Algerian Government; ***education:*** Univ. of Algiers, Econ., 1966, Doctorate in Econ., 1968; INSEE, Paris, 1969; ***political career:*** Minister of Trade, 1988-89, 1999-2001; Minister of the Budget, 1990-91; Minister of Finance, 2001-02, 2005-07; Presidential Advisor, 2001-05; Minister of Foreign Affairs, 2007-; ***office address:*** Ministry of Foreign Affairs, 1 Rue Ibn Batrane, El-Mouradia, Algiers, Algeria; ***phone:*** +213 (0)21 692333; ***fax:*** +213 (0)21 692161; ***URL:*** http://www.mae.dz.

MEDINA, Danillo; President, Government of the Dominican Republic; ***born:*** 1950; ***education:*** Instituto Tecnológico Santo Domingo (INTEC), (economics); ***party:*** Dominican Liberation Party; ***political career:*** Pres. of the Chamber of Deputies, 1994-95; Sec. of State of the Presidency, 1996-99, 2004-08; President, 2012-; ***office address:*** Office of the Presidency, Calle Moisés García, Santo Domingo, Dominican Republic; ***phone:*** +1 829 695 8000; ***fax:*** +1 829 688 2100; ***e-mail:*** prensa@presidencia.gov.do; ***URL:*** http://www.presidencia.gov.do.

MEDINA-MORA ICAZA, Eduardo; Ambassador, Embassy of Mexico in Washington; ***born:*** 30 January 1957, Federal District; ***education:*** Univ. Nacional Automoma de Mexico (UNAM), Law; ***political career:*** Coordinator of Advisores to the Undersec. of Fisheries; Legal Advisor to the National Board of Agriculture and Fisheries, and National Advisor to Coordinating Entrepreneurial Board; Attorney General, 2006-09; ***professional career:*** Amb. to the UK, 2009-12; Amb. to the US, 2012-; ***office address:*** Embassy of Mexico, 1911 Pennsylvania Ave, NW, Washington DC 20006, USA; ***fax:*** +44 (020) 7495 4035.

MEDVEDEV, Dmitry; Chair of the Council of Ministers, Government of the Russian Federation; ***born:*** 14 September 1965, Leningrad, Russian Federation; ***married:*** Svetlana Medvedev; ***children:*** Ilya (M); ***education:*** PhD (private law), Leningrad State Univ. (now called St. Petersburg State Univ.); ***political career:*** Consultant to Mayor of St Petersburg, 1990-95; Dep. Kremlin Chief of Staff, 1999-2003; Chief of Staff to President Putin, 2003-05; First Dep. Prime Minister in charge of social programmes, 2005-08; Pres.elect, March-May 2008, Pres., Russian Federation, May 2008-May 2012; Chair of the Council of Ministers, 2012-; ***professional career:*** Lecturer, St. Petersburg State Univ. 1991-99; Chmn., Gazprom, 2002-08; ***office address:*** Office of the Prime Minister, Krasnopresnenskaya 2, 103274 Moscow, Russian Federation; ***e-mail:*** president@gov.ru; ***URL:*** http://www.government.ru.

MEEHAN, Patrick; Congressman, Pennsylvania, 7th District, US House of Representatives; ***party:*** Republican; ***political career:*** Congressman, Pennsylvania, 7th District, 2011-; ***professional career:*** Lawyer; District Attorney of Delaware County; United States Attorney for the Eastern District of Pennsylvania; ***committees:*** House Cttees., Oversight and Government Reform; Homeland Security; Transportation and Infrastructure; ***office address:*** House of Representatives, 513 Cannon HOB, Washington DC 20515, USA; ***phone:*** +1 202 225 2011 .

MELROSE, H.M. Dianna; British High Commissioner, UK High Commission in Tanzania; ***born:*** Bulawayo, Zimbabwe; ***education:*** King's College, London, BA, Spanish and French; London Univ., MA, Latin American Studies, 1974; ***professional career:*** C.E. Heath & Co (Latin America) Ltd, 1975-78; British Council, 1978-79; Oxfam, 1980-98 (Policy Advisor, 1980-84, Head of Public Affairs Unit, 1984-92, Policy Director, 1993-98); joined FCO, Dep. Head of Policy Planning Staff, 1999-2000; Head of Policy Planning Staff, FCO, 2000-02; Head, Extractive Industries Transparency Initiative, Dpt. for Int'l. Development (DfID), 2002; Hd,, Int'l. Trade Dpt., DFID, 2003-06; Hd., Enlargement & SE Europe Grp., Europe Directorate, FCO, 2006-08; Amb. to Cuba, 2008-12; High Commissioner to Tanzania, 2012-; ***office address:*** British High Commission, PO Box 9200, Umoja House, Mirambo Street, Garden Avenue, Dar es Salaam, Tanzania; ***phone:*** +255 22 229 0000; ***e-mail:*** bhc.dar@fco.gov.uk; ***URL:*** http://www.britishembassy.gov.uk/cuba.

MENAN, Kodjo; Permanent Represent of Togo, United Nations; ***education:*** Univ. of Benin, Masters in Law; National Administration School of Lomé, Togo, Post-Grad. degree in Diplomacy; ***professional career:*** joined MFA, 1991; Most recently: Chargé d'affaires ai, Permanent Mission of Togo to the UN, 2002-07; Perm. Sec. of the Ministry of Foreign Affairs and Integration, 2007-09; Amb., Permanent Rep. of Togo to the UN, 2009-; ***office address:*** Permanent Mission of Togo to the UN, 112 East, 40th Street, New York, NY 10016, USA; ***phone:*** +1 656 502 8654; ***URL:*** http://www.untogo.org/.

MENENDEZ, Senator Robert; American, Senator for New Jersey, US Senate; ***born:*** 1 January 1954, New York City, NY, US; ***political career:*** NJ State Assembly, 1987-91; NJ State Senate, 1991-92; Congressman, New Jersey 13th District, US House of Representatives, 1992-06; House Democratic Caucus Chairman, 2002-06; US Senator, 2006-; ***committees:*** Senate Cttees. on Banking; Finance; Foreign Relations; ***office address:*** US Senate, 502 Hart Senate Office Building, Washington, DC 20510, USA; ***phone:*** +1 202 224 4744; ***URL:*** http://www.menendez.senate.gov.

MENZIES, Mark; MP for Fylde, UK Government; ***party:*** Conservative; ***political career:*** MP for Fylde, May 2010-; PPS, 2010-; ***committees:*** Scottish Affairs Select Cttee., 2010; ***office address:*** House of Commons, London, SW1A 0AA, United Kingdom; ***phone:*** +44 (0)20 7219 3000; ***e-mail:*** mark.menzies.mp@parliament.uk.

MENZIES, Ted; Minister of State for Finance, Government of Canada; ***born:*** 1952; ***political career:*** MP for Macleod, Alberta, 2004-; Parly. Sec. to the Minister of International Trade and to the Minister of International Cooperation, 2007; Parly. Sec. to the Minister of Finance, 2007-11; Minister of State for Finance, 2011-; ***professional career:*** Farmer; ***office address:*** House of Commons, Parliament Buildings, Wellington Street, Ottawa, Ontario K1A 0H8, Canada; ***phone:*** +1 613 943 5959; ***fax:*** +1 613 992 3674; ***URL:*** http://www.parl.gc.ca.

MEREDOV, Rashid; Deputy Chair and Minister of Foreign Affairs, Government of Turkmenistan; ***born:*** 1960; ***education:*** Moscow State Univ., law; ***political career:*** chief consultant, Ministry of Justice; head, law enforcing agencies, Office of the President of Turkmenistan, 1991; Head, Law Dept., Office of the President, 1993; Chmn., Law Cttee., Mejlis Turkmenistan, 1994; Dep. Dir., Turkmen National Inst. of Democracy & Human Rights, 1996; First Dep. Min. of Foreign Affairs, 1999; First Dep. Chairman, Mejlis of Turkemnistan, 1999, Chmn., 2001; Minister of Foreign Affairs of Turkmenistan, 2001; Dep. Chmn., Cabinet of Ministers, 2003-05; Deputy Chair and Minister of Foreign Affairs, 2007-; ***professional career:*** lecturer, civil law, Turkmen State Univ.; ***office address:*** Ministry of Foreign Affairs, pr. Makhtumkuli 83, Ashkhabad, Turkmenistan.

MERENTES, Nelson; Minister of Finance, Government of Venezuela; ***born:*** 1954; ***education:*** Mathematics, Ph.D; ***political career:*** Minister of Finance, 2001-02; Minister of Science and Technology, 2002-03; Minister of Finance, 2004-07; Minister of Planning & Finance, 2012-; ***professional career:*** Univ. Professor; Economist; Head, Central Bank of Venezuela; ***office address:*** Ministry of Finance, Edf Norte, piso 3 oficina 312, Centro Simón Bolívar, Caracas 1010, Venezuela; ***phone:*** +58 212 419406; ***fax:*** +58 212 481 5953; ***URL:*** http://www.mh.gov.ve.

MERKEL, Dr Angela; German, Chancellor, German Government; ***born:*** 17 July 1954, Hamburg, Germany; ***education:*** Univ. of Leipzig, degree in physics, 1973-78; Dr.rer.nat., 1986; ***party:*** CDU, 1990-; Leader, CDU, 2000-; ***political career:*** Mem., Democratic Awakening (DA), 1989; Press Spokeswoman for the DA, Dep. Press Spokeswoman, Govt. de Maiziere, 1990; Mem., CDU, 1990; Mem., Bundestag, 1990-; Minister for Women and Youth, 1991-94; Nat. Vice-Chwn., CDU, 1991-; Minister of the Environment, Nature Conservation and Nuclear Safety, 1994-98; Chwn., CDU; Chancellor, Nov. 2005-; ***professional career:*** Employed in the field of quantum chemistry, Central Inst. of Physical Chemistry, Acad. of Sciences, Berlin, 1978-90; ***publications:*** Der Preis des Überlebens. Gedanken und Gespräche über zukünftige Aufgaben der Umweltpolitik (The price of Survival: ideas and conversations about future tasks for environmental policy) 1997; ***recreations:*** reading, hiking, gardening; ***office address:*** Federal Chancellery, Willy-Brandt Strasse 1, 10557 Berlin, Germany; ***phone:*** +49 (0)30 18 40000; ***fax:*** +49 (0)30 18 400 2357; ***e-mail:*** angela.merkel@cdu.de.

MERKELY, Senator Jeff; Senator for Oregon, US Senate; ***education:*** Stanford Univ., International Relations; Princeton's Woodrow Wilson School of Public and International Affairs, Public Policy; ***political career:*** State Rep.,1998-09, Democratic Leader, 2003, Speaker, 2007; Senator for Oregon, 2009-; ***professional career:*** Nat. security analyst, Pentagon and Congressional Budget Office; Habitat for Humanity, Portland, Oregon, 1991; Dir. of Housing Development, Human Solutions; Pres., Oregon World Affairs Council; ***committees:*** Appropriations; Banking, Housing & Urban Affairs; Environment and Public Works; Budget; ***office address:*** US Senate, 313 Hart Senate Office Building, Washington DC 20510, USA; ***phone:*** +1 202 224 3753; ***e-mail:*** merkley.senate.gov/contact; ***URL:*** http://www.merkley.senate.gov/.

MERON, Judge Theodor; American, President, International Criminal Tribunal Yugoslavia; ***born:*** 28 April 1930; ***languages:*** English, French, Hebrew, Polish; ***education:*** Hebrew University, Jerusalem, MJ, 1954; Harvard, LLM, 1954, SJD, 1956; Legal qualification: Member of the Bar, New York State; ***interests:*** Armed conflict; Claims; Criminal Law; History & theory; Human rights; Organisations; State responsibility; Treaties; ***memberships:*** Institute of International Law; Council on Foreign Relations; ASIL; French Society of International Law; ILA, American Branch; AJIL, Co-Editor-in-Chief, 1993-98, now Honorary Editor; Board of Editors, Yearbook of International Humanitarian Law; ***professional career:*** *academic career:* New York University School of Law, Professor of International Law, 1977-, Charles L Denison Chair, 1994-78; Graduate Institute of International Studies, Geneva, Professor, 1991-95; Editor in Chief, AJIL, 1993-98; Visiting Professor at Harvard and at the University of California (Berkeley); Carnegie Lecturer, Hague Academy of International Law; Fellow, Rockefeller Foundation; Fellow, Max Planck Institute; Visiting Fellow, All Souls College, Oxford; Lectured at many universities and at the International Institute of Human Rights, Strasbourg; Helped establish the ICRC/Graduate Institute of International Studies seminars for University Professors on International Humanitarian Law; New York University, leads annual ICRC seminars for UN diplomats on International Humanitarian Law; Awarded 2004 Rule of Law Award by the IBA; Awarded 2006 Manley O Hudson Medal of the ASIL; *professional career:* Counselor on International Law, US Department of State; Served on advisory committees or boards of several human rights organisations, including Americas Watch and the International League for Human Rights; *diplomatic career:* Public Member of the US Delegation to the CSCE Conference on Human Dimensions, Copenhagen, 1990; Member of US Delegation to the Rome Conference on the Establishment of an ICC, 1998, involved in the drafting of the provisions on crimes, including war crimes and crimes against humanity; Served on preparatory commission for the establishment of the ICC, with particular responsibilities for the definition of the crime of aggression; Served on several committees of experts of the ICRC, including those on Internal Strife, on the Environment and Armed Conflicts, and on Direct Participation in Hostilities Under International Humanitarian Law;

Member of the steering committee of ICRC experts on Customary Rules of International Humanitarian Law; *judicial career:* Judge, ICTY, 2001-, President, 2003-05, 2011-; ***publications:*** Books: Investment Insurance in International Law, 1976; The United Nations Secretariat, 1977; Human Rights in International Law, 1984; Human Rights Law-Making in the United Nations, 1986; Human Rights in Internal Strife: Their International Protection, 1987; Human Rights and Humanitarian Norms as Customary Law, 1989; War Crimes Law Comes of Age: Essays, 1998; International Law in the age of Human Rights, 2004; The Humanization of International Law, 2006; Articles: Frequent contributor to the AJIL and other legal journals; ***office address:*** International Criminal Tribunal for the former Yugoslavia, Churchillplein 1, 2517 JW The Hague, The Netherlands; ***phone:*** +31 (0)70 512 8685.

MERSCH, Yves; Luxembourgeois, Member of the Executive Board, European Central Bank; ***born:*** 1 October 1949; ***professional career:*** admitted to the Bar, Luxembourg, 1974; Public Law Asst., Univ of Paris-South, 1974; Budget Asst., Min. of Finance, 1975; Asst., Int. Monetary Fund, Washington DC, USA, 1976-77; Min. of Finance, Fiscal Affairs and Structural Policies, 1977-80; Seconded to Min. of Foreign Affairs, UN Permanent Rep., New York, 1980; Advisor, Min. of Finance, Monetary Affairs and Int. Financial Relations, 1981; Govt. Cmnr., Luxembourg Stock Exchange, 1985; Dir., Treasury, 1989; Governor, Luxembourg Central Bank, 1998-2012; Mem., Governing Council of the European Central Bank (ECB), 2012-; ***office address:*** European Central Bank, Kaiserstrasse 29, D-60311 Frankfurt-am-Main, Germany; ***URL:*** http://www.ecb.int.

METCALFE, Stephen; MP for South Basildon and East Thurrock, UK Government; ***party:*** Conservative; ***political career:*** MP for South Basildon and East Thurrock, May 2010-; ***committees:*** Science and Technology Select Cttee., 2010-; ***office address:*** House of Commons, London, SW1A 0AA, United Kingdom; ***phone:*** +44 (0)20 7219 3000; ***e-mail:*** stephen.metcalfe.mp@parliament.uk.

MICA, John; American, Congressman, Florida Seventh District, US House of Representatives; ***born:*** 27 January 1943; ***married:*** Patricia S. Mica (née Szymanek), 1972; ***children:*** Clark (M), D'Anne (F); ***education:*** Univ. of Florida, BA; ***party:*** Rebublican; ***political career:*** Mem., US House of Representatives, 1992-; ***committees:*** Transportation and Infrastructure Cttees.; Chmn., Oversight and Government Reform; ***office address:*** House of Representatives, 436 Cannon House Street, Washington, DC 20515, USA; ***phone:*** +1 202 224 3121.

MICHEL, Alix James; President, Republic of Seychelles; ***born:*** 16 August 1944, Seychelles; ***parents:*** Simone Michel; ***married:*** Natalie Brigitte Nadège Michel (née Savvy); ***languages:*** English, French, Creole; ***education:*** Teacher Training Coll., Seychelles; ***party:*** Seychelles People's Progressive Front (SPPF); ***political career:*** mem., Exec. Cttee., Seychelles People's United Party (SPUP), predecessor of Seychelles People's Progressive Front (SPPF), 1974-77; Editor, The People; mem.,Central Exec. Cttee., SPPF. Dep. Sec. General, SPPF, 1984 and Sec.-Gen.,1994-; Minister of State, President's Office (Admin. and Information), 1977-79; Minister of Education and Information (Culture and Telecommunications), 1979-86; Minister of Education, Information and Youth (Culture and Sports), 1986-89; Minister of Finance, 1989-91; Minister of Finance and Information, 1991-93; First Designated Minister, Minister of Finance and Communications, Minister of Defence, 1993-96; Minister of Environment, 1996-98; Minister of Defence, Police and Risk and Disaster Management, 1996-2008; Minister of Finance and Communications, 1996-98; Vice Pres., Republic of Seychelles, 1996-98; Minister of Economic Planning, Minister of Environment and Transport, 1998-2004; Minister of Finance, 1998-2006; Minister of Internal Affairs, 1998-2007; Pres. 2006-; various portfolios, as of 2012: Defence, Legal Affairs, Information, Youth & Hydrocarbons; ***professional career:*** Seychelles Defence Forces, 1977-93; ***honours and awards:*** Outstanding Civilian Service Medal, US Army, 1995; ***recreations:*** reading, writing, poetry, aviation, photography; ***office address:*** Office of President, PO Box 55, State House, Victoria, Seychelles.

MIGUEL, Hon. Girlyn; Deputy Prime Minister and Minister of Education, Government of St. Vincent and the Grenadines; ***born:*** 1948; ***political career:*** MP, 1998-; Minister of Social Development, Family, Gender Affairs and Ecclesiastical Affairs, 2001-03; Minister of Agriculture, Lands and Fisheries, 2003-06; Minister of Education, 2006-, also Deputy Prime Minister, Dec. 2010-; ***office address:*** Ministry of Education, Government Buildings, Kingstown, St. Vincent and the Grenadines; ***phone:*** +1 784 456 1111.

MIKATI, Najib A.; Prime Minister, Government of Lebanon; ***born:*** 1955; ***education:*** MBA, American Univ. of Beirut; summer school programme, Harvard Univ. USA ; ***political career:*** Minister of Public Works and Transport, 1998-2004; Prime Minister, Apr. July 2005; Prime Minister, 2011-Apr. 2013; ***office address:*** Office of the Prime Minister, Council of Ministers, Al-Kasr Al-Houkoumi, Al-Sanayeh, Beirut, Lebanon.

MIKULSKI, Barbara Ann, BA; American, Democratic Conference Secretary, US Senate; ***born:*** 20 July 1936, Baltimore, MD, USA; ***parents:*** William Mikulski and Christine Mikulski (née Kutz); ***education:*** Inst. of Notre Dame, Baltimore, USA; Mt. St. Agnes Coll., Baltimore, BA, Sociology, 1958; Univ. of Maryland, Masters of Social Work, 1965; ***party:*** Democrat; ***political career:*** Baltimore City Cllr., 1971-76; US House of Reps., 1976-86; Senator for Maryland, US Senate, 1986-; Sec. of the Democratic Conference, US Senate, 1994-2004; ***professional career:*** Social Worker; ***committees:*** Health, Education, Labor and Pensions; Appropriations; Select Cttee. on Intelligence; ***honours and awards:*** Hon. LL.D, 1990; BETA Award, 1996; CREW Award, 1996; Most Trustworthy Politician, Baltimore Magazine, 1996; ***publications:*** Capitol Offense, 1996; Capitol Venture, 1997; Nine's Counting, 2000; ***office address:*** US Senate, 709 Hart Senate Office Building, Washington, DC 20510, USA; ***phone:*** +1 202 224 4654; ***URL:*** http://www.mikulski.senate.gov/.

MILAM TANG, Ignacio; Vice President, Government of Equatorial Guinea; ***born:*** June 1940; ***political career:*** Minister of Justice and Worship,1996-98; Minister of Youth and Sports, 1998-99; Second Vice-Pres. of the Chamber of People's Representatives; Dep. Prime Minister for the Civil Service and Administrative Coordination; Minister of State and Sec.-Gen. of the Presidency, 2003-06; Prime Minister, 2008-12; Vice President, 2012-; ***professional career:*** Amb. to Spain, 2006-08; ***office address:*** Office of the Vice President, Malabo, Equatorial Guinea; ***URL:*** http://www.guinea-equatorial.com.

MILANOVIC, Zoran; Prime Minister, Government of Croatia; ***born:*** 1966; ***languages:*** English, French, Russian; ***education:*** Univ. of Zagreb, Law Degree; ***party:*** Social Democratic Party of Croatia; ***political career:*** Prime Minister, Dec. 2011-; ***professional career:*** Diplomat; ***office address:*** Office of the Prime Minister, Trg Sv. Marka 2, Zagreb, Croatia; ***phone:*** +385 (0)1 456 9201.

MILIBAND, Ed; Leader of Her Majesty's Official Opposition, House of Commons; ***born:*** 1969; ***married:*** Justine Thornton, May 27 2011; ***s:*** 2; ***public role of spouse:*** Environmental Lawyer; ***party:*** Labour; ***political career:*** MP for Doncaster North, 2005-; Chancellor of the Duchy of Lancaster, Minister for the Cabinet Office, June 2007-Oct. 2008; Sec. of State for Energy and Climate Change, Oct, 2008-May 2010; Shadow Secretary of State for Energy and Climate Change, May 2010-Sept. 2010; Leader of Her Majesty's Official Opposition, Sept. 2010-; ***office address:*** House of Commons, London, SW1A 0AA, United Kingdom; ***e-mail:*** ed.miliband.mp@parliament.uk.

MILLER, Andrew; British, Member of Parliament for Ellesmere Port and Neston, House of Commons; ***born:*** 23 March 1949, Middlesex; ***education:*** LSE, Diploma, Industrial Relations; ***party:*** Labour Party, 1968-; ***political career:*** MP, Ellesmere Port and Neston, 1992-; Pres., Computing for Labour, 1993; Dir. of EURIM (European Informatics Market), 1994-98; Cncl. Mem. of EURIM, 1997-98; Chmn., Leadership Campaign Team, 1997-98; PPS, Dep. Trade and Industry, 2001-05; Chmn., NW Parliamentary Labour Party, 2001; Mem. the First Steps Team working with foreign office to promote relations with EU & prospective EU member states, specific responsibility for Hungary and Malta; ***interests:*** regional economy, occupational pensions, international trade union co-operation, science, communications information technology, environment, industry; ***memberships:*** Scientists for Labour, 1994-; Fabian Society; Action for Southern Africa (ACTSA), and previously Anti-Apartheid, 1992-; Honorary Life Mem., League Against Cruel Sports, 2000-; ***professional career:*** Technician, Dep. of Geology, Portsmouth Polytechnic, 1967-76; Trade Union Official, MSF, 1977-92; Dir., EURIM, 1994-98; ***committees:*** The Information Cttee., 1992-2001; Science and Technology Select Cttee., 1992-97; Vice-Chmn., Parliamentary Cttee., Science and Technology and Bd. Mem., Paliamentary Office of Science and Technology (POST); Parliamentary Labour Party Departmental Cttee. on Employment, 1994-; Parliamentary Labour Party Dep. Cttee on Environment, 1994-; Joint Vice-Chmn., Parliamentary Info.Technology Cttee., 1997-2005; Treasurer, Parliamentary and Scientific Cttee., 1997-00, and Vice-Pres., 2000-03; Joint human rights Cttee., 2001; Chmn., Parly. Information Technology Cttee., 2010-; Chmn., Regulatory Reform Select Cttee., 2005-10; Mem., Liaison Cttee., 2005-; Mem., Jt. Cttee. on Conventions, 2006-; Chmn., Parly. and Scientific Cttee., 2010-; Chair, Science & Technology Select Cttee, 2010-; ***trusteeships:*** Patron, Roadpeace, Chester Childbirth Trust, Parents Against Drug Abuse, 1994-; ***honours and awards:*** Officer's Cross of the Order of Merit of the Rep. of Hungary; ***publications:*** Information and Communication Technology Tools for Better Government, commissioned by the Cabinet Office Minister in prep. for Modernising Govt. White Paper; ***recreations:*** music, photography, tennis, cricket; ***office address:*** House of Commons, London, SW1A 0AA, United Kingdom; ***phone:*** +44 (0)20 7219 3796; ***e-mail:*** millera@parliament.uk; ***URL:*** http://www.andrew-miller-mp.co.uk.

MILLER, Candice S.; Congresswoman, Michigan 10th District, US House of Representatives; ***party:*** Republican Party; ***political career:*** Macomb County Treasurer; Michigan Secretary of State (two terms); Congresswoman, Michigan 10th District, US House of Representatives, 2002-; ***committees:*** House Adminstration, Chmn.; Homeland Security; Transportation and Infrastructure; ***office address:*** US House of Representatives, 508 Cannon House Office Building, Washington, DC 20515, USA.

MILLER, Gary; American, Congressman, California 42nd District, US House of Representatives; ***born:*** Arkansas, US; ***party:*** Republican Party; ***political career:*** CA State Assembly, 1995-98; Freshman Whip; US, House of Representatives, 1998-; ***committees:*** Financial Affairs Cttee.; Transportation and Infrastructure Cttee.; ***office address:*** House of Representatives, 436 Cannon House Building, Washington, DC 20515-6501, USA; ***phone:*** +1 202 224 3121.

MILLER, George; American, Congressman, California Seventh District, US House of Representatives; ***party:*** Democrat; ***political career:*** Mem., US House of Representatives, 1975-; ***committees:*** House Education and the Workforce Cttee.; ***office address:*** House of Representatives, 436 Cannon House Street, Washington, DC 20515-6501, USA; ***phone:*** +1 202 224 3121.

MILLER, Jeff; Congressman, Florida First District, US House of Representatives; ***party:*** Republican Party; ***political career:*** Congressman, Florida First District, US House of Representatives; ***committees:*** Armed Services; Chmn.,Veterans' Affairs; Permanent Select Cttee. on Intelligence; ***office address:*** House of Representatives, 436 Cannon House Street, Washington DC 20515-6501, USA; ***phone:*** +1 202 224 3121.

MILLER, Maria; Secretary of State for Culture, Olympics, Media and Sport; and Minister for Women and Equalities, House of Commons; ***born:*** 1964; ***party:*** Conservative; ***political career:*** MP for Basingstoke, 2005-; Shadow Minister for: Education, 2005-06, Family Welfare, 2006-07, Families, 2007-10; Parliamentary Under-Secretary of State (Minister for Disabled People), Department for Work and Pensions, 2010-12; Secretary of State for Culture, Olympics, Media and Sport; and Minister for Women and Equalities, 2012-; ***office address:*** Department of Culture, Media and Sport, 2-4 Cockspur Street, London, SW1Y 5DH, United Kingdom; ***phone:*** +44 (0)20 7211 6200; ***fax:*** +44 (0)20 7211 6210; ***URL:*** http://www.culture.gov.uk.

MILLETT, H.E. Peter; Ambassador, British Embassy in Jordan; ***professional career:*** British High Commissioner to Cyprus, 2005-10; Amb. to Jordan, 2010-; ***office address:*** British Embassy, PO Box 87, Abdoun, Amman, Jordan; ***phone:*** +962 6 592 3100; ***URL:*** http://ukinjordan.fco.gov.uk/.

MILLS, Karen; Administrator, Small Business Administration; ***education:*** Harvard Univ., AB, economics; Harvard Business School, MBA; ***political career:*** Chair, Maine Council on Competitivenss and the Economy, 2007; Administrator, Small Business Adminstration, 2009-, mem. of cabinet, 2012-; ***professional career:*** investor & business owner; president, MMP group; ***office address:*** Small Business Administration (SBA) , 409 Third Street, SW, Washington, DC 20416, USA; ***phone:*** +1 202 205 6740 ; ***fax:*** +1 202 205 6913; ***URL:*** http://www.sbaonline.sba.gov/.

MILLS, Nigel; MP for Amber Valley, UK Government; ***party:*** Conservative; ***political career:*** Councillor, Amber Valley Borough Council, 2004-08; MP for Amber Valley, May 2010-; ***committees:*** Administration, 2010-; Northern Ireland Affairs, 2011-; ***office address:*** House of Commons, London, SW1A 0AA, United Kingdom; ***phone:*** +44 (0)20 7219 3000; ***e-mail:*** nigel.mills.mp@parliament.uk.

MILQUET, Joelle; Deputy Prime Minister, Minister for the Interior, Government of Belgium; ***born:*** 17 February 1961; ***education:*** UCL, Law, 1984; Univ. of Amsterdam, post-grad studies in European Law; ***political career:*** Senator, 1995-99; MP, 1999-; President, Parti Social Chretien (PSC), 2000-2001, party changed name to Centre Démocrate Humaniste (CDH), May 2002-; MEP, 2006-; Deputy PM and Minister of Employment and Equal Opportunities in charge of Asylum and Migration Policy, 2008-Dec. 2011; Dep. Prime Minister, Minister for the Interior, Dec. 2011-; ***office address:*** Ministry of Interior, 66 rue Royale, 1000 Brussels, Belgium; ***phone:*** +32 (0)2 500 2048; ***fax:*** +32 (0)2 500 2036; ***e-mail:*** info@ibz.fgov.be; ***URL:*** http://www.ibz.fgov.be.

MILTENBERGER, Hon. J. Michael; Minister of Finance, Government of Northwest Territories, Canada; ***born:*** 17 March 1951, Ottawa, Canada; ***married:*** Jeri; ***children:*** Michaela (F); ***education:*** Univ. of Lethbridge, BA, Sociology; Arctic Coll. in Fort Smith, Cert. as a journeyman carpenter; ***political career:*** elected, MLA, 1995, re-elected, 1999; elected MLA for Thebacha, Fort Smith, 2003; elected to Cabinet, 1999, re-elected, 2001, 2003; Minister of Education, Culture and Employment, Minister Responsible for the Workers Compensation Board, Minister Responsible for the Public Utilities Board, Minister Responsible for Youth, 1999-2003; Minister of Health and Social Services, Minister Responsible for Seniors, Minister Responsible for Persons with Disabilities. 2003; Deputy Premier, Minister of Environment and Natural Resources, Minister Responsible for Workers Compensation Board, Minister Responsible for the Northwest Territories Housing Corporation, 2007-10; Deputy Premier, Minister of Environment and Natural Resources, Minister for Finance, Minister of Health & Social Services, 2010-11; Minister of Finance, Chairman of the Financial Management Board, Minister of Environment and Natural Resources, Minister Responsible for the Northwest Territories Housing Corporation, Government House Leader, 2011-; ***memberships:*** fmr. mem., Fort Smith Health Centre Bd. of Management; fmr. chmn., Western Arctic Leadership Program; Fmr. mem., Bd.of Dirs., Northwest Territories Assn. of Municipalities; mem., Royal Canadian Legion; mem., Senior Soc. and Fort Smith Metis Local 50; ***professional career:*** mgr., Childcare programs; Regional Superintendent, Health and Social Services in Fort Smith for 6 yrs.; ***clubs:*** Pelican Rapids Golf & Country Club; ***office address:*** Ministry of Finance, PO Box 1320, Yellowknife, NWT X1A 2L9, Canada; ***phone:*** +1 867 669 2355; ***fax:*** +1 867 669 0169; ***e-mail:*** michael_miltenberger@gov.nt.ca; ***URL:*** http://www.fin.gov.nt.ca.

MILTON, Anne; MP for Guildford, House of Commons; ***party:*** Conservative; ***political career:*** Local Councillor; MP for Guildford, 2005-; Shadow Minister for Tourism (Dept. for Culture, Media and Sport), Nov. 2006-July 2007; Shadow Minister for Health, July 2007-10; Parly. Under Sec. of State for Public Health, 2010-12; ***professional career:*** Nurse; ***office address:*** House of Commons, London, SW1A 0AA, United Kingdom; ***phone:*** +44 (0)20 7219 3000.

MIMICA, Neven; Commissioner, European Commission; ***education:*** Univ. of Zagreb, Faculty of Economics, 1976; ***party:*** Social Democratic Party of Croatia; ***political career:*** Entered government, 1997; Chief Negotiator with the EU, 2000-01; Minister of European Integration, 2001-03; Deputy Speaker, 2008; Deputy Prime Minister, 2011-13; Commissioner, Consumer Protection, European Commission, 2013-; ***office address:*** European Commission, rue de la Loi 200, B-1049 Brussels, Belgium.

MIRZIYAYOV, Shavkat; Prime Minister, Government of Uzbekistan; ***born:*** 1957; ***political career:*** Governor, Jizzakh Province, 1996-2001; Governor, Samarkand Region, 2001-03; Prime Minister, 2003-; ***office address:*** Office of the Prime Minister, Government House, 700008 Tashkent, Uzbekistan; ***phone:*** +998 71 239 8295; ***fax:*** +998 71 239 8601; ***URL:*** http://www.gov.uz/.

MISICK, Charles Washington; Minister of Finance, Investment & Trade, Government of Turks & Caicos; ***education:*** College of Arts, Science & Technology; Kennedy School of Government, Harvard Univ.; ***political career:*** Chief Minister, 1992; Minister of Economic Development, Physical Planning, Finance & Tourism; Leader of the Opposition, 2003; Minister of Finance, Investment & Trade, 2012-; ***office address:*** Ministry of Finance, Investment & Trade, Grand Turk, Turks & Caicos Islands.

MITCHELL, Andrew John Bower; British, MP for Sutton Coldfield, UK Government; ***born:*** 1956; ***parents:*** Sir David Mitchell and Lady Pam Mitchell (née Howard); ***married:*** Sharon Denise Mitchell (née Bennett), 1985; ***children:*** Hannah (F), Rosie (F); ***languages:*** French; ***education:*** Jesus Coll., Cambridge Univ. (MA Hons., Cantab.); ***party:*** Conservative Party; ***political career:*** Cons. Parly. Candidate contesting Sunderland South, 1983; MP (Cons.) for Gedling, 1987-97; Appointed Parly. Private Sec. to Min. of State at Foreign Office, 1988-90; Sec., "One Nation" Gp. of Conservative MPs, 1989-; Parly. Private Sec. to Sec. of State of Energy, 1990-92 and to Leader of the House of Lords, 1992-93; Vice-Chmn. of the Conservative Party, 1992-93; Asst. Govt. Whip, 1992-3; Govt. Whip & Lord Cmnr. of HM Treasury, 1993-95; Min. for Social Security, 1995-97; MP, Sutton Coldfield, 2001-; Shadow Sec. of State for Int. Dev., May 2005-May 2010; Sec. of State for International Development, May 2010-12; Parliamentary Secretary to the Treasury and Chief Whip, Sept.-Oct. 2012 (resigned); ***interests:*** finance and trade policy, policy for children, defence; ***professional career:*** British Army Officer, Short Service (Ltd.) Cmn., 1975; Pres., Cambridge Union, 1978; Chmn., Cambridge Univ. Conservatives, 1978; Lazard Brothers & Co., Limited (Merchant Bankers), 1979-87; Dir., Lazard Brothers & Co. Ltd; Dir., The Miller Insurance Gp., 1997-2001; Strategy Adviser to Anderson Consulting and Boots, 1997-; Dir., The C M Gp., 1998-2002; Adviser to the Bd., Hakluyt & Co, Dir. Financial Dynamics, 1998-2001; ***committees:*** Vice-chmn., Alexandra Rose Charity; ***clubs:*** Sutton Coldfield Conservative Club; Cambridge Union Soc.; Carlton & District Constitutional, The Balfour Club; ***office address:*** House of Commons, London, SW1A 0AA, United Kingdom; ***e-mail:*** andrew.mitchellmp@parliament.uk; ***URL:*** http://www.parliament.uk.

MITCHELL, Dr Austin (Vernon), MP, D.Phil, MA, O.N.Z.M.; British, Member of Parliament for Great Grimsby, House of Commons; ***born:*** 19 September 1934; ***married:*** Patricia Mitchell (née Jackson); Linda Mary Mitchell (née McDougall); ***children:*** Jonathan (M), Susan (F), Kiri (F), Hannah (F); ***public role of spouse:*** TV Producer, author, columnist; ***languages:*** French; ***education:*** Woodbottom County Sch., Bingley Grammar Sch., Manchester Univ., Oxford Univ.; ***party:*** Labour Party, 1956-; ***political career:*** MP (Lab.) for Grimsby, 1977-83; PPS to John Fraser (Minister of State for Prices and Consumer Protection), 1977-79; Opp. Whip, 1980-85; MP, Great Grimsby, 1983-; Opp. Front Bench Spokesman on Trade and Industry, 1987-89; ***interests:*** economy, poverty, trade and industry, accountancy and insolvency professions, legal reform, electoral reform, constitutional reform, consumer affairs, media and broadcasting; ***memberships:*** Political Studies Assn.; Nat. Union of Journalists; ***professional career:*** Lecturer in History, Univ. of Otago, N.Z., 1959-62; Sr. Lecturer in Politics, Univ. of Canterbury, 1962-67; Official Fellow, Nuffield Coll., Oxford, 1967-69; Journalist, Yorkshire TV, Leeds, 1969-71; Presenter, BBC, 1972-73; Journalist, Yorkshire TV, Leeds, 1973-77; Co Presenter, Target, Sky TV, 1989-98; ***committees:*** Mem., Treasury and Civil Service Select Cttee., 1983-87; Panel mem., Agriculture Select Cttee., 1997-2001; Environment Food & Rural Affairs Cttee., 2001-05; Public Accounts, 2005-; Yorkshire & the Humber, 2009-10; ***publications:*** New Zealand Politics in Action, 1962; Government by Party, 1966; Politics & People in New Zealand, 1969; The Whigs in Opposition, 1969; The Half Gallon Quarter Acre Pavlova Paradise, 1972; Yorkshire Jokes, 1973; Teach Thissen Tyke; Can Labour Win Again, 1979; Westminster Man, 1982; The Case for Labour, 1983; Four Years in the Death of the Labour Party, 1983; Britain: Beyond the Blue Horizon, 1989; Competitive Socialism, 1989; Accounting for Change, 1992; Corporate Governance Matters, 1996; The Common Fisheries Policy End or Mend?; Election '45, 1995; Last Time: Labour's Lessons from the Sixties, 1997; Fishermen, The Rise and Fall of Deep Water Trawling, 1997; Parliament in Pictures, 1999; Farewell my Lords, 1999; Austin Mitchell's Yorkshire Jokes, 2001; Pavlova Paradise Revisited, 2002; ***recreations:*** photography; ***office address:*** House of Commons, London, SW1A 0AA, United Kingdom; ***phone:*** +44 (0)1472 342145 / (0)20 7219 4559; ***fax:*** +44 (0)1472 251484 / (0)20 7219 4843; ***e-mail:*** mitchellav@parliament.uk / austinmitchellsyorkshirejokes@hotmail.co.uk; ***URL:*** http://www.austinmitchell.org.

MITCHELL, Hon. Fred; Minister of Foreign Affairs, Government of Bahamas; ***education:*** Antioch Univ.; MA, Harvard Univ; LLB, Univ. of Buckingham; ***political career:*** Minister of Foreign Affairs, 2002-07, 2012-; ***office address:*** Ministry of Foreign Affairs, East Hill St, PO Box N-3746, Nassau, Bahamas; ***phone:*** +1 242 322 7624; ***fax:*** +1 242 328 8212.

MITCHELL, Hon. Dr Keith Claudius, M.S., Ph.D; Grenadian, Prime Minister, Government of Grenada; ***born:*** 12 November 1946, Happy Hill, St Georges, Grenada; ***parents:*** Dowlyn Mitchell (dec'd) and Catherine Mitchell; ***married:*** Marietta Mitchell (née Cummings); ***children:*** Olinga (M); ***education:*** Univ. of West Indies, B.Sc., Mathematics and Chemistry, 1969-71; Howard Univ., MA, Mathematics, 1973-75; American Univ., Ph.D., Mathematics and Statistics, 1975-79; ***political career:*** MP, St. George's North West, 1984-95; General Sec., NNP, 1984-89., Leader, 1989-; Minister of Communication, Works, Public Utilities, Transportation, Civil Aviation & Energy, 1984-88; Minister of Communications, Works, Public Utilities, Co-operatives, Community Dev., Women's Affairs & Civil Aviation, NNP, 1988-89; Political Leader of the NNP, 1989; responsible for CARICOM, Science and Technology and Human Resource Development since first CARICOM Heads of Govt. Meeting, 1995-; Chmn., Ministerial Cncl. of the Assoc. of Caribbean States, 1996-97; Chmn. Bd. Governors, Caribbean Development Bank, 1997-98; Chmn., Community CARICOM, 1998; Prime Minister, Minister of Information and National Security, Minister of National Mobilisation and Minister of Finance, Trade and Industry, and Foreign Affairs, Carriacou and Petit Martinique Affairs, 1995-1999; Chmn., Organisation of Eastern Caribbean States (OECS), 2000-2002; Chmn., Regional Security System, 2001-2002; Prime Minister and Minister of National Security and Information, 1999-08; Minister of Information, Business and Private Sector Development, Human Resource Development, Information Communication Technology, Youth Development, 2006-08; Minister of Finance, 2007-08; Prime Minister, Minister of Finance, Energy, National Security, Public Administration, Disaster Preparedness, Home Affairs and Information, 2013-; ***professional career:*** Mem. Grenada Cricket Team, 1964-66; Captain combined Grenada and Leeward Youth Cricket Team, 1966; Captain Grenada Cricket Team, 1973; Teacher, The Presentation Boys Coll., 1972-73; Mathematics Professor, Howard Univ., 1977-83; Professional Statistical Consultant, Govt. and Private Corps. in the US; ***committees:*** Mem., CARICOM Prime Ministerial Sub-Cttee. on Cricket; ***trusteeships:*** supports many sporting events through personal sponsorships; ***publications:*** Textbooks for Caribbean O and A level Mathematics Students; ***recreations:*** playing cricket, competing with his Prime Minister's Eleven in friendly matches locally and regionally; ***office address:*** Office of the Prime Minister, Sixth Floor, Ministerial Complex, Botanical Gardens, St. George's, Grenada; ***phone:*** +1 473 440 2255/2265/2383; ***fax:*** +1 473 440 4116; ***e-mail:*** pmoffice@gov.gd.

MITTERLEHNER, Dr. Reinhold; Federal Minister of Economy, Family and Youth, Government of Austria; ***born:*** 10 December 1955; ***party:*** Austrian People's Party; ***political career:*** Federal Minister of Economy, Family and Youth, Dec. 2008-; ***office address:*** Ministry of Economy, Family and Youth, Stubenring 1, A-1010 Vienna, Austria; ***phone:*** +43 (0) 810 013571; ***URL:*** http://www.bmwfj.gv.at.

MNANGAGWA, Emmerson Dambudzo; Minister of Defence, Government of Zimbabwe; ***party:*** ZANU-PF; ***political career:*** Minister of State Security, 1982-88; Minister of Justice, Legal and Parly. Affairs, 1988-2000; Speaker, 2000-05; Minister of Rural Housing and Social Amenities, 2005-09; Minister of Defence, 2009-; ***office address:*** Ministry of Defence, 1st Floor, Manhumutapa Building, Samora Machel Avenue, Causeway, Harare, Zimbabwe; ***URL:*** http://www.mod.gov.zw.

MODERT, Octavie; Minister of Culture, Minister for Relations with Parliament, Delegate Minister to the Civil Service and Administrative Reform, Government of Luxembourg; ***born:*** 15 November 1966, Grevenmacher, Luxembourg; ***parents:*** Lucien Modert and Francine

Modert (née Hellers); ***married:*** Jean-Pierre Stronck; ***languages:*** English, French, German, Latin; ***education:*** LLM; MA, European Studies; ***party:*** CSV (Christian Democrat Party); ***political career:*** Sec. General, Cabinet of Ministers and Prime Minister's Office, 1998; Elected to the Chamber of Deputies, 2004; Sec. of State for Relations with Parliament, Sec. of State for Agriculture, Viticulture & Rural Dev., and Sec. of State for Culture, Higher Education & Research, 2004-09; Minister of Culture, Minister for Relations with Parliament, Delegate Minister to the Civil Service and Administrative Reform, 2009-; ***office address:*** Government of Luxembourg, 1 rue de la Congrégation, 1352 Luxembourg, Luxembourg; ***phone:*** +352 478 2525; ***fax:*** +352 22 29 10.

MODESTE-CURWEN, Hon. Dr Clarice; Minister of Health and Social Security, Grenada Government; ***born:*** 7 October 1945, Cumberland; ***married:*** Sandra Harvey, 1974; ***education:*** Mons Officer Cadet Sch., 1964; ***political career:*** served seven Governors as Private Sec., 1976-84; Official Sec. and Chief Administrator of the Office of the Governor, 1984-; Minister of Health and the Environment, 1998-04; Minister of Communications, Works & Transport, to 2007; Minister of Tourism, Civil Aviation, Culture and the Performing Arts, 2007-08; Minister of Health and Social Security, 2013-; ***interests:*** medical research; ***memberships:*** Mem., Advisory Bd., the Monash Inst. of Reproduction and Dev.; ***professional career:*** Teacher, Waltham Junior Secondary School, 1972-79; General Practitioner and Registrar served in the 11th Hussars (P.A.O.); Captain and ADC to the Governor of Victoria, Melbourne, 1967; in Ophthalmology, General Hospital, 1986-; worked in Market Research on leave of absence from Govt. of Victoria, Dir., Roy Morgan Research Ltd. and A.C. Nielsen, Sydney, 1989; ***committees:*** Grenada Medical Assoc. and is a mem. of St Mark's Development Cttee, the cttee for the Prevention of Blindness; Foundation for the Prevention of Blindness and is an advisor to the Victoria Women's Cooperative; ***honours and awards:*** Recognised by the Caribbean Council for the Blind for outstanding service to Grenada in the area of blindness prevention; OBE, 1977; LVO, 1988; CVO, 1998; Doctor of Laws honoris causa, Monash Univ., 1998; Fellow of Victorian Division of Inst. of Public Admin., Australia; ***office address:*** Ministry of Health, Ministerial Complex, Southern Wing 1st & 2nd Floors, Botanical Gardens, Tanteen, St. George's, Grenada; ***phone:*** +1 473 440 2649; ***URL:*** http://www.gov.gd/ministries/health.html.

MOHAMMED BEN AL HASSAN, HM Sidi; King, Morocco; ***born:*** 21 August 1963, Rabat; ***parents:*** late King H.M. Hassan II; ***married:*** Salma Bennani, 2002; ***children:*** Princess Lalla Khadija (F), Prince Moulay Al Hassan (M); ***education:*** Royal Coll., Baccalaureate, 1981; Univ. Mohammed V, Grad.; Univ. of judicial, economic & social studies, Rabat, 1985; First Cert., Political Sciences, 1987; Second Cert., high studies in public law, 1988; ***political career:*** King of Morocco, 1999-; ***professional career:*** Coordinator of Services, General Headquarters of the Armed Forces, 1985; ***honours and awards:*** Dr. in Law, Univ. of Nice-Antipolis in France, Oct. 1993; ***office address:*** Royal Palace, Palais Royal, Rabat, Morocco.

MOHAMUD, Hassan Sheikh; President, Government of Somalia; ***born:*** 1955; ***political career:*** civic activist; founder, Peace and Development Party, 2010; MP, leader of Peace & Development Party, 2012-; President, Government of Somalia, 2012-; ***professional career:*** founder, Somali Inst. of Management and Administration Development (now Simad Univ.), Mogadishu, 1999, dean, 1999-2009; ***office address:*** Office of the President, People's Palace, Mogadishu.

MOK, Dr. Mareth; Senior Minister of the Environment, Government of Cambodia; ***born:*** 20 January 1948, Takeo, Cambodia; ***parents:*** Mok Meas and Yang Soyat; ***married:*** Chhea Lang; ***children:*** Chandara (M), Chansothea (M), Chankarona (M), Chanvirak (M); ***languages:*** English, French; ***education:*** Ph.D., Agronomy and Biology, Paul Sabatier Univ. Toulouse, France, 1974; ***party:*** Cambodian People Party; ***political career:*** Perm. Dep. Governor Phnom Penh Municipality, 1980; Vice Minister of the Ministry of Agriculture, Fishery and Forestry, 1989; Sec. of State for the Secretariat of Environment and Senior Minister, Minister for the Ministry of the Environment, 1993-; ***honours and awards:*** National Construction Gold Medal; Thipadin (National Merit); Sena (National Merit); Mohasena (National Merit); Great Cross of Royal Order Mohasereywath; ***publications:*** Book on Agriculture; ***clubs:*** Golf; ***recreations:*** sport; ***office address:*** Ministry of the Environment, 48 Preah Shihanouk, Tonle Basac, Chamkar Mon, Phnom-Penh, Cambodia; ***phone:*** +855 (0)23 213908; ***fax:*** +855 (0)23 212540.

MOLEWA, Edna; Minister of Water & Environmental Affairs, Government of South Africa; ***born:*** 23 March 1957; ***party:*** Chairperson, African Nat. Congress (ANC) Women's League, NW Province, Provincial Treasurer; mem., ANC Women's League Nat. Exec. Cncl., 2003-; ***political career:*** MEC for Tourism, Env. & Conservation in NW Province, 1996-98; MEC for Agriculture, Conservation & Env. in the North West Province, 2000-04; Premier, North West Province, April 2004-09; Minister of Social Development, 2009-12; Minister of Water & Environmental Affairs, 2012-; ***committees:*** mem., Provincial Exec. cttee., 1996-; ***office address:*** Ministry of Water & Environmental Affairs, Private Bag X313, Pretoria 0001, South Africa.

MOMO JOHNSON, H.E. Wesley; Ambassador, Liberian Embassy in the UK; ***education:*** BSc., St Francis Coll., Brooklyn, New York, USA, 1975; MBA, Long Island, Univ., New York, USA, 1977; ***political career:*** Vice Chmn. and Vice Head of State, National Transitional Gov., 2003-06
; ***professional career:*** Consul General to New York, USA, 1980-81; Amb. to the United Kingdom; ***office address:*** Liberian Embassy, 23 Fitzroy Square, London, W1 6EW, United Kingdom; ***phone:*** +44 (0)20 7221 1036; ***URL:*** http://www.embassyofliberia.org.uk.

MONI, Dr Dipi; Minister of Foreign Affairs, Government of Bangladesh; ***parents:*** M.A. Wadud (dec'd); ***education:*** Johns Hopkins University School of Public Health, USA; Dhaka Medical College, Bangladesh; University of London; ***party:*** Bangladesh Awami League; ***political career:*** Minister of Foreign Affairs, 2009-; ***office address:*** Ministry of Foreign Affairs, Topkhana Road, Dhaka, Bangladesh; ***phone:*** +880 (0)2 236020; ***fax:*** +880 (0)2 411281; ***e-mail:*** pspmo@bangla.net; ***URL:*** http://www.mofabd.org.

MONIZ, Ernest; Secretary of Energy, US Government; ***education:*** Boston College, Physics,; Stanford Univ., Doctorate, Theoretical Physics; ***political career:*** Assoc. Dir. for Science, Office of Science and Technology Policy, Office of the President, 1995-97; Under Sec., Dept. of Energy, 1997-2001; US Sec. of Energy, 2013-; ***professional career:*** Fac. mem., Massachusetts Inst. of Technology (MIT), 1973-; Cecil & Ida Green Professor of Physics and Engineering Systems, MIT; ***office address:*** Department of Energy, 1000 Independence Ave., SW, Washington, DC 20585, USA; ***phone:*** +1 202 586 5575;
URL: http://www.energy.gov/.

MONTEBOURG, Arnaud; Minister for Productive Recovery, Government of France; ***born:*** 1962, Nievre, France; ***parents:*** Michel Montebourg and Leila Montebourg (née Ould Cadi); ***married:*** Horteuse Montebourg (née de Labriffe), 31 May 1997; ***political career:*** MP, Assemblée Nationale, 1997-; Minister of Productive Recovery, 2012-; ***professional career:*** Lawyer, 1990-; ***honours and awards:*** First Secretary of the Lawyers Stage's Conference, 1993; ***office address:*** L'Assemblée Nationale, 126 rue de l'université, 75355 Paris, France; ***phone:*** +33 (0)1 40 63 60 00.

MONTORO ROMERO, Cristobal Ricardo; Minister of Finance and Public Administration, Government of Spain; ***born:*** 20 July 1950, Jaén; ***education:*** Doctorate in Economics; ***party:*** Group of the European People's Party (Christian Democrats) and European Democrats; ***political career:*** Dep. for Madrid during the Vth and VIth Parly. Sessions and Dep. for Jaén during the VIIth Parly. Session; Sec. of State for the Economy, 1996-2000; Minister of the Treasury, 2000-04; MEP, 2004; Minister of Finance and Public Administration, 2011-; ***memberships:*** Mem., Governing Bd. of the Assoc. of Economists of Madrid; ***professional career:*** Prof. and Head of Dept. of Applied Economics, Univ. of Cantabria; Dir. of Studies and of the Journal of the Inst. of Economic Studies; Prof., Applied Economics, Madrid Autonomous Univ.; Prof., Applied Economics, Univ. of San Pablo-CEU; Dep. Dir. of Studies, Banco Atlántico; ***committees:*** Mem., Financial, Fiscal and Economic Climate Cttees. of the CEOE (Spaninsh Confederation of Business Organisations); Mem., Nat. Exec. Cttee. of the Popular Party; ***office address:*** Ministry of Economy and Finance, Paseo de la Catellana 162, 28071 Madrid, Spain; ***phone:*** +91 583 8348; ***URL:*** http://www.minhac.es.

MOON, Madeleine; MP for Bridgend, House of Commons; ***born:*** 1950; ***party:*** Labour; ***political career:*** Councillor, Bridgend Borough Cncl., 1991-; MP for Bridgend, 2005-; ***committees:*** Environment, Food and Rural Affairs, 2005-07; Welsh Affairs, 2005-06; Defence, 2009-; ***office address:*** House of Commons, London, SW1A 0AA, United Kingdom; ***e-mail:*** moonm@parliament.uk.

MOORE, Christlyn; Minister of Justice, Government of Trinidad & Tobago; ***education:*** Sir Hugh Wooding Law School; ***political career:*** Minister of Justice; ***professional career:*** litigator, both criminal and civil; Renaissance Chambers; Instructing Attorney, Commission of Enquiry, 1990 attempted coup; appears on behalf of the Attorney General; ***office address:*** Ministry of Justice, Tower C, Levels 19-21, International Waterfront Complex, #1 Wrightson Road, Port of Spain, Trinidad & Tobago; ***URL:*** http://www.moj.gov.tt/.

MOORE, James; Minister of Canadian Heritage and Official Languages, Government of Canada; ***education:*** BA, Univ. of Northern British Columbia; ***political career:*** MP for Port Moody, Westwood, Port Coquitlam in British Columbia, 2000-; Parly. Sec. to the Minister of Public Works and Government Services and for the Pacific Gateway and the Vancouver-Whistler Olympics, 2006-08; Minister of Canadian Heritage and Official Languages, 2008-; ***office address:*** House of Commons, Parliament Buildings, Wellington Street, Ottawa, Ontario K1A 0H8, Canada; ***phone:*** +1 613 943 5959; ***fax:*** +1 613 992 3674; ***URL:*** http://www.parl.gc.ca.

MOORE, Rt. Hon. Michael; British, Secretary of State for Scotland, UK Government; ***born:*** 3 June 1965, Northern Ireland; ***education:*** Strathallan Sch., Perthshire; Jedburgh Grammar Sch.; Edinburgh Univ., hons. degree, Politics and Modern History; ***party:*** Liberal Democrat; ***political career:*** MP for Tweeddale, Ettrick and Lauderdale 1997-2005; Spokesman for Scotland, Industry, Employment and Health, 1997-99; Spokesman for Transport 1999-2001; Campaign Chmn., Scottish Parly. Elections in 1999 and 2003; Dep. Lib. Dem. Foreign Affairs Spokesman 2001-05; Spokesman for Scotland 2001; Dep. Leader, Scottish Liberal Democrats, 2002-; Researcher for Archy Kirkwood; MP for Berwickshire, Roxburgh and Selkirk, 2005-; Lib. Dem Defence Spokesman, 2005-06; Lib. Dem. Spokesman on Foreign Affairs 2006-07; Lib. Dem. Spokesman for International Development, 2007-10, Scotland and Northern Ireland 2008; Secretary of State for Scotland, 2010-, also ministerial support to the Deputy Prime Minister in the Cabinet Office, 2010-; ***professional career:*** Scottish chartered accountant, Coopers and Lybrand; ***committees:*** British Council Advisory Board; Programme Cttee. of the Ditchley Foundation; Advisory Board of the John Smith memorial Trust; Gov. and Vice-Chair, Westminster Foundation for Democracy; ***recreations:*** rugby, hill walking; ***office address:*** Scottish Office, Dover House, 66 Whitehall, London, SW1A 2AU, United Kingdom; ***phone:*** +44 (0)20 7219 3000;
e-mail: michaelmooremp@parliament.uk; ***URL:*** http://www.michaelmoore.org.uk.

MOORE, Michael Kenneth; New Zealander, Director General, World Trade Organization (WTO); ***born:*** 1949; ***political career:*** former Junior Vice-Pres., Labour Party; MP (Lab.) for Eden 1972-75; MP (Lab.) for Papanui 1978-84; MP (Lab.) for Christchurch North 1984-; Minister for External Relations and Trade, Deputy Minister of Finance; Prime Minister 1990; Leader of the Opposition 1991-1993; Opp. spokesman, 1993-99; ***professional career:*** Former social worker; former abbatoir worker; Dir. Gen., World Trade Org., 1999-2002; Amb. to the USA, 2010-; ***publications:*** A Pacific Parliament; The Added Value Economy; Beyond Today; On Balance; Hard Labour; ***office address:*** World Trade Organization, Centre William Rappard, 154 rue de Lausanne, CH 1211 Geneva 12, Switzerland.

MORAES, Claude; MEP, European Parliament; ***born:*** 22 October 1965; ***education:*** LSE, London, UK, International Law; Birkbeck College, UK, M.Sc.; Dundee University, LL.B; ***party:*** Labour Party, UK; Party of European Socialists, European Parliament; ***political career:*** MEP for London; Deputy Leader, Labour MEPs, 2009-; ***interests:*** labour market, civil liberties, justice & home affairs policy, immigration & refugee policy, human rights; ***professional career:*** Lawyer; Director of an NGO (Charity); Policy Officer, TUC; Political Advisor, House of Commons; ***committees:*** Justice and Home Affairs Cttee., Socialist &

Democrats Spokesperson; Pres., EP Intergroup on Anti-Racism, 2004-; Pres., EP Intergroup on Ageing; ***trusteeships:*** Cncl. Mem., Liberty (NCCL, UK); ***honours and awards:*** FRSA; ***publications:*** (Jointly) Politics of Migration, 2004; Social Work and Minorities, 1994; Perspectives on Migration, 2005; ***office address:*** European Parliament, Rue Wiertz, B-1047 Brussels, Belgium; ***URL:*** http://www.claudemoraes.net.

MORALES, Evo; President, Republic of Bolivia; ***born:*** 25 October 1959; ***education:*** Secondary Schooling at Colegio Beltrán Ávila de Oruro, Bolivia; ***political career:*** Pres., Planning Cttee., Six Federations of the Tropic Cochambino, 1996; Leader of the Movement towards Socialism (MAS); Presidential candidate for Bolivia, July 2002; President, 2005-; ***professional career:*** Farmer and llama herder; ***office address:*** Palacio Legislativo, Plaza Murillo, La Paz, Bolivia; ***URL:*** http://www.presidencia.gov.bo.

MORALES CARAZO, Jaime; Vice President, Government of Nicaragua; ***born:*** 1936; ***political career:*** Negotiator, Sapoa peace process; Dep., National Assembly, 2002-07, 2012-Vice-Pres., Government of Nicaragua, 2007-; ***office address:*** Office of the Vice-President, Av. Bolivar y dupla sur, Managua, Nicaragua; ***URL:*** http://www.presidencia.gob.ni/.

MORAN, Jerry; American, Senator, Kansas, US Senate; ***party:*** Republican Party; ***political career:*** Mem., Kansas State Senate, eight years, Majority Leader; Mem., US House of Representatives,seven terms, -2010; Mem., US Senate, 2010-; ***committees:*** Senate: Banking, Housing and Urban Affairs; Veterans' Affairs; ***office address:*** Senate, Russell Senate Office Building, Room 354, Washington, DC 20510, USA; ***phone:*** +1 202 224 6521; ***URL:*** http://www.moran.senate.gov/.

MORDAUNT, Penny; MP for Portsmouth North, UK Government; ***party:*** Conservative; ***political career:*** MP for Portsmouth North, May 2010-; ***committees:*** European Scrutiny Select Cttee., 2010-; Defence, 2010-; Arms Export Controls, 2011; ***office address:*** House of Commons, London, SW1A 0AA, United Kingdom; ***phone:*** +44 (0)20 7219 3000; ***e-mail:*** penny.mordaunt.mp@parliament.uk.

MORDEN, Jessica; MP for Newport East, House of Commons; ***born:*** 1968; ***party:*** Labour; ***political career:*** MP for Newport East, 2005-; ***committees:*** Constitutional Affairs/Justice, 2005-10; Modernisation of the House of Commons, 2005-06; Welsh Affairs, 2005-07, 2010-; ***office address:*** House of Commons, London, SW1A 0AA, United Kingdom; ***e-mail:*** mordenj@parliament.uk.

MORENO, Dr Luis Alberto; President, Inter-American Development Bank; ***born:*** 3 May 1953, Philadelphia, USA; ***married:*** Gabriela Febres-Cordero, 1970; ***public role of spouse:*** Former Min. of Economic Development in Venezuela; ***languages:*** Spanish; ***education:*** Florida Int. Univ., Bachelor in Business Admin. and Economics, 1971-75; Thunderbird Univ., Phoenix, Arizona, MBA, American Graduate Sch. of Int. Management, 1976-77; Harvard Univ. Neiman Fellow, 1990-91; ***political career:*** Minister of Economic Development 1992-94; Campaign Manager of Andres Pastran 1994; ***professional career:*** Division Man., Praco, Colombia, 1977-82; Exec. Producer of nationwide nightly news program, and other entertainment and children's programming, 1982-90; Pres., Inst. de Foment Industrial, 1991-92; Telecommunication advisor and private conslt., Luis Carlos Sarmiento Org., Bogota, Colombia, 1994-97; Ptnr., Westsphere Andean Advisors, 1997-98; Ambassador of Colombia to the USA, 1998-2005; Pres., Inter-American Development Bank, 2005-; ***honours and awards:*** major television awards; decorations include: Orden de Boyaca en el Grado de Gran Cruz, 2002; 2012 Clinton Gobal Citizen Award for Leadership in Public Service; ***office address:*** Inter-American Development Bank, 1300 New York Avenue, NW , Washington, DC 20577, USA.

MORENO TOSCANO, Ambassador Carmen; Mexican, Executive Secretary, Inter-American Commission on Women; ***professional career:*** Diplomat; Mexican Ambassador to Costa Rica & Guatemala; Perm. Rep. of Mexcio to the OAS; Eminent Amb., 1994; Dir., UN International Research and Training Institute for the Advancement of Women (UN-INSTRAW, now part of UN-Women), 2003-09; Exec. Sec., Inter-American Commission on Women, 2009-; ***office address:*** Inter-American Commission of Women , 1889 F. Street, N.W. , Washington, DC 20006, USA.

MORGAN, Alasdair, MSP; MSP for South of Scotland, Scottish Parliament; ***born:*** 21 April 1945, Perthshire, UK; ***married:*** Anne Morgan (née Gilfillan), 28 August 1969; ***children:*** Gillian (F), Fiona (F); ***education:*** Breadalbane Academy, Aberfeldy; Univ. of Glasgow, MA (hons); ***party:*** Scottish National Party; ***political career:*** MP, Galloway and Upper Nithsdale, 1997-2001; MSP, 1999-; SNP Westminster Parly Group Leader, 1999-2001; Shadow Minister for Finance, 2001-03; Chief Whip & Business Manager, 2005-07; Dep., Presiding Officer, Scottish Parliament, 2007-; ***interests:*** rural affairs, transport; ***recreations:*** hill walking; ***office address:*** Scottish Parliament, Edinburgh, EH99 1SP, United Kingdom; ***e-mail:*** alasdair.morgan.msp@scottish.parliament.uk.

MORGAN, Most Rev. Dr Barry; Archbishop, Church of Wales; ***born:*** 31 January 1947, Neath, Wales; ***parents:*** Rees Haydn and Gwyneth; ***married:*** Hilary (née Lewis), 22 August 1969; ***children:*** Jonathan (M), Lucy (F); ***languages:*** Welsh, French; ***education:*** Univ. Coll. London, BA, 1969; Selwyn Coll. Cambridge, BA, 1972, MA, 1974; Univ. of Wales, Ph.D., 1986; Wescott House, Cambridge, 1970; ***memberships:*** Tairgwaith Workingmen's Club; ***professional career:*** Chaplain, Bryn-y-Don Community Sch., 1972-75; Curate of St Andrews major w Michaelston-le-Pit, 1972-75; Lecturer in Theology, Univ. of Wales, Cardiff, 1975-77; Chaplain and Lecturer, St Michael's Coll. Llandaff, 1975-77; Warden, Church Hostel, Bangor, 1977-84; Chaplain and Lecturer in Theology, Univ. of Wales, Bangor, 1977-84; In-service Training Advisor, 1978-84; Dir. of Ordinands, 1982-84; Canon of Bangor Cathedral, 1983-84; Rector, Wrexham, 1984-86; Archdeacon of Meirionnydd and Rector of Criccieth w Treflys, 1986-93; Bishop of Bangor, 1993-99; Bishop of Llandaff, 1999-; Archbishop of Wales, 2003-; ***honours and awards:*** Fellow of Cardiff, Bangor, Lampeter and UWIC, Swansea and Carmarthen Univs.; Pres., Welsh Centre for Int. Affairs, 2004; ***publications:*** O Ddydd i Ddydd, (1980); Pwyllgor Darlleniadau Beiblaidd Cyngor Eglwysi Cymru, History of the Church Hostel and Anglican Chaplaincy at University College of North Wales, Bangor, (1986); Concepts of Mission and Ministry in Anglican Chaplaincy Work, (1988); Ministry in the Church in Wales - the shape of things to come? (2002); Strangely Orthodox - R S Thomas and his Poetry of Faith (2006); ***recreations:*** golf; ***office address:*** Llys Esgob, Cathedral Green, Llandaff, Cardiff, CF5 2YE, United Kingdom; ***phone:*** +44 (0)29 2056 2400; ***fax:*** +44 (0)29 2056 8410; ***e-mail:*** archbishop@churchinwales.org.uk.

MORGAN, Nicky; MP for Loughborough, UK Government; ***education:*** Oxford Univ.; ***party:*** Conservative; ***political career:*** MP for Loughborough, May 2010-; PPS, 2010-12; Assist. Gov. Whip, 2012-; ***professional career:*** Solicitor; ***office address:*** House of Commons, London, SW1A 0AA, United Kingdom; ***phone:*** +44 (0)20 7219 3000; ***e-mail:*** nicky.morgan.mp@parliament.uk.

MORGAN OF ELY, Baroness Eluned; Member, House of Lords; ***born:*** 16 February 1967, Cardiff, Wales; ***children:*** Arwel (M), Gwenllian (F); ***languages:*** French, Spanish, Welsh; ***education:*** Atlantic Coll.; Univ. of Hull; ***party:*** Labour Party; Socialist Group in the European Parl.; ***political career:*** Labour MEP for Mid and West Wales 1994-99, re-elected, MEP for Wales, 1999-2004 and again 2004; Mem., House of Lords, 2011-; ***interests:*** devolution, tourism, minority languages, business; ***memberships:*** AEEU; European Movement; Amnesty International; Nicaragua Solidarity Campaign; BECTU; ***professional career:*** former researcher, S4C and BBC; ***committees:*** Mem., Cttee. on Regional Development; Mem., Industry, Research and Energy Cttee.; Mem., European Parliament's delegation with the Mashreq countries and the Gulf; Chair., Cymdeithas Cledwyn; ***trusteeships:*** Patron, Cartrefi Cymru Charity; ***honours and awards:*** Fellow, Trinity College, Carmarthen; ***recreations:*** walking, reading, audio books; ***office address:*** House of Lords, London, SW1A 0PW, United Kingdom; ***phone:*** +44 (0)20 7219 3000; ***URL:*** http://www.elunedmorgan.org.uk.

MORI, Emmanuel 'Manny'; President, Federated States of Micronesia; ***political career:*** Senator, 1999-2007; President, May 2007-; ***professional career:*** Exec.Vice Pres., Bank of the Federated States of Micronesia, 1997-99; ***office address:*** Office of the President, PO Box PS 53, Palikir, 96941 FM Pohnpei, Federated States of Micronesia; ***phone:*** +691 320 2228; ***URL:*** http://www.fsmgov.org/.

MORIN, Herve; Leader, Nouveau Centre Party; ***born:*** 17 August 1961; ***party:*** Nouveau Centre; ***political career:*** MP, 1998-; Technical Adviser to the Ministry of Defence, 1993; Minister of Defence, Gov. of France, 2007-10; ***office address:*** Le Nouveau Centre, 84 rue de Grenelle, 75007 Paris, France; ***phone:*** +30 (0)1 44 39 28 00; ***URL:*** http://www.nouveaucentre.fr.

MORRICE, Graeme; MP for Livingston, UK Government; ***party:*** Labour; ***political career:*** Councillor, West Lothian District Council, 1987-; MP for Livingston, May 2010-; PPS, 2010-; ***committees:*** Scottish Affairs, 2011-12; ***office address:*** House of Commons, London, SW1A 0AA, United Kingdom; ***phone:*** +44 (0)20 7219 3000; ***e-mail:*** graeme.morrice.mp@parliament.uk.

MORRIS, Anne Marie; MP for Newton Abbot, UK Government; ***party:*** Conservative; ***political career:*** Councillor, West Sussex County Council, 2005-07; MP for Newton Abbot, May 2010-; ***professional career:*** Lawyer; ***office address:*** House of Commons, London, SW1A 0AA, United Kingdom; ***phone:*** +44 (0)20 7219 3000; ***e-mail:*** annemarie.morris.mp@parliament.uk.

MORRIS, David; MP for Morecambe and Lunesdale, UK Government; ***party:*** Conservative; ***political career:*** MP for Morecambe and Lunesdale, May 2010-; ***committees:*** Science and Technology Select Cttee., 2010-12; ***office address:*** House of Commons, London, SW1A 0AA, United Kingdom; ***phone:*** +44 (0)20 7219 3000; ***e-mail:*** david.morris.mp@parliament.uk.

MORRIS, Grahame; MP for Easington, UK Government; ***party:*** Labour; ***political career:*** Councillor, Easington District Council, 1987-2003; MP for Easington, May 2010-; PPS, 2010-; ***committees:*** Health Select Cttee., 2010-; ***office address:*** House of Commons, London, SW1A 0AA, United Kingdom; ***phone:*** +44 (0)20 7219 3000; ***e-mail:*** grahame.morris.mp@parliament.uk.

MORRIS, James George; MP for Halesowen and Rowley Regis, UK Government; ***education:*** BA, Univ. of Birmingham; Postgraduate research, Oxford Univ.; MBA, Cranfield School of Management; ***party:*** Conservative; ***political career:*** MP for Halesowen and Rowley Regis, May 2010-; ***professional career:*** Small businessman in computer software; chief executive of think tank; ***committees:*** Communities and Local Government, 2010-; ***office address:*** House of Commons, London, SW1A 0AA, United Kingdom; ***phone:*** +44 (0)20 7219 7080; ***e-mail:*** james.morris.mp@parliament.uk.

MORRIS OF YARDLEY, Baroness Estelle; British, Member, House of Lords; ***born:*** 17 June 1952; ***party:*** Labour Party; ***political career:*** Opp. Spokesperson for Education, 1995-97; Parly. Under-Sec. of State for Education and Employment, 1997-98; Minister of State, Dept. for Education and Employment, 1998-2001; MP, Birmingham Yardley, 1992-2001, re-elected MP for Birmingham Yardley, 2001-02; Secretary of State for Education and Skills, 2001-02; Minister of State for the Arts, 2002-05; mem., House of Lords, May 2005-; ***interests:*** education, training, housing; ***office address:*** House of Lords, London, SW1A 0PW, United Kingdom; ***phone:*** +44 (0)20 7219 3000.

MORRISON, The Hon. Sara Antoinette Sibell Frances; Vice-President Emeritus, World Wide Fund for Nature; ***born:*** 9 August 1934, London; ***parents:*** Viscount Long of Wraxall and Laura Duchess of Malborough (née Chateris); ***married:*** Hon. Charles Andrew Morrison, 1954 (Diss'd 1984); ***languages:*** French; ***political career:*** Wiltshire County Cllr., 1959-1971; ***professional career:*** Gen. Electric Co., 1975-98 (Dir., 1980-98); Non-Exec. Dir.: Abbey Nat. Plc., 1979-95; Carlton TV, 1992-; Kleinwort Charter Trust, 1993-2001; Chmn., Nat. Council for Voluntary Organisations (formerly Nat. Council of Social service), 1977-81; Nat. Adv. Council on Employment of Disabled People, 1981-84; County Cllr. then Alderman, Wilts., 1961-71; Chmn., Wilts. Assn. of Youth Clubs, 1958-63; Wilts Community Council, 1965-70; Vice-Chmn., Nat. Assn. of Youth Clubs, 1969-71; Conservative Party Organisation, 1971-75; Mem., Governing Bd., Volunteer Centre, 1972-77; Nat. Consumer Council, 1975-77;

Bd., Fourth Channel TV Co., 1980-85; Governing Council, Family Policy Studies Centre, 1983-; Nat. Radiological Protection Bd., 1989-; Council, PSI, 1980-93; Governing Body, Imperial Coll., London, 1986-2001; UK Round Table on Sustainable Development, 1995-98; Chmn., WWF UK, 1998-2002; Pro-Chancellor, Univ. of Bath, 2000-; Acting Pres. and Vice Pres. of World Wide Fund for Nature, 2000, now Vice-pres. Emeritus, WWF; ***committees:*** Annan Cttee. of Enquiry into Broadcasting, 1974-77; Video Appeals Cttee. (Video Recordings Act, 1984), 1985-; ***honours and awards:*** Hon. Fellow, Imperial Coll., London, 1993; FRSA; Hon. DBA Coventry, 1994; Hon. LLD De Montford, 1998; ***URL:*** http://www.wwf.org.uk/.

MORSI, Mohammed; Former President, Government of Egypt; ***education:*** BSc. 1975, MSc. 1978, Cairo Univ. Egypt (Engineering); PhD, Univ. of Southern California. USA, 1982 ; ***party:*** Freedom and Justice Party; ***political career:*** Independent MP, 2000-05; President, June 2012-ousted July 2013; ***professional career:*** Assist. Prof., California State Univ., USA, 1982-85; Prof., Zagazig Univ. Egypt; ***office address:*** Office of the President, Al Etehadia Building, Heliopolis, Cairo, Egypt; ***URL:*** http://www.presidency.gov.eg.

MOSCOVICI, Pierre; French, Minister of Economy and Finance, Government of France; ***born:*** 16 September 1957, Paris, France; ***parents:*** Serge Moscovici and Marie Moscovici; ***education:*** Masters in Econ., 1978; Masters in Political Sciences, 1978; Masters in Advanced Macroeconomy, 1979; Masters in Philosophy, 1980; ***party:*** Socialist Group in the European Parliament; ***political career:*** General Chmn., Cmn. for the computerisation of local Communities for the Prime Minister, 1985; Sec. Gp. if Experts of the Socialist Party, 1986-88; Technical Advisor, Education and Financial Questions, Minister of Nat, Education, 1988-90; Nat. Sec. to the Socialist Party Studies, 1992-94; Treas., Socialist Party, 1992-94; Nat. Sec., Socialist Party Studies, 1992; Head of Modernisation Dept. for Public Service and Finance at the Gen. Cmn.; Nat. Assembly Dep. for Doubs, Mem., Nat. Bd. and Nat. Cncl. of Socialist party, 1995-97; Municipal Cllr. of Montbéliard, 1995-; MEP, 1994-97, 2004; Mem., General Cncl. of Doubs, 1994; Mem., Regional Cncl. of France-Comté, 1997; Dep. Minister of European Affairs, 1997; Minister of Economy and Finance, Government of France, 2012-; ***professional career:*** Lecturer then Prof., IEP, Paris, 1984-94; Auditor, then Cllr., Court of Accounts, 1984-94; Prof., ENSAE, Lecturer, ENA, 1989-93; Prof., Univ. of Paris IX Dauphine, 1992-95; ***publications:*** L'Heure des choix, pour une économie politique, 1991; A la recherche de la gauche perdue, 1994; Quelle économie pour quel emploi?, 1995; L'urgence, plaidoyer pour une autre politique, 1997; ***office address:*** Ministry of the Economy, Finance and Industry, 139 rue de Bercy, 75012 Paris Cedex 12, France; ***phone:*** +33 (0)1 40 04 04 04; ***fax:*** +33 (0)1 43 43 75 97; ***URL:*** http://www.minefi.gouv.fr/.

MOSLEY, Stephen; MP for City of Chester, UK Government; ***party:*** Conservative; ***political career:*** MP for City of Chester, May 2010-; ***committees:*** Science and Technology Select Cttee., 2010-; Jt. Cttee. on the Draft Communications Data Bill, 2012-; ***office address:*** House of Commons, London, SW1A 0AA, United Kingdom; ***phone:*** +44 (0)20 7219 3000; ***e-mail:*** stephen.mosley.mp@parliament.uk.

MOTA SOARES, Pedro Mota; Minister of Solidarity and Social Security, Government of Portugal; ***political career:*** MP; Sec.-Gen., CDS/PP party, 2002-05, Dep. Leader; Minister of Solidarity and Social Security, 2011-; ***professional career:*** Assist. Lecturer, Fac. of Law, Lusofona Humanities and Technologies Univ.; Senior Assoc. lawyer, Nobre Guedes, Mota Soares e Associados; ***office address:*** Ministry of Social Security and Work, Praha de Londres 2, 16° Andar, 1049-056 Lisbon, Portugal.

MOTEGI, Toshimitsu; Minister of Economy, Trade and Industry, Government of Japan; ***political career:*** State Minister for Science & Tech. Policy, Okinawa & Northern Territories Affairs, 2003-07; Minister of State for Financial Services, Minister for Administrative Reform, Minister for Civil Service Reform, 2008-11; Minister of Economy, Trade and Industry, Minister of State for the Corporation in support of Compensation for Nuclear Damage, Minister for Nuclear Incident Economic Countermeasures, Minister in charge of Industrial Competitiveness, 2012-; ***office address:*** Ministry of Economy, Trade and Industry, 1-3-1 Kasumigaseki, Chiyoda-ku, Tokyo 100, Japan; ***phone:*** +81 3 3501 1511; ***fax:*** +81 3 3501 2081; ***URL:*** http://www.meti.go.jp.

MOUSOUROULIS, Constantinos ; Minister of Merchant Marine and Aegean, Government of Greece; ***political career:*** MP, 2009-; Minister of Merchant Marine and Aegean, 2012-; ***professional career:*** European Commission, 1987-2004; Board, European Investment Bank; ***office address:*** Ministry of Merchant Marine and Aegean, 150 Gregoriou Lambraki str., 18535 Pireaus, Greece; ***phone:*** +30 (0)1 412 1211; ***URL:*** http://www.yen.gr.

MOVSISYAN, Armen; Minister of Energy, Government of Armenia; ***born:*** 1962; ***education:*** Yerevan Poly. Institute, 1978-83; SU All Union of Light Industry, 1984-89; ***party:*** Republican Party of Armenia; ***political career:*** Ministry of Energy, 1997-2000; Dep. Minister of Energy, 2000-01; Minister of Energy, 2001; Minister of Energy and Natural Resources, 2007-; ***office address:*** Ministry of Energy, Government House 2, Republic Square, 375010 Yerevan, Armenia; ***phone:*** +374 10 521964.

MOWAT, David; MP for Warrington South, UK Government; ***party:*** Conservative; ***political career:*** MP for Warrington South, May 2010-; ***committees:*** Scottish Affairs Select Cttee., 2010-; ***office address:*** House of Commons, London, SW1A 0AA, United Kingdom; ***phone:*** +44 (0)20 7219 3000; ***e-mail:*** david.mowat.mp@parliament.uk.

MRKIC, Ivan; Minister of Foreign Affairs, Government of Serbia; ***born:*** 30 May 1953, Belgrade; ***education:*** Belgrade Univ. Law School, 1977; ***political career:*** Chief of Cabinet to President Dobrica Cosic, 1992; State Sec., MFA, 2012; Minister of Foreign Affairs, 2012-; ***professional career:*** joined Federal Secretariat for Foreign Affairs, 1978; UN Disarmament Fellowship; Desk Editor, Dept. for In. Orgs. of the Fed. Sec. for Foreign Affairs, 1979-82; Political Attaché, SFRY Mission to the UN, 1990-92; Chargé d'Affairs, Embassy of the FRY, then Amb., 1993-99; Amb., Federal Ministry for Foreign Affairs; Amb. of the Rep. of Serbia to Japan, 2006-11; ***office address:*** Ministry of Foreign Affairs, 24-26 Kneza Milosa Street, 11000 Belgrade, Serbia; ***phone:*** +381 11 3616-333; ***fax:*** +381 11 3618-366; ***URL:*** http://www.mfa.gov.rs/.

MSWATI III, HM King; Sovereign, Swaziland; ***born:*** 1968; ***parents:*** King Sobhuza II; ***education:*** Sherborne School, UK; ***political career:*** King of Swaziland, 1986-; ***office address:*** Royal Palace, Mbabane, Swaziland.

MUDIE, George; British, Member of Parliament for Leeds East, House of Commons; ***born:*** 6 February 1945; ***party:*** Labour Party, 1962-; ***political career:*** Leader, Leeds City Cncl.; Treasurer, HM's Household and Dep. Chief Whip, 1997; MP, Leeds East, 1992-; ***interests:*** local government, industry, training; ***professional career:*** Trade Union Official; ***office address:*** House of Commons, London, SW1A 0AA, United Kingdom; ***phone:*** +44 (0)20 7219 3000; ***e-mail:*** mudieg@parliament.uk.

MUELLER, Robert; American, Director, Federal Bureau of Investigation; ***born:*** New York City; ***education:*** Princeton Univ., 1966; New York Univ., masters degree, International Relations, 1967; Univ. of Virginia Law Sch., law degree, 1973; ***professional career:*** United States Marine Corps; Acting Dep. Attorney General, US Dept. of Justice; Dir., Federal Bureau of Investigation; ***honours and awards:*** Bronze Star; two Navy Commendation Medals; Purple Heart; Vietnamese Cross of Gallantry; ***office address:*** Federal Bureau of Investigation, 935 Pennsylvania Avenue, NW, Room 7972, Washington, DC 20535, USA.

MUGABE, Robert Gabriel; Zimbabwean, President of the Republic of Zimbabwe, Zimbabwe African National Union; ***born:*** 1924; ***parents:*** Gabriel and Bona (née Shonhiwa); ***s:*** 1; ***d:*** 2; ***languages:*** Shona, Ndebele, English; ***education:*** Kutama; Fort Hare; Univ. of London; ***party:*** Zimbabwe African National Union, 1963-; ***political career:*** Chaired the inaugural congress of the Nat. Democratic Party, 1960; Acting Sec.-Gen. and Publicity Sec., ZAPU, 1962; Founder mem., Zimbabwe African Nat. Union (ZANU), 1963; Detained, 1963-64; imprisoned, 1964-74; Re-activated the armed liberation struggle after escaping what was then Rhodesia, 1975; Joint Leader, Patriotic Front, 1976-80; First Sec. and Pres. of ZANU (PF), 1977-; Leader, ZANU deleg., Lancaster House Conference, 1979; first Prime Minister of Zimbabwe, 1980-88; pronounced policy of reconciliation and national unity, 1980; Pres. of Republic of Zimbabwe, 1988-; ***professional career:*** Teacher, 1942-60, 1952-55; Lecturer, Chalimbana Teacher Training Coll., Zambia, 1955-1958; Lecturer, Saint Mary's Teacher Training Coll., Takoradi, Ghana, 1958-1960; ***committees:*** Chairman, NAM, 1986-1989; Chairman, OAU Ad-Hoc Committee on Angola; First Chairman of SADC Organ on Defence, Politics and Security; Chairman, World Solar Commission; Chairman OAU, 1997-; ***trusteeships:*** Zimbabwe Cricket Union; Child Survival and Development Foundation; Friends of a Catholic University in Zimbabwe; Red Cross; St. John's Ambulance; St. Anne's Hospital; Daramombe Mission; 21st Feburary Youth Movement; Cambridge Scholarship Trust; ***honours and awards:*** Hon. LLD, Ahmadou Bello, Moorhouse, Univ. Zimbabwe, Edinburgh, St. Augustine College, Massachusetts, Moscow, Michigan, Solusi; Hon. D. Science, Belgrade; Hon D. LItt, Africa Univ., Hon. D. Civil Laws,Mauritius; Hon D. Commerce, Fort Hare; Hon. D. Tech., National University of Science and Technology; Africa Prize for Leadership for the Sustainable End of Hunger, 1988; Jawaharlal Nehru Award, 1989; Olympic Order of Gold, 1995; Order of Jamaica, 1996; ***office address:*** Office of the President & Cabinet, P Bag 7700, Causeway, Harare, Zimbabwe; ***phone:*** +263 (0)4 707098 / 9.

MUHITH, Abul Maal Abdul; Minister of Finance, Government of Bangladesh; ***education:*** BA (Hons.) in English Literature, MA, Dhaka Univ. Bangladesh; Oxford Univ., UK; Harvard Univ., USA; ***party:*** Bangladesh Awami League; ***political career:*** Minister of Finance, 2009-; ***office address:*** Ministry of Finance, Bangladesh Secretariat, Bldg 7 (3rd Flr), Dhaka 1000, Bangladesh; ***phone:*** +880 2 861 5950; ***fax:*** +880 2 861 5581; ***URL:*** http://www.mof.gov.bd.

MUJICA , Jose; President, Government of Uruguay; ***born:*** 1935; ***party:*** Broad Front; ***political career:*** Political prisoner, 1972-85; Senator, 1999-; Minister of Livestock, Agriculture, and Fisheries, 2005-08; President of Uruguay, Nov. 2009, took office March 2010-; ***office address:*** Office of the President, Avda Dr. Luis Alberto de Herrera 3350, Montevideo, Uruguay; ***phone:*** +598 2487 2110; ***e-mail:*** presidente@presiencia.gub.uy; ***URL:*** http://www.presidencia.gub.uy.

MUKANTABANA, Séraphine; Minister for Refugees and Disaster Management, Government of Rwanda; ***political career:*** secondary school teacher; Refugee community, Congo-Brazzaville, 1994, returned to Rwanda, 2011; refugee repatriation projects; Commissioner, Rwanda Demobilisation & Reintegration Commission, -2013; Minister for Refugees and Disaster Management, 2013-; ***office address:*** Ministry of Refugee Affairs and Disaster Management, Kigali, Rwanda.

MUKHERJEE, Shri Pranab; President, Government of India; ***born:*** 11 December 1935; ***party:*** Indian National Congress (INC); ***political career:*** Minister of Defence, 2004-06; Minister of External Affairs, 2006-09; Ministry of Finance, 2009-12; President, July 2012-; ***professional career:*** Teacher; Journalist; Lawyer; ***office address:*** Office of the President, Rashtrapati Bhavan, New Delhi 110 004, India; ***phone:*** +91 11 2301 5321; ***fax:*** +91 11 2301 7290; ***e-mail:*** poi_gen@rb.nic.in; ***URL:*** http://presidentofindia.nic.in.

MULARONI, Antonella; Secretary of State for Foreign Affairs, Government of San Marino; ***born:*** 1961; ***education:*** Law Degree; ***political career:*** Sec. of State for Foreign and Political Affairs, Telecommunications and Transport, -2013; Captain Regent, 2013-; ***office address:*** Office of the Captains Regent, Palazzo Pubblico, 47031, San Marino; ***phone:*** +378 882259.

MULHOLLAND, Greg; MP for Leeds North West, House of Commons; ***party:*** Liberal Democrat; ***political career:*** Local Councillor for Leeds North West; MP for Leeds North West, 2005-; ***committees:*** Work and Pensions, 2005-10; Public Administration, 2010- ; ***office address:*** House of Commons, London, SW1P 0AA, United Kingdom; ***phone:*** +44(0)20 7219 3000; ***e-mail:*** greg.mulholland.mp@parliament.uk.

MULLEE, H.E. Patrick; Ambassador, British Embassy in Ecuador; ***professional career:*** Posting to Venezuela, 1977-80; Latin America and Africa Floater, 1980-84; FCO Policy Planning Staff, 1985-88; Vice Consul, Costa Rica, 1988-91; 2nd Sec., Barbados, 1991-95; Dep.Hd. Personnel Management Unit; 1995 - 1997; Eastern Caribbean Desk, 1997-2000; Dep. Hd. of Mission and Consul, Peru, 2000-03; Human Resources Mgr., Directorate General for Defence and Intelligence, 2003-08; Ambassador to Uruguay, 2008-13; Ambassador to Ecuador, 2013-; ***office address:*** British Embassy, Citiplaza Building, Naciones Unidas Ave and Republica de El Salvador 14th Floor , Quito, Ecuador; ***phone:*** +593 (0)2 2970800/970801; ***fax:*** +593 (0)2 2970809; ***e-mail:*** britemq@uio.satnet.net; ***URL:*** https://www.gov.uk/government/world/ecuador.

MUMBENGEGWI, Hon. Simbarashe Simbanenduku; Minister of Foreign Affairs, Government of the Republic of Zimbabwe; ***born:*** 20 July 1945, Chivi, Zimbabwe; ***parents:*** Chivandire Mumbengegwi and Dzivaidzo Shuvai Mumbengegwi; ***married:*** Emily Mumbengegwi (née Charasika), 18 July 1983; ***children:*** Chivandire (M), Tandiwe (F), Dzivaidzo (F), Haruperi (F), Liniah (F); ***public role of spouse:*** Psychologist; ***languages:*** English, Shona; ***education:*** Monash Univ., Melbourne, Aus., BA, Politics & History, 1971; Dip. Ed. 1972; M.Ed. 1973-76; Univ. of Zimbabwe, MA in Public Admin., 1987-90 (part time); ***party:*** ZANU-PF; ***political career:*** MP., 1980-90; Dep. Minister of Foreign Affairs, 1981-82; Minister of Water Resources and Development, 1982; Minister of National Housing, 1982-84; Minister of Public Construction and National Housing, 1984-88; Minister of Transport, 1988-90; Minister of Foreign Affairs, 2005-; ***professional career:*** Secondary sch. teacher, Zvishavane, Secondary sch. teacher and Univ. tutor, Melbourne, Australia, 1966-78; Amb. and Perm, Rep. to the UN, NY, 1990-95; Vice Pres., UN General Assembly, 1990-91; Mem. UN Security Council, 1991-92. Pres., UN Security Council, 1991; Amb. to Belgium, The Netherlands, Luxembourg and Perm. Rep. to the EU, 1995; Perm. Rep. to OPCW, 1997-99; Alternate Gov. of the Common Fund for Commodities, Amsterdam, 1998-99; Chmn. of the African, Caribbean and Pacific Grp. of States Cttee. on Sugar, 1997-98; Ambassador (formerly High Commissioner) for the Republic of Zimbabwe to the UK, 1999-2005; ***recreations:*** reading, photography, tennis, jogging, golf, swimming; ***office address:*** Ministry of Foreign Affairs, Basement, Munhumutapa Building, Samora Machel Avenue, PO Box 4240, Harare, Zimbabwe; ***phone:*** +263 (0)4 727005; ***fax:*** +263 (0)4 705161.

MUNDELL, David; Member of Parliament, House of Commons; ***party:*** Conservative; ***political career:*** mem., South of Scotland, Scottish Parliament; MP for Dumfriesshire, Clydesdale and Tweedale, 2005-; Shadow Secretary of State for Scotland, 2005-10; Parly. Under Secretary of State, Scotland Office, 2010-; ***committees:*** Vice-chair, All Party Group, Scotch Whisky and Spirits Group 2005-10; Vice-chair, All Party Group, West Coast Main Line Group 2005-10; mem., Select Cttee., Scottish Affairs 2005-10; ***office address:*** House of Commons, London, SW1P 0AA, United Kingdom; ***phone:*** +44 (0)20 7219 3000.

MUNN, Meg; Member of Parliament for Sheffield Heeley, House of Commons; ***born:*** 24 August 1959, Sheffield, UK; ***parents:*** Reginald Munn (dec'd) and Lillian Munn (née Seward); ***married:*** Dennis Bates; ***education:*** Rowlinson Comprehensive Sch., Sheffield; BA (Hons) Language, York Univ., 1981; MA, Social Work,, Nottingham Univ., 1986; Certificate in Management Studies, 1995; Diploma in Management Studies, 1997; ***party:*** Labour Party Co-operative Party; ***political career:*** Cllr., Nottingham City Cncl., 1987-91; MP, Sheffield Heeley, 2001-; PPS Dept. of Education & Skills, 2003-05; Parly. Under Sec. of State, DTI, 2005-06; Parly. Under Sec. of State, DCLG, 2006-07; Parly. Under Sec. of State, FCO, 2007-08; ***interests:*** social welfare, social affairs, co-operative issues, European affairs, small business; ***professional career:*** Assistant Director, City of York Cncl., 1999-2000; ***committees:*** Education and Skills Select Cttee., 2001-03; Procedure Select Cttee., 2001-02; Pres., Cooperative Congress, 2006; Chair, All Party Methodist Cttee., 2008-; Chair, All Party Kurdistan Region in Iraq Cttee., 2008-; Chair, Westminster Foundation for Democracy, 2008-10, Vice-Chair, 2010-; Vice-Chair, All Party Women in Enterprise Cttee., 2009-; Chair, All Party Child Protection Cttee., 2010-; Vice-Chair, All Party Engineering & IT Cttee., 2010-; ***office address:*** PO Box 4333, Sheffield, S8 2EY, United Kingdom; ***phone:*** +44 (0)114 258 2010; ***fax:*** +44 (0)114 258 6622; ***e-mail:*** meg.munn.mp@parliament.uk; ***URL:*** http://www.megmunnmp.org.uk.

MUNT, Tessa; MP for Wells, UK Government; ***born:*** 16 October 1959, Sutton, Surrey, England; ***parents:*** Paul Mitchell Vasey and Jean Vasey; ***children:*** Emma (F), Harry (M); ***party:*** Liberal Democrat; ***political career:*** MP for Wells, May 2010-; ***committees:*** Education Select Cttee., 2010-12; Administration Cttee., 2010-; ***office address:*** House of Commons, London, SW1A 0AA, United Kingdom; ***phone:*** +44 (0)20 7219 3000; ***e-mail:*** tessa.munt.mp@parliament.uk.

MUNTEANU, Igor; Ambassador, Embassy of the Republic of Moldova in the USA; ***education:*** B.Sc., State Univ. of Moldova, 1989; MA, Political Sciences and Institutional Analysis, SNSPA, Romania, 1992; Ph.D in Law, Int. Free Univ. of Moldova, 2003; ***professional career:*** Amb. to USA; ***office address:*** Embassy of the Republic of Moldova, 2101 S Street, NW, Washington, DC 20008, USA; ***phone:*** +1 202 667 1130; ***fax:*** +1 202 667 1204; ***e-mail:*** washington@mfa.md; ***URL:*** http://www.sua.mfa.md/about-embassy-en.

MURDOCH, Rupert, AC; Company Chairman and Chief Executive Officer, News Corporation Ltd.; ***born:*** 1931, Melbourne, Australia; ***education:*** Oxford Univ.; ***professional career:*** Worked at the Daily Express; took control of News Limited 1954, later acquiring The Daily Mirror and The Australian; acquired News of the World and Sun; purchased The News from Hearst, 1973; purchased Times newspapers and the predecessors to Harper Collins; acquired Twentieth Century Fox Film Studio, 1985, and six Fox Television Stations; launched British Sky Broadcasting, 1989, currently Chmn.; Chmn., CEO, Exec. Dir., News Corporation Ltd; ***honours and awards:*** Companion of the Order of Australia, 1984; ***office address:*** News Corporation Ltd. (The), 2 Holt Street, Sydney 2010, NSW, Australia; ***phone:*** +61 2 9288 3000.

MURERWA, Dr Herbert Muchemwa; Zimbabwean, Minister of Lands and Land Resettlement, Zimbabwean Government; ***born:*** 1941; ***parents:*** Gamanya Murerwa; ***married:*** Ruth Chipo Dhliwayo, 1969; ***children:*** Simbarashe (M), Mudiwa (F), Gamuchirayi (F), Tapiwa (F), Danai (F); ***languages:*** Shona, English; ***education:*** George Williams Coll. BA; Harvard, MEd.; ED.D.; ***party:*** Zimbabwe African National Union; ***political career:*** Minister of Environment and Tourism, 1990-95; Minister of Industry and Commerce, 1995-96; Minister of Finance, 1996-01, 2002-04, 2004-07; Minister of Higher Education and Technology, 2001-2002; Minister of Industry and Trade, 2002; Minister of Lands and Land Resettlement, 2009-; ***professional career:*** Teacher, 1963-64; YMCA Dir., 1965-69; Econ. Affairs Officer, UN Econ. Cmn. for Africa, 1978-80; Permanent Sec., High Cmnr. for Zimbabwe to UK, 1984-89; ***office address:*** Ministry of Lands, Ground Floor, Ngungunyana Building, 1 Borrowdale Road, Private Bag 7701, Causeway, Samora Machel Ave., Harare, Zimbabwe; ***phone:*** 263 (0)4 706081; ***fax:*** +263 (0)4 792750.

MURILLO KARAM, Jesus; Attorney General, Government of Mexico; ***born:*** 1947; ***education:*** Autonomous Univ. of Hidalgo, BA, Law; ***political career:*** Senator, 2006-09; Pres., Government Commission; Mem., Jursidictional and Justice Commissions of Mexico City; Sec.-Gen., PRI National Exec. Cttee.; Fed. Rep. & Pres., Chamber of Deputies, 2012-; Secretary of Justice, 2012-; ***office address:*** Office of the Attorney General, Reforma No 211, 2 piso, Col. Guerrero, Deleg. , Cuauhtémoc 06300, Mexico; ***phone:*** +52 55 5346 2600; ***fax:*** +52 55 5346 2760.

MURKOWSKI, Lisa; Senator for Alaska, US Senate; ***education:*** Georgetown Univ., degree in Economics, 1980, Willamette College of Law, law degree, 1985; ***political career:*** mem., State House of Representatives, 1998-2002; Senator for Alaska, US Senate, 2002-; ***committees:*** Senate Energy and Natural Resources Cttee.; Appropriations Cttee.; Indian Affairs Cttee.; Health, Education, Labor and Pensions Cttee.; ***office address:*** US Senate, 322 Hart Senate Office Building, Washington, DC 20510, USA; ***URL:*** http://www.murkowski.senate.gov/public/.

MURPHY, Christopher S.; Congressman, Connecticut, US House of Representatives; ***education:*** Williams College, Massachusetts, grad. maj. in history and political science; UConn Law School, Hartford, Connecticut, 2002; ***political career:*** Mem., Connecticut HOR, 1998-2002; Senator, Connecticut Senate, 2002-06; Mem., US House of Reps., 2007-; ***professional career:*** Real estate and banking lawyer, Ruben, Johnson & Morgan, 2002-2006; ***committees:*** Jt. Economic Cttee.; Foreign Relations; Health, Education, Labor & Pensions; ***office address:*** US Senate, SD-B40A Dirksen Senate Office Building, Washington, DC 20510, USA; ***phone:*** +1 202 225 4041; ***URL:*** http://www.murphy.senate.gov.

MURPHY, Conor; Minister for Social Development, Northern Ireland Assembly; ***born:*** 1963; ***party:*** Sinn Féin; ***political career:*** mem., Northern Ireland Assembly for Newry and Armagh, 1998; MP for Newry and Armagh, 2005-; Minister for Social Development, NI Assembly, May 2007-11; ***office address:*** Constituency Office, 1 Kilmorey Terrace, Patrick Street, Newry, BT35 6DW, United Kingdom; ***e-mail:*** murphyc@parliament.uk.

MURPHY, Jim; British, Shadow Secretary of State for Defence, House of Commons; ***born:*** 23 August 1967, Glasgow; ***married:*** Claire Cook; ***education:*** Milnerton High Sch., Cape Town; ***party:*** Labour Party; ***political career:*** MP, Eastwood, 1997-; Government Whip, 2002-05; Parly. Sec., Cabinet Office, 2005-06; Minister of State for Employment and Welfare Reform, 2006-07; Minister of State with responsibility for Europe, 2007-08; Sec. of State for Scotland, Oct. 2008-May 2010; Shadow Secretary of State for Scotland, May 2010-Sept. 2010; Shadow Secretary of State for Defence, Oct. 2010-; ***interests:*** economy, int. affairs, family policy; ***office address:*** House of Commons, London, SW1A 0AA, United Kingdom; ***phone:*** +44 (0)20 7219 3000; ***e-mail:*** jimmurphymp@parliament.uk; ***URL:*** http://www.jimmurphymp.com.

MURPHY, Rt. Hon. Paul Peter, MP; British, MP for Torfaen, British Government; ***born:*** 25 November 1948, Abersychan, Pontypool, Gwent; ***parents:*** Ronald Murphy and Marjorie Murphy (née Gough); ***education:*** Oriel Coll., Oxford Univ., MA; ***party:*** Labour Party; ***political career:*** Sec., Torfaen Constituency Lab. Party, 1971-87; MP (Labour) Torfaen, 1987-; PPS to Rt. Hon. Alan Williams MP; Opp. Front Bench Spokesman on Welsh Affairs, 1988; Opp. Front Bench Spokesman on Northern Ireland, 1994; Fmr. Opp. Spokesman on Foreign Affairs; Minister of State, Northern Ireland Office, 1997-99; Privy Cllr., 1999; Sec. of State for Wales, 1999-2003; Sec. of State for Northern Ireland, 2003-05; Secretary of State for Wales, 2008-09; ***memberships:*** TGWU; ***professional career:*** Management Trainee, CWS, 1970-71; Lecturer, History and Govt., Ebbw Vale Coll., 1971-87; mem., Torfaen Borough Cncl., 1973-87; Chmn., Torfaen Borough Cncl. Finance Cttee., 1976-86; ***committees:*** PLP Welsh Gp., 1987-; Chmn., Parliamentary Intelligence and Security Cttee., 2005-08; ***honours and awards:*** Knight of St. Gregory; Hon. Fellow, Oriel Coll. Oxford; Hon. Fellow, Gyndwr (Wrexham) Univ.; ***clubs:*** St. Joseph's; St. Dias; Oxford and Cambridge Club; ***recreations:*** classical music, cooking; ***office address:*** House of Commons, London, SW1P 0AN, United Kingdom; ***e-mail:*** paul.murphy.mp@parliament.uk.

MURPHY, Philip D.; Ambassador , US Embassy in Germany; ***education:*** Harvard Univ., USA, 1979; The Wharton School, Univ. of Pennsylvania; ***professional career:*** Amb. to Germany 2009-; ***office address:*** Embassy of the United States of America, Neustädtische Kirchstraße 4-5, 10117 Berlin, Germany; ***phone:*** +49 (0)30 830 50; ***fax:*** +49 (0)30 238 6290; ***URL:*** http://www.usembassy.de.

MURPHY, Scott; Congressman, New York 20th Dist., US House of Representatives; ***born:*** 1970, Columbia, Missouri; ***education:*** Harvard; ***political career:*** Mem., US HOR, 2009-; ***professional career:*** Business entrepreneur; Aide to Gov. Mel Carnahan; Dep. Chief of Staff to Gov. Roger Wilson, Missouri; Fndr., Advantage Capital Partners, 2001; ***office address:*** House of Representatives, 120 Cannon HOB, Washington DC 20515, USA; ***phone:*** +1 202 225 5514; ***URL:*** http://scottmurphy.house.gov/.

MURRAY, Ian, MP; MP for Edinburgh South, House of Commons; ***party:*** Labour; ***political career:*** Councillor, Edinburgh City Council 2003-10; MP for Edinburgh South, May 2010-; Shadow Minister, Business, Innovation and Skills, 2011-; ***committees:*** Environmental Audit, 2010-; Business, Innovation and Skills, 2010-11; Arms Export Controls, 2010-12; ***office address:*** House of Commons, London, SW1A 0AA , United Kingdom; ***phone:*** +44 (0)20 7219 3000; ***e-mail:*** ian.murray.mp@parliament.uk.

MURRAY, Patty, BA; Senator for Washington, US Senate; ***born:*** 10 October 1950, Bothell, Washington, USA; ***married:*** Rob Murray, 1972; ***children:*** Sara (F), Randy (M); ***education:*** Washington State Univ., BA, 1972; ***party:*** Democrat; ***political career:*** Washington State Senator; US Senator for Washington, 1992-; Dep. Minority Whip; Democratic Conference Sec., 2007-; ***professional career:*** Bd. of Dirs., Shoreline Sch. District; ***committees:*** Appropriations; Budget; Health, Education, Labor and Pension; Veterans

Affairs; Rules and Administration; Jt. Cttee. on Printing; Democratic Leadership, Conference Secretary; *honours and awards:* honoured by numerous orgs. incl. Congressional Youth Leadership Cncl., United Jewish Appeal, Nat. Farmer's Union, US Cttee. for UNICEF, Cttee. for Education Funding; *office address:* US Senate, 173 Russell Senate Office Building, Washington, DC 20510, USA; *phone:* +1 202 224 2621; *fax:* +1 202 224 2262; *URL:* http://www.murray.senate.gov.

MURRAY, Sheryll; MP for South East Cornwall, UK Government; *born:* 1956; *party:* Conservative; *political career:* MP for South East Cornwall, May 2010-; *committees:* Environmental Audit, 2010-; *office address:* House of Commons, London, SW1A 0AA, United Kingdom; *phone:* +44 (0)20 7219 3000; *e-mail:* sheryll.murray.mp@parliament.uk.

MURRISON, Andrew; Member of Parliament for South West Wiltshire, House of Commons; *born:* 1961, Colchester, Essex; *parents:* William Murrison RD (dec'd) and Marion Murrison (née Horn); *married:* Jenny Murrison (née Munden); *public role of spouse:* Physiotherapist; *education:* The Harwich Sch.; Bristol and Cambridge Univ.; *party:* Conservative Party; *political career:* MP, Westbury, 2001-10, South West Wiltshire, 2010-; Shadow Health Minister, 2003-07; Shadow Defence Minister, 2007-10; PPS to Andrew Lansley as Secretary of State for Health, 2010-12; Parly. Under-Sec. of State (International Security Strategy), Ministry of Defence, 2012-; *professional career:* Surgeon Commander, Royal Navy; called up to serve as Medical Officer, Iraq, 2003; *office address:* House of Commons, London, SW1A 0AA, United Kingdom; *phone:* +44 (0)20 7219 8337; *e-mail:* murrisona@parliament.uk; *URL:* http://www.parliament.uk.

MUSCAT, Dr Joseph; Prime Minister, Government of Malta; *born:* 1974; *education:* Univ. of Malta; Univ. of Bristol; *political career:* Education Sec., Partit Laburista; National Commission for Fiscal Morality, 1997-98; MP, 2004; Leader, Partit Laburista, 2008; Prime Minister, 2013-; *professional career:* journalist; investment adviser; *office address:* Office of the Prime Minister, Auberge de Castille, Valletta VLT 2000, Malta; *e-mail:* joseph.muscat@gov.mt.

MUSEVENI, Lt.-Gen. Yoweri Kaguta; Ugandan, President, Government of Uganda; *born:* 1944; *parents:* Amos Kaguta Museveni and Esteeri Museveni (née Kokundeka); *married:* Janet Museveni (née Kataaha); *s:* 1; *d:* 3; *public role of spouse:* Founder, Ugandan Women's Effort to Save Orphans; *languages:* English, Swahili; *education:* Univ. of Dar-es-Salaam, Tanzania, Pol. Sci., Econ. and Law; *political career:* Research Asst., Office of Milton Obote, former Pres., 1970-71; exile, Tanzania 1971-79; formed Front for National Salvation, participated in invasion of Uganda, 1979; Minister of Defence, interim Govt. of late Prof. Yusuf Lule, 1980; removed by his successor Pres. Godfrey Binaisa; Vice-Chmn., following replacement of Govt. by Military Commission, 1980; formed National Resistance Army, waged war against Obote Regime, following Obote's return to power in 1980, 1981-86; Pres. of Uganda 1986-; *interests:* regional integration of African countries; *professional career:* Cattle Farmer; *honours and awards:* Pearl of Africa, Class One; *publications:* What is Africa's Problem?, Speeches, 1992; Sowing the Mustard Seed, Autobiography, Macmillan, 1997; *recreations:* football; *office address:* Office of the President, Parliament Buildings, PO Box 7168 , Kampala, Uganda; *phone:* +256 41 254881/9; *fax:* +256 41 235462; *URL:* http://www.statehouse.go.ug/.

MUSHARRAF, General Pervez; Former President, Islamic Republic of Pakistan; *born:* 11 August 1943, Delhi; *parents:* Syed Musharaff-ud-Din (dec'd); *married:* Sehba Musharraf, 28 December 1968; *languages:* Turkish; *education:* Saint Patrick's High Sch., Karachi and Forman Christian Coll., Lahore; Command and Staff Coll., Quetta and the Nat. Defence Coll., graduate; Royal Coll. of Defence Studies, UK; *political career:* Pres. & Chief Exec. of Pakistan, 1999-2002; elected PM, Oct. 2002; Pres., 2002-08; *professional career:* Pakistan Military Academy, 1961; commissioned in Artillery Regiment, 1964; volunteered and served seven years in the Special Service Group 'Commandos', participated as Co. Cmdr. in Commando Battalion, 1971; Brigadier, Infantry Brigade and Armoured Div. Artillery; Major Gen., Infantry Div., 1991; Lt. General, Strike Corps., 1995; served on various important staff and instructional appointments, including Dep. Military Sec. at Military Secretary's Branch, mem. of Directing Staff at the Command and Staff Coll., Quetta and the Nat. Defence Coll.; Dir. General Military Operations at General HQ; General and Chief of Army Staff, 1998-; *committees:* Chmn., Joint Chiefs of Staff Cttee., 1999-2001; *honours and awards:* Imtiazi Sanad for gallantry; *recreations:* squash, badminton, golf, water sports, canoeing, sailing, reading, military history; *office address:* c/o PML-Q, Central Secretariat, Parliament Lodges, Islamabad, Pakistan.

MUSHIKIWABO, Louise; Rwandan, Minister of Foreign Affairs and Co-operation, Government of Rwanda; *born:* 1961; *education:* Univ. of Delaware, USA; *political career:* Minister of Information; Minister of Foreign Affairs & Cooperation; *honours and awards:* Outstanding Humanitarian Award, American Univ., School of International Studies, 2004; *publications:* Rwanda Means the Universe, 2006; numerous articles; collaborated on many documentary films; *office address:* Ministry of Foreign Affairs, PO Box 179, Kigali, Rwanda; *URL:* http://www.minaffet.gov.rw/.

MUSTILL, Lord Michael John, PC, LLD, FBA; British; *born:* 10 May 1931; *languages:* English; *education:* Cambridge University, BA, 1955, Law, Doctor of Laws; Legal qualification: Barrister; *political career:* Mem., House of Lords, 1992-; *interests:* Claims; Dispute settlement; Jurisdiction; History & theory; Litigation; *memberships:* British Academy; American Law Institute; *professional career:* academic career: Cambridge University, Goodhart Visiting Professor in Legal Science; Part-time teacher of law at various institutions; professional career: Barrister, 1955-78; Vice-President, Court of Arbitration, International Chamber of Commerce; Panellist, ICSID Panel of Arbitrators; judicial career:High Court Judge, 1978-85; Lord Justice of Appeal, 1989-91; Lord of Appeal, 1991-97; More than 100 arbitrations as Chairman and Member; *publications:* Books: Commercial Arbitration, co-author, 1982, 2nd ed, 1992, companion volume, 2001; Charterparties & Bills of Lading, co-editor, 17th ed, 1964, 18th ed, 1974, 19th ed, 1984; Marine Insurance, Joint Editor, 1981; Articles: Sjoratts forenigen I Goteborg; Arkiv for Sjorett; Current Legal Problems; Arbitration International; Israel Law Review; Asia Pacific Law Review; Juridsisk Tidskrift; *office address:* Essex Court Chambers, 24 Lincoln's Inn Fields, London, WC2A 3EG, UK; *phone:* +44 (0)207 813 8000; *fax:* +44 (0)207 813 8080; *e-mail:* lpaterson@essexcourt.net.

MUTORWA, Hon. John; Minister of Agriculture, Water and Forestry, Namibian Government; *political career:* Minister of Basic Education, Sport and Culture, to 2004; Minister of Youth, National Service, Sport and Culture, 2004-08; Minister of Agriculture, Water and Forestry, 2008-; *office address:* Ministry of Agriculture, Water and Forestry, Private Bag 13184, Windhoek, Namibia; *phone:* +264 61 208 7111; *fax:* +26461 229961.

MUTSEKWA, Giles; Minister of National Housing and Social Amenities, Government of Zimbabwe; *born:* 1948; *education:* Diploma in Business Management; Diploma in Transport Management; *party:* Movement for Democratic Change; *political career:* Sec. for Security and Intelligence (MDC); MP for Mutare North, 2000-08; MP for Dangamvura/Chikanga, 2008-; Co-Minister of Home Affairs, Feb. 200-June 2010; Minister of National Housing and Social Amenities, June 2010-; *professional career:* Army Major (Retired); *office address:* Ministry of National Housing and Social Amenities, 6th Floor, Kaguvi Building, Harare, Zimbabwe.

MVOUBA, Isidore; Minister of State, Minister for Transport, Civil Aviation and Merchant Marine, Government of the Republic of the Congo; *born:* 1954; *party:* Congolese Labour Party ; *political career:* Minister of Transport, Civil Aviation, and Merchant Navy, Co-ordinator for Government Action, 2002-04; Prime Minister, 2004-09 (poition abolished); Minister of State, Minister for Transport, Civil Aviation and Merchant Marine, 2009-; *professional career:* Railway Engineer; *office address:* Office of the Minister of State, PO Box 2096, Brazzaville, Republic of Congo.

MWANDOSYA, Prof. Mark; Minister without Portfolio, Government of Tanzania; *political career:* Minister of Communications and Transport; Minister of State in the Vice President's Office, 2006-08; Minister of Water and Irrigation, 2008-12; Minister without portfolio, May 2012-; *office address:* National Assembly, PO Box 941, Dodoma, Tanzania.

MYASNIKOVICH, Mikhail; Prime Minister, Government of Belarus; *born:* May 1950; *political career:* Deputy Prime Minister, 1995-2001; Prime Minister, Dec. 2010-; *professional career:* Engineer; Chmn. National Academy of Sciences; *office address:* Office of the Prime Minister, Council of Ministers, Independent Square, 220010 Minsk, Belarus; *phone:* +375 (8)172 226016; *fax:* +375 (8)172 226665.

N

NAILATIKAU, H.E. Brigadier General Ratu Epeli; Fijian, President, Government of Fiji; *born:* 1941; *married:* Adi Koila, 1981; *education:* Queen Victoria School, Fiji; officer training in New Zealand and Australia; Foreign Service course, Oxford, 1969-70; Australian Army College, 1976; Australian Joint Services Staff College, 1980; *political career:* Deputy Prime Minister and Minister for Fijian Affairs, 2000-03; Minister of Foreign Affairs and External Trade, 2007-08; Chair of the Great Council of Chiefs, Minister for Indigenous and Multi-Ethnic Affairs, Minister for Provincial Development, 2008; President of Fiji, 2009; *professional career:* Royal Fiji Military Forces, 1962; commissioned in Fiji Infantry Regiment, 1963; seconded to First Battalion, Royal New Zealand Infantry Regiment, Malaysia and Borneo, 1966; ADC to Govr. of Fiji, 1968-69; Fiji equerry to The Prince of Wales during the Fiji Independence visit, 1970; 2nd Secy., High Commission, Canberra, 1970-72; 2nd Secy., Mission to UN, 1973-74; Fiji equerry to the Queen during her visit, 1977; Commanding Officer, Fiji Battalion, Fiji Infantry Regiment serving with UN Interim Force in Lebanon (UNIFIL), 1978-79; Senior Plans Officer, UNIFIL HQ, Lebanon, 1981; Chief of Staff, Royal Fiji Military Forces, 1981-82 (Commander, 1982-87); Ambassador to Court of St. James's, Denmark, Federal Republic of Germany, Israel, the Holy See and Egypt, 1988-; *honours and awards:* Lieutenant of Victoria Order 1977; Officer of Most Excellent Order of the British Empire 1979; Officer of Order of St. John of Jerusalem 1985; Meritorious Service Decoration 1988; *office address:* PO Box 2513, Government Buildings, Suva, Fiji; *phone:* +679 3314 244; *fax:* +679 3301 645; *e-mail:* info@fiji.gov.fj; *URL:* http://www.fiji.gov.fi.

NAKAO, Takehiko; President, Asian Development Bank; *born:* 1956; *education:* Univ. of Tokyo, economics; Univ. of California, Berkeley, MBA; *political career:* Vice Minister of Finance for International Affairs, Ministry of Finance of Japan, -2013; *professional career:* joined Ministry of Finance, 1978, various senior positions incl. Dir.-Gen., International Bureau; economist & advisor, IMF, 1994-97; Minister, Embassy of Japan, Washington DC, USA, 2005-11; Visiting Prof., Univ. of Tokyo, 2010-11; Pres., Asian Development Bank, 2013-; *office address:* Asian Development Bank, 6 ADB Avenue, Mandaluyong City 1550, Manila, Philippines; *URL:* http://www.adb.org.

NALBANDIAN, Edward; Minister of Foreign Affairs, Government of Armenia; *born:* 1956; *d:* 1; *languages:* Arabic, English, French, Russian; *education:* Moscow State Inst. of Int. Relations, 1978; Ph.D. in political science, USSR Nat. Academy of Sciences, Inst. of Oriental studies, 1988; *political career:* Minister of Foreign Affairs of the Republic of Armenia, April 2008-; *professional career:* various diplomatic postings incl.: USSR Embassy, Lebanon, 1978-83; Chargé d'Affaires in Egypt for Armenia, 1992-93; Armenian Ambassador to Egypt, 1994-98; Amb. to France, 1999-2008; Amb. to Israel, 2000-08 (resident in Paris); Amb to Andorra, 2004-08; Int. org. of Francophony, Special Representative of the President of RA, 2006; *honours and awards:* USSR award of Friendship of Nations, 1982; Commander of the Legion of Honor of the French Republic, 2001; Armenian Medal of Mkhitar Gosh, 2001; Decoration of the Grand Cross of Saint Gregory of the Holy See, 2003; *office address:* Ministry of Foreign Affairs, Republic Square, Government House 2, Yerevan, Armenia.

NAMGYAL WANGCHUK, King Jigme Khesar; King, Kingdom of Bhutan; ***born:*** 1980; ***parents:*** Jigme Singye Wangchuk and Tshering Yangdon; ***education:*** Wheaton Coll., Massachusetts; Magdalene, Oxford, M.Phil., Politics; ***professional career:*** King of Bhutan, December 2006-; ***office address:*** Office of the King, Tashichhodzong, Thimphu, Bhutan; ***phone:*** +975 2 22521; ***fax:*** +975 2 22079.

NANDI-NDAITWAH, Netumbo; Minister of Foreign Affairs, Government of Namibia; ***born:*** 1952; ***political career:*** political activist, exiled; senior SWAPO member; Pres., Namibian National Women's Org., 19991-94; Mem., National Assembly, 1990-; Dep. Minister of Foreign Affairs, 1990-96; Dir-Gen. for Women's Affairs, Office of the President, 1996-2000; Minister for Women; Minister of Information; Minister of Environment & Tourism, 2010-12; Minister of Foreign Affairs, 2012-; ***office address:*** Ministry of Foreign Affairs, Government Buildings, 4th Floor, East Wing, Private Bag 13347, Windhoek, Namibia; ***phone:*** + 264 61 282 9111; ***fax:*** + 264 61 223937 ; ***URL:*** http://www.mfa.gov.na.

NANDY, Lisa; MP for Wigan, UK Government; ***party:*** Labour; ***political career:*** Councillor, London Borough of Hammersmith and Fulham Council, 2006-10; MP for Wigan, May 2010-; PPS to Tessa Jowell as Shadow Minister for London and the Olympics, 2011-12; Shadow Minister for Children and Families, 2012-; ***committees:*** Education Select Cttee., 2010-12; ***office address:*** House of Commons, London, SW1A 0AA, United Kingdom; ***phone:*** +44 (0)207219 3000; ***e-mail:*** lisa.nandy.mp@parliament.uk.

NAPOLITANO, President Giorgio; Italian, President , Republic of Italy; ***born:*** 29 June 1925, Naples, Italy; ***education:*** Naples Univ., Doctor in Law, 1942-47; ***party:*** Former member, Partito Comunista Italiano (PCI, Italian Communist Party); ***political career:*** Student activist-communist and anti-fascist; Co-founder of student movement, Naples Univ. and nationally, 1945-46; fmr. Secy. Communist Federations of Naples and Caserta; Mem. for Naples - Caserta, Chamber of Deputies, 1953-63, 1968-1996; mem. Leadership of PCI, from 10th Congress; Chmn., PCI Parly. Gp., 1981-86; mem., Italian delegation to the NATO Assembly, 1984-89; MEP, 1989-92; Speaker, Italian Chamber of Deputies, 1992-94; Pres., Italian Cncl. of European Movement, 1995-; Minister of the Interior, 1996-98; MEP, 1999-2004; Senator for Life, 2005-; President of Italy, 2006-; ***committees:*** Head of Southern Cttee. of Central Cttee. of PCI; Head of Cttee. on Mass Work; mem., Central Cttee. from 8th Congress of PCI; Head of Cultural Cttee. of Central Cttee. of PCI; mem., Cttee. on Trade and Industry; mem., Cttee. on Labour; mem., Central Cttee. of PCI; mem., Cttee. on Budget and Planning, 1987; mem., Foreign Affairs Cttee., 1987-92; Chmn., Special Cttee. for the Reorganisation of the Radio and Television Sector, 1995-96; Chmn., Constitutional Cttee. of the European Parliament, 1999-2004; ***publications:*** Interview on the PCI, 1975; Halfway through the Crossing, 1979; Beyond the Old Borders - The Future of Left and Europe, 1989; The Reformist Choice, 1990; Europe and America after 1989 - the Collapse of Communism, the Problems of the Left, 1992; Dove va la Repubblica, 1994; Europa politica - Il difficile approado di un lungo percorso, 2003; Dal Pci al socialismo europeo - Un'autobriografia politica, 2005; ***office address:*** Palazzo del Quirinale, 00187 Rome, Italy; ***phone:*** +39 (0)6 46991; ***fax:*** +39 (0)6 4699 3125; ***URL:*** http://www.quirinale.it.

NAPOLITANO, Grace F.; American, Congresswoman, California 38th District, US House of Representatives; ***party:*** Democrat; ***political career:*** CA State Assembly, 1992-98; Mem., US House of Representatives, 1998-; ***committees:*** Natural Resources; Transportation and Infrastructure; ***office address:*** House of Representatives, 436 Cannon House Street, Washington, DC 20515-6501, USA; ***phone:*** +1 202 224 3121.

NAPOLITANO, Janet; Secretary of Homeland Security, US Government; ***born:*** 29 November 1957, New York City, NY, USA; ***education:*** Santa Clara Univ., California, Truman Scholar and graduate summa cum laude; Univ. of Virginia law school; ***party:*** Democratic Party; ***political career:*** Attorney General, Arizona, 1998; Governor, State Government of Arizona, 2002-09; US Secretary of Homeland Security, 2009-; ***professional career:*** Attorney, Arizona; ***office address:*** Department of Homeland Security, Washington DC 20528, USA; ***URL:*** http://www.dhs.gov/dhspublic.

NAPTHINE, Hon. Dr Denis; Premier, Government of Victoria; ***born:*** 1952; ***political career:*** MLA, Portland, 1988-2002; Leader of the Opp., 1999-2002; MLA, South-West Coast, 2002-; Shadow Minister for Rural and Regional Development, 2002; Shadow Minister for State & Regional Development, 2002-04; Shadow Minister for Rural & Regional Development, 2004-05;. Shadow Minister for Agriculture (Including Forestry), 2005-06; Shadow Minister for Water, 2005-06; Shadow Minister for Agriculture, 2006; Shadow Minister for Ports & Shadow Minister for Racing, 2006-10. Shadow Minister for Regional and Rural Development, 2006-08; Shadow Minister for Regional Cities, 2008-10; Leader of the Liberal Party, 2013-; Leader, Victorian Liberal Nationals Coalition, 2013-; Premier, March 2013-; ***office address:*** Office of the Premier, Level 1, Treasury Place, Melbourne, VIC 3002, Australia; ***URL:*** http://www.premier.vic.gov.au/.

NARESH YADAV, Ram; Governor, Madhya Pradesh; ***born:*** 1928; ***party:*** Indian National Congress; ***political career:*** Chief Minister, Uttar Pradesh, 1977-79; Governor of Madhya Pradesh, 2011-; ***professional career:*** Lawyer; ***office address:*** Office of the Governor, Raj Bhavan, Bhopal, India.

NASEBY, Lord; British, Backbencher, House of Lords; ***born:*** 25 November 1936, Bromley, Kent, UK; ***married:*** Lady Naseby (née Ann Appleby), 3 September 1960; ***children:*** Julian R.L. (M), Jocelyn C.L. (M), Susannah (F); ***languages:*** French; ***education:*** Bedford Sch.; St. Catharine's Coll., Cambridge; ***party:*** Conservative Party; ***political career:*** MP for Northampton South, 1974-97; Dep. Speaker and Chmn. of Ways and Means, 1992-98; Backbencher, House of Lords; ***interests:*** South & Southeast Asia, NHS, trade and industry; ***professional career:*** Chmn., Tunbridge Wells Equitable Soc.; Chmn., Invesco Recovery Trust plc, 2011; ***honours and awards:*** Privy Cllr.; Sri Lanka Ratna Award; Hon. Fellowship in History, Univ. of Northampton; ***publications:*** Helping the Exporter; The Disaster of Direct Labour; ***clubs:*** MCC; All England Tennis; Royal St. George's G.C.; John of Gaunt G.C.; Carlton Club; Lord Taverners; Northamptonshire County Cricket Club, Pres.; ***recreations:*** tennis, golf, cricket, history, Patron, Naseby Battlefield Trust; ***office address:*** House of Lords, London, SW1A 0PW, United Kingdom; ***phone:*** +44 (0)20 7219 5353; ***fax:*** +44 (0)20 7219 5613.

NASH, Lord John Stoddard; Member, House of Lords; ***political career:*** Mem., House of Lords, 2013-; Parly. Under Sec., (Dept. of Education), 2013-; ***professional career:*** Dir., Stourbridge Properties Ltd.; Dir., Signature Hotel Group Ltd.; Dir., Future Academies; ***office address:*** House of Lords, London, SW1A 0PW, United Kingdom; ***phone:*** +44 (0)20 7219 5353.

NASH, Pamela; MP for Airdrie and Shotts, UK Government; ***party:*** Labour; ***political career:*** MP for Airdrie and Shotts, May 2010-; PPS to various shadow secretaries of state, 2011-; ***committees:*** Science and Technology Select Cttee., 2010-; Scottish Affairs, 2012-; ***office address:*** Constituency Office, 100 Stirling Street, Airdre, ML6 0AS, United Kingdom; ***phone:*** +44 (0)1236 753795; ***e-mail:*** pamela.nash.mp@parliament.uk.

NATALEGAWA, Raden Mohammad (Marty); Minister of Foreign Affairs, Government of Indonesia; ***education:*** London School of Economics and Political Science, 1984; Corpus Christi College, Univ. of Cambridge, UK, 1985; Australian National Univ., 1993; ***political career:*** Minister of Foreign Affairs, 2009-; ***professional career:*** Amb. to the United Kingdom; Perm. Rep. to the UN, 2007-09; ***office address:*** Ministry of Foreign Affairs, Jalan Taman Pejambon 6, Jakarta 10410, Indonesia; ***phone:*** +62 (0)21 3441 508; ***URL:*** http://www.deplu.go.id.

NATH, Kamal; Minister of Urban Development, Government of India; ***born:*** 18 November 1946, Kanpur, Uttar Pradesh, India; ***parents:*** Mahendra Nath and Leela Nath; ***married:*** Alka Nath, 2 January 1973; ***children:*** Nakul (M), Bakul (M); ***languages:*** English; ***education:*** St. Xavier's Coll., Calcutta, B.Commerce; ***party:*** Indian National Congress; ***political career:*** Joined Indian National Congress as youth worker, 1968; MP for Chhindwara Constituency, 1980-; Indian rep. at UN General Assembly, 1982 and 1983; Delegate at Int. Parly. Union Conferences, Nicaragua 1987, Guatemala 1988 and Cyprus 1990; Union Cncl. of Ministers: Minister of Environment and Forests, 1991-94; Textile Minister, 1995; Minister, Commerce & Industry; Minister of Road Transport and Highways, 2009-10; Minister of Urban Development, 2011-; ***interests:*** rural development; ***professional career:*** Pres., Bd. of Governors, Inst. of Management Technology, Ghaziabad; ***committees:*** Chmn., Madhya Pradesh Child Devel. Council; ***trusteeships:*** Patron, Bharat Yuvak Samaj; ***publications:*** India's Environmental Concerns; ***clubs:*** Calcutta Cricket & Football Clubs; ***recreations:*** listening to music; ***office address:*** Ministry of Urban Development, Nirman Bhavan, New Delhi 110 011, India; ***phone:*** +91 (0)11 301 9377; ***fax:*** +91 (0)11 301 4459; ***e-mail:*** knath@knath.com; ***URL:*** http://www.muepa.nic.in.

NAVRACSICS, Tibor; Deputy Prime Minister, Government of Hungary; ***born:*** 13 June 1966; ***languages:*** English, Serbian, Croatian; ***education:*** LLB., 1990, Higher degree as a Judge, 1992; PhD, Political Science, 2000; ***political career:*** MP, 2006-; Deputy Prime Minister, Minister of Justice and Administration, 2010-; ***professional career:*** Municipal Court, City of Veszprém; Assist. Prof. Univ. of Economics, Budapest; ***office address:*** Ministry of Justice, Szalay u. 16, 1055 Budapest, Hungary; ***phone:*** +36 (0)1 441 3003; ***fax:*** +36 (0)1 268 3702; ***URL:*** http://www.lm.hu.

NAZARBAYEV, Nursultan Abisevich, DSc (Econ); Kazakh, President, Republic of Kazakhstan; ***born:*** July 6 1940, Chemolgan, Kashelen District; ***education:*** Technical College, Karaganda integrated iron-and-steel works, 1967; Hon. Academician of the International Engineering Academy; Dsc, economics; ***political career:*** Party activities, 1977-84; Chmn., Council of Ministers of the Republic, 1984-89; First Secy., Central Cttee. of the Communist Party of Kazakhstan, 1989; Chmn., Supreme Council of the Republic of Kazakhstan, 1990 (elected by the Supreme Council); President of the Republic of Kazakhstan, 1991-; ***professional career:*** Iron founder, furnace attendant, metallurgical engineer, Karagandy integrated iron-steel works 1960-77; ***office address:*** Office of the President, 11 Mira Street, 473000 Astana, Kazakhstan.

NCHIMBI, Dr Emmanuel; Minister of Home Affairs, Government of Tanzania; ***born:*** 1971; ***education:*** Inst. of Dev. Management; Commonwealth Open Univ., Msc, 2001; Mzumbe Univ., MBA, 2003; Commonwealth Open Univ., Ph.D, Management, 2003; ***political career:*** District Commissioner, Regional Administration & Local Governments, 2003-05; Dep. Minister, Labour, Employment and Youth Dev., 2006-08; Dep. Minister, Ministry of Information, Culture & Sports, 2006; Dep. Minister, Ministry of Defence and National Service, 2008; Minister of Home Affairs, to date; ***office address:*** Ministry of Home Affairs, PO Box 77954, Dar es Salaam, Tanzania; ***phone:*** +255 754 003 388; ***e-mail:*** enchimbi@parliament.go.tz.

NCUBE, Welshman; Deputy Prime Minister, Government of Zimbabwe; ***born:*** 1961; ***education:*** BL, LLB, MPhil (Law), Univ. of Zimbabwe; ***party:*** Sec. Gen., Movement for Democratic Change; ***political career:*** MP for Bulawayo, 2000-08; Minister for Industry and Commerce, Feb. 2009-11; Deputy Prime Minister, 2011-; ***professional career:*** Professor of Law, Univ. of Zimbabwe; ***office address:*** Parliament Buildings, Box CY 298, Causeway, Harare, Zimbabwe.

NDEBELE, Joel Sibusiso; Minister of Correctional Services, Government of South Africa; ***born:*** 17 October 1948; ***education:*** Univ. of Zululand, Library Science, 1970-72; Univ. of South Africa, BA, Int. Politics & African Politics, 1982-83; BA, Dev. Admin. & Politics, 1985; ***political career:*** Chairperson, ANC in KwaZulu-Natal Province, 2002; Premier, KwaZulu-Natal Province, April 2004; Minister of Transport, 2009-12; Minister of Correctional Services, 2012-; ***committees:*** mem., Nat. Exec. Cttee. (NEC) of the African Nat. Congress (ANC); mem., Provincial Exec. Cttee. & the Provincial Working Cttee. of the ANC, 1994-; ***trusteeships:*** Founder & Chairperson, African Renaissance Trust; ***office address:*** Department of Correctional Services, Private Bag X853, Pretoria 0001, South Africa; ***URL:*** http://www.dcs.gov.za.

NDIAYE, Aly Ngouille; Minister of Mines and Energy, Government of Senegal; ***education:*** Thies Polytechnic School of Senegal; Illinois Inst. of Technology, Chicago; ***political career:*** Minister of Mines and Energy, 2012-; ***professional career:*** Business; Loan Director, Banque de l'Habitate du Sénégal; set up Djollof Microfinance Scheme; ***office***

address: Ministry of Mines and Energy, avenue André Peytavin 122 bis, BP 4037, Dakar, Senegal; **phone:** +221 33 889 5757; **fax:** +221 33 822 554; **URL:** http://www.industrie.gouv.sn.

NDIAYE, Mankeur; Minister of Foreign Affairs, Government of Senegal; **born:** 1960; **party:** Independent; **political career:** Minister of Foreign Affairs, Oct. 2012-; **professional career:** Ambassador, 2003-12, incl. Ambassador to France; **office address:** Ministry of Foreign Affairs, 1 place de l'Indépendance, BP 4044, Dakar, Senegal; **phone:** +221 33 889 1300; **fax:** +221 33 823 54 96; **URL:** http://www.diplomatie.gouv.sn.

NDONGO, Jacques Fame; Minister of Higher Education, Government of Cameroon; **born:** 14 November 1950, Nkolandom; **education:** Bac Philo, Yaoundé, 1969; Diploma ESJ, Lille, France, 1972; Univ. of Yaoundé, BA, 1972, MA, 1973; Univ. of Lille, Further studies diploma (DEA), 1976, Ph.D., 1978; Assistant, Univ. of Yaoundé, 1978; Univ. of Paris VII, Ph.D., 1984, junior lecturer, 1988, senior lecturer, 1992, professor, 1992; **political career:** Head of Mission, Communication for President Biya, Civil Cabinet, 1984-; Minister of Communications, 2000-04; Minister for Higher Education, 2004-; **professional career:** Head, national column, Cameroon Press Agency, 1972-74; Exec. Editor-in-chief, Cameroon Tribune, 1974-78; Dir., Ecole Supérieure des Sciences et Techniques de l'information et de la Communication, 1981-92; Rector, Univ. of Yaoundé I, 1988; Head, Dept. of Communication for Africa, ESSTIC, 1993-; Head, Hospital Centre of Univ. of Yaoundé, 1999-; Head, Cameroon Radio and Television, 2000-; **honours and awards:** Traditional chief (3rd degree), Nkolandom; **publications:** L'esthétique romanesque de Mongo Beti, 1985, Présence Africaine, Paris; Le Price et le Scribe, 1988, (Epi d'Or), Berger Levrault, Paris; Nnanga Kon (Translation from French), 1989, Editions Sopecam; La Communication par les signaux en milieu rural. Le cas du Cameroun., 1991, Editions Sopecam; Un regard africain sur la communication, 1983, Editions St Paul; Espace de Lumère, 2000, Presses Univ. de Yaoundé; Le temps des Titans, 2002, Presse Univ. de Yaoundé; Paul Biya ou l'incarnation de la rigeur, 1983, Editions Sopecam; Le Renouveau camerounais, 1983, Editions ESSTI; **office address:** Ministry of Higher Education, c/o Central Post Office, Yaoundé, Cameroon.

NDONG SIMA, Raymond; Prime Minister, Government of Gabon; **born:** 23 January 1955; **party:** Gabonese Democratic Party; **political career:** Minister of Agriculture, Livestock and Rural Development, 2009-11; Prime Minister, 2012-; **office address:** Office of the Prime Minister, BP 546, Libreville, Gabon; **phone:** +241 177 8981.

NEGRUTA, Vaceslav; Minister of Finance, Government of Moldova; **born:** 1972; **party:** Liberal Democratic Party of Moldova; **political career:** Minister of Finance, 2009-; **professional career:** Economist; **office address:** Ministry of Finance, Cosmonautilor 7, MD2005, Chisinau, Moldova; **phone:** +373 22 233575; **fax:** +373 22 228610; **e-mail:** cancelaria@minfin.moldova.md; **URL:** http://www.mf.gov.md.

NEILL, Bob, MP; Member of Parliament for Bromley and Chislehurst, House of Commons; **born:** 24 June 1952; **education:** LSE, law; **political career:** Cllr., London Borough of Havering; mem., GLC; Member, GLA, May 2000-08; MP for Bromley and Chislehurst, June 2006-; Shadow Minister for London, July 2007-08; Deputy Chmn., Conservative Party, July 2008-; Shadow Local Government Minister, 2008-10, also Planning, 2009-10; Parly. Under Secretary of State, Dept. of Communities & Local Government, 2010-12; **memberships:** Board Member, London Regional Arts Council 2003; **professional career:** Barrister, specialising in criminal law; Non-Exec. Bd. Dir., North-East London Strategic Health Authority, 2002-06; **committees:** Select Cttee. on Constitutional Affairs 2006-; **office address:** House of Commons, London, SW1A 0AA, United Kingdom.

NELSON, Bill; Senator for Florida, US Senate; **born:** 29 September 1942, Miami, Florida, USA; **married:** Grace Nelson; **education:** Melbourne's public schools; **party:** Democrat; **political career:** Florida Legislature, 1972-78; Mem., US Senate; **professional career:** Captain, US Army; Treas., Insurance Cmnr. and State Fire Marshal, 1995-00; **committees:** Budget; Commerce; Finance; Intelligence; Special Cttee. on Aging, 2013-; **office address:** Office of Senator Bill Nelson, US Senate, 716 Hart Senate Office Building, Washington, DC 20510, USA; **phone:** +1 202 224 5274; **URL:** http://www.billnelson.senate.gov/.

NEMATOV, H.E. Ilhom; Ambassador Extraordinary of Uzbekistan to the US, Embassy of Uzbekistan; **education:** Ph.D, economics; **political career:** Adviser to the Minister of Foreign Affairs, 1999-2000; Dep. Minister of Foreign Affairs, 2000-08; **professional career:** Fellow, Diplomatic Academy of the Ministry of Foreign Affairs, 1989-92; various diplomatic postings, MFA and missions abroad, 1992-97; Amb. Extraordinary & Plenipotentiary of Uzbekistan to India, 1997-99; Amb. Extraordinary & Pleniotentiary of Usbekistan to the Russian Federation, 2008-10; Amb. Extraordinary and Plenipotentiary of the Rep, of Uzbekistan to the US, 2010-; **office address:** Embassy of Uzbekistan to the US, 1746 Massacusetts Avenue, NW, Washington DC 20036-1903, USA; **URL:** http://www.uzbekistan.org.

NESBITT, Her Excellency Wanda L.; Ambassador, US Embassy in Namibia; **born:** Philadelphia, Pennsylvania, USA; **education:** Univ. of Pennsylvania, BA, Int. Relations and French; National War Coll., 1996-97; **professional career:** Vice-Consul, Port-au-Prince, Haiti, 1982-83; Vice-Consul, Paris, France, 1983-85; Bureau of Latin America Affairs, Washington, DC, 1986-88; Regional Consular Officer, Kinshasa, Zaire, 1990-92; Bureau of Consular Affairs, 1992-93; Bureau of Legislative Affairs, 1995-97; Dep. Chief of Mission, Kigali, Rwanda, 1997-99; Dep. Chief of Mission, Dar es Salaam, Tanzania, 2001; US Ambassador to Madagascar, 2002-04; Dir., Senior Level Assignments Div., Bureau of Human Resources, 2004-05; Principal Dep.Assist. Sec., Bureau of Consular Affairs, 2005-07, Amb., US Embassy in Cote d'Ivoire, 2007-10; Amb. to Namibia, 2010-; **office address:** US Embassy, 14 Lossen Street, Private Bag 12029, Windhoek, Namibia; **phone:** +264 61 221601; **fax:** +264 61 229 792; **e-mail:** kopfgb@state.gov; **URL:** http://www.usembassy.namib.com.

NETANYAHU, Benjamin, B.Sc; Israeli, Prime Minister, Government of Israel; **born:** 21 October 1949, Tel-Aviv, Israel; **parents:** Professor Benzion Netanyahu and Cela Netanyahu (dec'd) ; **married:** Sara; **children:** Noa (F), Yair (M), Avner (M); **education:** M.I.T., B.Sc., Architecture, M.Sc., Management Studies; **party:** Likud Party, Leader, 1993-99, 2005-; **political career:** Mem., First Israeli Delegation to US-Israel Strategic Talks 1984; Ambassador to UN 1984-88; Dpty. Ambassador to US 1982-84; Dep. Minister of Foreign Affairs 1988-90; Dep. Minister in Prime Minister's Office 1990-92; Leader, Likud Party 1993-; Prime Minister of Israel, 1996-99 (as PM signed Hebron and Wye River Agreements); Minister of Finance, 2003-06; Leader of the Opposition; 2005-; Prime Minister, 2009-; Minister of Foreign Affairs, 2013-; **professional career:** Soldier and Officer, Elite Unit, Israel Defense Forces 1967-72; consulting & management positions in industry in US and Israel; Dir. of Jonathan Institute, Jerusalem; **publications:** Editor of 'Terrorism: How the West Can Win' (1986), 'International Terrorism: Challenge and Response' (1981), Letters of Jonathan Netanyahu (1978); articles have appeared in The New York Times, The Wall Street Journal, The Washington Post, The Los Angeles Times, Le Monde, Time Magazine; 'A Place Among The Nations: Israel and the World', Bantam Books (1993); 'Fighting Terrorism: How Democracies Can Defeat Domestic and International Terrorism', Farrah, Straus & Giroux (1995); **office address:** Office of the Prime Office, 3 Kaplan Street, PO Box 187, Kiryat Ben-Gurion, Jerusalem 91919, Israel; **phone:** +972 2 670 5555; **fax:** +972 2 651 2631; **e-mail:** doar@pmo.gov.il; **URL:** http://www.pmo.gov.il/.

NETO, Dr António Domingos Pitra Costa; Minister of Public Administration Employment and Social Security, Angolan Government; **parents:** Costa António and Pereira Bravo Neto (née Catarina); **married:** Pitra Costa Neto (née Graça); **s:** 2; **d:** 4; **political career:** Minister of Labour, Public Administration and Social Security, Angola, 1997-2008, now known as Minister of Public Administration, Employment and Social Security; **interests:** international affairs and regional issues; **professional career:** Lawyer, teacher, lecturer in Faculty of Law; **publications:** technical publications on administrative and good governance issues; **recreations:** sports, music, literature; **office address:** Ministry of Public Administration, Employment and Social Security, Rua 17 de Septembro, 32, Luanda, Angola; **phone:** +244 339656; **fax:** +244 339656.

NEUBERGER, Baroness Julia, DBE; Member, House of Lords; **children:** Harriet (F), Matthew (M); **education:** Newnham Coll., Cambridge; Leo Baeck Coll., London; Harkness Fellowship, Harvard Medical School, 1991-92; **party:** Liberal Democrats; **political career:** mem., House of Lords, 2004-; created a Life Peer, 2004; **memberships:** Human Fertilisation and Embryology Authority, 1991-95; Medical Research Council, 1995-2000; Bd. of Visitors of Memorial Church, Harvard Univ. ; Central Ethical Compliance Gp., Unilever, 2003-09; Advisory Panel, Review of the Regulatory Framework for Legal Services in England and Wales, 2004-; Advisory Cncl., Centre for Reform, 2002; Advisory Bd., Clore Duffield, Leadership Programme, 2004; Vice Pres., Barnados, 2005; Bd. Mem., Jewish Care, 2005-06; Pres., Liberal Judaism; Bd. Mem., Jewish Policy Research, 2006; **professional career:** Rabbi, South London Liberal Synagogue, 1977-89; visiting Fellow, research ethics cttees., King's Fund Inst., 1989-91; Visiting Fellow, Harkness Fellowship, Harvard Medical School, 1991-92; Chwn., Camden & Islington Community Health Services NHS Trust, 1993-97; Chancellor, Univ. of Ulster, 1994-2000; Chief Exec., King's Fund, 1997-2004; Civil Service Commissioner, 2001-2002; Consultant, Clore Duffield Foundation, 2004-; Bd. Mem., VHI Healthcare, Ireland, 2005-; Bloomberg Prof. of Divinity, Harvard Univ., 2006; PM's Champion for Volunteering, 2007-09; Senior Rabbi, West London Synagogue, 2011-; **committees:** mem., Cttee. on Standards in Public Life, 2001-04; Health Cmn., Social Market Foundation, 2003-05; Advisory Cttee., Internal Centre for Health & Society UCL, 2003-04; mem., Advisory Cttee., trustees of the Sainsbury Centre for Mental Health, 2004-; Chwn., Cmn. for the Future of Volunteering, 2006-08; **trusteeships:** Imperial War Museum, 1999-2006; Patron, North London Hospice, 2000-; Cecil and Irene Roth Charitable Trust, 2000-; Booker Prize Foundation, 2002-; Walter and Liesel Schwab Charitable Trust, 2003; Urban Village Project, 2004-09; British Council, 2004-06; Urban Village, 2004-09; **honours and awards:** Hon. Doctorates from 14 universities; Hon. Fellow, Mansfield College, Oxford, 1997-;Hon. Fellow, CIPFA, 2002; Hon. Fellow, Royal Coll. of Physicians, 2004; Hon. Fellow, Queen's Nursing Instit., 2003; Hon. Fellow, Royal Coll. of General Practitioners, 2005-; Hon. Fellow, Royal College of Psychiatrists, 2005; **publications:** Baroness Neuberger is the author of several books on Judaism, women, healthcare, ethics and on caring for dying people including most recently 'The Moral State We're In' and 'Not Dead Yet'; **recreations:** gardening, family life, opera, Irish life, swimming; **office address:** House of Lords, London, SW1A 0PW, United Kingdom; **phone:** +44 (0)20 7219 2716; **fax:** +44 (0)20 7219 0620; **e-mail:** neubergerj@parliament.uk.

NEUBERGER OF ABBOTSBURY, Rt. Hon. the Lord; President, Supreme Court of the United Kingdom; **education:** Christ Church, Oxford Univ.; **political career:** Raised to the peerage, 2007; **professional career:** Lincoln's Inn, Called to the Bar, 1974; Queen's Counsel, 1987; Bencher for Lincoln's Inn, 1993; Recorder, 1990-96; High Court Judge, Chancery Division; Supervisory Judge for the Midland, Wales and Chester and Western Circuits, 2000-04; Lord Justice of Appeal, 2004; Lord of Appeal in Ordinary, 2007; President, The Supreme Court, 2013-; **office address:** Supreme Court of the United Kingdom, Parliament Square, London, SW1P 38D, United Kingdom; **URL:** http://www.supremecourt.gov.uk.

NEUMANN, Bernd; Minister of State to the Federal Chancellor, German Government; **born:** 1942; **political career:** Mem., Bremen State Assembly, 1971-87; MP, 1987-; Minister of State in the Federal Chancellery and Commissioner for Cultural and Media Affairs, 2005-; **professional career:** Teacher; **office address:** Federal Chancellery , Bundeskanzleramt, Willy-Brandt Str. 1 , 10557 Berlin, Germany; **phone:** +49 (0)1888 4000; **fax:** +49 (0)1888400 2357 .

NEVIN, Michael; High Commissioner, British High Commission in Malawi; **professional career:** career diplomat, postings in Japan, Malawi; Various positions FCO; Dep. High Commissioner, Nairobi, 2008-12; High Commissioner, Lilongwe, Malawi, Sept. 2012-; **office address:** British High Commission, PO Box 30042, Lilongwe 3, Malawi.

NEWLOVE, Helen Margaret; Member, House of Lords; **party:** Conservative; **political career:** Mem., House of Lords, 2010-; **professional career:** Campaigner against anti-social behaviour; **office address:** House of Lords, London, SW1A 0PW, United Kingdom; **phone:** +44 (0)20 7219 3000; **fax:** +44 (0)20 7219 5979; **URL:** http://www.parliament.uk.

NEWMAN, Campbell; Premier, Government of Queensland; **education:** Univ. of New South Wales; MBA, Univ. of Queensland, AUstralia; Royal Military College Duntroon; **political career:** Lord Mayor of Brisbane, 2004-11; MP, Premier, March 2012-

; ***professional career:*** Army Major; Civil Engineer; ***office address:*** Office of the Premier, Brisbane Albert Street QLD 4002, Queensland, 4000, Australia; ***URL:*** http://www.the premier.qld.gov.au.

NEWMARK, Brooks; MP for Braintree, House of Commons; ***married:*** Lucy; ***children:*** 5; ***education:*** Harvard College (BA Hons History), Worcester College, Oxford (Politics, Research Graduate), and Harvard Business School (MBA); ***political career:*** MP for Braintree, 2005-; Opposition Whip 2007-10; Government Whip, 2010-; ***professional career:*** Vice Pres, Lehman Brothers Inc., 1984-87; Dir., Newmark Brothers Ltd., 1987-92; Dir., Stellican Ltd., 1992-98; Sr. Partner, Apollo Management LP, 1998-2005; ***committees:*** Mem., Science and Technology Select Cttee., 2005-07; Mem., Treasury Select Cttee., 2006-07; Finance and Services, 2009-11; ***office address:*** House of Commons, London, SW1P 0AA, United Kingdom; ***phone:*** +44 (0)20 7219 3464; ***e-mail:*** brooks.newmark.mp@parliament.uk; ***URL:*** http://www.brooksnewmark.com.

NEWTON, Sarah; MP for Truro and Falmouth, UK Government; ***political career:*** Councillor, London Borough of Merton Council; MP for Truro and Falmouth, May 2010-; ***committees:*** Administration, 2010-; Science and Technology, 2012-; ***office address:*** House of Commons, London, SW1A 0AA, United Kingdom; ***phone:*** +44 (0)20 7219 3000; ***e-mail:*** sarah.newton.mp@parliament.uk.

NG, Dr Eng Hen; Minister for Defence, Government of Singapore; ***born:*** 10 December 1958; ***married:*** Ivy Lim Swee Lian; ***public role of spouse:*** Pediatrician and geneticist; ***education:*** Nat. Univ. of Singapore, M.B.B.S. with distinctions in Social Medicine and Public Health, 1982; Master in Medicine (Surgery) 1987; ***political career:*** Acting Minister for Manpower, 2003; Minister for Manpower and Second Minister for Education, 2003-07; Minister for Education and Second Minister for Defence, 2007-11; Minister for Defence, 2011-; ***professional career:*** Consultant Surgeon, Singapore General Hospital, 1992-97; Private Practice, Mount Elizabeth Hospital, 1997-2001 ; ***recreations:*** jogging, golf, reading; ***office address:*** Ministry of Defence, MINDEF Building, Gombak Drive, Off Upper Bukit Timah Road , Singapore 669645, Singapore; ***phone:*** +65 6760 8844; ***fax:*** +65 6233 6667; ***URL:*** http://www.mindef.gov.sg.

NGAFUAN, Dr Augustine; Minister of Foreign Affairs, Government of Liberia; ***born:*** April 7 1970, Monrovia, Liberia; ***education:*** Accountancy, Booker Washington Inst., Margibi County, Liberia; MBA, Univ. of Rochester, New York, USA, 2004; Certificate in Central Banking, Federal Reserve Bank of New York, 2005; ***political career:*** Minister of Finance, 2008-12; Minister of Foreign Affairs, 2012-; ***office address:*** Ministry of Foreign Affairs, PO Box 10-9002, Mamba Point, 1000 Monrovia 10, Liberia; ***phone:*** +231 226763; ***URL:*** http://www.mofa.gov.lr.

NGHIMTINA, Hon. Erikki; Minister of Works and Transport, Namibian Government; ***political career:*** Minister of Defence, to 2004; Minister of Mines and Energy, 2004-10; Minister of Works and Transport, 2010-; ***office address:*** Ministry of Works and Transport, Private Bag 13341, Windhoek, Namibia; ***e-mail:*** initialsurname@mod.gov.na; ***URL:*** http://www.mod.gov.na/.

NGUYEN THI DOAN ; Vice President, Government of Vietnam; ***education:*** Hanoi Univ. of Commerce, economics; Ph.D, economics; ***political career:*** Mem., Communist Party of Vietnam, Central Cttee., 1996; mem., Central Cttee., Supervisory Commission, 1999; Vice-Pres., Government of Vietnam, 2007-; ***professional career:*** lecturer, Hanoi Univ. of Commerce, Rector; ***office address:*** Office of the Vice President, Hoang Hoa Tham, Hanoi, Vietnam.

NHEMA, Francis; Minister of Environment and Tourism, Government of Zimbabwe; ***born:*** 1959; ***education:*** Strathclyde Univ., Scotland; ***political career:*** MP, Shurugwi District; Minister of Environment and Tourism; Minister of Environment, 2009-; ***office address:*** Ministry of Environment and Tourism, Karigamombe Centre, P. Bag 8853, Causeway, Harare, Zimbabwe.

NHIAL, Lt. Gen. Nhial Deng; Minister of Foreign Affairs, Government of South Sudan; ***born:*** 1952; ***parents:*** the late William Deng Nhial; ***education:*** Univ. of Khartoum, law; ***political career:*** Regional Affairs Minister; Defence Minister; Mem., Leadership Council, Sudan People's Liberation Movement; South Sudanese Minister of SPLA and Veterans Affairs, 2008-11; Minister of Foreign Affairs, South Sudan, 2011-; ***office address:*** Minister of Foreign Affairs, Juba, South Sudan.

NICHOLAS, Hon. Graydon; Lieutenant Governor, Government of New Brunswick; ***born:*** Tobique First Nation, New Brunswick; ***education:*** B.Sc., St. Francis Xavier Univ.; Bachelor of Law, Univ. of New Brunswick , 1971; MA, in Social Work, Wilfrid Laurier Univ., 1974; ***political career:*** Lieutenant Governor, 2009-; ***professional career:*** Union of New Brunswick Indians, Chmn., 1976-80, Pres. 1980-88; Provincial Court Judge; ***office address:*** Office of the Lieutenant Governor, PO Box, 6000, Fredericton, New Brunswick, Canada; ***phone:*** +1 506 453 2505; ***URL:*** http://www.gnb.ca/lg/index-e.asp.

NICHOLSON, Senator Arnold, QC; Minister for Foreign Affairs and Foreign Trade, Government of Jamaica; ***political career:*** Attorney General; Minister of Legal Affairs; Minister for Foreign Affairs and Foreign Trade, 2011-; ***office address:*** Ministry of Foreign Affairs and Trade, 21 Dominica Drive, Kingston 5, Jamaica; ***phone:*** +1 876 926 4220; ***URL:*** http://www.mfaft.gov.jm.

NICHOLSON OF WINTERBOURNE, Baroness , MEP; Member of the European Parliament and Member of the House of Lords; ***born:*** 16 October 1941, Oxford, UK; ***parents:*** Sir Godfrey Nicholson Bt. MP and The Lady Katharine (née Lindsay); ***married:*** Sir Michael Harris Caine (dec'd); ***children:*** Richard (M), Amar Kanim (M), Amanda (F); ***languages:*** French; ***education:*** St. Mary's School, Wantage; The Royal Academy of Music; The Royal College of Music; ***party:*** Liberal Democratic Party; mem., Group of the Alliance of Liberals and Democrats for Europe; ***political career:*** MP, 1987-97; MEP, South Region, 1999-; Mem. of House of Lords; Rapporteur for Kashmir; Rapporteur for Romania, 2004-07; Mem., EU Election Observation Mission, Palestine, 2005; Azerbaijan, 2005; Lebanon, 2005; Afghanistan, 2005; Iraq, Jan, & Dec. 2005; Armenia, 2007; Chief Observer, EU Election Observation Mission, Yemen, 2006; Parly. mission to Saudi Arabia, Oct. 2004; Jordan, July 2005; India, June 2006; Pakistan, June 2006; Israel and Palestine, Dec. 2006; Lebanon, March 2007; ***interests:*** foreign affairs, defence, international development, aid, human rights, intellectual property, data protection; Founder, East-Unesco Standing Conference on European-Islamic Dialogue; ***memberships:*** Dpty. Chmn., The Duke of Edinburgh's Award 30th Anniv. Tribute 1986; Dpty. Chmn., The Duke of Edinburgh's Award Int. Project 1987; Chmn., Friends of the Duke of Edinburgh's Award Scheme 1988-; Council Mem., The Howard League; Vice-Pres., The Small Farmers' Assn.; Advisory Bd. Mem., Women of Tomorrow Awards; Chmn., Advisory Cttee., The Carnegie UK Trust ADAPT (Access for Disables People to Arts Premises Today); Pres., West Regional Assn. for the Deaf; Dir., Cities in Schools; The Royal Academy of Music Appeal Cttee.; Council Mem., PITCOM (Parly. Information Technology Cttee.); Mem., Centre for Policy Studies, Royal Inst. of Int. Affairs; Fellow Elect, Industry and Parl. Trust (IBM): Patron, The Devon Care Trust Patron, CRUSAID; Pres., Hatherliegh District Branch, Save The Children Fund; Pres., Plymouth and West Devon Cassette Talking Newspaper; elected MP (Cons.) for Torridge and West Devon 1987-; Vice-Moderator, Movement for the Ordination of Women 1991-; Vice-Pres., Conservative Disability Grp. 1991; Vice-Chmn., All-Party Grp. on Penal Affairs 1992; Alt. Mem., UK Delegation to Western European Union and the Council of Europe; Special Envoy of the World Health Organisation; Vice Pres, of the Family Farmers' Association; Board of Advisers for the New York University Center for Dialogues, Islamic World - U.S. - The West; Vice Pres.of the Local Government Group for Europe; Vice Pres. of Mary Hare School for the severely and profoundly deaf children and young people; American Bar Association's Middle East North Africa Council; Patron of the Beethoven Piano Society of Europe; Patron of Saferworld; Board Mem., American Islamic Congress; Fellow of the Royal Society for the encouragement of the Arts, Manufactures and Commerce; Organising Cttee. of the New Arab Woman Forum; ***professional career:*** Computer Software Designer, Software Tutor, Systems Analyst, Computer Consultant, ICL 1962-66; Computer Consultant, John Tyzack & Partners 1967-69; General Management and Computer Consultant, McLintock, Mann & Whinney Murray 1969-73; joined The Save The Children Fund 1974, Dir. of Fundraising 1977-85; Vice-Chmn., Cons. Party with special responsibility for women 1983-87; Mem. of Parliament, Conservative, for Devon West and Torridge, Parly. Private Secy. to Min. of State, Ministry of Agriculture, Food and Fisheries, and at the Home Office 1987 and 1992-; Left the Conservative Party and joined the Liberal Democrat Party 1995; Lib Dem Parly. Spokesman on Human Rights and Overseas Aid 1995-; received working peerage, 1997-; Dir., Nicholson Productions Ltd.; ***committees:*** Britain in Europe Council; Cttee. on Foreign Affairs; Responsible for gender mainstreaming for the Foreign Affairs Cttee.; Vice Pres., Cttee. on Foreign Affairs, 2004-07; Subcttee. on Human Rights; Delegation for Relations with Iran; Substitute Mem., Delegation for Relations with the Mashreq Countries; Substitute Mem., Cttee. on Budgets; Mem., Euro-Mediterranean Parly. Assembly Delegation; Mem., Working Grp. on the Establishment of a Euro-Mediterranean University; ***trusteeships:*** AMAR Int. Charitable Foundation; The Suzy Lamplugh Trust; Ross McWhirter Foundation; Patron, Hospice Care Trust, N. Devon; Patron of The Winsford Trust; Patron of the Zambia Society Trust; ***honours and awards:*** Hon. Doctorate (N. London Univ.); The Carrie Prize for African Writing (Africagst), The Booker Prize Foundation; - Hon. Doctorate of the Univ. of Birmingham; Hon. Doctorate of the London Metropolitan Univ.; Hon. Doctorate of the 'Victor Babes University' Univ. of Timisora; Hon. Doctorate of the 'Dimitrie Cantemir' Christian Univ., Bucharest; ***publications:*** Why does the West Forget, 1993; Secret Society, 1996; ***clubs:*** Reform Club; Pall Mall; St. Stephen's Constitutional Club; Blyth Conservative Club (Life Mem); Tavistock Conservative Club; Okehampton, Torrington and Bideford Conservative Clubs; ***office address:*** House of Lords, London, SW1A 0PQ, United Kingdom; ***phone:*** +44 (0)20 7828 4992; ***fax:*** +44 (0)20 7828 4991.

NÍ CHUILÍN, Carál; MLA for Belfast North, Northern Ireland Assembly; ***party:*** Sinn Féin; ***political career:*** MLA for Belfast North, 2007-; Minister for Culture, Arts and Leisure, 2011-; ***office address:*** Northern Ireland Assembly, Causeway Exchange, 1-7 Bedford Street, Belfast, BT1 7FB, Northern Ireland; ***phone:*** +44 (0)28 9025 8825.

NIEBEL, Dirk; Minister of Economic Co-operation and Development, German Government; ***party:*** Gen. Sec., FDP; ***political career:*** Mem., German Bundestag; 1998; Federal Minister of Economic Cooperation and Development, 2009-; ***office address:*** Ministry for Economic Co-operation, Europahaus, Stresemannstrasse 94, 10963 Berlin, Germany; ***phone:*** +49 (0)30 25030; ***URL:*** http://www.bmz.de.

NIELSEN, Holger K., Ph.D; Minister of Taxation, Government of Denmark; ***born:*** 23 April 1950, Ribe, Denmark; ***party:*** Socialistisk Folkeparti (Socialist People's Party); ***political career:*** Member of the Folketing (Parl.), 1981, 84 & 1987-; Minister of Taxation, 2012-; ***memberships:*** Mem. of the European Affairs Cttee.; Mem. of the Economic and Political Affairs Cttee. Member of the Foreign Policy Cttee.; Chairman of the Socialist People's Party; ***office address:*** Ministry of Taxation, Nicolai Eigtveds Gade 28, 1402 Copenhagen K, Denmark; ***phone:*** +45 3392 3392; ***fax:*** +45 3393 2518; ***URL:*** http://www.skm.dk.

NIETO, Enrique Pena; President, Government of Mexico; ***born:*** 1966, Atlacomulco, Mexico; ***education:*** BA, Univ. Panamericana; MA, EGADE Business School; ***party:*** Institutional Revolutionary Party; ***political career:*** Governor, Mexico State, 2002-11; President, July 2012-; ***office address:*** Office of the President, Los Pinos, Puerta 1, Col. San Miguel Chapultepec, 11850 Mexico, DF, Mexico; ***phone:*** +52 55 5277 7455; ***fax:*** +52 55 5510 3717; ***URL:*** http://www.presidencia.gob.mx.

NIINISTÖ, Sauli Väinämö; Finnish, President, Government of Finland; ***born:*** 24 August 1948, Salo, Finland; ***parents:*** Váino Niinistö and Hilkka Helena Heimo (née Heimo); ***married:*** Marja-Leena Niinistö (née Alanko), 1974 (dec'd 1995); ***children:*** Nuutti (M), Matias (M); ***education:*** Matriculated, 1967; LL.M. Univ. of Turku, 1974; Snr. Lawyer, 1977; ***party:*** National Coalition Party (KOK); ***political career:*** mem., Salo City Cncl., 1977-; Chmn., Salo City Cncl., 1989-92; MP, 1987-;Mem., Grand Committee, 1987-90;Dep. Mem. of the Finance Committee, 1991-93; Chmn. Parliamentary Council of the Bank of Finland, 1995-; Parliamentary Trustee of the Bank of Finland, 1995; Dep. Mem. Jt committee of the European Parliament, 1993-94; Dep. PM, Minister of Justice, 1995-96; Dep. PM, -2002; Minister of Finance, 1996-04; President of Finland, 2012-; ***professional career:*** Owner, law office, Salo, 1978-88; Turku Court of Appeal, 1976-87; Appeal Court Justice of the Turku Court of Appeal, 1994-95; Vice-Pres., European Investment Bank, 2004-12; ***committees:***

Chmn. Constitutional Law, 1993-94; Mem. Constitutional Law, 1987-90 & 1993-94;Mem. of the Committee for Ordinary Law, 1987-93; ***office address:*** Office of the President, Mariankatu 2, 00170 Helsinki, Finland; ***phone:*** +358 (0)9 661133; ***fax:*** +358 (0)9 638247; ***e-mail:*** presidnetti@tpk.fi.

NIINISTÖ, Ville; Minister of Environment, Government of Finland; ***born:*** 30 July 1976; ***education:*** Univ. of Turku, Finland; ***party:*** Green League; ***political career:*** Turku City Council; NP, 2007-; Minister of Environment, 2011-; ***office address:*** Ministry of the Environment, Kasarmikatu 25, P.O.Box 380, 00131 Helsinki, Finland; ***phone:*** +358 (0)9 1991 9308; ***fax:*** +358 (0)9 1991 9323; ***e-mail:*** name.surname@vyh.fi; ***URL:*** http://www.environment.fi.

NIKOLIC, Tomislav; President, Serbian Government; ***born:*** 1953; ***education:*** As.C., Civil Engineering; ***party:*** founder, Progressive Party, 2008; ***political career:*** Deputy Prime Minister, Serbia; Dep. Prime Minister, Federal Rep. of Yugoslavia, 1996-2000; Pres., Serbia, 2012-; ***office address:*** Office of the President, Andricev venac 1, 11 000 Belgrade, Serbia; ***phone:*** +381 11 363 2121; ***e-mail:*** Tomislav.Nikolic@gov.yu; ***URL:*** http://www.predsednik.rs.

NIKSIC, Nermin; Prime Minister, Government of the Bosniac-Croat Federation; ***education:*** Faculty of Law, Univ. of Mostar, 1986; ***party:*** Social Democratic Party of Bosnia and Herzegovina; ***political career:*** Member of the House of Representatives of Bosnia and Herzegovina, 2000-07; Prime Minister, 2011-; ***professional career:*** Lawyer; ***office address:*** Office of the Prime Minister, Marsala Tita 16, 71000 Sarajevo, Zmaja od Bosne 3, Bosnia and Herzegovina; ***phone:*** +387 (0)33 650457; ***fax:*** +387 (0)33 664816.

NIMROD, Hon. Elvin G.; Deputy Prime Minister, Attorney General, Grenada Government; ***born:*** Carriacou; ***education:*** Hillsborough Government Primary School; Brooklyn college, BA, Political Science; John Lay college of Criminal Justice, MA Criminal Justice; New York Law School, Juris Doctorate degree; Hugh Wooding Law School, Trinidad, Legal Education Certificate, 1992; ***political career:*** Legal Affairs, Local Government, Carriacou and Petit Martinique Affairs; Minister of Labour, 1999; Minister of Foreign Affairs, International Trade and Minister of Carriacou and Petit Martinique Affairs, 1999-08; also Attorney General from 2006-08; Deputy Prime Minister, Attorney General, Minister for Legal Affairs, Labour, Local Government, Carricou and Martinique Affairs, 2013-; ***professional career:*** Teacher, Mt. Pleasant Government Primary School, Carriacou; Called to the Bar in Grenada, 1993; ***office address:*** Ministry of Legal Affairs, Communal House, 414 H A Blaize Street, St. George's, Grenada; ***phone:*** +1 473 440 2962; ***fax:*** +1 473 435 2964; ***e-mail:*** legalaffais@spiceisle.com; ***URL:*** http://www.gov.gd/ministries/legalaffairs.html.

NISBETT, Patrice; Minister of Foreign Affairs, Homeland Security, Labour, Justice and Legal Affairs, Government of St. Kitts; ***born:*** 1971; ***education:*** Univ. of West Indies, law; ***political career:*** MP; Minister of Foreign Affairs, Homeland Security, Labour, Justice and Legal Affairs; ***professional career:*** called to Bar, 1995; ***office address:*** House of Assembly, PO Box 164, Basseterre, St. Kitts.

NISHANI, Dr Bujar; President, Government of Albania; ***born:*** 29 September 166; ***languages:*** English; ***education:*** Military Academy, 1988; Law Faculty, of Univ. of Tirana, Albania, 2004; ***political career:*** Minister of Justice, 2009-11; Minister of the Interior, 2011-12; President, 2012-; ***professional career:*** Lecturer, Skanderbeg Military Academy; Dept. of Foreign Relations; ***office address:*** Office of the President, Bulevardi Dëshmorët e Kombit, Tirana, Albania; ***phone:*** +355 (0)4 228313; ***fax:*** +355 (0)4 233761; ***e-mail:*** presec@presec.tirana.al; ***URL:*** http://www.president.al.

NIXON, Jeremiah W. (Jay); Governor, Missouri, USA; ***education:*** Univ. of Missouri-Columbia, Undergrad. and Law degrees; ***political career:*** State Senator, 1986-92; Missouri Attorney General, 1992-08; Governor of Missouri, 2009-; ***professional career:*** Attorney; ***office address:*** Office of the Governor, Missouri Capitol Building, Room 216, PO Box 720,, Jefferson City, Missouri, MO 65102-0720, USA; ***phone:*** +1 573 751 3222; ***fax:*** +1 573 751 1495; ***e-mail:*** mogov@mail.state.mo.us; ***URL:*** http://www.gov.mo.gov.

N'JIE-SAIDY, Isatou; Gambian, Vice-President and Secretary of State for Women's Affairs, Gambian Government; ***born:*** 15 March 1952, Kuntaya, The Gambia; ***languages:*** English, French; ***education:*** Yundum Teacher's Training College, 1974; Research Instit. for Mgmnt. Science, RVB, Delft, The Netherlands, Post Grad. Dipl. in Industrial Mgmnt.; Univ. Cott. of Swansea, Wales, M.Sc Econ, 1988; ***political career:*** Ex-officio mem., National Women's Cncl., 1990-96; Administrator, Women's Bureau, 1990-96; Sec. of State for Health, Social Welfare and Women's Affairs, 1996-2001; Vice-Pres. and Sec. of State for Women's Affairs, 1997- ; ***memberships:*** Gambia Coll. Cncl., 1992-95; Royal Victoria Hospital Mgmnt. Bd., 1994-95; ***professional career:*** Teacher, 1970-72, 74-76; Indigenous Business Advisory Service (IBAS), 1976-83; Dep. Exec. Sec., Women's Bureau, National Women's Cncl., 1983-89; ***honours and awards:*** Grand Officer of the Republic of the Gambia, 2000; Grand Commander of the Rep. of the Gambia, 2001; ***recreations:*** reading; documentary and historical films; travel; ***office address:*** Office of the Vice President, State House, Banjul, The Gambia; ***phone:*** +220 227605; ***fax:*** +220 224012.

NKURUNZIZA, Pierre; President, Burundi; ***born:*** 1964, Ngozi province; ***political career:*** Hutu former rebel leader; leader, FDD, 2001; sole presidential candidate, August 2005; President of Burundi, 2005-; ***professional career:*** teacher; ***office address:*** Office of the President, Blvd de l'Uprona, Rohero I, BP 1870, Bujumbura, Burundi.

NOKES, Caroline; MP for Romsey and Southampton North, UK Government; ***party:*** Conservative; ***political career:*** Councillor, Test Valley Borough Council, 1999-; MP for Romsey and Southampton North, May 2010-; ***committees:*** Environmental Audit, 2010-; Works of Art, 2011-; ***office address:*** House of Commons, London, SW1A 0AA, United Kingdom; ***phone:*** +44 (0)20 7219 3000; ***e-mail:*** caroline.nokes.mp@parliament.uk.

NONIS, Dr Chris; High Commissioner, Sri Lankan High Commission; ***education:*** Royal Free Hospital, Univ. of London, medicine; ***memberships:*** Royal College of Physicians; Fellow, Royal Society of Medicine; ***professional career:*** businessman; Chair, Mackwoods; High Commissioner, Sri Lanka High Commission, London, 2011-; ***office address:*** Sri Lanka High Commission, 13 Hyde Park Gardens, London, W2 2LU, United Kingdom; ***URL:*** http://www.srilankahighcommission.co.uk/.

NONOO, H.E. Houda; Ambassador, Bahrain Embassy to the United States; ***born:*** 7 September 1964 , Bahrain; ***s:*** 2; ***education:*** City of London Polytechnic, BA, Accounting; International Univ. of Europe,Waterford, UK, MBA ; ***political career:*** Mem., Shura Council, 2006-; ***interests:*** factory working conditions; the rights of women and children; family and domestic law; the plight of domestic workers ; ***memberships:*** Founding mem., Bahrain Human Rights Watch Society (BHRWS), 2004-, Gen. Sec.2005-; ***professional career:*** Financial Director, Gourmet; Fin. Dir., Jetflair Int'l., UK; MD, Gulf Computer Services, Bahrain, 1993-; Ambassador to the USA, 2008-; ***committees:*** Mem., Cttee. for Finance and Economic Affairs, Shura Cncl., 2006-; ***office address:*** Embassy of Bahrain, 3502 International Drive NW, Washington DC 20008, USA; ***phone:*** +1 202 342 1111; ***fax:*** +1 202 362 2192; ***e-mail:*** information@bahrainembassy.org; ***URL:*** http://www.bahrainembassy.org.

NOONAN, Michael; Minister of Finance, Government of Ireland; ***education:*** BA, HDipEd, St. Patrick's Teacher Training Coll., Dublin Univ. Coll. Dublin; ***party:*** Fine Gael; ***political career:*** TD, Dáil Éireann; Minister for Justice, 1982-86; Minister of Industry & Commerce, Health, 1994-97; Leader, Fine Gael, 2002-03; Minister of Finance, 2011-; ***office address:*** Department of Finance, Upper Merrion Street, Dublin 2, Ireland; ***phone:*** +353 (0)1 676 7571; ***e-mail:*** michael.noonan@oireachtas.ie.

NORLAND, H.E. Richard; Ambassador, US Embassy in Georgia; ***professional career:*** Dep. Chief of Mission, Riga, Latvia, 2003-05; Dep. Chief of Mission, Kabul, Afghanistan, 2005-07; Amb., Tashkent, Uzbekistan, 2007-10; Amb. Tblisi, Georgia, 2011-; ***office address:*** US Embassy, George Balanchine Street, 0130 Tbilisi, Georgia; ***phone:*** +995 (8)32 227000; ***fax:*** +995 (8)32 532310; ***URL:*** http://georgia.usembassy.gov.

NORMAN, Jesse; MP for Hereford and South Herefordshire, UK Government; ***party:*** Conservative; ***political career:*** MP for Hereford and South Herefordshire, May 2010-; ***committees:*** Treasury Select Cttee., 2010-; ***office address:*** House of Commons, London, SW1A 0AA, United Kingdom; ***phone:*** +44 (0)20 7219 3000; ***e-mail:*** jesse.norman.mp@parliament.uk.

NORONHA NASCIMENTO, Dr. Luis António; Chief Justice, Supreme Court of Justice of Portugal; ***born:*** 1943, Oporto, Portugal; ***memberships:*** Mem., Nat. Cncl. of the Assn. of Portuguese Judges, 1984-88, Pres., 1992-96; ***professional career:*** Dep. Prosecutor, Paredes, Pombal e Santo Tirso; Judge, Trancoso, Marco de Canavezes, Vila Nova de Famalicão, Vila Nova de Gaia and Oporto; Spokesman for the High Council of the Judiciary, Vice Pres., 2001-04; Supreme Court Judge, 1998-; ***office address:*** Supreme Court of Justice, Praça do Comércio, 1149-012 Lisbon, Portugal; ***URL:*** http://www.stj.pt.

NORTH, Walter; Ambassador to Papua New Guinea, US Embassy; ***education:*** Harvard Univ.; George Washington Univ.; Lawrence Univ.; ***professional career:*** Mission Director, India, Indonesia and Zamiba. Overseas postings include Ethiopia & Bangladesh; Mission Director, USAID, Egypt; US Ambassador to Papua New Guinea, 2012-; ***office address:*** Embassy of the US, PO Box 1492, Port Moresby, Papua New Guinea.

NORTON, Eleanor Holmes; American, Congresswoman, District of Columbia, At Large, US House of Representatives; ***education:*** Antioch College, Ohio; Yale Univ., law, American Studies; ***party:*** Democrat; ***political career:*** Congresswoman, District of Columbia, US House of Representatives, currently in 11th term; ***professional career:*** Professor of Law; board member; Chair, US Equal Employment Opportunity Commission; ***committees:*** Oversight and Government Reform; Transportation and Infrastructure; ***office address:*** US House of Representatives, 2136 Rayburn House Office Building, Washington, DC 20515-5100, USA; ***phone:*** +1 202 225 8050.

NOVAK, Alexander; Minister of Energy, Government of the Russian Federation; ***born:*** 1971; ***education:*** Norilsk Industrial Inst.; Lomonosov Moscow State Univ.; ***political career:*** Norilsk Deputy Mayor for Economics and Finance, 2000-02, Norilsk First Dep. Mayor, 2000-02; Dep. Gov. of Krasnoyarsk Territory, 2002-07; Deputy Minister of Finance, 2008-12; Minister of Energy, 2012-; ***professional career:*** various positions, Zavenyagin Steel Combine, Norilsk, 1988-97; Dep. Dir., Norilsk Co. Transpolar Branch, 1999-2000; ***office address:*** Ministry of Energy, Bolshaya Ordinka Street 24/26, 101000 Moscow, Russia.

NOWOTNY, Ewald; Austrian, Governor, Österreichische Nationalbank; ***education:*** Univ. of Vienna, Ph.D; ***political career:*** MP, 1978-99; Chmn., Finance & Banking Cttee., 1985-99; mem., Austrian delegation to the Parly. Assembly of the WEU, 1994-99; ***professional career:*** Chmn., Austrian Postal Savings Bank, 1974-78; Prof. of Economics, Univs. of Harvard, Darmstadt and Linz; Prof. of Economics & Dir. of the Inst. for Fiscal & Monetary Policy, Wirtschaftsuniversität, Vienna, 1982-99; Vice-Chmn. of the Bd. of Dirs., European Investment Bank, Vice-President, EIB, 1999-2003; CEO, Austrian BAWAG P.S.K. Group, 2006-07; Governor, Österreichische Nationalbank, 2008-; ***office address:*** Österreichische Nationalbank, Otto-Wagner Platz 3, A-1090 Vienna, Austria; ***fax:*** +43 (0)1 40420 2398; ***e-mail:*** oenb.info@oenb.co.at; ***URL:*** http://www.oenb.at.

NOYER, Christian; French, Governor, Banque de France; ***born:*** 6 October 1950, Soisy, France; ***education:*** Univ. of Rennes, degree in law, 1971; Univ. de Paris, postgraduate degree in law, 1972; Inst. of Political Science, diploma, 1972; Ecole Nationale d'Administration, 1974-76; ***memberships:*** Alternate Mem., G-7 and G-10, 1993-95; Mem., Working Party No.3, OECD, 1993-95; Chmn., Paris Club of Creditor Countries, 1993-97; Pres., BIS, 2010-; ***professional career:*** Naval Officer, 1973; French Treasury, 1976; Financial Attaché, French Delegation to the EC, Brussels, 1980-82; Chief of Banking Office, Chief of Export Credit Office, French Treasury, 1982-85; Econ. Adviser to Minister for Econ. Affairs and Finance (E. Balladur), 1986-88; Dep. Dir., Int. Multilateral Issues, Treasury, 1988-90; Dep. Dir., Treasury Debt. Management, Monetary and Banking Issues, 1990-92; Dir., Dept. of Public Holdings and Public Financing, 1992-93; Chief of Staff of Minister for Econ. Affairs and Finance, 1993; Alternate Governor, IMF and World Bank, 1993-95; Dir. of Treasury, 1993-95; Chief of Staff of Minister for Econ. Affairs and Finance, 1995-97; Dir., Min. of Econ.

Affairs, Finance and Industry, 1997-98; Vice-Pres., European Central Bank, 1998-2002; current military position: Commander (Reserve Officer); Gov., Banque de France, to date; ***committees:*** Alternate Mem., European Monetary Cttee., 1988-90, Mem., 1993-95, 1998; Mem., European Econ. and Financial Cttee., 1999-2002; ***honours and awards:*** Off. of the Légion d'Honneur, France; Kt. of the Nat. Order of Merit, France; Cmdr., Nat. Order of the Lion, Senegal; Gran Cruz de la Order del Merito Civil (Spain), 2002; ***publications:*** Various articles, Banks, the rules of the game, 1990; ***office address:*** Banque de France, 1 rue la Vrillière, 75001 Paris, France; ***URL:*** http://www.banque-france.fr/.

NUJOMA, Utoni; Minister of Justice, Government of Namibia; ***born:*** 1952; ***parents:*** Sam Nujoma; ***education:*** Law, Univ. of Warwick, UK, 1991; Lund Univ., Sweden, 1995; ***political career:*** Dep. Minister of Justice, 2005-10; Minister of Finance, 2010-12; Minister of Justice, 2012-; ***office address:*** Ministry of Justice, Government Buildings, 4th Floor, East Wing, Private BAg 13347, Windhoek, Namibia; ***phone:*** +264 61 282 9111.

NUMANOVIC, Suad; Minister of Human and Minority Rights , Government of Montenegro; ***born:*** 27 April 1960; ***parents:*** Salih Numanovic and Kima Numanovic; ***children:*** Eldin (M), Armin (M), Amaz (M), Elma (F); ***languages:*** English; ***education:*** Fac. of Medicine, Belgrade, specialising in Internal Medicine; ***party:*** DPS, Democratic Party of Socialists; ***political career:*** Minister of Natural Disasters and Emergencies, 2005-06; Minister without Portfolio, 2006-09; Employment Minister, 2009-12; Minister of Human and Minority Rights, 2012-; ***professional career:*** Medical Practitioner; ***office address:*** Ministry of Human Rights, ul Jovana Tomajevica 66, Podgorica, Montenegro; ***phone:*** +381 (0)81 242230; ***fax:*** +381 (0)81 225 592; ***e-mail:*** snumanovic@mn.yu.

NUNES, Devin; Congressman, California 21st District, US House of Representatives; ***education:*** California Polytechnic State Univ., San Luis Obispo, BSc., Agricultural Business, MSc., Agriculture; ***party:*** Republican Party; ***political career:*** Congressman, California 21st District, US House of Representatives; ***committees:*** Ways and Means; Permanent Select Cttee. on Intelligence; ***office address:*** US House of Representatives, 1017 Longworth HOB, Washington, DC 20515, USA; ***phone:*** +1 202 225 2523.

NUNEZ FABREGA, Fernando; Minister of Foreign Affairs, Government of Panama; ***political career:*** Secretary of Anti-Corruption, 2009-11; Governor, Coclé, 2011-13; Minister of Foreign Affairs, 2013-; ***office address:*** Ministry of Foreign Affairs, Altos del Cerro Ancón, Panama 4, Republic of Panama.

NUTTALL, David; MP for Bury North, UK Government; ***political career:*** Councillor, Rotherham Metropolitan Borough Council, 1992-96, 2004-06; MP for Bury North May 2010-; ***committees:*** Procedure, 2010-; ***office address:*** House of Commons, London, SW1A 0AA, United Kingdom; ***phone:*** +44 (0)20 7219 3000;
e-mail: david.nuttall.mp@parliament.uk.

NWANZE, Kanayo; President, International Fund for Agricultural Development; ***education:*** Univ. of Ibadan, B.Sc., Agricultural Science, Nigeria, 1971; Kansas State University, USA, Doctorate in Agricultural Entomology, 1975; ***professional career:*** Dir-Gen., Africa Rice Centre (WARDA); Consultative Group on International Agricultural Research (CGIAR); Vice-Pres., IFAD, 2007-09, President, 2009-; ***office address:*** IFAD, Via Panole di Dono 44, Rome 00142, Italy; ***URL:*** http://www.ifad.org/.

O

OAKESHOTT OF SEAGROVE BAY, Lord Matthew; British, Member, House of Lords; ***born:*** 10 January 1947, Guildford, United Kingdom; ***parents:*** Keith Robertson Oakeshott CMG and Eva Jill Oakeshott; ***married:*** Dr. Pippa Poulton, 2 October 1976; ***children:*** Rachel Jill (F), Joseph Andrew (M), Luke Christopher (M); ***languages:*** French, German, Spanish; ***education:*** Charterhouse; Nuffield Coll., Oxford, M.A. First Class Hons., PPE, 1968; ***party:*** Labour, 1963-80; SDP/Liberal Democrats 1981-; ***political career:*** Oxford City Cllr., 1972-76; contested Horsham & Crawley, 1974; contested Cambridge, 1983; former Special Adviser to Roy Jenkins; Mem., House of Lords, 2000-; Liberal Democrat Treasury Spokesman, 2001-; Liberal Democrat Work and Pensions Spokesman, 2004-; ***interests:*** Economic affairs, pensions, housing, overseas development; ***professional career:*** M.D OLIM Ltd.; Investment Dir., Value and Income Trust plc; former Dir. Warburg Investment Man.; ***committees:*** SDP National Cttee. 1981-2; House of Lords Economic Affairs Select Cttee., 2001-04; Commons and Lords Joint Cttee., on Lords Reforms, 2003-04; ***trusteeships:*** Chmn., Coltstaple Trust; ***publications:*** Lord Matthew contributed a chapter to By-elections in British Politics, 1975; ***clubs:*** Arsenal F.C.; ***recreations:*** music, elections, supporting Arsenal; ***office address:*** House of Lords, London, SW1A 0PW, United Kingdom; ***phone:*** +44 (0)20 7219 3000.

OBAMA, President Barack; President, US Government; ***born:*** 4 August 1961, Hawaii; ***married:*** Michelle Obama; ***children:*** Natasha (F), Malia (F); ***public role of spouse:*** Lawyer; ***education:*** Columbia Univ., 1983; Harvard Law School, 1991; ***political career:*** leader, Illinois state senate; US Senator for the state of Illinois, 2004-08; Presidential candidate, 2008; President of the USA, 2009-; ***professional career:*** Community Organiser; Civil Rights Attorney; ***office address:*** The White House, 1600 Pennsylvania Avenue, NW, Washington, DC 20500, USA; ***phone:*** +1 202 456 1414; ***fax:*** +1 202 456 2461;
e-mail: president@whitehouse.gov; ***URL:*** http://www.whitehouse.gov/.

OBHRAI, Deepak; Parliamentary Secretary, Government of Canada; ***political career:*** MP for Calgary East, Alberta, 1997-; Parly. Sec. for Foreign Affairs, 2006-; Parly. Sec. to the Minister of International Co-operation, 2008-11; Parly. Sec. to the Minister of Foreign Affairs, 2011-; ***office address:*** House of Commons, Parliament Buildings, Wellington Street, Ottawa K1A 0A6, Ontario, Canada; ***phone:*** +1 613 943 5959; ***fax:*** +1 613 992 3674;
URL: http://www.parl.gc.ca.

O'BRIEN, Stephen; British, MP for Eddisbury, House of Commons; ***born:*** 1 April 1957; ***parents:*** David O'Brien and Rothy O'Brien; ***married:*** Gemma O'Brien (née Townshend), 1986; ***children:*** James (M), Angus (M), Clara (F); ***public role of spouse:*** Nurse and Researcher; ***languages:*** French; ***education:*** Emmanuel Coll., Cambridge Univ.; Coll. of Law, Chester; ***party:*** Conservative; ***political career:*** PPS, Rt. Hon. Michael Ancram QC, MP; Chmn., Conservative & Unionist Party, 2000-01; PPS, Shadow Foreign Sec., Rt. Hon. Francis Maude MP, 1999-2000; MP, Eddisbury; Acting Dir. of Office of Leader of H.M. Official Opposition, 2001; Opposition Whip, 2001-2002; Shadow Financial Sec. to the Treasury, 2002; Shadow Paymaster General, 2002-03; Shadow Secretary of State for Industry, 2003-2005; Shadow Minister of Health, 2005-10; Parly. Under-Sec. of State for International Development, May 2010-12; ***interests:*** competitiveness, trade & industry, international development, Northern Ireland, agriculture, health, education, constitutional affairs; ***memberships:*** Law Society; Assoc. Mem., British Irish Parly. Assn; Chmn., Chichester Conservation Assn., 1998-99; ***committees:*** Chmn., All Party Malaria, Tanzania, Uganda and Heavily Indebted Poor Countries Cttee.; Vice-Chmn., Jubilee 2000 Groups; Select Cttee. Mem., Education & Employment and Education Sub-Cttee., 1999-2001; Sec., Conservative Backbench Northern Ireland Cttee.; Sec., Conservative Backbench Trade & Industry Cttee.; Mem., Conservative Party National Membership Cttee. ; ***clubs:*** Constitutional & Conservative Club; ***recreations:*** classical pianist, conductor, fell-walking, golf; ***office address:*** House of Commons, London, SW1A 0AA, United Kingdom; ***phone:*** +44 (0)20 7219 6315; ***e-mail:*** obriens@parliament.uk.

OCHOA JR., Paquito; Executive Secretary, Government of the Philippines; ***education:*** AB Economics, Univ. of Santo Tomas; LL. B. Ateneo School of Law; ***political career:*** City Administrator, Quezon City, 2001-10; Executive Secretary, 2010-; ***office address:*** Office of the Executive Secretary, 1F Premier Guest House, Malacanan Palace, JP Laurel St., San Miguel 1005, Manila, Philippines; ***phone:*** +63 2 733 7759; ***URL:*** http://www.op.gov.ph.

O'CONNOR, Brendan; Minister for Employment, Skills and Training, Government of Australia; ***born:*** 1962, London, UK; ***education:*** BA, LLB (Monash); Harvard, Trade Union Program Diploma; ***political career:*** Mem. for Burke, Victoria, 2001-03; Mem. for Gorton, Victoria, (following redistribution), 2003-; Minister for Employment Participation, 2007-09; Minister for Home Affairs, 2009-11, also Minister for Justice, Minister for Privacy and Freedom of Information; Minister for Human Services, Minister Assisting for School Education, 2011; Minister for Immigration and Citizenship, 2013; Minister for Employment, Skills and Training, 2013-; ***committees:*** Mem, ALP Caucus Cttees.on Social Policy; Development and Living Standards, 2002-; Dep. Chmn., National Security Cttee., 2004-; HOR Economics Cttee., 2004-; ***office address:*** Department of Employment, PO Box 9879, Canberra ACT 2601, Australia; ***phone:*** +61 2 6121 6000; ***fax:*** +61 2 6121 7542; ***URL:*** http://www.deewr.gov.au.

O'CONNOR, Hon. Gordon; Chief Whip, Canadian Government; ***party:*** Conservative; ***political career:*** MP, House of Commons, 2004-; Critic, National Defence, 2004-06; Minister of National Defence, 2006-07; Minister of National Revenue, 2007-08; Chief Whip, 2008-; ***office address:*** House of Commons, Parliament Buildings, Wellington Street, Ottawa, ON K1A 0A6, Canada.

O'DONNELL, Lord Augustine Thomas; Member, House of Lords; ***political career:*** Member, House of Lords, 2012-; ***professional career:*** Lecturer in Economics, Univ. of Glasgow, 1975-79; UK Board Mem. IMF and World Bank, 1997-98; Head of the Home Civil Service, 2005-11; Visiting Prof., Univ. Coll. London;
Visiting Prof., London School of Economics; ***honours and awards:*** Knight Commander of the Order of the Bath, 2005; Knight Grand Cross of the Order of the Bath, 2011; ***office address:*** House of Lords, London, SW1A 0AA, United Kingdom.

O'DONNELL, Fiona; MP for East Lothian, House of Commons; ***party:*** Labour; ***political career:*** MP for East Lothian, May 2010-; Shadow Minister, Environment, Food and Rural Affairs, 2011-12; ***committees:*** Scottish Affairs Select Cttee., 2010-11; International Dev., 2012-; Arms Export Controls, 2012-; ***office address:*** House of Commons, London, SW1A 0AA, United Kingdom; ***phone:*** +44 (0)20 7219 3000;
e-mail: fiona.odonnell.mp@parliament.uk.

O'DOWD, John; MLA for Upper Bann, Northern Ireland Assembly; ***party:*** Sinn Féin; ***political career:*** MLA for Upper Bann, 2003-; Sinn Féin Group leader in the Assembly, 2007-11; Minister for Education, 2011-; ***office address:*** Northern Ireland Assembly, Parliament Buildings, Ballymiscaw, Belfast, BT14 3XX, United Kingdom.

ODUNTON, Nii A.; Secretary General, International Seabed Authority; ***education:*** M.Sc., Mineral Economics and Mine Finance, Henry Krumb School of Mines, Columbia University, 1974; ***professional career:*** Economic Affairs Officer, Dept. of Int. Economic Social Affairs, UN Secretariat New York, 1980-83; Secretary General, International Seabed Authority, 2009-; ***office address:*** International Seabed Authority, 14-20 Port Royal Street, Kingston, Jamaica; ***URL:*** http://www.isa.org.jm.

OETTINGER, Gunther H.; European Commissioner for Energy, European Commission; ***born:*** 15 October 1953, Stuttgart; ***education:*** Tubingen, Law and Economics, First State Law Exam., 1978; Second State Law Exam., 1982; ***political career:*** District Cllr., Ludwigsburg, 1979-93; Chmn., CDU in Ditzingen, 1977-85; Mem., Parliament of the State of Baden-Wurttemberg, 1984-; Chmn., CDU District Assn. North Wurttemberg, 2001-05; State Chmn., CDU, Baden-Wurttemberg, 2005-; Minister-Pres., Baden-Wurttemberg, 2005-10; European Commissioner for Energy, 2010-; ***professional career:*** Legal clerk then lawyer, auditing and tax consultancy firm, 1982-88; lawyer and exec. dir., 1988-2005 ; ***office address:*** European Commission, rue de la Loi 200, B-1049 Brussels, Belgium; ***phone:*** +32 (0)2 299 1111; ***URL:*** http://www.europa.eu.

O'FARRELL, Barry; Premier, Government of New South Wales; ***education:*** BA, Australian National Univ., Canberra, Australia; ***party:*** NSW Liberal Leader, 2007-; ***political career:*** MP, 1995-; Premier, 2011-; ***office address:*** Premier's Department, Level 39, Governor Macquarie Tower, 1 Farrer Place, Sydney, NSW, Australia; ***phone:*** +61 2 9228 5555; ***fax:*** info@premiers.nsw.gov.au; ***e-mail:*** info@premiers.nsw.gov.au;
URL: http://www.premiers.nsw.gov.au.

Off-One

OFFORD, Matthew; MP for Hendon, UK Government; ***party:*** Conservative; ***political career:*** Councillor, London Borough of Barnet Council, 2002-; MP for Hendon, May 2010-; ***office address:*** House of Commons, London, SW1A 0AA, United Kingdom; ***phone:*** +44 (0)20 7219 3000; ***e-mail:*** matthew.offord.mp@parliament.uk.

OGIO, Michael, GCMG CBE; Governor-General, Papua New Guinea; ***born:*** 1942; ***political career:*** Leader, People's Democratic Movement; Deputy Prime Minister and Minister of Forests; Acting Gov. General, 2010, elected Governor General, 2011-; ***office address:*** Office of the Governor General, NCD, Papua New Guinea.

O'GRADY, Frances; Secretary General, Trades Union Congress; ***born:*** 1959; ***education:*** BA Hons. Manchester Univ.; Dip. in Industrial Relations and Trade Union Studies, Middlesex Polytechnic UK; ***professional career:*** Dep. Sec.-Gen., TTUC, 2003-13; Sec.-Gen., TUC, 2013-; ***office address:*** Trades Union Congress, Congress House, Great Russell Street, London, WC1B 3LS, United Kingdom; ***phone:*** +44 (0)20 7636 4030; ***e-mail:*** info@tuc.org.uk; ***URL:*** http://www.tuc.org.uk/.

OHENE AGYEKUM, Daniel; Ambassador of Ghana to the US, Embassy of Ghana; ***born:*** 1942; ***political career:*** Minister, National Democratic Congress, 1993-99; Greater Accra Regional Minister, 1996-99; Minister in Chieftaincy Affairs, 1999-2000; Regional Chmn., NDC Party, 2001; ***professional career:*** Ghana Foreign Service; career diplomat; Amb. to the US, 2009-; ***office address:*** Embassy of Ghana, 3512 International Drive, NW , Washington, DC 20008, USA; ***phone:*** +1 202 686 4520; ***fax:*** +1 202 686 4527; ***URL:*** http://www.ghanaembassy.org/.

OHIN, Elliott; Minister of Foreign Affairs, Government of Togo; ***education:*** Univ. of Bordeaux, engineering; Paris, MSc., computer science; Sullivan Univ., Kentucky Univ., MBA; ***party:*** UFC; ***political career:*** Minister of Foreign Affairs, 2010-; ***professional career:*** Speedway SuperAmerica, petroleum corp.,; ***office address:*** Ministry of Foreign Affairs, BP 900, Place du Monument aux Morts, Lomé, Togo; ***phone:*** +228 221 2910; ***fax:*** +228 221 3974; ***URL:*** http://www.diplomatie.gouv.tg/.

OHLSSON, Birgitta; Minister for EU Affairs, Swedish Government; ***born:*** 1975; ***education:*** Stockholm Univ., 1994-97; ***political career:*** Chair, Liberal Youth Org., 1999-2002; Mem., Riksdag, 2002-2010; Minister for EU Affairs, 2010-; ***office address:*** Ministry of European Affairs, Swedish Government Offices, SE-103 333 Stockholm, Sweden; ***phone:*** +46 (0)8 405 1000.

OHSAN BELLEPEAU, Monique; Vice President, Government of Mauritius; ***party:*** Mauritian Labor Party; ***political career:*** Pres., Mauritian Labor Party; Vice Pres., Government of Mauritus, 2010-, Acting Pres., March-July 2012; ***professional career:*** journalist; broadcaster; ***office address:*** Office of the President, State House, Port Louis, Mauritius; ***phone:*** +230 454 3021; ***fax:*** +230 464 5370.

OKADA, Katsuya; Deputy Prime Minister , Government of Japan; ***born:*** 1953, Yokkaichi, Mie Prefecture, Japan; ***education:*** MP, 1990-; Faculty of Law, Univ. of Tokyo, 1976-; ***party:*** Democratic Party of Japan; ***political career:*** Minister for Foreign Affairs, 2009-10; Deputy Prime Minister, Minister of Reform of Administration, Social Security, Tax and Civil Services, 2011-13; ***office address:*** Deputy Prime Minister's Office, 1-6-1 nagata-cho, Chiyoda-ku, Tokyo, Japan; ***phone:*** +81 (0)3 3581 3111; ***URL:*** http://www.kantai.go.jp.

OKONJO-IWEALA, Dr. Ngozi; Minister of Finance, Government of Nigeria; ***education:*** Harvard Univ.; Massachusetts Institute of Technology, USA; ***political career:*** Minister of Finance, 2003-06; Minister of Foreign Affairs, 2006; Minister of Finance, 2011-; ***professional career:*** Man. Dir., World Bank, 2007-11; ***office address:*** Ministry of Finance, Ahmadu Bello Way, Central Business District, PMB 14, Garki, Abuja, Nigeria; ***phone:*** +234 9 234 6932.

OLDFATHER, Irene, MSP; MSP for Cunninghame South, Scottish Parliament; ***languages:*** French; ***education:*** Univ. Stathclyde, B.A. Hons. Politics, 1976; Univ. Arizona, Postgraduate, Accumulated Credit, 1978; Univ. Strathclyde, M.Sc. Politics, 1983; ***party:*** Labour; ***political career:*** Elected Mem. of North Ayrshire Cncl.; North Ayrshire Council's European Spokesperson; Management, Research and Policy Posts at Glasgow District Cncl., Housing Dept.; Political Researcher for Alex Smith MEP, South of Scotland, 1990-98; MSP, Cunninghame South, 1999-; ***memberships:*** Vice-Chmn, Cross Party Gp. on Tobacco Control; ***professional career:*** Asst. to Prof. Richard Rose, Brookings Inst., Washington, DC, 1976; Researcher at Dumbarton Cncl. on Alcohol, 1976-77; Research Officer at Strathclyde Regional Cncl.,1978-79; Convention of Scottish Local Authorities (CoSLA) European Members Network; Rep. CoSLA on EMU at Ministerial Meetings; Chwn., Convention of Scottish Local Authorities, Task Gp. on Economic and Monetary Union; Chwm., ECOS/Ouverture II Programme of Regional Aid Between East and West Europe; Writing, Producing and Presenting the Parl Audio Programme - "A Week in Europe" from the European Parl. London Office; Vice-Chwn., West Scotland European Consortium; Freelance Writer/Broadcaster specialising in European Affairs, 1994-98; Bd. of Management, James Watt Further and Higher Education Coll.; Vice Chwn., Aryshire International; Mem. of Aryshire Education Business Partnership; Part Time Lecturer, Paisley Univ., 1996-98; ***committees:*** Scottish Mem., European Cttee. of the Regions; Dep. Convenor, European Cttee., Scottish Parly.; North Aryshire Cncl. European Spokesperson and Vice Chwm. of the Cncl. Educational Cttee.; ***publications:*** The Effects of the Clayson Report on Drinking Habits, 1977; Homesteading at the Glenelg Quadrant, Glasgow, 1982; Additionally - The Problems of ERDF Funding in Scotland, 1991; The European Monetary System, 1992; The West Lothian Question - Fact or Fiction?, 1994, The Herald; EU Budget - The Need to Deal With Fraud in the Euro Wing?, 1995, The Herald, The Scotsman; Is Britain Failing to Punch its Weight in the Euro Ring?, 1995, The Scotsman; The Common Agricultural Policy - the Need for Review, 1995, The Herald; Women's Representation - Analysis of the Representation across National Parliment, 1995; Flexibility, the Key to Constitutional Change, 1995, The Herald; Britain Sabre Rattling in the European Beef Crisis, 1996, The Scotsman; Is Monetary Union a German Plot?, 1996, Scotland on Sunday; Strasbourg Diary, Comparison of British and EU Attitudes to the IGC, 1996, Scotland on Sunday; Anniversary of an Unhappy Marriage of Inconvenience, Britain and the EU, 1997, Scotland on Sunday; Tiger - An Endangered Species? South Korea's Laboured Unrest, 1997, Scotland on Sunday; Major Researches EU Balancing Act with Chirac, 1996, Scotland on Sunday; Dutch Lead the Way to Intergration, 1997, Scotland on Sunday; Achieving Broad Popular Support, 1998; The Euro, How Can Scotland Face Up to the Challenge?, 1998, Scotland Europa Research Paper No.14; ***office address:*** Sovereign House, Academy Road, Irvine, KA12 8RL, United Kingdom; ***phone:*** +44 (0)1294 313078; ***fax:*** +44 (0)1294 313605.

OLEKAS, Juozas, CSc. (Medical); Lithuanian, Minister of Defence, Government of Lithuania; ***born:*** 30 October 1955, Russia; ***education:*** Vilnius Univ., BA, 1980, Faculty of Medicine, MD, 1981, Ph.D., 1987; ***political career:*** Mem., Seimas of the Lithuanian reform movement Sajudis, 1988-90; Mem., Lithuanian Socialdemocratic Party, 1989; Mem., Supreme Cncl. of the USSR, 1989-90; Mem., Health Cttee. of the Supreme Cncl. of the USSR, 1989-90; Minister of Health Care, 1990-92; Mem., WHO European RCIS Cttee., 1992-93; Advisor of MP, 1993-96; Mem., Seimas, 1996-2000; Vice Chmn., Delegations of the Seimas for relations with Taiwan, Japan, 1996-2000; Chmn. Lithuanian Trade Union Center, 1997-; Vice Chmn. Lithuanian Socialdemocratic Party, 1999-; Mem. Seimas, 2000-04; Head, Social Democratic Coalition, the Seimas, 2001-; Vice-Pres., Parly. Assembly, Cncl. of Europe, 2002-03; Minister of Health Care, 2003-04; Mem., Seimas, 2004-; Head, Parly. Gp. Lithuanian Social Democratic Party of Seimas, 2004-; Head, Seimas Delegation, NATO Parly. Assembly, 2004-; Minister of Defence, 2006-08, 2012-; ***professional career:*** Vilnius Univ. 1985-90; Dpty. Pres., Lithuanian Union of Physicians; ***committees:*** Mem., Cttee. for European Affairs, Seimas, 2000-03; Vice-Chmn., Cttee. for Health Affairs, Seimas, 2000-2001; Mem., Cttee. for Health Affairs, 2004-; ***office address:*** Ministry of Defence, Totoriu 25/3, 2001 Vilnius , Lithuania; ***phone:*** +370 5 273 5519; ***URL:*** http://www.kam.lt.

OLLERENSHAW, Eric; MP for Lancaster and Fleetwood, UK Government; ***party:*** Conservative; ***political career:*** Mem., Greater London Assembly, 2000-04; MP for Lancaster and Fleetwood, May 2010-; ***office address:*** House of Commons, London, SW1A 0AA, United Kingdom; ***phone:*** +44 (0)20 7219 3000; ***e-mail:*** eric.ollerenshaw.mp@parliament.uk.

O'LOAN, Baroness Nuala; Member, House of Lords; ***political career:*** Mem., House of Lords, 2009-; ***professional career:*** Chair, Human Rights Inquiry, Equality and Human Rights Commission, 2008-; ***office address:*** House of Lords, London, SW1A 0PW, United Kingdom; ***phone:*** +44 (0)20 7219 3000; ***fax:*** +44 (0)20 7219 5979; ***URL:*** http://www.parliament.uk.

OLSEN, Oystein; Governor, Norges Bank; ***born:*** 1952; ***professional career:*** Research Dept., Statistics Norway, 1977-90; Dep. Dir. Gen., Economic Policy Dept., Ministry of Finance, 1994-96; Professor, Norwegian School of Management, 1993-99; Head, Research Dept., Statistics Norway, 1996-99, Dir.-Gen., 2005-10; Governor, Norges Bank, 2011-; ***office address:*** Norges Bank, PO Box 1179, Sentrum , N-0107 Oslo, Norway.

O'MALLEY, Martin; Governor, State of Maryland; ***born:*** 1963; ***education:*** Law school; ***political career:*** Mem., Baltimore City Council, 3rd District, 1991-99; Baltimore City Mayor, 1999-2006; Governor of Maryland, 2006-; ***professional career:*** Prosecutor, State's Attorney of Baltimore City; ***office address:*** State House, Annapolis, Maryland 21401-1925, USA; ***phone:*** +1 410 974 3901; ***fax:*** +1 410 974 3275; ***e-mail:*** governor@gov.state.md.us; ***URL:*** http://www.gov.state.md.us.

OMIROU, Yiannakis; Turkish Cypriot, President, House of Representatives; ***born:*** 19 September 1951, Paphos, Cyprus; ***parents:*** Lazaros Omirou and Eleni Omirou; ***languages:*** English; ***education:*** Law, Nat. and Kapodistriakon Univ., Athens, Greece; ***party:*** Leader of the Movement of Social Democrats, EDEK; ***political career:*** President of the House of Representatives, 2011-; ***interests:*** eurosocialism, socialism today; ***professional career:*** Lawyer; ***recreations:*** reading, football; ***office address:*** House of Representatives, Dyiavaharlal Nehrou, Omerou Avenue, 1402 Nicosia, Cyprus; ***phone:*** +357 (0)2 303451; ***fax:*** +357 (0)2 366611; ***URL:*** http://www.parliament.cy.

ONA, Enrique; Secretary of Health, Government of the Philippines; ***political career:*** Secretary of Health, 2010-; ***professional career:*** President of the Transplantation Society of the Philippines, 1989-; Exec. Dir., National Kidney and Transplant Institute,1999-2010; ***office address:*** Department of Health, San Lazaro Compound, Rizal Avenue, Santa Cruz, Manila, Philippines; ***phone:*** +63 2 743 8301-23; ***URL:*** http://www.doh.gov.ph.

O'NEILL, H.E. Michael; Ambassador, British Embassy in Qatar; ***professional career:*** Special Rep. to Sudan, 2007-10; Head of Mission, Helmand Provincial Reconstruction Team, ISAF Senior Civilian Representative, Regional Command South-West, Afghanistan, 2010-12; Amb. to Qatar, 2012-; ***office address:*** British Embassy, PO Box 3, Doha, Qatar; ***phone:*** +974 442 1991; ***fax:*** +974 443 8692; ***e-mail:*** bembcomm@qatar.net.qa; ***URL:*** http://ukinqatar.fco.gov.uk.

O'NEILL, Michelle; Minister for Agriculture and Rural Development, Northern Ireland Assembly; ***party:*** Sinn Féin; ***political career:*** MLA for Mid Ulster, 2007-; Mayor of Dungannon and South Tyrone, 2010-; Minister for Agriculture and Rural Development, 2011-; ***office address:*** Northern Ireland Assembly, Parliament Buildings, Ballymiscaw, Belfast, BT4 3XX, United Kingdom.

O'NEILL OF BENGARVE, Baroness; Member of the House of Lords; ***political career:*** Mem., House of Lords; ***memberships:*** Fellow, British Academy; Fellow, Academy of Medical Sciences; Hon. Fellow, Royal Society; ***office address:*** House of Lords, London, SW1A 0PQ, United Kingdom; ***phone:*** +44 (0)20 7219 3000; ***fax:*** +44 (0)20 7219 5979.

ONEK, Hilary; Minister of Disaster Management and Refugees, Government of Uganda; ***political career:*** Minister of Agriculture, Animal Husbandry and Fisheries, 2006-09; Minister of Energy and Minerals, 2009-11; Minister of Internal Affairs, 2011-13; Ministe of Disaster Management and Refugees, 2013-; ***professional career:*** Engineer; ***office address:*** c/o Office of the Prime Minister, Parliament Building, PO Box 7168, Kampala, Uganda ; ***phone:*** +256 41 4254 881; ***fax:*** +256 41 4235 459.

BIOGRAPHIES

ONGKILI, Maximus Johnity; Minister of Energy, Green Technology and Water, Government of Malaysia; ***party:*** United Sabah Party; ***political career:*** opposition politician, imprisoned 1991; MP; Minister of Science, Technology & Innovation, 2008-13; Minister of Energy, Green Technology & Water, 2013-; ***office address:*** Ministry of Energy, Green Technology & Water, Blok E4/5, Kompleks Pentadbiran Kerajaan Persekutuan, 62668 Putrajaya, Malaysia; ***phone:*** +60 3 8883 6000; ***URL:*** http://www.ktak.gov.my.

ONKELINX, Laurette; Deputy Prime Minister and Minister for Social Affairs and Public Health, Government of Belgium; ***born:*** 2 October 1958, Ougrée, Belgium; ***education:*** ULB, LL.B, 1976-81; ***party:*** Parti Socialiste (P.S., Socialist Party); ***political career:*** PS-Dep., district of Liège 1988; Chmn., Interfed. Cmn. of Socialist Women; mem., PS Party Office, 1988; Vice-Pres., House of Representatives; Minister for Social Integration, Health & Environment 1992-93; Minister-Pres., Govt. of the French Community 1993-99, in charge of Civil Service, Childhood and Health 1993-95, in charge of Education, Audiovisual Media, Youth Assistance & Health 1995-99; Deputy Prime Minister, Minister for Employment, 1999-2004; Dep. PM, Min. of Justice, 2004-07; Minister of Social Affairs and Public Health, 2007-; ***professional career:*** Lecturer, Administrative Sciences, 1982-85; Barrister, Court of Liège, 1981-; ***committees:*** Chmn., Justice Cttee., House of Representatives; ***publications:*** Preface of G.Revage's book "La vie d'une minimexée", Continuons le débat; Théâtre du jeune public; ***office address:*** Ministry of Social Affairs, 66 rue de la Loi, B-1040 Brussels, Belgium; ***phone:*** +32 (0)2 210 4511; ***fax:*** +32 (0)2 230 3895; ***URL:*** http://minsoc.fgov.be.

ONLEY, Hon. David C.; Lieutenant Governor, Province of Ontario; ***born:*** 1950; ***education:*** BA, Political Science, Univ. of Toronto, 1975; ***political career:*** Lieutenant Governor of Ontario, 2007-; ***interests:*** disability issues ; ***professional career:*** TV news presenter; ***office address:*** Office of the Lieutenant Governor of Ontario, Room 131, Legislative Building, Queen's Park, Toronto, Ontario, M7A 1A1, Canada; ***phone:*** +1 416 325 7780; ***e-mail:*** ltgov@gov.on.ca; ***URL:*** http://www.lt.gov.on.ca.

ONWURAH, Chinyelu; MP for Newcastle upon Tyne Central, House of Commons; ***party:*** Labour; ***political career:*** MP for Newcastle upon Tyne Central, May 2010-; Shadow Minister, Business, Innovation and Skills, Oct. 2010-; ***committees:*** Business, Innovation and Skills Select Cttee., 2010; ***office address:*** House of Commons, London, SW1A OAA, United Kingdom; ***phone:*** +44 (0)20 7219 3000; ***e-mail:*** chi.onwurah.mp@parliament.uk.

OPPERMAN, Guy; MP for Hexham, UK Government; ***party:*** Conservative; ***political career:*** Councillor, Wiltshire, 1995-99; MP for Hexham, May 2010-; PPS, 2012-; ***committees:*** Unopposed Bills (Panel), 2011-; ***office address:*** House of Commons, London, SW1A 0AA, United Kingdom; ***phone:*** +44 (0)20 7219 3000; ***e-mail:*** guy.opperman.mp@parliament.uk.

OPREA, Gabriel; Vice Prime Minister, Government of Romania; ***born:*** 1961; ***education:*** Univ. of Bucharest, law, Ph.D; ***political career:*** Minister, Ministry of Administration & Interior, 2008-09;Minister, Ministry of National Defence, 2009-12; Senator, Romanian Parliament, 2012-; Vice PM, Dec. 2012-; ***office address:*** Chamber of Deputies, Palatul Parlamentului, St. Izvor 2-4, Sector 5, 050563 Bucharest, Romania.

OPSTELTEN, Ivo; Minister of Security and Justice, Netherlands Government; ***born:*** 1944; ***education:*** Univ. of Leiden, Law; ***political career:*** Mayor, of: Dalen, 1972-77, Doorn, 1987-80, Delfzijl, 1980-87; Dir.-Gen., Public Order and Safety, Ministry of the Interior, 1987; Mayor of Utrecht,, 1992-87; Mayor of Rotterdam , 1999-2008; Acting Mayor of Tilburg, 2009-10; negotiator & mediator in discussions resulting in the formation of the Rutte government, 2010; Minister of Security and Justice, Rutte-Verhagen Government, Oct. 2010-Nov. 2012, Minister of Security and Justice, Rutte-Asscher Government, Nov. 2012-; ***office address:*** Schedeldoekshaven 100, 2511 EX The Hague, Netherlands; ***URL:*** http://www.justitie.nl.

OQILOV, Oqil; Prime Minister, Government of Tajikistan; ***born:*** 2 February 1944, Khujand City; ***parents:*** Gaybullo Ogilov and Mohinisso (née Zokirova); ***married:*** Rano Mansurova, 1968; ***children:*** Muzaffar (M), Masuda Olimova (F), Mavzuna Inoyatova; ***languages:*** Russian; ***education:*** Moscow Engineering-construction Institute, 1967; Academy of Social Science, Moscow, 1980; ***political career:*** Minister of Construction of the Republic of Tajikistan, Dushanbe, 1993-94; Dep. Prime Minister of the Republic of Tajikistan, Dushanbe, 1994-96; First Dep. Chmn. of Lenenabad Region, Khujand, 1996-99; Prime Minister of the Republic of Tajikistan 1999-; ***professional career:*** Engineer-Constructor; ***office address:*** Office of the Prime Minister, pr. Rudaki 80, Dushanbe, Tajikistan; ***phone:*** +992 372 215110; ***fax:*** +992 372 211510.

ORBÁN, Viktor; Hungarian, Prime Minister, Government of Hungary; ***born:*** 1963, Székesfehérvár, Hungary; ***married:*** Anikó Lévai; ***children:*** 5; ***education:*** Lóránd Eötvös Univ., Faculty of Law, 1982-87; Pembroke Coll., Oxford, UK, history of philosophy of English liberal politics, 1989; ***party:*** Fiatal Demokraták Szövetsége (FIDESZ, Federation of Young Democrats); ***political career:*** Anticommunist Co-founder of Hugarian opposition group, Federation of Young Democrates (FIDESZ), 1988, Spokesman, 1989 ; One of the opposition leaders who carried on talks about the Transition with the Communist authority; MP, 1990-; Vice-Pres. Liberal Int. 1992-; Mem., Bureau of the Liberal Int., 1993; Pres., FIDESZ, 1993-; Leader of FIDESZ Parl. Group, 1990-94; Prime Minister, 1998-2002, May 2010-; ***professional career:*** Researcher, Middle-Europe Research Gp., 1989-91; ***committees:*** Chmn., Cttee. on European Integration Affairs of the Hungarian Parl., 1994-98; ***publications:*** National Policy, 1988-98; ***office address:*** Office of the Prime Minister, Kossuth Lajos tér 1-3, 1055 Budapest, Hungary; ***phone:*** +36 (0)1 268 3000; ***fax:*** +36 (0)1 441 4702; ***URL:*** http://www.kancellaria.gov.hu.

ORECK, Bruce; Ambassador, US Embassy in Finland; ***education:*** BA, The Johns Hopkins Univ.; JD, Louisiana State Univ.; Masters of Law (Taxation), New York Univ.; ***professional career:*** Lawyer; Real estate developer; Founder, Zero Carbon Initiative; Amb. to Finland, 2009-; ***office address:*** Embassy of the United States of America, Itäinen Puistotie 14b, 00140 Helsinki, Finland; ***phone:*** +358 (0)9 171931; ***fax:*** +358 (0)9 174681; ***URL:*** http://finland.usembassy.gov.

OREN, H.E. Dr. Michael B.; Ambassador, Embassy of Israel in the USA; ***born:*** New Jersey, USA; ***education:*** Princeton and Columbia grad.; ***professional career:*** Officer, Israel Defense Forces; Officer, paratroopers, during Lebanon War; Liaison Officer, US Sixth Fleet during the Gulf War; IDF spokesman, 2nd Lebanon War and Gaza operation of Jan. 2009; Visiting prof., Harvard, Yale and Georgetown Univs.; Contributor, The Wall Street Journal, The New York Times and The New Republic; Advisor, Israeli delegation to the UN; Dir., Inter-Religious Affairs; briefed US Govt. on Middle Eastern Affairs; Israeli Amb. to Washington, 2009-; ***honours and awards:*** Lady Davis Fellow of Hebrew Univ.; Moshe Dayan Fellow, Tel-Aviv Univ.; Distinguished Fellow, Shalem Center, Jerusalem; ***publications:*** Six Days of War: June 1967 and the Making of the Modern Middle East; Power, Faith, and Fantasy: America in the Middle East, 1776 to the Present; ***office address:*** Embassy of Israel, 3514 International Drive, NW, , Washington, DC 20008, USA; ***phone:*** +1 202 364 5500; ***fax:*** +1 202 364 5607; ***e-mail:*** ask@israelemb.org; ***URL:*** http://www.israelemb.org/.

ORESHARSKI, Plamen; Prime Minister, Government of Bulgaria; ***education:*** Higher Inst. of Finances and Economics; ***political career:*** Finance Minister, 2005-09; Prime Minister, 2013-; ***professional career:*** Mem., Governing Council of the Bulgarian Stock Exchange, 1995-97; Board mem., UniCredit Bulbank, 1997-2000; Professor of Finance, Univ. for National and World Economy, Sofia; ***office address:*** Office of the Prime Minister, 1 Boulevard Knjaz Dondukov, 1194 Sofia, Bulgaria; ***phone:*** +359 (0)2 8501; ***URL:*** http://www.government.bg.

ORTEGA, Daniel; President, Nicaragua; ***born:*** 11 November 1945; ***political career:*** joined Sandinista's, 1963, leading role in guerilla war against Anastasio Somozo; imprisoned several times; President of Nicaragua, 1979-90; President, 2007-; ***office address:*** Office of the President, Av. Bolivar y dupla sur, Managua, Nicaragua; ***URL:*** http://www.presidencia.gob.ni/.

OSBORNE, Rt. Hon. George; Chancellor of the Exchequer, House of Commons; ***born:*** 23 May 1971; ***parents:*** Sir Peter Osborne and Lady Osborne; ***married:*** The Hon. Frances Victoria Osborne (née Howell), 4 April 1998; ***children:*** Luke Benedict Osborne (M), Liberty Kate Osborne (F); ***education:*** St Paul's Sch., London; Davidson Coll., North Carolina; Magdalen Coll., Oxford Univ., History; ***party:*** Conservative Party; ***political career:*** MP, Tatton, 2001-; Opposition Whip, 2003-; Shadow Chief Sec. to the Treasury, 2004-05; Shadow Chancellor of the Exchequer, May 2005-May 2010; Chancellor of the Exchequer, 2010-; ***professional career:*** Special Adviser, MAFF, 1995-97; ***committees:*** House of Commons Select Cttee. on Public Accounts; ***office address:*** Chancellor of the Duchy of Lancaster, 70 Whitehall, London, SW1A 2AS, United Kingdom; ***phone:*** +44 (0)20 7270 0400; ***e-mail:*** contact@georgeosborne.co.uk; ***URL:*** http://www.georgeosborne.co.uk.

OSBORNE, Sandra; Member of Parliament for Ayr, Carrick & Cumnock, House of Commons; ***born:*** 23 February 1956; ***parents:*** Thomas Clark and Isabella Clark; ***married:*** Alastair Osborne, 20 Febuary 1982; ***education:*** Camphill Senior Secondary, Paisley; Annesland Coll., Jordanhill Coll., Strathclyde Univ., Dip., Comm. Ed., Dip. in Equality and Discrimination, M.Sc., Equality and Discrimination; ***party:*** Labour Party; ***political career:*** MP, Ayr, 1997-2005; MP, Ayr, Carrick & Cumnock, 2005-; ***professional career:*** fmr. community worker; ***committees:*** European Scrutiny Select Cttee., 2004-10, 2011-; Foreign Affairs Select Cttee., 2005-10; Sec., All Party Colombia Gp., 2005; Sec., All Party Women, Peace and Security Gp., 2006; Defence Select Cttee., 2010-; Panel of Chairs, 2011-; ***office address:*** House of Commons, Westminster, London, SW1A 0AA, United Kingdom; ***phone:*** +44 (0)20 7219 3000; ***e-mail:*** osbornes@parliament.uk.

OSORIO, Néstor; President, Economic and Social Council; ***professional career:*** Colombian Planning Dept.; Perm. Rep to Int'l. Coffee Org., 1978-94; Perm. Rep. to the World Trade Org., 1994-99; Special Advisor to this Gov. on Coffee and Trade Affairs, 2000-02; Exec. Dir., International Coffee Org., 2002-2010; Perm. Rep. of Columbia to the UN, 2010; Pres., Economic and Social Council, 2013-; ***office address:*** Economic and Social Council, UN, UN Plaza, New York, NY 10017, USA; ***URL:*** http://www.un.org.

OSORIO CHONG, Miguel Angel; Secretary of the Interior, Government of Mexico; ***born:*** 1964; ***education:*** Univ. of the State of Hidalgo, Law; ***political career:*** Sec., PRI National Executive Cttee.; Fed. Rep., 59th Session, 2003-05; Governor of the State of Hidalgo, 205-11; Secretary of the Interior, 2012-; ***office address:*** Secretariat of the Interior, Bucareli 99, Col. Juárez, 06600 Mexico, DF, Mexico; ***phone:*** +52 55 5566 8188; ***fax:*** +52 55 5703 2171.

OSOTIMEHIN, Dr Babatunde; Executive Director, UNFPA; ***education:*** Univ. of Ibadan, Nigeria, medicine,1972; Univ. of Brimingham, UK, doctorate in medicine, 1979; ***political career:*** Minister of Health, Nigerian Government; ***professional career:*** Prof., Univ. of IBadan, 1980, Head, Dept. of Clinical Pathology, Provost, College of Medicine, 1990-94; Dir.-Gen., Nigerian National Agency for the Control of AIDS; Currently, Under-Secretary-General of the United Nations; also Exec, Dir., United Nations Population Fund (UNFPA), 2011-; ***office address:*** UNFPA, 220 East 42nd Street, New York, NY 10017, USA; ***URL:*** http://www.unfpa.org/.

OSSEIRAN, Inaan; Ambassador, Embassy of Lebanon in the UK; ***languages:*** English, French, Italian, Spanish; ***education:*** Lebanese and French Law, Masters Degree in Int. Private and Public Law, Saint Joseph Univ., Beirut; ***professional career:*** Charge d'Affaires, in Madrid, Spain, 1997-99; Consul General to Milan, Italy, 1999-2004; Amb, to Switzerland, 2004-07; Amb. to London, UK, 2007-; ***office address:*** Lebanese Embassy, 21 Kensington Palace Gardens, London, W8 4QM, United Kingdom; ***phone:*** +44 (0)20 7229 7265; ***fax:*** +44 (0)20 7243 1699; ***e-mail:*** emb.leb@btinternet.com; ***URL:*** http://www.lebaneseembassy.org.uk.

ØSTERGAARD, Morten; Minister for Science, Innovation and Higher Education, Government of Denmark; ***born:*** 17 June 1976, Århus, Denmark; ***education:*** MSc., Political Science, Aarhus Univ., 2006; ***party:*** Social Liberal Party; ***political career:*** MP, 2005-; Minister for Science, Innovation and Higher Education, 2011-; ***office address:*** Ministry of Science, Technology and Innovation, Bredgade 43, 1260 Copenhagen K, Denmark; ***phone:*** +45 3392 9700; ***fax:*** +45 3332 3501; ***e-mail:*** vtu@vtu.dk; ***URL:*** http://www.vtu.dk.

OTHMANI, Saad-Eddine El; Minister of Foreign Affairs & Co-operation, Government of Morocco; ***born:*** 1956; ***education:*** Hassan II Univ. of Casablanca, medicine, psychiatry; Univ. of Rabat, Islamic Studies; ***political career:*** Head, Justice & Development Party, 2008; Vice-Pres., House of Reps., 2010-11; Minister of Foreign Affairs, 2012-; ***office address:*** Ministry of Foreign Affairs & Co-operation, Avenue Franklin Roosevelt, Rabat, Morocco; ***phone:*** +212 37 761763,; ***URL:*** http://www.maec.gov.ma/.

OTTAWAY, Richard; British, Member of Parliament for Croydon South, House of Commons; ***born:*** 1945; ***parents:*** Christopher Ottaway and Grace Ottaway (née Luckin); ***married:*** Nichola E. Kisch, 1982; ***education:*** Bristol Univ., LL. B. Hons; ***party:*** Conservative Party; ***political career:*** MP (Cons) for Nottingham North, June 1983-87; PPS to Michael Heseltine MP; Pres., Bd., of Trade and Dep., Prime Minister, 1992-95; Govt. Whip, 1995-97; Chmn., All Party Gp. on Population & Dev., 1992-95; Opp. Spokesman on Local Government, London & Transport, 1997-99; Shadow Defence Spokesman, 1999-00; Treasury Spokesman, 2000-01; MP, Croydon South, 1992-; ***memberships:*** Population Concern; ***professional career:*** Joined RN, 1962, commissioned, 1966, RNC Dartmouth, 1966-67, served with Western Fleet, 1967-70; Bristol Univ., 1970-74; articled, 1974; admitted Solicitor, 1977; Dir., Coastal Europe Ltd, 1988-1995; ***committees:*** Founder Chmn., All Party Parly. UK-Malaysia Gp.; All Party Parly. Olympic Gp.; All Party Parly. Gp. for Population, Development and Reproductive Health; mem. Intelligence and Security Cttee., Vice Chmn., 1922 Cttee. Bd., Conservative Party, 2006; Foreign Affairs Select Cttee., 2003-04, Chair, 2010-; Defence, 2004-05; Liaison, 2010-; ***publications:*** Combating International and Maritime Fraud; Pay late, Pay Interest; Less People, Less Pollution; ***clubs:*** Royal Corinthian Yacht Club; Royal London Yacht Club; ***recreations:*** skiing, yacht racing, jazz; ***office address:*** House of Commons, London, SW1A 0AA, United Kingdom; ***phone:*** +44 (0)20 7219 6392; ***e-mail:*** ottawayr@parliament.uk; ***URL:*** http://www.richardottaway.com.

OTTER, C.L. 'Butch'; Governor, State of Idaho, USA; ***born:*** 3 May 1942; ***education:*** College of Idaho (now Albertson College of Idaho), BA Political Science, 1967; ***party:*** Republican Party; ***political career:*** Mem., Idaho Hse. of Reps., 1973-76; Lt. Governor, State of Idaho; Mem., US House of Representatives, 2000-06; Governor, State of Idaho, 2007-; ***professional career:*** Idaho Army National Guard's 116th Armored Cavalry, 1968-73; Mem., Bd. of Dir., J.R. Simplot Company; Dir., Food Products Div., J. R. Simplot; Pres., Simplot Livestock; Pres. Simplot Int'., to 1993; ***committees:*** Energy and Commerce Cttee.; ***office address:*** Office of the Governor, State Capitol, West Wing, 700 West Jefferson, 2nd Floor, PO Box 83720, Boise, Idaho 83720-0034, USA; ***phone:*** +1 208 334 2100; ***fax:*** +1 208 334 2175; ***URL:*** http://www.gov.idaho.gov/ourgov.

OUATTARA, Dr Alassane Dramane; Ivorian, President, Government of Cote d'Ivoire; ***born:*** 1942; ***married:*** Barbara Jean Davis, 1966; ***education:*** Degree in Business Administration, Drexel; Inst. of Technology, Philadelphia, USA 1965; Masters Degree in Economics, Univ. of Pennsylvania, USA 1967; Doctorate in Economics, Univ. of Philadelphia, USA 1972; ***political career:*** President, Dec. 2010-; ***professional career:*** Economist, International Monetary Fund, Washington DC, USA, 1968-73; with Central Bank of West African States: Commissioner, 1973-75, Special Advisor to the Governor and Director of Studies, 1975-82, Vice Governor, 1983-84, Governor; with International Monetary Fund: Dir., African Dept., 1984-, Adviser to the General Manager and the Manager of the African Dept., 1987-; ***committees:*** Pres., Co-ordination Cttee. for Multilateral Payment Arrangements (CNUCED) 1979-80; Mem., Administrative Council of the Global Economic Action Institute; Adviser to the Cttee. on Multinational Corporations; ***honours and awards:*** Commander of the Order of the Lion of Senegal; Commander of the Order of Mono of Toga; Commander of the National Order of Niger; Officer of the National Order of the Ivory Coast; ***publications:*** Numerous articles on currency, trade and finance; ***office address:*** Office of the President, 01 BP 1354, Abidjan, Côte d'Ivoire; ***phone:*** +225 2031 4000; ***fax:*** +225 2031 4540.

OUEDRAOGO, Desiré Kadre, M Econ. Sc; President, ECOWAS Commission; ***born:*** 1953, Sanmatenga, Burkina Faso; ***married:*** (married); ***education:*** Sch. of Commerce, France; Univ. of Paris (Sorbonne); ***political career:*** Prime Minister, 1996-2001; ***professional career:*** Former lecturer, Univ. of Ougadougou; mem. staff, Tinancial Div., Solidarity Funds and Community Devt., 1980; Econ. Affairs Counsellor, Min. of Commerce and Industrial Devt., 1977-80; Financial Counsellor and Exec. Sec., ECOWAS, 1983; Dep. Gov., Cen. Bank of West African States, 1993; Pres., ECOWAS Commission, 2012-; ***office address:*** ECOWAS, 101 Yakubu Gowon Crescent, Asokoro District P.M.B. , 401 Abuja, Nigeria.

OULD ABDELAZIZ, Gen. Mohamed; President, Government of Mauritania; ***born:*** 1956; ***education:*** Royal Military Academy, Morocco; ***political career:*** Presidential Chief of Staff, 2007; Coup leader, August 2008; President, 2008-April 09, re-elected July 2009-; ***professional career:*** Army, 1977-; founder the presidential guard unit, BASEP; ***office address:*** Office of the President, Nouakchott, Mauritania; ***URL:*** http://www.mauritania.mr.

OWADA, Judge Hisashi; Japanese, Judge, International Court of Justice; ***born:*** 18 September 1932; ***languages:*** Japanese, English, French, German, Russian; ***education:*** University of Tokyo, BA, 1955; University of Cambridge, LLB, 1956, Humanitarian Student in International Law, 1958; Legal qualification: Judge; ***interests:*** Armed conflict; Criminal Law; Dispute settlement; Economic law; Jurisdiction; Organisations; Law of the Sea; Treaties; ***memberships:*** Institute of International Law; Honorary Member, ASIL; Executive Board, ILA, Japanese Branch; Member emeritus, Executive Board, Japanese Society of International Law; ***professional career:*** *academic career:* Tokyo University, Adjunct Professor, 1963-88; Harvard Law School, Visiting Professor, 1979-81, 1987, 1989, 1999-2002; Columbia Law School, Adjunct Professor, 1994-98; New York University Law School, Inge Rennert Distinguished Visiting Professor, 1994-98; Waseda University Graduate School, Professor, 1999-2003; New York University Global Law School, Professor, 1998-; *professional career:* Senior Adviser to President of the World Bank, 1999-2003; President, Japan Institute of International Affairs, 1999-2003; *governmental career:* Private Secretary to Prime Minister of Japan, 1976-78; Director-General of Treaties Bureau (Principal Legal Adviser), Ministry of Foreign Affairs, 1984-87; Deputy Minister for Foreign Affairs, 1989-91; Vice-Minister for Foreign Affairs, 1991-93; Adviser to Minister for Foreign Affairs, 1993-94, 1999-2003; *diplomatic career:* Ambassador and Permanent Representative of Japan to OECD, 1988-89; Ambassador and Permanent Representative of Japan to the UN, 1994-98; Judicial career: Judge, ICJ, 2003-; Member, PCA, 2001-; ***publications:*** Books: US-Japan Economic Interaction in an Independent World, 1981; Japanese Perspectives on Asian Security, 1982; Practice of Japan in International Law, 1984; From Involvement to Engagement: A New Course for Japanese Foreign Policy, 1994; Diplomacy, 1997; Treatise on International Relations, 2003; Articles: Japanese Annual of International Law; Japanese Journal of International Law and Diplomacy; Singapore Yearbook of International Law; International Security; ***office address:*** International Court of Justice, Carnegieplein 2, 2517 KJ The Hague, The Netherlands; ***phone:*** +31 (0)70 302 2323; ***fax:*** +31 (0)70 364 9928; ***e-mail:*** mail@ici-cij.org.

OWEN, Albert; Member of Parliament for Ynys Môn, House of Commons; ***born:*** 1959; ***political career:*** MP for Ynys Môn, 2001-; ***interests:*** Welsh affairs, economic dev., welfare; ***committees:*** Welsh Affairs, 2001-10; Energy & Climate Change, 2010-; ***office address:*** House of Commons, London, SW1A 0AA, United Kingdom; ***phone:*** +44 (0)20 7219 8415; ***fax:*** +44 (0)20 7219 8415; ***e-mail:*** albert.owen.mp@parliament.uk.

OWEN, H.E. Jane; Ambassador, British Embassy in Norway; ***professional career:*** Dir., UK Trade and Investment, British High Commission in India, 2006-10; Amb. to Norway, 2010-; ***office address:*** British Embassy, Thomas Heftyesgate 8, 0244 Oslo, Norway; ***phone:*** +47 2313 2700; ***fax:*** +47 2313 2741; ***e-mail:*** britemb@online.no; ***URL:*** http://ukinnorway.fco.gov.uk/en.

OWENS, William L.; Congressman, New York Dist. 23, US House of Representatives; ***education:*** Law; ***political career:*** US Congressman, 2009-; ***professional career:*** US Air Force; Captain, Platttsburg Air Force Base; Lawyer; Mging. Ptnr., Stafford, Owens; ***committees:*** Armed Services; Homeland Security; ***office address:*** US House of Representatives, 2366 Rayburn HOB, Washington, DC 20515, USA; ***phone:*** +1 202 225 4611; ***URL:*** http://owens.house.gov/.

P

PABRIKS, Artis; Deputy Prime Minister, Minister of Economics, Minister of Defence, Government of Latvia; ***education:*** Univ. of Latvia, history degree; Univ. of Aarhus, Denmark, Ph.D, political science; ***political career:*** MP, 2004-; Parly sec., Ministry of Foreign Affairs; Minister of Foreign Affairs, July 2004-08; Deputy Prime Minister, Minister of Economics, Minister of Defence, 2010-; ***professional career:*** researcher; lecturer; professor; ***office address:*** Ministry of Economics, Brivibas bulv. 55, Riga 1519, Latvia; ***phone:*** +371 701 3101; ***fax:*** +371 728 0882; ***URL:*** http://www.lem.gov.lv.

PAET, Urmas; Minister of Foreign Affairs, Government of Estonia; ***born:*** 20 April 1974, Tallinn, Estonia; ***parents:*** Juri Paet and Silja Paet; ***married:*** Tiina; ***languages:*** English, German, Russian; ***education:*** Univ. of Tartu, Political Sciences; ***party:*** Vice, Chmn., Estonian Reform Party; ***political career:*** Tallinn City Govt., 1999-2003; Minister of Culture, 2003-05; Minister of Foreign Affairs, 2005-; ***office address:*** Ministry of Foreign Affairs, Islandi Väljak 1, 15049 Tallinn, Estonia; ***phone:*** +372 637 7092; ***fax:*** +372 637 7097; ***e-mail:*** vminfo@mfa.ee; ***URL:*** http://www.vm.ee.

PAGE, H.E. Andrew; Ambassador, UK Embassy in Slovenia; ***born:*** 17 September 1965; ***languages:*** French, Russian, Ukrainian, Slovene; ***professional career:*** Joined FCO, 1990; 2nd Sec., Kiev, 1993-96; Press Officer, Midle East, Terrorism, 1996-98; Hd. of South Africa Section, 1998-2000; Secondment to Quai d'Orsay (Africa Directorate), Paris, 2000-01; First Sec. (Political), 2001-04; Dep. Hd., Russia, South Caucasus and Central Asia Directorate, 2004-08; Amb., Slovenia, 2009-; ***office address:*** UK Embassy, 4th Floor Trg Republike 3, 1000 Ljubljana, Slovenia; ***phone:*** +386 1 200 3920; ***fax:*** +386 1 425 0174; ***e-mail:*** info@british-embassy.si; ***URL:*** http://www.ukinslovenia.fco.gov.uk.

PAHOR, Borut; President, Government of Slovenia; ***born:*** 2 November 1963; ***languages:*** English, French, Italian, Serbo-croat; ***party:*** Socialist Group in the European Parliament; ***political career:*** Mem., National Assembly; Leader, League of Communists - Party of Democratic Reform, then Social Democrats (SD); Chmn., National Assembly, 2000-04; MEP, 2004-08; Prime Minister, 2008-11; President of Slovenia, 2012-; ***committees:*** European Parliament's Cttee. on Budgetary Control; EP Cttee. on Constitutional Affairs; Substitute, EP Cttee. on Foreign Affairs; Vice-Chmn., delegation to the EU-Croatia Jt. Parly. Cttee.; ***office address:*** Office of the President, Erjavceva 17, 1000 Ljubljana, Slovenia.

PAICE, Rt. Hon. Sir James, MP; British, Minister of State, Department for Environment Food and Rural Affairs, UK Government; ***born:*** 1949, Suffolk, UK; ***married:*** (married); ***education:*** Framlingham Coll., Suffolk; Writtle Agricultural Coll.; ***party:*** Conservative Party; ***political career:*** Conservative Candidate for Caernarvon, 1979; Parly. Private Sec. to Baroness Trumpington; MP, South East Cambridgeshire, 1987-; PPS to John Gummer, Minister of Agriculture, Fisheries of Food, 1990-92; Dept. of Environment, 1993-94; Parly Under Sec. of State, Dept. of Employment, 1994-95; Dept. Education and Employment, 1995-97; Opp. Spokesman for Agriculture, Fisheries and Food, 1997-2001; Opp. Spokesman on Home Affairs, 2001-04; Shadow Sec. of State for Agricultural and Rural Affairs, 2004-05; Shadow Minister for Agriculture and Rural Affairs, 2005-2010; Minister of State, Department for Environment, Food and Rural Affairs, 2010-12; ***professional career:*** Gp. Training Officer, United Framlingham Farmers Ltd.; Gen. Mgr. and Exec. Dir., Framlingham Management and Training Services Ltd.; He served on MSC Area Manpower Board for Norfolk and Suffolk; European Council of Young Farmers for three years; Suffolk Coastal District Council, 1970-83; Chmn., Eye Constituency Young Conservatives, 1975; held various posts in Eye and Suffolk Coastal Conservative Assoc.; ***committees:*** Backbench Horticulture and Markets Sub-cttee.; Select Cttee. on Employment, 1987-89; Sec. of the Backbench Employment Cttee, 1988-89; Chair, Racing & Bloodstock Cttee., 1992-94; ***honours and awards:*** Privy Councillor; Knight Bachelor; ***office address:*** House of Commons, London, SW1A 0AA, United Kingdom; ***phone:*** +44 (0)20 7219 3000; ***e-mail:*** hcinfo@parliament.uk.

PAISLEY, Ian, Jr.; MP for North Antrim , House of Commons; *born:* 1966; *parents:* Lord Bannside, (Rev'd. Ian Paisley); *party:* Democratic Unionist Party; *political career:* Mem. of the Northern Ireland Assembly for North Antrim, 1998-2010; MP at Westminster for North Antrim, 2010-; *committees:* Northern Ireland Affairs, 2010-; *office address:* House of Commons, London, SW1A 0AA, United Kingdom; *phone:* +44 (0)20 7219 3000.

PAISLEY, Rev. Ian; See Lord Bannside.

PALIN, Governor Sarah; Fmr. Governor, State of Alaska; *born:* February 1964, Sandpoint, Idaho; *married:* Todd Palin; *children:* Piper (F), Trig (M), Track (M), Bristol (F), Willow (F); *public role of spouse:* Commercial Fisherman; *education:* Univ. of Idaho, journalism; *party:* Republican; *political career:* Mayor, Wasilia City Cncl.; Pres. Alaska Conference of Mayors; Governor of Alaska, 2006-09; Republican Candidate for Vice-President, USA, 2008; *professional career:* Sports reporter; contributor to Fox News, 2010-; *committees:* Chmn., Alaska's Oil and Gas Conservation Cmn.; Interstate Oil and Gas Compact Cmn.; *office address:* c/o The Republican Party, Republican National Committee, 310 First Street, SE, Washinton DC 20003, USA.

PALMER, H.E. Larry; Ambassador, Embassy of the United States in Barbados; *education:* BA, Emory Univ.; Master of Education in African History, Texas Southern Univ.; Doctorate of Higher Education Administration and African Studies, Indiana Univ. in Bloomington; *professional career:* Amb. to Honduras; Amb. to Barbados, 2012-; *office address:* Embassy of the United States, Canadian Imperial Bank of Commerce Building, Broad Street, Bridgetwon, PO Box 302, Barbados; *phone:* +1 246 436 4950; *URL:* http://barbados.usembassy.gov.

PALMER, Lord Monroe, OBE; Member, House of Lords; *party:* Liberal Democrat Party; *political career:* Councilor, Barnet Council, London; mem., House of Lords. 2011-; *office address:* House of Lords, London, SW1A 0PW, United Kingdom; *phone:* +44 (0)20 7219 3000.

PANAGIOTOPOULOS, Panos; Minister of Defence, Government of Greece; *political career:* Minister of Employment and Social Protection, to 2006; Minister of Defence, June 2012-; *office address:* Ministry of Defence, Pentagon, Mesogeion, Athens, Greece; *phone:* +30 (0)10 655 5911; *e-mail:* minister@mod.gr; *URL:* http://www.mod.gr.

PANDOR, Grace Naledi; Minister of Home Affairs, Government of South Africa; *born:* 7 December 1953; *education:* Univ. of Botswana and Swaziland, Cert. in Education, BA in History, 1977; Univ. of London, Masters in Education, 1978; Univ. of Stellenbosch, Masters degree, General Linguistics, 1997; *political career:* Mem. of Parliament, 1994-; Mem., National Executive Cttee. of the ANC; Minister of Education, 2004-09; Minister of Science and Technology, 2009-12; Minister of Home Affairs, 2012-; *professional career:* Teacher in London and Botswana; Snr. Lecturer, Academic Support Programme, Univ. of Cape Town; political exile; Chancellor, Cape Technikon, 2002 *office address:* Department of Home Affairs, Private Bag X741, Pretoria 0001, South Africa.

PANETTA, Leon; American, Chairman, Panetta Institute; *born:* June 1938, Monterey; *married:* Sylvia Marie Varni, 1962; *education:* Univ. of Santa Clara, BA in Political Science, 1960, law degree, 1963; *political career:* Dir., Central Intelligence Agency, 2009-11; Secretary of Defense, 2011-13; *professional career:* Army intelligence officer, 1964-66; Exec. Asst. to New York City Mayor John Lindsay; Legislative Aide to Thomas Kuchel; Head of US Office for Civil Rights during the Nixon Administration; practised law; Mem., HOR, 1977-93; Dir, Office of Management and Budget 1993-94; Chief of Staff to Pres. Clinton, 1994-97; Leon & Sylvia Panetta Institute for Public Policy, California State Univ., Monterey; Chmn., Panetta Institute, 2013-; *committees:* House Budget Cttee. 1979-93, Chmn., 1989-93; Iraq Study Group, 2006; *honours and awards:* Army Commendation Medal; *office address:* Panetta Institute for Public Policy, 100 Campus Center, Building 86E, California State University, Monterey Bay, Seaside, CA 93955, USA; *phone:* +1 831 582 4200; *URL:* http://www.panettainstitute.org/.

PANITCHPAKDI, Supachai, BA, MA, Ph.D,NIDA; Thai, Secretary General, UNCTAD; *born:* 30 May 1946; *education:* Netherlands, BA., Econ., MA. Econ., Ph.D. Development Planning; Hon. Doctorate, Economics Development, NIDA; *party:* Democrat; *political career:* MHR., 1986, 1995, 1996; Dep. Min. of Finance, 1986; Member of the National Legislative Assembly, 1991; Senator, 1992; Dep. Prime Minister, 1992-2000; *professional career:* Director General, World Trade Organization, 2002-05; Sec.-Gen., UNCTAD, 2005-; *honours and awards:* Knight Grand Cordon (Special Class) of the Most Exalted Order of the White Elephant; *office address:* UNCTAD, Palais des Nations, 8-14 Avenue de la Paix, CH 1211 Geneva 10, Switzerland.

PAPOULIAS, Karolos; Greek, President, Greece; *born:* 4 June 1929, Ioannina, Epirus, Greece; *parents:* Major Gen. Grigorios Papoulias; *married:* May Panou; *education:* Univs. of Athens, Munich, Cologne (Doctorate in Law); *political career:* Co-Founder, Socialist Democratic Union; Mem., Central Cttee., PASOK 1974-; Secy., International Relations Cttee., PASOK 1975-85 (representative of PASOK, Permanent Secretariate of Socialist and Progressive Parties, Mediterranean Region); MP for Ioannina 1977-2004; Alternative Minister for Foreign Affairs 1981-85; Minister for Foreign Affairs 1985-89; Alternative Minister of National Defence 1989-90; Pres.-in-office, EU; Pres. of Greece, 2005-; *memberships:* Secy.-Gen., Inst. for Mediterranean Studies; Pres. Ethnikos Athletic Union; Pres., Assn. for the Greek Linguistic Heritage; *professional career:* Lawyer; Munich Inst. for South-Eastern Europe; *committees:* Chmn., Standing Cttee. on Defence and Foreign Affairs, during Simitis Admin.; *publications:* Synopsis of Greek Resistance; several articles published in foreign newspapers and magazines; *office address:* Office of the President, Stissichorou 17-Leoforos Vass. Georgiou B8, 106 74 Athens, Greece.

PARADIS, Hon. Christian; Minister of Industry, Government of Canada; *education:* BA, civil law, Univ. of Sherbrooke; MA, corporate law, Laval Univ.; *political career:* MP, 2006-; Parly. Sec. to the Minister of Natural Resources, 2006-07; Secretary of State, Agriculture, 2007-08; Minister of Public Works and Government Services, 2008-10; Minister of Natural Resources, 2010-11; Minister of Industy, Minister of State for Agriculture, 2011-;

office address: House of Commons, Parliament Buildings, Wellington Street, Ottawa, Ontario, K1A 0A6, Canada; *phone:* +1 613 943 5959; *fax:* +1 613 992 3674; *URL:* http://www.parl.gc.ca.

PARISH, Neil; Member, European Parliament; *party:* Conservative Party; *political career:* MEP for South West England, 2004; MP, Tiverton and Honiton, 2010-; *committees:* Environment, Food and Rural Affairs, 2010-; *office address:* House of Commons, London, SW1A 0AA, United Kingdom; *e-mail:* neil.parish.mp@parliament.uk; *URL:* http://www.parliament.uk.

PARK, Geun-hye; President, Republic of Korea; *parents:* President Park Chung-hee; *education:* Engineering Degree, Sogang Univ., Seoul; *political career:* Mem., National Assembly, 1998-; President, 2013-; *office address:* Office of the President, Cheong Wa Dae, 1 Sejonj-no, Jongo-gu, Seoul, Republic of Korea; *URL:* http://www.cwd.go.kr.

PARK, Suk-hwan; Ambassador, Embassy of the Republic of Korea in the United Kingdom; *professional career:* Amb. to the UK, 2012-; *office address:* Embassy of the Republic of Korea, 60 Buckingham Gate, London, SW1E 6AJ, United Kingdom; *phone:* +44 (0)20 7227 5500; *fax:* +44 (0)20 7227 5503; *URL:* http://gbr.mofat.go.kr/eng/eu/gbr/main/index.jsp .

PARMINTER, Baroness Kathryn; Member, House of Lords; *party:* Liberal Democrat; *political career:* Mem., House of Lords, 2010-; *professional career:* Chief Exec., Campaign to Protect Rural England, 1998-2004; *office address:* House of Lords, London, SW1A 0PW, United Kingdom; *phone:* +44 (0)20 7219 3000; *fax:* +44 (0)20 7219 5979.

PARNELL, Governor Sean; Governor, State of Alaska; *education:* Pacific Lutheran Univ., Business Admin.; Univ. of Puget Sound School of Law (now Seattle Univ. School of Law), J.D.; *party:* Republican; *political career:* Alaska HOR, 1992-96; State Senator, 1996-2000; Lieutenant Gov., Alaska, 2006-09; Governor, 2009-; *professional career:* Attorney, licensed to practice law in Alaska and Washington, D.C., 1987-; Law practice, Anchorage; *committees:* House Finance Cttee., Senate Finance Cttee., Energy Council; *office address:* Office of the Governor, PO Box 110001, Juneau, AK 99811-0001, USA; *phone:* +1 907 465 3500; *URL:* http://www.gov.state.ak.us/.

PARTS, Juhan; Minister of Economic Affairs and Communications, Government of Estonia; *born:* 27 August 1966, Tallinn, Estonia; *languages:* English, Estonian, Russian; *education:* Univ. of Tartu, Law, 1991; *party:* Leader, Union for the Republic Res Publica; *political career:* Dep. Sec.-Gen., Ministry of Justice, 1992-98; Mem., Governing Bd., European Org. of Supreme Audit Institutions, 1998-2002; Auditor General, 1998-2002; Prime Minister, 2003-05; Minister of Economic Affairs and Communications, 2007-; *recreations:* football; *office address:* Ministry of Economic Affairs, 15161 Tallinn, Estonia.

PASSOS COEHLO, Pedro Manuel; Portuguese, Prime Minister, Government of Portugal; *born:* 1964; *education:* Lusiada Univ., Lisbon, Economics; *party:* Social Democratic Party (PSD); *political career:* Mem., National Council of Social Democratic Youth; Dep. Leader & Spokesperson, Social Democratic Party, Portuguese Parliament, 1991; Councillor, Amadora City Council, 1997-2001; Leader, Social Democratic Party (PSD), 2010-; Prime Minister, 2011-; *office address:* Prime Minister's Office, Presidência do Conselho de Ministros, Rua da Imprensa à Estrela 4, 1200 Lisbon, Portugal; *URL:* http://www.portugal.gov.pt/.

PASTOR, Ed; American, Congressman, Arizona Fourth District, US House of Representatives; *party:* Democrat; *political career:* Dep. Chief Whip, 1999-; Mem., US House of Representatives, 1992- ; *committees:* House Appropriations Cttee.; *office address:* House of Representatives, 436 Cannon House Street, Washington, DC 20515-6501, USA; *phone:* +1 202 224 3121.

PATEL, Priti; MP for Witham, UK Government; *education:* Keele Univ.; Univ. of Essex; *party:* Conservative; *political career:* MP for Witham, May 2010-; *committees:* Members' Expenses, 2011-; Public Admin., 2011-; *office address:* House of Commons, London, SW1A 0AA, United Kingdom; *phone:* +44 (0)20 7219 3000; *e-mail:* priti.patel.mp@parliament.uk.

PATERSON, Rt. Hon. Owen; British, Secretary of State for Environment, Food and Rural Affairs, British Government; *born:* 24 June 1956, Whitchurch, Shropshire; *parents:* Alfred Paterson (dec'd) and Cynthia Paterson (dec'd); *married:* Rose (née Ridley), January 1980; *languages:* French, German; *education:* Radley College, Corpus Christi College, Cambridge; National Leathersellers College, Northampton; *party:* Conservative Party; *political career:* PA to John Biffen MP, 1987, to Christopher Prout, 1989; Parly. Candidate, Wrexham, 1992; MP, North Shropshire, 1997-; Shadow Sec. of State for Northern Ireland, 2007-2010; Sec. of State for Northern Ireland, May 2010-12; Secretary of State for Environment, Food and Rural Affairs, 2012-; *professional career:* Man. Dir., British Leather Co., 1996-99; *office address:* Department of Environment, Food and Rural Affairs, Nobel House, 17 Smith Street, London, SW1P 3JR, United Kingdom; *phone:* +44 (0)20 7238 6951; *e-mail:* patersono@parliament.uk; *URL:* http://www.defra.gov.uk/.

PATIÑO AROCA, Ricardo; Minister of Foreign Affairs, Trade and Integration, Government of Ecuador; *born:* 1955; *education:* Autonomous Metropolitan Univ., Iztapalapa, Mexico City; MA, Int. Univ. of Andalusia, Spain; *political career:* Minister for Policy Coordination, 2007-10; Minister of Foreign Affairs, Trade and Integration, 2010-; *office address:* Ministry of Foreign Affairs, Trade and Integration, Carrión 10-40, Avienda 10 de Agosto y Carrión, Quito, Ecuador; *phone:* +593 (0)2 299 3284 / 3285; *fax:* +593 (0)2 227025; *e-mail:* webmaster@mmrree.gov.ec; *URL:* http://www.mmrree.gov.ec/.

PATO, Rimbink; Minister of Foreign Affairs, Government of Papua New Guinea; *party:* United Party; *political career:* MP, 2012; Minister of Foreign Affairs, 2012-; *professional career:* lawyer; property investor; *office address:* Ministry of Foreign Affairs, 2nd Floor Somare Foundation Building, Independence Drive, PO Box 422 , Waigani NCD, Papua New Guinea.

PATRICK, Deval; Governor, Commonwealth of Massachusetts; ***education:*** Harvard, grad., 1978; Harvard Law School ; ***political career:*** Governor, Commonwealth of Massachusetts, 2006-; ***professional career:*** NAACP Legal Defense and Education Fund; Hill & Barlow, 1986-1994, partner, 1990-94; Assistant Attorney General for Civil Rights, 1994-97; Chmn., Texaco's Equality and Fairness Task Force, 1997-99; Vice President and General Counsel, Texaco, 1999-2001; Executive Vice Pres. & Gen. Counsel, Coca-Cola Company, 2001-06, Corp. Sec., 2002-06; ***office address:*** State House, Boston, MA 02133, USA; ***phone:*** +1 617 725 4005; ***fax:*** +1 617 727 9725; ***URL:*** http://www.mass.gov/.

PATRIOTA, Antonio; Minister of External Relations, Government of Brazil; ***born:*** April 1954, Rio de Janeiro, Brazil; ***education:*** Brazil's Diplomatic Academy; ***political career:*** Minister of External Relations, 2011-; ***professional career:*** Served at Brazil's Permanent Mission to the United Nations in New York, 1994-99; Deputy Permanent Representative to the World Trade Organization, 1998-99; Served at Brazil's Permanent Mission to the International Organizations in Geneva, 1999-2003; Amb. to the USA, 2007-09; ***office address:*** Ministry of External Relations, Esplanada Ministerios, Pal. Itamaraty, 70170-900 Brasilia DF, Brazil; ***phone:*** +55 (0)61 224 3129; ***fax:*** +55 (0)61 226 1762; ***e-mail:*** webmaster@mre.gov.br; ***URL:*** http://www.mre.gov.br.

PATTERSON, Anne W.; American, Ambassador, US Embassy in Egypt; ***born:*** 1949, Fort Smith, Arkansas; ***married:*** David R. Patterson; ***children:*** Edward (M), Andrew (M); ***education:*** Wellesley College; Univ. of North Carolina; ***professional career:*** Joined the Foreign Service, 1973; Desk Officer, Nicaragua; Ecuador, 1974-77; Economic Counsellor, Riyadh, Saudi Arabia, 1984-88; Dir., Office of Andean Affairs, 1991-93; Dep. Assistant Sec. for Central America and the Caribbean, 1993-95; Principal Dep. Assistant Sec. for Inter American Affairs, 1996; US Ambassador to El Salvador, 1997-2000; US Ambassador to Colombia, 2000-2004; Acting Permanent Representative to the US Mission to the UN, 2004-06; Assist. Sec. of State for Int'l. Narcotics and Law Enforcement Affairs. 2006-07; Amb. to Pakistan, 2007-11; Amb. to Egypt, 2011-; ***honours and awards:*** Dept. of State's Superior Honor Award, 1981 and 1988; Meritorious Honor Award, 1977 and 1983; Presidential award, 1993; ***office address:*** American Embassy, North Gate, 8 Kamal El-Din Salah Street, Cairo, Egypt; ***phone:*** +20 (0)2 797 3300; ***fax:*** +20 (0)2 797 3200; ***URL:*** http://cairo.usembassy.gov.

PATTERSON, Ambassador Robert; US Ambassador, Embassy of the US, Turkmenistan; ***professional career:*** career office, Senior Foreign Service; joined state dept., 1985, assignments in Central and Eastern Europe, the North Caucasus, Russia, the USSR, East Africa; Head various political sections at US embassies incl. Hungary, Ukraine & Armenia; Counselor, Somalia Affairs, US Embasy, Nairobi, Kenya; US Amb. to Turkmenistan, 2011-; ***office address:*** Embassy of the US, 1984 Street, Ashgabat, Turkmenistan.

PAUL, Rand; Member, US Senate; ***education:*** Georgia Baptist Medical Center; Duke Univ.; ***party:*** Republican; ***political career:*** Mem., US Senate, 2010-; ***professional career:*** Ophthalmologist; ***committees:*** Foreign Relations; Health, Education, Labor and Pensions; Homeland Security & Government Affairs; Small Business & Entrepreneurship; ***office address:*** US Senate, 208 Russell Senate Office Building, Washington DC 20510, USA; ***phone:*** +1 202 224 4343; ***URL:*** http://www.paul.senate.gov/.

PAULWELL, Hon. Phillip Feanny; Jamaican, Minister of Mining, Energy and ICT, Government of Jamaica; ***born:*** 14 January 1962, Jamaica; ***parents:*** Wesley Paulwell; ***children:*** Terry-Ann (F); ***education:*** EXCED Community Coll., St. Andrew, Jamaica, 1981-83; Univ. W.I., LL.B, 1983-86; Norman Manley Law Sch., Univ. W.I., Cert. Legal Education, 1986-88; ***party:*** People's National Party (PNP); ***political career:*** Senator and Minister of State, Min. of Industry, Investment and Commerce, 1995-97; M.P. and Minister of Commerce and Technology, 1997-2000; Minister of Commerce, Science and Technology, 2000-07; Minister of Mining, Energy and ICT, 2011-; ***professional career:*** Legal Officer, Jamaica Commodity Trading Co., 1988-91; M.D./Trade Administrator, Jamaica Trade Bd., 1991-93; Exec. Dir., Jamaican Fair Trading Cmn., 1993-95 ; ***recreations:*** dancing; ***office address:*** Ministry of Energy and Mining, PCJ Building, 36 Trafalgar Road, Kingston 10, Jamaica; ***phone:*** +1 876 929 8990; ***fax:*** +1 876 960 1623; ***e-mail:*** info@mem.gov.jm.

PAVLUTS, Daniels; Minister for Economics, Government of Latvia; ***languages:*** English, French, German; ***education:*** BA, Jāzeps Vītols Latvian Academy of Music, 1999; City University (UK), Post-Graduate Diploma in Cultural Management, 2000; Harvard Univ., USA, 2007; ***political career:*** State Sec., Ministry of Culture, 2003-06; Minister for Economics, 2011-; ***office address:*** Ministry of Economy, Brivibas bulv. 55, Riga LV-1519, Latvia; ***phone:*** +371 6701 3101; ***URL:*** http://www.lem.gov.lv.

PAWAR, Shri Sharad; Minister of Agriculture, Food & Civil Supplies, Consumer Affairs & Public Distribution, Government of India; ***born:*** 12 December 1940, Baramati; ***parents:*** Govindrao Pawar and Sharda Bai G. Pawar; ***married:*** Pratibha Pawar; ***political career:*** mem., Maharashtra Legislative Assembly, 1967-91; Gen.-Sec., Pradesh Congress Cttee., Maharashtra Sec., Congress Legislature Party, Maharashtra, 1967-91; Minister of State, Home, Food, Civil Supplies, Rehabilitation, Publicity, Youth Welfare & Sports, Maharashtra, 1972-74; Minister, Education, Agriculture, Industries, Home, Labour & Youth Welfare, Maharashtra, 1974-78; Chief Minister, Maharashtra, 1978-80, 1988-91, 1993-95; Leader of the Opposition, Maharshtra Legislative Assembly, 1981-86; Pres., Congress, 1982-87; Elected to 8th Lok Sabha, 1984-85; Union Cabinet Minister, Defence, 1991-93; Mem., Maharashtra Legislative Cncl., 1993-95; Leader of the Oppostion, Maharashtra Legislative Cncl., 1995-96; re-elected to 11th Lock Sabha, 1996, re-elected to 12th Lok Sabha, 1998, 13th Lok Sabha, 1999; Leader of the Opposition, Lok Sabha, 1998; Leader, NCP Parly. Party, 1999; fmr. Federal Defence Minister; Food and Agricultural Minister, 2004-; ***interests:*** Agriculture, horticulture, economics, irrigation, energy, finance, sport; ***professional career:*** Agriculturist; ***committees:*** mem., Cttee. on Science & Tech., Environment and Forests, 1996-97; mem., Gen. Purposes Cttee., Cttee. on External Affairs, Consultative Cttee., Ministry of Human Resource Dev., 1998-99; mem., Cttee. on Agriculture, Gen. Purposes Cttee., 1999-2000; mem., Cttee. on Ethics, 2000-01; ***recreations:*** reading, travelling; ***office address:*** Ministry of Agriculture, Food & Civil Supplies, Consumer Affairs & Public Distribution, Room No. 120, Krishi Bhavan, New Delhi, India; ***phone:*** +91 (0)11 2373 7670.

PAWSEY, Mark; MP for Rugby, House of Commons; ***party:*** Conservative; ***political career:*** Councillor, Rugby Borough Council, 2002-07; MP for Rugby, May 2010-; ***committees:*** Communities and Local Government, 2010-; ***office address:*** House of Commons, London, SW1A 0AA, United Kingdom; ***phone:*** +44 (0)20 7219 3000; ***e-mail:*** mark.pawsey.mp@parliament.uk.

PAXMAN, H.E. Giles, LVO (1989); British Ambassador to Spain and Andorra, HM Diplomatic Service; ***born:*** 15 November 1951; ***parents:*** Arthur Keith Paxman and Joan McKay Paxman; ***married:*** Segégolène Cayol, 1980; ***children:*** Julia (F), Lauren (F), Alice (F); ***education:*** Malvern College; New College, Oxford; ***professional career:*** First Secretary, UKREP Brussels; Counsellor, Economic and Commercial Affairs, Rome; Counsellor, Political and Institutional Affairs, EU, Brussels; Head of Chancery, Singapore; Worked on Environment, Consumer Affairs and the Internal Market, Brussels; Minister and Dep. Head of Mission, Paris; Ambassador, British Embassy in Mexico, 2006-09; Amb. to Spain and Andorra, 2009-; ***office address:*** British Embassy, Torre Espacio, Paseo de la Castellana 259-D, 28010 Madrid, Spain; ***phone:*** +34 91 714 6300; ***fax:*** +34 91 714 6302; ***e-mail:*** enquiries.madrid@fco.gov.uk; ***URL:*** http://www.ukinspain.com.

PEAKE, Karolina; Deputy Prime Minister, Government of the Czech Republic; ***born:*** 10 October 1975; ***education:*** Charles Univ., Czech Republic; ***party:*** Civic Democratic Party, 1997-98; Public Affairs, 2007-12; LIDEM, 2012-; ***political career:*** Mem. Chamber of Deputies, 2010-; Deputy Prime Minister, Minister in Charge of the Government Legislative Council and Minister for the Fight against Corruption, 2012-; ***professional career:*** Lawyer; ***office address:*** Office of the Deputy Prime Minister, Nabr. Eduarda Benese 4, 118 01 Prague, Czech Republic; ***phone:*** +420 2 2400 2224; ***fax:*** +420 2 2481 0231; ***URL:*** http://www.vlada.cz.

PEARCE, Teresa; MP for Erith and Thamesmead, UK Government; ***party:*** Labour; ***political career:*** Councillor, London Borough of Bexley Council, 1998-2002; MP for Erith and Thamesmead, May 2010-; ***committees:*** Work and Pensions, 2010-; Treasury, 2011-; ***office address:*** House of Commons, London, SW1A 0AA, United Kingdom; ***phone:*** +44 (0)20 7219 3000; ***e-mail:*** teresa.pearce.mp@parliament.uk.

PEDRAZA SIERRA, Wilfredo; Minister of the Interior, Government of Peru; ***political career:*** Minister of the Interior, 2012-; ***professional career:*** lawyer; Coordinator, Special Investigations Unit, Truth & Reconciliation Commission; Head, National Penitentiary Inst.; ***office address:*** Ministry of the Interior, Plaza 30 de Agosto No. 150, San Isidro, Lima 27, Peru.

PEILLON, Vincent; Minister of National Education, Government of France; ***born:*** 1960; ***education:*** teacher; Research Dir., CNRS, 2002-04; ***party:*** Socialist Party; ***political career:*** MEP, 2004-2012; Deputy for the Somme, Assemblée Nationale, 1997-2002; Minister of National Education, 2012-; ***office address:*** Ministry of National Education, 110 rue Grenelle, 75317 Paris cedex 07, France; ***phone:*** +33 (0)1 55 55 10 10; ***URL:*** http://www.education.gouv.fr.

PEIRIS, Prof. G.L.; Minister of Foreign Affairs, Government of Sri Lanka; ***born:*** 13 August 1946; ***education:*** Bachelor of Laws, First Class Honours Ceylon, 1967; Doctor of Philosophy, Oxford, 1971; Doctor of Philosophy, Sri Lanka, 1974; ***political career:*** Minister of Justice, Constitutional Affairs, Ethnic Affairs and Nat. Integration and Dep. Minister of Finance and Planning, 1994; Minister of Industrial Development and Constitutional Affairs; & Dep. Minister of Finance & Planning, 2000-02; Constitutional Affairs, Ethnic Affairs and Nat. Integration; Minister of Enterprise Dev., Industrial Policy and Investment Promotion; & Minister of Constitutional Affairs , 2002-04; Chief Negotiator in the Government's Peace Process, 2002-04; Minister of Export Development and International Trade, 2007-10; Minister of Foreign Affairs, 2010-; ***professional career:*** University of Sri Lanka, Assist. Lecturer in Law, 1968-71; Lecturer in Law, 1971-75; Assoc. Prof. of Law 1975-79; Acting Dean of the Faculty of Law, 1977; Head of Dept. of Law, 1978-; Prof. of Law, 1979; Dean of the Faculty of Law, 1983-88; ***publications:*** Various books inc. Recent Development in Administrative Law, 1988; Essays on Commonwealth Administrative Law; Recent Trends in the Commonwealth Law of Evidence, 1989; Towards Equity, a collection of speeches, 2000; ***office address:*** Ministry of Foreign Affairs, Republic Building, Colombo 01, Sri Lanka; ***phone:*** +94 11 232 5371; ***e-mail:*** minister@formin.gov.lk; ***URL:*** http://www.simfa.gov.lk.

PELOSI, Nancy; American, Democratic Leader, US House of Representatives; ***education:*** Grad., Trinity Coll., Washington, D.C., 1962; ***party:*** Democrat; ***political career:*** Congresswoman, California Eighth District, US House of Representatives, 1987-; Democratic Whip, US HOR, 2001-02; Democratic Leader, US HOR, 2002-06; Speaker of the House of Representatives (first woman Speaker), 2007-10; Democratic Leader, US HOR, 2011-; ***office address:*** House of Representatives, U.S. Capitol, Washington DC 20515, USA; ***phone:*** +1 202 225 0100; ***URL:*** http://www.house.gov.

PENCE, Mike; Governor, State of Indiana; ***education:*** Indiana Univ. School of Law, 1986, JD; ***party:*** Republican Party; ***political career:*** Mem., US House of Representatives, 2000-12; Chmn., Republican Conference, 2009-10; Governor, State of Indiana, 2012-; ***committees:*** served on Foreign Affairs; Judiciary; Agriculture & Small Business Cttees.; ***office address:*** Office of the Governor, Statehouse Room 206, 200 W. Washington Street, Indianapolis, IN 46204, USA; ***phone:*** +1 317 232 4567; ***URL:*** http://www.in.gov/gov/.

PENDRY OF STALYBRIDGE, Lord Tom; British, Baron, House of Lords; ***born:*** 1934; ***married:*** Moira Anne Smith, 1966 (separated); ***s:*** 1; ***d:*** 1; ***education:*** St. Augustine's, Ramsgate; Oxford Univ.; ***party:*** Labour Party; ***political career:*** Opposition Whip, 1971-74; Lord Commissioner of the Treasury, 1974, resigned 1977; Under Sec. of State for NI, 1978-79; Shadow Spokesman NI, 1979-81; Opp. spokesman on overseas development, 1981; Opp. spokesman on regional affairs and devolution, 1982; Opp. spokesman on Sport and Tourism, 1992-97; MP, Stalybridge & Hyde, 1970-2001; Elevated to the House of Lords, May 2001-; ***interests:*** sport, tourism and industrial relations; ***memberships:*** Chmn., All Party Sports Group & All Party Tourism Group; Chmn. of the Football Foundation; Pres., Music Users' Council; Patron, National Federation of Football Supporters; ***committees:*** Formerly:- Members' Interest Select Cttee., Select Cttee for the Environment, Chmn., PLP Sports Cttee.,

PLP Films Cttee.; Vincents; ***clubs:*** Lords' Taverners; Garrick; ***recreations:*** Sport: formerly Royal Air Force boxing champion; Colony champion (Hong Kong 1957). Boxed for Oxford Univ.; ***office address:*** House of Lords, London, SW1A 0PW, United Kingdom; ***phone:*** +44 (0)20 7219 3000; ***fax:*** +44 (0)20 7219 5679; ***e-mail:*** hlinfo@parliament.uk; ***URL:*** http://www.parliament.uk.

PENNING, Michael; MP for Hemel Hempstead, House of Commons; ***party:*** Conservative Party; ***political career:*** MP for Hemel Hempstead, 2005-; Parliamentary Under Secretary of State (Roads and Motoring), 2010-12; Minister of State, Northern Ireland Office, 2012-; ***office address:*** House of Commons, London, SW1P 0AA, United Kingdom; ***phone:*** +44 (0)20 7219 3000.

PENROSE, John; MP for Weston Super Mare, House of Commons; ***education:*** BA (Hons), Law, Cambridge Univ. 1983-86; MBA, Columbia Univ, New York, USA; ***party:*** Conservative Party; ***political career:*** MP for Weston-Super-Mare, 2005; PPS to Oliver Letwin MP, 2006-08; Shadow Business Minister, 2009-10; Parly. Under Sec. of State (Tourism and Heritage), 2010-12; ***professional career:*** Risk Manager, J P Morgan, 1986-90; McKinsey & Company Strategic Management Consultant 1992-94; Commercial Dir., Thomson Publishing, 1995-96; Pres., EMA Schools Group, Pearson PLC, 1996-00; ***office address:*** House of Commons, London, SW1P 0AA, United Kingdom; ***phone:*** +44 (0)20 7219 3000; ***e-mail:*** john@johnpenrose.org.

PERCIASEPE, Bob; Acting Administrator, US Environmental Protection Agency, US Government; ***education:*** Cornell Univ.; Maxwell School of Syracuse Univ.; ***political career:*** various senior positions within state and municipal government, incl. Sec. of Environment for the State of Maryland; Senior EPA official, administration of President Bill Clinton; Dep. Administrator, US Environmental Protection Agency, 2009-, Acting Administrator, 2013-; ***interests:*** environment; ***professional career:*** CEO, National Audubon Society (environmental org.); ***office address:*** US Environmental Protection Agency, Ariel Rios Building, 1200 Pennsylvania Avenue, NW, Washington, DC 20460, USA; ***URL:*** http://www.epa.gov.

PERCY, Andrew; MP for Brigg and Goole, UK Government; ***education:*** Univ. of York; Univ. of Leeds; ***party:*** Conservative; ***political career:*** MP for Brigg and Goole, May 2010-; ***professional career:*** Teacher; ***committees:*** Regulatory Reform, 2010-; Standing Orders, 2011-; ***office address:*** House of Commons, London, SW1A 0AA, United Kingdom; ***phone:*** +44 (0)20 7219 3000; ***e-mail:*** andrew.percy.mp@parliament.uk.

PEREIRA NEVES, Dr Jose Maria; Prime Minister, Cape Verde; ***born:*** 28 March 1960, Santa Catarina, Cape Verde; ***education:*** School of Business Administration, São Paulo, Brazil, Public Admin. degree; ***party:*** Leader, African Party of the Independence of Cape Verde (Partido Africano da Independencia de Cabo Verde); ***political career:*** Deputy of the Nation, Vice Pres., National Assembly; Prime Minister, Minister of Finance, Planning and Regional Development 2001-; ***professional career:*** Dir., Nat. Centre for Public Administration Training; Consultant, Organizational Development, Administration of Human resources and Professional Training; Lecturer on Organizations, Administration of Conflicts and Leadership; ***office address:*** Office of the Prime Minister, Palácio do Governo, Av Cidade Lisboa, Praia, Sao Tiago, Cape Verde; ***phone:*** +238 610513; ***URL:*** http://www.governo.cv.

PERES, Shimon; President, State of Israel; ***born:*** 1923, Belorussia; ***married:*** Sonia Peres (née Gelman); ***education:*** Ben Shemen Agricultural Sch.; Harvard Univ. (Business Admin.); ***party:*** Israel Labour Party; Kadima from 2005; ***political career:*** Dir.-Gen., Ministry of Defence 1953-59; mem. of the Knesset since 1959; Dep. Minister of Defence 1959-65; Minister without Portfolio 1969-70; Minister of Posts & Transport 1970-74; Minister of Information 1974; Minister of Defence 1974-77; Acting Prime Minister 1977; Chmn. of Israel Labour Party & Leader of the Opposition 1977-84; Prime Minister 1984-86; Vice Prime Minister and Foreign Minister 1987-88; Vice Premier and Minister of Finance 1989-90; Leader of Labour Party until 1992; Minister of Foreign Affairs 1992-95; Prime Minister 1995-96; Minister of Regional Co-operation, 1999-01; Minister of Foreign Affairs and Dep. Prime Minister, 2001-2003; Dep. Prime Minister and Minister for the Development of the Negev and Galilee, 2005-07; President, State of Israel, 2007-; ***memberships:*** Chmn., Yad Ben-Gurion; Vice-Pres., Socialist International 1978-; ***committees:*** Chmn., Peres Institute for Peace; ***honours and awards:*** Legion of Honour by the French Govt., 1959; Nobel Peace Prize, 1994; ***publications:*** The Next Phase (1965); David's Sling (1970); Tomorrow is now (1978); From These Men (1979); Antebe Diary (1991); and many articles, mainly political; The New Middle East (1993); ***office address:*** Office of the President, Hanassi Street , Jerusalem 92188, Israel; ***phone:*** +972 2 670 7211; ***fax:*** +972 2 561 0037; ***URL:*** http://www.president.gov.il.

PERETZ, Amir; Minister of Environmental Protection, Government of Israel; ***born:*** 9 March 1952; ***party:*** Labour Party to 1999; founded Am Ehad (One Nation), 1999; merged with Labour Party, 2004; Leader, Labour Party, 2005-07; ***political career:*** Mayor of Sderot, 1983-88; Mem. of the Knesset, 1988-; Chairman, General Federation of Labourers, 1995-2005; Minister of Defence and Deputy PM, 2006-07; Minister of Environmental Protection, 2013-; ***professional career:*** Israeli Army; Farmer; ***office address:*** Ministry of Environmental Protection, PO Box 34033, 95464 Jerusalem , Israel; ***phone:*** +972 2 655 3777; ***URL:*** http://www.environment.gov.il.

PEREZ MOLINA, Otto; President, Guatemala; ***born:*** 1951; ***party:*** Patriotic Party; ***political career:*** President of Guatemala, 2011-; ***professional career:*** military; ***office address:*** Office of the Presidency, Guatemala City, Guatemala; ***URL:*** http://www.guatemala.gob.gt.

PERHAM, The Right Rev. Michael Francis, MA, Hon DPHil, FRSCM, Bishop of Gloucester; Member, House of Lords; ***born:*** 8 November 1947, Dorchester, Dorset; ***parents:*** Raymond Maxwell Perham and Marcelle Winifred Perham (née Barton); ***married:*** Alison Perham (née Grove), 1982; ***d:*** 4; ***education:*** Hardye's School, Dorchester; Keble College, Oxford Univ., BA, 1974, MA, 1978; Cuddesdon Theological College, Oxford, 1974-76; Hon. Doc. of Philosophy, Univ. of Glos., 2007; Ordained Deacon, Canterbury Cathedral, 1976; Ordained Priest, Canterbuy Cathedral, 1977; Ordained Bishop, St. Paul's Cathedral, 2004; ***political career:*** Mem., House of Lords, 2009-; ***memberships:*** Secretary of the C. of E. Doctrine Commission, 1979-84; Mem., C. of E. Liturgical Commission, 1986-2001; mem., Archbishops' Commission on Church Music, 1988-1992; Mem., General Synod of the C. of E., 1989-92, 1993-; Chmn., Praxis, 1990-97; Chmn., Cathedrals' Liturgy Group, 1994-2001; Mem., Cathedrals' Fabric Commission for the England, 1996-2001; Mem., Archbishops' Council of the Church of England, 1999-2004; Fellow, Woodward Corp., 2000-04; Chair, Business Cttee. of the General Synod, 2001-04; Chmn., Hospital Chaplaincies Council, 2007-2010; Vice-Chair, Mission and Public Affairs Council of the Church of England, 2007-10; Mem., Governing body of SPCK, 2001-, Chair, 2006-; Hon. Fellow, Royal School of Church Music, 2003-; Dir., Gloucester Heritage Urban Regeneration Co., 2004-; Pres., Alcuin Club, 2005-; Bishop Protector, European Province of the Society of Saint Francis, 2005-; Pres., Retired Clergy Assn., 2007-; Pro-Chancellor & Mem. of the Council of the Univ. of Gloucestershire, 2007-; Chmn., Governors of Ripon College Cuddesdon, 2009-; Pres., Affirming Catholicism, 2010-; ***professional career:*** Assist. Curate of St Mary's Addington, Croydon, 1976-81; Domestic Chaplain to the Bishop of Winchester, 1981-84; Rector of the Oakdale TEam Ministry, Poole, 1984-92; Canon Residentiary and Precentor of Norwich Cathedral, 1992-98; Vice-Dean of Norwich, 1995-98; (last) Provost of Derby, 1998-2000; Dean of Derby, 2000-04; (40th) Bishop of Gloucester, 2004-; ***publications:*** Numerous, including most recently: A New Handbook of Pastoral Liturgy, 2000, SPCK; Signs of Your Kingdom, 2003, SPCK; Glory in our Midst, 2005, SPCK; To Tell Afresh, 2010, SPCK; The Hospitality of God, 2011, SPCK (with Mary Gray-Reeves); ***office address:*** Diocese Office, 2 College Green, Gloucester, GL1 2LR, United Kingdom; ***phone:*** +44 (0)1452 410022; ***e-mail:*** bshpglos@glosdioc.org.uk; ***URL:*** http://www.parliament.uk.

PERKINS, Toby; MP for Chesterfield, UK Government; ***party:*** Labour; ***political career:*** MP for Chesterfield, May 2010-; Shadow Minister, Education, Oct. 2010-11; Shadow Minister, Business, Innovation and Skills, 2011-; ***committees:*** Communities and Local Government, Select Cttee., 2010-; Jt. Cttee. on Statutory Instruments 2010-; ***office address:*** House of Commons, London, SW1A 0AA, United Kingdom; ***phone:*** +44 (0)20 7219 3000; ***e-mail:*** toby.perkins.mp@parliament.uk.

PERLMUTTER, Ed; Congressman, 7th Dist. Colorado, US House of Representatives; ***education:*** Univ. of Colorado at Boulder, 1975; ***political career:*** Colorado State Senator for Dist. 20, 1994-06; President Pro Tem of the Senate, 2001-02; Mem., US HOR, 2007-; ***office address:*** House of Representatives, 415 Cannon House Office Building , Washington, DC 20515, USA; ***phone:*** +1 202 225 2645; ***fax:*** +1 202 225 5278.

PERRY, Claire; MP for Devizes, UK Government; ***party:*** Conservative; ***political career:*** MP for Devizes, May 2010-; PPS to Sec. of State for Defence, 2011-; ***committees:*** Justice Select Cttee., 2010-11; ***office address:*** House of Commons, London, SW1A 0AA, United Kingdom; ***phone:*** +44 (0)20 7219 3000; ***e-mail:*** claire.perry.mp@parliament.uk.

PERRY, Rick; Governor, State of Texas; ***born:*** 4 March 1950, West Texas, USA; ***married:*** Anita Perry; ***children:*** 2; ***education:*** Texas A&M Univ., degree in animal science, 1972; ***party:*** Republican; ***political career:*** mem., Texas House of Representatives, 1985-90; Texas Cmnr. of Agriculture, 1991-98; Governor, 2000-; ***memberships:*** lifetime mem., American Legion Post 75; ***professional career:*** US Air Force, 1972-77; ***committees:*** Appropriations and Calendars Cttees., 1985-90; ***honours and awards:*** voted one of Texas' 'top Legislators' by Dallas Morning News, 1989; ***office address:*** Office of the Governor, State Capitol, PO Box 12428, Austin, TX 78711-2428, USA; ***URL:*** http://www.governor.state.tx.us/.

PERSAD-BISSESSAR, Kamla; Trinidadian, Prime Minister, Government of Trinidad and Tobago; ***born:*** 22 April 1952, Siparia, Trinidad and Tobago; ***married:*** Dr. Gregory Bissessar, 1973; ***education:*** Legal Education Certificate; LL.B.; BA; ***party:*** United National Congress; ***political career:*** Alderman, St. Patrick County Cncl., 1987-91; UNC Senator, 1994-95; MP for Siparia, 1995; Attorney Gen. and Minister of Legal Affairs, 1995-96, Minister of Legal Affairs, 1996-99; Minister of Education, 1999-2002; Prime Minister, 2010-; ***professional career:*** Social Worker, Church of England Children's Society, London; Teacher, St. Andrew High Sch., Kingston, Jamaica, Lakshmi Girls High Sch., Trinidad; Lecturer, Dept. of Language and Linguistics, Univ. of West Indies; Consultant Lecturer, Jamaica Coll. of Insurance; Attorney at Law, opened own practice, -1995; ***committees:*** Chair, Ctte. to reform the Domestic Violence Act; Chair Joint Select Cttee. of Parly. on the Ombudsman; Chair, Parly. Questions Cttee.; Chair, Task Force on State Co.s; Chair, Cttee. to review Marriage Laws; Founding Mem. Policy Advisory Cttee. of the UN World Intellectual Property Organisation; ***honours and awards:*** Certificate of Merit for, Loyal and Dedicated Service to the Community, Min. of Community Development, Distinguished Services, International Biographical Centre, UK; ***office address:*** Office of the Prime Minister, Level 16, Eric Williams Finance Building, Eric Williams Complex, Independence Square, Port-of-Spain, Trinidad and Tobago; ***phone:*** +1 868 652 2045; ***fax:*** +1 868 628 7818; ***URL:*** http://www.opm.gov.tt.

PESEVSKI, Vladimir; Deputy Prime Minister with responsibility for the Economy, Government of Macedonia; ***languages:*** English, Russian; ***education:*** BA, MA, Faculty for Electrical Engineering at the Ss. Cyril and Methodius Univ., Skopje; MA, Business Admin., Univ. of Sheffield, UK, 2001; ***political career:*** Deputy Prime Minister with responsibility for the Economy, 2009-; ***office address:*** Office of the Deputy Prime Minister, Blvd. Ilinden bb, 1000 Skopje, Republic of Macedonia.

PETERS, Elizabeth Dipuo; Minister of Energy, Government of South Africa; ***born:*** 13 May 1960, Kimberley, RSA; ***children:*** Boitumelo (F), Kgomotso (F); ***languages:*** Setswana, Afrikaans, Xhosa, Sotho, English, Sepedi; ***education:*** Univ. of the North, BA, Social Work, 1987; Certificate in Development of Public Policy and Governance, Univ. of Western Cape, 1995; Certificate in Executive Management from the Univ. of Cape Town, Graduate School of Business, 2002; Certificate in International Policy Management, Havana Cuba, 2002; ***political career:*** Mem. National Assembly, 1994-96; Chief Whip of Northern Cape Provincial Legislature, 1997-99; MEC of Health, 1999-2004; Premier, Northern Cape Province, April 2004-09; Minister of Energy, 2009-; ***interests:*** better life for all, with emphasis on programs for the very poor; ***committees:*** African National Congress Women's League National Executive Cttee.,2002-; African National Congress (ANC) National Executive Cttee., 1997-2007;

clubs: Kimberley Club; *recreations:* reading, physical fitness training, watching rugby and soccer; *office address:* Ministry of Energy, Mineralia Centre, 228 Visagie Street, Pretoria 0001, South Africa; *URL:* http://www.dme.gov.za.

PETERS, Rt. Hon. Winston Raymond, BA, LL.B; New Zealander, Leader, New Zealand First Party; *born:* 1945, Whangarei, Northland; *education:* Auckland Univ., BA (History and Political Science), LLB; Diplomas for teaching at both primary and secondary levels; *party:* New Zealand First Party; *political career:* Dominian Cllr., National Party 1976-78; MP for Hunua 1978-81; Opposition Spokesman on Maori Affairs, Transport, Railways, Civil Aviation and Meteorological Services, 1984-; MP for Tauranga, 1990-; Minister of Maori Affairs, 1990-91; Minister in Charge of the Iwi Transition Agency; Founder and Leader, New Zealand First Party, 1993-; Dep. PM and Treasurer, 1996-98; MP for Tauranga, 1990-05; Foreign Minister, Minister for Racing, Associate Minister for Senior Citizens 2005-08 ; *professional career:* teacher; practised law, 1981-84; *committees:* Privileges Cttee.; Finance and Expenditure Select Cttee.; *recreations:* sport, reading, fishing, skiing; *office address:* New Zealand First Party, Parliament Buildings, Wellington, New Zealand.

PHAM BINH MINH ; Minister of Foreign Affairs, Government of Vietnam; *political career:* Central Cttee., Communist Party of Vietnam; Dep. Minister of Foreign Affairs, 2007-11; Minister of Foreign Affairs, 2011-; *professional career:* Amb., Dep. Perm. Rep. of Vietnam to the UN, 1999; Amb., Dep. Chief of Mission of the EMbassy of Vietnam in the US, 2001-03; *office address:* Ministry of Foreign Affairs, 1 Ton That Dam Street, Ba Dinh District, Hanoi, Vietnam; *URL:* http://www.mofa.gov.vn.

PHANG, Ha-Nam; Minister of Employment and Labour, Government of the Republic of Korea; *education:* BA, in English, Korea Univ. of Foreign Studies, 1982; MA, in Sociology, Vanderbilt Univ., 1990; Ph.D, in Sociology, Univ. of Wisconsin-Madison, USA, 1995; *political career:* Minister of Employment and Labour, 2013-; *office address:* Ministry of Employment and Labour, Government Complex II, 47 Gwanmun-ro, Gwacheon-si, Gyeonggi-do, Republic of Korea; *URL:* http://www.moel.go.kr.

PHICHIT, Maj. Gen. Douangchay; Deputy Prime Minister, People's Republic of Laos; *political career:* Minister of National Defence; Deputy Prime Minister and Minister of National Defence, 2006-; *office address:* Ministry of National Defence, National Assembly, 1 That-Luang Square, Vientiane, Laos.

PHILIPPE, H.R.H King , Duke of Brabant; King of the Belgians; *born:* 15 April 1960, Brussels; *parents:* HM King Albert II and HM Queen Paola; *education:* Trinity College Oxford, Constitutional History, 1983; Stanford Univ. MA, Political Science, 1985; *professional career:* Royal Military Academy, 1979-81; Training as a pilot for the Belgian Airforce, 1981; Training as a Paratrooper, 1982-83, promoted to the rank Captain in 1983, and to the rank Colonel in 1989; Hon. President, of the Belgian Foreign Trade Office (BFTB), 1993-2003; Hon. Chmn., National Council for Sustainable Development, 1997-; Mem., Senate, 1994-; Major-General, 2001; Hon. Chmn., Board of the Foreign Trade Agency (replacing BFTB), 2003-; Hon. Chmn., Belgian Investment Co. for Developing Countries, (BIO), 2003-; Hon. Chmn., European Chapter, Club of Rome, 2004-; Hon. Chmn., Int'l. Polar Foundation, 2004-; King of the Belgians following the abdication of his father King Albert II, July 2013-; *honours and awards:* Hon. Doct., Katholieke Univ., Leuven, 2002; *recreations:* civilian helicopter pilot, sports, reading; *office address:* Cabinet of the King, Palais Royal/Koninklijk Paleis, Rue de Bréderode, B-1000 Brussels, Belgium.

PHILLIPS, Douglas George; Commissioner, Yukon Territory; *political career:* MLA, 1985-2000; Official Opposition House Leader, 1996-2000; Commissioner, 2010-; *office address:* Office of the Commissioner, 211 Hawkins Street, Whitehorse, Yukon, Canada.

PHILLIPS, Dr. Peter; Deputy Prime Minister, Government of Jamaica; *political career:* Minister of National Security; Deputy Prime Minister, Minister of Finance, Planning and Public Service, Dec. 2011-; *office address:* Office of the Deputy Prime Minister, 1 Devon Road, Kingston 10, Jamaica; *phone:* +1 876 926 1590; *URL:* http://www.cabinet.gov.jm.

PHILLIPS, Stephen; MP for Sleaford and North Hykeham, UK Government; *party:* Conservative; *political career:* MP for Sleaford and North Hykeham, May 2010-; *committees:* European Scrutiny, 2010-; *office address:* House of Commons, London, SW1A 0AA, United Kingdom; *phone:* +44 (0)20 7219 3000; *e-mail:* stephen.phillips.mp@parliament.uk.

PHILLIPS OF WORTH MATRAVERS, Lord; Member, House of Lords; *born:* 1938; *political career:* Mem., House of Lords, 1999-, as President of the Supreme Court, disqualified from participation 2009-13; *professional career:* Lord of Appeal in Ordinary, 1999-2000; Master of the Rolls 2000-05; Hd. of Civil Justice; Lord Chief Justice of England and Wales, 2005-; Senior Law Lord, 2008; Pres., Supreme Court of the United Kingdom, 2009-12; *committees:* Draft Voting Eligibility (Prisoners) Bill , 2013-; *honours and awards:* Kt., 1987; PC., 1995; *office address:* House of Lords, London, SW1A 1AA, United Kingdom.

PHILLIPSON, Bridget; MP for Houghton and Sunderland South, UK Government; *party:* Labour; *political career:* MP for Houghton and Sunderland South, May 2010-; *committees:* Home Affairs Select Cttee., 2010-; Procedure, 2010-11; *office address:* House of Commons, London, SW1A 0AA, United Kingdom; *phone:* +44 (0)20 7219 3000; *e-mail:* bridget.phillipson.mp@parliament.uk.

PHOOKO, Hon. Dr. Motlocheloa; Minister of Public Service, Government of Lesotho; *born:* 1939; *political career:* MP, 2002; Minister of Health and Social Welfare, 2002-07; Appointed Senator, 2007; Minister in the PM's Office, 2007-11; Minister of Public Service, 2012-; *professional career:* Medicine; *office address:* Ministry of Public Service, PO Box 527, Maseru 100, Lesotho; *URL:* http://www.lesotho.gov.ls/.

PIANKALI, Omer; Ambassador, Embassy of Gabon in the UK; *professional career:* Amb. to Libya and accredited to Tunisia; Amb. to United Kingdom and accredited to Ireland, Sweden, Denmark, Norway and Finland, 2011-; *office address:* Embassy of the Republic of Gabon, 27 Elvaston Place, London, SW7 5NL, United Kingdom; *phone:* +44 (0)20 7823 9986; *fax:* +44 (0)20 7584 0047.

PICARDO, Fabian; Chief Minister, Government of Gibraltar; *born:* 18 February 1972; *education:* Oriel College, Oxford Univ; Inns of Court School of Law, Gray's Inn, London; *party:* Gibraltar Socialist Labour Party; *political career:* Chief Minister, 2011-; *professional career:* Called to the Bar, 1994; *office address:* Office of the Chief Minister, No 6 Convent Place, Gibraltar; *phone:* +350 2007 0071.

PICKERSGILL, Hon. Robert Dixon; Minister of Water, Land, Environment and Climate Change, Government of Jamaica; *party:* People's National Party (PNP); *political career:* Minister of Mining and Energy, 1997-2002; Minister of Transportation and Works, 2002-; Minister of Housing and Water, 2006; Minister of Water, Land, Environment and Climate Change, 2011-; *office address:* Ministry of Water, 25 Dominica Drive, The Towers, Jamaica; *phone:* +1 876 926 1691; *URL:* http://mtw.gov.jm.

PICKLES, Rt. Hon. Eric; British, Secretary of State for Communities and Local Government, UK Government; *born:* 1952; *party:* Conservative Party; *political career:* Cllr., Bradford, 1979-91, Leader, 1988-90; Leader, Conservative Group, 1987-91; PPS to Minister of Industry, 1993; Vice-Chmn., Conservative Party, 1993-; MP, Brentwood and Ongar, 1992-; Shadow Minister for Transport and Spokesman for London, 2001: Shadow Minister for Local Government and the Regions, 2002-07; Shadow Sec. of State for Communities and Local Government, 2007-09; Chairman of the Conservative Party, Jan. 2009-; Secretary of State for Communities and Local Government, May 2010-; *committees:* Conservative Nat. Advisory Cttee. on Local Govt., 1985-93, Chmn., 1992-93; *office address:* Department for Transport, Local Government and the Regions, Eland House, Bressenden Place, London, SW1E 5DU, United Kingdom; *phone:* +44 (0)20 7219 3000; *e-mail:* hcinfo@parliament.uk; *URL:* http://www.ericpickles.com.

PIEBALGS, Andris; Latvian, European Commissioner for Development, European Commission; *born:* 1957; *education:* Physics, Latvia Univ; *political career:* MP, Latvia; Minister of Education, 1990-93; Chair, Budget and Finance Cttee., 1990-93; Finance Minister, 1994-95; Energy Commissioner, European Commission, 2004-10; Development Commissioner, 2010-; *professional career:* Ambassador of Latvia in Estonia, 1995; Ambassador of Latvia to the EU, 1998-2003; *office address:* European Commission, 200 rue de la Loi, B-1049 Brussels, Belgium; *URL:* http://www.europa.eu.

PIERLUISI, Pedro; Resident Commissioner for Puerto Rico, US House of Representatives; *born:* 1959, San Juan, Puerto Rico; *education:* Tulane Univ., BA in American History, 1981; George Washington Univ., J.D., 1984; *political career:* Sec. of Justice (Attorney General), 1993-97; Resident Commissioner of Puerto Rico, 2009-; *professional career:* Private Attorney, Washington, D.C., 1984-90; Lawyer, Puerto Rico, 1990-93; Dir., Puerto Rico Homebuilders Assn., 1993-2003; Partner, O'Neill & Borges law firm, 1997-; Dir.,Univ. of Puerto Rico Foundation, 1997-2001; Dir., José Jaime Pierluisi Foundation (dedicated to his slain brother), Pres., 2003-06; Arbitrator, American Arbitration Assn.'s Int'l. Centre for Dispute Resolution; *committees:* Ethics; Judiciary; Natural Resources; *office address:* House of Representatives, 1218 Longworth, Washington, DC 20515, USA; *URL:* http://pierluisi.house.gov/.

PIERROT, Marcelle; Prefect, Guadeloupe; *born:* 1949, Trois-Rivières, Guadeloupe; *education:* Institute of Political Studies, Bordeaux; *political career:* long standing career in service of the state, most recently: Prefect, Lot, 2007; Prefect, Tarn, 2009; Prefect, Vosges, 2011; Prefect, Guadeloupe, 2012-; *honours and awards:* Officier de la Légion d'honneur; Officier de l'Order National du Mérite; IEP Bordeaux; *office address:* Prefecture, Palais d'Orléans, rue Lardenoy, 97109 Basse-Terre, Guadeloupe; *URL:* http://www.guadeloupe.pref.gouv.fr/.

PILLAY, Navanethem; UN High Commissioner; *born:* 1941; *education:* BA, LLB, Natal Univ., South Africa; Master of Law, Doctorate of Juridical Science, Harvard Univ., USA; *professional career:* Vice-Pres. of the Univ. of Durban Westville, South Africa; Judge of the South African High Court; Judge and President on the International Criminal Tribunal for Rwanda; Judge on the International Criminal Court in the Hague; United Nations High Commissioner for Human Rights, 2008-; *office address:* Office of the United Nation as High Commissioner for Human Rights, Palais Wilson, 52 Rue des Paquis, 1201 Geneva, Switzerland; *URL:* http://www.ohchr.org.

PINARD, Hon. Yvon, BA, LL.L; Canadian, Judge, Federal Court of Canada; *born:* 1940; *married:* Renee Chaput, 1964; *d:* 2; *education:* Immaculate Conception Sch., Drummondville. Sherbrooke Univ., BA, LL.L; *political career:* Mem., House of Commons, 1974; Parl. Sec. to Pres. of Privy Cncl., 1977; Pres. of H.M. Privy Cncl. for Canada, and Government House Leader, Mar. 1980-84; *professional career:* Called to Quebec Bar, 1964; Founder, Drummond Centre Caisse d'Entraide Economique; Judge of Federal Court of Canada, Trial Div. and Mem., ex officio, Federal Court of Appeal, 1984-; *office address:* Federal Court of Canada, Ottawa, ON K1A 0H9, Canada.

PINCHER, Christopher; MP for Tamworth, UK Government; *party:* Conservative; *political career:* MP for Tamworth, May 2010-; *committees:* Energy and Climate Change Select Cttee., 2010-; Armed Forces Bill, 2011-; Standing Orders, 2011-; *office address:* House of Commons, London, SW1A 0AA, United Kingdom; *phone:* +44 (0)20 7219 7169; *e-mail:* christopher.pincher.mp@parliament.uk.

PINDA , Rt. Hon. Mizengo Kayanza Peter; Prime Minister, Government of Tanzania; *born:* 1948; *education:* Univ. of Dar es Salaam, law; *political career:* MP, 2000-; Minister of State, in the President's Office Regional Administration and Local Government,2000-08; Prime Minister, 2008-; *office address:* Office of the Prime Minister, Magogoni Road, P.O. Box 3021, Dar es Salaam, Tanzania; *phone:* +255 22 211 2850; *fax:* +255 22 211 3439.

PIÑERA, Sebastián; President, Government of Chile; ***born:*** December 1 1949, Santiago, Chile; ***parents:*** José Piñera Carvallo; ***married:*** Cecilia Morel Montes; ***s:*** 2; ***d:*** 2; ***education:*** Pontifical Catholic Univ. of Chile, economics, 1971; MA and doctorate in economics, Harvard Univ.; ***party:*** Pres. National Renewal Party, 2001-04; ***political career:*** Senator, 1990-98; President, March 2010-; ***professional career:*** Teacher; Businessman; ***office address:*** Office of the President, Palacio de la Moneda, Santiago, Chile; ***phone:*** +56 (0)2 690 4000; ***URL:*** http://www.presidencia.gob.cl.

PING, Jean; Chair, African Union Commission; ***born:*** 24 November 1942, Omboué (Etimboué), Gabon; ***languages:*** French, English, Myéné; ***education:*** Univ. of Paris (Panthéon-Sorbonne), Doctorate in Econ.; ***political career:*** Minister of Information, Post and Telecommunication, Tourism and Leisure, Parastatal Reform, in charge of Relations with the Parliament, Official Speaker of the Government, 1990; Minister of Mining, ENergy and Hydraulic Resources, 1990-91, 1992-94; Minister of Foreign Affairs and Co-operation, 1994; Dep. Minister of Finance, 1994-97; Minister of Planning, Environment and Tourism, 1997-99; Snr. Minister in charge of Foreign Affairs, Co-operation and Franacophony, 1999-2006; Vice Prime Minister in Charge of Foreign Affairs, Co-operation, Francophony and Regional Integration, 2006-07; ***professional career:*** Administrator, Office of the Under-Director General in charge of Education, UNESCO, 1972-77; Sector for External Relations and Cooperation, UNESCO, 1977-78; First Counsellor, Embassy to France, 1978; Amb. Ex. & Plen., Perm, Delegate to UNESCO, 1978-12; Chair, AU Commission, to date; ***honours and awards:*** Commander of the Equatorial Star, Gabon; Commander of the Legion of Honour, France; Grand Officer of the Legion of Honour, France; Officer of the Pleiades, Order of the Francophony; Grand Cross of Merit, Portugal; Grand Officer of Wissam Al Alaoui, Morocco; Doctor Honoris Causa of the Chinese Diplomatic Institute; Doctor Honoris Causa of the African Studies; Institute of the Academy of Science of Moscow, Russia; Chinese Diplomatic Institute; Grand Cross of the Order of Bernado Higgius, Chili; ***publications:*** Author of various articles and reports on the national and international level; Globalisation, Peace, Democracy and Development in Africa: The Gabonese Experience, L' Harmattan, Paris, 2002; translated into Russian in 2004; Et l'Afrique brillera de milles feux. Ed. L'Harmattan, Paris, 2009; ***office address:*** African Union, PO Box 3243, Addis Ababa, Ethiopia.

PINTO DA COSTA, Manuel; President, Sao Tome and Principe; ***political career:*** President, Sao Tome, 1975-1990, re-elected 2011-; ***office address:*** Office of the President, Palácio dos Congressos, C.P., 181, Sao Tomé; ***phone:*** +239 222986-22; ***fax:*** +239 222835; ***URL:*** http://www.presidencia.st/.

PIRES, Emilia; Minster of Finance, Government of Timor-Leste; ***education:*** Latrobe Univ., maths; Univ. of Melbourne, government studies; LSE, MSc.; ***political career:*** Minister of Finance, East Timor, 2007-; ***professional career:*** civil servant, Government of Victoria, Australia; Senior Aid Management Specialist, World Bank; Senior Advisor to the Timor-Leste Ministry of Planning and Finance; UNMIT Senior Coordination Advisor; ***office address:*** Ministry of Finance, Bldg. No. 5, Government House, Dili, Timor-Leste; ***URL:*** http://www.mof.gov.tl/.

PIVA MESEN, Alfio; First Vice President, Government of Costa Rica; ***born:*** 1940; ***education:*** Ph.D, Univ. of Milan, Italy; ***political career:*** First Vice President; ***office address:*** Ministry of Presidency and Planning, Apdo. 520 Zapote, San José, Costa Rica; ***phone:*** +506 224 4092; ***fax:*** +506 253 6984.

PLAISANT, François-Marcel, CMG; French, Life Ambassador, French Government; ***born:*** 1932, Paris, France; ***parents:*** Marcel Plaisant and Geneviève Plaisant (née Brochet-Auchère); ***married:*** Renée Plaisant (née Charbaut), 1968; ***children:*** Béatrice (F), Francois-Claude (M); ***languages:*** German, English; ***education:*** Paris, Diplomé IEP; Diplomé d'Etudes Supérieures de Droit Public; Ecole Nationale d'Administration; ***professional career:*** Algeria peace talks, 1960-64; French Deleg. to NATO, 1965-68; 1st Sec., French Embassy, Bonn; Expert with the French Deleg. to the Quadripartite talks on Berlin, 1969-73; Counsellor, French Deleg. to the CSCE, Geneva, 1973-74; Head of Central European Desk, Paris 1976-78; Plenipotentiary Minister, Dep. Dir., Europe, 1978-79; Minister-Counsellor (DCM) French Embassy, Washington, 1980-81; Ambassador of France, South Africa, 1982-83; Dir., Europe, 1984; Ambassador to Greece, 1987; Ambassador, Head of the French Deleg. to Vienna, negotiations on Conventional Forces in Europe; Ambassador to Switzerland, 1991; Dep. Sec.-Gen., Foreign Min., 1993; Diplomatic adviser to the Govt., 1993; Ambassador to China, 1993-96; Life Ambassador of France, 1996; Dep. Pres., Friends of the Diplomatic Archives, 2007; ***honours and awards:*** Officier de la Légion d'Honneur; Commandeur de l'Ordre National du Mérite; Großes Bundesverdienstkreuz, Fed. Rep. of Germany; Commandeur de l'Order des Arts et des Lettres, 2008, CMG; ***publications:*** Various research papers on French Literature of the XVIth/XVIIth Century; Raconte-moi l'ambassadeur et le consul, 1997; Le ministère des affaires étrangères, 2000; The Ministry of Foreign Affairs, 2001; ***clubs:*** Association Guillaume BUDE; Société Saint-Simon; Societé d'histoire Diplomatique.

PLASTERK, Ronald; Minister of the Interior and Kingdom Relations, Netherlands Government; ***born:*** 1957; ***education:*** Leiden Univ., biology, doctorate in maths and natural sciences; Calif. Inst. of Technology; ***political career:*** Minister of Education, Culture and Science, 2007; Mem., House of Reps.; Party spokesperson; Minister of the Interior and Kingdom Relations, Nov. 2012-; ***professional career:*** research; various professorships; Dir., Hubrecht Laboratory, Netherlands Inst. for Developmental Biology, Utrecht, 2000-07; Professor of Developmental Genetics, Biomedical Centre, Univ. of Utrecht, 2000-07 ; ***office address:*** Ministry of the Interior and Kingdom Relations, Schedeldoekshaven 200, 2511 EZ The Hague, Netherlands.

PLATZECK, Matthias; German, Minister President, State of Brandenburg; ***born:*** 29 December 1953, Potsdam, Germany; ***education:*** Engineer biomedical cybernetics; ***political career:*** Co-founder of ARGUS (Potsdam citizens grp., 1987), Foundation for Environment and Nature Protection of East Germany (SUN, 1990), Bundnis 90 (parly. wing of the citizens movement 1991); Mem., Central Round Table 1989-90; Min. without portfolio Feb-May 1990; Min. for Environment, Nature Protection and Regional Planning of Brandenburg 1990-; elect. to GDR Parliament (Volkskammer) 1990, to All-German Parliament (Bundestag) 1990, (Land of) Brandenburg Parliament (Landtag, 1990-), Acting Council of Budnis 90 (Geschäftsfuhrender Ausschuss, 1991); Prime Minister, Brandenburg, 2002-; ***office address:*** Office of the Ministerpräsident, Heinrich-Mann-Allee 107, 14473 Potsdam, Germany.

PLEVNELIEV, Rosen; President, Government of Bulgaria; ***born:*** 14 May 1964; ***languages:*** English, German; ***education:*** Technical Univ., Sofia, 1989; ***political career:*** Minister of Regional Development, July 2009-11: President, Nov. 2011-; ***professional career:*** Founder and manager of several construction companies and projects; ***office address:*** Office of the President, 2 Boulevard Knjaz Dondukov, Sofia 1123, Bulgaria; ***phone:*** +359 2 83839; ***fax:*** +359 2 980 4484; ***e-mail:*** press@president.bg; ***URL:*** http://www.president.bg.

PLIBERSEK, Tanya; Minister for Health, Australian Government; ***political career:*** Member for Sydney; Minister for Housing and the Status of Women, 2007-10; Minister for Human Services, Minister for Social Inclusion, 2010-11; Minister of Health, 2011-; ***office address:*** Department of Health, Box 9848, Canberra, ACT 2601, Australia; ***phone:*** +61 2 6289 1555; ***URL:*** http://www.health.gov.au.

PLICANIC, Dr Senko; Minister of Justice and Public Administration, Government of Slovenia; ***born:*** 1963; ***political career:*** Minister of Justice & Public Administration, 2012-; ***professional career:*** Visiting researcher, Fulbright Scholarship, Berkeley School of Law; Visiting prof., Fulbright fellowship, Golden Gate Univ. School of Law; Assoc. Prof. of Law, Fac. of Law, Ljubliana; Dir., Inst. of Public Admin.; ***office address:*** Ministry of Justice, Zupanciceva 3, 1000 Ljubljana, Slovenia.

PLOUMEN, Lilianne; Minister for Foreign Trade and Development Cooperation, Netherlands Government; ***born:*** 1962; ***education:*** Erasmus Univ., Rotterdam; ***political career:*** Chair, Labour Party (PvdA), 2007-12; Minister for Foreign Trade and Development Cooperation, Rutte-Asscher gov., Nov. 2012-; ***professional career:*** marketing; market research; founder, Ploument Projecten, 1995; fundraising coordinator, Mamma Cash, 1995, dir., 1996-2001; development org., Cordaid, dir., international programmes; ***office address:*** Ministry of Foreign Affairs, PO Box 20061, 2500 EB The Hague, Netherlands; ***phone:*** +31 (0)70 348 6486.

POCOCK, H.E. Dr Andrew, CMG; High Commissioner, British High Commission in Nigeria; ***professional career:*** Dep. High Commissioner, Australia, 1997-2001; British High Commissioner in Tanzania, 2003-06; British Ambassador to Zimbabwe, 2006-09; High Commissioner in Canada, 2010-12; High Commissioner to Nigeria, Amb. to Equatorial Guinea, and Perm. Rep. to the Economic Community of West African States (ECOWAS), 2013-; ***office address:*** British High Commission, 19 Torrens Close, Mississippi, Maitama Abuja, Nigeria; ***phone:*** +234 9 4622200 ; ***URL:*** https://www.gov.uk/government/world/organisations/british-high-commission-abuja.

POFALLA, Ronald; Head of Federal Chancellery, German Government; ***education:*** Univ. of Cologne; ***party:*** CDU; ***political career:*** Sec. Gen., CDU, 2005-09; Head of Federal Chancellery and Ministry of Internal Affairs, 2009-11; Head of Federal Chancellery, 2011-; ***professional career:*** Lawyer; ***office address:*** Federal Chancellery, Bundeskanzleramt, Willy-Brandt Str. 1, 10557 Berlin, Germany; ***phone:*** +49 (0)1888 4000; ***URL:*** http://www.bundeskanzler.de.

POGUE, Donald C.; Chief Judge, United States Court of International Trade (USCIT); ***education:*** Dartmouth College, magna cum laude, Phi Beta Kappa; graduate work, University of Essex, UK; Yale Law School, JD; Yale University., M.Phil.; ***professional career:*** lawyer, Kestell, Pogue, & Gould; Chmn., Connecticut's Commission on Hospitals and Health Care; Judge, Connecticut's Superior Court; Judge, United States Court of International Trade (USCIT), 1995, Chair, Court's Long Range Planning Committee & Court's Budget Cttee., Chair, Judicial Conference's Committee on the Administrative Office, Chief Judge, 2010; ***office address:*** US Court of International Trade (USCIT), One Federal Plaza, New York, NY 10278-0001, USA.

POHAMBA, Hifikepunye; Namibian, President, Government of Namibia; ***born:*** 1935; ***education:*** Anglican Holy Cross Mission School, Onamunhama; ***political career:*** Organiser, SWAPO; in exile three times; opened SWAPO office, Lusaka; Dpty. Administrative Secy., Central Cttee., Tanga Consultative Congress, 1969; SWAPO Chief Representative for Northern Africa, 1971-75; Secy. for Finance, Politbureau at enlarged meeting of executive, Lusaka, 1975; Chief of Operations, SWAPO, Lusaka, 1979-80; operated at SWAPO HQ, Luanda, 1981-89; Departmental Head of Finance and Administration in Election Directorate, Namibia, 1989; Min. of Home Affairs, 1990; Minister of Lands, Resettlement and Rehabilitation, to 2004; President of Namibia, 2004-; ***professional career:*** Tsumeb Corporation 1956-60; ***office address:*** Office of the President, State House, Private Bag 13339, Windhoek, Namibia; ***phone:*** +264 61 220010; ***URL:*** http://www.op.gov.na.

POILIEVRE, Pierre; Parliamentary Secretary to the Minister of Transport, Government of Canada; ***born:*** 1979; ***education:*** Univ. of Calgary; ***political career:*** MP for Nepean, Carleton, Ontario, 2004-; Parly. Sec. to the President of the Treasury Board, 2006-07; Parly. Sec. to the Prime Minister and the Minister of Intergovernmental Affairs, 2007-11; Parly. Sec. to the Minister of Transport, Infrastructure and Communities and for the Federal Economic Development Agency for Southern Ontario, 2011-; ***office address:*** House of Commons, Parliament Buildings, Wellington Street, Ottawa K1A 0A6, Ontario, Canada; ***phone:*** +1 613 943 5959; ***fax:*** +1 613 992 3674; ***URL:*** http://www.parl.gc.ca.

POINT, Steven L. , OBC; Lieutenant Governor, Government of British Colombia; ***education:*** Bachelor of Law, Univ. of British Columbia, 1985 ; ***political career:*** Lieutenant Governor, 2007-; ***professional career:*** Provincial Court Judge, 1999; ***office address:*** Office of the Lieutenant Governor, 1401 Rockland Avenue, Victoria, BC, V8S 1V9, Canada; ***phone:*** +1 250 387 2080.

POLOZ, Stephen S.; Governor, Bank of Canada; ***education:*** BA, economics, Queen's Univ., 1978; MA, 1979, Ph.D., 1982, economics, Univ. of Western Ontario, Canada; ***professional career:*** Senior positions, Bank of Canada, 1981-95; Managing Editor, BCA

Research, 1995-99; Vice Pres. and Chief Economist, Export Development Canada (EDC), 1999-2004; Snr. Vice Pres. Corporate Affairs and Chief Economist, EDC, 2004-08; Snr. Vice Pres, Financing EDC, 2008-10; Pres. and Chief Executive Office, EDC, 2011-13; Governor and Chmn. of the Board of Directors, Bank of Canada, 2013-; ***office address:*** Bank of Canada, 234 Wellington Street, Ottawa, Ontario K1A 0G9, Canada; ***phone:*** +1 613 782 8111; ***fax:*** +1 613 782 8655; ***e-mail:*** paffairs@bankofcanada.ca; ***URL:*** http://www.bankofcanada.ca.

POLYE, Don; Treasury Minister, Government of Papua New Guinea; ***party:*** Triumph Heritage Empowerment Party, leader; ***political career:*** MP, 2002-; Dep. PM, 2010; Foreign Minister; Finance Minister; Treasury Minister; Minister of Border Development; ***office address:*** Treasury, Vulupindi Haus, PO Box 710, Waigani, NCD, Papua New Guinea; ***phone:*** +675 328 8452; ***fax:*** 675 328 8431; ***URL:*** http://www.treasury.gov.pg.

PONCE CEVALLOS , Javier; Minister of Agriculture, Aquaculture, Livestock and Fisheries, Government of Ecuador; ***education:*** Univ. Central del Ecuador, Sociology and Politics; Univ. de Vincennes, Paris, Media and Sociology and Cultural Creation; ***political career:*** Private Sec. to the President of the Republic, 2007; Minister of National Defence, 2008-12; Minister of Agriculture, Aquaculture, Livestock and Fisheries, 2012-; ***professional career:*** Columnist, El Universo and HOY; Editor, Encyclopedia Planeta; Dir., Study into Cooperation for the Development of Ecuador; Sec.-Gen., Ecumenical Project Cttee.; Hd., Rural Development / Communication; National Sec., Rural Development; ***office address:*** Ministry of Agriculture, Avenida Amazonas y ELoy Alfarom, Quito, Ecuador; ***phone:*** +593 (0)2 504433; ***fax:*** +593 (0)2 504922; ***e-mail:*** rtipan@sica.gov.ec; ***URL:*** http://www.magap.gov.ec.

PONTA, Victor; Prime Minister, Government of Romania; ***born:*** 1972; ***political career:*** Mem., Chamber of Deputies, 2004-; Minister-Degelate for Relations with Parliament, 2008-09; Prime Minister, May 2012-; ***office address:*** Office of the Prime Minister, Iata Victoriei 1, Sector 1, 71291 Bucharest, Romania; ***URL:*** http://www.gov.ro.

PONYO MAPON, Augustin Matata; Prime Minister, Government of the Democratic Republic of the Congo; ***born:*** 1964; ***political career:*** Minister of Finance, 2010-; Prime Minister, 2010-; ***office address:*** Prime Minister's Office, Boulevard du 30 Juin, BO 12997, Kinshasa, Democratic Republic of Congo; ***phone:*** +243 12 31197.

POOTS, Edwin; Minister of Health, Social Services and Public Safety, Northern Ireland Assembly; ***party:*** Democratic Unionist; ***political career:*** mem., Lagan Valley, Northern Ireland Assembly; Minister of Culture, Arts and Leisure, May 2007-10; Minister of the Environment, 2010-11; Minister of Health, Social Services and Public Safety, 2011-; ***professional career:*** Farmer; ***office address:*** Northern Ireland Assembly, Parliament Buildings, Stormont, Belfast, BT4 3XX, United Kingdom; ***phone:*** +44 (0)28 9052 1130.

POPAT, Lord Dolar Amarshi; Member, House of Lords; ***political career:*** Mem., House of Lords, 2010-; ***professional career:*** Businessman; Chief Exec., TLC Group; ***office address:*** House of Lords, London, SW1A 0PW, United Kingdom; ***phone:*** +44 (0)20 7219 3000; ***fax:*** +44 (0)20 7219 5979; ***URL:*** http://www.parliament.uk.

POPE, Neil; Australian, Administrator, Norfolk Island; ***born:*** 1949; ***political career:*** Mem., Victoria Legislative Assembly, 1982-92; Minister, Gov. of John Cain and Joan Kirne; Victorian Minister for Labour, 1988-92; Minister for Youth Affairs, 1988-91; Minister for School Education,1992; Administrator of Norfolk Island, 2012-; ***professional career:*** MD, Neil Pope & Associates, consultancy practice; ***office address:*** Office of the Administrator, South Pacific 2899, Norfolk Island; ***URL:*** http://www.norfolk.gov.nf/.

POPOVA, Margaritia; Vice President, Government of Bulgaria; ***born:*** 15 May 1956; ***education:*** Law, Sofia Univ, Bulgaria, 1989; Postgraduate Studies, Georgetown Univ. Washington, USA, 1998; ***political career:*** Minister of Justice, July 2009-11; Vice President, 2011-; ***professional career:*** Admin Head, District Prosecutor of the District Prosecutor's Office, Sofia, 1996-2006; 2001-04;Part-time Lecturer, Ministry of Interior, 2001-04: Lecturer, Nat. Inst. of Justice, 2005-; Prosecutor, Supreme Prosecutor's Office of Cassation, 2006; ***office address:*** Office of the Vice President, 2 Boulevard Knjaz Dondukov, Sofia 1123, Bulgaria; ***phone:*** +359 2 83839; ***fax:*** +359 2 980 4484; ***e-mail:*** press@president.bg; ***URL:*** http://www.president.bg.

POPOVSKI, Nikola; Minister of Foreign Affairs, Government of Macedonia; ***born:*** 24 May 1962, Macedonia; ***languages:*** English; ***education:*** Fac. of Economics, Skopje, MA; ***party:*** Social Democratic Union of Macedonia (SDUM); Sec. Gen., 1991-93; Vice-Pres., 1993-95 and 2000-2003; ***political career:*** MP, 1992-; Mem., Parly. Assembly of the Cncl. of Europe, 1993-2002; Chmn., Parliamentary Gp., Social Democratic Union of Macedonia, 1998-2002; Pres., Parliament of Republic of Macedonia, 2002-03; Minister of Finance, 2004-July 2006; Minister of Foreign Affairs, 2011-; ***committees:*** Foreign Policy Cttee., 1992-94; Environment, Youth and Sports Cttee., 1995-98; Financing and Budget Cttee., 1998-2002; ***office address:*** Ministry of Foreign Affairs, Dame Gruev br. 6, 1000 Skopje, Macedonia; ***phone:*** +389 2 311 0330 ; ***e-mail:*** mnr@mnr.gov.mk; ***URL:*** http://www.mfa.gov.mk.

PORTILLO, Michael Denzil Xavier; British, Broadcaster and former MP; ***born:*** 1953, London; ***parents:*** Luis Gabriel Portillo and Cora Portillo (née Waldegrave Blyth); ***married:*** Carolyn Claire Portillo (née Eadie), 1982; ***languages:*** Spanish, Italian, French; ***education:*** Harrow County Sch. for Boys; Peterhouse, Cambridge Univ., MA, History, (1st Class Hons.); ***party:*** Conservative Party; ***political career:*** Conservative Research Dept., 1976-79; Special Adviser, Sec. of State for Energy, 1979-81; Special Adviser to Sec. of State for Trade and Industry, 1983; Special Adviser, Chancellor of the Exchequer, 1983-84; MP, Enfield Southgate, 1984-97; mem., Energy Select Cttee., 1985-86; PPS to Sec. of State for Transport, 1986; Govt. Whip, 1986-87; Parly. Sec., DHSS, 1987-88; Minister of Public Transport, 1988-90; Minister for Local Govt and Inner Cities, Dept. of the Environment, 1990-92; Chief Sec. to the Treasury, 1992-94; Sec. of State for Employment, 1994-95; Sec. of State for Defence, 1995-97; MP, Kensington and Chelsea, 1999-2005; Shadow Chancellor of the Exchequer, 2000-2001; ***professional career:*** Ocean Transport and Trading Co. Ltd, 1975-76; Kerr McGee Oil (UK) Ltd, 1981-83; TV Broadcaster; ***honours and awards:*** Privy Counsellor; ***clubs:*** Savile; Chelsea Arts Club; ***office address:*** Conservative Party, 25 Victoria Street, London, SW1H 0DL, United Kingdom.

PORTMAN, Rob; American, Senator for Ohio, US Senate; ***party:*** Republican; ***political career:*** Assoc. Counsel to the Pres., then Dir. of the White House Office of Legislative Affairs, 1989-91; Asst. Maj. Whip; Mem., US House of Representatives, 1993-2005; US Trade Representative, 2005-06; Director, Office of Management and Budget, 2006-07; Mem., US Senate, 2010-; ***professional career:*** Associate, Patton Boggs, 1984-86; Associate, then Partner, Graydon, Head and Ritchey, 1986-89, 1991-93; ***committees:*** Finance; Budget; Energy and Natural Resources; Homeland Security and Governmental Affairs; ***office address:*** US Senate, 338 Russell Senate Office Building, Washington, DC 20510, USA; ***phone:*** +1 202 224 3353; ***URL:*** http://www.portman.senate.gov.

POTOCNIK, Janez; Commissioner for Environment, European Commission; ***education:*** Ph.D. in Economics, Faculty of Economics, Univ. of Ljubljana, 1993; ***political career:*** Head of Negotiating Team of the Rep. of Slovenia for Accession to the EU, 1998-2004; Ministerial Counsellor, resp. for European Affairs, 2001-02; Minister for European Affairs, 2002-04; European Commissioner for Science and Research, 2004-10; European Commissioner for Environment, 2010-; ***professional career:*** Assist. Dir., RS Institute for Social Planning, Ljubljana, 1984-87; Senior Researcher, Inst. for Economic Research, Ljubljana, 1988-93; Dir., Inst. of Microeconomic Analysis & Dev., 1993-2001; ***office address:*** European Commission, rue de la Loi 200, 1040 Brussels, Belgium; ***phone:*** +32 (0)2 299 1111; ***URL:*** http://www.europa.eu.

POULTER, Daniel; MP for Central Suffolk and North Ipswich, UK Government; ***party:*** Conservative; ***political career:*** Councillor, Hastings Borough Council 2006-07; MP for Central Suffolk and North Ipswich, May 2010-; Parly. Under-Sec. of State, Dept. of Health, 2012-; ***committees:*** Health, 2011-12; ***office address:*** House of Commons, London, SW1A 0AA, United Kingdom; ***phone:*** +44 (0)20 7219 3000; ***e-mail:*** daniel.poulter.mp@parliament.uk.

POUND, Stephen; British, Member of Parliament for Ealing North, House of Commons; ***born:*** 3 July 1948; ***education:*** TUC, Postal Studies; LSE, B.Sc., Econs.; ***party:*** Labour Party; ***political career:*** MP, Ealing North, 1997-; PPS to 2005-2010; Opp. Assist. Whip, 2010- Shadow Minister for Northern Ireland, 2010; ***interests:*** Ireland, Poland; ***recreations:*** walking, football; ***office address:*** House of Commons, London, SW1A 0AA, United Kingdom; ***phone:*** +44 (0)20 7219 4312; ***e-mail:*** stevepoundmp@parliament.uk; ***URL:*** http://www.stevepound.org.uk.

POWELL, Lucy; MP for Manchester Central, British Government; ***political career:*** Deputy Chief of Staff for Ed Miliband; MP for Manchester Central, Nov. 2012-; ***professional career:*** NESTA, the UK's innovation agency, 2007-10; ***office address:*** House of Commons, London, SW1 0AA, United Kingdom; ***phone:*** +44 (0)20 7219 3000.

POWELL, Nancy J.; Ambassador, US Embassy in India; ***born:*** Cedar Falls, Iowa, USA; ***languages:*** French, Nepali, Urdu; ***professional career:*** high school social studies teacher, Dayton, Iowa; Nepal Desk Officer and Refugee Assistance Officer, US Foreign Service, Washington, DC; US Foreign Service assignments in Pakistan, Nepal, and Canada; Dep. Chief of Mission, Lome, Togo, 1990-92; Consul General, Calcutta, India, and Political Counselor, New Delhi, 1993-95; US Amb. to Uganda, 1997-99; Dep. Chief of Mission, US Embassy, Dhaka, Bangladesh, 1995-97; Principal Dep. Asst. Sec. for African Affairs, 1999-01; Acting Asst. Sec. for African Affairs, 2001; US Ambassador to Ghana, 2001-02; US Amb. to Pakistan, 2002-04; US Amb. to Nepal, 2007-10; Amb. to India, 2012-; ***office address:*** American Embassy, Shanti Path, Chanakyapuri 110021, New Delhi 110 021, India; ***phone:*** +91 11 2419 8000; ***fax:*** +91 11 2419 0017; ***URL:*** http://newdelhi.usembassy.gov.

PRAET, Peter; Member of the Executive Board, European Central Bank; ***education:*** Univ. libre de Bruxelles, economics, BA, MA, Ph.D; ***professional career:*** Research Assist, Inst. for European Studies, 1976-77; Economist, IMF, USA, 1978-80; Prof. of economics, Univ. Libre de Bruxelles, 1980-87; Chief Economist, Générale de Banque (later Fortis Bank), 1987-99; Exec. Dir., Nationale Bank van Belgie, 2000-11; mem., Board of the Banking, Finance & Insurance Commission, 2002-11; Mem., Exec. Board, European Central Bank, 2011-; ***office address:*** European Central Bank, Kaisterstrasse 29, Frankfurt-am-Main D-60311, Germany; ***URL:*** http://www.ecb.int.

PRAMMER, Barbara; Austrian, President, Austrian Nationalrat; ***born:*** 1954; ***party:*** Sozialdemokratische Partei Österreichs (SPÖ, Social Democratic Party); ***political career:*** Minister of Women's Issues and Consumer Protection 1991-2000; President of National Council, 2006-; ***office address:*** Nationalrat, Dr. Karl Renner-Ring 3, A-1017 Vienna, Austria; ***phone:*** +43 (0)1 401100; ***fax:*** +43 (0)1 40110/2345; ***URL:*** http://www.parlinkom.gv.at.

PRASHAR, Baroness; Chair, Judicial Appointment Commission; ***born:*** 29 June 1948, Kenya; ***parents:*** Nauria Lal Prashar and Durga Devi Prashar; ***married:*** Vijay Kumar Sharma, July 1973; ***public role of spouse:*** Solicitor, Senior Partner; ***languages:*** English, Hindi, Punjabi; ***education:*** BA Hons. Dip, Social Administration; ***political career:*** Crossbencher; Mem., House of Lords; ***interests:*** social policy, criminal justice, education, human rights; ***memberships:*** Fellow, Royal Soc. of Arts; Fellow, National School of Government; Fellow, City and Guilds; Hon. Pres., Local Govt. Assn.; Pres., UKCISA; Cncl. for Int. Education; RSA India Chapter; Community Foundation Network; Kalpana Chalwa Foundation; ***professional career:*** Fmr. Dir.: Runnymede Trust; Fmr. Dir., Nat. Cncl. for Voluntary Organisations; First Civil Service Commissioner; Non-exec. Dir., ITV; Non-exec. Dir., Cabinet Office; ***committees:*** Fmr. Chmn., Parole Board of England and Wales; Chmn., Judicial Appointments Commission; ***trusteeships:*** Governor, Fmr. Chmn. Nat. Literary Trust; Fmr. Chllr., De Monfort Univ.; Chmn., Royal Cmmw. Soc.; The Ditchley Foundation; Gov. and Mem. of the Management Cttee., Cumberland Lodge; Ashridge College; Amb., National Aids Trust; Pattron, Tara Arts; ***honours and awards:*** CBE, 1995; Peerage, 1999; ***clubs:*** Royal Cmmw. Soc.; ***recreations:*** reading, golf, music and walking; ***office address:*** House of Lords, London, SW1A 0PQ, United Kingdom; ***phone:*** +44 (0)20 7219 3000.

PRASIDH, Cham; Minister of Commerce, Government of Cambodia; *born:* 15 May 1951, Phnom Penh; *parents:* Ung You Y and Tan Koui Hong; *married:* Tep Bopha Prasidh; *public role of spouse:* Chief of Bureau of Ministry of Commerce; *languages:* English, French; *education:* Bachelor Degree, Commerce & Economics; *political career:* Senior Minister; Minister of Commerce; Vice Minister, Min. of Finance; *committees:* mem., Central Cttee., CPP; *honours and awards:* Royal Order of the Kingdom of Cambodia; *recreations:* golf, tennis, table tennis, volley ball; *office address:* Ministry of Commerce, 20 A-B Norodom Blvd., Phnom Penh, 12205, Cambodia; *phone:* +855 (0)23 213288; *fax:* +855 (0)23 213288; *e-mail:* champrasidh@hotmail.com; *URL:* http://www.moc.gov.kh.

PREMAJAYANTHA, Susil, MP; Minister of the Environment and Natural Resources, Government of Sri Lanka; *born:* 10 January 1955; *parents:* S.A.D. Karunapala and T.M. Gunawathi Perera; *married:* Vijitha Chandralatha Ranasinghe, May 1983; *children:* S.A.D. Lahiru Devinda (M), S.A.D. Saminda Lakmal (M), S.A.D. Indiwari Kanchanamala (F); *languages:* Sinhala, English; *education:* Univ. of Colombo, Bachelor of Law, 1982; Postgraduate Inst. of Management, Sri Jayawardanapura Univ., Master of Public Administration; *party:* Sec. Gen., United People's Freedom Alliance; *political career:* Dep. Chmn., Sri-Jayawardanapura-Kotte Urban Council, 1991-93; Council Member, Western Province, 1993-94; Minister of Western Province, 1994-95; Chief Minister of Western Province, 1995-98; 1999-2000; Minister of Education, 2000-01; MP, 2001-04; Minister of Power and Energy, 2004-05; Minister of Education, 2006-10; Minister of Petroleum Industries, 2010-12; Minister of the Environment and Natural Resources, 2013-; *professional career:* Attorney-at-law; Banker, Bank of Ceylon; *committees:* Executive Board, UNESCO, 2007-; Chmn., Sri Lanka National Commission for UNESCO; *recreations:* music, cricket; *office address:* Ministry of the Environment, 82, Sampathpaya, Rajamalwatta Road, Battaramulla, Sri Lanka; *URL:* http://www.gov.lk.

PRENTICE, H.E. Christopher; Ambassador, British Embassy in Rome; *professional career:* Amb. to Jordan, 2002-06; Amb. at Large for the Sudan Peace Process and UK Special Representative, 2006-07; Amb. to Iraq, 2007-09; Amb. to Italy, 2011-; *office address:* British Embassy, Via XX Settembre 80a, 00187 Rome, Italy; *phone:* +39 06 4220 0001; *fax:* +39 06 487 3324; *e-mail:* InfoRome@fco.gov.uk; *URL:* http://ukinitaly.fco.gov.uk/en.

PRESCOTT OF KINGSTON UPON HULL, Rt. Hon. Lord John Leslie, MP; British, Member, House of Lords; *born:* 1938; *married:* Pauline Prescott (née Tilston), 1964; *children:* David (M), Jonathon (M); *education:* Hull Univ., B.Sc. Econ.; Oxford Univ., Dip. Econ./Pol.; *party:* Labour Party; *political career:* MP (Lab.) for Kingston upon Hull (East), 1970-2010; PPS to the Sec. of State for Trade, 1974-76; Mem., Cncl.of Europe, 1973-75; Leader, Labour Del. to European Parl., 1976-79; Dep. Opposition Spokesman on Transport, 1979-81; on Regional Affairs and Devolution, 1981-83; elected to Shadow Cabinet and appointed Opposition Spokesman on Transport, 1983-84 and 1988-93; Opposition Spokesman on Employment, 1984-87; Opposition Spokesman on Energy, 1987-88; Mem., Nat. Executive Cttee. (NEC), 1991-; Opposition Spokesman on Employment, 1993-94; Dep. leader of the Labour Party, 1994-2007; Dep. Prime Minister, and Sec. of State for the Environment, Transport and the Regions, May 1997-2001; Deputy Prime Minister, 2001-June 2007; First Secretary of State, 2001-06; Mem., House of Lords , July 2010-; *memberships:* RMT; *professional career:* Seaman, Merchant Navy, 1955-64; Education, 1964-68; Trade Union Official, Nat. Union of Seamen, 1968-70; *publications:* Not Wanted On Voyage: A report of the 1966 seamen's strike (1966); Alternative Regional Strategy: A framework for discussion (1982); Planning for Full Employment (1985); Real Needs - Local Jobs (1987); Moving Britain into the 1990s (1989); Moving Britain into Europe (1991); Full Steam Ahead (1993); Financing Infrastructure Investment (1994); Jobs and Social Justice (1994); *office address:* House of Lords, London, SW1A 0PW, United Kingdom; *phone:* +44 (0)20 7219 3000.

PRICE, Tom; Congressman, Sixth district of Georgia, US House of Representatives; *education:* Univ. of Michigan, MD; Emory Univ., Orthopaedic Surgery resid.; *political career:* Georgia Senate, Minority Whip, then Republican Majority Leader in 2002; US House of Representatives, 2005-; Chmn., HOR Republican Policy Cttee., 2011-13; *professional career:* private practice, orthopaedic clinic, Atlanta; Asst. Professor, Emory Univ. School of Medicine; Medical Dir., Orthopaedic Clinic, Grady Memorial Hospital, Atlanta; *committees:* HOR: Budget; Ways and Means; Education & the Workforce; *office address:* US House of Representatives, 506 Cannon House Office Building, Washington, DC 20515, USA; *phone:* +1 202 225 4501; *fax:* +1 202 225 4656; *URL:* http://www.tomprice.house.gov.

PRIMAROLO, Dawn; British, Member of Parliament for Bristol South, House of Commons; *born:* 2 May 1954; *education:* Bristol Univ.; *party:* Labour Party; *political career:* MP, Bristol South, 1987-; Opp. Spokesperson on Health, 1992-94; Shadow Health Min., 1992-94; Shadow Treasury Spokeswoman, 1994-; Financial Sec. to the Treasury, 1997-99; Paymaster Gen., 1999; Minister of State, Dept. of Health, 2007-09; Minister of State for Children, Young People and Families, 2009-10; Second Deputy Chairman, Ways and Means and Deputy Speaker, 2010-; Shadow Minister for Children, Young People and Families, 2010-; *interests:* defence, economic policy, European policy, employment, social security, women's rights, health; *professional career:* Legal Sec.; Administrator; Advice Worker; Cllr., Avon County, 1985-87; *office address:* House of Commons, London, SW1A 0AA, United Kingdom; *phone:* +44 (0)20 7219 3000; *e-mail:* primarolod@parliament.uk.

PRINGLE, Mike; Member for Edinburgh South, Scottish Parliament; *born:* 25 December 1945, Northern Rhodesia (Zambia); *parents:* Robert Pringle and Pauline Pringle; *married:* Maggie Pringle (née Birkett), 16 October 1971; *children:* Iain (M), Kevin (M); *education:* Edinburgh Academy, 1959-64; Napier Coll., Edinburgh; *party:* Scottish Liberal Democrats; *political career:* Cllr. in South Morningside, 1992-2003; MSP for Edinburgh South, May 2003-; mem., The Scottish Parliament Corporate Body; Party Spokesperson on Community Safety; *interests:* justice, sport, Free Tibet Campaign, ; *memberships:* mem., Servas; *professional career:* Barclay's Bank; Royal Bank of Scotland; owner, takeaway/bakery business; *recreations:* cinema, theatre, Hearts FC, holidaying in Scotland, collecting wine; *office address:* Scottish Parliament, Edinburgh, EH99 1SP, United Kingdom; *phone:* +44 (0)131 348 5788; *fax:* +44 (0)131 348 6489.

PRISK, Mark; Minister of State, UK Government; *education:* B.Sc. Hons, Land Management, Univ. of Reading; *party:* Conservatives; *political career:* MP, Hertford & Stortford, 2001-; Shadow Financial Secretary, 2002-03; Paymaster General, 2003-04; Opposition Whip, 2004-05; Shadow Minister for Business Enterprise, 2005-09; Shadow Minister for Business, 2009-10; Minister of State, Department for Business, Innovation and Skills, May 2010-12; Minister of State, Housing, Department for Communities and Local Government, 2012-; *interests:* defence, education, planning, development, small businesses; *professional career:* Graduate surveyor, Knight Frank, 1983-85; Derrick Wade & Waters, 1985-91; Principal, The Mark Prisk Connection, 1991-97; mp² consultancy, 1997-2001; *committees:* Welsh Affairs, 2001-05; Regulatory Reform, 2008-09; *recreations:* Music, piano, rugby, cricket, theatre, architecture, hiking, choral singing (vice-chair, The Parliament Choir, 2008-); *office address:* House of Commons, London, SW1A 0AA, United Kingdom; *phone:* +44 (0)20 7219 3000; *e-mail:* hcinfo@parliament.uk; *URL:* http://www.markprisk.com.

PRITCHARD, Mark; MP for The Wrekin, House of Commons; *political career:* Local Councillor; MP for The Wrekin, 2005-; *interests:* Rural Affairs; Defence; Health; Education; *committees:* Jt. Cttee. on National Security Strategy, 2010-; *office address:* House of Commons, London, SW1P 0AA, United Kingdom; *phone:* +44 (0)20 7219 3000.

PRITZKER, Penny; Secretary of Commerce, US Government; *education:* Harvard Univ., economics; Stanford Univ., JD, MBA; *political career:* mem., President's Council for Jobs and Competitiveness; mem., Economic Recovery Advisory Board; Secretary of Commerce, June 2013-; *professional career:* civic and busines leader; 25 years in real estate, hospitality, senior living, financial services; CEO, PSP Capital Partners; Board mem., incl. La Salle Bank Corp., Hyatt Hotels; *honours and awards:* Woodrow Wilson Award for Public Service; *office address:* Department of Commerce, 1401 Constitution Ave., NW, Washington, DC 20230-0001, USA; *phone:* +1 202 482 2000; *URL:* http://www.commerce.gov/.

PROVOPOULOS, Georgios A.; Governor, Bank of Greece; *born:* 1950; *education:* Univ. of Athens, economics; Essex Univ., economics, MA, Ph.D; *professional career:* Assoc. Prof., Univ. of Athens, Dept. of Economics, 1979-2007; Dep. Gov., Bank of Greece, 1990-93; Gen. Man, Foundation of Economic & Industrial Research, 1993-97; Economic Adviser, Alpha Bank, 1994-2004; Chmn., CEO, Emporiki Bank, 2004-06; Vice-Chmn. & MD, Piraeus Bank, 2006-08; Gov., Bank of Greece, 2008-; mem., Gov. Council, ECB; *office address:* Bank of Greece, 21 E Venizelos Avenue , GR-102 50 Athens, Greece; *URL:* http://www.bankofgreece.gr.

PRYOR, Mark; Senator for Arkansas, US Senate; *born:* 10 January 1963; *education:* University of Arkansas, BA, History, and law degree; *party:* Democratic Party; *political career:* mem., Arkansas State House of Representatives, 1990-98; Arkansas Attorney General, 1998; Senator for Arkansas, US Senate, 2003-; *committees:* Appropriations Cttee.; Commerce, Science and Transportation; Small Business and Entrepreneurship; Homeland Security and Governmental Affairs; Ethics; Rules and Administration; *office address:* US Senate, 217 Russell Senate Office Building, Washington, DC 20510, USA; *URL:* http://www.pryor.senate.gov/public/.

PUGH, John; Member of Parliament for Southport, House of Commons; *party:* Liberal Democrat Party; *political career:* MP for Southport, 2001-; *memberships:* Mem., Sefton Cncl.; *office address:* House of Commons, London, SW1A 0AA, United Kingdom; *phone:* +44 (0)20 7219 3000; *e-mail:* pughj@parliament.uk; *URL:* http://www.parliament.uk.

PURRYAG, Rajkeswur; President, Mauritius; *born:* 1947; *party:* Mauritian Labour Party; *political career:* MP; Gov. Minister of Social Security, 1980-82; Minister of Health, 1984-86; Minister of Economic Planning, 1995-97; Dep. PM & Minister of Foreign Affairs, 1997-2000; Speaker of Parliament, 2005-12; Pres. of Mauritius, 2012-; *professional career:* Attorney at law; *office address:* Office of the President, Sate House, Port Louis, Mauritius; *phone:* +230 454 3021; *fax:* +230 464 5370; *URL:* http://ncb.intnet.mu/presid/.

PUSIC, Vesna; Minister of Foreign and European Affairs, Government of Croatia; *education:* Faculty of Philosophy, Zagreb, 1976; *party:* Croatian People's Party; *political career:* MP, 2000-; Minister of Foreign and European Affairs, 2011-; First Deputy Prime Minister, 2012-; *professional career:* Co-founder and director of the Erasmus Guild; *office address:* Ministry of Foreign Affairs, Trg Nikole Subica Zrinskog 7-8, 10000 Zagreb, Croatia; *phone:* +385 (0)1 456 9964; *fax:* +385 (0)1 492 0149; *URL:* http://www.mvp.hr.

PUTIN, Vladimir; President, Russian Federation; *born:* 7 October 1952, Leningrad (now St. Petersburg); *parents:* Vladimir Putin (dec'd) and Maria Putina; *married:* Ludmila Putina, 1983; *languages:* English, German; *education:* Leningrad State Univ., Law Degree, 1975; St. Petersburg Mining Univ., Ph.D, Economics, 1997; *political career:* Dep. Chmn., City Govt., 1994-96; Dep. Presidential Business Mgr., 1996-97; Head of the President's Main Audit Directorate and Presidential Dep. Chief of Staff, 1997-98; Acting Prime Minister of Russian Federation, 1999-2000; President of Russian Federation, 2000-Mar. 2008; Prime Minister of Russian Federation, 2008-12; President, Russian Federation, 2012-; *professional career:* State Security Committee (KGB), 1975-90; Advisor to Rector, Leningrad State Univ., 1990, and to the Mayor of Leningrad, 1990-91; Adviser to the Chmn. of Leningrad City Cncl., 1990; Chmn., St. Petersburg City Council Cttee. for External Relations, 1991-96; First Dep. Mayor, St. Petersburg City Council, 1994-96; Dep. Head, General Management Dept. of Presidential Admin., 1996-97; Dep. Chief of Staff, Kremlin, Chief of the Central Supervision and Inspections Directorate, 1997-98; First Dep. Chief of Staff., Kremlin, 1998; Dir., Federal Security Service (FSB), 1998-99; Sec., Security Cncl., 1999; *committees:* Chmn., Cttee. for foreign relations of the St. Petersburg Mayor's Office, 1991-94; Chmn., Cttee. for external relations, 1994-96; *publications:* First Person (autobiography), 2000; *recreations:* mountain skiing, judo; *office address:* Office of the President, Staraya pl. 42, 103132 Moscow, Russian Federation; *URL:* http://www.president.kremlin.ru.

Q

QAHTAN, Abdul-Qader; Minister of the Interior, Government of Yemen; ***born:*** 1952; ***education:*** Yemeni Police College, law; Ain Shams Univ., Egypt, law, Masters, Ph.D; ***party:*** Islah Party; ***political career:*** Security Office, rank of Major-general; Secuity Manager, Taiz; Interpol commander; Minister of the Interior, 2011-; ***professional career:*** San'aa Univ.; ***office address:*** Ministry of the Interior, Almatar Road, Sana'a, Yemen.

QUIGLEY, Mike; Congressman, Illinois 5th Dist., US House of Represenatives; ***education:*** Roosevelt Univ; Univ. of Chicago, Master's degree, Public Policy; Loyola Univ., Law degree; ***party:*** Democrat; ***political career:*** Mem., Cook County Bd. of Cmnrs.; Congressman, 2009-; ***professional career:*** Adjunct Prof. of Political Science, Loyola Univ., and Roosevelt Univ.; Lawyer, for 20 years; ***committees:*** Judiciary; Oversight and Government Reform; ***honours and awards:*** Environmental awards from Audubon Society and Sierra Club; ***office address:*** US House of Representatives, 1319 Longworth HOB, Washington DC 20515, USA; ***phone:*** +1 202 225 4081; ***URL:*** http://quigley.house.gov/.

QUINLAN, H.E. Gary; Ambassador, Australian Mission to the United Nations; ***education:*** BA (Hons.), Univ. of Newcastle; ***professional career:*** Amb. to Singapore, 2001-05; Dep. Chief of Mission to USA, 2005-09; Perm. Rep. to the UN, New York, 2009-; ***office address:*** Australian Mission to the United Nations, 150 East 42nd Street, 33rd Floor, New York, NY 10017-5612, USA; ***phone:*** +1 212 351 6600; ***fax:*** +1 212 351 6610; ***e-mail:*** australia@un.int; ***URL:*** http://www.AustraliaUN.org.

QUINN, Governor Patrick; Governor, State of Illinois, USA; ***born:*** December 16, 1948; ***education:*** Georgetown Univ., Edmund A. Walsh School of Foreign Service, 1971; Northwestern Univ. School of Law, Juris Doctor, 1980; ***political career:*** Cmnr., Cook County Bd. of Tax Appeals, 1982-86; Illinois State Treasurer, 1991-95; Lt. Gov., 2002-09; appointed Governor of Illiinois, 2009-; ***professional career:*** Tax attorney; Revenue Director, City of Chicago, 1986; ***office address:*** Office of the Governor, 207 State House, Springfield, Illinois 62706, USA; ***phone:*** +1 217 782 0244; ***fax:*** +1 217 524 4049; ***e-mail:*** governor@state.il.us; ***URL:*** http://www.illinois.gov/gov.

QUINN, Ruairi; Irish, Minister of Education and Skills, Government of Ireland; ***born:*** 2 April 1946, Dublin; ***parents:*** Malachi Quinn and Julia Hoey; ***married:*** Nicola Underwood, 1969 (dec'd 1987); Liz Allam, 1990; ***children:*** Malachi (M), Sine (F), Conan (M); ***languages:*** French; ***education:*** UCD, Dublin, B.Arch.; ***party:*** Labour Party; ***political career:*** Mem., Dail Eireann, 1977-81, 1982-; Mem., Seanad Eireann, 1976 & 1981; Minister of State, Environment, 1982-83; Minister for Labour, 1984-87; Minister for Public Service, 1986-87; Dublin Dir. of Local Elections, 1991; Alderman, Dublin City Cncl., 1991-93; Dublin Dir., European Elections, 1994; Minister for Enterprise & Employment, 1993-94; Minister for Finance, 1994-97; Dep. Leader, Labour Party, 1990-97; Leader, Irish Labour Party, 1997-2002; Treasurer, Party of European Socialists, 2001-; TD, Dublin South East and Spokesperson on European Affairs and relations with the Party of European Socialists (PES); Minister of Education and Skills, Feb. 2011; ***professional career:*** Architect; ***committees:*** Chmn., Campaign Cttee., Mary Robinson's Presidential Campaign, 1990; ***office address:*** Department of Education, Marlborough Street, Dublin 1, Ireland; ***phone:*** +353 (0)1 889 6400; ***e-mail:*** ruairi.quinn@oireachtas.ie; ***URL:*** http://www.education.ie.

QURESHI, Yasmin; MP for Bolton South East, UK Government; ***party:*** Labour; ***political career:*** MP for Bolton South East, May 2010-; ***committees:*** Justice Select Cttee., 2010-; Political and Constitutional Reform, 2011; Joint Committee on Privacy and Injunctions, 2011-12; ***office address:*** House of Commons, London, SW1A 0AA, United Kingdom; ***phone:*** +44 (0)20 7219 3000; ***e-mail:*** yasmin.qureshi.mp@parliament.uk.

R

RABBITTE, Pat; Minister of Community, Rural and Gaeltacht Affairs, Government of Ireland; ***born:*** 18 May 1949, Claremorris, Co. Mayo, Ireland; ***married:*** Derry (née McDermott); ***education:*** Univ. College., Galway, BA, HDipEd., LLB; ***political career:*** Pres., UCG Students' Union, 1970-71; Pres., Union of Students in Ireland, 1972-74; Nat. Sec., Irish Transport and General Workers Union, 1975-89; Mem., Irish Parliament, 1989-; Minister of State to the Gvt. at the Dept. of Enterprise, Trade and Employment, 1994-97; Dublin County Cncl., 1985-91; Labour Party Spokesperson on Enterprise, Trade and Employment, 1999-2002; Leader, Irish Labour Party, 2002-07; Justice Spoksperson, 2007-11; Minister of Community, Rural and Gaeltacht Affairs, Feb. 2011-; ***office address:*** Dáil Éireann, Leinster House, Dublin 2, Ireland; ***phone:*** +353 (0)1 618 3772; ***fax:*** +353 (0)1 618 4032; ***e-mail:*** pat.rabbitte@oireachtas.ie; ***URL:*** http://www.pobail.ie.

RADEBE, Jeff, LL.M; South African, Minister of Justice and Constitutional Development, South African Government; ***born:*** 18 February 1953, Durban, South Africa; ***parents:*** Fishela Radebe and Thembani Conco; ***married:*** Bridgette; ***children:*** Vukani (M), Mandisa (F); ***public role of spouse:*** Businesswoman; ***languages:*** Zulu, English, German, Xhosa; ***education:*** studied law, Univ. of Zululand; LL.M, int. law, Karl Marx Univ., Leipzig, 1981; Lenin Int. Sch., Moscow, Russian Federation, 1985; military training with Umkhonto we Sizwe (MK); ***party:*** ANC; SACP; ***political career:*** Member of the South African Students Organisation (Saso), and co-founder of the KwaMashu Youth Organisation 1972; joined the ANC underground during the student uprisings, 1976; left for Mozambique on the instruction of the ANC, 1977; represented the ANC in Tanzania, Zambia and Lesotho 1981-86; created underground ANC and SACP structures inside South Africa from Lesotho, giving political direction to activists; arrested in South Africa in 1986 under the Terrorism Act, and sentenced to ten years imprisonment, released in after six on appeal in 1990; active, ANC's political dept. on Robben Island, later Head of Dept., 1990; Dpty. Chmn., ANC Southern Natal, and sec., of the interim leadership group of the SACP 1991; Min. for Public Works 1994-99; Chmn., Regional ANC Peace Forum; Chmn., Nelson Mandela Millennium Fund, 1998; Min. of Public Enterprises, 1999-2004; Minister of Transport, 2004-09; Minister of Justice and Constitutional Development, 2009-; ***memberships:*** Mem., Business Trust, 1998-; ***professional career:*** served legal articles, Durban, 1976; Radio Journalist, Radio Freedom, Dar es Salaam, Tanzania, two years; Project Co-ordinator for the Nat. Assoc. of Democratic Lawyers (Nadel), 1990; Chllr., Eastern Cape Technikon, 1995-; ***committees:*** Chmn., Mandela's 80th Birthday Cttee.; Nat. Exec. Cttee., ANC.; Central Cttee., SACP; Mem., South African Exec. Cttee. (NEC) of the ANC and Provincial Exec. Cttee. (PEC) of KwaZulu-Natal; serves on the Natal Regional Dispute Resolution Cttee.; ***trusteeships:*** Chmn., Makana Trust; Chmn., Nelson Mandela Millenium Fund; ***honours and awards:*** Hon. Doctorate in Humane Letters, Chicago State Univ., 1996; ***office address:*** Ministry of Justice and Constitutional Development, Presidia Buiding, corner Paul Kruger and Pretorius Streets, Pretoria 0001, South Africa; ***phone:*** +27 (0)12 315 1111; ***URL:*** http://www.doj.gov.za.

RADER, Randall R.; Chief Judge, US Court of Appeals; ***education:*** Brigham Young Univ., AB, English, 1974; George Washington Univ. Law School, JD, 1978; ***professional career:*** Professor of Law; Counsel in the House of Representatives Interior, Appropriations, and Ways and Means Committees, 1975-80; Minority and Majority Chief Counsel to Subcommittees of the U.S. Senate Committee on the Judiciary; Appt to United States Claims Court (now the U. S. Court of Federal Claims), 1988; Apptd. to United States Court of Appeals for the Federal Circuit by President George H. W. Bush in 1990, Chief Justice, 2010-; ***office address:*** US Court of Appeals, 717 Madison Place, NW, Washington DC 20439, USA; ***phone:*** +1 202 275 8000; ***URL:*** http://www.cafc.uscourts.gov/.

RADICE, Lord Giles Heneage; British, Member, House of Lords; ***born:*** 4 October 1936; ***married:*** Lisanne Koch, 1971; ***education:*** Winchester; Magdalen Coll., Oxford; ***party:*** Labour Party; ***political career:*** MP, Chester-le-Street, 1973-83; PPS to Rt. Hon. Shirley Williams MP, 1978-79; Chmn., Parly. Labour Party Employment Gp., 1979-80, Opp.Spokesman on Employment, 1981-83, on Education, 1983-87; MP, Durham North, 1983-2001; ***professional career:*** Dir. Research Dept., GMWU 1966-73; MP (Lab.); Chmn. European Movement, 1995-2001; Bd. Mem., Britain in Europe, 1999-2005; ***committees:*** Mem. of Select Cttees. on Expenditure 1974-79, Procedure 1977-79, Employment 1979-81; Treasury 1987-95; Chmn., Public Services Select Cttee., 1995-97; Chmn., Treasury Select Cttee., 1997-2001; Chmn. House of Lords EU Economic and Monetary Sub Cttee, 2002-06; Mem., Lords EU Sub Cttee. on External Affairs, 2011-; Chmn., British Assoc. to Central and Eastern Europe, 1997-2008; Franco-British Council, 2002-07; Chmn. Policy Network, 2007-09; ***honours and awards:*** Elevated to the House of Lords, as Baron Radice, of Chester-le-Street in the County of Durham, May 2001-; Order of Merit, German Federal Rep., 1996; Chevalier, l'Ordre national Légion d'Honneur, 2004; ***publications:*** Will Thorne: Constructive Militant (with E. A. Radice) (1974); The Industrial Democrats: Trade Unions in an Uncertain World (1978); Socialists in the Recession (1986); Labour's Path to Power - The New Revisionism (1989); various Fabian Socy. pamphlets; Offshore, 1992; The New Germans, 1995; Editor, What Needs to Change, 1996; Friends and Rivals, 2002; Diaries 1980-2001, 2004; The Tortoise and the Hares, 2008; Trio, Blair, Brown and Mandelson, 2010; ***office address:*** House of Lords, London, SW1A 0PA, United Kingdom; ***phone:*** +44 (0)20 7219 3000; ***fax:*** +44 (0)20 7219 5679.

RADMANOVIC, Nejobsa; President, Government of Bosnia & Herzegovina; ***born:*** October 1949; ***education:*** Univ. of Belgrade; ***party:*** Alliance of Independent Social Democrats; ***political career:*** Rotating President of Bosnia & Herzegovina, 2006-; ***office address:*** Office of the President, Musala 5, 71000 Sarajevo, Bosnia & Herzegovina; ***phone:*** +387 3366 4941; ***URL:*** http://www.predsjednistvohih.ba.

RAFINI, Brigi; Prime Minister, Government of Niger; ***born:*** 1953; ***education:*** National School of Administration (ENA), Niamey, Niger; ***party:*** Nigerien Party for Democracy and Socialism; ***political career:*** Minister of Agriculture; Prime Minister, Apr. 2011-; ***office address:*** Office of the Prime Minister, BP 893, Niamey, Niger; ***phone:*** +227 20 72269; ***fax:*** +227 20 723859.

RAITT, Lisa; Minister of Labour, Government of Canada; ***born:*** 1968; ***education:*** St. Francis Xavier Univ., Nova Scotia; Masters, in Chemistry, Univ. of Guelph; LL.B, Osgoode Hall Law School; ***party:*** Conservative; ***political career:*** MP for Halton, Ontario, 2008-; Minister of Natural Resources, 2008-10; Minister of Labour, 2010-; ***professional career:*** Called to the Ontario Bar, 1998; ***office address:*** House of Commons, Parliament Buildings, Wellington Street, Ottawa, Ontario, K1A 0A6, Canada; ***phone:*** +1 613 943 5959.

RAJAPAKSA, Mahinda; President, Government of Sri Lanka; ***born:*** Weeraketiya, Sri Lanka; ***education:*** Nalanda Coll., Thurstan Coll., Colombo; ***political career:*** Elected MP for Beliatta, 1970; Minister for of Labour; Minister of fisheries; Minister of Ports and Shipping; PM and Minister of Highways, 2004-05; President, 2005-; Minister of Defence; Finance; Religious Affairs and Moral Upliftment, to date; ***professional career:*** Lawyer; ***committees:*** Pres., Sri Lankan Cttee. for Solidarity with Palestine; ***honours and awards:*** Prof. Emeritus, Vishva Bharathi Univ. of Calcutta; Sri Rohana Janaranjana, Malwatte Chapter; ***office address:*** Office of the President, Old Parliament Building, Colombo Fort, Sri Lanka.

RAJASA, Hatta; Co-ordinating Minister for Economy, Government of Indonesia; ***party:*** National Mandate Party; ***political career:*** Minister of Research and Technology, 2001-04; Minister of Transport, 2004-09; Co-ordinating Minister for Economy, 2009-; ***office address:*** Ministry of Finance, Jalan Lapangan Banteng Temur 4, Jakarta Pusat, Indonesia; ***phone:*** +62 (0)21 372758; ***URL:*** http://www.depkeu.go.id/ind.

RAJOY BREY, Mariano; Spanish, Prime Minister, Government of Spain; ***born:*** 27 March 1955, Santiago de Compostela, Spain; ***education:*** Univ. of Santiago, law; ***political career:*** Vice-Pres., Regional Cncl., Alianza Popular (AP); Pres., AP in Pontevedra; Pres., Local Cncl., AP; MP for Galician Autonomous Community, 1981; Dir., Institutional Relations, Galicia Cncl.; Vice-Pres., Cncl. of Galicia, 1986-87; Vice-Sec., Popular Party (PP); MP for Pontevedra in the V and VI Legislature; Minister for Public Admin., 1996-98; Minister for Education and Culture,

1999-2000; First Vice-Pres. & Minister for the Cabinet Office; First Vice-Pres. and Minister of the Interior, 2001-04; Leader, Partido Popular, 2004-; Prime Minister, Nov. 2011-; ***professional career:*** Property Registrar ; ***committees:*** mem., Standing Cttee. of the AP, 1987; mem., Nat. Exec. Cttee. for the PP, 1989-; ***office address:*** Prime Minister's Chancellery, Complejo de la Moncloa, Edif. INIA, Avda. de Hierro s/n, 28071 Madrid, Spain; ***phone:*** +34 91 335 3535; ***e-mail:*** portal.presidencia@mp.boe.es; ***URL:*** http://www.la-moncloa.es.

RAKHMONOV, Emomali Sharipovich; President, Republic of Tajikistan; ***born:*** 5 October 1952, Dangara, Tajikistan; ***political career:*** Dir., Sivkhoz, Dangar Region, Tajikistan, 1988-92; chair, Kulyab Regional Exec., 1992-94; Pres., Republic of Tajikistan, 1994-; ***professional career:*** Manager of a cotton farm; ***office address:*** Office of the President, pr. Rudaki 80, 734023 Dushanbe, Tajikistan.

RAMADHAR, Prakash; Minister of Legal Affairs, Government of Trinidad & Tobago; ***party:*** COP; ***political career:*** MP, 2010-; Ministry of Legal Affairs, 2010-; ***professional career:*** Attorney-at-law; ***office address:*** Ministry of Legal Affairs, 72-74 South Quay, Port of Spain, Trinidad and Tobago; ***phone:*** +1 868 625 4586; ***fax:*** +1 868 625 9803; ***URL:*** http://www.legal.gov.tt.

RAMBACHAN, Dr Surujarattan; Minister of Local Government & Minister of Works, Government of Trinidad & Tobago; ***party:*** UNC; ***political career:*** founding mem., Org. for National Reconstruction, Dep. Political Leader; Senator; MP, 2010-; Minister of Foreign Affairs, 2010-11; Minister of Foreign Affairs and Communications, 2011-12; Minister of Local Government, 2012-; Minister of Works & Infrastructure, 2013-; ***professional career:*** Amb. to Brazil; ***office address:*** Ministry of Local Government, Kent House, Long Circular Road, Maraval, Trinidad and Tobago; ***phone:*** +1 868 628 1325; ***fax:*** +1 868 622 7410; ***URL:*** http://www.localgov.gov.tt/.

RAMGOOLAM, Dr. The Hon. Navinchandra, GCSK, FRCP; Prime Minister, Government of Mauritius; ***born:*** 14 July 1947; ***parents:*** Rt. Hon. Sir Seewoosagur Ramgoolam, GCMG, PC, 1st Prime Minister of Mauritius (dec'd) and Lady Sushil Ramgoolam (dec'd); ***married:*** Veena Ramgoolam (née Brizmohun), 1979; ***education:*** Royal Coll. of Surgeons, Dublin, Ireland; LSE, LL.B (Hons; Hon. Fellow, 1998), UK; Inns of Court Sch. of Law, LRCP, LRCSI, 1975; called to the Bar, Inner Temple, 1993; ***party:*** Mauritius Labour Party (MLP); ***political career:*** MP, 1991-95; Leader of Opp., 1991-95; Prime Minister, Mauritius, 1995-2000, 2005-; ***professional career:*** Doctor and Lawyer; ***honours and awards:*** Honorary Fellow (LSE 1998); Dr Honoris Causa, Univ. of Mauritius 1998, Aligarh Muslim Univ. India, 1998, Jawaharlall Nehru Univ, India, 2005; Grand Officier de la Légion d'Honneur, France, 2006; Honorary Freeman of Rodrigues, 2007; Wilberforce Medal, Wilberforce Lecture Trust, UK, 2007; Rajiv Gandhi Award, 2007; Pravasi Bharatiya Samman Award, India, 2008; Grand Commander of the Order of the Star and Key of the Indian Ocean, Government of Mauritius, 2008; Prix Louise Michel, CEPS, Paris, 2008; Doctor of Science (Honoris Causa), Padmashree Dr D.Y. Patil University, Mumbai, 2009; Fellow of the Royal College of Physicians, London, 2009; ***recreations:*** reading, water-skiing; ***office address:*** Office of the Prime Minister, Treasury Building, Intendance Street, Port Louis, Mauritius; ***phone:*** +230 207 9452/53; ***fax:*** +230 201 2578; ***e-mail:*** primeminister@mail.gov.mu.

RAMLOGAN, Anand; Attorney General, Government of Trinidad & Tobago; ***born:*** 1972; ***education:*** Univ. of the West Indies; Queen Mary & Westfield College; Univ. of Westminister; ***political career:*** Appointed Senator, 2010; Attorney General, 2010-; ***professional career:*** Attorney, private practice; established own chambers, Freedom House; ***office address:*** Office of the Attorney General, Cabildo Chambers, Cor. Sackville & St. Vincents Street, Port of Spain, Trinidad and Tobago; ***phone:*** +1 868 623 7010 / 625 6531; ***fax:*** +1 868 625 0470; ***URL:*** http://www.ag.gov.tt/.

RAMOTAR, Hon. Donald; President, Government of Guyana; ***born:*** 1950; ***education:*** BSc., economics, Univ. of Guyana; ***party:*** Gen. Sec., People's Progressive Party - Civic Party, 1997-; ***political career:*** President, Dec. 2011-; ***professional career:*** Economist; ***office address:*** Office of the President, New Garden Street, Bourda, Georgetown, Guyana; ***phone:*** +592 225 7051; ***e-mail:*** hpssec@gmail.com; ***URL:*** http://www.op.gov.gy.

RAMSAUER, Dr Peter; Minister of Transport, Building and Urban Affairs, German Government; ***born:*** 1954; ***party:*** CSU; ***political career:*** Minister of Transport, Building and Urban Affairs, 2009-; ***office address:*** Ministry of Transport, Platz der Republik 1, 11011 Berlin, Germany; ***phone:*** +49 (0)30 227-0; ***fax:*** +49 (0)30 227 363 6878.

RANDALL, John; Member of Parliament for Uxbridge and South Ruiship, House of Commons; ***born:*** 5 August 1955, Ealing, UK; ***parents:*** Alec Albert Randall and Joyce Margaret Randall (née Gore); ***married:*** Katherine Frances Randall (née Gray), 25 October 1986; ***children:*** Peter (M), David (M), Elizabeth (F); ***languages:*** French, Russian, Serbo-Croatian; ***education:*** London Univ., Sch. of Slavonic & East European Studies, BA (Hons) Serbo-Croat Language and Literature; ***party:*** Conservative Party; ***political career:*** MP, Uxbridge, 1997-; Opposition Whip, 2000-03, 2003-05; Opposition Assistant Chief Whip, 2005-10; Deputy Chief Whip (Treasurer of HM Household), 2010-; ***interests:*** environment, foreign affairs; ***professional career:*** Managing Dir., Randalls at Uxbridge Ltd.; Tour Leader, Limosa Holidays; ***clubs:*** Uxbridge Conservative Club; ***recreations:*** ornithology & wildlife, opera, sport; ***office address:*** House of Commons, London, SW1A 0AA, United Kingdom; ***phone:*** +44 (0)20 7219 6885; ***e-mail:*** randallj@parliament.uk.

RANDERSON, Baroness Jenny; Member, House of Lords; ***party:*** Welsh Liberal Democrats; ***political career:*** Mem., National Assembly for Wales, Cardiff Central, 1999-; Minister for Culture, Sport and the Welsh Language, 2000-03; Vice pres., Liberal Democrats; Welsh Liberal Democrat Shadow Minister for Economy, Education and Transport; Mem., House of Lords, 2011-; Parly. Under Sec. of State, Wales Office, 2012-; ***committees:*** Enterprise and Learning Cttee.; Legislation Cttee. Number 2; Standards of Conduct Cttee.; ***office address:*** House of Lords, London, SW1A 0PW, United Kingdom; ***phone:*** +44 (0)20 7219 3000; ***e-mail:*** jenny.randerson@wales.gov.uk.

RANKIN, H.E. John; High Commissioner, British High Commission in Sri Lanka; ***professional career:*** Counsellor and Deputy Head of Mission, Dublin, Rep. of Ireland, 1999-2003; Consul General, Boston, USA, 2003-2007; High Commissioner to Sri Lanka and the Maldives, 2011-; ***office address:*** British High Commission, 389 Bauddhaloka Mawatha, Colombo 7, Sri Lanka; ***phone:*** +94 11 539 0639; ***fax:*** +94 11 539 0694; ***e-mail:*** bhctrade@slt.lk; ***URL:*** http://ukinsrilanka.fco.gov.uk/en.

RANN, H.E. Michael David, JP; High Commissioner, Australian High Commission; ***born:*** 1953; ***education:*** Auckland Univ. ; ***party:*** Labor Party of South Australia; ***political career:*** MP, South Australian Parliament, 1985-; Minister for Employment & Furthe Education, Youth Affairs, 1989-92; Minister for Business and Regional Development; Deputy Leader, Leader of the Opposition, 1996-2002; Premier, South Australia, 2002-11, also Minister for the Arts, Economic Development, Sustainability and Climate Change, and Social Inclusion; ***professional career:*** High Commissioner to the UK, 2012-; ***honours and awards:*** Companion of the New Zealand Order of Merit (CNZM); ***office address:*** Australian High Commission, Australia House, Strand, London, WC2B 4LA, United Kingdom; ***phone:*** +44 (0)20 7379 4334; ***fax:*** +44 (0)20 7240 5333; ***URL:*** http://www.uk.embassy.gov.au/lhlh/aboutus.html.

RÄSÄNEN, Päivi; Minister of the Interior, Government of Finland; ***born:*** 19 December 1959; ***education:*** Licentiate of Medicine, Univ. of Helsinki, 1984; ***party:*** Christian Democrats; ***political career:*** MP, 1995-; Minister of the Interior, 2010-; ***professional career:*** Physician; ***office address:*** Ministry of the Interior, Kirkkokatu 12, P.O. Box 26, 00023 Government, Finland; ***phone:*** +358 (0)9 160 2812; ***fax:*** +358 (0)9 160 2927; ***URL:*** http://www.intermin.fi.

RASI-ZADE, Artur Tair; Prime Minister, Republic of Azerbaijan; ***education:*** mechanical engineering; ***political career:*** Dept. Hd., Cttee., Communist Party, 1981-86; First Dep. PM, 1986-92, 1996; Aide to Pres. of Azerbaijan, 1996; Prime Minister, 1996-; ***professional career:*** engineer; ***office address:*** Office of the Prime Minister, Lermontov Street 63, 37006 Baku, Azerbaijan; ***phone:*** +994 (0)12 957528.

RASMUSSEN, Anders Fogh; Danish, Secretary General, NATO; ***born:*** 26 January 1953; ***parents:*** Knud Rasmussen and Martha Rasmussen (née Fogh); ***married:*** Anne-Mette Rasmussen (née Jacobsen), 1978; ***children:*** Henrik (M), Maria (F), Christina (F); ***languages:*** English; ***education:*** Univ. of Aarhus, economics, 1978; ***party:*** Liberal Party; ***political career:*** MP, 1978-; Vice-Chmn., Liberal Party, 1985-98; Minister for Taxation, 1987-92; Minister for Economic Affairs, 1990-92; Parly. Spokesman for Liberal Party, 1992-98; Chmn., Liberal Gp. in the Parl., 1998-2001; Pres. Liberal Party, 1998-; Vice-Chmn., Foreign Policy Bd., 1998-2001; Prime Minister, Denmark Govt., 2001-09; ***interests:*** economic and foreign policy; ***professional career:*** Economic Consultant, Danish Federation of Crafts and Small Industries, 1978-87; Secretary General, NATO, 2009-; ***committees:*** Vice-Chmn., Folketing's Housing Cttee., 1981-86; Mem., Folketing's Fiscal Affairs Cttee., 1982-87; Chmn., Liberal Party's Education Cttee., 1984-; Mem., Man. Cttee. of the Parly. Liberal Party, 1984-87 and 1992-2001; Vice-Chmn., Folketing's Economic and Political Affairs Cttee., 1993-98; Mem., Folketing's Fiscal Affairs Cttee., 1994-98; ***honours and awards:*** Grand Cross of the Portuguese Order of Merit, 1992; Commander of the first class of the Order of the Dannebrog, Danish Medal of Merit in Gold, Grand Cross of the German Order of Merit, 2002; Grand Cross of the Order of Merit of the Republic of Poland, 2003; Grand Cross of the Order of the Oak Crown of Luxembourg, 2003; Grand Cross of the Order of Nicaragua, 2003; The Great Cross of the Order Pedro Joaquí Chamorro, 2003; Ordinul Steaua Romaniei Mare Cruce, 2004; Grand Dutch Gedeminas, 2004, Lithuania; The Three-Star Order, 2005, Latvia; The Order of Stara Planina, 1st Class, Bulgaria, 2006; Grand Cross of the Nordstjarneorden, Sweden, 2007; Grand Cross of the Order of the South Cross, Brazil, 1007; Adam Smith Award, 1993; Liberal of the Year, Jongeren Organisatie Vrijheid en Democratie, Holland, 2002; Doctor H.C., George Washington Univ., 2002; Hon. Doctor of Laws, Hampden-Sydney Coll., Virginia, 2003; The European Leader, The European Promotional Competition "Euro Leader", 2003; European of the Year, The Danish European Movement, 2003; The Robert Schuman Medal, Gp. of the European People's Party & European Democrats in the European Parliament, 2003; Ordinus Steaua României Mare Cruce, 2004; Grand Dutch Gedeminas, 2004 (L.i.G.l - Lithuania); The Three Star Order, 2005, Latvia; The Best Leader in Denmark 2005, (Leaders in Scandinavia) Politician of the Year, 2005, (Dansk Erhvervssakhenslutning); Chevalier du Saint-Chinian, 2007; ***publications:*** Opgør med Skattesystemet; Fra socialstat til minimalstat; ***office address:*** North Atlantic Treaty Organization, Blvd. Leopold III, B 1110 Brussels, Belgium; ***URL:*** http://www.nato.int.

RASMUSSEN, Lars Løkke; Leader, Venstre Party; ***born:*** 15 May 1964; ***married:*** Sólrun Løkke Rasmussen; ***education:*** LL.B., Univ. of Copenhagen, 1992; ***party:*** Leader, Venstre; ***political career:*** National Chmn., Young Liberals, 1986-89; mem., Græsted-Gilleleje Municipal Council, 1986-97; MP, 1994-; Vice-Chair, Liberal Party, 1998; County Mayor of Frederiksborg County, 1998-2001; Minister for the Interior and Health, 2001-07; Minister of Finance, 2007-09; Prime Minister, 2009-11; ***publications:*** Foreningshåndbogen (The Association Manual), 1994; Hvis jeg bli'r gammel (If I Get Old), 1997; Løkkeland - Lars Løkke Rasmussen's Denmark, 2006; ***office address:*** Venstre Party, Søllerødvej 30, 2840 Holte, Denmark; ***phone:*** +45 4580 2233; ***fax:*** +45 4580 3830; ***e-mail:*** venstre@venstre.dk; ***URL:*** http://www.venstre.dk.

RASUL, Zalmay; Minister of Foreign Affairs, Government of Afghanistan; ***born:*** 1942; ***languages:*** French,, English,, Italian,, Pashto; ***political career:*** National Security Advisor of the Islamic Republic of Afghanistan; Minister of Foreign Affairs, 2010- ; ***office address:*** Ministry of Foreign Affairs, Malak Azghar Road, Kabul, Afghanistan; ***phone:*** +93 20 210 0366; ***URL:*** http://mfa.gov.af.

RAVI, Vayalar; Minister of Overseas Indian Affairs, Government of India; ***born:*** 1937; ***education:*** BA, MA; ***party:*** Indian National Congress; ***political career:*** Mem., Lok Sabha, 1971-79; mem., Kerala Legislative Assembly, 1982-91; mem., Rajya Sabha, 1994-; Minister for Overseas Indians Affairs, 2004-; Minister of Parliamentary Affairs, 2008-11; Minister of Civil Aviation, 2011-12, Minister of Micro, Small and Medium Enterprises, 2012-; ***office address:*** Ministry of Overseas Indians Affairs, New Delhi 110 011, India.

RAYNSFORD, Rt. Hon. Wyvill Richard Nicolls (Nick), MP; British, MP for Greenwich and Woolwich, House of Commons; ***born:*** 1945; ***parents:*** Wyvill John Macdonald Raynsford (dec'd) and Patricia Howell Raynsford (dec'd) (née Dunn); ***married:*** Anne Elizabeth Raynsford (née Jelley), 1968; ***children:*** Catherine Patricia (F), Laura Anne (F), Helen Daphne (F); ***languages:*** French; ***education:*** Chelsea Sch. of Art (Dip. Ad. Fine Art); MA (Cantab) History; ***party:*** Labour Party; ***political career:*** Councillor, London Borough of Hammersmith and Fulham, 1971-75; MP, for Fulham, 1986-87; MP, Greenwich 1992-97; Labour Spokesman on London, 1993-97; Shadow Housing Minister, 1994-97; MP, Greenwich and Woolwich, 1997-; Parly. Under-Sec. of State, Dept. of Environment, 1997-99; Minister of State, for Housing, Planning and London, July-Sept. 1999; Minister of State for Housing and Planning, July 1999- June 2001; Minister of State for Local and Regional Government, 2001-05; ***professional career:*** A.C. Nielsen Co. Ltd (Market Research), 1966-68; Socy. for Co-operative Dwellings, 1972-73; SHAC Housing Aid Centre, 1973-86; Raynsford and Morris, Housing Consultants, 1987-92; Chmn., Strategic Forum for Construction and Dep. Chmn., Construction Industry Council; Pres., Labour Housing Group; Pres., National Home Improvement Council; Pres., Youthbuild; Pres., Constructionarium; Vice-Pres., Town and Country Planning Assn.; Chmn., NHBC Foundation; Chmn Fire Protection Association Council; Chmn., Public Scrutiny; Chmn., London Open House Supporters at Large Group; Chmn., Rockpools; Non-exec. dir., Hometrack; ***committees:*** Members' Expenses, 2011-; ***honours and awards:*** Hon. Fellow of: Institution of Civil Engineers and the Institute of Structural Engineers, the Royal Institute of British Architects, the Royal Town Planning Institute, the Royal Institute of Chartered Surveyors and the Chartered Institute of Housing; ***publications:*** A Guide to Housing Benefit, 1982, 7th edition 1986; Contributor to journals inc. Building; Roof; Municipal Journal; ***recreations:*** photography; ***office address:*** House of Commons, London, SW1A 0AA, United Kingdom; ***phone:*** +44 (0)20 7219 2773; ***fax:*** +44 (0)20 7219 2619; ***e-mail:*** nick.raynsford.mp@parliament.uk.

RECKLESS, Mark; MP for Rochester and Strood, UK Government; ***party:*** Conservative; ***political career:*** Councillor, Medway Council 2007-; MP for Rochester and Strood, May 2010-; ***committees:*** Home Affairs Select Cttee., 2010-; ***office address:*** House of Commons, London, SW1A 0AA, United Kingdom; ***phone:*** +44 (0)20 7219 3000; ***e-mail:*** mark.reckless.mp@parliament.uk.

REDDY, Jaipal; Minister of Science and Technology, Government of India; ***born:*** 16 January 1942; ***education:*** Osmania Univ., Hyderabad, Bachelor of Journalism, MA; ***party:*** Indian National Congress Party (INC); ***political career:*** Minister, Information & Broadcasting, Culture, May 2004-06; Minister of Urban Development, 2006-11; Minister of Petroleum and Natural Gas, 2011-12; Minister of Science and Technology, Minister of Earth Sciences, 2012-; ***professional career:*** Agriculturist; ***recreations:*** reading; ***office address:*** Ministry of Science and Technology, Technology Bhavan, New Mehrauli Road, New Delhi 110 016, India; ***phone:*** +91 11 2656 7373; ***URL:*** http://www.mst.nic.in.

REDFORD, Alison, QC; Premier, Government of Alberta; ***education:*** Univ. of Saskatchewan, Coll. of Law, 1988; ***political career:*** MLA for Calgary-Elbow, 2008-; Minister of Justice and Attorney General, 2008-11; Premier, 2011-; ***office address:*** Office of the Premier, Legislative Building, Room 307, 10800 - 97 Avenue, Edmonton, Alberta, T5K 2B6, Canada; ***phone:*** +1 780 427 2251; ***fax:*** +1 780 427 1349; ***e-mail:*** Premier@gov.ab.ca; ***URL:*** http://www.gov.ab.ca/premier.

REDING, Viviane; Luxembourgeois, Vice President and Commissioner, European Commission; ***born:*** 1951, Esch-sur Alzette, Luxembourg; ***education:*** Sorbonne, Paris, France, Dr., human sciences; ***political career:*** MP, Luxembourg, 1979-89; Mem., Office of the Chamber of Deputies; MP, BENELUX; Mem., North Atlantic Assembly; Leader, Christian Democrat/Conservative Gp.; Communal Cllr., City of Esch, 1981-99; Nat. Pres., Christian Social Women, 1988-93; MEP, 1989-99; Head, Luxembourg Delegation to EPP; Mem., EPP Gp. Office; Vice-Pres., PCS, 1995-00; Mem., European Cmn., Education, Culture, Youth, Media and Sport, 1999-04; Cmnr. for Information Society and Media, 2004-09; Vice Pres., Cmnr. for Justice, Fundamental Rights and Citizenship, 2009-; ***professional career:*** Journalist, Editorialist, Luxemburger Wort, 1978-99; Pres., Luxembourg Union of Journalists, 1986-98; ***committees:*** Pres., Social Cttee.; Pres., Petitions Cttee., 1989-92; Pres., Cultural Affairs Cttee., 1992-99; Vice-Pres., Social Cttee., 1992-94; Vice-Pres., Civil Liberties and Internal Affairs Cttee., 1997-99; ***honours and awards:*** St George's Cross, Genrealitat of Catalunya, 1992; Gold Medal of European Merit, 2001; Dr honoris causa; Hu Chen Univ.,Taipei, Univ. of Torino, Univ. of Genoa, 2004; Robert Schuman Medal, 2004; Prince of Asturias Int. Cooperation Prize, 2004; Officer of the French Legion of Honour, 2005; Gloria Artis Medal of Honor, Poland. 2005; ***office address:*** European Commission, Rue de la Loi 200, B-1049 Brussels, Belgium; ***phone:*** +32 2 298 1600; ***fax:*** +32 2 299 9201; ***e-mail:*** viviane.reding@cec.eu.int; ***URL:*** http://ec.europa.eu/.

REDWOOD, Rt. Hon. John Alan, MP; British, MP for Wokingham, House of Commons; ***born:*** 1951; ***parents:*** William Charles Redwood and Amy Redwood (née Champion); ***married:*** Gail Felicity Redwood (née Chippington), 1974 (Div'd 2004); ***languages:*** French, Spanish; ***education:*** Kent Coll., Canterbury, MA; Magdalen Coll., Oxford, DPhil; ***party:*** Conservative Party; ***political career:*** County Cllr., Oxfordshire County Cncl., 1973-77; Head, PM's Policy Unit, 1983-85; MP, Wokingham, 1987-; Minister for Corporate Affairs, Dept. of Trade and Industry, 1989-90; Minister of State DTI, 1990-92; Minister of State, Dept. of Environment, 1992-93; Sec. of State for Wales, 1993-95; Ran for the Conservative Leadership, 1995 and 1997; Shadow Sec. of State for Trade & Industry, 1997-99; Shadow Sec. of State for Environment, Transport and the Regions, 1999-00; Head, Parliamentary Campaigns Unit., July 2000-June 2001; Shadow Secretary of State for Deregulation, 2004-05; ***interests:*** Europe, the economy, wider ownership; ***professional career:*** Fellow, Tutor, Lecturer, All Souls Coll, Oxford, 1972-73; Investment Analyst, Robert Fleming & Co., 1973-77; Investment Mgr., later Dir., N M Rothschild, 1977-83; Dir. and Head of Overseas Privatisation, N M Rothschild, 1986-87; Dir., later Non-Exec. Chmn., Norcros PLC., 1985-89; Prof., Middlesex Univ. Business Sch., 2000-; non-exec. Dir., BNB Resources Plc., 2001-07; non-exec. Chmn., Concentric Plc, 2003-07; Chmn. Pan Asset Capital Management Ltd., 2007-09; ***committees:*** Chmn. Economic Competitiveness Policy Review, 2005-09; Chmn., Backbench Economic Affairs Cttee.; ***honours and awards:*** Fellow, All Souls Coll., Oxford Univ., 1972-86, 2003-05, 2007-; ***publications:*** Reason, Ridicule and Religion; Going for Broke; Value for Money Audits, co-author; Controlling Public Industries co-author; Equity for Everyman; Public Enterprise in Crisis; Popular Capitalism; The Global Marketplace; Our Currency, Our Country; The Death of Britain; Stars & Strife; Just Say "No"; Third Way Which Way?; Singing the Blues; Superpower Struggles; I Want to Make a Difference; After the Credit Crunch; ***recreations:*** water sports, village cricket; ***office address:*** House of Commons, London, SW1A 0AA, United Kingdom; ***phone:*** +44 (0)20 7219 3000; ***e-mail:*** redwoodj@parliament.uk; ***URL:*** http://www.johnredwood.com.

REED, Jack; American, Senator for Rhode Island, US Senate; ***born:*** 1949, Providence, Rhode Island, USA; ***education:*** US Military Academy, West Point, B.Sc., 1971; JFK Sch. of Govt., Harvard Univ., Masters of Public Policy, 1973; Harvard Law Sch., 1982; ***party:*** Democrat; ***political career:*** Rhode Island Senate, 1984-91; US House of Representatives, 1991-97; US Senator for Rhode Island, 1996-; ***professional career:*** served in the 82nd Airborne Division, Fort Bragg, North Carolina 1973-77; Assoc. Prof., Dept. of Social Sciences, West Point; Sutherland, Asbill and Brennan, Washington D.C. law firm; Edwards & Angell, Providence, Rhode Island law firm; ***committees:*** US Senate: Armed Services; Banking, Housing & Urban Affairs; Appropriations; ***office address:*** US Senate, 728 Hart Senate Office Building, Washington, DC 20510, USA; ***phone:*** +1 202 224 4642; ***fax:*** +1 202 224 6253; ***URL:*** http://www.reed.senate.gov.

REED, Jamie; MP for Copeland, House of Commons; ***born:*** 1973; ***party:*** Labour; ***political career:*** MP for Copeland, 2005-; Shadow Minister, Environment, Food and Rural Affairs, Oct. 2010-11; Shadow Minister, Health, 2011-; ***office address:*** House of Commons, London, SW1A 0AA, United Kingdom.

REED, Steve; MP for Croydon North, British Parliament; ***education:*** Sheffield Univ.; ***political career:*** Leader, Lambeth Council, 2006-12; MP for Croydon North, 2012-; ***professional career:*** Educational publishing; ***office address:*** House of Commons, London, SW1A 0AA, United Kingdom; ***phone:*** +44 (0)20 7219 3000.

REES-MOGG, Jacob; MP for North East Somerset, UK Government; ***born:*** 1969; ***parents:*** William Rees-Mogg; ***education:*** Trinity Coll., Oxford Univ.; ***party:*** Conservative Party; ***political career:*** MP for North East Somerset, May 2010-; ***professional career:*** Founder, Somerset Capital Management; ***committees:*** Procedures, 2010-; European Scrutiny, 2010-; ***office address:*** House of Commons, London, SW1A 0AA, United Kingdom; ***phone:*** +44 (0)20 7219 3000; ***URL:*** http://www.parliament.uk.

REEVELL, Simon; MP for Dewsbury, UK Government; ***party:*** Conservative; ***political career:*** MP for Dewsbury, May 2010-; ***committees:*** Scottish Affairs, 2010-; ***office address:*** House of Commons, London, SW1A 0AA, United Kingdom; ***phone:*** +44 (0)20 7219 3000; ***e-mail:*** simon.reevell.mp@parliament.uk.

REEVES, Rachel; Shadow Chief Secretary to the Treasury, House of Commons; ***party:*** Labour; ***political career:*** MP for Leeds West, 2010-; Shadow Minister, Work and Pensions, Oct. 2010-11; Shadow Chief Secretary to the Treasury, 2012-; ***committees:*** Business, Innovation and Skills Select Cttee., 2010-; ***office address:*** House of Commons, London, SW1A 0AA, United Kingdom; ***phone:*** +44 (0)20 7219 3000; ***e-mail:*** rachel.reeves.mp@parliament.uk.

REGMI, Khil Raj; Prime Minister, Government of Nepal; ***born:*** 1949; ***political career:*** Interim Prime Minister, 2013-; ***professional career:*** Chief Justice, 2011-13; ***office address:*** Central Secretariat, Singha Durbar, Kathmandu, Nepal; ***phone:*** +977 1 422 8555; ***fax:*** +977 1 422 7286.

REHMAN, H.E. Sherry; Ambassador of Pakistan to the US, Embassy of Pakistan; ***political career:*** Central Info. Sec., Pakistan Peoples Party; Federal Minister for Information and Broadcasting, 2008-09; Federal Minister, -2011; ***interests:*** democracy; women; empowerment; media freedom; human rights; ***professional career:*** Journalist; Founding Chair, Jinnah Institute; Chair, Pakistan Red Crescent Soc; Amb. of Pakistan to the US, Nov. 2011-; ***office address:*** Embassy of the Islamic Republic of Pakistan, 3517 International Court, NW, Washington DC, 20008, USA; ***phone:*** +1 202 243 6500; ***URL:*** http://www.embassyofpakistanusa.org/.

REHN, Olli; Finnish, Vice President, European Commission; ***born:*** 31 March 1962, Mikkeli, Finland; ***married:*** Merja Rehn; ***children:*** Silva (F); ***languages:*** English, French, German, Swedish; ***education:*** Studies in economics, int. relations and journalism, Macalester College, St Paul, Minnesota, USA, 1982-83; Master of Soc. Sc. political science, Univ. of Helsinki, 1989; Univ. of Oxford, D.Phil., (int. political economy), 1996; ***party:*** Dep. Chmn., Centre Party of Finland; ***political career:*** City Council of Helsinki, 1988-94; MP, 1991-95; Special Adviser to the PM of Finland, 1992-93; MEP, 1995-96; Hd. of Cabinet, the European Commission, 1998-2002; Economic Policy Adviser to Finnish PM, 2003-04; Mem. of the European Commission, responsible for Enterprise and the Information Society, 2004; Mem. of the European Commission responsible for Enlargement, 2004-2010; Commissioner for Economic and Monetary Affairs, 2010-; ***memberships:*** Vice-Pres., European Movement of Finland, 1996-98; ***professional career:*** Columnist in several newspapers and magazines, 1985-; Chmn., Football League of Finland, 1996-97; Prof. and Director of Research, Dept. of Political Science and Centre for European Studies, Univ. of Helsinki; ***honours and awards:*** Commissioner of Year 2006 (E.Voice); Alumni of Year 2011, Univ., of Helsinki; ***publications:*** Europe's Next Frontier, 2006; ***recreations:*** rock and jazz, reading, reading; ***office address:*** European Commission, rue de la Loi 200, B-1049 Brussels, Belgium; ***phone:*** +32 (0)2 295 7957; ***fax:*** +32 (0)2 295 8561; ***URL:*** http://www.europa.eu.int/comm/commission_barroso/rehn/index_en.htm.

REID, Alan; Member of Parliament for Argyll & Bute, House of Commons; ***born:*** 7 August 1954; ***education:*** Ayr Academy; B.Sc. (Hons), Strathclyde Univ.; ***party:*** Liberal Democrat Party; ***political career:*** Cllr., Renfrew District Cncl, 1988-96; MP for Argyll & Bute, 2001-; ***memberships:*** AUT; ***professional career:*** Computer Programmer; ***committees:*** Scottish Affairs, 2010-; ***office address:*** House of Commons, London, SW1A 0AA, United Kingdom; ***phone:*** +44 (0)20 7222 7999; ***fax:*** +44 (0)20 7799 2170; ***e-mail:*** reida@parliament.uk; ***URL:*** http://www.argyllandbute-libdems.org.uk.

REID, Harry; American, Senator (Nevada), US Senate; ***born:*** 1939, Searchlight, Nevada, USA; ***parents:*** Harry Reid and Inez Reid; ***married:*** Landra Reid (née Gould), 1959; ***children:*** Lana (F), Rory (M), Leif (M), Josh (M), Key (M); ***education:*** Utah State Univ., 1961; George Washington Univ., Law degree; ***party:*** Democrat; ***political career:*** Nevada State Assembly, 1968; State Lt. Governor, 1970; US House of Representatives, 1983; US Senator for Nevada, 1986-; Assist. Majority Leader (Democratic Whip), 1998-2003; Assist. Minority Leader (Democratic Whip), 2003-2004; Minority Leader, 2004-207; Majority Leader, 2007-; ***professional career:*** City Attorney, Henderson, Nevada; Chmn., Nevada Gaming Cmn., 1977-82; ***committees:*** Environment and Public Works Cttee.; Appropriations Cttee.; Ageing Cttee.; Indian Affairs Cttee.; Vice-Chmn., Select Cttee. on Ethics; Chmn., Democratic Policy Cttee.; ***office address:*** United States Senate, 528 Hart Senate Office Building, Washington, DC 20510, USA; ***phone:*** +1 202 224 3542; ***URL:*** http://www.reid.senate.gov.

REID OF CARDOWAN, Rt. Hon. Lord John, MP, Ph.D; British, Member, House of Lords; ***born:*** 8 May 1947; ***parents:*** Thomas Reid (dec'd) and Mary Reid (dec'd) (née Murray); ***married:*** Catherine Reid (née McGowan), 1969 (dec'd); Carine Adler, 2002; ***children:*** Kevin (M), Mark (M); ***languages:*** French; ***education:*** Stirling Univ., History (Hons), Ph.D., Economic History; ***party:*** Labour Party; ***political career:*** Researcher for Labour Party, Scotland, 1979-1983; Political Adv. to Rt. Hon. Neil Kinnock MP, Leader of Opposition, 1983-85; full-time Official for Trade Unionists for Labour, 1985-87; MP, Motherwell North, 1987-97; MP, Hamilton North and Bellshill, 1997-2005; Minister of State for the Armed Forces, 1997-98; Minister of Transport, 1998-99; Sec. of State for Scotland, 1999-2001; Secretary of State for Northern Ireland, 2001-02; Party Chmn. & Minister without Portfolio, 2002-2003; Leader of the House of Commons and Pres. of the Cncl., 2003; Secretary of State for Health, June 2003-2005; MP, Airdrie and Shotts, 2005-10; Sec. of State for Defence, May 2005-06; Home Secretary, May 2006-June 2007; Member, House of Lords, 2010-; ***interests:*** defence, foreign affairs, the economy; ***professional career:*** Chair, Institute of Security and Resilience Studies; Chmn., Celtic Football Club ; ***committees:*** fmr. Joint Vice Chmn. of All-Party Gps.: Uganda, Belize, Azerbaijan and Russia; Mem. Balkans, Central Asia and Latin-American All-Party Gps.; ***honours and awards:*** Fellow of the Armed Forces Parly. Scheme; Hon Prof University College London; ***recreations:*** football, crossword puzzles; ***office address:*** House of Lords, London, SW1A 0AA, United Kingdom; ***phone:*** +44 (0)20 7219 3000.

REILLY, Dr James; Minister for Health, Government of Ireland; ***party:*** Fine Gael; ***political career:*** TD for Dublin North, 2007-; Minister for Health and Children, 2011-; ***professional career:*** General Practitioner; ***office address:*** Department of Health, Hawkins House, Hawkins Street, Dublin 2, Ireland; ***phone:*** +353 (0)1 635 4000; ***fax:*** +353 (0)1 635 4001; ***e-mail:*** info@health.gov.ie; ***URL:*** http://www.dohc.ie.

REINESCH, Gaston; Governor, Banque Centrale de Luxembourg; ***born:*** 1958; ***education:*** LSE, economics; ***professional career:*** Visiting Prof., Univ. of Luxembourg; Dir. Gen., Ministry of Finance, 1995-2012; Governor, Central Bank of Luxembourg, 2013-; mem., Gov. Council, ECB, 2013-; ***office address:*** Banque Centrale de Luxembourg, 2 boulevard Royal, L-2983, Luxembourg; ***URL:*** http://www.bcl.lu.

REINFELDT, Fredrik; Prime Minister, Government of Sweden; ***born:*** August 1965; ***public role of spouse:*** Local Council Chairwoman; ***education:*** B.Sc., Business Administration and Economics, Stockholm Univ., 1990; ***party:*** Moderate Party; ***political career:*** MP, 1991-; Prime Minister, Sept. 2006-; ***office address:*** Prime Minister's Office, Rosenbad 4, 103 33 Stockholm, Sweden; ***phone:*** +46 (0)8 763 1000; ***fax:*** +46 (0)8 723 1171.

RELVAS, Miguel; Minister Assistant and Minister of Parliamentary Affairs, Government of Portugal; ***born:*** 1961; ***party:*** Social Democratic Party (PSD); ***political career:*** MP, 1985-2009; Sec. of State for Local Admin, 15th Const. gov; Minister Assist. and of Parly. Affairs, 2011-; ***professional career:*** businessman, CEO of various co's; ***office address:*** National Assembly, Palácio de S. Bento, 1249-068 Lisbon, Portugal.

REMENGESAU, Thomas, Jr; President, Palau; ***born:*** 1956, Koror, Palau; ***education:*** Grand Valley State Univ., Michigan, USA; ***political career:*** Senator, Palau National Congress, 1984-92; Vice-President and Minister of Administration, 1992-2000; President, 2001-08, 2013-; ***office address:*** Office of the President, PO Box 100, PW 96940, Koror, Palau.

RENNARD, Lord Christopher John; Member of the House of Lords; ***born:*** 8 July 1960; ***married:*** Ann McTegart; ***education:*** Liverpool Blue Coat School, Liverpool Univ.; ***party:*** LDP; ***political career:*** Organiser Liverpool Mossley Hill Liberals, 1982-84; Area Agent for East Midlands Liberals, 1984-88; Mem., House of Lords; Dir. of Campaigns & Elections, Liberal Democrats, 1988-2003; Chief Exec., Liberal Democrats, 2003-09; mem., Lib. Dem. Front Bench teams on Constitutional Affairs and Communities and Local Government; ***honours and awards:*** MBE, 1989; Created Life Peer, 1999; ***recreations:*** cooking, wine, France; ***office address:*** House of Lords, London, SW1A 0PQ, United Kingdom; ***phone:*** +44 (0)20 7219 6717; ***e-mail:*** rennardc@parliament.uk.

RENTON OF MOUNT HARRY, Lord Ronald Timothy; British, Member of the House of Lords; ***born:*** 28 May 1932, London, UK; ***parents:*** Ronald Kenneth Duncan Renton CBE and Eileen Renton MBE (née Torr); ***married:*** Alice Renton (née Fergusson), 1960; ***children:*** Christian Louise Gudgeon (F), Katherine Chelsea Etherington (F), Penelope Sally Rosita (F), Alexander James Torr (M), Daniel Charles Antony (M); ***public role of spouse:*** Author and Arboriculturalist; ***languages:*** French, Italian; ***education:*** Eton (King's Scholar); Magdalen Coll., Oxford (Roberts Gawen Scholar), MA; ***party:*** Conservative Party; ***political career:*** Vice-Pres., Cons. Trade Unionists, 1978-79, Pres., 1980-84; PPS to Rt. Hon. John Biffen MP, 1979-81; PPS to Rt. Hon. Sir Geoffrey Howe, MP, 1983-84; Parly. Under-Sec. of State, FCO, 1984; Minister of State, FCO, 1985-87; Minister of State, Home Office, 1987-89; Govt. Chief Whip, 1989-90; Minister for the Arts, 1990-92; Minister of State and Minister for the Civil Service, 1990-92; Cons. MP for Mid-Sussex, 1974-97; Mem., House of Lords, 1997-; ***interests:*** arts and heritage, the environment, finance; ***memberships:*** APEX Gen. Advisory Cncl., BBC, 1982-84; Governing Cncl., Roedean Sch., 1982-97; Mem., Advisory Bd. of the Know-How Fund for Central and Eastern Europe; Mem., Devt. - Parnham Trust; Mem., Criterion Theatre Trust; Vice-Chmn., British Cncl., 1992-98, Bd. Mem., 1998-99; Chmn., Outsider Art, 1995-2002; ***professional career:*** Joined Tennant Sons & Co. Ltd, 1954; Tennants' Subsidiaries, Canada, 1957-62; Dir., C. Tennant Sons & Co. Ltd. and Managing Dir., Tennant Trading Ltd., 1964-73; Dir., Silvermines Ltd., 1967-84; Australia and New Zealand Banking Gp., 1967-76; Fellowship Industry and Parl. Trust Ltd, 1977-79; Fleming Continental European Investment Trust, 1992-99, Chmn, 1999-2007; Mem., BBC Gen. Adv. Cncl., 1982-84; Vice-Chmn., British Cncl., 1992-97; Mem., British Cncl. Board, 1997-99; Founder (with Mick Jagger), Nat. Music Day; Chmn., Outsider Art Archive, 1995-2000; Chmn., Sussex Downs Conservation Bd., 1998-2005; Pres., Governing Council, Brighton College, 2007-; Partner, Mount Harry Vines, 2006-; ***committees:*** Mem., Select Cttee. on Nationalised Industries ,1974-79; Vice-Chmn., Cons. Parly. Trade Cttee., 1974-79; Mem. Select Cttee. on Nat. Heritage; Chmn., Cons. Foreign and C'wealth Cncl., 1983-84; Chmn., All Party Cttee. on Hong Kong; Chmn., Sub-Cttee., Agriculture and Environment, House of Lords EC Cttee., 2004-07; Chmn., South Downs Jt. Cttee., 2005-09; Chmn., House of Lords Information Cttee., 2007-; House of Lords Constitution Cttee., 2010-; ***trusteeships:*** Mental Health Foundation, 1985; Pres. Governing Cncl. of Roedean Sch., 1998- (Mem., 1984-98); Mem. of Parnham Trust's Devt. Cncl.; Mem. of Know-How Fund Advisory Bd.; Trustee of Brighton West Pier, 1999-2005; Mem., Council of Univ. of Sussex, 2000-08; ***honours and awards:*** Privy Cllr.; Bowland Award for eminent contriution to Areas of Outstanding Natural Beauty, 2000-; ***publications:*** The Dangerous Edge, 1994; Hostage to Fortune, 1997; Chief Whip, 2004; ***clubs:*** Garrick, London; ***recreations:*** writing, listening to opera, cycling, sea fishing; ***office address:*** House of Lords, London, SW1A 0PW, United Kingdom; ***phone:*** +44 (0)20 7219 3000; ***fax:*** +44 (0)20 7219 5679; ***e-mail:*** rentont@parliament.uk.

REYNDERS, Didier; Deputy Prime Minister, Minister for Foreign Affairs, Foreign Trade and European Affairs, Government of Belgium; ***born:*** 6 August 1958, Liege; ***married:*** Bernadette Reynders (née Prignon), 1981; ***public role of spouse:*** Judge; ***languages:*** Dutch, English, French; ***education:*** Inst. Saint Jean Berchmans, Liège, Latin-Greek Humanities; Univ. of Liège, LL.B, 1981; ***party:*** Mouvement Réformateur (MR); ***political career:*** Chief of Staff Cabinet of the Dep. Prime Minister, Minister of Justice and Institutional Reforms, 1987-88; Town Cllr., Liège 1988; Leader, PRL gp. in the Provincial Council of Liége, 1991; Vice-Chmn., PRL 1992; Dep., House of Representatives, 1992; Mem. of the House, 1992-99; Head of the PRL Gp., Liège City Cncl. 1995-; Chmn., PRL-FDF Gp. in the Chamber, 1995; Chmn., Féd. Provinciale et d'Arrondissement de Liège, PRL 1995-; Minister of Finance, 1999-; Chmn., Euro Grp., 2001; Chmn., Ecofin, 2001; Chmn., G10, 2002-; Deputy Prime Minister, 2004-; Pres., Mouvement Réformateur (MS), 2004; Mem. of the bureau and treasurer of the Liberal International, 2005-; Minister of Institutional Reform, 2007-Dec. 2011; Deputy Prime Minister, Minister for Foreign Affairs, Foreign Trade and European Affairs, Dec. 2011-; ***professional career:*** Lawyer, 1981-85; Gen. Manager, Local Authority Dept., Min. of the Région Wallonne 1985-88; Chmn., Belgian Nat. Railway Co., (SNCB-NMBS) 1986-91; Chmn., Nat. Airport Co. 1991-93; Chmn. of the Bd. of Dirs., SEFB Record Bank, June 1992-July 1999; Lecturer, Hautes Ecoles Commerciales (business coll.), Liège; Staff mem., Public Law Dept., Univ. of Liège; ***honours and awards:*** Chevalier de l'Ordre de Leopold; ***office address:*** Ministry of Foreign Affairs, 15 rue de Petit Carmes, 1000 Brussels, Belgium; ***phone:*** +32 (0)2 501 8111; ***fax:*** +32 (0)2 514 3067; ***e-mail:*** info@diplobel.orf; ***URL:*** http://www.didier-reynders.org.

REYNOLDS, Emma; MP for Wolverhampton North East, UK Government; ***party:*** Labour; ***political career:*** MP for Wolverhampton North East, May 2010-; Shadow Minister, Foreign and Commonwealth Affairs, Oct. 2010-11; ***committees:*** Foreign Affairs Select Cttee., 2010; Arms Export Control, 2010-11; ***office address:*** House of Commons, London, SW1A 0AA, United Kingdom; ***phone:*** +44 (0)20 7219 3000; ***e-mail:*** emma.reynolds.mp@parliament.uk.

REYNOLDS, Jonathan; MP for Stalybridge and Hyde, UK Government; ***party:*** Labour; ***political career:*** Councillor, Tameside Council, 2007-; MP for Stalybridge and Hyde, May 2010-; ***committees:*** Science and Technology Select Cttee., 2010-12; Finance and Services, 2010-12; Standing Orders, 2011-; ***office address:*** House of Commons, London, SW1A 0AA, United Kingdom; ***phone:*** +44 (0)20 7219 3000; ***e-mail:*** jonathan.reynolds.mp@parliament.uk.

RIBEIRO, Lord Bernard; Member, House of Lords; ***party:*** Conservative Party; ***political career:*** Mem., House of Lords, 2011-; ***professional career:*** Consultant Surgeon; Chmn., Research Review Panel, Pelican Cancer Foundation; ***honours and awards:*** Raised to the peerage as Baron Ribeiro, of Achimota in the Republic of Ghana and of Ovington in the County of Hampshire; ***office address:*** House of Lords, London, SW1A 0PW, United Kingdom; ***phone:*** +44 (0)20 7219 3000.

RICE, Ambassador Susan; US Permanent Representative to the United Nations; ***political career:*** US Assist. Sec. of State for African Affairs, 1997-2001; ***professional career:*** Dir. for International Orgs. and Peacekeeping, National Security Council, 1993-95; Special Assist. to President Clinton, 1995-97; Senior Dir., African Affairs, National Security Council, the White House, 1995-97; Senior Fellow, Brookings Institution, 2002-09; Senior Advisor for National Security Affairs on the Obama for America Campaign; Permanent Representative of US to the UN, 2009-; ***office address:*** Permanent Mission of the US to the UN, 799 United Nations Plaza, New York, NY 10017-3505, USA; ***phone:*** +1 212 415 4000; ***fax:*** +1 212 415 4443; ***URL:*** http://usun.state.gov/.

RICH, Roland; Australian, Executive Head, United Nations Democracy Fund; ***professional career:*** Diplomat; Academic; Legal Adviser to International Orgs.; Australian Defence College; Research Fellow, National Endowment for Democracy, Washington DC, 2005; Dir., Centre for Democratic Institutions, Australian National Univ., 1998-2005; Exec. Head, UNDEF, 2007-; ***office address:*** UNDEF, 1 United Nations Plaza, Room DC1 1300, New York, NY 10017, USA; ***URL:*** http://www.un.org/democracyfund/.

RICHARDS, Sir Francis Neville; British, Director, Centre for Studies in Security and Diplomacy; ***born:*** 1945; ***parents:*** Sir Brooks Richards (dec'd) and Lady Richards (dec'd) (née Williams); ***married:*** Gillian Richards (née Nevill), 1971; ***children:*** Joanna Catherine (F), James Nevill (M); ***languages:*** Russian, French; ***education:*** Eton College; Cambridge Univ., MA, History and Economics; ***professional career:*** Regular Army (Royal Green Jackets), 1967-69; Third (later Second) Sec., Embassy, Moscow, 1971-73; Second (later First)

Sec., UK Delegation to MBFR talks, Vienna, 1973-76; Foreign and Commonwealth Office (FCO), 1976-85; Economic - Commercial Cllr., New Delhi, 1985-88; Head, South Asia Dept., FCO, 1988-90; High Commissioner, Windhoek, 1990-92; Minister, Moscow, 1992-95; Asst. Under Sec. of State, (Central & Eastern Europe) FCO, 1995-97; Deputy Under Secretary of State, Foreign and Commonwealth Office, 1998; Director, GCHQ, 1998-2003; Governor and Commander in Chief, Gibraltar, 2003-06; Hon. Snr. Fellow, Univ. of Birmingham; Former Chmn., Bletchley Park Trust; Chmn., National Security Inspectorate; Chmn., Int. Advisory Boad, Altimo SA, 2007-; *trusteeships:* Trustee, Imperial War Museum, Dep. Chmn. 2009-; *honours and awards:* Commander, Royal Victorian Order (CVO) 1990; Companion, Order of St. Michael & St. George CMG, 1993; KCMG, 2002; Knight of Order of St. John, 2003; Hon, Doctor of the University, Univ. of Birmingham, 2012; Hon. Colonel of Cat Sp Regt RLC (TA), 2012; *clubs:* Special Forces; Brooks's; *recreations:* riding, travel; *office address:* Imperial War Museum, Lambeth Road, London, SE1 6HZ, United Kingdom.

RICKETTS, Sir Peter; Ambassador of the UK to France, British Embassy, Paris; *professional career:* Numerous diplomatic postings incl. Singapore and Hong Kong; Cabinet Office, 2000, Chmn., Joint Intelligence Cttee., 2000, FCO Political Director; UK Perm. Rep. to NATO in Brussels, 2003; Perm. Under Sec. & Head of the Diplomatic Service, FCO, 2006-10; National Security Advisor; Amb. to France, 2012-; *office address:* Embassy of the UK to France, 35 rue de Faubourg Saint Honoré, 75383 Paris Cedex 08, France; *URL:* http://ukinfrance.fco.gov.uk/en/.

RIDLEY, Viscount Matthew White, DL; Member, House of Lords; *party:* Conservative; *political career:* Mem., House of Lords, 2013-; *professional career:* Author; Chmn. Northern Rock, 2004-07; *office address:* House of Lords, London, SW1A 0AA, United Kingdom; *phone:* +44 (0)20 7219 3000.

RIFKIND, Rt. Hon. Malcolm Leslie, KCMG,QC, MP; British, MP for Kensington, House of Commons; *born:* 21 June 1946; *parents:* Elijah Rifkind and Ethel Rifkind (née Cohen); *married:* Edith Amalia Rifkind (née Steinberg), 1970; *education:* George Watson's Coll., Edinburgh Univ., LL.B, M.Sc.; *party:* Conservative; *political career:* Conservative MP for Edinburgh Pentlands, 1974-1997; Opposition Front Bench Spokesman on Scottish Affairs, 1975-76: Hon. Pres., Scottish Young Conservatives, 1976-77; Mem., Select Cttee. on Overseas Development, 1977-79; Sec., Cons. Parly. Foreign and Commonwealth Affairs Cttee., 1977-79; Minister for Home Affairs and the Environment at the Scottish Office, 1979-82; Parly. Under-Secy. of State, FCO, 1982-83, Minister of State, FCO, 1983-86; Queen's Counsel, 1985; Privy Councillor, 1986; Secy. of State for Scotland, 1986-90; Secy. of State for Transport, 1990-92; Secretary of State for Defence, 1992-95; Secy. of State for Foreign and Commonwealth Affairs, 1995-97; Pres., Scottish Conservatives; MP for Kensington and Chelsea, 2005-10, Kensington, 2010-; Shadow Sec. of State for Work and Pensions, May 2005; Chmn., Intelligence and Security Cttee., 2010-; *memberships:* Royal Company of Archers, Queen's Body Guard for Scotland, 1992; *professional career:* Lectured at Univ. of Rhodesia, 1967-68; Visiting Pro, Institute for Advance Studies in the Humanities, Edinburgh Univ., 1998; Admitted to the Scottish Bar 1970 ; *clubs:* Pratt's; *recreations:* walking, reading, field sports; *office address:* House of Commons, London, SW1A 0AA, United Kingdom.

RIMSEVICS, Ilmars; Governor, Bank of Latvia; *born:* 1965; *education:* Riga Technical Univ.; St. Lawrence Univ., USA; Clarkson Univ., USA, MBA; *professional career:* Manager, Foreign Operations Dept., Latvijas Zemes Banka, Head, Securities Dept., 1990-92; Dep. Gov., Supreme Council of the Republic of Latvia, 1992-2001, Chmn. of the Board, 1992-; Governor, 2001-; *office address:* Bank of Latvia, K Valdemara iela 2A, Riga LV-1050, Latvia; *URL:* http://www.bank.lv.

RINKEVICS, Edgars; Minister of Foreign Affairs, Government of Latvia; *born:* 21 September 1973; *education:* BA, 1995, MA, in political science, 1997, Univ. of Latvia; *party:* Zatlers' Reform Party; *political career:* Minister for Foreign Affairs, 2011-; *office address:* Ministry of Foreign Affairs, K.Valdemara iela 3, Riga LV-1395, Latvia; *phone:* +371 6701 6201; *e-mail:* mfa.cha@mfa.gov.lv; *URL:* http://www.am.gov.lv.

RIORDAN, Linda; MP for Halifax, House of Commons; *born:* 1953; *party:* Labour/Co-operative; *political career:* MP for Halifax, 2005-; *committees:* Environmental Audit, 2005-10; Crossrail Bill, 2006-07; Procedure, 2006-10; Justice, 2008-12; Chairmen's Panel/Panel of Chairs, 2010-; *office address:* House of Commons, London, SW1A 0AA, United Kingdom.

RISBY OF HAVERHILL, Lord Richard; British, Member, House of Lords; *born:* 1946; *education:* Cape Town Univ.; Magdalene Coll., Cambridge; *party:* Conservative Party; *political career:* Parly. candidate, Ashton-Under-Lyne, 1983; MP, Bury St. Edmunds, 1992-97; PPS to Sir Patrick Mayhew MP, 1994-95, to Tim Eggar MP, to Nicholas Soames MP, to James Arbuthnot MP; MP, West Suffolk, 1997-2010; Mem., House of Lords, 2011-; *professional career:* Co. Man. Dir.; *office address:* House of Lords, London, SW1A 0PW, United Kingdom; *phone:* +44 (0)20 7219 3000; *e-mail:* richardspring@richardspring.com.

RISCH, James E.; Senator for Idaho, US Senate; *political career:* State senator (11 terms); Three years as the Lieutenant Governor and President of the Senate, to 2006; Governor, 2006-07; Lt. Gov., 2007; US Senator, 2008-; *professional career:* Ada County Prosecuting Attorney; *committees:* Energy & Natural Resources; Foreign Relations; Select Cttee. on Intelligence; Select Cttee. on Ethics; Small Business & Enterprise; *office address:* US Senate, Washington, USA; *URL:* http://www.risch.senate.gov.

RISIKKO, Paula; Minister of Health and Social Services, Government of Finland; *born:* 1960; *education:* Doctor of Science (Health Care); *party:* National Coalition Party; *political career:* Mem., Seinäjoki City Cncl. 2001-; MP, 2003-; Minister of Health and Social Services, Apr. 2007-; *professional career:* Nurse; *office address:* Ministry of Health and Social Services, PO Box 33, FI-00023 Government, Helsinki, Finland; *phone:* +358 9 16001; *e-mail:* kirjaamo.stm@stm.fi; *URL:* http://www.stm.fi.

RITCHIE, Margaret; MP for South Down, British Parliament; *party:* Social Democratic and Labour Party; Leader 2010-11; *political career:* Down District Council member, 1985-; MLA, South Down; Minister for Social Development, May 2007-10; MP for South Down, 2010-; *committees:* Environment, Food and Rural Affairs, 2012-; *office address:* Constituency Office, 32 Saul Street, Downpatrick, BT30 6NQ, United Kingdom; *phone:* +44 (0)28 9052 1333; *e-mail:* margaret.ritchie.mp@parliament.uk.

RITZ, Gerry; Member of Parliament for Battlefords, Lloydminster, Canadian House of Commons; *political career:* MP for Battlefords, Lloydminster, 1997-; Minister of Agriculture and Agri-Food and Minister of the Canadian Wheat Board, 2007-; *office address:* House of Commons, Parliament Buildings, Ottawa, ON K1A 0A6, Canada.

RIVAS, Dante; Minister of the Environment, Government of Venezuela; *born:* 1975; *education:* Univ. of Los Andes, Merida State; *political career:* Minister of the Environment, 2013-; *professional career:* Geographer; *office address:* Ministry of the Environment, Torre Sur, Piso 18, Centro Simón Bolívar, Caracas 1010, Venezuela; *URL:* http://www.danterivas.org.

RIVKIN, H.E. Charles; Ambassador, US Embassy in France; *education:* BA, Yale Univ. USA, 1984; MBA, Harvard Univ., USA 1988; *professional career:* President and CEO, The Jim Henson Company; Amb. to France and Monaco, 2009-; *office address:* American Embassy, 2 avenue Gabriel, 75008 Paris, France; *phone:* +33 (0)1 43 12 22 22; *fax:* +33 (0)1 42 66 97 83; *URL:* http://france.usembassy.gov.

RIVLIN, Reuven; Knesset Member, Parliament of Israel; *born:* 1939, Jerusalem. Israel; *education:* Hebrew Univ. of Jerusalem, L.L.B. degree; *party:* Likud; *political career:* Knesset Member, 1988-; Minister of Communications, 2001-2003; Knesset Speaker, 2003-06, 2009-13; *memberships:* Fmr. mem., of the Jerusalem Muncipal Cncl.; Mem., El Al Exec. Cncl., 1981-86; Chmn., Likud Organization, 1988-93; Chmn. of the Jerusalem Branch of the Herut Movement, 1986-; *professional career:* Legal Adviser, Chmn. and team mgr. of the Betar Jerusalem Sports Assn.; *committees:* Knesset Cttee.; Foreign Affairs and Defense; Constitution, Law and Justice; State Control; Anti-Drug Abuse; Education and Culture; Advancement of the Status of Women; Cttee. for Appointing Judges; Cttee. for the Examination of the Maccabia Bridge Disaster; Parly. Inquiry cttee. on the Continuing Financial Crisis of the Local Govts; Parly. Inquiry Cttee. on Violence in Sports; *trusteeships:* Fmr. mem. of the Bd. of Trustees for the Khan Theater and a mem. of the Bd. of Trustees of the Israel Museum in Jerusalem; *office address:* The Knesset, Qiyat Ben-Gurion, 91950 Jerusalem, Israel.

ROA, Ruth Tapia; Secretary-General of Defence, Government of Nicaragua; *political career:* Sec.-Gen. of Defence; *professional career:* Spokeswoman, Nicaraguan Supreme Court; Ambassador of Nicaragua to France; *office address:* Ministry of Defence, Del Hotel Intercontinental 2 c. al Sur, 1 c. Oeste, Managua, Nicaragua; *phone:* +505 266 3580; *URL:* http://www.midef.gob.ni/.

ROBATHAN, Andrew; British, Member of Parliament for South Leicestershire, House of Commons; *born:* 17 July 1951; *parents:* Douglas and Sheena (née Gimson); *married:* Rachael Maunder, 1991; *children:* Kit (M), Camilla (F); *languages:* French, German; *education:* Merchant Taylors Sch., Northwood; Oriel Coll., Oxford, BA, (Modern History, 1973, MA); RMA, Sandhurst; *party:* Conservative Party; *political career:* Cllr., Hammersmith and Fulham, 1990-92; PPS to Iain Sproat MP; MP, Blaby, 1992-10; Shadow Minister for Dept. of Trade and Industry, 2002-03; Shadow Minister for Int. Dev., 2003; Shadow Minister for Defence, 2004-05; Dep. Chief Whip, 2005-10; MP for South Leicestershire, 2010-; Parly. Under Sec. of State for Defence Personnel, Welfare and Veterans, 2010-12; Minister of State for the Armed Forces, 2012-; *interests:* transport, defence, environment, Northern Ireland; *memberships:* Captain, HOC Tug of War Team, 1995-2000; Captain, HOC Clay Pigeon Team, 1997-2007; *professional career:* Army Officer, 1974-89, 1991; *committees:* Mem., Employment Select Cttee., 1992-94; Chmn. Cons. Def. Ctte. 1994-95, Vice Chmn. 1997-01; Vice-Chmn., Conservative Northern Ireland Cttee.; Mem. Int. Development Cttee. 1997-2002; *trusteeships:* The Halo Trust, 1999-06, Chmn., 2003-06; *honours and awards:* Freeman of the City of London; *office address:* House of Commons, London, SW1A 0AA, United Kingdom; *phone:* +44 (0)20 7219 3000; *e-mail:* hcinfo@parliament.uk.

ROBERTS, Dr Carl; High Commissioner, Antigua and Barbuda High Commission; *professional career:* High Commissioner of Antigua and Barbuda in the UK, 2004-; *office address:* High Commission of Antigua and Barbuda, Antigua House, 15 Thayer Street, London, W1M 5LD, United Kingdom; *phone:* +44 (0)20 7486 7073/5; *fax:* +44 (0)20 7486 9970; *e-mail:* antiguabarbudaUK@hotmail.com.

ROBERTS, John G., Jr.; Chief Justice, United States Supreme Court; *born:* 27 January 1955, Buffalo, NY; *education:* Harvard College, A.B., 1976; Harvard Law School, J.D., 1979; *professional career:* Associate Counsel to President Reagan, White House Counsel's Office, 1982-86; Practiced law in Washington D.C., 1986-89 and 1993-2003; Principal Deputy Solicitor General, U.S. Department of Justice, 1989-93; US Court of Appeals for the District of Columbia Circuit, 2003-05; Chief Justice of the USA, 2005-; *office address:* Supreme Court of the United States, Supreme Court Building, One First Street, NE, Washington, DC 20543, USA; *phone:* +1 202 479 3211; *URL:* http://www.supremecourt.gov/.

ROBERTS, Pat; American, Senator for Kansas, US Senate; *born:* 20 April 1936, Topeka, Kansas, USA; *parents:* Wes Roberts (dec'd) and Ruth Patrick Roberts (dec'd); *married:* Franki Roberts; *children:* David (M), Ashleigh (F), Anne-Wesley (F); *education:* Kansas State Univ., grad., 1958; *party:* Republican; *political career:* joined staff of Kansas Senator, 1967; Admin. Asst. to First District Congressman, 1969; US House of Representatives for eight terms, Kansas 1st District, 1980 onwards; US Senator for Kansas, 1996-; *professional career:* US Marine Corps, 1958-1962; Reporter and Editor for several Arizona newspapers, 1962-1967; *committees:* Chmn., Agriculture, Nutrition and Forestry Cttee.; Select Cttee. on Ethics; Finance; Health, Education, Labor and Pensions; Rules and

Administration; ***honours and awards:*** recipient of many tax-cutting awards; ***office address:*** US Senate, 302 Hart Senate Office Building, Washington, DC 20510, USA; ***phone:*** +1 202 224 4774; ***fax:*** +1 202 224 3514; ***URL:*** http://www.roberts.senate.gov.

ROBERTS OF CONWY, Lord; Member of the House of Lords; ***born:*** 10 July 1930; ***parents:*** Rev. E.P. Roberts and Margaret; ***married:*** Enid (née Williams), 1956; ***languages:*** German, Welsh; ***education:*** Harrow Sch.; Univ. Coll., Oxford; ***party:*** Conservative Party; ***political career:*** MP, Conwy, 1970-97; Privy Cllr., 1991; Mem. of House of Lords; ***professional career:*** Television executive; ***honours and awards:*** knighted, 1990; ***office address:*** House of Lords, London, SW1A 0PQ, United Kingdom; ***phone:*** +44 (0)20 7219 3000; ***fax:*** +44 (0)20 7219 5979.

ROBERTSON, Angus; MP for Moray, House of Commons; ***education:*** Broughton High Sch, Edinburgh, 1981-87; Aberdeen Univ., MA (Hons), Politics and International Relations, 1987-91; ***party:*** SNP; ***political career:*** MP, Moray, 2001-; ***memberships:*** SNP International Bureau; ***professional career:*** BBC Reporter, Austria; ***office address:*** House of Commons, London, SW1P0AA, United Kingdom.

ROBERTSON, Hugh; Minister of State for Sport and Tourism, UK Government; ***born:*** 9 October 1962, Canterbury, UK; ***married:*** Anna Copson, 17 May 2002; ***children:*** James (M); ***public role of spouse:*** Art Valuer; ***education:*** The Kings Sch., Canterbury; Land Management, Reading Univ.,1982-85; RMA Sandhurst, 1985-86; ***party:*** Conservative Party; ***political career:*** MP, Faversham and Mid Kent, 2001-; Cons. Whip, 2002-04; Sports Spokesman, 2004-05; Shadow Sports and Olympic Minister, 2005-10; Gov., Westminster Foundation for Democracy, 2005-08; Parly. Under Sec. of State (Sport and the Olympics), 2010-12; Minister of State for Sport and Tourism, 2012-; ***interests:*** foreign affairs, defence, fruit farming, sports; ***professional career:*** Army officer, 1985-95, (active service: Northern Ireland 1987, UN Cyprus, 1988, Gulf War, 1991, Bosnia, 1994); Schroder Investment Management, 1995-2001, (Assist. Dir., 1999-2001); ***honours and awards:*** Armourers' and Brasiers' Prize, 1986; Sultan of Brunel's Personal Order of Merit; Fellow, Royal Geographical Soc.; ***office address:*** House of Commons, London, SW1A 0AA, United Kingdom; ***phone:*** +44 (0)20 7219 3000; ***e-mail:*** hcinfo@parliament.uk; ***URL:*** http://www.parliament.uk.

ROBERTSON, John; MP for Glasgow North West, Scottish Parliament; ***political career:*** MP, Glasgow Anniesland, 2000-05, Glasgow North West, 2005-; PPS, 2005-; ***committees:*** Scottish Affairs, 2001-05; European Scrutiny, 2003-05; Energy and Climate Change, 2009-;Chairmen's Panel/Panel of Chairs, 2010-; ***office address:*** House of Commons, London, SW1A 0AA, United Kingdom; ***phone:*** +44 (0)20 7219 6964; ***fax:*** +44 (0)20 7219 1096; ***e-mail:*** robertsonjo@parliament.uk.

ROBERTSON, Laurence; British, Member of Parliament for Tewkesbury, House of Commons; ***born:*** 29 March 1958; ***parents:*** James Robertson and Jean Robertson (née Larkin); ***married:*** Susan Robertson; ***education:*** St. James C.E. Secondary; Farnworth Grammar; Bolton Inst. of Higher Education; ***party:*** Conservative Party; ***political career:*** Party Candidate, Makerfield, 1987, Ashfield, 1992; MP, Tewkesbury, 1997-; Opp. Whip's Office, 2001-03; Shadow Industry Minister, 2003-05; Shadow Northern Ireland Minister, 2005-10; ***interests:*** constitution, education, economy, European policy (anti-federalist), Northern Ireland, the countryside; ***professional career:*** Industrialist; ***committees:*** Environment Audit, 1997-99; Social Security Select Cttee., 1999-01; European Scrutiny Cttee., 1999-01; 1922 Executive, 1999-2001; Northern Ireland, 2010-; Liaison, 2010-; ***recreations:*** horse racing, golf, the countryside; ***office address:*** House of Commons, London, SW1A 0AA, United Kingdom; ***phone:*** +44 (0)20 7219 3000; ***e-mail:*** robertsonl@parliament.uk.

ROBINSON, Hon. Eric; Minister of Aboriginal and Northern Affairs, Government of Manitoba; ***married:*** Catherine Robinson; ***children:*** Shaneen (F); ***political career:*** NDP critic for Native Affairs and for the aboriginal Justice Enquiry; Worked at the Assembly of First Nations and the Brotherhood of Indian Nations, among other aboriginal organisations; Researcher, Aboriginal Justice Enquiry; Elected NDP MLA for Rupertersland, 1993, 1995; Minister of Aboriginal and Northern Affairs, also Minister charged with the administration of The Communities Economic Development Fund Act, 1999-2003; Pres., Vice.Pres. and dir. of many political organisations; Minister of Culture, Heritage and Tourism, Minister responsible for Sport, 2003-; Acting Minister of Aboriginal Affairs and Northern Affairs, Acting Minister charged with the administration of The Communities Economic Development Fund Act, 2008-2010; Deputy Premier, Minister of Aboriginal and Northern Affairs, Minister responsible for Sport, Aboriginal Education and the East Side Road Authority, 2010-; ***professional career:*** Broadcaster and Producer, CBC North Country, Churchill and Thompson in Cree and English; Worked for Native Communications Incorporated broadcasting in northern and southern Manitoba; Founder, Native Media Network; Facilitator and Master of ceremonies for many traditional and cultural events; ***publications:*** co-author, Infested Blanket; ***office address:*** Ministry of Aboriginal and Northern Affairs, 344 Legislative Building, 450 Broadway Avenue, Winnipeg, Manatoba R3C 0V8, Canada; ***e-mail:*** minem@leg.gov.mb.ca; ***URL:*** http://www.gov.mb.ca/.

ROBINSON, Rt. Hon. Geoffrey, MP; British, Member of Parliament for Coventry North West, House of Commons; ***born:*** 1938; ***married:*** Marie Elena Giorgio, 1968; ***s:*** 1; ***d:*** 1; ***languages:*** French, German, Italian; ***education:*** Cambridge Univ.; Yale Univ.; ***party:*** Labour Party; ***political career:*** Labour Party Research Asst., Transport House, 1965-68; Opp. Spokesman on Science, 1982/83; Opp. Spokesman on Regional Affairs, 1983-85; Opp. Spokesman on Industry, 1984-87; Paymaster General, 1997-98; MP, Coventry North-West, 1976- ; ***professional career:*** Snr. Exec., Industrial Reorganisation Corp. 1968-70; Financial Controller, British Leyland 1970-72; Man. Dir., Leyland Innocenti 1972-73; Chief Exec., Jaguar Cars, Coventry 1973-75; Unpaid Chief Exec., Triumph Motorcycles (Meriden) Ltd. 1978-80; ***publications:*** The Unconventional Minister; ***recreations:*** reading, gardening, watching football; ***office address:*** House of Commons, London, SW1A 0AA, United Kingdom; ***phone:*** +44 (0)20 7219 3000; ***e-mail:*** robinsong@parliament.uk.

ROBINSON, Peter David, MP; British, First Minister, Northern Ireland Assembly; ***born:*** 1948; ***parents:*** David McCrea Robinson and Sheila Robinson (née Lyttle); ***married:*** Iris Robinson (née Collins), 1970; ***children:*** Johnathan (M), Gareth (M), Rebekah (F); ***public role of spouse:*** Mayor of Castlereagh, Member of Castlereagh Borough Council, Mem. of N.I. Assembly, MP for Strangford; ***languages:*** French; ***education:*** Annadale Grammar Sch.; Castlereagh F.Ed. Coll.; ***party:*** Ulster Democratic Unionist Party; ***political career:*** Founding Mem., Ulster Democratic and Unionist Party, DUP, Exec. Mem., 1973; Mem. of Castlereagh Borough Council, 1977-, Alderman, 1977; Dep. Mayor, Castlereagh Borough Cncl., 1978-79, elected Mayor, Castlereagh, 1986; DUP MP, East Belfast, 1979-2010; Dep. Leader of DUP, 1981-87, 1988; elected Northern Ireland Assembly, 1982-86; Mem., Northern Ireland Forum, 1996-; elected to Northern Ireland Assembly, Belfast East, 1998-; Minister for Regional Development, NI Assembly, 2000-02 (NI Assembly suspended); Minister for Finance, NI Assembly, May 2007-June 2008; Leader, Democratic Unionist Party, May 2008-; First Minister, June 2008-; ***interests:*** Northern Ireland, terrorism, housing, shipbuilding, aviation; ***memberships:*** Sports Cncl. for Northern Ireland; British-American Parly. Assn.; ***professional career:*** Estate Agent; Chmn., Crown Publications; ***committees:*** Mem., Sports Cncl. for Northern Ireland, 1991; Northern Ireland Affairs Cttee., House of Commons, 1994; Chmn., Northern Ireland Assembly Environment Cttee.; Sec. Central Exec. Cttee., DUP, 1974-79, Gen. Sec., 1975-79; ***publications:*** The North Answers Back, 1970; Capital Punishment for Capital Crime, 1978; Self Inflicted, 1980; Ulster in Peril, 1981; Savagery and Suffering, 1981; Ulster the Facts, 1982; A War to be Won, 1983; Its Londonderry, 1984; Carson, Man of Action, 1985; Ulster The Prey, 1986; Hands Off the UDR; The Case for the Proscription of Provisional Sinn Fein; Their Cry was 'No Surrender'; The Union Under Fire, 1995; ***office address:*** Northern Ireland Assembly, Parliament Buildings, Belfast, BT4 3XX, United Kingdom; ***URL:*** http://www.peterrobinson.org.

ROBY, Martha; Congresswoman, Alabama (2nd District), House of Representatives; ***education:*** New York Univ., music, 1998; Cumberland School of Law, Samford Univ., 2001; ***party:*** Republican; ***political career:*** Montgomery City Council; Mem., HOR, 2010-; ***memberships:*** Alabama and Mississippi Bar Assns.; ***professional career:*** lawyer, Copeland, Franco, Screws & Gill, PA; ***committees:*** Agriculture; Armed Services; Education and the Workforce; ***office address:*** House of Representatives, 414 Cannon HOB, Washington DC 20515, USA; ***phone:*** +1 202 225 2901; ***URL:*** http://roby.house.gov/.

ROCKEFELLER IV, John D. (Jay); American, Senator for West Virginia, US Senate; ***born:*** 18 June 1937; ***married:*** Sharon Rockefeller (née Percy), 1967; ***children:*** John (M), Valerie (F), Charles (M), Justin (M); ***education:*** Phillips Exeter Acad.; Int. Christian Univ., Tokyo, Japanese, 1957-60; Harvard Univ., B.A., Far Eastern Languages and History, 1961; Yale Univ., Chinese; ***party:*** Democrat; ***political career:*** elected to West Virginia House of Delegates, 1966; West Virginia Sec. of State, 1968; Governor of West Virginia, 1976-84; US Senator of West Virginia, 1984-; ***professional career:*** VISTA volunteer, 1965-65; Pres., Wesleyan Coll., 1973-76; ***committees:*** US Senate: Commerce, Science & Transportation; Finance; Select Cttee. on Intelligence; Veterans' Affairs; Jt. Cttee. on Taxation; ***honours and awards:*** Named Gubnernatorial Father of the Year, May 1979; selected by Time Magazine as `New Generation of Leaders', 1975; ***clubs:*** Rotary Int.; ***office address:*** US Senate, 531 Hart Senate Office Building, Washington, DC 20510, USA; ***phone:*** +1 202 224 6472; ***URL:*** http://www.rockefeller.senate.gov.

RODGERS, Cathy McMorris; Congresswoman, Washington's Fifth District, US House of Representatives; ***education:*** Pensacola Christian Coll., Florida, BA pre-law; Univ. of Washington, MBA; ***political career:*** Washington State Representative, 7th District, House Republican leader; US House of Representatives, 2005-; ***committees:*** Washington State Rep. cttees: Chwn., Commerce and Labor; Joint Legislative Audit and Review; Government; US House of Rep. cttees: Armed Services; Resources; Education and Workforce; ***office address:*** US House of Representatives, 1708 Longworth House Office Building, Washington, DC 20515, USA; ***phone:*** +1 202 225 2006; ***fax:*** +1 202 225 3392.

RODGERS OF QUARRY BANK, Rt. Hon. Lord William Thomas, PC; British, Member, House of Lords; ***born:*** 1928; ***parents:*** William Arthur Rodgers and Gertrude Helen Rodgers (née Owen); ***married:*** Silvia (née Szulman), 1955; ***d:*** 3; ***public role of spouse:*** Author; ***education:*** Magdalen College, Oxford, MA; ***party:*** Liberal Democrats; ***political career:*** MP (Lab), 1962-81; MP (SDP), 1981-83; Parliamentary Under-Sec. for Economic Affairs, 1964-67; Parliamentary Under-Sec. for Foreign Affairs, 1967-68; Leader UK Delegation to Council of Europe, 1967-68; Minister of State, Board of Trade, 1968-69; Minister of State, Treasury, 1969-70; Minister of State for Defence 1974-76; Sec. of State for Transport, 1976-79; one of the four founders of the Social Democratic Party, 1981; Vice-Pres., SDP, 1982-87; Mem. House of Lords; Lib. Dem Spokesman on Home Affairs, Lords; Leader of the Lib. Dems. in the House of Lords, 1998-01; ***professional career:*** Dir.-Gen., Royal Inst. of British Architects, 1987-94; Chmn., Advertising Standards Authority, 1995-2000; ***committees:*** Chmn., House of Commons Select Cttee. Trade and Industry, 1971-74; ***publications:*** The People into Parliament (1966); Editor, Hugh Gaitskell (1964); The Politics of Change (1982); Editor, Government and Industry: A Business Guide (1986); Fourth Among Equals (2000); ***office address:*** House of Lords, London, SW1A 0PQ, United Kingdom; ***phone:*** +44 (0)20 7219 3000; ***fax:*** +44 (0)20 7219 5979; ***e-mail:*** hlinfo@parliament.uk.

RODRIGUES-BIRKETT, Carolyn; Minister of Foreign Affairs, Government of Guyana; ***born:*** 16 September 1973, Santa Rosa, Region One, Guyana; ***education:*** BA, Univ. of Guyana; ***political career:*** Minister of Amerindian Affairs, 2001-08; Minister of Foreign Affairs, 2008-; ***office address:*** Ministry of Foreign Affairs, Takuba Lodge, 254 South Road and New Garden Streets, Georgetown, Guyana; ***phone:*** +592 226 1607 / 225 6467; ***fax:*** +592 225 9192; ***e-mail:*** minfor@sdnp.org.gy; ***URL:*** http://www.minfor.gov.gy.

ROGER, Michel; Minister of State, Government of Monaco; ***born:*** March 1949; ***political career:*** Municipal Councillor, Poitiers, 1983-2001; Minister of State, March 2010-; ***professional career:*** Lawyer; Lecturer; Mem., Principality of Monaco's Supreme Court, 2007-10; ***office address:*** Ministry of State, Place de la Visitation, MC 9800 , Monaco; ***phone:*** +377 98 98 80 00; ***fax:*** +377 98 98 82 17; ***e-mail:*** sgne@goub.mc; ***URL:*** http://www.gouv.mc/.

ROGERS, Harold 'Hal'; American, Congressman, Kentucky Fifth District, US House of Representatives; ***education:*** Univ. of Kentucky, BA; Univ. of Kentucky Law School, LL.B; ***party:*** Republican; ***political career:*** Mem., US House of Representatives, 1980-;

professional career: Kentucky & North Carolina National Guard, 1957-64; **committees:** Chmn., House Appropriations Cttee.; **office address:** House of Representatives, 436 Cannon House Street, Washington, DC 20515-6501, USA; **phone:** +1 202 224 3121.

ROGERS, Mike; Congressman, Michigan 8th District, US House of Representatives; **party:** Republican Party; **political career:** Michigan Senate, 1995; Mem., US House of Representatives, 2000-; **professional career:** commissioned officer, US army; FBI special agent; **committees:** Energy and Commerce Cttee.; Perm. Select Ctte. on Intelligence, Chmn.; **office address:** House of Representatives, Washington, DC 20515, USA.

ROGERS, Mike; Congressman, Alabama 3rd District, US House of Representatives; **education:** Jacksonville State University in Jacksonville, Alabama, undergraduate degree in Political Science, Masters of Public Administration; **party:** Republican Party; **political career:** Congressman, Alabama 3rd District, US House of Representatives, 2002-; **committees:** Agriculture; Armed Services; Education and the Workforce; **office address:** US House of Representatives, 514 Cannon House Office Building, Washington, DC 20515, USA.

ROGERSON, Dan; MP for North Cornwall, House of Commons; **born:** 1975; **party:** Liberal Democrat; **political career:** Councillor, Bedford Borough Cncl., 1999-2002; MP for North Cornwall, 2005-; **committees:** Environment, Food and Rural Affairs, 2005-; **office address:** House of Commons, London, SW1A 0AA, United Kingdom.

ROHEE, Hon. Clement J.; Minister of Home Affairs, Government of Guyana; **political career:** Minister of Foreign Trade & International Cooperation, to 2006; Minister of Home Affairs, 2006-; **office address:** Ministry of Home Affairs, 6 Brickdam, Georgetown, Guyana; **phone:** +592 226 5064; **fax:** +592 226 8426; **URL:** http://www.sdnp.org.gy/moh/.

ROHRABACHER, Dana; American, Congressman, California 46th District, US House of Representatives; **party:** Republican; **political career:** Fmr. Special Asst. to President Reagan; Mem., US House of Representatives, 1988-; **committees:** House Space, Science & Technology Cttee.; House Foreign Affairs Cttee.; **office address:** House of Representatives, 436 Cannon House Street, Washington, DC 20515-6501, USA; **phone:** +1 202 224 3121.

RONCAGLIOLO, Rafael; Minister of Foreign Affairs, Government of Peru; **born:** 1944; **political career:** Politician; Sec. Gen., Transparencia del Peru, 1994-2002; Minister of Foreign Affairs, 2011-; **professional career:** sociologist; univ. professor; visiting prof., Univ. de Quebec; Univ. Iberoamericana de Mexico; Univ. Catolica Ecuador; **office address:** Ministry of Foreign Affairs, Palacio de Torre Tagle, Jr. Ucayali 363 , Lima 1, Peru; **phone:** +51 (0)1 427 3860; **fax:** +51 (0)1 426 3266; **URL:** http://www.rree.gob.pe.

RONDEAU, Jim; Minister of Healthy Living, Youth and Seniors, Government of Manitoba; **education:** B.Ed., Univ. of Winnipeg, Canada; **party:** New Democratic Party; **political career:** Minister of Industry, Econ. Dev. and Mines; Minister of Science, Technology, Energy and Mines, 2004-09; Minister of Healthy Living, Youth and Seniors, 2009-; **office address:** Ministry of Healthy Living, Youth and Seniors, 310 Legislative Building, 450 Broadway Avenue, Winnipeg, Manitoba, R3C 0V8, Canada; **URL:** http://www.gov.mb.ca/.

RONIS, Aivis; Latvian, Minister of Transport, Government of Latvia; **born:** 20 May 1968, Kuldiga, Latvia; **languages:** English, Russian, Swedish; **education:** Latvian, State Univ. Riga, Latvia, MA, Philosophy and Soc. Science, 1986-1991; Columbia Univ. NY, USA, Research Fellow, Fulbright Scholar, 1999-2000; **political career:** Minister of Foreign Affairs, 2010; Minister of Transport, 2011-; **professional career:** Snr. Editor, Informative Daily News Programme, Latvian State TV, 1989-91; Chief Desk Officer; Asst. to Minister of Foreign Affairs; Press Sec., Min. of Foreign Affairs, 1991-93; First Sec., Emb. of Latvia, Sweden, 1993-95; Undersecretary of State, Min. of Foreign Affairs, 1995-2000; Amb. Ex. & Plen. to Rep. of Turkey, 1999-2000; Amb. Ex. & Plen. to USA and Mexico, 2000-2005; **recreations:** fmr. Latvian youth chess champion; **office address:** Ministry of Transport, Gogola iela 2, Riga LV-1743, Latvia; **phone:** +371 6722 6922; **fax:** +371 6721 7180; **URL:** http://www.sam.gov.lv.

ROOS, H.E. John V.; Ambassador, American Embassy in Japan; **education:** Stanford Univ., USA; Stanford Law School, USA; **professional career:** Lawyer; Senior Partner at Wilson Sonsini Goodrich & Rosati; Amb. to Japan, 2009-; **office address:** US Embassy, 10-5, Akasaka 1-chome, Minato-ku (107-8420), Tokyo, Japan; **phone:** +81 (0)3 3224 5000; **fax:** +81 (0)3 3505 1862; **URL:** http://japan.usembassy.gov.

ROSENTHAL, Gert; Permanent Representative to the UN, Government of Guatemala; **born:** 11 September 1935; **education:** Univ. of California, Berkeley; B.A. Econ., 1957, M.A., 1959; **political career:** Minister of Foreign Affairs, 2006-08; Permanent Representative to the UN, 2008-; **professional career:** Economist, National Council. of Econ. Planning, 1960-64; Head, Economic Development Div., Nat. Council of Econ. Planning (CNPE), 1965; Gen. Sec., CNPE, 1969-70, 1973-74; Dir. in Mexico, Econ. Cmn. for Latin America and the Caribbean (CEPAL), 1974-85; Adj. Exec. Sec., CEPAL, 1985-87; Exec. Sec., CEPAL, 1988-97; Guatemalan Permanent Rep. at the UN, 1999-; Independent Government Advisor, 2005-06; **office address:** Guatemala Delegation to the UN, 57 Park Avenue, New York, NY 10016, USA; **phone:** +1 212 679 4760; **fax:** +1 212 685 8741; **URL:** http://www.un.int/guatemala/.

ROSINDELL, Andrew; Member of Parliament for Romford, House of Commons; **born:** 17 March 1966, Rush Green, Romford, UK; **parents:** Frederick William Rosindell and Eileen Rosina Rosindell (née Clark); **education:** Rise Park Sch., 1971-77; Marshalls Park Secondary Sch., 1977-83; **party:** Conservative Party; **political career:** joined Conservative Party and Young Conservatives, 1981; Chmn, Romford Young Conservatives, 1983-84; Chmn, Greater London Young Conservatives, 1987-88; Cllr., for the Chase Cross Ward of the London Borough of Havering, 1990-2002; UK Y.C. rep. to the Int. Young Democrat Union and the Democrat Youth Community of Europe, 1991-95; Int. Sec. of the Young Conservatives, UK, 1991-98; Co-ordinator, "Freedom Training Programme" with the Conservative Party Int. office and Westminster Foundation For Democracy, 1993-98; Chmn, Nat. Young Conservatives, 1993-94;

Chmn, European Young Conservatives, 1993-97; Exec. Sec., Int. Young Democrat Union, 1994-98; Chmn, Int. Young Democrat Union, 1998-2002; Chmn, Romford Conservative Assoc. 1998-2001; Pres., Havering Park Ward Conservatives, 2000-; Pres., Caribbean Young Democrat Union, 2001-; Armed Forces Parly. Scheme, Royal Marines, 2002-03; MP, Romford, 2001-; Vice Chmn., Conservative Party, 2004-05; Armed Forces Parly. Scheme, Royal Air Force, 2005-07; Opposition Whip, 2005; British Army, 2009; Shadow Home Affairs Minister and Spokesman on Animal Welfare, 2007-10; **interests:** foreign affairs, Europe, overseas terrritories and Crown dependencies, international development, constitutional reform, law and order, defence, local govt., elderly people, animal welfare; **memberships:** Mem., St. Edward The Confessor Church, Romford Market Place; Mem., London Accident Prevention Council, 1990-95; Mem., Standing Advisory Cncl For Religious Education in Havering, 1990-2000; Vice-Pres., Romford & District Scout Assoc., 1995-; Exec. Mem., Int. Democrat Union (IDU), 1998-2002; Hon. Mem., Konservativ Ungdom, Denmark, 1998-2002; Chmn., North Romford Community Area Forum, 1998-2002; Mem., Royal Society of St. George, 2000-; Mem., Overseas Territories All Party Gp., 2001-, Sec., 2009; Sec., Iceland All Party GP., 2001-; Sec., Falkland Islands All Party Gp., 2001-; Sec., Gibraltar All Party Gp., 2001-2002; Sec., Australia & New Zealand All Party Gp., 2001-; Jt. Treasurer, Danish All Party Gp., 2001-; Hon. mem., Falklands Islands Assn., 2002-; Mem., APPG, Cycling; Sec., All Party Parly. Manx Group, 2002-05, Chmn., 2005-; Mem., of the following All Party Parly Groups: Cayman Islands, Bahrain, Bermuda, Canada, St. Helena, Norway, Malta, Sweden, Finland, Turks & Caicos Islands, Kuwait, Qatar; Chmn., Conservative Friends of Gibraltar, 2002-; Pres., Romford Air Training Corps, 2002-; Chmn., Montserrat Grp., 2005-; Sec., APP Lichtenstein Gp., 2004-; Chmn., APP Greyhound Gp., 2006-; Vice-Chmn., APP Channel Islands Gp., 2006-; Sec., APP British Virgin Islands Gp., 2006-; Mem., Commonwealth Parly. Assn., 2001-; Mem., Inter-Parly. Union, 2001-; Alderman, London Borough of Havering, 2007-; Chmn., St. George's Day Group, 2007; Chmn., Flag Group, 2008; **professional career:** Researcher and journalist, 1986-97; Governor, Dame Tipping Church of England Sch., Havering-atte-Bower, 1990-2002; Research Asst. to Vivian Bendall MP (Ilford North); Dir., European Foundation, 1997-99; Int. Dir., European Foundation, 1999-; **committees:** Mem., National Union Executive Cttee. of the Conservative; Vice-Chmn., Housing Cttee., London Borough of Havering, 1996-97; Mem., Deregulation & Regulatory Reform Select Cttee., 2001-05; Jt Cttee. on Statutory Instruments, 2002-03; Constitutional Affairs Select Cttee., 2004-05; Mem., Northern Ireland Grand Cttee., 2006-08; Armed Forces Parly. Army Scheme, 2009-; Chmn., St George's Day, APPG, 2007; Chmn., Flag, APPG, 2008; Sec., South Pacific Islands APPG, 2008; Foreign Affairs, 2010-; **trusteeships:** Patron, Constitutional Monarchy Assn., 2002-; Patron, Justice for Dogs, 2002-; Patron, Remus Memorial Horse Sanctuary. 2004-; **honours and awards:** Mayor's Award For Community Action in recognition of charity work, 1978; **publications:** Co-author, Defending Our Great Heritage, 1993; **clubs:** Hon. Mem., East Anglian Staffordshire Bull Terrier Club; Hon. Mem., Romford Conservative and Constitutional Club; Mem., Royal Air Forces Assoc. Club; Mem., Romford Royal British Legion; Mem., North Romford Community Assoc., Collier Row; Vice-Pres., Romford Football Club, 2002-; Hon. Mem., Havering-atte-Bower Cricket Club, 2001-; Hon. Mem., Romford Model Railway Society; **office address:** House of Commons, London, SW1A 0AA, United Kingdom; **phone:** +44 (0)20 7219 8475; **fax:** +44 (0)20 7219 1960; **e-mail:** andrew@rosindell.com; **URL:** http://www.andrew.rosindell.com.

ROS-LEHTINEN, Ileana; American, Congresswoman, Florida 18th District, US House of Representatives; **born:** 1952; **party:** Republican; **political career:** Mem., US House of Representatives, 1989-; **committees:** Chmn., Foreign Affairs; **office address:** House of Representatives, 436 Cannon House Building, Washington DC 20515, USA; **phone:** +1 202 224 3121.

ROSLER, Philipp; Minister of Health, German Government; **education:** Hannover Medical School; **party:** FDP; **political career:** Minister for Economics, Labour and Transport of Lower Saxony, Feb.-Oct. 2009; Minister of Health, 2009-; **professional career:** Physician; **office address:** Ministry of Health, FriedrichStr. 108, 10117 Berlin, Germany; **phone:** +49 (0)30 206400; **URL:** http://www.bmg.bund.de.

ROTHERAM, Steve; MP for Liverpool, Walton, UK Government; **party:** Labour; **political career:** Councillor, Liverpool City Council, 2002-; Lord Mayor of Liverpool; MP for Liverpool, Walton, May 2010-; **committees:** Communities and Local Government, 2011; Culture, Media and Sport, 2011; **office address:** House of Commons, London, SW1A 0AA, United Kingdom; **phone:** +44 (0)20 7219 3000; **e-mail:** steve.rotheram.mp@parliament.uk.

ROUHANI, Hassan; President, Government of Iran; **languages:** Arabic, English, French, German, Russian; **education:** Univ. of Tehran, Iran; MPhil., PhD., Glasgow Caledonian Univ.; **political career:** President, June 2013-; **professional career:** Cleric; Head, Expediency Council, Strategic Research Centre; **office address:** Office of the President, Pasteur Avenue 13168-43311, Tehran, Iran; **phone:** +98 21 614451; **URL:** http://www.president.ir.

ROUPAKIOTIS, Antonis; Minister of Justice, Transparency and Human Rights, Government of Greece; **political career:** Minister of Labour and Social Security, 2012; Minister of Justice, Transparency and Human Rights, 2012-; **professional career:** Lawyer; **office address:** Ministry of Justice, 96 Mesogeion str,, 115 27 Athens, Greece; **phone:** +30 (0)10 771 1019; **URL:** http://www.ministryofjustice.gr.

ROUSE, Ruth Elizabeth; Ambassador, Grenada High Commission; **born:** 30 January 1963; **education:** German Foundation for Int. Dev., Berlin, Germany, Dip. in Int. Relations and Econ. Co-operation, 1987; Diplomatic Academy, London, Post Graduate Programme in Diplomacy, Practice, Procedures, Dynamics, 1989; Carleton Univ., Ottawa, Canada, BA., French & Spanish, 1996; Univ. of Westminster, MA, Diplomatic Studies, 2002; **professional career:** Desk Officer (Africa and Middle East Affairs), Political and Econ. Div., Min. of Foreign Affairs, Grenada, 1982-83; Protocol Officer (Protocol and Consular Div.), Min. of Foreign Affairs, Grenada, 1983-90; Second Sec., (Protocol, Culture and Dev. Affairs), OECS High Cmn., Ottawa, Canada, 1990-96; Chief of Protocol, Min. of Foreign Affairs, Grenada, 1996-99; High Cmnr. for Grenada, UK, 1999; High Commissioner (non-resident), South Africa; Permanent Represenative of Grenada to the UN; High Commissioner to the UK, 2008-; **honours and awards:** Independence Award for Outstanding Public Service, 1998; **office address:**

Grenada High Commission, 5 Chandos Street, London, W1G 9DG, United Kingdom; **phone:** +44 (0)20 7631 4277; **fax:** +44 (0)20 7631 4272; **e-mail:** grenada@high-commission.demon.co.uk.

ROUSSEFF, Dilma; President, Government of Brazil; **born:** 1947; **parents:** Pedro Rousseff; **party:** Workers Party (PT); **political career:** Minister of Mining and Energy, 2003-05; Chief of Staff of the Presidency, 2005-2010; President, 2010-; **office address:** Office of the Presidency, Palacio do Planalto, 30 Andar , 70150-900 Brasilia DF, Brazil; **phone:** +55 (0)61 411 1202; **fax:** +55 (0)61 411 2222; **URL:** http://www.planalto.gov.br.

ROY, Frank; British, Member of Parliament for Motherwell and Wishaw, House of Commons; **born:** 29 August 1958; **education:** Glasgow Caledonian Univ.; **party:** Labour Party; **political career:** PA to Helen Liddell MP, 1994; PPS to Rt. Hon. Helen Liddell MP, Dep. Sec. of State for Scotland, 1998-99; PPS to Rt. Hon. John Reid MP, Sec. of State for Scotland, 1999-2001; MP, Motherwell and Wishaw, 1997-; Asst. Govt Whip, 2005-06; Govt. Whip, 2006-10; **interests:** consumer affairs, social security legislation, foreign affairs; **professional career:** Steelworker; **committees:** Foreign Affairs, 2010-; **office address:** House of Commons, London, SW1A 0AA, United Kingdom; **phone:** +44 (0)20 7219 3000; **e-mail:** royf@parliament.uk.

ROY, Lindsay, MP; MP for Glenrothes, British Government; **born:** 1949; **political career:** MP for Glenrothes Nov. 2008-; **professional career:** Pres., The Headmaster's Association of Scotland; Rector, Kirkcaldy High School; **committees:** Scottish Affairs, 2009-; Public Administration, 2010-; **office address:** House of Commons, London, SW1A 0AA, United Kingdom; **phone:** +44 (0)20 7219 3107; **e-mail:** lindsay.roy.mp@parliament.uk.

ROYALL OF BLAISDON, Baroness Janet Anne; Shadow Leader of the Opposition, House of Lords; **born:** 20 August 1955, Gloucester, UK; **parents:** Basil Oscar Royall and Myra Jessie Albutt; **public role of spouse:** Energy Expert; **languages:** French, Spanish; **education:** BA Hons., French and Spanish, Westfield Coll., Univ. of London; **party:** Labour; **political career:** Mem., House of Lords; Chief Whip, Feb. 2008-Oct 2008; Lord Pres. of the Council, Oct. 2008-June 2009; Leader of the House of Lords, Sept. 2008-May 2010; Chancellor of the Duchy of Lancaster, June 2009-May 2010; Leader of the Opposition in the House of Lords, May 2010-; **interests:** foreign policy, development, health, penal reform, public policy; **professional career:** European Commission: Mem. Neil Kinnock Cabinet, 1995-2001, Euro. Cmnr for Transport, 1995-99; vice-Pres., of the Cmn., 1999-01; Press & Communications Dept., 2001-03; Head of Office in Wales, 2003-05; **honours and awards:** raised to peerage, 2004; **recreations:** gardening, swimming, reading; **office address:** House of Lords, London, United Kingdom; **phone:** +44 (0)20 7219 3107.

ROYCE, Ed; American, Congressman, California 40th District, US House of Representatives; **party:** Republican; **political career:** California State Senate, 1982; Mem., US House of Representatives, 1992-; Asst. Whip, 1999; **committees:** Financial Services; Foreign Affairs, Chmn.; **office address:** House of Representatives, 436 Cannon House Street, Washington, DC 20515-6501, USA; **phone:** +1 202 224 3121.

RUANE, Chris; Member of Parliament for Vale of Clwyd, House of Commons; **born:** 18 July 1958, St. Asaph; **parents:** Michael Ruane (dec'd) and Esther Ruane; **married:** Gill Roberts; **education:** Univ. of Wales, Aberystwyth (history & politics); Liverpool Univ., PGCE; **party:** Labour Party; **political career:** MP, Vale of Clwyd, 1997-; Parly. Private Sec. to Sec. of State for Wales, Nov. 2002-Mar. 2007; PPS to Caroline Flint MP, Minister of State for Emplyment and Welfare Reform, Oct. 2007-Jan. 2008, Minister for Housing, Jan.-Oct. 2008; PPS to David Miliband MP, Foreign Secretary, 2009-10; PPS to Ed Balls MP, Shadow Home Secretary, 2010-11, Shadow Chancellor, 2011-; Chair, Welsh Grp. Parly. Labour Party; **professional career:** Previously Dep. Headteacher; Pres. of local NUT; **committees:** Welsh Affairs Select Cttee. 1999-2002; All Party Objective One Group; Chair, N. Wales grp. of Labour MPs, 2002-; Chair, APPG on Heart Disease, 2002; **office address:** House of Commons, London, SW1A 0AA, United Kingdom; **phone:** +44 (0)20 7219 6378; **e-mail:** ruanec@parliament.uk.

RUBIO, Marco; Senator for Florida, US Senate; **political career:** Mem., Florida House of Reps., 2000-08; US Senate, 2010-; **committees:** Commerce; Science and Transportation; Foreign Relations; Intelligence; Small Business and Entrepreneurship; **office address:** US Senate, 317 Hart Senate Office Building, Washington DC 20510, USA; **phone:** +1 202 224 3041; **URL:** http://www.rubio.senate.gov.

RUDD, Amber; MP for Hastings and Rye, UK Government; **party:** Conservative; **political career:** MP for Hastings and Rye, May 2010-; **committees:** Environment, Food and Rural Affairs Select Cttee., 2010-; **office address:** House of Commons, London, SW1A 0AA, United Kingdom; **phone:** +44 (0)20 7219 3000; **e-mail:** amber.rudd.mp@parliament.uk.

RUDD, Hon. Kevin; Prime Minister, Government of Australia; **party:** Australian Labor Party (ALP); **political career:** Mem. for Griffith, HOR, 1998-; Federal Labor's Shadow Cabinet, 2001-07; Fed. Labor Leader and Leader of the Opposition, 2006-07; Prime Minister, 2007-June 2010; Minister of Foreign Affairs, Sept. 2010-resigned Feb. 2012; Prime Minister, June 2013-; **professional career:** Joined Dept. of Foreign Affairs and Trade, 1981; Embassy postings in Stockholm and Beijing; Policy Planning Bureau; Chief of Staff to Wayne Goss, Qld. State opposition leader, to 1989; Dir.-Gen., Cabinet Office, Qld. State Govt., 1992-95; Consultant, KPMG; **office address:** Office of the Prime Minister, 3-5 National Circuit, Barton, ACT 2660, Australia; **phone:** +61 2 6271 5111; **fax:** +61 2 6271 5414; **URL:** http://www.pm gov.au.

RUDDOCK, Joan Mary, B.Sc, ARCS; British, Member of Parliament for Lewisham, Deptford, House of Commons; **born:** 28 December 1943; **married:** Keith Ruddock, 1963 (dec'd); Frank Doran MP, 2010; **education:** Pontypool Grammar School for Girls; Imperial College, Univ. of London, BSc., botany, 1965; **party:** Labour Party; **political career:** MP for Lewisham Deptford, 1987-; Vice-Pres. SERA (Socialist Environment and Resources Assoc.); Shadow Transport Minister, 1989-92; Shadow Home Affairs Minister, 1992-94; Shadow Minister for Environmental Protection, 1994-97; Parly. Under-Sec. of State for Women 1997-98; Parly. Under Sec., Dept. for Environment, Food and Rural Affairs, 2007-08, DECC, 2008-09;

Minister of State, DECC, 2009-10; Shadow Minister for Energy and Climate Change, 2010; **interests:** environment, women, foreign affairs, Afghanistan, Palestine; **memberships:** Mem., British Delegation to Council of Europe and Western European Union, 1988-89; TGWU; Inter-Parliamentary Union, 2001-; **professional career:** Dir., Shelter, 1968-73; Dir., Oxford Housing Aid Centre, 1973-77; Special programmes officer, Manpower Services Cmn., Berkshire County Cncl, 1977-79; Mgr., Citizens Advice Bureau, Reading, 1979-86; Chair, CND, 1981-85; **committees:** Modernisation of the House of Commons Select Cttee., 2001-05; Vice-Chair, Afghanistan Gp., 2002-; Environment, Food and Rural Affairs Select Cttee., 2003-05; Vice-chair, Globe UK Gp., 2003-07; Vice-Chair, Equalities Gp., 2004-07; Internat. Development Select Cttee., 2005-07; Vice-Chair, Renewable and Sustainable Energy Gp., 2005-07;Chair, Compassion in Dying Gp., 2005-07; Hon. Treas., PLP London Regional Gp., 2005-; Women, Peace and Security Gp., 2006-07; **honours and awards:** Hon. Fellow, Goldsmith's Coll., London Univ.; Hon. Fellow, Laban, London; **office address:** House of Commons, London, SW1A 0AA, United Kingdom; **phone:** +44 (0)20 7219 4153; **e-mail:** joan.ruddock.mp@parliament.uk.

RUFFLEY, David; British, MP for Bury St. Edmunds, House of Commons; **born:** 18 April 1962; **education:** Queens' Coll., Cambridge Exhibitioner, 1981; Foundation Scholar, 1983; First Class Honours Historical Tripos Part 1; BA (Law, 1985) and MA (1988); **party:** Conservative Party; **political career:** Special Advisor to the Sec. of State for Education, 1991-92, to the Home Sec., 1992-93, to the Chllr. of the Exchequer, 1993-96; MP for Bury St. Edmunds, 1997-; H. M. Opposition Treasury Whip, 2004-05; Shadow Minister for Welfare Reform, 2005; **professional career:** Solicitor; Sch. Governor; **committees:** Mem., Treasury Affairs Select Cttee., 1998-2004, 2005, 2010-; Sec. of Backbench Finance Cttee., 1999-2001; **office address:** House of Commons, London, SW1A 0AA, United Kingdom; **phone:** +44 (0)20 7219 2880; **e-mail:** ruffleyd@parliament.uk.

RUSSELL, Bob; British, Member of Parliament for Colchester, House of Commons; **born:** 31 March 1946, Colchester; **education:** Myland Primary Sch., St Helena Secondary Modern Sch., North East Essex Technical Coll.; **party:** Liberal Democratic Party; **political career:** MP for Colchester, 1997-; **professional career:** Reporter, Essex County Standard and the weekly Colchester Gazette, 1963; News Editor, Braintree and Witham Times, 1966; Editor Maldon and Burnham Standard, 1968; Sub-Editor, London Evening News and Evening Standard, 1969-1973; Press Officer, Post Office Telecommunications/British Telecom, 13 years; Publicity Officer, Univ. of Essex, 1986-97; **committees:** Home Affairs, 1998-2005, 2006-10; Catering, 2000-01; Regulatory Reform, 2005-06; Armed Forces Bill, 2005-06, 2011; Chairmen's Panel 2009-10; Administration, 2010-11; Defence, 2011-; **office address:** House of Commons, London, SW1A 0AA, United Kingdom; **phone:** +44 (0)1206 506600; **e-mail:** brooksse@parliament.uk; **URL:** http://www.bobrussell.org.uk.

RUSSELL, Michael, MSP; Member of Scottish Parliament for South of Scotland, Scottish Parliament; **born:** 9 August 1953, Bromley, Kent; **parents:** Thomas Stevenston Russell (dec'd) and Jean Marjorie Haynes (dec'd); **married:** Cathleen Russell (née MacAskill), 1980; **public role of spouse:** Primary Head teacher; **languages:** French, Gaelic; **education:** Marr Coll., Troon, Ayrshire; Edinburgh Univ., MA, Scottish History and Literature; trained for Priesthood of Scottish Episcopal Church; **party:** Scottish National Party, 1974-; **political career:** Clydesdale SNP candidate for UK Parl., 1987; Chief Exec., SNP, 1994-99; ran election campaign for SNP, 1995-99; Mem. Scottish Parl. for South of Scotland, 1999-2003; Shadow Minister for Children and Education , SNP Spokesman on Culture, Broadcasting and Gaelic; Member of Scottish Parliament for South of Scotland, 2007-; Minister for Environment, 2007-09; Minister for External Affairs, Culture and Constitution, 2009; Cabinet Secretary for Education & Lifelong Learning, 2009-; **interests:** achieving independence for Scotland, developing Scottish Parliament and extending its powers, culture and broadcasting issues, Gaelic language, environment.; **memberships:** Celtic Film and TV Assn.; Erisuay Pony Soc.; **professional career:** Creative Producer, Church of Scotland, 1974-77; Dir., Cinema Sgire, Western Isles Islands Cncl., 1977-81; Founder and First Dir., Int. Celtic Film and TV Festival, 1981-83; Chief Exec., Network Scotland Ltd., 1983-91; Dir., Eala Bhan Ltd., 1991-; **trusteeships:** Fmr. Dir., Glasgow and Inverness Film Theatres; Fmr. Trustee, Celtic Film and TV Assn.; **publications:** A Poem of Remote Lives: the enigma of Werner Kissling, 1997, NWP; In Waiting: Travels in the Shadow of Edwin Muir, 1998, NWP; A Different Country, 2002, Biriwn; Stop the World, 2004, Edmor; Grasping the Thistle, Dennis Macleod, 2006; The Next 016 Thing, 2007; The Price of Innocence, Iain McNie, 2007; **clubs:** Glasgow Art Club; **office address:** Scottish Parliament, Edinburgh, EH99 1SP, United Kingdom; **phone:** +44 (0)131 348 5944; **fax:** +44 (0)131 348 5601; **e-mail:** michael.russel.msp@scottish.parliament.ulc.

RUTLEY, David; MP for Macclesfield, UK Government; **party:** Conservative; **political career:** MP for Macclesfield, May 2010-; PPS to Damian Green, 2010-; **committees:** Treasury Select Cttee., 2010-; **office address:** House of Commons, London, SW1A 0AA, United Kingdom; **phone:** +44 (0)20 7219 3000; **e-mail:** david.rutley.mp@parliament.uk.

RUTTE, Dr Mark; Dutch, Prime Minister, Government of the Netherlands; **born:** 14 February 1967, The Hague, Netherlands; **education:** Univ. of Leiden, history; **political career:** mem., VVD party executive, 1993-97; MP, 2003-; State Secretary for Social Affairs and Employment, 2002-04; State Secretary for Education, Culture and Science, 2004-06; Leader, VVD, 2006-; Prime Minister, Oct. 2010-, tendered resignation of full cabinet, April 2012, New coalition sworn in in November 2012; **office address:** Prime Minister's Office, Postbus 20001, 2500 EA The Hague, Netherlands; **URL:** http://www.minaz.nl.

RYALL, Tony, MP; Minister of Health and State-Owned Enterprises, New Zealand Government; **born:** November 1964; **married:** Kara Ryall; **education:** Massey Univ., B.Business Studies, 1987, Dipl. Business Studies; **political career:** MP for Bay of Plenty, 1990-; Min. for State Owned Enterprises, Min. Responsible for Radio New Zealand, Min. in charge of the Audit Dept., Assoc. Min. of Justice, 1997-99; Min. of Local Government, Min. of Youth Affairs, 1998-99; Min. of Justice, Min. Responsible for Housing New Zealand Ltd., 1999; Opposition Spokesperson on Justice, Housing, Timberlands and SILNA, 1999-2008; Minister of Health and State Services, 2008-13; Minister of Health and State-Owned Enterprises, 2013-; **interests:** finance, transport, education; **professional career:** Accountant, senior credit analyst; **committees:** Chair of Finance and Expenditure Select

Cttee., 1996; *office address:* Ministry of Health, 133 Molesworth Street, Wellington, New Zealand; *phone:* +64 4 496 2000; *fax:* +64 4 496 2340; *e-mail:* tony.ryall@national.org.nz; *URL:* http://www.tonyryall.co.nz.

RYAN, Eamon; Leader, Green Party; *born:* 1963, Dublin; *education:* Univ. College Dublin, Bachelor of Commerce; *party:* Leader, Green Party, 2011-; *political career:* Elected to Dáil 2002; Green Party spokesperson for Transport and Enterprise, Trade and Employment; Minister for Communications, Energy and Natural Resources, 2007-11; *professional career:* Founder and Manager, Irish Cycling Safaris and Belfield Bike shop; *committees:* Advisory Cttee. of the Dublin Transport Office; Fmr. mem., Jt. Oireachtas Cttee. for Communication, Marine and Natural Resources; *office address:* Green Party, 16/17 Suffolk Street, Dublin 2, Ireland; *phone:* +353 (0)1 679 0012; *fax:* +353 (0)1 679 7168; *e-mail:* info@greenparty.ie; *URL:* http://www.greenparty.ie.

RYAN, Paul; American, Congressman, Wisconsin First District, US House of Representatives; *born:* Janesville, Wisconsin, US; *married:* Janna Ryan (née Little), 2 Dec. 2000; *party:* Republican; *political career:* Mem., US House of Representatives, 1998-; *committees:* Budget; Chmn., Ways and Means Cttee.; *office address:* House of Representatives, 1217 Longworth House Office Building, Washington, DC 20515, USA; *phone:* +1 202 224 3121.

RYDER, Guy; Executive Director, International Labour Office; *born:* 1956; *education:* Univ. of Cambridge; Univ. of Liverpool; *professional career:* TUC; Sec., Industry Trade Section, International Fed. of Commercial, Clerical, Professional and Technical Employees, 1985; Assist. Dir., & Dir., Geneva Office, Internat. Confed. of Free Trade Unions, 1988-93; ILO, 1998-99; Gen. Sec, ICFTU, 2002-06; Gen. Sec., International Trade Union Confederation, 2006-10; Exec. Dir., ILO, 2010-; *office address:* ILO, 4 route des Morillons, CH 1211 Geneva 22, Switzerland; *phone:* +41 (0)22 799 61 11; *fax:* +41 (0)22 799 86 85; *URL:* http://www.ilo.org.

RYOO, Kihl-jae; Minister of Unification, Government of South Korea; *education:* BA, in Political Science, 1984, MA, in Political Science, 1987, Ph.D., in Political Science,1995, Korea Univ.; *political career:* Policy Advisor to the Ministry of Unification, 2009-13; Minister of Unification, 2013-; *professional career:* Mem., of the Diplomacy and Security Division at the Ideas for Korea, 2010-13; Pres. of the Korean Association of North Korean Studies, 2013; *office address:* Ministry of Unification, Central GOvernment Complex, 209 Sejong-daero (Sejong-ro), Jongno-gu, Seoul, Republic of Korea.

S

SAAID, Dr Abdi Farah Shirdon; Prime Minister, Government of Somalia; *political career:* Prime Minister, Oct. 2012-; *professional career:* government economist; businessman; *office address:* Office of the Prime Minister, Mogadishu, Somalia.

SAAKASHVILI, Mikheil; President, Georgia; *born:* 1967, Tbilisi, Georgia; *languages:* English, French, Ukrainian, Russian; *education:* Studied in Ukraine, France and Columbia University Law School, USA; *political career:* MP, 1995-; Minister of Justice, 2000-01; President of Georgia, 2004-; *professional career:* Lawyer; *office address:* State Chancery, 7 Ingorkva Street, 380034 Tbilisi, Georgia; *phone:* +995 (8)32 990070; *fax:* +995 (8)32 998887; *e-mail:* media@president.gov.ge; *URL:* http://www.parliament.ge.

SABLAN, Gregorio Kilili Camacho; Congressman-at-large for Northern Mariana Islands, US House of Representatives; *born:* 19 January 1955, Saipan, NM; *education:* University of Guam; Berkeley, California; *party:* Democrat; *political career:* Elected to 3rd NMI Legislature; Special Assist. to US Senator Daniel K. Inouye; Exec. Dir., Commonwealth Election Cmn.; first Northern Mariana Islands Congressman-at-Large, US House of Representatives, 2009-; *professional career:* served the administration of Gov. Carlos S. Camacho; served the Froilan C. Tenorio administration; served in Pedro P. Tenorio's administration; *committees:* Agriculture; Natural Resources; *office address:* US House of Representatives, 423 Cannon HOB , Washington, DC 20515, USA; *phone:* +1 202 225 2646; *URL:* http://www.sablan.house.gov.

SACCOMANNI, Fabrizio; Minister of the Economy and Finance, Government of Italy; *education:* Bocconi Univ., Italy; Princeton Univ., USA; *political career:* Minister of the Economy and Finance, Apr. 2013-; *professional career:* Bank of Italy, 1967-; Dir. Gen., 2006-13; International Monetary Fund, 1970-75; Chmn. foreign exchange policy cttee., European Monetary Inst., 1991-97; Vice Pres., European Bank for Reconstruction and Development, 2003-06; *publications:* Managing international financial sStability: Nation tamers versus global tigers, 2008; *office address:* Ministry of Economy and Finance, Via XX Settembre 97, 00187 Rome, Italy; *phone:* +39 06 59971; *URL:* http://www.finanze.it.

SACKS OF ALDGATE, Lord Jonathan; Member, House of Lords; *education:* Gonville & Caius Coll., Cambridge Univ.; New College, Oxford Univ.; King's Coll., London, PhD; Jews' Coll. London; *political career:* Mem. House of Lords, 2009-; *professional career:* Chief Rabbi, United Hebrew Congregations of the Commonwealth, 1991-; *office address:* House of Lords, London, SW1A 0OW, United Kingdom; *phone:* +44 (0)20 7219 3000; *fax:* +44 (0)20 7219 5979; *URL:* http://www.parliament.uk.

SADANG, Elbuchel; Minister of Finance, Government of Palau; *political career:* Director, National Treasury; Minister of Finance; Presidential Chief of Staff, -2013; Finance Minister, 2013-; *office address:* Ministry of Finance, PO Box 6011, 96940 Koror, Palau.

SALAM, Tamam; Prime Minister, Government of Lebanon; *parents:* Saeb Salam; *political career:* Minister of Culture, 2005-09; Prime Minister, Apr. 2013-; *office address:* Prime Minister's Office, Council of Ministers, Al-Kasr Al-Houkoumi, Al-Sanayeh, Beirut, Lebanon; *phone:* +961 1 814777 / 862006.

SALAMÉ, Riad; Governor, Banque du Liban; *education:* American Univ. of Beirut, economics; *professional career:* various positions, Merrill Lynch Beirut, 1973-93, most recently Vice-Pres., and Financial Advisor, Merrill Lynch, Paris; Governor, Banque du Liban, 1993-; *office address:* Banque du Liban, PO Box 11-5544, Hamra Street, Beirut, Lebanon; *phone:* +961 1 341230/ 1 341239; *fax:* +961 1 747600; *e-mail:* bdit@bdl.gov.lb; *URL:* http://www.bdl.gov.lb.

SALEH, Osman Muhammad; Minister of Foreign Affairs, Government of Eritrea; *political career:* Minister of Education, to 2007; Minister of Foreign Affairs, 2007-; *office address:* Ministry of Foreign Affairs, PO Box 190, Asmara, Eritrea; *phone:* +291 1 12 71 08; *fax:* +291 1 12 37 88.

SALIH, Major General Bakri Hassan; Minister of Republic Affairs, Government of Sudan; *political career:* Minister of the Presidential Affairs, 1998-2000; Minister of Defence, 2000-2005; Minister of Republic Affairs, 2005-; *office address:* Ministry of Republic Affairs, Khartoum, Sudan.

SALL, Macky; President, Government of Senegal; *born:* 1961; *political career:* Minister of Mines, Energy and Hydraulics, 2001-03; Minister of the Interior; 2003-04; Prime Minister, 2004-07; Pres. of the National Assembly; President, March 2012-; *office address:* Office of the President, Immeuble Administratif, ave Léopold Sédar Senghor, BP 168, Dakar, Senegal.

SALMOND, Rt. Hon. Alexander Elliot Anderson, MSP MP; First Minister, Scottish Parliament; *born:* 1954, Linlithgow; *parents:* Robert Salmond and Mary Salmond (née Milne); *married:* Moira Salmond (née McGlashan), 1981; *education:* Linlithgow Academy; St. Andrews Univ. (MA Hons. Economics and Mediaeval History); *party:* Scottish National Party; *political career:* Deputy Leader Scottish National Party (SNP) 1987-90; MP for Banff and Buchan 1987-2010; Leader, SNP, 1990-2000, and 2004-; MSP, Banff and Buchan 1999-2001, 2007-; First Minister, Scottish Parliament, May 2007-; *memberships:* Nat. Exec. Cttee. Scottish Nat. Party; Scottish Centre for Economic & Social Research; *professional career:* Asst. Economist, Govt. Economic Services, 1978-80; Economist, Royal Bank of Scotland, 1980-87; visiting Prof., Economics, Univ. of Strathclyde; *committees:* Energy Select Cttee, 1987-92; *publications:* Numerous articles and conference papers on economics of the oil industry; *recreations:* golf, reading; *office address:* Scottish Parliament , Hollyrood, Edinburgh, EH99 1SP, Scotland; *phone:* +44 (0)131 348 5000; *fax:* +44 (0)131 348 5601; *URL:* http://www.scotland.gov.uk.

SAMAD ABDULLAH, Dr Abdul; Minister of Foreign Affairs, Government of the Maldives; *born:* 1946; *education:* Leningrad Medical Inst.; Royal Tropical Medicine Inst., Belgium, Masters, Public Health; *political career:* Minister of Foreign Affairs, 2012-; *professional career:* international public servant; Dir., Gen., Health Services, Helath Ministry; many positions, WHO, most recently, Coordinator of Communicable Disease Control, Regional Office, New Delhi; joined Maldives Foreign Services, 2008; High Commissioner to the People's Rep. of Bangladesh; *office address:* Ministry of Foreign Affairs, Boduthakurufaanu Magu, Malé 20077, Maldives; *URL:* http://foreign.gov.mv.

SAMARAS, Antonis, MBA, BA(Econ); Greek, Prime Minister, Government of Greece; *born:* 1951; *parents:* Constaninos Samaras and Eleni Samaras (née Zannas); *married:* Georgia Samaras (née Kritikou); *languages:* English, French, Italian; *education:* Amherst College, BA(Econ), 1970-74; Harvard Univ., MBA, 1974-76; *party:* Leader New Democrats; *political career:* Elected MP for Messinia 1977, 81, 85, 89, 90 and 1993 elections; Minister of Finance in the Tzanetaki Cabinet 1989-; Minister for Foreign Affairs 1989-92; MEP, 2004-07; Minister of Culture, 2009; Prime Minister, June 2012-; *committees:* Pres. of Political Spring Party June 1993-; *office address:* Office of the Prime Minister, 15 Vassilissis Sophias Ave, 106 74 Athens, Greece; *phone:* +30 (0)10 338 5372; *e-mail:* mail@primeminister.gr; *URL:* http://www.primeminister.gr.

SAMBO, Namadi; Vice President, Government of Nigeria; *education:* BSc. MSc. (Architecture) Ahmadu Bello, Univ. Zaria, Nigeria; *political career:* Governor of Kaduna State, 2007-10; Vice President, 2010-; *professional career:* Architect; *office address:* Office of the Vice President, Federal Secretariat PhaseII, Shehu Shagari Way, Abuja, Nigeria; *phone:* +234 9 234 9909.

SAMHENG, Ith; Minister of Social Affairs, Labour, Vocational Training and Youth Rehabilitation, Government of Cambodia; *born:* 1 August 1954, Prey Veng, Cambodia; *parents:* Sam Sieng and Sok Cheng; *s:* 2; *languages:* English, French; *education:* Rubber Processing Chemical Lab. Inst. of Social Science & Labour Management, grad., 1973; *party:* Cambodian's People Party; *political career:* Leader, Cambodian's People Party (CPP); Minister of Social Affairs, Labour, Vocational Training and Youth Rehabilitation, to date; *interests:* peaceful society, non-discrimination, development, no poverty; *professional career:* Business Administration; *committees:* Central cttee., CPP; *honours and awards:* Medal, Kingdom Honour; *clubs:* Cambodia golf assn.; *recreations:* golf; *office address:* Ministry of Social Affairs, Labour, Vocational Training and Youth Rehabilitation, #788 Monivong Blvd, Phnom-Penh, Cambodia; *phone:* +855 (0)23 725191; *fax:* +855 (0)23 725191; *e-mail:* mosacry@camnet.com.kh.

SÁNCHEZ, Linda T.; Congresswoman, California 39th District, US House of Representatives; *party:* Democratic Party; *political career:* Congresswoman, California 39th District, US House of Representatives; *committees:* Ethics; *office address:* US House of Representatives, 1007 Longworth Building, Washington, DC 20515, USA.

SANCHEZ, Loretta; American, Congresswoman, California 47th District, US House of Representatives; ***party:*** Democratic Party; ***political career:*** Mem., US House of Representatives, 1996-; ***committees:*** Armed Services; Homeland Security; ***office address:*** House of Representatives, 436 Cannon House Street, Washington, DC 20515-6501, USA; ***phone:*** +1 202 224 3121.

SANCHEZ CEREN, Salvador; Vice President, Government of El Salvador; ***born:*** June 1944; ***party:*** Frente Farabundo Martí para la Liberación Nacional (FMLN); ***political career:*** Vice President; ***professional career:*** School Teacher; ***office address:*** Office of the Vice-President, Alameda Nauel Enrique Araujo 5505, San Salvadaor, El Salvador; ***phone:*** +503 248 9108/10; ***fax:*** +503 243 9951; ***e-mail:*** casapres@casapres.gob.sv; ***URL:*** http://www.casapres.gob.sv/.

SANDERS, Adrian; British, Member of Parliament for Torbay, House of Commons; ***born:*** 25 April 1959, Paignton, Devon; ***parents:*** John Sanders and Helen Sanders (dec'd); ***married:*** Alison Sanders (née Nortcliffe), 17 February 1991; ***education:*** Torquay Boys Grammar School; ***party:*** Liberal Democratic Party; ***political career:*** Torbay Borough Councillor 1984-86; Association of Liberal Councillors, 1986-89; Liberal Democrats Whips Office, 1989-90; Lib. Dem. Spokesman for Local Govt. and Housing; MP, Torbay, 1997-2003; Lib. Dem. spokesman on Tourism, 2003-05; Deputy Chief Whip, 2005-; ***interests:*** housing, charities, diabetes, tourism; ***memberships:*** Diabetes UK; ***committees:*** mem., ODPM, Select Cttee., 2003-05; mem., DCMS Select Cttee., 2005-; Selection, 2006-10; Modernisation of the House of Commons, 2006-08; ***clubs:*** Paignton Club; ***recreations:*** travel, soccer, film, music; ***office address:*** House of Commons, London, SW1A 0AA, United Kingdom; ***phone:*** +44 (0)20 7219 6304; ***e-mail:*** asanders@parliament.uk.

SANDERS, Bernie; American, Senator for Vermont, US Senate; ***education:*** University of Chicago, grad.1964; ***party:*** Independent; ***political career:*** Mayor, Burlington, Vermont, 1981-89; Mem., US House of Representatives, 1991-2006; Senator, US Senate, 2006-; ***memberships:*** Fndr. & Chmn., Progressive Caucus; ***committees:*** House Banking and Financial Services Cttee.; House Govt. Reform and Oversight Cttee.; Senate Cttees: Budget; Veterans; Energy; Environment; and Health, Education, Labor and Pensions; ***office address:*** US Senate, Hart Senate Office Building, Washington, DC 20510-4103, USA; ***URL:*** http://www.senate.gov/.

SANDERSON OF BOWDEN, Lord, Baron Charles Russell, Life Peer; British, Member of the House of Lords; ***born:*** 30 April 1933; ***parents:*** Charles Plummer Sanderson and Evelyn Martha Sanderson (née Gardiner); ***married:*** Frances Elizabeth (née Macaulay); ***children:*** Charles David (M), Andrew Bruce (dec'd) (M), Elizabeth Claire (F), Frances Georgina (F); ***education:*** St. Mary's Sch., Melrose; Glenalmond Coll.; Scottish Coll. of Textiles, Galashiels; Bradford Coll., Bradford; ***party:*** Conservative Party; ***political career:*** Min. of State, Scottish Office, 1987-90; Spokesman on all Scottish Office matters, House of Lords, 1987-90; Chmn., Scottish Conservative Party, 1990-93; Mem., House of Lords; ***professional career:*** SCUA: Vice-Pres., 1975-77, Pres., 1977-79; Nat. Union of Conservative Assns., 1979-86; Chmn., Nat. Union Exec. Cttee., 1981-86; Dir. Clydesdale Bank, 1993-2004, Chmn., 1999-2004; Chmn., Scottish Mortgage Trust, 1993-2003; ***committees:*** Chmn., Nat. Union Exec. Cttee., 1981-86; Chmn. Scottish Peers Assn., 1998-2000; ***trusteeships:*** Chmn., Abbotsford Trust, 2008-; ***honours and awards:*** Knighthood, 1981; Life Peerage, 1985; Hon. Degree, Glasgow Univ.; Hon. Degree, Napier Univ.; ***clubs:*** The Hon. Company of Edinburgh Golfers, Caledonian Club; ***recreations:*** golfing, fishing, photography; ***office address:*** House of Lords, London, SW1A 0PW, United Kingdom; ***phone:*** +44 (0)1835 822736; ***fax:*** +44 (0)1835 823272.

SANDOVAL, Brian; Governor, State of Nevada; ***education:*** Univ. of Nevada, BA, 1986; Ohio state Univ. Moritz College of Law, 1989; ***political career:*** Attorney General; Governor of Nevada, Nov. 2010-; ***professional career:*** law practice; chmn., Nevada Gaming Commission; ***office address:*** Office of the Governor, Capitol Building, Carson City, NV 89701, USA; ***phone:*** +1 775 684 5670; ***URL:*** http://gov.nv.gov/.

SANDYS, Laura; MP for South Thanet, UK Government; ***party:*** Conservative; ***political career:*** MP for South Thanet, May 2010-; ***committees:*** Energy and Climate Change Select Cttee., 2010-; Joint Committee on the Draft House of Lords Reform Bill, 2011-12; ***office address:*** House of Commons, London, SW1A 0AA, United Kingdom; ***phone:*** +44 (0)20 7219 3000; ***e-mail:*** laura.sandys.mp@parliament.uk.

SANG, Truong Tan; President, Government of Vietnam; ***political career:*** Mayor, Ho Chi Minh City; Party Chief, Ho Chi Minh City; Mem., leadership, Communist Party; President, Government of Vietnam, June 2011-; ***office address:*** Office of the President, Hanoi, Vietnam.

SANTOS, Juan Manuel; President, Government of Colombia; ***education:*** Cadet, Naval School, Cartagena; Economícs and Business Administration; LSE and Harvard, Post grad degrees in Economics, Economic Development and Public Administration; Fulbright scholar at the Fletcher School of Law and Diplomacy; Neiman Foundation grant to Harvard Univ.; ***political career:*** Min. of Foreign Trade; Min. of Finance and Public Credit; Minister of Defence, 2006-09; President, 2010-; ***professional career:*** Head of the Colombian Delegation to the International Coffee Organisation, London, for nine years; Pres., UNCTAD, 1992-96; Pres., CEPAL, 1997-99; Pres., Corporación Andina de Fomento (CAF), 2001-02; ***office address:*** Office of the President, Carrera 8a, No. 7-26, Santafé de Bogotá, Colombia; ***phone:*** +57 1 266 9300; ***URL:*** http://www.presidencia.gov.co.

SANTOS LOPEZ, Samuel; Minister of Foreign Affairs, Government of Nicaragua; ***born:*** 1938; ***political career:*** Mayor, Managua; Mem., FSLN National Reconstruction Government, 1975-85; Sec. of Finance, FSLN Party, 1992; Mem., National Sandinist Assembly, -2006; Minister of Foreign Affairs, 2007-; ***professional career:*** Businessman, director of several companies; real estate; ***office address:*** Ministry of Foreign Affairs, Kilometro 3 1/2, carretera sur, Managua, Nicaragua; ***URL:*** http://www.cancilleria.gob.ni/.

SANTOS PEREIRA, Alvaro; Minister of Economy and Employment, Government of Portugal; ***born:*** 1972; ***education:*** Univ. of Coimbra, Economics; Simon Fraser Univ., Vancouver, Canada, Ph.D, Economics; ***political career:*** Minister of Economy and Employment, Gov. of Portugal, 2011-; ***professional career:*** lecturer; visiting prof., Dept. of Economics, Univ. of BC, Canada; lecturer, Univ. of York, UK; ***office address:*** Ministry of Economy & Employment, Rua da Horta Seca 15, 1200-221 Lisbon, Portugal.

SAPIN, Michel; French, Minister of Labour, Employment & Professional Training, Government of France; ***born:*** 9 April 1952; ***education:*** National Sch. of Admin., 1980; ***political career:*** Nat. Assembly Dep. of the Indre, 1981-86; Sec., Nat. Assembly, 1983-84; Vice-Pres., Nat. Assembly, 1984-85; Nat. Assembly Dep. of Hauts-de-Seine, 1986-91; re-elected Dep. and Chmn., Cttee. for Law of the Nat. Assembly, 1988-91; Minister Delg. for Justice, 1991-92; Minister of Economy and Finances, 1992-93; Mem., Council for Monetary policy of the Banque de France, 1994-95; Mayor d'Argenton-sur-Creuse, 1995, re-elected 2001; Gen. Cllr. of the Indre, 1998; Pres., Centre Regional Council, 1998; First Vice-Pres. of the Assoc. of the Regions of France, 1998-2000; Vice-Pres., Centre Regional Council, 2000-2001; Mayor, Argenton-sur-Creuse, 2002-04, 2007-; Pres., RCentral Regional Council, 2004-07; Minister of Civil Service and Admin. Reform, 2000-2002; Minister for Labour, Employment and Professional Training, 2012-; ***office address:*** Assemblée Nationale, Palais Bourbon, 126 rue de l'Université, 75355, Cédex 07 SP, Paris, France.

SARGEANT, Carl; Assembly Member for Alyn and Deeside, National Assembly of Wales; ***political career:*** National Assembly of Wales mem. for Alyn and Deeside, May 2003-; Labour Chief Whip and Deputy Business Manager, 2007; Minister for Social Justice and Local Government, 2009-11; Minister for Local Government and Communities, 2011-13; Minister for Housing and Regeneration, 2013-; ***office address:*** National Assembly for Wales, Cardiff Bay, Cardiff, United Kingdom; ***phone:*** +44 (0)29 2082 5111.

SARGSYAN, Serge; President, Government of Armenia; ***born:*** 1954, Artsakh (Nagorno-Karabakh); ***education:*** Yerevan State Univ., 1971-76; ***political career:*** Head of Propaganda Section, Second Sec., then First Sec., Komsomol Youth Party's City Cttee. of Stepanakert, Asst. to First Sec., Karabakh Regional Cttee., 1979-88; Head of the Artsakh (Karabakh) Self Defence Cttee., 1988-93; Dep., National Assembly of the Republic of Armenia, 1990-93; Minister of Defence, Republic of Armenia, 1993-95; Head of the State Dept. of National Security, Minister of Nat. Security, 1995-96; Minister of Internal Affairs and National Security, 1996-99; Chief of Staff of the Pres., and Sec. of National Security Council, 1999-2000; Minister of Defence, 2000-07; Prime Minister, 2007-08; President of Armenia, 2008-; ***professional career:*** Turner, Yerevan Electro-technical Factory, 1975-79; ***honours and awards:*** Holder of First Degree 'Fighting Cross' Order; Knight of the 'Gold Eagle' Order; ***office address:*** Office of the President, Republic Square, Government House 1, Yerevan, Armenia.

SARGSYAN, Tigran; Prime Minister, Republic of Armenia; ***born:*** 1960; ***political career:*** Prime Minister, Republic of Armenia, 2008-; ***professional career:*** Chmn., Armenian Bankers' Assn., 1995-98; Chmn., Bank of the Republic of Armenia, 1998-2008; ***office address:*** Prime Minister's Office, Republic Square, Government House 1, Yerevan, Armenia.

SARKOZY, Nicolas; French, Ex Officio Member, Constitutional Court, Republic of France; ***born:*** 28 January 1955, Paris, France; ***married:*** Marie-Dominique Culioli, 1982 (Div'd 1996); Cécilia Ciganer-Albéniz, 1996 (Div'd 2007); Carla Bruni , 2008; ***education:*** Master's degree in private law, 1978; Barrister's Diploma, 1981; Institut des Études Politiques, 1979-81; ***party:*** UMP, Union pour un Mouvement Populaire (formerly the RPR); ***political career:*** Mem., Neuilly-sur-Seine Town Council, 1977; Mayor, Neuilly-sur-Seine, 1983-; Vice-Chmn., Hauts-de-Seine General House, with resp. for culture, 1986-88; Nat. Sec., RPR, with resp. for Youth & Training, 1988, with resp. for Leisure, Youth & Training, 1989; Co-Dir., union list for European Elections, 1989; Dep. Sec. Gen., RPR, resp. for federations, 1992-93; mem., political office of RPR, 1993-; interim Pres., RPR, April-Oct. 1999; head of list, RPR-DL for European elections, June 1999; Dpty. (RPR), National Assy., Hauts-de-Seine, 1988- (re-elected 1993, 1995, 1997); Min. of the Budget, 1993-95; Min. of Communication, 1994-95; Gov. Spokesman, 1993-95; Mem., finance cttee; Sec. Gen., RPR party, 1998-99; Minister of the Interior, Internal Security and Local Freedoms, 2002-04; Minister of State, Minister of Economy, Finance & Industry, 2004-05; Pres., Union pour un Mouvement Populaire (UMP), 2004-; Minister of the Interior and Regional Development, 2005-07; President, Republic of France, 2007-12; Co Prince, Andorra, 2007-12; Ex-Officio Mem., Constitutional Court, 2012-; ***professional career:*** Barrister; ***publications:*** Au bout de la passion, l'équilibre, 1995; Libre, 2001; La République, les religions, l'espérance, 2004; Georges Mandel, moine de la politique, 1994; ***office address:*** c/o Union pour un Mouvement Populaire, 55, rue La Boétie, 75384 Paris Cedex 08, France; ***phone:*** +33 (0)1 40 76 60 00; ***URL:*** http://www.u-m-p.org.

SARWAR, Anas; MP for Glasgow Central, UK Government; ***party:*** Labour; ***political career:*** MP for Glasgow Central, May 2010-; Deputy Leader, Scottish Labour, 2011-; ***committees:*** International Development Select Cttee., 2010-12; Arms Export Control, 2010-12; ***office address:*** House of Commons, London, SW1A 0AA, United Kingdom; ***phone:*** +44 (0)20 7219 3000; ***e-mail:*** anas.sarwar.mp@parliament.uk.

SASAE, H.E. Kenichiro; Ambassador, Embassy of Japan in the US; ***professional career:*** Dir.-Gen., Asian and Oceania Affairs Bureau, 2005-08; Dep. Minister for Foreign Affairs, 2008-10; Vice Minister for Foreign Affairs, 2010-12; Amb. to the USA, 2012-; ***office address:*** Embassy of Japan, 2520 Massachusetts Avenue NW, Washington DC 20008, USA; ***phone:*** +1 202 939 6700; ***URL:*** http://www.us.emb-japan.go.jp/english/html/index.html.

SASSOON, Lord James; Member, House of Lords; ***political career:*** Mem. House of Lords, 2010-; Commercial Sec., HM Treasury 2010-13; ***office address:*** HM Treasury, London, SW1A 2HQ, United Kingdom; ***phone:*** +44 (0)20 7270 4350; ***URL:*** http://www.hm-treasury.gov.uk.

SASSOU-NGUESSO, General Denis; Congolese, President of the Republic and Head of Government, Republic of Congo; ***born:*** 1943; ***political career:*** 1st Vice-Pres., Military Cttee. of PCT (Parti Congolais du Travail) 1977-79; Minister of National Defence; President 1979-92; President 1997-. Chmn., OAU, 2006-; ***office address:*** Office of the President, Palais du Peuple, BP 2006, Brazzaville, Republic of Congo.

SATA, Michael C.; President, Government of Zambia; ***born:*** 1937; ***political career:*** municipal councillor; governor of Lusaka under President Kenneth Kaunda; joined MMD party 1991, organising secretary; MMD Minister of Local Government, Labour and Health; Minister without Portfolio, -2001; Formed Patriotic Front, 2001; contested presidential elections, 2001, 2006, 2008; President of Zambia, 2011-; ***office address:*** Office of the President, PO Box 30208, Lusaka, Zambia; ***URL:*** http://www.statehouse.gov.zm.

SATYBALDIYEV, Zhantoro; Prime Minister, Government of Kyrgyzstan; ***born:*** March 1956; ***political career:*** Governor of Osh; Minister of Communications and Transportation; Deputy Prime Minsiter, 2010-11; Prime Minister, 2012-; ***office address:*** Office of the Prime Minister, Dom Pravitelstva, 720003 Bishkek, Kyrgyzstan; ***URL:*** http://www.government.gov.kg.

SAUVÉ, Jean-Marc; Vice-President, Council of State of France; ***born:*** 28 May 1949 , Templeux-le-Guérard, Somme; ***education:*** Instit. of Political Studies, Paris; Doctorate, Economics; ENA; ***professional career:*** Dir., gen. admin. Ministry of Justice, 1983-88; Dir., Civil Liberties and Legal Affairs, Ministry of the Interior, 1988-94; Prefect, Aisne, 1994-95; Counsellor of State, 1995; Sec. Gen. of the Govt., 1995-2006; Vice Pres., Conseil d'Etat, 2006-; ***committees:*** Pres., Bd. of Dir., Acad. of France in Rome, 1999-2008; Mem., Bd. of Dirs., Louvre Museum, 2002-08; ***office address:*** Conseil d'État , 1 place du Palais-Royal, 75100 Paris, France; ***phone:*** +33 (0)1 40 20 80 50; ***URL:*** http://www.conseil-etat.fr/.

SAVARIN, Hon. Charles Angelo; Minister of National Security, Immigration and Labour, Government of Dominica; ***born:*** 2 October 1943, Portsmouth, Dominica; ***s:*** 1; ***d:*** 4; ***education:*** Ruskin Coll., Oxford Univ., UK; ***party:*** Dominica Labour Party (DLP); ***political career:*** Senator, House of Assembly 1979-85; Minister without Portfolio, Prime Minister's Office 1983-85; MP for Roseau Central Constituency, 1995-2005; Leader of the Freedom Party 1996-2000; Minister for Tourism 2000-05; Minister for Foreign Affairs, Trade, Labour and the Public Service 2005-07; Minister for Public Utilities, Energy and Ports and the Public Service 2007-09; Minister for National Security, Immigration and Labour and the Public Service 2009-; ***professional career:*** Asst. Master, Dominica Grammar School 1963-70; Gen. Sec., Dominica Civil Services Assoc., 1966-83; Minister Councillor, Dominica High Commissioner, London, 1985-86; Amb., Perm. Rep. to the EU, 1986-93; Amb. to the Kingdom of Belgium, the Grand Duchy of Luxenburg, the Swiss Federation and Perm. Rep. to the UN Office in Geneva, 1986-1993; Gen. Man., Nat. Dev. Corporation, 1993-95; ***office address:*** Ministry of National Security, 5th Floor Financial Centre, Kennedy Avenue, Roseau, Dominica; ***phone:*** +767 266 8960; ***fax:*** +767 448 8960.

SAVILLE OF NEWDIGATE, Rt. Hon. Lord; Member, House of Lords; ***education:*** BA, BCL, Brasenose College, Oxford Univ.; ***political career:*** Mem. of House of Lords, 1997-, as Justice of the Supreme Court, disqualified from participtaion 2009-10; ***professional career:*** Called to the Bar (Middle Temple), 1962-; Queen's Counsel, 1975; Judge of the High Court, 1985; Lord Justice of Appeal, 1994; Lord of Appeal in Ordinary, 1997-2009; Justice of the Supreme Court of the United Kingdom, 2009-; ***office address:*** House of Lords, London, SW1 0AA, United Kingdom.

SAWFORD, Andy; MP for Corby and East Northamptonshire, British Government; ***education:*** Durham Univ., 1997; ***party:*** Labour Party; ***political career:*** MP for Corby and East Northamptonshire, Nov. 2012-; ***office address:*** House of Commons, London, SW1A 0AA, United Kingdom; ***phone:*** +44 (0)20 7219 3000.

SAYASONE, Lt. Gen. Choummaly; President, Lao People's Democratic Republic; ***born:*** 1936; ***party:*** Head, Lao People's Revolutionary Party, 2006-; ***political career:*** Defence Minister; Vice President, Lao People's Democratic Republic; President, June 2006-; ***office address:*** Office of the President, Presidential Buildings, Sethathirath Road, Vientiane, Laos.

SCALIA, Antonin ; Associate Justice, US Supreme Court; ***born:*** 11 March 1936, Trenton, New Jersey; ***education:*** Georgetown Univ., and Univ. of Fribourg, Switzerland, A.B; Harvard Law School, LL.B. ; ***professional career:*** private practice, Cleveland, Ohio, 1961-67; Prof. of Law, Univ. of Virginia, 1967-71; Prof. of Law, Univ. of Chicago, 1977-82; General Counsel, US Office of Telecommunications Policy, 1971-72; Assist. Attorney General, Office of Legal Counsel, 1974-77; Judge, US Court of Appeals, District of Columbia Circuit, 1982-86; Assoc. Justice, Supreme Court, 1986-; ***committees:*** Chmn., American Bar Association's Section of Administrative Law, 1981-82; Chmn., Administrative Conference of the US, 1972-1974; ***office address:*** Supreme Court, One First Street, NE, Washington, DC 20543, USA; ***phone:*** +1 202 479 3211; ***URL:*** http://www.supremecourt.gov/.

SCALISE, Steve; Congressman, Louisiana 1st District, US House of Representatives; ***born:*** October 6, 1965, New Orleans, USA; ***education:*** Louisiana State Univ., Computer Science with Political Science; ***party:*** Republican; ***political career:*** Louisiana Legislature, 12+ years; Mem., US HOR, 1st Dist. Louisiana, 2008-; ***professional career:*** Systems engineer; ***committees:*** Energy and Commerce; ***office address:*** House of Representatives, 1205 Longworth House Office Building, Washington, DC 20515, USA.

SCARCE, H.E. Rear Admiral Kevin, AO CSC RANR; Governor, South Australia; ***born:*** 1952 , Adelaide, SA; ***education:*** Univ. of New England, Bachelor of Financial Admin.; Univ. of New South Wales, Master of Management Economics; National Defense Univ., Washington DC, M.Sc., National Security Strategy; ***professional career:*** Joined Royal Australian Navy, 1968; HMAS Sydney, Vietnam; naval courses, UK, 1973; served at sea, HMA Ships Vendetta, Yarra, and Duchess; Aust. Embassy, 1979-82; Supply Officer, HMAS Perth; promoted to Commander, 1985; posted to Canberra, 1985-87; Supply Officer, Naval Air Station HMAS Albatross; promoted to Captain; Fleet Supply Officer, Fleet Headquarters; Commanding Officer, HMAS Cerberus, 1995-97; Naval Training Commander, 1997- 98; Commander Logistics - Navy, 1997-99; Support Commander Australia - Navy Support Command Australia, 1999-2000; Head, Maritime Systems, 2000-03; Acting Under Secretary Defence Materiel Org., 2003-04; Retired from the Royal Australian Navy, 2004; Chief Exec., South Australian Government Defence Unit and Chmn., Defence Industry Advisory Bd., 2004-05; Advisor, Port Adelaide Maritime Corp., 2006-07; Governor, South Australia, 2008-; ***honours and awards:*** Conspicuous Service Cross, Australia Day,1994; Mem. Military Division of the Order of Australia, Queen's Birthday List 2001; Officer of the Military Division of the Order of Australia, Australia Day 2004; ***office address:*** Government House, GPO Box 2373 , Adelaide 5001 , Australia; ***e-mail:*** governors.office@saugov.sa.gov.au; ***URL:*** http://www.governor.sa.gov.au/.

SCHATZ, Brian; Senator for Hawaii, US Senate; ***born:*** 1972; ***political career:*** mem., Hawaii State House of Reps., 1998-2006; Chmn., Democratic Party of Hawaii, 2008-10; Lieutenant Gov., 2010-12; Senator, US Senate, 2012-; ***office address:*** US Senate, G11 Dirksen Senate Office Building, Washington, DC 20510, USA; ***phone:*** +1 202 224 3934; ***URL:*** http://www.senate.gov/senators/112/Schatz_Brian.htm.

SCHÄUBLE, Wolfgang; Minister of Finance, Federal Government of Germany; ***born:*** 18 September 1942; ***education:*** Freiburg and Hamburg Univs., Law and Econ.; ***party:*** Christian Democratic Union (CDU), 1965-; ***political career:*** Mem., Federal Govt. (Bundestag), 1972-; Mem., Parly. Assembly of the Cncl. of Europe, 1975-84; Fed. Minister of Special Tasks and Head of the Fed. Chancellery, then Fed. Minister of the Interior, 1984-89; Fed. Chmn., CDU, 1998-2000; Minister of the Interior, 2005-09; Minister of Finance, 2009-; ***professional career:*** Assist. lecturer, Freiburg Univ. and Rep. of the Vice-Chancellor on political education, 1966-70; Mem. of the tax authorities, Baden Wurttemberg, 1971; Barrister, Offenburg, 1978-84; ***committees:*** Chmn., CDU Special Cttee. for Sport, 1976-84; Parly. Sec., CDU/CSU Parly. Gp., Bundestag, 1981-84, Chmn., 1991-2000; Vice-Chmn., CDU/CSU parly gp. for foreign policy, security policy and European policy, 2002-2005; ***office address:*** Wilhelmstrasse 97, 10117 Berlin, Germany; ***phone:*** +49 (0)30 22420; ***fax:*** +49 (0)30 3342 3260; ***e-mail:*** poststelle@bmf.bund.de; ***URL:*** http://www.bundesfinanzministerium.de.

SCHEER, Hon. Andrew; Speaker, House of Commons, Canada; ***born:*** Ottawa, Ontario; ***education:*** Univ. of Ottawa; Univ. of Saskatchewan; ***party:*** Conservative; ***political career:*** MP for Regina-Qu'Appelle, 2004-; Deputy Speaker; Speaker, 2011-; ***office address:*** Office of the Speaker, House of Commons, Parliament Buildings, Wellington Street, Ottawa K1A 0A6, Ontario, Canada; ***phone:*** +1 613 943 5959; ***fax:*** +1 613 992 3674; ***URL:*** http://www.parl.gc.ca.

SCHIFF, Adam B.; Congressman, California 29th District, US House of Representatives; ***party:*** Democratic Party; ***political career:*** Mem., US House of Representatives, 2000-; ***committees:*** Appropriations; Perm. Select Cttee. on Intelligence; ***office address:*** US House of Representatives, Washington, DC 20515, USA; ***phone:*** +1 202 224 3121.

SCHINDLER, Christian P.; Director General, International Textile Manufacturers Federation; ***born:*** 1968, Germany; ***education:*** Univ. of Fribourg, Switzerland, Masters, Econ., 1994; Institute for Economic Policy, Univ. of Cologne, Ph.D, 2004; ***professional career:*** PA to two members of the German Bundestag, 1994-97; PA/Speechwriter to Pres., Federation of German Wholesale and Foreign Trade (BGA), 1998-2001; Economist, International Textile Manufacturers Fed.(ITMF), 2004-07; Dir.Gen., ITMF, 2007-; ***office address:*** ITMF, Wiedingstrasse 9, CH 8055 Zurich, Switzerland; ***phone:*** +41 44 283 6380; ***fax:*** +41 44 283 6389; ***e-mail:*** secretariat@itmf.org; ***URL:*** http://www.itmf.org.

SCHIPPERS, Edith; Minister of Health, Welfare and Sport, Netherlands Government; ***born:*** 1964; ***education:*** Univ. of Leiden, Political Sciences; Jawaharlal Nehru Univ., India; ***political career:*** personal assistant, House of Reps., 1993; Policy Officer, VVD parliamentary party, health, welfare and sport, 1994-97; MP, 2003-; Deputy Leader, VVD, 2006-; Minister of Health, Welfare and Sport, Rutte-Verhagen gov., October 2010-12; Minister of Health, Welfare and Sport, Rutte-Asscher gov., Nov. 2012-; ***professional career:*** Confederation of Netherlands Industry and Employers, 1997-2003; ***office address:*** Ministry of Health, Welfare and Sport, Parnassusplein 5, 2511 VX The Hague, Netherlands; ***URL:*** http://www.minvws.nl.

SCHMIED, Claudia; Minister of Education, Government of Austria; ***born:*** 10 May 1959, Vienna, Austria; ***education:*** Vienna Univ. of Economics and Business Administration, Ph.D, 1983; ***party:*** Social Democrat Party; ***political career:*** Federal Minister of Education, Science and Culture, Jan. 2007-; ***memberships:*** Kuratorium, Salzburg Festival; Supervisory Bd., Art for Art Theatre; Exec. Bd., Association Wiener Symphoniker; Chmn., Assn. for Society and Economic Science; Exec. Bd., BSA (Fed. of Social-Democratic Univ. grads.); ***professional career:*** Corp. Acct. Mgr., Investkredit, 1983-97, Head of Corp. Finance Dept., 1995-97; Economic policy advisor, Office of the Federal Minister and State Sec. of Finance, 1997-2000; Investkredit, 2000-04; Mem., Exec. Bd., Kommunalkredit Austria, 2004-; Mem., Exec. Bd., Dexia Kommunalkredit Bank, 2005-; ***office address:*** Ministry of Education , Minoritenplatz 5, 1014 Vienna, Austria; ***phone:*** +43 (0)1 53120-5000.

SCHMIT, Nicolas; Minister of Employment, Work and Immigration, Government of Luxembourg; ***born:*** 10 December 1953; ***education:*** Institut des Etudes Politique, Aix-en-Provence, Ph.D., Economics; Dipl. des Etudes Approfondies, International Relations; M.Litt. ; ***political career:*** Head of Cabinet of the Foreign Affairs Minister, 1984-89; Sec., Parly. Gp. of the LSAP, 1989; Adviser, Permanent Mission of Luxembourg at the EU, Brussels, 1990-91; Mem., Council of State, 1991; Head, Dept. of Internat. Economic Relations and Cooperation, Ministry of Foreign Affairs, 1992-98; Amb., Permanent Mission of Luxembourg at the EU, 1998; Minister-Delegate for Foreign Affairs and Immigration, 2004-09; Minister of Employment, Labour and Immigration, 2009-; ***office address:*** Ministry of Employment, 26 rue Zithe, 2763 Luxembourg, Luxembourg; ***phone:*** +352 247 86100; ***fax:*** +352 247 86108; ***e-mail:*** officielle.boite@mt.ebat.lu; ***URL:*** http://www.mte.public.lu.

SCHNEIDER-AMMANN, Johann; Federal Councillor, Government of Switzerland; ***born:*** 1952; ***education:*** electrical engineering, Dipl. El. Ing. ETH; ***political career:*** mem., National Council, for the FTP; Head, Fed. Dept. of Economic Affairs, Education & Research

(EAER), 2010-; ***professional career:*** Pres., Ammann Group; ***office address:*** Federal Department of Economic Affairs, Education & Research, Bundeshaus Ost, 3003 Berne, Switzerland; ***URL:*** http://www.wbf.admin.ch/.

SCHÖNBORN, Cardinal Christoph, OP, Dr.theol.; Archbishop, Vienna; ***born:*** 22 January 1945, Skalken, Bohemia; ***education:*** Walberberg, Bonn, Germany, philosophy, theology; Le Saulchoir, theology; Vienna, Austria, philosophy, psychology; Ecole Practique des Hautes Etudes, Sorbonne, France, Christianity, Byzantine and slav.; Dr., Paris, France, 1974; ***memberships:*** Mem., Int. Theological Cmn., 1980-85; ***professional career:*** joined the Dominican Order; Ordained Priest, Vienna, 1970; Student's Chaplain, Graz, 1973-75; Prof. for Catholic Dogmatic Theology, Fribourg, Switzerland, 1975-91; Editing Sec., Catechism of the Catholic Church, 1987-92; Ordained Auxiliary Bishop, Cathedral of St. Stephens, Vienna, Austria, 1991; Archbishop of Vienna, 1995; created Cardinal, 1998; elected Pres. of the Austrian Bishop's Conference, 1998; ***honours and awards:*** Goldenes Komturkreuz with star of decoration for merits for the region of Lower Austria, 1998; ***publications:*** Die Menschen, die Kirche, das Land Christentum als gesellschaftliche Herausforderung, 1998; Wähle das Leben. Die Christliche Moral nach dem Katechismus der Katholischen Kirche, 1998; Gott sandte seinen Sohn. Christologie, 2002, Sophrone de Jérusalem, 1972; The Mystery of the Incarnation, 1993; Introduction to the Catechism of the Catholic Church, Joseph Cardinal Ratzinger, 1994; God's Human Face. the Christ-Icon, 1994; From Death to Life. The Christian Journey, 1995; Living the Catechism of the Catholic Church. The Creed, 1995; Loving the Church, 1998; The Sacraments, 2000; Life in Christ, 2001; ***office address:*** Archbishop of Vienna, Rotenturmstraße 2, A-1010 Vienna, Austria; ***phone:*** +43 (0)1 5155 23724; ***fax:*** +43 (0)1 5155 23728.

SCHRÖDER, Dr Kristina; Minister for Family Affairs, Senior Citizens, Women and Youth, German Government; ***born:*** 3 August 1977, Wiesbaden, Germany; ***education:*** Ph.D., Johannes Gutenberg Univ. of Mainz; ***political career:*** MP, 2002-; Minister of Family Affairs, Senior Citizens, Women and Youth, 2009-; ***office address:*** Ministry of Family Affairs, Glinkastraße 24, 10117 Berlin, Germany; ***phone:*** +49 (0)30 18 5550; ***URL:*** http://www.bmfsfj.de.

SCHULTZ VAN HAEGEN-MAAS GEESTERANUS, Melanie; Minister of Infrastructure and the Environment, Netherlands Government; ***born:*** 1970; ***education:*** Public Admin., Univ. of Leiden and Rotterdam Erasmus Univ.; INSEAD, Fontainebleu; IEDC School of Management; ***political career:*** mem., municipal executive, Leiden, 1999-2002; State Secretary for Transport, Public Works and Water Management, 2002; Minister of Infrastructure and the Environment, Rutte-Verhagen government, 2010-12; Minister of Infrastructure and the Environment, Rutte-Asscher government, Nov. 2012-; ***office address:*** Ministry of Infrastructure and the Environment, Plesmanweg 1-6, 2597 JG The Hague, Netherlands; ***URL:*** http://english.verkeerenwaterstaat.nl/english/.

SCHULZ, Martin; German, President, European Parliament; ***born:*** 1955; ***party:*** Socialist Group in the European Parliament; ***political career:*** Municipal Cllr., Würselen, 1984-; Mayor of Würselen, 1987-88; Mem., SPD Bureau & Fed. Executive, 1999-; Mem., European Parly., 1994-; Chmn., SPD Group, Euro Parliament, 2000-04; First Vice-Chmn., Socialist Group, 2004-09, Chmn., S&D Group, 2009; Pres., European Parliament, Jan. 2012-; ***office address:*** European Parliament, Allée du Printemps, B.P. 1024, F-67070 Strasbourg Cedex, France; ***phone:*** +33 (0)3 88 17 40 01; ***fax:*** +33 (0)3 88 25 65 01; ***URL:*** http://www.europarl.europa.eu/.

SCHUMER, Charles; Senator for New York, US Senate; ***married:*** Iris Weinshall; ***children:*** Jessica (F), Alison (F); ***education:*** Harvard Coll., graduate; Harvard Law Sch. graduate; ***political career:*** New York State Assembly; Rep. for the Ninth Congressional District in Brooklyn and Queens, US House of Representatives; Senator for New York, US Senate; ***committees:*** Chair, Rules & Administration; Judiciary; Finance; Banking, Housing and Urban Affairs; ***office address:*** US Senate, 313 Hart Senate Office Building, Washington, DC 20510, USA; ***phone:*** +1 202 224 6542; ***fax:*** +1 202 224 2262; ***URL:*** http://www.schumer.senate.gov.

SCHWAB, Professor Klaus, KCMG; Founder and Executive Chairman, World Economic Forum; ***born:*** 30 March 1938, Ravensburg, Germany; ***married:*** Hilde Schwab, 1971; ***children:*** Olivier (M), Nicole (F); ***education:*** Humanistische Gymnasium, Ravensburg, 1957; Swiss Fed. Inst. of Technology, Dipl. Ing., 1962, Dr.Ing., 1966; Univ. of Fribourg, Switzerland, Lic.ès.sc.écon, 1963, Dr.rer.pol., 1967; Swiss John F. Kennedy School Govt., Harvard Univ., Master of Public Admin., 1967; ***memberships:*** co-founder and mem., Schwab Foundation for Social Entrepreneurship, Geneva; Bd. Mem., Lucerne Festival; Mem., Visiting Cttee., JFK School of Govt., Harvard Univ.; Mem., President's Cncl., Univ. of Tokyo; Mem., Advisory Bd., Foreign Policy, Washington D.C.; ***professional career:*** Experience on shop floor of several co's, 1958-62; Asst. to Dir. Gen. of the German Machine-building Assn., Frankfurt, 1963-66; Mem. of Managing Bd., Sulzer Escher Wyss AG, Zurich, 1967-70; Prof., Geneva Univ., 1972-2003; Founder & Exec. Chmn., World Economic Forum, 1971-; ***trusteeships:*** Peres Centre for Peace, Tel Aviv; ***honours and awards:*** Seven Honorary Doctorates; Honorary Knighthood (KCMG); Grand Cross of the National Order of Merit of Germany; Knight of the Légion d'Honneur of France; Golden Grand Cross of the National Order of Austria; Medal of Freedom of the Republic of Slovenia; National Order of the Republic of Poland, Commander's Cross with Star; Decoration of the First Degree for Outstanding Giving, Jordan; Hon. Professor, Ben-Gurion Univ. of the Negev, Israel; Hon. Doc. of Foreign Affairs, Univ. of Beijing, China; ***publications:*** Author of the Annual Global Competitiveness Report, along with numerous articles & 6 books, Overcoming indifference, 1994, NY Univ. Press; ***recreations:*** cross country ski marathon, high mountain climbing; ***office address:*** World Economic Forum, 91-93 route de la Capite, 1223 Cologny, Switzerland; ***phone:*** +41 (0)22 869 1212; ***fax:*** +41 (0)22 786 2744; ***e-mail:*** contact@weforum.org.

SCHWARZENBERG, Karel; Minister of Foreign Affairs, Government of the Czech Republic; ***born:*** 10 December 1937, Prague; ***parents:*** Prince Karl VI of Schwarzenberg and Princess Antonie von Fürstenberg; ***education:*** Universities of Vienna, Munich and Graz, Law and Silviculture Studies, 1957; ***party:*** Leader, TOP 09 party; ***political career:*** Mem., Collegium of Counsellors of President Václav Havel, 1990-; Chancellor, 1990-92; Senator, Parliament of the Czech Republic representing the 6th election district, 2006-; Mem., EU Affairs Cttee.; Chairman, Foreign Affairs, Defence and Security Cttee., 2006; Mem., Permanent Delegation of the Parliament to the Council of Europe, 2006; Minister of Foreign Affairs, 2007-09; First Deputy Prime Minister, 2010-12; Minister of Foreign Affairs, 2010-; ***professional career:*** Administration of family estates in Austria and Bavaria, 1965-; Pres., Int'l Helsinki Cttee. for Human Rights, 1984-91; returned to Czechoslavakia, 1989; ***office address:*** Ministry of Foreign Affairs, Loretánské námestí 5, Prague 1, Czech Republic; ***e-mail:*** info@mzv.cz; ***URL:*** http://www.mzv.cz.

SCOTLAND OF ASTHAL, Baroness , QC; Member, House of Lords; ***education:*** LLB (Hons), London; ***party:*** Labour Party; ***political career:*** Mem. of House of Lords; Parly. Under-Sec.of State, Foreign and Commonwealth Office, 1999-2001; parly. Sec. Lord Chancellor's Dept., 2001-2003; Alternate UK Gov. Rep., European Convention, 2002-03; Home Office, Minister of State for the Criminal Justice System and Law Reform, 2003-07; Spokesperson for DTI on Women and Equality Issues in the House of Lords; Attorney General, June 2007-10; Shadow Attorney General, 2010-11; ***memberships:*** The Millennium Commission, 1994-99; Patron, The Margaret Beaufort Inst.; GAP; The Frank Longford Charitable Trust; Sponsor, George Viner Memorial Fund Trust; Thomas More Soc.; Lawyers' Christian Fellowship; ***professional career:*** Called to the Bar, Middle Temple, 1977; received Silk, 1991; Bencher, 1997; Hon. Fellow, The Soc. of Advanced Legal Studies, Wolfson Coll. Cambridge and Cardiff Univ.; Mem. of the Bar of Antigua and Commonwealth of Dominica; Assist. Recorder, 1994; approved to sit as Dep. High Court Judge, Family Division; Door Tenant, Bridewell Chambers; Founder Mem. and Head of 1 Gray's Inn Square; former positions include, Her Majesty's Commissioners for Racial Equality, Hon. Pres., Trinity Hall Law Soc., Chmn. ILEA Disciplinary Tribunal, mem., BBC World Service Consultative Gp. Chmn. HMG Caribbean Advisory Gp., Dominican Rep., Cncl. of the British Commonwealth Ex-Service League; ***committees:*** Former mem. Bar Public Relations, Cttee.; Race Relations Cttee.; Professional Conduct Cttee.; Judicial Studies Bd. Ethnic Minority Advisory Cttee.; House of Commons Working Party on Child Abduction; Legal Advisory Panel on the National Consumer Cncl.; Ind. Cttee. for the Supervision of Standards of Telephone Information Services; Nat. Advisory Cttee. on Mentally Disordered Offenders; All Parly. Gp., on Breast Cancer; Parly. Labour Party Women's Gp.; House of Lords, All Party Parly. London Gp; All Party Parly. Gp. of CAFOD; All Party Parly. Gp for Children and the Lords' Prayer Gp.; ***honours and awards:*** Created Peer, Baroness Scotland of Asthal, of Asthal in the County of Oxfordshire, 1997; raised to Privy Council, July 2001; Hon. Doctorate, Univ. of Westminster, Univ. of Buckingham and Univ. of Leicester; Dame of the Sacred Military Constantinian Order of Saint George; Black Woman of the Year (Law), 1992; Peer of the Year, House Magazine, 2004; Peer of the Year, Channel 4 Political Awards, 2004; Parliamentarian of the Year, Political Studies Assoc. Awards, 2004; ***office address:*** House of Lords, London, SW1A 0PQ, United Kingdom; ***phone:*** +44 (0)20 7219 3000; ***fax:*** +44 (0)20 7219 5979.

SCOTT, Lee; MP for Ilford North, House of Commons; ***party:*** Conservative Party; ***political career:*** MP for Ilford North, 2005-; ***committees:*** Transport, 2005-08; Health, 2007-10; Panel of Chairs, 2011-; ***office address:*** House of Commons, London, SW1P 0AA, United Kingdom; ***phone:*** +44 (0)20 7219 3000.

SCOTT, Richard; Governor, State of Florida; ***education:*** Univ. of Missouri-Kansas City, BA, business admin.; Southern Methodist Univ., law; ***political career:*** Governor, State of Florida, Nov. 2010-; ***professional career:*** law, Johnson & Swanson, Dallas; founder, Columbia, later Columbia/HCA (healthcare); ***office address:*** Office of the Governor, PL 05 The Capitol, 400 South Monroe Street, Tallahassee FL 32399-0001, USA; ***URL:*** http://www.flgov.com/.

SCOTT, Tim; Senator for South Carolina, US Senate; ***education:*** Charleston Southern University, 1998; ***party:*** Republican; ***political career:*** Charleston County Council, 14 years; SC House of Representatives, 2008-2010, Chmn., Freshman Caucus, House Whip; Mem., US HOR, South Carolina 1st District, 2010-; ***committees:*** US Senate: Commerce, Science & Transportation; Energy, & Natural Resources; Health, Education, Labor & Pensions; Small Business & Entrpreneurship; Special Cttee. on Aging; ***office address:*** US Senate, 117 Hart Senate Office Building, Washington DC 20510, USA; ***URL:*** http://www.scott.senate.gov/.

SEABECK, Alison; MP for Plymouth Moor View, House of Commons; ***born:*** 1954; ***party:*** Labour; ***political career:*** MP for Plymouth Devonport, 2005-; Assist. Govt. Whip, 2007-08; PPS Sec. of State for Transport, 2008-10; Shadow Minister, Communities and Local Government, Oct. 2010-11; Shadow Minister, Defence, 2011-; ***office address:*** House of Commons, London, SW1A 0AA, United Kingdom.

SEBASTIAN, Sir Cuthbert, GCME, OBE; Governor General, St. Kitts; ***education:*** BSc., Mount Allison Univ., Canada, 1953; MD, M. of Surgery, Dalhousie Univ., Canada, 1958; ***political career:*** Governor General, St. Christopher and Nevis, 1996-; ***professional career:*** Royal Air Force, 1944-45; Med. Supt., Cunningham Hosp., St. Kitts, 1966; Med. Supt. Joseph N. France Gen. Hospital, 1967-80; CMO, St. Christopher and Nevis, 1980-83; Private medical practitioner, 1983-95; ***office address:*** Government House, Basseterre, St. Kitts and Nevis.

SEBELIUS, Kathleen; American, Secretary of Health and Human Services, United States Government; ***born:*** 15 May 1948, Ohio, USA; ***married:*** Gary Sebelius; ***education:*** Univ. of Kansas, Master's Degree, Public Administration; ***party:*** Democrat; ***political career:*** Kansas Department of Corrections, 1975; Kansas House of Representatives from 1987-94; Kansas Insurance Commissioner, 1994-03; Governor of Kansas, 2003-09; US Secretary of Health and Human Services, 2009-; ***memberships:*** Kansas Governmental Ethics Commission; ***honours and awards:*** one of the Top Ten Public Officials in America, 2001, Governing Magazine; ***office address:*** Department of Health and Human Services, 200 Independence Ave., SW,, Washington, DC 20201, USA; ***phone:*** +1 202 619 0257; ***fax:*** +1 202 690 6247; ***URL:*** http://www.hhs.gov/.

SEBUTINDE, Justice Julia, LLB, LLM; Ugandan, Member, International Court of Justice; ***born:*** 28 February 1954; ***languages:*** English; ***education:*** Makerere University, Uganda, LLB 1977, Law; University of Edinburgh, LLM, 1990, Law; Law Development Centre, Kampala, Diploma in Legal Practice, 1978; University of Colombo, Commonwealth Certificate in

Sec-Sem

Legislative Drafting, 1983; National Judicial College, University of Reno, Certificate in Alternate Dispute Resolution Skills, 1997; Legal qualification: LLB, LLM, Diploma in Legal Practice; ***interests:*** Armed conflict; Criminal Law; Dispute settlement; Human rights; Organisations; State responsibility; Treaties; Gender justice in domestic and international courts; ***memberships:*** Uganda Women Judges Association, 1996-; International Women Judges Association, 1996-; Advocates International, 1988-; Advocates International (Uganda), 1988-; ***professional career:*** *governmental career:* Republic of Uganda, Principal State Attorney/Principal Legislative & Parliamentary Counsel, 1978-91, drafting expert in drafting Treaty for the establishment of the Inter-Governmental Association for Drought and Development and in drafting and amendment of the Treaty and Rules for the establishment of the Preferential Trade Area for Eastern and Southern Africa, later COMESA; Commonwealth Expert for the Republic of Namibia, responsible for repeal and replacement of apartheid legislation and training of local legislative drafters and for advising Parliament, 1991-96; *judicial career:* Judge, High Court of Uganda, 1996-2011; Chairperson, Judicial Commission of Inquiry into Corruption in the Uganda Police Force, 1999-2000; Chairperson, Judicial Commission of Inquiry into the Purchase of M1-24 Military Helicopters by Ugandan Ministry of Defence, 2001; Chairperson, Judicial Commission of Inquiry into Corruption in the Uganda Revenue Authority, 2002-04; Justice, UN Special Court for Sierra Leone, 2005-09; Mem., International Court of Justice, 2012-; ***office address:*** International Court of Justice, The Peace Palace, 2517 KJ The Hague, Netherlands; ***phone:*** +31 (0)70 302 2337; ***fax:*** +31 (0)70 364 9928.

SECCOMBE, Baroness Joan Anna Dalziel, DBE; British, Member of the House of Lords; ***born:*** 3 May 1930, Birmingham, UK; ***parents:*** Robert John Owen and Olive Barlow Owen (née Hall Wright); ***married:*** Henry Lawrence Seccombe, 1950; ***children:*** Philip Stanley (M), Robert Murray (M); ***education:*** St. Martin's, Solihull; ***party:*** Conservative Party; ***political career:*** Councillor, West Midlands County Cncl., 1977-81; Vice-Chmn. Nat. Union of Conservative and Unionist Assocs., 1984-87; Chmn., 1987-88; Mem. of Exec., 1975-97; Chmn. Conservative Party Annual Conference, Blackpool, 1987; Vice-Chmn., Conservative Party with special responsibility for Women, 1987-97; Mem., House of Lords; Opposition Spokesperson for, Education and Skills, 2003-04, Legal Affairs, 2003-, Home Affairs, 2004-; Opposition Whip, Education, Northern Ireland, 1997-2001; Opposition, Dep, Chief Whip, 2001-; ***interests:*** women's issues; family; criminal justice; ***professional career:*** JP, Solihull, 1968-2000, Chmn. of Bench, 1981-84; Vice Pres., Inst. of Trading Standards Admin., 1992-; Governor, Nuffield Hospitals, 1988-2001, Dep. Chmn., 1993-2001; Mem., Heart of England Tourist Bd., 1977-81, Chmn., Marketing Sub-Cttee., 1979-81; Mem., Women's Nat. Commission, 1984-90; Chmn., Trustees of Nuffield Hospitals Pension Scheme, 1992-2001; ***committees:*** Chmn., West Midlands Conservative Women's Cttee., 1975-78; Chmn., Lord Chancellor's Advisory Cttee., 1975-93; Chmn., Trading Standards Cttee., 1979-81; Chmn., Women's Nat. Cttee., 1981-84; House of Lords Cttees., Offices, 1992-94, 1998-2001, Broadcasting, 1994-97, Personal Bills, 1994-97; mem., Sub-Cttees. on, Administration and Works, 1992-94, 2000-02, Finance and Staff, 1994-97 ; ***honours and awards:*** DBE, 1984; Raised to the peerage, 1991; Extra Baroness in Waiting to HM The Queen, 2004-; ***clubs:*** Pres., St Enedoc Golf Club, 1992; ***recreations:*** golf, skiing, needlework; ***office address:*** House of Lords, London, SW1A 0PQ, United Kingdom; ***phone:*** +44 (0)20 7219 4558; ***fax:*** +44 (0)20 7219 6069; ***e-mail:*** seccombej@parliament.uk.

SEFCOVIC, Marcos; Vice President and Commissioner, European Commission; ***born:*** 1966; ***education:*** Univ. of Economics, Bratislava, Slovakia; Moscow State Inst. of International Relations; Comenius Univ.; Stanford Univ., USA; ***political career:*** Mem., EC, responsible for Education, Training, Culture & Youth, 2009-10; Vice-Pres. of the EC, responsible for Inter-Institutional Relations and Administration, 2010-; ***professional career:*** various diplomatic posits.; Amb., Slovak Embassy, Tel Aviv, Israel, 1999; MFA, Slovak Republic, 2002-04; Amb., Slovak Perm. Rep. to the EU, 2004; ***office address:*** European Commission, rue de la loi 200, B-1049 Brussels, Belgium; ***URL:*** http://www.europa.eu.

SEIN, Lt. Gen. (retd.) Thein; President, Government of Myanmar; ***political career:*** Prime Minister, 2007-11; President, 2011-; ***professional career:*** Army Career with rank of General; ***office address:*** Office of the President, Botahtaung Tsp, Rangoon, Myanmar; ***URL:*** http://www.myanmar.com.

SEKERAMAYI, Dr Sydney Tigere; Zimbabwean, Minister of State for National Security in the President's Office, Government of Zimbabwe; ***born:*** 1944; ***parents:*** Samuel Kupara Sekeramayi and Mazorwangu Sekeramayi (née Mutamba); ***married:*** Mercy Tsitsi Nyepudzai Sekeramayi (née Chihuri), 1983; ***children:*** Chipo (F), Farai (F), Tapiwa (F), Takudzwa (F), Tariro (F), Simukai (M), Shungu (M); ***languages:*** Shona, English, Swedish; ***education:*** MB, ChB, DTM; ***party:*** ZANU PF; ***political career:*** Minister of Lands, Resettlement and Rural Devt., 1980-82; Minister of State for Defence in the Prime Minister's Office, 1982-84; Minister of Health, 1984-88; Minister of State for Nat. Security, 1988-01; Minister of Mines and Energy, 2000-2001; Minister of Defence, 2001-09; Minister of State for National Security in the President's Office, 2009-; ***interests:*** consolidating national sovereignty, building strong national economy to stimulate rapid socio-economic development of the people; ***recreations:*** tennis, football; ***office address:*** Ministry of State Security, 4th Floor, Chaminuka Building, 5th Street, PO Box 2278, Causeway, Harare, Zimbabwe; ***phone:*** +263 (0)4 700501; ***URL:*** http://www.gta.gov.zw.

SEKIMIZU, Koji; Japanese, Secretary General, International Maritime Organization; ***born:*** 1952; ***professional career:*** Ship Inspector, Ministry of Transport, Japan, Chief Officer, Dep. Dir., Environment Division; Foreign Affairs, 1984-86; Dep. Dir., Safety Standards Div., Maritime Technology & Safety Bureau, Ministry of Transport, 1986-89; joined IMO, 1989, Head of the Technology Section, 1992, Maritime Safety Division,-1997, Senior Dep. Dir., Marine Environment Division, 1997, Dir., 2000, Dir., Maritime Division, 2004, Sec. Gen., IMO, 2011-; ***office address:*** International Maritime Organization, 4 Albert Embankment, London, SE1 7SR, United Kingdom.

SELAKOVIC, Nikola; Minister of Justice and Public Administration, Government of Serbia; ***born:*** 1983; ***education:*** Belgrade Fac. of Law; ***political career:*** Mem., Serbian Progressive Party, 2008-, mem., Exec. Board, Pres., Legal Council; Minister of Justice and Public Administration, 2012-; ***office address:*** Ministry of Justice, 22-26 Nemanjina Street, Belgrade, Republic of Serbia; ***phone:*** +381 11 361 6548; ***fax:*** +381 11 361 6419; ***URL:*** http://www.mpravde.gov.rs/.

SELINGER, Hon. Gregory; Premier, Government of Manitoba; ***married:*** Claudette Selinger (née Toupin); ***education:*** London School of Economics, Ph.D.; Queen's Univ., MA; Univ., of Manitoba, B.Sc., Social Science; ***political career:*** City Cllr., St. Boniface; Appointed to the Finance Portfolio, 1999; Minister of Finance; Minister responsible for French Language Services; Minister responsible for the Civil Service, and MLA for St Boniface; Premier, President of the Executive Council, Minister of Federal-Provincial Relations, Minister responsible for Francophone Affairs, 2010-; ***professional career:*** Assoc. Prof., Faculty of Social Work, Univ. of Manitoba; taught courses in social policy and community development; City Cllr., St Boniface; Served on the Bd., St. Boniface Hosp. and the St. Boniface Museum and as Pres. of the Old St. Boniface Residents' Assn.; coached soccer, basketball, Notre Dame Community Club, the YMCA; ***committees:*** Chmn, Winnipeg City Cttee. of Finance and Administration; ***office address:*** Office of the Premier, 204 Legislative Building, 450 Broadway, Winnipeg, Manitoba R3C 0V8, Canada; ***e-mail:*** premier@leg.gov.mb.ca; ***URL:*** http://www.gov.mb.ca.

SELKIRK OF DOUGLAS, Lord James Alexander, PC, QC, MSP; British, Member, House of Lords; ***born:*** 31 July 1942; ***married:*** Hon. Priscilla Susan (née Buchan), 1974; ***education:*** Univs. of Tours and Pau, courses in French; Balliol Coll., Oxford, MA, Modern History; Edinburgh Univ. (LLB Scots Law); passed Company Commander's course in the Army at Warminster; Capt. 2nd Bn Lowland Volunteers (Cameronian Officer); ***party:*** Conservative; ***political career:*** Edinburgh Town Councillor, 1972-74; MP (Cons.) for Edinburgh West, 1974-97; Opposition then Govt. Whip, 1977-1981; PPS to Malcolm Rifkind, 1983-87; Parly. Under Sec. at the Scottish Office, 1987-95; Minister of State, 1995-97; Life Peer, appointed 1997; MSP for Lothians, 1999-2007 (May elections); Business Manager of the Scottish Conservative Grp. of MSPs, 1999-2001; Principal Home Affairs Spokesman for the Scottish Conservative Gp. of MSPs, 2001-03; Spokesman for the Cons. Gp., MSPs & Dep. Convener of Education Cttee. 2003-07; ***interests:*** education, housing, health, local government, home affairs, law and order, consumer issues, transport, arts, culture, sport, environment, forestry, natural heritage and planning; ***memberships:*** Life Mem., National Trust for Scotland (member Cncl 1977-82); Mem., Royal Company of Archers and Dep. Keeper of Holyrood Palace, -2008; Chmn., Edinburgh Support Gp. of Hope and Homes for Children Charity, 2002-07; Hon. Pres., Scottish Amateur Boxing Assoc., 1975-99; Pres., Royal Commonwealth Socy. (Scotland), 1979-87 and Scottish National Cncl .UN Assoc., 1981-87; Pres., The Scottish Veterans' Garden City Assn. Charity, 1992-; ***professional career:*** Scots Advocate and Interim Procurator Fiscal Depute, 1968-76; Privy Counsellor and Queen's Counsel, 1995-; Pres., International Rescue Corp 1995-; Dir., Douglas-Hamilton (D Share) Ltd., 1997-; Pres., Scottish Garden City Assn., 2007-; ***committees:*** Scottish Select Cttee. for Scottish Affairs 1981-83; Hon. Sec., Cons. Parly. Constitutional Cttee. and Cons. Parly. Aviation Cttee. 1983-; Chairman, Scottish Parly. All-Party Penal Affairs Cttee. 1983; ***honours and awards:*** Hon. Air Cmdr. of No 603 (City of Edinburgh) Squadron; Appointed Life Peer, Lord Selkirk of Douglas, 1997; ***publications:*** Motive for a Mission: The Story Behind Hess's Flight to Britain (1971); The Air Battle for Malta: The Diaries of a Fighter Pilot (1981); Roof of the World: Man's First Flight over Everest (1983); The Truth about Rudolf Hess (1993); After You Prime Minister (2009); ***clubs:*** New (Edinburgh); Hon. Company of Edinburgh Golfers; ***recreations:*** everything to do with Scotland, boxing, golf, modern history; ***office address:*** House of Lords, London, SW1 0AA, United Kingdom; ***phone:*** +44 (0)207 219 2131.

SELLAL, Abdelmalek; Prime Minister, Algerian Government; ***born:*** 1 August 1948; ***political career:*** Minister of the Interior, for Local Communities and the Environment, Algerian Cabinet, 1998-99; Minister of Youth and Sports, 2000-2002; Minister of Public Works, 2002-2003; Minister of Transport, 2003-04; Minister of Water Resources, 2004-12; Prime Minister, 2012-; ***office address:*** Office of the Prime Minister, rue Docteur Saadane, Algiers, Algeria; ***phone:*** +213 (0)21 731200; ***fax:*** +213 (0)21 717929; ***URL:*** http://www.cg.gov.dz.

SELOUS, Andrew; Member of Parliament for Bedfordshire South West, House of Commons; ***born:*** 1962; ***married:*** Harriet Victoria; ***children:*** Camilla (F), Laetitia (F), Maria (F); ***education:*** LSE Industry & Trade BSc, 1984; ***party:*** Conservative Party; ***political career:*** MP, Bedfordshire South West, 2001-; ***professional career:*** Underwriter, Great Lakes, 1991-; ***committees:*** Work and Pensions, 2001-05; Ecclesiastical Committee, 2010; ***office address:*** House of Commons, London, SW1A 0AA, United Kingdom; ***phone:*** +44 (0)20 7219 8134; ***e-mail:*** andrew.selous.mp@parliament.uk; ***URL:*** http://www.parliament.uk; http://www.andrewselous.org.uk.

SEMASHKO, Vladimir I.; First Deputy Prime Minister, Government of Belarus; ***education:*** Belarusian Polytechnic Inst., 1972; ***political career:*** Minister of Energy, 2001-03; Acting Dep. PM, 2003; First Dep. PM, June 2004-; ***professional career:*** Engineer; ***office address:*** First Deputy Prime Minister's Office, Council of Ministers, Independent Square, 220010 Minsk, Belarus.

SEMETA, Algirdas Gediminas; Commissioner, European Commission; ***born:*** 1962; ***education:*** Vilnius Univ., Faculty of Economic Cybernetics and Finance, 1985; ***political career:*** Minister of Finance, 1997-99, 2008-09; European Commissioner for Taxation, Customs Union, Audit and Anti-Fraud, 2009-; ***office address:*** European Commission, rue de la Loi 200, B-1049 Brussels, Belgium; ***phone:*** +32 (0)2 299 1111; ***URL:*** http://www.europa.eu.

SEMJEN, Zsolt; Deputy Prime Minister, Government of Hungary; ***education:*** Pázmány Péter Catholic Univ.; Eötvös Loránd Univ. ; ***party:*** Christian Democratic People's Party; ***political career:*** Dep. state secretary with responsibility for church affairs in the Ministry for National Cultural Heritage; Dep. Prime Minister, Minister of General Affairs, 2010-; ***office address:*** Office of the Deputy Prime Minister, Kossuth Lajos tér 4, 1055 Budapest, Hungary; ***phone:*** +36 (0)1 268 3000,; ***fax:*** +36 (0)1 268 3050; ***URL:*** http://www.kancellaria.gov.hu.

BIOGRAPHIES

Sen-Sha

SENTAMU, Most Rev and Rt Hon. Dr John Tucker, LLB, Dip. L.P., MA, Ph.D, FRSA, Privy Councillor; Archbishop of York; ***born:*** 10 June 1949; ***education:*** Makerere Univ., Kampala; Law Dev. Centre; Selwyn College, Cambridge; Ridley Hall Theological College; ***political career:*** Mem., House of Lords; ***memberships:*** Mem., NACRO Young Offenders Cttee., 1985-95; Mem., Stephen Lawrence Judicial Inquiry, 1997-99; Pres. & Chair, London Marriage Guidance Council, 2000-04; Chair, NHS Sickle Cell & Thalassaemia Screening Prog., 2001-; Chair, Damilola Taylor Murder Review, 2002; Mem., Birmingham Hospital NHS Trust, 2002; Chair, EC1 New Deal for Communities, 2002-04; Pres., Youth for Christ; Pres., YMCA England; ***professional career:*** Assist. Chaplain, Selwyn College, Cambridge, 1979; Chaplain, HM Remand Centre, Latchmere House, 1979-82; Curate, St Andrew, Ham, 1979-82; Curate, St. Paul, Herne Hilll, 1982-83; Priest in Charge, Holy Trinity, Tulse Hill, 1983-84; Vicar, Upper Tulse Hill, St. Mattias, 1983-84; Vicar, Holy Trinity and St. Matthias, Tulse Hill, 1985-96; Priest in Charge, St. Saviour, Brixton, 1987-89; Hon. Canon, Southwark Cathedral, 1993-96; Bishop of Stepney, 1996-2002; Bishop of Birmingham, 2002-05; Archbishop of York, 2005-; ***honours and awards:*** Hon. Degrees from: Open Univ., 2001; Univ. of Gloucester, 2002; Univ. of Birmingham, 2003; Univ. of Leicester, 2005; Univ. of Hull, 2007; Univ. of Sheffield, 2007; Univ. of the West Indies, 2007; Birmingham City Univ., 2008; Univ. of Cambridge, 2008; Northumbria Univ., 2008; Univ. of Nottingham, 2008; Wycliffe College, Toronto, 2009; Teesside Univ., 2009. Other awards: Freeman of the City of London, 2000; Fellow, Univ. Coll. Christ Church Canterbury, 2001; Fellow, Queen Mary College, Univ. of London, 2001; Midlander of the Year, 2003; Hon. Fellow, Selwyn Coll., Cambridge, 2005; Chancellor, York St. John Univ., 2006-; Yorkshire Man of the Year, 2007; Speaker of the Year, 2007; Master Bencher (Hons), Gray's Inn, 2007; Freeman of the City of Montego Bay, 2007; Chancellor, Univ. of Cumbria, 2007-; Mem., Yorkshire Soc., 2009-; Hon. Dr., Univ. of York, 2010; Univ. of Leeds, LL.D (Hon), 2010; Univ. of the South, Tennessee, DD (Hon.) Sewanee, 2010; DD (Hon), Univ. of London, 2010; Visit York's Tourism Ambassador, 2010; ***recreations:*** music, cooking, reading, athletics, rugby, football; ***office address:*** Bishopthorpe Palace, Bishopthorpe, York, YO23 2GE, United Kingdom; ***phone:*** +44 (0)1904 707021; ***fax:*** +44 (0)1904 709204; ***e-mail:*** office@archbishopof york.org.

SEO, Nam-soo; Minister of Education, Government of South Korea; ***education:*** BA, in Philosophy, Seoul National Univ., 1975; MA., in Education, Univ. of Illinois, 1985; MA, in Public Administration, Seoul National Univ., 1988; Ph.D. in Education, Dongguk Univ., 1996; ***political career:*** Minister of Education. 2013-; ***professional career:*** Visiting scholar and researcher, Korean Educational Dev. Inst., 2008-12; President, Uiduk Univ., 2012-13; ***office address:*** Ministry of Education, 77-6 Sejong-no, Jongno-gu, 110 760 Seoul, South Korea; ***phone:*** +82 2 2100 6060; ***fax:*** +82 2 7 2100 6579; ***URL:*** http://english.mest.go.kr.

SEPULVEDA, H.E. Judge Bernardo, GCMG (Hon); Mexican, Vice-President, International Court of Justice; ***born:*** 14 December 1941; ***languages:*** Spanish, English; ***education:*** National University of Mexico, Licenciado en Derecho, 1964, magna cum laude; University of Cambridge, LLM, 1966, Diploma in International Law, 1965, Dissertation: "Collective security in the Inter-American System", 1965; ***interests:*** Armed conflict; Dispute settlement; Economic law; Organisations; State responsibility; ***memberships:*** ILA, Mexican Branch, President, 2002-; ***professional career:*** *academic career:* El Colegio de México, Professor of International Law, 1967-; Hague Academy of International Law, lecturer on responsibility of States, 2002; *professional career:* General Counsel of Grupo ICA, 1997-2004, the largest Mexican engineering and construction corporation; In that capacity, participated in a number of national and international arbitrations, including Aucoven v República Bolivariana de Venezuela (ICSID), 2003; Member, ILC, 1996-; *governmental career:* Secretary of Foreign Relations of Mexico, 1982-88; Head of Department of International Affairs, Secretary of the Treasury of Mexico, 1976-81; President of Mexican delegations to the UNGA and the OAS as well as of other international regional and global organizations; Co-chair of the Binational Commission, an intergovernmental organization dealing with all matters of interest in the relationship between Mexico and the US; As Foreign Secretary was responsible for Mexican participation in the Central American peace process in the 1980s; For those purposes and together with Venezuela, Colombia and Panama, established the Contadora Group as a diplomatic instrument to bring peace and stability to the area; Together with the Foreign Ministers of Argentina, Brazil, Colombia, Panama, Peru, Uruguay and Venezuela, took part in the creation of the Group of Eight, now the Rio Group, an institution devoted to promote Latin American cooperation; Under its auspices, Presidential Summits have taken place since 1987; *diplomatic career:* Ambassador of Mexico to the US and the UK; Participant in a number of Mexican delegations to UN Conferences, including UN Conference on the Law of the Sea, Vienna Conference on the Law of Treaties and several UN Conferences on Disarmament; Member of Mexican delegation to the 1981 Cancun Meeting of Heads of State and government; President of the UN Commission on Transnational Corporations, 1980; Rapporteur of the UN's Inter-governmental Working Group on a Code of Conduct for Transnational Corporations; Mexican representative to the UN Commission on Transnational Corporations, 1977-81; Member of Mexican delegation to the annual meetings of the IMF, the World Bank and the Interamerican Development Bank, as well as the Group of 24; *judicial career:* ICJ, Judge, 2005-, ad hoc Judge in the Avena Case, 2004, Vice-Pres., 2012-; Member of the Panel of Arbitrators of the ICDR; Member of the ITA; Member of the Commission of Arbitration of the Mexican Chamber of Commerce; Chairs an ICC arbitration panel; Mem., UN Int. Law Commission, 1996-2005; Mem., Int. Court of Justice Chamber of Summary Procedure; mem. of the Int. Court of Justice Budget and Admin. Cttee.; Pres., Latin American Soc. of Int. Law, elected in February 2010; ***honours and awards:*** Hon. Fellow of Queens' College, Univ. of Cambridge, 1990; Hon. Doctorate, Univ. of San Diego, 1982, and the Univ. of Leningrad (now St. Petersburg), 1987; Rockefeller Foundation Fellowship, 1964-66; Principe de Asturias Prize in the field of international co operation, 1984;. Unesco awarded him the Simón Bolivar Prize, 1985; Recipient of a number of orders, decorations and medals awarded by foreign governments, which include, the Knights Grand Cross of the Order of Saint Michael and Saint George; the Grand Cross, Order of Isabel la Católica; the Grand Cross, Order of General San Martin; Ribbon, Order of Kwang Wha; the Grand Cross, Order of Cristo; Order of the Republic of Egypt, First Class; the Grand Cross of the Order of Cruzeiro do Sul; the Grand Cordon, Order of the Rising Sun; Grand Officer, Ordre de la Légion d'Honneur; ***publications:*** Books: Foreign Investment in Mexio, 1973; Articles: Proceedings of the ASIL; Foro Internacional; Revista Mexicana de Politica Exterior; Anuario Mexicano de Derecho Internacional; Comercio Exterior; Este País; ***office address:*** International Court of Justice, Peace Palace - new wing, Carnegieplein 2, 2517 KJ The Hague, The Netherlands; ***phone:*** +31 (70) 302 24 52; ***fax:*** +31 (70) 302 24 09; ***e-mail:*** b.sepulveda@icj-cij.org.

SERETSE, Hon. Tebelelo; Ambassador, Embassy of Botswana; ***political career:*** Ministry of Works, Transport and Communications, to 2004; ***professional career:*** Amb. to the USA, 2011-; ***office address:*** Embassy of the Republic of Botswana, 1531-33 New Hampshire Avenue, NW, Washington DC 20036, USA; ***phone:*** +1 202 244 4990; ***fax:*** +1 202 244 4164; ***URL:*** http://www.botswanaembassy.org.

SERYAEV, HE Yazmurad N.; Ambassador, Embassy of Turkmenistan in the UK; ***professional career:*** Head of the European Countries Dept., Foreign Ministry; Diplomatic posting to Kazakhstan, 1999-2000; Diplomatic posting to Russia, 2000-2; Amb. of Turkmenistan to the UK, 2003-; ***office address:*** Embassy of Turkmenistan, 2nd Floor South, St George's Hse, 14/17 Wells Street, London, W1P 3FP, United Kingdom; ***phone:*** +44 (0)20 7255 1071; ***fax:*** +44 (0)20 7323 9184.

SESSIONS, Jeff; American, Senator for Alabama, US Senate; ***born:*** 24 December 1946, Hybart, Alabama, USA; ***married:*** Mary Sessions (née Blackshear); ***children:*** Mary Abigail (F), Ruth (F), Sam (M); ***education:*** Huntingdon Coll., BA, 1969; Univ. of Alabama, Juris Dr., 1973; ***party:*** Republican; ***political career:*** US Senator for Alabama, 1996-; ***memberships:*** Nat. Cncl. on the Arts; ***professional career:*** Practitioner of Law, Guin Bouldin & Porch, Russellville, Alabama, 1973-75; Officer - Capt., US Army Reserves, 1973-86; Asst. US Attorney for the Southern District of Alabama, 1975-77; Stockman and Bedsole, Mobile, Alabama, 1977-81; US Attorney, 1981-93; Stockman, Bedsole and Sessions, 1993-94; State Attorney General, 1995-97; ***committees:*** Budget; Judiciary Cttee.; Chmn., Subcttee. on Youth Violence; Joint Economic Cttee.; Caucus on Int. Narcotics Control; Cttee. on Health, Education, Labour and Pensions; Cttee. on Armed Services; Environment and Public Works; ***trusteeships:*** Huntingdon Coll. Bd. of Trustees; Bd. of Overseers, Samford University; ***recreations:*** lay leader and Sunday school teacher at his family's church; Chmn. of his church's Admin. Bd.; delegate, annual Alabama Methodist Conference, 1987; ***office address:*** US Senate, 335 Russell Senate Office Building, Washington, DC 20510, USA; ***phone:*** +1 202 224 4124; ***fax:*** +1 202 224 3149.

SESSIONS, Pete; American, Congressman, Texas 32nd District, US House of Representatives; ***party:*** Republican; ***political career:*** mem., US House of Representatives, 1996-; ***professional career:*** Southwestern Bell Telephone Company; ***committees:*** House Rules Cttee., Chmn.; ***office address:*** House of Representatives, 436 Cannon House Street, Washington, DC 20515-6501, USA; ***phone:*** +1 202 224 3121.

SEWELL, Terri; Congresswoman, House of Representatives; ***education:*** Princeton University, graduating cum laude in 1986; Marshall/Commonwealth Scholarship, Masters degree with first class Honors, Oxford University, 1988; graduate, Harvard Law School, editor of the Civil Rights Civil Liberties Law Review; ***party:*** Democrat; ***political career:*** HOR, Alabama 7th District, 2010-; ***professional career:*** lawyer; ***committees:*** Agriculture; Space and Technology; ***office address:*** 1133 Longworth HOB, Washington DC 20515, USA; ***URL:*** http://sewell.house.gov/.

SHACKLETON OF BELGRAVIA, Baroness Fiona; Member, House of Lords; ***education:*** Exeter Univ.; ***party:*** Conservative Party; ***political career:*** Mem., House of Lords, 2010-; ***professional career:*** Solicitor; Partner, Farrer and Co.; Partner, Payne Hicks Beach, 2001-; ***office address:*** House of Lords, London, SW1A 0PW, United Kingdom; ***phone:*** +44 (0)20 7219 3000.

SHAH, Dr Rajiv; Administrator, USAID; ***education:*** Univ. of Pennsylvania Medical School, medicine; Wharton School of Business, Masters, health economics; London School of Economics; Univ. of Michigan; ***professional career:*** Bill & Melinda Gates Foundation, incl. director of Agricultural Development, Global Development Program, Director of Strategic Opportunities; joined Obama Administration; Undersecretary for research, education & economics & chief scientist at the US Department of Agriculture; launched the National Institute of Food & Agriculture; Feed the Future food security initiative; Administrator, USAID, 2009-; ***office address:*** United States Agency for International Development (USAID) , Ronald Reagan Bldg, 1300 Pennsylvania Ave, NW, Washington, DC 20523-1000, USA; ***phone:*** +1 202 712 4810; ***URL:*** http://www.usaid.gov/.

SHAHEEN, Jeanne; American, Senator for New Hampshire, US Senate; ***born:*** 28 January 1947, St. Charles, MO, USA; ***married:*** Bill Shaheen; ***education:*** Shippensburg Univ., Pennsylvania, USA, BA, 1969; Univ. of Mississippi, MA, 1973; ***party:*** Democrat; ***political career:*** State Senate, New Hampshire, 1990; Governor, New Hampshire, 1996-2003; US Senator for New Hampshire, 2009-; ***professional career:*** managed several statewide campaigns; Teacher; owned a small business; ***committees:*** US Senate: Foreign Relations; Appropriations; Armed Services; Small Business; ***office address:*** US Senate, 520 Hart Senate Office Building, Washington DC 20510, USA; ***phone:*** +1 202 224 2841; ***URL:*** http://www.shaheen.senate.gov.

SHALOM, Silvan; Deputy Prime Minister, Minister of for Regional Development, the Negev and Galilee, Government of Israel; ***born:*** 1958, Tunisia; ***education:*** Ben-Gurion Univ., B.A., Econ.; Tel Aviv Univ., LL.B, M.A. in Public Policy; ***party:*** Likud Party; ***political career:*** Dir.-Gen., Min. of Energy; Elected to the Knesset, 1992; Dep. Minister of Defense, 1997-98; Minister of Science, 1998-99; Minister of Finance and Dep. Prime Minister, 2001-2003; Minister of Foreign Affairs and Deputy Prime Minister, 2003-06; Deputy Prime Minister, Minister of for Regional Development, the Negev and Galilee, 2009-; ***professional career:*** Journalist; Chmn. of the Bd., Israel Electric Co., 1990-92; Dep. Chmn., Public Cncl. of Youth Exchange, 1992-93 ; ***committees:*** Mem. of the Knesset Cttee. on Econ. Affairs; Finance; State Control; Status of Women, 1992-96; Chmn. of the Knesset Cttee. on Energy; sub-cttee. on Capital Markets, 1992-96; Mem. of the Knesset Cttee. on Econ. Affairs; Finance; State Control; Status of Women; Constitution, Law and Justice; Dep.Chmn. of the Knesset Sub-cttee. on Capital Markets, 1996-97; Mem., Knesset Foreign Affairs & Defense cttee; Education and Culture Cttee.; Joint Cttee. for the Defense budget; Special Legislative Cttee. for not Renewing the Emergency Situation, 1999-01; ***publications:*** Has published articles in daily newspapers; ***office address:*** Ministry of Energy & Water, Derekh Petah Tikva 48, Tel Aviv 61171, Israel; ***URL:*** http://www.mni.gov.il.

SHANNON, Jim; Member, Northern Ireland Assembly; ***born:*** 25 March 1955; ***parents:*** Richard James Shannon and Mona Rhoda Rebecca Shannon; ***children:*** Jamie (M), Ian (M), Luke (M); ***party:*** Democratic Unionist; ***political career:*** Ardsborough Cncl, 1985-; Mem. of Forum for Political Dialogue, 1996-98; Mayor of Ards Borough, 1991-92; Mem., Strangford, 2010-; ***interests:*** conservation, culture, country sports, shooting; ***memberships:*** Royal British Legion; ***professional career:*** Self Employed, Pork-Retailer; ***honours and awards:*** G.S.M; ***recreations:*** field sports, country sports, football; ***office address:*** Constituency Office: 34A Frances Street, Newtownards, County Down, B723 7DN, United Kingdom; ***phone:*** +44 (0)28 9182 7990; ***fax:*** +44 (0)28 9182 7991; ***e-mail:*** jim.shannon.mp@parliament.uk.

SHAPPS, Grant; Minister without Portfolio (Minister of State) & Chairman of the Conservative Party, UK Government; ***party:*** Conservative; ***political career:*** MP for Welwyn Hatfield, 2005-; Vice-Chmn., Campaigning, 2006-; Shadow Minister for Housing; Minister of State, Department for Communities and Local Government, 2010-12; Minister without Portfolio (Minister of State); Chairman of the Conservative Party, 2012-; ***professional career:*** Chmn., PrintHouse Corporation; ***office address:*** House of Commons, London, SW1P 0AA, United Kingdom; ***phone:*** +44 (0)20 7219 8497.

SHARIF, Mian Muhammad Nawaz; Prime Minister, Government of Pakistan; ***born:*** 1949; ***education:*** Gov. College Univ., Lahore; Punjab Univ., Law College; ***political career:*** Chief Minister of Punjab, 1985; Opposition leader, Pakistan Muslim Leageu, 1988-90; Prime Minister, 1990-93, 1998-99; Pres., Pakistan Muslim League; exile, Saudi Arabia, 1999-2007; Prime Minister of Pakistan, 2013-; ***office address:*** Office of the Prime Minister, F6/5 Cabinet Division, Cabinet Block, Constitution Avenue, Islamabad, Pakistan ; ***URL:*** http://www.pakistan.gov.pk/.

SHARIFOV, Abid; Deputy Prime Minister, Government of Azerbaijan; ***born:*** 6 January 1940, Sheki, Azerbaijan; ***parents:*** Godja Sharifov and Nabiya Sharifov; ***married:*** Sadayat Sharifov (née Ibragimova), 25 January 1957; ***children:*** Elchin (M), Tarana (F); ***public role of spouse:*** Teacher; ***languages:*** Russian, Azeri; ***political career:*** Government Official; Deputy Prime Minister, to date; ***professional career:*** Builder, Head of Construction Co.; ***honours and awards:*** Sign of Honour; October Revolution; Honoured Transport Builder of the USSR; Honoured Builder of the Azerbaijan Republic; ***office address:*** Office of the Prime Minister, Lermontov St 68, 370066 Baku, Azerbaijan; ***phone:*** +994 (0)12 927728.

SHARKEY, Lord John; Member, House of Lords; ***party:*** Liberal Democrat Party; ***political career:*** Mem., House of Lords, 2011-; ***professional career:*** Dir., Sharkey Associates Limited; ***office address:*** House of Lords, London, SW1A , United Kingdom; ***phone:*** +44 (0)207219 3000.

SHARMA, Alok; MP for Reading West, UK Government; ***party:*** Conservative; ***political career:*** MP for Reading West, May 2010-; ***committees:*** Science and Technology Select Cttee., 2010-11; ***office address:*** House of Commons, London, SW1A 0AA, United Kingdom; ***phone:*** +44 (0)20 7219 3000; ***e-mail:*** alok.sharma.mp@parliament.uk.

SHARMA, Anand; Minister of Commerce and Industry, Government of India; ***born:*** 1953; ***education:*** Faculty of Law, Himachal Pradesh University, Shimla, India; ***party:*** Indian National Congress; ***political career:*** Minister of Commerce and Industry; Minister of Textiles, 2011-; ***office address:*** Ministry of Commerce and Industry, Udyog Bhavan, New Delhi 110 001, India; ***phone:*** +91 11 301 0261; ***URL:*** http://commin.nic.in.

SHARMA, HE Kamalesh; Secretary-General, Commonwealth Secretariat; ***children:*** 2; ***education:*** Delhi Univ.; Cambridge Univ.; ***professional career:*** Indian Foreign Service, 1965-2001, Amb. and Perm. Rep. to the UN in Geneva, 1988-90; Amb. and the Indian Perm. Rep. to the UN in New York, 1997-2002; Special Representative of the UN Sec.-Gen. to Timor Leste, 2002-04; High Commissioner to UK, 2004-08; Commonwealth, Sec.-Gen., April 2008-; ***honours and awards:*** Hon. Doc. of Laws, De Montford Univ; Fellow, Harvard Univ.; Chancellor, Queen's Univ., Belfast; ***publications:*** Mille Fleurs - Poetry From Around The World; Imagining Tomorrow - Rethinking the Global Challenge; ***recreations:*** spiritual and mystical traditions, literature, cosmology, cricket, Indian and Western classical music, jazz; ***office address:*** Commonwealth Secretariat, Marlborough House, Pall Mall, London, SW1Y 5HX, United Kingdom; ***phone:*** +44 (0)20 7747 6500.

SHARMA, Virendra; MP for Ealing Southall, British Government; ***political career:*** Councillor, London Borough of Ealing Council; Mayor; MP for Ealing Southall, July 2007-; ***committees:*** Joint Committee on Human Rights, 2007-10, 2010-; Justice, 2007-09; International Development, 2009-10; Health, 2010-; ***office address:*** House of Commons, London, SW1A 2AH, United Kingdom; ***phone:*** +44 (0)20 7219 3000; ***e-mail:*** sharmav@parliament.uk.

SHATTER, Alan; Minister of Justice and Equality, Government of Ireland; ***party:*** Fine Gael; ***political career:*** TD for Dublin, 1981-2002, 2007-; Minister for Justuce and Equality, 2011-; ***professional career:*** Solicitor; Author; ***office address:*** Department of Justice, Equality and Law Reform, 72-76 St. Stephen's Green, Dublin 2, Ireland; ***phone:*** +353 (0)1 602 8202; ***fax:*** +353 (0)1 661 5461; ***e-mail:*** info@justice.ie; ***URL:*** http://www.justice.ie.

SHAW OF NORTHSTEAD, Lord; British, Member of the House of Lords; ***born:*** 9 October 1920, Leeds, UK; ***parents:*** Norman Shaw and Dorothea Shaw; ***married:*** Joan Mary Louise Shaw (née Mowat), 25 April 1951; ***s:*** 3; ***education:*** Sedbergh Sch.; ***party:*** Conservative; ***political career:*** MP, 1960-64, 1966-92; MEP, 1974-79; Mem., House of Lords; ***memberships:*** FCA; JP; ***professional career:*** Chartered Accountant; ***honours and awards:*** Kt., 1982; Life Peer, 1994; ***clubs:*** Carlton; ***office address:*** House of Lords, London, SW1A 0PQ, United Kingdom; ***phone:*** +44 (0)20 7219 3000; ***fax:*** +44 (0)20 7219 5979.

SHEA, Gail; Minister of National Revenue, Government of Canada; ***political career:*** MP PEI Government, Minister for Community Affairs, 2000-2003; Minister of Transportation and Public Works, 2003-; Minister responsible for the Status of Women, 2003-06; MP, Canadian Federal Gov. 2008-; Minister for Fisheries and Oceans, 2008-11; Minister of National Revenue, 2011-; ***office address:*** House of Commons, Parliament Buildings, Wellington Street, Ottawa, Ontario, K1A 0A6, Canada.

SHEA, Joan; Minister of Advanced Education and Skills, Government of Newfoundland and Labrador; ***education:*** Memorial Univ., Newfoundland, degree in Social Work, 1987; Univ. of Toronto, Masters degree in Social Work, 1990; ***political career:*** Minister of Human Resources, Labour and Employment, Minister responsible for Newfoundland and Labrador Housing and the Status of Women, 2003-06; Minister of Education, and Minister Responsible for the Status of Women, 2006-09; Minister of Child, Youth and Family Services, 2009-10; Minister of Education, 2010-11; Minister of Advanced Education and Skills, Minister responsible for Status of Persons with Disabilities and for Youth Engagement, 2012-; ***memberships:*** exec. mem., Assn. of Social Workers; mem., Social Workers Cttee. of Examiners; ***professional career:*** Adult Probation Officer, Dept. of Justice, 1987; Parole Officer, Correctional Services of Canada, 1990; Parole Officer, West Coast Correctional Centre, 1996; volunteer with Candian Mental Health Assn.; served as exec., Union of Solicitor General Employees (USGE); served as Girl Guides, Canada Deputy Area Cmnr.; Area Training Coordinator for southwest region; ***clubs:*** founding mem., Stephenville Gymnastics Club; ***office address:*** Confederation Building, P.O. Box 8700, St. John's, A1B 4J6, NL, Canada.

SHEERMAN, Barry John, MP; British, Member of Parliament for Huddersfield, House of Commons; ***born:*** 1940, Sunbury-on-Thames, Middlesex, England; ***parents:*** A. William Sheerman and Florence Sheerman; ***married:*** Pamela Elizabeth, 28 August 1965; ***s:*** 1; ***d:*** 3; ***languages:*** French; ***education:*** Hampton Grammar Sch.; Kingston Tech. Coll.; B.Sc. Econ.; London Sch. of Econ. (M.Sc.); ***party:*** Labour Co-operative Party; ***political career:*** Shadow Minister Employment and Education, 1983-87; Shadow Minister Home Affairs, Deputy to Roy Hattersley, 1987-92; Shadow Minister for Disability Rights, 1992-94; Co-Chmn., Parliamentary Group for Manufacturing Industry, 1993-; Co-Chmn., All Party British Manufacturing Group; Chmn., Nat. Educational Research and Development Trust; Chmn., Parly. Reform Group; Chmn., Labour Forum on Criminal Justice, 1987-92; Co-Chmn., Sec. to Parliamentary group for sustainable waste management, 1994-; Chmn., Urban Mines, 1995; Networking for Industry, now Policy Connect; Chmn. Interparle, 1998; Mem., Sec. of State's Manufacturing Task Force 1999-; MP, (Lab. and Co-op.) for Huddersfield 1979-; ***interests:*** entrepreneurship, education, environment; ***memberships:*** Fellow, RSA & RSG; Fellow, City and Guilds Institute; Fellow, Chartered Inst. of Wastes Management; ***professional career:*** Univ. lecturer 1966-79; ***committees:*** Public Accounts Cttee. 1980-83; Chmn., Cross Party Advisory Gp. on Preparation for EMU, 1999- ; Vice Chmn., Joint Cttee. on Financial Services and Markets, 1999; Chmn., Parly. Labour Party Trade Cttee.; Trustee and Chmn., Parly. Advisory Cncl., Transport Safety; Chmn., Select Cttee. on Education & Employment 1999-2001; Chair, Education and Skills Select Cttee., 2001; Chair, Children, Schools and Families Select Cttee., 2001-10; Liaison, 2002-10; ***trusteeships:*** Nat. Children's Centre; ***publications:*** Harold Laski: A Life on the Left, 1993; Hamish Hamilton, Viking-Penguin. Seven Steps to Justice 1992; Education and Training: A Policy for Labour 1987; ***clubs:*** Royal Cmmw. Soc.; ***recreations:*** walking, social entrepreneurship; ***office address:*** House of Commons, London, SW1A 0AA, United Kingdom; ***phone:*** +44 (0)20 7219 3000; ***e-mail:*** sheermanb@parliament.uk.

SHEIN, H.E. Dr Ali Mohamed; President of Zanzibar, Chairman of Revolutionary Council, Zanzibar; ***born:*** 1948; ***education:*** Vorenzh State Univ., USSR; Odessa State Univ., Medical Biochemicstry, Masters; Medical School, Univ. of Newcastle, UK, Ph.D; ***political career:*** founding mem., political party, Chama cha Mapinduzi; MP, 1995; Dep. Minister of Health, 1995; Mem., National Exec. Cttee. of Chama cha Mapinduzi-NEC, 1997-; elected mem., House of Reps., Zanzibar, 2000; Minister of State in the President's Office Responsible for Constitutional Affairs & Good Governance, 2000; Vice-Pres., 2001; mem., Central Cttee. of CCM, 2001-; elected vice-pres., Zanzibar, 2005-10; Pres., 2010-; ***office address:*** Office of the President, State House, PO Box 2422, Zanzibar, Tanzania; ***phone:*** +255 24 223 0815; ***URL:*** http://www.ikuluzanzibar.go.tz/.

SHELBROOKE, Alec; MP for Elmet and Rothwell, UK Government; ***party:*** Conservative; ***political career:*** Councillor, Leeds City Council 2004-; MP for Elmet and Rothwell, May 2010-; ***office address:*** House of Commons, London, SW1A 0AA, United Kingdom; ***phone:*** +44 (0)20 7219 3000; ***e-mail:*** alec.shelbrooke.mp@parliament.uk.

SHELBY, Richard C., BA, LL.B.; Senator for Alabama, US Senate; ***born:*** 6 May 1934, Birmingham, Alabama, USA; ***married:*** Annette Shelby (née Nevin); ***children:*** Richard Jr. (M), Claude Nevin (M); ***education:*** Univ. of Alabama, BA, 1957; LL.B, 1963; ***party:*** Republican; ***political career:*** Alabama State Senator, 1970-78; US Representative, 1979-87; US Senator for Alabama, 1987-; ***professional career:*** Lawyer, 1963-78; City Prosecutor, Tuscaloosa, Alabama, 1963-71; US Magistrate, Northern District of Alabama, 1966-70; Special Asst. Attorney General, State of Alabama, 1969-71; ***committees:*** Appropriations; Banking, Housing and Urban Affairs Cttee.; Rules and Administration; ***honours and awards:*** Spirit of Enterprise Award, US Chamber of Commerce; Courageous Vote Award, National Taxpayers Union; Guardian of Small Business Award, Nat. Federation of Independent Business; Taxpayers Friend; Friend of the Family; Guardian of the Seniors' Rights; ***office address:*** US Senate, 110 Hart Senate Office Building, Washington, DC 20510, USA; ***phone:*** +1 202 224 5744.

SHEPHERD, Richard Charles Scrimgeour, MP; British, Member of Parliament for Aldridge-Brownhills, House of Commons; ***born:*** 6 December 1942, Aberdeen; ***parents:*** Late Alfred Shepherd and Davida Sophia Shepherd (née Wallace); ***education:*** London Sch. of Economics; MSc., Economics, The Johns Hopkins School of Advanced International Studies; ***party:*** Conservative Party; ***political career:*** Mem., South East Economic Planning Council, 1970-74; Personal Asst. to Edward Taylor MP (Glasgow Cathcart), 1974 general election; MP, Aldridge-Brownhills, 1979-; ***professional career:*** Underwriting Mem. Lloyd's, 1974-94; Founded Shepherd Foods (London) Ltd., 1969; Dir., Partridges of Sloane Street, 1973-; Man. Dir., Shepherds Foods (London) Ltd.; Co-Chmn., Campaign for Freedom of Information; some journalism work; Shareholder in Cottonrose Ltd.; ***committees:*** Mem. of Treasury and Civil Service Select Cttee., 1979-; Sec. Cons. Parly. European Affairs and Industry Cttees., 1980-81;

Mem., Public Admin. Cttee., 1997-2000; Mem., Modernisation of the House of Commons, 1997-2010; Vice-Chmn., Conservative Party Cttee. for Constitutional Affairs, Scotland and Wales, 1999; Mem., Jt. Cttee. on Human Rights, 2001-; ***honours and awards:*** The Spectators Award as: Backbencher of the Year, 1987, Parliamentarian of the year, 1995, Campaign for Freedom of Information, 1988; ***clubs:*** Carlton; Beefsteak; Chelsea Arts; ***office address:*** House of Commons, London, SW1A 0AA, United Kingdom; ***phone:*** +44 (0)20 7219 5004; ***e-mail:*** shepherdr@parliament.uk.

SHERIDAN, James; Member of Parliament for Paisley and Renfrewshire, House of Commons; ***married:*** Jean Sheridan; ***party:*** Labour Party; ***political career:*** Local Authority Councillor, 1999-2002 Renfrewshire Council); MP, West Renfrewshire, 2001-2005 (Constituency Abolished); MP, Paisley and Renfrewshire North, 2005-10; MP, Paisley and Renfrewshire, 2010-; ***committees:*** Information, 2001-04; Broadcasting, 2003-05; Public Accounts, 2003-05; Armed Forces Bill, 2005-06; International Development, 2007-09; Chairmen's Panel/Panel of Chairs, 2009-; Culture, Media and Sport, 2010-; ***office address:*** Constituency Office: Mirren Court Three, 123 Renfrew Road, Paisley, Renfrewshire, PA3 4EA, United Kingdom; ***phone:*** +44 (0)141 847 1457; ***e-mail:*** sheridanj@parliament.uk; ***URL:*** http://www.james-sheridan-mp.org.uk.

SHERLOCK, Baroness Maeve; Member, House of Lords; ***political career:*** Mem., House of Lords, 2010-; ***professional career:*** Mem., Equality and Human Rights Commission, 2007-; ***office address:*** House of Lords, London, SW1A 0PW, United Kingdom; ***phone:*** +44 (0)20 7219 3000; ***URL:*** http://www.parliament.gov.

SHERMAN, Brad; American, Congressman, California 27th District, US House of Representatives; ***party:*** Democratic Party; ***political career:*** mem., US House of Representatives, 1991-; ***professional career:*** Fmr. Accountant; ***committees:*** Financial Services; Foreign Affairs; ***office address:*** House of Representatives, 436 Cannon House Street, Washington, DC 20515-6501, USA; ***phone:*** +1 202 224 3121.

SHETTY, Salil; Indian, Secretary General, Amnesty International; ***born:*** 3 February 1961; ***education:*** Bangalore Univ., India, B.Comm., 1981; Indian Inst. of Management, Ahmedabad, MBA, 1981-83; LSE, UK, MA, Social Policy & Planning, (Distinction, recipient of Titmuss Prize), 1991; ***interests:*** monitoring & evaluation, basic education, policy advocacy; ***professional career:*** Consultant, Karntaka State Industrial Investment & Dev. Corp. (Bangalore), 1982; Area Marketing Mngr., Wipro Ltd., Bombay, 1983-85; selected to Indian Civil Services, 1985; Regional Field Dir., ActionAid India, 1986-90; Exec. Dir., ActionAid India (Bangalore), 1991-95; Country Dir., ActionAid Kenya (Nairobi), with additional responsibility for ActionAid Tanzania & Africa-wide technology, 1995-98; Chief Exec., ActionAid, 1998-10; Sec. Gen., Amnesty International , June 2010-; ***office address:*** Amnesty International, Peter Benenson House, 1 Easton Street, London, WC1X 0DW, United Kingdom; ***phone:*** +44 (0)20 7413 5500; ***fax:*** +44 (0)20 7956 1157; ***e-mail:*** amnestyis@amnesty.org; ***URL:*** http://www.amnesty.org.

SHIMMIN, Hon. John; Minister of Economic Development, Government of the Isle of Man; ***born:*** Douglas, Isle of Man; ***parents:*** George Samuel Shimmin and Jacqueline Pamela Shimmin; ***married:*** Maureen Valerie (née O'Hara), 1986; ***children:*** Andrew (M), Peter (M); ***education:*** St. Ninians High Sch., IOM; Worcester Coll. of Higher Education, B.Ed. (Hons), 1978-82; ***political career:*** Chair, IOM Post Office; Minister of Transport, 2001-05; Minister of Home Affairs, 2005-07; Minister of Local Government and the Environment, 2007-09; Minister of Food Agriculture and the Environment, 2009-12; Minister of Economic Development, 2012-; ***interests:*** education, constitution, economy, ICT, environment; ***memberships:*** Former Pres. Tamworth Branch and I.O.M. Branch of NAS/UWT; ***professional career:*** Teacher of Physical Education, Maths, and Pastoral Care, 1982-96; ***committees:*** Constitutional Affairs; ***trusteeships:*** Relate; Alcohol Advisory; Douglas, Development Partnership; ***clubs:*** Cronkbourne Sports and Social Club; ***recreations:*** sports, family; ***office address:*** Department of Economic Development, Murray House, Mount Havelock, Douglas, Isle of Man, IM1 2SF, United Kingdom; ***e-mail:*** john.shimmin@gov.im.

SHINDE, Sushil Kumar; Minister of the Interior, Government of India; ***born:*** 1947; ***education:*** B.A.(Hons.); LL.B ; ***party:*** Indian National Congress; ***political career:*** Mem., Maharashtra Legislative Assembly serving as Minister of Finance and Minister of Planning; mem., Lok Sabha, 1999-; Minister of Power; Minister of the Interior, 2012-; ***professional career:*** Lawyer; ***office address:*** Ministry of Interior, Room 26, North Block, New Delhi 110 001, India; ***phone:*** +91 11 2309 2462; ***URL:*** http://mha.nic.in.

SHINSEKI , Gen. (Ret'd.) Eric K; Secretary of Veterans Affairs, US Government; ***education:*** US Military Acad., B.Sc., 1965; Duke Univ., MA, English Literature; US Army Command and General Staff College, and the National War College, Armor Officer Advanced Course; ***political career:*** US Secretary of Veteran Affairs, 2009-; ***professional career:*** Various command and staff assignments in the USA and overseas, including two combat tours with the 9th and 25th Infantry Divisions in the Republic of Vietnam. Served at Schofield Barracks, Hawaii and Fort Shafter, US Army Pacific; Ten years based in Europe, incl. as Dep. Chief of Staff for Support, Allied Land Forces, Southern Europe as part of Allied Command Europe; Cmdr. 1st Cavalry Div., Fort Hood, Texas, 1994-95; Lieutenant Gen., Dep. Chief of Staff for Operations and Plans, US Army, 1996-97; Commanding Gen., US Army Europe; Cmdr., Allied Land Forces Central Europe; Cmdr., NATO Stabilization Force, Bosnia-Herzegovina, 1997-98; Vice Chief-of-Staff, 1998-99; Chief of Staff, 1999-; ***honours and awards:*** Defense Distinguished Service Medal; Distinguished Service Medal; Legion of Merit (with Oak Leaf Clusters); Bronze Star Medal with "V" Device (with 2 Oak Leaf Clusters); Purple Heart (with Oak Leaf Cluster); Meritorious Service Medal (with 2 Oak Leaf Clusters); Air Medal, Army Commendation Medal (with Oak Leaf Cluster); Army Achievement Medal; Parachutist Badge; Ranger Tab; Office of the Secretary of Defense Identification Badge; Joint Chiefs of Staff Identification Badge; Army Staff Identification Badge; ***office address:*** Department of Veterans' Affairs, 810 Vermont Ave, NW, Washington, DC 20420, USA; ***phone:*** +1 202 273 5700; ***fax:*** +1 202 273 6705; ***URL:*** http://www.va.gov.

SHIPLEY, Lord John, OBE; Member, House of Lords; ***party:*** Liberal Democrat; ***political career:*** Local Gov. Councillor, Newcastle upon Tyne; Mem. House of Lords, 2010-; ***office address:*** House of Lords, London, SW1A 0PW, United Kingdom; ***phone:*** +44 (0)20 7219 3000; ***fax:*** +44 (0)20 7219 5979; ***URL:*** http://www.parliament.uk.

SHIVUTE, Peter; Chief Justice, Supreme Court of Namibia; ***born:*** 25 September 1963, Namibia; ***education:*** Trinity Hall College, Cambridge, LL.B (Hons), 1991; Univ. of Warwick, LL.M, 1996; ***professional career:*** Magistrate, Republic of Zambia, to 1988; Magistrate, Namibian Judiciary, 1991-95, 1996-2000; Acting Judge, then Judge, High Court of Namibia, 2000-03; Judge-President, High Court, 2003-04; Chief Justice, Supreme Court of Namibia, 2004-; ***office address:*** Supreme Court, Private Bag 13398, Windhoek, Namibia; ***phone:*** +264 61 279900; ***URL:*** http://www.superiorcourts.org.na/supreme/.

SHUKER, Gavin; MP for Luton South, House of Commons; ***party:*** Labour/Co-operative; ***political career:*** MP for Luton South, May 2010-; Shadow Minister, Environment, Food and Rural Affairs, 2011-; ***committees:*** Transport, 2010-11; ***office address:*** House of Commons, London, SW1A 0AA, United Kingdom; ***phone:*** +44 (0)20 7219 3000; ***e-mail:*** gavin.shuker.mp@parliament.uk.

SHUMLIN, Peter; Governor, State of Vermont; ***political career:*** Vermont House of Reps., 1990-92; Senate, 1992-2002, Democratic Leader, 1996-, President Pro-tempore, 1997; Senate, 2006-2010; Governor of Vermont, 2010-; ***office address:*** Office of the Governor, 109 State Street, Pavilion, Montpelier, VT 05609-0101, USA; ***URL:*** http://governor.vermont.gov/.

SHUSTER, Bill; American, Congressman, Pennsylvania Ninth District, US House of Representatives; ***education:*** BA, Political Science & History; American Univ. in Washington, MBA; ***party:*** Republican; ***political career:*** mem., US House of Representatives, 1973-; ***committees:*** Transportion and Infrastructure Cttee., 2001-, Chmn.; Armed Forces Cttee.; ***office address:*** House of Representatives, 436 Cannon House Street, Washington, DC 20515-6501, USA; ***phone:*** +1 202 224 3121.

SHUVALOV, Igor; First Deputy Prime Minister, Russian Government; ***born:*** 1967; ***political career:*** Dep. Minister of State Property, 1998; Chmn., Russian Federal Property Fund, 1998-2000; Head of Government Administration, 2000; Aide to President, 2003; Dep. Chief of the President's Executive Office, 2003; First Dep. Prime Minister, 2008, re-appointed 2012; ***office address:*** Council of the Federation, Bolshaya Dmitrovka 26, Moscow, Russian Federation.

SIBAL, Kapil; Minister of Communications and Information Technology, Government of India; ***born:*** 1948; ***education:*** MA, History, University of Delhi, India; LL.M, Harvard Law School, USA; ***party:*** Indian National Congress; ***political career:*** Mem., Rajya Sabha, 1998-2004; mem., Lok Sabha, 2004-; Minister of Science and Technology and Minister in the Department of Ocean Development, 2004-08; Minister of Human Resource Development, 2009-12; Minister of Communications and Information Technology, 2011-; Minister of Law and Justice, 2013-; ***office address:*** Ministry of Communications and Information Technology, Sanchar Bhavan, 20 Asoka Road, New Delhi 110 001, India; ***URL:*** http://www.moc.gov.in.

SIDIBÉ, Michel; Malian, Executive Director, UNAIDS; ***born:*** 1952; ***languages:*** French, English; ***professional career:*** Country Dir., Terre des Hommes (international development federation), Mali; UNICEF, 1987-2001; Dir., Country & Regional Support Dep., UNAIDS, 2001, Dep. Exec. Dir. of Programmes, 2007-; Assist. Sec.-Gen. of UN, 2007-09, Under Sec.-Gen., 2009-; Dir., Grassroots Soccer (HIV/AIDS prevention foundation); ***office address:*** UNAIDS, 20 Avenue Appia, CH-1211 Geneva 27, Switzerland; ***phone:*** +41 (0) 22 791 3666; ***fax:*** +41 (0)22 791 4187; ***URL:*** http://www.unaids.org.

SIHAMONI, King Norodom; King and Supreme Commander of Cambodia, Kingdom of Cambodia; ***born:*** 1953; ***parents:*** King Sihanouk (dec'd) and Monique Sihanouk; ***education:*** Prague High Sch.; National Conservatory, music and dance; North Korea, cinematography; ***professional career:*** Ambassador to UNESCO, 1992-2004; King of Cambodia, October 2004-; ***office address:*** Office of the King, Royal Palace, Phnom Penh, Cambodia.

SIKORSKI, Radoslaw; Minister for Foreign Affairs, Government of Poland; ***born:*** 1963; ***education:*** MA, PPE, Oxford Univ., UK; ***political career:*** Deputy Defence Minister, 1992; Under Sec. of State, Min. of Foreign Affairs, 1998-2001; Senator, 2005-07; MP, 2007-; Minister for National Defence, 2005-07; Minister of Foreign Affairs, 2008-; ***professional career:*** Writer and Broadcaster; Resident Fellow, American Instit. of Enterprise, Washington, 2002-05; Exec. Dir., New Atlantic Initiative, 2002-05; Editor, European Outlook, to date; ***office address:*** Ministry of Foreign Affairs, Aleja J.Ch. Szucha 25, 00-580 Warsaw, Poland; ***phone:*** +48 22 623 9000; ***fax:*** +48 22 629 0287; ***e-mail:*** mszdpi@warman.com.pl.

SILUANOV, Anton; Minister of Finance, Russian Government; ***born:*** 1963; ***education:*** Moscow Finance Inst.; ***political career:*** Dep. Finance Minister, 2003-04, 2005-11; Acting Finance Minister, Sep. 2011; Finance Minister, Dec. 2011-; ***professional career:*** Economist; senior economist, Finance Ministry, 1985-87; Soviet Army, 1987-89; Chief Economist and Adviser, Ministry of Finance, 1989-92; Dep. Head of Dept., Economy & Finance Ministry, 1992; Dept. Head, Budget Board, Finance Ministry, 1992-97; Mem., Bd., Finance Ministry, 2001; Head of the Dept. for Macro Economic Policy and Banking, 2003; ***office address:*** Ministry of Finance, ul. Ilyinka 9, 109097 Moscow, Russia; ***phone:*** +7 495 298 9101; ***fax:*** +7 495 925 0889; ***URL:*** http://www.minfin.ru.

SILVA DE LAPUERTA, Rosario; Judge, Court of Justice of the European Union; ***born:*** 1954; ***education:*** Universidad Complutense, Madrid, Spain; ***professional career:*** State Attorney, Legal Service, Ministry of Transport, Torurism and Communication; State Attorney, MFA; Chief State Attorney, State Legal Services; Judge, Court of Justice of the European Union, 2003-; ***office address:*** Court of Justice of the European Union, Rue du Fort Niedergrunewald, L-2925, Luxembourg; ***URL:*** http://www.curia.europa.eu.

SIMMONDS, Mark; Member of Parliament for Boston and Skegness, House of Commons; ***born:*** 12 April 1964; ***married:*** Lizbeth Josefina Hanomancin-Garcia, 1994; ***children:*** Oliver (M), Isabella (F), Oriana (F); ***education:*** Worksop Coll., Nottingham and Trent Polytechnic; ***party:*** Conservative Party; ***political career:*** Cllr., London Borough of Wandsworth, 1990-94; MP, Boston & Skegness, 2001-; PPS to Michael Ancram, 2001-03; Sec., All Party Parly. Gp. Latin America, 2001-; Shadow Minister for Education, 2003-04; Shadow Minister for International Dev., 2004-05; Shadow Minister for Foreign Affairs, 2004-05; Shadow Minister for Health, 2007-10; PPS to Sec. of State for Environment, Food and Rural Affairs, 2010-12; Parly. Under-Sec. of State, FCO, 2012-; ***interests:*** education, agriculture, foreign affairs; ***memberships:*** Chartered Surveyor; ***committees:*** Environmental Audit, 2001-03; Education and Skills, 2001-03; ***clubs:*** Naval and Military; ***recreations:*** reading, history, tennis, rubgy, family; ***office address:*** House of Commons, London, SW1A 0AA, United Kingdom; ***phone:*** +44 (0)20 7219 6254; ***fax:*** +44 (0)20 7219 1746; ***e-mail:*** simmondsm@parliament.uk; ***URL:*** http://www.marksimmondsmp.org.

SIMPSON, David; MP for Upper Bann, House of Commons; ***born:*** 1959; ***party:*** Democratic Unionist Party; ***political career:*** MLA for Upper Bann, 2003-; MP for Upper Bann, 2005-; ***committees:*** Joint Committee on Statutory Instruments and Commons Committee on Statutory Instruments, 2006-09; Transport, 2007-09; Northern Ireland Affairs, 2009-; ***office address:*** House of Commons, London, SW1A 0AA, United Kingdom.

SIMPSON, Keith; British, Member of Parliament for Mid Norfolk, House of Commons; ***born:*** 29 March 1949, Norwich; ***parents:*** Harry Simpson and Jean Simpson (née Day); ***married:*** Pepi Simpson (née Hollingworth), 4 August 1984; ***children:*** George (M); ***education:*** Univ. of Hull, BA (Hons); King's College London; ***party:*** Conservative Party; ***political career:*** National Vice-Chmn., Federation of Conservative Students, 1972-73; Head of Overseas and Defence Section, Conservative Research Department, 1986-88; Special Adviser to Sec. of State for Defence, 1988-90; MP for Mid Norfolk, 1997-; Conservative whip, 1999-2001; Conservative Frontbench Agriculture Spokesman, 2001-02; Conservative Frontbench Defence Spokesman, 2002-05; Conservative frontbench Foreign Office Spokesman, 2005-; ***interests:*** defence, foreign affairs, business, rural affairs; ***memberships:*** Rusi, IISS; ***professional career:*** Dir., Cranfield Security Studies Institute, 1991-97; ***publications:*** The Old Contemptibles; History of the German Army; A Nation in Arms; The War the Infantry Knew; ***office address:*** House of Commons, London, SW1A 0AA, United Kingdom; ***phone:*** +44 (0)20 7219 4053; ***e-mail:*** keithsimpsonmp@parliament.uk.

SIMPSON, Dr Richard, MSP; Shadow Public Health Minister, Scottish Parliament; ***born:*** 22 October 1942, Edinburgh, Scotland; ***parents:*** John Taylor Simpson and Margaret Norah Simpson (née Coates); ***married:*** Christine Margaret Simpson (née MacGregor), 6 February 1967; ***education:*** Edinburgh Univ.; ***party:*** Labour; ***political career:*** Mem., Scottish Parly., 1999-2003; Dep. Minister for Justice, 2001-2003; ***interests:*** health; ***memberships:*** British Medical Assn. (BMA); Fellow of Royal Coll. Psychiatrists; mem., Royal Coll. of General Practitioners; ***professional career:*** Medical Practitioner, GP and Psychiatrist, 1966-99; Dir. of Forth Valley Primary Care Research Group; Consultant Psychiatrist in addictions, West Lothian; ***committees:*** Scottish Parl. Finance; Scottish Parl. Health and Community Care ; ***honours and awards:*** Hon. Prof., Univ. of Stirling; ***publications:*** Over 30 medical research papers and four chapters in books on psychology and on prostate disease; ***clubs:*** Stirling Rugby Football Club; Elie Golf House Club; ***recreations:*** golf, swimming, classical music; ***office address:*** Scottish Parliament, Edinburgh, Scotland; ***e-mail:*** richard.simpson@hushmail.com.

SIMPSON-MILLER, Hon. Portia Lucretia F; Jamaican, Prime Minister, Jamaican Government; ***born:*** 1945, St Catherine, Jamaica; ***education:*** Union Institute, Miami, Florida, BA, Public Administration; Diploma and Certificate (Computer Programming and Public Relations), Jamaica Commercial Institute; ***party:*** People's National Party (PNP); ***political career:*** Vice-Pres., PNP, 1978; Cllr., Kingston and St. Andrew Corp., 1974-76; MP for South-West St. Andrew, 1976-80 and 1989-; PNP spokesperson on women's affairs, pensions, social security and consumer affairs, 1983-89; President of PNP's Women's Movement and leader of movement's delegation at Decade Forum, Nairobi, Kenya, 1985; Minister of Labour, Welfare and Sport, 1989-93; Minister of Labour and Welfare, 1993-95; Minister of Labour, Social Security and Sports, 1995-2000; Minister of Tourism and Sports, 2000-02; Minister of Local Government, 2003-05; Minister of Local Government, Community Development and Sport, 2005-06; Prime Minister, Minister of Defence, Sports and Women's Affairs, 2006-07; Prime Miister, Minister of Defence, Development, Information and Sports, Dec. 2011-; ***professional career:*** Various positions as secretary and social worker; during 1970s, Parly. Secy., Office of the Prime Minister and Min. of Local Govt., People's National Party (PNP); Activist for the establishment of the Bureau of Women's Affairs and legislation benefiting women and children (inc. Status of Children Act), 1972-80; ***committees:*** Exec. Cncl. and National Exec. Cncl., People's National Party; ***office address:*** Office of the Prime Minister, 1 Devon Road, Kingston 6, Jamaica; ***phone:*** +1 876 927 9941; ***fax:*** +1 876 927 9941; ***URL:*** http://www.cabinet.gov.jm.

SIMSEK, Mehmet; Turkish, Minister of Finance, Government of Turkey; ***born:*** 1967, Batman, Turkey; ***parents:*** Hasan and Mehdiye; ***married:*** Esra Simsek; ***education:*** M.Phil. in Finance and Economics, Univ. of Exeter, UK; B.Sc. in Economics, Univ. of Ankara, Turkey; ***party:*** Justice and Development Party; ***political career:*** MP for Gaziantep, 2007-; State Minister for Economic Affairs, 2007-09; Minister of Finance, 2009-; ***professional career:*** Snr. Economist, US Embassy, Ankara, 1993-97; Equity Researcher, UBS Securities, New York, 1997-98; Chief Economist and Bank Analyst, Deutsche-Bender Securities, Istanbul, 1998-2000; Chief Economist and Strategist for Emerging Europe, Middle East and Africa Region, Merrill Lynch, UK, 2000-07; ***office address:*** Ministry of Finance, Ilkadim Cad., 2 Dikmen Yolu, Ankara, Turkey; ***phone:*** +90 (9)312 425 0080; ***e-mail:*** mermet.sinsek@gmail.com; ***URL:*** http://www.maliye.gov.tr.

SINGER, Miroslav; Governor, Czech National Bank; ***born:*** 1964; ***education:*** Univ. of Economics, Prague; post grad. fellowship, Univ. of Pittsburg, Ph.D; ***professional career:*** Researcher & Lecturer, Economics Institute of the Academy of Sciences of the Czech Rep. & the Centre for Economic Research & Graduate Education at Charles Univ.; Chief Economist, Expandia Finance, 1995; MD, Expandia Investment Co., 1998-99; MD, Expandia Holding, 2000-01; Dir., PricewaterhouseCoopers Czech Rep., 2001-05; Vice-Gov., Czech National Bank, 2005-10, Governor, 2010-; ***office address:*** Czech National Bank, Na Príkope 28, 11503 Prague 1, Czech Republic; ***URL:*** http://www.cnb.cz.

SINGH, Dr. Manmohan; Prime Minister, Government of India; ***born:*** 26 September 1932; ***d:*** 3; ***education:*** Cambridge & Oxford Univ.; ***party:*** Indian National Congress; ***political career:*** mem., Rajya Sabha, 1991-; Finance Minister, 1991-96; Leader of the Opposition, 1998-2004; Prime Minister of India, May 2004-; Minister for Planning, Personnel, Public Grievances and Pensions; Atomic Energy and Space, 2004-; Minister of Finance, Nov. 2008-; Minister of Railways, 2011-; ***office address:*** Prime Minister's Office, Room 152, South Block, New Delhi 110001, India; ***phone:*** +91 (0)11 2301 2312.

SISON, HE Michele; Ambassador, US Embassy in Lebanon; ***professional career:*** career member, US Senior Foreign Service; US Ambassador to the United Arab Emirates, 2004-08; Amb. to Lebanon, 2008-10; Assist. Chief of Mission, Baghdad, 2011-12; Amb. to Sri Lanka, 2012-; ***office address:*** US Embassy, 210 Galle Road, Kollupitiya, (PO Box 106) , Colombo 3, Sri Lanka; ***URL:*** http://srilanka.usembassy.gov/.

SISOULIT, Thongloun; Deputy Prime Minister, Minister of Foreign Affairs, People's Republic of Laos; ***political career:*** Deputy Prime Minister, President of the State Planning Committee; Deputy Prime Minister, Minister of Foreign Affairs, April 2006-; ***office address:*** Office of the Deputy Prime Minister, 1 That-Luang Square, Vientiane, Laos.

SISSOKO, Django; Prime Minister, Government of Mali; ***born:*** 1947; ***political career:*** Minister of Justice, 1984-88; Sec.-Gen. of Presidency; Ombudsman, 2011-12; Prime Minister, 2013-; ***office address:*** Office of the Prime Minister, BP 97, quartier du Fleuve, Bamako, Mali; ***phone:*** +223 2022 5534; ***fax:*** +223 2029 9403.

SISULU, Dr L.N.; Minister of Public Service and Administration, South African Government; ***born:*** 10 May 1954, Johannesburg, Gauteng; ***education:*** Military Training, specialising in Intelligence, 1977-79; BA Degree and Dip. in Education, Univ. of Swaziland, 1980; BA Hons degree, history, Univ. of Swaziland, 1981; MA, Centre for Southern African Studies, Univ. of York, 1982; M Phil (later upgraded to D Phil), Centre for Southern African Studies, Univ. of York, 1989; ***political career:*** detained for political activities, 1975-76; joined Umkontho we Sizwe (MK), worked in underground structures, ANC in exile, 1977-87; Chief Administrator, ANC at Codesa 1, 1991; Administrator, Intelligence Dept. of Intelligence and Security, ANC, 1992; Mem., Parl. for the ANC, 1994-; Dep. Minister, Home Affairs, 1996-2001; Minister of Intelligence, 2001-04; Minister of Housing, 2004-09; Minister of Defence and Military Veterans, 2009-12; Minister of Public Service and Administration, 2012-; ***memberships:*** UN Fellow, Centre for Human Rights, Geneva, 1992; ***professional career:*** Teacher, Mazini Central high Sch., 1981; Lecturer, Dept. of History, Univ. of Swaziland, 1982; Sub Editor, The Times of Swaziland, 1983; Lecturer, Manzini Teacher Training Coll., 1985-87; Chief Examiner, History for Junior Cert. Examinations Syndicate Botswana, Lesotho and Swaziland, 1985-87; Personal Asst. to Jacab Zuma, ANC Head of Intelligence, 1990; Consultant, Nat. Children's Rights Cttee., Unesco, 1992; Dir., Govan Mbeki Research Fellowship, Univ. of Fort Hare, 1993; Sr. Research Fellow, Govan Mbeki Fellowship, Univ. of Fort Hare, 1993; Man., Sub-council on Intelligence Transitional Exec. Council (TEC), 1994; ***committees:*** Mem., Parl. Joint Standing Cttee. on Intelligence, 1995-; Mem., Mangt. Cttee., Policing Org. and Mangt. Course, PDM, Univ. of Witwatersrand, 1993; ***honours and awards:*** Human Rights Centre Fellowship, Geneva, 1992; ***publications:*** 'Women, Work and the Liberation Struggle in the 1980s' in R. Cohen (ed) Themes in Twentieth Century South Africa, Oxford University Press, 1991; ***office address:*** Ministry of Public Service, Private Bag X884, Pretoria 0001, South Africa; ***URL:*** http://www.dpsa.gov.za.

SITHOLE, Hon. Majozi; Minister of Finance, Government of Swaziland; ***political career:*** Minister of Econ. Planning & Dev., 1998-00; Minister for Finance 2000-; ***office address:*** Ministry of Finance, PO Box 433, Mbabane, Swaziland; ***phone:*** +268 404 2142/2145; ***fax:*** +268 404 3187.

SJOSTROM, Olof Carl; Swedish, Consul General of Monaco in Sweden; ***born:*** 1940; ***parents:*** Prof. Gunnar Sjöström and Margareta Ljungberg; ***married:*** Marianne Sjöström (née Vigre), 1965; ***children:*** J. Carl F. (M), Louise M. Andersson (F); ***public role of spouse:*** Journalist; ***languages:*** English, German, French; ***education:*** Univ. of Lund, MBA; Univ. of Grenoble; ***professional career:*** Svenska Handelsbanken, Stockholm, New York, Gothenburg, 1967-71, Head of Int. Dept., Gothenburg, 1965-71; Götaverken AB, Gothenburg, Mem. Exec. Cttee, 1971-72; AB Volvo, CFO, 1972-1974; Sr. Vice-Pres. and Mem. Exec.Cttee.of Volvo Gp. of Cos., 1974-80; Atlas Copco AB, Stockholm, Dep. Gp. Pres., 1980-85; Östgöta Enskilda Bank, Pres. and CEO, 1985-88; Salomon Brothers Int., London, New York, Sr. advisor 1989-1998. Former Chmn. and Bd. mem. of companies and foundations in Sweden and abroad active within manufacturing industries, trade, research, real estate, capital management, agriculture, arts, Church of Sweden. Former advisor president of the Republic of Zambia. Today chm Pomona-gruppen AB, Stockholm, Industricentralen AB, Stockholm, and bd mem. Wassum AB, Stockholm, Saracakis Grp of Cies SA, Athens; Monaco's Consul General in Sweden; ***committees:*** Foundation for Strategic Research, Capital Cttee.; Church of Sweden Capital Cttee.; ***publications:*** Karl XIV Johan - The founder of modern Sweden; Sweden and the Common Market; articles in newspapers and magazines; ***office address:*** Consulat Général de la Principauté de Monaco, Grev Turegatan 14, SE 11446 Stockholm, Sweden; ***phone:*** +46 (0)8 229320; ***mobile:*** +46 703 985577; ***e-mail:*** olof.sjostrom@telia.com.

SKELEMANI, Phandu T.C.; Botswanan, Minister of Foreign Affairs, Government of Botswana; ***born:*** 5 January 1945; ***parents:*** Phandu Skelemani and Manadi Skelmani Phandu; ***married:*** Kelebone D. Skelemani; ***public role of spouse:*** Deputy Permanent Secretary; ***languages:*** Ikalanga, English, Setswana, Ndebele, Shona; ***party:*** Botswana Democratic Party; ***political career:*** Attorney General, 1992-2003; Minister of Foreign Affairs, 2008-; ***memberships:*** Botswana Diamond Valuing Co., Debswana; ***professional career:*** Attorney Gen., 1992-; ***committees:*** Law Reform, Parly. Privileges, Cttee. on Assurances and Govt. Motions; ***honours and awards:*** Presidential Order of Honour; ***clubs:*** Rotary Club, British Airways Exec. Club; ***recreations:*** walking; ***office address:***

Ministry of Foreign Affairs and International Cooperation, Private Bag 00368, Gaborone, Botswana; ***phone:*** +267 3600 700; ***fax:*** +267 313366; ***e-mail:*** mofaic@registry.gov.bw; ***URL:*** http://www.gov.bw/government/ministry_of_foreign_affairs.html.

SKELMERSDALE, Lord, 7th Baron Roger Bootle-Wilbraham; British, Member of the House of Lords; ***born:*** 2 April 1945, Cove, Farnborough, Hants. UK; ***parents:*** Brigadier Lionel Bootle-Wilbraham 6th baron Skelmersdale and Ann Bootle-Wilbraham (née Quilter); ***married:*** Christine Joan (née Morgan), 1972; ***children:*** Andrew (M), Carolyn Ann (F); ***public role of spouse:*** Lecturer on horticultural matters; Managing Director, Broadleigh Nurseries Ltd; ***languages:*** Dutch, French; ***education:*** Eton College and Lord Wandsworth Coll., Basingstoke; Somerset Farm Inst.; Hadlow Coll; ***party:*** Conservative; ***political career:*** Lord-in-Waiting (Govt. Whip) 1981-86. Spokesman for Dept. of the Environment; Dept. of Transport; Dept. of Energy; Min. of Agriculture, Fisheries and Food; Foreign and Commonwealth Office; Office of Arts and Libraries 1981-86; Parly. Under-Secy. of State, Dept. of the Environment 1986-87; Under-Sec. of State, Dept. of Health & Social Security 1987-88; Under-Sec. of State, Dept. of Social Security 1988-89; Under-Sec. of State, Northern Ireland Office 1989-90; Dep. Chmn., of Cttees., House of Lords 1991-95; Parliamentary Affairs Consultant 1992-2002; Deputy Speaker, House of Lords, 1994-2003; Opposition Whip (specialising in health matters), 2002-05; Opposition Spokesman for Work and Pensions, 2005-09; Shadow Minister for Home Affairs, 2009-10; ***memberships:*** Vice-Chmn., Cncl. for Environmental Conservation 1979-81; Pres., Somerset Trust for Nature Conservation 1980-; British Naturalists Assn. 1979-95; Chmn., The Stroke Assn. 1993-2003; ***professional career:*** Proprietor, Broadleigh Gardens, 1972-73; Man. Dir., Broadleigh Nurseries Ltd, 1973-81, Dir., 1992-; ***office address:*** House of Lords, London, SW1A 0PW, United Kingdom; ***phone:*** +44 (0)20 7219 3224; ***fax:*** +44 (0)20 7630 0088; ***e-mail:*** skelmersdaler@parliament.uk.

SKERRIT, Hon. Roosevelt; Prime Minister, Minister for Finance, Foreign Affairs and Social Security, Government of Dominica; ***born:*** 8 June 1972; ***education:*** Clifton Dupigny Community Coll., 1990-92; New Mexico State Univ., Dipl. in Secondary Education, 1995; Univ. of Mississippi, BA (Hons) Double Major in Psychology & English, 1997; ***party:*** Political Leader, Dominica Labour Party (DLP); ***political career:*** elected to House of Assembly, 2000; Minister for Education, Sports & Youth Affairs, 2000-04; Prime Minister and Minister for Finance and Planning and Caribbean Affairs, Jan. 2004-; PM and Minister of Finance, Planning, National Security and Overseas Nationals, 2005-, Minister of Foreign Affairs and Social Security, 2007-; ***memberships:*** Chief Adviser, Movement for the Social, Educational & Cultural Advancement, Veille Case, Dominica; Chmn., Labour Party Vielle Case Constituency Assn.; mem., UNESCO Exec. Bd.; mem., Cncl. of the Univ. of West Indies; ***professional career:*** teacher, lecturer; Pres., Dominica Student's Assn., New Mexico State Univ.; Pres., Caribbean Student's Assn., Univ. of Mississippi; Orientation Leader & Adviser to the Univ. of Mississippi Int. Prog. Office; ***committees:*** mem., UWI Finance & Gen. Purpose Cttee.; mem., UWI Strategy Cttee.; mem., Standing Order Cttee.; Govt.'s Rep., UWI Non-Campus Territories Bd.; ***honours and awards:*** Guiness Book of World Records entry for Youngest Prime Minister; ***clubs:*** Vieille Case Sports Club; ***recreations:*** lawn tennis, music, reading; ***office address:*** Prime Minister's Office, Financial Centre, Kennedy Avenue, Roseau, Dominica; ***phone:*** +767 448 2401 ext.3300; ***fax:*** +767 448 4506; ***e-mail:*** pmoffice@cwdom.dm.

SKIDMORE, Chris; MP for Kingswood, UK Government; ***party:*** Conservative; ***political career:*** MP for Kingswood, May 2010-; ***professional career:*** Journalist; ***committees:*** Health, 2010-; ***office address:*** House of Commons, London, SW1A 0AA, United Kingdom; ***phone:*** +44 (0)20 7219 3000; ***e-mail:*** chris.skidmore.mp@parliament.uk.

SKINNER, Dennis Edward; British, Member of Parliament for Bolsover, House of Commons; ***born:*** 1932; ***parents:*** Tony Skinner and Lily Skinner (née Dudley); ***married:*** Mary Skinner, 1960; ***s:*** 1; ***d:*** 2; ***education:*** Tupton Hall Grammar Sch.; Ruskin Coll., Oxford; ***party:*** Labour Party; ***political career:*** Pres. Derbyshire NUM 1966-70; Mem., Clay Cross Council 1960-72, Derbyshire CC 1966-70; Chair, Labour Party 1988-89; Mem., Labour Party National Exec. Cttee. (NEC) 1991-; MP, Bolsover 1970-; ***memberships:*** National Exec., Labour Party; ***professional career:*** Miner 1949-70; ***recreations:*** walking, cycling; ***office address:*** House of Commons, London, SW1A 0AA, United Kingdom; ***e-mail:*** skinnerd@parliament.uk.

SKOTNIKOV, Judge Leonid; Russian, Member, International Court of Justice; ***born:*** 1951; ***education:*** Diploma, International Law, Moscow Institute of International Relations, 1974; Fellow, Center for International Affairs, Harvard Univ., 1990; ***professional career:*** Officer, Consular Depart., Ministry of Foreign Affairs, USSR, 1974-77; Officer, Permanent Mission of the USSR to the UN, 1977-81; Officer, 1981-86, then Head of Division, 1987-91, Legal Department, MFA, Dir., 1991-92; Amb. Extraordinary and Plenipotentiary of the Russian Federation to the Netherlands, 1992-98; Dir., Legal Depart., Member of the Collegium, MFA, 1998-2001; Amb., Perm. Rep. of the Russian Federation to the UN Office and other international organizations in Geneva; Mem., International Court of Justice, 2006-; ***office address:*** International Court of Justice, Peace Palace, 2517 KJ The Hague, Netherlands.

SKOURIS, Vassilios; President, Court of Justice of the EU; ***born:*** 1948; ***education:*** Free Univ., Berlin, law, 1970; Hamburg Univ., constitutional and administrative law, doctorate, 1973; ***political career:*** Minister of Internal Affairs, 1989, 1996; ***professional career:*** Assistant Professor, Hamburg University, 1972-77; Professor of Public Law, Bielefeld University, 1978; Professor of Public Law, University of Thessaloniki, 1982; Dir., Centre for International and European Economic Law, Thessaloniki, 1997-2005; Pres., Greek Association for European Law, 1992-94; President, Greek Economic and Social Council, 1998; Judge, Court of Justice, 1999-, President, 2003-; ***office address:*** Court of Justice of the European Union, Rue du Fort Niedergrunewald, L-2925, Luxembourg.

SLATER, Hon. Douglas; Minister of Foreign Affairs and International Affairs, Government of St. Vincent and the Grenadines; ***education:*** Univ. of West Indies, medicine, public health administration; Univ. of Havana; ***political career:*** Minister of Health and the Environment,-2010; Minister of Foreign Affairs, International Trade & Consumer Affairs, Dec. 2010-; ***professional career:*** Medicine in Guyana, Jamaica and St Vincent and the Grenadines; ***office address:*** Ministry of Foreign Affairs, Bay Street, Kingstown, St. Vincent and the Grenadines; ***phone:*** +1 784 456 1721.

SLAUGHTER, Andrew, MP; MP for Hammersmith, House of Commons; ***born:*** 29 September 1960, London, UK; ***parents:*** Alfred Frederick Slaughter and Marie Frances Slaughter (née Berry); ***education:*** Latymer Upper School, London; Univ. of Exeter Coll. of Law; Inns of Court Sch. of Law; ***party:*** Labour; Co-operative Party; ***political career:*** Councillor, London Borough of Hammersmith and Fulham, 1986-; MP for Ealing, Acton and Shepherd's Bush, 2005-10, Hammersmith, 2010-; PPS to Dr. Stephen Ladyman MP, 2005-07; PPS to Lord Jones of Birmingham as Minister of State, FCO and Department for Business, Enterprise and Regulatory Reform, 2007-08; PPS to Lord Malloch-Brown as Minister of State, FCO, 2007-09; Shadow Minister, Justice, Oct. 2010-; ***interests:*** Housing, education, transport; ***professional career:*** Barrister, Bridewell Chambers, 1993-; ***committees:*** Regulatory Reform Select Cttee., 2005-07; Children, Schools and Families, 2007-09; Court of Referees, 2007-10; Communities and Local Government, 2009-10; London, 2009-10; Joint Committee on Human Rights, 2010; ***office address:*** House of Commons, London, SW1A 0AA, United Kingdom; ***phone:*** +44 (0)20 7219 4990; ***fax:*** +44 (0)20 7219 6775; ***e-mail:*** slaughter@parliament.uk.

SLINN, David; Ambassador, British Embassy in Croatia; ***professional career:*** British Ambassador to North Korea, 2002-06, Amb. to Croatia, 2011-; ***office address:*** British Embassy, Ivana Lucica 4, Zagreb, Croatia; ***phone:*** +385 (0)1 600 9100; ***fax:*** +385 (0)1 600 9111; ***e-mail:*** british.embassyzagreb@fco.gov.uk; ***URL:*** http://ukincroatia.fco.gov.uk/en.

SLIPPER, Hon. Peter Neil; MP for Fisher, Australian Government; ***education:*** BA, LLB, Queensland; ***political career:*** MP for Fisher, Queensland, 1984-87, 1993-; Parly. Sec. to the Minister for Finance and Administration, 1998-2004; Speaker of the House of Representatives, 2011-12; ***professional career:*** Solicitor; Barrister; ***office address:*** House of Representatives, Parliament House, Canberra, ACT 2600, Australia.

SMITH, Rt. Hon. Andrew David, MP; British, MP for Oxford East, House of Commons; ***born:*** 1951; ***parents:*** David Smith and Georgina Smith (née Lowe); ***married:*** Val Smith (née Lambert), 1976; ***s:*** 1; ***public role of spouse:*** Oxford City Councillor; ***education:*** Univ. of Oxford, BA, BPhil; ***party:*** Labour Party; ***political career:*** MP, Oxford East, 1987-; Opp. Spokesman on Higher Education, 1988-1992; Opp. Spokesman, Treasury & Economic Affairs, 1992-94; Shadow Chief Sec. to Treasury, 1994-96; Shadow Transport Sec., July 1996-97; Minister for Employment, Welfare to Work and Equal Opportunities, Dept. for Education & Employment, 1997-99; Chief Sec. to Treasury, 1999-2001; Chief Sec. to Treasury, 2001-2002; re-elected to Oxford East 2001-; Secretary of State for Work and Pensions, 2002-04; ***interests:*** employment, economy, environment, automotive industry, education, retail trade, young people, overseas aid and dev., Europe; ***professional career:*** City Cllr., Oxford City Cncl., 1976-87; Officer, Co-operative Soc., 1979-87; Chmn., Recreation Cttee., 1980-83; Chmn., Planning Cttee., 1985-87; Chmn., Governors of Oxford Brookes Univ., 1987-93; ***committees:*** All-Party Cttee. on Overseas Aid and Devt., 1987-; Standing Cttee. on Education Reform Bill, 1987-88; Standing Cttee. on Finance Bill, 1988-92; Select Cttee. on Social Service, 1988; Standing Cttee. on Finance Bill, 1992-96; South East, 2009-10; ***clubs:*** Blackbird Leys Community Centre; ***recreations:*** gardening, walking, cycling; ***office address:*** House of Commons, London, SW1 0AN, United Kingdom; ***e-mail:*** smithad@parliament.uk.

SMITH, Angela; MP for Penistone and Stocksbridge, House of Commons; ***born:*** 1961; ***party:*** Labour; ***political career:*** MP for Sheffield Hillsborough, 2005-10; MP for Penistone and Stocksbridge, 2010-; Shadow Deputy Leader of the House of Commons, 2011-; ***office address:*** House of Commons, London, SW1A 0AA, United Kingdom; ***phone:*** +44 (0)114 283 1855; ***e-mail:*** smithac@parliament.uk.

SMITH, Chloe; Parliamentary Secretary, Cabinet Office, UK Government; ***education:*** BA, English Literature, Univ. of York ; ***party:*** Conservative Party; ***political career:*** MP for Norwich North, July 2009-; Economic Secretary, Oct. 2011-12; Parly. Sec., Cabinet Office, 2012-; ***professional career:*** Management Consultant, Deloitte; ***committees:*** Work and Pensions, 2009-10; Public Accounts, 2011-12; ***office address:*** House of Commons, London, SW1A 0AA, United Kingdom; ***phone:*** +44 (0)20 7219 3000.

SMITH, Christopher H.; American, Congressman, New Jersey Fourth District, US House of Representatives; ***party:*** Republican; ***political career:*** mem., US House of Representatives, 1980-; chair, several caucuses; author of several laws incl. The Trafficking Victims Protection act of 2000 and Stem Cell Therapeutic and Research Act of 2005; ***committees:*** Foreign Affairs, Co-Chmn.; ***office address:*** House of Representatives, 436 Cannon House Street, Washington, DC 20515-6501, USA; ***phone:*** +1 202 224 3121.

SMITH, H.E. Daniel B.; Ambassador, US Embassy in Greece; ***languages:*** German, Swedish, Turkish; ***education:*** BA, Univ. of Colorado; Ph.D, MA, Stanford Univ. USA; ***professional career:*** Amb. to Greece, 2010-; ***office address:*** Embassy of the United States of America, 91 Vassilissis Sophias Blvd, 10160, Athens, Greece; ***phone:*** +30 (0)10 721 2951; ***fax:*** +30 (0)10 645 6282; ***e-mail:*** AthensAmEmb@state.gov; ***URL:*** http://athens.usembassy.gov.

SMITH, Henry; MP for Crawley, UK Government; ***party:*** Conservative; ***political career:*** Councillor, West Sussex County Council, 1997-; Councillor, Crawley Borough Council, 2002-04; MP for Crawley, May 2010-; ***committees:*** European Scrutiny, 2010-; ***office address:*** House of Commons, London, SW1A 0AA, United Kingdom; ***phone:*** +44 (0)20 7219 3000; ***e-mail:*** henry.smith.mp@parliament.uk.

SMITH, James B.; Ambassador to Saudi Arabia, US Embassy; ***professional career:*** 28-year career, US Air Force, trained as fighter pilot, numerous operational assignments and combat missions, promoted to Brigadier General, 1998, retired 2002; exec., Ratheo Co.; Ambassador to the Kingdom of Saudi Arabia, 2009-; ***office address:*** Embassy of the US, Collector Road M, Riyadh Diplomatic Quarter or American Embassy, Unit 61307, Riyadh 11693, Saudi Arabia.

SMITH, Julian; MP for Skipton and Ripon, UK Government; ***party:*** Conservative; ***political career:*** MP for Skipton and Ripon, May 2010-; ***committees:*** Scottish Affairs Select Cttee., 2010-; ***office address:*** House of Commons, London, SW1A 0AA, United Kingdom; ***phone:*** +44 (0)20 7219 3000; ***e-mail:*** julian.smith.mp@parliament.uk.

SMITH, Lamar S.; American, Congressman, Texas 21st District, US House of Representatives; ***education:*** Methodist Univ. School of Law; ***party:*** Republican Party; ***political career:*** Bexar County commissioner; Texas State Rep.; mem., US House of Representatives, 1987-; ***committees:*** Judiciary Cttee.; Homeland Security; Science, Space and Technology, Chmn.; ***office address:*** US House of Representatives, 436 Cannon House Street, Washington, DC 20515-6501, USA; ***phone:*** +1 202 224 3121.

SMITH, Nick; Minister of Conservation and Housing, Government of New Zealand; ***born:*** 1964; ***party:*** National Party; ***political career:*** MP, 1990-; Minister of Environment, Minister of Accident Compensation Board, 2008-12, Minister of Local Government, 2011-12; Minister of Conservation, 2013-; Minister of Housing, 2013-; ***professional career:*** Engineer; ***office address:*** Department of Conservation, 84 Boulcott Street, Wellington, New Zealand; ***phone:*** +64 (0)4 917 7400 ; ***fax:*** +64 (0)4 917 7523; ***e-mail:*** library@mfe.govt.nz; ***URL:*** http://www.mfe.govt.nz.

SMITH, Nick; Member of Parliament, House of Commons; ***party:*** Labour; ***political career:*** MP, Blaenau Gwent, 2010-; ***committees:*** Public Accounts, 2010-; ***office address:*** House of Commons, London, SW1A 0AA, United Kingdom; ***phone:*** +44 (0)20 7219 7018; ***e-mail:*** nick.smith.mp@parliament.uk.

SMITH, Owen; Shadow Secretary of State for Wales, House of Commons; ***party:*** Labour; ***political career:*** MP for Pontypridd, May 2010-; Shadow Minister, Wales, Oct. 2010-11; Shadow Minister, Treasury, 2011-12; Shadow Secretary of State for Wales, Chair, National Policy Forum, 2012-; ***committees:*** Welsh Affairs Select Cttee., 2010-11; ***office address:*** Constituency Office, Morgan Street, Pontypridd, CF37 2DS, United Kingdom; ***phone:*** +44 (0)1443 401122; ***e-mail:*** owen.smith.mp@parliament.uk.

SMITH, Sir Robert, Bt; British, MP for Aberdeenshire West & Kincardine, House of Commons; ***born:*** 15 April 1958; ***parents:*** Sir William Gordon Smith (dec'd) and Lady Diana Smith; ***married:*** Fiona Anne Smith (née Cormack), 13 August 1993; ***children:*** Helen (F), Kirsty (F), Elizabeth (F); ***education:*** Merchant Taylors' School, Northwood; Univ. of Aberdeen; ***party:*** Liberal Democratic Party; ***political career:*** Contested Aberdeen North, 1987 (SDP/Alliance); elected to serve the Upper Donside ward of Aberdeen Council, 1995-97; Vice Convener, Grampian Joint Police Board, 1995-97; Scottish Education Spokesman, 1995-97; Lib. Dem. Spokesman for Scotland on Police & Prisons, 1997-2001; MP for AberdeenshireWest and Kincardine, 1997-; Spokesman on Transport and the Environment, 1997-99; Liberal Democrat Scottish Affairs Spokesman, 1999-2001; Scottish Whip, 1999-2001; Lib. Dem. Dep. Chief Whip, House Commons, 2001-06; Vice Chmn., All Party Group, UK Offshore Oil & Gas Industry; Whip, 2008-10; ***interests:*** farming and tourism as affected by the pound against the euro, high fuel prices and impact of foot and mouth disease, jobs dependent on the offshore oil and gas industry; ***memberships:*** twice served as mem. of Aberdeen Univ. Court; ***professional career:*** formerly Mgr. of the family estate, near Chapel of Garioch, Aberdeenshire; ***committees:*** Scottish Affairs Select Cttee., 1999-2001; Trade and Ind. Select Cttee., 2001-05; Procedures Cttee., 2001-10; Accommodation and Works, 2003-05; International Development, 2007-09; Energy and Climate Change, 2009-; ***recreations:*** hill walking, sailing; ***office address:*** Constituency Office, 6 Dee Street, Banchory, Kincardineshire, AB31 5ST, United Kingdom; ***phone:*** +44 (0)1330 820330; ***fax:*** +44 (0)1330 820338; ***e-mail:*** bobsmith@cix.co.uk.

SMITH, Stephen; Minister of Defence, Government of Australia; ***education:*** Univ. of Western Australia, BA, LL.B; London Univ., LL.M; ***political career:*** PPS to the Attorney General of Western Australia, 1983-87; Special Adviser to the Prime Minister; Sr., Adviser to the Dep., Prime Minister and Treasurer; State Sec., Western Australian Branch of the Australian Labor Party, 1987-90; Federal Mem. for Perth, 1993-; Shadow Minister for Trade, 1996-97, Resources and Energy, 1997-98, Communications, 1998-2001; Shadow Minister for Health, 2001-03; Shadow Minister for Immigration, 2003-07; Minister for Foreign Affairs, 2007-10; Minister of Defence, 2010-; ***professional career:*** Barrister and Solicitor; Lecturer and Tutor in Law; ***committees:*** Mem., Parly. Jt. Standing Cttee on Foreign Affairs, Defence, and Trade; Mem., Standing Cttee., on Banking, Finance and Public Admin. of the House of Representatives.; Mem., Standing Cttee. on Primary Industries, Resources and Rural and Regional Affairs; Chair, Jt. Parly. Cttee. on Corp. and Securities, 1994-96; ***office address:*** Department of Defence, Russell Offices, Canberra, ACT 2600, Australia; ***phone:*** +61 2 6265 9111; ***fax:*** +61 2 6273 4118; ***URL:*** http://www.dbcde gov.au.

SMITH OF BASILDON, Baroness Angela Evans; British, Member, House of Lords; ***born:*** 7 January 1959; ***education:*** Leicester Polytechnic, BA Hons., Public Admin.; ***party:*** Labour Party; ***political career:*** MP, Basildon, 1997-10; Parly. Under-Sec., Northern Ireland Office, 2005-06; Dept. for Communities and Local Government 2006-10; PPS to the Prime Minister, June 2007-10; Mem., House of Lords, 2010-; Opposition Spokesperson for Energy and Climate Change, 2010-; ***interests:*** crime and crime prevention, fire service and fire prevention, consumer protection, animal welfare, int. dev.; ***memberships:*** Mem. of Amnesty Int. and RSPCA, amongst others; ***committees:*** Mem., Standing Cttees. on Nat. Minimum Wage Bill, 1998, Wild Mammals Bill, 1998, Crime and Disorders Bill, 1998, Sexual Offenders Bill, 1999; Officer, All Party Parly. Groups on Animal Welfare, Charities and Voluntary Sector, Hospices, PPL Int. Dev. Cttee.; ***recreations:*** Coronation Street, reading, plays; ***office address:*** House of Lords, London, SW1A 0PW, United Kingdom; ***phone:*** +44 (0)20 7219 3000.

SMITH OF CLIFTON, Lord; British, Member of the House of Lords; ***born:*** 14 June 1937, London, UK; ***parents:*** Arthur James Smith and Vera Gladys Smith (née Cross); ***married:*** Julia Smith (née Bullock), 1979; Brenda Smith (née Eustace), 1960 (div'd. 1973); ***children:*** Adam (M), Gideon (M), Naomi (F); ***public role of spouse:*** Town Councillor; ***languages:*** French; ***education:*** London Sch. of Economics; ***party:*** Liberal Democrat; ***political career:*** Front bench spokesman on Northern Ireland, 1999-; Mem., House of Lords; ***interests:*** Northern Ireland, higher education, constitutional affairs, laboratory animals; ***memberships:*** Political Studies Assoc.; ***professional career:*** Univ. Teacher; Vice-Chllr., Univ. of Ulster, 1991-99; ***committees:*** British-Irish Interparly. Assembly; Chmn., Select Cttee. on Animals in Scientific Proceedures, 2001-2002; Democratic Audit Cttee.; ***honours and awards:*** Knighted, 1996; Peerage, 1997; Ac.SS, 2000; ***publications:*** Anti-Politics, 1972; The Politics of the Corporate Economy, 1979; The Fixers, 1996; ***clubs:*** Reform Club; ***recreations:*** water-colour painting, writing; ***office address:*** House of Lords, London, SW1A 0PW, United Kingdom; ***phone:*** +44 (0)20 7219 3000; ***fax:*** +44 (0)20 7219 5979; ***e-mail:*** smitht@parliament.uk.

SNOWDON, Hon. Warren; Minister for Defence Science and Personnel, Australian Government; ***political career:*** Member for Northern Territory; Minister of Defence Science and Personnel, 2007-09; Minister for Indigenous, Rural and Regional Health, and Regional Services Delivery, 2009-10; Minister for Defence Personnel, Material and Science, 2010; Minister for Indigenous Health, Rural and Regional Health and Local Government, 2010-11; Minister for Defence Science and Personnel, Minister for Veterans' Affairs, Minister for Indigenous Health, Minister assisting the PM on the Centenary of ANZAC, 2011-; ***office address:*** Department of Defence, Russell Offices, Canberra, ACT 2600, Australia; ***phone:*** +61 2 6265 9111; ***URL:*** http://www.defence.gov.au.

SNYDER, Rick; Governor, State of Michigan; ***education:*** Univ. of Michigan, Bachelor's degree, 1977, MBA, 1979, JD, 1982; ***political career:*** Governor, State of Michigan, 2010-; ***professional career:*** Coopers & Lybrand; various positions, Gateway Computers, incl. Pres., CEO, -1997; founder, Healthcare Media Inc.; Chair, Michigan economic Development Corp., 1999; ***office address:*** Office of the Governor, PO Box 30013, Lansing, Michigan 48909, USA; ***phone:*** +1 517 373 3400; ***URL:*** http://www.michigan.gov/snyder/.

SOAMES, Hon. (Arthur) Nicholas (Winston); British, Member of Parliament for Mid Sussex, House of Commons; ***born:*** 12 February 1948; ***education:*** Eton Coll.; ***party:*** Conservative Party; ***political career:*** Personal Asst. to Sir James Goldsmith, 1974-76; Personal Asst. to US Senator, 1976-78; MP, Crawley, 1983-97; PPS to Minister of State for Employment and Chmn. of Conservative Party, 1984-86; PPS to Sec. of State for Environment, 1987; Parly. Sec., Min. of Agriculture, Fisheries and Food, 1992-94; Minister of State for the Armed Forces, 1994-97; MP, Mid Sussex, 1997-; ***committees:*** Sec., Conservative Foreign Affairs Cttee., 1986-87; Public Administration, 1999; Joint Committee on Consolidation of Bills Etc, 2001-10; Standards and Privileges, 2006-10; ***honours and awards:*** Equerry to HRH Prince of Wales, KG, 1970-72; ***office address:*** House of Commons, London, SW1A 0AA, United Kingdom; ***phone:*** +44 (0)20 7219 3000; ***e-mail:*** hcinfo@parliament.uk.

SOBKÓW, Witold; Ambassador to the UK, Embassy of Poland; ***born:*** 17 February 1961; ***married:*** (divorced); ***children:*** Alexander (M), Hanna Sinéad (F); ***education:*** Warsaw Univ., Dept. of English Language and Literature, MA, 1979-1984, Dept. of Italian Language and Literature, MA; Islamic Studies, London Univ., 1999; ***professional career:*** Lecturer, Warsaw Univ., Neophilological Dept., 1984-1991; Dep. Head of the European Dept. and Advisor to the Minister, Ministry of Foreign Affairs, 1991-93; Minister Plenipotentiary and Deputy Head of Mission, Embassy of the Rep. of Poland, London, 1993-2000; Deputy Head, West European Dept., 2000-2001; Dir. for Non-European Countries and the UN System, July 2001-Oct. 2001; Sr. Advisor to the Minister on European Affairs, Oct. 2001-Sept. 2002; Consultant, board of Polish Diplomatic Digest, Oct. 2001-Sept. 2002; mem., Monitoring Cttee., gov. project of Poland's promotion abroad, Oct. 2001-Sept. 2002; Ambassador to Ireland, Sept. 2002-06; Ambassador to London, 2012-; ***office address:*** Embassy of Poland, 47 Portland Place, London, W1B 1JH, United Kingdom; ***phone:*** +44 0870 774 2700; ***fax:*** +44 (0)20 7323 4018; ***URL:*** http://london.polemb.net/.

SOEVNDAL, Villy; Minister of Foreign Affairs, Government of Denmark; ***born:*** 4 April 1952, Linde, Denmark; ***education:*** Kolding Teacher Training Coll., Denmark; ***party:*** The Socialist People's Party; ***political career:*** Minister for Foreign Affairs, 2011-; ***office address:*** Ministry of Foreign Affairs, Asiatisk Plads 2, 1448 Copenhagen K, Denmark; ***phone:*** +45 3392 0000; ***fax:*** +45 3254 0533; ***e-mail:*** um@um.dk; ***URL:*** http://www.um.dk.

SOLHJELL, Bård Vegar; Minister of the Environment, Government of Norway; ***born:*** 1971; ***education:*** Univ. of Oslo; Univ. of Bergen; ***party:*** Socialist Left Party, currently vice-chairman; ***political career:*** Party Sec., Socialist Left Party, 2001-05State Sec. at the Prime Minister's Office, 2005-07; Minister of Education, 2007-09; MP, 2009-12; Minister of the Environment, 2012-; ***office address:*** Ministry of Environment & International Development, Myntgaten 2, PB 8013 Dep, 0030 Oslo, Norway; ***phone:*** +47 22 24 57 01; ***fax:*** +47 22 24 60 34; ***e-mail:*** miljovernministeren@md.dep.no; ***URL:*** http://www.odin.dep.no/md.

SOLOMON SCHOFIELD, Vaughn; Lieutentant Governor, Government of Saskatchewan; ***born:*** October 1943; ***languages:*** Spanish; ***education:*** Univ. of Saskatchewan; ***political career:*** Lieutenant Governor of Saskatchewan, March 2012-; ***professional career:*** Businesswoman; Pres. and CEO, Western Group of Companies; ***office address:*** Government House, 4607 Dewdney Avenue, Regina SK S3P 3V7, Canada; ***phone:*** +1 306 787 4070.

SOLOMONT, Alan D.; Ambassador, US Embassy in Spain; ***education:*** Tufts Univ., Political Science and Town Planning; Univ. of Massachusetts in Lowell, Nursing; ***political career:*** Pres., Nat. Finance Cmn., Democrat Party, 1997-98; Campaign aide to Barack Obama; ***memberships:*** Mem., Corp. for Nat. and Community Service, 2000-, Pres., 2009-; ***professional career:*** Pres., Solomont Bailis Ventures; Co-Founder, HouseWorks; Fndr. and Dir.Gen., Angel Healthcare Investors; Visiting Lecturer, Tufts. Univ.; Ambassador to Spain, 2010-; ***office address:*** US Embassy, Serrano 75, 28006 Madrid, Spain; ***phone:*** +34 91 587 2200; ***fax:*** +34 91 587 2303; ***URL:*** http://www.embusa.es.

SOMMARUGA, Simonetta; Federal Councillor, Government of Switzerland; ***born:*** 1960; ***education:*** Lucerne Academy of Music; Fribourg Academy of Music; ***political career:*** Local Cllr., Koniz, 1997-2005; National Council of Switzerland, 1999; elected to Council of States, Bern, 2003-10; Federal Councillor, 2010; ***professional career:*** Mgr.,

Swiss Consumer Protection Foundation, 1993-99, Pres., 2000-10; ***office address:*** Federal Department of Justice, Bundeshaus West, 3003 Berne, Switzerland; ***phone:*** +41 (0)31 322 2111; ***URL:*** http://www.ejpd.admin.ch/.

SONG, Judge Sang-Hyun; Korea, President, International Criminal Court; ***born:*** 21 December 1941; ***languages:*** English, Korean, German, French; ***education:*** Seoul National University Law School, LLB, 1963; Cornell University Law School, JSD, 1970, maritime law of the sea; Legal qualification: Qualified to practice law in Korea; ***interests:*** Criminal Law; Dispute settlement; Economic law; Jurisdiction; Law of the Sea; ***memberships:*** Korean Bar Association, 1964 -; President, Korean International Trade Law Association, 1991-94; President, Korean Intellectual Property Research Society, 1986-96; President, Korean Law Professors Association, 1999-2005; ***professional career:*** *academic career:* Seoul National University, Professor of Law and Dean of Law School, 1972-; Harvard Law School, Visiting Professor, 1991, 1995, 1999, and 2003; New York University Law School, Member of Global Law Faculty, 1994-99; University of Melbourne, Faculty of Law, Professorial Fellow with title of Professor, 2002-; *professional career:* Practising attorney, 1970-72; *governmental career:* Advisor to the Supreme Court of Korea, 1979-2003; Advisor to the Minister of Justice, 1981-2003; Member, The Prime Minister's Committe on Clean Government, 1989-93; Member, The Prime Minister's Commission on Youth Protection, 2001-05; Presidential Commission for Judicial Reform, 2005-06; *diplomatic career:* Vice President, UNICEF/Korea, 1999-; *judicial career:* Judge, ICC, President; Conciliator, Seoul Central District Court, 1994-2000; Arbitrator for the Korean Commercial Arbitration Board, 1982-; Member, Arbitration Consultative Commission, WIPO, 1994-; Military Judge, 1964-67; ***publications:*** Books: Korean Law on Civil Procedure and Evidence, 1976, revised, 2004; Korean Law in the Global Economy, 1996; Korean Maritime Law, 1993, revised, 2004; Articles: Seoul National University Law Journal; Korean Bar Association Journal; UCLA Pacific Basin Law Journal; Pacific Rim Law and Policy Journal; Kobe Law Journal; ***office address:*** International Criminal Court, Maanweg 174, 2516 AB, The Hague, The Netherlands; ***phone:*** +31 (0)70 515 8208; ***fax:*** +31 (0)70 515 8789; ***e-mail:*** koreansong@hotmail.com.

SORIA, José Manuel; Minister of Industry, Energy & Tourism, Government of Spain; ***born:*** 1958; ***education:*** Economics & Business Studies; ***political career:*** MP, Las Palmas, 10th legislature; Pres., Partido Popular, Canary Islands, 1999-; PP parly. group, Canary Islands, 2003; mem., Regional parly., 2003-; Vice-Pres. & Treasury Minister, Canary Islands gov., 2007-2010; Pres., Cabildo de Gran Canaria, 2003-07; Mayor of Las Palmas de Gran Canaria, 1995-2003; Minister of Industry, Energy & Tourism, 2012-; ***office address:*** Ministry of Industry, Energy and Tourism, Po de la Castellana 160, 28071 Madrid, Spain; ***URL:*** http://www.minetur.gob.es/.

SORO, Guillaume Kigbafori; Vice President, Government of Côte d'Ivoire; ***party:*** New Forces; ***political career:*** former student leader; involved in 2002 rebellion; served under reconciliation government of Charles Konan Banny; Prime Minister, 2007-12; Vice President, 2012-; ***office address:*** Office of the Vice President, 01 BP 1354, Abidjan 01, Côte d'Ivoire; ***phone:*** +225 2031 4000; ***fax:*** +225 2031 4540; ***URL:*** http://www.cotedivoirepr.ci.

SOTOMAYOR, Sonia; Associate Justice, US Supreme Court; ***born:*** 25 June 1954, Bronx, New York; ***education:*** Princeton Univ., B.A. summa cum laude, 1976; Yale Law School, J.D., 1979, editor of the Yale Law Journal; ***professional career:*** Assist. Dist. Attorney, New York County, 1979-84; Associate then partner, Pavia & Harcourt, New York City, 1984-92; Judge, U.S. District Court, Southern District of New York, 1992-98; Judge, US Court of Appeals, Second Circuit, 1998-2009; Associate Justice, Supreme Court, 2009- ; ***office address:*** Supreme Court Building, One First Street, NE, Washington, DC 20543, USA; ***phone:*** +1 202 479 3211; ***fax:*** +1 202 479 2971; ***URL:*** http://www.supremecourtus.gov/.

SOUBRY, Anna; MP for Broxtowe, UK Government; ***party:*** Conservative; ***political career:*** MP for Broxtowe, May 2010-; PPS to Minister of State for Health, 2010-12; Parly. Under-Sec. of State, Dept. of Health, 2012-; ***committees:*** Justice Select Cttee., 2010; ***office address:*** House of Commons, London, SW1A 0AA, United Kingdom; ***phone:*** +44 (0)20 7219 3000; ***e-mail:*** anna.soubry.mp@parliament.uk.

SOULSBY, Sir Peter; MP for Leicester South, House of Commons; ***party:*** Labour Party; ***political career:*** Leader, Leicester City Council; MP for Leicester South, 2005-; Shadow Minister, Environment, Food and Rural Affairs, Oct. 2010; ***honours and awards:*** Kt. 1999; ***office address:*** House of Commons, London, SW1P 0AA, United Kingdom; ***phone:*** +44 (0)20 7219 3000.

SOULSBY OF SWAFFHAM PRIOR, Lord; Member, House of Lords; ***born:*** 23 June 1926; ***education:*** Queen Elizabeth Grammar School, Penrith, 1943; Univ., of Edinburgh, MRCVS, 1948; DVSM, 1949, Ph.D, 1952; Univ. of Cambridge, MA, 1954; C.Biol.F.I.Biol, 1998; ***political career:*** Mem., House of Lords; ***interests:*** parasitic diseases; immunology of parasitic infections; livestock dev. in the developing world; biotechnology; animal welfare; higher education; environmental issues; science and technology; biotechnology; ***memberships:*** Mem., Research Grant Boards: Nat. Institutes of Health, Washington DC, Tropical Medicine and Parasitology Study Section, 1968-72; Chmn., Study Grp. on Parasitic Diseases, Walter Reed Army Inst. of Research, Washington DC, 1973-77; Scientific Advisory Panel, Pan American Health Org. Zoonosis Centre, Buenos Aires, 1974-85; Chmn., Animal Research Grants Board, Agricultural & Food Research Cncl., 1985-88; Chmn., Veterinary Advisory Cttee., Horserace Betting Levy Board, 1985-97; ***professional career:*** University Lecturer, Univ. of Bristol, 1952-54, Univ. of Cambridge, 1954-64; Prof. of Parasitology, Univ. of Pennsylvania, Philadelphia and Chmn., graduate grp. in Parasitology, 1964-78, Chmn., Dept, of Pathobiology, 1965-78; Prof. of Animal Pathology, Univ. of Cambridge and Dean of Veterinary Medicine, 1978-93; Professorial Fellow, Wolfson Coll., Cambridge, 1978-93, Emeritus Fellow, 1993-, Hon. Fellow, 2004-; Advisory and Consultant to various national and international orgs. inc. WHO, FAO, PAHO, UNDP, NATO, ODA and Govs. of Sri Lanka, Malaysia, Iran, PR China, India and Univs. of Queensland, Pretoria, West Indies and St. George's Grenada; Leader of Overseas Science and Technology Expert Missions to Washington DC., 1993 and the PR of China, both with respect to biotechnology; ***committees:*** House of Lords Select Cttee. on Science and Technology; Vice Pres. All Party Grp. on Animal Welfare; Pres., Pet Advisory Cttee., Patron, Fund for the Replacement of Animals in Medical Experiments; Pres., Parliamentary and Scientific Cttee., 2004-08; ***honours and awards:*** Honorary Degrees: Univ. of Pennyslyvania, AM, 1972; DSc, 1985; Univ. of Edinburgh, DVMS, 1990; Univ. of Leon, Spain, DVM, 1993; Univ. of Peradeniya, Sri Lanka, DSc, 1994; Univ. of Glasgow, DVM&S, 2001; Univ. of Liverpool, DVSc, 2004; St. George's Univ., Grenada, D.Sc., 2006; Many other awards inc. Pres., Royal Soc. of Medicine, 1998-2002; Hon. Fellow, Inst. of Biology, 2003; Hon. Fellow, Royal College of Pathologists, 2005; Univ. Lincoln, D.Sc., 2007; Pres., Windward Islands Research & Education Foundation, 2008-; ***publications:*** Author and co-author of 14 books and some 200 articles in scientific journals.; ***office address:*** House of Lords, London, SW1A 0PQ, United Kingdom; ***phone:*** +44 (0)20 7219 8500; ***fax:*** +44 (0)20 7219 8602.

SOUVIRON CRESPO, Maria Beatriz; Ambassador, Bolivian Embassy; ***born:*** 1966, La Paz, Bolivia; ***professional career:*** Public sector and development projects 1993-2003; Fundraiser, 2003-06; Amb. to the UK, 2006-; ***office address:*** Bolivian Embassy, 106 Eaton Square, London, SW1W 9AD, United Kingdom; ***phone:*** +44 (0)20 7235 4248.

SPARKES, H. E. Andrew; Ambassador, British Embassy, Kathmandu; ***education:*** Cambridge Univ.; ***professional career:*** joined Foreign Office, 1983, various roles incl. postings in Malaysia, Israel, Lebanon, Mozambique, Bangkok; Dep. Head of Mission & Consul Gen., Jakarta, 1999-2001; Dep.High Commissioner & Consul General, Johannesburg/Pretoria, 2001-04; Amb., UK Embassy in D.R. of Congo, 2004-07; Amb., Rep. of Kosovo, 2008-10; Secondment to the EU, Dep. Head, EULEX Rule of Law Mission in Kosovo, 2010-13; Amb., Nepal, 2013-; ***office address:*** Embassy of the United Kingdom, PO Box 106, Lainchaur, PO Box 106, Kathmandu, Nepal; ***phone:*** +977 1 410583; ***fax:*** +977 1 411789; ***URL:*** http://ukinnepal.fco.gov.uk/en/.

SPEIER, Jackie; Congresswoman, Calif. 12th Dist. , US House of Representatives; ***education:*** Univ. of Calif., Davis, BA, Political Science; Univ. Calif., Hastings College of the Law, J.D.; ***political career:*** Mem., Calif. State Legislator, 18 years; US Congresswoman, 2008-; ***professional career:*** San Mateo Count Bd. of Supervisors for six years; ***committees:*** Financial Services; Oversight and Government Reform; Select Cttee. on Energy Independence and Global Warming; ***office address:*** House of Representatives, 211 Cannon HOB, Washington, DC. 20515, USA; ***phone:*** +1 202 225 3531; ***URL:*** http://speier.house.gov/.

SPELLAR, John; British, MP for Warley, British Government; ***born:*** 5 August 1947; ***education:*** St. Edmund Hall., Oxford Univ., BA, Philosophy, Politics, Econs.; ***party:*** Labour Party, 1966-; ***political career:*** MP, Birmingham Northfield, 1982-83, Warley, 1992- ; Opp. Whip, 1992-94; Opp. Spokesman on Northern Ireland, 1994-95; Parly. Under-Sec. of State, Ministry of Defence, 1997-99; Minister of State, MoD, 1999-2001; Minister for Transport, 2001-2003; Minister of State, Northern Ireland Office, 2003-05; Opposition Spokesman on Defence, 1995-97; Shadow Minister, Foreign and Commonwealth Affairs, Oct. 2010-; ***interests:*** industry, construction, defence; ***professional career:*** Nat. Office, EETPU; ***office address:*** House of Commons, London, SW1A 0AA, United Kingdom; ***phone:*** +44 (0)20 7219 3000; ***e-mail:*** hcinfo@parliament.uk.

SPELMAN, Rt. Hon. Caroline; British, Member of Parliament, House of Commons; ***born:*** 1958, Bishops Stortford, UK; ***parents:*** Marshall Cormack and Helen Cormack (née Greenfield); ***married:*** Mark Gerald Spelman, 27 April 1987; ***public role of spouse:*** Management Consultant; ***languages:*** French, German; ***education:*** London Univ.; ***party:*** Conservative Party; ***political career:*** Parly. Candidate for Bassetlaw; Frontbench Spokesman for Health & Women's Issues; MP, Meriden, 1997-; Shadow Sec. of State for International Development, 2001-03; Shadow Sec. of State for the Env., 2003; Shadow Sec. of State for Local Government and Communities, 2003-07; Chairman of the Conservative Party, 2007-09; Shadow Sec. of State for Communities and Local Government, Jan. 2009-May 2010; Secretary of State for Environment, Food and Rural Affairs, 2010-12; ***interests:*** agriculture, environment, international development; ***trusteeships:*** Oxford-Kilburn Club; Snowdon Trustee; ***publications:*** Author of several publications; A Green and Pleasant Land, Bow Grp. Paper (1991); The non-food user of Agricultural raw materials (1994); ***recreations:*** cooking, gardening, tennis; ***office address:*** House of Commons, London, SW1A 0AA, United Kingdom; ***phone:*** +44 (0)20 7219 3000; ***e-mail:*** spelmanc@parliament.uk; ***URL:*** http://www.carolinespelman.com.

SPENCER, Hon. Baldwin; Prime Minister, Government of Antigua and Barbuda; ***born:*** Green Bay; ***political career:*** Prime Minister, Minister of Foreign Affairs, Minister of National Security, Minister of Barbuda Affairs, Minister of Information and Public Broadcasting, Minister of Ecclesiastical Affairs, March 2004-07; PM, Minister of Foreign Affairs and Foreign Trade, National Security, Barbuda Affairs, Ecclesiastical Affairs, Public Utilities and Energy, 2007-; ***office address:*** Office of the Prime Minister, Queen Elizabeth Highway, St John's, Antigua; ***phone:*** +1 268 462 4956; ***fax:*** +1 268 462 3225; ***e-mail:*** pmo@antiguagov.ag; ***URL:*** http://www.antiguagov.com/pm.htm.

SPENCER, Mark; MP for Sherwood, UK Government; ***party:*** Conservative; ***political career:*** Councillor, Gedling District Council 2003-; Councillor, Nottinghamshire County Council, 2005-; MP for Sherwood, 2010- ; ***committees:*** Environmental Audit, 2010-; ***office address:*** House of Commons, London, SW1A 0AA, United Kingdom; ***phone:*** +44 (0)20 7219 3000; ***e-mail:*** mark.spencer.mp@parliament.uk.

SPERLING, Gene B.; Director, National Economic Council; ***education:*** Univ. of Minnesota; Yale Law School; Wharton Business School; ***professional career:*** Senior Fellow for Economic Policy, Center for American Progress; Counselor, US Dept. of the Treasury; NEC Director and principal economic policy advisor, President Clinton, 1997-2001; Dir., National Economic Council and Assist. to the President for Economic Policy, to President Obama, 2011-; ***office address:*** National Economic Council (NEC), The White House, Washington, DC 20502, USA; ***URL:*** http://www.whitehouse.gov/administration/eop/nec/.

SPICER, Lord (William) Michael (Hardy), MA; British, Member, House of Lords; ***born:*** 1943; ***parents:*** Brigadier Leslie Hardy Spicer and Muriel Winefred Alice Spicer (née Carter); ***married:*** Ann (née Hunter), 1967; ***children:*** Edward Sinclair Hardy (M), Antonia Hardy (F), Annabel Jane Hardy (F); ***education:*** Sacre Coeur, Vienna; Gaunts House Preparatory Sch.; Wellington Coll.; Cambridge Univ., Economics, MA; ***party:*** Conservative Party; ***political career:*** Deputy Chairman, Conservative Party, 1983; Minister of Aviation,

1984-88; Minister Coal & Electricity, 1988-90; Minister of Housing, 1990; Chmn., 1922 Cttee., 2001-; MP South Worcestershire 1974-97, West Worcestershire, 1997-2010; Mem., House of Lords, 2010-; ***interests:*** defence, foreign affairs, economics; ***professional career:*** Asst. to Editor of The Statist, 1964-66; Conservative Research Dept. (organising Party's contacts with academics and business consultancies), 1966-68; Dir., Conservative Systems Research Centre, 1968-70; Man. Dir., Economic Models Ltd. & Pres., Economic Models Corp. (Delaware), 1970; Governor, Wellington Coll.; Pres., Assoc. of Electricity Producers, 1998-; ***committees:*** Chmn., Assn. of Independent Electricity Producers, 1991-98; Chmn., Parly. Office of Science and Technology, 1991-92; Chmn., Parly. and Scientific Cttee., 1996-99; mem., Treasury Select Cttee.; Chmn Treasury Sub Cttee., 1997-2001; Chmn. 1922 Cttee., 2001-; ***honours and awards:*** Knight Bachelor; ***publications:*** 6 novels and A Treaty Too Far and Challenge Of The East; ***recreations:*** painting, writing, tennis (Chmn./captain, Lords & Commons Tennis Club, 1997-2007), bridge; ***office address:*** House of Lords, London, SW1A 0AA, United Kingdom; ***phone:*** +44 (0)20 7219 3000; ***URL:*** http://www.sirmichaelspicer.net.

SPIELMANN, Judge Dean, LLM; Luxembourgish, President, European Court of Human Rights; ***born:*** 26 October 1962; ***languages:*** Luxembourgeois, French, German, English; ***education:*** Université Catholique de Louvain, Licence en droit, 1988; University of Cambridge, Master of Laws (International Law), 1990, Foreign and Commonwealth Scholar; Legal qualification: Judge; Barrister, Luxembourg Bar, Avocat, 1989-92, Avocat à la Cour, 1992-2004; ***interests:*** Criminal Law; Jurisdiction; Human rights; Litigation; ***memberships:*** Institut Grand-Ducal, Membre agrégé, 2002-05, Membre effectif, 2005-; National Committee of the Association Henri Capitant des Amis de la Culture juridique francaise; Founding member and former member of the Advisory committee of the European Criminal Bar Association; Former member of the Common Core of European Private Law (Trento Group); Société française pour le droit international; International Association of Criminal Law; Committee member of the Union belgo-luxembourgeoise de droit pénal; ASIL; Foundation Internationale Pénale Pénitentiaire; ***professional career:*** *academic career:* Université Catholique de Louvain, Assistant Lecturer and Research Assistant, 1991-97, Criminal Law and Seminar in Criminal Law and Human Rights; Université du Luxembourg, Lecturer in Criminal Law, Criminal Procedure and Business Criminal Law, 1996-2004; University of Nancy 2, Lecturer, 1997-; Institut Universitaire International, Luxembourg, Lecturer, 1999-; Ministry of Justice, Luxembourg, Instructor in Private International Law, 1994-2001; University of Padua, Venice, Guest Lecturer, 1998; Numerous lectures and conferences on human rights at various universities and under a project of the Law Society of England and Wales; *professional career:* As counsel, represented applicants inter alia before the Council of Europe human rights protection organs (European Commission and Court of Human Rights) and also the European Court of Justice; Member of the European Union Network of Independent Experts in Fundamental Rights, 2002-04; Former Member of the Human Rights Committee of the CCBE; Member of the Criminal Law Committee of the CCBE, 2003-04; Member of the Advisory Commission of Human Rights, Luxembourg. 2000-04; *judicial career:* Judge, ECHR, 2004-, Vice-Pres., 2012, Pres., 2012-; ***publications:*** Books: Monographs concerning the European Convention of Human Rights: La Convention européenne des droits de l'homme et le droit luxembourgeois, co-author, 1991; L'effet potential de la Convention européenne des droits de l'homme entre personnes privées, 1995; Le Luxembourg devant la Cour européenne des droits de l'homme (Recueil de jurisprudence 1995-2003), 2003; Monographs concerning Luxembourgish law: Bibliographie juridique luxembourgeoise, co-author, 1989; Recueil de la jurisprudence administrative du Conseil d'Etat luxembourgeois, co-author, 1996; Bibliographie juridique luxembourgeoise (1989-1996), co-author, 2nd ed, 1997; Le secret bancaire et l'entraide judicaire internationale pénale au Grand-Duché de Luxembourg, in "Les Dossiers du Journal des Tribunaux", 2nd ed, 1999; Droit pénal général luxembourgeois, co-author, 2002, 2nd ed, 2004; Monographs concerning Comparative and Foreign law: L'infraction inachevée en droit pénal comparé, co-author, 1997; Droit pénal général [belge], co-author, 3rd ed, 2003; Articles: Annales de droit de Louvain; Annales de droit luxembourgeois; Annuaire international des droits de l'homme; Bulletin du Centre de Documentation communale; Bulletin du Cercle François Laurent; Bulletin Droit et Banque; Bulletin des droits de l'homme; Documentaçao de Direito Comparado; Droit bancaire et financier; Feuille de liaison de la conferencé Saint-Yves; Journal des Tribunaux; Pasicrisie luxembourgeoise; Public Procurement Law Review; Revue de droit pénal et de criminologie; Revue internationale de droit pénal; Revue trimestrielle des droits de l'Homme; Travaux de l'Association Henri Capitant; ***office address:*** European Court of Human Rights, F-67075 Strasbourg, France; ***phone:*** +33 (0)3 9021 5079; ***fax:*** +33 (0)3 8841 2730; ***e-mail:*** dean.spielmann@echr.coe.int; ***URL:*** http://www.echr.coe.int/.

SPINDELEGGER, Dr. Michael; Federal Minister of Foreign Affairs, Government of Austria; ***born:*** December 21 1959 ; ***education:*** Doctor of Law, Univ. of Vienna, 1983; ***political career:*** MP, Federal Chamber, 1992-93; MP, Nat. Assembly, 1993-95; MEP, 1995-96; MP, Nat. Assembly, 1996-; Federal Minister of Foreign Affairs, Dec. 2008-; ***office address:*** Ministry of Foreign Affairs, Minoritenplatz 8, 1014 Vienna, Austria; ***phone:*** +43 (0)1 501150; ***URL:*** http://www.bmaa.gv.at.

SPIRIC, Dr. Nikola; Minister of the Treasury and Finance, Council of Ministers, Bosnia and Herzegovina; ***born:*** 4 September 1956, Drvar, Bosnia and Herzegovina; ***married:*** Nada Jovana; ***children:*** Aleksandar (M); ***education:*** Univ. of Sarajevo, M.Sc. and Ph.D., monetary and public finance; ***party:*** Alliance of Independent Social Democrats; ***political career:*** Rep., Parly. Assembly, B&H. 1999-2000; Dep. Minister of Human Rights and Refugees in Cncl. of Ministers B&H, 2000; Chmn., House of Peoples of Parly. Assembly of B&H, 2001-02; Chmn., Dep. Chmn., House of Representatives, Parly. Assembly of B&H, 2002-06; Chmn., Council of Ministers of B&H, 2006-; Speaker, Parly. Assembly, Prime Minister, 2007-11; Minister of the Treasury and Finance, 2011-; ***professional career:*** Researcher at the Economic Inst., Sarajevo, 1980-92; Prof. of monetary and public finance at the Faculty of Economy, Banja Luka Univ., 1992-; ***honours and awards:*** Decoration o St. Sava, I order; Decoration of Flag of Republika Srpska with golden wreath; Golden medal from the Parliament of Greece; ***office address:*** Office of the Chairman, Council of Ministers, Trg Bosne i Hercegovine 1, , 71000 Sarajevo, Bosnia and Herzegovina; ***phone:*** +387 (0)3320 5345; ***URL:*** http://www.vijeceministara.gov.ba.

SSEKANDI, Edward; Vice President, Government of Uganda; ***education:*** LLB, Univ. of East Africa; Diploma in legal practice, Law Development Centre, Kampala; ***political career:*** Speaker; 2000-10; Vice President, 2011-; ***professional career:*** Law Lecturer, Law Development Centre, Kampala, and Makerere Univ.; ***office address:*** Office of the Vice President, PO Box 7359, Kampala, Uganda; ***phone:*** +256 41 345915; ***fax:*** +256 41 346102; ***e-mail:*** vp@statehouse.go.ug; ***URL:*** http://www.statehouse.go.ug.

ST. EDMUNDSBURY AND IPSWICH, Rt Rev the Lord Bishop of; Member, House of Lords; ***born:*** 1950; ***political career:*** Mem., House of Lords; ***professional career:*** Bishop of Stockport, 2000-07; Bishop of St Edmundsbury and Ipswich, 2007-; ***office address:*** House of Lords, London, SW1A 0PW, United Kingdom.

STABENOW, Debbie; American, Senator for Michigan, US Senate; ***born:*** 29 April 1950; ***children:*** Todd (M), Michelle (F); ***education:*** Michigan State Univ., BA, 1972, MA, 1975; ***political career:*** elected to Ingham County Bd. of Commission, 1974, Chwn. of the Bd., 1977-78; Michigan House of Representatives, 1979-90; served in the State Senate, 1991-94; Mem., US House of Representatives, 1996-2000; Senator, US Senate, 2000-; Democratic Conference Secretary, 2004-06; ***interests:*** education in public schools, fiscal responsibility in govt., tax relief for middle class families, preservation of natural resources, reducing the cost of prescription drugs, protecting the future of Social Security and Medicare; ***memberships:*** Mem., Bipartisan Centrist Coalition; Mem., Grace United Methodist Church; ***professional career:*** worked with youth in the public schs.; ***committees:*** Chair, Agriculture, Nutrition and Forestry; Budget; Energy and Natural Resources; Finance; ***honours and awards:*** named one of the "10 Powerhouses" in Washington by George magazine; recipient of over 60 awards for her leadership on behalf of families and small businesses inc. United States Jaycees Outstanding Young American Award; National Cttee. to Preserve Social Security and Medicare recognised her with its top award; Nat. Assoc. for Home Care named her a Home Health Hero; ***office address:*** United States Senate, 702 Hart Senate Office Building, Washington, DC 20510, USA; ***phone:*** +1 202 224 4822; ***URL:*** http://www.stabenow.senate.gov.

STAGG, Richard; Ambassador, British Embassy in Afghanistan; ***professional career:*** British Amb. to Bulgaria, 1998-2001; High Commissioner to India, 2007-11; Amb. to Afghanistan, 2012-; ***office address:*** British Embassy, 15th Street, Roundabout Wazir Akbar Khan, PO Box 334, Kabul, Afghanistan; ***phone:*** +93 70 102000; ***fax:*** +93 70 102250; ***e-mail:*** britishembassy.kabul@fco.gov.uk; ***URL:*** http://ukinafghanistan.fco.gov.uk/en.

STANLEY, Rt. Hon. Sir John Paul, PC; British, Member of Parliament for Tonbridge and Malling, House of Commons; ***born:*** 1942; ***married:*** Susan Elizabeth Giles, 1968; ***s:*** 2; ***d:*** 1; ***education:*** Lincoln Coll.; Oxford Univ., MA; ***party:*** Conservative Party; ***political career:*** PPS to Rt. Hon. Mrs. Margaret Thatcher, 1976-79; Minister for Housing and Construction, 1979-83; Minister of State for the Armed Forces, 1983-87; Minister of State, Northern Ireland Office, 1987-88; MP, Tonbridge and Malling, 1974-; ***professional career:*** Research Assoc. of the Int. Inst. for Strategic Studies, 1968-69; Rio Tinto-Zinc Corp. Ltd., 1969-79; ***committees:*** Mem., House of Commons Select Cttee. for Foreign Affairs, 1992-; Arms Export Controls, 2011-; ***publications:*** The Int. Trade in Arms (1972); ***office address:*** House of Commons, London, SW1A 0AA, United Kingdom; ***phone:*** +44 (0)20 7219 3000; ***e-mail:*** hcinfo@parliament.uk.

STAVRESKI, Zoran; Deputy Prime Minister in charge of Economic Affairs, Government of Macedonia; ***born:*** 29 October 1964; ***languages:*** English; ***education:*** Ss. Cyril and Methodius Univ., Fac. of Economics, Skopje, BA Econ., 1987, MA, 1997; ***political career:*** Undersec., Ministry of Finance, 2000-01; Dep. PM. in charge of Economic Affairs, 2006-; ***professional career:*** Researcher, then Dir., Research Directorate, Central Bank of Macedonia, 1993-2000; Senior Consultant to the World Bank, 2001-06; ***office address:*** Government of Macedonia, Blvd. Ilinden bb, 1000 Skopje, Macedonia; ***phone:*** +389 2 3118 022/ 3115 455; ***fax:*** +389 2 3112 561 / 3115 285; ***URL:*** http://www.gov.mk/.

STEDMAN-SCOTT, Baroness Deborah; Member, House of Lords; ***political career:*** Mem. House of Lords, 2010-; ***professional career:*** Chief Exec., Tomorrow's People; ***office address:*** House of Lords, London, SW1A 0PW, United Kingdom; ***phone:*** +44(0)20 7219 3000; ***fax:*** +44 (0)20 7219 5979; ***URL:*** http://www.parliament.uk.

STEEL OF AIKWOOD, Rt. Hon. Sir David Martin Scott, KT, KBE, PC, DL; British, Member, House of Lords; ***born:*** 31 March 1938, Kirkcaldy, Fife, Scotland; ***parents:*** The Very Rev. Dr. David Steel and Sheila Steel (née Martin); ***married:*** Judith Mary Steel (née MacGregor), 1962; ***s:*** 2; ***d:*** 1; ***languages:*** French, Swahili; ***education:*** George Watson's Coll. and Edinburgh Univ., MA, 1960, LL.B, 1962; ***party:*** Liberal Democratic Party; ***political career:*** Pres., Edinburgh Univ. Liberals, 1959; Students Rep. Cncl., 1960; Asst. Sec., Scottish Liberal Party, 1962-64; MP (Lib.) for Roxburgh, Selkirk & Peebles since 1965, Tweeddale, Ettrick and Lauderdale since 1983; Liberal Chief Whip, 1970-75; Leader of the Liberal Party, 1976-88; Mem., Parly. Deleg. to UN General Assembly, 1967, Sponsor, Private Mem's Bill to reform Law on Abortion, 1966-67; Mem. Privy Cncl., 1977; Pres., Liberal Int., 1994-96; Dep. Leader, Liberal Democrat Party, House of Lords, 1997-99; Presiding Officer of the Scottish Parliament; mem., Lothians, Scottish Parliament, 1999-2003, (retired); ***professional career:*** Rector, Univ. of Edinburgh, 1982-85; Visiting Fellow, Yale, 1987; Journalist and broadcaster, BBC Scotland; Chmn., the Countryside Movement, 1995-97; founder Bd. Mem. Int. Inst. for Democracy and Electoral Assistance, 1995- ; ***committees:*** Pres., Anti-Apartheid Movement of GB, 1966-69; Chmn., Shelter, Scotland, 1969-73; ***honours and awards:*** Hon. Dr., Univ. of Stirling 1991; Commander's Cross of the Order of Merit (Germany) 1992; Hon. D. Litt, of Buckingham 1994; Hon. Doctorate, Heriot-Watt Univ., 1996; raised to the peerage as Baron Steel of Aikwood, of Ettrick Forest in The Scottish Borders, 1997; Hon. LL.D, Univ. of Edinburgh, 1999; Hon. LL.D., Univ. of Strathclyde, 2000; Hon. D.Univ., The Open Univ., 2001; Hon. LL.D., Aberdeen Univ., 2001; Legion d'Honneur (France), 2003; Hon. LL.D., St. Andrews Univ., 2003, Glasgow Caledonian Univ., 2004; Knight of the Thistle, 2004; Hon. LL.D, Brunel Univ., 2010; ***publications:*** Contribution to various newspapers, Boost for the Borders, 1964; Out of Control, 1968; No Entry, 1969; Liberal Way Forward, 1975; A New Political Agenda, 1976; Militant for the Reasonable Man, 1977; A New Majority for a New Parliament, 1978; The High Ground of Politics, 1979; A House Divided, 1980; David Steel's Border Country, 1985; Partners in One Nation, 1985; Mary Stuart's Scotland, Judy Steel,

1987; The Time Has Come, David Owen, 1987; Against Goliath (Autobiography), 1989; *recreations:* classic cars, fishing, restoration of C16th Peel Tower; *office address:* House of Lords, London, SW1A 0PW, United Kingdom.

STEFANSSON, H.E. Gudmundur A.; Ambassador, Embassy of Iceland in Washington; *professional career:* Radio Producer; Editor; Police Officer; Amb. to Sweden, 2005-11; Amb. to the USA, 2011-; *office address:* Embassy of Iceland, 1156 15th St., NW, Suite 1200, Washington, DC 20005, USA; *phone:* +1 202 265 6653; *fax:* +1 202 265 6656; *e-mail:* icemb.wash@utn.stjr.is; *URL:* http://www.iceland.is/iceland-abroad/us.

STEINER, Achim; German, Executive Director, UN Environment Programme; *born:* 1961; *education:* BA, Oxford; MA, Univ. of London; German Development Institute; Harvard Business School; *professional career:* Director General, World Conservation Union, 2001-06; Exec. Dir., UNEP, 2006-; *office address:* UNEP, P.O. Box 30552, 00100 Nairobi, Kenya; *phone:* +254 (0)20 762 4001/2.

STEINMEIER, Dr Frank Walter; Head of the Parliamentary Group of the Social Democratic Party; *born:* 5 January 1956; *education:* Justus Liebig Univ., Law and Political Science, second state law examination, 1986; *party:* SPD; *political career:* Desk officer for media law and policy, State Chancellery of Lower Saxony, 1991; Head of Office, Minister Pres. of Lower Saxony, 1993-94; Head of Dept. for Guidelines on Policy, Departmental Co-ordination and Planning, 1994-96; State Sec., Fed. Chancellery and Cmnr. for the Federal Intelligence Services, 1998-99; Head of the Federal Chancellery, 1999-2005; Federal Minister of Foreign Affairs, 2005-07-, Vice Chancellor and Minister of Foreign Affairs, 2007-09; *professional career:* Military Service, 1974-76; Legal training, Frankfurt Main and Giessen, 1983-86; Academic Assist. to Chair of Public Law and Political Science, Dept. of Law Univ. of Giessen, 1986-91; *office address:* Parliamentary Group of the Social Democratic Party, Platz der Republik 1,, Berlin 11011, Germany.

STEPHEN, Lord Nicol, MSP; British, Member, House of Lords; *born:* 23 March 1960, Aberdeen; *parents:* R.A. Nicol Stephen and Sheila G. Stephen; *married:* Caris J. Doig; *children:* Mharni (F), Macleod (M), Mirrhyn (F), Drummond (M); *education:* Aberdeen Univ. LL.B; Edinburgh Univ., Dip L.P.; *party:* Leader, Scottish Liberal Democrats, 2005-08; *political career:* Councillor, Grampian Regional Council, 1982-91; MP for Kincardine & Deeside, 1991-92; mem., Aberdeen South, Scottish Parliament, 1999-2011; Dep. Minister of Enterprise and Lifelong Learning, 1999-2000; Deputy Minister for Education and Young People, 2000-03; Minister for Transport, 2003-05; Dep. First Minister and Minister for Enterprise and Lifelong Learning, 2005-07; Mem., House of Lords, 2011-; *interests:* education, health, economy; *memberships:* Law Society of Scotland; Aberdeen Chamber of Commerce; *professional career:* Solicitor; Senior Corporate Finance Manager; Project Manager; Company Director; *clubs:* Deeside Golf Club; *recreations:* golf; *office address:* House of Lords, London, SW1A 0PW, United Kingdom; *phone:* +44 (0)20 7219 3000.

STEPHENSON, Andrew; MP for Pendle, UK Government; *party:* Conservative; *political career:* Councillor, Macclesfield Borough Council 2003-07; MP for Pendle, May 2010-; *office address:* House of Commons, London, SW1A 0AA, United Kingdom; *phone:* +44 (0)20 7219 3000; *e-mail:* andrew.stephenson.mp@parliament.uk.

STEPISNIK, Stanko; Minster of Economic Development & Technology, Government of Slovenia; *education:* engineering; economics; *political career:* Dep., National Assembly, 2011; Minister of Economic Development and Technology, 2013-; *professional career:* EMO; ITC Celje; Dir., EMO-Orodjarna, d.o.o., 1984-2012; *office address:* Ministry of Economic Development, Kotnikova 5, 1000 Ljubljana, Slovenia; *URL:* http://www.vlada.si/.

STEVENS, Glenn; Governor, Reserve Bank of Australia; *education:* Univ. of Sydney, BEc. Hons; Univ. of Western Ontario, MA; *professional career:* Research Dept., Reserve Bank of Asutralia; Vising Scholar and various posits., Federal Reserve Bank of San Francisco; Head of Economic Analysis Dept., 1992-95; Head of International Dept., 1995-96; Assist. Gov., Reserve Bank of Australia, 1996-2001; Dep. Gov., 2001-06; Governor, 2006-; *office address:* Reserve Bank of Australia, 65 Martin Place, Sydney, NSW 2000, Australia; *URL:* http://www.rba.gov.au.

STEVENSON, John; Member of Parliament, House of Commons; *party:* Conservatives; *political career:* Councillor, Carlisle City Council 1999-2010; MP, Carlisle, 2010-; *office address:* House of Commons, London, SW1A 0AA, United Kingdom; *phone:* +44 (0)20 7219 3000; *e-mail:* john.stevenson.mp@parliament.uk.

STEWART, Bob; MP for Beckenham, UK Government; *party:* Conservative; *political career:* MP for Beckenham, May 2010-; *committees:* Defence Select Cttee., 2010-; Arms Export Controls, 2011-; *office address:* House of Commons, London, SW1A 0AA, United Kingdom; *phone:* +44 (0)20 7219 3000; *e-mail:* bob.stewart.mp@parliament.uk.

STEWART, Iain; MP for Milton Keynes South, UK Government; *party:* Conservative; *political career:* Councillor, Shenley Brook End and Tattenhoe Parish Council 2005-; MP for Milton Keynes South, May 2010-; *committees:* Transport Select Cttee., 2010-; *office address:* House of Commons, London, SW1A 0AA, United Kingdom; *phone:* +44 (0)20 7219 3000; *e-mail:* iain.stewart.mp@parliament.uk.

STEWART, H.E. Karen; Ambassador, US Embassy in Laos; *professional career:* Amb. to Belarus, Sept. 2006-10; Amb to Laos, 2010-; *office address:* US Embassy, Box 114, Rue Bartholonie, Vientiane, Laos PDR; *phone:* +856 21 212581; *URL:* http://laos.usembassy.gov.

STEWART, Rory; MP for Penrith and The Border, UK Government; *party:* Conservative; *political career:* MP for Penrith and The Border, May 2010-; *committees:* Foreign Affairs Select Cttee., 2010-; *office address:* House of Commons, London, SW1A 0AA, United Kingdom; *phone:* +44 (0)20 7219 3000; *e-mail:* rory.stewart.mp@parliament.uk.

STIJEPOVIC, Slavoljub; Minister of Education and Sport, Government of Montenegro; *born:* 2 May 1959, Titograd; *parents:* Vitomir Stijepovic and Zagorka Stijepovic; *married:* Ljiljana Stijepovic (née Milosavljevic), Jan 1986; *children:* Vladimir (M), Dragana (F); *education:* Graduated Lawyer, Law Faculty in Podgorica; *party:* Democratic Party of Socialists of Montenegro; *political career:* Dep. Minister of Labour and Social Welfare, 1991-96; Minister Without Portfolio, 1996-98; Minister of Sport, 1998-2001; Mem., Exec. Bd. and Mem., Municipality Bd. of Democratic Party of Socialists-Podgorica; Mem., Exec. Bd. and Mem., Supreme Bd. of Democratic Party of Socialist of Montenegro; Minister of Sports; Minister of Labour and Social Care; Minister of Education and Sport, 2010-; *memberships:* Mem., Exec. bd., Football Assoc. of Montenegro, to date; *professional career:* Independent Law Officer and Head of General Law and Self Managing Service, Construction Enterprise, Prvoborac Herceg Novi, 1984-91; former Pres., Assembly of Secretariat for Physical Culture of Municipality Titograd; former Gen. Sec. of Football Assoc. of Montenegro; former Dep. Pres., Football Assoc. of Montenegro; former Pres., Management Bd., Airline Company, Montenegro Airlines; former Pres., Management Bd., AD Zetatrans, Podgorica; former Pres., Assembly of AD Jugopetrol Kotor; Pres., Management Bd., Employment Agency of Montenegro, to date; *recreations:* sport; *office address:* Ministry of Education, Ul. Vuka Karadzica 3/IV, 81000 Podgorica, Montenegro.

STÖGER, Alois; Federal Minister of Health, Government of Austria; *born:* 3 September 1960, Linz, Austria; *political career:* Local Councillor, 1997-; Town Councillor, 2003-08; Federal Minister of Health, Dec. 2008-; *office address:* Ministry of Health, Radetzkystrasse 2, 1030 Vienna, Austria; *phone:* +43 (0)1 711000; *URL:* http://www.bmgf.gv.at.

STOLTENBERG, Jens; Norwegian, Prime Minister, Government of Norway; *born:* 16 March 1959, Oslo, Norway; *married:* Ingrid (née Schulerud); *children:* 2; *education:* Univ. of Oslo, Cand.oecon., 1987; *party:* Labour; *political career:* Info. Officer, Oslo Lab. Party, 1981; mem., AUF central board, 1979-89; mem., the party's central board, 1985-; Leader., Lab. League of Youth (AUF), 1985-89; Pres., Int. Union of Socialist Youth, (IUSY), 1985-89; Headed the Brundtland govts. cmn. on male roles, 1986; Leader, mem., Royal Cmn. on the Role of Men, 1986-88; Dep. mem., the Storting, 1989-93; mem., Defence Cmn., 1990-92; Leader, Oslo Labour Party, 1990-92; State Sec., Ministry of Environment, 1990-91; elected Dep. Chmn., Labour Party at its Nat. Congress, 1992; Dep. Leader, Labour Party, 1992-; mem., Storting, 1993-; Minister of Trade and Energy, 1993-96; Minister of Finance, 1996-97; MP, 1997-99; Prime Minister, 2000-01; Leader of the Labour Party 2002-; Prime Minister, Oct. 2005-; *professional career:* Journalist, Labour Party newspaper Arbeiderbladet, 1979-81; Exec. Officer, research dept., Central Bureau of Statistics, 1989-90; Lecturer, econ., Oslo Univ., 1989-90; *committees:* mem., Central Exec. Cttee. of the Labour Party, 1985-; Chmn., Energy and Environment Cttee., 1997-; leader, standing cttee., oil and energy affairs,1997-2000; mem., Sortings standing cttee., social affairs, 1991-93; *office address:* Office of the Prime Minister , Akersgaten 42, PB 8001 Dep, 0030 Oslo, Norway; *phone:* +47 2224 9090; *fax:* +47 2224 9500; *e-mail:* statsministeren@smk.dep.no; *URL:* http://www.odin.dep.no/smk.

STORELLA, Mark C.; US Ambassador, Embassy of the US, Lusaka; *professional career:* career member of the Senior Foreign Service. Most recently: Dep. PM. Rep. at the US Mission to the UN, Geneva; Senior Co-ordinator for Iraqi Refugees and Internally Displaced Persons, US Embassy, Baghdad; Amb. of Zambia, 2010-, also US Rep. , COMESA, 2010-; *office address:* Embassy of the US, Corner Independence and United Nations Avenues, Lusaka, Zambia; *phone:* +260 1 250955; *fax:* +260 1 252225; *URL:* http://www.zambia.usembassy.gov.

STOREY, Lord Mike, OBE, CBE; Member, House of Lords; *party:* Liberal Democratic Party; *political career:* Leader, Liverpool City Council, 1998-2005; Lord Mayor of Liverpool, 2009-2010; Mem., House of Lords, 2010-; *office address:* House of Lords, London, SW1A 0PW, United Kingdom; *phone:* +44 (0)20 7219 3000.

STOURNARAS, Yannis; Minister of Finance, Government of Greece; *education:* BSc., economics, Univ. of Athens, 1978, MPhil., DPhil., Oxford Univ. UK; *political career:* Minister of Finance, 2012-; *professional career:* Research fellow and lecturer at St Catherine's Coll. Oxford Univ., 1982-86; Special advisor, Ministry of Economy and Finance, 1986-89; Special advisor to the Bank of Greece, 1989-94; Professor of Economics, Univ. of Athens, 1989-; Man. Dir., Kappa Securities, 2005-08; *office address:* Ministry of Finance, Athens, Greece.

STOWELL OF BEESTON, Baroness Tina; Member, House of Lords; *party:* Conservative Party; *political career:* Mem., House of Lords, 2011-; *professional career:* Civil Servant, Ministry of Defence; British Embassy, Washington DC; Press Office at 10 Downing Street; Head of Communications, BBC Trust; Head of Corporate Affairs, BBC, 2008-10; *honours and awards:* MBE, 1996; *office address:* House of Lords, London, SW1A 0PW, United Kingdom; *phone:* +44 (0)20 7219 3000.

STRATHCLYDE, Rt. Hon. Lord Thomas Galloway Dunlop du Roy de Blicquy Galbraith; British, Member, House of Lords; *born:* 1960; *education:* Univ. of East Anglia, BA; Univ. d'Aix-en-Provence, France; *political career:* Govt. Whip, House of Lords, 1988-89; Spokesman on Trade and Industry, 1988-89; Parly. Under-Sec. of State, Dept. of Employment and Minister for Tourism, 1989-90; Parly. Under-Sec., Dept. of the Environment, 1990; Parly Under Sec, Scottish Office Minister for Agriculture and Fisheries, 1990-92; Under Sec. Dept of the Environment, 1992-93; Minister of State, Dept. of Trade and Industry, Minister for Consumer Affairs and Small Firms, 1993-94; Govt. Chief Whip in the House of Lords (Captain of the Gentlemen at Arms), 1994-97; Opp. Chief Whip, House of Lords, 1997; Shadow Leader of the House of Lords, 1999-May 2010; Leader of the House of Lords, Chancellor of the Duchy of Lancaster, May 2010-13; *professional career:* Bain Clarkson Ltd., 1982-88; *office address:* House of Lords, London, SW1A 0PQ, United Kingdom; *phone:* +44 (0)20 7219 3236; *fax:* +44 (0)20 7219 0304.

STRAW, Rt. Hon. Jack, MP; British, MP for Blackburn, House of Commons; *born:* 1946; *parents:* Walter Arthur Straw and Joan Ormston (née Gilbey); *married:* Alice Elizabeth Perkins (née Perkins), 1978; *children:* William (M), Charlotte (F); *education:* Brentwood Sch.; Univ. of Leeds, LL.B, 1967; Inns of Court Sch. of Law (Called to the Bar, Inner Temple,

1972); ***party:*** Labour Party; ***political career:*** Cllr. (Lab.), Islington, 1971-78; Deputy Leader, Inner London Education Authority, 1973-74; Special adviser to Sec. of State for Social Services, Rt. Hon. Barbara Castle, 1974-76; Special Adviser to Sec. of State for Environment, Rt. Hon. Peter Shore, 1976-77; MP (Lab.) for Blackburn, 1979-; Opp. Spokesman on the Treasury, 1980-83, and on Environment, 1983-87; Shadow Education Sec., 1987-92; Shadow Environment Sec., (Local Gov't and Housing), 1992-94; Shadow Home Sec., 1994-97; Sec. of State for the Home Dept., 1997-2001; Secretary of State for Foreign and Commonwealth Affairs, 2001-06; Leader of the House of Commons, 2006-07; Secretary of State for Justice and Lord Chancellor, June 2007-May 2010; Shadow Secretary of State for Justice and Shadow Lord Chancellor, May 2010-Sept. 2010; ***memberships:*** Inner Temple; GMWU; ***professional career:*** Pres., Nat. Union of Students, 1969-71; Barrister, 1972-74; Staff of World in Action, Granada TV, 1977-79; ***committees:*** Member, Council of the Institute for Fiscal Studies, 1983; ***honours and awards:*** Visiting Fellow, Nuffield College, Oxford; Inner Temple Law Scholarship, 1972; Fellow, Royal Statistical Soc., 1996-; Bencher, Inner Temple, 1997-; Hon. Vice-Pres., Blackburn Rovers FC, 1998-; LL.D. h.c., Univ. of Leeds, 1999; LL.D, Brunel Univ., 2007; ***publications:*** Granada Guildhall Lecture, 1969; Univ. of Leeds Convocation Lecture, 1978; 'Putting Blackburn Back to Work', 1983; 'Policy and Ideology', 1993; regular contributor to The Times, Guardian, Independent and Tribune newspapers; ***recreations:*** walking, music, cooking puddings, football supporter; ***office address:*** House of Commons, London, SW1A 0AA, United Kingdom; ***phone:*** +44 (0)20 7270 3000; ***e-mail:*** strawj@parliament.uk; ***URL:*** http://www.parliament.uk.

STREETER, Gary, MP; British, MP, South West Devon, House of Commons; ***born:*** 1955, East Devon, England; ***married:*** Janet Streeter; ***children:*** Tamsin (F), Gareth (M); ***education:*** Kings College, Univ. of London, LL.B, 1977; ***party:*** Conservative Party; ***political career:*** MP, Plymouth Sutton, 1992-97; Parly. Private Sec. to Solicitor General, 1993; Parly. Private Sec., to the Attorney General, 1994-95; Government Minister, Whips Office, 1995-96; Jr. Minister, Lord Chancellor's Dept, 1996; Parly. Private Sec. to John Major, 1997; MP, SW Devon, 1997-; Shadow Minister for Europe on the Opposition Front Bench, 1997-98; Shadow Sec. of State of Int. Dev., 1998-2001; Vice Chmn., Conservative Party, 2001-02; Foreign Affairs spokesman, 2003-04; Chmn., Conservative Party International Office, 2005-; ***interests:*** law and order, family, moral and social issues, developing world, building democracy; ***professional career:*** articled to a large City of London firm of solicitors until 1980; Solicitor, Foot & Bowden, Plymouth, 1980, Partner, 1984-98; Councillor, Plymouth City Council, 1986-89; Housing Chmn., 1989-91; ***committees:*** Environment Select Cttee., 1992-93; ODPM Select Cttee., 2002-04; Home Affairs Select Cttee., 2005-10; Jt. Cttee. on Security, 2010-; Ecclesiastical Cttee., 2010; ***honours and awards:*** Gelf Award for top law student, 1977; ***office address:*** House of Commons, London, SW1A 0AA, United Kingdom; ***phone:*** +44 (0)20 7219 3000; ***e-mail:*** mail@garystreeter.co.uk; ***URL:*** http://www.garystreeter.co.uk.

STRIDE, Mel; MP for Central Devon, UK Government; ***education:*** Oxford Univ.; ***party:*** Conservative; ***political career:*** MP for Central Devon, May 2010-; PPS; ***office address:*** House of Commons, London, SW1A 0AA, United Kingdom; ***phone:*** +44 (0)20 7219 3000; ***e-mail:*** mel.stride.mp@parliament.uk.

STRINGER, Graham; British, Member of Parliament for Blackley and Broughton, House of Commons; ***born:*** 17 February 1950; ***education:*** Univ. of Sheffield, B.Sc. (Hons), Chemistry; ***party:*** Labour Party; ***political career:*** MP, Manchester Blackley, 1997-2010, Blackley and Broughton, 2010-; ***professional career:*** Chmn., Manchester Airport plc.; ***committees:*** Environment, Transport and Regional Affairs, 1997-99; Modernisation of the House of Commons, 2006; Science and Technology, 2006-07, 2010-; Innovation, Universities and Skills, 2007-10, Transport 2011-; ***office address:*** House of Commons, London, SW1A 0AA, United Kingdom; ***phone:*** +44 (0)20 7219 3000; ***e-mail:*** hcinfo@parliament.uk.

STUART, Freundel; Prime Minister, Government of Barbados; ***education:*** Univ. of the West Indies, degrees in Law and Political Science; ***party:*** Democratic Labour Party; ***political career:*** Deputy Prime Minister, Attorney General and Minister of Home Affairs; Prime Minister, Minister of Home Affairs, Minister of National Security, Attorney General, Oct. 2010-; ***professional career:*** Attorney-at-Law; ***office address:*** Office of the Prime Minister, Government Headquarters, Bay Street, St. Michael, Barbados; ***phone:*** +1 246 436 3179; ***URL:*** http://primeminister.gov.bb.

STUART, Gisela; British, Member of Parliament for Birmingham, Edgbaston, House of Commons; ***born:*** 26 November 1955; ***education:*** Manchester Polytechnic, Business Studies; London Univ., LL.B; ***party:*** Labour Party; ***political career:*** MP, Birmingham, Edgbaston, 1997-; PPS, Home Office, 1998; Parly.-under-Sec., Dept. of Health, 1999-; Praesidium, Convention, Future of Europe; Chair, All Party Group Transatlantic & International Security; ***interests:*** pensions, criminal justice system, international security; ***committees:*** Mem., Social Security Cttee., 1997-98; Foreign Affairs Cttee., 2001-10; Defence Select Cttee., 2010-; ***trusteeships:*** Trustee, Henry Jackson Society; ***publications:*** The Making of Europe's Constitution, Fabian Society; House Magazine, Editor; ***office address:*** House of Commons, London, SW1A 0AA, United Kingdom; ***phone:*** +44 (0)20 7219 3000; ***e-mail:*** stuartg@parliament.uk.

STUART, Graham; MP for Beverley and Holderness, House of Commons; ***born:*** 1962; ***party:*** Conservative; ***political career:*** Councillor, Cambridge City Cncl., 1998; MP for Beverley and Holderness, 2005-; ***committees:*** Education, 2010-; Liaison, 2010-; ***office address:*** House of Commons, London, SW1A 0AA, United Kingdom; ***e-mail:*** graham.stuart.mp@parliament.uk.

STUBB, Alexander; Minister of Foreign Affairs, Finnish Government; ***born:*** 1968; ***education:*** BA, MA, Ph.D; ***party:*** National Coalition Party; ***political career:*** MEP, 2004-08; European Affairs and Minister of Foreign Affairs, April 2008-; ***office address:*** Ministry of Foreign Affairs, Merikasarmikatu, PO Box 176, 00161 Helsinki, Finland.

STUNELL, Andrew; Member of Parliament, House of Commons; ***born:*** 24 November 1942, Sutton, Surrey; ***parents:*** Robert Stunell (dec'd) and Trixie (née Thompson); ***married:*** Gillian Stunell; ***children:*** Judith (F), Kari (F), Peter (M), Mark (M), Daniel (M); ***public role of spouse:*** Educational Researcher; ***education:*** Kingston Polytechnic; Manchester Univ., Liverpool Polytechnic; ***party:*** Liberal Democratic Party; ***political career:*** Chester City Councillor, 1979-90; Cheshire County Council, 1981-91; Liberal Democrat Grp. Leader, Cheshire CC, 1981-87; Vice Chmn. Assoc. of County Councils, 1985-90; Mem., Stockport Metropolitan Borough Council, 1994-2002; MP, Hazel Grove, 1997-; Dep. Chief Whip, 1997-2001; Chief Whip, 2001-06; Shadow Secretary of State for Communities and Local Government, 2006-08; Chair, Local Election Campaign Team, 2008; Parly. Under Sec. of State, Dept. for Communities and Local Government, 2010-12; ***memberships:*** Vice Pres., Local Government Association, Vice Pres., Macclesfield Canal Soc., Pres., Goyt Valley Rail Users Group; ***professional career:*** CWS Architects Dept., Manchester, 1965-67; Snr. Architectural Assistant, Runcorn New Town, 1967-81; Assoc. of Liberal Democrat Cllrs., 1985-97; ***honours and awards:*** OBE; ***publications:*** various including, Energy: Clean and Green to 2050, Sept. 1999; Nuclear Waste: Cleaning Up the Mess, Sept.2001; Homes for All, Sept. 2007; ***office address:*** House of Commons, London, SW1A 0AA, United Kingdom; ***phone:*** +44 (0)20 7219 5136; ***fax:*** +44 (0)20 7222 2302; ***e-mail:*** enquiries@andrewstunell.org.uk; ***URL:*** http://www.andrewstunell.otg.uk.

STURDY, Julian; MP for York Outer, UK Government; ***party:*** Conservative; ***political career:*** Councillor, Harrogate Borough Council, 2002-07; MP for York Outer, May 2010-; ***committees:*** Transport Select Cttee., 2010-; ***office address:*** House of Commons, London, SW1A 0AA, United Kingdom; ***phone:*** +44 (0)20 7219 3000; ***e-mail:*** julian.sturdy.mp@parliament.uk.

STURGEON, Nicola, MSP; MSP for Glasgow Govan, Scottish Parliament; ***born:*** 19 July 1970, Irvine, Scotland; ***education:*** Glasgow Univ., LLB (Hons), 1992, Dip. in Legal Practice, 1993; ***party:*** Scottish National Party; ***political career:*** mem., Glasgow Govan, Scottish Parliament, 1999-: Cabinet Secretary, Health and Wellbeing, 2007-; Deputy First Minister; Deputy Party Leader; ***professional career:*** Solicitor, Drumchapel Law Centre, Glasgow; ***office address:*** Scottish Parliament, Edinburgh, EH99 1SP, United Kingdom; ***phone:*** +44 (0)131 348 5695; ***fax:*** +44 (0)131 348 6475; ***e-mail:*** nicola.sturgeon.msp@scottish.parliament.uk.

STUTHERS, Stan; Minister of Finance, Government of Manitoba; ***political career:*** Minister of Conservation; Minister of Agriculture, Food and Rural Initiatives, 2010-11; Minister of Finance, 2012-; ***office address:*** Ministry of Finance, 165 Legislative Building, 450 Broadway Avenue, Winnipeg, Manitoba, R3C 0V8, Canada; ***e-mail:*** minagr@leg.gov.mb.ca; ***URL:*** http://www.gov.mb.ca/.

STYLIANIDIS, Evripidis; Minister of the Interior, Government of Greece; ***born:*** 8 April 1966; ***languages:*** German; ***education:*** Studied Law, Democritus University of Thrace, 1984-89; PhD in constitutional law, Law School, Univ. of Hamburg, 1991-94; ***political career:*** Minister for National Education and Religious Affairs, 2007-09; Minister of Transport and Communications, 2009; Minister of the Interior, June 2012-; ***office address:*** Ministry of the Interior, 27 Stadiou str., 10183 Athens, Greece; ***phone:*** +30 (0)10 322 3521; ***e-mail:*** info@ypes.gr; ***URL:*** http://www.ypes.gr.

SUBBARAO, Dr. Duvvuri; Governor, Reserve Bank of India; ***born:*** August 11 1949; ***education:*** B.Sc (Hons) in Physics, Indian Inst. of Technology, Kharagpur;.M.Sc in Physics, Indian Inst. of Technology; MS, in Economics, Ohio State Univ., USA; a Humphrey fellow, MIT, USA, 1982-83; Ph.D. in Economics; ***professional career:*** Economist in the World Bank, 1999-2004; Sec. Prime Minister's Economic Advisory Council, 2005-07; Finance Sec., Ministry of Finance, 2007-08; Governor, Reserve Bank of India, 2008-, due to retire in Sept. 2013; ***office address:*** Reserve Bank of India, PO Box 10007, Central Office Building, Shahid Bhagat Singh Road, Mumbai 400 001, Maharashtra, India; ***phone:*** +91 2022 266 1602; ***fax:*** +91 2022 265 8269; ***e-mail:*** rbiprd@giasbm01.vsnl.net.in; ***URL:*** http://www.rbi.org.in.

SUBRAMANIAM, Dr S.; Minister of Health, Government of Malaysia; ***party:*** Malaysian Indian Congress; ***political career:*** MP, 2004-; Minister of Human Resources, 2008-13; Minister of Health, 2013-; ***office address:*** Ministry of Health, Ibu Pejabat KKM Blok, Pusat Pentadbiran Kerajaan Persekutuan, 62590 Putrajaya, Malaysia; ***URL:*** http://www.moh.gov.my.

SUGA, Yoshihide; Chief Cabinet Secretary, Government of Japan; ***party:*** Liberal Democratic Party; ***political career:*** Mem., House of Representatives, 1993-; Minister of Internal Affairs and Telecommunications, Minister of State for Privatisation of the Postal Service, 2005-06; Minister for INternal Affairs and Communications, Minister for Privatization of the Postal Services, 2006-11; Chief Cabinet Secretary, Minister in charge of Strengthening National Security, 2012-; ***office address:*** House of Representatives, 7-1 Nagata-cho, 1-chome, Chiyoda-ku, Tokyo 100-8960, Japapn; ***phone:*** +81 (0)3 5253 5111.

SUGAR OF CLAPTON, Lord Alan; Member, House of lords; ***born:*** 24 March 1947, Hackney, London; ***children:*** 3; ***political career:*** Mem., House of Lords, 2009-; Government Enterprise Champion 2009-10; ***professional career:*** Founder and Chmn., Amstrad, 1968-2008; Chmn., Tottenham Hotspur FC, 1991-2001; Presenter, BBC TV The Apprentice, 2005-; ***honours and awards:*** Raised to the peerage as Baron Sugar, of Clapton in the London Borough of Hackney, 2009; ***office address:*** House of Lords , London, SW1A 0PW, United Kingdom; ***phone:*** +44 (0)20 7219 3000; ***fax:*** +44 (0)20 7219 5979; ***URL:*** http://www.parliament.uk.

SUH, Seong-hwan; Minister for Land, Infrastructure and Transport, Government of the Republic of Korea; ***political career:*** Minister of Land, Infrastructure and Transport, 2013-; ***professional career:*** Dir. of Education Inst., Int. Campus, Yonsei Univ., 2012; ***office address:*** Ministry of Land, Infrastructure and Transport, Government Complex Sejong, A-Dong, 11 Doum6-Ro, Sejong CIty, 339-012, Republic of Korea; ***phone:*** +82 44 201 4672; ***fax:*** +82 44 860 9500; ***URL:*** http://english.mltm.go.kr.

SULEIMAN, General Michel; President, Government of Lebanon; ***born:*** 21 November 1948, Amshit in Jbeil ; ***married:*** Wafaa Sleiman; ***children:*** Rita (F), Lara (F), Charbel (M); ***languages:*** English, French; ***education:*** BA, politics and administrative sciences, Lebanese Univ., 1980; ***political career:*** President, May 2008-; ***professional career:*** Army career; Commander of the armed forces, 1998-2008; ***honours and awards:*** Nat. Order of the Cedar (Grand Cordon); Lebanese Order of Merit (Extraordinary Grade); Medal of King Abdul

Aziz; Italian Order of Merit (Grand Cross); Collar of Moubarak the Great; ***office address:*** Presidential Palace, P.O. Box 40001, Baabda, Lebanon; ***phone:*** +961 1 424961; ***e-mail:*** president_office@presidency.gov.lb; ***URL:*** http://www.presidency.gov.lb.

SULEYMANOV, H.E. Elin; Ambassador, Embassy of Azerbaijan, Washington DC; ***education:*** Moscow State Univ., Russia; Univ. of Toledo, Ohio; Fletcher School of Law and Diplomacy, Massachusetts; ***professional career:*** Diplomatic Service; Consul General to Los Angeles, 2006-2011; Amb. to the USA, 2011-; ***office address:*** Embassy of Azerbaijan, 2741 34th Street, NW, Washington, DC 20008-3027, USA; ***phone:*** +1 202 337 3500; ***fax:*** +1 202 337 5911; ***URL:*** http://www.azembassy.com/.

SUTCLIFFE, Gerry; British, Member of Parliament for Bradford South, House of Commons; ***born:*** 13 May 1953; ***education:*** Bradford and Ilkley Community Coll.; ***party:*** Labour Party, 1978-; ***political career:*** Cllr., Bradford, 1982-94, Leader, 1990-94; Dep. Branch Sec., GPMU, 1980-94; Asst. Govt. Whip, 1999-; MP, Bradford South, 1994-; Govt. Whip, 2001-03; Parly.Under-Sec. of State, Dep. of Trade & Industry, 2003-07; Parly. Under Sec., Dept. for Culture, Media and Sport, 2007-10; Shadow Minister for Culture, Media and Sport, 2010; Shadow Minister, Home Affairs, Oct. 2010-11; ***interests:*** economy, environment, education, transport; ***committees:*** Culture, Media and Sport, 2011-; ***office address:*** Consistuency, 3rd Floor, 76 Kirkgate, Bradford, BD1 1S2, United Kingdom; ***phone:*** +44 (0)1274 400007; ***fax:*** +44 (0)1274 400020; ***e-mail:*** sutcliffeg@parliament.uk.

SUTLEY, Nancy; Chair, Council on Environmental Quality, US Government; ***education:*** Cornell Univ., Bachelors; Harvard, Masters in Public Policy; ***professional career:*** Senior Policy Advisor to the EPA Regional Administrator in San Francisco and special assistant to the Administrator in Washington, D.C.; Energy Advisor to California Governor Gray Davis; Dep. Sec. for policy and intergovernmental relations, California EPA, 1999-2003; Dep. Mayor for Energy and Environment, City of Los Angeles, 2003-08; Chair, Council on Environmental Quality, 2009-; ***office address:*** Council on Environmental Quality, 722 Jackson Place, NW, Washington, DC 20503, USA; ***phone:*** +1 202 395 5750; ***fax:*** +1 202 456 6546; ***URL:*** http://www.whitehouse.gov/ceq/.

SUYANTO, Djoko; Minister for Political and Security Affairs, Government of Indonesia; ***political career:*** Minister for Political and Security Affairs, 2008-; ***professional career:*** Commander-in-Chief, Nat. Armed Forces of Indonesia, 2006-07; ***office address:*** Ministry for Political and Security Affairs, Jalan Jenderal Gatot Subroto, 10270 Jakarta, Indonesia.

SVABY, Daniel; Judge, Court of Justice of the European Union; ***education:*** University of Bratislava, Doctor of Laws; ***professional career:*** Judge, District Court, Bratislava; Judge, Appeal Court, Bratislava, also Vice-President; acting Judge, responsible for commercial law cases, Supreme Court; Mem., European Commission of Human Rights, Strasbourg; Judge, Constitutional Court, 2000-04; Judge, Court of First Instance, 2004-09; Judge, Court of Justice of the EU, 2009-; ***office address:*** Court of Justice of the European Union, Rue du Fort Niedergrunewald, L-2925, Luxembourg.

SVEINSSON, Gunnar; Minister of Foreign Affairs, Government of Iceland; ***born:*** 9 June 1968; ***education:*** Univ. of Iceland, 1995; ***party:*** Progressive Party; ***political career:*** MP, 2009-; Minister of Foreign Affairs, 2013-; ***office address:*** Minister of Foreign Affairs, Raudarárstígur 25, 150 Reykjavík, Iceland; ***phone:*** +354 545 9900; ***fax:*** +354 562 2373; ***e-mail:*** external@utn.stjr.is; ***URL:*** http://www.mfa.is .

SWALES, Ian; MP for Redcar, UK Government; ***party:*** Liberal Democrat; ***political career:*** MP for Redcar, May 2010-; ***committees:*** Public Accounts Select Cttee., 2010-; European Scrutiny, 2010-; ***office address:*** House of Commons, London, SW1A 0AA, United Kingdom; ***phone:*** +44 (0)20 7219 3000; ***e-mail:*** ian.swales.mp@parliament.uk.

SWAYNE, Desmond; British, Member of Parliament for New Forest West, House of Commons; ***born:*** 1957; ***education:*** Univ. of St. Andrews; ***party:*** Conservative Party; ***political career:*** Parly. Candidate, Pontypridd, 1987, West Bromwich, 1992; MP, New Forest West, 1997-; Parly. Secretary to the Treasury and Chief Whip, 2012-; ***professional career:*** School Teacher, 1981-87; Banker, 1987-97; ***office address:*** House of Commons, London, SW1A 0AA, United Kingdom; ***phone:*** +44 (0)20 7219 3000; ***e-mail:*** hcinfo@parliament.uk.

SWEE SAY, Lim; Minister in the Prime Minister's Office, Government of Singapore; ***born:*** 1955; ***married:*** Elaine Cheong; ***children:*** Shu Ming (F), Wen Zhe (M); ***public role of spouse:*** software engineer and computer sales manager, -1991; ***education:*** Catholic High School; National Jr. Coll.; Singapore Armed Forces Scholarship, Electronics, computer and Systems Engineering degree, Loughborough Univ. of Technology, UK, 1976; Masters in Management, Stanford Sloan programme, Stanford Univ., 1991; ***party:*** People's Action Party (PAP), 1996; ***political career:*** elected as one of six MPs representing Tanjong Pagar Gp. Representation Constituency (GRC), 1996; Chmn., Young PAP, 1999-; Minister of State for Communications and Information Technology and Minister of State for Trade and Industry, 1999-; Acting Minister for the Environment, 2000; Represented Holland-Bukit Panjang GRC, 2001-; Advisor, Buona Vista and commonwealth Division, to date; Acting Minister for the Environment and Minister of State for Communications and Information Technology, 2001-2002, Minister for the Environment, 2001-04; Minister in the Prime Minister's Office and Second Minister for National Development, 2004-; ***professional career:*** served in Civil Service, 20 yrs.; associated with dev. of info. technology, Singapore, 1970s-; worked on computer simulation projects and undertook applied research in software engineering, Ministry of Defence, 1977-84; joined National Computer Bd. (NCB), 1984, served as CEO, 1986-91, Chmn., 1994-98; Dep. Managing Dir., Economic Dev. Bd. of Singapore, based in New York, 1991-93, Man. Dir., 1994-96; Dep. Sec.-Gen., National Trades Union Congress, 1997-99; ***committees:*** Mem., Cttee. on Singapore's Competitiveness, 1997-98, Chmn., subcttee. on Manpower Dev.; Mem., PAP Central Exec. Cttee., 1999-; ***recreations:*** golf, spending time with his family; ***office address:*** Prime Minister's Office, Orchard Road, Istana Office Wing, Singapore 228231, Singapore; ***phone:*** +65 6737 5133; ***fax:*** +65 6835 6261; ***URL:*** http://www.pmo.gov.sg.

SWINFEN, Lord; Member, House of Lords; ***born:*** 14 December 1938; ***parents:*** Lord Swinfen and Mary Aline Swinfen (née Farmar); ***married:*** Patricia Anne Swinfen (née Blackmore), 1962; ***children:*** Charles (M), Georgina (F), Katherine (F), Arabella (F); ***education:*** Westminster; Sandhurst; ***party:*** Conservative; ***political career:*** Mem., House of Lords; ***interests:*** telemedicine, disability, defence; ***office address:*** House of Lords, London, SW1A 0PW, United Kingdom; ***phone:*** +44 (0)20 7219 3500; ***fax:*** +44 (0)20 7219 5979.

SWINNEY, John, MSP; SCO, Member for North Tayside, Scottish Parliament; ***born:*** 13 April 1964, Edinburgh, Scotland; ***s:*** 1; ***d:*** 1; ***education:*** Univ. of Edinburgh, MA, Politics, 1986; ***party:*** Scottish National Party (SNP); ***political career:*** Nat. Sec., SNP, 1986-92; Dep. Leader (Sr. Vice Convener), SNP, 1998-2000 ; MP, North Tayside, 1997-2001 ; Dep. Leader, Scottish Opposition and Shadow Minister for Enterprise and Lifelong Learning, 1999-2000; MSP, North Tayside, 1999-; Leader (National Convener) of the Scottish National Party, 2000-04; Leader of the Scottish opposition, 2000-04; Shadow Minister for Finance and Public Services, 2005-07; Cabinet Secretary, Finance and Sustainable Growth, 2007-; ***professional career:*** Strategic Planning Principal, Scottish Amicable; Business and Econ. Dev. consultant; ***committees:*** Convener, Scottish Parl. Enterprise and Lifelong Learning Cttee., 1999-2000; Convener, European and External Relations Cttee., 2004-05; ***recreations:*** hill walking, cycling; ***office address:*** Constituency Office, 35 Perth Street, Blairgowrie, Scotland, PH10 6DL, United Kingdom; ***phone:*** +44 (0)1250 876576; ***fax:*** +44 (0)1250 876991; ***e-mail:*** john.swinney.msp@scottish.parliament.uk.

SWINSON, Jo; MP for East Dunbartonshire , House of Commons; ***born:*** 5 February 1980, Glasgow; ***education:*** LSE, BSc, Management, 2000; ***party:*** Liberal Democrat; ***political career:*** MP for Dunbartonshire East, 2005-; Shadow Scottish Sec., 2006-07; Shadow Spokesperson, Women and Equality, 2007; Shadow Min. of State for Foreign Affairs, 2008-10; PPS to Vince Cable, Secretary of State for Business, Innovation & Skills, 2010-12; PPS to Nick Clegg, Dep. PM, Lord President of the Council, 2012; Parliamentary Under-Secretary of State (Minister for Employment Relations and Consumer Affairs), Dept. for Business, Innovation and Skills, 2012-; ***office address:*** House of Commons, London, SW1A 0AA, United Kingdom; ***phone:*** +44 (0)20 7219 8088; ***e-mail:*** swinsonj@parliament.uk; ***URL:*** http://www.joswinson.org.uk.

SWIRE, Rt. Hon. Hugo; Minister of State, UK Government; ***born:*** 30 November 1959, London; ***parents:*** Humphrey Swire (dec'd) and the Marchioness Townshend (née Montgomerie); ***married:*** Alexandra (Sasha) Swire (née Nott); ***children:*** Saffron (F), Siena (F); ***education:*** Eton; St Andrews Univ., 1978-79; Royal Military Academy, Sandhurst; ***party:*** Conservative Party; ***political career:*** stood as Conservative and Unionist candidate for Greenock and Inverclyde, Scotland, 1997 election; MP, East Devon, 2001-; PPS to Rt. Hon. Theresa May MP, 2003; Opposition Whip to Dept. of FCO and Office of the Dep. Prime Minister; Shadow Minister for the Arts, 2004; Shadow Minister for Culture, Media and Sport, 2005-10; Chmn., Conservative Middle East Council; Minister of State, Northern Ireland Office, 2010-12; Minister of State, South East Asia / Far East, India and Nepal, Latin America, Falklands, Australasia and Pacific, Commonwealth, FCO, 2012-; ***memberships:*** National Farmers Union; Countryside Alliance; Chmn., All Party Parly. United Arab Emirates Gp.; Vice-Chmn., All-Party Parly. Lebanon Gp., All-Party World Heritage Sites Gp.; Treasurer, All-Party Parly. Oman Gp.; Royal British Legion; Vice-Pres. Grenadier Guards Assn. (Wessex Branch); ***professional career:*** 1st Battalion Grenadier Guards, 1979-83; Hd. of Dev., The Nat. Gallery; Financial Consultant, Streets Financial Ltd.; Co-founder Man. Dir., Int. News Services & Prospect Films; Dir., Sotheby's, London, 1992-2002; Charity Auctioneer; Non-Exec. Chmn., PhotoMe plc., to date; Consultant, Aon Professional Risks, to date; Non-Exec. Dir., Symphony Environmental Technologies PLC; ***committees:*** Speaker's Advisory Cttee. on works of Art, 2001, Chmn., 2005-; Sec., Conservative Middle East Cncl.; Pres., Western Area Conservatives Clubs Cncl.; ***trusteeships:*** Heritage and Works of Art Trust, House of Commons; Council of the RNLI; Patron, West of England School and College for young people with little or no sight; Patron, Devon Link Up; ***honours and awards:*** Fellow, Royal Society of Arts; ***office address:*** House of Commons, London, SW1A 0AA, United Kingdom; ***phone:*** +44 (0)20 7219 8173; ***URL:*** http://www.hugoswire.com.

SYMS, Robert; Member of Parliament for Poole, House of Commons; ***born:*** 15 August 1956; ***parents:*** Raymond Syms and Mary Syms; ***married:*** Fiona Syms (née Mellersh), 2000 (Sep. 2008); Nicky Syms, 1991 (div'd 1999); ***children:*** Imogen Poppy (F), Nicholas Robert Charles (M); ***education:*** Colston's Sch., Bristol; ***party:*** Conservative Party; ***political career:*** Mem., North Wilts District Cncl., 1983-87; Mem., Wiltshire County Cncl., 1985-97; PPS to Chmn. of Conservative Party 1999; Shadow Frontbench Spokesman on Dept. of Environment, Transport & Regions 1999-; MP, Poole, 1997-; Shadow spokesman on Environment Transport and Regions, 1999-01; Vice-Chmn. of the Conservative Party, 2001-04; Opposition Whip, 2003-04; Shadow Spokesman, Office Dep. PM, 2004-; ***professional career:*** Co. Dir., Man. Dir., Building & Plant Hire Gp., Chippenham, Wilts; ***committees:*** Health Select Cttee., 1997-2000, 2007-10; Transport Select Cttee., 2002-03; Liaison, 2010-12; Regulatory Reform, 2010-12; ***honours and awards:*** Fellow of the Chartered Inst. of Building (FCIOB); ***office address:*** House of Commons, London, SW1A 0AA, United Kingdom; ***phone:*** +44 (0)20 7219 3000; ***e-mail:*** symsr@parliament.uk.

SYNNOTT, Sir Hilary Nicholas, KCMG; Senior Consulting Fellow, International Institute for Strategic Studies; ***born:*** 20 March 1945, Somerset, England; ***parents:*** Commander J.N.N. Synnott DSC, RN (dec'd) and F.E. Synnott (dec'd); ***married:*** Anne Synnott (née Clarke), 28 April 1973; ***public role of spouse:*** Mem., UK Council of Psychotherapists; MBE, 1989; ***languages:*** French, German, Italian; ***education:*** Beaumont Coll.; Royal Navy Coll., Dartmouth; Peterhouse, Cambridge, MA; ***memberships:*** C.Eng and MIEE, 1971; ***professional career:*** Royal Navy, 1962-73; HM Diplomatic Service, 1973-2004, served in Paris, Bonn and Amman; Hd., Western Europe Dept. and later of Security Coordination Dept., FCO, 1989-93; Dep. High Cmnr., New Delhi, 1993-96; Dir., South and South-East Asia, FCO, 1996-98; British High Cmnr. to Pakistan, 2000-03; Regional Coordinator for Southern Iraq, Coalition Provisional Authority (CPA), 2003-04; Senior Fellow, Int. Inst. for Strategic Studies, 2004-; Eric Lane Fellow, Clare Coll. Cambridge, 2007; mem., Atlantic Council Task Force on Pakistan, 2008; ***honours and awards:*** KCMG, 2002; CMG, 1997; Hon. Fellow, Peterhouse Cambridge; ***publications:*** Bad Days in Basra, 2008, I.B. Tauris; The Causes and Consequences of South Asia's Nuclear Tests, 1999, Oxford University Press; State-building in Southern Iraq, IISS, 2005; Transforming Pakistan, 2009, Routledge/IISS; ***office address:*** International Institute for Strategic Studies, Arundel House, 13-15 Arundel Street, London, WC2R 3DX, United Kingdom.

T

TAHA, Ali Osman Mohamed; First Vice President, Sudanese Government; ***party:*** National Congress Party; ***political career:*** Foreign Minister, 1995-98; Second Vice Pres., 2005-11; First Vice-Pres., 2011-; ***office address:*** First Vice President, People's Palace, PO Box 281, Khartoum, Sudan; ***phone:*** +249 1177 6603 / 777583; ***fax:*** +249 1177 1724 / 787676.

TAJANI, Antonio; Italian, Vice President and Commissioner, European Commission; ***born:*** 1953; ***education:*** Law; ***party:*** Forza Italia; ***political career:*** Mem., European Parliament, 1994-; Vice-Pres., European People's Party; Vice-Pres. for Transport, EU Commission, 2008-09; Vice Pres. and Commissioner for Industry and Entrepreneurship, 2009-; ***office address:*** European Parliament, 60 Rue Wiertz, P.O.B. 1047, B-1047 Brussels, Belgium; ***phone:*** +32 (0)2 284 2111; ***fax:*** +32 (0)2 284 9075; ***URL:*** http://ec.europa.eu/.

TAK-SING TSANG ; Secretary for Home Affairs, Executive Council of Hong Kong; ***education:*** University of Hong Kong, Master's in International and Public Affairs; MA, Comparative Literature; Harvard, Nieman Fellow, 1994-95; ***political career:*** Mem., Central Policy Unit, 1998-2007; Hong Kong Deputy, National People's Congress; Secretary for Home Affairs, Exec. Cncl. of HKSAR, 2007-; ***professional career:*** Journalist; ***office address:*** Home Affairs Bureau, 31/F Southorn Centre, 130 Hennessy Road, Wanchai, Hong Kong; ***phone:*** +852 2835 2277; ***fax:*** +852 2840 1902; ***URL:*** http://www.info.gov.hk/hab.

TAKSOE-JENSEN, Peter; Ambassador, Danish Embassy in New York; ***education:*** Law Degree, Univ. of Copenhagen, Denmark; ***professional career:*** Under-Sec. for Legal Affairs and Head of Legal Service, Danish Ministry of Foreign Affairs, 2003-08 ; Assistant Sec.-Gen. for Legal Affairs, UN, 2008-10; Amb. to the US, 2010-; ***office address:*** Embassy of Denmark, 3200 Whitehaven St., N.W., Washington DC, 20008, USA; ***phone:*** +1 202 234 4300; ***URL:*** http://www.ambwashington,um.dk.

TALABANI, Jalal; President, Iraq; ***born:*** 1933; ***education:*** Law degree, Baghdad Univ.; ***political career:*** founder mem., Kurdistan Students Union; founder mem., Patriotic Union of Kurdistan, 1975-2005; President of Iraq, 2005-; ***office address:*** Office of the President, Baghdad, Iraq.

TAMI, Mark, MP; MP for Alyn and Deeside, House of Commons; ***born:*** 1962; ***party:*** Labour Party; ***political career:*** MP for Alyn and Deeside, 2001-; ***committees:*** Selection, 2010-; Joint Committee on Security, 2011-; Administration, 2012-; ***office address:*** House of Commons, London, SW1A 0AA, United Kingdom; ***e-mail:*** tamim@parliament.uk.

TAN, Namik; Ambassador to the US, Turkish Embassy; ***born:*** 1956; ***education:*** Ankara Univ.; ***political career:*** Spokesperson, MFA, 2004-07; Dep. Undersecretary of the MFA, 2009; ***professional career:*** joined Ministry of Foreign Affairs, 1982; Second Sec., Moscow, 1984-87; First Sec., Abu Dhabi, 1988-89; Dep. Chief of Cabinet to the Turkish Pres., 1990-91; Counselor, Turkish Emb., Washington, 1991-95, First Counselor, 1997-2001; Head of the Dept. for the Americas, 2001; Amb. of Turkey to Israel 2007-09; Amb. of Turkey to the US, 2010-; ***office address:*** Turkish Embassy, 2525 Massachusetts Ave., NW, Washington, DC 20006, USA; ***phone:*** +1 202 612 6700; ***fax:*** +1 202 612 6744; ***URL:*** http://www.turkishembassy.org/.

TANIGAKI, Sadakazu; Minister of Justice, Japanese Government; ***born:*** 7 March 1945, Kyoto, Japan; ***education:*** Univ. of Tokyo, Law Dept., 1972; ***political career:*** Mem. of House of Representatives, 1983-; Minister of State for Science and Technology, 1997-98; Minister for Financial Reconstruction, 2000; Chmn. of the Nat. Public Safety Commission, Minister of State (Industrial Revitalisation Corporation, Food Safety Commission and Related Matters, 2003-04; Minister of Finance, 2004-08; Minister of Ocean Policy, 2009; Minister of Justice 2013-; ***professional career:*** Attorney-at-law; ***committees:*** Chmn., Standing Cttee. on Communications, 1991-93; Chmn., Standing Cttee. on Rules and Administration, 1995-96; Chmn., Financial Reconstructin Cmn., 2000; Chmn., National Public Safety Cmn., 2002-03; ***office address:*** Ministry of Justice, 1-1-1 Kasumigaseki, Chiyoda-ku, Tokyo 100, Japan; ***phone:*** +81 (0)3 3592 7011; ***URL:*** http://www.mpj.go.jp.

TAN KENG YAM, Dr Tony; Singaporean, President, Republic of Singapore; ***born:*** 7 February 1940; ***married:*** Mary Chee Bee Kiang; ***education:*** St. Patrick's Sch., 1947-56; St. Joseph's Instn., 1957-58; First Class Honours, Physics degree, Univ. of Singapore, 1962; M.Sc. specialising in Operations Research, Massachusetts Inst. of Technology, 1962-64; awarded a Research Scholarship to Univ. of Adelaide (Ph.D. Applied Mathematics), 1965-67; ***political career:*** MP for Sembawang Constituency, 1979; Senior Minister of State (Education), 1979-80; Minister of Education, 1980; Minister for Trade and Industry, 1981-84, concurrently Minister-in-charge, Nat. Univ. of Singapore and the Nanyang Technological Inst.; Minister for Finance, and concurrently Minister for Trade and Industry, 1983-85; Minister for Education, 1985-91; Finance, Education and Health, 1985; Minister of Trade and Industry, 1985-86; Chmn., Peoples' Action Party (PAP); Dep. Prime Minister and Minister for Defence, 1995-2006; President, Republic of Singapore, 2011-; ***professional career:*** Teacher, Physics Dept., Univ. of Singapore, 1 yr; Lecturer in Mathematics, Univ. of Singapore, 1967; Sub-Man., Oversea-Chinese Banking Corporation, 1969, apptd. Gen.-Man., 1978, Chmn. and CEO, 1991-; Vice-Chancellor, Nat. Univ. of Singapore, 1980 ; ***committees:*** Chmn., NTUC Investment and Co-operatives Cttee., 1979; Mem., Central Exec. Cttee. of the People's Action Party, 1981-; ***trusteeships:*** Chmn., Bd. of Trustees, NTUC Income, 1980-91; ***honours and awards:*** Medal of Honour, National Trades Union Congress, 1988; ***recreations:*** golf, swimming; ***office address:*** Office of the President, Istana Singapore, Orchard Road, 238823, Singapore; ***phone:*** +65 6737 5522; ***fax:*** +65 6735 3135; ***URL:*** http://www.istana.gov.sg.

TAPSELL, Sir Peter, MA, MP; British, Member of Parliament for Louth and Horncastle, Father of the House of Commons, House of Commons; ***born:*** 1930, Hove, Sussex; ***parents:*** Eustace Bailey Tapsell (dec'd) and Jessie Maxwell Tapsell (dec'd) (née Hannay); ***married:*** Hon. Cecilia Hawke, 1963-1971; Gabrielle Mahieu, 1974; ***education:*** Merton Coll., Oxford, BA (1st Class) Modern History, 1953, Hon. Postmaster, 1953, MA, 1957, Hon. Fellow, 1989; Librarian, Oxford Union, 1953; represented Oxford Union on debating tour of USA, 1954; Trustee of Oxford Union, 1985-93; ***party:*** Conservative; ***political career:*** Conservative Research Dept., Social Services and Agriculture, 1954-57; PA to PM Sir Anthony Eden, 1955; Contested Wednesbury by-election, 1957; Con. MP, Nottingham West, 1959-64, Horncastle, Lincs., 1966-83; Con. Front Bench Spokesman, Foreign and Commonwealth Affairs, 1976-77, Treasury and Economic Affairs, 1977-78; Con. MP, Lindsey East, Lincs., 1983-97; MP, Louth and Horncastle, 1997-; Father of the House of Commons, 2010-; Appt. Privy Counsellor, 2011; ***memberships:*** Court of Univ. of Nottingham, 1959-1964; Jt. Chmn., British-Caribbean Assoc., 1963-64; Vice Pres., Tennyson Socy., 1966-; Hon. Treas., Anglo-Chinese Parly. Gp., 1974-77; Hon. Mem., Brunei Govt. Investment Advisory Bd., 1976-88; Trilateral Commission, 1979-99; Council of Inst. for Fiscal Studies, 1983-2005; Deputy Chmn., Mitsubishi Trust Oxford Foundation, 1988-; Mem., Business Advisory Council of United Nations, 2001-06; ***professional career:*** Subaltern, Royal Sussex Regt., Middle East, 1948-50; Studied warfare in Kenya, Cyprus, the Congo and Vietnam; Financial Adviser to the late Sir Omar Saifuddin, Sultan of Brunei, 1968-88; Mem., London Stock Exchange, 1957-1990; Int. Partner, James Capel & Co., 1960-1990; Adviser to several Central Banks and int. companies on their management of int. reserves; Specialist in bond and currency markets; Adviser to Japanese companies with world-wide interests; ***committees:*** Unopposed Bills (Panel), 2004-; ***honours and awards:*** Brunei Dato, 1971; Hon. Fellow Merton College, Oxford, 1989; Hon. Life Mem., 6th Squadron RAF, 1971; Kt., 1985; The Spectator Backbencher of the Year, 1993; The Spectator Parliamentarian of the Year, 2004; ***clubs:*** Athenaeum; Carlton; Hurlingham; Chmn., Coningsby Club, 1957-58; ***recreations:*** travel in the Third World, mountain walking, reading history; ***office address:*** House of Commons, London, SW1A 0AA, United Kingdom; ***phone:*** +44 (0)20 7219 3000; ***fax:*** +44 (0)20 7219 4484.

TAUBIRA, Christiane; French, Keeper of the Seals and Minister of Justice, Government of France; ***born:*** 2 February 1952; ***political career:*** Leader, Walwari Creole Movement; Mem., Nat. Assembly for French Guiana, 1993-2012; MEP, 1994-99; Minister for Justice and Keeper of the Seals, 2012-; ***memberships:*** Mem., South American Deleg., 1994-; ***professional career:*** teacher; Dir., National Conservatory of Arts and Careers, French Guiana; Dir., Agric. Cooperation Antilles-French Guiana, 1982-85; Dir., Technical Assistance for Small Scale Fishing, 1985-90; Dir., Office of Co-op. and Foreign Trade (OCCE), 1990-93; ***committees:*** Mem., Dev. and Co-operation Cttee.; ***office address:*** Minister of Justice, 13 place Vendôme, 75042 Paris Cedex 01, France; ***phone:*** +33 (0)1 44 77 61 15; ***fax:*** +33 (0)1 44 77 70 20; ***URL:*** http://www.justice.gouv.fr.

TAYLOR, Duncan, CBE; Governor, Cayman Islands; ***political career:*** Governor, 2010-; ***professional career:*** Dep. Consul-General and Dep. Head of Post in New York; Amb. to Barbados and the Eastern Caribbean, 2006-10; ***office address:*** Governor's Office, Suite 202, 2nd Floor The Smith Road Centre, Smith Road, George Town, Grand Cayman, KY1 1003, Cayman Islands.

TAYLOR, Elaine; Deputy Premier, Government of Yukon; ***education:*** Univ. of Alberta; ***political career:*** MLA, 2002-; Minister of Culture and Tourism, Minister responsible for Women's Affairs, and Public Service Cmn.; Deputy Premier, 2008-; currently (2013) also: Minister of Community Services, Minister responsible for the Public Service Commission, Minister responsible for the Women's Directorate; Minister responsible for the French Language Service Directorate; ***office address:*** Ministry of Community Services, Yukon Government Administration Building, Whitehorse, Yukon, Canada; ***phone:*** +1 867 667 8262; ***fax:*** +1 867 667 8424.

TAYLOR OF GOSS MOOR, Lord Matthew Owen John, MA; British, Member, House of Lords; ***born:*** 3 January 1963; ***parents:*** Ken Taylor and Jill Taylor (née Black); ***married:*** Vicky Taylor; ***children:*** Arthur (M), Jacob (M); ***education:*** Treliske Sch., Truro; Univ. Coll. Sch.; Lady Margaret Hall, Oxford Univ.; ***party:*** Liberal Democrat; ***political career:*** Economic Policy Researcher, Parly. Lib. Party, 1986-87; Chmn., Parly. Youth Affairs Lobby, 1987-89; MP (Lib.) for Truro & St. Austell, 1987-2010; (Lib.) Energy Spokesman, 1987-88; Liberal Democrat Spokesman on Local Government and Housing, 1988-89; Trade and Industry, 1989-90; Education, 1990-92; Chmn., Lib. Dem. Communications, 1989-92; Chmn., Lib Dem. Campaigns and Communications, 1992-94; Environment Spokesman, 1994-99; Economy Spokesman, 1999-2003; Parly. Party Chmn., Lib. Dem., 2003-2005; Social Exclusion Spokesman, 2006-07; Special Adviser to the Govt. on Rural Economy and Affordable Rural Housing, 2007-08; Mem., House of Lords, 2010-; ***professional career:*** Pres., Oxford Univ. Student Union, 1985-86; Chmn., National Housing Fed., 2009-; ***committees:*** Environment Select Cttee., 1996-97; ***office address:*** House of Lords, London, SW1A 0AA, United Kingdom; ***phone:*** +44 (0)20 7219 3000; ***URL:*** http://www.matthewtaylor.info.

TAYLOR OF HOLBEACH, Lord John; Member, House of Lords; ***party:*** Conservative; ***political career:*** Opposition Whip, 2006-10; Opposition Spokesperson for: Environment, 2006-07, Wales, 2006-07, Work and Pensions, 2006-10, Environment, Food and Rural Affairs, 2007-10; Government Whip, 2010-11; Government Spokesperson for: Cabinet Office, 2010-11, Energy and Climate Change, 2010-11, Work and Pensions, 2010-11; Parliamentary Under-Secretary of State and Government Spokesperson: Department for Environment, Food and Rural Affairs, 2011-12; Dept. of Home Affairs, 2012-; ***office address:*** House of Lords, London, SW1A 0PW, United Kingdom; ***e-mail:*** taylorjlparliament.uk.

TEATHER, Sarah; Minister of State, Department for Education, UK Government; ***education:*** Cambridge Univ.; ***political career:*** Islington Cncl., 2002-03: MP for Brent East, 2003-10, Brent Central, 2010-; Shadow Sec. for Communities and Local Gov., 2005-06; Shadow Sec. for Education and Skills, 2006-07; Shadow Innovation, Universities and Skills Sec., 2007; Shadow Business and Enterprise, 2007-08: Shadow Secretary of State for Business,

Enterprise and Regulatory Reform, 2008-10, also Shadow Minister for Housing, 2008-10; Minister of State, Department for Education, 2010-12; ***office address:*** House of Commons, London, SW1A 0AA, United Kingdom; ***URL:*** http://www.sarahteather.org.uk.

TEEVEN, Fredrik; Secretary of State for Security and Justice, Netherlands Government; ***born:*** 1958; ***education:*** Auditors course, Tax & Customs Admin. Training Centre, Utrecht; Amsterdam Free Univ., Dutch Law; Univ. of Twente, Masters Degree in Public Management; ***party:*** VVD; ***political career:*** MP, 2002-03, 2006-; State Secretary for Security and Justice, Rutte-Verhagen gov., 2010-12; State Secretary for Security and Justice, Rutte-Asscher gov., Nov. 12- (abroad he will be known as the Minister for Migration); ***professional career:*** Fiscal investigator; Public Prosecutor, Amsterdam District Court, 1993; Prosecutor, War Crimes, National Public Prosecutors' Office, 2003-04; team leader/public prosecutor, Amsterdam Schipol Airport, 2004-06; ***office address:*** Ministry of Justice, Schedeldoekshaven 100, 2511 EX The Hague, Netherlands; ***URL:*** http://www.justitie.nl.

TEIKMANIS, H.E. Andris; Ambassador, Latvian Embassy in the UK; ***languages:*** English, French, German, Russian; ***education:*** Law, Latvian State Univ., 1983; ***professional career:*** Amb. at Large to the Council of Europe, 1995-99; Amb. to Germany, 2002-07; Under Sec. of State, Ministry of Foreign Affairs, 2004-08; Amb. to the Russian Federation, 2008-11; Sec. of State, Ministry of Foreign Affairs, 2008-13; Amb. to the United Kingdom, 2013-; ***office address:*** Embassy of the Republic of Latvia, 45 Nottingham Place, London, W1M 3FE, United Kingdom; ***phone:*** +44 (0)20 7312 0040; ***fax:*** +44 (0)20 7312 0042; ***e-mail:*** latemb@dircon.co.uk; ***URL:*** http://www.mfa.gov.lv/en/london/embassy.

TEIXEIRA DA CRUZ, Paula; Minister of Justice, Government of Portugal; ***born:*** 1960; ***education:*** Law; ***party:*** Social Democratic Party; ***political career:*** Councillor, Lisbon City Council, 1998-2002; Chmn., Municipal Assembly of Lisbon, 2005-2009; Minister of Justice, 2011-; ***professional career:*** lawyer; Teacher, Administrative Law, Lisbon Fac. of Law & Free Univ. of Lisbon, 1983-87; Inst. for Finance & Tax Studies, -92; mem., High Council of the Public Prosecutor's Office, 1999-2003; Mem., General Council of the Bar Assoc., 2002-05; Mem., Supreme Judicial Council, 2003-05; ***office address:*** Ministry of Justice, Rua do Ouro 6, 1149-019 Lisbon, Portugal; ***URL:*** http://www.mj.gov.pt.

TELAVI, Willy; Prime Minister, Government of Tuvalu; ***political career:*** Home Affairs Minister; Prime Minister, Dec. 2010-; ***professional career:*** career policeman; police commissioner of Tuvalu, 1993-2009; ***office address:*** Office of the Prime Minister, Vaiaku, Funafuti, Tuvalu; ***phone:*** +688 20250.

TEMER, Michel; Brazilian, Vice President, Government of Brazil; ***born:*** 23 September 1940, Tietê, State of São Paulo, Brazil; ***parents:*** Miguel Elias Temer Lulia and March Barbar Lulia; ***children:*** Maristela (F), Clarissa (F), Luciana (F); ***education:*** São Paulo (USP) Univ., Brazil, Law, 1959-63; Catholic Pontifical Univ. (PUC), SP, Brazil, Ph.D. in Law, 1974; ***party:*** Partido do Movimento Democrático Brasileiro (PMDB, Brazilian Democratic Movement Party); ***political career:*** Advisor to Sec. Education, State of São Paulo (SP), Brazil, 1963-64; Attorney Gen., State of SP; Chief Attorney Gen., State of SP, 1983-84 & 1992; Federal Dep., PMDB, State of SP, Brazil, Constitutional Assembly, 1987-91; Pres. of Chamber of Deps., Sec. of Govt., State of SP, 1993-94; Federal Dep., State of SP, Brazil, Revision Congress, 1993-95; Federal Dep., State of SP, Brazil, 1995-; Leader of PMDB for National Congress, 1995-96; Interim Pres. of Republic of Brazil, 27-31 January 1998 and 15 June 1999; Vice President, Jan. 2011-; ***professional career:*** Technical Scientific Dir., Schoolbook Foundation, State of SP; Sec., Public Security, State of SP, 1984-86 & 1992-93; Attorney General, State of São Paulo; Pres., Chamber of Deputies, 1997-98, 1999-00; ***honours and awards:*** Brigadeiro Tobias de Aguiar Medal, Military Police, 1985; Centenário do Corpo de Bombeiros Medal, Military Police, 1986; Distinction Prize, Parly. Cat., 1987; Mérito Internacional de Engenharia de Segurança do Trabalho, Ibero-American Assn. of Eng. of Safety in Work, 1987; Lawyer of the Year, golden sword and scale distinction, Brazilian Lawyers Assn., 1988; Armed Forces Order of Merit, Cmdr. Grade, 1996; Naval Order of Merit, Grand Officer Grade, 1996; Military Order of Merit, Grand Officer Grade, 04, 1997; Rio Branco Order (Min. of Foreign Relations), Grand Cross Grade, 04, 1997; Alferes Joaquim José da Silva Xavier Medal, Govt. of the Federal District, 05, 1997; Air Force Order of Merit, Grand Officer Grade, 09, 1997; Military Judiciary Order of Merit, 04, 1998; Paraguay Nat. Order of Merit, Grand Cross; Portuguese Honorific Order, Grand Cross; Legion of Honor, France; Honorary Citizen Title for the municipalities of Capivari-SP, Cerquilho-SP, Jundiaí-SP, Praia Grande-SP, Capela do Alto-SP, Lupérico-SP, Guareí-SP, Barretos-SP, Duartina-SP, Lucianopolis-SP and São José do Rio Preto-SP; Military Order of Merit, 04, 1999; Brasília Order of Merit, Grand Master, 04, 1999; Order of Dannebrog, Grand Cross, Denmark Reign, 05, 1999; Military Federal Public Prosecution Order of Merit, Grand Cross, 10, 1999; Medalha Comemorativa do Sesquicentenário de Nascimento de Rui Barbosa, Ministry of Culture, Casa de Rui Barbosa Foundation, 11, 1999; Colar do Mérito Seabra Fagundes, São Paulo Court of Accounts, 11, 1999; ***publications:*** numerous articles published in specialised magazines and periodicals, Federal Territory in the Brazilian Constitutions, Revista dos Tribunais, 1975; Elements of Constitutional Law, 13th edition, Malheiros, 1977; Your Rights in the Constitutional Assembly, 1989; Constitution and Politics, Malheiros, 1994; ***office address:*** Office of the Vice President, Palacio do Planalto, 30 Andar, 70150-900 Brasilia DF, Brazil; ***phone:*** +55 (0)61 411 1202; ***fax:*** +55 (0)61 411 2222.

TEO, Chee Hean; Minister for Defence, Government of Singapore; ***born:*** 27 December 1954; ***married:*** Chew Poh Yim; ***s:*** 1; ***d:*** 1; ***education:*** St Michael's School and St Joseph's Inst.; received commission, Singapore Armed Forces Training Inst., 1973; awarded President's Scholarship and SAF Scholarship, BSc., Univ. of Manchester Inst. of Science and Technology, 1976; MSc., Computing Science, Imperial Coll., London, 1977; Masters, Public Administration, Kennedy School of Govt., Harvard Univ., 1986; ***political career:*** MP, Marine Parade Gp. of Representation Constituency (GRC), 1992-97; Minister of State in the Ministries of Finance, Communications and Defence; Acting Minister for the Environment and Sr. Minister of State for Defence, 1995; Minister for Environment and Second Minister for Defence, 1996; MP for the Pasir Ris (FRC), 1997-2001; elected MP, Pasir-Ris Punggol GRC, 2001-; Minister for Education and Second Minister for Defence, 1997-2003; Minister for Defence, 2003-; Minister in Charge of the Civil Service, 2003-; ***professional career:*** joined Singapore Armed Forces (SAF), 1972; various command and staff appointments, Republic of Singapore Navy; Chief of Navy, Singapore Navy, 1991; Rear Admiral, 1991-92; ***honours and awards:*** Littauer Fellow, Harvard Univ., 1986; ***office address:*** Ministry of Defence, MINDEF Building, Gombak Drive, 669638, Singapore; ***phone:*** +65 6760 8828.

TEPARAK, H.E. Pasan; Ambassador Extraordinary and Plenipotentiary of Thailand to the UK, Embassy of Thailand; ***born:*** 1961; ***education:*** Thammasat Univ., Thailand, BA, MA; ***professional career:*** joined Ministry of Foreign Affairs, 1984-; Dep. Dir.-Gen., Dept. of Protocol, 2003-06; Consul-General, Royal Thai Consulate-General, 2006-11; Minister, Royal Thai Embassy, Canberra, 2011; Amb. attached to the MFA, 2011-12; Amb. Extraordinary and Plen. to the UK and Northern Ireland, 2012-; ***office address:*** Royal Thai Embassy, 29-30 Queen's Gate, London, SW7 5JB, United Kingdom; ***URL:*** http://www.thaiembassyuk.org.uk/.

TERRACCIANO, H.E. Pasquale; Ambassador, Italian Embassy in the UK; ***born:*** May 1946, Naples, Italy; ***professional career:*** First Sec. to NATO, Brussels, 1989-92; First Counsellor, in London, 1996-2000; Head, Press and Information Service, spokesman, Ministry of Foreign Affairs, 2004-06; Amb. to London, 2013-; ***office address:*** Italian Embassy, 14 Three Kings Yard, Davies Street, London, W1K 4EH, United Kingdom; ***phone:*** +44 (0)20 7312 2200; ***fax:*** +44 (0)20 7312 2230; ***e-mail:*** emblondon@embitaly.org.uk; ***URL:*** http://www.amblondra.esteri.it.

TESTER, Senator Jon; Senator, United States Senate; ***born:*** 21 August 1956; ***education:*** College of Great Falls, BSc. Music, 1978; ***political career:*** Montana Legislature, 1997-2005; Pres., Montana Senate, 2005-06; US Senate, Jan. 2007-; ***professional career:*** Farmer; Music Teacher; ***committees:*** Appropriations; Banking, Housing and Urban Affairs; Homeland Security & Governmental Affairs; Indian Affairs; Veterans' Affairs; ***office address:*** United States Senate, Dirksen Senate Office Building, Washington, DC 20510, USA; ***phone:*** +1 202 224 2644 ; ***fax:*** +1 202 224 8594; ***URL:*** http://www.tester.senate.gov.

THABANE, Hon. Motsoahae Thomas; Prime Minister, Government of Lesotho; ***party:*** All Basotho Convention; ***political career:*** Minister of Foreign Affairs, 1998-2002; Minister of Home Affairs, 2002-04; Minister of Communications, Science and Technology, 2004-07; Prime Minister, Minister of Defence, Police and National Security, 2012-; ***office address:*** Prime Minister's Office, PO Box 527, Maseru 100, Lesotho; ***phone:*** +266 2231 1000; ***fax:*** +266 2231 0444.

THACI, Hashim; Prime Minister, Government of Kosovo; ***born:*** 1968; ***education:*** University of Pristina; ***party:*** Democratic Party of Kosovo; ***political career:*** Prime Minister, 2008-; ***office address:*** Office of the Prime Minister, Rruga Nena Tereze, p.n. 10 000 Pristina, Republic of Kosovo; ***URL:*** http://www.kuvendikosoves.org.

THAHANE, Hon. Dr. Thahane Timothy; Minister of Energy, Meteorology and Water Affairs, Government of Lesotho; ***born:*** 1940; ***education:*** Memorial Univ. of Newfoundland, BA, Economics, B.Comm.; Univ. of Toronto, Masters, Economics; ***political career:*** Senator, 2002-; Minister of Finance & Dev. Planning, 2002; Minister of Energy, Meteorology and Water Affairs, 2012-; ***professional career:*** World Bank, 15 years; Ambassador to the US, 1978-80; Dep. Gov., South African Reserve Bank, 1996-2001; ***honours and awards:*** LLD, Honoris Causa, Memorial Univ. of St. Johns; ***office address:*** Ministry of Energy and Natural Resources, PO Box 426, Maseru, Lesotho; ***phone:*** +266 2232 3163; ***URL:*** http://www.lesotho.gov.ls/mnfinance.htm.

THAMMAVONG, Thongsing; Prime Minister, Government of Laos; ***party:*** Lao People's Revolutionary Party (LPRP); ***political career:*** Mem. of the LPRP Politburo, 1991-; Pres., National Assembly, 2006-10; Prime Minister, 2010-; ***office address:*** Office of the Prime Minister, Lane Xang Avenue, Vientiane, Laos PDR; ***phone:*** +856 21 213652.

THAN, Chhay; Senior Minister, Minister of Planning, Government of Cambodia; ***born:*** 21 October 1947, Takeo, Cambodia; ***parents:*** Chhay Thol and Duong Eth; ***married:*** Say Yi, 1967 (Dec'd); ***children:*** Chhay Ridhisen (M), Chhay Kalyane (F), Chhay Satia (M), Chhay Phalkun (F); ***languages:*** English, French; ***education:*** Phnom Penh Univ. of Cambodia, Business Studies; ***party:*** Cambodian People's Party (CPP); ***political career:*** Senior Minister, Minister of Planning, to date; ***professional career:*** Financial Accountant; ***honours and awards:*** Kingdom medal; ***office address:*** Ministry of Planning, 386 Preah Monivong Blvd. , Phnom-Penh, Cambodia; ***phone:*** +855 (023) 212049; ***fax:*** +855 (023) 217045; ***URL:*** http://www.mop.gov.kh.

THARMAN, Shanmugaratnam; Deputy Prime Minister and Minister for Finance and Manpower, Government of Singapore; ***married:*** Jane Yumiko Ittogi; ***public role of spouse:*** Chair of Singapore Art Museum; ***education:*** London School of Economics and Cambridge Univ., MPhil in Economics; Masters in Public Admin., Harvard Univ., USA, Littauer Fellow award; ***political career:*** Snr. Minister of State, Min. for Trade and Industry and Min. for Education, 2001-03; Minister of Education, 2003-08; Minister for Finance, 2007-, also now Deputy Prime Minister, 2011-, and Minister for Manpower, 2011-; ***professional career:*** Man. Dir., Monetary Authority of Singapore (MAS); ***office address:*** Ministry of Finance, 100 High Street #06-03, The Treasury, Singapore 179343, Singapore.

THEPKANJANA, Phongthep; Thai, Deputy Prime Minister, Minister of Education, Social and Legal Affairs, Government of Thailand; ***born:*** 13 November 1958, Samut Sakhon; ***education:*** Thammasat Univ., L.L.B.; George Washington Univ., MA Comparative Law, Foreign Practice; The School of Thai Bar, Barrister at Law; George Washington Univ., MA, Comparative Law, American Practice; Office of the Civil Service Cmn., High Ranking Exec. Training Program; ***political career:*** Dep. Sec.-Gen., Office of the Judicial Affairs, 1992-94; Spokesman, Ministry of Justice; Dep. Spokesman, Office of the Prime Minister, 1995-96; Mem., Constitution Drafting Assembly, 1996-97; Dep. Sec.-Gen., Thai Rak Thai Party, 1998-2001; Mem., House of Representatives, 2001; Minister of Justice, 2001-2002; Dep. Leader, Thai Rak Thai Party, 2001-07 (party disbanded); Minister to the Prime Minister's Office, 2002; Minister of Energy, 2002-03; Minister of Justice, 2003-05; Banned from political office as former member of Thai Rak Thai Party, 2007-12; Deputy Prime Minister, Minister of Legal and Social Affairs, 2012-; ***professional career:*** Assoc., Baker and McKenzie, 1981-82; Judge Trainee, 1984-85; Judge, Sakon Nakhon, Provincial Court, 1985-87; Judge attached to the Ministry working as Asst. Judge of the Supreme Court, 1987-88; Judge attached to the Ministry working as Dir., Legal Affairs Division, 1988-91; Judge, Samut Prakan Provincial Court, 1991-92; Chief Judge attached to the Ministry working as Chief Judge of Nonthaburi Provincial Court, 1994-95; Chief Judge attached to the Ministry working as Chief Judge of Chonburi Provincial Court, Juvenile and Family Division, 1995; *office address:* Ministry of Education, 319 Chandakasem Palace, Ratchadamnoen Road, Bangkok , Thailand; *URL:* http://www.moe.go.th/.

THESSIN, James; Ambassador to Paraguay, US Embassy; *education:* Catholic Univ. of Washington D.C.; Harvard Univ. School of Law; *professional career:* Attorney; career mem., Senior Executive Service; Assist Legal Adviser, Management, Human Rights & Refugee Affairs, Dept. of State; Attorney-Advisor for Political Military Affairs, Dept. of State; Deputy Legal Adviser, Dept. of State, 1990-; US Amb. to Paraguay, 2011-; *office address:* US Embassy, 1776 Mariscal Lopez Ave, Casilla Postal 402, Asunción, Paraguay.

THINLEY, Jigme; Prime Minister, Government of Bhutan; *born:* 9 September 1952, Zangling, Bumthang, Central Bhutan; *children:* 3; *education:* BA, St. Stephen's Coll. Delhi Univ. India, 1974; MPA, Pennsylvania State Univ. USA, 1976; *party:* President, Bhutan Harmony Party; *political career:* Minister of Foreign Affairs, 1998-2003; Chmn. of the Cabinet; Minister of Home & Cultural Affairs, 2003-07; Prime Minister, 1998-99, 2003-04, March 2008-; *professional career:* Perm. Rep. of the Kingdom of Bhutan to the UN's Office and other Int. Organizations in Geneva. Accredited simultaneously as Ambassador to Austria, Denmark, the European Union, Finland, the Netherlands, Norway, Sweden and Switzerland, 1994-98; Chairman, Ugyen Wangchuck Institute of Conservation and Environment (NWICE), 2009-; Chairperson, Royal Education Council, 2009-; *recreations:* gardening, archery, golf; *office address:* Office of the Prime Minister, PO Box 139 Gyelyong Tshogduthimpu, Thimphu, Bhutan.

THOMAS, Clarence; Associate Justice, US Supreme Court; *born:* 23 June 1948, Georgia; *education:* Holy Cross College, A.B., cum laude; Yale Law School, J.D., 1974; *professional career:* law practice, Missouri, 1974-; Assist. Attorney Gen., of Missouri, 1974-77; Attorney, Monsanto Company, 1977-79; Legislative Assist. to Senator John Danforth, 1979-81; Assist. Sec. for Civil Rights, U.S. Dept of Education, 1981-82; Chmn., U.S. Equal Employment Opportunity Cmn., 1982-90; Judge, US Court of Appeals, District of Columbia Circuit, 1990-91; Associate Justice of the Supreme Court, 1991- ; *office address:* Supreme Court Building, One First Street, NE, Washington, DC 20543, USA; *phone:* +1 202 479 3211; *URL:* http://www.supremecourt.gov/.

THOMAS, Gareth Richard; Member of Parliament for Harrow West, House of Commons; *party:* Labour Party; *political career:* MP, Harrow West, 1997-; PPS to Sec. of State for Education, Rt. Hon. Charles Clarke MP, 1999-2003; Parly. Under Sec. of State, Dept. for Int. Development, 2003-08; Minister of State, Dept. of Business, Enterprise & Regulatory Reform, 2008-09; Shadow Minister (jointly with International Development), 2010; Shadow Minister, Business, Innovation and Skills, Oct. 2010-11; Shadow Minister in the Cabinet Office, 2011-; *interests:* energy, environment, co-operatives, education; *publications:* 'Energy at the Crossroads', Fabian Society, 2001; *recreations:* canoeing, Rugby Union, jazz, triathlons; *office address:* House of Commons, London, SW1A 0AA, United Kingdom; *phone:* +44 (0)20 7219 4243; *e-mail:* thomasgr@parliament.uk.

THOMAS, Gwenda; Constituency Member for Neath, National Assembly for Wales; *party:* Labour; *political career:* mem., Nat. Assembly for Wales, Neath; Dep. Minister for Social Services, 2009-11; Dep. Minister for Children and Social Services, 2011-; *office address:* National Assembly for Wales, Cardiff Bay, Cardiff, CF99 1NA, United Kingdom; *phone:* +44 (0)29 2089 8750; *fax:* +44 (0)29 2089 8380.

THOMAS OF GRESFORD, Lord; Member of the House of Lords; *political career:* Mem., House of Lords, 1996-; Shadow Attorney General, 2004-06; Shadow Lord Chancellor, 2006-07; Shadow Attorney General 2007-10; Shadow Spokesperson for Justice 2007-10; *office address:* House of Lords, London, SW1A 0PQ, United Kingdom; *phone:* +44 (0)20 7219 3000; *fax:* +44 (0)20 7219 5979.

THOMAS OF WALLISWOOD, Baroness , OBE, DL; Member of the House of Lords; *born:* 20 December 1935, London; *parents:* John Arrow and Ebba Arrow (née Roll); *married:* David Churchill Thomas, 1958; *s:* 1; *d:* 2; *public role of spouse:* Former member of HM Diplomatic Service; *languages:* French, Spanish; *education:* Cranbourne Chase Sch.; Lady Margaret Hall, Oxford; *party:* Liberal Democrat; *political career:* County Councillor, Surrey, 1985-97; Chwm., Highways and Transport Cttee., 1993-96; Mem. House of Lords, 1994; Spokesperson on Transport, 1994-2001; chwn., of County Council, 1996-97; Spokesperson on Women's Issues, 2001; *committees:* House of Lords Select Cttee. on European Union: Sub-Cttee., E. 2001-04; Sub-Cttee., G, (Chmn.), 2004-07; mem., House of Lords Select Cttee. on European Union, 2004-07; *honours and awards:* OBE, 1989; DL, 1996; *office address:* c/o House of Lords, London, SW1A 0PW, United Kingdom; *phone:* +44 (0)20 7219 3599; *fax:* +44 (0)20 7219 0638; *e-mail:* thomass@parliament.uk.

THONDAMAN, Arumugam Ramanathan; Minister of Livestock and Rural Communities, Government of Sri Lanka; *political career:* Minister of Housing and Plantation Infrastructure; Minister of Livestock and Rural Communities, 2010-; *office address:* Ministry of Livestock and Rural Communities, 45 St Michael's Road, PO Box 562, Colombo 03, Sri Lanka; *phone:* +94 11 254 1369; *URL:* http://www.gov.lk.

THORNBERRY, Emily; MP for Islington South and Finsbury, House of Commons; *born:* 1960; *party:* Labour; *political career:* MP for Islington South and Finsbury, 2005-; Shadow Minister, Health, Oct. 2010-11; Shadow Attorney General, 2011-; *office address:* House of Commons, London, SW1A 0AA, United Kingdom; *e-mail:* thornberrye@parliament.uk.

THORNE, David; Ambassador, US Embassy in Italy; *languages:* Italian; *education:* BA, Yale Univ., 1966; MA in Journalism, Columbia Univ., 1971 ; *professional career:* Co-founder, Adviser Investments; former Pres., Board mem., Institute of Contemporary Art in Boston; Amb. to Italy, 2009-; *office address:* US Embassy, via Vittorio Veneto 121, 00187 Rome, Italy; *phone:* +39 06 46741; *fax:* +39 06 488 2672; *URL:* http://rome.usembassy.gov .

THORNING-SCHMIDT, Helle; Prime Minister, Government of Denmark; *born:* 1966; *married:* Stephen Kinnock; *public role of spouse:* Head, World Economic Forum; *languages:* English, French; *education:* BA, Univ. of Copenhagen, 1994; MA, College of Europe, Bruges, Belgium; *party:* Leader, Social Democrats, 2005-; *political career:* Mem., European Parliament, 1999-2004; MP, 2005-; Prime Minister, Oct. 2011-; *office address:* Office of the Prime Minister, Christiansborg, Prins Jørgens Gård 11, 1218 Copenhagen K, Denmark; *phone:* +45 3392 3300; *fax:* +45 3311 1665; *e-mail:* stm@stm.dk; *URL:* http://www.stm.dk.

THORNTON, H.E. James; High Commissioner to Zambia, British High Commission; *education:* Oxford Univ.; *professional career:* joined Foreign & Commonwealth Office, 1989; postings include: New York, Algiers, Mexico City, London, Abidjan, Sudan, Paris; High Commissioner to Zambia, 2012-; *office address:* British High Commission, 5210 Independence Avenue, P.O Box 50050, 15101 Ridgeway , Lusaka, Zambia.

THUNE, John; American, Senator for South Dakota and Chmn. Rep. Policy Cttee., US Senate; *party:* Republican; *political career:* mem., US House of Representatives, 1996-2003; Senator for South Dakota, US Senate, 2004-; Chmn., Rep. Policy Cttee., 2009-; *committees:* Commerce, Science and Transportation; Finance; Chmn., Senate Republican Conference; *office address:* 383 Russell, Senate Office Building, Washington, DC 20510, USA; *URL:* http://www.thune.senate.gov.

TIANGAYE, Nicolas; Prime Minister, Government of the Central African Republic; *born:* 1956; *political career:* Pres. of the National Transitional Council, 2003-05; Prime Minister, 2013-; *professional career:* Lawyer; *office address:* Office of the Prime Minister , Bangui, Central African Republic; *URL:* http://www.rcainfo.org.

TIAO, Luc-Adolphe; Prime Minister, Government of Burkina Faso; *born:* June 1954; *education:* Univ. of Ouagadougou, Burkina Faso; *party:* Congress for Democracy and Progress; *political career:* Prime Minister, 2011-; *professional career:* Amb. to France, 2008-11; *office address:* Office of the Prime Minister, BP 7027, Ouagadougou, Burkina Faso; *phone:* +226 5032 4889; *fax:* 226 5031 4761; *URL:* http://www.primature.gov.bf/republic/fgouvernement.htm.

TILLICH, Stanislaw; Prime Minster, State Government of Saxony; *born:* 1959; *education:* Technical Univ. Dresden, construction engineering; *party:* CDU; *political career:* mem., Kamenz Municipal Council, 1987-89, Dep. Chmn., 1989; Mem., GDR People's Assembly, 1990; Observer, Euro. Parliament, 1991-94; mem., European Parliament, 1994-99; Minister of Federal European Affairs; Plenipotentiary, Free State of Saxony for Federal Affairs; Chief of the State Chancellery, 2002; State Minister for Environment and Agriculture; Saxon State Minister of Finances, 2007-08; Prime Minister, Sate of Saxony, 2008-; *office address:* Office of the Prime Minister, Saxon State Chancellery, 01905 Dresden, Germany; *phone:* +49 (0)351 564 0; *URL:* http://www.sachsen.de/.

TIMERMAN, Héctor M.; Minister of Foreign Affairs, International Trade and Religion, Government of Argentina; *born:* 16 December 1953, Buenos Aires; *education:* Columbia Univ., New York, Master's in International Affairs, 1981; *political career:* Minister of Foreign Affairs, International Trade and Religion, 2011-; *memberships:* Co-Fndr. & Bd. Mem., Human Rights Watch, New York, 1981-89; Dir., Fund for Free Expression, London, 1983-89; Bd. of Dirs., Permanent Assembly for Human Rights, Buenos Aires, 2002-04; Pres., Bd. of Dirs., Int'l. Coalition of Historic Sites Museums of Conscience; *professional career:* Journalist; Writer for Noticias and Ámbito Financiero; Co-dir., Debate; Host of television and radio programmes; Contributor to The New York Times, Newsweek, The Nation, and The Los Angeles Times; Lecturer on Human Rights, New York, 1979-83, 2005-06; Exiled in the USA, 1978-84; Consul General, New York, 2004-07; Amb. to USA, 2007-; *publications:* co-author of "Torture", New Press, 2005; *office address:* Ministry of Foreign Affairs, Esmeralda 1212, 1007 Buenos Aires, Argentina; *phone:* +54 (0)11 4819 7000; *fax:* +54 (0)11 4819 7501; *e-mail:* web@cancilleria.gov.ar; *URL:* http://www.mrecic.gov.ar.

TIMMERMANS, Drs Frans; Minister of Foreign Affairs, Netherlands Government; *born:* 1961; *education:* Radboud Univ., Nijmegen; Univ. of Nancy; *political career:* various postings, Ministry of Foreign Affairs, 1987; Mem., House of Reps., 1998; Minister for European Affairs, 2007-10; Spoksepserson on Foreign Policy, PvdA, 2010-12; Minister of Foreign Affairs, 2012-; *office address:* Ministry of Foreign Affairs & Development Co-operation, Bezuidenhoutseweg 67, 2500 EB The Hague, Netherlands; *URL:* http://www.minbuza.nl.

TIMMS, Stephen Creswell; British, MP for East Ham, House of Commons; *born:* 29 July 1955; *education:* Cambridge Univ., MA, M.Phil.; *party:* Labour Party; *political career:* Cncl. Leader, London Borough of Newham, 1990-94; MP, Newham East, 1994-97; MP, East Ham, 1997-; Financial Sec., HM Treasury, 1999-2001; Minister for Schools, Dept. for Education and Skills, 2001-02; Minister of State for Energy, E-Commerce and Postal Services, 2002-05; Minister for Pensions, 2005-06; Chief Secretary to the Treasury, May 2006-June 2007; Minister for Competitiveness, 2007-08; Minister for Employment and Welfare Reform, 2008; Financial Sec., HM Treasury, 2008-10; concurrently Minister for Digital Britain, 2009-10; Shadow Financial Secretary, 2010-; Shadow Minister for Business, Innovation and Skills, 2010; Shadow Minister, Work and Pensions, Oct. 2010-; *interests:* treasury, East London regeneration, education; *professional career:* Telecoms Analyst; *office address:* House of Commons, London, SW1A 0AA, United Kingdom; *phone:* +44 (0)20 7219 3000; *e-mail:* stephen@stephentimms.org.uk.

TIMOFTI, Nicolae; President, Republic of Moldova; *born:* 1949; *party:* Independent; *political career:* President, Government of Moldova, 2012-; *professional career:* Judge; Chmn., Supreme Magistrates Council, -2012; *office address:* Office of the President, Stefan cel Mare 154, Krishinev, Moldova; *phone:* +373 2 234793; *URL:* http://www.president.md.

TIMPSON, Edward; MP for Crewe and Nantwich, House of Commons; *parents:* John Timpson and Alex Timpson; *married:* Julia Timpson; *education:* Durham University; *party:* Conservative; *political career:* MP for Crewe and Nantwich, May 2008-; PPS to

Theresa May, Home Secretary, 2010-12; Parly. Under-Sec. of State, Dept. of Education, 2012-; ***professional career:*** Called to the Bar, 1998, specialising in family law; ***office address:*** House of Commons, London, SW1 0AA, United Kingdom; ***phone:*** +44 (0)20 7219 8027.

TINE, Augustin; Minister of Armed Forces, Government of Senegal; ***political career:*** Political activist; Left Parti democratique senegalais, joined Macky Sall, Alliance for the Republic (APR);Minister of Armed Forces, 2012-; ***professional career:*** Dentist; ***office address:*** Ministry of Armed Forces, Immeuble Administratif, 8e étage, BP 4041, Dakar, Senegal; ***phone:*** +221 33 849 7612; ***fax:*** +221 33 823 6338; ***URL:*** http://www.forcesarmees.gouv.sn.

TIPTON, Scott; Congressman, US House of Representatives; ***party:*** Republican; ***political career:*** Congressman, HOR, Colorado 3rd District, 2010-; ***committees:*** Agriculture; Small Business; Natural Resources; ***office address:*** 128 Cannon HOB, Washington 20515, USA; ***URL:*** http://tipton.house.gov/.

TIZZANO, Professor Antonio; Italian, Judge, Court of Justice of the European Union; ***born:*** 1 January 1940; ***languages:*** Italian, French, English; ***education:*** University of Naples, Law Faculty, Graduate, Magna cum laude, 1962; Legal qualification: Professor; ***interests:*** Dispute settlement; Economic law; Jurisdiction; Human rights; Litigation; Organisations; ***memberships:*** Société française pour le droit international; Association Henri Capitant des amis de la culture juridique française; Società italiana di diritto internazionale; Associazione italiana di diritto comparato; Istituto Affari Internazionali; ***professional career:*** *academic career:* University of Naples, Assistant at the Law Faculty, 1962-67, Professor of European Community Law, 1979-92; National University of Somalia, Mogadishu and the University of Catania, Professor of International Law, 1969-77; Courses at The Hague Academy of International Law, 1987; University of Rome "La Sapienza", Professor of European Community Law, 1993-; Lecturer at numerous Italian and foreign universities; Rapporteur at many international Colloquia; *professional career:* Principal adviser of the Romanian Government in the framework of the ECPHARE programme for the approximation of the legislation in view of the adhesion of Romania to the EU, 1995-97; *governmental career:* Member of the Committee of independent experts established by the European Parliament and by the European Commission for the examination of the financial administration of the Commission, 1999; Member of the working party set up by the European University Institute, Florence, to draw up for the European Commission a report on the reorganisation of the Treaties of the EU, 2000-; Member of Council Research, European University Institut (Florence), 2003-; *diplomatic career:* Legal adviser to the Italian Permanent Representation to the European Communities, Brussels, 1984-92; Member of the Italian delegation in several negotiations and in the Intergovernmental Conferences for the Adhesion of Spain and Portugal to the EEC, 1985, for the Single European Act, 1985-86, and for the Maastricht Treaty on the EU, 1990-92; *judicial career:* Advocate General at the Court of Justice of European Communities; ***publications:*** Books: La Corte di Giustizia delle Comunità Europee, 1967; La Politica Mediterranea delle CEE, 1981; Professioni Servizi Nella CEE, 1985; Problematica del Diritto delle Comunità Europee, 1992; Codice dell'Unione Europea, 1st ed, 1995, 5th ed, 2005; Il Diritto Privato dell'Unione Europea, 2000; Il Trattato di Nizza, 2003; Una Costituzione per L'Europa, 2004; Trattati dell'Unione Europea e della Comunità Europea, 2004; Articles: Il Foro Italiano; Cahiers de droit européen; Pouvoirs; Revue du Marché Commun; The Italian Yearbook of International Law; Revue du Droit de L'Union Européenne; Rivista di diritto internazionale; L'Actualité juridique-Droit administratif; Contratto e Impresa/Europa; La Comunità Internazionale; Il Diritto dell'Unione Europea; ***office address:*** Court of Justice of the European Communities, Boulevard Adenauer, L-2925, Luxembourg; ***phone:*** +352 4303 2220; ***fax:*** +352 4303 2060; ***e-mail:*** Antonio.tizzano@curia.eu.int.

TOBBACK, Louis; Belgian, Mayor, Leuven, Belgium; ***born:*** 3 May 1938, Leuven, Belgium; ***parents:*** Jean Tobback and Maria Tobback (née Melis); ***married:*** Jenny Tobback (née Depus); ***public role of spouse:*** Barrister; ***languages:*** Dutch, French, English, German, Italian; ***education:*** Univ. of Brussels (VUB), Licentiate of Romanic Philology, 1962; ***party:*** Socialist Party; ***political career:*** Mem. of the Public Centre of Social Welfare, Cncl. of Leuven, 1965-70; Town Cllr. of Leuven, 1971-, Alderman 1971-76; MP for the constituency of Leuven 1974-91; Chmn. of the Flemish Socialist Gp. in the House of Representatives, 1978-88; Senator for the constituency of Leuven 1991-2003; Minister of the Interior, of the Modernisation of Public Services and of the Nat. Cultural and Scientific Instns., 1988-92; Minister of the Interior and of Civil Public Servants, 1992-94; Chmn, Flemish Socialist Party, 1994-98; Mayor of Leuven, 1995-; Vice Prime Minister and Minister of the Interior, 1998; Mayor of Leuven 1995-; Minister of State; ***professional career:*** Teacher of French, Koninklijk Atheneum, Leuven, 1962-74; ***office address:*** Office of the Mayor, Professor Van Overstraetenplein 1, 3000 Leuven, Belgium; ***phone:*** +32 (0)16 272211; ***e-mail:*** louis.tobback@leuven.be.

TOEWS, Hon. Victor Eric, QC; Minister of Public Safety, Government of Canada; ***married:*** Lorraine Toews; ***education:*** Univ. of Manitoba, Bachelor of Laws, 1976; ***political career:*** Min. of Labour, 1995; MLA for Rossmere; Min. of Justice and Attorney-Gen., Keeper of the Great Seal, Min. Responsible for Constitutional Affairs, 1997-99; Opposition critic for Justice, 2001-06; Minister of Justice and Attorney General of Canada, 2006-07; President of the Treasury Board, 2007-10; Minister of Public Safety, 2010-; ***professional career:*** Crown Counsel, Dept. of the Attorney Gen., 1977; QC, 1991; ***office address:*** House of Commons, Parliament Building, Wellington Street, Ottawa, Ontario, KA1 0A6, Canada.

TOLLEY, Anne; Minister of Police, Corrections, Deputy Leader of the House, Government of New Zealand; ***political career:*** MP for East Coast, 1999-; Minister for Education, Minister for Tertiary Education and Minister Responsible for ERO, 2008-11; Minister of Police, Corrections, Deputy Leader of the House, 2011-; ***office address:*** Ministry of Police, Charles Fergusson Building, Bowen Street, Wellington, New Zealand; ***phone:*** +64 (0)4 463 9700.

TOMADO, Dr. Carlos Alfonso; Minister of Labour, Employment and Human Resources, Government of Argentina; ***born:*** 4 May 1948; ***education:*** Univ. of Buenos Aires, Law, 1973; Univ. de Castilla La Mancha and Univ. of Bologna, Postgrad studies in Industrial Relations, 2000; ***political career:*** National Dir. of Work Relations, 1987-89; Sec. of Work; Minister of Labour, Employment and Human Resources, 2003-; ***office address:*** Ministry of Labour, Employment and Human Resources, Avenue Leandro N. Alem 650, 1001 Buenos Aires, Argentina; ***phone:*** +54 (0)11 4310 6000; ***fax:*** +54 (0)11 4310 6424; ***e-mail:*** consultas@trabajo.gov.ar; ***URL:*** http://www.trabajo.gov.ar.

TOMBLIN, Earl Ray; Governor, West Virginia; ***born:*** 1952; ***education:*** West Virginia Univ.; MBA, Marshall Univ.; ***political career:*** elected to West Virginia House of Delegates, 1974-190; mem., West Virginia Senate, 1980-; Pres., Senate, 1995-; Lt. Gov., 2000-2010; Gov. of West Virginia, 2010-; ***office address:*** Office of the Governor, 1900 Kanawha Boulevard E., Charleston WV 25305, USA; ***URL:*** http://www.state.wv/.

TOMI, Vincente Ehate; Prime Minister, Government of Equatorial Guinea; ***born:*** 1968; ***political career:*** Minister of Transport, Technology, Posts and Telecommunications; Prime Minister, Minister in Charge of Administrative Co-ordination, 2012-; ***office address:*** Office of the Prime Minister, Malabo, Equatorial Guinea; ***URL:*** http://guinea-equatorial.com.

TOMKA, Judge Dr Peter; Slovak, President, International Court of Justice; ***born:*** 1 June 1956; ***languages:*** Czech, Slovak, English, French, Russian; ***education:*** Charles University, Prague, LLM, 1979, Civil Law (summa cum laude), Doctor Juris, 1981, PhD, 1985, International Law, thesis on "Codification of International Law"; Institut de Droit de la Paix et du Développement, Nice, 1984-85; ***interests:*** Claims; Criminal Law; Dispute settlement; Jurisdiction; History & theory; Litigation; Organisations; State responsibility; Law of the Sea; Territory/boundaries; Treaties; ***memberships:*** Czechoslovak Society of International Law, 1981-92, Learned Secretary, 1986-91; ILA, Czechoslovak Branch, 1988-2001, Secretary, 1988-91; Slovak Society of International Law, 1982-, Honorary President, 2004-; ASIL, 2000-; ESIL, 2004-; International Arbitration Institute, 2005-; ***professional career:*** *academic career:* Charles University, Faculty of Law, Assistant, 1980-84, Reader, 1984-86, Adjunct Reader, 1986-91, Public International Law; Comenius University, Bratislava, Faculty of Law, Adjunct Reader, 1997-99, Public International Law; *professional career:* Agent of Slovakia in the Gabčikovo-Nagymaros Project (Hungary/Slovakia) case (ICJ), 1993-2003; Expert of Slovakia in Ceskoslovenská obchodní banka v the Slovak Republic (ICSID case No ARB/97/4), 1997-99; Member, ILC, 1999-2002; *governmental career:* Ministry of Foreign Affairs, Czechoslovakia, Assistant Legal Adviser, 1986-90, Head of Public International Law Division, 1990-91; Legal Adviser, Permanent Mission of Czechoslovakia to the UN, 1991-92; Legal Adviser and Director of International Law Department, Ministry of Foreign Affairs, Slovakia, 1997-98; Legal Adviser and Director General for Legal and Consular Affairs, Slovakia, 1998-99; *diplomatic career:* Ambassador-Deputy Permanent Representative of Slovakia to the UN, 1993-94; Ambassador-Acting Permanent Representative of Slovakia to the UN, 1994-97; Ambassador-Permanent Representative of Slovakia to the UN, 1999-2003; UNGA Sixth Committee, Chairman, 1997, (International Convention for the Suppression of Terrorist Bombings), Representative of Czechoslovakia, 1990-92, Representative of Slovakia, 1993-2002; President of the Ninth Meeting of States Parties to UN Convention on Law of the Sea, 1999; Chairman, Committee of Legal Advisers on Public International Law, Council of Europe, 2001-02; Chairman, ad hoc Committe on the International Convention against the Reproductive Cloning of Human Beings, 2002; Preparatory Commission for the International Sea-Bed Authority and ITLOS, Representative of Czechoslovakia, 1987-92, Representative of Slovakia, 1993-94; Head of Slovakian Delegation to the Assembly of the International Sea-Bed Authority, 1994-96; Preparatory Commission, ICC, Vice-Chairman, 1998, Representative of Slovakia, 1999-2002; Alternate Head of Delegation of Slovakia, Diplomatic Conference on the Establishment of the International Criminal Court, 1998; *judicial career:* Judge, ICJ, 2003-, Vice-Pres., 2009-12, Pres., 2012-; Arbitrator, Iron Rhine Railway case (Belgium/Netherlands), 2003-05; Member, PCA, 1994-; List of Arbitrators under Annex VII of UN Law of the Sea Convention, 2004-; Panel of Arbitrators maintained by ICSID, 2005-; ***publications:*** Articles: AJIL, Právník; Several in books; ***office address:*** International Court of Justice, Peace Palace, Carnegleplein 2, 2517 KJ The Hague, The Netherlands; ***phone:*** +31 (0)70 302 2323; ***fax:*** +31 (0)70 302 2409; ***e-mail:*** p.tomka@icj-cij.org; ***URL:*** http://www.Icj-cij.org.

TOMLINSON, Justin; MP for North Swindon, UK Government; ***party:*** Conservative; ***political career:*** Councillor, Swindon Borough Council, 2000-; MP for North Swindon, May 2010-; ***office address:*** House of Commons, London, SW1A 0AA, United Kingdom; ***phone:*** +44 (0)20 7219 3000; ***e-mail:*** justin.tomlinson.mp@parliament.uk.

TOMLINSON OF WALSALL, Lord, Baron John Edward; British, Member, House of Lords; ***born:*** 1939; ***married:*** Marianne Tomlinson (née Somar), 1963 (div'd); Paulette Tomlinson (née Fuller), 1996; ***s:*** 3; ***d:*** 1; ***languages:*** French; ***education:*** Westminster City Sch.; Co-operative Coll.; Brunel Univ.; Warwick Univ.; ***party:*** Labour; ***political career:*** MP (Lab.) for Meriden, 1974-79; PPS to the Prime Minister, 1975-76; Parly. Under-Sec. of State, FCO, 1976-79; Parly. Sec., Min. of Overseas Devt., 1977-79; MEP for Birmingham West, 1984-99; Mem., House of Lords; ***professional career:*** Sec., Sheffield Co-operative Party, 1962-68; Head of Research Dept., Amalgamated Union of Engineering Workers, 1968-70; Lecturer in Industrial Relations, 1970-74; Head of Dept. of Social Studies, Solihull Coll. of Technology; Pres., British Fluoridation Society; Chair, Advisory Bd., London School of Commerce, 2005-; Chair, Assoc. of Independent Higher Education Providers, 2006-; Chair of Gov., Anglia Ruskin Univ., 2011-; ***committees:*** Hansard Soc., Labour Movement in Europe; House of Lords, European Union Select Cttee.; Mem., British deleg. to Council of Europe and Western European Union; ***trusteeships:*** Industry and Parliament Trust, to 2007; ***honours and awards:*** Hon. LL.D., Univ. of Birmingham; Hon. Fellowship, Univ. of Wales Inst. Cardiff; ***publications:*** Left, Right: The March of Political Extremism in Britain; ***recreations:*** walking, watching sport; ***office address:*** House of Lords, London, SW1A 0PQ, United Kingdom; ***phone:*** +44 (0)20 7219 3000; ***fax:*** +44 (0)20 7219 5979.

TONG, H.E. Anote; President and Minister of Foreign Affairs, Republic of Kiribati; ***born:*** 1952; ***education:*** Canterbury Univ.; London School of Economics; ***political career:*** President of Kiribati, July 2003-; also Minister of Foreign Affairs and Immigration; ***office address:*** Office of the President, PO Box 68, Bairiki, Tarawa, Kiribati; ***phone:*** +686 21183; ***fax:*** +686 21145.

TOOMEY, Patrick J.; American, Senator for Pennsylvania, US Senate; ***education:*** Harvard Univ.; ***party:*** Republican; ***political career:*** mem., US House of Representatives, 1998-2004; mem., US Senate, 2011-; ***professional career:*** Fmr. Vice-Pres. & Dir., Chemical Bank of

New York; ***committees:*** Budget; Banking, Housing & Urban Affairs; Commerce, Science & Transportation; Joint Economic ; ***office address:*** US Senate, 502 Hart Senate Office Building, Washington, DC 20510, USA; ***phone:*** +1 202 224 4254; ***URL:*** http://www.toomey.senate.gov.

TOPE, Lord; Member of the House of Lords; ***born:*** 30 November 1943, Plymouth, UK; ***parents:*** Leslie Tope and Winifred Tope (née Merrick); ***married:*** Margaret Tope (née East), 1972; ***children:*** Andrew (M), David (M); ***education:*** Whitgift School, South Croydon, UK; ***party:*** Liberal Democrats; ***political career:*** Vice-Chmn. National League of Young Liberals, 1971-73, Pres, 1973-75; Liberal MP for Sutton & Cheam, 1972-74; Cllr., London Borough of Sutton, 1974-; Liberal Democrat Leader, London Borough of Sutton, 1974-99; Leader of the Council, 1986-99; Pres. London Liberal Democrats, 1991-2000; Assn. of London Govt., Vice-chmn., 1997-99; Local Gov. Assn.: Vice-Pres., 1997-2005; House of Lords: Liberal Democrat Education Spokesperson, 1994-2000; Asst. Whip, 1996-99; Vice Chmn. All Party Parly. Libraries Gp., 1998-; Vice Chmn., Britain-Bermuda Parly. Gp.; Mem., House of Lords; Greater London Authority; Liberal Democrat Leader, 2000-06; mem., Mayor of London's Advisory Cabinet, 2000-08; Metropolitan Police Authority, 2000-08; Communities & Local Gov. Spokesperson, 2009-10; Co-Chair, Lib. Dem Communities & Local Government, Parly. Cttee., 2010-; ***professional career:*** Unilever Ltd., 1961-69; Air Products Ltd., 1970-72; Dep. Gen. Sec., Voluntary Action Camden, 1975-90; ***committees:*** Leader, Cncl. & Chmn. of Policy & Resources Cttee., LB of Sutton, 1986-99, Exec. Councillor, 1999-; London Boroughs Assn. Policy & Finance Cttee., 1986-95, Chmn., 1994-95; Assn. of Metropolitan Authorities, Policy Cttee., 1989-95; Leaders' Cttee., 1995 London Fire & Civil Defence Authority, 1995-97; Vice-chmn., European & Int. Panel, 1997-99, Vice Chmn., European & Int. Executive, 1999-; EU Cttee. of the Regions, 1994-, Bureau Mem., 1996-, Pres., ELDR Gp.,1998-2002 , Vice-Chmn., Institutional Affairs Cmn., 1998-2002; Chair, Constitutional Affairs & European Governance Cttee., 2002-04; Select Cttee. on Relations between Central & Local Govt., 1995-96; London Assembly; Metropolitan Police Authority, Chair of Finance, Planning & Best Value Cttee., 2000-02; Chair, Finance Cttee., 2002-08; ***office address:*** House of Lords, London, SW1A 0PW, United Kingdom; ***e-mail:*** graham.tope@sutton.gov.uk.

TOTH, Tibor; Executive Secretary, Preparatory Commission for the Comprehensive Nuclear-Test-Ban Treaty Organization; ***professional career:*** Amb. and Permanent Rep. of Hungary to the UN in Geneva, 1990-93; Chair, negotiations on Biological Weapons Convention, 1992-2004; negotiator, Chemical Weapons Convention provisions, Executive Council,1992; Amb. and Permanent Rep. of Hungary to the UN in Vienna, 1997-2001; Amb. and Permanent Rep. of Hungary to the UN in Geneva, 2003-05; Exec. Sec., Preparatory Commission, CTBTO, 2005-; ***office address:*** Preparatory Commission for the Comprehensive Nuclear-Test-Ban Treaty Organization, PO Box 1200, A-1400 Vienna, Austria; ***e-mail:*** info@ctbto.org; ***URL:*** http://www.ctbto.org.

TOUHIG, Lord (James) Don, MP; British, Member, House of Lords; ***born:*** 5 December 1947, Abersychan, Gwent; ***married:*** Jennifer Hughes, 1968; ***children:*** Matthew (M), Charlotte (F), James (M), Katie (F); ***education:*** St Francis Sch., Abersychan; Eaast Monmouth College; ***party:*** Labour Party, 1962-; ***political career:*** Cllr., Gwent County, 1973-95; MP (Lab. and Co-op.) Islwyn, 1995-2010; PPS to Rt Hon. Gordon Brown, MP, as Chancellor of the Exchequer, 1997-99; Assist. Gov. Whip, 1999-2001; Parly. Under Sec. of State for Wales, 2001-05; Parly. Under Sec. of State and Minister for Veterans, Min. of Defence, 2005-06; Mem., House of Lords, 2010-; ***interests:*** health (NHS), education, home affairs, treasury (economy, tax), local govt., employment; ***memberships:*** TGWU; Pres., Homestart; Islwyn Drug and Alcohol Project; National OAP Assn. of Wales; Caerphilly CB Access Gp.; MENSA; MENCAP; Amnesty Int.; Islwyn Credit Union; ***professional career:*** Apprentice radio and TV engineer; journalist, 1968-95; Editor, Free Press of Monmouthshire, 1976-90; General Manager, Free Press Group of Newspapers, 1988-92; Gen.Mgr., Bailey Gp., 1992-93; Bailey Print, 1993-95; ***committees:*** fmr. Chmn., Gwent Finance Cttee.; Parly. and Scientific Cttee.; Sec., Welsh Gp. of Labour MPs, 1995-99; Mem., Select Cttee., Welsh Affairs, 1996-97; Sec., All-Party Police Gp., 1996-99; Chair, All Party Alcohol Abuse Gp., 1996-01; Mem., Labour Party Departmental Cttees. for: Home Affairs, 1997-2001, Trade and ind., 1997-2001, the Treasury, 1997-2001, Health, 1997-2001; ***trusteeships:*** Mem., Medical Cncl. on Alcoholism; ***honours and awards:*** Papal Knight of the Order of St. Sylvester; ***recreations:*** reading, cooking, music, walking; ***office address:*** House of Lords, London, SW1A 0PW, United Kingdom; ***phone:*** +44 (0)20 7219 3000; ***fax:*** +44 (0)20 7219 5979; ***e-mail:*** touhigd@parliament.uk; ***URL:*** http://www.dontouhig.org.uk.

TOURAINE, Marisol; Minister for Social Affairs and Health, Government of France; ***born:*** 1959, Paris, France; ***party:*** Socialist Party; ***political career:*** Gen. Cllr., Montbazon; Mem., Assmblée Nationale, 1997-2002, 2007-12; Socialist National Secretary for Social Affairs; Gen. Cllr., Idre-et-Loire, 1998-, Vice-Pres., Council, 2008-11, Pres., 2011-; Minister for Social Affairs and Health, 2012-; ***office address:*** L'Assemblée Nationale, 126 rue de l'université, 75355 Paris, France; ***phone:*** +33 (0)2 47 34 90 90.

TOURÉ, Aminata; Minister of Justice, Government of Senegal; ***born:*** 1962; ***political career:*** human rights activist; election campaigner; Director, cabinet of President Macky Sall, 2010; Minister of Justice, 2012-; ***professional career:*** Head, Marketing and Communication Dept., SOTRAC (public transport), Dakar; Dir., Senegalese Association for Family Wellbeing; United Nations Population Fund, 2003-10, incl. Director Human Rights, New York; ***office address:*** Ministry of Justice, Immeuble Administratif, 7e étage, BP 4030, Dakar, Senegal; ***phone:*** +221 33 823 5024; ***fax:*** +221 33 823 2727 ; ***URL:*** http://www.justice.gouv.sn.

TOURÉ, Dr. Hamadoun; Secretary-General, International Telecommunication Union; ***born:*** 1953; ***education:*** MA, Electrical Engineering, Technical Inst. of Electronics and Telecommunications of Leningrad; Ph.D, Univ. of Electronics, Telecommunications and Informatics of Moscow; ***professional career:*** engineer; various positions, International Telecommunications Satellite Org., 1986-96; Regional Gen. Mgr., ICO Global Communications, 1996-98; Dir., BDT, 1998-2006; Sec.-Gen., Int. Telecommunication Union, 2007- ; ***office address:*** International Telecommunication Union , Place des Nations, CH 1211 Geneva 20, Switzerland; ***URL:*** http://www.itu.int.

TOWICHUKCHAIKUL, Surapong; Minister of Foreign Affairs, Government of Thailand; ***education:*** engineering; ***political career:*** Minister of Foreign Affairs, 2011-; Deputy Prime Minister, 2012-; ***office address:*** Ministry of Foreign Affairs, Wang Saranrom, Bangkok 10200, Thailand.

TRAAVIK, H.E. Kim; Ambassador , Norwegian Embassy in the UK; ***professional career:*** Counsellor at the UN Embassy in Brussels, 1994-97; Amb. to OSCE, 1997-99 Sate Sec., Ministry of Foreign Affairs, 2001-05; Amb. to NATO, 2006-10; Amb.to the United Kingdom, 2010-; ***office address:*** Embassy of Norway, 25 Belgrave Square, London, SW1X 8QD, United Kingdom; ***phone:*** +44 (0)20 7591 5500; ***URL:*** http://www.norway.org.uk.

TRAORÉ, Dioncounda; Interim President, Republic of Mali; ***born:*** 1942; ***political career:*** Minister of the Civil Service, Labour, & Reform, 1992; Minister of Defence, 1993; Minister of State for Foreign Affairs, 1994-97; Pres., National Assembly, 2007-; Interim President, 2012-; ***office address:*** Office of the President, Bamako, Mali.

TREADELL, Vicki; British High Commissioner, New Zealand; ***born:*** 1960, Malaysia; ***professional career:*** Diplomat, postings include Islamabad, Kuala Lumpur, and most recently Deputy High Commissioner, Mumbai, India, 2007-11; High Commissioner, New Zealand, 2011-; ***office address:*** British High Commission, 44 Hill Street, Wellington 6011, New Zealand; ***URL:*** http://ukinnewzealand.fco.gov.uk/en/.

TREDINNICK, David, MP; British, Member of Parliament for Bosworth, House of Commons; ***born:*** 19 January 1950; ***parents:*** Stephen Victor Tredinnick and Evelyn Tredinnick (née Wates); ***married:*** Rebecca Jane Tredinnick (née Shott); ***children:*** Thomas (M), Sophie (F); ***education:*** Graduate Business Sch., Cape Town Univ., MBA; St. John's Coll., Oxford Univ., MLitt.; ***political career:*** Political Research, 1981-85 (Res. Asst. to Kenneth Warren MP and Angela Rumbold CBE, MP); Treasurer, Parly. Gp. for Alternative & Complimentary Medicine, 1989-2002; Chmn., British Atlantic Gp. of Young Politicians, 1989-91; Parly. Private Sec. to Ministry of State for Wales, 1991-94; Co-Chmn., Future of Europe Trust, 1991-95; MP, Bosworth, 1987-; Co-Chmn., Parly. Gp. for Integrated Healthcare, 2002-; ***professional career:*** Trainee, E.B. Savory Milln & Co, 1972-73; Account Exec., Quadrant Int. Salesman, Kalle Infotec, 1976-66; Sales Mgr., Word Processing, 1977-78; Consultant, Baird Communications, New York, 1978-79; Marketing Mgr., Q 1 Europe Ltd., 1979-81; Dir., Malden Mitcham Properties, 1995-; Chmn., Anglo-East European Trading Co., 1990-98; Chmn., Ukrainian Business Agency, 1992-97; ***committees:*** Sec., Conservative Backbench Defence Cttee. and Foreign Affairs Cttees., 1990-91; Chmn., Jt. Cttee. on Statutory Instruments, 1997-2005; Chmn., Select Cttee. on Statutory Instruments, 1997-2005; Health, 2010-; ***publications:*** Protecting the Police, 1982; Policing and Public Order in a Multi-Racial Britain, 1986; ***office address:*** House of Commons, London, SW1A 0AA, United Kingdom; ***e-mail:*** tredinnickd@parliament.uk.

TREES, Lord Alexander John; Member, House of Lords; ***education:*** School of Veterinary Studies, Univ. of Edinburgh; PhD; ***political career:*** Mem., House of Lords, 2012-; ***professional career:*** Professor of Veterinary Parasitology; Dean of the Faculty of Veterinary Science, Univ. of Liverpool, 2001-08; Pres., Royal College of Veterinary Surgeons, 2009-10; mem., Exec. Cttee. of the World Assoc. for the Advancement of Veterinary Parasitology; Chmn., Moredun Research Inst., 2011-; ***office address:*** House of Trees, London, SW1 0AA, United Kingdom; ***phone:*** +44 (0)20 7219 5353.

TRICKETT, Jon Hedley; British, Shadow Minister of State (Cabinet Office), House of Commons; ***born:*** 2 July 1950; ***education:*** Univ. of Hull, BA; Univ. of Leeds, MA; ***party:*** Labour Party; ***political career:*** MP, Hemsworth, 1996-; Shadow Minister of State (Cabinet Office), Oct. 2010-11; Shadow Minister for the Cabinet Office, 2011-; ***interests:*** regional and local government, industry, the economy, sport, culture; ***professional career:*** Plumber; Builder; ***office address:*** House of Commons, London, SW1A 0AA, United Kingdom; ***phone:*** +44 (0)20 7219 3000; ***e-mail:*** trickettj@parliament.uk; ***URL:*** http://www.epolitix.com/webminister/jon-trickett.

TRONCOSO, Carlos Morales; Minister of Foreign Affairs, Government of Dominican Republic; ***political career:*** member and leader Presidential Reformist Counsel, -Dec. 2008; mem., monetary board of the Dominican Republic; vice-pres., Dominican Republic, 1986-94; Minister of Foreign Affairs, 1994-96, 2004-; ***professional career:*** Extraordinary & Plenipotentiary Amb. of the Dominican Republic to the USA, 1989-1990; ***office address:*** Ministry of Foreign Affairs, Avda Independencia 752, Santo Domingo DN, Dominican Republic; ***phone:*** +1 809 535 6280; ***fax:*** +1 809 533 5772; ***e-mail:*** correspondencia@serex.gov.do; ***URL:*** http://www.serex.gov.do.

TRUE, Lord Nicholas; Member, House of Lords; ***education:*** Peterhouse Coll. Cambridge Univ.; ***party:*** Conservative Party; ***political career:*** Royal Borough of Richmond-upon-Thames Council, Councillor 1986-90, 1998-, Dep. Leader 2002-06, Leader of the Opposition 2006-10, Leader of the Council, 2010-; Mem., House of Lords, 2010-; ***honours and awards:*** CBE, 1993; ***office address:*** House of Lords, London, SW1A 0PW, United Kingdom; ***phone:*** +44 (0)20 7219 3000.

TRURO, Rt Rev the Lord Bishop of; Member, House of Lords; ***education:*** Univ. of Southampton; King's Coll. London Univ.; ***political career:*** Mem., House of Lords, 2013-; ***professional career:*** Ordained, 1980-; Bishop of Sherborne, 2001-08; Bishop of Truro, 2009-; ***office address:*** House of Lords, London, SW1A 0AA, United Kingdom; ***phone:*** +44 (0)20 7219 3000.

TRUSS, Elizabeth; MP for South West Norfolk, UK Government; ***party:*** Conservative; ***political career:*** Councillor, London Borough of Greenwich Council 2006-10; MP for South West Norfolk, May 2010-; Parly. Under Sec. of State, Dept. for Education, 2012-; ***office address:*** House of Commons, London, SW1A 0AA, United Kingdom; ***phone:*** +44 (0)20 7219 3000; ***e-mail:*** elizabeth.truss.mp@parliament.uk.

TRUSS, Hon. Warren; Leader of The Nationals, Government of Australia; ***born:*** 8 October 1948, Queensland; ***political career:*** Chair, Kingaroy Shire Council, 1983-90; Mem. House of Representatives for Wide Bay, Queensland, 1990-; Shadow Minister for Consumer Affairs,

1994-96; Dep. Leader of the House, 1997-98; Minister for Customs and Consumer Affairs, 1997-98; Minister for Community Services, 1998-99; Minister for Agriculture, Fisheries and Forestry, 1999-2005; Minister of Transport and Regional Services, 2005-06; Minister for Trade, 2006-07; Shadow Minister for Trade, Transport, Regional Development and Local Gvt., 2007-; Leader, The Nationals, 2007-; Shadow Minister for Infrastructure and Transport, 2010-; ***memberships:*** Mem., Queensland Graingrowers' Assn. State Cncl., 1979-90; Chair, Sugar Coast Burnett Regional Tourism Board, 1985-89; ***professional career:*** Farmer; ***office address:*** Parliament House, Canberra ACT 2600, Australia; ***phone:*** +61 2 6277 4482; ***fax:*** +61 2 6277 8569; ***e-mail:*** w.truss.mp@aph.gov.au.

TSAFTSARIS, Athanasios; Minister of Rural Development and Food, Government of Greece; ***political career:*** Minister of Rural Development and Food, 2012-; ***professional career:*** Prof. and chmn., Dept. of Genetics and Plant Breeding, Aristotle Univ. of Thessaloniki; Mem.,Board of Directors, Centre for Research and Technology - Hellas (CE.R.T.H.); Dir., Inst. of Applied Biosciences of Centre for Research and Technology - Hellas (CE.R.T.H.); ***publications:*** Author of over 200 research papers published int. journals; ***office address:*** Ministry of Rural Development and Food, 2-6 Acharnon Str., 10483 Athens, Greece; ***URL:*** http://www.minagric.gr.

TSANG YOK-SING, Jasper; President, Legislative Council, Government of Hong Kong; ***political career:*** Non-Official Member, Executive Council of Hong Kong, to 2008; President, Legislative Council, 2008-; ***office address:*** Executive Council, Central Government Offices, Lower Albert Road, Hong Kong.

TSENG YUNG-FU ; Minister of Justice, Government of Taiwan; ***political career:*** Minister of Justice, 2010-; ***professional career:*** Chief Prosecutor, Yunlin District Prosecutors Office, 1989-92; Chief Prosecutor, Chiayi District Prosecutors Office, 1992-93; Chief Prosecutor, Tainan District Prosecutors Office, 1993-96; Chief Prosecutor, Taipei District Prosecutors Office, 1997-99; Head Prosecutor, Supreme Prosecutors Office, 2000-10; Acting Prosecutor Gen., Supreme Prosecutors Office, 2010; ***office address:*** Ministry of Justice, 130 Chingking South Road, Section 1, Taipei, Taiwan; ***URL:*** http://www.moj.gov.tw/.

TSUNG CHUN-WAH, John; Financial Secretary, Government of Hong Kong SAR; ***education:*** Massachusetts Institute of Technology, architecture; Boston State College, Masters in Bilingual Education; Harvard's Kennedy School of Government, Masters in Public Administration; ***political career:*** Secretary, Department of Commerce, Industry and Technology, HKSAR, 2003-06; Dir., Chief Executive's Office, 2006-07; Financial Sec., HKSAR, 2007-; ***professional career:*** Teacher, Boston Public Schools; joined Hong Kong civil service, 1982; Administrative Assistant to the Financial Secretary; Assistant Director-General of Trade; Private Secretary to the Governor; Director General, London Economic and Trade Office; Commissioner of Customs and Excise; Sec. for Planning and Lands; Permanent Sec. for Housing, Planning and Lands; ***office address:*** Office of the Financial Secretary, Kowloon, Hong Kong.

TSVANGIRAI, Morgan; Prime Minister, Government of Zimbabwe; ***born:*** 1952, Gutu, Zimbabwe; ***political career:*** Helped form the MDC, 1999; charged with treason, 2000, 2002, 2003; MDC win parliamentary election 2008; Presidentital candidate 2008, stood down in run off election due to the intimidation of supporters of MDC; Prime Minister, Sept. 2008-; ***professional career:*** Miner; Sec.-Gen., Zimbabwe Congress of Trade Unions; ***office address:*** Movement for Democratic Change, Harvest Hse, 6th Floor, N.Mandela Ave/Angwa St., Harare, Zimbabwe; ***phone:*** +263 (0)91 240023; ***URL:*** http://www.mdczimbabwe.org.

TUCCARO, The Hon. George; Commissioner, Government of Northwest Territories; ***born:*** 1950; ***political career:*** Commissioner of Northwest Territories, 2010-; ***professional career:*** Announcer, CBC North Radio, Yellowknife, 1971-79; Communications Officer, Dept. of Indian and Northern Affairs, 1979; Co-ordinator of Aboriginal Languages Programming, 1981; documentary producer; coordinator, Cultural Industries Program; radio host, CBC North Radio, Trails End; TV anchor, North Beat; founder, GLT communications; ***office address:*** Commissioner of the Northwest Territories, P.O. Box 1320, Yellowknife, NT X1A 2L9, Canada; ***phone:*** +1 867 873 7400; ***e-mail:*** commissioner@gov.nt.ca.

TUIATUA TUPUA TAMASESE EFI, Afioga; Head of State, Samoa; ***born:*** 1 March 1938, Apia, Samoa; ***parents:*** Afioga Tupua Tamasese Meaole and Nove Irene Gustava Taisi Nelson; ***education:*** Victoria Univ., Wellington, New Zealand; ***political career:*** MP, 1966- (under title name Tufuga of Asau); Minister of Works (under title name Tupuola of Leulumoega), 1970-72; re-elected MP, 1973-75; re-appointed Minister of Works; re-elected MP, 1976; elected prime minister, 1976, held position - 1981; re-elected to parly., became first leader of the Opposition, 1982; re-elected MP for Anoamaa East (under title Tuiatua Tupua Tamasese), 2001-04; mem., Council of Deputies, 2004-07; Head of State, 2007- ; ***publications:*** several learned papers and articles; ***office address:*** Office of the Head of State, Government House, Vailima, Apia, Samoa; ***phone:*** +685 20438.

TUN HUSSEIN, Hishamuddin bin; Minister of Defence, Malaysian Government; ***education:*** LL.B., Univ. of Wales, Aberystwyth, UK, 1984; LL.M., London School of Economics, 1988; ***party:*** United Malays National Organisation; ***political career:*** Minister for Youth and Sports, 2000-04; Minister of Education, 2004-09; Minister of Home Affairs and Internal Security, 2009-12; Minister of Defence, 2012-; ***office address:*** Ministry for Defence, Wisma Pertahanan, Jalan Padang Tembak, 50634 Kuala Lumpur, Malaysia; ***phone:*** +60 (0)3 8886 8000; ***URL:*** http://www.mod.gov.my.

TUN RAZAK, Datuk Seri Najib; Prime Minister and Minister of Finance, Malaysian Government; ***political career:*** Minister of Defence, 2000-08; Minister of Finance, 2008-, Prime Minister, 2009-; ***office address:*** Prime Minister's Office, Main Block, Perdana Putra Building, Federal Gov. Admin. Centre, 62502 Putrajaya, Malaysia; ***e-mail:*** ppm@pmo.gov.my; ***URL:*** http://www.pmo.gov.my.

TUOMIOJA, Erkki Sakari; Finnish, Minister for Foreign Affairs, Finnish Government; ***born:*** 1 July 1946; ***languages:*** Swedish, English, French, German; ***education:*** MSc., 1971, MSc., in Economics and Business Administration 1974, Helsinki School of Economics; Licentiate in Social Sciences 1980, Dr. in Social Sciences, Univ. of Helsinki, 1996; ***party:*** Social Democratic Party of Finland; ***political career:*** Mem., Helsinki City Cncl., 1969-79; MP, 1970-79, 1991-; Dep. Mayor of Helsinki, 1979-91; Mem., Foreign Affairs Cttee.; Chmn., Grand Cttee.; Mem., Finnish Deleg. to the Nordic Cncl.; Minister of Trade and Industry for Finnish Govt., 1999-00; Pres., Council of Baltic Sea States, July 2002-June 2003; Minister for Foreign Affairs, 2000-07, 2011-; ***publications:*** 18 books on history and current affairs; ***office address:*** Ministry of Foreign Affairs, PO Box 176, FIN-00161, Helsinki, Finland; ***phone:*** +358 (0)9 16005; ***URL:*** http://www.formin.finland.fi.

TUPOU VI, HRH King Goerge; King of Tonga; ***born:*** 12 July 1959; ***parents:*** King George Tupou V; ***married:*** Nanasipau?u Tuku?aho; ***children:*** 3; ***political career:*** Minister of Defence, Minister of Foreign Affairs, 1998-2004; Prime Minister, 2000-06; King of Tonga, March 2012-; ***professional career:*** Tonga Defence Services (Naval), 1982, Lieutenant-Commander, 1987; High Commissioner to Australia, 2008-12; ***office address:*** Office of the Head of State, Niku'alofa, Tonga.

TURIA, Hon. Tariana; Minister of Whanau Ora; Disability Issues, Government of New Zealand; ***married:*** Hori Turia; ***political career:*** fmr. List MP with portfolio's of Maori Health and Youth Issues; Minister of State, Assoc. Minister of Maori Affairs (Social Development), Corrections, Health, Housing, Social Services and Employment (Social Services), 1999-2002; Co-Leader of the Maori Pary, 2004-; Minister of the Community and Voluntary Sector and Associate Minister of Health and Associate Minister of Social Development, Nov. 2008-; Minister of Disability Issues, March 2009-11; Minister of Whanau Ora; Disability Issues, 2011-; ***professional career:*** Mem., evaluation team for first pilot cervical screening project for Maori women; Mem., team that est. Te Awa Youth Trust (first marae based training est. in 1980); Mem., two Task Forces to est. Kura Kaupapa Maori; ***committees:*** Perm. Mem., Maori Affairs Select Cttee.; Health Select Cttee.; Primary Production Cttee.; ***office address:*** House of Representatives, Parliament Buildings, Wellington, New Zealand.

TURNER, Andrew; Member of Parliament for Isle of Wight, House of Commons; ***parents:*** Eustace Albert Turner and Joyce Mary Turner (née Lowe); ***education:*** Rugby; Keble Coll. Oxford; Birmingham Univ.; Henley Mgt. Coll.; ***party:*** Conservative; ***political career:*** mem. Oxford City Cncl. 1979-96; Sheriff of Oxford, 1994-5; MP, Isle of Wight, 2001-; Vice Chmn., Conservative Party, 2004; Vice Pres., Assoc. of Conservative Clubs; Shadow Minister for Charities, 2005-06; ***memberships:*** FRSA; ***professional career:*** Teacher of Economics and Geography, 1977-84; Conservative Research Dept., 1984-86; Special Adviser to Sec. of State for Social Services, 1986-87; Founding Dir., Grant Maintained Schools Foundation, 1987-97; Education Consultant, 1997-2000; Head of Education Policy and Resources, London Borough of Southwark, 2000-01; ***committees:*** Constitutional Reform, 2010-; ***clubs:*** Royal Solent Yacht Club; Ryde Rowing Club; Bembridge Sailing Club; Seaview Yacht Club; ***office address:*** 24 The Mall, Carisbrooke Road, Newport, IW, PO30 1BW, United Kingdom; ***phone:*** +44 (0)1983 530808; ***fax:*** +44 (0)1983 822266; ***e-mail:*** mail@islandmp.com; ***URL:*** http://www.islandmp.com.

TURNER, Dr Christian; High Commissioner, British High Commission in Kenya; ***professional career:*** FCO, Dep. Dir. Middle East and North Africa, 2008-09; FCO, Director Middle East and North Africa, 2009-12; High Commissioner to Kenya, 2012-; ***office address:*** British High Commission, Upper Hill Road, Nairobi, Kenya; ***phone:*** +254 2 284 4000; ***fax:*** +254 2 284 4077; ***e-mail:*** bhcinfo@iconnect.co.ke; ***URL:*** http://www.ukinkenya.fco.gov.uk.

TURNER, Karl; MP for Kingston Upon Hull East, UK Government; ***party:*** Labour; ***political career:*** MP for Kingston Upon Hull East, May 2010-; ***professional career:*** Barrister; ***committees:*** Justice, 2010-; ***office address:*** House of Commons, London, SW1A 0AA, United Kingdom; ***phone:*** +44 (0)20 7219 3000; ***e-mail:*** karl.turner.mp@parliament.uk.

TURTELBOOM, Annemie; Minister of Justice, Government of Belgium; ***born:*** 22 November 1967; ***education:*** Catholic Univ. of Leuven, Economics; ***political career:*** Deputy, Chamber of Reps, 2003-; Town Councillor, Puurs; Minister for Immigration and Asylum policy, 2008-09; Minister of the Interior, 2009-11; Minister of Justice, Dec. 2011-; ***office address:*** Ministry of Justice, 115 boulevard de Waterloo, 1000 Brussels, Belgium; ***phone:*** +32 (0)2 542 6604 / +32 (0)2 538 7039; ***e-mail:*** info@just.fgoc.br; ***URL:*** http://www.just.fgov.be.

TUSK, Donald; Prime Minister, Government of Poland; ***born:*** 22 April 1957, Gdansk, Poland; ***married:*** Malgorzata Tusk; ***children:*** Michal (M), Katarzyna (F); ***education:*** MA, Univ. of Gdansk, 1980; ***party:*** Leader, Civic Platform Party; ***political career:*** MP, Gdynia-Słupsk, 2001-05, Gdańsk, 2005-07, Warsaw, 2007-; Vice Speaker, the Sejm, 2001-05; Prime Minister, Nov. 2007-; ***professional career:*** Historian; ***office address:*** Office of the Prime Minister, Al. Ujazdowskie 1/3, 00-583 Warsaw, Poland; ***phone:*** +48 22 694 6000; ***e-mail:*** cirinfo@kprm.gov.pl; ***URL:*** http://www.kprm.gov.pl.

TUTU, Archbishop Desmond Mpilo, O.M.S.G, D.D., F.K.C.; South African, Archbishop Emeritus; ***born:*** 7 October 1931, Klerksdorp, Transvaal; ***married:*** Nomalizo Leah (née Shenxane), 2 July 1955; ***children:*** Trevor Thamsanqa (M), Theresa Thandeka (F), Naomi Nontombi (F), Mpho Andrea (F); ***education:*** Johannesburg Bantu High Sch., 1945-50; Teacher's Diploma, Pretoria Bantu Normal Coll.,1951-53; Univ. of South Africa, BA 1954; St. Peter's Theological Coll., Rosettenville, Ordination Training, Licentiate in Theology, 1958-60; King's Coll., Univ. of London, B.D. Hon., 1965; Univ. of London, M.Th.; ***memberships:*** Africa Leadership Forum, Nigeria; African Health Organisation; Africare;Afro Pentecost Winterthur, Switzerland; Anglican Students Federation; Beyond War Foundation; Campaigns for Human Rights; Cape Town Olympic Bid 2004; Carnegie Commission for Preventing the Deadliest Conflicts; Center for Attitudinal Healing; Center for Politics and Economics at Claremont Graduate; Center for the Study of Conflict; Centre for politics & Economics, Claremont University Center, CA, USA; Children of War; Childright Worldwide, Initiative to stop child exploitation; CIT, TecAfrica; Citizens Third Hague Peace Conference in May 1999; Civicus, World Alliance for Citizen Participation; Civilian based Defence Association; Claremont University Center, California, USA; Committee of 100 for 100 Tibet; Community Health Education & Reconstruction Training; Earth Council; Forum of Democratic Leaders in the Asia Pacific Region; plus numerous others too great to mention; ***professional career:*** Schoolmaster, 1954-57; ordained Deacon 1960; ordained Priest 1961-; P/T Curate at St Alban's, London, 1962-65; P/T Curate, St Mary's, Bletchingley, Surrey, UK 1966; Lecturer,

Theological Seminary, Alice, Cape, 1967-69; Univ. Lecturer, UBLS Roma, Lesotho, 1970-72; Assoc. Dir., World Cncl. of Churches, Theological Education Fund, 1972-75; Gen. Sec., South African Cncl. of Churches, 1978-85; Dean of Johannesburg 1975-76; Bishop of Lesotho, 1976-78, and of Johannesburg, 1985-6; Visiting Prof., Anglican Studies, New York General Theological Seminary, 1984; Archbishop of Cape Town and Metropolitan, Church of the Province of Southern Africa,1986-96; Pres., All Africa Conference of Churches, 1987-; also Chllr., Univ. of the Western Cape, 1988-; Chair, Truth and Reconciliation Commission, South Africa, 1995-8; Archbishop Emeritus of Cape Town, 1996-; Visiting Prof., Candler Sch. of Theology, Emory Univ., Atlanta GA, USA 1998-2000; ***trusteeships:*** Chmn., African European Institute; Benevolence through Education; Children's Trust; Christian Development Trust; Desmond Tutu Education Trust; Chmn., Educational Opportunities Council; Equal Opportunity Foundation; Kagiso Trust; Phelps Stokes Fund; Chmn., Project Vote; Sached Trust; South African Human Rights Commission; Tshezi Trust; University/Western Cape, Community Law; Plus Patron of numerous organisations.; ***honours and awards:*** Recipient of various Hon. degrees from univs. in numerous countries; Onassis Award; Family of Man Gold Medallion, 1983; Nobel Peace Prize, 1984; Martin Luther King Jr Humanitarian Award, USA, 1984; Order of Merit of Brazilia, 1987; Order of the Southern Cross, Brazil, 1987; Pacem in Terris Peace and Freedom Award from the Quad Cities, USA, 1987; Palmes d'Or; The Greek Order of St Dennis of Zante, USA, 1990; Peace Prize International Community of UNESCO Athens, 1997; President's Award, Glassborough State College, USA, 1986; President's Award, International Public Relations Association, 1992; President's Medal, Claremont Graduate School, CA, USA, 1990; Prix d'Athene, 1980; Mexican Order of the Aztec Eagle, Insignia Grade, Mexico, 1997; Third World Prize (joint recipient), 1989; Toastmasters International communication & Leadership Award, South Africa, 1997; USA President's Award, Glassboro State College, NJ, USA, 1986; Grand Cross of Merit, Germany, 1996; SOS Kinderdorf Gold Badge of Honour, RSA, 1998; The Freedom of the Journal, Journal of Theology for Southern Africa, RSA, 1998; The Immortal Chaplains Humanity Award, Minneapolis, USA, 1998; William L. Dunfey Award for Excellence in the Humanities, NH, USA, 1998; Youth Advocacy Program Humanity Award, Columbus OH, USA, 1998; Freedom of the City, Cape Town, South Africa, 1998; ***publications:*** Crying in the Wilderness, 1982; Hope and Suffering, 1983; The Words of Desmond Tutu, 1989; The Rainbow People of God, 1994; An African Prayer Book, 1995; The Essential Desmond Tutu, 1997; No Future without Forgiveness, 1999; also many forewords and other contributions to books and journals; ***office address:*** PO Box 1092, Milnerton, Cape Town 7435, South Africa; ***phone:*** +27 (0)21 552 7524; ***fax:*** +27 (0)21 552 1529; ***e-mail:*** mpilo@africa.com.

TWIGG, Derek; British, MP for Halton, House of Commons; ***born:*** 9 July 1959, Widnes; ***children:*** Sean (M), Megan (F); ***education:*** Bankfield High Sch., Widnes; Halton Coll. of Further Education, Widnes; ***party:*** Labour Party; ***political career:*** Chair., Halton Constituency Labour Party, 1985-96; Chair of Housing, 1987-93; Chair of Finance, 1993-96; MP, Halton, 1997-; PPS to Rt. Hon. Helen Liddell MP, Minister of State for Energy & Competitiveness in Europe, 1999-2000; PPS to Rt. Hon. Stephen Byers MP, Minister of State at DTLR, 2001-2002; Asst. Gov. whip, 2002-03; Gov. whip, 2003-05; Parly. Sec., Dept. of Transport, 2005-;07; Parly. Under Sec. of State, Min. of Defence, 2007-08; Shadow Minister, Health, Oct. 2010-11; ***interests:*** economy, education, employment, poverty, housing, health; ***memberships:*** GMB Trade Union; ***professional career:*** Political Consultant; Civil Servant ; ***committees:*** Mem., Public Accounts Cttee., 1998-99; ***recreations:*** sport, walking, reading military history; ***office address:*** Constituency Address, F2, Moor Lane Business Centre, Moor Lane, Widnes, WA8 7AQ, United Kingdom; ***phone:*** +44 (0)151 424 7030; ***fax:*** +44 (0)151 495 3800; ***e-mail:*** derek.twigg.mp@parliament.uk; ***URL:*** http://www.derek.twigg.org.uk.

TWIGG, Stephen; British, Shadow Secretary of State for Education, House of Commons; ***born:*** 25 December 1966, Enfield, London, UK; ***education:*** Balliol Coll., Oxford, PPE; ***party:*** Labour Party; ***political career:*** Cllr., Islington, 1992-96; Mem., London Gp. of Labour MPs; Chief Whip, 1994; Research Assistant to Margaret Hodge MP; Mem. Make Votes Count; Chair, Labour Campaign for Electoral Reform; Cncl. Mem., Electoral Reform Soc.; MP, Enfield Southgate, 1997-2005; Dep. Leader; Shadow Minister, Foreign and Commonwealth Affairs, 2010; Shadow Secretary of State for Education, 2011-; ***interests:*** education, democratic reform, home and foreign affairs; ***memberships:*** Exec. Mem., General Sec., Fabian Soc., 1996; Hon. Pres. British Youth Cncl.; Mem., Manufacturing, Science and Finance Union; ***professional career:*** Amnesty International UK; NCVO; Rowland Gp.; Sch. Governor, Merryhill Primary Sch., Southgate Secondary Sch.; Dir, Foreign Policy Centre; Dir., Crime Concern; ***committees:*** Mem., Select Cttee. for Education and Employment, 1999-2001; ***trusteeships:*** Patron, Body Positive; ***publications:*** The Cross We Bear- Electoral Reform for Local Government; The Moderniser's Dilemma- Radicalism in the Age of Blair; ***office address:*** House of Commons, London, SW1A 0AA, United Kingdom; ***e-mail:*** stephen.twigg.mp@parliament.uk; ***URL:*** http://www.stephentwigg.com.

TYMOSHENKO, Yulia; Former Prime Minister, Government of Ukraine; ***born:*** 27 November 1960; ***education:*** Dnipropetrovsk State Univ., Economics; ***party:*** All-Ukrainian Union (Batkivshchyna); ***political career:*** MP; Leader, All-Ukrainian Union "Batkivshchyna", 1999-; Vice PM of Ukraine, 1999-2001; Prime Minister, Feb.-Sept. 2005, 2007-10; currently imprisoned for alleged abuse of office, sentenced to seven-year prison term in 2011, charges she claims are politically motivated; ***professional career:*** Commercial Dir., then Gen. Dir., Ukrainian Petrol, 1991-95; Dir., United Energy Systems of Ukraine, 1995-97; ***committees:*** Co-Chmn., Power of the People electoral cmn., 2004.

TYRIE, Andrew; MP for Chichester, House of Commons; ***born:*** 15 January 1957; ***parents:*** Derek Tyrie (dec'd) and Patricia Tyrie; ***education:*** Trinity Coll., Oxford Univ., MA; Coll. of Europe, Bruges, Belgium; Wolfson Coll., Cambridge Univ., M.Phil.; ***party:*** Conservative Party; ***political career:*** Conservative Research Dept., 1983-84; Special Adviser to the Sec. of State for the Environment, 1985, Minister for Arts, 1985-86, advisor to Chllr. of the Exchequer, 1986-90; MP, Chichester, 1997-; Shadow Financial Sec., 2003-04; Shadow Paymaster General, 2004-05; ***professional career:*** BP, 1981-83; Snr. Econ., EBRD, 1992-97; ***committees:*** Select Cttee. on Public Admin., 1997-2001; Public Accounts Cmn., 1997; Standing Cttee., Financial Services & Markets Bill & Finance Bill, 2000; Treasury Cttee., 2001-03; Exec. Cttee., of 1922 Cttee., 2005-06; Constitutional Affairs Select Cttee., 2005-10; Liaison, 2010-; ***honours and awards:*** Fellow of Nuffield Coll., Oxford, 1990-91; Woodrow Wilson Scholar, 1990; ***publications:*** Reforming the Lords: A Conservative Approach, 1998; Leviathan at Large: the new regulator for the financial markets, Martin McElwee, 2000; Mr Blair's Poodle: an agenda for reviving the House of Commons, 2000; Back From the Brink, 2001; Statism by Stealth: New Labour, New Collectivism, Martin McElwee, 2002; Axis of Instability: America, Britain and the New World Order after Iraq, 2003; Mr. Blair's Poodle goes to War; the House of Commons, Congress and Iraq, 2004; Pruning the Politicians: The case for a smaller House of Commons, 2004, Conservative Mainstream; The Prospects for Public Spending, 1996; Sense on EMU, 1998; Mr Blair's Poodle goes to War: The House of Commons, Congress and Iraq, 2004, Centre for Policy Studies; The Conservative Party's proposals for the funding of political parties , 2006, The Conservative Party; One Nation Again, 2006, Centre for Policy Studies; ***clubs:*** MCC, RAC; ***recreations:*** golf; ***office address:*** House of Commons, London, SW1A 0AA, United Kingdom; ***phone:*** +44 (0)20 7219 6371; ***e-mail:*** andrew.tyrie.mp@parliament.uk.

U

UDALL, Mark; American, US Senator for Colorado, US Senate; ***party:*** Democrat; ***political career:*** Dep. Regional Whip, 1999; mem., US House of Representatives, 1999-2009; US Senator for Colorado, 2009-; ***committees:*** Armed Services; Energy & Natural Resources; Select Cttee. on Intelligence; ***office address:*** US Senate, 328 Hart Senate Office Building, Washington, DC 20510, USA; ***phone:*** +1 202 224 5941; ***URL:*** http://www.markudall.senate.gov/.

UDALL, Tom; American, Senator for New Mexico, US Senate; ***born:*** 18 May 1948, Tucson, Arizona; ***parents:*** Stewart Udall; ***married:*** Jill Z. Udall (née Cooper); ***children:*** Amanda Cooper Noel (F); ***public role of spouse:*** Former Mew Mexico Deputy Attorney General; ***education:*** Prescott Coll., Arizona, BA, 1970; Cambridge Univ., UK, LL.B, 1975; Univ. of New Mexico Law Sch., Juris Dr, 1977; ***party:*** Democrat; ***political career:*** mem., US House of Representatives, 1998-Jan. 2009; US Senator, 2009-; ***memberships:*** Pres., Nat. Assn. of Attorney Generals; ***professional career:*** Law Clerk, Santa Fe 1977; Asst. US Attorney 1978-81; private law practice, Santa Fe 1981; Chief Counsel, New Mexico Health & Environment Dept 1983; ptnr. & shareholder, Miller, Stratvert, Torgerson & Schlenker, Albuquerque 1985-90; New Mexico Attorney Gen, 1990-98; ***committees:*** US Senate: Appropriations; Foreign Relations; Environment & Public Works; Indian Affairs; Rules and Administration; Commission on Security & Cooperation in Europe; International Narcotics Control Caucus; ***office address:*** US Senate, 110 Hart Senate Office Building, Washington, DC 20510, USA; ***phone:*** +1 202 224 6621; ***URL:*** http://www.tomudall.senate.gov.

UMAROV, H.E. Kairat; Ambassador, Embassy of the Republic of Kazakhstan in the USA; ***languages:*** English, French; ***education:*** Almaty Pedagogical Inst. of Foreign Languages; ***political career:*** Dep. Foreign Minister, 2009-13 ; ***professional career:*** Amb. to India, 2004-09 and concurrently Amb. to Sri Lanka, 2008-09; Amb. to USA, 2013-; ***office address:*** Embassy of the Republic of Kazakhstan, 1401 16th Street, NW Washington DC, 20036, USA ; ***phone:*** +1 202 232 5488; ***URL:*** http://www.kazakhembus.com.

UMBELINA NETO, Natalia Pedro da Costa; Minister of Foreign Affairs, Cooperation and Communities, Government of Sao Tome e Principe; ***education:*** Univ. d'Aix-Marseille III, France; Centre National de la Recherche Scientifique, France; ***political career:*** Sec. of the Regional Government of Principe for Social Affairs; Minister of Foreign Affairs, Cooperation and Communities, 2012-; ***professional career:*** Inspector of Education: Sec. Gen., National Commission of UNESCO; ***office address:*** Ministry of Foreign Affairs, Avda 12 de Julho, CP 111, Sao Tome.

UMUNNA, Chuka; MP for Streatham, UK Government; ***party:*** Labour; ***political career:*** MP for Streatham, May 2010-; Shadow Minister, Business, Innovation and Skills, 2011-; ***committees:*** Treasury Select Cttee., 2010-11; ***office address:*** House of Commons, London, SW1A 0AA, United Kingdom; ***phone:*** +44 (0)20 7219 3000; ***e-mail:*** chuka.umunna.mp@parliament.uk.

UNDERWOOD, The Honourable Peter, AC; Governor , Tasmania; ***married:*** Frances Underwood BA, Dip Ed, A Mus A, MACE ; ***children:*** 4, 3 stepchildren; ***public role of spouse:*** Principal of the Friends' Junior School, Hobart (Ret'd); ***education:*** University of Tasmania; ***political career:*** Governor of Tasmania, 2008-; ***interests:*** teaching; ***professional career:*** Law practice, Hobart, Tasmania; judge, Supreme Court of Tasmania, 1984-2004; Dep. Pres., Australian Defence Force Discipline Appeal Tribunal from 1996-2007; Pres., Australian Inst. of Judicial Admin., 2002-04; Chief Justice, Supreme Court of Tasmania, 2004-08; Chair of the National Judicial College of Australia, 2007; ***honours and awards:*** Hon. Doctor of Laws degree, Univ. of Tasmania, 2001; Officer of the Order of Australia for service to the judiciary and to the law, 2002; Companion of the Order of Australia for service to the judiciary, to legal scholarship and administration, to law reform in the areas of civil and criminal procedure, and to the community of Tasmania. 2009; ***office address:*** Government House, Lower Domain Road, Hobart, Tasmania, Australia; ***URL:*** http://www.govhouse.tas.gov.au.

UPPAL, Paul; MP for Wolverhampton South West, UK Government; ***party:*** Conservative; ***political career:*** MP for Wolverhampton South West, May 2010-; PPS to Minister of State for Univeristies and Science, 2012-; ***professional career:*** Businessman; ***committees:*** Environmental Audit, 2011-; ***office address:*** House of Commons, London, SW1A 0AA, United Kingdom; ***phone:*** +44 (0)20 7219 3000; ***e-mail:*** paul.uppal.mp@parliament.uk.

UPTON, Fred; American, Congressman, Michigan Sixth District, US House of Representatives; ***party:*** Republican Party; ***political career:*** mem., US House of Representatives, 1986-; ***committees:*** Chmn., Energy and Commerce Cttee.; ***office address:*** House of Representatives, 436 Cannon House Street, Washington, DC 20515-6501, USA; ***phone:*** +1 202 224 3121.

URIBE ESCOBAR, José Dario; Director General, Banco de la Republica, Colombia; ***born:*** 1958, Medellin, Colombia; ***education:*** Univ. of Illinois, M.Sc. Econ., 1989; Ph.D Econ., 1992; ***professional career:*** Technical Manager, Banco de la Republica, 1998-2004; Dir. Gen., Banco de la Republica, 2005-; ***office address:*** Banco de la Republica, Piso 5°, Carrera 7 14-78 , Bogotá, Colombia; ***phone:*** +57 1 3430190 / 1 3360200; ***fax:*** +57 1 2861686 / 1 3347128; ***URL:*** http://www.banrep.gov.co.

URPILAINEN, H.E. Jutta; Minister of Finance, Government of Finland; ***born:*** August 1975; ***education:*** University of Jyväskylä; ***party:*** Social Democratic Party; ***political career:*** Minister of Finance, Deputy Prime Minister, June 2011-; ***professional career:*** Teacher; ***office address:*** Ministry of Finance, Snellmaninkatu 1A, P.O.Box 28, 00023 Government, Helsinki, Finland; ***phone:*** +358 (0)9 160 3099; ***fax:*** +358 (0)9 160 4755; ***e-mail:*** name.surname@vm.vn.fi; ***URL:*** http://www.ministryoffinance.fi/vm.

V

VAIPULU, Lord Samiu; Deputy Prime Minister, Government of Tonga; ***born:*** 1953; ***political career:*** MP, 1987-90, 1993-2002, 2005-; Minister for Justice, 2009-10; Deputy Prime Minister, Minister of Justice (2010-11) and Minister of Transport & Works, 2010-; ***professional career:*** tourism; ***office address:*** Legislative Assembly, PO Box 901, Nuku'alofa, Tonga.

VAIZEY, Hon. Edward Henry Butler; MP for Wantage, House of Commons; ***born:*** 5 June 1968; ***parents:*** John Vaizey (the late Baron Vaizey of Greenwich) and Marina Alandra Vaizey CBE; ***children:*** Joseph (M), Martha (F); ***education:*** Merton College, Oxford Univ., MA, 1986-89; City Univ., Dip. Law, 1992; Inns of Court, School of Law, 1993, called to the Bar, Middle Temple, 1993; ***political career:*** Desk Officer, Conservative Research Dept., 1989-91; Dir., Public Policy Unit, 1996-97; Chief Speech Writer to Leader of the Opposition (Conservative Party), 2004; MP for Wantage and Didcot, 2005-10; MP for Wantage, 2010-; Shadow Culture Minister, 2006-10; Parliamentary Under Secretary of State (Culture, Communications and Creative Industries), 2010-11; Parly. Under-Sec. of State, Culture, Media and Sport, 2010-; ***interests:*** the arts, science and technology, environment, energy and architecture; ***professional career:*** Barrister, 1993-96; Dir., Politics International, 1997-98; Dir., Consolidated Communications, 1998-2003; Non Exec. Dir., Edexcel Ltd., 2007-; ***committees:*** Modernisation Select Cttee., 2005-06; Environmental Audit Select Cttee., 2006-07; Dep. Chmn., Conservative Globalisation and Global Poverty Policy Group, 2006; mem., Reform Advisory Board; Reform Research Trust; Armed Forces Parliamentary Scheme (Royal Marines); Conservative Friends of Israel; Industry and Parliamentary Trust; ***trusteeships:*** Trident Trust, 1998-2007; Patron: Friends of St Mary's Church, Buckland; CHANT; The Abbey. Parliamentary Patron: Hansard Society; ***publications:*** A Blue Tomorrow, Ed. with Michael Gove and Nicholas Boles, 2001; The Blue Book on Transport, Ed. with Michael McManus, 2002; The Blue Book on Health, Ed., 2002; ***clubs:*** Soho House, Didcot Conservative Club; ***recreations:*** horse riding, watching Chelsea Football Club and Didcot Town Football Clubs; ***office address:*** House of Commons, London, SW1A 0AA, United Kingdom; ***phone:*** +44 (0)20 7219 3000; ***e-mail:*** vaizeye@parliament.uk.

VALCAREL SISO, Ramon Luis; Spanish, President, Committee of the Regions; ***born:*** 1954; ***education:*** Univ. of Murcia, Arts & Philosophy; ***political career:*** joined Popular Alliance, 1982; Mem., Murcia City Council, 1987; Pres., People's Party of the Murcia Region, 1991-; Pres., Autonomous Community of Murcia, 1995-; Mem., Committee of the Regions, 1995, various positions, Pres., 2012-; ***office address:*** Committee of the Regions, Batiment Jacques Delors, Rue Belliard 99-101, B-1040 Brussels, Belgium; ***URL:*** http://cor.europa.eu.

VALCOURT, Hon. Bernard, PC, BA, LLB; Canadian, Federal Minister of Aboriginal Affairs and Northern Development, Government of Canada; ***born:*** 1952; ***education:*** Académie St. Joseph; Coll. St. Louis-Maillet; University of New Brunswick; ***political career:*** MP, 1984-; Parliamentary Secy., Minister of State for Science and Technology; Minister of Revenue 1985-86; Minister of State for Small Business and Tourism 1986-87; Minister of State for Indian Affairs and Northern Development 1987-89 (resigned); Minister of Consumer and Corporate Affairs 1989-90; Minister of Fisheries and Oceans 1990-91; Minister of Employment and Immigration 1991; Minister of State for the Atlantic Canada Opportunities Agency, 2011-13; Federal Minister of Aboriginal Affairs and Northern Development, 2013-; ***memberships:*** Canadian Bar Assn.; New Brunswick Lawyers Assn; ***professional career:*** Law practice; ***office address:*** House of Commons, Ottawa, Ontario, K1A 0A6, Canada.

VALE DE ALMEIDA, Ambassador Joao; Ambassador, Head of the Delegation, European Union to the US; ***born:*** 1957, Lisbon, Portugal; ***education:*** Univ. of Lisbon; ***professional career:*** journalist; joined European Commission, 1982; held several senior positions within EC; Head of Cabinet of EC President José Manuel Barroso, 2004-09; Dir., External Relations, EC; Head of the Delegation of the EU to the US, 2010-; ***office address:*** Delegation of the EU to the US, 2300 M Street, NW, Washington, DC 20037, USA; ***URL:*** http://www.eurunion.org/.

VALLS, Manuel; Minister of the Interior, Government of France; ***born:*** 1962, Barcelona, Spain; ***education:*** Univ. Paris I Tolbiac, history; ***political career:*** Regional Cllr., Ile-de-France, 1986-92; Dep. Mayor, Argenteuil, 1988; Vice-Pres., Regional Council Ile de France, 1988-2002; Dep. Interministerial Adviser, Winter Olympics, Albertville, 1991-93; Mayor of Evry, 2001; Dep., Essonne, 2002-; Minister of the Interior, 2012-; ***office address:*** Assemblée Nationale, 126 rue de l'Université, Paris 07 SP, France.

VANDE LANOTTE (SP), Johan; Minister for Economy, Consumers and the North Sea, Government of Belgium; ***political career:*** Dep. Prime Minister, Minister for Interior; Dep. Prime Minister, 2011; Deputy Prime Minister, Minister for Economy, Consumers and the North Sea, Dec. 2011-; ***office address:*** Ministry for the Economy, Rue des Colonies 56, 1000 Brussels, Belgium.

VAN DEN ASSUM, H.E. Laetitia; Ambassador, Dutch Embassy in the United Kingdom; ***education:*** Law and Int. Relations, Amsterdam Univ., Netherlands; Columbia Univ., USA; ***professional career:*** Amb. to Thailand, Cambodia, Laos and Myanmar, 1995-2000; Amb. to South Africa, Lesotho and Swaziland, 2000-04; Amb. to Kenya, Seychelles and Somalia, 2006-11; Amb. to Mexico and Belize, 2011-12; Amb. to the UK, 2012-; ***office address:*** Embassy of the Kingdom of the Netherlands, 38 Hyde Park Gate, London, SW7 5DP, United Kingdom; ***phone:*** +44 9)020 7590 3200; ***fax:*** +44 (0)20 7225 0947; ***e-mail:*** lon@minbuza.nl; ***URL:*** http://unitedkingdom.nlembassy.org.

VAN LAARHOVEN, Dr J.P.R.; Secretary General, Benelux Economic Union; ***born:*** 1951; ***education:*** M.Sc., Ph.D., Univ. of Nijmegen; ***professional career:*** Scientific Researcher, Catholic Univ. of Nijmegen, 1977; Acting Head, Experimental & Chemical Endocrinoloyg Dept. and of the Lab. for Endocrinology, International Medicine, St. Radboud Hospital, Nijmegen, Business Mgr, Laboratory/Clinical Pharmacy units; EMMB, Board of Dirs., St.Anna Care Group, Geldrop, 2002; Sec.-Gen., Benelux Economic Union, 2007-; ***office address:*** Benelux Economic Union, 39 Rue de la Regence, 1000 Brussels, Belgium; ***URL:*** http://www.benelux.int.

VAN LE, Hieu; Australian, Lieutenant-Governor, South Australia; ***born:*** Vietnam; ***education:*** Univ.of Adelaide, grad. Economics and Accountancy, MBA in Business Administration; ***political career:*** Lieutenant Governor, South Australia, 2007-; ***professional career:*** Lecturer, Financial Services Institute of Australasia (Finsia); Lecturer, Adelaide Institute of TAFE; Snr. Mgr., Australian Securities and Investments Commission (ASIC), to date; South Australian Multicultural and Ethnic Affairs Commission (SAMEAC), 1997-2007, Dep. Chmn., 2004-07, Chmn., 2007- ; ***office address:*** Government House, GPO Box 2373 , Adelaide SA 5001 , Australia; ***e-mail:*** governors.office@saugov.sa.gov.au; ***URL:*** http://www.governor.sa.gov.au/.

VAN LOAN, Peter; Leader of the Government in the House of Commons, Government of Canada; ***education:*** MA. in international relations, Univ. of Toronto, Canada; ***political career:*** MP, 2004-; Minister of Intergovernmental Affairs and Minister for Sport, 2006-07; Leader of the Government in the House of Commons and Minister for Democratic Reform, 2007-08; Minister of Public Safety, 2008-10; Minister of International Trade, 2010-; Minister of the Asia-Pacific Gateway, 2010; Leader of the Government in the House of Commons, 2011-; ***office address:*** House of Commons, Parliament Buildings, Wellington Street, Ottawa, Ontario, K1A 0A6, Canada; ***phone:*** +1 613 943 5959; ***fax:*** +1 613 992 3674.

VAN RAEPENBUSCH, Sean; President, Civil Service Tribunal, Court of Justice of the EU; ***born:*** 1956; ***education:*** Free Univ. of Brussels, law; Doctor of Laws; ***professional career:*** Head, Legal Service, SA du canal et des installations maritimes de Bruxelles, 1979-84; Commission of the EC; mem., Legal Services, Commission of the EC, 1988-94; Legal Secretary, Court of Justice of the European Communities, 1994-2005; Lecturer, Univ. of Charleroi, 1989-91; Lecturer, Univ. of Mons Hainault, 1991-97; Lecturer, Univ. of Liège, 1989-91; EU, 1995-2005; Lecturer, Free Univ. of Brussels, 2006-; Judge, Civil Service Tribunal, 2005-, President, 2011-; ***office address:*** Court of Justice of the European Union, Rue du Fort Niedergrunewald, L-2925, Luxembourg.

VAN RIJN, Martin; State Secretary for Health, Welfare and Sport, Netherlands Government; ***born:*** 1956; ***education:*** Erasmus Univ., Rotterdam; ***political career:*** various policy and managerial positions, Ministry of Housing and Spatial Planning, 1980-2000; Dir-Gen., Management and Personnel Policy, Ministry of the Interior and Kingdom Relations, 2000; Dir-Gen. for Health Care, Ministry of Health, Welfare and Sport, 2003-08; State Sec. for Health, Welfare and Sport, Rutte-Asscher gov., Nov. 2012-; ***office address:*** Ministry of Health, Welfare and Sport, PO Box 20350, 2500 EJ The Hague, Netherlands; ***phone:*** +31 (0)70 340 7890.

VAN ROMPUY, Herman; Belgian, President, European Union; ***born:*** 31 October 1947, Etterbeek; ***parents:*** Victor Van Rompuy and Germaine Van Rompuy (née Geens); ***married:*** Windels Geertrui; ***languages:*** French, English, Dutch; ***education:*** Greek-Latin grammar sch., Sint-Jan Berchmanscollege, Brussels, 1965; Bachelor of philosophy, Catholic Univ of Leuven, 1968; Master's degree of economics, 1971; ***party:*** CVP; ***political career:*** Nat. Vice-Pres. CVP Youth 1973-77; Adviser to the cabinets of former Prime Min., Leo Tindemans and Min. of Finance, Gaston Geens; Dir. Centre d'études économiques, politiques et sociales of PSC-CVP 1980-88; Senator 1988-95; Secy. of State for Finance and for small and medium Enterprises; Pres., Nat. CVP 1988-93; Dep. Prime Minister and Minister of the Budget 1993-99; Prime Minister, Dec. 2008-Nov. 2009; Pres., European Union, Jan. 2010-; ***interests:*** economic policy; ***professional career:*** Attaché at study-department of the National Bank of Belgium, 1972-75; Adviser at the Cabinet of Prime Minister L. Tindemans, 1975-1978; Adviser of the Cabinet of Finance, Minister G. Geens, 1978-80; Dir. of the Centre for Political, Economic and Social Studies, 1980-88; Professor at the Trade Sch. Anwerp, 1980-87; Professor at the Flemish Sch. of Economics in Brussels, 1982-2008; ***committees:*** mem., Nat. CVP Bureau, 1978-; ***publications:*** 'De kentering der tijden' (The turn of times), Lannoo; 'Hopen na 1984' (Hope after 1984), Het Davidsfonds, Horizonreeks, 1984; 'Het christendom. Een modern gedachte', (Christianity. A moderne reflection), Het Davidsfonds, Forumreeks, 1990; De binnenkant op een Kier-avonden zonder politiek-lannoo, 2000; Haiku Poexiecentrum, 2010; ***office address:*** Office of the President, rue de la Loi 175, B-1048 Brussels, Belgium; ***phone:*** +32 (0)2 2811 6737; ***URL:*** http://www.europa.eu.

VAN SCHALKWYK, Marthinus; Minister of Tourism, Government of South Africa; ***born:*** 10 November 1959; ***education:*** Rand Afrikaans Univ., B. Proc degree, BA, Political Science, MA, Political Science; ***political career:*** MP for Randburg, 1990-98; Media Director, National Party, 1994 election campaign; Premier, Western Cape Province, 2002-04; Minister of Environmental Affairs & Tourism, 2004-09; Minister of Tourism, to date; ***professional career:*** Lecturer in Political Science, Rand Afrikaans Univ. and Univ. of Stellenbosch; ***office***

address: Department of Tourism, Private Bag X447, 0001 Pretoria, South Africa; **phone:** +27 12 310 3611; **fax:** +27 12 322 0082; **e-mail:** pmakwakwa@ozone.pwv.gov.za; **URL:** http://www.environment.gov.za/.

VARA, Shailesh; MP for North West Cambridgeshire, House of Commons; **born:** 1960; **education:** Brunel Univ. ; **party:** Conservative Party; **political career:** MP for North West Cambridgeshire, 2005-; Shadow Dep. Leader of the House, 2006-10; Assist. Government Whip, 2010-; **professional career:** Solicitor ; **committees:** Mem., Campaign Group Fen Project, 2005-10; Vice-Pres., Huntingdon CCC, 2007; Chmn., Conservative Parly. Friends of India, 2008-10; Vice-Chmn., Conservative Chinese Parliamentary Group, 2009-10; Environment, Food and Rural Affairs Cttee., 2005-06; Administration, 2010-11; Finance and Services, 2011-; **honours and awards:** Hon. Fellow, Brunel Univ., 2010; **recreations:** travel, cricket, tae kwon do; **office address:** House of Commons, London, SW1A 0AA, United Kingdom.

VARADKAR, Dr Leo; Minister of Transport, Tourism and Sport, Government of Ireland; **party:** Fine Gael; **political career:** TD for Dublin West, 2007-; Minister for Transport, Tourism and Sport, 2011-; **professional career:** General Practitioner; **office address:** Department of Transport, Transport House, 44 Kildare St., Dublin 2, Ireland; **phone:** +353 (0)1 670 7444; **fax:** ; **URL:** http://www.transport.ie.

VARELA RODRIGUEZ, Juan Carlos; Vice President and Foreign Minister, Government of Panama; **born:** 12 December 1963; **education:** Tech. Instit. of Georgia, USA, Indust. Eng.; **political career:** Campaign mgr., 1994; Presidential candidate 2008; Vice-President and Minister of Foreign Affairs, Govt. of Panama, 2009-; **professional career:** Dir., Grupo Varela, 1985-2008; **office address:** Ministry of Foreign Affairs, Amador, Edificio No. 1, Panama 4, Republic of Panama; **phone:** +507 228 2815/0927; **fax:** +507 228 2716; **URL:** http://www.mire.gob.pa/.

VARGA, Mihály; Minister of National Economy, Hungarian Government; **political career:** Minister of Finance, 2001-02; Minister without portfolio, 2012-13; Minister of National Economy, Chief Negotiator on the EU Budget, 2013-; **office address:** Ministry of Finance, Jòzef Nádor tér 2-4, 1051 Budapest, Hungary; **phone:** +36 (0)1 318 2006; **fax:** +36 (0)1 318 2570.

VARMA, Yatindra Nath; Attorney General, Government of Mauritius; **born:** 1974; **party:** Mauritius Labour Party; **political career:** MP, 2005-; Attorney General, 2010-; **professional career:** lawyer; Mem., Mauritian Bar, 2001; **committees:** Chair, Parly. Cttee. on Commission Against Corruption, 2008-10; **office address:** Office of the Attorney General, 2nd Floor, R. Seeneevassen Building, Port Louis, Mauritius; **phone:** +230 212 2139 / 0544; **fax:** +230 212 6742; **URL:** http://attorneygeneral.gov.mu.

VASAN, G.K.; Minister of Shipping, Government of India; **born:** 1964; **party:** Indian National Congress; **political career:** Minister of State, Ministry of Statistics and Programme Implementation, 2006-09; Minister of Shipping, 2009-; **office address:** Ministry of Shipping, Mahasagar Bhawan, Block 12, CGO Complex, Lodhi Road, New Delhi 110 003, India; **phone:** +91 11 301 3964.

VASSILIOU, Androulla; Cypriot, Commissioner, European Parliament; **born:** 1943; **married:** George Vassiliou; **public role of spouse:** Fmr. President of Cyprus; **education:** law; **political career:** mem., House of Representatives, Cyprus, 1996-2006; EU Commissioner for Health, April 2008-09; EU Commissioner for Education, Multilingualism and Youth, 2009-; **professional career:** legal adviser, Standard Chartered Bank; legal advisers, Bank of Cyprus; **office address:** European Commission, rue de la loi 200, 1049 Brussels, Belgium; **phone:** +32 (0)2 299 1111; **fax:** +32 (0)2 299 1970; **URL:** http://www.europa.eu.int.

VAZ, Keith, MP; British, Member of Parliament for Leicester East, House of Commons; **born:** 26 November 1956, Aden, Yemen; **parents:** Anthony Vaz and Merlyn Vaz (née Pereira); **married:** Maria Fernandes, 3 April 1993; **children:** Luke Swraj (M), Sahara (dec'd 1993) (F), Anjali Olga Verona (F); **public role of spouse:** President, Mental Health Tribunal; Council Member, The Law Society; **education:** Latymer Upper Sch., Hammersmith; Gonville & Caius Coll., Cambridge, Law, BA, 1979, MA, 1987, M.C.F.I., 1988; **party:** Labour Party, 1980-; **political career:** Chmn., Labour Party Race Action Gp., 1983-; Parly. Candidate, Richmond & Barnes, General Election, 1983; Euro-Parly. Candidate, West Surrey, 1984; MP, Leicester East, 1987-; Vice-Chair, Tribune Gp., MPs, 1992 and Treasurer, 1994; Shadow Jr. Environment Minister, 1992-97; Rep. of Central Regional Gp. of MPs, Labour Party Regional Exec., 1994-96; Shadow Jr. Environment Minister, 1992-97; PPS to the Attorney Gen. and Solicitor Gen., 1997-99; Parly. Sec. Lord Chancellor's Dept., 1999; Minister of State for Europe, Foreign and Commonwealth Office, 1999-2001; Mem., National Exec. Cttee., the Labour Party, 2007-; Chmn., Ethnic Minority Taskforce, 2006-; **memberships:** UNISON, 1985-; Court of Cncl., Loughborough Univ. and Leicester Univ.; Pres., Leicester & South Leicester, RSPCA, 1988-99; Nat. Advisory Bd. of Crime Concern, 1989-94; Pres., Leicester Kidney Patients Assn., 2000; **professional career:** Solicitor for London Borough of Richmond-upon-Thames, 1982; Sr. Solicitor, London Borough of Islington, 1982-85; Solicitor, Highfields and Belgrave Law Centre, Leicester, 1985-87; Governor, St Patrick's RC Sch., 1985-89; Governor, Regent Coll., 1998; Solicitor, Highfields and Belgrave Law Centre, Leicester, 1985-87; Pres., India Dev. Gp. (UK) Ltd., 1992-; Vice-Chmn., British Cncl., 1998-99; Governor, Regent Coll., 1998; Governor, Cmmw. Inst., 1998-99; **committees:** Most recently: Select ctte., Constitutional Affairs, 2003-07; Liaison, 2007-; Jt. Cttee. on National Security Strategy, 2010-; **trusteeships:** Patron, Ginger Bread, 1990-; Patron, Family Courts Campaign, 1991; Trustee, Centre for Local Econ. Strategies, 1994; Patron, UN Year of Tolerance, 1995; Patron, LASS, 1991-; Patron, Leicester Rowing Club, 1992-; Patron, Asian Business Club, 1998-; Patron Naz Project, London, 1999-; Patron, Asian Donors Appeal, 2000; Patron, Labour Party Race Action Gp., 2000-; Patron, Next Steps Foundation, 2003-; **honours and awards:** Asian of the Year, 1988; **publications:** Law Reform Now; **office address:** House of Commons, London, SW1A 0AA, United Kingdom; **phone:** +44 (0)20 7219 5605; **fax:** +44 (0)20 7219 3922.

VAZ, Valerie; MP for Walsall South, UK Government; **party:** Labour; **political career:** Councillor, London Borough of Ealing Council, 1986-90; MP for Walsall South, May 2010-; **committees:** Health, 2010-; Regulatory Reform, 2010-; **office address:** House of Commons, London, SW1A 0AA, United Kingdom; **phone:** +44 (0)20 7219 3000; **e-mail:** valerie.vaz.mp@parliament.uk.

VEGA, Gaspar; Deputy Prime Minister, Government of Belize; **party:** United Democratic Party; **political career:** Minister of Natural Resources and the Environment, 2008-12; Deputy Prime Minister, Minister of Natural Resources and Agriculture, 2012-; **office address:** Ministry of Natural Resources, Market Square, Belmopan, Belize; **phone:** +501 822 2226; **fax:** +501 822 2333; **e-mail:** info@mnrei.gov.bz; **URL:** http://www.mnrei.gov.bz.

VELLA, George; Minister of Foreign Affairs, Government of Malta; **born:** 1942; **party:** Labour Party; **political career:** MP, 1978-; Perm. Rep., Council of Europe, 1992; Spokesperson on Foreign Affairs; Dep. PM, 1996-98; Minister of Foreign Affairs, 2012-; **office address:** Ministry of Foreign Affairs, Palazzo Parisio, Merchant's Street, Valletta VLT 1171, Malta; **URL:** http://www.foreign.gov.mt/.

VENNER, Sir K. Dwight; Governor and Chairman, Eastern Caribbean Central Bank; **education:** Univ. of the West Indies, BSc., MSc., Economics; **professional career:** Junior Research Fellow, Institute of Social & Economic Research, Univ. of the West Indies, Lecturer in Economics, 1974-81; Dir. of Finance & Planning, St. Lucia Gov., 1981-89; Gov. and Chmn., Eastern Caribbean Central Bank, 1989-; **committees:** Board of Directors, Caribbean Knowledge and Learning Network; member, Commission for Growth and Development, World Bank; Chairman, OECS Economic Union Task Force Committee; Chair, UWI Open Campus Council; **honours and awards:** Commander of the British Empire (CBE), 1996; Distinguished Graduate of the University of the West Indies, 1998; Knight Commander of the Most Excellent Order of the British Empire (KBE), St Vincent and The Grenadines; Hon. Doctor of Laws from the University of the West Indies, 2003; **office address:** Eastern Caribbean Central Bank, PO Box 89, Basseterre, St. Kitts and Nevis.

VERBEKE, H.E. Johan; Ambassador, Belgian Embassy in the UK; **born:** 1951; **education:** Ghent Univ. , Belgium, law and philosophy; Yale, USA, Master of Laws ; **professional career:** assistant professor of European Law; joined Diplomatic Corps; Beirut, 1982; Amman, 1984; Bujumbura, 1985; Santiago de Chile,1988; spokesman, Min.of Foreign Affairs, 1990; EUduring the Belgian EU-Presidency, 1993; Dep. Chief of Mission, Washington, 1994; Dep. Dir.-Gen. for Political Affairs, Min. of Foreign Affairs, 1998-2000; Chef de Cabinet, Min. of Foreign Affairs, 2000-04; Permanent Rep. to the UN, 2004-08; Amb. to the UK, 2010-; **office address:** Embassy of Belgium, 17 Grosvenor Crescent, London, SW1X, United Kingdom; **phone:** +44 (0)20 7470 3700; **fax:** +44 (0)20 7470 3795 / 3710; **e-mail:** uk@diplobel.org; **URL:** http://www.diplomatie.be/london.

VERMA, Baroness Sandip; Member, House of Lords; **party:** Conservative; **political career:** Raised to peerage, 2006; Opp. Whip, 2006-10; Opposition spokesperson, 2006-10; Gov. Whip, 2010-12; Gov., Spokesperson, 2010-12; Parly.under-Sec. of State and Government Spokesperson, Dept. of Energy and Climate Change, 2012-; **office address:** House of Lords, London, SW1A 0PW, United Kingdom; **phone:** +44 (0)20 7219 5216; **e-mail:** vermas@parliament.uk; **URL:** http://www.parliament.uk.

VICKERS, Martin; MP for Cleethorpes, UK Government; **party:** Conservative; **political career:** Councillor, North East Lincolnshire Council; MP for Cleethorpes, May 2010-; **office address:** House of Commons, London, SW1A 0AA, United Kingdom; **phone:** +44 (0)20 7219 3000; **e-mail:** martin.vickers.mp@parliament.uk.

VIDEGARAY CASO, Luis; Secretariat of Finance and Public Credit, Government of Mexico; **born:** 1968; **education:** Instituto Tecnologico Autonomo de Mexico; Massachusetts Inst. of Technology, US, Ph.D, economics; **political career:** Gov. Adviser; Finance Sec., Government of the State of Mexico, 2005-09; National Coordinator of Sec. of State Finances, 2008-09; MP, 2009-11; Pres., Budget and Public Account Commission, 2009-11; Secretariat of Finance and Public Credit, 2012-; **office address:** Secretariat of Foreign Affairs, Palacio National Primer Patio Mariano, 3 Fl. Of. 3045, Col. Centro, Cuauhtemoc 06000, Mexico DF; **phone:** +52 55 5542 2213; **fax:** +52 55 5228 1142.

VIERA, Mauru Luiz Iecher; Ambassador , Embassy of Brazil in the USA; **education:** Universidade Federal Fluminense, Brazil, 1973; Univ. of Michigan, USA; Cambridge Univ., UK; Université de Nancy, France ; **professional career:** Amb. to Argentina, 2004-10; Amb. to USA, 2011-; **office address:** Embassy of Brazil, 3006 Massachusetts Avenue, NW, Washington, DC 20008, USA; **phone:** +1 202 238 2700; **fax:** +1 202 238 2827; **e-mail:** webmaster@brasilemb.org; **URL:** http://www.brasilemb.org.

VIGENIN, Kritian; Minister of Finance, Government of Bulgaria; **born:** 1975; **education:** Univ. of National and World Economy, Sofia, 1998; Harvard Univ., USA, 2001; **political career:** MEP, 2007-13; Minister of Finance, 2013-; **office address:** Ministry of Finance, 2 Aleksander Zhendov St., 113 Sofia, Bulgaria; **phone:** +359 (0)2 737987.

VILKS, Andris; Minister of Finance, Government of Latvia; **born:** June 1963; **education:** Univ. of Latvia, 1986; **party:** Civic Union; **political career:** Minister of Finance, 2010-; **professional career:** Chief Economist, SEB Banka, 2007-09; **office address:** Ministry of Finance, LV 1510 Riga, Latvia.

VILLIERS, Theresa, MP; British, Minister of State for Northern Ireland, UK Government; **born:** 1968, London, UK; **married:** Sean Wilken, June 1999; **education:** Sarum Hall Sch.; Francis Holland Sch.; Univ. of Bristol, UK, first class law degree; Jesus Coll., Oxford, UK, BCL; Inns of Crt. Sch. of Law; **party:** Conservative & Unionist Party; **political career:** Spokeswoman on Economic Affairs, European Parl., 1999-2004; MP for Chipping Barnet. 2005-; Shadow Chief Secretary to the Treasury, 2005-07; Shadow Secretary of State for Transport, 2007-May 2010; Minister of State for Transport, May 2010-12; Minister of State for Northern Ireland, 2012-; **interests:** transport, the economy, environmental issues and the green belt, Cyprus; **professional career:** Barrister, Lincoln's Inn, London, UK, 1993-95;

lecturer in law, King's Coll., London, UK, 1995-99; *publications:* author of various legal texts, Waiver, Variation and Estoppel, Sean Wilken; *office address:* Northern Ireland Office, 11 Millbank, London, SW1P 4PN, United Kingdom; *URL:* http://www.nio.gov.uk.

VILOVIC, Ranko; Chair, United Nations Peacebuilding Commission; *professional career:* Head of the Consular Dept., MFA, -1992; Counselor, Croatian Emb., Bern, Swizterland, 1992-93; Head of Croatian Consulate, Zurich, 1993-95; Head, Dept. for Peace & Security, 1995-98; Minister Counselor, Permanent Mission to the OSCE, UN and International Organizations in Vienna, 1998-2002; Head of the Dept. for Northern & Western Europe, MFA, 2002-04; Head of the UN Dept., 2004-08; Dep. Perm. Rep. of Croatia to the UN, 2008-09, Perm. Rep., 2009-; *office address:* UN Peacebuilding Commission, First Ave. at 46th Street, New York, NY 10017, USA; *URL:* http://www.un.org/en/peacebuilding/.

VILSACK, Tom; American, Secretary of Agriculture, US Government; *born:* 13 December 1950, Pittsburgh, PA, USA; *education:* Hamilton Coll., Clinton, NY, USA, BA, history, 1972; Union Univ.'s Albany Law Sch., law degree, 1975; *party:* Democrat; *political career:* Mayor of Mt. Pleasant, IA, 1987; elected to State Senate of IA, 1992; Governor, Iowa, 1998-2006; US Secretary of Agriculture, 2009-; *interests:* creating new opportunities for children, working families and communities, water-monitoring to ensure cleaner water, providing stable power supplies, relief from high cost of prescription drugs, long-term care to Iowans, health care coverage to uninsured children; *professional career:* practised law, Mt. Pleasant, IA, 1975-98; *committees:* Mem., NGA's Exec. Cttee. ; *clubs:* Pres., Mt. Pleasant's Rotary Club; *office address:* State Capitol Building, Des Moines, IA 20319-0001, USA; *phone:* +1 515 281 5211; *URL:* http://www.usda.gov.

VIMONT, H.E. Pierre; Executive Secretary General, European External Action Service; *born:* 1949; *education:* Law degree; Institute of Political Studies grad.; National School of Administration (ENA) grad.; *professional career:* Joined the Foreign Service in 1977; London posting, 1978-81; Press and Information Office, Min. of Foreign Affairs, 81-85; seconded to Institute for East-West Security, New York, 1985-86; Permanent Rep.of France to the European Communities, Brussels, 1986-90; chief of staff to the minister delegate for European affairs, 1990-93; Dir. for development and scientific, technical and educational cooperation; Dir. for cultural, scientific and technical relations; Dep. Dir. Gen., Cultural, Scientific and Technical Relations Dept., 1996-97; Dir., European Cooperation, 1997-99; Amb. and permanent rep. to the EU, 1999-2002; Chief of staff to the minister of foreign affairs, 2002-07; Ambassador to the USA, 2007-10; Executive Sec.-Gen., European External Action Service, 2011-; *office address:* EU External Action Service, 1046 Brussels, Belgium; *URL:* http://eeas.europa.eu/.

VINCENT-ROSTOWSKI, Jan; Deputy Prime Minister and Minister of the Economy, Government of Poland; *born:* 30 April 1951, London, UK; *parents:* Roman Rostowski; *languages:* English, French, Russian, Spanish; *education:* BSc., Int. Relations, 1972, MA, Economy and History, 1973, Univ. College London; MSc., Economics, 1975, LSE; *political career:* Active in the Polish Solidarity Campaign, a London based Solidarity support group, 1980s; Advisor to the Polish Deputy Prime Minister and Finance Minister, 1989-91; Minister of Finance, 2007-12; Deputy Prime Minister and Minister of the Economy, 2012-; *professional career:* Lecturer, London Univ. 1998-95; In the early 90s, advisor to the Russian Federation on macroeconomic policy; Prof. of Economics and head of the Dept. of Economics, Central European Univ. in Budapest, 1995-2000 and 2005-2006 (Post suspended following appointment as Polish Finance Minster.); Co-founders of the Center for Social and Economic Research (CASE) and mem.of its Supervisory Council; Economic Advisor to the National Bank of Poland, 2002-04; Economic Advisor to PEKAO SA Bank, 2004; *publications:* Co-edited the academic journal, "Communist Economies" (later known as "Communist Economies & Economic Transformation" and "Post Communist Economies"; Many academic papers on European enlargement, monetary policy, currency policy and the transformation of post communist economies; *office address:* Ministry of Economy, pl. Trzech Krzyzy 5, 00-507 Warsaw, Poland; *phone:* +48 22 693 5000; *URL:* http://web.mg.gov.pl/portalout.

VIRANT, Dr Gregor; Minister of the Interior, Government of Slovenia; *born:* 1969; *political career:* Minister of Public Administration, 2004-08; Chmn., Rally for the Republic, 2008-11; :eader., Civic List, 2011-; Dep., National Assembly, 2011-; Minister of the Interior, 2013-; *office address:* Ministry of the Interior, Stefanova 2, 1000 Ljubljana, Slovenia; *phone:* +386 1 472 5125; *URL:* http://www.mnz.si/.

VIRKKUNEN, Henna; Minister of Public Administration and Local Government, Government of Finland; *party:* National Coalition Party; *political career:* MP, 2007-; Minister of Education and Science, 2008-10, 2010-11; Minister of Public Administration and Local Government, 2011-; *office address:* Ministry of Finance, Kirkkokaut 12, PO Box 26 , 00023 Helsinki, Finland.

VISCO, Ignazio; Governor, Banca d'Italia; *born:* 1949; *education:* Univ. of Rome, economics; Univ. of Philadelphia, economics, MA, Ph.D ; *professional career:* Economic Research Dept., Bank of Italy, 1974-97, Head of Dept., 1990-97; Chief Economist & Head of the Economics Dept., OECD, 1997-2002; Dept. Dir. Gen., Bank of Italy, 2007-11; Chmn., International Relations Cttee., ESCB, 2009-10; Gov., Bank of Italy, 2011-; Gov. Council, ECB; Chmn., Jt. Governing Board of the Insurance Supervisory Authority, 2013-; *office address:* Banca d'Italia, Via Nazionale 91, 00184 Rome, Italy; *URL:* http://www.bancaditalia.it.

VITTER, David; American, Senator for Louisiana, US Senate; *party:* Republican Party; *political career:* mem., US House of Representatives, 1999-04; US Senate, 2004-; *committees:* Former mem. House of Representatives Appropriations and Budget Cttees.; *office address:* US Senate, 516 Hart Senate Office Building, Washington, DC 20510, USA; *phone:* +1 202 224 4623; *URL:* http://www.vitter.senate.gov.

VON DANWITZ, Thomas; Judge, Court of Justice of the European Union; *born:* 1962; *education:* Doc. of Law, Bonn; *professional career:* Prof. of German Public Law and European Law, 1996-2003; Dean, Fac. of Law, Ruhr Univ., Bochum, 2000-01; Prof. of Germana Public Law and European Law, Univ. of Cologne, 2003-06; Dir., Institute of Public Law and

Administrative Science, 2006; Visiting Professor; Judge, Court of Justice of the European Union, 2006-; *office address:* Court of Justice of the European Union, Rue du Fort Niedergrunewald, L-2925, Luxembourg.

VON DER LEYEN, Ursula; Minister of Labour and Social Affairs, Federal Government of Germany; *born:* 8 October 1958; *education:* Göttengen, Münster, Econ., 1980; London School of Economics, 1978; Medical School of Hanover, 1987; Masters Degree in Public Health, 2001; *political career:* Mem., CDU, State Assembly of Lower Saxony, 2003-05; Mem. of the Presidium of the CDU, 2004-; Minister for Social Affairs, Women, Family Affairs and Health, Lower Saxony, 2003-05; Federal Minister of the Family, Senior Citizens, Women and Youth, 2005-10; Minister of Labour and Social Affairs, 2010-; *professional career:* Assist. Doctor, Medical School of Hanover, 1988-92; Academic, Dept. of Epidemiology, Social Medicine and Health System Research, Med. School of Hanover, 1998-2002; *committees:* Chwmn., Family Affairs Cttee. of the CDU, 2005-; *office address:* Ministry of Labour and Social Affairs, Wilhelmstrasse 49, 10117 Berlin, Germany; *phone:* +49 (0)30 185270; *fax:* +49 (0)30 18 527 1830; *e-mail:* poststelle@bmas.bund.de; *URL:* http://www.bmvg.de.

VORACHITH, Bounyang; Vice President, Government of Laos; *political career:* Deputy Prime Minister, Permanent Member of the Cabinet; Prime Minister, 2001-06; Vice President, 2006-; *office address:* Office of the Vice President, Setharthirath Road, Vientiane, Laos.

VROUTSIS, Ioannis; Minister of Labour and Social Security, Government of Greece; *education:* Kapodestrian Univ. of Athens; Panteio Univ. of Athens; *political career:* Minister of Labour, Social Security and Providence, 2012-; *professional career:* Economist; *office address:* Ministry of Labour and Social Security, 40 Pireos str.,, 104 37 Athens, Greece; *phone:* +30 (0)10 529 5000; *URL:* http://www.ypakp.gr.

VUCIC, Aleksandar; First Deputy Prime Minister, Government of Serbia; *born:* 1970; *political career:* Sec.-Gen., Radical Party; Minister of Information, 1998; joined Progressive Party, Dep. Pres., Pres, 2012-; First Dep. Prime Minister, 2012-; *office address:* Office of the Deputy Prime Minister, Nemanjina 11, 11000 Belgrade, Serbia.

VUJANOVIC, Filip; President of Montenegro; *born:* 1 September 1954; *party:* Democratic Party of Socialists; *political career:* Minister of Justice; Minister of Interior; Prime Minister, 1998-2002; President of the Parliament of Montenegro, 2003, President of State, 2003-; *professional career:* Lawyer; *office address:* Office of the President of Montenegro, Bld. Svetog Petra Cetinjskog 12, 81000 Podgorica, Montenegro; *URL:* http://www.predsjednik.me/.

VUJCIC, Boris; Governor, Croatian National Bank; *born:* 1964; *education:* Zagreb Faculty of Economics, Ph.D; *professional career:* Assist. Lecturer, Faculty of Economic, Zagreb, 1989-97, Assist. Prof., 1997-03, Professor, 2003-; Fulbright Fellow, Michigan State Univ., USA, 1994-95; Visiting Prof., Zagreb Faculty of Science, 2004-; Dep. Chief Negotiator with the EU, 2005-; Dir., Croatian National Bank Research Dept., 1996-2000, Dep. Gov., 2000-2012, Governor, 2012-; *office address:* Croatian National Bank, Trg hrvatskih velikana 3, HR-10000 Zagreb, Croatia; *URL:* http://www.hnb.hr.

W

WADDAULAH, HM Sir Haji Hassanal Bolkiah Mu'izzaddin; Sultan of Brunei, Prime Minister, Minister of Defence and Minister of Finance, Brunei Darussalem Government; *born:* 15 July 1946, Darussalam, Brunei; *education:* Victoria Inst., Kuala Lumpur, Malaysia, 1961-63; Royal Military Academy, Sandhurst, UK, 1963-67; *political career:* Head of State for Brunei, 1967-; Prime Minister, 1984-; Minister of Home Affairs, 1984-86; Minister of Defence, 1986-; Minister of Finance, 2002-; *office address:* Office of the Prime Minister, 1100 Bandar Seri Bagawan, Brunei Darussalam; *phone:* +673 (0)2 386000.

WADE-GERY, Sir Robert, KCMG, KCVO, MA, BA; British, Fellow, All Souls Coll., Oxford; *born:* 1929, Oxford, UK; *parents:* Henry Theodore Wade-Gery and Vivian Wade-Gery (née Whitfield); *married:* Sarah Wade-Gery (née Marris), 1962; *children:* William (M), Laura (F); *languages:* French, Spanish; *education:* Winchester (scholar); New Coll., Oxford (scholar) (first class honours in Classical Honour Moderations and Litterae Humianiores, Greats); *memberships:* Royal Inst. of Int. Affairs, London; Int. Inst. of Strategic Studies; *professional career:* British Foreign (now Diplomatic) Service, 1951-87; Foreign Office, 1951-54; 3rd, then 2nd Sec., Bonn, 1954-57; Foreign Office, 1957-60; 1st Sec., Tel Aviv, 1961-64; Foreign Office, 1964-67, Saigon, 1967-68; Cllr. and Sec. of Duncan Cttee. on Overseas Representation, Cabinet Office, London, 1968-69; Bank of England, 1969-70; FCO, 1970-71; Under-Sec., Central Policy Review Staff, Cabinet Office, 1971-73; Min., Madrid, 1973-77; Min., Moscow, 1977-79; Dep. Sec., Cabinet Office, 1979-82; British High Cmnr. in India, 1982-87; Vice-Chmn., Barclays de Zoete Wedd, 1993-97, Barclays Capital, 1997-99 (Exec Dir. since 1987); Sr. Consultant to British Invisibles, London, 1999-2001, Barclays Private Bank, 1999-2002; Dir., Barclays Bank, Spain 1989-2001; Dir., India Index Fund 1992-2004; Fellow, All Souls Coll., Oxford, 1951-73, 1987-89 and 1997-; *honours and awards:* CMG, 1979; KCMG, 1982; KCVO, 1983; Hon. Fellow, New Coll., Oxford; *clubs:* Boodle's, London; Beefsteak; *recreations:* walking, sailing, travel, history; *office address:* All Souls College, Oxford, OX1 4AL, United Kingdom; *phone:* +44 (0)1451 821115; *fax:* +44 (0)1451 822496.

WAFFA-OGOO, Hon. Susan; Minister of Foreign Affairs, Government of Gambia; *political career:* Minister of Fisheries, Natural Resources and the Environment; Minister of Tourism and Culture, 2005-07; Minister of Foreign Affairs, International Co-operation and Gambians Abroad, 2012-; *professional career:* Permanent Representative of the Gambia to the United Nations, 2009-12; *office address:* Ministry of Foreign Affairs, 4 Marina Parade, Banjul, Gambia; *phone:* +220 4228 291.

WAHEED HASSAN MANIK, Dr Mohamed; President, Government of the Maldives; *education:* BA, American Univ., Beirut, Lebanon; MA, Ph.D., Stanford Univ., USA; *political career:* Vice President, 2008-12; President, Commander in Chief of the Armed Forces and Police, 2012-; *professional career:* Joined UNICEF, 1992, Head of Education in Tanzania, Head of Education, Bangladesh, UNICEF Headquarters in New York, senior advisor coordinating global policy for UNICEF; *office address:* Office of the President, Malé, Maldives.

WAITE, Terry, CBE; British, President, Y Care International; *born:* 31 May 1939, Cheshire, England; *married:* Frances Waite; *children:* 4; *education:* higher education in London; *professional career:* Education Advisor to the Anglican Bishop of Bristol, England -1969; Provincial Training Advisor, first African Anglican Archbishop of Uganda, Rwanda and Burundi, 1969-72; Int. Consultant to a Roman Catholic Medical Order, 1972-80; Archbishop of Canterbury's Private Staff, Lambeth Palace with responsibility for Archbishop's diplomatic and ecclesiastical changes, 1980-92; early 1980s negotiated release of sev. hostages from Iran; taken hostage, Lebanon, 1987-91, solitary confinement for first 4 years; elected Fellow Commoner, Trinity Hall Cambridge, 1991; Founder Pres., Y Care, Int. Dev. Wing of the British YMCA, 1994-; Pres., Emmaus UK, 1998; Ambassador for WWF-UK; Mem. Advisory Bd., Gorton Monastery, 2003-; lecturer, writer and broadcaster appearing in North and South America, Australia and New Zealand, South Africa and throughout Europe; Founder Chmn., Hostage UK, 2005-; *trusteeships:* Patron of: Butler Trust; Bury St. Edmunds Volunteer Centre, Save Our Parsonages, The Bridge Project Sudbury Appeal, The Romany Society, Lewisham Environment Trust, Suffolk Branch of Far East Prisoners of War Society, COFEPOW (Children and Families of the Far East Prisoners of War), One World Broadcasting Trust, Warrington Male Voice Choir, The One to One Children's Fund; Prisons Video Trust, Underprivileged Children's Charity, Bristol, Tymes Trust (the Young ME Sufferers Trust), and many other organisations; *honours and awards:* MBE, 1982; Templeton UK Award, 1985; Doctor of Civil Law Univ. of Kent at Canterbury, 1986; CBE, 1992; Roosevelt Four Freedoms Medal, 1992; Doctor of Civil Law, Univ. of the City of London, 1992; Doctor of Law, Univ. of Durham, 1992; Doctor of Law, Univ. of Sussex, 1992; DHC, Yale Divinity Sch., 1992; Freedom of Canterbury, and Lewisham, 1992; Hon. LHD, Wittenberg Univ., 1992; Doctor of Humane Letters, Univ. of Southern Florida, 1992; Doctor of Law, Liverpool Univ., 1992; Doctor of Humane Letters Virginia Commonwealth Univ., 1996; Hon. Doctor of Philosophy, Anglia Poly. Univ. (now Angela Ruskin Univ.), 2001; Hon. Doctor of Letters, Nottingham Trent Univ., 2001, De Montfort Univ, 2005 ; *publications:* contributed articles to many journals and periodicals e.g. Readers Digest and the Kipling Journal; contributed articles and forewords to many books, Taken on Trust, 1991; Footfalls in Memory, 1995; Travels With a Primate, 2000; *office address:* Trinity Hall, Cambridge, CB2 1TJ, United Kingdom.

WAJED, Hasina; Bangladeshi, Prime Minister, Bangladeshi Government; *born:* 28 September 1947, Tungipara, Bangladesh; *parents:* Bangabandhu Sheikh Mujibur Rahman and Begum Fazilatunnesa; *married:* M.A. Wazed Miah; *public role of spouse:* Scientist; *education:* Univ. of Dhaka, graduate, 1973; *party:* Awami League; *political career:* Elected Pres., Awami League, 1981; Leader of the Opp., Parl.; Prime Minister of the People's Republic of Bangladesh, with Portfolios for Armed Forces Division, Cabinet Division, Special Affairs, Defence, Establishment, 1996-2001; Prime Minister, Minister for Energy and Power, Housing and Public Works, Women's Affairs, Religious Affairs and Armed Forces Division, Jan. 2009-; *memberships:* Chief, Students' Union, Eden Girls' Coll., Bangladesh; mem., Students' League of Dhaka Univ., Sec., Chattra League unit, Rokeya Hall; Pres., Eden Intermediate Girls' Coll. Chattra League; *office address:* Prime Minister's Office, Old Sandshad Bhaban, Belgaon, Dhaka, Bangladesh.

WALKER, Charles; MP for Broxbourne, House of Commons; *born:* 1967; *party:* Conservative; *political career:* Councillor, Wandsworth Borough Cncl., 2002-; MP for Broxbourne, 2005; *committees:* Scottish Affairs, 2005-10; Public Administration, 2007-11; Chairmen's Panel/Panel of Chairs, 2010-; Standing Orders, 2011-; *office address:* House of Commons, London, SW1A 0AN, United Kingdom; *e-mail:* charles.walker.mp@parliament.uk.

WALKER, Robin; MP for Worcester, UK Government; *party:* Conservative; *political career:* MP for Worcester, May 2010-; *committees:* Welsh Affairs, 2011-; *office address:* House of Commons, London, SW1A 0AA, United Kingdom; *phone:* +44 (0)20 7219 3000; *e-mail:* robin.walker.mp@parliament.uk.

WALKER, Scott; Governor, State of Wisconsin; *education:* Marquette Univ.; *party:* Republican; *political career:* State Assembly, 1993; elected to Milwaukee County Exec., 2002-2010; Governor of Wisconsin, 2010-; *office address:* Office of the Governor, 115 East State Capitol, Madison, WI 53702, USA; *URL:* http://www.wisgov.state.wi.us/.

WALKER OF GESTINGTHORPE, Rt Hon Sir Robert; Member, House of Lords; *education:* Trinity College, Cambridge Univ.; *political career:* Member, House of Lords, 2002-, as Justice of the Supreme Court, disqualified from participation 2009-13; *professional career:* Lord Justice of Appeal, 1997-2002; Lord of Appeal in Ordinary in 2002-2009; Justice of the Supreme Court of the United Kingdom, 2009-13; *honours and awards:* raised to the peerage as The Lord Walker of Gestingthorpe, 2002; *office address:* House of Lords, London, SW1A 0PW, United Kingdom.

WALLACE, Ben; MP for Lancaster and Wyre, House of Commons; *party:* Conservative Party; *political career:* mem., Lancaster & Wyre, 2005-10; Shadow Minister for Scotland, 2007-10; mem., Wyre & Preston, 2010-; PPS to Kenneth Clarke, 2010-; *professional career:* Army; *committees:* Scottish Affairs, 2005-10; *office address:* House of Commons, London, SW1A 0AA, United Kingdom; *phone:* +44 (0)20 7219 3000.

WALLACE OF SALTAIRE, Lord; British, Member of the House of Lords; *married:* Helen Wallace; *children:* Edward (M), Harriet (F); *public role of spouse:* Centennial Professor, European Institute, London School of Economics; *education:* Cambridge Univ., UK, History; Cornell Univ., Political Science, Ph.D, 1968; *political career:* Mem., House of Lords, 1995-; Speaker for the Liberal Democrats on Defence and Foreign Affairs; Gov. Whip and Spokesmen for FCO, Home Office (Security and Police and Ministry of Defence), 2010-; *memberships:*

Upper Wharfedale Agricultural Soc.; Wensleydale Railway Assoc.; *professional career:* Lecturer in Govt., Univ. of Manchester, 1967-77; Dir. of Studies, Royal Inst. of Int. Affairs, London, 1978-90; Walter F. Hallstein Fellow, St Antony's Coll., Oxford, 1990-95; Concurrently Prof., Int. Studies, Central European Univ., Budapest, 1994-97; Consultant, British Govt., Dutch Govt., EC, Brookings Inst., The Club of Rome; Research Dir., Transatlantic Policy Network, 1993-95, Advisor, 1995-2005; Prof. Int. Relations, LSE, 1997-2006, now Emeritus Prof.; *committees:* Mem., Lords Select Cttee. on European Communities, 1997-2001; Chair, Sub-Cttee. on Justice and Home Affairs, 1997-2000; *honours and awards:* Hon. Dr., Univ. Libre de Bruxelles, 1992; Ordre pour la Mérite, France, 1995; Legion d'Honneur, France, 2006; *publications:* Regional Integration; the West European Experience, 1994; Opening the door; the enlargement of the EU and Nato, 1997; occasional contributor, BBC, CNN, the Financial Times and the Guardian; Policy Making in the European Union (with Helen Wallace), 5th ed., 2005; Rethinking European Order (with Robin Niblett) 2001; *clubs:* Saltaire Tennis Club; *recreations:* singing, walking, gardening; *office address:* House of Lords, London, SW1A 0PW, United Kingdom; *phone:* +44 (0)20 7219 3000; *fax:* +44 (0)20 7219 5979; *e-mail:* hlinfo@parliament.uk; *URL:* http://www.parliament.uk.

WALLACE OF TANKERNESS, Lord James (Jim) Robert, QC, MSP, MA, LL.B; British, Advocate General for Scotland, Office of the Advocate General for Scotland; *born:* 1954; *parents:* John F.T. Wallace and Grace H. Wallace (née Maxwell); *married:* Rosemary Wallace (née Fraser), 1983; *children:* Helen (F), Clare (F); *education:* Downing Coll., Cambridge; Edinburgh Univ; *party:* Liberal Democrat Party; *political career:* elected MP (Lib.) for Orkney and Shetland, 1983-2001; Lib. Spokesman on Energy, 1983-85, on Fisheries, 1983-87, on Defence, 1985-87; Dep. Lib. Whip, 1985-87; Chief Whip, 1987-88, First Chief Whip, 1988-92; Lib. Dem. Spokesman on Employment, 1988-92, on Fisheries, 1988-97, on Scotland, 1992-; Leader of Scottish Liberal Democrats, 1992-2005; MSP, Orkney, 1999-07; Dep. First Minister and Minister for Justice, 1999-2003; Dep. First Minister and Minister for Enterprise and Lifelong Learning, 2003-05; Raised to the House of Lords, 2007-; Advocate General for Scotland, 2010-; *interests:* constitutional reform, fisheries, energy, renewable energy; *memberships:* Faculty of Advocates; *professional career:* Called to Scottish Bar, 1979; QC (Scotland), 1997; *committees:* Mem., House of Commons Procedure Cttee., 1988-92; House of Lords Constitution Cttee., 2008-; *honours and awards:* Privy Councillor, 2000; *publications:* Pamphlet (co-ed.), A New Deal for Rural Scotland (1983); *clubs:* Caledonian; Scottish Liberal; *recreations:* golf, music; *office address:* House of Lords, London, SW1A 0PW, United Kingdom; *e-mail:* wallacej@parliament.uk.

WALLEY, Joan Lorraine, MP; British, Member of Parliament for Stoke-on-Trent North, House of Commons; *born:* 1949; *parents:* Arthur Simeon Walley and Mary (née Pass); *married:* Jan Ostrowski, 1980; *s:* 2; *languages:* German; *education:* Hull Univ., University College Wales; *political career:* Lab. MP, 1987-; Environment Spokeswoman, 1988-89; Transport Spokeswoman, 1989-96; *interests:* environment, transport; *memberships:* Inst. of Environmental Health Officers, Vice-Pres.; *professional career:* Alcoholics Recovery Project, 1970-73; Planning Department, Swansea City Cncl., 1974-77; Wandsworth Borough Cncl., 1977-78; NACRO: Nat. Assn. for the Care and Resettlement of Offenders, 1978-82; *committees:* Parly. Football Cttee.; Environmental Audit, 2010-; Liaison, 2010-; Members' Expenses, 2011-; *trusteeships:* West Midlands Home Safety Council; *recreations:* walking, swimming, music, football; *office address:* House of Commons, London, SW1A 0AA, United Kingdom; *phone:* +44 (0)20 7219 4524; *fax:* +44 (0)20 7219 4397.

WALLIN, Stefan; Minister of Defence, Government of Finland; *born:* 1967; *education:* Master of Social Sciences; *party:* Swedish People's Party, Leader, 2006-; *political career:* MP, 2007-; Minister of the Environment, and Minister at the Ministry for Foreign Affairs (Nordic co-operation), Jan.-Apr. 2007; Minister of Culture and Sport, Apr. 2007-11; Minister of Defence, 2011-; *office address:* Ministry of Defence, Fabianinkatu 2, FI-00131Government, Helsinki, Finland; *e-mail:* opmkirjaamo@minedu.fi; *URL:* http://www.defmin.fi.

WALPOLE, Hon. Alice; Ambassador, British Embassy in Luxembourg; *professional career:* Consul-General, Basra, Iraq, 2009-11; British Amb. to Luxembourg, 2011-; *office address:* British Embassy, 5, Boulevard Joseph II, L-1840 Luxembourg, Luxembourg; *phone:* +352 229864; *fax:* +352 229867; *e-mail:* britemb@pt.lu; *URL:* http://ukinluxembourg.fco.gov.uk/en.

WALTER, Hon. Matthew Joseph; Minister of Agriculture, Fisheries and Forestry, Government of Dominica; *born:* 12 December 1955, Paix Bouche, Dominica; *education:* Kuru Kuru Cooperative Coll., Dipl. in Management, 1981; Dominica Teacher's Coll., Univ. of the West Indies and Local, Cert. in Teaching, 1989; *party:* Dominica Labour Party, 1979-; *political career:* Minister for Community Development & Gender Affairs, 2000-07; Minister of Agriculture, Fisheries and Forestry, 2007-; *professional career:* Teaching Assistant, 1979-89; Assist. Teacher, 1989-95; *office address:* Ministry of Agriculture, Government Headquarters, Kennedy Avenue, Roseau, Dominica; *phone:* +1 767 448 2401 ; *fax:* +1 767 449 8220; *e-mail:* walterr@cwdom.dm.

WALTER, Robert; British, Member of Parliament for North Dorset, House of Commons; *born:* 30 May 1948; *parents:* Richard Walter (dec'd 2001) and Irene Walter; *married:* Sally Walter (née Middleton), 1970 (dec'd, 1995); *children:* Elizabeth (F), Charles (M), Alexander (M); *education:* Warminster School; Univ. of Aston, Birmingham, UK, B.Sc. 1971; *party:* Conservative Party; *political career:* Chmn., Conservative Gp. for Europe, 1992-95, Vice-Pres., 1995-; MP, North Dorset, 1997-; British-Irish Inter Parly. Body, 1997-; Opposition Spokesman on Constitutional Affairs and Wales, 1999-2001; Mem., Parly. Assembly of Cncl. of Europe, 2001-; Mem., European Security and Defence Assembly, 2001-, Pres., 2009-; Pres., Federated Group of Christian Democrats and European Democrats, European Security and Defence Assembly, 2006-08; appointed by Prime Minister, Rt. Hon. David Cameron MP, to head the United Kingdom delegation to the Parly Assembly of the Council of Europe, 2011; Chmn., European Democratic Group and a Vice-President of the Assembly, 2011-;Chmn., British Group of the Inter-Parliamentary Union, 2011-; All-Party Parly. Groups inc. Vice-Chair, Human Rights Group; Chmn., Belgian Group; Treasurer of the Russia Group and Turkey Group; Vice-Chairman of the Croatia Group and Sweden Group; *memberships:* Mem. of various All Party Parly. Gps.: Vice-Chmn., Human Rights Gp; Vice-Chmn., Lupus Gp; Treasurer,

Bitish-Japanese Gp, British-Caribbean Gp, Voluntary Sector Gp; Mem., Free Trade Gp; Vice-Chmn., Consumer Safety Int.; Rear-Commodore, House of Commons Yacht Club; ***professional career:*** Int. Banker & farmer; fmr. mem., London Stock Exchange; fmr. Dir., Aubrey G. Lanston & Co. Inc.; ***committees:*** Backbench Cttees.: Vice Chmn., Agriculture, 1997-99; Sec., European Affairs, 1997-99; Health Select Cttee. 1997-99; Int. Dev. Select Cttee., 2001-03; Econ. Affairs and Culture, Science and Educ. cttees., Parly. Assembly, Cncl. of Europe, 2001-; Defense Cttee., European Security and Defence Assembly, to date; Treasury Select Cttee. 2003-05; Mem., European Standing Cttee.B (European Legis.), 2001-05; Mem., Executive of the 1922 Cttee., 2002-05; Chmn., Defence Cttee., European Security and Defence Assembly, 2006-08; ***trusteeships:*** Chmn. of Governors, Tachbrook Sch., 1980-98; ***honours and awards:*** Freeman of the City of London, 1983-; Liveryman of the Worshipful Company of Needlemakers; ***clubs:*** Vice-Pres., Society of Dorset Men; Patron, Gillingham and Shaftesbury Agricultural Society; ***office address:*** House of Commons, London, SW1A 0AA, United Kingdom; ***phone:*** +44 (0)20 7219 6981; ***fax:*** +44 (0)20 7219 2608; ***e-mail:*** robert.walker.mp@parliament.uk; ***URL:*** http://www.bobwaltermp.com.

WANGCHUK, Khandu; Minister of Economic Affairs, Government of Bhutan; ***political career:*** Minister of Trade and Industry; Minister of Foreign Affairs, to 2007; Chairman of the Cabinet, 2007; Minister of Economic Affairs, 2008-; ***office address:*** Ministry of Economic Affairs, Tashichhodzong, PO Box 117, Thimphu, Bhutan.

WAQA, Baron; President, Government of Nauru; ***born:*** 1959; ***political career:*** MP, 2003-; Minister of Education, May-Aug. 2003, 2004-07; President, 2013-; ***office address:*** Office of the President, Government Offices, Yaren, Nauru; ***phone:*** +674 444 3100; ***fax:*** +674 444 3199; ***URL:*** http://www.naurugov.nr.

WARD, David; MP for Bradford East, UK Government; ***party:*** Liberal Democrat; ***political career:*** Councillor, Bradford Metropolitan District Council, 1984-; MP for Bradford East, May 2010-; ***committees:*** Business, Innovation and Skills Select Cttee. 2010-12; Education, 2012-; ***office address:*** House of Commons, London, SW1A 0AA, United Kingdom; ***phone:*** +44 (0)20 7219 3000; ***e-mail:*** david.ward.mp@parliament.uk.

WARNER, Lord; Member of the House of Lords; ***born:*** 8 September 1940; ***parents:*** Albert Warner and Laura Warner; ***married:*** Suzanne Elisabeth Warner (née Reeder), 1990; ***children:*** Andrew Simon (M), Joel James Stephen (M), Justine Emma (F); ***public role of spouse:*** Non-Executive Director of the Environment Agency; ***education:*** Dulwich College, Univ. California, Berkley; ***party:*** Labour; ***political career:*** Sr. policy advisor to the Home Sec.; Chmn., Youth Justice Bd. for England & Wales; Chmn., Nat. Cncl. for Voluntary Organisations (NCVO); Mem., House of Lords; Parly. Undersec. for Health, 2003-04; Minister of State for NHS Reform Dept. of Health, 2005-06 ; Mem. of Gov. Commission, Funding of Social Care, 2010-11; ***interests:*** law & order, children's issues, health & social care; ***professional career:*** Sr. Civil Servant; Dir. of Social Services; Management Consultant; ***committees:*** Mem., House of Lords Select Cttee. on Science and Technology, 2008-; ***recreations:*** theatre, films, sport, reading; ***office address:*** House of Lords, London, SW1A 0PQ, United Kingdom; ***phone:*** +44 (0)20 7219 3000; ***fax:*** +44 (0)20 7219 5979.

WARNER, Mark; Senator for Virginia, US Senate; ***born:*** 15 December 1954, Indianapolis, Indiana, USA; ***married:*** Lisa Warner (née Collis); ***education:*** George Washington Univ., 1977; Harvard Law Sch., graduated 1980; ***party:*** Democrat; ***political career:*** Governor, State of Virginia, to 2006; Senator for Virginia, US Senate, 2009-; ***memberships:*** chair, Virginia Foundation for Independent Colleges; chair, Virginia Math and Science Coalition; co-chair, Virginia's Communities in Schools Foundation; mem., Boards of: Virginia Union Univ., George Washington Univ., Appalachian Sch. of Law; chair, Democratic Party of Virginia, 1993-95; ***professional career:*** founding partner, Columbia Capital Corp.; founding Chair, Virginia Health Care Foundation; founded Virginia High-Tec Partnership, 1997; ***office address:*** US Senate, 475 Russell Senate Office Building, Washington DC 20510, USA; ***phone:*** +1 202 224 2023; ***URL:*** http://www.warner.senate.gov.

WARREN, Elizabeth; Senator of Massachusetts, US Senate; ***party:*** Democrat; ***political career:*** US Senate, 2012-; ***professional career:*** Professor of Law, Harvard Law School; ***office address:*** US Senate, 2 Russel Courtyard, Washington DC 25010, USA; ***phone:*** +1 202 224 4543; ***URL:*** http://www.warren.senate.gov.

WARSI, Baroness Sayeeda Hussain; Senior Minister of State (Jointly FCO & Department for Communities and Local Government), UK Government; ***political career:*** Mem., House of Lords, 2007-; Shadow Minister for Community Cohesion 2007-10, Social Action 2007-10; Minister without Portfolio, 2010-12; Co-Chairman of the Conservative Party; Senior Minister of State (Jointly Foreign and Commonwealth Office and Department for Communities and Local Government), 2012-; ***interests:*** cities, cohesion, women's empowerment, charities, Pakistan, Dubai; ***office address:*** House of Lords, London, SW1A 0PW, United Kingdom.

WARWICK OF UNDERCLIFFE, Baroness; Member, House of Lords; ***born:*** 16 July 1945, Bradford, Yorkshire; ***parents:*** Jack and Olive; ***married:*** Dr Sean Young, 06 June 1969; ***education:*** Bedford Coll., Univ. of London, BA (Hons), 1964-67; ***party:*** Labour Party; ***political career:*** Mem., House of Lords; ***memberships:*** Fellow RSA, 1984; ***professional career:*** Chief Exec., Universities UK; ***honours and awards:*** Hon D.Litt, Bradford Univ.; Hon Doctor of the Open Univ.; Doctor of Science (SocSc) h.c., Royal Holloway Univ. of London; ***office address:*** House of Lords, London, SW1A 0PW, United Kingdom; ***phone:*** +44 (0)20 7219 3000; ***fax:*** +44 (0)20 7219 5679; ***e-mail:*** hlinfo@parliament.uk; ***URL:*** http://www.parliament.uk.

WASIRA, Stephen Masato; Tanzanian, Minister of State in the Office of the President, Government of Tanzania; ***born:*** 1945; ***education:*** BA (International Studies and Economics); MPA (Master of Public Administration); American Univ., Washington DC; ***party:*** CCM; ***political career:*** Minister of Water, 2006-07; Minister of Agriculture, Food Security and Co-operatives, 2007-10; Minister of State in the President's Office, 2010-; ***professional career:*** Community Dev. Asst., 1964-69; District Exec. Secy., TANU 1969-73; MP 1970-75; Dpty. Min. of Agriculture 1973-75; Regional Commissioner 1975-82; Diplomat, Washington DC 1982-86; MP 1985-90; Dpty. Min., Local Govt. and Cooperatives 1987-86; Min. of Agriculture and Livestock Development 1989-; ***committees:*** Foreign Affairs Cttee. 1985-; ***office address:*** Office of the President , Dar es Salaam, Tanzania.

WASSERMAN SCHULTZ, Debbie; Congresswoman, 20th District, Florida, US House of Representatives; ***education:*** Univ. of Florida, Bach. degree in Political Science, 1988, Master's, 1990; ***political career:*** Florida House of Representatives, 1992-2000, House Democratic Leader Pro Tempore, and Floor Leader; Florida State Senate, 2000-04; US House of Representatives, 2005-; Snr. Democratic Whip; ***committees:*** Florida Legislature: House Cttee. on Higher Education, 1994-96; Current US House of Representatives: Budget; Judiciary; ***office address:*** US House of Representatives, 118 Cannon House Office Building, Washington, DC 20515, USA; ***phone:*** +1 202 225 7931; ***fax:*** +1 202 226 2052.

WATERS, Maxine; American, Congresswoman, California Thirty-Fifth District, US House of Representatives; ***education:*** BA, California State University, Los Angeles, USA; ***party:*** Democratic Party; ***political career:*** Chief Dep., Los Angeles City Council; mem., California State Assembly, 1976-90, Democratic Caucus Chair; Chair, Congressional Black Caucus (CBC), 1997-98; Chief Dep. Whip, Democratic Party; Mem., US House of Representatives, 1988-; ***professional career:*** Teacher; Volunteer Co-ordinator, Head Start programme; ***committees:*** House: Financial Services; Judiciary; ***office address:*** House of Representatives, 436 Cannon House Street, Washington, DC 20515, USA; ***phone:*** +1 202 224 3121.

WATKINSON, Angela; Member of Parliament for Hornchurch & Upminster, House of Commons; ***born:*** 1941; ***education:*** Wanstead county high sch.; Public administration, Anglia University; ***party:*** Conservative Party; ***political career:*** MP, Upminster, 2001-10; MP for Hornchurch and Upminster, 2010-; Gpv. Whip, 2010-12; ***memberships:*** Upminster Conservative Assn.; ***professional career:*** Banking and Local Gov.; ***committees:*** Governor, Gaynes, Sacred Heart of Mary sch.; ***office address:*** House of Commons, London, SW1A 0AA, United Kingdom; ***phone:*** +44 (0)20 7219 3000; ***e-mail:*** watkinsona@parliament.uk; ***URL:*** http://www.parliament.uk; http://www.angelawatkinsonmp.com.

WATSON, Tom; MP for West Bromwich East, House of Commons; ***married:*** Siobhan Charlotte Corby; ***education:*** King Charles I School, Kidderminster; ***party:*** Labour Party; ***political career:*** MP, West Bromwich East, 2001-; PPS to Paymaster Gen., 2003-05; Defence Minister, 2005; Government Whip 2007; Cabinet Office Minister, 2008; Labour Party Deputy Chair; Campaign Coordinator, 2011-resigned July 2013; ***professional career:*** Fundraising officer, Save the Children; Political Officer, AEEU ; ***committees:*** Mem., Home Affairs Select Cttee., 2001-03; Culture, Media & Sport, 2009-12; ***office address:*** House of Commons, London, SW1A 0AA, United Kingdom; ***phone:*** +44 (0)20 7219 8123; ***fax:*** +44 (0)20 7219 1943 / 0121 5532043; ***e-mail:*** tom.watson.mp@parliament.uk; ***URL:*** http://www.tom-watson.co.uk.

WATSON OF INVERGOWRIE, Lord; Member of the House of Lords; ***married:*** Clare; ***public role of spouse:*** IT Consultant; ***education:*** Heriot-Watt Univ., BA Hons., Economics, 1974; ***political career:*** Trade Union Official (ASTMS/MSF), 1977-89; Labour MP for Glasgow Central, 1989-97; Labour MSP for Glasgow Cathcart, 1999-2005; Intro. the Protection of Wild Mammals (Scotland) Bill, March 2000 (Royal Assent 2002); Minister for Tourism, Culture & Sport, 2001-03; Intro. to House of Lords as Lord Watson of Invergowrie, 1997-; ***professional career:*** Adult Education Lecturer (WEA), 1974-77; official, ASTMS/MSF trade union, 1977-89; Dir., PS Communication Consultants Ltd., Edinburgh, 1997-99; Dir., Dundee United FC, 2003-05; ***committees:*** Convener of Finance Cttee., 1999-2001; Mem., Housing, Social Inclusion and Voluntary Sector Cttee., 1999-2001; Enterprise and Culture Cttee., 2003-05; Public Petitions Cttee., 2003-05; ***honours and awards:*** Visiting Research Fellow, Dept. of Govt., Strathclyde Univ., 1996-2002; Hon. doctorate, Abertay Univ., Dundee, 1998; ***publications:*** three books on Dundee United, Year Zero: An Inside View of the Scottish Parliament, Febuary 2001; ***office address:*** House of Lords, London, SW1A 0PQ, United Kingdom; ***phone:*** +44 (0)20 7219 8731; ***e-mail:*** watsonm@parliament.uk.

WATT, H.E. James W.; British Ambassador to Egypt; ***born:*** 5 November 1951; ***parents:*** Anthony James MacDonald Watt (dec'd) and Sona Elvey Watt (née White); ***married:*** Elizabeth Ghislane Villeneuve, 1980; Amal Saad, 2004; ***children:*** Louis (M), Clelia (F); ***languages:*** Arabic, French, Italian, Spanish; ***education:*** Ampleforth College, UK; BA in modern languages, Oxford Univ., 1973 ; ***professional career:*** HM Diplomatic Service, 1977-; Amb. to Lebanon, 2003-06; Amb. to Jordan, 2006-11; Amb. to Egypt, 2011-; ***honours and awards:*** CVO, 1997; ***clubs:*** The Athenaeum; ***office address:*** British Embassy, 7 Ahmed Ragheb Street, Garden City, Cairo, Egypt; ***phone:*** +20 (0)2 794 0850; ***fax:*** +20 (0)2 794 0859; ***e-mail:*** james.watt@fco.gov.uk; ***URL:*** http://ukinegypt.fco.gov.uk/en.

WATTS, Dave; British, Member of Parliament for St. Helens North, House of Commons; ***born:*** 26 August 1951; ***party:*** Labour Party; ***political career:*** Leader, St. Helens Borough Cncl.; MP, St. Helens North, 1997-; PPS, 1999-2005; Asst. Govt. Whip, 2005-10; ***committees:*** Finance & Service, 1997-2001, 2005-06; Foreign Affairs, 2010-12; Administration, 2010-; Arms Export Controls, 2011-12; ***office address:*** House of Commons, London, SW1A 0AA, United Kingdom; ***phone:*** +44 (0)20 7219 3000; ***e-mail:*** wattsd@parliament.uk.

WAXMAN, Henry; American, Congressman, California 30th District, US House of Representatives; ***education:*** UCLA, USA, BA, political science; UCLA Law School, JD; ***party:*** Democratic Party; ***political career:*** California State Assembly (three terms); mem., US House of Representatives; ***interests:*** health; ***committees:*** Energy and Commerce; ***office address:*** House of Representatives, 436 Cannon House Street, Washington, DC 20515-6501, USA; ***phone:*** +1 202 224 3121.

WEATHERLEY, Mike; MP for Hove, UK Government; ***party:*** Conservative; ***political career:*** Councillor, Crawley Borough Council, 2006-07; MP for Hove, May 2010-; ***committees:*** Administration, 2010-; ***office address:*** House of Commons, London, SW1A 0AA, United Kingdom; ***phone:*** +44 (0)20 7219 3000; ***e-mail:*** mike.weatherley.mp@parliament.uk.

WEBB, Senator Jim; Senator for Virginia, United States Senate; ***born:*** 9 February 1946; ***education:*** Univ. of Southern Calif., 1963-64; US Naval Academy, grad. 1968; Georgetown Univ. Law School, J.D., 1975; ***political career:*** US Senator for Virginia, 2007-; ***professional career:*** US Marines, 1968-72; author, screenwriter and journalist; lawyer; Sec. of the Navy, 1987-88; ***office address:*** United States Senate, 248 Russell Senate Office Building, Washington, DC 20510, USA; ***phone:*** +1 202 224 4024; ***URL:*** http://www.webb.senate.gov.

WEBB, Prof. Steve; British, Minister for State, Department for Energy and Climate Change, UK Government; ***born:*** 18 July 1965, Birmingham; ***married:*** Helen Webb; ***children:*** Charlotte (F), Dominic (M); ***education:*** Hertford College, Oxford, First Class Honours Degree, PPE; ***party:*** Liberal Democratic Party; ***political career:*** MP for Northavon, 1997-10, for Thornbury and Yate, 2010-; Shadow Health Secretary, 2005-Asst. Lib. Dem. Spokesman for Social Security and Welfare State, 1997-99; Chief Spokesman, Social Security, 1999-2001; Shadow Sec. of State for Work and Pensions, 2001-05; Shadow Sec. of State for Health, 2005-06; Chair, Election Manifesto Team, 2007-08; Shadow Sec. for Environment, Energy, Food and Rural Affairs, 2008; Shadow Sec. for Energy and Climate Change, 2008-09; Shadow Sec. for Work and Pension, 2009-10; Minister of State, Dept. for Work and Pensions, May 2010-; ***memberships:*** Mem. Commission on Social Justice; Amnesty Int.; World Development Org.; Lib.Dem. Tax & Benefits Working Gp.; ***professional career:*** Economist, Institute for Fiscal Studies, 1986-95; Professor of Social Policy at Bath University, 1995-97; ***committees:*** Ecclesiastical; All Party Gps: Camping and Traveller Management; Christians in Parliament; E-Democracy; Myodil; Nuclear Energy; Occupational Pensions; Post Offices; Poverty; Social Science and Policy; Pensioner Incomes; Internet; Infertility; Chair, Manifesto Writing Group, 2006-07; ***honours and awards:*** Winner of the 2005 inaugural Hansard Society E-Democracy Award; ***publications:*** For Richer, For Poorer: The Changing Distribution of Income in the UK 1961 - 1991 (1994, Institute for Fiscal Studies); Contributor to The Orange Book - Reclaiming Liberalism, (2004); Author of a chapter in The Future of the NHS (2006), ed. Michelle Tempest; ***recreations:*** oboe, church organist, internet/computing; ***office address:*** House of Commons, London, SW1A 0AA, United Kingdom; ***phone:*** +44 (0)20 7219 4378; ***e-mail:*** webbs@parliament.uk; ***URL:*** http://www.stevewebb.org.uk; (blog) http://www.webbsteve.blogspot.com.

WEEKERS, Mr Drs F.H.H.; Dutch, Secretary of State for Finance, Netherlands Government; ***born:*** 17 October 1967, Weert, Netherlands; ***languages:*** English, German, French; ***education:*** Doctoral Degree in Law; Doctoral Degree in Econ.; ***party:*** VVD; ***political career:*** City Cllr., 1994-2003, 2008-10; MP, 1998-2002, 2003-; State Secretary for Finance, Rutte-Verhagen gov., 2010-12; State Secretary for Finance, Rutte-Asscher gov., Nov. 2012-; ***professional career:*** Attorney, admitted to the bar in Roermond; ***committees:*** Justice/Legal Affairs; European Affairs: Budget; Finance; Public Health; Social Affairs; Transport; ***office address:*** Korte Voorhout 7, Postbus 20201, 2500 EE The Hague, Netherlands; ***URL:*** http://www.minfin.nl.

WEI OF SHOREDITCH, Lord Nathanael; Member, House of Lords; ***party:*** Conservative; ***political career:*** Mem., House of Lords, 2010-; Gov. Adviser, Big Society, 2010-; ***professional career:*** Founding Mem., Teach First; Founder, Future Leaders; ***honours and awards:*** Raised to the peerage, 2010; ***office address:*** House of Lords, London, SW1A 0PW, United Kingdom; ***phone:*** +44 (0)20 7219 3000; ***fax:*** +44 (0)20 7219 5979; ***URL:*** http://www.parliament.uk.

WEIDMANN, Dr Jens; President, Deutsche Bundesbank; ***born:*** 1968; ***education:*** Univ. de Droit, d'Economie et des Sciences, Aix-Marseille III & the Rheinische Friedrich-Wilhelms Univ., Bonn, economics; Bonn Univ., Ph.D; ***professional career:*** IMF, 1997-99; Sec. Gen., German Council of Economic Experts, 1999-2003; Head, Deutssche Bundesbankk's Monetary Policy and Analysis Division & Dep. Head, Economics Dept., 2003-06; Head, Dept. for Economic & Fiscal Policy, Federal Chancellor's Office, 2006-11; Pres., Deutsche Bundesbank, 2011-; Mem., Gov. Council, ECB, 2011-; Gov., IMF, 2011-; Mem., Board of Directors, Bank for International Settlements, 2011-; Mem., Steering Cttee. of the Financial Stability Board, 2011-; Mem., Steering Cttee., European Systemic Risk Board, 2011-; ***office address:*** Deutsche Bundesbank, Wilhelm Epstein Straße 14, 60431 Frankfurt am Main, Germany; ***URL:*** http://www.bundesbank.de.

WEINTRAUB, Ellen; Chair, Federal Election Commission; ***education:*** Yale College, BA, cum laude; Harvard Univ., J.D.; ***professional career:*** mem., New York and District of Columbia bars; mem., Supreme Court bar; Litigator, Cahill Gordon & Reindel; Counsel, Perkins Coie LLP; mem, Federal Election Commission, 2002, chair, 2003, 2013; ***office address:*** Federal Election Commission, 999 E Street, NW, Washington, DC 20463, USA; ***phone:*** +1 202 694 1100; ***fax:*** +1 202 219 3880; ***URL:*** http://www.fec.gov/.

WEIR, Michael; Member of Parliament for Angus, House of Commons; ***born:*** 24 March 1957, Arbroath; ***children:*** 2; ***education:*** Arbroath High School; LLB, Aberdeen Univ.; ***party:*** SNP; ***political career:*** District Cllr., 1984-88; MP, Angus, 2001-; SNP Spokesperson, 2004-; ***professional career:*** solicitor ; ***recreations:*** history, organic gardening; ***office address:*** Scottish Nationalist Party, 6 North Charlotte Street, Edinburgh, EH2 4 JH, United Kingdom; ***phone:*** +44 (0)131 226 3661; ***fax:*** +44 (0)131 226 7373; ***e-mail:*** mike.weir.mp@angussnp.org; ***URL:*** http://www.xjr60.dial.pipex.com.

WELBY, ARCHBISHOP OF CANTERBURY, The Most Rev. and the Rt. Hon. Justin; Archbishop of Canterbury; ***married:*** Caroline Welby (née Eaton); ***languages:*** French; ***education:*** Trinity College, Cambridge Univ.; St John's College, Durham Univ.; ***political career:*** Mem., House of Lords, 2013-; ***professional career:*** Elf Aquitaine; Treasurer, Enterprise Oil PLC, 1984-89; Ordained as a Deacon, 1992; Ordained as a Priest, 1993; Dean of Liverpool, 2007-11; Bishop of Durham, 2011-13; Archbishop of Canterbury, March 2013-; ***office address:*** Lambeth Palace, Lambeth Palace Rd, Lambeth, London, SE1 7JU, United Kingdom; ***phone:*** +44 (0)20 7898 1200.

WENAWESER, Ambassador Christian; Ambassador Extraordinary and Plenipotentiary Permanent Representative of Liechtenstein , United Nations; ***born:*** 1963; ***education:*** Zurich Univ., 1982-87, Licentiate, 1987; Scholarship, Swiss National Foundation; Diplomatic Training, MFA, 1991-92; ***professional career:*** Diplomatic Officer, Office of Foreign Affairs, Liechtenstein; Counsellor and Dep. Perm. Rep. of Liechtenstein, 1998-2002; Permanent Rep. of Liechtenstein to the UN, 2002-; Chmn., Special Working Group on the Crime of Aggression, 2003-09; Vice-Chair, Working Group on Security Council Reform, 2004-05; Vice-Pres., 61st Session of the UN General Assembly, 2006-07; President, Assembly of States Parties to the Rome Statue of the International Criminal Court (ICC), 2008-; ***office address:*** Permanent Mission of Liechtenstein to the UN, 633 Third Avenue, 27th Floor, New York NY 10017, USA.

WENSLEY, H.E. Penelope, AO; Governor, State of Queensland, Australia; ***married:*** Stuart McCosker; ***d:*** 2; ***education:*** Univ. of Queensland, BA Hons., English and French Lit.; ***professional career:*** joined the Australian Foreign Service, 1968; postings to Paris 1969-73, Mexico City 1975-77, Wellington New Zealand 1982-5, Consul-General, Hong Kong 1986-8; Amb. and Perm. Rep. to the UN, Geneva, 1993-6, 1991-92; Amb. for Environment, 1992-96; Amb. and Perm. Rep. to the UN, New York, 1997-2001; High Cmnr. to India and non-resident Amb. to Bhutan, 2001-04; Amb. to France, and non-resident Amb. to Algeria, Mauritania, Morocco and Monaco, 2005-08; Governor of Queensland, 2008-; ***honours and awards:*** Qld. Univ. Alumnus of the Year 1994; Hon. Dr. of Philosophy, Univ. of Qld., 1994; Officer of the Order of Australia (AO), 2001; Hon. Dr. of Philosophy, Griffith University, 2008; ***office address:*** Government House, GPO Box 434, Brisbane, Queensland 4001, Australia; ***phone:*** +61 (0)7 3858 5700; ***fax:*** +61 (0)7 3858 5701; ***URL:*** http://www.govhouse.qld.gov.au/.

WESCOT-WILLIAMS, Sarah; Prime Minister, Government of Sint Maarten; ***party:*** Leader, Democratic Party; ***political career:*** Mem., Executive Council, Sint Maarten, 1991-93, 1995-97, 1999-; Mem., Legislative Council, 1995-; Chair, Permanent Commission for Constitutional Affairs of the Legislature; Prime Minister, October 10, 2010-; ***office address:*** Office of the Prime Minister, Philipsburg, Sint Maarten.

WESSEX, HRH The Earl of; Earl of Wessex; ***born:*** 10 March 1964; ***parents:*** HRH The Prince Philip, Duke of Edinburgh and HRH Queen Elizabeth II; ***married:*** HRH Countess of Wessex (née Sophie Rhys-Jones), 19 June 1999; ***children:*** Lady Louise Alice Elizabeth Mary (F), James Alexander Philip Theo, Viscount Severn (M); ***education:*** Gordonstoun; Jesus Coll. Cambridge, MA, History, 1990; ***professional career:*** Royal Marines; Really Useful Theatre Company; Dir. Ardent Productions; undertaking Royal engagements in UK and abroad; Patron of many organisations including The Duke of Edinburgh's Award, The Duke of Edinburgh's International Award Assoc, Commonwealth Games Federation, British Paralympic Assoc., City of Birmingham Symphony Orchestra and Symphony Chorus, ADC Theatre, Cambridge, Globe Theatre, Saskatchewan, Canada, Haddo Arts Trust, London Mozart Players, National Youth Music Theatre, National Youth Orchestras of Scotland, National Youth Theatre, The Royal Exchange Theatre Co., Badminton Scotland, Snow Sport GB, Orpheus Trust, Northern Ballet; Chetham School of Music; Royal Wolverhampton School, Lincoln Cathedral, Beacon Arts Theatre Greenock, Hall for Cornwall; Oglander Roman Villa; Royal Fleet Auxillary Assn; Commodore in Chief, Royal Fleet Auxiliary; Royal Honorary Colonel, The Royal Wessex Yeomanry, The London Regiment, Royal Colonel 2 Bn. Rifles; Colonel-in-Chief, Saskatchewan Dragons, Prince Edward Island Regiment, the Hastings and Prince Edward Regiment; Honorary Air Commodore RAF Waddington; ***trusteeships:*** The Duke of Edinburgh's Award; The Duke of Edinburgh's International Award Foundation. Chmn., International Award Council; Chancellor Univ. of Bath; Honorary Liveryman Worshipful Company of Haberdashers, Gardeners, Fuellers; ***recreations:*** real tennis, horse riding, sailing, skiing, badminton; ***office address:*** Bagshot Park, Bagshot, Surrey, GU19 5PL, United Kingdom; ***phone:*** +44 (0)126 707040; ***e-mail:*** jebsmed.severn@ntlbusiness.com.

WESSEX, HRH The Countess of; Countess of Wessex; ***parents:*** Christopher Rhys-Jones and Mary Rhys-Jones; ***married:*** The Earl of Wessex, 19 June 1999; ***children:*** Lady Louise Alice Elizabeth Mary (F), James Alexander Philip Theo, Viscount Severn (M); ***professional career:*** Public Relations; Patron of many organisations including, Brendoncare Foundation, Central School of Ballet, CHASE Children's Hospice Service, Childline, Craft Guild of Chefs, Disability Initiative, Dyslexia Institute, Friends of Southwark Cathedral, Friends of the Royal London Hospital Whitechapel, Greater London Fund for the Blind, Hallé Concerts Soc., Healing Foundation, Lions Club Int., London Children's Flower Soc., MENCAP, Meningitis Trust, Moor House School, Nat. Autistic Soc., New Haven Trust, Peckham Settlement, RNID, Royal Coll. of Speech and Language Therapists, Royal School for Deaf Children, St Mary's Wrestwood Children's Trust, Sunderland AFC Foundation, Tomorrow's People, Vision 2020, Wessex Heartbeat; Grand Pres. St John Ambulance, Pres., Brainwave; Pres., Girl Guiding UK; Colonel in Chief, Lincoln and Welland Regiment, Royal Alberta Light Horse and Queen Alexandra's Royal Army Nursing Corps; ***committees:*** Advisory Cttee.; ***office address:*** Bagshot Park, Bagshot, GU19 5PL, United Kingdom; ***phone:*** +44 (0)1276 707044.

WESTCOTT, Dr Nicholas, CMG; Managing Director for Africa, European External Action Service; ***born:*** 20 July 1956; ***languages:*** French, Swahili; ***education:*** Sidney Sussex College, Cambridge, BA (History), 1977; Univ. of Dar es Salaam, Tanzania, Research Associate, 1979-80; Sidney Sussex College, Cambridge, PhD (African Studies), 1982; ***professional career:*** Joined FCO, 1982; Secondment to EC, Brussels, 1984-85; First Sec., UK Permanent Rep. to the EC, 1985-89; Europe Communities Dept (Internal), FCO, 1990-91; European Correspondent and Head of CFSP Unit, 1992-93; Dep. High Cmnr., Dar es Salaam, 1993-96; Hd. of Economic Relations Dept, 1996-98; Counsellor, Resource Planning Dept, 1999; Minister-Counsellor, British Embassy, Washington, 1999-2002; Chief Information Officer, FCO, 2002-07; High Cmnr. to Ghana, and Ambassador (non-resident) to Cote d'Ivoire, Burkina Faso, Niger and Togo, 2008-11; MD for Africa, European External Action Service, 2011-; ***honours and awards:*** Companion of the Order of St Michael and St George, 1998; ***office address:*** EEAS, Africa Dept., rue de la Science, 1040 Brussels, Belgium.

WESTERWELLE, Dr Guido; Vice-Chancellor and Minister of Foreign Affairs, German Government; ***education:*** Law, Univ. of Bonn, 1987; Doctoral degree in law, FernUniversität Hagen; ***party:*** FDP; ***political career:*** GDP Party Chmn., 2001-; Vice-Chancellor and Minister of Foreign Affairs, 2009-; ***office address:*** Ministry of Foreign Affairs, Werderscher Markt 1, 10117 Berlin, Germany; ***phone:*** +49 (0)30 5000; ***fax:*** +49 (0)1888 173402; ***URL:*** http://www.auswaertiges-amt.de.

WESTMACOTT, Sir Peter John, KCMG LVO; Ambassador, British Embassy USA; ***born:*** 23 December 1950; ***married:*** Susie Nemazee; ***children:*** Oliver Thomas (M), Laura Jane (F), Rupert John (M); ***professional career:*** entered FCO, 1972; Third Sec., Middle Eastern Dept., FCO, 1972-73; Second Sec., Tehran, 1974-78; on loan to European Cmn., FCO, 1978-80; First Sec., Economic, Paris, 1980-84; First Sec., European Community Dept., FCO, 1984; PS/Minister of State, FCO, 1984-87; Head of Chancery, Ankara, 1987-90; Dep. Private Sec. to HRH The Prince of Wales, 1990-93; Counsellor, Political and Public Affairs, Washington, 1993-97; Dir. Americas, FCO, 1997-2000; Deputy Under Sec., Wider World, FCO, 2000-2001; British Amb. to Turkey, 2002-06; British Amb. to France, 2007-11; Amb. to the USA, 2012-; ***office address:*** British Embassy, 3100 Massachusetts Avenue NW, Washington, DC 20008, USA; ***phone:*** +1 202 588 6500; ***fax:*** +1 202 588 7870; ***URL:*** http://ukinusa.fco.gov.uk/.

WHARTON, James; MP for Stockton South, UK Government; ***party:*** Conservative; ***political career:*** MP for Stockton South, May 2010-; ***committees:*** Public Accounts Select Cttee., 2010-; ***office address:*** House of Commons, London, SW1A 0AA, United Kingdom; ***phone:*** +44 (0)20 7219 3000; ***e-mail:*** james.wharton.mp@parliament.uk.

WHEATCROFT OF BLACKHEATH, Baroness Patience; Member, House of Lords; ***party:*** Conservative Party; ***political career:*** Mem., House of Lords, 2010-; ***professional career:*** Dep. City Editor, Mail on Sunday; Business and City Editor, The Times; Editor, Sunday Telegraph; Editor-in-chief, The Wall Street Journal Europe; Non-exec. dir., Barclays Plc & Shaftesbury plc, 2008-09; ***office address:*** House of Lords, London, SW1A 0PW, United Kingdom; ***phone:*** +44 (0)20 7219 3000.

WHEELER, Graeme; Governor, Reserve Bank of New Zealand; ***professional career:*** New Zealand Treasury; various positions, World Bank, 1997-2010, incl. Vice-Pres. & Treasurer, 2001-06. Man. Dir., Operations, 2006-10; Advisory Business, US, 2010-12; Governor, Reserve Bank of New Zealand, 2012-; ***office address:*** Reserve Bank of New Zealand, 2 The Terrace, PO Box 2498 , Wellington 6011, New Zealand.

WHEELER, Heather; MP for South Derbyshire, UK Government; ***party:*** Conservative; ***political career:*** Councillor, London Borough of Wandsworth Council, 1982-86; Councillor, South Derbyshire District Council,1995-; MP for South Derbyshire, May 2010-; ***committees:*** Standards & Privileges Parly. Select Cttee., 2010-; Communities & Local Gov. Parly Select Cttee., 2011-; ***office address:*** House of Commons, London, SW1A 0AA, United Kingdom; ***phone:*** +44 (0)20 7219 3000; ***e-mail:*** heather.wheeler.mp@parliament.uk.

WHEELER, Baroness Margaret; Member, House of Lords; ***political career:*** Mem., House of Lords, 2010-; ***professional career:*** Fmr. mem., Commission on Social Justice; ***office address:*** House of Lords, London, SW1A 0PW, United Kingdom; ***phone:*** +44 (0)20 7219 3000; ***fax:*** +44 (0)20 7219 5979; ***URL:*** http://www.parliament.uk.

WHITE, H.E. Barry; Ambassador, US Embassy in Norway; ***education:*** Harvard Coll. USA; J.D., Harvard Law Sch., USA; ***professional career:*** Chmn. and Managing Partner, (CEO), Foley Hoag LLP; Amb. to Norway, 2009-; ***office address:*** US Embassy, Drammensveien 18, 0244 Oslo, Norway; ***phone:*** +47 2244 8550; ***fax:*** +47 2243 8377; ***e-mail:*** irc@usa.no; ***URL:*** http://norway.usembassy.gov.

WHITE, Chris; MP for Warwick and Leamington, UK Government; ***party:*** Conservative; ***political career:*** Councillor, Warwick District Council, 2007-; MP for Warwick and Leamington, May 2010-; ***committees:*** International Development Select Cttee., 2010-; Arms Export Controls, 2010-; ***office address:*** House of Commons, London, SW1A 0AA, United Kingdom; ***phone:*** +44 (0)20 7219 3000; ***e-mail:*** chris.white.mp@parliament.uk.

WHITEFORD, Eilidh; MP for Banff and Buchan, UK Government; ***party:*** Scottish National Party; ***political career:*** MP for Banff and Buchan, May 2010-; SNP Spokesperson, 2010-; ***committees:*** Scottish Affairs Select Cttee., 2010-; ***office address:*** House of Commons, London, SW1A 0AA, United Kingdom; ***phone:*** +44 (0)20 7219 3000; ***e-mail:*** eilidh.whiteford.mp@parliament.uk.

WHITEHEAD, Dr Alan; British, Member of Parliament for Southampton Test, House of Commons; ***born:*** 15 September 1950; ***married:*** Sophie Whitehead (née Wronska), 1979; ***children:*** Patrick (M), Isabel (F); ***languages:*** French; ***education:*** Southampton Univ., B.A., Ph.D.; ***party:*** Labour Party; ***political career:*** Leader, Southampton City Cncl., 1984-92; PPS, Baroness Blackstone 1999-2001; MP, Southampton Test, 1997-; Parly. Under-Sec. of State, Dept. of Transport, Local Government and the Regions, 2001-02; ***interests:*** further and higher education, environment, transport, local and regional govt.; ***professional career:*** Lecturer; Prof. of Public Policy, Southampton Inst., 1992-97; ***committees:*** currently: Standards & Privileges, 2005-; Energy & Climate Change, 2009-; Environmental Audit, 2010-; ***office address:*** Constituency Office, 20-22 Southampton Street, Southampton, SO15 3FD, United Kingdom; ***phone:*** +44 (0)23 8023 1942; ***e-mail:*** whiteheada@parliament.uk; ***URL:*** http://www.alan-whitehead.org.uk.

WHITEHOUSE, Senator Sheldon; US Senator for Rhode Island, US Senate; ***born:*** 20 October 1955; ***education:*** Yale; Univ. of Virginia School of Law; ***political career:*** Policy Advisor, and Counsel, Office of the Governor of Rhode Island; R.I.US Attorney, 1994-98; Attorney General, 1999-2003; US Senator, 2007-; ***committees:*** Budget; Environment & Public Works; HELP; Judiciary; Special Cttee. on Aging; ***office address:*** United States Senate, 717 Hart Senate Office Building, Washington, DC 20510, USA; ***phone:*** +1 202 224 2921; ***URL:*** http://www.whitehouse.senate.gov.

WHITFIELD, Ed; American, Congressman, Kentucky First District, US House of Representatives; ***party:*** Republican; ***political career:*** mem., US House of Representatives, 1994-; ***committees:*** Energy and Commerce Cttee.; ***office address:*** House of Representatives, 436 Cannon House Street, Washington, DC 20515-6501, USA; ***phone:*** +1 202 224 3121.

WHITTAKER, Craig; MP for Calder Valley, UK Government; ***party:*** Conservative; ***political career:*** Councillor, Heptonstall Parish Council, 1998-2003; Councillor, Calderdale Metropolitan Borough Council, 2003-04, 2007-10; MP for Calder Valley, May 2010-; ***committees:*** Education Select Cttee., 2010-; Unopposed Bills (Panel), 2011-; Joint Committee on the Draft Communications Data Bill, 2012-; ***office address:*** House of Commons, London, SW1A 0AA, United Kingdom; ***phone:*** +44 (0)20 7219 3000; ***e-mail:*** craig.whittaker.mp@parliament.uk.

WHITTINGDALE, John; MP for Maldon, House of Commons; ***born:*** 16 October 1959, Dorset, UK; ***parents:*** John Whittingdale and Margaret Whittingdale (née Napier); ***married:*** Ancilla Whittingdale (née Murfitt), 8 September 1990 (Div'd Sept. 08); ***children:*** Henry (M), Alice (F); ***education:*** Sandroyd School, Wiltshire: Winchester College; Univ. College, London; ***political career:*** Political Sec. to Prime Minister, 1988-90; Private Sec. to Rt. Hon. Margaret Thatcher, 1990-92; MP, South Colchester and Maldon, 1992-97; MP, Maldon and Chelmsford East, 1997-2010; Opposition Whip, 1997-98; Conservative Treasury Spokesman, 1998-99; PPS to the Leader of the Opposition, 1999-2001; Shadow Sec. of State for Trade and Industry, 2001-2002; Shadow Sec. of State for Culture, Media and Sport, 2002-04; Shadow Sec. of State for Agriculture, 2004-05; Shadow Sec. of State for Culture, Media and Sport, 2005-07; MP for Maldon, 2010-; Chmn., All Party Ukraine Parly Gp., 2010-; Chmn., All Party Writers Gp, 2010-; Chmn., All Party Intellectual Property Gp., 2010-; Jt. Chmn., All Party Electronic Games Gp., 2010-; ***committees:*** Chmn., House of Commons Culture, Media and Sport Select Cttee., 2005-; Parly. Mem., Conservative Party Board, 2006-10; Vice Chmn., Conservative 1922 Cttee., 2006; Liaison, 2005-; ***honours and awards:*** OBE, 1990; ***recreations:*** music, cinema; ***office address:*** House of Commons, London, SW1A 0AA, United Kingdom; ***phone:*** +44 (0)20 7219 3000; ***e-mail:*** john.whittingdale.mp@tory.org.uk.

WHITTY, Lord; Member of the House of Lords; ***born:*** 15 June 1943; ***parents:*** Frederick James and Kathleen May (née Lavender); ***married:*** Angela Forrester, 1993; Tanya Gibson, 1970 (Diss'd 1987); ***children:*** Michael Sean (M), Daniel James (M); ***languages:*** French, German; ***education:*** Latymer Sch.; St John's Coll., Cambridge; ***party:*** Labour; ***political career:*** General Sec., Labour Party, 1985-94; European Co-ordinator, Labour Party, 1994-97; Government Whip, Foreign Affairs, Education, 1997-98; Parly. Under Sec. (Transport) DETR, 1998-2001; Parly. Under Sec., Food, Farming and Rural Affairs, DEFRA, 2001-05; Mem., House of Lords; ***interests:*** employment, environment; ***professional career:*** Civil Servant, Trade Union Officer; Chair, Consumer Focus (formerly National Consumer Council), 2006-; Non-exec. dir., Environment Agency, 2006-10; ***honours and awards:*** Privy Councillor, 2005; ***office address:*** House of Lords, London, SW1A 0PQ, United Kingdom; ***phone:*** +44 (0)20 7219 3118; ***fax:*** +44 (0)20 7219 5979; ***e-mail:*** whittyl@parliament.uk.

WICKER, Roger F.; American, US Senator, US Senate; ***born:*** July 5, 1951; ***education:*** Univ.of Mississippi, B.A., 1973, J.D., 1975; ***party:*** Republican; ***political career:*** member of the Mississippi state senate, 1988-1994; mem., US House of Representatives, 1994-2007; Senator, US Senate, 2007-; ***professional career:*** Air Force Reserve Officer Training Corps; United States Air Force, 1976-1980; United States Air Force Reserve, 1980-2003; public defender, Lee County, Miss., 1984-1987; ***committees:*** Armed Services; Budget; Commerce, Science & Transportation; Environment and Public Works; Joint Economic Cttee.; ***office address:*** US Senate, 487 Russell Senate Office Building , Washington, DC 20510, USA; ***phone:*** +1 202 224 6253; ***URL:*** http://www.wicker.senate.gov.

WIGGIN, Bill, MP; MP for North Herefordshire, House of Commons; ***born:*** 1966; ***party:*** Conservative; ***political career:*** MP for Leominster, 2001-10, for North Herefordshire, 2010-; Shadow Secretary of State for Wales, 2003-05; Shadow Minister for Environment, Food & Rural Affairs, 2005-09; Assist. Gov. Whip, 2010-12; ***professional career:*** Banker; ***committees:*** Welsh Affairs, 2001-03; Environment, Food and Rural Affairs Select Cttee, 2002-05; Selection, 2012-; ***office address:*** House of Commons, London, SW1A 0AA, United Kingdom; ***e-mail:*** bill.wiggin.mp@parliament.uk.

WIGHTMAN, Andrew; Ambassador, British Embassy in the Republic of Korea; ***languages:*** French, Korean; ***education:*** BA, Edinburgh Univ.; ***professional career:*** Dep. Amb, to Italy; Amb. to the Republic of Korea, 2011-; ***office address:*** British Embassy, Taepyeongno 40, 4 Jeong-dong, Jung-gu, Seoul 100-120, South Korea; ***phone:*** +82 2 3210 5500; ***fax:*** +82 2 725 1738; ***e-mail:*** bembassy@britain; ***URL:*** https://www.gov.uk/government/world/organisations/british-embassy-seoul.

WIGLEY, Lord Dafydd; British, Member, House of Lords; ***born:*** 1943; ***parents:*** Elfyn Edward Wigley, BA, FSAA, FIMT and Myfanwy Wigley LL.B; ***married:*** Elinor Bennett Wigley (née Owen), 1967; ***public role of spouse:*** International Harpist; ***languages:*** Welsh, French; ***education:*** Caernarfon Grammar Sch; Rydal Sch.; Manchester Univ., BSc; ***party:*** Plaid Cymru (Welsh National Party); ***political career:*** Cllr, Merthyr Tydfil County Borough Cncl, 1972-74; Plaid Cymru MP for Caernarfon, 1974-2001; Party Spokesman on Economic & Industrial Affairs; Pres. Plaid Cymru, 1981-84; Main Sponsor, Disabled Persons Act, 1981; Chmn. All-Party Reform Group, 1983-87; Vice-Chmn. All-Party Social Services Group, 1985-87; Plaid Cymru Whip, 1987; Pres., 1991-2010; Vice Chair, All Party Disablement Group, 1992-2001; Candidate, European Parliament Elections, North Wales Constituency, 1994; Leader of the Opposition, National Assembly of Wales, 1999-2000; Member, House of Lords, 2011-; ***memberships:*** Pres., Spastic Socy, in Wales, 1985-88; mem., Mencap Profound Mental Handicap Study Cttee, 1987-97; Vice-Pres., Wales Cncl. for the Disabled; Pres., Mencap in Wales, 1991-; ***professional career:*** Finance Staff, Ford Motor Co., 1964-67; Chief Cost Accountant & Financial Planning Mgr., Mars Ltd., 1967-71; Financial Controller, Hoover Ltd., 1971-74; Vice-Pres., Fed. of Industrial Dev. Assns., 1985-2001; Chmn., ADC Ltd., 1984-; Chair, Advisory Bd., Univ. of Wales Bangor; Pres., South Caernarfon Creamery, 1989-; ***committees:*** mem., Commons Select Cttee on Welsh Affairs, 1983-87; Economic Development Cttee., National Assembly, 2000-; Culture Cttee., NA, 2000-; Audit Cttee., NA, 1999-, Chair, 2002-; ***honours and awards:*** Fellow, Univ. of Bangor, Wales; Privy Cllr., 1997; Hon. Doctor of Law, Univ. of Wales, 2002; ***publications:*** An Economic Plan for Wales (1970); Agenda I'R IAITH, (1988); Report on Tourism in Wales (1987); O Ddifri (1992); Dal Ati (1993); A Democratic Wales in a United Europe (1995); A Real Choice for Wales; Ymaen ir Wal (2001); ***recreations:*** chess, football, swimming, tennis; ***office address:*** House of Lords, London, SW1A 0PW, United Kingdom; ***phone:*** +44 (0)20 7219 3000.

WIJNERMAN, Adelien; Minister of Finance, Government of Suriname; ***political career:*** Minister of Finance, 2011-; ***professional career:*** economist; ***office address:*** Ministry of Finance, Onafhankelukheidsplein #3, Paramaribo, Suriname.

WILDASH, H. E. Richard; Ambassador, British Embassy in Angola; *born:* 24 December 1955, Ealing, London; *parents:* Arthur Ernest Wildash and Sheila Howard Wildash; *married:* Elizabeth Jane Wildash (née Walmsley), August 1981; *children:* Bethany (F), Joanna (F); *education:* St. Paul's Sch., Barnes; Corpus Christi Coll., Cambridge; *memberships:* MCIL, FRGS; *professional career:* Third Sec., British Embassy, East Berlin, 1979; Third Sec., British Embassy, Abidjan, 1981; First Sec., British High Cmn., Harare, 1988; First Sec., British High Comn., New Delhi, 1994; Dep. High Cmnr., British High Cmnr., Kuala Lumpur, 1998; British High Cmn., Cameroon, 2002-05; British Amb. to Equatorial Guinea, Gabon, Central African Republic & Chad, 2002-06; British High Cmnr., Malawi, 2005-10: Amb. to Angola, 2010-; *honours and awards:* LVO; *recreations:* travel, arts; *office address:* RJWILDASH 031869, BFPO 5329, HA4 6EP, United Kingdom; *e-mail:* Richard.Wildash@fco.gov.uk / wildash@tuskerfish.co.uk.

WILDERS, Geert; Member of Parliament, Netherlands Government; *party:* People's Party for Freedom and Democracy, 1989-2004; Leader, Party for Freedom, 2006-; *political career:* Mem., Tweede Kamer, 1998-; *office address:* Tweede Kamer, The Netherlands Parliament, The Hague, Netherlands.

WILLEM-ALEXANDER, Prince of Orange; Dutch, King of the Netherlands; *born:* 27 April 1967; *parents:* Prince Claus (dec'd) and HM Queen Beatrix of the Netherlands; *married:* Queen Máxima (née Zorreguieta), 2002; *children:* Catharina-Amalia, Princess of Orange (F), Princess Alexia (F), Princess Ariane (F); *education:* Nieuwe Baarnse School, Baarn; Baarns Lyceum; Eerste Vrijzinnig Christelijk Lyceum, The Hague; Atlantic College, Llantwit Major, Wales, International Baccalaureate, 1985; military service; Leiden University, history, 1987-93; *professional career:* military service, 1985-87; Military Pilot's licence, 334 Transport Squadron, Royal Netherlands Air Force; 1993; Commodore, Royal Netherlands Navy reserve; Brigadier General, Royal Netherlands Army reserve; Commodore, Royal Netherlands Air Force reserve; Brigadier General, Royal Military Constabulary reserve; Aide-de-Camp Extraordinary to Her Majesty the Queen; Became King on the abdication of his mother Queen Beatrix, April 30 2013-; *office address:* Paleis Noordeinde 68, 2500 GK The Hague, Netherlands; *URL:* http://www.koninklijkhuis.nl/.

WILLETTS, Rt. Hon. David; British, Minister of State for Universities and Science, Department for Business, Innovation and Skills, UK Government; *born:* 9 March 1956, Birmingham, United Kingdom; *parents:* John Willetts and Hilary Willetts; *married:* Sarah Willetts (née Butterfield), 1986; *children:* Matthew (M), Imogen (F); *public role of spouse:* Artist; *languages:* German; *education:* King Edward's School, Birmingham; Christ Church, Oxford, First Class Hons. Degree, Politics, Philosophy and Econs.; *party:* Conservative Party; *political career:* Research Asst. to Nigel Lawson MP, 1978; Official, HM Treasury, 1978-84; Mem., Margaret Thatcher's Downing Street Policy Unit, 1984-86; Dir. of Studies, Centre for Policy Studies, 1987-92; Consultant Dir., Conservative Research Dept., 1987-92; MP, Havant, 1992-; PPS to Sir Norman Fowler, 1993-94; Treasury Whip, 1994-95; PS, Office of Public Service, 1995-96; Paymaster General, 1996; Opp. Spokesman on Employment, 1997; Chair., Conservative Research Dept., 1997-; Shadow Sec. of State for Education and Employment, 1998-99, Social Security, 1999-; Shadow Secretary of State for Work and Pensions, 2001-2005; Shadow Sec. of State for Trade and Industry, May-Dec. 2005; Shadow Sec. of State for Education and Skills, Dec. 2005-07; Shadow Sec. of State for Innovation, Universities and Skills, 2007-10; Minister of State for Universities and Science, Department for Business, Innovation and Skills, 2010-; *interests:* economic policy, health, social security, education; *professional career:* Dir., Retirement Security Ltd., 1988-94; Dir., Electra Corp. Ventures Ltd., 1988-94; Visiting Gellow, Nuffield College, Oxford, 1999-; mem., Global Commission on Ageing, 2000-; visiting Prof., Cass Business School, 2004-; *committees:* Social Security Cttee., 1992-93; mem., Conservative Policy Bd., 2001-; Hd., Conservative Policy Co-ordination, 2003-04; *publications:* Modern Conservation, 1992, Penguin; Civic Conservatism, 1994, Social Market Foundation; Blair's Gurus, 1996; Why Vote Conservative, 1997; Welfare to Work, 1998; After the Landslide, 1999, Centre for Policy Studies; Browned-Off: What's Wrong with Gordon Brown's Social Policy, 2000; Tax Credits: Do they add up?, 2002, Politea; Old Europe? Demographic Change & Pension Reform, 2003, Centre for European Reform; Left Out, Left Behind, 2003, Policy Exchange; *clubs:* Hurlingham Club; *recreations:* swimming, reading, cycling; *office address:* Ministry of State for Universities and Science, Department for Business, Innovation and Skills, 1 Victoria Street, London, SW1H 0ET, United Kingdom; *e-mail:* willettsd@parliament.uk; *URL:* http://www.davidwilletts.org.

WILLIAM OF WALES, DUKE OF CAMBRIDGE, HRH Prince; see Cambridge, Duke of.

WILLIAMS, Eliud; President, Government of Dominica; *born:* 1948; *education:* MBA, Univ. of West Indies, 1995; *political career:* Perm. Sec., Ministry of Health and Social Security, 1992-96; Perm. Sec., Ministry of Agriculture and the Environment, 1996-2000; Perm. Sec., Ministry of Communications, Works and Housing, 2000-08; President, 2012-; *professional career:* Dir. Gen., Eastern Caribbean Telecommunications Authority; Chmn., Rural Enterprise Project; *office address:* Office of the President, Government Headquarters, Morne Bruce, Roseau, Dominica; *phone:* +1 767 448 8968.

WILLIAMS, Hywel; MP for Arfon, House of Commons; *education:* Psychology BSc, Univ. Wales Cardiff, 1974; *party:* Plaid Cymru; *political career:* MP, Caernarfon, 2001-10; MP, Arfon, 2010-; *professional career:* Freelance Dir. Consultant, 1991-; *committees:* Chairman's Panel, 2005-; Science & Technology, 2012-; *office address:* Plaid Cymru, 18 Park Grove, Cardiff, CF1 3BN, United Kingdom; *e-mail:* hywel.williams.mp@parliament.uk.

WILLIAMS, Kirsty; Constituency Member for Brecon & Radnor, National Assembly for Wales; *party:* Leader, Welsh Liberal Democrats; *political career:* mem., the Nat. Assembly for Wales, Brecon and Radnor; *committees:* Chair, Standards of Conduct Cttee.; Mem., Economic Development & Transport Cttee.; *office address:* National Assembly for Wales, Cardiff Bay, Cardiff, CF99 1NA, United Kingdom; *phone:* +44 (0)29 2089 8358; *fax:* +44 (0)29 2089 8359; *e-mail:* kirsty.williams@wales.gov.uk.

WILLIAMS, Mark; MP for Ceredigion, House of Commons; *born:* 1966; *party:* Liberal Democrat; *political career:* MP for Ceredigion, 2005-; *professional career:* Teacher; *committees:* Welsh Affairs, 2005-; *office address:* House of Commons, London, SW1A 0AA, United Kingdom; *e-mail:* williamsmf@parliament.uk.

WILLIAMS, Roger; British, Member of Parliament for Brecon & Radnorshire, House of Commons; *born:* 1948; *married:* Penny Williams; *children:* 2; *education:* Christ Coll., Brecon; Selwyn Coll., Cambridge; *party:* Liberal Democrat Party; *political career:* County Cllr., for 20 years; past Vice-chmn., Powys TEC; MP for Brecon & Radnorshire, 2001-; Liberal Democrat Dep. Shadow Spokesman for Rural Affairs, 2002-05, 2006-10; Whip, 2004-07; Shadow Wales Secretary, 2007-10; Whip, 2008-10; *interests:* agriculture, education, economic dev., rural issues, broadcasting, miner's compensation, illegal meat imports; *memberships:* Fmr. Chmn, Mid Wales Agri-Food Partnership; Past Chmn., Brecon and Radnor NFU; Mem., Farmers Union of Wales; Mem. Country Landowners and Business Assn.; fmr. mem., Brecon Beacons Nat. Park; fmr. mem., Dev. Bd. for Rural Wales; *professional career:* Farmer; Lay Sch. Inspector, to date; *committees:* Standing Cttee. for the Animal Health Bill; Welsh Affairs Select Cttee., 2001-05; Environment, Food and Rural Affairs, 2005-10; Science & Technology, 2010-; *office address:* House of Commons, London, SW1A 0AA, United Kingdom; *phone:* +44 (0)20 7219 8145 / (0)1874 625739; *fax:* +44 (0)20 7219 1747 / (0)1874 625635; *e-mail:* williamsr@parliament.uk; williamsr@cix.co.uk; *URL:* http://www.rogerwilliams.org.uk; http://www.epolitix.com/webminster/roger-williams.

WILLIAMS, Stephen; MP for Bristol West, House of Commons; *born:* 11 October 1966; *education:* Mountain Ash Comprehensive, Glamorgan; Bristol University; *political career:* MP for Bristol West, 2005-; Lib. Dem., Shadow Public Health Minister, 2005-06; Lib. Dem., Shadow Further and Higher Education, 2006-07; Lib. Dem., Shadow Children, Schools and Families, 2007; Shadow Secretary of State for Innovation, Universities and Skills, 2009-10; *interests:* taxation, education, preventative health care, arts, civil rights; *memberships:* Mem. Chartered Institute of Taxation; WWF; Amnesty International; National Trust; Friends of the Earth; Bristol Civic Society; Stonewall; *professional career:* Tax Consultant; *committees:* Education and Skills Select Cttee., 2005-08; Public Accounts Cttee., 2005-06; Political & Constitutional Reform, 2010-; Members' Expenses, 2011-; *office address:* House of Commons, London, SW1P 0AA, United Kingdom; *phone:* +44 (0)20 7219 3000; *e-mail:* stephen.williams.mp@parliament.uk.

WILLIAMS OF ELVEL, Lord Charles Cuthbert Powell; Member, House of Lords; *born:* 9 February 1933; *parents:* Dr. N. P. Williams DD (dec'd) and Muriel de Lérisson Williams (née Cazenove); *married:* Jane Gillian (née Portal), 1975; *education:* Westminster; Christ Church, Oxford, BA, 1955, MA; London Sch. of Economics; *political career:* Opposition Front Bench Spksmn. on: Trade and Industry 1987-92; Defence 1990-97; the Environment 1992-97; Dep. Leader of the Opposition in the House of Lords, 1989-92; *interests:* banking, finance, environment; *professional career:* Nat. Service, 1955-57; BP, 1958-64; Bank of London and Montreal, 1964-66; Eurofinance SA, Paris, 1966-70; Baring Bros., 1970-77, MD 1971-77; Chmn., Price Cmn., 1977-79; MD., Henry Anhsbacher & Co. Ltd., 1979-82, Henry Ansbacher Holdings 1982-85; Dir. Mirror Gp. Newspapers plc, 1985-92; *committees:* Ecclesiastical Cttee., 1997-; Select Cttee on the EU, 1999-2002, 2009-; Chmn., Academy of St. Martin-in-the-Fields, 1988; Pres. Campaign for the Protection of Rural Wales, 1989-95; *honours and awards:* CBE, 1980; PC, 2013; *publications:* The Last Great Frenchman: a life of General de Gaulle, 1993; Bradman: an Australian Hero, 1996; Adenauer: the Father of the New Germany, 2000; Pétain, 2005; Harold Macmillan, 2009; *clubs:* MCC, Reform; *recreations:* cricket, music; *office address:* House of Lords, London, SW1A 0PW, United Kingdom; *phone:* +44 (0)20 7219 6054; *fax:* +44 (0)20 7219 5979; *e-mail:* williamscc@parliament.uk.

WILLIAMS OF OYSTERMOUTH, The Rt. Rev. and the Rt. Hon. the Lord Rowan Douglas; Archbishop of Canterbury, Church of England; *born:* 14 June 1950, Swansea Valley, Wales; *married:* Jane Paul, 1981; *s:* 1; *d:* 1; *public role of spouse:* Lecturer on theology; *education:* Christ's Coll., Cambridge, BA, Theology, 1971, MA, 1975; Wadham Coll., Oxford, D.phil, 1975; DD, 1989; *party:* Crossbencher; *political career:* Raised to the Peerage, 2013; *professional career:* Lecturer, Mirfield Theological Coll., 1975; Deacon, 1977; Priest, 1978; Tutor, Westcott House, Cambridge, 1977-80; Hon. Curate, Chesterton St. George, Ely, 1980-83; Lecturer in Divinity, Cambridge, 1980-86; Dean & Chaplain, Clare Coll., Cambridge, 1984-86; Prof., Theology, Oxford, 1986-1992; Bishop of Monmouth, 1992; Archbishop, Wales, 2000; elected Archbishop of Canterbury, July 2002, enthroned, Feb., 2003-March 2013; *honours and awards:* Fellow, British Academy, FRSL; *publications:* various books on history of theology and spirituality; *recreations:* music, fiction, languages; *office address:* House of Lords, London, SW1A 0PW, United Kingdom; *phone:* +44 (0)20 7219 5353.

WILLIAMSON, Chris; MP for Derby North, House of Commons; *party:* Labour; *political career:* Councillor, Derby City Council, 1991-; MP for Derby North, May 2010-; Shadow Minister, Communities and Local Government, Oct. 2010-; *committees:* Communities and Local Government Select Cttee., 2010; *office address:* House of Commons, London, SW1A 0AA, United Kingdom; *phone:* +44 (0)20 7219 3000; *e-mail:* chris.williamson.mp@parliament.uk.

WILLIAMSON, Gavin; MP for South Staffordshire, UK Government; *party:* Conservative; *political career:* Councillor, North Yorkshire County Council, 2001-05; MP for South Staffordshire, May 2010-; PPS, 2011-; *office address:* House of Commons, London, SW1A 0AA, United Kingdom; *phone:* +44 (0)20 7219 3000; *e-mail:* gavin.williamson.mp@parliament.uk.

WILLIAMSON, Hon. Maurice; New Zealander, Minister of Building and Construction; Customs; Statistics; Land Information, New Zealand Government; *born:* 6 March 1951, Auckland, New Zealand; *education:* Auckland Univ., B.Sc Physics & Mathematics, 1970-74; Post graduate studies, Computer Science, applied Mathematics, Political Science and Education; *party:* National Party; *political career:* Former Minister of Transport, Minister of Research, Science and Technology, Minister of Statistics, Minister of Local Government, Minister of Communications and Minister for Information Technology; Minister of Building and Construction; Customs; Statistics; Small Business, Nov. 2008-11; Minister of Building and Construction; Customs; Statistics; Land Information, 2011-; ***memberships:*** Pakuranga Rotary Club; Int'l. Federation of Operations Research Societies; Fellow, New Zealand Computer Socy., 1995; ***professional career:*** Teacher Part time, 1973-74; Corporate Planning Div., Air New Zealand, Ops research analyst, planning analyst, dept. supervisor, 1975-87; ***honours and awards:*** Awarded Chartered Institute of Transport Award for the Most Meritorious Paper prepared and delivered to the institute in 1994-95; ***clubs:*** Auckland toastmasters Club Communicator of the Year 1993; ***recreations:*** sailing, tennis, music, photography, follower of rugby and cricket; ***office address:*** Parliament Buildings, Wellington, New Zealand.

WILLIAMSON OF HORTON, Lord , GCMG, CB, PC; British, Member, House of Lords; ***born:*** 8 May 1934, Whitstable, Kent; ***parents:*** Samuel Charles Williamson and Marie Williamson (née Denney); ***married:*** Patricia Williamson (née Smith), 6 September 1961; ***s:*** 2; ***languages:*** French; ***education:*** Exeter Coll., Oxford; ***political career:*** Dep. Sec., UK Cabinet Office, 1983-87; Sec. Gen., European Cmn., 1987-97; Mem., House of Lords; Convenor (leader) of the Ind. Crossbench Peers, 2004-07; ***professional career:*** Non Exec. Dir., Whitbread Plc, 1998-2005; ***trusteeships:*** Thomson Foundation, 2001-06; ***honours and awards:*** GCMG, CB and PC; Commandeur Légion d'Honneur, France; Knight Commander's Cross, Order of Merit, Germany; ***office address:*** House of Lords, London, SW1A 0PW, United Kingdom; ***phone:*** +44 (0)20 7219 3583.

WILLOTT, Jenny; MP for Cardiff Central, House of Commons; ***political career:*** MP for Cardiff Central, 2005-; Shadow Minister for Youth Affairs, 2006-07; Deputy Chief Whip, 2006-08; Shadow Minister for Justice, 2008; Shadow Secretary of State for Work and Pensions, 2008-09; Shadow Chancellor of the Duchy of Lancaster, 2009-10; Assist. Gov. Whip, 2012-; ***office address:*** House of Commons, London, SW1P 0AA, United Kingdom; ***phone:*** +44 (0)20 7219 3000; ***e-mail:*** willottj@parliament.uk.

WILLS, Lord Michael; British, Member, House of Lords; ***born:*** 20 May 1952; ***education:*** Univ. of Cambridge; ***party:*** Labour Party; ***political career:*** MP, North Swindon, 1997-2010; Parly.-under-Sec., DTI; Parly.-under-sec., Education & Employment, 1999-2001; Parly.-under-Sec., LCD, 2001-03; Minister of State, Min. of Justice, 2007-10; Mem., House of Lords, 2010-; ***professional career:*** TV Producer; ***recreations:*** family; ***office address:*** House of Lords, London, SW1A 0AA, United Kingdom; ***phone:*** +44 (0)20 7219 3000; ***URL:*** http://www.michaeldwills.co.uk.

WILSON, Caroline; Consul-General, British Consulate in Hong Kong; ***education:*** MA, (Law) Downing Coll., Univ. of Cambridge; MA, (EEuropean Community Law), Universite Libre de Bruxelles; ***professional career:*** Minister Counsellor (Economic), British Emb in Moscow, 2008-12; Consul General, Hong Kong, 2012-; ***office address:*** British Consulate General, No 1 Supreme Court Road, Central, Hong Kong, Hong Kong; ***phone:*** +852 2901 3000; ***fax:*** +852 2901 3066; ***e-mail:*** political@britishconsulate.org.hk, commercial@britishconsulate.org.hk;
URL: https://www.gov.uk/government/world/organisations/british-consulate-general-hong-kong.

WILSON, Phil, MP; MP for Sedgefield, British Government; ***party:*** Labour; ***political career:*** Political Researcher; MP for Sedgefield, July 2007-; PPS, 2008-10; Opp. Whip, 2010-; ***committees:*** Public Accounts Cttee., 2007-10; Regulatory Reform Cttee., 2007-10; North East, 2009-10; ***office address:*** House of Commons, London, SW1 0AA, United Kingdom; ***phone:*** +44 (0)20 7219 3000; ***e-mail:*** phil.wilson.mp@parliament.uk.

WILSON, Rob; MP for Reading East, House of Commons; ***education:*** Reading Univ.; ***party:*** Conservative; ***political career:*** Local Councillor, Reading; MP for Reading East, 2005-; Shadow Min., Higher Education, 2007-09; Opp. Whip, 2009-10; PPS to Jeremy Hunt, 2010-; ***professional career:*** Businessman, Health and Communications Sectors; ***office address:*** House of Commons, London, SW10 0AA, United Kingdom; ***phone:*** +44 (0)20 7219 2498; ***e-mail:*** robwilsonmp@parliament.uk.

WILSON, Sammy; MLA and MP for East Antrim; ***born:*** 4 April 1953, Belfast, Northern Ireland; ***parents:*** Alexander Wilson and Mary Wilson; ***education:*** BA, Economics and Politics, Queen's Univ. Belfast, 1972-75; DipEd., Stranmillis Coll., Belfast, 1975-76; ***party:*** Democratic Unionist Party, 1975-; ***political career:*** DUP, Press Officer, 1982-89; Belfast City Cncl., 1981-; Belfast Lord Mayor, 1986 and 2000; Mem., Northern Ireland Forum, 1996; MLA, Belfast East, 1998-2003; MLA, East Antrim, 2003; MP East Antrim, 2005-; mem., Policing Board, 2005-06; DUP Spokesperson for Education and Skills and Policing; ***interests:*** supporter of academic selection in schools, socio-economic issues, housing; ***professional career:*** Head of Economics, Grosvenor Grammar Sch., 1977-98; ***committees:*** Northern Ireland Affairs Cttee., 2005-09; ***recreations:*** reading, motorcycling, gardeing; ***office address:*** DUP East Antrim Constituency Office, 116 Main Street, Larne, Co. Antrim, NI, BT40 1RG, United Kingdom; ***phone:*** +44 (0)28 2826 7722; ***fax:*** +44 (0)28 2826 9922; ***e-mail:*** lewisp@parliament.uk.

WILSON OF CULWORTH, Rt. Hon. Lord Nicholas; Justice of the Supreme Court of the United Kingdom; ***born:*** 1945; ***education:*** Worcester Coll., Oxford Univ.; ***professional career:*** Barrister; High Court Judge, 1993-2005; Lord Justice of Appeal, 2005-11; Justice of the Supreme Court of the United Kingdom, 2011-; ***office address:*** UK Supreme Court, Parliament Square, London, SW1P 3BD, United Kingdom; ***phone:*** +44 (0)20 7860 1980; ***fax:*** +44 (0)20 7760 1401.

WILSON OF TILLYORN, Lord David; British, Member, House of Lords; ***born:*** 1935; ***parents:*** Rev. William Skinner Wilson and Enid Wilson; ***married:*** Natasha Helen Mary Wilson (née Alexander), 1967; ***s:*** 2; ***education:*** Trinity Coll., Glenalmond; Keble Coll., Oxford, Grad. in Modern History, 1958; Chinese language studies, Hong Kong Univ., 1960-62; visiting scholar, Columbia Univ., NY; Ph.D., London Univ., 1973; ***political career:*** Mem., House of Lords; ***memberships:*** Fellow, Royal Society of Edinburgh 2000-03, President, 2008-; ***professional career:*** Entered Foreign Service, 1958; South-East Asia Dept., Foreign Office; Third Sec., Vientiane; Third, then Second Sec. Peking, 1963-65; First Sec., Foreign Office, Far Eastern Dept., -1968 (resigned); Exec. Editor, *The China Quarterly*, Contemporary China Institute, School of Oriental and African Studies of London Univ., 1968; rejoined Diplomatic Service, 1974, Cabinet Office, 1977; Political Adviser, Governor of Hong Kong, 1977-81; Head of Southern European Dept., FCO 1981-84; Asst. Under-Sec. of State responsible for Asia and the Pacific, FCO 1984-87; Governor and Commander-in-Chief of Hong Kong, 1987-92; Mem., Governing Body, School of Oriental and African studies, 1992-97; Chmn., Scottish Hydro Electric plc (later Scottish and Southern Energy Plc), 1993-2000; Chmn., Scottish Cttee., British Council, Mem., of British Council Board, 1993-2002; Chancellor's Assessor, Univ., of Aberdeen, 1993-97; Council, Glenalmond Coll., 1994-2005 (Chmn., Council, 2000-05); Chancellor, Univ. of Aberdeen, 1997-; Vice Pres., Royal Scottish Geographical Society, 1996-; Fellow, Royal Society of Edinburgh, 2000-; Mem., Bd. of Martin Currie Pacific Trust, 1993-2003; Master of Peterhouse, Cambridge, 2002-08; Dep. Vice Chancellor, Univ. of Cambridge, 2005-08; ***committees:*** Chmn., Int. Cttee., 2001-02; ***trusteeships:*** Nat. Museum of Scotland, 1999-2006, Chmn., 2002-06; Scotland's Churches Scheme, 1999-2002; Carniegie Trust for the Univs. of Scotland, 2000-; ***honours and awards:*** GMG, 1985; KCMG 1987; GCMG, 1991; KT 2000 Hon. LLD, Aberdeen Univ. 1990; Hon. D.Litt, Sydney Univ. 1991; Hon. D. Litt Univ. of Abertay, Dundee, 1994; Hon. LLD, Chinese Univ. of Hong Kong, 1996; Hon. D.Litt., Univ. of Hong Kong, 2006; Hon. Fellow, Keble College, Oxford; FRSE; ***clubs:*** Alpine; New (Edinburgh); Royal Northern and Univ. (Aberdeen); ***recreations:*** theatre, hill walking, reading; ***office address:*** House of Lords, London, SW1A 0PW, United Kingdom.

WINCHESTER, Rt Rev the Lord Bishop of; Member, House of Lords; ***political career:*** Member, House of Lords, 2012-; ***professional career:*** Head, Church Mission Society; Member, General Synod; Bishop of Winchester, 2012-; ***office address:*** House of Lords, London, SW1A 0AA , United Kingdom; ***phone:*** +44 (0)20 7219 5353.

WINNICK, David Julian; British, Member of Parliament for Walsall North, House of Commons; ***born:*** 26 June 1933; ***education:*** LSE, London Univ. Diploma, Social Admin.; ***party:*** Labour Party; ***political career:*** Cllr., Willesden London Borough, 1959-64, Brent London Borough, 1964-66; MP, Croydon South, 1966-70; Mem., Commons Select Cttee. on Environment, 1979-83, on Home Affairs, 1983-87, 1997-; on Procedure, 1988-97; Mem. British-Irish Inter-Parly. Body, 1990-; British Co-Chair, 1997-; MP, Walsall North, 1979-; ***committees:*** Home Affairs, 1982-87, 1997-; ***office address:*** House of Commons, London, SW1A 0AA, United Kingdom; ***phone:*** +44 (0)20 7219 3000/5003; ***e-mail:*** winnickd@parliament.uk.

WINTERTON, Rt. Hon. Rosie; British, Commons Shadow Chief Whip, House of Commons; ***born:*** 10 August 1958; ***education:*** Univ. of Hull, BA Hons., History; ***party:*** Labour Party; ***political career:*** Constituency Personal Asst. to John Prescott, 1980-86; Parly. officer for Southwark Cncl., 1986-88; Parly. officer for the Royal College of Nursing, 1988-90; Managing Dir., Connect Public Affairs, 1990-94; Head of John Prescott's Private Office, 1994-97; Head of Party Leadership Campaign Team; Parly. Sec. in Lord Chllr's. Dept., 2001; MP, Doncaster Central, 1997-; Minister of State Dept. of Health, 2003-07; Minister of State, Dept. of Transport, 2007-08; Minister of State, Dept. of Works and Pensions, 2008-09; Shadow Leader of the House of Commons and Lord Privy Seal, 2010; Shadow Minister for Women, 2010; Commons Shadow Chief Whip, Oct. 2010-; ***interests:*** regional policy, employment, transport; ***memberships:*** TGWU; ***professional career:*** Man. Dir., CPA; ***recreations:*** sailing, reading; ***office address:*** House of Commons, London, SW1A 0AA, United Kingdom; ***phone:*** +44 (0)20 7219 3000; ***e-mail:*** rosie.winterton.mp@parliament.uk.

WISELER, Claude; Minister of Sustainable Development and Infrastructures, Government of Luxembourg; ***born:*** 30 January 1960; ***education:*** Univ. de Paris III (new Sorbonne), MA, Modern Literature, 1983; Univ. de Paris-Sorbonne, Ph.D; ***political career:*** Adviser to the Ministries of Family and Social Welfare, Civil Service and Tourism, 1989-99; Sec. Gen., Christian Social Party (CSV), 1995-2000; Deputy for the Central Regional, 2000-; Alderman, Ville de Luxembourg, 2000-04; Minister of Civil Service & Administrative Reform, Minister of Public Works, 2004-09; Minister of Sustainable Development and Infrastructure, 2009-; ***professional career:*** Language teacher, Athenée de Luxembourg and Central Technical College, 1983-87; ***committees:*** Vice-Pres., Parly. Gp. of the CSV; Vice-Pres., National Education Cmn.; Vice-Pres., Professional Training Cmn.; Vice-Pres., Sports Cmn.; ***office address:*** Ministry of Sustainable Development and Infrastructures , 4 blvd F.D. Roosevelet, 2940 Luxembourg, Luxembourg; ***phone:*** +352 2478 3300; ***fax:*** +352 462709; ***URL:*** http://www.environnement.public.lu/index.html.

WISHART, Peter; Member of Parliament for Perth and North Perthshire, House of Commons; ***education:*** Queen Anne High Sch., Dunfermline, Fife Moray House Coll. of Education, Community Education 1984; ***party:*** SNP; ***political career:*** MP, North Tayside, 2001-05; MP, Perth and North Perthshire, 2005-; SNP Spokesperson, 2001-10; ***committees:*** Works of Art, 2011-; ***office address:*** 35 Perth Street, Blairgowrie, PH10 6DL, United Kingdom; ***phone:*** +44 (0)1250 876576 / 01738 639598; ***fax:*** +44 (0)1250 876991 / 01738 587637; ***e-mail:*** wishartp@parliament.uk; ***URL:*** http://www.petewishartmp.com.

WITKOWSKI, Jacques; Prefect, Mayotte; ***born:*** 1963; ***political career:*** Dep. Prefect, Cotes-d'Armor, 1998; Dir, Cabinet of Regional Prefect, Reunion, 2000; Polynesia; Sec.-Gen., Prefecture, Finistere, 2008; Prefect, Mayotte, 2013-; ***office address:*** Prefecture, Dzagudzi, Mayotte; ***URL:*** http://www.mayotte.pref.gouv.fr/.

WOLDE GIORGIS, Lt. Girma; President, Federal Democratic Republic of Ethiopia; ***born:*** 1925, Addis Ababa, Ethiopia; ***languages:*** Amharic, English, French, Italian, Tigrigna, Oromiffa; ***education:*** The Scola di Principe Piemonte, Italian Sch., Addis Ababa, 1937-40; Guenet Military School Graduate Sub-Lieutenant, 1944; School of Social Science, The Netherlands; Cert. in Air Traffic Management, Sweden, Cert. in Air Traffic Control, Canada; ***political career:*** Dir.-Gen., Ministry of Commerce, Industry and Planning, 1959; Elected Mem., House of People's Representatives, 2000-; mem., Economic Sub-cttee; Pres., Federal Democratic Republic of Ethiopia; ***memberships:*** Bd. Mem., Ethiopian Chamber of Commerce, 1967; Mem., Council of People's Representatives of FDRE; Bd. Mem., Ethiopian Red Cross Society, 1982; ***professional career:*** enlisted as soldier, Ethiopian Army Communications, 1941, training at Guenet Military Academy, promoted to Second-Lieutenant, 1944; transferred to Ethiopian Air Force, 1946; assist. instructor, air navigation & air traffic control training, 1948; Head of Technical Services, Civil Aviation Authority, 1949; Head, Civil Aviation of the Federated Gov. in Eritrea, 1955; Dir.-Gen., Ethiopian Civil Aviation, 1958; Bd. Mem., Ethiopian Airlines, 1958; Mem., Civil Advisory Council to Military gov., 1974, then mgr., Import & Export Enterprise; First-Vice Commissioner, Peace Commission, 1976; Head of Logistics, ICRC, Demobilization of X-Army persons, 1990; founded LEM-Ethiopia, An Environmental Society, 1992; ***office address:*** Office of the President, PO Box 23698 Code 1000, Addis Ababa, Ethiopia; ***phone:*** +251 (11) 551 1000.

WOLFF, Alejandro D.; Ambassador, US Embassy in Chile; ***languages:*** French, Spanish; ***education:*** Univ. of California at Los Angeles, 1978; ***professional career:*** Amb. and Dep. Perm. U.S. Rep. to the UN, 2005-10; Amb. to Chile, 2010-; ***office address:*** US Embassy, Avenida Andrés Bello 2800, Las Condes, Santiago, Chile; ***phone:*** +56 (0)2 232 2600; ***fax:*** +56 (0)2 339 3710; ***e-mail:*** infous@state.gov; ***URL:*** http://santiago.usembassy.gov.

WOLFSON OF APSLEY GUISE, Lord Simon; Member, House of Lords; ***party:*** Conservative; ***political career:*** Mem. House of Lords 2010-; ***professional career:*** Chief Exec., NEXT plc; ***office address:*** House of Lords, London, SW1A 0PW, United Kingdom; ***phone:*** +44 (0)20 7219 3000; ***fax:*** +44 (0)20 7219 5979; ***URL:*** http://www.parliament.uk.

WOLLASTON, Sarah; MP for Totnes, UK Government; ***party:*** Conservative; ***political career:*** MP for Totnes, May 2010-; ***committees:*** Health Select Cttee., 2010-; ***office address:*** House of Commons, London, SW1A 0AA, United Kingdom; ***phone:*** +44 (0)20 7219 3000; ***e-mail:*** sarah.wollaston.mp@parliament.uk.

WOLZFELD, H.E. Jean-Louis; Luxembourgeois, Ambassador, Embassy of Luxembourg in the USA; ***born:*** 5th July 1951; ***professional career:*** Ambassador to Japan, 1986-93; Permanent Representative of Luxembourg to the United Nations, 1993-98; Political Dir., Ministry of Foreign Affairs, 1998-2003; Ambassador to the UK, 2003-08; Amb. to the USA, 2012-; ***office address:*** Embassy of Luxembourg, 2200 Massachusetts Avenue, NW Washington 20008, USA; ***phone:*** +1 202 265 4171; ***fax:*** +1 202 328 8270; ***URL:*** http://washington.mae.lu/en.

WONG, Hon. Penny; Australian, Minister of Finance and Deregulation, Government of Australia; ***born:*** Sabah, Malaysia; ***education:*** Univ. of Adelaide, BA and a Law Degree (Hons); Grad.Dip. in Law Practise; ***political career:*** Delegate, ALP State Convention (SA) 1989-94, 1996-; Dep.Chwmn., ALP Platform Cttee. (SA) 1990-94; Mem., ALP State Executive (SA) 1996-99; Mem., ALP National Policy Cttee. on Industry, Infrastructure and Regional Development 1998-2000; Delegate, ALP National Conference 2000. Labor Senator for South Australia, 2002-; Shadow Minister for Employment and Workforce Participation, and Shadow Minister for Corporate Governance and Responsibility, 2004-07; Shadow Minister for Public Administration and Accountability, 2006-07; Minister for Climate Change and Water, 2007-10; Minister of Finance and Deregulation, 2010-; Leader of the Government in the Senate, 2013-; ***professional career:*** Industrial officer, Construction, Forestry, Mining and Energy Union, 1990-96; Ministerial advisor to the Carr government in New South Wales; Barrister and solicitor 1996-2000; Legal officer 2000-02; ***office address:*** Department of Finance and Deregulation, John Gorton Building, King Edward Terrace, Parkes, Canberra ACT 0221, Australia; ***phone:*** +61 (0)2 6215 2222; ***URL:*** http://www.finance.gov.au.

WOOD, Leanne; Leader, Plaid Cymru; ***born:*** 13 December 1971, Rhondda, Wales; ***parents:*** Jeffrey Wood and Avril Wood (née James); ***children:*** Cerys Amelia (F); ***languages:*** English; ***education:*** Tonypandy Comprehensive Sch.; Univ. of Glamorgan, BA Hons, Public Admin.; Cardiff Univ., Diploma in Social Work; ***party:*** Plaid Cymru - The Party of Wales; ***political career:*** Local Councillor, Rhondda Cynon Taf, 1995-1999; Parly. candidate, Rhondda, 1997 and 2001; National Assembly of Wales mem. for South Wales Central, May 2003-; Leader, Plaid Cymru, 2012-; ***interests:*** social exclusion, women and youth issues, international affairs, criminal justice and drugs; ***memberships:*** UNISON; Amnesty; Palestine Solidarity Campaign; CND; Welsh Language Soc.; NAPO; ***professional career:*** Probation officer; women's aid support worker; Univ. lecturer, social work and social policy; ***committees:*** Social Justice and Regeneration; Equal Opportunities; Chair, Cwm Cynon Women's Aid Management Cttee.; ***recreations:*** gardening, travelling, reading; ***office address:*** National Assembly for Wales, Cardiff Bay, Cardiff, CF99 1NA, United Kingdom; ***phone:*** +44 (0)29 20 898256; ***fax:*** +44 (0)29 2089 8257; ***e-mail:*** leanne.wood@wales.gov.uk.

WOOD, Mike; British, Member of Parliament for Batley and Spen, House of Commons; ***born:*** 3 March 1946; ***education:*** Univ. of Southampton; Leeds Univ., BA, CQSW; ***party:*** Labour Party; ***political career:*** MP, Batley and Spen, 1997-; ***interests:*** poverty, housing, transport, environment, the welfare state; ***professional career:*** social worker; probation officer; ***recreations:*** walking, reading, ornithology, music; ***office address:*** House of Commons, London, SW1A 0AA, United Kingdom; ***phone:*** +44 (0)20 7219 3000; ***e-mail:*** woodm@parliament.uk.

WOOD, HE Sebastian; Ambassador, British Embassy in Beijing; ***born:*** 1961; ***languages:*** Mandarin; ***professional career:*** FCO, Director Asia Pacific, 2005-08; Amb. to the People's Republic of China, 2010-; ***office address:*** British Embassy, 11 Guang Hua Lu, Jian Guo Men Wai, Beijing 100600, People's Republic of China; ***phone:*** +86 (10) 5192 4000; ***URL:*** http://ukinchina.fco.gov.uk/en.

WOOD OF ANFIELD, Lord Stewart; Member, House of Lords; ***born:*** 25 March 1968; ***parents:*** Brian James Wood and Gisela Wood; ***married:*** Camilla Bustani, 1998; ***children:*** Luca (M), Matias (M); ***languages:*** French, German; ***education:*** Univ. College, Oxford Univ., Philosophy, Politics and Economics, 1989; Fulbright Scholar, Harvard Univ., 1990; PhD, Harvard Univ., 1997; Junior Research Fellow, St John's College, Oxford Univ., 1995-96; ***party:*** Labour Party; ***political career:*** Special Adviser on the Chancellor of the Exchequer's Council of Economic Advisers at HM Treasury, 2001-07; Special Adviser to the Prime Minister, 2007-10; Adviser to Ed Miliband, Leader of HM Opposition, 2010; Mem., House of Lords, 2011-; Shadow Minister without portfolio (Cabinet Office), Oct. 2011-; ***memberships:*** Community Trade Union; Mem. of Cooperative Party; ***professional career:*** Fellow and Tutor in Politics, Magdalen College, Oxford Univ., 1995-; Visiting Fellow, Nuffield College, Oxford Univ., 2011-; ***trusteeships:*** Trustee of the English Stage Company (Royal Court Theatre); ***honours and awards:*** Fulbright Scholar, 1989-90; ***publications:*** Options for Britain: A Strategic Policy Review, 1996 (edited by David Halpern, Stewart Wood, Stuart White and Gavin Cameron); Business, Government and Labour Market Policy in Britain and Germany, in David Soskice and Peter Hall eds., Varieties of Capitalism: The Institutional Foundations of Comparative Advantage, 2001; Labour Market Regimes Under Threat? Sources of Continuity in Germany, Britain, and Sweden", in Paul Pierson ed., The New Politics of the Welfare State, 2001; ***office address:*** House of Lords, London, SW1, United Kingdom; ***phone:*** +44 (0)20 7219 7304; ***e-mail:*** stewart.wood@parliament.uk.

WOODCOCK, John; MP for Barrow and Furness, House of Commons; ***party:*** Labour/Co-operative; ***political career:*** MP for Barrow and Furness, May 2010-; Shadow Minister, Transport, Oct. 2010-; ***committees:*** Defence Select Cttee., 2010; Arms Export Controls, 2010-; ***office address:*** House of Commons, London, SW1A 0AA, United Kingdom; ***phone:*** +44 (0)20 7219 3000; ***e-mail:*** john.woodcock.mp@parliament.uk.

WOODWARD, Rt. Hon. Shaun; British, MP, House of Commons; ***born:*** 1958; ***education:*** Jesus Coll., Cambridge; ***party:*** Conservative Party -2001; Labour Party 2001-; ***political career:*** Dir. of Communications, Conservative Central Office, 1990-92; Mem., Conservative Foreign Affairs Forum; MP, Witney, 1992-2001; left Conservative party and joined Labour, 2001; MP for St Helens South, 2001-; Parly. Sec., Northern Ireland Office, 2005-06; Minister for Creative Industries and Tourism, 2006-June 2007; Secretary of State for Northern Ireland, June 2007-May 2010; Shadow Secretary of State for Northern Ireland, May 2010-Oct. 2011; ***memberships:*** AMICUS; ***professional career:*** Broadcaster; Univ. Lecturer; BBC TV Journalist; ***committees:*** Jt. Select Cttee. on Human Rights, 2001-05; ***office address:*** House of Commons, London, SW1A 0AA, United Kingdom; ***phone:*** +44 (0)20 7210 3000; ***e-mail:*** woodwardsh@parliament.uk; ***URL:*** http://www.shaunwoodward.com.

WOOLMER OF LEEDS, Lord Kenneth John; British, Member, House of Lords; ***born:*** 25 April 1940, Curby, UK; ***married:*** Janice (née Chambers), 23 September 1961; ***children:*** John (M), Kevin (M), David (M); ***education:*** Kettering Grammar Sch.; Leeds Univ., BA (Econ.); ***party:*** Labour Party; ***political career:*** MP (Lab.) for Batley and Morley, 1979-83; Mem., Front Bench Opposition Spokesman on Trade, Aviation and Shipping, 1981-83; Mem., House of Lords; ***professional career:*** Jr. Research Fellow, Univ. of the West Indies, 1961-62; Teacher, London County Cncl., 1963; Lecturer, Sch. of Econ., Leeds Univ, 1963-66, and 1968-79; Lecturer, Ahmadu Bello Univ., Nigeria, 1966-68; Cllr., Leeds City Cncl., 1970-78, and West Yorkshire Metropolitan County Cncl., 1973-80; Principal, Halton Gill Assocs., 1983-96; Dir., MBA Programmes, Leeds Univ. Business Sch., 1991-96; Dir., Leeds United A.F.C., 1992-97; Dean of External Relations, Leeds Univ. Business Sch., 1996-97, and Dean, 1997-2000; Dir., Halton Gill Consulting Ltd., 1999-2001; Ptnr., Halton Gill Assocs., 1999-2000; Ptnr., Anderson McGraw, 2000-06; ***committees:*** House of Commons Select Cttee. on the Treasury and Civil Service, 1980-81; Mem., House of Lords EU Select Cttee, 2001; EU Select Cttee., 2001-06; Subcttee. B 'Internal Market', 1999-20006, Chmn., 2001-06; EU Select Cttee. A Economic & Financial Affairs and International Trade; ***honours and awards:*** Baron, Lord Woolmer of Leeds, 1999; ***recreations:*** watching football and cricket; ***office address:*** House of Lords, London, SW1A 0PW, United Kingdom; ***e-mail:*** woolmerk@parliament.uk.

WORCESTER, Rt Rev the Lord Bishop of; Bishop of Worcester; ***education:*** BSc, 1977, MA, 1994, St Chad's College, Durham Univ.; PGCE. 1979, Keble College, Oxford Univ.; PhD, 2002, Durham Univ.; ***political career:*** Member, House of Lords, 2012-; ***professional career:*** Teacher; Bishop of Huntingdon, 2003-08; Bishop of Worcester, 2008-; ***office address:*** House of Lords, London, SW1A 0AA , United Kingdom; ***phone:*** +44 (0)20 7219 5353.

WORTHINGTON, Baroness Bryony; Member, House of Lords; ***party:*** Labour Party; ***political career:*** Mem., House of Lords, 2011-; ***professional career:*** Promoting environmental change; ***office address:*** House of Lords, London, SW1A 0PW, United Kingdom; ***phone:*** +44 (0)20 7219 3000.

WRIGHT, David; MP for Telford, House of Commons; ***born:*** 22 December 1966, Telford; ***parents:*** Kenneth William Wright and Heather Wright; ***married:*** Lesley Wright (née Insole); ***education:*** Wolverhampton Polytechnic, Degree in Humanities; ***party:*** Labour; ***political career:*** Councillor, Wrekin District Council, 1989-97; Town Councillor, Oakengates, 1989-2000; MP, Telford, 2001- PPS to Rosie Winterton MP, Dept. of Health, 2001-05; PPS to David Miliband, Office of the Dep. PM, 2005-06; PPS, -09; Assist. Gov. Whip, 2009-10; Opp. Whip, 2010-11; ***memberships:*** Mem., Chartered Inst. of Housing; ***professional career:*** Worked thirteen yrs. on the dev. of housing and regeneration strategies for local communities, Sandwell, West Midlands; Sch. Governor, Wombridge Primary Sch., eight yrs.; active in the dev. and growth of local Credit Unions; ***office address:*** House of Commons, London, SW1A OPQ, United Kingdom; ***phone:*** +44 (0)20 7219 8331; ***fax:*** +44 (0)20 7219 1979; ***e-mail:*** wrightda@parliament.uk.

WRIGHT, Iain, MP; MP for Hartlepool, House of Commons; ***political career:*** Councillor; MP for Hartlepool, September 2004-; Parly. Under-Sec. of State, Dept. for Communities and Local Government, 2007-09; Parliamentary Under-Secretary of State, Department for Children, Schools and Families, 2009-10; Shadow Minister for Education, Oct. 2010-11; Shadow Minister for Business, Innovation and Skills, 2011-; ***office address:*** House of Commons, London, SW1A 0AA, United Kingdom; ***e-mail:*** iain.wright.mp@parliament.uk.

WRIGHT, Jeremy; MP for Kenilworth and Southam, House of Commons; ***married:*** Yvonne Wright (née Salter); ***party:*** Conservative; ***political career:*** MP for Rugby and Kenilworth, 2005-10; MP for Kenilworth and Southam, 2010-; Opp. Whip, 2007-10; Gov. Whip, 2010-12; Parly. Under Sec. of State, Ministry of Justice, 2012-; ***professional career:*** Criminal Law Barrister; ***committees:*** Constitutional Affairs Select Cttee.; ***trusteeships:*** Community Development Fund; ***office address:*** House of Commons, London, SW1P 0AA, United Kingdom; ***phone:*** +44 (0)20 7219 2008.

WRIGHT, Simon; MP for Norwich South, UK Government; ***party:*** Liberal Democrat; ***political career:*** Councillor, North Norfolk District Council; MP for Norwich South, May 2010-; PPS, 2011-; ***committees:*** Environmental Audit, 2010-; ***office address:*** House of Commons, London, SW1A 0AA, United Kingdom; ***phone:*** +44 (0)20 7219 3000; ***e-mail:*** simon.wright.mp@parliament.uk.

WYANT, Gordon, QC; Minister of Justice and Attorney General, Government of Saskatchewan; *political career:* City Councillor, 2003-2009, numerous cttees.; MLA, 2010-; Minister of Justice and Attorney Genral, Deputy Government House Leader, 2012-; *office address:* Ministry of Justice, 1874 Scarth Street, Regina, Saskatchewan, S4P 3V7, Canada; *phone:* +1 306 787 8971; *fax:* +1 306 787 5830; *URL:* http://www.justice.gov.sk.ca/.

WYDEN, Ron; Senator for Oregon, US Senate; *married:* Laurie Wyde; *children:* Adam (M), Lilly (F); *education:* Univ. of California, Santa Barbara; Stanford Univ., BA; Univ. of Oregon Law Sch., Law degree, 1974; *party:* Democrat; *political career:* US House of Representatives; US Senator for Oregon, 1996-; *professional career:* Dir., Oregon Legal Services for the Elderly; Co-Dir., Oregon Gray Panthers; Oregon State Bd. of Examiners of Nursing Home Administrators; *committees:* US Senate: Energy & Natural Resources; Finance; Budget; Select Cttee. on Intelligence; Select Cttee. on Aging; Joint Cttee. on Taxation; *honours and awards:* Senator of the Year, Nat. Assn. of Police Organisations, 1997; *office address:* US Senate, 223 Dirksen Senate Office Building, Washington, DC 20510, USA; *phone:* +1 202 224 5244; *fax:* +1 202 224 2262; *URL:* http://www.wyden.senate.dov.

WYNNE, Kathleen; Premier, Ontario; *born:* 1953; *education:* Queen's Univ., BA; Univ. of Toronto, MA; Ontario Inst. for Studies in Education; *party:* Ontario Liberal Party; *political career:* Mem., Legislative Assembly of Ontario, Don Valley West, 2003-; Minister of Municipal Affairs and Housing, Minister of Aborginal Affairs, -12; Leader, Ontario Liberal Party, 2013-; Premier, Ontario, 2013-, also Minister of Agriculture and Foods, 2013-; *office address:* Office of the Premier, Room 281, Legislative Building, Queen's Park, Toronto M7A 1A1, Canada; *phone:* +1 416 325 1941; *fax:* +1 416 325 7578; *URL:* http://www.premier.gov.on.ca/.

X

XI, Jinping; President, People's Republic of China; *born:* 1953, Shaanxi Province, China; *parents:* Xi Zhongxun; *education:* Tsinghua Univ., Chemical Eng.; *political career:* Communist party positions, Shaanxi, Hebei, Zhejiang and Fujian; CCP Party Leader, Shanghai, 2007-; Mem., CCP Politburo, 2007-; Vice-President, People's Republic of China, 2008-13; President elect, 2012; President, March 2013-; *office address:* Communist Party of China, Zhongnanhai , Beijing, China.

XIAOCHUAN, Zhou; Governor, People's Bank of China; *born:* 1948; *education:* Beijing Chemical Engineering Instit., grad., 1975; Tsinghua Univ., Ph.D, 1985; *political career:* Assist. Minister, Ministry of Foreign Trade & Econ.Cooperation, 1986-89; mem., State Econ. System Restructuring Cttee., 1986-91; *professional career:* Vice Pres., Bank of China, 1991-95; Dep. Governor, PBC and Administrator of the State Admin.of Foreign Exchange, 1996-98; Chmn., China Securities Regulatory Cmn., 2000; Gov., People's Bank of China (PBC), 2002-; Chmn., Monetary Policy Cttee. of the PBC, 2003-; *office address:* People's Bank of China, 32 Chengfang St., Xi Cheng District, Beijing, China.

XUE, Judge Hanqin; Chinese, Member, International Court of Justice; *born:* 15 September 1955; *languages:* Chinese, English; *education:* Beijing Foreign Languages Studies University, BA, 1980; Columbia University School of Law, LLM, 1983, JSD, 1995; Beijing University, Department of Law, diploma in international law, 1982; Chinese National Lawyer's Qualification examination, 1988; Legal qualification: Doctor of Law; *interests:* Claims; Environment law; Jurisdiction; Human rights; Organisations; State responsibility; Law of the Sea; Space; Territory/boundaries; Treaties; *memberships:* Institut de Droit International, Associate Member, 2005-; Chinese Society of International Law, 1995-, Council Member, 1997, Vice-President, 2000-; China Law Society, Council Member, 1997-; Chinese Society of Private International Law, Vice-President and Council Member, 1995-; Chinese Yearbook of International Law, Board Member, 1993-; ILA, Consultant to Committee on Water Resources, 1993-; *professional career:* Beijing University, Adjunct-Professor of Law, 1994-; Beijing Foreign Affairs College, Professor of Law, 1998-; ILC, Member, 2002-; ILA, Consultant to Committee on Water Resources, 1993-; *governmental career:* Ministry of Foreign Affairs, Law and Treaty Department, Director-General, 1999-2003, Deputy Director-General, 1994-99, Division Chief, 1988-94, Deputy Division Chief, 1984-88, Legal Officer, 1980-84; Ambassador of the People's Republic of China to the Netherlands, 2003-08; Permanent Representative of the People's Republic of China to OPCW, 2003-08, Ambassador to ASEAN, 2008-10; Numerous international conference and treaty negotiatons; Mem., ICJ, 2010-; *publications:* Books: Commentary on the Charter of the United Nations, co-editor, 1999; A Complete Compilation of Treaties on Trade and Economy between China and Foreign Countries, co-editor, 1996; International Law, 1995; Chapter on State Responsibility in "International Law", 2000; Transboundary Damage in International Law, 2003; Chapter on China in "National Treaty Law and Practice", co-author, 2005; Articles: Studies of International Affairs; Chinese Yearbook of International Law; Colarado Journal of International Environmental Law and Policy; Peace, Justice and Law; Pacific Journal; Proceedings of the ASIL; Austrian Review of International and European Law; Chinese Journal of International Law; National Treaty Law and Practice; *office address:* International Court of Justice, Peace Palace, Carnegieplein 2, 2517 KJ The Hague, The Netherlands; *fax:* +31 (0)70 3551 651; *e-mail:* xue_hanqin@mfa.gov.cn / hqxue@yahoo.com.

Y

YAACOB, Assoc. Prof. Ibrahim; Minister of Information, Communication and the Arts, Government of Singapore; *born:* 3 October 1955, Singapore; *education:* Civil Engineering degree, Univ. of Singapore, 1980; PhD, Stanford Univ., USA, 1989; *political career:* elected as one of four MPs, Jalan Besar Gp. Representation Constituency (GRC), 1997-99; Parly. Sec. for Communications, 1998 (became Communications and Information Technology, 1999); Sr. Parly. Sec., 2001-; re-elected as one five MPs for Jalan Besar GRC, 2001-; Minister of State for the Ministry of Community Dev. and Sports, 2001; Acting Minister of Community Dev. and Sports and Minister in charge of Muslim Affairs, 2002; Minister for Community Development and Sports and Minister-in-charge of Muslim Affairs, 2003-04; Minister for the Environment and Water Resources and Minister-in-charge of Muslim Affairs, 2004-11; Minister of Information, Communication and the Arts, 2011-; *memberships:* fmr. youth Mem., Muslim Missionary Society of Singapore (Jamiyah); Mem., MUIS Council, 1992-96; Bd. Mem., Yayasan Mendaki, 1993; Bd. Mem., People's Assoc., to date; Bd. Mem., National Heritage Bd., Civil Service Coll., STV12 Pte Ltd and Temasek Polytechnic; Mem., Feedback Unit Supervisory Panel, 1998-2002; *professional career:* fmr. Structural Engineer, consulting firm Bylander Meinhardt Partnership; Post-Doctoral Fellow, Cornell Univ., 1989; Research Scientist, Dept. Civil Engineering, National Univ. of Singapore, 1990; tenure track position, Dept. of Industrial and Systems Engineering, 1991, Sr. Lecturer, 1993, obtained tenure, 1997; volunteer tutor for the council for the Dev. of Singapore Muslim Community (Yayasan Mendaki), 1983; actively involved with Muslim Religious Council of Singapore (MUIS) and Assoc. of Muslim Professionals, 1990; Council Mem., Central Singapore Community Development Council (CDC), 1997, second Chmn., 2000; one of Unit's Dep. Chmn., Feedback Unit Supervisory Panel, 1998-2002; Dep. Chmn., Yayasan Mendaki, 1994 and Chmn., 2002-; Chmn., Jalan Besar Town Council, 1999-2001; First Mayor, Central Singapore CDC, 2001; on secondment from National Univ. of Singapore, to date; *committees:* fmr. Mem., Singapore 21 Cttee.; First Chmn., Singapore Broadcasting Authority's Malay Programmes Advisory Cttee., 1995-2001; Mem., Inter-Ministry Cttee. on Dysfunctional Family, Delinquents and Drug Abuse, 1994, Chmn., Sub-Cttee. on Drug Abuse; Mem., Govt. Parly. Cttee. (GPC) for Ministry of Information and the Arts and Ministry of Community Dev., 1997; Mem., Inter-Ministerial Cttee. (IMC) on Ageing Population and Singapore Talent Recruitment (STAR) Cttee.; *trusteeships:* elected Trustee, NTUC Income, 1998; *recreations:* reading, listening to music, meeting people; *office address:* Ministry of Information, Communication and the Arts, 140 Hill Street, 02-02 MICA Building, Singapore 179369, Singapore; *URL:* http://www.mica.gov.sg.

YAAKOB, Ismail Sabri bin; Minister of Agriculture, Government of Malaysia; *political career:* MP, 2004-; Minister of Youth and Sports, 2008-09; Minister of Domestic Trade, Co-operatives and Consumerism, 2009-13; Minister of Agriculture, 2013-; *office address:* Ministry of Agriculture, Level 17, Wisma Tani, 28 Persiaran Perdana, 62624 Putrajaya, Malaysia.

YADAV, President Ram Baran; President, Nepal; *born:* 4 February 1948, Dhanusha, Nepal; *education:* Calcutta Medical Coll., and School of Tropical Medicine, Univ. of Calcutta, Medicine; *political career:* Chairman of Ward No. 9, Sapahi Panchayat, 1987-90; arrested and jailed for three months during the Jana Andolan, 1990; Minister of State for Health, 1991-94; Mem., House of Reps., 1999-2007; Minister of Health, 1999-2007; Mem., Dhanusa 5, Constituent Assembly, 2008; President of Nepal, 2008-; *office address:* Office of the President, Shital Niwas, Maharajganj, Kathmandu , Nepal.

YAHIA, Habib Ben; Tunisian, Secretary General, Arab Maghreb Union; *born:* 1938; *political career:* Minister of Foreign Affairs, 1963; Sec. of State in the MFA, 1988; Minister of Foreign Affairs, 1991; Minister of Defence, 1997; Minister of Foreign Affairs, 1999-2004; Minister to the President, 2005; *professional career:* Diplomat, including: Amb. of Tunisia, Abu Dhabi, 1976; Amb. to Japan, 1977; Ambassador to the USA, 1981; Sec. Gen., Arab Maghreb Union, 2006-; *office address:* Arab Maghreb Union, 14 rue Tensift, Agdal Rabat, Morocco; *URL:* http://www.maghrebarabe.org.

YAKOVENKO, H.E. Alexander V.; Ambassador , Embassy of the Russian Federation; *political career:* Dep. Minister of Foreign Affairs, 2005-11; *professional career:* Dep. Perm. Rep. of the Russian Federation to Int. Organizations in Vienna, 1997-2000; Spokesman of MFA of Russia, Dir. of the Info. and Press Dept., MFA, 2000-05; Amb. to the UK, 2011-; *office address:* Embassy of the Russian Federation, 13 Kensington Palace Gardens, London, W8 4QX, United Kingdom; *phone:* +44 (0)20 7229 3628; *fax:* +44 (0)20 7727 8625; *e-mail:* info@rusemb.org; *URL:* http://www.rusemb.org.uk.

YANG, Philemon; Prime Minister, Government of Cameroon; *born:* 1947; *political career:* Minister of Mines and Energy, 1979-84; Prime Minister, 2009-; *professional career:* Amb. to Canada, 1984-2004; *office address:* Office of the Prime Minister, c/o the Central Post Office, Yaoundé, Cameroon; *phone:* +237 2223 5750; *e-mail:* spm@spm.gov.cm; *URL:* http://www.spm.gov.cm.

YANUKOVYCH, Victor; President, Government of Ukraine; *born:* July 1950, Donetsk Region, Ukraine; *languages:* Russian, Ukrainian; *education:* Doctor of Economics, 2000; *party:* Party of the Regions; *political career:* Governor of Donetsk; Prime Minister, Ukraine, 2002-04; Presidential Candidate, 2004; Prime Minister, July 2006-07; President, Feb. 2010; *professional career:* Coal mining industry transport executive; *office address:* Office of the President, 11 Bankova Street, 252005 Kiev, Ukraine; *phone:* +380 44 255 7333.

YAPA, Anura Priyadharshana, MP; Minister of Petroleum Industries, Government of Sri Lanka; *born:* 18 January 1959; *education:* Nalanda Coll., Colombo; *political career:* Minister of Health and Women's Affairs, North Eastern Province, Prov. Cncl., 1993; MP, 1994-; Dep. Minister of Posts, Telecommunications and Media, 1997-00; Minister of Media, 2000-01; Dep. Minister of Education and Higher Education, 2001-04; Minister of Plantation Industries, 2004-05; Minister of Information and Mass Media, 2005-09; Minister of Investment

Promotion and Enterprise Development, 2009-10; Minister of the Environment, 2010-13; Minister of Petroleum Industries, 2013-; ***professional career:*** Attorney at Law, Public Notary, Justice of the Peace; ***office address:*** Ministry of Petroleum, 80 Sir Ernest de Silva Mawatha, Colomboo 07, Sri Lanka; ***e-mail:*** secoffice@menr.lk; ***URL:*** http://www.gov.lk.

YASSIN, Tan Sri Dato' Haji Muhyiddin bin Haji Mohd; Deputy Prime Minister, Malaysian Government; ***party:*** United Malays National Organisation; ***political career:*** Minister of Youth and Sports, 1995-2000; Minister of Domestic Trade and Consumer Affairs, 2000-04; Minister of Agriculture, 2004-08; Minister of International Trade and Industry, 2008-09; Deputy Prime Minister and Minister of Education, 2009- ; ***office address:*** Prime Minister's Department, Blok Utama, Bangunan Perdan Putra, Pusat Pentadbiran Kerajaan Persekutuan, 65502, Malaysia; ***phone:*** +60 (0)3 8888 1957; ***URL:*** http://www.pmo.gov.my.

YAZICI, Hayati; Minister of State and Minister of Customs and Trade, Government of Turkey; ***born:*** 23 May 1952; ***education:*** School of Law, Istanbul Univ., 1975; ***party:*** Justice and Development Party (AKP); ***political career:*** MP for Istanbul Province, 2007-; Deputy Prime Minister, Minister of State responsible for Labour and the Istanbul 2010 European Capital of Culture Agency; Minister of State, 2011-, Minister of Customs and Trade, 2011-; ***professional career:*** Lawyer and Judge; ***office address:*** Turkish Grand Assembly, Ankara, Turkey.

YELICH, Lynne; Federal Minister of State for Western Economic Diversification, Government of Canada; ***born:*** 1953; ***political career:*** MP for Blackstrap, Saskatchewan, 2000-; Parly. Sec. to the Minister of Human Resources and Social Development, 2006-08; Minister of State for Western Economic Diversification, 2008-12; Federal Minister of State for Western Economic Diversification, 2013-; ***office address:*** House of Commons, Wellington Street, Ottawa, Ontario, K1A 0A6, Canada; ***phone:*** +1 613 943 5959; ***fax:*** +1 613 992 3674; ***URL:*** http://www.parl.gc.ca.

YEO, Timothy Stephen Kenneth, MA, MP; British, MP for South Suffolk, House of Commons; ***born:*** 1945, London, UK; ***parents:*** Dr. Kenneth John Yeo and Norah Margaret Yeo (née Richardson); ***married:*** Diane Helen Yeo (née Pickard), 1970; ***children:*** Jonathan Christopher Yeo (M), Emily Claire Yeo (F); ***public role of spouse:*** Chief Executive, Chelsea & Westminster Hospital Charities; ***languages:*** French; ***education:*** Charterhouse Sch.; Emmanuel Coll., Cambridge Univ., MA Hons.; ***party:*** Conservative Party; ***political career:*** Contested Bedwelty, 1974; Con. MP, South Suffolk, 1983-; Jt. Sec., Cons. Party Back Bench Finance Cttee., 1984-87; Mem., Commons Select Cttee. on Social Services, 1985-88; P.P.S. to Rt. Hon. Douglas Hurd MP, Foreign Sec., 1988-90; Under-Sec. of State, Dept. of the Environment, 1990-92, Dept. of Health, 1992-93; Minister of State for Environment and Countryside, Dept. of Environment, 1993-94; Opp. Spokesman on Environment and Local Govt., 1997-98; Shadow Sec. of State for Agriculture, Fisheries and Food, 1998-2001; Shadow Secretary of State for Culture, Media and Sport, 2001-2002; Shadow Sec. of State for Trade and Industry. 2002-03; Shadow Sec. of State for Health & Education, 2003-04; Shadow Sec. of State for Environment and Transport, 2003-05; ***interests:*** economic issues; ***memberships:*** Soc. of Investment Analysts, 1969-81; ***professional career:*** Asst. Treasurer, Bankers Trust Co., 1970-73; Dir., Worcester Engineering Co., 1975-86; Dir., The Spastics Soc., 1980-83; Chmn., Charities VAT Reform Gp., 1982-88, Pres., 1988-90; Chmn., Tadworth Court Children's Hospital, 1983-90; Vice-Pres., Int. Voluntary Service, 1984; ***committees:*** Treasury Select Cttee., 1996-97; Chmn., Environmental Audit Select Cttee., 2005-10; Liaison, 2006; Chair, Energy & Climate Change, 2010-; Liasion, 2010-; Joint Cttee. on National Security Strategy, 2010-; ***trusteeships:*** Britain-Tanzania Trust; ***publications:*** Public Accountability and Regulation of Charities; ***clubs:*** Royal & Ancient Golf Club of St. Andrews; ***recreations:*** golf, skiing; ***office address:*** House of Commons, London, SW1A 0AA, United Kingdom; ***phone:*** +44 (0)20 7219 3000; ***fax:*** +44 (0)20 7219 4857.

YILDIZ, Taner; Minister of Energy and Natural Resources, Government of Turkey; ***born:*** 1962; ***education:*** Istanbul Technical University; ***party:*** Justice and Development Party; ***political career:*** MP, 2002-; Minister of Energy and Natural Resources, 2009-; ***office address:*** Ministry of Energy and Natural Resources, Inonu Bulvari 27, Ankara, Turkey.

YILMAZ, Cevdet; Minister of Development, Government of Turkey; ***born:*** 1967; ***education:*** MA, Univ. of Denver, USA; Doctorate in Education, Bilkent Univ.; ***political career:*** MP, 2007-; Minister of State responsible for the State Planning Organization and the Turkish Statistical Institute, 2009-11; Minister of Development, 2011-; ***office address:*** Ministry of State, Eski Basbakanlik, Ankara, Turkey; ***phone:*** +90 (9)312 413 7000.

YING-JEOU, President Ma; President, Republic of China (Taiwan); ***born:*** July 13 1950, Hong Kong; ***education:*** National Taiwan Univ., LL.B, 1972; New York Univ., LL.M., 1976; Harvard Law School, SJD, 1981; ***political career:*** Minister of Resesarch, Development and Evaluation Cmn., 1988-91; Dep. Minister of Mainland Affairs Cncl., 1991-93; Minister of Justice, 1993-96; Minister without Portfolio, 1996-97; Mayor, Taipai City, 1998-2006; Chmn., Kuomintang, 2005-07; President, Republic of China, Taiwan, 2008-; ***professional career:*** Legal Consultant, First Nat. Bank of Boston, 1980-81; Assoc. Lawyer, Cole and Deits, New York, 1981; Research Consultant, Univ., of Maryland Sch. of Law, 1981; Assoc. Prof. of Law, Nat. Chengchi Univ., 1998; ***office address:*** Office of the President, 122 Chungking Road, Section 1, Taipei, Taiwan; ***phone:*** +886 2 311 3731; ***fax:*** +886 2 311 1604.

YOO, Jeong-bok; Minister of Security and Public Administration, Government of South Korea; ***born:*** June 1957; ***education:*** BA., Political Science, Yonsei Univ.; MA, Public Admin., Seoul Nat. Univ.; Doctoral Program in Political Science, Yonsei Univ.; ***political career:*** Mayor of Gimpo City, Gyeonggi Province; MP, 2004-; Minister of Security and Public Administration, 2013-; ***office address:*** Ministry of Security and Public Administration, 209 Sejong-daero (Sejong-ro), Jongno-gu, Seoul, Republic of Korea; ***phone:*** +82 2 2100 3399; ***URL:*** http://www.mopas.go.kr.

YOO, Jin-ryong; Minister of Culture, Sports and Tourism, Government of Republic of Korea; ***born:*** September 1956; ***education:*** BA, Commerce and Trade, 1979, MA, in Public Administration,1987, Seoul National Univ.; Ph.D. Public Admin. Hanyang Univ., 2005; ***political career:*** Minister of Culture, Sports and Tourism, 2013-; ***professional career:*** Mem., Arts Council Korea, 2008-10; Pres., Leisure Design Forum Inc., 2008-12; Dean, Hallyu Graduate School, Catholic Univ. of Korea, 2012; ***office address:*** Ministry of Culture, Sports and Tourism, 215 Changgyeonggung-ro, Jongno-gu, Seoul 110-360, Republic of Korea; ***phone:*** +82 2 3704 9114; ***URL:*** http://www.mcst.go.kr.

YOON, Sang-jick; Ministry of Trade, Industry and Energy, Government of the Republic of Korea; ***education:*** BA, in International Economics, 1981, MA, in Political Science, 1984, Seoul National Univ.; MA, in Law, Korea Univ. Graduate School, 1996; LL.M., 1998, S.J.D., 2007, Univ. of Wisconsin-Madison, USA; ***political career:*** Vice Minister for Industry and Technology, Ministry of Knowledge Economy, 2011-13; Minister of Trade, Industry and Energy, 2013-; ***office address:*** Minister of Industry, Trade and Energy, 47, Gwanmoonro, Gwacheon-si, Gyeong gi-do, Republic of Korea; ***URL:*** http://www.mke.go.kr.

YOON, Seong-kyu; Minister of Environment, Government of the Republic of Korea; ***education:*** BSc., Mechanical Engineering, Hanyang Univ, 1979; MSc., Clausthal Univ. of Technology, Germany; MSc., Environmental Engineering, Hanyang Univ., 2007; Ph.D., Environmental Engineering, Hanyang Univ., 2013; ***political career:*** Minister of Environment, 2013-; ***professional career:*** Dir., Center for Waste Eco-Energy and Greenhouse Gases, 2009-13; ***office address:*** Ministry of Environment, Government Complex Sejong, 11 Doum6-Ro, Sejong City 339-012, Republic of Korea; ***phone:*** +82 044 201 6570; ***URL:*** http://eng.me.go.kr.

YORK, KG, KCVO EARL OF INVERNESS AND BARON KILLYLEAGH, HRH The Duke of; Duke of York; ***born:*** 19 February 1960; ***parents:*** HRH The Prince Philip, Duke of Edinburgh and HM Queen Elizabeth II; ***married:*** Sarah (née Ferguson), 23 July 1986 (Div'd 1996); ***children:*** HRH Princess Beatrice (F), HRH Princess Eugenie (F); ***education:*** Gordonstoun Sch., Scotland; ***professional career:*** Royal Navy Pilot, saw active service in the Falklands conflict; Patron of many organisations including: National Maritime Museum, Greenwich; Commonwealth Society for the Deaf; Royal Philharmonic Orchestra; Oman Britain Friendship Association; National Association of Hospital & Community Friends; ***office address:*** Buckingham Palace, London, SW1A 1AA, United Kingdom.

YOUNG, Bill (C.W.); American, Congressman, Florida Tenth District, US House of Representatives; ***party:*** Republican Party; ***political career:*** Florida State Senate; Mem., US House of Representative, 1970- ; ***professional career:*** founder, National Bone Marrow Donor Program; ***committees:*** Appropriations; ***office address:*** US House of Representatives, 436 Cannon House Street, Washington, DC 20515, USA; ***phone:*** +1 202 225 5961.

YOUNG, H.E. Sir Colville Norbert, G.C.M.G., M.B.E., Ph.D, J.P(S); Belizean, Governor-General, Belize; ***born:*** 20 November 1932, Belize City; ***parents:*** Henry Oswald Young and Adney Wilhelmina Young (née Waite); ***married:*** Lady Norma (née Trapp), 4 January 1956; ***children:*** Carlton Norman (M), Maureen Emily Alegria (F), Colville Ludwig Jr. (M), Lynn Raymond (M); ***languages:*** English, Spanish; ***education:*** St. Michael's Coll., 1946-50; First Class Teacher's Certificate, 1955; B.A. (English, Hons) Univ. of London/Univ. Coll. of the West Indies, 1961; D.Phil (Linguistics) Univ. of York, 1973; ***memberships:*** Mem., Soc. for Caribbean Linguistics; Assn. for Belize Archaeology; Caribbean Teachers of English Assn.; ***professional career:*** Lecturer in linguistics, St. Johns Coll., Univ. Coll. of Belize and in universities in the US; Organiser or participant in numerous conferences and workshops dealing with Belizean language; Principal, St. Michael's Coll., Belize, 1974-76; Lecturer in English and General Studies, Belize Technical Coll., Belize, 1976-86; Pres., Univ. Coll. of Belize, 1986-90; Lecturer, Univ. of Belize, 1990-93; ***trusteeships:*** Fmr. trustee, Belize Library Assn.; Patron, Baron Bliss Trust; Scouts Assn. of Belize; Belize Historical Soc.; ***honours and awards:*** Arts Faculty Prize UCWI, 1959; Student of the Year UCWI, 1960; apptd, Justice of the Peace, 1958; MBE, 1986; Outstanding Teacher's Award, Anglican Cathedral Coll., 1987; Prime Minister's Citation for contribution to Belizean Culture, 1988; Fulbright Scholar; Mem., Jury Panel for Gabriela Mistral Inter-American Cultural Prize, Music 1992; GCMG, 1994; Belize, Ministry of Education distinguished Service Award; JP (Sen.), 1994; Hon. Doctorate, York Univ. 2003; Hon. Doctorate of Humane Letters, Univ. of North Florida 2006; Hon. Doctorate of Laws, Univ. of the West Indies, 2006; ***publications:*** Creole Proverbs of Belize (1980, revised 1988); From One Caribbean Corner (1983); Caribbean Corner Calling (1988); Language and Education in Belize (1989); Pataki Full (1990); Poetry and Drama in various anthologies; Articles in Belizean Affairs, Journal of Belizean Affairs, Belcast Journal, Caribbean Dialogue, Handbook on World Education; ***recreations:*** creative writing (poetry, plays, short stories), collecting and arranging Belizean folk songs, steel band music, composing music (Composer and Librettist, Tiger Dead); ***office address:*** Office of the Governor General, P O Box 173, Belmopan, Belize; ***phone:*** +501 822 2521/ 822 3081; ***fax:*** +501822 2050; ***e-mail:*** gougenbz@btl.net.

YOUNG, Don; American, Congressman, Alaska at Large, US House of Representatives; ***born:*** 1933; ***education:*** BA, Chico State College, 1958; ***party:*** Republican; ***political career:*** Mem., US House of Representatives, 1974-; ***professional career:*** US Army, 1955-57; ***committees:*** Natural Resources; Transportation and Infrastructure Cttees.; ***office address:*** House of Representatives, 436 Cannon House Building, Washington, DC 20515, USA; ***phone:*** +1 202 224 3121.

YOUNG, Rt. Hon. Sir George, Bt., MP; British, Parliamentary Secretary to the Treasury and Chief Whip, House of Commons; ***born:*** 1941; ***married:*** Aurelia Nemon Stuart, 1964; ***education:*** Eton; Christ Church, Oxford; ***political career:*** Cllr., Lambeth Borough Cncl., 1968-71; Mem., Greater London Cncl., 1970-73; Chmn., Acton Housing Assn., 1972-79; Cons. MP for Ealing, Acton, 1974-97; Parly. Under Sec. of State, Dept. of Health and Social Security, 1979-81; Under-Sec. of State for the Environment, 1981-86; Minister for Housing and Planning, 1990-95; Sec. of State for Transport, 1995-97; Opp. Front Bench Spokesman for Defence, 1997-98; Cons. MP for North West Hants, 1997-; Shadow Leader of the House of Commons and Constitutional Affairs, 1998-2001; Shadow Leader of the House of Commons, Sept. 2009-May 2010; Leader of the House of Commons, Lord Privy Seal, May 2010-Sept. 2012; Parliamentary Secretary to the Treasury and Chief Whip, 2013-; ***professional career:*** Economist, Nat. Econ. Dev. Office, 1966-67; Kobler Research Fellow, Univ. of Surrey, 1967-69; Econ. Adviser, Post Office Corp., 1969-74; Comptroller of the Household, 1990; ***committees:*** Chmn. Standards and Privileges Cttee., 2001-09; Liaison, 2002-09; Reform of the House of Commons, 2009; ***trusteeships:*** Trustee, Guinness Trust, 1986-90; ***publications:***

Accommodation Services in the UK 1970-80, 1970; Tourism: Blessing or Blight?, 1973; *office address:* House of Commons, London, SW1A 0AA, United Kingdom; *phone:* +44 (0)20 7219 3000; *e-mail:* sirgeorge@sirgeorgeyoung.org.uk; *URL:* http://www.sirgeorgeyoung.org.uk.

YOUNG, H.E. Marianne; High Commissioner, British High Commission in Namibia; *professional career:* International Journalist; High Commissioner to Namibia, 2011-; *office address:* British High Commission, PO Box 22202, 116 Robert Mugabe Avenue, Windhoek, Namibia; *phone:* +264 61 274800; *fax:* +264 61 228895; *e-mail:* windhoek.general@fco.gov.uk; *URL:* http://ukinnamibia.fco.gov.uk/en/.

YOUNG, H.E. Stephen M.; Consul-General, US Consulate in Hong Kong; *education:* BA, Wesleyan Univ., 1973; MA, 1974, Ph.D. in history, 1980, Univ. of Chacago; *professional career:* US Ambassador to Kyrgyzstan, 2003-05; Consul-General to Hong Kong and Macau, 2010-; *office address:* US Consulate, 26 Garden Road, Hong Kong, Hong Kong; *phone:* +852 2523 9011; *fax:* +852 2845 1598; *URL:* http://www.hongkong.usconsulate.gov.

YOUNG OF NORWOOD GREEN, Lord Anthony; Member, House of Lords; *political career:* mem., House of Lords, 2004-; Parly. Under Sec., Minister for Skills & Apprenticeships, Dept. for Innovation, Universities and Skills, Oct. 2008-June 2009; Minister for Postal Affairs and Employment Relations, Dept. for Business, Innovation and Skills, 2009-10; Government Whip, 2008-10; Opposition Spokesperson for Business, Innovation and Skills, 2010-; *professional career:* Telecommunications apprentice at the Post Office; elected a Union Branch Officer in 1967; elected Gen. Sec., National Communications Union (NCU) in 1989; Following the NCU's merger with the Postal Workers he was initially joint Gen. Sec. then Senior Dep. Gen. Sec., combined Communication Workers' Union; Joined the General Council of the Trades Union Congress (TUC) in 1989, served as President of the General Council of the TUC, 2001-2002; Governor, BBC, 1998-2002; mem., Armed Forces Pay Review Board, 2005-08; *honours and awards:* elevated to the peerage as Lord Young of Norwood Green in the London Borough of Ealing, 2004; *office address:* House of Lords, London, SW1A 0PW, United Kingdom.

YOUNG OF OLD SCONE, Baroness; Member of the House of Lords; *born:* 8 April 1948, Perth, Scotland; *parents:* George Young and Mary Young; *education:* MA Hons Classics, Edinburgh Univ., 1966-70; Dip-Sec. Science, Strathclyde Univ.; *party:* unaffiliated; *political career:* Mem., House of Lords; *interests:* environment, health, civil liberties, health and social care; *memberships:* IHM; Vice Pres. RSPB; Birdlife International; Flora + Fauna International; Pres., Beds., Cambs. & Northants., Wildlife Trust; *professional career:* Chief Exec., Diabetes UK; Chancellor, Cranfield Univ.; *committees:* previously Climate Change Adaption Cttee.; *trusteeships:* Institute of Public Policy Research; *honours and awards:* Hon. Degrees, Hertfordshire Univ., Aberdeen Univ., York Univ., Cranfield Univ., Stirling Univ., Open Univ., St. Andrews Univ., Gloucestershire Uni., Exeter Uni.; *recreations:* cinema, gardening, ornithology, dressage; *office address:* House of Lords, London, SW1A 0PQ, United Kingdom; *phone:* +44 (0)20 7219 3100; *fax:* +44 (0)20 7219 5679.

YOUNGER OF LECKIE, Viscount; Member, House of Lords; *born:* 11 November 1955; *parents:* Viscount Younger of Leckie (George Younger) and Diana, Viscountess Younger of Leckie (Diana Rhona née Tuck); *married:* Jennie Wootton, 1988; *children:* Emily Evelyn (F), Alice Elizabeth (F), Alexander William George (M); *public role of spouse:* MD & Global Head of Marketing and Communications, Deutsche Bank; *party:* Conservative; *political career:* Chair, Buckingham Conservative Constituency Assn. 2006-10; Mem., Assn of Conservative Peers 2006-; Elected Hereditary Peer, House of Lords, 2010-; Chair, Milton Keynes Conservatives, 2011-; Parliamentary Under Secretary of State, 2013-; *memberships:* Royal Company of Archers (Queen's Bodyguard for Scotland); Dir., Highland Society of London; Mem., Assoc. of MBAs and Institute of Marketing (MCIM); *office address:* House of Lords, London, SW1A 0PW, United Kingdom; *phone:* +44 (0)20 7219 3000; *fax:* +44 (0)20 7219 5979; *e-mail:* jeg.younger@virgin.net; *URL:* http://www.parliament.uk.

YOUSSEF, Dr. Al-Haj Adam; Second Vice President, Government of Sudan; *born:* 1955; *education:* BSc., Univ. of Khartoum; *party:* National Congress Party; *political career:* Governor of the Northern State, 1995-97; Governor of Dafur, 1997-99; Minister of Agriculture and Forestry; Second Vice Pres., 2011-; *professional career:* University Professor; *office address:* Office of the Second Vice President, People's Palace, PO Box 281, Khartoum, Republic of Sudan; *phone:* +249 1 8377 8426.

YUBAMRUNG, Dr Chalerm; Deputy Prime Minister, responsible for the Ministry of the Interior, Government of Thailand; *born:* 1947; *party:* Pheu Thai Party; *political career:* MP; Health Minister; Interior Minister; Justice Minister; Leader of the Oppostiion, 2009-11; Deputy Prime Minister; *office address:* Ministry of the Interior, Thanon Atsadang, Bangkok 10200, Thailand.

YUDHOYONO, President Susilo Bambang; President, Government of Indonesia; *languages:* English; *education:* Masters degree, USA; *party:* Democratic Party; *political career:* Minister of Mines and Energy, 1999-2000; Co-ordinating Minister for Political Affairs, Social and Security Affairs, 2000-01; President, Sept. 2004-; *professional career:* Army General; *office address:* Office of the President, Istana Merdeka, Jakarta, Indonesia; *URL:* http://www.dpr.go.id.

YUN, Byung-se; Minister of Foreign Affairs and Trade, Government of South Korea; *born:* August 1953; *education:* College of Law, Seoul Nat. Univ., 1976; 1978 Graduate School of Law, Seoul Nat. Univ., 1978; MA., The School of Advanced International Studies (SAIS), The Johns Hopkins University, Maryland, USA, 1983; *political career:* Minister of Foreign Affairs, 2013-; *professional career:* Visiting Professor, Graduate School of Int. Studies, Sogang Univ. Seoul; *office address:* Ministry of Foreign Affairs and Trade, 60 Sajik-ro 8-gil, Seoul 110 787, South Korea; *URL:* http://www.mofat.go.kr.

YUSGIANTORO, Dr. Ir. Purnomo; Minister of Defence, Government of Indonesia; *political career:* Ministerial Adviser, 1993-98; Minister of Energy and Mineral Resources, 2000-09; Pres. of the Conference and Secretary-General of OPEC, 2004; Minister of Defence, 2009-; *professional career:* lecturer and teacher; Lecturer, Atma Jaya Jakarta, Prof., 2002-; Gov., then Sec. Gen and President, OPEC, 2004; *office address:* Ministry of Defence, Jalan Merdeka Selatan 13-14, Jakarta 10110, Indonesia; *phone:* +62 (0)21 345 6184; *URL:* http://www.hankam.go.id.

YUSUF, Dr Abdulqawi; Somali, Member, International Court of Justice; *born:* 12 September 1948; *languages:* Somali, English, French, Italian, Arabic; *education:* Somali National University, Faculty of Law, Laurea di Dottore in Giurisprudenza, 1973; Graduate Institute of International Studies, University of Geneva, Docteur ès sciences politiques (International Law), 1980; University of Florence, Post-Graduate studies in International Law and Relations, 1976-77; Centre for Studies and Research in International Law, Hague Academy of International Law, Certificate, 1974; Legal qualification: PhD in International Law; Barrister, Supreme Court of Somalia, 1974-80; *interests:* Dispute settlement; Economic law; Environment law; Jurisdiction; Organisations; Law of the Sea; Territory/boundaries; Treaties; Intellectual property; *memberships:* Institut de Droit International; Founder and General Editor, African Yearbook of International Law; Founding Member, African Association of International Law; Founding Member and Member of the Governing Board, African Foundation for International Law; Commission on Environmental Law, World Conservation Union; *professional career:* academic career: Faculty of Law, Somali National University, Lecturer in International Law, 1974-80, Chairman, Public Law Department, 1976-78; Faculté de Droit, Université de Genève, Assistant Professor, 1981-83; Visiting lecturer on public international law and international economic law at the University of Sienna, L'Institut universitaire d'études du développement, Geneva, University of Florence, University of Milan-Bocconi, the International Development Law Institute, Rome, University of Turin, the UNITAR Fellowship Programme in International Law, the Hague Academy of International Law; Governmental career: UNESCO, Director of the Office of International Standards and Legal Affairs, 2001-; UNIDO, Special Adviser and Assistant Director-General for African Affairs, 1998-2001, Legal Adviser and Director of the Legal Service, 1994-98; UNCTAD, Representative and Head, New York Office 1992-94, Head, Legal Policies Section, Technology Progamme, Geneva, 1992; Legal Adviser, Dir., Office of International Standards and Legal Affairs, UNESCO, 2001-09; Member, International Court of Justice, 2009-; *diplomatic career:* Somali representative to the Third UN Conference on the Law of the Seas, 1975-80; Member, Somali delegation to the Afro-Asian Legal Consultative Committee, 1975-76; Member, Somali delegation to OAU and Arab-League meetings, 1974-76; *judicial career:* Judge ad hoc, ICJ; *publications:* Numerous; *office address:* International Court of Justice, The Peace Palace, 2517 KJ The Hague, Netherlands.

YVON, H.E. Christopher; Ambassador, British Embassy in Macedonia; *professional career:* FCO, Dep. Head, Int. Organisations Dept., 2001-10; Amb. to Macedonia, 2010-; *office address:* British Embassy, Dimitrija Chupovski 26, 4th Floor, Skopje 1000, Macedonia; *phone:* +389 2329 9299; *fax:* +389 2311 7555; *e-mail:* beskopje@mt.net.mk; *URL:* http://ukinmacedonia.fco.gov.uk/en.

Z

ZAHAWI, Nadhim; MP for Stratford-on-Avon, UK Government; *born:* 1967; *party:* Conservative; *political career:* Local Councillor, Wandsworth, 1994-2006; MP for Stratford-on-Avon, May 2010-; *professional career:* European Marketing Dir., Smith & Brooks Ltd.; Co-founder and CEO, YouGov plc, 2000-2010; *committees:* Business, Innovation and Skills, 2010-; Arms Export Controls, 2010-; Jt. Cttee. on Privacy and Injunctions, 2011-12; *office address:* House of Commons, London, SW1A 0AA, United Kingdom; *phone:* +44 (0)20 7219 3000; *URL:* http://www.zahawi.com.

ZAHID HAMIDI, Dr. Ahmad; Minister of Home Affairs, Government of Malaysia; *education:* Universiti Putra Malaysia; *party:* United Malays National Organisation (UMNO); *political career:* Minister of Defence, 2009-13; Minister of Home Affairs & Internal Security, 2013-; *office address:* Ministry of Home Affairs, Blok D2, Pusat Pentadbiran Kerajaan Persekutuan, 62546 Putrajaya, Malaysia; *URL:* http://www.moha.gov.my.

ZAK, Leocardia I.; Director, US Trade & Development Agency; *education:* Mount Holyoke College; Northeastern Univ. School of Law, JD; *professional career:* Adjunct Prof.of Law, Boston Univ. School of Law; Georgetown Univ. Law Center; partner, Mintz, Levin, Cohn, Ferris, Glovsky and Popeo; Gen. Counsel, USTDA, 2000-06, Dep. Dir., 2006-09; Director, 2010-; *office address:* US Trade & Development Agency, 1000 Wilson Boulevard, Suite 1600, Arlington, VA 22209, USA; *phone:* +1 703 875 4357; *URL:* http://www.ustda.gov/.

ZAKHAILWAL, Dr Omar; Minister of Finance, Government of Afghanistan; *born:* 1968; *education:* BA, (economics), Univ. of Winnipeg, Canada; MA, Queen's Univ., Canada; Doctorate, Carleton Univ. Canada; *political career:* Minister of Finance, 2009-; *office address:* Ministry of Finance, Pashtunistan Watt, Kabul, Afghanistan; *phone:* +93 20 210 2099; *URL:* http://www.mof.gov.af.

ZANNER, Ambassador Lamberto; Secretary General, OSCE; *professional career:* career diplomat; Head of Disarmament, Arms Control and Cooperative Security at NATO, 1991-97; Chair., negotiations on the adaptation of the Treaty on Conventional Armed Forces in Europe, 1997-2000; Perm. Rep. of Italy to the Executive Council of the Organization for the Prohibition of Chemical Weapons in The Hague, 2000-02; Dir., Conflict Prevention Centre of the OSCE, 2002-06; UN Special Rep. to Kosovo and Head of the UN Interim Administration Mission in Kosovo (UNNMIK), 2008-11; *office address:* OSCE, Wallnerstrasse 6, A-1010 Vienna, Austria; *phone:* +43 (0)1 5143 66000; *fax:* +43 (0)1 5143 66996; *URL:* http://www.osce.org.

ZANONATO, Flavio; Minister of Economic Development, Government of Italy; ***political career:*** Mayor of Padua, 1993-99, 2004-13; Minister of Economic Development, Apr. 2013-; ***office address:*** Ministry of Economic Development, Via Molise, 2, 00187 Rome, Italy; ***phone:*** +39 06 4204 3486; ***URL:*** http://www.sviluppoeconomico.gov.it.

ZANTOVSKY, Michael; Czech, Ambassador , Embassy of the Czech Republic in the UK; ***born:*** 1949; ***married:*** Kristina Zantovsky; ***education:*** Charles Univ., Prague; McGill Univ., Montreal; research fellow, Psychiatric Research Inst., Prague; ***political career:*** Senator, 1996-2002; ***professional career:*** Correspondent with Reuters 1988; Mem., independent cultural initiative The Open Dialogue, 1989; founding mem., revived Czech chapter of P.E.N., the international writers organization; Founding Mem. then Press Spokesman of Civic Forum, 1989; Adviser and Press Secy. to President Václav Havel 1990; President's Director of Policy 1991-; Ambassador of Czechoslovakia to the USA 1992-, Amb. of the Czech Republic to the USA 1993-97; Amb. to Israel, 2009-09, Amb. to the United Kingdom, 2009; ***office address:*** Embassy of the Czech Republic, 26 Kensington Palace Gardens, London, W8 4QY, United Kingdom; ***phone:*** +44 (0)20 7243 1115; ***fax:*** +44 (0)20 7727 9654; ***e-mail:*** london@embassy.mzv.cz; ***URL:*** http://www.mzv.cz/london.

ZARDARI, President Asif Ali; President, Pakistan; ***born:*** 22 July 1955, Karachi, Pakistan; ***parents:*** Hakim Ali Zardari; ***married:*** Benazir Bhutto (dec'd); ***children:*** Bakhtawar (F), Asifa (F), Bilawal (M); ***public role of spouse:*** Former PM of Pakistan; ***political career:*** Mem., National Assembly; Imprisoned 1990-93; Minister of the Environment, 1993-96; Imprisoned 1997-2004; Co-Chmn.(with son Bilawal), PPP, 2007-; President of Pakistan, 2008-; ***office address:*** Office of the President, Aiwan-e-Sadr, Islamabad, Pakistan; ***phone:*** +92 (0)51 820606; ***fax:*** +92 51 921 1018; ***URL:*** http://www.pak.gov.pk/.

ZARIFI, Hamrokhon; Minister of Foreign Affairs, Government of the Republic of Tajikistan; ***born:*** 25 December 1948; ***parents:*** Kurbon Zaripov and Guldasta Zaripov; ***married:*** Kadirya Nabieva; ***children:*** Siyuush (M), Rakhshonak (F); ***languages:*** English, Persian, Russian; ***education:*** Kulyab State Univ., Grad. Physical and Mathematical Fac., 1971; ***political career:*** Coordinator, Kulyab Regional Exec. Cttee., 1974-84; various posts in the Party organisation and in the Govt. of Tajikistan, 1984-93; Minister of Foreign Affairs, 2007-; ***professional career:*** Lecturer, Kulyab State Univ, 1971-74; scientist, Physical and Technical Scientific Reserarch Instit., Dushanbe, 1971-74; joined Ministry of Foreign Affairs, 1993; Dep. Minister of Foreign Affairs, 1995-96; Permanent Rep. to the UN and other organisations in Vienna, and Head of the Tajikistan Delegation to the OSCE 1996-2003; Head of Mission to the European Communities, 1997-2003; Amb. Ex. & Pleni. to Austria, 1997-2003, to Switzerland, 1998-2003 and to Hungary, 1999-2002; Amb. of Tajikistan to USA, 2003-07; ***clubs:*** University Club, USA; ***office address:*** Ministry of Foreign Affairs, 42 Rudaki Street, Dushanbe, Tajikistan.

ZDROJEWSKI, Bogdan; Minister of Culture and National Heritage, Government of Poland; ***born:*** 1957, Klodzko, Poland; ***children:*** Karolina (F), Stanislaw (M); ***public role of spouse:*** Councillor and chair of the City Council in Wroclaw; ***education:*** Wrocław Univ., philosophy, 1983, cultural studies, 1985; ***party:*** Civic Platform, Dec. 2006-Nov.2007 chairman of the Parliamentary Group of Civic Platform; ***political career:*** Mem., Independent Students Union (NZS - chmn. 1982-84), 1980-85; Founder and manager of Social Research Center to Regional Election Commission NSZZ "S" Dolny Śląsk, 1989-90; Mayor of Wrocław, 1990-2001; Councilor, City Council in Wrocław, 1990-2001; Senator, 1997-2000; Mem., National Bd., Civic Platform, 2001-06; Chmn., Parly. Gp. of Civic Platform, 2006-07; Minister of Culture and National Heritage, 2007-; ***memberships:*** mem., Local Territorial Council to the President of the Republic of Poland, 1993-95; Kredyt Bank SA Council. 1994-97; Board of Supervisors in Foundation of The National Ossoliński Institute (Ossolineum). 1996-2001; Board of Supervisors in Foundation in Support of Local Democracy, 1995-; The Largest Polish Cities Presidents Convent and Council of Academical Chancellors of Wrocław and Opole; ***professional career:*** Academy of Econ., 1983-89; Wroclaw Univ., 1989-90; ***committees:*** Wrocław Civil Committee "Solidarity" 1989-90; Hon. Chmn., Dolny Śląsk (Lower Silesia) Civil Committee, 1995-97; Chmn., National Conference of Civil Committee, 1996-7; ***honours and awards:*** First laureate of the Andrzej Baczkowski Award for an"exemplary public service officer during daily work and crisis" 1997; winner of the Leader of Europe award, 1998; Sancti Silvestri order from pope John Paul II , 1998; Federal Cross I Class (Das Verdienstkreuz 1 Klasse), the Oder of Merit of the Federal Republic of Germany, from German President in 2001; Golden Cross of Merit from the President of Poland in 2002; ***publications:*** Co-editor of Komunikaty; Przedruki; Victoria, Przemysl kultury w rozwoju regionalnym i lokalnym - doswiadczenia wroclawskie, 2002, The Institute for Market Economics; Bogdan Zdrojewski poleca Wroclaw, 2006; ***office address:*** Ministry of Culture and National Heritage, ul. Krakowskie Przedmiescie 15/17, 00-071 Warsaw, Poland; ***phone:*** +48 22 42 10 349; ***fax:*** +48 22 82 61 922.

ZEMAN, Ing. Milos; Czech, President, Czech Republic; ***born:*** 28 September 1944, Kolin, Central Bohemia; ***married:*** Ivana Zeman; ***children:*** Katerina (F), David (M); ***education:*** Prague Sch. of Economics, Grad., Extramural studies, 1969; ***party:*** Founder, Hon. Chmn., Party of Citizen Rights SPOZ; ***political career:*** Elected Federal Assembly, Czech and Slovak Federal Republic, 1990; Party Chmn., (CSSD), 1993-2007; Mem. for North Moravian, Chamber of Deputies, CR Parl., 1996; Chmn./Speaker, CR Parl., 1996; Prime Minister, Czech Republic, 1998-2002; President, Czech Rep., 2013-; ***memberships:*** Civic Forum Assembly, 1989; ***professional career:*** Physical Education Organisation, 1970-84; Agricultural Organisation, 1984-89; ***committees:*** Chmn., Budget Cttee., 1990; Chmn., CSSD Prague Municipal Cttee., 1992; ***office address:*** Office of the President, Prague Castle, Prague 119 08 1, Czech Republic; ***phone:*** +420 224 371111; ***fax:*** +420 2 2481 0231; ***e-mail:*** posta@vlada.ck.

ZENON, H.E. Alexandros; High Commissioner, Cyprus High Commission in the UK; ***born:*** January 1953, Limassol, Cyprus; ***education:*** LLB, Univ. of Athens, Greece; DEA post graduate degree, Paris IV-Sorbonne Univ. Paris France; Dip., Int. Inst. of Public Admin., Paris, France; ***professional career:*** Amb. to Italy, Switzerland, Malta and San Marino, 2000-05; Acting Perm. Sec., Ministry of Foreign Affairs, Nicosia, 2006-07; Perm. Sec., Ministry of Foreign Affairs, Nicosia, 2007-08; High Commissioner to the UK, 2008-; ***office address:*** High Commission of the Republic of Cyprus, 13 St. James's Square, London, SW1Y 4LB, United Kingdom; ***phone:*** +44 220 7499 8272; ***fax:*** +44 22 7491 0691; ***URL:*** http://www.mfa.gov.cy/highcomlondon.

ZHAMISHEV, Bolat; Minister of Finance, Government of Kazakhstan; ***born:*** 1957; ***education:*** Kazakh Agricultural Inst., 1981; Ph.D. in Economics; ***political career:*** Minister of Finance, 2007-; ***professional career:*** Dep. Chmn., Nat. Bank of the Republic of Kazakhstan, 2003-04; ***office address:*** Ministry of Finance, 60 Republic Square, 473000 Astana, Kazakhstan; ***phone:*** +7 3172 280065; ***fax:*** +7 3172 324089; ***URL:*** http://www.minfin.kz.

ZHANG, Gaoli; Vice Premier, State Council, People's Republic of China; ***education:*** Xiamen Univ., China; ***political career:*** Mem., Political Bureau, CPC Central Cttee; sec., CPC Tianjin Municipal Cttee, 2007-12; Mem., Standing Cttee., Political Bureau, CPC Central Ctee; sec., CPC Tianjin Municipal Cttee, 2012-13; Mem., Standing Cttee., Political Bureau, CPC Central Cttee.; vice premier, State Council; dep. sec., Leading Party Members' Group, State Council, 2013-; ***office address:*** Office of the Vice Premier, State Council Secretariat, Beijing, China.

ZIDAN, Ali; Prime Minister, Government of Libya; ***political career:*** Prime Minister, 2012-; ***professional career:*** Diplomat; ***office address:*** Office of the Prime Minister, Tripoli, Libya.

ZIENTS, Jeffrey; Deputy Director, Office of Management and Budget; ***education:*** Duke Univ., Political Science, summa cum laude; ***political career:*** Dep. Dir. for Management, Office for Management and Budget, 2009-, Acting Dir., to date; ***professional career:*** twenty years of business experience; Mgt. consultant; Bain & Co & Mercer Mgt. Consulting; CEO; entrepreneur; founder, investment firm; co-founder, Urban Alliance Foundation; ***office address:*** Office of Management and Budget, 725 17th Street, NW, Room 9026, Washington, DC 20503, USA; ***phone:*** +1 202 395 3080; ***fax:*** +1 202 395 3888; ***URL:*** http://www.whitehouse.gov/omb/.

ZILLE, Helen; Premier, Government of Western Cape; ***political career:*** activist; political campagner; joined the former Democratic Party; Elected to Provincial Parliament, 1999; Minister of Education, Western Cape province, 1999-2001; leader of the opposition, Western Cape Legislature, 2001-04; Member, National Parliament, 2004-06; Mayor of Cape Town, 2006; leader, Democratic Alliance; Premier, Western Cape Province, 2009-; ***professional career:*** Political correspondent, Rand Daily Mail; worked in several NGOs and activist orgs., 1980s-, incl. the Open Society Foundation, the Independent Media Diversity Trust; Black Sash; ***office address:*** Office of the Premier, 142 Long Street, Cape Town, South Africa.

ZLATANOVA, Zinaida; Deputy Prime Minister, Government of Bulgaria; ***party:*** BSP; ***political career:*** Deputy Prime Miinister, Minister in charge of EU funds, Minister of Justice, 2013; ***office address:*** Ministry of Justice, 1 Slavjaska st., 1000 Sofia, Bulgaria; ***phone:*** +359 (0)2 869 3274; ***URL:*** http://www.mjeli.government,bg.

ZUMA, Jacob Gedleyihlekisa; President, South Africa; ***born:*** 12 April 1942, Inkandla, KwaZulu, Natal; ***married:*** Sizakele Khumalo, 1973; Nkosazana Dlamini-Zuma (Div'd 1998); Kate Mantsho Zuma (Dec'd 2000); Nompumelelo Ntuli, 2008; ***children:*** 18; ***party:*** African National Congress (ANC), 1958-; ***political career:*** active mem., Umkhonto we Sizwe; Dep. Chief then Chief Representative, ANC in Mozambique, 1977-84; Head of Underground Structures, ANC, 1987; Chief, Intelligence Dept., ANC, 1988; Chmn., Southern Natal, 1990; Dep. Sec.-Gen., ANC, 1991; Nat. Chmn., ANC, 1994; Chmn., ANC in KwaZulu Natal, 1994; Dep. Pres., ANC, 1997-; Dep. Pres., South African Government, 1999-; Leader of Govt. Business, Nat. Assembly, 1999-sacked June 2005; President of the ANC. Dec. 2007-; President of South Africa, May 2009-; ***memberships:*** MEC, Economic Affairs and Tourism; Nat. Chmn., African Nat. Congress; Mem., ANC, NWC, NEC; ***committees:*** ANC Nat. Exec. Cttee., 1977; ANC Political Military Cttee.; ANC Political Cttee.; mem., Exec. Cttee. of Economic Affairs and Tourism, KwaZulu Natal Provincial Govt., 1994; ***trusteeships:*** Peace and Reconstruction Foundation, KwaZulu Natal; Jacob Zuma Bursary Fund; ***honours and awards:*** Nelson Mandela Award for Outstanding Leadership, 1998; ***office address:*** Office of the President, Union Buildings, West Wing, Government Avenue, Pretoria 0002, South Africa; ***phone:*** +27 (0)21 461 9468; ***e-mail:*** communications@po.gov.za; ***URL:*** http://www.anc.org.za.

ZWIEFELHOFER, Thomas; Deputy Prime Minister, Government of Liechtenstein; ***education:*** Law studies and a Ph.D.,Univ. of St. Gallen; University of Liechtenstein; ***party:*** Patriotic Union; ***political career:*** Deputy Prime Minister, Minister of Interior, Justice and Economy, 2013-; ***professional career:*** Lawyer; ***office address:*** Ministry of the Interior, Regierungsgebaude, 9490 Vaduz, Liechtenstein; ***URL:*** http://www.liechtenstein.li.

CARDIFF COUNCIL			
03186194	2014		
A & H	£699.00		

4204260

STANDARD TIME ZONES OF THE WORLD

| -12 | -11 | -10 | -9 | -8 | -7 | -6 | -5 | -4 | -3 | -2 | -1 |

BEAUFORT SEA

CHUKCHI SEA

Alaska

Admundsen Gulf

Baffin Bay

Greenland

GREEN

Jan N

NOR

ICELAND

Faroe Is.

BERING SEA

Hudson Bay

CANADA

LABRADOR SEA

UN

IRELAND

NORTH PACIFIC OCEAN

NORTH ATLANTIC OCEAN

St. Pierre & Miquelon

PORTUGAL SP

UNITED STATES

The Azores

MOROCC

Bermuda

Madeira

MEXICO

Gulf of Mexico

BAHAMAS

Canary Is.

Western Sahara

International Date Line

Midway Islands

Johnston Atoll

Hawaii

CUBA

Cayman Is.

JAMAICA

HAITI

DOM. REPUBLIC

Puerto Rico

Anguilla

Guadeloupe

Martinique

CAPE VERDE

MAURITANIA

BELIZE

GUATEMALA HONDURAS

EL SALVADOR NICARAGUA

CARIBBEAN SEA

SENEGAL

THE GAMBIA

GUINEA-BISSAU

GUINEA

COSTA RICA PANAMA

TRINIDAD & TOBAGO

VENEZUELA

SIERRA LEONE

COTE D IVOIR

LIBERIA

COLOMBIA

GUYANA

SURINAME

French Guiana

EQUATOR

ECUADOR

Galapagos Islands

Ascension

KIRIBATI

PERU

BRAZIL

Tokelau Islands

SAMOA American Samoa

Wallis and Futuna

TONGA Niue (NZ)

French Polynesia

Cook Islands

Pitcairn Islands

BOLIVIA

PARAGUAY

CHILE

St. Helena

Easter Island

URUGUAY

THE WORLD

Scale 1:85,000,000

| 0 | 1000 | 2000Km |

| 0 | 500 | 1000miles |

Correct along the Meridians and the Equator

Plate Carrée Projection (WGS84 Datum)

ARGENTINA

SOUTH ATLANT

OCEAN

SOUTH PACIFIC OCEAN

Falkland Islands

South Georgia and the South Sandwich Is.

SCOTIA SEA

AMUNDSEN SEA

BELLINGSHAUSEN SEA

WEDDELL SEA

| -12 | -11 | -10 | -9 | -8 | -7 | -6 | -5 | -4 | -3 | -2 | -1 |